ESV

STUDY BIBLE

ENGLISH STANDARD VERSION

ESV

STUDY BIBLE

ENGLISH STANDARD VERSION

CROSSWAY

WHEATON, ILLINOIS - WWW.ESVBIBLE.ORG

ESV Text Edition: 2011

Library of Congress Catalog Card Number 2008020094

Printed in China
Published by Crossway
Wheaton, Illinois 60187, U.S.A.
www.crossway.org

Crossway is a not-for-profit publishing ministry that exists solely for the purpose of publishing the Good News of the Gospel and the Truth of God's Word, the Bible. A portion of the purchase price of every ESV Bible is donated to help support Bible distribution ministry around the world.

The ESV Bible is free online and on mobile devices everywhere worldwide, including a selection of free Bible resources, at www.esvbible.org.

RRD 24 23 22 21 20 19 18 17 16 15
17 16 15 14 13 12 11 10 9 8 7 6

Contents

Continued on the following page

Articles and Resources

Illustrations

Abbreviations

General

c.	about, approximately	i.e.	that is
cf.	compare, confer	KJV	King James Version
ch., chs.	chapter(s)	lit.	literally
d.	died	LXX	Septuagint
e.g.	for example	MT	Masoretic Text
esp.	especially	NT	New Testament
ESV	English Standard Version	OT	Old Testament
etc.	and so on	par.	parallel passage(s)
ff.	following verse(s)	p., pp.	page(s)
Gk.	Greek	v., vv.	verse(s)
Hb.	Hebrew	vs.	versus

Books of the Bible

Genesis	Gen.	Nahum	Nah.
Exodus	Ex.	Habakkuk	Hab.
Leviticus	Lev.	Zephaniah	Zeph.
Numbers	Num.	Haggai	Hag.
Deuteronomy	Deut.	Zechariah	Zech.
Joshua	Josh.	Malachi	Mal.
Judges	Judg.	Matthew	Matt.
Ruth	Ruth	Mark	Mark
1 Samuel	1 Sam.	Luke	Luke
2 Samuel	2 Sam.	John	John
1 Kings	1 Kings	Acts	Acts
2 Kings	2 Kings	Romans	Rom.
1 Chronicles	1 Chron.	1 Corinthians	1 Cor.
2 Chronicles	2 Chron.	2 Corinthians	2 Cor.
Ezra	Ezra	Galatians	Gal.
Nehemiah	Neh.	Ephesians	Eph.
Esther	Est.	Philippians	Phil.
Job	Job	Colossians	Col.
Psalms	Ps.	1 Thessalonians	1 Thess.
Proverbs	Prov.	2 Thessalonians	2 Thess.
Ecclesiastes	Eccles.	1 Timothy	1 Tim.
Song of Solomon	Song	2 Timothy	2 Tim.
Isaiah	Isa.	Titus	Titus
Jeremiah	Jer.	Philemon	Philem.
Lamentations	Lam.	Hebrews	Heb.
Ezekiel	Ezek.	James	James
Daniel	Dan.	1 Peter	1 Pet.
Hosea	Hos.	2 Peter	2 Pet.
Joel	Joel	1 John	1 John
Amos	Amos	2 John	2 John
Obadiah	Obad.	3 John	3 John
Jonah	Jonah	Jude	Jude
Micah	Mic.	Revelation	Rev.

Books of the Apocrypha

Bel and the Dragon	Bel and Dragon	2 Maccabees	2 Macc.
Sirach (Ecclesiasticus)	Sir.	Tobit	Tob.
2 Esdras	2 Esd.	Wisdom of Solomon	Wisd. Sol.
1 Maccabees	1 Macc.		

INTRODUCTION:
A USER'S GUIDE TO THE ESV STUDY BIBLE

Purpose and Vision

The ESV Study Bible was created to help people understand the Bible in a deeper way—that is, to encounter the timeless truth of God's Word as a powerful, compelling, life-changing reality. To accomplish this purpose, the ESV Study Bible combines the best and most recent evangelical scholarship with the ESV Bible text, which, as an "essentially literal" translation, is especially suited for Bible study. The result is the most comprehensive study Bible ever published—with completely new notes, maps, illustrations, charts, timelines, articles, and other features. Created by an exceptional team of 95 evangelical Christian scholars and teachers, the ESV Study Bible contains more than 2 million words of Bible text and insightful explanation and teaching—equivalent to a 20-volume Bible resource library. (See the complete list of contributors on pp. 13–18.)

The purpose and vision of the ESV Study Bible, then, is first and foremost to honor the Lord: (1) in terms of the excellence, beauty, and accuracy of its content and design, and (2) in terms of helping people come to a deeper understanding of the Bible, of the gospel, and of Jesus Christ as their Lord and Savior.

Divine Words and Merely Human Words

The ESV Study Bible contains two kinds of words. The first kind is the actual words of the Bible, which are the very words of God to us. These are printed in the larger font at the top of each page. The second kind is the study notes, which are merely human words. These are printed in the smaller font at the bottom of each page. The difference in font sizes serves to remind readers that the words of the Bible itself are infinitely more valuable than the words of the notes. The words of the Bible are the words of our Creator speaking to us. They are completely truthful (Ps. 119:160; Prov. 30:5; Titus 1:2; Heb. 6:18); they are pure (Ps. 12:6); they are powerful (Jer. 23:29; Heb. 4:12; 1 Pet. 1:23); and they are wise and righteous (Ps. 19:7–11). God's people should read these words with reverence and awe (Deut. 28:58; Ps. 119:74; Isa. 66:2), and with joy and delight (Ps. 19:7–11; 119:14, 97, 103; Jer. 15:16). Through these words God gives us eternal life (John 6:68; 1 Pet. 1:23) and daily nourishes our spiritual lives in this present world (Deut. 32:46; Matt. 4:4). The words of the study notes are useful because they help to explain the words of the Bible, but they must never become a substitute for the Bible itself.

The best way to use a study Bible, therefore, is always to begin and end with the words of the Bible. We should always begin by reading the Bible's actual words, seeking with our hearts and our minds to understand these words and apply them to our lives. Then, after starting with the words of the Bible itself, we can turn to the study notes and many other study Bible resources for information about the background to the text, for the meaning of puzzling words or phrases, and for connections to other parts of the Bible. Finally, we should return again to the Bible itself, reading it with a new and deeper understanding, asking God to speak through his Word to our lives and to draw us near to himself.

The Purpose of the ESV Study Bible Notes

The purpose of the notes in the ESV Study Bible is to provide significant explanatory help for Christians who want to understand the Bible in a deeper way. To that end, the notes provide the following types of helpful content:

1. Explanation of the Bible text, especially with regard to the meaning of specific words and phrases in their immediate context and in relation to the Bible as a whole.

2. Brief summary notes at the beginning of each new section, explaining the meaning and purpose of the section. These correspond to the outline for each book of the Bible, and are shaded within the notes to help identify the structure of each book.
3. A summary of how specific Bible texts fit into the overall history of salvation as this unfolds throughout the Old Testament.
4. Explanation of puzzling events, words, and phrases that are often misunderstood.
5. Background descriptions of historical and archaeological information, providing a contextual framework to help illuminate and understand the text.
6. Explanation of key Greek and Hebrew words (usually given in their lexical form), to provide insight into the meaning of key words in the original languages of the Bible.
7. Presentation of significant alternative interpretations of important Bible passages.
8. Explanation of key texts that are crucial for the understanding of Christian doctrine, theology, and ethics.
9. Interaction with and responses to challenges concerning the truthfulness, historicity, or believability of specific Bible passages.
10. Application to life today for selected key passages.

The Understanding and Teaching of God's Word

With this purpose in mind, the ESV Study Bible carries forward a centuries-old tradition of "explaining," "expounding," or "teaching" the Word of God. This process of teaching God's Word is found even within the Bible itself. For example, when Moses spoke the words of Deuteronomy to the people of Israel, he told them, "You shall *teach* them diligently to your children, and shall talk of them when you sit in your house, and when you walk by the way, and when you lie down, and when you rise" (Deut. 6:7). Similarly, when Ezra and the Levites read the Book of the Law to the exiles who had returned from Babylon, they "helped the people to understand . . . and they gave the sense, so that the people understood . . ." (Neh. 8:7–8). In the early church, Philip was sent to the Ethiopian eunuch to help him understand what he was reading from Isaiah (Acts 8:26–40). And the apostle Paul, in city after city, spent his time "*teaching* the word of God" (Acts 18:11; cf. 15:35; 20:20, 27). Likewise, throughout the history of the church, God has raised up people to teach the Word (cf. 1 Cor. 12:28; Eph. 4:11).

The ESV Study Bible stands within this historic stream and was created specifically to provide *explanation* and *teaching*—to help people come to a deeper understanding of God's Word and the gospel, and to provide a resource for the edification and strengthening of God's people around the world.

Doctrinal Perspective

The doctrinal perspective of the ESV Study Bible is that of classic evangelical orthodoxy, in the historic stream of the Reformation. The notes are written from the perspective of confidence in the complete truthfulness of the Bible. In passages where errors or contradictions have been alleged, possible solutions to these challenges have been proposed. At times the notes also summarize interpretations that are inconsistent with classic evangelical orthodoxy, indicating how and why such views are in conflict with Scripture. Within that broad tradition of evangelical orthodoxy, the notes have sought to represent fairly the various evangelical positions on disputed topics such as baptism, the Lord's Supper, spiritual gifts, the future of ethnic Israel, and questions concerning the millennium and other events connected with the time of Christ's return.

Additional Content: Introductions and Articles

In addition to the explanatory notes, the ESV Study Bible contains an abundance of other helpful material, including:

- Extensive *introductions* to each section and book of the Bible, focusing on authorship and date of writing, the historical setting, key themes, literary features, and detailed outlines.
- Background studies on the *history and archaeology* of the ancient world, the *canon* of the Old and New Testaments, the reliability of *ancient manuscripts*, and the nature of the *original Bible languages* (Hebrew, Aramaic, and Greek).
- A compact overview of *themes in the history of salvation* that are found throughout the OT, indicating how these themes ultimately find fulfillment in Christ.
- A series of articles on the major *doctrines* and *ethical teachings* of Scripture.
- A summary of the basic differences in doctrine and the understanding of the Bible within Christianity, including *Evangelical Protestantism*, *Liberal Protestantism*, *Eastern Orthodoxy*, and *Roman Catholicism*.
- A description of the other *world religions* (modern Judaism, Islam, Hinduism, Buddhism, and Confucianism).
- An overview of the teachings of prominent *cults*, explaining how and where they depart from Scripture and classic evangelical Christianity.

Other Unique Features

The ESV Study Bible is also unique with respect to a number of newly created study Bible features. Among these unique features are:

- *Over 200 all-new full-color maps*, created with the latest satellite imagery, digital technology, and cartographic techniques. Based on extensive research and the most recent biblical archaeological scholarship, the maps are printed in full color throughout the Bible, helping to make the events, people, and places of the Bible come to life.
- *More than 40 all-new illustrations*, created specifically for the ESV Study Bible, including full-color renderings of important biblical structures, cities, and objects, shown in precise, accurate detail. These unique dimensional drawings were carefully researched and precisely rendered by architectural illustrators.
- *200-plus charts* offering key insights and analysis in clear, concise outline form, located along with the notes throughout the Bible.

Using the Cross-reference System

The ESV Study Bible includes *80,000 cross-references* and an *extensive concordance*, which together encourage easy location of important words, passages, and biblical themes. There are several kinds of cross-references. References to specific words or phrases appear as, e.g., "ver. 7" (within the same chapter), "ch. 9:6" (within the same book), or "Heb. 4:2." Brackets (e.g., "[ch. 9:6]") denote passages with a similar theme. "See" denotes less direct references (e.g., "See Jn. 8:26"). "Cited" denotes passages quoted in or from other parts of Scripture. "(Heb.)" or "(Gk.)" indicates that the similarity of a cross-referenced passage is clearer in the original Hebrew or Greek than in English.

The ESV Online Study Bible

The ESV Study Bible is being published simultaneously in print form and online. The online edition is available free to all who purchase a copy of the print edition. The online edition includes additional features, such as the ability to create personal online notes; to search and follow interactive links between notes, maps, articles, charts, timelines, illustrations, and cross-references; to listen to audio recordings of the ESV; as well as additional resources not included in the print edition. (For information on accessing the online edition, go to www.esvbible.org.)

The ESV Bible and the ESV Study Bible

Lastly, the ESV Study Bible uses the "essentially literal" ESV (English Standard Version) Bible translation as the foundational text for creating the study Bible notes and other features. Emphasizing word-for-word accuracy, literary excellence, and depth of meaning, the ESV Bible is especially suited to be the basic text for a study Bible. First published in 2001, the ESV Bible translation work involved more than 100 Bible scholars and advisors, including: (1) the 14-member Translation Oversight Committee; (2) more than 50 leading Bible Scholars; and (3) a 50-plus-member Advisory Council—all of whom are committed to historic Christian orthodoxy. Many of the ESV translation team also participated in the creation of the ESV Study Bible. The ESV Bible is available worldwide in more than 120 editions and bindings. (For more information, go to www.esv.org.)

Goal and Vision

As mentioned at the beginning of this introduction, the goal and vision of the ESV Study Bible is, first and foremost, to honor the Lord and his Word: (1) in terms of the excellence, beauty, and accuracy of its content and design, and (2) in terms of helping people to come to a deeper understanding of the Bible, of the gospel, and of Jesus Christ as their Lord and Savior. Because Crossway is a not-for-profit publishing ministry, all receipts from the ESV Study Bible are used to further the support of this goal and vision.

We are very aware, however, that anything we do will always be less than perfect and subject to error. Yet we know that God still uses imperfect and inadequate things to his honor and praise. And so to our triune God (Father, Son, and Holy Spirit), and to his people, we offer our work of creating and publishing the ESV Study Bible—with the prayer that our Lord would guard and protect from any error or deficiency that may unintentionally be in these pages; and with the prayer that by God's grace the ESV Study Bible may prove useful in bringing many to Christ and for the building up of his church worldwide, for this generation, for generations to come, and for eternity.

Soli Deo Gloria!—To God alone be the glory!

Lane T. Dennis
Executive Editor

Wayne Grudem
General Editor

Contributors

Editorial Oversight Committee

The following people comprise the Editorial Oversight Committee, which developed the concept, selected the contributors, and provided general oversight and final approval of the ESV Study Bible content and design.

Executive Editor
Lane T. Dennis
Crossway
Ph.D., Northwestern University

General Editor
Wayne Grudem
Phoenix Seminary
Ph.D., The University of Cambridge

Theological Editor
J. I. Packer
Regent College (Canada)
D.Phil., The University of Oxford

Old Testament Editor
C. John Collins
Covenant Theological Seminary
Ph.D., The University of Liverpool

New Testament Editor
Thomas R. Schreiner
The Southern Baptist Theological Seminary
Ph.D., Fuller Theological Seminary

Project Director, Managing Editor
Justin Taylor
Crossway
Ph.D. candidate, The Southern Baptist Theological Seminary

Study Note Contributors

The following people were responsible for writing the ESV Study Bible notes, as indicated below for each book of the Bible. In many cases more than one person contributed to the writing of the notes for specific books, and the notes for each of the books involved many levels of review and editing. The final notes as they appear in the ESV Study Bible, therefore, are the result of a collaborative effort, and in some cases may include content or views differing from those of individual contributors.

Genesis
T. Desmond Alexander
Union Theological College (Belfast)
Ph.D., The Queen's University of Belfast

Exodus
Kenneth Laing Harris
Covenant Theological Seminary
Ph.D., The University of Liverpool

Leviticus
John Currid
Reformed Theological Seminary (Charlotte)
Ph.D., The University of Chicago
Nobuyoshi Kiuchi
Tokyo Christian University
Ph.D., Council for National Academic Awards (UK)
Jay A. Sklar
Covenant Theological Seminary
Ph.D., The University of Gloucestershire

Numbers
Gordon J. Wenham
Trinity Theological College (Bristol)
Ph.D., King's College, The University of London

Deuteronomy
Paul Barker
Holy Trinity Doncaster (Australia)
Ph.D., The University of Gloucestershire

Joshua
V. Philips Long
Regent College (Canada)
Ph.D., The University of Cambridge

Judges
David M. Howard Jr.
Bethel Seminary (St. Paul)
Ph.D., The University of Michigan

Ruth
Ronald Bergey
Faculté Libre de Théologie Réformée (France)
Ph.D., Dropsie University

1 and 2 Samuel
David Toshio Tsumura
Japan Bible Seminary (Tokyo)
Ph.D., Brandeis University

1 and 2 Kings
Iain W. Provan
Regent College (Canada)
Ph.D., The University of Cambridge

1 and 2 Chronicles
Brian E. Kelly
Canterbury Christ Church University (England)
Ph.D., The University of Bristol

Ezra
J. Gordon McConville
The University of Gloucestershire
Ph.D., The University of Sheffield

Nehemiah
J. Gordon McConville
The University of Gloucestershire
Ph.D., The University of Sheffield

Esther
Barry G. Webb
Moore Theological College (Australia)
Ph.D., The University of Sheffield

Job
Kenneth Laing Harris
Covenant Theological Seminary
Ph.D., The University of Liverpool

August Konkel
Providence College and Seminary (Manitoba)
Ph.D., Westminster Theological Seminary

Psalms
C. John Collins
Covenant Theological Seminary
Ph.D., The University of Liverpool

Proverbs
Duane A. Garrett
The Southern Baptist Theological Seminary
Ph.D., Baylor University

Kenneth Laing Harris
Covenant Theological Seminary
Ph.D., The University of Liverpool

Ecclesiastes
Max F. Rogland
Erskine Theological Seminary
Ph.D., Leiden University

Song of Solomon
C. John Collins
Covenant Theological Seminary
Ph.D., The University of Liverpool

Andrew Stewart
M.A., Covenant Theological Seminary

Isaiah
Raymond C. Ortlund Jr.
Immanuel Church (Nashville)
Ph.D., The University of Aberdeen

Jeremiah
Paul R. House
Beeson Divinity School, Samford University
Ph.D., The Southern Baptist Theological Seminary

Lamentations
Paul R. House
Beeson Divinity School, Samford University
Ph.D., The Southern Baptist Theological Seminary

Ezekiel
David J. Reimer
The University of Edinburgh
D.Phil., The University of Oxford

Daniel
Iain M. Duguid
Grove City College
Ph.D., The University of Cambridge

Paul D. Wegner
Phoenix Seminary
Ph.D., King's College, The University of London

Hosea
Robert I. Vasholz
Covenant Theological Seminary
Th.D., The University of Stellenbosch

Joel
W. Brian Aucker
Covenant Theological Seminary
Ph.D., The University of Edinburgh

Amos
John Oswalt
Wesley Biblical Seminary
Ph.D., Brandeis University

Obadiah
Paul R. Raabe
Concordia Seminary (St. Louis)
Ph.D., The University of Michigan

Jonah
Mark D. Futato
Reformed Theological Seminary (Orlando)
Ph.D., The Catholic University of America

Micah
W. Brian Aucker
Covenant Theological Seminary
Ph.D., The University of Edinburgh

Dennis R. Magary
Trinity Evangelical Divinity School
Ph.D., The University of Wisconsin, Madison

Nahum
Walter A. Maier III
Concordia Theological Seminary (Ft. Wayne)
Ph.D., Harvard University

Habakkuk
Paul D. Wegner
Phoenix Seminary
Ph.D., King's College, The University of London

Zephaniah
David W. Baker
Ashland Theological Seminary
Ph.D., The University of London

Haggai
W. Brian Aucker
Covenant Theological Seminary
Ph.D., The University of Edinburgh

Zechariah
Iain M. Duguid
Grove City College
Ph.D., The University of Cambridge

Malachi
Gordon P. Hugenberger
Park Street Church (Boston)
Ph.D., C.N.A.A., College of St. Paul and Mary/Oxford Centre for Postgraduate Hebrew Studies

Matthew
Michael J. Wilkins
Talbot School of Theology, Biola University
Ph.D., Fuller Theological Seminary

Mark
Hans F. Bayer
Covenant Theological Seminary
Ph.D., The University of Aberdeen

Luke
Wayne Grudem
Phoenix Seminary
Ph.D., The University of Cambridge

Thomas R. Schreiner
The Southern Baptist Theological Seminary
Ph.D., Fuller Theological Seminary

John
Andreas J. Köstenberger
Southeastern Baptist Theological Seminary
Ph.D., Trinity Evangelical Divinity School

Acts
John B. Polhill
The Southern Baptist Theological Seminary
Ph.D., The Southern Baptist Theological Seminary

Romans
Thomas R. Schreiner
The Southern Baptist Theological Seminary
Ph.D., Fuller Theological Seminary

1 Corinthians
Frank S. Thielman
Beeson Divinity School, Samford University
Ph.D., Duke University

2 Corinthians
Scott J. Hafemann
Gordon-Conwell Theological Seminary
D.Theol., Eberhard-Karls-Universitat Tübingen

Galatians
Simon J. Gathercole
The University of Cambridge
Ph.D., The University of Durham

Ephesians
S. M. Baugh
Westminster Seminary California
Ph.D., The University of California, Irvine

Philippians
Sean M. McDonough
Gordon-Conwell Theological Seminary
Ph.D., The University of St. Andrews

Colossians
Clinton E. Arnold
Talbot School of Theology, Biola University
Ph.D., The University of Aberdeen

1 and 2 Thessalonians
Colin Nicholl
Research scholar
Ph.D., The University of Cambridge

1 and 2 Timothy
Ray Van Neste
Union University
Ph.D., The University of Aberdeen

Titus
Ray Van Neste
Union University
Ph.D., The University of Aberdeen

Philemon
Clinton E. Arnold
Talbot School of Theology, Biola University
Ph.D., The University of Aberdeen

Hebrews
David W. Chapman
Covenant Theological Seminary
Ph.D., The University of Cambridge

James
Grant R. Osborne
Trinity Evangelical Divinity School
Ph.D., The University of Aberdeen

1 Peter
Thomas R. Schreiner
The Southern Baptist Theological Seminary
Ph.D., Fuller Theological Seminary

2 Peter
Doug Oss
Assemblies of God Theological Seminary
Ph.D., Westminster Theological Seminary

Thomas R. Schreiner
The Southern Baptist Theological Seminary
Ph.D., Fuller Theological Seminary

1, 2, and 3 John
Robert W. Yarbrough
Trinity Evangelical Divinity School
Ph.D., The University of Aberdeen

Jude
Doug Oss
Assemblies of God Theological Seminary
Ph.D., Westminster Theological Seminary

Thomas R. Schreiner
The Southern Baptist Theological Seminary
Ph.D., Fuller Theological Seminary

Revelation
Dennis E. Johnson
Westminster Seminary California
Ph.D., Fuller Theological Seminary

Article Contributors

The following articles are included in the ESV Study Bible, written by the person(s) indicated after the title of each article.

Introduction: A User's Guide to the ESV Study Bible
Lane T. Dennis
Crossway
Ph.D., Northwestern University

Wayne Grudem
Phoenix Seminary
Ph.D., The University of Cambridge

Overview of the Bible: A Survey of the History of Salvation
Vern S. Poythress
Westminster Theological Seminary
D.Theol., The University of Stellenbosch

The Theology of the Old Testament
C. John Collins
Covenant Theological Seminary
Ph.D., The University of Liverpool

Introduction to the Pentateuch
Gordon J. Wenham
Trinity Theological College (Bristol)
Ph.D., King's College, The University of London

Introduction to the Historical Books
David M. Howard Jr.
Bethel Seminary (St. Paul)
Ph.D., The University of Michigan

Introduction to the Poetic and Wisdom Literature
David J. Reimer
The University of Edinburgh
D.Phil., The University of Oxford

Introduction to the Prophetic Books
Paul R. House
Beeson Divinity School, Samford University
Ph.D., The Southern Baptist Theological Seminary

The Time Between the Testaments
J. Julius Scott Jr.
Wheaton College, retired
Ph.D., The University of Manchester

The Roman Empire and the Greco-Roman World at the Time of the New Testament
David W. Chapman
Covenant Theological Seminary
Ph.D., The University of Cambridge

Jewish Groups at the Time of the New Testament
John C. DelHousaye
Phoenix Seminary
Ph.D., Fuller Theological Seminary

The Theology of the New Testament
Thomas R. Schreiner
The Southern Baptist Theological Seminary
Ph.D., Fuller Theological Seminary

Reading the Gospels and Acts
Darrell L. Bock
Dallas Theological Seminary
Ph.D., The University of Aberdeen

Reading the Epistles
Thomas R. Schreiner
The Southern Baptist Theological Seminary
Ph.D., Fuller Theological Seminary

God's Plan of Salvation
Mark Dever
Capitol Hill Baptist Church (Washington)
Ph.D., The University of Cambridge

Biblical Doctrine: An Overview (13 Articles)
Erik Thoennes
Talbot Theological Seminary, Biola University
Ph.D., Trinity Evangelical Divinity School

Biblical Ethics: An Overview (13 Articles)
Wayne Grudem
Phoenix Seminary
Ph.D., The University of Cambridge

Daniel R. Heimbach
Southeastern Baptist Theological Seminary
Ph.D., Drew University

C. Ben Mitchell
Trinity Evangelical Divinity School
Ph.D., The University of Tennessee

Craig Mitchell
Southwestern Baptist Theological Seminary
Ph.D., Southwestern Baptist Theological Seminary

Interpreting the Bible: An Introduction
Daniel Doriani
Central Presbyterian Church (St. Louis)
Ph.D., Westminster Theological Seminary

Interpreting the Bible: A Historical Overview
John Hannah
Dallas Theological Seminary
Ph.D., The University of Texas at Dallas

Reading the Bible Theologically
J. I. Packer
Regent College (Canada)
D.Phil., The University of Oxford

Reading the Bible as Literature
Leland Ryken
Wheaton College
Ph.D., The University of Oregon

Reading the Bible in Prayer and Communion with God
John Piper
Bethlehem Baptist Church (Minneapolis)
D.Theol., The University of Munich

Reading the Bible for Personal Application
David Powlison
Westminster Theological Seminary
Ph.D., The University of Pennsylvania

Reading the Bible for Preaching and Public Worship
R. Kent Hughes
College Church (Wheaton, IL), retired
D.Min., Trinity Evangelical Divinity School

The Canon of the Old Testament
Roger T. Beckwith
Research scholar
D.D., The University of Oxford

The Canon of the New Testament
Charles E. Hill
Reformed Theological Seminary (Orlando)
Ph.D., The University of Cambridge

The Apocrypha
Roger T. Beckwith
Research scholar
D.D., The University of Oxford

The Reliability of the Old Testament Manuscripts
Paul D. Wegner
Phoenix Seminary
Ph.D., King's College, The University of London

The Reliability of the New Testament Manuscripts
Daniel B. Wallace
Dallas Theological Seminary
Ph.D., Dallas Theological Seminary

Archaeology and the Reliability of the Old Testament
John Currid
Reformed Theological Seminary (Charlotte)
Ph.D., The University of Chicago

Archaeology and the Reliability of the New Testament
David W. Chapman
Covenant Theological Seminary
Ph.D., The University of Cambridge

The Original Languages of the Bible: Hebrew and Aramaic
Peter J. Williams
Tyndale House (Cambridge)
Ph.D., The University of Cambridge

The Original Languages of the Bible: Greek
David Alan Black
Southeastern Baptist Theological Seminary
D.Theol., The University of Basel

The Septuagint
Peter J. Gentry
The Southern Baptist Theological Seminary
Ph.D., The University of Toronto

How the New Testament Quotes and Interprets the Old Testament
C. John Collins
Covenant Theological Seminary
Ph.D., The University of Liverpool

Roman Catholicism
Gregg R. Allison
The Southern Baptist Theological Seminary
Ph.D., Trinity Evangelical Divinity School

Eastern Orthodoxy
Robert Letham
Wales Evangelical School of Theology
Ph.D., The University of Aberdeen

Liberal Protestantism
Bruce A. Ware
The Southern Baptist Theological Seminary
Ph.D., Fuller Theological Seminary

Evangelical Protestantism
Bruce A. Ware
The Southern Baptist Theological Seminary
Ph.D., Fuller Theological Seminary

Evangelical Protestantism and Global Christianity
Harold A. Netland
Trinity Evangelical Divinity School
Ph.D., Claremont Graduate School

The Bible and Contemporary Judaism
Marvin R. Wilson
Gordon College
Ph.D., Brandeis University

The Bible and Other World Religions
Harold A. Netland
Trinity Evangelical Divinity School
Ph.D., Claremont Graduate School

The Bible and Islam
Timothy C. Tennent
Asbury Theological Seminary
Ph.D., The University of Edinburgh

The Bible and Religious Cults
Ron Rhodes
Reasoning from the Scriptures Ministries
Th.D., Dallas Theological Seminary

History of Salvation in the Old Testament
Vern S. Poythress
Westminster Theological Seminary
D.Theol., The University of Stellenbosch

The ESV Study Bible benefited greatly from the work of a wide range of other contributors and consultants. The following list first indicates the specific kind of contribution, followed by a list of those who contributed or consulted in this area.

Other Contributors

Literary Features
Leland Ryken
Wheaton College
Ph.D., The University of Oregon

Maps
David Barrett (www.biblemapper.com)

Illustrations
Maltings Partnership (Derby, England)

Geography Editor
Barry J. Beitzel
Trinity Evangelical Divinity School
Ph.D., Dropsie University

Archaeological and Architectural Reconstruction Editor
Leen Ritmeyer
Ritmeyer Archaeological Design
Ph.D., The University of Manchester

Old Testament Archaeology Editor
John Currid
Reformed Theological Seminary (Charlotte)
Ph.D., The University of Chicago

New Testament Archaeology Editor
David W. Chapman
Covenant Theological Seminary
Ph.D., The University of Cambridge

Assistant Editor for Research
Travis Buchanan
M.Div., Phoenix Seminary

Consultants

Old Testament Consultants
W. Brian Aucker
Covenant Theological Seminary
Ph.D., The University of Edinburgh

Kenneth Laing Harris
Covenant Theological Seminary
Ph.D., The University of Liverpool

Paul R. House
Beeson Divinity School, Samford University
Ph.D., The Southern Baptist Theological Seminary

David J. Reimer
The University of Edinburgh
D.Phil., The University of Oxford

Gordon J. Wenham
Trinity Theological College (Bristol)
Ph.D., King's College, The University of London

New Testament Consultants
Darrell L. Bock
Dallas Theological Seminary
Ph.D., The University of Aberdeen

John C. DelHousaye
Phoenix Seminary
Ph.D., Fuller Theological Seminary

Grant R. Osborne
Trinity Evangelical Divinity School
Ph.D., The University of Aberdeen

Robert H. Stein
The Southern Baptist Theological Seminary
Ph.D., Princeton Theological Seminary

Archaeological Consultant
James K. Hoffmeier
Trinity Evangelical Divinity School
Ph.D., The University of Toronto

Old Testament Charts and Timelines Consultants
W. Brian Aucker
Covenant Theological Seminary
Ph.D., The University of Edinburgh

Kenneth Laing Harris
Covenant Theological Seminary
Ph.D., The University of Liverpool

Gregory R. Perry
Covenant Theological Seminary
Ph.D., Union Theological Seminary (Richmond)

Paul D. Wegner
Phoenix Seminary
Ph.D., The University of London

New Testament Charts and Timelines Consultants
James M. Hamilton Jr.
The Southern Baptist Theological Seminary
Ph.D., The Southern Baptist Theological Seminary

John C. DelHousaye
Phoenix Seminary
Ph.D., Fuller Theological Seminary

Ethics Consultant
Robert A.J. Gagnon
Pittsburgh Theological Seminary
Ph.D., Princeton Theological Seminary

Cults Consultant
Robert M. Bowman Jr.
Institute for Religious Research
M.A., Fuller Theological Seminary

PREFACE
TO THE ENGLISH STANDARD VERSION

The Bible

"This Book [is] the most valuable thing that this world affords. Here is Wisdom; this is the royal Law; these are the lively Oracles of God." With these words the Moderator of the Church of Scotland hands a Bible to the new monarch in Britain's coronation service. These words echo the King James Bible translators, who wrote in 1611: "God's sacred Word . . . is that inestimable treasure that excelleth all the riches of the earth." This assessment of the Bible is the motivating force behind the publication of the English Standard Version.

Translation Legacy

The English Standard Version (ESV) stands in the classic mainstream of English Bible translations over the past half-millennium. The fountainhead of that stream was William Tyndale's New Testament of 1526; marking its course were the King James Version of 1611 (KJV), the English Revised Version of 1885 (RV), the American Standard Version of 1901 (ASV), and the Revised Standard Version of 1952 and 1971 (RSV). In that stream, faithfulness to the text and vigorous pursuit of accuracy were combined with simplicity, beauty, and dignity of expression. Our goal has been to carry forward this legacy for a new century.

To this end each word and phrase in the ESV has been carefully weighed against the original Hebrew, Aramaic, and Greek to ensure the fullest accuracy and clarity and to avoid under-translating or overlooking any nuance of the original text. The words and phrases themselves grow out of the Tyndale–King James legacy, and most recently out of the RSV, with the 1971 RSV text providing the starting point for our work. Archaic language has been brought to current usage and significant corrections have been made in the translation of key texts. But throughout, our goal has been to retain the depth of meaning and enduring language that have made their indelible mark on the English-speaking world and have defined the life and doctrine of the church over the last four centuries.

Translation Philosophy

The ESV is an "essentially literal" translation that seeks as much as possible to capture the precise wording of the original text and the personal style of each Bible writer. As such, its emphasis is on "word-for-word" correspondence, at the same time taking into account differences of grammar, syntax, and idiom between current literary English and the original languages. Thus it seeks to be transparent to the original text, letting the reader see as directly as possible the structure and meaning of the original.

In contrast to the ESV, some Bible versions have followed a "thought-for-thought" rather than "word-for-word" translation philosophy, emphasizing "dynamic equivalence" rather than the "essentially literal" meaning of the original. A "thought-for-thought" translation is of necessity more inclined to reflect the interpretative opinions of the translator and the influences of contemporary culture.

Every translation is at many points a trade-off between literal precision and readability, between "formal equivalence" in expression and "functional equivalence" in communication, and the ESV is no exception. Within this framework we have sought to be "as literal as possible" while maintaining clarity of expression and literary excellence. Therefore, to the extent that plain English permits and the meaning in each case allows, we have sought to use the same English word for important recurring words in the original; and, as far as grammar and syntax allow, we have rendered Old Testament passages cited in the New in ways that show their correspondence. Thus in each of these areas, as well as throughout the Bible as a whole, we have sought to capture the echoes and overtones of meaning that are so abundantly present in the original texts.

As an essentially literal translation, then, the ESV seeks to carry over every possible nuance of meaning in the original words of Scripture into our own language. As such, the ESV is ideally suited for in-depth study of the Bible. Indeed, with its emphasis on literary excellence, the ESV is equally suited for public reading and preaching, for private reading and reflection, for both academic and devotional study, and for Scripture memorization.

Translation Principles and Style

The ESV also carries forward classic translation principles in its literary style. Accordingly it retains theological terminology—words such as "grace," "faith," "justification," "sanctification," "redemption," "regeneration," "reconciliation," "propitiation"—because of their central importance for Christian doctrine and also because the underlying Greek words were already becoming key words and technical terms in New Testament times.

The ESV lets the stylistic variety of the biblical writers fully express itself—from the exalted prose that opens Genesis, to the flowing narratives of the Historical Books, to the rich metaphors and dramatic imagery of the Poetic Books, to the ringing rhetorical indictments in the Prophetic Books, to the smooth elegance of Luke, to the profound simplicities of John and the closely reasoned logic of Paul.

In punctuating, paragraphing, dividing long sentences, and rendering connectives, the ESV follows the path that seems to make the ongoing flow of thought clearest in English. The biblical languages regularly connect sentences by frequent repetition of words such as "and," "but," and "for," in a way that goes beyond the conventions of literary English. Effective translation, however, requires that these links in the original be reproduced so that the flow of the argument will be transparent to the reader. We have therefore normally translated these connectives, though occasionally we have varied the rendering by using alternatives (such as "also," "however," "now," "so," "then," or "thus") when they better capture the sense in specific instances.

In the area of gender language, the goal of the ESV is to render literally what is in the original. For example, "anyone" replaces "any man" where there is no word corresponding to "man" in the original languages, and "people" rather than "men" is regularly used where the original languages refer to both men and women. But the words "man" and "men" are retained where a male-meaning component is part of the original Greek or Hebrew. Likewise, the word "man" has been retained where the original text intends to convey a clear contrast between "God" on the one hand and "man" on the other hand, with "man" being used in the collective sense of the whole human race (see Luke 2:52). Similarly, the English word "brothers" (translating the Greek word *adelphoi*) is retained as an important familial form of address between fellow Jews and fellow Christians in the first century. A recurring note is included to indicate that the term "brothers" (*adelphoi*) was often used in Greek to refer to both men and women, and to indicate the specific instances in the text where this is the case. In addition, the English word "sons" (translating the Greek word *huioi*) is retained in specific instances because the underlying Greek term usually includes a male-meaning component and it was used as a legal term in the adoption and inheritance laws of first-century Rome. As used by the apostle Paul, this term refers to the status of all Christians, both men and women, who, having been adopted into God's family, now enjoy all the privileges, obligations, and inheritance rights of God's children.

The inclusive use of the generic "he" has also regularly been retained, because this is consistent with similar usage in the original languages and because an essentially literal translation would be impossible without it.

In each case the objective has been transparency to the original text, allowing the reader to understand the original on its own terms rather than on the terms of our present-day culture.

The Translation of Specialized Terms

In the translation of biblical terms referring to God, the ESV takes great care to convey the specific nuances of meaning of the original Hebrew and Greek terms. First, concerning terms that refer to God in the Old Testament: God, the Maker of heaven and earth, introduced himself to the people of Israel with a special personal name, the consonants for which are YHWH (see Exodus 3:14–15). Scholars call this the "Tetragrammaton," a Greek term referring to the four Hebrew letters YHWH. The exact pronunciation of YHWH is uncertain, because the Jewish people considered the personal name of God to be so holy that it should never be spoken aloud. Instead of reading the word YHWH, they would normally read the Hebrew word *'adonay* ("Lord"), and the ancient translations into Greek, Syriac, and Aramaic also followed this practice. When the vowels of the word *'adonay* are placed with the consonants of YHWH, this results in the familiar word *Jehovah* that was used in some earlier English Bible translations. As is common among English translations today, the ESV usually renders the personal name of God (YHWH) with the word LORD (printed in small capitals). An exception to this is when the Hebrew word *'adonay* appears together with YHWH, in which case the two words are rendered together as "the Lord [in lower case] GOD [in small capitals]." In contrast to the personal name for God (YHWH), the more general name for God in Old Testament Hebrew is *'elohim* and its related forms of *'el* or *'eloah*, all of which are normally translated "God" (in lower case letters). The use of these different ways to translate the Hebrew words for God is especially beneficial to the English reader, enabling the reader to see and understand the different ways that the *personal* name and the *general* name for God are both used to refer to the *One True God* of the Old Testament.

Second, in the New Testament, the Greek word *Christos* has been translated consistently as "Christ." Although the term originally meant "anointed," among Jews in New Testament times the term came to designate the Messiah, the great Savior that God had promised to raise up. In other New Testament contexts, however, especially among Gentiles, *Christos* ("Christ") was on its way to becoming a proper name. It is important, therefore, to keep the context in mind in understanding the various ways that *Christos* ("Christ") is used in the New Testament. At the same time, in accord with its "essentially literal" translation philosophy, the ESV has retained consistency and concordance in the translation of *Christos* ("Christ") throughout the New Testament.

Third, a particular difficulty is presented when words in biblical Hebrew and Greek refer to ancient practices and institutions that do not correspond directly to those in the modern world. Such is the case in the translation of *'ebed* (Hebrew) and *doulos* (Greek), terms which are often rendered "slave." These terms, however, actually cover a range of relationships that require a range of renderings—either "slave," "bondservant," or "servant"—depending on the context. Further, the word "slave" currently carries associations with the often brutal and dehumanizing institution of slavery in nineteenth-century America. For this reason, the ESV translation of the words *'ebed* and *doulos* has been undertaken with particular attention to their meaning in each specific context. Thus in Old Testament times, one might enter slavery either voluntarily (e.g., to escape poverty or to pay off a debt) or involuntarily (e.g., by birth, by being captured in battle, or by judicial sentence). Protection for all in servitude in ancient Israel was provided by the Mosaic Law. In New Testament times, a *doulos* is often best described as a "bondservant"—that is, as someone bound to serve his master for a specific (usually lengthy) period of time, but also as someone who might nevertheless own property, achieve social advancement, and even be released or purchase his freedom. The ESV usage thus seeks to express the nuance of meaning in each context. Where absolute ownership by a master is in view (as in Romans 6), "slave" is used; where a more limited form of servitude is in view, "bondservant" is used (as in 1 Corinthians 7:21–24); where the context indicates a wide range of freedom (as in John 4:51), "servant" is preferred. Footnotes are generally provided to identify the Hebrew or Greek and the range of meaning that these terms may carry in each case.

Fourth, it is sometimes suggested that Bible translations should capitalize pronouns referring to deity. It has seemed best not to capitalize deity pronouns in the ESV, however, for the following reasons: first, there is nothing in the original Hebrew and Greek manuscripts that corresponds to such capitalization; second, the practice of capitalizing deity pronouns in English Bible translations is a recent innovation, which began only in the mid-twentieth century; and, third, such capitalization is absent from the KJV Bible and the whole stream of Bible translations that the ESV seeks to carry forward.

A fifth specialized term, the word "behold," usually has been retained as the most common translation for the Hebrew word *hinneh* and the Greek word *idou*. Both of these words mean something like

"Pay careful attention to what follows! This is important!" Other than the word "behold," there is no single word in English that fits well in most contexts. Although "Look!" and "See!" and "Listen!" would be workable in some contexts, in many others these words lack sufficient weight and dignity. Given the principles of "essentially literal" translation, it is important not to leave *hinneh* and *idou* completely untranslated, and so to lose the intended emphasis in the original languages. The older and more formal word "behold" has usually been retained, therefore, as the best available option for conveying the original sense of meaning.

Textual Basis and Resources

The ESV is based on the Masoretic text of the Hebrew Bible as found in *Biblia Hebraica Stuttgartensia* (2nd ed., 1983), and on the Greek text in the 1993 editions of the *Greek New Testament* (4th corrected ed.), published by the United Bible Societies (UBS), and *Novum Testamentum Graece* (27th ed.), edited by Nestle and Aland. The currently renewed respect among Old Testament scholars for the Masoretic text is reflected in the ESV's attempt, wherever possible, to translate difficult Hebrew passages as they stand in the Masoretic text rather than resorting to emendations or to finding an alternative reading in the ancient versions. In exceptional, difficult cases, the Dead Sea Scrolls, the Septuagint, the Samaritan Pentateuch, the Syriac Peshitta, the Latin Vulgate, and other sources were consulted to shed possible light on the text, or, if necessary, to support a divergence from the Masoretic text. Similarly, in a few difficult cases in the New Testament, the ESV has followed a Greek text different from the text given preference in the UBS/Nestle-Aland 27th edition. Throughout, the translation team has benefited greatly from the massive textual resources that have become readily available recently, from new insights into biblical laws and culture, and from current advances in Hebrew and Greek lexicography and grammatical understanding.

Textual Footnotes

The footnotes that accompany the ESV text are an integral part of the ESV translation, informing the reader of textual variations and difficulties and showing how these have been resolved by the ESV translation team. In addition to this, the footnotes indicate significant alternative readings and occasionally provide an explanation for technical terms or for a difficult reading in the text.

Publishing Team

The ESV publishing team includes more than a hundred people. The fourteen-member Translation Oversight Committee has benefited from the work of more than fifty biblical experts serving as Translation Review Scholars and from the comments of the more than fifty members of the Advisory Council, all of which has been carried out under the auspices of the Crossway Board of Directors. This hundred-plus-member team shares a common commitment to the truth of God's Word and to historic Christian orthodoxy and is international in scope, including leaders in many denominations.

To God's Honor and Praise

We know that no Bible translation is perfect or final; but we also know that God uses imperfect and inadequate things to his honor and praise. So to our triune God and to his people we offer what we have done, with our prayers that it may prove useful, with gratitude for much help given, and with ongoing wonder that our God should ever have entrusted to us so momentous a task.

Soli Deo Gloria!—To God alone be the glory!

*The Translation Oversight Committee**

*A complete list of the Translation Oversight Committee, the Translation Review Scholars, and the Advisory Council, is available upon request from Crossway.

Overview of the Bible: A Survey of the History of Salvation

How does the Bible as a whole fit together? The events recorded in the Bible took place over a span of thousands of years and in several different cultural settings. What is their unifying thread?

One unifying thread in the Bible is its divine authorship. *Every book of the Bible is God's word.* The events recorded in the Bible are there because God wanted them recorded, and he had them recorded with his people and their instruction in mind: "For whatever was written in former days was written for our instruction, that through endurance and through the encouragement of the Scriptures we might have hope" (Rom. 15:4).

God's Plan for History

The Bible also makes it clear that *God has a unified plan for all of history.* His ultimate purpose, "a plan for the fullness of time," is "to unite all things in him [Christ], things in heaven and things on earth" (Eph. 1:10), "to the praise of his glory" (Eph. 1:12). God had this plan even from the beginning: "remember the former things of old; for I am God, and there is no other; I am God, and there is none like me, declaring the end from the beginning and from ancient times things not yet done, saying, 'My counsel shall stand, and I will accomplish all my purpose'" (Isa. 46:9–10). "When the fullness of time had come," when the moment was appropriate in God's plan, "God sent forth his Son, born of woman, born under the law, to redeem those who were under the law" (Gal. 4:4–5).

The work of Christ on earth, and especially his crucifixion and resurrection, is the climax of history; it is the great turning point at which God actually accomplished the salvation toward which history had been moving throughout the OT. The present era looks back on Christ's completed work but also looks forward to the consummation of his work when Christ will come again and when there will appear "new heavens and a new earth in which righteousness dwells" (2 Pet. 3:13; see Rev. 21:1–22:5).

The unity of God's plan makes it appropriate for him to include *promises and predictions* at earlier points in time, and then for the *fulfillments* of these to come at later points. Sometimes the promises take *explicit* form, as when God promises the coming of the Messiah, the great Savior whom Israel expected (Isa. 9:6–7). Sometimes the promises take *symbolic* form, as when God commanded animal sacrifices to be offered as a symbol for the forgiveness of sins (Leviticus 4). In themselves, the animal sacrifices were not able to remove sins permanently and to atone for them permanently (Heb. 10:1–18). They pointed forward to Christ, who is the final and complete sacrifice for sins.

Christ in the Old Testament

Since God's plan focuses on Christ and his glory (Eph. 1:10), it is natural that the promises of God and the symbols in the OT all point forward to him. "For all the promises of God find their Yes in him [Christ]" (2 Cor. 1:20). When Christ appeared to the disciples after his resurrection, his teaching focused on showing them how the OT pointed to him: "And he said to them, 'O foolish ones, and slow of heart to believe all that the prophets have spoken! Was it not necessary that the Christ should suffer these things and enter into his glory?' And beginning with Moses and all the Prophets, he interpreted to them in all the Scriptures the things concerning himself" (Luke 24:25–27). One could also look at Luke 24:44–48: "Then he said to them, 'These are my words that I spoke to you while I was still with you, that everything written about me in the Law of Moses and the Prophets and the Psalms must be fulfilled.' Then he opened their minds to understand the Scriptures, and said to them, 'Thus it is written, that the Christ should suffer and on the third day rise from the dead, and that repentance and forgiveness of sins should be proclaimed in his name to all nations, beginning from Jerusalem. You are witnesses of these things.'"

When the Bible says that "he opened their minds to understand *the Scriptures*" (Luke 24:45), it cannot mean just a few scattered predictions about the Messiah. It means the OT as a whole, encompassing all three of the major divisions of the OT that the Jews traditionally recognized. "The Law of Moses" includes Genesis to Deuteronomy. "The Prophets" include both the "former prophets" (the historical books Joshua, Judges, 1–2 Samuel, and 1–2 Kings) and the "latter prophets" (Isaiah, Jeremiah, Ezekiel, and the 12 Minor Prophets, Hosea–Malachi). "The Psalms" is representative of the third grouping by the Jews, called the "Writings." (The book of Daniel was placed in this group.) At the heart of understanding all these OT books is the truth that they point forward to the suffering of Christ, his resurrection, and the subsequent spread of the gospel to "all nations" (Luke 24:47). The OT as a whole, through its promises, its symbols, and its pictures of salvation, looks forward to the actual accomplishment of salvation that took place once for all in the life, death, and resurrection of Jesus Christ.

The Promises of God

In what ways does the OT look forward to Christ? First, it directly points forward through *promises of salvation and promises concerning God's commitment to his people.* God gave some specific promises in the OT relating to the coming of Christ as the Messiah, the Savior in the line of David. Through the prophet Micah, God promises that the Messiah is to be born in Bethlehem, the city of David (Mic. 5:2), a prophecy strikingly fulfilled in the NT (Matt. 2:1–12). But God often gives more general promises concerning a future great day of salvation, without spelling out all the details of how he will accomplish it (e.g., Isa. 25:6–9; 60:1–7). Sometimes he promises simply to be their God (see Gen. 17:7).

One common refrain is that, "I will be their God, and they shall be my people" (cf. Jer. 31:33; Hos. 2:23; Zech. 8:8; 13:9; Heb. 8:10). Variations on this broad theme may sometimes focus more on the people and what they will be, while at other times they focus on God and what he will do. God's promise to "be their God" is really his comprehensive commitment to be with his people, to care for them, to discipline them, to protect them, to supply their needs, and to have a personal relationship with them. If that commitment continues, it promises to result ultimately in the final salvation that God works out in Christ.

The principle extends to all the promises in the OT. "For all the promises of God find their Yes in him [Christ]" (2 Cor. 1:20). Sometimes God gives immediate, temporal blessings. These blessings are only a foretaste of the rich, eternal blessings that come through Christ: "Blessed be the God and Father of our Lord Jesus Christ, who has blessed us in Christ with every spiritual blessing in the heavenly places" (Eph. 1:3).

Warnings and Curses

God's relation to people includes not only blessings but also warnings, threatenings, and cursings. These are appropriate because of God's righteous reaction to sin. They anticipate and point forward to Christ in two distinct ways. First, *Christ is the Lamb of God, the sin-bearer* (John 1:29; 1 Pet. 2:24). He was innocent of sin, but became sin for us and bore the curse of God on the cross (2 Cor. 5:21; Gal. 3:13). Every instance of the wrath of God against sin, and his punishments of sin, looks forward to the wrath that was poured out on Christ on the cross.

Second, *Christ at his second coming wars against sin and exterminates it.* The second coming and the consummation are the time when the final judgment against sin is executed. All earlier judgments against sin anticipate the final judgment. Christ during his earthly life anticipated this final judgment when he cast out demons and when he denounced the sins of the religious leaders.

Covenants

The promises of God in the OT come in the context not only of God's commitment to his people but also of instruction about the people's commitment and obligations to God. Noah, Abraham, and others whom God meets and addresses are called on to respond not only with trust in God's promises but with lives that begin to bear fruit from their fellowship with God. The relation of God to his people is summed up in various *covenants* that God makes with people. A covenant between two human beings is a binding commitment obliging them to deal faithfully with one another (as with Jacob and Laban in Gen. 31:44). When God makes a covenant with man, God is the sovereign, so he specifies the obligations on both sides. "I will be their God" is the fundamental obligation on God's side, while "they shall be my people" is the fundamental obligation on the human side. But then there are variations in the details.

For example, when God first calls Abram he says, "Go from your country and your kindred and your father's house to the land that I will show you" (Gen. 12:1). This commandment specifies an obligation on the part of Abram, an obligation on the human side. God also indicates what he will do on his part: "And I will make of you a great nation, and I will bless you and make your name great, so that you will be a blessing" (Gen. 12:2). God's commitment takes the form of promises, blessings, and curses. The *promises and blessings* point forward to Christ, who is the fulfillment of the promises and the source of final blessings. The *curses* point forward to Christ both in his bearing the curse and in his execution of judgment and curse against sin, especially at the second coming.

The obligations on the human side of the covenants are also related to Christ. Christ is fully man as well as fully God. As a man, he stands with his people on the human side. He fulfilled the obligations of God's covenants through his perfect obedience (Heb. 5:8). He received the reward of obedience in his resurrection and ascension (see Phil. 2:9–10). The OT covenants on their human side thus point forward to his achievement.

By dealing with the wrath of God against sin, Christ changed a situation of alienation from God to a situation of peace. He reconciled believers to God (2 Cor. 5:18–21; Rom. 5:6–11). He brought personal intimacy with God, and the privilege of being children of God (Rom. 8:14–17). This intimacy is what all the OT covenants anticipated. In Isaiah, God even declares that his servant, the Messiah, will *be* the covenant for the people (see Isa. 42:6; 49:8).

Offspring

It is worthwhile to focus on one specific element in OT covenants, namely, the promise concerning offspring. In making a covenant with Abram, God calls on him to "walk before me, and be blameless" (Gen. 17:1). That is a human obligation in the covenant. On the divine side, God promises that he will make Abram "the father of a multitude of nations" (Gen. 17:4), and he renames him Abraham (Gen. 17:5). The covenant with Abraham in fact extends beyond Abraham to his posterity: "And I will establish my covenant between me and you and *your offspring after you* throughout their generations for an *everlasting* covenant, to be God to you and to your offspring after you. And I will give to you and to your offspring after you the land of your sojournings, all the land of Canaan, for an everlasting possession, and I will be their God" (Gen. 17:7–8).

The promises made to Abraham are exceedingly important within the OT because they are the foundation for the nation of Israel. The history after Abraham shows that Abraham had a son, Isaac, in fulfillment of God's promise to Sarah. Isaac was the immediate result of God's promise of offspring who will inherit the land. Isaac in turn had a son, Jacob, and Jacob was the father of 12 sons who in turn multiplied into the 12 tribes of Israel. The nation of Israel became the next stage in the offspring that God promised.

But how does this relate to Christ? Christ is the descendant of David and of Abraham, as the genealogy in Matthew indicates (Matt. 1:1). Christ is the offspring of Abraham. In fact, he is the offspring in a uniquely emphatic sense: "Now the promises were made to Abraham and to his offspring. It does not say, 'And to offsprings,' referring to many, but referring to one, 'And to your offspring,' *who is Christ*" (Gal. 3:16; see notes on Gen. 22:15–18).

Abraham was told to "walk before me, and be blameless" (Gen. 17:1). Abraham was basically a man of faith who trusted God (Gal. 3:9; Heb. 11:8–12, 17–19). But Abraham also had his failures and sins. Who will walk before God and be blameless in an ultimate way? Not Abraham. Not anyone else on earth either, except Christ himself (Heb. 4:15). All the other candidates for being "offspring" of Abraham ultimately fail to be blameless. Thus the covenant with Abraham has an unbreakable tie to Christ. Christ is the ultimate offspring to whom the other offspring all point. One may go down the list of offspring: Isaac, Jacob, then the sons of Jacob. Among these sons, Judah is their leader who will have kingship (Gen. 49:10). David is the descendant of Abraham and Judah; Solomon is the descendant of David; and then comes Rehoboam and the others who descend from David and Solomon (Matt. 1:1–16).

Christ is not only the descendant of all of them by legal right; he is also superior to all of them as the uniquely blameless offspring. Through Christ believers are united to him and thereby themselves become "Abraham's offspring" (Gal. 3:29). Believers, Jews and Gentiles alike, become heirs to the promises of God made to Abraham and his offspring: "There is neither Jew nor Greek, there is neither slave nor free, there is no male and female, for you are all one in Christ Jesus. And if you are Christ's, then you are Abraham's offspring, heirs according to promise" (Gal. 3:28–29).

Christ as the Last Adam

Christ is not only the offspring of Abraham, but—reaching back farther in time to an earlier promise of God—the offspring of the woman: "I will put enmity between you [the serpent] and the woman, and between your offspring and her *offspring*; he shall bruise your head, and you shall bruise his heel" (Gen. 3:15). The conquest over the serpent, and therefore the conquest of evil and the reversal of its effects, is to take place through the offspring of the woman. One can trace this offspring down from Eve through Seth and his godly descendants, through Noah, and down to Abraham, where God's promise takes the specific form of offspring for Abraham (see Luke 3:23–38, which traces Jesus' genealogy all the way back to Adam). Thus Christ is not only the offspring of Abraham but the last Adam (1 Cor. 15:45–49). Like Adam, he represents all who belong to him. And he reverses the effects of Adam's fall.

Shadows, Prefigures, and "Types"

The NT constantly talks about Christ and the salvation that he has brought. That is obvious. What is not so obvious is that the same is true of the OT, though it does this by way of *anticipation*. It gives us "shadows" and "types" of the things that were to come (see 1 Cor. 10:6, 11; Heb. 8:5).

For example, 1 Corinthians 10:6 indicates that the events the Israelites experienced in the wilderness were "examples for us." And 1 Corinthians 10:11 says, "Now these things happened to them as an example, but they were written down for our instruction, on whom the end of the ages has come." In 1 Corinthians 10:6 and 11, the Greek word for "example" is *typos*, from which derives the English word "type" (cf. Rom. 5:14).

A "type," in the language of theology, is *a special example, symbol, or picture that God designed beforehand, and that he placed in history at an earlier point in time in order to point forward to a later, larger fulfillment*. Animal sacrifices in the OT prefigure the final sacrifice of Christ. So these animal sacrifices were "types" of Christ. The temple, as a dwelling place for God, prefigured Christ, who is the final "dwelling place" of God, and through whom God comes to be with his people (Matt. 1:23; John 2:21). The OT priests were types of Christ, who is the final high priest (Heb. 7:11–8:7).

Fulfillment takes place preeminently in Christ (Eph. 1:10; 2 Cor. 1:20). But in the NT those people who are "in Christ," who place their trust in him and experience fellowship with his person and his blessings, receive the benefits of what he has accomplished, and therefore one can also find anticipations or "types" in the OT that point forward to the NT church, the people in the NT who belong to Christ. For example, the OT temple not only prefigured Christ, whose body is the temple (John 2:21), but prefigured the church, which is also called a temple (1 Cor. 3:16–17), because it is indwelt by the Holy Spirit. Some OT symbols also may point forward especially to the consummation of salvation that takes place in the new heaven and the new earth yet to come (2 Pet. 3:13; Rev. 21:1–22:5). Old Testament Jerusalem prefigured the new Jerusalem that will come "down out of heaven from God" (Rev. 21:2).

Christ the Mediator

The Bible makes it clear that ever since the fall of Adam into sin, sin and its consequences have been the pervasive problem of the human race. It is a constant theme running through the Bible. Sin is rebellion against God, and it deserves death: "the wages of sin is death" (Rom. 6:23). God is holy, and no sinful human being, not even a great man like Moses, can stand in the presence of God without dying: "you cannot see my face, for man shall not see me and live" (Ex. 33:20). Sinful man needs a *mediator* who will approach God on his behalf. Christ, who is both God and man, and who is innocent of sin, is the only one who can serve: "there is one mediator between God and men, the man Christ Jesus, who gave himself as a ransom for all" (1 Tim. 2:5–6).

Though there is only one mediator in an ultimate sense, in a subordinate way various people in the OT serve in some kind of mediatorial capacity. Moses is one of them. He went up to Mount Sinai to meet God while all the people waited at the bottom of the mountain (Exodus 19). When the people of Israel were terrified at hearing God's audible voice from the mountain, they asked for Moses to bring them God's words from then on (Ex. 20:18–21). God approved of the arrangement involving Moses bringing his words to the people (Deut. 5:28–33).

But if there is only one mediator, as 1 Timothy 2:5 says, how could Moses possibly serve in that way? Moses was not the ultimate mediator, but he *prefigured* Christ's mediation. Because Moses was sinful, he could not possibly have survived the presence of God without forgiveness, that is, without having a sinless mediator on his own behalf. God welcomed Moses into his presence only because, according to the plan of God, Christ was to come and make atonement for Moses. The benefits of Christ's work were reckoned beforehand for Moses' benefit. And so it must have been for all the OT saints. How could they have been saved otherwise? God is perfectly holy, and they all needed perfection. Perfection was graciously reckoned to them because of Christ, who was to come.

That means that *there is only one way of salvation*, throughout the OT as well as in the NT. Only Christ can save us. "And there is salvation in no one else, for there is no other name under heaven given among men by which we must be saved" (Acts 4:12). The instances of salvation in the OT all depend on Christ. And in the OT, salvation frequently comes through a *mediator*, a person or institution that stands between God and man. All the small instances of mediation in the OT prefigure Christ. How else could it be, since there is only one mediator and one way of salvation?

So understanding of the unity of the Bible increases when one pays attention to *instances where God brings salvation*, and *instances where a mediator stands between God and man*. These instances include not only cases where God brings *spiritual* salvation in the form of personal fellowship, spiritual intimacy, and the promise of eternal life with God. They also include instances of *temporal*, external deliverance—"salvation" in a physical sense, which prefigures salvation in a spiritual sense. And indeed, salvation is not *merely* spiritual. Christians look forward to the resurrection of the body and to "new heavens and a new earth in which righteousness dwells" (2 Pet. 3:13). Personal salvation starts with renewal of the heart, but in the end it will be comprehensive and cosmic in scope. The OT, when it pays attention to physical land and physical prosperity and physical health, anticipates the physicality of the believer's prosperity in the new heavens and the new earth.

Instances of mediators in the OT include prophets, kings, and priests. *Prophets* bring the word of God from God to the people. *Kings*, when they submit to God, bring God's rule to bear on the people. *Priests* represent the people in coming before God's presence. Christ is the final prophet, king, and priest who fulfills all three functions in a final way (Heb. 1:1–3). One can also look at *wise men*, who bring God's wisdom to others; *warriors*, who bring God's deliverance from enemies; and *singers*, who bring praise to God on behalf of the people and speak of the character of God to the people.

Mediation occurs not only through human figures, but through institutions. *Covenants* play a mediatorial role in bringing God's word to the people. The *temple* brings God's presence to the people. The *animal sacrifices* bring God's forgiveness to the people. In reading the Bible one should look for ways in which God brings his word and his presence to people through *means* that he establishes. All these means perform a kind of mediatorial role, and because there is only one mediator, it is clear that they all point to Christ. ◂

THE
OLD TESTAMENT

The Theology of the Old Testament

When it comes to describing "the theology of the Old Testament," not everyone is convinced that there is a single theology represented in these diverse books. Many scholars have, however, tried to find a point of unity for all the books, often by proposing a single unifying theme, such as *covenant*, or *the kingdom of God*, or *the Messiah*, or *God himself*. These proposals do provide genuine insights, but they are often too oversimplified to do justice to the variety of materials in the OT.

It will be more fruitful to understand the OT as a whole in terms of an unfolding story, with a number of basic components: *monotheism*, *creation and fall*, *election and covenant*, *covenant membership*, and *eschatology*. This article will first explain these components, so that we can summarize the overarching story. Then we will consider briefly how the various parts of the OT relate to this unfolding story, and consider how this provides a link to the NT authors' stance toward the OT. The goal is to articulate some of the beliefs that will enable the careful reader to profit more fully from reading the OT books themselves.

The Components of the Story

1. *Monotheism.* There is only one true God, who made heaven and earth and all mankind. He made a material world that he is happy with, and he made it a fit place for human beings to live, and love, and serve. Every human being needs to know and love this God, whose spotless moral purity, magnificent power and wisdom, steadfast faithfulness, and unceasing love are breathtakingly beautiful. This one God rules over all things, and he will vindicate his own goodness and justice (in his own time). In ruling, God has not limited himself to working within the natural properties of what he has made, for he can go (and has gone) beyond these properties to do mighty deeds both in creation and in caring for his people.

The OT invites Israel, not simply to acknowledge the existence of this one true God, but to commit themselves to him in exclusive loyalty and love, centering their lives on the inestimable privilege of knowing him (Deut. 6:4–9). The fundamental character of this God is explained in Exodus 34:6–7, which focuses on his steadfast love and mercy (a passage frequently echoed in the rest of the OT). The OT also affirms that God is "righteous," i.e., morally pure and perfect. Although this righteousness certainly results in God's work of punishing evildoers and vindicating his own moral character, the term commonly emphasizes God's reliability in keeping his promises (e.g., Ps. 71:2; 116:5).

The OT does not explicitly describe God as a trinity. Rather, with its references to God's Spirit (e.g., Gen. 1:2), its use of "us/our" for God (e.g., Gen. 1:26), and its indications or hints of a divine Messiah (e.g., Ps. 110:5; Isa. 9:6; cf. Ezek. 34:15, 23), it lays the groundwork for the fuller declaration of divine triunity that is found in the NT (Matt. 28:19; 1 Cor. 12:4–6; 2 Cor. 13:14).

2. *Creation and fall.* The one Creator God made the first human beings, Adam and Eve, with dignity and purpose; their calling was to live faithfully to God and to spread the blessings of Eden throughout the earth. Because Adam and Eve betrayed God's purpose, all people since the fall are beset with sins and weaknesses that only God's grace can redeem and heal.

3. *Election and covenant.* The one true God chose a people for himself and bound himself to them by his covenant (Ex. 19:4–6; Deut. 7:6–11). This covenant expressed God's intention to save the people, and through them to bring light to the rest of the world, in order to restore all things to their proper functioning in the world God made. The land of Israel was to be a kind of reconstituted Eden, which would flourish as the people's faithfulness flourished (or languish if the people were unfaithful). God's covenants generally involve one person who represents the whole people (e.g., Adam, Noah, Abraham, David): the rest of the people experience the covenant by virtue of their inclusion in the community represented. The representative is required to embody the ideal of covenant faithfulness as a model for those on whose behalf he has acted.

4. *Covenant membership.* In his covenant, God offers his grace to his people: the forgiveness of their sins, the shaping of their lives in this world to reflect his own glory, and a part to play in bringing light to the Gentiles. Each member of God's people is responsible to lay hold of this grace from the heart: to believe the promises (see Paul's use of Abraham and David as examples of faith in Rom. 4:1–25; cf. also Heb. 11:1–40), and then to grow in obeying the commands, and to keep on doing so all their lives long. Those who lay hold in this way are the faithful. These people, as distinct from the unfaithful among them, enjoy the full benefits of God's love. Each Israelite is a member of a people, a corporate entity; the members have a mutual participation in the life of the people as a whole. Thus the spiritual and moral well-being of the whole affects the well-being of each of the members, and each member contributes to the others by his own spiritual and moral life. Thus each one shares the joys and sorrows of the others, and of the whole. Historical judgments upon the whole people often come because too many of the members are unfaithful; these judgments do not, however, bring the story of God's people to an end but serve rather to purify and chasten that people (often by removing unbelieving members).

It is important for Christian readers to sharpen their grasp of how the OT uses words such as "salvation" and "judgment." When the OT speaks of God "redeeming" his people (e.g., Ex. 15:13) or "saving" them (e.g., Ex. 14:30), it refers to God's gracious dealings for the sake of this corporate entity, the people: he calls it, he protects it, he purifies it, in order to foster the conditions under which the life of its members may flourish. The OT can also speak of God giving "salvation" or "redemption" to particular persons (e.g., Ps. 3:2, 7; 19:14). Generally in the OT, however, such expressions refer to members of the people experiencing the benefits of covenant membership, whether that be forgiveness of sins, or deliverance from some trouble or persecution, or something else—tracing everything back to the grace of God that led him to make the covenant originally and now to keep it in effect. When Christians speak of personal salvation, they usually are thinking of individuals in isolation, and so have a much narrower meaning in mind; they should consider whether the NT usage is closer to the OT usage than they might have realized hitherto, including both every aspect of their lives and their connections to other believers, and thus extending to a wider range of experience than simply their souls.

The "law," given through Moses, plays a vital role in the OT. It is uniformly presented as an object of delight and admiration (e.g., Psalm 119) because it is a gift from a loving and gracious God. The law is never presented in the OT as a list of rules that one must obey in order to be right with God; rather, it is God's fatherly instruction, given to shape the people he has loved and saved into a community of faith, holiness, and love, bound together by mutual support and care. The various laws, with their penalties for infractions and provisions for repayment, were designed to protect that community from the failures of its members; and the moral guidelines gave specific form to what the restored image of God would look like in the agrarian culture of ancient Israel. Right at the heart of this system is worship at the sanctuary, with its provisions for atonement and forgiveness for those who have gone astray. Sadly, only in a very few instances in the OT do we see anything that even remotely matches this ideal, whether on a large scale (Josh. 22:1–34 is an excellent example, distinctive for its rarity) or on a small one (e.g., Boaz in the book of Ruth, who embodies the Lord's own kindness to a foreign-born "proselyte"). The prophets anticipated an era, after Judah's return from exile in Babylon, in which God's people would really take the law into their own hearts (e.g., Ezek. 36:25–27); the covenant renewal that the postexilic community experienced was, however, only a brief foretaste of that expectation. (Interpreters debate the way in which this relates to the spread of Christianity among the Gentiles—is it focused primarily on *Israel* laying hold of the covenant properly, or does it describe the new arrangement that Jesus' resurrection brought in?—but that is outside the scope of this article.)

5. *Eschatology.* The story of God's people is headed toward a glorious future in which all kinds of people will come to know the Lord and join his people. This was the purpose for which God called Abraham (Gen. 12:1–3), and for which he appointed Israel (Ex. 19:4–6). It is part of the dignity of God's people that, in God's mysterious wisdom, their personal faithfulness contributes to the story getting to its goal (cf. Deut. 4:6–8).

The OT develops its idea of a Messiah (eventually clarified as the ultimate heir of David) in the light of these components. The earliest strands of the messianic idea speak of an offspring who will undo the work of the Evil One and bless the Gentiles by bringing them into his kingdom (Gen. 3:15; 22:17–18; 24:60); the idea that kings will descend from Abraham (Gen. 17:6, 16) and Jacob (Gen. 35:11) becomes focused on the tribe of Judah, to which the obedience of the peoples will be brought (Gen. 49:10). The kings in David's line carry this idea forward. They are to embody the people: just as the people as a whole is God's son (Ex. 4:22–23), so also the Davidic king is God's son (2 Sam. 7:14; Ps. 89:26–27). The promise of a lasting dynasty for David (2 Sam. 7:16) becomes the expectation that a final heir of his line will one day arise, take his Davidic throne (in "the last days"), and lead his people in the great task of bringing light to the Gentiles (e.g., Ps. 2:8; 72:8–11, 17 [using Gen. 22:18]; Isa. 9:6–7; 11:1–10; see note on Isa. 42:1–9 concerning the servant of the Lord).

The Parts of the OT in Relation to the Story

The OT is thus the story of the one true Creator God, who called the family of Abraham to be his remedy for the defilement that came into the world through the sin of Adam and Eve. God rescued Israel from slavery in Egypt in fulfillment of this plan, and established them as a theocracy for the sake of displaying his existence and character to the rest of the world. God sent his blessings and curses upon Israel in order to pursue that purpose. God never desisted from that purpose, even in the face of the most grievous unfaithfulness in Israel.

This overarching story serves as a grand narrative or worldview story for Israel: each member of the people was to see himself or herself as an *heir* of this story, with all its glory and shame; as a *steward* of the story, responsible to pass it on to the next generation; and as a *participant*, whose faithfulness could play a role, by God's mysterious wisdom, in the story's progress.

Some who have seen this category of Israel's story as a key to OT theology have argued for reading the entire OT *as a story*. This does not help the reader, for the very obvious reason that not everything in the OT is narrative or "story." For example, there are *laws* (in the Pentateuch), whose purpose was to protect equity and civility in the theocracy by guiding judges in what penalties to impose and by specifying the minimum standard of behavior necessary to preserve the theocracy (many of the specific laws do not intend to spell out the moral ideal for the members of Israel, which comes from likeness to God in the creation account and from the goal of community holiness; the "perfection" of the laws consisted in the way they serve the social fabric of God's people); there is *wisdom* (in the books of Job, Proverbs, and Ecclesiastes, as well as in the Psalms), which helps the members to live well daily; there are *songs* (esp. the Psalms) that the people of God should sing in corporate worship; there are *poems* (esp. the Song of Solomon; cf. Prov. 5:15–20) celebrating such wonders as romantic love; and lots more. Therefore it is better to speak of reading the parts of the OT *in relation to* its overarching story. That is, we can see the parts in relation to the Big Story that unifies the whole. The Proverbs help people to live their little stories in such a way as to contribute to the Big Story. The Psalms—many of which explicitly recount parts of the Big Story—help people live as faithful members of the worshiping corporate entity, the people of God. The Prophets keep recalling the Big Story, the direction in which Israel's story is headed, calling their audiences to live faithfully in its light. The Big Story tells us that God's purpose is to restore our humanity to its proper function, and thus it reminds each person of the human nature he shares with every other human being, and of the duty and benefit of seeking the good of others. For example, enjoying the love of a faithful spouse is a way of experiencing renewed humanity—a way that displays God's goodness to the rest of the world (as in the Song of Solomon).

All of these factors explain why it is possible for the NT authors both to say that the Sinai covenant is done away with (see below), because it was focused on the theocracy, which had an end in mind from the beginning (when the Gentiles would receive the light in large measure)—and at the same time to affirm that this covenant has embedded in it principles that cannot pass away, because they are part of the larger story of which the Sinai covenant is one chapter.

The OT as Christian Scripture

The OT presents itself, then, as a story that is headed somewhere. The OT closes with both anxiety and hope under Persian rule (see Malachi). The books of the Second Temple period (between the Old and New Testaments) continue this notion of Israel as God's people chosen for a purpose, but not all strands of this material make clear what that purpose is. Some of these Second Temple books offer endings for the story (e.g., in the Qumran community as the elect); but the faithful were looking for more. (For more information on the Second Temple period, see The Time between the Testaments, pp. 1783–1785.) The NT authors, most of whom were *Jewish* Christians, saw themselves as heirs of the OT story, and as authorized to describe its proper completion in the death and resurrection of Jesus and the messianic era that this ushered in. These authors appropriated the OT as Christian Scripture, and they urged their audiences (many of whom were *Gentile* Christians) to do the same. There is debate over just how the NT authors used the OT as Scripture (see How the New Testament Quotes and Interprets the Old Testament, pp. 2605–2607), but the simplest summary of the NT authors' stance would be to say that they saw the OT as constituting the earlier chapters of the story in which Christians are now participating.

This construct, of earlier and later chapters in the story of God's work for his people, allows us to understand how the OT era and the Christian era will have elements both of continuity and of discontinuity. The OT had looked forward to an internationalized people of God, without explaining exactly how that would connect to the theocracy of Israel (see note on Ps. 87:4–6). The theocracy defined the people of God as predominantly coming from a particular ethnic group in a particular land; Gentile converts ("sojourners") were protected (Ex. 12:49; 20:10; 22:21; Lev. 19:10) but could not be full-status members of the theocratic community (cf. Deut. 14:21; 15:3; Num. 34:14–15, which shows that land was allocated to Israelites alone). The NT abolishes the distinction (Eph. 2:19), because the theocracy as such is no longer in existence and many of its provisions are done away with (cf. Acts 10:34–35; Heb. 9:11–14). At the same time, the character of the one Creator God, and his interest in restoring the image of God in human beings, transcends the specific arrangements of the theocracy: hence the moral commands of God apply to Christians as they did to the faithful in Israel (cf. Rom. 13:8–10). ◂

Old Testament Timeline: An Overview*

The following dates (all B.C.) are close approximations based on correlating dates between the Bible and other ancient Near Eastern sources (largely from Assyrian accession lists, Babylonian king-lists, or Egyptian historical sources). Often dates can be confirmed between the Assyrian and Babylonian Empires by narratives recording contacts between these two countries.

Patriarchs to Judges (c. 2166–1030)

	1446 Date for Exodus**	1260 Date for Exodus**
Abraham	2166–1991	2000–1825
Isaac	2066–1886	1900–1720
Jacob	2006–1859	1840–1693
Joseph	1915–1805	1749–1639
Moses' birth	1526	1340
Exodus	1446	1260
Desert wanderings	1446–1406	1260–1220
Entrance into Canaan	1406	1220
Period of the judges	1375 to 1050–1030	1210 to 1050–1030

United Monarchy (c. 1050–931)

	Dates	Notes
Saul's reign	1050–1030 to 1010	Numerals relating to Saul's age and length of reign may be missing in the Hebrew text (see 1 Sam. 13:1)***
David's reign	1010–971	
Solomon's reign	971–931	

Divided Monarchy to Exile (931–586)

Kingdom divided	931	See The Divided Kingdom, pp. 622–623
Syro-Ephraimite war	740–732	Pekah (Israel) and Rezin (Syria) pressure Jotham and Ahaz (Judah) to join their opposition to Tiglath-pileser III (Assyria)
Fall of Samaria (Israel)	722	Shalmaneser V (727–722) and Sargon II (722–705) of Assyria
Josiah's reforms	628	
Battle of Carchemish	605	Daniel and three friends exiled to Babylon
Jerusalem attacked	597	Nebuchadnezzar II takes exiles to Babylon including Jehoiachin and Ezekiel
Fall of Jerusalem (Judah)	586	Nebuchadnezzar II takes more exiles to Babylon

Return from Exile (539–445)

Fall of Babylon	539	Cyrus of Persia (539–530)
1st return of exiles to Jerusalem	538	
Temple building begins	536	
Temple completed	516	Darius I (522–486)
Esther in palace of Xerxes	478	Xerxes I/Ahasuerus (485–464)
2nd return of exiles to Jerusalem under Ezra	458	Artaxerxes I (464–423)
3rd return of exiles to Jerusalem under Nehemiah	445	

**See also Historical Books Timeline, p. 385; and The Divided Kingdom, pp. 622–623.*

***See The Date of the Exodus, p. 33.*

****Possible dates for the beginning of Saul's reign are calculated based on other data in the OT: e.g., David's age at accession and length of reign (2 Sam. 5:4–5); Ish-bosheth's age when he became king (2 Sam. 2:10); and Jonathan's probable age in relation to both Ish-bosheth and David, presuming that Jonathan was Saul's firstborn son (1 Sam. 14:49; 31:2) and was at least 20 when referred to as a commander of troops early in Saul's reign (1 Sam. 13:2).*

THE DATE OF THE EXODUS

The following material summarizes some of the arguments for an early date (1446 B.C.) and a later date (c. 1260) of the exodus. The archaeological claims of each side have all been challenged by the other side, but the details of such responses are not included here.

Arguments for an Early Date of the Exodus

These arguments are used to support an "early date" (about 1446 B.C.) for the exodus:

1. First Kings 6:1 says, "In the four hundred and eightieth year after the people of Israel came out of the land of Egypt, in the fourth year of Solomon's reign over Israel . . . he began to build the house of the LORD." The currently accepted date for the fourth year of Solomon's reign is 967/966 B.C., and 480 years before that would be 1446. This is supported by 1 Chronicles 6:33–37, which names 18 generations from Korah (in the time of Moses) to Heman (in the time of David), which then requires 19 generations from Moses to Solomon. Nineteen generations in 480 years works out to an average of 25.3 years per generation, a reasonable number that gives confirmation to an actual 480 years in 1 Kings 6:1.

2. In Judges 11:26, Jephthah's message to the king of the Ammonites says that Israel had already lived in Canaan for "300 years." This message is dated to around 1100 B.C., which would yield a date of around 1400 for entrance into the land of Canaan, which is consistent with a 1446 exodus.

3. Archaeological data from Jericho, Ai, and Hazor have been claimed to show evidence of destruction in the late fifteenth century B.C., which is consistent with a 1446 exodus and 1406 conquest of Canaan. But there is no evidence of occupation of Jericho in the thirteenth century (as would be required by a later date for the exodus).

4. The Amarna Letters show that Canaanite kings in the late fifteenth century B.C. wrote letters to Pharaoh pleading for help against the *'apiru* who were "taking over" the lands of Canaan. This is consistent with dating the beginning of the conquest by Israel at 1406.

5. Exodus 1:11, which mentions the building of "Raamses," should not be dated to c. 1270 B.C. (as a "late date" view would hold), because the remarkable multiplication of Israel (Ex. 1:12–22) and the birth of Moses (Ex. 2:2) both occur after Exodus 1:11. But if Moses was "eighty years old" (Ex. 7:7) when he led the people out of Egypt, this would put the exodus at least 80 years after the building of Raamses, or 1190 B.C., which is far too late on either scheme. In fact, the Merneptah Stele (an inscribed tombstone-like stone slab) describes a military triumph over Israel in Canaan in 1211–1209 B.C.

6. With an early date for the exodus, the time of the Judges takes about 350 years. This is generally consistent with the book of Judges itself, where a simple addition of the length of the reigns of the individual judges gives just over 400 years, and this can be reduced to 350 if there was overlapping of some reigns, but it cannot reasonably be reduced to as little as 170 years, as would be required by the proposed later date for the exodus.

Arguments for a Later Date of the Exodus

In favor of a "later date" (c. 1260 B.C.) are the following arguments:

1. Exodus 1:11 says the Israelites "built for Pharaoh store cities, Pithom and Raamses." But the city of Raamses (also spelled Rameses; the Egyptian Pi-Rameses) was built by Raamses II, who reigned 1279–1213 B.C. This city is not mentioned in any earlier archaeological records from Egypt. Therefore the Israelites were still in Egypt around 1270 B.C. when Raamses was built. In addition, the other geographical terms in Exodus—e.g., Pithom, Migdol, *Yam Sup* (the "Red Sea"), etc.—are all attested in thirteenth-century Egyptian texts, whereas they are not attested in the period of the early date.

2. First Kings 6:1 probably uses the expression "480 years" as a representative number to stand for 12 idealized generations of 40 years each. But in reality the period covered 12 generations of only 25 years each, or 300 years. Subtracting 300 years from 966 B.C. gives an exodus about 1266.

3. Egypt had imperial control over Canaan from about 1400–1250 B.C. But there is no Egyptian record of any military conflicts with Israel over that land until the Merneptah Stele, which refers to a victory over Israel around 1211–1209 B.C.

4. The Bible contains almost no mention of conflict with Egypt in Joshua or Judges, which would be strange if the Israelites entered Canaan in 1406 B.C., when the Egyptian Empire had control over Canaan. This makes a late date for the exodus more likely, since Egyptian influence over Canaan was minimal after about 1200 B.C.

5. The covenant forms used at the time of Moses in the biblical narratives show significant parallels to ancient Near Eastern covenants in the thirteenth century but not in the fifteenth century B.C.

6. Archaeological discoveries in Canaan show the complete destruction of some cities (such as Hazor) in the later thirteenth century B.C., which would fit with a date of c. 1260 for the exodus. Further, site surveys seem to show that there was a huge migration into the hill country areas of Canaan in the thirteenth century B.C. There also appear to have been technological innovations in this later period, such as terracing of the land, newer pottery styles, and plaster-lined silos, that favor the later date for Israel's occupation.

Conclusion

Both the early date and the late date are supported by established evangelical scholars today. In this Study Bible, both the early date (1446 B.C.) and the later date (c. 1260) are included. ◂

The Hebrew Calendar Compared to the Gregorian (Modern) Calendar

The Hebrew calendar was composed of 12 lunar months, each of which began when the thin crescent moon was first visible at sunset. They were composed of approximately 29/30 days and were built around the agricultural seasons. Apparently some of the names of the months were accommodated from Babylon following the time that the Israelites were exiled there.

Hebrew Month	*Gregorian (Modern) Month*	*Biblical References*
First Month: Abib (Preexile) Nisan (Postexile)	March–April	Ex. 13:4; 23:15; 34:18; Deut. 16:1; Neh. 2:1; Est. 3:7 (cf. Gen. 8:13; Ex. 12:2, 18; 40:2, 17; Lev. 23:5; Num. 9:1; 20:1; 28:16; 33:3; Josh. 4:19; 1 Chron. 12:15; 27:2, 3; 2 Chron. 29:3, 17; 35:1; Ezra 6:19; 7:9; 8:31; 10:17; Est. 3:7, 12; Ezek. 29:17; 30:20; 45:18, 21; Dan. 10:4)
Festivals: 14th: Passover (Ex. 12:18; Lev. 23:5) 15th–21st: Unleavened Bread (Ex. 12:14–20; Lev. 23:6) 16th: First Fruits (Lev. 23:9–11)		
Second Month: Ziv (Preexile) Iyyar (Postexile)	April–May	1 Kings 6:1, 37 (cf. Gen. 7:11; 8:14; Ex. 16:1; Num. 1:1, 18; 9:11; 10:11; 1 Chron. 27:4; 2 Chron. 3:2; 30:2, 13, 15; Ezra 3:8)
Festival: 14th: Later Passover (Num. 9:10–11)		
Third Month: Sivan	May–June	Est. 8:9 (cf. Ex. 19:1; 1 Chron. 27:5; 2 Chron. 15:10; 31:7; Ezek. 31:1)
Festivals: 4th: Pentecost [Feast of Weeks] (Lev. 23:15–16)		
Fourth Month: Tammuz	June–July	Ezek. 8:14 (cf. 2 Kings 25:3; 1 Chron. 27:7; Jer. 39:2; 52:6; Ezek. 1:1; Zech. 8:19)
Fifth Month: Ab	July–August	Not mentioned by name in the Bible (cf. Num. 33:38; 2 Kings 25:8; 1 Chron. 27:8; Ezra 7:8, 9; Jer. 1:3; 28:1; 52:12; Ezek. 20:1; Zech. 7:3, 5; 8:19)
Sixth Month: Elul	August–September	Neh. 6:15 (cf. 1 Chron. 27:9; Ezek. 8:1; Hag. 1:1, 15)
Seventh Month: Ethanim (Preexile) Tishri (Postexile)	September–October	1 Kings 8:2 (cf. Gen. 8:4; Lev. 16:29; 23:24, 27, 34, 39, 41; 25:9; Num. 29:1, 7, 12; 2 Kings 25:25; 1 Chron. 27:10; 2 Chron. 5:3; 7:10; 31:7; Ezra 3:1, 6; Neh. 7:73; 8:2, 14; Jer. 28:17; 41:1; Ezek. 45:25; Hag. 2:1; Zech. 7:5; 8:19)
Festivals: 1st: Trumpets (Lev. 23:24; Num. 29:1) 10th: Day of Atonement (Lev. 16:29–34; 23:27–32) 15th–21st: Booths (Lev. 23:34–40) 22nd: Solemn assembly (Lev. 23:36)		
Eighth Month: Bul (Preexile) Marchesvan (Postexile)	October–November	1 Kings 6:38 (cf. 1 Kings 12:32, 33; 1 Chron. 27:11; Zech. 1:1)
Ninth Month: Chislev (Kislev)	November–December	Neh. 1:1; Zech. 7:1 (cf. 1 Chron. 27:12; Ezra 10:9; Jer. 36:9, 22; Hag. 2:10, 18)
Festival: 25th: Dedication (John 10:22)		
Tenth Month: Tebeth	December–January	Est. 2:16 (cf. Gen. 8:5; 2 Kings 25:1; 1 Chron. 27:13; Ezra 10:16; Jer. 39:1; 52:4; Ezek. 24:1; 29:1; 33:21; Zech. 8:19)
Eleventh Month: Shebat	January–February	Zech. 1:7 (cf. Deut. 1:3; 1 Chron. 27:14)
Twelfth Month: Adar*	February–March	Ezra 6:15; Est. 3:7, 13; 8:12; 9:1, 15, 17, 19, 21 (cf. 2 Kings 25:27; 1 Chron. 27:15; Jer. 52:31; Ezek. 32:1; 32:17)

**Periodically, a 13th month was added so that the lunar calendar would account for the entire solar year.*

Introduction to the Pentateuch

The Name of the Pentateuch

The Pentateuch (Gk. "five-volumed") consists of the first five books of the Bible, i.e., Genesis through Deuteronomy. The Hebrew term for it is *torah* ("law" or "instruction"), so this is how the NT refers to it (Gk. *nomos*, "law"). In the Hebrew Bible, the law is the first of the three major sections, and sometimes *nomos* may refer to the whole OT (e.g., John 10:34). Although the Pentateuch contains many laws, it is essentially narrative with episodes of law-giving, but in the broader sense of *torah* all the Pentateuch can be seen as instruction, for it teaches as much through the history it records as by the law it gives. Another name for the Pentateuch found in some translations is "the five books of Moses." This is also an apt description in that the books of Exodus to Deuteronomy provide a biography of Moses, and traditionally he has been seen as their main author.

The Pentateuch as Foundational to the Whole Bible

The Pentateuch is not simply the beginning of the Bible; it is also the foundation of the Bible. It serves to orient the reader for reading the rest of the biblical story line. It introduces the key promises that show God's purposes in history and that lay the groundwork for the coming of Christ. Its theological ideas and ethical principles inform the rest of the Bible so that the subsequent books assume its authority and appeal to it as they evaluate people's deeds and character. These points are illustrated briefly here:

1. *Orientation.* The beginning of a book sets its tone and gives clues to the author's perspective. Genesis did this for the ancient world of polytheism by explaining that the world is created and controlled by only one God, not by a crowd of competing gods and goddesses. Similarly it speaks to today's readers, who often are essentially atheists (whether consciously or unconsciously): it shows them what it means to believe that behind all the phenomena of nature and the laws of science there is an all-powerful, loving God who controls all that happens.

2. *Divine purposes.* The Pentateuch shows God's intentions for his creation by describing what the world was like when he first created man and woman in the garden of Eden. Their sin sets back the divine program but does not defeat it, for God later calls Abraham and promises him descendants, land, and most important of all, blessing through his descendants to all the nations. These promises are more fully developed in the later books of the Pentateuch.

3. *Theology and ethics.* The Pentateuch gives insight into God's character and his ethical standards. It illustrates both his benevolence and his righteousness. He cares for mankind, creating man in his own image, providing him with food, and protecting human life from violent assault. Yet at the same time he demands moral behavior, from keeping the Sabbath to refusing adultery or theft. Tales of punishment, from the flood (Genesis 6–9) to the golden calf (Exodus 32), demonstrate the danger of disregarding divine standards.

Content

A review of the contents of the Pentateuch shows that its center of gravity is *the law-giving at Sinai*. All of Exodus 19 to Numbers 10 is devoted to the events that occurred in the vicinity of Sinai: the declaration of the Ten Commandments, the building of the tabernacle, the laws governing sacrifice, entry to the tabernacle, and the celebration of the festivals. Closer examination of this central section suggests that its climax is *God's glory filling the newly built tabernacle* (Ex. 40:34–38) as a visible demonstration of his choice of and intimacy with Israel—a restoration of the situation in the garden of Eden, where God walked with Adam and Eve (Gen. 3:8).

But the outer frame of the books of Exodus to Deuteronomy is constituted by *the life of Moses*. Exodus 2 tells of his birth and providential upbringing in the Egyptian court, while Deuteronomy 34 describes his death. Exodus 3–15 describes his call to lead his people and the establishment of his authority over Pharaoh in the eyes of the Israelites (Ex. 14:31). Moses' approaching death colors all the final chapters of the Pentateuch. He is told to prepare for his death in Numbers 27, and the whole of Deuteronomy consists of his last appeals to the nation to serve the Lord faithfully. To this end he preaches three sermons and recites two poems (Deuteronomy 32; 33) before he is granted a vision of the Promised Land and dies (Deuteronomy 34).

The book of Genesis serves as an introduction to the rest of the Pentateuch. It explains the context for Moses' life and ministry. It gives the origin of the nation of Israel and its tribes, and explains how they came to be living in Egypt though their ancestors had been promised the land of Canaan. The people of Israel are to bring blessing to the nations, and the opening chapters of Genesis show the desperate need of the nations for blessing. The first avalanche of sin led to the universal judgment of the flood. The new start with Noah and his sons was again derailed, first by the sin of Ham (Gen. 9:20–29) and then by the Tower of Babel (Gen. 11:1–9). In this general way Genesis explains the situation that Moses confronted, and various episodes in the lives of the patriarchs also show parallels to Moses' experience, e.g., Abraham's exodus from Egypt (Gen. 12:10–20).

Time Span

It is striking that the earliest events in the Bible are dated more precisely than the later ones. For example, the different stages of the flood are dated to the exact day of the year (Gen. 7:11; 8:4, 5; see chart, p. 63). The ages of the pre-flood heroes at the fathering of their firstborn and at their death are carefully noted in Genesis 5. Taking these figures at face value, Archbishop Usher (1581–1656) calculated that the creation of the world occurred in 4004 B.C. Using similar principles, Orthodox Jews hold that the year 2000 was the year 5760 (i.e., 5,760 years since creation).

Such a venerable interpretative approach cannot be glibly dismissed, but most conservative interpreters today believe that it does not account well enough for the literary conventions of Moses' day. For example, the genealogies do not claim to include every generation, and may skip any number of them (see note on Gen. 5:1–32; also Introduction to Genesis: Genesis and Science). With respect to the long lives of the antediluvians (those who lived before the flood), some scholars think these numbers should be understood as their actual ages in years, while others think their ages expressed in multiple centuries may have a symbolic significance, in line with the practices of other ancient peoples (see note on Gen. 5:1–32). It is best to admit one's ignorance here; yet at least it can be said that Moses used these numbers to make a point about the antiquity and reality of his audience's forbears.

However, the dating of the Israelite patriarchs by the internal numbering system of the OT is not so problematic. Conservative biblical scholars think it is likely that Abraham, Isaac, and Jacob lived in the late third and early second millennium B.C., and that the Israelites entered Egypt either in the early nineteenth century B.C. (consistent with an early date for the exodus; see Ex. 12:40) or else in the seventeenth or sixteenth century B.C., during the Egyptian second Intermediate Period (1640–1532 B.C.). The Hyksos Dynasty that ruled during this time came from outside Egypt and therefore could have welcomed Hebrews like Joseph and his family to play a prominent part in Egyptian life.

The date of the exodus from Egypt is likewise controversial. Combining the biblical and extrabiblical evidence points to Solomon's temple being built in 967 or 966 B.C. According to 1 Kings 6:1, Solomon began to build the temple 480 years after the exodus. If the author intended "480 years" as a literal designation, then working backward suggests the exodus would have been in 1447 or 1446 B.C., which is the date preferred by many conservative OT scholars today. However, on the basis of the description of the events surrounding the exodus (such as building the cities of Pithom and Raamses), most Egyptologists prefer a date in the 1200s—preferably after 1279 B.C. but certainly before 1209, when an Egyptian monument mentions that Israel was established as a people in the land of Canaan. If there is symbolism in the designation "480 years," then it is possible that the exodus took place in the early 1200s B.C. rather than in the mid-1400s. (For arguments on both sides of this debate, see The Date of the Exodus, p. 33.)

Composition

For more than 2,000 years, readers of the Pentateuch assumed that Moses was its author (cf. Mark 7:10). This was a natural conclusion to draw from its contents, for most of the laws are said to have been given to Moses by God (e.g., Lev. 1:1), and indeed some passages are explicitly said to have been written down by Moses (see Deut. 31:9, 24). The account of his death could have been recorded by someone else, though some held it was a prophetic account by Moses himself (Deuteronomy 34).

But in the late eighteenth century, critical scholars began challenging the assumption of Mosaic authorship. They argued that several authors were responsible for writing the Pentateuch. These authors supposedly wrote many centuries after Moses, and were separated from each other in time and location. Complicated theories were developed to explain how the Pentateuch grew as different authors' accounts were spliced and adjusted by a series of editors. According to these critical scholars, it was likely that the Pentateuch reached its final form in the fifth century B.C., nearly a millennium after Moses.

In the late twentieth century this type of critical theory was strongly attacked, not just by conservative scholars but also by those brought up on such theories. They argue that the theories are too complicated, self-contradictory, and ultimately unprovable. It is much more rewarding and less speculative to focus interpretative effort on the final form of the text. So there is a strong move to abandon the compositional theories of the nineteenth and early twentieth centuries for simpler hypotheses. Thus some critical scholars would see the Pentateuch being an essentially fifth-century B.C. creation. Others suggest earlier dates. But none of these suggestions can really be proven.

The Pentateuch does undoubtedly claim to be divine in origin, mediated through Moses. Thus Moses should be looked to as the original human author. Indeed, as stated above, the Pentateuch looks like a life of Moses, with an introduction. But this need not mean that he wrote every word of the present Pentateuch. It seems likely that the spelling and the grammar of the Pentateuch were revised to keep it intelligible for later readers. Also, a number of features in the text look like clarifications for a later age. But this is quite different from supposing that the Pentateuch was essentially composed in a later age. Rather, it should be seen as originating in Moses' time but undergoing some slight revision in later eras so later readers could understand its message and apply it to their own situations.

Theme

The theme of the Pentateuch is announced in Genesis 12:1–3, the call of Abraham: "Go from your country . . . to the land that I will show you. And I will make of you a great nation, and I will bless you . . . and in you all the families of the earth shall be blessed." Here God promises Abraham four things: (1) a land to live in; (2) numerous descendants ("a great nation"); (3) blessing (divinely granted success) for himself; and (4) blessing through him for all the nations of the world. God's benefit for the nations is the climax or goal of the promises: the preceding promises of land, descendants, and personal blessing are steps on the way to the final goal of universal blessing.

Each time God appears to the patriarchs, the promises are elaborated and made more specific. For example, the promise of an unidentified "land" in Genesis 12:1 becomes "this land" in Genesis 12:7 and "all the land of Canaan, for an everlasting possession" in Genesis 17:8.

The fulfillment of these promises to Abraham constitutes the story line of the Pentateuch. It is a story of gradual and often difficult fulfillment. The birth of children to produce a great nation is no easy matter: the patriarchs' wives—Sarah, Rebekah, and Rachel—all have great trouble conceiving (Gen. 17:17; 25:21; 30:1). But by the time they enter Egypt, Jacob's family numbers 70 (Gen. 46:27; Ex. 1:5). After many years in Egypt they have become so numerous that the Egyptians perceive them as a threat (Ex. 1:7–10), and when the first census is taken, they total 603,550 fighting men (Num. 1:46).

Similarly the promise of land is very slow in being fulfilled. Abraham acquires a well at Beersheba, and a burial plot for Sarah at Hebron (Gen. 21:30–31; 23:1–20). Jacob bought some land near Shechem (Gen. 33:19), but then late in life he and the rest of the family emigrated to Egypt (Genesis 46–50). The book of Exodus begins with the hope of a quick return to Canaan, but the stubbornness of Pharaoh delays Israel's departure. Their journey through the Sinai wilderness is eventful, and after about a year they reach Kadesh on the very borders of Canaan. There, scared by the report of some of the spies, the people rebel against Moses and the God-given promises, so they are condemned to wander in the wilderness for 40 years (Numbers 13–14). And of course the Pentateuch ends with Moses dying outside the Promised Land and the people hoping to enter it.

For these reasons the theme of the Pentateuch has been described as "the *partial* fulfillment of the promises to the patriarchs." Such a description certainly fits the climactic promise that through Abraham and his descendants all the families of the earth would be blessed. The closest fulfillment of this in the Pentateuch is Joseph saving Egypt and the surrounding lands from starvation in the seven-year famine. But later on, Israel is seen as a threat by other peoples in the region such as the Moabites, Midianites, and Amorites. It is not apparent how or when all the peoples of the world will be blessed. At the end of the Pentateuch that, like the promise of land, still awaits fulfillment.

But the promise of blessing to the patriarchs and their descendants is abundantly fulfilled within the Pentateuch—despite their frequent lack of faith and their willful rebellion. For example, after Abraham has lied about his wife and allowed her to be taken by a foreign king, the pair escape, greatly enriched (Genesis 12; 20). Jacob, forced to flee from home after cheating his father, eventually returns with great flocks and herds to meet a forgiving brother (Genesis 27–33). The nation of Israel breaks the first two commandments by making the golden calf, yet enjoys the privilege of God dwelling among them in the tabernacle (Exodus 32–40). The Pentateuch is thus *a story of divine mercy to a wayward people*.

However, alongside this account of God's grace must be set *the importance of the law and right behavior*. The opening chapters of Genesis set out the pattern of life that everyone should follow: monogamy, Sabbath observance, rejection of personal vengeance and violence—principles that even foreigners living in ancient Israel were expected to observe. But Israel was chosen to mediate between God and the nations and to demonstrate in finer detail what God expected of human society, so that other peoples would exclaim, "What great nation has a god so near to it . . . ? And what great nation is there, that has statutes and rules so righteous as all this law . . . ?" (Deut. 4:7–8).

To encourage Israel's compliance with all the law revealed at Sinai, it was embedded in a covenant. This involved Israel giving its assent to the Ten Commandments and the other laws on worship, personal behavior, crime, and so on. Obedience to these laws guaranteed Israel's future blessing and prosperity, whereas disobedience would be punished by crop failure, infertility, loss of God's presence, defeat by enemies, and eventually exile to a foreign land (see Leviticus 26; Deuteronomy 28).

These covenantal principles—that *God will bless Israel when she keeps the law and punish her when she does not*—pervade the rest of the OT. The book of Joshua demonstrates that fidelity to the law led to the successful conquest of the land, while the books of Judges and Kings show that Israel's apostasy to other gods led to defeat by her enemies. The argument of the prophets is essentially that Israel's failure to keep the law puts her at risk of experiencing the divine punishments set out in Leviticus 26 and Deuteronomy 28.

From NT times, Christians have seen the promises in the Pentateuch as finding their ultimate fulfillment in Christ. Jesus is the offspring of the woman who bruises the serpent's head (Gen. 3:15). He is the one through whom "all the families of the earth shall be blessed" (Gen. 12:3). He is the star and scepter who shall rise out of Israel (Num. 24:17). More than this, many heroes of the OT have been seen as types of Christ. Jesus is the second Adam. He is the true Israel (Jacob), whose life sums up the experience of the nation.

But preeminently Jesus is seen as the new and greater Moses. As Moses declared God's law for Israel, so Jesus declares and embodies God's word to the nations. As Moses suffered and died outside the land so that his people could enter it, so the Son of God died on earth so that his people might enter heaven. It was observed that the filling of the tabernacle with the glory of God was the climax of the Pentateuch (Ex. 40:34–38). So too "the Word became flesh and dwelt among us, and we have seen his glory" (John 1:14). The goal of the entire Bible is that humans everywhere should glorify the God whose glory has confronted them. Lost sight of in Eden, this goal reappears through Moses, on its way to final fulfillment through Christ. ◂

INTRODUCTION TO

GENESIS

Author, Title, and Date

The English title "Genesis" comes from the Greek translation of the Pentateuch and means "origin," a very apt title because Genesis is all about origins—of the world, of the human race, of sin, and of the Jewish people. The Hebrew title is translated "In the Beginning," using the first phrase in the book.

Traditionally Genesis, like the rest of the Pentateuch, has been ascribed to Moses. The other books of the Pentateuch relate Moses' life and his role in bringing Israel to the borders of Canaan, and parts of these books are expressly said to have been written by Moses (e.g., Num. 33:2; Deut. 31:24). Genesis is clearly an introduction to the books that follow, so it is natural to suppose that if Moses was responsible for their composition, he must also have been the author of Genesis (cf. John 5:46). This understanding of the Pentateuch's origin was the view of Jews and Christians from pre-Christian times until the nineteenth century.

But as explained in the Introduction to the Pentateuch, pp. 35–37, this traditional view came to be rejected in the nineteenth and twentieth centuries by most critical scholars, who believed that Genesis and the other books had been composed over a long period of time and reached their final form in the fifth century B.C. In recent decades, however, scholars have become increasingly uncertain about these ideas. It has been recognized that the arguments for the late composition of the Pentateuch out of a variety of sources are flimsy and far from being cast-iron proofs. This is not to deny that the book of Genesis contains post-Mosaic elements, such as the place names "Dan" and "Ur of the Chaldeans" (Gen. 14:14; 15:7), or that the Hebrew of Genesis has been modernized somewhat, but this is to be expected in a sacred text preserved for the instruction of later generations. If they were to understand the text, place names and archaic language would have had to be revised.

Throughout the OT period, the stories of Genesis would have been a great encouragement to faith. Readers must envisage these stories being read to the people at the great festivals in Jerusalem, or recited by visiting Levites in the villages throughout the land. Hearing them, the people of David's time could rejoice that the promises to Abraham about inheriting the land from the border of Egypt to the Euphrates River (15:18) had more or less been fulfilled in their day. On the other hand, in exile in Babylon, the Jews could have drawn comfort from the fact that the land of Canaan was promised to them forever (17:8). And when the exiles started to return, they felt that those promises were being fulfilled (Nehemiah 9). So it is possible that the stories were slightly updated as they were retold, but there is no evidence of substantial changes being made.

In fact, Genesis seems to reflect very well its origin in the second millennium B.C. (Moses lived in the 1500s or 1300s). For example, the flood story finds its best parallels in the Atrahasis and Gilgamesh epics and in the Sumerian flood story, which were composed c. 1600 B.C., while the genealogies of Genesis 5 and 11 find a parallel in the Sumerian King List, dated about 1900 B.C. As far as the patriarchal stories are concerned, many features show that they are at home in the early second millennium. Their names are typical of that period, and many family customs correspond to what is known from that era. The rise of Joseph to be vizier (chief adviser) of Egypt, though not mentioned in Egyptian texts, is quite feasible in the era of the Hyksos (Semitic rulers of Egypt, c. 1600 B.C.). Whatever date is preferred for Moses and the composition of the Pentateuch, several centuries must have separated him from the patriarchs, during which the stories about them were presumably passed on by word of mouth, or perhaps by some kind of early written record that is now lost. In any case, these parallels confirm that the history recorded in Genesis is quite reliable.

Place in the Pentateuch

The first five books of the Bible are called by the Jews "the Law," and by Christians "the Pentateuch" or "the Five Books of Moses." The overall theme of the Pentateuch is God's covenant with Israel through Moses, which established Israel as a theocracy (a nation where God's directives rule the civil, social, and religious spheres) for the sake of the whole world. In view of the authorship discussion above, it is reasonable to consider the first audience of the Pentateuch to be Israel in the wilderness (either the generation that left Egypt or their children). Genesis, as the first volume of this first section of the Bible, orients the reader to the rest of the Pentateuch, and thus to the rest of the Bible. It explains in story form the nature and character of God, and the place of man in God's creation. It offers an analysis of sin and its consequences, and describes God's reaction to it (and thus shows why the true religion must be redemptive). It records the call of Abraham, through whom all the nations of the world will be blessed, and traces the birth and careers of the forefathers of the nation of Israel, leading to Israel in Egypt. The fact that Yahweh is the universal Creator shows why Israel can have a message for all mankind. At the same time Genesis sets out models of behavior, both in its opening chapters and in the examples of the patriarchs' faithful obedience.

Genesis is therefore a book of instruction, and this is why Jews include it in the Law, for the Hebrew word *torah*, usually translated "law," has the broader sense of "instruction." It can rightly be considered the "First Book of Moses" because of its role as the prelude to the following four books, Exodus to Deuteronomy, which are structured around the life of Moses. As explained in the Introduction to the Pentateuch, pp. 35–37, the first five books of the Bible are foundational to the rest, and Genesis is the foundation of the Pentateuch.

Arrangement of the Book

Genesis divides into two major sections: (1) the primeval history of the world before Abraham (chs. 1–11); (2) the history of the patriarchs (chs. 12–50). The proportions of the two sections are significant: essentially chapters 1–11 are setting the stage for the main drama, namely, God's dealings with Abraham, Isaac, Jacob, and his sons—the subject of chapters 12–50.

Genesis is about beginnings and generations. Starting with the divine ordering of creation, it follows for many generations a family line that takes the reader from Adam to Jacob and his sons (see diagram, p. 41). This family line forms the backbone of Genesis, links its disparate elements into a cohesive whole, and explains the distinctive literary features that set it apart from other OT narrative books.

One of the hallmarks of Genesis is the heading or title "These are the generations of . . ." (2:4; 5:1 with slight variant; 6:9; 10:1; 11:10; 11:27; 25:12; 25:19; 36:1; 36:9; 37:2; see chart below). Each heading functions like a zoom lens by focusing attention on a smaller part of the total picture that has been shown in the preceding section, and the heading thus serves as an introduction to the following section. As Genesis describes how the earth's population increases over many generations, the reader's attention is constantly being directed toward one particular person in each generation and his descendants.

The Generations of Genesis

Primeval History (1:1–11:26)			
Introduction	**General heading**	**Specific heading**	**Section introduced**
2:4	These are the generations of	the heavens and the earth	2:4–4:26
5:1	These are the generations of	Adam	5:1–6:8
6:9	These are the generations of	Noah	6:9–9:29
10:1	These are the generations of	the sons of Noah	10:1–11:9
11:10	These are the generations of	Shem	11:10–26
Patriarchal History (11:27–50:26)			
11:27	These are the generations of	Terah	11:27–25:11
25:12	These are the generations of	Ishmael	25:12–18
25:19	These are the generations of	Isaac	25:19–35:29
36:1, 9	These are the generations of	Esau	36:1–37:1
37:2	These are the generations of	Jacob	37:2–50:26

Another important feature of Genesis is its particular interest in genealogies. Although these can be off-putting for modern readers, lacking the dramatic tension of the narrative episodes, they contribute in a special way to the structure of Genesis (as well as to its sense of history; see Genesis and History). Different types of genealogy are used: linear and segmented. Genesis has two *linear genealogies* that cover 10 generations, naming only one ancestor in each generation. These play an important role in linking major narrative sections. The period of Adam and Eve is linked to Noah by the genealogy in chapter 5. A similar genealogy in 11:10–26 connects Noah's son Shem with Abraham. While the linear genealogies are integral to the central family line, Genesis has a number of *segmented genealogies* that perform a subsidiary function within the book. Giving limited information about characters of secondary interest, the segmented genealogies provide branched family trees that usually cover only a few generations (see 10:1–32; 25:12–18; 36:1–8; 36:9–43). Whereas the linear genealogies take readers swiftly from "A" to "B" as part of a longer journey, the segmented genealogies are cul-de-sacs (see diagram to the right).

The Genealogies of Genesis

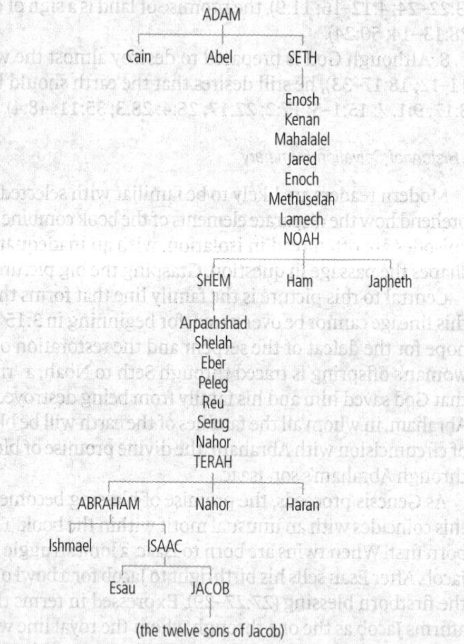

Theme

The theme of Genesis is creation, sin, and re-creation. It tells how God created the world as very good, but that it was destroyed in the flood as a result of man's disobedience. The new world after the flood was also spoiled by human sin (ch. 11). The call of Abraham, through whom all the nations would be blessed, gives hope that God's purpose will eventually be realized through Abraham's descendants (ch. 49).

Key Themes

1. The Lord God, being both transcendent and immanent, having created the earth to be his dwelling place, commissions human beings as his priestly vice-regents or representatives so that they might fill the earth and caringly govern the other creatures (1:1–2:25).

2. Abandoning their priestly and royal duties, the human couple rebel against God and betray him by acting on the serpent's suggestions; their willful disobedience radically affects human nature and the harmonious order of creation (3:1–24; 6:5–6).

3. God graciously announces that the woman's offspring will redeem humanity from the serpent's tyranny. Genesis then traces a unique family line, highlighting how its members enjoy a special relationship with God and are a source of blessing to a world that lies under the curse of God (3:15; 4:25; 5:2; 6:8–9; 11:10–26; 12:1–3; 17:4–6; 22:16–18; 26:3–4, 24; 27:27–29; 28:14; 30:27–30; 39:5; 49:22–26).

4. As a result of the man's disobedience, his unique relationship with the ground degenerates, resulting in hard toil and even famine. While Genesis graphically illustrates the effects of this broken relationship, it also portrays the special family line as bringing relief from such hardship (3:17–19; 5:29; 9:20; 26:12–33; 41:1–57; 47:13–26; 50:19–21).

5. While the woman's punishment centers on pain in bearing children (3:16), women play an essential role in continuing the unique family line; with God's help even barrenness is overcome (11:30; 21:1–7; 25:21; 29:31–30:24; 38:1–30).

6. The corruption of human nature causes families to be torn apart as brotherly affection is replaced by resentment and hatred (4:1–16; 13:5–8; 25:22–23, 29–34; 27:41–45; 37:2–35). Although Genesis highlights the reality of family strife, the members of the family line have the potential to be agents of reconciliation (13:8–11; 33:1–11; 45:1–28; 50:15–21).

7. Whereas exile from Eden and dispersion throughout the earth are used by God to punish the wicked (3:22–24; 4:12–16; 11:9), the promise of land is a sign of divine favor (12:1–2, 7; 13:14–17; 15:7–21; 26:2–3; 28:13–14; 50:24).

8. Although God is prepared to destroy almost the whole of humanity because of its corruption (6:7, 11–12; 18:17–33), he still desires that the earth should be populated by persons who are righteous (1:28; 8:17; 9:1, 7; 15:1–5; 17:2; 22:17; 26:4; 28:3; 35:11; 48:4).

History of Salvation Summary

Modern readers are likely to be familiar with selected parts of Genesis. Most, however, struggle to comprehend how the disparate elements of the book combine to form a unified account. Consequently, individual episodes are often read in isolation, with an inadequate appreciation of how the larger literary context shapes the passage in question. Grasping the big picture of Genesis is very important.

Central to this picture is the family line that forms the backbone of the entire book. The importance of this lineage cannot be overstated, for beginning in 3:15 the offspring of the woman becomes the source of hope for the defeat of the serpent and the restoration of the earth and everything in it. In due course the woman's offspring is traced through Seth to Noah, a "righteous man" (6:9) who found favor with God, so that God saved him and his family from being destroyed in the flood. From Noah the family line moves to Abraham, in whom all the families of the earth will be blessed (12:1–3). When God establishes the covenant of circumcision with Abraham, the divine promise of blessing is linked to a future royal descendant traced through Abraham's son Isaac.

As Genesis proceeds, the promise of blessing becomes intimately connected with the firstborn son. Yet this coincides with an unusual motif within the book. The status of firstborn does not always go to the son born first. When twins are born to Isaac, a long struggle takes place between Esau and his younger brother Jacob. After Esau sells his birthright to Jacob for a bowl of stew (25:29–34), Jacob deceptively gets from Isaac the firstborn blessing (27:27–29). Expressed in terms that echo God's promise to Abraham, this blessing affirms Jacob as the one through whom the royal line will continue.

Joseph's promotion over Reuben to the status of firstborn, along with his dreams, initially indicates that the potential royal line will continue through him. Although he is sold into slavery by his brothers, his subsequent governorship of Egypt confirms that God is with him. Later, when the family is reunited and Jacob pronounces the blessing of the firstborn on Joseph's younger son, Ephraim, the future royal line is linked to the descendants of Ephraim (48:13–19). Genesis, however, contains an interesting twist. In spite of Joseph's importance, his older brother Judah undergoes a remarkable transformation, and kingship is also associated with his descendants (49:8–12).

Beyond Genesis, the line of Ephraim assumes leadership of Israel when Joshua leads the people into the land of Canaan. In the time of Samuel, however, the Ephraimites are rejected when God chooses David to establish the first dynasty in Israel (see Ps. 78:67–72). Eventually, the divine promises linked to the family line in Genesis come to fulfillment in Jesus Christ, the incarnate Son of God who becomes by adoption "the son of David, the son of Abraham" (Matt. 1:1; see Acts 3:25–26; Gal. 3:16). By looking forward to a special King who will mediate God's blessing to humanity, Genesis provides the foundation on which the rest of the Bible stands.

In saying that Genesis points forward to Jesus Christ, one must be careful because Genesis does not provide a full-grown Christology. What begins in Genesis as a divine promise of salvation linked to the woman's offspring is expanded throughout the rest of the OT. Nevertheless, the ideas that are introduced in Genesis are fully consistent with the final reality.

While the concept of *the nations' being blessed through a future King* is at the heart of Genesis, other related themes are also developed. One of the most important of these is the divine promise to Abraham that he will become a *great nation* (Gen. 12:2). Central to this are the twin concepts of *land* and *descendants*, both being essential components of nationhood.

This emphasis on a nation has to be understood in the light of God's purpose for the earth. It is to be his dwelling place, where he will live surrounded by a human population of royal priests. When Adam and Eve betray God, however, they forfeit their special status. Later, when God comes to dwell among the Israelites, they as a nation are given the opportunity to be a royal priesthood (Ex. 19:6). Unfortunately, they never fully realize all that God wants them to be. Yet even through failure, they provide an indication of how the earth should be under God's rule.

With the coming of Jesus Christ, the national theocracy of Israel is replaced by an international royal priesthood that includes Jews, Samaritans, and Gentiles (1 Pet. 2:9). Although the church becomes the dwelling place of God on earth, evil still remains. Only after the return of Christ and the final judgment will all things be restored and a new earth be created. At that time the new Jerusalem will mark the completion of the divine project that began in Genesis. John's vision of the new earth in Revelation 21–22 has close affinities with Genesis 1–2.

(For an explanation of the "History of Salvation," see the Overview of the Bible, pp. 23–26. See also History of Salvation in the Old Testament: Preparing the Way for Christ, pp. 2635–2661.)

Genesis and History

Clearly all the events in Genesis long predate the time of Moses—this is so with the patriarchs (chs. 12–50) and much more so with the primeval period (chs. 1–11). Further, there are important parallels between chapters 1–11 and stories of ancient times from Mesopotamia (e.g., creation and flood). Since these stories are generally called "myths," some suggest that this is the right category for the stories in chapters 1–11. Some even argue that the stories of the patriarchs are legends, with only a loose connection to actual people and events. In order to sort through these issues, the first question is whether Genesis claims to record "history."

In order to address this issue, it is crucial to have a good, clear, and precise definition of "history." In ordinary language, the word simply refers to an account of events that the author believes to have happened; in and of itself, the label "history" makes no comment about whether the account is complete, unbiased, free from divine activity, in strict chronological sequence, or with or without figurative and imaginative (sometimes called mythological) elements.

With this definition, it is easy to see that Genesis aims to record actual events rather than mythical events. The book explains to its Jewish audience how their ancestors came to be in Egypt; the genealogies connect Jacob and his children with the ancient generations, going back to Adam and Eve, the original pair of humans. Further, the book is *narrative prose,* whose main function in the Bible is to recount history. The creation account, 1:1–2:3, is stylistically different from the rest of the book; it is *exalted prose,* and its historicity is assumed elsewhere in the Bible (e.g., Ps. 136:4–9). (See Genesis and Science.)

The similarities of Genesis 1–11 to the Mesopotamian stories actually support the conclusion that these chapters intend to record history. The Mesopotamian stories clearly aim to celebrate actual historical events, but they do so in "mythological" terms. The Genesis stories are fundamentally different, however, in that they recount the activities of the one true God. Genesis, like the Mesopotamian stories, provides the opening act of a grand narrative that conveys a particular worldview. In order to provide the necessary grounding for this worldview, the author needed to use real events (albeit theologically interpreted). In this way Genesis aims to provide a true record of these events, in harmony with the biblical worldview. That worldview includes the notions that Yahweh, the deity of Israel, is the universal Creator of heaven and earth, who made mankind to know and love him; that all mankind fell through the disobedience of Adam and Eve; and that God chose Israel to be the vehicle by which all mankind would receive the blessing of knowing the true God. Clearly, that worldview requires the events of Genesis to be historical.

At the same time, it is not possible to answer all questions arising from Genesis. For example, faithful interpreters of the book disagree on just how long Adam lived before Abraham, or even how long the creation period lasted (see Genesis and Science). There is not enough material here for a complete life of Abraham. Even the name of the pharaoh that Joseph served is not mentioned. It is possible through archaeological research to locate some of the Genesis events in ancient Near Eastern history, at least in order to offer a plausible scenario for them. But it remains true that Moses has not sought to provide a comprehensive retelling of ancient days; his purpose lay elsewhere.

Genesis and Science

The relation of Genesis to science is primarily a question of how one reads the accounts of creation and fall (chs. 1–3) and of the flood (chs. 6–9). What kind of "days" does Genesis 1 describe? How long ago is this supposed to have happened? Were all species created as they are now? Were Adam and Eve real people? Are all people descended from them? How much of the earth did Noah's flood cover? How much impact did it have on geological formations?

Faithful interpreters have offered arguments for taking the creation week of Genesis 1 as a regular week with ordinary days (the "calendar day" reading); or as a sequence of geological ages (the "day-age" reading); or as God's "workdays," analogous to a human workweek (the "analogical days" view); or as a literary device to portray the creation week *as if* it were a workweek, but without concern for temporal sequence (the "literary framework" view). Some have suggested that Genesis 1:2, "the earth was without form and void," describes a condition that resulted from Satan's primeval rebellion, which preceded the creation week (the "gap theory"). There have been other readings as well, but these five are the most common.

None of these views requires denying that Genesis 1 is historical, so long as the discussion in the section on Genesis and History is kept in mind. Each of these readings can be squared with other biblical passages that reflect on creation. The most important of these is Exodus 20:11, "in six days the LORD made heaven and earth, the sea, and all that is in them, and rested on the seventh day": since this passage echoes Genesis 1:1–2:3, the word "day" here need mean only what it means in Genesis 1. Therefore, it does not *require* an ordinary-day interpretation, nor does it *preclude* an ordinary-day interpretation. The arguments for and against these different views involve detailed treatment of the Hebrew (going far beyond the question of the meaning of "day"), and assessing these arguments would go beyond the goal of this discussion.

A further question involves the genealogies: do they describe direct father-to-son descent, or do they allow for gaps? The Hebrew term "father" can be used of a distant ancestor, and "son" can refer to a distant descendant. Likewise, "to father" can mean "to become the ancestor of." In other words, the conventions for Hebrew genealogies allow for gaps; genealogies are not given to indicate a length of time.

These issues become less pressing when it is recalled that no biblical passage ever actually purports to count up the length of the creation week (outside of Ex. 20:11) and that no biblical author adds up the life spans in the genealogies to compute absolute time.

Should Genesis 1 be called a "scientific account"? Again, it is crucial to have a careful definition. Does Genesis 1 record a true account of the origin of the material universe? To that question, the answer must be yes. On the other hand, does Genesis 1 provide information in a way that corresponds to the purposes of modern science? To this question the answer is no. Consider some of the challenges. For example, the term "kind" does not correspond to the notion of "species"; it simply means "category," and could refer to a species, or a family, or an even more general taxonomic group. Indeed, the plants are put into two general categories, small seed-bearing plants and larger woody plants. The land animals are classified as domesticable stock animals ("livestock"); small things such as mice, lizards, and spiders ("creeping things"); and larger game and predatory animals ("beasts of the earth"). Indeed, no species, other than man, gets its proper Hebrew name. Not even the sun and moon get their ordinary Hebrew names (1:16). The text says nothing about the process by which "the earth brought forth vegetation" (1:12), or by which the various kinds of animals appeared—although the fact that it was in response to God's command indicates that it was not due to any natural powers inherent in the material universe itself.

This account is well cast for its main purpose, which was to enable a community of nomadic shepherds in the Sinai desert to celebrate the boundless creative goodness of the Creator; it does not say why, e.g., a spider is different from a snake, nor does it comment on what genetic relationship there might be between various creatures. At the same time, when the passage is received according to its purpose, it shapes a worldview in which science is at home (probably the only worldview that really makes science possible). This is a concept of a world that a good and wise God made, perfectly suited for humans to enjoy and to rule. The things in the world have natures that people can know, at least in part. Human senses and intelligence are the right tools for discerning and saying true things about the world. (The effects of sin, of course, can interfere with this process.)

It is clear that Adam and Eve are presented as real people. Their role in the story, as the channel by which sin came into the world, implies that they are seen as the headwaters of the human race. The image of God distinguishes them from all the animals, and is a special bestowal of God (i.e., not a purely "natural" development). It is no wonder that all human beings share capacities for language, moral judgment, rationality, and appreciation for beauty, unlike and beyond the powers observed in the animals; any science that ignores this fact does not faithfully describe reality. The biblical worldview leads one to expect as well that all humans now share a need for God and a bent toward sin, as well as a possibility for faith in the true God.

One must take similar care in reading the flood story. The notes will discuss the extent to which Moses intended to describe the flood's coverage of the globe. Certainly the description of the flood implies that it was widespread and catastrophic, but there are difficulties in making confident claims that the account is geared to answering the question of just how widespread. Thus, it would be incautious to attribute to the flood all the geological formations observed today—the strata, the fossils, the deformations, and so on. Geologists agree that catastrophic events, such as volcanic eruptions and large-scale floods, have had great impact on the landscape; it is questionable, though, whether these events can in fact achieve all that might be claimed for them. Again, such matters do not come within the author's own scope, which is to stress the interest that God has in all mankind.

Thus, even though it is wrong to use Genesis as if it were directly furnishing information in modern scientific form, it is nonetheless crucial to affirm its historical account and its God-centered worldview in order to provide a proper foundation for doing good science.

Reading Genesis in the Twenty-first Century

The book of Genesis originated thousands of years ago—a fact easily forgotten when it is read in a modern English translation. It was composed in an age and culture far removed from the experiences of most modern readers. Due allowance must be made for this distance between text and reader. While modern English translations attempt to bridge this gap, it is not always possible to replicate the nuances and wordplays of the Hebrew original. Moreover, Genesis employs literary techniques not commonly used today. Woven into stories set in an ancient Near Eastern culture, these features present obstacles that can be overcome only through patient study of the text.

Interpreting Genesis is further complicated by the fact that it is also the inspired Word of God. This leads some readers to suppose that this infallible text will be omniscient, like its divine author. They then look for answers to questions that Genesis is not trying to answer. Yet like any other part of the Bible, Genesis is limited and selective in the information that it conveys; it does not tell readers everything that they could possibly want to know. Frequently, readers may ask questions, legitimate in themselves, that are not answered by the text. Genesis does not tell, for instance, how the serpent came to be God's enemy or where Cain found a wife. Such questions could be multiplied many times. Consequently, one's natural curiosity must be correctly channeled, for the inspired author of Genesis intentionally communicates only certain things. Yet the text does not cease to be the Word of God simply because it is limited in what it tells the reader; it need not be exhaustive in order to be true.

These observations regarding the limitations of Genesis as a literary text are especially important when one turns to its opening chapters. The sections on Genesis and History and Genesis and Science show why it is right to say that these chapters are meant to convey history, and that they present a worldview that gives science its proper home. At the same time, this is not the same as saying that they offer their message in a form that modern readers are accustomed to reading. To read Genesis well, it is helpful to have some understanding of ancient literary forms. Thus, it would be hasty to conclude that Genesis conflicts with a proper understanding of either science or historiography (whose standard conclusions at any given time are also liable to revision). Put simply, the author of Genesis writes to celebrate the fact that God made the world, not to explain the details of how he made it.

This difference in approach means that Genesis 1 does not address the mechanics of creation. Rather, it simply says that God brought the heavens and the earth into being by means of his spoken word ("And God said"); and it explains that God ordered the earth in terms of time and space, revealing that people were originally created by God and appointed by God to be his representatives on earth, to rule it for his glory and the benefit of all creation. To the extent that scientists deny that God is the Creator of all things, a fundamental conflict will exist between the foundation and conclusions of such scientific work and the Bible. At the same time, to the extent that the focus of science is on understanding and describing the world that God created, no conflict between the Bible and scientific work needs to exist. Understood in terms of what the author of Genesis seeks to communicate, science as well as the Bible have a valuable and legitimate place. But as divine revelation, Genesis provides knowledge that cannot be discovered by human investigation. Were it otherwise, there would be no need for Genesis to be a part of the Bible.

The modern reader receives Genesis best, then, when he or she cooperates with Moses' own purpose in writing the book. It is the front end of the grand narrative of creation, fall, and redemption—a narrative that has reached a glorious point in the resurrection of Jesus, the down payment of its even more glorious consummation. The story is of a good world made by a good God and man's role in that world, the story of how the stain of sin affects everything, the story of how God intends to reverse those effects. Thus, the life that one lives in the body, one's connection to all mankind, one's connection to and responsibility for the created world, one's dependence on God's grace—all are founded on the story that begins in Genesis. The Christian economy, like the covenant made at Sinai, involves a need for moral purity, lived in the body; physical ordinances by which God communicates his grace; a community to which the faithful are bound—all affirming God's original creation intent. Further, Genesis offers a paradigm for God's dealings with his creation, namely, the representative: Adam represented mankind and the world, and the consequences of his fall pass to all those whom he represented. This provides the framework for the Christian understanding of how Jesus does his representative work, which will have consequences both for the people he represents and for the rest of creation.

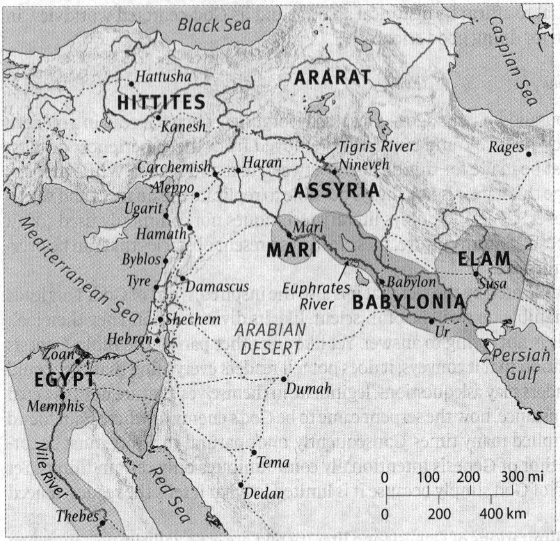

The Near East at the Time of Genesis
c. 2000 B.C.
The book of Genesis describes events in the ancient Near East from the beginnings of civilization to the relocation of Jacob's (Israel's) family in Egypt. The stories of Genesis are set among some of the oldest nations in the world, including Egypt, Assyria, Babylonia, and Elam.

Literary Features

As already mentioned, Genesis is a history book, with its history packaged in literary forms.

Genesis is an anthology of diverse forms. It is more highly unified than most anthologies, however, because all of the material falls into the overall genre of historical narrative. But in turn, the history is not packaged as it is in the history books with which modern readers are familiar. Instead, the book of Genesis is primarily a collection of what may be called hero stories—episodic tales focused on a central character with whom the reader is to sympathize—with interspersed genealogies. The first three chapters belong to a genre known as the story of origins. Genesis also has affinities with the epic genre because the story is one of universal history (chs. 1–11) and the origins of the nation of Israel (chs. 12–50).

A literary approach to the book of Genesis requires that the reader think correctly about the currently recognized concept of a literary "hero." This approach has three crucial principles: (1) real life provides the materials for a hero, but the image of the hero is always achieved by a selection and distillation of items drawn from a larger body of information about a person; (2) cultures celebrate heroes as a way of codifying their own ideals, values, and virtues; and (3) literary heroes are representative of the culture producing them and, in some ways, of people universally. The heroes in these stories are not always "heroic": they are simply the human center of attention in the story; their actions are brave or cowardly or noble or base, or (more often) a complex mixture of all these characteristics. As the narrative proceeds, the reader should be struck with the *contingencies*—that is, the episodes could have turned out differently, perhaps even should have turned out differently. God's providential care for his people uses their imperfections to achieve his purposes for them. The original audience would then see their own situations as permeated with God's purpose, and would thus learn to embrace their lives as a gift from God, to be lived as he directs. An example is the servant's finding Rebekah to be Isaac's wife (ch. 24). Any of these events could have turned out differently, and then Isaac and Rebekah would never have married—perhaps, in view of 24:3–8, Isaac would not have married at all, and then where would the promises to Abraham be? But God kept his promise (one is not obligated to think that everything the servant did was right), and the first readers could learn to see themselves under God's care as the result of reflection on what took place. The modern Christian reader is likewise the heir and beneficiary of this story.

Unifying literary motifs include: (1) The characterization of God and the story of his dealings with people. (2) The sinfulness of the human race and individuals within it. (3) The story of the unfolding plan of God to redeem a people for himself despite human waywardness. (4) The " hero story" as the nearly constant genre. (5) Characters, characters, characters: as one reads Genesis, one is continually drawn into encounters with unforgettable characters and their stories, and lessons about wisdom and folly that can be learned from them.

Outline

I. Primeval History (1:1–11:26)
   A. God's creation and ordering of heaven and earth (1:1–2:3)
   B. Earth's first people (2:4–4:26)
      1. The man and woman in the sanctuary of Eden (2:4–25)
      2. The couple rebels against God (3:1–24)
      3. Adam and Eve's sons (4:1–26)
   C. Adam's descendants (5:1–6:8)
      1. The family line from Adam to Noah (5:1–32)
      2. The wickedness of humanity (6:1–8)
   D. Noah's descendants (6:9–9:29)
      1. Noah and the flood (6:9–9:19)
      2. The cursing of Canaan (9:20–29)
   E. The descendants of Noah's sons (10:1–11:9)
      1. The clans, languages, lands, and nations (10:1–32)
      2. The Tower of Babel (11:1–9)
   F. Shem's descendants (11:10–26)

II. Patriarchal History (11:27–50:26)
   A. Terah's descendants (11:27–25:18)
      1. A brief introduction to Terah's family (11:27–32)
      2. Abram's migration to Canaan (12:1–9)
      3. Abram in Egypt (12:10–20)
      4. Abram and Lot separate (13:1–18)
      5. Abram's rescue of Lot (14:1–24)
      6. God's covenant with Abram (15:1–21)
      7. The birth of Ishmael (16:1–16)
      8. The covenant of circumcision (17:1–27)
      9. The destruction of Sodom (18:1–19:29)
      10. Lot's relationship with his daughters (19:30–38)
      11. Abimelech takes Sarah into his harem (20:1–18)
      12. The birth of Isaac (21:1–21)
      13. Abimelech makes a treaty with Abraham (21:22–34)
      14. The testing of Abraham (22:1–19)
      15. Nahor's children (22:20–24)
      16. The death and burial of Sarah (23:1–20)
      17. A wife for Isaac (24:1–67)
      18. The death of Abraham (25:1–11)
      19. The genealogy of Ishmael (25:12–18)
   B. Isaac's descendants (25:19–37:1)
      1. The birth of Esau and Jacob (25:19–26)
      2. Esau sells his birthright (25:27–34)
      3. Isaac in Gerar (26:1–35)
      4. Isaac blesses Jacob (27:1–45)
      5. Jacob is sent to find a wife (27:46–28:9)
      6. Jacob at Bethel (28:10–22)
      7. Jacob meets Rachel and Laban (29:1–14)
      8. Jacob marries Leah and Rachel (29:15–30)
      9. Jacob's children (29:31–30:24)
      10. Jacob prepares to return to Canaan (30:25–31:18)
      11. Laban accuses Jacob in Gilead (31:19–55)
      12. Jacob prepares to meet Esau again (32:1–21)

13. Jacob encounters God at Peniel (32:22–32)
14. Jacob is reconciled with Esau (33:1–20)
15. The rape of Dinah (34:1–31)
16. Jacob's onward journey to Hebron (35:1–29)
17. Esau's descendants in Edom (36:1–37:1)

C. Jacob's descendants (37:2–50:26)
   1. Joseph is sold into slavery (37:2–36)
   2. Judah and Tamar (38:1–30)
   3. Joseph in Egypt (39:1–23)
   4. Joseph and the king's prisoners (40:1–23)
   5. Joseph interprets Pharaoh's dreams (41:1–57)
   6. The brothers' first journey to Egypt (42:1–38)
   7. Joseph's brothers return to Egypt (43:1–34)
   8. Benjamin is accused of stealing (44:1–34)
   9. Joseph discloses his identity (45:1–28)
   10. Jacob's family relocates to Egypt (46:1–27)
   11. Jacob's family settles in Egypt (46:28–47:12)
   12. Joseph oversees the famine response in Egypt (47:13–26)
   13. Jacob requests to be buried in Canaan (47:27–31)
   14. Jacob's blessing of Joseph, Ephraim, and Manasseh (48:1–22)
   15. Jacob blesses his 12 sons (49:1–28)
   16. The death and burial of Jacob (49:29–50:14)
   17. Joseph reassures his brothers (50:15–21)
   18. The death of Joseph (50:22–26)

GENESIS

Chapter 1

1[a]Job 38:4-7; Ps. 33:6; 136:5; Isa. 42:5; 45:18; John 1:1-3; Acts 14:15; 17:24; Col. 1:16, 17; Heb. 1:10; 11:3; Rev. 4:11
2[b]Jer. 4:23

The Creation of the World

1 In the [a]beginning, God created the heavens and the earth. 2 The earth was [b]without
form and void, and darkness was over the face of the deep. And the Spirit of God was
hovering over the face of the waters.

1:1–11:26 *Primeval History.* The first eleven chapters of Genesis differ from those that follow. Chapters 12–50 focus on one main family line in considerable detail, whereas chs. 1–11 could be described as a survey of the world before Abraham. These opening chapters differ not only in their subject matter from ch. 12 onward, but also because there are no real parallels to the patriarchal stories in other literatures. In contrast to the patriarchal stories, however, other ancient nonbiblical stories do exist recounting stories about both creation and the flood. The existence of such stories, however, does not in any way challenge the authority or the inspiration of Genesis. In fact, the nonbiblical stories stand in sharp contrast to the biblical account, and thus help readers appreciate the unique nature and character of the biblical accounts of creation and the flood. In other ancient literary traditions, creation is a great struggle often involving conflict between the gods. The flood was sent because the gods could not stand the noise made by human beings, yet they could not control it. Through these stories the people of the ancient world learned their traditions about the gods they worshiped and the way of life that people should follow. Babylonian versions of creation and flood stories were designed to show that Babylon was the center of the religious universe and that its civilization was the highest achieved by mankind.

Reading Genesis, readers can see that it is designed to refute these delusions. There is only one God, whose word is almighty. He has only to speak and the world comes into being. The sun and moon are not gods in their own right, but are created by the one God. This God does not need feeding by man, as the Babylonians believed they did by offering sacrifices, but he supplies man with food. It is human sin, not divine annoyance, that prompts the flood. Far from Babylon's tower (Babel) reaching heaven, it became a reminder that human pride could neither reach nor manipulate God.

These principles, which emerge so clearly in Genesis 1–11, are truths that run through the rest of Scripture. The unity of God is fundamental to biblical theology, as is his almighty power, his care for mankind, and his judgment on sin. It may not always be obvious how these chapters relate to geology and archaeology, but their theological message is very clear. Read in their intended sense, they provide the fundamental presuppositions of the rest of Scripture. These chapters should act as eyeglasses, so that readers focus on the points their author is making and go on to read the rest of the Bible in light of them.

1:1–2:3 *God's Creation and Ordering of Heaven and Earth.* The book of Genesis opens with a majestic description of how God first created the heavens and earth and then how he ordered the earth so that it may become his dwelling place. Structured into seven sections, each marked by the use of set phrases, the entire episode conveys the picture of the all-powerful, transcendent God who sets everything in place with consummate skill in conformity to his grand design. The emphasis is mainly on how God orders or structures everything. The structure of the account is as follows: after giving the setting (1:1–2), the author describes the six workdays (1:3–31) and the seventh day, God's Sabbath (2:1–3). Each of the six workdays follows the same pattern: it begins with "and God said," and closes with "and there was evening and there was morning, the *n*th day." After declaring that God is the Creator of all things (1:1), the focus of the rest of Genesis 1 (beginning at 1:3) is mainly on God bringing things into existence by his word and ordering the created things ("let the waters . . . be gathered together," 1:9), rather than on how the earth was initially created (1:1). Different features indicate this. For example, vegetation is mentioned on day 3, prior to the apparent creation of the sun on day 4. Readers concerned with how to compare this passage with a modern scientific perspective should consult Introduction: Genesis and Science. Viewed in its ancient Near Eastern context, Genesis 1 says that God created everything, but it is also an account of how God has structured creation in its ordered complexity. Readers are introduced in the first three days to Day, Night, the Heavens, Earth, Seas—all these items, and only these, being specifically named by God. In days 4–6 the three distinctive regions are populated: the Heavens with lights and birds; the Seas with fish and swarming creatures; and the Earth with livestock and creeping things. God finally gives authority to human beings, as his vice-regents, to govern all these living creatures. Genesis 1 establishes a hierarchy of authority. Humanity is divinely commissioned to govern other creatures on God's behalf, the ultimate purpose being that the whole earth should become the temple of God, the place of his presence, and should display his glory.

1:1 In the beginning. This opening verse can be taken as a *summary*, introducing the whole passage; or it can be read as the *first event*, the origin of the heavens and the earth (sometime before the first day), including the creation of matter, space, and time. This second view (the origin of the heavens and the earth) is confirmed by the NT writers' affirmation that creation was from nothing (Heb. 11:3; Rev. 4:11). **God created.** Although the Hebrew word for "God," *'Elohim*, is plural in form (possibly to express majesty), the verb "create" is singular, indicating that God is thought of as one being. Genesis is consistently monotheistic in its outlook, in marked contrast to other ancient Near Eastern accounts of creation. There is only one God. The Hebrew verb *bara'*, "create," is always used in the OT with God as the subject; while it is not always used to describe creation out of nothing, it does stress God's sovereignty and power. **Heavens and the earth** here means "everything." This means, then, that "In the beginning" refers to the beginning of everything. The text indicates that God created everything in the universe, which thus affirms that he did in fact create it *ex nihilo* (Latin "out of nothing"). The effect of the opening words of the Bible is to establish that God, in his inscrutable wisdom, sovereign power, and majesty, is the Creator of all things that exist.

1:2 The initial description of the **earth** as being **without form and void**, a phrase repeated within the OT only in Jer. 4:23, implies that it lacked order and content. The reference to **darkness . . . over the face of the deep** points to the absence of light. This initial state will be transformed by God's creative activity: **the Spirit of God was hovering**. This comment creates a sense of expectation; something is about to happen. There is no reason to postulate that a long time elapsed between Gen. 1:1 and 1:2, during which time the earth became desolate and empty. Critical scholars argue that the word "deep" (Hb. *tehom*) is a remnant of Mesopotamian mythology from the creation account called Enuma Elish. Marduk, in fashioning the universe, had also to vanquish Tiamat, a goddess of chaos. These scholars believe that the Hebrew God had to conquer the chaos deity Tiamat in the form of the "deep" (notice the similarity of

3 And God said, [c]"Let there be light," and there was light. 4 And God saw that the light was
good. And God separated the light from the darkness. 5 God called the light Day, and the
darkness he called Night. And there was evening and there was morning, the first day.
6 And God said, [d]"Let there be an expanse[1] in the midst of the waters, and let it separate
the waters from the waters." 7 And God made[2] the expanse and [e]separated the waters that
were under the expanse from the waters that were [f]above the expanse. And it was so.
8 And God called the expanse Heaven.[3] And there was evening and there was morning,
the second day.
9 And God said, [g]"Let the waters under the heavens be gathered together into one place,
and let the dry land appear." And it was so. 10 God called the dry land Earth,[4] and the waters
that were gathered together he called Seas. And God saw that it was good.
11 And God said, [h]"Let the earth sprout vegetation, plants[5] yielding seed, and fruit trees
bearing fruit in which is their seed, each according to its kind, on the earth." And it was so.
12 The earth brought forth vegetation, plants yielding seed according to their own kinds,
and trees bearing fruit in which is their seed, each according to its kind. And God saw that
it was good. 13 And there was evening and there was morning, the third day.
14 And God said, "Let there be lights in the expanse of the heavens to separate the day
from the night. And let them be for [i]signs and for [j]seasons,[6] and for days and years, 15 and
let them be lights in the expanse of the heavens to give light upon the earth." And it was
so. 16 And God [k]made the two great lights—the greater light to rule the day and the lesser

3 [c]2 Cor. 4:6
6 [d]Job 37:18; Ps. 136:5; Jer. 10:12; 51:15
7 [e]Prov. 8:27-29 [f]Ps. 148:4
9 [g]Job 38:8-11; Ps. 33:7; 136:6; Jer. 5:22; 2 Pet. 3:5
11 [h]Ps. 104:14
14 [i]Jer. 10:2; Ezek. 32:7, 8; Joel 2:30, 31; 3:15; Matt. 24:29; Luke 21:25 [j]Ps. 104:19
16 [k]Deut. 4:19; Ps. 136:7-9

[1] Or *a canopy;* also verses 7, 8, 14, 15, 17, 20 [2] Or *fashioned;* also verse 16 [3] Or *Sky;* also verses 9, 14, 15, 17, 20, 26, 28, 30; 2:1 [4] Or *Land;* also verses 11, 12, 22, 24, 25, 26, 28, 30; 2:1 [5] Or *small plants;* also verses 12, 29 [6] Or *appointed times*

the two words *tehom* and "Tiamat"). There are many linguistic reasons, however, for doubting a direct identification between the two. In any event, there is no conflict in Genesis or in the rest of the Bible between God and the deep, since the deep readily does God's bidding (cf. 7:11; 8:2; Ps. 33:7; 104:6).

1:3–5 And God said. In ch. 1 the absolute power of God is conveyed by the fact that he merely speaks and things are created. Each new section of the chapter is introduced by God's speaking. This is the first of the 10 words of creation in ch. 1. **Let there be light.** Light is the first of God's creative works, which God speaks into existence. **the light was good** (v. 4). Everything that God brings into being is good. This becomes an important refrain throughout the chapter (see vv. 10, 12, 18, 21, 25, 31). **God called the light Day** (v. 5). The focus in v. 5 is on how God has ordered time on a weekly cycle; thus, "let there be light" may indicate the dawning of a new day. God is pictured working for six days and resting on the Sabbath, which is a model for human activity. Day 4 develops this idea further: the lights are placed in the heavens for signs and seasons, for the purpose of marking days and years and the seasons of the great festivals such as Passover. This sense of time being structured is further emphasized throughout the chapter as each stage of God's ordering and filling is separated by evening and morning into specific days. **there was evening and there was morning, the first day.** The order—evening, *then* morning—helps the reader to follow the flow of the passage: after the workday (vv. 3–5a) there is an evening, and then a morning, implying that there is a nighttime (the worker's daily rest) in between. Thus the reader is prepared for the next workday to dawn. Similar phrases divide ch. 1 into six distinctive workdays, while 2:1–3 make a seventh day, God's Sabbath. On the first three days God creates the environment that the creatures of days 4–6 will inhabit; thus, sea and sky (day 2) are occupied by fish and birds created on day 5 (see chart below). By a simple reading of Genesis, these days must be described as days in the life of God, but how his days relate to human days is more difficult to determine (cf. Ps. 90:4; 2 Pet. 3:8). See further Introduction: Genesis and Science.

Location	Inhabitants
1. Light and dark	4. Lights of day and night
2. Sea and sky	5. Fish and birds
3. Fertile earth	6. Land animals (including mankind)
7. Rest and enjoyment	

1:6–8 waters. Water plays a crucial role in ancient Near Eastern creation literature. In Egypt, for example, the creator-god Ptah uses the preexistent waters (personified as the god Nun) to create the universe. The same is true in Mesopotamian belief: it is out of the gods of watery chaos—Apsu, Tiamat, and Mummu—that creation comes. The biblical creation account sits in stark contrast to such dark mythological polytheism. In the biblical account, water at creation is no deity; it is simply something God created, and it serves as material in the hands of the sole sovereign Creator. As light was separated from darkness, so waters are separated to form an **expanse** (vv. 6–7), which God calls **Heaven** (v. 8). As the ESV footnote illustrates by offering the alternative term "sky," it is difficult to find a single English word that accurately conveys the precise sense of the Hebrew term *shamayim*, "heaven/heavens." In this context, it refers to what humans see above them, i.e., the region that contains both celestial lights (vv. 14–17) and birds (v. 20).

1:9–13 Two further regions are organized by God: the **dry land** forming **Earth**, and the **waters** forming **Seas** (vv. 9–10). These are the last objects to be specifically named by God. God then instructs the earth to bring forth **vegetation** (vv. 11–12). While the creation of vegetation may seem out of place on day 3, it anticipates what God will later say in vv. 29–30 concerning food for both humanity and other creatures. The creation of distinctive locations in days 1–3, along with vegetation, prepares for the filling of these in days 4–6.

1:14–19 This section corresponds closely with the ordering of Day and Night on the first day, involving the separation of light and darkness (vv. 3–5). Here the emphasis is on the creation of **lights** that will govern time, as well as providing **light upon the earth** (v. 15). By referring to them as the **greater light** and **lesser light** (v. 16), the text avoids using terms that were also proper names for pagan deities linked to the sun and the moon. Chapter 1 deliberately undermines pagan ideas regarding nature's being controlled by different deities. (To the ancient pagans of the Near East, the gods were personified in various elements of nature. Thus, in Egyptian texts, the gods Ra and Thoth are personified in the sun and the moon, respectively.) The term **made** (Hb. *'asah*, v. 16), as the ESV footnote shows, need only mean that God "fashioned" or "worked on" them; it does not of itself imply that they did not exist in any form before this. Rather, the focus here is on the way in which God has ordained the sun and moon to order and define the passing of time according to his purposes. Thus the references to **seasons** (v. 14) or "appointed times" (ESV footnote) and to **days and years** are probably an allusion to the appointed times and patterns in the Hebrew calendar for worship, festivals, and religious observance (Ex. 13:10; 23:15).

1:16 and the stars. The immense universe that God created (see note on

18 [l]Jer. 31:35
21 [m]Ps. 104:25, 26
22 [n]ch. 8:17; 9:1
26 [o]ch. 3:22; 11:7; Isa. 6:8 [p]ch. 5:1; 9:6; 1 Cor. 11:7; Eph. 4:24; Col. 3:10; James 3:9 [q]ch. 9:2; Ps. 8:6-8; James 3:7
27 [r]ch. 2:18, 21-23; 5:2; Mal. 2:15; Matt. 19:4; Mark 10:6
28 [s]ch. 9:1, 7

light to rule the night—and the stars. 17 And God set them in the expanse of the heavens
to give light on the earth, 18 to [l]rule over the day and over the night, and to separate the
light from the darkness. And God saw that it was good. 19 And there was evening and there
was morning, the fourth day.
20 And God said, "Let the waters swarm with swarms of living creatures, and let birds[1]
fly above the earth across the expanse of the heavens." 21 So [m]God created the great sea
creatures and every living creature that moves, with which the waters swarm, according
to their kinds, and every winged bird according to its kind. And God saw that it was good.
22 And God blessed them, saying, [n]"Be fruitful and multiply and fill the waters in the seas,
and let birds multiply on the earth." 23 And there was evening and there was morning,
the fifth day.
24 And God said, "Let the earth bring forth living creatures according to their kinds—
livestock and creeping things and beasts of the earth according to their kinds." And it
was so. 25 And God made the beasts of the earth according to their kinds and the livestock
according to their kinds, and everything that creeps on the ground according to its kind.
And God saw that it was good.
26 Then God said, [o]"Let us make man[2] in our image, [p]after our likeness. And [q]let them have
dominion over the fish of the sea and over the birds of the heavens and over the livestock
and over all the earth and over every creeping thing that creeps on the earth."

27 So God created man in his own image,
in the image of God he created him;
[r]male and female he created them.

28 And God blessed them. And God said to them, [s]"Be fruitful and multiply and fill the

[1] Or *flying things*; see Leviticus 11:19–20 [2] The Hebrew word for *man* (*adam*) is the generic term for mankind and becomes the proper name *Adam*

Isa. 40:25–26) is mentioned here only in a brief phrase, almost as if it were an afterthought. The focus of Genesis 1 is on the earth; the focus of the rest of the Bible is on man (male and female) as the pinnacle of God's creation and the object of his great salvation.

1:20–23 Having previously described the creation of the **waters** and the **expanse of the heavens**, this section focuses on how they are filled with appropriate creatures of different kinds. As reproductive organisms, they are blessed by God so that they may be fruitful and fill their respective regions.

1:21 The term for **great sea creatures** (Hb. *tannin*) in various contexts can denote large serpents, dragons, or crocodiles, as well as whales or sharks (the probable sense here). Some have suggested that this could also refer to other extinct creatures such as dinosaurs. Canaanite literature portrays a great dragon as the enemy of the main fertility god Baal. Genesis depicts God as creating large sea creatures, but they are not in rebellion against him. He is sovereign and is not in any kind of battle to create the universe.

1:24–31 This is by far the longest section given over to a particular day, indicating that day 6 is the peak of interest for this passage. The final region to be filled is the dry land, or Earth (as it has been designated in v. 10). Here a significant distinction is drawn between all the living creatures that are created to live on the dry land, and human beings. Whereas vv. 24–25 deal with the "living creatures" that the earth is to bring forth, vv. 26–30 concentrate on the special status assigned to humans.

1:24–25 livestock and creeping things and beasts of the earth. These terms group the land-dwelling animals into three broad categories, probably reflecting the way nomadic shepherds would experience them: the domesticatable stock animals (e.g., sheep, goats, cattle, and perhaps camels and horses); the small crawlers (e.g., rats and mice, lizards, spiders); and the larger game and predatory animals (e.g., gazelles, lions). This list is not intended to be exhaustive, and it is hard to know where to put some animals (e.g., the domestic cat). See further Introduction: Genesis and Science.

1:26 Let us make man in our image. The text does not specify the identity of the "us" mentioned here. Some have suggested that God may be addressing the members of his court, whom the OT elsewhere calls "sons of God" (e.g., Job 1:6) and the NT calls "angels," but a significant objection is that man is not made in the image of angels, nor is there any indication that angels participated in the creation of human beings. Many Christians and some Jews have taken "us" to be God speaking to himself, since God alone does the making in Gen. 1:27 (cf. 5:1); this would be the first hint of the Trinity in the Bible (cf. 1:2).

1:27 There has been debate about the expression **image of God**. Many scholars point out the idea, commonly used in the ancient Near East, of the king who was the visible representative of the deity; thus the king ruled on behalf of the god. Since v. 26 links the image of God with the exercise of dominion over all the other creatures of the seas, heavens, and earth, one can see that humanity is endowed here with authority to rule the earth as God's representatives or vice-regents (see note on v. 28). Other scholars, seeing the pattern of **male and female**, have concluded that humanity expresses God's image in relationship, particularly in well-functioning human community, both in marriage and in wider society. Traditionally, the image has been seen as the capacities that set man apart from the other animals—ways in which humans resemble God, such as in the characteristics of reason, morality, language, a capacity for relationships governed by love and commitment, and creativity in all forms of art. All these insights can be put together by observing that the *resemblances* (man is like God in a series of ways) allow mankind to *represent* God in ruling, and to establish worthy *relationships* with God, with one another, and with the rest of the creation. This "image" and this dignity apply to *both* "male and female" human beings. (This view is unique in the context of the ancient Near East. In Mesopotamia, e.g., the gods created humans merely to carry out work for them.) The Hebrew term *'adam*, translated as **man**, is often a generic term that denotes both male and female, while sometimes it refers to man in distinction from woman (2:22, 23, 25; 3:8, 9, 12, 20): it becomes the proper name "Adam" (2:20; 3:17, 21; 4:1; 5:1). At this stage, humanity as a species is set apart from all other creatures and crowned with glory and honor as ruler of the earth (cf. Ps. 8:5–8). The events recorded in Genesis 3, however, will have an important bearing on the creation status of humanity.

1:28 As God had blessed the sea and sky creatures (v. 22), so too he blesses humanity. **Be fruitful and multiply.** This motif recurs throughout Genesis in association with divine blessing (see 9:1, 7; 17:20; 28:3; 35:11; 48:4) and serves as the basis of the biblical view that raising faithful children is a part of God's creation plan for mankind. God's creation plan is that the whole earth

earth and subdue it, and have dominion over the fish of the sea and over the birds of the
heavens and over every living thing that moves on the earth." 29 And God said, "Behold, I
have given you every plant yielding seed that is on the face of all the earth, and every tree
with seed in its fruit. [t]You shall have them for food. 30 And [u]to every beast of the earth and
to every bird of the heavens and to everything that creeps on the earth, everything that
has the breath of life, I have given every green plant for food." And it was so. 31 [v]And God
saw everything that he had made, and behold, it was very good. And there was evening
and there was morning, the sixth day.

The Seventh Day, God Rests

2 Thus the heavens and the earth were finished, and [w]all the host of them. 2 And [x]on
the seventh day God finished his work that he had done, and he rested on the seventh
day from all his work that he had done. 3 So God blessed the seventh day and made it holy,
because on it God rested from all his work that he had done in creation.

The Creation of Man and Woman

4 [y]These are the generations
of the heavens and the earth when they were created,
in the day that the LORD God made the earth and the heavens.

5 When no [z]bush of the field[1] was yet in the land[2] and no small plant of the field had
yet sprung up—for the LORD God had not caused it to rain on the land, and there was

[1] *Or open country* [2] Or *earth*; also verse 6

29 [t]ch. 9:3; Ps. 104:14, 15; 145:15, 16
30 [u]Ps. 147:9
31 [v]Eccles. 7:29; 1 Tim. 4:4

Chapter 2

1 [w]Deut. 4:19; Ps. 33:6
2 [x]Ex. 20:8-11; 31:17; Deut. 5:12-14; Heb. 4:4
4 [y]ch. 1:1
5 [z][ch. 1:11, 12]

should be populated by those who know him and who serve wisely as his vice-regents or representatives. **subdue it, and have dominion**. The term "subdue" (Hb. *kabash*) elsewhere means to bring a people or a land into subjection so that it will yield service to the one subduing it (Num. 32:22, 29). Here the idea is that the man and woman are to make the earth's resources beneficial for themselves, which implies that they would investigate and develop the earth's resources to make them useful for human beings generally. This command provides a foundation for wise scientific and technological development; the evil uses to which people have put their dominion come as a result of Genesis 3. **over every living thing**. As God's representatives, human beings are to rule over every living thing on the earth. These commands are not, however, a mandate to exploit the earth and its creatures to satisfy human greed, for the fact that Adam and Eve were "in the image of God" (1:27) implies God's expectation that human beings will use the earth wisely and govern it with the same sense of responsibility and care that God has toward the whole of his creation.

1:31 Having previously affirmed on six occasions that particular aspects of creation are "good" (vv. 4, 10, 12, 18, 21, 25), God now states, after the creation of the man and the woman, that **everything** he has made is **very good**; the additional **behold** invites the reader to imagine seeing creation from God's vantage point. While many things do not appear to be good about the present-day world, this was not so at the beginning. Genesis goes on to explain why things have changed, indicating that no blame should be attributed to God. Everything he created was very good: it answers to God's purposes and expresses his own overflowing goodness. Despite the invasion of sin (ch. 3), the material creation retains its goodness (cf. 1 Tim. 4:4).

2:1–3 These verses bring to a conclusion the opening section of Genesis by emphasizing that God has completed the process of ordering creation. The repeated comment that God **rested** does not imply that he was weary from labor. The effortless ease with which everything is done in ch. 1 suggests otherwise. Rather, the motif of God's resting hints at the purpose of creation. As reflected in various ancient Near Eastern accounts, divine rest is associated with temple building. God's purpose for the earth is that it should become his dwelling place; it is not simply made to house his creatures. God's "activities" on this day (he **finished**, "rested," "blessed," "made it holy") all fit this delightful pattern. The concept of the earth as a divine sanctuary, which is developed further in 2:4–25, runs throughout the whole Bible, coming to a climax in the future reality that the apostle John sees in his vision of a "new heaven and a new earth" in Rev. 21:1–22:5. **God blessed the seventh day and made it holy** (Gen. 2:3). These words provide the basis for the obligation that God placed on the Israelites to rest from their normal labor on the Sabbath day (see Ex. 20:8–11). There is no evening-followed-by-morning refrain for this day, prompting many to conclude that the seventh day still continues (which seems to underlie John 5:17; Heb. 4:3–11).

2:4–4:26 *Earth's First People.* Centered initially on the garden of Eden, the episodes that make up this part of Genesis recount how God's ordered creation is thrown into chaos by the human couple's disobedience. The subsequent story of Cain and Abel and then Lamech (ch. 4) shows the world spiraling downward into violence, which precipitated the flood (6:11, 13). These events are very significant for understanding not only the whole of Genesis but all of the Bible.

2:4–25 *The Man and Woman in the Sanctuary of Eden.* The panoramic view of creation in ch. 1 is immediately followed by a complementary account of the sixth day that zooms in on the creation of the human couple, who are placed in the garden of Eden. In style and content this section differs significantly from the previous one; it does not contradict anything in ch. 1, but as a literary flashback it supplies more detail about what was recorded in 1:27. The picture of a sovereign, transcendent deity is complemented by that of a God who is both immanent and personal. The two portrayals of God balance each other, together providing a truer and richer description of his nature than either does on its own. In a similar way, whereas ch. 1 emphasizes the regal character of human beings, ch. 2 highlights their priestly status.

2:4 These are the generations of. This is the first of 11 such headings that give structure to the book of Genesis (cf. 5:1, which varies slightly; 6:9; 10:1; 11:10; 11:27; 25:12; 25:19; 36:1; 36:9; 37:2; see Introduction: Arrangement of the Book). Each heading concentrates on what comes forth from the object or person named. The earliest translators of Genesis into Greek (in the Septuagint) used the word *genesis* to render the Hebrew word for "generations" (Hb. *toledot*); from this is derived the title "Genesis." The rest of the verse is artfully arranged in a mirror (or chiastic) form, the parts of the two poetic lines corresponding to each other in reverse order: **heavens** (A), **earth** (B), **when they were created** (C), **in the day that** the Lord God **made** (C'), **earth** (B'), **heavens** (A'). This form unifies the two parts of the chiasmus, hereby inviting the reader to harmonize 2:5–25 with 1:1–2:3. **LORD God**. Throughout 1:1–2:3 the generic word "God" was used to denote the deity as the transcendent Creator. The reader is now introduced to God's personal name, "Yahweh" (translated as "LORD" because of the ancient Jewish tradition of substituting in Hb. the term that means "Lord" [*'Adonay*] for "Yahweh" when reading the biblical text). The use of "Yahweh" throughout this passage underlines the personal and relational nature of God. The precedent for translating this as "LORD" and not "Yahweh" in English is found in the Septuagint's customary translation (Gk. *Kyrios*, "Lord"). That translation was then quoted many times by the NT

5[a]ch. 3:23
7[b]ch. 3:19, 23; 18:27; Ps. 103:14; Eccles. 12:7; 1 Cor. 15:47 [c]ch. 7:22; Job 33:4; Isa. 2:22 [d]Job 27:3 [e]Cited 1 Cor. 15:45
8[f]ver. 15; ch. 13:10; Isa. 51:3; Ezek. 28:13; 31:8; Joel 2:3
9[g]ch. 3:22; Rev. 2:7; 22:2, 14 [h]ver. 17
11[i]ch. 10:7, 29; 25:18; 1 Sam. 15:7
14[j]Dan. 10:4
15[k]ver. 8

no man [a]to work the ground, **6** and a mist[1] was going up from the land and was watering
the whole face of the ground— **7** then the LORD God formed the man of [b]dust from the
ground and [c]breathed into his [d]nostrils the breath of life, and [e]the man became a living
creature. **8** And the LORD God planted a [f]garden in Eden, in the east, and there he put the
man whom he had formed. **9** And out of the ground the LORD God made to spring up every
tree that is pleasant to the sight and good for food. [g]The tree of life was in the midst of the
garden, [h]and the tree of the knowledge of good and evil.
10 A river flowed out of Eden to water the garden, and there it divided and became four
rivers. **11** The name of the first is the Pishon. It is the one that flowed around the whole
land of [i]Havilah, where there is gold. **12** And the gold of that land is good; bdellium and
onyx stone are there. **13** The name of the second river is the Gihon. It is the one that flowed
around the whole land of Cush. **14** And the name of the third river is the [j]Tigris, which
flows east of Assyria. And the fourth river is the Euphrates.
15 The LORD God took the man [k]and put him in the garden of Eden to work it and keep

[1] *Or spring*

authors, who also used the Greek term *Kyrios*, "Lord," rather than "Yahweh" for God's name. (For more on the name "Yahweh," see notes on Ex. 3:14; 3:15.)

2:5–7 These verses concentrate on God's creation of a human male, amplifying 1:26–31 in particular. The main action here is God's "forming" of the man (2:7); vv. 5–6 describe the conditions as the action took place. The term **land** (Hb. *'erets*) can refer to the whole earth (cf. ESV footnote), to dry land (cf. 1:10), or to a specific region (cf. 2:11–13). To show the continuity with ch. 1 (see note on 2:4), and in view of the mention of **rain**, the ESV rendering ("land") is best. The location of this land is some unnamed place, just as the rainy season was about to begin, and thus when the ground was still dry, and without any **bush of the field**. These conditions prevailed before the creation of man, suggesting that the lack of growth was related to the absence of a man to irrigate the land (which would be the normal way in dry conditions to bring about growth). **then the LORD God formed the man of dust from the ground** (v. 7). The verb "formed" (Hb. *yatsar*) conveys the picture of a potter's fashioning clay into a particular shape. The close relationship between the man and the ground is reflected in the Hebrew words used to denote them, *'adam* and *'adamah*, respectively. **breathed into his nostrils the breath of life** (v. 7). Here God breathes life—physical, mental, and spiritual—into the one created to bear his image. **living creature.** The same term in Hebrew is used in 1:20, 24 to denote sea and land creatures. While human beings have much in common with other living beings, God gives humans alone a royal and priestly status and makes them alone "in his own image" (1:27). (See Paul's quotation of this passage in 1 Cor. 15:45.)

2:8–9 God provides a suitable environment for the man by planting a **garden in Eden, in the east**. The name "Eden," which would have conveyed the sense of "luxury, pleasure," probably denotes a region much greater than the garden itself. God formed the man in the "land" (see vv. 5–7), and then **put** him in the garden (cf. v. 15). The earliest translation into Greek (the Septuagint) used the word *paradeisos* (from which comes the English term "paradise"; cf. note on Luke 23:39–43) to translate the Hebrew term for "garden," on the understanding that it resembled a royal park. The abundance of the garden is conveyed by the observation that it contained **every tree that is pleasant to the sight and good for food** (Gen. 2:9), which is an ironic foreshadowing of 3:6 (see note there). Two trees, however, are picked out for special mention: **the tree of life** and **the tree of the knowledge of good and evil** (2:9). Since relatively little is said about these trees, any understanding of them must be derived from the role that they play within the account of Genesis 2–3, especially ch. 3. On "tree of life," see note on 3:22–24; on "tree of knowledge," see note on 2:17.

2:10–14 The general description of the **river** that **flowed out of Eden** dividing into **four rivers** (v. 10) implies that Eden had a central location. In spite of the very specific details provided, however, Eden's location remains a mystery. While the names **Tigris** and **Euphrates** (v. 14) are associated with the two rivers that surround Mesopotamia, the rivers **Pishon** and **Gihon**, as well as the regions of **Havilah** and **Cush** (vv. 11, 13), have not been satisfactorily identified (see map to the right). The reference to **gold** and **onyx** (vv. 11, 12) suggests that the land is rich in resources; these materials are later associated with the making of the tabernacle and temple.

2:15–16 The overall picture of Eden presented in the preceding verses suggests that the park-like garden is part of a divine sanctuary. **The man** is **put** in the garden **to work it and keep it**. The term "work" (Hb. *'abad*; cf. v. 5; 3:23; 4:2, 12; Prov. 12:11; 28:19) denotes preparing and tending, and "keep" (Hb. *shamar*) adds to that idea. Since this command comes before Adam sinned, work did not come as a result of sin, nor is it something to be avoided. Productive work is part of God's good purpose for man in creation. Later, the same two verbs are used together of the work undertaken by the priests and Levites in the tabernacle ("minister" or "serve" [Hb. *'abad*] and "guard" [Hb. *shamar*]; e.g., Num. 3:7–8; 18:7). The man's role is to be not only a gardener but also a guardian. As a priest, he is to maintain the sanctity of the garden as part of a temple complex. **And the LORD God commanded the man.** The fact that the command was given to Adam implies that God gave "the man" a leadership role, including the responsibility to guard and care for ("keep") all of creation (Gen. 2:15)—a role that is also related to the leadership responsibility of Adam for Eve as his wife (cf. v. 18, "a helper fit for him"). (On the NT understanding of the relationship between husband and wife, see Eph. 5:22–33.)

The Garden of Eden

Genesis describes the location of Eden in relation to the convergence of four rivers. While two of the rivers are unknown (the Pishon and the Gihon), the nearly universal identification of the other two rivers as the Tigris and the Euphrates suggests a possible location for Eden at either their northern or southern extremes.

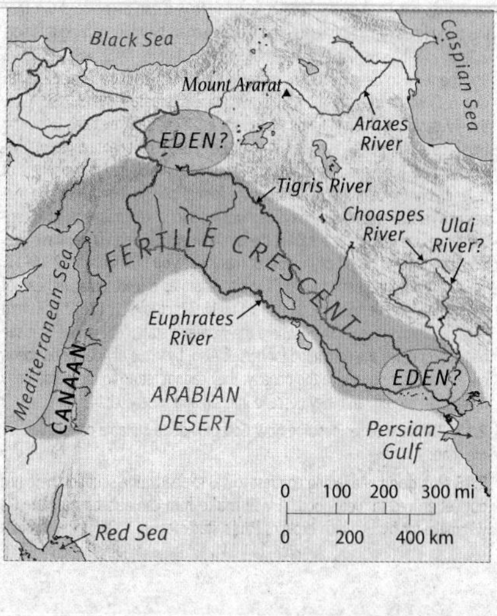

it. **16** And the LORD God commanded the man, saying, "You may surely eat of every tree of
the garden, **17** but of the tree of the knowledge of good and evil [l]you shall not eat, for in
the day that you eat[1] of it you [m]shall surely die."

18 Then the LORD God said, "It is not good that the man should be alone; [n]I will make
him a helper fit for[2] him." **19** [o]Now out of the ground the LORD God had formed[3] every
beast of the field and every bird of the heavens and [p]brought them to the man to see what
he would call them. And whatever the man called every living creature, that was its name.
20 The man gave names to all livestock and to the birds of the heavens and to every beast of
the field. But for Adam[4] there was not found a helper fit for him. **21** So the LORD God caused
a [q]deep sleep to fall upon the man, and while he slept took one of his ribs and closed up
its place with flesh. **22** And the rib that the LORD God had taken from the man he made[5]
into a woman and brought her to the man. **23** Then the man said,

> "This at last is [r]bone of my bones
> and flesh of my flesh;
> she shall be called Woman,
> because she was [s]taken out of Man."[6]

24 [t]Therefore a man shall leave his father and his mother and hold fast to his wife, and
they shall become one flesh. **25** And the man and his wife were both naked and were not
ashamed.

[1] Or *when you eat* [2] Or *corresponding to*; also verse 20 [3] Or *And out of the ground the LORD God formed* [4] Or *the man* [5] Hebrew *built* [6] The Hebrew words for *woman* (*ishshah*) and *man* (*ish*) sound alike

17 [l]ch. 3:1-3, 11, 17 [m]Rom. 6:23; James 1:15
18 [n]1 Cor. 11:9; 1 Tim. 2:13
19 [o]ch. 1:20, 24 [p]Ps. 8:6
21 [q]ch. 15:12; 1 Sam. 26:12
23 [r]ch. 29:14; Judg. 9:2; 2 Sam. 5:1; 19:13; [Eph. 5:28-30] [s]1 Cor. 11:8
24 [t]Cited Matt. 19:5; Mark 10:7; 1 Cor. 6:16; Eph. 5:31; [Ps. 45:10; 1 Cor. 7:10, 11]

2:17 While God generously permitted the man to eat from every tree of the garden, God prohibited him from eating from **the tree of the knowledge of good and evil** (v. 17). The fruit of this tree has been variously understood as giving (1) sexual awareness, (2) moral discrimination, (3) moral responsibility, and (4) moral experience. Of these possibilities, the last is the most likely: by their obedience or disobedience the human couple will come to know good and evil by experience. Experience gained by "fearing the LORD" (Prov. 1:7) is wisdom, while that gained by disobeying God is slavery. **In the day** implies fixed certainty rather than absolute immediacy (e.g., 1 Kings 2:42). See note on Gen. 3:4–5. **you shall surely die** (2:17). What kind of "death" does this threaten: physical, spiritual, or some combination? The Hebrew word can be used for any of these ideas, and the only way to find out is by reading to see what happens as the story unfolds. (See note on 3:4–5.)

Theologians have discussed whether the instructions in 2:16–17, together with the instructions in 1:28–30, should be called God's "covenant" with Adam. Some have denied it, observing that the Hebrew word for "covenant" (*berit*) is not used until 6:18; others have added to this the insistence that covenants have to do with redemption. In reply, it can be pointed out that the thing itself can be present, even if the ordinary word identifying it is not: 2 Sam. 7:4–17 says nothing about a covenant, but Ps. 89:3, 28, 34, 39 all use the term to describe God's promise to David. The same happens with Hos. 6:7, which refers to a covenant with Adam (see note there). Also, Gen. 9:1–17 describes Noah in terms that clearly echo 1:28–30, explicitly using the word "covenant": Noah is a kind of new Adam, i.e., a covenant representative. Finally, there is no evidence that biblical covenants are limited to the sphere of redemption: the term simply describes the formal binding together of two parties in a relationship, on the basis of mutual personal commitment, with consequences for keeping or breaking the commitment. The man (Adam) receives this covenant on behalf of the rest of mankind: **you** is singular in 2:16–17, which provides the basis for Paul's use of Adam as a representative head of the human race, parallel to Christ, in 1 Cor. 15:22; cf. Rom. 5:12–19. The word "you" is plural in Gen. 3:1–5, where the woman's statement shows that she has appropriated the command for herself. Also, by virtue of Adam's disobedience, his offspring receive the penalty: they cannot return to the garden any more than he can, and they descend into sin and misery (ch. 4).

2:18–25 These verses describe how God provides a suitable companion for the man.

2:18 Not good is a jarring contrast to 1:31; clearly, the situation here has not yet arrived to "very good." **I will make him** can also be translated "I will make *for* him," which explains Paul's statement in 1 Cor. 11:9. In order to find the man a **helper fit for him**, God brings to him all the livestock, birds, and beasts of the field. None of these, however, proves to be "fit for" the man. "Helper" (Hb. *'ezer*) is one who supplies strength in the area that is lacking in "the helped." The term does not imply that the helper is either stronger or weaker than the one helped. "Fit for him" or "matching him" (cf. ESV footnote) is not the same as "like him": a wife is not her husband's clone but complements him.

2:20 The man gave names. By naming the animals, the man demonstrates his authority over all the other creatures. **Adam.** See note on 5:1–2.

2:23–24 When no suitable companion is found among all the living beings, God fashions a woman from the man's own flesh. The text highlights the sense of oneness that exists between the man and the woman. Adam joyfully proclaims, **"This at last is bone of my bones and flesh of my flesh."** This terminology is used elsewhere of blood relatives (29:14). This sentence and the story of Eve's creation both make the point that marriage creates the closest of all human relationships. It is also important to observe that God creates only one Eve for Adam, not several Eves or another Adam. This points to heterosexual monogamy as the divine pattern for marriage that God established at creation. Moreover, the kinship between husband and wife creates obligations that override even duty to one's parents (**therefore a man shall leave his father and his mother and hold fast to his wife**, 2:24). In ancient Israel, sons did not move away when they married, but lived near their parents and inherited their father's land. They "left" their parents in the sense of putting their wife's welfare before that of their parents. The term "hold fast" is used elsewhere for practicing covenant faithfulness (e.g., Deut. 10:20; see how Paul brings these texts together in 1 Cor. 6:16–17); thus, other Bible texts can call marriage a "covenant" (e.g., Prov. 2:17; Mal. 2:14). Paul's teaching on marriage in Eph. 5:25–32 is founded on this text. The sense of being made for each other is further reflected in a wordplay involving the terms "man" and "woman"; in Hebrew these are, respectively, *'ish* and *'ishshah*. As a result of this special affiliation, Gen. 2:24 observes that when a man leaves his parents and takes a wife, **they shall become one flesh**, i.e., one unit (a union of man and woman, consummated in sexual intercourse). Jesus appeals to this verse and 1:27 in setting out his view of marriage (Matt. 19:4–5).

2:25 naked and . . . not ashamed. This final description in vv. 18–25 offers a picture of innocent delight and anticipates further developments in the story. The subject of the couple's nakedness is picked up in 3:7–11, and a play on the similar sounds of the words "naked" (Hb. *'arummim*) and "crafty" (3:1, Hb. *'arum*) links the end of this episode with the start of the next.

Chapter 3
1 [u]Matt. 10:16; 2 Cor. 11:3; Rev. 12:9; 20:2
3 [v]ch. 2:17
4 [w]ver. 13; John 8:44; [2 Cor. 11:3]
6 [x]1 Tim. 2:14 [y]ver. 12, 17; Hos. 6:7
7 [z]ver. 5 [a]ch. 2:25
8 [b][Ps. 139:1-12; Jer. 23:23, 24]
10 [c]ver. 7; ch. 2:25

The Fall

3 Now [u]the serpent was more crafty than any other beast of the field that the LORD
God had made.
He said to the woman, "Did God actually say, 'You[1] shall not eat of any tree in the garden'?" **2** And the woman said to the serpent, "We may eat of the fruit of the trees in the
garden, **3** but God said, [v]'You shall not eat of the fruit of the tree that is in the midst of
the garden, neither shall you touch it, lest you die.'" **4** [w]But the serpent said to the woman,
"You will not surely die. **5** For God knows that when you eat of it your eyes will be opened,
and you will be like God, knowing good and evil." **6** So when the woman saw that the tree
was good for food, and that it was a delight to the eyes, and that the tree was to be desired
to make one wise,[2] she took of its fruit [x]and ate, and she also gave some to her husband
who was with her, [y]and he ate. **7** [z]Then the eyes of both were opened, [a]and they knew that
they were naked. And they sewed fig leaves together and made themselves loincloths.
8 And they heard the sound of the LORD God walking in the garden in the cool[3] of the
day, and the man and his wife [b]hid themselves from the presence of the LORD God among
the trees of the garden. **9** But the LORD God called to the man and said to him, "Where are
you?"[4] **10** And he said, "I heard the sound of you in the garden, and I was afraid, [c]because
I was naked, and I hid myself." **11** He said, "Who told you that you were naked? Have you

[1] In Hebrew *you* is plural in verses 1–5 [2] Or *to give insight* [3] Hebrew *wind* [4] In Hebrew *you* is singular in verses 9 and 11

3:1–24 *The Couple Rebels against God.* The sudden and unexplained arrival of a cunning serpent presents a challenge of immense importance to the human couple. Their choice is to disregard God's instructions, an act of willful rebellion that has terrible consequences for the whole of creation. As a result, God's creation is thrown into disorder, with chaotic effects that result from the disruption of all the harmonious relationships that God had previously established.

3:1 The speaking **serpent** is suddenly introduced into the story with minimum detail. Nothing is mentioned about its origin, other than that it is one of the beasts **of the field**. Although the serpent is eventually portrayed as God's enemy, the initial introduction is full of ambiguity regarding its true nature. While the brief comment that it is the craftiest of the beasts possibly indicates potential danger, the Hebrew term *'arum* does not carry the negative moral connotations of the English words "crafty" and "cunning." Similarly, the serpent's initial question may have sounded quite innocent, although it deliberately misquotes God as saying that the couple must **not eat of any tree in the garden**. Did the serpent merely misunderstand what God had said? In these ways the subtlety of the serpent's approach to the woman is captured by the narrator. It is noteworthy that the serpent also deliberately avoids using God's personal name "Yahweh" ("LORD") when he addresses the woman. Here is another hint that his presence in the garden presents a threat. Although his initial words appear deceptively innocent, his subsequent contradiction of God leaves no doubt about the serpent's motive and purpose. The text does not indicate when or how the serpent became evil. As the narrative proceeds, it becomes clear that more than a simple snake is at work here; an evil power is using the snake (see note on v. 15). As indicated by God's declaration that "everything he had made . . . was very good" (1:31), clearly evil entered the created world at some unknown point after God's work of creation was completed. Likewise, nothing in the Bible suggests the eternal existence of evil (see notes on Isa. 14:12–15; Ezek. 28:11–19).

3:2–3 The woman's response largely echoes the divine instruction given in 2:16–17 regarding the tree of knowledge (for more on the meaning of the covenant, see note on 2:17), although she fails to identify the tree clearly as the tree of the knowledge of good and evil and adds the comment **neither shall you touch it**. These minor variations are possibly meant to convey, even at this stage, that the woman views God's instructions as open to human modification.

3:4–5 The serpent not only directly contradicts what God has said but goes on to present the fruit of the tree as something worth obtaining: by eating it, the couple will be **like God, knowing good and evil**. The irony of the serpent's remarks should not be overlooked. The couple, unlike the serpent, has been made in the image of God (1:26–27). In this way they are already like God. Moreover, being in the image of God, they are expected to exercise authority over all the beasts of the field, which includes the serpent. By obeying the serpent, however, they betray the trust placed in them by God. This is not merely an act of disobedience; it is an act of treachery. Those who were meant to govern the earth on God's behalf instead rebel against their divine King and obey one of his creatures. **You will not surely die**. It is sometimes claimed that the serpent is correct when he says these things to the couple, for they do not "die"; Adam lives to be 930 years old (5:5). Further, their eyes are opened (3:7) and God acknowledges in v. 22 that "the man has become like one of us in knowing good and evil." Yet the serpent speaks half-truths, promising much but delivering little. Their eyes are indeed opened, and they come to know something, but it is only that they are naked. They know good and evil by experience, but their sense of guilt makes them afraid to meet God; they have become slaves to evil. And while they do not cease to exist physically, they are expelled from the garden-sanctuary and God's presence. Cut off from the source of life and the tree of life, they are in the realm of the dead. What they experience outside of Eden is not life as God intended, but spiritual death.

3:6 when the woman saw. Like all the other trees in the garden, the tree of the knowledge of good and evil was "pleasant to the sight and good for food" (2:9). The irony is that somehow the serpent has made the woman discontent with the permitted trees, focusing her desire on this one. Its deadly appeal to her, apparently, is its ability **to make one wise** (see note on 2:17)—wise, however, not according to the "fear of the LORD" (Prov. 1:7; 9:10). **she also gave some to her husband who was with her**. The fact that Adam was "with her" and that he knowingly **ate** what God had forbidden indicates that Adam's sin was both an act of conscious rebellion against God and a failure to carry out his divinely ordained responsibility to guard or "keep" (Gen. 2:15) both the garden and the woman that God had created as "a helper fit for him" (2:18, 20). The disastrous consequences of Adam's sin cannot be overemphasized, resulting in the fall of mankind, the beginning of every kind of sin, suffering, and pain, as well as physical and spiritual death for the human race.

3:7–13 Eating the fruit transforms the couple, but not for the better. Now ashamed of their nakedness (cf. 2:25), they attempt to clothe themselves. Conscious of the Lord God's presence, they hide. When confronted by God regarding the tree of the knowledge of good and evil, the man blames the woman, who in turn blames the serpent.

3:9 the LORD God called to the man . . . , "Where are you?" Both "man" and "you" are singular in Hebrew. God thus confronts Adam first, holding him primarily responsible for what happened, as the one who is the representative (or "head") of the husband-and-wife relationship, established before the fall (see note on 2:15–16).

eaten of the tree of which I commanded you not to eat?" **12** The man said, [d]"The woman
whom you gave to be with me, she gave me fruit of the tree, and I ate." **13** Then the LORD
God said to the woman, "What is this that you have done?" The woman said, [e]"The serpent
deceived me, and I ate."

14 The LORD God said to the serpent,

"Because you have done this,
cursed are you above all livestock
and above all beasts of the field;
on your belly you shall go,
and [f]dust you shall eat
all the days of your life.
15 I will put enmity between you and the woman,
and between your offspring[1] and [g]her offspring;
[h]he shall bruise your head,
and you shall bruise his heel."

16 To the woman he said,

"I will surely multiply your pain in childbearing;
[i]in pain you shall bring forth children.
[j]Your desire shall be for[2] your husband,
and he shall [k]rule over you."

17 And to Adam he said,

"Because you have listened to the voice of your wife
and have eaten of the tree

[1] Hebrew *seed*; so throughout Genesis [2] Or *against*

12 [d]ch. 2:18; Job 31:33
13 [e]ver. 4; 2 Cor. 11:3; 1 Tim. 2:14
14 [f]Isa. 65:25; Mic. 7:17
15 [g]Isa. 7:14; Mic. 5:3; Matt. 1:23, 25; Luke 1:34, 35; Gal. 4:4; 1 Tim. 2:15 [h]Rom. 16:20; Heb. 2:14; Rev. 20:1-3, 10
16 [i][John 16:21] [j]ch. 4:7; Song 7:10 [k]1 Cor. 11:3; 14:34; Eph. 5:22-24; Col. 3:18; 1 Tim. 2:11, 12; Titus 2:5; 1 Pet. 3:1, 5, 6

3:14–15 God addresses the serpent first. Verse 1 declared the serpent "more crafty" (Hb. *'arum*); now God declares it more **cursed** (Hb. *'arur*). Indicted for its part in tempting the woman, the serpent will be viewed with contempt from now on. This is conveyed both literally and figuratively by the serpent's going on its **belly** and eating **dust**. Having deceived the woman, the serpent will have ongoing hostility with the woman, which will be perpetuated by their respective **offspring**.

3:15 While many modern commentators interpret this part of the curse as merely describing the natural hostility that exists between men and snakes, it has traditionally been understood as pointing forward to the defeat of the serpent by a future descendant of the woman, and this interpretation fits well with the words and the context. This defeat is implied by the serpent's being bruised in the head, which is more serious than the offspring of Eve being bruised in the heel. For this reason, v. 15 has been labeled the "Protoevangelium," the first announcement of the gospel. This interpretation requires that the serpent be viewed as more than a mere snake, something which the narrative itself implies, given the serpent's ability to speak and the vile things he says. While the present chapter does not explicitly identify the serpent with Satan, such an identification is a legitimate inference and is clearly what the apostle John has in view in Rev. 12:9 and 20:2. The motif of the **offspring** of the woman is picked up in Gen. 4:25 with the birth of Seth; subsequently, the rest of Genesis traces a single line of Seth's descendants, observing that it will eventually produce a king through whom all the nations of the earth will be blessed (see Introduction: History of Salvation Summary). **he shall bruise your head, and you shall bruise his heel**. Some interpreters have suggested that by saying "he" and "his," the intended meaning is that one particular offspring is in view. Within the larger biblical framework, this hope comes to fulfillment in Jesus Christ, who is clearly presented in the NT as overcoming Satan (Heb. 2:14; 1 John 3:8; cf. Matt. 12:29; Mark 1:24; Luke 10:18; John 12:31; 16:11; 1 Cor. 15:24; Col. 2:15), while at the same time being bruised.

3:16 By way of punishing the woman for her sin of disobedience, God pronounces that she will suffer **pain** (Hb. *'itstsabon*) in the bearing of children. This strikes at the very heart of the woman's distinctiveness, for she is the "mother of all living" (v. 20). **Your desire shall be for your husband, and he shall rule over you**. These words from the Lord indicate that there will be an ongoing struggle between the woman and the man for leadership in the marriage relationship. The leadership role of the husband and the complementary relationship between husband and wife that were ordained by God before the fall have now been deeply damaged and distorted by sin. This especially takes the form of inordinate desire (on the part of the wife) and domineering rule (on the part of the husband). The Hebrew term here translated "desire" (*teshuqah*) is rarely found in the OT. But it appears again in 4:7, in a statement that closely parallels 3:16—that is, where the Lord says to Cain, just before Cain's murder of his brother, that sin's "desire is for you" (i.e., to master Cain), and that Cain must "rule over it" (which he immediately fails to do, by murdering his brother, as seen in 4:8). Similarly, the ongoing result of Adam and Eve's original sin of rebellion against God will have disastrous consequences for their relationship: (1) Eve will have the sinful "desire" to oppose Adam and to assert leadership over him, reversing God's plan for Adam's leadership in marriage. But (2) Adam will also abandon his God-given, pre-fall role of leading, guarding, and caring for his wife, replacing this with his own sinful, distorted desire to "rule" over Eve. Thus one of the most tragic results of Adam and Eve's rebellion against God is an ongoing, damaging conflict between husband and wife in marriage, driven by the sinful behavior of both in rebellion against their respective God-given roles and responsibilities in marriage. (See notes on Eph. 5:21–32 for the NT pattern for marriage founded on the redemptive work of Christ.)

3:17–19 God's punishment of the man involves his relationship with the very ground from which he was formed (see note on 2:5–7). Because he has eaten that which was prohibited to him, he will have to struggle to eat in the future. Given the abundance of food that God provided in the garden, this judgment reflects God's disfavor. Adam will no longer enjoy the garden's abundance but will have to work the ground from which he was taken (3:23; see note on 2:8–9). The punishment is not work itself (cf. 2:15), but rather the hardship and frustration (i.e., "pain," *itstsabon*; cf. 3:16) that will accompany the man's labor. To say that the **ground** is **cursed** (Hb. *'arar*, v. 17) and will bring forth **thorns and thistles** (v. 18) indicates that the abundant productivity that was seen in Eden will no longer be the case. Underlying this judgment is a disruption of the harmonious relationship that originally existed between humans and nature.

[l]of which I commanded you,
'You shall not eat of it,'
[m]cursed is the ground because of you;
[n]in pain you shall eat of it all the days of your life;
18 thorns and thistles it shall bring forth for you;
and you shall eat the plants of the field.
19 By the sweat of your face
you shall eat bread,
till you return to the ground,
for out of it you were taken;
[o]for you are dust,
and [p]to dust you shall return."

20 The man called his wife's name Eve, because she was the mother of all living.[1] 21 And
the LORD God made for Adam and for his wife garments of skins and clothed them.
22 Then the LORD God said, [q]"Behold, the man has become like one of us in knowing
good and evil. Now, lest he reach out his hand [r]and take also of the tree of life and eat,
and live forever—" 23 therefore the LORD God sent him out from the garden of Eden [s]to
work the ground from which he was taken. 24 He drove out the man, and at the east of
the garden of Eden he placed the [t]cherubim and a flaming sword that turned every way
to guard the way to the tree of life.

Cain and Abel

4 Now Adam knew Eve his wife, and she conceived and bore Cain, saying, "I have gotten[2] a man with the help of the LORD." 2 And again, she bore his brother Abel. Now
Abel was a keeper of sheep, and Cain a worker of the ground. 3 In the course of time Cain
brought to the LORD an offering of [u]the fruit of the ground, 4 and Abel also brought of [v]the
firstborn of his flock and of their fat portions. And the LORD [w]had regard for Abel and his

[1] *Eve* sounds like the Hebrew for *life-giver* and resembles the word for *living* [2] *Cain* sounds like the Hebrew for *gotten*

17 [l]ch. 2:17 [m]ch. 5:29; [Rom. 8:20-22] [n]Eccles. 2:22, 23
19 [o]ch. 2:7; Ps. 103:14 [p]Job 34:15; Ps. 104:29; Eccles. 3:20; 12:7; Rom. 5:12
22 [q]ver. 5 [r]ch. 2:9
23 [s]ch. 2:5
24 [t]Ps. 18:10; 104:4; Heb. 1:7; [Ex. 25:18-22; Ezek. 28:11-16]

Chapter 4

3 [u]Lev. 2:12; Num. 18:12
4 [v]Ex. 13:12; Num. 18:17; Prov. 3:9 [w]Heb. 11:4

3:19 Further, the man's body will **return to the ground** (v. 19), i.e., it will die (which was not true of the original created order; cf. Rom. 5:12). For this reason, the Bible looks forward to a time when nature will be set free from the consequences of human sin; i.e., nature will no longer be the arena of punishment, and it will finally have glorified human beings to manage it and bring out its full potential (Rom. 8:19–22).

3:20–21 God's words of judgment on the serpent, woman, and man are immediately followed by two observations that possibly convey a sense of hope. First, the man names his wife **Eve** (v. 20), which means "life-giver" (see ESV footnote). Second, God clothes the couple (v. 21). While this final action recognizes that the human couple is now ashamed of their nakedness in God's presence, as a gesture it suggests that God still cares for these, his creatures. Because God provides **garments** to clothe Adam and Eve, thus requiring the death of an animal to cover their nakedness, many see a parallel here related to (1) the system of animal sacrifices to atone for sin later instituted by God through the leadership of Moses in Israel, and (2) the eventual sacrificial death of Christ as an atonement for sin.

3:22–24 The couple is expelled **from the garden**. God begins a sentence in v. 22 and breaks off without finishing it—for the man to **live forever** (in his sinful condition) is an unbearable thought, and God must waste no time in preventing it ("therefore the LORD God sent him out from the garden"). The **tree of life**, then, probably served in some way to confirm a person in his or her moral condition (cf. Prov. 3:18; 11:30; 13:12; Rev. 2:7; 22:2, 14, 19). According to Gen. 2:15, the man was put in the garden to work it and keep or guard it. Outside the garden the man will have to work the ground, but the task of keeping or guarding the garden is given to the **cherubim** (3:24). By allowing themselves to be manipulated by the serpent, the couple failed to fulfill their priestly duty of guarding the garden. Consequently, their priestly status is removed from them as they are put out of the sanctuary. The placing of cherubim to the **east of the garden** is reflected in the tabernacle and temple, where cherubim were an important component in the structure and furnishings (see The Ark of the Covenant, p. 184).

4:1–26 *Adam and Eve's Sons.* This chapter shows mankind plunging further into sin, with Cain murdering his brother and his descendant Lamech taking indiscriminate revenge. Although they have been expelled from the garden of Eden, Adam and Eve are enabled by God to have two sons. With them rests the hope of an offspring who will overcome the serpent. When Cain callously murders his righteous brother Abel, however, evil seems to triumph. Any hope that Cain's descendants will reverse this trend appears remote when Lamech boasts of killing a man simply for striking him. Against this background the brief announcement of Seth's birth to replace Abel offers fresh hope.

4:1 Eve's reference to the Lord's **help** when **Cain** is born conveys a sense of optimism. The serpent may yet be overthrown by the offspring of the woman.

4:2–5 Although Cain and Abel have contrasting occupations and present different types of offerings to God, the present episode is not designed to elevate herdsmen over farmers, or animal offerings over plant offerings. One way to explain why God **had regard for Abel and his offering**, but not for Cain, is to posit that Abel's offering, being of the **firstborn of his flock**, is a more costly offering, expressing greater devotion. Another way to explain the difference is first to observe that both offerings are recognizable parts of the later Levitical system: for Cain's offering of **the fruit of the ground** (v. 3), cf. Deut. 26:2 (an offering expressing consecration), and for Abel's offering of the firstborn of his flock, cf. Deut. 15:19–23 (a kind of peace offering, a meal in God's presence). But at no point does the Bible suggest that offerings work automatically, as if the worshiper's faith and contrition did not matter; and Cain's fundamentally bad heart can be seen in his resentment toward his brother and in his uncooperative answers to God in the rest of the passage. Several NT texts derive legitimate inferences from this narrative, namely, that Cain demonstrated an evil heart by his evil deeds, while Abel demonstrated a pious heart by his righteous deeds (1 John 3:12); and that Abel offered his sacrifice by faith and was commended as righteous for that reason (Heb. 11:4).

4:6–7 The Lord's words challenge Cain to do better. He still has the possibility of turning, evidently with God's help, to please God. To succeed in doing this,

offering, 5 but [x]for Cain and his offering he had no regard. So Cain was very angry, and his
face fell. 6 The LORD said to Cain, "Why are you angry, and why has your face fallen? 7 [y]If
you do well, will you not be accepted?[1] And if you do not do well, sin is crouching at the
door. [z]Its desire is for[2] you, but you must rule over it."

8 Cain spoke to Abel his brother.[3] And when they were in the field, Cain rose up against his
brother Abel and [a]killed him. 9 Then the LORD said to Cain, "Where is Abel your brother?"
He said, [b]"I do not know; am I my brother's keeper?" 10 And the LORD said, "What have
you done? The voice of your brother's blood [c]is crying to me from the ground. 11 And now
[d]you are cursed from the ground, which has opened its mouth to receive your brother's
blood from your hand. 12 When you work the ground, it shall no longer yield to you its
strength. You shall be a fugitive and a wanderer on the earth." 13 Cain said to the LORD,
"My [e]punishment is greater than I can bear.[4] 14 Behold, [f]you have driven me today away
from the ground, and [g]from your face I shall be hidden. I shall be a fugitive and a wanderer
on the earth, [h]and whoever finds me will kill me." 15 Then the LORD said to him, "Not so!
If anyone kills Cain, vengeance shall be taken on him [i]sevenfold." And the LORD [j]put a
mark on Cain, lest any who found him should attack him. 16 Then Cain went away from
the presence of the LORD and settled in the land of Nod,[5] east of Eden.

17 Cain knew his wife, and she conceived and bore Enoch. When he built a city, he called
the name of the city after the name of his son, Enoch. 18 To Enoch was born Irad, and Irad
fathered Mehujael, and Mehujael fathered Methushael, and Methushael fathered Lamech.
19 And Lamech took two wives. The name of the one was Adah, and the name of the other
Zillah. 20 Adah bore Jabal; he was the father of those who dwell in tents and have livestock.
21 His brother's name was Jubal; he was the father of all those who play the lyre and pipe.
22 Zillah also bore Tubal-cain; he was the forger of all instruments of bronze and iron. The
sister of Tubal-cain was Naamah.

[1] Hebrew *will there not be a lifting up* [of your face]? [2] Or *against* [3] Hebrew; Samaritan, Septuagint, Syriac, Vulgate add *Let us go out to the field* [4] Or *My guilt is too great to bear* [5] *Nod* means *wandering*

5 [x][Prov. 21:27]
7 [y]Eccles. 8:12, 13; Isa. 3:10, 11; Rom. 2:6-11 [z]ch. 3:16
8 [a]Matt. 23:35; Heb. 12:24; 1 John 3:12; Jude 11
9 [b]John 8:44
10 [c]Heb. 12:24; [Rev. 6:10]
11 [d]Deut. 27:24; [Num. 35:33]
13 [e]ch. 19:15
14 [f]Job 15:20-24 [g]2 Kgs. 24:20; Ps. 51:11; 143:7; Jer. 52:3 [h]ch. 9:6; Num. 35:19
15 [i]Ps. 79:12 [j][Ezek. 9:4, 6; Rev. 14:9, 11]

however, he must overcome the domination of **sin**, presented here as a wild beast seeking to devour Cain (cf. note on 3:16).

4:8 The brevity of the report of Abel's murder underlines the coldness of Cain's action. Jealousy, probably coupled with anger at God, causes him to slay his own brother without pity. The heinousness of this spiteful murder reveals that sin has mastered Cain.

4:9 am I my brother's keeper? When the Lord confronts Cain with his crime, his coldhearted nature causes him to deny any knowledge about his brother. Cain shows no sign of remorse.

4:10–12 Cain's punishment is linked to his crime. He will no longer be able to cultivate the soil (vv. 11–12) because his brother's blood cries out to God **from the ground** (v. 10). Cain's sentence adds to the alienation between man and the ground that has already been introduced in 3:17–18. Underlying these punishments is a principle that recurs throughout Scripture: human sin has a bearing on the fertility of the earth. Whereas God intended humanity to enjoy the earth's bounty, sin distances people not only from God himself but also from nature (see note on 3:17–19). Genesis 4:10 is the likely background for the NT's use of the phrase "the blood of Abel" as the paradigm for an innocent victim crying for justice (Matt. 23:35; Luke 11:51; Heb. 12:24).

4:13–16 Cain is immediately conscious of the severity of his punishment. He is to be alienated from both the ground and God. While this may seem like a very lenient sentence, it meant that Cain would become **a fugitive and a wanderer on the earth** (v. 14). Alienated from the rest of human society, Cain fears that others will have such a dread of him that anyone finding him **will kill** him (v. 14). The reader is not told who those others might be. By way of reassuring Cain, the Lord states that **sevenfold** vengeance will come on anyone who kills him (v. 15). **the LORD put a mark on Cain**. In spite of much scholarly speculation, the precise nature of the mark is uncertain. It must have been something visible, but that is all that can be said. Like his parents, who were sent out of the garden, Cain is forced to move away **from the presence of the LORD** (and Moses seems to be implying that this is true of Cain's offspring as well, since vv. 17–24 lack any mention of God). Presumably Cain moves farther to the **east of Eden** (v. 16). Cain settles in a region that is appropriately known as **Nod** (location unknown), which in Hebrew means "wandering."

4:17–24 These verses provide selective information about Cain's descendants, concluding with a description of Lamech (v. 19), who boasts of having taken revenge "seventy-sevenfold" by killing a man who wounded him. Seven generations on from Cain, Lamech resembles his ancestor, but seems to be worse.

4:17 Cain knew his wife. No explanation is given as to the origin of Cain's wife. As is often the case in Genesis, the limited and selective nature of the account leaves the reader with unanswered questions (see Introduction: Reading Genesis in the Twenty-first Century). Presumably, Cain married his sister—a reasonable assumption, since the whole human race descends from Adam and Eve (and the laws later forbidding this practice, such as in Lev. 18:9, would not have been relevant at this stage; cf. Gen. 5:4). **he built a city**. The precise identity of the city-builder is open to debate. While Cain would appear to be the builder (on the basis that it is named after **his son, Enoch**), the Hebrew text could also be taken as indicating that Enoch was the builder. Although the opening two chapters make no specific mention of a "city," the early readers of Genesis would have automatically assumed that the instruction to fill the earth implies that humanity would establish a city or cities around, and then spreading out from, Eden. While this was part of God's design for the earth, Genesis observes that some people engage in city building without any reference to God (see esp. 11:1–9).

4:18–22 Five generations after Cain, **Lamech** is born (v. 18). His immediate descendants are associated with animal breeding, music, and metalwork, all of which are noteworthy cultural and technological developments (vv. 20–22). Whereas Abel is linked to sheep (v. 2), the herds of **Jabal** also include cattle, donkeys, and possibly camels (v. 20). (Pre-flood genealogies are well attested in the ancient Near East, in particular, in Mesopotamian texts. The Sumerian King List records lists of monarchs who ruled the land before the "Great Deluge." The founding of cities was one of the primary industries of these pre-flood rulers. Such parallels confirm the historicity of the biblical pre-flood account.)

4:23–24 The new developments of vv. 20–22 are overshadowed by Lamech's

24[k]ver. 15
26[l]1 Chr. 1:1; Luke 3:38 [m]ch. 5:6 [n]Ps. 116:17; Zeph. 3:9; Zech. 13:9
Chapter 5
1[o]See ch. 1:26, 27
3[p]ch. 4:25
4[q]For ver. 4-32, see 1 Chr. 1:1-4; Luke 3:36-38
5[r]ch. 3:19

23 Lamech said to his wives:

"Adah and Zillah, hear my voice;
you wives of Lamech, listen to what I say:
I have killed a man for wounding me,
a young man for striking me.
24 [k]If Cain's revenge is sevenfold,
then Lamech's is seventy-sevenfold."

25 And Adam knew his wife again, and she bore a son and called his name Seth, for she
said, "God has appointed[1] for me another offspring instead of Abel, for Cain killed him."
26 To [l]Seth also a son was born, and he called his name [m]Enosh. At that time people began
[n]to call upon the name of the LORD.

Adam's Descendants to Noah

5 This is the book of the generations of Adam. When God created man, [o]he made him
in the likeness of God. 2 Male and female he created them, and he blessed them and
named them Man[2] when they were created. 3 When Adam had lived 130 years, he fathered
a son in his own likeness, after his image, and [p]named him Seth. 4 [q]The days of Adam after
he fathered Seth were 800 years; and he had other sons and daughters. 5 Thus all the days
that Adam lived were 930 years, [r]and he died.

[1] *Seth* sounds like the Hebrew for *he appointed* [2] Hebrew *adam*

boast of having **killed a man** for **wounding** or **striking** him (v. 23). Lamech's response is out of proportion to the injury, showing his inordinate vengefulness. This, like his bigamy (v. 19), reveals his depravity. His behavior reveals that the line of Cain is dominated by those who have no regard for the lives of others or respect for the principle of monogamy that 2:23–24 endorses (see note there). Later laws in the Pentateuch insist on proportional punishment: in the case of murder, a maximum of life for life (Ex. 21:23). **sevenfold . . . seventy-sevenfold**. Lamech is boasting that his vengeful passion makes him safer than Cain (Gen. 4:15), who had protection only from God. "Seventy-sevenfold" is a picturesque statement for extravagant excess; cf. Matt. 18:22 (see ESV footnote).

4:25–26 The final verses of this section suddenly jump back to Adam and Eve in order to report the birth of their third son, **Seth**. Eve's remark, **God has appointed for me another offspring instead of Abel**, is clearly an allusion back to the offspring of the woman in 3:15. The potential of Seth's birth is immediately underlined by the observation, **At that time people began to call upon the name of the LORD**, i.e., to seek him in (public) worship. Details are not given, but the implication may be that this calling on the Lord's name began in Adam's own family circle.

5:1–6:8 *Adam's Descendants.* This section of Genesis falls into two distinctive parts. Whereas 5:1–32 is largely a genealogy that traces a single line of descendants from Adam to Noah, naming only one person in each generation, 6:1–8 provides a worldwide picture of increasing human wickedness. The contrast between these two elements is not simply between the particular and the universal but, more importantly, between righteousness and evil.

5:1–32 *The Family Line from Adam to Noah.* After a brief introduction, which echoes elements of ch. 1, this passage follows a particular line of descendants from Adam to Noah. The chapter's layout is dominated by a distinctive literary structure that is repeated for each of those specifically mentioned in each generation. The pattern may be set out as follows: *When A had lived X years, he fathered B. A lived Y years after he fathered B and had other sons and daughters. Thus all the days of A were Z (= X + Y) years, after which he died* (see chart, p. 60). Since the word "fathered" in a genealogy can mean "fathered an ancestor of," it is possible that this genealogy skips any number of generations; certainly the literary conventions allow for this. That omissions do actually occur appears from comparing, for example, the genealogy of Moses in Ex. 6:16–20 with that of Joshua in 1 Chron. 7:23–27: undoubtedly the genealogy for Moses has been compressed (cf. also Ezra 7:1–5 with 1 Chron. 6:4–14). At three points in Gen. 5:3–31, the pattern is briefly broken to introduce additional information involving Adam–Seth, Enoch, and Lamech–Noah. One of the most striking aspects of the passage is the great age of the first people in Genesis. (Other ancient Near Eastern texts attribute even longer lives to earlier generations; e.g., the Sumerian King List mentions kings who reign—interestingly, before a flood—for periods of 28,800, 36,000, and 43,200 years.) Given that the life span of people today (and at least since the flood) is much shorter than the life span of those listed from Adam to Noah, the question is often raised as to whether the remarkable longevity of these patriarchs as given in 5:1–32 should be taken at face value or whether their longevity has some other explanation. Some have suggested that the figures should be understood as symbolic (e.g., that they may be related to various astronomical periods); or that the numbers are encoded with some unknown honorary significance; or that the figures were calculated by a different numeric method (e.g., that they should be divided by a factor of 5, plus, in some cases, the addition of the number 7 or 14). No writer, however, has offered a convincing alternative explanation, and none of the proposed alternatives can be substantiated with any certainty. The traditional understanding is that the numbers should be taken at face value, often assuming that something changed in the cosmology of the earth or in the physiology of humans (or in both) after the flood, resulting in a rapid decline in longevity, finally stabilizing at a "normal" life span in the range of 70 years or 80 years (see Ps. 90:10). In any case, one clear implication of these genealogies is that these people actually lived (regardless of how long), and that they actually died.

5:1–2 The heading that introduces 5:1–6:8 differs from all the others (see note on 2:4) by referring to a **book**. This was probably something like a clay tablet that preserved the contents of 5:1–21 and possibly 11:10–26, although there the pattern is somewhat abbreviated. The book is named after **Adam** (Hb. *'adam*). The same Hebrew word is also translated in 5:1 by **man** and in 5:2 by **Man**. This reflects the fact that Hebrew *'adam* may function as a proper name, a common noun denoting a male individual, and a generic noun denoting male and female human beings (see notes on 1:26; 1:27; 2:15–16). **the likeness of God** (5:1). See note on 1:27.

5:3–5 The linear list of descendants begins with **Adam** and then proceeds to name his son **Seth**. As 4:25 records, Seth is Adam's third-born son. This line is clearly presented as offering an alternative to the line of seven generations linked to Cain in 4:17–18. But whereas Cain's line leads to a killer in the seventh generation, the comparable generation in Seth's line produces Enoch, who walked with God and did not die (see note on 5:22–24). **fathered a son in his own likeness, after his image**. From the normal pattern of the genealogy, the phrase "fathered Seth" would be expected here. The additional material introduces the idea that Seth resembles Adam. While this implies that Seth is made, like Adam, in the divine image, it also suggests that he images his father as well; Seth's line, however, is certainly portrayed more positively than that of Cain.

6 When Seth had lived 105 years, [s]he fathered Enosh. 7 Seth lived after he fathered Enosh
807 years and had other sons and daughters. 8 Thus all the days of Seth were 912 years,
and he died.
9 When Enosh had lived 90 years, he fathered Kenan. 10 Enosh lived after he fathered
Kenan 815 years and had other sons and daughters. 11 Thus all the days of Enosh were
905 years, and he died.
12 When Kenan had lived 70 years, he fathered Mahalalel. 13 Kenan lived after he fathered
Mahalalel 840 years and had other sons and daughters. 14 Thus all the days of Kenan were
910 years, and he died.
15 When Mahalalel had lived 65 years, he fathered Jared. 16 Mahalalel lived after he fathered
Jared 830 years and had other sons and daughters. 17 Thus all the days of Mahalalel were
895 years, and he died.
18 When Jared had lived 162 years he fathered [t]Enoch. 19 Jared lived after he fathered
Enoch 800 years and had other sons and daughters. 20 Thus all the days of Jared were 962
years, and he died.
21 When Enoch had lived 65 years, he fathered Methuselah. 22 Enoch [u]walked with God[1]
after he fathered Methuselah 300 years and had other sons and daughters. 23 Thus all the days
of Enoch were 365 years. 24 Enoch [u]walked with God, and he was not,[2] [v]for God took him.
25 When Methuselah had lived 187 years, he fathered Lamech. 26 Methuselah lived after
he fathered Lamech 782 years and had other sons and daughters. 27 Thus all the days of
Methuselah were 969 years, and he died.

[1] Septuagint *pleased God* [2] Septuagint *was not found*

6 [s]ch. 4:26
18 [t]Jude 14
22 [u]ver. 24; ch. 6:9; [Mic. 6:8; Mal. 2:6]
24 [u][See ver. 22 above] [v]Heb. 11:5; [2 Kgs. 2:11]

5:22–24 The usual pattern of the genealogy (see note on vv. 1–32) is altered with the substitution of the expression **Enoch walked with God**. This is then developed further in v. 24 when the expected phrase "and he died" is replaced by the comment **and he was not, for God took him**. In this passage, and in certain other contexts in Genesis (e.g., 3:8; 6:9; 17:1; 24:40; 48:15), the Hebrew verb for "walked" is a distinctive form that conveys the sense of an ongoing intimacy with God. Remarkably, because of this special relationship, Enoch does not die (cf. Elijah, 2 Kings 2:1–12). The narrator's desire to highlight this fact may explain why the present genealogy, unlike the one in Gen. 11:10–26, regularly mentions that "X died."

5:27 According to the dates given, it is possible to conclude that **Methuselah** died in the year of the flood.

Genealogies: Showing Age at Fatherhood and Age at Death

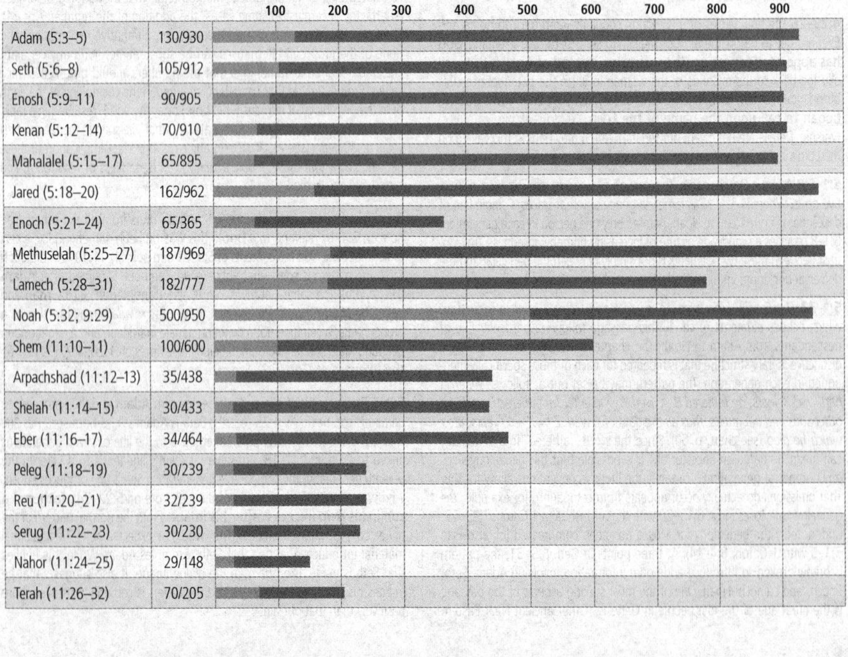

29[w]ch. 3:17
32[x]ch. 6:10 [y]ch. 10:21
Chapter 6
3[z]1 Pet. 3:19, 20; [Neh. 9:30; Gal. 5:16, 17] [a]Ps. 78:39
5[b]Ps. 14:2, 3 [c]ch. 8:21; Job 14:4; 15:14; Ps. 51:5; Jer. 17:9; Matt. 15:19; Rom. 3:23
6[d]1 Sam. 15:11; 2 Sam. 24:16; Joel 2:13; [Num. 23:19; 1 Sam. 15:29] [e]Isa. 63:10; Eph. 4:30
8[f]ch. 19:19; Ex. 33:12, 13, 16, 17

28 When Lamech had lived 182 years, he fathered a son 29 and called his name Noah,
saying, "Out of the ground [w]that the LORD has cursed, this one shall bring us relief[1] from
our work and from the painful toil of our hands." 30 Lamech lived after he fathered Noah
595 years and had other sons and daughters. 31 Thus all the days of Lamech were 777
years, and he died.
32 After Noah was 500 years old, Noah fathered [x]Shem, Ham, and [y]Japheth.

Increasing Corruption on Earth

6 When man began to multiply on the face of the land and daughters were born to them,
2 the sons of God saw that the daughters of man were attractive. And they took as their
wives any they chose. 3 Then the LORD said, [z]"My Spirit shall not abide in[2] man forever, [a]for
he is flesh: his days shall be 120 years." 4 The Nephilim[3] were on the earth in those days,
and also afterward, when the sons of God came in to the daughters of man and they bore
children to them. These were the mighty men who were of old, the men of renown.
5 [b]The LORD saw that the wickedness of man was great in the earth, and that every
[c]intention of the thoughts of his heart was only evil continually. 6 And [d]the LORD regretted that he had made man on the earth, and it [e]grieved him to his heart. 7 So the LORD
said, "I will blot out man whom I have created from the face of the land, man and animals
and creeping things and birds of the heavens, for I am sorry that I have made them." 8 But
Noah [f]found favor in the eyes of the LORD.

[1] *Noah* sounds like the Hebrew for *rest* [2] Or *My Spirit shall not contend with* [3] Or *giants*

5:28–31 The genealogical pattern is disrupted by the inclusion of Lamech's explanation for the name **Noah**. Lamech's comment on the name "Noah" (Hb. *noakh*), which strictly speaking means "rest" (Hb. *nuakh*), introduces the related concept of "comfort" (Hb. *nakham*). Lamech expects that Noah will bring both rest and comfort from the **painful toil** of working the soil (see 3:17–19). Lamech's **777 years** provides an interesting point of contact with his namesake in 4:18–24 and seventy-sevenfold vengeance.

5:32 Although this verse gives the impression of continuing the genealogical pattern used in vv. 3–31, the naming of three sons, **Shem, Ham, and Japheth**, brings the list to an end. A similar ending draws to a conclusion the genealogy of Shem in 11:10–26.

6:1–8:22 A flood story, included in the Epic of Gilgamesh, has been found in the Mesopotamian literature. It has many similarities to the biblical account of the flood. A certain man named Utnapishtim built an ark, loaded it with animals, and survived a torrential rain. The relationship of the two accounts, if any, is uncertain, although the appearance of a flood story in Mesopotamia gives some support and confirmation to the historicity of the biblical event. That is, the existence of such stories elsewhere indicates that the Bible indeed preserves the memory of a momentous event, as does the Mesopotamian account. There are also key differences between the biblical and Mesopotamian stories, particularly in regard to what motivated God or the gods to bring the flood.

6:1–8 *The Wickedness of Humanity.* The very specific list of descendants in ch. 5 is immediately followed by this short passage that explains why God sent a flood to punish the whole of humanity. But this passage concludes by recognizing that, in contrast to everyone else, Noah (introduced in 5:28–32) finds favor in God's eyes.

6:1–2 man began to multiply. The motif of multiplying is first introduced by God in 1:28, where it is presented in a very positive light and viewed as necessary to fulfill God's plans for the earth. The present passage, however, reveals that this God-mandated task leads to increasing wickedness on the earth as the population expands. This problem is exacerbated by the coming together of the **sons of God** and the **daughters of man** (6:2). The identity of both groups is uncertain, and various solutions have been advocated, although none has gained universal support. Various scholars have proposed that the "sons of God" are (1) fallen angels (cf. Job 1:6; some, however, suggest that this contradicts Mark 12:25, though the reference in Mark is to angels in heaven; see also 2 Pet. 2:4–5; Jude 5–6); or (2) tyrannical human judges or kings (in the ungodly line of Lamech, possibly demon-possessed); or (3) followers of God among the male descendants of Seth (i.e., the godly line of Seth, but who married the ungodly daughters of Cain). Though it would be difficult to determine which of these three views may be correct, it is clear that the kind of relationship described here involved some form of grievous sexual perversion, wherein the "sons of God" **saw** and with impunity **took** any women ("daughters of man") that they wanted. The sequence here in Gen. 6:2 ("saw . . . attractive [good] . . . took") parallels the sequence of the fall in 3:6 ("saw . . . good . . . took"). In both cases, something good in God's creation is used in disobedience and sinful rebellion against God, with tragic consequences. Only Noah stands apart from this sin. (See note on 1 Pet. 3:19.)

6:3 God announces that because of the immoral nature of people, their **days shall be 120 years**. There are two possible interpretations of this number of years: either the lives of human beings will no longer exceed 120 years, or the coming of the flood is anticipated in 120 years. While the latter interpretation is simpler, the former interpretation is appealing, and would be true as a generalization even though some of those who live after the flood (e.g., Abraham) enjoy lives in excess of 120 years.

6:4 Nephilim. The meaning of this term is uncertain. It occurs elsewhere in the OT only in Num. 13:33, where it denotes a group living in Canaan. If both passages refer to the same people, then the Israelite spies (Num. 13:33) are expressing their fears of the Canaanites by likening them to the ancient **men of renown**. Although in Hebrew *Nepilim* means "fallen ones," the earliest Greek translators rendered it *gigantes*, "giants." This idea may have been mistakenly deduced from Num. 13:33; one must be cautious about reading it back into the present passage. The Nephilim were **mighty men** or warriors and, as such, may well have contributed to the violence that filled the earth (see Gen. 6:13).

6:5 This verse concisely describes the universal intensity and pervasiveness of human wickedness.

6:6–7 the LORD regretted . . . it grieved him to his heart. The Hebrew verb rendered "regretted" (Hb. *nakham*) is sometimes translated "repent," and sometimes as "feel sorrow, be grieved." God is grieved over his creation, which he at first saw as very good (1:31) but which is now filled with sin (see notes on 1 Sam. 15:11; 15:29; Jonah 3:10). The destruction of **man and animals and creeping things and birds of the heavens** suggests that this will be a reversal of God's creative work. The resulting flood reflects this, for the dry land is submerged under water, subsequently to reappear, as in Gen. 1:9. **from the face of the land**. On the extent of the flood, see note on 6:17.

6:8 Noah is distinguished from the rest of humanity. Apart from Noah, the only other person in the OT who is described as finding **favor in the eyes of the LORD** is Moses, in Ex. 33:17 (and possibly Abraham; cf. Gen. 18:3). Placed on a par with Moses, Noah is rescued from the looming annihilation.

Noah and the Flood

9 These are the generations of Noah. [g]Noah was a righteous man, [h]blameless in his generation. Noah [i]walked with God. 10 And Noah had three sons, Shem, Ham, and Japheth.
11 Now the earth was corrupt in God's sight, and the earth was filled with violence. 12 And
God [j]saw the earth, and behold, it was corrupt, [k]for all flesh had corrupted their way on
the earth. 13 And God said to Noah, [l]"I have determined to make an end of all flesh,[1] for
the earth is filled with violence through them. Behold, I will destroy them with the earth.
14 Make yourself an ark of gopher wood.[2] Make rooms in the ark, and cover it inside and
out with pitch. 15 This is how you are to make it: the length of the ark 300 cubits,[3] its
breadth 50 cubits, and its height 30 cubits. 16 Make a roof[4] for the ark, and finish it to a
cubit above, and set the door of the ark in its side. Make it with lower, second, and third
decks. 17 [m]For behold, I will bring a flood of waters upon the earth to destroy all flesh in
which is the breath of life under heaven. Everything that is on the earth shall die. 18 But
[n]I will establish my covenant with you, and you shall come into the ark, you, your sons,
your wife, and your sons' wives with you. 19 And of every living thing of all flesh, you
shall bring two of every sort into the ark to keep them alive with you. They shall be male
and female. 20 Of the birds according to their kinds, and of the animals according to their
kinds, of every creeping thing of the ground, according to its kind, two of every sort shall
come in to you to keep them alive. 21 Also take with you every sort of food that is eaten,
and store it up. It shall serve as food for you and for them." 22 [o]Noah did this; he did all
that God commanded him.

7 Then the LORD said to Noah, [p]"Go into the ark, you and all your household, for I
have seen that [q]you are righteous before me in this generation. 2 Take with you seven
pairs of all [r]clean animals,[5] the male and his mate, and a pair of the animals that are not

9 [g]ch. 7:1; Ezek. 14:14, 20; 2 Pet. 2:5 [h]Job 1:1, 8; Luke 1:6 [i]ch. 5:22, 24; [Heb. 11:7]
12 [j]Ps. 14:2, 3; 53:2, 3 [k]Job 22:15-17
13 [l]Ezek. 7:2, 3, 6
17 [m]ch. 7:4; 2 Pet. 2:5
18 [n]ch. 9:9, 11
22 [o]Heb. 11:7; [Ex. 40:16]

Chapter 7

1 [p]Matt. 24:38, 39; Luke 17:26, 27; Heb. 11:7; 1 Pet. 3:20; 2 Pet. 2:5 [q]ch. 6:9
2 [r]ch. 8:20; [Lev. 11]

[1] Hebrew *The end of all flesh has come before me* [2] An unknown kind of tree; transliterated from Hebrew [3] A *cubit* was about 18 inches or 45 centimeters
[4] Or *skylight* [5] Or *seven of each kind of clean animal*

6:9–9:29 *Noah's Descendants.* Centered on Noah and his descendants, this section of Genesis is dominated by the account of the flood that brings about a renewal of the earth, which has similarities to 1:1–2:3. While the land is cleansed of the defilement caused by human wrongdoing and a new start is made possible by God, the people's nature has not been transformed, as the final short episode in 9:20–28 reveals. The inclination of the human heart is still toward evil.

6:9–9:19 *Noah and the Flood.* This long section recounts how Noah and his immediate family are rescued from the flood. By echoing ch. 1, the whole process is presented as the undoing of creation and then the "re-creation" of the earth as it emerges from the flood. But after the flood not everything returns to a pristine condition. Human nature is not renewed.

6:9 These are the generations of Noah. A new heading introduces this section of Genesis (see note on 2:4). Noah's personal righteousness explains why he is warned about the forthcoming deluge. The Hebrew for **blameless** conveys the sense of being perfect, without evident flaw (although not necessarily sinless). **walked with God.** See note on 5:22–24. Like Noah, Abraham is later required by God to walk before him and be blameless (see 17:1). The positive attributes listed here are rarely ascribed to human beings in the OT.

6:11–12 In contrast to Noah, **the earth was corrupt in God's sight.** These verses confirm what has already been indicated in vv. 1–7. Here, however, particular emphasis is given to the **violence** that fills the earth. The mention of "corruption" here may lie behind Paul's "bondage to corruption" (Rom. 8:21): the creation suffers as mankind corrupts its way, and as God punishes that corruption. Originally delegated to govern the earth on God's behalf, humans have aggressively and viciously asserted their rule over others, including both people and other living creatures. The ancient Near Eastern epics of Gilgamesh and Atrahasis also tell of a flood sent to punish human beings. In those stories, however, it is merely the disruptive noise of humanity that leads to their destruction. Genesis emphasizes that God destroys the people he has created because of their immoral behavior.

6:13–17 In a long speech, God gives Noah directions for the construction of an **ark** (v. 14) that will be sufficiently large to house his family and a variety of other living creatures.

6:15 In modern measurements, the ark would have been around 450 feet (140 m) long, 75 feet (23 m) wide, and 45 feet (14 m) high, yielding a displacement of about 43,000 tons (about 39 million kg). The inside capacity would have been 1.4 million cubic feet (39,644 cubic m), with an approximate total deck area of 95,700 square feet (8,891 square m).

6:17 Everything that is on the earth shall die. Although God intends the flood to destroy every person and his remarks have a strong universal emphasis, this in itself does not necessarily mean that the flood had to cover the whole earth. Since the geographical perspective of ancient people was more limited than that of contemporary readers, it is possible that the flood, while universal from their viewpoint, did not cover the entire globe. Indeed, Genesis implies that prior to the Tower of Babel incident (see 11:1–9), people had not yet spread throughout the earth. Many interpreters, therefore, argue that a huge regional flood may have been all that was necessary for God to destroy all human beings. The expression "all the earth" (7:3; cf. 8:9, "the whole earth") does not exclude such a possibility: later, "all the earth" came to Joseph to buy grain (41:57), with "all the earth" clearly referring to the eastern Mediterranean seaboard. In support of the view that the flood covered all the earth, other interpreters point out that the text says that "all the high mountains under the whole heaven were covered" (7:19) and that the water was "fifteen cubits" above the tops of the mountains. If "the mountains of Ararat" (8:4) refers to the range that includes present-day Mount Ararat in Turkey (elevation 16,854 feet or 5,137 m), the amount of water necessary to cover it would be at least 16,854 feet above sea level.

6:18–22 God indicates that he will establish a **covenant** with Noah (see notes on 9:9–11; 9:12–17). By taking into the ark two of **every living thing,** including birds, animals, and creeping things, Noah displays the caring oversight that people were expected to have for other living creatures.

7:1–5 Having made the ark according to God's direction, Noah is now told to embark. He is instructed to take on board **seven pairs of all clean animals** and **a pair of the animals that are not clean.** On the distinction between clean and unclean creatures, see Lev. 11:1–47 and Deut. 14:4–20. Since after the flood some clean animals will be offered as sacrifices (see Gen. 8:20) and some will be eaten as food (see 9:3), to ensure their survival it was necessary to have more than one pair of each kind in the ark.

4[s]ver. 12, 17; [Job 37:11-13] [t]ch. 6:17
5[u]ch. 6:22
11[v]ch. 8:2; Prov. 8:28; [Amos 9:6] [w]ch. 8:2; 2 Kgs. 7:19; Isa. 24:18; Mal. 3:10; [Ps. 78:23]
15[x]ch. 6:20
16[y]ver. 2, 3
17[z]ver. 4, 12

clean, the male and his mate, **3** and seven pairs[1] of the birds of the heavens also, male and
female, to keep their offspring alive on the face of all the earth. **4** For in seven days [s]I will
send rain on the earth forty days and forty nights, [t]and every living thing[2] that I have
made I will blot out from the face of the ground." **5** [u]And Noah did all that the LORD had
commanded him.

6 Noah was six hundred years old when the flood of waters came upon the earth. **7** And
Noah and his sons and his wife and his sons' wives with him went into the ark to escape
the waters of the flood. **8** Of clean animals, and of animals that are not clean, and of birds,
and of everything that creeps on the ground, **9** two and two, male and female, went into
the ark with Noah, as God had commanded Noah. **10** And after seven days the waters of
the flood came upon the earth.

11 In the six hundredth year of Noah's life, in the second month, on the seventeenth
day of the month, on that day all the [v]fountains of the great deep burst forth, and [w]the
windows of the heavens were opened. **12** And rain fell upon the earth forty days and forty
nights. **13** On the very same day Noah and his sons, Shem and Ham and Japheth, and Noah's
wife and the three wives of his sons with them entered the ark, **14** they and every beast,
according to its kind, and all the livestock according to their kinds, and every creeping
thing that creeps on the earth, according to its kind, and every bird, according to its kind,
every winged creature. **15** They [x]went into the ark with Noah, two and two of all flesh in
which there was the breath of life. **16** And those that entered, male and female of all flesh,
went in [y]as God had commanded him. And the LORD shut him in.

17 The flood [z]continued forty days on the earth. The waters increased and bore up the

[1] Or *seven of each kind* [2] Hebrew *all existence*; also verse 23

7:11–12 A peculiar feature of the flood narrative is the number of detailed chronological notices (cf. 8:4–5, 13–14). By pinpointing the exact date of the flood within Noah's life, the text underlines that it was a real event. **all the fountains of the great deep burst forth, and the windows of the heavens were opened** (7:11). Powerful imagery is used here to capture the intensity of the flood. From below and above, water poured out to cover the land. **Rain fell** continuously for **forty days and forty nights** (v. 12).

7:16 The safety of those in the ark depended on both human and divine action. **the LORD shut him in**. The use of the personal name "Yahweh" ("LORD"; see note on 2:4) underscores God's special relationship with Noah.

7:17–24 The devastating results of the flood are described, fulfilling the judgment that God had previously pronounced. **the waters prevailed on the earth 150 days** (v. 24). The figure of 150 days, which includes the 40 days of rain mentioned in v. 12, is repeated in 8:3. In both places it denotes the five-month period that falls between the detailed chronological notices given in 7:11 (marking the very start of the flood on the 17th day of the second month) and 8:4 (when the ark comes to a place of rest on the 17th day of the seventh month). It will be a further seven months before the land is sufficiently dry for those in the ark to disembark safely (see 8:13–14). On the depth of the flood (**above the mountains**), see note on 6:17.

Chronology of Noah's Time in the Ark

Dates are in the form of month, day, and Noah's year, as given in the text. Hence, 2/10/600 means the tenth day of the second month in Noah's 600th year. Months are calculated at 30 days each. Dates in parentheses are extrapolations from dates explicitly given in the text.

	Reference	Event	Date	Day
	7:4,10	Announcement of the flood 7 days in advance	(2/10/600)	Sunday
Waters prevail: 150-day period	7:11,13	Flood begins; Noah and family enter the ark	2/17/600	Sunday
	7:12	Flood lasts 40 days and ends	(3/27/600)	Friday
	8:4	Ark rests on mountains of Ararat after waters prevail and abate for 150 days total	7/17/600	Friday
Waters abate: 150-day period	8:5	Mountaintops eventually become visible	10/1/600	Wednesday
	8:7	Raven sent out (after 40 days of mountaintop visibility)	(11/10/600)	Sunday
	8:8	Dove sent out	(11/17/600)	Sunday
	8:10	Dove's second flight (7 days later); returns with olive leaf	(11/24/600)	Sunday
	8:12	Dove's third flight (7 days later); does not return	(12/1/600)	Sunday
	8:3	Waters fully abated; end of second 150-day period	(12/17/600)	Wednesday
Earth dries: 70-day period	8:13	Noah eventually removes the covering of the ark	1/1/601	Wednesday
	8:14–19	Earth dried out; Noah leaves ark	2/27/601	Wednesday
Total time in ark: 370 days				

ark, and it rose high above the earth. 18 The waters prevailed and increased greatly on the
earth, and the ark floated on the face of the waters. 19 And the waters prevailed so mightily on the earth that all the high mountains under the whole heaven were covered. 20 The
waters prevailed above the mountains, covering them fifteen cubits[1] deep. 21 And [a]all flesh
died that moved on the earth, birds, livestock, beasts, all swarming creatures that swarm
on the earth, and all mankind. 22 Everything on the dry land [b]in whose nostrils was the
breath of life died. 23 He blotted out every living thing that was on the face of the ground,
man and animals and creeping things and birds of the heavens. They were blotted out
from the earth. Only [c]Noah was left, and those who were with him in the ark. 24 And the
waters prevailed on the earth 150 days.

The Flood Subsides

8 But God [d]remembered Noah and all the beasts and all the livestock that were with
him in the ark. And [e]God made a wind blow over the earth, and the waters subsided.
2 [f]The fountains of the deep and [f]the windows of the heavens were closed, the rain from
the heavens was restrained, 3 and the waters receded from the earth continually. At the end
[g]of 150 days the waters had abated, 4 and in the seventh month, on the seventeenth day of
the month, the ark came to rest on the mountains of [h]Ararat. 5 And the waters continued
to abate until the tenth month; in the tenth month, on the first day of the month, the tops
of the mountains were seen.
6 At the end of forty days Noah opened the window of the ark that he had made 7 and sent
forth a raven. It went to and fro until the waters were dried up from the earth. 8 Then he
sent forth a dove from him, to see if the waters had subsided from the face of the ground.
9 But the dove found no place to set her foot, and she returned to him to the ark, for the
waters were still on the face of the whole earth. So he put out his hand and took her and
brought her into the ark with him. 10 He waited another seven days, and again he sent forth
the dove out of the ark. 11 And the dove came back to him in the evening, and behold, in
her mouth was a freshly plucked olive leaf. So Noah knew that the waters had subsided
from the earth. 12 Then he waited another seven days and sent forth the dove, and she did
not return to him anymore.
13 In the six hundred and first year, in the first month, the first day of the month, the
waters were dried from off the earth. And Noah removed the covering of the ark and looked,
and behold, the face of the ground was dry. 14 In the second month, on the twenty-seventh
day of the month, the earth had dried out. 15 Then God said to Noah, 16 "Go out from the
ark, [i]you and your wife, and your sons and your sons' wives with you. 17 Bring out with
you every living thing that is with you of all flesh—birds and animals and every creeping
thing that creeps on the earth—that they may swarm on the earth, and [j]be fruitful and
multiply on the earth." 18 So Noah went out, and his sons and his wife and his sons' wives
with him. 19 Every beast, every creeping thing, and every bird, everything that moves on
the earth, went out by families from the ark.

God's Covenant with Noah

20 Then Noah built an altar to the LORD and took some of every clean animal and some of
every clean bird and offered burnt offerings on the altar. 21 And when the LORD smelled [k]the

[1] A *cubit* was about 18 inches or 45 centimeters

21 [a]ver. 4; ch. 6:13, 17; 2 Pet. 3:6
22 [b]ch. 2:7
23 [c]2 Pet. 2:5

Chapter 8

1 [d]ch. 19:29; 30:22; Ex. 2:24; 1 Sam. 1:19 [e]Ex. 14:21
2 [f]ch. 7:11
3 [g]ch. 7:24
4 [h]2 Kgs. 19:37; Isa. 37:38; Jer. 51:27
16 [i]ch. 7:13
17 [j]ch. 1:22, 28; 9:1
21 [k]Ex. 29:18, 25, 41; Lev. 1:9, 13, 17; See Ezek. 16:19; 20:41; 2 Cor. 2:15; Eph. 5:2; Phil. 4:18

8:1 God remembered Noah. This marks the turning point in the flood story. When the Bible says that God "remembers" someone or his covenant with someone, it indicates that he is about to take action for that person's welfare (cf. 9:15; 19:29; 30:22; Ex. 2:24; 32:13; Ps. 25:6–7; 74:2). All life on the land having been destroyed, God now proceeds to renew everything, echoing what he did in Genesis 1. **God made a wind blow over the earth.** The Hebrew word for wind, *ruakh*, is also sometimes translated "Spirit" (e.g., 1:2; 6:3). While the context normally enables the reader to distinguish *ruakh* meaning "wind" from *ruakh* meaning "Spirit," the present verse intentionally echoes 1:2.

8:2–4 In v. 2 God puts into reverse the process started in 7:11. The waters both rose and abated during the period of **150 days** (see note on 7:17–24). **Mountains of Ararat** indicates a range of mountains of which Mount Ararat (in modern Turkey) is the highest. The text does not name the specific mountain on which the ark came to rest.

8:5–14 The slow, gradual process by which the **waters** receded and the land **dried out** (v. 14) is captured by the detailed account of Noah's releasing a **raven** (v. 7) and then a **dove** (vv. 8–12). As in ch. 1, the dry land emerges from the waters.

8:15–17 God's instructions to Noah are reminiscent of ch. 1, especially the statement that Noah and his family are to **be fruitful and multiply on the earth** (see 1:28).

8:18–19 In obedience to God, Noah goes out of the ark with his family and all the creatures.

8:20–22 Noah's first recorded act on emerging from the ark is to build an **altar to the LORD** (v. 20). On it he presents whole-burnt offerings, using

pleasing aroma, the LORD said in his heart, "I will never again [l]curse[1] the ground because
of man, for [m]the intention of man's heart is evil from his youth. [n]Neither will I ever again
strike down every living creature as I have done. **22** [o]While the earth remains, seedtime and
harvest, cold and heat, summer and winter, [p]day and night, shall not cease."

9 And God blessed Noah and his sons and said to them, [q]"Be fruitful and multiply and
fill the earth. **2** [r]The fear of you and the dread of you shall be upon every beast of the
earth and upon every bird of the heavens, upon everything that creeps on the ground and
all the fish of the sea. Into your hand they are delivered. **3** [s]Every moving thing that lives
shall be food for you. And [t]as I gave you the green plants, I give you everything. **4** But you
shall not eat flesh with its [u]life, that is, its blood. **5** And for your lifeblood I will require a
reckoning: [v]from every beast I will require it and [w]from man. From his fellow man I will
require a reckoning for the life of man.

6 [x]"Whoever sheds the blood of man,
by man shall his blood be shed,
[y]for God made man in his own image.

7 And you,[2] be fruitful and multiply, increase greatly on the earth and multiply in it."
8 Then God said to Noah and to his sons with him, **9** "Behold, [z]I establish my covenant
with you and your offspring after you, **10** and with every living creature that is with you,
the birds, the livestock, and every beast of the earth with you, as many as came out of
the ark; it is for every beast of the earth. **11** [a]I establish my covenant with you, that never
again shall all flesh be cut off by the waters of the flood, and never again shall there be a
flood to destroy the earth." **12** And God said, [b]"This is the sign of the covenant that I make

[1] Or *dishonor* [2] In Hebrew *you* is plural

21 [l]ch. 3:17; 6:17 [m]ch. 6:5; Ps. 58:3; Rom. 1:21; [Matt. 15:19] [n]ch. 9:11, 15; Isa. 54:9
22 [o]Jer. 5:24 [p]Jer. 33:20, 25

Chapter 9

1 [q]ch. 1:22, 28; 8:17
2 [r][Ps. 8:6-8; James 3:7]
3 [s]Deut. 12:15; 1 Tim. 4:3, 4 [t]ch. 1:29
4 [u]Lev. 17:10, 11, 14; Deut. 12:16, 23; 1 Sam. 14:33; Acts 15:20, 29
5 [v]Ex. 21:28 [w]ch. 4:10, 11
6 [x]Ex. 21:12, 14; Lev. 24:17; Num. 35:31, 33; [Matt. 26:52; Rev. 13:10] [y]ch. 1:27; 5:1; James 3:9
9 [z]ch. 6:18; 8:20-22
11 [a]Isa. 54:9, 10
12 [b]ch. 17:11

some of the clean animals and birds. While this is undoubtedly intended to express gratitude for divine deliverance, it is also an act of atonement. This is a normal aspect of **burnt offerings** (see Lev. 1:3–17, esp. v. 4) and is supported by the mention of the **pleasing aroma** (Gen. 8:21; cf. Lev. 1:9, 13, 17). The Hebrew term for "pleasing," *nikhoakh*, conveys the idea of rest and tranquility. It is related to the name "Noah" (Hb. *noakh*) and is probably used here in order to remind the reader of Lamech's remarks in Gen. 5:29. It also has the sense of "soothing." The burnt offering soothes God's anger at human sin, so although human nature has not been changed by the flood, God's attitude has changed. Notice how 8:21 (**for the intention of man's heart is evil from his youth**) echoes very closely 6:5 ("every intention of the thoughts of his heart was only evil continually"). In spite of the human propensity to sin, atonement through sacrifice is possible, securing a peaceful relationship between the Lord and humanity. **I will never again curse the ground** (8:21). The clear force of the Hebrew text is that God will not send another flood; he is not revoking the curse pronounced in 3:17, which continues to be in place (the words for "curse" are different; see ESV footnote). This short comment about the effect of sacrifice underlines the importance of sacrifice in the Bible's plan of salvation.

9:1–4 While God's speech here closely parallels 1:28–30, two important changes are introduced. First, the positive instruction to exercise dominion over the living creatures is replaced by the negative comment that they will **fear** and **dread** human beings. Second, whereas the emphasis was previously on people's eating from plants, humans are now given permission to be carnivorous. While God now permits the taking of animal life for food, the animal's blood remains sacred and is not to be consumed, as an acknowledgment that all life is from God (see Lev. 17:12–14).

9:5–6 Following his comments about the killing of animals, God addresses the issue of homicide. Violence by "all flesh" (v. 11), i.e., by man and animals, prompted God to send the flood (6:11, 13). If human nature has not improved after the flood (6:5; 8:21), how is violence to be prevented in the future? This legal enactment is the answer: **From his fellow man I will require a reckoning for the life of man**. This means that any animal or person that takes a human life will be held accountable by God, working through human representatives (e.g., Ex. 20:13; 21:28). **Whoever sheds the blood of man, by man shall his blood be shed**. Here the principle of *talion*, a life for a life, is applied (see Ex. 21:23). This measured response is preferable to Lamech's seventy-sevenfold vengeance (Gen. 4:24). Human life is to be valued so highly that it is protected by this system of punishment because **God made man in his own image**, and so to murder another human being is to murder what is most like God, and is thus implicitly an attack on God himself. Many would see this statement as establishing the moral principle permitting the death penalty in cases of murder—with the understanding that the person charged would have been justly tried and his guilt established beyond any reasonable doubt (cf. the OT requirement of two or three witnesses, Deut. 19:15; repeated in the NT, e.g., Matt. 18:16; Heb. 10:28). A further requirement is that such a death-penalty verdict must always be carried out under the jurisdiction of the established authorities (cf. Deut. 19:15–21; Rom. 13:1–5). The difficulty of establishing guilt beyond any reasonable doubt and the difficulty of ensuring justice in a modern, complex urban society (as compared to an ancient village-based society) underscore the great care and caution that must be taken in applying this principle today.

9:7 God's speech ends as it began in v. 1, repeating what was said in 8:17 and echoing 1:28. God wants humanity to flourish and not to be destroyed by violence or another flood. This positive view of population growth (cf. note on 1:28) stands in sharp contrast to the Babylonian flood story, which ends with the gods taking measures to inhibit mankind from filling the earth.

9:9–11 God outlines the **covenant** he is now establishing with all living creatures, having mentioned it briefly before the flood in 6:18. This is the first covenant explicitly named in Genesis (see note on 2:17); a similar covenant is later established with Abraham and his descendants in ch. 17. A covenant formally binds two parties together in a relationship, on the basis of mutual personal commitment, with consequences for keeping or breaking the commitment. God makes this kind of covenant with a group of people by covenanting with one who represents them: everyone else then experiences the covenant by virtue of being included "in" the representative (see note on 12:3); here, the animals are included as well as Noah's descendants, showing Noah to be a kind of new Adam. Emphasizing that the covenant is for all living creatures, God states that there will never again be **a flood to destroy the earth** (9:11).

9:12–17 Different covenants have appropriate signs or symbols linked to them. Circumcision is the sign of the covenant with Abraham (ch. 17), and the Sabbath is the sign of the covenant with Israel at Mount Sinai (Ex. 31:12–17). On this occasion God's designated **sign** is the rainbow (Gen. 9:13). Its presence, when rain clouds are in the sky, will be a visible reminder of God's

between me and you and every living creature that is with you, for all future generations:
13 I have set [c]my bow in the cloud, and it shall be a sign of the covenant between me and
the earth. 14 When I bring clouds over the earth and the bow is seen in the clouds, 15 [d]I will
remember my covenant that is between me and you and every living creature of all flesh.
And the waters shall never again become a flood to destroy all flesh. 16 When the bow is in
the clouds, I will see it and remember [e]the everlasting covenant between God and every
living creature of all flesh that is on the earth." 17 God said to Noah, "This is the sign of the
covenant that I have established between me and all flesh that is on the earth."

Noah's Descendants

18 The sons of Noah who went forth from the ark were [f]Shem, Ham, and Japheth. (Ham
was the father of Canaan.) 19 These three were the sons of Noah, and [g]from these the people
of the whole earth were dispersed.[1]

20 Noah began to be a man of the soil, and he planted a vineyard.[2] 21 He drank of the wine
and became drunk and lay uncovered in his tent. 22 And Ham, the father of Canaan, saw
the nakedness of his father and told his two brothers outside. 23 Then Shem and Japheth
took a garment, laid it on both their shoulders, and walked backward and covered the
nakedness of their father. Their faces were turned backward, and they did not see their
father's nakedness. 24 When Noah awoke from his wine [h]and knew what his youngest son
had done to him, 25 he said,

> [i]"Cursed be Canaan;
> [j]a servant of servants shall he be to his brothers."

26 He also said,

> "Blessed be the LORD, the God of Shem;
> and let Canaan be his servant.
> 27 May God enlarge Japheth,[3]
> and let him dwell in the tents of Shem,
> and let Canaan be his servant."

28 After the flood Noah lived 350 years. 29 All the days of Noah were 950 years, and he
died.

[1] *Or from these the whole earth was populated* [2] *Or Noah, a man of the soil, was the first to plant a vineyard* [3] *Japheth* sounds like the Hebrew for *enlarge*

13 [c]Ezek. 1:28; [Rev. 4:3; 10:1]
15 [d][Lev. 26:42, 45; 1 Kgs. 8:23; Ezek. 16:60]
16 [e]ch. 17:7, 13, 19
18 [f]ch. 5:32; 10:1
19 [g]ch. 10:32
24 [h][Hab. 2:15]
25 [i]Deut. 27:16 [j]Josh. 9:23; Judg. 1:28; 1 Kgs. 9:20, 21

everlasting covenant (v. 16). It is not necessary to think that rainbows first began to exist at this time; in any case, God says that he will now use rainbows as a sign of this covenant. This sign should not be interpreted as symbolizing that God has hung up his warrior's **bow**, since there is no hint of that meaning in the text.

9:18–19 These verses, which bring the flood story to an end, anticipate the next two episodes. The reference to Ham's son **Canaan** (v. 18) prepares for the events of vv. 20–29. The mention of people's being **dispersed** over the **whole earth** (v. 19) is developed in ch. 10.

9:20–29 *The Cursing of Canaan.* This unusual episode provides an unexpected sequel to the flood story. After the flood and the "new creation" comes another fall, by Noah—a sort of second Adam, in that he (like Adam) is father of the whole human race. It also anticipates similar activity by Lot's daughters after the destruction of Sodom (19:30–38). Noah's drunkenness and Ham's indiscretion result in contrasting announcements regarding the futures of Shem, Japheth, and Ham's son Canaan.

9:20 The reference to Noah as a **man of the soil** and his success in growing vines points to a fresh start after the flood (see note on 5:28–31).

9:21–23 became drunk. The brevity of the description of Noah's drunkenness is an indication of disapproval. Ham's actions, however, are the object of serious criticism because Ham unashamedly looks on the **nakedness of his father** in the tent and then reports this to his brothers (v. 22). There is no indication, however, that perverse sexual behavior was involved in addition to Ham seeing his father drunk and naked. Though the text does not explicitly state what happened, it is clear that Ham humiliated and dishonored his father and that he apparently sought to make his brothers a party to that humiliation. Instead, Ham's brothers make every effort to avoid seeing Noah's naked body, as readers are told twice that they approached him **backward** (v. 23). The response of Shem and Japheth is in sharp contrast to Ham's actions, as the brothers honor their father despite his foolish behavior (Ex. 20:12).

9:24–27 The designation of Ham as the **youngest son** (v. 24) is peculiar, given that he is always listed after Shem and before Japheth. Possibly, for some unexplained reason, the traditional order of names does not reflect the birth sequence of the boys. **Cursed be Canaan**. Noah's reaction to Ham's action is to curse Canaan, Ham's son. This outcome has clearly been anticipated in the narration, for twice previously it has been mentioned, in each context unnecessarily, that Ham is the father of Canaan (vv. 18, 22). **a servant of servants shall he be**. This passage was wrongly appealed to in past centuries to justify the enslavement of African people, resulting in grievous abuse, injustice, and inhumanity to people created in the image of God. Noah's curse of Canaan, which focuses on his being a servant, anticipates the judgment that will later befall the Canaanites (cf. Deut. 7:1–3 with Gen. 10:15–19). This, coupled with the fact that the curse falls on Canaan alone and not on Ham's other children (who settled in northern Africa), shows how illegitimate it was to use this text to justify enslaving African people. (For more on the overall biblical position on slavery, see notes on 1 Cor. 7:21; Eph. 6:5; Col. 3:22–25; 1 Tim. 1:10.) Shem, however, is given pride of place, as is implied by Noah's remark that Japheth will **dwell in the tents of Shem** (Gen. 9:27).

9:28 The report of Noah's death continues the pattern used throughout Genesis 5 to describe the total age and death of Adam and his descendants.

10:1–11:9 *The Descendants of Noah's Sons.* The next main section of Genesis outlines developments after the flood, focusing on how humanity becomes divided into different nations.

Chapter 10
2[k]For ver. 1-5, see 1 Chr. 1:5-7; Ezek. 38:1-6
4[l]Ps. 72:10; Ezek. 38:13 [m]Num. 24:24; Isa. 23:1, 12; Dan. 11:30
5[n]Isa. 11:11; Jer. 2:10; 25:22; Ezek. 27:6; Zeph. 2:11

Nations Descended from Noah

10 These are the generations of the sons of Noah, Shem, Ham, and Japheth. Sons were
born to them after the flood.
2 [k]The sons of Japheth: Gomer, Magog, Madai, Javan, Tubal, Meshech, and Tiras. 3 The
sons of Gomer: Ashkenaz, Riphath, and Togarmah. 4 The sons of Javan: Elishah, [l]Tarshish,
[m]Kittim, and Dodanim. 5 From these [n]the coastland peoples spread in their lands, each
with his own language, by their clans, in their nations.

10:1–32 *The Clans, Languages, Lands, and Nations.* This entire passage sets out, largely in the form of lists, how the descendants of Noah's three sons populate different regions of the earth. Additional details of special interest are occasionally added. This genealogical-geographical passage is describing a process that covered a long time, as family clans migrated to particular regions (see map below). The ancestor after whom the clan or tribe is named may not have lived in the region that later bears his name. Each of the three main parts of this section concludes with a reference to clans, languages, and nations (vv. 5, 20, 31).

10:1 These are the generations of. This distinctive formula marks the start of a new section in Genesis (see note on 2:4).

10:2–5 Japheth's descendants are listed first. **From these the coastland peoples spread** (v. 5). This is the only additional remark that is made

Table of Nations
c. 2200 B.C.
Many of the people groups mentioned in Genesis 10 can be identified with relative certainty. In general, the descendants of Ham settled in North Africa and the eastern Mediterranean coast, the descendants of Shem in Mesopotamia and Arabia, and the descendants of Japheth in Europe and the greater area of Asia Minor.

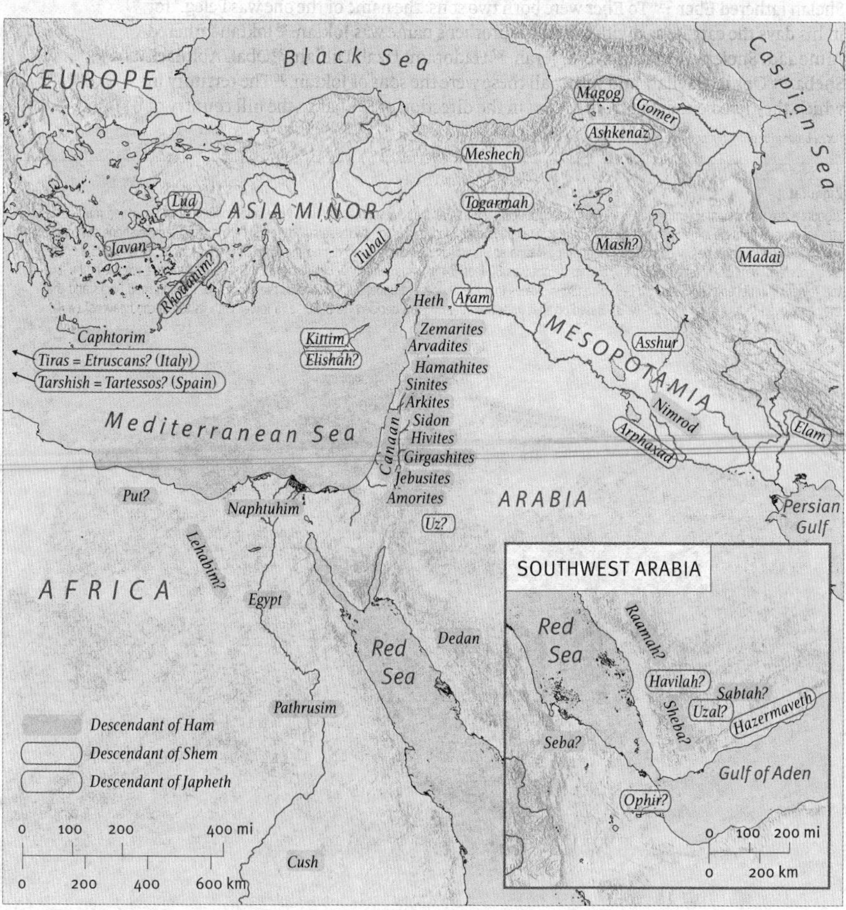

6 [o]The sons of Ham: Cush, Egypt, Put, and Canaan. 7 The sons of Cush: Seba, Havilah,
Sabtah, Raamah, and Sabteca. The sons of Raamah: Sheba and Dedan. 8 Cush fathered
Nimrod; he was the first on earth to be a mighty man.[1] 9 He was a mighty hunter before
the LORD. Therefore it is said, "Like Nimrod a mighty hunter before the LORD." 10 The
beginning of his kingdom was [p]Babel, Erech, Accad, and Calneh, in [q]the land of Shinar.
11 From that land he went into Assyria and built Nineveh, Rehoboth-Ir, Calah, and 12 Resen
between Nineveh and Calah; that is the great city. 13 [r]Egypt fathered Ludim, Anamim,
Lehabim, Naphtuhim, 14 Pathrusim, Casluhim (from whom[2] the Philistines came), and
[s]Caphtorim.
15 [t]Canaan fathered Sidon his firstborn and Heth, 16 and the Jebusites, the Amorites, the
Girgashites, 17 the Hivites, the Arkites, the Sinites, 18 the Arvadites, the Zemarites, and
the Hamathites. Afterward the clans of the Canaanites dispersed. 19 And the territory of
the Canaanites extended from Sidon in the direction of Gerar as far as Gaza, and in the
direction of Sodom, Gomorrah, Admah, and Zeboiim, as far as Lasha. 20 These are the sons
of Ham, by their clans, their languages, their lands, and their nations.
21 To Shem also, the father of all the children of Eber, the elder brother of Japheth,
children were born. 22 The [u]sons of Shem: Elam, Asshur, Arpachshad, Lud, and Aram.
23 The sons of Aram: Uz, Hul, Gether, and Mash. 24 Arpachshad fathered [v]Shelah; and
Shelah fathered Eber. 25 [w]To Eber were born two sons: the name of the one was Peleg,[3] for
in his days the earth was divided, and his brother's name was Joktan. 26 Joktan fathered
Almodad, Sheleph, Hazarmaveth, Jerah, 27 Hadoram, Uzal, Diklah, 28 Obal, Abimael,
Sheba, 29 [x]Ophir, Havilah, and Jobab; all these were the sons of Joktan. 30 The territory in
which they lived extended from Mesha in the direction of Sephar to the hill country of

[1] *Or he began to be a mighty man on the earth* [2] *Or from where* [3] *Peleg means division*

6 [o]For ver. 6-8, see 1 Chr. 1:8-10
10 [p]ch. 11:9 [q]ch. 11:2
13 [r]For ver. 13-18, see 1 Chr. 1:11-16
14 [s]Deut. 2:23; Jer. 47:4; Amos 9:7
15 [t][ch. 15:18-21]
22 [u]For ver. 22-29, see 1 Chr. 1:17-25
24 [v]ch. 11:12; Luke 3:35, 36
25 [w]1 Chr. 1:19
29 [x]1 Kgs. 9:28; 10:11

Ziggurat

Ziggurats are monumental temple-towers found throughout the area of ancient Mesopotamia. They were commonly built of sun-dried mud and straw bricks held in position with bitumen as mortar. Stairways ascended to the top of these structures, where a small temple/shrine sat on the summit. The illustration below depicts the Ziggurat of Nanna at Ur, which was constructed during the reign of Ur-Nammu (c. 2113–2095 B.C.). Its area covered 150 x 200 feet (46 x 61 m), and its height was 80 feet (24 m). It is commonly believed that this type of structure was being built in the Tower of Babel episode (Gen. 11:1–9). The text indicates that the builders of Babel had discovered the process of making mud bricks and that they employed "bitumen for mortar" (v. 3). Based on that invention, the builders decided "to build . . . a tower with its top in the heavens" (v. 4).

32[y]ver. 1; ch. 9:19
Chapter 11
2[z]ch. 10:10; 14:1, 9; Isa. 11:11; Dan. 1:2; Zech. 5:11
3[a]ch. 14:10; Ex. 2:3
4[b]Deut. 1:28
5[c]ch. 18:21
7[d]ch. 1:26; [Ps. 2:4]
8[e]ch. 10:25, 32; Luke 1:51
9[f]ch. 10:10

the east. 31 These are the sons of Shem, by their clans, their languages, their lands, and
their nations.
32 These are the clans of the sons of Noah, according to their genealogies, in their nations,
[y]and from these the nations spread abroad on the earth after the flood.

The Tower of Babel

11 Now the whole earth had one language and the same words. 2 And as people migrated
from the east, they found a plain in [z]the land of Shinar and settled there. 3 And they
said to one another, "Come, let us make bricks, and burn them thoroughly." And they had
brick for stone, [a]and bitumen for mortar. 4 Then they said, "Come, let us build ourselves a
city and a tower [b]with its top in the heavens, and let us make a name for ourselves, lest we
be dispersed over the face of the whole earth." 5 And [c]the LORD came down to see the city
and the tower, which the children of man had built. 6 And the LORD said, "Behold, they are
one people, and they have all one language, and this is only the beginning of what they
will do. And nothing that they propose to do will now be impossible for them. 7 Come,
[d]let us go down and there confuse their language, so that they may not understand one
another's speech." 8 So [e]the LORD dispersed them from there over the face of all the earth,
and they left off building the city. 9 Therefore its name was called [f]Babel, because there the

concerning them; it associates Japheth's descendants with the coastal regions and islands of the Mediterranean Sea.

10:6–20 Ham's descendants receive considerably more attention than those of Japheth and Shem. Among them figure many of Israel's enemies, such as the Egyptians, Babylonians, Philistines, and various Canaanite groups. Ham's immediate sons are **Cush, Egypt, Put, and Canaan** (v. 6). Cush and Put are the regions to the south and west of Egypt, respectively. **Cush fathered Nimrod** (v. 8). This association may seem unusual given that Cush is linked geographically with Africa, and Nimrod with Mesopotamia. Nimrod is of particular interest for several reasons. He is linked to the great cities of Babel (i.e., Babylon; see note on 11:9) and Nineveh in Assyria, whose inhabitants at a later stage would descend in destructive power on the kingdoms of Israel and Judah. The military might of the Assyrians and Babylonians may account for the related observations that Nimrod was a **mighty man** (i.e., warrior) and a **mighty hunter** (10:8, 9). These descriptions, one of which is linked with irony to the expression **before the LORD** (10:9), are probably to be viewed negatively. Nimrod's aggression as a person runs totally counter to what God had intended when at creation he commissioned humanity to be his vice-regents or representatives. **Babel . . . in the land of Shinar** (v. 10). These details link Nimrod with the Tower of Babel episode (see 11:2, 9). Nimrod's kingdom is the antithesis of what God desired. **the great city** (10:12). This probably denotes a region that included both Nineveh and Calah (see Jonah 3:3). The detailed list of Canaan's descendants includes cities that play a significant role in later episodes in Genesis. The specific mention of **Sodom** and **Gomorrah** (Gen. 10:19) provides a possible link between the actions of Ham in 9:22 and of the men of Sodom in 19:4–8. The designation "Canaanite" is sometimes used to cover all the different groups mentioned in 10:15–19 (e.g., 28:1).

10:21–32 These verses list the descendants of **Shem**. These are the people with whom Israelites felt the most affinity, for Abraham was descended from Shem. Insofar as they can be identified, many of these are Arabian tribes or kingdoms. From the outset, Shem's great-grandson **Eber** is selected for special attention (v. 21), being mentioned even before Shem's own sons are named (v. 22). The designation "Hebrew" (Hb. *'ibri*; see 14:13) is derived from "Eber" (Hb. *'eber*). By way of underlining his importance, readers are informed that he called one of his sons **Peleg** (which may be taken to mean "division"), **for in his days the earth was divided** (10:25). This is probably an allusion to the Tower of Babel incident (11:1–9). The line of Shem's descendants from Arpachshad to Peleg is repeated with additional information in 11:11–19.

11:1–9 *The Tower of Babel.* This episode is significantly more important than its length suggests. It presents a unified humanity using all its resources to establish a city that is the antithesis of what God intended when he created the world. The tower is a symbol of human autonomy, and the city builders see themselves as determining and establishing their own destiny without any reference to the Lord. (The tower story may also be a polemic against Mesopotamian mythology. *Eridu Genesis*, a fragmentary text found at Ur, Nippur, and Nineveh, describes the goddess Nintur's calling for humanity to build cities and to congregate in one place. Her desire, according to this text, is that humans be sedentary and not nomadic. Yahweh demands just the opposite, so that the earth would become populated.)

11:1 The opening description of the **whole earth** having **one language** indicates that the present episode is not placed chronologically after the events narrated in ch. 10, which specifically mention nations and languages. This incident, however, may have occurred during the broad period covered in ch. 10, especially if it is linked to the naming of Peleg in 10:25 (see note on 10:21–32).

11:2–4 Come, let us build ourselves a city . . . and let us make a name for ourselves. The Babel enterprise is all about human independence and self-sufficiency apart from God. The builders believe that they have no need of God. Their technology and social unity give them confidence in their own ability, and they have high aspirations, constructing a **tower with its top in the heavens** (11:4). Contrary to God's plan that people should fill the earth (e.g., 1:22, 28; 9:1, 7), the city-building project is designed to prevent the population from being **dispersed over the face of the whole earth** (11:4). By showing God's continued interest in his creatures, this episode provides the setting for the call of Abram out of this very region, to be the vehicle of blessing to the whole world.

11:5–8 With irony, the narrator points out that it was necessary for the Lord to come **down** in order to **see the city and the tower** (v. 5). Acknowledging the potential danger of a unified, self-confident humanity (v. 6), God intervenes by confusing their language so that they cannot understand one another. This has the desired effect of dispersing the people throughout the world (vv. 8–9).

11:9 This verse links the name of the city, **Babel** (Hb. *babel*), with the verb *balal*, which means "to confuse, to mix, to mingle." But *babel* is also the name used in the OT for the city of Babylon. As a city, Babylon symbolizes humanity's ambition to dethrone God and make the earth its own (see Revelation 17–18).

Genesis 11:4

Action	Purpose	Desire
They built a city . . .	. . . in order not to be dispersed over the face of the whole earth.	Security
They built a tower with its top in the heavens . . .	. . . in order to make a name for themselves.	Praise

LORD confused[1] the language of all the earth. And from there the LORD dispersed them
over the face of all the earth.

Shem's Descendants

10 [g]These are the generations of Shem. When Shem was 100 years old, he fathered
Arpachshad two years after the flood. 11 And Shem lived after he fathered Arpachshad
500 years and had other sons and daughters.
12 When Arpachshad had lived 35 years, he fathered Shelah. 13 And Arpachshad lived
after he fathered Shelah 403 years and had other sons and daughters.
14 When Shelah had lived 30 years, he fathered Eber. 15 And Shelah lived after he fathered
Eber 403 years and had other sons and daughters.
16 When Eber had lived 34 years, he fathered Peleg. 17 And Eber lived after he fathered
Peleg 430 years and had other sons and daughters.
18 When Peleg had lived 30 years, he fathered Reu. 19 And Peleg lived after he fathered Reu
209 years and had other sons and daughters.
20 When Reu had lived 32 years, he fathered Serug. 21 And Reu lived after he fathered Serug
207 years and had other sons and daughters.
22 When Serug had lived 30 years, he fathered Nahor. 23 And Serug lived after he fathered
Nahor 200 years and had other sons and daughters.
24 When [h]Nahor had lived 29 years, he fathered Terah. 25 And Nahor lived after he fathered
Terah 119 years and had other sons and daughters.
26 When [h]Terah had lived 70 years, he fathered Abram, Nahor, and Haran.

[1] *Babel* sounds like the Hebrew for *confused*

10[g][ch. 10:22]; For ver. 10-26, see 1 Chr. 1:17-27
24[h]Josh. 24:2
26[h][See ver. 24 above]

11:10–26 *Shem's Descendants.* Resembling the list of Adam's descendants in 5:3–31, the present linear genealogy traces Noah's line through Shem down to Terah, the father of Abram, Nahor, and Haran. While the pattern is almost identical to that used in ch. 5, the final element, "*Thus all the days of A were Z years, and he died*," is missing. Also, unlike ch. 5, no additional information is inserted. Consequently, the list moves swiftly from Shem to Terah. While the periods mentioned are still unusually long, they gradually become somewhat shorter. The length of time during which these men live is much shorter than is recorded for men living before the flood (cf. 5:1–32). This is similar to the pattern found in a clay tablet from the Mesopotamian city of Uruk, called the Sumerian King List (see note on 5:1–32). It was inscribed by a scribe during the reign of King Utukhegal, about 2100 B.C. It tells of kings who reigned for extremely long times. A flood then came, and subsequent kings ruled for vastly shorter times.

11:26 The regular pattern of the genealogy is broken with the naming of Terah's three sons. Before this, only the son through whom the linear genealogy is traced is specifically named in each generation. **Abram** comes first in the list because the ongoing family line is traced through him.

11:27–50:26 *Patriarchal History.* The narrative now moves from the general survey of humanity to the specific family from which Israel comes. The narrative style becomes severely matter-of-fact. The narrator devotes much more time to describing the lives of the characters: whereas chs. 1–11 covers many generations in only 11 chapters, the patriarchal history deals with only four generations in 39 chapters. It begins with Abraham and goes on to his son Isaac, and Isaac's two sons Jacob and Esau; the final section focuses on Jacob's sons, especially Joseph. Here the specifics of being Israel are made clear: the land, the people, the blessing, and the calling. The Sinai (or Mosaic) covenant, which the first audience for these chapters receives, will provide the setting in which Israel is to put these patriarchal promises into practice. Throughout these chapters the readers will see how God has preserved the members of his chosen family, whose calling it is to walk with him, to be the headwaters of a special people and to be the channel by which blessing comes to the entire world.

11:27–25:18 *Terah's Descendants.* A new heading, identified by the expression "these are the generations of," introduces the next main section of Genesis (see note on 2:4). These chapters focus on the immediate family of Terah. Special attention is given to Abram because the unique family line of Genesis is continued through him.

11:27–32 *A Brief Introduction to Terah's Family.* Various details pertinent to understanding the subsequent narrative are given: the death of Lot's father, Haran (v. 28); the relocation of the family from southern to northern Mesopotamia (v. 31); and the inability of Abram's wife to have children (v. 30).

11:27 Abram will later have his name changed to "Abraham" (see 17:5).

11:28 Ur of the Chaldeans is unquestionably the ancient city in southern Babylonia, the remains of which are located at Tell el-Muqayyar in modern Iraq. See illustration, p. 71. Archaeological investigations by Leonard Woolley from 1922–1934 uncovered evidence of a highly developed urban culture in the time of Abram, a culture that developed around 2000 B.C. The term "Chaldeans" probably dates from the period 1000–500 B.C. and has been added to distinguish this Ur from similarly named cities in northern Mesopotamia (see Introduction: Author, Title, and Date). "Chaldeans" refers to the Kaldu people who settled in southern Babylonia from about 1200 B.C. onward.

11:29 The name **Sarai** is later changed to "Sarah" (see 17:15). Sarai's barrenness is an obvious barrier to the continuation of Abram's family line. The initial barrenness of the patriarchs' wives is a recurring motif in Genesis (see 25:21; 29:31).

11:31–32 According to the Kultepe Texts from the nineteenth century B.C. (texts composed by Assyrian traders who clearly understood such matters), **Haran** was an important crossroads and commercial center in the ancient Near East.

11:31 Although Terah's ambition is to move his family **from Ur** to **Canaan**, they do not complete the journey, but settle in northern Mesopotamia at **Haran** (the location in Turkey is now called Eskiharran, "old Harran"). The spelling of the town name "Haran" in Hebrew is quite distinct from the name of Terah's third son. (This is the Bible's first reference to "the land of Canaan." But the Ebla archives, found in northern Syria in the 1970s, contain clay tablets dating to c. 2300 B.C. They make mention of certain geographical places found in Scripture, such as Sodom and Zeboiim, two cities in the episode of the war of the kings [Gen. 14:1–16]. In addition, the first time the name "Canaan" is used in extrabiblical literature is at Ebla, in tablets that predate the biblical writings by centuries.)

11:32 By way of completing this short introduction to Terah's family, the narrative records his death at the age of **205**. If Abram was born when

29 [j]ch. 17:15 [j]ch. 22:20
31 [k]ch. 12:1 [l]ch. 15:7; Josh. 24:2; Neh. 9:7; Acts 7:2, 4
Chapter 12
1 [m]Acts 7:3; Heb. 11:8
2 [n]ch. 17:6; 18:18; [Gal. 3:14]
3 [o]ch. 27:29; Num. 24:9

Terah's Descendants

27 Now these are the generations of Terah. Terah fathered Abram, Nahor, and Haran;
and Haran fathered Lot. 28 Haran died in the presence of his father Terah in the land of his
kindred, in Ur of the Chaldeans. 29 And Abram and Nahor took wives. The name of Abram's
wife was [j]Sarai, and the name of Nahor's wife, [j]Milcah, the daughter of Haran the father
of Milcah and Iscah. 30 Now Sarai was barren; she had no child.
31 Terah [k]took Abram his son and Lot the son of Haran, his grandson, and Sarai his daughter-in-law, his son Abram's wife, and they went forth together [l]from Ur of the Chaldeans
to go into the land of Canaan, but when they came to Haran, they settled there. 32 The days
of Terah were 205 years, and Terah died in Haran.

The Call of Abram

12 Now [m]the LORD said[1] to Abram, "Go from your country[2] and your kindred and your
father's house to the land that I will show you. 2 [n]And I will make of you a great nation,
and I will bless you and make your name great, so that you will be a blessing. 3 [o]I will bless

[1] *Or had said* [2] *Or land*

Terah was 70 years old (see v. 26), and if Abram was 75 years old when he departed for Canaan (see 12:4), then Terah died 60 years after Abram's departure (70 + 75 + 60 = 205). In Acts 7:4, however, Stephen says that Abram left Haran *after* the death of Terah. A simple way to resolve the chronological difficulty is to suppose that Stephen was following an alternative text (represented today in the Samaritan Pentateuch), which says that Terah died at the age of 145.

12:1–9 *Abram's Migration to Canaan.* After the essential background information in 11:27–32, this section moves swiftly to highlight God's invitation to Abram to become a source of blessing for the rest of humanity. (The name "Abram" appears in a text from Dilbat, and "Abraham" in the Egyptian Execration Texts [20th–19th centuries B.C.]. Other names from the patriarchal period, such as "Terah," "Nahor," and "Benjamin," are also known from the Mari texts [18th century B.C.].)

12:1–3 The divine speech that suddenly and unexpectedly introduces this section is exceptionally important, for it sets the agenda not only for Abram's life but also for his descendants. By focusing on how divine blessing will be mediated through Abram to **all the families of the earth**, it marks an important turning point within the book of Genesis. The repetition of the verb **bless** (vv. 2–3) underscores the hope that through **Abram** people everywhere may experience God's favor, reversing the predominantly negative experience of chs. 3–11. God's plans for Abram have both national and international dimensions, which are developed in the episodes that follow.

12:1 God's invitation to Abram challenges him to abandon the normal sources of personal identity and security: his family and country. To obey, Abram must trust God implicitly; all human support is largely removed. The promised outcomes are conditional on Abram's obedience. **said**. In Acts 7:2–3, Stephen has God calling Abram *before* he lived in Haran; the ESV footnote, "had said," shows that the grammar allows for this reading.

12:2 God's purpose for Abram, that he become **a great nation**, stands in obvious tension with Sarai's barrenness and the summons to leave his homeland. Abram is challenged by God to establish a new humanity. **make your name great**. This was the failed aspiration of the tower builders (11:4).

12:3 Although Abram is called to be a blessing to others, much rests on how they treat him. Those who are positive toward Abram will experience God's favor; the one who despises Abram will know God's displeasure. The text speaks of **those who bless** (plural) but of **him who dishonors** (singular), emphasizing that many more will be blessed than cursed. Indeed, such will be the influence of Abram that **all the families of the earth shall be blessed** in him. This promise is later reaffirmed to Isaac and Jacob (see 22:18; 26:4; 28:14). **in you**. This may simply indicate "*by means of* you," but it is more likely that this expression is designating Abram as the covenantal representative for a people. To be "in" some person, then, is to be a member of that people for whom that person is the representative (cf. 2 Sam. 19:43; 20:1). This seems to be the way Paul takes it in Gal. 3:8–9, where "in you" becomes "along with Abraham"; it would also explain the origin of the NT expression "in Christ."

The City of Ur

The ancient city of Ur lies 186 miles (300 km) southeast of modern Baghdad on a bend of the original course of the Euphrates River. Major excavations took place at the site in 1922–1934 under the direction of Sir Leonard Woolley. Ur became an important city in Mesopotamia near the end of the third millennium B.C. The governor of Ur, a man named Ur-Nammu (c. 2113–2095 B.C.), brought the city to great prominence. He took the titles "King of Ur, King of Sumer and Akkad." Thus was founded the Third Dynasty of Ur (2113–2006 B.C.). This period was one of great peace and prosperity, the high point of the city's existence. This diagram of the city represents the Third Dynasty of Ur, and it includes a central palace and a temple complex. The latter has as its center the Ziggurat of Ur-Nammu (see p. 68) that is dedicated to the moon god Nanna. Ur was the birthplace of the Hebrew patriarch Abraham (Gen. 11:27–32), and the plan below represents the city that he would have been familiar with.

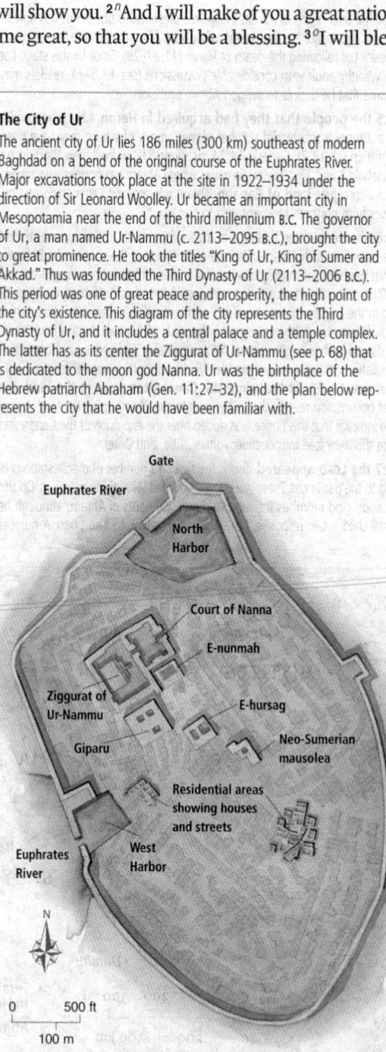

those who bless you, and him who dishonors you I will curse, and [p]in you all the families
of the earth shall be blessed."[1]
4 So Abram went, as the LORD had told him, and Lot went with him. Abram was seventy-
five years old when he departed from [q]Haran. 5 And Abram took Sarai his wife, and Lot his
brother's son, and all their possessions that they had gathered, and the people that they
had acquired in Haran, and they set out to go to the land of Canaan. When they came to
the land of Canaan, 6 Abram [r]passed through the land to the place at Shechem, to [s]the
oak[2] of [t]Moreh. At that time [u]the Canaanites were in the land. 7 Then the LORD appeared
to Abram and said, [v]"To your offspring I will give this land." So he built there an altar to
the LORD, who had appeared to him. 8 From there he moved to the hill country on the east

[1] Or *by you all the families of the earth shall bless themselves* [2] Or *terebinth*

3 [p]ch. 18:18; 22:18; 26:4; 28:14; Jer. 4:2; Acts 3:25; Gal. 3:16; Cited Gal. 3:8
4 [q]ch. 11:31
6 [r][Heb. 11:9] [s]ch. 13:18 [t]Deut. 11:30; Judg. 7:1 [u]ch. 13:7
7 [v]ch. 13:15; 17:8; Ex. 33:1; Ps. 105:9-12; [Num. 32:11]; Gal. 3:16

12:4 The brief report of Abram's response presents his obedience as immediate and unquestioning. **Lot went with him**. Abram may have been responsible for Lot following the death of Haran (11:27–28). Since by this stage Lot is a wealthy adult with considerable possessions (see 13:5–6), readers may assume that he desires to support Abram's mission.

12:5 the people that they had acquired in Haran. Abram had under his authority a substantial number of men, many of whom may have been herdsmen (cf. 13:7). Genesis 14:14 mentions 318 trained men "born in his household," and 17:12 refers to males whom Abram has bought with money from a foreigner. **land of Canaan**. Abram migrates with everything he possesses from northern Mesopotamia to Canaan.

12:6 Shechem is the first of a number of locations in Canaan mentioned in association with Abram. (The site of Shechem is the modern Tel Balatah, which has been extensively excavated. A major settlement here begins around 1900 B.C. Its importance in the patriarchal period is confirmed by its mention in the Egyptian Execration Texts and in the Khu-Sebek inscription, which both date to the 19th century B.C.) **the oak of Moreh**. As a seminomadic herdsman with a large retinue, Abram probably camped away from urban populations; these locations are identified by distinctive natural features (e.g., trees; see 13:18). **At that time the Canaanites were in the land**. This brief observation reveals that other people already occupied the land. It may also indicate that this notice was added after the expulsion of the Canaanites from this area (see Introduction: Author, Title, and Date).

12:7 the LORD appeared. This is the first of a number of manifestations of God to the patriarchs. These are often associated with divine promises. On this occasion God promises the land to the descendants of Abram, although he is still childless. In response, Abram builds an **altar to the LORD**. A number of altars are constructed by the patriarchs at different locations (see 13:18; 22:9; 26:25; 33:20; 35:7). They are a common feature of the patriarchal period because no central sanctuary existed before the exodus from Egypt. Before the construction of the tabernacle, God was not perceived as ordinarily dwelling on the earth. These altars are places where God may be encountered in worship (Ex. 20:24).

12:8 From Shechem, Abram migrates southward to a location between **Bethel** and **Ai**, before going much farther in the direction of Egypt. (Excavations at the site of Beitan, which is probably to be identified as biblical Bethel, have revealed a flourishing Canaanite city during the patriarchal period of the Middle Bronze Age [c. 2000–1500 B.C.]. The city contained four well-fortified gate complexes with a massive fortification wall [about 11.5 feet/3.5 m thick]. A large Canaanite sanctuary has been discovered immediately inside the city wall.)

12:9 The Negeb is the southern region of Canaan (Hb. *negeb* means "south").

12:10–20 *Abram in Egypt*. A severe famine in Canaan forces Abram to seek refuge in Egypt. Because of the Nile River, the land of Egypt was better placed to provide food for man and beast during a time of drought. The events described in this section raise many questions that go unanswered, creating a sense of ambiguity as to how the behavior of everyone involved should be judged. As is common in biblical stories, the narrator gives no direct evaluation of the participants' actions, leaving the reader to figure out the ethical questions. In this passage, the first readers (Israel following Moses) would have seen how God kept his promise to Abram, in spite of all threats, and in spite of the morally dubious actions even of Abram himself.

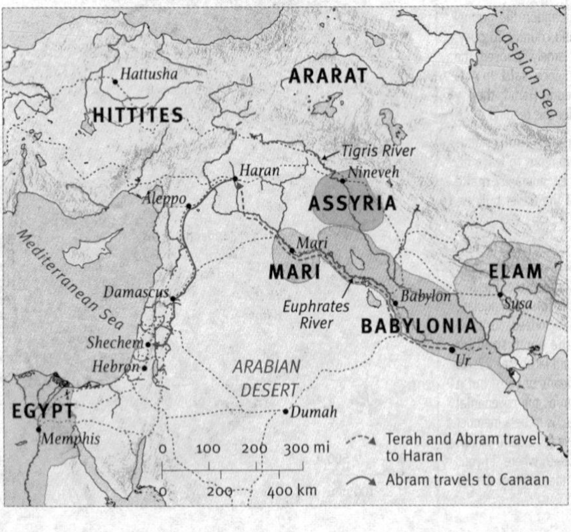

Abram Travels to Canaan
c. 2091/1925 B.C.
Abram was born in Ur, a powerful city in southern Babylonia. Abram's father, Terah, eventually led the family toward the land of Canaan but decided to settle in Haran (see Gen. 11:27–31). After Terah's death, the Lord called Abram to go "to the land that I will show you" (Canaan), which he promises to give to Abram's descendants. See note on Gen. 11:32.

8[w]ch. 28:19
10[x]ch. 26:1; 43:1
12[y]See ch. 20:1-18; 26:6-11
17[z]1 Chr. 16:21; Ps. 105:14

Chapter 13
1[a]ch. 12:9
2[b]ch. 24:35; [Ps. 112:1-3; Prov. 10:22]
4[c]ch. 12:7, 8
6[d]ch. 36:6, 7
7[e]ch. 26:20 [f]ch. 12:6
8[g][1 Cor. 6:1-8] [h][Acts 7:26]
9[i]ch. 20:15; 34:10

of [w]Bethel and pitched his tent, with Bethel on the west and Ai on the east. And there he
built an altar to the LORD and called upon the name of the LORD. 9 And Abram journeyed
on, still going toward the Negeb.

Abram and Sarai in Egypt

10 Now [x]there was a famine in the land. So Abram went down to Egypt to sojourn there,
for the famine was severe in the land. 11 When he was about to enter Egypt, he said to
Sarai his wife, "I know that you are a woman beautiful in appearance, 12 and when the
Egyptians see you, they will say, 'This is his wife.' Then they [y]will kill me, but they will let
you live. 13 Say you are my sister, that it may go well with me because of you, and that my
life may be spared for your sake." 14 When Abram entered Egypt, the Egyptians saw that the
woman was very beautiful. 15 And when the princes of Pharaoh saw her, they praised her
to Pharaoh. And the woman was taken into Pharaoh's house. 16 And for her sake he dealt
well with Abram; and he had sheep, oxen, male donkeys, male servants, female servants,
female donkeys, and camels.
17 But the LORD [z]afflicted Pharaoh and his house with great plagues because of Sarai,
Abram's wife. 18 So Pharaoh called Abram and said, "What is this you have done to me?
Why did you not tell me that she was your wife? 19 Why did you say, 'She is my sister,'
so that I took her for my wife? Now then, here is your wife; take her, and go." 20 And
Pharaoh gave men orders concerning him, and they sent him away with his wife and
all that he had.

Abram and Lot Separate

13 So Abram went up from Egypt, he and his wife and all that he had, and Lot with
him, [a]into the Negeb.
2 [b]Now Abram was very rich in livestock, in silver, and in gold. 3 And he journeyed on from
the Negeb as far as Bethel to the place where his tent had been at the beginning, between
Bethel and Ai, 4 to [c]the place where he had made an altar at the first. And there Abram
called upon the name of the LORD. 5 And Lot, who went with Abram, also had flocks and
herds and tents, 6 so that [d]the land could not support both of them dwelling together; for
their possessions were so great that they could not dwell together, 7 [e]and there was strife
between the herdsmen of Abram's livestock and the herdsmen of Lot's livestock. At that
time [f]the Canaanites and the Perizzites were dwelling in the land.
8 Then Abram said to Lot, [g]"Let there be no strife between you and me, and between
your herdsmen and my herdsmen, [h]for we are kinsmen.[1] 9 [i]Is not the whole land before

[1] Hebrew *we are men, brothers*

12:11–13 Fearful that his life will be endangered because of Sarai's beauty, Abram devises a ruse, based on a half-truth (see 20:12). Abram's selfish actions imply that he thinks God is unable to protect him. Yet when the plan backfires, it is the Lord who rescues him (12:17).

12:15 Pharaoh is the title given to the king of Egypt, not a personal name.

12:16 Some biblical scholars have maintained that the mention of **camels** in Genesis is anachronistic, on the assumption that they were not domesticated until about 1100 B.C. Archaeological finds of camel bones, however, suggest that some camels were in use by humans as early as the third millennium B.C. While the evidence is limited, it is hardly surprising, given the use to which camels were put. In Genesis they usually appear in passages that involve long-distance journeys through or close to deserts (see 24:10–64; 31:17, 34; 37:25). The scarcity of camels in the period of the patriarchs made them a luxury of great worth, and thus their listing here (and elsewhere) may serve to emphasize Abram's wealth.

12:17 Pharaoh's taking of **Sarai** brings divine punishment on him and **his house**. This event (**plagues**; cf. Ex. 11:1) prefigures the exodus from Egypt when God punishes another pharaoh for his mistreatment of Abram's descendants.

13:1–18 *Abram and Lot Separate.* Expelled from Egypt, Abram retraces his steps northward, through the Negeb, back to the hill country between Bethel and Ai where he had previously built an altar (12:8). Competition for pasture soon leads to strife between the herdsmen of Abram and Lot. When Abram magnanimously offers Lot first choice of the land, Lot opts for the fertile Jordan Valley. Afterward, the Lord reaffirms that Abram's descendants will possess all of Canaan.

13:2–6 These verses emphasize the wealth of both Abram and Lot, describing how the hill country east of Bethel is unable to sustain the **livestock** of both men.

13:7 The pressure on pastureland may well have been increased by the fact that **the Canaanites and the Perizzites were dwelling in the land**. Cf. the similar notice in 12:6.

Abraham's Timeline

Event	Age of Abraham	Genesis
Abram departs from Haran, enters Canaan	75	12:4–5
Abram fathers Ishmael with Hagar	85–86	16:3–4
Abraham fathers Isaac with Sarah	100	21:5
Abraham's wife Sarah dies	137	23:1
Abraham's son Isaac marries Rebekah	140	25:20
Abraham dies	175	25:7

you? Separate yourself from me. If you take the left hand, then I will go to the right, or
if you take the right hand, then I will go to the left." 10 And Lot lifted up his eyes and saw
that the [j]Jordan Valley was well watered everywhere like [k]the garden of the LORD, like
the land of Egypt, in the direction of [l]Zoar. (This was before the LORD [m]destroyed Sodom
and Gomorrah.) 11 So Lot chose for himself all the Jordan Valley, and Lot journeyed east.
Thus they separated from each other. 12 Abram settled in the land of Canaan, while Lot
settled among the cities of the valley and moved his tent as far as Sodom. 13 Now the men
of Sodom [n]were wicked, great sinners against the LORD.

14 The LORD said to Abram, after Lot had separated from him, "Lift up your eyes and
look from the place where you are, [o]northward and southward and eastward and westward, 15 for all the land that you see I will give [p]to you and [q]to your offspring forever.
16 [r]I will make your offspring as the dust of the earth, so that if one can count the dust
of the earth, your offspring also can be counted. 17 Arise, walk through the length and
the breadth of the land, for I will give it to you." 18 So Abram moved his tent and came
and [s]settled by the [t]oaks[1] of Mamre, which [u]are at Hebron, and there he built an altar
to the LORD.

Abram Rescues Lot

14 In the days of Amraphel king of [v]Shinar, Arioch king of Ellasar, Chedorlaomer
king of [w]Elam, and Tidal king of Goiim, 2 these kings made war with [x]Bera king of
Sodom, Birsha king of Gomorrah, Shinab king of [y]Admah, Shemeber king of [y]Zeboiim, and
the king of Bela (that is, Zoar). 3 And all these joined forces in the Valley of Siddim ([z]that
is, the Salt Sea). 4 Twelve years they had served Chedorlaomer, but in the thirteenth year
they rebelled. 5 In the fourteenth year Chedorlaomer and the kings who were with him
came and defeated the [a]Rephaim in [b]Ashteroth-karnaim, the [c]Zuzim in Ham, the [d]Emim
in Shaveh-kiriathaim, 6 and the [e]Horites in their hill country of Seir as far as [f]El-paran on

[1] Or *terebinths*

10 [j]ch. 19:17, 25, 28; Deut. 34:3; 1 Kgs. 7:46; [Matt. 3:5] [k]ch. 2:8; Isa. 51:3; Ezek. 28:13; Joel 2:3 [l]ch. 14:2, 8; 19:22 [m]ch. 19:24, 25
13 [n]ch. 18:20; Ezek. 16:49; 2 Pet. 2:7, 8
14 [o]ch. 28:14
15 [p]ch. 17:8; 28:13; 35:12; Acts 7:5 [q]ch. 12:7; 15:18; 24:7; 26:4; Deut. 34:4; 2 Chr. 20:7
16 [r]ch. 22:17; 28:14; 32:12; Num. 23:10; [1 Kgs. 3:8]; See ch. 15:5
18 [s]ch. 14:13 [t]ch. 12:6 [u]ch. 35:27

Chapter 14

1 [v]ch. 10:10; 11:2 [w]ch. 10:22; Isa. 11:11; Acts 2:9
2 [x]ver. 8; ch. 13:10; 19:22 [y]Deut. 29:23
3 [z]Num. 34:12; Deut. 3:17; Josh. 3:16
5 [a]ch. 15:20; Deut. 2:11; 3:11 [b]Deut. 1:4 [c][Deut. 2:20] [d]Deut. 2:10, 11
6 [e]Deut. 2:12, 22 [f][ch. 21:21; Num. 12:16; 13:3]

13:10 the Jordan Valley was well watered everywhere. Lot's experience with the effects of famine (12:10, probably from drought) makes his choice of the fertile Jordan Valley understandable. **like the garden of the LORD.** A reference to the garden of Eden, which was also well watered (see 2:10). This description of the Jordan Valley predates the destruction of **Sodom and Gomorrah**, which may have adversely affected the suitability of this area for flocks and herds. The precise location of these cities is unknown; one possibility is the plain southeast of the Dead Sea.

13:11–13 Lot's decision to settle **among the cities of the valley** brings him into the vicinity of Sodom. Lot is later found living in the city (see 14:12; 19:3–11), having abandoned his tent-dwelling lifestyle. After parting company from Abram, Lot now resides close to a city whose population is described as **wicked, great sinners against the LORD**. Cf. chs. 18–19.

13:14–17 Expanding on 12:7, this divine speech emphasizes not only the extent of the land that Abram's descendants will inherit but also how numerous they will be. **As the dust of the earth** (13:16) is one of three similes used by God to illustrate the large number of offspring that Abram will have (cf. 15:5; 22:17). At this stage, Abram still has no children.

13:18 Abram relocates to near **Hebron** (also known as Kiriath-arba; see 23:2), setting up his tent by the **oaks of Mamre**. Since one of Abram's allies is "Mamre the Amorite" (14:13), the oaks are probably named after him (see note on 12:6). **altar.** See note on 12:7. During the Middle Bronze Age (c. 2000–1500 B.C.), when the patriarchs lived, Hebron was, for its day, a major settlement in the Judean hills. It covered between six and seven acres, was heavily fortified, and contained some large public buildings. A cuneiform tablet discovered there from this time period indicates that Hebron was a capital city of a Canaanite kingdom.

14:1–24 *Abram's Rescue of Lot.* After separating from Abram and settling in Sodom, Lot is taken captive by an alliance of four kings who invade the Jordan Valley and defeat a local confederation of five kings. See map, p. 75. When Abram learns of his nephew's abduction from Sodom, he marshals a small force and, after pursuing the invaders northward, successfully recovers Lot and a large quantity of plunder. Abram's subsequent encounter with the kings of Sodom and Salem provides an interesting insight into his future aspirations in light of God's promises. Although Abram can compete militarily against powerful kings, he rejects the use of power to achieve God's purpose. Thus he does not use force to take control of the land of Canaan. This section falls into three parts: (1) vv. 1–12, the events leading up to Lot's abduction; (2) vv. 13–16, Lot's rescue by Abram; and (3) vv. 17–24, Abram's meeting with the kings of Sodom and Salem.

14:1–12 Alternative names are given in this passage for a number of locations. This suggests that an older account has been reworded for inclusion here in Genesis (see Introduction: Author, Title, and Date).

14:1–3 A brief summary introduces the rival alliances of kings. Such alliances were a common and recurring aspect of politics in the ancient Near East. The kings mentioned here have not yet been identified in sources outside the Bible, but their names correspond with known names or name types appropriate to the regions from which they may have come. **Shinar** is Babylonia (see 10:10). The location of **Ellasar** is uncertain, although the king's name, **Arioch**, is found in texts from the ancient cities of Mari and Nuzi; this might suggest that Ellasar is in northern Mesopotamia. **Elam** was an ancient state lying to the east of southern Babylonia. **Tidal** is possibly a Hittite name. **Goiim** in Hebrew means "nations." **Zoar** probably lay at the southern edge of the Valley of Jericho (see 19:22–23).

14:3 The **Salt Sea** is the Dead Sea.

14:4 After **twelve years** of subjugation, the kings of the Jordan Valley gain independence for one year.

14:5–7 Under the leadership of **Chedorlaomer**, the invading kings display their military strength by defeating a number of different tribal groups. The six locations reveal that the invaders moved southward along the King's Highway in Transjordan as far as the Gulf of Aqaba before turning northward, eventually arriving at **Hazazon-tamar** (v. 7), also known as Engedi (see 2 Chron. 20:2). When this episode was edited for inclusion in Genesis, **En-mishpat** was known as **Kadesh**.

14:8–11 The five kings of the Jordan Valley fail to repel the alliance of eastern kings. Consequently, the cities of **Sodom** and **Gomorrah** are plundered.

7[g] ch. 16:14; 20:1; Num. 13:26 [h] 2 Chr. 20:2

the border of the wilderness. 7 Then they turned back and came to En-mishpat (that is,
[g]Kadesh) and defeated all the country of the Amalekites, and also the Amorites who were
dwelling [h]in Hazazon-tamar.
8 Then the king of Sodom, the king of Gomorrah, the king of Admah, the king of
Zeboiim, and the king of Bela (that is, Zoar) went out, and they joined battle in the Valley
of Siddim 9 with Chedorlaomer king of Elam, Tidal king of Goiim, Amraphel king of
Shinar, and Arioch king of Ellasar, four kings against five. 10 Now the Valley of Siddim

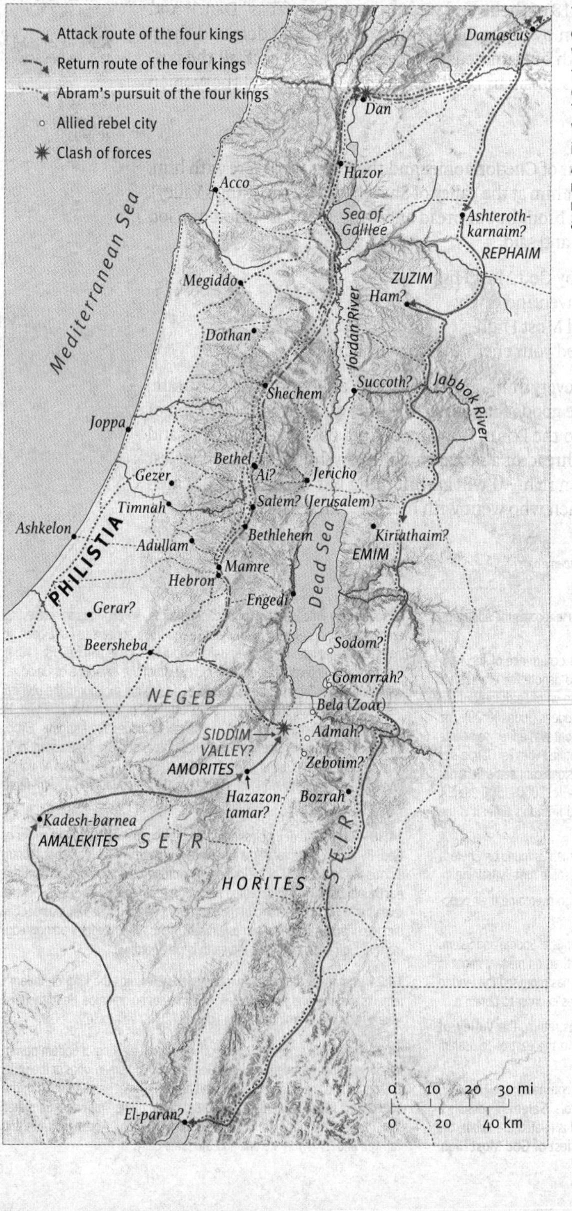

The Battle at the Valley of Siddim

c. 2085/1920 B.C.

When five Canaanite cities rebelled against their four Mesopotamian overlords, the four kings led a campaign to reassert their control over the region. The campaign culminated in a battle in the Siddim Valley, and Abram's nephew Lot, who was living in Sodom, was captured and carried off. When Abram was informed of Lot's capture, he and his men pursued the four kings to Dan, where they recaptured Lot and chased the fleeing forces as far as Hobah, north of Damascus.

was full of [i]bitumen pits, and as the kings of Sodom and Gomorrah fled, some fell into
them, and the rest fled [j]to the hill country. 11 So the enemy took [k]all the possessions of
Sodom and Gomorrah, and all their provisions, and went their way. 12 They also took
Lot, [l]the son of Abram's brother, [m]who was dwelling in Sodom, and his possessions, and
went their way.
13 Then one who had escaped came and told Abram the Hebrew, [n]who was living by
the [o]oaks[1] of Mamre the Amorite, brother of Eshcol and of Aner. These were allies of
Abram. 14 When Abram heard that his kinsman had been taken captive, he led forth his
trained men, [p]born in his house, 318 of them, and went in pursuit as far as [q]Dan. 15 And
he divided his forces against them by night, he and his servants, and defeated them
and pursued them to Hobah, north of Damascus. 16 Then he brought back all the possessions, and also brought back his kinsman Lot [r]with his possessions, and the women
and the people.

Abram Blessed by Melchizedek

17 After his return from the defeat of Chedorlaomer and the kings who were with him,
the king of Sodom went out to meet him at the Valley of Shaveh (that is, the [s]King's Valley).
18 And [t]Melchizedek king of Salem brought out bread and wine. (He was [u]priest of [v]God
Most High.) 19 And he blessed him and said,

[w]"Blessed be Abram by God Most High,
[x]Possessor[2] of heaven and earth;
20 and blessed be God Most High,
who has delivered your enemies into your hand!"

And Abram gave him [y]a tenth of everything. 21 And the king of Sodom said to Abram,
"Give me the persons, but take the goods for yourself." 22 But Abram said to the king of
Sodom, [z]"I have lifted my hand[3] to the LORD, God Most High, Possessor of heaven and
earth, 23 that [a]I would not take a thread or a sandal strap or anything that is yours, lest
you should say, 'I have made Abram rich.' 24 I will take nothing but what the young men
have eaten, and the share of the men who went with me. Let [b]Aner, Eshcol, and Mamre
take their share."

[1] Or *terebinths* [2] Or *Creator*; also verse 22 [3] Or *I have taken a solemn oath*

10 [i]ch. 11:3; Ex. 2:3 [j]ch. 19:17, 30
11 [k]ver. 16, 21
12 [l]ch. 12:5 [m]ch. 13:12
13 [n]ch. 13:18 [o]ch. 12:6
14 [p]ch. 15:3; 17:12, 13, 23, 27; Eccles. 2:7 [q]Judg. 18:29
16 [r]ver. 11, 12
17 [s]2 Sam. 18:18
18 [t]Heb. 7:1 [u]Ps. 110:4; Heb. 5:6, 10; 7:1, 11, 17 [v]Ps. 57:2; Acts 16:17
19 [w]Heb. 7:6, 7 [x]Matt. 11:25
20 [y]Heb. 7:4; [ch. 28:22]
22 [z]Ex. 6:8; Num. 14:30; Deut. 32:40; Ezek. 20:5, 6, 15, 23, 28; Dan. 12:7; Rev. 10:5, 6
23 [a][Esth. 9:15, 16]
24 [b]ver. 13

14:12 Paralleling the general report of v. 11, this verse records the abduction of **Lot** and his **possessions** from **Sodom**.

14:13–16 Abram the Hebrew. This is the first occurrence of the term "Hebrew" in the Bible and is probably used here to denote the ethnicity of Abram (see note on 10:21–32). **Dan** (14:14). The town of Laish in northern Canaan was renamed "Dan" in the period of the judges (Judg. 18:29). The use of the name "Dan" here indicates that this account was edited sometime later (see note on Gen. 14:1–12). (Dan is to be identified with Tel Dan, a site extensively excavated since the 1960s. A large and significant settlement has been uncovered here from the Middle Bronze Age [c. 2000–1500 B.C.]. A monumental mud-brick arched gateway was found from this time; it is the earliest of its kind ever found.)

14:14 trained men. The Hebrew word for "trained men" is found only here in the OT. The context implies that they may have had some military training.

14:15 A nighttime assault enables Abram's forces to overcome their opponents, who flee northward.

14:17–24 By contrasting Abram's reactions to the kings of Sodom and Salem, this passage underlines his reliance on God rather than on military might in order to gain possession of Canaan. Although God has promised the land to Abram, the patriarch will not adopt violent strategies in order to obtain it.

14:17 The **king of Sodom** greets Abram on his return. The **Valley of Shaveh**, also known as the **King's Valley**, lay to the east of Jerusalem (see 2 Sam. 18:18).

14:18 Melchizedek (which means "king of righteousness"; see Heb. 7:2) generously provides a meal for the returning victors. **Salem** is possibly a shortened version of "Jerusalem" (see Ps. 76:2) and is related to *shalom*, the Hebrew word for "peace" (see Heb. 7:2). **He was priest of God Most High**. Although very little is known about Melchizedek, he provides an interesting example of a priest-king linked to Jerusalem. There appears to have been an expectation that later kings of Jerusalem should resemble him (see Ps. 110:4). The book of Hebrews presents Jesus Christ, from the royal line of David, as belonging to the "order of Melchizedek" and therefore superior to the Levitical priests (Heb. 5:5–10; 6:20–7:17). "God Most High" in Hebrew is *'El 'Elyon*. *'El* is the common Semitic term for "God." To this is added the attribute *'Elyon*, meaning "Most High." Elsewhere in Genesis other attributes are added to *'El* (e.g., in Gen. 16:13 "God of seeing" translates *'El Ro'i*; in 17:1 "God Almighty" translates *'El Shadday*; in 21:33 "Everlasting God" translates *'El 'Olam*). These different names highlight different aspects of God's nature.

14:19–20 Melchizedek's blessing attributes Abram's victory to the power of God. By giving Melchizedek **a tenth of everything** (i.e., a tithe), Abram affirms the truthfulness of Melchizedek's words. **Possessor of heaven and earth**. Although God has created the whole earth to be his temple, Genesis reveals that God's ownership of the earth is rejected by those who do not obey him (see Introduction: Key Themes). In light of this, Melchizedek's acknowledgment of God's authority over the earth is noteworthy.

14:21 In marked contrast to Melchizedek's blessing, the king of Sodom's remarks are surly and small-minded: he expresses no gratitude. He "dishonors" Abram, and this is ominous in the light of 12:3 ("I will curse").

14:22–24 Abram's rejection of the offer made by the king of Sodom powerfully affirms that he is depending on God and not on human kings or their gifts in order to become a "great nation" and acquire a great name (see 12:2). **the LORD, God Most High**. By prefixing the divine name "Yahweh" (translated "LORD"; see note on 2:4) to *'El 'Elyon*, "God Most High," Abram indicates that Yahweh and *'El 'Elyon* are one and the same deity.

God's Covenant with Abram

15 After these things the word of the LORD came to Abram in a vision: [c]"Fear not,
Abram, I am [d]your shield; your reward shall be very great." 2 But Abram said, "O
Lord GOD, what will you give me, for I continue[1] childless, and the heir of my house is
Eliezer of Damascus?" 3 And Abram said, "Behold, you have given me no offspring, and
[e]a member of my household will be my heir." 4 And behold, the word of the LORD came
to him: "This man shall not be your heir; [f]your very own son[2] shall be your heir." 5 And he
brought him outside and said, "Look toward heaven, and [g]number the stars, if you are able
to number them." Then he said to him, [h]"So shall your offspring be." 6 And [i]he believed
the LORD, and [j]he counted it to him as righteousness.

7 And he said to him, "I am the LORD who [k]brought you out from Ur of the Chaldeans
[l]to give you this land to possess." 8 But he said, "O Lord GOD, [m]how am I to know that I
shall possess it?" 9 He said to him, "Bring me a heifer three years old, a female goat three
years old, a ram three years old, a turtledove, and a young pigeon." 10 And he brought
him all these, [n]cut them in half, and laid each half over against the other. But [o]he did not
cut the birds in half. 11 And when birds of prey came down on the carcasses, Abram drove
them away.

12 As the sun was going down, a [p]deep sleep fell on Abram. And behold, dreadful and
great darkness fell upon him. 13 Then the LORD said to Abram, "Know for certain [q]that
your offspring will be sojourners in a land that is not theirs and will be servants there,
and [r]they will be afflicted for [s]four hundred years. 14 But [t]I will bring judgment on the
nation that they serve, and afterward [u]they shall come out with great possessions. 15 As for
you, you shall go to your fathers in peace; [v]you shall be buried in a good old age. 16 And
they shall come back here in the fourth generation, for [w]the iniquity of the Amorites [x]is
not yet complete."

17 When the sun had gone down and it was dark, behold, a smoking fire pot and a flaming torch passed between these pieces. 18 On that day the LORD made a covenant with

[1] Or *I shall die* [2] Hebrew *what will come out of your own loins*

Chapter 15
1 [c]ch. 26:24; Dan. 10:12; Luke 1:13, 30 [d]Ps. 3:3; 18:2; 84:11; 119:114
3 [e]ch. 14:14
4 [f]ch. 17:16
5 [g]Ps. 147:4 [h]ch. 22:17; 26:4; Ex. 32:13; Deut. 1:10; 10:22; 1 Chr. 27:23; Heb. 11:12; Cited Rom. 4:18
6 [i]Rom. 4:9, 22; Gal. 3:6; James 2:23 [j]Cited Rom. 4:3; [Ps. 106:31]
7 [k]ch. 11:31; 12:1; Neh. 9:7, 8; Acts 7:2-4 [l]Ps. 105:42, 44
8 [m][Judg. 6:17; 2 Kgs. 20:8; Ps. 86:17; Isa. 7:11-13; Luke 1:18]
10 [n]Jer. 34:18, 19 [o]Lev. 1:17
12 [p]ch. 2:21
13 [q]Acts 7:6, 7 [r]Ex. 1:11, 12; 3:7 [s]Acts 7:6; [Ex. 12:40, 41; Gal. 3:17]
14 [t]Ex. 6:6 [u]Ex. 12:36; Ps. 105:37
15 [v]ch. 25:8
16 [w]1 Kgs. 21:26; Amos 2:9 [x][Dan. 8:23; Matt. 23:32; 1 Thess. 2:16]

15:1–21 *God's Covenant with Abram.* This chapter falls into two closely related sections: vv. 1–6 address Abram's concern that he is still childless; vv. 7–21 focus on Abram's desire to have a divine pledge that the land of Canaan will belong to his descendants. Both elements are essential components of nationhood. God's conditional promise in 12:2 that Abram will become a "great nation" is now guaranteed by a covenant, although the fulfillment will not take place until several centuries after Abram's death.

15:1–6 Abram receives a sign from God that he will have many descendants.

15:1 After these things links this episode to the one immediately preceding. In ch. 14 Abram rejected the offer from the king of Sodom for the victory spoils as a reward. In response, God now states that Abram's **reward shall be very great**. By rejecting the use of human wealth to achieve greatness (14:22–24), Abram demonstrates his willingness to wait for God to provide. **in a vision**. Although it is not certain, the initial vision may have taken place at night. In 15:5 God brings Abram out of his tent to count the stars.

15:2 the heir of my house is Eliezer of Damascus. This individual, whose name means "God is help," is not named elsewhere. The context suggests that he is a trusted member of Abram's household, possibly a slave, who came from Damascus. Yet the Hebrew text is somewhat obscure, and other interpretations are possible. Abram could have acquired him on the journey from Haran to Canaan.

15:6 This key verse in Genesis is quoted four times in the NT (Rom. 4:3, 22; Gal. 3:6; James 2:23). Faith in God is something that everyone in the Bible was expected to exercise. It entails trust in or confident reliance on God (see notes on John 1:12–13; Heb. 11:1), based on the truthfulness of his words, and it will lead to obeying his commands. A person's faith or lack of it is most apparent in crises such as Abram was facing. He believed God would give him a son despite many years of childlessness. **counted . . . as righteousness**. "Righteousness" is the fundamental OT virtue characterized by a godly life lived in conformity with the law. It is the righteous who enjoy God's favor. Here the narrator underlines the significance of faith, in that before Abram has proved himself righteous by his deeds, he is counted (that is, regarded) as righteous because of his faith.

15:9–17 The ritual described here is possibly a type of oath that involves a self-curse if not fulfilled; God will become like the dead animals if he does not keep his word (see Jer. 34:18–19). Another interpretation, however, is that the ritual is an acted sign in which the sacrificial animals symbolize Abram's descendants (all of Israel), the "birds of prey" (Gen. 15:11) signify their enemies (unclean nations), and the "fire pot" and "torch" (v. 17) represent God's presence. The promises of vv. 13–16 look forward to God's being in the midst of the Israelites after they come out of Egypt.

15:13–16 Four hundred years is probably to be understood as a round figure (cf. Acts 7:6). This anticipates the length of the Israelites' oppression by the Egyptians before the exodus from Egypt. **and afterward they shall come out with great possessions**. This promise, given by the Lord to Abram (soon to be called "Abraham"; Gen. 17:5), was fulfilled 600 to 800 years later at the time of the exodus (Ex. 12:35–36). **for the iniquity of the Amorites is not yet complete** (Gen. 15:16). The Amorites are one of the main population groups in Canaan and are frequently listed alongside the Canaanites and others (see vv. 19–21). (See notes on Genesis 10, where the Amorites are included among the descendants of Ham.) God's comment implies that the Amorites will be dispossessed of their land as an act of divine punishment. At that time, their accumulated iniquity will be so great that God will no longer tolerate their presence in the land. On the destruction of the Canaanites, see Introduction to Joshua: The Destruction of the Canaanites.

15:17 When the sun had gone down. The final part of the ritual occurs after sunset. Since vv. 1–6 assume a nighttime setting, Abram may have spent much of the day preparing the animals. **a smoking fire pot and a flaming torch**. These are taken to be symbolic of God's presence, which is often associated with fire (e.g., Ex. 13:21–22).

15:18–21 These verses provide a brief summary, affirming the significance of what has taken place, by stating, **On that day the LORD made a covenant with Abram**. This covenant, which differs from the covenant described in ch. 17, is introduced using a Hebrew idiom that literally means "to cut a covenant." (For description of a covenant, see note on 9:9–11.)

Abram, saying, [y]"To your offspring I give[1] this land, from [z]the river of Egypt to the great
river, the river Euphrates, 19 the land of the Kenites, the Kenizzites, the Kadmonites, 20 the
Hittites, the Perizzites, the Rephaim, 21 the Amorites, the Canaanites, the Girgashites and
the Jebusites."

Sarai and Hagar

16 [a]Now Sarai, Abram's wife, had borne him no children. She had a female Egyptian
servant whose name was [b]Hagar. 2 And Sarai said to Abram, "Behold now, the LORD
has prevented me from bearing children. Go in to my servant; it may be that I shall obtain
children[2] by her." And Abram listened to the voice of Sarai. 3 So, after Abram [c]had lived ten
years in the land of Canaan, Sarai, Abram's wife, took Hagar the Egyptian, her servant, and
gave her to Abram her husband as a wife. 4 And he went in to Hagar, and she conceived.
And when she saw that she had conceived, [d]she looked with contempt on her mistress.[3]
5 And Sarai said to Abram, "May the wrong done to me be on you! I gave my servant to
your embrace, and when she saw that she had conceived, she looked on me with contempt. May [e]the LORD judge between you and me!" 6 But Abram said to Sarai, "Behold,
your servant is in your power; do to her as you please." Then Sarai dealt harshly with her,
and she fled from her.
7 The angel of the LORD found her by a spring of water in the wilderness, the spring on
the way to [f]Shur. 8 And he said, "Hagar, servant of Sarai, where have you come from and
where are you going?" She said, "I am fleeing from my mistress Sarai." 9 The angel of the
LORD said to her, "Return to your mistress and submit to her." 10 The angel of the LORD
also said to her, [g]"I will surely multiply your offspring so that they cannot be numbered
for multitude." 11 And the angel of the LORD said to her,

"Behold, you are pregnant
and shall bear a son.
You shall call his name Ishmael,[4]
[h]because the LORD has listened to your affliction.

18 [y]ch. 12:7; 13:15; 24:7; 26:4; Num. 34:2; Deut. 34:4; Neh. 9:8 [z]Ex. 23:31; Deut. 1:7; Josh. 1:4

Chapter 16

1 [a]ch. 15:2, 3 [b]ch. 21:9; Gal. 4:24
3 [c]ch. 12:5
4 [d][1 Sam. 1:6, 7]
5 [e]ch. 31:53; 1 Sam. 24:12
7 [f]ch. 25:18; Ex. 15:22
10 [g]ch. 17:20; 21:18; See ch. 25:12-18
11 [h][ch. 29:32]

[1] Or *have given* [2] Hebrew *be built up*, which sounds like the Hebrew for *children* [3] Hebrew *her mistress was dishonorable in her eyes*; similarly in verse 5
[4] *Ishmael* means *God hears*

God unconditionally pledges that Abram's **offspring** will possess **this land**. The reference to both offspring and land links this covenant with the earlier conditional promise that Abram would become a great nation (12:2). **from the river of Egypt to the great river, the river Euphrates**. While the location of the northern boundary is clear, the designation "river of Egypt" is somewhat ambiguous. It could refer to the Wadi el Arish (midway between Israel and the Nile; Num. 34:5, however, uses a slightly different expression for this). Alternatively, "river" could refer to the eastern branch of the Nile. (But the distinctive Hebrew term for the Nile is not used here.) While others occupied the land when the divine covenant was given, this promise was probably fulfilled for a time in the reign of Solomon (see 1 Kings 4:21).

16:1–16 *The Birth of Ishmael.* Impatient for an heir, Sarai seeks to resolve the problem of her barrenness by having her maidservant, Hagar, bear a child on her behalf, a custom mentioned in other ancient Near Eastern texts. Subsequent tensions between Sarai and Hagar cause the latter to run away. By sending an angel-messenger, the Lord persuades Hagar to return, probably thus leading Abram to think that the child soon to be born, Ishmael, might indeed be the promised son (cf. 17:18). Theologically, this episode emphasizes the hearing and seeing nature of God, and his mercy.

16:2 Abram listened to the voice of Sarai. The Hebrew idiom implies that Abram obeyed Sarai. Abram is possibly criticized here for conceding too readily to his wife's request (see v. 6).

16:3 as a wife. Hagar's status within Abram's household is changed from servant to wife, although this does not place her on a par with Sarai (see note on 25:5–6). While the OT records occasions when particular individuals have more than one wife, such instances are almost always fraught with complications and difficulties. The taking of multiple wives is never encouraged in the Bible (see 2:24; Deut. 17:17) and usually arises out of peculiar circumstances. (For more on polygamy, see Marriage and Sexual Morality, pp. 2543–2545.)

16:4 Hagar's ability to conceive causes her to look down on Sarai.

16:5–7 Sarai initially directs her anger at Abram, who acquiesces in the situation, permitting Sarai to deal **harshly** with Hagar. The human solution to Sarai's barrenness creates new problems.

16:7 The angel of the LORD. The Hebrew word for "angel" may also be translated "messenger." There is an element of mystery about this figure. In 19:1 the "two angels" who arrive at Sodom resemble human beings (in 18:2 they are called "men"). When "the angel of the LORD" speaks, his words are perceived as being God's words. Therefore, the impression is given that the angel is identical with God. On this basis some Christians believe that "the angel of the LORD" is the preincarnate Christ. Others, however, hold that the reference here is to an angel who has been commissioned to speak as God's representative, and so the angel's words are God's words. **the spring on the way to Shur**. Hagar's flight takes her in the direction of Egypt, her homeland. The location of the spring/well is clarified in 16:14, when it is named "Beer-lahai-roi." It "lies between Kadesh and Bered."

16:9 submit to her. Hagar is commanded by God to transform her attitude toward her mistress, Sarai; instead of despising her, she is to submit to her authority.

16:10 By way of encouragement, the angel of the Lord promises Hagar that she will have numerous descendants; cf. 17:20; 25:12–18.

16:11 Ishmael means "God hears." Hagar's harsh treatment by Sarai has not gone unobserved by God.

16:12 The angel promises Hagar that her son will become a strongly independent person. Unlike his mother, he will not need to be servile toward others, but he will live a life of hostility toward others.

12[l]Job 39:5-8; [ch. 21:20] [j]ch. 25:18
13[k][ch. 32:30; Ex. 19:21; 33:20; Judg. 13:22]
14[l]ch. 24:62; 25:11 [m]ch. 14:7; 20:1; Num. 13:26
Chapter 17
1[n]ch. 6:9; Deut. 18:13; Job 1:1; Ps. 119:1; Matt. 5:48
2[o]ch. 12:2; 13:16; 22:17
3[p]ver. 17
4[q]Rom. 4:11, 12, 16
5[r]Neh. 9:7 [s]Cited Rom. 4:17

12 He shall be [i]a wild donkey of a man,
his hand against everyone
and everyone's hand against him,
and he shall dwell [j]over against all his kinsmen."

13 So she called the name of the LORD who spoke to her, "You are a God of seeing,"[1] for she
said, [k]"Truly here I have seen him who looks after me."[2] 14 Therefore the well was called
[l]Beer-lahai-roi;[3] it lies between [m]Kadesh and Bered.
15 And Hagar bore Abram a son, and Abram called the name of his son, whom Hagar
bore, Ishmael. 16 Abram was eighty-six years old when Hagar bore Ishmael to Abram.

Abraham and the Covenant of Circumcision

17 When Abram was ninety-nine years old the LORD appeared to Abram and said to
him, "I am God Almighty;[4] walk before me, and be [n]blameless, 2 that I may make
my covenant between me and you, and [o]may multiply you greatly." 3 Then Abram [p]fell on
his face. And God said to him, 4 "Behold, my covenant is with you, and you shall be [q]the
father of a multitude of nations. 5 No longer shall your name be called Abram,[5] but [r]your
name shall be Abraham,[6] [s]for I have made you the father of a multitude of nations. 6 I will

[1] Or *You are a God who sees me* [2] Hebrew *Have I really seen him here who sees me?* or *Would I have looked here for the one who sees me?* [3] *Beer-lahai-roi* means *the well of the Living One who sees me* [4] Hebrew *El Shaddai* [5] *Abram* means *exalted father* [6] *Abraham* means *father of a multitude*

16:13 Hagar is impressed by the perceptiveness of God as revealed through his angel-messenger. This is seen in the name she gives to the Lord; she calls him **God of seeing** (Hb. *'El Ro'i*). **here I have seen him who looks after me**. Although this could imply that Hagar actually saw God himself, her remarks may also be interpreted as denoting an inner perception; she perceives that God sees or "looks after" her.

16:14 Beer-lahai-roi means "well of the Living One who sees me."

16:15 By naming Ishmael, Abram publicly acknowledges him as his son and heir.

16:16 eighty-six years old. Ishmael is born 11 years after Abram settled in the land of Canaan (see chart, p. 73).

17:1–27 *The Covenant of Circumcision.* Thirteen years after the birth of Ishmael, the Lord appears to Abram. In a series of speeches God announces that he will establish an eternal covenant with Abram and his offspring. This covenant will involve Abram as the father of many nations; consequently, his name is changed to "Abraham." The sign of the covenant is circumcision. In the future this covenant will be established with Isaac but not Ishmael (although the latter, by being circumcised, will enjoy some of the benefits of the covenant). Most of the chapter consists of a divine speech that focuses on the part to be played by God (vv. 4–8), Abraham (vv. 9–14), and Sarah (vv. 15–16). The nature and contents of the covenant distinguish it from the covenant of ch. 15, which is solely about future nationhood.

17:1–2 God Almighty (Hb. *'El Shadday*). Like many other divine names in Genesis, the common Semitic word for "God," *'El*, is followed by a term that highlights a particular attribute of God (see note on 14:18). *'El Shadday* emphasizes God's power, which in this context will enable Sarai to bear Abram a son. Two closely related instructions are given to Abram, challenging him (1) to maintain an ongoing relationship with God and (2) to be faultless or perfect. **walk before me**. A distinctive verbal form in Hebrew is used here to underline the ongoing nature of this activity (see note on 5:22–24). **be blameless**. The Hebrew term for "blameless" (*tamim*) is also used of sacrificial animals, which were to be without blemish. Noah, with whom God also made a covenant, is also described in 6:9 as a blameless man who walked with God. **that I may make my covenant**. The manner in which God introduces this covenant distinguishes it from the formally unconditional covenant already made in ch. 15. (Of course, there is an implied condition in ch. 15: Abram must continue to believe God's promises, and he must father offspring.) Here, however, a conditional dimension is explicit, indicating that this covenant will benefit only those who walk before God and are blameless (see note on 17:19).

17:4–5 the father of a multitude of nations. These words summarize the covenant being established by God. Everything else that God says in the rest of the chapter expands on this core affirmation. To underline their importance, these words are repeated at the end of v. 5. **your name shall be Abraham, for I have made you the father of a multitude of nations**. The transformation of Abram's name to "Abraham" encapsulates the purpose of the covenant. Although the term "father" normally denotes a biological relationship, the Bible contains examples of its being used metaphorically. Joseph describes himself as "father to Pharaoh" (45:8; cf. Judg. 17:10, where Micah invites a young Levite to be his "father"). The concept of Abraham's being the "father of a multitude of nations" is probably related to the earlier divine promise that "in you all the families of the earth shall be blessed" (Gen. 12:3). As a father figure, Abraham will have a profound influence on others, including those who are not his biological children.

17:6 I will make you exceedingly fruitful. This promise echoes the divine blessing given at creation (1:28) and later repeated to Noah after the flood (9:1). **kings shall come from you**. Fruitfulness is associated with human beings' exercising dominion over the earth on God's behalf (1:28; 9:1–7). God's covenant with Abraham anticipates the reestablishment of the

Four Kinds of Abraham's Offspring

Offspring	Explanation	Examples
Natural, physical offspring	Physical descendants of Abraham	Ishmael, Isaac, the sons of Keturah (and by extension Esau, Jacob, etc.)
Natural, yet special offspring	Physical descendants of Abraham especially tied to God's elective and saving purposes	Isaac (by extension Jacob and the entire nation of Israel)
Promised offspring	The true, unique offspring of Abraham	A distinctive line of offspring, starting earlier with Seth and continuing through Noah, Abraham, Isaac, Israel, and David, culminating in Jesus Christ (Gal. 3:16)
Spiritual offspring	Those united with Christ (the promised offspring)	Jews and Gentiles who trust in the Messiah

make you exceedingly fruitful, and I will make [t]you into nations, and [u]kings shall come
from you. 7 And I will [v]establish my covenant between me and you and your offspring
after you throughout their generations for an everlasting covenant, [w]to be God to you
and to your offspring after you. 8 And [x]I will give to you and to your offspring after you
the land of your sojournings, all the land of Canaan, for an everlasting possession, and
[y]I will be their God."

9 And God said to Abraham, "As for you, you shall keep my covenant, you and your
offspring after you throughout their generations. 10 This is my covenant, which you shall
keep, between me and you and your offspring after you: Every male among you shall be
circumcised. 11 You shall be circumcised in the flesh of your foreskins, and it shall be a
[z]sign of the covenant between me and you. 12 He who is [a]eight days old among you shall
be circumcised. Every male throughout your generations, whether born in your house or
[b]bought with your money from any foreigner who is not of your offspring, 13 both he who
is born in your house and he who is bought with your money, shall surely be circumcised.
So shall my covenant be in your flesh an everlasting covenant. 14 Any uncircumcised male
who is not circumcised in the flesh of his foreskin shall be cut off from his people; he has
broken my covenant."

Isaac's Birth Promised

15 And God said to Abraham, "As for Sarai your wife, you shall not call her name Sarai,
but Sarah[1] shall be her name. 16 I will bless her, and moreover, I will [c]give[2] you a son by
her. I will bless her, and [d]she shall become nations; kings of peoples shall come from her."
17 Then Abraham [e]fell on his face [f]and laughed and said to himself, "Shall a child be born
to a man who is a hundred years old? Shall Sarah, who is ninety years old, bear a child?"
18 And Abraham said to God, "Oh that Ishmael might live before you!" 19 God said, "No, but
[g]Sarah your wife shall bear you a son, and you shall call his name [h]Isaac.[3] I will establish
my covenant with him as an everlasting covenant for his offspring after him. 20 As for
Ishmael, I have heard you; behold, I have blessed him and will make him fruitful and
[i]multiply him greatly. He [j]shall father twelve princes, and [k]I will make him into a great

[1] *Sarai* and *Sarah* mean *princess* [2] Hebrew *have given* [3] *Isaac* means *he laughs*

6 [t]ch. 35:11 [u]ver. 16
7 [v]Gal. 3:17 [w]Heb. 11:16; [ch. 26:24; 28:13]
8 [x]ch. 12:7; 13:15; Ps. 105:11 [y]Ex. 6:7; Lev. 26:12
11 [z]Acts 7:8; Rom. 4:11
12 [a]Lev. 12:3; Luke 1:59; 2:21; Phil. 3:5 [b][Ex. 12:48, 49]
16 [c]ch. 18:10 [d]ch. 35:11
17 [e]ver. 3 [f]ch. 21:6; Rom. 4:19; [John 8:56]
19 [g]ch. 18:10; 21:2; Gal. 4:23, 28 [h]ch. 21:3
20 [i]ch. 16:10 [j]See ch. 25:12-16 [k]ch. 21:13, 18

creation mandate (i.e., Abraham is "another Adam," a covenant representative). Through this covenant the negative effects of the fall will ultimately be reversed.

17:7 for an everlasting covenant. The covenant will be ongoing in nature, extending from one generation to the next.

17:10–14 These verses introduce circumcision as God's appointed sign of the covenant.

17:10 Circumcision is not a Hebrew invention. For example, it was used in Egypt from very early periods as an act of ritual purity (apparently a requirement for men who would work in an Egyptian temple). Some tomb scenes from as early as the Old Kingdom (c. 2575–2134 B.C.) depict the practice.

17:11 You shall be circumcised in the flesh of your foreskins. Circumcision, which involves cutting off the foreskin of the penis, creates a mark that would not normally be visible to others. The nature of the **sign** suggests that it was intended to focus attention on the importance of Abraham's offspring, the royal line through which blessing would come.

17:12 eight days old. To ensure that the covenant extends to the next generation, all newborn male children are to be circumcised at eight days of age.

17:12–13 All the male members of Abraham's household are to be circumcised. The covenant is not about establishing racial purity, since males who are not Abraham's offspring are included. Nor is it about social status; no distinction is drawn between those born in Abraham's household and those bought with money.

17:14 shall be cut off from his people. Every uncircumcised male was excluded from the benefits of belonging to the covenant. Circumcision distinguished those who believed in the importance of the divine promises to Abraham from those who did not. This created a major theological problem for the early church as more and more Gentiles believed in Jesus Christ as Savior and Lord. While some Jewish believers argued that circumcision was necessary for salvation (see chart, p. 2248), Paul contended that "righteousness" comes through faith and that circumcision of the heart is what matters, not circumcision of the foreskin (see Rom. 2:25–29; 1 Cor. 7:18–19; Gal. 6:15).

17:15–16 The name **Sarai** is changed to an alternative form, **Sarah**; both forms mean "princess." **I will give you a son by her**. God Almighty will overcome Sarah's barrenness and provide a son for Abraham. **kings of peoples**. See note on 17:6.

17:17 laughed and said to himself. Abraham's reaction indicates that he considers God's promise that Sarah will bear a son as, to say the least, highly improbable. They are too old to have children.

17:19 Isaac means "he laughs." The motif of laughter occurs in a number of passages associated with the birth of Isaac. In v. 17 and 18:12–15, Abraham and Sarah, respectively, laugh out of unbelief that a son will be born to them, but there may be an element of incredulous joy in these instances as well. The joy of giving birth to Isaac causes Sarah to laugh (21:6). Cf. Ishmael's laughter (21:9). **I will establish my covenant with him**. Echoing what has been said in 17:7, this verse clarifies that the eternal covenant will be "established" with Isaac, but not Ishmael (see vv. 20–21). Here an important distinction is drawn between those with whom the covenant is "established," and those who may receive particular benefits of the covenant. While Ishmael and the other male members of Abraham's household are circumcised, the continuation of the covenant is linked to a unique line of Abraham's descendants that continues through Isaac (see Introduction: History of Salvation Summary; cf. chart, p. 79). This line eventually leads to Jesus Christ, through whom God's blessing is mediated in a saving way to others.

17:20 Although God favors the yet-to-be-born Isaac over Ishmael, the latter is still blessed by God with the promise that he will become a **great nation** (see 25:12–18).

nation. **21** But [l]I will establish my covenant with Isaac, [m]whom Sarah shall bear to you at
this time next year."
22 When he had finished talking with him, [n]God went up from Abraham. **23** Then Abraham
took Ishmael his son and all those born in his house or bought with his money, every
male among the men of Abraham's house, and he circumcised the flesh of their foreskins
that very day, as God had said to him. **24** Abraham was ninety-nine years old when he
was circumcised in the flesh of his foreskin. **25** And Ishmael his son was thirteen years old
when he was circumcised in the flesh of his foreskin. **26** That very day Abraham and his son
Ishmael were circumcised. **27** And all the men of his house, those born in the house and
those bought with money from a foreigner, were circumcised with him.

18 And the LORD appeared to him by the [o]oaks[1] of Mamre, as he sat at the door of
his tent in the heat of the day. **2** He lifted up his eyes and looked, and behold, three
men were standing in front of him. [p]When he saw them, he ran from the tent door to
meet them and bowed himself to the earth **3** and said, "O Lord,[2] if I have found favor in
your sight, do not pass by your servant. **4** Let a [q]little water be brought, and wash your feet,
and rest yourselves under the tree, **5** while I bring a morsel of bread, that [r]you may refresh
yourselves, and after that you may pass on—[s]since you have come to your servant." So
they said, "Do as you have said." **6** And Abraham went quickly into the tent to Sarah and
said, "Quick! Three seahs[3] of fine flour! Knead it, and make cakes." **7** And Abraham ran to
the herd and took a calf, tender and good, and gave it to a young man, who prepared it
quickly. **8** Then he took curds and milk and the calf that he had prepared, and set it before
them. And he stood by them under the tree while they ate.
9 They said to him, "Where is Sarah your wife?" And he said, "She is [t]in the tent." **10** The
LORD said, "I will surely return to you [u]about this time next year, and [v]Sarah your wife
shall have a son." And Sarah was listening at the tent door behind him. **11** Now [w]Abraham
and Sarah were old, advanced in years. The way of women had ceased to be with Sarah.
12 [x]So Sarah laughed to herself, saying, [y]"After I am worn out, and [z]my lord is old, shall
I have pleasure?" **13** The LORD said to Abraham, "Why did Sarah laugh and say, 'Shall I
indeed bear a child, now that I am old?' **14** [a]Is anything too hard[4] for the LORD? [b]At the
appointed time I will return to you, about this time next year, and Sarah shall have a
son." **15** But Sarah denied it,[5] saying, "I did not laugh," for she was afraid. He said, "No,
but you did laugh."
16 Then the men set out from there, and they looked down toward Sodom. And Abraham

[1] *Or terebinths* [2] *Or My lord* [3] A *seah* was about 7 quarts or 7.3 liters [4] *Or wonderful* [5] *Or acted falsely*

21 [l]ch. 26:2-5 [m]ch. 21:2
22 [n]ch. 35:13

Chapter 18

1 [o]ch. 13:18; 14:13
2 [p]ch. 19:1; [Heb. 13:2]
4 [q]ch. 19:2; 24:32; 43:24; [Luke 7:44; John 13:14]
5 [r]Judg. 19:5; [Ps. 104:15] [s]ch. 19:8; 33:10
9 [t]ch. 24:67
10 [u]ver. 14; 2 Kgs. 4:16 [v]ch. 17:19, 21; 21:2; Cited Rom. 9:9
11 [w]ch. 17:17; Rom. 4:19; Heb. 11:11, 12
12 [x][ch. 17:17] [y][Luke 1:18] [z]1 Pet. 3:6
14 [a]Job 42:2; Jer. 32:17, 27; Zech. 8:6; Matt. 19:26; Luke 1:37 [b]ver. 10

17:23–27 Through repeated references to circumcision, these verses underline the fact that Abraham conscientiously fulfilled God's instructions to him.

18:1–19:29 *The Destruction of Sodom.* Genesis 18–19 forms a unified narrative that divides into a number of distinct episodes, coalescing around the rescue of Lot from the divine destruction of Sodom. There are three main sections: (1) 18:1–15, the Lord appears to Abraham at Mamre; (2) 18:16–33, Abraham intercedes on behalf of Lot's family; and (3) 19:1–29, Lot is rescued from Sodom.

18:1–15 This passage, unlike some other biblical texts that recount divine appearances, provides a detailed description of how the Lord appears to Abraham. In doing so it highlights the generous nature of Abraham as he shows hospitality to three "men." This theme of generous hospitality reappears in ch. 19 in connection with Lot.

18:1 Although 13:18 reports that Abram settled at the **oaks of Mamre** many years earlier, he is still dwelling in a **tent** (cf. Heb. 11:9).

18:2 three men. Abraham's actions suggest that he viewed the men as exceptionally important. **he ran.** In the Middle East, an elderly man of some social standing would not normally respond in this way to visitors. **bowed himself to the earth.** While this may have been a common mode of greeting others (see 19:1), it shows that Abraham regards the visitors as worthy of great respect.

18:3 O Lord. The term here (Hb. *'Adonay*) is a distinctive one for God in the OT (e.g., 20:4). The polite term of respect "my lord" (Hb. *'adoni*) has a slight difference of spelling, affecting the last vowel (e.g., 23:6). The ESV text renders the Hebrew, while the footnote represents the different spelling. If the spelling in the Hebrew text is correct—and there is no reason to doubt it—then Abraham recognizes that one of his visitors is a divine manifestation. This explains Abraham's part in the conversation of 18:22–33.

18:4–5 Although Abraham speaks of a **little water** (v. 4) and a **morsel of bread** (v. 5), he proceeds to prepare a substantial meal.

18:6–8 These verses detail the preparations of the meal, underlining the expense to which Abraham goes in order to cater lavishly to his visitors. **he stood by them.** Abraham does not eat with the men, but like a servant, he waits on them. The events of vv. 2–8 (and 19:1–3) are probably alluded to in Heb. 13:2.

18:9–15 These verses center on Sarah and the promise that she will have a son in about 12 months.

18:11 The way of women had ceased to be with Sarah. Focusing on Sarah's age, this comment underlines that she has now ceased to have menstrual cycles, indicating that her reproductive years have ended.

18:12–15 So Sarah laughed to herself. Given her personal circumstances, Sarah laughs in disbelief at the idea of bearing a son to Abraham. Her reaction mirrors her husband's in 17:17. Although Sarah was hidden from the men, her response does not go unnoticed by the Lord, who asks, **Is anything too hard for the LORD?** Despite Sarah's negative situation, she still honors Abraham by using a title of dignity and respect: **my lord.** First Peter 3:6 notes this as indicating her pattern of submitting to and obeying her husband.

18:16–33 In this section the prospect of Sodom's destruction is revealed by the Lord to Abraham. Out of concern for Lot, Abraham intercedes with God regarding his nephew and his family. The ensuing conversation underlines

went with them to set them on their way. 17 The LORD said, [c]"Shall I hide from Abraham
what I am about to do, 18 seeing that Abraham shall surely become a great and mighty
nation, and all the nations of the earth shall be [d]blessed in him? 19 For I have [e]chosen[1] him,
that he may command his children and his household after him to keep the way of the
LORD by doing righteousness and justice, so that the LORD may bring to Abraham what
he has promised him." 20 Then the LORD said, "Because [f]the outcry against Sodom and
Gomorrah is great and their sin is very grave, 21 [g]I will go down to see whether they have
done altogether[2] according to the outcry that has come to me. And if not, [h]I will know."

Abraham Intercedes for Sodom

22 [i]So the men turned from there and went toward Sodom, but Abraham [j]still stood
before the LORD. 23 Then Abraham drew near and said, [k]"Will you indeed sweep away the
righteous with the wicked? 24 Suppose there are fifty righteous within the city. Will you
then sweep away the place and not spare it for the fifty righteous who are in it? 25 Far be
it from you to do such a thing, to put the righteous to death with the wicked, [l]so that the
righteous fare as the wicked! Far be that from you! [m]Shall not the Judge of all the earth
do what is just?" 26 And the LORD said, [n]"If I find at Sodom fifty righteous in the city, I will
spare the whole place for their sake."

27 Abraham answered and said, [o]"Behold, I have undertaken to speak to the Lord, I who
am but dust and ashes. 28 Suppose five of the fifty righteous are lacking. Will you destroy
the whole city for lack of five?" And he said, "I will not destroy it if I find forty-five there."
29 Again he spoke to him and said, "Suppose forty are found there." He answered, "For the
sake of forty I will not do it." 30 Then he said, "Oh let not the Lord be angry, and I will speak.
Suppose thirty are found there." He answered, "I will not do it, if I find thirty there." 31 He
said, "Behold, I have undertaken to speak to the Lord. Suppose twenty are found there."
He answered, "For the sake of twenty I will not destroy it." 32 Then he said, [p]"Oh let not
the Lord be angry, and I will speak again but this once. Suppose ten are found there." He
answered, "For the sake of ten I will not destroy it." 33 And the LORD went his way, when
he had finished speaking to Abraham, and Abraham returned to his place.

[1] Hebrew *known* [2] *Or they deserve destruction; Hebrew they have made a complete end*

17 [c][Ps. 25:14; Amos 3:7; John 15:15]
18 [d]ch. 12:3; 22:18; 26:4; Acts 3:25; Gal. 3:8
19 [e][Amos 3:2]
20 [f]ch. 4:10; 19:13; [Isa. 3:9; Ezek. 16:49, 50; James 5:4]
21 [g]ch. 11:5, 7; Ex. 3:8 [h]Josh. 22:22
22 [i]ver. 16; ch. 19:1 [j]ver. 1; [Ps. 106:23; Jer. 18:20]
23 [k]ch. 20:4; Num. 16:22; 2 Sam. 24:17
25 [l][Job 8:20] [m]Deut. 32:4; Job 8:3; 34:10; Rom. 3:5, 6
26 [n]Jer. 5:1; Ezek. 22:30; [Isa. 65:8]
27 [o][Luke 18:1]
32 [p]Judg. 6:39

that the destruction of Sodom and the other cities of the plain is fully justified because of the inhabitants' overwhelming wickedness (see also 13:13). Had there been as few as 10 righteous people in Sodom, the city would have been spared. Abraham's intercession for the Gentile cities of Sodom and Gomorrah is in line with his calling to be the vehicle of blessing to the whole world. See map below.

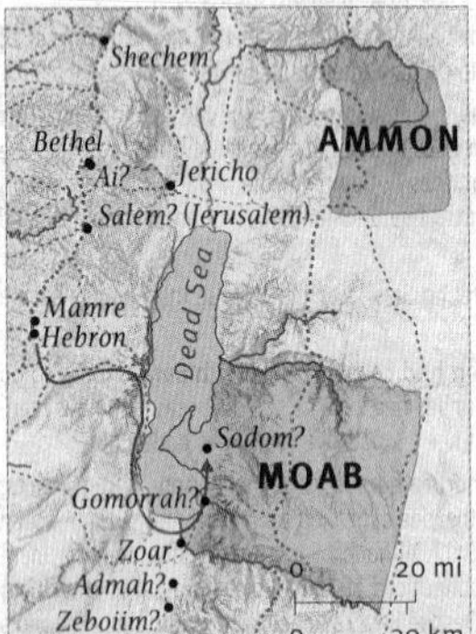

The Destruction of Sodom and Gomorrah
c. 2067/1901 B.C.
At Abraham's request, the Lord spared Lot and his family from the destruction that came upon Sodom and Gomorrah. Afterwards, Lot's two daughters feared that their isolation would result in the end of their family line and they plotted to get their father drunk in order that they might conceive children by him. Each daughter bore a son, from whom the Moabites and the Ammonites were descendants.

18:17–19 God chooses to disclose to Abraham what he is **about to do** (v. 17), on the grounds that Abraham has a unique role to fulfill regarding his own descendants and **all the nations of the earth** (v. 18).

18:21 I will go down to see. These words reveal that the decision to destroy the cities of the plain was undertaken with careful scrutiny of the evidence. This remark should not be interpreted as indicating limited knowledge on the part of God, any more than do the similar and ironic words in 11:5. All that is implied is God's direct attention to the matter.

18:23–25 Abraham's response to God's revelation is probably prompted by his concern for Lot, although Lot is not mentioned specifically. But the main issue for Abraham is, will God destroy the righteous alongside the wicked? Knowing that God must be true to his nature, Abraham poses the question, **Shall not the Judge of all the earth do what is just?**

18:26–33 As Abraham engages with God on the fate of the righteous in Sodom, different scenarios are presented whereby the hypothetical number of righteous in the city is gradually reduced from 50 to 10 (vv. 26–32). God eventually affirms that **for the sake of ten I will not destroy it** (v. 32). The principle has been established that God will not punish the righteous along with the wicked. As the next chapter reveals, only Lot and two of his children are actually rescued from the destruction of Sodom.

19:1–29 Following the events recorded in ch. 18, this passage underscores the reason for Sodom's destruction. The men of Sodom are contrasted with Lot, who seeks to protect the two "visitors" from being sexually molested. Lot's hospitality toward the two men parallels that of Abraham.

19:1–3 The two angels. From the context, these are the two men who accompanied the Lord in ch. 18, but subsequently separated from him (see 18:22). **Lot was sitting in the gate of Sodom**. The opening scene parallels the start of ch. 18, although the setting is now urban rather than rural. Subtle differences in the reporting of these parallel events may be significant.

God Rescues Lot

19 The [q]two angels came to Sodom in the evening, and Lot was sitting in the gate of
Sodom. When Lot saw them, he rose to meet them and bowed himself with his
face to the earth 2 and said, "My lords, [r]please turn aside to your servant's house and spend
the night [s]and wash your feet. Then you may rise up early and go on your way." They
said, [t]"No; we will spend the night in the town square." 3 But he pressed them strongly;
so they turned aside to him and entered his house. And he made them a feast and baked
unleavened bread, and they ate.
4 But before they lay down, the men of the city, the men of Sodom, both young and old,
all the people to the last man, surrounded the house. 5 [u]And they called to Lot, "Where
are the men who came to you tonight? [v]Bring them out to us, that we [w]may know them."
6 Lot went out to the men at the entrance, shut the door after him, 7 and said, "I beg you,
my brothers, do not act so wickedly. 8 [x]Behold, I have two daughters who have not known
any man. Let me bring them out to you, and do to them as you please. Only do nothing to
these men, for they have come under the shelter of my roof." 9 But they said, "Stand back!"
And they said, "This fellow [y]came to sojourn, and [z]he has become the judge! Now we will
deal worse with you than with them." Then they pressed hard against the man Lot, and
drew near to break the door down. 10 But the men reached out their hands and brought Lot
into the house with them and shut the door. 11 And they struck with [a]blindness the men
who were at the entrance of the house, both small and great, so that they wore themselves
out groping for the door.
12 Then the men said to Lot, "Have you anyone else here? Sons-in-law, sons, daughters,
or anyone you have in the city, [b]bring them out of the place. 13 For we are about to destroy
this place, [c]because the outcry against its people has become great before the LORD, and
the LORD has sent us to destroy it." 14 So Lot went out and said to his sons-in-law, who were
to marry his daughters, [d]"Up! Get out of this place, for the LORD is about to destroy the
city." But he seemed to his sons-in-law to be jesting.
15 As morning dawned, the angels urged Lot, saying, "Up! Take your wife and your two
daughters who are here, lest you be swept away in the punishment of the city." 16 But he
lingered. So the men seized him and his wife and his two daughters by the hand, [e]the LORD
being merciful to him, and they brought him out and set him outside the city. 17 And as
they brought them out, one said, "Escape for your life. [f]Do not look back or stop anywhere
in the [g]valley. Escape to the hills, lest you be swept away." 18 And Lot said to them, "Oh, no,
my lords. 19 Behold, your servant has found favor in your sight, and you have shown me
great kindness in saving my life. But I cannot escape to the hills, lest the disaster overtake
me and I die. 20 Behold, this city is near enough to flee to, and it is a little one. Let me escape
there—is it not a little one?—and my life will be saved!" 21 He said to him, "Behold, I grant
you this favor also, that I will not overthrow the city of which you have spoken. 22 Escape

Chapter 19
1 [q]ch. 18:22
2 [r]Heb. 13:2; [Judg. 4:18] [s]See ch. 18:4 [t][Luke 24:28]
5 [u]Isa. 3:9; [ch. 13:13] [v]Judg. 19:22 [w]Rom. 1:24, 27; Jude 7
8 [x][Judg. 19:24]
9 [y]ch. 13:12 [z]Ex. 2:14
11 [a][2 Kgs. 6:18; Acts 13:11]
12 [b]2 Pet. 2:7, 9; [Rev. 18:4, 5]
13 [c]ch. 18:20
14 [d]Num. 16:21, 26, 45; Jer. 51:6
16 [e][Ps. 34:22]
17 [f]ver. 26; [Matt. 24:16-18] [g]ch. 13:10

Like Abraham, Lot greets the two men by bowing before them and offering them hospitality. Since it is evening, he invites them to **spend the night** in his house. Lot, like Abraham, also provides a meal for the visitors, and there is no report of his wife assisting. **Unleavened bread** implies that it was baked in haste. By resembling Abraham, Lot demonstrates that he is righteous, unlike the men of Sodom (a theme developed in 2 Pet. 2:7–8).

19:4 the men of the city. Every male in Sodom, **both young and old**, was involved in the assault on the two visitors. They had become a gang seeking an orgy of rape.

19:5 that we may know them. In Hebrew the verb "to know" (Hb. *yada'*) sometimes denotes sexual intercourse (e.g., 4:1, 17, 25; 19:8; cf. Judg. 19:22). The context implies that the men of Sodom intend to have homosexual relations with the two visitors, hence the origin of the term "sodomy." Lot's earlier insistence (Gen. 19:3) that the visitors should not spend the night in the square indicates that he feared for their safety. By acting so wickedly against defenseless strangers, the entire community invites divine punishment.

19:6–9 Lot's readiness to protect the two men from the mob surrounding his house is commendable. In desperation he offers his two unmarried **daughters** as substitutes—a shocking, cowardly, and inexcusable act (even if he intended this only as a bluff, or expected the offer to be rejected). The reaction of the crowd only confirms the truly evil nature of their intentions.

19:9 The crowd's hostility is now directed at Lot. While he addresses them as "brothers" (v. 7), they see him and resent him as a foreigner who **has become the judge**.

19:10–11 Having failed to persuade the mob, Lot himself needs to be rescued. The angels strike blind the men nearest the door of Lot's house.

19:12–14 The angels announce to Lot the imminent destruction of the city and instruct him to warn his relatives. His sons-in-law, however, treat Lot's words as a joke.

19:16 he lingered. Even Lot is slow to grasp the seriousness of the situation. Of necessity, in a display of divine mercy, the men physically pull Lot and his family out of the city.

19:17–23 Since the entire valley will be destroyed, Lot is told to **escape to the hills**. He pleads, however, to be permitted to take refuge in a small city in the valley. His request is granted, a further indicator of God's mercy in the context of extensive judgment.

there quickly, for I can do nothing till you arrive there." Therefore the name of the city was called [h]Zoar.[1]

God Destroys Sodom

23 The sun had risen on the earth when Lot came to Zoar. 24 Then [i]the LORD rained on Sodom and Gomorrah sulfur and fire from the LORD out of heaven. 25 And he overthrew those cities, and all the valley, and all the inhabitants of the cities, and what grew on the ground. 26 But Lot's wife, behind him, looked back, and she became [j]a pillar of salt.

27 And Abraham went early in the morning to the place where he had [k]stood before the LORD. 28 And he looked down toward Sodom and Gomorrah and toward all the land of the valley, and he looked and, behold, the smoke of the land went up like the smoke of a furnace.

29 So it was that, when God destroyed the cities of the valley, God [l]remembered Abraham and sent Lot out of the midst of the overthrow when he overthrew the cities in which Lot had lived.

Lot and His Daughters

30 Now Lot went up out of Zoar and [m]lived in the hills with his two daughters, for he was afraid to live in Zoar. So he lived in a cave with his two daughters. 31 And the firstborn said to the younger, "Our father is old, and there is not a man on earth to come in to us after the manner of all the earth. 32 Come, let us make our father drink wine, and we will lie with him, that we may preserve offspring from our father." 33 So they made their father drink wine that night. And the firstborn went in and lay with her father. He did not know when she lay down or when she arose.

34 The next day, the firstborn said to the younger, "Behold, I lay last night with my father. Let us make him drink wine tonight also. Then you go in and lie with him, that we may preserve offspring from our father." 35 So they made their father drink wine that night also. And the younger arose and lay with him, and he did not know when she lay down or when she arose. 36 Thus both the daughters of Lot became pregnant by their father. 37 The firstborn bore a son and called his name Moab.[2] [n]He is the father of the Moabites to this day. 38 The younger also bore a son and called his name Ben-ammi.[3] [o]He is the father of the Ammonites to this day.

Abraham and Abimelech

20 From there Abraham journeyed toward the territory of the Negeb and lived between [p]Kadesh and Shur; and he [q]sojourned in [r]Gerar. 2 And Abraham said of Sarah his wife, [s]"She is my sister." And Abimelech king of Gerar sent and took Sarah. 3 [t]But God

[1] *Zoar* means *little* [2] *Moab* sounds like the Hebrew for *from father* [3] *Ben-ammi* means *son of my people*

22 [h]ch. 14:2
24 [i]Deut. 29:23; Jer. 20:16; 50:40; Lam. 4:6; Amos 4:11; Zeph. 2:9; Luke 17:29; 2 Pet. 2:6
26 [j]Luke 17:32
27 [k]ch. 18:22
29 [l]See ch. 8:1
30 [m]ver. 17, 19
37 [n]Deut. 2:9
38 [o]Deut. 2:19

Chapter 20

1 [p]ch. 16:7, 14 [q]ch. 26:3 [r]ch. 26:6
2 [s]See ch. 12:13-20; 26:7-11
3 [t]Ps. 105:14

19:24–25 the LORD rained on Sodom and Gomorrah sulfur and fire from the LORD out of heaven (v. 24). These words emphasize the divine nature of the punishment, the consequence of which is the total destruction of all the inhabitants of Sodom and Gomorrah and all the vegetation (v. 25). The theme of universal destruction echoes the flood story. This judgment on Sodom and Gomorrah, the flood of chs. 6–9, and the later destruction of the Canaanites when the people of Israel entered the Promised Land (Deut. 20:16–18) all vividly demonstrate God's righteous wrath against sin, his mercy in rescuing the godly from destruction, and the certainty of the final judgment to come (cf. 2 Pet. 2:4–10).

19:26 Lot's wife disregards the angel's instruction not to look back (v. 17) and is transformed into a **pillar of salt**, engulfed perhaps in the fiery matter raining in molten lumps from the sky.

19:27–29 The narrative jumps away from Lot to focus briefly on Abraham, reminding the reader of his intercession for Lot and his family (18:20–33).

19:30–38 *Lot's Relationship with His Daughters.* The last unsavory episode in the life of Lot describes how he becomes the father of the Moabites and Ammonites. It has a number of parallels with the last episode of the flood story (9:20–27).

19:30 Although Lot had asked to escape to **Zoar** (vv. 20, 22), the destruction of the valley fills him with such fear that he leaves the city and moves away to live **in the hills**. There he and his **daughters** inhabit a **cave**. Archaeological surveys have revealed that caves around the Dead Sea often served as places of refuge.

19:31–36 Lot's two daughters fear that the isolated location chosen by their father will prevent them from having husbands. Having lost everything else, Lot may have wished to protect his daughters. They, however, devise a plan whereby they will have intercourse with their father in order to have children. Consequently, Lot is manipulated by his daughters, who make him drunk. Ironically, although they have intercourse with him on consecutive nights, Lot has no knowledge of this taking place.

19:37–38 This unseemly episode explains the origin of the **Moabites** and **Ammonites**.

20:1–18 *Abimelech Takes Sarah into His Harem.* Abimelech's actions place in jeopardy the fulfillment of God's promise to Abraham that Sarah will bear him a son. Closely resembling the earlier taking of Sarah by Pharaoh (12:10–20), this account presupposes the reader's knowledge of that event.

20:1 No specific reason is given for Abraham's relocation to **Gerar**, in the northern Negeb. Abraham and Sarah are unknown to the inhabitants of the region.

20:2 She is my sister. This comment presupposes that the reader is familiar with 12:11–13, which explains the rationale behind Abraham's words. Evidently Sarah looked much younger than her real age. **Abimelech king of Gerar**. Abimelech, which means "my father is king," appears to have been

3 [u]Job 33:15, 16; Matt. 1:20; 2:12
4 [v]ch. 18:23; [1 Chr. 21:17]
6 [w]ch. 39:9; Ps. 51:4
7 [x]1 Sam. 7:5; Job 42:8 [y][Num. 16:32, 33]
11 [z]Prov. 16:6 [a]ch. 12:12; 26:7
12 [b][ch. 11:29]
13 [c]ch. 12:1 [d]ch. 12:13
14 [e]ch. 12:16
15 [f]ch. 13:9; 34:10
16 [g][ver. 5] [h][ch. 24:65]
17 [i][James 5:16]
18 [j][ch. 12:17]

Chapter 21
1 [k]1 Sam. 2:21 [l]ch. 17:19; 18:10, 14
2 [m]Heb. 11:11; [Gal. 4:22] [n]ch. 17:21
3 [o]ch. 17:19
4 [p]Acts 7:8

came to Abimelech [u]in a dream by night and said to him, "Behold, you are a dead man
because of the woman whom you have taken, for she is a man's wife." **4** Now Abimelech
had not approached her. So he said, [v]"Lord, will you kill an innocent people? **5** Did he
not himself say to me, 'She is my sister'? And she herself said, 'He is my brother.' In the
integrity of my heart and the innocence of my hands I have done this." **6** Then God said
to him in the dream, "Yes, I know that you have done this in the integrity of your heart,
and it was I who kept you from sinning [w]against me. Therefore I did not let you touch
her. **7** Now then, return the man's wife, [x]for he is a prophet, so that he will pray for you,
and you shall live. But if you do not return her, know that you shall surely die, you [y]and
all who are yours."

8 So Abimelech rose early in the morning and called all his servants and told them all
these things. And the men were very much afraid. **9** Then Abimelech called Abraham and
said to him, "What have you done to us? And how have I sinned against you, that you have
brought on me and my kingdom a great sin? You have done to me things that ought not to
be done." **10** And Abimelech said to Abraham, "What did you see, that you did this thing?"
11 Abraham said, "I did it because I thought, [z]'There is no fear of God at all in this place, and
[a]they will kill me because of my wife.' **12** Besides, [b]she is indeed my sister, the daughter of
my father though not the daughter of my mother, and she became my wife. **13** And when
[c]God caused me to wander from my father's house, I said to her, 'This is the kindness you
must do me: at every place to which we come, [d]say of me, "He is my brother."'"

14 Then Abimelech [e]took sheep and oxen, and male servants and female servants, and
gave them to Abraham, and returned Sarah his wife to him. **15** And Abimelech said, "Behold,
[f]my land is before you; dwell where it pleases you." **16** To Sarah he said, "Behold, I have given
[g]your brother a thousand pieces of silver. It is [h]a sign of your innocence in the eyes of all[1]
who are with you, and before everyone you are vindicated." **17** Then [i]Abraham prayed to
God, and God healed Abimelech, and also healed his wife and female slaves so that they
bore children. **18** For the LORD [j]had closed all the wombs of the house of Abimelech because
of Sarah, Abraham's wife.

The Birth of Isaac

21 The LORD [k]visited Sarah as he had said, and the LORD did to Sarah [l]as he had promised. **2** And Sarah [m]conceived and bore Abraham a son in his old age [n]at the time
of which God had spoken to him. **3** Abraham called the name of his son who was born to
him, whom Sarah bore him, [o]Isaac.[2] **4** And Abraham [p]circumcised his son Isaac when he

[1] Hebrew *It is a covering of eyes for all* [2] *Isaac* means *he laughs*

a common royal name. The same name is mentioned in ch. 26 (see note on 26:1–2) and is given to later biblical figures.

20:3–6 But God came to Abimelech. God intervenes to ensure that Abimelech does not touch Sarah. In contrast to 12:10–20, this episode emphasizes in a variety of ways the important point that Sarah has not had intercourse with the king; otherwise, Abimelech could be the father of the son born to Sarah in 21:1–3. **in a dream by night**. Throughout Genesis dreams are often used as a medium of divine revelation (see 28:12; 31:10–11; 37:5–9; 40:5–8; 41:1).

20:7 Abraham is the first person in the Bible to be designated a **prophet**. In this context, attention is drawn to his ability to intercede on behalf of others, one of the characteristics of a great prophet (Jer. 15:1); cf. his actions in Gen. 18:22–33.

20:9 Abimelech rightly challenges Abraham for deceiving him about the status of Sarah his wife. The term **great sin** sometimes denotes adultery.

20:11 There is no fear of God at all in this place. Abraham's response betrays both his lack of faith in God and his misjudgment of the people of Gerar. The whole episode reveals that the king and his servants were God-fearing (see vv. 5, 8, 16).

20:12–13 Besides, she is indeed my sister. Abraham's explanation, which is a half-truth, does not excuse his behavior. **at every place to which we come**. Abraham regularly resorted to this wife-sister ruse (v. 12) for his own self-protection. Genesis 12 and 20 reveal that it did not always work. Only God's intervention protects Abraham's relationship with Sarah, a point that should not be lost on the first audience (cf. note on 12:10–20).

20:14–16 Abimelech's generosity, on top of his innocence, contrasts sharply with Abraham's self-serving deception regarding the truth about Sarah. The king's actions are a very public affirmation that he has not acted inappropriately toward Sarah, and thus he is not the father of any children she may have.

20:17–18 The healing of **Abimelech** and the restoration of **his wife and female slaves so that they** may once again have **children** underlines God's power over fertility. By noting that these things are restored, the narrator prepares the way for the birth of Isaac (21:1–3). By observing that Abraham prays, the narrative picks up on the theme of God's blessing being mediated through Abraham (see 12:3).

21:1–21 *The Birth of Isaac.* In fulfillment of God's promise, Sarah bears Abraham a son, who is named Isaac. In due course Isaac is confirmed as Abraham's heir, when God instructs Abraham to send Hagar and Ishmael away. While Isaac takes priority over Ishmael, God does not abandon Hagar and her son.

21:1 as he had promised. See 17:16, 19, 21.

21:2 at the time of which God had spoken to him. See 18:10, 14.

21:3 Isaac. The name was announced by God to Abraham in 17:19 (see note for the meaning of the name).

21:4 Isaac is **circumcised** by **Abraham** in fulfillment of God's instructions in 17:12.

was eight days old, [q]as God had commanded him. 5 [r]Abraham was a hundred years old
when his son Isaac was born to him. 6 And Sarah said, [s]"God has made laughter for me;
everyone who hears will laugh over me." 7 And she said, "Who would have said to Abraham
that Sarah would nurse children? [t]Yet I have borne him a son in his old age."

God Protects Hagar and Ishmael

8 And the child grew and was weaned. And Abraham made a great feast on the day that
Isaac was weaned. 9 But Sarah [u]saw the son of Hagar the Egyptian, whom she had borne
to Abraham, [v]laughing.[1] 10 So she said to Abraham, [w]"Cast out this slave woman with her
son, for the son of this slave woman shall not be heir with my son Isaac." 11 And the thing
was very displeasing to Abraham on account of his son. 12 But God said to Abraham, "Be
not displeased because of the boy and because of your slave woman. Whatever Sarah says
to you, do as she tells you, for [x]through Isaac shall your offspring be named. 13 And I will
make [y]a nation of the son of the slave woman also, because he is your offspring." 14 So
Abraham rose early in the morning and took bread and a skin of water and gave it to Hagar,
putting it on her shoulder, along with the child, and sent her away. And she departed and
wandered in the wilderness of [z]Beersheba.

15 When the water in the skin was gone, she put the child under one of the bushes. 16 Then
she went and sat down opposite him a good way off, about the distance of a bowshot, for
she said, "Let me not look on the death of the child." And as she sat opposite him, she lifted
up her voice and wept. 17 And God heard the voice of the boy, and the angel of God called
to Hagar from heaven and said to her, "What troubles you, Hagar? Fear not, for God has
heard the voice of the boy where he is. 18 Up! Lift up the boy, and hold him fast with your
hand, for I will make him into a great nation." 19 Then [a]God opened her eyes, and she saw
a well of water. And she went and filled the skin with water and gave the boy a drink.
20 And God was with the boy, and he grew up. He lived in the wilderness [b]and became an
expert with the bow. 21 He lived in the wilderness of Paran, and his mother took a wife for
him from the land of Egypt.

A Treaty with Abimelech

22 At that time [c]Abimelech and Phicol the commander of his army said to Abraham,
[d]"God is with you in all that you do. 23 Now therefore swear to me here by God that you will
not deal falsely with me or with my descendants or with my posterity, but [e]as I have dealt
kindly with you, so you will deal with me and with the land where you have sojourned."
24 And Abraham said, "I will swear."

25 When Abraham reproved Abimelech about a well of water that Abimelech's servants

[1] Possibly *laughing in mockery*

4 [q]ch. 17:10, 12
5 [r]ch. 17:1, 17; Rom. 4:19
6 [s][Isa. 54:1; Gal. 4:27]
7 [t]ch. 18:11, 12
9 [u]ch. 16:1, 15 [v][Gal. 4:29]
10 [w]Cited Gal. 4:30
12 [x]Cited Rom. 9:7; Heb. 11:18
13 [y]ver. 18; ch. 16:10; 17:20
14 [z]ver. 31
19 [a]Num. 22:31; 2 Kgs. 6:17, 18, 20; [Luke 24:16, 31]
20 [b]ch. 16:12
22 [c]ch. 20:2; [ch. 26:1, 26] [d][ch. 26:28]
23 [e]ch. 20:14

21:5–7 These verses underline the unexpected nature of Isaac's birth. Abraham and Sarah are both very old.

21:8 on the day that Isaac was weaned. Isaac was probably two or three years old.

21:9 The Hebrew verb translated **laughing** is ambiguous and may be interpreted as denoting either "mocking" or "playing." The verbal form used here possibly favors "mocking." Galatians 4:29 follows this interpretation. Ishmael was probably making fun of Isaac's role as Abraham's promised son.

21:10 Although Ishmael is Abraham's son, Sarah does not want him to be an **heir** alongside **Isaac**. Paul uses Sarah's words in his "allegory" of the two covenants, Gal. 4:30.

21:11–13 While Abraham is reluctant to send Ishmael away, God reassures him that this is for the best.

21:12 through Isaac shall your offspring be named. Even though Ishmael is older than Isaac, God confirms that Isaac will take priority over Ishmael (see 17:19). The importance of this is picked up in Rom. 9:7 and Heb. 11:18.

21:14 putting it on her shoulder, along with the child. While these words might suggest that Ishmael was placed on Hagar's shoulder, this is hardly likely, since Ishmael is about 16 years old (see 16:16; 21:5, 8) at this time. The last thing Abraham did was to give Ishmael to Hagar, probably after "putting it" (the bread and water) on Hagar's shoulder. The Hebrew term for "child" (Hb. *yeled*) may denote an older teenager; it is used, e.g., of Joseph in 37:30. **wilderness of Beersheba**. Water was difficult to find in this region. Man-made wells appear to have been the main source of water (see 21:30; 26:18–22). On "Beersheba," see note on 21:31.

21:15–16 When the water in the skin is exhausted and no other supply has been found, Hagar weeps in despair.

21:17–18 God's intervention saves **Hagar** and confirms to her that her son will become a **great nation** (v. 18), echoing the promise given to Abraham in v. 13. **God heard the voice of the boy** (v. 17). Although this passage avoids using his personal name, "Ishmael" means "God hears" (see 16:11). Although it was Ishmael's misbehavior that led to the expulsion from Abraham's household, God reaffirms his promise: "I will make him into a great nation" (21:18).

21:21 wilderness of Paran. The central region in northern Sinai.

21:22–34 *Abimelech Makes a Treaty with Abraham.* Acknowledging Abraham's power, Abimelech establishes with him a treaty intended to protect both parties.

21:22–23 Abimelech. See note on 20:2. **God is with you in all that you do**. Abimelech attributes Abraham's success to God.

21:25–30 Before sealing the treaty, Abraham raises the contentious issue of ownership of a **well**. The **covenant** or treaty was designed to prevent conflict

25 [f][ch. 26:15, 18, 20-22]
27 [g]ch. 26:31
31 [h]ch. 26:33
33 [i]ch. 4:26; 12:8 [j]Isa. 40:28; [Ps. 90:2]

Chapter 22

1 [k]1 Cor. 10:13; Heb. 11:17; James 1:12, 13; 1 Pet. 1:6, 7
2 [l]2 Chr. 3:1

[f]had seized, **26** Abimelech said, "I do not know who has done this thing; you did not tell me,
and I have not heard of it until today." **27** So Abraham took sheep and oxen and gave them
to Abimelech, and the two men [g]made a covenant. **28** Abraham set seven ewe lambs of the
flock apart. **29** And Abimelech said to Abraham, "What is the meaning of these seven ewe
lambs that you have set apart?" **30** He said, "These seven ewe lambs you will take from my
hand, that this[1] may be a witness for me that I dug this well." **31** Therefore [h]that place was
called Beersheba,[2] because there both of them swore an oath. **32** So they made a covenant at
Beersheba. Then Abimelech and Phicol the commander of his army rose up and returned
to the land of the Philistines. **33** Abraham planted a tamarisk tree in Beersheba and [i]called
there on the name of the LORD, [j]the Everlasting God. **34** And Abraham sojourned many
days in the land of the Philistines.

The Sacrifice of Isaac

22 After these things [k]God tested Abraham and said to him, "Abraham!" And he said,
"Here I am." **2** He said, "Take your son, your only son Isaac, whom you love, and go
to [l]the land of Moriah, and offer him there as a burnt offering on one of the mountains
of which I shall tell you." **3** So Abraham rose early in the morning, saddled his donkey,
and took two of his young men with him, and his son Isaac. And he cut the wood for the
burnt offering and arose and went to the place of which God had told him. **4** On the third
day Abraham lifted up his eyes and saw the place from afar. **5** Then Abraham said to his
young men, "Stay here with the donkey; I and the boy[3] will go over there and worship and

[1] Or *you* [2] *Beersheba* means *well of seven* or *well of the oath* [3] Or *young man*; also verse 12

between the two parties. The gift of **seven ewe lambs** to Abimelech confirms Abraham's ownership of the well.

21:31 In light of Abraham's gift to Abimelech, the name **Beersheba** probably means "well of seven"; however, given that the Hebrew words for "seven" (*sheba'*) and "oath" (*shebu'ah*) are similar, it could also mean "well of the oath." Perhaps the name was chosen because it embraced both concepts. Given Abraham's seminomadic lifestyle and the need for him to dig a well, no settlement probably existed at this location in his time. When a permanent settlement was later established in this area, the name of the well was given to it (see 26:33). The town of Beersheba, located in the northern Negeb, became famous as marking the southern boundary of Israel (e.g., Judg. 20:1; 1 Sam. 3:20).

21:32 land of the Philistines. The use of the term "Philistines" here is generally taken to be anachronistic, since the name is normally associated with non-Canaanites from the Aegean region who inhabited southwest Canaan from about 1180 B.C. onward—nearly a thousand years after Abraham's time. (In 1 Samuel the Philistines are portrayed as the main opponents of the Israelites.) In light of this, the term may be used here and elsewhere to replace an earlier, obscure term; Genesis contains various examples of such modernizations (see note on Gen. 14:13–16; also Introduction: Author, Title, and Date). Alternatively, archaeological evidence from various sites in Canaan points to the possibility that some people from the Aegean region (esp. Crete and Cyprus) may have already been settled in southwest Canaan. This raises the possibility that Abraham and Isaac (see ch. 26) had dealings with people who came from the same area as the later Philistines.

21:33 Everlasting God (Hb. *'El 'Olam*). In Hebrew *'El* is the common Semitic term for "God," followed by the attribute "of everlastingness" (Hb. *'Olam*). See note on 14:18.

22:1–19 *The Testing of Abraham.* This episode brings to a climax God's ongoing interaction with Abraham, resulting in an important divine oath. The conditional promises of 12:1–3 are now unconditionally guaranteed as a result of Abraham's preparedness to sacrifice his son. Put to the test, Abraham displays remarkable trust in God, especially when the death of Isaac would appear to contradict all that God had promised to Abraham. The passage conveys two truths for its original audience: (1) it shows the kind of faith that Abraham had, and commends it for Israel; and (2) it shows that "substitution" is a part of the "atoning sacrifices" that God will direct Israel to offer (see note on 22:13). This further enables the people of Israel to see their very existence, even in the desert, as part of God's plan, which they must embrace. James 2:21–22 says that by Abraham's works here, his faith (from Gen. 15:6) was "completed," i.e., brought to its full and proper expression. This shows that "justified" in James 2:21 probably has the sense "shown to be righteous," rather than the sense "counted righteous" often found in Paul's writings (see note on James 2:21).

22:1 God tested Abraham. The particular form of the verb "tested" makes this phrase a summary of the whole passage and clarifies the meaning of the events. The genuineness of Abraham's obedience to God is tested. While it is not unknown for God to test individuals, testing must be clearly distinguished from tempting. God does not tempt anyone to do evil (see note on James 1:13); he does, however, test the commitment of people (e.g., Ex. 15:25; 16:4).

22:2 your only son Isaac, whom you love. With the departure of Ishmael from Abraham's household, Isaac had become Abraham's only son. As such, he was held with much affection by his father. **land of Moriah**. According to 2 Chron. 3:1, Solomon constructed the temple on Mount Moriah in Jerusalem. While Genesis 22 does not specify that the sacrifice of Isaac took place at or near Jerusalem, v. 14 possibly implies such a connection. A **burnt offering** involved the entire sacrifice being consumed by fire. The outcome of the incident makes it clear that God never intended the directive to be fulfilled. Thus, taken as a whole (in terms of both the command and the outcome), the incident cannot be seen to conflict with God's moral law. Because this was by far the greatest demand that God could have made of Abraham, it confirmed the depth of the Patriarch's commitment. Abraham was willing to kill his own son, although as the author of Hebrews observes (Heb. 11:17–19), he prepared to do so believing that God was able to bring Isaac back to life again (see note on Gen. 22:5–8).

22:3 Abraham rose early in the morning. Abraham promptly responds to the challenge placed before him.

22:4 On the third day. It requires about two days to travel on foot from Beersheba to Jerusalem, a distance of about 45 miles (72 km) "as the crow flies." Elsewhere, two days also represents the time set aside to prepare for a special encounter with God on the third day (see Ex. 19:11). Perhaps this sets the pattern for the significant "third day" (cf. Matt. 16:21; 1 Cor. 15:4).

22:5–8 I and the boy will . . . come again to you. While Abraham is committed to sacrificing Isaac, he plans to do so in the belief that both of them will return (see Heb. 11:17–19). **God will provide . . . the lamb**. It is unclear whether Abraham is speaking ironically here (Isaac is the "lamb"), or whether he is expressing faith that somehow God will preserve his son. As it turns out, God does provide a substitute for Isaac (see note on Gen. 22:13).

come again to you." 6 And Abraham took the wood of the burnt offering and [m]laid it on
Isaac his son. And he took in his hand the fire and the knife. So they went both of them
together. 7 And Isaac said to his father Abraham, "My father!" And he said, "Here I am, my
son." He said, "Behold, the fire and the wood, but where is the lamb for a burnt offering?"
8 Abraham said, [n]"God will provide for himself the lamb for a burnt offering, my son." So
they went both of them together.
9 When they came to the place of which God had told him, Abraham built the altar there
and laid the wood in order and bound Isaac his son and [o]laid him on the altar, on top of
the wood. 10 Then Abraham reached out his hand and took the knife to slaughter his son.
11 But the angel of the LORD called to him from heaven and said, "Abraham, Abraham!"
And he said, "Here I am." 12 He said, [p]"Do not lay your hand on the boy or do anything
to him, for [q]now I know that you fear God, seeing you have not withheld your son, your
only son, from me." 13 And Abraham lifted up his eyes and looked, and behold, behind
him was a ram, caught in a thicket by his horns. And Abraham went and took the ram
and offered it up as a burnt offering instead of his son. 14 So Abraham called the name of
that place, [r]"The LORD will provide";[1] as it is said to this day, "On the mount of the LORD
it shall be provided."[2]
15 And the angel of the LORD called to Abraham a second time from heaven 16 and said,
[s]"By myself I have sworn, declares the LORD, because you have done this and have not
withheld your son, your only son, 17 I will surely bless you, and I will surely multiply your
offspring [t]as the stars of heaven and [u]as the sand that is on the seashore. And your offspring shall possess [v]the gate of his[3] enemies, 18 and [w]in your offspring shall all the nations
of the earth be blessed, [x]because you have obeyed my voice." 19 So Abraham returned to
his young men, and they arose and went together to [y]Beersheba. And Abraham lived at
[y]Beersheba.
20 Now after these things it was told to Abraham, "Behold, [z]Milcah also has borne children to your brother Nahor: 21 [a]Uz his firstborn, [b]Buz his brother, Kemuel the father of
Aram, 22 Chesed, Hazo, Pildash, Jidlaph, and Bethuel." 23 ([c]Bethuel fathered Rebekah.) These
eight Milcah bore to Nahor, Abraham's brother. 24 Moreover, his concubine, whose name
was Reumah, bore Tebah, Gaham, Tahash, and Maacah.

[1] *Or will see* [2] *Or he will be seen* [3] *Or their*

6 [m][John 19:17]
8 [n][John 1:29, 36; 1 Pet. 1:19; Rev. 5:12]
9 [o]Heb. 11:17; James 2:21
12 [p][Mic. 6:7, 8] [q][ch. 26:5]
14 [r]ver. 8
16 [s]Ps. 105:9; Luke 1:73; Heb. 6:13
17 [t]Jer. 33:22; See ch. 15:5 [u]See ch. 13:16 [v]ch. 24:60; Ps. 127:5
18 [w]ch. 12:3; 18:18; 26:4; Gal. 3:8; Cited Acts 3:25 [x]ver. 3; ch. 26:5
19 [y]ch. 21:31
20 [z]ch. 11:29
21 [a]Job 1:1 [b]Jer. 25:23
23 [c]ch. 24:15

22:11 the angel of the LORD. See note on 16:7. The repetition of the name **Abraham, Abraham** underscores the urgency of the intervention (cf. 22:1).

22:12 now I know that you fear God. Abraham's action confirms his faithful obedience to God. While Abraham's faith was earlier the means by which God counted him as righteous (15:6), that faith is now "active along with his works," and the faith is "completed by his works" (James 2:21–23), so that his faith resulted in obedience, which is its expected outcome. On God's knowledge, see note on Gen. 18:21.

22:13 behind him was a ram. Although Abraham has passed the test, God provides a ram so that it may be sacrificed as a **burnt offering**. In Genesis such sacrifices are associated with solemn promises made by God (see 8:20–22). **instead of his son**. The fact that a ram died in the place of Isaac has led many Christian interpreters to see introduced here the principle of substitutionary atonement, which would later become a reality in the substitutionary sacrificial death of Christ on the cross, as "the Lamb of God, who takes away the sin of the world" (John 1:29).

22:14 Echoing Abraham's earlier comment to Isaac in v. 8, the location is named **The LORD will provide**. On the basis of this, the belief developed (**as it is said to this day**) that God would provide the sacrifice necessary to atone for sin. **the mount of the LORD**. This probably denotes the hill on which the temple was later built in Jerusalem (see Isa. 2:3).

22:15–18 The divine oath recorded in these verses should not be overlooked, for it brings to a climax a process that started with the conditional promises made by God to Abraham in 12:1–3. **By myself I have sworn**. The fact that God swears by himself gives to these words a unique authority, assuring Abraham that they will indeed be fulfilled (see Heb. 6:13–18). The oath falls into two parts: whereas the first half focuses on Abraham's many descendants, the second part concentrates on a single descendant who will overcome **his enemies** (Gen. 22:17) and mediate blessing to **all the nations of the earth** (v. 18). Although the second half of the oath is often taken to refer to all of Abraham's descendants, Genesis as a whole is interested in tracing a single unique line of offspring that will eventually bring forth a special King who will rule over the Gentiles (see Introduction: History of Salvation Summary), and the reference to "*his* enemies" points in this direction (see note on 3:15). This is why Paul (Gal. 3:16) can insist on one offspring, who is "Christ" (i.e., the Messiah; cf. Gen. 3:15; 24:60 for "offspring" as a particular descendant). And this explains why Isaac is clearly set apart from Ishmael as Abraham's heir. From the perspective of the whole Bible, this oath to Abraham comes to fulfillment in Jesus Christ (Acts 3:25–26; Gal. 3:16).

22:16–17 because you . . . have not withheld your son, your only son. The central focus of God's words to Abraham is on the way in which Abraham's actions are a vindication of his faith (see Rom. 4:3, 22–23; Gal. 3:6; James 2:23). Many also see an allusion in Rom. 8:32 to this verse.

22:20–24 *Nahor's Children.* Genealogies often demarcate major sections of material in Genesis. These verses, which function like a minor genealogy, divide the main part of the Abraham story (chs. 12–22) from several episodes that serve as an appendix to the life of Abraham: the death and burial of Sarah (ch. 23); the acquisition of a wife for Isaac (ch. 24); and the death of Abraham (25:1–11). The special reference to **Rebekah** in 22:23 anticipates the events of ch. 24 when Abraham sends a servant to Paddan-aram to find a bride for Isaac from among his relatives. **concubine** (22:24). See note on 25:5–6.

23:1–20 *The Death and Burial of Sarah.* As the story of Abraham's life draws to a conclusion, this chapter records how Abraham buys a cave in Hebron to be a burial place for Sarah. By acquiring this plot of land, Abraham not only establishes future rights to it for his family but puts down a marker that his

Chapter 23
2[d]ch. 35:27; Josh. 14:15; Judg. 1:10 [e]ver. 19
4[f]ch. 17:8; 1 Chr. 29:15; Ps. 105:12; Heb. 11:9, 13 [g]Acts 7:5
10[h]ch. 34:20, 24; Ruth 4:1
15[i]Ex. 30:13; Ezek. 45:12
16[j]1 Chr. 21:25; Jer. 32:9; Zech. 11:12
17[k]ch. 25:9; 49:29-32; 50:13
20[l][Ruth 4:7-10; Jer. 32:10-14]

Sarah's Death and Burial

23 Sarah lived 127 years; these were the years of the life of Sarah. **2** And Sarah died at
[d]Kiriath-arba (that is, [e]Hebron) in the land of Canaan, and Abraham went in to
mourn for Sarah and to weep for her. **3** And Abraham rose up from before his dead and said
to the Hittites,[1] **4** [f]"I am a sojourner and foreigner among you; [g]give me property among
you for a burying place, that I may bury my dead out of my sight." **5** The Hittites answered
Abraham, **6** "Hear us, my lord; you are a prince of God[2] among us. Bury your dead in the
choicest of our tombs. None of us will withhold from you his tomb to hinder you from
burying your dead." **7** Abraham rose and bowed to the Hittites, the people of the land. **8** And
he said to them, "If you are willing that I should bury my dead out of my sight, hear me
and entreat for me Ephron the son of Zohar, **9** that he may give me the cave of Machpelah,
which he owns; it is at the end of his field. For the full price let him give it to me in your
presence as property for a burying place."
10 Now Ephron was sitting among the Hittites, and Ephron the Hittite answered Abraham
in the hearing of the Hittites, of all who [h]went in at the gate of his city, **11** "No, my lord,
hear me: I give you the field, and I give you the cave that is in it. In the sight of the sons
of my people I give it to you. Bury your dead." **12** Then Abraham bowed down before the
people of the land. **13** And he said to Ephron in the hearing of the people of the land, "But
if you will, hear me: I give the price of the field. Accept it from me, that I may bury my dead
there." **14** Ephron answered Abraham, **15** "My lord, listen to me: a piece of land worth four
hundred [i]shekels[3] of silver, what is that between you and me? Bury your dead." **16** Abraham
listened to Ephron, and Abraham [j]weighed out for Ephron the silver that he had named
in the hearing of the Hittites, four hundred shekels of silver, according to the weights
current among the merchants.
17 So [k]the field of Ephron in Machpelah, which was to the east of Mamre, the field with
the cave that was in it and all the trees that were in the field, throughout its whole area,
was made over **18** to Abraham as a possession in the presence of the Hittites, before all who
went in at the gate of his city. **19** After this, Abraham buried Sarah his wife in the cave of
the field of Machpelah east of Mamre (that is, Hebron) in the land of Canaan. **20** The field
and the cave that is in it [l]were made over to Abraham as property for a burying place by
the Hittites.

[1] Hebrew *sons of Heth;* also verses 5, 7, 10, 16, 18, 20 [2] Or *a mighty prince* [3] A *shekel* was about 2/5 ounce or 11 grams

descendants are to be associated with the land of Canaan, as God had already promised (12:7; 13:14–17; 15:18–21).

23:2 Kiriath-arba, which means "town of four" (see Josh. 14:15), was later known as **Hebron** (see Judg. 1:10, 20).

23:3 Hittites. The designation "Hittite" was used in the ancient Near East to refer to at least three different groups of people. Those mentioned in Genesis are probably to be distinguished from the Hittites associated with Anatolia and Syria. Presumably Abraham addressed the leaders of the Hittites who were assembled at the gate of Hebron. The city gate was commonly the location where public decisions were formally made and transactions between individuals were ratified (see Ruth 4:1–11).

23:4 a sojourner and foreigner among you. Abraham's description of himself emphasizes his immigrant status. Even after 62 years of seminomadic existence in Canaan, Abraham has no permanent location to call his own. This is all the more noteworthy in light of God's repeated promises to Abraham that his descendants will possess all the land of Canaan. The author of Hebrews develops the idea that Abraham chose to go on living in tents because he was looking for a city "whose designer and builder is God" (Heb. 11:9–10).

23:6 In contrast to Abraham's own assessment of his status, the Hittites recognize his special relationship with God and accord him the title **prince of God**. Abraham was probably well known to the inhabitants of Hebron, for he had a long association with this location (see 13:18). Out of deep respect for Abraham, they generously offer him the use of one of the **choicest** of their own **tombs** for the burial of Sarah.

23:8–10 Acknowledging their generosity, Abraham politely asks the Hittites to permit **Ephron the son of Zohar** (v. 8) to sell to him at full value **the cave of Machpelah** (v. 9) as a burial place. Although Ephron is present when these discussions take place at the city gate (v. 10), Abraham first seeks permission from the Hittite population as a whole. This may have been necessary either because Abraham himself was not a Hittite or because the transfer of property from one individual to another required the involvement of a third party. According to tradition, the cave of Machpelah is located beneath the present Mosque of Abraham in Hebron.

23:11–16 Although Ephron's initial response is to offer the field and cave to Abraham for free, this may not have been his true intention, because the second time he offers it, he also casually injects what he would consider a fair price (v. 15). Abraham insists that he will pay the full value of the property. It is important that Abraham buy the property because an actual sale ensures that Abraham has full legal title to the burial plot. When Ephron sets the price at **four hundred shekels of silver** (v. 15), Abraham willingly accepts and weighs out the amount. Since the weight of a shekel could vary (see the comment **according to the weights current among the merchants**, v. 16), it is impossible to be certain about the precise value of the field and cave. It is often suggested, on the basis of comparisons with 1 Kings 16:24 and Jer. 32:9, that this was a high price to pay, but one cannot be sure. (This type of purchase contract for the cave of Machpelah was quite similar to legal texts from the period found among the Babylonians and the Anatolian Hittites.)

23:17–19 Mamre. See note on 13:18.

23:20 Abraham's purchase of the **field** and **cave** meant that his descendants would own this land in perpetuity. Abraham, Isaac, Jacob, Rebekah, and Leah would later be laid to rest in this cave.

Isaac and Rebekah

24 Now Abraham was old, well advanced in years. And the LORD [m]had blessed Abraham
in all things. 2 And Abraham said to his servant, [n]the oldest of his household, who
had charge of all that he had, [o]"Put your hand under my thigh, 3 that I may make you
swear by the LORD, the God of heaven and God of the earth, that [p]you will not take a wife
for my son from the daughters of the Canaanites, among whom I dwell, 4 [q]but will go to
my country and to my kindred, and take a wife for my son Isaac." 5 The servant said to
him, "Perhaps the woman may not be willing to follow me to this land. Must I then take
your son back to the land from which you came?" 6 Abraham said to him, "See to it that
you do not take my son back there. 7 The LORD, the God of heaven, [r]who took me from
my father's house and from the land of my kindred, and who spoke to me and swore to
me, [s]'To your offspring I will give this land,' [t]he will send his angel before you, and you
shall take a wife for my son from there. 8 But if the woman is not willing to follow you,
then [u]you will be free from this oath of mine; only you must not take my son back there."
9 So the servant [v]put his hand under the thigh of Abraham his master and swore to him
concerning this matter.
10 Then the servant took ten of his master's camels and departed, taking all sorts of

Chapter 24

1 [m]ver. 35; ch. 13:2
2 [n][ch. 15:2] [o]ver. 9; ch. 47:29
3 [p]ch. 26:34, 35; 27:46; Deut. 7:3; [2 Cor. 6:14]
4 [q][ch. 28:2]
7 [r]ch. 12:1 [s]See ch. 12:7 [t]Ex. 23:20, 23; 33:2; [Heb. 1:14]
8 [u]See Josh. 2:17-20
9 [v]ver. 2

24:1–67 *A Wife for Isaac.* The account of how Rebekah becomes Isaac's wife forms one of the longest episodes in the book of Genesis. Displaying exceptional narrative skill, the author highlights how God controls events so that, after a long journey from Canaan to northern Mesopotamia, Abraham's servant is guided to Rebekah. (The journey from Hebron, where Sarah was buried [23:19], to Nahor [in the district of Haran], where Rebekah lived [24:10], was approximately 550 miles or 900 km along ancient routes, a journey that would have taken Abraham's servant approximately 21 days to travel; a man traveling alone could go an average of 25 miles a day or so, faster than a caravan, whose travel speed would be about 17–23 miles per day.) See map to the left. Then, like Abraham, Rebekah must leave her family and country in an act of faith in order to journey to Canaan and marry Isaac, whom she has never met. Genesis's first audience would marvel at how God orchestrated the servant's faithfulness, Rebekah's positive response, and some unlikely events (e.g., v. 15) to bring about the marriage; they would be better able to see their very existence as the result of God's guiding hand.

Journeys to Paddan-aram

c. 2026/1860 B.C.

When Isaac was 40 years old, Abraham sent his eldest servant back to Paddan-aram, the land of his relatives, to obtain a wife for Isaac. The servant found Rebekah, the granddaughter of Abraham's brother Nahor, and brought her back to Isaac, who was living in the Negeb. Later, Jacob would make this same journey as he fled from his brother Esau.

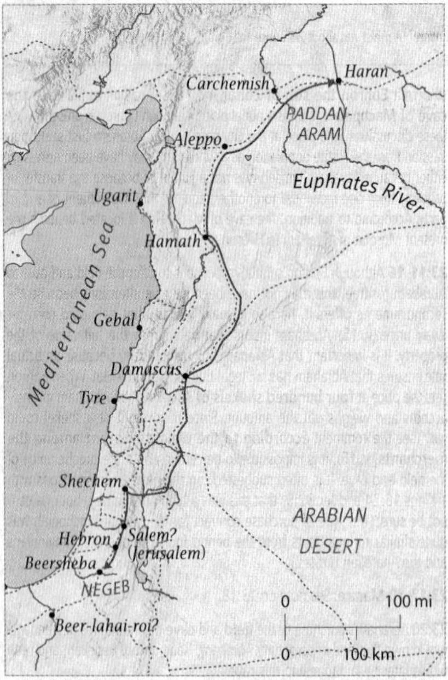

24:1 The observation that **the LORD had blessed Abraham in all things** confirms the special relationship between God and Abraham.

24:2–6 Abraham is deeply concerned that Isaac should not marry a Canaanite; he fears that this will draw him away from worshiping the Lord. From ch. 9 onward, the **Canaanites** are frequently portrayed as being wicked (see notes on 9:24–27; 10:6–20; 13:11–13). Abraham entrusts the important task of finding a **wife** for Isaac to his most reliable servant, **the oldest of his household, who had charge of all that he had** (24:2). To place his servant under oath, Abraham instructs him to **put your hand under my thigh** (v. 2). On the significance of this action, see note on v. 9. In spite of having left Haran in northern Mesopotamia almost a hundred years earlier, Abraham refers to it as **my country** (v. 4). He hopes that a wife may be found for Isaac from among his relatives there. Although Abraham insists that Isaac's wife should come from his **kindred** in Mesopotamia (v. 4), he emphasizes that Isaac himself should not return there (v. 6). Isaac's future is to be in Canaan, for God has promised this land to Abraham's descendants. Later, Abraham's grandson Jacob will get wives from the same region (29:1–28).

24:9 the servant put his hand under the thigh of Abraham. Since striking one's thigh was possibly understood as a sign of remorse and submission (see Jer. 31:19; Ezek. 21:12), the placing of one's hand under the thigh of another may have indicated submission to that person's strength and authority. In any case, by undertaking this action, the servant binds himself to obey Abraham's request.

24:10 camels. See note on 12:16. **Mesopotamia** (lit., "between the rivers") was the Greek title for the entire region between the Euphrates and Tigris Rivers. Here "Mesopotamia" is a translation for the Hebrew expression *'Aram naharayim*, meaning "Aram of the two rivers," an expression that denotes more precisely only the northwestern part of Mesopotamia. The **city of Nahor**, probably to be identified with Nakhur (which is mentioned in ancient texts that were recovered from Mari on the Euphrates), was located near Haran in northern Mesopotamia (see note on 11:31). "Nahor" is also the name of Terah's father (11:25) and Abraham's brother (see 11:26–27; 22:20). The use of the same name for both a city and a person is not unusual; settlements are sometimes named after people, and people are sometimes named after places.

choice gifts from his master; and he arose and went to [w]Mesopotamia[1] to the city of Nahor.
11 And he made the camels kneel down outside the city by the well of water at the time
of evening, the time when [x]women go out to draw water. 12 And he said, "O LORD, [y]God
of my master Abraham, [z]please grant me success today and show steadfast love to my
master Abraham. 13 Behold, [a]I am standing by the spring of water, and the daughters of
the men of the city are coming out to draw water. 14 Let the young woman to whom I shall
say, 'Please let down your jar that I may drink,' and who shall say, 'Drink, and I will water
your camels'—let her be the one whom you have appointed for your servant Isaac. [b]By
this[2] I shall know that you have shown steadfast love to my master."

15 Before he had finished speaking, behold, Rebekah, who was born to Bethuel the
son of [c]Milcah, the wife of Nahor, Abraham's brother, came out with her water jar on
her shoulder. 16 The young woman [d]was very attractive in appearance, a maiden[3] whom
no man had known. She went down to the spring and filled her jar and came up. 17 Then
the servant ran to meet her and said, "Please give me a little water to drink from your
jar." 18 She said, "Drink, my lord." And she quickly let down her jar upon her hand and
gave him a drink. 19 When she had finished giving him a drink, she said, "I will draw
water for your camels also, until they have finished drinking." 20 So she quickly emptied
her jar into the trough and ran again to the well to draw water, and she drew for all his
camels. 21 The man gazed at her in silence to learn whether the LORD had prospered his
journey or not.

22 When the camels had finished drinking, the man took a gold ring weighing a half
shekel,[4] and two bracelets for her arms weighing ten gold shekels, 23 and said, "Please tell
me whose daughter you are. Is there room in your father's house for us to spend the night?"
24 She said to him, [e]"I am the daughter of Bethuel the son of Milcah, whom she bore to
Nahor." 25 She added, "We have plenty of both straw and fodder, and room to spend the
night." 26 [f]The man bowed his head and worshiped the LORD 27 and said, "Blessed be the
LORD, [g]the God of my master Abraham, who has not forsaken [h]his steadfast love and his
faithfulness toward my master. As for me, the LORD [i]has led me in the way to the house
of my master's kinsmen." 28 Then the young woman ran and told her mother's household
about these things.

29 Rebekah had a brother whose name was [j]Laban. Laban ran out toward the man, to
the spring. 30 As soon as he saw the ring and the bracelets on his sister's arms, and heard
the words of Rebekah his sister, "Thus the man spoke to me," he went to the man. And
behold, he was standing by the camels at the spring. 31 He said, "Come in, [k]O blessed of
the LORD. Why do you stand outside? For I have prepared the house and a place for the
camels." 32 So the man came to the house and unharnessed the camels, and gave [l]straw and
fodder to the camels, and there was [m]water to wash his feet and the feet of the men who
were with him. 33 Then food was set before him to eat. But he said, "I will not eat until I
have said what I have to say." He said, "Speak on."

34 So he said, "I am Abraham's servant. 35 The LORD [n]has greatly blessed my master, and
he has become great. He has given him flocks and herds, silver and gold, male servants
and female servants, camels and donkeys. 36 And Sarah my master's wife [o]bore a son to my
master when she was old, and [p]to him he has given all that he has. 37 [q]My master made me

[1] Hebrew *Aram-naharaim* [2] Or *By her* [3] Or *a woman of marriageable age* [4] A *shekel* was about 2/5 ounce or 11 grams

10 [w]Deut. 23:4; Judg. 3:8
11 [x]1 Sam. 9:11; John 4:7
12 [y]ver. 27, 42, 48 [z]ch. 27:20
13 [a]ver. 43
14 [b]See ch. 15:8
15 [c]ch. 11:29; 22:23
16 [d]ch. 26:7
24 [e]ver. 15; ch. 22:23
26 [f]ver. 48, 52; Ex. 4:31
27 [g]ver. 12, 42, 48 [h]ch. 32:10; Ps. 98:3 [i]ver. 48
29 [j]ch. 25:20; 28:2; 29:5
31 [k][ch. 26:29; Judg. 17:2; Ruth 3:10]
32 [l]ch. 43:24; Judg. 19:21 [m]See ch. 18:4
35 [n]ver. 1
36 [o]ch. 21:2 [p]ch. 25:5
37 [q]ver. 3-8

24:12–14 The servant (like Abraham) has faith in the Lord and prays for guidance. The conditions set by the servant reveal that he is seeking a wife who has a generous and caring disposition similar to that of God, who shows **steadfast love** to Abraham (v. 12). The specific request in v. 14 is not the ordinary way to ask for guidance—the servant might better have asked for wisdom to discern the best wife for Isaac rather than to probe into what God had providentially **appointed**. Nevertheless, God graciously honors the request (cf. Gideon's fleece, Judg. 6:36–40) as his means of directing events.

24:16 The description of Rebekah as **a maiden whom no man had known** confirms that she is a virgin, creating the expectation that she may well be the one intended by God to be Isaac's wife.

24:17–20 Rebekah's actions exactly mirror what the servant had earlier prayed for (v. 14).

24:27–28 God's swift answer to the servant's prayer evokes an immediate response of worship and praise.

24:29 The actions of **Laban**, Rebekah's brother, suggest that he has taken on the day-to-day responsibility of overseeing the family. While Laban's father Bethuel is still alive (cf. v. 50), his lack of involvement in the narrative suggests that he may well be incapacitated, possibly through old age.

24:34–49 The long speech by the servant closely repeats much of what has already been narrated in the first part of the chapter. Additional minor details are occasionally included; for example, v. 47 reveals that the gold ring mentioned in v. 22 was put on Rebekah's nose.

swear, saying, 'You shall not take a wife for my son from the daughters of the Canaanites,
in whose land I dwell, 38 but you shall go to my father's house and to my clan and take
a wife for my son.' 39 I said to my master, 'Perhaps the woman will not follow me.' 40 But
he said to me, 'The LORD, [r]before whom I have walked, will send his angel with you and
[s]prosper your way. You shall take a wife for my son from my clan and from my father's
house. 41 Then you will be free from my oath, when you come to my clan. And if they will
not give her to you, you will be free from my oath.'
42 "I came today to the spring and said, [t]'O LORD, the God of my master Abraham, if now
you [s]are prospering the way that I go, 43 behold, I am standing [u]by the spring of water. Let
the virgin who comes out to draw water, to whom I shall say, "Please give me a little water
from your jar to drink," 44 [v]and who will say to me, "Drink, and I will draw for your camels
also," let her be the woman whom the LORD has appointed for my master's son.'
45 "Before I had finished [w]speaking in my heart, behold, Rebekah came out with her water
jar on her shoulder, and she went down to the spring and drew water. I said to her, 'Please
let me drink.' 46 She quickly let down her jar from her shoulder and said, 'Drink, and I will
give your camels drink also.' So I drank, and she gave the camels drink also. 47 Then I asked
her, 'Whose daughter are you?' She said, 'The daughter of Bethuel, Nahor's son, whom
Milcah bore to him.' [x]So I put the ring on her nose and the bracelets on her arms. 48 [y]Then
I bowed my head and worshiped the LORD and blessed the LORD, [t]the God of my master
Abraham, who had led me by the right way[1] to take [z]the daughter of my master's kinsman
for his son. 49 Now then, if you are going to [a]show steadfast love and faithfulness to my
master, tell me; and if not, tell me, that I may turn to the right hand or to the left."
50 Then Laban and Bethuel answered and said, "The thing has come from the LORD; we
cannot [b]speak to you bad or good. 51 Behold, Rebekah is before you; take her and go, and
let her be the wife of your master's son, [c]as the LORD has spoken."
52 When Abraham's servant heard their words, [y]he bowed himself to the earth before the
LORD. 53 And the servant brought out jewelry of silver and of gold, and garments, and gave
them to Rebekah. He also gave to her brother and to her mother costly ornaments. 54 And
he and the men who were with him ate and drank, and they spent the night there. When
they arose in the morning, he said, [d]"Send me away to my master." 55 Her brother and her
mother said, "Let the young woman remain with us a while, at least ten days; after that
she may go." 56 But he said to them, "Do not delay me, since the LORD has prospered my
way. Send me away that I may go to my master." 57 They said, "Let us call the young woman
and ask her." 58 And they called Rebekah and said to her, "Will you go with this man?" She
said, "I will go." 59 So they sent away Rebekah their sister and [e]her nurse, and Abraham's
servant and his men. 60 And they blessed Rebekah and said to her,

"Our sister, may you [f]become
thousands of ten thousands,
and [g]may your offspring possess
the gate of those who hate him!"[2]

61 Then Rebekah and her young women arose and rode on the camels and followed the
man. Thus the servant took Rebekah and went his way.
62 Now Isaac had returned from [h]Beer-lahai-roi and was dwelling in the Negeb. 63 And
Isaac went out [i]to meditate in the field toward evening. And he lifted up his eyes and saw,
and behold, there were camels coming. 64 And Rebekah lifted up her eyes, and when she
saw Isaac, she dismounted from the camel 65 and said to the servant, "Who is that man,

40 [r]ch. 17:1 [s]ver. 21
42 [t]ver. 12, 27 [s][See ver. 40 above]
43 [u]ver. 13
44 [v]ver. 14, 18
45 [w]1 Sam. 1:13
47 [x][Ezek. 16:11, 12]
48 [y]ver. 26, 52 [t][See ver. 42 above] [z][ch. 22:23]
49 [a]ch. 47:29; Josh. 2:14
50 [b]ch. 31:24; 2 Sam. 13:22
51 [c]See ver. 13-15, 42-46
52 [y][See ver. 48 above]
54 [d]ver. 56, 59
59 [e]ch. 35:8
60 [f]ch. 17:16 [g]ch. 22:17
62 [h]ch. 16:14; 25:11
63 [i]Ps. 77:12; 143:5

[1] Or *faithfully* [2] Or *hate them*

24:50–51 The thing has come from the LORD . . . as the LORD has spoken. Rebekah's brother and father acknowledge that the providential nature of all that has taken place convincingly indicates that Rebekah should become Isaac's **wife**. This is clearly God's will.

24:53 The gifts confirm what the servant has earlier said about Abraham's wealth (see v. 35).

24:60 they blessed Rebekah. The hopes expressed in this brief blessing echo the divine oath made to Abraham in 22:17, emphasizing both many descendants and a special descendant who will conquer his enemies (**those who hate him**; see note on 22:15–18).

24:63 Isaac went out. This is another divinely directed event, which allows for Isaac to be the first person to meet Rebekah when they arrive at Isaac's homeland.

24:65 she took her veil and covered herself. It was customary for a woman to cover her face with a veil during the period of betrothal.

walking in the field to meet us?" The servant said, "It is my master." So she took her veil
and covered herself. 66 And the servant told Isaac all the things that he had done. 67 Then
Isaac brought her into the tent of Sarah his mother and took Rebekah, and she became
his wife, and he loved her. So Isaac was [j]comforted after his mother's [k]death.

Abraham's Death and His Descendants

25 Abraham took another wife, whose name was Keturah. 2 [l]She bore him Zimran,
Jokshan, Medan, Midian, Ishbak, and Shuah. 3 Jokshan fathered Sheba and Dedan.
The sons of Dedan were Asshurim, Letushim, and Leummim. 4 The sons of Midian were
Ephah, Epher, Hanoch, Abida, and Eldaah. All these were the children of Keturah. 5 [m]Abra-
ham gave all he had to Isaac. 6 But to the sons of his concubines Abraham gave gifts, and while
he was still living he [n]sent them away from his son Isaac, eastward [o]to the east country.
7 These are the days of the years of Abraham's life, 175 years. 8 Abraham [p]breathed his
last and [q]died in a good old age, an old man and full of years, and was gathered to his
people. 9 Isaac and Ishmael [r]his sons buried him in the cave of Machpelah, in the field of
Ephron the son of Zohar the Hittite, east of Mamre, 10 the field [s]that Abraham purchased
from the Hittites. [t]There Abraham was buried, with Sarah his wife. 11 After the death of
Abraham, God blessed Isaac his son. And Isaac settled at [u]Beer-lahai-roi.
12 These are the generations of Ishmael, Abraham's son, [v]whom Hagar the Egyptian,
Sarah's servant, bore to Abraham. 13 [w]These are the names of the sons of Ishmael, named in
the order of their birth: [x]Nebaioth, the firstborn of Ishmael; and [x]Kedar, Adbeel, Mibsam,
14 Mishma, Dumah, Massa, 15 Hadad, [y]Tema, [z]Jetur, [z]Naphish, and Kedemah. 16 These are
the sons of Ishmael and these are their names, by their villages and by their encampments,
[a]twelve princes according to their tribes. 17 (These are the years of the life of Ishmael: 137
years. He [b]breathed his last and died, and was gathered to his people.) 18 [c]They settled
from Havilah to [d]Shur, which is opposite Egypt in the direction of Assyria. He settled[1]
over against all his kinsmen.

The Birth of Esau and Jacob

19 These are the generations of Isaac, Abraham's son: [e]Abraham fathered Isaac, 20 and
Isaac was forty years old when he took Rebekah, [f]the daughter of Bethuel the Aramean
of [g]Paddan-aram, [h]the sister of Laban the Aramean, to be his wife. 21 And Isaac prayed to
the LORD for his wife, because she was barren. And [i]the LORD granted his prayer, and

[1] Hebrew *fell*

67 [j]ch. 37:35; 38:12 [k]ch. 23:2

Chapter 25

2 [l]1 Chr. 1:32, 33
5 [m]ch. 24:36
6 [n]ch. 21:14 [o][Judg. 6:3]
8 [p]ver. 17; ch. 35:29; 49:33 [q]ch. 15:15
9 [r]ch. 35:29
10 [s]ch. 23:16; 50:13 [t]ch. 49:30, 31
11 [u]ch. 16:14; 24:62
12 [v]ch. 16:15
13 [w]1 Chr. 1:29-31 [x]Isa. 60:7
15 [y]Job 6:19; Isa. 21:14 [z]1 Chr. 5:19
16 [a]ch. 17:20
17 [b]ver. 8
18 [c]1 Sam. 15:7 [d]ch. 16:7; 20:1; Ex. 15:22
19 [e]Matt. 1:2
20 [f]ch. 22:23 [g]See ch. 28:2 [h]ch. 24:29
21 [i]2 Sam. 21:14; 24:25; 1 Chr. 5:20; 2 Chr. 33:13; Ezra 8:23

24:67 and she became his wife. This is another key event leading toward the fulfillment of the promise to make of Abraham a great nation.

25:1–11 *The Death of Abraham.* These verses form the final part of the narrative that started in 11:27. To complete this major section of Genesis, some additional information is provided about Abraham, concluding with the report of his death and burial. The details, most of which are of secondary importance, are included for completeness.

25:1–4 Abraham took another wife. Only minimum information is given regarding Abraham's relationship with **Keturah**. Like Hagar, she has the status of a "concubine" (see 1 Chron. 1:32; also note on Gen. 25:5–6). No indication is given as to when this relationship was established; it possibly existed before the death of Sarah, but this remains uncertain. Reflecting the culture of the ancient Near East, it was not unknown for men to take "second" wives, but this was usually an action of those who were wealthy. The precise status of the "second" wife could vary, depending on the nature of the relationship; she might, e.g., be the maidservant of the first wife (see 16:1–3; 29:24, 29; 30:3, 9).

25:5–6 These verses highlight Isaac's position as Abraham's main heir by noting that (1) **Abraham gave all he had to Isaac** (v. 5), and (2) **the sons of** Abraham's **concubines** were sent away (v. 6). "Concubines" probably refers to Hagar and Keturah, who both bore Abraham children, although neither woman shares the status of Sarah, Abraham's first wife. The term "concubine" (Hb. *pilegesh*) may give the impression that no formal relationship existed between Abraham and these women. Yet since their sons are publicly recognized as Abraham's children, some type of formal relationship evidently existed. In Judg. 19:9, the father of a man's concubine is designated as his "father-in-law," suggesting that a form of marriage has taken place between the man and the woman. But the sons of Hagar and Keturah are clearly distinguished from Isaac (see also 1 Chron. 1:28–34).

25:9–10 the cave of Machpelah . . . that Abraham purchased. See ch. 23 for the account of how Abraham bought this burial site.

25:12–18 *The Genealogy of Ishmael.* Before proceeding to recount in detail the events associated with Isaac's immediate family, a short section is devoted to naming the 12 sons of Ishmael, who became chieftains of tribes in Arabia. This information confirms that God's promise in 17:20 was fulfilled.

25:12 These are the generations of. See note on 2:4.

25:19–37:1 *Isaac's Descendants.* A new heading, identified by the expression "these are the generations of," introduces the next main section of Genesis (see note on 2:4). While these chapters focus on the immediate family of Isaac, special attention is given to Jacob because the unique family line of Genesis is continued through him. This section of Genesis has been skillfully composed through the use of particular themes and through the structural arrangement of the material into a mirror-image pattern.

25:19–26 *The Birth of Esau and Jacob.* This section plays an important role by introducing Isaac and Rebekah's twin sons, who become the central characters in chs. 25–36. Significantly, the account of their birth is proleptic in nature, i.e., it anticipates future developments in the story.

25:20 The repeated use of the term **Aramean** and the designation of their dwelling place as **Paddan-aram** (meaning "plain of Aram") indicate that Abraham's family was considered to be Arameans. In Deut. 26:5 a patriarch (more likely Jacob than Abraham) is described as a "wandering Aramean."

25:21 Like Sarah, **Rebekah** is also **barren**. But the Lord responds to Isaac's prayer, and Rebekah conceives.

Rebekah his wife conceived. 22 The children struggled together within her, and she said,
"If it is thus, why is this happening to me?"[1] So she went [j]to inquire of the LORD. 23 And
the LORD said to her,

> [k]"Two nations are in your womb,
> and two peoples from within you[2] shall be divided;
> [l]the one shall be stronger than the other,
> [m]the older shall serve the younger."

24 When her days to give birth were completed, behold, there were twins in her womb.
25 The first came out red, [n]all his body like a hairy cloak, so they called his name Esau.
26 Afterward his brother came out with [o]his hand holding Esau's heel, so [p]his name was
called Jacob.[3] Isaac was sixty years old when she bore them.
27 When the boys grew up, Esau was [q]a skillful hunter, a man of the field, while Jacob
was a quiet man, [r]dwelling in tents. 28 Isaac loved Esau because [s]he ate of his game, but
Rebekah loved Jacob.

Esau Sells His Birthright

29 Once when Jacob was cooking stew, Esau came in from the field, and he was exhausted.
30 And Esau said to Jacob, "Let me eat some of that red stew, for I am exhausted!" (Therefore
his name was called Edom.[4]) 31 Jacob said, "Sell me your birthright now." 32 Esau said, "I am
about to die; of what use is a birthright to me?" 33 Jacob said, "Swear to me now." So he swore
to him and [t]sold his birthright to Jacob. 34 Then Jacob gave Esau bread and lentil stew, and
he ate and drank and rose and went his way. Thus Esau despised his birthright.

God's Promise to Isaac

26 Now there was a famine in the land, besides [u]the former famine that was in the
days of Abraham. And Isaac went to Gerar to [v]Abimelech king of the [w]Philistines.
2 And the LORD appeared to him and said, "Do not go down to Egypt; dwell [x]in the land

[1] Or *why do I live?* [2] Or *from birth* [3] *Jacob* means *He takes by the heel*, or *He cheats* [4] *Edom* sounds like the Hebrew for *red*

22 [j][1 Sam. 9:9]
23 [k]ch. 17:16; 24:60 [l][2 Sam. 8:14]; See Obad. 18-21 [m]ch. 27:29, 40; Cited Rom. 9:12
25 [n]ch. 27:11, 16, 23
26 [o]Hos. 12:3 [p]ch. 27:36
27 [q]ch. 27:3, 5 [r]Heb. 11:9
28 [s]ch. 27:4, 7, 9
33 [t]Heb. 12:16

Chapter 26

1 [u]ch. 12:10 [v]ch. 20:2 [w]ch. 21:34
2 [x]ch. 12:1

25:22–23 The observation that the **children struggled together within her** (v. 22) introduces one of the main themes of chs. 25–36. The relationship between the twin boys will be largely hostile. Conflict between brothers is a recurring motif in Genesis, beginning with Cain and Abel, and is a constant reminder of the negative impact of the fall on human existence. Yet the divine revelation that **the older shall serve the younger** (25:23) prepares the reader to expect that Jacob will have a significant role to play in the development of the unique family line in Genesis. Normally, younger brothers were subservient to the firstborn male, who enjoyed special privileges associated with the concept of primogeniture. On this reversal of human expectations, see Rom. 9:7–13.

25:25 red. See note on v. 30.

25:26 holding Esau's heel, so his name was called Jacob. The name "Jacob" (cf. ESV footnote) not only resembles the Hebrew term for "heel" (*'aqeb*) but also has the connotation of "deceiver." To grasp someone by the heel was apparently a figure of speech meaning "to deceive." The motif of deception appears in a number of episodes associated with Jacob. **Isaac was sixty years old**. The twins are born 15 years before the death of Abraham, which is recorded in vv. 7–8. Occasionally in Genesis, for specific reasons, some events are narrated out of chronological order, as here.

Isaac's Timeline

Event	Age of Isaac	Genesis
Isaac's mother Sarah dies	37	23:1
Isaac marries Rebekah	40	25:20
Isaac fathers Jacob and Esau with Rebekah	60	25:26
Isaac's father Abraham dies	75	25:7
Isaac's brother Ishmael dies	123	25:17
Isaac sends Jacob to Laban in Haran	137	28:5
Isaac's grandson Joseph is born	151	30:25; 31:38–41
Isaac dies	180	35:28

25:27–34 *Esau Sells His Birthright.* This episode centers on Esau's dismissive attitude toward his birthright. While Jacob may be criticized for exploiting his brother in a moment of weakness, Esau is indifferent toward his firstborn status. He does not grasp the significance of all that God has promised to fulfill through the unique line descended from Abraham, of which he is the natural heir.

25:27–28 The contrast between Esau and Jacob is reflected in their personalities. The manlier, outdoor-oriented Esau is loved by his father, whereas the quieter, domesticated nature of Jacob makes him his mother's favorite.

25:30 In Hebrew the name **Edom** is similar to the word **red**.

25:31–32 The Nuzi texts from the fifteenth century B.C. in Mesopotamia give evidence for transferable birthrights, mentioning one particular case in which a man sells his birthright for a sheep.

25:34 Thus Esau despised his birthright. Esau was contemptuous of his special firstborn status. On the basis of this, Heb. 12:16 describes Esau as "unholy." Esau did not appreciate that his birthright was linked to God's plan of redemption for the whole world.

26:1–35 *Isaac in Gerar.* The events recorded in this section probably took place after the death of Abraham, when Esau and Jacob were young men. Much of this chapter closely resembles episodes from the life of Abraham. This chapter also confirms that the divine promises to Abraham are passed on to Isaac.

26:1–2 besides the former famine that was in the days of Abraham. The narrator alludes to the famine mentioned in 12:10. On that occasion Abraham went down to Egypt. Isaac, however, is instructed to remain in **Gerar**, having just moved there because of the famine. **Abimelech**. See note on 20:2. Since the events of this chapter are difficult to date precisely, it is possible that this is the same king mentioned in chs. 20–21. It is perhaps

of which I shall tell you. 3 [y]Sojourn in this land, and [z]I will be with you and will bless you,
for [a]to you and to your offspring I will give all these lands, and I will establish [b]the oath
that I swore to Abraham your father. 4 [c]I will multiply your offspring as the stars of heaven
and will give to your offspring all these lands. And [d]in your offspring all the nations of
the earth shall be blessed, 5 because [e]Abraham obeyed my voice and kept my charge, my
commandments, my statutes, and my laws."

Isaac and Abimelech

6 So Isaac settled in Gerar. 7 When the men of the place asked him about his wife, [f]he
said, "She is my sister," for [g]he feared to say, "My wife," thinking, "lest the men of the place
should kill me because of Rebekah," because [h]she was attractive in appearance. 8 When he
had been there a long time, Abimelech king of the Philistines looked out of a window and
saw Isaac laughing with[1] Rebekah his wife. 9 So Abimelech called Isaac and said, "Behold,
she is your wife. How then could you say, 'She is my sister'?" Isaac said to him, "Because I
thought, 'Lest I die because of her.'" 10 Abimelech said, "What is this you have done to us?
One of the people might easily have lain with your wife, and [i]you would have brought
guilt upon us." 11 So Abimelech warned all the people, saying, "Whoever touches this man
or his wife shall surely be put to death."

12 And Isaac sowed in that land and reaped in the same year a hundredfold. The LORD
[j]blessed him, 13 and the man became rich, and gained more and more until he became very
wealthy. 14 He had possessions of flocks and herds and many servants, so that the Philistines
[k]envied him. 15 (Now the Philistines had stopped and filled with earth all the wells [l]that
his father's servants had dug in the days of Abraham his father.) 16 And Abimelech said to
Isaac, "Go away from us, for you are much mightier than we."

17 So Isaac departed from there and encamped in the Valley of Gerar and settled there.
18 And Isaac dug again the wells of water that had been dug in the days of Abraham his
father, which the Philistines had stopped after the death of Abraham. And [m]he gave them
the names that his father had given them. 19 But when Isaac's servants dug in the valley
and found there a well of spring water, 20 the herdsmen of Gerar [n]quarreled with Isaac's
herdsmen, saying, "The water is ours." So he called the name of the well Esek,[2] because
they contended with him. 21 Then they dug another well, and they quarreled over that
also, so he called its name Sitnah.[3] 22 And he moved from there and dug another well, and
they did not quarrel over it. So he called its name Rehoboth,[4] saying, "For now the LORD
has made room for us, and we shall be fruitful in the land."

23 From there he went up to Beersheba. 24 And the LORD appeared to him the same night
and said, [o]"I am the God of Abraham your father. [p]Fear not, for [q]I am with you and will
bless you and multiply your offspring for my servant Abraham's sake." 25 So he [r]built an
altar there and called upon the name of the LORD and pitched his tent there. And there
Isaac's servants dug a well.

26 When Abimelech went to him from Gerar with Ahuzzath his adviser and [s]Phicol the

3 [y]ch. 20:1; Heb. 11:9 [z]ch. 28:15 [a]See ch. 13:15 [b][Mic. 7:20]; See ch. 22:16-18
4 [c]Cited Ex. 32:13; See ch. 15:5 [d]See ch. 12:3
5 [e]ch. 22:18
7 [f]ch. 12:13; 20:2, 13 [g][Prov. 29:25] [h]ch. 24:16
10 [i]ch. 20:9
12 [j]ver. 3; ch. 24:1, 35
14 [k][Eccles. 4:4]
15 [l]ch. 21:30
18 [m]ch. 21:31
20 [n]ch. 21:25
24 [o]ch. 17:7; 24:12; 28:13; Ex. 3:6 [p]ch. 15:1; See Ps. 27:1-3 [q]ch. 28:15; 31:3; [ch. 21:22, 23]
25 [r]ch. 12:7; 13:18
26 [s]ch. 21:22

[1] Hebrew may suggest an intimate relationship [2] *Esek* means *contention* [3] *Sitnah* means *enmity* [4] *Rehoboth* means *broad places*, or *room*

more likely, however, that he is the son or grandson of the Abimelech known to Abraham. **Philistines**. See note on 21:32.

26:3–5 The Lord instructs Isaac to remain in Canaan, with the promise that he will be blessed for doing so. **I will establish the oath that I swore to Abraham**. This undoubtedly refers to the oath recorded in 22:16–18, the substance of which is repeated here (see note on 22:15–18). Not only is Isaac heir to the promises made by God to Abraham, but their fulfillment is intimately linked to him and his descendants. **kept my charge, my commandments, my statutes, and my laws**. The various terms used here, which are elsewhere often associated with the law and instructions given at Mount Sinai, underline that Abraham's obedience to God was unreserved.

26:6–7 Being new to the region of Gerar, Isaac adopts the same ruse that Abraham earlier used in both Egypt (12:10–12) and Gerar (20:1–18).

26:8 saw Isaac laughing with Rebekah. In this context the Hebrew verb "to laugh" implies laughing as they caress affectionately. The narrator deliberately chooses this verb to create a play on the name "Isaac," which means "he laughs." Abimelech sees Isaac "being himself" with Rebekah and draws the obvious conclusion that they are married.

26:12–13 The LORD blessed him. Blessing is always an indication of divine favor. Consequently, Isaac **became very wealthy**.

26:15 The Philistines may have closed up the **wells** to discourage seminomadic herdsmen from grazing their livestock in this region.

26:17 Isaac relocates from the city of Gerar to the **Valley of Gerar**, a region under the control of Gerar but not adjacent to the city.

26:19–22 Since **water** was a vital commodity in this arid region, disputes over the ownership of wells were common (see 21:25). The names of the wells, **Esek** ("contention," 26:20), **Sitnah** ("enmity," v. 21), and **Rehoboth** ("broad places/room," v. 22), reflect the events associated with them.

26:23–25 Isaac's servants dug a well. Years earlier Abraham had dug a well at Beersheba (see 21:30), but it was later filled in by the Philistines (26:15).

26:26–31 Abimelech comes to Isaac in order to establish a **covenant** (v. 28) or treaty with him, guaranteeing peaceful coexistence. This arises from a change

commander of his army, 27 Isaac said to them, "Why have you come to me, seeing that you
hate me and [t]have sent me away from you?" 28 They said, "We see plainly that the LORD
has been with you. So we said, let there be a sworn pact between us, between you and us,
and let us make a covenant with you, 29 that you will do us no harm, just as we have not
touched you and have done to you nothing but good and have sent you away in peace.
[u]You are now the blessed of the LORD." 30 So he made them a feast, and they ate and drank.
31 In the morning they rose early and [v]exchanged oaths. And Isaac sent them on their way,
and they departed from him in peace. 32 That same day Isaac's servants came and told him
about the well that they had dug and said to him, "We have found water." 33 He called it
Shibah;[1] therefore the name of the city is [w]Beersheba to this day.
34 When Esau was forty years old, he took [x]Judith the daughter of Beeri the Hittite to
be his wife, and Basemath the daughter of Elon the Hittite, 35 and [y]they made life bitter[2]
for Isaac and Rebekah.

Isaac Blesses Jacob

27 When Isaac was old and [z]his eyes were dim so that he could not see, he called Esau
his older son and said to him, "My son"; and he answered, "Here I am." 2 He said,
"Behold, I am old; I do not know the day of my death. 3 [a]Now then, take your weapons,
your quiver and your bow, and go out to the field and hunt game for me, 4 and prepare for
me delicious food, such as I love, and bring it to me so that I may eat, that my soul [b]may
bless you before I die."
5 Now Rebekah was listening when Isaac spoke to his son Esau. So when Esau went to
the field to hunt for game and bring it, 6 Rebekah said to her son Jacob, "I heard your father
speak to your brother Esau, 7 'Bring me game and prepare for me delicious food, that I
may eat it and bless you before the LORD before I die.' 8 Now therefore, my son, [c]obey my
voice as I command you. 9 Go to the flock and bring me two good young goats, so that I
may prepare from them delicious food for your father, such as he loves. 10 And you shall
bring it to your father to eat, [d]so that he may bless you before he dies." 11 But Jacob said to
Rebekah his mother, "Behold, [e]my brother Esau is a hairy man, and I am a smooth man.
12 Perhaps my father [f]will feel me, and I shall seem to be mocking him and bring [g]a curse
upon myself and not a blessing." 13 His mother said to him, [h]"Let your curse be on me, my
son; only obey my voice, and go, bring them to me."
14 So he went and took them and brought them to his mother, and his mother prepared

[1] *Shibah* sounds like the Hebrew for *oath* [2] Hebrew *they were bitterness of spirit*

27 [t]ver. 16
29 [u]ch. 24:31
31 [v]ch. 21:31
33 [w]ch. 21:31; 22:19
34 [x][ch. 28:9; 36:2, 3]
35 [y]ch. 27:46

Chapter 27

1 [z]ch. 48:10; 1 Sam. 3:2
3 [a]ch. 25:27, 28
4 [b]ch. 10:25; 48:9, 15; 49:28; Deut. 33:1
8 [c]ver. 13
10 [d]ver. 4
11 [e]ch. 25:25
12 [f]ver. 21, 22 [g][Deut. 27:18]
13 [h][1 Sam. 25:24; 2 Sam. 14:9; Matt. 27:25]

of heart by Abimelech, who now acknowledges the Lord's presence with Isaac. A similar treaty was made in the time of Abraham (21:22–32). **Phicol** (26:26) is possibly the same individual mentioned in 21:22. Alternatively, "Phicol" could be a family name or title and here refer to someone else.

26:32–33 The ratification of the treaty coincides with the discovery of **water** in a **well** being dug by **Isaac's servants** (v. 32). Consequently, the well is called **Shibah** (Hb. *shib'ah*, v. 33), which resembles the Hebrew word for "oath" (*shebu'ah*). **Beersheba**. See note on 21:31.

26:34–35 By emphasizing the **Hittite** origin of Esau's wives, v. 34 probably implies that Esau has not chosen them wisely. This is confirmed by the observation that they **made life bitter for Isaac and Rebekah** (v. 35).

27:1–45 *Isaac Blesses Jacob.* Genesis records in detail two important occasions when patriarchs, nearing death, pronounce special blessings on their firstborn sons (27:1–46; 49:1–27). In this present account, Isaac's intention to bless Esau is subverted by Rebekah, who helps Jacob receive the blessing of the firstborn. This event not only builds on the earlier incident when Esau sells his birthright to Jacob (25:29–34), but also develops the divine statement in 25:23 that the older will serve the younger. Although Rebekah's actions involved deception, the text simply reports what Rebekah did without condoning or commenting on her actions. Nevertheless, the first audience again would see the ways in which God in his sovereignty uses all kinds of actions (good, bad, and mixed) to bring his people to the place in which they find themselves.

27:1–2 Isaac is introduced as both **old** and blind. Both factors are important in light of subsequent events. Believing he was near to death, Isaac decides that the time has come to bless his firstborn son, Esau. Such blessings were very important, for as prayers addressed to God they were viewed as shaping the future of those blessed. Isaac's blindness enables Jacob to avoid detection when he pretends to be Esau. It may also be implied that Isaac's physical loss of sight reflects an inner blindness that makes him oblivious to Esau's shortcoming and God's purpose for Jacob (25:23). Isaac's motivation for blessing Esau is possibly driven by a desire for "delicious food" (27:4) rather than a true assessment of his character.

27:4 that my soul may bless you before I die. The paternal blessing that Isaac wishes to give to Esau is important because it will establish the identity of the heir to the divine promises given to Abraham and Isaac. In light of this, the "firstborn" line will eventually lead to a royal descendant through whom all the nations of the earth will be blessed. This link between firstborn and blessing is emphasized in a wordplay involving both terms. In Hebrew, "firstborn" is *bekorah*, whereas "blessing" is *berakah*. Much of the story involving Esau and Jacob centers on these concepts and how the younger twin, Jacob, acquires both the firstborn birthright and the related paternal blessing.

27:5–10 Rebekah was listening. The narrator unambiguously states that Rebekah instigates and coordinates the deception undertaken by Jacob. This mitigates, but does not remove, Jacob's guilt in deceiving his father.

27:11–13 When **Jacob** expresses concern about being discovered, **Rebekah** states that she will bear any **curse** placed on him. Rebekah's desire for Jacob to receive the blessing of the firstborn is no doubt motivated by her special love for him (see 25:28).

27:11 From birth, Esau was clearly distinguished from Jacob by his **hairy** appearance (see 25:25).

15 [i]ver. 27
21 [j]ver. 12
23 [k]ver. 16 [l]Heb. 11:20
25 [m]ver. 10
27 [l][See ver. 23 above]
[n][Hos. 14:6]
28 [o]Deut. 33:13; Zech. 8:12; [ch. 49:25; 2 Sam. 1:21] [p]Deut. 7:13; 33:28; Joel 2:19
29 [q][ch. 49:8] [r][2 Sam. 8:14] [s]ch. 12:3; Num. 24:9
34 [t]Heb. 12:17
36 [u]ch. 25:26 [v]ch. 25:33
37 [w]ver. 29; [2 Sam. 8:14]

delicious food, such as his father loved. 15 Then Rebekah took the [i]best garments of Esau
her older son, which were with her in the house, and put them on Jacob her younger son.
16 And the skins of the young goats she put on his hands and on the smooth part of his
neck. 17 And she put the delicious food and the bread, which she had prepared, into the
hand of her son Jacob.

18 So he went in to his father and said, "My father." And he said, "Here I am. Who are
you, my son?" 19 Jacob said to his father, "I am Esau your firstborn. I have done as you told
me; now sit up and eat of my game, that your soul may bless me." 20 But Isaac said to his
son, "How is it that you have found it so quickly, my son?" He answered, "Because the
LORD your God granted me success." 21 Then Isaac said to Jacob, "Please come near, that
I [j]may feel you, my son, to know whether you are really my son Esau or not." 22 So Jacob
went near to Isaac his father, who felt him and said, "The voice is Jacob's voice, but the
hands are the hands of Esau." 23 And he did not recognize him, because [k]his hands were
hairy like his brother Esau's hands. [l]So he blessed him. 24 He said, "Are you really my son
Esau?" He answered, "I am." 25 Then he said, "Bring it near to me, [m]that I may eat of my
son's game and bless you." So he brought it near to him, and he ate; and he brought him
wine, and he drank.

26 Then his father Isaac said to him, "Come near and kiss me, my son." 27 So he came near
and kissed him. And Isaac smelled the smell of his garments [l]and blessed him and said,

"See, [n]the smell of my son
is as the smell of a field that the LORD has blessed!
28 May God give you of [o]the dew of heaven
and of the fatness of the earth
and [p]plenty of grain and wine.
29 Let peoples serve you,
and nations [q]bow down to you.
[r]Be lord over your brothers,
and may your mother's sons bow down to you.
[s]Cursed be everyone who curses you,
and blessed be everyone who blesses you!"

30 As soon as Isaac had finished blessing Jacob, when Jacob had scarcely gone out from
the presence of Isaac his father, Esau his brother came in from his hunting. 31 He also
prepared delicious food and brought it to his father. And he said to his father, "Let my
father arise and eat of his son's game, that you may bless me." 32 His father Isaac said to
him, "Who are you?" He answered, "I am your son, your firstborn, Esau." 33 Then Isaac
trembled very violently and said, "Who was it then that hunted game and brought it to
me, and I ate it all before you came, and I have blessed him? Yes, and he shall be blessed."
34 As soon as Esau heard the words of his father, [t]he cried out with an exceedingly great
and bitter cry and said to his father, "Bless me, even me also, O my father!" 35 But he said,
"Your brother came deceitfully, and he has taken away your blessing." 36 Esau said, [u]"Is
he not rightly named Jacob?[1] For he has cheated me these two times. [v]He took away my
birthright, and behold, now he has taken away my blessing." Then he said, "Have you not
reserved a blessing for me?" 37 Isaac answered and said to Esau, "Behold, [w]I have made him

[1] *Jacob means He takes by the heel, or He cheats*

27:19–27 I am Esau your firstborn (v. 19). This is an outright lie, and in violation of God's later command in Ex. 20:16. Isaac's reaction to Jacob's assertion suggests that he is not immediately convinced that this is Esau. The subsequent conversation adds to the drama of the story (Gen. 27:20–26). Isaac is eventually persuaded when he smells Esau's clothing (v. 27), which Jacob had earlier put on (v. 15).

27:29 Let peoples serve you, and nations bow down to you. Isaac's blessing for his "firstborn" goes far beyond requesting an abundance of material necessities (v. 28). Here Isaac asks for universal sovereignty, embracing not only immediate family but also peoples and nations. This blessing clearly builds on the divine promise to Abraham that kings will be among his descendants (17:6). **Cursed be everyone who curses you, and blessed be everyone who blesses you!** These words, which echo God's promise to Abraham in 12:3, develop a motif in Genesis whereby God's blessing or favor is mediated to others through members of the unique line. This blessing, however, is excluded from those who disdain God's chosen ones.

27:30–36 When Esau returns to discover what has happened, he is filled with anger toward his brother (see v. 41). In response to Isaac's comment that Jacob deceived him, Esau observes, **Is he not rightly named Jacob? For he has cheated me these two times** (v. 36). Esau alludes here to the wordplay on the name "Jacob," which means "to deceive/cheat" (see note on 25:26). From Esau's perspective, Jacob has cheated him out of both his birthright (see 25:29–34) and his blessing, although Esau willingly forfeited his birthright to Jacob (see 25:33).

lord over you, and all his brothers I have given to him for servants, and [x]with grain and
wine I have sustained him. What then can I do for you, my son?" 38 Esau said to his father,
"Have you but one blessing, my father? Bless me, even me also, O my father." And [t]Esau
lifted up his voice and wept.
39 Then Isaac his father answered and said to him:

"Behold, [y]away from[1] the fatness of the earth shall your dwelling be,
and away from[2] the dew of heaven on high.
40 By your sword you shall live,
and you [z]shall serve your brother;
but when you grow restless
[a]you shall break his yoke from your neck."

41 Now Esau [b]hated Jacob because of the blessing with which his father had blessed him,
and Esau said to himself, [c]"The days of mourning for my father are approaching; [d]then I
will kill my brother Jacob." 42 But the words of Esau her older son were told to Rebekah.
So she sent and called Jacob her younger son and said to him, "Behold, your brother Esau
comforts himself about you by planning to kill you. 43 Now therefore, my son, obey my
voice. Arise, flee to Laban my brother in Haran 44 and stay with him a while, until your
brother's fury turns away— 45 until your brother's anger turns away from you, and he forgets what you have done to him. Then I will send and bring you from there. Why should
I be bereft of you both in one day?"
46 Then Rebekah said to Isaac, [e]"I loathe my life because of the Hittite women.[3] [f]If Jacob
marries one of the Hittite women like these, one of the women of the land, what good
will my life be to me?"

Jacob Sent to Laban

28 Then Isaac called Jacob [g]and blessed him and directed him, [f]"You must not take
a wife from the Canaanite women. 2 [h]Arise, go to Paddan-aram to the house of
[i]Bethuel your mother's father, and take as your wife from there one of the daughters of
Laban your mother's brother. 3 [j]God Almighty[4] bless you and make you fruitful and multiply
you, that you may become a company of peoples. 4 May he give [k]the blessing of Abraham
to you and to your offspring with you, that you may take possession of [l]the land of your
sojournings that God gave to Abraham!" 5 Thus Isaac sent Jacob away. And he went to
Paddan-aram, to Laban, the son of Bethuel the Aramean, the brother of Rebekah, Jacob's
and Esau's mother.

Esau Marries an Ishmaelite

6 Now Esau saw that Isaac had blessed Jacob and sent him away to Paddan-aram to take
a wife from there, and that as he blessed him he directed him, "You must not take a wife

[1] Or *Behold, of* [2] Or *and of* [3] Hebrew *daughters of Heth* [4] Hebrew *El Shaddai*

37 [x]ver. 28
38 [t][See ver. 34 above]
39 [y]ver. 28; ch. 36:6, 7
40 [z]ch. 25:23; [2 Sam. 8:14]; See Obad. 18-21 [a][2 Kgs. 8:20-22]
41 [b][ch. 37:4] [c]ch. 50:3, 4, 10 [d][Amos 1:11; Obad. 10]
46 [e]ch. 26:34, 35; 28:8 [f]ch. 24:3

Chapter 28

1 [g]ver. 6 [f][See ch. 27:46 above]
2 [h]Hos. 12:12 [i]ch. 22:23
3 [j]See ch. 17:1
4 [k]See ch. 12:2, 3 [l]ch. 17:8; 36:7; 37:1

27:40 you shall break his yoke from your neck. Although Jacob has been given authority over his older twin brother, Isaac indicates that Esau will eventually free himself from his brother's control. Later, Esau's descendants settle outside the Promised Land, to the east of the Jordan River (see note on 32:3–5), eventually taking control of Seir, which is later named "Edom" (see note on 36:1–37:1).

27:41–45 I will kill my brother Jacob (v. 41). When Rebekah learns of Esau's desire to murder his brother, she encourages Jacob to take refuge in northwestern Mesopotamia (**Haran**) with her brother **Laban** (vv. 42–43). Fratricide is a common theme in Genesis.

27:46–28:9 *Jacob Is Sent to Find a Wife*. This section, which continues the account of Jacob's deception of Isaac, focuses on the issue of finding an appropriate wife for Jacob and presupposes a knowledge of the earlier comment in 26:34–35 about Esau's choice of wives. Isaac and Rebekah encourage Jacob to get a wife from among their relatives who are living in northwest Mesopotamia. Their advice to Jacob in turn prompts Esau to take another wife, on this occasion from Ishmael's family.

27:46 the Hittite women. Rebekah is probably alluding here to Esau's wives (see 26:34–35), although she could be referring to Hittite women in general. She may have deliberately raised this issue in order to provide a rationale for sending Jacob away, conscious of Esau's desire to kill him.

28:1–2 In response to Rebekah's negative observation about Hittite wives, Isaac instructs Jacob to **take a wife** from Laban's family. (Abraham issued similar instructions in 24:3–4.) This advice, which coincides with Rebekah's desire that Jacob should flee from Esau, requires Jacob to go to **Paddan-aram** (28:2; see note on 25:20). Although Rebekah specifically mentions Hittite wives, Isaac expands on this by referring to **Canaanite women** (28:1), a broader designation that would have included the Hittites (see note on 10:6–20).

28:3–4 Isaac's blessing of Jacob, as in 27:29, not only echoes the divine promises to Abraham but explicitly requests that **God Almighty** (28:3; see note on 17:1–2) will **give the blessing of Abraham** (28:4) to Jacob. Although Jacob is being sent away to Haran in northwest Mesopotamia, Isaac anticipates that he will return to Canaan in order to take possession of the land divinely given to Abraham. **make you fruitful and multiply you**. See note on 1:28. **a company of peoples**. This echoes the motif of Abraham as father of many nations (see 17:4–6) and is repeated in 35:11.

28:6–9 Having heard his father's instruction to Jacob that he should not take

from the Canaanite women," 7 and that Jacob had obeyed his father and his mother and
gone to Paddan-aram. 8 So when Esau saw [m]that the Canaanite women did not please Isaac
his father, 9 Esau went to Ishmael and took as his wife, besides the wives he had, [n]Mahalath
the daughter of Ishmael, Abraham's son, the sister of [o]Nebaioth.

Jacob's Dream

10 Jacob left [p]Beersheba and went toward [q]Haran. 11 And he came to a certain place
and stayed there that night, because the sun had set. Taking one of the stones of the
place, he put it under his head and lay down in that place to sleep. 12 And he [r]dreamed,
and behold, there was a ladder[1] set up on the earth, and the top of it reached to heaven.
And behold, [s]the angels of God were ascending and descending on it! 13 And behold,
[t]the LORD stood above it[2] and said, [u]"I am the LORD, the God of Abraham your father
and the God of Isaac. [v]The land on which you lie I will give to you and to your offspring.
14 Your offspring shall be like [w]the dust of the earth, and you shall spread abroad to the
west and to the east and to the north and to the south, and in you and [x]your offspring
shall all the families of the earth be blessed. 15 Behold, [y]I am with you and will keep you
wherever you go, and [z]will bring you back to this land. For I will [a]not leave you until
I have done what I have promised you." 16 Then Jacob awoke from his sleep and said,
"Surely the LORD is [b]in this place, and I did not know it." 17 And he was afraid and said,
"How awesome is this place! This is none other than the house of God, and this is the
gate of heaven."

18 So early in the morning Jacob took the stone that he had put under his head and
set it up [c]for a pillar [d]and poured oil on the top of it. 19 He called the name of that place
[e]Bethel,[3] but the name of the city was Luz at the first. 20 Then Jacob [f]made a vow, saying,
"If God will be with me and will keep me in this way that I go, and will give me bread to
eat and clothing to wear, 21 [g]so that I come again to my father's house in peace, [h]then the
LORD shall be my God, 22 and this stone, which I have set up for a pillar, [i]shall be God's
house. And [j]of all that you give me I will give a full tenth to you."

[1] *Or a flight of steps* [2] *Or beside him* [3] *Bethel means the house of God*

8 [m]ch. 24:3; 26:35
9 [n][ch. 36:3] [o]ch. 25:13; 36:3
10 [p]ch. 21:31; 26:33 [q][Acts 7:2]
12 [r][Num. 12:6; Job 33:15, 16] [s][John 1:51]
13 [t][ch. 35:1; 48:3] [u]ch. 26:24 [v]ch. 35:12; See ch. 13:14-16
14 [w]See ch. 13:16 [x]See ch. 12:3
15 [y]ch. 26:24; 31:3 [z]ch. 35:6 [a]1 Kgs. 8:57
16 [b]Ex. 3:5; Josh. 5:15
18 [c]ch. 31:13, 45; 35:14; [1 Sam. 7:12; 2 Sam. 18:18] [d][Lev. 8:10, 11; Num. 7:1]
19 [e]ch. 35:7; Judg. 1:23, 26
20 [f]ch. 31:13
21 [g][Judg. 11:31; 2 Sam. 15:7-9] [h]Deut. 26:17
22 [i]ch. 35:7, 14 [j]ch. 14:20; Lev. 27:30-33

a **Canaanite** wife, Esau seeks to make amends for his earlier actions. To gain his parents' approval, he marries one of Ishmael's daughters. Esau, however, still retains his two Hittite wives.

28:10–22 *Jacob at Bethel.* Through an extraordinary dream, Jacob encounters the Lord. This experience has a dramatic effect on him as the Lord confirms that the divine promises to Abraham will be established through him. This encounter with God is later matched by a similar event on Jacob's return to Canaan (32:22–32). Both events take place at crucial points in the life of Jacob, as he is departing from and returning to Canaan.

28:10 Leaving **Beersheba**, Jacob sets out to travel the 550 miles (900 km) to **Haran** (see note on 11:31).

28:12 As he rests overnight, Jacob has a dream, which centers on a **ladder set up on the earth, and the top of it reached to heaven**. The Hebrew term translated "ladder" could possibly denote a stairway (see ESV footnote) similar to those found on ancient ziggurats (see illustration, p. 68). What matters most is not the precise shape of this structure but its purpose; it provides a bridge between heaven and earth, revealing that God is still committed to making the earth his dwelling place (see Introduction: History of Salvation Summary). Jesus identifies himself as the ladder linking earth and heaven (John 1:51). While human beings want to ascend to heaven (as reflected in the Tower of Babel story, Genesis 11), God is interested in making the earth his temple-city.

28:13–15 The expression **the LORD stood above it** (v. 13) could also be rendered "the LORD stood beside him" (ESV footnote). Jacob's reaction in v. 16 suggests that he perceived God as being with him on earth rather than in heaven. The Lord's words loudly echo the divine promises made to Abraham (12:3, 7; 13:14–16; 17:7–8; 18:18; 22:17–18) and Isaac (26:4). In an act of grace, God states that he will not abandon Jacob but will fulfill these promises to him.

28:16–17 Surely the LORD is in this place (v. 16). Jacob's affirmation of the Lord's presence indicates that he considers God to be resident in this location. Consequently, he describes it as the **house of God** (v. 17). The associated phrase **gate of heaven** (v. 17) possibly implies that this is the entrance to the divine city. Since Jacob names the location "Bethel" (v. 19), which means "house of God," the idea of God's being present on earth is clearly dominant in his thinking. (The idea of a gate into heaven is a common one in ancient Near Eastern literature. For example, one of the titles given to a high priest of Thebes in Egypt was "The Opener of the Gates of Heaven.")

28:18 Although Jacob commemorates this special event by setting up a **pillar** and consecrating it with **oil**, it is noteworthy that he does not build an altar. This is a further indication that he has not yet fully accepted the Lord as his God. While the practice of setting up pillars was common in Canaanite worship, Deut. 16:22 prohibits it. Years later, after his faith-transforming encounter with God at Penuel (Gen. 32:22–32), Jacob returns to Bethel in order to construct an altar (35:1–7).

28:19 the name of the city was Luz at the first. The city's name continued to be "Luz" until the Israelites occupied Canaan many centuries later (see 35:6; 48:3; Josh. 18:13; Judg. 1:23, 26). The actual location called "Bethel" by Jacob probably lay outside the city of Luz (see Josh. 16:2).

28:20–21 If God will be with me . . . , then the LORD shall be my God. The conditional nature of Jacob's vow reveals that he is still ambivalent regarding his commitment to the Lord. Although God reveals himself to Jacob at Bethel, it will require a further personal encounter before Jacob fully trusts in the Lord (see 32:22–32).

28:22 this stone . . . shall be God's house. Jacob promises that he will construct a sanctuary for God, the consecrated stone being the first part of the process. Temple building becomes an important part of the duties undertaken by the royal line descended from Jacob. **I will give a full tenth to you**. Centuries later, Israelite worshipers give a tenth of their income to God

Jacob Marries Leah and Rachel

29 Then Jacob went on his journey and came to [k]the land of the people of the east.
2 As he looked, he saw a well in the field, and behold, three flocks of sheep lying
beside it, for out of that well the flocks were watered. The stone on the well's mouth was
large, 3 and when all the flocks were gathered there, the shepherds would roll the stone
from the mouth of the well and water the sheep, and put the stone back in its place over
the mouth of the well.

4 Jacob said to them, "My brothers, where do you come from?" They said, [l]"We are from
Haran." 5 He said to them, "Do you know Laban the son of Nahor?" They said, "We know
him." 6 He said to them, "Is it well with him?" They said, "It is well; and see, Rachel his
daughter is coming with the sheep!" 7 He said, "Behold, it is still high day; it is not time
for the livestock to be gathered together. Water the sheep and go, pasture them." 8 But they
said, "We cannot until all the flocks are gathered together and the stone is rolled from the
mouth of the well; then we water the sheep."

9 While he was still speaking with them, [m]Rachel came with her father's sheep, for she
was a shepherdess. 10 Now as soon as Jacob saw Rachel the daughter of Laban his mother's
brother, and the sheep of Laban his mother's brother, Jacob came near and rolled the stone
from the well's mouth and watered the flock of Laban his mother's brother. 11 Then Jacob
kissed Rachel and wept aloud. 12 And Jacob told Rachel that he was [n]her father's kinsman,
and that he was Rebekah's son, [o]and she ran and told her father.

13 As soon as Laban heard the news about Jacob, his sister's son, [o]he ran to meet him and
embraced him and kissed him and brought him to his house. Jacob told Laban all these
things, 14 and Laban said to him, [p]"Surely you are my bone and my flesh!" And he stayed
with him a month.

15 Then Laban said to Jacob, "Because you are my kinsman, should you therefore serve

Chapter 29
1 [k]Num. 23:7; Judg. 6:3
4 [l]ch. 27:43
9 [m]Ex. 2:16, 17
12 [n]ch. 13:8; 14:14, 16 [o][ch. 24:28, 29]
13 [o][See ver. 12 above]
14 [p]ch. 2:23; 37:27; Judg. 9:2; 2 Sam. 5:1; 19:12, 13; 1 Chr. 11:1

as an expression of their commitment to him; this is regularly referred to as a tithe.

29:1–14 *Jacob Meets Rachel and Laban.* Aspects of this episode parallel the earlier account of the journey of Abraham's servant to Paddan-aram in order to find a wife for Isaac (ch. 24). While both accounts involve providential encounters at a well, subtle differences exist. Whereas Abraham's servant prays for guidance, Jacob is not recorded as praying. In ch. 24, Rebekah's willingness to water the camels proves decisive in establishing her identity as Isaac's future wife. On this occasion, Jacob's willingness to water Laban's herd establishes a special relationship between the two men.

29:1 the people of the east. This is an unusual way of referring to the inhabitants of Paddan-aram in northwest Mesopotamia. In Genesis, however, the "east" is often associated with those who are expelled or move away from God's presence (3:23–24; 4:16; 21:14; 25:6). This brief comment possibly signals that Jacob's relatives do not worship the Lord.

29:2–3 These verses provide information about the process by which herds were normally watered at this well. In particular, attention is drawn to the large stone that covered the well's mouth.

29:4–6 When Jacob discovers that the shepherds are from **Haran** (v. 4), he inquires after his uncle, **Laban the son of Nahor** (v. 5). Strictly speaking, Laban is Nahor's grandson. The Hebrew term for "son" may denote any male descendant. In the NT Jesus is described as the "son of David" (Matt. 1:1), even though David lived about 1,000 years earlier.

29:6 Providentially, Laban's daughter, **Rachel**, is spotted bringing her herd to the well. Rachel means "ewe," an appropriate name for a shepherdess (v. 9).

29:10 Jacob came near and rolled the stone from the well's mouth. Jacob demonstrates extraordinary strength in being able to move the stone.

29:11–14 Jacob kissed Rachel (v. 11), probably as an act of family affection rather than of romance (cf. v. 13). Jacob discloses his identity to Rachel (v. 12), who in turn introduces him to her father, **Laban**. The warmth of the family reunion is shown by the way Laban embraces and kisses his nephew Jacob (v. 13).

29:15–30 *Jacob Marries Leah and Rachel.* Jacob's journey to Paddan-aram to find a wife results in his obtaining not one, but two. The episode is full

Jacob's Timeline

Event	Age of Jacob	Genesis
Jacob's grandfather Abraham dies	15	25:7
Jacob sent to Laban in Haran	77	28:5
Jacob marries Leah and Rachel	84	29:21–30; 30:1, 22–26
Jacob fathers Joseph with Rachel	91	30:22–24
Jacob flees from Laban to Canaan	97	ch. 31
Jacob's son Joseph sold into slavery	108	37:12–36
Jacob's father Isaac dies	120	35:28–29; cf. 25:26 with 35:28
Jacob reunites with Joseph and moves his family to Egypt	130	chs. 46–47; cf. 47:9, 28
Jacob dies	147	47:28

18[q]ch. 30:26; 31:41; [Hos. 12:12]
20[q][See ver. 18 above]
22[r]Judg. 14:10; [John 2:1, 2]
24[s]See ch. 30:9-12
27[t][Judg. 14:12]
29[u]See ch. 30:3-7
30[v]ver. 20; ch. 31:41
31[w]Deut. 21:15 [x][ch. 30:22]
32[y]ch. 31:42; Ex. 3:7; 4:31; Deut. 26:7
34[z][Num. 18:2, 4]
35[a]Matt. 1:2; [ch. 49:8]

Chapter 30

1[b]ch. 29:31
2[c][ch. 16:2; 1 Sam. 1:5]

me for nothing? Tell me, what shall your wages be?" **16** Now Laban had two daughters.
The name of the older was Leah, and the name of the younger was Rachel. **17** Leah's eyes
were weak,[1] but Rachel was beautiful in form and appearance. **18** Jacob loved Rachel. And
he said, [q]"I will serve you seven years for your younger daughter Rachel." **19** Laban said, "It
is better that I give her to you than that I should give her to any other man; stay with me."
20 So Jacob [q]served seven years for Rachel, and they seemed to him but a few days because
of the love he had for her.

21 Then Jacob said to Laban, "Give me my wife that I may go in to her, for my time is
completed." **22** So Laban gathered together all the people of the place and [r]made a feast.
23 But in the evening he took his daughter Leah and brought her to Jacob, and he went in
to her. **24** (Laban gave[2] [s]his female servant Zilpah to his daughter Leah to be her servant.)
25 And in the morning, behold, it was Leah! And Jacob said to Laban, "What is this you
have done to me? Did I not serve with you for Rachel? Why then have you deceived me?"
26 Laban said, "It is not so done in our country, to give the younger before the firstborn.
27 [t]Complete the week of this one, and we will give you the other also in return for serving
me another seven years." **28** Jacob did so, and completed her week. Then Laban gave him his
daughter Rachel to be his wife. **29** (Laban gave [u]his female servant Bilhah to his daughter
Rachel to be her servant.) **30** So Jacob went in to Rachel also, and he loved Rachel more than
Leah, and served Laban [v]for another seven years.

Jacob's Children

31 When the LORD saw that Leah was [w]hated, [x]he opened her womb, but Rachel was
barren. **32** And Leah conceived and bore a son, and she called his name Reuben,[3] for she
said, "Because the LORD [y]has looked upon my affliction; for now my husband will love
me." **33** She conceived again and bore a son, and said, "Because the LORD has heard that I
am hated, he has given me this son also." And she called his name Simeon.[4] **34** Again she
conceived and bore a son, and said, "Now this time my husband will be [z]attached to me,
because I have borne him three sons." Therefore his name was called Levi.[5] **35** And she
conceived again and bore a son, and said, "This time I will praise the LORD." Therefore
she called his name [a]Judah.[6] Then she ceased bearing.

30 When Rachel saw that [b]she bore Jacob no children, she envied her sister. She said to
Jacob, "Give me children, or I shall die!" **2** Jacob's anger was kindled against Rachel,
and he said, "Am I in the place of God, [c]who has withheld from you the fruit of the womb?"

[1] Or *soft* [2] Or *had given*; also verse 29 [3] *Reuben* means *See, a son* [4] *Simeon* sounds like the Hebrew for *heard* [5] *Levi* sounds like the Hebrew for *attached* [6] *Judah* sounds like the Hebrew for *praise*

of irony. Having deceived his father by pretending to be the firstborn, Jacob himself is now deceived by his uncle Laban into marrying his firstborn daughter, Leah. Afterward, Laban permits Jacob to marry Rachel, but only on the understanding that Jacob will work for another seven years in order to pay the bride-price for her.

29:15–18 These verses set the scene by providing information essential for the development of the story. The brief descriptions of **Leah** and **Rachel** are sufficient to explain why Jacob loves Rachel.

29:18 I will serve you seven years for your younger daughter Rachel. In the ancient Near East it was customary for a prospective husband to give the bride's father a substantial gift of money, known as the bride-price. Jacob indicates that he is prepared to work for Laban in order to give the equivalent of seven years' wages for Rachel.

29:22 made a feast. Feasting was an important element of ancient Near Eastern weddings.

29:23 in the evening. It was dark or nearly dark when Leah was introduced to Jacob for the consummation of their marriage, and darkness in a world without artificial lighting can be pitch-black. At this stage, Jacob did not realize that Leah was the bride. She may also have come to him wearing a veil, the sign of a betrothed woman (see 24:65).

29:24 The mention of **Zilpah** here anticipates later developments when she will become a substitute wife for Leah (see 30:9–13).

29:25 Only **in the morning** does Jacob realize that he has been deceived by Laban.

29:26 to give the younger before the firstborn. Laban's remarks are highly ironic in light of Jacob's earlier deception of his father.

29:27 Complete the week of this one. The wedding celebrations lasted for seven days. Laban persuades Jacob to complete this process with Leah on the understanding that he will then be able to marry Rachel. This would also give ample opportunity for Leah to conceive a child.

29:29 The mention of **Bilhah** here anticipates later developments, for she will bear children on behalf of Rachel for Jacob (30:3–8).

29:31–30:24 *Jacob's Children.* These verses report the birth of 11 sons and one daughter to Jacob. Not surprisingly, given his unexpected marriage to Leah, Jacob's domestic scene is fraught with tension. Laban's deception and manipulation of Jacob creates years of discord between his two daughters.

29:31 When the LORD saw that Leah was hated. From the outset, Jacob had loved **Rachel** (v. 18). Undoubtedly, he found it difficult to love Leah, given the events that had brought them together, and Rachel probably also loathed her sister for the same reason. Yet their treatment of Leah causes the Lord to favor her over Rachel. While Leah is able to have children, Rachel is **barren**. As Genesis frequently highlights, the Lord is ultimately the One who creates human life.

29:32–35 Leah bears Jacob four **sons**. As the ESV footnotes reveal, each son's name is associated with a wordplay involving a comment made by Leah: **Reuben** ("see," v. 32), **Simeon** ("hear," v. 33), **Levi** ("attach," v. 34), and **Judah** ("praise," v. 35).

30:1–2 Rachel's barrenness causes further tensions to surface within Jacob's household. When Rachel demands **children** from Jacob (v. 1), he places the

3 Then she said, "Here is my servant [d]Bilhah; go in to her, so that she may give birth [e]on
my behalf,[1] that even I may have children[2] through her." 4 So she gave him her servant
Bilhah as a wife, and Jacob went in to her. 5 And Bilhah conceived and bore Jacob a son.
6 Then Rachel said, "God has [f]judged me, and has also heard my voice and given me a son."
Therefore she called his name Dan.[3] 7 Rachel's servant Bilhah conceived again and bore
Jacob a second son. 8 Then Rachel said, "With mighty wrestlings[4] I have wrestled with my
sister and have prevailed." So she called his name [g]Naphtali.[5]
9 When Leah saw that she had ceased bearing children, she took her servant Zilpah and
[h]gave her to Jacob as a wife. 10 Then Leah's servant Zilpah bore Jacob a son. 11 And Leah
said, [i]"Good fortune has come!" so she called his name [i]Gad.[6] 12 Leah's servant Zilpah bore
Jacob a second son. 13 And Leah said, "Happy am I! For women [j]have called me happy." So
she called his name Asher.[7]
14 In the days of wheat harvest Reuben went and found [k]mandrakes in the field and
brought them to his mother Leah. Then Rachel said to Leah, "Please give me some of your
son's mandrakes." 15 But she said to her, "Is it a small matter that you have taken away my
husband? Would you take away my son's mandrakes also?" Rachel said, "Then he may lie
with you tonight in exchange for your son's mandrakes." 16 When Jacob came from the field
in the evening, Leah went out to meet him and said, "You must come in to me, for I have
hired you with my son's mandrakes." So he lay with her that night. 17 And God listened
to Leah, and she conceived and bore Jacob a fifth son. 18 Leah said, "God has given me my
wages because I gave my servant to my husband." So she called his name Issachar.[8]
19 And Leah conceived again, and she bore Jacob a sixth son. 20 Then Leah said, "God has
endowed me with a good endowment; now my husband will honor me, because I have
borne him six sons." So she called his name [l]Zebulun.[9] 21 Afterward she bore a daughter
and called her name Dinah.
22 Then God [m]remembered Rachel, and God listened to her and [n]opened her womb.
23 She conceived and bore a son and said, "God has taken away [o]my reproach." 24 And she
called his name Joseph,[10] saying, [p]"May the LORD add to me another son!"

Jacob's Prosperity

25 As soon as Rachel had borne Joseph, Jacob said to Laban, "Send me away, that I may
go to my own home and country. 26 Give me my wives and my children [q]for whom I have

3 [d]ch. 29:29 [e]ch. 50:23
6 [f][ch. 49:16]
8 [g][Matt. 4:13]
9 [h]ver. 4; ch. 29:24
11 [i][ch. 49:19]
13 [j][Luke 1:48]
14 [k]Song 7:13
20 [l][Matt. 4:13]
22 [m]See ch. 8:1 [n]ch. 29:31; [Ps. 127:3]
23 [o]Luke 1:25; [1 Sam. 1:6; Isa. 4:1]
24 [p]ch. 35:17
26 [q]ch. 29:20, 30

[1] Hebrew *on my knees* [2] Hebrew *be built up*, which sounds like the Hebrew for *children* [3] *Dan* sounds like the Hebrew for *judged* [4] Hebrew *With wrestlings of God* [5] *Naphtali* sounds like the Hebrew for *wrestling* [6] *Gad* sounds like the Hebrew for *good fortune* [7] *Asher* sounds like the Hebrew for *happy* [8] *Issachar* sounds like the Hebrew for *wages*, or *hire* [9] *Zebulun* sounds like the Hebrew for *honor* [10] *Joseph* means *May he add*, and sounds like the Hebrew for *taken away*

blame on **God** (v. 2). While recognizing God's role in this situation, however, Jacob does not pray for Rachel, as his father Isaac had done for Rebekah (see 25:21–22).

30:3–8 To overcome her barrenness, Rachel offers Jacob her servant **Bilhah** as a substitute wife (v. 3). This practice, which was also carried out by Abraham and Sarah (see 16:1–4), was part of ancient Near Eastern culture. (E.g., the Nuzi texts from the 15th century B.C. treat the concept of marriage, and many of these texts deal with the issue of childlessness and provisions for new wives.) Children born to the substitute, or second, wife were regarded as belonging to the main, or first, wife. In this way, continuity of the family line was preserved. For this reason, Rachel names the two boys born to Bilhah (30:6, 8). Once again each name involves wordplay, **Dan** and **Naphtali** being associated with the verbs "judge" and "wrestle" (see ESV footnotes).

30:14–16 These verses, which recount Leah's conception of Issachar, highlight the intensity of the dispute between the two sisters. On this occasion Leah buys from Rachel the right to lie with Jacob. Having agreed to this with her sister, she says to Jacob, **I have hired you with my son's mandrakes**. The Hebrew term translated here as "mandrakes" (*duda'im*, possibly "love fruits") is usually understood to denote the plant *mandragora officinarum*, a species long regarded as having unusual properties. Unfortunately, no explanation is given as to why Rachel is so eager to have these mandrakes; the context suggests that she may have viewed the plant as increasing female fertility. This and other proposals, however, must be treated with caution.

30:17–21 God listened to Leah (v. 17). Although it is observed in 29:35 that Leah "ceased bearing" after the birth of Judah, she obviously wishes to have more children. God grants her wish, enabling her to have two more sons and a daughter. Once more, the names of the sons, **Issachar** (30:18) and **Zebulun** (v. 20), are deliberately chosen to reflect events surrounding their births: "Issachar" is related to the concept of "wages" and "Zebulun" to the concept of "honor." The birth of **Dinah** (v. 21) is briefly mentioned, anticipating the events recorded in ch. 34.

30:22–24 God remembered Rachel (v. 22). After many years of waiting, Rachel eventually bears Jacob a son. (On God's "remembering," see note on 8:1.) The repetition of "God" in 30:22 emphasizes that he is the One who has enabled Rachel to conceive and give birth. This is reinforced when Rachel acknowledges that **God has taken away my reproach** (v. 23). Since throughout Genesis fertility is often associated with divine blessing, a woman's inability to bear children could be interpreted as reflecting divine disapproval. Given the resentment that existed between the sisters, Leah may well have taunted Rachel over her inability to bear children. As with all the other sons born to Jacob, Joseph's name is derived from a remark made by his mother; in Hebrew **Joseph** (v. 24) sounds like the verb "add to." For the sad answer to her prayer, see 35:16–20.

30:25–31:18 *Jacob Prepares to Return to Canaan.* Having completed 14 years of service to Laban, Jacob looks to return to his family in Canaan. Laban, however, is reluctant to lose Jacob's service, which has brought him considerable wealth. The events narrated in this section illustrate how God's blessing is mediated through Jacob, but only to those who bless him. By mistreating Jacob, Laban is eventually disadvantaged.

28[r]ch. 29:15
29[s]ch. 31:6, 38-40
30[t]ver. 43 [u][1 Tim. 5:8]
32[v]ch. 31:8
37[w]See ch. 31:8-12
38[x][Ex. 2:16]
43[y]ver. 30 [z]ch. 24:35; 26:13, 14
Chapter 31
2[a]ch. 4:5
3[b]ver. 13; ch. 28:15; 32:9

served you, that I may go, for you know the service that I have given you." 27 But Laban said
to him, "If I have found favor in your sight, I have learned by divination that[1] the LORD
has blessed me because of you. 28 [r]Name your wages, and I will give it." 29 Jacob said to him,
[s]"You yourself know how I have served you, and how your livestock has fared with me. 30 For
you had little before I came, [t]and it has increased abundantly, and the LORD has blessed
you wherever I turned. But now when shall I [u]provide for my own household also?" 31 He
said, "What shall I give you?" Jacob said, "You shall not give me anything. If you will do
this for me, I will again pasture your flock and keep it: 32 let me pass through all your flock
today, removing from it every speckled and spotted sheep and every black lamb, and the
spotted and speckled among the goats, and [v]they shall be my wages. 33 So my honesty will
answer for me later, when you come to look into my wages with you. Every one that is not
speckled and spotted among the goats and black among the lambs, if found with me, shall
be counted stolen." 34 Laban said, "Good! Let it be as you have said." 35 But that day Laban
removed the male goats that were striped and spotted, and all the female goats that were
speckled and spotted, every one that had white on it, and every lamb that was black, and
put them in the charge of his sons. 36 And he set a distance of three days' journey between
himself and Jacob, and Jacob pastured the rest of Laban's flock.

37 Then [w]Jacob took fresh sticks of poplar and almond and plane trees, and peeled white
streaks in them, exposing the white of the sticks. 38 He set the sticks that he had peeled
in front of the flocks in the troughs, that is, the [x]watering places, where the flocks came
to drink. And since they bred when they came to drink, 39 the flocks bred in front of
the sticks and so the flocks brought forth striped, speckled, and spotted. 40 And Jacob
separated the lambs and set the faces of the flocks toward the striped and all the black
in the flock of Laban. He put his own droves apart and did not put them with Laban's
flock. 41 Whenever the stronger of the flock were breeding, Jacob would lay the sticks in
the troughs before the eyes of the flock, that they might breed among the sticks, 42 but
for the feebler of the flock he would not lay them there. So the feebler would be Laban's,
and the stronger Jacob's. 43 Thus the man [y]increased greatly and [z]had large flocks, female
servants and male servants, and camels and donkeys.

Jacob Flees from Laban

31 Now Jacob heard that the sons of Laban were saying, "Jacob has taken all that was
our father's, and from what was our father's he has gained all this wealth." 2 And
Jacob saw [a]that Laban did not regard him with favor as before. 3 Then the LORD said to
Jacob, [b]"Return to the land of your fathers and to your kindred, and I will be with you."
4 So Jacob sent and called Rachel and Leah into the field where his flock was 5 and said

[1] Or *have become rich and*

30:27–30 learned by divination. The narrator does not specify the precise method by which Laban discovers that the Lord has blessed him because of Jacob. The Israelites were later prohibited by God from practicing divination (Deut. 18:10) because it sought to provide knowledge by inappropriate methods (e.g., interpreting omens, using supernatural powers). Laban's use of divination is sinful, even though the information obtained is accurate. **the LORD has blessed me because of you**. In Genesis, all the members of the special line descended from Abraham are portrayed as mediating God's blessing to others (see Introduction: History of Salvation Summary). **Name your wages**. For 14 years Jacob has served Laban in order to pay the bride-price for Leah and Rachel. Having fulfilled this obligation, which has financially benefited Laban well beyond what he might have expected, Jacob now wants to provide for his own household. Laban, conscious of how Jacob has enriched him and eager to retain his services, asks Jacob to name his wages for remaining with him.

30:31–34 As payment for his services, Jacob asks Laban to allocate to him all the **speckled and spotted sheep** and **goats**, along with **every black lamb**. Their distinctive markings allow these animals to be easily distinguished from those that belong to Laban.

30:35 Having agreed on the wages, Laban secretly removes all the animals allocated to Jacob and gives them to his **sons**. Yet again, Laban's deceitful nature influences his treatment of Jacob.

30:37–39 To recover the loss of speckled and spotted sheep and goats, Jacob attempts to manipulate the breeding process of the flocks by placing **fresh sticks of poplar and almond and plane trees** (v. 37) in the troughs where the flocks were watered. These sticks, which have **peeled white streaks in them** (v. 37), correspond to the genetic makeup of the flocks, producing animals that are **striped, speckled, and spotted** (v. 39). The text should not be understood to imply any causal relationship between the sticks and the newborn animals.

30:40 Jacob separates his animals from those of Laban.

30:41–42 Jacob adopts a selective breeding policy to ensure that the striped, speckled, and spotted sheep and goats come from the strongest animals in Laban's flocks.

30:43 Having arrived in Paddan-aram with only his staff (see 32:10), Jacob becomes very rich. The brief description of his possessions resembles earlier summaries of Abraham's wealth (see 12:16; 24:35; also note on 26:12–13).

31:1–3 Jacob's growing **wealth** becomes a source of friction within Laban's family (v. 1). Even Laban's own attitude toward Jacob changes (v. 2). Against this background, the Lord instructs Jacob to **return** to Canaan (v. 3).

31:4–13 In a long speech, Jacob explains to Rachel and Leah his reasons for returning to his homeland. In doing so he contrasts the actions of their father with the God of his father: **your father does not regard me with favor**

to them, [c]"I see that your father does not regard me with favor as he did before. But the
God of my father [d]has been with me. 6 [e]You know that I have served your father with all
my strength, 7 yet your father has cheated me and changed my wages [f]ten times. But God
did not permit him to harm me. 8 If he said, [g]'The spotted shall be your wages,' then all
the flock bore spotted; and if he said, 'The striped shall be your wages,' then all the flock
bore striped. 9 Thus God has [h]taken away the livestock of your father and given them to
me. 10 In the breeding season of the flock I lifted up my eyes and saw in a dream that the
goats that mated with the flock were striped, spotted, and mottled. 11 Then the angel of
God said to me in the dream, 'Jacob,' and I said, 'Here I am!' 12 And he said, 'Lift up your
eyes and see, all the goats that mate with the flock are striped, spotted, and mottled, for [i]I
have seen all that Laban is doing to you. 13 I am the God of Bethel, [j]where you anointed a
pillar and made a vow to me. Now [k]arise, go out from this land and return to the land of
your kindred.' " 14 Then Rachel and Leah answered and said to him, "Is there [l]any portion
or inheritance left to us in our father's house? 15 Are we not regarded by him as foreigners?
For [m]he has sold us, and he has indeed devoured our money. 16 All the wealth that God
has taken away from our father belongs to us and to our children. Now then, whatever
God has said to you, do."

17 So Jacob arose and set his sons and his wives on camels. 18 He drove away all his livestock,
all his property that he had gained, the livestock in his possession that he had acquired in
[n]Paddan-aram, to go to the land of Canaan to his father Isaac. 19 Laban had gone to shear
his sheep, and Rachel stole her father's [o]household gods. 20 And Jacob tricked[1] Laban the
Aramean, by not telling him that he intended to flee. 21 He fled with all that he had and
arose and crossed the [p]Euphrates,[2] and [q]set his face toward the hill country of Gilead.

22 When it was told Laban on the third day that Jacob had fled, 23 he took his kinsmen
with him and pursued him for seven days and followed close after him into the hill country
of Gilead. 24 But God came to Laban the Aramean [r]in a dream by night and said to him,
"Be careful not to say anything to Jacob, [s]either good or bad."

25 And Laban overtook Jacob. Now Jacob had pitched his tent in the hill country, and
Laban with his kinsmen pitched tents in the hill country of Gilead. 26 And Laban said to
Jacob, "What have you done, that you have [t]tricked me and driven away my daughters like
captives of the sword? 27 Why did you flee secretly [t]and trick me, and did not tell me, so
that I might have sent you away with mirth and songs, with tambourine and lyre? 28 And
why did you not permit me [u]to kiss my sons and my daughters farewell? Now you have
done foolishly. 29 It is [v]in my power to do you harm. But the [w]God of your[3] father spoke to
me last night, saying, 'Be careful not to say anything to Jacob, [x]either good or bad.' 30 And

[1] Hebrew *stole the heart of*; also verses 26, 27 [2] Hebrew *the River* [3] The Hebrew for *your* is plural here

5 [c]ver. 2 [d]ver. 3
6 [e]ver. 38-40; ch. 30:29
7 [f]ver. 41; [Num. 14:22; Neh. 4:12; Job 19:3; Zech. 8:23]
8 [g]ch. 30:32
9 [h]ver. 1
12 [i][Ex. 3:7]
13 [j]See ch. 28:18-22 [k]ver. 3; ch. 32:9
14 [l][2 Sam. 20:1; 1 Kgs. 12:16]
15 [m]ch. 30:26; See ch. 29:15-20, 27
18 [n]ch. 25:20; 28:2, 6, 7
19 [o]ver. 30, 34; [Judg. 17:5; 1 Sam. 15:23; 19:13; Ezek. 21:21; Hos. 3:4; Zech. 10:2]
21 [p]Ex. 23:31; Ps. 72:8 [q]2 Kgs. 12:17; Luke 9:51
24 [r]See ch. 20:3 [s]ch. 24:50; Num. 24:13; 2 Sam. 13:22
26 [t]ver. 20
27 [t][See ver. 26 above]
28 [u]ver. 55; Ruth 1:9, 14; 1 Kgs. 19:20; Acts 20:37
29 [v]Deut. 28:32; Neh. 5:5 (Heb.); Prov. 3:27; Mic. 2:1 [w]ver. 42, 53; ch. 28:13 [x]ver. 24

as he did before. But the God of my father has been with me (v. 5). While Laban has exploited Jacob for his own advantage, God has consistently worked against Laban's schemes. **God of Bethel** (v. 13). At Bethel, God had promised to be with Jacob (28:15). Some 20 years later, Jacob acknowledges God's faithfulness (31:5). God now instructs Jacob to return to the land of his kindred.

31:14–16 In their response, **Rachel** and **Leah** also contrast their father's actions with those of God (cf. note on 31:4–13). Whereas the former has in practice disinherited them (vv. 14–15), God has provided for them and their children (v. 16).

31:19–55 *Laban Accuses Jacob in Gilead.* Fearful that Laban will prevent him from leaving Paddan-aram, Jacob escapes when his father-in-law is away shearing sheep. When Laban discovers what has happened, he pursues Jacob, catching up with him in Gilead. Accusation and counteraccusation eventually result in the making of a treaty that guarantees protection to both parties.

31:19 Rachel stole her father's household gods. "Household gods" translates the Hebrew word *terapim*. In spite of their being mentioned quite often in the Bible, knowledge of these objects is vague, the term often being translated as "images/idols." In this instance, since Laban later refers to them as "gods" in v. 30, they may have been small figurines depicting particular gods. The narrator does not explain why Rachel took her father's "gods." Perhaps she believed that this would prevent him from using their power to overcome Jacob. Possibly she thought that they would bring her good fortune. Maybe she wanted them only for their inherent value, given that they may have been made of costly metal. Whatever the reason, it later becomes evident that Jacob had no knowledge of their misappropriation (v. 32).

31:20 Jacob tricked Laban. The Hebrew idiom translated here as "tricked" is literally "stole the heart" (ESV footnote). The repetition of the verb "steal" in vv. 19–20 highlights one of the important themes of this passage. Although Jacob takes only what rightly belongs to him, Laban later accuses him of having stolen everything that is now in his possession (v. 43).

31:21 hill country of Gilead. The region lies to the east of the Jordan River, several hundred miles south of Paddan-aram.

31:22–24 Laban catches up with Jacob about 10 days after his initial departure. By this stage Jacob, with his family and livestock, has reached Gilead.

31:26–30 Laban seeks to portray Jacob in a poor light by contrasting his secretive flight with Laban's desire to have a joyful send-off. **The God of your father** (v. 29). Although Laban acknowledges that God has spoken to him (see v. 24), he refuses to acknowledge God as his own; he is the God of Isaac. To underline this point, Laban asks Jacob, **Why did you steal my gods?** (v. 30).

31:26 Laban falsely charges Jacob with having forced his **daughters** to go with him. But Rachel and Leah had willingly agreed to accompany their husband (v. 16).

30[y]ver. 19; Judg. 18:24
32[z][ch. 44:9]
35[a][Lev. 19:32]
37[b]ver. 54
39[c][Ex. 22:12]
41[d]ch. 29:27, 28 [e]ver. 7
42[f]Ps. 124:1, 2 [g]ver. 53 [h]See ch. 29:32 [i]ver. 29
44[j]ch. 26:28 [k]Josh. 24:27
45[l]ch. 28:18
48[m]ver. 44
49[n]Judg. 11:29, 34
50[o]Judg. 11:10; 1 Sam. 12:5; Jer. 42:5; Mic. 1:2; [Job 16:19]
52[p]ver. 43, 44

now you have gone away because you longed greatly for your father's house, but why
did you [y]steal my gods?" **31** Jacob answered and said to Laban, "Because I was afraid, for I
thought that you would take your daughters from me by force. **32** [z]Anyone with whom you
find your gods shall not live. In the presence of our kinsmen point out what I have that is
yours, and take it." Now Jacob did not know that Rachel had stolen them.

33 So Laban went into Jacob's tent and into Leah's tent and into the tent of the two female
servants, but he did not find them. And he went out of Leah's tent and entered Rachel's.
34 Now Rachel had taken the household gods and put them in the camel's saddle and sat
on them. Laban felt all about the tent, but did not find them. **35** And she said to her father,
"Let not my lord be angry that I cannot [a]rise before you, for the way of women is upon
me." So he searched but did not find the household gods.

36 Then Jacob became angry and berated Laban. Jacob said to Laban, "What is my offense?
What is my sin, that you have hotly pursued me? **37** For you have felt through all my goods;
what have you found of all your household goods? Set it here before my kinsmen and [b]your
kinsmen, that they may decide between us two. **38** These twenty years I have been with
you. Your ewes and your female goats have not miscarried, and I have not eaten the rams
of your flocks. **39** What was torn by wild beasts I did not bring to you. I bore the loss of it
myself. [c]From my hand you required it, whether stolen by day or stolen by night. **40** There
I was: by day the heat consumed me, and the cold by night, and my sleep fled from my
eyes. **41** These twenty years I have been in your house. [d]I served you fourteen years for your
two daughters, and six years for your flock, and [e]you have changed my wages ten times.
42 [f]If the God of my father, the God of Abraham and the [g]Fear of Isaac, had not been on
my side, surely now you would have sent me away empty-handed. [h]God saw my affliction
and the labor of my hands and [i]rebuked you last night."

43 Then Laban answered and said to Jacob, "The daughters are my daughters, the children are my children, the flocks are my flocks, and all that you see is mine. But what can I
do this day for these my daughters or for their children whom they have borne? **44** Come
now, [j]let us make a covenant, you and I. [k]And let it be a witness between you and me."
45 So Jacob [l]took a stone and set it up as a pillar. **46** And Jacob said to his kinsmen, "Gather
stones." And they took stones and made a heap, and they ate there by the heap. **47** Laban
called it Jegar-sahadutha,[1] but Jacob called it Galeed.[2] **48** Laban said, [m]"This heap is a witness between you and me today." Therefore he named it Galeed, **49** [n]and Mizpah,[3] for he
said, "The LORD watch between you and me, when we are out of one another's sight. **50** If
you oppress my daughters, or if you take wives besides my daughters, although no one is
with us, see, [o]God is witness between you and me."

51 Then Laban said to Jacob, "See this heap and the pillar, which I have set between you
and me. **52** [p]This heap is a witness, and the pillar is a witness, that I will not pass over this
heap to you, and you will not pass over this heap and this pillar to me, to do harm. **53** The

[1] Aramaic *the heap of witness* [2] Hebrew *the heap of witness* [3] *Mizpah* means *watchpost*

31:35 To prevent Laban from having access to the camel's saddle, where his "gods" are hidden, Rachel tells her father that **the way of women is upon** her. This refers to a woman's regular menstrual discharge. Although Laban has accused Jacob of deception, his own daughter is the principal culprit. The picture of Rachel sitting on and concealing Laban's "gods" emphasizes the total impotence of such idols.

31:36–42 Jacob responds sharply to Laban's unproven accusation of theft by recounting the scrupulous manner in which he cared for Laban's herds. During 20 years of arduous labor Jacob never once took advantage of Laban, even when the latter sought to mistreat him.

31:42 the God of Abraham and the Fear of Isaac. The term "Fear," as a metonym, is clearly a substitute for "God." Possibly, since Isaac treated God with reverential fear, God could be designated as the "One Feared" or the "Fear" of Isaac. Another possibility is the idea that Isaac's God induced fear in others (see, e.g., the reaction of Abimelech in 26:10–11, 28–29).

31:43–44 In spite of Jacob's observations, Laban continues to claim ownership of everything that Jacob has taken (v. 43). Then, in a gesture possibly intended to save face, Laban invites Jacob to make a **covenant** or treaty with him (v. 44). The pretext for the treaty is Laban's supposed desire to protect the future of his daughters and grandchildren (see v. 50).

31:45–46 Two separate "witnesses" are set up, one by Jacob and the other by his kinsmen. Jacob uses one **stone** to create a **pillar** (v. 45), similar to what he did earlier at Bethel (28:18, 22). His **kinsmen** pile up **stones** to form a **heap** (31:46). The creation of two witnesses may have been intended to underline the seriousness of the oath. More likely, the two witnesses reflect in some way the deities worshiped by Jacob and Laban. Jacob's single stone stands in marked contrast to the heap of stones set up by Laban and his relatives. Jacob's monotheistic faith is set alongside the polytheism of Laban. Since ancient Near Eastern treaties normally involved the gods as witnesses, the treaty between Jacob and Laban also required divine witnesses. Because Jacob is not prepared to compromise his monotheistic faith, two witnesses are established.

31:47–49 The Aramaic expression **Jegar-sahadutha** and the Hebrew term **Galeed** both mean "witness heap." **Mizpah**, meaning "watchtower," became the name of a settlement north of the Jabbok River; it was the hometown of Jephthah (see Judg. 11:11). The name "Mizpah" was also given to an important city located on the boundary between Israel and Judah, 8 miles (13 km) northwest of Jerusalem (see Judges 20).

God of Abraham and the God of Nahor, the God of their father, judge between us." So Jacob
swore by the [q]Fear of his father Isaac, 54 and Jacob offered a sacrifice in the hill country and
called [r]his kinsmen to eat bread. They ate bread and spent the night in the hill country.
55[1] Early in the morning Laban arose and kissed [s]his grandchildren and his daughters
and blessed them. Then Laban departed and returned home.

Jacob Fears Esau

32 Jacob went on his way, and the angels of God met him. 2 And when Jacob saw them
he said, "This is God's [t]camp!" So he called the name of that place [u]Mahanaim.[2]
3 And Jacob sent[3] messengers before him to Esau his brother in the land of [v]Seir, the

[1] Ch 32:1 in Hebrew [2] *Mahanaim* means *two camps* [3] Or *had sent*

53 [q]ver. 42
54 [r]ver. 37
55 [s]ver. 28, 43
Chapter 32
2 [t][Josh. 5:14; Luke 2:13] [u]Josh. 21:38; 2 Sam. 2:8; 17:24, 27; 1 Kgs. 2:8
3 [v]ch. 36:8, 9; Deut. 2:5; Josh. 24:4

32:1–21 *Jacob Prepares to Meet Esau Again.* After separating peacefully from Laban, Jacob prepares to meet his estranged brother Esau. Jacob is naturally hesitant about how he will be received some 20 years after fleeing from Esau in order to avoid being killed by him. Jacob's preparations are intended to promote a peaceful reconciliation.

32:1–2 These two verses provide an interesting, if somewhat enigmatic, interlude between Jacob's encounters with Laban and Esau. The reference to the **angels of God** (v. 1) is reminiscent of Jacob's dream at Bethel (28:12), the only other place in the whole of the OT where this same expression is used. Similarly, Jacob's observation, **This is God's camp** (32:2), parallels his previous comment about Bethel's being "the house of God" (28:17). Since camps were mobile, unlike houses, Jacob's remark suggests that God has sent his angels to accompany Jacob safely back to the land of Canaan. **Mahanaim** (32:2) means "two camps," possibly alluding to God's camp and Jacob's camp. The motif of "two camps" reappears in vv. 7, 10.

32:3–5 Jacob sent messengers before him. The Hebrew term for "messengers" (*mal'ak*) denotes "angels" in v. 1. **in the land of Seir, the country of Edom.** This region lies to the east of Canaan in Transjordan. According to 36:6–8, **Esau** settled here after Jacob returned to Canaan. Esau was obviously drawn to this region before Jacob returned and may have already separated himself from his father Isaac, who is living at Mamre, near Hebron (see 35:27). "Seir" (Hb. *Se'ir*) recalls "hairy" (Hb. *Sa'ir*), and "Edom" (Hb. *'Edom*) recalls

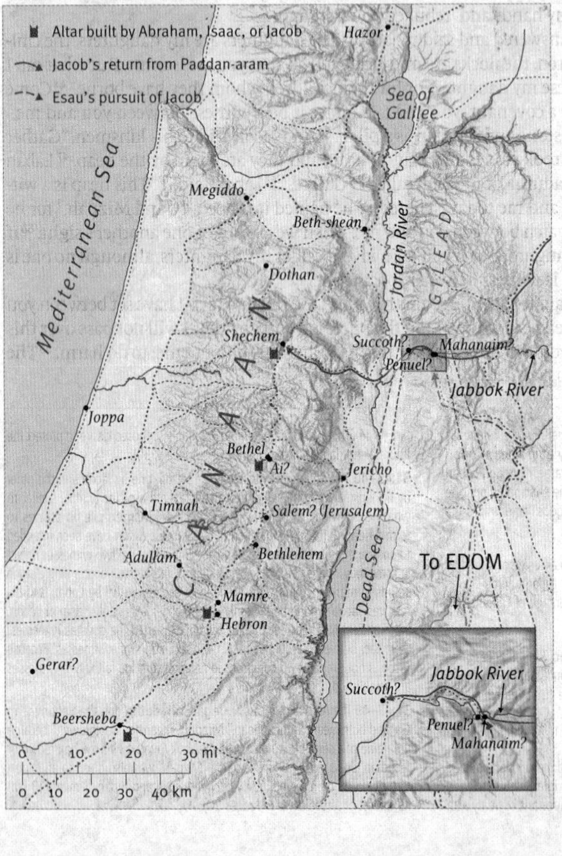

Jacob Returns to Canaan
c. 1976/1810 B.C.
After acquiring wealth in Paddan-aram, Jacob returned to Canaan. He came to Mahanaim, where he sent his household ahead of him and crossed the Jabbok alone. There he wrestled with a mysterious man until morning and named the place Peniel (also called Penuel). Jacob then encountered his brother Esau, who had come from Edom to meet him. After the two were reconciled, Esau returned to Edom, while Jacob journeyed to Canaan.

5 [w]ch. 33:8, 15
6 [x]ch. 33:1
7 [y]ch. 35:3
9 [z]ch. 28:13; 31:42, 53 [a]ch. 31:3, 13
10 [b][2 Sam. 7:18]
11 [c][Prov. 18:19]
12 [d]ch. 28:13-15
13 [e]ch. 43:11; [Prov. 17:8; 18:16; 19:6; 21:14]
22 [f]Deut. 2:37; 3:16; Josh. 12:2
24 [g]Hos. 12:3, 4

country of Edom, 4 instructing them, "Thus you shall say to my lord Esau: Thus says your
servant Jacob, 'I have sojourned with Laban and stayed until now. 5 I have oxen, donkeys,
flocks, male servants, and female servants. I have sent to tell my lord, in order that [w]I may
find favor in your sight.'"
6 And the messengers returned to Jacob, saying, "We came to your brother Esau, and
[x]he is coming to meet you, and there are four hundred men with him." 7 Then Jacob was
[y]greatly afraid and distressed. He divided the people who were with him, and the flocks
and herds and camels, into two camps, 8 thinking, "If Esau comes to the one camp and
attacks it, then the camp that is left will escape."
9 And Jacob said, [z]"O God of my father Abraham and God of my father Isaac, O LORD
who [a]said to me, 'Return to your country and to your kindred, that I may do you good,'
10 [b]I am not worthy of the least of all the deeds of steadfast love and all the faithfulness
that you have shown to your servant, for with only my staff I crossed this Jordan, and now
I have become two camps. 11 Please deliver me from the hand of my brother, from the hand
of Esau, for [c]I fear him, that he may come and attack me, the mothers with the children.
12 But [d]you said, 'I will surely do you good, and make your offspring as the sand of the sea,
which cannot be numbered for multitude.'"
13 So he stayed there that night, and from what he had with him he took [e]a present for
his brother Esau, 14 two hundred female goats and twenty male goats, two hundred ewes
and twenty rams, 15 thirty milking camels and their calves, forty cows and ten bulls, twenty
female donkeys and ten male donkeys. 16 These he handed over to his servants, every drove
by itself, and said to his servants, "Pass on ahead of me and put a space between drove and
drove." 17 He instructed the first, "When Esau my brother meets you and asks you, 'To
whom do you belong? Where are you going? And whose are these ahead of you?' 18 then
you shall say, 'They belong to your servant Jacob. They are a present sent to my lord Esau.
And moreover, he is behind us.'" 19 He likewise instructed the second and the third and
all who followed the droves, "You shall say the same thing to Esau when you find him,
20 and you shall say, 'Moreover, your servant Jacob is behind us.'" For he thought, "I may
appease him[1] with the present that goes ahead of me, and afterward I shall see his face.
Perhaps he will accept me."[2] 21 So the present passed on ahead of him, and he himself
stayed that night in the camp.

Jacob Wrestles with God

22 The same night he arose and took his two wives, his two female servants, and his eleven
children,[3] and crossed the ford of the [f]Jabbok. 23 He took them and sent them across the
stream, and everything else that he had. 24 And Jacob was left alone. And [g]a man wrestled

[1] Hebrew *appease his face* [2] Hebrew *he will lift my face* [3] Or *sons*

"red" (Hb. *'admoni*), from 25:25. The tone of Jacob's message to Esau is very deferential. Twice describing Esau as **my lord**, Jacob wants to **find favor** (32:5) in his brother's **sight** (see note on v. 18).

32:6 four hundred men with him. A force of this size suggests that Esau plans to attack Jacob. Genesis 14 recounts how Abraham, with a force of 318 men, successfully went to battle against four kings.

32:7–8 Out of fear of Esau, Jacob divides his family and possessions into **two camps** (v. 7). Jacob's actions, while understandable from a human perspective, reflect his inability to trust God fully for protection. The motif of "two camps," however, has already been introduced in vv. 1–2 with reference to God's protective presence.

32:9–13 Jacob's prayer, prompted by fear of Esau, expresses deep gratitude to God and a humble recognition that Jacob is unworthy of God's **steadfast love** and **faithfulness** (v. 10; see Ex. 34:6). Ironically, because God has prospered him so abundantly, Jacob is able to divide everything that he has into **two camps** (Gen. 32:10). Once again the motif of "two camps" is picked up (see vv. 1–2). **O LORD** (v. 9). This is the first time Jacob addresses God using his special name, "Yahweh," translated here "LORD" (see note on 2:4). **make your offspring as the sand of the sea** (32:12). Genesis does not specify when this divine promise was made to Jacob. At Bethel God speaks of Jacob's offspring being like the "dust of the earth" (28:14; see 13:16). On another occasion God could have compared Jacob's descendants to the sand of the sea, for he uses this image in his oath to Abraham (see 22:17).

32:13–21 To demonstrate his goodwill, Jacob sends Esau various droves of animals as a present.

32:18 your servant Jacob . . . my lord Esau. Jacob's deferential attitude is noteworthy, given earlier statements about the older serving the younger (see 25:23) and Isaac's blessing, which speaks of Jacob's being lord over his brothers (27:29).

32:22–32 *Jacob Encounters God at Peniel.* This passage records a nighttime encounter between God and Jacob. Jacob is transformed by this extraordinary meeting, which is marked by the changing of his name from "Jacob" to "Israel."

32:22–23 ford of the Jabbok. Jacob's journey has brought him to the Jabbok River, which flows westward into the Jordan Valley about 24 miles (39 km) north of the Dead Sea.

32:24 a man wrestled. The unexpected and sudden introduction of this man, who wrestles in the dark with Jacob, captures something of the event itself. By the time their contest comes to an end, Jacob is convinced that his opponent is God himself (see v. 30). This is not improbable, given that God had previously come to Abraham in human form (18:1–15). The story contains an interesting wordplay in Hebrew: God wrestles (*ye'abeq*) with Jacob (*ya'aqob*) by the Jabbok (*yabboq*).

with him until the breaking of the day. 25 When the man saw that he did not prevail against
Jacob, he touched his hip socket, and Jacob's hip was put out of joint as he wrestled with
him. 26 Then he said, "Let me go, for the day has broken." But Jacob said, [h]"I will not let
you go unless you bless me." 27 And he said to him, "What is your name?" And he said,
"Jacob." 28 Then he said, [i]"Your name shall no longer be called Jacob, but Israel,[1] for [j]you
have striven with God and [k]with men, and have prevailed." 29 Then Jacob asked him, "Please
tell me your name." But he said, [l]"Why is it that you ask my name?" And there he blessed
him. 30 So Jacob called the name of the place Peniel,[2] saying, "For [m]I have seen God face to
face, and yet my life has been delivered." 31 The sun rose upon him as he passed [n]Penuel,
limping because of his hip. 32 Therefore to this day the people of Israel do not eat the sinew
of the thigh that is on the hip socket, because he touched the socket of Jacob's hip on the
sinew of the thigh.

Jacob Meets Esau

33 And Jacob lifted up his eyes and looked, and behold, [o]Esau was coming, and four
hundred men with him. So he divided the children among Leah and Rachel and
the two female servants. 2 And he put the servants with their children in front, then Leah
with her children, and Rachel and Joseph last of all. 3 He himself went on before them,
[p]bowing himself to the ground seven times, until he came near to his brother.
4 [q]But Esau ran to meet him and embraced him [r]and fell on his neck and kissed him, and
they wept. 5 And when Esau lifted up his eyes and saw the women and children, he said,
"Who are these with you?" Jacob said, [s]"The children whom God has graciously given your
servant." 6 Then the servants drew near, they and their children, and bowed down. 7 Leah
likewise and her children drew near and bowed down. And last Joseph and Rachel drew
near, and they bowed down. 8 Esau said, "What do you mean by [t]all this company[3] that
I met?" Jacob answered, [u]"To find favor in the sight of my lord." 9 But Esau said, "I have
enough, my brother; keep what you have for yourself." 10 Jacob said, "No, please, if I have
found favor in your sight, then accept my present from my hand. [v]For I have seen your
face, which is like seeing the face of God, and you have accepted me. 11 Please accept my
[w]blessing that is brought to you, because God has dealt graciously with me, and because
I have enough." Thus he [x]urged him, and he took it.

[1] *Israel* means *He strives with God*, or *God strives* [2] *Peniel* means *the face of God* [3] Hebrew *camp*

26 [h][Luke 18:1]; See Matt. 15:21-28
28 [i]ch. 35:10; 2 Kgs. 17:34 [j]Hos. 12:3, 4 [k]ch. 33:4
29 [l]Judg. 13:18
30 [m]ch. 16:13; Ex. 24:10, 11; Deut. 5:24; Judg. 6:22; 13:22; [Ex. 33:20; Isa. 6:5]
31 [n]Judg. 8:8, 17; 1 Kgs. 12:25

Chapter 33

1 [o]ch. 32:6
3 [p]ch. 18:2; 42:6; 43:26
4 [q]ch. 32:28 [r]ch. 45:14
5 [s]ch. 48:9; Ps. 127:3; Isa. 8:18
8 [t]ch. 32:16 [u]ver. 15; ch. 32:5
10 [v]ch. 18:1; 19:1
11 [w]2 Kgs. 5:15 [x][2 Sam. 13:25, 27; 2 Kgs. 5:23]

32:25 Jacob's hip was put out of joint. Jacob's injury highlights not only the strength of his opponent but also his own resolve to prevail.

32:26 I will not let you go unless you bless me. Jacob's determination to be blessed is demonstrated by his reluctance to release his opponent, even when his thigh is dislocated.

32:28 Your name shall no longer be called Jacob, but Israel. From the context, "Israel" is probably to be understood as meaning "he strives with God"; the alternative meaning is "God strives" (see ESV footnote), but the context makes this less likely. Hosea 12:3–4 reflects on this event. The renaming of Jacob brings to a climax a lifetime of struggling with others (see Gen. 25:22). Through all this, Jacob has finally come to realize the importance of being blessed by God. The events of the preceding years have changed Jacob. The God of his father has now become his God (32:9; see also 28:21). (This is the first mention of the name "Israel" in the Bible. In extrabiblical literature, it first appears in the "Israel Stele" of Pharaoh Merneptah of the late 13th century B.C. The text says: "Israel lies desolate; its seed is no more." Obviously by this early date the name was being used for a people and not merely for an individual.)

32:30 Jacob called the name of the place Peniel, saying, "For I have seen God face to face, and yet my life has been delivered." "Peniel" means "face of God." Jacob's encounter with God fills him with awe. When later Moses asks to see God's glory, he is told, "You cannot see my face, for man shall not see me and live" (Ex. 33:20). In light of this, either Jacob's encounter is a remarkable exception or, alternatively, the expression "face to face" should be understood as a figure of speech for intimacy with God. In Ex. 33:11, God speaks to Moses "face to face," but in both cases the phrase can imply a close personal encounter, or possibly a vision of the brightness of God's glory, without suggesting a literal vision of God's face.

32:31 Penuel is a variant spelling of "Peniel."

33:1–20 *Jacob Is Reconciled with Esau.* The account of Jacob's reconciliation with Esau comes as the sequel to Jacob's encounter with God at Penuel. Esau's affectionate embrace of his brother and Jacob's deferential attitude ensure a successful reunion.

33:1–3 With **Esau** in sight, **Jacob** arranges his wives and **children** in order of importance, with pride of place being given to **Rachel** and **Joseph**, the only one of Jacob's sons to be named here (v. 2). Jacob's special treatment of Joseph becomes an important theme later in Genesis (see ch. 37).

33:3 Jacob slowly approaches Esau, **bowing himself to the ground seven times**. Jacob's actions are clearly intended to express his submission to Esau. Jacob's behavior is noteworthy, especially given the earlier divine revelation that the older would serve the younger (25:23).

33:4 Esau ran to meet him. The unreserved manner in which Esau greets and embraces Jacob reveals that he holds no animosity toward his brother. The description of their reconciliation may well have influenced Jesus' account of the lost son returning to his father (see Luke 15:20).

33:8 All this company that I met refers to the droves of animals that Jacob had sent ahead to Esau (see 32:13–21).

33:10 For I have seen your face, which is like seeing the face of God, and you have accepted me. Jacob draws a remarkable parallel between his earlier encounter with God and his meeting with Esau. Like God, Esau shows unmerited favor to Jacob.

33:11 Please accept my blessing. In this context, Jacob's blessing refers to the tangible present of livestock that he gives to Esau. Previously, Jacob had deprived Esau of the blessing of the firstborn. While Jacob cannot restore

12 Then Esau said, "Let us journey on our way, and I will go ahead of[1] you." **13** But Jacob
said to him, "My lord knows that the children are frail, and that the nursing flocks and
herds are a care to me. If they are driven hard for one day, all the flocks will die. **14** Let my
lord pass on ahead of his servant, and I will lead on slowly, at the pace of the livestock that
are ahead of me and at the pace of the children, until I come to my lord [y]in Seir."

15 So Esau said, "Let me leave with you some of the people who are with me." But he said,
"What need is there? [z]Let me find favor in the sight of my lord." **16** So Esau returned that
day on his way to [a]Seir. **17** But Jacob journeyed to [b]Succoth, and built himself a house and
made booths for his livestock. Therefore the name of the place is called Succoth.[2]

18 And Jacob came safely[3] to the city of [c]Shechem, which is in the land of Canaan, on his
way from Paddan-aram, and he camped before the city. **19** And from the sons of [d]Hamor,
Shechem's father, [e]he bought for a hundred pieces of money[4] the piece of land on which
he had pitched his tent. **20** There he erected an altar and called it El-Elohe-Israel.[5]

The Defiling of Dinah

34 Now [f]Dinah the daughter of Leah, whom she had borne to Jacob, went out to see the
women of the land. **2** And when Shechem the son of [g]Hamor the Hivite, the prince
of the land, saw her, he seized her and lay with her and humiliated her. **3** And his soul was
drawn to Dinah the daughter of Jacob. He loved the young woman and spoke tenderly to
her. **4** So Shechem [h]spoke to his father Hamor, saying, "Get me this girl for my wife."

5 Now Jacob heard that he had defiled his daughter Dinah. But his sons were with his
livestock in the field, so Jacob held his peace until they came. **6** And Hamor the father of
Shechem went out to Jacob to speak with him. **7** The sons of Jacob had come in from the
field as soon as they heard of it, and the men were indignant and [i]very angry, because he
[j]had done an outrageous thing in Israel by lying with Jacob's daughter, [k]for such a thing
must not be done.

8 But Hamor spoke with them, saying, "The soul of my son Shechem longs for your[6]
daughter. Please give her to him to be his wife. **9** Make marriages with us. Give your daughters to us, and take our daughters for yourselves. **10** You shall dwell with us, and [l]the land
shall be open to you. Dwell and [m]trade in it, and [n]get property in it." **11** Shechem also said
to her father and to her brothers, [o]"Let me find favor in your eyes, and whatever you say

[1] Or *along with* [2] *Succoth* means *booths* [3] Or *peacefully* [4] Hebrew *a hundred qesitah;* a unit of money of unknown value [5] *El-Elohe-Israel* means *God, the God of Israel* [6] The Hebrew for *your* is plural here

14 [y]ch. 32:3
15 [z]ver. 8; ch. 34:11; 47:25; Ruth 2:13
16 [a]ch. 32:3
17 [b]Josh. 13:27; Judg. 8:5; Ps. 60:6
18 [c]Josh. 24:1; Judg. 9:1; Ps. 60:6; Acts 7:16
19 [d]Acts 7:16 [e]Josh. 24:32; John 4:5

Chapter 34

1 [f]ch. 30:21
2 [g]Acts 7:16
4 [h][Judg. 14:2]
7 [i]ch. 49:7 [j]Josh. 7:15; Judg. 20:6 [k]ver. 31; ch. 20:9; 2 Sam. 13:12
10 [l]ch. 13:9; 20:15 [m]ver. 21; ch. 42:34 [n]ch. 47:27
11 [o]See ch. 33:15

this particular blessing to Esau, he seeks to make restitution by giving him another blessing, which comes from God's blessing of Jacob.

33:12–14 While **Esau** desires to have his brother return with him (v. 12), Jacob politely refuses, using the travel-weariness of his children and livestock as an excuse (v. 13). Yet again, Jacob addresses Esau as **my lord** and refers to himself as **servant** (v. 14). **until I come to my lord in Seir**. Apparently Jacob still does not fully trust Esau, and has no intention of following him to Seir (see v. 17). From the point where Esau and Jacob met, the shortest route to the northern border of Seir was approximately 100 miles or 161 km to the south, while Succoth was only 4 miles or 6.4 km to the west.

33:17–18 The story contains an unexpected twist at this point, for Jacob had earlier indicated to Esau that he would follow him to Seir (v. 14). Jacob, however, relocates to Succoth and then Shechem. **Succoth** (v. 17) is in the Jordan Valley near where the Jabbok River joins the Jordan River. **Shechem** (v. 18), about 20 miles (32 km) west of Succoth, was the first place named in connection with Abraham's arrival in Canaan (see 12:6).

33:19 from the sons of Hamor, Shechem's father. The reference to Shechem links this episode with the next, where he is one of the central characters in the story. **hundred pieces of money**. The Hebrew term rendered here "money" (*qesitah*) is used rarely in the OT (see Josh. 24:32; Job 42:11); the precise value is uncertain.

33:20 altar. Previously, Abraham had built an altar at Shechem. Possibly, Jacob reconstructs this earlier altar, for the Hebrew verb used to describe his action is not the usual one for building altars. Since this is the first altar mentioned in connection with Jacob, it signals his commitment to worship the Lord. This is reinforced by the name he gives the altar: **El-Elohe-Israel** means "God, the God of Israel." Jacob identifies the God worshiped at this altar as the One whom he had encountered at Peniel and who had changed his name.

34:1–31 *The Rape of Dinah.* Almost as soon as Jacob returns to Canaan, an incident threatens the future security of his whole family. While the rape of Dinah by Shechem is inexcusable, the punishment meted out by Simeon and Levi far exceeds the crime. While they are reluctant to acknowledge any fault on their part, Jacob is very conscious of how their actions have endangered his entire household. Furthermore, circumcision, which was intended by God to bring divine blessing, leads on this occasion to death and destruction. All of this takes place without any reference to God.

34:1 Dinah's association with the **women of the land** possibly carries negative connotations. The only other occurrence of this expression in Genesis comes in 27:46, when Rebekah speaks out against Jacob's marrying "one of the women of the land."

34:2–4 Hamor the Hivite, the prince of the land (v. 2), was clearly a figure of some importance in Shechem. His status later allowed him to persuade all the men of the city to be circumcised. While Hamor's son **Shechem** (v. 4) is initially drawn to Dinah by lust, he now desires to hold on to her as his wife.

34:7 Dinah's brothers are justifiably enraged at the way Shechem has treated their sister.

34:8–9 Although Hamor comes to speak to Jacob (v. 6), the latter appears to be pushed aside by his sons. They are the ones who engage in discussion with Hamor and Shechem.

34:11–12 In an attempt to win over Dinah's family, Shechem offers a generous

to me I will give. 12 Ask me for as great a [p]bride price[1] and gift as you will, and I will give
whatever you say to me. Only give me the young woman to be my wife."
13 The sons of Jacob answered Shechem and his father Hamor deceitfully, because he had
defiled their sister Dinah. 14 They said to them, "We cannot do this thing, to give our sister
to one who is uncircumcised, for [q]that would be a disgrace to us. 15 Only on this condition
will we agree with you—that you will become as we are by every male among you being
circumcised. 16 Then we will give our daughters to you, and we will take your daughters to
ourselves, and we will dwell with you and become one people. 17 But if you will not listen
to us and be circumcised, then we will take our daughter, and we will be gone."
18 Their words pleased Hamor and Hamor's son Shechem. 19 And the young man did
not delay to do the thing, because he delighted in Jacob's daughter. Now [r]he was the most
honored of all his father's house. 20 So Hamor and his son Shechem [s]came to the gate of
their city and spoke to the men of their city, saying, 21 "These men are at peace with us; let
them dwell in the land and [t]trade in it, for behold, the land is large enough for them. Let
us take their daughters as wives, and let us give them our daughters. 22 Only on this condition will the men agree to dwell with us to become one people—when every male among
us is circumcised as they are circumcised. 23 Will not their livestock, their property and all
their beasts be ours? Only let us agree with them, and they will dwell with us." 24 And all
who went out of the gate of his city listened to Hamor and his son Shechem, and every
male was circumcised, all who [u]went out of the gate of his city.
25 On the third day, when they were sore, two of the sons of Jacob, [v]Simeon and Levi,
[w]Dinah's brothers, took their swords and came against the city while it felt secure and killed
all the males. 26 They killed Hamor and his son Shechem with the sword and took Dinah out
of Shechem's house and went away. 27 The sons of Jacob came upon the slain and plundered
the city, because they had defiled their sister. 28 They took their flocks and their herds, their
donkeys, and whatever was in the city and in the field. 29 All their wealth, all their little
ones and their wives, all that was in the houses, they captured and plundered.
30 Then Jacob said to Simeon and Levi, [x]"You have brought trouble on me [y]by making
me stink to the inhabitants of the land, [z]the Canaanites and the Perizzites. [a]My numbers
are few, and if they gather themselves against me and attack me, I shall be destroyed, both
I and my household." 31 But they said, "Should he treat our sister like a prostitute?"

God Blesses and Renames Jacob

35 God said to Jacob, "Arise, go up to [b]Bethel and dwell there. Make an altar there to
the God who appeared to you [c]when you fled from your brother Esau." 2 So Jacob
said to his [d]household and to all who were with him, "Put away [e]the foreign gods that are

[1] Or *engagement present*

12 [p]Ex. 22:16, 17; 1 Sam. 18:25; [Deut. 22:29]
14 [q]Josh. 5:9
19 [r][1 Chr. 4:9]
20 [s]See Ruth 4:1
21 [t]ver. 10; ch. 42:34
24 [u][ch. 23:10]
25 [v]See ch. 49:5-7 [w]ch. 29:33, 34; 30:21
30 [x]Josh. 7:25 [y]Ex. 5:21; 1 Sam. 13:4; 27:12; 2 Sam. 10:6; 16:21; 1 Chr. 19:6 (Heb.) [z]ch. 13:7; 15:20, 21 [a]1 Chr. 16:19; Ps. 105:12

Chapter 35
1 [b]ch. 28:19 [c]ch. 27:43
2 [d]ch. 18:19; Josh. 24:15 [e][ch. 31:19; Josh. 24:23; 1 Sam. 7:3]

bride price and gift. This was a normal part of marriage arrangements in the ancient Near East. He is willing to give them whatever they ask.

34:13 deceitfully. The Hebrew term used here (*mirmah*) implies treachery. Although Jacob's sons resemble their father, whose name means "he deceives" (see 25:26), their actions here are about to go beyond anything he has done.

34:14–17 As a precondition for marriage between Dinah and Shechem, her brothers request that the men of Shechem become **circumcised** (v. 15; see note on 17:11). In ch. 17 circumcision is introduced as the sign of the eternal covenant that God established with Abraham. Those who are circumcised acknowledge Abraham as their father. While Jacob's sons are right to insist that circumcision is necessary in order for both groups to become **one people** (v. 16), their intention, as revealed in subsequent events, is otherwise.

34:21 These men are at peace with us. Hamor and Shechem are utterly deceived by Jacob's sons.

34:25 two of the sons of Jacob, Simeon and Levi. Although all of Jacob's sons were involved in the deception of Hamor and Shechem, only Simeon and Levi are involved in the slaughter of **all the males**. While all the brothers are involved in plundering the city, Jacob later attaches particular guilt to Simeon and Levi for the massacre of the men of Shechem (v. 30). This is later reflected in 49:5–7 and explains why both brothers are passed over in favor of their younger sibling Judah.

34:30 Jacob's condemnation of Simeon and Levi focuses not on the morality of their actions but on the possible consequences for his household. Out of anger at what has happened, **the Canaanites and the Perizzites** may attack Jacob's household.

35:1–29 *Jacob's Onward Journey to Hebron.* Jacob moves by stages from Shechem to Bethel, eventually coming to Hebron, where his father Isaac is still alive. During this journey a number of incidents occur that either bring to a close previous episodes or anticipate later developments in Genesis. Ending with the death of Isaac, this chapter marks the passing of one generation while preparing for the next. Transformed by the experiences of Bethel and Peniel, Jacob is now in a position to assume the mantle of his father as the one through whom the divine promises to Abraham will be continued.

35:1–5 Jacob relocates from Shechem to Bethel.

35:1 Jacob had only set up a pillar at Bethel when God appeared to him (28:18). By returning to **Bethel** and building **an altar there**, Jacob acknowledges that God has been faithful to him (see 28:20–22).

35:2–3 Jacob's instructions are intended to prepare his household for entering God's presence; **Bethel** (v. 3) is the "house of God." They must rid themselves of **foreign gods** (v. 2). As emphasized later in the first prohibition of the Ten Commandments, those who worship the Lord must not have other gods (see Ex. 20:3). Rachel's theft of her father's household gods suggests that polytheistic beliefs existed within Jacob's household. These must be eradicated. The

2[f]Ex. 19:10
3[g]ch. 32:7, 24 [h]ch. 28:20; 31:3
4[i]Josh. 24:26; Judg. 9:6
6[j]ch. 28:19
7[k]ver. 1
8[l]ch. 24:59
10[m][ch. 17:5, 15] [n]ch. 32:28
11[o]See ch. 17:1 [p]ch. 28:3; 48:4 [q]ch. 17:5, 6, 16; 26:4
12[r]ch. 12:7; 13:15; 17:8; 26:3; 28:13
13[s]ch. 17:22
14[t]ch. 28:18; 31:45
15[u]ch. 28:19

among you and [f]purify yourselves and change your garments. 3 Then let us arise and go
up to Bethel, so that I may make there an altar to the God [g]who answers me in the day of
my distress and [h]has been with me wherever I have gone." 4 So they gave to Jacob all the
foreign gods that they had, and the rings that were in their ears. Jacob hid them under
[i]the terebinth tree that was near Shechem.

5 And as they journeyed, a terror from God fell upon the cities that were around them,
so that they did not pursue the sons of Jacob. 6 And Jacob came to [j]Luz (that is, Bethel),
which is in the land of Canaan, he and all the people who were with him, 7 and there he
built an altar and called the place El-bethel,[1] because [k]there God had revealed himself to
him when he fled from his brother. 8 And [l]Deborah, Rebekah's nurse, died, and she was
buried under an oak below Bethel. So he called its name Allon-bacuth.[2]

9 God appeared[3] to Jacob again, when he came from Paddan-aram, and blessed him.
10 And God said to him, "Your name is Jacob; [m]no longer shall your name be called Jacob,
but [n]Israel shall be your name." So he called his name Israel. 11 And God said to him, [o]"I
am God Almighty:[4] be [p]fruitful and multiply. [q]A nation and a company of nations shall
come from you, and kings shall come from your own body.[5] 12 [r]The land that I gave to
Abraham and Isaac I will give to you, and I will give the land to your offspring after you."
13 Then God [s]went up from him in the place where he had spoken with him. 14 And Jacob
[t]set up a pillar in the place where he had spoken with him, a pillar of stone. He poured out
a drink offering on it and poured oil on it. 15 So Jacob called the name of the place where
God had spoken with him [u]Bethel.

The Deaths of Rachel and Isaac

16 Then they journeyed from Bethel. When they were still some distance[6] from Ephrath,
Rachel went into labor, and she had hard labor. 17 And when her labor was at its hardest, the

[1] *El-bethel means God of Bethel* [2] *Allon-bacuth means oak of weeping* [3] *Or had appeared* [4] *Hebrew El Shaddai* [5] *Hebrew from your loins* [6] *Or about two hours' distance*

members of Jacob's household must **purify** themselves (Gen. 35:2). While no details are given here, later Israelite tradition emphasized the importance of purification rituals, some of which involved the washing of clothes. This may explain Jacob's final instruction to change **garments** (v. 2; see Ex. 19:10). **who answers me in the day of my distress** (Gen. 35:3). The present tense, "answers," here indicates that God has consistently responded to Jacob in every time of trouble.

35:4 the rings that were in their ears. It is not clear whether these earrings were worn by the people or by the foreign gods; some ancient Near Eastern evidence indicates that idols could have earrings. Jacob probably buried these cultic objects so that their location would not be easily discovered.

35:5 a terror from God. While the precise nature of this terror is unknown, other passages in Genesis record how fear of God is used to protect the patriarchs (e.g., 20:8; 26:28–29). Jacob's fears expressed in 34:30 are answered by God's protection, in spite of the excessive vengeance shown by Simeon and Levi (34:25).

35:6–15 These verses describe what happens when Jacob returns to Bethel; three separate events take place: Jacob builds the altar as instructed (v. 7); Deborah dies and is buried (v. 8); and God appears to Jacob again (vv. 9–15).

35:6 Luz (that is, Bethel). See note on 28:19.

35:7 called the place El-bethel. This probably refers to the altar. "El-bethel," meaning "God of Bethel," resembles in form the name that Jacob gave to the altar at Shechem (33:20).

35:8 Deborah, Rebekah's nurse, received a brief mention in 24:59, although this is the first time that her name is given. Her presence with Jacob may suggest that she had been sent to him by Rebekah in fulfillment of her promise in 27:45.

35:9–13 These verses bring the account of Jacob's developing relationship with God to an important climax. Jacob's return to Bethel is accompanied by further divine appearances.

35:9 blessed him. This not only confirms the blessing of 32:29 but more importantly places Jacob on a par with Abraham and Isaac, of whom similar affirmations were made (see 24:1; 25:11).

35:10 God's statement here confirms the importance of the transformation that has taken place in Jacob's life. On the change of Jacob's name to **Israel**, see note on 32:28.

35:11–12 God's second statement emphasizes that Jacob is now heir to the divine promises first given to Abraham and then to Isaac. **I am God Almighty**. This is how God revealed himself to Abraham (see note on 17:1–2) and is the divine name used by Isaac when he blesses Jacob in 28:3. Much of God's speech closely resembles what he says to Abraham in 17:5–6 and what Isaac requests for Jacob in 28:3–4. **be fruitful and multiply**. This instruction goes back to the very creation of humanity (see note on 1:28). **A nation and a company of nations shall come from you**. While Isaac refers to a "company of peoples" (28:3), God's comment reveals that he has more than the nation of Israel in view. Given the close connection with the divine promises made to Abraham, this seems to be a development of the idea that Abraham would be the father of many nations (17:4–6). **kings shall come from your own body**. The promise of royal descendants is first given to Abraham in 17:6. This royal theme reappears in Joseph's dreams (37:6–10), showing that the ultimate fulfillment of this divine promise will come through Jacob's descendants. **The land that I gave** (35:12). The divine promise of the land, which goes back to the call of Abraham in 12:1–3, is renewed to include Jacob and his descendants.

35:14–15 pillar. See note on 28:18. **drink offering**. This is the only mention in Genesis of such an offering. Later references suggest that wine was used (e.g., Ex. 29:40; Lev. 23:13; Num. 15:1–10).

35:16–20 Jacob travels south from **Bethel**, undoubtedly with the intention of going to Mamre (Hebron). His journey is disrupted, however, when **Rachel** dies while giving birth. The name that Rachel gives her newborn son, **Ben-oni** (v. 18), is potentially ambiguous (see ESV footnote): it probably means "son of my sorrow," to signify the tragic consequences surrounding his birth, but it could also mean "son of my strength" (see 49:3 for "strength" in this sense). Jacob deliberately changes the name and removes the ambiguity. **Benjamin** (35:18) means "son of my right hand." **on the way to Ephrath (that is, Bethlehem)**. Jewish tradition locates the tomb between Bethlehem and Jerusalem. This tradition, however, can be traced back only to the fourth

midwife said to her, "Do not fear, for [v]you have another son." 18 And as her soul was departing (for she was dying), she called his name Ben-oni;[1] [w]but his father called him Benjamin.[2]
19 So [x]Rachel died, and she was buried on the way to [y]Ephrath (that is, Bethlehem), 20 and
Jacob set up a pillar over her tomb. It is [z]the pillar of Rachel's tomb, which is there to this
day. 21 Israel journeyed on and pitched his tent beyond the tower of Eder.
22 While Israel lived in that land, Reuben went and [a]lay with Bilhah his father's concubine. And Israel heard of it.
Now the sons of Jacob were twelve. 23 The sons of Leah: [b]Reuben (Jacob's firstborn),
Simeon, Levi, Judah, Issachar, and Zebulun. 24 The sons of Rachel: Joseph and Benjamin.
25 The sons of Bilhah, Rachel's servant: Dan and Naphtali. 26 The sons of Zilpah, Leah's servant:
Gad and Asher. These were the sons of Jacob who were born to him in Paddan-aram.
27 And Jacob came to his father Isaac at [c]Mamre, or [d]Kiriath-arba (that is, Hebron), where
Abraham and Isaac had sojourned. 28 Now the days of Isaac were 180 years. 29 And Isaac
breathed his last, and he died [e]and was gathered to his people, old and full of days. And
[f]his sons Esau and Jacob buried him.

Esau's Descendants

36 These are the generations of Esau (that is, [g]Edom). 2 Esau [h]took his wives from the
Canaanites: Adah the daughter of Elon the Hittite, [i]Oholibamah the daughter of
Anah the daughter[3] of Zibeon the Hivite, 3 and [j]Basemath, Ishmael's daughter, the sister
of Nebaioth. 4 And Adah bore to Esau, [k]Eliphaz; Basemath bore Reuel; 5 and Oholibamah
bore Jeush, Jalam, and Korah. These are the sons of Esau who were born to him in the
land of Canaan.
6 Then Esau took his wives, his sons, his daughters, and all the members of his household,
his livestock, all his beasts, and all his property that he had acquired in the land of Canaan.
He went into a land away from his brother Jacob. 7 [l]For their possessions were too great for
them to dwell together. [m]The land of their sojournings could not support them because
of their livestock. 8 So Esau settled in [n]the hill country of Seir. ([o]Esau is Edom.)

17 [v]ch. 30:24
18 [w][Luke 1:59, 60]
19 [x]ch. 48:7 [y]Ruth 1:2; 4:11; Mic. 5:2; Matt. 2:6, 16-18
20 [z]1 Sam. 10:2; [2 Sam. 18:18]
22 [a]ch. 49:4; 1 Chr. 5:1; [2 Sam. 16:22; 20:3; 1 Cor. 5:1]
23 [b]For ver. 23-26, see ch. 46:8-27; Ex. 1:2-4
27 [c]ch. 13:18; 23:19 [d]ch. 23:2; Josh. 14:15; 15:13
29 [e]ch. 15:15; 25:8 [f]ch. 25:9; 49:31

Chapter 36

1 [g]ch. 25:30
2 [h]ch. 26:34 [i]ver. 14, 18, 25
3 [j][ch. 28:9]
4 [k]ver. 10; 1 Chr. 1:35
7 [l]ch. 13:6 [m]ch. 17:8; 23:4; 28:4; 37:1; Heb. 11:9
8 [n]See ch. 32:3 [o]ver. 1, 19

[1] *Ben-oni* could mean *son of my sorrow*, or *son of my strength* [2] *Benjamin* means *son of the right hand* [3] Hebrew; Samaritan, Septuagint, Syriac *son*; also verse 14

century A.D. The ESV footnote, "about two hours' distance," locates Rachel's grave somewhere north of Jerusalem, which fits with Jer. 31:15.

35:18 her soul was departing. This is one place in the OT where the word "soul" (Hb. *nepesh*) denotes what gives life to the body.

35:21 The location of the **tower of Eder** is uncertain, although the context suggests that it lay between Bethlehem and Hebron. Since "Eder" means "flock" or "herd," this tower may have been used by shepherds.

35:22–23 Reuben went and lay with Bilhah his father's concubine. While Reuben's action may have been prompted by inappropriate lust, it challenged Jacob's position as head of the household. As the firstborn son, Reuben may also have viewed his action as establishing his authority over his brothers (see 2 Sam. 16:20–23). Yet it had the opposite effect (see 1 Chron. 5:1–2; also note on Gen. 48:3–7). Although initially Jacob takes no immediate action against Reuben—implied by the narrator's brief comment, **Israel heard of it**—he later denies Reuben his preeminence as the firstborn (49:3–4). Although Jacob's actions run counter to the provisions for inheritance in Deut. 21:15–17, the unseemly behavior of Reuben means that he will not inherit what he otherwise would have received.

35:26 These were the sons of Jacob who were born to him in Paddan-aram. Strictly speaking (see vv. 16–20), Benjamin was not born in Paddan-aram, but this is a general summary statement.

35:27 Mamre, or Kiriath-arba (that is, Hebron). See notes on 13:18; 23:2.

35:28–29 In spite of hinting and evidently believing that his death was imminent in 27:1–2, Isaac has remained alive during Jacob's 20 years of exile in Paddan-aram. The report of Isaac's death, like that of Abraham in 25:7–10, marks the end of an era and brings to a natural conclusion the main narrative section that began with 25:19. According to 49:30–31, Isaac was **buried** in the cave at Machpelah.

36:1–37:1 *Esau's Descendants in Edom.* Largely through genealogy-like lists, this chapter provides a brief description of Esau and his descendants. This information, which concludes the narrator's interest in Esau, precedes the much fuller and more important account of Jacob's descendants. The location of this material resembles 25:12–18, where information about Ishmael's descendants comes before the longer account of Isaac's family. The author of Genesis usually writes about minor characters before concentrating in detail on the main participants of the unique family line. Particular attention is given to the presence of both "chiefs" and "kings" among Esau's descendants, who coexist alongside the Horites, the original inhabitants of Seir. Eventually, however, Esau's descendants assume control of Seir, renaming it "Edom."

36:1–8 These verses, which are more narrative than genealogy, anticipate and explain the summary description of Esau that comes in v. 9. Repeated references to Canaan underline that these events occurred during Esau's time in Canaan, when five sons and some daughters were born to him. Then, because the land was unable to support the livestock of both Esau and Jacob (see 13:5–6 for a similar scenario), the former relocated outside Canaan in the hill country of Seir, southeast of the Dead Sea.

36:1 These are the generations of. See note on 2:4. **Esau (that is, Edom).** On the origin of the name "Edom," see note on 25:30.

36:2–3 The names of Esau's wives here—**Adah**, **Oholibamah** (v. 2), and **Basemath** (v. 3)—are not the same as those mentioned in 26:34 and 28:9. According to 26:34, Esau married Judith (the daughter of Beeri) and Basemath (the daughter of Elon). According to 28:9, he later also married Mahalath (the daughter of Ishmael). No simple solution enables the two lists to be harmonized, although various possibilities exist: e.g., (1) Esau may have married more than three women; (2) the same woman may have been known by two different names (e.g., Basemath may also have been known as Adah; both are listed as the daughter of Elon); or (3) the same name may have been given to two separate women (e.g., Basemath, which means "perfume," may have been a common female name).

9 [p]ver. 43
10 [q]ver. 4
12 [r]Num. 24:20; 1 Sam. 15:2, 3
14 [s]ver. 2
15 [t]Ex. 15:15 [u]ver. 11, 12
17 [v]ver. 13
18 [w]ver. 14
19 [x]ver. 1, 8
20 [y]For ver. 20-28, see 1 Chr. 1:38-42 [z]ch. 14:6; Deut. 2:12, 22
25 [a]ver. 2
29 [b]ver. 20
31 [c]For ver. 31-43, see 1 Chr. 1:43-54
37 [d][ch. 26:22]
41 [e][Num. 33:42]
43 [f]ver. 9

9 These are the generations of Esau the father of [p]the Edomites in the hill country of
Seir. 10 These are the names of Esau's sons: [q]Eliphaz the son of Adah the wife of Esau, Reuel
the son of Basemath the wife of Esau. 11 The sons of Eliphaz were Teman, Omar, Zepho,
Gatam, and Kenaz. 12 (Timna was a concubine of Eliphaz, Esau's son; she bore [r]Amalek to
Eliphaz.) These are the sons of Adah, Esau's wife. 13 These are the sons of Reuel: Nahath,
Zerah, Shammah, and Mizzah. These are the sons of Basemath, Esau's wife. 14 These are
the sons of [s]Oholibamah the daughter of Anah the daughter of Zibeon, Esau's wife: she
bore to Esau Jeush, Jalam, and Korah.

15 These are [t]the chiefs of the sons of Esau. [u]The sons of Eliphaz the firstborn of Esau:
the chiefs Teman, Omar, Zepho, Kenaz, 16 Korah, Gatam, and Amalek; these are the chiefs
of Eliphaz in the land of Edom; these are the sons of Adah. 17 These are the sons of [v]Reuel,
Esau's son: the chiefs Nahath, Zerah, Shammah, and Mizzah; these are the chiefs of Reuel
in the land of Edom; these are the sons of Basemath, Esau's wife. 18 These are the sons of
[w]Oholibamah, Esau's wife: the chiefs Jeush, Jalam, and Korah; these are the chiefs born
of Oholibamah the daughter of Anah, Esau's wife. 19 These are the sons of Esau ([x]that is,
Edom), and these are their chiefs.

20 [y]These are the sons of [z]Seir the Horite, the inhabitants of the land: Lotan, Shobal,
Zibeon, Anah, 21 Dishon, Ezer, and Dishan; these are the chiefs of the Horites, the sons of
Seir in the land of Edom. 22 The sons of Lotan were Hori and Hemam; and Lotan's sister
was Timna. 23 These are the sons of Shobal: Alvan, Manahath, Ebal, Shepho, and Onam.
24 These are the sons of Zibeon: Aiah and Anah; he is the Anah who found the hot springs
in the wilderness, as he pastured the donkeys of Zibeon his father. 25 These are the children
of Anah: Dishon and [a]Oholibamah the daughter of Anah. 26 These are the sons of Dishon:
Hemdan, Eshban, Ithran, and Cheran. 27 These are the sons of Ezer: Bilhan, Zaavan, and
Akan. 28 These are the sons of Dishan: Uz and Aran. 29 These are the chiefs of the Horites:
the [b]chiefs Lotan, Shobal, Zibeon, Anah, 30 Dishon, Ezer, and Dishan; these are the chiefs
of the Horites, chief by chief in the land of Seir.

31 [c]These are the kings who reigned in the land of Edom, before any king reigned over
the Israelites. 32 Bela the son of Beor reigned in Edom, the name of his city being Dinhabah.
33 Bela died, and Jobab the son of Zerah of Bozrah reigned in his place. 34 Jobab died, and
Husham of the land of the Temanites reigned in his place. 35 Husham died, and Hadad
the son of Bedad, who defeated Midian in the country of Moab, reigned in his place, the
name of his city being Avith. 36 Hadad died, and Samlah of Masrekah reigned in his place.
37 Samlah died, and Shaul of [d]Rehoboth on the Euphrates[1] reigned in his place. 38 Shaul
died, and Baal-hanan the son of Achbor reigned in his place. 39 Baal-hanan the son of Achbor
died, and Hadar reigned in his place, the name of his city being Pau; his wife's name was
Mehetabel, the daughter of Matred, daughter of Mezahab.

40 These are the names of the chiefs of Esau, according to their clans and their dwelling places, by their names: the chiefs Timna, Alvah, Jetheth, 41 Oholibamah, Elah, [e]Pinon,
42 Kenaz, Teman, Mibzar, 43 Magdiel, and Iram; these are the chiefs of Edom (that is, Esau,
the father of [f]Edom), according to their dwelling places in the land of their possession.

[1] Hebrew *the River*

36:9–43 Although this section begins with a heading identical to that found in v. 1, by a clever use of genealogical information vv. 9–43 reveal that Esau's descendants established themselves as the dominant group in Seir.

36:9–14 This section, which lists Esau's five sons and 10 grandsons, prepares the reader for vv. 15–19. **concubine** (v. 12). See note on 25:5–6.

36:15–19 Esau's sons and grandsons produce 14 **chiefs**. While all the names listed here appear in vv. 9–14, the inclusion of **Korah** among the sons of Eliphaz (v. 16) is unexpected. Korah is not included in the earlier list of Eliphaz's sons (v. 11); possibly he is a grandson of Eliphaz. "Korah" is also the name given to a son of Oholibamah (vv. 14, 18). Since chiefs were normally tribal leaders, these verses indicate that Esau became the father of 14 tribes.

36:20–30 This section lists five chiefs associated with the **Horites**, the original inhabitants of **Seir**. By placing the five chiefs of Seir alongside the 14 chiefs of Esau (vv. 15–19), the narrator signals that Esau's descendants became the dominant force in the region of Seir (see Deut. 2:12, 22).

36:31–39 These are the kings who reigned in the land of Edom, before any king reigned over the Israelites. A number of kings emerge from among Esau's descendants. Although the kings listed here succeed one another, the list probably records a series of dynasties, each associated with a particular city. The author of v. 31 either lived after the Israelite monarchy was a reality or clearly anticipated that one would be established. The pattern of tribal leaders eventually being replaced by kings was repeated in ancient Israel.

36:40–43 These verses list a number of Edomite chiefs, **according to their clans and their dwelling places** (v. 40). The distinctive feature of this section is the mention of "dwelling places." These chiefs are associated with particular regions, which possibly bore their names, although the evidence for this is limited. This list of Edomite chiefs is repeated in 1 Chron. 1:51–54.

Joseph's Dreams

37 Jacob lived in [g]the land of his father's sojournings, in the land of Canaan.
2 These are the generations of Jacob.
Joseph, being seventeen years old, was pasturing the flock with his brothers. He was
a boy with the sons of Bilhah and Zilpah, his father's wives. And Joseph brought [h]a bad
report of them to their father. 3 Now Israel loved Joseph more than any other of his sons,
because he was [i]the son of his old age. And he made him [j]a robe of many colors.[1] 4 But
when his brothers saw that their father loved him more than all his brothers, they hated
him and could not speak peacefully to him.
5 Now Joseph had a dream, and when he told it to his brothers they hated him even
more. 6 He said to them, "Hear this dream that I have dreamed: 7 Behold, we were binding sheaves in the field, and behold, [k]my sheaf arose and stood upright. And behold, your
sheaves gathered around it and [l]bowed down to my sheaf." 8 His brothers said to him, "Are
you indeed to reign over us? Or are you indeed to rule over us?" So they hated him even
more for his dreams and for his words.
9 Then he dreamed another dream and told it to his brothers and said, "Behold, I have
dreamed another dream. Behold, the sun, the moon, and eleven stars were bowing down
to me." 10 But when he told it to his father and to his brothers, his father rebuked him
and said to him, "What is this dream that you have dreamed? Shall I and [m]your mother
and your brothers indeed come [n]to bow ourselves to the ground before you?" 11 And [o]his
brothers were jealous of him, [p]but his father kept the saying in mind.

[1] See Septuagint, Vulgate; or (with Syriac) *a robe with long sleeves*. The meaning of the Hebrew is uncertain; also verses 23, 32

Chapter 37
1 [g]See ch. 36:7
2 [h][1 Sam. 2:23, 24]
3 [i]ch. 44:20 [j]ver. 23, 32
7 [k]ch. 42:6, 9 [l]ch. 43:26; 44:14
10 [m][ch. 35:18] [n]ver. 7, 9
11 [o]Acts 7:9 [p][Luke 2:19, 51]

37:1 This verse provides a transition from Esau's family to Jacob's. Whereas Esau's descendants dwell in Seir (alongside the Horites), **Jacob** settles in **Canaan** (like his father Isaac).

37:2–50:26 *Jacob's Descendants.* The last main section of Genesis further develops the theme of a regal line descended from Abraham. While royalty is initially ascribed to Joseph, and is later linked to his younger son Ephraim, future kingship is also associated with the line of Judah. As immediate heir to the patriarchal promises, Joseph, the governor of Egypt, mediates divine blessing to many people. Genesis, however, anticipates a time when the leadership of Israel will pass from the tribe of Ephraim to the tribe of Judah (see Ps. 78:67–68). This story serves the first readers by explaining how they came to be in Egypt, namely, through God's mysterious use of evil and noble deeds to bring about his purpose (cf. Gen. 50:20).

37:2–36 *Joseph Is Sold into Slavery.* Joseph is the second youngest son of Jacob. But his father bestows on him privileges normally given to the firstborn. Joseph's royal dreams further antagonize his older brothers, who cannot accept that he will reign over them. When the opportunity presents itself, they sell Joseph into slavery in Egypt.

37:2 These are the generations of. See note on 2:4. **Joseph brought a bad report of them to their father**. Joseph's action not only alienates him from his brothers but implies that his behavior is more righteous than theirs, something largely borne out by future events.

37:3 As previously indicated, Joseph is Jacob's favorite (see note on 33:1–3). **the son of his old age**. Since Benjamin is actually the last son born to Jacob, the unusual Hebrew expression "son of old age" (there is no explicit word for "his" in the Hebrew text) may denote someone who displays exceptional maturity while still young or perhaps the son closest to Jacob in his old age. Jacob may have recognized Joseph's leadership potential early in life. **robe of many colors**. The Hebrew expression used to denote this cloak is used elsewhere only of a garment worn by King David's daughter Tamar (see 2 Sam. 13:18). The actual design of the cloak is uncertain; as the ESV footnote explains, the translation here is based on the understanding of the Septuagint translators (Gk. *poikilos*, "many-colored"). The alternative is "a robe with long sleeves" (cf. the text and ESV footnote of 2 Sam. 13:18, which uses the same Hebrew expression).

37:4–5 Jealousy leads to division and deep animosity within Jacob's family (v. 4). **Joseph had a dream** (v. 5). Although it is not specified here, in Genesis dreams are normally associated with divine revelations (see 20:3; 28:12; 31:10–11; 40:5–8; 41:1).

Joseph's Timeline

Event	Age of Joseph	Genesis
Joseph's father Jacob moves family from Haran to Canaan	6	31:17–21
Joseph sold to Potiphar in Egypt	17	ch. 37
Joseph interprets dreams of cupbearer and baker in prison	28	ch. 40
Joseph's grandfather Isaac dies	29	35:28–29
Joseph interprets Pharaoh's dreams, is released from prison	30	41:1–36
Seven years of plenty; sons Manasseh and Ephraim born during this time	30–37	41:47–52
Seven years of famine; two years into the famine Joseph reconciles with his brothers and father	37–44	41:53–47:26
Joseph's father Jacob dies	56	47:28
Joseph dies	110	50:22–26

12[q]See ch. 33:18
14[r]ch. 13:18; 35:27
17[s]2 Kgs. 6:13
18[t][Ps. 37:12, 32]
20[u]ver. 26
21[v]ch. 42:22
22[w]ver. 29, 30
23[x]ver. 3
24[y][Jer. 38:6; Lam. 3:53]
25[z]Job 6:19; Isa. 21:13
[a][ver. 28, 36; ch. 39:1]
[b]ch. 43:11; Jer. 8:22; 46:11

Joseph Sold by His Brothers

12 Now his brothers went to pasture their father's flock near [q]Shechem. 13 And Israel
said to Joseph, "Are not your brothers pasturing the flock at Shechem? Come, I will send
you to them." And he said to him, "Here I am." 14 So he said to him, "Go now, see if it is
well with your brothers and with the flock, and bring me word." So he sent him from the
Valley of [r]Hebron, and he came to Shechem. 15 And a man found him wandering in the
fields. And the man asked him, "What are you seeking?" 16 "I am seeking my brothers," he
said. "Tell me, please, where they are pasturing the flock." 17 And the man said, "They have
gone away, for I heard them say, 'Let us go to [s]Dothan.'" So Joseph went after his brothers
and found them at [s]Dothan.

18 They saw him from afar, and before he came near to them [t]they conspired against
him to kill him. 19 They said to one another, "Here comes this dreamer. 20 Come now, [u]let
us kill him and throw him into one of the pits.[1] Then we will say that a fierce animal has
devoured him, and we will see what will become of his dreams." 21 But when [v]Reuben heard
it, he rescued him out of their hands, saying, "Let us not take his life." 22 And Reuben said
to them, "Shed no blood; throw him into this pit here in the wilderness, but do not lay a
hand on him"—[w]that he might rescue him out of their hand to restore him to his father.
23 So when Joseph came to his brothers, they stripped him of his robe, [x]the robe of many
colors that he wore. 24 And they took him and [y]threw him into a pit. The pit was empty;
there was no water in it.

25 Then they sat down to eat. And looking up they saw a [z]caravan of [a]Ishmaelites coming
from Gilead, with their camels bearing [b]gum, balm, and myrrh, on their way to carry it

[1] Or *cisterns*; also verses 22, 24

37:8 Joseph's brothers intuitively interpret Joseph's first dream as indicating that he will **reign over** them (later fulfilled in his rule over Egypt). The dream adds to the brothers' jealous hatred of Joseph, for his father has already dressed him in special attire.

37:9–11 The second dream reinforces the expectation that Joseph will exercise authority over the rest of his family. **Shall I and your mother** (v. 10). When Joseph had this dream, his mother Rachel was probably dead (see 35:16–19); "your mother" refers to Leah. While Joseph's brothers later bow down to him (42:6; 43:26; 44:14), there is no specific mention of his parents' doing this, although possibly his father did so in 47:28–31 (see note).

37:12–14 Joseph's brothers have taken the family flocks northward from Hebron to find better pasture. **Shechem**. See note on 33:17–18 and map to the right.

37:15–17 Since his brothers have moved farther north, Joseph travels from Shechem to **Dothan**, a journey of about 16 to 20 miles (26 to 32 km), in order to find them.

37:18–20 they conspired against him to kill him. Fratricide is one of the most depraved aspects of fallen humanity (see 4:8; 27:41). **this dreamer**. The brothers' comment is full of sarcasm; the Hebrew expression implies "master/owner of the dreams."

37:21–22 Reuben, the eldest of the brothers, argues against killing Joseph, so that he might **restore him to his father**. Reuben possibly hopes to regain his father's favor so that he will be confirmed as the firstborn (see note on 35:22–23), or perhaps Reuben has no other motive than to show mercy to Joseph. Unknown to Reuben, his plan is undermined when his brothers sell Joseph to passing traders. When he later returns to get Joseph, he is not there (37:29).

37:25 they sat down to eat. This underlines the callousness of the brothers, who have just thrown their brother into a pit. **caravan of Ishmaelites**. These traders, who originate from the Sinai Peninsula, are traveling south in the direction of Egypt. Although they are initially identified as Ishmaelites (a broad category covering various people groups), in vv. 28 and 36 they are designated more specifically as Midianites. **coming from Gilead**. See note on 31:21. **camels**. See note on 12:16. (Apparently this was a known activity in the region: e.g., one Ugaritic text, from the 14th century B.C., tells of a man in Syria being sold by his comrade to a passing caravan of Egyptians—who stripped him of his goods and abandoned him.)

Joseph and His Brothers
c. 1900/1730 B.C.

Jacob sent Joseph from Hebron to Shechem to find his brothers, who had been pasturing their father's flock. When Joseph arrived, he learned that his brothers had gone on to Dothan, so he went there and found them. His brothers threw him into a pit and later sold him to some Ishmaelite spice traders on their way from Gilead to Egypt. The traders took Joseph to Egypt and sold him to Potiphar, the captain of Pharaoh's guard.

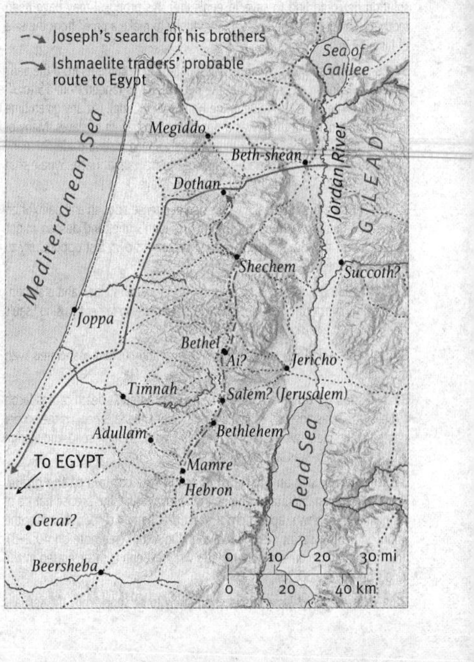

down to Egypt. 26 Then Judah said to his brothers, "What profit is it [c]if we kill our brother
and conceal his blood? 27 Come, let us sell him to the Ishmaelites, and [d]let not our hand be
upon him, for he is our brother, our own flesh." And his brothers listened to him. 28 Then
[e]Midianite traders passed by. And they drew Joseph up and lifted him out of the pit, and
[f]sold him to the Ishmaelites for twenty shekels[1] of silver. They took Joseph to Egypt.
29 When Reuben returned to the pit and saw that Joseph was not in the pit, he [g]tore
his clothes 30 and returned to his brothers and said, "The boy [h]is gone, and I, where shall
I go?" 31 Then they took [i]Joseph's robe and slaughtered a goat and dipped the robe in the
blood. 32 And they sent the robe of many colors and brought it to their father and said,
"This we have found; please identify whether it is your son's robe or not." 33 And he identified it and said, "It is my son's robe. [j]A fierce animal has devoured him. Joseph is without
doubt torn to pieces." 34 Then Jacob tore his garments and put sackcloth on his loins and
mourned for his son many days. 35 All his sons and all his daughters [k]rose up to comfort
him, but he refused to be comforted and said, "No, [l]I shall go down to Sheol to my son,
mourning." Thus his father wept for him. 36 Meanwhile [m]the Midianites had sold him in
Egypt to Potiphar, an officer of Pharaoh, [n]the captain of the guard.

Judah and Tamar

38 It happened at that time that Judah went down from his brothers and [o]turned aside
to a certain [p]Adullamite, whose name was Hirah. 2 There Judah saw the daughter
of a certain Canaanite whose name was [q]Shua. He took her and went in to her, 3 and she
conceived and bore a son, and he called his name [r]Er. 4 She conceived again and bore a son,
and she called his name [r]Onan. 5 Yet again she bore a son, and she called his name [r]Shelah.
Judah[2] was in Chezib when she bore him.
6 And Judah took a wife for Er his firstborn, and her name was Tamar. 7 But Er, Judah's
firstborn, [s]was wicked in the sight of the LORD, and the LORD put him to death. 8 Then
Judah said to Onan, "Go in to [t]your brother's wife and [u]perform the duty of a brother-in-

[1] A *shekel* was about 2/5 ounce or 11 grams [2] Hebrew *He*

26 [c]ver. 20
27 [d][1 Sam. 18:17]
28 [e]ver. 36; Judg. 8:22, 24 [f]ch. 45:4; Ps. 105:17; Acts 7:9
29 [g]ch. 44:13; Num. 14:6; 2 Sam. 1:11; 3:31; Job 1:20
30 [h]ch. 42:13, 32, 36; 44:31; Jer. 31:15; Lam. 5:7
31 [i]ver. 23
33 [j]ver. 20; ch. 44:28
35 [k][2 Sam. 12:17] [l]ch. 42:38; 44:29, 31
36 [m]ver. 28; [ver. 25; ch. 39:1] [n]ch. 40:3, 4; 41:10, 12

Chapter 38

1 [o]ver. 16; ch. 19:3; 2 Kgs. 4:8 [p]1 Sam. 22:1; 2 Sam. 23:13; 1 Chr. 11:15; Mic. 1:15
2 [q][1 Chr. 2:3]
3 [r]ch. 46:12; Num. 26:19, 20
4 [r][See ver. 3 above]
5 [r][See ver. 3 above]
7 [s]1 Chr. 2:3
8 [t]Matt. 22:24; Mark 12:19; Luke 20:28 [u]See Deut. 25:5-10

37:26–27 Judah said to his brothers. Although Judah exhibits compassion by not wanting to kill Joseph (and he may have been seeking any possible solution he could find to save Joseph's life), his proposal may have been motivated by greed as he sees an opportunity to make a profit from the sale of his brother.

37:28 twenty shekels of silver. Mesopotamian documents from the early second millennium B.C. reveal that the price of slaves ranged from 15 to 30 shekels (20 shekels is the value in the Hammurabi Code). (At any given time in the history of Egypt there was a significant substratum of slaves. Many of these were captives of war, but there was also a large slave trade. So many of the slaves came from "Asia"—Canaan, Mesopotamia, Hatti, Syria—that the word "Asiatic" became synonymous with "slave.")

37:29–30 tore his clothes. A visible sign of intense anguish and pain, often linked to mourning. **where shall I go?** Reuben's grief and despair might center not on the loss of Joseph himself but on his own lost opportunity to regain his father's favor (see note on vv. 21–22).

37:31–33 Jacob's deception by his sons, using Joseph's cloak and a slaughtered **goat**, mirrors the way Jacob had deceived his own father by using Esau's cloak and two goatskins (see 27:15–16).

37:34 put sackcloth on his loins. A common custom associated with mourning.

37:35 I shall go down to Sheol. The report of Joseph's death causes Jacob to believe that his grief will continue through the afterlife. "Sheol" is the proper name for the place where people go after death, though solid knowledge about the afterlife was lacking at this time.

37:36 Potiphar was **an officer of Pharaoh, the captain of the guard.** Potiphar holds an important position in the royal court. The precise nature of his post is not known, apart from the fact that he had responsibility for the imprisonment of senior members of the king's staff (see note on 40:2–3). This factor will become important later when Joseph is incarcerated in the king's prison (see 39:20).

38:1–30 *Judah and Tamar.* Readers are likely to be shocked by the sexually oriented content of this chapter, with its references to spilled semen and prostitution. Nevertheless, the unsavory account of Judah's relationship with Tamar, which interrupts the ongoing story of Joseph's time in Egypt, fulfills an important role in Genesis, for it focuses on the continuation of Judah's family line and concludes with a birth account in which a firstborn twin is pushed aside by his younger brother. In light of preceding episodes, these features highlight the potential importance of Judah's line through Perez (v. 29). Later, in ch. 49, kingship will be associated with Judah's descendants, and biblical history reveals that from Perez comes the Davidic dynasty (see Ruth 4:18–22). Although this chapter shows Judah at his worst, it also accounts for a remarkable transformation in his life, which comes through in the remaining episodes of the Joseph story. Further, Judah provides a stark contrast to the chaste Joseph in Genesis 39: though he suffered for his chastity, Joseph's behavior is the right way to bring blessing to the Gentiles.

38:1–2 A sense of foreboding is conveyed through Judah's separation from the rest of his family, his friendship with **Hirah** (v. 1; a native of the Canaanite city of Adullam, about 12 miles [19 km] southwest of Bethlehem), and his marriage to an unnamed **Canaanite** woman, the **daughter** of **Shua** (v. 2). In Genesis, marriages to Canaanites are never applauded (see 24:3; 26:34–35; 28:1).

38:6–7 Judah is instrumental in arranging Er's marriage to **Tamar** (v. 6). The reference to Er's death is tantalizingly brief (v. 7), and the precise nature of his wickedness is not disclosed. No information on Tamar's background is provided, although it is likely that she was a Canaanite.

38:8 Judah instructs his second son **Onan** to fulfill the custom of "levirate marriage," which required a brother to marry his brother's childless widow and give her children. Brief details about this obligation are given in Deut. 25:5–10. It plays an important role in the book of Ruth (Ruth 1:11–13; 4:1–12; see also Matt. 22:24–25; Luke 20:28). Judah is eager that Tamar should have a son to continue the firstborn line of Er. Since Genesis has a particular interest in the "firstborn," this concern is noteworthy. The motif of firstborn also figures prominently in the birth account at the end of the chapter.

38:9 Onan knew that the offspring would not be his. While publicly Onan appears to fulfill his father's request, in private he refuses to father a

11 [v][Ruth 1:12, 13] [w]Lev. 22:13
12 [x]ch. 24:67; 37:35; 2 Sam. 13:39 [y]Judg. 14:1
14 [z][ver. 19; ch. 24:65] [a]ver. 21 [b]ver. 26
18 [c]ver. 25
19 [d]ver. 14
21 [e]ver. 14
24 [f]Judg. 19:2

law to her, and raise up offspring for your brother." 9 But Onan knew that the offspring
would not be his. So whenever he went in to his brother's wife he would waste the semen
on the ground, so as not to give offspring to his brother. 10 And what he did was wicked
in the sight of the LORD, and he put him to death also. 11 Then Judah said to Tamar his
daughter-in-law, [v]"Remain a widow in your father's house, till Shelah my son grows up"—
for he feared that he would die, like his brothers. So Tamar went and remained [w]in her
father's house.

12 In the course of time the wife of Judah, Shua's daughter, died. When Judah [x]was comforted, he went up to [y]Timnah to his sheepshearers, he and his friend Hirah the Adullamite.
13 And when Tamar was told, "Your father-in-law is going up to Timnah to shear his sheep,"
14 she took off her widow's garments [z]and covered herself with a veil, wrapping herself
up, and sat at the entrance to [a]Enaim, which is on the road to Timnah. For she saw that
Shelah was grown up, [b]and she had not been given to him in marriage. 15 When Judah
saw her, he thought she was a prostitute, for she had covered her face. 16 He turned to her
at the roadside and said, "Come, let me come in to you," for he did not know that she was
his daughter-in-law. She said, "What will you give me, that you may come in to me?" 17 He
answered, "I will send you a young goat from the flock." And she said, "If you give me a
pledge, until you send it—" 18 He said, "What pledge shall I give you?" She replied, [c]"Your
signet and your cord and your staff that is in your hand." So he gave them to her and went
in to her, and she conceived by him. 19 Then she arose and went away, and taking off [d]her
veil she put on the garments of her widowhood.

20 When Judah sent the young goat by his friend the Adullamite to take back the pledge
from the woman's hand, he did not find her. 21 And he asked the men of the place, "Where
is the cult prostitute[1] who was at [e]Enaim at the roadside?" And they said, "No cult prostitute has been here." 22 So he returned to Judah and said, "I have not found her. Also, the
men of the place said, 'No cult prostitute has been here.'" 23 And Judah replied, "Let her
keep the things as her own, or we shall be laughed at. You see, I sent this young goat, and
you did not find her."

24 About three months later Judah was told, "Tamar your daughter-in-law [f]has been
immoral.[2] Moreover, she is pregnant by immorality."[3] And Judah said, "Bring her out, and

[1] Hebrew *sacred woman*; a woman who served a pagan deity by prostitution; also verse 22 [2] Or *has committed prostitution* [3] Or *by prostitution*

child on behalf of Er. **he would waste the semen on the ground**. Onan engaged in *coitus interruptus*, not self-gratification—as some early rabbis mistakenly thought. A detailed explanation for his action is not given, but selfishness is the most likely explanation: he probably feared that a son born to Tamar would be privileged over all other sons born to him, reducing the importance of his own family line and reducing his share of Judah's inheritance. (Although the circumstances are different, Ruth 4:5–6 provides another example of a man refusing to undertake the duty of levirate marriage.)

38:10 Onan's hypocritical behavior causes God to punish him by **death**.

38:11 Following the deaths of his two eldest sons, Judah protects his remaining son, **Shelah**, by sending Tamar back to her own family, under the pretext that one day she will marry Shelah. He treats Tamar as if she were dangerous, while it was actually the evil of the two sons that brought about their deaths.

38:12 Some time later Judah becomes a widower. After a period of mourning he travels to **Timnah**. Two locations are known by this name, but this one is probably located in the southern hill country of Judah (see Josh. 15:57).

38:13–14 Having waited in vain for Judah to fulfill his promise regarding Shelah (v. 11), Tamar decides to take action. She puts off **her widow's garments** and covers herself **with a veil**, possibly intending at first to remind Judah that she is betrothed to Shelah (see note on 24:65). She then goes to the entrance to **Enaim** in the hope of meeting her father-in-law. The location of Enaim, whose name means "two springs" or "eyes," is unknown; it probably ought to be distinguished from "Enam," mentioned in Josh. 15:34. Given Tamar's veil and Judah's inability to recognize her, it is ironic that these events should take place at a location known as "eyes."

38:15 When Judah sees Tamar, he assumes that she is a prostitute, **for she had covered her face**, thus effectively achieving anonymity. Since betrothed women wore veils, Judah's belief that Tamar is a **prostitute** would not have been simply based on her covered face. Her lone presence by the roadside possibly contributed to his assumption; Jer. 3:2 links "waysides" with prostitution.

38:16–18 Judah's request for sexual intercourse reinforces the reader's perception of him as a man driven by personal gratification. Having knowingly deceived Tamar by sending her away, he now takes advantage of her for his own pleasure. Tamar's request, **What will you give me . . . ?** (v. 16), plays on Judah's refusal to give her Shelah. Judah's offer of a **young goat** (v. 17) results in Tamar's taking from Judah his **signet**, **cord**, and **staff** in **pledge** (v. 18). From experience, she knows that he is not a man to be trusted. The "signet" may have been a small cylinder seal that was worn on a cord around the neck. The seal was rolled over soft clay to give a unique impression, identifying the owner; the seal was often perforated for suspension by the cord.

38:19 Tamar returns home and resumes her status as a widow.

38:21 Hirah searches for Tamar in vain. Ironically, Hirah's description of Tamar as a **cult prostitute** introduces into the account a religious dimension linked to fertility rituals. The term used by Hirah (Hb. *qedeshah*) is rarely used in the OT (see Deut. 23:17; Hos. 4:14), possibly because it resembles Hebrew words associated with holiness.

38:24–26 The report of Tamar's **immorality** produces an outburst of righteous indignation that prompts Judah to demand that she should **be burned** to death (v. 24). When Judah discovers that he was responsible for Tamar's pregnancy, he acknowledges her righteousness in contrast to his own failure (v. 26). This marks an important turning point for Judah.

38:27–30 Knowing that Tamar has **twins**, the midwife ties a **scarlet thread** (v. 28) on the hand of **Zerah** so that she can identify him as the firstborn, the one who **came out first**. But before Zerah is fully born, his twin brother breaks out in front of him. Consequently, in the light of the midwife's observation, he

[g]let her be burned." 25 As she was being brought out, she sent word to her father-in-law,
"By the man to whom these belong, I am pregnant." And she said, "Please identify whose
these are, [h]the signet and the cord and the staff." 26 Then Judah identified them and said,
[i]"She is more righteous than I, since [j]I did not give her to my son Shelah." And he did not
know her again.
27 When the time of her labor came, there were twins in her womb. 28 And when she was
in labor, one put out a hand, and the midwife took and tied a scarlet thread on his hand,
saying, "This one came out first." 29 But as he drew back his hand, behold, his brother came
out. And she said, "What a breach you have made for yourself!" Therefore his name was
called [k]Perez.[1] 30 Afterward his brother came out with the scarlet thread on his hand, and
his name was called [k]Zerah.

Joseph and Potiphar's Wife

39 Now Joseph had been brought down to Egypt, and [l]Potiphar, an officer of Pharaoh,
the captain of the guard, an Egyptian, [m]had bought him from the [n]Ishmaelites who
had brought him down there. 2 [o]The LORD was with Joseph, and he became a successful
man, and he was in the house of his Egyptian master. 3 His master saw that the LORD was
with him and that the LORD [p]caused all that he did to succeed in his hands. 4 So Joseph
[q]found favor in his sight and attended him, and he made him overseer of his house [r]and
put him in charge of all that he had. 5 From the time that he made him overseer in his

[1] *Perez means a breach*

24 [g]Lev. 21:9; [Deut. 22:21; John 8:5]
25 [h]ver. 18
26 [i]1 Sam. 24:17 [j]ver. 14
29 [k]ch. 46:12; Num. 26:20; 1 Chr. 2:4; Matt. 1:3
30 [k][See ver. 29 above]

Chapter 39

1 [l]ch. 37:36 [m]ch. 37:28 [n]ch. 37:25
2 [o]ver. 21; Acts 7:9; [ch. 21:22; 26:24, 28; 28:15; 1 Sam. 16:18; 18:14, 28]
3 [p]2 Chr. 26:5; Ps. 1:3
4 [q]ver. 21; ch. 19:19; 33:10 [r]ver. 8

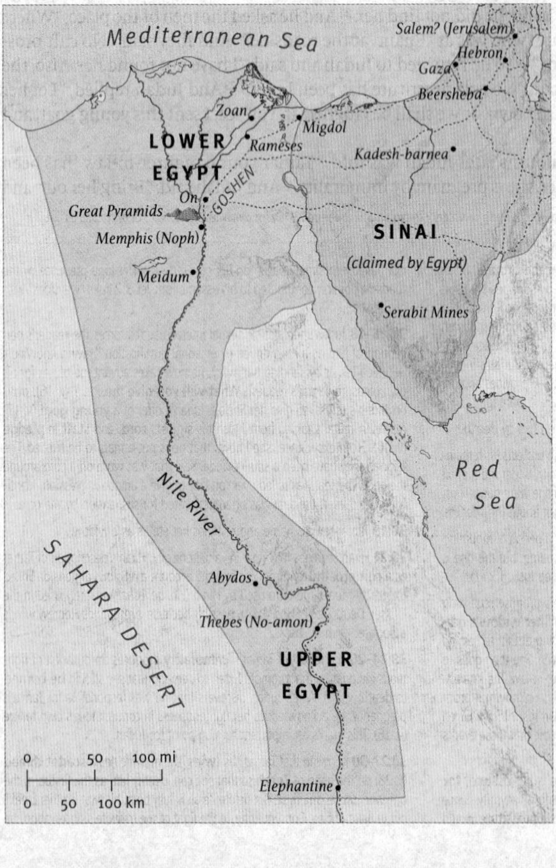

Egypt at the Time of Joseph
c. 1900/1730 B.C.
Joseph arrived in Egypt during the reign of the Twelfth Dynasty, arguably the zenith of Egypt's power. Shortly before this era, Upper and Lower Egypt had been unified under one ruler, and now Egyptian influence expanded south and east. The regular flooding of the Nile River provided a relatively stable supply of food and offered some degree of protection from the famines suffered by other lands of the ancient Near East.

5 [s][ch. 30:27]
6 [t][ch. 29:17; 1 Sam. 16:12]
8 [u]ver. 4
9 [v]2 Sam. 12:13; Ps. 51:4
10 [w][Prov. 1:10]
12 [x][Prov. 7:13, 18]
20 [y]Ps. 105:18

house and over all that he had, the LORD blessed the Egyptian's house [s]for Joseph's sake;
the blessing of the LORD was on all that he had, in house and field. 6 So he left all that he
had in Joseph's charge, and because of him he had no concern about anything but the
food he ate.
Now Joseph was [t]handsome in form and appearance. 7 And after a time his master's wife
cast her eyes on Joseph and said, "Lie with me." 8 But he refused and said to his master's
wife, "Behold, because of me my master has no concern about anything in the house, and
[u]he has put everything that he has in my charge. 9 He is not greater in this house than I
am, nor has he kept back anything from me except you, because you are his wife. How
then can I do this great wickedness and [v]sin against God?" 10 And as she spoke to Joseph
day after day, he [w]would not listen to her, to lie beside her or to be with her.
11 But one day, when he went into the house to do his work and none of the men of
the house was there in the house, 12 [x]she caught him by his garment, saying, "Lie with
me." But he left his garment in her hand and fled and got out of the house. 13 And as
soon as she saw that he had left his garment in her hand and had fled out of the house,
14 she called to the men of her household and said to them, "See, he has brought among
us a Hebrew to laugh at us. He came in to me to lie with me, and I cried out with a
loud voice. 15 And as soon as he heard that I lifted up my voice and cried out, he left his
garment beside me and fled and got out of the house." 16 Then she laid up his garment
by her until his master came home, 17 and she told him the same story, saying, "The
Hebrew servant, whom you have brought among us, came in to me to laugh at me.
18 But as soon as I lifted up my voice and cried, he left his garment beside me and fled
out of the house."
19 As soon as his master heard the words that his wife spoke to him, "This is the way your
servant treated me," his anger was kindled. 20 And Joseph's master took him and [y]put him

is called **Perez** (v. 29), which means "breach." Viewed in the light of Genesis as a whole, the unusual nature of this brief birth account, especially with its focus on the identity of the firstborn, suggests that something significant will develop in the line of Perez.

39:1–23 *Joseph in Egypt.* The Lord's presence with Joseph in Egypt enables him to find favor with first Potiphar and then the keeper of the prison. While Joseph's refusal to lie with Potiphar's wife results in his being wrongly imprisoned, his personal integrity is not compromised. Implicit in this account is the idea that God's presence with Joseph is linked to Joseph's commitment to the Lord.

39:1 This verse, which echoes 37:36, reintroduces Joseph as the main character of the story. He continues as such till the book ends.

39:2–5 The LORD was with Joseph. Right at the outset, God's presence with Joseph is unambiguously affirmed. Although God never speaks directly to him (as he did to Abraham, Isaac, and Jacob), Joseph's life in Egypt is governed by God's providential care (see 50:20). **he became a successful man**. In spite of having been sold into slavery, Joseph prospers, being promoted to the position of **overseer** of Potiphar's **house**. The repeated references to **the LORD** in these verses emphasize that Joseph's success is due to God's presence with him. By indicating that divine blessing comes through Joseph, the narrator picks up on one of the important elements of the promises made to the patriarchs (see, e.g., 12:3; 18:18; 22:17; 30:27).

39:6–9 handsome in form and appearance (v. 6). This echoes 29:17, describing Joseph's mother Rachel. This brief observation explains why Potiphar's **wife** (39:7) is drawn to him. Joseph's refusal to **lie** (i.e., sexually, vv. 7–8) with her contrasts sharply with the behavior of Reuben and Judah (35:22; 38:15–18). His integrity does not permit him to betray his master by committing adultery. **sin against God**. Joseph rightly recognizes that to give in to Potiphar's wife not only would be an offense against his master, who has trusted him with everything he owns, but would equally be an offense "against God" (cf. Ps. 51:4a). Joseph exercises authority without seeing this as an opportunity to betray or exploit others. (The motif of the "spurned seductress" appears elsewhere in ancient Near Eastern literature. In Egypt, the story called the "Tale of Two Brothers" tells of two brothers, one of whom spurns the advances of the other's wife.)

39:10–12 he would not listen to her. Joseph consistently rejects the advances of Potiphar's wife. **But one day**, in the course of doing his normal work, Potiphar's wife catches Joseph **by his garment**. Unable to free himself, Joseph flees, leaving his **garment in her hand**. As in 37:31–33, Joseph's garment plays an important role in the story and, as before, is used to deceive other people.

39:13–15 While Potiphar is still absent, his wife convinces the **men of her household** to side with her. **he has brought among us a Hebrew to laugh at us**. She combines three elements in order to maximize her case against Joseph: (1) she places some of the blame on her husband, for he was responsible for Joseph's presence in the household; (2) by emphasizing Joseph's non-Egyptian origin, she exploits a long-standing racial tension that existed between native Egyptians and foreigners from Canaan; and (3) she portrays Joseph's action as being directed against the entire household, and not simply her. "Laugh" recalls 21:9 and 26:8, where it has the connotations of "making fun of someone" and "caressing," respectively. Concerning the term "Hebrew," see note on 10:21–32.

39:16–19 With Joseph's **garment** as evidence (v. 16), Potiphar's wife tells to her husband with significant variations what she has already told the men of her household. Once again she focuses on the non-Egyptian background of Joseph (**Hebrew**, v. 17), her husband's poor judgment in bringing him into the household (**whom you have brought**, v. 17), and Joseph's exploitation of her (**laugh at me**, v. 17; contrast v. 14, where she speaks of "laugh at us"). To place further pressure on her husband, she describes Joseph as **your servant** (v. 19).

39:20–23 The swiftness with which the narrator reports the imprisonment of Joseph mirrors what happened in reality. As a slave, Joseph had no legal rights. While the reader is not immediately conscious of the significance of Joseph's being imprisoned **where the king's prisoners were confined** (v. 20), this will prove significant for future developments. (The law codes of the ancient Near East, including OT legislation, do not employ punishment by imprisonment in jail. Yet the practice is well known and attested in ancient Egyptian literature; therefore, this story fits well with the culture of ancient Egypt.) By echoing much of the language of vv. 2–5, these verses imply that Joseph's experience in prison paralleled his earlier experience in Potiphar's house. Because of the Lord's presence with him, Joseph prospers (v. 23).

into the [z]prison, the place where the king's prisoners were confined, and he was there in
prison. 21 But [a]the LORD was with Joseph and showed him steadfast love [b]and gave him
favor in the sight of the keeper of the prison. 22 And the keeper of the prison [c]put Joseph
in charge of all the prisoners who were in the prison. Whatever was done there, he was
the one who did it. 23 The keeper of the prison paid no attention to anything that was in
Joseph's charge, because [d]the LORD was with him. And whatever he did, the LORD made
it succeed.

Joseph Interprets Two Prisoners' Dreams

40 Some time after this, the [e]cupbearer of the king of Egypt and his baker committed
an offense against their lord the king of Egypt. 2 And Pharaoh was angry with his
two officers, the chief cupbearer and the chief baker, 3 [f]and he put them in custody in the
house of the captain of the guard, in the prison where Joseph was confined. 4 The captain
of the guard appointed Joseph to be with them, and he attended them. They continued
for some time in custody.

5 And one night they both dreamed—the cupbearer and the baker of the king of Egypt,
who were confined in the prison—each his own dream, and each dream with its own interpretation. 6 When Joseph came to them in the morning, he saw that they were troubled.
7 So he asked Pharaoh's officers who were with him in custody in his master's house, [g]"Why
are your faces downcast today?" 8 They said to him, [h]"We have had dreams, and there is
no one to interpret them." And Joseph said to them, [i]"Do not interpretations belong to
God? Please tell them to me."

9 So the chief cupbearer told his dream to Joseph and said to him, "In my dream there
was a vine before me, 10 and on the vine there were three branches. As soon as it budded, its
blossoms shot forth, and the clusters ripened into grapes. 11 Pharaoh's cup was in my hand,
and I took the grapes and pressed them into Pharaoh's cup and placed the cup in Pharaoh's
hand." 12 Then Joseph said to him, [j]"This is its interpretation: [k]the three branches are three
days. 13 In three days Pharaoh will [l]lift up your head and restore you to your office, and you
shall place Pharaoh's cup in his hand as formerly, when you were his cupbearer. 14 Only
remember me, when it is well with you, and please do me the kindness to mention me to
Pharaoh, and so get me out of this house. 15 For [m]I was indeed stolen out of the land of the
Hebrews, and [n]here also I have done nothing that they should put me into the pit."

16 When the chief baker saw that the interpretation was favorable, he said to Joseph,
"I also had a dream: there were three cake baskets on my head, 17 and in the uppermost
basket there were all sorts of baked food for Pharaoh, but the birds were eating it out of
the basket on my head." 18 And Joseph answered and said, [o]"This is its interpretation: the
three baskets are three days. 19 [p]In three days Pharaoh will lift up your head—from you!—
and [q]hang you on a tree. And the birds will eat the flesh from you."

20 [z]ch. 40:3, 5; [ch. 40:15; 41:14]
21 [a]ver. 2; Acts 7:9, 10 [b]Ex. 3:21; 11:3; 12:36
22 [c]ch. 40:4
23 [d]ver. 2, 3

Chapter 40

1 [e]Neh. 1:11
3 [f][ch. 39:20]
7 [g][Neh. 2:2]
8 [h]ch. 41:15 [i]ch. 41:16; Dan. 2:28, 47
12 [j]ver. 18; ch. 41:12; [Dan. 2:36] [k][ch. 41:26, 27]
13 [l]2 Kgs. 25:27; Jer. 52:31; [ver. 19, 20, 22; Ps. 3:3]
15 [m]ch. 37:28 [n]ch. 39:20
18 [o]See ver. 12
19 [p]ver. 13 [q]ver. 22

40:1–23 ***Joseph and the King's Prisoners.*** The events recorded in this chapter take place some time after Joseph's imprisonment began. Two senior royal attendants are imprisoned for offending Pharaoh. With God's help, Joseph interprets their dreams, predicting that one of them will be reinstated but the other put to death. These events prepare the way for Joseph to be later summoned from prison to interpret Pharaoh's dreams.

40:1 committed an offense against. In 39:9 the same Hebrew verb is translated "sin against." In contrast to Joseph, who refused to sin against God, the **cupbearer** and **baker** have sinned against **their lord**, who as **king of Egypt** enjoyed divine status. The repetition of the rarely used expression "king of Egypt" emphasizes the seriousness of their offense. The primary duties of the cupbearer and baker, as their titles suggest, were to provide the king with drink and food, respectively; as royal attendants they had unique access to him, and they were trusted to keep him from being poisoned.

40:2–3 two officers. The Hebrew terms (*saris* and *sar*) used to denote the status of the **cupbearer** and **baker** are identical to those used of Potiphar (see 37:36; 39:1). **captain of the guard**. This same title is given to Potiphar in 37:36 and 39:1. Since Potiphar's name is not used in this context, however, the captain is probably another person.

40:4 The narrator continues to observe parallels between Joseph's experience in prison and what happened in Potiphar's house (see 39:4). In prison, as in Potiphar's house, Joseph waited on a captain of the guard and was appointed to manage the affairs of his house.

40:5–8 In the ancient Near East, **dreams** were often viewed as a medium of divine revelation. But because of their imprisonment, the cupbearer and baker no longer have access to the "magicians" and "wise men" who might have been able to provide an interpretation (see 41:8). Joseph's question, **Do not interpretations belong to God?** (40:8), recalls his own experience of dreams. Years later, Daniel, another exiled Hebrew, also interpreted dreams in a foreign context (see Dan. 2:25–45; 4:19–27).

40:9–11 Not only does the cupbearer's dream mention **three branches** (v. 10), but the related activities are grouped in threes.

40:12–15 Joseph perceives that the **three branches** symbolize **three days** (v. 12). The observation that **Pharaoh will lift up your head** (v. 13) introduces a motif that reappears in vv. 19 and 20. **remember me** (v. 14). See note on v. 23. **that they should put me into the pit** (v. 15). While Joseph's remark relates to Egypt, his mention of "the pit" recalls for the reader what his brothers did to him in Canaan (see 37:20, 22, 24, 28, 29).

40:18–19 In three days Pharaoh will lift up your head—from you! Joseph's interpretation repeats the motif of lifting up someone's head (see v. 13). On this occasion, however, it has tragic consequences. Whether or not

20 On the third day, which was Pharaoh's [r]birthday, he made a feast for all his servants
and [s]lifted up the head of the chief cupbearer and the head of the chief baker among
his servants. 21 [t]He restored the chief cupbearer to his position, and [u]he placed the cup
in Pharaoh's hand. 22 But he [v]hanged the chief baker, as Joseph had interpreted to them.
23 Yet the chief cupbearer did not remember Joseph, but forgot him.

Joseph Interprets Pharaoh's Dreams

41 After two whole years, Pharaoh dreamed that he was standing by the Nile, 2 and
behold, there came up out of the Nile seven cows attractive and plump, and they
fed in the reed grass. 3 And behold, seven other cows, ugly and thin, came up out of the
Nile after them, and stood by the other cows on the bank of the Nile. 4 And the ugly, thin
cows ate up the seven attractive, plump cows. And Pharaoh awoke. 5 And he fell asleep and
dreamed a second time. And behold, seven ears of grain, plump and good, were growing
on one stalk. 6 And behold, after them sprouted seven ears, thin and [w]blighted by the east
wind. 7 And the thin ears swallowed up the seven plump, full ears. And Pharaoh awoke,
and behold, it was a dream. 8 So in the morning [x]his spirit was troubled, and he sent and
called for all the [y]magicians of Egypt and all its wise men. Pharaoh told them his dreams,
but there was none who could interpret them to Pharaoh.

9 Then the chief cupbearer said to Pharaoh, "I remember my offenses today. 10 When
Pharaoh was [z]angry with his servants [a]and put me and the chief baker in custody in the
house of the captain of the guard, 11 [b]we dreamed on the same night, he and I, each having a dream with its own interpretation. 12 A young Hebrew was there with us, a servant
of the captain of the guard. When we told him, [c]he interpreted our dreams to us, giving
an interpretation to each man according to his dream. 13 And [d]as he interpreted to us, so
it came about. I was restored to my office, and the baker was hanged."

14 [e]Then Pharaoh sent and called Joseph, and they [f]quickly brought him [g]out of the pit.
And when he had shaved himself and changed his clothes, he came in before Pharaoh.
15 And Pharaoh said to Joseph, "I have had a dream, and there is no one who can interpret
it. [h]I have heard it said of you that when you hear a dream you can interpret it." 16 Joseph
answered Pharaoh, [i]"It is not in me; [j]God will give Pharaoh a favorable answer."[1] 17 Then
Pharaoh said to Joseph, "Behold, [k]in my dream I was standing on the banks of the Nile.
18 Seven cows, plump and attractive, came up out of the Nile and fed in the reed grass.
19 Seven other cows came up after them, poor and very ugly and thin, such as I had never
seen in all the land of Egypt. 20 And the thin, ugly cows ate up the first seven plump cows,
21 but when they had eaten them no one would have known that they had eaten them, for
they were still as ugly as at the beginning. Then I awoke. 22 I also saw in my dream seven

[1] Or (compare Samaritan, Septuagint) *Without God it is not possible to give Pharaoh an answer about his welfare*

20 [r]Matt. 14:6; Mark 6:21 [s]ver. 13, 19
21 [t]ver. 13 [u]Neh. 2:1
22 [v]ver. 19

Chapter 41

6 [w][Ezek. 17:10; 19:12]; Hos. 13:15
8 [x]Ps. 77:4; Dan. 2:1, 3 [y]ver. 24; Ex. 7:11, 22; [Dan. 1:20; 2:2; 4:7; Matt. 2:1]
10 [z]ch. 40:2, 3 [a][ch. 39:20]
11 [b]ch. 40:5
12 [c]See ch. 40:12-19
13 [d]ch. 40:21, 22
14 [e]Ps. 105:20 [f][Dan. 2:25] [g][1 Sam. 2:8; Ps. 113:7, 8]
15 [h]ver. 12; Dan. 5:16
16 [i]Dan. 2:30 [j]ch. 40:8; Dan. 2:22, 28, 47
17 [k]See ver. 1-7

the idiom requires decapitation, the baker's corpse was to be hung **on a tree** so that the **birds** could feast on it, reflecting the imagery of his dream.

40:20–22 Pharaoh's birthday may refer to his actual birthday or to the anniversary of his accession, when amnesties were more often granted. As Joseph revealed, the heads of both men are **lifted up** (v. 20).

40:23 In spite of Joseph's specific request in v. 14, **the chief cupbearer did not remember Joseph, but forgot him**. The reader knows that God will "remember" Joseph, as he does other figures in Genesis (8:1; 19:29; 30:22).

41:1–57 *Joseph Interprets Pharaoh's Dreams.* This lengthy episode recounts Joseph's dramatic rise in status from being a prisoner in the king's jail to becoming the chief administrator of Egypt, second only to Pharaoh himself. Central to this is Joseph's ability to interpret Pharaoh's dreams, which anticipate seven years of plenty followed by seven years of famine. Later this will play an important part in bringing Joseph's brothers to Egypt. Joseph's God-given administrative ability is immediately recognized by Pharaoh and prompts his promotion. Throughout this chapter, Joseph consistently acknowledges God as the source of his special gifting.

41:1–7 Pharaoh's two dreams share a common pattern of abundance followed by scarcity. The repetition of this theme in two separate dreams troubles Pharaoh and alerts him to their peculiar nature.

41:1 After two whole years. These events take place two years after the chief cupbearer has been released from prison. Joseph is now 30 years old (see v. 46) and has been in Egypt for about 12 or 13 years (see 37:2). (See chart, p. 114.)

41:8–13 The inability of Pharaoh's officials to interpret the dreams prompts the **chief cupbearer** to **remember** Joseph and his capacity to accurately interpret dreams (see 40:5–22).

41:8 the magicians of Egypt. These were probably cultic officials who interpreted omens and signs—not to be confused with modern illusionists who perform to entertain. The fact that Joseph is very successful with dream interpretation—because "interpretations belong to God" (40:8)—leads one to believe that Joseph is defeating the Egyptians on their own turf.

41:12 Joseph's non-Egyptian origin is indicated by the expression **a young Hebrew**. See 14:13; also note on 10:21–32.

41:14 The brevity of this verse conveys the speed with which Joseph was brought from prison to Pharaoh's court. Protocol required that he be **shaved** and clothed before entering Pharaoh's presence. The expression **out of the pit** graphically illustrates what it was like for Joseph to be incarcerated in prison.

41:15–16 Joseph responds to Pharaoh by unambiguously stating that **God**, not Joseph, is the one who will **answer** Pharaoh's request (cf. 40:8).

41:17–24 Pharaoh's description of the dreams repeats, almost word for word, what has been reported by the narrator in vv. 1–8. This repetition underlines the importance of the dreams.

ears growing on one stalk, full and good. 23 Seven ears, withered, thin, and blighted by the
east wind, sprouted after them, 24 and the thin ears swallowed up the seven good ears. And
[l]I told it to the magicians, but there was no one who could explain it to me."
25 Then Joseph said to Pharaoh, "The dreams of Pharaoh are one; [m]God has revealed
to Pharaoh what he is about to do. 26 The seven good cows are seven years, and the seven
good ears are seven years; the dreams are one. 27 The seven lean and ugly cows that came
up after them are seven years, and the seven empty ears blighted by the east wind are
also [n]seven years of famine. 28 It is as I told Pharaoh; [o]God has shown to Pharaoh what he
is about to do. 29 There will come [p]seven years of great plenty throughout all the land of
Egypt, 30 but after them there will arise [q]seven years of famine, and all the plenty will be
forgotten in the land of Egypt. [r]The famine will consume the land, 31 and the plenty will
be unknown in the land by reason of the famine that will follow, for it will be very severe.
32 And the doubling of Pharaoh's dream means that the [s]thing is fixed by God, and God
will shortly bring it about. 33 Now therefore let Pharaoh select a discerning and wise man,
and set him over the land of Egypt. 34 Let Pharaoh proceed to appoint overseers over the
land and take one-fifth of the produce of the land[1] of Egypt during the seven plentiful
years. 35 And [t]let them gather all the food of these good years that are coming and store
up grain under the authority of Pharaoh for food in the cities, and let them keep it. 36 That
food shall be a reserve for the land against the seven years of famine that are to occur in
the land of Egypt, so that the land may not perish through the famine."

Joseph Rises to Power

37 This proposal pleased Pharaoh and all his servants. 38 And Pharaoh said to his servants,
"Can we find a man like this, [u]in whom is the Spirit of God?"[2] 39 Then Pharaoh said to
Joseph, "Since God has shown you all this, there is none so discerning and wise as you are.
40 [v]You shall be over my house, and all my people shall order themselves as you command.[3]
Only as regards the throne will I be greater than you." 41 And Pharaoh said to Joseph, "See,
[w]I have set you over all the land of Egypt." 42 Then Pharaoh [x]took his signet ring from his
hand and put it on Joseph's hand, and [y]clothed him in garments of fine linen [z]and put a
gold chain about his neck. 43 And he made him ride in his second chariot. [a]And they called
out before him, "Bow the knee!"[4] Thus he set him [b]over all the land of Egypt. 44 Moreover,
Pharaoh said to Joseph, "I am Pharaoh, and [c]without your consent no one shall lift up hand
or foot in all the land of Egypt." 45 And Pharaoh called Joseph's name Zaphenath-paneah.
And he gave him in marriage Asenath, the daughter of Potiphera priest of On. So Joseph
went out over the land of Egypt.
46 Joseph was thirty years old when he [d]entered the service of Pharaoh king of Egypt. And
Joseph went out from the presence of Pharaoh and went through all the land of Egypt.
47 During the seven plentiful years the earth produced abundantly, 48 and he gathered up
all the food of these seven years, which occurred in the land of Egypt, and put the food
in the cities. He put in every city the food from the fields around it. 49 And Joseph stored

24 [l]ver. 8; [Dan. 4:7]
25 [m][Dan. 2:28, 29, 45; Rev. 4:1]
27 [n][2 Kgs. 8:1]
28 [o]ver. 25
29 [p]ver. 47
30 [q]ver. 54; ch. 45:6 [r]ch. 47:13
32 [s]Num. 23:19; Isa. 14:24; 46:10, 11
35 [t]ver. 48
38 [u]Num. 27:18; Dan. 4:8, 18; 5:11, 14
40 [v]Ps. 105:21; Acts 7:10
41 [w]ch. 42:6
42 [x]Esth. 3:10; 8:2, 8, 10 [y][Esth. 8:15] [z]Ezek. 16:11; [Dan. 5:7, 29]
43 [a][Esth. 6:9] [b]ver. 40; ch. 42:6; 45:8, 9, 26
44 [c][Ps. 105:21, 22]
46 [d]1 Sam. 16:21; 1 Kgs. 12:6, 8; Dan. 1:19

[1] Or *over the land and organize the land* [2] Or *of the gods* [3] Hebrew *and according to your command all my people shall kiss the ground* [4] *Abrek*, probably an Egyptian word, similar in sound to the Hebrew word meaning *to kneel*

41:25–36 Joseph's speech falls into two parts. Emphasizing the divine origin of the dreams, Joseph interprets their meaning to Pharaoh in vv. 25–32. He stresses that the twofold revelation indicates that they will be fulfilled soon. In vv. 33–36 Joseph outlines the action that Pharaoh ought to take in order to prepare for the seven years of famine. Joseph's instructions are sufficiently detailed to impress Pharaoh deeply.

41:38 the Spirit of God. Pharaoh recognizes that Joseph is enabled by God to perceive things hidden from others. He ascribes this ability to a divine presence within Joseph. While Pharaoh undoubtedly interpreted this according to his own religious outlook, the early readers of Genesis would have understood Joseph's divine empowerment as being consistent with what they recognized as a recurring feature within Israelite religion. On various occasions God empowered people for special service by giving them his Spirit (see, e.g., Ex. 31:3; Judg. 3:10; 1 Sam. 16:13).

41:40–41 Joseph is made the "vizier," to govern **all** the people of **Egypt**, second only to Pharaoh himself. (A document from the Tomb of Rekhmire in the Late Bronze Age tells of the duties of the vizier in Egypt. He is the "grand steward of all Egypt," and all activities of state are under his control.)

41:42–43 To signify Joseph's special appointment, Pharaoh presents him with his royal **signet ring**, dresses him appropriately, and provides royal transport (v. 43).

41:44 It was not unknown for Semites to attain high positions in the Egyptian government. For example, during the first half of the second millennium B.C., an "Asiatic" (see note on 37:28) named Hur became superintendent of the Royal Seal (or "chancellor") of Egypt. Hur is well known from numerous scarab-seals of the seventeenth and sixteenth centuries B.C.

41:45 called Joseph's name Zaphenath-paneah. The provision of an Egyptian name and a wife completes the process by which Pharaoh fully integrates Joseph into the royal court. Joseph's marriage to **Asenath, the daughter of Potiphera priest of On**, would have completed his assimilation into Egypt. By marrying into a prominent priestly family, Joseph would gain additional acceptance.

49[e]ch. 22:17; Judg. 7:12; 1 Sam. 13:5; Ps. 78:27
50[f]ch. 46:20; 48:5
52[g][ch. 49:22; Hos. 13:15]
54[h]Ps. 105:16; Acts 7:11 [i]ver. 30
56[j]ch. 42:6; [ch. 47:14, 20, 24]
57[k]ver. 54, 56

Chapter 42

1[l]Acts 7:12
2[m]ch. 43:8
4[n]ch. 35:18 [o]ver. 38
6[p]ch. 41:41 [q]ch. 37:7, 9, 10
7[r]ver. 30
9[s]ch. 37:5, 9 [t]ver. 7, 30
13[u]ver. 32; See ch. 37:30

up grain in great abundance, [e]like the sand of the sea, until he ceased to measure it, for
it could not be measured.
50 Before the year of famine came, [f]two sons were born to Joseph. Asenath, the daughter
of Potiphera priest of On, bore them to him. **51** Joseph called the name of the firstborn
Manasseh. "For," he said, "God has made me forget all my hardship and all my father's
house."[1] **52** The name of the second he called Ephraim, "For God has [g]made me fruitful in
the land of my affliction."[2]
53 The seven years of plenty that occurred in the land of Egypt came to an end, **54** and [h]the
seven years of famine began to come, [i]as Joseph had said. There was famine in all lands,
but in all the land of Egypt there was bread. **55** When all the land of Egypt was famished,
the people cried to Pharaoh for bread. Pharaoh said to all the Egyptians, "Go to Joseph.
What he says to you, do."
56 So when the famine had spread over all the land, Joseph opened all the storehouses[3]
and [j]sold to the Egyptians, for the famine was severe in the land of Egypt. **57** Moreover,
all the earth came to Egypt to Joseph to buy grain, because the famine was severe [k]over
all the earth.

Joseph's Brothers Go to Egypt

42 When [l]Jacob learned that there was grain for sale in Egypt, he said to his sons,
"Why do you look at one another?" **2** And he said, "Behold, I have heard that there
is grain for sale in Egypt. Go down and buy grain for us there, that we may [m]live and not
die." **3** So ten of Joseph's brothers went down to buy grain in Egypt. **4** But Jacob did not send
Benjamin, [n]Joseph's brother, with his brothers, for [o]he feared that harm might happen
to him. **5** Thus the sons of Israel came to buy among the others who came, for the famine
was in the land of Canaan.
6 Now Joseph was governor [p]over the land. He was the one who sold to all the people
of the land. And Joseph's brothers came and [q]bowed themselves before him with their
faces to the ground. **7** Joseph saw his brothers and recognized them, but he treated them
like strangers and [r]spoke roughly to them. "Where do you come from?" he said. They
said, "From the land of Canaan, to buy food." **8** And Joseph recognized his brothers, but
they did not recognize him. **9** And Joseph [s]remembered the dreams that he had dreamed
of them. [t]And he said to them, "You are spies; you have come to see the nakedness of the
land." **10** They said to him, "No, my lord, your servants have come to buy food. **11** We are all
sons of one man. We are honest men. Your servants have never been spies."
12 He said to them, "No, it is the nakedness of the land that you have come to see." **13** And
they said, "We, your servants, are twelve brothers, the sons of one man in the land of Canaan,
and behold, the youngest is this day with our father, and one [u]is no more." **14** But Joseph
said to them, "It is as I said to you. You are spies. **15** By this you shall be tested: by the life
of Pharaoh, you shall not go from this place unless your youngest brother comes here.
16 Send one of you, and let him bring your brother, while you remain confined, that your
words may be tested, whether there is truth in you. Or else, by the life of Pharaoh, surely
you are spies." **17** And he put them all together in custody for three days.

[1] *Manasseh* sounds like the Hebrew for *making to forget* [2] *Ephraim* sounds like the Hebrew for *making fruitful* [3] Hebrew *all that was in them*

41:50–52 The names of the two boys reveal that Joseph has not entirely forgotten the past. While the name **Manasseh** (v. 51), which has the sense of "forget," reflects how things have moved on for Joseph, it ironically also recalls his **father's** household. The name **Ephraim** (v. 52), which means "twice fruitful," recalls the recurring theme of being **fruitful** (see note on 1:28).

41:54–57 As predicted in Pharaoh's dreams, the seven years of plenty are followed by a **famine** that extends well beyond the borders of Egypt. Joseph's preparations, however, ensure that food is available for the Egyptians and **all the earth** (v. 57; i.e., all the eastern Mediterranean region; cf. note on 6:17).

42:1–38 *The Brothers' First Journey to Egypt.* Shortage of food in Canaan forces Jacob to send his sons to Egypt, but Benjamin, Joseph's younger brother, remains at home, for Jacob fears losing him, too. When Joseph finally encounters his brothers again, he deliberately conceals his identity. After accusing them of being spies, he holds Simeon hostage, sending the others back to Canaan on the understanding that they will return with Benjamin. Naturally, Jacob is very reluctant to permit this.

42:6–9 About 20 years have passed since his brothers last saw Joseph at age 17 (see chart, p. 114). While Joseph recognizes them, not surprisingly, they remain oblivious to the true identity of the Egyptian governor who questions them regarding their motive for visiting Egypt. **bowed themselves before him** (v. 6). The brothers' obeisance is clearly interpreted by Joseph as fulfilling his earlier dreams (37:5–11). The narrator underlines this by observing that **Joseph remembered the dreams** (42:9). Speaking through an interpreter (v. 23) and without disclosing his true identity, Joseph accuses his brothers of being **spies** who have come to assess Egyptian defenses against invasions. **the nakedness of the land** (v. 9). An idiom that alludes to the locations where Egypt would be most vulnerable to attack.

42:10–17 In their attempt to deny the charge of being spies (which is issued three times: vv. 9, 12, 14), Joseph's brothers mention that their younger

18 On the third day Joseph said to them, "Do this and you will live, [v]for I fear God: 19 if
you are honest men, let one of your brothers remain confined where you are in custody,
and let the rest go and carry [w]grain for the famine of your households, 20 and [x]bring your
youngest brother to me. So your words will be verified, and you shall not die." And they
did so. 21 Then they said to one another, [y]"In truth we are guilty concerning our brother,
in that we saw the distress of his soul, when he begged us and we did not listen. That is
why this distress has come upon us." 22 And Reuben answered them, [z]"Did I not tell you
not to sin against the boy? But you did not listen. So now [a]there comes a reckoning for his
blood." 23 They did not know that Joseph understood them, for there was an interpreter
between them. 24 Then he turned away from them and [b]wept. And he returned to them
and spoke to them. And he took Simeon from them and bound him before their eyes.
25 [c]And Joseph gave orders to fill their bags with grain, and to replace every man's money
in his sack, and to give them provisions for the journey. This was done for them.

26 Then they loaded their donkeys with their grain and departed. 27 And as [d]one of them
opened his sack to give his donkey fodder at [e]the lodging place, he saw his money in the
mouth of his sack. 28 He said to his brothers, "My money has been put back; here it is in
the mouth of my sack!" At this their hearts failed them, and they turned trembling to one
another, saying, "What is this that God has done to us?"

29 When they came to Jacob their father in the land of Canaan, they told him all that had
happened to them, saying, 30 "The man, the lord of the land, [f]spoke roughly to us and took
us to be spies of the land. 31 But we said to him, 'We are honest men; we have never been
spies. 32 We are twelve brothers, sons of our father. One [g]is no more, and the youngest is
this day with our father in the land of Canaan.' 33 Then the man, the lord of the land, said
to us, [h]'By this I shall know that you are honest men: leave one of your brothers with me,
and take [i]grain for the famine of your households, and go your way. 34 Bring your youngest
brother to me. Then I shall know that you are not spies but honest men, and I will deliver
your brother to you, and you shall [j]trade in the land.'"

35 [k]As they emptied their sacks, behold, every man's bundle of money was in his sack.
And when they and their father saw their bundles of money, they were afraid. 36 And Jacob
their father said to them, "You have [l]bereaved me of my children: Joseph is no more, and
Simeon is no more, and now you would take Benjamin. All this has come against me."
37 Then Reuben said to his father, "Kill [m]my two sons if I do not bring him back to you.
Put him in my hands, and I will bring him back to you." 38 But he said, "My son shall not
go down with you, for [n]his brother is dead, and he is the only one left. [o]If harm should
happen to him on the journey that you are to make, [p]you would bring down my gray
hairs with sorrow to Sheol."

Joseph's Brothers Return to Egypt

43 Now the famine was [q]severe in the land. 2 And when they had eaten the grain that
they had brought from Egypt, their father said to them, "Go again, buy us a little
food." 3 But Judah said to him, "The man solemnly warned us, saying, 'You shall not see my

18 [v]Lev. 25:43; Neh. 5:15
19 [w]ver. 33
20 [x]ver. 34; ch. 43:5; 44:23
21 [y][Job 36:8, 9]; See ch. 37:23-28
22 [z]ch. 37:21 [a]ch. 9:5; 2 Chr. 24:22; [1 Kgs. 2:32; Ps. 9:12; Luke 11:50, 51]
24 [b]ch. 43:30
25 [c]ch. 44:1
27 [d]ver. 35; ch. 43:21 [e]Ex. 4:24; Jer. 9:2
30 [f]ver. 7, 9
32 [g]ver. 13
33 [h]ver. 15, 19, 20 [i]ver. 19
34 [j]ch. 34:10, 21
35 [k]ver. 27; ch. 43:21
36 [l]ch. 43:14
37 [m][ch. 46:9]
38 [n]ver. 13, 32, 36; ch. 37:33; 44:28 [o]ver. 4; ch. 44:29 [p]ch. 37:35; 44:31

Chapter 43

1 [q]ch. 41:54, 57

brother is **this day with our father** (v. 13). Seizing on this reference to Benjamin, Joseph demands that the brothers prove their trustworthiness by sending for their brother (v. 16). Then, by way of demonstrating his authority over them, Joseph has them placed **in custody for three days** (v. 17).

42:18–26 By way of concession, motivated by his **fear** of **God** (v. 18), Joseph permits all the brothers to return to Canaan, apart from Simeon (v. 19). In Joseph's hearing the brothers interpret their present dilemma as a punishment for their heartless treatment of Joseph in the past (vv. 21–23). Their words so move Joseph that he withdraws from their presence to weep (v. 24). Upon his return, Joseph sends away all the brothers, except Simeon, having instructed his servant to replace **every man's money in his sack** (v. 25).

42:27–28 Later, when they stop for the night, one of the brothers discovers that his **money** has been replaced **in the mouth of his sack** (v. 27). This apparently inexplicable occurrence evokes considerable apprehension. The brothers interpret it as something **that God has done** (v. 28), with the intention of bringing further harm to them. Running through this section of the story is the idea that those who perpetrate evil cannot evade punishment forever. The brothers' consciences clearly trouble them.

42:35 The unexpected discovery of **every man's bundle of money** in his sack naturally fills the brothers and their father with fear. The extraordinary event would make others think that they have taken the grain from Egypt without paying for it, or even that they had sold Simeon for cash.

42:36–38 In light of all that has happened, Jacob is reluctant to go down to Egypt, being exceptionally anxious about the possibility of losing **Benjamin** (v. 36). Reuben's response does little to reassure his father (v. 37). Jacob is unlikely to entrust Benjamin to someone who cares so little for the lives of his own sons. Jacob emphatically states, **My son shall not go down with you** (v. 38).

42:38 Sheol. See note on 37:35.

43:1–34 *Joseph's Brothers Return to Egypt.* The ongoing famine eventually forces Jacob to send his sons back to Egypt with Benjamin. When the brothers return, they are unexpectedly invited to dine at Joseph's house. Taken by surprise, they suspect that this may be a ploy to enslave them because of the money in their sacks. The lavish meal prepares the way for Joseph's disclosure of himself to his brothers, which comes in the next chapter.

43:1–10 Judah takes the lead in successfully persuading his father to permit the brothers to take Benjamin with them to Egypt. His approach differs mark-

face unless your [r]brother is with you.' 4 If you will send our brother with us, we will go down
and buy you food. 5 But if you will not send him, we will not go down, for the man said to
us, 'You shall not see my face, unless your brother is with you.'" 6 Israel said, "Why did you
treat me so badly as to tell the man that you had another brother?" 7 They replied, "The man
questioned us carefully about ourselves and our kindred, saying, 'Is your father still alive?
Do you have another brother?' What we told him was in answer to these questions. Could
we in any way know that he would say, 'Bring your brother down'?" 8 And Judah said to
Israel his father, "Send the boy with me, and we will arise and go, that we may [s]live and not
die, both we and you and also our little ones. 9 I will be a pledge of his safety. From my hand
you shall require him. [t]If I do not bring him back to you and set him before you, then let me
bear the blame forever. 10 If we had not delayed, we would now have returned twice."

11 Then their father Israel said to them, "If it must be so, then do this: take some of the
choice fruits of the land in your bags, and carry a present down to the man, a little [u]balm
and a little honey, gum, myrrh, pistachio nuts, and almonds. 12 Take double the money
with you. Carry back with you the money [v]that was returned in the mouth of your sacks.
Perhaps it was an oversight. 13 Take also your brother, and arise, go again to the man. 14 May
[w]God Almighty[1] [x]grant you mercy before the man, and may he send back your other brother
and Benjamin. And as for me, [y]if I am bereaved of my children, I am bereaved."

15 So the men took this present, and they took double the money with them, and
Benjamin. They arose and went down to Egypt and stood before Joseph.

16 When Joseph saw Benjamin with them, he said to the [z]steward of his house, "Bring
the men into the house, and slaughter an animal and make ready, for the men are to dine
with me at noon." 17 The man did as Joseph told him and brought the men to Joseph's
house. 18 And the men were afraid because they were brought to Joseph's house, and they
said, "It is because of the money, which was replaced in our sacks the first time, that we are
brought in, so that he may assault us and fall upon us to make us servants and seize our
donkeys." 19 So they went up to the steward of Joseph's house and spoke with him at the
door of the house, 20 and said, [a]"Oh, my lord, [b]we came down the first time to buy food.
21 And [c]when we came to the lodging place we opened our sacks, and there was each man's
money in the mouth of his sack, our money in full weight. So we have brought it again
with us, 22 and we have brought other money down with us to buy food. We do not know
who put our money in our sacks." 23 He replied, "Peace to you, do not be afraid. Your God
and the God of your father has put treasure in your sacks for you. I received your money."
Then he brought Simeon out to them. 24 And when the man had brought the men into
Joseph's house and [d]given them water, and they had washed their feet, and when he had
given their donkeys fodder, 25 they prepared [e]the present for Joseph's coming at noon, for
they heard that they should eat bread there.

26 When Joseph came home, they brought into the house to him the present that they
had with them and [f]bowed down to him to the ground. 27 And he inquired about their
welfare and said, "Is your father well, the old man [g]of whom you spoke? Is he still alive?"
28 They said, "Your servant our father is well; he is still alive." And they [h]bowed their heads
and prostrated themselves. 29 And he lifted up his eyes and saw his brother Benjamin, [i]his
mother's son, and said, "Is this your youngest brother, [g]of whom you spoke to me? God be
gracious to you, my son!" 30 Then Joseph hurried out, for [j]his compassion grew warm for
his brother, and he sought a place to weep. And he entered his chamber and [k]wept there.
31 Then he washed his face and came out. And [l]controlling himself he said, "Serve the food."
32 They served him by himself, and them by themselves, and the Egyptians who ate with

[1] Hebrew *El Shaddai*

3 [r]ch. 42:20; 44:23
8 [s]ch. 42:2
9 [t]ch. 42:37; 44:32
11 [u]See ch. 37:25
12 [v]ch. 42:25, 27, 35
14 [w]See ch. 17:1 [x][Neh. 1:11] [y]ch. 42:36
16 [z]ver. 19; ch. 44:1, 4; [ch. 24:2; 39:4]
20 [a]ch. 44:18 [b]ch. 42:3, 10
21 [c]ch. 42:27
24 [d]See ch. 18:4
25 [e]ver. 11
26 [f]ch. 42:6; See ch. 37:5-11
27 [g]ch. 42:11, 13
28 [h]ver. 26
29 [i]ch. 35:18 [g][See ver. 27 above]
30 [j]1 Kgs. 3:26; [Jer. 31:20] [k]ch. 42:24
31 [l]ch. 45:1

edly from that of Reuben (see 42:37). First, he repeats in quick succession what **the man** (i.e., Joseph) **said**, emphasizing that he will not see them unless their brother is with them (vv. 3–5). Second, Judah offers himself as a **pledge** for the **safety** of Benjamin (v. 9). He will take full personal responsibility and bear the blame if anything should happen to him.

43:15–17 Joseph invites his brothers to dine with him at his house.

43:30–31 his compassion grew warm for his brother. Drawn to Benjamin after two decades of being apart, Joseph swiftly retires to his chamber to weep (v. 30). After refreshing himself, he returns and the meal begins (v. 31).

43:32 by himself. Joseph eats apart from his brothers as a means of maintaining his guise, since as the narrator observes, it was an **abomination to the Egyptians** to **eat** with these foreigners, the **Hebrews** (see notes on 10:21–32; 14:13–16).

him by themselves, because the Egyptians could not eat with the Hebrews, for that is [m]an
abomination to the Egyptians. 33 And they sat before him, the firstborn according to his
birthright and the youngest according to his youth. And the men looked at one another
in amazement. 34 [n]Portions were taken to them from Joseph's table, but Benjamin's portion was [o]five times as much as any of theirs. And they drank and were merry[1] with him.

Joseph Tests His Brothers

44 Then he commanded [p]the steward of his house, [q]"Fill the men's sacks with food, as
much as they can carry, and put each man's money in the mouth of his sack, 2 and
put my cup, the silver cup, in the mouth of the sack of the youngest, with his money for
the grain." And he did as Joseph told him.
3 As soon as the morning was light, the men were sent away with their donkeys. 4 They
had gone only a short distance from the city. Now Joseph said to his [r]steward, "Up, follow
after the men, and when you overtake them, say to them, 'Why have you repaid evil for
good?[2] 5 Is it not from this that my lord drinks, and [s]by this that he practices divination?
You have done evil in doing this.'"
6 When he overtook them, he spoke to them these words. 7 They said to him, "Why does
my lord speak such words as these? Far be it from your servants to do such a thing! 8 Behold,
[t]the money that we found in the mouths of our sacks we brought back to you from the land
of Canaan. How then could we steal silver or gold from your lord's house? 9 [u]Whichever
of your servants is found with it shall die, and we also will be [v]my lord's servants." 10 He
said, "Let it be as you say: he who is found with it shall be my servant, and the rest of you
shall be innocent." 11 Then each man quickly lowered his sack to the ground, and each
man opened his sack. 12 And he searched, beginning with the eldest and ending with the
youngest. And the cup was found in Benjamin's sack. 13 Then they [w]tore their clothes, and
every man loaded his donkey, and they returned to the city.
14 When Judah and his brothers came to Joseph's house, he was still there. They [x]fell
before him to the ground. 15 Joseph said to them, "What deed is this that you have done?
Do you not know that a man like me [y]can indeed practice divination?" 16 And Judah said,
"What shall we say to my lord? What shall we speak? Or how can we clear ourselves? God
has found out [z]the guilt of your servants; behold, we are [a]my lord's servants, both we and
he also in whose hand the cup has been found." 17 But he said, "Far be it from me that I
should do so! Only the man in whose hand the cup was found shall be my servant. But as
for you, go up in peace to your father."

[1] Hebrew *and became intoxicated* [2] Septuagint (compare Vulgate) adds *Why have you stolen my silver cup?*

32 [m]ch. 46:34; Ex. 8:26
34 [n][2 Sam. 11:8] [o][ch. 45:22]

Chapter 44

1 [p]ver. 4; See ch. 43:16 [q]ch. 42:25
4 [r]ver. 1
5 [s]ver. 15; ch. 30:27; [2 Kgs. 21:6; 2 Chr. 33:6]
8 [t]ch. 43:21
9 [u][ch. 31:32] [v]ver. 16
13 [w]ch. 37:29
14 [x]ch. 37:7, 9, 10; 42:6; 43:26, 28
15 [y]ver. 5
16 [z]ch. 37:18; [Num. 32:23] [a]ver. 9

43:33–34 Joseph's feelings for Benjamin result in his being given portions that are **five times** those given to his brothers.

44:1–34 *Benjamin Is Accused of Stealing.* Still disguising his true identity from his brothers, Joseph sends them away after the meal. But he gives instructions that his silver cup should be placed in the sack of Benjamin in order to accuse him of theft. Later, when the cup is found in Benjamin's sack, the brothers are forced to return and face Joseph once more. When Joseph threatens to hold on to Benjamin, Judah pleads passionately in a long speech that he should become Joseph's slave in place of Benjamin. Judah's action reveals how much his character has changed from when he proposed selling Joseph into slavery.

44:1–2 As in 42:25, Joseph instructs the **steward** to place **each man's money** into the **mouth of his sack**. Additionally, Joseph's silver cup is to be put into Benjamin's sack. Joseph does this with the intention of accusing Benjamin of theft.

44:3–5 my lord . . . practices divination (v. 5). Since these remarks are set in the context of an elaborate ruse, it is impossible to know whether they should be taken as reflecting something that Joseph actually did. Joseph clearly intends that his brothers should believe that he has powers of supernatural discernment (see v. 15). For further comments on divination, see note on 30:27–30.

44:6–10 When the brothers are charged with theft (v. 6), they naturally deny doing anything wrong (v. 7). On the contrary, they appeal to their honesty in bringing back the money found previously in their sacks (v. 8). Confident of their innocence, they propose that anyone found hiding the cup should be put to death, with all of them becoming slaves to the steward (v. 9; the Hebrew term for **servants** also denotes "slaves," and this is probably the implication here). In reply, Joseph's steward adopts a more lenient approach, merely requiring that only the guilty person be enslaved (v. 10).

44:11–13 they tore their clothes (v. 13). This was an outward sign of inner anguish and grief, often associated with mourning (cf. 37:29). Previously, in 37:29, Jacob tore his clothes upon learning of Joseph's "death."

44:14–17 When Judah and his brothers came to Joseph's house (v. 14). The narrator isolates Judah from his brothers, drawing attention to him—possibly not only because he has become their spokesman but also anticipating his offer to take Benjamin's place as Joseph's slave. **Do you not know that a man like me can indeed practice divination?** (v. 15). Building on what his steward had said earlier regarding the silver cup (see v. 5), Joseph portrays himself as having the ability to discover secrets hidden from others. This may also be a ploy on Joseph's part in order to elicit information from the brothers. Now that he has created the impression that he can discover knowledge with divine help, his brothers may feel that they can no longer conceal their past actions. For this reason, Judah remarks, **God has found out the guilt of your servants** (v. 16). In all probability Judah has in mind the brothers' treatment of Joseph, for he knows that they are innocent of taking the silver cup. The brothers are convinced that God is now holding them to account for their actions against Joseph. On behalf of all the brothers, Judah speaks to Joseph.

44:16 lord's servants. That is, slaves. See note on 44:6–10.

18[b] ch. 43:20 [c] Ex. 32:22 [d] ch. 41:40
20[e] ver. 30; [ch. 43:8] [f] [ch. 37:3]
21[g] ch. 42:15, 20; 43:3, 5
22[h] [ver. 31]
23[i] ch. 43:3
25[j] ch. 43:2
27[k] ch. 46:19
28[l] ch. 37:33
29[m] ch. 42:36, 38 [n] ch. 42:4, 38
32[o] ch. 43:9

Chapter 45

1[p] ch. 43:31; [Esth. 5:10]
3[q] Acts 7:13
4[r] ch. 37:28
5[s] ch. 50:20; Ps. 105:16, 17
6[t] ch. 41:30 [u] Ex. 34:21; Deut. 21:4; 1 Sam. 8:12; [Isa. 30:24]
8[v] ver. 26; ch. 41:43

18 Then Judah went up to him and said, [b]"Oh, my lord, please let your servant speak a
word in my lord's ears, and [c]let not your anger burn against your servant, for [d]you are like
Pharaoh himself. 19 My lord asked his servants, saying, 'Have you a father, or a brother?'
20 And we said to my lord, 'We have a father, an old man, [e]and a young brother, [f]the child of
his old age. His brother is dead, and he alone is left of his mother's children, and his father
loves him.' 21 Then you said to your servants, [g]'Bring him down to me, that I may set my
eyes on him.' 22 We said to my lord, 'The boy cannot leave his father, for if he should leave
his father, [h]his father would die.' 23 Then you said to your servants, [i]'Unless your youngest
brother comes down with you, you shall not see my face again.'

24 "When we went back to your servant my father, we told him the words of my lord.
25 And when [j]our father said, 'Go again, buy us a little food,' 26 we said, 'We cannot go down.
If our youngest brother goes with us, then we will go down. For we cannot see the man's
face unless our youngest brother is with us.' 27 Then your servant my father said to us, 'You
know that my wife bore me [k]two sons. 28 One left me, and I said, [l]"Surely he has been torn
to pieces," and I have never seen him since. 29 If you [m]take this one also from me, [n]and harm
happens to him, you will bring down my gray hairs in evil to Sheol.'

30 "Now therefore, as soon as I come to your servant my father, and the boy is not with
us, then, as his life is bound up in the boy's life, 31 as soon as he sees that the boy is not with
us, he will die, and your servants will bring down the gray hairs of your servant our father
with sorrow to Sheol. 32 For your servant became a pledge of safety for the boy to my father,
saying, [o]'If I do not bring him back to you, then I shall bear the blame before my father all
my life.' 33 Now therefore, please let your servant remain instead of the boy as a servant to
my lord, and let the boy go back with his brothers. 34 For how can I go back to my father if
the boy is not with me? I fear to see the evil that would find my father."

Joseph Provides for His Brothers and Family

45 Then Joseph could not [p]control himself before all those who stood by him. He
cried, "Make everyone go out from me." So no one stayed with him when Joseph
made himself known to his brothers. 2 And he wept aloud, so that the Egyptians heard it,
and the household of Pharaoh heard it. 3 And Joseph said to his brothers, [q]"I am Joseph!
Is my father still alive?" But his brothers could not answer him, for they were dismayed
at his presence.

4 So Joseph said to his brothers, "Come near to me, please." And they came near. And
he said, "I am your brother, Joseph, [r]whom you sold into Egypt. 5 And now do not be distressed or angry with yourselves because you sold me here, [s]for God sent me before you
to preserve life. 6 For the famine has been in the land these two years, and there are [t]yet
five years in which there will be neither [u]plowing nor harvest. 7 And God sent me before
you to preserve for you a remnant on earth, and to keep alive for you many survivors. 8 So
it was not you who sent me here, but God. He has made me a father to Pharaoh, and lord
of all his house and [v]ruler over all the land of Egypt. 9 Hurry and go up to my father and

44:18 In this verse, which introduces one of the longest recorded speeches in Genesis, Judah begs Joseph for the opportunity to speak to him in private in order to ask an important favor of him. The tone of his opening words expresses total deference, for Judah recognizes that Joseph is **like Pharaoh himself**.

44:19–29 Judah summarizes for Joseph, mainly by quoting what different people said, the process that led to Benjamin's being in Egypt. In doing so he highlights why his father will be so distraught at not having Benjamin returned to him.

44:29 Sheol. See note on 37:35.

44:30–34 please let your servant remain instead of the boy. Building on what he has already said, Judah petitions Joseph to let Benjamin return to his father in Canaan in order to prevent him from dying of grief at the loss of a second son. To make this possible, Judah offers to take Benjamin's place and become Joseph's slave (v. 33). For Judah, this would be preferable to witnessing his father's distress if Benjamin remained in Egypt (v. 34). The selfless attitude of Judah stands in sharp contrast to what he previously displayed when arguing that Joseph should be sold into slavery (see 37:26–27). On that occasion, Judah cared little about the impact that this would have on his **father**. **Sheol**. See note on 37:35.

45:1–28 *Joseph Discloses His Identity.* Moved by Judah's speech, Joseph is unable to restrain his emotions. To the consternation of his shocked brothers, he reveals that he is Joseph. In a long speech he attempts to dissipate their sense of guilt by stressing God's role in sending him to Egypt in order to preserve the lives of his family. With the famine set to continue for another five years, Joseph sends his brothers back to Canaan in order to bring the rest of his family to Egypt. The narrator makes no comment on whether Joseph's overall strategy with his brothers was right, and it is unclear just what Moses expected his audience to think. Probably he was more interested in the consequences: the brothers were led to acknowledge their guilt in the matter of Joseph, and also to be concerned for their father and their youngest brother. Further, this is what enables the reconciliation between them and Joseph. The first audience would recognize the value of courageous self-sacrifice and reconciliation, not simply on the family level, but on the level of the whole people of God—values that they would themselves need to practice in order to meet the claims of their calling.

45:8 father to Pharaoh. This is probably not a specific title that was given to Joseph but rather a designation he uses in order to mark out his role as someone who is committed to Pharaoh's well-being. For a similar use of the term "father," see note on 17:4–5.

say to him, 'Thus says your son Joseph, God has made me lord of all Egypt. Come down to
me; do not tarry. 10 [w]You shall dwell in the land of Goshen, and you shall be near me, you
and your children and your children's children, and your flocks, your herds, and all that
you have. 11 [x]There I will provide for you, for there are yet five years of famine to come, so
that you and your household, and all that you have, do not come to poverty.' 12 And now
your eyes see, and the eyes of my brother Benjamin see, that it is [y]my mouth that speaks
to you. 13 You must tell my father of all my honor in Egypt, and of all that you have seen.
Hurry and [z]bring my father down here." 14 Then he fell upon his brother Benjamin's neck
and wept, and Benjamin wept upon his neck. 15 And he kissed all his brothers and wept
upon them. After that his brothers talked with him.
16 When the report was heard in Pharaoh's house, "Joseph's brothers have come," it pleased
Pharaoh and his servants. 17 And Pharaoh said to Joseph, "Say to your brothers, 'Do this: load
your beasts and go back to the land of Canaan, 18 and take your father and your households,
and come to me, and [a]I will give you the best of the land of Egypt, and you shall eat the fat
of the land.' 19 And you, Joseph, are commanded to say, 'Do this: take [b]wagons from the land
of Egypt for your little ones and for your wives, and bring your father, and come. 20 Have
no concern for[1] your goods, for the best of all the land of Egypt is yours.'"
21 The sons of Israel did so: and Joseph gave them [b]wagons, according to the command
of Pharaoh, and gave them provisions for the journey. 22 To each and all of them he gave
[c]a change of clothes, but to Benjamin he gave three hundred shekels[2] of silver and [d]five
changes of clothes. 23 To his father he sent as follows: ten donkeys loaded with the good
things of Egypt, and ten female donkeys loaded with grain, bread, and provision for his
father on the journey. 24 Then he sent his brothers away, and as they departed, he said to
them, [e]"Do not quarrel on the way."
25 So they went up out of Egypt and came to the land of Canaan to their father Jacob.
26 And they told him, "Joseph is still alive, and he is ruler over all the land of Egypt." And his
heart became numb, for he did not believe them. 27 But when they told him all the words
of Joseph, which he had said to them, and when he saw [f]the wagons that Joseph had sent
to carry him, the spirit of their father Jacob revived. 28 And Israel said, "It is enough; Joseph
my son is still alive. I will go and see him before I die."

Joseph Brings His Family to Egypt

46 So Israel took his journey with all that he had and came to [g]Beersheba, and offered
sacrifices [h]to the God of his father Isaac. 2 And God spoke to Israel [i]in visions of the
night and said, "Jacob, Jacob." And he said, "Here I am." 3 Then he said, "I am God, [j]the God
of your father. Do not be afraid to go down to Egypt, for there I will [k]make you into a great

[1] Hebrew *Let your eye not pity* [2] A *shekel* was about 2/5 ounce or 11 grams

10 [w]ch. 46:34; 47:1, 4, 6, 27; 50:8; Ex. 8:22; [ch. 47:11; Josh. 10:41]
11 [x]ch. 47:12; 50:21
12 [y][ch. 42:23]
13 [z]Acts 7:14
18 [a]ch. 47:6
19 [b]ch. 46:5
21 [b][See ver. 19 above]
22 [c][2 Kgs. 5:5, 22, 23] [d][ch. 43:34]
24 [e][ch. 42:22]
27 [f]ver. 19, 21; ch. 46:5

Chapter 46

1 [g]ch. 21:31, 33; 26:33; 28:10 [h]ch. 26:24, 25; 28:13; 31:42
2 [i]ch. 15:1; Job 33:14, 15
3 [j]ch. 28:13 [k]ch. 35:11; [ch. 12:2; Ex. 1:7, 9; Deut. 26:5]

45:10 land of Goshen. The precise location of Goshen is disputed; it was probably a region in the eastern delta area of the Nile suitable for herdsmen, in the area of the Wadi Tumilat. This Goshen should be distinguished from the one mentioned in Josh. 10:41; 11:16; 15:51. Joseph chooses the region of Goshen because of its suitability for herdsmen and its close proximity to him. This location probably also lessened the likelihood of Jacob's family being absorbed into Egyptian society (as Joseph had been), enabling them to retain their ethnic and religious distinctiveness. (The Egyptian text Papyrus Anastasis VI tells of Pharaoh Merneptah, in approximately 1220 B.C., allowing Edomite nomads to live in Goshen "to keep themselves and their flocks alive in the territory of the king.")

45:21–24 Joseph lavishes gifts on his brothers, treating Benjamin with exceptional generosity, and sends them away with additional gifts for his father. **three hundred shekels of silver** (v. 22). Previously Joseph had been sold into slavery for a mere 20 shekels (37:28). Joseph's admonition, **Do not quarrel on the way** (45:24), may have been necessary for his brothers; but the narrator records it in light of his purpose to promote unity among the people of God who read this (see note on vv. 1–28).

45:25–28 Unsurprisingly, Jacob struggles to believe that Joseph not only is alive but is also **ruler over all . . . of Egypt** (v. 26). Through time, however, he is persuaded that this is true, especially by the gifts that Joseph has sent. He then consents to visit Joseph (v. 28).

46:1–27 *Jacob's Family Relocates to Egypt.* This section falls into two distinct parts: the itinerary for Jacob's journey to Egypt (vv. 1–7); and a register, based on genealogical information, of those who were members of Jacob's family when they settled in Egypt (vv. 8–27).

46:1 Setting out (possibly from Hebron; see 37:14), Jacob travels south to **Beersheba**, where his father Isaac (see 26:23–33) and grandfather Abraham (21:22–34) lived for a time. (For more on Beersheba, see note on 21:31.)

46:2–4 Before Jacob leaves for Egypt, God speaks to him in a vision at **night** (v. 2). Previously God had prohibited Isaac from going to Egypt during a time of famine (26:1–5). Given this earlier prohibition and what had happened to Abraham in Egypt during another famine (12:10–20), Jacob may well have been reluctant to go there. God had promised that Abraham would become a **great nation** (12:2), and this theme runs throughout chs. 12–50. **I myself will go down with you** (46:4). God had made and kept similar promises when Jacob went to Paddan-aram (see 28:15). **I will also bring you up again** (46:4) is both a promise of the exodus from Egypt like 15:13–16 and a reassurance that Jacob himself will be buried in the Promised Land. God reassures Jacob that his journey to Egypt will not undermine the divine promises that center on Canaan. Although Jacob will die in Egypt (49:33), he will then be buried with his ancestors, Abraham and Isaac, in Canaan (49:29–50:13). While the patriarchs died before witnessing the fulfillment of God's redemptive purposes for the whole world, they believed that their eternal destiny was secure because of their relationship with God (see Heb. 11:12–16, 39).

nation. **4** I myself will go down with you to Egypt, and I will also [l]bring you up again, and
[m]Joseph's hand shall close your eyes."
5 Then Jacob set out from Beersheba. The sons of Israel carried Jacob their father, their
little ones, and their wives, in the wagons [n]that Pharaoh had sent to carry him. **6** They
also took their livestock and their goods, which they had gained in the land of Canaan,
and [o]came into Egypt, Jacob and all his offspring with him, **7** his sons, and his sons' sons
with him, his daughters, and his sons' daughters. All his offspring he brought with him
into Egypt.
8 [p]Now [q]these are the names of the descendants of Israel, who came into Egypt, Jacob
and his sons. [r]Reuben, Jacob's firstborn, **9** and the sons of Reuben: Hanoch, Pallu, Hezron,
and Carmi. **10** The sons of Simeon: Jemuel, Jamin, Ohad, Jachin, Zohar, and Shaul, the son
of a Canaanite woman. **11** The sons of [s]Levi: Gershon, Kohath, and Merari. **12** The sons of
[t]Judah: Er, Onan, Shelah, Perez, and Zerah (but [u]Er and Onan died in the land of Canaan);
and the sons of [v]Perez were Hezron and Hamul. **13** [w]The sons of Issachar: Tola, Puvah, Yob,
and Shimron. **14** The sons of Zebulun: Sered, Elon, and Jahleel. **15** These are the sons of Leah,
[x]whom she bore to Jacob in Paddan-aram, together with his daughter Dinah; altogether
his sons and his daughters numbered thirty-three.
16 The sons of Gad: Ziphion, Haggi, Shuni, Ezbon, Eri, Arodi, and Areli. **17** [y]The sons of
Asher: Imnah, Ishvah, Ishvi, Beriah, with Serah their sister. And the sons of Beriah: Heber
and Malchiel. **18** [z]These are the sons of Zilpah, [a]whom Laban gave to Leah his daughter;
and these she bore to Jacob—sixteen persons.
19 The sons of Rachel, Jacob's wife: Joseph and Benjamin. **20** And [b]to Joseph in the land
of Egypt were born Manasseh and Ephraim, whom Asenath, the daughter of Potiphera
the priest of [c]On, bore to him. **21** And [d]the sons of Benjamin: Bela, Becher, Ashbel, Gera,
Naaman, Ehi, Rosh, Muppim, Huppim, and Ard. **22** These are the sons of Rachel, who were
born to Jacob—fourteen persons in all.
23 The son[1] of Dan: Hushim. **24** [e]The sons of Naphtali: Jahzeel, Guni, Jezer, and Shillem.
25 [f]These are the sons of Bilhah, [g]whom Laban gave to Rachel his daughter, and these she
bore to Jacob—seven persons in all.
26 All the persons belonging to Jacob who came into Egypt, who were his own descendants, not including Jacob's sons' wives, were sixty-six persons in all. **27** And the sons of
Joseph, who were born to him in Egypt, were two. [h]All the persons of the house of Jacob
who came into Egypt were seventy.

[1] Hebrew *sons*

4 [l]ch. 15:16; 28:15; 48:21; 50:24; Ex. 3:8 [m]ch. 50:1
5 [n]ch. 45:19, 21, 27
6 [o]Josh. 24:4; Ps. 105:23; Isa. 52:4; Acts 7:14, 15
8 [p]For ver. 8-11, see Ex. 6:14-16 [q]Ex. 1:1-5 [r]Num. 26:5; 1 Chr. 5:1-3
11 [s]1 Chr. 6:1
12 [t]1 Chr. 2:3; 4:21 [u]ch. 38:3, 7, 10 [v]ch. 38:29; 1 Chr. 2:5
13 [w]1 Chr. 7:1
15 [x]See ch. 29:32-35; 30:1-21
17 [y]1 Chr. 7:30
18 [z]See ch. 30:10-13 [a]ch. 29:24
20 [b]ch. 41:50-52 [c]ch. 41:45
21 [d]See Num. 26:38-40; 1 Chr. 7:6-12; 8:1
24 [e]1 Chr. 7:13
25 [f]See ch. 30:5-8 [g]ch. 29:29
27 [h]Ex. 1:5; Deut. 10:22; [Acts 7:14]

46:5–7 These verses underline that Jacob took with him to Egypt everything that he possessed, including all the members of his family. These general comments prepare for the more detailed register of family members that comes in vv. 8–27. (An illustration of what this would have looked like comes from the Beni Hasan Mural from the 19th century B.C., which was found in an Egyptian tomb. It depicts a group of Asiatics as they travel into Egypt. The group brought animals, weapons, and musical instruments. All the men are bearded, and they wear clothes with elaborate designs.)

46:8–27 The register of Jacob's family is organized according to his wives, beginning with Leah's children (vv. 8–15) and proceeding to those of Zilpah (vv. 16–18), Rachel (vv. 19–22), and Bilhah (vv. 23–25). Verses 26–27 appear to provide a concluding summary, although the lists and associated numbers present difficulties (see note on vv. 26–27). Since v. 20 includes Joseph and his sons, who were already in Egypt, it is not simply recording those who migrated there with Jacob at this particular time.

46:8–15 Associated with Leah are six sons, one daughter, 25 grandsons, and two great-grandsons—a total of 34. To reduce this to "thirty-three" (v. 15), some scholars have speculated that the name **Ohad** (v. 10) should be removed, since it does not appear in the parallel lists of Num. 26:12–13 and 1 Chron. 4:24. Alternatively, it could be argued that **Dinah** (Gen. 46:15), the only daughter mentioned, should be omitted from the final count. Yet at least two of the grandsons, **Er** and **Onan**, died in Canaan (v. 12; see 38:2–10), and it seems unlikely that Perez's two sons, **Hezron** and **Hamul** (46:12), were born before Jacob moved to Egypt. These observations indicate that the 33 mentioned at the end of v. 15 were not derived simply from the names listed, and the number 33 is not intended as a total of the list just given. Although **Reuben** (v. 8) was the first son to be born to Jacob, the official status of **firstborn** was transferred to Joseph (see 1 Chron. 5:1–2). **his sons and his daughters numbered thirty-three**. The reference to daughters here is puzzling, since only one daughter, Dinah, is mentioned in the preceding list. This is another indication that 33 may not be intended as the total of the names in Gen. 46:8–14, but represents some other method of counting.

46:16–18 Serah is the only other granddaughter named in the register. Her name is required in order to make up the final total of **sixteen persons** (v. 18).

46:20 On Joseph's wife and sons, see note on 41:45.

46:26–27 The relationship between the numbers **sixty-six** (v. 26) and **seventy** (v. 27) presents another difficulty. The four totals linked to Jacob's wives in vv. 8–25 add up to 70 (i.e., 33, 16, 14, and 7), which is the figure recorded in v. 27 (cf. Deut. 10:22). Yet Gen. 46:26 mentions 66 persons as belonging to Jacob, excluding his sons' wives, none of whom is named in the preceding verses. The difference between the two figures cannot be: (1) Jacob's four wives, because Rachel died in Canaan (35:16–20); (2) Joseph, Ephraim, and Manasseh, who were already in Egypt; or (3) Er and Onan, who died in Canaan. These observations indicate that the numbers given should be treated with caution, a point reinforced by the fact that the earliest Greek translation (the Septuagint) adjusts upward the number of sons born to Joseph from two to nine and consequently totals the number of Jacob's descendants in Egypt as 75 and not 70 (see Acts 7:14 and its note). It looks as if the Hebrew manuscript tradition from which the translators worked was not unanimous

Jacob and Joseph Reunited

28 He had sent Judah ahead of him to Joseph to show the way before him in Goshen,
and they came [i]into the land of Goshen. 29 Then Joseph prepared his chariot and went
up to meet Israel his father in Goshen. He presented himself to him and [j]fell on his neck
and wept on his neck a good while. 30 Israel said to Joseph, [k]"Now let me die, since I have
seen your face and know that you are still alive." 31 Joseph said to his brothers and to his
father's household, [l]"I will go up and tell Pharaoh and will say to him, 'My brothers and
my father's household, who were in the land of Canaan, have come to me. 32 [m]And the
men are shepherds, for they have been keepers of livestock, and they have brought their
flocks and their herds and all that they have.' 33 When Pharaoh calls you and says, [m]'What
is your occupation?' 34 you shall say, [m]'Your servants have been keepers of livestock [n]from
our youth even until now, both we and our fathers,' in order that you may dwell [o]in the
land of Goshen, for every shepherd is [p]an abomination to the Egyptians."

Jacob's Family Settles in Goshen

47 So Joseph [q]went in and told Pharaoh, "My father and my brothers, with their flocks
and herds and all that they possess, have come from the land of Canaan. They are now
in [r]the land of Goshen." 2 And from among his brothers he took five men and [s]presented
them to Pharaoh. 3 Pharaoh said to his brothers, [t]"What is your occupation?" And they said
to Pharaoh, [u]"Your servants are shepherds, as our fathers were." 4 They said to Pharaoh,
[v]"We have come to sojourn in the land, for there is no pasture for your servants' flocks, for
the famine is severe in the land of Canaan. And now, please let your servants dwell [w]in the
land of Goshen." 5 Then Pharaoh said to Joseph, "Your father and your brothers have come
to you. 6 The land of Egypt is before you. Settle your father and your brothers [x]in the best
of the land. [y]Let them settle in the land of Goshen, and if you know any [z]able men among
them, put them in charge of my livestock."
7 Then Joseph brought in Jacob his father and stood him before Pharaoh, [a]and Jacob
blessed Pharaoh. 8 And Pharaoh said to Jacob, "How many are the days of the years of your
life?" 9 And Jacob said to Pharaoh, "The days of the years of my [b]sojourning are 130 years.
[c]Few and evil have been the days of the years of my life, and [d]they have not attained to
the days of the years of the life of my fathers in the days of their [b]sojourning." 10 And Jacob
[e]blessed Pharaoh and went out from the presence of Pharaoh. 11 Then Joseph settled his
father and his brothers and gave them a possession in the land of Egypt, in the best of
the land, in the land of [f]Rameses, [g]as Pharaoh had commanded. 12 And Joseph [h]provided

28 [i]See ch. 45:10
29 [j][ch. 45:14]
30 [k][Luke 2:29, 30]
31 [l]ch. 47:1
32 [m]ch. 47:3
33 [m][See ver. 32 above]
34 [m][See ver. 32 above] [n]ch. 37:12 [o]ver. 28 [p]ch. 43:32; Ex. 8:26

Chapter 47

1 [q]ch. 46:31 [r]See ch. 45:10
2 [s]Acts 7:13
3 [t]ch. 46:33 [u]ch. 46:32, 34
4 [v]ch. 15:13; Deut. 26:5 [w]ch. 46:34
6 [x]ch. 45:18 [y]ver. 4 [z]Ex. 18:21, 25
7 [a]ver. 10
9 [b]1 Chr. 29:15; Ps. 39:12; 119:19, 54; Heb. 11:9, 13 [c]Job 14:1; [Ps. 39:4, 5; James 4:14] [d]ch. 11:32; 25:7; 35:28
10 [e]ver. 7
11 [f]Ex. 1:11; 12:37; [ch. 45:10] [g]ver. 6
12 [h]ch. 45:11; 50:21

at this point. Perhaps 70 is treated here as a round number, representing the ideal, conveying the idea that all Israel went down to Egypt.

46:28–47:12 *Jacob's Family Settles in Egypt.* Joseph uses his God-given administrative skills to ensure that his family settles safely in Egypt. Having previously decided that the land of Goshen would be the best location for them (see note on 45:10), through skillful preparation and diplomacy, Joseph ensures that Pharaoh confirms this choice of territory.

46:28 Once again the narrator observes that **Judah** took the lead. Judah's role as the leader of his brothers anticipates the blessing that his father will bestow on him (see 49:8–12; also Num. 2:9; 7:12; 10:14).

46:31–34 Joseph gives advice to his brothers, anticipating that they will be summoned into Pharaoh's presence. To ensure that they will be given the land of Goshen, he instructs them to say that they are **keepers of livestock** (i.e., cattle and sheep, v. 32) and that this is their traditional occupation (v. 34). This information may also have been designed to reassure Pharaoh that Joseph's family would not endanger national security. **every shepherd is an abomination to the Egyptians** (v. 34). The precise reason for the Egyptians' aversion toward shepherds is not known, although it may have a religious dimension related to the offering of sacrifices (see Ex. 8:26). This may also be linked to the refusal of Egyptians to eat with Hebrews (see Gen. 43:32).

47:1–6 Having primed his brothers, Joseph introduces **five** of them to Pharaoh (v. 2), mentioning that his family is **now in the land of Goshen** (v. 1). When his brothers subsequently respond to Pharaoh's question, they conclude by requesting that they be permitted to **dwell** in **Goshen** (v. 4). Pharaoh graciously grants their request (v. 6).

47:7–10 Joseph introduces his father Jacob to Pharaoh. The record of this meeting is framed by the repeated comment that **Jacob blessed Pharaoh** (vv. 7, 10). While this could be interpreted as merely denoting words spoken by way of greeting and saying farewell, the image of Jacob blessing Pharaoh takes on special significance when viewed within the context of Genesis as a whole. Genesis presents the special line associated with Abraham and his seed as mediating God's blessing to others (see Introduction: History of Salvation Summary). **How many are the days of the years of your life?** (v. 8). Pharaoh's inquiry about Jacob's age may have been motivated by the belief that longevity was a sign of divine favor. **Few and evil have been . . . the years of my life** (v. 9). In this response Jacob perhaps alludes to those events that have made his life less than happy: e.g., his treatment of Esau, and his sons' deception of him regarding Joseph. While Jacob is now 130 years old, Abraham and Isaac lived to be 175 and 180, respectively. The Hebrew term translated **sojourning** implies that Jacob and his fathers had no permanent abode. This concept is developed along theological lines by the author of Hebrews, who views the patriarchs as looking forward to inhabiting a "city that has foundations, whose designer and builder is God" (Heb. 11:10). Jacob's comments may indicate that he anticipated something better to come.

47:11–12 Joseph allocates land to his family in the **land of Rameses**. Previously, the designation "land of Goshen" has been used to denote the territory where they were to dwell (e.g., 45:10; 46:28). The name "Rameses" is most often associated with the great thirteenth-century-B.C. Egyptian king Rameses II. While it is possible that the actual name "Rameses" goes back to the time of Joseph, this may be an example of a later term's being substituted for an earlier name (see, e.g., the use of "Dan" in 14:14; also Introduction: Author, Title, and Date).

14[j]ch. 41:56
15[j]ver. 19
19[k][Neh. 5:2, 3]
22[l][Ezra 7:24]
24[m]ch. 41:34
25[n]See ch. 33:15
26[o]ver. 22
27[p]See ch. 45:10 [q]ch. 46:3
28[r][ver. 9]
29[s]Deut. 31:14; 1 Kgs. 2:1 [t]See ch. 33:15 [u]ch. 24:2

his father, his brothers, and all his father's household with food, according to the number
of their dependents.

Joseph and the Famine

13 Now there was no food in all the land, for the famine was very severe, so that the
land of Egypt and the land of Canaan languished by reason of the famine. 14 [j]And Joseph
gathered up all the money that was found in the land of Egypt and in the land of Canaan,
in exchange for the grain that they bought. And Joseph brought the money into Pharaoh's
house. 15 And when the money was all spent in the land of Egypt and in the land of Canaan,
all the Egyptians came to Joseph and said, "Give us food. [j]Why should we die before your
eyes? For our money is gone." 16 And Joseph answered, "Give your livestock, and I will give
you food in exchange for your livestock, if your money is gone." 17 So they brought their
livestock to Joseph, and Joseph gave them food in exchange for the horses, the flocks, the
herds, and the donkeys. He supplied them with food in exchange for all their livestock
that year. 18 And when that year was ended, they came to him the following year and said
to him, "We will not hide from my lord that our money is all spent. The herds of livestock
are my lord's. There is nothing left in the sight of my lord but our bodies and our land.
19 Why should we die before your eyes, both we and our land? [k]Buy us and our land for
food, and we with our land will be servants to Pharaoh. And give us seed that we may live
and not die, and that the land may not be desolate."

20 So Joseph bought all the land of Egypt for Pharaoh, for all the Egyptians sold their
fields, because the famine was severe on them. The land became Pharaoh's. 21 As for the
people, he made servants of them[1] from one end of Egypt to the other. 22 [l]Only the land of
the priests he did not buy, for the priests had a fixed allowance from Pharaoh and lived on
the allowance that Pharaoh gave them; therefore they did not sell their land.

23 Then Joseph said to the people, "Behold, I have this day bought you and your land for
Pharaoh. Now here is seed for you, and you shall sow the land. 24 And at the harvests you
shall give a [m]fifth to Pharaoh, and four fifths shall be your own, as seed for the field and
as food for yourselves and your households, and as food for your little ones." 25 And they
said, "You have saved our lives; [n]may it please my lord, we will be servants to Pharaoh."
26 So Joseph made it a statute concerning the land of Egypt, and it stands to this day, that
Pharaoh should have the fifth; [o]the land of the priests alone did not become Pharaoh's.

27 Thus Israel settled in the land of Egypt, [p]in the land of Goshen. [q]And they gained
possessions in it, and were fruitful and multiplied greatly. 28 And Jacob lived in the land of
Egypt seventeen years. [r]So the days of Jacob, the years of his life, were 147 years.

29 And [s]when the time drew near that Israel must die, he called his son Joseph and said
to him, "If now [t]I have found favor in your sight, [u]put your hand under my thigh and

[1] Samaritan, Septuagint, Vulgate; Hebrew *he removed them to the cities*

47:13–26 *Joseph Oversees the Famine Response in Egypt.* This detailed description of Joseph's handling of the response to the famine in Egypt draws attention to how the lives of the people are saved and how they commit themselves to serving Pharaoh.

47:13–14 The **famine** is so **severe** and prolonged that the Egyptians eventually run out of **money** to buy **grain**.

47:15–17 When all their **money is gone**, the Egyptians appeal to Joseph for help (v. 15). He responds by offering to buy their **livestock** (v. 16). This sustains the Egyptians for another **year** (v. 17).

47:18–25 With no money and no livestock, the Egyptians resort to selling their land and themselves, as debt-slaves, to Pharaoh. They also ask for seed in order to sustain themselves for the future. Joseph willingly grants these requests. While some scholars believe that Joseph exploits the people's poverty, the response of the people, **You have saved our lives** (v. 25), shows that in these terrible circumstances the Egyptians view Joseph positively. From their perspective, Joseph provides seed on the understanding that they may keep for themselves **four fifths** of the harvest (v. 24). While Pharaoh's share of one **fifth** may seem excessive, this must be viewed in light of the people's having no other means of sustaining themselves. In such circumstances a less scrupulous administrator might have placed an even heavier burden on the poor.

47:27–31 *Jacob Requests to Be Buried in Canaan.* While the Egyptians struggle to survive during the famine, Jacob's family is portrayed as growing and prospering. Jacob's request to be buried in Canaan emphasizes that the family's future lies there.

47:27 gained possessions in it, and were fruitful and multiplied greatly. This brief statement encapsulates the positive experience of Jacob's family in Egypt. The motif of being fruitful and multiplying first appears in 1:22, 28 and recurs throughout Genesis, usually in association with divine blessing (see 9:1, 7; 17:20; 28:3; 35:11; 48:4).

47:28–31 Jacob's imminent death, at the age of **147**, dominates the final episodes of Genesis. His desire to be buried in Canaan is later fulfilled, a detailed description being given in 49:29–50:14. **put your hand under my thigh** (47:29). See note on 24:9. **bowed himself upon the head of his bed**. Jacob bows—possibly in worship, or possibly in gratitude to Joseph (which would fulfill Joseph's predictive dream in 37:9–11; see note there), or possibly because of frailty. By not explaining why Jacob bowed, Genesis allows all these interpretations. Hebrews 11:21 refers to this, citing the Septuagint, which has Jacob bowing on "the head of his staff" (see ESV footnote; the difference between the words in Hebrew is very small, since they have exactly the same consonants and only two vowels are different: Hb. *hammittah* is "the bed," while *hammatteh* is "the staff").

[v]promise to deal kindly and truly with me. [w]Do not bury me in Egypt, 30 but let me lie with
my fathers. Carry me out of Egypt and [x]bury me in their burying place." He answered, "I
will do as you have said." 31 And he said, "Swear to me"; and he swore to him. Then [y]Israel
bowed himself upon the head of his bed.[1]

Jacob Blesses Ephraim and Manasseh

48 After this, Joseph was told, "Behold, your father is ill." So he took with him his
two sons, Manasseh and Ephraim. 2 And it was told to Jacob, "Your son Joseph has
come to you." Then Israel summoned his strength and sat up in bed. 3 And Jacob said to
Joseph, [z]"God Almighty[2] appeared to me at [a]Luz in the land of Canaan and blessed me,
4 and said to me, 'Behold, I will make you fruitful and multiply you, and I will make of you
a company of peoples and will give this land to your offspring after you [b]for an everlasting
possession.' 5 And now your [c]two sons, who were born to you in the land of Egypt before
I came to you in Egypt, [d]are mine; Ephraim and Manasseh shall be mine, as Reuben and
Simeon are. 6 And the children that you fathered after them shall be yours. They shall be
called by the name of their brothers in their inheritance. 7 As for me, when I came from
Paddan, to my sorrow [e]Rachel died in the land of Canaan on the way, when there was
still some distance[3] to go to Ephrath, and I buried her there on the way to Ephrath (that
is, Bethlehem)."

8 When Israel saw Joseph's sons, he said, "Who are these?" 9 Joseph said to his father, [f]"They
are my sons, whom God has given me here." And he said, "Bring them to me, please, that
[g]I may bless them." 10 Now [h]the eyes of Israel were dim with age, so that he could not see.
So Joseph brought them near him, [i]and he kissed them and embraced them. 11 And Israel
said to Joseph, [j]"I never expected to see your face; and behold, God has let me see your offspring also." 12 Then Joseph removed them from his knees, and he bowed himself with his
face to the earth. 13 And Joseph took them both, Ephraim in his right hand toward Israel's
left hand, and Manasseh in his left hand toward Israel's right hand, and brought them
near him. 14 [k]And Israel stretched out his right hand and laid it on the head of Ephraim,
who was the younger, and his left hand on the head of Manasseh, [l]crossing his hands (for
Manasseh was the firstborn). 15 And he blessed Joseph and said,

"The God [m]before whom my fathers Abraham and Isaac walked,
the God who has been my shepherd all my life long to this day,
16 [n]the angel who has [o]redeemed me from all evil, bless the boys;
and in them let [p]my name be carried on, and the name of my fathers
Abraham and Isaac;
and let them [q]grow into a multitude[4] in the midst of the earth."

17 When Joseph saw that his father [r]laid his right hand on the head of Ephraim, it displeased him, and he took his father's hand to move it from Ephraim's head to Manasseh's

[1] Hebrew; Septuagint *staff* [2] Hebrew *El Shaddai* [3] *Or about two hours' distance* [4] *Or let them be like fish for multitude*

29 [v]ch. 24:49 [w][ch. 50:25]
30 [x]ch. 49:29; 50:5, 13
31 [y]ch. 48:2; 1 Kgs. 1:47; [Heb. 11:21]

Chapter 48

3 [z]See ch. 17:1 [a]ch. 28:13, 19; 35:6, 9
4 [b]ch. 17:8
5 [c]ch. 41:50-52; 46:20 [d]Josh. 13:7; 14:4; 17:17
7 [e]See ch. 35:9-19
9 [f][ch. 33:5] [g]ch. 49:25, 26; Heb. 11:21; [ch. 27:4]
10 [h][ch. 27:1] [i]ch. 27:27
11 [j][ch. 37:33; 45:26]
14 [k]ver. 17 [l]ver. 19
15 [m]ch. 17:1; 24:40
16 [n]ch. 28:15; 31:11, 13, 24; Ex. 23:20 [o]Isa. 44:22, 23; 49:7; 63:9; [2 Sam. 4:9; Ps. 34:22; 121:7] [p]Amos 9:12; Acts 15:17 [q][Num. 26:34, 37]
17 [r]ver. 14

48:1–22 *Jacob's Blessing of Joseph, Ephraim, and Manasseh.* When Jacob is very old and close to death, he pronounces a variety of blessings on all his sons. The first part of this process is recorded in this chapter and focuses specifically on Joseph and his two sons, Manasseh and Ephraim. Immediately following this, all of Jacob's other sons gather around his bed in order to be blessed (ch. 49). While chs. 48 and 49 stand together, the events of 48:1–22 set Joseph and his younger son Ephraim apart from all the other brothers. In particular, Ephraim receives from Jacob the blessing of the firstborn, indicating that the special line traced throughout Genesis will continue through his descendants (see Introduction: History of Salvation Summary). Various elements within ch. 48 are reminiscent of how Jacob was blessed by his father Isaac (27:1–40).

48:1–2 The opening verses suggest that **Joseph** merely comes with his **two sons** to visit his **father** who is **ill**. There is no hint at this stage of the important developments that are about to take place.

48:3–7 Jacob speaks to Joseph, picking up on three distinctive issues. First, he refers to the theophany (his vision of God) at Bethel, recalling the all-important promises made to him by God (see 28:13–15). Second, Jacob elevates his grandsons **Ephraim and Manasseh** to the status of full sons, on par with **Reuben and Simeon** (48:5). Later, this will result in Joseph's descendants, through Ephraim and Manasseh, being viewed as two separate tribes. Consequently, when the land of Canaan is allocated, Joseph through his descendants receives one-sixth of the territory. This double portion of the inheritance confirms that Joseph was designated the "firstborn" in place of Reuben (see 1 Chron. 5:1–2; also note on Gen. 35:22–23). By naming Ephraim before Manasseh (cf. 48:1), Jacob anticipates what will transpire in vv. 13–19. Third, Jacob recalls the death of Joseph's mother, **Rachel** (v. 7), following their return from northern Mesopotamia (see note on 35:16–20). **Paddan** is an abbreviated form of "Paddan-aram" (see note on 25:20).

48:8–10 Like the eyesight of his father Isaac, Jacob's eyesight has deteriorated in old **age** (see 27:1). For this reason he finds it difficult to clearly identify Joseph's two sons.

48:13–20 The blessing of Joseph is intimately linked to the blessing of his two sons. By placing his **right hand** on the head of **Ephraim** (v. 13), however, Jacob gives him priority over his older brother **Manasseh** (see 41:51–52). Although Joseph protests, thinking his father has mistakenly placed his right hand on the wrong head (48:17–18), Jacob is emphatic that Ephraim should be blessed as the firstborn ahead of Manasseh (v. 19). Subsequent history

head. **18** And Joseph said to his father, "Not this way, my father; since this one is the firstborn, put your right hand on his head." **19** But his father refused and said, [r]"I know, my
son, I know. He also shall become a people, and he also shall be great. Nevertheless, [s]his
younger brother shall be greater than he, and his offspring shall become a multitude[1] of
nations." **20** So he blessed them that day, saying,

> "By you Israel will pronounce blessings, saying,
> [t]'God make you as Ephraim and as Manasseh.'"

Thus he put Ephraim before Manasseh. **21** Then Israel said to Joseph, "Behold, I am about
to die, but [u]God will be with you and will bring you again to the land of your fathers.
22 Moreover, I have given to [v]you rather than to your brothers one mountain slope[2] that I
took from the hand of the Amorites with my sword and with my bow."

Jacob Blesses His Sons

49 [w]Then Jacob called his sons and said, "Gather yourselves together, that I may tell
you what shall happen to you [x]in days to come.

2 "Assemble and listen, O sons of Jacob,
listen to Israel your father.

3 "Reuben, you are [y]my firstborn,
my might, and the [z]firstfruits of my strength,
preeminent in dignity and preeminent in power.
4 Unstable as water, you shall not have preeminence,
because you [a]went up to your father's bed;
then you defiled it—he went up to my couch!

5 [b]"Simeon and Levi are brothers;
weapons [c]of violence are their swords.
6 Let my soul come not into their council;
[d]O my glory, [e]be not joined to their company.
For in their anger they killed men,
and in their willfulness they [f]hamstrung oxen.
7 Cursed be their anger, for it is fierce,
and their wrath, for it is cruel!
I will [g]divide them in Jacob
and scatter them in Israel.

8 "Judah, [h]your brothers shall praise you;
[i]your hand shall be on the neck of your enemies;
[j]your father's sons shall bow down before you.

19 [r][See ver. 17 above] [s]Num. 1:33, 35; 2:19, 21; Deut. 33:17
20 [t][Ruth 4:11, 12]
21 [u]ch. 46:4; 50:24
22 [v]Josh. 24:32; John 4:5

Chapter 49

1 [w]For ver. 1-27, see Deut. 33:6-25 [x]Num. 24:14; Deut. 4:30; 31:29; Isa. 2:2; Jer. 23:20; Dan. 2:28; 10:14; Hos. 3:5
3 [y]ch. 29:32 [z]Deut. 21:17
4 [a]ch. 35:22; 1 Chr. 5:1
5 [b]ch. 29:33, 34 [c]ch. 34:25, 26
6 [d][Ps. 16:9; 57:8] [e][Ps. 26:9] [f]Josh. 11:6, 9; 2 Sam. 8:4
7 [g]See Num. 3:5-13; Josh. 19:1-9; 1 Chr. 4:24-39
8 [h]ch. 29:35; [ch. 27:29] [i][Job 16:12] [j]1 Chr. 5:2

[1] Hebrew *fullness* [2] Or *one portion of the land;* Hebrew *shekem,* which sounds like the town and district called *Shechem*

reveals that the Ephraimites become one of the leading tribes, with Joshua guiding the people into the Promised Land. But the Ephraimites are later rejected by God in favor of Judah (see Ps. 78:67–71).

48:21–22 Jacob anticipates that after his death, his family will return to the land of Canaan (v. 21). To Joseph alone he bequeaths **one mountain slope** that he has taken by force from the Amorites (v. 22), possibly referring to 34:25–29 (cf. 33:18–19; and Joseph's burial place, Josh. 24:32).

49:1–28 *Jacob Blesses His 12 Sons.* Close to death, Jacob pronounces on each of his sons a blessing that, reflecting something of their past actions, tells how their descendants will prosper in the future. Passing from oldest to youngest, with one exception, Jacob clearly anticipates that Judah and Joseph will outshine their brothers in importance; together their blessings make up about half of Jacob's speech. The pronouncements are presented using poetic imagery and language, sometimes with wordplays, which occasionally make them difficult to interpret precisely.

49:1–2 After blessing Joseph and his two sons, Jacob summons all his other **sons** together in order to indicate their future destinies. Jacob's words are viewed by the narrator as being more than mere wishes; there is a predictive element to them, for they concern **days to come,** that is, "in the distant future" (sometimes translated "in the latter days"; see note on Isa. 2:2).

49:3–4 Although **Reuben** as the **firstborn** ought to be preeminent, his special standing within the family is forfeited because of his shocking behavior with Jacob's servant wife, Bilhah (see note on 35:22–23).

49:5–7 Jacob's pronouncement regarding **Simeon and Levi** centers on their violent disposition. Undoubtedly, this relates back to their treatment of the men of Shechem whom they massacred on account of the humiliation of their sister Dinah (ch. 34). Distancing himself from their fierce anger and cruel wrath, Jacob indicates that their descendants will be scattered throughout the other tribes (49:7). As a result, their strength will be dissipated, preventing them from bringing destruction on Israel. In fulfillment of this, the Levites (whose inheritance will be their ministry at the sanctuary) receive 48 cities distributed throughout all the tribal areas (Num. 18:23–24; 35:1–8; Josh. 21:1–45) and the Simeonites obtain land within the territory taken by Judah (Josh. 19:1–9). These arrangements prevented either tribe from dominating the rest.

49:8–12 Judah receives a long and positive blessing from his father, permeated with statements that highlight positive qualities of leadership. As with the other blessings, Jacob's remarks project the personal qualities that Judah has already displayed onto his future descendants. Remarkably, while royalty has been associated chiefly with Joseph from ch. 37 onward, Judah is portrayed as being held in high esteem by his brothers—his **father's sons**

9 Judah is [k]a lion's cub;
from the prey, my son, you have gone up.
[l]He stooped down; he crouched as a lion
and as a lioness; who dares rouse him?
10 The [m]scepter shall not depart from Judah,
nor the ruler's staff [n]from between his feet,
until tribute comes to him;[1]
and to him shall be the obedience of the peoples.
11 Binding his foal to the vine
and his donkey's colt to the choice vine,
he has washed his garments in wine
and his vesture in the blood of grapes.
12 His [o]eyes are darker than wine,
and his teeth whiter than milk.

13 [p]"Zebulun shall dwell at the [q]shore of the sea;
he shall become a haven for ships,
and his border shall be at Sidon.

14 [r]"Issachar is a strong donkey,
crouching between the sheepfolds.[2]
15 He saw that a resting place was good,
and that the land was pleasant,
so he bowed his shoulder to bear,
and [s]became a servant at forced labor.

16 [t]"Dan shall [u]judge his people
as one of the tribes of Israel.
17 Dan [v]shall be a serpent in the way,
a viper by the path,
that bites the horse's heels
so that his rider falls backward.
18 I [w]wait for your salvation, O LORD.

19 [x]"Raiders shall raid [y]Gad,[3]
but he shall raid at their heels.

[1] By a slight revocalization; a slight emendation yields (compare Septuagint, Syriac, Targum) *until he comes to whom it belongs*; Hebrew *until Shiloh comes*, or *until he comes to Shiloh* [2] Or *between its saddlebags* [3] *Gad* sounds like the Hebrew for *raiders* and *raid*

9 [k]Rev. 5:5; [Deut. 33:22; Hos. 5:14] [l][Num. 23:24; 24:9]
10 [m]Num. 24:17; Zech. 10:11 [n]Deut. 28:57
12 [o]Prov. 23:29
13 [p][Deut. 33:18, 19]; Josh. 19:10, 11 [q][Deut. 1:7; Josh. 9:1; Judg. 5:17]
14 [r]Judg. 5:16; [1 Chr. 12:32]
15 [s]Josh. 16:10
16 [t][Deut. 33:22] [u]ch. 30:6
17 [v]Judg. 18:27
18 [w]Ps. 25:5; 119:166, 174; Isa. 25:9; Mic. 7:7; [Luke 2:25]
19 [x][Deut. 33:20] [y]See 1 Chr. 5:18-22

shall bow down before him (49:8). More than this, the nations will bring tribute to him, and to one of his descendants **shall be the obedience of the peoples** (v. 10). In these words Jacob predicts the great empire of David, and the greater kingdom of Christ, the second David. This sets the tone for the chief aspect of messianic expectation in the OT: the way that Abraham's blessing will come to the Gentiles will be by the ultimate heir of David reigning and incorporating the Gentiles into his benevolent empire. This explains why the installation of Jesus as the Davidic king is so important in the NT, with the implication that the long-awaited time of enlightening the Gentiles has finally arrived (e.g., Matt. 28:18–20; Rom. 1:1–6; 15:12). By way of emphasizing Judah's potential royal status, he is compared to a **lion** (Gen. 49:9). In addition, one of his descendants will hold a **scepter** and **ruler's staff**, the symbols of kingship (v. 10). If the phrase **until tribute comes to him** (v. 10) is taken to mean "until Shiloh comes" (see ESV footnote), then it could be an allusion to the departure of the ark of the covenant from Shiloh in the time of Samuel, when the tribe of Judah, in the person of David, replaced the tribe of Ephraim as Israel's leading tribe (see Ps. 78:59–72, which summarizes the events recorded in the books of Samuel). Associated with the future Judahite king is a time of prolific grape harvest (Gen. 49:11). The picture presented here accords with later statements that link the Davidic dynasty with agricultural prosperity (e.g., Ps. 72:16; Amos 9:11–15). The royal line of Judah culminates with Jesus Christ (Matt. 1:1–16).

49:13 Zebulun is listed here before Issachar, although according to 30:17–20 Issachar was born before Zebulun. Since Zebulun's territory did not actually extend to the Mediterranean Sea (cf. Josh. 19:10–16), Jacob's remarks are difficult to interpret. Yet major trading routes from the coast, which lay about 10 miles (16 km) to the west, ran through the tribal region of Zebulun, providing an outlet to the sea, and involvement by Zebulunites in the coastal commerce of exporting and importing—and thus living in Sidon by the sea—may be the substantive fulfillment of Jacob's poetic words. Furthermore, if the name "Sidon" (one of Phoenicia's leading cities) is used here as a collective term to refer to Phoenicia in general, then the statement that **his border shall be at Sidon** is quite apt.

49:14–15 Although Jacob's blessing of **Issachar** emphasizes the strength of his descendants, it also indicates that like a **donkey** they will be forced to work for others—but precisely what situation is envisaged is unclear.

49:16–18 Jacob sees in **Dan** and his descendants both positive and negative attributes. Their snakelike behavior (v. 17) is later reflected in their assault on the unsuspecting inhabitants of Laish (Judges 18). **Dan shall judge** (Gen. 49:16). The name "Dan" is a play on the Hebrew word "judge" (see 30:6). **I wait for your salvation, O LORD** (49:18). Jacob's pronouncements are interrupted here by a brief prayer that highlights his concern for his descendants. Without divine deliverance they will not survive.

49:19 The descendants of **Gad**, located in the region of Gilead, east of the Jordan River, will be attacked by raiders. Of necessity the Gadites will become skillful warriors who use stealth to fend off the invaders. In Hebrew "Gad" sounds like the terms **raiders** (Hb. *gedud*) and **raid** (Hb. *gud*).

20[z][Deut. 33:24]
21[a][Deut. 33:23]
22[b]ch. 41:52; Josh. 17:14, 18
23[c][ch. 37:24, 28; 39:20]
24[d]Job 29:20 [e]Ps. 132:2, 5; Isa. 1:24 [f]Ps. 23:1; 80:1 [g]Isa. 28:16; Eph. 2:20; 1 Pet. 2:4; [Deut. 32:4]
25[h]ch. 35:3; 50:17 [i]ch. 17:1; 35:11 [j]Deut. 33:13
26[k]Deut. 33:15; Hab. 3:6 [l]Deut. 33:16
27[m][Judg. 20:21, 25; Ezek. 22:27] [n]Zech. 14:1; [Ezek. 39:10]
29[o]ver. 33; ch. 25:8 [p]ch. 47:30 [q]ch. 50:13; [ch. 23:9]
30[r]See ch. 23:16-18
31[s]ch. 23:19; 25:9 [t]ch. 35:29
33[u]ver. 29

20 [z]"Asher's food shall be rich,
and he shall yield royal delicacies.

21 [a]"Naphtali is a doe let loose
that bears beautiful fawns.[1]

22 "Joseph is [b]a fruitful bough,
a fruitful bough by a spring;
his branches run over the wall.[2]
23 The archers [c]bitterly attacked him,
shot at him, and harassed him severely,
24 yet [d]his bow remained unmoved;
his arms[3] were made agile
by the hands of the [e]Mighty One of Jacob
(from there is [f]the Shepherd,[4] [g]the Stone of Israel),
25 [h]by the God of your father who will help you,
by [i]the Almighty[5] [j]who will bless you
with blessings of heaven above,
blessings of the deep that crouches beneath,
blessings of the breasts and of the womb.
26 The blessings of your father
are mighty beyond the blessings of my parents,
up to the bounties [k]of the everlasting hills.[6]
May they be [l]on the head of Joseph,
and on the brow of him who was set apart from his brothers.

27 [m]"Benjamin is a ravenous wolf,
in the morning devouring the prey
and at evening [n]dividing the spoil."

Jacob's Death and Burial

28 All these are the twelve tribes of Israel. This is what their father said to them as he
blessed them, blessing each with the blessing suitable to him. 29 Then he commanded
them and said to them, "I am to be [o]gathered to my people; [p]bury me with my fathers
[q]in the cave that is in the field of Ephron the Hittite, 30 in the cave that is in the field at
Machpelah, to the east of Mamre, in the land of Canaan, [r]which Abraham bought with the
field from Ephron the Hittite to possess as a burying place. 31 [s]There they buried Abraham
and Sarah his wife. There [t]they buried Isaac and Rebekah his wife, and there I buried
Leah— 32 the field and the cave that is in it were bought from the Hittites." 33 When Jacob
finished commanding his sons, he drew up his feet into the bed and breathed his last and
[u]was gathered to his people.

[1] Or *he gives beautiful words, or that bears fawns of the fold* [2] Or *Joseph is a wild donkey, a wild donkey beside a spring, his wild colts beside the wall* [3] Hebrew *the arms of his hands* [4] Or *by the name of the Shepherd* [5] Hebrew *Shaddai* [6] A slight emendation yields (compare Septuagint) *the blessings of the eternal mountains, the bounties of the everlasting hills*

49:20 Jacob briefly indicates that **Asher's** descendants will enjoy a prosperous future. Their territory along the coastal plain of Acco provides fertile land and harbors for trade.

49:21 Compared to a graceful **doe**, the tribe of **Naphtali** will flourish, nourished by the rich natural resources of upper Galilee.

49:22–26 Jacob reserves his longest blessing for **Joseph**, confirming his special standing among the brothers. The references to God (using a variety of divine titles), along with the emphasis on blessing, give this pronouncement an added dimension. By describing Joseph as **fruitful** (v. 22), Jacob may be subtly alluding to Ephraim, whose name means "twice fruitful" (see note on 41:50–52). In spite of his brothers' hostility toward him (49:23), Joseph has survived, sustained by the **Mighty One of Jacob** (v. 24). Anticipating the future, Jacob prays that Joseph's descendants will experience blessing upon blessing, blessings that exceed those shown to Abraham and Isaac (vv. 25–26). **who was set apart from his brothers** (v. 26). Jacob's final remark may compare Joseph to the Nazirites, the holiest laypeople in Israel (Numbers 6), or it may simply be referring to his leading role among his brothers.

49:27 Using the image of a **wolf**, Jacob reveals that the descendants of **Benjamin** will be aggressive warriors (e.g., 1 Chron. 8:40; 12:2).

49:28 Jacob's blessing of his sons emphasizes the contribution that each will make to the **twelve tribes of Israel**. While the unity of the 12 is assumed, the tribes of Judah and Joseph are clearly distinguished from all the others in terms of their leadership role within the nation. This outcome reflects in large measure how Joseph and Judah are portrayed within chs. 37–50. Beyond Genesis, the tribes of Ephraim and Judah are consistently portrayed as taking the lead, with the latter eventually providing the Davidic dynasty.

49:29–50:14 *The Death and Burial of Jacob.* Focusing on the death and burial of Jacob, this section falls into two parts. In 49:29–33 Jacob instructs his sons to bury him in Canaan. The process by which the sons fulfill this request is then recorded in 50:1–14. Jacob's desire to be buried in Hebron reflects his belief that, as God has consistently promised, the future for his descendants will be in Canaan and not Egypt.

49:29–33 In his last instruction to his sons, Jacob asks to be buried with his **fathers** in the **cave** purchased by Abraham from **Ephron the Hittite**

50 Then Joseph [v]fell on his father's face and wept over him and kissed him. **2** And Joseph
commanded his servants the physicians to [w]embalm his father. So the physicians
embalmed Israel. **3** Forty days were required for it, for that is how many are required for
embalming. And the Egyptians [x]wept for him seventy days.
4 And when the days of weeping for him were past, Joseph spoke to the household
of Pharaoh, saying, [y]"If now I have found favor in your eyes, please speak in the ears of
Pharaoh, saying, **5** 'My father made me swear, saying, "I am about to die: in my tomb [z]that
I hewed out for myself in the land of Canaan, there shall you bury me." Now therefore, let
me please go up and bury my father. Then I will return.'" **6** And Pharaoh answered, "Go
up, and bury your father, as he made you swear." **7** So Joseph went up to bury his father.
With him went up all the servants of Pharaoh, the elders of his household, and all the
elders of the land of Egypt, **8** as well as all the household of Joseph, his brothers, and his
father's household. Only their children, their flocks, and their herds were left [a]in the land
of Goshen. **9** And there went up with him both chariots and horsemen. It was a very great
company. **10** When they came to the threshing floor of Atad, which is beyond the Jordan,
[b]they lamented there with a very great and grievous lamentation, and he [c]made a mourning for his father seven days. **11** When the inhabitants of the land, the Canaanites, saw the
mourning on the threshing floor of Atad, they said, "This is a grievous mourning by the
Egyptians." Therefore the place was named Abel-mizraim;[1] it is beyond the Jordan. **12** Thus
his sons did for him as he had commanded them, **13** for [d]his sons carried him to the land of
Canaan and buried him in the cave of the field at Machpelah, to the east of Mamre, which
Abraham [e]bought with the field from Ephron the Hittite to possess as a burying place.
14 After he had buried his father, Joseph returned to Egypt with his brothers and all who
had gone up with him to bury his father.

God's Good Purposes

15 When Joseph's brothers saw that their father was dead, they said, "It may be that Joseph
will hate us and pay us back for all the evil that we did to him." **16** So they sent a message to
Joseph, saying, "Your father gave this command before he died: **17** 'Say to Joseph, "Please
forgive the transgression of your brothers and their sin, because they did evil to you."' And
now, please forgive the transgression of the servants of [f]the God of your father." Joseph
wept when they spoke to him. **18** His brothers also came and [g]fell down before him and

[1] *Abel-mizraim* means *mourning* (or *meadow*) *of Egypt*

Chapter 50
1 [v]ch. 46:4
2 [w]ver. 26; [2 Chr. 16:14; Mark 16:1; Luke 23:56; John 19:39, 40]
3 [x][ver. 10; Num. 20:29; Deut. 34:8; 1 Sam. 31:13; Job 2:13]
4 [y]ch. 47:29; See ch. 33:15
5 [z]2 Chr. 16:14; Isa. 22:16; Matt. 27:60
8 [a]See ch. 45:10
10 [b][2 Sam. 1:17; Acts 8:2] [c][ver. 3]
13 [d]ch. 49:29, 30; [Acts 7:16] [e]ch. 23:16
17 [f]ch. 49:25
18 [g][ch. 37:7, 10]

(v. 29). The account of the cave's purchase is recorded in ch. 23 (see notes). The burials of **Abraham** (49:30) and **Isaac** (v. 31) are recounted in 25:8–10 and 35:27–29. While Jacob indicates that **Rebekah** and **Leah** were also buried at **Machpelah** (49:30), this information is not recorded elsewhere in Genesis. **was gathered to his people** (v. 33). This idiom, commonly used in connection with dying, seems to reflect a belief in being reunited with others in the afterlife.

50:1–3 Joseph arranges for Jacob's body to be **embalmed** (v. 2). This was necessary in order to delay the normal process of putrefaction and so enable Jacob's corpse to be transported to Hebron. Mummification was not practiced by the Hebrews, and so Joseph entrusts the task to Egyptian **physicians** (v. 2). Since embalming was normally a religious practice involving priests, Joseph may have deliberately chosen to use physicians in order to distinguish his father's beliefs from those of the Egyptian priests. Apart from Jacob, the only other person in the Bible who was embalmed is Joseph (see v. 26). The **seventy days** of mourning reflects Egyptian royal practice according to some ancient sources (e.g., Herodotus, *History* 2.86; but 72 days in Diodorus of Sicily, *Histories* 1.72), suggesting that Jacob is being shown very high honor; for the Israelites the period of mourning was normally between seven and 30 days. It is unclear, however, whether the two periods mentioned are consecutive or concurrent.

50:4–6 Joseph seeks permission from Pharaoh to **bury** his father in **Canaan**.

50:7–9 Probably as a result of the high esteem in which Joseph was held, the funeral procession comprises a large number of prominent Egyptian officials and public figures.

50:10–11 Coming to the **threshing floor of Atad**, the funeral procession halts to mourn for **seven days**. The precise location is not known. The expression **beyond the Jordan** (v. 11) is sufficiently ambiguous to place Atad in either Canaan or Transjordan. Threshing floors were normally on an elevated place so that the wind could be used to separate the chaff from the grain. The week of mourning made such an impact on the local population that they named the place **Abel-mizraim** (v. 11), which means "the mourning of Egypt" (ESV footnote).

50:12–14 These verses confirm that Jacob's request in 49:29–32 was carried out. Abraham's purchase of the **cave** at **Machpelah** (50:13) is recorded in ch. 23.

50:15–21 *Joseph Reassures His Brothers.* Following the burial of Jacob, the brothers are fearful that Joseph will take revenge on them for all the evil that they did to him.

50:15–17 Afraid to address Joseph face-to-face, the brothers send a **message**, confessing their guilt and seeking his forgiveness.

50:18–21 Probably encouraged by news of Joseph's reaction to their message, the **brothers came and fell down before him**. Once again, their obeisance and words, **Behold, we are your servants**, fulfill Joseph's dreams (37:5–10). Echoing what he had said previously (see 45:5–9), Joseph stresses that God transformed their **evil** into **good** and that as a result, many people have been **kept alive**. This principle that God ultimately overrules human sin for his glory and the ultimate good of mankind is important in Scripture. The crucifixion is the prime example of it (Acts 3:13–26; Rom. 8:28). Joseph's gracious, forgiving attitude unites the family. Like the lives of Jacob and Esau, Joseph's life was marred by deadly hatred between brothers. In both cases the story ends with the offended brother's offering full forgiveness to those who had mistreated him (Gen. 33:4).

said, "Behold, we are your servants." **19** But Joseph said to them, "Do not fear, for [h]am I in
the place of God? **20** As for you, you meant evil against me, but [i]God meant it for good, to
bring it about that many people[1] should be kept alive, as they are today. **21** So do not fear;
[j]I will provide for you and your little ones." Thus he comforted them and spoke kindly
to them.

The Death of Joseph

22 So Joseph remained in Egypt, he and his father's house. Joseph lived 110 years. **23** And
Joseph saw Ephraim's children [k]of the third generation. The [l]children also of Machir the
son of Manasseh were [m]counted as Joseph's own.[2] **24** And Joseph said to his brothers, "I am
about to die, but [n]God will visit you and bring you up out of this land to the land [o]that he
swore to Abraham, to Isaac, and to Jacob." **25** Then [p]Joseph made the sons of Israel swear,
saying, "God will surely visit you, and you shall carry up my bones from here." **26** So Joseph
died, being 110 years old. They [q]embalmed him, and he was put in a coffin in Egypt.

[1] Or *a numerous people* [2] Hebrew *were born on Joseph's knees*

19 [h]ch. 30:2; [2 Kgs. 5:7]
20 [i]ch. 45:5, 7
21 [j]ch. 45:11; 47:12
23 [k][Job 42:16; Ps. 128:6] [l]Num. 32:39; 1 Chr. 7:14, 15 [m][ch. 30:3]
24 [n]ch. 15:14; 46:4; 48:21; Ex. 3:16, 17; [Heb. 11:22] [o]ch. 15:18; 26:3; 28:13; 35:12; 46:4
25 [p]Ex. 13:19; Josh. 24:32
26 [q]See ver. 2

50:22–26 *The Death of Joseph.* The final 60 years of Joseph's life in Egypt are passed over in almost complete silence. Apart from briefly mentioning the birth of some children, this final section of Genesis focuses on the death of Joseph. As it brings the account of his earthly life to a conclusion, it looks to the future, anticipating the time when God will bring the Israelites out of Egypt and return them to the land of Canaan.

50:22–23 Joseph lives long enough to see the grandchildren or great-grandchildren of Ephraim; the precise sense of **third generation** is disputed.

50:24–26 With death imminent, Joseph makes arrangements for his **bones** to be taken to Canaan. Unlike his father Jacob (see 49:29–32), Joseph does not focus on the burial site at Machpelah. Rather, he confidently affirms that God will lead the Israelites out of Egypt to Canaan. When this happens, Joseph wants his bones to be transported there. Later, Moses fulfills this instruction (Ex. 13:19), and Joseph's remains are eventually buried at Shechem (Josh. 24:32). **embalmed**. See note on Gen. 50:1–3. Now the first audience of Genesis has the relevant parts of the backstory to the book of Exodus, which relates events much closer to their own time and indeed part of their own experience.

INTRODUCTION TO

EXODUS

Title

Exodus is the second of the first five books of the OT, which are referred to collectively as either "Torah" ("law," "instruction" in Hb.) or "Pentateuch" ("five-volumed" in Gk.). The English title "Exodus" is taken from the Septuagint and the Greek noun *exodos*, "a going out" or "departure," the major event of the first half of the book, in which the Lord brings Israel out of Egypt. The Hebrew title, "Names," is taken from the first line of the text, "These are the names of the sons of Israel who came to Egypt with Jacob" (1:1).

Author

The authorship and composition of the book of Exodus cannot be taken in isolation from the rest of the Torah/Pentateuch. The shape of the book of Exodus bears this out as it opens with a list of names referring to characters and events narrated in the book of Genesis (Ex. 1:1–6) and closes with an assembled tabernacle that is filled with the glory of the Lord (40:34–38) without Israel having received full instructions for how they are to serve the Lord in it (see Lev. 1:1ff.). For further discussion of these matters in relation to what have traditionally been referred to as "the five books of Moses," see Introduction to the Pentateuch, pp. 35–37.

Like most books of the OT, Exodus does not explicitly refer to its authorship or composition as a book. However, its genre and content have traditionally led to the conclusion that it was written by Moses as an authoritative record both of its events and of the covenant instruction that the Lord revealed through him. While the reasons for this assessment of Exodus include the explicit references to Moses either writing (see 24:4; 34:28) or being commanded to write (see 17:14), they are not exhausted by it. The genre of Exodus is typically understood to be "historical narrative" since it presents the material as events, speeches, and covenant instructions that took place in Israel's history. As a narrative, the book of Exodus focuses on specific aspects of the history in order to emphasize certain points for its intended audience (something that all narrative about historical events necessarily does, even if merely through what it selects as important). Exodus emphasizes throughout the book that Yahweh (the Lord; see notes on 3:14; 3:15) has remembered his covenant with Israel, will bring them out of Egypt, and will instruct them on how to live as his people as he dwells in their midst. Integral to this emphasis is the way Exodus also shows that Yahweh has chosen to reveal his purposes, lead his people out of Egypt, and instruct them on how they are to live, through Moses. Thus, while Moses probably did not write everything in the Pentateuch (e.g., the narrative of his death in Deuteronomy 34), and while there also appears to be language and references that have been updated for later readers, the book of Exodus is best read as recorded and composed primarily by Moses.

Date and Historical Context

The date of Israel's exodus from Egypt is the primary chronological problem for Exodus; the book contains few clues to solve it. While the narrative refers to the cities that the people of Israel were building in Egypt (Pithom and Raamses, 1:11) and the length of their time in Egypt (430 years, 12:40), it does not include the names of any of the kings of Egypt to which it refers (nor does the book of Genesis record the name of the pharaoh "who knew Joseph"; cf. Ex. 1:8). The content of the book clearly indicates that the exodus and its time of year are important for Israel's identity since Israel's calendar was reoriented around the month in which they came out of Egypt (12:2), but Exodus refers to these events as if its hearers/readers were familiar with them and thus selects and shapes the details of the account in accord with its communicative purpose.

As indicated in the article on the date of the exodus (p. 33), some scholars, working from the figure of 480 years (1 Kings 6:1) for the time since the exodus to Solomon's fourth year (c. 966 B.C.), calculate a date of c. 1446 B.C. for Israel's departure from Egypt. Others, because Exodus 1:11 depicts Israel working on a city called Raamses, argue that this points to the exodus occurring during the reign of Raamses II in Egypt (c. 1279–1213 B.C.), possibly around the year 1260 B.C.

Whatever the date of the exodus, the question is not necessarily about whether the numbers given in the OT are reliable but rather about trying to understand their function according to the conventions by which an author in the ancient Near Eastern context would have used them. Any attempt to determine the date of the exodus necessarily includes the interpretation of both the references in the OT and the relevant records and artifacts from surrounding nations in the ancient Near East. That is, because the OT was first given in an ancient Near Eastern setting, the interpreter's first task is to understand, as much as possible, what an ancient Israelite would have thought the text meant. Scholars are not always sure that they can answer this question when it comes to details about dates and numbers; fortunately, the message of Exodus is plain nevertheless.

The geography of Egypt, Sinai, and the route of the exodus is another important matter for the book of Exodus that involves a similar process of trying to identify the references in the narrative to the landscape and cities with what is known or has been discovered about their location in relation to the current landscape. For a possible route of the exodus, see map, p. 143.

Theme

The overarching theme of Exodus is the fulfillment of God's promises to the patriarchs that he would make their descendants a great nation. This is carried out despite the opposition of the greatest superpower in the ancient world of the time, Egypt, and despite the unbelief and disobedience of the people themselves. Exodus shows that the success of the exodus must be ascribed first to the power and character of God, who remembers his promises, punishes sin, and forgives the penitent. Second, it highlights both the faithfulness of Moses, who follows divine instructions exactly, and his prayerfulness. It is his prayer, e.g., that leads to victory over Amalek (17:8–16) and his intercession that persuades God to pardon the people after they had begun worshiping the golden calf (chs. 32–34).

Purpose, Occasion, and Background

Exodus is the second book in the Pentateuch and picks up the narrative of Genesis by focusing on the time when the sons of Jacob (1:1–6) have grown into the people of Israel (1:8). The first half of the book records events that fulfill the promise to Abraham that his descendants would sojourn in a land that was not their own, be afflicted for 400 years, and then come out by the Lord's hand with numerous possessions (Gen. 15:13–14). The narrative of Israel's preservation in and exodus out of Egypt is sometimes referred to as being like a second creation account both because the vocabulary seems to evoke the first chapters of Genesis (see Ex. 1:7) and because it is through Abraham's descendants that the Lord has promised to bless all nations and thus to restore his presence and purposes in the world (Gen. 12:1–3).

The second half of the book narrates the events surrounding the covenant being revealed, confirmed, broken, and renewed (Exodus 19; 24; 32–34; 35–40) and records the covenant instructions that the Lord revealed to Israel through Moses at Mount Sinai (chs. 20–23; 25–31). The instructions begin with the Ten Commandments (20:1–21) and include a lengthy section detailing the specifics for the construction of the tabernacle and its service (25:1–31:18). But this is not the totality of the Lord's covenant instructions, which are recorded further in both Leviticus and Numbers before Israel finally leaves the region of Mount Sinai for the land of Canaan (Num. 10:11ff.).

Numbers describes how the generation who came out of Egypt ended up wandering in the wilderness instead of entering Canaan. Then the book of Deuteronomy records Moses' reaffirmation of the covenant instructions recorded in Exodus through Numbers and appeals to the next generation who will enter the land to keep the commandments by fearing the Lord and walking in his ways (Deut. 8:6).

Historical Reliability of the Exodus

Doubts have often been cast on the historical reliability of the exodus account. It is true that no remains of the Israelites have been found in the area of Goshen in the eastern Nile delta or in the wilderness of Sinai. But in neither area would such remains be expected to survive. The mud-built huts of the Israelites have long been destroyed by repeated flooding, and, wandering through the wilderness, the people would not have left buildings or other permanent traces. It thus is unreasonable to expect such archaeological evidence. Furthermore, one should not expect to find extrabiblical texts regarding Israel's stay and departure from Egypt, because the story is negative about Egypt. Egyptian texts are quite propagandistic and would not mention such a defeat.

Nevertheless there is plenty of data that seems to corroborate the biblical account: (1) It is most unlikely that a nation should invent a story of its origins as slaves in a neighboring country. (2) The second millennium B.C. was an era when there were many foreigners in Egypt, some of whom were employed making bricks for building projects. (3) The name of the city Raamses is unlikely to have originated or have been remembered later. (4) Some have argued that the sequence of plagues related in Exodus fits with the (ecological) situation that accompanies and follows the annual flooding of the Nile. (This need not imply that the plagues were purely "natural.") (5) The organization of the covenant texts in the Pentateuch (e.g., Exodus 20) fits the pattern of second-millennium-B.C. treaties, not later ones. (6) The tent-tabernacle has many parallels in Egypt and Canaan from the second millennium. Indeed traces of a tent shrine dating from about 1150 B.C. have been found in the wilderness at Timna, not far from the route of the Israelite wanderings. (7) A stele (an inscribed tombstone-like stone slab) from the Egyptian pharaoh Merenptah, c. 1209 B.C., mentions that he had conquered the people of Israel in an invasion of Canaan. This would fit with an exodus from Egypt some time before this and demonstrates that Israel was already settled as a people in Canaan.

This archaeological evidence makes skepticism about the historicity of the biblical account of the exodus unwarranted. This is not to deny that the story is told to make theological points: much historical writing is motivated by the desire to teach lessons from the past. Nor does the archaeological evidence require one to believe that the book of Exodus gives a complete and full account of what happened: there are obviously many gaps and events that are passed over. But the evidence does make it unreasonable to challenge the central affirmation of OT faith: "I am the LORD your God, who brought you out of the land of Egypt, out of the house of slavery" (20:2).

Key Themes

The events and instructions narrated in the book of Exodus are explicitly framed as the Lord remembering his covenant promises to Abraham (2:24; 3:6, 14–17; 6:2–8). The promises include land, numerous offspring, and blessing for both Abraham's descendants and the nations (Gen. 12:1–3), which are rooted in the covenant relationship with the Lord: "I will establish my covenant between me and you and your offspring after you . . . and I will be their God" (Gen. 17:7–8). The covenant promises in Genesis were made with Abraham and reaffirmed with Isaac and Jacob. Exodus highlights the role that Moses fills as the covenant mediator through whom the Lord reveals his purposes to his people and sustains the covenant relationship. Each of these aspects will be described briefly in relation to key themes in Exodus.

1. *Offspring.* As was noted above, the Lord promised Abraham that he would have innumerable offspring (Gen. 15:5) who would also be afflicted for 400 years in a foreign land and come out with great possessions (Gen. 15:13). Through Joseph, the Lord brings 70 individuals into the land of Egypt (Ex. 1:1–6) who became numerous (1:7) even amid affliction (1:8–12) and were brought out of Egypt as a large multitude (12:37–38). Exodus also focuses on how the people of Israel are shown to be Abraham's offspring, both in the faithful actions of some of its members (the midwives fear God not Pharaoh, 1:15–22) and particularly by the fact that the Lord repeatedly refers to them as "my people" in his words to Israel (3:7) and before Pharaoh (5:1). The Lord is indicating both to Pharaoh and to the people that, although they have been enslaved in Egypt for a long time, it is his covenant promise to them as Abraham's offspring that truly governs their identity.

2. *Land.* The entrance into the land of Canaan is not realized within the events narrated in Exodus, but the promise of the land is held before Israel as *a place of provision* that is "flowing with milk and honey" (3:17) and also as *a place they will inherit* and where they will live as the Lord's people (6:7–8). The promise of the land is significant for what Israel's response in certain situations reveals about their understanding of both the Lord's presence and his promise to bring them to Canaan. When the people are hungry after coming out of Egypt and wish they were back in slavery by the "meat pots" (16:3), the contrast between where they are headed and what they long for in Egypt shows that they have not yet taken to heart what the Lord's deliverance is to signify for them. Their prospects in Canaan are declared to depend on their fidelity in serving the Lord alone (23:23–32), which the Israelites also have not taken fully to heart, as demonstrated by the incident of the golden calf before they ever set foot in Canaan (32:1–6).

3. *Blessing.* The Lord's promise to bless all nations through Abraham looks forward to how Israel's life is to mediate the presence of the Lord to the nations around them (they are to be "a kingdom of priests," "a holy

nation," 19:6). Israel is to live before God in the world, obeying the covenant instructions that he will reveal to them (see Deut. 4:6–8). The events of the plagues and exodus present the opportunity for people back in Egypt and the surrounding nations to join the Lord's people in response to what they have either experienced (thus Israel goes out a "mixed multitude," Ex. 12:38) or what they have heard (e.g., Josh. 2:10). The "recognition formula" (see note on Ex. 7:5) includes the expectation that the Egyptians will know that Israel's God is the true God (7:5; 14:4, 18).

4. *Covenant mediator.* A key theme of Exodus is that Moses is the one who is called by God to mediate between the Lord and his people. A key indicator of whether Israel will desire to live as the Lord's people is seen in how they respond to Moses as the one who speaks on the Lord's behalf. The story of Moses begins with his preservation at birth (2:1–10) and in Midian (2:11–22) but is highlighted through the Lord's presence and speech in his call at the burning bush (3:1–4:17) and then in the fact that the Lord speaks to Moses alone in Egypt (e.g., 7:1), calls Moses alone up to Mount Sinai (19:20; 24:2), listens to Moses' intercession on behalf of the people (32:11–14), speaks with Moses "face to face" (34:29–35), and has Moses oversee the assembling of the tabernacle (40:16–33) and the consecration of both it and the priests who will serve in it (40:9–15).

5. *Covenant presence.* The presence of the Lord is highlighted throughout the book of Exodus: he appears to Moses in the burning bush (3:1–4:17); he comes down on Mount Sinai in the sight of the people (19:16–20); he reveals himself to the leaders of Israel (24:9–11); he shows Moses his glory and declares his covenant character (34:1–10). Furthermore, a large part of the second half of the book focuses on the instructions for (25:1–31:17) and assembling of the tabernacle (35:1–40:33), in which the Lord promises to dwell among his people (29:43–46; 40:34–38). Just as the ground on which Moses stood at the burning bush was holy because of the Lord's presence, so it is also his presence among his people that will make them holy. And in light of the covenant breach with the golden calf (32:1–6), Exodus ends with the lingering question of just how a sinful people will live with a holy God in her midst, which is a question that the instruction recorded in Leviticus will begin to address.

History of Salvation Summary

Within the story of man's salvation, the book of Exodus describes a great forward step. The book of Genesis showed the plight of the human race and its need for salvation. The call of Abraham began the process of divine rescue. Then Jacob's migration to Egypt seemed to put the plan aside. But in a most dramatic fashion Exodus shows the divine plan reactivated. Heaven-sent plagues force the Egyptians to let Israel go. Then, accompanied by the cloud of God's presence, they travel toward the promised land of Canaan. Pausing en route at Mount Sinai, they hear God declare to them his laws and seal his covenant with them. Israel is already God's people by virtue of the promises to Abraham; this covenant establishes the people as a theocracy, in which the covenant specifies the operations of the civil and social, as well as religious, aspects of Israel's life. Despite their prompt disregard of their covenantal relationship in the worship of the golden calf, the covenant is renewed and the tabernacle is built, a pledge of God's continuing presence with them. The book ends with the glory of God filling the tabernacle, ready to lead the people to the Promised Land.

The NT sees the OT exodus story as the pattern for the ministry and death of Christ. In him God "dwelt [lit., "tabernacled"] among us, and we have seen his glory" (John 1:14). Jesus sojourned in Egypt, and then came out, fulfilling the pattern of Israel (Matt. 2:15, using Hos. 11:1). At the Last Supper, a Passover meal (cf. Exodus 12–13), Jesus referred to "the new covenant in my blood" (Luke 22:20), echoing Moses' words in Exodus 24:8. He also described his death as the exodus (ESV, "departure"; Gk. *exodos*) that he would accomplish at Jerusalem (Luke 9:31). As Jesus reenacted the exodus in his own life and death, so must his followers. Baptism into his death identifies the believer with the Israelites' passage through the Red Sea, and partaking of his spiritual food and drink identifies the believer with their experiences in the wilderness (1 Cor. 10:1–3). Finally, in heaven, believers shall sing the Song of Moses and the Lamb (Rev. 15:3; cf. Exodus 15). (For an explanation of the "History of Salvation," see the Overview of the Bible, pp. 23–26. See also History of Salvation in the Old Testament: Preparing the Way for Christ, pp. 2635–2661.)

Literary Features

Exodus is an adventure story par excellence. It features a cruel villain (Pharaoh), an unlikely hero (Moses), overwhelming disasters (the plagues), a spectacular deliverance (crossing the Red Sea), a long journey (through the wilderness), a mountaintop experience (where Moses received the Ten Commandments), and a grand finale (the presence of God coming down to the ark of the covenant, filling the tabernacle with glory). The story features unexpected setbacks and unpredictable delays, magic tricks (from Pharaoh's sorcerers) and

The Journey to Mount Sinai
1446/1260 B.C.
Among the many theories regarding the route of the exodus, the traditional route to Jebel Musa is considered by many scholars to be the most plausible. Beginning at Rameses, the Israelites journeyed to Succoth, but these two sites are the only ones on the route identified with certainty. From there they traveled to Etham and Pi-hahiroth, where they crossed the Red Sea. From there they traveled to Marah, Elim, Rephidim, and finally Mount Sinai.

miracles, feasts and festivals, music and dancing, and many close encounters with the living God. God's purpose in all of this was to show his glory by fulfilling the promises he made to his people in the covenant. The exodus is the archetypal deliverance of the OT—the definitive salvation event that established the identity of Israel as the people of God and demonstrated the character of their Deliverer as the God who saves.

The basic framework of the book is epic. Epics begin with a nation in crisis, and this epic opens with the Israelites languishing in slavery and their would-be deliverer born under the threat of death by drowning. The story proceeds along epic lines, with a cosmic confrontation between good and evil that is happily resolved through a mighty act of rescue and a long journey to freedom. Moses is the heroic (albeit imperfect) national leader who serves as the human instrument of a divine deliverance. Like many epics, Exodus is also the story of the founding of a nation. This helps to explain how the second half of the book connects to the first: once the people of God are delivered from bondage, they meet to receive a national constitution (the Ten Commandments) and to establish a place for their national assembly (the tabernacle). Within its epic framework, Exodus also contains a wealth of subgenres: rescue story, calling story, human-divine encounter, diplomatic negotiation, plague story, genealogy, institution of a festival, song of victory, travelogue, miracle story, legal code, case law, covenant renewal ceremony, architectural blueprint, garment design, building narrative.

Outline

I. Exodus of Israel from Egypt (1:1–18:27)
  A. Setting: Israel in Egypt (1:1–2:25)
    1. The sons of Jacob become the people of Israel (1:1–7)
    2. New pharaoh, new situation (1:8–2:25)
  B. Call of Moses (3:1–4:31)
    1. Burning bush: call of Moses (3:1–4:17)
    2. Moses returns from Midian to Egypt (4:18–31)
  C. Moses and Aaron: initial request (5:1–7:7)
    1. Initial request (5:1–21)
    2. God promises to deliver Israel from Egypt (5:22–6:9)
    3. Moses and Aaron: narrative synopses and genealogy (6:10–30)
    4. Moses encouraged (7:1–7)

- D. Plagues and exodus (7:8–15:21)
  1. Moses and Aaron before Pharaoh: initial sign (7:8–13)
  2. First plague: water to blood (7:14–25)
  3. Second plague: frogs (8:1–15)
  4. Third plague: gnats (8:16–19)
  5. Fourth plague: flies (8:20–32)
  6. Fifth plague: Egyptian livestock are killed (9:1–7)
  7. Sixth plague: boils (9:8–12)
  8. Seventh plague: hail (9:13–35)
  9. Eighth plague: locusts (10:1–20)
  10. Ninth plague: darkness (10:21–29)
  11. Tenth plague: final sign (11:1–15:21)
- E. Journey (15:22–18:27)
  1. Water problem: Marah (15:22–27)
  2. Food problem: manna (16:1–36)
  3. Water problem: Massah and Meribah (17:1–7)
  4. Passage problem: Israel defeats Amalek (17:8–16)
  5. Judgment problem: Jethro advises Moses (18:1–27)

II. Covenant at Sinai (19:1–40:38)

- A. Setting: Sinai (19:1–25)
- B. Covenant words and rules (20:1–23:33)
  1. The Ten Commandments (20:1–21)
  2. Worship instructions: against idols and for an altar (20:22–26)
  3. Detailed legislation (21:1–23:19)
  4. Commands for the conquest (23:20–33)
- C. Covenant confirmed (24:1–18)
- D. Instructions for the tabernacle (25:1–31:17)
  1. Request for contributions (25:1–9)
  2. Ark of the covenant (25:10–22)
  3. Table for the bread of the Presence (25:23–30)
  4. Golden lampstand (25:31–40)
  5. Tent of the tabernacle (26:1–37)
  6. Bronze altar (27:1–8)
  7. Court of the tabernacle (27:9–19)
  8. Oil for the lamp (27:20–21)
  9. Garments for the priests (28:1–43)
  10. Consecration of the priests (29:1–37)
  11. Offering and promises of the tabernacle (29:38–46)
  12. Altar of incense (30:1–10)
  13. Census offering (30:11–16)
  14. Bronze basin (30:17–21)
  15. Anointing oil and incense (30:22–38)
  16. Craftsmen (31:1–11)
  17. Sabbath (31:12–17)
- E. Moses receives the tablets (31:18)
- F. Covenant breach, intercession, and renewal (32:1–34:35)
  1. Covenant breach: the golden calf (32:1–35)
  2. Moses intercedes for the people (33:1–23)
  3. Covenant renewal: new tablets (34:1–35)
- G. Tabernacle: preparation for the presence (35:1–40:38)
  1. Moses prepares the people (35:1–36:7)
  2. Tabernacle construction (36:8–39:43)
  3. Tabernacle assembled (40:1–33)
  4. The glory of the Lord (40:34–38)

EXODUS

Chapter 1
1[a]For ver. 1-4, see Gen. 35:23-26; 46:8-26
5[b]Gen. 46:27; Deut. 10:22
6[c]Gen. 50:26
7[d]Deut. 26:5; Acts 7:17; [Gen. 46:3]
8[e]Cited Acts 7:18
9[f]Ps. 105:24
10[g]Ps. 83:3, 4 [h]Ps. 105:25; Acts 7:19
11[i]ch. 3:7; Gen. 15:13; Deut. 26:6 [j]ch. 2:11; 5:4, 5; 6:6, 7; Ps. 81:6 [k][2 Chr. 16:4] [l][ch. 12:37; Gen. 47:11]
13[m]See ch. 5:7-19
14[n][ch. 2:23; 6:9; Num. 20:15; Acts 7:19, 34]

Israel Increases Greatly in Egypt

1 [a]These are the names of the sons of Israel who came to Egypt with Jacob, each with
his household: 2Reuben, Simeon, Levi, and Judah, 3Issachar, Zebulun, and Benjamin,
4Dan and Naphtali, Gad and Asher. 5All the descendants of Jacob were [b]seventy persons;
Joseph was already in Egypt. 6Then [c]Joseph died, and all his brothers and all that generation.
7[d]But the people of Israel were fruitful and increased greatly; they multiplied and
grew exceedingly strong, so that the land was filled with them.

Pharaoh Oppresses Israel

8Now there arose a new king over Egypt, [e]who did not know Joseph. 9And he said to
his people, "Behold, [f]the people of Israel are too many and too mighty for us. 10[g]Come,
[h]let us deal shrewdly with them, lest they multiply, and, if war breaks out, they join our
enemies and fight against us and escape from the land." 11Therefore they set taskmasters
over them [i]to afflict them with heavy [j]burdens. They built for Pharaoh [k]store cities, Pithom
and [l]Raamses. 12But the more they were oppressed, the more they multiplied and the
more they spread abroad. And the Egyptians were in dread of the people of Israel. 13So
they ruthlessly made the people of Israel [m]work as slaves 14and [n]made their lives bitter
with hard service, in mortar and brick, and in all kinds of work in the field. In all their
work they ruthlessly made them work as slaves.
15Then the king of Egypt said to the Hebrew midwives, one of whom was named Shiphrah

1:1–18:27 *Exodus of Israel from Egypt.* The entirety of the first half of the book of Exodus is focused on the exodus of the people of Israel out of Egypt: the setting (1:1–2:25), leadership (3:1–6:30), signs (7:1–15:21), and journey (15:22–18:27).

1:1–2:25 *Setting: Israel in Egypt.* The opening section sets the stage for the rest of the book by describing: the connection to the narrative of Genesis (Ex. 1:1–7), the oppression that has arisen under a new pharaoh (1:8–22), the preservation of Moses at birth (2:1–10) and later in Midian (2:11–22), and the declaration of God's intimate knowledge of Israel's suffering and God's faithfulness to his covenant with Abraham and his descendants (2:23–25).

1:1–7 *The Sons of Jacob Become the People of Israel.* This section links the events of Joseph bringing Jacob and all his brothers to Egypt (see Gen. 46:8–26) and the death of that generation (see Gen. 50:26) with their descendants living in Egypt.

1:1 the sons of Israel who came to Egypt with Jacob. Two names are used to refer to the same person: Israel and Jacob. The dual reference reminds the reader of the previous narrative in Genesis where God declared that Jacob would be called Israel (Gen. 32:28; 35:10) and connects the narrative of Exodus with the promise that God would be faithful to the covenant that he made with Abraham and reaffirmed with Jacob (Gen. 35:11–12). God's faithfulness to remember and fulfill his covenant promises is a central theme in the book of Exodus (Ex. 2:24; 3:6–8, 15–17; 4:5; 6:2–8; and also 32:13).

1:2–4 The names of the sons of Jacob (aside from Joseph) are given in the order of their birth with respect to who bore them (i.e., Leah, Rachel, Bilhah, and Zilpah). The same list of names (with the addition of Joseph) is found in Gen. 35:23–26 with the name of the mother listed before her sons.

1:5 seventy persons. On the relationship between this number and the 75 given in Stephen's speech (Acts 7:14), see note on Gen. 46:26–27.

1:7 The Hebrew phrase translated **the people of Israel** is the same phrase rendered as "the sons of Israel" in v. 1. Since the narrative has just referred to the death of Joseph and all his generation (v. 6), the focus shifts here from the specific 12 sons of Jacob to their offspring who have become the people of Israel. The vocabulary used to describe their growth (they were **fruitful, multiplied**, and **the land was filled with them**) parallels that of God's command to mankind at creation (Gen. 1:28) as well as his later reiteration to Jacob (Gen. 35:11).

1:8–2:25 *New Pharaoh, New Situation.* The coming to power (1:8) and death (2:23) of a new king of Egypt frame this section, which describes both how the peaceful existence of Jacob's family in Egypt turned into one of oppression through enslavement (1:8–22) and how these circumstances became the context in which God preserved the life of Moses (2:1–22).

1:8 The reference to a new leader in Egypt **who did not know Joseph** presumes that the reader is familiar with the narrative of Joseph's entry, problems, and rise to power in Egypt (see Genesis 37–50, esp. 41:37–45).

1:11 The description of the taskmasters who were put in place **to afflict** Israel echoes the vocabulary of God's covenant with Abraham in which he foretold that his offspring would sojourn in a foreign land and "be afflicted for four hundred years" (Gen. 15:13). It is commonly accepted today that the site of **Raamses** is located at Qantir in the eastern Nile delta about 12 miles (19 km) south of Tanis. Excavations have confirmed this identification. During the second millennium B.C., a massive settlement of Asiatic foreigners lived here. (On the "Asiatics," see note on Gen. 37:28.) In addition, a factory has been discovered at the site; it produced decorated glazed tiles. Pottery fragments found in the factory bear the name Raamses. **Pithom** is probably located at Tell el Retabe, about 17 miles (27 km) southeast of Raamses.

1:15–22 The **Hebrew midwives** (v. 15) show through their defiant actions that they **feared God** (vv. 17, 21) more than they feared the **king of Egypt** (v. 17). For the narrator to say this twice shows that he commends them for

and the other Puah, 16 "When you serve as midwife to the Hebrew women and see them on
the birthstool, if it is a son, you shall kill him, but if it is a daughter, she shall live." 17 But
the midwives [o]feared God and did not do as the king of Egypt commanded them, but
let the male children live. 18 So the king of Egypt called the midwives and said to them,
"Why have you done this, and let the male children live?" 19 The midwives said to Pharaoh,
"Because the Hebrew women are not like the Egyptian women, for they are vigorous and
give birth before the midwife comes to them." 20 [p]So God dealt well with the midwives. And
the people multiplied and grew very strong. 21 And because the midwives feared God, [q]he
gave them families. 22 Then Pharaoh commanded all his people, [r]"Every son that is born to
the Hebrews[1] you shall cast into [s]the Nile, but you shall let every daughter live."

The Birth of Moses

2 Now a [t]man from the house of Levi went and took as his wife a Levite woman. 2 The
woman conceived and bore a son, and [u]when she saw that he was a fine child, she hid
him three months. 3 When she could hide him no longer, she took for him a basket made
of bulrushes[2] and daubed it with bitumen and pitch. She put the child in it and placed
it among the [v]reeds by the river bank. 4 And [w]his sister stood at a distance to know what
would be done to him. 5 Now the daughter of Pharaoh came down to bathe at the river,
while her young women walked beside the river. She saw the basket among the reeds and
sent her servant woman, and she took it. 6 When she opened it, she saw the child, and
behold, the baby was crying. She took pity on him and said, "This is one of the Hebrews'
children." 7 Then his sister said to Pharaoh's daughter, "Shall I go and call you a nurse
from the Hebrew women to nurse the child for you?" 8 And Pharaoh's daughter said to
her, "Go." So the girl went and called the child's mother. 9 And Pharaoh's daughter said
to her, "Take this child away and nurse him for me, and I will give you your wages." So
the woman took the child and nursed him. 10 When the child grew older, she brought

[1] Samaritan, Septuagint, Targum; Hebrew lacks *to the Hebrews* [2] Hebrew *papyrus reeds*

17 [o]Prov. 16:6; [Dan. 3:16-18; 6:13; Acts 5:29]
20 [p][Eccles. 8:12]
21 [q][1 Sam. 2:35; 2 Sam. 7:11, 27; 1 Kgs. 2:24; 11:38; Ps. 127:1]
22 [r]Acts 7:19 [s]Gen. 41:1

Chapter 2

1 [t]ch. 6:20; Num. 26:59; 1 Chr. 23:14
2 [u]Acts 7:20; Heb. 11:23
3 [v]ver. 5; Isa. 19:6
4 [w]ch. 15:20; Num. 26:59

their faith. Also, this narrative names so few people (not even naming the pharaohs!) that it is probably a further display of the narrator's approval of the women's deeds that he gives their names, **Shiphrah** and **Puah** (v. 15), a detail unnecessary for describing the events themselves. The faithfulness of the midwives is also an indication that there were those among the people of Israel who feared God after all the years of enslavement and before there was any knowledge of God's call of Moses. The exemplary actions of the midwives signify a central theme of the book of Exodus: Israel is called to fear God above any other ruler, nation, or circumstance.

1:16 The use of the term **"son"** (vv. 16, 22) is thematic for chs. 1–15. In an attempt to prevent a possible future rebellion, the king of Egypt here calls for all the male children of Israel to be killed at birth. When God instructs Moses about what he will say to Pharaoh, he refers to Israel as his "firstborn son" (4:22) and warns that refusal to listen will lead to the death of Egypt's firstborn (4:23), which comes about in the tenth plague (12:29–30).

1:19 When challenged as to why they did not carry out the pharaoh's decrees, the midwives gave an answer that some have called deceptive. It is uncertain that the reply is, strictly speaking, untrue; nor is it clear whether this is all that the women said. The narrator simply commends the women for refusing to comply with Pharaoh's murderous scheme. Some would argue that, with such an evil plan, Pharaoh had forfeited any right to expect obedience (or complete truthfulness) from his subjects. Exodus, however, reports these events without giving any moral evaluation, its chief purpose being to help its readers rejoice that God had wonderfully preserved his people from Pharaoh.

1:22 Pharaoh chooses to **let every daughter live** because he is primarily worried about the threat of Israel's sons joining with a foreign army against Egypt (v. 10). However, it is the faithfulness of some of Israel's daughters who fear God more than Pharaoh that is highlighted here (Shiphrah and Puah) and in the following narrative (Moses' mother and sister in 2:1–10); they are part of the means by which God will eventually bring his people out of slavery. Furthermore, it is ironic that Pharaoh's own daughter is also one who acts to preserve the life of Moses, through whom God will bring Israel out of Egypt.

2:1–22 This section narrates two different points at which Moses' life was preserved: as an infant (vv. 1–10) and as a young man (vv. 11–22). Clearly, the book of Exodus intends to narrate the setting, events, and characters in each case as the actual events of Moses' preservation. In the NT, these two particular narrative motifs will converge in the events of Jesus' preservation from Herod through the flight to Egypt (Matt. 2:13–23). It is crucial for the first audience to know how God preserved Moses from several dangers: this story, together with the account of God's call on Moses (Ex. 3:1–4:17), should enable the people of Israel to embrace Moses as God's authorized "prince and judge" (2:14), as well as lawgiver.

2:2 she saw that he was a fine child. The Hebrew is lit., "she saw him, that he was good." This may refer simply to Moses' being "healthy." Some have seen here an echo of the creation account (1:7); this would fit with the way the opening events in the book of Exodus act as a creation-like account for the birth of Israel as a nation.

2:3 The birth account of Moses contains several words that are likely influenced by or borrowed from Egyptian, like the terms used for a **basket made of bulrushes** and **reeds**.

2:7–9 As someone from the population of slaves in Egypt, it took significant courage for Moses' **sister** to presume to speak to **Pharaoh's daughter** (v. 7). Her bold move ends up bringing about a situation that surely Moses' mother could not have imagined possible when she hid him: she is paid **wages** to nurse her own son (v. 9).

2:10 Moses. In Hebrew, the name sounds like the verb *mashah*, "to draw out" (see ESV footnote). The name may also be related to the common Egyptian word for "son." Since Pharaoh's daughter clearly knows that Moses is a Hebrew child (vv. 6–9), it is possible that she chose the name for both its Hebrew ("drawn out of water") and Egyptian ("son") senses. The irony of such a dual reference would be that her action not only prefigures but is also a part of the means that God uses to "draw" Israel as his "son" out of Egypt (Hos. 11:1). The narrator tells nothing of what it was like for Moses in Pharaoh's household: Did Pharaoh know of Moses' origin? Why did he allow one of his daughters to adopt a child at all? Did the daughter marry? The attentive reader may guess at answers to these questions, but the absence of further comment probably shows that the narrator did not intend to supply

10[x]Acts 7:21; [Heb. 11:24] [y]2 Sam. 22:17; Ps. 18:16
11[z]Acts 7:23; Heb. 11:24-26 [a]See ch. 1:11
12[b]Acts 7:24
13[c]Acts 7:23-28
14[d][Luke 12:14]
15[e]Acts 7:29; Heb. 11:27 [f]Gen. 24:11; 29:2
16[g]ch. 3:1 [h]Gen. 24:11; 29:10; 1 Sam. 9:11
17[i][Gen. 29:10]
18[j]Num. 10:29; [ch. 3:1; 4:18; 18:1, 5, 9, 12]
19[i][See ver. 17 above]
20[k]Gen. 31:54; 43:25
21[l]ch. 4:25; 18:2
22[m]ch. 18:3 [n]Acts 7:29; [Heb. 11:13, 14]
23[o][ch. 7:7]; Acts 7:23, 30 [p][Deut. 26:7] [q]ch. 3:9; Gen. 18:20, 21; James 5:4
24[r]ch. 6:5 [s]Ps. 105:8, 42; 106:45 [t]Gen. 15:14; 46:4
25[u]ch. 3:7; 4:31; [Luke 1:25] [v][ch. 3:16]
Chapter 3
1[w]ch. 4:27; 18:5; 24:13; Num. 10:33; 1 Kgs. 19:8
2[x]For ver. 2-10, see Acts 7:30-35 [y]Isa. 63:9

him to Pharaoh's daughter, and he became [x]her son. She named him Moses, "Because,"
she said, "I [y]drew him out of the water."[1]

Moses Flees to Midian

11 One day, [z]when Moses had grown up, he went out to his people and looked on their
[a]burdens, and he saw an Egyptian beating a Hebrew, one of his people.[2] **12** He looked this
way and that, and seeing no one, he [b]struck down the Egyptian and hid him in the sand.
13 When [c]he went out the next day, behold, two Hebrews were struggling together. And
he said to the man in the wrong, "Why do you strike your companion?" **14** He answered,
[d]"Who made you a prince and a judge over us? Do you mean to kill me as you killed the
Egyptian?" Then Moses was afraid, and thought, "Surely the thing is known." **15** When
Pharaoh heard of it, he sought to kill Moses. But [e]Moses fled from Pharaoh and stayed in
the land of Midian. And he sat down by [f]a well.
16 Now the [g]priest of Midian had seven daughters, and [h]they came and drew water and
filled the troughs to water their father's flock. **17** The shepherds came and drove them away,
but Moses stood up and saved them, and [i]watered their flock. **18** When they came home to
their father [j]Reuel, he said, "How is it that you have come home so soon today?" **19** They
said, "An Egyptian delivered us out of the hand of the shepherds and even drew water for
us and [i]watered the flock." **20** He said to his daughters, "Then where is he? Why have you
left the man? Call him, that he may [k]eat bread." **21** And Moses was content to dwell with the
man, and he gave Moses his daughter [l]Zipporah. **22** She gave birth to a son, and he called
his name [m]Gershom, for he said, "I have been a [n]sojourner[3] in a foreign land."

God Hears Israel's Groaning

23 [o]During those many days the king of Egypt died, and the people of Israel [p]groaned
because of their slavery and cried out for help. [q]Their cry for rescue from slavery came up to
God. **24** And [r]God heard their groaning, and God [s]remembered his covenant with [t]Abraham,
with Isaac, and with Jacob. **25** God [u]saw the people of Israel—and God [v]knew.

The Burning Bush

3 Now Moses was keeping the flock of his father-in-law, Jethro, the priest of Midian, and
he led his flock to the west side of the wilderness and came to Horeb, the [w]mountain
of God. **2** [x]And [y]the angel of the LORD appeared to him in a flame of fire out of the midst

[1] *Moses* sounds like the Hebrew for *draw out* [2] Hebrew *brothers* [3] *Gershom* sounds like the Hebrew for *sojourner*

these details. It would seem likely that the daughter never told Pharaoh the truth about Moses' origin, but this can only be surmised.

2:11 when Moses had grown up. In Acts 7:23 Stephen gives Moses' age at this time as 40 (reflecting Jewish interpretative tradition). Even after a life preserved from the affliction of slavery, and privileged by what he would have received as a part of Pharaoh's house, Moses identifies himself with the Hebrew slaves as **his people**.

2:14 Who made you a prince and a judge over us? The words of the Hebrew man foreshadow the repeated grumbling that Moses will encounter when he leads Israel out of Egypt (see 5:21; 14:11, 12; 15:24; 16:2–3; 17:3). Acts 7:27 quotes these words from the Septuagint, which renders them "a ruler and a judge."

2:15 In sitting down **by a well**, Moses repeats the actions through which both Isaac (through Abraham's servant, Gen. 24:11ff.) and Jacob (Gen. 29:2ff.) interacted with women who would become their wives.

2:18 Reuel is later referred to as "Jethro" (3:1; 4:18; 18:1). Clearly both names refer to the same person: the priest of Midian (2:16) who is Moses' father-in-law.

2:19 The reference to Moses as an **Egyptian** indicates an aspect of tension in the narrative: while Moses bore enough signs of his Egyptian upbringing for Reuel's daughters to assume his ethnic identity, he was also known as a Hebrew (v. 6) and chose to identify himself with the Hebrew slaves (v. 11). However, through the events of vv. 11–15, Moses becomes alienated from both the people of his birth (v. 14) and his Egyptian household (v. 15).

2:23–25 These verses function with 1:1–7 to frame the opening section with the reminder that the offspring of **Abraham**, **Isaac**, and **Jacob** will not be defined by their years of slavery, but by their **covenant** relationship with the **God** who has **heard** their cries (and who **saw** and **knew** their affliction) and **remembered** his promises.

2:23 many days. Acts 7:30 takes this period as 40 years (cf. Ex. 2:11; 7:7).

2:24 remembered. See note on Gen. 8:1.

3:1–4:31 *Call of Moses.* This section focuses primarily on the call of Moses at the burning bush (3:1–4:17) but also includes narration of certain events related to Moses' return from Midian to Egypt: the peaceful departure from Jethro (4:18–20), the Lord's reminder and further instruction to Moses (4:21–23), the preservation of Moses' life by Zipporah (4:24–26), and the arrival of Aaron before Moses met with the elders of Israel (4:27–31).

3:1–4:17 *Burning Bush: Call of Moses.* At the burning bush, God reveals himself, his promises, and his purposes to Moses (3:1–22) and also demonstrates his power both through and for Moses (4:1–17). The call of Moses marks the beginning of the role that he will fill as the one who will mediate between the Lord and his people, and it is recorded in detail here, in part to remind Israel that following the Lord necessitates fidelity to the covenant which he revealed through Moses (chs. 20–23).

3:1 Horeb, the mountain of God. The mountain where Moses has arrived is also referred to as "Mount Sinai" (see 19:11). "Horeb" is typically understood as either another name for Mount Sinai or as a term that refers to the region in which the mountain was located. Mount Sinai becomes known as "the mountain of God" through the events that are about to unfold in the narrative of Exodus: God calls Moses from the burning bush at the mountain; Aaron meets Moses here when he returns from Midian (4:27); and God meets with Moses on the mountain when Israel comes out of Egypt and gives him the law (ch. 19).

3:2 Where **the angel of the LORD** appears in the OT, he is often described

of a bush. He looked, and behold, the bush was burning, yet it was not consumed. 3 And
Moses said, "I will turn aside to see this great sight, why the bush is not burned." 4 When
the LORD saw that he turned aside to see, [z]God called to him [a]out of the bush, "Moses,
Moses!" And he said, "Here I am." 5 Then he said, "Do not come near; [b]take your sandals
off your feet, for the place on which you are standing is holy ground." 6 And he said, [c]"I
am the God of your father, the God of Abraham, the God of Isaac, and the God of Jacob."
And Moses hid his face, for [d]he was afraid to look at God.
7 Then the LORD said, [e]"I have surely seen the affliction of my people who are in Egypt
and have heard their cry because of their [f]taskmasters. I know their sufferings, 8 and [g]I
have come down to deliver them out of the hand of the Egyptians and [h]to bring them up
out of that land to a [i]good and broad land, a land [j]flowing with milk and honey, to the
place of [k]the Canaanites, the Hittites, the Amorites, the Perizzites, the Hivites, and the
Jebusites. 9 And now, behold, [l]the cry of the people of Israel has come to me, and I have
also seen the [m]oppression with which the Egyptians oppress them. 10 [n]Come, I will send
you to Pharaoh that you may bring my people, the children of Israel, out of Egypt." 11 But
Moses said to God, [o]"Who am I that I should go to Pharaoh and bring the children of
Israel out of Egypt?" 12 He said, [p]"But I will be with you, and this shall be the sign for you,
that I have sent you: when you have brought the people out of Egypt, [q]you shall serve
God on this mountain."
13 Then Moses said to God, "If I come to the people of Israel and say to them, 'The God

4 [z]ch. 19:3 [a]Deut. 33:16
5 [b]Josh. 5:15; [ch. 19:12; Eccles. 5:1]
6 [c]ch. 4:5; Gen. 28:13; 1 Kgs. 18:36; Cited Matt. 22:32; Mark 12:26; [Luke 20:37] [d][1 Kgs. 19:13; Isa. 6:1, 2, 5]
7 [e]ch. 2:23-25; Neh. 9:9; Ps. 106:44 [f]ch. 5:13, 14
8 [g]Gen. 11:5, 7; 18:21 [h]ch. 6:6; 12:51; [Gen. 50:24] [i]Deut. 1:25; 8:7, 8, 9 [j]ch. 13:5; 33:3; Lev. 20:24; Num. 13:27; Deut. 26:9, 15; Jer. 11:5; 32:22; Ezek. 20:6 [k]Gen. 15:18-21
9 [l]ch. 2:23 [m]ch. 1:11-14, 22
10 [n][Ps. 105:26; Mic. 6:4]
11 [o]ch. 6:12; [1 Sam. 18:18; Isa. 6:5, 8; Jer. 1:6]
12 [p]ch. 4:12, 15; Deut. 31:8, 23; Josh. 1:5 [q]See ch. 19

as acting or speaking in a manner that suggests he is more than simply an angel or messenger and that he is closely identified with God himself (e.g., Gen. 22:11–18). Here he appears to Moses in a **flame of fire**, which is a sign of God's presence throughout the events narrated in the book of Exodus: in the pillar of fire and cloud that leads and protects the Israelites (Ex. 13:21–22); in the signs of God's presence on Mount Sinai (19:18); and in the tabernacle (40:38). The angel also protects Israel when they come out of Egypt (14:19), and God promises that he will go before Israel into the land of Canaan (23:20; 33:2). In 3:4 this angel of God is identified as "the LORD" and "God."

3:5 Do not come near; take your sandals off your feet. The instructions to Moses are followed by a reason that emphasizes the **place** where he is **standing**. The very ordinariness of the location helps make the point that it is **holy ground**, not because of any special properties of the place but only because of God's presence. This is representative of a theme in Exodus: God is holy, and he is the one who makes or declares places and people to be holy—and each is properly understood or treated as holy only in its relation to God. The instructions given to Moses here at the burning bush are also given to his successor Joshua when he meets the "commander of the army of the LORD" as Israel is preparing to take Jericho (see Josh. 5:13–15).

3:6 Although Moses is in exile from his household in Egypt (2:15) and somewhat estranged from the people of his birth (2:14), God reveals himself as **the God of your father** and makes it clear that Moses' identity is framed primarily by his being an offspring of **Abraham** and thus belonging to the people to whom God has pledged himself by covenant (see 2:23–25). Jesus quotes from this verse (Matt. 22:32), affirming that Abraham, Isaac, and Jacob still live.

3:7–9 God tells Moses of his intimate knowledge of Israel's affliction (**I have . . . seen, heard, know**; see also 2:23–25) and indicates his covenant promises and identification with them by referring to the Hebrew slaves as **my people** (also 3:10), which is also what the Lord will instruct Moses to say before Pharaoh (e.g., 5:1).

3:11–12 Who am I . . . ? Moses' initial question is surely sensible, and God does not reprove him for asking it (v. 11). However, God does not answer Moses' question in the way that he asks it, but instead says, **"I will be with you"** indicating that his presence with Moses is essential to the call (v. 12). When the OT says that God is "with" someone, it stresses God's power that enables the person to carry out his calling (cf. 4:12; Gen. 26:3). God also promises that the very place where they are speaking will become a confirming **sign** to Moses when he brings the people out and they serve God **on this mountain** (see Ex. 3:1).

3:13 What is his name? Given the polytheism and pantheism of the surrounding Egyptian culture, it was essential to know the identity of the one true God (**the God of your fathers**). Further, in ancient cultures, to know the name of someone was to know something very essential about that person. Though Moses is apparently not familiar with God's name, this does not mean that the personal name of God was unknown to the Hebrews prior to Moses (see e.g., Gen. 4:26; 9:26; 12:8; 26:25; 28:16; 30:27; cf. Ex. 3:15); it may have meant that the name had been lost or had fallen into disuse during the centuries of slavery in Egypt, or that the name had not been used extensively or fully understood before this time. (See further notes on 6:2–8 and 6:3–8.)

Three Stages of Moses' Life

Location	Age	Reference
Egypt	0–40	Ex. 2:11; Acts 7:23
Midian	41–80	Ex. 2:15; 7:7; Acts 7:29–30
The wilderness	81–120	Deut. 31:2; 34:7; cf. Num. 14:33–34; Deut. 29:5

Covenantal Call and Dialogue

Moses' Questions and Concerns	Yahweh's Responses and Signs
Who am I that I should go? (3:11).	I will be with you; when you come out of Egypt, you will serve me on this mountain (3:12).
What is your name, that I may tell the people who sent me? (3:13).	I AM WHO I AM: Yahweh, the God of your fathers Abraham, Isaac, and Jacob (3:14–15).
How would the people believe that you have sent me? (4:1).	Yahweh turns Moses' rod into a serpent then back into a rod (4:2–4); Yahweh makes Moses' hand leprous then heals it (4:6–7); Yahweh instructs Moses to turn water from the Nile into blood (4:9).
I am not eloquent; I am slow of speech (4:10).	I, Yahweh, am the one who made your mouth (4:11).
Please send someone else (4:13).	Aaron will go with you; you will speak my words to him and he will speak to the people for you (4:15–16).

of your fathers has sent me to you,' and they ask me, 'What is his name?' what shall I say to
them?" 14 God said to Moses, "I AM WHO I AM."[1] And he said, "Say this to the people of Israel,
[r]'I AM has sent me to you.'" 15 God also said to Moses, "Say this to the people of Israel, 'The
LORD,[2] the [s]God of your fathers, the God of Abraham, the God of Isaac, and the God of Jacob,
has sent me to you.' This is [t]my name forever, and thus I am to be remembered throughout
all generations. 16 Go and [u]gather the elders of Israel together and say to them, 'The LORD,
the God of your fathers, the God of Abraham, of Isaac, and of Jacob, has appeared to me,
saying, [v]"I have observed you and what has been done to you in Egypt, 17 and I promise
that [w]I will bring you up out of the affliction of Egypt to the land of the Canaanites, the
Hittites, the Amorites, the Perizzites, the Hivites, and the Jebusites, a land [w]flowing with
milk and honey."' 18 And [x]they will listen to your voice, and you and the elders of Israel
[y]shall go to the king of Egypt and say to him, 'The LORD, the God of the Hebrews, has
[z]met with us; and now, please let us go a three days' journey into the wilderness, that we
may sacrifice to the LORD our God.' 19 But I know that the king of Egypt [a]will not let you
go unless compelled [b]by a mighty hand.[3] 20 So [c]I will stretch out my hand and strike Egypt
with [d]all the wonders that I will do in it; [e]after that he will let you go. 21 And [f]I will give
this people favor in the sight of the Egyptians; and when you go, you shall not go empty,
22 but each woman shall ask of her neighbor, and any woman who lives in her house, for
[g]silver and gold jewelry, and for clothing. You shall put them on your sons and on your
daughters. So [h]you shall plunder the Egyptians."

Moses Given Powerful Signs

4 Then Moses answered, "But behold, they will not believe me or listen to my voice, for
they will say, 'The LORD did not appear to you.'" 2 The LORD said to him, "What is that
in your hand?" He said, [i]"A staff." 3 And he said, "Throw it on the ground." So he threw

[1] Or *I AM WHAT I AM*, or *I WILL BE WHAT I WILL BE* [2] The word *LORD*, when spelled with capital letters, stands for the divine name, *YHWH*, which is here connected with the verb *hayah*, "to be" in verse 14 [3] Septuagint, Vulgate; Hebrew *go, not by a mighty hand*

14[r]ch. 6:3; Ps. 68:4; John 8:58; Heb. 13:8; Rev. 1:4; 4:8
15[s]ver. 6 [t]Hos. 12:5; [Ps. 135:13]
16[u]ch. 4:29 [v]ch. 4:31; Gen. 50:24; [Luke 1:68]
17[w]ver. 8
18[x]ch. 4:31 [y]ch. 5:1 [z]Num. 23:3, 4, 15, 16
19[a]ch. 5:2; 7:4 [b]ch. 6:1; 13:3
20[c]Deut. 6:22; Neh. 9:10; Jer. 32:20; Acts 7:36; See ch. 7–12 [d]ch. 4:21 [e]ch. 12:31
21[f]ch. 11:2, 3; 12:35, 36; [Gen. 15:14]
22[g][ch. 33:6] [h][Ezek. 39:10]
Chapter 4
2[i]ver. 17, 20

3:14 I AM WHO I AM. In response to Moses' question ("What is [your] name?" v. 13), God reveals his name to be "Yahweh" (corresponding to the four Hebrew consonants *YHWH*). The three occurrences of "I AM" in v. 14 all represent forms of the Hebrew verb that means "to be" (Hb. *hayah*), and in each case are related to the divine name Yahweh (i.e., "the LORD"; see note on v. 15). The divine name Yahweh has suggested to scholars a range of likely nuances of meaning: (1) that God is self-existent and therefore not dependent on anything else for his own existence; (2) that God is the creator and sustainer of all that exists; (3) that God is immutable in his being and character and thus is not in the process of becoming something different from what he is (e.g., "the same yesterday and today and forever," Heb. 13:8); and (4) that God is eternal in his existence. While each of these points is true of God, the main focus in this passage is on the Lord's promise to be with Moses and his people. The word translated "I am" (Hb. *'ehyeh*) can also be understood and translated as "I will be" (cf. ESV footnote). Given the context of Ex. 3:12 ("I will be with you"), the name of Yahweh ("the LORD") is also a clear reminder of God's promises to his people and of his help for them to fulfill their calling. In each of these cases, the personal name of God as revealed to Moses expresses something essential about the attributes and character of God.

3:15 The LORD. Though some modern translations keep "Yahweh" in English, the ESV follows the tradition of replacing Yahweh by "the LORD" (with small capital letters). This practice goes back to the first Greek translation in the third century B.C., the Septuagint, which renders Yahweh by *kyrios* "Lord," a usage that was also quoted extensively in the Greek NT. In this way, translating this term as "the LORD" also shows the links with the NT, which calls Christ "Lord," thereby identifying him with the God of the OT. When Jesus says, "Before Abraham was, I am" (John 8:58, using the Gk. found in Ex. 3:14), the Pharisees show by their desire to stone him that they understood Jesus to be claiming identity with the God who had revealed himself to Moses. (Cf. the table of "I am" statements in John, p. 2041.)

3:16–17 Go and gather the elders of Israel together and say to them. This is the first direct charge to Moses related to the role he will fulfill as the one through whom the Lord will speak to Israel (see 4:15–16; 7:2; 19:3; 20:19–21; 24:3; 34:29–35).

3:18 To someone as powerful as the **king of Egypt**, Moses making a request in the name of **the LORD, the God of the Hebrews** would look ridiculous. What god would choose to be identified with a nation of slaves and then also presume to make a request from the king of the nation that has enslaved them? Given all the other equally true things that God could have told Moses to say to designate him (e.g., the Lord, the God who has created the heavens and the earth), he is evidently making the point to both Egypt and Israel that he has chosen to identify with the people of his covenant even when they appear to have little value in the eyes of the nation they serve except as forced labor. **that we may sacrifice to the LORD our God.** The Lord frames the request to Pharaoh in terms of his people being able to worship him, as he will throughout the plagues: "Let my people go, that they may serve me" (7:16; 8:1, 20; 9:1, 13; 10:3). This signifies to Israel that their freedom from slavery is governed by the promises and purposes of the covenant relationship with the Lord, and it shows Pharaoh that the nature of this relationship supersedes any claim *he* has on Israel.

3:19 The might or strength of God's **hand** is the means by which he will bring Israel out of Egypt. This image for God's power working in the world to save his people recurs throughout the narrative of the plagues and the exodus (see 6:1; 7:4; 9:3; 13:3). The use of the image may represent intentional irony because ancient Egyptian texts often described the power of Pharaoh by saying that he had a "strong hand/arm" to destroy his enemies.

3:22 God tells Moses not only that Israel will be brought out of Egypt but also that they will **plunder the Egyptians**. The description must have seemed inconceivable to Moses. Plundering in the ancient Near East was what victorious armies did to cities they defeated. God describes a situation in which Israel will not only be released from the most powerful nation in the region, but the people will also be given the spoils of Egypt by **each woman** of Israel simply asking for them from **her neighbor**. The precious materials that Israel carries out of Egypt will, among other things, become part of what they will use to construct the tabernacle (see 35:4–9, 20–29).

4:1–17 This section narrates the dialogue between God and Moses regarding the signs he will perform before Israel and Pharaoh; it is framed by explicit references that bring Moses' staff into focus (vv. 2, 17). The staff serves as a sign that God will be with Moses and will bring about what he has promised through him.

4:3–9 The three signs indicate the extent of the Lord's power and prefigure the

it on the ground, and it became a serpent, and Moses ran from it. 4 But the LORD said to
Moses, "Put out your hand and catch it by the tail"—so he put out his hand and caught
it, and it became a staff in his hand— 5 "that they may [j]believe that the LORD, [k]the God of
their fathers, the God of Abraham, the God of Isaac, and the God of Jacob, has appeared
to you." 6 Again, the LORD said to him, "Put your hand inside your cloak."[1] And he put his
hand inside his cloak, and when he took it out, behold, his hand was [l]leprous[2] like snow.
7 Then God said, "Put your hand back inside your cloak." So he put his hand back inside
his cloak, and when he took it out, behold, [m]it was restored like the rest of his flesh. 8 "If
they will not believe you," God said, "or listen to the first sign, they may believe the latter
sign. 9 If they will not believe even these two signs or listen to your voice, you shall take
some water from the Nile and pour it on the dry ground, and the water that you shall take
from the Nile [n]will become blood on the dry ground."
10 But Moses said to the LORD, "Oh, my Lord, I am not eloquent, either in the past or
since you have spoken to your servant, but [o]I am slow of speech and of tongue." 11 Then
the LORD said to him, "Who has made man's mouth? Who makes him mute, or deaf, or
seeing, or blind? Is it not I, the LORD? 12 Now therefore go, and [p]I will be with your mouth
and teach you what you shall speak." 13 But he said, "Oh, my Lord, please send someone
else." 14 Then the anger of the LORD was kindled against Moses and he said, "Is there not
Aaron, your brother, the Levite? I know that he can speak well. Behold, [q]he is coming out
to meet you, and when he sees you, he will be glad in his heart. 15 [r]You shall speak to him
and [s]put the words in his mouth, and [p]I will be with your mouth and with his mouth
and will teach you both what to do. 16 [t]He shall speak for you to the people, and he shall
be your mouth, and [u]you shall be as God to him. 17 And take in your hand [v]this staff, with
which you shall do the signs."

Moses Returns to Egypt

18 Moses went back to [w]Jethro his father-in-law and said to him, "Please let me go back
to my brothers in Egypt to see whether they are still alive." And Jethro said to Moses, "Go
in peace." 19 And the LORD said to Moses in Midian, "Go back to Egypt, for [x]all the men
who were seeking your life are dead." 20 So Moses took [y]his wife and his sons and had
them ride on a donkey, and went back to the land of Egypt. And Moses took [z]the staff of
God in his hand.
21 And the LORD said to Moses, "When you go back to Egypt, see that you do before

5 [j]ch. 19:9 [k]See ch. 3:6
6 [l]Num. 12:10; 2 Kgs. 5:27
7 [m][2 Kgs. 5:14]
9 [n]ch. 7:19
10 [o][ch. 6:12; Jer. 1:6]
12 [p][ch. 3:12; Isa. 50:4; Jer. 1:9; Ezek. 33:22; Matt. 10:19, 20; Mark 13:11; Luke 12:11, 12; 21:15]
14 [q]ver. 27
15 [r]ch. 7:1, 2 [s]Num. 22:38; 23:5, 12, 16; Deut. 18:18; 2 Sam. 14:3, 19; Isa. 51:16 [p][See ver. 12 above]
16 [t]ver. 30 [u][ch. 7:1; 18:19]
17 [v]ver. 2; ch. 7:15
18 [w][ch. 2:18]
19 [x]ch. 2:15, 23; [Matt. 2:20]
20 [y]ch. 18:2-4 [z]ch. 17:9; Num. 20:8, 9

[1] Hebrew *into your bosom*; also verse 7 [2] *Leprosy* was a term for several skin diseases; see Leviticus 13

realms of the plagues to come: creatures of the earth (staff to a serpent), people (Moses' hand becoming leprous), and the elements of nature (water to blood).

4:3–4 A staff turning into a snake was not a normal part of Moses' experience, and his initial response (**Moses ran**) is natural and sensible. However, since it is the Lord who has instructed him, the otherwise foolish response of picking up the snake **by the tail** (v. 4) becomes not only sensible but faithful as well.

4:5 Although God states that the signs will be given so that Israel **may believe that the LORD, the God of their fathers . . . has appeared** to Moses, they are also intended as confirmation to Moses himself. In light of the Lord's gracious response to his questions, for which he has not been reproved up to this point, Moses is also responsible to act faithfully in response to what the Lord has promised about his purposes for Israel.

4:10–12 Egyptian magicians acted as Pharaoh's advisers and were known for being proud of their considerable powers of speech. When Moses protests that he is **slow of speech and of tongue** (v. 10), he is raising a relevant concern if he is going to address Pharaoh and his court. However, as the Lord signified in making Moses' hand leprous and then restoring it, he has power to work in and through that which he has created, including Moses' **mouth** (vv. 11–12). Cf. Jeremiah's call (Jer. 1:4–10).

4:14 The Lord has not reproved Moses for his questions but has responded by revealing his person and purposes. When the narrative states that **the anger of the LORD was kindled against Moses**, it indicates to the reader that Moses was also responsible for doing what God had told him. Still, however, the Lord accommodates Moses by granting Aaron as his spokesman while also continuing to call him to lead Israel out of Egypt.

4:16 He shall speak. The instructions to Moses and Aaron here describe the responsibilities of a prophet (see 7:1–2), who is called to speak exclusively and exhaustively what God reveals (see Deut. 18:18–22; 1 Sam. 3:17–20). Typically, a prophet is both the recipient and deliverer of God's message, but in this case Aaron is the recipient and deliverer of Moses' message. When God says that Moses **shall be as God** to Aaron, he is calling both of these men to faithfulness in their respective roles of relating what he reveals. From his upbringing, Moses was likely already familiar with someone being the **"mouth"** of another person. In ancient Egypt, there was a high official called "the mouth of the king" whose job was to mediate between the "god" Pharaoh and the people of Egypt by speaking Pharaoh's words unaltered to the people.

4:18–31 *Moses Returns from Midian to Egypt.* This section is brief but significant for what it shows in the transition from Moses' exile in Midian to his return to Egypt. In each subsection there is a focus on the Lord's masterful speech or action: he informs Moses that he can return to Egypt (vv. 18–20); he reminds Moses of his call before Pharaoh and foretells the outcome (vv. 21–23); he seeks Moses' life (vv. 24–26); and he sends Aaron to encourage and assist Moses (vv. 27–31).

4:21 I will harden his heart. The heart refers to the whole of the intellect, will, and emotions from which a person acts. The various Hebrew verbs used to describe the hardening of Pharaoh's heart all refer to a desire to act contrary to the Lord rather than in accord with him. (See chart, p. 151.) The hardening of Pharaoh's heart is referred to throughout chs. 4–14 with the implication that Pharaoh is answerable for his own actions (e.g., 8:15). However, the Lord states here that it is *his* sovereign hand that ultimately governs the events. This is also indicated by the recurring "as the LORD had said" (see 7:13; 8:15, 18; 9:12, 35). Though one might conclude that, if God hardens someone's

21[a]ch. 3:20 [b]ch. 7:13, 22; 8:15, 32; 9:12, 35; 10:1; 14:8; Rom. 9:17, 18; [Deut. 2:30; Josh. 11:20; Isa. 63:17]
22[c]Hos. 11:1 [d]Jer. 31:9
23[e]ch. 11:5; 12:29
24[f][Num. 22:22; 1 Chr. 21:16] [g][Gen. 17:14]
25[h]ch. 2:21 [i]Josh. 5:2, 3
27[j]ver. 14 [k]See ch. 3:1
28[l]ver. 15, 16 [m]See ver. 3-9
29[n]ch. 3:16
30[o]ver. 16
31[p]ver. 8, 9; ch. 3:18 [q]See ch. 3:16 [r]ch. 2:25; 3:7 [s]ch. 12:27; Gen. 24:26; 1 Chr. 29:20

Chapter 5
1[t]ch. 10:9
2[u][2 Kgs. 18:35; Job 21:15]

Pharaoh all the [a]miracles that I have put in your power. But [b]I will harden his heart, so
that he will not let the people go. 22 Then you shall say to Pharaoh, 'Thus says the LORD,
[c]Israel is my [d]firstborn son, 23 and I say to you, "Let my son go that he may serve me." If
you refuse to let him go, behold, I [e]will kill your firstborn son.'"
24 At a lodging place on the way [f]the LORD met him and [g]sought to put him to death.
25 Then [h]Zipporah took a [i]flint and cut off her son's foreskin and touched Moses'[1] feet with
it and said, "Surely you are a bridegroom of blood to me!" 26 So he let him alone. It was then
that she said, "A bridegroom of blood," because of the circumcision.
27 The LORD said to Aaron, "Go into the wilderness [j]to meet Moses." So he went and
met him at the [k]mountain of God and kissed him. 28 And Moses [l]told Aaron all the words
of the LORD with which he had sent him to speak, and all [m]the signs that he had commanded him to do. 29 Then Moses and Aaron [n]went and gathered together all the elders
of the people of Israel. 30 [o]Aaron spoke all the words that the LORD had spoken to Moses
and did the signs in the sight of the people. 31 And the people [p]believed; and when they
heard that the LORD had [q]visited the people of Israel and that he had [r]seen their affliction,
[s]they bowed their heads and worshiped.

Making Bricks Without Straw

5 Afterward Moses and Aaron went and said to Pharaoh, "Thus says the LORD, the God
of Israel, 'Let my people go, that they may hold [t]a feast to me in the wilderness.'" 2 But
Pharaoh said, [u]"Who is the LORD, that I should obey his voice and let Israel go? I do not

[1] Hebrew *his*

heart, the latter is not answerable for his actions, this is not the biblical view, and certainly here the narrative is also careful to point out that Pharaoh also hardened his own heart (8:15, 32; 9:34). The sinner remains responsible for his sin. Cf. Rom. 9:16–18.

4:22–23 Israel had been in Egypt for over 400 years (see 12:40), and the people were enslaved for the better part of the time, which meant that they had no possessions or land to pass down as an inheritance. When the Lord instructs Moses to tell Pharaoh "**Israel is my firstborn son**," he is indicating that he has remembered his covenant with Abraham (see Gen. 15:13–21) and that he will bring his people to the land promised as an inheritance to their fathers (see Gen. 15:16; 28:15; 48:21; 50:24). He is also asserting that Israel's true identity extends back to a time and relationship that predates the many years they had been in Egypt's service—a claim that Pharaoh will ignore to the peril of his own and all of Egypt's firstborn (see Ex. 12:29–32). Israel as a whole is God's "son," and all individual Israelites are also "sons" (Deut. 14:1). For the Davidic king as God's "son" and "firstborn," embodying and representing the people, see notes on Ps. 2:7; 89:26–28.

4:24–26 The events narrated in these verses are significant not only for what they tell but also for what they *show*. Not only has the Lord remembered his covenant promises (2:24), but his people are also called to remember the conditions of the covenant. Moses is held responsible for the provisions of the covenant with Abraham that required him to circumcise his sons (Gen. 17:9–14). Failure to be circumcised may lead to being "cut off" (some form of severe punishment from God; see notes on Gen. 17:14; Ex. 12:15; Lev. 7:11–36; Num. 9:6–14). Moses' failure to circumcise his son could have led to his death, had it not been for his wife's action. Once again, Moses' life is preserved through the actions of another, this time through his wife **Zipporah**.

4:27 Aaron is sent to meet Moses **at the mountain of God**, which is also the place where Moses first received the call to lead Israel out of Egypt and which, when they have come out, will become a sign that it is God who has brought them out (see 3:1 and note).

5:1–7:7 *Moses and Aaron: Initial Request.* This section describes Moses' and Aaron's initial audience and request before Pharaoh (5:1–21) and the Lord's promises and encouragement in light of the response (5:22–6:9; 7:1–7). It also includes a genealogy of Moses and Aaron that records their particular antecedents in light of the roles that they will fill when Israel is brought out of Egypt (6:10–30).

5:1–21 *Initial Request.* Moses' and Aaron's initial audience with Pharaoh bears out what the Lord has foretold about Pharaoh's response (vv. 1–19; see 3:19; 4:21) and foreshadows the challenge that Moses and Aaron will face in leading the people of Israel (5:20–21).

5:1 The phrase **thus says the LORD** introduces Moses' and Aaron's words when the narrative explicitly recounts (1) the Lord's instructions to them or (2) their actual speech to Pharaoh (see 7:17; 8:1, 20; 9:1, 13; 10:3; 11:4). As a statement of authority, the form of the phrase was used in the ancient Near East (note Pharaoh's own appropriation of it in 5:10). For the Hebrew prophets it became a standard reminder to both messenger and recipient that the words came from and would be acted upon by the Lord (see Isa. 38:1, 5; Jer. 2:2).

5:2 I do not know the LORD. Pharaoh's response becomes thematic in

The Hardening of Pharaoh's Heart

Declarations	Hardenings		
I [Yahweh] will harden Pharaoh's heart.	Yahweh hardened the heart of Pharaoh.	Pharaoh's heart was hardened.	Pharaoh hardened his heart.
4:21			
7:3			
		7:13	
		7:14	
		7:22	
			8:15
		8:19	
			8:32
		9:7	
	9:12		
			9:34
		9:35	
	10:1		
	10:20		
	10:27		
	11:10		
14:4			
		14:5	
	14:8		

know the LORD, and moreover, [v]I will not let Israel go." 3 Then they said, "The [w]God of the
Hebrews has met with us. Please let us go a three days' journey into the wilderness that we
may sacrifice to the LORD our God, lest he fall upon us with pestilence or with the sword."
4 But the king of Egypt said to them, "Moses and Aaron, why do you take the people away
from their work? Get back to your [x]burdens." 5 And Pharaoh said, "Behold, [y]the people of
the land are now many,[1] and you make them rest from their burdens!" 6 The same day
Pharaoh commanded the [z]taskmasters of the people and their [a]foremen, 7 "You shall no
longer give the people straw to make bricks, as in the past; let them go and gather straw
for themselves. 8 But the number of bricks that they made in the past you shall impose on
them, you shall by no means reduce it, for they are idle. Therefore they cry, 'Let us go and
offer sacrifice to our God.' 9 Let heavier work be laid on the men that they may labor at it
and pay no regard to lying words."

10 So the [b]taskmasters and the foremen of the people went out and said to the people,
"Thus says Pharaoh, 'I will not give you straw. 11 Go and get your straw yourselves wherever you can find it, but your work will not be reduced in the least.'" 12 So the people were
scattered throughout all the land of Egypt to gather stubble for straw. 13 The [c]taskmasters
were urgent, saying, "Complete your work, your daily task each day, as when there was
straw." 14 And the foremen of the people of Israel, whom Pharaoh's [c]taskmasters had set
over them, were beaten and were asked, "Why have you not done all your task of making
bricks today and yesterday, as in the past?"

15 Then the foremen of the people of Israel came and cried to Pharaoh, "Why do you
treat your servants like this? 16 No straw is given to your servants, yet they say to us, 'Make
bricks!' And behold, your servants are beaten; but the fault is in your own people." 17 But
he said, "You are idle, you are idle; that is why you say, 'Let us go and sacrifice to the
LORD.' 18 Go now and work. No straw will be given you, but you must still deliver the
same number of bricks." 19 The foremen of the people of Israel saw that they were in
trouble when they said, "You shall by no means reduce your number of bricks, your daily
task each day." 20 They met Moses and Aaron, who were waiting for them, as they came
out from Pharaoh; 21 and [d]they said to them, "The LORD look on you and judge, because
you have made us stink in the sight of Pharaoh and his servants, and have put a sword
in their hand to kill us."

22 Then Moses turned to the LORD and said, "O Lord, why have you done evil to this
people? Why did you ever send me? 23 For since I came to Pharaoh to speak in your name,
he has done evil to this people, and you have not delivered your people at all."

[1] Samaritan *they are now more numerous than the people of the land*

2 [v]ch. 3:19
3 [w]ch. 3:18; 7:16; 9:1, 13
4 [x]ch. 1:11
5 [y]ch. 1:7, 9
6 [z]ch. 3:7 [a]ver. 14, 15, 19
10 [b]ch. 3:7
13 [c]ch. 3:7
14 [c][See ver. 13 above]
21 [d]ch. 6:9

the Lord's descriptions of what the plagues are to signify for Egypt: "that you may know that I am the LORD" (8:10; see also 7:5, 17; 8:22; 9:14, 29; 10:2; 11:7). The sense of the word "know" here is similar to its use in the declaration that the Lord "knew" Israel's suffering (see 2:25): it is not simply the knower's cognitive recognition or acknowledgment but also the inclination or posture of the knower in relation to what is known. As Pharaoh's opening question makes clear (**"Who is the LORD, that I should obey his voice . . . ?"**), his statement that he does not "know" the Lord is as much about defiance against his claims as it is about ignorance of his identity.

5:3 lest he fall upon us. This reason is not explicitly included in the narrative of what God told Moses to say, although it is clearly implied by the authority of the Lord: Egypt will be held responsible and judged for obstructing Israel's ability to obey.

5:6–8 The role of **taskmasters** is well known from Egyptian texts. An account from the time of Rameses II (13th century B.C.) records that 40 "stable masters" were assigned a quota of 2,000 bricks. The walls of the Rekhmire Chapel in Thebes (15th century B.C.) bear a famous scene that depicts the process of brick making in Egypt.

5:10 Thus says Pharaoh. In contrast to "Thus says the LORD" (see v. 1), Pharaoh is both denying the power of the Lord's words and asserting the authority of his own.

5:15–16 Israel's foremen refer to themselves before Pharaoh as **your servants**, which is highlighted by its repetition and stands in stark contrast to the fact that the Lord has called Israel "my people" (v. 1). In addition to the plagues functioning so that Egypt will know that it is the Lord who acts (see v. 2), the lengthy process to come is also merciful to Israel, for the people are in need of learning to trust the Lord who is at work on their behalf.

5:21 The anger expressed by Israel's foremen is the second instance of resistance to Moses' help and leadership (see 2:14) and another foreshadowing of things to come (see 14:11–12; 15:24; 16:2; 17:2–3).

5:22–6:9 *God Promises to Deliver Israel from Egypt.* After the first audience with Pharaoh results in his defiance and further hardship for Israel (5:1–21), Moses asks the Lord why he has done this (5:22–23) and the Lord responds by emphasizing that he will be present with his people and will bring about their deliverance in faithfulness to his covenant (6:1–9).

5:22–23 Although the Lord had promised that he would deliver his people (3:8) and that Pharaoh would resist letting them go (3:19–20; 4:21), the shape and time frame of the events about to unfold were unknown to Moses. His first encounter with Pharaoh seemed to have brought **evil** (Hb. *ra'a'*, the same word translated "trouble" in 5:19) by making Israel's situation and Pharaoh's disposition worse than it had been.

God Promises Deliverance

6 But the LORD said to Moses, "Now you shall see what I will do to Pharaoh; for with a
strong hand he will send them out, and with [e]a strong hand he will [f]drive them out
of his land."
2God spoke to Moses and said to him, [g]"I am the LORD. **3**I appeared to Abraham, to Isaac,
and to Jacob, as [h]God Almighty,[1] but by my name the [i]LORD I did not make myself known
to them. **4**[j]I also established my covenant with them [k]to give them the land of Canaan, the
land in which they lived as sojourners. **5**Moreover, [l]I have heard the groaning of the people
of Israel whom the Egyptians hold as slaves, and I have remembered my covenant. **6**Say
therefore to the people of Israel, [m]'I am the LORD, and [n]I will bring you out from under the
burdens of the Egyptians, and I will deliver you from slavery to them, and [o]I will redeem
you with an outstretched arm and with great acts of judgment. **7**I [p]will take you to be my
people, and [q]I will be your God, and you shall know that [m]I am the LORD your God, who
has brought you out [n]from under the burdens of the Egyptians. **8**I will bring you into
[r]the land that I [s]swore to give to Abraham, to Isaac, and to Jacob. I will give it to you for a
possession. [m]I am the LORD.'" **9**Moses spoke thus to the people of Israel, but they [t]did not
listen to Moses, because of their broken spirit and harsh slavery.
10So the LORD said to Moses, **11**"Go in, tell Pharaoh king of Egypt to let the people of
Israel go out of his land." **12**But Moses said to the LORD, "Behold, the people of Israel
have [t]not listened to me. How then shall Pharaoh listen to me, for [u]I am of uncircumcised lips?" **13**But the LORD spoke to Moses and Aaron and gave them a charge about the
people of Israel and about Pharaoh king of Egypt: to bring the people of Israel out of
the land of Egypt.

[1] Hebrew *El Shaddai*

Chapter 6
1[e]ch. 3:19; 13:3 [f]ch. 11:1; 12:33, 39
2[g][Isa. 42:8; Mal. 3:6]
3[h]Gen. 17:1 [i]Ps. 68:4; 83:18; [John 8:58; Rev. 1:4, 8]
4[j]Gen. 15:18; 17:4, 7 [k]Gen. 17:8; 28:4
5[l]ch. 2:24
6[m][Isa. 42:8; Mal. 3:6] [n]ch. 7:4; Deut. 26:8; Ps. 136:11, 12; [ch. 3:17] [o]ch. 15:13; Deut. 7:8; 2 Kgs. 17:36; 1 Chr. 17:21; Neh. 1:10
7[p]Deut. 4:20; 7:6; 14:2; 26:18; 2 Sam. 7:24; [1 Pet. 2:9] [q]ch. 29:45, 46; Gen. 17:8; Lev. 22:33; Deut. 29:13; [Rev. 21:7] [m][See ver. 6 above] [n][See ver. 6 above]
8[r]ch. 32:13; Gen. 15:18; 26:3; 28:13; 35:12; Ezek. 20:6, 42 [s][Gen. 14:22; Deut. 32:40; Ezek. 20:5, 6; 47:14] [m][See ver. 6 above]
9[t]ch. 5:21; [Acts 7:25]
12[t][See ver. 9 above] [u]ver. 30; ch. 4:10; Jer. 1:6; [Jer. 6:10; Ezek. 44:7]

6:1–9 The Lord reaffirms to Moses (see 5:22–23) that he will bring his people out of Egypt, which is emphasized throughout this section by the numerous first-person statements (e.g., **I will bring you out . . . I will deliver you . . . and I will redeem you**; 6:6).

6:1 With a strong hand refers to what **the LORD** will do in order to bring Israel out of Egypt (which 3:19–20 and 13:3 make explicit), not to the manner in which Pharaoh will send them. The Hebrew verb translated **"he will send them out"** is also translated "he will let you go" (3:20) and is the same verb (*shallakh*) used repeatedly in the command to Pharaoh, "Let my people go" (e.g., 8:1).

6:2–8 The repeated declaration of God's presence and identity, **"I am the LORD,"** frames the section (vv. 2, 6, 8) and emphasizes the significance of the plagues for Israel: the same **God Almighty** who made a covenant with **Abraham**, **Isaac**, and **Jacob** (vv. 3–4) has heard the cries of their descendants and **remembered** his covenant (v. 5); he is the one who revealed himself to Moses (see 3:14–15) and who will bring them out of Egypt into the land he had promised to their fathers (6:6–8). Regarding the stress here on the Lord's faithfulness, see further "I will be with you" in 3:12 and the note on 3:14.

6:3–8 I appeared. God did indeed appear to Abraham, Isaac, and Jacob, as indicated in a number of places in Genesis (e.g., Gen. 24:3, 7, 12; 26:22; 27:27; 28:21). **but by my name the LORD I did not make myself known to them**. In light of this statement, some have suggested that the patriarchs did not actually know the name Yahweh. It is probably best, however, to understand this statement as explaining that the patriarchs did not fully understand and experience the essential character of God as represented by the name Yahweh ("the LORD"), as this was first understood more fully by Moses when the Lord appeared to him at the burning bush (see Ex. 3:1–22). Thus in 3:12–15 God had revealed himself to Moses in a far deeper way, promising Moses, "I will be with you," and revealing the significance of his covenant identity as Yahweh ("the LORD"). Here then (in 6:6–8), God reaffirms his commitment to his people and his covenant identity in repeated affirmations, stating three times that he is **the LORD**—that is, he is the God of the covenant who will act in a decisive way on behalf of his people: "I will bring you out" (v. 6); "I will deliver you" (v. 6); "I will redeem you" (v. 6); "I will take you to be my people" (v. 7); "I will be your God" (v. 7); "I will bring you into the land" (v. 8); and "I will give it to you for a possession" (v. 8).

6:6 redeem. See note on 15:13.

6:7 When the Lord says, **"I will take you to be my people, and I will be your God,"** he is expressing the central idea of Israel's relationship with him (see Deut. 4:20; 7:6). He will bring them into a personal relationship with himself, a relationship of great blessing, protection, and joy. When he says, **"and you shall know that I am the LORD your God,"** he is indicating that he will reveal himself to Israel through his acts on their behalf (see Ex. 10:2). This expression, common in Exodus, is called the "recognition formula"; see note on 7:5. Although it is addressed to Israel here, several similar statements (without the designation "your God") are directed to Pharaoh during the course of the plagues (see 5:2; 7:5, 17).

6:10–30 *Moses and Aaron: Narrative Synopses and Genealogy.* The genealogy of Moses and Aaron (vv. 14–25) is framed by opening and closing sections, which nearly mirror each other (vv. 10–13, 26–30). The function of the genealogy is to preserve the particular history of Moses and Aaron as the ones through whom the Lord brought Israel out of Egypt (as vv. 26–27 make clear) and also of Aaron's sons who would become the heads of the priestly line in Israel (vv. 23, 25).

6:10–13 The content of this section is repeated in vv. 26–30, but reversed in sequence:

Moses (vv. 10–12)
  Moses and Aaron (v. 13)
    genealogy (vv. 14–25)
  Aaron and Moses (vv. 26–27)
Moses (vv. 28–30).

Aside from highlighting the genealogy, the shape of this frame also appears to emphasize the particular role of Moses as the one who interacts directly with the Lord (vv. 10–12, 28–30) in addition to his role with Aaron in carrying out what the Lord commands (vv. 13, 26–27).

6:12 I am of uncircumcised lips (cf. v. 30). It is difficult to determine whether Moses intends something significantly different from his plea of being "slow of speech and of tongue" (4:10). The vocabulary may be meant to evoke the incident involving circumcision in 4:24–26. If so, Moses could be implying that he feels not only physically unable to speak (4:10) but also personally unfit or "unclean" to fulfill the task (cf. Isa. 6:5).

The Genealogy of Moses and Aaron

14 These are the heads of their fathers' houses: the [v]sons of Reuben, the firstborn of
Israel: Hanoch, Pallu, Hezron, and Carmi; these are the clans of Reuben. 15 The [w]sons of
Simeon: Jemuel, Jamin, Ohad, Jachin, Zohar, and Shaul, the son of a Canaanite woman;
these are the clans of Simeon. 16 These are the names of the [x]sons of Levi according to
their generations: Gershon, Kohath, and Merari, the years of the life of Levi being 137
years. 17 The [y]sons of Gershon: Libni and Shimei, by their clans. 18 The [z]sons of Kohath:
Amram, Izhar, Hebron, and Uzziel, the years of the life of Kohath being 133 years. 19 The
[a]sons of Merari: Mahli and Mushi. These are the clans of the Levites according to their
generations. 20 [b]Amram took as his wife Jochebed his father's sister, and she bore him Aaron
and Moses, the years of the life of Amram being 137 years. 21 [c]The sons of Izhar: Korah,
Nepheg, and Zichri. 22 The [d]sons of Uzziel: Mishael, Elzaphan, and Sithri. 23 Aaron took
as his wife Elisheba, the daughter of [e]Amminadab and the sister of [f]Nahshon, and she
bore him [g]Nadab, Abihu, Eleazar, and Ithamar. 24 The [h]sons of Korah: Assir, Elkanah, and
Abiasaph; these are the clans of the Korahites. 25 Eleazar, Aaron's son, took as his wife one
of the daughters of Putiel, and [i]she bore him Phinehas. These are the heads of the fathers'
houses of the Levites by their clans.

26 These are the Aaron and Moses [j]to whom the LORD said: "Bring out the people of Israel
from the land of Egypt [k]by their hosts." 27 It was they who spoke to Pharaoh king of Egypt
about bringing out the people of Israel from Egypt, this Moses and this Aaron.

28 On the day when the LORD spoke to Moses in the land of Egypt, 29 the LORD said to
Moses, [l]"I am the LORD; [m]tell Pharaoh king of Egypt all that I say to you." 30 But Moses said
to the LORD, "Behold, [n]I am of uncircumcised lips. How will Pharaoh listen to me?"

Moses and Aaron Before Pharaoh

7 And the LORD said to Moses, "See, I have made you like [o]God to Pharaoh, and your
brother Aaron shall be your [p]prophet. 2 [q]You shall speak all that I command you, and
your brother Aaron shall tell Pharaoh to let the people of Israel go out of his land. 3 But [r]I
will harden Pharaoh's heart, and though I [s]multiply my signs and wonders in the land of
Egypt, 4 Pharaoh will not listen to you. Then I will lay my hand on Egypt and bring my
hosts, my people the children of Israel, out of the land of Egypt by great acts of judgment.
5 The Egyptians [t]shall know that I am the LORD, when I stretch out my hand against Egypt
and bring out the people of Israel from among them." 6 Moses and Aaron did so; they did
just as the LORD commanded them. 7 Now Moses was [u]eighty years old, and Aaron eighty-
three years old, when they spoke to Pharaoh.

8 Then the LORD said to Moses and Aaron, 9 "When Pharaoh says to you, [v]'Prove yourselves

14 [v]Gen. 46:9; 1 Chr. 5:3
15 [w]Gen. 46:10; 1 Chr. 4:24
16 [x]Gen. 46:11; Num. 3:17; 1 Chr. 6:1, 16
17 [y]Num. 3:18; 1 Chr. 6:17; 23:7
18 [z]Num. 3:19; 26:57; 1 Chr. 6:2, 18
19 [a]Num. 3:20; 1 Chr. 6:19; 23:21
20 [b]See ch. 2:1
21 [c]Num. 16:1; 1 Chr. 6:37, 38
22 [d]Lev. 10:4; Num. 3:30
23 [e]Ruth 4:19, 20; 1 Chr. 2:10; Matt. 1:4; Luke 3:33 [f]Num. 1:7; 2:3; 7:12, 17; 10:14; Matt. 1:4; Luke 3:32 [g]Lev. 10:1; Num. 3:2; 26:60; 1 Chr. 6:3; 24:1
24 [h]1 Chr. 6:22, 23, 37
25 [i]Num. 25:7, 11; Josh. 24:33; Ps. 106:30
26 [j]ver. 13 [k]ch. 7:4; 12:17, 51; Num. 33:1
29 [l]See ver. 2 [m]ver. 11; [ch. 7:2]
30 [n][Isa. 6:5]; See ver. 12

Chapter 7

1 [o]ch. 4:16 [p]Gen. 20:7; [1 Sam. 9:9]
2 [q][ch. 4:15; 6:29]
3 [r]See ch. 4:21 [s]ch. 11:9; Ps. 135:9; See Ps. 78:43-51; 105:26-36
5 [t]ver. 17; ch. 8:10, 22; 14:4, 18
7 [u][Deut. 29:5; 31:2; 34:7; Acts 7:23, 30]
9 [v][Isa. 7:11; John 2:18; 4:48; 6:30]

6:14–25 The beginning of the genealogy looks as if the sons or **heads** of the household of Jacob's sons will be listed in the order of their birth (v. 14a). However, after naming the sons of **Reuben** (v. 14b) and **Simeon** (v. 15), it stops to focus on the **sons of Levi** (v. 16) and in particular on **Aaron, Moses** (v. 20), and Aaron's sons (vv. 23, 25). The genealogy functions primarily to preserve (1) the family history of Moses and Aaron as the ones through whom the Lord led Israel out of Egypt, and (2) the history of Aaron's sons as those who were called to be priests in Israel (see 28:1). Other figures in the genealogy are likely included because of their roles in events narrated in the book of Numbers: the **sons of Korah** (Ex. 6:24) eventually become jealous of Aaron's role as priest and rebel (Num. 16:1–50); and Aaron's grandson **Phinehas** (Ex. 6:25) is later noted for his act of faithfulness in relation to Israel's Baal worship at Peor (Num. 25:1–9). Like many Biblical genealogies, this one does not aim to include every single generation. It only lists four generations from Jacob to Moses (Levi-Kohath-Amram-Moses); compare 1 Chronicles 7, which lists 12 generations from Jacob to Joshua.

6:26–27 These verses are structured to highlight the central statement that it was this particular Moses and Aaron who went before Pharaoh.

7:1–7 *Moses Encouraged.* The Lord reaffirms several things from his earlier conversations with Moses: he has provided Aaron to act like Moses' **prophet** in speaking to Pharaoh (7:1–2; see 4:16); he will **harden Pharaoh's heart** (7:3; see 4:21); and he will bring Israel out of Egypt by his **hand** (7:4–5; see 3:19–20).

7:5 The Egyptians shall know that I am the LORD. This statement recalls Pharaoh's earlier response ("Who is the LORD . . . ? I do not know the LORD . . ."; see 5:2) and is repeated as an explicit purpose of the plagues (see 7:17; 8:10, 22; 14:4, 18). In English, this phrase might seem simply equivalent to the Egyptians knowing "that I am God." While the plagues surely signify this, the Hebrew term translated as "the LORD" is the name by which God revealed himself to Moses at the burning bush (3:14–15) and thus refers to the Egyptians knowing who he is, namely, "that I am Yahweh," Israel's covenant God. While the successive plague narratives offer further descriptions of Yahweh (see 8:10, 22; 9:14, 29; 11:7), their central purpose is to focus on his self-revelation through his mighty acts. This "recognition formula" describes the Lord's revealing himself as Israel's God, to both Israel (6:7; 10:2; 16:12; 29:46; cf. Deut. 4:35; 7:9) and Egypt (Ex. 7:5, 17; 8:22; 14:4, 18). Outside of Exodus, the recognition formula is common in Ezekiel, where God vindicates himself, especially before his unbelieving people, but also before the nations (e.g., Ezek. 28:22; 36:23).

7:8–15:21 *Plagues and Exodus.* This section includes the initial sign that Moses and Aaron perform before Pharaoh (7:8–13), the nine plagues (7:14–10:29) leading up to the lengthy account and instructions surrounding the tenth plague and the exodus (11:1–13:16), and the crossing of the Red Sea and subsequent celebration (13:17–15:21).

7:8–13 *Moses and Aaron before Pharaoh: Initial Sign.* Although Moses and Aaron had already requested that Pharaoh let Israel go (see 5:1–3), they had not yet performed any of the signs the Lord had given them. This section

by working a miracle,' then you shall say to Aaron, 'Take your staff and cast it down before
Pharaoh, that it may become a serpent.'" [10]So Moses and Aaron went to Pharaoh and did
just as the LORD commanded. Aaron cast down his staff before Pharaoh and his servants,
and it became a serpent. [11]Then Pharaoh summoned the wise men and the sorcerers, and
they, the [w]magicians of Egypt, also [x]did the same by their secret arts. [12]For each man cast
down his staff, and they became serpents. But Aaron's staff swallowed up their staffs. [13]Still
[r]Pharaoh's heart was hardened, and he would not listen to them, [r]as the LORD had said.

The First Plague: Water Turned to Blood

[14]Then the LORD said to Moses, "Pharaoh's heart is hardened; he refuses to let the people
go. [15][y]Go to Pharaoh in the morning, as he is going out to the water. Stand on the bank
of the Nile to meet him, and take in your hand [z]the staff that turned into a [a]serpent.
[16]And you shall say to him, 'The [b]LORD, the God of the Hebrews, sent me to you, saying,
"Let my people go, [c]that they may serve me in the wilderness." But so far, you have not
obeyed. [17]Thus says the LORD, "By this [d]you shall know that I am the LORD: behold, with
the staff that is in my hand I will strike the water that is in the Nile, and [e]it shall turn
into blood. [18]The fish in the Nile shall die, and the Nile will stink, and the Egyptians will
[f]grow weary of drinking water from the Nile."'" [19]And the LORD said to Moses, "Say to
Aaron, 'Take your staff and [g]stretch out your hand over the waters of Egypt, over their
rivers, their canals, and their ponds, and all their pools of water, so that they may become
blood, and there shall be blood throughout all the land of Egypt, even in vessels of wood
and in vessels of stone.'"

[20]Moses and Aaron did as the LORD commanded. In the sight of Pharaoh and in the
sight of his servants he [h]lifted up the staff and struck the water in the Nile, and all the
[i]water in the Nile turned into blood. [21]And the fish in the Nile died, and the Nile stank,
so that the Egyptians [j]could not drink water from the Nile. There was blood throughout
all the land of Egypt. [22]But [k]the magicians of Egypt did the same by their secret arts. So

11[w]Gen. 41:8 [x]ver. 12, 22; ch. 8:7, 18; 9:11; 2 Tim. 3:8
13[r][See ver. 3 above]
15[y]ch. 8:20; 9:13 [z]ch. 4:2, 17; 17:5 [a]ch. 4:3
16[b]ch. 3:18; 5:3; 9:1, 13 [c]ch. 3:12, 18; 5:1, 3
17[d]ver. 5 [e]ch. 4:9; [Rev. 16:4]
18[f]ver. 21, 24
19[g]ch. 8:5, 6, 16, 17; 9:22; 10:12, 21; 14:16, 21, 26
20[h]ch. 17:9 [i]Ps. 78:44; 105:29
21[j]ver. 18, 24
22[k]ver. 11

narrates briefly an initial sign that precedes the plagues: Aaron's staff turns into a serpent.

7:9 The **staff** signifies for Moses and Aaron that God is the one working the signs through them on Israel's behalf (see 4:1–17), and it will continue to serve in this manner throughout the plagues to come. See chart, p. 156.

7:11–12 This is the first of three times where the **magicians of Egypt** see the sign that Aaron performs and then do **the same by their secret arts** (also v. 22; 8:7). The Hebrew word translated "magician" is most likely derived from an Egyptian title that refers to a lector priest: someone who acted as a magician in service to the gods of Egypt and was also considered a teacher of wisdom. Egyptian texts are filled with descriptions of priests performing extraordinary feats, including turning inanimate objects into animals. Talc 2 of the Westcar Papyrus tells of a priest who made a wax crocodile that came to life when he threw it in a lake. The narrative of Exodus does not seek to provide any further explanation of the means by which the magicians performed these signs (whether by trickery, evil supernatural powers, a combination of these, etc.). In each case, the description focuses instead on events that indicate that, although the magicians were able to wield or utilize power to perform the sign, they did not have mastery or authority over it. Here, this is shown by the fact that **Aaron's staff swallowed up their staffs**.

7:13 The recurring references to the hardness of **Pharaoh's heart** signify that the Lord is sovereign over and governs the events (see 4:21; 7:3; and chart, p. 151), that Pharaoh is held responsible for his refusal to acknowledge what the signs reveal (see also 8:15, 32), and also that the readers or hearers of Exodus are being called to see these things and to keep from hardening their own hearts. Psalm 95 uses this phrase from the exodus narrative to warn Israel in its worship ("do not harden your hearts," Ps. 95:8) and subsequently, the book of Hebrews uses Psalm 95 to call the church to continue in Christ by faith (Heb. 3:7–4:13).

7:14–25 *First Plague: Water to Blood.* After separate instances in which Moses and Aaron made the initial request to let Israel go (5:1–3) and performed the first sign of the Lord's power (7:8–13), the Lord now instructs them to warn Pharaoh that his failure to let Israel go will result in a sign that bears not only the evidence of the Lord's power but also the physical effects of the Lord's judgment on Egypt.

7:14 Then the LORD said to Moses. This phrase heads the narrative of each plague (see 8:1, 16, 20; 9:1, 8, 13; 10:1, 21; 11:1). It not only indicates the sequence of the plagues but also signifies that the events are governed by the word of the Lord spoken to Moses. **Pharaoh's heart is hardened**. Even before the first plague, the Lord said he would harden Pharaoh's heart (4:21; 7:3), and in response to the sign of Aaron's staff, Pharaoh signified the state of his heart by refusing to listen (7:13).

7:15 Since **the Nile** was the water in which Moses was most likely placed by his mother and drawn out of by Pharaoh's daughter (2:1–10), there may be intentional irony in the fact that through Moses the first plague will affect the waters of the Nile.

7:16 The LORD, the God of the Hebrews. The Lord identifies himself with the people of Israel even though they are slaves (see note on 3:18), referring to them also as **"my people"** (cf. 3:7). To the king of a powerful nation like Egypt, the Lord's identification with an enslaved people would seem to indicate that he had no power or authority to make such a request. However, the Lord will reveal through the plagues and exodus that he has power over all the earth (see 9:14, 29) and that his deliverance of Israel stems from his steadfast love for them and faithfulness to his covenant promises and not to Israel's size, wealth, or power as a nation (cf. Deut. 7:6–11).

7:17 By this you shall know that I am the LORD. Although this statement and the others like it (8:10, 22; 9:14, 29; 10:2) are most often spoken to Pharaoh and Egypt (7:5; 14:4, 8), it first appears in Exodus where the Lord is speaking to Moses about Israel (6:7).

7:19 even in vessels of wood and . . . stone. The extent of the first plague shows that it cannot be explained simply as the result of natural causes.

7:22–25 This is the second time that the **magicians** are described as having done **the same by their secret arts** (v. 22; see also vv. 11–12 and note; 8:7). The repeated vocabulary highlights the effects of this on Pharaoh, whose **heart remained hardened** (7:22; see v. 14) and who did not take the sign or what it signified **to heart** (v. 23). The description of the Egyptian people digging for water (v. 24) and the time frame of **seven full days** (v. 25) indicate what was being shown to Pharaoh: although the magicians repeated the sign, they did not have the power to reverse the effects of the plague or to cleanse the water of the Nile.

[l]Pharaoh's heart remained hardened, and he would not listen to them, as [m]the LORD had
said. 23 Pharaoh turned and went into his house, and he did not take even this to heart.
24 And all the Egyptians dug along the Nile for water to drink, for they could not drink
the water of the Nile.
25 Seven full days passed after the LORD had struck the Nile.

The Second Plague: Frogs

8 [1] Then the LORD said to Moses, "Go in to Pharaoh and say to him, 'Thus says the LORD,
"Let my people go, that [n]they may serve me. 2 But if you [o]refuse to let them go, behold,
I will plague all your country with [p]frogs. 3 The Nile shall swarm with frogs that shall
come up into your house and into [q]your bedroom and on your bed and into the houses of
your servants and your people,[2] and into your ovens and your kneading bowls. 4 The frogs
shall come up on you and on your people and on all your servants."'" 5 [3] And the LORD
said to Moses, "Say to Aaron, [r]'Stretch out your hand with your staff over the rivers, over
the canals and over the pools, and make frogs come up on the land of Egypt!'" 6 So Aaron
stretched out his hand over the waters of Egypt, and [s]the frogs came up and covered the
land of Egypt. 7 But [t]the magicians did the same by their secret arts and made frogs come
up on the land of Egypt.

[1] Ch 7:26 in Hebrew [2] Or *among your people* [3] Ch 8:1 in Hebrew

22 [l]ver. 13 [m]ver. 3, 4
Chapter 8
1 [n]ver. 20; ch. 3:12, 18
2 [o]ch. 7:14; 9:2 [p][Rev. 16:13]
3 [q]Ps. 105:30
5 [r]See ch. 7:19
6 [s]Ps. 78:45; 105:30
7 [t]See ch. 7:11

8:1–15 *Second Plague: Frogs.* After Pharaoh's refusal to heed the sign of the water of the Nile turned to blood, the Lord commands Moses and Aaron to perform a second plague, also from the Nile: frogs will come up to cover the land (vv. 1–7). Although Pharaoh recognizes the power represented in the plague and pleads with Moses, he further hardens his heart when there is relief from its effects (vv. 8–15).

8:3–4 The account of the second plague emphasizes that the effects will extend beyond the water of the Nile: the frogs will come up **into** the **house**, **bedroom**, and **bed**, into the **ovens** and **kneading bowls**, and even **on** all of the inhabitants of Egypt.

8:7 This is the third time that the magicians observed the sign Aaron performed and then **did the same by their secret arts** (see 7:11–12 and note; 7:22). In each case, the narrator offers no further comment or qualification of the magicians' work but instead focuses on how the following events illustrate the supremacy of the Lord's power. Part of the narrative tension is that Pharaoh and his court begin to recognize some of what is being revealed, though

The Battle between Yahweh and the Rulers of Egypt

Exodus records the instructions and events of the plagues for the purpose of showing how the Lord revealed both his person and his power through delivering Israel from Egypt. The plagues fall on areas of life supposedly protected by Egypt's gods, thus demonstrating the Lord's power over the gods of the world's mightiest nation. The narrative of the plagues is therefore not necessarily an exhaustive account of everything that happened but is shaped in order to communicate the aspects of each plague that are necessary for its purpose. For example, the section describing the third plague (8:16–19) does not record either the instruction or the event of Moses and Aaron going before Pharaoh, but the fact that the magicians seek to reproduce the sign (v. 18) indicates that it is likely they performed it initially in the presence of Pharaoh and his court. Each of the sections on the third, sixth, and ninth plagues are similar in their brevity and style, which also lends to the shape of three cycles of three plagues leading up to the tenth and final plague.

	Type of Plague	Reference	Warning?	Time of Warning	Instruction	Agent	Staff?	Pharaoh promises to let people go?	Pharaoh's heart hardened?
1st Cycle	1. Nile to blood	7:14–25	Yes	In the morning	Go to Pharaoh; Stand	Aaron	Yes	–	Yes
	2. Frogs from the Nile	8:1–15	Yes	–	Go in to Pharaoh	Aaron	Yes	Yes	Yes
	3. Dust to gnats	8:16–19	–	–	–	Aaron	Yes	–	Yes
2nd Cycle	4. Flies	8:20–32	Yes	Early in the morning	Present yourself to Pharaoh	God	–	Yes	Yes
	5. Egyptian livestock die	9:1–7	Yes	–	Go in to Pharaoh	God	–	–	Yes
	6. Boils	9:8–12	–	–	–	Moses	–	–	Yes
3rd Cycle	7. Hail	9:13–35	Yes	Early in the morning	Present yourself before Pharaoh	Moses	–	Yes	Yes
	8. Locusts	10:1–20	Yes	–	Go in to Pharaoh	Moses	Yes	Yes	Yes
	9. Darkness	10:21–29	–	–	–	Moses	Yes	Yes	Yes
	10. Death of firstborn	11:1–10; 12:29–32	Yes	–	–	God	Yes	Yes	Yes

8 Then Pharaoh called Moses and Aaron and said, [u]"Plead with the LORD to take away the
frogs from me and from my people, and [v]I will let the people go to sacrifice to the LORD."
9 Moses said to Pharaoh, "Be pleased to command me when [u]I am to plead for you and for
your servants and for your people, that the frogs be cut off from you and your houses and
be left only in the Nile." **10** And he said, "Tomorrow." Moses said, "Be it as you say, so [w]that
you may know that [x]there is no one like the LORD our God. **11** The frogs shall go away from
you and your houses and your servants and your people. They shall be left only in the Nile."
12 So Moses and Aaron went out from Pharaoh, and Moses cried to the LORD about the
frogs, as he had agreed with Pharaoh.[1] **13** And the LORD did according to the word of Moses.
The frogs died out in the houses, the courtyards, and the fields. **14** And they gathered them
together in heaps, and the land stank. **15** But when Pharaoh saw that there was a [y]respite,
he [z]hardened his heart and would not listen to them, as the LORD had said.

The Third Plague: Gnats

16 Then the LORD said to Moses, "Say to Aaron, [a]'Stretch out your staff and strike the
dust of the earth, so that it may become gnats in all the land of Egypt.'" **17** And they did
so. Aaron stretched out his hand with his staff and struck the dust of the earth, and [b]there
were gnats on man and beast. All the dust of the earth became gnats in all the land of
Egypt. **18** The [c]magicians tried by their secret arts to produce gnats, but they could not. So
there were gnats on man and beast. **19** Then the magicians said to Pharaoh, "This is [d]the
finger of God." But Pharaoh's heart was hardened, and he would not listen to them, as
the LORD had said.

The Fourth Plague: Flies

20 Then the LORD said to Moses, [e]"Rise up early in the morning and present yourself to
Pharaoh, as he goes out to the water, and say to him, 'Thus says the LORD, [f]"Let my people
go, that they may serve me. **21** Or else, if you will not let my people go, behold, I will send
swarms of flies on you and your servants and your people, and into your houses. And the
houses of the Egyptians shall be filled with swarms of flies, and also the ground on which
they stand. **22** But on that day [g]I will set apart the land of Goshen, where my people dwell,

[1] *Or which he had brought upon Pharaoh*

8 [u]ver. 28, 30; ch. 9:28; 10:17, 18; [Num. 21:7; 1 Kgs. 13:6; Acts 8:24] [v]ver. 25-28; ch. 10:8, 24; 12:31, 32
9 [u][See ver. 8 above]
10 [w]ver. 22; ch. 7:17 [x]ch. 9:14; Deut. 33:26; 2 Sam. 7:22; 1 Chr. 17:20; Ps. 86:8; Isa. 46:9; Jer. 10:6, 7
15 [y][Eccles. 8:11] [z]ver. 32; ch. 7:14; 9:7, 34; 10:1
16 [a]See ch. 7:19
17 [b]Ps. 105:31
18 [c]See ch. 7:11
19 [d]ch. 31:18; Ps. 8:3; Luke 11:20
20 [e]ch. 7:15; 9:13 [f]ver. 1
22 [g]ch. 9:4; 11:7; [Mal. 3:18]

Pharaoh will never fully relent even in light of all the plagues and even after the death of his own firstborn son.

8:8 Pharaoh's request that Moses and Aaron **plead with the LORD to take away the frogs** (v. 8) represents a tacit admission that the magicians of Egypt were powerless to do this (see v. 7). Pharaoh acted as if it were *his* prerogative to keep Israel or to **let the people go**, but his request to Moses is also an implicit admission that this power belonged to the Lord alone.

8:12 Moses cried to the LORD on Egypt's behalf, in accord with the stipulations he had allowed Pharaoh to set (vv. 9–11). Moses' intercession for Egypt (v. 29; 9:33; 10:18) prepares for and prefigures the way that he will intercede on Israel's behalf once they have gone out of Egypt (see 15:25; 17:4; 32:11–14; 33:12–16).

8:13 The fact that **the LORD did according to the word of Moses** stands in distinct contrast to the inefficacy of the magicians of Egypt.

8:14–15 Although Pharaoh **hardened his heart** in light of the relief from the frogs (v. 15), it is the people of Egypt who must clean up the mess (just as they had to dig for water after the first plague). **The land stank** (v. 14) would have been a potent reason to question whether their king had made the right choice. The disastrous effects of Pharaoh's refusal to heed the warnings of the plagues become gradually more evident to those who are suffering because of his disobedience (see v. 19; 10:7).

8:15 The narrative of each plague opens with the phrase "and the LORD said to Moses" (see 7:14); the fulfillment of the plague or the hardening of Pharaoh's heart is often followed by the phrase **"as the LORD had said"** (see 7:13, 22; 8:19; also 9:12, 35), further underscoring that the events are governed by the word of the Lord.

8:16–19 *Third Plague: Gnats.* The description of the third plague is sparse and similar to those of the sixth (9:8–12) and ninth plagues (10:21–29), which are also brief and begin with the Lord's instruction to Moses about the plague itself (see chart, p. 156). The brevity of this section brings the response of the magicians into sharp focus (8:18–19).

8:18–19 Up to this point the **magicians** of Egypt had been able to use **their secret arts** to replicate the signs done by Aaron (see 7:11–12 and note; 7:22; 8:7). In each case they had been unable to overpower the sign (the serpents) or reverse its effects (water to blood; frogs on the land). But now that they are unable to produce gnats from dust they say to Pharaoh, **"This is the finger of God"** (v. 19). The narrative of the plagues highlights the way that some of Pharaoh's servants (see also 10:7) begin to recognize what he fails to see: the God who sent Moses and Aaron has shown that he has power over Egypt and that Pharaoh's persistent defiance is harming his own people.

8:20–32 *Fourth Plague: Flies.* The fourth plague is the first to focus on the distinction between the effects on Egypt and on Israel (vv. 22–24). Although Pharaoh has been reluctant to acknowledge either the damage caused by the plagues or what they represent, he begins to plead with Moses more often in order to gain relief (see v. 8) while still refusing to listen to the command to let Israel go.

8:20–21 In the Lord's message to Pharaoh he refers to Israel as **my people** (v. 20; see 3:7) and to Egypt as **your people** (8:21) and prefigures the distinction he will make (in the fourth plague) between Israel and Egypt (vv. 22–24).

8:22 The **land of Goshen** (perhaps the area of the eastern delta in Egypt) was originally given to Jacob and his family by the pharaoh who had known and honored Joseph (Gen. 47:4–6; cf. Gen. 45:10; 46:28). He had given the Israelites this territory in part because they and their means of livelihood were abhorrent to the Egyptians (see Gen. 43:32; 46:34). The distinction that the Lord will make between Goshen and Egypt would have seemed entirely contrary to what the Egyptians considered to be the worth of each nation. **that you may know that I am the LORD in the midst of the earth**. The Lord states repeatedly that the plagues have the purpose that Pharaoh (and the Egyptians) would know who he is (see note on Ex. 7:5). Both translation

so that no swarms of flies shall be there, [h]that you may know that I am the LORD in the
midst of the earth.[1] 23 Thus I will put a division[2] between my people and your people.
Tomorrow this sign shall happen."'" 24 And the LORD did so. [i]There came great swarms
of flies into the house of Pharaoh and into his servants' houses. Throughout all the land
of Egypt the land was ruined by the swarms of flies.
25 Then Pharaoh called Moses and Aaron and said, "Go, sacrifice to your God within the
land." 26 But Moses said, "It would not be right to do so, for the offerings we shall sacrifice
to the LORD our God are an [j]abomination to the Egyptians. If we sacrifice offerings [j]abomi-
nable to the Egyptians before their eyes, will they not stone us? 27 We must go [k]three days'
journey into the wilderness and sacrifice to the LORD our God [l]as he tells us." 28 So Pharaoh
said, "I will let you go to sacrifice to the LORD your God in the wilderness; only you must
not go very far away. [m]Plead for me." 29 Then Moses said, "Behold, I am going out from
you and I will plead with the LORD that the swarms of flies may depart from Pharaoh,
from his servants, and from his people, tomorrow. Only let not Pharaoh [n]cheat again by
not letting the people go to sacrifice to the LORD." 30 So Moses went out from Pharaoh and
prayed to the LORD. 31 And the LORD did as Moses asked, and removed the swarms of flies
from Pharaoh, from his servants, and from his people; not one remained. 32 But Pharaoh
[o]hardened his heart this time also, and did not let the people go.

The Fifth Plague: Egyptian Livestock Die

9 Then the LORD said to Moses, [p]"Go in to Pharaoh and say to him, 'Thus says [q]the LORD,
the God of the Hebrews, "Let my people go, that they may serve me. 2 For if you refuse to
let them go and still hold them, 3 behold, [r]the hand of the LORD will fall with a very severe
plague upon your livestock that are in the field, the horses, the donkeys, the camels, the
herds, and the flocks. 4 [s]But the LORD will make a distinction between the livestock of Israel
and the livestock of Egypt, so that nothing of all that belongs to the people of Israel shall
die."'" 5 And the LORD set a time, saying, "Tomorrow the LORD will do this thing in the
land." 6 And the next day the LORD did this thing. [t]All the livestock of the Egyptians died,
but not one of the livestock of the people of Israel died. 7 And Pharaoh sent, and behold,
not one of the livestock of Israel was dead. But [u]the heart of Pharaoh was hardened, and
he did not let the people go.

The Sixth Plague: Boils

8 And the LORD said to Moses and Aaron, "Take handfuls of soot from the kiln, and let
Moses throw them in the air in the sight of Pharaoh. 9 It shall become fine dust over all the
land of Egypt, and become [v]boils breaking out in sores on man and beast throughout all

[1] *Or that I the LORD am in the land* [2] Septuagint, Vulgate; Hebrew *set redemption*

22 [h]ver. 10; ch. 7:17
24 [i]Ps. 78:45; 105:31; [Isa. 7:18]
26 [j][Gen. 43:32; 46:34]
27 [k]ch. 3:18 [l]ch. 3:12
28 [m]See ver. 8
29 [n]ver. 15; [Jer. 42:20, 21]
32 [o]ver. 15

Chapter 9

1 [p]ch. 8:1, 2 [q]See ch. 7:16
3 [r]ch. 7:4
4 [s]ch. 8:22; 11:7
6 [t][ver. 19]
7 [u]ch. 7:14
9 [v]Lev. 13:18; Deut. 28:27; 2 Kgs. 20:7; Job 2:7; Isa. 38:21; Rev. 16:2

options for this phrase (see ESV footnote on 8:22) focus on the identity (see 3:14–15) and presence (see 6:2–8) of Yahweh, who is at work on behalf of his people.

8:25–27 When Pharaoh offers the qualified response that Israel may go and serve God **within the land** (v. 25), Moses responds first with the logistical problems that should have been obvious to Pharaoh (v. 26) before he gives the reason that really governs his inability to accept the lesser offer: Israel must go out to serve the Lord **as he tells us** (v. 27).

8:28 Despite the ruin that the flies had brought on Egypt (v. 24) and what it represented about the Lord's power, Pharaoh still seeks to govern the extent to which he would let Israel go (**only you must not go very far away**) before he asks for Moses to intercede for him.

8:32 After Moses' intercession brought relief from the flies, **Pharaoh hardened his heart this time also**, just as he had after the relief from the frogs (see v. 15).

9:1–7 *Fifth Plague: Egyptian Livestock Are Killed.* The fifth plague is the second to make a distinction between Israel and Egypt (see 8:22–23) and the first to bring about death in Egypt as the specific effect of the plague.

9:1 The LORD instructs Moses once again to refer to him before Pharaoh as **the God of the Hebrews** (see 3:18; 7:16). In light of the distinction between Israel and Egypt in the fourth plague and also here in the fifth, the reference should have begun to hammer home to Pharaoh that Yahweh's identification with Israel indicated his favor on them—but also that this did not mean that God's power and authority were limited to the Hebrew people.

9:3 The reference to **the hand of the LORD** is another thematic statement in the account of the exodus (see note on 3:19) that makes explicit what the events are meant to show to both Egypt and to Israel: it is the Lord who is at work to bring Israel out of Egypt.

9:5 Tomorrow. When Pharaoh was asked to set the time of relief for the second plague, he requested that it be done "tomorrow" (see 8:10). Moses then used the same time frame in his plea for relief from the fourth plague (8:29). Now, the Lord again uses it for the timing of the plague on Egypt's livestock.

9:7 The fact that Pharaoh sends someone to check on whether Israel had been spared from this fifth plague, and then responds as he does, both illustrates and contributes further to the hardness of his heart.

9:8–12 *Sixth Plague: Boils.* The description of the sixth plague is similar to that of the third in both its brevity and the way it focuses on the magicians of Egypt (see 8:16–19; and chart, p. 156).

9:8 After Aaron performs the initial sign (7:10) and the first three plagues (7:19; 8:3, 16), and the Lord's agency alone is described in the fourth and fifth (8:24; 9:6), here the Lord commands **Moses** to be the one to bring about the sign. As the events continue to unfold, the narrative shows Moses maturing in the role that the Lord had called him to at the burning bush (3:1–4:17).

9:9 The **boils** of the sixth plague are the first effect to impact the inhabitants

the land of Egypt." 10 So they took soot from the kiln and stood before Pharaoh. And Moses
threw it in the air, and it became boils breaking out in sores on man and beast. 11 And [w]the
magicians could not stand before Moses because of the boils, for the boils came upon the
magicians and upon all the Egyptians. 12 [x]But the LORD hardened the heart of Pharaoh,
and he did not listen to them, as [y]the LORD had spoken to Moses.

The Seventh Plague: Hail

13 Then the LORD said to Moses, [z]"Rise up early in the morning and present yourself before
Pharaoh and say to him, 'Thus says the LORD, the God of the Hebrews, "Let my people go,
that they may serve me. 14 For this time I will send all my plagues on you yourself,[1] and
on your servants and your people, so [a]that you may know that there is none like me in
all the earth. 15 For by now I could have put out my hand and struck you and your people
with pestilence, and you would have been cut off from the earth. 16 [b]But for this purpose
I have raised you up, to show you my power, so [c]that my name may be proclaimed in all
the earth. 17 [d]You are still exalting yourself against my people and will not let them go.
18 Behold, about this time tomorrow I will cause very heavy hail to fall, such as never has
been in Egypt from the day it was founded until now. 19 Now therefore send, [e]get your
livestock and all that you have in the field into safe shelter, for every man and beast that
is in the field and is not brought home will die when the hail falls on them."'" 20 Then
whoever feared the word of the LORD among the servants of Pharaoh hurried his slaves
and his livestock into the houses, 21 but whoever did not pay attention to the word of the
LORD left his slaves and his livestock in the field.

22 Then the LORD said to Moses, "Stretch out your hand toward heaven, so that there
may be [f]hail in all the land of Egypt, on man and beast and every plant of the field, in the
land of Egypt." 23 Then Moses stretched out his staff toward heaven, and the [g]LORD sent
thunder and hail, and fire ran down to the earth. And the LORD rained hail upon the land
of Egypt. 24 There was hail and fire flashing continually in the midst of the hail, very heavy
hail, such as had never been in all the land of Egypt since it became a nation. 25 The hail
struck down everything that was in the field in all the land of Egypt, both man and beast.
And the hail [h]struck down every plant of the field and broke every tree of the field. 26 [i]Only
in the land of Goshen, where the people of Israel were, was there no hail.

27 Then Pharaoh sent and called Moses and Aaron and said to them, "This time [j]I have
sinned; the [k]LORD is in the right, and I and my people are in the wrong. 28 [l]Plead with the

[1] Hebrew *on your heart*

11 [w]See ch. 7:11; 2 Tim. 3:9
12 [x]See ch. 4:21 [y]ch. 4:21
13 [z]ch. 7:15; 8:20
14 [a]ch. 8:10
16 [b]Cited Rom. 9:17; [ch. 10:1, 2; 11:9; 14:17; Prov. 16:4] [c][Ps. 83:18]; Isa. 63:12
17 [d][Neh. 9:10]
19 [e][ver. 4]
22 [f]Rev. 16:21
23 [g]Ps. 78:47, 48; 105:32; [Josh. 10:11; 1 Sam. 12:17; Ps. 18:13; 148:8; Isa. 30:30; Ezek. 38:22; Rev. 8:7]
25 [h]Ps. 78:47; 105:33
26 [i]ver. 4, 6; ch. 8:22; 10:23; 11:7; 12:13; [Isa. 32:18]
27 [j]ch. 10:16 [k]2 Chr. 12:6; Ps. 129:4; 145:17; Lam. 1:18; Dan. 9:14
28 [l]See ch. 8:8

of Egypt directly. The progression of the plagues continues to grow both in what they show of the Lord's power and in the proximity of their effects on the lives of Pharaoh and his people.

9:11 Pharaoh originally summons his **magicians** to contest the significance of the signs performed by Moses and Aaron (7:11). While they are able to reproduce some of the first signs (7:11, 22; 8:7), they could not overpower them (7:12) or reverse their effects (7:24; 8:8). When the magicians are unable to produce gnats, they confess to Pharaoh what has been signified throughout, "This is the finger of God" (see 8:19). In the sixth plague, the effects of the Lord's power are embodied in the magicians themselves who **could not stand before Moses because of the boils**.

9:13–35 *Seventh Plague: Hail.* In the progression of the narrative, the seventh plague is highlighted by both the length and content of its description. The extended section of the Lord's words to Pharaoh is particularly significant: it is the first and only time the Lord explicitly explains to Pharaoh the power and purposes of the plagues (vv. 14–17), and it is also the first time he offers Pharaoh a way to avoid the effects of the plague (vv. 18–19).

9:14–16 The repeated reference to the earth in these verses underscores the Lord's message: although Pharaoh considered himself to be a representative of divine power, the plagues have revealed that there is no one like the Lord **in all the earth** (v. 14; see v. 29); that it was only by the Lord's mercy that Egypt had not yet been destroyed **from the earth** (v. 15); and that Pharaoh was ultimately raised up by the Lord's power and for the proclamation of his name **in all the earth** (v. 16, also cited by the apostle Paul on the purposes behind God's absolute sovereignty, Rom. 9:17).

9:14 this time. The Lord indicates the increasing intensity and proximity of the effects of this plague, but when Pharaoh uses the same phrase to qualify his repentance (v. 27) it is clear that he has still not taken any of the plagues to heart. The Hebrew phrase translated **"on you yourself"** is literally "on your heart" (see ESV footnote) and is likely an intended wordplay with the continued reference to the state of Pharaoh's heart (vv. 34–35) and the hearts of his servants (v. 34; see vv. 20–21).

9:18–21 hail . . . such as never has been in Egypt from the day it was founded until now (v. 18; also v. 24). Several of the plagues involved elements that would have occurred naturally to some degree in the land of Egypt (e.g., frogs, flies, hail, locusts), but in each case the details (related to the timing, concentration, location, severity, or even the means of relief) were meant to signify that the Lord had supernaturally brought them on Egypt. The provision of a way to find **safe shelter** from the hail (v. 19) was a test to indicate who had taken the plagues to heart and thus **feared the word of the LORD** (v. 20). The reference to those who **did not pay attention to the word of the LORD** draws into focus the wordplay on the state of the heart of Pharaoh and his servants (see v. 14) as the Hebrew phrase is literally, "whoever did not set his heart to the word of the Lord."

9:27 This time I have sinned. Pharaoh's qualified admission echoes the opening words from the Lord's explanation of the plague ("this time," v. 14), but indicates that he has drawn the wrong conclusion (see also 10:17). Pharaoh has sinned in response to each plague, refusing to listen to the word of the Lord, and Egypt stands under judgment as a result.

LORD, for there has been enough of God's thunder and hail. I will let you go, and you shall
stay no longer." 29 Moses said to him, "As soon as I have gone out of the city, [m]I will stretch
out my hands to the LORD. The thunder will cease, and there will be no more hail, so that
you may know that [n]the earth is the LORD's. 30 But as for you and your servants, [o]I know
that you do not yet fear the LORD God." 31 (The flax and the barley were struck down, for
the barley was in the ear and the flax was in bud. 32 But the wheat and the emmer[1] were
not struck down, for they are late in coming up.) 33 So Moses went out of the city from
Pharaoh and [m]stretched out his hands to the LORD, and the thunder and the hail ceased,
and the rain no longer poured upon the earth. 34 But when Pharaoh saw that the rain and
the hail and the thunder had ceased, he sinned yet again and [p]hardened his heart, [q]he
and his servants. 35 So [r]the heart of Pharaoh was hardened, and he did not let the people
of Israel go, just as the LORD had spoken through Moses.

The Eighth Plague: Locusts

10 Then the LORD said to Moses, "Go in to Pharaoh, for I have hardened his heart
and the heart of his servants, that I may show these signs of mine among them,
2 and [s]that you may tell in the hearing of your son and of your grandson how I have dealt
harshly with the Egyptians and what signs I have done among them, [t]that you may know
that I am the LORD."
3 So Moses and Aaron went in to Pharaoh and said to him, "Thus says the LORD, the
God of the Hebrews, 'How long will you refuse to [u]humble yourself before me? Let my
people go, that they may serve me. 4 For if you refuse to let my people go, behold, tomorrow I will bring [v]locusts into your country, 5 and they shall cover the face of the land, so
that no one can see the land. And they shall [w]eat what is left to you after the hail, and they
shall eat every tree of yours that grows in the field, 6 and they shall fill [x]your houses and
the houses of all your servants and of all the Egyptians, as neither your fathers nor your
grandfathers have seen, from the day they came on earth to this day.'" Then he turned
and went out from Pharaoh.
7 Then Pharaoh's servants said to him, "How long shall this man be a snare to us? Let the
men go, that they may serve the LORD their God. Do you not yet understand that Egypt
is ruined?" 8 So Moses and Aaron were brought back to Pharaoh. And he said to them,

[1] A type of wheat

29 [m]1 Kgs. 8:22, 38; Ps. 143:6; Isa. 1:15 [n]Ps. 24:1; 1 Cor. 10:26; [Deut. 10:14]
30 [o]Isa. 26:10
33 [m][See ver. 29 above]
34 [p]See ch. 7:14 [q]1 Sam. 6:6
35 [r]See ch. 4:21

Chapter 10

2 [s][ch. 13:8, 14; Deut. 4:9; 6:20-22; Ps. 78:5-7; Joel 1:3] [t]ch. 7:17
3 [u]1 Kgs. 21:29
4 [v]Lev. 11:22; Prov. 30:27; Joel 1:4; 2:25; Rev. 9:3
5 [w]ch. 9:32
6 [x][ch. 8:3, 21; Joel 2:9]

9:31–32 The explanation about crops in Egypt indicates that Pharaoh took comfort from what remained in his land rather than acknowledging the destruction that had already come.

9:34 he . . . hardened his heart, he and his servants. The repetition highlights Pharaoh's responsibility. His defiance leads the way for the defiance of his servants and brings about the destruction of his land. As the plagues progress, some of Pharaoh's servants begin to recognize that he is exercising his rule at their expense rather than in their best interest (see 8:19; 10:7; 11:8).

9:35 The two references to the **heart of Pharaoh** represent both his responsibility for his actions (v. 34) and the sovereign governance over the events by the Lord (v. 35; see also 10:1).

10:1–20 *Eighth Plague: Locusts.* The eighth plague ties together the events and narrative of plagues seven through nine: the locusts of the eighth plague finish off what the hail of the seventh has left behind (see 9:31–32), and the language describing the effect of the locusts "covering the face of the land" prefigures the darkness of the ninth (10:21). Where the Lord explained his purposes more explicitly to Pharaoh in the seventh (see 9:14–17), here he indicates again to Moses that the plagues are not solely for Egypt but primarily for what they reveal to the people of Israel (10:2; see also 6:7).

10:1 I have hardened his heart and the heart of his servants. This is only the second plague narrative (cf. 7:14) that begins with a statement about the condition of Pharaoh's heart. The point is clear: Yahweh governs the events (see 9:34–35). Hereafter in the plague and exodus narrative it is usually the Lord who is referred to as hardening the heart of Pharaoh (see note on 4:21; also chart, p. 151).

10:2 The Lord has Moses tell Pharaoh several times that the purpose of the plagues is **that you may know that I am the LORD** (see note on 7:5). Here in the preface to the eighth plague, the Lord addresses these words to Moses and reminds him that this is also his purpose for Israel (see 6:7)—and that what is signified in the plagues will become a part of the regular celebration in Israel of who the Lord is and what he has done for his people (**that you may tell in the hearing of your son and of your grandson**).

10:5 The description of the locusts as covering **the face of the land, so that no one can see the land** (also v. 15) prefigures the darkness that is to come in the ninth plague (vv. 21–23). Although each of the plagues has signified judgment through the threat of disease and/or death in some measure, the seventh through the ninth plagues intensify the warning and prefigure the judgment of death that is to come with the final plague.

10:6 from the day they came on earth to this day. Like the hail of the seventh plague, the Lord makes it clear that, although swarms of locusts were not unknown in the history of Egypt, the warning, timing, and extent of this plague indicate that it should not be interpreted as simply a regular and expected part of their normal experience.

10:7 Like the magicians in 8:19, some of **Pharaoh's servants** recognize what the plagues signify and make the bold move to suggest strongly to Pharaoh that he is not acting on behalf of his people as a ruler should.

10:8–11 Pharaoh listens to his servants (v. 7) and for the first time calls Moses and Aaron back into his presence before the plague has begun (v. 8). However, as in his post-plague pleading with Moses, Pharaoh responds to Moses' answer (v. 9) with an offer of only qualified obedience to the Lord's command (v. 10) and then sends them out in the anger of offended pride (v. 11). Contrary to what all of the plagues have indicated, Pharaoh continues to act as if he has unqualified authority over Israel.

8 [y] ver. 24
9 [z] ch. 5:1; [ch. 3:18]
10 [a] ver. 24
12 [b] See ch. 7:19 [c] ver. 4, 5
14 [d] Ps. 78:46; 105:34
[e] Joel 2:2
15 [f] Ps. 105:35
16 [g] ch. 9:27
17 [h] See ch. 8:8
18 [i] ch. 8:30; 9:33
19 [j] [Joel 2:20]
20 [k] See ch. 4:21
21 [l] ver. 12 [m] Ps. 105:28
23 [n] [ch. 8:22; 9:4, 6]
24 [o] ver. 8 [p] ver. 10
27 [q] ver. 20
29 [r] [Heb. 11:27]

[y]"Go, serve the LORD your God. But which ones are to go?" **9** Moses said, "We will go with
our young and our old. We will go with our sons and daughters and with our flocks and
herds, for [z]we must hold a feast to the LORD." **10** But he said to them, "The LORD be with
you, if ever I let you and your [a]little ones go! Look, you have some evil purpose in mind.[1]
11 No! Go, the men among you, and serve the LORD, for that is what you are asking." And
they were driven out from Pharaoh's presence.
12 Then the LORD said to Moses, [b]"Stretch out your hand over the land of Egypt for
the locusts, so that they may come upon the land of Egypt and [c]eat every plant in the
land, all that the hail has left." **13** So Moses stretched out his staff over the land of Egypt,
and the LORD brought an east wind upon the land all that day and all that night. When
it was morning, the east wind had brought the locusts. **14** [d]The locusts came up over
all the land of Egypt and settled on the whole country of Egypt, [e]such a dense swarm
of locusts as had never been before, nor ever will be again. **15** They covered the face of
the whole land, so that the land was darkened, and [f]they ate all the plants in the land
and all the fruit of the trees that the hail had left. Not a green thing remained, neither
tree nor plant of the field, through all the land of Egypt. **16** Then Pharaoh hastily called
Moses and Aaron and said, [g]"I have sinned against the LORD your God, and against you.
17 Now therefore, forgive my sin, please, only this once, and [h]plead with the LORD your
God only to remove this death from me." **18** So [i]he went out from Pharaoh and pleaded
with the LORD. **19** And the LORD turned the wind into a very strong west wind, which
lifted the locusts and drove them [j]into the Red Sea. Not a single locust was left in all
the country of Egypt. **20** But the LORD [k]hardened Pharaoh's heart, and he did not let the
people of Israel go.

The Ninth Plague: Darkness

21 Then the LORD said to Moses, [l]"Stretch out your hand toward heaven, that there may
be [m]darkness over the land of Egypt, a darkness to be felt." **22** So Moses stretched out his
hand toward heaven, and there was pitch darkness in all the land of Egypt three days.
23 They did not see one another, nor did anyone rise from his place for three days, but [n]all
the people of Israel had light where they lived. **24** Then Pharaoh called Moses and said,
[o]"Go, serve the LORD; [p]your little ones also may go with you; only let your flocks and your
herds remain behind." **25** But Moses said, "You must also let us have sacrifices and burnt
offerings, that we may sacrifice to the LORD our God. **26** Our livestock also must go with
us; not a hoof shall be left behind, for we must take of them to serve the LORD our God,
and we do not know with what we must serve the LORD until we arrive there." **27** But the
LORD [q]hardened Pharaoh's heart, and he would not let them go. **28** Then Pharaoh said to
him, "Get away from me; take care never to see my face again, for on the day you see my
face you shall die." **29** Moses said, "As you say! [r]I will not see your face again."

[1] Hebrew *before your face*

10:17 When Pharaoh pleads with Moses and Aaron that his sin be forgiven **only this once**, the Hebrew is similar to his earlier qualified admission, "This time I have sinned" (9:27; see also 9:14) and indicates again that he recognizes neither the nature of his actions nor the gravity of what the plagues represent. **remove this death from me**. Pharaoh's description of the effect of the locusts as "death" is apt because of what has happened to Egypt's crops and also for the way it foreshadows the death to come in the final plague.

10:19 Red Sea. See note on 13:18.

10:21–29 *Ninth Plague: Darkness.* The ninth plague is significant both for its immediate effects and for what it represents. The "darkness to be felt" immobilizes the inhabitants of Egypt from any normal pattern of living for three full days and is a foreboding warning of the death that waits in the final plague.

10:23 After the locusts of the eighth plague are described as covering "the face" (vv. 5, 15) of the land so that no one could "see the land" (v. 5) because it was "darkened" (v. 15), the plague of darkness now has the effect that the people of Egypt **did not see one another**. The extended night that Egypt endures **for three days** prefigures the death to come, both in the way that darkness was often associated with the realm of death and for how the final plague will come at midnight (11:4; 12:29).

10:24 Pharaoh once again offers a qualification to what the Lord has asked in order to have some way of still tethering Israel to Egypt as his labor force. He has told them to go and sacrifice: "within the land" (8:25), without "your little ones" (10:9–11), and then here without **your flocks and your herds**. The Lord's words to Pharaoh have always framed Israel's going out as having the purpose "that they may serve me" (see 7:16; 8:1; etc. and also 3:12, 18), indicating also that this service would be primarily worship (see 5:1; 10:9, 25–26). Pharaoh stands in continual defiance of what the Lord is calling Israel to do in terms of the location, people, and provisions for serving him.

10:27–29 The narrative of each plague ends with either a description like this on the state of **Pharaoh's heart** (8:32; 9:7; 10:20) or a declaration that events had transpired according to the word of the Lord (8:15, 19; 9:12, 35), and once with a reference to the time elapsed (7:25). The interchange between Pharaoh and Moses in 10:28 may indicate that the warning of the tenth plague (11:4–8) comes while Moses is still in Pharaoh's presence. The threefold reference to Pharaoh's **face** plays on the description of the darkening of the land by the locusts (see 10:5, 15) and on the effects of the thick darkness on the people of Egypt (vv. 21–23) and, as Moses' final statement makes clear, forewarns of the finality of the plague to come: **I will not see your face again**.

A Final Plague Threatened

11 The LORD said to Moses, "Yet [s]one plague more I will bring upon Pharaoh and
upon Egypt. Afterward he will let you go from here. [t]When he lets you go, he will
drive you away completely. 2 Speak now in the hearing of the people, that [u]they ask, every
man of his neighbor and every woman of her neighbor, for silver and gold jewelry." 3 [v]And
the LORD gave the people favor in the sight of the Egyptians. Moreover, the man Moses
was very great in the land of Egypt, in the sight of Pharaoh's servants and in the sight of
the people.
4 So Moses said, "Thus says the LORD: [w]'About midnight I will go out in the midst of
Egypt, 5 and every firstborn in the land of Egypt shall die, from the firstborn of Pharaoh
who sits on his throne, even to the firstborn of the slave girl who is [x]behind the handmill,
and all the firstborn of the cattle. 6 [y]There shall be a great cry throughout all the land of
Egypt, such as there has never been, nor ever will be again. 7 But not a dog shall growl
[z]against any of the people of Israel, either man or beast, that you may know that the LORD
[a]makes a distinction between Egypt and Israel.' 8 And [b]all these your servants shall come
down to me and bow down to me, saying, 'Get out, you and all the people who follow
you.' And after that I will go out." And he went out from Pharaoh in hot anger. 9 Then the
LORD said to Moses, [c]"Pharaoh will not listen to you, that [d]my wonders may be multiplied
in the land of Egypt."
10 Moses and Aaron did all these wonders before Pharaoh, and the LORD [e]hardened
Pharaoh's heart, and he did not let the people of Israel go out of his land.

The Passover

12 The LORD said to Moses and Aaron in the land of Egypt, 2 [f]"This month shall be for
you the beginning of months. It shall be the first month of the year for you. 3 Tell
all the congregation of Israel that on the tenth day of this month every man shall take a
lamb [g]according to their fathers' houses, a lamb for a household. 4 And if the household is
too small for a lamb, then he and his nearest neighbor shall take according to the number

Chapter 11
1 [s][ch. 4:23] [t]ch. 12:31, 33, 39
2 [u]ch. 3:22; 12:35
3 [v]ch. 3:21; 12:36
4 [w]ch. 12:29; [Job 34:20; Amos 4:10]
5 [x]Matt. 24:41; Luke 17:35
6 [y]ch. 12:30; [Amos 5:16, 17]
7 [z][ch. 8:22; 9:4] [a]ch. 9:4
8 [b]ch. 12:33
9 [c]ch. 3:19; 7:4; 10:1 [d]ch. 7:3
10 [e]See ch. 4:21

Chapter 12
2 [f]ch. 13:4; 23:15; 34:18; Deut. 16:1
3 [g]ver. 21

11:1–15:21 *Tenth Plague: Final Sign.* The section that describes the tenth and final plague includes extended accounts that relate to: the warning (11:1–10); the instructions for Israel's Passover and the Feast of Unleavened Bread (12:1–28); the plague (12:29–32); the exodus (12:33–42); the statute for the Passover (12:43–51); the command to consecrate the firstborn and celebrate the Feast of Unleavened Bread (13:1–16); how Israel went out of Egypt (13:17–22); the events of the Red Sea (14:1–31); and the songs of Moses (15:1–18) and Miriam (15:19–21).

11:1–10 The Lord both prepares Israel for going out of Egypt (vv. 1–3) and once again warns Pharaoh of the plague that is to come (vv. 4–8). The section ends with a final statement that Moses and Aaron had done all that the Lord asked them and that Pharaoh would not listen because the Lord had hardened his heart (vv. 9–10).

11:1 Yet one plague more I will bring upon Pharaoh and upon Egypt. Although the Lord told Moses at the outset that Pharaoh would not listen because of his hardened heart (see 3:19–20; 4:21), the Lord only now reveals when the plagues would end. The plague narratives show Moses continually maturing in his role as Israel's leader, as one who is called to act in light of the Lord's promises even though he does not know exactly how and when the Lord will bring Israel out of Egypt.

11:2–3 The Lord instructs Israel to ask the Egyptians **for silver and gold**, a fulfillment of what he told Moses at the burning bush (3:21–22). In addition, the fact that **Moses** was considered **very great** by both **Pharaoh's servants** and **the people** in Egypt is a fulfillment of the Lord's promise at the burning bush: "I will be with you" (3:12, 15).

11:4 The descriptions of the third, sixth, and ninth plagues each begin with the Lord simply instructing Moses to perform the sign (8:16; 9:8; 10:21; see chart, p. 156). The descriptions of the other plagues always include the words to Pharaoh "thus says the LORD" and the instruction to "let my people go" (see 7:16, 17; 8:1, 20; 9:1, 13; 10:3). The warning here indicates the finality of the tenth plague when Moses says, "**Thus says the LORD**," and then describes the forthcoming effects of the plague without any further request to let Israel go.

11:5 When the Lord spoke to Moses as he was preparing to go back to Egypt, he referred to Israel as "my firstborn son" (4:22) and indicated that Pharaoh's refusal would result in the death of his **firstborn** (4:23). Since Pharaoh leads as his people's representative, the plagues have extended not simply to him but also to his people, a fact which becomes even more poignant in the final plague when **every firstborn in the land of Egypt shall die**.

11:7 The LORD makes a distinction between Egypt and Israel from the very beginning by referring to Israel as "my people" (see 3:7; 5:1) and identifying himself with them as "the God of the Hebrews" (3:18; 5:3). This distinction is further revealed to Pharaoh through the plagues (see 8:22–23; 9:4, 26; 10:23) and is grounded not in anything inherent in either nation but in the Lord's sovereign governance over all nations and particularly in his steadfast love for and covenant promises to Abraham (see Deut. 7:6–11).

11:8 The narrative does not tell the reader explicitly why Moses **went out from Pharaoh in hot anger**. As the one who has interacted with Pharaoh throughout and even pleaded with the Lord on his behalf, it may be that Moses found Pharaoh's persistent pride infuriating because of the devastating effect it would have on the people of Egypt (cf. note on 9:34).

12:1–28 Where the Lord had made a distinction in earlier plagues by protecting Israel's land, livestock, and people from the effects he brought upon Egypt, the people of Israel are now called to act faithfully in order to appropriate the means by which the Lord will "pass over" them during the tenth plague. The Lord's instructions to Moses and Aaron look beyond simply the events of the tenth plague and describe how the Passover and the Feast of Unleavened Bread will be celebrated by Israel in the Promised Land.

12:2 The events of the plagues and exodus are so significant for Israel's identity as an emerging nation that the **month** they come out of Egypt will become for them **the first month of the year**. (Cf. The Hebrew Calendar, p. 34.)

12:3–4 Just as the plague will result in the death of a firstborn in every house in Egypt (see v. 30), Israel is given instructions for a lamb to be sacrificed on behalf of every **household**.

5[h]Lev. 22:19-21; Deut. 17:1; Mal. 1:8, 14; Heb. 9:14
6[i]ver. 18; Lev. 23:5; Num. 9:3; 28:16; Josh. 5:10; Ezra 6:19
7[j]ver. 22
8[k]ch. 23:18; 34:25; Num. 9:11; Deut. 16:3; 1 Cor. 5:8
9[l]Deut. 16:7; 2 Chr. 35:13
10[m]ch. 23:18; 29:34; 34:25; Deut. 16:4; [Lev. 7:15]
11[n][Luke 12:35; Eph. 6:14; 1 Pet. 1:13] [o]ver. 27; Lev. 23:5; Deut. 16:5; [1 Cor. 5:7]
12[p]ver. 23; ch. 11:4, 5 [q]Num. 33:4 [r]ch. 6:2; Isa. 43:11
13[s][Heb. 11:28]
14[t]ch. 13:9 [u]ver. 17, 24, 43; ch. 13:10; 2 Kgs. 23:21
15[v]ch. 13:6, 7; 23:15; 34:18, 25; Lev. 23:6; Num. 28:17; Deut. 16:3, 8; [1 Cor. 5:7, 8] [w][Gen. 17:14; Num. 9:13]
16[x]Lev. 23:7, 8; Num. 28:18, 25
17[y]ch. 13:3 [z]ver. 51; ch. 7:4
18[a]Lev. 23:5; Num. 28:16
19[b]ver. 15

of persons; according to what each can eat you shall make your count for the lamb. **5** Your
lamb shall be [h]without blemish, a male a year old. You may take it from the sheep or from
the goats, **6** and you shall keep it until the [i]fourteenth day of this month, when the whole
assembly of the congregation of Israel shall kill their lambs at twilight.[1]

7 "Then they shall take some of the blood and put it on the [j]two doorposts and the lintel
of the houses in which they eat it. **8** They shall eat the flesh that night, roasted on the fire;
with [k]unleavened bread and bitter herbs they shall eat it. **9** Do not eat any of it raw or boiled
in water, but [l]roasted, its head with its legs and its inner parts. **10** And [m]you shall let none
of it remain until the morning; anything that remains until the morning you shall burn.
11 In this manner you shall eat it: with [n]your belt fastened, your sandals on your feet, and
your staff in your hand. And you shall eat it in haste. [o]It is the LORD's Passover. **12** For [p]I will
pass through the land of Egypt that night, and I will strike all the firstborn in the land of
Egypt, both man and beast; and on [q]all the gods of Egypt I will execute judgments: [r]I am
the LORD. **13** [s]The blood shall be a sign for you, on the houses where you are. And when
I see the blood, I will pass over you, and no plague will befall you to destroy you, when I
strike the land of Egypt.

14 "This day shall be [t]for you a memorial day, and you shall keep it as a feast to the LORD;
throughout your generations, as a [u]statute forever, you shall keep it as a feast. **15** [v]Seven
days you shall eat unleavened bread. On the first day you shall remove leaven out of your
houses, for if anyone eats what is leavened, from the first day until the seventh day, [w]that
person shall be cut off from Israel. **16** On the first day you shall hold a [x]holy assembly, and
on the seventh day a holy assembly. No work shall be done on those days. But what everyone needs to eat, that alone may be prepared by you. **17** And you shall observe the Feast of
Unleavened Bread, for [y]on this very day I brought your [z]hosts out of the land of Egypt.
Therefore you shall observe this day, throughout your generations, as a statute forever. **18** [a]In
the first month, from the fourteenth day of the month at evening, you shall eat unleavened
bread until the twenty-first day of the month at evening. **19** [b]For seven days no leaven is to
be found in your houses. If anyone eats what is leavened, [b]that person will be cut off from

[1] Hebrew *between the two evenings*

12:7 they shall take some of the blood and put it on the two doorposts. The practice would indicate that the members of the household had followed the Lord's instructions and were consecrated to him; but the Israelites, in light of the developed sacrificial system, would find the blood of the slain lamb to be a vivid reminder that a life had to be sacrificed in place of those in the home.

12:8 The Passover lamb is to be eaten **with unleavened bread**. This reflects the coming events in which Israel is sent out of Egypt so quickly that they have to pack up their dough before it is leavened (vv. 34, 39).

12:9–10 Israel is to prepare their Passover lambs by roasting them "on the fire" (v. 8), and they are to **burn** anything that remains of the meal in the morning (v. 10). Although the reasons for these instructions are not stated explicitly, the reference to the meal as "the LORD's" (v. 11; see also v. 27) indicates that it is to be treated as holy.

12:11 Similar to the instruction about unleavened bread (v. 8), Israel is to eat the Passover dressed in a manner that symbolizes their being sent out of Egypt in the middle of the night (vv. 31–34).

12:12 The seventh plague had been a forewarning that the Lord has authority over **both man and beast** (9:25), but where the hail had affected only those who remained in the field, the tenth plague would strike **all the firstborn in the land of Egypt**. The Lord has stated repeatedly that the central purpose of the plagues is that both Egypt and Israel would know who he is: **"I am the LORD"** (see 3:13–15; 6:2–8; 7:5, 17). What is being displayed in judgment on Egypt's land, animals, people, king, and **gods** is also revealing to Israel that Yahweh is the only true God of heaven and earth and he is acting on their behalf. The events of the Passover are the ultimate demonstration of God's holy judgment of Egypt in its stubborn rejection of Yahweh, of God's great love for his people Israel, and of his power that is infinitely greater than all the power of Pharaoh and his kingdom (cf. Rom. 9:17, 22–24).

12:13 Since the Lord had shown clearly in previous plagues that he could distinguish between the people of Egypt and Israel (e.g., 8:22; 9:4), the **blood** placed on the doorway of the houses of Israel was to function both as the **sign** that they were a part of the Lord's people and also as the seal or means to appropriate the Lord's protection from the plague (see also 12:21–23).

12:14–20 The instructions in this section relate particularly to the way that Israel will celebrate the Feast of Unleavened Bread in the Promised Land.

12:15 The consequence of eating something leavened during the seven days is that a **person shall be cut off from Israel** (also v. 19). This suggests that eating leavened bread during the Passover was a serious sin. Although being "cut off" is stated as the consequence for a number of violations of the law (e.g., not being circumcised, Gen. 17:14; eating part of the sacrifice while unclean, Lev. 7:20–21; committing incest, Lev. 20:17), the majority of the contexts where it is mentioned do not state explicitly whether this refers to an action that Israel is to carry out or whether it is something known and acted upon by the Lord (see note on Ex. 31:14–15). In the context of the instructions for the Passover, it is possible that the addition of being cut off from the congregation of Israel (12:19) indicates that Israel was to remove a person from the celebration of the Passover if and when they knew the restriction had been broken. However, even where such an action may be intended, it would have been grounded primarily in what being cut off represented about the person's state before the Lord and thus would have been a merciful warning against disregarding the covenant lest the person continue in such a state and be cut off forever. Sometimes it appears that God's judgment brings about the offender's premature death. (See also note on Lev. 7:11–36; cf. notes on Gen. 17:14; Lev. 22:1–3; Num. 9:6–14; Ps. 37:9.)

12:19 a sojourner or a native of the land. See vv. 43–49. The sojourners were non-Israelites, living among Israel; often they were converts to the Lord. These rules are not just for the first Passover in Egypt; they prescribe how the

the congregation of Israel, [c]whether he is a sojourner or a native of the land. 20 You shall
eat nothing leavened; in all your dwelling places you shall eat unleavened bread."
21 Then Moses called all the elders of Israel and said to them, "Go and select lambs for
yourselves [d]according to your clans, and kill the Passover lamb. 22 Take a bunch of [e]hyssop
and [f]dip it in the blood that is in the basin, and touch [g]the lintel and the two doorposts
with the blood that is in the basin. [h]None of you shall go out of the door of his house until
the morning. 23 [i]For the LORD will pass through to strike the Egyptians, and when he sees
the blood on [g]the lintel and on the two doorposts, the LORD will pass over the door and
[j]will not allow the destroyer to enter your houses to strike you. 24 You shall observe this
rite as a statute for you and for your sons forever. 25 And when you come to the land that
the LORD will give you, [k]as he has promised, you shall keep this service. 26 And [l]when
your children say to you, 'What do you mean by this service?' 27 you shall say, [m]'It is the
sacrifice of the LORD's Passover, for he passed over the houses of the people of Israel in
Egypt, when he struck the Egyptians but spared our houses.'" And the people [n]bowed
their heads and worshiped.
28 Then the people of Israel went and did so; as the LORD had commanded Moses and
Aaron, so they did.

The Tenth Plague: Death of the Firstborn

29 [o]At midnight the [p]LORD struck down all the firstborn in the land of Egypt, [q]from the
firstborn of Pharaoh who sat on his throne to the firstborn of the captive who was in the
dungeon, and all the firstborn of the livestock. 30 And Pharaoh rose up in the night, he
and all his servants and all the Egyptians. And there was [r]a great cry in Egypt, for there
was not a house where someone was not dead. 31 Then he summoned Moses and Aaron
by night and said, "Up, go out from among my people, [s]both you and the people of Israel;
and go, serve the LORD, as you have said. 32 [t]Take your flocks and your herds, as you have
said, and be gone, and bless me also!"

The Exodus

33 [u]The Egyptians were urgent with the people to send them out of the land in haste. For
they said, "We shall all be dead." 34 So the people took their dough before it was leavened,
their kneading bowls being bound up in their cloaks on their shoulders. 35 The people of
Israel had also done as Moses told them, for they had [v]asked the Egyptians for silver and
gold jewelry and for clothing. 36 [w]And the LORD had given the people favor in the sight
of the Egyptians, so that [x]they let them have what they asked. Thus they plundered the
Egyptians.
37 And the [y]people of Israel journeyed from [z]Rameses to Succoth, [a]about six hundred
thousand men on foot, besides women and children. 38 A [b]mixed multitude also went up
with them, and very much livestock, both flocks and herds. 39 And they baked unleavened
cakes of the dough that they had brought out of Egypt, for it was not leavened, because

19 [c]ver. 48, 49
21 [d]ver. 3
22 [e]Lev. 14:6; Num. 19:18; Ps. 51:7; Heb. 9:19 [f]Heb. 11:28 [g]ver. 7 [h][Isa. 26:20]
23 [i]ver. 12, 13 [g][See ver. 22 above] [j]Heb. 11:28; [Ezek. 9:6; Rev. 7:3; 9:4]
25 [k]ch. 3:8, 17
26 [l]ch. 13:8, 14; Deut. 6:20; 32:7; Josh. 4:6, 21; Ps. 78:3-6
27 [m]ver. 11, 21 [n]ch. 4:31
29 [o]ch. 11:4 [p]Num. 8:17; 33:4; Ps. 78:51; 105:36; 135:8; 136:10 [q]ch. 4:23; 11:5
30 [r]ch. 11:6; [Amos 5:16, 17]
31 [s][ch. 10:9-11]
32 [t][ch. 10:24-26]
33 [u]ch. 6:1; 11:1, 8; Ps. 105:38
35 [v]ch. 3:22; 11:2
36 [w]ch. 3:21; 11:3 [x]Gen. 15:14; Ps. 105:37
37 [y]Num. 33:3, 5 [z]Gen. 47:11; [ch. 1:11] [a][ch. 38:26; Num. 1:46; 2:32; 11:21; 26:51]
38 [b]Lev. 24:10, 11; Num. 11:4; [Neh. 13:3]

festival is to be celebrated when Israel arrives in Canaan and has foreigners living among them.

12:21 After Pharaoh offers qualified obedience to the Lord's request, including attempts to restrict the place (8:25), participants (10:8–11), and provision (10:24–26) for serving him, there is tragic irony in the fact that Israel's first sacrifice (**kill the Passover lamb**) is in the land of Egypt and signifies the judgment that will come upon it.

12:22 hyssop. A bushy shrub used as a brush in a variety of cleansing ceremonies (see Lev. 14:4–7; Num. 19:6, 18; Ps. 51:7; cf. John 19:29).

12:23 when he sees the blood. See notes on vv. 7, 13.

12:26–27 when your children say to you . . . you shall say. Israel's identity as the people whom the Lord had brought out of Egypt was to be formed not only through faithful participation in the celebration of the Passover but also by proper narration of what it signifies.

12:30 The elders of Israel had been called to act on behalf of their households (v. 21) so that every "house" would appropriate the means for protection (v. 22); Pharaoh's refusal to obey the Lord results in there being **not a house where someone was not dead**. In each case, the leaders acted as representatives through whom the consequences of either their faithfulness or unfaithfulness were extended to their respective "houses."

12:35–36 Israel's obedience in asking **for silver and gold jewelry and for clothing** (v. 35) fulfills not only what the Lord had promised to Moses at the burning bush (3:22) but also what he had originally promised to Abraham, that his descendants would come out (of Egypt) "with great possessions" (Gen. 15:14).

12:37 While the sons of Jacob and their families arrived in Egypt with 70 persons (see 1:5), the people of Israel who were going out of the land now numbered more than **six hundred thousand . . . , besides women and children**. This would suggest a total company of about 2 million. On the large numbers in the Pentateuch, see Introduction to Numbers, p. 260.

12:39 The celebration of Israel's exodus from Egypt (see vv. 14–20; 13:3–10) will involve the seemingly unimportant but historically particular event of having to bake **unleavened cakes of the dough** (see 12:34). Israel's inability to prepare **any provisions for themselves** is merciful because Yahweh will continually demonstrate his provision for them in this context. As the narrative will make clear, Israel is still in need of fully believing and appropriating this truth during the journey to Sinai (see 15:24; 16:2; 17:2–3).

39[u][See ver. 33 above] [c][Deut. 16:3]
41[d]Gal. 3:17; [Gen. 15:13; Acts 7:6]
42[e]See Deut. 16:1-6
44[f][Gen. 17:12, 13]
45[g]Lev. 22:10
46[h]Num. 9:12; Cited John 19:36
47[i]ver. 6
48[j]Num. 9:14 [k]ver. 19
49[l]Num. 9:14; 15:15, 16 [j][See ver. 48 above]
51[m]ver. 41; Acts 13:17 [n]ver. 17

Chapter 13
2[o]ver. 12, 13, 15; ch. 22:29, 30; 34:19; Lev. 27:26; Num. 3:13; 8:16, 17; 18:15; Deut. 15:19; Cited Luke 2:23
3[p]ch. 12:42; Deut. 16:3 [q]ch. 3:19; 6:1 [r]See ch. 12:8
4[s]ch. 23:15; 34:18; Deut. 16:1
5[t]ch. 3:8; 23:23; 33:2; 34:11; Josh. 12:8; 24:11 [u]ch. 6:8 [v]See ch. 3:8 [w]ch. 12:25, 26
6[x]ch. 12:15, 16
8[y]See ch. 12:26

[u]they were thrust out of Egypt and [c]could not wait, nor had they prepared any provisions
for themselves.
40 The time that the people of Israel lived in Egypt was 430 years. **41** At the end of [d]430
years, on that very day, all the hosts of the LORD went out from the land of Egypt. **42** It was
a night of watching by the LORD, to bring them out of the land of Egypt; so this same
night is a [e]night of watching kept to the LORD by all the people of Israel throughout
their generations.

Institution of the Passover

43 And the LORD said to Moses and Aaron, "This is the statute of the Passover: no foreigner shall eat of it, **44** but every slave[1] that is [f]bought for money may eat of it after you
have circumcised him. **45** [g]No foreigner or hired worker may eat of it. **46** It shall be eaten in
one house; you shall not take any of the flesh outside the house, and [h]you shall not break
any of its bones. **47** [i]All the congregation of Israel shall keep it. **48** [j]If a stranger shall sojourn
with you and would keep the Passover to the LORD, let all his males be circumcised. Then
he may come near and keep it; he [k]shall be as a native of the land. But no uncircumcised
person shall eat of it. **49** There shall be [l]one law for the native and for the [j]stranger who
sojourns among you."
50 All the people of Israel did just as the LORD commanded Moses and Aaron. **51** And on that
very day the [m]LORD brought the people of Israel out of the land of Egypt by their [n]hosts.

Consecration of the Firstborn

13 The LORD said to Moses, **2** [o]"Consecrate to me all the firstborn. Whatever is the first to
open the womb among the people of Israel, both of man and of beast, is mine."

The Feast of Unleavened Bread

3 Then Moses said to the people, [p]"Remember this day in which you came out from
Egypt, out of the house of slavery, [q]for by a strong hand the LORD brought you out from
this place. [r]No leavened bread shall be eaten. **4** Today, in the month of [s]Abib, you are going
out. **5** And when the LORD brings you into [t]the land of the Canaanites, the Hittites, the
Amorites, the Hivites, and the Jebusites, which [u]he swore to your fathers to give you, a
land [v]flowing with milk and honey, [w]you shall keep this service in this month. **6** [x]Seven
days you shall eat unleavened bread, and on the seventh day there shall be a feast to the
LORD. **7** Unleavened bread shall be eaten for seven days; no leavened bread shall be seen
with you, and no leaven shall be seen with you in all your territory. **8** [y]You shall tell your

[1] Or *servant*; the Hebrew term *'ebed* designates a range of social and economic roles (see Preface)

12:41 The reference to Israel as the **hosts of the LORD** (also vv. 17, 51; 7:4) evokes a military image (see 15:4). The pharaoh "who did not know Joseph" (1:8) had originally enslaved Israel because he feared they would form a military alliance with one of Egypt's enemies (1:10). Although Israel probably had enough people to stage a military coup (12:37), the plagues and the exodus signified that it was the Lord who would fight on behalf of his people (cf. 14:14). When Israel is equipped for battle, it is not to fight Egypt but to be ready to go into the land the Lord has promised them (13:18).

12:43–49 The statutes related to the Passover were necessary in light of the "mixed multitude" that went out of Egypt with Israel (v. 38). Participation in the feasts that would be formative for Israel's life in the land required that a person be identified as a part of the Lord's people by letting **all his males be circumcised** (v. 48). In the NT church, there is a parallel in that baptism (the sign of membership in God's people) would ordinarily precede participating in the Lord's Supper. Similarly here, circumcision is required prior to eating the Passover.

12:46 you shall not break any of its bones. This is probably the text John 19:36 has in mind as fulfilled in the death of Jesus on Passover (John may have combined this text with Ps. 34:20; see notes on Ps. 34:15–22 and John 19:36).

13:1–16 As the Passover in 12:1–27 looks forward to Israel's life in the land, these verses call the people of Israel to faithfulness in celebrating the Feast of Unleavened Bread (13:3–10) and consecrating all their firstborn (vv. 2, 11–16).

13:2 In addition to the yearly sacrifice of the Passover (see 12:1–13), Israel is also called to **consecrate** to the Lord **all the firstborn** in Israel, whether animal or human. The instructions for how and why this is to be carried out are given in 13:11–16. This reminds Israel that, when the Egyptian firstborn died in the tenth plague, the Israelites were spared (v. 15). "Consecrate" means "make holy by giving to God." Thus the firstborn of sacrificial animals, such as sheep and cattle, had to be sacrificed. However, firstborn donkeys and humans had to be redeemed: a lamb was offered in sacrifice instead of them (vv. 12–13).

13:3 The repeated statement that the Lord brought his people out **by a strong hand** (also vv. 9, 14, 16) frames the instruction of this section and acts as the grounds upon which Israel is called to be faithful in keeping both the Feast of Unleavened Bread (vv. 3, 9) and the consecration of all the firstborn (vv. 14, 16). As a reminder of the Lord's power, it also seems intended to encourage Israel to fear the Lord and not the nations who inhabit the land of Canaan (see vv. 5, 11).

13:5 The instruction of vv. 2–16 focuses on the time when the Lord will bring Israel **into the land of the Canaanites** (also v. 11). With the repeated statement that the Lord brought Israel out of Egypt "by a strong hand" (see v. 3), Moses encourages Israel to see that faithfulness to these two statutes is a part of being formed to fear the Lord and not the nations who inhabit the land.

13:6–7 These instructions relate to the Feast of Unleavened Bread, which is initiated by the celebration of Passover and is observed for **seven days** (see 12:14–20).

13:8 Israel is called once again (see 12:26) not only to faithfully participate

son on that day, 'It is because of what the LORD did for me when I came out of Egypt.'
9 And it shall [z]be to you as a sign on your hand and as [a]a memorial [z]between your eyes,
that the law of the LORD may be in your mouth. For with a strong hand the LORD has
brought you out of Egypt. 10 [b]You shall therefore keep this statute at its appointed time
from year to year.
11 "When the LORD brings you into the land of the Canaanites, [c]as he swore to you and
your fathers, and shall give it to you, 12 [d]you shall set apart to the LORD all that first opens
the womb. All the firstborn of your animals that are males shall be the LORD's. 13 [e]Every
firstborn of a donkey you shall redeem with a lamb, or if you will not redeem it you shall
break its neck. Every [f]firstborn of man among your sons you shall redeem. 14 [g]And when
in time to come your son asks you, 'What does this mean?' you shall say to him, [h]'By a
strong hand the LORD brought us out of Egypt, from the house of [i]slavery. 15 For when
Pharaoh stubbornly refused to let us go, the [j]LORD killed all the firstborn in the land of
Egypt, both the firstborn of man and the firstborn of animals. Therefore I sacrifice to the
LORD all the males that first open the womb, but [k]all the firstborn of my sons I redeem.'
16 [l]It shall be as a mark on your hand or frontlets between your eyes, for [m]by a strong hand
the LORD brought us out of Egypt."

Pillars of Cloud and Fire

17 When Pharaoh let the people go, God did [n]not lead them by way of the land of the
Philistines, although that was near. For God said, "Lest the people [o]change their minds
when they see war and return to Egypt." 18 But God [p]led the people around by the way
of the wilderness toward the Red Sea. And the people of Israel went up out of the land
of Egypt equipped for battle. 19 Moses took the bones of Joseph with him, for Joseph[1]
had made the sons of Israel solemnly swear, saying, [q]"God will surely visit you, and you
shall carry up my bones with you from here." 20 And [r]they moved on from Succoth and
encamped at Etham, on the edge of the wilderness. 21 And [s]the LORD went before them by
day in a pillar of cloud to lead them along the way, and by night in a pillar of fire to give
them light, that they might travel by day and by night. 22 The pillar of cloud by day and
the pillar of fire by night did not depart from before the people.

[1] Samaritan, Septuagint; Hebrew *he*

9 [z]Deut. 6:8; 11:18; [Num. 15:39; Matt. 23:5] [a]ch. 12:14, 24
10 [b][ch. 12:14, 17, 24, 43]
11 [c]ver. 5
12 [d]ver. 2
13 [e]ch. 34:20 [f]Num. 3:46, 47; 18:15, 16
14 [g]See ch. 12:26 [h]ver. 3, 16 [i]ver. 3
15 [j]ch. 12:29 [k]ver. 13
16 [l]ver. 9 [m]ver. 14
17 [n][Ps. 107:7] [o]ch. 14:11, 12; [Neh. 9:17]; See Num. 14:1-4
18 [p]ch. 14:2; [Deut. 32:10]; See Num. 33:6-49
19 [q]Gen. 50:25; Josh. 24:32; Heb. 11:22; [Acts 7:16]
20 [r]ch. 12:37; Num. 33:6
21 [s]ch. 14:19, 24; 40:38; Num. 10:34; 14:14; Deut. 1:33; Neh. 9:12, 19; Ps. 78:14; 99:7; 105:39; 1 Cor. 10:1; [Isa. 4:5]; See Num. 9:15-23

in the statutes of the Lord but also to tell their children what they mean: **You shall tell your son on that day** (also 13:14).

13:9 The Lord's statutes were to be so normative and governing for life in Israel that they would be like marks **on your hand** and **between your eyes** (also v. 16). In a wordplay related to the part of the body responsible for both eating and speaking (the mouth), faithfulness is described as having the result **that the law of the LORD may be in your mouth**; that is, you will always be saying it to yourself or teaching your children (Deut. 6:7; Ps. 1:2).

13:11–16 set apart to the LORD all that first opens the womb (v. 12). This was another way in which Israel's pattern of everyday life was to reflect the fact that they were the people that the Lord had brought out of Egypt (see also 34:19–20). Every firstborn was regarded as belonging to the Lord. Firstborn animals were to be sacrificed, redeemed by the sacrifice of another animal, or killed (13:12–15). Firstborn children were to be redeemed (v. 13) by the sacrifice of a lamb. Like the Passover (see 12:26) and the Feast of Unleavened Bread (13:8–9), parents were to be faithful in both the doing and the telling of consecration: **And when in time to come your son asks you, "What does this mean?" you shall say . . .** (vv. 14–15).

13:17 Although the Lord has clearly shown through the plagues that he can bring his people victoriously through **the land of the Philistines**, he mercifully chooses to take them on another route that will not lead to immediate armed conflict. However, this route will result in Israel being hemmed in between the Red Sea and Pharaoh's army of chariots (see 14:5–9) and will call them to a different sort of challenge. Before the Lord calls Israel to trust that he will fight *through* them (as he will do with the Amalekites in 17:8–16), he will show them once again how he will fight *for* them (see 14:13–14).

13:18 toward the Red Sea. In the accounts of the crossing of the sea (15:4; Deut. 11:4; Ps. 106:7, 9, 22) the water is often referred to as *Yam Sup*, which is also the Hebrew phrase in this verse. Some modern scholars interpret *Yam Sup* as "Sea of Reeds/Papyrus" because the term *sup* refers to the reeds growing along the Nile River (Ex. 2:3). Because papyrus does not grow along the Red Sea/Gulf of Suez, some scholars have concluded that the *Yam Sup* is one of the marshy lakes in the eastern delta region north of the Red Sea. Support for this is claimed from the Egyptian document Papyrus Anastasis III, which describes a "papyrus lake" not far from the city of Rameses that could be identified with the *Yam Sup* of the Exodus account. Many scholars have concluded from this that the Israelites crossed a marshy area of a lake rather than a large body of water such as the Red Sea. Other scholars disagree, proposing that *sup* is not related to the Egyptian word "papyrus" but rather to a word that means "end" (Hb. *sop*). And, thus, the *yam sup* would literally mean "the sea of the end," that is, the sea at the end of the land of Egypt (i.e., the Red Sea). The Septuagint translates *yam sup* into Greek as *tēn erythran thalassan* (lit., "the red sea") here and elsewhere. In addition, every certain reference to *yam sup* in the Bible refers to the Red Sea or its northern extensions in the Gulfs of Aqaba and Suez (e.g., 1 Kings 9:26; Jer. 49:21). This suggests that the name *Yam Sup* is best understood to denote the Red Sea/Gulf of Suez and, therefore, the Israelites crossed this major body of water when they fled Egypt.

13:19 Taking the **bones of Joseph** carried out his last wishes (Gen. 50:24–25); it reaffirmed for Israel that God had kept the promises he had made so long before. Hebrews 11:22 sees Joseph's desire to be buried in the Promised Land as evidence of his "faith" in God's future blessings, including "a better country, that is, a heavenly one" (Heb. 11:16; cf. Heb. 11:1, 10, 13–16, 39–40).

13:21–22 Throughout the events of Exodus, **cloud** and **fire** accompany and signify the presence of the Lord: at the burning bush (3:2), in giving the people manna (16:10), on Mount Sinai (19:18), and in the tabernacle (40:38).

Chapter 14
2 [t]ch. 13:18, 20; Num. 33:7, 8 [u]Jer. 44:1
4 [v]See ch. 4:21 [w]Rom. 9:17, 22, 23; See ch. 9:16 [x]ch. 7:5
5 [y]Ps. 105:25
7 [z]ch. 15:4; [Isa. 31:1]
8 [v][See ver. 4 above] [a]ch. 6:1; 13:3, 9, 16; Num. 33:3; Deut. 26:8; Acts 13:17; [ch. 3:19]
9 [b]ch. 15:9; Josh. 24:6 [c]ver. 2
10 [d]Josh. 24:7; Neh. 9:9
11 [e]Ps. 106:7; [ch. 13:17]
12 [f]ch. 5:21; 6:9
13 [g]2 Chr. 20:15, 17; Isa. 41:10, 13, 14 [h][ver. 30]
14 [i]ver. 25; Deut. 1:30; 3:22; 20:4; Josh. 10:14, 42; 23:3; 2 Chr. 20:15, 29; Neh. 4:20 [j][Isa. 30:15]
16 [k]See ch. 7:19
17 [l][ver. 4, 8] [m]ver. 4
18 [n]ch. 7:5 [m][See ver. 17 above]
19 [o]ch. 23:20; 32:34; Num. 20:16; Isa. 63:9; [ch. 13:21]

Crossing the Red Sea

14 Then the LORD said to Moses, 2 “Tell the people of Israel to [t]turn back and encamp
in front of Pi-hahiroth, between [u]Migdol and the sea, in front of Baal-zephon; you
shall encamp facing it, by the sea. 3 For Pharaoh will say of the people of Israel, ‘They are
wandering in the land; the wilderness has shut them in.’ 4 And [v]I will harden Pharaoh’s
heart, and he will pursue them, and I will [w]get glory over Pharaoh and all his host, [x]and
the Egyptians shall know that I am the LORD.” And they did so.
5 When the king of Egypt was told that the people had fled, the [y]mind of Pharaoh and
his servants was changed toward the people, and they said, “What is this we have done, that
we have let Israel go from serving us?” 6 So he made ready his chariot and took his army
with him, 7 and took [z]six hundred chosen chariots and all the other chariots of Egypt with
officers over all of them. 8 And [v]the LORD hardened the heart of Pharaoh king of Egypt,
and he pursued the people of Israel while [a]the people of Israel were going out defiantly.
9 The [b]Egyptians pursued them, all Pharaoh’s horses and chariots and his horsemen and his
army, and overtook them [c]encamped at the sea, by Pi-hahiroth, in front of Baal-zephon.
10 When Pharaoh drew near, the people of Israel lifted up their eyes, and behold, the
Egyptians were marching after them, and they feared greatly. And the people of Israel
[d]cried out to the LORD. 11 They [e]said to Moses, “Is it because there are no graves in Egypt
that you have taken us away to die in the wilderness? What have you done to us in bringing
us out of Egypt? 12 Is not this what [f]we said to you in Egypt: ‘Leave us alone that we may
serve the Egyptians’? For it would have been better for us to serve the Egyptians than to
die in the wilderness.” 13 And Moses said to the people, [g]“Fear not, stand firm, and see the
salvation of the LORD, which he will work for you today. For [h]the Egyptians whom you
see today, you shall never see again. 14 [i]The LORD will fight for you, and you have only [j]to
be silent.”
15 The LORD said to Moses, “Why do you cry to me? Tell the people of Israel to go forward. 16 [k]Lift up your staff, and [k]stretch out your hand over the sea and divide it, that the
people of Israel may go through the sea on dry ground. 17 And [l]I will harden the hearts of
the Egyptians so that they shall go in after them, and [m]I will get glory over Pharaoh and
all his host, his chariots, and his horsemen. 18 And the Egyptians [n]shall know that I am the
LORD, [m]when I have gotten glory over Pharaoh, his chariots, and his horsemen.”
19 [o]Then the angel of God who was going before the host of Israel moved and went
behind them, and the pillar of cloud moved from before them and stood behind them,

14:1–31 With statements that echo his words to Moses before the plagues (see vv. 4, 8, 17, 18; 4:21; 7:3–5), the Lord indicates that the coming events are governed by his power and purposes. Although the Lord tells Moses that he will “get glory over Pharaoh” (14:4), he does not tell him just how Israel will be delivered. Between the time of the plagues in Egypt (7:14–12:32) and the journey to Sinai (15:22–18:27), the events at the Red Sea show Moses as a maturing leader who trusts the word of the Lord (see 14:13–14), as they also illustrate Israel’s need to do the same (see vv. 10–12).

14:2 The body of water that Israel is about to cross is called “the Red Sea” in 13:18 and 15:4 and is referred to simply as “**the sea**” in this section. The exact route of the exodus is uncertain, but it is likely that they crossed the Red Sea at its northern end (see map, p. 143).

14:4 The content of this verse is repeated nearly verbatim in the narrative (vv. 17–18) and echoes the Lord’s words to Moses both before and during the plagues: **I will harden Pharaoh’s heart** (cf. 4:21; 7:3, etc.), **I will get glory over Pharaoh** (cf. 7:16), and **the Egyptians shall know that I am the LORD** (cf. 7:5).

14:5 When the Egyptians refer to letting Israel go by saying, “**What is this we have done . . . ?**” they exhibit the hardness of heart that the Lord said he would bring about (see vv. 4, 8, 17). The question also resembles the way Israel will wrongly attribute their circumstances to Moses in the face of Egypt’s pursuit (see v. 11).

14:7 The possession of **chariots** represented a significant advantage in ancient Near Eastern warfare; Egypt was proficient in the use of chariots, as indicated by the distinction of **six hundred chosen chariots** in addition to all the others. Pharaoh was coming out against what appeared to be a wandering and trapped nation with his most prestigious and imposing force.

14:10 The reference to Israel seeing Egypt’s army and fearing **greatly** is thematic for this section. Through the plagues (and continuing on their journey to Sinai), Yahweh calls Israel to fear him over any other nation or battle force (see vv. 13, 31).

14:11 What have you done to us . . . ? Note the similar mistake that the Egyptians make with reference to their own actions (v. 5). This incident between the people and Moses was prefaced by earlier events (2:14; 5:21) and also prefigures those to come (15:24; 16:2; 17:3).

14:12 When the people of Israel say, “**it would have been better for us to serve the Egyptians than to die in the wilderness**,” they are viewing their circumstances without reference to the fact that the Lord himself brought them to this place. As revealed throughout Israel’s history, the Lord is merciful in never leaving his people simply to themselves or to their circumstances. As both Daniel and his three friends will later assert (see Dan. 3:16–18; 6:10), whatever the Lord calls his people to face as a result of fearing him is in fact better than simply remaining alive.

14:13 Fear not. Israel is being called once again not to fear any other nation or circumstance (see v. 10) but to fear the Lord (see v. 31).

14:17–18 References to the Lord getting **glory over Pharaoh** (see also v. 4) come on either side of the statement that **the Egyptians shall know that I am the LORD**. Although the plagues have continually revealed that the Lord—and not Pharaoh—is due honor, the victory over Pharaoh’s chariots in the Red Sea will be known powerfully in Egypt and throughout the surrounding nations (see 9:16; 15:14–16).

14:19 the angel of God. See note on 3:2.

20 coming between the host of Egypt and the host of Israel. And there was the cloud and
the darkness. And it lit up the night[1] without one coming near the other all night.
21 Then Moses [k]stretched out his hand over the sea, and the LORD drove the sea back by
[p]a strong east wind all night and [q]made the sea dry land, and the waters were [r]divided.
22 And [s]the people of Israel went into the midst of the sea on dry ground, the waters being
[t]a wall to them on their right hand and on their left. 23 The Egyptians pursued and went in
after them into the midst of the sea, all Pharaoh's horses, his chariots, and his horsemen.
24 And in the morning watch the LORD in the pillar of fire and of cloud looked down on
the Egyptian forces and threw the Egyptian forces into a panic, 25 clogging[2] their chariot
wheels so that they drove heavily. And the Egyptians said, "Let us flee from before Israel,
for the [u]LORD fights for them against the Egyptians."
26 Then the LORD said to Moses, [v]"Stretch out your hand over the sea, that the water may
come back upon the Egyptians, upon their chariots, and upon their horsemen." 27 [w]So Moses
stretched out his hand over the sea, and the sea [x]returned to its normal course when the
morning appeared. And as the Egyptians fled into it, the LORD [y]threw[3] the Egyptians into
the midst of the sea. 28 The [z]waters returned and covered the chariots and the horsemen;
of all the host of Pharaoh that had followed them into the sea, [a]not one of them remained.
29 But the [b]people of Israel walked on dry ground through the sea, the waters being a wall
to them on their right hand and on their left.
30 Thus the LORD [c]saved Israel that day from the hand of the Egyptians, and Israel saw
the Egyptians dead on the seashore. 31 [d]Israel saw the great power that the LORD used
against the Egyptians, so the people feared the LORD, and they [e]believed in the LORD and
in his servant Moses.

The Song of Moses

15 Then Moses and the people of Israel [f]sang this song to the LORD, saying,

[g]"I will sing to the LORD, for he has triumphed gloriously;
the horse and his rider[4] he has thrown into the sea.
2 [h]The LORD is my strength and my [i]song,
and he has become [j]my salvation;
this is my God, and I will praise him,
[k]my father's God, and [l]I will exalt him.
3 The LORD is [m]a man of war;
[n]the LORD is his name.

4 [o]"Pharaoh's chariots and his host he cast into the sea,
and his chosen [p]officers were sunk in the Red Sea.
5 The [q]floods covered them;
they [r]went down into the depths like a stone.

[1] Septuagint *and the night passed* [2] Or *binding* (compare Samaritan, Septuagint, Syriac); Hebrew *removing* [3] Hebrew *shook off* [4] Or *its chariot*; also verse 21

21 [k][See ver. 16 above] [p]ch. 15:10 [q]Ps. 66:6 [r]ch. 15:8; Neh. 9:11; Ps. 74:13; 78:13; 106:9; 114:3; Isa. 51:10; 63:12; [Josh. 3:16; 4:23; Isa. 10:26; 11:15, 16]
22 [s]ver. 29; ch. 15:19; Num. 33:8; Ps. 66:6; Isa. 63:13; 1 Cor. 10:1; Heb. 11:29; [Ps. 77:19] [t]Ps. 78:13; [Hab. 3:10]
25 [u]ver. 14
26 [v]ver. 16, 21
27 [w]ver. 21 [x][Josh. 4:18] [y]ch. 15:1, 7; Deut. 11:4; Ps. 78:53; Heb. 11:29
28 [z][Hab. 3:8-13] [a]Ps. 106:11
29 [b]See ver. 22
30 [c]Ps. 106:8, 10
31 [d]Ps. 92:9-11; [ver. 13] [e]Ps. 106:12; [John 2:11; 11:45]

Chapter 15

1 [f]Ps. 106:12; [Judg. 5:1; 2 Sam. 22:1] [g]ver. 21
2 [h]Ps. 18:1, 2; 59:17; 118:14; 140:7; Isa. 12:2 [i]Deut. 10:21; Ps. 109:1 [j]Ps. 18:46; Hab. 3:18 [k]ch. 3:6, 15, 16 [l]2 Sam. 22:47; Ps. 34:3; 99:5, 9; 118:28; 145:1; Isa. 25:1
3 [m]Ps. 24:8; Rev. 19:11 [n]ch. 3:15; 6:3; Ps. 83:18; Isa. 42:8; Mal. 3:6
4 [o]ch. 14:28 [p]ch. 14:7
5 [q]ver. 10; ch. 14:28 [r]Neh. 9:11

14:22 The image of the **waters** as a wall is a vivid indication of the protection given by the water on each side (cf. 1 Sam. 25:16; Jer. 15:20). The text presents the event as a demonstration of the Lord's "great power" (Ex. 14:31) including how the waters "returned and covered the chariots and horsemen" of Egypt (v. 28). Thus the text is clear that this is not a purely natural event. Similar events will take place when Joshua leads Israel across the Jordan into the land of Canaan (Josh. 3:14–17), when Elijah and Elisha cross the Jordan together on the way to Elijah being taken (2 Kings 2:8), and when Elisha returns across the Jordan alone (2 Kings 2:14).

14:31 they believed in the LORD and in his servant Moses. Since the Lord has chosen Moses as the one through whom he will reveal his word, it is necessary for Israel to learn to follow Moses as a consequence of learning to fear the Lord (see vv. 10, 13).

15:1–21 This section includes a celebration of the Lord's deliverance in song (vv. 1–18), followed by the women playing tambourines and dancing and Miriam singing the first lines of the song (vv. 19–21).

15:1–18 The song of praise is a celebration of the triumph over Pharaoh's army in the Red Sea as representative of the Lord's power and rule. It is similar to other songs or psalms in both the OT and NT that celebrate particular events that reveal God's character: e.g., Deborah and Barak's song in response to victory over Sisera and Jabin of Canaan (Judg. 5:1–31); Hannah's song at the birth of Samuel (1 Sam. 2:1–10); Mary's response to the angel's news and Elizabeth's greeting (Luke 1:46–55); and Zechariah's prophecy after the birth of John the Baptist (Luke 1:68–79).

15:1 the horse and his rider he has thrown into the sea. The drowning of Pharaoh's army by the hand of the Lord is the central event celebrated by the song, and it is referred to with various images: "cast into the sea" and "sunk in the Red Sea" (v. 4); "floods covered them," and "they went down . . . like a stone" (v. 5); "the sea covered them; they sank like lead" (v. 10); "the earth swallowed them" (v. 12).

15:2 The singular reference to **my father's God** echoes the Lord's words to Moses at the burning bush, which indicate that this phrase refers to "the God of Abraham, the God of Isaac, and the God of Jacob" (3:6) and equips Israel also to say of him, **"this is my God."**

15:4 Red Sea. See note on 13:18.

6 [s]Your right hand, O LORD, glorious in power,
your right hand, O LORD, [t]shatters the enemy.
7 In the [u]greatness of your majesty you overthrow your adversaries;
you send out your fury; it [v]consumes them like stubble.
8 At the [w]blast of your nostrils the waters piled up;
the [x]floods stood up in a heap;
the deeps congealed in the heart of the sea.
9 The enemy said, [y]'I will pursue, I will overtake,
I [z]will divide the spoil, my desire shall have its fill of them.
I will draw my sword; my hand shall destroy them.'
10 You [a]blew with your wind; the [b]sea covered them;
they sank like lead in the mighty waters.
11 [c]"Who is like you, O LORD, among the gods?
Who is like you, majestic in holiness,
awesome in [d]glorious deeds, [e]doing wonders?
12 You stretched out [f]your right hand;
the earth swallowed them.
13 "You have [g]led in your steadfast love the people whom [h]you have redeemed;
you have [i]guided them by your strength to your holy abode.
14 [j]The peoples have heard; they tremble;
pangs have seized the inhabitants of Philistia.
15 Now are the chiefs of Edom [k]dismayed;
trembling seizes the leaders of [l]Moab;
[m]all the inhabitants of Canaan have melted away.
16 Terror and [n]dread fall upon them;
because of the greatness of your arm, they are still [o]as a stone,
till your people, O LORD, pass by,
till the people pass by whom [p]you have purchased.
17 You will bring them in and [q]plant them on your own mountain,
the place, O LORD, which you have made for your abode,
[r]the sanctuary, O Lord, which your hands have established.
18 [s]The LORD will reign forever and ever."

19 For when [t]the horses of Pharaoh with his chariots and his horsemen went into the sea, [u]the LORD brought back the waters of the sea upon them, but the people of Israel walked on dry ground in the midst of the sea. 20 Then [v]Miriam [w]the prophetess, the [x]sister of Aaron, took a tambourine in her hand, and [y]all the women went out after her with tambourines and dancing. 21 And Miriam sang to them:

[z]"Sing to the LORD, for he has triumphed gloriously;
the horse and his rider he has thrown into the sea."

6 [s]ver. 12; Ps. 118:15, 16; Isa. 51:9 [t]Ps. 2:9; Rev. 2:27
7 [u]Deut. 33:26 [v][Isa. 5:24; 47:14; Mal. 4:1]
8 [w]ch. 14:21, 22; 2 Sam. 22:16; Job 4:9; Ps. 18:15; [2 Thess. 2:8] [x]Ps. 78:13; [Josh. 3:16; Hab. 3:10]
9 [y]ch. 14:9 [z]Gen. 49:27; Judg. 5:30; Isa. 53:12; Luke 11:22
10 [a]ch. 14:21; [Isa. 11:15; 40:24] [b]ver. 5; ch. 14:28
11 [c]Deut. 3:24; 1 Sam. 2:2; 2 Sam. 7:22; 1 Kgs. 8:23; 2 Chr. 6:14; Jer. 10:6 [d][Isa. 6:3; Rev. 4:8] [e]Ps. 77:14
12 [f]ver. 6
13 [g]Ps. 77:20 [h]Ps. 77:15 [i]Ps. 78:54
14 [j]Num. 14:14; Deut. 2:25; Josh. 2:9, 10; 9:24
15 [k][Deut. 2:4] [l]Num. 22:3 [m]Josh. 2:9, 11, 24; 5:1
16 [n]Deut. 2:25; 11:25 [o]1 Sam. 25:37 [p]Ps. 74:2; [1 Pet. 2:9]
17 [q]Ps. 44:2; 80:8; [Jer. 32:41] [r]Ps. 78:54; 132:13, 14
18 [s]Ps. 10:16; 29:10; 45:6; 146:10; Rev. 11:15
19 [t]ch. 14:23 [u]ch. 14:28, 29
20 [v]Mic. 6:4 [w][Judg. 4:4; 2 Kgs. 22:14; Neh. 6:14; Luke 2:36] [x]ch. 2:4; Num. 26:59 [y]Judg. 11:34; 1 Sam. 18:6; Ps. 68:25; 149:3; 150:4
21 [z]ver. 1

15:6 The reference to the Lord's **right hand** (v. 12; cf. v. 16) takes up God's words to Moses describing the means by which Israel would come out of Egypt (see 6:1; 7:4–5).

15:9 While the words of **the enemy** refer first of all to the actions of the Egyptians (**pursue, overtake**; see 14:9) who intended to bring Israel back to serve as slaves (see 14:5), they also extend beyond the particular events of the Red Sea and are representative of the pride and desire of any adversary of the Lord and his people (i.e., **divide the spoil, destroy**).

15:11 In light of the events that have taken place, the rhetorical questions of this verse imply that there is no one **among the gods** of the nations like the LORD (see also 12:12; 20:3). In a similar song, Hannah proclaims the complementary answers to the questions of this verse: "There is none holy like the LORD; there is none besides you; there is no rock like our God" (1 Sam. 2:2).

15:13–18 These verses, like the song as a whole (see v. 9), describe Israel's journey out of Egypt and into the land of Canaan. They anticipate the fear that will befall the surrounding peoples, the Philistines, Edomites, and Moabites, as well as the Canaanites. **your own mountain, the place . . . you have made for your abode** (v. 17). In one sense the whole hilly country of Canaan is to be God's dwelling. But his "abode" may be a more specific reference to the hill of Jerusalem, where God's temple will stand.

15:13 redeemed. This term refers to God's dealings for the sake of his people, rescuing them from danger and fostering the conditions in which their faithfulness may flourish; cf. 6:6; Ps. 74:2; 77:15; 106:10; Isa. 52:9; 62:12. See note on Isa. 41:14.

15:16 purchased. An image for the way that God "acquired" his people through great deeds; cf. Ps. 74:2.

15:21 Miriam leads the women in singing a verse that repeats the first verse of the song (see v. 1).

Bitter Water Made Sweet

22 Then Moses made Israel set out from the Red Sea, and they went into the wilderness
of [a]Shur. They went three days in the wilderness and found no water. 23 When they came
to [b]Marah, they could not drink the water of Marah because it was bitter; therefore it was
named Marah.[1] 24 And the people [c]grumbled against Moses, saying, "What shall we drink?"
25 And he [d]cried to the LORD, and the LORD showed him a log,[2] and he [e]threw it into the
water, and the water became sweet.
There the LORD[3] made for them a statute and a rule, and there he [f]tested them, 26 saying,
[g]"If you will diligently listen to the voice of the LORD your God, and do that which is right
in his eyes, and give ear to his commandments and keep all his statutes, I will put none of
the [h]diseases on you that I put on the Egyptians, for I am the LORD, [i]your healer."
27 Then [j]they came to Elim, where there were twelve springs of water and seventy palm
trees, and they encamped there by the water.

Bread from Heaven

16 They [k]set out from Elim, and all the congregation of the people of Israel came to
the wilderness of Sin, which is between Elim and Sinai, on the fifteenth day of the
second month after they had departed from the land of Egypt. 2 And the whole congregation of the people of Israel [l]grumbled against Moses and Aaron in the wilderness, 3 and
the people of Israel said to them, [m]"Would that we had died by the hand of the LORD in
the land of Egypt, [n]when we sat by the meat pots and ate bread to the full, for you have
brought us out into this wilderness to kill this whole assembly with hunger."
4 Then the LORD said to Moses, "Behold, I am about to rain [o]bread from heaven for you,
and the people shall go out and gather a day's portion every day, that I may [p]test them,

[1] *Marah* means *bitterness* [2] Or *tree* [3] Hebrew *he*

22 [a]Gen. 16:7; 25:18; 1 Sam. 15:7
23 [b][Ruth 1:20]
24 [c]ch. 16:2; 17:3
25 [d]ch. 14:10; 17:4 [e][2 Kgs. 2:21; 4:41] [f]ch. 16:4; Deut. 8:2, 16; Judg. 2:22; 3:1, 4; Ps. 66:10
26 [g]See Lev. 26:3-13; Deut. 7:12-15 [h]Deut. 28:27, 60 [i]ch. 23:25; Ps. 103:3; 147:3; Hos. 6:1
27 [j]Num. 33:9

Chapter 16

1 [k]Num. 33:10, 11
2 [l]ch. 15:24; 17:3; 1 Cor. 10:10
3 [m][Num. 20:3-5] [n]Num. 11:4, 5
4 [o]Neh. 9:15; Ps. 78:24, 25; 105:40; John 6:31, 32; 1 Cor. 10:3 [p]See ch. 15:25

15:22–18:27 *Journey.* Israel journeys from Egypt to Rephidim and responds to difficulties like the need for water (15:22–27; 17:1–7) and food (16:1–36). The narrative also includes two difficult situations the people face while encamped at Rephidim (see 17:1): the external attack by another nation (17:8) and the internal question of how to help the people make decisions according to the Lord's statutes (18:1–27). From Rephidim Israel will make their final short journey to the wilderness of Sinai (see 19:2).

15:22–27 *Water Problem: Marah.* The people of Israel respond to a lack of water at Marah in a manner similar to their grumbling against Moses at the Red Sea (14:10–12). They do not yet trust that the Lord's presence with them is sufficient for their protection and provision, which will be a recurring struggle in the journey to Sinai (see 16:2–3; 17:2–3) and ultimately lead to the situation through which this generation of Israel will be not be allowed to enter Canaan (Num. 14:1–4).

15:22–24 With the large number of people and livestock coming out of Egypt (see 12:37–38), the inability to find drinkable **water** is a significant problem (15:22–23). However, Israel has just experienced the Lord's power over the waters of the Red Sea and thus their choice to grumble **against Moses** about the lack of something to **drink** (v. 24) is ironic. The signs in Egypt confirmed Moses as the Lord's choice to lead Israel, and Israel needs to faithfully appropriate what has been revealed to them (see vv. 25–26).

15:24–26 grumbled. Though the people of Israel had just seen the power of the Lord unforgettably demonstrated, they nonetheless forgot and failed to trust the Lord. In contrast to their unbelief, Moses **cried to the LORD** to deliver the people from their distress. **the LORD showed him a log**. In response to Moses' cry for help, the Lord intervenes by causing the water to become **sweet**. Although some have proposed a naturalistic explanation for this, it seems more likely that it was entirely the Lord's direct intervention ("the LORD showed" Moses what to do). The purpose of the event at Marah is made clear in vv. 25a and 26: **There the LORD made for them a statute and . . . tested them**. The statute was to demonstrate, by means of testing, the principle (**a rule**) that if the people would **diligently listen to the voice of the LORD**, he would graciously care for them as their healer.

15:25–26 The **statute** calls Israel to give heed to all that he has commanded (e.g., Passover, the Feast of Unleavened Bread, and the consecration of the firstborn) and all that he will reveal further, which requires implicitly that the people follow Moses as the one through whom they will "listen to the voice of the LORD." The Lord's reference to himself as **your healer** indicates that Israel has already been graciously spared from what happened to the **Egyptians** and that faithfulness is the means by which they will continue to appropriate the blessings of the covenant relationship with the Lord (see 23:25; Deut. 7:15). The statute given here is the seed of that which Moses will give the next generation of Israel before they enter the land (see Deut. 7:12–15).

15:27 Elim (cf. Num. 33:9) was perhaps an oasis in Wadi Gharandel. With its **twelve springs** and **seventy palm trees** it signified to Israel once again that, since the Lord is leading them, they should not conclude too quickly that they know the meaning of their circumstances, especially when they cannot yet see how the Lord will work on their behalf (e.g., parting the Red Sea).

16:1–36 *Food Problem: Manna.* After setting out from Elim, Israel complains against Moses for lack of food; in response, the Lord graciously provides both manna and quail. The provision of manna includes instructions about gathering it that will shape Israel's life in the pattern of work and rest, as will be revealed more fully at Mount Sinai.

16:2 Although the people **grumbled against Moses and Aaron**, Moses will make it clear that their complaint is really against—and is heard by—the Lord (see note on v. 7).

16:3 The theme **by the hand of the LORD** describes how the Lord delivered Israel (see 6:1; 7:4–5; 13:3). When the people of Israel wish that they had **died** by his hand rather than being delivered by it, they show that they have not understood what his power on their behalf reveals about his person and the fulfillment of his promises to Abraham, Isaac, and Jacob. This incident is not the first time they have longed for what they had in Egypt (see 14:12), and it foreshadows another such incident during the period of wandering in the wilderness (see Num. 20:3–5).

16:4 The provision of **bread from heaven** was meant to signify not simply the satisfaction of Israel's physical needs but also that their whole lives were to be sustained by the Lord and governed by his word: **that I may test them, whether they will walk in my law or not**. Moses makes this point clear to the next generation (Deut. 8:3), and in response to the request for a manna-like sign shortly after he has fed five thousand, Jesus makes the same point about himself when he says, "I am the bread that came down from heaven" (John 6:41, 43–58).

whether they will walk in my law or not. 5 On the sixth day, when they prepare what they bring in, [q]it will be twice as much as they gather daily." 6 So Moses and Aaron said to all the people of Israel, [r]"At evening [s]you shall know that it was the LORD who brought you out of the land of Egypt, 7 and in the morning you shall see the [t]glory of the LORD, because he has heard your grumbling against the LORD. For [u]what are we, that you grumble against us?" 8 And Moses said, "When the LORD gives you in the evening meat to eat and in the morning bread to the full, because the LORD has heard your grumbling that you grumble against him—[v]what are we? Your grumbling is not [w]against us but against the LORD."

9 Then Moses [x]said to Aaron, "Say to the whole congregation of the people of Israel, [y]'Come near before the LORD, for he has heard your grumbling.'" 10 And as soon as Aaron spoke to the whole congregation of the people of Israel, they looked toward the wilderness, and behold, the [t]glory of the LORD appeared in the cloud. 11 And the LORD said to Moses, 12 "I [z]have heard the grumbling of the people of Israel. Say to them, 'At [a]twilight you shall eat meat, and [b]in the morning you shall be filled with bread. Then you shall know that I am the LORD your God.'"

13 In the evening [c]quail came up and covered the camp, and in the morning [d]dew lay around the camp. 14 And when the dew had gone up, there was on the face of the wilderness a fine, flake-like thing, fine as frost on the ground. 15 When the people of Israel saw it, they said to one another, [e]"What is it?"[1] For they [f]did not know what it was. And Moses said to them, [g]"It is the bread that the LORD has given you to eat. 16 This is what the LORD has commanded: 'Gather of it, each one of you, as much as he can eat. You shall each take an [h]omer,[2] according to the number of the persons that each of you has in his tent.'" 17 And the people of Israel did so. They gathered, some more, some less. 18 But when they measured it with an omer, [i]whoever gathered much had nothing left over, and whoever gathered little had no lack. Each of them gathered as much as he could eat. 19 And Moses said to them, "Let no one leave any of it over till the morning." 20 But they did not listen to Moses. Some left part of it till the morning, and [j]it bred worms and stank. And Moses was angry with them. 21 Morning by morning they gathered it, each as much as he could eat; but when the sun grew hot, it melted.

22 On [k]the sixth day they gathered twice as much bread, two omers each. And when all the leaders of the congregation came and told Moses, 23 he said to them, "This is what the LORD has commanded: 'Tomorrow is a day of [l]solemn rest, a holy Sabbath to the LORD; bake what you will bake and boil what you will boil, and all that is left over lay aside to be kept till the morning.'" 24 So they laid it aside till the morning, as Moses commanded them, and [m]it did not stink, and there were no worms in it. 25 Moses said, "Eat it today, for [l]today is a Sabbath to the LORD; today you will not find it in the field. 26 Six days you shall gather it, but on the seventh day, which is a Sabbath, there will be none."

27 On the seventh day some of the people went out to gather, but they found none. 28 And the LORD said to Moses, [n]"How long will you refuse to keep my commandments and my

5 [q]ver. 22
6 [r]ver. 12, 13 [s]ch. 6:7; [Num. 16:28-30]
7 [t]ch. 40:34; Num. 16:19; 1 Kgs. 8:10, 11; [ch. 13:21; 14:24] [u]Num. 16:11
8 [v]ver. 7 [w][Num. 14:27; 1 Sam. 8:7; Luke 10:16; Rom. 13:2]
9 [x][ch. 4:14-16] [y]Num. 16:16
10 [t][See ver. 7 above]
12 [z]ver. 8 [a]ver. 6 [b]ver. 7
13 [c]Num. 11:31; Ps. 78:27, 28; 105:40 [d]Num. 11:9
15 [e]ver. 31 [f]Deut. 8:3 [g]Deut. 8:3; See ver. 4
16 [h]ver. 36
18 [i]Cited 2 Cor. 8:15
20 [j][ver. 24]
22 [k]ver. 5
23 [l]ch. 35:2, 3; Gen. 2:3; Lev. 23:3; See ch. 20:8-11; 31:14-17
24 [m][ver. 20]
25 [l][See ver. 23 above]
28 [n][Ps. 78:10; Ezek. 20:13]

[1] Or *"It is manna."* Hebrew *man hu* [2] An *omer* was about 2 quarts or 2 liters

16:6 Although the plagues are described to Pharaoh as taking place so that the Egyptians would know "that I am the LORD" (see note on 7:5), the Lord first said that the signs would serve a similar purpose for Israel (see 6:7; 10:2), and their complaints against Moses bear evidence that they are still in need of coming to **know** and appropriate **that it was the LORD who brought you out of the land of Egypt** (see also 16:12).

16:7 Moses repeatedly stresses that the people's **grumbling** is both **against the LORD** (also twice in v. 8) and **heard** by him (also vv. 8, 9, 12), regardless of how they choose to describe their situation (see vv. 2–3). Since the people are responding to the Lord's power as if it is disconnected from his person (see v. 3), Moses says that they will see **the glory of the LORD** (v. 10), which is a manifestation of his presence (see 24:16–17; 40:34–35).

16:15 It is the bread that the LORD has given you to eat. See note on v. 4. The name "manna" appears to be related by similar sound to the expression **"What is it?"** (see ESV footnote).

16:18 gathered much . . . gathered little. Paul cites this text in 2 Cor. 8:15 to encourage the Corinthian Christians to give generously for the poor Jewish Christians in Judea; there is no point in hoarding the good gifts of God.

16:20 An integral aspect to Israel showing that they will walk in the law of the Lord (v. 4) is whether or not they will **listen to Moses**, whom the Lord has chosen to lead them.

16:22–30 The instructions for gathering manna for six days and resting on the seventh as a **holy Sabbath** (v. 23) begin to shape Israel in the pattern of regular work and rest that the Lord will reveal further to Moses through the fourth commandment (20:8–11; see also 31:13–17). This pattern embodies trust in the Lord's provision for something Israel has no part in producing; later, when Israel has settled in the land and is depending more on its own labor, the regular Sabbath rest will be seen as an expression of divine mercy.

16:24 The contrast between the manna that people saved until morning on other days (v. 20) and what they kept for the Sabbath (without **stink** and **worms**) illustrates that the manna's condition is controlled, as their lives should be, by the word of the Lord (see v. 28).

laws? 29 See! The LORD has given you the Sabbath; therefore on the sixth day he gives you
bread for two days. Remain each of you in his place; let no one go out of his place on the
seventh day." 30 So the people [o]rested on the seventh day.
31 Now the house of Israel called its name [p]manna. It was [q]like coriander seed, white, and
the taste of it was like wafers made with honey. 32 Moses said, "This is what the LORD has
commanded: 'Let an omer of it be kept throughout your generations, so that they may see
the bread with which I fed you in the wilderness, when I brought you out of the land of
Egypt.'" 33 And Moses said to Aaron, "Take a [r]jar, and put an omer of manna in it, and place
it before the LORD to be kept throughout your generations." 34 As the LORD commanded
Moses, so Aaron placed it before [s]the testimony to be kept. 35 The people of Israel [t]ate the
manna forty years, till they came to a habitable land. They ate the manna till [u]they came
to the border of the land of Canaan. 36 (An omer is [v]the tenth part of an ephah.)[1]

Water from the Rock

17 [w]All the congregation of the people of Israel moved on from the wilderness of Sin
by stages, according to the commandment of the LORD, and camped at Rephidim,
but there was no water for the people to drink. 2 [x]Therefore the people quarreled with
Moses and said, "Give us water to drink." And Moses said to them, "Why do you quarrel
with me? Why do you [y]test the LORD?" 3 But the people thirsted there for water, and [z]the
people grumbled against Moses and said, "Why did you bring us up out of Egypt, to kill us
and our children and our livestock with thirst?" 4 So Moses cried to the LORD, "What shall
I do with this people? They are almost ready [a]to stone me." 5 And the LORD said to Moses,
"Pass on before the people, taking with you some of the elders of Israel, and take in your
hand the staff with [b]which you struck the Nile, and go. 6 [c]Behold, I will stand before you
there on the rock at Horeb, and you shall strike the rock, and water shall come out of it, and
the people will drink." And Moses did so, in the sight of the elders of Israel. 7 And he called
the name of the place [d]Massah[2] and [e]Meribah,[3] because of the quarreling of the people of
Israel, and because they tested the LORD by saying, "Is the LORD among us or not?"

Israel Defeats Amalek

8 [f]Then Amalek came and fought with Israel at Rephidim. 9 So Moses said to [g]Joshua,
"Choose for us men, and go out and fight with Amalek. Tomorrow I will stand on the

[1] An *ephah* was about 3/5 bushel or 22 liters [2] *Massah* means *testing* [3] *Meribah* means *quarreling*

30 [o]Luke 23:56
31 [p]ver. 15 [q]Num. 11:7, 8
33 [r]Heb. 9:4
34 [s]ch. 25:16, 21; 26:33, 34; 27:21; 30:6, 26, 36; 40:21
35 [t]Deut. 8:2, 3; Neh. 9:20, 21 [u]Josh. 5:12
36 [v]Lev. 5:11; 6:20

Chapter 17

1 [w]ch. 16:1; Num. 33:12, 14
2 [x]Num. 20:3, 4 [y]Deut. 6:16; Ps. 78:18, 41; 95:8, 9; Isa. 7:12; Matt. 4:7; 1 Cor. 10:9; Heb. 3:8, 9
3 [z]ch. 15:24; 16:2
4 [a]Num. 14:10; 1 Sam. 30:6; 2 Chr. 24:21; Matt. 23:37; Luke 13:34; John 8:59; 10:31-33; 11:8; Acts 7:58; 14:5, 19; 2 Cor. 11:25; Heb. 11:37; [Josh. 9:25; 1 Kgs. 21:13]
5 [b]ch. 7:20
6 [c]Num. 20:8-11; Deut. 8:15; Neh. 9:15; Ps. 78:15, 16, 20; 105:41; 114:8; Isa. 43:20; 48:21; 1 Cor. 10:4
7 [d]Ps. 95:8 [e]Num. 20:13; Ps. 81:7; 95:8
8 [f]Deut. 25:17; 1 Sam. 15:2
9 [g]ch. 24:13; 32:17; 33:11

16:32–34 These verses contain instructions about keeping a jar of manna and placing it **before the LORD** (vv. 32–33), which is described as being carried out when Aaron **placed it before the testimony** (v. 34). The "testimony" refers to the two tablets of the Ten Commandments (see 31:18; 34:28–29) that will be placed in the ark (see 25:16), which at this point in the narrative has not yet been built (see 25:10–22; 37:1–9).

16:35 The reference to the fact that Israel ate **manna till they came to the border of the land of Canaan** indicates that at least this verse was written after Israel had finished its wandering in the wilderness (see Josh. 5:12).

17:1–7 *Water Problem: Massah and Meribah.* Israel grumbles against Moses a third time out of concern for physical provision (see 15:24–25; 16:2–3). The events of this quarrel are similar to those that will take place at the same location and through which Moses will not be allowed to enter Canaan (see Num. 20:2–13).

17:2 The people again **quarrel** with Moses, who describes their actions as their daring to **test the LORD** (see also v. 7). After experiencing the plagues, the crossing of the Red Sea, and the Lord's provision of both water (15:25, 27) and food (16:13–14), the people of Israel show a hardness of heart like Pharaoh and the Egyptians, which is precisely how Ps. 95:7–9 describes these events.

17:6 at Horeb. See note on 3:1. **I will stand before you there on the rock**. A further example of the Lord's promise to Moses, "I will be with you" (3:12). The Lord's presence presumably was manifested in the pillar of cloud (see 13:21–22), providing protection for Moses from the quarreling people of Israel, but also as a demonstration of God's power, producing fear and awe among the people. The trustworthiness of God's promise to provide for his people is dramatically demonstrated, as Moses obeys God's command to strike the rock and the Lord provides water for his people. In light of God's promise to stand there "on the rock," some interpreters see a close identification between the presence of God and the rock itself. The command, **you shall strike the rock**, is thus understood to be God's command to Moses to strike God himself, with the result that God himself is the source of the life-giving water that flowed from the rock. This incident probably provides the background in the NT when Paul says "the rock was Jesus" (1 Cor. 10:4; see note on Num. 20:2–13).

17:7 The place where these events happened will bear names for Israel that reflect these events (**Massah** means *testing* and **Meribah** means *quarreling*, see ESV footnotes) and thus act as a reminder for the people (see Ps. 95:7–9; cf. Heb. 3:7–4:13).

17:8–16 *Passage Problem: Israel Defeats Amalek.* While Israel is camped at Rephidim (v. 8; cf. v. 1), the people face their first battle when they are attacked by the people of Amalek, who inhabited the northern Sinai peninsula (Gen. 14:7; Num. 13:29).

17:9 This is the first mention of **Joshua**, who acts as an assistant to Moses (see 24:13; 33:11). He will be among the few who are faithful in the wilderness (see Num. 14:6–9, 30) and will succeed Moses, leading Israel into Canaan (see Deut. 34:9; Josh. 1:1–9).

17:9–13 The focus on Moses' **hand(s)** (vv. 9, 11, 12) manifests two things that the people of Israel need to take to heart: (1) Moses is the one whom the Lord has chosen to lead Israel (notice that Moses' hands relate to who **prevailed**; v. 11); and (2) the Lord is responsible for working their deliverance through Moses (signified by the **staff of God** in Moses' hand [v. 9] and the fact that his hands **grew weary** [v. 12], showing his human weakness).

9[h]ch. 4:20
10[g][See ver. 9 above] [i]ch. 24:14; 31:2
11[j][1 Tim. 2:8]
12[i][See ver. 10 above]
13[g][See ver. 9 above]
14[g][See ver. 9 above] [k]Num. 24:20; Deut. 25:19; 1 Sam. 15:3, 7; 30:1, 17; 2 Sam. 8:12
15[l][Judg. 6:24]
16[k][See ver. 14 above]
Chapter 18
1[m][ch. 2:18] [n]ver. 12; ch. 2:16
3[o]ch. 4:20; Acts 7:29 [p]ch. 2:22 [q]Ps. 39:12; Heb. 11:13
5[r]See ch. 3:1
7[s]Gen. 14:17; 18:2; 19:1; 1 Kgs. 2:19 [t][Gen. 29:13; 33:4]; 2 Sam. 19:39
8[u]See Neh. 9:9-15; Ps. 78:12-28, 42-53; 106:7-12
10[v]Gen. 14:20; 2 Sam. 18:28; Luke 1:68
11[w]1 Chr. 16:25; 2 Chr. 2:5; Ps. 95:3; 97:9; 135:5 [x]Neh. 9:10; [Ps. 119:21; Dan. 4:37; Luke 1:51]
12[y]Deut. 12:7; 14:26; 1 Chr. 29:22; [ch. 24:11; Gen. 31:54]

top of the hill with [h]the staff of God in my hand." 10 So [g]Joshua did as Moses told him,
and fought with Amalek, while Moses, Aaron, and [i]Hur went up to the top of the hill.
11 Whenever Moses [j]held up his hand, Israel prevailed, and whenever he lowered his hand,
Amalek prevailed. 12 But Moses' hands grew weary, so they took a stone and put it under
him, and he sat on it, while Aaron and [i]Hur held up his hands, one on one side, and the
other on the other side. So his hands were steady until the going down of the sun. 13 And
[g]Joshua overwhelmed Amalek and his people with the sword.
14 Then the LORD said to Moses, "Write this as a memorial in a book and recite it in the
ears of [g]Joshua, that [k]I will utterly blot out the memory of Amalek from under heaven."
15 And Moses [l]built an altar and called the name of it, The LORD Is My Banner, 16 saying,
"A hand upon the throne[1] of the LORD! [k]The LORD will have war with Amalek from generation to generation."

Jethro's Advice

18 [m]Jethro, [n]the priest of Midian, Moses' father-in-law, heard of all that God had done
for Moses and for Israel his people, how the LORD had brought Israel out of Egypt.
2 Now Jethro, Moses' father-in-law, had taken Zipporah, Moses' wife, after he had sent her
home, 3 along with her [o]two sons. The name of the one was Gershom ([p]for he said, [q]"I have
been a sojourner[2] in a foreign land"), 4 and the name of the other, Eliezer[3] (for he said, "The
God of my father was my help, and delivered me from the sword of Pharaoh"). 5 Jethro,
Moses' father-in-law, came with his sons and his wife to Moses in the wilderness where
he was encamped at the [r]mountain of God. 6 And when he sent word to Moses, "I,[4] your
father-in-law Jethro, am coming to you with your wife and her two sons with her," 7 Moses
[s]went out to meet his father-in-law and bowed down and [t]kissed him. And they asked
each other of their welfare and went into the tent. 8 Then Moses told his father-in-law [u]all
that the LORD had done to Pharaoh and to the Egyptians for Israel's sake, all the hardship
that had come upon them in the way, and how the LORD had delivered them. 9 And Jethro
rejoiced for all the good that the LORD had done to Israel, in that he had delivered them
out of the hand of the Egyptians.
10 Jethro said, [v]"Blessed be the LORD, who has delivered you out of the hand of the
Egyptians and out of the hand of Pharaoh and has delivered the people from under the
hand of the Egyptians. 11 Now I know that [w]the LORD is greater than all gods, because in
this affair they [x]dealt arrogantly with the people."[5] 12 And Jethro, Moses' father-in-law,
brought a burnt offering and sacrifices to God; and Aaron came with all the elders of Israel
to eat bread with Moses' father-in-law [y]before God.

[1] A slight change would yield *upon the banner* [2] *Gershom* sounds like the Hebrew word for *sojourner* [3] *Eliezer* means *My God is help* [4] Hebrew; Samaritan, Septuagint, Syriac *behold* [5] Hebrew *with them*

17:14–16 No explicit reason is given for the severity of the Lord's judgment on **Amalek**. A later reference to the event (Deut. 25:17–19) says that Amalek "did not fear God," having attacked the people of Israel who were trailing behind and tired from the journey. The Amalekites still posed a threat to Israel in the days of Saul and David (1 Sam. 15:3). For a longer discussion of a similar matter, see Introduction to Joshua: The Destruction of the Canaanites.

18:1–27 *Judgment Problem: Jethro Advises Moses.* After all of Israel's difficulties, this section highlights Jethro's peaceful relationship with Moses (vv. 1–6), his response to what the Lord has done (vv. 7–12), and his counsel (vv. 13–27).

18:1 Jethro, the priest of Midian, Moses' father-in-law (see 3:1; 4:18). Although it would have been possible to refer to him simply as "Jethro" after 18:1, the narrative highlights his relationship to Moses. He is referred to as "Jethro, Moses' father-in-law" repeatedly in the opening verses (vv. 2, 5, 6) and then most often as "his/Moses' father-in-law" (vv. 7, 8, 12, 14, 15, 17, 24, 27). In light of the difficulty of both Egypt and the journey to Rephidim, Jethro's coming to meet Moses displays a relational posture of peace and encouragement, similar to when Aaron met Moses "at the mountain of God" (see v. 5) on his return from Midian (see 4:27–31).

18:2 Zipporah was last mentioned traveling with Moses on the way back to Egypt (see 4:20, 24–26), and the narrative does not include a description of the situation in which Moses **sent her home** (probably for her safety). The interchange between Jethro and Moses appears to signify a relationship of peace and goodwill.

18:3–4 In contrast to the place names that have marked Israel's grumbling with Moses and testing of the Lord (see 15:23; 17:7), this aside in the narrative mentions the names of Moses' sons. This serves to remind Moses (and Israel) of his time as a **sojourner** (18:3; see 2:22) in another land and that Yahweh, the **God** of his **father**, was his **help** (18:4; see 3:6).

18:5 Since the provision of water from a rock takes place at Horeb (see 17:6) while Israel is camped at Rephidim (17:1, 8), the reference to Moses being **encamped at the mountain of God** seems to indicate that the events of this chapter occur at the same place. It is from here that Israel will make the short trip to the base of Mount Sinai (19:2).

18:8–12 After simply hearing about what the Lord had done on Israel's behalf, Jethro's words and actions represent a more faithful response than came from many of those who had experienced the events in Egypt (not to mention Egypt itself, as well as Amalek). When he says, **"Now I know that the LORD is greater than all gods"** (v. 11), he echoes the purpose that the Lord said the plagues were to have for both Israel (6:7) and Egypt (7:5, 17). When Jethro brings a **burnt offering and sacrifices** and eats **before God** with Moses, Aaron, and the elders, he prefigures the pattern of life that the Lord will reveal further at Mount Sinai (see Deut. 12:5–7).

13 The next day Moses sat to judge the people, and the people stood around Moses from
morning till evening. 14 When Moses' father-in-law saw all that he was doing for the people,
he said, "What is this that you are doing for the people? Why do you sit alone, and all the
people stand around you from morning till evening?" 15 And Moses said to his father-in-
law, "Because [z]the people come to me to inquire of God; 16 [a]when they have a dispute, they
come to me and I decide between one person and another, and I [b]make them know the
statutes of God and his laws." 17 Moses' father-in-law said to him, "What you are doing is
not good. 18 You and the people with you will certainly wear yourselves out, for the thing
is too heavy for you. [c]You are not able to do it alone. 19 Now obey my voice; I will give you
advice, and God be with you! You shall [d]represent the people before God and [e]bring their
cases to God, 20 and you shall warn them about the statutes and the laws, and make them
know [f]the way in which they must walk and [g]what they must do. 21 Moreover, look for
[h]able men from all the people, men who fear God, who are trustworthy and hate a bribe,
and place such men over the people as chiefs of thousands, of hundreds, of fifties, and of
tens. 22 And [i]let them judge the people at all times. [j]Every great matter they shall bring
to you, but any small matter they shall decide themselves. So it will be easier for you, and
they will [k]bear the burden with you. 23 If you do this, God will direct you, you will be [l]able
to endure, and all this people also will go to their place in peace."

24 So Moses listened to the voice of his father-in-law and did all that he had said. 25 [m]Moses
chose able men out of all Israel and made them heads over the people, chiefs of thousands,
of hundreds, of fifties, and of tens. 26 And [n]they judged the people at all times. Any hard
case they brought to Moses, but any small matter they decided themselves. 27 Then Moses
let his father-in-law depart, and [o]he went away to his own country.

Israel at Mount Sinai

19 On the third new moon after the people of Israel had gone out of the land of Egypt,
on that day they [p]came into the wilderness of Sinai. 2 They set out from [q]Rephidim
and came into the wilderness of Sinai, and they encamped in the wilderness. There Israel
encamped before [r]the mountain, 3 while [s]Moses went up to God. [t]The LORD called to him
out of the mountain, saying, "Thus you shall say to the house of Jacob, and tell the people
of Israel: 4 [u]You yourselves have seen what I did to the Egyptians, and how [v]I bore you on
eagles' wings and brought you to myself. 5 Now therefore, if you will indeed obey my voice
and keep my covenant, you shall be [w]my treasured possession among all peoples, for [x]all
the earth is mine; 6 and you shall be to me a [y]kingdom of priests and [z]a holy nation. These
are the words that you shall speak to the people of Israel."

7 So Moses came and called the elders of the people and set before them all these words
that the LORD had commanded him. 8 [a]All the people answered together and said, "All
that the LORD has spoken we will do." And Moses reported the words of the people to the

15 [z][Lev. 24:12; Num. 15:34]
16 [a]ch. 24:14; Deut. 17:8; [2 Sam. 15:2, 3; 1 Cor. 6:1] [b]Deut. 4:5; 5:1
18 [c]Num. 11:14, 17; Deut. 1:9, 12
19 [d]ch. 4:16; [ch. 20:19; Deut. 5:5] [e]Num. 27:5
20 [f]Ps. 143:8 [g]Deut. 1:18
21 [h]Deut. 1:15; 16:18; See 2 Chr. 19:5-10; [Acts 6:3]
22 [i]ver. 26 [j]Lev. 24:11; Num. 15:33; 27:2; 36:1; Deut. 1:17; 17:8 [k]Num. 11:17
23 [l]ver. 18
25 [m]Deut. 1:15
26 [n]ver. 22
27 [o][Num. 10:29, 30]

Chapter 19

1 [p]Num. 33:15
2 [q]ch. 17:1, 8 [r]See ch. 3:1
3 [s]ch. 20:21; [Acts 7:38] [t]ch. 3:4
4 [u]Deut. 29:2 [v]Deut. 32:11, 12; Isa. 63:9; Rev. 12:14
5 [w]Deut. 7:6; 14:2; 26:18; Ps. 135:4; Mal. 3:17; Titus 2:14 [x]ch. 9:29; Deut. 10:14; Job 41:11; Ps. 24:1; 50:12; 1 Cor. 10:26
6 [y]1 Pet. 2:5, 9; Rev. 1:6; 5:10; 20:6 [z]Lev. 20:26; Deut. 7:6; 14:21; 26:19; 28:9; Isa. 62:12; 1 Pet. 2:9
8 [a]ch. 24:3, 7; Deut. 5:27; 26:17

18:13–26 In his advice Jethro upholds Moses' role as the one through whom Israel would **know the statutes of God and his laws** (v. 16) while also helping him find a faithful and workable way to have others **bear the burden** of judging the people (v. 22), thus ensuring the people's well-being.

19:1–40:38 *Covenant at Sinai.* The second half of Exodus focuses on the events at Mount Sinai and the content of the law revealed to Moses. The narrative includes: the preparation of the people (19:1–25); the Ten Commandments and other laws (20:1–23:19); the instructions for entering the land (23:20–33); the confirmation of the covenant (24:1–18); the instructions relating to the tabernacle (25:1–31:18; 35:1–3); the breach, intercession, and renewal of the covenant (32:1–34:35); and the assembling of the tabernacle (35:4–40:38).

19:1–25 *Setting: Sinai.* Israel arrives at Sinai, where the rest of the events of Exodus will take place and where the Lord will reveal his covenant through Moses. Chapter 19 focuses on the instructions that the Lord gives to Moses in order to prepare Israel for his presence at Mount Sinai.

19:1–3 When Israel comes to the **wilderness of Sinai** and camps at **the mountain** (vv. 1–2), it is the fulfillment of the sign the Lord promised to Moses at the burning bush—that he would bring the people out of Egypt and they would "serve God on this mountain" (3:12). **On the third new moon** puts their arrival at Sinai about seven weeks after the exodus. This coincides with the Feast of Weeks (Pentecost), which among other things celebrates the giving of the law (Lev. 23:15–21).

19:4–6 The Lord calls Israel to be faithful to his **covenant** even before he has revealed all of its particulars (v. 5). What they **have seen** in Egypt (v. 4) reminds them that God's covenant relationship with them is prior to and essential for their living as his people.

19:6 When the Lord calls Israel **a kingdom of priests and a holy nation**, he is not referring exclusively to the role that Aaron and his sons will fill as priests (28:1) but also to what Israel's life as a whole is to represent among the nations. By keeping the covenant (19:5), the people of Israel would continue both to set themselves apart from, and also to mediate the presence and blessing of the Lord to, the nations around them (see Gen. 12:3; Deut. 4:6; note on Isa. 61:5–7). When Peter applies these terms to the church (see 1 Pet. 2:5, 9), he is explaining that the mixed body of Jewish and Gentile believers inherit the privileges of Israel, and he is calling the believers to persevere in faithfulness so that those around them "may see your good deeds and glorify God on the day of visitation" (1 Pet. 2:12).

LORD. 9 And the LORD said to Moses, "Behold, I am coming to you [b]in a thick cloud, that
[c]the people may hear when I speak with you, and may also [d]believe you forever."
When Moses told the words of the people to the LORD, 10 the LORD said to Moses, "Go to
the people and [e]consecrate them today and tomorrow, and let them [f]wash their garments
11 and be ready for the third day. For on the third day [g]the LORD will come down on Mount
Sinai in the sight of all the people. 12 And you shall set limits for the people all around, saying, 'Take care not to go up into the mountain or touch the edge of it. [h]Whoever touches
the mountain shall be put to death. 13 No hand shall touch him, but he shall be stoned or
shot;[1] whether beast or man, he shall not live.' When [i]the trumpet sounds a long blast,
they shall come up to the mountain." 14 So Moses [j]went down from the mountain to the
people and [e]consecrated the people; [f]and they washed their garments. 15 And he said to
the people, "Be ready for the [k]third day; [l]do not go near a woman."
16 On the morning of the [k]third day there were [m]thunders and lightnings and [n]a thick
cloud on the mountain and a very loud [o]trumpet blast, so that all the people in the camp
[p]trembled. 17 Then [q]Moses brought the people out of the camp to meet God, and they
took their stand at the foot of the mountain. 18 Now [r]Mount Sinai was wrapped in smoke
because the LORD had descended on it in fire. The smoke of it went up like the smoke of
a kiln, and [s]the whole mountain trembled greatly. 19 And as the [o]sound of the trumpet
grew louder and louder, Moses spoke, and [t]God answered him in thunder. 20 The LORD
came down on Mount Sinai, to the top of the mountain. And the LORD called Moses to
the top of the mountain, and Moses went up.
21 And the LORD said to Moses, "Go down and warn the people, lest they break through
to the LORD [u]to look and many of them perish. 22 Also let the priests who come near to
the LORD [v]consecrate themselves, lest the LORD [w]break out against them." 23 And Moses
said to the LORD, "The people cannot come up to Mount Sinai, for you yourself warned
us, saying, [x]'Set limits around the mountain and consecrate it.'" 24 And the LORD said to
him, "Go down, and come up bringing Aaron with you. But do not let the priests and the
people [y]break through to come up to the LORD, lest he break out against them." 25 So Moses
went down to the people and told them.

The Ten Commandments

20 [z]And [a]God spoke all these words, saying,
2 [b]"I am the LORD your God, who brought you out of the land of Egypt, out of the
house of slavery.

[1] That is, shot with an arrow

9 [b]ch. 20:21; 24:16; Deut. 4:11; Ps. 18:11; 97:2; [Matt. 17:5] [c]Deut. 4:12, 36; [John 12:28, 29] [d]ch. 14:31
10 [e]Lev. 11:44, 45; [Josh. 3:5] [f][Gen. 35:2; Lev. 15:5]
11 [g]ch. 34:5; [Deut. 33:2]
12 [h]Cited Heb. 12:20
13 [i]ver. 16, 19
14 [j]ver. 3 [e][See ver. 10 above] [f][See ver. 10 above]
15 [k]ver. 11 [l][1 Sam. 21:4, 5; 1 Cor. 7:5]
16 [k][See ver. 15 above] [m]Ps. 77:18; Heb. 12:18; Rev. 4:5; 8:5; 11:19 [n]ver. 9 [o]ver. 13 [p]Heb. 12:21
17 [q]Deut. 4:10
18 [r]ch. 24:17; Judg. 5:5; [Ps. 144:5; Isa. 6:4; Rev. 15:8] [s]Ps. 68:8; Heb. 12:26
19 [o][See ver. 16 above] [t]Neh. 9:13; Ps. 81:7
21 [u][ch. 3:6; 1 Sam. 6:19]
22 [v]Lev. 10:3 [w]2 Sam. 6:8; 1 Chr. 13:11
23 [x]ver. 12; [Josh. 3:4]
24 [y]2 Sam. 6:8; 1 Chr. 13:11

Chapter 20

1 [z]For ver. 1-17, see Deut. 5:6-21 [a]Deut. 5:22
2 [b]Lev. 26:13; Ps. 81:10; Hos. 13:4

19:9 that the people may hear when I speak with you. The sights and sounds of the Lord's presence on Mount Sinai are emphasized throughout the section (see also vv. 11, 16–19) and were to signify further that Moses was the one through whom the Lord was revealing his word to Israel.

19:10–13 Through the instructions to **consecrate** the people (vv. 10–11) and to **set limits** (vv. 12–13), the Lord is preparing Israel for the pattern of worship that will be embodied in the tabernacle (see 26:31–37). The mountain is to be set apart because it will be made holy by the Lord's presence on it (19:11). The Hebrew verb translated "consecrate" is lit. "to set apart as holy" and indicates that Moses is to prepare Israel to come before a holy God. While most of the specifics are not given, the call to **wash their garments** (v. 10) indicates that consecration includes setting aside or altering aspects of daily living in preparation to meet God (see v. 17).

19:15 It is not clear whether the instruction to **not go near a woman** was included in or implied by the Lord's instruction to Moses. The purpose of consecration (see vv. 10–13) indicates that the rationale likely includes abstaining from sex as an aspect of setting oneself apart to meet with God (cf. Lev. 15:16–18), not because of anything presumed to be inherently unacceptable in either sex or women.

19:16–20 All the sights (**lightnings and a thick cloud**, v. 16; **smoke** and **fire**, v. 18) and sounds (**thunders** and **a very loud trumpet blast**, vv. 16, 19) signify the Lord's presence (v. 18); the experience was to be a continual reminder to Israel that the Lord had spoken to Moses (see vv. 18–21).

19:22–24 The reference to **the priests** precedes the Lord's instructions that Aaron and his sons will fill the role (see 28:1). If Aaron's sons are being referred to here, they are grouped together with **the people** as those who are restricted from coming up on the mountain. **break out against them.** I.e., kill them (cf. Lev. 10:1–2; 2 Sam. 6:6–8).

20:1–23:33 *Covenant Words and Rules.* This section records what will later be referred to as the Book of the Covenant (24:7) and includes: the Ten Commandments (20:1–21); instructions on worship (20:22–26; 23:10–19); rules and principles for community life (21:1–23:9); and instructions for entering the land of Canaan (23:20–33).

20:1–21 *The Ten Commandments.* (See note on Deut. 5:1–21.) The Ten Commandments or "ten words" (see ESV footnote at Ex. 34:28) are highlighted as the core of the covenant stipulations revealed to Moses; they define the life that the Lord calls his people to live before him (20:1–11) and with each other (vv. 12–17). The commandments are not exhaustive even in the areas to which they relate, but indicate to Israel how to remain faithful to the Lord. After Israel has wandered in the wilderness for forty years, Moses will restate the commandments to the generation that is about to enter the land of Canaan (see Deut. 5:6–21 and notes). NT authors assume the applicability of these commands in shaping the moral life of both Jewish and Gentile Christians (e.g., Rom. 13:9–10; Eph. 6:2).

20:1 When **God spoke all these words**, he did so in such a way that all the people could hear. Cf. the repeated description of the sights and sounds of the Lord's presence on Mount Sinai (19:16–20; 20:18); and "I have talked with you from heaven" (v. 22).

20:2 I am the LORD your God, who brought you out of . . . Egypt. As a preface to the Ten Commandments and the rest of the law, this description

3 [c]"You shall have no other gods before[1] me.
4 [d]"You shall not make for yourself a carved image, or any likeness of anything that is in
heaven above, or that is in the earth beneath, or that is in the water under the earth. 5 [e]You
shall not bow down to them or serve them, for I the LORD your God am [f]a jealous God,
[g]visiting the iniquity of the fathers on the children to the third and the fourth generation
of those who hate me, 6 but showing steadfast love to thousands[2] of those who love me
and keep my commandments.
7 [h]"You shall not take the name of the LORD your God in vain, for the LORD will not
hold him guiltless who takes his name in vain.
8 [i]"Remember the Sabbath day, to keep it holy. 9 [j]Six days you shall labor, and do all your
work, 10 but the [k]seventh day is a Sabbath to the LORD your God. On it you shall not do
any work, you, or your son, or your daughter, your male servant, or your female servant,
or your livestock, or the [l]sojourner who is within your gates. 11 For [m]in six days the LORD
made heaven and earth, the sea, and all that is in them, and rested on the seventh day.
Therefore the LORD blessed the Sabbath day and made it holy.
12 [n]"Honor your father and your mother, [o]that your days may be long in the land that
the LORD your God is giving you.
13 [p]"You shall not murder.[3]

[1] *Or besides* [2] *Or to the thousandth generation* [3] The Hebrew word also covers causing human death through carelessness or negligence

3 [c]2 Kgs. 17:35; Jer. 25:6; 35:15
4 [d]Lev. 26:1; Deut. 27:15; Ps. 97:7; [Acts 17:29]
5 [e]ch. 23:24; Josh. 23:7 [f]ch. 34:14; Deut. 4:24; 6:15; Josh. 24:19; Nah. 1:2 [g]ch. 34:7; Num. 14:18; [Ps. 79:8; 109:14; Isa. 65:6, 7; Jer. 32:18]
7 [h]Lev. 19:12; [Matt. 5:34, 35; James 5:12]
8 [i]Lev. 19:3, 30; 26:2; See ch. 31:13-17
9 [j]ch. 23:12; 34:21; 35:2; Lev. 23:3; Luke 13:14
10 [k]ch. 16:26; 31:15; Gen. 2:2, 3; Ezek. 20:12; See Num. 15:32-36 [l]See Neh. 13:16-19
11 [m]See Gen. 1:1–2:3
12 [n]Lev. 19:3; Cited Matt. 15:4; 19:19; Mark 7:10; 10:19; Luke 18:20; Eph. 6:2; [Jer. 35:18, 19] [o]Eph. 6:3
13 [p]Cited Matt. 5:21; 19:18; Rom. 13:9; [Gen. 9:5, 6; 1 John 3:15]

signifies that Israel's call to covenant faithfulness is preceded by and based upon the Lord's acts on their behalf in covenant relationship. Israel's obedience to the commandments is the means by which they are to appropriate and enjoy what the Lord has already done by delivering them from Egypt and taking them to be his possession. The Lord will use the deliverance from Egypt to identify himself throughout Israel's history, often to call them to remember what he has done for them and to live accordingly (e.g., Judg. 6:8; 1 Sam. 10:18; Ps. 81:10; Jer. 34:13).

20:3 You shall have no other gods. Yahweh demands exclusive covenant loyalty. As the one true God of heaven and earth, Yahweh cannot and will not tolerate the worship of any "other gods" (cf. 22:20; 23:13, 24, 32); in other words, monotheism, the worship of the one true God, is the only acceptable belief and practice. **before me**. This Hebrew expression has been taken to mean "in preference to me," or "in my presence," or "in competition with me." Most likely, "in my presence" (i.e., worshiping other gods in addition to the Lord) is the intended sense here, in view of (1) the creation account (Gen. 1:1–2:3), which makes any "other gods" irrelevant (since only the Lord is active); (2) the events in Egypt, in which the Lord displayed his superiority to "other gods" (cf. Ex. 12:12; 15:11; Ezek. 20:7–8); and (3) the persistent call to worship Yahweh alone (Ex. 22:20; 23:13, 24, 32–33; cf. Deut. 6:13–15). Even though this commandment does not comment on whether these "other gods" might have some real existence, Moses' statement to a later generation makes clear that only "the LORD is God; there is no other besides him" (Deut. 4:35, 39; see also Ps. 86:10; Isa. 44:6, 8; 45:5, 6, 18; and 1 Cor. 8:4–6). See also note on Deut. 5:7.

20:4–6 You shall not make for yourself a carved image. The gods of both Egypt and Canaan were often associated with some aspect of creation and worshiped as, or through, an object that represented them. The Lord has made it clear, through the plagues and the exodus, that he has power over every aspect of creation because the whole earth is his (9:29; 19:5), and thus he commands Israel to refrain from crafting an image of anything in **heaven** or **earth** for worship (20:4–5a). The prohibition is grounded in the fact that the Lord is a jealous God (see 34:14; Deut. 6:15), and that the Lord has no physical form, and should not be thought to be localized in one (Deut. 4:15–20). Israel saw what happened to Egypt when Pharaoh refused to acknowledge what was being revealed about the Lord; here Israel is warned against doing the same, while also being reassured that their God is merciful and gracious (see Ex. 34:6–7).

20:5–6 a jealous God. God the Creator is worthy of all honor from his creation. Indeed, his creatures (mankind esp.) are functioning properly only when they give God the honor and worship that he deserves. God's jealousy is therefore also his zeal for his creatures' well-being. **visiting the iniquity of the fathers on the children**. Human experience confirms that immoral behavior on the part of parents often results in suffering for their children and grandchildren. This is one of the grievous aspects of sin, that it harms others besides the sinner himself. But this general principle is qualified in two ways: First, it applies only to **those who hate me**, i.e., to those who persist in unbelief as enemies of God. The cycle of sin and suffering can be broken through repentance. Second, the suffering comes to **the third and the fourth generation**, while God shows **steadfast love** (v. 6) to another group of people, namely, to **thousands of those who love me and keep my commandments** (i.e., to the thousandth generation; see ESV footnote, and cf. Deut. 7:9).

20:7 Taking the Lord's name **in vain** (see note on Deut. 5:11) refers primarily to someone taking a deceptive oath in God's name or invoking God's name to sanction an act in which the person is being dishonest (Lev. 19:12). It also bans using God's name in magic, or irreverently, or disrespectfully (Lev. 24:10–16). The Lord revealed his name to Moses (Ex. 3:14–15), and he has continued to identify himself in connection with his acts on Israel's behalf (see 6:2, 6–8). Yahweh is warning Israel against using his name as if it were disconnected from his person, presence, and power.

20:8–11 Israel is to **remember the Sabbath day** by keeping it **holy** (v. 8; see notes on Deut. 5:12–15). The Lord had already begun to form the people's life in the rhythm of working for **six days** (Ex. 20:9) and resting on the **seventh day** as a **Sabbath** (v. 10) through the instructions for collecting manna (see 16:22–26). Here the command is grounded further in the way that it imitates the Lord's pattern in creation (20:11; see Gen. 2:1–3). Every aspect of Israel's life is to reflect that the people belong to the Lord and are sustained by his hand. The weekly pattern of work and rest is to be a regular and essential part of this (see Ex. 31:12–18). In Deut. 5:15, Moses gives another reason for observing the day: it recalls their redemption from slavery in Egypt.

20:12 Honor your father and your mother. The word "honor" means to treat someone with the proper respect due to the person and their role. With regard to parents, this means (1) treating them with deference (cf. 21:15, 17); (2) providing for them and looking after them in their old age (for this sense of honor, see Prov. 3:9). Both Jesus and Paul underline the importance of this command (Mark 7:1–13; Eph. 6:1–3; 1 Tim. 5:4). This is the only one of the Ten Commandments with a specific promise attached to it: **that your days may be long**—meaning not just a long life, but one that is filled with God's presence and favor. See note on Deut. 5:16.

20:13–15 The sixth through eighth commandments present general prohibitions not to **murder** (v. 13; see note on Deut. 5:17), **commit adultery** (v. 14), or **steal** (v. 15). In doing so, they set minimum standards for Israel to be a just society and indicate the context in which the people will be called further to be holy and to love the Lord with all their heart, soul, and might (Deut. 6:4–9), and their neighbors with goodwill and generosity (Lev. 19:18). Thus, while the prohibition against stealing is a basic principle of justice in Israel's national life, the people are called to do more than refrain from taking

14 [q]"You shall not commit adultery.
15 [r]"You shall not steal.
16 [s]"You shall not bear false witness against your neighbor.
17 [t]"You shall not covet [u]your neighbor's house; [v]you shall not covet your neighbor's
wife, or his male servant, or his female servant, or his ox, or his donkey, or anything that
is your neighbor's."
18 Now when all the people saw [w]the thunder and the flashes of lightning and the sound
of the trumpet and the mountain smoking, the people were afraid[1] and trembled, and
they stood far off 19 and said to Moses, [x]"You speak to us, and we will listen; but do not let
God speak to us, lest we die." 20 [y]Moses said to the people, "Do not fear, for God has come
to [z]test you, that the fear of him may be before you, that you may not sin." 21 The people
stood far off, while Moses drew near to the [a]thick darkness where God was.

Laws About Altars

22 And the LORD said to Moses, "Thus you shall say to the people of Israel: 'You have
seen for yourselves that I have [b]talked with you from heaven. 23 [c]You shall not make gods
of silver to be with me, nor shall you make for yourselves gods of gold. 24 An altar of earth
you shall make for me and sacrifice on it your burnt offerings and your peace offerings,
your sheep and your oxen. [d]In every place where I cause my name to be remembered I will
come to you and [e]bless you. 25 [f]If you make me an altar of stone, [g]you shall not build it of
hewn stones, for if you wield your tool on it you profane it. 26 And you shall not go up by
steps to my altar, that your nakedness be not exposed on it.'

Laws About Slaves

21 "Now these are the [h]rules that you shall set before them. 2 [i]When you buy a Hebrew
slave,[2] he shall serve six years, and in the seventh he shall go out free, for nothing.
3 If he comes in single, he shall go out single; if he comes in married, then his wife shall

[1] Samaritan, Septuagint, Syriac, Vulgate; Masoretic Text *the people saw* [2] Or *servant;* the Hebrew term *'ebed* designates a range of social and economic roles; also verses 5, 6, 7, 20, 21, 26, 27, 32 (see Preface)

14 [q]Lev. 18:20; Deut. 22:22; Prov. 6:32; 1 Cor. 6:9; Heb. 13:4; Cited Matt. 5:27; Rom. 13:9
15 [r]Lev. 19:11; Eph. 4:28; Cited Matt. 19:18; Rom. 13:9
16 [s]ch. 23:1; Prov. 19:5, 9; 21:28; 24:28; 25:18; Cited Matt. 19:18; See Deut. 19:16-20
17 [t]Luke 12:15; Eph. 5:3, 5; Cited Rom. 7:7; 13:9; [Col. 3:5; Heb. 13:5] [u]Mic. 2:2 [v]Jer. 5:8; Matt. 5:28
18 [w]Heb. 12:18
19 [x]Deut. 5:25, 27; 18:16; Gal. 3:19, 20; Heb. 12:19
20 [y][1 Sam. 12:20] [z][Gen. 22:1]; Deut. 13:3
21 [a]Deut. 4:11; 2 Sam. 22:10; 1 Kgs. 8:12; Ps. 18:9; 97:2
22 [b]Deut. 4:36; Neh. 9:13; Heb. 12:25
23 [c][ch. 32:31; 2 Kgs. 17:33; Ezek. 20:39; Zeph. 1:5]
24 [d]Deut. 12:5, 11; 14:23; 16:6, 11; 26:2; 1 Kgs. 8:29; 9:3; 2 Chr. 6:6; 7:16; 12:13; Ezra 6:12; Neh. 1:9; Ps. 74:7; Jer. 7:10, 12 [e]Deut. 7:13
25 [f]Deut. 27:5; Josh. 8:31 [g][1 Kgs. 5:17; 1 Chr. 22:2]

Chapter 21

1 [h]ch. 24:3; Deut. 4:14; 6:1
2 [i]Deut. 15:12; Jer. 34:14; See Lev. 25:39-41

another person's possessions. They are to embody the Lord's love for them by loving the stranger and sojourner as themselves (Lev. 19:33–34). When Jesus refers to the law in the Sermon on the Mount ("you have heard that it was said," Matt. 5:21ff.), he is correcting not the intended purpose of the OT law but the mistaken presumption that these laws (or their interpretation) were meant to be exhaustive of what it meant to live as a child of the kingdom of heaven. (E.g., as Jesus made clear, simply refraining from murder does not fulfill the law when a person disdains his brother as a fool; or simply refraining from adultery does not fulfill the law when a man lusts after a woman; see Matt. 5:21–24, 27–28; and note on Matt. 5:21–48.)

20:16 Acting as a **false witness** (see 23:1–3) suggests a legal trial in which false testimony could lead to punishment for one's **neighbor**. Bearing "false witness" is condemned in Scripture for its disastrous effects among people and its utter disregard for God's character (see Prov. 6:16–19; 12:22; 19:5, 9). The Lord's righteousness and justice were to be reflected in Israel's life as a nation, which was thus to exclude speaking falsely, especially for the sake of gaining something at the expense of another person and perverting justice.

20:17 While the previous four commandments focus on actions committed or words spoken (vv. 13–16), the tenth commandment warns against allowing the heart to **covet . . . anything that is your neighbor's**. When a person covets, he allows the desire for that which is coveted to govern his relationship with other people; this may become the motivation for murder, stealing, or lying either to attain the desired thing or to keep it from someone else. Because of the way that coveting values a particular thing over trust in and obedience to the Lord as the provider, it is also a breach of the first commandment, which the apostle Paul makes clear when he refers to coveting as idolatry (Eph. 5:5; Col. 3:5).

20:18–20 The last time Israel had experienced a sign of **thunder** and **lightning**, it was in the context of the plague of hail sent on Egypt (see 9:23–26). Moses tells the people not to **fear** that God would kill them (20:20), explaining that God is testing them so that their life in the land might be governed by the **fear** of the Lord (see Deut. 6:2).

20:22–26 *Worship Instructions: Against Idols and for an Altar.* Together with 23:10–19, these verses frame the first section of laws following the Ten Commandments (21:1–23:9) and focus on Israel's worship. Israel's relationship with the Lord is her first priority (see the sequence of the Ten Commandments). This is reflected again here in that these religious regulations precede those on relating to one's neighbor. These rules give more detailed explanations of the obligations implied by the first and second commandments (20:3–6).

21:1–23:19 *Detailed Legislation.* This section contains basic guidelines for living together as a just society while also calling the people to live as those who are set apart to the Lord. The specific laws are not intended to be exhaustive but are to result in a way of life characterized by justice and civility among the people of God, so that they are free to pursue moral excellence.

21:1 The word translated **rules** could also be rendered "rulings" or "judgments," i.e., decisions by a judge that could be used to mediate particular disputes between people in Israel.

21:2–11 All of these rules pertain to slaves in Israel and seek to govern the movement of people in and out of a household in a way that is just—both for them and for the household of which they have been a part. Israelites are to remember what life was like in Egypt and to avoid oppressing one another in the same manner (see Lev. 25:35–46). Although the restitution for slaves is governed by their social situation, their identity as full human beings, rather than mere possessions, is assumed, since they are not included in the laws governing the loss of property (see Ex. 21:33–22:15). (Cf. notes on 1 Cor. 7:21; Eph. 6:5; Col. 3:22–25; Philem. 18–19.)

21:2 Just as the rhythm of Israel's life is to be six days of work and then a Sabbath of rest to the Lord (20:8–11), so there will be patterns of giving rest to a **slave** after **six years** of service, to the land after six years of cultivation (see 23:10–11; Lev. 25:1–6), and to both people and land in the Year of Jubilee—after seven sets of seven years (see Lev. 25:8–22). Israel's life is to image the pattern set by the Lord in creation (Gen. 2:1–3), so that they will continually trust him for their provision.

go out with him. 4 If his master gives him a wife and she bears him sons or daughters, the
wife and her children shall be her master's, and he shall go out alone. 5 But [j]if the slave
plainly says, 'I love my master, my wife, and my children; I will not go out free,' 6 then his
master shall bring him to [k]God, and he shall bring him to the door or the doorpost. And
his master shall bore his ear through with an awl, and he shall be his slave forever.
7 "When a man [l]sells his daughter as a slave, she shall not go out as the male slaves do.
8 If she does not please her master, who has designated her[1] for himself, then he shall let
her be redeemed. He shall have no right to sell her to a foreign people, since he has broken
faith with her. 9 If he designates her for his son, he shall deal with her as with a daughter.
10 If he takes another wife to himself, he shall not diminish her food, her clothing, or [m]her
marital rights. 11 And if he does not do these three things for her, she shall go out for nothing, without payment of money.
12 [n]"Whoever strikes a man so that he dies shall be put to death. 13 [o]But if he did not lie
in wait for him, but God let him fall into his hand, then [p]I will appoint for you a place to
which he may flee. 14 But if a man willfully attacks another to kill him by cunning, [q]you
shall take him from my altar, that he may die.
15 "Whoever strikes his father or his mother shall be put to death.
16 [r]"Whoever steals a man and sells him, and anyone found [s]in possession of him, shall
be put to death.
17 [t]"Whoever curses[2] his father or his mother shall be put to death.
18 "When men quarrel and one strikes the other with a stone or with his fist and the
man does not die but takes to his bed, 19 then if the man rises again and walks outdoors
with his staff, he who struck him shall be clear; only he shall pay for the loss of his time,
and shall have him thoroughly healed.
20 "When a man strikes his slave, male or female, with a rod and the slave dies under his
hand, he shall be avenged. 21 But if the slave survives a day or two, he is not to be avenged,
for the [u]slave is his money.
22 "When men strive together and hit a pregnant woman, so that her children come out,
but there is no harm, the one who hit her shall surely be fined, as the woman's husband

[1] Or *so that he has not designated her* [2] Or *dishonors*; Septuagint *reviles*

5 [j]Deut. 15:16, 17
6 [k][Ps. 82:6; John 10:34, 35]
7 [l]Neh. 5:5
10 [m]1 Cor. 7:5
12 [n]Gen. 9:6; Lev. 24:17; Num. 35:30, 31; [Matt. 26:52]
13 [o]Deut. 19:4, 5; See Num. 35:22-25 [p]Num. 35:11; Deut. 4:41-43; 19:2, 3; See Josh. 20:2-9
14 [q]See 1 Kgs. 2:28-34
16 [r]Deut. 24:7; 1 Tim. 1:10 [s]ch. 22:4
17 [t]Lev. 20:9; Deut. 27:16; Cited Matt. 15:4; Mark 7:10; [Prov. 20:20; 30:11]
21 [u][Lev. 25:45, 46]

21:5–6 Debt was the most common reason that people became slaves. To employ a destitute person as a slave could be seen as a benevolent act, as it guaranteed him food and shelter and some income (Gen. 47:23–25). The security provided by a good employer could lead some slaves to choose to remain in that status permanently.

21:7–11 If a poor family could not afford the costs of a normal wedding, the father might "sell" his daughter to a rich man as his "slave," i.e., as a secondary wife like Zilpah and Bilhah (Gen. 29:24, 29). As wives from poor families, they could face exploitation—which these laws aim to prevent.

21:12–32 These laws relate to situations in which someone has been injured by another person (vv. 12–27) or by an animal (vv. 28–32).

21:13 The reference to **a place to which he may flee** looks forward to the cities of refuge that the Lord will prescribe (see Num. 35:9–15) in order to protect someone who killed unintentionally—until their case can be judged.

21:16 This instruction, repeated in Deut. 24:7, indicates that the people of Israel were called to justice not only in the way they treated slaves but also in the manner by which a person could become a slave.

21:17 This rule is placed among other commandments that deal with either death or physical harm. Its placement here, along with the prescription of the death penalty, highlights the gravity of the command to honor one's parents (20:12; cf. Mark 7:9–10). As earlier instructions have already indicated, Israel's faithfulness to the Lord is to be formed not simply through its worship but also in the life of the household (Ex. 12:26; 13:8; cf. also Deut. 4:9; 6:7).

21:20–21 These verses provide a general rule relating to cases in which a slave has been severely beaten by his master (**strikes his slave . . . with a rod**). The instruction not to avenge a slave who survives such a beating because **the slave is his money** relates only to the financial circumstances of the one he serves; it is neither a description of how a slave as a person is to be understood, nor a prescription for how a slave is to be treated. The expectation for how Israelites were to treat one another (and particularly those who were typically oppressed or overlooked) is indicated in the repeated statements at the end of this section of laws: "You shall not wrong a sojourner or oppress him" (22:21–24; 23:6–9).

21:22–25 These verses contain phrases that are difficult to interpret. The ESV offers a traditional understanding in the text and a more recent view in the footnote. The situation in view is a brawl between men. A pregnant woman nearby is accidentally hit. This results in either a premature live birth or a miscarriage where the child dies (**her children come out**; the plural "children" is probably a plural of indefiniteness, allowing for either a single or a multiple birth). This much is clear, but interpreters disagree about the exact meaning of the Hebrew traditionally rendered **there is no harm . . . there is harm**, and **the judges determine** (see ESV footnote for the alternative reading). According to the traditional view, "harm" is suffered by either the woman or her baby. Depending on the extent of loss (death of the baby, injury to the baby, injury to the mother), the man who caused the injury shall pay "as the judges determine," presumably according to the "eye-for-eye" principle. As the preceding and following laws show (vv. 26–32), "eye for eye" was not taken literally. It was simply a formula for proportionate punishment or compensation. One implication, however, is that the death of the baby seems to be judged according to the same principles that apply to the taking of other human life (e.g., the death of the mother). The alternative view understands the obscure terms quite differently (see ESV footnote). This view presupposes that the baby has died, and the issue is who is to pay the penalty for the death of the baby and the injury to the mother. In a fight, it may not be obvious who is responsible for the damaging blow. If the offender is identifiable, he alone must pay for the loss of life—as much as the husband demands (cf. v. 30). If the offender cannot be identified, the community (**you**) **shall pay**. This principle also applies to compensation for injuries the woman may have suffered (according to the "eye-for-eye" principle as noted above). By either interpretation, the OT attributes human personhood to the developing baby in the womb (cf. Ps. 51:5 and note; 71:5–6 and note; 139:13–16); but

shall impose on him, and [v]he shall pay as the [w]judges determine. 23 But if there is harm,[1]
then you shall pay [x]life for life, 24 [y]eye for eye, tooth for tooth, hand for hand, foot for foot,
25 burn for burn, wound for wound, stripe for stripe.

26 "When a man strikes the eye of his slave, male or female, and destroys it, he shall let
the slave go free because of his eye. 27 If he knocks out the tooth of his slave, male or female,
he shall let the slave go free because of his tooth.

28 "When an ox gores a man or a woman to death, the [z]ox shall be stoned, and its flesh
shall not be eaten, but the owner of the ox shall not be liable. 29 But if the ox has been
accustomed to gore in the past, and its owner has been warned but has not kept it in,
and it kills a man or a woman, the ox shall be stoned, and its owner also shall be put to
death. 30 If [a]a ransom is imposed on him, then [v]he shall give for the redemption of his life
whatever is imposed on him. 31 If it gores a man's son or daughter, he shall be dealt with
according to this same rule. 32 If the ox gores a slave, male or female, the owner shall give
to their master [b]thirty shekels[2] of silver, and [z]the ox shall be stoned.

Laws About Restitution

33 "When a man opens a pit, or when a man digs a pit and does not cover it, and an ox or
a donkey falls into it, 34 the owner of the pit shall make restoration. He shall give money
to its owner, and the dead beast shall be his.

35 "When one man's ox butts another's, so that it dies, then they shall sell the live ox and
share its price, and the dead beast also they shall share. 36 Or if it is known that the ox has
been accustomed to gore in the past, and its owner has not kept it in, he shall repay ox for
ox, and the dead beast shall be his.

22 [3] "If a man steals an ox or a sheep, and kills it or sells it, he shall repay five oxen for
an ox, and [c]four sheep for a sheep. 2 [4] If a thief is found [d]breaking in and is struck
so that he dies, there shall be no bloodguilt for him, 3 but if the sun has risen on him, there
shall be bloodguilt for him. He shall surely pay. If he has nothing, then [e]he shall be sold
for his theft. 4 If the stolen beast [f]is found alive in his possession, whether it is an ox or a
donkey or a sheep, [g]he shall pay double.

5 "If a man causes a field or vineyard to be grazed over, or lets his beast loose and it feeds
in another man's field, he shall make restitution from the best in his own field and in his
own vineyard.

6 "If fire breaks out and catches in thorns so that the stacked grain or the standing grain
or the field is consumed, he who started the fire shall make full restitution.

7 "If a man gives to his neighbor money or goods to keep safe, and it is stolen from the
man's house, then, if the thief is found, [g]he shall pay double. 8 If the thief is not found,
the owner of the house shall come near to God to show whether or not he has put his
hand to his neighbor's property. 9 For every breach of trust, whether it is for an ox, for a
donkey, for a sheep, for a cloak, or for any kind of lost thing, of which one says, 'This is it,'

[1] *Or so that her children come out and it is clear who was to blame, he shall be fined as the woman's husband shall impose on him, and he alone shall pay. If it is unclear who was to blame . . .* [2] A *shekel* was about 2/5 ounce or 11 grams [3] Ch 21:37 in Hebrew [4] Ch 22:1 in Hebrew

22 [v][Deut. 22:18, 19] [w][Job 31:11]
23 [x]Deut. 19:21
24 [y]Lev. 24:20; Deut. 19:21; Cited Matt. 5:38
28 [z]Gen. 9:5
30 [a]ch. 30:12; Num. 35:31, 32 [v][See ver. 22 above]
32 [b][Zech. 11:12, 13; Matt. 26:15] [z][See ver. 28 above]

Chapter 22

1 [c]2 Sam. 12:6; [Prov. 6:31; Luke 19:8]
2 [d]Matt. 24:43
3 [e][ch. 21:2]
4 [f]ch. 21:16 [g][ver. 1]
7 [g][See ver. 4 above]

the law also distinguishes between death due to willful murder and death due to negligence (see Ex. 21:12–14, 28–32). However understood, this law demonstrates the Bible's concern to protect life, including life in the womb.

21:23–25 The general principle in Israel is that restitution for a life taken or harmed shall be **life for life, eye for eye, tooth for tooth . . . stripe for stripe** (see also Lev. 24:17–22; Deut. 19:21). In relation to taking human life, the rule is grounded in humanity being made in God's image (see Gen. 9:6) and in the way that bloodshed defiles the land in which a holy God dwells with his people (see Num. 35:30–34). A number of scholars now hold that, as the surrounding context makes clear, the principle is not applied literally in every case, but the application of the principle takes into account differing circumstances (see Ex. 21:12–14, 19, 21, 26–28, 30). In Matt. 5:38–42 Jesus shows that this principle, which was meant to guide judges in assessing damages, was never intended as the rule for ordinary interpersonal relationships (in which the faithful should seek to imitate God's own generosity).

21:28–29 In situations where an animal gores and kills a person, the instruction that it **shall be stoned** is another illustration for Israel that human life is to be understood as holy to the Lord (see also 19:12–13).

21:33–22:15 These laws relate to loss of animals and property.

21:33–36 Irresponsible action (like not covering a pit, v. 33) and previous knowledge (like an ox's tendency to gore, v. 36) are to be taken into consideration when stipulating the sort of restitution that is required.

22:2–3 if the sun has risen on him. This condition distinguishes between what is permissible retaliation when a thief is caught breaking in during the night (v. 2) vs. during the day (v. 3). The stipulation protects both the one who is surprised by a thief at night (v. 2) and the thief himself, who could be identified during the day and should be brought to the judges for punishment (vv. 3b, 4).

22:7–13 In addition to laws governing damage to or theft of property *owned* by a person, this section describes circumstances in which a person has been given either property or animals by another for safekeeping, and what was entrusted to him has been stolen (vv. 7–9) or injured (vv. 10–13).

22:9 In this case, lying about being the victim of a thief is the means by which a person acts like a thief and takes his neighbor's property (also in v. 12). Thus, the person must **pay double to his neighbor**, which is the

the case of both parties shall come before God. The one whom God condemns shall pay
double to his neighbor.
10 "If a man gives to his neighbor a donkey or an ox or a sheep or any beast to keep safe,
and it dies or is injured or is driven away, without anyone seeing it, 11 [h]an oath by the LORD
shall be between them both to see whether or not he has put his hand to his neighbor's
property. The owner shall accept the oath, and he shall not make restitution. 12 But if [i]it
is stolen from him, he shall make restitution to its owner. 13 If it is torn by beasts, let him
bring it as evidence. He shall not make restitution for what has been torn.
14 "If a man borrows anything of his neighbor, and it is injured or dies, the owner not
being with it, he shall make full restitution. 15 If the owner was with it, he shall not make
restitution; if it was hired, it came for its hiring fee.[1]

Laws About Social Justice

16 [j]"If a man seduces a virgin[2] who is not betrothed and lies with her, he shall give the
bride-price[3] for her and make her his wife. 17 If her father utterly refuses to give her to him,
[j]he shall pay money equal to the [k]bride-price for virgins.
18 [l]"You shall not permit a sorceress to live.
19 [m]"Whoever lies with an animal shall be put to death.
20 [n]"Whoever sacrifices to any god, other than the LORD alone, shall be devoted to
destruction.[4]
21 [o]"You shall not wrong a sojourner or oppress him, for you were sojourners in the land
of Egypt. 22 [p]You shall not mistreat any widow or fatherless child. 23 If you do mistreat them,
and they [q]cry out to me, I will surely [r]hear their cry, 24 and my wrath will burn, and I will kill
you with the sword, and [s]your wives shall become widows and your children fatherless.
25 [t]"If you lend money to any of my people with you who is poor, you shall not be like a
moneylender to him, and you shall not exact interest from him. 26 [u]If ever you take your
neighbor's cloak in pledge, you shall return it to him before the sun goes down, 27 for that
is his only covering, and it is his cloak for his body; in what else shall he sleep? And if he
[q]cries to me, I will hear, for I am [v]compassionate.
28 [w]"You shall not revile God, nor [w]curse a ruler of your people.
29 "You shall not delay to offer from the fullness of your harvest and from the outflow
of your presses. [x]The firstborn of your sons you shall give to me. 30 [y]You shall do the same
with your oxen and with your sheep: [z]seven days it shall be with its mother; on the eighth
day you shall give it to me.
31 [a]"You shall be consecrated to me. Therefore [b]you shall not eat any flesh that is torn
by beasts in the field; [c]you shall throw it to the dogs.
23 [d]"You shall not spread a false report. You shall not join hands with a wicked man
to be a [e]malicious witness. 2 You shall not fall in with the many to do evil, nor shall
you bear witness in a lawsuit, siding with the many, so as to pervert justice, 3 [f]nor shall you
be partial to a poor man in his lawsuit.

[1] Or *it is reckoned in* (Hebrew *comes into*) its hiring fee [2] Or *a girl of marriageable age*; also verse 17 [3] Or *engagement present*; also verse 17 [4] That is, set apart (devoted) as an offering to the Lord (for destruction)

11 [h]Heb. 6:16
12 [i]Gen. 31:39
16 [j]Deut. 22:28, 29
17 [j][See ver. 16 above] [k]Gen. 34:12; 1 Sam. 18:25
18 [l]Lev. 19:26, 31; 20:27; Deut. 18:10, 11; 1 Sam. 28:3, 9
19 [m]Lev. 18:23; 20:15; Deut. 27:21
20 [n][Num. 25:2, 7, 8; Josh. 23:16]; See Deut. 13:1-15; 17:2-5
21 [o]ch. 23:9; Lev. 19:33; Deut. 10:18, 19; Jer. 7:6; Zech. 7:10; Mal. 3:5
22 [p]Deut. 24:17; 27:19; Ps. 94:6; Isa. 1:17, 23; 10:2; Ezek. 22:7; Zech. 7:10; James 1:27
23 [q]Job 34:28; Luke 18:7 [r]Ps. 18:6; 145:19; [James 5:4]
24 [s]Ps. 109:9; Lam. 5:3
25 [t]Lev. 25:35-37; Deut. 23:19, 20; Neh. 5:7; Ps. 15:5; Prov. 28:8; Ezek. 18:8, 13, 17; 22:12
26 [u]Deut. 24:13, 17; Prov. 20:16; Ezek. 18:7, 16; Amos 2:8; [Prov. 22:27]
27 [q][See ver. 23 above] [v]ch. 34:6; 2 Chr. 30:9; Neh. 9:17
28 [w]Cited Acts 23:5; [2 Sam. 19:21; Eccles. 10:20; Jude 8]
29 [x]See ch. 13:2
30 [y]Deut. 15:19 [z]Lev. 22:27
31 [a]ch. 19:6; Lev. 11:44, 45 [b]Lev. 22:8; Ezek. 4:14; 44:31 [c][Matt. 7:6]

Chapter 23

1 [d][Lev. 19:11; Ps. 15:3; 101:5] [e]Deut. 19:16-18; Ps. 35:11; [1 Kgs. 21:10, 13; Matt. 26:59-61; Acts 6:11, 13]
3 [f]Lev. 19:15; [Deut. 1:17]

restitution required of a thief (see v. 4). The person would say **"this is it"** to indicate, "this is the item in dispute."

22:16–17 This rule relates to the practice of a man paying a **bride-price** to his future father-in-law in order to marry his **virgin** daughter. Although the expression referring to the one who **seduces** the daughter most likely implies some mutual consent, the consequence focuses on the responsibility of the man to provide, both through marrying the woman (unless the father **utterly refuses**, v. 17) and by paying her father (see Deut. 22:28–29). Since the bride-price was equivalent to several years' wages, Ex. 22:17 amounts to the threat of huge damages in the case of premarital intercourse.

22:18–20 These rules each carry the penalty of death because they are contrary to Israel being a holy people who worship a holy God: the presence of a **sorceress** (v. 18; see Lev. 20:26–27), having sex with an **animal** (Ex. 22:1; see Lev. 18:23), and offering **sacrifices** to other gods (Ex. 22:20; see 20:3; 23:13) are all things that make Israel unclean and are reasons that the Lord is about to judge the nations in Canaan (see Lev. 20:22–26).

22:21–23:9 The instruction for Israel not to wrong or oppress **a sojourner** frames this section (22:21; 23:9), which seeks to help the people recognize that they are called beyond keeping the basic rules for a civil society, to embodying the very character of the Lord in caring for those who are easily oppressed and even those who may be predisposed against them (see 23:4–5).

22:22 Through his prophets, the Lord will repeatedly denounce the mistreatment of the **widow** and the **fatherless child** in Israel and Judah (e.g., Isa. 1:17, 23; Jer. 5:28; 7:5–7; 22:3; Zech. 7:10).

22:25–27 Amos 2:8 condemns Israel for openly ("beside every altar") flouting this law.

23:1–3, 6–8 These sections complement one another and warn Israel against acting to **pervert justice** (vv. 2, 6) by being a false witness (see 20:16). The structures of civil and religious life in Israel were meant to represent the evaluation of the Lord and to form the people according to his character, which is

4[g]“If you meet your enemy’s ox or his donkey going astray, you shall bring it back to
him. 5 If you see the donkey of one who hates you lying down under its burden, you shall
refrain from leaving him with it; you shall rescue it with him.
6[h]“You shall not pervert the justice due to your poor in his lawsuit. 7[d]Keep far from a
false charge, and [i]do not kill the innocent and righteous, for [j]I will not acquit the wicked.
8[k]And you shall take no bribe, for a bribe blinds the clear-sighted and subverts the cause
of those who are in the right.
9[l]“You shall not oppress a sojourner. You know the heart of a sojourner, for you were
sojourners in the land of Egypt.

Laws About the Sabbath and Festivals

10[m]“For six years you shall sow your land and gather in its yield, 11 but the seventh year
you shall let it rest and lie fallow, that the poor of your people may eat; and what they
leave the beasts of the field may eat. You shall do likewise with your vineyard, and with
your olive orchard.
12[n]“Six days you shall do your work, but on the seventh day you shall rest; that your ox
and your donkey may have rest, and the son of your servant woman, and the alien, may
be refreshed.
13[o]“Pay attention to all that I have said to you, and make no mention of the names of
other gods, nor let it be heard on your lips.
14[p]“Three times in the year you shall keep a feast to me. 15[q]You shall keep the Feast of
Unleavened Bread. As I commanded you, you shall eat unleavened bread for seven days
at the appointed time in the month of [r]Abib, for in it you came out of Egypt. [s]None shall
appear before me empty-handed. 16 You shall keep [t]the Feast of Harvest, of the firstfruits
of your labor, of what you sow in the field. You shall keep the [u]Feast of Ingathering at the
end of the year, when you gather in from the field the fruit of your labor. 17[p]Three times
in the year shall all your males appear before the Lord GOD.
18[v]“You shall not offer the blood of my sacrifice with anything leavened, or let the fat
of my feast remain until the morning.
19“The best of the [w]firstfruits of your ground you shall bring into the house of the
LORD your God.
[x]“You shall not boil a young goat in its mother’s milk.

Conquest of Canaan Promised

20[y]“Behold, I send an angel before you to guard you on the way and to bring you to the
place that I have prepared. 21 Pay careful attention to him and obey his voice; [z]do not rebel
against him, [a]for he will not pardon your transgression, for my name is in him.
22“But if you carefully obey his voice and do all that I say, then [b]I will be an enemy to
your enemies and an adversary to your adversaries.

4[g][Deut. 22:1, 4; Prov. 25:21; Matt. 5:44; Rom. 12:20; 1 Thess. 5:15]
6[h]Deut. 27:19; Eccles. 5:8; Isa. 10:1, 2; Jer. 5:28, 29; Mal. 3:5
7[d][See ver. 1 above] [i]Deut. 27:25; [Prov. 17:26] [j]ch. 34:7
8[k]Deut. 16:19; [1 Sam. 8:3; 2 Chr. 19:7; Ps. 26:10; Prov. 17:23; Isa. 1:23; 5:23; 33:15]
9[l]See ch. 22:21
10[m]Lev. 25:3, 4
12[n]See ch. 20:9
13[o]Deut. 4:9; Josh. 22:5; 23:7; Hos. 2:17; Zech. 13:2
14[p]ver. 17; ch. 34:23; Deut. 16:16
15[q]See ch. 12:15 [r]ch. 13:4 [s]ch. 34:20; Deut. 16:16
16[t]ch. 34:22; See Lev. 23:9-21 [u]Deut. 16:13; See Lev. 23:34-44
17[p][See ver. 14 above]
18[v]ch. 12:8; 34:25; Lev. 2:11
19[w]ch. 34:26; Lev. 2:12; 23:10, 17; Num. 18:12, 13; Deut. 26:2, 10; Neh. 10:35; Ezek. 44:30 [x]ch. 34:26; Deut. 14:21
20[y]ch. 14:19; 33:2, 14; Josh. 5:13, 14; 6:2; Isa. 63:9
21[z]Ps. 78:40, 56 [a][ch. 32:34; 34:7; Num. 14:35; Josh. 24:19]
22[b]Gen. 12:3; Deut. 30:7; Jer. 30:20

why the warnings are grounded in the judgment of the Lord: **for I will not acquit the wicked** (23:7; see 34:7).

23:4–5 Israel is called beyond merely keeping the civil laws, to act in ways that represent love for an **enemy** (v. 4) or **one who hates** them (v. 5; see Lev. 19:18).

23:6 The warning not to **pervert the justice due** includes the refusal to take advantage of the **poor** in a **lawsuit** (v. 6) as well as to show partiality to them by altering testimony (v. 3).

23:10–19 See note on 20:22–26.

23:10 The pattern of work and rest that is to frame Israel’s week (see v. 12) is also to be applied to the pattern of years (see Lev. 25:2–7).

23:12 As is true for anything that the Lord commands, keeping the Sabbath as a day of **rest** (20:8–11) is good not only for the individual who is responsible to act faithfully but also for others, in this case for all those who are a part of the household (cf. Mark 2:27).

23:14–17 This section reaffirms the celebration of the **Feast of Unleavened Bread** (v. 15; see 12:15–20; 13:3–10) and introduces the **Feast of Harvest** and the **Feast of Ingathering** (23:16), which are explained in further detail later (see Lev. 23:9–22).

23:19 The reason for this rule is not made explicit here or in the other places where it is repeated (see 34:26; Deut. 14:21). Boiling a **young goat in its mother’s milk** may have been a pagan religious ceremony practiced by the nations in Canaan as a way to induce fertility. Alternatively it may be seen as a gross violation of the natural order: the young goat should drink its mother’s milk and gain life from it, not be cooked in it.

23:20–33 *Commands for the Conquest.* The Lord promises to send his angel before the people into Canaan (vv. 20, 23) and calls them to obey him by driving the nations out, by destroying their places of worship, and by being faithful in serving him alone.

23:20–22 The **angel** who will go before Israel is described in ways that closely identify him with God: the Lord tells Israel not to **rebel against him** (v. 21) because **he will not pardon your transgression** and because **my name is in him** (v. 21, implying God’s nature and character), and that to **obey his voice** is to **do all that I say** (v. 22). When Joshua finally leads the people into the land, he meets a figure outside Jericho referred to as “the commander of the army of the LORD” who speaks nearly identical words as those spoken to Moses at the burning bush (see 3:2; Josh. 5:13–15); both his title and drawn sword seem to identify him with the angel who has protected Israel (see Ex. 14:19) and who is promised here to go before them into Canaan (see also 33:2).

23 [y]"When my angel goes before you and brings you [c]to the Amorites and the Hittites
and the Perizzites and the Canaanites, the Hivites and the Jebusites, and I blot them out,
24 you shall [d]not bow down to their gods nor serve them, [e]nor do as they do, but [f]you shall
utterly overthrow them and break their [g]pillars in pieces. 25 You [h]shall serve the LORD your
God, and [i]he[1] will bless your bread and your water, and [j]I will take sickness away from
among you. 26 [k]None shall miscarry or be barren in your land; I will fulfill the [l]number of
your days. 27 I will send [m]my terror before you and will throw into [n]confusion all the people
against whom you shall come, and I will make all your enemies turn their backs to you.
28 And [o]I will send hornets[2] before you, which shall drive out the Hivites, the Canaanites,
and the Hittites from before you. 29 [p]I will not drive them out from before you in one
year, lest the land become desolate and the wild beasts multiply against you. 30 Little by
little I will drive them out from before you, until you have increased and possess the land.
31 [q]And I will set your border from the Red Sea to the Sea of the Philistines, and from the
wilderness to the Euphrates,[3] for [r]I will give the inhabitants of the land into your hand,
and you shall drive them out before you. 32 [s]You shall make no covenant with them and
their gods. 33 They shall not dwell in your land, lest they make you sin against me; for if
you serve their gods, [t]it will surely be a snare to you."

The Covenant Confirmed

24 Then he said to Moses, "Come up to the LORD, you and Aaron, [u]Nadab, and Abihu,
and [v]seventy of the elders of Israel, and worship from afar. 2 Moses [w]alone shall
come near to the LORD, but the others shall not come near, and the people shall not come
up with him."

3 Moses came and told the people all the words of the LORD and [x]all the rules.[4] And all
the people answered with one voice and said, [y]"All the words that the LORD has spoken
we will do." 4 And [z]Moses wrote down all the words of the LORD. He rose early in the
morning and built an altar at the foot of the mountain, and twelve [a]pillars, according to
the twelve tribes of Israel. 5 And he sent young men of the people of Israel, who offered
burnt offerings and sacrificed peace offerings of oxen to the LORD. 6 And [b]Moses took half
of the blood and put it in basins, and half of the blood he threw against the altar. 7 Then
he took the Book of the Covenant and read it in the hearing of the people. And they said,
[x]"All that the LORD has spoken we will do, and we will be obedient." 8 [c]And Moses took
the blood and threw it on the people and said, "Behold the blood of the covenant that the
LORD has made with you in accordance with all these words."

9 Then Moses and Aaron, Nadab, and Abihu, and [d]seventy of the elders of Israel [e]went

[1] Septuagint, Vulgate *I* [2] *Or the hornet* [3] Hebrew *the River* [4] *Or all the just decrees*

23 [y][See ver. 20 above] [c]See ch. 13:5
24 [d]ch. 20:5 [e]Lev. 18:3; Deut. 12:30, 31 [f]ch. 34:13; Num. 33:52; Deut. 7:5, 25; 12:3 [g]See Deut. 16:22
25 [h]Deut. 6:13; 10:12, 20; 11:13; 13:4; Josh. 22:5; Matt. 4:10 [i]Deut. 7:13; 28:5, 8 [j]ch. 15:26; Deut. 7:15
26 [k]Deut. 7:14 [l][Job 5:26; Ps. 55:23]
27 [m]Deut. 2:25; Josh. 2:9 [n]Deut. 7:23
28 [o]Deut. 7:20; Josh. 24:12
29 [p]Deut. 7:22
31 [q]Gen. 15:18; Num. 34:3; Deut. 11:24; Josh. 1:4; [1 Kgs. 4:21, 24; Ps. 72:8] [r]Josh. 21:44; Judg. 1:4; 11:21
32 [s]ch. 34:12, 15; Deut. 7:2
33 [t]ch. 34:12; Deut. 7:16; Josh. 23:13; Judg. 2:3; Ps. 106:36

Chapter 24

1 [u]ch. 28:1; See ch. 6:23 [v]Num. 11:16
2 [w]ver. 13, 15, 18
3 [x]ch. 21:1 [y]ch. 19:8; Deut. 5:27
4 [z]Deut. 31:9 [a]Gen. 28:18; 31:45; [ch. 23:24]
6 [b]Heb. 9:18, 19
7 [x][See ver. 3 above]
8 [c]Cited Heb. 9:19, 20; [Heb. 13:20; 1 Pet. 1:2]
9 [d]Num. 11:16 [e][ver. 1]

23:24 you shall not bow down to their gods. See note on 20:3.

23:25–26 Among the gods worshiped in both Egypt and Canaan were those believed to have control over crops, health, or fertility. The Lord made it clear through the signs in Egypt that he has power over all of life and he calls Israel to serve him alone, promising the people blessings through the provisions of food and health (v. 25; see also 15:26) and offspring (23:26).

24:1–18 *Covenant Confirmed.* This section describes three different aspects of the covenant being confirmed: (1) Moses leads the people of Israel in sacrificing to the Lord and reconfirming the covenant with them (vv. 3–8); (2) Moses, Aaron and his sons, and the elders worship the Lord and eat before him (vv. 1–2, 9–11); and (3) Moses and Joshua go further up the mountain in order for Moses alone to enter the cloud of the Lord's presence (vv. 12–18).

24:1–2 The distinctions explained in relation to the Lord's presence on Mount Sinai are preparing Israel for the tabernacle. The three groups of people represent three different levels of proximity to the Lord's presence: (1) the people **shall not come up** (v. 2); (2) Moses, Aaron and his sons, and the elders will **worship from afar** (v. 1); and (3) Moses **alone shall come near to the LORD** (v. 2).

24:4 This is one of three references in Exodus to Moses writing (also 34:28) or being commanded to write (17:14; see also Deut. 31:9).

24:5 The narrative of Exodus has already referred to **burnt offerings** (10:25; 18:12) and **peace offerings** (20:24), but the Lord had not yet prescribed their practice or described their function for Israel. While Israel likely had some familiarity with the function of sacrifice, the people manifest their need for the Lord's further instructions when they offer burnt offerings and peace offerings to the golden calf (see 32:6).

24:6–8 The reasons for the covenant-confirming actions of **blood** thrown **against the altar** (v. 6) and **on the people** (v. 8) are not made explicit, but they probably signify the cleansing and atonement aspects of each. The blood links the altar and the people, symbolizing the union of God and Israel in the covenant. The Lord had called Israel to keep his covenant as the means to serving as a kingdom of priests and a holy nation (19:4–6), and here he anoints and inaugurates them to live as such (see Heb. 9:18–22).

24:7 The **Book of the Covenant** most likely refers to both the Ten Commandments (20:1–21) and the commands and rules that follow (20:22–23:33).

24:8 the blood of the covenant. When Jesus uses this phrase of the cup in the Last Supper (Matt. 26:28; Mark 14:24), he is likening the Christian communion meal to the OT peace offering (see note on Ex. 24:9–11; cf. also 1 Cor. 10:17–18).

24:9–11 Moses, Aaron and his sons, and 70 of the elders partake in what the peace offering (v. 5) signifies: fellowship and communion in the presence of God. The description focuses on the fact that the men **saw the God of Israel** (vv. 9–11) and remained unharmed. According to 33:20 "man shall not see me and live," so the "seeing" here in 24:10 was something different from that of 33:20; cf. 33:23, which perhaps denotes a partial, as opposed to a full and complete, vision of God (see notes on Matt. 5:8; John 1:18; Rev. 22:4).

10[f]Gen. 32:30; Judg. 13:22; Isa. 6:1, 5; [ch. 33:20, 23; John 1:18; 1 Tim. 6:16; 1 John 4:12, 20] [g]Ezek. 1:26; 10:1
11[h][ch. 18:12; Gen. 31:54]
12[i]ver. 2, 15, 18 [j]ch. 31:18; 32:15, 16; Deut. 5:22
13[k]ch. 33:11; [ch. 17:9, 10] [l]See ch. 3:1
14[m]ch. 17:10, 12; 31:2
15[n]ch. 19:9, 16; [Matt. 17:5]
16[o]ch. 16:10; Lev. 9:23; Num. 14:10; 16:42
17[p]ch. 3:2; 19:18; Deut. 4:36; Heb. 12:18, 29
18[q]ch. 34:28; Deut. 9:9, 18, 25; 10:10

Chapter 25

2[r]For ver. 1-7, see ch. 35:4-9 [s]ch. 35:5, 21, 29; 36:2; Judg. 5:2; 1 Chr. 29:5; [Ezra 1:6; 2:68; 3:5; 7:16]; Neh. 11:2; [2 Cor. 8:12; 9:7]
4[t]ch. 26:1, 31, 36
5[u]ch. 26:14
6[v]ch. 27:20 [w]ch. 30:7, 23, 34; 31:11
7[x]ch. 28:4, 15
8[y]Heb. 9:1, 2; See ch. 36:1-4 [z]ch. 29:45; 1 Kgs. 6:13; 2 Cor. 6:16; Rev. 21:3
9[a]ver. 40 [b]ch. 26:1
10[c]ch. 37:1-3; Deut. 10:3; Heb. 9:4

up, 10 and they [f]saw the God of Israel. There was under his feet as it were a pavement of
[g]sapphire stone, like the very heaven for clearness. 11 And he did not lay his hand on the
chief men of the people of Israel; they beheld God, and [h]ate and drank.
12 The LORD said to Moses, [i]"Come up to me on the mountain and wait there, that I may
give you the [j]tablets of stone, with the law and the commandment, which I have written
for their instruction." 13 So Moses rose with his assistant [k]Joshua, and Moses went up [l]into
the mountain of God. 14 And he said to the elders, "Wait here for us until we return to you.
And behold, Aaron and [m]Hur are with you. Whoever has a dispute, let him go to them."
15 Then Moses went up on the mountain, and [n]the cloud covered the mountain. 16 [o]The
glory of the LORD dwelt on Mount Sinai, and the cloud covered it six days. And on the
seventh day he called to Moses out of the midst of the cloud. 17 Now the appearance of
the glory of the LORD was like a [p]devouring fire on the top of the mountain in the sight of
the people of Israel. 18 Moses entered the cloud and went up on the mountain. And Moses
[q]was on the mountain forty days and forty nights.

Contributions for the Sanctuary

25 The LORD said to Moses, 2 [r]"Speak to the people of Israel, that they take for me
a contribution. From [s]every man whose heart moves him you shall receive the
contribution for me. 3 And this is the contribution that you shall receive from them: gold,
silver, and bronze, 4 [t]blue and purple and scarlet yarns and fine twined linen, goats' hair,
5 tanned [u]rams' skins, goatskins,[1] acacia wood, 6 [v]oil for the lamps, [w]spices for the anointing
oil and for the fragrant incense, 7 onyx stones, and stones for setting, for the [x]ephod and
for the breastpiece. 8 And let them make me a [y]sanctuary, that [z]I may dwell in their midst.
9 [a]Exactly as I show you concerning the pattern of the [b]tabernacle, and of all its furniture,
so you shall make it.

The Ark of the Covenant

10 [c]"They shall make an ark of acacia wood. Two cubits[2] and a half shall be its length, a
cubit and a half its breadth, and a cubit and a half its height. 11 You shall overlay it with

[1] Uncertain; possibly *dolphin skins*, or *dugong skins*; compare 26:14 [2] A *cubit* was about 18 inches or 45 centimeters

The description of the clear surface they saw **under his feet** may indicate that this is all they saw of God.

24:13–14 This is the first time **Joshua** is referred to as Moses' **assistant** (also 33:11; Josh. 1:1). **Hur** helped Aaron hold up Moses' hands during the battle with Amalek (Ex. 17:10–12).

24:17–18 like a devouring fire. God's presence is often signified in Exodus by fire (see also 3:2; 13:21–22; 19:18; 40:38; cf. Deut. 4:24; 9:3). Moses enters the **cloud** as the one with whom the Lord has chosen to meet, and therefore he is not destroyed (see Ex. 24:9–11).

25:1–31:17 *Instructions for the Tabernacle.* The instructions for the tabernacle (25:1–31:17) and the description of the instructions being carried out (35:4–40:38) make up the majority of the second half of the book of Exodus. The Lord said of Israel, "I will take you to be my people, and I will be your God" (6:7), and the focus on the tabernacle is grounded in the fact that it is the means through which the Lord chose to dwell in the midst of his people (see 25:8; 29:45). The level of detail in the instructions emphasizes that Israel is to worship the Lord according to his word and that the materials, design, and layout of the tabernacle signify how Israel is to relate to the Lord, who is both holy and in their midst. For example, the objects inside the tabernacle where the Lord will meet with his people are made of or overlaid with pure gold (in contrast to the materials outside the tent, which are made of bronze and silver). Although the instructions include a significant level of detail, the details are not exhaustive enough for the reader to be sure precisely how every aspect was to be made (Moses is repeatedly "shown" how to make it, 25:9). The inclusion of the details may also have been meant to ensure that any early Israelite hearing the instructions read aloud would recognize that the tabernacle in their midst was indeed the one revealed to Moses, for him to oversee in construction. At the same time, there are two important keys to understanding the symbolism of the tabernacle. First, the tabernacle is seen as a tented palace for Israel's divine king. He is enthroned on the ark of the covenant in the innermost Holy of Holies (the Most Holy Place). His royalty is symbolized by the purple of the curtains and his divinity by the blue. The closer items are to the Holy of Holies, the more valuable are the metals (bronze→silver→gold) of which they are made. The other symbolic dimension is Eden. The tabernacle, like the garden of Eden, is where God dwells, and various details of the tabernacle suggest it is a mini-Eden. These parallels include the east-facing entrance guarded by cherubim, the gold, the tree of life (lampstand), and the tree of knowledge (the law). Thus God's dwelling in the tabernacle was a step toward the restoration of paradise, which is to be completed in the new heaven and earth (Revelation 21–22).

25:1–9 *Request for Contributions.* Israel's ability to make a **contribution** for the sanctuary was most likely possible through the precious metals and materials that the people brought out of Egypt according to the promise of the Lord (see 3:21–22; 11:2; 12:35–36).

25:8 A **sanctuary** is a "holy place," which, like the ground at the burning bush, is made holy by the Lord's presence (3:5). The presence of the Lord in Israel's **midst** will be borne out in the arrangement of the camp around the tabernacle (see Num. 2:1–34).

25:9 Israel is to follow the **pattern** for the sanctuary **exactly** as the Lord shows Moses (also v. 40; 26:30; 27:8) both because the fear of the Lord is shown through fidelity to what he commands and also because the particulars of the sanctuary are meant to teach the people what it means to have a holy God dwell among them.

25:10–22 *Ark of the Covenant.* The instructions for the sanctuary begin with the **ark** (see 37:1–9), which is God's throne, from where he will meet and speak with Moses (25:22). The special function of the ark is borne out in several ways: its pieces are to be overlaid with or made of **pure gold** (vv. 11–14, 17–18); it will contain the **testimony** (v. 16) that the Lord will give Moses, that is, the tablets of the Ten Commandments; and it is to be the only item in the Most Holy Place (see 26:33).

[d]pure gold, inside and outside shall you overlay it, and you shall make on it a molding of
gold around it. 12 You shall cast four rings of gold for it and put them on its [e]four feet, two
rings on the one side of it, and two rings on the other side of it. 13 You shall make poles
of acacia wood and overlay them with gold. 14 And you shall put the poles into the rings
on the sides of the ark to carry the ark by them. 15 The [f]poles shall remain in the rings of
the ark; they shall not be taken from it. 16 [g]And you shall put into the ark the [h]testimony
that I shall give you.
17 [i]"You shall make a mercy seat[1] of pure gold. Two cubits and a half shall be its length,
and a cubit and a half its breadth. 18 And you shall make two cherubim of gold; of [j]ham-
mered work shall you make them, on the two ends of the mercy seat. 19 Make one cherub
on the one end, and one cherub on the other end. [k]Of one piece with the mercy seat shall
you make the cherubim on its two ends. 20 [l]The cherubim shall spread out their wings
above, overshadowing the mercy seat with their wings, their faces one to another; toward
the mercy seat shall the faces of the cherubim be. 21 And you shall put the mercy seat on the
top of the ark, and in the ark you shall put the testimony that I shall give you. 22 [m]There
I will meet with you, and from above the mercy seat, from [n]between the two cherubim
that are on the ark of the testimony, I will speak with you about all that I will give you in
commandment for the people of Israel.

The Table for Bread

23 [o]"You shall make a table of acacia wood. Two cubits shall be its length, a cubit its
breadth, and a cubit and a half its height. 24 You shall overlay it with [p]pure gold and make
a molding of gold around it. 25 And you shall make a rim around it a handbreadth[2] wide,
and a molding of gold around the rim. 26 And you shall make for it four rings of gold, and
fasten the rings to the four corners at its four legs. 27 Close to the frame the rings shall lie,

[1] Or *cover* [2] A *handbreadth* was about 3 inches or 7.5 centimeters

11 [d]ver. 24, 25; ch. 30:3, 4; 37:2
12 [e]ch. 37:3
15 [f]1 Kgs. 8:8
16 [g][Deut. 31:26; 1 Kgs. 8:9] [h]See ch. 16:34
17 [i]ch. 37:6; Heb. 9:5
18 [j]ver. 31; ch. 37:7, 17, 22; Num. 8:4; 10:2
19 [k]ch. 37:8
20 [l]1 Kgs. 8:7; 1 Chr. 28:18; Heb. 9:5
22 [m]ch. 29:42, 43; 30:6, 36; Lev. 16:2; Num. 17:4 [n]Num. 7:89
23 [o]For ver. 23-29, see ch. 37:10-16; [1 Kgs. 7:48; 2 Chr. 4:8; Heb. 9:2]
24 [p]ver. 11

The Ark of the Covenant

The ark of the covenant (Ex. 25:10–22; 37:1–9) was the only piece of furniture in the Most Holy Place; the ark and its contents were kept hidden from view at all times. The ark itself was a wooden chest, overlaid with pure gold, measuring 3.75 feet long, 2.25 feet wide, and 2.25 feet high (1.1 m x 0.7 m x 0.7 m). It contained within it the two stone tablets of the Testimony (the Ten Commandments). The author of Hebrews adds that it also contained "a golden urn holding the manna, and Aaron's staff that budded" (Heb. 9:4). The ark was not to be touched by human hands. Two wooden poles, overlaid with gold, were used to transport it and were not to be removed from the ark. The mercy seat, or atonement cover, was a solid golden slab that fitted perfectly on top of the ark. The golden cherubim, which were hammered out of the same piece of gold, had wings outstretched over the mercy seat and faces that looked downward (in reverent awe). It was here, from between the cherubim, that God spoke to Moses, the representative of the people of Israel. Ancient iconography often depicts cherubim as having a lion-like body, wings, and a human face.

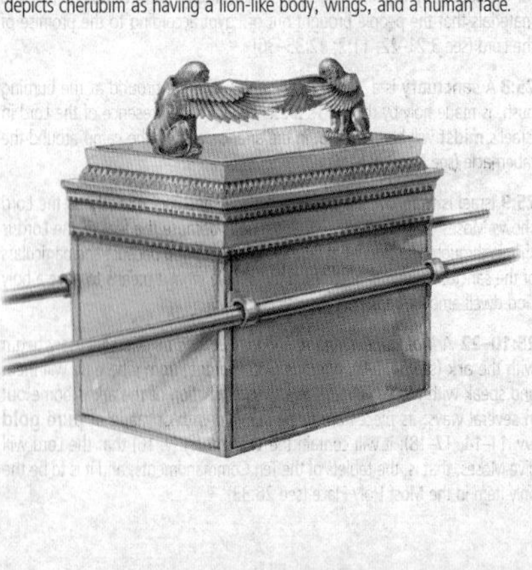

25:17–22 The **mercy seat** (v. 17) and the **two cherubim** (vv. 18–20) are to be made of gold and fashioned as one piece, which will act as the cover for the ark (v. 21; see illustration to the left). The noun translated "mercy seat" (Hb. *kapporet*) may be related to the verb that typically has the sense "to make atonement" (Hb. *kipper*) and is thus sometimes translated as "atonement cover." The instructions here focus on the fact that it is **from above the mercy seat, from between the two cherubim** that the Lord will speak to Moses (v. 22; see also Num. 7:89). For this reason, the Lord is sometimes referred to in the OT as being "enthroned" upon the cherubim (Ps. 80:1; also 1 Sam. 4:4; 2 Sam. 6:2; Isa. 37:16). Cherubim are the traditional guardians of holy places. Archaeological finds from non-

The Table for the Bread of the Presence

The wooden table, overlaid with pure gold (Ex. 25:23–30; 37:10–16), was 3 feet long, 1.5 feet wide, and 2.25 feet high (1 m x 0.5 m x 0.7 m). It held the 12 loaves (Lev. 24:5–9) of the bread of the Presence, which were holy (1 Sam. 21:4). Wooden poles, overlaid with gold, were inserted through the rings of the table when the table was transported.

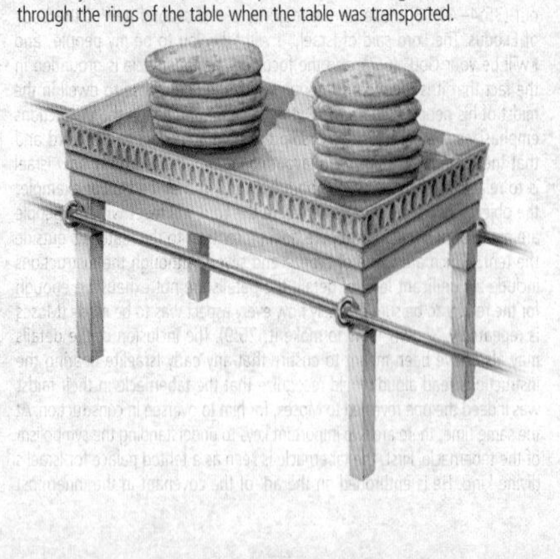

as [q]holders for the poles to carry the table. 28 You shall make the poles of acacia wood, and
overlay them with gold, and the table shall be carried with these. 29 And you shall make its
plates and [r]dishes for incense, and its flagons and bowls with which to pour drink offerings; you shall make them of pure gold. 30 And you shall set the [s]bread of the Presence on
the table before me regularly.

The Golden Lampstand

31 [t]"You shall make a lampstand of pure gold. The lampstand shall be made of hammered work: its base, its stem, its cups, its calyxes, and its flowers shall be of one piece
with it. 32 And there shall be six branches going out of its sides, three branches of the
lampstand out of one side of it and three branches of the lampstand out of the other
side of it; 33 three cups made like almond blossoms, each with calyx and flower, on one
branch, and three cups made like almond blossoms, each with calyx and flower, on the
other branch—so for the six branches going out of the lampstand. 34 And on the lampstand itself there shall be four cups made like almond blossoms, with their calyxes and
flowers, 35 and a calyx of one piece with it under each pair of the six branches going out
from the lampstand. 36 Their calyxes and their branches shall be of one piece with it, the
whole of it a single piece of hammered work of pure gold. 37 You shall make seven lamps
for it. And the lamps [u]shall be set up so as [v]to give light on the space in front of it. 38 Its
tongs and their trays shall be of pure gold. 39 It shall be made, with all these utensils, out
of a talent[1] of pure gold. 40 And [w]see that you make them after the pattern for them, which
is being shown you on the mountain.

The Tabernacle

26 "Moreover, [x]you shall make the [y]tabernacle with ten curtains of [z]fine twined linen
and blue and purple and scarlet yarns; you shall make them with cherubim [z]skill-
fully worked into them. 2 The length of each curtain shall be twenty-eight cubits,[2] and the
breadth of each curtain four cubits; all the curtains shall be the same size. 3 Five curtains
shall be coupled to one another, and the other five curtains shall be coupled to one another.

[1] A *talent* was about 75 pounds or 34 kilograms [2] A *cubit* was about 18 inches or 45 centimeters

27 [q]ch. 26:29; 30:4; 36:34; 37:14, 27; 38:5
29 [r]ch. 37:16; Num. 4:7
30 [s]Lev. 24:5, 6
31 [t]For ver. 31-39, see ch. 37:17-24; [1 Kgs. 7:49; Zech. 4:2; Heb. 9:2; Rev. 1:12]
37 [u]Lev. 24:2-4; 2 Chr. 13:11 [v]Num. 8:2
40 [w]ver. 9; ch. 26:30; 27:8; Num. 8:4; Acts 7:44; Cited Heb. 8:5; [1 Chr. 28:11, 19]

Chapter 26

1 [x]For ver. 1-37, see ch. 36:8-38 [y]ch. 25:9 [z]ver. 31, 36; ch. 28:6, 15; 36:8, 35; 39:3, 8

Israelite societies suggest that these sometimes looked like winged bulls or lions with human heads.

25:23–30 *Table for the Bread of the Presence.* The **table** (see 37:10–16) is one of three items in the Holy Place (see 40:4–5); like all the items, its pieces are to be either overlaid with **gold** (25:24–26, 28) or made of it (v. 29; see illustration on p. 184). The **bread of the Presence** consisted of 12 flat loaves of bread, symbolizing the 12 tribes of Israel (Lev. 24:5–9). Facing the lampstand, they enjoyed the perpetual light of divine blessing.

25:31–40 *Golden Lampstand.* The **lampstand** (see 37:17–24) is the second of three items in the Holy Place; like the other pieces in the tabernacle, it is made of **pure gold** (25:31; see illustration to the right). The lamp provides light within the tabernacle, and the priests will be instructed to keep it burning regularly (see 27:20–21; Lev. 24:1–4). Its description in terms of cups, calyxes, and flowers shows that it was a symbolic tree, recalling the tree of life in Eden.

25:40 Hebrews 8:5 cites this text in support of its argument that the tent was a faithful copy of the heavenly realities Moses saw on the mountain. From the perspective of the author of Hebrews, the tent had its purpose in the history of God's people, but that purpose is now finished, and the (probably Jewish Christian) audience must not think of relying on it as if it were a divinely sanctioned substitute for Christian faithfulness.

26:1–37 *Tent of the Tabernacle.* This section describes the curtains, frames, and bars (vv. 1–30) that would make up the **tabernacle** (see 36:8–38), which was divided into two sections internally (the Most Holy Place and the Holy Place, 26:31–34) with a screen for the entrance (vv. 36–37). See the illustration of the tabernacle tent (p. 186). The tent's external dimensions were 45 feet long, 15 feet wide, and 15 feet high (or 13.7 m by 4.6 m by 4.6 m). It was surrounded by a screened courtyard 50 yards by 25 yards (or 45.7 m by 22.9 m); see 27:9–19.

26:1 The **cherubim** (also 25:18) are likely included in the design to signify that the tabernacle is the place on earth where the God of heaven has chosen to dwell with Israel. When Adam and Eve are sent out of the garden, cherubim are placed at the entrance to ensure that the couple do not eat from the tree of life in their fallen state (Gen. 3:22–24). Since the cherubim are incorporated on the curtains of the tabernacle and on the veil that separates the Most Holy Place where God will be present (Ex. 26:31), they may represent a similar warning.

The Golden Lampstand

The golden lampstand (Ex. 25:31–40) was made of pure gold, hammered out of one solid piece. Resting on a base, the central stem had six branches, three on either side, together carrying seven lamps. The lampstand with its branches was modeled on a flowering almond tree.

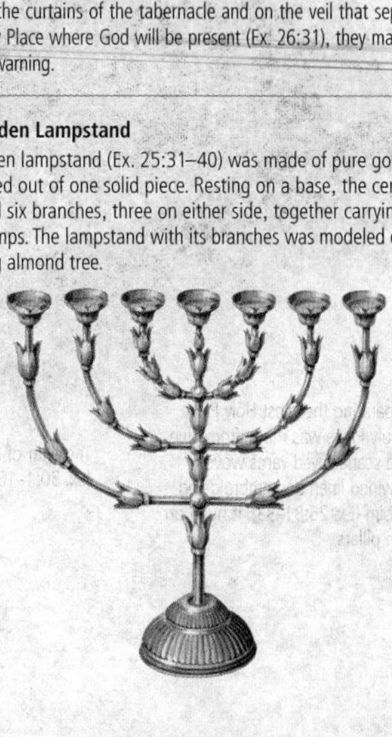

4 And you shall make loops of blue on the edge of the outermost curtain in the first set.
Likewise you shall make loops on the edge of the outermost curtain in the second set.
5 Fifty loops you shall make on the one curtain, and fifty loops you shall make on the edge
of the curtain that is in the second set; the loops shall be opposite one another. 6 And you
shall make fifty clasps of gold, and couple the curtains one to the other with the clasps,
so that the tabernacle may be a single whole.

7 "You shall also make [a]curtains of goats' hair for a tent over the tabernacle; eleven curtains shall you make. 8 The length of each curtain shall be thirty cubits, and the breadth
of each curtain four cubits. The eleven curtains shall be the same size. 9 You shall couple
five curtains by themselves, and six curtains by themselves, and the sixth curtain you shall
double over at the front of the tent. 10 You shall make fifty loops on the edge of the curtain
that is outermost in one set, and fifty loops on the edge of the curtain that is outermost
in the second set.

11 "You shall make fifty clasps of bronze, and put the clasps into the loops, and couple
the tent together that it may be a single whole. 12 And the part that remains of the curtains
of the tent, the half curtain that remains, shall hang over the back of the tabernacle. 13 And
the extra that remains in the length of the curtains, the cubit on the one side, and the
cubit on the other side, shall hang over the sides of the tabernacle, on this side and that
side, to cover it. 14 [b]And you shall make for the tent a covering of tanned [c]rams' skins and
a covering of goatskins on top.

7 [a]ch. 36:14
14 [b]ch. 36:19 [c]ch. 25:5

THE TABERNACLE TENT

The entire tent was 45 feet (13.7 m) long, 15 feet (4.6 m) wide, and 15 feet (4.6 m) high. It was a wooden skeletal structure, overlaid with gold, with no solid roof or front wall (Ex. 26:15–29). Five wooden bars (overlaid with gold) passed through rings attached to each frame (Ex. 26:26–30).

The Most Holy Place was a 15-foot (4.6-m) cube, containing only the ark of the covenant (Ex. 25:10–22; 37:1–9). It was here that Yahweh would descend to meet with his people in a cloud theophany (divine appearance). The high priest could enter only once a year, on the Day of Atonement (see note on Heb. 9:7).

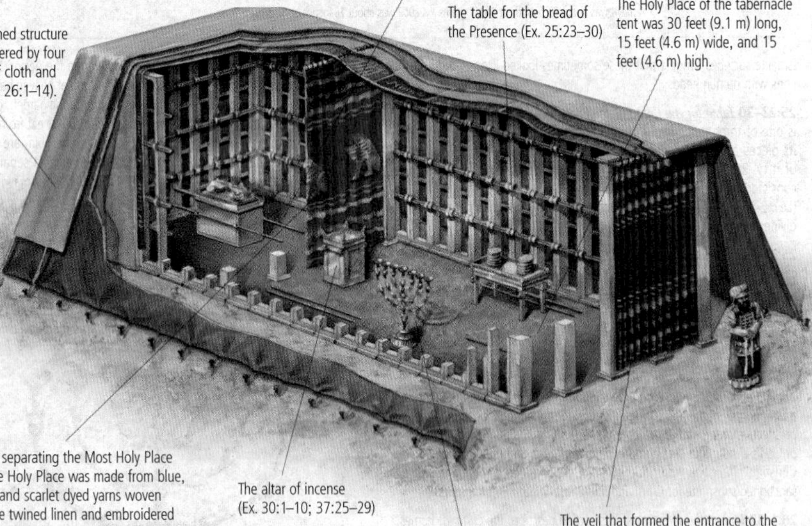

The framed structure was covered by four layers of cloth and skin (Ex. 26:1–14).

The table for the bread of the Presence (Ex. 25:23–30)

The Holy Place of the tabernacle tent was 30 feet (9.1 m) long, 15 feet (4.6 m) wide, and 15 feet (4.6 m) high.

The veil separating the Most Holy Place from the Holy Place was made from blue, purple, and scarlet dyed yarns woven with fine twined linen and embroidered with cherubim (Ex. 26:31–33). It hung on four golden pillars.

The altar of incense (Ex. 30:1–10; 37:25–29)

The golden lampstand (Ex. 25:31–40; 37:17–24)

The veil that formed the entrance to the tabernacle was similar to the veil separating the Holy Place from the Most Holy Place, except that cherubim were not embroidered on it. It was suspended on five golden pillars (Ex. 26:36–37).

29 [d]See ch. 25:27
30 [e]See ch. 25:40
31 [f]ch. 36:35; [Lev. 16:2; 2 Chr. 3:14; Matt. 27:51; Heb. 9:3] [g]ver. 1
33 [f][See ver. 31 above] [h]See ch. 16:34
34 [i]ch. 25:21; 40:20
35 [j]ch. 40:22; Heb. 9:2 [k]ch. 40:24
36 [l]ch. 27:16; 36:37 [m]ver. 1, 31; ch. 25:4 [g][See ver. 31 above]

Chapter 27

1 [n]For ver. 1-8, see ch. 38:1-7; [Ezek. 43:13]
2 [o]ch. 29:12; 30:2; [Lev. 4:7, 30; 1 Kgs. 1:50; Ps. 118:27] [p][Num. 16:38]
3 [q][1 Sam. 2:13]

15 "You shall make upright frames for the tabernacle of acacia wood. 16 Ten cubits shall
be the length of a frame, and a cubit and a half the breadth of each frame. 17 There shall
be two tenons in each frame, for fitting together. So shall you do for all the frames of the
tabernacle. 18 You shall make the frames for the tabernacle: twenty frames for the south
side; 19 and forty bases of silver you shall make under the twenty frames, two bases under
one frame for its two tenons, and two bases under the next frame for its two tenons; 20 and
for the second side of the tabernacle, on the north side twenty frames, 21 and their forty
bases of silver, two bases under one frame, and two bases under the next frame. 22 And
for the rear of the tabernacle westward you shall make six frames. 23 And you shall make
two frames for corners of the tabernacle in the rear; 24 they shall be separate beneath, but
joined at the top, at the first ring. Thus shall it be with both of them; they shall form the
two corners. 25 And there shall be eight frames, with their bases of silver, sixteen bases; two
bases under one frame, and two bases under another frame.

26 "You shall make bars of acacia wood, five for the frames of the one side of the tabernacle, 27 and five bars for the frames of the other side of the tabernacle, and five bars for
the frames of the side of the tabernacle at the rear westward. 28 The middle bar, halfway
up the frames, shall run from end to end. 29 You shall overlay the frames with gold and
shall make their rings of gold for [d]holders for the bars, and you shall overlay the bars
with gold. 30 Then you shall erect the tabernacle [e]according to the plan for it that you were
shown on the mountain.

31 [f]"And you shall make a veil of blue and purple and scarlet yarns and [g]fine twined linen.
It shall be made with cherubim [g]skillfully worked into it. 32 And you shall hang it on four
pillars of acacia overlaid with gold, with hooks of gold, on four bases of silver. 33 And you
shall hang [f]the veil from the clasps, and bring [h]the ark of the testimony in there within
the veil. And the veil shall separate for you the Holy Place from the Most Holy. 34 [i]You shall
put the mercy seat on the ark of the testimony in the Most Holy Place. 35 And [j]you shall set
the table outside the veil, and the [k]lampstand on the south side of the tabernacle opposite
the table, and you shall put the table on the north side.

36 "You shall make a [l]screen for the entrance of the tent, of [m]blue and purple and scarlet
yarns and [g]fine twined linen, embroidered with needlework. 37 And you shall make for
the screen five pillars of acacia, and overlay them with gold. Their hooks shall be of gold,
and you shall cast five bases of bronze for them.

The Bronze Altar

27 "You shall make the [n]altar of acacia wood, five cubits[1] long and five cubits broad.
The altar shall be square, and its height shall be three cubits. 2 And you shall make
[o]horns for it on its four corners; its horns shall be of one piece with it, and [p]you shall overlay
it with bronze. 3 You shall make pots for it to receive its ashes, and shovels and basins and
[q]forks and fire pans. You shall make all its utensils of bronze. 4 You shall also make for it a
grating, a network of bronze, and on the net you shall make four bronze rings at its four
corners. 5 And you shall set it under the ledge of the altar so that the net extends halfway
down the altar. 6 And you shall make poles for the altar, poles of acacia wood, and overlay

[1] A *cubit* was about 18 inches or 45 centimeters

26:7–14 In addition to the fine linen curtains that make up the inner part of the tabernacle, there are also **curtains of goats' hair** (v. 7), **a covering of tanned rams' skins and a covering of goatskins** (v. 14) that cover the tabernacle.

26:30 The details given here as well as for other elements are not exhaustive, which is also indicated when the Lord repeats the command that Moses shall follow the pattern or plan he was **shown on the mountain** (see 25:9, 40; 27:8).

26:31 The colors and design of the **veil** are the same as the curtains on top of the tabernacle (v. 1).

26:33–35 The **Most Holy Place** will contain only the **ark of the testimony**, separated by a veil from the **Holy Place**, which will include the altar of incense (see 30:1–10) in addition to the **lampstand** and **table** already mentioned (see 25:23–40).

27:1–8 *Bronze Altar.* This **altar** made of wood and overlaid with **bronze** is referred to later by its function: "the altar of burnt offering" (see 38:1–7). The altar was placed before the door of the tabernacle with the bronze basin between them (40:6–7) and they were the only two items inside the court around the tabernacle (see illustration of the bronze altar, p. 188). This is the altar where the priests will offer the sacrifices that the Lord commands Israel to bring to him (see Lev. 1:1–7:38).

27:2 The altar is to be made with **horns** on each corner. The function and significance of the horns are not explained, but they are referred to when both Adonijah and Joab take hold of them in order to seek refuge from Solomon (see 1 Kings 1:50; 2:28).

them with bronze. 7 And the poles shall be put through the rings, so that the poles are on
the two sides of the altar when it is carried. 8 You shall make it hollow, with boards. [r]As it
has been shown you on the mountain, so shall it be made.

The Court of the Tabernacle

9 [s]"You shall make the court of the tabernacle. On the south side the court shall have
hangings of fine twined linen a hundred cubits long for one side. 10 Its twenty pillars and
their twenty bases shall be of bronze, but the hooks of the pillars and their fillets shall be
of silver. 11 And likewise for its length on the north side there shall be hangings a hundred
cubits long, its pillars twenty and their bases twenty, of bronze, but the hooks of the pillars
and their fillets shall be of silver. 12 And for the breadth of the court on the west side there
shall be hangings for fifty cubits, with ten pillars and ten bases. 13 The breadth of the court
on the front to the east shall be fifty cubits. 14 The hangings for the one side of the gate shall
be fifteen cubits, with their three pillars and three bases. 15 On the other side the hangings
shall be fifteen cubits, with their three pillars and three bases. 16 For the gate of the court
there shall be [t]a screen twenty cubits long, of blue and purple and scarlet yarns and fine
twined linen, embroidered with needlework. It shall have four pillars and with them four
bases. 17 All the pillars around the court shall be filleted with silver. Their hooks shall be of
silver, and their bases of bronze. 18 The length of the court shall be a hundred cubits, the
breadth fifty, and the height five cubits, with hangings of fine twined linen and bases of
bronze. 19 All the utensils of the tabernacle for every use, and all its pegs and all the pegs
of the court, shall be of bronze.

Oil for the Lamp

20 [u]"You shall command the people of Israel that they bring to you pure beaten olive
oil for the light, that a lamp may regularly be set up to burn. 21 [v]In the tent of meeting,
[w]outside the veil that is before the testimony, Aaron and his sons shall tend it from evening
to morning before the LORD. It shall be a statute forever to be observed throughout their
generations by the people of Israel.

The Priests' Garments

28 "Then bring near to you [x]Aaron your brother, and his sons with him, from among
the people of Israel, to serve me as priests—Aaron and Aaron's sons, [y]Nadab and
Abihu, Eleazar and Ithamar. 2 [z]And you shall make holy garments for Aaron your brother,
for glory and for beauty. 3 You shall speak to all the [a]skillful, whom I have filled with a spirit

8 [r]See ch. 25:40
9 [s]For ver. 9-19, see ch. 38:9-20
16 [t]ch. 26:36
20 [u]Lev. 24:1-4
21 [v]ch. 25:22; 29:42; 30:36 [w]See ch. 26:31

Chapter 28

1 [x]Num. 18:7; Heb. 5:4 [y]See ch. 6:23
2 [z]ver. 40; ch. 29:29; 31:10; 39:1, 2; Lev. 8:7, 30; Num. 20:26, 28; See ch. 29:5-9
3 [a]ch. 31:6; 35:10, 25; 36:1

27:9–19 *Court of the Tabernacle.* The **court of the tabernacle** (see 38:9–20) encloses both the tabernacle and the bronze basin and altar of burnt offering (see illustration of the tabernacle, pp. 190–191).

27:10–11 The materials for constructing the court will include the precious metals **bronze** and **silver** (also vv. 17–19)—lesser metals than the pure gold prescribed for the elements inside the tabernacle (25:10–40), since they are farther from the Most Holy Place, where the Lord dwells.

The Bronze Altar

The bronze altar for burnt offerings (Ex. 27:1–8; 38:1–7) stood in the outer courtyard with its poles removed. It was a hollow wooden box, overlaid with bronze, measuring 4.5 feet high and 7.5 feet long and wide (1.4 m x 2.3 m x 2.3 m). There was a bronze grating on the top and on the sides of the altar.

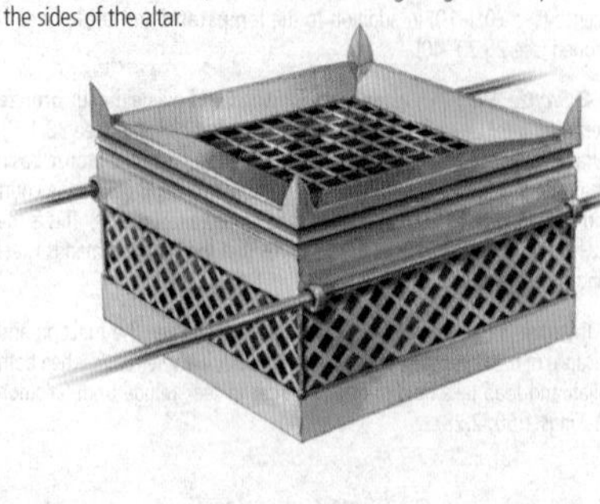

27:13 The instructions for the court include mention of the fact that the tabernacle and its court will be set up with the **front to the east**. The sanctuary, like the garden of Eden, is entered from the east (Gen. 3:24).

27:20–21 *Oil for the Lamp.* In addition to the sacrifices that will be prescribed, the people of Israel are also to bring **olive oil** for the **lamp** that is in the tabernacle (see 25:31–40).

28:1–43 *Garments for the Priests.* This section includes the command that Aaron and his sons will serve the Lord as **priests** (v. 1) and describes the **holy garments** that are to be made for Aaron (vv. 2–39) and his sons (vv. 40–43).

28:1 The names of **Aaron's sons** are recorded in the genealogy of Aaron and Moses (6:23), preserving their lineage as those who were to serve as priests. The sons are listed here with the slight difference that they are set in pairs: **Nadab and Abihu, Eleazar and Ithamar**. The reference to Nadab and Abihu together seems to highlight the pair and prepare the reader to interpret the events of their death (see Lev. 10:1–2) in light of their participation in the events of Exodus (see Ex. 24:9–11).

28:2 for glory and for beauty. Aaron's garments, like the tabernacle and its elements, are made from precious materials and decorated with vivid colors representing the glory of the Lord who is present in the midst of his people. (See the illustration on p. 208.)

4[b]ver. 15 [c]ver. 6 [d]ver. 31 [e]ver. 39; [Lev. 8:7]
5[f]ch. 25:3
6[g]For ver. 6-12, see ch. 39:2-7
8[h]ver. 27, 28; ch. 29:5; 39:5; Lev. 8:7
12[i]ver. 29, 30 [j][Num. 16:40; Josh. 4:7; Zech. 6:14]
15[k]For ver. 15-28, see ch. 39:8-21
17[l][Ezek. 28:13; Rev. 21:19, 20]
27[m]ver. 8
29[n]ver. 12, 30 [o]See ver. 12
30[p]Lev. 8:8; Num. 27:21; Deut. 33:8; 1 Sam. 28:6; Ezra 2:63; Neh. 7:65; [1 Sam. 23:9; 30:7, 8]
31[q]For ver. 31-37, see ch. 39:22-31

of skill, that they make Aaron's garments to consecrate him for my priesthood. 4 These are
the garments that they shall make: a [b]breastpiece, an [c]ephod, [d]a robe, [e]a coat of checker
work, [e]a turban, and [e]a sash. They shall make holy garments for Aaron your brother and
his sons to serve me as priests. 5 They shall receive [f]gold, blue and purple and scarlet yarns,
and fine twined linen.

6 [g]"And they shall make the ephod of gold, of blue and purple and scarlet yarns, and
of fine twined linen, skillfully worked. 7 It shall have two shoulder pieces attached to its
two edges, so that it may be joined together. 8 And the [h]skillfully woven band on it shall
be made like it and be of one piece with it, of gold, blue and purple and scarlet yarns, and
fine twined linen. 9 You shall take two onyx stones, and engrave on them the names of
the sons of Israel, 10 six of their names on the one stone, and the names of the remaining
six on the other stone, in the order of their birth. 11 As a jeweler engraves signets, so shall
you engrave the two stones with the names of the sons of Israel. You shall enclose them
in settings of gold filigree. 12 And you shall set the two stones on the shoulder pieces of
the ephod, as stones of remembrance for the sons of Israel. And [i]Aaron shall bear their
names before the LORD on his two shoulders [j]for remembrance. 13 You shall make settings
of gold filigree, 14 and two chains of pure gold, twisted like cords; and you shall attach the
corded chains to the settings.

15 [k]"You shall make a breastpiece of judgment, in skilled work. In the style of the ephod
you shall make it—of gold, blue and purple and scarlet yarns, and fine twined linen shall
you make it. 16 It shall be square and doubled, a span[1] its length and a span its breadth.
17 [l]You shall set in it four rows of stones. A row of sardius,[2] topaz, and carbuncle shall be the
first row; 18 and the second row an emerald, a sapphire, and a diamond; 19 and the third row
a jacinth, an agate, and an amethyst; 20 and the fourth row a beryl, an onyx, and a jasper.
They shall be set in gold filigree. 21 There shall be twelve stones with their names according
to the names of the sons of Israel. They shall be like signets, each engraved with its name,
for the twelve tribes. 22 You shall make for the breastpiece twisted chains like cords, of pure
gold. 23 And you shall make for the breastpiece two rings of gold, and put the two rings
on the two edges of the breastpiece. 24 And you shall put the two cords of gold in the two
rings at the edges of the breastpiece. 25 The two ends of the two cords you shall attach to
the two settings of filigree, and so attach it in front to the shoulder pieces of the ephod.
26 You shall make two rings of gold, and put them at the two ends of the breastpiece, on its
inside edge next to the ephod. 27 And you shall make two rings of gold, and attach them
in front to the lower part of the two shoulder pieces of the ephod, at its seam above the
[m]skillfully woven band of the ephod. 28 And they shall bind the breastpiece by its rings to
the rings of the ephod with a lace of blue, so that it may lie on the skillfully woven band of
the ephod, so that the breastpiece shall not come loose from the ephod. 29 [n]So Aaron shall
bear the names of the sons of Israel in the breastpiece of judgment on his heart, when he
goes into the Holy Place, to bring them to regular [o]remembrance before the LORD. 30 And
in the breastpiece of judgment [p]you shall put the Urim and the Thummim, and they shall
be on Aaron's heart, when he goes in before the LORD. Thus Aaron shall bear the judgment
of the people of Israel on his heart before the LORD regularly.

31 [q]"You shall make the robe of the ephod all of blue. 32 It shall have an opening for the

[1] A *span* was about 9 inches or 22 centimeters [2] The identity of some of these stones is uncertain

28:5 gold, blue and purple and scarlet yarns. These are the same colors as the materials and yarns used in the tabernacle (25:11, 24, 31; 26:1). These materials imply that the priests are close to God and act as his representatives to the people (e.g., in overseeing sacrifices, in pronouncing blessings, in teaching God's word, in administering justice, and in their example of holiness).

28:9–30 The priestly mediation is two-way: God to Israel and Israel to God. The jewels on Aaron's robes represent the 12 tribes of Israel, on whose behalf Aaron enters God's presence. The **ephod** (vv. 6–14) is to have **two onyx stones,** each engraved with six of the names of the sons of Israel. The **breastpiece of judgment** (vv. 15–30) is to have 12 different stones set in four rows of three, each with the name of one of the 12 tribes. The ephod and the breastpiece together represent the value that the Lord places upon his people as a whole nation (six names each on two onyx stones), and as individual tribes (each named on an individual precious stone). Note how similar stones adorn the new Jerusalem (Rev. 21:12–21). These two pieces of Aaron's clothing also indicate that he is to act as a representative on behalf of the 12 tribes **before the LORD** in order to bring them to **remembrance** (Ex. 28:12, 29).

28:30 The **Urim and the Thummim** (see note on 1 Sam. 14:41–42) are to be placed in the breastpiece of judgment and carried before the Lord, but their function is not fully explained. From several contexts where they are referred to in the OT, it appears that the Urim and Thummim, whatever they were, were used in seeking the Lord's decision on particular matters (see Num. 27:21; 1 Sam. 28:6; Ezra 2:63; see also 1 Sam. 23:9; 30:7–8).

THE TABERNACLE AND COURT

The tabernacle was a portable temple—a "tent of meeting"—within a movable courtyard (Exodus 25–31; 35–40). It was constructed after the pattern that Yahweh revealed to Moses on Mount Sinai, and was assembled in the desert as Moses led the Israelites from Egypt to the Promised Land. For an enlargement of the tent itself, see p. 186. The tabernacle courtyard was 150 feet (46 m) long and 75 feet (23 m) wide, totaling 11,250 square feet (1,045 square meters).

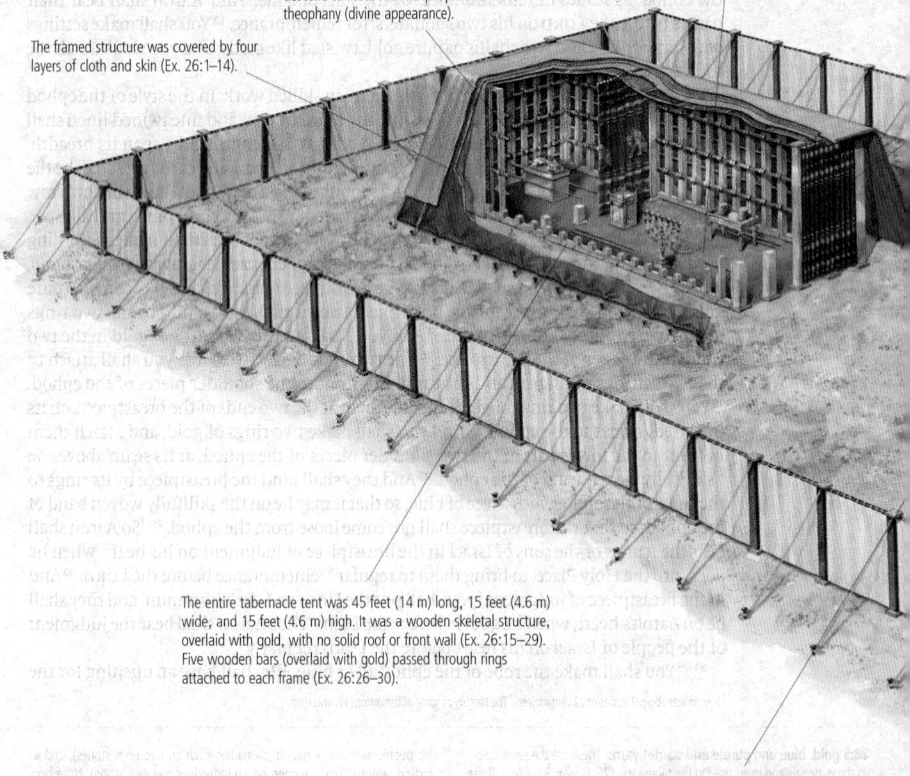

The Holy Place of the tabernacle tent was 30 feet (9.1 m) long, 15 feet (4.6 m) wide, and 15 feet (4.6 m) high. It housed the table (Ex. 25:23–30), the golden lampstand (Ex. 25:31–40; 37:17–24), and the altar of incense (Ex. 30:1–10; 37:25–29).
The Most Holy Place of the tabernacle tent was a 15-foot (4.6-m) cube, containing only the ark of the covenant (Ex. 25:10–22; 37:1–9). It was here that Yahweh would descend to meet with his people in a cloud theophany (divine appearance).
The framed structure was covered by four layers of cloth and skin (Ex. 26:1–14).
The entire tabernacle tent was 45 feet (14 m) long, 15 feet (4.6 m) wide, and 15 feet (4.6 m) high. It was a wooden skeletal structure, overlaid with gold, with no solid roof or front wall (Ex. 26:15–29). Five wooden bars (overlaid with gold) passed through rings attached to each frame (Ex. 26:26–30).
The bronze basin with its stand was for ceremonial washings (Ex. 30:17–21; 38:8).

Tabernacle and Court Architectural Plan

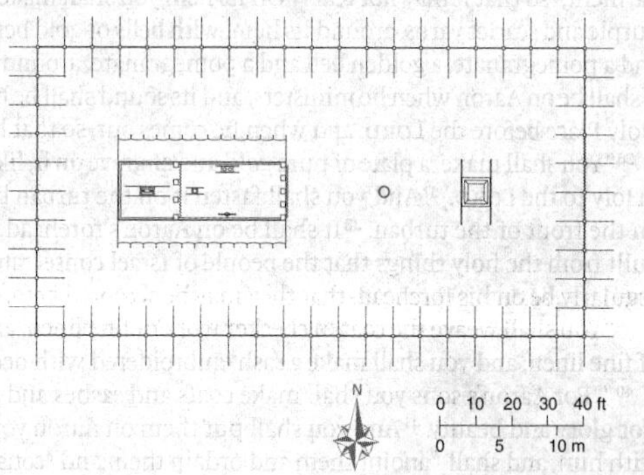

The veil separating the Holy Place from the tabernacle courtyard was similar to the veil separating the Holy Place from the Most Holy Place, except that cherubim were not embroidered on it (Ex. 26:36–37). It hung on five golden pillars.

The bronze altar, also known as the altar of burnt offering (Ex. 27:1–8; 38:1–7), was made from a hollow wooden box (7.5 feet/2.3 m long and wide, and 4.5 feet/1.4 m high), overlaid with bronze. It had four horns at its corners. It was transported by means of two poles on its journey through the wilderness.

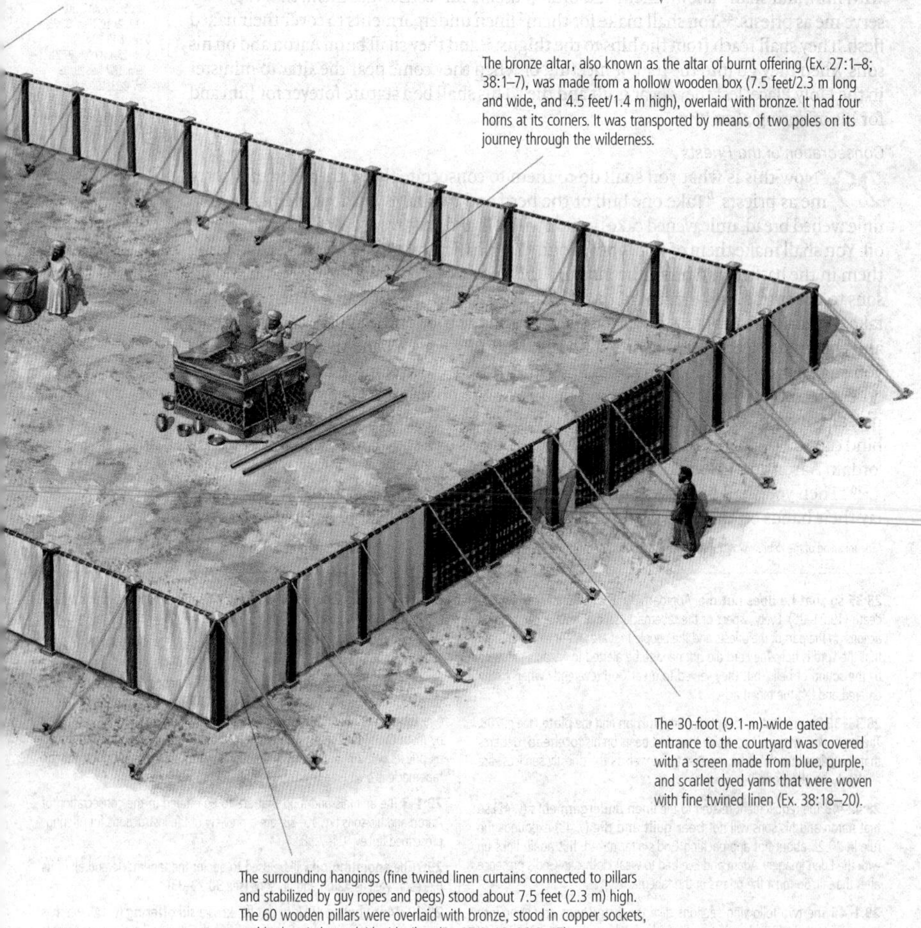

The 30-foot (9.1-m)-wide gated entrance to the courtyard was covered with a screen made from blue, purple, and scarlet dyed yarns that were woven with fine twined linen (Ex. 38:18–20).

The surrounding hangings (fine twined linen curtains connected to pillars and stabilized by guy ropes and pegs) stood about 7.5 feet (2.3 m) high. The 60 wooden pillars were overlaid with bronze, stood in copper sockets, and had capitals overlaid with silver (Ex. 27:9–19; 38:9–17).

head in the middle of it, with a woven binding around the opening, like the opening in a
garment,[1] so that it may not tear. 33 On its hem you shall make pomegranates of blue and
purple and scarlet yarns, around its hem, with bells of gold between them, 34 a golden bell
and a pomegranate, a golden bell and a pomegranate, around the hem of the robe. 35 And
it shall be on Aaron when he ministers, and its sound shall be heard when he goes into the
Holy Place before the LORD, and when he comes out, so that he does not die.
36 "You shall make [r]a plate of pure gold and engrave on it, like the engraving of a signet,
[s]'Holy to the LORD.' 37 And you shall fasten it on the turban by a cord of blue. It shall be
on the front of the turban. 38 It shall be on Aaron's forehead, and Aaron shall [t]bear any
guilt from the holy things that the people of Israel consecrate as their holy gifts. It shall
regularly be on his forehead, that they may be accepted before the LORD.
39 "You shall weave the coat in checker work of fine linen, and you shall make a turban
of fine linen, and you shall make a sash embroidered with needlework.
40 [u]"For Aaron's sons you shall make coats and sashes and caps. You shall make them
[v]for glory and beauty. 41 And you shall put them on Aaron your brother, and on his sons
with him, and shall [w]anoint them and ordain them and [x]consecrate them, that they may
serve me as priests. 42 You shall make for them [y]linen undergarments to cover their naked
flesh. They shall reach from the hips to the thighs; 43 and they shall be on Aaron and on his
sons when they go into the tent of meeting or when they come near the altar to minister
in the Holy Place, lest they [z]bear guilt and die. [a]This shall be a statute forever for him and
for his offspring after him.

Consecration of the Priests

29 "Now this is what you shall do to them to consecrate them, that they may serve
me as priests. [b]Take one bull of the herd and two rams without blemish, 2 [c]and
unleavened bread, unleavened cakes mixed with oil, and unleavened wafers smeared with
oil. You shall make them of fine wheat flour. 3 You shall put them in one basket and bring
them in the basket, and bring the bull and the two rams. 4 You shall bring Aaron and his
sons to the entrance of the tent of meeting and [d]wash them with water. 5 Then [e]you shall
take the garments, and put on Aaron the coat and the robe of the ephod, and the ephod,
and the breastpiece, and gird him with the [f]skillfully woven band of the ephod. 6 [g]And
you shall set the turban on his head and put the holy crown on the turban. 7 You shall
take [h]the anointing oil and pour it on his head and anoint him. 8 Then you [i]shall bring
his sons and put coats on them, 9 and you shall gird Aaron and his sons with [j]sashes and
bind caps on them. And [k]the priesthood shall be theirs by a statute forever. Thus you shall
[l]ordain Aaron and his sons.
10 "Then you shall bring the bull before the tent of meeting. [m]Aaron and his sons shall
lay their hands on the head of the bull. 11 Then you shall kill the bull before the LORD at

[1] The meaning of the Hebrew word is uncertain; possibly *coat of mail*

36 [r]Lev. 8:9 [s]Zech. 14:20
38 [t]Lev. 10:17; Num. 18:1; [Isa. 53:11; Ezek. 4:4-6; John 1:29; Heb. 9:28; 1 Pet. 2:24]
40 [u]ch. 39:27-29, 41; [Ezek. 44:17, 18] [v]ver. 2
41 [w]ch. 29:7; 30:30; 40:13, 15; Lev. 10:7 [x]ch. 29:9; Heb. 7:28; [Lev. 21:10]
42 [y]Lev. 6:10; 16:4; [Ezek. 44:18]
43 [z]Lev. 5:1, 17; 20:19 [a]ch. 27:21

Chapter 29
1 [b]Lev. 8:2
2 [c]Lev. 2:4; See Lev. 6:20-22
4 [d]ch. 40:12; Lev. 8:6; [Heb. 10:22]
5 [e]ch. 28:2-4 [f]ch. 28:8
6 [g]ch. 28:36, 37; Lev. 8:9; [Num. 6:7]
7 [h]ver. 21; ch. 28:41; 30:25; Lev. 8:12, 30; 10:7; 21:10; Num. 35:25
8 [i]Lev. 8:13
9 [j]ch. 28:4, 39 [k]ch. 27:21; Num. 18:7 [l]ver. 29, 33; Lev. 8:33; 16:32; See ch. 28:41
10 [m]ver. 15, 19; Lev. 1:4; 8:14

28:35 so that he does not die. Approaching God carelessly can lead to death (19:21–25). Every aspect of the tabernacle service involves intentional actions on the part of the priests and the people that are meant to teach Israel that the Lord is holy. The Lord did not need to be alerted to Aaron's presence by the sound of bells, but they served to greet God reverently when Aaron entered and left the tabernacle.

28:36–38 For an artist's conception of the **turban** and the **plate**, see p. 208. The inscription on the plate, which the priest bears on his **forehead**, declares that the priest and those he represents, as well as the priestly services, are all **"Holy to the LORD."**

28:42–43 The requirement related to the **linen undergarments** (v. 42) so that Aaron and his sons will not **bear guilt and die** (v. 43) expounds the rule in 20:26 about not approaching God's altar naked. This again links up with the Eden imagery. Adam and Eve had to wear clothes in God's presence after the fall. So must the priests in the tabernacle.

29:1–46 The two following sections give the instructions on (1) how to **consecrate** Aaron and his sons to serve the Lord as priests (vv. 1–37), and (2) how they were to make the daily offerings (vv. 38–46). The Lord will **consecrate** the tabernacle and priests (v. 44), and through them, his people (vv. 42b–46).

29:1–37 *Consecration of the Priests.* Aaron and his sons are to be consecrated to serve the Lord as priests in a manner that reflects some of the regular service they will perform as priests on behalf of the people (see Lev. 1:1–7:38): preparation (Ex. 29:1–9), a sin offering (vv. 10–14), two burnt offerings—one for the Lord (vv. 15–18) and one for ordination (vv. 19–28), followed by instructions for the practice and perpetuation of ordaining Aaron's sons as priests (vv. 29–37). These instructions will not be carried out until the tabernacle is built (see Lev. 8:1–9:24).

29:1–3 The animals and food that are to be offered in the consecration of Aaron and his sons (vv. 10–28) are a preview of the instructions for offerings prescribed in Lev. 1:1–7:38.

29:7 The **anointing oil** will be used to anoint the tabernacle and all of its pieces as well as Aaron and his sons (see 30:22–33).

29:10–14 The **bull** (v. 10) is to be offered as a **sin offering** (v. 14), which is described as having the function of purifying the altar and making atonement for it (v. 36; see also Lev. 4:1–12).

12[n]Lev. 8:15 [o]See ch. 27:2
13[p]Lev. 3:3, 4
14[q]Lev. 4:11, 12, 21; Num. 19:3, 5; Heb. 13:11 [r]ver. 36; ch. 30:10
15[s]ver. 1; Lev. 8:18 [t]ver. 19; Lev. 1:4; 8:14
17[u]Lev. 8:20
18[v]ver. 25, 41; See Gen. 8:21
19[w]ver. 1; Lev. 8:22 [t][See ver. 15 above]
21[x]ver. 7
22[y]ver. 13 [z]Lev. 7:37; 8:28, 31, 33
23[a]ver. 2, 3; Lev. 8:26
24[b]Lev. 7:30; 8:27, 29; Num. 5:25; 6:20
25[c]Lev. 6:22; 8:28 [d]ver. 18, 41
26[e]Lev. 8:29 [f]ver. 22 [g]ver. 24
27[h]Lev. 7:31, 34; 10:14, 15; Num. 18:11, 18 [i]Lev. 7:32, 34; 10:15; Num. 18:11 [f][See ver. 26 above]
28[j]Lev. 10:15 [g][See ver. 26 above]
29[k]Num. 18:8; [Num. 20:26, 28] [l]ver. 9
30[m]Lev. 8:33, 35
31[n]Lev. 8:31
32[o][Matt. 12:4]
33[p]Lev. 10:14, 15, 17 [q]Lev. 22:10

the entrance of the tent of meeting, 12 and [n]shall take part of the blood of the bull and put
it on the [o]horns of the altar with your finger, and the rest of[1] the blood you shall pour out
at the base of the altar. 13 And you shall take all [p]the fat that covers the entrails, and the
long lobe of the liver, and the two kidneys with the fat that is on them, and burn them
on the altar. 14 But the flesh of the bull and its skin and its dung you shall burn with fire
[q]outside the camp; [r]it is a sin offering.

15 "Then [s]you shall take one of the rams, and [t]Aaron and his sons shall lay their hands
on the head of the ram, 16 and you shall kill the ram and shall take its blood and throw
it against the sides of the altar. 17 Then you shall [u]cut the ram into pieces, and wash its
entrails and its legs, and put them with its pieces and its head, 18 and burn the whole ram
on the altar. It is a burnt offering to the LORD. It is a [v]pleasing aroma, a food offering[2] to
the LORD.

19 [w]"You shall take the other ram, [t]and Aaron and his sons shall lay their hands on the
head of the ram, 20 and you shall kill the ram and take part of its blood and put it on
the tip of the right ear of Aaron and on the tips of the right ears of his sons, and on the
thumbs of their right hands and on the great toes of their right feet, and throw the rest
of the blood against the sides of the altar. 21 Then you shall take part of the blood that is
on the altar, and of the [x]anointing oil, and sprinkle it on Aaron and his garments, and on
his sons and his sons' garments with him. He and his garments shall be holy, and his sons
and his sons' garments with him.

22 "You shall also take the fat from the ram and the fat tail and the [y]fat that covers the
entrails, and the long lobe of the liver and the two kidneys with the fat that is on them,
and the right thigh (for it is a ram of [z]ordination), 23 and [a]one loaf of bread and one cake
of bread made with oil, and one wafer out of the basket of unleavened bread that is before
the LORD. 24 You shall put all these on the palms of Aaron and on the palms of his sons,
and [b]wave them for a wave offering before the LORD. 25 Then [c]you shall take them from
their hands and burn them on the altar on top of the burnt offering, as a [d]pleasing aroma
before the LORD. It is a food offering to the LORD.

26 "You shall take the [e]breast of the ram of Aaron's [f]ordination and [g]wave it for a wave
offering before the LORD, and it shall be your portion. 27 And you shall consecrate the
[h]breast of the wave offering that is waved and the [i]thigh of the priests' portion that is
contributed from the ram of [f]ordination, from what was Aaron's and his sons'. 28 It shall
be for Aaron and his sons as a [j]perpetual due from the people of Israel, for it is a [g]contribu-
tion. It shall be a [g]contribution from the people of Israel from their peace offerings, their
contribution to the LORD.

29 "The holy garments of Aaron [k]shall be for his sons after him; they shall [l]be anointed
in them and ordained in them. 30 The son who succeeds him as priest, who comes into the
tent of meeting to minister in the Holy Place, shall wear them [m]seven days.

31 "You shall take the ram of ordination and [n]boil its flesh in a holy place. 32 And Aaron
and his sons shall eat the flesh of the ram and the [o]bread that is in the basket in the entrance
of the tent of meeting. 33 [p]They shall eat those things with which atonement was made at
their ordination and consecration, but an [q]outsider shall not eat of them, because they are

[1] Hebrew *all* [2] Or *an offering by fire*; also verses 25, 41

29:15–18 The first of the two **rams** (v. 15) is to be offered as a **burnt offering** (v. 18), which is the same offering later described in Leviticus as atoning for the sin of the one who offers it (see Lev. 1:3–9).

29:19–28 The **other ram** (v. 19) is offered as a **ram of ordination** (vv. 22, 27), which differs in at least two respects from the burnt offering (vv. 15–18). First, some of the blood is placed on Aaron and his sons before it is thrown against the altar (v. 20) as well as then being sprinkled on their clothes along with anointing oil in order to consecrate both the priests and their garments (v. 21). Second, rather than burning the whole ram on the altar, certain parts are offered to the Lord together with bread (vv. 22–25) and the breast is eaten by the priests (vv. 26–28).

29:20 Since Aaron and his sons were dressed in their priestly garments, the blood is placed on the **ears**, **thumbs**, and **great toes**, the exposed parts representing the whole. The specification of the **right** member of each of these body parts is probably connected to the way that the right hand is considered the place of honor (see Gen. 48:17–19). As in Ex. 24:6–8, putting the blood on the priests and on the altar serves to link them closely to God. It may also be seen to purify them from sin.

29:27–28 This instruction looks forward to the sacrifices that the people will bring and indicates that in **peace offerings** the breast and the right thigh are consecrated to the priest (see Lev. 7:29–36).

29:31–34 This section instructs the priests that their portion of the **ram of ordination** (see vv. 26–28) has to be treated as holy in terms of where it is cooked and eaten, who is able to eat it, and for how long it may be kept.

holy. 34 And if any of the flesh for the ordination or of the bread remain until the morning,
then you shall [r]burn the remainder with fire. It shall not be eaten, because it is holy.
35 "Thus you shall do to Aaron and to his sons, according to all that I have commanded
you. Through [s]seven days shall you ordain them, 36 and every day you shall offer a [t]bull as
a sin offering for atonement. Also you shall purify the altar, when you make atonement
for it, and shall [u]anoint it to consecrate it. 37 Seven days you shall make atonement for
the altar and consecrate it, and the [v]altar shall be most holy. [w]Whatever touches the altar
shall become holy.
38 "Now this is what you shall offer on the altar: [x]two lambs a year old [y]day by day regularly. 39 One lamb you shall offer [z]in the morning, and the other lamb you shall offer [a]at
twilight. 40 And with the first lamb a tenth measure[1] of fine flour mingled with a fourth
of a hin[2] of beaten oil, and a fourth of a hin of wine for a drink offering. 41 The other lamb
you shall offer [a]at twilight, and shall offer with it a grain offering and its drink offering, as
[b]in the morning, for a [c]pleasing aroma, a food offering to the LORD. 42 It shall be a [d]regular
burnt offering throughout your generations at the entrance of the tent of meeting before
the LORD, [e]where I will meet with you, to speak to you there. 43 There I will meet with
the people of Israel, and it shall be [f]sanctified by my glory. 44 I will consecrate the tent of
meeting and the altar. [g]Aaron also and his sons I will consecrate to serve me as priests. 45 [h]I
will dwell among the people of Israel and will be their God. 46 And they shall know that
[i]I am the LORD their God, who brought them out of the land of Egypt that I might dwell
among them. I am the LORD their God.

The Altar of Incense

30 [j]"You shall make [k]an altar on which to burn incense; you shall make it of acacia
wood. 2 A cubit[3] shall be its length, and a cubit its breadth. It shall be square, and
two cubits shall be its height. [l]Its horns shall be of one piece with it. 3 You shall [m]overlay
it with pure gold, its top and around its sides and its horns. And you shall make a molding of gold around it. 4 And you shall make two golden rings for it. Under its molding on
two opposite sides of it you shall make them, and they shall be [n]holders for poles with

[1] Possibly an *ephah* (about 3/5 bushel or 22 liters) [2] A *hin* was about 4 quarts or 3.5 liters [3] A *cubit* was about 18 inches or 45 centimeters

34 [r]Lev. 8:32
35 [s]Lev. 8:33-35
36 [t]ver. 14; ch. 30:10 [u]ch. 30:26, 28, 29; 40:10
37 [v]ch. 40:10 [w]ch. 30:29; [Matt. 23:19]
38 [x]Num. 28:3; 1 Chr. 16:40; 2 Chr. 2:4; 13:11; 31:3; Ezra 3:3 [y][Dan. 8:11-13; 9:27; 12:11]; Heb. 10:11
39 [z]2 Kgs. 16:15; Ezek. 46:13-15 [a]1 Kgs. 18:29, 36; Ezra 9:4, 5; Ps. 141:2; Dan. 9:21
41 [a][See ver. 39 above] [b]ch. 30:9; 40:29 [c]ver. 18, 25
42 [d]Num. 28:6 [e]See ch. 25:22
43 [f]ch. 40:34; [1 Kgs. 8:11; 2 Chr. 5:14; 7:1-3; Ezek. 43:5; Hag. 2:7, 9; Mal. 3:1]
44 [g]Lev. 21:15; 22:9, 16
45 [h]ch. 25:8; Lev. 26:12; Zech. 2:10; 2 Cor. 6:16; Rev. 21:3
46 [i]ch. 20:2

Chapter 30

1 [j]For ver. 1-5, see ch. 37:25-28 [k]ch. 40:5; Lev. 4:7; Rev. 8:3
2 [l]See ch. 27:2
3 [m]ch. 39:38; 40:5, 26; Num. 4:11
4 [n]See ch. 25:27

The Altar of Incense

The wooden altar, overlaid with pure gold (Ex. 30:1–10; 37:25–28), was 3 feet high, and 1.5 feet long and wide (1 m x 0.5 m x 0.5 m). It stood in the Holy Place before the veil which separated the Holy Place from the Most Holy Place. It was transported by means of wooden poles which were overlaid with gold and inserted through rings attached to the sides of the altar.

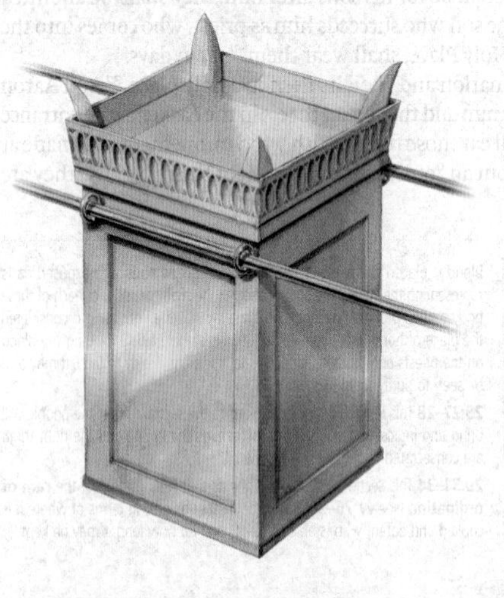

29:35–37 The ordination process is to take place over **seven days** (see Lev. 8:33–36).

29:38–46 *Offering and Promises of the Tabernacle.* This section includes instructions for the **morning** and **twilight** sacrifice of a **burnt offering**, which was to be the regular service of the priests (vv. 38–42a). It closes with the reminder that, in all that has been prescribed for the tabernacle and its service, it is the Lord who meets with, dwells among, and sanctifies his people (vv. 42b–46). In their repetition of first-person statements (e.g., **I will meet**), these verses echo the Lord's reminder to Moses after the first request before Pharaoh (see 6:1–9).

30:1–10 *Altar of Incense.* The **altar** for burning **incense** is similar in construction to the altar for burnt offering (27:1–8), except that it is smaller and is overlaid with **pure gold** (30:3) since it is one of the three pieces that serve in the Holy Place.

30:6–8 The altar is to be placed in the Holy Place before the **veil** that separates it from the Most Holy Place and the ark of the testimony (v. 6; see illustration of the tabernacle tent, p. 186). Aaron is to burn incense on the altar as an offering before the Lord in the morning and the evening, which correspond to the times when he is also to tend the lamps (vv. 7–8; see 27:21).

30:9 The prohibition against the priests offering **unauthorized incense**, like all the other tabernacle regulations, emphasizes that the Lord is holy (see Lev. 10:1–3). The holiness of the incense means that it must not be made for any other purpose (see Ex. 30:34–38).

30:11–16 *Census Offering.* Every person numbered in a census is to give **half a shekel** (v. 13) for the service of the tabernacle (v. 16). The instructions emphasize that it is to be understood as an **offering to the LORD** (vv. 13–14), either as a **ransom** (v. 12) or to **make atonement for your lives** (vv. 15–16).

30:12 The fact that the ransom is explained as averting a **plague** warns Israel against allowing a census to replace their dependence upon the Lord. Pride in

which to carry it. 5 You shall make the poles of acacia wood and overlay them with gold.
6 And you shall put it in front of the veil that is above the ark of the testimony, in front of
the [o]mercy seat that is above the testimony, where I will meet with you. 7 And Aaron shall
[p]burn fragrant incense on it. Every morning when he [q]dresses the lamps he shall burn it,
8 and when Aaron sets up the lamps at twilight, he shall burn it, a regular incense offering
before the LORD throughout your generations. 9 You shall not offer [r]unauthorized incense
on it, or a burnt offering, or a grain offering, and you shall not pour a drink offering on
it. 10 [s]Aaron shall make atonement on its horns once a year. With the blood of the [t]sin
offering of atonement he shall make atonement for it once in the year throughout your
generations. It is most holy to the LORD."

The Census Tax

11 The LORD said to Moses, 12 [u]"When you take the census of the people of Israel, then
each shall give [v]a ransom for his life to the LORD when you number them, that there be
no plague among them when you number them. 13 Each one who is numbered in the
census shall give this: half a shekel[1] according to the [w]shekel of the sanctuary (the [x]shekel
is twenty gerahs),[2] [y]half a shekel as an offering to the LORD. 14 Everyone who is numbered
in the census, from twenty years old and upward, shall give the LORD's offering. 15 The
rich shall not give more, and the poor shall not give less, than [y]the half shekel, when you
give the LORD's offering to make atonement for your lives. 16 You shall take the atonement
money from the people of Israel and shall [z]give it for the service of the tent of meeting,
that it may bring the people of Israel to [a]remembrance before the LORD, so as to make
atonement for your lives."

The Bronze Basin

17 The LORD said to Moses, 18 "You shall also make a [b]basin of bronze, with its stand of
bronze, for washing. [b]You shall put it between the tent of meeting and the altar, and you
shall put water in it, 19 with which Aaron and his sons [c]shall wash their hands and their
feet. 20 When they go into the tent of meeting, or when they come near the altar to minister,
to burn a food offering[3] to the LORD, they shall wash with water, so that they may not die.
21 They shall wash their hands and their feet, so that they may not die. It shall [d]be a statute
forever to them, even to him and to his offspring throughout their generations."

The Anointing Oil and Incense

22 The LORD said to Moses, 23 "Take the [e]finest spices: of liquid myrrh 500 shekels, and of
sweet-smelling cinnamon half as much, that is, 250, and 250 of [f]aromatic cane, 24 and 500
of cassia, according to the shekel of the sanctuary, and a [g]hin[4] of olive oil. 25 And you shall
make of these a sacred anointing oil blended as by the [h]perfumer; it shall be a [i]holy anointing oil. 26 [j]With it you shall anoint the tent of meeting and the ark of the testimony, 27 and
the table and all its utensils, and the lampstand and its utensils, and the altar of incense,
28 and the altar of burnt offering with all its utensils and the [k]basin and its stand. 29 You
shall consecrate them, that they may be most holy. [l]Whatever touches them will become
holy. 30 [m]You shall anoint Aaron and his sons, and consecrate them, that they may serve
me as priests. 31 And you shall say to the people of Israel, 'This shall be my holy anointing oil throughout your generations. 32 It shall not be poured on the body of an ordinary
person, and you shall make no other like it in composition. [n]It is holy, and it shall be holy
to you. 33 [o]Whoever compounds any like it or whoever puts any of it on an outsider shall
be cut off from his people.'"

[1] *A* shekel *was about 2/5 ounce or 11 grams* [2] *A* gerah *was about 1/50 ounce or 0.6 gram* [3] *Or* an offering by fire [4] *A* hin *was about 4 quarts or 3.5 liters*

6 [o]ch. 25:21, 22
7 [p]ver. 34; ch. 31:11; 37:29; 40:27; 1 Sam. 2:28; 1 Chr. 23:13; 2 Chr. 2:4; 29:11; Luke 1:9 [q]See ch. 27:20, 21
9 [r]Lev. 10:1
10 [s]Lev. 16:18; 23:27 [t]ch. 29:36
12 [u]Num. 1:2-4; 26:2; 2 Sam. 24:2 [v]ch. 21:30; Num. 31:50; [Ps. 49:7]
13 [w]ch. 38:24; Lev. 5:15; 27:3, 25 [x]Lev. 27:25; Num. 3:47; 18:16; Ezek. 45:12 [y]ch. 38:26; Matt. 17:24; [Gen. 24:22]
15 [y][See ver. 13 above]
16 [z]See ch. 38:25-31 [a][ch. 28:12; 39:7; Num. 16:40]
18 [b]ch. 40:7, 30; [1 Kgs. 7:38]
19 [c]ch. 40:31, 32; Ps. 26:6; [Isa. 52:11; Heb. 10:22]
21 [d]See ch. 27:21
23 [e]Song 4:14; Ezek. 27:22 [f]Ezek. 27:19
24 [g]ch. 29:40
25 [h]ch. 37:29 [i]ch. 37:29; Num. 35:25; Ps. 89:20; 133:2
26 [j]ch. 40:9; Lev. 8:10; Num. 7:1
28 [k]ch. 40:11
29 [l]ch. 29:37
30 [m]See ch. 29:7
32 [n]ver. 25, 37
33 [o]ver. 38

numbers appears to be the reason for the adverse judgment on David's census (see 2 Sam. 24:1–17; 1 Chron. 21:1–17).

30:17–21 *Bronze Basin.* The **basin of bronze** is for the priests to wash themselves before serving either in the tent of meeting or at the altar for burnt offering. It is placed between them in the court of the sanctuary (see illustration of the tabernacle and its court, pp. 190–191). The basin may also have been used to wash the sacrifices (Lev. 1:9).

30:20–21 so that they may not die. See note on 28:35.

30:22–38 *Anointing Oil and Incense.* This section gives instructions for making the **anointing oil** (vv. 22–33) and **incense** (vv. 34–38). Since the oil is used to consecrate the elements of the tabernacle and the priests (vv. 26–30) and the incense is to be burned on the altar inside the Holy Place (v. 36), the section repeatedly emphasizes that each is to be treated as **holy** (vv. 25, 29, 31, 32) and not to be used for any other purpose (vv. 32, 37).

30:33–38 shall be cut off from his people. See note on 12:15.

34 The LORD said to Moses, [p]"Take sweet spices, stacte, and onycha, and galbanum, sweet
spices with pure frankincense (of each shall there be an equal part), 35 and make an [q]incense
blended as by the [r]perfumer, [s]seasoned with salt, pure and holy. 36 You shall beat some of it
very small, and put part of it before the testimony in the tent of meeting [t]where I shall meet
with you. [u]It shall be most holy for you. 37 And the incense that you shall make [v]according
to its composition, you shall not make for yourselves. It shall be for you holy to the LORD.
38 [w]Whoever makes any like it to use as perfume shall be cut off from his people."

Oholiab and Bezalel

31 The LORD said to Moses, 2 "See, I have called by name [x]Bezalel the son of Uri, son
of [y]Hur, of the tribe of Judah, 3 and I have [z]filled him with the Spirit of God, with
ability and intelligence, with knowledge and all craftsmanship, 4 to devise artistic designs,
to work in gold, silver, and bronze, 5 in cutting stones for setting, and in carving wood, to
work in every craft. 6 And behold, I have appointed with him [a]Oholiab, the son of Ahisamach,
of the tribe of Dan. And I have given to all able men [b]ability, that they may make all that
I have commanded you: 7 [c]the tent of meeting, and [d]the ark of the testimony, and [e]the
mercy seat that is on it, and all the furnishings of the tent, 8 [f]the table and its utensils,
and [g]the pure lampstand with all its utensils, and [h]the altar of incense, 9 and [i]the altar of
burnt offering with all its utensils, and [j]the basin and its stand, 10 and [k]the finely worked
garments,[1] the holy garments for Aaron the priest and the garments of his sons, for their
service as priests, 11 and [l]the anointing oil and the fragrant [m]incense for the Holy Place.
According to all that I have commanded you, they shall do."

The Sabbath

12 And the LORD said to Moses, 13 "You are to speak to the people of Israel and say, 'Above
all you shall keep my Sabbaths, for this is a sign between me and you throughout your
generations, that you may know that I, the LORD, sanctify you. 14 You shall keep the Sabbath,
because it is holy for you. Everyone who profanes it shall be put to death. [n]Whoever does
any work on it, that soul shall be cut off from among his people. 15 [o]Six days shall work be
done, but [p]the seventh day is a Sabbath of solemn rest, holy to the LORD. [n]Whoever does any
work on the Sabbath day shall be put to death. 16 Therefore the people of Israel shall keep
the Sabbath, observing the Sabbath throughout their generations, as a covenant forever.
17 [q]It is a sign forever between me and the people of Israel that [r]in six days the LORD made
heaven and earth, and [s]on the seventh day he rested and was refreshed.'"

18 And he gave to Moses, when he had finished speaking with him on Mount Sinai, the
[t]two tablets of the testimony, tablets of stone, written with [u]the finger of God.

The Golden Calf

32 When the people saw that Moses [v]delayed to come down from the mountain, the
people gathered themselves together to Aaron and said to him, [w]"Up, make us
gods who shall [x]go before us. As for this Moses, the man who brought us up out of the

[1] Or *garments for worship*

34 [p]ver. 7; ch. 25:6; 37:29
35 [q]ver. 25 [r]See ver. 25 [s][Lev. 2:13]
36 [t]See ch. 25:22 [u][ch. 40:10]
37 [v]ver. 32
38 [w]ver. 33

Chapter 31

2 [x]ch. 35:30; 36:1; 1 Chr. 2:20 [y]ch. 17:10, 12; 24:14
3 [z]ch. 35:31; [1 Kgs. 7:14]
6 [a]ch. 35:34 [b]ch. 28:3; 35:10, 35; 36:1
7 [c]See ch. 36:8-38 [d]See ch. 37:1-5 [e]See ch. 37:6-9
8 [f]See ch. 37:10-16 [g]See ch. 37:17-24 [h]See ch. 37:25-28
9 [i]See ch. 38:1-7 [j]ch. 38:8
10 [k]ch. 35:19; 39:1, 41
11 [l]ch. 30:25, 31; 37:29 [m]ch. 30:7, 34
14 [n]ch. 35:2; [Jer. 17:27]; See Num. 15:32-36
15 [o]See ch. 20:9 [p]ch. 16:23; 20:10; Gen. 2:2 [n][See ver. 14 above]
17 [q]ver. 13 [r]Gen. 1:31 [s]Gen. 2:2; Heb. 4:4, 10
18 [t]ch. 24:12; 32:15, 16; Deut. 4:13; 5:22; 9:10, 11; [2 Cor. 3:3] [u]See ch. 8:19

Chapter 32

1 [v]ch. 24:18; Deut. 9:9 [w]ver. 23; Cited Acts 7:40 [x]ch. 13:21

31:1–11 *Craftsmen.* This section names **Bezalel** (v. 2) and **Oholiab** (v. 6) as those whom the Lord had prepared to work in every craft he had prescribed for the construction of the tabernacle and all its elements (see 35:30–36:2).

31:3–5 Bezalel is described as being **filled . . . with the Spirit of God,** which means here that he has been equipped to fulfill the particular task to which he was called: **with ability and intelligence . . . to devise . . . to work** (vv. 3b–4). The expression "filled with the Spirit" appears in 28:3; 35:31; Deut. 34:9; Mic. 3:8, each time with the idea of God fitting the person for a task that serves the well-being of God's people; this is the likely background for the NT expression; e.g., Luke 1:15, 41; Acts 2:4; Eph. 5:18.

31:12–17 *Sabbath.* This section explicitly reminds Israel of what the instructions about the tabernacle signify: remembering the **Sabbath** by keeping it **holy** is integral to Israel's life as the people who are sanctified (or "made holy") by the Lord (see 20:8–11; 35:1–3). This passage grounds Israel's Sabbath observance both in creation (31:17; cf. 20:11), which Israel shares with all mankind, and in God's special choice of Israel ("sanctify," 31:13; "covenant forever," v. 16). The form of the fourth commandment in Exodus (20:8–11) stresses the first, while that in Deuteronomy (Deut. 5:12–15) stresses the second. This section shows that there is no tension between the two emphases.

31:14–15 The parallel statements regarding **whoever does any work on the Sabbath** indicates that putting a person **to death** (v. 15) is to signify the reality of **that soul** being **cut off from among his people** (v. 14). The judgment that "one shall be cut off from among his people" occurs a number of times in the law without indicating precisely what is meant (see 12:15 and note; cf. Lev. 17:10; Num. 9:13). Although the judgment at times appears to include death at the hand of the congregation when the offender is known to them (as prescribed here), it also indicates at times that the person would be killed directly by the Lord (see Ex. 30:38; Lev. 10:1–3), or suffer some other kind of separation from covenant benefits.

31:18 *Moses Receives the Tablets.* This brief statement declares that the Lord gave Moses the **tablets of the testimony** (the Ten Commandments), which was the purpose for which he had called him up to the mountain (see 24:12).

32:1–34:35 *Covenant Breach, Intercession, and Renewal.* Between the instructions for the tabernacle (25:1–31:17) and their being carried out

2 [y][ch. 12:35, 36]; See Judg. 8:24-27
4 [z]Deut. 9:16; Neh. 9:18; Ps. 106:19; Acts 7:41; [Judg. 17:3, 4] [a]1 Kgs. 12:28
5 [b][2 Kgs. 10:20]
6 [c]Cited 1 Cor. 10:7 [d]Gen. 26:8; [Judg. 21:21]
7 [e]Deut. 9:12 [f]Judg. 2:19; [Hos. 9:9]
8 [g]ch. 20:3, 4, 23; Deut. 9:16
9 [h]ch. 33:3, 5; 34:9; Deut. 9:6, 13; 31:27; 2 Chr. 30:8; Acts 7:51; [Isa. 48:4]
10 [i]Deut. 9:14 [j]ch. 22:24 [k]ch. 33:3 [l]Num. 14:12
11 [m]Deut. 9:18, 26-29; Ps. 106:23; [Ps. 74:1, 2]
12 [n][Deut. 32:27]; See Num. 14:13-16 [o]See ver. 14
13 [p]Gen. 22:16; Heb. 6:13 [q]Gen. 12:7; 13:15; 15:7, 18; 26:4; 28:13; 35:11, 12; 48:16
14 [r]Ps. 106:45; [1 Chr. 21:15; Jer. 18:8; 26:13, 15, 19; Amos 7:3, 6; Jonah 3:10; 4:2]
15 [s]Deut. 9:15 [t]ch. 34:29
16 [u]ch. 31:18
17 [v]ch. 17:9, 10; 24:13; 33:11
18 [w]Jer. 51:14

land of Egypt, we do not know what has become of him." 2 So Aaron said to them, "Take
off the [y]rings of gold that are in the ears of your wives, your sons, and your daughters,
and bring them to me." 3 So all the people took off the rings of gold that were in their ears
and brought them to Aaron. 4 [z]And he received the gold from their hand and fashioned
it with a graving tool and made a golden[1] calf. And they said, [a]"These are your gods, O
Israel, who brought you up out of the land of Egypt!" 5 When Aaron saw this, he built an
altar before it. And Aaron [b]made a proclamation and said, "Tomorrow shall be a feast to
the LORD." 6 And they rose up early the next day and offered burnt offerings and brought
peace offerings. And [c]the people sat down to eat and drink and rose up [d]to play.
7 And the LORD said to Moses, [e]"Go down, for your people, whom you brought up out
of the land of Egypt, have [f]corrupted themselves. 8 They have turned aside quickly out of
the way that [g]I commanded them. They have made for themselves a golden calf and have
worshiped it and sacrificed to it and said, 'These are your gods, O Israel, who brought
you up out of the land of Egypt!'" 9 And the LORD said to Moses, "I have seen this people,
and behold, [h]it is a stiff-necked people. 10 Now therefore [i]let me alone, that [j]my wrath
may burn hot against them and [k]I may consume them, in order that [l]I may make a great
nation of you."
11 But [m]Moses implored the LORD his God and said, "O LORD, why does your wrath
burn hot against your people, whom you have brought out of the land of Egypt with
great power and with a mighty hand? 12 [n]Why should the Egyptians say, 'With evil intent
did he bring them out, to kill them in the mountains and to consume them from the face
of the earth'? Turn from your burning anger and [o]relent from this disaster against your
people. 13 Remember Abraham, Isaac, and Israel, your servants, to whom you [p]swore by
your own self, and said to them, [q]'I will multiply your offspring as the stars of heaven,
and all this land that I have promised I will give to your offspring, and they shall inherit
it forever.'" 14 And the LORD [r]relented from the disaster that he had spoken of bringing
on his people.
15 Then [s]Moses turned and went down from the mountain with the [t]two tablets of the
testimony in his hand, tablets that were written on both sides; on the front and on the back
they were written. 16 [u]The tablets were the work of God, and the writing was the writing of
God, engraved on the tablets. 17 When [v]Joshua heard the noise of the people as they shouted,
he said to Moses, "There is a noise of war in the camp." 18 But he said, "It is not the sound
of [w]shouting for victory, or the sound of the cry of defeat, but the sound of singing that I

[1] Hebrew *cast metal*; also verse 8

(35:1–40:33) is a section of narrative that illustrates Israel's need for the sanctifying work of the Lord: the people of Israel break the covenant (32:1–35), the Lord responds in anger, but Moses intercedes for the people (33:1–23), and the Lord renews the covenant (34:1–35).

32:1–35 *Covenant Breach: The Golden Calf.* After hearing the Lord speak from Mount Sinai (see 20:22) and agreeing to keep the covenant (see 24:3, 7), the people of Israel become impatient with the length of time Moses is up on the mountain and break the covenant by making an idol and worshiping it with offerings and a feast (32:1–6). The rest of the account focuses on Moses' actions: upon coming down the mountain he breaks the tablets in anger (vv. 15–19), destroys the idol (v. 20), receives from Aaron a lame, self-serving explanation of the event (vv. 21–24), and executes judgment (vv. 25–29) before going back up the mountain to intercede for the people again (vv. 30–34). While illustrating the unfaithfulness of many of the people, the account highlights the faithful maturing of Moses as a leader and shows him bearing aspects of the Lord's character.

32:1 make us gods who shall go before us. In the NT, Stephen's response before the high priest recounts aspects of Israel's history and says of this event that Israel "thrust [Moses] aside, and in their hearts they turned to Egypt" (Acts 7:39).

32:4 These are your gods, O Israel, who brought you up out of the land of Egypt. The plurals "these" and "gods" may indicate that Israel considered the **calf** to be another god alongside the Lord (see Aaron's proclamation of a "feast to the LORD" in v. 5). Whatever the people may have thought, their words and their actions are clearly out of accord with both the first (20:3) and second commandments (20:4–6). This incident also prefigures one of the most disastrous acts in Israel's later history, when Jeroboam I speaks the same words before two golden calves, which he sets up for the specific purpose of creating an alternative to worshiping the Lord in Jerusalem (see 1 Kings 12:26–28).

32:6 The people offered **burnt offerings** and **peace offerings** to the calf, which are the same offerings they had made to the Lord at the base of Mount Sinai just before they confirmed their commitment to keeping his covenant (see 24:5). **the people sat down to eat and drink and rose up to play.** In 1 Cor. 10:7 Paul cites this to show that simply being a part of God's people is not enough; God's own people must show faithful loyalty to him, and avoid thinking that mixing pagan practices into their lives is harmless.

32:10–14 Moses responds to the Lord's statement about destroying the people and making a nation out of *him* (v. 10), appealing to God's own reputation among the Gentiles (whom God intends to bless through Israel, cf. 19:6; Gen. 12:2–3) and his promises to Abraham (Ex. 32:11–13). Moses' intercession on behalf of the people results in the Lord's relenting from consuming them entirely (v. 14; see also Num. 14:12–21). However, Moses himself will be a means of judgment on some of the people (Ex. 32:26–29), and the Lord will judge them further through a plague (v. 35).

32:11 In his intercession for the people, Moses argues the Lord's words back to him when he refers to Israel as **"your people, whom you have brought out of the land of Egypt"** (see v. 7).

32:16 the writing was the writing of God. See 31:18.

hear." 19 And as soon as he came near the camp and [x]saw the calf and the dancing, Moses'
anger burned hot, and he threw the tablets out of his hands and broke them at the foot of
the mountain. 20 He took the calf that they had made and burned it with fire and ground
it to powder and scattered it on the water and made the people of Israel drink it.
21 And Moses said to Aaron, [y]"What did this people do to you that you have brought
such a great sin upon them?" 22 And Aaron said, "Let not the anger of my lord burn hot.
[z]You know the people, that they are set on evil. 23 For [a]they said to me, 'Make us gods
who shall go before us. As for this Moses, the man who brought us up out of the land
of Egypt, we do not know what has become of him.' 24 So [b]I said to them, 'Let any who
have gold take it off.' So they gave it to me, and I threw it into the fire, and out came
this calf."
25 And when Moses saw that the people had broken loose (for Aaron had let them break
loose, [c]to the derision of their enemies), 26 then Moses stood in the gate of the camp and
said, "Who is on the LORD's side? Come to me." And all the sons of Levi gathered around
him. 27 And he said to them, "Thus says the LORD God of Israel, 'Put your sword on your
side each of you, and go to and fro from gate to gate throughout the camp, and each of
you [d]kill his brother and his companion and his neighbor.'" 28 And the sons of Levi did
according to the word of Moses. And that day about three thousand men of the people
fell. 29 And Moses said, "Today you have been [e]ordained for the service of the LORD, each
one at the cost of his son and of his brother, so that he might bestow a blessing upon you
this day."
30 The next day Moses said to the people, [f]"You have sinned a great sin. And now I will go
up to the LORD; [g]perhaps I can make atonement for your sin." 31 So Moses returned to the
LORD and said, "Alas, [f]this people has sinned a great sin. They have [h]made for themselves
gods of gold. 32 But now, if [i]you will forgive their sin—but if not, please [j]blot me out of
[k]your book that you have written." 33 But the LORD said to Moses, [l]"Whoever has sinned
against me, I will blot out of my book. 34 [m]But now go, lead the people to the place about
which I have spoken to you; [n]behold, my angel shall go before you. Nevertheless, in the
day when I visit, I will visit their sin upon them."
35 Then the LORD sent a plague on the people, because they made the calf, the one that
Aaron made.

The Command to Leave Sinai

33 The LORD said to Moses, "Depart; go up from here, you [o]and the people whom you
have brought up out of the land of Egypt, to the land of which I swore to Abraham,
Isaac, and Jacob, saying, 'To [p]your offspring I will give it.' 2 I will send an [q]angel before you,
[r]and I will drive out the Canaanites, the Amorites, the Hittites, the Perizzites, the Hivites,
and the Jebusites. 3 [s]Go up to a land flowing with milk and honey; [t]but I will not go up
among you, [u]lest I consume you on the way, for you are a [v]stiff-necked people."

19 [x]Deut. 9:16, 17, 21
21 [y][Gen. 20:9]
22 [z][ch. 14:11; 15:24; 16:2, 20; 17:2, 4; 1 Sam. 15:24]
23 [a]ver. 1
24 [b]ver. 2-4
25 [c][ver. 12]
27 [d][Num. 25:5; Deut. 33:9]
29 [e][Zech. 13:3; Matt. 10:37; Luke 14:26]; See Num. 25:11-13; Deut. 13:6-10
30 [f]See ver. 21; [1 Sam. 12:20] [g]2 Sam. 16:12; Amos 5:15
31 [f][See ver. 30 above] [h]ch. 20:23
32 [i][Num. 14:19] [j][Rom. 9:3] [k]Ps. 56:8; 69:28; 139:16; Dan. 12:1; Phil. 4:3
33 [l]Ezek. 18:4, 20
34 [m]ch. 33:12 [n]See ch. 14:19

Chapter 33
1 [o]ch. 32:7 [p]ch. 32:13; See Gen. 12:7
2 [q]See ch. 14:19 [r]See ch. 13:5
3 [s]See ch. 3:8 [t][ver. 15-17] [u]ch. 32:10; Num. 16:21, 45 [v]See ch. 32:9

32:19 When **Moses' anger burned hot**, his response images the Lord's (v. 10) and highlights the fact that Aaron has not handled the situation appropriately (see v. 22). When he throws down the **tablets** and breaks them, it is an apt picture of what the people have done in worshiping the calf.

32:20 The significance of making the people drink the **water** is not explained. It may represent (1) a further step in the destruction and desecration of the idol to have the people digest and pass it; or (2) a step in the shaming of the Israelites for their folly in worshiping the calf; or (3) a type of test, something like the test for adultery in Num. 5:16–22, exposing degrees of guilt.

32:24 As painful as it is, due to the gravity of the circumstances, there is humor in Aaron's feeble attempt to distance himself from responsibility by claiming that he merely threw the metal into the fire **and out came this calf** (see v. 4).

32:27 each of you kill his brother and his companion and his neighbor. It is not clear precisely what Moses' instruction to the Levites meant in terms of whether there was any sort of discerning whom they were to kill. Given the Lord's words to Moses in v. 33 about "whoever has sinned against me," it seems unlikely that the Levites' choices were random.

32:33–34 The Lord affirms the presumption in Moses' request that the Lord determines whose names will be in his **book**, a reality which is referred to in both the OT and NT in various ways: "the book of the living" (Ps. 69:28), "the book" (Dan. 12:1), "names . . . written in heaven" (Luke 10:20), "the book of life" (Phil. 4:3).

33:1–23 ***Moses Intercedes for the People.*** After the incident with the golden calf (32:1–35), this chapter narrates the tension of the events as the Lord says he will not go among his people (33:1–6), and the existence of a temporary tent of meeting raises questions about the future of the tabernacle (vv. 7–11). It is in this context that Moses continues to mature in the role of covenant representative as he intercedes again (see 32:9–14) for the people of Israel (33:12–23).

33:1–8 The Lord instructs Moses to lead the people toward the land of Canaan and promises again that **an angel** will go before them (see 23:20), but because Israel is a **stiff-necked people** (also 33:5; 32:9; 34:9), the Lord says that he will not **go up among** them, so as not to destroy them. When Moses intercedes on Israel's behalf, he will ask that the Lord go with Israel particularly because of their condition and their need for his pardon (see 34:8–9).

4 When the people heard this disastrous word, they [w]mourned, and [x]no one put on his
ornaments. 5 For the LORD had said to Moses, "Say to the people of Israel, 'You are a [v]stiff-
necked people; if for a single moment I should go up among you, I would [y]consume you.
So now [x]take off your ornaments, that I may know what to do with you.'" 6 Therefore the
people of Israel stripped themselves of their ornaments, from Mount Horeb onward.

The Tent of Meeting

7 Now Moses used to take the tent and pitch it outside the camp, far off from the camp,
and [z]he called it the tent of meeting. And everyone who [a]sought the LORD would go out
to the tent of meeting, which was outside the camp. 8 Whenever Moses went out to the
tent, all the people would rise up, and [b]each would stand at his tent door, and watch
Moses until he had gone into the tent. 9 When Moses entered the tent, the [c]pillar of cloud
would descend and stand at the entrance of the tent, and the LORD[1] would speak with
Moses. 10 And when all the people saw the pillar of cloud standing at the entrance of the
tent, all the people would rise up and worship, each at his tent door. 11 Thus [d]the LORD
used to speak to Moses face to face, as a man speaks to his friend. When Moses turned
again into the camp, his [e]assistant Joshua the son of Nun, a young man, would not depart
from the tent.

Moses' Intercession

12 Moses said to the LORD, "See, [f]you say to me, 'Bring up this people,' but you have not
let me know whom you will send with me. Yet you have said, [g]'I know you by name, and
you have also found favor in my sight.' 13 Now therefore, if I have found favor in your sight,
please [h]show me now your ways, that I may know you in order to find favor in your sight.
Consider too that this nation is [i]your people." 14 And he said, [j]"My presence will go with
you, and [k]I will give you rest." 15 And he said to him, [l]"If your presence will not go with
me, do not bring us up from here. 16 For how shall it be known that I have found favor in
your sight, I and your people? [m]Is it not in your going with us, [n]so that we are distinct, I
and your people, from every other people on the face of the earth?"
17 And the LORD said to Moses, "This very thing that you have spoken I will do, [o]for you
have found favor in my sight, and I know you by name." 18 Moses said, "Please [p]show me
your glory." 19 And he said, [q]"I will make all my goodness pass before you and will proclaim
before you my name 'The LORD.' And [r]I will be gracious to whom I will be gracious, and
will show mercy on whom I will show mercy. 20 But," he said, "you cannot see my face, for
[s]man shall not see me and live." 21 And the LORD said, "Behold, there is a place by me where
you shall stand on the rock, 22 and while my glory passes by I will put you in a [t]cleft of the
rock, and I will [u]cover you with my hand until I have passed by. 23 Then I will take away
my hand, and you shall see my back, but my face shall [v]not be seen."

[1] Hebrew *he*

4 [w]Num. 14:39 [x][Ezek. 24:17, 23; 26:16]
5 [v][See ver. 3 above] [y]ch. 32:12 [x][See ver. 4 above]
7 [z]ch. 29:42, 43 [a]Deut. 4:29; 2 Sam. 21:1; 1 Chr. 16:10, 11; Ps. 40:16
8 [b][Num. 16:27]
9 [c]See ch. 13:21
11 [d]Num. 12:8; Deut. 34:10; See Gen. 32:30 [e]ch. 17:9, 10; 24:13; 32:17
12 [f]ch. 32:34 [g]ver. 17
13 [h]Ps. 25:4; [Ps. 103:7] [i]Deut. 9:29; [Joel 2:17]
14 [j]Josh. 1:5; Isa. 63:9; See ch. 40:34-38 [k]Deut. 3:20; Josh. 21:44; 22:4; 23:1; [Ps. 95:11]
15 [l][ver. 1-3]
16 [m]Num. 14:14 [n]ch. 19:5, 6; 1 Kgs. 8:53
17 [o]ver. 12, 13
18 [p][ver. 20; 1 Tim. 6:16]
19 [q]Ps. 31:19; Jer. 31:14; [ch. 34:5-7] [r]Cited Rom. 9:15
20 [s]Gen. 32:30; Deut. 5:24; Judg. 6:22, 23; 13:22; Isa. 6:5; Rev. 1:17; [ch. 24:10, 11]
22 [t]Isa. 2:21 [u]Ps. 91:1, 4
23 [v]ver. 20; John 1:18; 1 Tim. 6:16; 1 John 4:12

33:7–11 The description of this **tent of meeting** being located **far off** and **outside the camp** (v. 7) contrasts with the description of the tabernacle as the place where the Lord was to "dwell in their midst" (25:8). This section steps off the main story line and introduces tension in the narrative related to how the covenant breach (ch. 32) and the Lord's response (33:1–6) will affect the existence of the sanctuary that has been described (25:1–31:17). The remainder of the section hangs with expectant hope in light of the Lord's abiding presence in the **pillar of cloud** (see 13:21; 14:19; 24:15) and the continued relationship with Moses, to whom he speaks **face to face** (33:8–11). The people's focus on Moses whenever he would go in and out of the camp foreshadows the way that his intercession (vv. 12–18; 34:8–9) will be the means by which the Lord commits himself to come back into their midst.

33:12–16 Moses intercedes again on behalf of the people (see 32:11–13, 30–32) and appeals both to the special relationship that he has with the Lord and to the fact that **this nation is your people** (33:13). Although God has drawn back from destroying all the people, he has promised only to send an angel to lead them into the land. This is not good enough for Moses, who demands that the Lord himself accompany them (v. 15). God accepts his plea, and his presence is demonstrated personally to Moses in 33:17–34:28 and publicly by the construction of the tabernacle (chs. 35–40).

33:17–18 Moses' request to see the Lord's **glory** (v. 18; see note on 16:7) should be interpreted primarily in light of his role as covenant representative on behalf of the people and not simply as for the sake of his own experience, however much he desired it as a personal blessing. In response to the Lord saying that he will go with his people (33:17), Moses is asking him to signify his presence as he did when the covenant was confirmed at Mount Sinai (see 24:9–11, 15–18) and maybe even more particularly to pledge that he will dwell among his people in the tabernacle so that both it and the people would be "sanctified by [his] glory" (29:43–46).

33:19 The Lord's words appear to be a response to Moses' requests—that the Lord would show him his ways (v. 13) and his glory (v. 18). The description points forward to the event of the Lord's self-declaration that is to come: **"I will make all my goodness pass before you and will proclaim before you my name 'The LORD'** (see 34:5–6) **. . . I will be gracious . . . and will show mercy"** (see 34:6). Paul cites this in Rom. 9:15 to show that, when God shows mercy, it is because he has chosen to do so.

Moses Makes New Tablets

34 The LORD said to Moses, [w]"Cut for yourself two tablets of stone like the first, [x]and I
will write on the tablets the words that were on the first tablets, [y]which you broke.
2 Be ready by the morning, and come up in the morning to Mount Sinai, and present
yourself there to me [z]on the top of the mountain. 3 No [a]one shall come up with you, and
let no one be seen throughout all the mountain. Let no flocks or herds graze opposite
that mountain." 4 So Moses cut two tablets of stone like the first. And he rose early in the
morning and went up on Mount Sinai, as the LORD had commanded him, and took in his
hand two tablets of stone. 5 The LORD [b]descended in the cloud and stood with him there,
and [c]proclaimed the name of the LORD. 6 The LORD passed before him and proclaimed,
[d]"The LORD, the LORD, a God merciful and [e]gracious, slow to anger, and abounding in
steadfast [f]love and faithfulness, 7 [g]keeping steadfast love for thousands,[1] [h]forgiving iniquity and transgression and sin, but [i]who will by no means clear the guilty, [j]visiting the
iniquity of the fathers on the children and the children's children, to the third and the
fourth generation." 8 And Moses quickly [k]bowed his head toward the earth and worshiped.
9 And he said, "If now I have found favor in your sight, O Lord, please [l]let the Lord go in
the midst of us, for [m]it is a stiff-necked people, and pardon our iniquity and our sin, and
take us for [n]your inheritance."

The Covenant Renewed

10 And he said, "Behold, [o]I am making a covenant. Before all your people [p]I will do
marvels, such as have not been created in all the earth or in any nation. And all the people
among whom you are shall see the work of the LORD, for it is an [q]awesome thing that I
will do with you.

11 "Observe what I command you this day. Behold, [r]I will drive out before you the Amorites,
the Canaanites, the Hittites, the Perizzites, the Hivites, and the Jebusites. 12 [s]Take care, lest
you make a covenant with the inhabitants of the land to which you go, lest it become a
[t]snare in your midst. 13 You shall [u]tear down their altars and [v]break their pillars and cut
down their [w]Asherim 14 (for [x]you shall worship no other god, for the LORD, whose name
is Jealous, is a jealous God), 15 [s]lest you make a covenant with the inhabitants of the land,
and when they [y]whore after their gods and sacrifice to their gods and [z]you are invited, you
eat of his sacrifice, 16 and you take of [a]their daughters for your sons, and their daughters
[y]whore after their gods and make your sons whore after their gods.

17 [b]"You shall not make for yourself any gods of cast metal.

18 [c]"You shall keep the Feast of Unleavened Bread. Seven days you shall eat unleavened
bread, as I commanded you, at the time appointed in [d]the month Abib, for in the month
Abib you came out from Egypt. 19 [e]All that open the womb are mine, all your male[2] livestock, the firstborn of cow and sheep. 20 The [f]firstborn of a donkey you shall redeem with
a lamb, or if you will not redeem it you shall break its neck. All the firstborn of your sons
you shall redeem. And [g]none shall appear before me empty-handed.

[1] *Or to the thousandth generation* [2] Septuagint, Theodotion, Vulgate, Targum; the meaning of the Hebrew is uncertain

Chapter 34

1 [w]Deut. 10:1 [x]ver. 28; Deut. 10:2, 4 [y]ch. 32:19
2 [z]ch. 19:20
3 [a]ch. 19:12, 13, 21
5 [b]Num. 11:25; [1 Kgs. 8:10, 11] [c]ch. 33:19
6 [d]Num. 14:18; 2 Chr. 30:9; Neh. 9:17; Ps. 86:15; 103:8; 111:4; 112:4; 116:5; 145:8; Joel 2:13 [e]ch. 22:27 [f]Ps. 57:10; 108:4
7 [g]ch. 20:5, 6; Deut. 5:10; Jer. 32:18; Dan. 9:4 [h]Ps. 103:3; 130:4; Dan. 9:9; 1 John 1:9 [i]ch. 23:21; Josh. 24:19; Job 10:14; Nah. 1:3 [j]Deut. 5:9
8 [k]ch. 4:31; 12:27
9 [l]ch. 33:15, 16 [m]See ch. 32:9 [n]Deut. 32:9; Ps. 28:9; 33:12; 78:62; 94:14; Jer. 10:16; Zech. 2:12
10 [o]ver. 27; Deut. 5:2; 29:1 [p]Deut. 4:32-35; Josh. 6:20; 10:12, 13; 2 Sam. 7:23; Ps. 77:14; 78:12 [q]Deut. 10:21; Ps. 145:6; [Isa. 64:3]
11 [r]See ch. 13:5
12 [s]ch. 23:32; Deut. 7:2; Josh. 23:12, 13; Judg. 2:2 [t]See ch. 23:33
13 [u]Deut. 7:5; 12:3; Judg. 2:2; 6:25; 2 Chr. 34:3, 4 [v]ch. 23:24; 2 Kgs. 18:4; 23:14; 2 Chr. 31:1 [w]See Deut. 16:21
14 [x]ch. 20:3, 5
15 [s][See ver. 12 above] [y]Lev. 17:7; 20:5; Deut. 31:16; Judg. 2:17; Jer. 3:9; Ezek. 6:9 [z]Num. 25:2; Ps. 106:28; [1 Cor. 8:4, 7, 10; 10:27]
16 [a]Deut. 7:3, 4; 1 Kgs. 11:2; Ezra 9:2; Neh. 13:25 [y][See ver. 15 above]
17 [b]Lev. 19:4; Deut. 27:15; [ch. 32:4, 8]
18 [c]See ch. 12:15 [d]ch. 13:4
19 [e]See ch. 13:2
20 [f]ch. 13:13; Num. 18:15 [g]ch. 23:15; Deut. 16:16

34:1–35 *Covenant Renewal: New Tablets.* The Lord calls Moses back up to Mount Sinai and proclaims further his covenant name and character (vv. 1–10) before reaffirming some of the stipulations related to worship and renewing the covenant with Moses and Israel (vv. 11–28). When Moses comes down to speak the words of the covenant to the people, he does not know that his role as the one through whom the Lord will speak is also reaffirmed through his shining face (vv. 29–35).

34:3 This brief statement of restrictions focuses on the fact that Moses alone is to be seen **throughout all the mountain**, which seems a more strict warning than when the law was initially given (see 19:12, 17).

34:6–7 The Lord's proclamation of his name and the declaration of his character becomes a central confessional passage for the OT (e.g., see Neh. 9:17, 31; Ps. 86:15; 103:8; Jonah 4:2; Joel 2:13). This confession describes the Lord's gracious character in preserving Israel as a whole for the sake of God's overall purpose and in sparing those individuals who look to him in true faith (e.g., see note on Ps. 32:1–5). Moses will argue these very words back to the Lord when he intercedes for the people after their rebellion following the spies' report on Canaan (see Num. 14:18–19). The description emphasizes the **merciful and gracious** character of the Lord (see Ex. 33:19), whose **steadfast love** and forgiveness extends to **thousands** (probably of generations, cf. Deut. 7:9; and note on Ex. 20:5–6) in contrast to the few generations upon whom he visits iniquity. Moses will appeal to Israel's need for the Lord's gracious and merciful presence so that he might forgive them and take them as his inheritance (see 34:9). On **visiting the iniquity of the fathers on the children**, see notes on 20:5–6 and Deut. 5:9–10.

34:9 for it is a stiff-necked people (cf. note on 33:1–8). It is because of the people's very stubbornness toward God that Moses makes this request.

34:11–16 The instructions here in relation to **the inhabitants of the land** reinforce the earlier command of 23:23–33 and emphasize that Israel **shall worship no other god** (34:14–16). The instructions are particularly relevant in the light of the manufacture and worship of the golden calf, which has just happened.

34:17 cast metal. This is the same Hebrew word used of the "golden" calf (see ESV footnote at 32:4).

21 [h]See ch. 20:9
22 [i]ch. 23:16; Deut. 16:10, 13
23 [j]ch. 23:14, 17; Deut. 16:16
24 [k]ch. 33:2; Deut. 7:1; Ps. 78:55; 80:8; See ch. 23:27-31 [l]Deut. 12:20; 19:8 [m][Prov. 16:7]
25 [n]See ch. 12:8 [o]See ch. 12:10
26 [p]See ch. 23:19 [q]Deut. 14:21
27 [r]ver. 10
28 [s]See ch. 24:18 [t][ver. 1; ch. 31:18; 32:16; Deut. 4:13; 10:2, 4]
29 [u]ch. 32:15 [v]2 Cor. 3:7; [Matt. 17:2]
30 [w]ver. 29
32 [x]ch. 24:3
33 [y]2 Cor. 3:13
34 [z]2 Cor. 3:16
35 [a]ver. 29

Chapter 35

1 [b]ch. 34:32
2 [c]ch. 31:15; See ch. 20:9
3 [d]ch. 16:23
5 [e]For ver. 5-9, see ch. 25:2-7 [f]See ch. 25:2

21 [h]“Six days you shall work, but on the seventh day you shall rest. In plowing time and
in harvest you shall rest. 22 [i]You shall observe the Feast of Weeks, the firstfruits of wheat
harvest, and the Feast of Ingathering at the year’s end. 23 [j]Three times in the year shall all
your males appear before the LORD God, the God of Israel. 24 For I will [k]cast out nations
before you and [l]enlarge your borders; [m]no one shall covet your land, when you go up to
appear before the LORD your God three times in the year.
25 [n]“You shall not offer the blood of my sacrifice with anything leavened, [o]or let the sacrifice of the Feast of the Passover remain until the morning. 26 [p]The best of the firstfruits
of your ground you shall bring to the house of the LORD your God. [q]You shall not boil a
young goat in its mother’s milk.”
27 And the LORD said to Moses, “Write these words, for in accordance with these words
[r]I have made a covenant with you and with Israel.” 28 [s]So he was there with the LORD forty
days and forty nights. He neither ate bread nor drank water. And he [t]wrote on the tablets
the words of the covenant, the Ten Commandments.[1]

The Shining Face of Moses

29 When Moses came down from Mount Sinai, with [u]the two tablets of the testimony
in his hand as he came down from the mountain, Moses did not know that the skin of his
face [v]shone because he had been talking with God.[2] 30 Aaron and all the people of Israel
saw Moses, and behold, the skin of his face [w]shone, and they were afraid to come near him.
31 But Moses called to them, and Aaron and all the leaders of the congregation returned to
him, and Moses talked with them. 32 Afterward all the people of Israel came near, and he
[x]commanded them all that the LORD had spoken with him in Mount Sinai. 33 And when
Moses had finished speaking with them, he put a [y]veil over his face.
34 Whenever Moses [z]went in before the LORD to speak with him, he would remove the
veil, until he came out. And when he came out and told the people of Israel what he was
commanded, 35 the people of Israel would see the face of Moses, that the skin of Moses’
face was [a]shining. And Moses would put the veil over his face again, until he went in to
speak with him.

Sabbath Regulations

35 Moses assembled all the congregation of the people of Israel and said to them,
[b]“These are the things that the LORD has commanded you to do. 2 [c]Six days work
shall be done, but on the seventh day you shall have a Sabbath of solemn rest, holy to the
LORD. Whoever does any work on it shall be put to death. 3 [d]You shall kindle no fire in all
your dwelling places on the Sabbath day.”

Contributions for the Tabernacle

4 Moses said to all the congregation of the people of Israel, “This is the thing that the
LORD has commanded. 5 [e]Take from among you a contribution to the LORD. [f]Whoever is

[1] Hebrew *the ten words* [2] Hebrew *him*

34:27–35 These verses are the background for Paul’s contrast (2 Cor. 3:7–18) between the effects of Moses’ ministry (which produced “death,” because of the people’s unbelief) and of his own ministry (which produced “life,” because the Spirit made it effectual). Paul adapted Ex. 34:34 in 2 Cor. 3:16; and in 2 Cor. 3:17 he was probably explaining that the “Lord” of the Exodus passage is the Spirit, who brings freedom.

34:30 they were afraid to come near him. The people respond to the effect of Moses’ meeting with the Lord in a manner similar to when they heard God speak from Mount Sinai (see 20:19). However, it is the glory of the Lord in their midst that is meant to sanctify both the tabernacle and the people (see 29:43), which is how Paul later describes the work of the Spirit in the life of one who has turned to the Lord (see 2 Cor. 3:16–18).

34:35 Like the pillar of cloud over the temporary tent of meeting (see 33:7–11), the skin of Moses’ face **shining** is a sign to the people that it is the Lord who is speaking with Moses, just as he did on Mount Sinai.

35:1–40:38 *Tabernacle: Preparation for the Presence.* The final section describes the preparation (35:1–36:7), construction (36:8–39:43), and assembling (40:1–33) of the tabernacle, which is then filled by the glory of the Lord (40:34–38). The order in which the construction of the elements of the sanctuary is narrated corresponds to the order in which Moses was instructed to assemble them when the tabernacle was finally erected (see 40:2–15). The length of the account of the work underlines its importance. The assembly of the tabernacle is the visible guarantee of God’s continuing presence with and care of Israel.

35:1–36:7 *Moses Prepares the People.* Moses prepares the people to carry out the instructions for the tabernacle by reaffirming the need to keep the Sabbath (35:1–3), calling for the contribution of materials and craftsmen (35:10–19), and setting Bezalel and Oholiab over the work (35:30–36:1). The people respond by bringing their contributions (35:20–29), such that the craftsmen have more than they need and Moses has to restrain them from giving more (36:2–7).

35:1–3 The instructions for the tabernacle end with a section on keeping the Lord’s Sabbaths (see 31:12–17), and the description of the fulfillment of those instructions begins with Moses calling the people to keep the **Sabbath** (35:2–3). Israel is to embody faithfulness **to the LORD** by keeping the Sabbath **holy** while they are building his sanctuary.

35:5–19 The lists of the materials needed (vv. 5–9; see 25:3–7) and the objects to be constructed (35:10–19) presume a familiarity with the instructions

of a generous heart, let him bring the LORD's contribution: gold, silver, and bronze; 6 blue
and purple and scarlet yarns and fine twined linen; goats' hair, 7 tanned rams' skins, and
goatskins;[1] acacia wood, 8 oil for the light, spices for the anointing oil and for the fragrant
incense, 9 and onyx stones and stones for setting, for the ephod and for the breastpiece.
10 "Let [g]every skillful craftsman among you come and make all that the LORD has commanded: 11 [h]the tabernacle, its tent and its covering, its hooks and its frames, its bars, its
pillars, and its bases; 12 [i]the ark with its poles, the mercy seat, and the [j]veil of the screen;
13 [k]the table with its poles and all its utensils, and the [l]bread of the Presence; 14 [m]the lampstand also for the light, with its utensils and its lamps, and the [n]oil for the light; 15 [o]and
the altar of incense, with its poles, [p]and the anointing oil and the [q]fragrant incense, and
[r]the screen for the door, at the door of the tabernacle; 16 [s]the altar of burnt offering, with
its grating of bronze, its poles, and all its utensils, the [t]basin and its stand; 17 [u]the hangings of the court, its pillars and its bases, and the screen for the gate of the court; 18 [v]the
pegs of the tabernacle and the pegs of the court, and their [w]cords; 19 the [x]finely worked
garments for ministering[2] in the Holy Place, the holy garments for Aaron the priest, and
the garments of his sons, for their service as priests."
20 Then all the congregation of the people of Israel departed from the presence of Moses.
21 And they came, [y]everyone whose heart stirred him, and everyone whose spirit moved
him, [z]and brought the LORD's contribution to be used for the tent of meeting, and for all
its service, and for the holy garments. 22 So they came, both men and women. All who were
of a willing heart brought brooches and earrings and signet rings and armlets, all sorts
of gold objects, every man dedicating an offering of gold to the LORD. 23 And [a]every one
who possessed [b]blue or purple or scarlet yarns or fine linen or goats' hair or tanned rams'
skins or goatskins brought them. 24 [c]Everyone who could make a contribution of silver or
bronze brought it as the LORD's contribution. And every one who possessed acacia wood
of any use in the work brought it. 25 And every [d]skillful woman spun with her hands, and
they all brought what they had spun in blue and purple and scarlet yarns and fine twined
linen. 26 All the women [y]whose hearts stirred them to use their skill spun the goats' hair.
27 And the [e]leaders brought onyx stones and stones to be set, for the ephod and for the
breastpiece, 28 and spices and oil for the light, and for the anointing oil, and for the fragrant
incense. 29 [f]All the men and women, the people of Israel, whose heart moved them to bring
anything for the work that the LORD had commanded by Moses to be done brought it as
a freewill offering to the LORD.

Construction of the Tabernacle

30 [g]Then Moses said to the people of Israel, "See, the LORD has called by name Bezalel
the son of Uri, son of Hur, of the tribe of Judah; 31 and he has filled him with the Spirit of
God, with [h]skill, with intelligence, with knowledge, and with all craftsmanship, 32 to devise
artistic designs, to work in gold and silver and bronze, 33 in cutting stones for setting, and
in carving wood, for work in every skilled craft. 34 And he has inspired him to teach, both
him and Oholiab the son of Ahisamach of the tribe of Dan. 35 He has [h]filled them with
skill to do every sort of work done by an engraver or by a designer or by an embroiderer
in blue and purple and scarlet yarns and fine twined linen, or by a weaver—by any sort
of workman or skilled designer.

36 "Bezalel and Oholiab and [i]every craftsman in whom the LORD has put skill and
intelligence to know how to do any work in the construction of the sanctuary shall
work in accordance with all that the LORD has commanded."

[1] The meaning of the Hebrew word is uncertain; also verse 23; compare 25:5 [2] Or *garments for worship*; see 31:10

10 [g]ver. 25; ch. 28:3; 31:6; 36:1, 2
11 [h]See ch. 26:1-30
12 [i]See ch. 25:10-16 [j]ch. 26:31, 33; 39:34; 40:3, 21; Num. 4:5
13 [k]See ch. 25:23-29 [l]ch. 25:30
14 [m]See ch. 25:31-39 [n]ch. 27:20
15 [o]See ch. 30:1-10 [p]See ch. 30:23-33 [q]See ch. 30:34-38 [r]ch. 26:36
16 [s]See ch. 27:1-8 [t]See ch. 30:18-21
17 [u]See ch. 27:9-17
18 [v]ch. 27:19 [w]ch. 39:40
19 [x]ch. 31:10
21 [y]See ch. 25:2 [z]ch. 36:3
23 [a][1 Chr. 29:8] [b]ver. 6, 7; ch. 25:4, 5
24 [c]ch. 36:3, 6
25 [d]ver. 10
26 [y][See ver. 21 above]
27 [e][1 Chr. 29:6-8; Ezra 2:68]
29 [f]ch. 36:3
30 [g]For ver. 30-34, see ch. 31:1-6
31 [h][1 Kgs. 7:14; 2 Chr. 2:14]
35 [h][See ver. 31 above]

Chapter 36

1 [i]ch. 28:3; 31:6; 35:10, 25

for the tabernacle, which Moses must have relayed to the people at some point (see 34:32).

35:10 The call for contributions is not simply for materials but also for **every skillful craftsman** (see vv. 25–26; 36:1).

35:20–29 The description of all the contributed materials emphasizes the people's willingness of **heart** (vv. 21–22, 26, 29), which indicates that they are responding in accordance with the initial call for contributions (v. 5; see 36:3–7) and shows their penitence for making the golden calf.

35:30–36:1 This section refers to **Bezalel** and **Oholiab** (cf. 31:1–6), who will oversee the designs and construction of every aspect related to the tabernacle, as those whom the Lord has **filled . . . with skill** (see 35:31, 34, 35). It also describes the **skill** of **every craftsman** who will help as the Lord enables them (also 36:2). In the same way that the Lord enabled his people to contribute the materials for the sanctuary (see 25:1–9), he has also prepared or empowered some of them with the skills required to craft the sanctuary.

35:31 he has filled him with the Spirit of God. See 31:3–5 and note.

2 [j] See ch. 25:2
3 [k] ch. 35:24 [l] See ch. 35:29
5 [m] [2 Chr. 31:10; 2 Cor. 8:2, 3]
6 [n] ver. 3
8 [o] For ver. 8-19, see ch. 26:1-14
20 [p] For ver. 20-34, see ch. 26:15-29 [q] ch. 25:5, 28; 30:5

2 And Moses called Bezalel and Oholiab and every craftsman in whose mind the LORD had
put skill, everyone [j] whose heart stirred him up to come to do the work. 3 And they received
from Moses all the [k] contribution that the people of Israel had brought for doing the work
on the sanctuary. They still kept bringing him [l] freewill offerings every morning, 4 so that
all the craftsmen who were doing every sort of task on the sanctuary came, each from the
task that he was doing, 5 and said to Moses, [m] "The people bring much more than enough
for doing the work that the LORD has commanded us to do." 6 So Moses gave command,
and word was proclaimed throughout the camp, "Let no man or woman do anything more
for the [n] contribution for the sanctuary." So the people were restrained from bringing, 7 for
the material they had was sufficient to do all the work, and more.
8 [o] And all the craftsmen among the workmen made the tabernacle with ten curtains.
They were made of fine twined linen and blue and purple and scarlet yarns, with cherubim
skillfully worked. 9 The length of each curtain was twenty-eight cubits,[1] and the breadth
of each curtain four cubits. All the curtains were the same size.
10 He[2] coupled five curtains to one another, and the other five curtains he coupled to
one another. 11 He made loops of blue on the edge of the outermost curtain of the first
set. Likewise he made them on the edge of the outermost curtain of the second set. 12 He
made fifty loops on the one curtain, and he made fifty loops on the edge of the curtain
that was in the second set. The loops were opposite one another. 13 And he made fifty
clasps of gold, and coupled the curtains one to the other with clasps. So the tabernacle
was a single whole.
14 He also made curtains of goats' hair for a tent over the tabernacle. He made eleven
curtains. 15 The length of each curtain was thirty cubits, and the breadth of each curtain four
cubits. The eleven curtains were the same size. 16 He coupled five curtains by themselves,
and six curtains by themselves. 17 And he made fifty loops on the edge of the outermost
curtain of the one set, and fifty loops on the edge of the other connecting curtain. 18 And
he made fifty clasps of bronze to couple the tent together that it might be a single whole.
19 And he made for the tent a covering of tanned rams' skins and goatskins.
20 [p] Then he made the upright frames for the tabernacle of [q] acacia wood. 21 Ten cubits
was the length of a frame, and a cubit and a half the breadth of each frame. 22 Each frame
had two tenons for fitting together. He did this for all the frames of the tabernacle. 23 The
frames for the tabernacle he made thus: twenty frames for the south side. 24 And he made
forty bases of silver under the twenty frames, two bases under one frame for its two tenons, and two bases under the next frame for its two tenons. 25 For the second side of the
tabernacle, on the north side, he made twenty frames 26 and their forty bases of silver, two
bases under one frame and two bases under the next frame. 27 For the rear of the tabernacle
westward he made six frames. 28 He made two frames for corners of the tabernacle in the
rear. 29 And they were separate beneath but joined at the top, at the first ring. He made
two of them this way for the two corners. 30 There were eight frames with their bases of
silver: sixteen bases, under every frame two bases.
31 He made bars of acacia wood, five for the frames of the one side of the tabernacle, 32 and
five bars for the frames of the other side of the tabernacle, and five bars for the frames of
the tabernacle at the rear westward. 33 And he made the middle bar to run from end to

[1] A *cubit* was about 18 inches or 45 centimeters [2] Probably Bezalel (compare 35:30; 37:1)

36:2–7 The earnest response of the people to the request for contributions (see 35:20–29), such that they had to be **restrained from bringing** any more (36:6), is a fitting response to the Lord who has been gracious and merciful in renewing his covenant with them (33:12–34:27).

36:8–39:43 *Tabernacle Construction.* This section narrates the construction of the tent of the tabernacle (36:8–38) and its furniture (37:1–29), the pieces outside the tent (38:1–8) and the court (38:9–20), the priestly garments for Aaron and his sons (39:1–31), and also a record of the amount of precious metals used in construction of the tabernacle (38:21–31). The description closes with a summary statement that emphasizes not only that all the elements related to the tabernacle were finished but that the people had done so according to the word of the Lord through Moses (39:32–43).

36:8–38 This section describes the construction of the pieces of the tent of the tabernacle according to the instructions given to Moses (see 26:1–37): the **curtains** (36:8–9) that are then put together so that the **tabernacle was a single whole** (vv. 10–13), the other **curtains** of skins to cover over the tabernacle (vv. 14–19), the **frames** for each side (vv. 20–30) and their **bars** (vv. 31–34), and the pieces for the **veil** and the **screen for the entrance** (vv. 35–38). See illustration of the tabernacle tent, p. 186.

36:10 Throughout the construction of the tabernacle, the narrative refers to

end halfway up the frames. 34 And he overlaid the frames with gold, and made their rings
of gold for holders for the bars, and overlaid the bars with gold.
35 [r]He made the veil of blue and purple and scarlet yarns and fine twined linen; with
cherubim skillfully worked into it he made it. 36 And for it he made four pillars of acacia
and overlaid them with gold. Their hooks were of gold, and he cast for them four bases
of silver. 37 He also made a screen for the entrance of the tent, of blue and purple and
scarlet yarns and fine twined linen, embroidered with needlework, 38 and its five pillars
with their hooks. He overlaid their capitals, and their fillets were of gold, but their five
bases were of bronze.

Making the Ark

37 [s]Bezalel made the ark of acacia wood. Two cubits[1] and a half was its length, a cubit
and a half its breadth, and a cubit and a half its height. 2 And he overlaid it with
pure gold inside and outside, and made a molding of gold around it. 3 And he cast for it
four rings of gold for its [t]four feet, two rings on its one side and two rings on its other
side. 4 And he made poles of acacia wood and overlaid them with gold 5 and put the poles
into the rings on the sides of the ark to carry the ark. 6 And he made a mercy seat of pure
gold. Two cubits and a half was its length, and a cubit and a half its breadth. 7 And he made
two cherubim of gold. He made them of hammered work on the two ends of the mercy
seat, 8 one cherub on the one end, and one cherub on the other end. Of one piece with the
mercy seat he made the cherubim on its two ends. 9 The cherubim spread out their wings
above, overshadowing the mercy seat with their wings, with their faces one to another;
toward the mercy seat were the faces of the cherubim.

Making the Table

10 [u]He also made the table of acacia wood. Two cubits was its length, a cubit its breadth,
and a cubit and a half its height. 11 And he overlaid it with pure gold, and made a molding
of gold around it. 12 And he made a rim around it a handbreadth[2] wide, and made a molding of gold around the rim. 13 He cast for it four rings of gold and fastened the rings to the
four corners at its four legs. 14 Close to the frame were the rings, as holders for the poles to
carry the table. 15 He made the poles of acacia wood to carry the table, and overlaid them
with gold. 16 And he made the vessels of pure gold that were to be on the table, its plates
and dishes for incense, and its bowls and flagons with which to pour drink offerings.

Making the Lampstand

17 [v]He also made the lampstand of pure gold. He made the lampstand of hammered
work. Its base, its stem, its cups, its calyxes, and its flowers were of one piece with it. 18 And
there were six branches going out of its sides, three branches of the lampstand out of one
side of it and three branches of the lampstand out of the other side of it; 19 three cups made
like almond blossoms, each with calyx and flower, on one branch, and three cups made like
almond blossoms, each with calyx and flower, on the other branch—so for the six branches
going out of the lampstand. 20 And on the lampstand itself were four cups made like almond
blossoms, with their calyxes and flowers, 21 and a calyx of one piece with it under each pair
of the six branches going out of it. 22 Their calyxes and their branches were of one piece
with it. The whole of it was a single piece of hammered work of pure gold. 23 And he made

[1] A *cubit* was about 18 inches or 45 centimeters [2] A *handbreadth* was about 3 inches or 7.5 centimeters

35 [r]For ver. 35-38, see ch. 26:31-37

Chapter 37

1 [s]For ver. 1-9, see ch. 25:10-20
3 [t]ch. 25:12
10 [u]For ver. 10-16, see ch. 25:23-29
17 [v]For ver. 17-24, see ch. 25:31-39

the person doing the task simply as **he**; this is probably Bezalel (see 37:1), the one whom the Lord called to oversee the work (35:30–34).

37:1–29 The pieces described in this chapter are those that will be inside the tent of the tabernacle: the **ark** (vv. 1–9) is the only piece in the Most Holy Place (26:34), which is separated by a veil from the **table** (37:10–16), the **lampstand** (vv. 17–24), and the **altar of incense** (vv. 25–29) in the Holy Place (see 26:33–34; 40:3–5, 21–27).

37:1–9 The **ark** (see 25:10–20) will become "the ark of the testimony" once Moses fulfills the Lord's command to put the testimony (the tablets of the Ten Commandments) in the ark when the tabernacle is finally assembled (see 25:16; 40:20). See illustration of the ark, p. 184. The importance of the ark as the central piece of the tabernacle and the place where the Lord will meet with Moses (see 25:22) is signified further by the explicit reference to **Bezalel** as the one who made it, since he was specifically called and "filled with the Spirit of God" to oversee the work (see 35:30–34).

37:10–16 The **table** is constructed here, but the bread of the Presence that is central to its function (see 25:23–29) will be placed on it only when the tabernacle is finally assembled (see 40:23). See illustration of the table, p. 184.

37:17–24 lampstand of pure gold. See 25:31–39 and illustration, p. 185.

25[w]For ver. 25-28, see ch. 30:1-5
29[x]ch. 30:23, 24, 34, 35 [y]ch. 30:7
Chapter 38
1[z]For ver. 1-7, see ch. 27:1-8
8[a]ch. 30:18 [b]1 Sam. 2:22; [Num. 4:23; 8:24]
9[c]For ver. 9-20, see ch. 27:9-19

its seven lamps and its tongs and its trays of pure gold. 24 He made it and all its utensils
out of a talent[1] of pure gold.

Making the Altar of Incense

25 [w]He made the altar of incense of acacia wood. Its length was a cubit, and its breadth
was a cubit. It was square, and two cubits was its height. Its horns were of one piece with
it. 26 He overlaid it with pure gold, its top and around its sides and its horns. And he made
a molding of gold around it, 27 and made two rings of gold on it under its molding, on
two opposite sides of it, as holders for the poles with which to carry it. 28 And he made the
poles of acacia wood and overlaid them with gold.

29 [x]He made the holy anointing oil also, and the [y]pure fragrant incense, blended as by
the perfumer.

Making the Altar of Burnt Offering

38 [z]He made the altar of burnt offering of acacia wood. Five cubits[2] was its length,
and five cubits its breadth. It was square, and three cubits was its height. 2 He made
horns for it on its four corners. Its horns were of one piece with it, and he overlaid it with
bronze. 3 And he made all the utensils of the altar, the pots, the shovels, the basins, the
forks, and the fire pans. He made all its utensils of bronze. 4 And he made for the altar a
grating, a network of bronze, under its ledge, extending halfway down. 5 He cast four rings
on the four corners of the bronze grating as holders for the poles. 6 He made the poles of
acacia wood and overlaid them with bronze. 7 And he put the poles through the rings on
the sides of the altar to carry it with them. He made it hollow, with boards.

Making the Bronze Basin

8 [a]He made the basin of bronze and its stand of bronze, from the mirrors of the [b]minis-
tering women who ministered in the entrance of the tent of meeting.

Making the Court

9 [c]And he made the court. For the south side the hangings of the court were of fine
twined linen, a hundred cubits; 10 their twenty pillars and their twenty bases were of
bronze, but the hooks of the pillars and their fillets were of silver. 11 And for the north
side there were hangings of a hundred cubits, their twenty pillars, their twenty bases
were of bronze, but the hooks of the pillars and their fillets were of silver. 12 And for the
west side were hangings of fifty cubits, their ten pillars, and their ten bases; the hooks
of the pillars and their fillets were of silver. 13 And for the front to the east, fifty cubits.
14 The hangings for one side of the gate were fifteen cubits, with their three pillars and
three bases. 15 And so for the other side. On both sides of the gate of the court were hangings of fifteen cubits, with their three pillars and their three bases. 16 All the hangings
around the court were of fine twined linen. 17 And the bases for the pillars were of bronze,
but the hooks of the pillars and their fillets were of silver. The overlaying of their capitals was also of silver, and all the pillars of the court were filleted with silver. 18 And the
screen for the gate of the court was embroidered with needlework in blue and purple
and scarlet yarns and fine twined linen. It was twenty cubits long and five cubits high
in its breadth, corresponding to the hangings of the court. 19 And their pillars were four
in number. Their four bases were of bronze, their hooks of silver, and the overlaying of
their capitals and their fillets of silver. 20 And all the pegs for the tabernacle and for the
court all around were of bronze.

[1] A *talent* was about 75 pounds or 34 kilograms [2] A *cubit* was about 18 inches or 45 centimeters

37:25–29 altar of incense. See 30:1–5 and illustration, p. 194. **anointing oil** and **incense**. See note on 30:22–38.

38:1–20 The pieces described are those outside the tent of the tabernacle but inside the **court** that surrounds it (vv. 9–20; see 27:9–19): the **altar of burnt offering** (38:1–7; see 27:1–8) is straight in line from the entrance of the court, with the **basin of bronze** (38:8; see 30:17–21) standing between it and the tabernacle (see illustration of the tabernacle and its court, pp. 190–191).

38:8 The description of the **basin** includes details about the objects from which the **bronze** was taken and the **women** who gave them. The **mirrors** would have been good quality and made of highly polished pieces of bronze that were most likely brought out of Egypt (see 12:36). The role of the women who **ministered in the entrance of the tent of meeting** would have been clear to the initial audience, but is not explained anywhere else in the OT and is referred to elsewhere only in connection with the sin of Eli's sons (see 1 Sam. 2:22).

Materials for the Tabernacle

21 These are the records of the tabernacle, [d]the tabernacle of the testimony, as they were
recorded at the commandment of Moses, the responsibility of the Levites [e]under the direction of Ithamar the son of Aaron the priest. 22 [f]Bezalel the son of Uri, son of Hur, of the
tribe of Judah, made all that the LORD commanded Moses; 23 and with him was [f]Oholiab
the son of Ahisamach, of the tribe of Dan, an engraver and designer and embroiderer in
blue and purple and scarlet yarns and fine twined linen.
24 All the gold that was used for the work, in all the construction of the sanctuary, the
gold from the offering, was twenty-nine talents and 730 shekels,[1] by [g]the shekel of the
sanctuary. 25 The silver from those of the congregation who were recorded was a hundred
talents and 1,775 shekels, by the shekel of the sanctuary: 26 a [g]beka[2] a head (that is, half a
shekel, by the shekel of the sanctuary), for everyone who was listed in the records, from
twenty years old and upward, for [h]603,550 men. 27 The hundred talents of silver were
for casting the [i]bases of the sanctuary and the bases of the veil; a hundred bases for the
hundred talents, a talent a base. 28 And of the 1,775 shekels he made hooks for the pillars
and overlaid their capitals and made fillets for them. 29 The bronze that was offered was
seventy talents and 2,400 shekels; 30 with it he made the [j]bases for the entrance of the tent
of meeting, [k]the bronze altar and the bronze grating for it and all the utensils of the altar,
31 the [l]bases around the court, and the [m]bases of the gate of the court, all the [n]pegs of the
tabernacle, and all the pegs around the court.

Making the Priestly Garments

39 From the [o]blue and purple and scarlet yarns they made [p]finely woven garments,[3]
for ministering in the Holy Place. They made the holy garments for Aaron, [q]as the
LORD had commanded Moses.
2 [r]He made the ephod of gold, blue and purple and scarlet yarns, and fine twined linen.
3 And they hammered out gold leaf, and he cut it into threads to work into the blue and
purple and the scarlet yarns, and into the fine twined linen, in skilled design. 4 They made
for the ephod attaching shoulder pieces, joined to it at its two edges. 5 And the skillfully
woven band on it was of one piece with it and made like it, of gold, blue and purple and
scarlet yarns, and fine twined linen, as the LORD had commanded Moses.
6 They made the onyx stones, enclosed in settings of gold filigree, and engraved like
the engravings of a signet, according to the names of the sons of Israel. 7 And he set them
on the shoulder pieces of the ephod to be stones of remembrance for the sons of Israel, as
the LORD had commanded Moses.
8 [s]He made the breastpiece, in skilled work, in the style of the ephod, of gold, blue and
purple and scarlet yarns, and fine twined linen. 9 It was square. They made the breastpiece
doubled, a span[4] its length and a span its breadth when doubled. 10 And they set in it four
rows of stones. A row of sardius, topaz, and carbuncle was the first row; 11 and the second
row, an emerald, a sapphire, and a diamond; 12 and the third row, a jacinth, an agate, and
an amethyst; 13 and the fourth row, a beryl, an onyx, and a jasper. They were enclosed in
settings of gold filigree. 14 There were twelve stones with their names according to the
names of the sons of Israel. They were like signets, each engraved with its name, for the
twelve tribes. 15 And they made on the breastpiece twisted chains like cords, of pure gold.
16 And they made two settings of gold filigree and two gold rings, and put the two rings
on the two edges of the breastpiece. 17 And they put the two cords of gold in the two rings
at the edges of the breastpiece. 18 They attached the two ends of the two cords to the two

[1] A *talent* was about 75 pounds or 34 kilograms; a *shekel* was about 2/5 ounce or 11 grams [2] A *beka* was about 1/5 ounce or 5.5 grams [3] Or *garments for worship* [4] A *span* was about 9 inches or 22 centimeters

21 [d]Num. 1:50, 53; 9:15; 10:11; 17:7, 8; 18:2; 2 Chr. 24:6; Acts 7:44; [ch. 16:34] [e]ch. 6:23; 28:1; Num. 4:28, 33
22 [f]ch. 31:2, 6
23 [f][See ver. 22 above]
24 [g]See ch. 30:13
26 [g][See ver. 24 above] [h]Num. 1:46
27 [i]ch. 26:19, 21, 25, 32
30 [j]ch. 26:37 [k]ch. 27:2-4
31 [l]ch. 27:10-12 [m]ch. 27:16, 17 [n]ch. 27:19

Chapter 39

1 [o]ch. 35:23, 25 [p]ver. 41; ch. 31:10; 35:19 [q]ch. 28:2-4
2 [r]For ver. 2-7, see ch. 28:6-12
8 [s]For ver. 8-21, see ch. 28:15-28

38:21–31 This section represents an official record (v. 21) of those who oversaw the work of the tabernacle (vv. 22–23) and of the precious materials **gold** (v. 24), **silver** (vv. 25–28), and **bronze** (vv. 29–31) that were used in its construction.

38:26 The record of a **beka a head** of silver (see ESV footnote) for each person **twenty years old and upward** appears to indicate that Israel had already been numbered and that atonement money had already been collected (see 30:12–16).

39:1–31 This section describes the **garments** for Aaron and his sons, including: the **ephod** (vv. 2–7; see 28:6–12), the **breastpiece** (39:8–21; see 28:15–28), and the **robe** (39:22–26; see 28:31–34); the **coats** and other pieces of **linen** (39:27–29; see 28:39–40); and the **plate of the holy crown** (39:30–31; see 28:36–37). See illustration, p. 208. After the

settings of filigree. Thus they attached it in front to the shoulder pieces of the ephod.
19 Then they made two rings of gold, and put them at the two ends of the breastpiece, on
its inside edge next to the ephod. 20 And they made two rings of gold, and attached them
in front to the lower part of the two shoulder pieces of the ephod, at its seam above the
skillfully woven band of the ephod. 21 And they bound the breastpiece by its rings to the
rings of the ephod with a lace of blue, so that it should lie on the skillfully woven band of
the ephod, and that the breastpiece should not come loose from the ephod, as the LORD
had commanded Moses.

22 [t]He also made the robe of the ephod woven all of blue, 23 and the opening of the robe
in it was like the opening in a garment, with a binding around the opening, so that it
might not tear. 24 On the hem of the robe they made pomegranates of blue and purple
and scarlet yarns and fine twined linen. 25 They also made bells of pure gold, and put the
bells between the pomegranates all around the hem of the robe, between the pomegranates— 26 a bell and a pomegranate, a bell and a pomegranate around the hem of the robe
for ministering, as the LORD had commanded Moses.

27 [u]They also made the coats, woven of fine [v]linen, for Aaron and his sons, 28 and the
[v]turban of fine linen, and the caps of fine linen, and the linen undergarments of fine
twined linen, 29 and the sash of fine twined linen and of blue and purple and scarlet yarns,
embroidered with needlework, as the LORD had commanded Moses.

30 [w]They made the plate of the holy crown of pure gold, and wrote on it an inscription,
like the engraving of a signet, "Holy to the LORD." 31 And they tied to it a cord of blue to
fasten it on the turban above, as the LORD had commanded Moses.

32 Thus all the work of the tabernacle of the tent of meeting was finished, and the people
of Israel did [x]according to all that the LORD had commanded Moses; so they did. 33 Then
they brought the tabernacle to Moses, the tent and all its utensils, its hooks, its frames, its
bars, its pillars, and its bases; 34 the covering of tanned rams' skins and goatskins, and the
[y]veil of the screen; 35 the ark of the testimony with its poles and the mercy seat; 36 the table
with all its utensils, and the bread of the Presence; 37 [z]the lampstand of pure gold and its
lamps with the lamps set and all its utensils, and the oil for the light; 38 [a]the golden altar,
the anointing oil and the fragrant incense, and [b]the screen for the entrance of the tent;
39 the bronze altar, and its grating of bronze, its poles, and all its utensils; the basin and its
stand; 40 [c]the hangings of the court, its pillars, and its bases, and the [d]screen for the gate
of the court, its [e]cords, and its pegs; and all the utensils for the service of the tabernacle,
for the tent of meeting; 41 the finely worked garments for ministering in the Holy Place,
the holy garments for Aaron the priest, and the garments of his sons for their service as
priests. 42 [f]According to all that the LORD had commanded Moses, so the people of Israel
had done all the work. 43 And Moses saw all the work, and behold, they had done it; as the
LORD had commanded, so had they done it. Then Moses [g]blessed them.

The Tabernacle Erected

40 The LORD spoke to Moses, saying, 2 "On the [h]first day of the first month you shall
[i]erect the tabernacle of the tent of meeting. 3 And you shall put in it the ark of the
testimony, and you shall [j]screen the ark with the veil. 4 And [k]you shall bring in the table
and arrange it, and [l]you shall bring in the lampstand and set up its lamps. 5 [m]And you shall
put the golden altar for incense before the ark of the testimony, and set up the screen for
the door of the tabernacle. 6 [n]You shall set the altar of burnt offering before the door of
the tabernacle of the tent of meeting, 7 [o]and place the basin between the tent of meeting
and the altar, and put water in it. 8 And you shall set up the court all around, and hang up
the screen for the gate of the court.

9 "Then you shall take the [p]anointing oil and anoint the tabernacle and all that is in it,
and consecrate it and all its furniture, so that it may become holy. 10 You shall also anoint

22 [t]For ver. 22-26, see ch. 28:31-34
27 [u]ch. 28:39, 40, 42 [v]Ezek. 44:18
28 [v][See ver. 27 above]
30 [w]ch. 28:36, 37; 29:6
32 [x]ver. 42, 43; ch. 25:40
34 [y]ch. 35:12
37 [z][ch. 25:31]
38 [a]ch. 30:3; 37:26; 40:5, 26 [b]ch. 26:36; 36:37
40 [c]See ch. 27:9-15; 38:9-17 [d]ch. 27:16; 38:18 [e]ch. 35:18
42 [f]ch. 35:10
43 [g]Lev. 9:22, 23; Josh. 22:6; 2 Sam. 6:18; 1 Kgs. 8:14; 2 Chr. 6:3; 30:27; See Num. 6:23-27

Chapter 40

2 [h][ch. 12:2; 13:4] [i]ver. 17; ch. 26:30
3 [j]ver. 21; [ch. 35:12]
4 [k]ver. 22; ch. 26:35 [l]ver. 24, 25
5 [m]ver. 26; [ch. 39:38]
6 [n]ver. 29
7 [o]ver. 30; ch. 30:18
9 [p]ch. 30:26

description of each piece, it is emphasized that it was made **as the LORD had commanded Moses** (39:1, 5, 7, 21, 26, 29, 31).

39:32–43 This section narrates the fact that the people completed **all the work of the tabernacle** (v. 32) and then brought the pieces to Moses (vv. 33–41). The section is framed by repetitive statements that emphasize that **the people of Israel did according to all that the LORD had commanded Moses** (vv. 32, 42–43; see 40:16).

40:1–33 *Tabernacle Assembled.* The Lord once again speaks to Moses and instructs him as to when and how he is to set up (vv. 2–8) and anoint the tabernacle (vv. 9–15), which tasks he then carries out (vv. 16–33).

[q]the altar of burnt offering and all its utensils, and consecrate the altar, [r]so that the altar
may become most holy. 11 You shall also anoint the basin and its stand, and consecrate it.
12 [s]Then you shall bring Aaron and his sons to the entrance of the tent of meeting and shall
wash them with water 13 and put on Aaron the holy garments. And you shall anoint him
and consecrate him, that he may serve me as priest. 14 You shall bring his sons also and put
coats on them, 15 [t]and anoint them, as you anointed their father, that they may serve me
as priests. And their anointing shall admit them to a [u]perpetual priesthood throughout
their generations."

16 This Moses did; according to all that the LORD commanded him, so he did. 17 In the
first month in the second year, on the first day of the month, [v]the tabernacle was erected.
18 Moses erected the tabernacle. He laid its bases, and set up its frames, and put in its poles,
and raised up its pillars. 19 And he spread the tent over the tabernacle and put the covering
of the tent over it, as the LORD had commanded Moses. 20 He [w]took the testimony and put
it into the ark, and put the poles on the ark and set the mercy seat above on the ark. 21 And
he brought the ark into the tabernacle and [x]set up the veil of the screen, and screened [y]the
ark of the testimony, as the LORD had commanded Moses. 22 [z]He put the table in the tent
of meeting, on the north side of the tabernacle, outside the veil, 23 and arranged the bread
on it before the LORD, as the LORD had commanded Moses. 24 [a]He put the lampstand in the
tent of meeting, opposite the table on the south side of the tabernacle, 25 [b]and set up the
lamps before the LORD, as the LORD had commanded Moses. 26 [c]He put the golden altar in
the tent of meeting before the veil, 27 and burned fragrant incense on it, as the LORD had
commanded Moses. 28 [d]He put in place the screen for the door of the tabernacle. 29 [e]And
he set the altar of burnt offering at the entrance of the tabernacle of the tent of meeting,
and offered on it the burnt offering and the [f]grain offering, as the LORD had commanded
Moses. 30 [g]He set the basin between the tent of meeting and the altar, and put water in it
for washing, 31 with which Moses and [h]Aaron and his sons [i]washed their hands and their

10 [q]ch. 30:28 [r]ch. 29:37
12 [s]See Lev. 8:1-13
15 [t]ch. 28:41; 29:7 [u]Num. 25:13
17 [v]ver. 2; Num. 7:1
20 [w]ch. 25:16; See ch. 16:34
21 [x]ver. 3; See ch. 35:12 [y]ver. 3, 20
22 [z]ver. 4; ch. 26:35
24 [a]ch. 26:35
25 [b]ver. 4; ch. 25:37
26 [c]ver. 5; ch. 30:6, 7
28 [d]ver. 5; ch. 26:36
29 [e]ver. 6 [f]ch. 29:41; 30:9
30 [g]ver. 7
31 [h]ch. 30:19, 20 [i]ch. 30:21

The High Priest's Holy Garments

The illustration depicts the holy garments worn by the high priests (Exodus 28; 39).

The *turban* of fine linen held a plate of pure shining gold, on which were engraved the Hebrew words for "Holy to YHWH."

The *ephod* (a colorful linen torso garment held by a skillfully woven waistband) had two shoulder pieces, each holding an onyx stone. The names of the 12 sons of Israel were engraved on these two stones. The cloth *breastpiece of judgment* had four rows, each with three precious stones. Each of these stones had engraved upon it the name of one of the tribes of Israel. The breastpiece also contained the Urim and the Thummim, and was attached to the ephod by gold chains and rings. The blue *robe* was worn under the ephod (Lev. 8:7–8); colorful imitation pomegranates lined the hem of the robe, alternating with golden bells. The white *coat* or tunic of checkered weave and fine linen was probably held by the embroidered sash under the robe.

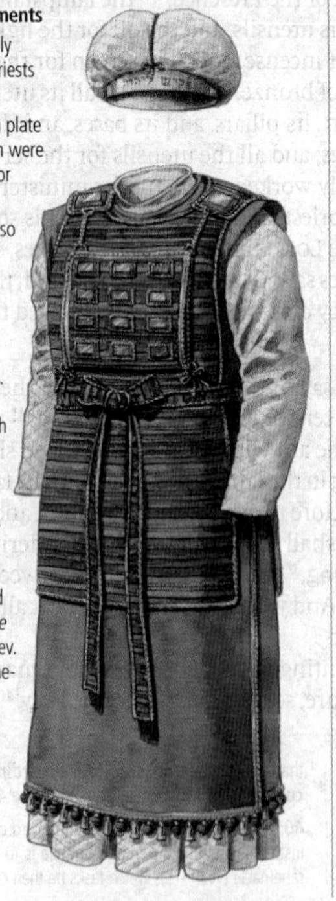

40:12–15 The anointing of **Aaron and his sons** commanded here is described in Lev. 8:1–13.

40:16–33 In correspondence to the repeated concluding statements that the people had done all that the Lord had commanded through Moses in constructing the tabernacle and its pieces (see 39:1, 5, 7, 21, 26, 29, 31, 32–42), this section emphasizes that when he erected the tabernacle, Moses did **according to all that the LORD commanded him** (40:16); it repeats that he did **as the LORD had commanded** (vv. 19, 21, 23, 25, 27, 29, 32–33) and that he **finished the work** (v. 33). The people's strict obedience to God's commands demonstrated their repentance after the golden calf disaster and made possible the fulfillment of God's promise to dwell among them (vv. 34–38).

40:34–38 *The Glory of the Lord.* The repetition in the narrative of these verses emphasizes the point that the Lord is present with all his glory in the midst of his people: the **tabernacle** (vv. 34, 35, 36, 38) was to be the **tent of meeting** (v. 34) where the Lord's presence was signified by the **cloud** (vv. 34–38) and **fire** (v. 38), so that they might be sanctified by **the glory of the LORD** (vv. 34, 35; see note on 16:7) and know that he was their God who had brought them out of the land of Egypt in order that he might dwell among them (see 29:43–46). When Solomon built the temple, "the glory filled the house of the LORD" (1 Kings 8:10–11, echoing these verses).

33 [j]ver. 8; ch. 27:9, 16 [k][Heb. 3:2, 5]
34 [l]See ch. 13:21 [m]ch. 29:43; Lev. 16:2; Num. 9:15; [1 Kgs. 8:10, 11; 2 Chr. 5:13, 14; 7:2; Isa. 6:4; Hag. 2:7, 9; Rev. 15:8]
36 [n]Num. 9:17; 10:11; [Neh. 9:19]
37 [o]See Num. 9:19-22

feet. 32 When they went into the tent of meeting, and when they approached the altar, they
washed, as the LORD commanded Moses. 33 [j]And he erected the court around the tabernacle
and the altar, and set up the screen of the gate of the court. So [k]Moses finished the work.

The Glory of the LORD

34 Then [l]the cloud covered the tent of meeting, and [m]the glory of the LORD filled the
tabernacle. 35 And Moses was not able to enter the tent of meeting because the cloud settled
on it, and the glory of the LORD filled the tabernacle. 36 Throughout all their journeys,
[n]whenever the cloud was taken up from over the tabernacle, the people of Israel would
set out. 37 But [o]if the cloud was not taken up, then they did not set out till the day that it
was taken up. 38 For the cloud of the LORD was on the tabernacle by day, and fire was in it
by night, in the sight of all the house of Israel throughout all their journeys.

INTRODUCTION TO LEVITICUS

Author, Date, and Title

The authorship of Leviticus is closely related to the larger question of who wrote the Pentateuch. As discussed in Introduction to the Pentateuch: Composition, p. 36, the Pentateuch itself clearly presents Moses as the mediator between the Lord and Israel at this point in Israel's history (e.g., 1:1). Moreover, it also states explicitly that Moses wrote down at least some portions of the Pentateuch (Deut. 31:9, 24). These factors indicate at the least that Moses is the primary source for the Pentateuch's material, and at the most that he is also its primary author. With regard to Leviticus in particular, the Lord is described as "speaking to" Moses over 30 different times, and in many of these instances he then goes on to command Moses to "speak" the words he has just heard to the Israelites (Lev. 1:1–2; 4:1; 6:8–9; etc.). This again indicates that Moses is the source of Leviticus, if not its author. (For other views, see Introduction to the Pentateuch: Composition, p. 36.) This in turn suggests a date for the book in or near the time of Moses, which would be in the fifteenth or thirteenth century B.C., depending on when one dates the exodus (see The Date of the Exodus, p. 33).

The Hebrew name for Leviticus, taken from the beginning of the book, is *wayyiqra'*, meaning "and he called." The English name "Leviticus" can be traced back to the Septuagint (the Gk. translation), in which the book is called *leyitikon*, meaning "things concerning Levites." (This title may incorrectly suggest that the material of the book concerns only what priests do. As will become apparent, Leviticus is about much more than priestly duties.)

Theme

The book of Leviticus is a further and deeper unfolding of the divine-human relationship codified on Mount Sinai. On the one hand, it assumes that Israel is sinful and impure. On the other hand, it describes how to deal with sin and impurity so that the holy Lord can dwell in the people's midst.

Purpose, Occasion, and Background

Leviticus should be considered a continuation of Exodus. The second part of Exodus is devoted to building the tabernacle (Exodus 25–40), the purpose of which is to manifest the Lord's glory among the people (see Ex. 29:42–46; Lev. 9:23). The entire content of Leviticus was given less than a month after the construction of the tabernacle, between the first month of the year (Ex. 40:1, 34–35; Lev. 1:1) and the second month of the year (Num. 1:1) following the exodus from Egypt.

Interpretative Issues

Leviticus is a difficult book, mainly because modern readers have no firsthand experience of ancient rituals and the worship practices of the tabernacle. For this reason, readers should be aware of the potential pitfall of imposing concepts or distinctions that are foreign to the biblical text itself. With this general warning in mind, several particular interpretative issues may be mentioned.

Ritual and ethical commands. To begin, there is some debate about how to understand the relationship between the "ritual" regulations of chapters 1–16 and what are commonly called the "moral/ethical" commands of chapters 17–27. It is not uncommon for modern readers to see "ritual" and "ethics" as two very separate matters and thus to view these two sections of the book as quite different and distinct. Leviticus, however, is more nuanced than that. While it may be true that not every "ethical" law of chapters 17–27 involves a ritual, it is not true that every "ritual" law of chapters 1–16 is disconnected from ethics. In fact, the whole of the book is concerned with Israel's being "holy" to the Lord, and the ritual laws of chapters 1–16 are just as important in this regard as are the laws of chapters 17–27. From the perspective of Leviticus, there is no such thing as a "nonethical" ritual law. As a result, it is unwise to see chapters 1–16 and chapters 17–27 as two unrelated sections of material. Both are equally concerned with Israel's holiness to the Lord.

Unclean, clean, holy. Leviticus also often uses the language of "unclean," "clean," and "holy" differently than today. With "unclean" and "clean," for example, most modern readers are tempted to think of that which is "nonhygienic" or "hygienic." In Leviticus, however, these words do not refer to hygiene at all. Rather, they refer to "ritual states." (The word "holy" is also used in many contexts to describe a ritual state.) Understanding the concept of ritual states is very important to understanding Leviticus as a whole.

Leviticus sets forth three basic ritual states: the unclean, the clean, and the holy. On the one hand, these categories guide the community with reference to the types of actions a person may (or may not) engage in, or the places that a person may (or may not) go. Those who are unclean, e.g., may not partake of a peace offering (7:20), while those who are clean may (7:19). (A modern analogy might be that of registering to vote: a person who is "registered" may vote, whereas a person who is "unregistered" may not.) There is a distinction to be made between "ritual states" and "moral states." One who is in the ritual state of holiness is not necessarily more personally righteous than a person who is simply clean or unclean (just as a person who is "registered" to vote is not necessarily more righteous than a person who is not).

How ritual purity relates to moral purity. Even though ritual states and moral states are different, the ritual states also seemed to represent or symbolize grades of moral purity. The highest grade of moral purity was that of the Lord himself, who was "holy" and who dwelt in the "Holy of Holies." By constantly calling the Israelites to *ritual* purity in all aspects of life, the Lord was reminding them of their need for also seeking after *moral* purity in all aspects of life (20:24–26).

Interpreting the rituals and ceremonies. A further challenge in Leviticus is how to interpret the various rituals and ceremonies. In particular, how should the individual acts and objects that make up a ritual be understood? Answering this question can be difficult, for the simple reason that Leviticus rarely explains what various ritual actions or objects mean. (One of the few exceptions is 17:11, where sacrificial animal blood is said to be the "life" of the animal.) Some help is provided, however, by asking questions about the *general* function(s) and the *specific* function(s) of the ritual. *Generally* speaking, rituals may function in several ways: e.g., to address aspects of the human condition (such as impurity or sinfulness), to serve as a way for the offerer to express emotions or desires to the Lord, and to underscore various truths about the Lord or the human condition. (In many instances, one ritual may accomplish all of these things.) It is helpful to ask which of these general functions is in view in the ritual being considered. Related to this, one should also ask, "What is the *specific* goal/function of this particular ritual as a whole?" Answering these two questions provides an interpretative framework in which to understand the individual actions of the ritual (much as a paragraph is an interpretative framework for the sentences in it). For example, if a ritual as a whole is meant to express an emotion (general), and more specifically to express praise (specific), then the individual actions or objects of the ritual should somehow contribute to this goal. Though this approach may still leave some questions unanswered, it will usually provide helpful guidelines and protect readers from some of the interpretative excesses of the past.

Another interpretative issue is how one should understand various concepts such as uncleanness, cleanness, and holiness. Great debate accompanies this issue, for the simple reason that Leviticus often provides various laws concerning cleanness and uncleanness without giving an explicit rationale of why something or someone is clean or unclean (e.g., ch. 12). Traditionally, commentators have thought that the rationale behind these rules was to be found in hygienic concerns, polemics against Canaanite religious customs, or the symbolic meaning of "death." (For these and other views, see notes on chs. 11–15.) Of these options, uncleanness as symbolic of death appears to be the only proposal that sufficiently covers many (as opposed to just some) of the cases of uncleanness. (If this is correct, then holiness—which is the polar opposite of uncleanness—could often symbolize "life.")

NT relevance of commands in Leviticus. What do these legislative texts of Leviticus have to do with the church today? At this point, only a broad picture may be presented, and it will be painted in three brushstrokes, merely offering examples of the value of Leviticus for the Christian believer. First, the sacrificial system of Leviticus has ceased for the people of God; it has been fulfilled in the coming of Christ (cf. Heb. 9:1–14, 24–28; 10:1–14). Yet studying these laws is important because they enable the reader to understand how the work of Christ saves people, since the sacrifices point to different aspects of the meaning of Christ's sacrifice of himself.

Second, the festal calendar of Israel enumerated in Leviticus (Lev. 23:1–44) has strongly shaped the Christian church's traditional calendar. The three main national pilgrim feasts of Israel are the Feast of Unleavened Bread, the Feast of Harvest, and the Feast of Booths. For those churches that follow the traditional calendar, these celebrations find their climax in Good Friday, Easter, and Pentecost. To fully understand the Christian celebrations, one must see their initial purpose in the OT. At the same time, some aspects of the legislation in Leviticus (such as the laws regulating clean and unclean foods) had the goal of separating Israel from the other nations. Although this separation has been done away with in the Christian era, these laws still teach the people of God to be morally clean (see note on 11:1–47).

Third, the entire Levitical Holiness Code (chs. 17–27) deals with sanctification, i.e., the idea of holiness affecting how one lives in the covenant community. The NT applies to Christians the same principle of life stated in Leviticus 11:44, "be holy, for I am holy" (quoted in 1 Pet. 1:16). In fact, many of the moral requirements reflected in the Holiness Code reveal the kinds of moral conduct that are still either pleasing or displeasing to God (cf., e.g., Lev. 19:11–18, 35–36). On the other hand, several details of the Holiness Code concern more symbolic aspects of holiness that should no longer be followed in the Christian era (such as laws prohibiting garments of two kinds of cloth, 19:19; prohibiting the shaving of the edges of one's beard, 21:5; and excluding people with physical defects from presenting offerings, 21:17–23). Further, the NT envisions a people of God that transcends national boundaries, and thus it dissolves the bond between the specifically theocratic system of government that was OT Israel. Therefore, current civil governments need not replicate the civil laws specific to the Mosaic theocracy (such as capital punishment for adultery in 20:10 or for blasphemy in 24:16, or the Sabbath year and Jubilee year in 25:1–22), although of course all governments must pursue justice (and Leviticus may certainly help Christians develop their notions of justice).

Key Themes

1. The holy Lord is present in the midst of his people (Ex. 40:34; Lev. 1:1). The people of Israel must therefore properly address their sin and impurity and must strive for personal holiness.

2. In order to approach God, worshipers must be wholehearted in their devotion (1:1–6:7; 22:17–30).

3. Those who are called to be spiritual leaders, such as priests, bear a heavier responsibility than do the laypeople (chs. 4; 21). In addition to the outward holiness that the priests are granted when ordained, they are constantly commanded to maintain inner holiness (chs. 8; 9; 10; 21).

4. As seen in the Day of Atonement ritual (ch. 16), the total cleansing of sins and uncleanness is done when the innermost part of the tent of meeting is purified. Ultimate purification of uncleanness is impossible from the human side.

5. Atonement is a gracious act of the Lord by which sins and impurities can be dealt with (17:11).

History of Salvation Summary

The book of Leviticus is concerned with what it means to be the holy people of a holy God: it provides instruction for conduct, both in private and as members of the body of God's people, and it details the ways in which the sacrifices and priesthood are to be administered as God's gracious provision for his people's failures. Without doubt, the death and resurrection of Jesus Christ is the culmination of salvation history, according to which he fulfilled the goals of the various offerings, the holy objects, the role of the chief priest, and the holy feasts. He also, by his resurrection, entered into his Davidic kingship and has initiated the era in which the people of God include the Gentiles and are no longer defined as a nation-state. Because of this, Christ's atoning work made obsolete the literal observance of not only the animal sacrifices and offerings but also the temple worship as a whole.

But as long as believers continue to bear their sinful nature (which they do until they die), the atoning grace of Christ does not make Leviticus irrelevant to NT believers, since principles can still be learned from the underlying laws in this book. In fact, NT writers such as the apostles Paul and Peter employ language taken from Leviticus in their exhortations to believers to follow Christ (e.g., offerings, the tabernacle, priesthood, and feasts). NT authors use the burnt offering (1 Pet. 1:19), sin offering (e.g., Rom. 8:3; Heb. 5:3; 13:11; 1 Pet. 3:18; 1 John 2:2; 4:10), and guilt offering (possibly 1 Cor. 15:3, using Isa. 53:10) to explain what Jesus accomplished on the cross, and the peace offering to explain the Christian Lord's Supper (1 Cor. 10:16–18). Thus, the book of Leviticus serves as a constant reminder of the person and work of Jesus Christ and challenges believers to apply his gospel. (For an explanation of the "History of Salvation," see the Overview of the Bible, pp. 23–26. See also History of Salvation in the Old Testament: Preparing the Way for Christ, pp. 2635–2661.)

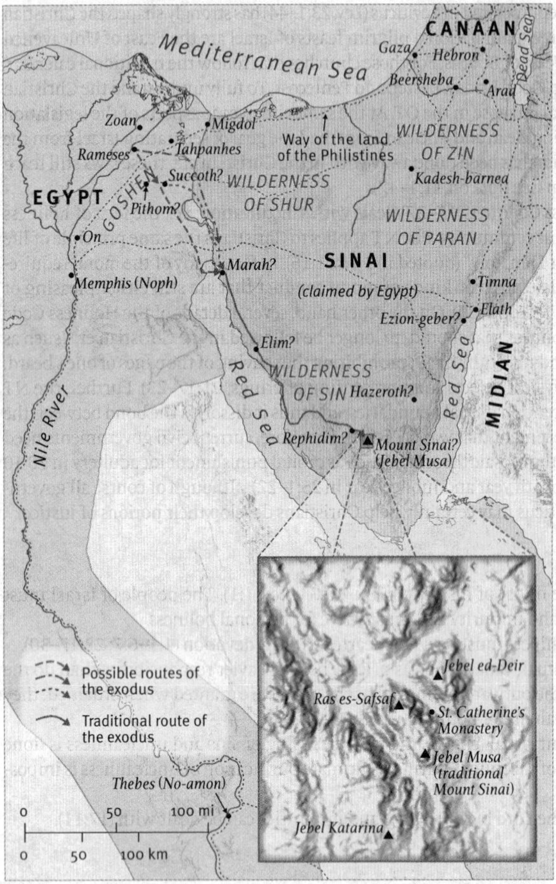

The Setting of Leviticus
c. 1446/1260 B.C.
The book of Exodus finishes with Moses and Israel having constructed and assembled the tabernacle at the base of Mount Sinai. The book of Leviticus primarily records the instructions the Lord gives to Moses from the tent of meeting, but also includes narrative of a few events related to the tabernacle.

Literary Features

Though on the surface Leviticus is a handbook of laws and regulations, it is actually much more than this. Composed as Israel was preparing to become a settled nation in a promised land, the book has affinities with utopian literature. Literary utopias both describe how people live in an ideal society and also offer an explanation of the institutions and practices that produce the society that is pictured. Leviticus outlines how people should live in God's ideal commonwealth, explaining the practices (the rules and regulations that God commands) and the institutional scaffolding (the Levitical priesthood) that produce God's intended good society. Additional genres include manual for worship, law code, community health regulations, liturgical calendar, and narrative.

The primary rhetorical form of Leviticus is oracular directive from a divine Lawgiver—a series of commands that come from the authoritative voice of God. The commands are addressed by God to Moses, with the formula "and the LORD spoke to Moses" repeated over 30 times. It thus becomes clear that Leviticus is meant to be received as the very words of the Lord that are intended to direct his covenant people in holy living.

Literary realism is present in the form of a total lack of inhibition in discussing such matters as the slaughter of animals, human diseases, bodily functions, and sexual behavior. A good reading strategy is to imagine stories and human experiences of people living within the system—experiences such as the terror of discovering some type of contamination in one's home and having to report it to the priests and perhaps dismantle the house (14:33–47).

Outline

I. Five Major Offerings (1:1–6:7)
   A. The burnt offering (1:1–17)
   B. The grain offering (2:1–16)
   C. The peace offering (3:1–17)
   D. The sin offering (4:1–5:13)
   E. The guilt offering (5:14–6:7)

II. Handling of the Offerings (6:8–7:38)
   A. The burnt offering (6:8–13)
   B. The grain offering (6:14–23)
   C. The sin offering (6:24–30)
   D. The guilt offering (7:1–10)
   E. The peace offering (7:11–36)
   F. Summary (7:37–38)

III. The Establishment of the Priesthood (8:1–10:20)
   A. The ordination of Aaron and his sons (8:1–36)
   B. The first tabernacle service (9:1–24)
   C. The Nadab and Abihu incident (10:1–20)

IV. The Laws on Cleanness and Uncleanness (11:1–15:33)
   A. Clean and unclean creatures (11:1–47)
   B. Uncleanness of a childbearing mother (12:1–8)
   C. Leprous diseases and their purification (13:1–14:57)
   D. Discharges from male and female reproductive organs (15:1–33)

V. The Day of Atonement Ritual (16:1–34)

VI. The Handling and Meaning of Blood (17:1–16)

VII. The Call to Holiness (18:1–22:33)
   A. Prohibitions against pagan practices (18:1–30)
   B. Call to holiness (19:1–37)
   C. Punishment for disobedience (20:1–27)
   D. Holiness of the priests (21:1–24)
   E. Holiness of the offerings (22:1–33)

VIII. Holy Times (23:1–25:55)
   A. Holy feasts (23:1–44)
      1. Introduction and weekly Sabbath (23:1–3)
      2. The Passover (23:4–8)
      3. The Firstfruits (23:9–14)
      4. The Weeks (23:15–22)
      5. The Trumpets (23:23–25)
      6. The Day of Atonement (23:26–32)
      7. The Booths (23:33–36)
      8. Summary of the annual feasts (23:37–44)
   B. Oil and bread of the Presence (24:1–9)
   C. The case of a blasphemer (24:10–23)
   D. The sabbatical year and Jubilee (25:1–22)
   E. Laws of redemption (25:23–55)

IX. Blessings and Curses (26:1–46)

A. Fundamental conditions (26:1–2)
B. Blessings for obedience (26:3–13)
C. The first stage (26:14–17)
D. The second stage (26:18–20)
E. The third stage (26:21–22)
F. The fourth stage (26:23–26)
G. The fifth stage (26:27–39)
H. Conditions and confession within the covenant (26:40–46)

X. Vows and Dedication (27:1–34)

A. The case of persons (27:1–8)
B. The case of animals (27:9–13)
C. The case of a house (27:14–15)
D. The case of land (27:16–25)
E. The case of the firstborn (27:26–27)
F. The case of devoted things (27:28–29)
G. The case of tithes (27:30–33)
H. Postscript (27:34)

LEVITICUS

Chapter 1
1[a]Ex. 19:3 [b]Ex. 40:34, 35
2[c]ch. 22:18, 19
3[d]See Ex. 12:5
4[e]ch. 3:2, 8, 13; 4:4, 15, 24, 29, 33; 8:14, 18, 22; 16:21; Ex. 29:10, 15, 19 [f]ch. 22:21, 27; [Isa. 56:7; Rom. 12:1; Phil. 4:18]

Laws for Burnt Offerings

1 [a]The LORD called Moses and spoke to him [b]from the tent of meeting, saying, 2"Speak
to the people of Israel and say to them, [c]When any one of you brings an offering to the
LORD, you shall bring your offering of livestock from the herd or from the flock.
3"If his offering is a burnt offering from the herd, he shall offer [d]a male without blemish.
He shall bring it to the entrance of the tent of meeting, that he may be accepted before the
LORD. 4 [e]He shall lay his hand on the head of the burnt offering, and it shall be [f]accepted

1:1–6:7 *Five Major Offerings.* Leviticus describes five major offerings, each with its own characteristics (see chart below). (Though not evident in the chart, what is done with the blood and how the remaining flesh is handled varies according to the sinner's standing before the Lord when the offering is a sin offering.) While each offering has its own emphasis, the five offerings have common or overlapping elements, especially the use of blood and "a pleasing aroma."

1:1–17 *The Burnt Offering.* Cf. 6:8–13. The burnt offering is the most costly offering there is, since it is completely burned up with nothing left (except for the skin, which the priest kept). The motive for offering the burnt offering is assumed, not specified, but other references to the sacrifices show that it is offered on such occasions as thanksgiving, penitence, vows, and self-dedication. Instead of focusing on the motive, this text focuses on more fundamental aspects of the sacrifices, such as the symbolism of the shedding of blood and the burning. The mention of "a pleasing aroma" (1:9, 13, 17) implies that the sacrifice results in the Lord's favor toward the offerer. This could happen in sin contexts, such as Noah's offering burnt offerings after the flood to appease the wrath of God that was still present after he had destroyed so many of his creatures (Gen. 8:20). This could also happen in praise or thanksgiving contexts, such as the psalmist's presenting costly and pleasing burnt offerings as acts of praise for the Lord's deliverance (Ps. 66:13, 15). One is also reminded by this sacrifice of Paul's exhortation to Christians to present their bodies as sacrifices to the Lord (Rom. 12:1). In Leviticus 1, three options are provided regarding the material of the sacrifice—a bull, small livestock (such as a sheep or a goat), and a bird—but all were to be from the offerer's own prior possession (v. 2).

1:1–2 Following on the heels of Ex. 40:34–35, Lev. 1:1 relates that the Lord spoke to Moses **from the tent of meeting**, i.e., the tabernacle (cf. Exodus 26). This introduces the material up to Lev. 7:34, but probably beyond that as well. Verse 2 of ch. 1 mentions that domestic animals are to be offered, which relates to the cases that come next—the bull (vv. 3–9) and small cattle (vv. 10–13)—and also to the animal offered as a peace offering in ch. 3 (see 3:1).

1:3–4 The bull offered by the worshiper must be **without blemish**, i.e., without any physical defects (22:22–24) that would lessen its value and make it an unworthy animal to present to the Lord (cf. Mal. 1:8). **lay his hand**. This gesture is also found in the peace offering (Lev. 3:2, 8, 13) and the sin offering (4:4, 15, 24, 29, 33). While its symbolism is debated, it probably serves to establish some sort of relationship between the offerer and animal so that the animal is **accepted** on his or her behalf. **shall be accepted . . . to make atonement for him.** This not only introduces 1:5 but is the purpose of the whole ritual up to v. 9. "Make atonement" (Hb. *kipper*) is of fundamental importance for what the ritual achieves by the shedding of blood, burning of the flesh, etc. While some take this Hebrew term as referring to expiation (the removal of sin) as opposed to propitiation (the appeasement of wrath), both realities seem to be involved. On the one hand, sin calls forth God's wrath and results in the offerer's needing to be ransomed (17:11) so that the Lord's wrath is appeased (propitiation). In this way, the sacrificial animal dies instead of the offerer. On the other hand, sin is also defiling and must be removed (expiation). The offerings that "make atonement" are the burnt offering, the sin offering (4:26), and the guilt offering (5:16), but not the grain offering or the peace offering.

Five Major Offerings

Name	Emphasis	Focus is on the general procedure or reasons for the offerings	Focus is on the proper handling, eating, or disposal of the offerings
Burnt Offering	underscores prayers of petition or praise	ch. 1	6:8–13
Grain Offering	pleasing aroma; often mirrors emphasis of the offering it accompanies	ch. 2	6:14–23
Peace Offering	fellowship with the Lord by having a communion meal	ch. 3	7:11–36
Sin Offering	atonement of a committed sin; metaphor of purification	4:1–5:13	6:24–30
Guilt Offering	atonement of a committed sin; metaphor of compensation for wrongdoing	5:14–6:7	7:1–10

for him [g]to make atonement for him. 5 Then he shall kill the bull before the LORD, and
Aaron's sons the priests shall bring the blood [h]and throw the blood against the sides of
the altar that is at the entrance of the tent of meeting. 6 Then he shall flay the burnt offering and cut it into pieces, 7 and the sons of Aaron the priest shall put fire on the altar and
[i]arrange wood on the fire. 8 And Aaron's sons the priests shall arrange the pieces, the head,
and the fat, on the wood that is on the fire on the altar; 9 but its entrails and its legs he
shall wash with water. And the priest shall burn all of it on the altar, as [j]a burnt offering,
a food offering[1] with a [k]pleasing aroma to the LORD.

10 "If his gift for a burnt offering is from the flock, from the sheep or goats, he shall
bring a male without blemish, 11 [l]and he shall kill it on the north side of the altar before
the LORD, and Aaron's sons the priests shall throw its blood against the sides of the altar.
12 And he shall cut it into pieces, with its head and its fat, and the priest shall arrange them
on the wood that is on the fire on the altar, 13 but the entrails and the legs he shall wash
with water. And the priest shall offer all of it and burn it on the altar; it is [j]a burnt offering,
a food offering with [k]a pleasing aroma to the LORD.

14 "If his offering to the LORD is a burnt offering of birds, then he shall bring his offering of [m]turtledoves or pigeons. 15 And the priest shall bring it to the altar and wring off its
head and burn it on the altar. Its blood shall be drained out on the side of the altar. 16 He
shall remove its crop with its contents[2] and cast it [n]beside the altar on the east side, in the
place for ashes. 17 He shall tear it open by its wings, but [o]shall not sever it completely. And
the priest shall burn it on the altar, on the wood that is on the fire. It is a burnt offering,
a food offering with a pleasing aroma to the LORD.

Laws for Grain Offerings

2 "When anyone brings a [p]grain offering as an offering to the LORD, his offering shall be
of fine flour. [q]He shall pour oil on it and put frankincense on it 2 and bring it to Aaron's
sons the priests. And he shall take from it a handful of the fine flour and oil, with all of its
frankincense, and the priest shall burn this as its [r]memorial portion on the altar, a food

[1] *Or an offering by fire; so throughout Leviticus* [2] *Or feathers*

4 [g]ch. 4:20, 26, 31, 35; Num. 15:25; 2 Chr. 29:23, 24; [ch. 9:7; 16:24]
5 [h]ch. 3:8; 2 Chr. 35:11; Heb. 12:24; 1 Pet. 1:2
7 [i][Gen. 22:9]
9 [j]ch. 2:3, 9, 10, 11, 16; 3:5, 9, 11, 14, 16; 4:35; Ex. 29:18, 25, 41 [k]See Gen. 8:21
11 [l]ver. 5
13 [j][See ver. 9 above] [k][See ver. 9 above]
14 [m]ch. 5:7; 12:8; [Luke 2:24]
16 [n]ch. 6:10
17 [o][Gen. 15:10]

Chapter 2

1 [p]ch. 6:14; 9:17; Num. 15:4 [q]ver. 15
2 [r]ver. 9, 16; ch. 5:12; 6:15; 24:7; [Acts 10:4]

1:5–9 After slaughtering the animal, all the ritual acts—such as throwing the **blood against the sides of the altar** (v. 5), flaying and cutting the animal into **pieces** (v. 6), preparing **fire** (v. 7), and burning all the pieces (vv. 8–9)—are to be performed by **Aaron's sons**, who represent the Lord (being holy in their professional capacity; see ch. 8). Thus atonement is achieved through both the sacrifice and the priests who represent the Lord. This underscores that atonement is a divine activity. **food offering** (1:9). This is not a specific name of an offering but a more general term for what is "consumed" by the Lord in the fire. In other offerings, it is often coupled with a **pleasing aroma** (v. 9; Hb. *reakh nikhoakh*, cf. Gen. 8:21). The word "pleasing" implies the Lord's favorable acceptance (Lev. 1:3–4) of the offerer's sacrifice. Paul uses the Greek for this expression, rendered "fragrant offering," as an image for both Christ's self-sacrifice (Eph. 5:2) and the generosity of Christians (Phil. 4:18).

1:10–13 When the offerer desires to offer a **sheep** or a goat, his animal ought to be **without blemish** (v. 10). The priest's procedure is similar to offering the bull (vv. 3–9). The laying on of a hand is assumed but not mentioned. **north side of the altar** (v. 11). This specification applies not only to the case of the small cattle but may also indicate the place of slaughter for the bull in v. 5.

1:14–17 The priest is to **wring off** the bird's **head** (v. 15) and **tear it open by its wings, but . . . not sever it completely** (v. 17). These directions can be taken as pointing to the intention to keep the bird's shape as intact as possible before burning it; this, at least, would make up for its smallness. Despite its smallness, the bird burnt offering achieves the same goal as a **pleasing aroma to the LORD** (v. 17). Again, casting it **beside the altar on the east side** may also apply to the cases of the herd and flock (v. 16).

2:1–16 *The Grain Offering.* Cf. 6:14–23. Grain offerings typically consisted of four elements: (1) fine flour; (2) oil; (3) frankincense; and (4) salt (see 2:11–13). They could be brought either uncooked (vv. 1–3) or cooked (vv. 4–10). The priest would not burn the entire offering but only a handful as a "memorial portion" (see note on vv. 1–3). The grain offering would ordinarily be offered with a burnt or peace offering and probably served the same purpose as the offering it accompanied, whether for petition or for praise.

2:1–3 The use of **fine flour** as well as the costly spice **frankincense** suggests that the Israelites were to present their very best to the Lord. The priest was to burn a **handful** of the offering as a **memorial portion** to the Lord (v. 2). The language of remembrance is used in the Bible to refer to the Lord's favor (Ps. 8:3). This "memorial portion," then, would have served as the Israelites' way of asking the Lord to "remember" them with favor as they made their request or offered their praise.

Sacrifices

Name of Sacrifice	Types of Animal	Hand-laying	Use of Blood	Priestly Portions	Lay Portions
Burnt	Cattle, sheep, goats, birds	Yes	Poured on altar sides	No	No
Peace	Cattle, sheep, goats	Yes	Poured on altar sides	Yes	Yes
Sin	Cattle, sheep, goats, birds	Yes	Smeared on altars, sprinkled inside tent	Yes, usually	No
Guilt	Rams	Probably	Poured on altar sides	Yes	No

[s]offering with a pleasing aroma to the LORD. 3 But the [t]rest of the grain offering shall be
for Aaron and his sons; [u]it is a most holy part of the LORD's food offerings.
4 "When you bring a grain offering baked in the oven as an offering, it shall be [v]unleav-
ened loaves of fine flour mixed with oil or unleavened wafers smeared with oil. 5 And if
your offering is a grain offering [w]baked on a griddle, it shall be of fine flour unleavened,
mixed with oil. 6 You shall break it in pieces and pour oil on it; it is a grain offering. 7 And
if your offering is a grain offering cooked in a pan, it shall be made of fine flour with oil.
8 And you shall bring the grain offering that is made of these things to the LORD, and when
it is presented to the priest, he shall bring it to the altar. 9 And the priest shall take from
the grain offering its memorial portion and burn this on the altar, a food [x]offering with a
[y]pleasing aroma to the LORD. 10 But the [z]rest of the grain offering shall be for Aaron and
his sons; [z]it is a most holy part of the LORD's food offerings.
11 "No grain offering that you bring to the LORD shall be made with [a]leaven, for you
shall burn no leaven nor any honey as a food offering to the LORD. 12 [b]As an offering of
firstfruits you may bring them to the LORD, but they shall not be offered on the altar for
a pleasing aroma. 13 You [c]shall season all your grain offerings with salt. You shall not let
the [d]salt of the covenant with your God be missing from your grain offering; [e]with all
your offerings you shall offer salt.
14 "If you offer a grain offering of firstfruits to the LORD, you shall offer for the grain
offering of your firstfruits fresh [f]ears, roasted with fire, crushed new grain. 15 And [g]you
shall put oil on it and lay frankincense on it; it is a grain offering. 16 And the priest shall
burn as its [h]memorial portion some of the crushed grain and some of the oil with all of
its frankincense; it is a food offering to the LORD.

Laws for Peace Offerings

3 "If his offering is [i]a sacrifice of peace offering, if he offers an animal from the herd,
male or female, [j]he shall offer it [k]without blemish before the LORD. 2 And [l]he shall lay
his hand on the head of his offering and kill it at the entrance of the tent of meeting, and
Aaron's sons the priests shall throw the blood against the sides of the altar. 3 And from the
sacrifice of the peace offering, as a food offering to the LORD, he shall offer [m]the fat covering
the entrails and all the fat that is on the entrails, 4 [n]and the two kidneys with the fat that is
on them at the loins, and the long lobe of the liver that he shall remove with the kidneys.
5 Then Aaron's sons [o]shall burn it on the altar on top of the burnt offering, which is on the
wood on the fire; it is a food offering with a pleasing aroma to the LORD.
6 "If his offering for a sacrifice of peace offering to the LORD is an animal from the flock,
male or female, he shall offer it [k]without blemish. 7 If he offers a lamb for his offering, then
he shall offer it before the LORD, 8 lay his hand on the head of his offering, and kill it in
front of the tent of meeting; and Aaron's sons shall throw its blood against the sides of the

2 [s]See ch. 1:9
3 [t]ch. 7:9; 10:12, 13 [u][Ex. 40:10]
4 [v]Ex. 29:2
5 [w]ch. 6:21; 7:9; [1 Chr. 23:29; Ezek. 4:3]
9 [x]See ch. 1:9 [y][Phil. 4:18]
10 [z]ver. 3
11 [a]ch. 6:17; [Matt. 16:12; Mark 8:15; Luke 12:1; 1 Cor. 5:8; Gal. 5:9]
12 [b]See Ex. 23:19
13 [c]Col. 4:6 [d]Num. 18:19; [2 Chr. 13:5] [e]Ezek. 43:24
14 [f]ch. 23:14; [Josh. 5:11]
15 [g]ver. 1
16 [h]See ver. 2

Chapter 3

1 [i]ch. 17:5; 22:21; 23:19; Amos 5:22; See ch. 7:11-21, 29-34 [j]ver. 7, 12 [k]See Ex. 12:5
2 [l]See ch. 1:4
3 [m]ch. 4:8, 9; Ex. 29:13, 22
4 [n]ver. 10
5 [o]ch. 6:12
6 [k][See ver. 1 above]

2:4–10 Three types of breads are mentioned in these verses: those **baked in the oven** (v. 4), those **baked on a griddle** (v. 5), and those **cooked in a pan** (v. 7). Since the grain offering was holy, the remaining part was to go to the holy priests (v. 10).

2:11–13 Leaven and **honey** are both prohibited on the altar, though the text does not explain why. (It is assumed that leaven and honey could be presented as **firstfruits** [v. 12] because these were not burned on the altar [cf. Num. 18:12–13].) Various explanations for this prohibition have been put forward, e.g., that leaven represents "corruption" and is thus prohibited (cf. Matt. 16:6). Leviticus itself, however, provides no clues. By contrast, the reason for including **salt**, a preservative, seems clearer. It is described here as the **salt of the covenant** (Lev. 2:13), a phrase that is used elsewhere to refer to the permanence of a covenant relationship (Num. 18:19). It could thus serve to constantly remind Israel of the permanent nature of its covenant relationship with the Lord.

2:14–16 Up to this point the chapter has described the more common types of grain offerings. It concludes by describing a very specific type, namely, **a grain offering of firstfruits** (v. 14; cf. Ex. 23:16, 19; 34:26). It appears that one way of offering these was to rub the **ears** (or "heads") of the plant and for the resulting **grain** to be **roasted with fire** (Lev. 2:14; cf. 23:14; Josh. 5:11).

3:1–17 *The Peace Offering.* This offering achieves and expresses peace or fellowship between an offerer and the Lord. The ritual as a whole symbolizes a communion meal that is held between the offerer, the officiating priest, and the Lord. In OT times such meals were a means of affirming a covenant relationship (Gen. 26:28–30). Generally speaking, then, this offering was a time to remember and reaffirm the covenant relationship between the Lord and Israel (cf. 1 Cor. 10:16–18; 11:23–26). As with the burnt offering, there are various specific motives for offering a peace offering, ranging from petition to praise. In this chapter, though, the entire emphasis is on the procedure for the offering, with a special focus on the burning of the fat.

3:1–5 The procedure of this ritual involving a bull is the same as that of the burnt offering, up until the shedding of blood. Only the fatty parts of the animal, instead of all of it, are to be burned up. The **fat** in ancient Israel represented the very best part of the animal (cf. the "fat of the wheat," Num. 18:12). The "fat" would be like filet mignon, i.e., the most succulent and savory part of the animal. To present this to the Lord was a way of acknowledging that he was the One worthy of most honor. (When Eli allows his sons, as priests, to eat the fat of the sacrifices, he is rebuked for honoring his sons above the Lord [1 Sam. 2:29].)

3:6–17 Almost the same procedure is prescribed here for the offering of a sheep or a goat.

altar. 9 Then from the sacrifice of the peace offering he shall offer as a food offering to the
LORD its fat; he shall remove the whole [p]fat tail, cut off close to the backbone, and the fat
that covers the entrails and all the fat that is on the entrails 10 and the two kidneys with the
fat that is on them at the loins and the long lobe of the liver that he shall remove [q]with the
kidneys. 11 And the priest shall burn it on the altar as [r]a food offering to the LORD.
12 "If his offering is a goat, then he shall offer it before the LORD 13 and lay his hand on its
head and kill it in front of the tent of meeting, and the sons of Aaron shall throw its blood
against the sides of the altar. 14 Then he shall offer from it, as his offering for a food offering
to the LORD, the fat covering the entrails and all the fat that is on the entrails 15 and the two
kidneys with the fat that is on them at the loins and the long lobe of the liver that he shall
remove [q]with the kidneys. 16 And the priest shall burn them on the altar as a [r]food offering
with a pleasing aroma. [s]All fat is the LORD's. 17 It shall be a statute forever throughout your
generations, in all your dwelling places, that you eat neither [s]fat nor [t]blood."

Laws for Sin Offerings

4 And the LORD spoke to Moses, saying, 2 "Speak to the people of Israel, saying, [u]If anyone
sins unintentionally[1] in any of the LORD's commandments [v]about things not to be
done, and does any one of them, 3 if it is the anointed priest who [w]sins, thus bringing guilt
on the people, then he shall offer for the sin that he has committed [x]a bull from the herd
without blemish to the LORD for a sin offering. 4 He shall bring the bull to the [y]entrance of
the tent of meeting before the LORD and lay his hand on the head of the bull and kill the
bull before the LORD. 5 And the anointed priest [z]shall take some of the blood of the bull
and bring it into the tent of meeting, 6 and the priest shall dip his finger in the blood and
[z]sprinkle part of the blood seven times before the LORD in front of the veil of the sanctuary.
7 And the priest [a]shall put some of the blood on the horns of the altar of fragrant incense
before the LORD that is in the tent of meeting, and [b]all the rest of the blood of the bull he
shall pour out at the base of the altar of burnt offering that is at the entrance of the tent
of meeting. 8 And all the fat of the bull of the sin offering he shall remove from it, [c]the fat
that covers the entrails and all the fat that is on the entrails 9 [d]and the two kidneys with the
fat that is on them at the loins and the long lobe of the liver that he shall remove with the
kidneys 10 (just as these are taken from the ox of the sacrifice of the peace offerings); and
the priest shall burn them on the altar of burnt offering. 11 But [e]the skin of the bull and
all its flesh, with its head, its legs, its entrails, and its dung— 12 all the rest of the bull—he
shall carry [f]outside the camp to a clean place, to the ash heap, and shall [g]burn it up on a
fire of wood. On the ash heap it shall be burned up.
13 [h]"If the whole congregation of Israel sins unintentionally[2] and [i]the thing is hidden

[1] Or *by mistake*; so throughout Leviticus [2] Or *makes a mistake*

9 [p]ch. 9:19; Ex. 29:22
10 [q]ver. 4
11 [r]ch. 21:6, 8, 17, 21, 22; 22:7, 25; Num. 28:2; Ezek. 44:7; Mal. 1:7
15 [q][See ver. 10 above]
16 [r][See ver. 11 above] [s]ch. 7:23-25; 1 Sam. 2:15; Ezek. 44:7, 15
17 [s][See ver. 16 above] [t]ch. 7:26; 17:10, 14; 19:26; Gen. 9:4; Deut. 12:16, 23; 15:23; 1 Sam. 14:33; Acts 15:20, 29

Chapter 4

2 [u]ch. 5:15, 18; [Ps. 19:12]; See Num. 15:22-29 [v]ver. 13, 22, 27; ch. 5:17
3 [w][Heb. 7:27, 28] [x]ch. 9:2
4 [y]ch. 1:3, 4
5 [z]ver. 16, 17; ch. 5:9; 16:14; Num. 19:4; [Isa. 52:15]
6 [z][See ver. 5 above]
7 [a]ch. 8:15; 9:9; 16:18; [Ex. 39:38] [b]ch. 5:9; 8:15; 9:9; Ex. 29:12
8 [c]ch. 3:3
9 [d]ch. 3:4
11 [e]ch. 9:11; Ex. 29:14; Num. 19:5
12 [f]ch. 6:11; 10:4, 5; 14:3; 16:27; 24:14, 23; Ex. 29:14; 33:7 [g]Heb. 13:11
13 [h]Num. 15:24-26 [i]ch. 5:2-4

3:16–17 Since the peace offering was the one offering of which the offerer partook, it makes sense for this chapter to end by underscoring the two parts of the animal of which the offerer was never to partake, namely, the **fat** and the **blood**. The fat represented the very best part of the animal (see note on vv. 1–5). As such, it was to be given to the Lord as the One worthy of most honor (thus **all fat is the LORD's**). The blood was reserved for a very special purpose: atoning for the life of the Israelites. As a result, it too must not be consumed (see notes on 17:11; 17:12).

4:1–5:13 *The Sin Offering.* Cf. 6:24–30. In this section the focus of the sin offering (Hb. *khatta't*) is on making amends for one's broken relationship with the Lord, caused either by unintentionally violating one of the Lord's prohibitive commandments (4:1–35) or by failing to do something that one was required to do (5:1–13). (In other places the focus will be on addressing severe cases of uncleanness; e.g., 12:6; 14:19; 15:15, 30.) The sin offering is distinguished from other offerings in that the ritual can vary according to the sinner's position before the Lord (e.g., the type of animal required or what the priest does with the blood). In ch. 4 the ritual for the sin of the anointed priest and that of the whole congregation is basically the same, while the ritual for a leader and a common individual is the same. A core part of the ritual is the sprinkling of blood (4:6, 17). Since this is a purifying act (cf. 16:19), it implies that the holy objects are considered to be defiled by the sins of the people. Because of this—and the fact that this offering occurs to address uncleanness as well—some have preferred to call the offering a "purification offering" instead of a "sin offering." In either case, the offering deals with the sin or impurity of the offerer, culminating in the Day of Atonement ritual in ch. 16. In this regard it foreshadows the essence of the Messiah's atoning work on the cross.

4:1–21 This section prescribes how to deal with the sins of the anointed priest and the whole congregation. Blood is sprinkled **in front of the veil** that separates the outer and inner parts of the tabernacle, indicating that their sins have defiled the Most Holy Place. But since this is a regular occasion, and not the Day of Atonement ritual (ch. 16), the blood cannot be brought into the Most Holy Place. The ritual here shows that the priest and congregation as a corporate entity bear heavier responsibility before the Lord than an individual leader or layperson (so that a more costly animal is required for them to make atonement).

4:3 the anointed priest. Opinion is divided over whether this phrase refers to "the high priest" or to just any priest, though the former option is commonly favored.

4:13 If the whole congregation . . . sins unintentionally. For a possible biblical example, see Josh. 9:15, where Israel makes a covenant with the Gibeonites (who deceived the Israelites by hiding relevant facts from them). **realize their guilt**. The Hebrew term *'asham* is often translated "be guilty," but since sinners bring their animal only after they come to know their sin, it is more likely that the word refers to sinners "realizing their guilt" or "suf-

from the eyes of the assembly, and they do any one of the things that by the LORD's commandments ought not to be done, and they realize their guilt,[1] 14 [j]when the sin which they have committed becomes known, the assembly shall offer a bull from the herd for a sin offering and bring it in front of the tent of meeting. 15 And the elders of the congregation [k]shall lay their hands on the head of the bull before the LORD, and the bull shall be killed before the LORD. 16 Then [l]the anointed priest shall bring some of the blood of the bull into the tent of meeting, 17 and the priest shall dip his finger in the blood and sprinkle it seven times before the LORD in front of the veil. 18 And he shall put some of the blood on the horns of the altar that is in the tent of meeting before the LORD, and the rest of the blood he shall pour out at the base of the altar of burnt offering that is at the entrance of the tent of meeting. 19 And all its fat he shall take from it and burn on the altar. 20 Thus shall he do with the bull. As he did [m]with the bull of the sin offering, so shall he do with this. [n]And the priest shall make atonement for them, and they shall be forgiven. 21 And he shall carry the bull [f]outside the camp and burn it up as he burned the first bull; it is the sin offering for the assembly.

22 "When a leader sins, [o]doing unintentionally any one of all the things that by the commandments of the LORD his God ought not to be done, and realizes his guilt, 23 or [p]the sin which he has committed is made known to him, he shall bring as his offering a goat, a male without blemish, 24 and [q]shall lay his hand on the head of the goat and kill it in the place where they kill the burnt offering before the LORD; it is a sin offering. 25 [r]Then the priest shall take some of the blood of the sin offering with his finger and put it on the horns of the altar of burnt offering and pour out the rest of its blood at the base of the altar of burnt offering. 26 And all its fat he shall burn on the altar, like [s]the fat of the sacrifice of peace offerings. So [t]the priest shall make atonement for him for his sin, and he shall be forgiven.

27 "If [u]anyone of the common people sins unintentionally in doing any one of the things that by the LORD's commandments ought not to be done, and realizes his guilt, 28 [v]or the sin which he has committed is made known to him, he shall bring for his offering a goat, a female without blemish, for his sin which he has committed. 29 [w]And he shall lay his hand on the head of the sin offering and kill the sin offering in the place of burnt offering. 30 And the priest shall take some of its blood with his finger and put it on the horns of the altar of burnt offering and pour out all the rest of its blood at the base of the altar. 31 And [x]all its fat he shall remove, [y]as the fat is removed from the peace offerings, and the priest shall burn it on the altar for a [z]pleasing aroma to the LORD. [a]And the priest shall make atonement for him, and he shall be forgiven.

32 "If he brings a lamb as his offering for a sin offering, he shall bring [b]a female without blemish 33 [w]and lay his hand on the head of the sin offering and kill it for a sin offering in the place where they kill the burnt offering. 34 Then the priest shall take some of the blood of the sin offering with his finger and put it on the horns of the altar of burnt offering and pour out all the rest of its blood at the base of the altar. 35 And all its fat he shall remove [c]as the fat of the lamb is removed from the sacrifice of peace offerings, and the priest shall burn it on the altar, on top of the LORD's food offerings. [d]And the priest shall make atonement for him for the sin which he has committed, and he shall be forgiven.

5 "If anyone sins in that he hears a public [e]adjuration to testify, and though he is a witness, whether he has seen or come to know the matter, yet does not speak, he shall [f]bear his iniquity; 2 or [g]if anyone touches an unclean thing, whether a carcass of an unclean wild animal or a carcass of unclean livestock or a carcass of unclean swarming things, and it is

[1] *Or suffer for their guilt, or are guilty;* also verses 22, 27, and chapter 5

14 [j]ver. 23
15 [k]See ch. 1:4
16 [l]See ver. 5-12
20 [m]ver. 3 [n]Num. 15:25, 28
21 [f][See ver. 12 above]
22 [o]ver. 2, 13, 27
23 [p]ver. 14
24 [q]See ch. 1:4
25 [r]ver. 7, 18, 30, 34
26 [s]ver. 31; ch. 3:3, 5 [t]ver. 20, 31, 35; ch. 5:10, 13, 16, 18; 6:7; 14:18; 15:15
27 [u]ver. 2; Num. 15:27
28 [v]ver. 14, 23
29 [w]ver. 4, 15, 24; See ch. 1:4
31 [x]ch. 3:14 [y]ver. 10, 26; ch. 3:3 [z]ch. 1:9; See Gen. 8:21 [a]ver. 20, 26, 35
32 [b]ver. 28
33 [w][See ver. 29 above]
35 [c]ch. 3:3, 9 [d]ver. 20, 26, 31

Chapter 5

1 [e]1 Kgs. 8:31; Prov. 29:24; [1 Sam. 14:24, 26; Matt. 26:63] [f]ver. 17; ch. 7:18; 10:17; 17:16; 19:8; 20:17, 19; Num. 5:31; [Num. 9:13]
2 [g]ch. 11:24, 28, 31, 39; Num. 19:11, 13, 16

fering for their guilt" (and hence realizing it; see ESV footnote) (cf. Lev. 4:22, 27; 5:2, 3, 4, 5).

4:22–35 The **priest** atones for the sin of a **leader** or an individual by what he does with the **blood** at the **altar** of the **burnt offering** (v. 25) and by burning the **fat** on it (v. 26). The meat is not burned outside the camp, since it will be eaten by the priests (6:24–30).

5:1–6 The common element in the following four cases is that sinners either deliberately (v. 1) or unknowingly (vv. 2–4) fail to do something that is required. They might *fail to give testimony* (v. 1), which could prevent justice from being carried out. They might *fail to deal properly with ritual uncleanness* (vv. 2–3), which could lead to the Lord's tabernacle being defiled. Or they might *fail to fulfill an oath* (v. 4), which would result in the Lord's name being profaned (see note on 19:11–12). In any of these cases, once they realized their **guilt**, they were to confess their **sin** (5:5) and bring a **sin offering** so that the **priest** could **make atonement** for them (v. 6).

hidden from him and he has become unclean, and he realizes his guilt; 3 or if he touches
[h]human uncleanness, of whatever sort the uncleanness may be with which one becomes
unclean, and it is hidden from him, when he comes to know it, and realizes his guilt; 4 or
if anyone utters with his lips a [i]rash oath to do evil or to do good, any sort of rash oath
that people [j]swear, and it is hidden from him, when he comes to know it, and he realizes
his guilt in any of these; 5 when he realizes his guilt in any of these and [k]confesses the sin
he has committed, 6 he shall bring to the LORD as his compensation[1] for the sin that he
has committed, a female from the flock, a lamb or a goat, for a sin offering. And the priest
shall make atonement for him for his sin.

7 "But [l]if he cannot afford a lamb, then he shall bring to the LORD as his compensation
for the sin that he has committed two [m]turtledoves or two pigeons,[2] one for a sin offering
and the other for a burnt offering. 8 He shall bring them to the priest, who shall offer first
the one for the sin offering. He shall [n]wring its head from its neck [n]but shall not sever it
completely, 9 and he shall sprinkle some of the blood of the sin offering on the side of the
altar, while [o]the rest of the blood shall be drained out [p]at the base of the altar; it is a sin
offering. 10 Then he shall offer the second for a burnt offering according to the rule. [q]And
the priest shall make atonement for him for the sin that he has committed, and he shall
be forgiven.

11 "But if he cannot afford two turtledoves or two pigeons, then he shall bring as his offering for the sin that he has committed a [r]tenth of an ephah[3] of fine flour for a sin offering.
He [r]shall put no oil on it and shall put no frankincense on it, for it is a sin offering. 12 And
he shall bring it to [s]the priest, and the priest shall take a handful of it as its memorial portion and [t]burn this on the altar, on the LORD's food offerings; it is a sin offering. 13 Thus
[q]the priest shall make atonement for him for the sin which he has committed in any one
of these things, and he shall be forgiven. And the remainder[4] shall be for the priest, as in
the grain offering."

Laws for Guilt Offerings

14 The LORD spoke to Moses, saying, 15 [u]"If anyone commits a breach of faith and sins
unintentionally in any of the holy things of the LORD, [v]he shall bring to the LORD as his
compensation, a ram without blemish out of the flock, valued[5] in silver shekels,[6] according to the [w]shekel of the sanctuary, for a guilt offering. 16 He shall also make restitution
for what he has done amiss in the holy thing and [x]shall add a fifth to it and give it to the
priest. [q]And the priest shall make atonement for him with the ram of the guilt offering,
and he shall be forgiven.

17 [y]"If anyone sins, doing any of the things that by the LORD's commandments ought not
to be done, [z]though he did not know it, then realizes his guilt, he shall bear his iniquity.
18 [a]He shall bring to the priest a ram without blemish out of the flock, or its equivalent
for a guilt offering, and [q]the priest shall make atonement for him for the mistake that
he made unintentionally, and he shall be forgiven. 19 It is a guilt offering; he has indeed
incurred guilt before[7] the LORD."

6 [8]The LORD spoke to Moses, saying, 2 "If anyone sins and [b]commits a breach of faith
against the LORD by [c]deceiving his neighbor in [d]a matter of deposit or security, or
through robbery, or [e]if he has oppressed his neighbor 3 or [f]has found something lost and
lied about it, [g]swearing falsely—in any of all the things that people do and sin thereby—
4 if he has sinned and has realized his guilt and will restore [e]what he took by robbery or

[1] Hebrew *his guilt penalty*; so throughout Leviticus [2] Septuagint *two young pigeons*; also verse 11 [3] An *ephah* was about 3/5 bushel or 22 liters [4] Septuagint; Hebrew *it* [5] Or *flock, or its equivalent* [6] A *shekel* was about 2/5 ounce or 11 grams [7] Or *he has paid full compensation to* [8] Ch 5:20 in Hebrew

3 [h]See ch. 12; ch. 13; ch. 15
4 [i][Judg. 11:30, 31; 1 Sam. 14:24; 25:22; Mark 6:23; Acts 23:12] [j]Eccles. 5:2
5 [k]ch. 16:21; 26:40; Num. 5:7; Ezra 10:1; [Josh. 7:19]
7 [l]ch. 12:8; 14:21 [m]See ch. 1:14
8 [n]ch. 1:15, 17
9 [o]ch. 1:15 [p]ch. 4:7, 18, 30, 34
10 [q]See ch. 4:20, 26, 31, 35
11 [r]Num. 5:15
12 [s]ch. 2:2 [t]ch. 4:35
13 [q][See ver. 10 above]
15 [u]ch. 22:14; [Ezra 10:2] [v][Ezra 10:19] [w]See Ex. 30:13
16 [x]ch. 6:5; 22:14; 27:13, 15, 27, 31; Num. 5:7 [q][See ver. 10 above]
17 [y]ch. 4:2 [z]Num. 15:29; [Luke 12:48]
18 [a]ver. 15 [q][See ver. 10 above]

Chapter 6

2 [b]Num. 5:6 [c]ch. 19:11 [d]Ex. 22:7, 10 [e]ch. 19:13; Mic. 2:2
3 [f]Ex. 23:4; Deut. 22:1-3 [g]ch. 19:12; Ex. 22:11
4 [e][See ver. 2 above]

5:7–13 The provision of three possibilities for the **sin offering**, adjusted according to the sinner's economic situation, would ensure that all Israelites have the ability to present an atoning sacrifice, no matter how poor they might be.

5:14–6:7 *The Guilt Offering.* Cf. 7:1–10. The distinction between the offenses covered by the guilt offering and the offenses related to the sin offering is puzzling. In general, however, the offenses here appear to be more serious, as shown by the fact that the sacrificial animal is more costly (a male instead of a female) and that the sins are described as a "breach of faith" (5:15). The word translated "guilt offering" (Hb. *'asham*) is used elsewhere with the sense of "compensation/reparation for guilt" (5:6), and the offering as a whole serves to repair the relationship between sinners and the Lord. This has led some to call this a "reparation offering."

6:1–7 This case indicates the necessity of making reparation both to the damaged **neighbor** and to the Lord, and that when a person is seeking the Lord's forgiveness, he must also correct the wrong committed against his neighbor (cf. Matt. 5:23–26).

what he got by oppression or the deposit that was committed to him or the lost thing
that he found **5** or anything about which he has sworn falsely, he shall [h]restore it in full
and shall add a fifth to it, and give it to him to whom it belongs on the day he realizes his
guilt. **6** And he shall bring to the priest as his compensation to the LORD [i]a ram without
blemish out of the flock, or its equivalent for a guilt offering. **7** [j]And the priest shall make
atonement for him before the LORD, and he shall be forgiven for any of the things that
one may do and thereby become guilty."

The Priests and the Offerings

8 [1]The LORD spoke to Moses, saying, **9** "Command Aaron and his sons, saying, This is the
law of the burnt offering. The burnt offering shall be on the hearth on the altar all night
until the morning, and the fire of the altar shall be kept burning on it. **10** And [k]the priest
shall put on his linen garment and put his linen undergarment on his body, and he shall
take up the ashes to which the fire has reduced the burnt offering on the altar and put
them [l]beside the altar. **11** Then [m]he shall take off his garments and put on other garments
and carry the ashes [n]outside the camp to a clean place. **12** The fire on the altar shall be kept
burning on it; it shall not go out. The priest shall burn wood on it every morning, and he
shall arrange the burnt offering on it and shall burn on it [o]the fat of the peace offerings.
13 Fire shall be kept burning on the altar continually; it shall not go out.

14 "And this is the law of [p]the grain offering. The sons of Aaron shall offer it before the
LORD in front of the altar. **15** And one shall take from it a handful of the fine flour of the
grain offering and its oil and all the frankincense that is on the grain offering and burn
this as its [q]memorial portion on the altar, a pleasing aroma to the LORD. **16** And [r]the rest
of it Aaron and his sons shall eat. It shall be eaten unleavened [s]in a holy place. In the court
of the tent of meeting they shall eat it. **17** [t]It shall not be baked with leaven. [u]I have given
it as their portion of my food offerings. [v]It is a thing most holy, like the sin offering and
the guilt offering. **18** Every male among the children of Aaron may eat of it, as decreed
forever throughout your generations, from the LORD's food offerings. Whatever touches
them shall become holy."

19 The LORD spoke to Moses, saying, **20** [w]"This is the offering that Aaron and his sons
shall offer to the LORD on the day when he is anointed: a [x]tenth of an ephah[2] of fine flour
as a regular grain offering, half of it in the morning and half in the evening. **21** It shall be
made with oil [y]on a griddle. You shall bring it [z]well mixed, in baked[3] pieces like a grain
offering, and offer it for a pleasing aroma to the LORD. **22** The priest from among Aaron's
sons, who is anointed to succeed him, shall offer it to the LORD as decreed forever. [a]The
whole of it shall be burned. **23** Every grain offering of a priest shall be wholly burned. It
shall not be eaten."

24 The LORD spoke to Moses, saying, **25** "Speak to Aaron and his sons, saying, [b]This is the

[1] Ch 6:1 in Hebrew [2] An *ephah* was about 3/5 bushel or 22 liters [3] The meaning of the Hebrew is uncertain

5 [h]Num. 5:7; [ch. 5:16; 2 Sam. 12:6; Luke 19:8]
6 [i]ch. 5:15, 18
7 [j]See ch. 4:26
10 [k]ch. 16:4; Ezek. 44:18; See Ex. 28:39-43 [l]ch. 1:16
11 [m]ch. 16:23; Ezek. 42:14; 44:19 [n]See ch. 4:12
12 [o]ch. 3:3, 9, 14
14 [p]ch. 2:1; Num. 15:4
15 [q]ch. 2:2, 9
16 [r]ch. 2:3, 10; Ezek. 44:29; [1 Cor. 9:13] [s]ver. 26; ch. 10:12, 13
17 [t]ch. 2:11 [u]Num. 18:9 [v]ver. 25, 29; ch. 2:3; 7:1
20 [w]Ex. 29:1, 2 [x]ch. 5:11; Ex. 16:36
21 [y]ch. 2:5; 7:9 [z]ch. 7:12
22 [a]Ex. 29:25
25 [b]See ch. 4

6:8–7:38 *Handling of the Offerings.* This section focuses on issues related to the proper handling, eating, and disposal of the various sacrifices and offerings. The sacrifices and offerings are either "holy" or "most holy" and must therefore be treated with due respect. If this was not done, the offering would not count and the offender would be punished (cf. 7:18, 20–21).

6:8–13 *The Burnt Offering.* Cf. 1:3–17. This passage concerns the continual burnt offerings that were made every morning and every evening (Ex. 29:38–42). It explains how the **ashes** of this offering are to be handled each morning, which requires the proper attire for the activities both inside (Lev. 6:10) and outside (v. 11) the tabernacle complex. This passage also underscores that the **fire on the altar shall be kept burning** (vv. 9, 12–13); this requirement would in turn serve as a special exhortation to the priests to be faithful in their duties so that the worship of the Lord could continue without interruption.

6:14–23 *The Grain Offering.* The description in ch. 2 relates to what the worshiper does, while this section focuses on what the priests do.

6:14–18 After summarizing the law of ch. 2 in 6:14–15, these verses go on to underscore that the grain offering is **most holy** and must therefore be eaten by holy people (the **sons of Aaron**) in a **holy place** (**the court of the tent of meeting**) (vv. 16–18). It is imperative that the most holy status of the offering be respected.

6:19–23 These verses appear to describe a grain offering, offered by **Aaron and his sons**, that was to begin at the inauguration of the priesthood and then to continue as a **regular grain offering** (vv. 19–20; cf. Ex. 29:38–42). Since it appears that this was offered on behalf of the priests, it is not surprising that the high priest (**the priest . . . who is anointed**) would do this, since he would represent the priests as a whole. These verses also remind the priests of their continual need for the Lord's favor.

6:24–30 *The Sin Offering.* Cf. 4:1–5:13. Chapter 4 has already indicated that the meat of the sin offering is to be **burned up** when its blood has been taken into the **Holy Place** (4:3–21; cf. 6:30). These verses explain that the remaining meat of other sin offerings (4:22–35) is to be eaten by holy people (**priests**) in a **holy place** (6:26, 29). **blood . . . on a garment . . . earthenware vessel . . . bronze vessel**. Most interpreters believe that the blood itself was considered holy. Thus, the stipulations of vv. 27–28 are to ensure that holy blood does not leave the holy place.

law of the sin offering. [c]In the place where the burnt offering is killed shall the sin offering
be killed before the LORD; [d]it is most holy. 26 [e]The priest who offers it for sin shall eat it.
[f]In a holy place it shall be eaten, in the court of the tent of meeting. 27 Whatever touches
its flesh shall be holy, and when any of its blood is splashed on a garment, you shall wash
that on which it was splashed in a holy place. 28 And [g]the earthenware vessel in which it
is boiled [h]shall be broken. But if it is boiled in a bronze vessel, that shall be scoured and
rinsed in water. 29 Every male among the priests may eat of it; [d]it is most holy. 30 [i]But no
sin offering shall be eaten from which any blood is brought into the tent of meeting to
make atonement in the Holy Place; it shall be burned up with fire.

7 [j]"This is the law of the [k]guilt offering. [l]It is most holy. 2 [m]In the place where they kill the
burnt offering they shall kill the guilt offering, and its blood shall be thrown against
the sides of the altar. 3 And [n]all its fat shall be offered, the fat tail, the fat that covers the
entrails, 4 the two kidneys with the fat that is on them at the loins, and the long lobe of
the liver that he shall remove [o]with the kidneys. 5 The priest shall burn them on the altar
as a food offering to the LORD; it is a guilt offering. 6 [p]Every male among the priests may
eat of it. It shall be eaten in a holy place. [q]It is most holy. 7 The [r]guilt offering is just like
the sin offering; there is one law for them. The priest who makes atonement with it shall
have it. 8 And the priest who offers any man's burnt offering shall have for himself the
skin of the burnt offering that he has offered. 9 And [s]every grain offering baked [t]in the
oven and all that is prepared [u]on a pan or a griddle shall belong to the priest who offers
it. 10 And every grain offering, mixed with oil or dry, shall be shared equally among all
the sons of Aaron.

11 "And this is the law of the sacrifice of peace offerings that one may offer to the LORD.
12 If he offers it for a thanksgiving, then he shall offer with the thanksgiving sacrifice
[v]unleavened loaves mixed with oil, unleavened wafers smeared with oil, and loaves of
fine flour [w]well mixed with oil. 13 [x]With the sacrifice of his peace offerings for thanksgiving
he shall bring his offering with loaves of leavened bread. 14 And from it he shall offer one
loaf from each offering, as a [y]gift to the LORD. [z]It shall belong to the priest who throws
the blood of the peace offerings. 15 And the flesh of the sacrifice of his peace offerings [a]for
thanksgiving shall be eaten on the day of his offering. He shall not leave any of it until
the morning. 16 But [b]if the sacrifice of his offering is a vow offering or a freewill offering,
it shall be eaten on the day that he offers his sacrifice, and on the next day what remains
of it shall be eaten. 17 But what remains of the flesh of the sacrifice on the third day shall
be burned up with fire. 18 If any of the flesh of the sacrifice of his peace offering is eaten
on the third day, he who offers it shall not be accepted, neither shall it be credited to him.
It is [c]tainted, and he who eats of it shall bear his iniquity.

19 "Flesh that touches any unclean thing shall not be eaten. It shall be burned up with
fire. All who are clean may eat flesh, 20 but the person who eats of the flesh of the sacrifice
of the LORD's peace offerings [d]while an uncleanness is on him, that person shall be cut off
from his people. 21 And if anyone touches an unclean thing, whether [e]human uncleanness
or an [f]unclean beast or any [g]unclean detestable creature, and then eats some flesh from the
sacrifice of the LORD's peace offerings, that person shall be cut off from his people."

22 The LORD spoke to Moses, saying, 23 "Speak to the people of Israel, saying, [h]You shall
eat no fat, of ox or sheep or goat. 24 The fat of an animal [i]that dies of itself and the fat of
one that is torn by beasts may be put to any other use, but on no account shall you eat it.

25 [c]ch. 1:3, 5, 11; 4:24, 29, 33; [ch. 7:2] [d]ver. 17, 29
26 [e]ch. 10:17, 18; Num. 18:9, 19; Ezek. 44:27-29 [f]ver. 16
28 [g]ch. 11:32, 33; 15:12 [h][ch. 11:33; 15:12]
29 [d][See ver. 25 above]
30 [i]ch. 4:7, 11, 12, 18, 21; 16:27; Heb. 13:11; [ver. 26, 29; ch. 10:18]

Chapter 7

1 [j]See ch. 5:1–6:7 [k]ver. 37 [l]ch. 6:17, 25
2 [m]ch. 6:25
3 [n]ch. 3:3, 4, 9, 10, 14-16; 4:8, 9; Ex. 29:13, 22
4 [o]ch. 3:4
6 [p]ch. 6:18, 29 [q]ver. 1
7 [r]ch. 6:25, 26; 14:13
9 [s]ch. 2:3, 10; Num. 18:9; Ezek. 44:29 [t]ch. 2:7 [u]ch. 2:5; 6:21
12 [v]ch. 2:4; Num. 6:15 [w]ch. 6:21
13 [x]Amos 4:5
14 [y]Ex. 29:27, 28 [z]Num. 18:8, 11, 19
15 [a]ch. 22:29, 30
16 [b]ch. 19:6-8; 22:21
18 [c]ch. 19:7
20 [d]ch. 15:3; 22:3
21 [e]See ch. 12; ch. 13; ch. 15 [f]See ch. 11:24-28 [g]See ch. 11:10-23
23 [h]ch. 3:16, 17
24 [i]ch. 17:15; 22:8; Ex. 22:31; Deut. 14:21; Ezek. 4:14; 44:31

7:1–10 *The Guilt Offering.* The earlier passage (5:14–6:7) focused on *when* this was to be offered; this passage now focuses on *how* it is to be offered.

7:1–7 This ritual has some elements in common with each of the other offerings, but it is not identical to any of them. As in the sin offering, the remaining flesh goes to the **priest** and his family.

7:8–10 Having just described what portion of the guilt offering the priest receives (v. 7), these verses now proceed to discuss what portion the **priest** receives from the **burnt offering** (v. 8) and **grain offering** (vv. 9–10).

7:11–36 *The Peace Offering.* The peace offering is subdivided into three types, according to their associated motivations: **thanksgiving** (in response to God's favor toward the offerer; vv. 12, 13, 15), a **vow** (an offering in fulfillment of a vow; v. 16), and **freewill** (when there is no specific obligation to make an offering; v. 16). **cut off from his people** (vv. 20, 21, 25, 27). Some understand this to mean that the person is isolated from his relatives and family. Others, however, note that it is associated elsewhere with death (Ex. 31:14; Num. 4:18–20) and thus conclude that it refers to the premature death of the sinner. In either case, it was a severe penalty indeed. On the prohibition against eating **fat** and **blood** (Lev. 7:22–27), see note on 3:16–17. In the peace offering, the **breast** and **right thigh** (the choicest parts of an animal) go to the priests as a wave offering and a contribution. The reference to their anointing (7:35–36) anticipates ch. 8, on their ordination.

25 For every person who eats of the fat of an animal of which a food offering may be made to the LORD shall be cut off from his people. 26 Moreover, [j]you shall eat no blood whatever, whether of fowl or of animal, in any of your dwelling places. 27 Whoever eats any blood, that person shall be cut off from his people."

28 The LORD spoke to Moses, saying, 29 "Speak to the people of Israel, saying, [k]Whoever offers the sacrifice of his peace offerings to the LORD shall bring his offering to the LORD from the sacrifice of his peace offerings. 30 [l]His own hands shall bring the LORD's food offerings. He shall bring the fat with [m]the breast, that the breast may be waved as a wave offering before the LORD. 31 [n]The priest shall burn the fat on the altar, but [o]the breast shall be for Aaron and his sons. 32 And [o]the right thigh you shall give to the priest as a contribution from the sacrifice of your peace offerings. 33 Whoever among the sons of Aaron offers the blood of the peace offerings and the fat shall have the right thigh for a portion. 34 For the breast that is [o]waved and the thigh that is [o]contributed I have taken from the people of Israel, out of the sacrifices of their peace offerings, and [p]have given them to Aaron the priest and to his sons, as a perpetual due from the people of Israel. 35 This is the portion of Aaron and of his sons from the LORD's food offerings, from the day they were presented to serve as priests of the LORD. 36 The LORD commanded this to be given them by the people of Israel, [q]from the day that he anointed them. It is a perpetual due throughout their generations."

37 This is the law [r]of the burnt offering, of the grain offering, of the sin offering, [s]of the guilt offering, [t]of the ordination offering, and [u]of the peace offering, 38 which the LORD commanded Moses on Mount Sinai, on the day that he commanded the people of Israel [v]to bring their offerings to the LORD, in the wilderness of Sinai.

Consecration of Aaron and His Sons

8 [w]The LORD spoke to Moses, saying, 2 "Take Aaron and his sons with him, and [x]the garments and [y]the anointing oil and the bull of the sin offering and the two rams and the basket of unleavened bread. 3 And assemble all the congregation at the entrance of the tent of meeting." 4 And Moses did as the LORD commanded him, and the congregation was assembled at the entrance of the tent of meeting.

5 And Moses said to the congregation, [z]"This is the thing that the LORD has commanded to be done." 6 And Moses brought Aaron and his sons and washed them with water. 7 And he put [a]the coat on him and tied the sash around his waist and clothed him with the robe and put the ephod on him and tied the skillfully woven band of the ephod around him, binding it to him with the band.[1] 8 And he placed the breastpiece on him, and [b]in the breastpiece he put the Urim and the Thummim. 9 And he set [a]the turban on his head, and [c]on the turban, in front, he set the golden plate, the holy crown, as the LORD commanded Moses.

10 [d]Then Moses took the anointing oil and anointed the tabernacle and all that was in it, and consecrated them. 11 And he sprinkled some of it on the altar seven times, and anointed the altar and all its utensils and the basin and its stand, to consecrate them. 12 And [e]he

[1] Hebrew *with it*

26 [j]See ch. 3:17
29 [k]ch. 3:1
30 [l]ch. 3:3, 4, 9, 14 [m]See Ex. 29:24
31 [n]ch. 3:5, 11, 16 [o][ch. 9:21; Num. 6:20]
32 [o][See ver. 31 above]
34 [o][See ver. 31 above] [p]Ex. 29:28; Num. 18:18, 19
36 [q]ch. 8:12, 30; Ex. 40:13-15
37 [r]ch. 6:9, 14, 25 [s]ver. 1 [t]ch. 6:20; Ex. 29:1 [u]ver. 11
38 [v]ch. 1:2

Chapter 8

1 [w]See Ex. 29
2 [x]See Ex. 28:2-4 [y]See Ex. 30:23-25
5 [z]Ex. 29:4
7 [a]Ex. 28:4
8 [b]See Ex. 28:30
9 [a][See ver. 7 above] [c]ch. 21:12; Ex. 28:36, 37
10 [d]See Ex. 30:26-29
12 [e]ch. 21:10, 12; Ex. 30:30; Ps. 133:2

7:37–38 *Summary.* These verses now summarize the offerings described in 6:8–7:36.

8:1–10:20 *The Establishment of the Priesthood.* The book of Exodus ends with the construction of the tabernacle (Exodus 35–40), and Leviticus 1–7 provides a manual for sacrifice in the tabernacle. Now ch. 8 records the installation of the priesthood, and ch. 9 describes the first services in the tabernacle. Chapter 10 records an occasion when priests did not obey the words and instructions of the Lord in matters of worship.

8:1–36 *The Ordination of Aaron and His Sons.* This chapter describes the rite of priestly ordination as a fulfillment of the commands given in Exodus 28–29. It is a highly structured narrative divided into seven parts by the phrase "as the LORD commanded" (Lev. 8:4, 9, 13, 17, 21, 29, 36). The number seven often symbolizes completion in the OT, and in this chapter the sevenfold layout signifies that, by the end, the installation of the priests is fully done.

8:1–4 Aaron and his sons, along with their **garments**, will be consecrated by the offerings, **oil**, and **unleavened bread**. Nearly one-third of the uses of the term **commanded** (v. 4) in Leviticus can be found in ch. 8, pointing to the absolute command of the Lord and the complete loyalty of Moses. **entrance of the tent of meeting**. That is, the entrance to the screened-off courtyard.

8:5–9 Moses clothes Aaron and his sons with gorgeous garments, which not only cover their nakedness (Gen. 3:7; Ex. 20:26), but also represent the Lord's glory and beauty and the glorious task of mediating between the Lord and his people (Ex. 28:40). On **Urim** and **Thummim**, see note on Ex. 28:30.

8:10–13 God had commanded Moses to anoint the **tabernacle** and its **utensils** with **oil** (Ex. 30:22–33), to set apart these items for holy use.

poured some of the anointing oil on Aaron's head and anointed him to consecrate him.
13 And Moses brought Aaron's sons and clothed them with coats and tied sashes around
their waists and bound caps on them, as the LORD commanded Moses.
14 Then he brought [f]the bull of the sin offering, and Aaron and his sons [g]laid their
hands on the head of the bull of the sin offering. 15 And he[1] killed it, and [h]Moses took the
blood, and with his finger put it on the horns of the altar around it and purified the altar
and poured out the blood at the base of the altar and consecrated it to make atonement
for it. 16 [i]And he took all the fat that was on the entrails and the long lobe of the liver and
the two kidneys with their fat, and Moses burned them on the altar. 17 But [j]the bull and
its skin and its flesh and its dung he burned up with fire outside the camp, as the LORD
commanded Moses.
18 [k]Then he presented the ram of the burnt offering, and Aaron and his sons laid their
hands on the head of the ram. 19 And he killed it, and Moses threw the blood against the
sides of the altar. 20 He cut the ram into pieces, and Moses burned [l]the head and the pieces
and the fat. 21 He washed the entrails and the legs with water, and Moses burned the whole
ram on the altar. It was a burnt offering with a pleasing aroma, a food offering for the
LORD, as the LORD commanded Moses.
22 Then [m]he presented the other ram, the ram of ordination, and Aaron and his sons
laid their hands on the head of the ram. 23 And he killed it, and Moses took some of its
blood and [n]put it on the lobe of Aaron's right ear and on the thumb of his right hand and
on the big toe of his right foot. 24 Then he presented Aaron's sons, and Moses put some of
the blood on the lobes of their right ears and on the thumbs of their right hands and on
the big toes of their right feet. And Moses threw the blood against the sides of the altar.
25 Then he took the fat and the fat tail and all the fat that was on the entrails and the long
lobe of the liver and the two kidneys with their fat and the right thigh, 26 and out of the
basket of unleavened bread that was before the LORD he took one unleavened loaf and one
loaf of bread with oil and one wafer and placed them on the pieces of fat and on the right
thigh. 27 And he put all these in the hands of Aaron and in the hands of his sons and waved
them as a wave offering before the LORD. 28 Then Moses took them from their hands and
burned them on the altar with the burnt offering. This was an ordination offering with
a pleasing aroma, a food offering to the LORD. 29 And Moses took the breast and waved
it for a wave offering before the LORD. It was Moses' portion of the ram of ordination, as
the LORD commanded Moses.
30 Then [o]Moses took some of the anointing oil and of the blood that was on the altar and
sprinkled it on Aaron and his garments, and also on his sons and his sons' garments. So he
consecrated Aaron and his garments, and his sons and his sons' garments with him.
31 And Moses said to Aaron and his sons, "Boil the flesh at the entrance of the tent of
meeting, and there eat it and the bread that is in the basket of ordination offerings, as
I commanded, saying, 'Aaron and his sons shall eat it.' 32 And what remains of the flesh
and the bread you shall burn up with fire. 33 And you shall not go outside the entrance of
the tent of meeting for seven days, until the days of your ordination are completed, for it
[p]will take seven days to ordain you. 34 As has been done today, the LORD has commanded
to be done to make atonement for you. 35 At the entrance of the tent of meeting you shall
remain day and night for seven days, performing what the LORD has [q]charged, so that you

[1] Probably Aaron or his representative; possibly Moses; also verses 16–23

14 [f]Ezek. 43:19 [g]ch. 4:4
15 [h]ch. 4:7; Ezek. 43:20, 26; [Heb. 9:22]
16 [i]ch. 3:4; 4:8
17 [j]ch. 4:11, 12
18 [k]ver. 2
20 [l]ch. 1:8
22 [m]ver. 2
23 [n]See ch. 14:14-17
30 [o]Ex. 30:30; Num. 3:3
33 [p]Ezek. 43:25, 26
35 [q]Num. 3:7; 9:19; Deut. 11:1; 1 Kgs. 2:3; Zech. 3:7

8:14–17 Moses presents a **sin offering** on the altar for the purification of the priesthood and the altar.

8:18–21 Cf. Ex. 29:15–18 and Leviticus 1. **Aaron and his sons** dedicate themselves by offering a **ram** as a **burnt offering**. This animal, probably costlier than a goat (cf. 4:28 with 5:15, 18; 6:6), is in keeping with the greater responsibility that they bear before the Lord (see note on 4:1–21).

8:22–29 Cf. Ex. 22:19ff. The ritual relating to the second **ram** bears the nature of the peace offering. Whereas the first ram (Lev. 8:18–21) purified the altar and the priests in general, the second ram is for the sacrifice of installation. Placing its blood on the right extremities of the priests constitutes a form of merism, where the two extremities of the body stand for the whole person. Thus, it symbolizes total dedication and purification.

8:30 This is the second **anointing** with **oil**, and this time "sprinkling" of **blood** on **Aaron** and his **garments** is added. Since the latter rite is mostly performed on the tent and its utensils, Aaron and his sons are probably regarded as equivalent to those objects with regard to holiness and consecration.

8:31–36 This is a meal of covenant ratification. The ceremony symbolizes the bond between the Lord and his priesthood.

do not die, for so I have been commanded." 36 And Aaron and his sons did all the things
that the LORD commanded by Moses.

The LORD Accepts Aaron's Offering

9 [r]On the eighth day Moses called Aaron and his sons and the elders of Israel, 2 and
he said to Aaron, [s]"Take for yourself a bull calf for a sin offering and [t]a ram for
a burnt offering, both without blemish, and offer them before the LORD. 3 And say to
the people of Israel, [u]'Take a male goat for a sin offering, and a calf and a lamb, both a
year old without blemish, for a burnt offering, 4 and an ox and a ram for peace offerings, to sacrifice before the LORD, and [v]a grain offering mixed with oil, for [w]today the
LORD will appear to you.'" 5 And they brought what Moses commanded in front of the
tent of meeting, and all the congregation drew near and stood before the LORD. 6 And
Moses said, "This is the thing that the LORD commanded you to do, that the glory of
the LORD may appear to you." 7 Then Moses said to Aaron, "Draw near to the altar and
[x]offer your sin offering and your burnt offering and [y]make atonement for yourself and
for the people, and bring the offering of the people and make atonement for them, as
the LORD has commanded."

8 So Aaron drew near to the altar and killed the calf of the sin offering, which was for
himself. 9 [z]And the sons of Aaron presented the blood to him, and he dipped his finger in
the blood and [a]put it on the horns of the altar and poured out the blood at the base of the
altar. 10 [b]But the fat and the kidneys and the long lobe of the liver from the sin offering he
burned on the altar, [c]as the LORD commanded Moses. 11 [d]The flesh and the skin he burned
up with fire outside the camp.

12 Then he killed the burnt offering, and Aaron's sons handed him the blood, and he
[e]threw it against the sides of the altar. 13 [f]And they handed the burnt offering to him, piece
by piece, and the head, and he burned them on the altar. 14 [g]And he washed the entrails
and the legs and burned them with the burnt offering on the altar.

15 [h]Then he presented the people's offering and took the goat of the sin offering that
was for the people and killed it and [i]offered it as a sin offering, [j]like the first one. 16 And
he presented the burnt offering and offered it [k]according to the [l]rule. 17 And he presented
the [m]grain offering, took a handful of it, and burned it on the altar, [n]besides the burnt
offering of the morning.

18 Then he killed the ox and the ram, [o]the sacrifice of peace offerings for the people. And
Aaron's sons handed him the blood, and he threw it against the sides of the altar. 19 But
the fat pieces of the ox and of the ram, the fat tail and that which covers [p]the entrails and
the kidneys and the long lobe of the liver— 20 they put the fat pieces on the breasts, [q]and
he burned the fat pieces on the altar, 21 but the breasts and the right thigh Aaron waved
[r]for a wave offering before the LORD, as Moses commanded.

22 Then Aaron [s]lifted up his hands toward the people and [t]blessed them, and he came
down from offering the sin offering and the burnt offering and the peace offerings. 23 And
Moses and Aaron went into the tent of meeting, and when they came out they blessed the
people, and [u]the glory of the LORD appeared to all the people. 24 And [v]fire came out from
before the LORD and consumed the burnt offering and the pieces of fat on the altar, and
when all the people saw it, [w]they shouted and [x]fell on their faces.

Chapter 9

1 [r]Ezek. 43:27
2 [s]ch. 4:3; 8:14; Ex. 29:1 [t]ch. 8:18
3 [u]ch. 4:23; [Ezra 6:17]
4 [v]ver. 17; ch. 2:4 [w]ver. 6, 23; Ex. 29:43
7 [x]ch. 4:3; Heb. 5:1-3; 7:27; 9:7 [y]ch. 4:16, 20
9 [z]ch. 4:6; 8:15 [a]See ch. 4:7
10 [b]ch. 8:16 [c]ch. 4:8
11 [d]ch. 4:11, 12; 8:17
12 [e]ch. 1:5; 8:19
13 [f]ch. 8:20
14 [g]ch. 8:21
15 [h]ver. 3, 7; Heb. 2:17; 5:3 [i]See ch. 6:26 [j]ver. 8
16 [k]ch. 1:3, 10 [l]ch. 5:10
17 [m]ver. 4; ch. 2:1, 2 [n]Ex. 29:38, 39
18 [o]ch. 3:1, 12, 16
19 [p]ch. 3:3, 9, 14; 4:8; 7:3
20 [q]ch. 3:5, 16
21 [r]Ex. 29:24, 26; See ch. 7:30-34
22 [s][Luke 24:50] [t]Deut. 21:5; See Num. 6:23-27
23 [u]ver. 4, 6
24 [v][Judg. 6:21; 13:19, 20; 1 Kgs. 18:38; 1 Chr. 21:26; 2 Chr. 7:1] [w][Ezra 3:11] [x][1 Kgs. 18:39; 2 Chr. 7:3]

9:1–24 ***The First Tabernacle Service.*** Chapter 9 prescribes and describes the first tabernacle service after the ordination of Aaron and his sons. The requirement of various offerings assumes that both the priests and the people are sinful. The Lord manifests himself by miraculously burning the animals on the altar, thus indicating that he has accepted both the priests and the people (cf. Ex. 29:43–46). This chapter functions as a sequel to the Sinai event; just as God came down to deliver his covenant to his people, so now he descends upon his altar to dwell intimately with them.

9:1–4 After the seven days of the ordination service are concluded, then begins the inauguration of the daily sacrifices in the tabernacle. The first services conducted by Aaron as high priest are described in this chapter.

9:5–6 The purpose of this service is for the **glory of the LORD** (see note on Ex. 16:7; cf. Ex. 40:34–35) to be manifested both to the people and to the priests.

9:7–21 The **atonement** of the priests comes first (vv. 7–14), and then that of **the people** (vv. 15–21). As in other ceremonies, the atonement process moves from removing sinfulness (by the sin offering), to underscoring their petitions, praises, or both (by the burnt offering), and finally to communion (by the peace offering).

9:22–24 **Moses and Aaron** together enter the **tent**. Moses is "passing the torch" to Aaron; the priests will now mediate between the Lord and the people.

The Death of Nadab and Abihu

10 Now [y]Nadab and Abihu, the sons of Aaron, [z]each took his censer and put fire in
it and laid incense on it and offered [a]unauthorized[1] fire before the LORD, which
he had not commanded them. 2 And fire [b]came out from before the LORD and consumed
them, and they died before the LORD. 3 Then Moses said to Aaron, "This is what the LORD
has said: 'Among [c]those who are near me [d]I will be sanctified, and before all the people I
will be glorified.'" [e]And Aaron held his peace.
4 And Moses called Mishael and Elzaphan, the sons of [f]Uzziel the uncle of Aaron, and
said to them, "Come near; carry your brothers away from the front of the sanctuary and
out of the camp." 5 So they came near and carried them in their coats out of the camp, as
Moses had said. 6 And Moses said to Aaron and to Eleazar and Ithamar his sons, [g]"Do not
let the hair of your heads hang loose, and do not tear your clothes, lest you die, and [h]wrath
come upon all the congregation; but let your brothers, the whole house of Israel, bewail
the burning that the LORD has kindled. 7 [i]And do not go outside the entrance of the tent
of meeting, lest you die, [j]for the anointing oil of the LORD is upon you." And they did
according to the word of Moses.
8 And the LORD spoke to Aaron, saying, 9 [k]"Drink no wine or strong drink, you or your
sons with you, when you go into the tent of meeting, lest you die. It shall be a statute
forever throughout your generations. 10 You are to [l]distinguish between the holy and the
common, and between the unclean and the clean, 11 and [m]you are to teach the people of
Israel all the statutes that the LORD has spoken to them by Moses."
12 Moses spoke to Aaron and to Eleazar and Ithamar, his surviving sons: "Take the [n]grain
offering that is left of the LORD's food offerings, and eat it unleavened beside the altar,
for [o]it is most holy. 13 You shall eat it in a holy place, because it is your due and your sons'
due, from the LORD's food offerings, for [p]so I am commanded. 14 But the [q]breast that is
waved and the thigh that is contributed you shall eat in a clean place, you and your sons
and your daughters with you, for they are given as your due and your sons' due from the
sacrifices of the peace offerings of the people of Israel. 15 [r]The thigh that is contributed and
the breast that is waved they shall bring with the food offerings of the fat pieces to wave
for a wave offering before the LORD, and it shall be yours and your sons' with you as a due
forever, as the LORD has commanded."
16 Now Moses diligently inquired about [s]the goat of the sin offering, and behold, it
was burned up! And he was angry with Eleazar and Ithamar, the surviving sons of Aaron,
saying, 17 [t]"Why have you not eaten the sin offering in the place of the sanctuary, since
[o]it is a thing most holy and has been given to you that you may bear the iniquity of the
congregation, to make atonement for them before the LORD? 18 Behold, [u]its blood was
not brought into the inner part of the sanctuary. You certainly ought to have eaten it in
the sanctuary, [v]as I commanded." 19 And Aaron said to Moses, "Behold, [w]today they have

[1] Or *strange*

Chapter 10
1 [y]ch. 16:1; Ex. 6:23; 28:1; Num. 3:4; 26:61; 1 Chr. 24:2 [z][Num. 16:18] [a]Ex. 30:9
2 [b]ch. 9:24; Num. 16:35; [2 Sam. 6:7]
3 [c]ch. 21:17, 21 [d]Ezek. 28:22 [e][Ps. 39:9]
4 [f]Ex. 6:18, 22; Num. 3:19, 30
6 [g]ch. 13:45; 21:10; Ezek. 24:16, 17 [h]Num. 1:53; 16:22, 46; 18:5; Josh. 7:1; 22:18, 20
7 [i]ch. 21:12 [j]ch. 8:30
9 [k]Ezek. 44:21; [Num. 6:3, 20; Luke 1:15; 1 Tim. 3:3, 8]
10 [l]ch. 11:47; 20:25; Ezek. 22:26; 44:23
11 [m]ch. 14:57; Deut. 24:8; Neh. 8:2, 8, 9; [Jer. 18:18; Mal. 2:7]
12 [n]ch. 6:16; Num. 18:9, 10 [o]See ch. 6:17
13 [p]ch. 2:3; 6:16
14 [q]ch. 7:31, 34; Ex. 29:24, 26, 27; Num. 18:11
15 [r]ch. 7:31, 34
16 [s]ch. 9:3, 15
17 [t]ch. 6:26, 29 [o][See ver. 12 above]
18 [u]ch. 6:30 [v]ch. 6:26
19 [w]ch. 9:8, 12

10:1–20 *The Nadab and Abihu Incident.* The Lord's acceptance of Aaron's offering (ch. 9) is followed, on the same day, by an apparent rejection of it, and joy gives way to sorrow.

10:1–3 Nadab and Abihu, the eldest of Aaron's four sons, capriciously took censers of their own, put **incense** in them, and **offered unauthorized fire** (lit., strange or foreign fire; see ESV footnote) to **the LORD**. The offense lies in their doing it their own way instead of in a way authorized by the Lord, and as a result they were instantly killed. (This probably also involved entering—or trying to enter—the Most Holy Place [cf. 16:1–2] after drinking alcohol [cf. 10:8–11].) The point of the story is that God will not allow his holiness to be violated, not even by members of the high priest's family. **And Aaron held his peace**. He raised no vocal objection against God's justice in the death of his sons; perhaps he was simply dumbfounded.

10:4–7 The ordained priests, who are holy, ought not to mourn even for the death of their rebellious family members (but see note on 21:1–4).

10:8–11 This is the only time in Leviticus that God speaks directly to Aaron alone. God delineates three major roles for the priesthood: (1) **to distinguish between the holy** and the profane, (2) to separate the **clean** from the **unclean**, and (3) to **teach the people** the laws of God.

10:9 Wine and **strong drink** are forbidden while priests are "on duty," presumably so that they can faithfully carry out their responsibilities (vv. 10–11). Laypeople as well are discouraged from drunkenness in the sanctuary (cf. 1 Sam. 1:12–16).

10:10–11 The priests are crucial for enabling Israel to live faithfully to the covenant. On their task to **teach**, cf. also Deut. 33:10; Ezra 7:10; Neh. 8:1–12; Mal. 2:6–7.

10:12–15 Now that various offerings have been offered to the Lord, it is the priests' duty and privilege to partake of them, as was previously commanded.

10:16–20 The incident described here takes place on the final day of the installation of the priesthood. Moses discovers that **Eleazar and Ithamar** have not followed the regulations of sacrifice given by God (v. 16). It is dramatic because it follows so closely on the offense of Nadab and Abihu (vv. 1–3). Moses voices his anger; Aaron, however, intervenes on behalf of his two sons. He argues that the events of the day have been so exceptional as to show that it is too dangerous to perform the ritual. Aaron's defense displays his fear of the holiness of God, which Moses is glad to see in his brother.

offered their sin offering and their burnt offering before the LORD, and yet such things
as these have happened to me! If I had eaten the sin offering today, [x]would the LORD have
approved?" 20 And when Moses heard that, he approved.

Clean and Unclean Animals

11 And the LORD spoke to Moses and Aaron, saying to them, 2 "Speak to the people of
Israel, saying, [y]These are the living things that you may eat among all the animals
that are on the earth. 3 Whatever parts the hoof and is cloven-footed and chews the cud,
among the animals, you may eat. 4 Nevertheless, among those that chew the cud or part
the hoof, you shall not eat these: The camel, because it chews the cud but does not part the
hoof, is unclean to you. 5 And the [z]rock badger, because it chews the cud but does not part
the hoof, is unclean to you. 6 And the hare, because it chews the cud but does not part the
hoof, is unclean to you. 7 And the pig, because it parts the hoof and is cloven-footed but
does not chew the cud, [a]is unclean to you. 8 You shall not eat any of their flesh, and you
shall not touch their carcasses; they are unclean to you.

9 "These you may eat, of all that are in the waters. Everything in the waters that has fins
and scales, whether in the seas or in the rivers, you may eat. 10 But anything in the seas
or the rivers that does not have fins and scales, of the swarming creatures in the waters

19 [x]Jer. 6:20; 14:12; Hos. 9:4; Mal. 1:10, 13; 2:13

Chapter 11

2 [y]For ver. 1-47, see Deut. 14:3-20; [Matt. 15:11; Mark 7:15, 18; Acts 10:12-15; 11:6-9; Rom. 14:14; 1 Cor. 8:8; Col. 2:16, 21; Heb. 9:10]

5 [z]Ps. 104:18; Prov. 30:26

7 [a][Isa. 65:4; 66:3, 17]

11:1–15:33 *The Laws on Cleanness and Uncleanness.* Leviticus 10:10–11 defines the principal duties of the Israelite priesthood. One of these tasks is "to distinguish between the unclean and the clean." Chapters 11–15 apply this principle to a variety of areas of Israelite life and culture. Chapter 11 deals with the matter of foods that are clean and may be eaten, and foods that are unclean and may not be eaten. Chapter 12 treats the issue of cleanliness and purification after childbirth. The following two chapters (chs. 13–14) provide regulations concerning cleanliness in matters of fungi, skin diseases, and infections. Chapter 15 considers human bodily discharges that may cause a person to be unclean. These five chapters constitute a codified directory for Israel, and in particular for the priests, that defines what is clean and unclean in God's sight.

11:1–47 *Clean and Unclean Creatures.* This chapter explains which creatures were considered clean and which were considered unclean. The *rationale* of why a creature is placed in one category vs. the other has puzzled commentators throughout the ages, and there is still no consensus of opinion. Typical explanations include a concern for hygiene; a "death" motif (i.e., unclean animals were somehow more associated with death in the Israelite mind); and polemics against Canaanite customs. More recently, it has been argued that a creature is unclean when it does not conform to established norms (e.g., an Israelite's established norm for a four-legged creature would be a cow or a goat, since these were their herd and flock animals; a pig is thus unclean because, even though it has four legs, it is unlike the norm in that it does not chew the cud). In evaluating the above approaches, it is probably fair to say that no single one of them can provide a rationale that works for all the animals in this chapter. As a result, there might be a number of different reasons why an animal was considered clean or unclean. While the *rationale* of the classifications is still debated, the *purpose* of these laws is clear. In brief, they were to help Israel—as the Lord's holy people—to make distinctions between ritual cleanness and ritual uncleanness (vv. 46–47). Significantly, making these distinctions in the *ritual* realm would no doubt serve as a constant reminder to the people of their need for making the parallel distinctions in the *moral* realm as well. Further, adherence to these food laws expresses Israel's devotion to the Lord: just as he separated the Israelites from the other nations, so they must separate clean from unclean foods (20:24–26). This is why the restrictions can be removed in Acts 10:9–28, when the Jew vs. Gentile distinction is no longer relevant in defining the people of God (cf. also Mark 7:19; Col. 2:16–23; Heb. 9:1–14; 10:1–18). For Israel to obey these dietary restrictions also shows that the people honor the Creator, who has the right to decide how his creatures may be used. A "clean" animal is one "permitted" for food (Lev. 11:2). It is clear that classifying an animal as "unclean" is not the same as declaring that animal "evil": God cares for all beasts, clean and unclean alike (cf. Ps. 104:17–18; 147:9). Leviticus employs a simple and practical classification system for edible animals, based on readily observable features. It is geared to the kind of life that Israel will live in the land of Canaan, and it is not always easy to apply it to animals that Israelites did not normally encounter (for instance, the sturgeon, which modern rabbis consider to have the wrong kind of scales, is not included here). This system is good for its purpose, a purpose that is different from that of the modern zoologist's taxonomy. See the parallel list in Deut. 14:3–21 (with notes).

11:1–8 The first paragraph deals with land-dwelling animals. In order for a land animal to be considered "clean," it must meet two conditions: chewing the **cud** and being **cloven-footed**. In practical terms, these criteria permit Israel to eat hoofed mammals with two functional toes, including domestic beasts such as sheep, goats, and cattle, and wild ones such as antelopes (cf. Deut. 14:4–5). A horse, on the other hand, which has only one toe, is not clean. The diet of these animals is apparently not the basis of their cleanness or uncleanness. The passage itself says nothing about what the animals eat, and the **camel**, **rock badger** (hyrax), and **hare** are exclusively vegetarian but unclean. The **pig** is the only animal in this list that is not strictly vegetarian. (Many of the clean aquatic creatures of Lev. 11:9–12 are carnivorous.) The expression translated **chews the cud** can be applied to camels, rock badgers, and hares (vv. 4–6); based on the observable features of the animal, the thorough chewing of these animals looks like the cud-chewing of, say, cattle.

11:9–12 The presence of **fins** and **scales** is the mark for distinguishing between clean and unclean water-dwelling creatures. In practical terms, this limits the clean aquatic animals to what modern zoologists would call true fish; anything aquatic that **does not have fins and scales** (e.g., squid, shellfish) is unclean.

Spectrum of Conditions from Holy to Unclean

Holy				Unclean
Life				Death
Priests	Physically impaired priests	Clean non-priests	Unclean non-priests	Human corpses
Sacrificial animals	Blemished sacrificial animals	Clean animals	Unclean animals	Animal corpses

and of the living creatures that are in the waters, is [b]detestable to you. 11 You shall regard
them as detestable; you shall not eat any of their flesh, and you shall detest their carcasses.
12 Everything in the waters that does not have fins and scales is detestable to you.
13 "And these you shall detest among the birds;[1] they shall not be eaten; they are [b]detest-
able: [c]the eagle,[2] the bearded vulture, the black vulture, 14 the kite, [d]the falcon of any kind,
15 every raven of any kind, 16 the ostrich, the nighthawk, the sea gull, the [e]hawk of any kind,
17 the [f]little owl, the cormorant, the [g]short-eared owl, 18 the barn owl, the [h]tawny owl, the
carrion vulture, 19 the stork, the heron of any kind, the hoopoe, and [i]the bat.
20 "All winged insects that go on all fours are detestable to you. 21 Yet among the winged
insects that go on all fours you may eat those that have jointed legs above their feet, with
which to hop on the ground. 22 Of them you may eat: [j]the locust of any kind, the bald
locust of any kind, the cricket of any kind, and the grasshopper of any kind. 23 But all other
winged insects that have four feet are detestable to you.
24 "And by these you shall become unclean. Whoever touches their carcass shall be unclean
until the evening, 25 and whoever carries any part of their carcass [k]shall wash his clothes
and be unclean until the evening. 26 Every animal that parts the hoof but is not cloven-
footed or does not chew the cud is unclean to you. Everyone who touches them shall be
unclean. 27 And all that walk on their paws, among the animals that go on all fours, are
unclean to you. Whoever touches their carcass shall be unclean until the evening, 28 and
he who carries their carcass [k]shall wash his clothes and be unclean until the evening; they
are unclean to you.
29 "And these are unclean to you among the swarming things that swarm on the ground:
the mole rat, [l]the mouse, the great lizard of any kind, 30 the gecko, the monitor lizard, the
lizard, the sand lizard, and the chameleon. 31 These are unclean to you among all that
swarm. Whoever touches them when they are dead shall be unclean until the evening. 32 And
anything on which any of them falls when they are dead shall be unclean, whether it is an
article of wood or a garment or a skin or a sack, any article that is used for any purpose.
[m]It must be put into water, and it shall be unclean until the evening; then it shall be clean.
33 And if any of them falls into any earthenware vessel, all that is in it shall be unclean,
and you [n]shall break it. 34 Any food in it that could be eaten, on which water comes, shall
be unclean. And all drink that could be drunk from every such vessel shall be unclean.
35 And everything on which any part of their carcass falls shall be unclean. Whether oven
or stove, it shall be broken in pieces. They are unclean and shall remain unclean for you.
36 Nevertheless, a spring or a cistern holding water shall be clean, but whoever touches
a carcass in them shall be unclean. 37 And if any part of their carcass falls upon any seed
grain that is to be sown, it is clean, 38 but if water is put on the seed and any part of their
carcass falls on it, it is unclean to you.
39 "And if any animal which you may eat dies, whoever touches its carcass shall be unclean
until the evening, 40 and [o]whoever eats of its carcass shall wash his clothes and be
unclean until the evening. And whoever carries the carcass shall wash his clothes and
be unclean until the evening.

10 [b]ch. 7:21
13 [b][See ver. 10 above] [c]Job 39:26, 30
14 [d]Job 28:7
16 [e]Job 39:26
17 [f]Ps. 102:6 [g]Isa. 34:11
18 [h]Ps. 102:6; Isa. 34:11; Zeph. 2:14
19 [i]Isa. 2:20
22 [j]Ex. 10:4; Joel 1:4; [Matt. 3:4; Mark 1:6]
25 [k]ch. 13:6, 34; 14:8, 9, 47; 15:5; 16:26, 28; 17:15; Num. 19:10; 31:24
28 [k][See ver. 25 above]
29 [l]Isa. 66:17
32 [m]ch. 15:12
33 [n]ch. 6:28; 15:12
40 [o]ch. 17:15; 22:8; Deut. 14:21; Ezek. 4:14; 44:31

[1] Or *things that fly*; compare Genesis 1:20 [2] The identity of many of these birds is uncertain

11:13–19 Almost all the unclean **birds** are predators and carrion-eaters (i.e., ones contacting death and consuming blood). The term translated "bird" (Hb. *'op*) covers a variety of creatures that fly (see ESV footnote), and thus can include the **bat**.

11:20–23 Insofar as the **winged insects** have an ability to leave the ground, they are clean. For the **locust** and **grasshopper** as allowable food, cf. the diet of John the Baptist (Matt. 3:4).

Grades of Uncleanness

Tolerated	Punishable/Sinful
Discharges (Leviticus 12; 16)	Forgotten cleansing (Numbers 5–6; 19)
Skin diseases (Leviticus 13–14)	Idolatry, homicide, illicit sex (Leviticus 17–20; Numbers 35)

11:24–28 The law gradually introduces the theme of death as a defiling force (see "carcasses" in vv. 8, 11). The **carcass** of any unclean animal is defiling, i.e., it makes the person who **touches** it **unclean** for a period (**until the evening**).

11:29–35 Not only are these creatures unclean for food, but touching them **when they are dead** will also make one defiled.

11:36–38 It is uncertain why the water in **a spring or a cistern** is not contaminated by an unclean creature that falls into it. Perhaps it is because water in them is naturally flowing and is continuously refreshed and renewed. It may also be an exception because water is in such short supply in Palestine.

11:39–40 Even the clean quadrupeds are defiling after they have died.

41 [p]“Every swarming thing that swarms on the ground is detestable; it shall not be eaten.
42 Whatever goes on its belly, and whatever goes on all fours, or whatever has many feet,
any swarming thing that swarms on the ground, you shall not eat, for they are detestable.
43 [q]You shall not make yourselves detestable with any swarming thing that swarms, and
you shall not defile yourselves with them, and become unclean through them. 44 For I am
the LORD your God. Consecrate yourselves therefore, and [r]be holy, for I am holy. [q]You shall
not defile yourselves with any swarming thing that crawls on the ground. 45 [s]For I am the
LORD who brought you up out of the land of Egypt to be your God. [r]You shall therefore
be holy, for I am holy.”
46 This is the law about beast and bird and every living creature that moves through the
waters and every creature that swarms on the ground, 47 [t]to make a distinction between
the unclean and the clean and between the living creature that may be eaten and the living
creature that may not be eaten.

Purification After Childbirth

12 The LORD spoke to Moses, saying, 2 “Speak to the people of Israel, saying, If a woman
conceives and bears a male child, then [u]she shall be unclean seven days. [v]As at the
time of her menstruation, she shall be unclean. 3 And on the [w]eighth day the flesh of his
foreskin shall be circumcised. 4 Then she shall continue for thirty-three days in the blood
of her purifying. She shall not touch anything holy, nor come into the sanctuary, until
the days of her purifying are completed. 5 But if she bears a female child, then she shall
be unclean two weeks, as in her menstruation. And she shall continue in the blood of her
purifying for sixty-six days.
6 [u]“And when the days of her purifying are completed, whether for a son or for a daughter, she shall bring to the priest at the entrance of the tent of meeting a lamb a year old
for a burnt offering, and a pigeon or a turtledove for a sin offering, 7 and he shall offer it
before the LORD and make atonement for her. Then she shall be clean from the flow of
her blood. This is the law for her who bears a child, either male or female. 8 And if she cannot afford a lamb, then she shall take [x]two turtledoves or two pigeons,[1] [y]one for a burnt
offering and the other for a sin offering. [z]And the priest shall make atonement for her,
and she shall be clean.”

Laws About Leprosy

13 The LORD spoke to Moses and Aaron, saying, 2 “When a person has on the skin of his
body a [a]swelling or an eruption or a spot, and it turns into a case of leprous[2] disease
on the skin of his body, [b]then he shall be brought to Aaron the priest or to one of his sons

[1] Septuagint *two young pigeons* [2] *Leprosy* was a term for several skin diseases

41 [p][ver. 29]
43 [q]ch. 20:25
44 [r]ch. 19:2; 20:7, 26; 21:8; Ex. 19:6; Cited 1 Pet. 1:16; [1 Thess. 4:7] [q][See ver. 43 above]
45 [s]Ex. 6:7 [r][See ver. 44 above]
47 [t]ch. 10:10; 20:25

Chapter 12

2 [u][Luke 2:22] [v]ch. 15:19
3 [w]Gen. 17:12; Luke 1:59; 2:21; John 7:22, 23
6 [u][See ver. 2 above]
8 [x]ch. 1:14; 5:7; Cited Luke 2:24 [y]ver. 6 [z]ch. 4:26

Chapter 13

2 [a]ch. 14:56 [b]Deut. 24:8

11:44–45 For I am the LORD. This self-identification is used here for the first time in the book; it occurs frequently from ch. 18 on. **for I am holy**. Cf. 19:2; 20:26; 21:8. The Lord, who is himself holy, calls his people to **consecrate** themselves, i.e., dedicate themselves to holiness (Hb. *hitqaddesh*), and to **be holy**, i.e., practice a holy lifestyle. Cf. 20:7–8 and note. **who brought you up out of the land of Egypt**. Personal consecration (in which a person imitates God's own character) is a response to God's gracious initiative (cf. Ex. 20:2). First Peter 1:16 applies the same principle to Christian readers, portraying them as the heirs of this special status.

12:1–8 *Uncleanness of a Childbearing Mother.* A woman who has just given birth is considered unclean. The loss of blood signifies that one is incomplete and unclean. Three steps are required to move from defilement to purity: (1) the woman is to remain unclean for 7 or 14 days, depending on the gender of the child; (2) she then moves into the second stage, which lasts for 33 to 66 days in which she is neither pure nor impure; and (3) finally, she offers sacrifices in order to enter into full communion with the covenant people. The time of purification for the mother is twice as long if she gives birth to a female rather than a male. The reason is uncertain, although it may be that the female is *potentially* more unclean because of the probability of her menstruating and of her giving birth. In any event, there is no implication that the reason for the distinction is any kind of presumed "inferiority" of women.

12:8 lamb . . . two turtledoves. Cf. 5:11; and Luke 2:24, indicating the poverty of Jesus' parents.

13:1–14:57 *Leprous Diseases and Their Purification.* These chapters deal with a specific skin disease called *tsara'at*. Chapter 13 addresses cases of the disease on the human skin (13:1–46), followed by a case affecting clothes and articles (13:47–58). Chapter 14 gives the prescribed purificatory rite for the healed person (14:1–32) along with the purificatory rite for an afflicted house (14:33–53).

13:1–59 This chapter deals with uncleanness brought about by "leprosy." The ESV adopts the traditional rendering "leprosy" for the Hebrew *tsara'at*, but its exact modern equivalent is unclear (see ESV footnote on v. 2; cf. also Matt. 8:2 with ESV footnote), particularly in view of the fact that it manifests itself not only in humans but also in clothes and articles (Lev. 13:47–59), and even in the walls of houses (14:34–53). The term used in Leviticus is in fact generic: it could include many skin ailments, such as psoriasis, urticaria (hives), favus (which produces honeycomb-shaped crusts), and leukoderma (which produces white patches on the skin). What today is called leprosy (Hansen's disease) was unknown in the Near East at the time of Leviticus. Clear references to it do not occur until the late first millennium B.C.

13:1–8 Basic symptoms of a **leprous disease** are given in vv. 2–3 (**the hair in the diseased area has turned white** and **the disease appears to be deeper than the skin of his body**). **priest shall pronounce**. By this means, the priest makes the status of uncleanness official. The person receiving

the priests, 3 and the priest shall examine the diseased area on the skin of his body. And
if the hair in the diseased area has turned white and the disease appears to be deeper than
the skin of his body, it is a case of leprous disease. When the priest has examined him, he
shall pronounce him unclean. 4 But if the spot is white in the skin of his body and appears
no deeper than the skin, and the hair in it has not turned white, [c]the priest shall shut up
the diseased person for seven days. 5 And the priest shall examine him on the seventh
day, and if in his eyes the disease is checked and the disease has not spread in the skin,
then the [c]priest shall shut him up for another seven days. 6 And the priest shall examine
him again on the seventh day, and if the diseased area has faded and the disease has not
spread in the skin, then the priest shall pronounce him clean; it is only an eruption. And
[d]he shall wash his clothes and be clean. 7 But if the eruption spreads in the skin, after he
has shown himself to the priest for his cleansing, he shall appear again before the priest.
8 And the priest shall look, and if the eruption has spread in the skin, then the priest shall
pronounce him unclean; it is a leprous disease.

9 "When a man is afflicted with a leprous disease, he shall be brought to the priest, 10 and
the priest shall look. And if there is a [e]white swelling in the skin that has turned the hair
white, and there is raw flesh in the swelling, 11 it is a chronic leprous disease in the skin of
his body, and the priest shall pronounce him unclean. [f]He shall not shut him up, for he
is unclean. 12 And if the leprous disease breaks out in the skin, so that the leprous disease
covers all the skin of the diseased person from head to foot, so far as the priest can see,
13 then the priest shall look, and if the leprous disease has covered all his body, he shall
pronounce him clean of the disease; it has all turned white, and he is clean. 14 But when
raw flesh appears on him, he shall be unclean. 15 And the priest shall examine the raw flesh
and pronounce him unclean. Raw flesh is unclean, for it is a leprous disease. 16 But if the
raw flesh recovers and turns white again, then he shall come to the priest, 17 and the priest
shall examine him, and if the disease has turned white, then the priest shall pronounce
the diseased person clean; he is clean.

18 "If there is in the skin of one's body a [g]boil and it heals, 19 and in the place of the boil
there comes a white swelling or a [h]reddish-white spot, then it shall be shown to the priest.
20 And the priest shall look, and if it appears deeper than the skin and its hair has turned
white, then the priest shall pronounce him unclean. It is a case of leprous disease that has
broken out in the boil. 21 But if the priest examines it and there is no white hair in it and
it is not deeper than the skin, but has faded, then the priest shall shut him up seven days.
22 And if it spreads in the skin, then the priest shall pronounce him unclean; it is a disease.
23 But [i]if the spot remains in one place and does not spread, it is the scar of the boil, and
the priest shall pronounce him clean.

24 "Or, when the body has a burn on its skin and the raw flesh of the burn becomes a
spot, [j]reddish-white or white, 25 the priest shall examine it, and if the hair in the spot has
turned white and it appears deeper than the skin, then it is a leprous disease. It has broken
out in the burn, and the priest shall pronounce him unclean; it is a case of leprous disease.
26 But if the priest examines it and there is no white hair in the spot and it is no deeper
than the skin, but has faded, the priest shall shut him up seven days, 27 and the priest shall
examine him the seventh day. If it is spreading in the skin, then the priest shall pronounce
him unclean; it is a case of leprous disease. 28 But if the spot remains [k]in one place and does

4 [c][ver. 11]
5 [c][See ver. 4 above]
6 [d]See ch. 11:25
10 [e][Num. 12:10, 12; 2 Kgs. 5:27; 15:5; 2 Chr. 26:20, 21]
11 [f][ver. 4, 5]
18 [g]See Ex. 9:9
19 [h]ver. 24
23 [i]ver. 28
24 [j]ver. 19
28 [k]ver. 23

such a pronouncement must dwell outside the camp, as stated in vv. 45–46, until he or she becomes clean.

13:3 unclean (cf. v. 8). See Introduction: Interpretative Issues. This requires such persons to live outside the camp until they are free of their disease (vv. 45–46), and to present a sacrifice as part of a cleansing ceremony (14:1–32). Modern readers should not confuse this kind of "uncleanness" with "under God's condemnation," nor even with "excluded from the love of the community": the purpose of this law is to prevent what is unclean from coming into contact with what is holy (a contact that would be dangerous for the unclean person and for the whole community).

13:9–17 This is the case of a person with a severe, chronic skin condition. The patient has **raw flesh**, i.e., it is oozing, red, and active. His condition is easily recognizable, and therefore no quarantine is needed. The priest simply declares him ritually **unclean** and impure.

13:18–44 These rules deal with various cases of the leprous disease in relation to other common skin diseases or disorders, such as a **boil** (vv. 18–23), a **burn** (vv. 24–28), **itching disease** (vv. 29–37), **leukoderma** (vv. 38–39), and **baldness** (vv. 40–44). The **priest** is responsible for discerning whether or not the condition is one that makes a person unclean (cf. 10:10–11); this is one way in which the priesthood is to serve the well-being of the people.

13:45–46 The person with a skin disease is to tear his clothes, go about with

34[l]ver. 6
45[m]ch. 10:6 [n]Ezek. 24:17, 22; Mic. 3:7 [o][Lam. 4:15]
46[p]Num. 5:2; 12:14, 15; [2 Kgs. 7:3; 15:5; 2 Chr. 26:21; Luke 17:12]
47[q][Jude 23; Rev. 3:4]
51[r]ch. 14:44

not spread in the skin, but has faded, it is a swelling from the burn, and the priest shall
pronounce him clean, for it is the scar of the burn.
29 "When a man or woman has a disease on the head or the beard, 30 the priest shall
examine the disease. And if it appears deeper than the skin, and the hair in it is yellow and
thin, then the priest shall pronounce him unclean. It is an itch, a leprous disease of the
head or the beard. 31 And if the priest examines the itching disease and it appears no deeper
than the skin and there is no black hair in it, then the priest shall shut up the person with
the itching disease for seven days, 32 and on the seventh day the priest shall examine the
disease. If the itch has not spread, and there is in it no yellow hair, and the itch appears to
be no deeper than the skin, 33 then he shall shave himself, but the itch he shall not shave;
and the priest shall shut up the person with the itching disease for another seven days.
34 And on the seventh day the priest shall examine the itch, and if the itch has not spread
in the skin and it appears to be no deeper than the skin, then the priest shall pronounce
him clean. And [l]he shall wash his clothes and be clean. 35 But if the itch spreads in the skin
after his cleansing, 36 then the priest shall examine him, and if the itch has spread in the
skin, the priest need not seek for the yellow hair; he is unclean. 37 But if in his eyes the itch
is unchanged and black hair has grown in it, the itch is healed and he is clean, and the
priest shall pronounce him clean.
38 "When a man or a woman has spots on the skin of the body, white spots, 39 the priest
shall look, and if the spots on the skin of the body are of a dull white, it is leukoderma
that has broken out in the skin; he is clean.
40 "If a man's hair falls out from his head, he is bald; he is clean. 41 And if a man's hair
falls out from his forehead, he has baldness of the forehead; he is clean. 42 But if there is
on the bald head or the bald forehead a reddish-white diseased area, it is a leprous disease
breaking out on his bald head or his bald forehead. 43 Then the priest shall examine him,
and if the diseased swelling is reddish-white on his bald head or on his bald forehead,
like the appearance of leprous disease in the skin of the body, 44 he is a leprous man, he is
unclean. The priest must pronounce him unclean; his disease is on his head.
45 "The leprous person who has the disease shall wear torn clothes and [m]let the hair of
his head hang loose, and he shall [n]cover his upper lip[1] and cry out, [o]'Unclean, unclean.'
46 He shall remain unclean as long as he has the disease. He is unclean. He shall live alone.
His dwelling shall be [p]outside the camp.
47 "When there is a case of leprous disease in a [q]garment, whether a woolen or a linen
garment, 48 in warp or woof of linen or wool, or in a skin or in anything made of skin,
49 if the disease is greenish or reddish in the garment, or in the skin or in the warp or the
woof or in any article made of skin, it is a case of leprous disease, and it shall be shown
to the priest. 50 And the priest shall examine the disease and shut up that which has the
disease for seven days. 51 Then he shall examine the disease on the seventh day. If the
disease has spread in the garment, in the warp or the woof, or in the skin, whatever be
the use of the skin, the disease is a [r]persistent leprous disease; it is unclean. 52 And he
shall burn the garment, or the warp or the woof, the wool or the linen, or any article
made of skin that is diseased, for it is a persistent leprous disease. It shall be burned
in the fire.
53 "And if the priest examines, and if the disease has not spread in the garment, in the
warp or the woof or in any article made of skin, 54 then the priest shall command that they
wash the thing in which is the disease, and he shall shut it up for another seven days. 55 And
the priest shall examine the diseased thing after it has been washed. And if the appearance
of the diseased area has not changed, though the disease has not spread, it is unclean. You
shall burn it in the fire, whether the rot is on the back or on the front.

[1] Or *mustache*

an unadorned head, and have his beard and mouth covered. These are all signs of mourning in the OT (Ezek. 24:17, 22; Mic. 3:7). Here they symbolize that a person is ritually dead. Cf. Luke 17:12–13, where lepers "stood at a distance" and called for help from Jesus.

13:47–59 Except for the symptoms and actual treatments such as washing, the procedure of the examination in cases of **leprous disease in a garment** follows that of the cases for humans. Causes of such disease include various molds or fungi. When it becomes clear that the suspected area is affected by the disease, the treatment (i.e., **tear** or **burn** it) is destructive; the object must no longer be used, or has to be completely abandoned.

56 "But if the priest examines, and if the diseased area has faded after it has been washed,
he shall tear it out of the garment or the skin or the warp or the woof. 57 Then if it appears
again in the garment, in the warp or the woof, or in any article made of skin, it is spreading.
You shall burn with fire whatever has the disease. 58 But the garment, or the warp or the
woof, or any article made of skin from which the disease departs when you have washed
it, shall then be washed a second time, and be clean."

59 This is the law for a case of leprous disease in a garment of wool or linen, either in
the warp or the woof, or in any article made of skin, to determine whether it is clean or
unclean.

Laws for Cleansing Lepers

14 The LORD spoke to Moses, saying, 2 "This shall be the law of the leprous person for
the day of his cleansing. [s]He shall be brought to the priest, 3 and the priest shall go
[t]out of the camp, and the priest shall look. Then, if the case of leprous disease is healed in
the leprous person, 4 the priest shall command them to take for him who is to be cleansed
two live[1] clean birds and [u]cedarwood and [v]scarlet yarn and [w]hyssop. 5 And the priest shall
command them to kill one of the birds in an earthenware vessel over fresh[2] water. 6 He
shall take the live bird with the cedarwood and the scarlet yarn and the hyssop, and dip
them and the live bird in the blood of the bird that was killed over the fresh water. 7 And
he shall [x]sprinkle it [y]seven times on him who is to be cleansed of the leprous disease. Then
he shall pronounce him clean and shall [z]let the living bird go [a]into the open field. 8 And he
who is to be cleansed [b]shall wash his clothes and shave off all his hair and bathe himself in
water, and he shall be clean. And after that he may come into the camp, but [c]live outside
his tent seven days. 9 And [d]on the seventh day he shall shave off all his hair from his head,
his beard, and his eyebrows. He shall shave off all his hair, and then he [b]shall wash his
clothes and bathe his body in water, and he shall be clean.

10 "And on the eighth day he [e]shall take two male lambs without blemish, and one ewe
lamb a year old without blemish, and a [f]grain offering of three tenths of an ephah[3] of fine
flour mixed with oil, and one log[4] of oil. 11 And the priest who cleanses him shall set the
man who is to be cleansed and these things before the LORD, at the entrance of the tent of
meeting. 12 And the priest shall take one of the male lambs and [g]offer it for a guilt offering,
along with the log of oil, and [h]wave them for a wave offering before the LORD. 13 And he
shall kill the lamb [i]in the place where they kill the sin offering and the burnt offering,
in the place of the sanctuary. For [j]the guilt offering, like the sin offering, belongs to the
priest; [k]it is most holy. 14 The priest shall take some of the blood of the guilt offering, and
the priest shall put it [l]on the lobe of the right ear of him who is to be cleansed and on the
thumb of his right hand and on the big toe of his right foot. 15 Then the priest shall take
some of the log of oil and pour it into the palm of his own left hand 16 and dip his right
finger in the oil that is in his left hand and sprinkle some oil with his finger seven times
before the LORD. 17 And some of the oil that remains in his hand the priest shall put on the
lobe of the right ear of him who is to be cleansed and on the thumb of his right hand and
on the big toe of his right foot, on top of the blood of the guilt offering. 18 And the rest of
the oil that is in the priest's hand he shall put on the head of him who is to be cleansed.
[m]Then the priest shall make atonement for him before the LORD. 19 The priest shall offer
the sin offering, to make atonement for him who is to be cleansed from his uncleanness.
And afterward he shall kill the burnt offering. 20 And the priest shall offer the burnt offering and the [f]grain offering on the altar. [m]Thus the priest shall make atonement for him,
and he shall be clean.

[1] Or *wild* [2] Or *running;* Hebrew *living;* also verses 6, 50, 51, 52 [3] An *ephah* was about 3/5 bushel or 22 liters [4] A *log* was about 1/3 quart or 0.3 liter

Chapter 14

2 [s]Matt. 8:2, 4; Mark 1:40, 44; Luke 5:12, 14; 17:14
3 [t][2 Kgs. 7:10; Luke 17:12]
4 [u]Num. 19:6 [v]Heb. 9:19 [w]See Ex. 12:22
7 [x]Heb. 9:13 [y][2 Kgs. 5:10, 14] [z][ch. 16:22] [a]ver. 53; [ch. 17:5]
8 [b]ver. 47; See ch. 11:25 [c]Num. 12:15
9 [d][Num. 31:19] [b][See ver. 8 above]
10 [e][Matt. 8:4]; Mark 1:44; Luke 5:14 [f]Num. 15:4; See ch. 2
12 [g]ch. 5:18; 6:6, 7 [h]See Ex. 29:24
13 [i]ch. 1:5, 11; 4:4, 24 [j]ch. 7:7 [k]ch. 2:3; 7:6
14 [l][ch. 8:23; Ex. 29:20]
18 [m]See ch. 4:26
20 [f][See ver. 10 above] [m][See ver. 18 above]

14:1–32 Chapter 13 told how an unclean person is consigned to a place outside the camp. Chapter 14 explains how that person is readmitted into the covenant community.

14:1–9 Cedarwood, scarlet yarn, and **hyssop** all seem to have cleansing properties (see Num. 19:6) and are thus used in this two-bird ritual. The release of a live bird into the wilderness is reminiscent of the scapegoat in Lev. 16:6–10. The live bird being driven into the fields may symbolize the patient's disease being carried outside the camp of Israel.

14:10–20 This final series of sacrifices, focusing on cleansing at the sanctuary, restores the patient to full fellowship as a member of the covenant community. When the three standard offerings are presented—the sin offering, the burnt offering, and the grain offering—then the person has full restoration.

21[n]ch. 5:7, 11; 12:8 [h][See ver. 12 above]
22[o]See ch. 12:8
23[p]ver. 10, 11
24[q]ver. 12
25[r]For ver. 25-29, see ver. 14-18
30[s]ver. 22; ch. 15:15
31[m][See ver. 18 above]
32[t]ver. 10
34[u]Gen. 17:8; Num. 32:22; Deut. 32:49
35[v][Ps. 91:10; Zech. 5:4]
44[w]ch. 13:51, 52
47[x]See ch. 11:25
49[y]ver. 52 [z][ver. 4-6]

21 "But [n]if he is poor and cannot afford so much, then he shall take one male lamb
for a guilt offering [h]to be waved, to make atonement for him, and a tenth of an ephah
of fine flour mixed with oil for a grain offering, and a log of oil; 22 [o]also two turtledoves
or two pigeons, whichever he can afford. The one shall be a sin offering and the other
a burnt offering. 23 [p]And on the eighth day he shall bring them for his cleansing to the
priest, to the entrance of the tent of meeting, before the LORD. 24 [q]And the priest shall
take the lamb of the guilt offering and the log of oil, and the priest shall wave them for
a wave offering before the LORD. 25 And he shall kill the lamb of the guilt offering. [r]And
the priest shall take some of the blood of the guilt offering and put it on the lobe of the
right ear of him who is to be cleansed, and on the thumb of his right hand and on the
big toe of his right foot. 26 And the priest shall pour some of the oil into the palm of his
own left hand, 27 and shall sprinkle with his right finger some of the oil that is in his left
hand seven times before the LORD. 28 And the priest shall put some of the oil that is in
his hand on the lobe of the right ear of him who is to be cleansed and on the thumb of
his right hand and on the big toe of his right foot, in the place where the blood of the
guilt offering was put. 29 And the rest of the oil that is in the priest's hand he shall put
on the head of him who is to be cleansed, to make atonement for him before the LORD.
30 And he shall offer, of the [s]turtledoves or pigeons, whichever he can afford, 31 one[1] for
a sin offering and the other for a burnt offering, along with a grain offering. [m]And the
priest shall make atonement before the LORD for him who is being cleansed. 32 This is
the law for him in whom is a case of leprous disease, who cannot afford [t]the offerings
for his cleansing."

Laws for Cleansing Houses

33 The LORD spoke to Moses and Aaron, saying, 34 "When you come into the land of
Canaan, which I give you [u]for a possession, and I put a case of leprous disease in a house
in the land of your possession, 35 then he who owns the house shall come and tell the
priest, 'There seems to me to be some case of [v]disease in my house.' 36 Then the priest
shall command that they empty the house before the priest goes to examine the disease,
lest all that is in the house be declared unclean. And afterward the priest shall go in to
see the house. 37 And he shall examine the disease. And if the disease is in the walls of
the house with greenish or reddish spots, and if it appears to be deeper than the surface,
38 then the priest shall go out of the house to the door of the house and shut up the house
seven days. 39 And the priest shall come again on the seventh day, and look. If the disease
has spread in the walls of the house, 40 then the priest shall command that they take out
the stones in which is the disease and throw them into an unclean place outside the city.
41 And he shall have the inside of the house scraped all around, and the plaster that they
scrape off they shall pour out in an unclean place outside the city. 42 Then they shall take
other stones and put them in the place of those stones, and he shall take other plaster
and plaster the house.

43 "If the disease breaks out again in the house, after he has taken out the stones and
scraped the house and plastered it, 44 then the priest shall go and look. And if the disease
has spread in the house, it is a [w]persistent leprous disease in the house; it is unclean. 45 And
he shall break down the house, its stones and timber and all the plaster of the house, and
he shall carry them out of the city to an unclean place. 46 Moreover, whoever enters the
house while it is shut up shall be unclean until the evening, 47 and whoever sleeps in
the house [x]shall wash his clothes, and whoever eats in the house shall wash his clothes.

48 "But if the priest comes and looks, and if the disease has not spread in the house after
the house was plastered, then the priest shall pronounce the house clean, for the disease is
healed. 49 And for the [y]cleansing of the house he shall take [z]two small birds, with cedarwood

[1] Septuagint, Syriac; Hebrew *afford,* [31]*such as he can afford, one*

14:21–32 These sacrifices are a concession to the **poor** who **cannot afford** the animals of vv. 10–20. Birds are substituted for the expensive large animals, and the amount of grain required is two-thirds less than the normal amount. Cf. note on 12:8.

14:33–57 These laws regarding leprous disease in houses anticipate the time when Israel will settle in the Land of Promise and the people will be living in houses. Houses may become infected with **disease**; this latter term is a general word that may refer to things such as mold, mildew, and fungus. These are unclean and dangerous, and therefore must be eradicated. The priest determines what course of action is to be taken when such a problem occurs.

and scarlet yarn and hyssop, 50 and shall kill one of the birds in an earthenware vessel over
fresh water 51 and shall take the cedarwood and the hyssop and the scarlet yarn, along with
the live bird, and dip them in the blood of the bird that was killed and in the fresh water
and sprinkle the house seven times. 52 Thus he shall cleanse the house with the blood of the
bird and with the fresh water and with the live bird and with the cedarwood and hyssop
and scarlet yarn. 53 And he shall let the live bird go out of the city [a]into the open country.
So he shall [b]make atonement for the house, and it shall be clean."
54 This is the law for any case of leprous disease: for [c]an itch, 55 for [d]leprous disease in a
garment or in [e]a house, 56 and [f]for a swelling or an eruption or a spot, 57 to [g]show when it
is unclean and when it is clean. This is the law for leprous disease.

Laws About Bodily Discharges

15 The LORD spoke to Moses and Aaron, saying, 2 "Speak to the people of Israel and say
to them, [h]When any man has a discharge from his body,[1] his discharge is unclean.
3 And this is the law of his uncleanness for a discharge: whether his body runs with his
discharge, or his body is blocked up by his discharge, it is his uncleanness. 4 Every bed on
which the one with the discharge lies shall be unclean, and everything on which he sits shall
be unclean. 5 And anyone who touches his bed [i]shall wash his clothes and [j]bathe himself
in water and be unclean until the evening. 6 And whoever sits on anything on which the
one with the discharge has sat shall wash his clothes and bathe himself in water and be
unclean until the evening. 7 And whoever touches the body of the one with the discharge
shall wash his clothes and bathe himself in water and be unclean until the evening. 8 And
if the one with the discharge spits on someone who is clean, then he shall wash his clothes
and bathe himself in water and be unclean until the evening. 9 And any saddle on which
the one with the discharge rides shall be unclean. 10 And whoever touches anything that
was under him shall be unclean until the evening. And whoever carries such things shall
wash his clothes and bathe himself in water and be unclean until the evening. 11 Anyone
whom the one with the discharge touches without having rinsed his hands in water shall
wash his clothes and bathe himself in water and be unclean until the evening. 12 And an
[k]earthenware vessel that the one with the discharge touches shall be broken, and every
vessel of wood shall be rinsed in water.
13 "And when the one with a discharge is cleansed of his discharge, then [l]he shall count
for himself seven days for his cleansing, and wash his clothes. And he shall bathe his body
in fresh water and shall be clean. 14 And on the eighth day he shall take two [m]turtledoves
or two pigeons and come before the LORD to the entrance of the tent of meeting and give
them to the priest. 15 And the priest shall use them, [n]one for a sin offering and the other
for a burnt offering. [o]And the priest shall make atonement for him before the LORD for
his discharge.
16 [p]"If a man has an emission of semen, he shall bathe his whole body in water and
be unclean until the evening. 17 And every garment and every skin on which the semen
comes shall be washed with water and be unclean until the evening. 18 If a man lies with a
woman and has an emission of semen, both of them shall bathe themselves in water and
[q]be unclean until the evening.

[1] Hebrew *flesh*; also verse 3

53 [a]See ver. 7 [b]ver. 19, 20
54 [c]ch. 13:30
55 [d]ch. 13:47 [e]ver. 34
56 [f]ch. 13:2
57 [g]See ch. 10:10, 11

Chapter 15

2 [h]ch. 22:4; Num. 5:2; 2 Sam. 3:29
5 [i]See ch. 11:25 [j]ch. 16:26; 17:15
12 [k]ch. 6:28; 11:32, 33
13 [l]ver. 28; [ch. 14:8]
14 [m]See ch. 12:8
15 [n]ch. 14:30, 31 [o]ver. 30; See ch. 4:26
16 [p]ch. 22:4; Deut. 23:10
18 [q][1 Sam. 21:4]

15:1–33 *Discharges from Male and Female Reproductive Organs.* The rules in this chapter are symmetrically structured:

- a serious case of male discharge (vv. 2–15)
  - man's emission of semen (vv. 16–17)
    - sexual intercourse (v. 18)
  - female menstruation (vv. 19–24)
- a serious case of female discharge (vv. 25–30).

One characteristic of these regulations is their emphasis on the transmission of contagion from one person to another. Transmission of infection may occur in any number of ways: for example, by sitting on an object that a defiled person had previously sat on, by touching contaminated cooking utensils, and by having direct contact through touching or spitting. No matter how it happens, the person infected is required to separate and to undergo the purification ritual. It is clear that "unclean" is not the same as "sinful," but rather has to do with what is permitted (cf. note on 13:3). The Bible does not view the process of reproduction, with its associated bodily functions, as evil; this is part of the original good creation (even though human nature is severely damaged by the fall of Adam). Certainly the Creator of these functions has the right to tell his obedient creatures how and when to use them.

15:2 his body. The Hebrew *basar* (here, "body"; cf. ESV footnote, "flesh") is used euphemistically here for the "genitals." In fact, the same word is used in v. 19 of the female vagina.

15:16–18 The **emission of semen** is polluting, perhaps because it is the life liquid and its loss makes a man unclean.

19 "When a woman has a discharge, and the discharge in her body is blood, she shall be
in her menstrual impurity for seven days, and whoever touches her shall be unclean until
the evening. 20 [r]And everything on which she lies during her menstrual impurity shall be
unclean. Everything also on which she sits shall be unclean. 21 And whoever touches her
bed shall wash his clothes and bathe himself in water and be unclean until the evening.
22 And whoever touches anything on which she sits shall wash his clothes and bathe himself
in water and be unclean until the evening. 23 Whether it is the bed or anything on which
she sits, when he touches it he shall be unclean until the evening. 24 And [s]if any man lies
with her and her menstrual impurity comes upon him, he shall be unclean seven days,
and every bed on which he lies shall be unclean.

25 "If [t]a woman has a discharge of blood for many days, not at the time of her menstrual
impurity, or if she has a discharge beyond the time of her impurity, all the days of the
discharge she shall continue in uncleanness. As in the days of her impurity, she shall be
unclean. 26 Every bed on which she lies, all the days of her discharge, shall be to her as the
bed of her impurity. And everything on which she sits shall be unclean, as in the uncleanness of her menstrual impurity. 27 And whoever touches these things shall be unclean, and
shall wash his clothes and bathe himself in water and be unclean until the evening. 28 But
[u]if she is cleansed of her discharge, she shall count for herself seven days, and after that
she shall be clean. 29 And on the eighth day she shall take two [v]turtledoves or two pigeons
and bring them to the priest, to the entrance of the tent of meeting. 30 And the priest shall
use one for a sin offering and the other for a burnt offering. And the priest shall make
atonement for her before the LORD for her unclean discharge.

31 "Thus you shall keep the people of Israel separate from their uncleanness, lest they
die in their uncleanness by [w]defiling my tabernacle that is in their midst."

32 This is the law [x]for him who has a discharge and [y]for him who has an emission of
semen, becoming unclean thereby; 33 [z]also for her who is unwell with her menstrual impurity, that is, for anyone, [x]male or [a]female, who has a discharge, and for the [b]man who lies
with a woman who is unclean.

The Day of Atonement

16 The LORD spoke to Moses after [c]the death of the two sons of Aaron, when they
drew near before the LORD and died, 2 and the LORD said to Moses, "Tell Aaron your
brother not to [d]come at any time into the Holy Place inside the veil, before the mercy seat
that is on the ark, so that he may not die. For [e]I will appear in the cloud over the mercy
seat. 3 But in this way Aaron shall come into the Holy Place: [f]with a bull from the herd for

20 [r]See ver. 4-10
24 [s]ch. 18:19; [ch. 20:18]
25 [t]Matt. 9:20; Mark 5:25; Luke 8:43
28 [u]For ver. 28-30, see ver. 13-15
29 [v]See ch. 12:8
31 [w]Num. 5:3; 19:13, 20; Ezek. 5:11; 23:38
32 [x]ver. 2 [y]ver. 16
33 [z]ver. 19 [x][See ver. 32 above] [a]ver. 25 [b]ver. 24

Chapter 16

1 [c]ch. 10:1, 2
2 [d][Ex. 30:10; Heb. 9:7, 12, 24, 25; 10:19-22] [e]Ex. 25:22; 40:34, 35; [1 Kgs. 8:10-12]
3 [f]ch. 4:3

15:19–23 A woman who is menstruating is unclean, and her uncleanness may be transmitted to others. The structure of this passage corresponds to that of the male with a discharge earlier in the chapter.

15:24 If a man has sexual relations with a woman during her **menstrual** period, then he is considered **unclean** for **seven days**. That is the same length of time as is prescribed for the woman herself. It has often been alleged that this rule conflicts with 18:19 and 20:18, in which both parties are cut off from Israel. How are these statements to be harmonized? Perhaps the present verse deals only with the ritual implications of the act, or perhaps it is concerned with an inadvertent sexual act, whereas the later texts focus on a brazen breaking of the law. The texts simply seem to be dealing with different circumstances.

15:25–30 These laws are concerned with irregular or unnatural flows of blood from a female (cf. the woman who has a long-term "discharge of blood" in Matt. 9:20–22; Mark 5:25–34; Luke 8:43–48).

15:31–33 This section concludes with a warning and summary. **You** in v. 31 refers to Moses and Aaron (cf. v. 1 and 10:11). **defiling my tabernacle**. The presence of uncleanness in the camp constantly defiles the sanctuary; this idea prepares for the need for its cleansing in the Day of Atonement ritual (see 16:16).

16:1–34 *The Day of Atonement Ritual.* Occasioned by the death of Nadab and Abihu (ch. 10), the prescription sets out how—and for what purpose—Aaron the chief priest is to enter the Most Holy Place. The account ends with the institutionalization of the ritual (16:29–34). The nature of the ritual shows that purification for sins and uncleanness must be done from the innermost part of the tabernacle. All the other purificatory rituals hinge on the ceremony of this day. The sin offerings in this chapter in particular point to the work of Christ on the cross (see Heb. 9:7–14).

16:1–2 These verses explain the immediate occasion for the atonement-day ritual, implying that Nadab and Abihu's sin was not simply being drunk (cf. 10:9) but entering (or attempting to enter) the Most Holy Place (**inside the veil**).

16:3–10 The preparations and the general guidelines for the atonement-day ritual are now described. Aaron prepares **a bull . . . for a sin offering** and **a ram for a burnt offering** (atoning for the house of the priests). He also prepares **two male goats for a sin offering** and a **ram for a burnt offering** (atoning for the people). One of the two goats for the people's sin purifies the tent of meeting, while the other is presented alive to be sent away into the wilderness. As the ESV footnote explains, the meaning of **Azazel** (vv. 8, 10) is uncertain. Many take it to be a proper name (since it is parallel to **the LORD** in v. 8) and thus conclude that it is the name either of an otherwise unknown demon or of a place. The traditional explanation is that Azazel (Hb. *'aza'zel*) is a compound word, combining "goat" (Hb. *'ez*) with "going away" (Hb. *'azel*): the word would then mean "goat that goes away" (hence the conventional "scapegoat"). Each of these explanations has its difficulties; in any event, the idea is clear enough: the goat is sent out in order to take sin away from Israel.

a sin offering and [g]a ram for a burnt offering. **4** He shall put on [h]the holy linen coat and
shall have the linen undergarment on his body, and he shall tie the linen sash around his
waist, and wear the linen turban; these are the holy garments. [i]He shall bathe his body in
water and then put them on. **5** And he shall take from [j]the congregation of the people of
Israel two male goats for a sin offering, and one ram for a burnt offering.
6 "Aaron shall [k]offer the bull as a sin offering for himself and shall [l]make atonement
for himself and for his house. **7** Then he shall take the two goats and set them before the
LORD at the entrance of the tent of meeting. **8** And Aaron shall cast lots over the two goats,
one lot for the LORD and the other lot for [m]Azazel.[1] **9** And Aaron shall present the goat on
which the lot fell for the LORD and use it as a sin offering, **10** but the goat on which the lot
fell for [m]Azazel shall be presented alive before the LORD to make atonement over it, that
it may be sent away into the wilderness to [m]Azazel.
11 "Aaron shall present [k]the bull as a sin offering for himself, and shall make atonement
for himself and for his house. He shall kill the bull as a sin offering for himself. **12** And he
shall take [n]a censer full of coals of fire from the altar before the LORD, and two handfuls
of sweet incense beaten small, and he shall bring it inside the veil **13** [o]and put the incense
on the fire before the LORD, that the cloud of the incense may cover [p]the mercy seat that
is over the testimony, so that he does not die. **14** And [q]he shall take some of the blood of the
bull and sprinkle it with his finger on the front of the mercy seat on the east side, and in
front of the mercy seat he shall sprinkle some of the blood with his finger seven times.
15 "[r]Then he shall kill the goat of the sin offering that is for the people and bring its blood
[s]inside the veil and do with its blood as he did with the blood of the bull, sprinkling it
over the mercy seat and in front of the mercy seat. **16** Thus he shall [t]make atonement for
the Holy Place, because of the uncleannesses of the people of Israel and because of their
transgressions, all their sins. And so he shall do for the tent of meeting, which dwells with
them in the midst of their uncleannesses. **17** [u]No one may be in the tent of meeting from
the time he enters to make atonement in the Holy Place until he comes out and has made
atonement for himself and for his house and for all the assembly of Israel. **18** Then he shall
go out to the altar that is [v]before the LORD and [w]make atonement for it, and shall take
some of the blood of the bull and some of the blood of the goat, and put it on the horns of
the altar all around. **19** And he shall sprinkle some of the blood on it with his finger seven
times, and cleanse it and consecrate it from the uncleannesses of the people of Israel.
20 "And when he has made an end of [x]atoning for the Holy Place and the tent of meeting and the altar, he shall present the live goat. **21** And Aaron shall lay both his hands on
the head of the live goat, and confess over it all the iniquities of the people of Israel, and
all their transgressions, all their sins. And he shall [y]put them on the head of the goat and
send it away into the wilderness by the hand of a man who is in readiness. **22** The goat
shall [z]bear all their iniquities on itself to a remote area, and [a]he shall let the goat go free
in the wilderness.
23 "Then Aaron shall come into the tent of meeting and [b]shall take off the linen garments
that he put on when he went into the Holy Place and shall leave them there. **24** And he shall
bathe his body in water in a holy place and put on his garments and come out and [c]offer

[1] The meaning of *Azazel* is uncertain; possibly the name of a place or a demon, traditionally a scapegoat; also verses 10, 26

3 [g]ch. 1:10; 8:18
4 [h]ch. 6:10; 8:7; Ezek. 44:17, 18; See Ex. 28:39-43 [i]ch. 8:6, 7; Ex. 30:20
5 [j]ch. 4:14; Num. 29:11; 2 Chr. 29:21; Ezra 6:17
6 [k]Ezek. 45:22 [l]ver. 17, 24; ch. 9:7; Heb. 7:27, 28; 9:7
8 [m]ver. 26
10 [m][See ver. 8 above]
11 [k][See ver. 6 above]
12 [n]ch. 10:1; Num. 16:46; Rev. 8:3-5
13 [o]Ex. 30:1, 7, 8 [p]Ex. 25:21
14 [q]Heb. 9:13, 25; 10:4; See ch. 4:5, 6
15 [r]Heb. 2:17; 5:1; 9:7 [s]ver. 2; Heb. 6:19; 9:3, 7
16 [t]ver. 18; [Ex. 29:36; Ezek. 45:18; Heb. 9:22, 23]
17 [u][Luke 1:10, 21]
18 [v]ch. 1:5; 4:24 [w]ver. 16; ch. 4:7, 18; Ex. 30:6, 10
20 [x]ver. 16, 18; Ezek. 43:20; 45:20
21 [y][Isa. 53:6; 2 Cor. 5:21]
22 [z][Isa. 53:11, 12; John 1:29; Heb. 9:28; 1 Pet. 2:24] [a][ch. 14:7]
23 [b]See ch. 6:11
24 [c]ver. 3, 5

16:11–17 The atonement-day ritual starts with atonement for the priests (vv. 11–14) and then moves to atonement for the people (vv. 15–17). Aaron puts incense on the fire and it creates, literally, a **cloud**. The purpose of this act is to make the Most Holy Place misty and foggy to prevent Aaron from clearly seeing the presence of God. This is for Aaron's protection. **because of the uncleannesses of the people of Israel and because of their transgressions, all their sins** (v. 16). Some interpreters assume that this description of sins refers to heinous offenses that have not been dealt with by the rituals on ordinary occasions. But the emphasis of "all their sins" (see also v. 21) appears to require the interpretation that the sins and uncleannesses on the ordinary occasions are once again taken up on this occasion.

16:18–19 Presumably, **altar** here refers to the altar of burnt offering and not the incense altar (the purification of which is implied in v. 16b). The **blood** that has purified the mercy seat purifies this altar, thus restoring it to its pristine condition.

16:20–22 This rite of sending the guilt of all Israel into the desert is commonly understood to be another way of cleansing the people, in addition to the prior purification of the sanctuary (vv. 3–20). But it is possible to see the two rites consecutively, based on the understanding that "bearing iniquity" (or guilt) is part of the atonement (Hb. *kipper*) process. If so, the relationship between the two rites is that Aaron bears the iniquities in purifying the holy objects (cf. 10:17), and then he places them on the Azazel-goat, so that the latter takes them away into the wilderness.

16:23–25 Aaron leaves his Day of Atonement clothes inside the Holy Place because they are holy. They are not to be worn for the normal activity of the high priesthood.

his burnt offering and the burnt offering of the people and make atonement for himself
and for the people. 25 And [d]the fat of the sin offering he shall burn on the altar. 26 And he
who lets the goat go to [e]Azazel shall wash his clothes and [f]bathe his body in water, and
afterward he may come into the camp. 27 [g]And the bull for the sin offering and the goat for
the sin offering, whose blood was brought in to make atonement in the Holy Place, shall
be carried outside the camp. Their skin and their flesh and their dung shall be burned up
with fire. 28 And he who burns them shall wash his clothes and bathe his body in water,
and afterward he may come into the camp.

29 "And it shall be a statute to you forever that [h]in the seventh month, on the tenth day
of the month, you shall [i]afflict yourselves[1] and shall do no work, either [j]the native or the
stranger who sojourns among you. 30 For on this day shall atonement be made for you [k]to
cleanse you. You shall be clean before the LORD from all your sins. 31 [l]It is a Sabbath of solemn
rest to you, and you shall [i]afflict yourselves; it is a statute forever. 32 [m]And the priest who is
anointed and [n]consecrated as priest in his father's place [o]shall make atonement, wearing
the holy linen garments. 33 He shall make atonement for [p]the holy sanctuary, and he shall
make atonement for the tent of meeting and for [q]the altar, and he shall make atonement
for [r]the priests and for [s]all the people of the assembly. 34 And this shall be a statute forever
for you, that atonement may be made for the people of Israel [t]once in the year because of
all their sins." And Aaron[2] did as the LORD commanded Moses.

The Place of Sacrifice

17 And the LORD spoke to Moses, saying, 2 "Speak to Aaron and his sons and to all the
people of Israel and say to them, This is the thing that the LORD has commanded.
3 If any one of the house of Israel [u]kills an ox or a lamb or a goat in the camp, or kills it
outside the camp, 4 and [v]does not bring it to the entrance of the tent of meeting to offer it
as a gift to the LORD in front of the tabernacle of the LORD, bloodguilt shall be imputed
to that man. He has shed blood, and that man [w]shall be cut off from among his people.
5 This is to the end that the people of Israel may bring their sacrifices that they sacrifice [x]in
the open field, that they may bring them to the LORD, to the priest at the entrance of the
tent of meeting, and sacrifice them [y]as sacrifices of peace offerings to the LORD. 6 And the
priest shall [y]throw the blood on the altar of the LORD at the entrance of the tent of meeting and burn the fat [z]for a pleasing aroma to the LORD. 7 So they shall no more sacrifice
their sacrifices to goat demons, after whom they [a]whore. This shall be a statute forever for
them throughout their generations.

8 "And you shall say to them, Any one of the house of Israel, or of the strangers who sojourn
among them, who [b]offers a burnt offering or sacrifice 9 and [c]does not bring it to the entrance
of the tent of meeting to offer it to the LORD, [w]that man shall be cut off from his people.

Laws Against Eating Blood

10 "If any one of the house of Israel or of the strangers who sojourn among them [d]eats
any blood, I will [e]set my face against that person who eats blood and will cut him off from
among his people. 11 [f]For the life of the flesh is in the blood, and I have given it for you on

[1] Or *shall fast*; also verse 31 [2] Hebrew *he*

25 [d]ch. 4:8-10; Ex. 29:13
26 [e]ver. 8, 10 [f][ch. 15:5; 17:15]
27 [g]ch. 4:11, 12, 21; 6:30; Heb. 13:11, 12
29 [h]ch. 23:27; Num. 29:7 [i]ch. 23:32; Ps. 35:13; Isa. 58:3, 5; Dan. 10:12 [j]ch. 17:15; 18:26; 19:34; [Ex. 12:49]
30 [k]Ps. 51:2; Jer. 33:8; Heb. 10:1, 2; 1 John 1:7, 9
31 [l]ch. 23:32 [i][See ver. 29 above]
32 [m][ch. 21:10] [n]Ex. 29:29, 30; [Num. 20:28] [o]ver. 4
33 [p]ver. 16 [q]ver. 18 [r]ver. 6 [s]ver. 24
34 [t]Ex. 30:10; Heb. 9:7, 25

Chapter 17

3 [u][Deut. 12:5, 6, 13-15, 21]
4 [v]ver. 9 [w][Ex. 30:33]
5 [x]ch. 14:7, 53 [y]ch. 1:5
6 [y][See ver. 5 above] [z]See Gen. 8:21
7 [a]See Ex. 34:15
8 [b]ch. 1:2, 3
9 [c]ver. 4 [w][See ver. 4 above]
10 [d]See ch. 3:17 [e]ch. 20:3, 6; 26:17; Jer. 44:11; Ezek. 14:8; 15:7; [Ps. 34:16]
11 [f]ver. 14

16:26–28 The person who handles the Azazel-goat is assumed to have been defiled, presumably because he had contact with the uncleanness that the goat bore.

16:29–34 On the **tenth day** of the **seventh month** (Tishri, i.e., September/October), the Israelites and the strangers are to **afflict** themselves (v. 29; lit., "afflict or humble their souls"). This term expresses self-denial and self-mortification, connected with fasting and prayer (Ps. 35:13; Isa. 58:3; cf. Ezra 8:21). This is also a day that the people are not to work; it is a day of rest.

17:1–16 *The Handling and Meaning of Blood.* Chapter 17 deals with the handling of animals, beginning with a reminder that the blood of slain animals should be brought to the sanctuary (vv. 3–4). As the chapter progresses, deeper rationales for the instructions are gradually revealed: they are intended to prevent ongoing idolatry (v. 7), and the blood of a sacrificial animal is the "life" that takes the place of the offerer's death (vv. 11–14). Animal blood is not to be used by Israel indiscriminately as it was used among the pagans of the time.

17:1–9 If a person slaughters an animal either **in the camp** or **outside the camp** (v. 3) and does not bring the blood to the sanctuary (v. 4), that act is tantamount to human murder (though not identical to it). The immediate purpose for the prohibition is to prevent the people's idolatry in worshiping the **goat demons** (v. 7). Anyone who violates the prohibition is to be **cut off from his people** (v. 9).

17:10–12 These verses provide key insight into the understanding of sacrifice and atonement by explaining the meaning and significance of animal blood.

17:10 eats any blood. This probably refers to eating meat that still has the blood in it (cf. Gen. 9:4; Deut. 12:23).

17:11 The **blood** is here described as the **life** of the animal. The Hebrew

the altar [g]to make atonement for your souls, [h]for it is the blood that makes atonement
by the life. 12 Therefore I have said to the people of Israel, No person among you shall eat
blood, neither shall any stranger who sojourns among you eat blood.
13 "Any one also of the people of Israel, or of the strangers who sojourn among them, who
takes in hunting any beast or bird that may be eaten shall [i]pour out its blood and [j]cover it
with earth. 14 For the life of every creature[1] is its [k]blood: its blood is its life.[2] Therefore I have
said to the people of Israel, You shall not eat the blood of any creature, for the life of every
creature is its blood. Whoever eats it shall be cut off. 15 [l]And every person who eats what
dies of itself or what is torn by beasts, [m]whether he is a native or a sojourner, [n]shall wash
his clothes and [o]bathe himself in water and be unclean until the evening; then he shall be
clean. 16 But if he does not wash them or bathe his flesh, [p]he shall bear his iniquity."

Unlawful Sexual Relations

18 And the LORD spoke to Moses, saying, 2 "Speak to the people of Israel and say
to them, [q]I am the LORD your God. 3 [r]You shall not do as they do in the land
of Egypt, where you lived, and [s]you shall not do as they do in the land of Canaan, to
which I am bringing you. You shall not walk in their statutes. 4 [t]You shall follow my
rules[3] and keep my statutes and walk in them. [q]I am the LORD your God. 5 [t]You shall
therefore keep my statutes and my rules; [u]if a person does them, he shall live by them:
I am the LORD.
6 "None of you shall approach any one of his close relatives to uncover nakedness. I am
the LORD. 7 [v]You shall not uncover the nakedness of your father, which is the nakedness

[1] Hebrew *all flesh* [2] Hebrew *it is in its life* [3] Or *my just decrees*; also verse 5

11 [g][Matt. 26:28; Mark 14:24; Rom. 3:25; 5:9; Eph. 1:7; Col. 1:14, 20; Heb. 13:12; 1 John 1:7; Rev. 1:5] [h]Heb. 9:22
13 [i]Deut. 12:16, 24; 15:23 [j]Ezek. 24:7
14 [k]ver. 11; See Gen. 9:4
15 [l]See ch. 22:8 [m]See ch. 16:29 [n]See ch. 11:25 [o]ch. 15:5
16 [p][Num. 19:20]; See ch. 5:1

Chapter 18

2 [q]ch. 11:44; 19:4; 20:7; Ex. 6:6, 7
3 [r]Ezek. 20:7, 8; 23:8 [s]Ex. 23:24; Deut. 12:30, 31
4 [t]ver. 26; ch. 19:19, 37; 20:8, 22; 25:18; Deut. 4:1, 6; 5:1; 6:1; 12:1; Ezek. 20:19 [q][See ver. 2 above]
5 [t][See ver. 4 above] [u]Ezek. 20:11, 13, 21; Cited Rom. 10:5; Gal. 3:12; [Luke 10:28]
7 [v]For ver. 7-16, see ch. 20:11-21

reads literally: "And I, I have given it. . . ." This underscores the action of the Lord himself in granting the means of **atonement**; it is his gracious gift. **makes atonement by the life**. That is, by means of the life of the animal, which ransoms the life of the offerer from the deserved judgment of the Lord.

17:12 Therefore. Because the Lord has set aside the blood for the unique role of atonement (v. 11), the Israelites and all sojourners are prohibited from partaking of it.

17:13–14 These verses describe how to handle the blood of animals killed in the hunt (vv. 13–14), with v. 14 emphasizing the prohibition against consuming **blood** (cf. vv. 10–12).

17:15–16 A person who eats from these animals is **unclean**, probably because the animals that have died in these ways have not had their blood drained properly. Therefore, one who eats them becomes unclean and must be purified.

18:1–22:33 *The Call to Holiness.* This section applies the principle of holiness (19:1–2) to various aspects of Israelite life. Chapter 18 considers the realm of sexual behavior and how Israel is to act differently from the pagan nations. Chapters 19–20 give a variety of applications of holiness to Israel's existence: the manner in which the people treat the land, their neighbors, their parents, and all other things is to be distinct. Holiness is to affect every area of Israelite life. Chapters 21–22 specifically deal with the regulations regarding the holiness of the priesthood.

18:1–30 *Prohibitions against Pagan Practices.* The rules from ch. 18 onward aim to lead the people to holiness. Though the term "holy" or "holiness" is not mentioned in ch. 18, avoiding such conduct as practiced in Egypt and particularly in Canaan is the minimal requirement for the people to become holy. In reading the laws, it is important to see both their original context and their underlying and abiding principles. From the latter viewpoint, the laws in this chapter can be seen as commanding the people to avoid any action that ignores the order that God revealed in his creation. In this sense, the prohibited acts in this chapter are representative (i.e., nonexhaustive) examples.

18:1–5 The people are commanded not to imitate the customs of the Egyptians and the Canaanites, but to obey the Lord's rules and statutes.

18:5 if a person does them, he shall live by them. Two interrelated interpretative issues arise here. First, what is the meaning of "live"? Does it refer simply to retaining bodily life, or does it refer to life in God's pleasure, or does it refer to eternal life? Second, what is the connection between "doing" and "living"? In particular, does this verse imply that the doing *earns* the life (as the questioner in Luke 10:25 seems to imply)? In answer to the first question, when the Pentateuch speaks of "living" by keeping God's statutes and rules, it refers to enjoying life under God's pleasure (cf. Deut. 4:1; 8:1). In answer to the second question, when the OT stresses "doing," it always sees this as the right response to God's grace that provides both covenant relationship and moral instruction; it never presents obedience as the way of gaining that grace (it is the same as the NT in this respect: cf. Gal. 5:6; 1 John 2:3). Leviticus 18:5 is thus describing how the genuinely faithful guide their "walk" so that they can "abide in God's love" (cf. John 15:10). The echoes of this text in Deut. 4:1; 8:1; Neh. 9:29; Ezek. 20:11, 13, 21 all appear to assume this reading of the text. In Luke 10:25 ("Teacher, what shall I do to inherit eternal life?") the lawyer is taking the words of Lev. 18:5 to describe the way of earning eternal life. Jesus has him summarize the law (you must love the Lord and your neighbor), and then urges him, "Do this, and you will live" (Luke 10:28). Since the man wanted to "justify himself" (Luke 10:29), it is best to read this as Jesus' challenge to all who would use the law (improperly) as a means to earn life: they must obligate themselves to unswerving loving obedience in order to gain their righteousness, or else give up in despair. On the question of how Paul uses the text in Rom. 10:5 and Gal. 3:12, see notes there.

18:6–20 These laws prohibit a variety of sexual sins: incest (vv. 6–18), intercourse during menstruation (v. 19), and adultery (v. 20).

18:6–18 These laws prohibit sexual relations (**approach . . . to uncover nakedness**), and therefore marriage, between people who are too closely related, either by blood (mother, sister, granddaughter, aunt) or by marriage (stepmother, stepsister, stepdaughter, stepgranddaughter, sister-in-law, daughter-in-law, aunt by marriage). "Uncover nakedness" can at times merely refer to voyeurism (cf. Gen. 9:22–23), but in the OT it is most commonly a euphemism for sexual intercourse. No mention is made of the daughter, probably because that needs no comment (cf. Gen. 19:30–38), and this prohibition is already well known in the laws of other cultures. It is assumed that, gener-

of your mother; she is your mother, you shall not uncover her nakedness. **8** [w]You shall
not uncover the nakedness of your father's wife; it is your father's nakedness. **9** [x]You shall not
uncover the nakedness of your sister, your father's daughter or your mother's daughter,
whether brought up in the family or in another home. **10** You shall not uncover the nakedness of your son's daughter or of your daughter's daughter, for their nakedness is your
own nakedness. **11** You shall not uncover the nakedness of your father's wife's daughter,
brought up in your father's family, since she is your sister. **12** You shall not uncover the
nakedness of your father's sister; she is your father's relative. **13** You shall not uncover the
nakedness of your mother's sister, for she is your mother's relative. **14** You shall not uncover
the nakedness of your father's brother, that is, you shall not approach his wife; she is your
aunt. **15** [y]You shall not uncover the nakedness of your daughter-in-law; she is your son's
wife, you shall not uncover her nakedness. **16** [z]You shall not uncover the nakedness of
your brother's wife; it is your brother's nakedness. **17** You shall not uncover the nakedness
of a woman and of her daughter, and you shall not take her son's daughter or her daughter's daughter to uncover her nakedness; they are relatives; it is depravity. **18** And you shall
not take a woman as a [a]rival wife to her sister, uncovering her nakedness [b]while her sister
is still alive.

19 [c]"You shall not approach a woman to uncover her nakedness while she is in her menstrual uncleanness. **20** [d]And you shall not lie sexually with your neighbor's wife and so
make yourself unclean with her. **21** You shall not give any of your children to [e]offer them[1]
to [f]Molech, and so [g]profane the name of your God: I am the LORD. **22** [h]You shall not lie with
a male as with a woman; it is an abomination. **23** [i]And you shall not lie with any animal
and so make yourself unclean with it, neither shall any woman give herself to an animal
to lie with it: it is [j]perversion.

24 [k]"Do not make yourselves unclean by any of these things, [l]for by all these the nations
I am driving out before you have become unclean, **25** and the [m]land became unclean, so
that I punished its iniquity, and the land [n]vomited out its inhabitants. **26** But [o]you shall
keep my statutes and my rules and do none of these abominations, either the [p]native or
the stranger who sojourns among you **27** (for the people of the land, who were before you,
did all of these abominations, so that the land became unclean), **28** lest the land vomit you
out when you make it unclean, as it vomited out the nation that was before you. **29** For
everyone who does any of these abominations, the persons who do them shall be cut off
from among their people. **30** [q]So keep my charge never to practice [r]any of these abominable
customs that were practiced before you, and never to make yourselves unclean by them:
[s]I am the LORD your God."

[1] Hebrew *to make them pass through* [the fire]

8 [w]Deut. 22:30; 27:20; 1 Cor. 5:1; [Gen. 49:4; Amos 2:7]
9 [x][2 Sam. 13:12; Ezek. 22:11]
15 [y][Gen. 38:26; Ezek. 22:11]
16 [z][Gen. 38:8; Deut. 25:5; Matt. 22:24; Mark 12:19; Luke 20:28]
18 [a][1 Sam. 1:6] [b][Gen. 31:50]
19 [c][ch. 15:24; 20:18; Ezek. 18:6; 22:10]
20 [d]See Ex. 20:14
21 [e]ch. 20:2-5; Deut. 18:10 [f][1 Kgs. 11:7, 33; Acts 7:43] [g]ch. 19:12; 20:3; 21:6; 22:2, 32; Ezek. 36:20, 22; Mal. 1:12
22 [h]ch. 20:13; [Gen. 19:5; Judg. 19:22; Rom. 1:27; 1 Cor. 6:9, 10; 1 Tim. 1:9, 10]
23 [i]ch. 20:15, 16; Ex. 22:19 [j]ch. 20:12
24 [k]ver. 30; [Matt. 15:19, 20; Mark 7:21-23] [l]ch. 20:23; [Deut. 18:12]
25 [m]Num. 35:34; Jer. 2:7; Ezek. 36:17 [n]ch. 20:22
26 [o]See ver. 4, 5 [p]See ch. 16:29
30 [q]ch. 22:9 [r]ver. 3, 26; ch. 20:23; Deut. 18:9 [s]See ver. 2

ally speaking, Israelites will marry other Israelites, and these laws provide a boundary for how close such unions may be. There is some debate over just what motivates this system of requirements; certainly they enforce a distinction between family affection and erotic love as such—a distinction that protects the well-being of the community, and especially of its vulnerable members. This concern would not be limited to the Israelite theocracy and is therefore also applicable to Christians.

18:18 a rival wife to her sister. Some have taken this to be a general prohibition of bigamy (with "to her sister" in the sense of "to another woman"). Bigamy is indeed outside the creation ideal (Gen. 2:24), but elsewhere in this chapter the Hebrew term "sister" simply refers to a biological sister. Further, the laws of Israel do not always require the ethical ideal; often they simply set out the minimum level of civility that the Israelite theocracy can tolerate. Biblical narratives generally show polygamous marriages as unhappy ones, and allow the reader to draw the clear conclusion: e.g., Gen. 29:30–30:2 (Jacob's marriage to two sisters, at a time historically prior to this prohibition); 1 Sam. 1:2–7 (the two wives of Elkanah).

18:19 Leviticus offers no explanation for what motivates this law. Unlike most of the other sexual laws of this chapter, such as the ones dealing with adultery and homosexuality, this law is not repeated as prohibitive in the NT. In view of 15:19–24, the concern is probably the ceremonial uncleanness that the man will contract. In other words, the man who touches a woman in her menstrual condition becomes ritually unclean himself.

18:20 This prohibition follows from the seventh commandment (Ex. 20:14) and is universally applicable. **make yourself unclean with her**. Although not all uncleanness is sin, all sin makes a person unclean.

18:21 This refers to the cult of **Molech** (2 Kings 23:10; Jer. 32:35). The precise nature of the offering of **children** to this pagan god is uncertain. It may be that they are being given to the cult of Molech to train to be temple prostitutes, and that is why this passage is listed in a section dealing with sexual prohibitions. On the other hand, Roman authors describe the practice of sacrificing babies by fire in Carthage (a north African city founded by Phoenicians, who were part of Canaan), and thus this may indeed refer to this horrific custom.

18:22 You shall not lie with a male as with a woman. This prohibited all male homosexual activity (cf. 20:13; also note on Rom. 1:26–27). In the larger picture, such activity is utterly at odds with the creation ideal (see note on Gen. 2:23–24).

18:24–30 All the above-listed offenses are declared to be abominations to the Lord, and any one of them defiles not just the offender but also the **land**.

The LORD Is Holy

19 And the LORD spoke to Moses, saying, 2 “Speak to all the congregation of the people
of Israel and say to them, [t]You shall be holy, for I the LORD your God am holy. 3 [u]Every
one of you shall revere his mother and his father, and [v]you shall keep my Sabbaths: I am
the LORD your God. 4 [w]Do not turn to idols [x]or make for yourselves any gods of cast metal:
I am the LORD your God.
5 [y]“When you offer a sacrifice of peace offerings to the LORD, you shall offer it so [z]that
you may be accepted. 6 It shall be eaten the same day you offer it or on the day after, and
anything left over until the third day shall be burned up with fire. 7 If it is eaten at all on
the third day, it is [a]tainted; it will not be accepted, 8 and everyone who eats it shall [b]bear
his iniquity, because [c]he has profaned what is holy to the LORD, and that person shall be
cut off from his people.

Love Your Neighbor as Yourself

9 [d]“When you reap the harvest of your land, you shall not reap your field right up to its
edge, neither shall you gather the gleanings after your harvest. 10 And you shall not strip
your vineyard bare, neither shall you gather the fallen grapes of your vineyard. You shall
leave them for the poor and for the sojourner: I am the LORD your God.
11 [e]“You shall not steal; [f]you shall not deal falsely; you shall not lie to one another.
12 [g]You shall not swear by my name falsely, and so [h]profane the name of your God: I am
the LORD.
13 [i]“You shall not oppress your neighbor or rob him. [j]The wages of a hired worker shall
not remain with you all night until the morning. 14 [k]You shall not curse the deaf or put a
stumbling block before the blind, but you shall [l]fear your God: I am the LORD.
15 [m]“You shall do no injustice in court. You shall not be partial to the poor or defer to
the great, but in righteousness shall you judge your neighbor. 16 [n]You shall not go around
as a slanderer among your people, and you shall not [o]stand up against the life[1] of your
neighbor: I am the LORD.
17 [p]“You shall not hate your brother in your heart, but [q]you shall reason frankly with
your neighbor, lest you [r]incur sin because of him. 18 [s]You shall not take vengeance or bear
a grudge against the sons of your own people, but [t]you shall love your neighbor as yourself: I am the LORD.

[1] Hebrew *blood*

Chapter 19
2 [t]See ch. 11:44, 45
3 [u]See Ex. 20:12 [v]See Ex. 20:8
4 [w]ch. 26:1; 1 John 5:21; See Ex. 20:3-5 [x]Ex. 34:17; [Deut. 27:15]
5 [y]See ch. 7:15-18 [z]ch. 1:3; 22:19
7 [a]ch. 7:18
8 [b]See ch. 5:1 [c]ch. 22:15
9 [d]ch. 23:22; Deut. 24:19-21; [Ruth 2:15, 16]
11 [e]See Ex. 20:15 [f][ch. 6:2, 3; Eph. 4:15, 25; Col. 3:9]
12 [g]See Ex. 20:7 [h]See ch. 18:21
13 [i]ch. 6:2, 3 [j]Deut. 24:14, 15; Mal. 3:5; [James 5:4]
14 [k]Deut. 27:18 [l]ver. 32; ch. 25:17; Eccles. 5:7; 12:13; 1 Pet. 2:17
15 [m]Ex. 23:2, 3; Deut. 1:17; 16:19; 27:19; Ps. 82:2; Prov. 24:23; James 2:9; [2 Chr. 19:6, 7]
16 [n]Prov. 11:13; 20:19 [o]Ex. 23:1, 7; [Matt. 26:60, 61]; See 1 Kgs. 21:10-13; Acts 6:11-13
17 [p]1 John 2:9, 11; 3:15 [q]Prov. 27:5, 6; Matt. 18:15; Luke 17:3; Gal. 6:1; Eph. 5:11 [r][ch. 22:16; Rom. 1:32; 1 Tim. 5:22; 2 John 11]
18 [s]Prov. 20:22; Rom. 12:17, 19; Heb. 10:30 [t]Matt. 5:43; Cited Matt. 19:19; 22:39; Mark 12:31; Luke 10:27; Rom. 13:9; Gal. 5:14; James 2:8

19:1–37 *Call to Holiness.* In ch. 19 the Lord strongly commands the people (including the priests) to become holy in their practice, as he is holy (v. 2). One becomes practically holy by observing *all* the following negative and positive commandments. Some of the commandments in vv. 3–18 are similar to the Ten Commandments (Ex. 20:2–17), and the topics in this chapter show that holiness must be practiced in every sphere of one's life. Some of the rules are grounded in the fact that the Lord is the One who saved the Israelites from the bondage in Egypt. Many of these rules (e.g., Lev. 19:9–18) are oriented toward the Israelites' functioning as a loving community, serving one another's well-being.

19:1–4 Holiness here refers first and foremost to the essential nature of God. The term **holy** means “set apart, unique, and distinct,” and holiness in humans ordinarily refers to their being set apart for service to God (see note on Isa. 6:3). Human holiness is the imitation of God, i.e., becoming and acting like him.

19:5–8 Sacrifices are to be made in a specific way, namely, according to God's commands. If they are not carried out in the prescribed manner, then the offerer has **profaned** that which is **holy**.

19:9–10 Thorough harvesting may reflect coveting and greed. Caring for one's neighbor and helping provide for the **poor** and the **sojourner** displays holiness. (For a literal observance of these rules, and for kindness that goes well beyond the simple legal requirement, see Ruth 2.)

19:11–18 This section refers often to the Ten Commandments. Holiness requires that a person keep the Word of God and, in particular, the fundamental moral law enumerated in the Ten Commandments.

19:11–12 Dishonesty in human relationships is prohibited. When someone swore an oath, he would do so by invoking the name of the Lord. To **swear . . . falsely**, therefore, was to disregard the holiness of God's **name** and thus **profane** it.

19:13–14 The prohibition against oppression is exemplified by two cases: delay in paying the **wages** of the **hired worker** and insulting the physically disadvantaged.

19:15–16 Justice and righteousness must prevail in the Israelite legal system. No favoritism is permitted; the **poor** and the **great** are to be treated the same in a court of law.

19:17 To **hate** in one's **heart** is prohibited; one should rather **reason frankly** with his **neighbor** (cf. Prov. 27:5–6). The instruction is followed by a warning: **lest you incur sin because of him**. Scholars debate the relationship between reproof and incurring sin, but this probably has to do with a situation in which one who refuses to “reason frankly with his neighbor,” helping him to see his sin, would share in the guilt of the neighbor's sin when it is committed; it might also suggest that to fail to “reason frankly” will result in bitter feelings that will overflow into sinful action.

19:18 The instruction and warning of v. 17 is developed in a heightened way. **you shall love your neighbor as yourself**. To love one's neighbor as oneself is a fundamental principle of the Torah, God's law. Both Jesus and Paul teach that it is a foundational tenet for how believers are to treat one another (Matt. 22:39–40; Rom. 13:9; Gal. 5:14), while James calls this the “royal law” (James 2:8). In Matt. 5:43, Jesus cites a distortion of this rule in order to restore the rule to its rightful place.

You Shall Keep My Statutes

19 [u]"You shall keep my statutes. You shall not let your cattle breed with a different kind.
[v]You shall not sow your field with two kinds of seed, nor shall you wear a garment of cloth
made of two kinds of material.
20 "If a man lies sexually with a woman who is a slave, assigned to another man and not
yet ransomed or given her freedom, a distinction shall be made. They shall not be put to
death, because she was not free; 21 but [w]he shall bring his compensation to the LORD, to
the entrance of the tent of meeting, a ram for a guilt offering. 22 And the priest shall make
atonement for him with the ram of the guilt offering before the LORD for his sin that he
has committed, and he shall be forgiven for the sin that he has committed.
23 "When you come into the land and plant any kind of tree for food, then you shall regard
its fruit as forbidden.[1] Three years it shall be forbidden to you; it must not be eaten. 24 And
in the fourth year all its fruit shall be holy, an offering of praise to the LORD. 25 But in the
fifth year you may eat of its fruit, to increase its yield for you: I am the LORD your God.
26 [x]"You shall not eat any flesh with the blood in it. [y]You shall not interpret omens or
[z]tell fortunes. 27 [a]You shall not round off the hair on your temples or mar the edges of your
beard. 28 You shall not make any [b]cuts on your body for the dead or tattoo yourselves: I
am the LORD.
29 [c]"Do not profane your daughter by making her a prostitute, lest the land fall into
prostitution and the land become full of depravity. 30 [d]You shall keep my Sabbaths and
[e]reverence my sanctuary: I am the LORD.
31 [f]"Do not turn to mediums or necromancers; do not seek them out, and so make yourselves unclean by them: I am the LORD your God.
32 [g]"You shall stand up before the gray head and honor the face of an old man, and you
shall [h]fear your God: I am the LORD.
33 [i]"When a stranger sojourns with you in your land, you shall not do him wrong. 34 [j]You
shall treat the stranger who sojourns with you as the native among you, and [k]you shall love
him as yourself, for you were strangers in the land of Egypt: I am the LORD your God.
35 [l]"You shall do no wrong in judgment, in measures of length or weight or quantity.
36 [m]You shall have just balances, just weights, a just ephah, and a just hin:[2] I am the LORD
your God, who brought you out of the land of Egypt. 37 And [n]you shall observe all my
statutes and all my rules, and do them: I am the LORD."

Punishment for Child Sacrifice

20 The LORD spoke to Moses, saying, 2 "Say to the people of Israel, [o]Any one of the people
of Israel or of the strangers who sojourn in Israel who gives any of his children to
Molech shall surely be put to death. The people of the land shall stone him with stones.

19 [u]See ch. 18:4, 5 [v]Deut. 22:9-11
21 [w]ch. 5:15; 6:6, 7
26 [x]See ch. 3:17 [y]Deut. 18:10; 2 Kgs. 17:17 [z]2 Kgs. 21:6; 2 Chr. 33:6
27 [a]ch. 21:5; [Isa. 15:2; Jer. 9:26; 48:37]
28 [b]ch. 21:1, 4, 5; Deut. 14:1; 1 Kgs. 18:28; Jer. 16:6; 41:5; 47:5; 48:37
29 [c][Deut. 23:17]
30 [d]ver. 3; ch. 26:2; See Ex. 20:8 [e]Eccles. 5:1; [Matt. 21:12, 13; Mark 11:15-17; Luke 19:45, 46; John 2:14-16]
31 [f]ch. 20:6, 27; Deut. 18:11; Isa. 8:19; [Ex. 22:18; 1 Sam. 28:3, 7, 9; 1 Chr. 10:13; Acts 16:16]
32 [g]Prov. 20:29; [Lam. 5:12] [h]See ver. 14
33 [i]Ex. 22:21; 23:9; Mal. 3:5
34 [j]See ch. 16:29 [k]Deut. 10:19; See ver. 18
35 [l]See ver. 15
36 [m]Deut. 25:13, 15; Prov. 11:1; 16:11; 20:10; Ezek. 45:10; [Amos 8:5; Mic. 6:11]
37 [n]See ch. 18:4, 5

Chapter 20

2 [o]See ch. 18:21

[1] Hebrew *as its uncircumcision* [2] An *ephah* was about 3/5 bushel or 22 liters; a *hin* was about 4 quarts or 3.5 liters

19:19–37 Holiness means more than mere separation, but it always signifies that something is set apart in its proper sphere. In this section, this principle is applied in a variety of areas of life, such as in agricultural practice in which two different types of seeds are not to be planted together.

19:19 Two different kinds of domesticated animals are not to be crossbred, and two types of **cloth** are not to be woven together. Ceremonial holiness requires that things stay in their proper sphere, just as Israel must observe its separation from the nations (20:22–26).

19:20–22 The concept of holiness governs sexual relations in Israel. It requires that a fair judgment be conveyed in legal matters pertaining to adultery and promiscuity.

19:23–25 In the land of promise the **fruit** of the **tree** must not be eaten for the first **three years** (v. 23). **In the fourth year** it is **holy** and an **offering of praise to the LORD** (v. 24). Only **in the fifth** year can it be eaten (v. 25). **Forbidden** literally means "uncircumcised," and so the law of the land is being compared to circumcision. As a child is not to be circumcised before the eighth day, so the fruit on a tree is not to be plucked or eaten until after the third year.

19:26–31 These are all practices of the Canaanites. Holiness requires Israel not to act like the pagans in any areas of life.

19:33–34 Since the Israelites had been **strangers** in **Egypt** and knew what it was like, they ought to treat the strangers living among them just like themselves. In this regard the commandment in v. 18b is broadened beyond one's own countrymen to foreigners (cf. Luke 10:29–37).

19:35–36 In a summary way the rule in v. 15—avoid injustice and partiality; judge in righteousness—is taken up again and applied to commercial transactions.

19:37 observe all my statutes. This sums up the entire chapter. Cf. 18:5.

20:1–27 *Punishment for Disobedience.* The rules in ch. 20 have much in common with those in ch. 18. This chapter, however, sets forth and stresses the punishments for violating the rules. Special emphasis is laid on Molech worship and mediums/necromancers. Almost all the crimes listed are punishable by the death penalty. Only a few are to receive a lesser sentence, such as in 20:17–18, in which the perpetrator is excommunicated.

20:1–6 Worshipers of **Molech** ought to be stoned **to death** (v. 2). If that is not implemented, the Lord himself punishes them and their followers directly by cutting them off (vv. 4–5; i.e., by bringing them to a premature death himself; see note on 7:11–36). The Lord carries out the same punishment upon those who consult **mediums and necromancers** (20:6)—cf. 1 Sam. 28:9, where Saul consults the medium of En-dor.

3 [p]I myself will set my face against that man and will cut him off from among his people,
because he has given one of his children to Molech, to make my sanctuary [q]unclean and
[r]to profane my holy name. 4 And if the people of the land do at all close their eyes to that
man when he gives one of his children to Molech, and do not [s]put him to death, 5 then I
will set my face against that man and against his clan and will cut them off from among
their people, him and all who follow him in [t]whoring after Molech.
6 "If [u]a person turns to mediums and necromancers, whoring after them, [v]I will set my face
against that person and will cut him off from among his people. 7 [w]Consecrate yourselves,
therefore, and be holy, for I am the LORD your God. 8 [x]Keep my statutes and do them; [y]I am
the LORD who sanctifies you. 9 For [z]anyone who curses his father or his mother shall surely
be put to death; he has cursed his father or his mother; [a]his blood is upon him.

Punishments for Sexual Immorality

10 "If a [b]man commits adultery with the wife of[1] his neighbor, both the adulterer and
the adulteress shall surely be put to death. 11 [c]If a man lies with his father's wife, he has
uncovered his father's nakedness; both of them shall surely be put to death; their blood is
upon them. 12 [d]If a man lies with his daughter-in-law, both of them shall surely be put to
death; they have committed [e]perversion; their blood is upon them. 13 [f]If a man lies with a
male as with a woman, both of them have committed an abomination; they shall surely be
put to death; their blood is upon them. 14 [g]If a man takes a woman and her mother also, it
is depravity; he and they shall be burned with fire, that there may be no depravity among
you. 15 [h]If a man lies with an animal, he shall surely be put to death, and you shall kill the
animal. 16 [h]If a woman approaches any animal and lies with it, you shall kill the woman
and the animal; they shall surely be put to death; their blood is upon them.
17 [i]"If a man takes his sister, a daughter of his father or a daughter of his mother, and sees
her nakedness, and she sees his nakedness, it is a disgrace, and they shall be cut off in the
sight of the children of their people. He has uncovered his sister's nakedness, and he shall
bear his iniquity. 18 [j]If a man lies with a woman during her menstrual period and uncovers
her nakedness, he has made naked her fountain, and she has uncovered the fountain of
her blood. Both of them shall be cut off from among their people. 19 [k]You shall not uncover
the nakedness of your mother's sister or of your father's sister, for that is to make naked
[l]one's relative; they shall bear their iniquity. 20 [m]If a man lies with his uncle's wife, he has
uncovered his uncle's nakedness; they shall bear their sin; they shall die childless. 21 [n]If a
man takes his brother's wife, it is impurity.[2] He has uncovered his brother's nakedness;
they shall be childless.

You Shall Be Holy

22 [o]"You shall therefore keep all my statutes and all my rules and do them, that the land
where I am bringing you to live may not [p]vomit you out. 23 [q]And you shall not walk in the
customs of the nation that I am driving out before you, for they did all these things, and
therefore I detested them. 24 But [r]I have said to you, 'You shall inherit their land, and I will
give it to you to possess, a land [s]flowing with milk and honey.' I am the LORD your God,
[t]who has separated you from the peoples. 25 [u]You shall therefore separate the clean beast

[1] Hebrew repeats *if a man commits adultery with the wife of* [2] Literally *menstrual impurity*

3 [p]See ch. 17:10 [q]ch. 19:30; Ezek. 5:11; 23:38, 39 [r]See ch. 18:21
4 [s]Deut. 17:2, 3, 5
5 [t]See Ex. 34:15
6 [u]See ch. 19:31 [v]See ch. 17:10
7 [w]See ch. 11:44
8 [x]See ch. 18:4 [y]ch. 21:8, 15, 23; 22:32; Ex. 31:13; Ezek. 37:28
9 [z]See Ex. 21:17 [a]ver. 11, 12, 13, 16, 27; [2 Sam. 1:16; 1 Kgs. 2:32, 33, 37]
10 [b]ch. 18:20; Deut. 22:22; John 8:4, 5
11 [c]See ch. 18:8
12 [d]ch. 18:15 [e]ch. 18:23
13 [f]See ch. 18:22
14 [g]ch. 18:17; Deut. 27:23
15 [h]ch. 18:23; Ex. 22:19; Deut. 27:21
16 [h][See ver. 15 above]
17 [i]ch. 18:9; Deut. 27:22
18 [j]ch. 18:19; [ch. 15:24]
19 [k]ch. 18:12, 13 [l]ch. 18:6
20 [m]ch. 18:14
21 [n]ch. 18:16
22 [o]See ch. 18:4 [p]ch. 18:25, 28
23 [q]ch. 18:3, 24, 30; Deut. 9:5
24 [r]Ex. 3:17; 6:8 [s]See Ex. 3:8 [t]Ex. 33:16; 1 Kgs. 8:53; [Ex. 19:5; Deut. 7:6; 14:2; 1 Kgs. 8:53]
25 [u]See ch. 11:2-47; Deut. 14:4-20

20:7–8 This is the first time in Leviticus that the Lord is said to be the agent of sanctifying the people. The Lord **sanctifies** the Israelites by making them his holy people, set apart to be his own, giving them a holy status; now he calls on them to **consecrate** themselves and **be holy** (i.e., dedicate themselves to holiness in practice); see note on 11:44–45.

20:9 anyone who curses his father or his mother. Cursing one's parents is not merely using condescending or abusive language toward them but refers to a serious breach of a child's duty to honor his or her parents. It means "to make light of something," and is the exact opposite of "honoring" one's parents (Ex. 20:12); cf. Ex. 21:17. For the moral revulsion of such disrespect, cf. Prov. 20:20; 30:11, 17.

20:10–20 Each of these sexual activities has already been prohibited in ch. 18. They are repeated here because this section includes the punishment for each of the crimes: capital punishment (20:10–16), exile (vv. 17–18), or barrenness (vv. 19–21).

20:17 sees her nakedness. See note on 18:6–18.

20:22–26 This section of exhortations toward holiness concludes chs. 18–20 (cf. 20:22–24 with 18:3–5, 24–28). Moreover, in light of its reference to clean and unclean creatures in 20:25 (cf. ch. 11), this section may conclude not only chs. 18–20 but chs. 11–20 as well. **A land flowing with milk and honey** is a common scriptural description of Canaan (Ex. 13:5; 33:3; Num. 13:27; etc.). Egyptian texts such as the *Story of Sinuhe* also characterize Canaan as a productive, fertile land.

20:27 In v. 6, the one who consults a **necromancer** or a **medium** was to be put to death. In this verse, the necromancer or the medium is to be **put to death**. Why this verse appears in this place in the text is puzzling; it may

from the unclean, and the unclean bird from the clean. You shall not make yourselves
detestable by beast or by bird or by anything with which the ground crawls, which I have
set apart for you to hold unclean. 26 [v]You shall be holy to me, [w]for I the LORD am holy and
have separated you from the peoples, that you should be mine.
27 [x]"A man or a woman who is a medium or a necromancer shall surely be put to death.
They shall be [y]stoned with stones; [z]their blood shall be upon them."

Holiness and the Priests

21 And the LORD said to Moses, "Speak to the priests, the sons of Aaron, and say to
them, [a]No one shall make himself unclean for the dead among his people, 2 except
for his closest relatives, his mother, his father, his son, his daughter, his brother, 3 or his
virgin sister (who is near to him because she has had no husband; for her he may make
himself unclean). 4 He shall not make himself unclean as a husband among his people
and so profane himself. 5 [b]They shall not make bald patches on their heads, nor shave off
the edges of their beards, nor make any cuts on their body. 6 They shall be holy to their
God and [c]not profane the name of their God. For they offer the LORD's food offerings,
[d]the bread of their God; therefore they shall be holy. 7 [e]They shall not marry a prostitute
or a woman who has been defiled, neither shall they marry a woman [f]divorced from her
husband, for the priest is holy to his God. 8 You shall sanctify him, for he offers the bread
of your God. He shall be holy to you, for [g]I, the LORD, who sanctify you, [h]am holy. 9 And
the daughter of any priest, if she profanes herself by whoring, profanes her father; [i]she
shall be burned with fire.
10 [j]"The priest who is chief among his brothers, on whose head the anointing oil is
poured and who has been consecrated to wear the garments, [k]shall not let the hair of
his head hang loose nor tear his clothes. 11 He shall not [l]go in to any dead bodies nor
make himself unclean, even for his father or for his mother. 12 [m]He shall not go out of
the sanctuary, lest he [n]profane the sanctuary of his God, for the [o]consecration of the
anointing oil of his God is on him: I am the LORD. 13 And he shall take a wife in her
virginity.[1] 14 A widow, [p]or a divorced woman, or a woman who has been defiled, or a
prostitute, these he shall not marry. But he shall take as his wife a virgin[2] of his own
people, 15 that he may not profane his offspring among his people, for [g]I am the LORD
who sanctifies him."
16 And the LORD spoke to Moses, saying, 17 "Speak to Aaron, saying, None of your offspring
throughout their generations who has a blemish may [q]approach to offer the bread of his
God. 18 For no one who has a blemish shall draw near, a man [r]blind or lame, or one who has
a mutilated face [s]or a limb too long, 19 or a man who has an injured foot or an injured hand,
20 or a hunchback or a dwarf or a man with a [r]defect in his sight or an itching disease or scabs

[1] *Or a young wife* [2] Hebrew *young woman*

26 [v]Ex. 19:6 [w]ver. 7; See ch. 11:44
27 [x]See ch. 19:31 [y]ver. 2 [z]ver. 9

Chapter 21

1 [a]Ezek. 44:25
5 [b]Ezek. 44:20; [ch. 19:27, 28; Deut. 14:1]
6 [c]See ch. 18:21 [d]See ch. 3:11
7 [e]ver. 13, 14; Ezek. 44:22 [f]See Deut. 24:1-4
8 [g]ch. 22:9, 16 [h]See ch. 11:44
9 [i][Gen. 38:24]
10 [j]ch. 8:12; 16:32; Ex. 29:29, 30; Num. 35:25 [k]ch. 10:6
11 [l]Num. 19:14; [ver. 1, 2]
12 [m]ch. 10:7 [n]ver. 23 [o][ch. 8:9, 12, 30]
14 [p]ver. 7; Ezek. 44:22
15 [g][See ver. 8 above]
17 [q]ch. 10:3; [Num. 16:5; Ps. 65:4]
18 [r]ch. 22:22 [s][ch. 22:23]
20 [r][See ver. 18 above]

be because the act receives capital punishment, as do most of the other activities of the section.

21:1–24 *Holiness of the Priests.* Chapters 21–22 deal with the Lord's demand of holiness for the priests and the offerings. While priests have been ordained and are holy in terms of their office (ch. 8), that holiness is only an outward one; it does not necessarily mean that they have inner holiness of heart and conduct (see Introduction: Interpretative Issues). More stringent regulations of holiness are required of the priests because they work directly with the holy objects of the sanctuary.

21:1–4 For a layperson, coming into contact with **the dead** (as in attending a funeral) brings about defilement, though it is allowed (cf. Numbers 19). But ordinary **priests** (for high priests, see note on Lev. 21:10–15) are prohibited from coming into contact with the dead, **except** in the case of their **closest relatives** (v. 2). **his virgin sister** (v. 3). The assumption is that, once she marries, she is not regarded as one of his closest relatives, but comes under the care of her husband and his clan (see Gen. 2:24).

21:5–6 Priests were prohibited from making **bald patches on their heads**, shaving off the **edges of their beards**, or making **cuts on their body** (cf. 19:27–28). These acts are pagan mourning and burial practices. The priests of Israel oversee the ceremonial worship of the people, and therefore, no Canaanite ritual is to penetrate the priestly system. Even in burial practices the priests are to be holy.

21:7–8 The priest is required to be **holy** in the area of matrimony. He is to marry a woman of high moral character. She may not be a **prostitute**, because that is a defiling profession. He also is not to marry one who has been **divorced**. The text does not explain this latter prohibition; perhaps it acknowledges that even though divorce is allowed by the laws, a broken or failed marriage always carries an element of falling short of the creation ideal (see note on Deut. 24:1–4), and the priests are to embody the covenant ideal in their lives as well as their teaching (cf. Mal. 2:1–9).

21:10–15 The high **priest** is subject to stricter holiness regulations than is the ordinary priest. Thus, whereas a common priest may marry a **widow**, the high priest must marry a **virgin** (vv. 13–14). (Perhaps this rule is given to ensure that all the children in his home are his own.) The high priest may not participate in any mourning or burial activities (vv. 10–12; cf. note on vv. 1–4). This is to keep the high priest from uncleanness that he might otherwise bring into the inner parts of the sanctuary.

21:16–20 No priest who has a **blemish** may **approach** to offer sacrifices. The same requirement applies to sacrificial animals. Both the priest and the animal are to exemplify holiness and completeness (see 22:17–25).

or [t]crushed testicles. 21 No man of the offspring of Aaron the priest who has a blemish shall
come near to [u]offer the LORD's food offerings; since he has a blemish, he shall not come near
to offer the bread of his God. 22 He may eat the bread of his God, both of [v]the most holy and
of the [w]holy things, 23 but he shall not go through the veil or approach the altar, because he
has a blemish, that he may not [x]profane my sanctuaries, [y]for I am the LORD who sanctifies
them." 24 So Moses spoke to Aaron and to his sons and to all the people of Israel.

22 And the LORD spoke to Moses, saying, 2 "Speak to Aaron and his sons so that they
[z]abstain from the holy things of the people of Israel, which they [a]dedicate to me,
so that they do not [b]profane my holy name: I am the LORD. 3 Say to them, 'If any one of all
your offspring throughout your generations approaches the holy things that the people of
Israel dedicate to the LORD, while [c]he has an uncleanness, that person shall be cut off from
my presence: I am the LORD. 4 None of the offspring of Aaron who has a leprous disease or
a [d]discharge may eat of the holy things [e]until he is clean. [f]Whoever touches anything that
is unclean through contact with the dead or [g]a man who has had an emission of semen,
5 and [h]whoever touches a swarming thing by which he may be made unclean or [i]a person
from whom he may take uncleanness, whatever his uncleanness may be— 6 the person
who touches such a thing shall be unclean until the evening and shall not eat of the holy
things unless he has [j]bathed his body in water. 7 When the sun goes down he shall be clean,
and afterward he may eat of the holy things, because [k]they are his food. 8 [l]He shall not eat
what dies of itself or is torn by beasts, and so make himself unclean by it: I am the LORD.'
9 They shall therefore keep my charge, [m]lest they bear sin for it and die thereby when they
profane it: [n]I am the LORD who sanctifies them.

10 [o]"A lay person shall not eat of a holy thing; no foreign guest of the priest or hired
worker shall eat of a holy thing, 11 but if a priest buys a slave[1] as his property for money,
the slave[2] may eat of it, and [p]anyone born in his house may eat of his food. 12 If a priest's
daughter marries a layman, she shall not eat of the contribution of the holy things.
13 But if a priest's daughter is widowed or divorced and has no child and [q]returns to
her father's house, [r]as in her youth, she may eat of her father's food; yet no lay person
shall eat of it. 14 [s]And if anyone eats of a holy thing unintentionally, he shall add [t]the
fifth of its value to it and give the holy thing to the priest. 15 They [u]shall not profane the
holy things of the people of Israel, which they contribute to the LORD, 16 and so cause
them [m]to bear iniquity and guilt, by eating their holy things: [n]for I am the LORD who
sanctifies them."

Acceptable Offerings

17 And the LORD spoke to Moses, saying, 18 "Speak to Aaron and his sons and all the people
of Israel and say to them, [v]When any one of the house of Israel or of the sojourners in Israel
presents a burnt offering as his offering, for any of their vows or freewill offerings that they
offer to the LORD, 19 if it is to be accepted for you it shall be a [w]male without blemish, of
the bulls or the sheep or the goats. 20 [x]You shall not offer anything that has a blemish, for
it will not be acceptable for you. 21 And when anyone [y]offers a sacrifice of peace offerings
to the LORD [z]to fulfill a vow or as a freewill offering from the herd or from the flock, to be
accepted it must be perfect; there shall be no blemish in it. 22 Animals [a]blind or disabled
or mutilated or having a discharge or [b]an itch or scabs you shall not offer to the LORD or
give them to the LORD as a food [c]offering on the altar. 23 You may present a bull or a lamb
that has a part [d]too long or too short for a freewill offering, but for a vow offering it cannot

[1] Or *servant*; twice in this verse [2] Hebrew *he*

20 [t][Deut. 23:1]
21 [u]ver. 6
22 [v]ch. 2:3, 10; 6:17, 25; 7:1; 10:12, 17; 14:13; 24:9; Num. 18:9 [w]ch. 22:10, 12
23 [x]ver. 12 [y]ch. 22:9, 16

Chapter 22

2 [z][Num. 6:3] [a]ver. 3; Ex. 28:38; Deut. 15:19 [b][Num. 18:32]; See ch. 18:21
3 [c]ch. 7:20
4 [d]ch. 15:2 [e]ch. 14:2; 15:13 [f]Num. 19:11 [g]ch. 15:16
5 [h]ch. 11:24, 43, 44 [i]ch. 15:7, 19
6 [j][Heb. 10:22]; See ch. 15:5-11
7 [k]ch. 21:22; [Num. 18:11, 13]; See ch. 3:11
8 [l]See ch. 7:24
9 [m][Ex. 28:43]; See ch. 19:17 [n]ch. 21:8, 15, 23
10 [o]ch. 24:9; [1 Sam. 21:6; Matt. 12:4; Mark 2:26; Luke 6:4]
11 [p]Num. 18:11, 13
13 [q][Gen. 38:11; Ruth 1:8] [r]ch. 10:14; Num. 18:11, 19
14 [s]ch. 4:2; 5:15, 16, 18 [t]ch. 27:13, 15, 19
15 [u]ch. 19:8; Num. 18:32
16 [m][See ver. 9 above] [n][See ver. 9 above]
18 [v]ch. 1:2, 3, 10; Num. 15:14
19 [w]ch. 1:3, 10
20 [x]Deut. 15:21; 17:1; Mal. 1:8, 14; [Heb. 9:14; 1 Pet. 1:19]
21 [y]ch. 3:1, 6 [z]ch. 7:16; Num. 15:3, 8; Deut. 23:21, 23; Ps. 61:8; 65:1; Eccles. 5:4, 5
22 [a]ver. 20; ch. 21:18; Mal. 1:8 [b]ch. 21:20 [c]ch. 1:9, 13; 3:3, 5
23 [d]ch. 21:18

21:21–24 While the priests with physical defects cannot officiate in the priestly work, they are entitled to **eat** the divine food because of their lineage. **for I am the LORD who sanctifies them** (v. 23). Although "them" might refer to the priests with physical defects, the singular is used of such priests in vv. 17–23a, and the analogy with v. 15 suggests that "them" in v. 23 refers to **my sanctuaries**, which immediately precedes it.

22:1–33 *Holiness of the Offerings.* This chapter aims at guaranteeing the holiness of offerings, particularly against those who handle them (i.e., the priests and lay offerers). The offerings, just like the priest, ought to be physically without blemish (cf. vv. 21–22 with 21:17–22).

22:1–3 The potential cause of profaning the offerings lies in **uncleanness**. The heavy responsibility demanded of the priests is reflected in the phrase **cut off from my presence** (v. 3), which is more severe than the ordinary formula "cut off from his people." When a layman is cut off in the Levitical law, it is from among the people (19:8; 20:5), but the priest is exiled from the service in the tabernacle (i.e., in God's presence).

22:4–9 For the background of these rules, see 11:1–47; 13:1–59; 15:1–33; and 17:15. Contracting uncleanness is inevitable, but when purification has been made, one can eat the holy offering. If purification is not made and the offering is eaten, the offender forfeits his life.

be accepted. 24 Any animal that has its testicles bruised or crushed or torn or cut you shall
not offer to the LORD; you shall not do it within your land, 25 neither shall you offer as [e]the
bread of your God any such animals gotten from a foreigner. Since there is a [f]blemish in
them, because of their mutilation, they will not be accepted for you."
26 And the LORD spoke to Moses, saying, 27 [g]"When an ox or sheep or goat is born, it shall
remain seven days with its mother, and from the eighth day on it shall be acceptable as a
food offering to the LORD. 28 But you shall not kill an ox or a sheep [h]and her young in one
day. 29 And when you sacrifice a [i]sacrifice of thanksgiving to the LORD, you shall sacrifice
it so that you may be accepted. 30 It shall be eaten on the same day; [j]you shall leave none
of it until morning: I am the LORD.
31 [k]"So you shall keep my commandments and do them: I am the LORD. 32 [l]And you
shall not profane my holy name, that [m]I may be sanctified among the people of Israel. [n]I
am the LORD who sanctifies you, 33 who brought you out of the land of Egypt [o]to be your
God: I am the LORD."

25 [e]See ch. 3:11 [f]Mal. 1:14
27 [g]Ex. 22:30
28 [h][Deut. 22:6]
29 [i]ch. 7:12; Ps. 107:22; 116:17; Amos 4:5
30 [j]ch. 7:15
31 [k]ch. 19:37; Num. 15:40; Deut. 4:40
32 [l]See ch. 18:21 [m]ch. 10:3 [n]See ch. 20:8
33 [o]See Ex. 6:7

Feasts of the LORD

23 The LORD spoke to Moses, saying, 2 "Speak to the people of Israel and say to them,
[p]These are the appointed feasts of the LORD that you shall [q]proclaim as [r]holy convocations; they are my appointed feasts.

The Sabbath

3 [s]"Six days shall work be done, but on the seventh day is a Sabbath of solemn rest, a holy
convocation. You shall do no work. It is a Sabbath to the LORD in all your dwelling places.

Chapter 23

2 [p]ver. 4, 37; Num. 29:39; See Ex. 23:14-17 [q]Num. 10:10; Ps. 81:3; Joel 2:15 [r]Ex. 12:16
3 [s]ch. 19:3; Ex. 23:12; 31:15; 34:21; Luke 13:14; See Ex. 20:8-11; Deut. 5:12-15

22:10–16 For non-priests, the right of eating the holy offerings is conditioned on whether a person belongs to a priestly **house** (whether through purchase or by birth). Priests and their families subsisted on food from donations to the tabernacle. Who else may partake of that food? A **slave** purchased by a priest is included (v. 11), but a hired laborer is not. A **priest's daughter** may participate only until she is married outside the priestly family (vv. 12–13). The priests are to guard the holy food so that those unauthorized may not eat of it (vv. 15–16).

22:17–25 No **animal** is to be sacrificed if it is blemished. This parallels the requirements of priestly purity (21:17–23). Animals with defects are considered unholy and incomplete, and are therefore not to be offered to the Holy One.

22:26–28 The rationale for these laws is uncertain. Some argue that they perhaps have a polemical function against pagan ritual, in particular the fertility rites of the Canaanites. Others believe that they reflect the sanctity of the seven-day cycle in Israel. Yet others maintain that the laws simply show the high regard for all life that the Hebrews are to have (cf. Ex. 23:19; Deut. 20:19–20; 22:6–7).

22:29–30 A **thanksgiving** sacrifice was a type of peace offering (cf. 7:15). While other types of peace offerings could be eaten on the next day (7:16), this one was to be consumed **on the same day** (see also 7:15). This stricter rule could suggest that this offering was especially sacred or important.

23:1–25:55 *Holy Times.* Following chs. 18–22 (which addressed the theme of human behavioral holiness), these chapters address holiness in relation to time.

23:1–44 *Holy Feasts.* This chapter is a systematic presentation of the festal calendar in Israel (cf. Ex. 23:10–19; 34:18–26; Numbers 28–29; Deut. 16:1–17; see chart below). It is based on three national pilgrim festivals: the Feast of Unleavened Bread, the Feast of Harvest, and the Feast of Booths. The foundation of these three feasts is the Sabbath. Keeping this calendar sets Israel apart from all the surrounding nations.

23:1–3 *Introduction and Weekly Sabbath.* On the Lord's **appointed feasts**, people are to meet with the Lord. The **Sabbath** is a day of **solemn rest**. Therefore, **no work** is to be done on that day. This idea of "rest" is the basis for all the following feasts. The day is also one of **holy convocation**, i.e., of public assembly for worship (cf. the term in vv. 2, 4, 7, 21).

Holy Feasts

The Sabbath principle permeates each of these feasts, which are intended to express the divine-human relationship. Each feast requires (1) cessation from ordinary work and (2) dedication to the Lord by means of offerings.

Feast	Reference	General time of year	Specific time of year	Modern equivalent	Significance
Sabbath	23:3	Weekly	7th day	Saturday	Creation
Passover	23:4–8	Spring	14th of first month (Abib)	March/April (Easter)	Salvation
Firstfruits	23:9–14	Spring	16th of first month (Abib)	March/April (Easter)	Dedication
Weeks	23:15–21	Spring	1st of third month (Sivan)	Pentecost	Dedication
Trumpets	23:23–25	Fall	1st of seventh month (Tishri)	September	Solemn assembly; spiritual preparation
Day of Atonement	23:26–32	Fall	10th of seventh month (Tishri)	September/October	Redemption
Booths	23:33–36	Fall	15th–22nd of seventh month (Tishri)	September/October	Joyful remembrance of the Lord's historic guidance

The Passover

4 [p]"These are the appointed feasts of the LORD, the [t]holy convocations, which you shall
proclaim at the time appointed for them. 5 [u]In the first month, on the fourteenth day of the
month at twilight,[1] is the LORD's Passover. 6 And on the fifteenth day of the same month is
the Feast of Unleavened Bread to the LORD; for seven days you shall eat unleavened bread.
7 [v]On the first day you shall have a holy convocation; you shall not do any ordinary work.
8 But you shall present a food offering to the LORD for seven days. On the seventh day is a
holy convocation; you shall not do any ordinary work."

The Feast of Firstfruits

9 And the LORD spoke to Moses, saying, 10 "Speak to the people of Israel and say to them,
[w]When you come into the land that I give you and reap its harvest, you shall bring the
sheaf of [x]the firstfruits of your harvest to the priest, 11 and he shall [y]wave the sheaf before
the LORD, so that you may be accepted. On the day after the Sabbath the priest shall wave
it. 12 And on the day when you [y]wave the sheaf, you shall offer a [z]male lamb a year old
without blemish as a burnt offering to the LORD. 13 [a]And the grain offering with it shall
be two tenths of an ephah[2] of fine flour mixed with oil, a food offering to the LORD with a
pleasing aroma, [b]and the drink offering with it shall be of wine, a fourth of a hin.[3] 14 And
you shall eat neither bread nor grain [c]parched or [c]fresh until this same day, until you have
brought the offering of your God: it is a statute forever throughout your generations in
all your dwellings.

The Feast of Weeks

15 [d]"You shall count seven full weeks from the day after the Sabbath, from the day that
you brought the sheaf of the [y]wave offering. 16 You shall count [e]fifty days to the day after
the seventh Sabbath. Then you shall present a grain offering of [f]new grain to the LORD.
17 You shall bring from your dwelling places two loaves of bread to be waved, made of
two tenths of an ephah. They shall be of fine flour, and they shall be baked with leaven,
as [g]firstfruits to the LORD. 18 And you shall present with the bread seven lambs a year old
without blemish, and one bull from the herd and two rams. They shall be a burnt offering to the LORD, with their grain offering and their drink offerings, a food offering with
a pleasing aroma to the LORD. 19 And you shall offer one [h]male goat for a sin offering, and
two male lambs a year old as a sacrifice of [i]peace offerings. 20 And the priest shall [y]wave
them with the bread of the firstfruits as a wave offering before the LORD, with the two
lambs. [j]They shall be holy to the LORD for the priest. 21 And you shall make a proclamation
on the same day. You shall hold a holy convocation. You shall not do any ordinary work. It
is a statute forever in all your dwelling places throughout your generations.

22 "And [k]when you reap the harvest of your land, you shall not reap your field right up
to its edge, nor shall you gather the gleanings after your harvest. You shall leave them for
the poor and for the sojourner: I am the LORD your God."

The Feast of Trumpets

23 And the LORD spoke to Moses, saying, 24 "Speak to the people of Israel, saying, In [l]the
seventh month, on the first day of the month, you shall observe a day of solemn rest, [m]a

4 [p][See ver. 2 above] [t]Ex. 12:16
5 [u]Ex. 13:3, 10; 23:15; 34:18; Num. 9:2, 3; 28:16, 17; Josh. 5:10; 2 Kgs. 23:21; Ezra 6:19; [Num. 9:10, 11; 2 Chr. 30:2, 13, 15]; See Ex. 12:2-14; Deut. 16:1-8
7 [v]Ex. 12:16; Num. 28:18, 25
10 [w]Ex. 23:19; 34:26; Num. 15:18, 19; 28:26; Deut. 26:1, 2 [x]ver. 17
11 [y]ver. 15, 20; Ex. 29:24
12 [y][See ver. 11 above] [z]ch. 1:10
13 [a]ch. 2:14-16 [b]Ex. 29:40
14 [c][ch. 2:14]
15 [d]Ex. 34:22; Deut. 16:9 [y][See ver. 11 above]
16 [e]Acts 2:1 (Gk.) [f]Num. 28:26
17 [g]See ver. 10
19 [h]ch. 4:23, 28; Num. 28:30 [i]See ch. 3:1
20 [y][See ver. 11 above] [j]Num. 18:12; Deut. 18:4
22 [k]ch. 19:9, 10; Deut. 24:19; [Ruth 2:2, 3]
24 [l]Num. 29:1 [m]ch. 25:9

[1] Hebrew *between the two evenings* [2] An *ephah* was about 3/5 bushel or 22 liters [3] A *hin* was about 4 quarts or 3.5 liters

23:4–8 *The Passover.* It is also called **the Feast of Unleavened Bread** (cf. Luke 22:1). The basic rule is set out in Ex. 12:16–19. In addition to eating unleavened bread and doing no **ordinary work**, this rule adds another element, namely, presenting **a food offering to the LORD** (Lev. 23:8).

23:9–14 *The Firstfruits.* The rule applies to the life of the people in the Promised Land. For the relevant laws, see Ex. 23:15 and 34:18–20. The feast consists of two stages. It begins with the waving of the sheaves before the Lord. Then comes a series of sacrifices that include a whole **burnt offering**, a **grain offering**, and a **drink offering** (reflecting the grape harvest). These two acts are to dedicate and celebrate the entire harvest as a blessing from God given to his people.

23:15–22 *The Weeks.* The Feast of Weeks begins **fifty days** after the **sheaf of the wave offering** is brought to the priest (vv. 15–16). This feast is also called "the Feast of the Harvest" (Ex. 23:16) and "the day of the firstfruits" (Num. 28:26); in the NT it is called "Pentecost" (Acts 2:1, from the Gk. word for "fiftieth"). The purpose of this celebration is to recognize the Lord as the provider of all crops and as the One who deserves the firstfruits of all produce. The added rule concerning the **harvest** (Lev. 23:22) is also in tune with the generosity that is expected of the people on this occasion. In v. 22 God commands Israel not to forget the less fortunate during a time of national celebration of abundance.

23:23–25 *The Trumpets.* The trumpet blasts and a solemn assembly on the **first day** of the **seventh month** call the people to prepare for the most sacred month of the Hebrew calendar. In addition, the day marks the end of one agricultural year and the beginning of another. Postexilic Judaism celebrates this day as Rosh Hashanah, i.e., New Year's Day.

27[n]ch. 16:29, 30; Num. 29:7
29[o]See Ex. 30:33
34[p]Num. 29:12; Deut. 16:13; Ezra 3:4; Neh. 8:14; Ezek. 45:25; Hos. 12:9; Zech. 14:16; John 7:2
36[q]Num. 29:35; Neh. 8:18; John 7:37 [r]Num. 29:35; Deut. 16:8; 2 Kgs. 10:20; 2 Chr. 7:9; Neh. 8:18; Isa. 1:13; Joel 1:14; 2:15; Amos 5:21
37[s]ver. 2, 4
38[t]Num. 29:39
39[u]Ex. 23:16; Deut. 16:13
40[v]See Neh. 8:14-18 [w]Deut. 16:14, 15
41[x]See Num. 29:12-38
42[y]See Neh. 8:14-18
43[z]See Deut. 31:10-13
44[a]ver. 2

Chapter 24
1[b]Ex. 27:20, 21
4[c]Ex. 31:8; 39:37

memorial proclaimed with blast of trumpets, a holy convocation. 25 You shall not do any
ordinary work, and you shall present a food offering to the LORD."

The Day of Atonement

26 And the LORD spoke to Moses, saying, 27 "Now [n]on the tenth day of this seventh month
is the Day of Atonement. It shall be for you a time of holy convocation, and you shall afflict
yourselves[1] and present a food offering to the LORD. 28 And you shall not do any work on
that very day, for it is a Day of Atonement, to make atonement for you before the LORD
your God. 29 For whoever is not afflicted on that very day [o]shall be cut off from his people.
30 And whoever does any work on that very day, that person I will destroy from among his
people. 31 You shall not do any work. It is a statute forever throughout your generations in
all your dwelling places. 32 It shall be to you a Sabbath of solemn rest, and you shall afflict
yourselves. On the ninth day of the month beginning at evening, from evening to evening
shall you keep your Sabbath."

The Feast of Booths

33 And the LORD spoke to Moses, saying, 34 "Speak to the people of Israel, saying, [p]On
the fifteenth day of this seventh month and for seven days is the Feast of Booths[2] to the
LORD. 35 On the first day shall be a holy convocation; you shall not do any ordinary work.
36 For seven days you shall present food offerings to the LORD. [q]On the eighth day you shall
hold a holy convocation and present a food offering to the LORD. It is a [r]solemn assembly;
you shall not do any ordinary work.

37 [s]"These are the appointed feasts of the LORD, which you shall proclaim as times of holy
convocation, for presenting to the LORD food offerings, burnt offerings and grain offerings,
sacrifices and drink offerings, each on its proper day, 38 [t]besides the LORD's Sabbaths and
besides your gifts and besides all your vow offerings and besides all your freewill offerings,
which you give to the LORD.

39 "On the fifteenth day of the seventh month, when you have [u]gathered in the produce
of the land, you shall celebrate the feast of the LORD seven days. On the first day shall be
a solemn rest, and on the eighth day shall be a solemn rest. 40 And [v]you shall take on the
first day the fruit of splendid trees, branches of palm trees and boughs of leafy trees and
willows of the brook, and [w]you shall rejoice before the LORD your God seven days. 41 [x]You
shall celebrate it as a feast to the LORD for seven days in the year. It is a statute forever
throughout your generations; you shall celebrate it in the seventh month. 42 [y]You shall
dwell in booths for seven days. All native Israelites shall dwell in booths, 43 that [z]your
generations may know that I made the people of Israel dwell in booths when I brought
them out of the land of Egypt: I am the LORD your God."

44 Thus Moses [a]declared to the people of Israel the appointed feasts of the LORD.

The Lamps

24 [b]The LORD spoke to Moses, saying, 2 "Command the people of Israel to bring you
pure oil from beaten olives for the lamp, that a light may be kept burning regularly.
3 Outside the veil of the testimony, in the tent of meeting, Aaron shall arrange it from
evening to morning before the LORD regularly. It shall be a statute forever throughout
your generations. 4 He shall arrange the lamps on the [c]lampstand of pure gold[3] before
the LORD regularly.

[1] Or *shall fast*; also verse 32 [2] Or *tabernacles* [3] Hebrew *the pure lampstand*

23:26–32 *The Day of Atonement.* The **Day of Atonement** is on the **tenth day** of the **seventh month**. The special nature of this feast is marked by **now** in v. 27. Although ch. 16 already prescribed the ritual and explained what the people were to do on that day, the emphasis here is on the people's afflicting themselves (see note on 16:29–34), **not** doing **any work**, and the possibility of punishment if they do not observe the regulations of this day.

23:33–36 *The Booths.* The **Feast of Booths** was a weeklong feast that began on the **fifteenth day** of the **seventh month**. Since it celebrates the people's salvation from Egypt, it was fitting for them to cease from work and to worship before the Lord.

23:37–44 *Summary of the Annual Feasts.* Judging from v. 38, **the appointed feasts** in v. 37 refers to the six feasts over and above the weekly Sabbath. The purpose of these feasts is to help the people remember the Lord and his work on their behalf and to worship him appropriately. Verses 37–38 summarize the festal calendar, but vv. 39–44 return to a discussion of the Feast of Booths. These verses may simply be a further elaboration because of the lack of detail in the earlier explanation of the festival.

24:1–9 *Oil and Bread of the Presence.* The placement of this text directly after a discussion of the Israelite festal calendar (ch. 23) appears peculiar. But its placement here may be to remind the Israelites not to forget the daily tabernacle activities in light of the annual festivals just discussed.

Bread for the Tabernacle

5 "You shall take fine flour and bake twelve [d]loaves from it; two tenths of an ephah[1] shall
be in each loaf. 6 And you shall set them in two piles, six in a pile, [e]on the table of pure
gold[2] before the LORD. 7 And you shall put pure frankincense on each pile, that it may go
with the bread as a memorial portion as a food offering to the LORD. 8 [f]Every Sabbath day
Aaron shall arrange it before the LORD regularly; it is from the people of Israel as a covenant
forever. 9 And [g]it shall be for Aaron and his sons, and [h]they shall eat it in a holy place, since
it is for him a most holy portion out of the LORD's food offerings, a perpetual due."

Punishment for Blasphemy

10 Now an Israelite woman's son, whose father was an Egyptian, went out among the
people of Israel. And the Israelite woman's son and a man of Israel fought in the camp,
11 and the Israelite woman's son [i]blasphemed the [j]Name, and cursed. Then they [k]brought
him to Moses. His mother's name was Shelomith, the daughter of Dibri, of the tribe of
Dan. 12 And [l]they put him in custody, [m]till the will of the LORD should be clear to them.
13 Then the LORD spoke to Moses, saying, 14 [n]"Bring out of the camp the one who cursed,
and let all who heard him [o]lay their hands on his head, and let all the congregation stone
him. 15 And speak to the people of Israel, saying, Whoever curses his God shall [p]bear his
sin. 16 Whoever [q]blasphemes the name of the LORD shall surely be put to death. All the
congregation shall stone him. The sojourner as well as the native, when he blasphemes
the Name, shall be put to death.

An Eye for an Eye

17 [r]"Whoever takes a human life shall surely be put to death. 18 [s]Whoever takes an animal's life shall make it good, life for life. 19 If anyone injures his neighbor, [t]as he has done
it shall be done to him, 20 fracture for fracture, eye for eye, tooth for tooth; whatever injury
he has given a person shall be given to him. 21 [s]Whoever kills an animal shall make it good,
[r]and whoever kills a person shall be put to death. 22 You shall have the [u]same rule for the
sojourner and for the native, for I am the LORD your God." 23 So Moses spoke to the people
of Israel, and [v]they brought out of the camp the one who had cursed and stoned him with
stones. Thus the people of Israel did as the LORD commanded Moses.

The Sabbath Year

25 [w]The LORD spoke to Moses on Mount Sinai, saying, 2 "Speak to the people of Israel
and say to them, When you come into [x]the land that I give you, the land shall keep
a Sabbath to the LORD. 3 For six years you shall sow your field, and for six years you shall
prune your vineyard and gather in its fruits, 4 but in the seventh year there shall be a Sabbath

[1] An *ephah* was about 3/5 bushel or 22 liters [2] Hebrew *the pure table*

5 [d]Ex. 25:30
6 [e]Ex. 25:23, 24; 1 Kgs. 7:48; 2 Chr. 4:19; 13:11; Heb. 9:2
8 [f]1 Chr. 9:32; [Num. 4:7; 2 Chr. 2:4]
9 [g]1 Sam. 21:6; Matt. 12:4; Mark 2:26; Luke 6:4 [h][ch. 6:16; 8:31; 21:22; Ex. 29:33]
11 [i]See ver. 16 [j][Ex. 3:14, 15; Phil. 2:9] [k]Ex. 18:22, 26
12 [l][Num. 15:34] [m][Ex. 18:15, 16; Num. 27:5; 36:5, 6]
14 [n][ver. 23] [o][Deut. 13:9; 17:7]
15 [p]ch. 5:1; 20:17, 20; 22:9; Num. 9:13; [Ex. 20:7]
16 [q]ver. 11; 1 Kgs. 21:10, 13; Matt. 26:65, 66; Mark 14:63, 64; John 10:33
17 [r]Gen. 9:5, 6; Ex. 21:12; Num. 35:31; Deut. 19:11, 12
18 [s]Ex. 21:33, 34
19 [t]Ex. 21:23-25; Deut. 19:21; Matt. 5:38; 7:2
21 [s][See ver. 18 above] [r][See ver. 17 above]
22 [u]ch. 19:34; Ex. 12:49; Num. 15:16
23 [v][ver. 14]

Chapter 25

1 [w]ch. 26:46
2 [x]Ex. 23:10, 11; [ch. 26:34, 35; 2 Chr. 36:21]

24:5–9 The **twelve loaves** symbolize the 12 tribes of Israel as they stand in the presence of God. In Ex. 25:30 they are called "the bread of the Presence." New loaves are to be set out on each Sabbath without exception. This is important because it is a sign of the covenant between the 12 tribes of Israel and God.

24:10–23 *The Case of a Blasphemer.* This section interrupts the flow of divine instructions with a narrative; it indicates the way in which many of the case laws in Israel arose, as responses to specific situations. It also shows how to apply these case laws in new situations that come up, by analogy with the existing laws.

24:10–12 The command against blaspheming God's name has already been given, in Ex. 20:7 and 22:28. It is dealt with again in the present passage for two reasons: first, no penalty for it was provided in the previous prohibitions; second, the one who blasphemes in this case is not a full-fledged Israelite. The man is placed under temporary guard until judgment is passed.

24:13–16 The culprit is to be stoned outside **the camp** (v. 14). The laying on of **hands** prior to the stoning has been commonly explained in such a way that the congregation, having overheard the curse and become defiled, devolves the guilt onto the culprit, and his death makes atonement for the guilt. Alternatively, it may be taken as a gesture simply to indicate who it is that had cursed **the name of the LORD**.

24:17–23 These verses deal with the principle of *lex talionis* (Latin, "the law of retribution"). It is a form of ironic justice in which the punishment for the crime is found in the crime itself. The principle applies to everyone in Israel without exception (see Ex. 21:23–25; Deut. 19:21). It is unlikely that **fracture for fracture, eye for eye, tooth for tooth** actually implies mutilation as the punishment for the offender; rather, the value of the injured member will be the imposed fine (cf. Ex. 21:18–19). This law, when properly applied, guides the judges in assessing damages and sets a limit on the thirst for revenge. Since this is a rule for judges to follow, it should not be invoked in ordinary daily relationships (cf. Jesus' stance, Matt. 5:38).

25:1–22 *The Sabbatical Year and Jubilee Year.* This section is a sequel to ch. 23, which primarily dealt with the Hebrew festal calendar. Added to that calendar are these two celebrations based on the Sabbath principle (i.e., one in seven). Israel is required to keep these holy times as a symbol that they are a holy people.

25:1–7 Every **seventh year** is a sabbatical year, and no agricultural activities should be engaged in. The personified **land** suggests that the land (more than the Israelites) needs to **rest**. The Israelites may work the land for six years, but there is to be no organized farming in the seventh year. This practice is clearly a benefit to the soil, but it is also a recognition that all produce belongs to God and that he bestows it freely on his people.

of solemn rest for the land, a Sabbath to the LORD. You shall not sow your field or prune
your vineyard. 5 [y]You shall not reap what grows of itself in your harvest, or gather the
grapes of your undressed vine. It shall be a year of solemn rest for the land. 6 The Sabbath
of the land[1] shall provide food for you, for yourself and for your male and female slaves[2]
and for your hired worker and the sojourner who lives with you, 7 and for your cattle and
for the wild animals that are in your land: [z]all its yield shall be for food.

The Year of Jubilee

8 "You shall count seven weeks[3] of years, seven times seven years, so that the time of
the seven weeks of years shall give you forty-nine years. 9 Then you shall sound [a]the loud
trumpet on the tenth day of the seventh month. [b]On the Day of Atonement you shall
sound the trumpet throughout all your land. 10 And you shall consecrate the fiftieth year,
and [c]proclaim liberty throughout the land to all its inhabitants. It shall be a jubilee for
you, when each of you shall return to his property and each of [d]you shall return to his clan.
11 That fiftieth year shall be a jubilee for you; in it [e]you shall neither sow nor reap [y]what
grows of itself nor gather the grapes from the undressed vines. 12 For it is a jubilee. It shall
be holy to you. [f]You may eat the produce of the field.[4]

13 [d]"In this year of jubilee each of you shall return to his property. 14 And if you make a
sale to your neighbor or buy from your neighbor, [g]you shall not wrong one another. 15 [h]You
shall pay your neighbor according to the number of years after the jubilee, and he shall
sell to you according to the number of years for crops. 16 If the years are many, you shall
increase the price, and if the years are few, you shall reduce the price, for it is the number
of the crops that he is selling to you. 17 [i]You shall not wrong one another, but you shall
fear your God, for I am the LORD your God.

18 [j]"Therefore you shall do my statutes and keep my rules and perform them, and then
[k]you will dwell in the land securely. 19 [l]The land will yield its fruit, and [m]you will eat your
fill [k]and dwell in it securely. 20 And if you say, [n]'What shall we eat in the seventh year, if
[o]we may not sow or gather in our crop?' 21 I will [p]command my blessing on you in the
sixth year, so that it will produce a crop sufficient for three years. 22 [q]When you sow in the
eighth year, you will be eating some of [r]the old crop; you shall eat the old until the ninth
year, when its crop arrives.

Redemption of Property

23 "The land shall not be sold in perpetuity, for [s]the land is mine. For you are strangers
and sojourners with me. 24 And in all the country you possess, you shall allow a redemption of the land.

25 "If your brother becomes poor and sells part of his property, [t]then his nearest redeemer
shall come and redeem what his brother has sold. 26 If a man has no one to redeem it and

[1] That is, the Sabbath produce of the land [2] Or *servants* [3] Or *Sabbaths* [4] Or *countryside*

5 [y][2 Kgs. 19:29]; Isa. 37:30
7 [z]ver. 12
9 [a][ch. 23:24; Isa. 27:13] [b]ch. 23:24, 27
10 [c]Isa. 61:1; Jer. 34:8, 13, 15, 17; Ezek. 46:17; [Isa. 61:2; 63:4; Luke 4:19] [d]ch. 27:24; Num. 36:4
11 [e]ver. 4, 5 [y][See ver. 5 above]
12 [f]ver. 6, 7
13 [d][See ver. 10 above]
14 [g][ch. 19:33]
15 [h]ch. 27:18, 23
17 [i]ver. 36, 43; ch. 19:14, 32
18 [j]See ch. 18:4, 5 [k]ch. 26:5, 6; Deut. 12:10; [Prov. 1:33; Jer. 23:6; Ezek. 34:25, 28]
19 [l]Ps. 85:12; Ezek. 34:26, 27 [m]ch. 26:5; Deut. 11:15; [Joel 2:19, 26] [k][See ver. 18 above]
20 [n][Matt. 6:25, 31; Luke 12:22, 29] [o]ver. 4, 5
21 [p]Deut. 28:8
22 [q][2 Kgs. 19:29] [r]ch. 26:10
23 [s]Deut. 32:43; 2 Chr. 7:20; Ps. 85:1; Hos. 9:3; Joel 2:18; 3:2
25 [t]Ruth 2:20; 3:9, 12; 4:4, 6; Jer. 32:7, 8

25:8–12 The Hebrew word *yobel*, **jubilee** (v. 10), is related to a term that means "ram" or "ram's horn." The ram's horn (or **trumpet**) is to be sounded throughout Israel on the **Day of Atonement** to announce the beginning of the fiftieth year (v. 9). Jubilee is a year of release and **liberty** (v. 10). In that year, people are to **return** to their land possession, i.e., their ancestral **property** (v. 10). Israelites who sold themselves to indenture are also to be released and sent home. This provided a periodic restoration of the means to earn a living for each family in an agrarian society. (The jubilee did not equalize all possessions in Israel, however, since possessions such as cattle and money were not reallocated.) The prohibitions of the jubilee are the same as for the sabbatical year. The land is to lie fallow for two years in a row: the forty-ninth year (sabbatical year) and the fiftieth year (jubilee). This law prohibits the amassing of large estates, which would reduce many Israelites to tenant status on their ancestral land (cf. Isa. 5:8).

25:13–17 Basic guidelines for business are given. In selling or purchasing **property**, the **price** must be calculated according to how many **years** have passed since the jubilee, since it is not the estate itself that is to be sold or purchased but the amount of **crops** that can be harvested before the next jubilee. Since all the Israelites eventually **return** to their inherited land, the act of selling agricultural land essentially means leasing it (but see vv. 29–31 for land that could be sold permanently). The injunction **you shall not wrong one another** (vv. 14, 17) is idiomatic for the economic oppression of the poor and needy (cf. 19:33). There is to be no exploitation of fellow Israelites in land transactions.

25:18–22 This is an exhortation to keep God's law, which will bring rich blessings. These blessings include security in the land against external threats (vv. 18–19). God also promises to supply enough food during years of agricultural activity to cover periods in which the land lies fallow, such as during the sabbatical year (vv. 21–22).

25:23–55 *Laws of Redemption.* This section deals with the concept of redemption. If a person gets into difficulty or danger, then a relative (his "nearest redeemer," v. 25) is to redeem him from his dire straits (see note on Ruth 3:12–13). The various methods of redemption are explained.

25:23–24 The land is the Lord's, so one cannot sell his inherited land as though it were his permanent possession. The status of the Israelites is that of **strangers and sojourners with** the Lord. Thus they are tenants, so to speak, in the Promised Land. This principle is later applied to the believer's existence in this world (cf. Ps. 39:12; 1 Pet. 2:11).

25:25–28 If an Israelite is forced to sell his land temporarily, he and his family retain the right of redemption. The land may be redeemed in one

then himself becomes prosperous and finds sufficient means to redeem it, 27 let [u]him calculate the years since he sold it and pay back the balance to the man to whom he sold it,
and then return to his property. 28 But if he does not have sufficient means to recover it,
then what he sold shall remain in the hand of the buyer until the year of jubilee. In the
jubilee it shall [v]be released, and [w]he shall return to his property.
29 "If a man sells a dwelling house in a walled city, he may redeem it within a year of its
sale. For a full year he shall have the right of redemption. 30 If it is not redeemed within a
full year, then the house in the walled city shall belong in perpetuity to the buyer, throughout his generations; [v]it shall not be released in the jubilee. 31 But the houses of the villages
that have no wall around them shall be classified with the fields of the land. They may
be redeemed, and [v]they shall be released in the jubilee. 32 As for [x]the cities of the Levites,
the Levites may redeem at any time the houses in the cities they possess. 33 And if one of
the Levites exercises his right of redemption, then the house that was sold in a city they
possess shall be released in the jubilee. For the houses in the cities of the Levites are their
possession among the people of Israel. 34 But the fields [y]of pastureland belonging to their
cities may not be sold, for that is their possession forever.

Kindness for Poor Brothers

35 "If your brother becomes poor and cannot maintain himself with you, [z]you shall support him as though he were a stranger and a sojourner, and he shall live with you. 36 [a]Take
no interest from him or profit, but [b]fear your God, that your brother may live beside you.
37 [a]You shall not lend him your money at interest, nor give him your food for profit. 38 [c]I
am the LORD your God, who brought you out of the land of Egypt to give you the land
of Canaan, and to be your God.
39 [d]"If your brother becomes poor beside you and sells himself to you, you shall not
make him serve as a slave: 40 he shall be with you as a hired worker and as a sojourner. He
shall serve with you until the year of the jubilee. 41 [v]Then he shall go out from you, [e]he and
his children with him, and go back to his own clan and return [f]to the possession of his
fathers. 42 For they are [g]my servants,[1] whom I brought out of the land of Egypt; they shall
not be sold as slaves. 43 [h]You shall not rule over him [i]ruthlessly but [j]shall fear your God.
44 As for your male and female slaves whom you may have: you may buy male and female
slaves from among the nations that are around you. 45 [k]You may also buy from among the
strangers who sojourn with you and their clans that are with you, who have been born in
your land, and they may be your property. 46 You may bequeath them to your sons after
you to inherit as a possession forever. You may make slaves of them, but over your brothers
the people of Israel [l]you shall not rule, one over another ruthlessly.

Redeeming a Poor Man

47 "If a stranger or sojourner with you becomes rich, and [m]your brother beside him
becomes poor and sells himself to the stranger or sojourner with you or to a member of
the stranger's clan, 48 then after he is sold he may be redeemed. One of his brothers may
redeem him, 49 or his uncle or his cousin may [n]redeem him, or a close relative from his
clan may redeem him. Or if he [o]grows rich he may redeem himself. 50 He shall calculate
with his buyer from the year when he sold himself to him until the year of jubilee, and

[1] Hebrew *slaves*

27 [u]See ver. 50-52
28 [v]ch. 27:21 [w]ver. 13, 41
30 [v][See ver. 28 above]
31 [v][See ver. 28 above]
32 [x][Num. 35:2]; See Josh. 21:2-40
34 [y]Num. 35:2; 1 Chr. 13:2; [Acts 4:36, 37]; See Josh. 21:11-42; 1 Chr. 6:55-81
35 [z]Deut. 15:7, 8; [Ps. 41:1; 112:5, 9; Prov. 14:31; Acts 11:29; 1 John 3:17]
36 [a]See Ex. 22:25 [b]ver. 17, 43; Neh. 5:9; [Mal. 3:5]
37 [a][See ver. 36 above]
38 [c]ver. 42, 55; ch. 22:32, 33; 26:13
39 [d]Ex. 21:2; Deut. 15:12; 1 Kgs. 9:22; 2 Kgs. 4:1; Neh. 5:5
41 [v][See ver. 28 above] [e][Ex. 21:3] [f]ver. 13, 28
42 [g]ver. 55; [Rom. 6:22; 1 Cor. 7:23]
43 [h][Eph. 6:9; Col. 4:1] [i]Ex. 1:13, 14; Ezek. 34:4 [j]ver. 17, 36
45 [k]Isa. 14:1, 2; 56:3, 6
46 [l]Ex. 1:13, 14; Ezek. 34:4
47 [m]ver. 25, 35, 39
49 [n]See Neh. 5:1-5 [o]ver. 26, 47

of three ways: (1) a kinsman-redeemer buys back the land; (2) the seller himself is able to buy it back; or (3) it is restored to the rightful owner at the **jubilee**.

25:29–34 Houses in **walled** cities are not regulated by rights of **redemption** as are houses in unwalled **villages**. The former are not released at the jubilee, and their redemption is for only one year (not in perpetuity). Why this distinction is made is uncertain, although it may be that houses in walled settlements are considered privately owned, rather than part of a tribal inheritance. One exception to the rule is that houses belonging to **Levites** in their cities carry full rights of redemption.

25:35–38 Israelites are to show mercy to one another because they are recipients of God's mercy.

25:39–46 A further predicament is envisaged, namely, that an Israelite, becoming impoverished, had to sell himself to a fellow Israelite. In this case the poor man must not be treated like an ordinary **slave** (v. 39) but as a **hired worker** and a **sojourner** (v. 40). His right to return to his house at the **jubilee** means that he has sold just his labor, and not his status as a free Israelite, to his fellow Israelite. **ruthlessly** (vv. 43, 46). Treating a fellow Israelite like a slave is prohibited by language echoing the Israelites' hard labor in Egypt (cf. Ex. 1:13).

25:47–55 A Hebrew in dire financial straits may indenture himself to a **stranger or sojourner** in the land. Yet the Israelite retains his right of redemption. He may be **redeemed** by a kinsman or he may redeem himself if he gains sufficient means (vv. 48–49). In addition, his indenture ceases at the **jubilee** (v. 54). These verses demonstrate that the sojourner is required to keep the laws of Israel while residing in the land.

the price of his sale shall vary with the number of years. The time he was with his owner
shall be [p]rated as the time of a hired worker. 51 If there are still many years left, he shall
pay proportionately for his redemption some of his sale price. 52 If there remain but a few
years until the year of jubilee, he shall calculate and pay for his redemption in proportion
to his years of service. 53 He shall treat him as a worker hired year by year. [l]He shall not
rule ruthlessly over him in your sight. 54 And if he is not redeemed by these means, then
[q]he and his children with him shall be released in the year of jubilee. 55 For it is [r]to me that
the people of Israel are servants.[1] They are my servants whom I brought out of the land of
Egypt: I am the LORD your God.

Blessings for Obedience

26 "You shall not make [s]idols for yourselves or erect an [t]image or [u]pillar, and you shall
not set up a [v]figured stone in your land to bow down to it, for I am the LORD your
God. 2 [w]You shall keep my Sabbaths and reverence my sanctuary: I am the LORD.
3 [x]"If you walk in my statutes and observe my commandments and do them, 4 then [y]I will
give you your rains in their season, and the land shall yield its increase, and the trees of
the field shall yield their fruit. 5 [z]Your threshing shall last to the time of the grape harvest,
and the grape harvest shall last to the time for sowing. And [a]you shall eat your bread to
the full and [b]dwell in your land securely. 6 [c]I will give peace in the land, and [d]you shall lie
down, and none shall make you afraid. And [e]I will remove harmful beasts from the land,
[f]and the sword shall not go through your land. 7 You shall chase your enemies, and they
shall fall before you by the sword. 8 [g]Five of you shall chase a hundred, and a hundred of
you shall chase ten thousand, and your enemies shall fall before you by the sword. 9 [h]I will
turn to you and [i]make you fruitful and multiply you and will confirm my covenant with
you. 10 You shall eat [j]old store long kept, and you shall clear out the old to make way for
the new. 11 [k]I will make my dwelling[2] among you, and my soul shall not abhor you. 12 [l]And
I [m]will walk among you and will be your God, and you shall be my people. 13 [n]I am the
LORD your God, who brought you out of the land of Egypt, that you should not be their
slaves. [o]And I have broken the bars of your yoke and made you walk erect.

Punishment for Disobedience

14 [p]"But if you will not listen to me and will not do all these commandments, 15 if you
spurn my statutes, and if your soul abhors my rules, so that you will not do all my commandments, but [q]break my covenant, 16 then I will do this to you: I will visit you with
panic, with [r]wasting disease and fever that consume the eyes and make the heart ache. And
[s]you shall sow your seed in vain, for your enemies shall eat it. 17 I will [t]set my face against
you, and [u]you shall be struck down before your enemies. [v]Those who hate you shall rule
over you, and [w]you shall flee when none pursues you. 18 And if in spite of this you will not
listen to me, then I will discipline you again [x]sevenfold for your sins, 19 and I will break [y]the
pride of your power, and I [z]will make your heavens like iron and your earth like bronze.
20 And [a]your strength shall be spent in vain, for [b]your land shall not yield its increase, and
the trees of the land shall not yield their fruit.
21 [c]"Then if you walk contrary to me and will not listen to me, I will continue striking

[1] Or *slaves* [2] Hebrew *tabernacle*

50 [p]Job 7:1; Isa. 16:14; 21:16
53 [l][See ver. 46 above]
54 [q]ver. 41; Ex. 21:2, 3
55 [r]ver. 42

Chapter 26

1 [s]See ch. 19:4 [t]See Ex. 20:4, 5 [u]Ex. 23:24 [v]Num. 33:52; [Ezek. 8:10]
2 [w]ch. 19:30; See Ex. 20:8
3 [x]Deut. 11:13-15; 28:1-14; See ch. 18:4
4 [y]Ps. 67:6; 85:12; Ezek. 34:26, 27; 36:30; Joel 2:23, 24; Zech. 8:12; [ver. 20; Deut. 11:17]
5 [z][Amos 9:13] [a]See ch. 25:19 [b]See ch. 25:18
6 [c][1 Kgs. 4:25; 1 Chr. 22:9] [d]Job 11:19; Jer. 30:10; Zeph. 3:13 [e]Ezek. 34:25; [2 Kgs. 17:25; Isa. 35:9; Ezek. 5:17; 14:15] [f][Ezek. 14:17]
8 [g][Deut. 32:30; Josh. 23:10; Isa. 30:17]
9 [h]2 Kgs. 13:23 [i]Neh. 9:23
10 [j]ch. 25:22
11 [k]Ezek. 37:26-28; [Rev. 21:3]
12 [l]Ex. 29:45; Cited 2 Cor. 6:16 [m]Jer. 7:23; 11:4; 24:7; 30:22; Ezek. 11:20; 14:11; 36:28; 37:27; See Ex. 6:7
13 [n]See ch. 25:38 [o]Ezek. 34:27; [Jer. 27:2; 28:10, 13]
14 [p][Lam. 2:17; Mal. 2:2]; See Deut. 28:15-68
15 [q]ver. 44; Deut. 31:20
16 [r]Deut. 28:21 [s]Deut. 28:33, 51; Job 31:8; Jer. 5:17; Mic. 6:15
17 [t]See ch. 17:10 [u]Deut. 28:25; Judg. 2:14; Jer. 19:7 [v]Ps. 106:41 [w]Prov. 28:1; [ver. 36; Ps. 53:5]
18 [x]ver. 21, 24, 28; 1 Sam. 2:5; Ps. 119:164; Prov. 24:16
19 [y]Ezek. 30:6; [Jer. 13:9] [z]Deut. 28:23
20 [a][Ps. 127:1; Isa. 49:4] [b][Hag. 1:10]; See ver. 4
21 [c]ver. 27

26:1–46 *Blessings and Curses.* A principal element of a covenant document is a section of sanctions, i.e., blessings and curses that are dependent on how one keeps the covenant agreement. Often they appear at the close of a covenant document, and there they enumerate the sovereign's granting of rewards or punishments based on the vassal's obedience or disobedience. Verses 1–13 display the blessings if Israel obeys the covenant; vv. 14–39 pronounce curses.

26:1–2 *Fundamental Conditions.* These verses remind Israel what is at the heart of Israelite law: fidelity to God and the keeping of the Sabbath.

26:3–13 *Blessings for Obedience.* If Israel is faithful to the Word of God, then blessings of abundance will be theirs: rain, abundant crops, rich harvest, and protection from enemies (vv. 4–10). In addition, God will **make** them **fruitful and multiply** them (v. 9; cf. Gen. 1:28; 28:3; 35:11). All these blessings are visible manifestations of the Lord's presence (Lev. 26:11–12) as the Israelites live out their privilege as God's new humanity.

26:11–12 The apostle Paul uses these verses to describe the privileges of God's people as his temple (2 Cor. 6:16).

26:14–17 *The First Stage.* The reverse side of the blessings in vv. 4–7 is set out as punishment. **your soul abhors** (v. 15). The phrase appeared in v. 11, and here it refers to the Israelites' inner attitude to the Lord's commandments, and thus to the Lord himself.

26:18–20 *The Second Stage.* If the people continue to walk in disobedience, the Lord will target their **pride** and **power** by stopping the rain. **sevenfold** (v. 18). Rather than "seven times," it means "fully" or "completely." If the Hebrews refuse to alter their behavior as a result of the first series of judgments, these punishments will be added.

26:21–22 *The Third Stage.* This time the people's hardness of heart will be

you, sevenfold for your sins. 22 And [d]I will let loose the wild beasts against you, which shall
bereave you of your children and destroy your livestock and make you few in number, so
that [e]your roads shall be deserted.
23 "And [f]if by this discipline you are not turned to me [c]but walk contrary to me, 24 [g]then
I also will walk contrary to you, and I myself will strike you sevenfold for your sins. 25 And
[h]I will bring a sword upon you, that shall execute vengeance for the covenant. And if you
gather within your cities, [i]I will send pestilence among you, and you shall be delivered
into the hand of the enemy. 26 [j]When I break your supply[1] of bread, ten women shall bake
your bread in a single oven and shall dole out your bread again by weight, and [k]you shall
eat and not be satisfied.
27 "But [l]if in spite of this you will not listen to me, but walk contrary to me, 28 then I
will walk contrary to you [m]in fury, and I myself will discipline you [x]sevenfold for your
sins. 29 [n]You shall eat the flesh of your sons, and you shall eat the flesh of your daughters.
30 And [o]I will destroy your high places and cut down your incense altars and [p]cast your
dead bodies upon the dead bodies of your idols, and my soul will abhor you. 31 And I
will [q]lay your cities waste and will [r]make your sanctuaries desolate, and [s]I will not smell
your pleasing aromas. 32 And [t]I myself will devastate the land, so that your enemies who
settle in it shall be [u]appalled at it. 33 And [v]I will scatter you among the nations, and I will
unsheathe the sword after you, and your land shall be a desolation, and your cities shall
be a waste.
34 [w]"Then the land shall enjoy[2] its Sabbaths as long as it lies desolate, while you are in
your enemies' land; then the land shall rest, and enjoy its Sabbaths. 35 As long as it lies
desolate it shall have rest, the rest that it did not have on your Sabbaths when you were
dwelling in it. 36 And as for those of you who are left, [x]I will send faintness into their hearts
in the lands of their enemies. The [y]sound of a [z]driven leaf shall put them to flight, and they
shall flee as one flees from the sword, and they shall fall when none pursues. 37 They shall
stumble over one another, as if to escape a sword, though none pursues. And [a]you shall
have no power to stand before your enemies. 38 And you shall perish among the nations,
and the land of your enemies shall eat you up. 39 And those of you who are left shall [b]rot
away in your enemies' lands because of their iniquity, and also because of the iniquities
of their fathers they shall rot away like them.
40 "But if [c]they confess their iniquity and the iniquity of their fathers in their treachery that
they [d]committed against me, and also in walking contrary to me, 41 so that I walked contrary
to them and brought them into the land of their enemies—if then their [e]uncircumcised
heart is [f]humbled and they make amends for their iniquity, 42 then I will [g]remember my
covenant with Jacob, and I will remember my covenant with Isaac and my covenant with
Abraham, and I will [h]remember the land. 43 But [w]the land shall be abandoned by them and
enjoy its Sabbaths while it lies desolate without them, and they shall make amends for
their iniquity, because they spurned my rules and their soul abhorred my statutes. 44 Yet
for all that, when they are in the land of their enemies, [i]I will not spurn them, neither
will I abhor them so as to destroy them utterly and [j]break my covenant with them, for
I am the LORD their God. 45 But I will for their sake remember the covenant with their
forefathers, [k]whom I brought out of the land of Egypt [l]in the sight of the nations, that I
might be their God: I am the LORD."
46 [m]These are the statutes and rules and laws that the LORD made between himself and
the people of Israel through Moses [n]on Mount Sinai.

[1] Hebrew *staff* [2] Or *pay for*; twice in this verse; also verse 43

22 [d]Deut. 32:24; See ver. 6 [e]Judg. 5:6; Isa. 33:8; Lam. 1:4; Zech. 7:14
23 [f]Jer. 2:30; 5:3; See Amos 4:6-12 [c][See ver. 21 above]
24 [g]2 Sam. 22:27; Ps. 18:26
25 [h]Deut. 32:25; Jer. 14:12; 24:10; 29:17, 18; Ezek. 5:17; 6:3; 14:17; 29:8; 33:2 [i]Num. 14:12; Deut. 28:21
26 [j]Ps. 105:16; Isa. 3:1; Ezek. 4:16; 5:16; 14:13 [k]Isa. 9:20; Mic. 6:14; Hag. 1:6
27 [l]ver. 21, 24
28 [m]Isa. 59:18; 63:3; 66:15; Jer. 21:5; Ezek. 5:13, 15; 8:18 [x][See ver. 18 above]
29 [n]Deut. 28:53; Ezek. 5:10; [2 Kgs. 6:29; Lam. 4:10]
30 [o]2 Chr. 14:5; 34:3, 4, 7; See Ezek. 6:3-6 [p][2 Kgs. 23:20; 2 Chr. 34:5; Ezek. 6:5]
31 [q]Neh. 2:3; Jer. 4:7; See 2 Kgs. 25:4-10 [r]Ps. 74:7; Lam. 1:10; Ezek. 9:6; 21:2 [s]Jer. 6:20; See Isa. 1:11-15; Amos 5:21-23
32 [t]Jer. 9:11; 25:11, 18 [u]Deut. 28:37; 1 Kgs. 9:8; Jer. 18:16; 19:8; Ezek. 5:15
33 [v]Deut. 4:27; 28:64; Neh. 1:8; Ps. 44:11; Jer. 9:16; Ezek. 12:15; 20:23; 22:15; Zech. 7:14; [Luke 21:24]
34 [w]2 Chr. 36:21; See ch. 25:2
36 [x]Ezek. 21:7 [y]ver. 17 [z]Job 13:25
37 [a]Josh. 7:12, 13; Judg. 2:14
39 [b]Deut. 28:65; Ezek. 4:17; 24:23; 33:10; [Ezek. 6:9]
40 [c][Neh. 9:2; Prov. 28:13; 1 John 1:9]; See 1 Kgs. 8:33-36; Dan. 9:4-19 [d]ch. 6:2; Num. 5:6
41 [e]See Ex. 6:12 [f][1 Kgs. 21:29; 2 Chr. 12:6, 7; 32:26; 33:12, 13]
42 [g]Ex. 2:24; 6:5; Ps. 106:45; Ezek. 16:60 [h][Ps. 85:1]
43 [w][See ver. 34 above]
44 [i][Deut. 4:31; 2 Kgs. 13:23; Neh. 9:31; Rom. 11:2] [j]ver. 15
45 [k]ch. 22:33 [l]Ps. 98:2; Ezek. 20:9, 22
46 [m]ch. 27:34; Deut. 6:1; 12:1 [n]ch. 25:1

punished by **wild beasts** (cf. v. 6). From this section onward, the idea of walking **contrary to** the Lord (v. 21) appears frequently (vv. 23, 27, 40; cf. the complementary judgment theme of the Lord's walking contrary to them: vv. 24, 28, 41).

26:23–26 *The Fourth Stage.* This stage is characterized by the Lord's wrath that manifests itself in the sending of **sword** and **pestilence** on the people (cf. vv. 5–6, 8). For the first time, the deliverance of the people **into the hand of the enemy** is mentioned.

26:27–39 *The Fifth Stage.* This is the final set of curses. Intensification is clear in this last series as the people continue in their stubbornness and God increases his punishments. The final place for the covenant breakers will be in exile (v. 34).

26:27–33 The punishment includes an unbelievable form of cannibalism and the destruction of the religious centers, the **cities**, and the **land**. The Lord's wrath is actually carried out by the people's **enemies**.

26:34–39 All of this is followed by the Lord's ironical judgment that the evacuation of the people brings about a **rest** for the **land** (cf. 25:2–7). Once the covenant breakers are gone, then the land will **enjoy its Sabbaths**

Chapter 27
2[o][Judg. 11:30, 31, 39; 1 Sam. 1:11, 28; See Num. 30]
3[p]ver. 25; See Ex. 30:13
10[q]ver. 33
13[r]ver. 15, 19 [s]ch. 22:14
15[t]ver. 13 [s][See ver. 13 above]
18[u]ver. 23; ch. 25:15, 16
19[v]ver. 13 [s][See ver. 13 above]
21[w]ch. 25:28, 30, 31, 33, 41 [x]ver. 28 [y]Num. 18:14; Ezek. 44:29
22[z]ch. 25:10, 25
23[a]ver. 18
24[b]ch. 25:28

Laws About Vows

27 The LORD spoke to Moses, saying, **2** "Speak to the people of Israel and say to them,
If anyone [o]makes a special vow to the LORD involving the valuation of persons,
3 then the valuation of a male from twenty years old up to sixty years old shall be fifty
shekels[1] of silver, according to the [p]shekel of the sanctuary. **4** If the person is a female, the
valuation shall be thirty shekels. **5** If the person is from five years old up to twenty years
old, the valuation shall be for a male twenty shekels, and for a female ten shekels. **6** If
the person is from a month old up to five years old, the valuation shall be for a male five
shekels of silver, and for a female the valuation shall be three shekels of silver. **7** And if the
person is sixty years old or over, then the valuation for a male shall be fifteen shekels, and
for a female ten shekels. **8** And if someone is too poor to pay the valuation, then he shall
be made to stand before the priest, and the priest shall value him; the priest shall value
him according to what the vower can afford.

9 "If the vow[2] is an animal that may be offered as an offering to the LORD, all of it that
he gives to the LORD is holy. **10** [q]He shall not exchange it or make a substitute for it, good
for bad, or bad for good; and if he does in fact substitute one animal for another, then
both it and the substitute shall be holy. **11** And if it is any unclean animal that may not be
offered as an offering to the LORD, then he shall stand the animal before the priest, **12** and
the priest shall value it as either good or bad; as the priest values it, so it shall be. **13** [r]But if
he wishes to redeem it, he shall add a [s]fifth to the valuation.

14 "When a man dedicates his house as a holy gift to the LORD, the priest shall value it
as either good or bad; as the priest values it, so it shall stand. **15** [t]And if the donor wishes to
redeem his house, he shall add a [s]fifth to the valuation price, and it shall be his.

16 "If a man dedicates to the LORD part of the land that is his possession, then the valuation shall be in proportion to its seed. A homer[3] of barley seed shall be valued at fifty
shekels of silver. **17** If he dedicates his field from the year of jubilee, the valuation shall
stand, **18** but if he dedicates his field after the jubilee, then the priest shall [u]calculate the
price according to the years that remain until the year of jubilee, and a deduction shall be
made from the valuation. **19** [v]And if he who dedicates the field wishes to redeem it, then
he shall add a [s]fifth to its valuation price, and it shall remain his. **20** But if he does not wish
to redeem the field, or if he has sold the field to another man, it shall not be redeemed
anymore. **21** But the field, [w]when it is released in the jubilee, shall be a holy gift to the LORD,
like a field that has been [x]devoted. The priest shall be in [y]possession of it. **22** If he dedicates
to the LORD a field that he has bought, [z]which is not a part of his possession, **23** [a]then the
priest shall calculate the amount of the valuation for it up to the year of jubilee, and the
man shall give the valuation on that day as a holy gift to the LORD. **24** [b]In the year of jubilee
the field shall return to him from whom it was bought, to whom the land belongs as a

[1] A *shekel* was about 2/5 ounce or 11 grams [2] Hebrew *it* [3] A *homer* was about 6 bushels or 220 liters

(26:34). The verb "enjoy" is commonly used in reference to either God or man, but here it is employed as a personification. In this way, the land will be purified and will recover its holiness.

26:40–46 *Conditions and Confession within the Covenant.* God's rejection of Israel is not final. If the people repent, confess their sins, and walk humbly before God, then he will deliver them from exile and restore them to the Land of Promise. The people, however, have an **uncircumcised heart** (v. 41); this means that although the Israelites are circumcised in the flesh, their hearts are actually like the hearts of the pagan peoples.

27:1–34 *Vows and Dedication.* This final chapter of Leviticus sets out the means of redemption as it relates to vows made to the Lord and his sanctuary. The material appears to be an appendix or addendum to the book; it does not fit smoothly with the content of the previous Holiness Code. This does not mean that the chapter was added at a later time, but it was placed here at the end to underscore the importance of funding the sanctuary.

27:1–8 *The Case of Persons.* In Israel, a man may make a **vow** to the Lord dedicating himself or a member of his family. This pledge entails service in the sanctuary. However, because non-Levites cannot serve on the temple grounds, a person may be freed from this service by making a payment to the sanctuary. These verses establish the payment scale, perhaps determined by the customary prices for slaves.

27:9–13 *The Case of Animals.* One of the vows a man can make is to donate a clean **animal** to the sanctuary. No redemption of the animal is permitted once the animal has been donated. A person may also contribute an **unclean animal** for the service of the tabernacle. It is, however, not to be sacrificed. The priests may sell it in the markets and use the money for the sanctuary. If the original owner tries to buy it back, it will cost him 20 percent more than its **valuation** by the priests.

27:14–15 *The Case of a House.* This is a more expensive donation than that of an animal. Its value is estimated by the **priest**; to **redeem** it one must **add**, as in the animal case, **a fifth** to the value.

27:16–25 *The Case of Land.* Dedication of **land** is divided into two cases, that of inherited land (vv. 16–21) and that of purchased land (vv. 22–25). Since the land belongs to the Lord, only the crops can be donated to the Lord (which, in practice, means donating them to the priests). Hence the rules on the **jubilee** year apply as necessary (vv. 17–18; see 25:15–16). If the donor

possession. 25 Every valuation shall be according to [c]the shekel of the sanctuary: [d]twenty
gerahs[1] shall make a shekel.
26 "But a [e]firstborn of animals, which as a firstborn belongs to the LORD, no man may
dedicate; whether ox or sheep, it is the LORD's. 27 And if it is an unclean animal, then he
shall buy it back at the valuation, [f]and add a fifth to it; or, if it is not redeemed, it shall be
sold at the valuation.
28 "But [g]no devoted thing that a man devotes to the LORD, of anything that he has,
whether man or beast, or of his inherited field, shall be sold or redeemed; every devoted
thing is most holy to the LORD. 29 [h]No one devoted, who is to be devoted for destruction[2]
from mankind, shall be ransomed; he shall surely be put to death.
30 [i]"Every tithe of the land, whether of the seed of the land or of the fruit of the trees, is
the LORD's; it is holy to the LORD. 31 If a man wishes to redeem some of his tithe, he shall
add a fifth to it. 32 And every tithe of herds and flocks, every tenth animal of all that [j]pass
under the herdsman's staff, shall be holy to the LORD. 33 One shall not differentiate between
good or bad, [k]neither shall he make a substitute for it; and if he does substitute for it, then
both it and the substitute shall be holy; it shall not be redeemed."
34 [l]These are the commandments that the LORD commanded Moses for the people of
Israel [m]on Mount Sinai.

[1] A *gerah* was about 1/50 ounce or 0.6 gram [2] That is, set apart (devoted) as an offering to the Lord (for destruction)

25 [c]ver. 3 [d]See Ex. 30:13
26 [e]See Ex. 13:2
27 [f]ver. 11-13
28 [g]ver. 21; Josh. 6:17-19; 1 Sam. 15:21
29 [h][Num. 21:2; Judg. 11:35]
30 [i]Gen. 14:20; 28:22; Num. 18:21, 24; Deut. 14:28; 2 Chr. 31:5, 6, 12; Neh. 13:12; Mal. 3:8, 10
32 [j]Ezek. 20:37; [Jer. 33:13]
33 [k]ver. 10
34 [l]ch. 26:46 [m]ch. 25:1; 26:46

does not redeem the land when the Jubilee comes, then he forfeits the land to the priesthood. It becomes a binding donation.

27:26–27 *The Case of the Firstborn.* The **firstborn** of **man** or animal cannot be made the subject of a vow because the firstborn already **belongs to the LORD** (Ex. 13:2; 34:19–20).

27:28–29 *The Case of Devoted Things.* The **devoted thing** (Hb. *kherem*) belonged irreversibly to the Lord and could not be **ransomed**. This kind of devoting was part of Israel's war against the Canaanites (see notes on Deut. 2:34–35; Josh. 6:17); a blasphemer or idolater could also be devoted (Ex. 22:20; Deut. 13:15). Probably only recognized leaders had the authority to pronounce such a sentence.

27:30–33 *The Case of Tithes.* The **tithe** is already the Lord's; this law allows the rules for ordinary vows to govern the tithes as well (cf. vv. 9–13).

27:34 *Postscript.* The phrase **on Mount Sinai** appeared in 25:1 and 26:46, giving the impression that just chs. 25–27 were spoken on Mount Sinai. But the semantic range of **commandments** (Hb. *mitswot*), which probably includes "rules and statutes" (cf. 26:14–15), suggests that this verse refers to the entire content of Leviticus.

INTRODUCTION TO

NUMBERS

Author, Date, and Title

The composition of Numbers cannot be discussed just on its own, as it is an integral part of the Pentateuch, so for a fuller review see Introduction to the Pentateuch, pp. 35–37. The evidence for the authorship of Numbers itself fits in easily with the position suggested there. Moses himself is said to have written chapter 33 (Israel's wilderness itinerary). He is also said to have received the many laws Numbers contains.

Some have objected, however, that the narrator does not seem to be Moses himself; comments like "the man Moses was very meek" (12:3) seem to suggest this is biography rather than autobiography. In reply, it is fair to observe that clues as to when the book was written are sparse, but there are many indications of its antiquity.

These indications consist of similar texts, customs, or artifacts from places or periods close to the time of Moses and the wilderness wanderings. For example, a copper snake was found in a tent shrine at Timna dating from the twelfth century B.C. The snake makes one think of the episode in 21:4–9, and the tent shrine recalls the tabernacle. In the Jordan Valley an inscription was found that mentioned the prophet Balaam and his oracles. The boundaries of Canaan as defined in chapter 34 match those in Egyptian texts of the fifteenth to thirteenth centuries B.C. They do not correspond to the borders of the later state of Israel. The censuses find parallels in neighboring countries from the eighteenth to fourteenth centuries B.C. The organization of the Israelite camp has early Egyptian parallels. These are just some of the features that show the authenticity of the details of the book of Numbers.

The English title "Numbers" (Gk. *Arithmoi*) is borrowed from the name of the book in the Greek translation of the OT, the Septuagint. This title is based on the presence of census returns in chapters 1–4 and 26. The fifth word of the book in Hebrew, "in the wilderness" (Hb. *bemidbar*), constitutes its Hebrew title and perhaps gives a better summary of its contents.

Theme

The theme of Numbers is the gradual fulfillment of the promises to Abraham that his descendants would be the people of God and occupy the land of Canaan. The book shows the reality of God's presence with Israel in the cloud of fire over the tabernacle, but the repeated displays of unbelief by Israel delay the entry into Canaan and cost many lives. Nevertheless, by the end of the book, Israel is poised to enter the land.

Purpose, Occasion, and Background

Jews refer to the first five books of the Bible as "the Law" (Torah), and Christians call them the "Pentateuch" or "The Five Books of Moses." Numbers is the fourth volume in this series and relates Israel's journey from Mount Sinai to the borders of the Promised Land, summarizing some 40 years of the nation's history. The book begins with Israel making final preparations to leave Sinai. It then records their triumphal setting out, before relating a series of disasters in which the people grumbled about the difficulty of the journey and the impossibility of conquering Canaan. This response leads to God delaying the entry to Canaan by 40 years. The closing chapters of the book tell how the people at last set out again and reached the banks of the Jordan, poised to cross into the land promised to their forefathers.

Numbers thus relates a most important stage in the early history of Israel. Genesis begins with the creation of the world, but soon focuses on the life of the patriarchs and ends with their move to Egypt. Exodus

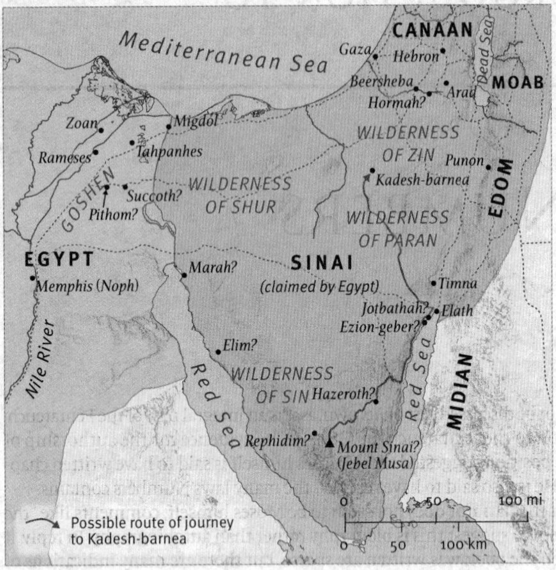

Journeys in the Wilderness
c. 1446/1260 B.C.
The book of Numbers details the Israelites' experience in the wilderness as they journeyed from Mount Sinai to Canaan. As with the exodus, it is difficult to establish the exact route that the Israelites took, but it is generally believed that they headed east from Mount Sinai until they reached the Red Sea, where they turned northward to the top of the gulf and on to Kadesh-barnea.

tells how they left Egypt and came to Sinai to receive the law. Leviticus contains some of these laws, and Numbers still more. Numbers also summarizes the 40 years in the wilderness, and Deuteronomy (the sequel to Numbers) has Moses expounding the laws and urging the people to obey them. Deuteronomy ends with Moses' death.

Another way of looking at the Pentateuch is as a biography of Moses (see Introduction to the Pentateuch, pp. 35–37). Numbers makes a vital contribution to this biography. First, it underlines *Moses' unique role as mediator between God and Israel.* As elsewhere in the Pentateuch, it is constantly reiterated that "the LORD spoke to Moses." And when this is challenged by his brother and sister, God himself intervenes: "With him [i.e., Moses] I speak mouth to mouth, clearly, and not in riddles, and he beholds the form of the LORD" (12:8). Second, it makes an astounding claim about *Moses' character*: "Now the man Moses was very meek, more than all the people who were on the face of the earth" (12:3; see note on 12:3–4). Third, it explains *why Moses never entered Canaan himself*: his failure to follow God's instruction precisely is tersely told (20:10–13), as is the subsequent death of his brother Aaron for supporting Moses' action (20:22–29). The book closes with the reader left in suspense about when and how Moses himself will die.

Numbers is to be classed as a historical work, not only because various details in it are corroborated by archaeological discoveries but also because it deliberately sets out to record what happened on the journey from Mount Sinai to the Jordan River. It does this to instruct future generations of readers with the lessons to be learned from the wilderness experience. It is saying in effect to the reader, "Your forefathers made many mistakes on their journey to Canaan; make sure you do not repeat them."

However, Numbers does not paint an entirely gloomy picture: the book encourages its readers as well as warns them. By the end of the book the people of Israel have conquered formidable opponents in the Transjordan (the land east of the Jordan River), taken possession of their territory, and are poised to cross the Jordan and enter the Promised Land. In this way the book shows how the promises to the patriarchs are being fulfilled (see Key Themes).

Key Themes

The theme of the Pentateuch is the gradual fulfillment of the promises to the patriarchs, and Numbers makes a notable contribution to the exposition of that theme. There are four elements to the patriarchal promise set out first in Genesis 12:1–3: (1) land, (2) many descendants, (3) covenant relationship with God, and (4) blessing to the nations. These four aspects of the promise all play a role in Numbers.

1. *The land.* The land of Canaan is the goal of the book of Numbers. It is broached in the first chapter, where

a census is taken of all the men who are able to go to war. Israel is being prepared to fight for the land. Chapter 10 sees them setting out from Sinai, led by the fire of God's presence. Chapter 13 relates their arrival at the southern border of the land and the mission of the spies. The spies' gloomy report causes Israel to lose heart about the land, and God sentences them to wander for 40 years in the wilderness. But the second half of the book shows the people again on the move toward the land, overcoming opposition and reaching the eastern border of Canaan, marked by the Jordan River (ch. 34). The last word from God in the book is both a command and a promise: each of the tribes of the people of Israel shall hold on to its own inheritance (36:9).

2. *Descendants.* Abraham had been promised that his descendants would be as many as the stars of heaven (Gen. 15:5). Jacob's family consisted of just 70 persons when he entered Egypt (Gen. 46:27). Now they have increased immensely. The first census showed that the fighting men numbered 603,550. That did not include women and children. Surveying their camp from a hilltop, Balaam declared, "Who can count the dust of Jacob or number the fourth part of Israel?" (Num. 23:10). Balaam went on to predict that Israel would become a powerful kingdom in its own right: "a star shall come out of Jacob, and a scepter shall rise out of Israel" (24:17).

3. *Covenant relationship with God.* The essence of the covenant was, "You shall be my people, and I will be your God." The Lord's presence with Israel is constantly brought out in the book of Numbers. There are the dramatic manifestations of his presence in the cloud that guided them or that appeared at moments of crisis (e.g., 9:15–23; 14:10). Then the design of the tabernacle and the harsh measures to be taken against intruders all emphasized the reality of God's holy presence (3:38). On the other hand, Israel was expected to trust God's promises and obey his laws. Failure to do so resulted in death for the individual and sometimes for large groups (e.g., 15:32–36; 25:6–9). Even Moses forfeited his right to enter the land because of disobedience (20:10–13). But despite Israel's persistent failure to keep to the law, God never forsakes them or goes back on his promises. They may have to wait an extra 40 years to enter the land, but eventually they do reach it. "The LORD is slow to anger and abounding in steadfast love" (14:18).

4. *Blessing to the nations.* This is the aspect of the promises that is least apparent in Numbers. To a greater or lesser degree, the nations that Israel encounters are all hostile: the Edomites refuse Israel passage; the Moabites try to have Israel cursed; Sihon and Og attack them and are defeated (chs. 21–22). Nevertheless Balaam recalls the phrasing of Genesis 12:3 when he says, "Blessed are those who bless you, and cursed are those who curse you" (Num. 24:9). The implication is that nations who treat Israel generously by blessing her will themselves be blessed.

Place in the Bible

The events of Numbers are often mentioned elsewhere in Scripture. Its episodes are taken as showcase examples of Israel's sinfulness and God's reaction to it. Deuteronomy relates the story of the spies (Numbers 13–14) to remind the new generation not to repeat the unbelief of their parents, who, having reached the border of Canaan, refused to enter it (Deut. 1:19–32). The book of Ezekiel draws on the laws of Numbers to demonstrate the guilt of Jerusalem and explain why it deserved to be destroyed. The Psalms refer to incidents from the wilderness wanderings (e.g., Ps. 95:8–11; 135:10–12), and Psalms 105 and 106 relate the story in more detail. The priestly blessing (Num. 6:24–26) seems to have inspired various psalmists (see Psalms 67, 120–134). These episodes are used both as reminders of God's goodness in the past (e.g., Ps. 136:16–22) and to encourage future loyalty to the law (Ps. 105:45).

The NT also draws on Numbers to make similar points for the Christian church. John 1:14 speaks of the Word dwelling (lit., "tabernacling") among believers. John 3:14 refers to the serpent Moses set up (Num. 21:4–9) as imaging Christ on the cross. Both Jude 11 and Revelation 2:14 see Balaam's error as a danger facing the early church. But it is the apostle Paul in 1 Corinthians 10:2–11 who makes the most use of Numbers. After mentioning the water and manna God had supplied in the wilderness (Num. 11:11–35; 20:2–13), he continues, "Nevertheless, with most of them God was not pleased, for they were overthrown in the wilderness [Numbers 11; 14; 16–17]. Now these things took place as examples for us, that we might not desire evil as they did. Do not be idolaters as some of them were. . . . We must not indulge in sexual immorality as some of them did, and twenty-three thousand fell in a single day [Numbers 25]. We must not put Christ to the test, as some of them did . . . and were destroyed by the Destroyer [21:5–9]. Now these things happened to them as an example, but they were written down for our instruction."

Parallels between Exodus and Numbers

Ex. 18:1	Advice from Moses' father-in-law	Advice from Moses' father-in-law	Num. 10:29
Ex. 15:22	Three-day journey to Sinai	Three-day journey from Sinai	Num. 10:33
Ex. 15:22–26	Complaint about water	Unspecified complaint	Num. 11:1–3
Exodus 16	Manna and quail	Manna and quail	Num. 11:4–15, 31–35
Exodus 18	Leaders appointed to assist Moses	Leaders appointed to assist Moses	Num. 11:16–30
Ex. 15:20–21	Miriam's song of praise	Miriam and Aaron rebel	Numbers 12
Ex. 17:8–16	Israel defeats Amalek	Israel defeated by Amalek	Num. 14:39–45
Ex. 17:1–7	Water from rock	Water from rock	Num. 20:1–13
Ex. 32:6	People sacrifice to other gods	People sacrifice to other gods	Num. 25:2
Ex. 32:27	Killing of apostates demanded	Killing of apostates demanded	Num. 25:5
Ex. 32:28–29	Levites' status enhanced	Levites' (Phinehas's) status enhanced	Num. 25:6–13
Ex. 32:35	Plague on the people	Plague on the people	Num. 25:9

History of Salvation Summary

Numbers continues the story of God's people, following them from Mount Sinai to the verge of the Jordan River. The book shows the steadfast purpose of God to fashion a people for himself who will display his image to the world, and out of which his appointed Savior will arise. The unfaithfulness of the members of that people puts God's steadfastness to the test; but whereas the unfaithful members suffer God's punishment, the people as a whole are preserved and shaped. (For an explanation of the "History of Salvation," see the Overview of the Bible, pp. 23–26. See also History of Salvation in the Old Testament: Preparing the Way for Christ, pp. 2635–2661.)

Literary Features

The overall genre of the book of Numbers is the historical chronicle. The largest quantity of material is narrative, and these parts require the usual attention to plot, character, and setting. Specific narrative types are also important. Numbers especially uses the travel story, with prominent motifs of conflict, danger, adventure, suspense, and testing. The travel story in Numbers begins as a quest story and ends as a story of wilderness wandering because of the sinfulness of the nation. The presence of Moses as a heroic leader makes the story a hero story as well.

Narrative accounts for only half of the book, however. The narrative sections alternate regularly with lists and collections of laws (comprising a religious instruction manual). Numbers is based on a predictable rhythm back and forth between sections of lists, instructions, and regulations on the one hand, and narrative material on the other (see diagram, p. 262). The non-narrative units should not be read as interruptions of the narrative, but as complementary material in a historical chronicle. The law-giving sections are often phrased in quasi-narrative terms as what God told Moses, following the formula "the LORD spoke to Moses." Additionally, the sections of regulations can be viewed as telling the "story" (though not in narrative form) of a nation's religious practices. The religious rituals and sacrifices express religious truths in visual form.

As a story of national destiny, Numbers also has the character of an epic. Moses is the epic hero who is representative of the nation. The main antagonists in the story of the nation are: (1) the physical locales in which the traveling group finds itself; (2) other nations with whom the Israelites come into contact; and (3) the nation itself (often in conflict with its leader, Moses). The dominant narrative motif is (to use John Milton's formula in *Paradise Lost*) "supernal grace contending with sinfulness of men."

The Large Numbers in the Pentateuch

The census lists recorded in Numbers 1 and 26 have been a matter of considerable debate among scholars since the early 1900s. The grand total of warriors recorded in Numbers 1:46 comes to 603,550—which is the same number recorded in the first census (Ex. 38:26), and very similar to the number in the third census recorded in Numbers 26:51, which was taken nearly 40 years after the first census in Numbers. Since these totals include only male warriors between the ages of 20 and 60 (excluding women, children, and older men), 603,550 warriors would suggest a total population of something more than 2 million.

The Problem. Three main problems have been raised regarding whether the actual number of Israelites who were delivered from Egypt and led by Moses through the wilderness for 40 years could have been this large. The first objection (1) suggests that it is difficult to imagine how so many people (more than 2 million) could have survived for 40 years in the wilderness, including their highly organized encampment around the tabernacle and their frequent relocation during these years. Though this certainly would not be impossible—given the fact of God's miraculous provision of manna, quail, and water, and given the cloud of God's presence—the sudden influx of such a large population would nonetheless have been difficult to assimilate into this geographic area. A second objection (2) suggests that the archaeological evidence for the overall population of the Promised Land just after the exodus seems to be well below 3 million. Related to this, other texts (e.g., Ex. 23:29–30; Deut. 7:6–7, 21) suggest that there were not enough Israelites to take possession of the Promised Land all at once. A third objection (3) suggests that some of the numbers in general seem to reflect mathematical oddities (most figures are rounded to even 100s) and that the ratio of adult males to firstborn males seems quite large (27 to 1).

Proposed Solutions. Briefly stated, the proposed solutions may be summarized under the following four explanations:

1. *The figures should be taken at face value.* In this case, it is assumed that the people were sustained, protected, and led by God's miraculous provision and presence during the 40 years in the wilderness; that the Promised Land was more fertile in ancient times; and that the number of firstborn sons (22,273; see Num. 3:43) corresponds to the number who were born during the 13-month period since the exodus. Those who support this position argue that the author of Numbers seems to be taking the numbers at face value, since they all add up correctly even when different methods of tabulation are used (cf. 1:46 with 2:32).

2. *The figures should be taken at face value but they correspond to the population of Israel at a later date, possibly in the time of David.* This suggestion, advocated mainly in the mid-twentieth century, has lost favor, largely because it does not correspond well with the apparent population in the time of David. Also, the tribes of Simeon had already been merged with the tribe of Judah in David's time, whereas the two tribes are clearly distinct in the lists in Numbers 1 and 26.

3. *The numbers were changed due to scribal misunderstanding.* This view suggests that the numbers were originally much smaller, but that larger numbers were substituted later due to scribal misunderstanding of the Hebrew word *'elep*, which can be translated either as "thousand" or "group" or "clan." Thus it has been proposed that a number that now appears in Hebrew as 46,500 (1:21) originally meant 46 groups totaling 500 persons. Following this hypothesis, there would have been a total of 598 families, with a total of 5,550 male warriors, yielding a total population of about 20,000. This hypothesis, however, presents other difficulties, as do other similar proposals based on the meaning of the Hebrew word *'elep*, one of which yields an estimated population of 140,000 and another that proposes a total population of 72,000. Those who support this general line of argument agree that it still needs refinement. They also agree that there is no one-size-fits-all solution for every OT case of what may seem to be very large numbers.

4. *The numbers are symbolic.* Two variations on the symbolic view are: (1) that the figures are based on "gematria," that is, the symbolic numerical value given to each of the letters in the Hebrew alphabet; or (2) that the figures correspond in a symbolic way to astronomical periods associated with the 12 tribes of Israel. Though some have argued that astronomical symbolism is hinted at in Joseph's dream (by the way in which the sun, moon, and 11 stars bowed down to Joseph), it is difficult to apply this symbolism in a comprehensive and consistent way.

Summary. Since these numbers claim to be census figures, the natural presupposition is that they are to be taken at face value. And although this presupposition is not without its difficulty, there is no obvious solution to the problems posed by these census figures. In any case, the theological message of this section in Numbers is clear—namely, (1) that every eligible adult male in Israel must be prepared and committed to fight in the Lord's army, and (2) that all the people of Israel who were delivered from Egypt are the elect people of God, but they must confirm God's choice by their wholehearted participation in the realization of their calling (see further Ex. 32:32–33; Ps. 87:6; Isa. 4:3; Dan. 12:1; Mal. 3:16).

Outline

Numbers consists of three major blocks of material describing the events and laws associated with three centers where Israel encamped for a significant time. These centers are Sinai (chs. 1–10), Kadesh (chs. 13–19), and the plains of Moab (chs. 22–36). They are linked by two short travelogues recording what occurred as Israel journeyed from one camp to the next.

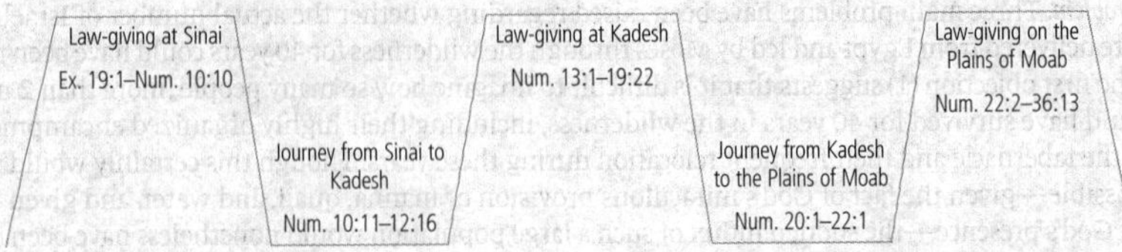

I. Israel Prepares to Enter the Land (1:1–10:10)
- A. The first census (1:1–46)
- B. The responsibilities of the Levites (1:47–54)
- C. Israel in camp and on the march (2:1–34)
- D. Two censuses of the Levites (3:1–4:49)
  - 1. Census of all male Levites (3:1–51)
    - a. The sons of Aaron (3:1–4)
    - b. The duties of the Levites (3:5–10)
    - c. Reason for the Levitical census (3:11–13)
    - d. The clans' numbers, positions, and responsibilities (3:14–39)
    - e. Redemption of the firstborn (3:40–51)
  - 2. Census of mature Levites (4:1–49)
    - a. The tasks of the Kohathites (4:1–20)
    - b. The tasks of the Gershonites (4:21–28)
    - c. The tasks of the Merarites (4:29–33)
    - d. The results of the second census (4:34–49)
- E. Cleansing the camp (5:1–6:27)
  - 1. Exclusion of the unclean from the camp (5:1–4)
  - 2. Atonement for perjury (5:5–10)
  - 3. Test of suspected adultery (5:11–31)
  - 4. Rules for Nazirites (6:1–21)
    - a. Definition of a Nazirite (6:1–6)
    - b. Nazirites and uncleanness (6:7–12)
    - c. Completion of a Nazirite vow (6:13–20)
    - d. Summary of the law (6:21)
  - 5. The priestly blessing (6:22–27)
- F. Offerings for the tabernacle (7:1–89)
- G. The lampstand (8:1–4)
- H. The dedication of the Levites (8:5–22)
- I. The retirement of the Levites (8:23–26)
- J. The second Passover (9:1–5)
- K. The delayed Passover (9:6–14)
- L. The moving cloud (9:15–23)
- M. The silver trumpets (10:1–10)

II. Marching from Sinai to Kadesh (10:11–12:16)
- A. Israel strikes camp at Sinai (10:11–28)
- B. Request to Hobab to accompany Israel (10:29–32)
- C. Three protests (11:1–12:16)
  - 1. Taberah (11:1–3)
  - 2. Kibroth-hattaavah (11:4–35)
  - 3. The uniqueness of Moses (12:1–16)

III. Forty Years near Kadesh (13:1–19:22)
- A. The mission of the spies and the national rebellion (13:1–14:45)
  - 1. Spies sent out (13:1–16)
  - 2. Mission accomplished (13:17–24)

3. The spies' report of their mission (13:25–33)
4. The people's reaction (14:1–12)
5. Moses' plea for forgiveness (14:13–19)
6. God's response to Moses' prayer (14:20–35)
7. Death of the faithless spies (14:36–38)
8. An unsuccessful attempt at conquest (14:39–45)

B. The law-giving at Kadesh (15:1–41)
1. Meal, oil, and wine to accompany sacrifice (15:1–16)
2. The dough offering (15:17–21)
3. Sacrifices for unintentional sins (15:22–31)
4. A sabbathbreaker executed (15:32–36)
5. Tassels on clothes (15:37–41)

C. The rebellion of Korah, Dathan, and Abiram (16:1–50)
1. The complaints of Korah, Dathan, and Abiram (16:1–15)
2. The death of the Kohathite supporters of Korah (16:16–19, 35–40)
3. The death of the ringleaders and their families (16:20–34)
4. Judgment averted by Aaron (16:41–50)

D. Aaron's blossoming staff (17:1–13)

E. Duties and privileges of priests and Levites (18:1–32)
1. Guard duties in and around the tabernacle (18:1–7)
2. The priests' income (18:8–20)
3. The Levites' income (18:21–24)
4. The tithe of the tithe (18:25–32)

F. Cleansing from death (19:1–22)
1. The recipe for producing the cleansing ash (19:1–10)
2. The cleansing procedure (19:11–22)

IV. Marching from Kadesh to the Plains of Moab (20:1–21:35)

A. Regrouping at Kadesh (20:1)
B. Rebellion at Meribah (20:2–13)
C. Encounter with Edom (20:14–21)
D. The death of Aaron (20:22–29)
E. First victory over the Canaanites (21:1–3)
F. The bronze snake (21:4–9)
G. Through Transjordan (21:10–20)
H. Victory over Sihon (21:21–30)
I. The campaign against Og, king of Bashan (21:31–35)

V. Israel in the Plains of Moab (22:1–36:13)

A. Balak, Balaam, and Israel (22:1–24:25)
1. Balak summons Balaam (22:1–6)
2. Balaam turns down Balak's first invitation (22:7–14)
3. Balaam accepts Balak's second invitation (22:15–21)
4. The donkey and the angel (22:22–35)
5. Balak greets Balaam (22:36–40)
6. Balaam blesses Israel three times (22:41–24:14)
   a. The first blessing (22:41–23:12)
   b. The second blessing (23:13–30)
   c. The third blessing (24:1–14)
7. Balaam's final oracle (24:15–19)
8. Three cryptic predictions (24:20–25)

B. Apostasy at Peor (25:1–18)

C. The second census (26:1–65)

D. Laws for the land (27:1–30:16)
1. The daughters of Zelophehad (27:1–11)
2. Joshua commissioned as Moses' successor (27:12–23)

3. Calendar of public sacrifices (28:1–29:40)
   a. The daily offering (28:1–8)
   b. The Sabbath offerings (28:9–10)
   c. The new moon sacrifices (28:11–15)
   d. The Feast of Unleavened Bread (28:16–25)
   e. The Feast of Weeks (Pentecost) (28:26–31)
   f. The first day of the seventh month (29:1–6)
   g. The Day of Atonement (29:7–11)
   h. The Feast of Booths (29:12–38)
   i. Clarification and summary (29:39–40)
4. The obligations of vows (30:1–16)
   a. Men and vows (30:1–2)
   b. Women and vows (30:3–5)
   c. Vows made by a woman before her marriage (30:6–8)
   d. Widows and divorcees (30:9)
   e. Vows made by a woman after her marriage (30:10–16)

E. Retribution on Midian (31:1–54)
1. The Lord's campaign of vengeance against Midian (31:1–12)
2. Moses' anger with his officers (31:13–18)
3. Purification for uncleanness (31:19–24)
4. Dividing the spoils (31:25–47)
5. Head count and atonement (31:48–54)

F. The settlement in Transjordan (32:1–42)

G. Summary of Israel's journey from Egypt to Canaan (33:1–56)

H. The boundaries of Canaan (34:1–15)
1. The southern border (34:1–5)
2. The western border (34:6)
3. The northern border (34:7–9)
4. The eastern border (34:10–15)

I. The distributors of the land (34:16–29)

J. Cities for the Levites (35:1–8)

K. The cities of refuge (35:9–34)
1. The selection and purpose of these cities (35:9–15)
2. Homicide that warrants the death penalty (35:16–21)
3. Homicide that does not deserve death (35:22–29)
4. Final points (35:30–34)

L. Zelophehad's daughters marry (36:1–13)

NUMBERS

Chapter 1
1[a]ch. 10:11, 12; Ex. 19:1 [b]Ex. 25:22
2[c]Ex. 30:12; 38:26; 2 Sam. 24:2; 1 Chr. 21:2; See ch. 26:2-51 [d]ver. 18, 20, 22; ch. 3:47; 1 Chr. 23:3, 24
3[e]ch. 14:29; Ex. 30:14 [f]Ex. 12:51
5[g]ch. 7:30
6[h]ch. 7:36
7[i]See Ex. 6:23
8[j]ch. 7:18
9[k]ch. 7:24
10[l]ch. 7:48; 1 Chr. 7:26 [m]ch. 7:54
11[n]ch. 7:60
12[o]ch. 7:66
13[p]ch. 7:72
14[q]ch. 7:42
15[r]ch. 7:78
16[s]ch. 26:9 [t]ch. 7:2; [Ex. 18:21, 25]; See 1 Chr. 27:16-22
17[u]1 Chr. 12:31; 16:41; 2 Chr. 28:15; 31:19; Ezra 8:20
20[v]For ver. 20-46, see ch. 2:3-32
21[w][ch. 26:7]
23[x][ch. 26:14]

A Census of Israel's Warriors

1 The LORD spoke to Moses [a]in the wilderness of Sinai, [b]in the tent of meeting, on the
first day of the second month, in the second year after they had come out of the land
of Egypt, saying, 2 [c]"Take a census of all the congregation of the people of Israel, by clans,
[d]by fathers' houses, according to the number of names, every male, head by head. 3 [e]From
twenty years old and upward, all in Israel who are able to go to war, you and Aaron shall
list them, [f]company by company. 4 And there shall be with you a man from each tribe,
each man being the head of the house of his fathers. 5 And these are the names of the men
who shall assist you. From Reuben, [g]Elizur the son of Shedeur; 6 from Simeon, [h]Shelumiel
the son of Zurishaddai; 7 from Judah, [i]Nahshon the son of Amminadab; 8 from Issachar,
[j]Nethanel the son of Zuar; 9 from Zebulun, [k]Eliab the son of Helon; 10 from the sons of Joseph,
from Ephraim, [l]Elishama the son of Ammihud, and from Manasseh, [m]Gamaliel the son
of Pedahzur; 11 from Benjamin, [n]Abidan the son of Gideoni; 12 from Dan, [o]Ahiezer the son
of Ammishaddai; 13 from Asher, [p]Pagiel the son of Ochran; 14 from Gad, Eliasaph the son of
[q]Deuel; 15 from Naphtali, [r]Ahira the son of Enan." 16 These were the ones [s]chosen from the
congregation, [t]the chiefs of their ancestral tribes, the heads of the clans of Israel.
17 Moses and Aaron took these men [u]who had been named, 18 and on the first day of the
second month, they assembled the whole congregation together, who registered themselves by clans, by fathers' houses, according to the number of names from twenty years
old and upward, head by head, 19 as the LORD commanded Moses. So he listed them in
the wilderness of Sinai.
20 The people of [v]Reuben, Israel's firstborn, their generations, by their clans, by their
fathers' houses, according to the number of names, head by head, every male from twenty
years old and upward, all who were able to go to war: 21 those listed of the tribe of Reuben
were [w]46,500.
22 Of the people of Simeon, their generations, by their clans, by their fathers' houses,
those of them who were listed, according to the number of names, head by head, every
male from twenty years old and upward, all who were able to go to war: 23 those listed of
the tribe of Simeon were [x]59,300.
24 Of the people of Gad, their generations, by their clans, by their fathers' houses, according

1:1–10:10 *Israel Prepares to Enter the Land.* Numbers tells how Israel moved from Mount Sinai to the Jordan Valley, the eastern border of the Promised Land. All the material in the first 10 chapters relates Israel's preparations for a war of conquest.

1:1–46 *The First Census.* This census has two purposes: (1) to demonstrate the fulfillment of the promise to Abraham that his descendants would be as numerous as the sand on the seashore (Gen. 22:17); and (2) to count the number of men over 20 years old who could fight. Both considerations should give the people confidence in their battle for the land.

1:1 The wilderness of Sinai is the area near Mount Sinai (see map, p. 258). Israel has been encamped there since Ex. 19:1 and will set out on their journey in Num. 10:11. **The tent of meeting**, otherwise known as the tabernacle and described in Exodus 25–31; 35–40, had been completed just one month earlier (Ex. 40:2) and now served as God's earthly dwelling in which he gave instructions to Moses. It thus reminded Israel of both Sinai and the garden of Eden.

1:3 All . . . able to go to war shows that the invasion of Canaan is imminent.

1:4–19 By appointing the chiefs of the tribes to count their own tribe, the census was begun on the very day it was commanded (v. 18).

1:20–46 The results of the census are recorded tribe by tribe. The number of men between the ages of 20 and 60 comes to a total of 603,550, which is the same number found in Ex. 38:26 (cf. Ex. 30:12–16); these are identified as **every man able to go to war in Israel** (see Num. 1:45–46). When women, children, and men under 20 and over 60 are included, the total population would probably have been about 2 million. This remarkable fulfillment of the promises should have given the people every confidence that the invasion of Canaan would succeed. (Regarding questions that have been raised concerning these large numbers, see Introduction: The Large Numbers in the Pentateuch).

to the number of the names, from twenty years old and upward, all who were able to go
to war: 25 those listed of the tribe of Gad were [y]45,650.
26 Of the people of Judah, their generations, by their clans, by their fathers' houses, according to the number of names, from twenty years old and upward, every man able to go to
war: 27 those listed of the tribe of Judah were [z]74,600.
28 Of the people of Issachar, their generations, by their clans, by their fathers' houses,
according to the number of names, from twenty years old and upward, every man able to
go to war: 29 those listed of the tribe of Issachar were [a]54,400.
30 Of the people of Zebulun, their generations, by their clans, by their fathers' houses,
according to the number of names, from twenty years old and upward, every man able to
go to war: 31 those listed of the tribe of Zebulun were [b]57,400.
32 Of the people of Joseph, namely, of the people of Ephraim, their generations, by their
clans, by their fathers' houses, according to the number of names, from twenty years old
and upward, every man able to go to war: 33 those listed of the tribe of Ephraim were
[c]40,500.
34 Of the people of Manasseh, their generations, by their clans, by their fathers' houses,
according to the number of names, from twenty years old and upward, every man able to
go to war: 35 those listed of the tribe of Manasseh were [d]32,200.
36 Of the people of Benjamin, their generations, by their clans, by their fathers' houses,
according to the number of names, from twenty years old and upward, every man able to
go to war: 37 those listed of the tribe of Benjamin were [e]35,400.
38 Of the people of Dan, their generations, by their clans, by their fathers' houses, according to the number of names, from twenty years old and upward, every man able to go to
war: 39 those listed of the tribe of Dan were [f]62,700.
40 Of the people of Asher, their generations, by their clans, by their fathers' houses, according to the number of names, from twenty years old and upward, every man able to go to
war: 41 those listed of the tribe of Asher were [g]41,500.
42 Of the people of Naphtali, their generations, by their clans, by their fathers' houses,
according to the number of names, from twenty years old and upward, every man able to
go to war: 43 those listed of the tribe of Naphtali were [h]53,400.
44 [i]These are those who were listed, whom Moses and Aaron listed with the help of the
chiefs of Israel, twelve men, each representing his fathers' house. 45 So all those listed of
the people of Israel, by their fathers' houses, from twenty years old and upward, every
man able to go to war in Israel— 46 all those listed were [j]603,550.

Levites Exempted

47 But [k]the Levites were not listed along with them by their ancestral tribe. 48 For the
LORD spoke to Moses, saying, 49 "Only the tribe of Levi you shall not list, and you shall
not take a census of them among the people of Israel. 50 [l]But appoint the Levites over the
tabernacle of the testimony, and over all its furnishings, and over all that belongs to it.
They are to carry the tabernacle and all its furnishings, and they shall take care of it [m]and
shall camp around the tabernacle. 51 [n]When the tabernacle is to set out, the Levites shall
take it down, and when the tabernacle is to be pitched, the Levites shall set it up. [o]And if
any outsider comes near, he shall be put to death. 52 The people of Israel shall pitch their
tents by their companies, each man in his own camp and [p]each man by his own standard.
53 But the Levites shall camp around the tabernacle of the testimony, so that there may be
no [q]wrath on the congregation of the people of Israel. [r]And the Levites shall keep guard
over the tabernacle of the testimony." 54 Thus did the people of Israel; they did according
to all that the LORD commanded Moses.

25 [y][ch. 26:18]
27 [z][ch. 26:22; 2 Sam. 24:9]
29 [a][ch. 26:25]
31 [b][ch. 26:27]
33 [c][ch. 26:37]
35 [d][ch. 26:34]
37 [e][ch. 26:41]
39 [f][ch. 26:43]
41 [g][ch. 26:47]
43 [h][ch. 26:50]
44 [i]ch. 26:64
46 [j]Ex. 38:26; [ch. 11:21; 26:51; Ex. 12:37]
47 [k]ch. 2:33; [ch. 26:57, 58, 62]; See ch. 3; ch. 4; 1 Chr. 6
50 [l]ch. 3:7, 8; Ex. 38:21; See ch. 4:15-33 [m]See ch. 3:23-38
51 [n]ch. 10:17, 21 [o]ch. 3:10, 38; 18:22; [1 Sam. 6:19; 2 Sam. 6:6, 7; 1 Chr. 13:10]
52 [p]ch. 2:2, 34
53 [q]ch. 8:19; 16:46; 18:5 [r]ch. 3:7, 8, 38; 8:26; 9:19, 23; 18:3-5; 31:30, 47; 1 Chr. 23:32; [2 Chr. 13:11]

1:26–27 Judah is the largest tribe. This, like its position in the camp (2:3) and leading the nation on the march (2:9), indicates Judah's preeminence among the tribes. David and Jesus came from the tribe of Judah.

1:47–54 *The Responsibilities of the Levites.* The **Levites**, the priestly tribe, were not included in the census because they had a more important job than fighting. They were responsible for the **tabernacle**, God's palace, the most vital part of the whole camp. Israel was the people of God, but without his presence with them in the tabernacle, there would have been no point to their existence. The Levites' task was to ensure God's continuing presence with Israel. They dismantled, carried, and reassembled the tabernacle (vv. 50–51). They also guarded it from intruders. Entry to the tabernacle by laypeople could lead to divine wrath breaking out and the death of many Israelites, so the Levites were told to execute any outsider breaking in (vv. 51–53). A similar

Chapter 2
2 [s]ch. 1:52
3 [t]See Ex. 6:23
9 [u]ch. 10:14-16

Arrangement of the Camp

2 The LORD spoke to Moses and Aaron, saying, 2 [s]"The people of Israel shall camp each
by his own standard, with the banners of their fathers' houses. They shall camp facing the tent of meeting on every side. 3 Those to camp on the east side toward the sunrise
shall be of the standard of the camp of Judah by their companies, the chief of the people
of Judah being [t]Nahshon the son of Amminadab, 4 his company as listed being 74,600.
5 Those to camp next to him shall be the tribe of Issachar, the chief of the people of Issachar
being Nethanel the son of Zuar, 6 his company as listed being 54,400. 7 Then the tribe of
Zebulun, the chief of the people of Zebulun being Eliab the son of Helon, 8 his company
as listed being 57,400. 9 All those listed of the camp of Judah, by their companies, were
186,400. [u]They shall set out first on the march.
10 "On the south side shall be the standard of the camp of Reuben by their companies,
the chief of the people of Reuben being Elizur the son of Shedeur, 11 his company as listed
being 46,500. 12 And those to camp next to him shall be the tribe of Simeon, the chief of the
people of Simeon being Shelumiel the son of Zurishaddai, 13 his company as listed being

threat had been made against anyone trying to approach God on Mount Sinai (Ex. 19:11–13; Heb. 12:18–29).

2:1–34 *Israel in Camp and on the March.* This chapter prescribes how the camp was to be arranged and the order in which the tribes were to march. At the center of the camp was the tabernacle. (Rameses II, in his campaigns in Syria [1275–1270 B.C.], employed a similar strategic layout. The pharaoh, who claimed to be divine, had his large tent pitched in the center of his military encampment.) Surrounding the tabernacle are the Levites: their arrangement is more closely described in ch. 3. They guarded the sanctuary from intrusions by unauthorized laypeople. Beyond the Levites the lay tribes are encamped. The 12 tribes were divided into four groups of three. In premier position, east of the tabernacle camp, were Judah with Issachar and Zebulun (2:2–9). Next in rank came the tribes camping to the south of the tabernacle, Reuben with Gad and Simeon (vv. 10–16). After them on the west came Ephraim with Benjamin and Manasseh (vv. 18–24). Finally, on the northern side of the tabernacle camp were Dan with Asher and Naphtali (vv. 25–34). The same sequence was to be maintained on the march. The Judah group headed the march, followed by the Reuben group. Then followed the Levites carrying the tabernacle. After them came the Ephraim group of tribes, and the Dan group brought up the rear (v. 31). See diagram below.

2:2 It is not known what Israel's tribal **banners** and standards looked like, though other ancient armies had them as well. **Facing** (lit., "opposite") could also be translated "at a distance from." A gap had to be kept between the lay tribes and the tabernacle.

Israel in Camp

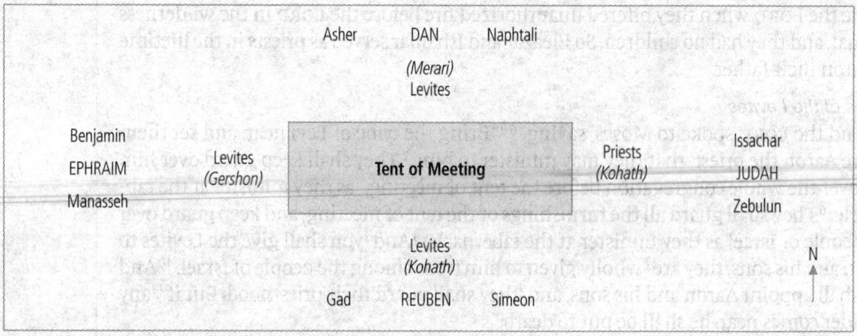

Israel on the March

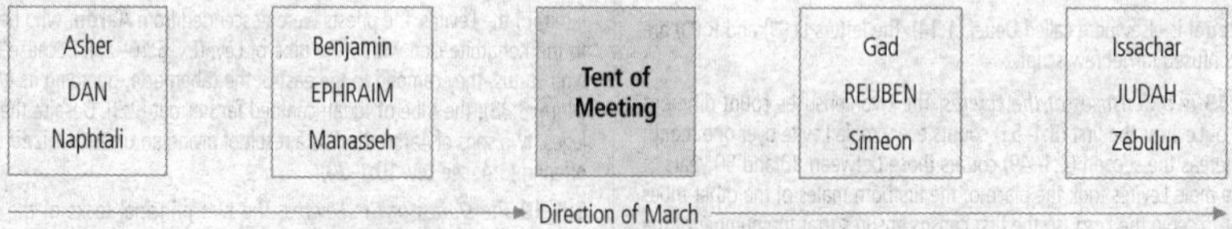

Both in camp and on the march, the tabernacle (guarded by the Levites) is always at the center, as God is at the heart of the nation. The Judah group has pride of place in the camp and leads the nation on the march (capital letters designate the lead tribe in each of the four groups).

59,300. 14 Then the tribe of Gad, the chief of the people of Gad being Eliasaph the son of
[v]Reuel, 15 his company as listed being 45,650. 16 All those listed of the camp of Reuben, by
their companies, were 151,450. [w]They shall set out second.
17 [x]"Then the tent of meeting shall set out, with the camp of the Levites in the midst of
the camps; as they camp, so shall they set out, each in position, standard by standard.
18 "On the west side shall be the standard of the camp of Ephraim by their companies,
the chief of the people of Ephraim being Elishama the son of Ammihud, 19 his company
as listed being 40,500. 20 And next to him shall be the tribe of Manasseh, the chief of the
people of Manasseh being Gamaliel the son of Pedahzur, 21 his company as listed being
32,200. 22 Then the tribe of Benjamin, the chief of the people of Benjamin being Abidan
the son of Gideoni, 23 his company as listed being 35,400. 24 All those listed of the camp of
Ephraim, by their companies, were 108,100. [y]They shall set out third on the march.
25 "On the north side shall be the standard of the camp of Dan by their companies, the
chief of the people of Dan being Ahiezer the son of Ammishaddai, 26 his company as listed
being 62,700. 27 And those to camp next to him shall be the tribe of Asher, the chief of the
people of Asher being Pagiel the son of Ochran, 28 his company as listed being 41,500.
29 Then the tribe of Naphtali, the chief of the people of Naphtali being Ahira the son of
Enan, 30 his company as listed being 53,400. 31 All those listed of the camp of Dan were
157,600. [z]They shall set out last, standard by standard."
32 These are the people of Israel as listed by their fathers' houses. All those listed in the
camps by their companies were [a]603,550. 33 But [b]the Levites were not listed among the
people of Israel, as the LORD commanded Moses.
34 Thus did the people of Israel. According to all that the LORD commanded Moses, [c]so
they camped by their standards, and so they set out, each one in his clan, according to his
fathers' house.

The Sons of Aaron

3 These are the generations of Aaron and Moses at the time when the LORD spoke with
Moses on Mount Sinai. 2 These are the names of the sons of Aaron: [d]Nadab the firstborn, and Abihu, Eleazar, and Ithamar. 3 These are the names of the sons of Aaron, [e]the
anointed priests, [f]whom he ordained to serve as priests. 4 [g]But Nadab and Abihu died
before the LORD when they offered unauthorized fire before the LORD in the wilderness
of Sinai, and they had no children. So Eleazar and Ithamar served as priests in the lifetime
of Aaron their father.

Duties of the Levites

5 And the LORD spoke to Moses, saying, 6 [h]"Bring the tribe of Levi near, and set them
before Aaron the priest, that they may minister to him. 7 They shall keep guard over him
and over the whole congregation before the tent of meeting, [i]as they minister at the tabernacle. 8 They shall guard all the furnishings of the tent of meeting, and keep guard over
the people of Israel as they minister at the tabernacle. 9 And [j]you shall give the Levites to
Aaron and his sons; they are [k]wholly given to him from among the people of Israel. 10 And
you shall appoint Aaron and his sons, and [l]they shall guard their priesthood. But if [m]any
outsider comes near, he shall be put to death."
11 And the LORD spoke to Moses, saying, 12 "Behold, [n]I have taken the Levites from among

14 [v][ch. 7:42, 47; 10:20]
16 [w]ch. 10:18-20
17 [x]ch. 10:17, 21
24 [y]ch. 10:22-24; [Ps. 80:2]
31 [z]ch. 10:25-27
32 [a]See ch. 1:46
33 [b]See ch. 1:47
34 [c][ch. 24:2, 5, 6]

Chapter 3

2 [d]See Ex. 6:23
3 [e]See Lev. 8 [f]See Ex. 28:41
4 [g]ch. 26:61; Lev. 10:1, 2; 1 Chr. 24:2
6 [h]ch. 1:50; 8:6; 18:2
7 [i]ch. 8:11, 15, 24, 26
9 [j]ch. 8:19; 18:6 [k]ch. 8:16
10 [l]ch. 18:7; [Rom. 12:7] [m]ver. 38; See ch. 1:51
12 [n]ver. 41; ch. 8:16; 18:6

2:14 Reuel is elsewhere called Deuel (1:14). The letters D (ד) and R (ר) are easily confused in Hebrew script.

3:1–4:49 *Two Censuses of the Levites.* The two censuses count different groups of Levites: the first (3:1–51) counts every male Levite over one month old, whereas the second (4:1–49) counts those between 30 and 50 years of age. The male Levites took the place of the firstborn males of the other tribes in order to serve the Lord, so the first census ensures that the number of the former matches the number of the latter. Transporting the tabernacle requires strength, so the second census aims to find if there are enough able-bodied male Levites for this task.

3:1–51 *Census of All Male Levites.* This census focuses on the Levites' ongoing role in Israel.

3:1–4 *The Sons of Aaron.* This census begins with the **priests**, the most holy family of the Levites. The priests were descended from **Aaron**, who belonged to the Kohathite clan within the tribe of Levi (Ex. 6:16–25). Because of their high status, they camped to the east of the tabernacle, guarding its entrance (Num. 3:38); the tribe of Judah camped farther out (2:3). Despite their privileges, two sons of Aaron **died** as a result of giving an **unauthorized** incense offering (3:4; see Lev. 10:1–20).

3:5–10 *The Duties of the Levites.* The two principal tasks of the Levites included: (1) guarding the tabernacle from intruders and (2) ministering **at the tabernacle** (i.e., transporting it from place to place). How this is to be done is explained in ch. 4.

3:11–13 *Reason for the Levitical Census.* In the last plague, every **firstborn** male Egyptian and every firstborn of their cattle died, but the Israelite boys and cattle were spared. So after this, all Israelite firstborn boys and cattle were dedicated to God. That meant the cattle were sacrificed and the boys should

13[o]See Ex. 13:2 [p]ch. 8:17; Ex. 13:12, 15
15[q]ver. 39; ch. 26:62; [ch. 1:47]
17[r]ch. 26:57; Gen. 46:11; Ex. 6:16; 1 Chr. 6:1, 16; 23:6
18[s]Ex. 6:17; 1 Chr. 6:17; 23:7
19[t]Ex. 6:18; 1 Chr. 6:2, 18; 23:12
20[u]Ex. 6:19; 1 Chr. 6:19; 23:21
23[v]ch. 1:53
25[w]ch. 4:24-26 [x]Ex. 25:9 [y]Ex. 26:7; 36:14 [z]Ex. 26:14 [a]Ex. 26:36
26[b]Ex. 27:9 [c]Ex. 27:16 [d]ver. 37; Ex. 35:18; 39:40
27[e]1 Chr. 26:23
30[f][Ex. 6:22; Lev. 10:4]
31[g]Ex. 25:10 [h]Ex. 25:23 [i]Ex. 25:31 [j]Ex. 27:1; 30:1

the people of Israel instead of every firstborn who opens the womb among the people of
Israel. The Levites shall be mine, 13 for [o]all the firstborn are mine. [p]On the day that I struck
down all the firstborn in the land of Egypt, I consecrated for my own all the firstborn in
Israel, both of man and of beast. They shall be mine: I am the LORD."
14 And the LORD spoke to Moses in the wilderness of Sinai, saying, 15 "List the sons of Levi,
by fathers' houses and by clans; [q]every male from a month old and upward you shall list."
16 So Moses listed them according to the word of the LORD, as he was commanded. 17 [r]And
these were the sons of Levi by their names: Gershon and Kohath and Merari. 18 And these
are the names of the sons of Gershon by their clans: [s]Libni and Shimei. 19 And the sons of
Kohath by their clans: [t]Amram, Izhar, Hebron, and Uzziel. 20 And the sons of Merari by their
clans: [u]Mahli and Mushi. These are the clans of the Levites, by their fathers' houses.
21 To Gershon belonged the clan of the Libnites and the clan of the Shimeites; these
were the clans of the Gershonites. 22 Their listing according to the number of all the males
from a month old and upward was[1] 7,500. 23 [v]The clans of the Gershonites were to
camp behind the tabernacle on the west, 24 with Eliasaph, the son of Lael as chief of the
fathers' house of the Gershonites. 25 And the [w]guard duty of the sons of Gershon in
the tent of meeting involved [x]the tabernacle, [y]the tent with [z]its covering, [a]the screen for
the entrance of the tent of meeting, 26 [b]the hangings of the court, [c]the screen for the door
of the court that is around the tabernacle and the altar, and [d]its cords—all the service
connected with these.
27 To Kohath belonged the clan of the [e]Amramites and the clan of the Izharites and the
clan of the Hebronites and the clan of the Uzzielites; these are the clans of the Kohathites.
28 According to the number of all the males, from a month old and upward, there were
8,600, keeping guard over the sanctuary. 29 The clans of the sons of Kohath were to camp
on the south side of the tabernacle, 30 with [f]Elizaphan the son of Uzziel as chief of the
fathers' house of the clans of the Kohathites. 31 And their guard duty involved [g]the ark,
[h]the table, [i]the lampstand, [j]the altars, the vessels of the sanctuary with which the priests

[1] Hebrew *their listing was*

have served God in the sanctuary (Ex. 11:4–13:15). But after the golden calf incident, the Levites took the place of the firstborn boys (Ex. 32:25–29).

3:14–39 *The Clans' Numbers, Positions, and Responsibilities.* The census results are listed by clan, specifying which parts of the tabernacle each clan was responsible for carrying and which side they had to guard (see diagram below). Most privileged were the **Kohathites (8,600)**, camping on the **south side** and responsible for the ark and other holy furniture. Next in privilege were the **Gershonites (7,500)**, camping on the **west** side and responsible for the curtains and hangings. Finally came the Merarites (**6,200**), camping on the **north side** and looking after the **frames**, **pegs**, etc. The total number of Levites (v. 39) is **22,000**, which is 300 less than the sum of the individual clans. The likeliest explanation is that, due to a copyist's error, the number of Kohathites should be 8,300, not 8,600. The numerals 6 and 3 are very similar in Hebrew. The location of the priests at the **east** side of the tabernacle guarding its entrance (v. 38) may anticipate the role of Jesus as high priest, giving his people access to God's presence in heaven (Hebrews 9–10).

Positions and Duties of the Levites

The Merarites camped on the north, guarding and carrying the structural components of the tent and the court (frames, bars, pillars, bases, pegs, cords, etc.).

The Gershonites camped on the west, guarding and carrying the coverings, hangings, and entrance screens of the tent and the courtyard.

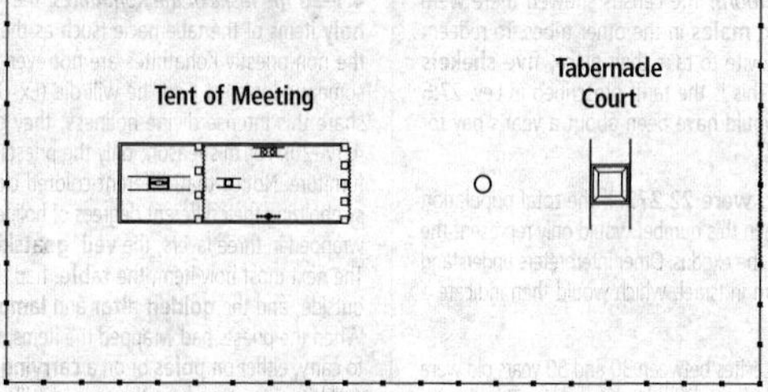

Moses and the priests camped on the east, guarding the tabernacle sanctuary and protecting Israel.

The Kohathites camped on the south, guarding and carrying the items within the tabernacle sanctuary (ark, table, lampstand, altars, vessels, and screen).

minister, and [k]the screen; all the service connected with these. 32 And Eleazar the son of
Aaron the priest was to be chief over the chiefs of the Levites, and to have oversight of
those who kept guard over the sanctuary.
33 To Merari belonged the clan of the Mahlites and the clan of the Mushites: these
are the clans of Merari. 34 Their listing according to the number of all the males from a
month old and upward was 6,200. 35 And the chief of the fathers' house of the clans of
Merari was Zuriel the son of Abihail. They were to camp on the north side of the tabernacle. 36 [l]And the appointed guard duty of the sons of Merari involved the [m]frames of
the tabernacle, [n]the bars, [o]the pillars, the bases, and all their accessories; all the service
connected with these; 37 also [p]the pillars around the court, with their bases and [q]pegs
and [r]cords.
38 Those who were to camp before the tabernacle on the east, before the tent of meeting
toward the sunrise, were Moses and Aaron and his sons, [s]guarding the sanctuary itself, to
protect[1] the people of Israel. And any outsider who came near was to be put to death. 39 All
those listed among the Levites, whom Moses and Aaron listed at the commandment of the
LORD, by clans, all the males from a month old and upward, were [t]22,000.

Redemption of the Firstborn

40 And the LORD said to Moses, "List all the firstborn males of the people of Israel, from
a month old and upward, taking the number of their names. 41 [u]And you shall take the
Levites for me—I am the LORD—instead of all the firstborn among the people of Israel,
and the cattle of the Levites instead of all the firstborn among the cattle of the people of
Israel." 42 So Moses listed all the firstborn among the people of Israel, as the LORD commanded him. 43 And all the firstborn males, according to the number of names, from a
month old and upward as listed were 22,273.
44 And the LORD spoke to Moses, saying, 45 [v]"Take the Levites instead of all the firstborn
among the people of Israel, and the cattle of the Levites instead of their cattle. The Levites
shall be mine: I am the LORD. 46 And [w]as the redemption price for the 273 of the firstborn
of the people of Israel, over and above the number of the male Levites, 47 you shall take
[x]five shekels[2] per head; you shall take them according to [y]the shekel of the sanctuary (the
shekel of twenty gerahs[3]), 48 and give the money to Aaron and his sons as the redemption
price for those who are over." 49 So Moses took the redemption money from those who
were over and above those redeemed by the Levites. 50 From the firstborn of the people
of Israel he took the money, [z]1,365 shekels, by the shekel of the sanctuary. 51 And Moses
[a]gave the redemption money to Aaron and his sons, according to the word of the LORD,
as the LORD commanded Moses.

Duties of the Kohathites

4 The LORD spoke to Moses and Aaron, saying, 2 "Take a census of the sons of Kohath
from among the sons of Levi, by their clans and their fathers' houses, 3 [b]from thirty
years old up to fifty years old, all who can come on duty, to do the work in the tent of

[1] Hebrew *guard* [2] A *shekel* was about 2/5 ounce or 11 grams [3] A *gerah* was about 1/50 ounce or 0.6 gram

31 [k]Ex. 26:36
36 [l]ch. 4:31, 32 [m]Ex. 26:15 [n]Ex. 26:26 [o]Ex. 26:32, 37
37 [p]Ex. 27:10 [q]Ex. 27:19 [r]ver. 26
38 [s]See ch. 1:53
39 [t][ver. 22, 28, 34; See ver. 46-49]
41 [u]ver. 12, 45
45 [v]ver. 12, 41
46 [w]ch. 18:15, 16; Ex. 13:13
47 [x]ch. 18:16; Lev. 27:6 [y]See Ex. 30:13
50 [z]ver. 46, 47
51 [a]ver. 48

Chapter 4

3 [b]ver. 23, 30, 35, 39, 43, 47; [ch. 8:24; 1 Chr. 23:3, 24, 27]

3:40–51 *Redemption of the Firstborn.* The census showed there were **273** fewer **Levites** than **firstborn males** in the other tribes. To redeem these 273 Israelites who had no Levite to take their place, **five shekels** (v. 47) per person had to be paid. This is the tariff prescribed in Lev. 27:6 for boys under five. Five shekels would have been about a year's pay for a herdsman.

3:43 all the firstborn males . . . were 22,273. If the total population was over 2 million, as some hold, then this number would only represent the number of firstborn males born since the exodus. Other interpreters understand this figure as the total of all firstborn in Israel, which would then indicate a much smaller total population.

4:1–49 *Census of Mature Levites.* Levites between 30 and 50 years old were responsible for moving the tabernacle from campsite to campsite. This chapter specifies what each Levitical clan must do (vv. 3–33) and then records their number (vv. 34–49). The instructions presuppose that the reader can visualize the tabernacle and its furniture. For a full description of the tabernacle, see Exodus 25–31 and notes, and The Tabernacle, pp. 190–191.

4:1–20 *The Tasks of the Kohathites.* The Kohathite priests handle the **most holy** items of the tabernacle (such as the ark, lampstand, and altars), but the non-priestly Kohathites are not even to look at them, lest they die. If someone looks at God, he will die (Ex. 33:20), and because these items share this intense divine holiness, they could prove equally lethal (Num. 4:17–20). For this reason, only the priests may wrap these pieces of sacred furniture. Notice that different-colored cloths are used for different items, symbolizing their different degrees of holiness. The **ark**, being most holy, was wrapped in three layers, the **veil**, **goatskin**, and **blue . . . cloth** (vv. 5–6). The next most holy item, the **table**, had three layers with **goatskin** on the outside, and the **golden altar** and **lampstand** had two layers (vv. 7–11). When the priests had wrapped the items, they were given to the Kohathites to carry, either on **poles** or on a **carrying frame** (vv. 6, 8, 10, 11, 12, 14). A Hittite document from the second millennium B.C. provides an analogy to OT texts that describe the work of Levites and priests, in that it describes two classes of people who watch over and take care of the temple: a priestly class and a non-priestly class. People in the latter group serve as aides to the former group.

meeting. 4 This is the service of the sons of Kohath in the tent of meeting: [c]the most holy
things. 5 When the camp is to set out, Aaron and his sons shall go in and take down [d]the
veil of the screen and cover [e]the ark of the testimony with it. 6 Then they shall put on it
a covering of goatskin[1] and spread on top of that a cloth all of blue, and shall put in its
[f]poles. 7 And over the [g]table of the bread of the Presence they shall spread a cloth of blue
and put on it the plates, the dishes for incense, the bowls, and the flagons for the drink
offering; [h]the regular showbread also shall be on it. 8 Then they shall spread over them a
cloth of scarlet and cover the same with a covering of goatskin, and shall [i]put in its poles.
9 And they shall take a cloth of blue and cover [j]the lampstand for the light, with its lamps,
its tongs, its trays, and all the vessels for oil with which it is supplied. 10 And they shall put
it with all its utensils in a covering of goatskin and put it on the carrying frame. 11 And over
[k]the golden altar they shall spread a cloth of blue and cover it with a covering of goatskin,
and shall put in its poles. 12 And they shall take all [l]the vessels of the service that are used in
the sanctuary and put them in a cloth of blue and cover them with a covering of goatskin
and put them on the carrying frame. 13 And they shall take away the ashes from the altar
and spread a purple cloth over it. 14 And they shall put on it all the utensils of the altar,
which are used for the service there, the fire pans, the forks, the shovels, and the basins, all
the utensils of the altar; and they shall spread on it a covering of goatskin, and shall put
in its poles. 15 And when Aaron and his sons have finished covering the sanctuary and all
the furnishings of the sanctuary, as the camp sets out, after that [m]the sons of Kohath shall
come to carry these, [n]but they must not touch the holy things, lest they die. These are the
things of the tent of meeting that the sons of Kohath are to carry.
16 "And Eleazar the son of Aaron the priest shall have charge of [o]the oil for the light, the
[p]fragrant incense, [q]the regular grain offering, and [r]the anointing oil, with the oversight
of the whole tabernacle and all that is in it, of the sanctuary and its vessels."
17 The LORD spoke to Moses and Aaron, saying, 18 "Let not the tribe of the clans of the
Kohathites be destroyed from among the Levites, 19 but deal thus with them, that they
may live and not die when they come near to [s]the most holy things: Aaron and his sons
shall go in and appoint them each to his task and to his burden, 20 [t]but they shall not go
in to look on the holy things even for a moment, lest they die."
21 The LORD spoke to Moses, saying, 22 "Take a census of the sons of Gershon also, by
their fathers' houses and by their clans. 23 [u]From thirty years old up to fifty years old, you
shall list them, all who can [v]come to do duty, to do service in the tent of meeting. 24 This
is the service of the clans of the Gershonites, in serving and bearing burdens: 25 [w]they
shall carry [x]the curtains of the tabernacle and the tent of meeting with [y]its covering and
the covering of goatskin that is on top of it and the screen for the entrance of the tent of
meeting 26 and the hangings of the court and the screen for the entrance of the gate of the
court that is around the tabernacle and the altar, and their cords and all the equipment
for their service. And they shall do all that needs to be done with regard to them. 27 All the
service of the sons of the Gershonites shall be at the command of Aaron and his sons, in all
that they are to carry and in all that they have to do. And you shall assign to their charge
all that they are to carry. 28 This is the service of the clans of the sons of the Gershonites
in the tent of meeting, and their guard duty is to be [z]under the direction of Ithamar the
son of Aaron the priest.
29 "As for the sons of Merari, you shall list them by their clans and their fathers' houses.
30 [u]From thirty years old up to fifty years old, you shall list them, everyone who can come
on duty, to do the service of the tent of meeting. 31 And [a]this is what they are charged to
carry, as the whole of their service in the tent of meeting: the frames of the tabernacle,
with its bars, pillars, and bases, 32 and the pillars around the court with their bases, pegs,
and cords, with all their equipment and all their accessories. And you shall [b]list by name
the objects that they are required to carry. 33 This is the service of the clans of the sons of

[1] The meaning of the Hebrew word is uncertain; compare Exodus 25:5

4 [c]ver. 19
5 [d]See Ex. 26:31 [e]Ex. 25:10, 16
6 [f]Ex. 25:13
7 [g]Ex. 25:23, 29, 30; 37:16; Lev. 24:6, 8 [h]2 Chr. 2:4
8 [i][Ex. 25:15, 28]
9 [j]See Ex. 25:31-39
11 [k]Ex. 30:1, 3
12 [l][1 Chr. 9:28, 29]
15 [m]ch. 7:9; 10:21; Deut. 31:9 [n]2 Sam. 6:6, 7; 1 Chr. 13:9, 10
16 [o]Ex. 25:6; 27:20; Lev. 24:2 [p]Ex. 25:6; 31:11 [q]Ex. 29:40, 41 [r]Ex. 31:11; See Ex. 30:23-33
19 [s]ver. 4
20 [t][Ex. 19:21; 1 Sam. 6:19]
23 [u]ver. 3 [v]ch. 8:24; [Ex. 38:8; 1 Sam. 2:22]
25 [w][ch. 3:25, 26] [x]See Ex. 26:1-6; 36:8-13 [y]Ex. 36:14, 19
28 [z]ver. 33
30 [u][See ver. 23 above]
31 [a]ch. 3:36, 37
32 [b]Ex. 38:21

4:21–28 *The Tasks of the Gershonites.* This section specifies the **curtains** of the tabernacle that the **Gershonites** are to carry. They were to be transported in two oxcarts (7:7).

4:29–33 *The Tasks of the Merarites.* The Merarites had to transport the planks, poles, bases, etc. These items, being heavier and bulkier than the curtains, required four oxcarts (7:8).

Merari, the whole of their service in the tent of meeting, [c]under the direction of Ithamar
the son of Aaron the priest."
34 And Moses and Aaron and the chiefs of the congregation listed the sons of the
Kohathites, by their clans and their fathers' houses, 35 [u]from thirty years old up to fifty
years old, everyone who could come on duty, for service in the tent of meeting; 36 and those
listed by clans were 2,750. 37 [d]This was the list of the clans of the Kohathites, all who served
in the tent of meeting, whom Moses and Aaron listed according to the commandment
of the LORD by Moses.
38 Those listed of the sons of Gershon, by their clans and their fathers' houses, 39 [u]from
thirty years old up to fifty years old, everyone who could come on duty for service in the
tent of meeting— 40 those listed by their clans and their fathers' houses were 2,630. 41 [e]This
was the list of the clans of the sons of Gershon, all who served in the tent of meeting, whom
Moses and Aaron listed according to the commandment of the LORD.
42 Those listed of the clans of the sons of Merari, by their clans and their fathers' houses,
43 [u]from thirty years old up to fifty years old, everyone who could come on duty, for service
in the tent of meeting— 44 those listed by clans were 3,200. 45 [f]This was the list of the clans
of the sons of Merari, whom Moses and Aaron listed according to the commandment of
the LORD by Moses.
46 All those who were listed of the Levites, whom Moses and Aaron and the chiefs of Israel
listed, by their clans and their fathers' houses, 47 [u]from thirty years old up to fifty years old,
everyone who could come to do the service of ministry and the service of bearing burdens
in the tent of meeting, 48 those listed were 8,580. 49 According to the commandment of the
LORD through Moses they were listed, [g]each one with his task of serving or carrying. Thus
they were listed by him, [h]as the LORD commanded Moses.

Unclean People

5 The LORD spoke to Moses, saying, 2 "Command the people of Israel that they [i]put out
of the camp everyone who is leprous[1] or has [j]a discharge and everyone who is [k]unclean
through contact with the dead. 3 You shall put out both male and female, putting them
outside the camp, that they may not defile their camp, [l]in the midst of which I dwell." 4 And
the people of Israel did so, and put them outside the camp; as the LORD said to Moses,
so the people of Israel did.

Confession and Restitution

5 And the LORD spoke to Moses, saying, 6 "Speak to the people of Israel, [m]When a man
or woman commits any of the sins that people commit by breaking faith with the LORD,

[1] *Leprosy* was a term for several skin diseases; see Leviticus 13

33 [c]ver. 28
35 [u][See ver. 23 above]
37 [d]ver. 2
39 [u][See ver. 23 above]
41 [e]ver. 22
43 [u][See ver. 23 above]
45 [f]ver. 29
47 [u][See ver. 23 above]
49 [g]ver. 15, 24, 31 [h]ver. 1, 21, 29

Chapter 5

2 [i]ch. 12:14; Lev. 13:46 [j]Lev. 15:2 [k]ch. 9:6, 10; 19:11, 13; 31:19; Lev. 21:1; [Hag. 2:13]
3 [l]See Lev. 26:11, 12
6 [m]Lev. 6:2, 3

4:34–49 *The Results of the Second Census.* Levites between 30 and 50 years old totaled **8,580**, just over a third of their total number of 22,000 (3:39). This chapter again shows preparations being made for the march into Canaan. It underlines once again the dangerous holiness of God: he cannot be approached casually. It also emphasizes the importance of the ministry of the Levites, who make possible the transport of the tabernacle to the land and who guard it from intrusion.

5:1–6:27 *Cleansing the Camp.* In preparation for the march to the Holy Land, the camp of Israel must be purged of all uncleanness. The concept of uncleanness (i.e., that which disgusts and angers God) is most important in the Bible, and in its OT form is explained most fully in Leviticus 11–16. (The NT shows that some things labeled unclean in the OT period, e.g., particular foodstuffs, were so designated for didactic reasons only until Christ came; see notes on Mark 7:19; Acts 15:1; 15:19–21; Gal. 2:11–12; 4:10; 5:1.) Uncleanness ranges in seriousness from mild uncleanness caused by marital intercourse (Lev. 15:18), to moderate uncleanness caused by skin disease (Leviticus 13), to severe uncleanness triggered by sins such as idolatry, adultery, and homicide. Severe uncleanness led to the Canaanites losing the land, and the same fate could befall Israel (Lev. 20:22–23). People who were unclean were forbidden to participate in worship, and their uncleanness could somehow infect the tabernacle, which would make it impossible for God to dwell there. The Day of Atonement was designed to cleanse the tabernacle once a year (Leviticus 16) in order to ensure God's continuing presence with his people. These regulations in Numbers 5–6 are preventative: they aim to eliminate uncleanness from the camp so that the tabernacle will remain pure and God will stay with his people as they journey to Canaan. The principle that only the purified can belong to the kingdom of heaven is reaffirmed in Eph. 5:5; Rev. 21:27; 22:14–15.

5:1–4 *Exclusion of the Unclean from the Camp.* The unclean are excluded from the tribal encampments of ch. 2 and must live in places such as caves or wilderness tents, separate from the people (cf. Lev. 13:46; 2 Kings 7:3).

5:2 leprous. The skin conditions involved are described in Leviticus 13. **dead**. On the uncleanness caused by death, see Num. 19:11–22. **discharge**. See notes on Leviticus 15.

5:5–10 *Atonement for Perjury.* This law extends the scope of Lev. 6:1–7, which deals with the case of someone stealing his neighbor's property and then taking an oath denying the fact. This amounts to taking God's name in vain (Ex. 20:7), a most serious offense. If the offender later recognizes his **guilt** and confesses it, he must return his neighbor's property plus 20 percent and offer a **ram** as a guilt offering. Verses 5–10 of Numbers 5 deal with the situation when there is none of the victim's family to receive the restored goods: in this case it is to go to the **priest** along with the sacrificial ram. Verses 9–10 generalize this principle: the priest who offers a sacrifice keeps for himself the parts that are not burnt. The NT affirms that reconciliation

7[n]Lev. 5:5; 26:40; [Josh. 7:19] [o]Lev. 6:5
8[p]Lev. 6:6, 7
9[q]ch. 18:19; Ex. 29:28; Lev. 6:17, 18; 7:6, 7, 9, 10, 14; Deut. 18:3, 4
13[r]Lev. 18:20 [s]John 8:4
15[t][Lev. 2:1, 15; 5:11] [u]1 Kgs. 17:18; Ezek. 29:16
18[v][1 Cor. 11:5-7]
21[w][Jer. 29:22]
22[x]Ps. 109:18 [y]See Deut. 27:15-26
25[z][Lev. 8:27]
26[a]Lev. 2:2, 9; 5:12

and that person realizes his guilt, 7 [n]he shall confess his sin that he has committed.[1] [o]And
he shall make full restitution for his wrong, adding a fifth to it and giving it to him to
whom he did the wrong. 8 But if the man has no next of kin to whom restitution may
be made for the wrong, the restitution for wrong shall go to the LORD for the priest,
in addition to [p]the ram of atonement with which atonement is made for him. 9 And
[q]every contribution, all the holy donations of the people of Israel, which they bring to
the priest, shall be his. 10 Each one shall keep his holy donations: whatever anyone gives
to the priest shall be his."

A Test for Adultery

11 And the LORD spoke to Moses, saying, 12 "Speak to the people of Israel, If any man's
wife goes astray and breaks faith with him, 13 if a man [r]lies with her sexually, and it is
hidden from the eyes of her husband, and she is undetected though she has defiled herself, and there is no witness against her, [s]since she was not taken in the act, 14 and if the
spirit of jealousy comes over him and he is jealous of his wife who has defiled herself, or
if the spirit of jealousy comes over him and he is jealous of his wife, though she has not
defiled herself, 15 then the man shall bring his wife to the priest and bring the offering
required of her, a tenth of an ephah[2] of barley flour. [t]He shall pour no oil on it and put no
frankincense on it, for it is a grain offering of jealousy, a grain offering of remembrance,
[u]bringing iniquity to remembrance.
16 "And the priest shall bring her near and set her before the LORD. 17 And the priest shall
take holy water in an earthenware vessel and take some of the dust that is on the floor of
the tabernacle and put it into the water. 18 And the priest shall set the woman before the
LORD and [v]unbind the hair of the woman's head and place in her hands the grain offering
of remembrance, which is the grain offering of jealousy. And in his hand the priest shall
have the water of bitterness that brings the curse. 19 Then the priest shall make her take
an oath, saying, 'If no man has lain with you, and if you have not turned aside to uncleanness while you were under your husband's authority, be free from this water of bitterness
that brings the curse. 20 But if you have gone astray, though you are under your husband's
authority, and if you have defiled yourself, and some man other than your husband has
lain with you, 21 then' (let the priest make the woman take the oath of the curse, and say
to the woman) [w]'the LORD make you a curse and an oath among your people, when the
LORD makes your thigh fall away and your body swell. 22 May this water that brings the
curse [x]pass into your bowels and make your womb swell and your thigh fall away.' And
the woman shall say, [y]'Amen, Amen.'
23 "Then the priest shall write these curses in a book and wash them off into the water
of bitterness. 24 And he shall make the woman drink the water of bitterness that brings
the curse, and the water that brings the curse shall enter into her and cause bitter pain.
25 And the priest shall take the grain offering of jealousy out of the woman's hand [z]and
shall wave the grain offering before the LORD and bring it to the altar. 26 And the priest
[a]shall take a handful of the grain offering, as its memorial portion, and burn it on the
altar, and afterward shall make the woman drink the water. 27 And when he has made her
drink the water, then, if she has defiled herself and has broken faith with her husband,
the water that brings the curse shall enter into her and cause bitter pain, and her womb

[1] Hebrew *they shall confess their sin that they have committed* [2] An *ephah* was about 3/5 bushel or 22 liters

with one's fellow man is required of those who would be at peace with God (Matt. 5:23–26; 6:14–15).

5:11–31 *Test of Suspected Adultery.* This ritual is an acted-out prayer that God would show whether a man's suspicions about his wife's fidelity were justified. Adultery, like other sexual sins, causes grievous uncleanness, and so must be eliminated from Israel. The test is designed to distinguish between actual-but-unwitnessed adultery (vv. 12–14a) and unwarranted suspicion (v. 14b). The actions all underline the seriousness of the sin of adultery. When an adulterous man and woman were caught in the act, they faced the death penalty in Israel (Deut. 22:22) and elsewhere in the ancient Near East. On this occasion the husband is merely suspicious. To confirm or dispel his suspicions the woman must offer a sacrifice (Num. 5:15–16), drink **water** containing **dust** from the **floor of the tabernacle** (i.e., dust from the presence of God; v. 17), and accept a **curse** against herself that her **womb swell** and her **thigh fall away** (vv. 19–22) if she is guilty. It is not clear exactly what this threat means (the focus is on the members of her body with which she may have sinned), but it could be a threat of a miscarriage. Ultimately, though, the guilty wife is threatened with childlessness, a catastrophe in Bible times, whereas the innocent is assured **she shall be free and shall conceive children** (v. 28; cf. Gen. 20:17–18).

5:15 grain offering. For the normal procedure, see Leviticus 2. The omission of **oil** and **frankincense** shows this is not a joyful occasion.

5:18 unbind the hair. An act of shaming, or perhaps of mourning (cf. Lev. 10:6; 21:10).

shall swell, and her thigh shall fall away, and the woman [b]shall become a curse among
her people. 28 But if the woman has not defiled herself and is clean, then she shall be free
and shall conceive children.

29 "This is the law in cases of jealousy, when a wife, [c]though under her husband's authority, goes astray and defiles herself, 30 or when the spirit of jealousy comes over a man and
he is jealous of his wife. Then he shall set the woman before the LORD, and the priest
shall carry out for her all this law. 31 The man shall be free from iniquity, but the woman
[d]shall bear her iniquity."

The Nazirite Vow

6 And the LORD spoke to Moses, saying, 2 "Speak to the people of Israel and say to them,
When either a man or a woman makes a special vow, the vow of [e]a Nazirite,[1] [f]to separate himself to the LORD, 3 he [g]shall separate himself from wine and strong drink. He shall
drink no vinegar made from wine or strong drink and shall not drink any juice of grapes
or eat grapes, fresh or dried. 4 All the days of his separation[2] he shall eat nothing that is
produced by the grapevine, not even the seeds or the skins.

5 "All the days of his vow of separation, no [h]razor shall touch his head. Until the time is
completed for which he separates himself to the LORD, he shall be holy. [i]He shall let the
locks of hair of his head grow long.

6 "All the days that he separates himself to the LORD [j]he shall not go near a dead body.
7 [k]Not even for his father or for his mother, for brother or sister, if they die, shall he make
himself unclean, because his separation to God is on his head. 8 All the days of his separation he is holy to the LORD.

9 "And if any man dies very suddenly beside him and he defiles his consecrated head,
then [l]he shall shave his head on the day of his cleansing; on the seventh day he shall shave
it. 10 [m]On the eighth day he shall bring two turtledoves or two pigeons to the priest to the
entrance of the tent of meeting, 11 and the priest shall offer one for a sin offering and the
other for a burnt offering, and make atonement for him, because he sinned by reason of
the dead body. And he shall consecrate his head that same day 12 and separate himself to the
LORD for the days of his separation and bring a male lamb a year old [n]for a guilt offering.
But the previous period shall be void, because his separation was defiled.

13 "And this is the law for the Nazirite, [o]when the time of his separation has been completed: he shall be brought to the entrance of the tent of meeting, 14 and he shall bring his
gift to the LORD, one male lamb a year old without blemish for a burnt offering, and one
ewe lamb a year old without blemish [p]as a sin offering, and one ram without blemish [q]as
a peace offering, 15 and a basket of unleavened bread, [r]loaves of fine flour mixed with oil,
and unleavened wafers smeared with oil, and their [s]grain offering and their [t]drink offerings. 16 And the priest shall bring them before the LORD and offer [u]his sin offering and his
burnt offering, 17 and he shall offer the ram as a sacrifice of peace offering to the LORD, with
the basket of unleavened bread. The priest shall offer also its grain offering and its drink
offering. 18 And the Nazirite [v]shall shave his consecrated head at the entrance of the tent
of meeting and shall take the hair from his consecrated head and put it on the fire that is
under the sacrifice of the peace offering. 19 And the priest shall take the [w]shoulder of the

[1] *Nazirite* means *one separated*, or *one consecrated* [2] Or *Naziriteship*

27 [b]Deut. 28:37; Jer. 24:9; 29:18, 22; 42:18; 44:12; Zech. 8:13
29 [c]ver. 19, 20
31 [d]Lev. 20:17, 19, 20

Chapter 6

2 [e]Judg. 13:5; [Acts 21:23] [f][Rom. 1:1]
3 [g]Amos 2:12; Luke 1:15
5 [h]Judg. 13:5; 16:17; 1 Sam. 1:11 [i]Ezek. 44:20; [1 Cor. 11:14]
6 [j]ch. 19:11, 16; Lev. 21:11
7 [k]Lev. 21:1, 2, 11
9 [l]Acts 18:18; 21:24
10 [m]Lev. 5:7; 14:22; 15:14, 29
12 [n]Lev. 5:6
13 [o]Acts 21:26
14 [p]Lev. 4:32 [q]Lev. 3:6
15 [r]Ex. 29:2; Lev. 2:4 [s]See Ex. 29:41 [t]ch. 15:5, 7, 10
16 [u]ver. 14
18 [v]Acts 18:18; 21:24
19 [w]1 Sam. 2:15

6:1–21 *Rules for Nazirites.* Nazirites were the most dedicated laypeople in the OT. Samson, Samuel, and John the Baptist were lifelong Nazirites, but usually a person took a vow to become a Nazirite for only a specific period of time.

6:1–6 *Definition of a Nazirite.* A **Nazirite** (see ESV footnote on v. 2) had to avoid cutting his or her **hair** (both men and women could be Nazirites, v. 2), not eat any product made from **grapes**, and avoid contact with any **dead body**.

6:7–12 *Nazirites and Uncleanness.* Death was a source of severe uncleanness, and contact with death compromised the Nazirite's status. It had to be remedied by offering three sacrifices (**sin**, **burnt**, and **guilt** offerings; Lev. 1:14–16; 5:7–10, 14–16) and by starting the period of the Nazirite vow all over again: **the previous period shall be void** (Num. 6:12). It is probably the issue of uncleanness that prompts the inclusion of the laws on the Nazirite at this point in the book (see 5:2–4).

6:7 his separation to God is on his head. The word here translated "separation" (Hb. *nezer*) is also used of the high priest's crown (Lev. 8:9). Both the priestly crown and the Nazirite's uncut hair reminded other people of their dedication to God's service. In this way the dedication of the Nazirites was a challenge to every Israelite to follow the Lord wholeheartedly.

6:13–20 *Completion of a Nazirite Vow.* When the period to which a Nazirite had dedicated himself was over, he had to bring three animal sacrifices (**burnt**, **sin**, and **peace** offerings; Lev. 1:10–13; 4:32–35; 3:6–11) and the customary accompanying **grain** and wine offerings (Lev. 2:4–13; Num. 15:1–10). Finally, the Nazirite shaved his head and burned his hair on the altar. His unshaven head marked his dedication to God, and by burning the hair he symbolically gave himself to God. **The shoulder of the ram** is given to the **priest**, in addition to his usual share of the sacrifice (the **breast** and the **thigh**; cf. Lev. 7:31–34).

19[x]Ex. 29:23, 24
20[y][ch. 5:25; Ex. 29:27, 28]
23[z]Lev. 9:22; Deut. 21:5; 1 Chr. 23:13
24[a]Ps. 134:3 [b]See Ps. 121:3-8
25[c]Ps. 31:16; 67:1; 80:3, 7, 19; 119:135; [Dan. 9:17]
26[d]Ps. 4:6
27[e]Deut. 28:10; 2 Chr. 7:14; Dan. 9:18, 19

Chapter 7

1[f]Ex. 40:17, 18 [g]Lev. 8:10, 11
2[h]ch. 1:4
7[i]ch. 4:25, 28
8[j]ch. 4:29, 31, 33
9[k]ch. 3:31; See ch. 4:4-15 [l][2 Sam. 6:13; 1 Chr. 15:5, 15]
10[m]Deut. 20:5; 1 Kgs. 8:63; 2 Chr. 7:5, 9; Ezra 6:16; Neh. 12:27
12[n]See Ex. 6:23

ram, when it is boiled, and one unleavened loaf out of the basket and one unleavened
wafer, and [x]shall put them on the hands of the Nazirite, after he has shaved the hair of his
consecration, 20 and the priest shall wave them for a wave offering before the LORD. [y]They
are a holy portion for the priest, together with the breast that is waved and the thigh that
is contributed. And after that the Nazirite may drink wine.
21 "This is the law of the Nazirite. But if he vows an offering to the LORD above his
Nazirite vow, as he can afford, in exact accordance with the vow that he takes, then he
shall do in addition to the law of the Nazirite."

Aaron's Blessing

22 The LORD spoke to Moses, saying, 23 "Speak to Aaron and his sons, saying, Thus [z]you
shall bless the people of Israel: you shall say to them,

24 The LORD [a]bless you and [b]keep you;
25 the LORD [c]make his face to shine upon you and be gracious to you;
26 the LORD [d]lift up his countenance[1] upon you and give you peace.

27 [e]"So shall they put my name upon the people of Israel, and I will bless them."

Offerings at the Tabernacle's Consecration

7 On the day when Moses had finished [f]setting up the tabernacle and had anointed and
[g]consecrated it with all its furnishings and had anointed and consecrated the altar with
all its utensils, 2 [h]the chiefs of Israel, heads of their fathers' houses, who were the chiefs of
the tribes, who were over those who were listed, approached 3 and brought their offerings
before the LORD, six wagons and twelve oxen, a wagon for every two of the chiefs, and for
each one an ox. They brought them before the tabernacle. 4 Then the LORD said to Moses,
5 "Accept these from them, that they may be used in the service of the tent of meeting, and
give them to the Levites, to each man according to his service." 6 So Moses took the wagons
and the oxen and gave them to the Levites. 7 Two wagons and four oxen [i]he gave to the
sons of Gershon, according to their service. 8 And four wagons and eight oxen [j]he gave
to the sons of Merari, according to their service, under the direction of Ithamar the son
of Aaron the priest. 9 But to the sons of Kohath he gave none, because they were charged
with [k]the service of the holy things that [l]had to be carried on the shoulder. 10 And the
chiefs offered offerings for the [m]dedication of the altar on the day it was anointed; and
the chiefs offered their offering before the altar. 11 And the LORD said to Moses, "They shall
offer their offerings, one chief each day, for the dedication of the altar."
12 He who offered his offering the first day was [n]Nahshon the son of Amminadab, of
the tribe of Judah. 13 And his offering was one silver plate whose weight was 130 shekels,[2]

[1] Or *face* [2] A *shekel* was about 2/5 ounce or 11 grams

6:21 *Summary of the Law.* **above his Nazirite vow**. If the ex-Nazirite had pledged to do more than keep the Nazirite abstention rules (6:3–7), he must fulfill those pledges too.

6:22–27 *The Priestly Blessing.* Placed here, this famous blessing shows that God's will is to bless every Israelite, not just the Nazirites. But God's blessing is mediated by the priests. The earliest archaeological discovery containing the covenantal name of God (Yahweh) in Jerusalem is a silver amulet containing this priestly blessing. It was found in a Judean tomb dating to the seventh or sixth century B.C.

6:24 The LORD bless you. God blesses by giving good harvests, peace, children, and his own presence (Lev. 26:3–13). **keep**. That is, "guard" and "protect."

6:25 his face to shine upon you. God's presence is like sunshine (Ps. 19:1–11). A shining face is a smiling face, a pledge of God's good favor (Ps. 80:3, 7, 19).

6:26 The "countenance" is the face or the expression of one's face. For God to **lift up his countenance** involves taking notice of and treating his people with favor. **Peace** (Hb. *shalom*) involves more than the English sense of "lack of war"; it means total well-being.

7:1–89 *Offerings for the Tabernacle.* **On the day when Moses had finished setting up the tabernacle** places these events a month before those described in chs. 1–6 (Ex. 40:2; Num. 1:1). If the opening chapters of Numbers had not been placed first, it would have been more difficult to grasp the significance of what is described in this chapter. Numbers 3–4 describes the duties of the priests and Levites; ch. 7 shows how the other tribes supported them. First, they supplied wagons and oxen to help the Levites carry the tabernacle. The Gershonites, carriers of the tabernacle curtains and hangings, were given two wagons and four oxen (4:25–26; 7:7). The Merarites—carriers of the poles, frames, and bases—were given four wagons and eight oxen (4:31–32; 7:8). The Kohathites, who carried the tabernacle furniture on shoulder poles, received none (v. 9).

7:10–88 On 12 successive days the chiefs of the 12 tribes (one chief per day) brought gifts to show their tribes' support for the official worship. Each tribe gave exactly the same thing: **one silver plate** and **one silver basin**, each filled with **flour mixed with oil**. They also offered **one golden dish . . . full of incense**. The low weight (4 ounces [113 g]) of the dish makes commentators think it may have been more like a ladle or spoon. Then there were a variety of animals to keep the regular sacrifices going. The summary of all the donations in vv. 84–88 shows that the animals were not sacrificed immediately after they were offered but were kept for the appropriate occasion. The exact repetition of the donations of each tribe underlines that all the tribes were equally committed to supporting the tabernacle. It is also noteworthy that, as in chs. 1–4, the tribe of Judah takes the lead (see notes on 1:26–27; 2:1–34).

one silver basin of 70 shekels, according to [o]the shekel of the sanctuary, both of them full
of fine flour mixed with oil for a [p]grain offering; 14 one golden dish of 10 shekels, full of
[q]incense; 15 [r]one bull from the herd, one ram, one male lamb a year old, for a burnt offering;
16 one male goat for a [s]sin offering; 17 and for [t]the sacrifice of peace offerings, two oxen, five
rams, five male goats, and five male lambs a year old. This was the offering of Nahshon
the son of Amminadab.

18 On the second day [u]Nethanel the son of Zuar, the chief of Issachar, made an offering.
19 He offered for his offering one silver plate whose weight was 130 shekels, one silver
basin of 70 shekels, according to the shekel of the sanctuary, both of them full of fine
flour mixed with oil for a grain offering; 20 one golden dish of 10 shekels, full of incense;
21 one bull from the herd, one ram, one male lamb a year old, for a burnt offering; 22 one
male goat for a sin offering; 23 and for the sacrifice of peace offerings, two oxen, five rams,
five male goats, and five male lambs a year old. This was the offering of Nethanel the son
of Zuar.

24 On the third day [v]Eliab the son of Helon, the chief of the people of Zebulun: 25 his
offering was one silver plate whose weight was 130 shekels, one silver basin of 70 shekels,
according to the shekel of the sanctuary, both of them full of fine flour mixed with oil for
a grain offering; 26 one golden dish of 10 shekels, full of incense; 27 one bull from the herd,
one ram, one male lamb a year old, for a burnt offering; 28 one male goat for a sin offering;
29 and for the sacrifice of peace offerings, two oxen, five rams, five male goats, and five male
lambs a year old. This was the offering of Eliab the son of Helon.

30 On the fourth day [w]Elizur the son of Shedeur, the chief of the people of Reuben: 31 his
offering was one silver plate whose weight was 130 shekels, one silver basin of 70 shekels,
according to the shekel of the sanctuary, both of them full of fine flour mixed with oil for
a grain offering; 32 one golden dish of 10 shekels, full of incense; 33 one bull from the herd,
one ram, one male lamb a year old, for a burnt offering; 34 one male goat for a sin offering;
35 and for the sacrifice of peace offerings, two oxen, five rams, five male goats, and five male
lambs a year old. This was the offering of Elizur the son of Shedeur.

36 On the fifth day [x]Shelumiel the son of Zurishaddai, the chief of the people of Simeon:
37 his offering was one silver plate whose weight was 130 shekels, one silver basin of 70
shekels, according to the shekel of the sanctuary, both of them full of fine flour mixed with
oil for a grain offering; 38 one golden dish of 10 shekels, full of incense; 39 one bull from
the herd, one ram, one male lamb a year old, for a burnt offering; 40 one male goat for a sin

13 [o]See Ex. 30:13 [p]ch. 8:8; See Ex. 29:41
14 [q]Ex. 30:34, 35
15 [r]Lev. 1:2, 3
16 [s]Lev. 4:23, 24
17 [t]Lev. 3:1
18 [u]ch. 1:8
24 [v]ch. 1:9
30 [w]ch. 1:5
36 [x]ch. 1:6

Dated Events from Exodus 40 to Numbers 10

Reference	Event	Date*	Event	Reference
Ex. 40:2	Tabernacle set up	1.1.2	Tabernacle set up	Num. 7:1
Lev. 1:1	Laws from tabernacle begin		Offerings for altar begin	Num. 7:3
Lev. 8:1	Ordination of priests begins			
Lev. 9:1	Ordination completed	8.1.2		
Lev. 10:1–3	Death of Nadab and Abihu			
Lev. 24:10–23	Blasphemer dies			
		12.1.2	Offerings for altar end	Num. 7:78
			Appointment of Levites	Num. 8:5
		14.1.2	Second Passover	Num. 9:2
		1.2.2	Census begins	Num. 1:1
		14.2.2	Delayed Passover	Num. 9:11
		20.2.2	Cloud moves	Num. 10:11

**The date formula is day.month.year. For example, 1.1.2 = the first day of the first month of the second year. All of these events occurred in the second year after the exodus. (For modern equivalents to the months see The Hebrew Calendar, p. 34.)*

42[y]ch. 1:14; [ch. 2:14]
48[z]ch. 1:10
54[a]ch. 1:10
60[b]ch. 1:11
66[c]ch. 1:12
72[d]ch. 1:13
78[e]ch. 1:15

offering; 41 and for the sacrifice of peace offerings, two oxen, five rams, five male goats, and
five male lambs a year old. This was the offering of Shelumiel the son of Zurishaddai.
42 On the sixth day [y]Eliasaph the son of Deuel, the chief of the people of Gad: 43 his
offering was one silver plate whose weight was 130 shekels, one silver basin of 70 shekels,
according to the shekel of the sanctuary, both of them full of fine flour mixed with oil for
a grain offering; 44 one golden dish of 10 shekels, full of incense; 45 one bull from the herd,
one ram, one male lamb a year old, for a burnt offering; 46 one male goat for a sin offering;
47 and for the sacrifice of peace offerings, two oxen, five rams, five male goats, and five male
lambs a year old. This was the offering of Eliasaph the son of Deuel.
48 On the seventh day [z]Elishama the son of Ammihud, the chief of the people of Ephraim:
49 his offering was one silver plate whose weight was 130 shekels, one silver basin of 70
shekels, according to the shekel of the sanctuary, both of them full of fine flour mixed with
oil for a grain offering; 50 one golden dish of 10 shekels, full of incense; 51 one bull from
the herd, one ram, one male lamb a year old, for a burnt offering; 52 one male goat for a sin
offering; 53 and for the sacrifice of peace offerings, two oxen, five rams, five male goats, and
five male lambs a year old. This was the offering of Elishama the son of Ammihud.
54 On the eighth day [a]Gamaliel the son of Pedahzur, the chief of the people of Manasseh:
55 his offering was one silver plate whose weight was 130 shekels, one silver basin of 70
shekels, according to the shekel of the sanctuary, both of them full of fine flour mixed with
oil for a grain offering; 56 one golden dish of 10 shekels, full of incense; 57 one bull from
the herd, one ram, one male lamb a year old, for a burnt offering; 58 one male goat for a sin
offering; 59 and for the sacrifice of peace offerings, two oxen, five rams, five male goats, and
five male lambs a year old. This was the offering of Gamaliel the son of Pedahzur.
60 On the ninth day [b]Abidan the son of Gideoni, the chief of the people of Benjamin: 61 his
offering was one silver plate whose weight was 130 shekels, one silver basin of 70 shekels,
according to the shekel of the sanctuary, both of them full of fine flour mixed with oil for
a grain offering; 62 one golden dish of 10 shekels, full of incense; 63 one bull from the herd,
one ram, one male lamb a year old, for a burnt offering; 64 one male goat for a sin offering;
65 and for the sacrifice of peace offerings, two oxen, five rams, five male goats, and five male
lambs a year old. This was the offering of Abidan the son of Gideoni.
66 On the tenth day [c]Ahiezer the son of Ammishaddai, the chief of the people of Dan: 67 his
offering was one silver plate whose weight was 130 shekels, one silver basin of 70 shekels,
according to the shekel of the sanctuary, both of them full of fine flour mixed with oil for
a grain offering; 68 one golden dish of 10 shekels, full of incense; 69 one bull from the herd,
one ram, one male lamb a year old, for a burnt offering; 70 one male goat for a sin offering;
71 and for the sacrifice of peace offerings, two oxen, five rams, five male goats, and five male
lambs a year old. This was the offering of Ahiezer the son of Ammishaddai.
72 On the eleventh day [d]Pagiel the son of Ochran, the chief of the people of Asher: 73 his
offering was one silver plate whose weight was 130 shekels, one silver basin of 70 shekels,
according to the shekel of the sanctuary, both of them full of fine flour mixed with oil for
a grain offering; 74 one golden dish of 10 shekels, full of incense; 75 one bull from the herd,
one ram, one male lamb a year old, for a burnt offering; 76 one male goat for a sin offering;
77 and for the sacrifice of peace offerings, two oxen, five rams, five male goats, and five male
lambs a year old. This was the offering of Pagiel the son of Ochran.
78 On the twelfth day [e]Ahira the son of Enan, the chief of the people of Naphtali: 79 his
offering was one silver plate whose weight was 130 shekels, one silver basin of 70 shekels,
according to the shekel of the sanctuary, both of them full of fine flour mixed with oil for
a grain offering; 80 one golden dish of 10 shekels, full of incense; 81 one bull from the herd,
one ram, one male lamb a year old, for a burnt offering; 82 one male goat for a sin offering;
83 and for the sacrifice of peace offerings, two oxen, five rams, five male goats, and five male
lambs a year old. This was the offering of Ahira the son of Enan.
84 This was the dedication offering for the altar on the day when it was anointed, from
the chiefs of Israel: twelve silver plates, twelve silver basins, twelve golden dishes, 85 each
silver plate weighing 130 shekels and each basin 70, all the silver of the vessels 2,400
shekels according to the shekel of the sanctuary, 86 the twelve golden dishes, full of incense,

weighing 10 shekels apiece according to the shekel of the sanctuary, all the gold of the
dishes being 120 shekels; 87 all the cattle for the burnt offering twelve bulls, twelve rams,
twelve male lambs a year old, with their grain offering; and twelve male goats for a sin
offering; 88 and all the cattle for the sacrifice of peace offerings twenty-four bulls, the rams
sixty, the male goats sixty, the male lambs a year old sixty. This was the dedication offering
for the altar after it [f]was anointed.
89 And when Moses went into the tent of meeting [g]to speak with the LORD, he heard
[h]the voice speaking to him from above the mercy seat that was on the ark of the testimony,
from between the two cherubim; and it spoke to him.

The Seven Lamps

8 Now the LORD spoke to Moses, saying, 2 "Speak to Aaron and say to him, When you set
up the lamps, the seven lamps shall give light in front of the lampstand." 3 And Aaron
did so: he set up its lamps in front of the lampstand, as the LORD commanded Moses. 4 And
[i]this was the workmanship of the lampstand, hammered work of gold. From its base to
its flowers, it was hammered work; according to the pattern that the LORD had shown
Moses, so he made the lampstand.

Cleansing of the Levites

5 And the LORD spoke to Moses, saying, 6 "Take the Levites from among the people of
Israel and cleanse them. 7 Thus you shall do to them to cleanse them: sprinkle the [j]water of
purification upon them, and [k]let them go with a razor over all their body, and wash their
clothes and cleanse themselves. 8 Then let them take a bull from the herd and [l]its grain
offering of fine flour mixed with oil, [m]and you shall take another bull from the herd for
a sin offering. 9 [n]And you shall bring the Levites before the tent of meeting [o]and assemble
the whole congregation of the people of Israel. 10 When you bring the Levites before the
LORD, the people of Israel [p]shall lay their hands on the Levites, 11 and Aaron shall offer
the Levites before the LORD as a wave offering from the people of Israel, that they may
do the service of the LORD. 12 Then the Levites [q]shall lay their hands on the heads of the
bulls, and you shall offer [r]the one for a sin offering and the other for a burnt offering to
the LORD to make atonement for the Levites. 13 And you shall set the Levites before Aaron
and his sons, and shall offer them as [s]a wave offering to the LORD.
14 "Thus you shall separate the Levites from among the people of Israel, and [t]the Levites
shall be mine. 15 And after that the Levites shall go in to serve at the tent of meeting, when
you have cleansed them and offered them as a [s]wave offering. 16 For they are [u]wholly given
to me from among the people of Israel. [v]Instead of all who open the womb, the firstborn
of all the people of Israel, I have taken them for myself. 17 [w]For all the firstborn among
the people of Israel are mine, both of man and of beast. On the day that I struck down all

88 [f]ver. 1, 10
89 [g]ch. 12:8; See Ex. 33:9-11 [h]See Ex. 25:22

Chapter 8

4 [i]Ex. 25:31
7 [j]ch. 19:9, 17; [Lev. 8:6] [k][Lev. 14:8, 9]
8 [l]Lev. 2:1; See Ex. 29:41 [m]ver. 12
9 [n][Ex. 29:4; 40:12] [o][Lev. 8:3]
10 [p][Lev. 1:4]
12 [q][Ex. 29:10] [r]ver. 8
13 [s]ver. 11, 21
14 [t]ch. 3:45; [ch. 16:9]
15 [s][See ver. 13 above]
16 [u]ch. 3:9 [v]ch. 3:12, 45
17 [w]See Ex. 13:2

Offerings from the Twelve Tribes

Day	Chief	Tribe
1	Nahshon	Judah
2	Nethanel	Issachar
3	Eliab	Zebulun
4	Elizur	Reuben
5	Shelumiel	Simeon
6	Eliasaph	Gad
7	Elishama	Ephraim
8	Gamaliel	Manasseh
9	Abidan	Benjamin
10	Ahiezer	Dan
11	Pagiel	Asher
12	Ahira	Naphtali

7:89 This verse emphasizes the awesome responsibility of Moses, who often **went into the tent of meeting to speak with the LORD**, and who then heard the **voice** of God **speaking to him**, in order to receive and communicate God's instructions for the people. This verse also reinforces the importance of the tabernacle, for it was there that Moses heard God speaking to him **from between the two cherubim**. For a description of the cherubim on the ark, see Ex. 25:10–22; see also The Ark of the Covenant, p. 184.

8:1–4 *The Lampstand.* It is described more fully in Ex. 25:31–40, and its construction is explained in Ex. 37:17–24; see also The Golden Lampstand, p. 185. This section gives instructions for its operation. The important point is that **the seven lamps . . . give light in front of the lampstand**, that is, that their light shines on the table opposite it in the tabernacle (see The Tabernacle Tent, p. 186) on which are 12 flat loaves of bread symbolizing the 12 tribes of Israel (Ex. 25:23–30). Light reflects the glorious presence of God, so this arrangement of the furniture in the tabernacle is a reminder of God's ongoing intention to bless the people of Israel (see notes on John 1:4–5; 8:12).

8:5–22 *The Dedication of the Levites.* Like the previous paragraph, this section tidies up points partially covered earlier. The duties of the Levites in transporting and guarding the tabernacle have already been covered in chs. 3–4. Now these verses explain how the Levites were inducted into these roles. The rites are not as elaborate as the ordination of the priests in Leviticus 8–9, probably because the Levites had lower status than the priests. Nevertheless, as

19[u][See ver. 16 above] [x]ch. 25:11, 13 [y]See ch. 1:53
21[z]ver. 7 [a]ver. 11, 12, 13, 15
24[b][ch. 4:3; 1 Chr. 23:3, 24, 27]
26[c]See ch. 1:53
Chapter 9
1[d][ch. 1:1]
3[e]See Lev. 23:5
6[f]ch. 5:2; 19:11, 16; [John 18:28] [g]ch. 27:2; Ex. 18:15, 19, 26
7[h]ver. 13

the firstborn in the land of Egypt I consecrated them for myself, 18 and I have taken the
Levites instead of all the firstborn among the people of Israel. 19 [u]And I have given the
Levites as a gift to Aaron and his sons from among the people of Israel, to do the service
for the people of Israel at the tent of meeting and [x]to make atonement for the people of
Israel, [y]that there may be no plague among the people of Israel when the people of Israel
come near the sanctuary."

20 Thus did Moses and Aaron and all the congregation of the people of Israel to the
Levites. According to all that the LORD commanded Moses concerning the Levites, the
people of Israel did to them. 21 And [z]the Levites purified themselves from sin and washed
their clothes, and [a]Aaron offered them as a wave offering before the LORD, and Aaron
made atonement for them to cleanse them. 22 And after that the Levites went in to do their
service in the tent of meeting before Aaron and his sons; as the LORD had commanded
Moses concerning the Levites, so they did to them.

Retirement of the Levites

23 And the LORD spoke to Moses, saying, 24 "This applies to the Levites: [b]from twenty-five
years old and upward they[1] shall come to do duty in the service of the tent of meeting.
25 And from the age of fifty years they shall withdraw from the duty of the service and serve
no more. 26 They minister[2] to their brothers in the tent of meeting [c]by keeping guard, but
they shall do no service. Thus shall you do to the Levites in assigning their duties."

The Passover Celebrated

9 And the LORD spoke to Moses in the wilderness of Sinai, [d]in the first month of the second year after they had come out of the land of Egypt, saying, 2 "Let the people of Israel
keep the Passover at its appointed time. 3 [e]On the fourteenth day of this month, at twilight,
you shall keep it at its appointed time; according to all its statutes and all its rules you shall
keep it." 4 So Moses told the people of Israel that they should keep the Passover. 5 And they
kept the Passover in the first month, on the fourteenth day of the month, at twilight, in
the wilderness of Sinai; according to all that the LORD commanded Moses, so the people
of Israel did. 6 And there were certain men who were [f]unclean through touching a dead
body, so that they could not keep the Passover on that day, and [g]they came before Moses
and Aaron on that day. 7 And those men said to him, "We are unclean through touching
a dead body. Why are we kept from bringing the LORD's [h]offering at its appointed time

[1] Hebrew *he*; also verses 25, 26 [2] Hebrew *He ministers*

this ceremony declares, the Levites had an important role to play. As explained earlier (Num. 3:40–43), the Levites substituted for the firstborn Israelites, and this point is repeated (8:16–18). By the Levites taking on this role, they are removing the risk of plague breaking out on the whole people (which would happen if an Israelite approached the sanctuary incorrectly; see v. 19). The ceremony involved several elements designed to **cleanse** the Levites: sprinkling with the **water of purification** (probably the liquid described in ch. 19), shaving the whole **body**, and washing **their clothes** (8:7). This cleansing process made them fit to be offered to God. The leaders of the congregation then laid hands on the Levites, symbolizing that the Levites are the representatives of the congregation (vv. 9–11). Then, like parts of a sacrifice, they are offered **as a wave offering** (v. 11). Parts of the peace offering were waved and then given to the priest (Lev. 7:28–34). "Sacrificial waving" is usually supposed to be a side-to-side movement, but how the Levites were "waved" is unclear. The ceremony was completed by offering two sacrifices (the burnt and sin offering) using bulls, the most valuable of sacrificial animals (Lev. 1:3–9; 4:1–21).

8:23–26 *The Retirement of the Levites.* At age 50 Levites were to retire from **the duty of the service** (i.e., the work involved in transporting the tabernacle) because carrying the tabernacle was too hard for older men. But they were allowed to continue to act as guards (vv. 25–26). In 4:23 it is said that Levites start their labor of carrying the tabernacle when they are 30 years old, but here they start at age 25 (8:24). The reason for the difference is unclear: maybe from the ages of 25 to 30 they were viewed as apprentices.

9:1–5 *The Second Passover.* The first Passover took place in Egypt just before the Israelites escaped. It was unique in that it occurred before the saving event of the exodus and the crossing of the Red Sea; all subsequent Passover celebrations recalled these momentous events, but inevitably many of the features of the first Passover were missing. So this **Passover**, celebrated a year later at **Sinai**, was the first of many that were essentially retrospective commemorations of the first Passover in **Egypt**. **On the fourteenth day** (vv. 3, 5). This places the celebration of the Passover between the events described in chs. 7–8 and the censuses of chs. 1–4. **according to all its statutes** (9:3). See Exodus 12–13, which both describes the original Egyptian Passover and gives many regulations about subsequent Passover celebrations.

9:6–14 *The Delayed Passover.* The regular **Passover** of the "first month" was carried out properly (v. 5), but some people could not join in because they were unclean through contact with a corpse. Death is one of the more potent sources of uncleanness (see ch. 19). As explained in ch. 5 (see notes there), uncleanness prevents those affected from living in the camp, let alone participating in worship. But failure to celebrate the Passover when one is able to do so is a serious sin, meriting being **cut off** (9:13). "Cut off" probably means dying suddenly and mysteriously as a divine punishment, though some interpreters think it sometimes may refer to excommunication from Israel or judicial execution. (For other offenses that merit this penalty, cf. Lev. 17:4, 9; 20:6, 18; Num. 15:30–31; 19:13.) Those affected by uncleanness were not *required* to celebrate the Passover at another time; nevertheless, they were *allowed* to keep it one month later than usual, following the standard procedures (9:11–12). **if a stranger sojourns among you** (v. 14). Resident aliens, though not obliged to keep the Passover, are welcome to observe it if they so desire. They *are* expected to observe the Sabbath and the Day of Atonement (Ex. 20:10; Lev. 16:29).

among the people of Israel?" 8 And Moses said to them, "Wait, that [i]I may hear what the
LORD will command concerning you."
9 The LORD spoke to Moses, saying, 10 "Speak to the people of Israel, saying, If any one of
you or of your descendants is unclean through touching a dead body, or is on a long journey,
he shall still keep the Passover to the LORD. 11 [j]In the second month on the fourteenth day
at twilight they shall keep it. [k]They shall eat it with unleavened bread and bitter herbs.
12 [l]They shall leave none of it until the morning, [m]nor break any of its bones; [n]according
to all the statute for the Passover they shall keep it. 13 But if anyone who is clean and is
not on a journey fails to keep the Passover, [o]that person shall be cut off from his people
because he did not bring the LORD's [p]offering at its appointed time; that man shall bear
his sin. 14 And if a stranger sojourns among you and would keep the Passover to the LORD,
according to the statute of the Passover and according to its rule, so shall he do. [q]You shall
have one statute, both for the sojourner and for the native."

The Cloud Covering the Tabernacle

15 [r]On the day that the tabernacle was set up, the cloud covered the tabernacle, the tent
of the testimony. And [s]at evening it was over the tabernacle like the appearance of fire
until morning. 16 So it was always: the cloud covered it by day[1] and the appearance of fire
by night. 17 And whenever the cloud [t]lifted from over the tent, after that the people of
Israel set out, and in the place where the cloud settled down, there the people of Israel
camped. 18 At the command of the LORD the people of Israel set out, and at the command
of the LORD they camped. [u]As long as the cloud rested over the tabernacle, they remained
in camp. 19 Even when the cloud continued over the tabernacle many days, the people of
Israel [v]kept the charge of the LORD and did not set out. 20 Sometimes the cloud was a few
days over the tabernacle, and according to the command of the LORD they remained in
camp; then according to the command of the LORD they set out. 21 And sometimes the
cloud remained from evening until morning. And when the cloud lifted in the morning,
they set out, or if it continued for a day and a night, when the cloud lifted they set out.
22 Whether it was two days, or a month, or a longer time, that the cloud continued over
the tabernacle, abiding there, the people of Israel [w]remained in camp and did not set out,
but when it lifted they set out. 23 At the command of the LORD they camped, and at the
command of the LORD they set out. [v]They kept the charge of the LORD, at the command
of the LORD by Moses.

The Silver Trumpets

10 The LORD spoke to Moses, saying, 2 "Make two silver trumpets. Of hammered work
you shall make them, and you shall use them for [x]summoning the congregation
and for breaking camp. 3 And when [y]both are blown, all the congregation shall gather
themselves to you at the entrance of the tent of meeting. 4 But if they blow only one, then
[z]the chiefs, the heads of the tribes of Israel, shall gather themselves to you. 5 When you

[1] Septuagint, Syriac, Vulgate; Hebrew lacks *by day*

8 [i]ch. 27:5
11 [j]See Ex. 12:6; 2 Chr. 30:2-15 [k]Ex. 12:8; [Deut. 16:3]
12 [l]Ex. 12:10 [m]Ex. 12:46; Cited John 19:36 [n]Ex. 12:43, 49
13 [o]Ex. 12:15; [Gen. 17:14] [p]ver. 7
14 [q]Ex. 12:48, 49
15 [r]Ex. 40:17, 34 [s]See Ex. 13:21
17 [t]ch. 10:11, 33, 34; Ex. 40:36
18 [u][1 Cor. 10:1]
19 [v]See ch. 1:53
22 [w]Ex. 40:36, 37
23 [v][See ver. 19 above]

Chapter 10

2 [x]Isa. 1:13; Joel 1:14; [Ps. 81:3]
3 [y]Jer. 4:5; Joel 2:15
4 [z]ch. 1:16; 7:2; Ex. 18:21

9:15–23 *The Moving Cloud.* The **cloud** of God's presence had led the people out of Egypt to Mount Sinai (Ex. 13:21–22; 19:9, 16). This hymn-like passage celebrates the relationship between God and Israel (or at least what that relationship was like when Israel was in an obedient mood). Wherever and whenever the cloud moved, the people followed. **At the command of the LORD they camped, and at the command of the LORD they set out** (Num. 9:23). The people had to be ready for immediate departure on any day, and they had to follow the Lord every day until the cloud stopped—which required continual obedience to God's visible guidance. (Notice, however, the disobedience of the people in Num. 14:1–4, when they refuse to "set out" to Canaan, and the disastrous consequences of their disobedience as seen in 14:11–45. But ch. 11 already shows that the people were not as full of faith as they should have been.)

9:15 the cloud covered the tabernacle. This visible evidence of God's presence (cf. Ex. 40:34–38) could be seen by all Israel. In the evening it was **like the appearance of fire until morning** and thus it gave continual testimony, day and night, to God's presence among his people.

10:1–10 *The Silver Trumpets.* How was Israel to move in step with the cloud of God's presence? A large group of people needed to be marshaled, or else any movement was bound to be chaotic. So the primary purpose of the trumpets was to signal when the different tribes were to set out (see vv. 5–7). But they are also to be used to summon the **congregation** (v. 3) or the **chiefs** (v. 4). Their use in **war** and on the festival days is also prescribed (vv. 9–10). But blowing the trumpets was more than just a way of summoning the people to come to the tabernacle or to follow the cloud; it was a kind of prayer, a plea to God to remember his people and their needs, **that you may be remembered before the LORD your God** (v. 9; cf. v. 10). **Two silver trumpets** (v. 2), according to Josephus (*Jewish Antiquities* 3.291), were just over a foot in length and flared. They are pictured on Titus's arch among the plunder he brought to Rome from Jerusalem. Two ways of blowing the trumpets are mentioned here: simply blowing (Num. 10:3–4, 7), and sounding an **alarm** (vv. 6–7). The difference is that blowing involves long notes, whereas sounding an alarm is done with staccato blasts. **On the day of your gladness** (v. 10) would include such occasions as festivals or victory celebrations after battle.

blow an alarm, [a]the camps that are on the east side shall set out. 6 And when you blow
an alarm the second time, [b]the camps that are on the south side shall set out. An alarm
is to be blown whenever they are to set out. 7 But when the assembly is to be gathered
together, [c]you shall blow a long blast, but you shall not [d]sound an alarm. 8 [e]And the sons
of Aaron, the priests, shall blow the trumpets. The trumpets shall be to you for a perpetual
statute throughout your generations. 9 And [f]when you go to war in your land against the
adversary who [g]oppresses you, then you shall [d]sound an alarm with the trumpets, that
you may be [h]remembered before the LORD your God, and you shall be saved from your
enemies. 10 [i]On the day of your gladness also, and at your appointed feasts and [j]at the
beginnings of your months, you shall blow the trumpets over your burnt offerings and
over the sacrifices of your peace offerings. They shall be [k]a reminder of you before your
God: I am the LORD your God."

Israel Leaves Sinai

11 In the second year, in the second month, on the twentieth day of the month, [l]the
cloud lifted from over the tabernacle of the testimony, 12 and the people of Israel [m]set out
by stages from the [n]wilderness of Sinai. And the cloud settled down in the [o]wilderness
of Paran. 13 They set out for the first time [p]at the command of the LORD by Moses. 14 The
standard of the camp of the people of Judah set out [q]first by their companies, and over
their company was [r]Nahshon the son of Amminadab. 15 And over the company of the tribe
of the people of Issachar was Nethanel the son of Zuar. 16 And over the company of the
tribe of the people of Zebulun was Eliab the son of Helon.

17 And when [s]the tabernacle was taken down, the sons of Gershon and the sons of Merari,
[t]who carried the tabernacle, set out. 18 And [u]the standard of the camp of Reuben set out by
their companies, and over their company was [v]Elizur the son of Shedeur. 19 And over the
company of the tribe of the people of Simeon was [w]Shelumiel the son of Zurishaddai. 20 And
over the company of the tribe of the people of Gad was [x]Eliasaph the son of [y]Deuel.

21 Then the Kohathites set out, [z]carrying the holy things, and [a]the tabernacle was set up
before their arrival. 22 And [b]the standard of the camp of the people of Ephraim set out by
their companies, and over their company was [c]Elishama the son of Ammihud. 23 And over the
company of the tribe of the people of Manasseh was [c]Gamaliel the son of Pedahzur. 24 And
over the company of the tribe of the people of Benjamin was [d]Abidan the son of Gideoni.

25 Then [e]the standard of the camp of the people of Dan, acting as the [f]rear guard of all
the camps, set out by their companies, and over their company was [g]Ahiezer the son of
Ammishaddai. 26 And over the company of the tribe of the people of Asher was [h]Pagiel the
son of Ochran. 27 And over the company of the tribe of the people of Naphtali was [i]Ahira
the son of Enan. 28 [j]This was the order of march of the people of Israel by their companies,
when they set out.

29 And Moses said to Hobab the son of [k]Reuel the Midianite, Moses' father-in-law, "We

5 [a]ver. 14; See ch. 2:3-9
6 [b]ver. 18; See ch. 2:10-16
7 [c]ver. 3 [d]Joel 2:1
8 [e]1 Chr. 15:24; 2 Chr. 13:12
9 [f]ch. 31:6; 2 Chr. 13:14; [Josh. 6:5] [g]Judg. 2:18; 4:3; 10:8, 12; 1 Sam. 10:18 [d][See ver. 7 above] [h]See Gen. 8:1
10 [i]ch. 29:1; 1 Chr. 15:24; 2 Chr. 5:12, 13; 7:6; 29:26-28; Ezra 3:10; Neh. 12:35 [j]Ps. 81:3; See ch. 28:11 [k]ver. 9
11 [l]ch. 9:17
12 [m][Ex. 40:36] [n]ch. 1:1; 9:5; Ex. 19:1, 2 [o]ch. 12:16; 13:3, 26; Gen. 21:21; Deut. 1:1
13 [p]ver. 5, 6; ch. 2:34
14 [q]See ch. 2:3-9 [r]For ver. 14-16, see ch. 1:7-9
17 [s]ch. 1:51 [t]See ch. 4:24-33; 7:6-8
18 [u]See ch. 2:10-16 [v]ch. 1:5
19 [w]ch. 1:6
20 [x]ch. 1:14 [y][ch. 2:14]
21 [z]ch. 7:9; See ch. 4:4-15 [a][ver. 17]
22 [b]See ch. 2:18-24 [c]ch. 1:10
23 [c][See ver. 22 above]
24 [d]ch. 1:11
25 [e]See ch. 2:25-31 [f][Josh. 6:9] [g]ch. 1:12
26 [h]ch. 1:13
27 [i]ch. 1:15
28 [j]ch. 2:34
29 [k]See Ex. 2:18

10:11–12:16 *Marching from Sinai to Kadesh.* As pointed out above, the book of Numbers alternates static sections devoted to law-giving and organization with travelogue. In chs. 10–12 Israel moves from the foot of Mount Sinai to Kadesh-barnea, an oasis on the southern border of Canaan. Initially all runs smoothly. "The cloud lifted . . . and the people of Israel set out" (10:11–12), just as 9:15–23 said they should. On the move, the people proceeded in the formation specified in ch. 2. The Judahite group of tribes headed the procession (10:13–16; cf. 2:1–9). They were followed by the Gershonite Levites with their two wagons loaded with the tabernacle curtains, and the Merarite Levites with four wagons loaded with poles and pegs (10:17; cf. 3:21–26, 33–37). These Levites preceded the Kohathites so that they could erect the tabernacle before the Kohathites arrived. Then the sacred furniture carried by the Kohathites could be installed immediately in the tabernacle (10:21). The Gershonites and Merarites were followed by the Reubenite tribes (10:18–20; cf. 2:10–16). Then right at the center of the procession came the most sacred items of tabernacle furniture, carried by the Kohathites (10:21; cf. 3:27–32). However, it appears that the ark itself went out in front of the whole procession (10:33); like the cloud, it symbolized and conveyed God's presence and his guidance of his people. The rear of the procession was brought up by the Ephraimite and Danite groups of tribes (10:22–28; cf. 2:18–31).

10:11–28 *Israel Strikes Camp at Sinai.* The people of Israel have been at Sinai for almost a full year (see Ex. 19:1). Israel now leaves Sinai to begin its journey to the Promised Land under the guidance and direction of the *shekinah* glory (i.e., the dwelling glory cloud). This text describes the striking of the Israelite camp and the order of march of the tribes.

10:12 and the people of Israel set out by stages from the wilderness of Sinai. One would expect the people to have felt tremendous excitement, pride, joy, and safety in God's protection when they set out in this great procession, with trumpets, banners, and, in the very front, the cloud of the presence of God himself. They were seeing dramatic evidence of the fulfillment of God's promises to Abraham hundreds of years earlier. Sadly, however, they soon complain (ch. 11), rebel (ch. 14), and oppose Moses' authority (ch. 16).

10:29–32 *Request to Hobab to Accompany Israel.* The relationship of **Hobab** and **Reuel** to Jethro (Ex. 3:1; 18:1–2) is uncertain. The least difficult solution is that Reuel and Jethro are alternative names of **Moses' father-in-**

are setting out for the place of which the LORD said, [l]'I will give it to you.' Come with us,
and we will do good to you, for [m]the LORD has promised good to Israel." 30 But he said
to him, "I will not go. I will depart to my own land and to my kindred." 31 And he said,
"Please do not leave us, for you know where we should camp in the wilderness, and you
will serve [n]as eyes for us. 32 And if you do go with us, [o]whatever good the LORD will do to
us, the same will we do to you."
33 So they set out from [p]the mount of the LORD three days' journey. And the ark of the
covenant of the LORD went before them three days' journey, to seek out [q]a resting place
for them. 34 [r]And the cloud of the LORD was over them by day, whenever they set out from
the camp.
35 And whenever the ark set out, Moses said, [s]"Arise, O LORD, and let your enemies
be scattered, and let those who hate you flee before you." 36 And when it rested, he said,
"Return, O LORD, to the ten thousand thousands of Israel."

The People Complain

11 And [t]the people complained in the hearing of the LORD about their misfortunes,
and when the LORD heard it, [u]his anger was kindled, and [v]the fire of the LORD
burned among them and consumed some outlying parts of the camp. 2 Then [w]the people
cried out to Moses, [x]and Moses prayed to the LORD, and the fire died down. 3 So the name
of that place was called [y]Taberah,[1] because the fire of the LORD burned among them.
4 Now the [z]rabble that was among them had a strong craving. And the people of Israel
also [a]wept again and said, [b]"Oh that we had meat to eat! 5 [c]We remember the fish we ate in
Egypt that cost nothing, the cucumbers, the melons, the leeks, the onions, and the garlic.
6 But now our strength is dried up, and there is nothing at all but this manna to look at."
7 Now [d]the manna was like coriander seed, and its appearance like that of bdellium. 8 [e]The
people went about and gathered it and ground it in handmills or beat it in mortars and
boiled it in pots and made cakes of it. [f]And the taste of it was like the taste of cakes baked
with oil. 9 [g]When the dew fell upon the camp in the night, the manna fell with it.
10 Moses heard the people [h]weeping throughout their clans, everyone at the door of his
tent. And the anger of the LORD blazed hotly, and Moses was displeased. 11 [i]Moses said
to the LORD, "Why have you dealt ill with your servant? And why have I not found favor
in your sight, that you lay the burden of all this people on me? 12 Did I conceive all this
people? Did I give them birth, that you should say to me, [j]'Carry them in your bosom, as a
[k]nurse carries a nursing child,' to the land [l]that you swore to give their fathers? 13 [m]Where
am I to get meat to give to all this people? For they weep before me and say, 'Give us meat,
that we may eat.' 14 [n]I am not able to carry all this people alone; the burden is too heavy
for me. 15 If you will treat me like this, kill me at once, if I find favor in your sight, that I
may not see my wretchedness."

[1] *Taberah* means *burning*

29 [l]Gen. 12:7 [m]Gen. 32:12; Ex. 3:8; 6:7, 8
31 [n][Job 29:15]
32 [o]ver. 29; [Judg. 1:16; 4:11]
33 [p]See Ex. 3:1 [q]Ps. 132:8; Jer. 31:2
34 [r]See Ex. 13:21
35 [s]Ps. 68:1, 2

Chapter 11

1 [t]Deut. 9:22 [u]Ps. 78:21 [v][ch. 16:35; Lev. 10:2; 2 Kgs. 1:12; Ps. 106:18; Rev. 13:13]
2 [w][ch. 21:7] [x][James 5:16]; See ch. 16:45-48
3 [y]Deut. 9:22
4 [z]See Ex. 12:38 [a]ch. 14:1 [b]Ps. 78:18; 106:14; 1 Cor. 10:6
5 [c][ch. 21:5; Ex. 16:3; Acts 7:39]
7 [d]Ex. 16:14, 31
8 [e]Ex. 16:16-18 [f][Ex. 16:31]
9 [g]Ex. 16:13, 14
10 [h][Zech. 12:12-14]
11 [i][1 Kgs. 19:4; Jonah 4:1-4, 9]
12 [j]Isa. 40:11; [Deut. 1:31] [k][Isa. 49:23; 1 Thess. 2:7] [l]Gen. 50:24; Ex. 13:5
13 [m][2 Kgs. 7:2; Matt. 15:33; Mark 8:4; John 6:7, 9]
14 [n]Ex. 18:18; Deut. 1:9, 12

law. This would make Hobab Moses' brother-in-law. In Judg. 4:11 Hobab's descendants are called Kenites, whereas here he is called a **Midianite**. Probably the Kenites were a subgroup of the Midianites. **The LORD has promised good to Israel**, that is, the land. **I will depart to my own land and to my kindred.** Hobab apparently rejects the offer of a share in Canaan (in stark contrast to Abraham's response to God's call; Gen. 12:1–4). It is not clear if Moses' subsequent entreaty persuaded him to change his mind, for the text does not say. In Numbers 25 and 31 the Midianites are fierce enemies of Israel, but in Judg. 1:16 and 4:11 the Kenites are Israel's allies, living in Canaan.

10:33–36 These verses describe the first three-day march from Sinai toward Kadesh led by the **cloud** and the **ark**. The repetition of **three days** emphasizes the short distance traveled; it does not imply the ark was separated from the main party by this distance. As the ark **set out** and **rested** (vv. 35–36), Moses expressed his confidence that God would bring Israel successfully into Canaan.

11:1–12:16 *Three Protests.* The whole people and their most senior figures complain about the difficulties of the journey to Canaan; by implication they are also complaining about Moses' leadership and God's promises. This pattern matches the problems of the journey from the Red Sea to Sinai. At that time, after a three-day trek, the people had complained about water, and now they complain again (Ex. 15:22–25; cf. Num. 10:33; 11:1–3). The next complaint is about food (Exodus 16; Num. 11:4–35). The final protest is about Moses' leadership (Ex. 17:1–7; Numbers 12).

11:1–3 *Taberah.* This is just a general complaint by the people. In judgment, **fire** breaks out in the **outlying parts of the camp** (cf. Lev. 10:2; Num. 16:35). As on other occasions, Moses' intercession halts God's judgment (Ex. 32:11–14, 31–32; Num. 12:13–15; 14:11–25). **Taberah** means burning (ESV footnote); like other place names in the Bible, it commemorates the events that occurred there.

11:4–35 *Kibroth-hattaavah.* The second popular protest concerns the manna that had been Israel's food ever since it was provided on the way to Sinai (Exodus 16). On the surface, the protest is merely about the monotony of the diet; underlying the complaint, however, is a yearning for the pleasures of **Egypt** (Num. 11:4–5) and a rejection of God's plans.

11:7 Bdellium is a pale yellow resin found in desert areas.

11:11–15 Moses can bear the complaining no more and protests to God about the burden of leading Israel by himself.

16[o][Ex. 24:1, 9] [p]Deut. 1:15; 16:18
17[q]ver. 25; ch. 12:5; Gen. 11:5; 18:21; Ex. 19:20 [r][2 Kgs. 2:9, 15; Neh. 9:20] [s]Ex. 18:22
18[t]Ex. 19:10 [u]See ver. 5
20[v][Ps. 78:29; 106:15] [w]ch. 21:5
21[x]Ex. 12:37; [ch. 1:46; Ex. 38:26]
22[y][ver. 13]
23[z]Isa. 50:2; 59:1 [a]ch. 23:19; Ezek. 12:25; 24:14
24[b]ver. 16
25[c]ver. 17
26[d][1 Sam. 20:26; Jer. 36:5]
28[e]ch. 26:65; Ex. 24:13; [ch. 13:8]; See ch. 13:16 [f][Mark 9:38; Luke 9:49]
29[g][1 Cor. 14:5]
31[h]Ex. 16:13; Ps. 78:26-28; 105:40
32[i]Ex. 16:36; [Ezek. 45:11]
33[j]Ps. 78:30, 31 [k][ch. 16:49]
34[l]Deut. 9:22

Elders Appointed to Aid Moses

16 Then the LORD said to Moses, "Gather for me [o]seventy men of the elders of Israel,
whom you know to be the elders of the people and [p]officers over them, and bring them
to the tent of meeting, and let them take their stand there with you. 17 [q]And I will come
down and talk with you there. And [r]I will take some of the Spirit that is on you and put
it on them, and [s]they shall bear the burden of the people with you, so that you may not
bear it yourself alone. 18 And say to the people, [t]'Consecrate yourselves for tomorrow, and
you shall eat meat, for you have wept in the hearing of the LORD, saying, "Who will give
us meat to eat? [u]For it was better for us in Egypt." Therefore the LORD will give you meat,
and you shall eat. 19 You shall not eat just one day, or two days, or five days, or ten days,
or twenty days, 20 but a whole month, [v]until it comes out at your nostrils and becomes
loathsome to you, because you have rejected the LORD who is among you and have wept
before him, saying, [w]"Why did we come out of Egypt?"'" 21 But Moses said, [x]"The people
among whom I am number six hundred thousand on foot, and you have said, 'I will give
them meat, that they may eat a whole month!' 22 [y]Shall flocks and herds be slaughtered
for them, and be enough for them? Or shall all the fish of the sea be gathered together
for them, and be enough for them?" 23 And the LORD said to Moses, [z]"Is the LORD's hand
shortened? Now you shall see whether [a]my word will come true for you or not."

24 So Moses went out and told the people the words of the LORD. [b]And he gathered seventy men of the elders of the people and placed them around the tent. 25 Then [c]the LORD
came down in the cloud and spoke to him, and took some of the Spirit that was on him
and put it on the seventy elders. And as soon as the Spirit rested on them, they prophesied.
But they did not continue doing it.

26 Now two men remained in the camp, one named Eldad, and the other named Medad,
and the Spirit rested on them. They were among those registered, but they [d]had not gone
out to the tent, and so they prophesied in the camp. 27 And a young man ran and told
Moses, "Eldad and Medad are prophesying in the camp." 28 And [e]Joshua the son of Nun,
the assistant of Moses from his youth, said, "My lord Moses, [f]stop them." 29 But Moses
said to him, "Are you jealous for my sake? [g]Would that all the LORD's people were prophets, that the LORD would put his Spirit on them!" 30 And Moses and the elders of Israel
returned to the camp.

Quail and a Plague

31 Then a [h]wind from the LORD sprang up, and it brought quail from the sea and let them
fall beside the camp, about a day's journey on this side and a day's journey on the other
side, around the camp, and about two cubits[1] above the ground. 32 And the people rose all
that day and all night and all the next day, and gathered the quail. Those who gathered
least gathered ten [i]homers.[2] And they spread them out for themselves all around the camp.
33 [j]While the meat was yet between their teeth, before it was consumed, the anger of the
LORD was kindled against the people, and [k]the LORD struck down the people with a very
great plague. 34 Therefore the name of that place was called [l]Kibroth-hattaavah,[3] because

[1] A *cubit* was about 18 inches or 45 centimeters [2] A *homer* was about 6 bushels or 220 liters [3] *Kibroth-hattaavah* means *graves of craving*

11:16–23 The Lord promises to meet Moses' need for assistance and the people's desire for an alternative to the manna. But God's apparent concession to the popular appetite will in fact prove to be a judgment, because they were in effect saying, **Why did we come out of Egypt?** (v. 20).

11:24–30 Moses' request for assistance is met as the Lord endows **seventy elders** with the gift of prophecy. Unlike Moses with his unique gift of prophecy (12:6–7), these elders prophesied only for a short time (**they did not continue doing it**), but this was enough to give them credibility as assistants to Moses. Their prophesying would have involved some kind of speaking under the influence of the Holy **Spirit**, showing their similarity to the prophet Moses (cf. notes on 1 Sam. 10:5; 1 Chron. 25:1–8). It is unclear whether or not **Eldad and Medad** were attached to the group of 70. In any case, they prophesied in a different place (**in the camp**), whereas the 70 had prophesied **around the tent** (Num. 11:24). This made their prophesying much more obvious to the other Israelites, which was a concern to Joshua (vv. 27–28). However, Moses' prayer—**Would that all the LORD's people were prophets**! (v. 29)—anticipates Joel's vision of the "day of the LORD," when "your sons and daughters shall prophesy" (Joel 2:28; cf. Acts 2:17). When this passage (like most of the OT) speaks of the work of the **Spirit** (Num. 11:17, 25–26), it is focusing primarily on the empowering of the Spirit for service to the people of God, more than an internal, personal experience.

11:31–34 Quail (small partridges) migrate north across the Sinai Peninsula in the spring and return in the fall, so although the Israelites had eaten some in the previous year (Ex. 16:13), these were not a regular dish. The migration of the second year was such that the Israelites were able to catch enormous quantities of quail: they were piled **two cubits** (3 feet or 0.9 m) high on the ground (Num. 11:31); thus anyone could collect at least **ten homers** (v. 32), roughly 60 bushels (480 dry gallons or 2,200 liters)! This greed was punished by **a very great plague** (v. 33). The form of the plague is unexplained, but it led to many deaths and the place being named **Kibroth-hattaavah**, "graves of craving" (v. 34).

there they buried the people who had the craving. **35** [m]From Kibroth-hattaavah the people
journeyed to [n]Hazeroth, and they remained at [n]Hazeroth.

Miriam and Aaron Oppose Moses

12 Miriam and Aaron spoke against Moses because of the Cushite woman whom he
had married, for he had married a Cushite woman. **2** And they said, "Has the LORD
indeed spoken only through Moses? [o]Has he not spoken through us also?" And [p]the LORD
heard it. **3** Now the man Moses was very meek, more than all people who were on the face
of the earth. **4** And suddenly the LORD said to Moses and to Aaron and Miriam, "Come
out, you three, to the tent of meeting." And the three of them came out. **5** And [q]the LORD
came down in a pillar of cloud and stood at the entrance of the tent and called Aaron and
Miriam, and they both came forward. **6** And he said, "Hear my words: If there is a prophet
among you, I the LORD make myself known to him [r]in a vision; I speak with him [s]in a
dream. **7** Not so with [t]my servant Moses. [u]He is faithful in all my house. **8** With him I speak
[v]mouth to mouth, clearly, and not in [w]riddles, and he beholds [x]the form of the LORD. Why
then were you not afraid to speak against my servant Moses?" **9** And the anger of the LORD
was kindled against them, and he departed.
10 When the cloud removed from over the tent, behold, [y]Miriam was [z]leprous,[1] like snow.
And Aaron turned toward Miriam, and behold, she was leprous. **11** And Aaron said to Moses,
"Oh, my lord, [a]do not punish us[2] because we have done foolishly and have sinned. **12** Let
her not be as one dead, whose flesh is half eaten away when he comes out of his mother's
womb." **13** And Moses cried to the LORD, "O God, please heal her—please." **14** But the LORD
said to Moses, "If her father had but [b]spit in her face, should she not be shamed seven days?
Let her be [c]shut outside the camp seven days, and after that she may be brought in again."
15 So Miriam [d]was shut outside the camp seven days, and the people did not set out on the
march till Miriam was brought in again. **16** After that the people set out from [e]Hazeroth,
and camped in [f]the wilderness of Paran.

[1] *Leprosy* was a term for several skin diseases; see Leviticus 13 [2] Hebrew *do not lay sin upon us*

35 [m]ch. 33:17 [n]ch. 12:16; 33:17, 18

Chapter 12

2 [o]Mic. 6:4 [p]ch. 11:1; 2 Kgs. 19:4; Isa. 37:4; Ezek. 35:12, 13; [Mal. 3:16]
5 [q]ch. 11:25; 16:19
6 [r]Gen. 46:2; Ezek. 1:1; Dan. 8:2; 10:8, 16; Luke 1:11, 22; Acts 10:11; 22:17, 18 [s]Gen. 20:6; 31:10, 11; 1 Kgs. 3:5; Job 33:15; Matt. 1:20; 27:19
7 [t]Ps. 105:26 [u]Heb. 3:2, 5
8 [v]ch. 7:89; [Ex. 33:11; Deut. 34:10; 1 Cor. 13:12] [w]Ps. 49:4; 78:2; Prov. 1:6 [x][Ex. 33:20, 23]
10 [y]Deut. 24:9 [z]See Lev. 13:10
11 [a][2 Sam. 19:19; 24:10; Prov. 30:32]
14 [b]Deut. 25:9; Job 30:10 [c]See Lev. 13:46
15 [d][2 Kgs. 15:5; 2 Chr. 26:20, 21; Luke 17:12]
16 [e]ch. 11:35; [ch. 33:18] [f]See ch. 10:12

12:1–16 *The Uniqueness of Moses.* After the protests of the people comes an even more painful challenge to Moses' authority. His brother Aaron, the high priest, and his sister Miriam, a prophetess (Ex. 15:20), contest his unique position. Once again their initial remarks, concerning Moses' Cushite wife, are only cover for their real complaint: **Has the LORD . . . spoken only through Moses?** (Num. 12:2).

12:1–2 Miriam and Aaron spoke against Moses. This represents a further challenge to Moses' supreme authority, which has many points in common with the previous two challenges (cf. 11:1, 4–6, and 11:10). **Cushite woman**. Nothing is known about "the Cushite woman" beyond this brief mention. She may be the same person as Zipporah (Ex. 2:16–22), though she is usually described as a Midianite. Some texts, however, suggest Midian and Cushan are the same (see Hab. 3:7). Since Cush normally refers to ancient Ethiopia, most interpreters think that "the Cushite woman" probably was Moses' second wife, and that she came from Ethiopia. This leads some commentators to suggest that racial or ethnic prejudice may have been involved, the objection being to someone of African descent. In any case it becomes clear that Miriam and Aaron's objection to "the Cushite woman" was a pretense, and that the real issue was their challenge to Moses' supreme authority.

12:3–4 very meek. The Hebrew term here translated "meek" (Hb. *'anaw*) is more often translated "humble, poor." The focus is more on Moses' attitude than on his demeanor. Some have argued that Moses could not have written in this way about himself, thereby challenging Moses' authorship of Numbers. It is clear, however, that the inclusion of this description of Moses' character is both accurate and necessary for understanding the account. **On the face of the earth** indicates that Moses was highly respected, certainly by Pharaoh and the people of Egypt, but also when he encountered other peoples during the 40 years in the wilderness (e.g., the defeat of the Amorites, 21:21–35; and Balaam and the dread of the Moabites, chs. 22–24). Here Moses relies on divine vindication rather than defending himself. Vindication comes quickly, as all **three** (**Miriam**, **Aaron**, and **Moses**) are summoned by God, who then points out Moses' unique qualities, as seen in the 11-line poem in 12:6–8. Christian readers may see in this description of Moses' unique mediating role a foreshadowing of Christ, the prophet greater than Moses (cf. Deut. 18:15; Acts 3:22; 7:37).

12:6–8 This sets Moses apart from the ordinary prophets, who receive their revelations in **vision** and **dream** (which thus involves much more imagery). By contrast, God speaks to Moses **mouth to mouth** (v. 8; that is, as one person facing another and conversing; cf. Ex. 33:11), which implies verbal communication, often extensive, as well as extended dialogue between God and Moses. **He is faithful in all my house** (Num. 12:7). In other words, he is like the trusted manager of a man's household, such as was Eliezer or Joseph (Gen. 24:2; 39:4). He is someone with whom the owner speaks directly and explicitly, **not in riddles** (Num. 12:8). **the form of the LORD** (v. 8). "Form" (Hb. *temunah*) is sometimes translated "likeness" (e.g., Ex. 20:4). At Sinai, Israel did not see God's likeness but only heard his voice (Deut. 4:12, 15). It is not entirely clear how seeing God's form or likeness differs from seeing his face (cf. Ex. 33:18–23), but it apparently involved a less intensive kind of vision. The point here is that Moses was allowed to see what most ordinary believers must wait for their death to see (Ps. 17:15). **Why then were you not afraid to speak against my servant Moses?** To oppose Moses, whom God had put in this position, was also to oppose God himself.

12:9–12 Moses' unique access to God should have been evident all along to Miriam and Aaron; their obtuseness prompts the **anger** of God. **leprous, like snow**. Biblical "leprosy" covers a variety of skin conditions, characterized by sores and peeling skin (see note on Lev. 13:1–59). The flakiness of Miriam's skin, not necessarily its whiteness, causes her affliction to be compared to snow and the skin of a stillborn child (Num. 12:12).

12:13–16 As final proof of Moses' status, his prayer for his sister's healing is immediately answered. But like other healed "lepers," she must **be shut outside the camp seven days** before being readmitted (see Lev. 14:1–9; Num. 5:2). This punishment is justified by comparison with family custom, where a child must be disciplined for shaming her father (12:14; see Deut. 25:9 for the shame of spitting).

Chapter 13
2 [g]ch. 32:8; See Deut. 1:22-25
3 [h]ver. 26; ch. 12:16; 32:8; Deut. 1:19; 9:23
6 [i]ch. 34:19; 1 Chr. 4:15 [j]ver. 30; ch. 14:6, 30; 26:65; 32:12; Deut. 1:36; See Josh. 14:6-15; 15:13-18; Judg. 1:12-15
8 [k]ver. 16; ch. 11:28; 14:6, 30, 38; Ex. 24:13; Deut. 32:44; [Neh. 8:17]
16 [k][See ver. 8 above]
17 [l]ver. 22, 29; ch. 21:1; Josh. 15:19; Judg. 1:15 [m]ver. 29; Judg. 1:9, 19
20 [n]Neh. 9:25, 35; Ezek. 34:14 [o]Deut. 31:6, 7, 23
21 [p]ch. 20:1; 33:36; 34:3; Josh. 15:1 [q]ch. 34:8
22 [m][See ver. 17 above] [r]See Josh. 14:15 [s]Josh. 15:14; Judg. 1:10 [t]ver. 33; Deut. 1:28; 2:10; 9:2; Josh. 11:21, 22 [u]Ps. 78:12, 43; Isa. 19:11, 13; 30:4; Ezek. 30:14
23 [v]ch. 32:9; Deut. 1:24, 25

Spies Sent into Canaan

13 The LORD spoke to Moses, saying, 2 [g]"Send men to spy out the land of Canaan, which I am giving to the people of Israel. From each tribe of their fathers you shall send a man, every one a chief among them." 3 So Moses sent them from [h]the wilderness of Paran, according to the command of the LORD, all of them men who were heads of the people of Israel. 4 And these were their names: From the tribe of Reuben, Shammua the son of Zaccur; 5 from the tribe of Simeon, Shaphat the son of Hori; 6 [i]from the tribe of Judah, [j]Caleb the son of Jephunneh; 7 from the tribe of Issachar, Igal the son of Joseph; 8 from the tribe of Ephraim, [k]Hoshea the son of Nun; 9 from the tribe of Benjamin, Palti the son of Raphu; 10 from the tribe of Zebulun, Gaddiel the son of Sodi; 11 from the tribe of Joseph (that is, from the tribe of Manasseh), Gaddi the son of Susi; 12 from the tribe of Dan, Ammiel the son of Gemalli; 13 from the tribe of Asher, Sethur the son of Michael; 14 from the tribe of Naphtali, Nahbi the son of Vophsi; 15 from the tribe of Gad, Geuel the son of Machi. 16 These were the names of the men whom Moses sent to spy out the land. And Moses called [k]Hoshea the son of Nun Joshua.

17 Moses sent them to spy out the land of Canaan and said to them, "Go up into [l]the Negeb and go up into [m]the hill country, 18 and see what the land is, and whether the people who dwell in it are strong or weak, whether they are few or many, 19 and whether the land that they dwell in is good or bad, and whether the cities that they dwell in are camps or strongholds, 20 and whether the land is [n]rich or poor, and whether there are trees in it or not. [o]Be of good courage and bring some of the fruit of the land." Now the time was the season of the first ripe grapes.

21 So they went up and spied out the land [p]from the wilderness of Zin to Rehob, [q]near Lebo-hamath. 22 They went up into [m]the Negeb and came to [r]Hebron. [s]Ahiman, Sheshai, and Talmai, the [t]descendants of Anak, were there. ([u]Hebron was built seven years before [u]Zoan in Egypt.) 23 And [v]they came to the Valley of Eshcol and cut down from there a branch with a single cluster of grapes, and they carried it on a pole between two of them; they also brought some pomegranates and figs. 24 That place was called the Valley of Eshcol,[1] because of the cluster that the people of Israel cut down from there.

Report of the Spies

25 At the end of forty days they returned from spying out the land. 26 And they came to Moses and Aaron and to all the congregation of the people of Israel in the wilderness

[1] *Eshcol* means *cluster*

13:1–19:22 *Forty Years near Kadesh.* The central section of the book of Numbers brings together events spanning 40 years, when the Israelites lived in and near Kadesh-barnea. Kadesh is a large oasis about 50 miles (80 km) southwest of Beersheba (see map, p. 258). It marked the southern limit of the land of Canaan, according to 34:4. So when Israel reached there, they were on the verge of entering the Promised Land. But as a result of the rebellion prompted by the spies' negative reports, God punished the people by making them wait 40 years to enter the land. A few important episodes from this period are recounted in chs. 13–19.

13:1–14:45 *The Mission of the Spies and the National Rebellion.* The significance of this episode is indicated by its length. It stands alongside the golden calf episode (Exodus 32–34) as one of the two great apostasies of the wilderness wanderings. On the former occasion, Israel broke the first two commandments (Ex. 20:3–6) and the Lord threatened to annihilate them and create a new people from Moses' descendants (Ex. 32:9–10). Only Moses' intercession persuaded God to relent (Ex. 32:11–14). This time the people turn their backs on the Promised Land and propose returning to Egypt. Again the Lord threatens their destruction, which is averted only by Moses' intercession.

13:1–16 *Spies Sent Out.* Twelve tribal leaders are selected to go from Paran to "spy out the land of Canaan" (v. 2) and to bring back a report concerning the quality of the land and the morale of its inhabitants, probably with the intention of strengthening the faith of the Israelites.

13:2 Note the reminder that the **land** has been promised by God.

13:4–16 This list of tribal leaders differs from that in chs. 1–2; perhaps younger, more energetic leaders were needed for the spying mission. In 13:16, **Hoshea** ("he saves") is renamed **Joshua** ("Yahweh saves"), anticipating the faith he shows in 14:6.

13:17–24 *Mission Accomplished.* The spies cover some 220 miles (354 km) from the **Negeb**, the arid region south of Beersheba, right up to the north, **Rehob, near Lebo-hamath**, about 47 miles (76 km) north of Damascus (v. 21).

13:20 Season of the first ripe grapes, i.e., late July.

13:22 Hebron is about 20 miles (32 km) south of Jerusalem. Theologically it is very significant as the burial place of the patriarchs and their wives (e.g., Genesis 23) and the place where God had promised the land to Abraham forever (Gen. 17:8). **the descendants of Anak**. Anak in Hebrew (*'anaq*) means "neck," and the Anakim were famous for their height (see Num. 13:33; Deut. 2:21; 9:2). **Zoan** is Tanis, in the Nile delta. It was the capital of Egypt in the time of the Israelite monarchy, but this verse must be referring to its earlier history. Tanis was founded in the early second millennium B.C., and excavations at Hebron demonstrate that the first fortified city dates to the Middle Bronze II period (c. 2000–1750 B.C.). The correspondence of dating is striking.

13:23 Eshcol ("cluster" in Hb.) cannot be precisely located, but grapes grow well in the Hebron area.

13:25–33 *The Spies' Report of Their Mission.* This report covers the same ground as the narration in vv. 17–24. But whereas the latter is straightforward and factual, the spies' account is lurid and exaggerated, calculated to dismay the hearers. Notice the description of the cities as **fortified and very large** (v. 28), and the long list of inhabitants (vv. 28–29). Archaeological excavation has confirmed that Canaanite cities of the Late Bronze Age were large and

of Paran, at [w]Kadesh. They brought back word to them and to all the congregation, and
showed them the fruit of the land. 27 And they told him, "We came to the land to which
you sent us. It [x]flows with milk and honey, [y]and this is its fruit. 28 [z]However, the people
who dwell in the land are strong, and the cities are fortified and very large. And besides,
we saw the descendants of Anak there. 29 [a]The Amalekites dwell in the land of the Negeb.
The Hittites, the Jebusites, and the Amorites dwell in the hill country. [b]And the Canaanites
dwell by the sea, and along the Jordan."

30 But [c]Caleb quieted the people before Moses and said, "Let us go up at once and occupy
it, for we are well able to overcome it." 31 [d]Then the men who had gone up with him said,
"We are not able to go up against the people, for they are stronger than we are." 32 So [e]they
brought to the people of Israel a bad report of the land that they had spied out, saying, "The
land, through which we have gone to spy it out, is a land that devours its inhabitants, and
[f]all the people that we saw in it are of great height. 33 And there we saw the [g]Nephilim (the
sons of Anak, who come from the [g]Nephilim), and we seemed to ourselves [h]like grasshoppers, and so we seemed to them."

The People Rebel

14 Then all the congregation raised a loud cry, and the people [i]wept that night. 2 And
all the people of Israel [j]grumbled against Moses and Aaron. The whole congregation
said to them, "Would that we had died in the land of Egypt! Or [k]would that we had died
in this wilderness! 3 Why is the LORD bringing us into this land, to fall by the sword? [l]Our

26[w]ch. 20:1, 16; 32:8; 33:36; Deut. 1:19; Josh. 14:6, 7
27[x]See Ex. 3:8 [y]Deut. 1:25
28[z]Deut. 1:28; 9:1, 2
29[a]ch. 14:43; Ex. 17:8 [b][ch. 14:25]
30[c][ch. 14:6, 24]
31[d]ch. 32:9; Deut. 1:28; Josh. 14:8
32[e]ch. 14:36, 37 [f][Amos 2:9]
33[g]Gen. 6:4 [h]Isa. 40:22

Chapter 14
1[i]ch. 11:4
2[j]ver. 27, 29, 33; ch. 16:41; Ex. 15:24; 16:2; 17:3; Ps. 106:25; [Josh. 9:18] [k][ver. 27-29]
3[l]ver. 31

The Journey of the Spies

When the Israelites first arrived at Kadesh-barnea, Moses dispatched 12 spies to scout out the Promised Land of Canaan. For 40 days the spies traveled throughout Canaan, from the Negeb to Rehob and back again—a distance of over 500 miles (805 km).

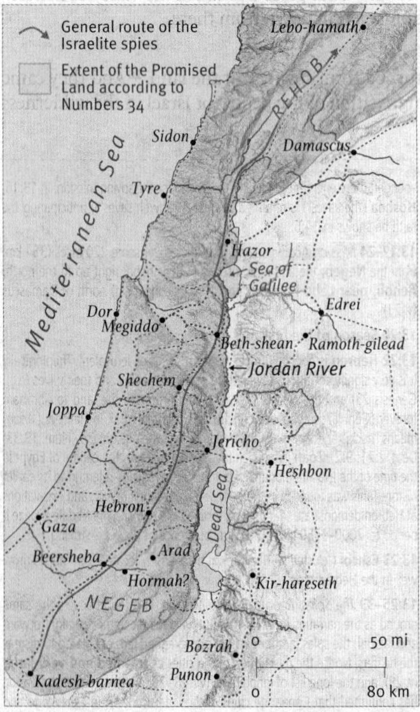

heavily defended. For example, the city of Hazor consisted of an upper city of 26 acres and a lower city of 160 acres. Estimates put the population at 40,000. Its defense walls were massively built of stone and mud brick; some of the walls measured as wide as 24 feet (7.3 m). The spies claim that the land **devours its inhabitants** (v. 32) and, to cap it off, that the tall Anakites are descended from the **Nephilim** (see note on Gen. 6:4) and therefore must be quite invincible. (Given the exaggerated tone of the spies' account, their reference to Nephilim is most likely an expression of their fear and an excuse for their disobedience, rather than an accurate statement indicating that the Nephilim were still living after the flood.) Scholars generally accept that the location of **Kadesh** is modern Tell 'Ain el-Qudeirat. This site, however, has revealed no remains before the tenth century B.C. This lack of evidence may be explained in a number of ways: (1) the identification may be incorrect; (2) earlier remains may not have been discovered yet; or (3) groups on the move like the Israelites may have left no remains to be discovered.

13:31 We are not able to go up against the people, for they are stronger than we are. This statement reflects lack of faith in the Lord, for the spies are evaluating the situation only from a human perspective. As a result, they have no courage. By contrast, trust in the Lord would produce genuine courage, as it does when the people of Israel are given a second opportunity to enter and conquer the Promised Land after 40 years of wandering in the wilderness (cf. Josh. 1:5–9).

14:1–12 *The People's Reaction.* The people react very strongly to this pessimistic view of their prospects. Their comments challenge both God's purposes and his power. God had promised them the land, but they dismiss it as impossible and suggest choosing a new leader to bring them back to Egypt (vv. 1–4).

14:6–9 Joshua and **Caleb** rightly term the popular reaction as rebellion **against the LORD** and urge them to have faith in God's power to bring them into the land (v. 9). For this they are threatened with stoning (v. 10), a form of execution prescribed for apostates (Lev. 20:2, 27; 24:23; Num. 15:36; Deut. 13:10).

14:6 tore their clothes. A typical sign of grief (Gen. 37:29, 34).

14:8 If the LORD delights in us, he will bring us into this land and give it to us. This statement from Joshua and Caleb stands in stark contrast to the cowardly statement from the other spies in 13:31. God's subsequent blessing on Joshua and Caleb (see 14:30, 38; 26:65) shows his approval of their faith.

14:11–12 The gravity of the sin is marked by God's proposal to destroy the **nation** and start again with **Moses**. A similar threat was made in Ex. 32:10.

14:13–19 *Moses' Plea for Forgiveness.* Moses prays here, as he did after

wives and our little ones will become a prey. Would it not be better for us to go back to
Egypt?" 4 And they said to one another, [m]"Let us choose a leader and [n]go back to Egypt."
5 Then [o]Moses and Aaron fell on their faces before all the assembly of the congregation
of the people of Israel. 6 [p]And Joshua the son of Nun and Caleb the son of Jephunneh,
who were among those who had spied out the land, tore their clothes 7 and said to all the
congregation of the people of Israel, [q]"The land, which we passed through to spy it out,
is an exceedingly good land. 8 If [r]the LORD delights in us, he will bring us into this land
and give it to us, [s]a land that flows with milk and honey. 9 Only [t]do not rebel against the
LORD. And [u]do not fear the people of the land, for [v]they are bread for us. Their protection
is removed from them, and the LORD is with us; do not fear them." 10 [w]Then all the congregation said to stone them with stones. But [x]the glory of the LORD appeared at the tent
of meeting to all the people of Israel.
11 And the LORD said to Moses, "How long will this people [y]despise me? And how long
will they not [z]believe in me, in spite of all the signs that I have done among them? 12 I
will strike them with the pestilence and disinherit them, and I [a]will make of you a nation
greater and mightier than they."

Moses Intercedes for the People

13 But [b]Moses said to the LORD, "Then the Egyptians will hear of it, for you brought
up this people in your might from among them, 14 and they will tell the inhabitants of
this land. [c]They have heard that you, O LORD, are in the midst of this people. For you, O
LORD, are seen face to face, and [d]your cloud stands over them and you go before them, in
a pillar of cloud by day and in a pillar of fire by night. 15 Now if you kill this people as one
man, then the nations who have heard your fame will say, 16 'It is because the LORD [e]was
not able to bring this people into the land that he swore to give to them that he has killed
them in the wilderness.' 17 And now, please let the power of the Lord be great as you have
promised, saying, 18 [f]'The LORD is slow to anger and abounding in steadfast love, forgiving
iniquity and transgression, but he will by no means clear the guilty, [g]visiting the iniquity
of the fathers on the children, to the third and the fourth generation.' 19 Please [h]pardon
the iniquity of this people, according to the greatness of your steadfast love, just [i]as you
have forgiven this people, from Egypt until now."

God Promises Judgment

20 Then the LORD said, "I have pardoned, [j]according to your word. 21 But truly, as I live,
and as all [k]the earth shall be filled with the glory of the LORD, 22 [l]none of the men who
have seen my glory and my signs that I did in Egypt and in the wilderness, and yet have
put me to the test these [m]ten times and have not obeyed my voice, 23 [n]shall see the land
that I swore to give to their fathers. And none of those who despised me shall see it. 24 But
my servant [o]Caleb, because he has a different spirit and has [p]followed me fully, I will bring
into the land into which he went, and his descendants shall possess it. 25 [q]Now, since the
Amalekites and the Canaanites dwell in the valleys, [r]turn tomorrow and set out for the
wilderness by the way to the Red Sea."
26 And the LORD spoke to Moses and to Aaron, saying, 27 "How long shall [s]this wicked
congregation grumble against me? [t]I have heard the grumblings of the people of Israel,
which they grumble against me. 28 Say to them, [u]'As I live, declares the LORD, [v]what you
have said in my hearing I will do to you: 29 [w]your dead bodies shall fall in this wilderness,

4 [m]Neh. 9:17 [n][Deut. 17:16; Acts 7:39]
5 [o]ch. 16:4, 22; 20:6
6 [p]ver. 30; ch. 13:6, 8
7 [q]ch. 13:27; Deut. 1:25
8 [r]Deut. 10:15; 2 Sam. 22:20; 1 Kgs. 10:9; Ps. 18:19; 22:8; Isa. 62:4 [s]See Ex. 3:8
9 [t]Josh. 22:16, 18, 19, 29 [u]Deut. 7:18; 20:3 [v]ch. 24:8; [Ps. 14:4; 74:14]
10 [w]Ex. 17:4 [x]See Lev. 9:23
11 [y]ver. 23; ch. 16:30 [z]Deut. 1:32; 9:23; Ps. 78:22, 32; 106:24; Heb. 3:18; [John 12:37]
12 [a]Ex. 32:10
13 [b]Ex. 32:12; [Deut. 9:28; 32:27; Ps. 106:23; Ezek. 20:9, 14]
14 [c]Ex. 15:14; Josh. 2:9, 10; 5:1 [d]See Ex. 13:21
16 [e]Deut. 9:28; [Josh. 7:9]
18 [f]See Ex. 34:6, 7 [g]See Ex. 20:5
19 [h]Ex. 34:9 [i]Ps. 78:38; 106:45
20 [j]Ps. 106:23; [James 5:16]; See 1 John 5:14-16
21 [k]Ps. 72:19; Hab. 2:14
22 [l]Deut. 1:35; Ps. 95:11; 106:26; Heb. 3:17, 18 [m][Gen. 31:7; Job 19:3]
23 [n]ch. 32:11; Ezek. 20:15; [ch. 26:64]
24 [o]ver. 6; ch. 13:6 [p]ch. 32:12; Josh. 14:8, 9
25 [q]ver. 43, 45; See ch. 13:29 [r]Deut. 1:40
27 [s]ver. 35 [t]Ex. 16:7, 12
28 [u]ver. 21, 23; ch. 26:65 [v][ver. 2]
29 [w]1 Cor. 10:5; Heb. 3:17

the making of the golden calf (Exodus 32), acting, as often in the Pentateuch, as a covenant mediator (cf. Num. 12:3–4). He points out that, were God to fulfill his threat to annihilate Israel, the nations would say that **the LORD was not able to bring this people into the land** (cf. Ex. 32:12). He reminds God that he promised Abraham that his descendants would inherit the land (cf. Ex. 32:13), and finally he quotes God's own description of his character to prove that he ought to forgive (Ex. 34:6–7; Num. 14:18–19).

14:20–35 *God's Response to Moses' Prayer.* God's response is somewhat surprising. On the one hand, he declares: **I have pardoned, according to your word** (i.e., he has drawn back from destroying Israel immediately). But that does not mean they can go ahead with their planned entry to Canaan. In fact, the disobedient Israelites will get what they asked for. They wanted to return to Egypt (v. 3); they are told to go into the wilderness by the Red Sea (v. 25). They said they did not want to enter the land because they would die there (vv. 2–3); they are told they will never enter it, but die in the wilderness (vv. 27–38). They feared that their **little ones . . . would become a prey** (see v. 3); but it is the children who in 40 years' time will enter the land (v. 31).

14:21 all the earth shall be filled with the glory of the LORD. God's purposes will not be defeated by human failure; he will certainly fulfill them. (See notes on Ps. 72:18–20; Isa. 6:3.)

14:29 All those **twenty years old and upward** are sentenced to die in the wilderness, because it was those over 20 who had been enrolled to fight (see 1:3) but had refused.

and [x]of all your number, listed in the census [y]from twenty years old and upward, who
have grumbled against me, 30 not one shall come into the land where I [z]swore that I would
make you dwell, [a]except Caleb the son of Jephunneh and Joshua the son of Nun. 31 [b]But
your little ones, who you said would become a prey, I will bring in, and they shall know
the land that [c]you have rejected. 32 But as for you, [w]your dead bodies shall fall in this
wilderness. 33 And your children [d]shall be shepherds in the wilderness [e]forty years and
shall [f]suffer for your faithlessness, until the last of your dead bodies lies in the wilderness.
34 [g]According to the number of the days in which you spied out the land, [h]forty days, a year
for each day, you shall bear your iniquity forty years, and you shall know my displeasure.'
35 [i]I, the LORD, have spoken. Surely this will I do to all [j]this wicked congregation who are
gathered together against me: in this wilderness they shall come to a full end, and there
they shall die."

36 [k]And the men whom Moses sent to spy out the land, who returned and made all the
congregation grumble against him by bringing up a bad report about the land— 37 the
men who brought up a bad report of the land—[l]died by plague before the LORD. 38 Of
those men who went to spy out the land, [m]only Joshua the son of Nun and Caleb the son
of Jephunneh remained alive.

Israel Defeated in Battle

39 When Moses told these words to all the people of Israel, the people [n]mourned greatly.
40 And they rose early in the morning and went up to the heights of the hill country,
saying, [o]"Here we are. We will go up to the place that the LORD has promised, for we
have sinned." 41 [p]But Moses said, "Why now are you transgressing the command of
the LORD, when that will not succeed? 42 [q]Do not go up, [r]for the Lord is not among
you, lest you be struck down before your enemies. 43 For there [s]the Amalekites and
the Canaanites are facing you, and you shall fall by the sword. Because you have turned
back from following the LORD, the LORD will not be with you." 44 [t]But they presumed
to go up to the heights of the hill country, although neither [u]the ark of the covenant
of the LORD nor Moses departed out of the camp. 45 Then [v]the Amalekites and the
Canaanites who lived in that hill country came down and defeated them and pursued
them, even to [w]Hormah.

29 [x]ch. 1:45; 26:64; Deut. 1:35 [y]ch. 1:3; Ex. 30:14
30 [z]See Gen. 14:22 [a]ver. 6, 38; See ch. 13:6
31 [b]ver. 3; Deut. 1:39 [c]Ps. 106:24
32 [w][See ver. 29 above]
33 [d]ch. 32:13; [Ps. 107:40] [e]Ps. 95:10; [Deut. 2:14] [f]Ezek. 23:35
34 [g]ch. 13:25 [h][Ezek. 4:6]
35 [i]ch. 23:19 [j]ver. 27
36 [k]ch. 13:32
37 [l]1 Cor. 10:10; Heb. 3:17; Jude 5
38 [m]ch. 26:65; See ch. 13:16
39 [n]Ex. 33:4
40 [o]Deut. 1:41
41 [p][2 Chr. 24:20]
42 [q]Deut. 1:42 [r][Deut. 31:17]
43 [s]ver. 25, 45; See ch. 13:29
44 [t]Deut. 1:43 [u][1 Sam. 4:3]
45 [v]ver. 43; [Deut. 1:44] [w]ch. 21:3; Judg. 1:17

14:36–38 *Death of the Faithless Spies.* Though all the adult Israelites were warned that they would die in the wilderness, the 10 faithless spies, who had incited the national apostasy, "died by plague" (v. 37; ironically, this uses one of the same Hebrew words used with reference to the Egyptian plagues—Hb. *maggepah*, "plague"; cf. Ex. 9:14). A similar fate befell many of those involved in the idolatry of the golden calf (Ex. 32:35). The story of the spies illustrates an important principle: when God forgives sin, he does not always eliminate the consequences of sin. In the case of Israel, God's forgiveness meant that it remained the people of God, in a corporate sense. The covenant made at Sinai—that the Lord would be their God and that Israel would be his people—was maintained. Yet the people still suffered for their sin: they did not enter Canaan, but died in the wilderness.

The Failed Entry into Canaan

After the Lord had condemned the people for refusing to enter Canaan, a group of Israelites changed their mind and tried to go up, even though neither Moses nor the ark of the covenant went with them. When they reached the hill country, they were beaten back by the Amalekites and Canaanites, who chased them all the way to Hormah.

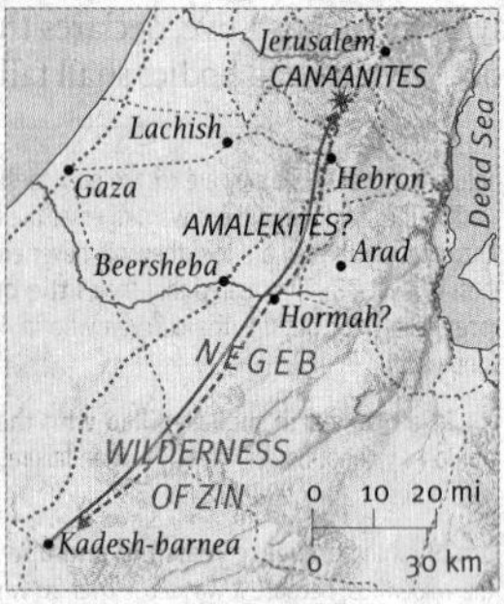

14:36–37 the men who brought up a bad report of the land . . . died by plague before the LORD. These men are prime examples of unbelief within the covenant people, and must be removed (see note on Isa. 1:24–28). Thus God judged the leaders (who "died by the plague before the LORD") because of the disastrous effect of their bad report (it **made all the congregation grumble** against Moses)—a dramatic reminder of the principle that God requires a higher level of accountability for those in leadership.

14:39–45 *An Unsuccessful Attempt at Conquest.* Despite the death of the spies, and despite Moses telling the people that they must die in the wilderness and not enter the land, they attempt a conquest. Their defeat, ironically at the hands of the **Amalekites** and **Canaanites** (cf. 13:29), fulfills Moses' warning.

14:45 Then the Amalekites and the Canaanites . . . came down and defeated them. In disobeying Moses' command (vv. 41–43), the Israelites "presume" (v. 44) to take matters into their own hands. Rather than accomplishing God's purposes, they encounter his judgment. **Hormah** (Hb. meaning "Destruction"; see 21:3) is a village on the southern border of Canaan (Josh. 15:30).

15:1–41 *The Law-giving at Kadesh.* At each place where Israel encamped for a long time, laws were given: at Sinai (Exodus 20—Numbers 9), Kadesh (Numbers 15), and the plains of Moab (Numbers 28–36). The Kadesh laws are the briefest and are mainly clarifications of the Sinai laws.

Laws About Sacrifices

15 The LORD spoke to Moses, saying, 2 “Speak to the people of Israel and say to
them, [x]When you come into the land you are to inhabit, which I am giving you,
3 and [y]you offer to the LORD from the herd or from the flock a food offering[1] or a burnt
offering or a sacrifice, [z]to fulfill a vow or as a freewill offering or [a]at your appointed
feasts, to make a [b]pleasing aroma to the LORD, 4 then [c]he who brings his offering shall
offer to the LORD [d]a grain offering of a tenth of an ephah[2] of fine flour, [e]mixed with a
quarter of a hin[3] of oil; 5 and you shall offer with the burnt offering, or for the sacrifice,
a quarter of a hin of [f]wine for the drink offering for each lamb. 6 [g]Or for a ram, you shall
offer for a grain offering two tenths of an ephah of fine flour mixed with a third of a
hin of oil. 7 And for the drink offering you shall offer a third of a hin of wine, a [b]pleas-
ing aroma to the LORD. 8 And when you offer a bull as a burnt offering or sacrifice, to
[z]fulfill a vow or for [h]peace offerings to the LORD, 9 then one shall offer [i]with the bull
a grain offering of three tenths of an ephah of fine flour, mixed with half a hin of oil.
10 And you shall offer for the drink offering half a hin of wine, as a food offering, a
pleasing aroma to the LORD.

11 [j]“Thus it shall be done for each bull or ram, or for each lamb or young goat. 12 As many
as you offer, so shall you do with each one, as many as there are. 13 Every native Israelite
shall do these things in this way, in offering a food offering, with a pleasing aroma to the
LORD. 14 And if a stranger is sojourning with you, or anyone is living permanently among
you, and he wishes to offer a food offering, with a pleasing aroma to the LORD, he shall do
as you do. 15 For the assembly, [k]there shall be one statute for you and for the stranger who
sojourns with you, a statute forever throughout your generations. You and the sojourner
shall be alike before the LORD. 16 One law and one rule shall be for you and for the stranger
who sojourns with you.”

17 The LORD spoke to Moses, saying, 18 [l]“Speak to the people of Israel and say to them,
When you come into the land to which I bring you 19 and when you eat of [m]the bread of the
land, you shall present a contribution to the LORD. 20 [n]Of the first of your dough you shall
present a loaf as a contribution; like a [o]contribution from the threshing floor, so shall you
present it. 21 [n]Some of the first of your dough you shall give to the LORD as a contribution
throughout your generations.

Laws About Unintentional Sins

22 [p]“But if you sin unintentionally,[4] and do not observe all these commandments that
the LORD has spoken to Moses, 23 all that the LORD has commanded you by Moses, from
the day that the LORD gave commandment, and onward throughout your generations,
24 then if it was done unintentionally [q]without the knowledge of the congregation, all the
congregation shall offer one bull from the herd for a burnt offering, a pleasing aroma to

Chapter 15
2 [x]ver. 18; Lev. 23:10; Deut. 26:1
3 [y]Lev. 1:2, 3 [z]Lev. 22:21; 27:2 [a]ch. 28:19, 27; Lev. 23:8, 12, 36; Deut. 16:10 [b]Ex. 29:18; Lev. 4:31; See Gen. 8:21
4 [c]Lev. 2:1; 6:14 [d]Ex. 29:40; Lev. 23:13 [e]ch. 28:5; Lev. 14:10
5 [f]ch. 28:7, 14
6 [g]ch. 28:12, 14
7 [b][See ver. 3 above]
8 [z][See ver. 3 above] [h]Lev. 7:11
9 [i]ch. 28:12, 14; See Lev. 6:14-17
11 [j]See ch. 28
15 [k]ver. 29, 30; ch. 9:14; Ex. 12:49
18 [l]ver. 2
19 [m][Josh. 5:11, 12]
20 [n]Deut. 26:2, 10; Neh. 10:37; Ezek. 44:30 [o]Lev. 2:14; See Lev. 23:10-17
21 [n][See ver. 20 above]
22 [p][Lev. 4:2]
24 [q][Lev. 4:13]

[1] Or *an offering by fire*; so throughout Numbers [2] An *ephah* was about 3/5 bushel or 22 liters [3] A *hin* was about 4 quarts or 3.5 liters [4] Or *by mistake*; also verses 24, 27, 28, 29

15:1–16 *Meal, Oil, and Wine to Accompany Sacrifice.* Leviticus 1–7, which explains how each type of sacrifice is to be conducted, does not explain that burnt offerings (Leviticus 1) and peace offerings (Leviticus 3) must be accompanied by appropriate quantities of meal, oil, and wine. This may be because such materials were not available in the wilderness. But **when you come into the land** (Num. 15:2), the situation will be different. Then these other products will be available and (along with animal sacrifices) must be offered to God. The imagery of sacrifice is drawn from that of a meal: the worshiper must act as the generous host and give to God all that he would give an important guest (Gen. 18:1–8). It was not that God needed food, but these gifts showed the worshiper's devotion (Ps. 50:12–15). The giving of these laws at this point is very telling. The entry into Canaan has just been delayed 40 years, and an attempt to enter has failed (Num. 14:20–45), so the question could be asked: would Israel ever enter the Promised Land? These laws emphatically answer *yes*. It is not a question of *if* they will enter the land, but rather *when* they will come in. In this way the laws reaffirm the land promise. Further, the continuing instructions show that God has indeed retained Israel as his people (see note on 14:36–38). But more than that, the laws are an assurance that their harvests in the land would be abundant, as they stipulate that large quantities must be offered with each animal. The sacrifice of a **lamb** must be accompanied by about half a gallon (1.9 liters) of **flour**, a quart (0.95 liters) of **oil**, and a quart (0.95 liters) of **wine** (15:4–5). At least double quantities are needed for a **bull** (vv. 8–10). Verses 14–16 allow Gentile immigrants to offer sacrifices, as long as they follow the same rules as the Israelites.

15:17–21 *The Dough Offering.* The book of Leviticus (19:24–25; 23:10–11) insists that the firstfruits of the crops must be given to God. This principle is now extended to baking. The first dough is given to the priests. Observant Jews today still remember this rule when they bake, by throwing a small lump of dough into the fire.

15:22–31 *Sacrifices for Unintentional Sins.* Sins by mistake (i.e., unpremeditated sins, or sins done when the person did not know the action was sinful; cf. Lev. 4:1–5:13) may be atoned for by offering a sin offering.

15:22–26 These verses recall the rule for a sin of the congregation (cf. Lev. 4:13–21).

the LORD, [r]with its grain offering and its drink offering, according to the rule, and [s]one
male goat for a sin offering. 25 [t]And the priest shall make atonement for all the congregation of the people of Israel, and they shall be forgiven, because it was a mistake, and they
have brought their offering, a food offering to the LORD, and their sin offering before
the LORD for their mistake. 26 And all the congregation of the people of Israel shall be
forgiven, and the stranger who sojourns among them, because the whole population was
involved in the mistake.
27 [u]"If one person sins unintentionally, he shall offer a female goat a year old for a sin
offering. 28 [v]And the priest shall make atonement before the LORD for the person who
makes a mistake, when he sins unintentionally, to make atonement for him, and he shall
be forgiven. 29 [w]You shall have one law for him who does anything unintentionally, for him
who is native among the people of Israel and for the stranger who sojourns among them.
30 [x]But the person who does anything with a high hand, whether he is native or a sojourner,
reviles the LORD, and that person shall be cut off from among his people. 31 Because he has
[y]despised the word of the LORD and has broken his commandment, that person shall be
utterly cut off; his iniquity shall be on him."

A Sabbathbreaker Executed

32 While the people of Israel were in the wilderness, they found a man [z]gathering sticks
on the Sabbath day. 33 And those who found him gathering sticks brought him to Moses
and Aaron and to all the congregation. 34 [a]They put him in custody, because it had not
been made clear what should be done to him. 35 And the LORD said to Moses, [b]"The man
shall be put to death; all the congregation shall [c]stone him with stones outside the camp."
36 And all the congregation brought him outside the camp and stoned him to death with
stones, as the LORD commanded Moses.

Tassels on Garments

37 The LORD said to Moses, 38 "Speak to the people of Israel, and tell them to [d]make tassels
on the corners of their garments throughout their generations, and to put a cord of blue
on the tassel of each corner. 39 And it shall be a tassel for you to look at and remember all
the commandments of the LORD, to do them, [e]not to follow[1] after your own heart and
your own eyes, which you are inclined [f]to whore after. 40 So you shall remember and do all
my commandments, and be [g]holy to your God. 41 [h]I am the LORD your God, who brought
you out of the land of Egypt to be your God: I am the LORD your God."

[1] Hebrew *to spy out*

24 [r]ver. 8-10 [s]ch. 28:15; Lev. 4:23
25 [t]Lev. 4:20
27 [u]Lev. 4:27, 28
28 [v]Lev. 4:35
29 [w]See ver. 15
30 [x][Deut. 17:12; Ps. 19:13; Heb. 10:26]
31 [y]2 Sam. 12:9; 2 Chr. 36:16; Prov. 13:13
32 [z]Ex. 35:3; See Ex. 20:8, 9
34 [a]Lev. 24:12
35 [b]Ex. 31:14, 15 [c]Lev. 24:14-16; Josh. 7:25; 1 Kgs. 21:13; Acts 7:58
38 [d]Deut. 22:12; [Matt. 23:5]
39 [e][Job 31:7; Eccles. 11:9; Ezek. 6:9] [f]Ps. 73:27; 106:39; [Ezek. 6:9]
40 [g]See Lev. 11:44
41 [h]Lev. 22:33; See Lev. 20:8

15:27–29 This is the rule for an individual (**one person**, cf. Lev. 4:27–35). Minor changes from Leviticus are introduced (e.g., the congregation must offer a bull and a goat, not just a bull, while the individual may offer only **a female goat a year old**, not a lamb). The reason for these changes is unclear. The fact that a sacrifice must be given even **for the person who makes a mistake**, or who **sins unintentionally**, implies that such sin still requires **atonement**, though it is not counted to be as serious as willful sin. An immigrant (**the stranger who sojourns among them**, Num. 15:29) may also seek atonement for unintentional sin (see also vv. 14–16).

15:30–31 Sins committed **with a high hand** must refer to deliberate, intentional sins, since these are contrasted with unintentional sins (vv. 22, 24, 27). A "high hand" suggests lifting up a hand in defiance against God, and such a sin cannot be atoned for (see Heb. 10:26–30). Those who sin consciously and deliberately **shall be cut off** (i.e., die suddenly and mysteriously as punishment from God; see Gen. 17:14; Ex. 12:15; 31:14; Num. 9:13 and note on 9:6–14).

15:32–36 *A Sabbathbreaker Executed.* This seems to be a case of sinning "with a high hand"—and publicly, too—so that the offender is actually executed, not just left to be "cut off" (cf. vv. 30–31), which applied only when the offender escaped human detection. In this case it is clear that the man has sinned, since all work **on the Sabbath** is prohibited (Ex. 20:10), including lighting a fire (Ex. 35:3). However, in this case the people did not know what his punishment should be: **it had not been made clear what should be done to him** (Num. 15:34). The mode of his execution underlines the importance of observing the Sabbath.

15:37–41 *Tassels on Clothes.* In the ancient world, **tassels** were worn by nobles and other high-class people. In Israel they are to be worn by everyone as a mark of their status as the chosen people. **Blue** was used in the tabernacle curtains and in the priests' vestments (Ex. 26:31; 28:31). So the blue threads reminded the Israelites that they were "a kingdom of priests and a holy nation" (Ex. 19:6). This meant they had to **remember and do all my commandments** (Num. 15:40). In particular, they had to avoid the mistake of the spies of following **after your own heart** (v. 39). There is a play on words with the expression **to follow**, for this verb (Hb. *tur*) means both "to spy" and "to follow," and thus alludes to the danger found in following their own whims rather than being absolutely loyal to the divine commandments. It seems that tassels were part of Jesus' clothing in observance of this requirement and that the "fringes" touched for healing by the sick in Matthew's Gospel would have been "tassels," since the same Greek word used for "tassel" in the Septuagint is also used in Matthew (Gk. *kraspedon*, "tassel" or "fringe"; see Matt. 9:20; 14:36).

16:1–50 *The Rebellion of Korah, Dathan, and Abiram.* This story heads a section concerned with demonstrating the privileges and mediatorial role of the priesthood. It begins with Korah overemphasizing one truth to the exclusion of others (which is what heretics and founders of cults commonly do). He claims that since "all in the congregation are holy," all have equal access to God (v. 3). As a result, he and his followers demand that they should have all the privileges of priests, to enter God's presence in the tabernacle itself. But God judged them swiftly, and the final episode ends with all the people crying out in fear, "we perish," and, "Everyone who comes near . . . to the tabernacle . . . shall die" (17:12, 13). They have learned that only the priests may approach the tabernacle, and this protects the rest of the nation

Korah's Rebellion

16 Now [i]Korah the son of Izhar, son of Kohath, son of Levi, and [j]Dathan and Abiram
the sons of Eliab, and On the son of Peleth, sons of Reuben, took men. 2 And they
rose up before Moses, with a number of the people of Israel, 250 chiefs of the congregation, chosen from the assembly, well-known men. 3 [k]They assembled themselves together
against Moses and against Aaron and said to them, [l]"You have gone too far! For [m]all in
the congregation are holy, every one of them, and the LORD is among them. Why then do
you exalt yourselves above the assembly of the LORD?" 4 When Moses heard it, [n]he fell on
his face, 5 and he said to Korah and all his company, "In the morning the LORD will show
[o]who is his,[1] and who is [p]holy, and will bring him near to him. The one [q]whom he chooses
he will [r]bring near to him. 6 Do this: take [s]censers, Korah and all his company; 7 put fire in
them and put incense on them before the LORD tomorrow, and the man whom the LORD
chooses shall be the holy one. [t]You have gone too far, sons of Levi!" 8 And Moses said to
Korah, "Hear now, you sons of Levi: 9 is it [u]too small a thing for you that the God of Israel
has [v]separated you from the congregation of Israel, to bring you near to himself, to do
service in the tabernacle of the LORD and to stand before the congregation to minister
to them, 10 and that he has brought you near him, and all your brothers the sons of Levi
with you? And would you seek the priesthood also? 11 Therefore it is against the LORD
that you and all your company have gathered together. What is [w]Aaron that you grumble
against him?"
12 And Moses sent to call Dathan and Abiram the sons of Eliab, and they said, "We will
not come up. 13 Is it [x]a small thing that you have brought us up out of [y]a land flowing
with milk and honey, to kill us in the wilderness, that you must also [z]make yourself a
prince over us? 14 Moreover, you have not brought us into a land flowing with milk and
honey, nor given us inheritance of fields and vineyards. Will you put out the eyes of these
men? We will not come up." 15 And Moses was very angry and said to the LORD, [a]"Do not
respect their offering. [b]I have not taken one donkey from them, and I have not harmed
one of them."
16 And Moses said to Korah, "Be present, you and all your company, [c]before the LORD,
you and they, and Aaron, tomorrow. 17 And [d]let every one of you take his censer and put
incense on it, and every one of you bring before the LORD his censer, [e]250 censers; you also,
and Aaron, each his censer." 18 So every man took his censer and put fire in them and laid
incense on them and stood at the entrance of the tent of meeting with Moses and Aaron.
19 Then Korah assembled all the congregation against them at the entrance of the tent of
meeting. [f]And the glory of the LORD appeared to all the congregation.
20 And the LORD spoke to Moses and to Aaron, saying, 21 [g]"Separate yourselves from
among this congregation, that I may consume them [h]in a moment." 22 And they [i]fell on
their faces and said, "O God, [j]the God of the spirits of all flesh, [k]shall one man sin, and will

[1] Septuagint *The LORD knows those who are his*

Chapter 16
1 [i]ch. 27:3; Ex. 6:16, 18, 21; Jude 11 [j]ch. 26:9
3 [k]Ps. 106:16-18 [l]ver. 7 [m]See Ex. 19:6
4 [n]ch. 14:5; 20:6
5 [o][2 Tim. 2:19] [p]ver. 3 [q]ch. 17:5; 1 Sam. 2:28; Ps. 105:26; [Ex. 28:1] [r]ch. 3:10; Lev. 10:3; Ps. 65:4; Ezek. 40:46; 44:15, 16
6 [s]Lev. 10:1
7 [t]ver. 3
9 [u]ver. 13; 1 Sam. 18:23; Isa. 7:13; [Ezek. 16:20] [v]ch. 8:14; Deut. 10:8
11 [w]Ex. 16:8; [1 Cor. 3:5]
13 [x]ver. 9 [y]See Ex. 3:8 [z]Ex. 2:14; Acts 7:27, 35
15 [a][Gen. 4:4, 5] [b]1 Sam. 12:3; [Acts 20:33; 2 Cor. 7:2]
16 [c]Ex. 16:9; 1 Sam. 12:3, 7
17 [d]ver. 6, 7 [e]ver. 35
19 [f]See Lev. 9:23
21 [g]ver. 45; [Gen. 19:17, 22; Jer. 51:6; Rev. 18:4] [h]Ex. 33:5; Ps. 73:19
22 [i]ver. 45; ch. 14:5; 20:6 [j]ch. 27:16; Job 12:10; Eccles. 12:7; Isa. 57:16; Zech. 12:1 [k][Gen. 18:23-25; 2 Sam. 24:17]

from death. This is outlined in the laws of ch. 18, which explain how the tribe of Levi has this vital role (18:1–7), and that the tithes and sacrificial portions that they receive are a reward for their important and dangerous service (18:8–32).

16:1–15 *The Complaints of Korah, Dathan, and Abiram.* After the leaders of the revolt are introduced (vv. 1–2), Korah targets his complaint against Aaron's high priesthood (vv. 3–11), and then the scene switches to Dathan and Abiram, who grumble about leaving the comforts of Egypt for death in the wilderness (vv. 12–15).

16:1 Korah was a Levite (but not a priest) from the Kohathite clan. They camped near the tribe of **Reuben** (2:10–11; 3:29), from which the other leaders (**Dathan**, **Abiram**, and **On**) came. This could explain their collaboration. On is not mentioned later in the story.

16:3 The claim that **all . . . are holy** could be based on the repeated call in the law to be holy (e.g., Lev. 11:45; 19:2; Num. 15:40). But this ethical holiness is not identical with priestly holiness, which confers the right to approach God in the offering of sacrifice and incense. When the Kohathites claim that Moses and Aaron **exalt** themselves, they show that they have missed the point, not understanding that the priesthood is a matter of God's own appointment (cf. Heb. 5:4).

16:8–11 The Levites already enjoy great privileges in serving in the tabernacle, so they should not **seek the priesthood also** (v. 10).

16:12–15 The Reubenite complaint is somewhat different from Korah's. The Reubenites object to dying in the **wilderness** instead of in Canaan or Egypt. This is rebellion against God's will and purpose akin to that provoked by the spies, who died in a plague (14:37). The complainers here will perish in even more spectacular fashion.

16:15 I have not taken one donkey from them. As Samuel would do later (see 1 Sam. 12:3–5), Moses professes that he is innocent of misusing his office for personal gain (see notes on 1 Sam. 8:3; 8:14–15; 12:3–6).

16:16–19, 35–40 *The Death of the Kohathite Supporters of Korah.* For a similar judgment on the unauthorized offering of incense, see Lev. 10:1–3.

16:20–34 *The Death of the Ringleaders and Their Families.* **And the earth opened its mouth and swallowed them up**. God executes swift judgment on those who thought they could assume the privileges of priesthood for themselves. **Sheol** (v. 33) is the place of the dead, often pictured as being under the earth (Gen. 37:35; Ps. 6:5; 9:17; Isa. 14:9–20).

you be angry with all the congregation?" **23** And the LORD spoke to Moses, saying, **24** "Say
to the congregation, Get away from the dwelling of Korah, Dathan, and Abiram."
25 Then Moses rose and went to Dathan and Abiram, and the elders of Israel followed
him. **26** And he spoke to the congregation, saying, [l]"Depart, please, from the tents of these
wicked men, and touch nothing of theirs, lest you be swept away with all their sins." **27** So
they got away from the dwelling of Korah, Dathan, and Abiram. And Dathan and Abiram
came out and stood [m]at the door of their tents, together with their wives, their sons, and
their little ones. **28** And Moses said, "Hereby you shall know that the LORD has sent me to
do all these works, and that it has not been [n]of my own accord. **29** If these men die as all
men die, or if they are visited by the fate of all mankind, [o]then the LORD has not sent me.
30 But if the LORD creates something new, and [p]the ground opens its mouth and swallows
them up with all that belongs to them, and they [q]go down alive into Sheol, then you shall
know that these men have despised the LORD."
31 [r]And as soon as he had finished speaking all these words, the ground under them split
apart. **32** And the earth opened its mouth and swallowed them up, with their households
and [s]all the people who belonged to Korah and all their goods. **33** So they and all that
belonged to them went down alive into Sheol, and the earth closed over them, and [t]they
perished from the midst of the assembly. **34** And all Israel who were around them fled at
their cry, for they said, "Lest the earth swallow us up!" **35** And [u]fire came out from the LORD
and consumed [v]the 250 men offering the incense.
36 [1] Then the LORD spoke to Moses, saying, **37** "Tell Eleazar the son of Aaron the priest
to take up the censers out of the blaze. Then scatter the fire far and wide, for they have
become holy. **38** As for the censers of [w]these men who have sinned at the cost of their lives,
let them be made into hammered plates as a covering for the altar, for they offered them
before the LORD, and they became holy. [x]Thus they shall be a sign to the people of Israel."
39 So Eleazar the priest took the bronze censers, which those who were burned had offered,
and they were hammered out as a covering for the altar, **40** to be a reminder to the people
of Israel, so [y]that no outsider, who is not of the descendants of Aaron, should draw near to
burn incense before the LORD, lest he become like Korah and his company—as the LORD
said to him through Moses.
41 But on the next day all the congregation of the people of Israel [z]grumbled against
Moses and against Aaron, saying, "You have killed the people of the LORD." **42** And when
the congregation had assembled against Moses and against Aaron, they turned toward the
tent of meeting. And behold, [a]the cloud covered it, and [b]the glory of the LORD appeared.
43 And Moses and Aaron came to the front of the tent of meeting, **44** and the LORD spoke
to Moses, saying, **45** [c]"Get away from the midst of this congregation, that I may consume
them in a moment." [d]And they fell on their faces. **46** And Moses said to Aaron, "Take your
censer, and put fire on it from off the altar and lay incense on it and carry it quickly to the
congregation and make atonement for them, for [e]wrath has gone out from the LORD; the
plague has begun." **47** So Aaron took it as Moses said and ran into the midst of the assembly.
And behold, the plague had already begun among the people. And he put on the incense
and made atonement for the people. **48** And he stood between the dead and the living, and
[f]the plague was stopped. **49** Now those who died in the plague were 14,700, [g]besides those
who died in the affair of Korah. **50** And Aaron returned to Moses at the entrance of the tent
of meeting, when the plague was stopped.

[1] Ch 17:1 in Hebrew

26 [l][Gen. 19:12-14; Isa. 52:11; 2 Cor. 6:17; Rev. 18:4]
27 [m][Ex. 33:8]
28 [n][Jer. 23:16; Ezek. 13:2, 17]
29 [o][1 Kgs. 22:28]
30 [p][Gen. 4:11] [q]ver. 33; Ps. 55:15
31 [r]ch. 26:10; 27:3; Deut. 11:6; Ps. 106:17
32 [s][ch. 26:11; 1 Chr. 6:22, 27]
33 [t]Jude 11
35 [u][ch. 11:1]; Lev. 10:2; Ps. 106:18 [v]ver. 17
38 [w]Prov. 20:2; Hab. 2:10; [1 Kgs. 2:23] [x]ch. 17:10; 26:10
40 [y]ch. 3:10; 2 Chr. 26:18
41 [z]See ch. 14:2
42 [a]Ex. 40:34 [b]ver. 19; See Lev. 9:23
45 [c]ver. 21, 24 [d]ver. 22
46 [e]ch. 8:19; 11:33; Lev. 10:6; 1 Chr. 27:24
48 [f]ver. 50; ch. 25:8; 2 Sam. 24:25; Ps. 106:30
49 [g]ch. 27:3

16:24 Get away from the dwelling of Korah, Dathan, and Abiram. This ominous warning builds suspense among the entire people of Israel, and especially among these three men and their families. God is preparing to punish them and affirm the leadership of Moses in a dramatic, public way.

16:33 and the earth closed over them. The judgment from God was swift and absolute. The form in which the judgment occurred also may have given a symbolic hint of their future condition, away from the presence of the Lord.

16:35 fire came out from the LORD and consumed the 250 men. See note on v. 33. God brings swift judgment, showing that no one should presume to come before his presence without God's own authorization (but cf. Heb. 10:19 with regard to believers in the new covenant).

16:39–40 A covering for the altar is mentioned in Ex. 38:2. This new one may have replaced or been put on top of the old one. It served as a reminder that **no outsider . . . should draw near to burn incense**.

16:41–50 *Judgment Averted by Aaron.* If the previous episode showed that non-priests offering incense provoked divine judgment, then this one shows that priests are indeed appointed to minister atonement. The plague provoked by the protest of **all the congregation** was stopped by **Aaron** holding a **censer** and standing **between the dead and the living** (v. 48).

Aaron's Staff Buds

17 [1] The LORD spoke to Moses, saying, 2 [h]"Speak to the people of Israel, and get from
them staffs, one for each fathers' house, from all their chiefs according to their
fathers' houses, twelve staffs. Write each man's name on his staff, 3 and write Aaron's name
on the staff of Levi. For there shall be one staff for the head of each fathers' house. 4 Then
you shall deposit them in the tent of meeting before the testimony, [i]where I meet with you.
5 And the staff of the man [j]whom I choose shall sprout. Thus I will make to cease from me
[k]the grumblings of the people of Israel, which they grumble against you." 6 Moses spoke
to the people of Israel. And all their chiefs gave him staffs, one for each chief, according
to their fathers' houses, twelve staffs. And the staff of Aaron was among their staffs. 7 And
Moses deposited the staffs before the LORD in [l]the tent of the testimony.

8 On the next day Moses went into the tent of the testimony, and behold, the staff of
Aaron for the house of Levi had sprouted and put forth buds and produced blossoms, and
it bore ripe almonds. 9 Then Moses brought out all the staffs from before the LORD to all
the people of Israel. And they looked, and each man took his staff. 10 And the LORD said
to Moses, "Put back [m]the staff of Aaron before the testimony, to be kept [n]as a sign for the
rebels, [o]that you may make an end of their grumblings against me, lest they die." 11 Thus
did Moses; as the LORD commanded him, so he did.

12 And the people of Israel said to Moses, "Behold, we perish, we are undone, we are
all undone. 13 [p]Everyone who comes near, who comes near to the tabernacle of the LORD,
shall die. Are we all to perish?"

Duties of Priests and Levites

18 So the LORD said to Aaron, "You and your sons and your father's house with you shall
[q]bear iniquity connected with the sanctuary, [r]and you and your sons with you shall
bear iniquity connected with your priesthood. 2 And with you bring your brothers also, the
tribe of Levi, the tribe of your father, that they may [s]join you and [t]minister to you while
you and your sons with you are before the tent of the testimony. 3 They shall keep guard
over you and [u]over the whole tent, [v]but shall not come near to the vessels of the sanctuary
or to the altar [w]lest they, and you, die. 4 They shall join you and keep guard over the tent
of meeting for all the service of the tent, [x]and no outsider shall come near you. 5 And you
shall [y]keep guard over the sanctuary and over the altar, [z]that there may never again be
wrath on the people of Israel. 6 [a]And behold, I have taken your brothers the Levites from
among the people of Israel. [b]They are a gift to you, given to the LORD, to do the service
of the tent of meeting. 7 And [c]you and your sons with you shall guard your priesthood
for all that concerns the altar and [d]that is within the veil; and you shall serve. I give your
priesthood as a gift,[2] and [e]any outsider who comes near shall be put to death."

8 Then the LORD spoke to Aaron, "Behold, [f]I have given you charge of the contributions

[1] Ch 17:16 in Hebrew [2] Hebrew *service of gift*

Chapter 17
2 [h][Ezek. 37:16]
4 [i]See Ex. 25:22
5 [j]ch. 16:5 [k]ch. 16:11
7 [l]ch. 18:2; Ex. 38:21; 2 Chr. 24:6; Acts 7:44
10 [m]Heb. 9:4 [n]ch. 16:38 [o]ver. 5
13 [p]See ch. 1:51

Chapter 18
1 [q]ver. 23; See Ex. 28:38 [r]ver. 23
2 [s][Gen. 29:34] [t]See ch. 3:6-10
3 [u]ch. 3:25, 31, 36 [v]ch. 16:40 [w]ch. 4:15
4 [x]See ch. 17:13
5 [y]ch. 3:38; Ex. 27:21; 30:7; Lev. 24:3 [z]See Lev. 10:6
6 [a]ch. 3:12, 45 [b]ch. 3:9; 8:19
7 [c]ch. 3:10 [d]Heb. 9:3, 6 [e]See ch. 1:51
8 [f]ch. 5:9; Lev. 7:32

17:1–13 *Aaron's Blossoming Staff.* This experiment is a symbolic reenactment of the Korah episode, which showed who had the right to approach God (16:5). The chief of each tribe puts his staff in front of the ark for a night to see what will happen to it. Nothing happened to the staffs, except for Aaron's, which "produced blossoms" and "bore ripe almonds" (17:8) overnight (hence miraculously). It may well be that flowering almonds are significant. Their white blossoms symbolize purity, holiness, and God himself, which are all associated with the priesthood.

17:6 The **twelve staffs** probably do not include Aaron's. There are 12 secular tribes in chs. 1 and 7, so Aaron's staff brings the number up to 13.

17:10 The miraculous **staff** was kept in the ark (which seems to be what **before the testimony** is meant by) as a **sign** and a warning (cf. note on Heb. 9:4).

17:12–13 The miracle of Aaron's staff seems to have finally convinced the people about the status of the priests and prepares the way for a statement of the priestly tribe's rights and privileges in ch. 18. The mediatorial role of the Aaronite high priests foreshadows the even greater role of Christ, the ultimate high priest (Hebrews 4–10).

18:1–32 *Duties and Privileges of Priests and Levites.* The preceding events have demonstrated the necessity of properly appointed mediators between God and Israel, if the nation's sins are not to lead to her destruction. This chapter sums up the duties of the priests (cf. Lev. 10:8–11) and Levites, and lays down the rewards that they are to receive for their service. Aaron's special status is underlined by God speaking directly to him (Num. 18:1, 8). Usually in Numbers God speaks to Moses, who then passes on his instruction to the appropriate people.

18:1–7 *Guard Duties in and around the Tabernacle.* In general, the priests, as the descendants of Aaron, must guard the interior of the tabernacle (vv. 5–7), and the Levites must guard its exterior (vv. 3–4). This is to prevent intrusion by any **outsider** (i.e., unauthorized person), who is to be executed if caught (vv. 4, 7). If a Levite should trespass into the area guarded by the priests, both Levite and priest will die (v. 3). These rigorous measures are designed **that there may never again be wrath on the people of Israel** (v. 5). In the future, the risk of divine judgment is limited to the priests and Levites, who **bear iniquity connected with your priesthood** (v. 1).

18:8–20 *The Priests' Income.* The income of priests is derived from the sacrifices and similar offerings. Most of the privileges listed here are mentioned elsewhere in the law, but here the rights are all brought together. First, there

made to me, all the consecrated things of the people of Israel. I have given them to you
[g]as a portion and to your sons as a perpetual due. 9 This shall be yours of the most holy
things, reserved from the fire: every offering of theirs, every grain offering of theirs and
every [h]sin offering of theirs and every [i]guilt offering of theirs, which they render to me,
shall be most holy to you and to your sons. 10 In a most holy place shall you eat it. Every
male may eat it; it is holy to you. 11 This also is yours: the contribution of their gift, all the
[j]wave offerings of the people of Israel. I have given them to [k]you, and to your sons and
daughters with you, as a perpetual due. [l]Everyone who is clean in your house may eat
it. 12 [m]All the best of the oil and all the best of the wine and of the grain, [n]the firstfruits
of what they give to the LORD, I give to you. 13 The first ripe fruits of all that is in their
land, [o]which they bring to the LORD, shall be yours. [l]Everyone who is clean in your house
may eat it. 14 [p]Every devoted thing in Israel shall be yours. 15 [q]Everything that opens the
womb of all flesh, whether man or beast, which they offer to the LORD, shall be yours.
Nevertheless, [r]the firstborn of man you shall redeem, and the firstborn of unclean animals
you shall redeem. 16 And their redemption price [s](at a month old you shall redeem them)
you shall fix at five shekels[1] in silver, according to the shekel of the sanctuary, [t]which is
twenty gerahs. 17 [u]But the firstborn of a cow, or the firstborn of a sheep, or the firstborn
of a goat, you shall not redeem; they are holy. You shall sprinkle their blood on the altar
and shall burn their fat as a food offering, with a pleasing aroma to the LORD. 18 But their
flesh shall be yours, as [v]the breast that is waved and as the right thigh are yours. 19 [w]All the
holy contributions that the people of Israel present to the LORD I give to you, and to your
sons and daughters with you, as a perpetual due. [x]It is a covenant of salt forever before
the LORD for you and for your offspring with you." 20 And the LORD said to Aaron, "You
shall have no inheritance in their land, neither shall you have any portion among them.
[y]I am your portion and your inheritance among the people of Israel.

21 [z]"To the Levites I have given every tithe in Israel for an inheritance, in return for their
service that they do, their service in the tent of meeting, 22 [a]so that the people of Israel do
not come near the tent of meeting, [b]lest they bear sin and die. 23 But [c]the Levites shall do
the service of the tent of meeting, [d]and they shall bear their iniquity. It shall be a perpetual
statute throughout your generations, and among the people of Israel they shall have no
inheritance. 24 For the tithe of the people of Israel, which [e]they present as a contribution
to the LORD, I have given to the Levites for an inheritance. Therefore I have said of them
that they shall have no inheritance [f]among the people of Israel."

25 And the LORD spoke to Moses, saying, 26 "Moreover, you shall speak and say to the
Levites, 'When you take from the people of Israel the tithe that I have given you from
them for your inheritance, then you shall present a contribution from it to the LORD, [g]a
tithe of the tithe. 27 [h]And your contribution shall be counted to you as though it were the
grain of the threshing floor, and as the fullness of the winepress. 28 So you shall also present a contribution to the LORD from all your tithes, which you receive from the people of
Israel. And from it you shall give the LORD's contribution to Aaron the priest. 29 Out of all
the gifts to you, you shall present every contribution due to the LORD; from each its best
part is to be dedicated.' 30 Therefore you shall say to them, 'When you have offered from

[1] A *shekel* was about 2/5 ounce or 11 grams

8 [g]Ex. 29:29; 40:13, 15
9 [h]Lev. 4:22, 27; 6:25, 26 [i]Lev. 7:7; 14:13
11 [j]Ex. 29:27, 28; Lev. 7:30, 34 [k]Lev. 10:14; [Deut. 18:3] [l][Lev. 22:2, 3, 11-13]
12 [m]Deut. 18:4 [n]Ex. 23:19; 34:26; Neh. 10:35, 36
13 [o]Ex. 22:29; Lev. 2:14; Deut. 26:2 [l][See ver. 11 above]
14 [p]Lev. 27:28
15 [q]See Ex. 13:2 [r]Ex. 13:13; 34:20
16 [s]ch. 3:47; Lev. 27:2, 6 [t]See Ex. 30:13
17 [u]Deut. 15:19
18 [v]Ex. 29:26, 28; Lev. 7:31, 32, 34
19 [w]ver. 11 [x]Lev. 2:13; 2 Chr. 13:5
20 [y]ver. 23, 24; Deut. 10:9; 12:12; 14:27; 18:1, 2; Josh. 13:33; 14:3; 18:7; Ezek. 44:28
21 [z]ver. 24, 26; Lev. 27:30, 32; Deut. 14:22; Neh. 10:37; 12:44; Heb. 7:5, 8, 9; [Gen. 14:20; 28:22]
22 [a]See ch. 1:51 [b]Lev. 22:9
23 [c]ch. 3:7 [d]ver. 1
24 [e]ver. 19, 26, 29 [f]ver. 20, 21, 26
26 [g]Neh. 10:38
27 [h]ver. 30

are the parts of those sacrifices that only priests could eat: the cereal, sin, and guilt offerings (vv. 8–10). Second are those sacrifices and other offerings that all clean members of the priestly families could eat (vv. 11–19). These include parts of the peace offerings (v. 11), firstfruits of the harvest (vv. 12–13), and firstborn animals (vv. 17–18). Firstborn humans and unclean animals cannot be sacrificed but instead must be redeemed. That means the parents must give five shekels for their firstborn son (v. 16; see also Ex. 13:1–2, 11–16).

18:19 Covenant of salt forever indicates a permanent and inviolable principle (cf. 2 Chron. 13:5). The significance of salt may be its qualities as a lasting preservative, well known throughout the ancient Near East, or its use as a seasoning of food, which would point to a shared meal between the two parties of the covenant as symbolic of their friendship and the binding nature of their agreement.

18:21–24 *The Levites' Income.* The income of the Levites comes from the **tithe** given by the other tribes. It is their reward for (1) their transporting of the tabernacle, (2) **their service in the tent of meeting** (v. 21), and (3) their shouldering the risk associated with holy things, **so that the people of Israel do not come near . . . and die** (v. 22). It also compensates them for having **no inheritance among the people of Israel** (vv. 23–24); that is, unlike other tribes, they had no tribal territory, only 48 cities scattered through the land (35:1–8). "I am your portion and your inheritance among the people of Israel" (18:20; cf. Deut. 10:9). Their tribal "inheritance" is not an allocation of land but their task of serving at the sanctuary for the sake of the people. The Levites do not need an allocation of tribal land because their service in the presence of the Lord, and the **tithe of the people of Israel**, is their more-than-sufficient inheritance.

18:25–32 *The Tithe of the Tithe.* The Levites had to give a tenth of their income to the priests. Indeed, as God's representatives the priests were to receive the **best** tenth of the tithe (vv. 29–30; cf. Lev. 22:18–25; Mal. 1:6–14; 3:6–10).

30[i]ver. 27
31[j][Matt. 10:10; Luke 10:7; 1 Tim. 5:17, 18]; See 1 Cor. 9:4-14
32[k]Lev. 19:8; 22:16 [l]Lev. 22:2, 15
Chapter 19
2[m]Deut. 21:3; 1 Sam. 6:7
3[n]Lev. 4:12; [Heb. 13:11]
4[o][Lev. 4:6, 17; 16:14, 19]; Heb. 9:13
5[p]Ex. 29:14; Lev. 4:11, 12
6[q]See Lev. 14:4, 6, 49
7[r]See Lev. 11:25
8[s]ver. 5 [r][See ver. 7 above]
9[t]Heb. 9:13 [u]Lev. 4:12; 6:11; 10:14 [v]ver. 13, 20, 21; ch. 31:23
10[r][See ver. 7 above]
11[w]ver. 16; See ch. 5:2; 9:6, 10; 31:19
12[x]ch. 31:19
13[y]ver. 20; Lev. 15:31 [z]See Ex. 30:33
15[a]ch. 31:20; Lev. 11:32
16[b]ver. 11 [c][Matt. 23:27; Luke 11:44]
17[d]Heb. 9:13
18[e]See Ex. 12:22
19[f]ver. 12

it the best of it, [i]then the rest shall be counted to the Levites as produce of the threshing floor, and as produce of the winepress. 31 And you may eat it in any place, you and your households, for it is [j]your reward in return for your service in the tent of meeting. 32 And you shall [k]bear no sin by reason of it, when you have contributed the best of it. But you shall not [l]profane the holy things of the people of Israel, lest you die.'"

Laws for Purification

19 Now the LORD spoke to Moses and to Aaron, saying, 2 "This is the statute of the law that the LORD has commanded: Tell the people of Israel to bring you a red heifer without defect, in which there is no blemish, [m]and on which a yoke has never come. 3 And you shall give it to Eleazar the priest, and [n]it shall be taken outside the camp and slaughtered before him. 4 And Eleazar the priest shall take some of its blood with his finger, and [o]sprinkle some of its blood toward the front of the tent of meeting seven times. 5 And the heifer shall be burned in his sight. [p]Its skin, its flesh, and its blood, with its dung, shall be burned. 6 And the priest shall take [q]cedarwood and hyssop and scarlet yarn, and throw them into the fire burning the heifer. 7 Then the priest [r]shall wash his clothes and bathe his body in water, and afterward he may come into the camp. But the priest shall be unclean until evening. 8 [s]The one who burns the heifer [r]shall wash his clothes in water and bathe his body in water and shall be unclean until evening. 9 And a man who is clean shall gather up [t]the ashes of the heifer and deposit them outside the camp in a [u]clean place. And they shall be kept for the water for [v]impurity for the congregation of the people of Israel; it is a sin offering. 10 And the one who gathers the ashes of the heifer [r]shall wash his clothes and be unclean until evening. And this shall be a perpetual statute for the people of Israel, and for the stranger who sojourns among them.

11 [w]"Whoever touches the dead body of any person shall be unclean seven days. 12 He [x]shall cleanse himself with the water on the third day and on the seventh day, and so be clean. But if he does not cleanse himself on the third day and on the seventh day, he will not become clean. 13 Whoever touches a dead person, the body of anyone who has died, and does not cleanse himself, [y]defiles the tabernacle of the LORD, [z]and that person shall be cut off from Israel; because the water for impurity was not thrown on him, he shall be unclean. His uncleanness is still on him.

14 "This is the law when someone dies in a tent: everyone who comes into the tent and everyone who is in the tent shall be unclean seven days. 15 And every [a]open vessel that has no cover fastened on it is unclean. 16 [b]Whoever in the open field touches someone who was killed with a sword or who died naturally, or touches a human bone or a [c]grave, shall be unclean seven days. 17 For the unclean they shall take [d]some ashes of the burnt sin offering, and fresh[1] water shall be added in a vessel. 18 Then a clean person shall take [e]hyssop and dip it in the water and sprinkle it on the tent and on all the furnishings and on the persons who were there and on whoever touched the bone, or the slain or the dead or the grave. 19 And the clean person shall sprinkle it on the unclean [f]on the third day and on the seventh day.

[1] Hebrew *living*

19:1–22 *Cleansing from Death.* Life and death are the two poles of existence inside and outside the Bible. Holiness, God, and life are associated in Scripture, whereas uncleanness, sin, and death also belong together (see chart, p. 229). Human corpses caused the gravest kind of pollution under the Mosaic system, affecting all who approached them. Thus those who have contact with the dead must keep away from the sanctuary and undergo cleansing. This rite is designed to provide ritual cleansing for all who have been near or touched corpses. This is especially relevant here in view of the numerous deaths reported in the preceding chapters (14:37; 15:36; 16:32, 35, 49) and those that follow (20:1, 28; 21:6, 35; 25:9; 31:7).

19:1–10 *The Recipe for Producing the Cleansing Ash.* **a red heifer without defect . . . on which a yoke has never come** (v. 2). Its youth shows its fullness of life, while its redness speaks of blood, the most effective agent of atonement. The redness of **cedarwood** and **scarlet** (v. 6) may also be significant. **Hyssop** (v. 6) is also used for cleansing (Ps. 51:7). The same ingredients are used in the cleansing of a leper (Lev. 14:4). The ashes are described as a **sin offering** (Num. 19:9), an offering designed to cleanse both the sanctuary and the worshiper (see Leviticus 4). Those engaged in making this cleansing ash paradoxically incur a mild uncleanness themselves (Num. 19:7–8, 10; see also v. 21).

19:11–22 *The Cleansing Procedure.* The process of the cleansing ash (see note on vv. 1–10) has two phases: it involves sprinkling **water** (with some ash in it) on the affected person or tent **on the third day** after contamination and also **on the seventh day**. On the seventh day he must also **bathe himself** and **wash his clothes**. The sprinkling does not have to be done by a priest, just a **clean person** (vv. 18–19). Failure to carry out this rite is serious: it **defiles the tabernacle**, and **that person shall be cut off** (i.e., die; see notes on 9:6–14; 15:30–31; see also 19:13, 20). Hebrews 9:13–14 notes that the blood of Christ is even more effective in its cleansing power: it will purify the conscience from dead works to serve the living God. These regulations were intended for Israel; now that Christ has come, Christians do not need purification rites such as these.

[g]Thus on the seventh day he shall cleanse him, and he shall [h]wash his clothes and bathe
himself in water, and at evening he shall be clean.
20 "If the man who is unclean does not cleanse himself, [i]that person shall be cut off from
the midst of the assembly, since he has defiled the sanctuary of the LORD. Because the
water for impurity has not been thrown on him, he is unclean. 21 And it shall be a statute
forever for them. The one who sprinkles the water for impurity shall wash his clothes,
and the one who touches the water for impurity shall be unclean until evening. 22 And
[j]whatever the unclean person touches shall be unclean, and anyone who touches it shall
be unclean until evening."

The Death of Miriam

20 And the people of Israel, the whole congregation, came [k]into the wilderness of
Zin in the first month, and the people stayed in Kadesh. And [l]Miriam died there
and was buried there.

The Waters of Meribah

2 [m]Now there was no water for the congregation. [n]And they assembled themselves together
against Moses and against Aaron. 3 And the people [o]quarreled with Moses and said, "Would
that we had perished [p]when our brothers perished before the LORD! 4 Why have you brought

19 [g][Lev. 14:9] [h]See Lev. 11:25
20 [i]See Ex. 30:33
22 [j][ver. 11; Hag. 2:13]

Chapter 20

1 [k]See ch. 13:21 [l]ch. 12:1; 26:59; Ex. 15:20
2 [m][Ex. 17:1] [n]ch. 16:19, 42
3 [o]ch. 14:2; [Ex. 17:2] [p]ch. 11:1, 33; 14:37; 16:32, 33, 35, 49

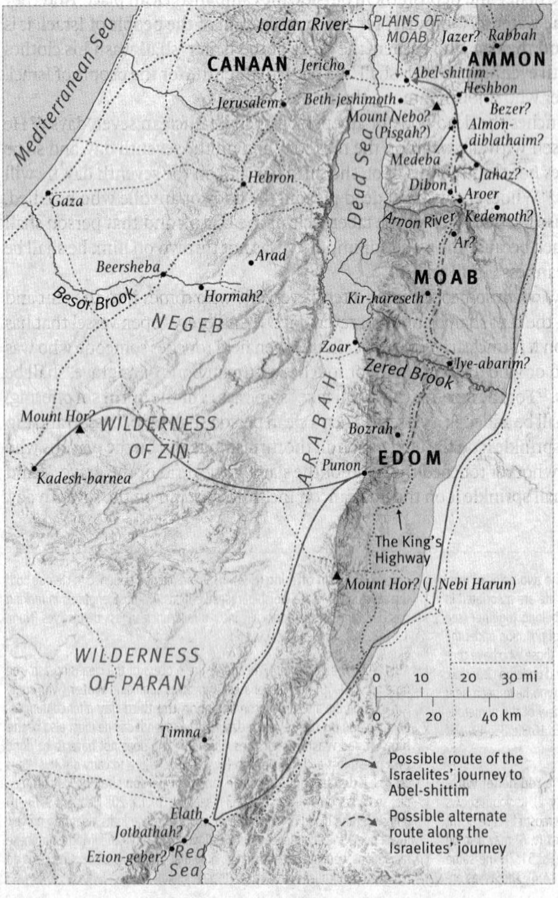

The Journey to Canaan
After many years of wandering in the wilderness as a consequence of their sin, the Israelites set out from Kadesh-barnea toward the Promised Land. It is difficult to know for certain the exact route they took from Kadesh-barnea to the plains of Moab, but it is possible that they followed a course that went around the lands of Edom and Moab along a desert route, after being refused passage through those lands—or they may have taken another route, through the heart of Edom and Moab along the King's Highway.

the assembly of the LORD into this wilderness, that we should die here, both we and our
cattle? 5 And [q]why have you made us come up out of Egypt to bring us to this evil place?
It is no place for grain or figs or vines or pomegranates, and there is no water to drink."
6 Then Moses and Aaron went from the presence of the assembly to the entrance of the
tent of meeting and [r]fell on their faces. [s]And the glory of the LORD appeared to them, 7 and
the LORD spoke to Moses, saying, 8 [t]"Take the staff, and assemble the congregation, you
and Aaron your brother, and tell the rock before their eyes to yield its water. So [u]you shall
bring water out of the rock for them and give drink to the congregation and their cattle."
9 And Moses took the staff [v]from before the LORD, as he commanded him.

Moses Strikes the Rock

10 Then Moses and Aaron gathered the assembly together before the rock, and he said to
them, [w]"Hear now, you rebels: shall we bring water for you out of this rock?" 11 And Moses
lifted up his hand and struck the rock with his staff twice, [u]and water came out abundantly,
and the congregation drank, and their livestock. 12 And the LORD said to Moses and Aaron,
"Because [x]you did not believe in me, [y]to uphold me as holy in the eyes of the people of
Israel, therefore you shall not bring this assembly into the land that I have given them."
13 [z]These are the waters of Meribah,[1] where the people of Israel quarreled with the LORD,
and through them he showed himself holy.

Edom Refuses Passage

14 [a]Moses sent messengers from Kadesh to [b]the king of Edom: "Thus says [c]your brother
Israel: You know all the hardship that we have met: 15 [d]how our fathers went down to
Egypt, [e]and we lived in Egypt a long time. [f]And the Egyptians dealt harshly with us and
our fathers. 16 And [g]when we cried to the LORD, he heard our voice and [h]sent an angel and
brought us out of Egypt. And here we are in Kadesh, a city on the edge of your territory.
17 [i]Please let us pass through your land. We will not pass through field or vineyard, [j]or
drink water from a well. We will go along the King's Highway. We will not turn aside to
the right hand or to the left until we have passed through your territory." 18 But Edom said

5 [q][Ex. 17:3]
6 [r]ch. 14:5; 16:4, 22, 45 [s]See Lev. 9:23
8 [t][Ex. 17:5] [u]See Ex. 17:6
9 [v]ch. 17:10
10 [w]Ps. 106:32, 33
11 [u][See ver. 8 above]
12 [x]ch. 27:14; Deut. 1:37; 3:26; 32:51 [y]Ezek. 20:41; 36:23; 38:16
13 [z]ch. 27:14; Ex. 17:7; Deut. 32:51; 33:8; Ps. 81:7; 95:8; 106:32
14 [a]Judg. 11:16, 17 [b]See Gen. 36:31-39 [c]Deut. 2:4, 8; 23:7; Obad. 10, 12
15 [d]Gen. 46:6; Acts 7:15 [e]See Ex. 12:40 [f]Ex. 1:11; Deut. 26:6
16 [g]Ex. 2:23; 3:7 [h]Ex. 3:2; 14:19; 23:20; 33:2
17 [i][ch. 21:22; Deut. 2:27] [j][ver. 19]

[1] *Meribah* means *quarreling*

20:1–21:35 *Marching from Kadesh to the Plains of Moab.* After a long time (nearly 40 years) of aimless wandering in the wilderness, Israel is ready to move and enter the Land of Promise. In this section one may see parallels with the earlier journeys from the Red Sea to Sinai and from Sinai to Kadesh (Exodus 13–19; Numbers 11–12). Most of the older generation have died out, and the younger ones are now taking over. Though not perfect, the younger generation are not so harsh in their complaints, nor do they show their fathers' readiness to contend against the leaders of the nation. Now it is those leaders—Moses and Aaron—who make the most serious mistakes.

20:1 *Regrouping at Kadesh.* Kadesh was last mentioned in 13:26, when the spies returned. **The wilderness of Zin** was the area first traversed by the spies (13:21), so it is just north of Kadesh. **in the first month**. The year is not mentioned, but according to 33:38, Aaron died in the fortieth year after the exodus, and this would fit here. The death of **Miriam** is a watershed. She was the sister of Moses, the preserver of his life (Ex. 2:4–8), and a prophetess (Ex. 15:20–21). She was clearly the leading woman of Israel (Numbers 12). It has often been noted that the leading woman of the NT was also called Miriam (English, "Mary").

20:2–13 *Rebellion at Meribah.* Complaints about lack of water characterized the journey from the Red Sea to Sinai (Ex. 15:22–27; 17:1–7), and now they occur again. In both situations Moses struck the rock with his staff. This is what he had been told to do in Ex. 17:6, but on this second occasion he had been told to speak to the rock (Num. 20:8). This deviation from carrying out God's instruction led to Moses' being condemned not to **bring this assembly into the land** (v. 12). Since this seems like a minor error, it has been suggested that it was Moses' anger (see v. 10) to which God took exception. But v. 12 seems to make it clear that it was carelessness in attending to God's command that was the real issue: **Because you did not believe in me, to uphold me as holy in the eyes of the people**. As the prime mediators of God's laws to Israel, Moses and Aaron had to be exemplary in their obedience. Their failure to follow the divine instruction exactly led to their forfeiting their right to enter Canaan. Some have suggested that another factor was involved: since God had told Moses in the earlier incident, "I will stand before you there on the rock" (Ex. 17:6), Moses should have known that God was present here on the rock as well; therefore Moses' speaking to the rock (Num. 20:8) would be actually speaking to God, and therefore when Moses **struck the rock with his staff twice** (v. 11), it was a serious manifestation of anger against God, and it is not surprising that God punished Moses severely (cf. note on 1 Cor. 10:3–4). Others hold that the emphasis here is on the difference between what God commanded and what Moses did; usually Moses did just what God commanded him, but not here. It was similar carelessness by Aaron's sons that led to their death in Lev. 10:1–3. The phraseology of Num. 20:12 also echoes that of the spy story, where God complains, "How long will they not believe in me?" (14:11). The people's unbelief led to their exclusion from the land; so did Aaron's and Moses' unbelief. **Meribah** means "quarreling." In Ex. 17:7, Rephidim was also nicknamed Meribah (see also Ps. 95:8).

20:14–21 *Encounter with Edom.* According to Gen. 25:24–26, Edom (Esau) was the twin brother of Jacob (Israel). This made the Edomites the people with whom Israel felt greatest affinity. Yet the history of Israelite/Edomite relations is one of tension, if not bitter hostility, as this story illustrates. Note the form of address: **your brother Israel** (Num. 20:14).

20:16 Kadesh, a city on the edge of your territory. In the second millennium B.C., Edom's main settlements were southeast of the Dead Sea, whereas Kadesh-barnea is a long way west of there, in northern Sinai. This suggests either that the Edomites were living west of the Dead Sea, or that another Kadesh is meant instead of Kadesh-barnea.

20:17–21 The King's Highway is the main trade route from Damascus to Arabia, passing through the Edomite heartlands on the high hills southeast of the Dead Sea. Israel wanted to travel along this road from south to north to bring them to the northern edge of the Dead Sea. Thwarted by the Edomites, **Israel turned away**, apparently making their way south toward the Gulf of

to him, "You shall not pass through, lest I come out with the sword against you." 19 And
the people of Israel said to him, "We will go up by the highway, [k]and if we drink of your
water, I and my livestock, [l]then I will pay for it. Let me only pass through on foot, nothing
more." 20 But he said, [m]"You shall not pass through." And Edom came out against them
with a large army and with a strong force. 21 Thus Edom [n]refused to give Israel passage
through his territory, so Israel [o]turned away from him.

The Death of Aaron

22 And they journeyed from [p]Kadesh, and the people of Israel, the whole congregation,
came to [q]Mount Hor. 23 And the LORD said to Moses and Aaron at Mount Hor, on the
border of the land of Edom, 24 [r]"Let Aaron be gathered to his people, for he shall not enter
the land that I have given to the people of Israel, because [s]you rebelled against my command at the waters of Meribah. 25 Take Aaron and Eleazar his son and bring them up to
Mount Hor. 26 And strip Aaron of his garments and put them on Eleazar his son. And
Aaron [r]shall be gathered to his people and shall die there." 27 Moses did as the LORD commanded. And they went up Mount Hor in the sight of all the congregation. 28 [t]And Moses
stripped Aaron of his garments and put them on Eleazar his son. And Aaron died there
[u]on the top of the mountain. Then Moses and Eleazar came down from the mountain.
29 And when all the congregation saw that Aaron had perished, [v]all the house of Israel
wept for Aaron thirty days.

Arad Destroyed

21 When [w]the Canaanite, the king of Arad, who lived in [x]the Negeb, heard that Israel
was coming by the way of Atharim, he fought against Israel, and took some of
them captive. 2 [y]And Israel vowed a vow to the LORD and said, "If you will indeed give
this people into my hand, then I will devote their cities to destruction."[1] 3 And the LORD
heeded the voice of Israel and gave over the Canaanites, and they devoted them and their
cities to destruction. So the name of the place was called [z]Hormah.[2]

The Bronze Serpent

4 From Mount Hor [a]they set out by the way to the Red Sea, [b]to go around the land of
Edom. And the people became impatient on the way. 5 And the people [c]spoke against God
and against Moses, [d]"Why have you brought us up out of Egypt to die in the wilderness?
For there is no food and no water, and [e]we loathe this worthless food." 6 [f]Then the LORD
sent fiery serpents among the people, and [g]they bit the people, so that many people of
Israel died. 7 [h]And the people came to Moses and said, "We have sinned, for we have spoken
against the LORD and against you. [i]Pray to the LORD, that he take away the serpents from

[1] That is, set apart (devote) as an offering to the Lord (for destruction); also verse 3 [2] *Hormah* means *destruction*

19 [k][ver. 17] [l]Deut. 2:6, 28
20 [m][Judg. 11:17; Amos 1:11]
21 [n][Deut. 2:29] [o][ch. 21:4; Deut. 2:8; Judg. 11:18]
22 [p]ch. 33:37 [q]ch. 21:4; 33:37
24 [r]ch. 27:13; Deut. 32:50; [ch. 31:2; Gen. 25:8] [s]ver. 12
26 [r][See ver. 24 above]
28 [t]Ex. 29:29, 30 [u]ch. 33:38; Deut. 32:50; [Deut. 10:6]
29 [v]Deut. 34:8

Chapter 21

1 [w]ch. 33:40; [Judg. 1:16] [x]See ch. 13:17
2 [y][Gen. 28:20; Judg. 11:30]
3 [z]ch. 14:45; Deut. 1:44; Josh. 19:4; Judg. 1:17
4 [a]ch. 20:22; 33:41 [b]Judg. 11:18
5 [c]Ps. 78:19 [d]Ex. 16:3; 17:3 [e][ch. 11:6]
6 [f]Deut. 8:15; 1 Cor. 10:9; [Isa. 14:29; 30:6] [g]Jer. 8:17
7 [h]Ps. 78:34; [ch. 11:2] [i][Ex. 8:8, 28; 1 Sam. 12:19; 1 Kgs. 13:6; Acts 8:24]

Aqaba (21:4) and then northward through the wilderness east of the King's Highway (see Deut. 2:1–8).

20:22–29 *The Death of Aaron.* Aaron's death fulfills the judgment pronounced on him and Moses in v. 12, namely, that they would not live to enter Canaan. Moses prepares to die in 27:12–23, but his death is not reported until Deuteronomy 34.

20:22–23 The location of **Mount Hor** is uncertain; it is probably somewhere north of the Gulf of Aqaba, if that is where **the border . . . of Edom** ran. "The Mount of the Prophet Aaron" near Petra is the traditional location.

20:26 gathered to his people. After death, one is reunited with one's deceased relatives, according to OT belief (see note on 2 Sam. 12:23; this expression also occurs in Gen. 25:8, 17; 35:29; 49:33; Num. 20:24; Deut. 32:50).

20:28 stripped Aaron . . . and put them on Eleazar his son. The death of Aaron meant that his son must succeed him as high priest. The importance of the high priest as supreme mediator between God and Israel is indicated by his garments: the ritual clothing of Eleazar marks his induction into this highest religious office. Hebrews makes much of the superiority of Christ's high priesthood over Aaron's (see Heb. 4:14–10:18).

21:1–3 *First Victory over the Canaanites.* The spying mission was followed by the death of the spies and an unauthorized attempt to enter Canaan, which ended in Israel's defeat at Hormah (14:36–45). However, the death of Aaron for his unbelief is followed by victory at Hormah. This marks the turning point: from now on, one victory after another will follow until they reach the Jordan, ready to enter the land of Canaan.

21:1 Notice that this battle was not an Israelite initiative; rather, **Israel** responded to an attack by **the king of Arad**. This point is made about other engagements in the Transjordan (the area east of the Jordan River): Israel responded to threats; it did not provoke the war (see vv. 21–23, 33–35; 25:17–18). Arad and Hormah were in the northern Negeb, but it is uncertain which archaeological sites these places are to be identified with. It is surprising to find this account set in the Negeb, for when last located, Israel was skirting the eastern frontier of Edom (20:21). Thus it is often suggested that the story of the victory at Hormah was placed here out of chronological sequence in order to highlight the change in Israel's fortunes after the death of Aaron. (Some, however, argue that this episode does fit sequentially into the whole narrative.)

21:2–3 devote their cities to destruction (v. 2). Canaanite cities that resist Israel are to be totally destroyed, according to Deut. 20:16–18 (see note). **Hormah** was the place this policy was first implemented. Its name, "Destruction," commemorates this (Num. 21:3).

21:4–9 *The Bronze Snake.* A new day may have dawned, but old habits are not eradicated. The people once again grumble about their food and are punished: this time by poisonous snakes. As an antidote, Moses makes a bronze snake, which cures anyone who looks at it.

9 [j]John 3:14, 15; [2 Kgs. 18:4]
10 [k]ch. 33:43, 44
11 [k][See ver. 10 above]
12 [l]Deut. 2:13
13 [m]ch. 22:36; Judg. 11:18
15 [n]ver. 28; Deut. 2:9, 18, 29; Isa. 15:1
16 [o][2 Sam. 20:14] [p][ch. 20:8; Ex. 17:6]
18 [q]See Gen. 49:10
20 [r][ch. 23:28]
21 [s]Deut. 2:26, 27; Judg. 11:19
22 [t][ch. 20:17]
23 [u]Deut. 29:7 [v]Deut. 2:32; Judg. 11:20
24 [w]Deut. 2:33; Josh. 12:1, 2; 24:8; Neh. 9:22; Ps. 135:11; 136:19, 20; Amos 2:9 [x]See Gen. 32:22
27 [y]See ch. 23:7

us." So Moses prayed for the people. **8** And the LORD said to Moses, "Make a fiery serpent
and set it on a pole, and everyone who is bitten, when he sees it, shall live." **9** So [j]Moses
made a bronze[1] serpent and set it on a pole. And if a serpent bit anyone, he would look at
the bronze serpent and live.

The Song of the Well

10 And the people of Israel set out and [k]camped in Oboth. **11** [k]And they set out from Oboth
and [k]camped at Iye-abarim, in the wilderness that is opposite Moab, toward the sunrise.
12 From there they set out and camped in [l]the Valley of Zered. **13** From there they set out
and camped on the other side of the Arnon, which is in the wilderness that extends from
the border of the Amorites, for the [m]Arnon is the border of Moab, between Moab and the
Amorites. **14** Therefore it is said in the Book of the Wars of the LORD,

> "Waheb in Suphah, and the valleys of the Arnon,
> **15** and the slope of the valleys
> that extends to the seat of [n]Ar,
> and leans to the border of Moab."

16 And from there they continued [o]to Beer;[2] that is the well of which the LORD said to
Moses, "Gather the people together, so that [p]I may give them water." **17** Then Israel sang
this song:

> "Spring up, O well!—Sing to it!—
> **18** the well that the princes made,
> that the nobles of the people dug,
> with [q]the scepter and with their staffs."

And from the wilderness they went on to Mattanah, **19** and from Mattanah to Nahaliel, and
from Nahaliel to Bamoth, **20** and from Bamoth to the valley lying in the region of Moab
by the top of Pisgah [r]that looks down on the desert.[3]

King Sihon Defeated

21 Then [s]Israel sent messengers to Sihon king of the Amorites, saying, **22** [t]"Let me pass
through your land. We will not turn aside into field or vineyard. We will not drink the
water of a well. We will go by the King's Highway until we have passed through your territory." **23** [u]But Sihon would not allow Israel to pass through his territory. He gathered all his
people together and went out against Israel to the wilderness and [v]came to Jahaz and fought
against Israel. **24** [w]And Israel defeated him with the edge of the sword and took possession
of his land from the Arnon to the [x]Jabbok, as far as to the Ammonites, for the border of the
Ammonites was strong. **25** And Israel took all these cities, and Israel settled in all the cities
of the Amorites, in Heshbon, and in all its villages. **26** For Heshbon was the city of Sihon
the king of the Amorites, who had fought against the former king of Moab and taken all
his land out of his hand, as far as the Arnon. **27** Therefore the [y]ballad singers say,

[1] Or *copper* [2] *Beer* means *well* [3] Or *Jeshimon*

21:9 bronze serpent. The Hebrew term translated "bronze" can also mean "copper" (see ESV footnote). The area through which the Israelites were traveling had copper mines, and archaeologists have found a 5-inch-long (13 cm) copper snake in a Midianite shrine at Timna, so it seems likely that copper is meant here. The redness of copper suggested atonement (see 19:1–10), so symbolically it was well chosen for this occasion. Jesus compares his own death on the cross to the uplifted serpent (John 3:14–15). By the time of King Hezekiah of Judah (c. 715 B.C.), this copper serpent had become an object of worship among the Israelites and had to be destroyed (2 Kings 18:4).

21:10–20 *Through Transjordan.* Israel's passage east of the Dead Sea, around the territory of Moab and through the land of the Amorites, is summarized here. Many of the places cannot be precisely located, but the general route is clear. The territory of Moab extended from the Zered River to the Arnon River on the eastern side of the Dead Sea. The Zered flows into the Dead Sea at its southern end, and the Arnon enters it about halfway up the eastern side.

21:14 The Book of the Wars of the LORD was perhaps a collection of ancient songs like the book of Jashar (see Josh. 10:13; 2 Sam. 1:18). The ESV represents the Hebrew text as it exists today for Num. 21:14–15. Because of the difficulty in understanding these verses, some have suggested that the text may have suffered from a copyist's error. Minor changes to the Hebrew text have been proposed, but none of the suggestions can be verified with any degree of certainty.

21:16–20 These verses summarize Israel's journey through the territory of the Amorites, who lived north of the Arnon on the eastern side of the Dead Sea, as is explained more fully in vv. 21–30. Verses 16–18 celebrate the finding of an abundant **well**.

21:21–30 *Victory over Sihon.* The Amorites occupied the Transjordan from the Arnon to the Jabbok (v. 24), so Israel had to pass through their territory, along **the King's Highway** (v. 22; see 20:17), to reach the northern end of the Dead Sea where they could cross the Jordan. But Sihon, king of the Amorites, came and fought Israel and was defeated (21:24). As a result, this was the first land that the Israelites settled (v. 25). Heshbon's name is modern Hesban; the absence of archaeological remains at Hesban from the conquest era suggests that the name may have been moved to that location from another site.

21:27–30 This old poem celebrates the capture of Moabite territory by **Sihon**. It is included in Numbers to show that the Israelites could justifiably

"Come to [z]Heshbon, let it be built;
let the city of Sihon be established.
28 For [a]fire came out from [z]Heshbon,
flame from the city of Sihon.
It devoured [n]Ar of Moab,
and swallowed[1] the heights of the Arnon.
29 [a]Woe to you, O Moab!
You are undone, O people of [b]Chemosh!
He has made his sons fugitives,
and his daughters captives,
to an Amorite king, Sihon.
30 So we overthrew them;
Heshbon, as far as [c]Dibon, perished;
and we laid waste as far as Nophah;
fire spread as far as [d]Medeba."[2]

King Og Defeated

31 Thus Israel lived in the land of the Amorites. 32 And Moses sent to spy out [e]Jazer, and
they captured its villages and dispossessed the Amorites who were there. 33 Then they
turned and went up by the way to Bashan. And Og the king of Bashan came out against
them, he and all his people, to battle [f]at Edrei. 34 [g]But the LORD said to Moses, "Do not
fear him, for I have given him into your hand, and all his people, and his land. And [h]you
shall do to him as you did to Sihon king of the Amorites, who lived at Heshbon." 35 So they

[1] Septuagint; Hebrew *the lords of* [2] Compare Samaritan and Septuagint; Hebrew *and we laid waste as far as Nophah, which is as far as Medeba*

27[z]See ch. 32:37
28[a]Jer. 48:45, 46 [z][See ver. 27 above] [n][See ver. 15 above]
29[a][See ver. 28 above] [b]Judg. 11:24; 1 Kgs. 11:7; 2 Kgs. 23:13; Jer. 48:7
30[c]ch. 32:3; Josh. 13:17; Isa. 15:2; Jer. 48:18; [ch. 33:45, 46] [d]1 Chr. 19:7; Isa. 15:2
32[e]ch. 32:1; Josh. 13:25; 2 Sam. 24:5; Jer. 48:32
33[f]Deut. 1:4; 3:1; Josh. 13:12
34[g]Deut. 3:2 [h]See ver. 24

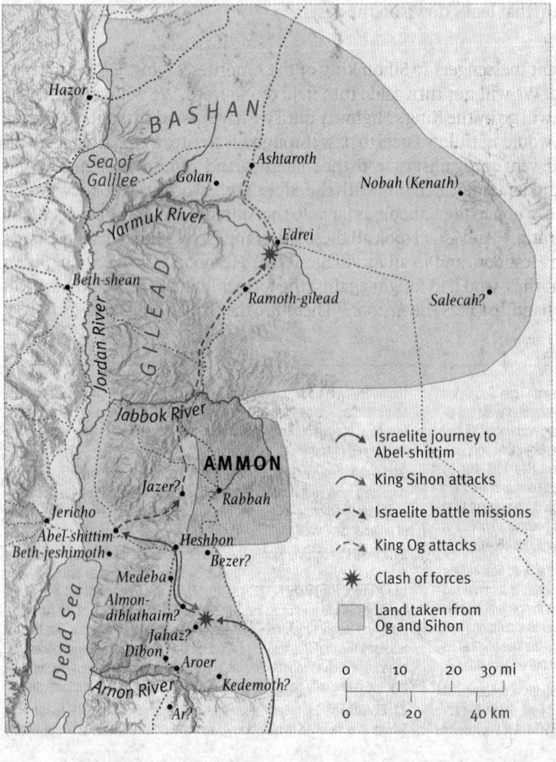

Israel Defeats Og and Sihon
As with Edom and Moab, the Israelites asked permission to pass through the territory of King Sihon, but he refused. When Sihon attacked the Israelites at Jahaz, the Israelites defeated him and captured his land. Later, Moses dispatched troops to capture Jazer, and then they turned north and were met by King Og's forces. They defeated Og's forces and took control of his land as well.

Chapter 22
1 [i]ch. 26:3, 63; 31:12; 33:48, 50; 35:1; 36:13
2 [j]Judg. 11:25
3 [k]Ex. 15:15
4 [l]ch. 31:8; Josh. 13:21
5 [m]Deut. 23:4; Josh. 24:9; Neh. 13:2; Mic. 6:5; 2 Pet. 2:15; Jude 11; Rev. 2:14 [n]Deut. 23:4; [ch. 23:7]
6 [o]ch. 23:7
7 [l][See ver. 4 above] [p][1 Sam. 9:7, 8; Mic. 3:11]
9 [q][Gen. 20:3; Job 33:15, 16]
12 [r]See ch. 23:20
17 [s]ver. 37; ch. 24:11 [t]ver. 11

defeated him and his sons and all his people, until he had no survivor left. And they possessed his land.

Balak Summons Balaam

22 Then [i]the people of Israel set out and camped in the plains of Moab beyond the
Jordan at Jericho. 2 And [j]Balak the son of Zippor saw all that Israel had done to the
Amorites. 3 And [k]Moab was in great dread of the people, because they were many. Moab was
overcome with fear of the people of Israel. 4 And Moab said to [l]the elders of Midian, "This
horde will now lick up all that is around us, as the ox licks up the grass of the field." So
Balak the son of Zippor, who was king of Moab at that time, 5 [m]sent messengers to Balaam
the son of Beor [n]at Pethor, which is near the River in the land of the people of Amaw,[1] to
call him, saying, "Behold, a people has come out of Egypt. They cover the face of the earth,
and they are dwelling opposite me. 6 [o]Come now, curse this people for me, since they are
too mighty for me. Perhaps I shall be able to defeat them and drive them from the land,
for I know that he whom you bless is blessed, and he whom you curse is cursed."
7 So the elders of Moab and [l]the elders of Midian departed with [p]the fees for divination
in their hand. And they came to Balaam and gave him Balak's message. 8 And he said to
them, "Lodge here tonight, and I will bring back word to you, as the LORD speaks to me."
So the princes of Moab stayed with Balaam. 9 [q]And God came to Balaam and said, "Who are
these men with you?" 10 And Balaam said to God, "Balak the son of Zippor, king of Moab,
has sent to me, saying, 11 'Behold, a people has come out of Egypt, and it covers the face of
the earth. Now come, curse them for me. Perhaps I shall be able to fight against them and
drive them out.'" 12 God said to Balaam, "You shall not go with them. You shall not curse
the people, for [r]they are blessed." 13 So Balaam rose in the morning and said to the princes
of Balak, "Go to your own land, for the LORD has refused to let me go with you." 14 So the
princes of Moab rose and went to Balak and said, "Balaam refuses to come with us."
15 Once again Balak sent princes, more in number and more honorable than these. 16 And
they came to Balaam and said to him, "Thus says Balak the son of Zippor: 'Let nothing
hinder you from coming to me, 17 [s]for I will surely do you great honor, and whatever you
say to me I will do. [t]Come, curse this people for me.'" 18 But Balaam answered and said to

[1] Or *the people of his kindred*

displace the Amorites from their land, for the Amorites had acquired it from the Moabites by force. It also helps to explain the king of Moab's anxiety about Israel that drove him to hire Balaam to curse Israel (see 22:4–6, and all of chs. 22–24). **Moab** had been defeated by Sihon, and Sihon had been defeated by Israel, so what hope has Moab?

21:29 Chemosh was the god of Moab (Judg. 11:24).

21:31–35 *The Campaign against Og, King of Bashan.* This is reported more fully in Deut. 3:1–11. This large area in northern Transjordan was later settled by three tribes (see Numbers 32). These victories scare the Moabites and reassure the Israelites that they will indeed be able to conquer Canaan.

22:1–36:13 *Israel in the Plains of Moab.* These chapters tell of Israel's lengthy encampment in the plains of Moab at the northern end of the Dead Sea. Here they prepared to cross the Jordan and enter Canaan proper. The events here match to some extent those at the other long encampments at Sinai and Kadesh: there is law-giving (chs. 28–36), a major apostasy (ch. 25), a census (ch. 26), and a battle (ch. 31). But these familiar features are preceded and followed by a very positive affirmation of the promise of the land. The prophecies of Balaam reaffirm Israel's destiny in a surprising and emphatic way (chs. 23–24), whereas the last word of God through Moses in 36:9 is: "for each of the tribes . . . of Israel shall hold on to its own inheritance." In this way the promise made to Abraham that the land of Canaan would be Israel's everlasting possession (Gen. 17:8) is reaffirmed. This theme will be strongly emphasized in the book of Deuteronomy.

22:1–24:25 *Balak, Balaam, and Israel.* This witty and amusing tale makes a serious point, namely, that the one true God is on Israel's side and therefore no human power can prevail against them (23:21–23). Even a pagan seer like Balaam can see this. Because Balaam is said to speak God's word (23:5; 24:2) and sounds pious (22:18, 38; 23:12), it is easy to suppose that the narrator views Balaam as a saint. But it seems more likely that the narrator's remarks about fees indicate that Balaam was indirectly asking for more, and that he was out to obtain as much as he could for his services (22:7, 18; see also 31:16; Deut. 23:4–5). Balaam's request to the second group of messengers to **stay here tonight** (Num. 22:19) was probably another expression of hoping for more; this account certainly presents Balaam as one "who loved gain from wrongdoing" (cf. 2 Pet. 2:15). It may seem surprising that God can use such a corrupt character to deliver his word, but he can even make a donkey speak (Num. 22:28–30)!

22:1–6 *Balak Summons Balaam.* Though Israel had not attacked **Moab**, but skirted their territory, the Moabite king **Balak** was so scared by their defeat of Sihon and Og that he summoned a man with an international reputation for blessing and cursing to defeat Israel by cursing them (v. 6). **Pethor** is in northern Syria **near the River** Euphrates, which is some 400 miles (644 km) by road north of Moab. **Amaw** is in the same area and is probably mentioned in nonbiblical texts. An eighth-century B.C. inscription found at the site of Deir Alla in Jordan begins with, "Inscription of **Balaam the son of Beor** [v. 5], the man who was a seer of the gods." This is certainly the same person spoken of in Numbers.

22:7–14 *Balaam Turns down Balak's First Invitation.* Though Balaam says God refused him permission to go, when Balak subsequently increases his offer, it suggests that the original messengers had reported to Balak that it might be a matter of cash (v. 15; cf. note on 22:1–24:25).

22:15–21 *Balaam Accepts Balak's Second Invitation.* The question of money figures much more prominently here (vv. 15–18), but again Balaam awaits God's permission. Happily for Balaam's pocketbook, God agrees, on condition that he only does **what I tell you** (v. 20).

the servants of Balak, [u]"Though Balak were to give me his house full of silver and gold, [v]I
could not go beyond the command of the LORD my God to do less or more. 19 So you, too,
[w]please stay here tonight, that I may know what more the LORD will say to me." 20 [q]And
God came to Balaam at night and said to him, "If the men have come to call you, rise, go
with them; [x]but only do what I tell you." 21 So Balaam rose in the morning and saddled
his donkey and went with the princes of Moab.

Balaam's Donkey and the Angel

22 But God's anger was kindled because he went, [y]and the angel of the LORD took
his stand in the way [z]as his adversary. Now he was riding on the donkey, and his two
servants were with him. 23 And the donkey saw the angel of the LORD standing in the
road, with a drawn sword in his hand. And the donkey turned aside out of the road and
went into the field. And Balaam struck the donkey, to turn her into the road. 24 Then the
angel of the LORD stood in a narrow path between the vineyards, with a wall on either
side. 25 And when the donkey saw the angel of the LORD, she pushed against the wall
and pressed Balaam's foot against the wall. So he struck her again. 26 Then the angel
of the LORD went ahead and stood in a narrow place, where there was no way to turn
either to the right or to the left. 27 When the donkey saw the angel of the LORD, she lay
down under Balaam. And Balaam's anger was kindled, and he struck the donkey with
his staff. 28 Then the LORD [a]opened the mouth of the donkey, and she said to Balaam,
"What have I done to you, that you have struck me these three times?" 29 And Balaam said
to the donkey, "Because you have made a fool of me. I wish I had a sword in my hand,
for then I would kill you." 30 And the donkey said to Balaam, "Am I not your donkey,
on which you have ridden all your life long to this day? Is it my habit to treat you this
way?" And he said, "No."

31 Then the LORD [b]opened the eyes of Balaam, and he saw the angel of the LORD standing in the way, with his drawn sword in his hand. And he bowed down and fell on his
face. 32 And the angel of the LORD said to him, "Why have you struck your donkey these
three times? Behold, I have come out [c]to oppose you because your way is perverse[1] before
me. 33 The donkey saw me and turned aside before me these three times. If she had not
turned aside from me, surely just now I would have killed you and let her live." 34 Then
Balaam said to the angel of the LORD, [d]"I have sinned, for I did not know that you stood
in the road against me. Now therefore, if it is evil in your sight, I will turn back." 35 And
the angel of the LORD said to Balaam, "Go with the men, [e]but speak only the word that I
tell you." So Balaam went on with the princes of Balak.

36 When Balak heard that Balaam had come, he went out to meet him at the city of Moab,
[f]on the border formed by the Arnon, at the extremity of the border. 37 And Balak said to
Balaam, "Did I not send to you to call you? Why did you not come to me? Am I not able to
[g]honor you?" 38 Balaam said to Balak, "Behold, I have come to you! Have I now any power
of my own to speak anything? [h]The word that God puts in my mouth, that must I speak."
39 Then Balaam went with Balak, and they came to Kiriath-huzoth. 40 And Balak sacrificed
oxen and sheep, and sent for Balaam and for the princes who were with him.

41 And in the morning Balak took Balaam and brought him up to Bamoth-baal, and
from there he saw a fraction of the people.

[1] Or *reckless*

18 [u]ch. 24:13 [v]ver. 38; ch. 23:26; [1 Kgs. 22:14; 2 Chr. 18:13]
19 [w]ver. 8
20 [q][See ver. 9 above] [x]ver. 35; ch. 23:12, 26; 24:13
22 [y][Ex. 4:24; 1 Chr. 21:16] [z]ver. 32
28 [a]2 Pet. 2:16
31 [b][Gen. 21:19; 2 Kgs. 6:17; Luke 24:16, 31]
32 [c]ver. 22
34 [d][1 Sam. 15:24; 26:21; 2 Sam. 12:13; Job 34:31, 32]
35 [e]ver. 20
36 [f]ch. 21:13
37 [g]ver. 17; ch. 24:11
38 [h]ver. 18

22:19 what more the LORD will say to me. It is hard to think that there was some part of v. 12 that Balaam did not understand. It is likely that he wanted the money and the honor that Balak offered (v. 17; cf. 2 Pet. 2:15).

22:22–35 ***The Donkey and the Angel.*** This is a hilarious put-down of Balaam's pretensions. The international expert on magic cannot see the angel, but his donkey can. And the angel upbraids him for his temper and cruelty. The whole episode reinforces the message that Balaam must **speak only the word that I tell you** (v. 35).

22:22 But God's anger was kindled, apparently because God knew that Balaam's heart was set on the money, in spite of God's strict instructions.

22:34–35 if it is evil in your sight. In view of the overall portrait of Balaam, this apparent submission is probably to be taken as insincere. Despite the clear statement both of God (see v. 12) and of the angel of the Lord in v. 32, Balaam continues to seek a way to get the money and honor that Balak had promised him (v. 17). Even though he had just been told that this was "perverse" (v. 32), he implicitly questions the veracity of this statement by saying "if it is evil" (v. 34). **The angel of the LORD** represents the manifestation of the presence and authority of the Lord himself (cf. Gen. 16:7; 18:1–2; Ex. 3:1–6).

22:36–40 ***Balak Greets Balaam.*** Balaam reasserts his intention to say only what God allows him to say (v. 38), despite the fee he has been offered.

22:36 The city of Moab (Hb. *'Ir-Mo'ab*) is located on the **Arnon,** which formed the northern border of Moab (21:13). **at the extremity of the bor-**

Chapter 23
1[i]ver. 29
2[j]ver. 14, 30
3[k]ver. 15 [l][ch. 24:1]
4[m]ver. 16
5[n]ver. 12, 16; ch. 22:38; Deut. 18:18; Isa. 51:16; 59:21; Jer. 1:9
7[o]ver. 18; ch. 24:3, 15, 20, 21, 23; Job 27:1; 29:1; Ps. 49:4; 78:2; Isa. 14:4; Mic. 2:4; [ch. 21:27] [p][ch. 22:5] [q][Gen. 29:1] [r]ch. 22:6
9[s][ch. 24:17] [t]Deut. 32:28 [u]Ex. 33:16; [Ezra 9:2; Esth. 3:8; Eph. 2:14]
10[v]See Gen. 13:16 [w]Ps. 37:37; 116:15; Rev. 14:13
11[x]ch. 22:11; 24:10; Deut. 23:5; Neh. 13:2
12[y]See ver. 5

Balaam's First Oracle

23 And Balaam said to Balak, [i]"Build for me here seven altars, and prepare for me
here seven bulls and seven rams." **2** Balak did as Balaam had said. And Balak and
Balaam [j]offered on each altar a bull and a ram. **3** And Balaam said to Balak, [k]"Stand beside
your burnt offering, and I will go. Perhaps the LORD will come [l]to meet me, and whatever
he shows me I will tell you." And he went to a bare height, **4** [m]and God met Balaam. And
Balaam said to him, "I have arranged the seven altars and I have offered on each altar a
bull and a ram." **5** And the LORD [n]put a word in Balaam's mouth and said, "Return to Balak,
and thus you shall speak." **6** And he returned to him, and behold, he and all the princes
of Moab were standing beside his burnt offering. **7** And Balaam [o]took up his discourse
and said,

"From [p]Aram Balak has brought me,
 the king of Moab [q]from the eastern mountains:
'Come, [r]curse Jacob for me,
 and come, denounce Israel!'
8 How can I curse whom God has not cursed?
 How can I denounce whom the LORD has not denounced?
9 For from the top of the crags [s]I see him,
 from the hills I behold him;
behold, [t]a people dwelling alone,
 and [u]not counting itself among the nations!
10 [v]Who can count the dust of Jacob
 or number the fourth part[1] of Israel?
Let me die [w]the death of the upright,
 and let my end be like his!"

11 And Balak said to Balaam, "What have you done to me? [x]I took you to curse my enemies,
and behold, you have done nothing but bless them." **12** And he answered and said, [y]"Must
I not take care to speak what the LORD puts in my mouth?"

[1] *Or dust clouds*

der. By meeting him as soon as he entered Moabite territory, Balak showed his respect for Balaam.

22:39 The location of **Kiriath-huzoth** is not known.

22:41–24:14 *Balaam Blesses Israel Three Times.* The first three attempts to persuade Balaam to curse Israel follow a similar pattern, though there are some significant deviations in the third. First, Balak takes Balaam to various high points in order to view Israel: Bamoth-baal (22:41), Pisgah (23:14), and Peor (23:28). Second, seven altars are built and seven bulls and rams are sacrificed at each place (23:1–2, 14, 29–30). Third, Balaam tells Balak to stay by the altars while he goes elsewhere to meet the Lord (23:3–5, 15–16), but on the third occasion the Spirit of God descends on him then and there (24:1–2). Fourth, Balaam pronounces a long, three-part blessing on Israel: the first two address Israel's wilderness situation, but the third looks forward to an Israelite king (23:7–10, 18–24; 24:3–9). Fifth, Balak reacts angrily to the blessing (23:11, 25; 24:10–11). Sixth, Balaam reasserts that he only has said what the Lord has told him (23:12, 26; 24:12–13). This pattern reinforces the point that Balaam's words, which are the opposite of what he was hired to say, are inspired by God and therefore must be reliable.

22:41–23:12 *The First Blessing.* Balaam's first blessing (23:7–10) reflects on why he has been summoned: to **curse . . . Israel** (23:7). In the biblical worldview, a curse can have a real effect on those denounced; it is not merely empty words. **Aram** is the region of Syria where Balaam came from. It is mentioned often in the OT and other ancient texts.

23:9 A people dwelling alone comments on Israel's sense of being a chosen people, different from other nations.

23:10 The dust of Jacob alludes to the fulfillment of the promise to the patriarchs (Gen. 13:16; 28:14). **Let my end be like his** is a prayer to be like Israel in life and death, which would partly fulfill the promise that in Abraham's descendants all the families of the earth would be blessed (Gen. 12:3; 22:18).

Balaam Blesses Israel

Concerned that the vast number of Israelites would overwhelm his land, King Balak of Moab summoned Balaam to come and curse them. Balaam traveled from the region of the Euphrates River, and Balak went out to meet him at a city on the Arnon River at the border of his land. Balak took Balaam to Bamoth-baal, Pisgah, and Peor to curse the Israelites, but each time Balaam blessed them.

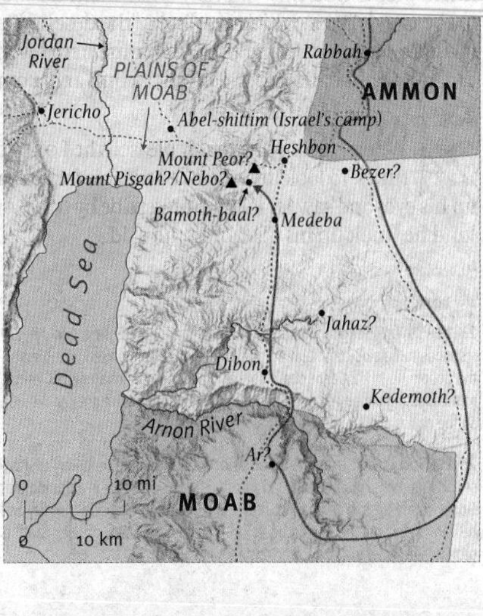

Balaam's Second Oracle

13 And Balak said to him, "Please come with me to another place, from which you may
see them. You shall see only a fraction of them and shall not see them all. Then curse
them for me from there." 14 And he took him to the field of Zophim, to the top of Pisgah,
[z]and built seven altars and offered a bull and a ram on each altar. 15 Balaam said to Balak,
[a]"Stand here beside your burnt offering, while I meet the LORD over there." 16 And the
LORD met Balaam and [b]put a word in his mouth and said, "Return to Balak, and thus shall
you speak." 17 And he came to him, and behold, he was standing beside his burnt offering,
and the princes of Moab with him. And Balak said to him, "What has the LORD spoken?"
18 And Balaam took up his discourse and said,

"Rise, Balak, and hear;
give ear to me, O son of Zippor:
19 [c]God is not man, that he should lie,
or a son of man, that he should change his mind.
Has he said, and will he not do it?
Or has he spoken, and will he not fulfill it?
20 Behold, I received a command to bless:
[d]he has blessed, and [e]I cannot revoke it.
21 [f]He has not beheld misfortune in Jacob,
nor has he seen trouble in Israel.
The LORD their God is with them,
and the shout of a king is among them.
22 [g]God brings them out of Egypt
and is for them like [h]the horns of the wild ox.
23 For there is no enchantment against Jacob,
no [i]divination against Israel;
now it shall be said of Jacob and Israel,
[j]'What has God wrought!'
24 Behold, a people! [k]As a lioness it rises up
and as a lion it lifts itself;
[l]it does not lie down until it has devoured the prey
and drunk the blood of the slain."

25 And Balak said to Balaam, "Do not curse them at all, and do not bless them at all."
26 But Balaam answered Balak, "Did I not tell you, [m]'All that the LORD says, that I must
do'?" 27 And Balak said to Balaam, [n]"Come now, I will take you to another place. Perhaps
it will please God that you may curse them for me from there." 28 So Balak took Balaam
to the top of [o]Peor, which overlooks [p]the desert.[1] 29 And Balaam said to Balak, [q]"Build for
me here seven altars and prepare for me here seven bulls and seven rams." 30 [r]And Balak
did as Balaam had said, and offered a bull and a ram on each altar.

Balaam's Third Oracle

24 When Balaam saw that it pleased the LORD to bless Israel, he did not go, as at [s]other
times, to look for omens, but set his face toward the wilderness. 2 And Balaam lifted
up his eyes and saw Israel [t]camping tribe by tribe. And [u]the Spirit of God came upon him,
3 and he [v]took up his discourse and said,

[1] Or *Jeshimon*

14[z]ver. 1, 2
15[a]ver. 3
16[b]ver. 5, 12
19[c]1 Sam. 15:29; Mal. 3:6; Rom. 11:29; Titus 1:2; Heb. 6:18; James 1:17
20[d]ch. 22:12; Gen. 12:2; 22:17 [e]ch. 22:18
21[f][Jer. 50:20]
22[g]ch. 24:8 [h]Deut. 33:17; Job 39:9-12; Ps. 22:21; 92:10
23[i]ch. 22:7 [j]Ps. 44:1
24[k]Gen. 49:9 [l]Gen. 49:27
26[m]See ch. 22:18
27[n]ver. 13
28[o]ch. 25:18; 31:16; Josh. 22:17; Ps. 106:28, 29; Hos. 9:10; [ch. 25:3, 5] [p]See ch. 21:20
29[q]ver. 1
30[r]ver. 2

Chapter 24

1[s]ch. 23:3, 15
2[t]See ch. 2:22-31 [u]Judg. 3:10; 1 Sam. 19:20, 23; 2 Chr. 15:1; 20:14
3[v]See ch. 23:7

23:13–30 *The Second Blessing.* Balaam's second blessing (vv. 18–24) responds to Balak's complaint that Balaam should have cursed, not blessed, the people (v. 11). Balaam observes that **God** does not **change his mind**, so the blessing already pronounced cannot be turned into a curse (vv. 19–20). So the nation will be free from disaster (v. 21).

23:19 God is not man, that he should lie. Balaam, even against his selfish intentions, must speak God's truth (cf. v. 26). Here he is affirming that God's truthfulness in general (cf. Titus 1:2; Heb. 6:18; God does not lie, and he cannot lie, for this would be contrary to his character) implies that his promises to Israel will also come to pass.

23:21 the shout of a king is among them. The king in view here is God himself, whose festivals are marked by shouts and trumpet blasts (e.g., 29:1).

23:23 Because God is with Israel, attempts to attack them with magic will fail.

23:24 lioness. This is a frightening image of Israel's military might and an indirect warning to Balak not to attack them.

24:1–14 *The Third Blessing.* Balaam's third blessing (vv. 3–9) is distinguished from the first two (see note on 22:41–24:14). The mention of the Spirit of God empowering Balaam (24:2) underlines the validity of this blessing, as do the opening lines of the blessing itself: **the man whose eye is opened . . .**

4 [w][Ezek. 1:28; 3:23; Rev. 1:10, 17]
6 [x][Ps. 1:3; Jer. 17:8] [y]Ps. 104:16; Isa. 61:3
7 [z][Jer. 51:13; Rev. 17:1] [a]1 Sam. 15:8 [b]2 Sam. 5:12; 1 Chr. 14:2
8 [c]See ch. 23:22 [d][ch. 14:9; 23:24] [e]Isa. 38:13; Jer. 50:17 [f]Ps. 45:5; Jer. 50:9
9 [g]ch. 23:24; Gen. 49:9 [h]Gen. 12:3; 27:29
10 [i][Job 27:23; Lam. 2:15; Ezek. 21:14, 17; 22:13] [j]See ch. 23:11
11 [k]ch. 22:17, 37
13 [l]ch. 22:18 [m]See ch. 16:28
14 [n][Mic. 6:5; Rev. 2:14] [o]See Gen. 49:1
15 [p][ch. 21:27]; See ch. 23:7
16 [q]Acts 7:48 [r]See ver. 4
17 [s][ch. 23:9]

"The oracle of Balaam the son of Beor,
the oracle of the man whose eye is opened,[1]
4 the oracle of him who hears the words of God,
who sees the vision of the Almighty,
[w]falling down with his eyes uncovered:
5 How lovely are your tents, O Jacob,
your encampments, O Israel!
6 Like palm groves[2] that stretch afar,
like gardens beside a river,
[x]like aloes [y]that the LORD has planted,
like cedar trees beside the waters.
7 Water shall flow from his buckets,
and his seed shall be [z]in many waters;
his king shall be higher than [a]Agag,
and [b]his kingdom shall be exalted.
8 God brings him out of Egypt
and is for him like the [c]horns of the wild ox;
he shall [d]eat up the nations, his adversaries,
and shall [e]break their bones in pieces
and [f]pierce them through with his arrows.
9 He crouched, he lay down like a lion
and [g]like a lioness; who will rouse him up?
[h]Blessed are those who bless you,
and cursed are those who curse you."

10 And Balak's anger was kindled against Balaam, and he [i]struck his hands together. And
Balak said to Balaam, [j]"I called you to curse my enemies, and behold, you have blessed
them these three times. 11 Therefore now flee to your own place. I said, [k]'I will certainly
honor you,' but the LORD has held you back from honor." 12 And Balaam said to Balak,
"Did I not tell your messengers whom you sent to me, 13 [l]'If Balak should give me his
house full of silver and gold, I would not be able to go beyond the word of the LORD, to
do either good or bad [m]of my own will. What the LORD speaks, that will I speak'? 14 And
now, behold, I am going to my people. Come, [n]I will let you know what this people will
do to your people [o]in the latter days."

Balaam's Final Oracle

15 [p]And he took up his discourse and said,

"The oracle of Balaam the son of Beor,
the oracle of the man whose eye is opened,
16 the oracle of him who hears the words of God,
and knows the knowledge of [q]the Most High,
who sees the vision of the Almighty,
[r]falling down with his eyes uncovered:
17 [s]I see him, but not now;
I behold him, but not near:

[1] Or *closed,* or *perfect;* also verse 15 [2] Or *valleys*

who hears the words of God, who sees the vision of the Almighty (vv. 3–4).

24:5–6 This picture of Israel's future prosperity in Canaan uses imagery drawn from the garden of Eden (see Gen. 2:9–10).

24:7 Water shall flow from his buckets. This continues the image of well-watered gardens. **his seed shall be in many waters**. Though this clause is difficult to interpret, it may refer to the fertility of the land or to the growth of Israel's population. **His king shall be higher than Agag** seems to be a prediction of Saul's defeat of Agag, the king of Amalek, Israel's oldest enemy (Ex. 17:8–16; 1 Sam. 15:1–9), though it may also refer to an otherwise unknown king.

24:8–9 These verses reiterate 23:22, 24 and add a reference to the patriarchal promise (Gen. 12:3; 27:29). Verse 9 of Numbers 24 implies, of course, that Balak, by demanding a curse on Israel, will himself be **cursed**. This logic inevitably leads to the final blessing on Israel, which ends with an explicit curse on Moab (see vv. 15–19).

24:15–19 *Balaam's Final Oracle.* This oracle begins like the previous one (cf. vv. 3–4 with vv. 15–16). But it rapidly becomes a prophecy about the rise of the Davidic dynasty, which conquered the surrounding peoples, including Moab (2 Sam. 8:2–12).

24:17 star . . . scepter. Symbols of kingship (see Gen. 49:10). **Sons of Sheth** should probably be identified with nomads who lived in Canaan. The Shutu are mentioned in Egyptian texts from 1900 B.C.

[t]a star shall come out of Jacob,
and [u]a scepter shall rise out of Israel;
it shall [v]crush the forehead[1] of Moab
and break down all the sons of Sheth.
18 [w]Edom shall be dispossessed;
[x]Seir also, his enemies, shall be dispossessed.
Israel is doing valiantly.
19 And one from Jacob shall exercise dominion
and destroy the survivors of cities!"

20 Then he looked on Amalek and [y]took up his discourse and said,

"Amalek was the first among the nations,
[z]but its end is utter destruction."

21 And he looked on the Kenite, and took up his discourse and said,

"Enduring is your dwelling place,
and your nest is set in the rock.
22 Nevertheless, Kain shall be burned
when Asshur takes you away captive."

23 And he took up his discourse and said,

"Alas, who shall live when God does this?
24 But ships shall come from [a]Kittim
and shall afflict Asshur and [b]Eber;
and he too [c]shall come to utter destruction."

25 Then Balaam rose and [d]went back to his place. And Balak also went his way.

Baal Worship at Peor

25 While Israel lived in [e]Shittim, [f]the people began to whore with the daughters of
Moab. 2 [g]These invited the people to the sacrifices of their gods, and the people ate
and bowed down to their gods. 3 So Israel yoked himself to Baal of Peor. And the anger of
the LORD was kindled against Israel. 4 And the LORD said to Moses, [h]"Take all the chiefs

[1] Hebrew *corners* [of the head]

17 [t]Matt. 2:2; Rev. 22:16 [u]Gen. 49:10 [v]Jer. 48:45; [2 Sam. 8:2]
18 [w][2 Sam. 8:14; Ps. 60:8, 9; Amos 9:12] [x]Gen. 32:3; 36:8
20 [y]See ch. 23:7 [z][Ex. 17:14; 1 Sam. 15:3, 8]
24 [a]Gen. 10:4; Dan. 11:30 [b]Gen. 10:21, 25 [c]ver. 20
25 [d][ch. 31:8]

Chapter 25

1 [e]ch. 33:49; Josh. 2:1; 3:1; Mic. 6:5 [f][ch. 31:16]
2 [g]Ex. 34:15, 16; Josh. 22:17; Ps. 106:28; Hos. 9:10; [1 Cor. 10:20]
4 [h]See Deut. 4:3

24:18 Seir is an alternative name for Edom.

24:19 the survivors of cities (or "survivors of Ir"). Ir ("city") could be short for the city of Moab, mentioned in 22:36. In this case this prophecy ends with another prediction of Moab's subjugation by the Davidic dynasty.

24:20–25 *Three Cryptic Predictions.* Balaam unexpectedly adds three short, cryptic oracles against the nations, which function as backhanded encouragement to Israel; her future will be secure through the destruction of her enemies.

24:20 The first oracle predicts the defeat of the Amalekites (cf. Ex. 17:8–16; 1 Sam. 15:18; 30:17), probably in the time of David.

24:21–22 The second oracle predicts the defeat of the Kenites by **Asshur**. The Kenites were on good terms with Israel (see Judg. 1:16; 4:11). Asshur is probably a tribe that lived in northern Sinai (Gen. 25:3, 18; 2 Sam. 2:9), not the well-known Assyria. But nothing further is known of their attacking the Kenites.

24:23–24 These verses are quite obscure. The passage appears to be a reference to the Philistines (**Kittim**) arriving on the coasts of Canaan in the twelfth century B.C. They afflicted **Asshur and Eber** before themselves coming **to utter destruction** at the hands of David. All these prophecies therefore seem to find their focus in the time of David. Christians have seen them as extending beyond the time of David to the time of the Second David, Jesus Christ, to whom all nations will bow (see Ps. 72:8–11).

24:25 Then Balaam rose and went back to his place. But this is not the end of the story of Balaam, for it is later discovered that he advised Balak to send women to seduce Israel and lead them away from allegiance to God (31:16; cf. Rev. 2:14). God's judgment came on Balaam in the war against Midian in Num. 31:8.

25:1–18 *Apostasy at Peor.* Balaam had delivered his final oracles at Peor (23:28). Now, at the foot of the mountain where Balaam had been prophesying, the Israelites start "whoring with the daughters of Moab" and sacrificing to their gods. The juxtaposition could not be more stark between the most exuberant visions of Israel's future and their present blatant infidelity to the law and the covenant. But this sort of inconsistency was not new. The same thing had happened at Sinai: while Moses was being given instructions on building the tabernacle, the people were making and worshiping the golden calf (Exodus 25–34). And at Kadesh the wonderful prospect of entry to the land was dashed by national unbelief (Numbers 13–14). These earlier episodes are alluded to here in ch. 25, and various details in this apostasy parallel earlier ones (e.g., the plagues, the consecration of the Levites/priest). What is missing here is the threat to destroy the whole nation or delay the entry to Canaan. God's plan is going to be implemented despite Israel's unfaithfulness. As Deut. 9:5 puts it, "Not because of your righteousness . . . are you going in to possess their land, but because of the wickedness of these nations . . . that he may confirm the word that the LORD swore to your fathers."

25:1 Shittim was the final encampment before the Israelites crossed the Jordan (see Josh. 2:1). This is possibly Tell el-Hammam, about 10 miles (16 km) east of Jericho. At this site there are impressive remains from the time of David, including massive outer walls, fortress towers, and a large, sloping embankment.

25:1–2 Whore . . . sacrifices of their gods . . . ate echoes the terms used in Ex. 34:15–16. The people were breaking the first commandment given after the golden calf apostasy.

25:3 Baal was the main Canaanite fertility god, whom **Israel** was constantly tempted to worship.

25:4–5 the fierce anger of the LORD. Drastic action (execution) was the

4 [i][Deut. 21:23; 2 Sam. 21:6; Gal. 3:13] [j]ver. 11; Deut. 13:17
5 [k][ch. 11:16; Ex. 18:21, 25] [l][Ex. 32:27]
6 [m]Joel 2:17
7 [n]Ps. 106:30 [o]Ex. 6:25
9 [p]Deut. 4:3; [1 Cor. 10:8]
11 [q][2 Cor. 11:2] [r]Deut. 32:16, 21; 1 Kgs. 14:22; Ps. 78:58; Zeph. 1:18; 3:8; 1 Cor. 10:22; [Ex. 20:5]
12 [s]Mal. 2:4, 5
13 [t]See 1 Chr. 6:4-15 [u]Ex. 40:15
15 [v]ch. 31:8; Josh. 13:21
17 [w]ch. 31:2, 7
18 [x]ch. 31:16; Rev. 2:14 [y]See ch. 23:28

Chapter 26
1 [z]ch. 25:9
2 [a]ch. 1:2, 3; Ex. 30:12; 38:25, 26
3 [b]ver. 63; See ch. 22:1
4 [c]ch. 1:1
5 [d]Gen. 46:8, 9; Ex. 6:14; 1 Chr. 5:1-3

of the people and [i]hang[1] them in the sun before the LORD, [j]that the fierce anger of the
LORD may turn away from Israel." 5 And Moses said to [k]the judges of Israel, [l]"Each of you
kill those of his men who have yoked themselves to Baal of Peor."
6 And behold, one of the people of Israel came and brought a Midianite woman to his
family, in the sight of Moses and in the sight of the whole congregation of the people of
Israel, while they were [m]weeping in the entrance of the tent of meeting. 7 [n]When Phinehas
[o]the son of Eleazar, son of Aaron the priest, saw it, he rose and left the congregation and
took a spear in his hand 8 and went after the man of Israel into the chamber and pierced
both of them, the man of Israel and the woman through her belly. Thus the plague on the
people of Israel was stopped. 9 Nevertheless, [p]those who died by the plague were twenty-
four thousand.

The Zeal of Phinehas

10 And the LORD said to Moses, 11 "Phinehas the son of Eleazar, son of Aaron the priest, has
turned back my wrath from the people of Israel, in that he [q]was jealous with my jealousy
among them, so that I did not consume the people of Israel in [r]my jealousy. 12 Therefore
say, [s]'Behold, I give to him my covenant of peace, 13 and it shall be to him and to [t]his
descendants after him the covenant of [u]a perpetual priesthood, because he was jealous
for his God and made atonement for the people of Israel.'"
14 The name of the slain man of Israel, who was killed with the Midianite woman, was
Zimri the son of Salu, chief of a father's house belonging to the Simeonites. 15 And the
name of the Midianite woman who was killed was Cozbi the daughter of [v]Zur, who was
the tribal head of a father's house in Midian.
16 And the LORD spoke to Moses, saying, 17 [w]"Harass the Midianites and strike them
down, 18 for they have harassed you with their [x]wiles, with which they beguiled you in
the matter of [y]Peor, and in the matter of Cozbi, the daughter of the chief of Midian, their
sister, who was killed on the day of the plague on account of Peor."

Census of the New Generation

26 [z]After the plague, the LORD said to Moses and to Eleazar the son of Aaron, the priest,
2 [a]"Take a census of all the congregation of the people of Israel, from twenty years
old and upward, by their fathers' houses, all in Israel who are able to go to war." 3 And Moses
and Eleazar the priest spoke with them [b]in the plains of Moab by the Jordan at Jericho,
saying, 4 "Take a census of the people,[2] from twenty years old and upward," as the LORD
[c]commanded Moses. The people of Israel who came out of the land of Egypt were:
5 [d]Reuben, the firstborn of Israel; the sons of Reuben: of Hanoch, the clan of the
Hanochites; of Pallu, the clan of the Palluites; 6 of Hezron, the clan of the Hezronites; of

[1] Or *impale* [2] *Take a census of the people* is implied (compare verse 2)

only possible way to obliterate the perversion of **Baal** worship (v. 2) and the accompanying prostitution with the daughters of Moab (v. 1), and so to assuage the Lord's fierce anger. **hang them in the sun**. This most likely refers to the ancient Near Eastern practice of impaling dead bodies on a stick after execution for heinous crimes, as a form of disgrace (rather than burying the bodies) and as a public warning to all who would be tempted to engage in such perversion themselves.

25:6 Publicly flouting this ban on liaisons with foreign women, a chief's son (v. 14) takes a **Midianite** princess (v. 15) into a tent near the tabernacle. Moabites and Midianites collaborated in hiring Balaam (22:4, 7), and evidently in the seduction of Israel also.

25:7–8 Phinehas, the high priest's son, goes after the chief's son and the princess (see v. 6) and executes them on the spot, perhaps in the very act of intercourse. This punishment without waiting for a trial corresponds to the Levites' slaughter of the golden calf worshipers (Ex. 32:25–28). In the case of the Levites, this led to their being set apart as the priestly tribe (Ex. 32:29). For his part, Phinehas was rewarded with heading a permanent priestly dynasty (Num. 25:10–13). Phinehas's grandfather **Aaron** had halted a **plague** by offering incense (16:46–50).

25:9 Though the **plague** was stopped by Phinehas's intervention (its start is hinted at in v. 3), still a huge number died. This parallels the plagues at Sinai and Kadesh (Ex. 32:35; Num. 14:37; 16:49).

25:16–18 The ongoing struggle with Midian is reported in ch. 31 and Judges 6–8.

26:1–65 *The Second Census.* The later chapters of Numbers are all concerned with Israel's future life in Canaan. Balaam has predicted a secure and prosperous future there. This census deals with establishing the relative size of the tribes so that they may each be given an appropriately sized holding (vv. 53–54). The first census (ch. 1) was primarily concerned with establishing the number of fighting men, but this issue is mentioned only once in this second census (in 26:2). The issue of territory probably also explains why the second census is so interested in the clans that make up each tribe—which are hardly mentioned in ch. 1. The total number of Israelites has changed very little between the censuses: 603,550 (first) and 601,730 (second). Even though the total may be similar, 26:64–65 stresses that the people being counted are quite different: only Joshua and Caleb figure in both totals. The tribal totals vary somewhat more than the overall total, but the most striking change is the fall in Simeon's total from 59,300 to 22,200 and the increase in Manasseh's from 32,200 to 52,700. The fall in Simeon's numbers could be partly due to the plague caused by Zimri, the Simeonite (25:9, 14), but there is no obvious explanation for the increase in Manasseh. (On interpreting the census numbers, see note on 1:20–46.)

26:1 Eleazar has now taken over from **Aaron**, his father, as high priest.

Carmi, the clan of the Carmites. 7 These are the clans of the Reubenites, and those listed
were [e]43,730. 8 And the sons of Pallu: Eliab. 9 The sons of Eliab: Nemuel, Dathan, and
Abiram. These are the Dathan and Abiram, [f]chosen from the congregation, who contended
against Moses and Aaron in the company of Korah, when they contended against the LORD
10 and [g]the earth opened its mouth and swallowed them up together with Korah, when
that company died, when the fire devoured 250 men, and [h]they became a warning. 11 But
[i]the sons of Korah did not die.

12 The sons of [j]Simeon according to their clans: of Nemuel, the clan of the Nemuelites;
of Jamin, the clan of the Jaminites; of Jachin, the clan of the Jachinites; 13 of Zerah, the clan
of the Zerahites; of Shaul, the clan of the Shaulites. 14 These are the clans of the Simeonites,
[k]22,200.

15 The sons of [l]Gad according to their clans: of Zephon, the clan of the Zephonites; of
Haggi, the clan of the Haggites; of Shuni, the clan of the Shunites; 16 of Ozni, the clan of
the Oznites; of Eri, the clan of the Erites; 17 of Arod, the clan of the Arodites; of Areli, the
clan of the Arelites. 18 These are the clans of the sons of Gad as they were listed, [m]40,500.

19 The sons of [n]Judah were Er and Onan; and Er and Onan died in the land of Canaan.
20 And the sons of Judah according to their clans were: of Shelah, the clan of the Shelanites;
of Perez, the clan of the Perezites; of Zerah, the clan of the Zerahites. 21 And the sons of
Perez were: of Hezron, the clan of the Hezronites; of Hamul, the clan of the Hamulites.
22 These are the clans of Judah as they were listed, [o]76,500.

23 The sons of [p]Issachar according to their clans: of Tola, the clan of the Tolaites; of Puvah,
the clan of the Punites; 24 of Jashub, the clan of the Jashubites; of Shimron, the clan of the
Shimronites. 25 These are the clans of Issachar as they were listed, [q]64,300.

26 The sons of [r]Zebulun, according to their clans: of Sered, the clan of the Seredites; of
Elon, the clan of the Elonites; of Jahleel, the clan of the Jahleelites. 27 These are the clans
of the Zebulunites as they were listed, [s]60,500.

28 The sons of [t]Joseph according to their clans: Manasseh and Ephraim. 29 [u]The sons of
Manasseh: of [v]Machir, the clan of the Machirites; and Machir was the father of Gilead; [w]of
Gilead, the clan of the Gileadites. 30 These are the sons of Gilead: of Iezer, the clan of the
Iezerites; of Helek, the clan of the Helekites; 31 and of Asriel, the clan of the Asrielites; and
of Shechem, the clan of the Shechemites; 32 and of Shemida, the clan of the Shemidaites;
and of Hepher, the clan of the Hepherites. 33 Now [x]Zelophehad the son of Hepher had
no sons, but daughters. And the names of the daughters of Zelophehad were Mahlah,
Noah, Hoglah, Milcah, and Tirzah. 34 These are the clans of Manasseh, and those listed
were [y]52,700.

35 These are the sons of Ephraim according to their clans: of Shuthelah, the clan of the
Shuthelahites; of Becher, the clan of the Becherites; of Tahan, the clan of the Tahanites.
36 And these are the sons of Shuthelah: of Eran, the clan of the Eranites. 37 These are the
clans of the sons of Ephraim as they were listed, [z]32,500. These are the sons of Joseph
according to their clans.

38 The sons of [a]Benjamin according to their clans: of Bela, the clan of the Belaites; of
Ashbel, the clan of the Ashbelites; of Ahiram, the clan of the Ahiramites; 39 of Shephupham,
the clan of the Shuphamites; of Hupham, the clan of the Huphamites. 40 And the sons
of Bela were Ard and Naaman: of Ard, the clan of the Ardites; of Naaman, the clan of
the Naamites. 41 These are the sons of Benjamin according to their clans, and those listed
were [b]45,600.

42 These are the sons of [c]Dan according to their clans: of Shuham, the clan of the
Shuhamites. These are the clans of Dan according to their clans. 43 All the clans of the
Shuhamites, as they were listed, were [d]64,400.

44 The sons of [e]Asher according to their clans: of Imnah, the clan of the Imnites; of
Ishvi, the clan of the Ishvites; of Beriah, the clan of the Beriites. 45 Of the sons of Beriah:

7 [e][ch. 1:21]
9 [f]ch. 1:16; 16:2
10 [g]See ch. 16:31-35 [h]ch. 16:38; [1 Cor. 10:6; 2 Pet. 2:6]
11 [i]Ex. 6:24; 1 Chr. 6:22; [ch. 16:32]
12 [j]Gen. 46:10; Ex. 6:15; 1 Chr. 4:24
14 [k][ch. 1:23]
15 [l]Gen. 46:16
18 [m][ch. 1:25]
19 [n]Gen. 46:12; 1 Chr. 2:3-5; See Gen. 38:3-10
22 [o][ch. 1:27]
23 [p]Gen. 46:13; 1 Chr. 7:1
25 [q][ch. 1:29]
26 [r]Gen. 46:14
27 [s][ch. 1:31]
28 [t]Gen. 46:20
29 [u]For ver. 29-37, see 1 Chr. 7:14-20 [v]Josh. 17:1 [w]ch. 36:1
33 [x]ch. 27:1; 36:11; Josh. 17:3
34 [y][ch. 1:35]
37 [z][ch. 1:33]
38 [a]Gen. 46:21; 1 Chr. 7:6; See 1 Chr. 8:1-5
41 [b][ch. 1:37]
42 [c]Gen. 46:23
43 [d][ch. 1:39]
44 [e]Gen. 46:17; 1 Chr. 7:30, 31

26:9–11 These verses recall the events in ch. 16.

26:11 But the sons of Korah did not die clarifies a possible misreading of 16:32.

26:19–21 sons of Judah. See Genesis 38.

26:28–37 Verse 28 reverses the order of **Ephraim** and **Manasseh** in 1:32–35. The detail given about Manasseh in 26:28–34 is striking. It is needed to explain the identity of **the daughters of Zelophehad** (v. 33), who are prominent in chs. 27 and 36. (See also note on 27:1–11.)

of Heber, the clan of the Heberites; of Malchiel, the clan of the Malchielites. 46 And the
name of the daughter of Asher was Serah. 47 These are the clans of the sons of Asher as
they were listed, [f]53,400.
48 The sons of [g]Naphtali according to their clans: of Jahzeel, the clan of the Jahzeelites;
of Guni, the clan of the Gunites; 49 of Jezer, the clan of the Jezerites; of Shillem, the clan
of the Shillemites. 50 These are the clans of Naphtali according to their clans, and those
listed were [h]45,400.
51 This was the list of the people of Israel, [i]601,730.
52 The LORD spoke to Moses, saying, 53 [j]"Among these the land shall be divided for
inheritance according to the number of names. 54 [k]To a large tribe you shall give a
large inheritance, and to a small tribe you shall give a small inheritance; every tribe shall
be given its inheritance in proportion to its list. 55 But the land shall be [l]divided by lot.
According to the names of the tribes of their fathers they shall inherit. 56 Their inheritance
shall be divided according to lot between the larger and the smaller."
57 [m]This was the list of the Levites according to their clans: of Gershon, the clan of the
Gershonites; of Kohath, the clan of the Kohathites; of Merari, the clan of the Merarites.
58 These are the clans of Levi: the clan of the Libnites, the clan of the Hebronites, the clan of
the Mahlites, the clan of the Mushites, the clan of the Korahites. And Kohath was the father
of Amram. 59 The name of Amram's wife was [n]Jochebed the daughter of Levi, who was born
to Levi in Egypt. And she bore to Amram Aaron and Moses and Miriam their sister. 60 [o]And
to Aaron were born Nadab, Abihu, Eleazar, and Ithamar. 61 [p]But Nadab and Abihu died
when they offered unauthorized fire before the LORD. 62 And those listed were [q]23,000,
every male from a month old and upward. For [r]they were not listed among the people of
Israel, because [s]there was no inheritance given to them among the people of Israel.
63 These were those listed by Moses and Eleazar the priest, who listed the people of Israel
[t]in the plains of Moab by the Jordan at Jericho. 64 [u]But among these there was not one of
those listed by Moses and Aaron the priest, who had listed the people of Israel in the wilderness of Sinai. 65 For the LORD had said of them, [v]"They shall die in the wilderness." Not
one of them was left, [w]except Caleb the son of Jephunneh and Joshua the son of Nun.

The Daughters of Zelophehad

27 Then drew near the daughters of [x]Zelophehad the son of Hepher, son of Gilead,
son of Machir, son of Manasseh, from the clans of Manasseh the son of Joseph. The
names of his daughters were: Mahlah, Noah, Hoglah, Milcah, and Tirzah. 2 And they stood
before Moses and before Eleazar the priest and before the chiefs and all the congregation,
at the entrance of the tent of meeting, saying, 3 "Our father [y]died in the wilderness. He was
not among the company of those who gathered themselves together against the LORD
[z]in the company of Korah, but [a]died for his own sin. And he had no sons. 4 Why should
the name of our father be taken away from his clan because he had no son? [b]Give to us a
possession among our father's brothers."
5 Moses [c]brought their case before the LORD. 6 And the LORD said to Moses, 7 "The daughters of Zelophehad [d]are right. [e]You shall give them possession of an inheritance among
their father's brothers and transfer the inheritance of their father to them. 8 And you shall

47 [f][ch. 1:41]
48 [g]Gen. 46:24; 1 Chr. 7:13
50 [h][ch. 1:43]
51 [i][ch. 1:46]
53 [j]Josh. 11:23; 14:1, 2; Ps. 105:44
54 [k]ch. 33:54; 35:8
55 [l]ch. 33:54; 34:13; Josh. 11:23; 14:2
57 [m]Gen. 46:11; See Ex. 6:16-19; 1 Chr. 6:1, 16-30
59 [n]Ex. 2:1, 2, 4; 6:20
60 [o]ch. 3:2; 1 Chr. 24:1
61 [p]ch. 3:4; Lev. 10:1, 2; 1 Chr. 24:2
62 [q][ch. 3:39] [r]ch. 1:49 [s]See ch. 18:20
63 [t]ver. 3; See ch. 22:1
64 [u][ch. 1:44; Deut. 2:14, 15]
65 [v]ch. 14:28, 29; 1 Cor. 10:5 [w]See ch. 13:6

Chapter 27

1 [x]ch. 26:33; 36:11; Josh. 17:3
3 [y]ch. 14:35; 26:64, 65 [z]ch. 16:1, 2 [a][Ezek. 18:4]
4 [b]Josh. 17:4
5 [c]Ex. 18:19
7 [d]ch. 36:5 [e]ch. 36:2

26:57–62 As in ch. 3, **Levites** over **a month old** are counted. Their number has increased from 22,000 to **23,000** (cf. 3:39; 26:62).

27:1–30:16 *Laws for the Land.* Chapters 27–30 are united by these laws for the land—particularly the inheritance rules and the celebrations of the festivals.

27:1–11 *The Daughters of Zelophehad.* These daughters have already been mentioned (in 26:33) without an obvious reason. Now it becomes clear why they were picked out. Their father had no sons to inherit his land. Under traditional rules, daughters did not inherit from their father. The father would provide a dowry for them when they were married, but his land and other possessions were divided among his sons. If he had no sons, his estate would pass to his nearest male relative. Verses 9–10 of ch. 27 spell out the order of precedence. But the daughters point out that in this situation the land could pass out of Zelophehad's family and his name could be forgotten. To prevent this from happening, the daughters ask that they be allowed to inherit. So a new rule is devised for the case of a man without sons, whereby his daughters will inherit before his brothers or uncles (v. 8).

27:1 Noah here (Hb. *No'ah*) is a woman's name and spelled differently from Noah (Hb. *Noakh*) in Genesis 6–9.

27:3–4 He was not . . . in the company of Korah (v. 3; see ch. 16). It is not clear why Zelophehad's daughters mention this episode. Perhaps those involved in Korah's rebellion lost their right to inherit, or perhaps these daughters just wanted to make clear that their father had not been among those notorious sinners. Nor is it clear why they raised the issue of their inheritance at this stage (27:4). Perhaps the census had led them to think about inheritance, as it was designed to assess the size of the tribes with a view to giving them sufficient land. Maybe the Manassites were already thinking of settling northern Transjordan after defeating Og, king of Bashan, there (21:31–35; 32:33–42). In any case, this request shows the faith of these women: they were sure that the land would be conquered and assigned.

speak to the people of Israel, saying, 'If a man dies and has no son, then you shall transfer
his inheritance to his daughter. 9 And if he has no daughter, then you shall give his inheritance to his brothers. 10 And if he has no brothers, then you shall give his inheritance to his
father's brothers. 11 And if his father has no brothers, then you shall give his inheritance
to the nearest [f]kinsman of his clan, and he shall possess it. And it shall be for the people
of Israel [g]a statute and rule, as the LORD commanded Moses.'"

Joshua to Succeed Moses

12 The LORD said to Moses, "Go up into [h]this mountain of Abarim and see the land that
I have given to the people of Israel. 13 When you have seen it, you also [i]shall be gathered
to your people, as your brother Aaron was, 14 [j]because you rebelled against my word in the
wilderness of Zin when the congregation quarreled, failing [k]to uphold me as holy at the
waters before their eyes." (These are [l]the waters of Meribah of Kadesh in the wilderness
of Zin.) 15 Moses spoke to the LORD, saying, 16 "Let the LORD, [m]the God of the spirits of all
flesh, appoint a man over the congregation 17 who [n]shall go out before them and come in
before them, who shall lead them out and bring them in, that the congregation of the LORD
may not be [o]as sheep that have no shepherd." 18 So the LORD said to Moses, "Take [p]Joshua
the son of Nun, a man [q]in whom is the Spirit, and [r]lay your hand on him. 19 Make him
stand before Eleazar the priest and all the congregation, and you shall [s]commission him in
their sight. 20 You shall invest him with some of your authority, [t]that all the congregation
of the people of Israel may obey. 21 And he shall stand before Eleazar the priest, who shall
inquire for him [u]by the judgment of the Urim before the LORD. At his word they shall go
out, and at his word they shall come in, both he and all the people of Israel with him, the
whole congregation." 22 And Moses did as the LORD commanded him. He took Joshua and
made him stand before Eleazar the priest and the whole congregation, 23 and he laid his
hands on him and [s]commissioned him as the LORD directed through Moses.

Daily Offerings

28 The LORD spoke to Moses, saying, 2 "Command the people of Israel and say to them,
'My offering, [v]my food for my food offerings, my [w]pleasing aroma, you shall be
careful to offer to me at its appointed time.' 3 [x]And you shall say to them, This is the food
offering that you shall offer to the LORD: two male lambs a year old without blemish, day

11 [f]See Ruth 4:3-6; Jer. 32:6-9 [g]ch. 35:29
12 [h]ch. 21:11; 33:44, 47; Deut. 32:49; [Deut. 3:27; 34:1]
13 [i]See ch. 20:24
14 [j]ch. 20:12, 24 [k]ch. 20:12, 13 [l]ch. 20:13; Deut. 32:51; [Ex. 17:7]
16 [m]See ch. 16:22
17 [n]Deut. 31:2; 1 Sam. 8:20; 18:13; 1 Kgs. 3:7; 2 Chr. 1:10; [Josh. 14:11] [o]1 Kgs. 22:17; Ezek. 34:5; Zech. 10:2; Matt. 9:36; Mark 6:34
18 [p]ch. 32:28 [q]Gen. 41:38; See Judg. 3:10 [r]Deut. 34:9
19 [s]Deut. 3:28; 31:7, 8
20 [t]See Josh. 1:16-18
21 [u]See Ex. 28:30
23 [s][See ver. 19 above]

Chapter 28

2 [v]See Lev. 3:11 [w]See Gen. 8:21
3 [x]For ver. 3-8, see Ex. 29:38-42

Calendar of Public Sacrifices

Occasion	Bulls	Rams	Lambs	Goats
Every day (28:3–8)			2	
Sabbath (28:9–10)			2	
1st day of month (28:11–15)	2	1	7	1
Unleavened Bread: each day (28:17–25)	2	1	7	1
Pentecost (Feast of Weeks) (28:26–31)	2	1	7	1
1st day of 7th month (29:1–6)	1	1	7	1
Day of Atonement (29:7–11)	1	1	7	1
Feast of Booths (29:12–38):				
1st day	13	2	14	1
2nd day	12	2	14	1
3rd day	11	2	14	1
4th day	10	2	14	1
5th day	9	2	14	1
6th day	8	2	14	1
7th day	7	2	14	1
8th day	1	1	7	1

27:12–23 *Joshua Commissioned as Moses' Successor.* The sin of Moses and Aaron at Meribah meant they could not enter the land, so a successor to Moses had to be appointed (20:10–13). The Lord designates Joshua as his successor (27:18). Then Joshua stands before Eleazar the high priest and Moses lays his hands on him, publicly declaring Joshua to be his successor (vv. 22–23).

27:12 Like Aaron, Moses must climb a **mountain** to die (cf. 20:22–29). From it he will see the promised **land**. This command is fulfilled in Deuteronomy 34.

27:20–21 some of your authority. Joshua will not have the direct communication with God that Moses had (12:1–8). Instead he will have to be instructed by **Eleazar** the high **priest**, who will use the **Urim** and Thummim to determine God's will (27:21). The Urim and Thummim were some sort of sacred lot and were part of the high priest's equipment (see Ex. 28:30; Lev. 8:8; cf. note on 1 Sam. 14:41–42).

28:1–29:40 *Calendar of Public Sacrifices.* Although Moses' days as mediator of revelation are numbered, he still is God's chosen vessel to pass on law to Israel. First among his final instructions are laws about public sacrifices (cf. other calendars, Ex. 23:10–19; 34:18–26; Leviticus 23; Deut. 16:1–17; cf. also The Hebrew Calendar, p. 34). These are the sacrifices offered in the tabernacle on a daily basis by the priests on behalf of the nation. Twice a day lambs are offered as a burnt offering (see Leviticus 1): one in the morning and another in the evening. On holy days, extra sacrifices are added. These chapters explain just what is required on which day. They are summarized in the chart to the left. To see how many sacrifices the priests would have to offer, one must add together all the offerings that are required for each reason. For example, on a Sabbath falling on the first day of a month, the priests would have to offer: two lambs (the daily offering) plus two lambs (the Sabbath offering) plus two bulls, one ram, seven lambs, and one goat (1st-day-of-the-month offering). Most of the sacrifices were burnt offerings (see Leviticus 1),

5 [y]ch. 15:4; Ex. 16:36 [z]Lev. 2:1 [a]Ex. 29:40
6 [b]Ex. 29:42; [Amos 5:25]
10 [c][Ezek. 46:4, 5]
11 [d]ch. 10:10; 1 Sam. 20:5; 1 Chr. 23:31; 2 Chr. 2:4; Ezra 3:5; Isa. 1:13, 14; Ezek. 45:17; 46:6; Hos. 2:11; Col. 2:16
12 [e]For ver. 12-14, see ch. 15:4-12
15 [f]ver. 22, 30; ch. 15:24; 29:11, 16, 19, 25
16 [g]Deut. 16:1; Ezek. 45:21; See Ex. 12:6
17 [h]Lev. 23:6; [Ex. 12:18]
18 [i]Ex. 12:16; Lev. 23:7
19 [j]ver. 31; ch. 29:8, 13; Lev. 22:20; Deut. 15:21; 17:1
22 [k]ver. 15, 30; ch. 29:22, 28, 31, 34, 38

by day, as a regular offering. 4 The one lamb you shall offer in the morning, and the other
lamb you shall offer at twilight; 5 also [y]a tenth of an ephah[1] of fine flour for [z]a grain offering, mixed [a]with a quarter of a hin[2] of beaten oil. 6 It is a [b]regular burnt offering, which
was ordained at Mount Sinai for a pleasing aroma, a food offering to the LORD. 7 Its drink
offering shall be a quarter of a hin for each lamb. In the Holy Place you shall pour out a
drink offering of strong drink to the LORD. 8 The other lamb you shall offer at twilight.
Like the grain offering of the morning, and like its drink offering, you shall offer it as a
food offering, with a pleasing aroma to the LORD.

Sabbath Offerings

9 "On the Sabbath day, two male lambs a year old without blemish, and two tenths of an
ephah of fine flour for a grain offering, mixed with oil, and its drink offering: 10 this is [c]the
burnt offering of every Sabbath, besides the regular burnt offering and its drink offering.

Monthly Offerings

11 [d]"At the beginnings of your months, you shall offer a burnt offering to the LORD:
two bulls from the herd, one ram, seven male lambs a year old without blemish; 12 also
[e]three tenths of an ephah of fine flour for a grain offering, mixed with oil, for each bull,
and two tenths of fine flour for a grain offering, mixed with oil, for the one ram; 13 and a
tenth of fine flour mixed with oil as a grain offering for every lamb; for a burnt offering
with a pleasing aroma, a food offering to the LORD. 14 Their drink offerings shall be half
a hin of wine for a bull, a third of a hin for a ram, and a quarter of a hin for a lamb. This
is the burnt offering of each month throughout the months of the year. 15 Also [f]one male
goat for a sin offering to the LORD; it shall be offered besides the regular burnt offering
and its drink offering.

Passover Offerings

16 [g]"On the fourteenth day of the first month is the LORD's Passover, 17 [h]and on the fifteenth day of this month is a feast. Seven days shall unleavened bread be eaten. 18 [i]On the
first day there shall be a holy convocation. You shall not do any ordinary work, 19 but offer
a food offering, a burnt offering to the LORD: two bulls from the herd, one ram, and seven
male lambs a year old; [j]see that they are without blemish; 20 also their grain offering of fine
flour mixed with oil; three tenths of an ephah shall you offer for a bull, and two tenths for
a ram; 21 a tenth shall you offer for each of the seven lambs; 22 also [k]one male goat for a sin
offering, to make atonement for you. 23 You shall offer these besides the burnt offering of
the morning, which is for a regular burnt offering. 24 In the same way you shall offer daily,
for seven days, the food of a food offering, with a pleasing aroma to the LORD. It shall be

[1] An *ephah* was about 3/5 bushel or 22 liters [2] A *hin* was about 4 quarts or 3.5 liters

but all the goats are sin offerings (see Leviticus 4). In addition to the animals being sacrificed, a grain offering of flour and oil, and a drink offering of wine had to be made. The size of the grain offering and drink offering varied with the animal being offered. Here the same quantities are prescribed as in Num. 15:4–10: a lamb must be accompanied by about half a gallon (1.9 liters) of flour, a quart (0.95 liters) of oil, and a quart (0.95 liters) of wine. At least double quantities are needed for a bull. These regulations make several points. First, they show the importance of the sacrificial system in Israel (cf. note on 15:1–16). In the limited time before his death, Moses explains what sacrifices must be offered in public worship on behalf of the whole nation. These are over and above the private sacrifices that a layperson may want to bring for personal reasons. Second, they are a strong assurance to Joshua that the nation will indeed inherit the land and become a prosperous agricultural community, able to provide for this lavish and expensive worship. It has been calculated that, over the course of a year, these sacrifices involved a total of 113 bulls, 1,086 lambs, over a ton of flour, and 1,000 bottles of oil and wine! Finally, this list of sacrifices underlines the importance of the sabbatical principle. Every seventh day is a Sabbath and marked by a doubling of the daily sacrifice, while the seventh month is marked by a huge number of extra sacrifices, especially during the Feast of Booths, which is clearly marked out as the biggest celebration of the year.

28:1–8 *The Daily Offering.* A lamb was offered in the **morning** and another in the evening at **twilight** (v. 4). This pattern of prayer in the morning and in the evening has carried on in Jewish and Christian practice throughout the centuries. **Pleasing** (or "soothing") **aroma** is a phrase that regularly describes the effect of sacrifice on God: it soothes his anger at sin (see Gen. 8:21).

28:9–10 *The Sabbath Offerings.* The extra burnt offerings on the Sabbath mean that twice as many are offered that day as on other days of the week.

28:11–15 *The New Moon Sacrifices.* The first of the month, indicated by the new moon, was an important festival; as many sacrifices were offered then as at Passover or Pentecost (see vv. 16–31). It was an occasion for family worship (1 Sam. 20:5–6; 2 Kings 4:23). It was like the Sabbath, a day when trading stopped (Amos 8:5; see also Col. 2:16).

28:16–25 *The Feast of Unleavened Bread.* This immediately followed **Passover**, which is celebrated **on the fourteenth day of the first month** (i.e., in late March or April).

28:17 Unleavened, that is, made without yeast (cf. Ex. 12:15–20).

28:18 Holy convocation is probably a gathering for worship. **Ordinary work**, lit., "work of labor." This seems to be a milder ban than the rule for the Sabbath and the Day of Atonement, when absolutely no work was permitted (see Lev. 23:3, 28; Num. 29:7).

28:19–24 These sacrifices are to be offered on each of the **seven days** of unleavened bread.

offered besides the regular burnt offering and its drink offering. 25 And [l]on the seventh
day you shall have a holy convocation. You shall not do any ordinary work.

Offerings for the Feast of Weeks

26 "On [m]the day of the firstfruits, when you offer a grain offering of new grain to the
LORD at your Feast of Weeks, you shall have a holy convocation. You shall not do any
ordinary work, 27 but offer a burnt offering, with a pleasing aroma to the LORD: [n]two
bulls from the herd, one ram, seven male lambs a year old; 28 also their grain offering of
fine flour mixed with oil, three tenths of an ephah for each bull, two tenths for one ram,
29 a tenth for each of the seven lambs; 30 with [o]one male goat, to make atonement for you.
31 Besides the regular burnt offering and its grain offering, you shall offer them and their
drink offering. [p]See that they are without blemish.

Offerings for the Feast of Trumpets

29 "On the first day of the seventh month you shall have a holy convocation. You shall
not do any ordinary work. [q]It is a day for you to blow the trumpets, 2 and you shall
offer a burnt offering, for a pleasing aroma to the LORD: one bull from the herd, one ram,
seven male lambs a year old without blemish; 3 also their grain offering of fine flour mixed
with oil, three tenths of an ephah[1] for the bull, two tenths for the ram, 4 and one tenth for
each of the seven lambs; 5 with [o]one male goat for a sin offering, to make atonement for
you; 6 besides [r]the burnt offering of the new moon, and its grain offering, and [s]the regular
burnt offering and its grain offering, and their drink offering, according to the rule for
them, for a pleasing aroma, a food offering to the LORD.

Offerings for the Day of Atonement

7 [t]"On the tenth day of this seventh month you shall have a holy convocation and [u]afflict
yourselves.[2] You shall do no work, 8 but you shall offer a burnt offering to the LORD, a pleasing aroma: one bull from the herd, one ram, seven male lambs a year old: [v]see that they
are without blemish. 9 And their grain offering shall be of fine flour mixed with oil, three
tenths of an ephah for the bull, two tenths for the one ram, 10 a tenth for each of the seven
lambs: 11 also [w]one male goat for a sin offering, besides [x]the sin offering of atonement, and
the regular burnt offering and its grain offering, and their drink offerings.

Offerings for the Feast of Booths

12 [y]"On the fifteenth day of the seventh month you shall have a holy convocation. You
shall not do any ordinary work, and you shall keep a feast to the LORD seven days. 13 And
[z]you shall offer a burnt offering, a food offering, with a pleasing aroma to the LORD, thirteen bulls from the herd, two rams, fourteen male lambs a year old; they shall be without
blemish; 14 and their grain offering of fine flour mixed with oil, three tenths of an ephah
for each of the thirteen bulls, two tenths for each of the two rams, 15 and a tenth for each
of the fourteen lambs; 16 also one male goat for a sin offering, besides the regular burnt
offering, its grain offering and its drink offering.

17 "On the second day twelve bulls from the herd, two rams, fourteen male lambs a year
old without blemish, 18 with the grain offering and the drink offerings for the bulls, for the
rams, and for the lambs, [a]in the prescribed quantities; 19 also one male goat for a sin offering,
besides the regular burnt offering and its grain offering, and their drink offerings.

[1] An *ephah* was about 3/5 bushel or 22 liters [2] Or *and fast*

25 [l]Ex. 12:16; 13:6; Lev. 23:8
26 [m]Ex. 23:16; 34:22; Lev. 23:10, 15; Deut. 16:10; [Acts 2:1]
27 [n][Lev. 23:18, 19]
30 [o]ver. 15, 22
31 [p]ver. 19

Chapter 29

1 [q]Lev. 23:24; See ch. 10:1-10
5 [o][See ch. 28:30 above]
6 [r]See ch. 28:11-15 [s]See ch. 28:3-8
7 [t]Lev. 16:29; 23:27 [u]ch. 30:13; Ps. 35:13; Isa. 58:5
8 [v]ver. 13, 17, 20, 23, 26, 29, 32, 36; See ch. 28:19
11 [w]See ch. 28:15 [x]Lev. 16:3, 5
12 [y]See Lev. 23:34
13 [z]Ezra 3:4
18 [a]ver. 21, 24, 27, 30, 33, 37; ch. 15:12; 28:7, 14

28:26–31 *The Feast of Weeks (Pentecost).* This took place seven weeks after Passover. It coincided with the grain festival in Israel, so it is called **the day of the firstfruits** (see also Lev. 23:15–22). This calendar (Num. 28:1–29:40) requires one more bull and one less ram than the Leviticus instruction, making it like the first of the month and the Feast of Unleavened Bread (Num. 28:25–26).

29:1–6 *The First Day of the Seventh Month.* Every new moon was a holy day (28:11–15), but since the seventh month of the year was holy, the first day of that month was especially holy. It was therefore marked by a **holy convocation**, no **ordinary work**, the blowing of **trumpets**, and almost twice as many sacrifices as on other new moon festivals. According to 10:10, blowing the trumpets at the festivals is a plea to God to remember Israel. For observant Jews even today, the days from the first to the tenth of the seventh month (the Day of Atonement) are the holiest in the year, when they search their consciences and confess their sins.

29:7–11 *The Day of Atonement.* This day is fully described in Leviticus 16. Here is simply a list of the principal sacrifices and a reminder of the laity's duties: to hold a **holy convocation and afflict yourselves** (i.e., fast) and **do no work**.

29:12–38 *The Feast of Booths.* This festival involved all the Israelites living in booths (i.e., temporary dwellings) for the week to remind themselves of their lifestyle in the wilderness (see Lev. 23:33–43). Once again, this calendar (Num. 28:1–29:40) focuses on the sacrifices offered by the priests. The large number of sacrifices offered during the eight days highlights its importance. Coming at the end of the agricultural year in October, the feast was an occasion to

20 "On the third day eleven bulls, two rams, fourteen male lambs a year old without blemish, 21 with the grain offering and the drink offerings for the bulls, for the rams, and for the lambs, in the prescribed quantities; 22 also one male goat for a sin offering, besides the regular burnt offering and its grain offering and its drink offering.

23 "On the fourth day ten bulls, two rams, fourteen male lambs a year old without blemish, 24 with the grain offering and the drink offerings for the bulls, for the rams, and for the lambs, in the prescribed quantities; 25 also one male goat for a sin offering, besides the regular burnt offering, its grain offering and its drink offering.

26 "On the fifth day nine bulls, two rams, fourteen male lambs a year old without blemish, 27 with the grain offering and the drink offerings for the bulls, for the rams, and for the lambs, in the prescribed quantities; 28 also one male goat for a sin offering; besides the regular burnt offering and its grain offering and its drink offering.

29 "On the sixth day eight bulls, two rams, fourteen male lambs a year old without blemish, 30 with the grain offering and the drink offerings for the bulls, for the rams, and for the lambs, in the prescribed quantities; 31 also one male goat for a sin offering; besides the regular burnt offering, its grain offering, and its drink offerings.

32 "On the seventh day seven bulls, two rams, fourteen male lambs a year old without blemish, 33 with the grain offering and the drink offerings for the bulls, for the rams, and for the lambs, in the prescribed quantities; 34 also one male goat for a sin offering; besides the regular burnt offering, its grain offering, and its drink offering.

35 [b]"On the eighth day you shall have a [c]solemn assembly. You shall not do any ordinary work, 36 but you shall offer a burnt offering, a food offering, with a pleasing aroma to the LORD: one bull, one ram, seven male lambs a year old without blemish, 37 and the grain offering and the drink offerings for the bull, for the ram, and for the lambs, in the prescribed quantities; 38 also one male goat for a sin offering; besides the regular burnt offering and its grain offering and its drink offering.

39 "These you shall offer to the LORD at your [d]appointed feasts, in addition to your [e]vow offerings and your freewill offerings, for your burnt offerings, and for your grain offerings, and for your drink offerings, and for your peace offerings."

40 [1] So Moses told the people of Israel everything just as the LORD had commanded Moses.

Men and Vows

30 Moses spoke to [f]the heads of the tribes of the people of Israel, saying, "This is what the LORD has commanded. 2 [g]If a man vows a vow to the LORD, or [h]swears an oath to bind himself by a pledge, he shall not break his word. [i]He shall do according to all that proceeds out of his mouth.

Women and Vows

3 "If a woman vows a vow to the LORD and binds herself by a pledge, while within her father's house in her youth, 4 and her father hears of her vow and of her pledge by which she has bound herself and says nothing to her, then all her vows shall stand, and every

[1] Ch 30:1 in Hebrew

35 [b][John 7:37] [c]See Lev. 23:36
39 [d]Lev. 23:2, 4; 1 Chr. 23:31; 2 Chr. 31:3; Ezra 3:5; Neh. 10:33; [Isa. 1:14] [e]Lev. 7:11, 16; 22:21, 23

Chapter 30
1 [f]ch. 1:4, 16; 7:2
2 [g]Deut. 23:21; Eccles. 5:4; See Lev. 27:2 [h]See Lev. 5:4 [i]Job 22:27; Ps. 22:25; 50:14; 66:13, 14; 116:14, 18; Nah. 1:15

thank God for the harvest and to pray for plenty of rain in the next year. In Israel, rain is expected only between October and April.

29:39–40 *Clarification and Summary.* Verse 39 functions as a footnote to the calendar of public sacrifices (28:1–29:40), clarifying that private sacrifices prompted by vows or other circumstances may be offered whenever they are needed. The calendar of public sacrifices simply lays down the essential offerings that must always be made.

30:1–16 *The Obligations of Vows.* In a crisis people often make a vow: "If God delivers me from X, I promise to do Y." There are many examples in the Bible (e.g., Gen. 28:20–22; 1 Sam. 1:11). The danger is that, when the crisis is over, the vow may not be fulfilled. Stern warnings about failing to fulfill a vow are found in Deut. 23:21–23 and Eccles. 5:4–6. These laws are concerned with defining those few circumstances in which a person may be excused from fulfilling a vow. Basically, a man is always obliged to fulfill his vow (Num. 30:2), but a woman may be excused if her father or husband (the leader of the family, who is assumed to have the authority to nullify such a vow) objects to her vow as soon as he hears about it (vv. 5, 8, 12, 14). But if the man, as the head of the family, hears of his daughter's vow or his wife's vow and does not object to it, then it stands and the woman is obliged to fulfill it (vv. 4, 7, 11, 13). The placement of this law here may seem surprising, but there are several reasons why it should come here. Vows are mentioned in 29:39, and they are often involved in the offering of a sacrifice. Also, war often prompts vows, and Israel is about to start its military campaign in Canaan. In addition, the conquest of Canaan depends on God keeping his promised word to Israel, and Israel must be equally strict in carrying out her promises to God.

30:1–2 *Men and Vows.* The general principle here is that whether a man makes a **vow** (to do something positive, like offer a sacrifice) or a **pledge** (to avoid or abstain from something), **he shall not break his word**.

30:3–5 *Women and vows.* Until married, a woman is under her father's authority. If she makes a vow and her father objects, she will be forgiven for not carrying it out.

pledge by which she has bound herself shall stand. 5 But if her father opposes her on the
day that he hears of it, no vow of hers, no pledge by which she has bound herself shall
stand. And the LORD will forgive her, because her father opposed her.
6 "If she marries a husband, while under her [j]vows or any thoughtless utterance of her
lips by which she has bound herself, 7 and her husband hears of it and says nothing to
her on the day that he hears, then her vows shall stand, and her pledges by which she
has bound herself shall stand. 8 But if, on the day that her husband comes to hear of it, he
opposes her, then he makes void her [j]vow that was on her, and the thoughtless utterance
of her lips by which she bound herself. [k]And the LORD will forgive her. 9 (But any vow of
a widow or of a divorced woman, anything by which she has bound herself, shall stand
against her.) 10 And if she vowed in her husband's house or bound herself by a pledge with
an oath, 11 and her husband heard of it and said nothing to her and did not oppose her, then
all her vows shall stand, and every pledge by which she bound herself shall stand. 12 But
if her husband makes them null and void on the day that he hears them, then whatever
proceeds out of her lips concerning her vows or concerning her pledge of herself shall
not stand. Her husband has made them void, and [l]the LORD will forgive her. 13 Any vow
and any binding oath to afflict herself,[1] her husband may establish,[2] or her husband may
make void. 14 But if her husband says nothing to her from day to day, then he establishes
all her vows or all her pledges that are upon her. He has established them, because he said
nothing to her on the day that he heard of them. 15 But if he makes them null and void
after he has heard of them, then [m]he shall bear her iniquity."
16 These are the statutes that the LORD commanded Moses about a man and his wife and
about a father and his daughter while she is in her youth within her father's house.

Vengeance on Midian

31 The LORD spoke to Moses, saying, 2 [n]"Avenge the people of Israel on the Midianites.
Afterward you shall [o]be gathered to your people." 3 So Moses spoke to the people,
saying, "Arm men from among you for the war, that they may go against Midian to execute
the LORD's vengeance on Midian. 4 You shall send a thousand from each of the tribes of
Israel to the war." 5 So there were provided, out of the thousands of Israel, a thousand
from each tribe, twelve thousand [p]armed for war. 6 And Moses sent them to the war, a
thousand from each tribe, together with Phinehas the son of Eleazar the priest, with the
vessels of the sanctuary and [q]the trumpets for the alarm in his hand. 7 They warred against
Midian, as the LORD commanded Moses, and [r]killed every male. 8 They killed the kings
of Midian with the rest of their slain, [s]Evi, Rekem, [t]Zur, Hur, and Reba, the five kings of
Midian. And they also killed [u]Balaam the son of Beor with the sword. 9 And the people of
Israel took captive the women of Midian and their little ones, and they took as plunder
all their cattle, their flocks, and all their goods. 10 All their cities in the places where they
lived, and all their [v]encampments, they burned with fire, 11 [w]and took all the spoil and all
the plunder, both of man and of beast. 12 Then they brought the captives and the plunder
and the spoil to Moses, and to Eleazar the priest, and to the congregation of the people
of Israel, at the camp on [x]the plains of Moab by the Jordan at Jericho.
13 Moses and Eleazar the priest and all the chiefs of the congregation went to meet them

6 [j]Ps. 56:12
8 [j][See ver. 6 above] [k]ver. 12
12 [l]ver. 8
15 [m]See Lev. 5:1

Chapter 31

2 [n]ch. 25:17 [o]See ch. 20:24
5 [p]ch. 32:27; Josh. 4:13
6 [q]ch. 10:6, 9; Lev. 23:24
7 [r][Deut. 20:13; Judg. 21:11; 1 Sam. 27:9; 1 Kgs. 11:15, 16]
8 [s]Josh. 13:21 [t]ch. 25:15 [u]Josh. 13:22
10 [v]Gen. 25:16
11 [w][Deut. 20:14; Josh. 8:2]
12 [x]See ch. 22:1

[1] *Or to fast* [2] *Or may allow to stand*

30:6–8 *Vows Made by a Woman before Her Marriage.* If a woman under a vow gets married, her new husband can cancel her vow.

30:9 *Widows and Divorcees.* They are not subject to the authority of a father or a husband, so their vows are binding.

30:10–16 *Vows Made by a Woman after Her Marriage.* These may be waived by a husband as soon as he hears of them, but if he **says nothing** they are binding (v. 14). If he later objects to them, he (and not the woman) is guilty and will suffer the penalty for breaking them.

31:1–54 *Retribution on Midian.* The Midianites were a group of nomadic tribes who inhabited the deserts on the fringes of Canaan. They were associated with the Ishmaelites, Amalekites, and Moabites. It is the Moabite Midianites who are the target here. Instigated by Balaam (v. 16), they had seduced the Israelites into worshiping Baal at Peor (ch. 25), so a brief but fierce military campaign is launched against them, for persuading Israelites to worship other gods is a capital offense, according to Deuteronomy 13. As the last campaign headed by Moses (Num. 31:1–2), this one sets precedents for the coming invasion of Canaan.

31:1–12 *The Lord's Campaign of Vengeance against Midian.* This campaign against the Midianites is punishment for their seduction of Israel away from her true Husband, the Lord (cf. 25:1–13).

31:6 Phinehas was the one who intervened in 25:7 and thereby halted the plague provoked by the worship of Baal. He went as chaplain to the army because his father, the high priest, had to keep away from the pollution caused by death in battle. **vessels of the sanctuary**. It is not clear exactly what is meant—possibly the priestly garments, the ark, or the Urim and Thummim.

31:8 The daughter of **Zur** was killed by Phinehas (25:15).

31:13–18 *Moses' Anger with His Officers.* Normally in wars outside Canaan,

14[y]ver. 48
15[z][1 Sam. 15:3]
16[a]ch. 25:2 [b]ch. 24:14; 2 Pet. 2:15; Rev. 2:14 [c]See ch. 23:28 [d]ch. 25:9
17[e]Judg. 21:11, 12
18[f]See Deut. 21:10-14
19[g]ch. 5:2 [h]See ch. 19:12, 22
23[i]ch. 19:9
24[j]See Lev. 11:25
27[k]Josh. 22:8; 1 Sam. 30:24
28[l][ch. 18:26]; See ver. 30-41, 47
30[m]See ver. 42-47 [n]See ch. 1:53
37[o]ver. 28
41[p][ch. 18:8, 19]
47[q]ver. 30
48[r]ver. 14

outside the camp. 14 And Moses was angry with [y]the officers of the army, the commanders
of thousands and the commanders of hundreds, who had come from service in the war.
15 Moses said to them, "Have you [z]let all the women live? 16 Behold, [a]these, [b]on Balaam's
advice, caused the people of Israel to act treacherously against the LORD in the incident
of [c]Peor, and so [d]the plague came among the congregation of the LORD. 17 Now therefore,
[e]kill every male among the little ones, and kill every woman who has known man by lying
with him. 18 But all the young girls who have not known man by lying with him [f]keep
alive for yourselves. 19 [g]Encamp outside the camp seven days. Whoever of you has killed
any person and [h]whoever has touched any slain, purify yourselves and your captives on
the third day and on the seventh day. 20 You shall purify every garment, every article of
skin, all work of goats' hair, and every article of wood."

21 Then Eleazar the priest said to the men in the army who had gone to battle: "This is
the statute of the law that the LORD has commanded Moses: 22 only the gold, the silver,
the bronze, the iron, the tin, and the lead, 23 everything that can stand the fire, you shall
pass through the fire, and it shall be clean. Nevertheless, it shall also be purified [i]with the
water for impurity. And whatever cannot stand the fire, you shall pass through the water.
24 You must [j]wash your clothes on the seventh day, and you shall be clean. And afterward
you may come into the camp."

25 The LORD said to Moses, 26 "Take the count of the plunder that was taken, both of
man and of beast, you and Eleazar the priest and the heads of the fathers' houses of the
congregation, 27 and [k]divide the plunder into two parts between the warriors who went
out to battle and all the congregation. 28 And levy for the LORD a tribute from the men of
war who went out to battle, [l]one out of five hundred, of the people and of the oxen and
of the donkeys and of the flocks. 29 Take it from their half and give it to Eleazar the priest
as a contribution to the LORD. 30 And from the people of Israel's half you shall take [m]one
drawn out of every fifty, of the people, of the oxen, of the donkeys, and of the flocks, of all
the cattle, and give them to the Levites [n]who keep guard over the tabernacle of the LORD."
31 And Moses and Eleazar the priest did as the LORD commanded Moses.

32 Now the plunder remaining of the spoil that the army took was 675,000 sheep, 33 72,000
cattle, 34 61,000 donkeys, 35 and 32,000 persons in all, women who had not known man
by lying with him. 36 And the half, the portion of those who had gone out in the army,
numbered 337,500 sheep, 37 and [o]the LORD's tribute of sheep was 675. 38 The cattle were
36,000, of which the LORD's tribute was 72. 39 The donkeys were 30,500, of which the LORD's
tribute was 61. 40 The persons were 16,000, of which the LORD's tribute was 32 persons.
41 And Moses gave the tribute, which was the contribution for the LORD, to Eleazar the
priest, [p]as the LORD commanded Moses.

42 From the people of Israel's half, which Moses separated from that of the men who had
served in the army— 43 now the congregation's half was 337,500 sheep, 44 36,000 cattle,
45 and 30,500 donkeys, 46 and 16,000 persons— 47 [q]from the people of Israel's half Moses
took one of every 50, both of persons and of beasts, and gave them to the Levites who kept
guard over the tabernacle of the LORD, as the LORD commanded Moses.

48 Then [r]the officers who were over the thousands of the army, the commanders of thousands and the commanders of hundreds, came near to Moses 49 and said to Moses, "Your

the women were spared (Deut. 20:14). But as these **women** were responsible for seducing the Israelites, they had to be killed. In addition, if **every male among the little ones** were killed, this would preclude the perpetuation of the Midianite people and eliminate the Midianites as a nation forever. Girls without sexual experience (Num. 31:18), who were not involved with the sin of Baal-peor, were allowed to live and marry Israelite warriors.

31:19–24 *Purification for Uncleanness.* Though the war had been ordered by God, and such wars are often called "holy wars," it nevertheless made the soldiers unclean. (See Introduction to Joshua: The Destruction of the Canaanites.) They had to undergo sprinkling with the **water** mixture described in ch. 19 and wait **outside the camp** for a week (Num. 31:19, 24). The spoils also had to be purified (vv. 22–23).

31:25–47 *Dividing the Spoils.* The initial division of the spoil of war was that half went to the soldiers and half to those who stayed behind (v. 27; cf. 1 Sam. 30:24). From their share of the spoils the soldiers had to give one-five-hundredth to the priests, and from their share the people had to give one-fiftieth to the Levites. Thus one-tenth of one percent of the total spoil went to the priests and one percent went to the Levites. A similar ratio is decreed in Num. 18:26 for the distribution of the tithes: the Levites give one-tenth of the tithe to the priests.

31:48–54 *Head Count and Atonement.* A check on the numbers returning from battle revealed no losses. But conducting a census demands the payment of ransom, normally half a *silver* shekel per head (Ex. 30:11–16). On this occasion they dedicate all the gold captured from the Midianites, 16,750 **gold . . . shekels** (Num. 31:52), on behalf of 12,000 warriors (v. 5). The gold may have been made into vessels for the tabernacle; at any rate it served to remind God of Israel's generosity and to ward off a plague, which a census could provoke (v. 54; cf. 2 Sam. 24:15).

servants have counted the men of war who are under our command, and there is not a man
missing from us. 50 And we have brought the LORD's offering, what each man found, articles
of gold, armlets and bracelets, signet rings, earrings, and beads, [s]to make atonement for
ourselves before the LORD." 51 And Moses and Eleazar the priest received from them the gold,
all crafted articles. 52 And all the gold of the contribution that they presented to the LORD,
from the commanders of thousands and the commanders of hundreds, was 16,750 shekels.[1]
53 [t](The men in the army had each taken plunder for himself.) 54 And Moses and Eleazar the
priest received the gold from the commanders of thousands and of hundreds, and brought
it into the tent of meeting, [u]as a memorial for the people of Israel before the LORD.

Reuben and Gad Settle in Gilead

32 Now the people of Reuben and the people of Gad had a very great number of livestock. And they saw the land of [v]Jazer and the land of Gilead, and behold, the place
was a place for livestock. 2 So the people of Gad and the people of Reuben came and said to
Moses and to Eleazar the priest and to the chiefs of the congregation, 3 [w]"Ataroth, [x]Dibon,
Jazer, Nimrah, Heshbon, Elealeh, Sebam, [y]Nebo, and Beon, 4 the land [z]that the LORD struck
down before the congregation of Israel, is a land for livestock, and your servants have
livestock." 5 And they said, "If we have found favor in your sight, let this land be given to
your servants for a possession. Do not take us across the Jordan."
6 But Moses said to the people of Gad and to the people of Reuben, "Shall your brothers go to the war while you sit here? 7 Why will you discourage the heart of the people of
Israel from going over into the land that the LORD has given them? 8 Your fathers did this,
[a]when I sent them from Kadesh-barnea to see the land. 9 For when they went up to the
Valley of Eshcol and saw the land, they discouraged the heart of the people of Israel from
going into the land that the LORD had given them. 10 [b]And the LORD's anger was kindled
on that day, and he swore, saying, 11 'Surely none of the men who came up out of Egypt,
[c]from twenty years old and upward, shall see the land that I swore to give [d]to Abraham,
to Isaac, and to Jacob, because they have not wholly followed me, 12 none except Caleb the
son of Jephunneh the [e]Kenizzite and Joshua the son of Nun, for [f]they have wholly followed the LORD.' 13 And the LORD's anger was kindled against Israel, and he made them
[g]wander in the wilderness forty years, until [h]all the generation that had done evil in the
sight of the LORD was gone. 14 And behold, you have risen in your fathers' place, a brood
of sinful men, to increase still more the fierce anger of the LORD against Israel! 15 For if
you [i]turn away from following him, he will again abandon them in the wilderness, and
you will destroy all this people."
16 Then they came near to him and said, [j]"We will build sheepfolds here for our livestock,
and cities for our little ones, 17 but [k]we will take up arms, ready to go before the people of
Israel, until we have brought them to their place. And our little ones shall live in the fortified
cities because of the inhabitants of the land. 18 [l]We will not return to our homes until each
of the people of Israel has gained his inheritance. 19 For we will not inherit with them on the
other side of the Jordan and beyond, [m]because our inheritance has come to us on this side
of the Jordan to the east." 20 So [n]Moses said to them, "If you will do this, if you will take up

50 [s]See Ex. 30:12
53 [t]ver. 32; Deut. 20:14
54 [u]Ex. 30:16

Chapter 32

1 [v]ver. 3, 35; See ch. 21:32
3 [w]ver. 34 [x]ver. 34; See ch. 21:30 [y]ver. 38; ch. 33:47; Deut. 32:49; 1 Chr. 5:8; Isa. 15:2; 46:1; Jer. 48:1, 22
4 [z]ch. 21:24, 34; [ver. 33]
8 [a]See ch. 13:3, 21-33; Deut. 1:22-28
10 [b]For ver. 10-12, see Deut. 1:34-36
11 [c]ch. 14:29 [d]See Gen. 50:24
12 [e]Josh. 14:6; 15:17 [f]ch. 14:24; Deut. 1:36; Josh. 14:8, 9
13 [g]See ch. 14:33-35 [h]ch. 26:64, 65
15 [i][Deut. 30:17; Josh. 22:16, 18; 2 Chr. 7:19, 20; 15:2]
16 [j]ver. 24
17 [k]Josh. 4:12, 13
18 [l]Josh. 22:4
19 [m]ver. 33; Josh. 12:1; 13:8
20 [n]Deut. 3:18; Josh. 1:13, 14; 4:12, 13

[1] A *shekel* was about 2/5 ounce or 11 grams

32:1–42 *The Settlement in Transjordan.* The conquest of the kings of Transjordan—Sihon and Og—was described in ch. 21. The high hills (2,500 feet [762 m]) of Transjordan made for excellent cattle grazing, so it must have seemed a good idea for some of the Israelites to settle there. The tribes of Reuben and Gad put their bid in first. However, since Transjordan south of the Sea of Galilee is outside the Promised Land, Moses is shocked by the request. He accuses the tribes of making the same mistake as the spies by rejecting God's promises (32:6–15). The tribes of Reuben and Gad insist that they fully support the conquest of Canaan: their fighting men will head the invasion force and not return to Transjordan until Canaan is won (vv. 16–27). Moses accepts this compromise (vv. 28–32). The subsequent settlement of Reuben and Gad is summarized. Part of the tribe of Manasseh also settled in northern Transjordan.

32:1 The land of Jazer means the land surrounding the village of Jazer. For possible locations of this and other places mentioned, see map, p. 320. **Gilead** normally means the hilly district south of the Jabbok River, but in vv. 39–40 it refers to the area north of the Jabbok.

32:3 These towns were part of Sihon's territory (see 21:2–32) and subsequently were incorporated into the tribal land of Reuben and Gad (32:34–38).

32:6–15 Moses gives a passionate summary of the spy episode (see chs. 13–14). He sees the reluctance of Reuben and Gad to enter Canaan as worse than that of their parents: **you have risen in your fathers' place . . . to increase still more the fierce anger of the LORD against Israel** (32:14). It could provoke God to abandon Israel entirely (v. 15). Perhaps these fears explain the readiness to punish the Transjordanian tribes in Josh. 22:12.

32:16–19 The tribes of Reuben and Gad modify their proposal. They will leave their **livestock** in **sheepfolds** and their **little ones** in **cities** (v. 16; "small villages" must be meant) while their adult fighting men head the army entering Canaan (v. 17). They **will not return** to Transjordan until the campaign is over (v. 18).

32:20–32 Moses accepts their offer but warns them that if they fail to live up

arms to go before the LORD for the war, 21 and every armed man of you will pass over the
Jordan before the LORD, until he has [o]driven out his enemies from before him 22 and the
land is subdued before the LORD; then after that you shall return and be free of obligation
to the LORD and to Israel, and [p]this land shall be your possession before the LORD. 23 But
if you will not do so, behold, you have sinned against the LORD, and [q]be sure your sin will
find you out. 24 [r]Build cities for your little ones and folds for your sheep, and do what you
have promised." 25 And the people of Gad and the people of Reuben said to Moses, "Your
servants will do as my lord commands. 26 [s]Our little ones, our wives, our livestock, and all
our cattle shall remain there in the cities of Gilead, 27 [t]but your servants will pass over,
every man who is [u]armed for war, before the LORD to battle, as my lord orders."

28 So [v]Moses gave command concerning them to Eleazar the priest and to [w]Joshua the
son of Nun and to the heads of the fathers' houses of the tribes of the people of Israel.
29 And Moses said to them, "If the people of Gad and the people of Reuben, every man
who is armed to battle before the LORD, will pass with you over the Jordan and the land
shall be subdued before you, then you shall give them the land of Gilead for a possession.
30 However, if they will not pass over with you armed, they shall have possessions among
you in the land of Canaan." 31 And the people of Gad and the people of Reuben answered,
"What the LORD has said to your servants, we will do. 32 We will pass over armed before
the LORD into the land of Canaan, and the possession of our inheritance shall remain
with us beyond the Jordan."

33 And [x]Moses gave to them, to the people of Gad and to the people of Reuben and to
the half-tribe of Manasseh the son of Joseph, the kingdom of Sihon king of the Amorites
and the kingdom of Og king of Bashan, the land and its cities with their territories, the
cities of the land throughout the country. 34 And the people of Gad built [y]Dibon, [z]Ataroth,
[a]Aroer, 35 Atroth-shophan, [b]Jazer, Jogbehah, 36 [c]Beth-nimrah and Beth-haran, [d]fortified cities, and folds for sheep. 37 And the people of Reuben built [e]Heshbon, [y]Elealeh, Kiriathaim,
38 [f]Nebo, and [g]Baal-meon ([h]their names were changed), and [c]Sibmah. And they gave other
names to the cities that they built. 39 And the sons of [i]Machir the son of Manasseh went to
Gilead and captured it, and dispossessed the Amorites who were in it. 40 And Moses [j]gave
Gilead to Machir the son of Manasseh, and he settled in it. 41 And [k]Jair the son of Manasseh
went and captured their villages, and called them Havvoth-jair.[1] 42 And Nobah went and
captured Kenath and its villages, and called it Nobah, after his own name.

Recounting Israel's Journey

33 These are the stages of the people of Israel, when they went out of the land of Egypt
by their companies under the leadership of Moses and Aaron. 2 Moses wrote down
their starting places, [l]stage by stage, by command of the LORD, and these are their stages

[1] *Havvoth-jair means the villages of Jair*

21 [o]ch. 33:52
22 [p]Deut. 3:12, 15, 16, 18; Josh. 1:15; 13:8, 32; 22:4, 9
23 [q][Gen. 44:16; Isa. 59:12]
24 [r]ver. 16; See ver. 34-38
26 [s]Josh. 1:14
27 [t]Josh. 4:12, 13 [u]ch. 31:5
28 [v]Josh. 1:13 [w]ch. 27:18
33 [x]Deut. 29:8; Josh. 12:6; 13:8; 22:4; See Deut. 3:12-17
34 [y]ver. 3 [z]ver. 3 [a]See Deut. 2:36
35 [b]ver. 1; See ch. 21:32
36 [c][ver. 3] [d]ver. 17
37 [e]ver. 3; ch. 21:27 [y][See ver. 34 above]
38 [f]See ver. 3 [g][ver. 3; Josh. 13:17; Jer. 48:23] [h][Ex. 23:13; Josh. 23:7] [c][See ver. 36 above]
39 [i]Gen. 50:23; 1 Chr. 7:14, 15
40 [j]Deut. 3:13, 15; Josh. 13:31; 17:1
41 [k]Deut. 3:14; See 1 Chr. 2:21-23

Chapter 33
2 [l]See ch. 9:17-23

to their promise, they will be assigned land in Canaan instead (v. 30). They assure him that they will keep their promise (vv. 31–32).

32:23 Your sin will find you out, that is, "you will suffer for your sin." This statement assumes that God, in his providential knowledge and sovereign oversight of all things, always knows whether his people are faithful and will not endure unfaithfulness among them.

32:33–42 Following this final summary about the settlement of **Reuben** and **Gad** in Transjordan (vv. 33–38), the settlement of part of the tribe of **Manasseh** in northern **Gilead** is mentioned (vv. 39–42). It is defined more fully in Josh. 13:29–31. It is unclear why this has not been discussed before. Maybe it was not thought to be as controversial as Reuben and Gad's proposal, because northern Gilead fell within the boundaries of Canaan (see Numbers 34).

32:34 Dibon and **Aroer** subsequently belonged to Reuben (Josh. 13:16–17), whereas Heshbon (Num. 32:37) subsequently belonged to **Gad** (Josh. 21:39).

33:1–56 *Summary of Israel's Journey from Egypt to Canaan.* This list of camping places is unexpected at this point in Numbers. What is its function and why is it here? It comes straight after the threat posed by the settlement in Transjordan, when it seemed that some tribes might not have wanted to enter the Promised Land. Further, this is the only part of the book that is explicitly said to be written by Moses: most of the book is said to have been given to Moses by God, but only this is said to have been recorded by him (v. 2). It therefore serves as Moses' testimony of what God has done for Israel during his lifetime. By mentioning Aaron's death in vv. 38–39, Moses indirectly reminds the people that he too will die soon because of his disobedience (see 20:10–13). But this is not to suggest that God has failed his people; rather, this list of places where Israel triumphed over her enemies, was fed and watered, received the law, and was preserved for 40 years in the wilderness is proof that the Lord can bring Israel into Canaan—provided that they do not imitate the unbelief of their forefathers. The list therefore concludes with an urgent plea to make sure that all pagan worship is eliminated from Canaan when they enter it (33:50–56). Seventeen of the names in this list occur only here, and nothing more is known than that Israel camped at those places. Even places that are named elsewhere cannot necessarily be firmly located. Though tradition places Sinai at Jebel Musa in the southern Sinai Peninsula, clues within the narrative may point to a more northerly location. But these geographical uncertainties do not affect the historical and theological point of the passage, namely, God's sovereign and merciful guidance of Israel from Egypt to Canaan. This chapter is a uniform and complete description that reflects the form of a military itinerary. Such military itineraries are widely attested in the countries bordering on the eastern Mediterranean Sea: in ancient Egypt, for example, those of Thutmose III (c. 1479–1425 B.C.), Amenophis II (c. 1427–1401), and Sethos I (c. 1306–1290) provide prime examples of this literary genre.

33:1–4 These verses summarize Exodus 2–12. **On their gods also the**

according to their starting places. 3 They [m]set out from Rameses in [n]the first month, on the
fifteenth day of the first month. On the day after the Passover, the people of Israel went
out [o]triumphantly in the sight of all the Egyptians, 4 while the Egyptians were burying
all their firstborn, [p]whom the LORD had struck down among them. [q]On their gods also
the LORD executed judgments.

5 So the people of Israel set out from Rameses and camped at [r]Succoth. 6 And they set
out from Succoth and camped at [s]Etham, which is on the edge of the wilderness. 7 And
they set out from Etham and turned back to [t]Pi-hahiroth, which is east of Baal-zephon,
and they camped before Migdol. 8 And they set out from before Hahiroth[1] and [u]passed
through the midst of the sea into the wilderness, and they [v]went a three days' journey in
the wilderness of Etham and camped at Marah. 9 And they set out from Marah and came
to [w]Elim; at Elim there were twelve springs of water and seventy palm trees, and they
camped there. 10 And they set out from Elim and camped by the Red Sea. 11 And they set
out from the Red Sea and camped in [x]the wilderness of Sin. 12 And they set out from the
wilderness of Sin and camped at Dophkah. 13 And they set out from Dophkah and camped
at Alush. 14 And they set out from Alush and camped at [y]Rephidim, where there was no
water for the people to drink. 15 And they set out from Rephidim and camped in the [z]wil-
derness of Sinai. 16 And they set out from the wilderness of Sinai and camped at [a]Kibroth-
hattaavah. 17 And they set out from Kibroth-hattaavah and camped at [b]Hazeroth. 18 And
they [c]set out from Hazeroth and camped at Rithmah. 19 And they set out from Rithmah
and camped at Rimmon-perez. 20 And they set out from Rimmon-perez and camped at
Libnah. 21 And they set out from Libnah and camped at Rissah. 22 And they set out from
Rissah and camped at Kehelathah. 23 And they set out from Kehelathah and camped at
Mount Shepher. 24 And they set out from Mount Shepher and camped at Haradah. 25 And
they set out from Haradah and camped at Makheloth. 26 And they set out from Makheloth
and camped at Tahath. 27 And they set out from Tahath and camped at Terah. 28 And they
set out from Terah and camped at Mithkah. 29 And they set out from Mithkah and camped
at Hashmonah. 30 And they set out from Hashmonah and camped at Moseroth. 31 And they
set out from Moseroth and camped at [d]Bene-jaakan. 32 And they set out from Bene-jaakan
and camped at [e]Hor-haggidgad. 33 And they set out from Hor-haggidgad and camped at
[e]Jotbathah. 34 And they set out from Jotbathah and camped at Abronah. 35 And they set
out from Abronah and camped at [f]Ezion-geber. 36 And they set out from Ezion-geber and
camped in the [g]wilderness of Zin (that is, Kadesh). 37 And they set out from [h]Kadesh and
camped at [i]Mount Hor, on the edge of the land of Edom.

38 And Aaron the priest went up [j]Mount Hor at the command of the LORD and died there,
in the fortieth year after the people of Israel had come out of the land of Egypt, on the first
day of the fifth month. 39 And Aaron was [k]123 years old when he died on Mount Hor.

40 And [l]the Canaanite, the king of Arad, who lived in the Negeb in the land of Canaan,
heard of the coming of the people of Israel.

41 And they set out from Mount Hor and camped at Zalmonah. 42 And they set out from
Zalmonah and camped at Punon. 43 And they set out from Punon and camped at [m]Oboth.
44 And they set out from Oboth and camped at [n]Iye-abarim, in the territory of Moab. 45 And
they set out from Iyim and camped at [o]Dibon-gad. 46 And they set out from Dibon-gad and
camped at Almon-diblathaim. 47 And they set out from Almon-diblathaim [p]and camped in
the mountains of Abarim, before Nebo. 48 And they set out from the mountains of Abarim
and camped in [q]the plains of Moab by the Jordan at Jericho; 49 they camped by the Jordan
from Beth-jeshimoth as far as [r]Abel-shittim in the plains of Moab.

[1] Some manuscripts and versions *Pi-hahiroth*

3 [m]Ex. 12:37 [n]Ex. 12:2; 13:4 [o]Ex. 14:8
4 [p]Ex. 12:29 [q]Ex. 12:12; [Isa. 19:1]
5 [r]Ex. 12:37
6 [s]Ex. 13:20
7 [t]Ex. 14:2, 9
8 [u]Ex. 14:22 [v]Ex. 15:22, 23
9 [w]Ex. 15:27
11 [x]Ex. 16:1
14 [y]Ex. 17:1
15 [z]Ex. 19:1, 2
16 [a]ch. 11:34
17 [b]ch. 11:35; 12:16
18 [c]ch. 12:16
31 [d][Deut. 10:6]
32 [e]Deut. 10:7
33 [e][See ver. 32 above]
35 [f]Deut. 2:8; 1 Kgs. 9:26; 22:48; 2 Chr. 8:17
36 [g]ch. 20:1; 27:14
37 [h]ch. 20:1, 14, 22 [i]ch. 20:23; 21:4; 34:7, 8
38 [j]ch. 20:25-28; Deut. 32:50; [Deut. 10:6]
39 [k][Ex. 7:7]
40 [l]ch. 21:1
43 [m]ch. 21:10
44 [n]ch. 21:11
45 [o]ch. 21:30; [ch. 32:34]
47 [p]Deut. 32:49
48 [q]ch. 22:1
49 [r]See ch. 25:1

LORD executed judgments (Num. 33:4). The defeat of Pharaoh (who was regarded as divine) and the plagues of Egypt demonstrated that the Lord is more powerful than all the gods of Egypt. And as the Lord had treated the Egyptian gods, so Israel was to abolish the worship of rival deities in Canaan (v. 52).

33:5–15 These verses summarize Ex. 12:37–19:2.

33:16–17 These verses sum up Israel's journeys in chs. 10–11.

33:18–29 This section of the wilderness journey is mentioned only here.

33:30–34 This section of the wilderness journey is also probably mentioned in Deut. 10:6–7, if the similar place names are in fact the same places.

33:35 Ezion-geber is probably at the northern end of the Gulf of Aqaba.

33:37–49 These verses sum up Israel's journeys in chs. 20–25.

33:50–56 This stern warning against religious syncretism and cultural assimilation is repeated often in Deuteronomy and Judges. It concludes with a warning that Israel herself will go into exile if she compromises: **I will do to you as I thought to do to them** (Num. 33:56). Its insistence that the land

Drive Out the Inhabitants

50 And the LORD spoke to Moses in the plains of Moab by the Jordan at Jericho, saying, 51 "Speak to the people of Israel and say to them, [s]When you pass over the Jordan into the land of Canaan, 52 then [t]you shall drive out [u]all the inhabitants of the land from before you and destroy all their [v]figured stones and destroy all their metal images and demolish all their high places. 53 And you shall take possession of the land and settle in it, for I have given the land to you to possess it. 54 [w]You shall inherit the land by lot according to your clans. [x]To a large tribe you shall give a large inheritance, and to a small tribe you shall give a small inheritance. Wherever the lot falls for anyone, that shall be his. According to the tribes of your fathers you shall inherit. 55 But if you do not drive out the inhabitants of the land from before you, then those of them whom you let remain shall be as [y]barbs in your eyes and thorns in your sides, and they shall trouble you in the land where you dwell. 56 And I will do to you [z]as I thought to do to them."

Boundaries of the Land

34 The LORD spoke to Moses, saying, 2 "Command the people of Israel, and say to them, When you enter [a]the land of Canaan [b](this is the land that shall fall to you for an inheritance, the land of Canaan as defined by its borders), 3 [c]your south side shall be from the wilderness of Zin alongside Edom, and your southern border shall run from the end of [d]the Salt Sea on the east. 4 And your border shall turn south of [e]the ascent of Akrabbim, and cross to Zin, and its limit shall be south of Kadesh-barnea. Then it shall go on to [e]Hazar-addar, and pass along to Azmon. 5 And the border shall turn [f]from Azmon to [g]the Brook of Egypt, and its limit shall be at the sea.

6 "For the western border, you shall have the Great Sea and its[1] coast. This shall be your western border.

7 "This shall be your northern border: from the Great Sea you shall draw a line to [h]Mount Hor. 8 From Mount Hor you shall draw a line [i]to Lebo-hamath, and the limit of the border shall be at [j]Zedad. 9 Then the border shall extend to Ziphron, and its limit shall be at [k]Hazar-enan. This shall be your northern border.

10 "You shall draw a line for your eastern border from Hazar-enan to Shepham. 11 And the border shall go down from Shepham to [l]Riblah on the east side of Ain. And the border shall go down and reach to the shoulder of [m]the Sea of Chinnereth on the east. 12 And the border shall go down to the Jordan, and its limit shall be at [n]the Salt Sea. This shall be your land as defined by its borders all around."

13 Moses commanded the people of Israel, saying, [o]"This is the land that you shall inherit by lot, which the LORD has commanded to give to the nine tribes and to the half-tribe. 14 [p]For the tribe of the people of Reuben by fathers' houses and the tribe of the people of Gad by their fathers' houses have received their inheritance, and also the half-tribe of Manasseh. 15 The two tribes and the half-tribe have received their inheritance beyond the Jordan east of Jericho, toward the sunrise."

List of Tribal Chiefs

16 The LORD spoke to Moses, saying, 17 "These are the names of the men who shall divide the land to you for inheritance: [q]Eleazar the priest and Joshua the son of Nun. 18 You shall

[1] Syriac; Hebrew lacks *its*

51 [s]Deut. 9:1; [Josh. 3:17]
52 [t]ch. 32:21 [u]Ex. 23:24, 33; 34:13; Deut. 7:2, 5; 12:3 [v]Lev. 26:1
54 [w]ch. 26:53, 55 [x]ch. 26:54; 35:8
55 [y]Josh. 23:13; Judg. 2:3; Ps. 106:34, 36
56 [z][Deut. 28:63]

Chapter 34

2 [a]Gen. 17:8; Ex. 3:8; Ps. 105:11 [b]ver. 13
3 [c]Josh. 15:1; See Gen. 15:18-21; Ezek. 47:13-21 [d]ver. 12; Gen. 14:3; Josh. 15:2
4 [e]Josh. 15:3
5 [f]Josh. 15:4 [g]Gen. 15:18; Josh. 15:4, 47; 1 Kgs. 8:65; 2 Kgs. 24:7; 1 Chr. 13:5; 2 Chr. 7:8; Isa. 27:12
7 [h]ch. 33:37
8 [i]ch. 13:21; 2 Kgs. 14:25; Ezek. 48:1 [j]Ezek. 47:15
9 [k]Ezek. 47:17
11 [l]2 Kgs. 23:33; Jer. 39:5 [m]Deut. 3:17; Josh. 11:2; 12:3; 19:35; Matt. 4:18; Luke 5:1
12 [n]ver. 3
13 [o]ver. 2; Josh. 14:1, 2
14 [p]ch. 32:33; Josh. 14:3
17 [q]Josh. 14:1; 19:51

must be divided among the tribes in proportion to their size and allocated by lot (v. 54) repeats the instruction of 26:53–56. The census had determined the size of the tribes; now the focus is on the land. Its boundaries will be defined in ch. 34, and the chiefs are appointed to oversee the allocation of the land (34:17–29).

34:1–15 *The Boundaries of Canaan.* The promise to Abraham was that his descendants would be given "all the land of Canaan" (Gen. 17:8). But hitherto the boundaries of Canaan have never been stated. The definition here, as the Lord gives it, corresponds to that found in Egyptian texts of the fifteenth to thirteenth centuries B.C., which is the era of Moses. In fact, Israel never occupied all this territory—it represents the *Promised* Land, not the subsequently occupied land, of Israel. The boundary is not always clear. Oversimplifying, Canaan consisted of the land between the Mediterranean and the Jordan plus modern Lebanon and a portion of modern Syria. See map, p. 320.

34:1–5 *The Southern Border.* The southern border of the Promised Land runs from the southern end of the Dead Sea (**the Salt Sea**), **south of Kadesh-barnea**, to the Mediterranean coast, west of Gaza (**the Brook of Egypt**).

34:6 *The Western Border.* The western border of the Promised Land is the Mediterranean (**the Great Sea**).

34:7–9 *The Northern Border.* The northern border of the Promised Land runs from the Mediterranean, north of Byblos, to **Hazar-enan**, perhaps an oasis on the edge of the desert somewhere east of Zedad.

34:10–15 *The Eastern Border.* The eastern border of the Promised Land is the hardest to define. From **Hazar-enan** it apparently runs southward along the edge of the desert before swinging westward to the Sea of Galilee (**Sea of Chinnereth**). From there it runs south along the Jordan to the Dead Sea.

34:16–29 *The Distributors of the Land.* These distributors are the tribal

take one [r]chief from every tribe to divide the land for inheritance. 19 These are the names
of the men: Of the tribe of Judah, Caleb the son of Jephunneh. 20 Of the tribe of the people
of Simeon, Shemuel the son of Ammihud. 21 Of the tribe of Benjamin, Elidad the son of
Chislon. 22 Of the tribe of the people of Dan a chief, Bukki the son of Jogli. 23 Of the people
of Joseph: of the tribe of the people of Manasseh a chief, Hanniel the son of Ephod. 24 And
of the tribe of the people of Ephraim a chief, Kemuel the son of Shiphtan. 25 Of the tribe of
the people of Zebulun a chief, Elizaphan the son of Parnach. 26 Of the tribe of the people of
Issachar a chief, Paltiel the son of Azzan. 27 And of the tribe of the people of Asher a chief,
Ahihud the son of Shelomi. 28 Of the tribe of the people of Naphtali a chief, Pedahel the son
of Ammihud. 29 These are the men whom the LORD commanded to divide the inheritance
for the people of Israel in the land of Canaan."

Cities for the Levites

35 The LORD spoke to Moses in [s]the plains of Moab by the Jordan at Jericho, saying,
2 [t]"Command the people of Israel to give to the Levites some of the inheritance of
their possession as cities for them to dwell in. And you shall give to the Levites pasturelands around the cities. 3 The cities shall be theirs to dwell in, and their pasturelands shall

18 [r]ch. 1:4, 16
Chapter 35
1 [s]See ch. 22:1
2 [t]Josh. 14:3, 4; 21:2; See Ezek. 45:1-5; 48:8-14

chiefs of the 10 tribes who will settle west of the Jordan. Thus no chiefs of Reuben and Gad are listed, because they are settling in Transjordan. The chiefs are mentioned in the order of the lands they eventually received from south to north. On this principle, Simeon, as the southernmost tribe, ought to precede Judah. But Judah, being the foremost tribe in the book of Numbers (see 2:2–9), actually heads the list. Apart from Caleb, chief of Judah, the other named chiefs are mentioned nowhere else in Scripture; nevertheless, they are important: **These are the men whom the LORD commanded to divide the inheritance for the people of Israel in the land of Canaan** (34:29).

35:1–8 *Cities for the Levites.* After the censuses for the secular tribes always come the censuses of the Levites (chs. 1–3; 26). The second census was for determining the size of the tribes so as to give them an appropriately sized territory. But the Levites were expressly excluded from inheriting land

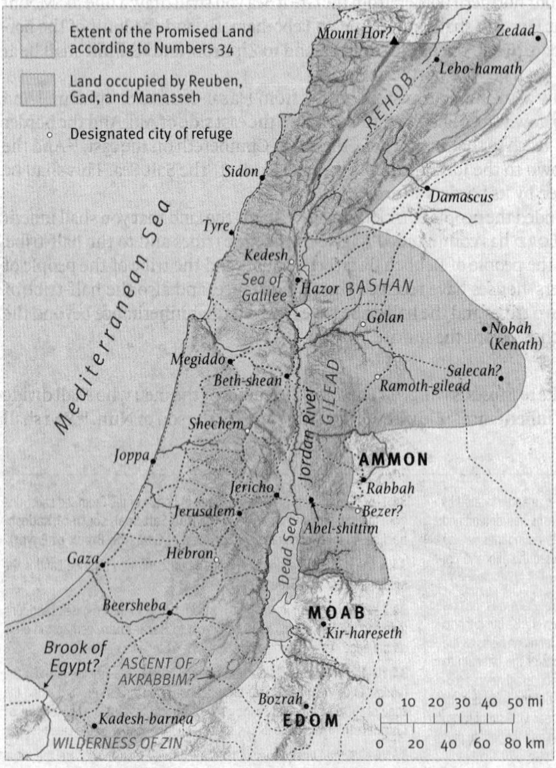

The Boundaries of the Promised Land
The original boundaries of the Promised Land as defined in Numbers 34 are somewhat different from the boundaries of the land that the Israelites eventually occupied. The original boundaries included the mountainous area north of Sidon and Damascus, but the Israelites never occupied this area during the settlement period. Conversely, the original boundaries did not include land east of the Jordan River, but the Israelites occupied this land after capturing it from Og and Sihon.

6 [u]ver. 13; Deut. 4:41, 42; Josh. 20:2, 7, 8; 21:3, 13, 21, 27, 32, 36, 38
7 [v]Josh. 21:41
8 [w]Josh. 21:3 [x]ch. 26:54; 33:54
10 [y]For ver. 10-12, see Deut. 19:2-4; Josh. 20:2-6
11 [z]Ex. 21:13
13 [a]See ver. 6
14 [b]Deut. 4:41; Josh. 20:8
15 [c]ch. 15:16
16 [d]Ex. 21:12, 14; Lev. 24:17; Deut. 19:11, 12
19 [e]Deut. 19:6, 12; Josh. 20:3, 5
20 [f]Ex. 21:14; Deut. 19:11
21 [e][See ver. 19 above]
22 [g]Ex. 21:13

be for their cattle and for their livestock and for all their beasts. 4 The pasturelands of the
cities, which you shall give to the Levites, shall reach from the wall of the city outward
a thousand cubits[1] all around. 5 And you shall measure, outside the city, on the east side
two thousand cubits, and on the south side two thousand cubits, and on the west side two
thousand cubits, and on the north side two thousand cubits, the city being in the middle.
This shall belong to them as pastureland for their cities.
6 “The cities that you give to the Levites shall be [u]the six cities of refuge, where you shall
permit the manslayer to flee, and in addition to them you shall give forty-two cities. 7 All
the cities that you give to the Levites shall be [v]forty-eight, with their pasturelands. 8 And
as for the cities that you shall give [w]from the possession of the people of Israel, [x]from the
larger tribes you shall take many, and from the smaller tribes you shall take few; each, in
proportion to the inheritance that it inherits, shall give of its cities to the Levites.”

Cities of Refuge

9 And the LORD spoke to Moses, saying, 10 “Speak to the people of Israel and say to them,
[y]When you cross the Jordan into the land of Canaan, 11 [z]then you shall select cities to be
cities of refuge for you, that the manslayer who kills any person without intent may flee
there. 12 The cities shall be for you a refuge from the avenger, that the manslayer may not
die until he stands before the congregation for judgment. 13 And the cities that you give
shall be your [a]six cities of refuge. 14 [b]You shall give three cities beyond the Jordan, and three
cities in the land of Canaan, to be cities of refuge. 15 These six cities shall be for refuge for
the people of Israel, and [c]for the stranger and for the sojourner among them, that anyone
who kills any person without intent may flee there.
16 [d]“But if he struck him down with an iron object, so that he died, he is a murderer.
The murderer shall be put to death. 17 And if he struck him down with a stone tool that
could cause death, and he died, he is a murderer. The murderer shall be put to death.
18 Or if he struck him down with a wooden tool that could cause death, and he died, he
is a murderer. The murderer shall be put to death. 19 [e]The avenger of blood shall himself
put the murderer to death; when he meets him, he shall put him to death. 20 And if he
pushed him out of hatred or hurled something at him, [f]lying in wait, so that he died, 21 or
in enmity struck him down with his hand, so that he died, then he who struck the blow
shall be put to death. He is a murderer. [e]The avenger of blood shall put the murderer to
death when he meets him.
22 “But if he pushed him suddenly without enmity, or hurled anything on him [g]without
lying in wait 23 or used a stone that could cause death, and without seeing him dropped it on

[1] A *cubit* was about 18 inches or 45 centimeters

(26:52–62). Nevertheless, they had to live somewhere and needed land to graze the livestock they received in tithes from the other tribes. Arrangements for the other tribes were discussed in 34:16–29, so now the Levites' needs are broached. Basically the Levites are assigned 48 cities (in reality, little villages) and their immediately surrounding grazing land. The grazing land stretched for **a thousand cubits** (500 yards [457 m]) from the city wall (35:4). This meant that if the "city" was very small, the grazing lands would stretch **two thousand cubits** in each direction (v. 5). Commentators assume that in the case of larger settlements, the pasturelands would still stretch 1,000 cubits outward from the city wall, but overall the total size of the settlement would be bigger. Among the Levitical cities are six cities of refuge, whose function is described in vv. 9–34. Forty-two other cities had to be chosen elsewhere, to make a total of 48. Big tribes had to have more Levitical cities, and small tribes had to have fewer cities (v. 8). Joshua 21 reports the fulfillment of this command, but most tribes ended up with four Levitical cities each.

35:9–34 *The Cities of Refuge.* The fact that this rule is mentioned at this point is explained by the mention of the cities of refuge in v. 6. The theological reason for the rule is given at the end of the section: "You shall not defile the land in which you live, in the midst of which I dwell" (v. 34). Canaan is the holy land, not because Israel lives there but because God dwells there. He is the preeminently holy one, and sin and death are in absolute opposition to him (see note on 5:1–6:27). If the land is made unclean by violent death, drastic measures have to be taken to make atonement; otherwise the Lord will forsake the land and Israel will be exiled. The cities of refuge and the laws associated with them show how cases of homicide are to be handled, in order to prevent the nation's being forsaken. The Israelite system of justice involved the injured party seeking relief in court from the aggressor. In the case of homicide, the male relative closest to the murder victim was expected to exact retribution. This is the situation envisaged in 35:11–15. In hot anger, the avenger may hunt down the killer and execute him. But the "manslayer" should run to the nearest city of refuge to stand trial "before the congregation," that is, the whole populace (or its representatives). The judges will then decide whether the killer deserves to be executed for his crime. The criteria are set out in vv. 16–24.

35:9–15 *The Selection and Purpose of These Cities.* **Six cities of refuge** were chosen: **three . . . beyond the Jordan** (Bezer, Ramoth-gilead, and Golan), and **three . . . in the land of Canaan** (Hebron, Shechem, and Kedesh). The law of refuge applied not just to the Israelites but also to the **stranger** and the **sojourner** (cf. 9:14; 15:15; 19:10; Lev. 16:29; 17:8, 15; 18:26; 20:2; 24:16).

35:16–21 *Homicide That Warrants the Death Penalty.* The common factor that links these examples is planning or premeditation. The killer in these cases had with him a lethal weapon (an iron tool or a stone), or he was known to hate his victim, or he lay in wait for him. These killings all count as murder, and the avenger of blood may execute the killer.

35:22–29 *Homicide That Does Not Deserve Death.* These are killings that are not planned but are the result of an accident or impulsive behavior. In

him, so that he died, though he was not his enemy and did not seek his harm, **24** then [h]the
congregation shall judge between the manslayer and [e]the avenger of blood, in accordance
with these rules. **25** And the congregation shall rescue the manslayer from the hand of the
avenger of blood, and the congregation shall restore him to his city of refuge to which he
had fled, and he shall live in it [i]until the death of the high priest [j]who was anointed with
the holy oil. **26** But if the manslayer shall at any time go beyond the boundaries of his city
of refuge to which he fled, **27** and [e]the avenger of blood finds him outside the boundaries
of his city of refuge, and the avenger of blood kills the manslayer, he shall not be guilty of
blood. **28** For he must remain in his city of refuge [i]until the death of the high priest, but
after the death of the high priest the manslayer may return to the land of his possession.
29 And these things shall be for [k]a statute and rule for you throughout your generations
in all your dwelling places.

30 "If anyone kills a person, the murderer shall be put to death on the [l]evidence of witnesses. But no person shall be put to death on the testimony of one witness. **31** Moreover,
you shall accept no ransom for the life of a murderer, who is guilty of death, but he shall be
put to death. **32** And you shall accept no ransom for him who has fled to his city of refuge,
that he may return to dwell in the land before the death of the high priest. **33** You shall not
[m]pollute the land in which you live, for blood [m]pollutes the land, and no atonement can
be made for the land for the blood that is shed in it, except [n]by the blood of the one who
shed it. **34** [o]You shall not defile the land in which you live, in the midst of which I dwell,
[p]for I the LORD dwell in the midst of the people of Israel."

Marriage of Female Heirs

36
The heads of the fathers' houses of the clan of the [q]people of Gilead the son of
Machir, son of Manasseh, from the clans of the people of Joseph, came near and
spoke before Moses and before the chiefs, the heads of the fathers' houses of the people
of Israel. **2** They said, [r]"The LORD commanded my lord to give the land for inheritance by
lot to the people of Israel, and [s]my lord was commanded by the LORD to give the inheritance of Zelophehad our brother to his daughters. **3** But if they are married to any of the
sons of the other tribes of the people of Israel, then their inheritance will be taken from
the inheritance of our fathers and added to the inheritance of the tribe into which they
marry. So it will be taken away from the lot of our inheritance. **4** And when [t]the jubilee of
the people of Israel comes, then their inheritance will be added to the inheritance of the
tribe into which they marry, and their inheritance will be taken from the inheritance of
the tribe of our fathers."

5 And Moses commanded the people of Israel according to the word of the LORD, saying,
"The tribe of the people of Joseph [u]is right. **6** This is what the LORD commands concerning
the daughters of Zelophehad: 'Let them marry whom they think best, [v]only they shall marry
within the clan of the tribe of their father. **7** The inheritance of the people of Israel shall

24 [h]ver. 12; Josh. 20:6 [e][See ver. 19 above]
25 [i]Josh. 20:6 [j]Ex. 29:7; Lev. 4:3; 21:10
27 [e][See ver. 19 above]
28 [i][See ver. 25 above]
29 [k]ch. 27:11
30 [l]Deut. 17:6; 19:15; Heb. 10:28; [Matt. 18:16; John 8:17; 2 Cor. 13:1; 1 Tim. 5:19]
33 [m]Ps. 106:38; Jer. 3:1, 2, 9; [Mic. 4:11] [n]See Gen. 9:6
34 [o]Lev. 18:25; Deut. 21:23 [p]See Ex. 29:45

Chapter 36

1 [q]ch. 26:29
2 [r]ch. 26:55; 33:54 [s]ch. 27:1, 7; Josh. 17:3, 4
4 [t]Lev. 25:10
5 [u][ch. 27:7]
6 [v]ver. 12

these cases **the congregation shall rescue the manslayer from the hand of the avenger of blood** (v. 25). However, the killer in this case is not deemed totally innocent: he is punished by being confined to one of the cities of refuge. If the avenger of blood finds him outside the boundaries of the city, he may kill him. The manslayer must stay there until the high priest dies.

35:30–34 *Final Points.* At least two **witnesses** are required for a murder conviction (v. 30; see also Deut. 19:15–21). The laws of Ex. 21:28–32 allow for ransom when someone is killed by a bull. In other words, instead of the bull's owner being put to death, the victim's family may accept monetary compensation (ransom) instead. Numbers 35 prohibits such an arrangement in these cases. **Ransom** is not permitted in the case of murder or less culpable homicide, for as v. 33 puts it, **no atonement can be made for the land for the blood that is shed in it, except by the blood of the one who shed it** (see also Gen. 9:5–6).

36:1–13 *Zelophehad's Daughters Marry.* In 27:1–11 Zelophehad's daughters had requested a change in inheritance rules, where a man had daughters but no sons. In this situation they had asked that daughters be allowed to inherit. This was granted. Now the heads of Zelophehad's clan see a snag: if these daughters marry husbands from another tribe, their land will become the property of that tribe. Then the tribe of Manasseh, to which Zelophehad belonged, will lose that land, because it will not revert to the original tribe in the year of **jubilee** (36:4). The Jubilee Year occurred every 50 years, and in it, land which had been sold returned to its original owner (Lev. 25:10–28). But this did not apply to land that was transferred through marriage. Normally when men married, there was no transfer of land; it stayed within the man's own tribe. But if a land-owning daughter married, the land would be transferred to her husband's family and tribe. To prevent tribal land being lost through intermarriage, Moses rules that Zelophehad's daughters must marry men from their own tribe (Num. 36:6). In this way tribal lands will be preserved: **every one of the people of Israel shall hold on to the inheritance of the tribe of his fathers** (v. 7). So important is this principle that it is repeated in v. 9. Happily this all worked out, for the daughters married their cousins (v. 11). This insistence that "every one . . . shall hold on to" his own inheritance is more than a legal obligation: it is a promise that the tribes will always live in their God-given land. In the words of Gen. 17:8, "I will give to you and to your offspring . . . all the land of Canaan, for an everlasting possession." This makes a fitting conclusion to a book whose principal interest is to show how Israel was brought to the verge of the Promised Land. But in another way the book leaves the reader in suspense. The last time the situation of the daughters of Zelophehad was discussed, there immediately followed the command to

7[w][1 Kgs. 21:3]
8[x]1 Chr. 23:22
11[y]ch. 27:1; Josh. 17:3
13[z]See ch. 22:1

not be transferred from one tribe to another, for every one of the people of Israel [w]shall
hold on to the inheritance of the tribe of his fathers. 8 And [x]every daughter who possesses
an inheritance in any tribe of the people of Israel shall be wife to one of the clan of the
tribe of her father, so that every one of the people of Israel may possess the inheritance of
his fathers. 9 So no inheritance shall be transferred from one tribe to another, for each of
the tribes of the people of Israel shall hold on to its own inheritance.'"

10 The daughters of Zelophehad did as the LORD commanded Moses, 11 [y]for Mahlah,
Tirzah, Hoglah, Milcah, and Noah, the daughters of Zelophehad, were married to sons of
their father's brothers. 12 They were married into the clans of the people of Manasseh the
son of Joseph, and their inheritance remained in the tribe of their father's clan.

13 These are the commandments and the rules that the LORD commanded through Moses
to the people of Israel [z]in the plains of Moab by the Jordan at Jericho.

Moses to go up the mountain to die (Num. 27:12). This command has still not been fulfilled, so Numbers requires a sequel. And that is provided by the book of Deuteronomy.

36:13 The book closes by reminding the reader that **the LORD commanded** its content **through Moses**, i.e., through the preeminent prophet (cf. 12:6–8). Israel's good lies in heeding these instructions. The very last word, in both Hebrew and English, is **Jericho**, looking forward to the first stage in the conquest (Josh. 2:1).

INTRODUCTION TO

DEUTERONOMY

Author and Title

The name "Deuteronomy" derives from the Greek for "second law," an early mistranslation of "copy of this law" in 17:18. In fact, Deuteronomy emphasizes that its laws are not a new law but rather the preaching of the original law given to Israel at Sinai.

Deuteronomy 31:9 records that Moses wrote down "this law," most likely referring to chapters 1–30. Certainly the bulk of these chapters is the speech of Moses to Israel in the plains of Moab at the end of the 40-year wilderness period and immediately preceding the conquest under Joshua. Later OT and NT statements also assume Mosaic authorship (cf. Josh. 23:6; 1 Kings 2:3; Mal. 4:4; Matt. 19:7–8; Rom. 10:19).

Date

There are two main issues related to the dating of this book. One is the date of the conquest, and hence of Moses' life. The dating of the conquest is disputed, with the two major positions placing it in the late fifteenth century B.C. (about 1406) or in the thirteenth century (about 1220; for further discussion, see Introduction to the Historical Books, pp. 385–387).

The second issue is the dating of the book itself. If Moses is the author, then the two issues are more or less the same. However, another widely held view is that the book should be dated long after Moses. Some would date the book to the time of King Josiah in the latter part of the seventh century B.C. (2 Kings 22:8–13). Certainly Josiah's reforms were advanced by the finding of a book, probably Deuteronomy, in the temple. However, this need not indicate that the book was written then. Others argue that while there may be material in Deuteronomy from the time of Josiah, it was subsequently edited in the exilic period of the sixth century B.C.

The view taken in these notes is that the book substantially dates from Moses himself, in agreement with its internal testimony (cf. Deut. 31:9, 24). The parallels with ancient treaties, especially the Hittite treaties from the second millennium, also point to an early date, thus around the fifteenth or thirteenth century B.C.

Structure

There are a number of similarities between the structure of Deuteronomy and ancient treaty documents. In particular, treaties from the Hittites of the second millennium and treaties from the Assyrians of the eighth century B.C. have clear affinities with the structure of Deuteronomy, though each with differences. Though Deuteronomy does not perfectly match the treaties of the Hittites, it is much closer in structure to them than to the later Assyrian treaties.

A simple summary of the treaty structure, with Deuteronomy's verses, is shown on the chart to the right.

Ancient Treaty Structure	Deuteronomy
Preamble	1:1–5
Historical Prologue	1:6–4:43
General Stipulations	4:44–11:32
Specific Stipulations	12:1–26:19
Blessings and Curses	27:1–28:68
Document Clause	31:9–29
Witnesses	32:1–47

Theme

Deuteronomy, the last installment of Moses' biography, contains his last three sermons and two prophetic poems about Israel's future. Reflecting on the nation's past mistakes, he urges the people not to repeat those mistakes when entering the Promised Land. Israel's entry fulfills the promises made to the patriarchs, but if the people fall into idolatry or fail to keep the law, they will be exiled.

Purpose, Occasion, and Background

Deuteronomy is largely a sermon, or set of sermons, preached by Moses to all of Israel shortly before his death and not long before the conquest of the land under the leadership of Joshua. It is a motivational sermon, urging Israel's faithful obedience to the covenant laws of Sinai given 40 years previously.

The circumstance of the sermon carries added significance because of Israel's failure, a generation earlier, to conquer the land starting at Kadesh-barnea on the southern border of Canaan (see 1:19–46). Now that they are back at the eastern border of the Promised Land, Deuteronomy seeks to ensure that such failure does not recur. The rhetorical style of the sermon motivates obedience by constantly reassuring them of God's faithfulness and his power to keep his promise of land. This faithfulness of God remains despite Israel's persistent sin, detailed at length (e.g., 1:19–46; 9:1–29). Thus Deuteronomy demonstrates that God's faithfulness results in mercy to his sinful people, for the sake of his promises to Abraham.

The theology of Deuteronomy is focused on convincing Israel to trust and obey, and to conquer the land. The uniqueness and incomparability of God is clearly argued (e.g., ch. 4). His power over other nations and armies is evident (e.g., 2:1–23). His grace and faithfulness are also stressed, with frequent reminders that the land is sworn by him on oath and is undeserved (9:4–6) and full of good things (e.g., 6:10–12).

The book's emphasis on the continuation of the covenant made at Sinai with the previous generation underscores the abiding significance of God's law for his people (e.g., see 5:1–3). The large central section of Deuteronomy (12:1–26:19) recites the law, consistently urging Israel to keep it. The law is wide-ranging, incorporating all areas of life—economics, family and sexual relationships, religious observance, leadership, justice, guidance, food, property, and warfare. To some extent, the detail of the laws fleshes out the great command of 6:5, that Israel is to love the Lord with all its heart, soul, and strength. Chapters 12–16 show what such total love of God will look like and, in many respects, provide examples of what the Ten Commandments (ch. 5) mean in practice.

Function of Deuteronomy in the Bible

Deuteronomy is an important book. It concludes the Pentateuch (the first five books of the Bible), drawing together many of its key themes. Deuteronomy brings together the patriarchal promises, the history of the exodus and wilderness, and the laws given at Sinai. It also provides a theological foundation for the history books that follow (esp. Joshua–2 Kings). The language of Deuteronomy is often found in these later books, so much so that they are sometimes referred to as the Deuteronomistic History. Deuteronomy is surely the key book undergirding the reforms of Josiah in 2 Kings 23 and is referred to by several of the prophets, especially Jeremiah and Hosea. Deuteronomy is also frequently quoted in the NT, most notably by Jesus in his wilderness temptations and by Paul in his letter to the Romans.

Deuteronomy and Ethics

The ethical application of OT law is a complex issue. There is no one rule that will cover the ethical application of all the laws in Deuteronomy; each law needs to be handled on a case-by-case basis. While many OT laws will not be kept by Christians to the letter, the laws embody important and abiding principles for Christian ethical behavior. Sometimes those OT principles are modified in the NT; often they are reinforced. For instance, the sacrificial system finds its fulfillment in the cross of Christ, but the principles of OT sacrifice are still instructive for Christians.

As a further example, the laws that define sexual morality and the principles underlying those laws are unchanged in the NT. Indeed, Jesus shows the deeper intent of the laws on sexual matters in the Sermon on the Mount (Matt. 5:27–30). However, the laws in Deuteronomy on warfare are not repeated for the NT church because God's people are no longer a nation and the land to be inherited is now heavenly (1 Pet. 1:4). Nonetheless, the principles of maintaining the holiness of God's people and of God judging sin remain unchanged.

It is important to recognize that there are different kinds of laws and rules in Deuteronomy. Many of

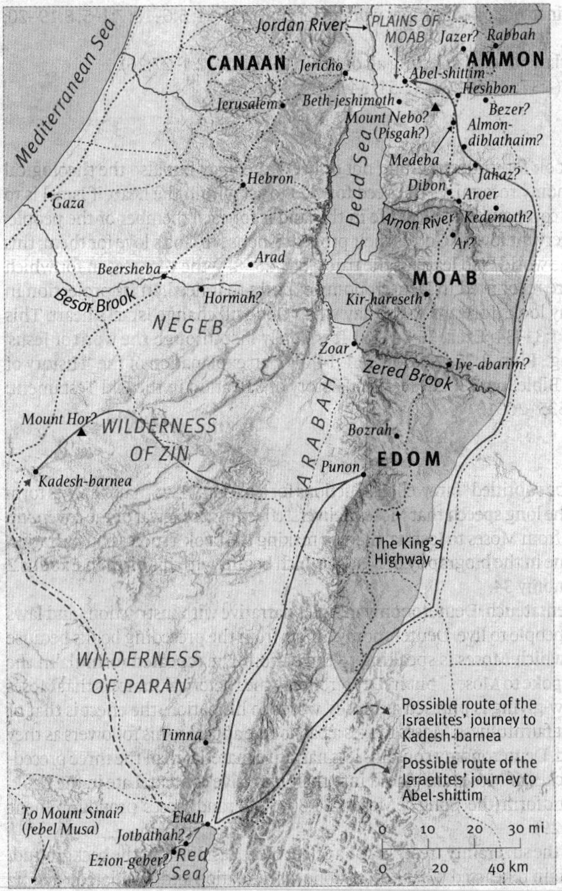

The Setting of Deuteronomy
c. 1406/1220 B.C.
The book of Deuteronomy recounts Moses' words to the Israelites as they waited on the plains of Moab to enter Canaan. Moses begins by reviewing the events of Israel's journey from Mount Sinai (or Mount Horeb) to the plains of Moab.

the specific laws, especially those that detail penalties that judges are to impose, do not intend to spell out the ethical ideals for God's people; their main function is to set the minimum standard of behavior needed to protect Israel's theocracy. The "perfection" (Ps. 19:7) of these laws consists in the way they preserve the social fabric of the theocracy. The ethical ideals for God's people ultimately come from the creation pattern (the "image of God") and from the goal of community holiness. (See the note on Deut. 24:1–4 for an example.) In addition, Deuteronomy constantly addresses the "heart" of its audience: embracing this law, seeking the good of this people, is the right response to God's grace and the embodiment of virtue.

Key Themes

1. The uniqueness of God (4:1–40).
2. The election of Israel (4:37–38; 7:6–8; 10:14–15; 14:2).
3. The goodness of the land that God has promised to give Israel (1:25; 6:10–11; 8:7–13; 11:8–15).
4. The faithfulness of God, despite Israel's sin, to keep his promise of land made originally to Abraham (1:8, 19–46; 7:1–26; 8:1–20; 9:1–10:11).
5. The power of God to defeat the enemies in the land (2:1–3:11; 4:1–40; 7:1–26).
6. Exhortations to Israel to love, serve, fear, and obey God (6:5; 10:12–13; 13:4).

7. Warnings against idolatry and instruction for proper worship of God (4:9–31; 5:6–10; 7:1–5; 8:19–20; 12:1–32; 13:1–18).
8. The comprehensiveness of the laws of God affecting all of life in the land (12:1–27:26).
9. The imminent death of Moses (1:37; 3:26; 4:21; 32:51; 34:1–12).

History of Salvation Summary

Deuteronomy is an important book for understanding not only OT theology but also the theological unity of both Testaments. Deuteronomy recognizes the need for God to act within the heart if Israel is to achieve faithful obedience to God's covenant. The ideal life in the land is for each member of the people, and the body as a whole, to display fervent love to God as their proper response to God's love for them; this is the means by which the rest of the world is to learn of the true God (4:5–8)—the very reason for which Israel exists. Israel's record of failure recounted in Deuteronomy exposes that need. In its projection in 4:29–31 and 30:1–20, Deuteronomy looks forward to the day when God will change Israel's heart. This longing recurs in the OT (e.g., Jer. 31:31–34; Ezek. 36:24–28). It is finally met through the work of Jesus' death and the giving of his Spirit (e.g., Rom. 2:25–29; Col. 2:11–14). (For an explanation of the "History of Salvation," see the Overview of the Bible, pp. 23–26. See also History of Salvation in the Old Testament: Preparing the Way for Christ, pp. 2635–2661.)

Literary Features

The book of Deuteronomy could be subtitled "farewell instructions for a nation." Two major events form the substance of Deuteronomy: (1) the long speech that Moses delivers, effecting a renewal of the covenant, and (2) the passing of the leadership from Moses to Joshua, thereby making the book a succession narrative. The book thus forms the final volume in the biography of Moses, which begins with his birth in Exodus 2 and ends with his death in Deuteronomy 34.

Like the preceding books of the Pentateuch, Deuteronomy mingles narrative with instructions and laws by which God wanted his covenant people to live. Deuteronomy differs from the preceding books because it is cast as a farewell discourse in which Moses is speaking to the nation. The repeated formula in the preceding three books is "the LORD spoke to Moses," but in Deuteronomy the rhetorical stance is that Moses speaks to the people. Because the law-giving is phrased as Moses' words to his nation, the effect is that of an extended exhortation to covenant faithfulness. Moses makes a passionate appeal to his followers as they are about to enter the Promised Land. Deuteronomy contains less narrative material than the three preceding books, but occasionally the speeches of Moses are placed into their narrative context. Late in the book, two formal discourses are cast in poetic form (the "Song of Moses," 31:30–32:47; and Moses' pronouncement of blessing on the nation, 32:48–33:29).

It is likely that the literary form of the suzerainty treaty of the ancient Near East lurks in the background. In a suzerainty treaty, a king or suzerain rehearsed what he had done for his nation and stipulated what he required in response. There is also an incipient note of anticipation, as it is understood that the instructions are given to a people on the verge of setting up a utopia—a good society governed by identifiable institutions and practices—in a promised land.

Outline

I. Prologue (1:1–5)

II. Moses' First Speech: Historical Prologue (1:6–4:43)

- A. Introduction to first speech (1:6–8)
- B. Encouragement to trust in the land of promise (1:9–18)
- C. Israel's failure at Kadesh recalled (1:19–46)
- D. Israel passes through Edom, Moab, and Ammon (2:1–23)
- E. Israel defeats Heshbon (2:24–37)
- F. Israel defeats Bashan (3:1–11)
- G. Distribution of Transjordanian land (3:12–17)
- H. Command to all Israelites to fight (3:18–22)
- I. Reiteration of Moses being denied entry into the land (3:23–29)

J. Exhortation to Israel (4:1–40)
K. Setting apart cities of refuge (4:41–43)

III. Moses' Second Speech: General Covenant Stipulations (4:44–11:32)
A. Introduction to Moses' second speech (4:44–49)
B. The Ten Commandments (5:1–21)
C. Israel requests Moses to mediate God's law (5:22–33)
D. The greatest commandment (6:1–25)
E. Exclusive relationship worked out in conquest and worship (7:1–26)
F. Learning the lessons of the wilderness (8:1–20)
G. Recounting the golden calf incident (9:1–10:11)
H. Exhortation (10:12–11:32)

IV. Moses' Second Speech: Specific Covenant Stipulations (12:1–26:19)
A. Proper worship (12:1–32)
B. Threats of idolatry (13:1–18)
C. Clean and unclean foods (14:1–21)
D. Tithes (14:22–29)
E. The sabbatical year (15:1–18)
F. Firstborn animals (15:19–23)
G. Feasts (16:1–17)
H. Leaders (16:18–18:22)
I. Protecting life (19:1–21:14)
J. Protecting sexual morality (21:15–23:14)
K. Various laws protecting property (23:15–24:22)
L. Laws on justice, marriage, and business (25:1–16)
M. Amalek (25:17–19)
N. Firstfruits and tithes (26:1–19)

V. Moses' Third Speech: Blessings and Curses (27:1–28:68)

VI. Moses' Third Speech: Final Exhortation (29:1–30:20)

VII. Succession of Leadership (31:1–34:12)
A. The commissioning of Joshua and the writing of the law (31:1–29)
B. The Song of Moses (31:30–32:47)
C. The blessing of Moses (32:48–33:29)
D. The death of Moses (34:1–12)

Deuteronomy

The Command to Leave Horeb

1 These are the words that Moses spoke to all Israel beyond the Jordan in the wilderness,
in [a]the Arabah opposite [b]Suph, between [c]Paran and Tophel, Laban, Hazeroth, and
Dizahab. 2 It is eleven days' journey from Horeb by the way of Mount Seir to [d]Kadesh-barnea.
3 [e]In the fortieth year, on the first day of the eleventh month, Moses spoke to the people of
Israel according to all that the LORD had given him in commandment to them, 4 after [f]he
had defeated Sihon the king of the Amorites, who lived in Heshbon, and [g]Og the king of
Bashan, who lived in Ashtaroth and in [h]Edrei. 5 Beyond the Jordan, [i]in the land of Moab,
Moses undertook to explain this law, saying, 6 "The LORD our God said to us in Horeb, [j]'You
have stayed long enough at this mountain. 7 Turn and take your journey, and go to [k]the
hill country of the Amorites and to all their neighbors in [a]the Arabah, [l]in the hill country
and in the lowland and in the Negeb and [l]by the seacoast, the land of the Canaanites, and
Lebanon, as far as the great river, the river Euphrates. 8 See, I have set the land before you.

Chapter 1
1 [a]ch. 3:17 [b][Num. 21:14] [c]1 Sam. 25:1
2 [d]ch. 2:14; 9:23; Num. 13:26; 32:8; 34:4
3 [e][Num. 33:38]
4 [f]See Num. 21:21-32 [g]See Num. 21:33-35 [h]ch. 3:1, 10; Josh. 12:4; 13:12
5 [i]ch. 29:1
6 [j]ch. 2:3; [Ex. 19:1; Num. 10:11]
7 [k][Num. 13:29] [a][See ver. 1 above] [l]Josh. 9:1

1:1–5 *Prologue.* This first, brief section provides the chronological and geographical setting of Deuteronomy, identifying the speaker and audience as well as summarizing that the book is an exposition of the law. It parallels the preamble sections of ancient covenant treaties.

1:1 The Hebrew name of Deuteronomy (*Debarim*; lit., "The words") is taken from the opening phrase, **These are the words**. This opening informs the reader that the bulk of Deuteronomy, up to the end of ch. 30, is the spoken words of Moses. **Moses** has been the leader of Israel since early in the book of Exodus, called by God to that role at the burning bush (Exodus 3). Deuteronomy is Moses' final speech before his death. **all Israel**. Deuteronomy emphasizes the unity of the people. **beyond the Jordan**. That is, east of the Jordan River, on the north end of the Dead Sea. Since leaving Egypt and crossing the Red Sea, Israel has been in the **wilderness** for 40 years (Exodus 14–15; see Ex. 15:22). **Arabah**. The low Jordan Valley and area surrounding the Dead Sea. **Suph . . . Dizahab**. These are places that Israel passed through en route to Moab. Numbers 12:16 mentions **Paran** and **Hazeroth**. Suph, **Tophel**, **Laban**, and Dizahab are not mentioned elsewhere in the OT.

1:2 Horeb is the name used in Deuteronomy for Mount Sinai (except see 33:2), where Israel received the commandments (Ex. 19:1–Num. 10:12). **Kadesh-barnea**. A town on the southern border of the Promised Land where Israel camped (Num. 13:26).

1:3–4 The juxtaposition of "eleven days" (v. 2) with **fortieth year** highlights the time lost in reaching the border of the Promised Land. The 40-year delay was God's punishment for Israel's failure to enter the land (Num. 14:33–34). As in Deut. 1:1, **Moses spoke**, here stressing his faithfulness in speaking **according to all that the LORD had given him in commandment to them**. Deuteronomy rarely distinguishes between God's words and Moses' words. **defeated Sihon**. See Num. 21:21–35. **Heshbon** and **Bashan** were east of the Jordan, north of where Deuteronomy is set (see Deut. 1:1, 5).

1:5 The repeated mention of **beyond the Jordan** (also v. 1) underscores that Israel is not yet in the Promised Land. (**Moab** is "beyond" the Jordan, i.e., on the east side, from the perspective of Canaan.) Unlike their fighting against Sihon and Og (v. 4), Israel had not fought against Moab en route to the Promised Land. **This law** refers to the entire law given to Israel at Sinai (Ex. 19:1–Num. 10:12). Moses' task is not simply to repeat that law but to expound it (in effect, to preach it) so that Israel will newly accept the law before crossing the Jordan to conquer the land. At Sinai, Israel verbally agreed to the covenant law's obligations (Ex. 24:3) but did not behave accordingly. Hence in Deuteronomy Moses exhorts Israel to a covenant renewal with God.

1:6–4:43 *Moses' First Speech: Historical Prologue.* Moses' first speech rehearses Israel's past failure at Kadesh near the beginning of the 40-year wilderness period as well as its passing through Edom, Moab, and Ammon without fighting, its successes over Heshbon and Bashan, and the distribution of those two lands. Chapter 4 is an exhortation that functions as a transition from the history in chs. 1–3 to the rehearsal of the Ten Commandments in ch. 5. The purpose of chs. 1–3 is not simply to retell history but to use history to persuade Israel to trust God so the land will be conquered. Deuteronomy 1:6–3:29 parallels the historical prologue of ancient covenant treaties (see Introduction: Structure). Chapter 4 does not readily parallel such treaties.

1:6–8 *Introduction to First Speech.* Moses' first speech, or sermon, begins by focusing on the land.

1:6 Deuteronomy typically names God as **the LORD our** (or your) **God**. "LORD" is Yahweh, the personal and covenantal name for God revealed to Moses (Ex. 3:14–15; see note on Gen. 2:4).

1:7 Turn. Israel left Sinai in Num. 10:11ff. **Amorites**. A general term for the occupants of the land. The descriptions of the land reflect its geography, roughly east to west. **Arabah**. See note on Deut. 1:1. The **hill country** is the ridge of higher mountains overlooking the Jordan Valley from the west. The **lowland** is the next strip of land to the west, with low, undulating hills. The **Negeb** is the arid land across the south, which becomes desert. **Seacoast** refers to the flat Mediterranean coastline. In general terms, the land is occupied by **Canaanites** (a term virtually synonymous at this time with "Amorites," mentioned earlier in the verse). **Lebanon** lies to the north. The **river Euphrates** lies even farther north and east. Cf. the description of the land in the promise to Abraham (Gen. 15:18–21).

1:8 See has a sense of urgency, for it is a time of decision: from the plains of Moab Israel can now survey the land before it. **Take possession of the land** is a common command in Deuteronomy (e.g., 1:21, 39; 2:24, 31; 3:18; 4:1, 5, 14, 22, etc.). **fathers**. See 1:11, 21; 4:1; 6:3; 10:11; 12:1; 26:7; 27:3; 29:25. The promise of land was made first **to Abraham**

Go in and take possession of the land that the LORD swore to your fathers, [m]to Abraham,
to Isaac, and to Jacob, to give to them and to their offspring after them.'

Leaders Appointed

9 "At that time [n]I said to you, 'I am not able to bear you by myself. 10 The LORD your God
has multiplied you, and behold, [o]you are today as numerous as the stars of heaven. 11 [p]May
the LORD, the God of your fathers, make you a thousand times as many as you are and
bless you, [q]as he has promised you! 12 [r]How can I bear by myself the weight and burden
of you and your strife? 13 [s]Choose for your tribes wise, understanding, and experienced
men, and I will appoint them as your heads.' 14 And you answered me, 'The thing that
you have spoken is good for us to do.' 15 So I took the heads of your tribes, wise and experienced men, [t]and set them as heads over you, commanders of thousands, commanders
of hundreds, commanders of fifties, commanders of tens, and officers, throughout your
tribes. 16 And I charged your judges at that time, 'Hear the cases between your brothers, and
[u]judge righteously between a man and his brother or the alien who is with him. 17 [v]You
shall not be partial in judgment. You shall hear the small and the great alike. You shall
not be intimidated by anyone, for [w]the judgment is God's. And the case that is too hard
for you, you shall [x]bring to me, and I will hear it.' 18 And I commanded you at that time
all the things that you should do.

Israel's Refusal to Enter the Land

19 "Then we set out from Horeb and [y]went through all that great and terrifying wilderness that you saw, on the way to the hill country of the Amorites, as the LORD our God
commanded us. And [z]we came to Kadesh-barnea. 20 And I said to you, 'You have come to
the hill country of the Amorites, which the LORD our God is giving us. 21 See, the LORD
your God has set the land before you. Go up, take possession, as the LORD, the God of your
fathers, has told you. [a]Do not fear or be dismayed.' 22 Then all of you came near me and
said, 'Let us send men before us, that they may explore the land for us and bring us word
again of the way by which we must go up and the cities into which we shall come.' 23 The
thing seemed good to me, and [b]I took twelve men from you, one man from each tribe.
24 And [c]they turned and went up into the hill country, and came to the Valley of Eshcol
and spied it out. 25 And they took in their hands some of the fruit of the land and brought
it down to us, and brought us word again and said, 'It is a good land that the LORD our
God is giving us.'

8 [m]Gen. 12:7; 13:14, 15; 15:18; 17:7, 8; 26:3, 4; 28:13, 14; 50:24
9 [n]Num. 11:14; [Ex. 18:18]
10 [o][ch. 10:22; 28:62]; See Gen. 15:5
11 [p][2 Sam. 24:3] [q]Gen. 12:2; 22:17; 26:3, 24
12 [r][1 Kgs. 3:8, 9]
13 [s][Ex. 18:21; Num. 11:16, 17]
15 [t]Ex. 18:25
16 [u]ch. 16:18; John 7:24
17 [v]ch. 16:19; Ex. 23:2, 3; Lev. 19:15; 2 Chr. 19:7; Prov. 24:23; 28:21; Mal. 2:9; James 2:1, 9 [w]2 Chr. 19:6; [Ex. 21:6] [x]Ex. 18:22, 26
19 [y]ch. 8:15; 32:10; Jer. 2:6; [Num. 10:12] [z]See ver. 2
21 [a]ch. 31:8; Josh. 1:9
23 [b]Num. 13:3
24 [c]See Num. 13:22-27

(Gen. 12:7; 15:18–21), reiterated **to Isaac** (Gen. 26:4), and then **to Jacob** (Gen. 28:13; 35:12; cf. Deut. 6:10; 9:5; 29:13; 30:20; 34:4). The promises to the three patriarchs included land for **their offspring after them**. Moses is emphasizing that the current generation of Israel is included in the promises and God intends to keep his promise of the land. Thus the patriarchal reference functions rhetorically to persuade Israel to go in and possess the land.

1:9–18 *Encouragement to Trust in the Land of Promise.* Before rehearsing the departure from Horeb as v. 6 anticipated, Moses recalls the appointment of tribal heads to help Moses judge and lead the people (Ex. 18:18–26; cf. Num. 11:14ff.). Rather than digressing from the theme of the land, this section reminds Israel that God has already been faithful to another part of the Abrahamic promises, namely, offspring.

1:10 numerous as the stars of heaven. Cf. the promise to Abraham of offspring (Gen. 15:5). Having just exhorted Israel regarding the promise of land in Gen. 15:18–21 (a promise yet to be fulfilled), Moses refers to a promise already fulfilled in order to stir up Israel's faith that God will keep the land promise.

1:12–18 The need for leaders to help Moses is tangible evidence that the promise to Abraham of offspring has been fulfilled. In the Exodus parallel (Ex. 18:13–26), Moses' father-in-law, Jethro, encourages Moses to appoint tribal **heads** to share in judging between disputants.

1:13 The process to **appoint** leaders involved the people nominating the judges and Moses confirming them; Ex. 18:25 simply summarizes that Moses chose them.

1:16–17 alien. Aliens were non-Israelites who resided in the land and accepted Israelite rule and law but did not own land and were hence vulnerable to oppression. Deuteronomy consistently upholds the equal rights of aliens and Israelites (e.g., 10:19; 14:29; 16:11, 14; 24:14, 17, 19–21; 26:11–13; 27:19). **You shall not be partial in judgment**. Impartiality is a prerequisite for good judgment as well as a characteristic of God himself (10:17).

1:19–46 *Israel's Failure at Kadesh Recalled.* This section rehearses Israel's failure to enter the land at Kadesh some 38 years previously (already alluded to in vv. 3–4; cf. Numbers 13–14) in order to warn the current generation not to repeat the sins of their parents. Israel is theologically at the same point as they were at Kadesh, namely, on the border of the Promised Land. The question is whether or not they will repeat the same mistake.

1:20–21 to you. Strictly speaking, the addressees at Kadesh were the parents of the current generation, who were either children at that time or were born afterward. However, the repetition of "you" throughout Deuteronomy (cf. 4:15; 5:3) treats the current generation as having been present through their parents and thus incorporates the current generation in their parents' sin. This pessimistically suggests that the current generation is no different from their predecessors (cf. 1:3). **Do not fear** is a common command in the Scriptures; God alone is to be feared (10:12; 13:4).

1:23–25 twelve men. See Num. 13:4–15. **The Valley of Eshcol** is close to Hebron and still renowned for its fruit. **good land**. See also Deut. 1:35; 3:25; 4:21–22; 6:18; 8:7, 10; 9:6; 11:17. Moses does not repeat all the details of what the spies said, particularly their "bad report" (Num. 13:32), or describe Caleb's positive minority report.

26 "Yet you would not go up, but rebelled against the command of the LORD your
God. 27 And [d]you murmured in your tents and said, 'Because the LORD [e]hated us he has
brought us out of the land of Egypt, [f]to give us into the hand of the Amorites, to destroy
us. 28 Where are we going up? [g]Our brothers have made our hearts melt, saying, [h]"The
people are greater and taller than we. The cities are great and fortified up to heaven.
And besides, we have seen [i]the sons of the Anakim there."' 29 Then I said to you, 'Do not
be in dread or afraid of them. 30 The LORD your God who goes before you [j]will himself
fight for you, just as he did for you in Egypt before your eyes, 31 and in the wilderness,
where you have seen how the LORD your God [k]carried you, as a man carries his son, all
the way that you went until you came to this place.' 32 Yet in spite of this word [l]you did
not believe the LORD your God, 33 [m]who went before you in the way [n]to seek you out a
place to pitch your tents, in fire by night and in the cloud by day, to show you by what
way you should go.

The Penalty for Israel's Rebellion

34 "And the LORD heard your words and was angered, and he swore, 35 [o]'Not one of these
men of this evil generation shall see the good land that I swore to give to your fathers,
36 [p]except Caleb the son of Jephunneh. He shall see it, and to him and to his children I will
give the land on which he has trodden, because he has wholly followed the LORD!' 37 Even
with me [q]the LORD was angry on your account and said, 'You also shall not go in there.
38 [r]Joshua the son of Nun, [r]who stands before you, he shall enter. [s]Encourage him, for he
shall cause Israel to inherit it. 39 And as for [t]your little ones, who you said would become
a prey, and your children, who today [u]have no knowledge of good or evil, they shall go
in there. And to them I will give it, and they shall possess it. 40 But as for you, [v]turn, and
journey into the wilderness in the direction of the Red Sea.'

41 "Then you answered me, [w]'We have sinned against the LORD. We ourselves will go up
and fight, just as the LORD our God commanded us.' And every one of you fastened on his
weapons of war and thought it easy to go up into the hill country. 42 And the LORD said to
me, [x]'Say to them, Do not go up or fight, [y]for I am not in your midst, lest you be defeated
before your enemies.' 43 So I spoke to you, and you would not listen; but you rebelled against
the command of the LORD and [z]presumptuously went up into the hill country. 44 [a]Then
the Amorites who lived in that hill country came out against you and chased you [b]as bees
do and beat you down in Seir as far as [c]Hormah. 45 And you returned and wept before the
LORD, but the LORD did not listen to your voice or give ear to you. 46 So [d]you remained at
Kadesh many days, the days that you remained there.

27 [d]Ps. 106:25; See Num. 14:1-4 [e]ch. 9:28 [f][Josh. 7:7]
28 [g]Josh. 14:8 [h]ch. 9:1, 2; See Num. 13:28-33 [i]See Num. 13:22
30 [j]ch. 3:22; Ex. 14:14, 25; Josh. 10:14, 42; 23:3, 10; [Neh. 4:20]
31 [k]ch. 32:11, 12; Ex. 19:4; Isa. 46:3, 4; 63:9; Hos. 11:3
32 [l]Ps. 106:24; Jude 5
33 [m]See Ex. 13:21 [n]Num. 10:33
35 [o]See ch. 2:15; Num. 14:20-30
36 [p]Num. 14:30; Josh. 14:9
37 [q]ch. 4:21; 32:51; 34:4; Num. 20:12; 27:13, 14; [Ps. 106:32]
38 [r]ch. 31:3, 7; Ex. 24:13; [1 Sam. 16:22] [s]ch. 31:7, 23; Num. 27:18-20
39 [t]Num. 14:3, 31 [u]Isa. 7:15, 16
40 [v]ch. 2:1; Num. 14:25
41 [w]Num. 14:40
42 [x]Num. 14:42 [y][ch. 31:17]
43 [z]Num. 14:44
44 [a]Num. 14:45 [b][Ps. 118:12; Isa. 7:18] [c]See Num. 21:3
46 [d]Num. 20:1, 22; Judg. 11:17

1:26 Yet. The positive report of the spies in v. 25 is sharply juxtaposed with the people's rebellion in v. 26. Deuteronomy highlights Israel's culpability, reinforcing the warning for the current generation not to follow in their parents' footsteps.

1:27–28 murmured. See Num. 14:1–4. This was not the only time Israel murmured in complaint during the 40-year wilderness period, though the word used here (Hb. *ragan*) is rare (cf. Ps. 106:25). **Because the LORD hated us**. In their sin, Israel attributed to God the opposite motive for his action (cf. Deut. 9:28, and the attitude of the people in Num. 14:1–4). The words attributed to the spies in Numbers (cf. Num. 13:28–29) are repeated by the people in Deuteronomy. **Anakim** were reputed to be giants (Num. 13:22, 28, 33; cf. Deut. 2:10, 11, 21; 9:2). Israel's fear expressed here is addressed by Moses in chs. 2–3.

1:29–31 Do not be . . . afraid. See v. 21. This exhortation is grounded in past experience of the plagues and the exodus from **Egypt** (see Exodus 7–14) and the **wilderness** provision (see also Deut. 1:33). **before your eyes . . . you have seen**. Even though this is the next generation (see note on vv. 20–21), Moses sees the nation as a unity and addresses his audience as though they were there with the previous generation. **carried you, as a man carries his son**. The image is tender and loving, repudiating the false claim of v. 27.

1:32–33 you did not believe. Unbelief parallels rebellion (v. 26). **fire by night and in the cloud by day**. See Ex. 13:21.

1:34–36 God's anger at Israel's sin resulted in the 40-year wilderness period, preventing the first generation from entering the land. God's mention of **good land** makes it clear that he agrees with the spies' report (v. 25) and rejects the people's ill-founded fear and unbelief. **Caleb** was one of the 12 spies who gave the minority report (Num. 13:30) and advocated entry into the land. **wholly followed**. See Num. 14:24.

1:37–38 Even with me. Moses' failure, which prevented his entry into the land, was not related to the spies' incident but occurred when he struck the rock in self-exalting anger at Meribah (see note on Num. 20:2–13). **on your account**. Moses says that his own sin was provoked by Israel. See also Deut. 3:26; 4:21; 32:51. **Joshua the son of Nun** is first mentioned in Ex. 17:9–14. He was Moses' assistant (Ex. 24:13) and one of the 12 spies (Num. 13:8). With Caleb, he advocated entry into the land (Num. 14:6–9). Joshua succeeded Moses as leader of Israel (Num. 27:18; Deut. 31:3).

1:39 have no knowledge of good or evil. The expression suggests very young children before they are old enough to distinguish between right and wrong. The need for discernment between good and evil is enforced in 30:15–20.

1:42–44 If God does not **fight** for Israel, defeat is assured (cf. v. 30). **you would not listen**. Israel stubbornly continues to refuse to heed God's word (see 9:6–7). **chased you as bees do**. Cf. Ex. 23:28. Instead of fighting for Israel, God now fights against it.

2:1–23 *Israel Passes through Edom, Moab, and Ammon.* Moses continues

The Wilderness Years

2 “Then we turned and journeyed into the wilderness in the direction of the Red Sea,
[e]as the LORD told me. And for many days we traveled around Mount Seir. 2 Then the
LORD said to me, 3 ‘You have been traveling around this mountain country [f]long enough.
Turn northward 4 and command the people, “You are about to pass through the territory
of [g]your brothers, the people of Esau, [h]who live in Seir; and [i]they will be afraid of you. So
be very careful. 5 Do not contend with them, for I will not give you any of their land, no,
not so much as for the sole of the foot to tread on, because [h]I have given Mount Seir to
Esau as a possession. 6 [j]You shall purchase food from them with money, that you may eat,
and you shall also buy water from them with money, that you may drink. 7 For the LORD
your God has blessed you in all the work of your hands. [k]He knows your going through
this great wilderness. [l]These forty years the LORD your God has been with you. You have
lacked nothing.”’ 8 So [m]we went on, away from our brothers, the people of Esau, who live
in Seir, away from [n]the Arabah road from [o]Elath and [p]Ezion-geber.
“And we turned and went in the direction of the wilderness of Moab. 9 And the LORD
said to me, [q]‘Do not harass Moab or contend with them in battle, for I will not give you
any of their land for a possession, because I have given [r]Ar to [s]the people of Lot for a possession.’ 10 ([t]The Emim formerly lived there, [u]a people great and many, and tall [v]as the
Anakim. 11 Like the Anakim they are also counted as [w]Rephaim, but the Moabites call
them Emim. 12 [x]The Horites also lived in Seir formerly, but the people of Esau dispossessed them and destroyed them from before them and settled in their place, [y]as Israel
did to the land of their possession, which the LORD gave to them.) 13 ‘Now rise up and go
over [z]the brook Zered.’ So we went over [z]the brook Zered. 14 And the time from our leaving
[a]Kadesh-barnea until we crossed [b]the brook Zered was thirty-eight years, [c]until the entire
generation, that is, the men of war, had perished from the camp, as the LORD had sworn
to them. 15 For indeed the hand of the LORD was against them, to destroy them from the
camp, until they had perished.
16 “So as soon as all the men of war had perished and were dead from among the people,
17 the LORD said to me, 18 ‘Today you are to cross the border of Moab at Ar. 19 And when
you approach the territory of the people of Ammon, [d]do not harass them or contend with
them, for I will not give you any of the land of the people of Ammon as a possession,
because I have given it to [e]the sons of Lot for a possession.’ 20 (It is also counted as a land of
[f]Rephaim. Rephaim formerly lived there—but the Ammonites call them Zamzummim—

Chapter 2
1 [e]ch. 1:40; Num. 14:25
3 [f]ch. 1:6
4 [g]ch. 23:7; Amos 1:11; Obad. 10, 12 [h]See Gen. 32:3 [i]See Num. 20:18-21
5 [h][See ver. 4 above]
6 [j]ver. 28
7 [k][Job 23:10] [l]See ch. 8:2-4
8 [m]Judg. 11:18 [n]See ch. 1:1 [o]1 Kgs. 9:26; [2 Kgs. 14:22; 16:6; 2 Chr. 26:2] [p]See Num. 33:35
9 [q]ver. 19, 29 [r]ver. 18; Num. 21:15; Isa. 15:1 [s]ver. 19; Gen. 19:36, 37
10 [t]Gen. 14:5 [u][ver. 21] [v]See Num. 13:22
11 [w]See Gen. 14:5
12 [x]ver. 22; Gen. 14:6; See Gen. 36:20-30 [y]Num. 21:24, 31, 35
13 [z][Num. 21:12]
14 [a]See ch. 1:2, 19 [b][Num. 21:12] [c]Num. 14:33, 35; 26:64; Ps. 78:33; 95:11; 106:26; Ezek. 20:15; [1 Cor. 10:5; Heb. 3:17]; See ch. 1:35
19 [d][ver. 9] [e]Gen. 19:36, 38
20 [f]See Gen. 14:5

to recount past history, jumping to near the end of the 40-year wilderness period and recalling Israel’s peaceful passage through three nations distantly related to it (see Num. 20:14–21:20). This passage reminds Israel of God’s care in bringing them so far and counters their fear of the inhabitants of the land (see Deut. 1:28) so that they now may enter the land.

2:1 Red Sea. This probably includes the Gulf of Aqaba, the northeastern arm of the Red Sea. **Mount Seir** is south of the Dead Sea, in the land of Edom (see 1:2).

2:2–4 the LORD said to me. This expression occurs seven times in chs. 1–3, giving Moses a prophetic role (i.e., as God’s authorized spokesman). **long enough**. See also 1:6. This formally announces the end of the 40-year wilderness wandering. **your brothers**. The nation of Edom was descended from Jacob’s twin brother, **Esau** (Gen. 25:30; 32:3; 36:1). Deuteronomy does not call the nation “Edom,” instead referring either to Seir or Esau, perhaps to stress the blood relationship. The Israelites need to **be very careful** not to provoke Edom against them (see Num. 20:18–21).

2:5 as a possession. This rare expression also occurs in vv. 9, 19 with respect to Moab and Ammon (and in v. 12 with respect to Israel’s future possession). God has given land to Edom, Moab, and Ammon and forbids Israel to attempt taking that land, presumably because of the blood relationships through Esau and Lot. The point is God’s ability to give and protect land, thus encouraging Israel to trust him.

2:6–7 Israel is not to be indebted to anyone other than God. This is a frequent theme in Deuteronomy (see 14:29; 15:10; 16:15; 24:19; 30:9). Israel **lacked nothing**, for God provided food and water when they ran short (Exodus 16–17; Numbers 11).

2:8 Elath and Ezion-geber were seaports on the Red Sea at the Gulf of Aqaba (see v. 1). The **Arabah road** ran from these towns northward to the Dead Sea. Israel is now heading in a northeasterly direction.

2:9 Moab, like Ammon (v. 19), was descended from **Lot**, Abraham’s nephew (Gen. 19:37).

2:10–12 This section, like vv. 20–23, is very important in Moses’ argument. The people whom God dispossessed in order to give Moab its land included the **Anakim** (also v. 21), the very people Israel feared (see 1:28). The point is that Israel has no reason to fear them. God is more powerful. **Rephaim**, like Anakim, were so **tall** that the people of Israel thought of them as “giants” (cf. Num. 13:32–33; see also Deut. 2:20; 3:11, 13). Both **Emim** and Rephaim are mentioned in Gen. 14:5. Edom’s possession is a model to encourage Israel. The **land of their possession** may refer only to the Transjordanian land Israel possessed already (Deut. 2:24–3:17). **Horites**. See Gen. 14:6; 36:20–30.

2:13–15 The wadi (or **brook**) **Zered** (a wadi is a river that usually flows only after rain) was the border between Edom and Moab. **thirty-eight years**. God’s decree after the spies incident, that the adult generation of Israel then living would die in the wilderness (Num. 14:22–23, 35), has been fulfilled. The **hand of the LORD** suggests pestilence (e.g., Ex. 9:3, 15; 1 Sam. 5:6–11).

2:20–23 See note on vv. 10–12. The **Zamzummim** are probably the same as the Zuzim (Gen. 14:5). **Avvim**. See Josh. 13:3 and 18:23. **Caphtorim**. See Gen. 10:14 and Jer. 47:4. Possibly Caphtor was Crete, the original home of the Philistines.

21 [g]a people great and many, and tall as the Anakim; but the LORD destroyed them before
the Ammonites,[1] and they dispossessed them and settled in their place, 22 as he did for the
people of Esau, who live in Seir, when he destroyed [h]the Horites before them and they
dispossessed them and settled in their place even to this day. 23 As for [i]the Avvim, who lived
in villages as far as [j]Gaza, [k]the Caphtorim, who came from Caphtor, destroyed them and
settled in their place.) 24 'Rise up, set out on your journey and [l]go over the Valley of the
Arnon. Behold, I have given into your hand Sihon the Amorite, king of [m]Heshbon, and his
land. Begin to take possession, and [n]contend with him in battle. 25 This day I will begin to
put [o]the dread and fear of you on the peoples who are under the whole heaven, who shall
hear the report of you and shall tremble and be in anguish because of you.'

The Defeat of King Sihon

26 "So I sent messengers from the wilderness of [p]Kedemoth to Sihon the king of [m]Heshbon,
[q]with words of peace, saying, 27 [r]'Let me pass through your land. I will go only by the road;
I will turn aside neither to the right nor to the left. 28 [s]You shall sell me food for money,
that I may eat, and give me water for money, that I may drink. Only let me pass through
on foot, 29 [t]as the sons of Esau who live in Seir and the Moabites who live in Ar did for me,
until I go over the Jordan into the land that the LORD our God is giving to us.' 30 But [u]Sihon
the king of [m]Heshbon would not let us pass by him, for the LORD your God [v]hardened
his spirit and made his heart obstinate, that he might give him into your hand, as he is
this day. 31 And the LORD said to me, 'Behold, I have begun to give Sihon and his land over
to you. Begin to take possession, that you may occupy his land.' 32 Then [w]Sihon came out
against us, he and all his people, to battle at Jahaz. 33 And [x]the LORD our God gave him
over to us, and [y]we defeated him and his sons and all his people. 34 And we captured all his
cities at that time and devoted to destruction[2] every [z]city, men, women, and children. We
left no survivors. 35 Only the livestock we took as spoil for ourselves, with the plunder of
the cities that we captured. 36 [a]From Aroer, which is on the edge of the Valley of the Arnon,
and from [b]the city that is in the valley, as far as Gilead, there was not a city too high for
us. [c]The LORD our God gave all into our hands. 37 Only to the land of the sons of Ammon
you did not draw near, that is, to all the banks of the river [d]Jabbok and the cities of the
hill country, whatever the LORD our God had forbidden us.

The Defeat of King Og

3 "Then we turned and went up the way to Bashan. And [e]Og the king of Bashan came
out against us, he and all his people, to battle at [f]Edrei. 2 But the LORD said to me, 'Do
not fear him, for I have given him and all his people and his land into your hand. And
you shall do to him as you did to [g]Sihon the king of the Amorites, who lived at Heshbon.'
3 So the LORD our God gave into our hand Og also, the king of Bashan, and all his people,
[h]and we struck him down until he had no survivor left. 4 And we took all his cities at that
time—there was not a city that we did not take from them—sixty cities, [i]the whole region

[1] Hebrew *them* [2] That is, set apart (devoted) as an offering to the Lord (for destruction)

21 [g][ver. 10]
22 [h]Gen. 14:6; See Gen. 36:20-30
23 [i]Josh. 13:3, 4 [j]Gen. 10:19; Jer. 25:20 [k]See Gen. 10:14
24 [l]Num. 21:13, 14; Judg. 11:18, 21 [m]Num. 21:27, 28, 30 [n][ver. 9]
25 [o]ch. 11:25; 28:10; See Ex. 15:14-16; Josh. 2:9-11
26 [p]Josh. 13:18; 1 Chr. 6:79 [m][See ver. 24 above] [q][ch. 20:10]
27 [r]Num. 21:21, 22; Judg. 11:19
28 [s]ver. 6; Num. 20:19
29 [t]ver. 5, 9; [ch. 23:3, 4; Num. 20:18; Judg. 11:17, 18]
30 [u]Num. 21:23 [m][See ver. 24 above] [v]See Ex. 4:21
32 [w]See Num. 21:23-30
33 [x][ch. 7:2] [y]ch. 29:7
34 [z]ch. 3:6
36 [a]ch. 3:12; 4:48; Josh. 12:2; 13:9, 16; 2 Kgs. 10:33 [b]Josh. 13:9, 16; 2 Sam. 24:5 [c]Ps. 44:3
37 [d]ch. 3:16; Gen. 32:22; Num. 21:24; Josh. 12:2; Judg. 11:22

Chapter 3

1 [e]ch. 29:7; Num. 21:33, 35 [f]See ch. 1:4
2 [g]See Num. 21:23-26, 34
3 [h]Num. 21:35
4 [i]1 Kgs. 4:13

2:24–37 *Israel Defeats Heshbon.* Moses recounts Israel's first conquest (see Num. 21:21–30).

2:24–25 The wadi **Arnon** (see note on vv. 13–15) flowed into the Dead Sea and marked the border between Moab to the south and Amorite territory and Ammon to the north. **Begin to take possession**. See 1:21. Even though Heshbon lies in Transjordan, in a sense its conquest marks the beginning of possessing the Promised Land (see Josh. 12:1–6). **Sihon the Amorite**. See note on Deut. 1:3–4. According to Gen. 15:16, the land would be given to Israel when the iniquity of the Amorites was complete, and now that time has come. Thus the defeat of various nations represents God's punishment for their iniquity (Deut. 18:12). (See Introduction to Joshua: The Destruction of the Canaanites.) In holy war, enemies **tremble** before the Lord (Ex. 15:14; see also Josh. 4:24–5:1).

2:26 Heshbon was a fertile land (Song 7:4), north of Moab and Ammon on the east of the Jordan River. The offer of **words of peace** does not seem to match the instruction to fight in Deut. 2:24. Perhaps Israel was reluctant to obey and fight.

2:30 God hardened his spirit and made his heart obstinate just as with Pharaoh during the series of plagues (Ex. 9:12; 10:1–2, 20, 27; 11:9–10; 14:4, 8, 17–18). **as he is this day**. Expressions like this occur regularly in Deuteronomy (Deut. 4:20, 38; 6:24; 8:18; 10:15; 29:28) to give Israel confidence in God's power and faithfulness.

2:32 Jahaz is mentioned in Josh. 13:18 and 21:36–37, along with Kedemoth (Deut. 2:26).

2:34–35 devoted to destruction. The total destruction of Sihon's cities and people reflects God's instructions for battle within the Promised Land (see note on 20:16–18). This emphasis is absent in the parallel account in Numbers 21. Since God is the victor, the spoils of battle belong to him and not to Israel, hence their destruction as an act of devotion to God.

2:36–37 Aroer was on the northern bank of the **Arnon**. **Gilead** is the name given generally to the Transjordanian territory. The **Jabbok** River (cf. Gen. 32:22) in part marked the border of Ammon and Gilead.

3:1–11 *Israel Defeats Bashan.* This section recounts Israel's second Transjordanian victory (see Num. 21:31–35). Like Sihon, Og was also an Amorite (Deut. 3:8).

of Argob, the kingdom of Og in Bashan. 5 All these were cities fortified with high walls, gates,
and bars, besides very many unwalled villages. 6 And [j]we devoted them to destruction,[1] as
we did to Sihon the king of Heshbon, devoting to destruction every [k]city, men, women,
and children. 7 But all the livestock and the spoil of the cities we took as our plunder. 8 So
we took the land at that time out of the hand of the two kings of the Amorites who were
beyond the Jordan, from the Valley of the Arnon to Mount Hermon 9 (the Sidonians call
[l]Hermon [m]Sirion, while the Amorites call it [n]Senir), 10 all the cities of the [o]tableland and all
Gilead and all Bashan, as far as [p]Salecah and Edrei, cities of the kingdom of Og in Bashan.
11 (For [q]only Og the king of Bashan was left of the remnant of [r]the Rephaim. Behold, his
bed was a bed of iron. Is it not in [s]Rabbah of the Ammonites? Nine cubits[2] was its length,
and four cubits its breadth, according to the [t]common cubit.[3])
12 "When we took possession of this land at that time, I gave to the Reubenites and the

[1] That is, set apart (devoted) as an offering to the Lord (for destruction); twice in this verse [2] A *cubit* was about 18 inches or 45 centimeters [3] Hebrew *cubit of a man*

6 [j]See ch. 7:2; Ps. 135:10-12 [k]ch. 2:34
9 [l]ch. 4:48; Josh. 11:3, 17; 12:5 [m]Ps. 29:6; [ch. 4:48] [n]1 Chr. 5:23; Song 4:8; Ezek. 27:5
10 [o]ch. 4:43; Josh. 13:9, 16, 17, 21; Jer. 48:8, 21 [p]Josh. 12:5; 13:11; 1 Chr. 5:11
11 [q]ch. 2:11, 20 [r]See Gen. 14:5 [s]2 Sam. 11:1; 12:26; Jer. 49:2; Ezek. 21:20; 25:5; Amos 1:14 [t][Rev. 21:17]

3:1 Bashan is the area northeast of the Sea of Galilee. **Edrei** was a town on the southern border of Bashan (see map below).

3:5–7 cities fortified. See 1:28. In recounting these victories, Moses seeks to persuade Israel to cross the Jordan, not fearing the enemy but trusting in God's power. **devoted them to destruction**. See note on 2:34–35.

3:8–10 Mount Hermon (9,232 feet/2,814 m) is a snowcapped mountain at Israel's northern border with Lebanon and Syria (see Ps. 42:6; 89:12; 133:3). The alternative names **Sirion** and **Senir** are also found in ancient Ugaritic, Hittite, and Assyrian documents. **Salecah** lay on the southeastern edge of **Bashan** (Josh. 12:5; 13:11).

3:11 Rephaim. See note on 2:10–12. **Rabbah**, capital of Ammon (2 Sam. 11:1; Amos 1:13–14), is modern-day Amman, Jordan. Og's **bed of iron** was over 13 feet (4 m) long and 6 feet (1.8 m) wide. This may refer to his coffin. The reference reminds Israel that the "giant" Rephaim have been killed and that Israel's fear of them (see Deut. 1:28) is unfounded. The **common cubit** (different from a royal cubit) was approximately 18 inches (46 cm).

3:12–17 *Distribution of Transjordanian Land.* These verses recapitulate the distribution of the lands of Sihon and Og to the tribes of Reuben, Gad, and half the tribe of Manasseh (Num. 32:1–42; 34:13–15). The repeat of this

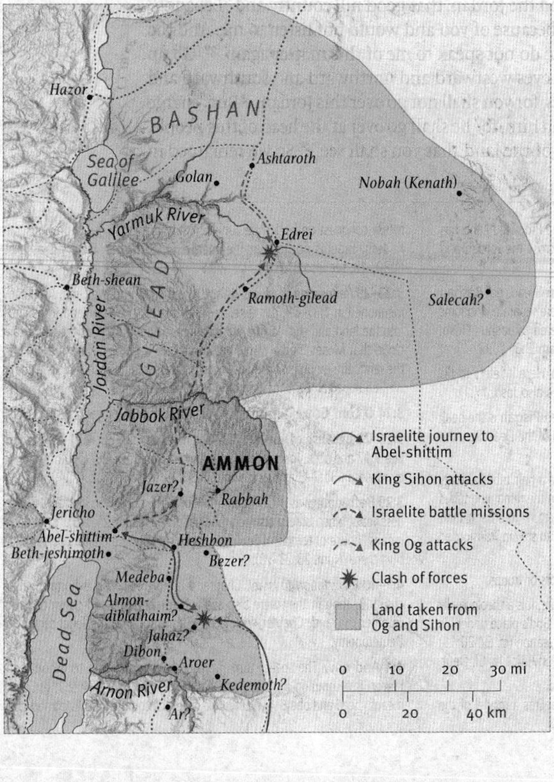

Israel Defeats Og and Sihon
Deuteronomy reviews how the Israelites defeated King Sihon when he refused them passage through his land and attacked them at Jahaz. Soon afterward, the Israelites spied out Jazer and captured it. As they headed north from Jazer, the Israelites were attacked by King Og's forces at Edrei, but they defeated him and took control of his land as well.

Gadites the territory beginning [u]at Aroer, which is on the edge of the Valley of the Arnon,
and half the hill country of Gilead with [v]its cities. **13** [w]The rest of Gilead, and all Bashan,
the kingdom of Og, that is, [x]all the region of Argob, I gave to the half-tribe of Manasseh.
(All that portion of Bashan is called the land of [r]Rephaim. **14** [y]Jair the Manassite took all the
region of Argob, that is, Bashan, as far as the border of [z]the Geshurites and the Maacathites,
and called the villages [a]after his own name, Havvoth-jair, as it is to this day.) **15** To Machir
[b]I gave Gilead, **16** and to the Reubenites [c]and the Gadites I gave the territory from Gilead
as far as the Valley of the Arnon, with the middle of the valley as a border, as far over as
the river Jabbok, [d]the border of the Ammonites; **17** the Arabah also, with the Jordan as the
border, from [e]Chinnereth as far as [f]the Sea of the Arabah, [g]the Salt Sea, under [h]the slopes
of Pisgah on the east.

18 "And I commanded you at that time, saying, 'The LORD your God has given you this
land to possess. [i]All your men of valor shall cross over armed before your brothers, the
people of Israel. **19** Only your wives, your little ones, and your livestock [j](I know that you
have much livestock) shall remain in the cities that I have given you, **20** [k]until the LORD
gives rest to your brothers, as to you, and they also occupy the land that the LORD your
God gives them beyond the Jordan. Then each of you may return to his possession which
I have given you.' **21** And I commanded [l]Joshua at that time, 'Your eyes have seen all that
the LORD your God has done to these two kings. So will the LORD do to all the kingdoms
into which you are crossing. **22** You shall not fear them, for it is [m]the LORD your God who
fights for you.'

Moses Forbidden to Enter the Land

23 "And I pleaded with the LORD at that time, saying, **24** 'O Lord GOD, you have only
begun to show your servant [n]your greatness and your mighty hand. For [o]what god is there
in heaven or on earth who can do such works and mighty acts as yours? **25** Please let me
go over and see [p]the good land beyond the Jordan, that good hill country and [q]Lebanon.'
26 But [r]the LORD was angry with me because of you and would not listen to me. And the
LORD said to me, [s]'Enough from you; do not speak to me of this matter again. **27** [t]Go up
to the top of Pisgah and lift up your eyes westward and northward and southward and
eastward, and look at it with your eyes, for you shall not go over this Jordan. **28** But [u]charge
Joshua, and encourage and strengthen him, for he shall go over at the head of this people,
and he shall put them in possession of the land that you shall see.' **29** So we remained in
[v]the valley opposite Beth-peor.

12 [u]See ch. 2:36 [v]See Num. 32:32-38; Josh. 13:8-13
13 [w]See Num. 32:39-42; Josh. 13:29-31 [x]1 Kgs. 4:13 [r][See ver. 11 above]
14 [y]Num. 32:41; [1 Chr. 2:22, 23] [z]Josh. 12:5; 13:11, 13; 2 Sam. 3:3; 10:6; 13:37, 38 [a]Num. 32:41
15 [b]Num. 32:39
16 [c][2 Sam. 24:5] [d]Num. 21:24; Josh. 12:2
17 [e]See Num. 34:11 [f]ch. 4:49; Josh. 3:16; 12:3; 2 Kgs. 14:25 [g]See Gen. 14:3 [h][Num. 21:15]
18 [i]Num. 32:20, 21; Josh. 1:14; 4:12
19 [j]Num. 32:1, 4
20 [k]Josh. 22:4
21 [l][Num. 27:18]
22 [m]See Ex. 14:14
24 [n]ch. 5:24; 11:2; 32:3; 1 Chr. 29:11 [o]See Ex. 15:11
25 [p]ch. 4:22; Ex. 3:8 [q][Josh. 1:4]
26 [r]See ch. 1:37 [s][2 Cor. 12:9]
27 [t]Num. 27:12, 13
28 [u]ch. 1:38; 31:3, 7; Num. 27:23
29 [v]ch. 4:46; 34:6

in Deuteronomy underscores that the possession of the Promised Land has begun, which should make Israel more confident to cross the Jordan and conquer the remaining land.

3:14 Cf. Num. 32:41, which implies Jair's villages were in Gilead, not **Bashan** (also Judg. 10:4). The **Geshurites** and **Maacathites** were separate kingdoms bordering Bashan to the west. They were not conquered by Joshua (Josh. 13:13) and remained independent in David's time (2 Sam. 3:3; 10:6).

3:15 Machir was the son of Manasseh (Gen. 50:23). Here it refers to his descendants, a subsection of the tribe of Manasseh (see also Josh. 17:1).

3:17 Chinnereth is another name for the Sea of Galilee. **Pisgah** is the peak of Mount Nebo, overlooking Jericho and the north end of the Dead Sea, the place where Moses dies (v. 27; 34:1–4).

3:18–22 *Command to All Israelites to Fight.* Two and a half tribes already possess their land, but they are commanded here to join the remaining tribes to conquer the land west of the Jordan and only then return to inhabit their Transjordanian land. Wives and children of all tribes are to stay in Transjordan and await the completed conquest.

3:18 men of valor. A military term, suggesting warriors or troops.

3:20 Though **rest** here conveys simply peace after warfare, it is a theologically rich term, suggesting the well-being of God's people in God's place under his rule. Thus the notion hints back to the seventh day of creation (cf. Ex. 20:11) and forward to a permanent rest (Ps. 95:7–11; Heb. 3:7–4:11). Cf. Deut. 12:10; 25:19; Josh. 1:13, 15; 21:44; 22:4; 23:1.

3:21–22 The conquests of Sihon and Og give the Israelites a model of the future conquest under Joshua. Unlike its experience 38 years previously at Kadesh, Israel is not to **fear** the enemy. If God **fights**, victory is assured (1:30, 42; see also 31:6, 8).

3:23–29 *Reiteration of Moses Being Denied Entry into the Land.* As already mentioned in 1:37–38, it is reiterated that the Lord had denied Moses entry into the land and that Joshua would succeed him. In light of the significant cloud that Moses' death would cast over Israel's enthusiasm for entry into the land, the emphasis here lies more on encouraging Joshua so that he is well-equipped to continue on from Moses' leadership.

3:24 O Lord GOD is a standard form for beginning a prayer (cf. 9:26).

3:26–28 because of you. See 1:37 and notes on 1:37–38; 4:21–22. **Pisgah**. See 3:17 and note. **Joshua** (see 1:38 and note on 1:37–38) is commissioned by Moses in 31:7–8 and by the Lord in 31:23. See also Josh. 1:1–9.

3:29 Beth-peor was the location of another act of rebellion in Israel's wilderness years, when Israel worshiped the Baal of Peor (Num. 25:1–5). "Beth-peor" means "house or temple of Peor," perhaps referring to the altars Balaam had built there (Num. 23:28–29).

4:1–40 *Exhortation to Israel.* Chapter 4 is more obviously exhortation than chs. 1–3, though they were also seeking to persuade and convince Israel to enter the land. Chapter 4 provides a transition into the legal section of Deuteronomy.

4:1 And now. The speech turns from recounting the past to exhortation. **Listen** is a common injunction in Deuteronomy (5:1; 6:3, 4; 9:1; etc.) and means "heed and obey." As is often the case, the command to listen and obey

Moses Commands Obedience

4 "And now, O Israel, listen to [w]the statutes and the rules[1] that I am teaching you, and
do them, [x]that you may live, and go in and take possession of the land that the LORD,
the God of your fathers, is giving you. 2 [y]You shall not add to the word that I command
you, nor take from it, that you may keep the commandments of the LORD your God that
I command you. 3 Your eyes have seen what the LORD did [z]at Baal-peor, for the LORD your
God destroyed from among you all the men who followed the Baal of Peor. 4 But you who
held fast to the LORD your God are all alive today. 5 See, I have taught you statutes and rules,
as the LORD my God commanded me, that you should do them in the land that you are
entering to take possession of it. 6 [a]Keep them and do them, for [b]that will be your wisdom
and your understanding in the sight of the peoples, who, when they hear all these statutes,
will say, 'Surely this great nation is a wise and understanding people.' 7 For [c]what great
nation is there that has [d]a god so near to it as the LORD our God is to us, whenever we call
upon him? 8 And what great nation is there, that has statutes and rules so [e]righteous as
all this law that I set before you today?

9 [f]"Only take care, and [g]keep your soul diligently, lest you forget the things that your
eyes have seen, and lest they depart from your heart all the days of your life. [h]Make them
known to your children and your children's children— 10 how on [i]the day that you stood
before the LORD your God at Horeb, the LORD said to me, [j]'Gather the people to me, that
I may let them hear my words, [k]so that they may learn to fear [l]me all the days that they
live on the earth, and that they may teach their children so.' 11 And [m]you came near and
stood at the foot of the mountain, while [n]the mountain burned with fire to the heart of
heaven, wrapped in darkness, cloud, and gloom. 12 Then [o]the LORD spoke to you out of
the midst of the fire. You heard the sound of words, [p]but saw no form; [q]there was only a
voice. 13 [r]And he declared to you his covenant, which he commanded you to perform, that
is, [s]the Ten Commandments,[2] [t]and he wrote them on two tablets of stone. 14 And [u]the LORD
commanded me at that time to teach you statutes and rules, that you might do them in
the land that you are going over to possess.

Idolatry Forbidden

15 [v]"Therefore watch yourselves very carefully. Since [w]you saw no form on the day that
the LORD spoke to you at Horeb out of the midst of the fire, 16 beware [x]lest you act corruptly [y]by making a carved image for yourselves, in the form of any figure, [z]the likeness
of male or female, 17 the likeness of any animal that is on the earth, the likeness of any

[1] Or *just decrees*; also verses 5, 8, 14, 45 [2] Hebrew *words*

Chapter 4
1 [w]See Lev. 18:4 [x]ch. 6:24; 8:1
2 [y]ch. 12:32; [Josh. 1:7; Prov. 30:6; Rev. 22:18, 19]
3 [z]See Num. 23:28; 25:3-9
6 [a]ch. 29:9 [b]Job 28:28; Ps. 111:10; Prov. 1:7; 9:10
7 [c]2 Sam. 7:23 [d]Ps. 34:18; 46:1; 145:18; 148:14; [James 4:8]
8 [e]Rom. 7:12
9 [f]ver. 23 [g][Prov. 4:23] [h]ch. 6:7; 11:19; 32:46; Gen. 18:19; See Ps. 78:4-6
10 [i]Ex. 19:9, 16; Heb. 12:18, 19 [j]ch. 31:12 [k]ch. 14:23; 17:19 [l]ch. 12:1; 31:13; 1 Kgs. 8:40
11 [m]Ex. 19:17 [n]ch. 5:22, 23; Ex. 19:18; 20:18, 21; [Ex. 24:16, 17]
12 [o]ver. 33, 36; ch. 5:4, 22; Ex. 20:1, 19 [p]ver. 15 [q]Ex. 20:22; [1 Kgs. 19:12; Job 4:16]
13 [r]ch. 9:9, 11 [s]Ex. 34:28 [t]See Ex. 24:12
14 [u]See Ex. 21–23
15 [v]Josh. 23:11 [w]ver. 12
16 [x]ver. 25 [y]ver. 23; ch. 5:8; Ex. 20:4; [Acts 17:29] [z]Rom. 1:23

carries a motive clause to encourage that behavior: **that you may live, and go in and take possession**. Land possession is not linked to military strategy or strength but to comprehensive obedience of **the statutes and the rules** that govern all aspects of life. As is common in Deuteronomy, mention of the land is qualified by reference to the patriarchs (**fathers**) in order to stimulate Israel's trust in God's faithfulness (see note on 1:8).

4:2 The authority and sufficiency of God's word is implied in the command **not add . . . nor take from**. Israel is to submit to God's entire word (see also 12:32). Such a command is necessary because of their persistent rebellion in the previous 40 years. For similar commands, see Prov. 30:6; Eccles. 3:14; Rev. 22:18–19.

4:3–4 Your eyes have seen. See also 3:21. **Baal-peor**. See 3:29 and note. **Held fast** describes faithfulness to a covenant, as in marriage (Gen. 2:24), and is commanded of all Israel (e.g., Deut. 10:20; 13:4). Those who held fast rejected pagan worship and are therefore **alive today** as an example of the promise of 4:1 (that those who obey will live) being fulfilled.

4:6 Part of the incentive to keep the commandments is missiological. Obedience will show to other nations Israel's **wisdom** and **understanding**, akin to the moral wisdom encouraged in Proverbs. Such wisdom will draw attention not only to Israel but ultimately to Israel's God (as epitomized by the queen of Sheba's visit with Solomon; 1 Kings 10), a pattern intended by the Abrahamic covenant (Gen. 12:3).

4:7–8 so near. In the verses following, the Lord's nearness at Mount Horeb is recalled, though v. 7 has in mind an ongoing nearness, notably in answering prayer. In Deuteronomy that nearness comes through God's word (30:14) and his presence in the midst of the people. See also 1 Kings 8:52. In comparison with other nations, Israel's **law** is emphasized as **righteous** in order to encourage Israel to keep the laws of the following chapters and not to regard them as unduly onerous.

4:9 take care. Like all fallen humans, Israel's natural tendency is to ignore, **forget**, or disobey. Their failure in the past 40 years adds testimony to this warning. **Make them known to your children**. See 6:7; 11:19. Each generation has the responsibility of instructing the next generation in the faith.

4:12 saw no form; there was only a voice. The emphasis here, and in the second commandment (5:8–9), is that worship of an image is prohibited, since God's self-revelation was audible, not visible. Despite this, notice "your eyes have seen" in 4:3, 9, and "before your eyes" in v. 34.

4:13–14 Though not the entirety of the Sinai **covenant**, the **Ten Commandments** (lit., "Ten Words") sum it up. They alone of God's commands were spoken audibly to all Israel and were written by God on the two stone tablets (Ex. 20:1, 18–19; 24:12). The emphasis on covenant stresses the relational nature of the law (cf. Ex. 19:5; 20:2). The **statutes and rules** are the other laws given at Sinai, spoken only to Moses, who was instructed to teach them to Israel (Exodus 21–Leviticus 27).

4:15–19 The absence of a visible form for God now gives reason for prohibiting the worship of idols and images (cf. the second commandment, 5:8–9).

winged bird that flies in the air, 18 the likeness of anything that creeps on the ground,
the likeness of any fish that is in the water under the earth. 19 And beware lest you raise
your eyes to heaven, and when you see [a]the sun and the moon and the stars, [b]all the host
of heaven, you be drawn away and bow down to them and serve them, things that the
LORD your God has allotted to all the peoples under the whole heaven. 20 But the LORD
has taken you and [c]brought you out of the iron furnace, out of Egypt, [d]to be a people
of his own inheritance, as you are this day. 21 Furthermore, [e]the LORD was angry with
me because of you, and he swore that I should not cross the Jordan, and that I should
not enter the good land that the LORD your God is giving you for an inheritance. 22 For
I must die in this land; [f]I must not go over the Jordan. But you shall go over and take
possession of [g]that good land. 23 [h]Take care, lest you forget the covenant of the LORD
your God, which he made with you, and [i]make a carved image, the form of anything
that the LORD your God has forbidden you. 24 For [j]the LORD your God is a consuming
fire, [k]a jealous God.

25 "When you father children and children's children, and have grown old in the land, [l]if
you act corruptly by making a carved image in the form of anything, and [m]by doing what
is evil in the sight of the LORD your God, so as to provoke him to anger, 26 I [n]call heaven
and earth to witness against you today, that you will soon utterly perish from the land that
you are going over the Jordan to possess. You will not live long in it, but will be utterly
destroyed. 27 And the LORD [o]will scatter you among the peoples, [p]and you will be left few
in number among the nations where the LORD will drive you. 28 And [q]there you will serve
gods of wood and stone, the work of human hands, [r]that neither see, nor hear, nor eat, nor
smell. 29 [s]But from there you will seek the LORD your God and you will find him, if you
search after him with all your heart and with all your soul. 30 When you are in tribulation,
and all these things come upon you [t]in the latter days, you will return to the LORD your
God and obey his voice. 31 For the LORD your God is [u]a merciful God. [v]He will not leave you
or destroy you or forget the covenant with your fathers that he swore to them.

The LORD Alone Is God

32 "For [w]ask now of the days that are past, which were before you, since the day that God
created man on the earth, and ask from one end of heaven to the other, whether such a
great thing as this has ever happened or was ever heard of. 33 [x]Did any people ever hear
the voice of a god speaking out of the midst of the fire, as you have heard, and still live?
34 Or has any god ever attempted to go and take a nation for himself from the midst of
another nation, by trials, [y]by signs, by wonders, and [z]by war, [a]by a mighty hand and [b]an
outstretched arm, and by great deeds of terror, all of which the LORD your God did for
you in Egypt before your eyes? 35 To you it was shown, [c]that you might know that the
LORD is God; [d]there is no other besides him. 36 [e]Out of heaven he let you hear his voice,

19 [a]ch. 17:3; Job 31:26-28 [b]2 Kgs. 17:16; 21:3; [Gen. 2:1]
20 [c]1 Kgs. 8:51; Jer. 11:4 [d]ch. 9:29; 32:9
21 [e]See ch. 1:37
22 [f]ch. 3:27 [g]ch. 3:25
23 [h]ver. 9 [i]ch. 5:8; Ex. 20:4; [Acts 17:29]
24 [j]Ex. 24:17; Cited Heb. 12:29; [ch. 9:3; Isa. 10:16-18; 29:6; 30:27, 30; Zeph. 1:18] [k][Isa. 42:8]; See Ex. 20:5
25 [l]ver. 16 [m]ch. 9:18; 2 Kgs. 17:17
26 [n]ch. 30:18, 19; 31:28; 32:1; Isa. 1:2; Jer. 2:12; 6:19; Mic. 6:2
27 [o]See Lev. 26:33 [p]ch. 28:62
28 [q]ch. 28:36, 64; Jer. 16:13 [r]Ps. 115:4-7; 135:15-17; Isa. 44:9; 46:7
29 [s]ch. 30:2, 3; Lev. 26:40-42; 2 Chr. 15:4; Neh. 1:9; Isa. 55:6, 7; Jer. 29:13, 14
30 [t]See Gen. 49:1
31 [u]Ex. 34:6; 2 Chr. 30:9; Neh. 9:31; Jonah 4:2 [v]ch. 31:6, 8; Josh. 1:5; 1 Chr. 28:20
32 [w]Job 8:8
33 [x]ver. 12; ch. 5:24, 26; Ex. 3:6; 19:21; [Gen. 32:30; Ex. 24:11; 33:20, 23; Judg. 6:22, 23; 13:22]
34 [y]ch. 26:8; Ex. 7:3; Jer. 32:21 [z]See Ex. 15:3-10 [a]ch. 7:8; 11:2; 26:8; 34:12 [b]Ex. 6:6; Jer. 32:21
35 [c][Ex. 10:2] [d]ver. 39; 1 Sam. 2:2; 2 Sam. 22:32; Isa. 45:5, 18, 22; 46:9; Cited Mark 12:32
36 [e]Ex. 19:9, 19; Neh. 9:13

4:20 The Lord's saving acts in bringing Israel out from slavery (**iron furnace**; see also 1 Kings 8:51; Jer. 11:4) in Egypt give cause to worship. **His own inheritance** suggests privilege and intimacy (see Deut. 9:26, 29). Israel is the Lord's inheritance; the land is Israel's inheritance (4:21, etc.), though the landless tribe of Levi has the Lord as their inheritance (10:9; 12:12; 18:1).

4:21–22 because of you. See notes on 1:37–38; 3:26–28. **good land**. The land was described as "good" by the spies (1:25; cf. 1:35). The repeated emphasis serves as encouragement to Israel to enter.

4:23–24 A return to the prohibition of idolatry. **Take care** again suggests the ease with which people fall into idolatry (see v. 19 and note on v. 9). From the iron furnace of Egypt (v. 20) to a **consuming fire** (cf. 5:25; 9:3): Israel's covenant relationship with the Lord is to be exclusive. God is **jealous** for his people's unqualified allegiance. This is in fact the language of love (see also 5:9; 6:15; 9:3; cf. Heb. 12:29).

4:25–26 Calling on elements of nature to testify to an oath is a common feature of ancient Near Eastern covenant documents. See also 30:19 and 31:28.

4:27–28 scatter. See 28:64–68. **few in number**. See 28:62. The punishment for idolatry is exile to a pagan land; God will hand Israel over to an idolatrous nation to continue the sinful practice (cf. Rom. 1:24, 26, 28). Sarcasm is expressed here that other gods **neither see, nor hear, nor eat, nor smell** (see Ps. 115:4–7; 135:15–17).

4:29–30 Exile is not the end. There remains hope of repentance and return (see 30:1–10). **with all your heart and with all your soul**. See note on 6:5. **obey his voice**. Returning to the Lord means forsaking the worship of visible forms and obeying his commands. See note on 4:12.

4:31 merciful. God's mercy does not compromise his jealous anger (v. 24; cf. 5:9–10; Ex. 34:6–7). In Deuteronomy, mercy is grounded in the Lord's faithfulness to the Abrahamic promises (9:27; 30:5, 20). God will maintain his **covenant** with Abraham, even if Israel forgets it (4:23; see Rom. 3:3–4). God also **swore** those promises under oath (Gen. 22:16; Heb. 6:13, 17–18). Cf. note on Deut. 1:8.

4:32–34 The Lord's approach to Israel at Sinai is the greatest event in any time (**since the day that God created man**) or any place (**one end of heaven to the other**). The theme of Israel's uniqueness resumes from vv. 5–20. **By a mighty hand and an outstretched arm** represents God's power (see 5:15; 7:19; 9:29; 11:2; 26:8; Ex. 3:19–20).

4:35–36 that you might know. The plagues were revelatory, so that Israel, as well as Pharaoh and Egypt, might know the Lord (Ex. 6:7). **there is no other**. See also Deut. 4:39; cf. 5:7; 6:4; 32:39. Deuteronomy asserts clear monotheism (belief in only one true God; see Mark 12:32). God is sovereign both in **heaven** and on **earth**.

that he might discipline you. And on earth he let you see his great fire, and [x]you heard
his words out of the midst of the fire. **37** And because [f]he loved your fathers and chose
their offspring after them[1] and brought you out of Egypt [g]with his own presence, by his
great power, **38** [h]driving out before you nations greater and mightier than you, to bring
you in, to give you their land for an inheritance, as it is this day, **39** know therefore today,
and lay it to your heart, that [i]the LORD is God in heaven above and on the earth beneath;
[j]there is no other. **40** [k]Therefore you shall keep his statutes and his commandments, which
I command you today, [l]that it may go well with you and with your children after you,
and that you may prolong your days in the land that the LORD your God is giving you
for all time."

Cities of Refuge

41 Then Moses [m]set apart three cities in the east beyond the Jordan, **42** that [n]the manslayer
might flee there, anyone who kills his neighbor unintentionally, without being at enmity
with him in time past; he may flee to one of these cities and save his life: **43** [o]Bezer in the
wilderness on the [p]tableland for the Reubenites, Ramoth in Gilead for the Gadites, and
Golan in Bashan for the Manassites.

Introduction to the Law

44 This is the law that Moses set before the people of Israel. **45** These are the testimonies,
the statutes, and the rules, which Moses spoke to the people of Israel when they came
out of Egypt, **46** beyond the Jordan [q]in the valley opposite Beth-peor, in the land of Sihon
the king of the Amorites, who lived at Heshbon, [r]whom Moses and the people of Israel
defeated when they came out of Egypt. **47** And they took possession of his land and the land
[s]of Og, the king of Bashan, the two kings of the Amorites, who lived to the east beyond
the Jordan; **48** [t]from Aroer, which is on the edge of the Valley of the Arnon, as far as Mount
[u]Sirion[2] (that is, [v]Hermon), **49** together with all the Arabah on the east side of the Jordan as
far as [w]the Sea of the Arabah, under the slopes of Pisgah.

The Ten Commandments

5 And Moses summoned all Israel and said to them, "Hear, O Israel, the statutes and the
rules that I speak in your hearing today, and you shall learn them and be careful to do
them. **2** [x]The LORD our God made a covenant with us in Horeb. **3** [y]Not with our fathers did
the LORD make this covenant, but with us, who are all of us here alive today. **4** The LORD
spoke with you [z]face to face at the mountain, out of the midst of the fire, **5** [a]while I stood
between the LORD and you at that time, to declare to you the word of the LORD. For [b]you
were afraid because of the fire, and you did not go up into the mountain. He said:

6 [c]"'I am the LORD your God, who brought you out of the land of Egypt, out of the
house of slavery.

[1] Hebrew *his offspring after him* [2] Syriac; Hebrew *Sion*

36 [x][See ver. 33 above]
37 [f]ch. 10:15 [g]Ex. 33:14; [Isa. 63:9]
38 [h]ch. 7:1; 11:23; Ex. 23:27, 28; 34:24; See ch. 9:1-5
39 [i]Josh. 2:11; 1 Kgs. 8:23; 2 Chr. 20:6; Eccles. 5:2 [j]1 Sam. 2:2; 2 Sam. 22:32; Isa. 45:5, 18, 22; 46:9; Cited Mark 12:32
40 [k]Lev. 22:31 [l]ch. 5:16; 6:2, 3; 11:9; 12:25, 28; 22:7; [Prov. 3:1, 2; 10:27]
41 [m]Num. 35:6, 14
42 [n]ch. 19:4
43 [o]Josh. 20:8; 21:36; 1 Chr. 6:78 [p]See ch. 3:10
46 [q]ch. 3:29 [r]ch. 1:4; Num. 21:24
47 [s]ch. 3:3, 4; Num. 21:33, 35
48 [t]See ch. 2:36 [u][ch. 3:9] [v]See ch. 3:9
49 [w]See ch. 3:17

Chapter 5

2 [x]ch. 4:23; Ex. 19:5
3 [y][Heb. 8:9]
4 [z][ch. 34:10; Ex. 33:11; Num. 14:14; Judg. 6:22]
5 [a]Ex. 20:21; [Gal. 3:19] [b]Ex. 19:16; 20:18; 24:2
6 [c]For ver. 6-21, see Ex. 20:2-17

4:37–39 Juxtaposed with God's universal sovereignty is his love of Abraham, Isaac, and Jacob (see notes on 1:8; 4:31). **loved**. A key, and unique, theme of Deuteronomy is the love of God for the patriarchs (here and 10:15), or for his people in general (5:10; 7:9, 12–13; 23:5), and Israel's reciprocal love for God (6:5; 7:9; 10:12; 11:1, 13, 22; 13:3; 19:9; 30:6, 16, 20). **as it is this day**. See note on 2:30. **know . . . and lay it to your heart**. Deuteronomy is constantly concerned with the state of Israel's heart (see 6:4–5; 7:17; 8:2, 17; 9:4; 10:16).

4:41–43 *Setting Apart Cities of Refuge.* Three cities, **Bezer**, **Ramoth**, and **Golan**, are set apart in Transjordan as places to which a person guilty of manslaughter can flee to evade revenge from the dead person's family (see also Num. 35:9–28). In Deut. 19:1–13, three more cities west of the Jordan are set apart for the same purpose.

4:44–11:32 *Moses' Second Speech: General Covenant Stipulations.* The first part of Moses' second speech largely consists of general covenant stipulations. More specific stipulations follow in chs. 12–16.

4:44–49 *Introduction to Moses' Second Speech.* These verses provide the geographical and historical setting of the second speech. See 2:24–3:29.

5:1–21 *The Ten Commandments.* As in Exodus 20–24, the Ten Commandments stand at the head of the law given at Sinai (see Ex. 20:1–17). In many respects, the detailed laws of Deuteronomy 12–26 follow the general pattern of the Ten Commandments, suggesting that the Ten Commandments function as a summary of God's requirements for his people. All but the Sabbath commandment (5:12–15) and the commandment against carved images (vv. 8–10) are explicitly reinforced in the NT.

5:1 Hear, O Israel often introduces new and important sections; cf. 4:1; 6:4; 9:1; 20:3. **Statutes and the rules** covers all the ethical teaching of Deuteronomy.

5:3 Not with our fathers . . . but with us. In reality, the Horeb covenant (Exodus 19–24) *was* made with the previous generation. However, generations are conflated to make a rhetorical point: the current generation is just as bound by the covenant at Horeb as their parents were. See notes on Deut. 1:20–21 and 1:29–31. See also 4:10; 11:2–9; 29:13–15.

5:5 you were afraid. See vv. 22–27.

5:6 The Ten Commandments begin with a statement of a preexisting relationship with the Lord (**your God**) and recognition of his prior action in saving Israel. Obedience to the Ten Commandments and laws in general therefore does not earn the relationship but is a response of faith to God's grace.

7 " 'You shall have no other gods before[1] me.
8 " 'You shall not make for yourself a carved image, or any likeness of anything that is
in heaven above, or that is on the earth beneath, or that is in the water under the earth.
9 You shall not bow down to them or serve them; for I the LORD your God am a jealous
God, visiting the iniquity of the fathers on the children to the third and fourth generation
of those who hate me, 10 but showing steadfast love to [d]thousands[2] of those who love me
and keep my commandments.
11 " 'You shall not take the name of the LORD your God in vain, for the LORD will not
hold him guiltless who takes his name in vain.
12 " 'Observe the Sabbath day, to keep it holy, as the LORD your God commanded you. 13 Six
days you shall labor and do all your work, 14 but [e]the seventh day is a Sabbath to the LORD
your God. On it you shall not do any work, you or your son or your daughter or your male
servant or your female servant, or your ox or your donkey or any of your livestock, or the
sojourner who is within your gates, [f]that your male servant and your female servant may
rest as well as you. 15 [g]You shall remember that you were a slave[3] in the land of Egypt, and
the LORD your God brought you out from there [h]with a mighty hand and an outstretched
arm. Therefore the LORD your God commanded you to keep the Sabbath day.
16 " 'Honor your father and your mother, as the LORD your God commanded you, [i]that
your days may be long, and that it may go well with you in the land that the LORD your
God is giving you.
17 [j]" 'You shall not murder.[4]
18 [j]" 'And you shall not commit adultery.
19 " 'And you shall not steal.
20 " 'And you shall not bear false witness against your neighbor.
21 " 'And you shall not covet your neighbor's wife. And you shall not desire your neigh-

[1] Or *besides* [2] Or *to the thousandth generation* [3] Or *servant* [4] The Hebrew word also covers causing human death through carelessness or negligence

10 [d]Ex. 20:6; Jer. 32:18
14 [e]Ex. 16:29, 30; Heb. 4:4 [f][Ex. 23:12]
15 [g]ch. 15:15; 16:12; 24:18, 22 [h]See ch. 4:34
16 [i]See ch. 4:40
17 [j]Matt. 5:21, 27; Luke 18:20; James 2:11
18 [j][See ver. 17 above]

5:7 no other gods. Exclusive worship of the Lord is an obvious corollary of his incomparability (4:35, 39). The Israelites were not the only monotheists in antiquity. The Egyptian Pharaoh Akhenaton (Amenophis IV, ruled c. 1350–1334 B.C.) worshiped the Aton, i.e., the sun god, as the only God. But this brand of monotheism is distinctly different: the Aton is personified in the sun, and he is impersonal and mechanistic. Yahweh is not part of creation; he is personal, ethical, and is in covenant with his people.

5:8 a carved image. The prohibition of images and likenesses derives from the argument of 4:12, 15–19, 23 that at Horeb, God's revelation was audible but not visible.

5:9–10 jealous. See 4:24 and note on 4:23–24. **visiting the iniquity**. This is not God punishing innocent children for up to four generations (see 7:10). Rather, up to four generations of **those who hate** God may suffer the effects of their ancestors' sins or even continue in the same sins. See also Ex. 34:6–7. The view that innocent children suffer for their parents' sins is opposed in Jer. 31:29–30 and Ezek. 18:2–4. **But** contrasts God's treatment of those who hate him with his treatment of those who love him. God's **steadfast love** far outlasts the effects of sin on subsequent generations.

5:11 To **take the name** is to utter it, as in an oath (cf. Ps. 16:4); **in vain** indicates "for a worthless purpose" (e.g., deceitfully). This commandment thus prohibits using God's name when making a vow or oath that is intentionally left unfulfilled. It also prohibits perjury, as well as the wrong attribution of character or motive to God (such as in Deut. 1:27).

5:12–14 Sabbath rest also applies to domestic animals and to **the sojourner who is within your gates** (v. 14), i.e., foreigners who take up permanent residence in Israel and accept its rules but cannot own land (see note on 1:16–17). The work prohibited is not defined here, but see Ex. 34:21; 35:3; Num. 15:32–36.

5:15 Unlike the parallel in Ex. 20:11 (which presents Sabbath keeping as imitating God's rest after the creation, cf. Gen. 2:1–3), the motivation for the **Sabbath** rest here is Israel's liberation from slavery. (Cf. Ex. 31:12–17, which brings together the themes of *creation* and *Israel as God's special covenant people* as the grounds for Sabbath observance.) Israel is frequently urged in Deuteronomy to **remember** their slavery **in the land of Egypt** as a spur to keeping the law (Deut. 15:15; 16:12; 24:18, 22). Remembering is often linked to obedience (7:18; 8:2, 18; 9:7; 11:2; 16:3; 24:9; 25:17; 32:7).

5:16 that your days may be long. See also 4:40; 5:33; 6:2; 11:9; 25:15; 30:18. This did not merely mean a long life, but one that experienced God's presence and favor: **that it may go well with you**. This motivation is absent in Ex. 20:12; see note on Deut. 1:5. (See also 4:40; 5:29, 33; 6:3, 18; etc.)

5:17 You shall not murder. The verb used here (Hb. *ratsakh*) includes both the unlawful or immoral killing of another human being (the specific meaning of the English word "murder") and also (see ESV footnote at Ex. 20:13) causing the death of another human being through careless or negligent behavior (as in Deut. 19:4–6; cf. Num. 35:22–25). This verb is never used in the OT of killing in war. The exact opposite of murder is commanded in Lev. 19:18, "You shall love your neighbor as yourself."

5:18 you shall not commit adultery. This specific prohibition is against having sexual relations with a person who is married to someone else, but it implies a broader concern for sexual purity shown in the detailed laws about other kinds of sexual sin (21:10–23:14). Both 5:21 and Matt. 5:28 show that God was concerned not only with outward conformity to this law but also with purity of heart.

5:19 you shall not steal. This command requires each Israelite to respect a neighbor's property (thus promoting honest labor as the means of earning wealth). A right to personal ownership of property is implied: the obligation not to steal a neighbor's animal (see v. 21) indicates that the neighbor has a right to keep the animal as personal property.

5:20 you shall not bear false witness. "Bearing witness" suggests a legal trial in which false testimony could lead to punishment for the **neighbor**, so the command prohibits a hateful lie. For detailed laws concerning false witness, see 19:16–21; 25:1–16; for a more general directive about truth-telling, see Lev. 19:11.

5:21 Unlike the parallel in Ex. 20:17, the **neighbor's wife** is listed first and with a different verb (**covet**) from the possessions of the husband (**desire**), setting her apart as no mere possession. God requires purity of heart with regard to the seventh (Deut. 5:18) and the tenth (5:21) commandments, and, by implication, all 10 (cf. Matt. 5:21–30).

bor's house, his field, or his male servant, or his female servant, his ox, or his donkey, or
anything that is your neighbor's.'
22 "These words the LORD spoke to all your assembly [k]at the mountain out of the midst
of the fire, the cloud, and the thick darkness, with a loud voice; and he added no more.
And [l]he wrote them on two tablets of stone and gave them to me. 23 And [m]as soon as you
heard the voice out of the midst of the darkness, while the mountain was burning with
fire, you came near to me, all the heads of your tribes, and your elders. 24 And you said,
'Behold, the LORD our God has shown us his glory and [n]greatness, and [o]we have heard his
voice out of the midst of the fire. This day we have seen God speak with man, and man
[p]still live. 25 Now therefore why should we die? For this great fire will consume us. [q]If we
hear the voice of the LORD our God any more, we shall die. 26 [p]For who is there of all flesh,
that has heard the voice of the living God speaking out of the midst of fire as we have, and
has still lived? 27 Go near and hear all that the LORD our God will say, and [r]speak to us all
that the LORD our God will speak to you, and we will hear and do it.'
28 "And the LORD heard your words, when you spoke to me. And the LORD said to me, 'I
have heard the words of this people, which they have spoken to you. [s]They are right in all
that they have spoken. 29 [t]Oh that they had such a heart as this always, to fear me and to
keep all my commandments, [u]that it might go well with them and with their descendants[1]
forever! 30 Go and say to them, "Return to your tents." 31 But you, stand here by me, and [v]I
will tell you the whole commandment and the statutes and the rules that you shall teach
them, that they may do them in the land that I am giving them to possess.' 32 You shall be
careful therefore to do as the LORD your God has commanded you. [w]You shall not turn
aside to the right hand or to the left. 33 [x]You shall walk in all the way that the LORD your
God has commanded you, that you may live, and [y]that it may go well with you, and that
you may live long in the land that you shall possess.

The Greatest Commandment

6 "Now this is [z]the commandment—the statutes and the rules[2]—that the LORD your
God commanded me to teach you, that you may do them in the land to which you are
going over, to possess it, 2 that [a]you may fear the LORD your God, you and your son and your
son's son, by keeping all his statutes and his commandments, which I command you, all the
days of your life, and [b]that your days may be long. 3 Hear therefore, O Israel, and be careful
to do them, that it may go well with you, and that you may multiply greatly, [c]as the LORD,
the God of your fathers, has promised you, in a land flowing with milk and honey.
4 "Hear, O Israel: [d]The LORD our God, the LORD is one.[3] 5 You [e]shall love the LORD your
God with all your heart and with all your soul and with all your might. 6 And [f]these words
that I command you today shall be on your heart. 7 [g]You shall teach them diligently to

[1] Or *sons* [2] Or *just decrees*; also verse 20 [3] Or *The LORD our God is one LORD*; or *The LORD is our God, the LORD is one*; or *The LORD is our God, the LORD alone*

22 [k]See ch. 4:11 [l]ch. 9:10, 11; Ex. 24:12
23 [m]See ch. 4:12
24 [n]See ch. 3:24 [o]Ex. 19:19 [p]See ch. 4:33
25 [q]ch. 18:16
26 [p][See ver. 24 above]
27 [r]See Ex. 20:19
28 [s]ch. 18:17
29 [t]ch. 32:29; Ps. 81:13; Isa. 48:18; [Matt. 23:37; Luke 19:42] [u]See ch. 4:40
31 [v]Gal. 3:19
32 [w]ch. 17:20; 28:14; Josh. 1:7; 23:6; 2 Kgs. 22:2; Prov. 4:27
33 [x]ch. 10:12; 30:16; Jer. 7:23; [Luke 1:6] [y]See ch. 4:40

Chapter 6

1 [z]ch. 4:1; 5:31; 12:1
2 [a]ch. 5:29; 10:12, 20; 13:4; Ps. 128:1; Eccles. 12:13 [b]See ch. 4:40
3 [c]Gen. 15:5; 22:17; 26:4; 28:14; Ex. 32:13
4 [d]Cited Mark 12:29; [Isa. 42:8; Zech. 14:9; John 17:3; 1 Cor. 8:4, 6]
5 [e]Cited Matt. 22:37; Mark 12:30; Luke 10:27; [2 Kgs. 23:25]
6 [f]ch. 11:18; 32:46; Ps. 37:31; Isa. 51:7; Jer. 31:33
7 [g]See ch. 4:9

5:22–33 *Israel Requests Moses to Mediate God's Law.* Having heard the Ten Commandments audibly, Israel fears continuing to hear the Lord's voice and requests Moses to relay to them all the following laws, a request to which the Lord consents.

5:22 Each of the **two tablets of stone** probably contained the full Ten Commandments, following ancient Near Eastern treaty practice. Both copies were later placed inside the ark of the covenant. The remainder of Israel's law was written by Moses in a book and kept beside the ark (31:24–26).

5:27 we will hear and do it. Israel's fear at hearing God's voice (see also Ex. 20:18–21) is accompanied by their pledge of obedience.

5:29 God's wish is that their holy and appropriate **fear** at the theophany of Horeb would become a permanent fear of the Lord in their hearts (see note on 1:20–21).

5:32–33 not turn aside to the right hand or to the left. God's way is likened to a straight path. See also 2:27; 17:11, 20; 28:14. **walk in all the way**. See also 8:6; 9:16; 10:12; 11:22; 19:9; 26:17; 28:9; 30:16; 31:29.

6:1–25 *The Greatest Commandment.* These verses contain one of the great commandments, namely, to love God with all of one's power (v. 5), which follows the famous statement of the uniqueness of God (v. 4). The section comprises general exhortations to obey and warnings not to disobey.

6:1–2 commandment . . . statutes . . . rules. See 5:31. **fear the LORD**. A common command in Deuteronomy. See 4:10; 5:29; 6:13, 24; 8:6; 10:12, 20; 13:4; 14:23; 17:19; 28:58; 31:12, 13. Cf. note on Prov. 1:7.

6:3 milk and honey. This description of the land is added incentive to obedience. See also 11:9; 26:9, 15; 27:3; 31:20.

6:4 Hear, O Israel. This verse is called the *Shema* from the Hebrew word for "Hear." **The LORD our God, the LORD is one** (see ESV footnote). The Lord alone is Israel's God, "the only one." It is a statement of exclusivity, not of the internal unity of God. This point arises from the argument of ch. 4 and the first commandment. While Deuteronomy does not argue theoretically for monotheism, it requires Israel to observe a practical monotheism (cf. 4:35). This stands in sharp contrast to the polytheistic Canaanites.

6:5 love. See 4:37. **all**. That the Lord alone is Israel's God leads to the demand for Israel's exclusive and total devotion to him. **heart . . . soul . . . might**. All Israelites in their total being are to love the Lord; "this is the great and first commandment" (Matt. 22:38). In Matt. 22:37, Mark 12:30, and Luke 10:27, Jesus also includes "mind." In early Hebrew, "heart" included what we call the "mind". "Might" indicates energy and ability.

6:6 on your heart. Cf. 4:39. The demand is for a heart that totally loves the Lord. Deuteronomy anticipates the new covenant, when God's words will be truly and effectively written on the heart (Jer. 31:31–34; also Deut. 30:6–8).

6:7–9 The two pairs of opposites (**sit/walk, lie down/rise**) suggest any

your children, and shall talk of them when you sit in your house, and when you walk by
the way, and when you lie down, and when you rise. 8 [h]You shall bind them as a sign on
your hand, and they shall be as frontlets between your eyes. 9 [i]You shall write them on the
doorposts of your house and on your gates.
10 "And when the LORD your God brings you into the land that he swore to your fathers,
to Abraham, to Isaac, and to Jacob, to give you—with great and good cities [j]that you did
not build, 11 and houses full of all good things that you did not fill, and cisterns that you
did not dig, and vineyards and olive trees that you did not plant—and when you eat and
are full, 12 [k]then take care lest you forget the LORD, who brought you out of the land of
Egypt, out of the house of slavery. 13 It is [l]the LORD your God you shall fear. Him you shall
serve and [m]by his name you shall swear. 14 You shall not [n]go after other gods, [o]the gods of
the peoples who are around you— 15 for [p]the LORD your God in your midst [q]is a jealous
God—[r]lest the anger of the LORD your God be kindled against you, and he destroy you
from off the face of the earth.
16 [s]"You shall not put the LORD your God to the test, [t]as you tested him at Massah. 17 You
shall [u]diligently keep the commandments of the LORD your God, and his testimonies and
his statutes, which he has commanded you. 18 [v]And you shall do what is right and good
in the sight of the LORD, that it may go well with you, and that you may go in and take
possession of the good land that the LORD swore to give to your fathers 19 [w]by thrusting
out all your enemies from before you, as the LORD has promised.
20 [x]"When your son asks you in time to come, 'What is the meaning of the testimonies
and the statutes and the rules that the LORD our God has commanded you?' 21 then you
shall say to your son, [y]'We were Pharaoh's slaves in Egypt. And the LORD brought us out of
Egypt with a mighty hand. 22 And [z]the LORD showed signs and wonders, great and grievous, against Egypt and against Pharaoh and all his household, before our eyes. 23 And he
brought us out from there, that he might bring us in and give us the land that he swore
to give to our fathers. 24 And the LORD commanded us to do all these statutes, [a]to fear the
LORD our God, [b]for our good always, that [c]he might preserve us alive, as we are this day.
25 And [d]it will be righteousness for us, if we are careful to do all this commandment before
the LORD our God, as he has commanded us.'

A Chosen People

7 "When the [e]LORD your God brings you into the land that you are entering to take possession of it, and clears away many nations before you, [f]the Hittites, the Girgashites,
the Amorites, the Canaanites, the Perizzites, the Hivites, and the Jebusites, seven nations
[g]more numerous and mightier than you, 2 [h]and when the LORD your God gives them over

8 [h]ch. 11:18; Prov. 3:3; 6:21; 7:3; See Ex. 13:9
9 [i]ch. 11:20; [Isa. 57:8]
10 [j]Josh. 24:13; [Josh. 11:13; Neh. 9:25; Ps. 105:44]
12 [k][Prov. 30:8, 9]
13 [l]Cited Matt. 4:10; Luke 4:8 [m]ch. 10:20; Josh. 2:12; Ps. 63:11; Isa. 45:23; 65:16; Jer. 12:16
14 [n]ch. 8:19; 11:16, 28; 13:2, 3; 28:14; Jer. 25:6 [o]ch. 13:7
15 [p]ch. 7:21 [q]See Ex. 20:5 [r]ch. 7:4; 11:17
16 [s]Cited Matt. 4:7; Luke 4:12 [t]ch. 9:22; 33:8; Ps. 95:8; [1 Cor. 10:9]; See Ex. 17:2-7
17 [u]ch. 11:22; Ps. 119:4
18 [v]See ch. 12:25
19 [w]Ex. 23:28-30; Num. 33:52, 53
20 [x]Ex. 12:26; 13:14
21 [y][Ex. 20:2]
22 [z]Ps. 135:9; See ch. 4:34
24 [a]ver. 2, 13 [b]ch. 10:13; Jer. 32:39 [c]ch. 4:1; 8:1; [Lev. 18:5; Ps. 41:2]
25 [d]ch. 24:13

Chapter 7

1 [e]ch. 31:3; Ps. 44:2, 3 [f]See Ex. 23:23 [g]ch. 4:38; 9:1; 11:23
2 [h]ver. 23; ch. 23:14

and every time, place, and activity. **bind them . . . write them**. Many Jews have fulfilled these commands literally with phylacteries (v. 8) and mezuzot (v. 9), i.e., boxes bound on the arm and forehead or attached to doorposts containing vv. 4–5 and other Scripture verses. See also 11:18–20.

6:10–12 that you did not. This repetition stresses the nature of the land as a good gift of God. All these things took time, effort, or a waiting period before they were finished or bore fruit. **eat and are full**. The land will be bountiful and satisfying. But such a gift is not without its risks, notably forgetfulness. To **forget** is less a memory problem than a moral one, a parallel to disobedience (8:11).

6:13 fear. See v. 2 and note on vv. 1–2. Jesus quotes this verse in his refusal to bow down to Satan in the wilderness (Matt. 4:10; Luke 4:8), demonstrating that he was God's perfect Son, whereas Israel had failed its wilderness tests. See also Deut. 6:16 and 8:3.

6:14–15 other gods. Deuteronomy's great fear—Israel's potential apostasy—is reiterated (cf. 4:16–19; 8:11–20). **jealous**. See 4:24 and note on 4:23–24.

6:16 You shall not put the LORD your God to the test. Testing God is an act of disobedience and a lack of trust in him. Israel's behavior at **Massah** (see Ex. 17:7) was a constant pattern in the wilderness (Num. 14:22). Jesus quoted this verse in his wilderness temptations (Matt. 4:7; Luke 4:12).

6:20–24 What is the meaning . . . ? This hypothetical question (cf. Ex. 12:26) elicits an answer that the law is set in the context of salvation from Egypt (see also the preface to the Ten Commandments, Deut. 5:6).

6:25 be righteousness for us. See also 24:13. This need not mean "righteousness as merited legal status," which would clash with God's gracious initiative (6:20–24; cf. 7:6–8). In context, the words mean "righteousness as the right response of obedience to God's covenant."

7:1–26 *Exclusive Relationship Worked Out in Conquest and Worship.* The emphases on the incomparability of the Lord and the demand for exclusive allegiance to him are now applied to Israel's conquest. See parallels in Ex. 23:20–33.

7:1 The **Hittites** (not the same group as those in Anatolia [Turkey]) are descended from Ham, like the other peoples listed in this verse (cf. Gen. 10:15–17). On **Amorites** and **Canaanites**, see Deut. 1:7. The **Perizzites** are associated with Canaanites in Gen. 13:7 and Judg. 1:4–5. The **Hivites** lived around Shechem, in Gibeonite territory and in the north, near Mount Hermon. The **Jebusites** were based in Jerusalem. Compare the lists in Deut. 20:17 (which omits the **Girgashites**); Josh. 3:10; 24:11. For a parallel to Deut. 7:1–6, see Ex. 34:11–16.

7:2 devote them to complete destruction. See 2:34–35; 20:10–18; and note on 20:16–18. **no covenant**. Israel's covenant with God is exclusive, and thus covenants with other nations are prohibited (cf. Joshua 9). **no mercy**. The listed nations (see Deut. 7:1) inhabit Israel's land promised by God. They are being punished for their sins (Gen. 15:16); the God of justice is using Israel as his executioner; and any mercy shown to those whom God is judging will

to you, and you defeat them, then you must [i]devote them to complete destruction.[1] [j]You
shall make no covenant with them and show no mercy to them. 3 [k]You shall not intermarry
with them, giving your daughters to their sons or taking their daughters for your sons,
4 for they would turn away your sons from following me, to serve other gods. [l]Then the
anger of the LORD would be kindled against you, and he would destroy you [m]quickly. 5 But
thus shall you deal with them: [n]you shall break down their altars and dash in pieces their
[n]pillars and chop down their [n]Asherim and [o]burn their carved images with fire.

6 "For [p]you are a people holy to the LORD your God. The LORD your God has chosen you
to be [p]a people for his treasured possession, out of all the peoples who are on the face of
the earth. 7 It was not because you were more in number than any other people that the
LORD set his love on you and chose you, for you were the fewest of all peoples, 8 but [q]it is
because the LORD loves you and is keeping [r]the oath that he swore to your fathers, that
the LORD has brought you out with a mighty hand and redeemed you from the house of
slavery, from the hand of Pharaoh king of Egypt. 9 Know therefore that the LORD your God
is God, [s]the faithful God [t]who keeps covenant and steadfast love with those who love him
and keep his commandments, to a thousand generations, 10 and [u]repays to their face those
who hate him, by destroying them. [v]He will not be slack with one who hates him. He will
repay him to his face. 11 [w]You shall therefore be careful to do the commandment and the
statutes and the rules that I command you today.

12 [x]"And because you listen to these rules and keep and do them, the LORD your God will
keep with you [y]the covenant and the steadfast love that he swore to your fathers. 13 He will
[z]love you, bless you, and multiply you. [a]He will also bless the fruit of your womb and the
fruit of your ground, your grain and your wine and your oil, the increase of your herds
and the young of your flock, in the land that he swore to your fathers to give you. 14 You
shall be blessed above all peoples. [b]There shall not be male or female barren among you
or among your livestock. 15 And the LORD will take away from you all sickness, and none
of the evil [c]diseases of Egypt, which you knew, will he inflict on you, but he will lay them
on all who hate you. 16 And [d]you shall consume all the peoples that the LORD your God
will give over to you. [e]Your eye shall not pity them, neither shall you serve their gods, for
that would be [f]a snare to you.

17 "If you say in your heart, 'These nations are greater than I. How can I dispossess them?'
18 [g]you shall not be afraid of them but you shall [h]remember what the LORD your God did
to Pharaoh and to all Egypt, 19 the great trials that your eyes saw, [i]the signs, the wonders,
the mighty hand, and the outstretched arm, by which the LORD your God brought you
out. So will the LORD your God do to all the peoples of whom you are afraid. 20 Moreover,
[j]the LORD your God will send hornets among them, until those who are left and hide

2 [i]ch. 20:17; Ex. 22:20; Lev. 27:29; Num. 21:2, 3 [j]Ex. 23:32; 34:12; Judg. 2:2; [ch. 20:10; Josh. 2:14; 9:18; Judg. 1:24]
3 [k]Ex. 34:16; Josh. 23:12, 13; 1 Kgs. 11:2; [Ezra 9:2]
4 [l]ch. 6:15 [m][ch. 4:26; 28:20]
5 [n]See Ex. 34:13 [o]ver. 25
6 [p]ch. 14:2; 26:19; 28:9; Ex. 19:6; 22:31; Jer. 2:3; Amos 3:2; 1 Pet. 2:9; See Ex. 19:5
8 [q]ch. 10:15; Isa. 43:4; 63:9; Jer. 31:3; Hos. 11:1; Mal. 1:2 [r]Ex. 32:13; Ps. 105:9-11; Luke 1:72, 73
9 [s]Isa. 49:7; 1 Cor. 1:9; 10:13; 2 Cor. 1:18; 1 Thess. 5:24; 2 Thess. 3:3; 2 Tim. 2:13; Heb. 10:23; 1 John 1:9 [t]ch. 5:10; Ex. 20:6; 2 Chr. 6:14; Neh. 1:5; 9:32; Dan. 9:4
10 [u]Job 34:11; Isa. 59:18; Nah. 1:2, 3 [v][2 Pet. 3:9]
11 [w]ch. 10:13
12 [x]For ver. 12-16, see ch. 28:1-14; Lev. 26:3-13 [y]Ps. 105:8; Luke 1:55, 72
13 [z][John 14:21] [a]ch. 30:9
14 [b]Ex. 23:26
15 [c]ch. 28:27, 60; Ex. 9:14; 15:26
16 [d]ver. 2 [e]ch. 13:8; 19:13, 21; 25:12 [f]ver. 25; ch. 12:30; Judg. 8:27; See Ex. 23:33
18 [g]ch. 1:29; 31:6 [h]Ps. 77:11; 105:5
19 [i]ch. 6:22; 11:3
20 [j]Ex. 23:28; Josh. 24:12

[1] That is, set apart (devote) as an offering to the Lord (for destruction)

not only compromise God's punishment but will also make Israel vulnerable to follow their evil ways (Deut. 7:16).

7:3–4 The prohibition of intermarriage would be unnecessary if all the Canaanites were destroyed. Intermarriage with those of other religions is the issue, not interracial marriage or ethnic cleansing. Israel is vulnerable to **turn away** from God (see esp. Solomon in 1 Kings 11:1–8). That is far more likely than Israelites converting their non-Israelite spouses to the Lord (cf. 2 Cor. 6:14–15).

7:5 All the paraphernalia of Canaanite religion is to be totally destroyed or it will be a snare to Israel (see v. 16 and note on 12:2–3). The **pillars** were made of stone. **Asherim** were wooden poles adorned with female fertility symbols (see note on Judg. 6:25–26).

7:6 For. This verse provides the reason for the preceding commands. **holy to the LORD**. At its heart, holiness means being exclusively separated to God. Hence Israel must have no association with pagan religion. **chosen**. See 4:37; 10:15; 14:2. **treasured possession**. See Ex. 19:5; Deut. 14:2; 26:18.

7:7–8 The Lord's **love** for Israel derives from his love for their **fathers**, the patriarchs (4:37), and not from their own merits. See also 9:4–5.

7:9–10 Unlike 5:9–10, there is no mention here of visiting iniquity to the third or fourth generations. Rather, God **repays to their face those who hate him**.

7:12 Though the **covenant** God made with Abraham had few conditions, Israel is obligated to keep the Sinai covenant laws for the Abrahamic covenant to remain in force. See Gen. 12:2–3; Deut. 28:4, 11–13.

7:13–15 The fulfillment of the Abrahamic covenant is described in terms of blessing. **Grain . . . wine and . . . oil** represent the three main crops (see also 11:14; 12:17; 14:23; 18:4; 28:51). **Evil diseases** may refer to the plagues against Egypt (Exodus 7–14), or more generally the diseases that were common afflictions in Egypt.

7:16 snare. See Ex. 10:7; 23:33; 34:12; Judg. 2:3; 8:27; 1 Sam. 18:21; Ps. 106:36.

7:17–18 Israel is warned three times (here, 8:17, and 9:4) not to **say in your heart** certain things that express fear (7:17) or pride (8:17; 9:4). The state of Israel's heart is a key issue in Deuteronomy (see 4:39; 6:6; and notes on 4:37–39; 6:6). The answer to each warning is "remember" (7:18; 8:18; 9:7). The antidote to wrong fear is to **remember what the LORD your God did**. Right fear means fearing God (see note on 5:29).

7:20 The **hornets** are either literal, or figuratively represent the "panic" of those chased by hornets; see Ex. 23:28, and note on Josh. 24:12 (cf. "bees" in Deut. 1:44).

themselves from you are destroyed. **21** You shall not be in dread of them, for the LORD your
God is [k]in your midst, [l]a great and awesome God. **22** [m]The LORD your God will clear away
these nations before you little by little. You may not make an end of them at once,[1] lest the
wild beasts grow too numerous for you. **23** [n]But the LORD your God will give them over to
you and throw them into great confusion, until they are destroyed. **24** And [o]he will give
their kings into your hand, and you shall [p]make their name perish from under heaven.
[q]No one shall be able to stand against you until you have destroyed them. **25** The carved
images of their gods [r]you shall burn with fire. You [s]shall not covet the silver or the gold
that is on them or take it for yourselves, lest you be [t]ensnared by it, for it is an abomination
to the LORD your God. **26** And you shall not bring an abominable thing into your house
and become devoted to destruction[2] like it. You shall utterly detest and abhor it, [u]for it is
devoted to destruction.

Remember the LORD Your God

8 "The whole commandment that I command you today [v]you shall be careful to do,
that you may live and multiply, and go in and possess the land that the LORD swore
to give to your fathers. **2** And you shall remember the whole way that the LORD your God
has led you [w]these forty years in the wilderness, that he might humble you, [x]testing you
[y]to know what was in your heart, [z]whether you would keep his commandments or not.
3 And he humbled you and [a]let you hunger and [b]fed you with manna, which you did not
know, nor did your fathers know, that he might make you know that [c]man does not live by
bread alone, but man lives by every word[3] that comes from the mouth of the LORD. **4** [d]Your
clothing did not wear out on you and your foot did not swell these forty years. **5** Know then
in your heart that, [e]as a man disciplines his son, the LORD your God disciplines you. **6** So
you shall keep the commandments of the LORD your God by walking in his ways and by
fearing him. **7** For the LORD your God is bringing you into a good land, [f]a land of brooks
of water, of fountains and springs, flowing out in the valleys and hills, **8** a land of wheat
and barley, [g]of vines and fig trees and pomegranates, a land of olive trees and honey, **9** a
land in which you will eat bread without scarcity, in which you will lack nothing, a land
whose stones are iron, and out of whose hills you can dig copper. **10** And you shall eat and
be full, and you shall bless the LORD your God for the good land he has given you.
11 "Take care lest you forget the LORD your God by not keeping his commandments and
his rules and his statutes, which I command you today, **12** [h]lest, when you have eaten and
are full and have built good houses and live in them, **13** and when your herds and flocks
multiply and your silver and gold is multiplied and all that you have is multiplied, **14** [i]then

[1] Or *quickly* [2] That is, set apart (devoted) as an offering to the Lord (for destruction); twice in this verse [3] Hebrew *by all*

21 [k]ch. 6:15; Num. 11:20; 14:14; Josh. 3:10 [l]ch. 10:17; Neh. 1:5; 4:14; 9:32; [ch. 28:58]
22 [m]Ex. 23:29, 30
23 [n]ver. 2
24 [o]Josh. 10:24, 42; 11:12; See Josh. 12:1 [p]See ch. 9:14 [q]ch. 11:25; Josh. 1:5; 10:8; 23:9
25 [r]ver. 5; ch. 12:3; [Ex. 32:20; 1 Chr. 14:12] [s][Josh. 7:1, 21] [t]See ver. 16
26 [u]ch. 13:17; Lev. 27:28; Josh. 6:17, 18; 7:1; [Mic. 4:13]

Chapter 8

1 [v]ch. 4:1; 5:32, 33; 6:1-3
2 [w]ch. 1:3; 2:7; 29:5; Amos 2:10 [x]ver. 16; Ex. 15:25 [y][2 Chr. 32:31] [z][Ex. 16:4; Judg. 3:4]
3 [a]Ex. 16:2, 3 [b]Ex. 16:12, 14, 15, 35; [Num. 11:6-9; 21:5] [c]Cited Matt. 4:4; Luke 4:4; [John 6:49-51]
4 [d]ch. 29:5; Neh. 9:21
5 [e]Prov. 3:12; Heb. 12:5, 6; [2 Sam. 7:14; Prov. 29:17; Hos. 10:10; Rev. 3:19]
7 [f]ch. 11:10-12
8 [g][Num. 20:5]
12 [h]ch. 6:11, 12; 28:47; 32:15; Prov. 30:9; Hos. 13:6
14 [i][1 Cor. 4:7]

7:22–23 little by little. See Ex. 23:29–30. This verse gives some theological interpretation to the book of Joshua. While Josh. 10:42 envisages a rapid conquest, Josh. 11:18 acknowledges that Joshua's wars took a long time. **Confusion** is a common feature of holy war (see Deut. 28:20; also Ex. 14:24; Josh. 10:10; 1 Sam. 5:9, 11; 14:20).

7:25–26 See note on v. 5. **Abomination** is an important word in Deuteronomy (see 12:31; 13:14; 14:3; 17:1, 4; 18:9, 12; 20:18; 22:5; 23:18; 24:4; 25:16; 27:15; 32:16). It denotes a significant sin, often with the sense of social or theological hypocrisy, and God's increased anger against it. **devoted to destruction**. See note on 2:34–35.

8:1–20 *Learning the Lessons of the Wilderness.* This chapter makes clear that the wilderness period was not only a punishment but also a test. While contrasting the deprivation of the wilderness with the abundance of the land, this chapter implies that the land itself is also a test. If the wilderness lesson is learned, it can be applied in the new situation of the land.

8:2–3 Remember is a key word in this chapter (also v. 18), along with its antonym "forget": vv. 11, 14, 19. Remembrance is demonstrated in obedience (see 5:15 and note). **testing you**. The wilderness test was to reveal the state of Israel's **heart**. This does not imply that God did not **know** but rather that he desired for Israel's heart to produce evidence of obedience. **Manna** literally means "What is it?" (Ex. 16:15); it was not to their liking (Num. 11:6; 21:5). The testing was also to teach Israel **that man does not live by bread alone, but man lives by every word that comes from the mouth of the LORD**. Real life derives directly from God and trusting his word ("word" could also be translated "thing spoken of"; see also ESV footnote). This was the learning that Israel needed in its heart (Deut. 8:2) if it was to pass the test in the land (e.g., v. 17). This is the first of three verses from Deuteronomy quoted by Jesus in his temptation, affirming his confidence and determined faithfulness toward God (Matt. 4:4; Luke 4:4; see also Deut. 6:13, 16).

8:4 clothing . . . foot. Cf. 29:5; Neh. 9:21.

8:5 Again the emphasis is on Israel's **heart**. The wilderness test was punishment for the generation that perished, but a loving act of discipline for the current generation. **disciplines**. See Prov. 3:11–12; Heb. 12:5–11.

8:7 The purpose of passing the test of v. 3 is because (**For**) Israel is entering an especially abundant land (vv. 7–10). Though the antithesis of the **good land**, the wilderness is the testing ground for life in the land.

8:10 The culmination of this hymn-like praise of the land is complete satisfaction. For that, Israel is to **bless the LORD**, i.e., praise him.

8:11 Satisfaction carries a warning: **Take care** (see 4:9, 23), the command that 8:7–10 has been working toward. **forget**. See note on vv. 2–3. For a parallel of vv. 7–11, see 6:10–12.

8:14 The danger is a **heart . . . lifted up**, namely, pride (see note on 7:17–18). In the land of plenty, pride comes from forgetting the wilderness (8:14–16) and failing to apply its lessons in the good land.

your heart be lifted up, and you [j]forget the LORD your God, who brought you out of the
land of Egypt, out of the house of slavery, 15 who [k]led you through the great and terrifying
wilderness, [l]with its fiery serpents and scorpions [m]and thirsty ground where there was
no water, [n]who brought you water out of the flinty rock, 16 who fed you in the wilderness
with [o]manna that your fathers did not know, that he might humble you and test you, [p]to
do you good in the end. 17 Beware [q]lest you say in your heart, 'My power and the might of
my hand have gotten me this wealth.' 18 You shall remember the LORD your God, for [r]it is
he who gives you power to get wealth, [s]that he may confirm his covenant that he swore
to your fathers, as it is this day. 19 And if you forget the LORD your God and go after other
gods and serve them and worship them, [t]I solemnly warn you today that you shall surely
perish. 20 Like the nations that the LORD makes to perish before you, [u]so shall you perish,
because you would not obey the voice of the LORD your God.

Not Because of Righteousness

9 "Hear, O Israel: you are [v]to cross over the Jordan today, to go in to dispossess nations
[w]greater and mightier than you, cities great and fortified up to heaven, 2 a people great
and tall, [x]the sons of the Anakim, [y]whom you know, and of whom you have heard it said,
'Who can stand before the sons of Anak?' 3 Know therefore today that he who [z]goes over
before you [a]as a consuming fire is the LORD your God. He will destroy them and subdue
them before you. [b]So you shall drive them out and make them perish quickly, as the LORD
has promised you.

4 [c]"Do not say in your heart, after the LORD your God has thrust them out before you,
'It is because of my righteousness that the LORD has brought me in to possess this land,'
whereas it is [d]because of the wickedness of these nations that the LORD is driving them
out before you. 5 [e]Not because of your righteousness or the uprightness of your heart are
you going in to possess their land, but because of the wickedness of these nations the
LORD your God is driving them out from before you, and that he may confirm [f]the word
that the LORD swore to your fathers, to Abraham, to Isaac, and to Jacob.

6 "Know, therefore, that the LORD your God is not giving you this good land to possess
because of your righteousness, for you are [g]a stubborn people. 7 Remember and do not
forget how you provoked the LORD your God to wrath in the wilderness. [h]From the day
you came out of the land of Egypt until you came to this place, you have been rebellious
against the LORD. 8 Even [i]at Horeb you provoked the LORD to wrath, and the LORD was so
angry with you that he was ready to destroy you. 9 [j]When I went up the mountain to receive
the tablets of stone, the tablets of the covenant that the LORD made with you, I remained

14 [j]Ps. 78:11; 106:21
15 [k]See ch. 1:19 [l]Num. 21:6; Isa. 30:6 [m]Hos. 13:5 [n]Ex. 17:6; Num. 20:11; Ps. 78:15; 114:8; [ch. 32:13]
16 [o]ver. 3; Ex. 16:15 [p][Jer. 24:5-7; Heb. 12:11]
17 [q][ch. 9:4]
18 [r][Prov. 10:22; Hos. 2:8] [s]ch. 7:8, 12
19 [t][ch. 4:26; 30:18]
20 [u][Dan. 9:11, 12]

Chapter 9

1 [v]ch. 11:31; 12:10; Josh. 1:11 [w]See ch. 4:38
2 [x]See Num. 13:22 [y]ch. 1:28
3 [z]ch. 31:3; [Josh. 3:11] [a]See ch. 4:24 [b]ch. 7:24; Ex. 23:29-31
4 [c][ch. 8:17] [d]ch. 18:12; Lev. 18:24, 25; 20:23; [ch. 20:18]
5 [e][Titus 3:5] [f]See Gen. 50:24
6 [g]ch. 10:16
7 [h]ver. 24; ch. 31:27; [Ex. 14:11; 15:24; 16:2; 17:2; Num. 11:4; 14:2, 11, 41; 20:2; 21:5; 25:2]
8 [i]Ex. 32:4; Ps. 106:19
9 [j]Ex. 24:12, 15

8:15 water out of the flinty rock. See Ex. 17:6 and Num. 20:8, 11. Massah is where Israel tested God (Deut. 6:16). In reality, Israel was being tested by God.

8:17 say in your heart. See 7:17 and note on 7:17–18. This verse puts into words the pride alluded to in 8:14 and is the climax of vv. 12–17.

8:18 Instead of forgetfulness (vv. 11, 14), Israel is to **remember**. See v. 2 and note on vv. 2–3; 5:15 and note. **it is he who gives you power**. This is an explicit corrective to the proud words in 8:17. Israel's future wealth will be evidence of God's faithfulness to keep covenant. **as it is this day**. See 2:30 and note.

8:19–20 The path of forgetfulness leads not only to pride (vv. 14, 17) but also to idolatry. When Israel commits idolatry, it acts like a pagan nation and so its destiny at God's hands will be **like** that of the **nations**.

9:1–10:11 *Recounting the Golden Calf Incident.* Continuing the theme of Israel's "heart" problem, this section speaks of Israel's stubbornness in sin and gives extended evidence of that stubbornness.

9:2 Anakim. See 1:28 and note on 1:27–28.

9:3 consuming fire. Cf. 4:24, where this expression was used of potential judgment against Israel. Here, the nations will be the object of God's consuming fire. **Quickly** contrasts with 7:22. Compared with their long settlement in the land, the Canaanites will disappear quickly, but by the timescale of the conquest it will be a slow process.

9:4–5 Do not say in your heart (see 7:17 and note on 7:17–18) alludes to Israel's pride and the heart as its source (cf. 8:17). In the ancient world, victory in battle was regarded as a reward for one's righteousness in the eyes of the gods. Israel is warned away from such thinking. While victory in the Promised Land is God's punishment of the nations' wickedness, that does not imply Israel's righteousness. Israel's possession of the land is due solely to God's faithfulness to the Abrahamic promises.

9:6 Yet again, the point is made (cf. vv. 4–5) that Israel's **righteousness** is not the cause of its being given the land. Israel is in fact **stubborn**, literally, "stiff-necked" (see also vv. 13, 27). The account of the golden calf is retold at length (vv. 7–21) to demonstrate Israel's stubbornness.

9:7 As with 7:17–18 and 8:17–20, the way to avoid saying wrong things in the heart (cf. 9:4) is to **remember**. Remembering their history of moral failure in the wilderness is humbling, countering Israel's potential pride. **wrath**. Various Hebrew words translated "wrath," "anger," "angry," and "hot displeasure" are used in ch. 9 (vv. 8, 18, 19, 20, 22). Verses 7–8 and 20–22 bracket the account of the golden calf. **From the day**. Israel's provocation of God began even before the people crossed the Red Sea (Ex. 14:11).

9:8 Even at Horeb, where they heard God's voice directly, Israel misbehaved. The retelling of the golden calf incident follows (cf. Exodus 32–34).

9:9–10 When I went up. See Ex. 24:12–18. **finger of God**. See Ex. 31:18. **all the words . . . spoken with you**. That is, the Ten Commandments (see Deut. 5:22).

on the mountain [k]forty days and forty nights. I neither ate bread nor drank water. 10 And
[l]the LORD gave me the two tablets of stone written with the finger of God, and on them
were all the words that the LORD had spoken with you on the mountain out of the midst
of the fire [m]on the day of the assembly. 11 And at the end of forty days and forty nights
the LORD gave me the two tablets of stone, the tablets of the covenant. 12 Then the LORD
said to me, [n]'Arise, go down quickly from here, for your people whom you have brought
from Egypt have acted corruptly. They have [o]turned aside quickly out of the way that I
commanded them; they have made themselves a metal image.'

The Golden Calf

13 [p]"Furthermore, the LORD said to me, 'I have seen this people, and behold, it is [g]a stubborn people. 14 [q]Let me alone, that I may destroy them and [r]blot out their name from under
heaven. And [s]I will make of you a nation mightier and greater than they.' 15 [t]So I turned
and came down from the mountain, and [u]the mountain was burning with fire. And the
two tablets of the covenant were in my two hands. 16 And [v]I looked, and behold, you had
sinned against the LORD your God. You had made yourselves a golden[1] calf. [w]You had
turned aside quickly from the way that the LORD had commanded you. 17 So I took hold
of the two tablets and threw them out of my two hands and broke them before your eyes.
18 Then I [x]lay prostrate before the LORD [y]as before, forty days and forty nights. I neither
ate bread nor drank water, because of all the sin that you had committed, [z]in doing what
was evil in the sight of the LORD to provoke him to anger. 19 For I was afraid of the anger
and hot displeasure that the LORD bore against you, so that he was ready to destroy you.
[a]But the LORD listened to me that time also. 20 And the LORD was so angry with Aaron
that he was ready to destroy him. And I prayed for Aaron also at the same time. 21 Then [b]I
took the sinful thing, the calf that you had made, and burned it with fire and crushed it,
grinding it very small, until it was as fine as dust. And I threw the dust of it into the brook
that ran down from the mountain.

22 "At [c]Taberah also, and at [d]Massah and at [e]Kibroth-hattaavah you provoked the LORD
to wrath. 23 And [f]when the LORD sent you from Kadesh-barnea, saying, 'Go up and take
possession of the land that I have given you,' then you rebelled against the commandment
of the LORD your God and [g]did not believe him or obey his voice. 24 [h]You have been rebellious against the LORD from the day that I knew you.

25 [x]"So I lay prostrate before the LORD for these forty days and forty nights, because the
LORD had said he would destroy you. 26 [i]And I prayed to the LORD, 'O Lord GOD, do not
destroy your people and your heritage, whom you have redeemed through your greatness,
whom you have brought out of Egypt with a mighty hand. 27 Remember your servants,
Abraham, Isaac, and Jacob. Do not regard the stubbornness of this people, or their wick-

[1] Hebrew *cast metal*

9 [k]Ex. 24:18; 34:28; [1 Kgs. 19:8; Matt. 4:2; Luke 4:1, 2]
10 [l]Ex. 31:18 [m]ch. 4:10; 10:4; 18:16; Ex. 19:17
12 [n]Ex. 32:7, 8 [o][ch. 31:29; Judg. 2:17]
13 [p]Ex. 32:9 [g][See ver. 6 above]
14 [q]Ex. 32:10 [r]ch. 7:24; 25:19; 29:20; Ex. 17:14 [s]Num. 14:12
15 [t]Ex. 32:15 [u]ch. 4:11; 5:23; Ex. 19:18
16 [v]Ex. 32:19 [w][ch. 31:29; Judg. 2:17]
18 [x]Ex. 34:28; [Ps. 106:23] [y]ver. 9; ch. 10:10 [z]ch. 4:25
19 [a]ch. 10:10; Ex. 32:14; 33:17
21 [b]Ex. 32:20
22 [c]Num. 11:1-3 [d]Ex. 17:7, [e]Num. 11:34
23 [f]Num. 13:3; 14:1-4 [g]Ps. 106:24, 25
24 [h]ver. 7; ch. 31:27
25 [x][See ver. 18 above]
26 [i]See Ex. 32:11-13

9:12 your people whom you have brought. God disowns Israel and passes them over to Moses (cf., e.g., 5:6, "I am the LORD your God, who brought you out . . ."). **quickly**. This heightens the contrast of Israel's sin with having so recently received the Ten Commandments.

9:13–15 This people is almost a contemptuous description of Israel, continuing God's disassociation from Israel (see v. 12). Moses' intercession for the makers of the golden calf is not described until v. 25, though it is alluded to in v. 19, in order to keep the theme of Israel's stubbornness uninterrupted through v. 24 (cf. Ex. 32:9–10, 15).

9:17 broke them. Breaking the tablets indicates the deliberate ending of the covenant relationship: an impulsive gesture of fury and despair, following God's words in vv. 12–14. A treaty of Esarhaddon, an Assyrian king (681–669 B.C.), forbids his vassal to destroy the treaty text, as this would be tantamount to rebellion.

9:18–20 This is the second period of **forty days and forty nights** (see vv. 9, 11). **the LORD listened to me**. This alludes to Moses' intercession (see vv. 25–29). **Aaron** was Moses' brother, the priest of Israel. Exodus 32–34 does not mention any intercession for Aaron.

9:21 sinful thing. Deuteronomy emphasizes Israel's act of sin (see also vv. 16, 18, 27). No mention is made here of forcing Israel to drink the water with the ground-up golden calf (cf. Ex. 32:20).

9:22–24 Horeb was not the only location where the Lord was provoked to anger. As v. 7 suggests, this is far from a complete list. **Taberah**. See Num. 11:1–3. **Massah**. See Ex. 17:7 and Deut. 6:16. **Kibroth-hattaavah**. See Num. 11:34–35; 33:16–17. **Kadesh-barnea**. See Deut. 1:19–32. **From the day** brackets the account beginning with v. 7. Being **rebellious** is the same as being stubborn.

9:25 forty days and forty nights. Given its placement in Ex. 32:11–14, it is unclear if this is the same period as in Deut. 9:18, or earlier (see vv. 9–11), as the following prayer implies.

9:26 O Lord GOD. See 3:24 and note. **your people . . . whom you have brought out** (see also 9:29). Moses counters the Lord's disowning of Israel in vv. 12–14 (see note on v. 12).

9:27–28 The primary basis of intercession for mercy is the Abrahamic promise (see 4:31 and note). No excuse for Israel's **sin** is given, for there is none. A second basis of intercession is God's reputation among the nations, not the least being Egypt. Two wrong statements might be made if Israel is destroyed. The first is that God is impotent to save; the second is that he **hated** Israel. Both are untrue (cf. 1:27; Ex. 32:12).

edness or their sin, 28 lest the land from which you brought us say, [j]"Because the LORD
was not able to bring them into the land that he promised them, and because he hated
them, he has brought them out to put them to death in the wilderness." 29 [k]For they are
your people and your heritage, whom you brought out by your great power and by your
outstretched arm.'

New Tablets of Stone

10 "At that time the LORD said to me, [l]'Cut for yourself two tablets of stone like the first,
and come up to me on the mountain and [m]make an ark of wood. 2 And I will write
on the tablets the words that were on the first tablets that you broke, and [n]you shall put
them in the ark.' 3 So I made an ark [o]of acacia wood, and [p]cut two tablets of stone like the
first, and went up the mountain with the two tablets in my hand. 4 And [q]he wrote on the
tablets, in the same writing as before, the Ten Commandments[1] [r]that the LORD had spoken
to you on the mountain out of the midst of the fire [s]on the day of the assembly. And the
LORD gave them to me. 5 Then I turned and [t]came down from the mountain and [u]put the
tablets in the ark that I had made. [v]And there they are, as the LORD commanded me."
6 (The people of Israel [w]journeyed from Beeroth Bene-jaakan[2] to Moserah. [x]There Aaron
died, and there he was buried. And his son Eleazar ministered as priest in his place. 7 [y]From
there they journeyed to Gudgodah, and from Gudgodah to Jotbathah, a land with brooks
of water. 8 At that time [z]the LORD set apart the tribe of Levi [a]to carry the ark of the covenant
of the LORD [b]to stand before the LORD to minister to him and [c]to bless in his name, to
this day. 9 [d]Therefore Levi has no portion or inheritance with his brothers. The LORD is his
inheritance, as the LORD your God said to him.)
10 [e]"I myself stayed on the mountain, as at the first time, forty days and forty nights, [f]and
the LORD listened to me that time also. The LORD was unwilling to destroy you. 11 [g]And
the LORD said to me, 'Arise, go on your journey at the head of the people, so that they may
go in and possess the land, which I swore to their fathers to give them.'

Circumcise Your Heart

12 "And now, Israel, [h]what does the LORD your God require of you, but [i]to fear the LORD
your God, [j]to walk in all his ways, [k]to love him, to serve the LORD your God with all your
heart and with all your soul, 13 and [l]to keep the commandments and statutes of the LORD,
which I am commanding you today [m]for your good? 14 Behold, [n]to the LORD your God
belong heaven and the heaven of heavens, [o]the earth with all that is in it. 15 Yet [p]the LORD
set his heart in love on your fathers and chose their offspring after them, you above all
peoples, as you are this day. 16 Circumcise therefore [q]the foreskin of your heart, and be no

[1] Hebrew *words* [2] *Or the wells of the Bene-jaakan*

28 [j]Num. 14:16
29 [k]ch. 4:20; 1 Kgs. 8:51; Neh. 1:10; [Ps. 95:7]
Chapter 10
1 [l]Ex. 34:1, 2 [m]Ex. 25:10
2 [n]Ex. 25:16, 21
3 [o]Ex. 25:10; 37:1 [p]Ex. 34:4
4 [q]Ex. 34:28 [r]Ex. 20:1 [s]See ch. 9:10
5 [t]Ex. 34:29 [u]Ex. 40:20 [v]1 Kgs. 8:9
6 [w]Num. 33:30, 31 [x][Num. 20:28; 33:38]
7 [y]Num. 33:32, 33
8 [z]Num. 3:6; 8:14; 16:9; [1 Chr. 23:13] [a]Num. 4:5, 15 [b]ch. 17:12; 18:5, 7 [c]ch. 21:5; Lev. 9:22; See Num. 6:23-26
9 [d]See Num. 18:20
10 [e]ch. 9:18, 25 [f]ch. 9:19
11 [g]Ex. 32:34; 33:1
12 [h][Mic. 6:8] [i]See ch. 6:2, 13 [j]See ch. 5:33 [k]See ch. 6:5
13 [l]ch. 7:11 [m]ch. 6:24
14 [n]1 Kgs. 8:27; 2 Chr. 6:18; Neh. 9:6; Ps. 115:16; Isa. 66:1 [o]Ex. 19:5; Ps. 24:1
15 [p]ch. 4:37; [ch. 7:7]
16 [q]ch. 30:6; Jer. 4:4; [Acts 7:51]

10:1 Rather than an explicit reply, the Lord's answer is demonstrated in the command to replace the two tablets of stone broken in 9:17. The new tablets are **like the first**, with the same words, writing, and commandments (10:2–4). Deuteronomy first mentions the **ark** here (see also 31:9, 25–26) as simply a chest or box made **of wood**; it is not described as the footstool of God's throne. The ark was constructed (Ex. 37:1–9) soon after the writing of the replacement tablets (Ex. 34:1–4; see Deut. 10:1–5; for instructions to build the ark, see Exodus 25). It was a common practice in the ancient Near East to deposit covenant documents in religious shrines, one copy for each party.

10:5 there they are. The covenant is still in place, despite Israel's persistent provocations to anger the Lord over the past 40 years.

10:6–9 Even though **Aaron** eventually **died**, Moses' prayer for him was answered (9:20). Moreover, Aaron's death did not end the priesthood. God continued to provide priests through Aaron's son, **Eleazar**, and the **tribe of Levi** (see Ex. 32:26–29; Num. 3:6–14; Deut. 21:5). Since this tribe owned no land (18:1–2), it is singled out for specific care and provision by the other tribes (e.g., 12:12, 18; 14:27). **Beeroth Bene-jaakan . . . Moserah**. See Num. 33:30–31. The location of Moserah is uncertain, but presumably it was close to Mount Hor (cf. Num. 20:27–28). **Gudgodah** is the same as Hor-haggidgad (Num. 33:32–33). **Jotbathah**. See Num. 33:33–34.

10:11 The command to **arise** and **go on your journey** indicates that with the tablets replaced and the ark built, Moses' intercession has been answered fully.

10:12–11:32 *Exhortation.* Having focused on the key commandments and *Shema* (6:4–5; see note on 6:4), and having repeatedly expressed concern at Israel's record of failure and its heart of fear and pride, Moses now exhorts the Israelites to get their hearts right.

10:12–13 And now marks a transition from history to exhortation. **what does the LORD your God require of you**. Cf. Mic. 6:8. Five commands follow, the central one of which is **love** (see Deut. 4:37; 6:5; and note on 4:37–39; also 11:1, 13, 22). **fear**. See note on 6:1–2. **walk in all his ways**. See 5:33 and note on 5:32–33. **serve**. See 6:13; 10:20; 11:13; 13:4. **keep**. See 4:40; 5:29; 6:24. **for your good**. Obedience is for the people's benefit in the end.

10:14–15 The contrast between **heaven of heavens, the earth with all that is in it** and Israel's fathers heightens the sense of astonishment at election and grace. **love on your fathers**. See 4:37 and 7:7–8; note on 4:37–39; cf. 10:12.

10:16 Circumcise therefore the foreskin of your heart. The mention of "offspring" (v. 15) recalls Genesis 17, where God instituted circumcision as his covenant sign for Abraham and his descendants (cf. Gen. 17:9–14). This verse explicitly recognizes Israel's need to change its heart (cf. Deut. 29:4; see also Jer. 4:4; 9:25–26; Rom. 2:25–29). Here, circumcision symbolizes removing the stubbornness that prevents the heart from properly loving God (cf. Ex. 6:12, where "uncircumcised lips" do not speak well; Jer. 6:10, where "uncircumcised

longer [r]stubborn. 17 For the LORD your God is [s]God of gods and [t]Lord of lords, [u]the great,
the mighty, and the awesome God, who is [v]not partial and takes no bribe. 18 [w]He executes
justice for the fatherless and the widow, and loves the sojourner, giving him food and
clothing. 19 [x]Love the sojourner, therefore, for you were sojourners in the land of Egypt.
20 [i]You shall fear the LORD your God. You shall serve him and [y]hold fast to him, and [z]by
his name you shall swear. 21 [a]He is your praise. He is your God, [b]who has done for you
these great and terrifying things that your eyes have seen. 22 Your fathers went down to
Egypt [c]seventy persons, and now the LORD your God has made you [d]as numerous as the
stars of heaven.

Love and Serve the LORD

11 [e]"You shall therefore love the LORD your God and [f]keep his charge, his statutes, his
rules, and his commandments always. 2 And consider today (since I am not speaking
to [g]your children who have not known or seen it), consider the discipline[1] of the LORD
your God, [h]his greatness, [i]his mighty hand and his outstretched arm, 3 [j]his signs and his
deeds that he did in Egypt to Pharaoh the king of Egypt and to all his land, 4 and what he
did to the army of Egypt, to their horses and to their chariots, [k]how he made the water of
the Red Sea flow over them as they pursued after you, and how the LORD has destroyed
them to this day, 5 and [l]what he did to you in the wilderness, until you came to this place,
6 and [m]what he did to Dathan and Abiram the sons of Eliab, son of Reuben, how the earth
opened its mouth and swallowed them up, with their households, their tents, and every
living thing that followed them, in the midst of all Israel. 7 For your eyes have seen [n]all
the great work of the LORD that he did.

8 "You shall therefore keep the whole commandment that I command you today, that
you may [o]be strong, and go in and take possession of the land that you are going over to
possess, 9 and [p]that you may live long in the land [q]that the LORD swore to your fathers to
give to them and to their offspring, [r]a land flowing with milk and honey. 10 For the land
that you are entering to take possession of it is not like the land of Egypt, from which you
have come, where you sowed your seed and irrigated it,[2] like a garden of vegetables. 11 [s]But
the land that you are going over to possess is a land of hills and valleys, which drinks water
by the rain from heaven, 12 a land that the LORD your God cares for. [t]The eyes of the LORD
your God are always upon it, from the beginning of the year to the end of the year.

13 "And if you will indeed obey my commandments that I command you today, [u]to love
the LORD your God, and to serve him with all your heart and with all your soul, 14 [v]he[3] will
give the rain for your land in its season, [w]the early rain and the later rain, that you may
gather in your grain and your wine and your oil. 15 [x]And he will give grass in your fields
for your livestock, and [y]you shall eat and be full. 16 Take care [z]lest your heart be deceived,

[1] Or *instruction* [2] Hebrew *watered it with your feet* [3] Samaritan, Septuagint, Vulgate; Hebrew *I*; also verse 15

16 [r]See ch. 9:6
17 [s]Josh. 22:22; Ps. 136:2; Dan. 2:47; 11:36 [t]Rev. 17:14; 19:16 [u]Neh. 9:32; See ch. 7:21 [v]2 Chr. 19:7; Job 34:19; Acts 10:34; Rom. 2:11; Gal. 2:6; Eph. 6:9; Col. 3:25; 1 Pet. 1:17
18 [w]Ps. 68:5; 146:9; [ch. 24:17; Ex. 22:22]
19 [x]Ex. 22:21; 23:9; Lev. 19:33, 34
20 [i][See ver. 12 above] [y]ch. 11:22; 13:4; 30:20 [z]See ch. 6:13
21 [a]Ps. 22:3; 109:1; Jer. 17:14 [b]2 Sam. 7:23; Ps. 106:21, 22
22 [c]Gen. 46:27; Ex. 1:5; [Acts 7:14] [d]ch. 28:62; Neh. 9:23; See Gen. 15:5

Chapter 11

1 [e]See ch. 6:5 [f][Ezek. 44:16]; See Lev. 8:35
2 [g]ch. 31:13 [h]ch. 3:24; 5:24 [i]See ch. 4:34
3 [j]ch. 6:22; 7:19
4 [k]Ex. 14:27, 28; 15:9, 10; Ps. 106:11
5 [l]See Ps. 78:14-40
6 [m]Num. 16:1, 31; 27:3; Ps. 106:17
7 [n]Judg. 2:7
8 [o]ch. 31:6, 7; Josh. 1:6, 7, 9, 18
9 [p]See ch. 4:40 [q]See Gen. 50:24 [r]Ex. 3:8
11 [s]ch. 8:7
12 [t][1 Kgs. 9:3; Jer. 24:6]
13 [u]See ch. 6:5
14 [v]ch. 28:12; Lev. 26:4 [w][Job 29:23; Jer. 5:24; Hos. 6:3; Joel 2:23; James 5:7]
15 [x]Ps. 104:14 [y]ch. 6:11; [Joel 2:19]
16 [z][Job 31:27]

ears" do not hear clearly). This is a command beyond any human's competence to fulfill (see Deut. 30:6). **stubborn**. See 9:6 and note.

10:17 Israel's heart needs correction because (**for**) God is **the awesome God**. **not partial**. See 1:17. The election of Israel (10:15) does not mean God will cut moral corners in showing special favors to Israel. He is a just God (v. 18).

10:18–19 The **fatherless**, the **widow**, and the **sojourner** are the main categories of landless people (in addition to the Levites). Deuteronomy commands special care for such people (e.g., 14:29; 16:11, 14; 24:17, 19–21; 27:19). **you were sojourners**. Israel's own experience in **Egypt** is a motivation for several laws in Deuteronomy (e.g., 15:15; 24:18, 22).

10:20 fear the LORD your God. Cf. vv. 12–13. **hold fast**. See 4:4 and note on 4:3–4.

10:22 down to Egypt seventy persons. See Gen. 46:27 and Ex. 1:5. **numerous as the stars of heaven**. Having referred to the election of Abraham in Deut. 10:15, Moses now speaks of the fulfillment of part of the Abrahamic promise (Gen. 15:5). See Deut. 1:10 and note.

11:1 therefore. The command to love is grounded in God's gracious rescue of Israel from Egypt (10:21–22). **love**. See 4:37; 6:5; and note on 4:37–39.

11:2 Moses addresses the adults of Israel on the basis that all had experienced the exodus and wilderness events, even though the adults who left Egypt had died in the wilderness. See 5:3 and note. **discipline**. See 8:5.

11:6 Dathan and Abiram, along with Korah who is unnamed here, rebelled against Moses' leadership in the wilderness (Num. 16:1–35).

11:7 your eyes have seen. See notes on v. 2 and 1:29–31. See also 3:21; 4:3, 9, 12; 7:19; 10:21; 29:2.

11:9 milk and honey. See 6:3. Again, both the goodness of the land as well as God's faithfulness to the Abrahamic promise provide incentives for Israel to enter and conquer.

11:10 irrigated it. Lit., "watered it with your feet" (see ESV footnote). The need for irrigation in Egypt implies lack of rain. The use of feet, possibly to turn water wheels, implies hard work.

11:11–15 The idyllic picture of the land (cf. 6:10–11; 8:7–10) recalls the description of Eden (Gen. 2:5–13) and is an added incentive to conquer it. **The eyes of the LORD your God are always upon it** suggests care and protection as well as bounty. **if you will indeed obey**. This command lies in the center of idyllic land descriptions, highlighting the centrality of obedience. **early rain and the later rain**. Both October/November and March/April rains are needed for good crops. **eat and be full**. See Deut. 6:10–11 and 8:12.

11:16–17 Take care lest. Abundance always carries warnings (6:12; 8:11–12), often expressed in terms of the heart (8:11–17). The deception

and you turn aside and [a]serve other gods and worship them; 17 then [b]the anger of the
LORD will be kindled against you, and he [c]will shut up the heavens, so that there will be
no rain, and the land will yield no fruit, and [d]you will perish quickly off the good land
that the LORD is giving you.
18 [e]"You shall therefore lay up these words of mine in your heart and in your soul, and
[f]you shall bind them as a sign on your hand, and they shall be as frontlets between your
eyes. 19 You shall teach them to your children, talking of them when you are sitting in your
house, and when you are walking by the way, and when you lie down, and when you rise.
20 [g]You shall write them on the doorposts of your house and on your gates, 21 [h]that your
days and the days of your children may be multiplied in the land that the LORD swore to
your fathers to give them, [i]as long as the heavens are above the earth. 22 For if [j]you will be
careful to do all this commandment that I command you to do, loving the LORD your God,
walking in all his ways, and [k]holding fast to him, 23 then the LORD [l]will drive out all these
nations before you, and you will [m]dispossess nations greater and mightier than you. 24 [n]Every
place on which the sole of your foot treads shall be yours. Your territory shall be [o]from the
wilderness to[1] the Lebanon and from the River, the river Euphrates, to the western sea.
25 [p]No one shall be able to stand against you. The LORD your God will lay [q]the fear of you
and the dread of you on all the land that you shall tread, [r]as he promised you.
26 [s]"See, I am setting before you today a blessing and a curse: 27 [t]the blessing, if you obey
the commandments of the LORD your God, which I command you today, 28 and [u]the curse,
if you do not obey the commandments of the LORD your God, but turn aside from the way
that I am commanding you today, [v]to go after other gods that you have not known. 29 And
when the LORD your God brings you into the land that you are entering to take possession
of it, you shall set [w]the blessing on Mount Gerizim and the curse on Mount Ebal. 30 Are
they not beyond the Jordan, west of the road, toward the going down of the sun, in the
land of the Canaanites who live in the [x]Arabah, opposite Gilgal, beside [y]the oak[2] of Moreh?
31 For you are [z]to cross over the Jordan to go in to take possession of the land that the LORD
your God is giving you. And when you possess it and live in it, 32 you shall be careful [a]to
do all the statutes and the rules that I am setting before you today.

The LORD's Chosen Place of Worship

12 [b]"These are the statutes and rules that you shall be careful to do in the land that the
LORD, the God of your fathers, has given you to possess, [c]all the days that you live
on the earth. 2 [d]You shall surely destroy all the places where the nations whom you shall
dispossess served their gods, [e]on the high mountains and on the hills and under every

[1] Hebrew *and* [2] Septuagint, Syriac; see Genesis 12:6. Hebrew *oaks, or terebinths*

16 [a]ver. 28; See ch. 6:14
17 [b]ch. 6:15 [c]1 Kgs. 8:35; 2 Chr. 6:26; 7:13; [ch. 28:23, 24; Lev. 26:19, 20; Amos 4:7; Zech. 14:17; Rev. 11:6] [d]ch. 4:26; 30:18; Josh. 23:15, 16
18 [e]See ch. 6:6 [f]See ch. 6:8
20 [g]ch. 6:9
21 [h]See ch. 4:40 [i]Ps. 89:29
22 [j]ch. 6:17 [k]See ch. 10:20
23 [l]See ch. 4:38 [m]ch. 9:1
24 [n]Josh. 1:3; [Josh. 14:9] [o]See Ex. 23:31
25 [p]See ch. 7:24 [q]ch. 2:25 [r]Ex. 23:27
26 [s]ch. 30:1, 15, 19
27 [t]See ch. 28:2-14
28 [u]See ch. 28:15-45 [v]See ch. 6:14
29 [w]ch. 27:12, 13; Josh. 8:33
30 [x]See ch. 1:1 [y]Judg. 7:1
31 [z]ch. 9:1; 12:10; Josh. 1:11
32 [a]ch. 5:32; 12:32

Chapter 12

1 [b]ch. 6:1 [c]ch. 4:10
2 [d]ch. 7:5; Ex. 34:13 [e]1 Kgs. 14:23; 2 Kgs. 16:4; 17:10; Jer. 3:6

here is probably wrongly thinking that the Canaanite fertility gods are the source of the rain, crops, and animals. **anger**. The warnings also lead to the threat of punishment (see chs. 6; 8). Here, if the Lord is not acknowledged as the provider of rain (11:14), he will cause the rain to stop (see 28:23–24; cf. 1 Kings 17:1).

11:18–21 On remembering and imparting **these words** to the next generation, see note on 6:7–9. **as long as the heavens are above the earth**. That is, forever.

11:24–25 on which the sole of your foot treads. See Josh. 1:3; cf. Deut. 2:5; 28:65. **territory**. See 1:7; Gen. 15:18; Josh. 1:3–4. **fear of you and the dread of you**. See Deut. 2:25, though the expression is not identical in Hebrew. The promise assumes Israel's faithfulness.

11:26 I am setting before you today. This expression, repeated in v. 32, brackets these verses and gives them an urgency for making the right decision. Though the conquest is the immediate concern, general obedience is the ultimate goal. The two options are summarized as **a blessing and a curse** (see chs. 27–28). On the decision, see 30:15, 19.

11:28 that you have not known. There has been no personal relationship with the Canaanite Baals, unlike with the Lord, who has entered a covenant relationship with Israel.

11:29 See 27:1–14 for details on this ceremony and the two mountains.

11:30 Arabah. See 1:1 and note; 1:7. **Gilgal**. See Josh. 4:19. The **oak of Moreh** is where the promise of land was first made to Abraham (Gen. 12:6). The ceremony will implicitly acknowledge fulfillment of that promise.

11:31–32 These verses conclude the general exhortations from chs. 5–11.

12:1–26:19 *Moses' Second Speech: Specific Covenant Stipulations.* Following the general stipulations of chs. 5–11, the commands and laws become more specific. The order of the stipulations in these chapters seems to purposely follow the order of categories in the Ten Commandments.

12:1–32 *Proper Worship.* Chapter 12 deals with proper worship, expanding the understanding of the first commandment about having no other gods ahead of the Lord.

12:1 statutes and rules. This exact expression occurs in 5:1; 11:32; 26:16, at the beginning and ending of the two main sections of stipulations.

12:2–3 destroy all the places where the nations . . . served their gods. In the conquest, most cities still stood, except for Jericho, Ai, and Hazor (Josh. 6:24; 8:28; 10:1; 11:12–14). The places that are to be destroyed are the worship centers. Canaanite religion, focused on fertility, set up its shrines on **mountains** and **hills** and under significant trees. Archaeological excavations at Hazor provide an example of a Late Bronze Age Canaanite temple. Within a central niche (or "holy of holies"), a male deity sat on a throne. Next to him was a row of standing stones, or stelae, one of which

green tree. 3 You shall tear down their altars and dash in pieces [f]their pillars and burn their
[g]Asherim with fire. You shall chop down the carved images of their gods and [h]destroy their
name out of that place. 4 [i]You shall not worship the LORD your God in that way. 5 But you
shall seek [j]the place that the LORD your God will choose out of all your tribes to put his
name and make his habitation[1] there. There you shall go, 6 and there you shall bring your
burnt offerings and your sacrifices, [k]your tithes and the contribution that you present, your
vow offerings, your freewill offerings, and the [l]firstborn of your herd and of your flock.
7 And [m]there you shall eat before the LORD your God, and [n]you shall rejoice, you and your
households, in all that you undertake, in which the LORD your God has blessed you.
8 "You shall not do according to all that we are doing here today, [o]everyone doing whatever
is right in his own eyes, 9 for you have not as yet come to [p]the rest and to the inheritance
that the LORD your God is giving you. 10 But when [q]you go over the Jordan and live in the
land that the LORD your God is giving you to inherit, [r]and when he gives you rest from
all your enemies around, so that you live in safety, 11 then to [j]the place that the LORD your
God will choose, to make his name dwell there, there you shall bring all that I command
you: your burnt offerings and your sacrifices, [k]your tithes and the contribution that you
present, and all your finest vow offerings that you vow to the LORD. 12 And [n]you shall rejoice
before the LORD your God, you and your sons and your daughters, your male servants and
your female servants, and the Levite that is within your towns, since [s]he has no portion or
inheritance with you. 13 [t]Take care that you do not offer your burnt offerings at any place
that you see, 14 but at [j]the place that the LORD will choose in one of your tribes, there you
shall offer your burnt offerings, and there you shall do all that I am commanding you.
15 "However, you may slaughter and eat meat within any of your towns, as much as
you desire, [u]according to the blessing of the LORD your God that he has given you. [v]The
unclean and the clean may eat of it, as of the gazelle and as of the deer. 16 [w]Only you shall
not eat the blood; you shall pour it out on the earth like water. 17 You may not eat within
your towns [k]the tithe of your grain or of your wine or of your oil, or the firstborn of your
herd or of your flock, or any of your vow offerings that you vow, or your freewill offerings
or the contribution that you present, 18 but [m]you shall eat them before the LORD your God
in [j]the place that the LORD your God will choose, you and your son and your daughter,

[1] *Or name as its habitation*

3 [f]See ch. 16:22 [g]See ch. 16:21 [h][Zeph. 1:4; Zech. 13:2]
4 [i]ver. 31
5 [j]ch. 16:2; 26:2; 1 Kgs. 8:29; 2 Chr. 7:12; [Josh. 18:1]
6 [k]ch. 14:22, 23; 15:19, 20 [l]ch. 14:23
7 [m]ch. 14:23, 26; 15:20 [n]ch. 14:26; 16:11, 14, 15; 26:11; 27:7; 28:8; Lev. 23:40
8 [o]Judg. 17:6; 21:25
9 [p]1 Kgs. 8:56; Ps. 95:11; [Heb. 4:8]
10 [q]See ch. 11:31 [r]ch. 25:19; Josh. 23:1; [2 Sam. 7:1; 1 Kgs. 5:4]
11 [j][See ver. 5 above] [k][See ver. 6 above]
12 [n][See ver. 7 above] [s]See Num. 18:20
13 [t]Lev. 17:3, 4; [1 Kgs. 12:28, 33]
14 [j][See ver. 5 above]
15 [u]ch. 16:17 [v]ch. 14:5; 15:22
16 [w]See Lev. 3:17
17 [k][See ver. 6 above]
18 [m][See ver. 7 above] [j][See ver. 5 above]

had a carving of upraised hands stretched in worship toward the sun god. **tear . . . dash . . . burn . . . chop**. See Deut. 7:5. **Asherim**. See note on 7:5. **destroy their name out of that place**. The name indicated the presence of the god. See 12:5.

12:4 Not only Canaanite worship practices are prohibited but also the syncretism of using such places and paraphernalia to worship the Lord.

12:5–6 the place. It is a single "place," in contrast to "places" in v. 2 (also vv. 13–14). Contrast Ex. 20:24–25. This place is unnamed, though centuries later it was clearly identified with Jerusalem. Until then, the "place" was where the tabernacle resided, which for much of that time was Shiloh (Josh. 18:1, 10; 22:12; Judg. 18:31; 1 Sam. 1:3, 24; 3:21; 4:3; Jer. 7:12, 14). **the LORD your God will choose**. See Deut. 12:11, 14, 18, 21, 26; 14:23, 24; 16:2, 6–7, 11; 26:2. In Deuteronomy, the Lord chooses Israel (7:6), the king (17:15), and the priests (18:5). **Put his name and make his habitation** anticipates the realized presence of God, though God is not limited to such a place (e.g., 1 Kings 8:27–30). **There you shall go** (also Deut. 12:6, 7, 14), rather than to the Canaanite places. **bring**. Israel's worship of "bringing" is in response to God's bringing Israel into the land. **offerings . . . sacrifices** (also v. 11). See Leviticus 1–7.

12:7 eat. The "peace offering" sacrifices were not totally burned up on the altar. Part of the animal was to be eaten by the offerer, the offerer's household, and the priests. **before the LORD your God**. That is, in his presence, where his name dwells (also vv. 12, 18). **rejoice** (also vv. 12, 18). Unlike other ancient religions, which attempted to win the gods' favor or to appease them, Israelite worship was marked by rejoicing in response to grace and blessing.

12:8–9 according to all that we are doing here today. Once the land is entered, the laws of worship, especially regarding its place, are to be stricter. **everyone doing whatever is right in his own eyes**. See Judg. 17:6; 21:25. **rest**. See Deut. 3:20 and note. In a sense, this anticipated place of worship will reflect the abiding rest of Israel in the land, which finally occurs only under David (2 Sam. 7:1).

12:12 rejoice. See v. 7, which included households in general. Now specific members of the households are mentioned, notably **servants** and **the Levite** (landless categories of people). Levites were scattered in various **towns** to serve each of the other tribes. They owned no land (**portion or inheritance**) and relied on the offerings and sacrifices for their survival (v. 19; Num. 26:62). In this way worship was to be corporate and caring.

12:13–14 Take care implies the ease with which Israel will disobey this command, as their subsequent history shows. The repetition of the command to offer sacrifices only **at the place that the LORD will choose** (see v. 5) underscores its seriousness. **in one of your tribes**. While this phrase could mean one place per tribal territory, v. 5 has already specified one place for the entire nation.

12:15 you may slaughter and eat meat within any of your towns. Possibly up to this point, any meat eaten was ordinarily sacrificial. Now, partly because of the distances that people would be from the central place for sacrifice (vv. 20–21), provision is made for non-sacrificial eating of meat. **as much as you desire**. On abundance in the land, see 6:10–11; 8:7–10; 11:11–15. **unclean and the clean**. This is a ceremonial distinction, not a moral one. Leviticus 12–15 defines certain people as unclean and therefore forbidden to eat sacrificial meat, but this would not apply to meat from non-sacrificial animals.

12:16 you shall not eat the blood. See Gen. 9:4 and Lev. 3:17. The blood is the life (Deut. 12:23–24) and is divinely earmarked for atonement for sin (Lev. 17:10–12). See also Acts 15:20.

12:17–19 tithe . . . offerings. See v. 11. **servant . . . and the Levite**. See note on v. 12.

your male servant and your female servant, and the Levite who is within your towns. And
[n]you shall rejoice before the LORD your God in all that you undertake. 19 [x]Take care that
you do not neglect the Levite as long as you live in your land.
20 "When the LORD your God [y]enlarges your territory, [z]as he has promised you, and you
say, 'I will eat meat,' because you crave meat, you may eat meat whenever you desire. 21 If
[a]the place that the LORD your God will choose to put his name there is too far from you,
[b]then you may kill any of your herd or your flock, which the LORD has given you, as I have
commanded you, and you may eat within your towns whenever you desire. 22 Just [c]as the
gazelle or the deer is eaten, so you may eat of it. [c]The unclean and the clean alike may eat
of it. 23 [d]Only be sure that you do not eat the blood, [e]for the blood is the life, and you shall
not eat the life with the flesh. 24 You shall not eat it; you shall pour it out on the earth like
water. 25 You shall not eat it, [f]that all may go well with you and with your children after
you, [g]when you do what is right in the sight of the LORD. 26 But the [h]holy things that are
due from you, and [i]your vow offerings, you shall take, and you shall go to [a]the place that
the LORD will choose, 27 and [j]offer your burnt offerings, the flesh and the blood, on the
altar of the LORD your God. The blood of your sacrifices shall be poured out on the altar
of the LORD your God, but the flesh you may eat. 28 Be careful to obey all these words that
I command you, [f]that it may go well with you and with your children after you forever,
when you do what is good and right in the sight of the LORD your God.

Warning Against Idolatry

29 "When [k]the LORD your God cuts off before you the nations whom you go in to dispossess, and you dispossess them and dwell in their land, 30 take care [l]that you be not ensnared
to follow them, after they have been destroyed before you, and that you do not inquire
about their gods, saying, 'How did these nations serve their gods?—that I also may do the
same.' 31 [m]You shall not worship the LORD your God in that way, for every [n]abominable
thing that the LORD hates they have done for their gods, for [o]they even burn their sons
and their daughters in the fire to their gods.
32[1] "Everything that I command you, you shall be careful to do. [p]You shall not add to
it or take from it.

13 "If a prophet or [q]a dreamer of dreams arises among you and gives you a sign or a
wonder, 2 and [r]the sign or wonder that he tells you comes to pass, and if he says, 'Let
us go after other gods,' which you have not known, 'and let us serve them,' 3 you shall not
listen to the words of that prophet or that dreamer of dreams. For the LORD your God [s]is
testing you, to know whether you love the LORD your God with all your heart and with
all your soul. 4 You shall [t]walk after the LORD your God and fear him and keep his commandments and obey his voice, and you shall serve him and [u]hold fast to him. 5 But [v]that

18 [n][See ver. 7 above]
19 [x]ch. 14:27; [2 Chr. 31:4]
20 [y]ch. 19:8 [z]ch. 11:24; 19:8, 9; Gen. 28:14; Ex. 34:24
21 [a]See ver. 5 [b]ver. 15
22 [c]ch. 14:5; 15:22
23 [d]See Lev. 3:17 [e]See Gen. 9:4
25 [f]ch. 4:40; [Eccles. 8:12; Isa. 3:10] [g]ch. 6:18; 13:18; Ex. 15:26; 1 Kgs. 11:38
26 [h][Num. 5:9, 10; 18:19] [i][1 Sam. 1:21] [a][See ver. 21 above]
27 [j]Lev. 1:5, 9, 13; 17:11
28 [f][See ver. 25 above]
29 [k]ch. 19:1; Josh. 23:4, 5
30 [l]ch. 7:16
31 [m]ver. 4; Lev. 18:3, 26, 30; [2 Kgs. 17:15] [n]ch. 7:25; 17:1; 18:12; 23:18; 25:16; 27:15 [o]2 Kgs. 17:31; Jer. 7:31; 19:5
32 [p]See ch. 4:2

Chapter 13

1 [q]Jer. 23:25, 32; 27:9; 29:8; Zech. 10:2
2 [r][ch. 18:22; Jer. 28:9]
3 [s]ch. 8:2
4 [t]2 Kgs. 23:3; 2 Chr. 34:31 [u]See ch. 10:20
5 [v]ch. 18:20; [Jer. 2:8; 14:14, 15; Zech. 13:3]

[1] Ch 13:1 in Hebrew

12:20–22 you may eat meat. See v. 15 and note.

12:23–24 do not eat the blood. See v. 16 and note.

12:26–27 Holy things are things set apart for God: sacrifices, offerings, tithes, objects of vows. See vv. 17–18. **The blood of your sacrifices shall be poured out on the altar**. E.g., Lev. 1:5.

12:30 take care that you be not ensnared. See 7:2; and notes on 7:5; 7:16.

12:31 You shall not worship . . . in that way (see v. 4). Canaanite worship is not only wrong, it is accompanied by **abominable** moral practices (see 7:25, and note on 7:25–26), not the least of which is child sacrifice. See 2 Kings 3:27; 16:3; 23:10; Jer. 7:31; 19:5; 32:35.

12:32 not add to it or take from it. See note on 4:2.

13:1–18 *Threats of Idolatry.* Three scenarios (vv. 1–5, 6–11, 12–18) are addressed in which people are encouraged to worship other gods.

13:1 Much of OT law is "case law," supposing a particular situation and its right response. Here, each situation is introduced with **if** (vv. 1, 6, 12). **prophet or a dreamer of dreams**. Both would lay claim to divine revelatory authority.

13:2 Two things must occur in this scenario. First, **the sign or wonder that he tells you comes to pass**. A miracle or sign in itself is not, however, proof of God's direction since these can be performed other than under God's power (see the Egyptian magicians [e.g., Ex. 7:22] and Simon the Sorcerer [Acts 8:9]). But a word that did not come to pass was a clear indication that the Lord did not give it and that its speaker was not the Lord's spokesman (Deut. 18:21–22). The second condition is that the oracle-monger says, **Let us go after other gods**. This theological test is essential.

13:3 For the LORD your God is testing you. The Lord is testing faithfulness to himself by allowing false prophets to appear among his people. The warning is that fulfilled signs and wonders can be deceptive, and when accompanied by false teaching, they are not from the Lord. **love**. See 4:37–39 and note.

13:4 walk . . . fear. See 10:12–13, 20 and notes there. **hold fast**. See note on 4:3–4.

13:5 Israel must not only refuse to listen to the **prophet** or **dreamer**, they must **put** that person **to death**. He has broken the first commandment, a breach made clearer by the phrase **who brought you out of the land of Egypt** (see 5:6–7). Even though the prophet or dreamer of dreams is used by God to test Israel, that person is not innocent. **purge the evil from your midst**. See 17:7, 12; 19:19; 21:21; 22:21; 24:7 (the death penalty is implied in these cases). Just as Israel is to destroy all pagans from the land, so are they to purge any apostate Israelites, like they would a contagious infection (cf. excommunication in 1 Cor. 5:13). Capital punishment therefore is not only retributive but also protective of the community.

prophet or that dreamer of dreams shall be put to death, because he has taught rebellion
against the LORD your God, who brought you out of the land of Egypt and redeemed
you out of the house of slavery, to make you leave the way in which the LORD your God
commanded you to walk. [w]So you shall purge the evil[1] from your midst.
6 [x]"If your brother, the son of your mother, or your son or your daughter or [y]the wife
you embrace[2] or your friend [z]who is as your own soul entices you secretly, saying, 'Let us
go and serve other gods,' [a]which neither you nor your fathers have known, 7 some [b]of the
gods of the peoples who are around you, whether near you or far off from you, from the
one end of the earth to the other, 8 you shall [c]not yield to him or listen to him, nor [d]shall
your eye pity him, nor shall you spare him, nor shall you conceal him. 9 But you shall kill
him. [e]Your hand shall be first against him to put him to death, and afterward the hand
of all the people. 10 [f]You shall stone him to death with stones, because he sought to draw
you away from the LORD your God, who brought you out of the land of Egypt, out of the
house of slavery. 11 And [g]all Israel shall hear and fear and never again do any such wickedness as this among you.
12 "If you hear in one of your cities, which the LORD your God is giving you to dwell
there, 13 that certain [h]worthless fellows have gone out among you and have drawn away
the inhabitants of their city, saying, 'Let us go and serve other gods,' which you have not
known, 14 then you shall inquire and make search and ask [i]diligently. And behold, if it be
true and certain that such an abomination has been done among you, 15 you shall surely
put the inhabitants of that city to the sword, devoting it to destruction,[3] all who are in
it and its cattle, with the edge of the sword. 16 You shall gather all its spoil into the midst
of its open square and [j]burn the city and all its spoil with fire, as a whole burnt offering
to the LORD your God. It shall be a [k]heap forever. It shall not be built again. 17 [l]None of
the devoted things shall stick to your hand, [m]that the LORD may turn from the fierceness
of his anger and show you mercy and have compassion on you and multiply you, [n]as
he swore to your fathers, 18 if you obey the voice of the LORD your God, [o]keeping all his
commandments that I am commanding you today, and doing what is right in the sight
of the LORD your God.

Clean and Unclean Food

14 "You are [p]the sons of the LORD your God. [q]You shall not cut yourselves or make any
[r]baldness on your foreheads for the dead. 2 For [s]you are a people holy to the LORD
your God, and the LORD has chosen you to be a people for his treasured possession, out
of all the peoples who are on the face of the earth.
3 [t]"You shall not eat any abomination. 4 [u]"These are the animals you may eat: the ox, the

[1] Or *evil person* [2] Hebrew *the wife of your bosom* [3] That is, setting apart (devoting) as an offering to the Lord (for destruction)

5 [w]ch. 17:7; 19:19; 21:21; 22:21; 24:7; [1 Cor. 5:13]
6 [x]ch. 17:2 [y]ch. 28:54, 56; Mic. 7:5 [z][1 Sam. 18:1, 3; 20:17] [a]ch. 28:64
7 [b]ch. 6:14
8 [c]Prov. 1:10 [d]See ch. 7:16
9 [e]ch. 17:7
10 [f]ch. 17:5; See Josh. 7:25
11 [g]ch. 17:13; 19:20; 21:21
13 [h]Judg. 19:22; 20:13; 1 Sam. 2:12; 25:17; 2 Sam. 16:7; 20:1; 1 Kgs. 21:10, 13
14 [i]ch. 17:4; 19:18
16 [j]Josh. 6:24 [k]Josh. 8:28; Jer. 49:2; [Isa. 17:1; 25:2; Jer. 30:18]
17 [l]Josh. 6:18 [m]Josh. 7:26 [n]See Gen. 50:24
18 [o]ch. 12:25, 28

Chapter 14

1 [p][Isa. 1:2; Hos. 1:10; John 1:12; Rom. 9:8, 26; Gal. 3:26] [q]See Lev. 19:28 [r][Isa. 15:2; 22:12; Ezek. 7:18; Amos 8:10]
2 [s]See ch. 7:6
3 [t]Ezek. 4:14; [Acts 10:13, 14]
4 [u]For ver. 4-20, see Lev. 11:2-23

13:6 In this second scenario, the stakes are higher in that the rebellious person may be a relative, spouse, **or your friend who is as your own soul**. Allegiance to the Lord is to take priority even over such close and beloved personal relations (cf. Luke 14:26–33).

13:8 The command **you shall not yield to him** suggests strong pressure being exerted by the person inviting to apostasy. **nor shall your eye pity him**. Cf. 7:2, where Israel is to show no mercy to Canaanite pagans; this treacherous Israelite is to be treated the same way. **nor shall you conceal him**. Loving the Lord with all one's heart and soul precludes protecting such a loved one.

13:11 Capital punishment is also a deterrent so that other Israelites do not act likewise (see note on v. 5).

13:12–13 The first two scenarios above assume a lack of success in the attempts to lead Israelites astray. The third scenario is when **certain worthless fellows** have succeeded in drawing **inhabitants of their city** away from the Lord.

13:14 you shall inquire and make search and ask diligently. The hearsay of v. 12 must be checked carefully to ensure it is **true and certain**, not mere rumor.

13:15–17 Not only the instigator but the whole **city** must be treated as if it were a Canaanite city within the land, for the city allowed the "worthless fellows" (v. 13) to continue leading people astray. **devoting it to destruction**. See 2:34–35; 7:2, and note on 20:16–18. The city is also to be burned, which in the land-conquest happened only to Hazor (Josh. 11:13). This law was carried out in the case of Gibeah's rebellion (Judg. 20:37–40). An **open square** or piazza was a common feature in Israelite cities. A good example is at Beersheba (Iron Age II), where the square measured 258 sq. yards (216 sq. m) and could have held hundreds of people and tons of material. **devoted things**. Israel was not to keep any of the spoil for themselves. Cf. Achan's sin (Josh. 7:10–15).

14:1–21 *Clean and Unclean Foods.* Israel's diet was to be distinctive, reflecting its own distinctiveness in God's election from among all nations (cf. Leviticus 11).

14:1–2 For a parallel, see Lev. 21:5–6. To call the people of God **sons** or "children of God" in the OT is rare, but not unknown (see Deut. 1:31; 8:5). Israel as a whole is God's "son" (Ex. 4:22–23; Hos. 11:1), and its members are also "sons" or "children" (cf. Isa. 1:2). **cut yourselves or make any baldness on your foreheads for the dead**. Probably both of these activities relate to pagan practices, the latter for mourning (Lev. 19:27–28; see also 1 Kings 18:28). Such practices are therefore forbidden to Israelites, who are **holy to the LORD**. See Deut. 7:6 and note.

14:3 Unclean animals are regarded as an **abomination** (see Leviticus 11; Deut. 7:25–26 and note; 12:15 and note). Clean and unclean animals are separated to illustrate the separation of Israel from other nations (14:2). The distinctions are not related to hygiene, nor are unclean animals hateful to God

7[v]Lev. 11:5; [Ps. 104:18; Prov. 30:26]
8[w][Lev. 11:26]
21[x]See Lev. 7:24 [y]See ch. 7:6 [z]See Ex. 23:19
22[a]See Num. 18:21
23[b]ch. 12:7; 15:20 [c]ch. 12:6 [d]ch. 4:10; 17:19
24[e]ch. 12:21
26[b][See ver. 23 above]
27[f]See ch. 12:19 [g]See Num. 18:20
28[h]ch. 26:12; [Amos 4:4]

sheep, the goat, 5 the deer, the gazelle, the roebuck, the wild goat, the ibex,[1] the antelope,
and the mountain sheep. 6 Every animal that parts the hoof and has the hoof cloven in
two and chews the cud, among the animals, you may eat. 7 Yet of those that chew the cud
or have the hoof cloven you shall not eat these: the camel, the hare, and the [v]rock badger,
because they chew the cud but do not part the hoof, are unclean for you. 8 And the pig,
because it parts the hoof but does not chew the cud, is unclean for you. Their flesh you
shall not eat, and [w]their carcasses you shall not touch.
9 "Of all that are in the waters you may eat these: whatever has fins and scales you may
eat. 10 And whatever does not have fins and scales you shall not eat; it is unclean for you.
11 "You may eat all clean birds. 12 But these are the ones that you shall not eat: the eagle,[2]
the bearded vulture, the black vulture, 13 the kite, the falcon of any kind; 14 every raven of any
kind; 15 the ostrich, the nighthawk, the sea gull, the hawk of any kind; 16 the little owl and
the short-eared owl, the barn owl 17 and the tawny owl, the carrion vulture and the cormorant, 18 the stork, the heron of any kind; the hoopoe and the bat. 19 And all winged insects
are unclean for you; they shall not be eaten. 20 All clean winged things you may eat.
21 [x]"You shall not eat anything that has died naturally. You may give it to the sojourner
who is within your towns, that he may eat it, or you may sell it to a foreigner. For [y]you are
a people holy to the LORD your God.
[z]"You shall not boil a young goat in its mother's milk.

Tithes

22 [a]"You shall tithe all the yield of your seed that comes from the field year by year. 23 And
before the LORD your God, in the place that he will choose, to make his name dwell there,
[b]you shall eat the tithe of your grain, of your wine, and of your oil, [c]and the firstborn of
your herd and flock, [d]that you may learn to fear the LORD your God always. 24 And if the
way is too long for you, so that you are not able to carry the tithe, when the LORD your
God blesses you, because [e]the place is too far from you, which the LORD your God chooses,
to set his name there, 25 then you shall turn it into money and bind up the money in your
hand and go to the place that the LORD your God chooses 26 and spend the money for whatever you desire—oxen or sheep or wine or strong drink, whatever your appetite craves.
And [b]you shall eat there before the LORD your God and rejoice, you and your household.
27 And you shall not neglect [f]the Levite who is within your towns, for [g]he has no portion
or inheritance with you.
28 [h]"At the end of every three years you shall bring out all the tithe of your produce in

[1] Or *addax* [2] The identity of many of these birds is uncertain

(cf. Ps. 104:17–18; 147:9 for God's care for them). When the gospel breaks down the separation between Israel and the Gentiles, all foods are declared clean (Mark 7:19; Acts 10:9–16, 28; cf. 1 Tim. 4:3–5).

14:4–8 Clean animals both have a cloven hoof and chew the cud. If only one criterion is met, the animal is unclean. Cleanness cannot be based on the animals' vegetarian diet, as the **camel**, **hare**, and **rock badger** are vegetarian as well.

14:9–10 For seafood to be clean, it needs both **fins and scales**.

14:11–20 While no summary criteria are given to distinguish **clean birds** from unclean, the unclean seem to be birds of prey. These eat carrion and blood, which are forbidden to Israelites (v. 21).

14:21 This verse shows the three levels of people in Israelite society. Israelites cannot eat **anything that has died naturally**, probably because the blood is still in the animal (see note on 12:16). However, a **sojourner** (see notes on 5:12–14; 10:18–19) can eat that dead animal, and it can also be sold to a **foreigner**. **holy to the LORD**. See 7:6; 14:2. **You shall not boil a young goat in its mother's milk** (also Ex. 23:19; 34:26). This prohibition may be a polemic against Canaanite magical practices. It is also an affront to God's creative design: kids (young goats) should be given life by drinking their mothers' milk, not be cooked in it (cf. Deut. 22:6–7).

14:22–29 *Tithes.* Giving a tithe (10 percent) was a practice as early as Abram (Gen. 14:20). See Lev. 27:30–33; Num. 18:8–32 for more specific aspects of the tithing laws. Moses stresses what to do with these tithes. By NT times, Jews gave a tithe to the Levites as well as a tithe for a feast.

14:23 in the place that he will choose. See 12:5–6 and note. **you shall eat**. Deuteronomy's emphasis on festive celebration of the land's blessing is seen here with an annual tithe party. The whole household (14:26) plus the Levites (v. 27) are to be included. The dedication of the **firstborn** child or animal is a common OT principle (see Ex. 13:1–2; 1 Sam. 1:11). **learn to fear**. Tithing does not mean the giving of the surplus. Tithing would teach Israel to fear or trust God that the remaining 90 percent was sufficient and that God would provide each year. Israel should have learned this fear through the provision of manna in the wilderness (Deut. 8:3).

14:24–26 if the way is too long for you. Distance from the central sanctuary is no excuse for not tithing, but to make the travel easier, converting the tithe into money is allowed. **when the LORD your God blesses you**. Underlining this whole legislation is a clear expectation of blessing. **wine or strong drink**. While condemning drunkenness, and forbidding priests to drink while in the sanctuary (Lev. 10:9), the Bible expects drinking at celebratory occasions such as weddings and worship (Gen. 9:21; Luke 22:17–18; John 2:1–10). **rejoice**. See Deut. 12:7 and note.

14:27 you shall not neglect the Levite. See notes on 10:6–9 and 12:12.

14:28–29 An additional **tithe** every third year is for the benefit of the landless, who are (potentially) poor. It is to be given to them **within your towns** and not at the central sanctuary (cf. v. 23). In a chapter emphasizing the holiness of Israel apart from other nations, the inclusion of the sojourner (cf. v. 21) shows the inclusiveness of Deuteronomy.

the same year and lay it up within your towns. 29 And the Levite, because [g]he has no portion or inheritance with you, and the sojourner, the fatherless, and the widow, who are
within your towns, shall come and eat and be filled, that [i]the LORD your God may bless
you in all the work of your hands that you do.

The Sabbatical Year

15 "At the end of [j]every seven years you shall grant a release. 2 And this is the manner
of the release: every creditor shall release what he has lent to his neighbor. He shall
not exact it of his neighbor, his brother, because the LORD's release has been proclaimed.
3 [k]Of a foreigner you may exact it, but whatever of yours is with your brother your hand
shall release. 4 [l]But there will be no poor among you; [m]for the LORD will bless you in the
land that the LORD your God is giving you for an inheritance to possess— 5 [n]if only you
will strictly obey the voice of the LORD your God, being careful to do all this commandment that I command you today. 6 For the LORD your God will bless you, [o]as he promised
you, and [p]you shall lend to many nations, but you shall not borrow, and [q]you shall rule
over many nations, but they shall not rule over you.
7 "If among you, one of your brothers should become poor, in any of your towns within
your land that the LORD your God is giving you, [r]you shall not harden your heart or shut
your hand against your poor brother, 8 but [s]you shall open your hand to him and lend him
sufficient for his need, whatever it may be. 9 Take care lest there be an unworthy thought
in your heart and you say, 'The seventh year, the year of release is near,' and your [t]eye look
grudgingly[1] on your poor brother, and you give him nothing, and he [u]cry to the LORD
against you, and [v]you be guilty of sin. 10 You shall give to him freely, and [w]your heart shall
not be grudging when you give to him, because [x]for this the LORD your God will bless you
in all your work and in all that you undertake. 11 For [y]there will never cease to be poor in
the land. Therefore I command you, [s]'You shall open wide your hand to your brother, to
the needy and to the poor, in your land.'
12 [z]"If your brother, a Hebrew man or a Hebrew woman, is sold[2] to you, he shall serve
you six years, and in the seventh year you shall let him go free from you. 13 And when you
let him go free from you, you shall not let him go empty-handed. 14 You shall furnish
him liberally out of your flock, out of your threshing floor, and out of your winepress. [a]As
the LORD your God has blessed you, you shall give to him. 15 [b]You shall remember that
you were a slave in the land of Egypt, and the LORD your God redeemed you; therefore I
command you this today. 16 But [c]if he says to you, 'I will not go out from you,' because he
loves you and your household, since he is well-off with you, 17 then you shall take an awl,

[1] Or *be evil*; also verse 10 [2] Or *sells himself*

29 [g][See ver. 27 above] [i]ch. 15:10; 24:19; Ps. 41:1; Prov. 14:21; 19:17; 22:9; Mal. 3:10

Chapter 15

1 [j]ch. 31:10; Neh. 10:31; [ver. 12; Ex. 23:10, 11; Lev. 25:2-4]
3 [k][ch. 23:20]
4 [l][ver. 11] [m]ch. 28:8
5 [n]ch. 28:1
6 [o]ch. 7:13; Ex. 23:25 [p]ch. 28:12, 44 [q]ch. 28:13; 1 Kgs. 4:21, 24; Ezra 4:20; [Prov. 22:7]
7 [r][1 John 3:17]
8 [s]Lev. 25:35; [Matt. 5:42; Luke 6:34, 35]
9 [t]ch. 28:54, 56; Prov. 23:6; 28:22; Matt. 20:15 [u]ch. 24:15 [v][Matt. 25:41, 42]
10 [w][2 Cor. 9:7] [x]Prov. 28:27; See ch. 14:29
11 [y][Matt. 26:11; Mark 14:7; John 12:8] [s][See ver. 8 above]
12 [z]Ex. 21:2; Jer. 34:14; [Lev. 25:39-41]
14 [a]ch. 8:18; 16:17
15 [b]See ch. 5:15
16 [c]Ex. 21:5, 6

15:1–18 *The Sabbatical Year.* The laws in these verses relate to the sabbatical year. See Ex. 23:10–11 and Lev. 25:1–7.

15:1–3 All debts between Israelites are to be cancelled (or merely deferred for one year) at the end of every seventh year regardless of the amount of debt or its term. Debts owed by foreigners are not subject to this release (cf. 14:21).

15:4–6 there will be no poor among you. Cf. v. 11. The ideal in v. 4 is in effect a command to be generous: "Let there be no poor among you." Since the land will be sufficiently blessed by God (v. 6), provided the economic laws are upheld (v. 5), there should be no one who is poor. Verse 11 perhaps expresses the reality that Israel will fail to fulfill the law and thus there will always be poor and the need for generosity. **you shall lend to many nations, but you shall not borrow**. Israel will be rich in blessing, if there is obedience (v. 5). See 28:43–44 for when there is disobedience.

15:7–8 one of your brothers. This law does not apply to the poor outside Israel. The cause of the fellow Israelite's poverty is not the issue, even if it is the result of squandering or foolishness. The command is internal: **you shall not harden your heart or shut your hand**. True obedience stems from the heart, and it may be costly to the Israelite in giving what is needed. The verbs **open** and **lend** are emphatic. Christians are also to be generous toward one another (cf. 1 John 3:17).

15:9–11 unworthy thought in your heart. See note on 4:37–39. If the sabbatical year is close, then any money lent is less likely to be repaid. So the command is to lend what is needed, regardless of the date of the next sabbatical year. **You shall give to him freely, and your heart shall not be grudging**. This reiterates 15:8, emphasizing a heart of generosity. **there will never cease to be poor**. See v. 4 and note on vv. 4–6. Cf. Matt. 26:11.

15:12 This section assumes that some Israelites might fall into desperate poverty and become, within Israel, slaves or "bondservants." This may suggest a failure by Israelites to be generous as commanded in vv. 1–11. The sabbatical year provides a limit to such slavery (cf. Ex. 21:2–6; Lev. 25:39–46). Slavery in Israel was therefore a short-term measure to help self-employed peasant farmers who could not pay their debts. Thus a rich landowner who offered a bankrupt peasant guaranteed employment and support until the sabbatical year was valued. Taking on such a "slave" was viewed as an act of charity (Gen. 47:21–25). Some "slaves" might find the secure status of employee so attractive that they became permanent slaves; see Deut. 15:16–17.

15:13–15 To prevent immediate return to being a slave, the slave owner is not to **let him go empty-handed** but to **furnish him liberally**. **As the LORD your God has blessed you**. Throughout this chapter, the blessing of God on Israel motivates obedience to these laws. **You shall remember that you were a slave**. The second motivation comes from Israel's experience of oppression in Egypt (see 5:15 and note).

15:16–17 In some cases, the slave may decide not to leave his master. In such a case, piercing with an awl marks permanent ownership. See Ex. 21:5–6; and note on Deut. 15:12.

19 [d]See Ex. 13:2
20 [e]ch. 12:7; 14:23, 26
21 [f]See Lev. 22:20
22 [g]ch. 12:15
23 [h]See Lev. 3:17

Chapter 16

1 [i]For ver. 1-8, see Ex. 12:2-39 [j]Ex. 13:4; 34:18
2 [k]Num. 28:19 [l]See ch. 12:5
3 [m]Ex. 13:6 [n]Ex. 12:11; [Isa. 52:12]
4 [o]Ex. 13:7 [p]Ex. 34:25
8 [q][Ex. 13:6] [r]Lev. 23:8, 36
9 [s]Ex. 23:16; 34:22; Lev. 23:15; Num. 28:26; [Acts 2:1]
10 [t]2 Chr. 8:13 [u]See ch. 26:1-11 [v]ch. 12:15; [1 Cor. 16:2]
11 [w]ch. 12:7, 12, 18; 14:26; See Neh. 8:9-12

and put it through his ear into the door, and he shall be your slave[1] forever. And to your
female slave[2] you shall do the same. 18 It shall not seem hard to you when you let him go
free from you, for at half the cost of a hired worker he has served you six years. So the LORD
your God will bless you in all that you do.
19 [d]"All the firstborn males that are born of your herd and flock you shall dedicate to
the LORD your God. You shall do no work with the firstborn of your herd, nor shear the
firstborn of your flock. 20 [e]You shall eat it, you and your household, before the LORD your
God year by year at the place that the LORD will choose. 21 [f]But if it has any blemish, if it
is lame or blind or has any serious blemish whatever, you shall not sacrifice it to the LORD
your God. 22 You shall eat it within your towns. [g]The unclean and the clean alike may eat
it, as though it were a gazelle or a deer. 23 [h]Only you shall not eat its blood; you shall pour
it out on the ground like water.

Passover

16 "Observe the [i]month of Abib and keep the Passover to the LORD your God, for [j]in
the month of Abib the LORD your God brought you out of Egypt by night. 2 And
you shall offer the Passover sacrifice to the LORD your God, from the flock or [k]the herd,
[l]at the place that the LORD will choose, to make his name dwell there. 3 You shall eat no
leavened bread with it. [m]Seven days you shall eat it with unleavened bread, the bread of
affliction—for you came out of the land of Egypt [n]in haste—that all the days of your life
you may remember the day when you came out of the land of Egypt. 4 [o]No leaven shall
be seen with you in all your territory for seven days, [p]nor shall any of the flesh that you
sacrifice on the evening of the first day remain all night until morning. 5 You may not
offer the Passover sacrifice within any of your towns that the LORD your God is giving
you, 6 but at the place that the LORD your God will choose, to make his name dwell in it,
there you shall offer the Passover sacrifice, in the evening at sunset, at the time you came
out of Egypt. 7 And you shall cook it and eat it at the place that the LORD your God will
choose. And in the morning you shall turn and go to your tents. 8 For [q]six days you shall
eat unleavened bread, and on the seventh day there shall be [r]a solemn assembly to the
LORD your God. You shall do no work on it.

The Feast of Weeks

9 [s]"You shall count seven weeks. Begin to count the seven weeks from the time the sickle
is first put to the standing grain. 10 Then you shall keep [t]the Feast of Weeks to the LORD your
God with [u]the tribute of a freewill offering from your hand, which you shall give [v]as the
LORD your God blesses you. 11 And [w]you shall rejoice before the LORD your God, you and your
son and your daughter, your male servant and your female servant, the Levite who is within

[1] Or *servant;* the Hebrew term *'ebed* designates a range of social and economic roles (see Preface) [2] Or *servant*

15:18 It shall not seem hard to you. This is a warning against greed.

15:19–23 *Firstborn Animals.* These verses deal with firstborn animals, which are to be dedicated to the Lord (see Ex. 13:2; Num. 18:15–18). Giving the firstborn is an expression of thanks and trust that more animals are to come. The animal is to be eaten in the central place (**before the LORD**; Deut. 15:20). However, the animal must be unblemished, like any sacrificial animal (e.g., Lev. 1:3). If blemished in any way, it is to be eaten for a normal, non-sacrificial meal (cf. Deut. 12:15–16 and notes there).

16:1–17 *Feasts.* This section deals with the three main Israelite feasts (see Ex. 23:14–17). If Deuteronomy's detailed laws are arranged in the order of the Ten Commandments, this section corresponds to the Sabbath law in Deut. 5:12 (cf. Lev. 23:3 for the Sabbath as the weekly day of public worship). On Passover, see Ex. 12:2–39; 34:18–25; Lev. 23:4–8; Num. 28:16–25. On the Feast of Weeks, see Lev. 23:15–22; Num. 28:26–31. On the Feast of Booths, see Lev. 23:33–43; Num. 29:12–40. All the feasts occur at the central place, a point repeatedly made in Deuteronomy 16 (see vv. 2, 6, 7, 11, 15, 16; also 12:5). For those who lived outside of Jerusalem, attendance at the feasts entailed several days of pilgrimage (Luke 2:41–52).

16:1 Abib. The first month (Ex. 12:2; Lev. 23:5), corresponding to March/April. On Jesus' crucifixion at **Passover**, see John 13:1; 19:31; 1 Cor. 5:7–8.

16:2 flock or the herd. In Deuteronomy, the Passover sacrifice need not be a lamb (cf. Ex. 12:3, 21).

16:3 eat no leavened bread. Unleavened Bread is the name of the seven-day feast after Passover (Ex. 23:15; cf. 12:15–20). **remember.** Remembrance leads to obedience (see Deut. 8:2–3 and note there).

16:5–6 You may not offer the Passover sacrifice within any of your towns. See note on 16:1–17. This may seem to reverse the provision of Ex. 12:21–24, which envisages the Passover being celebrated in homes. Deuteronomy, however, anticipates settlement in the land.

16:7 cook. The Passover sacrifice was to be roasted, not boiled (Ex. 12:8–9). **tents.** See Deut. 5:30. For this pilgrimage festival, Israelites needed to stay in temporary accommodations near the central sanctuary.

16:9–10 The Feast of Weeks is called the Feast of Harvest in Ex. 23:16. The **seven weeks** are counted **from the time the sickle is first put to the standing grain**, thus marking the end of the grain harvest. The Greek name for this festival is Pentecost, meaning 50 days, counting inclusively, or seven weeks (see Acts 2). A **freewill offering** is an expression of thankfulness for the blessing of harvest.

16:11–12 rejoice. See 12:7 and note. Landless people are again included (see 12:12 and note). The Israelites are called to **remember** their slavery in **Egypt**, a time when they were also landless (see 8:2–3 and note).

your towns, the sojourner, the fatherless, and the widow who are among you, at the place
that the LORD your God will choose, to make his name dwell there. 12 [x]You shall remember
that you were a slave in Egypt; and you shall be careful to observe these statutes.

The Feast of Booths

13 [y]"You shall keep the Feast of Booths seven days, when you have gathered in the produce
from your threshing floor and your winepress. 14 [z]You shall rejoice in your feast, you and
your son and your daughter, your male servant and your female servant, the Levite, the
sojourner, the fatherless, and the widow who are within your towns. 15 For [a]seven days you
shall keep the feast to the LORD your God at the place that the LORD will choose, because
the LORD your God will bless you in all your produce and in all the work of your hands,
so that you will be altogether joyful.

16 [b]"Three times a year all your males shall appear before the LORD your God at the place
that he will choose: at the Feast of Unleavened Bread, at the Feast of Weeks, and at the Feast
of Booths. [c]They shall not appear before the LORD empty-handed. 17 Every man [d]shall give
as he is able, [v]according to the blessing of the LORD your God that he has given you.

Justice

18 "You shall appoint [e]judges and officers in all your towns that the LORD your God
is giving you, according to your tribes, and they shall judge the people with righteous
judgment. 19 [f]You shall not pervert justice. [g]You shall not show partiality, [h]and you shall
not accept a bribe, for a bribe blinds the eyes of the wise and subverts the cause of the
righteous. 20 Justice, and only justice, you shall follow, that you may live and inherit the
land that the LORD your God is giving you.

Forbidden Forms of Worship

21 "You shall not plant any tree as [i]an Asherah beside the altar of the LORD your God that
you shall make. 22 And you shall not set up a pillar, which the LORD your God hates.

17 [j]"You shall not sacrifice to the LORD your God an ox or a sheep in which is a blemish,
any defect whatever, for that is an abomination to the LORD your God.

2 [k]"If there is found among you, within any of your towns that the LORD your God is
giving you, a man or woman who does what is evil in the sight of the LORD your God, [l]in
transgressing his covenant, 3 and has gone and served other gods and worshiped them, or
[m]the sun or the moon or any of the host of heaven, [n]which I have forbidden, 4 and it is told
you and you hear of it, then you shall inquire [o]diligently, and if it is true and certain that
such an abomination has been done in Israel, 5 then you shall bring out to your gates that
man or woman who has done this evil thing, and you [p]shall stone that man or woman to
death with stones. 6 [q]On the evidence of two witnesses or of three witnesses the one who
is to die shall be put to death; a person shall not be put to death on the evidence of one

12 [x]See ch. 5:15
13 [y]Ex. 23:16; See Lev. 23:34
14 [z]ver. 11; See Neh. 8:9-12
15 [a]Lev. 23:39
16 [b]ch. 31:11; Ex. 23:14, 17; 34:23 [c]Ex. 23:15
17 [d][Ezek. 46:5, 11; 2 Cor. 8:12] [v][See ver. 10 above]
18 [e]ch. 1:16; Num. 11:16; Josh. 1:10; 1 Chr. 23:4; 26:29
19 [f]ch. 27:19; Ex. 23:2, 6; Isa. 10:2; Amos 5:12; [Lev. 19:15]; See ch. 24:17 [g]See ch. 1:17 [h]See Ex. 23:8
21 [i]Ex. 34:13; Judg. 6:25; 1 Kgs. 14:15; 16:33; 2 Kgs. 13:6; 17:16; 2 Chr. 33:3

Chapter 17

1 [j]See Lev. 22:20
2 [k]For ver. 2-7, see ch. 13:6-14 [l]Josh. 7:11, 15; 23:16; Judg. 2:20; 2 Kgs. 18:12; Hos. 6:7; 8:1
3 [m]See ch. 4:19 [n][Jer. 7:31; 19:5; 32:35]
4 [o]ch. 13:14; 19:18
5 [p][Lev. 24:14, 16; Josh. 7:25]
6 [q][John 8:17]; See Num. 35:30

16:13 The **Feast of Booths** or Tabernacles is called the Feast of Ingathering in Ex. 23:16 and 34:22. Occurring in September/October, it focuses on the harvest of summer fruits such as dates, grapes, and olives. This is the feast in which the law was to be read every seventh year (Deut. 31:9–13).

16:14–15 rejoice. See v. 11 and notes on 12:7; 12:12. **altogether joyful**. The superabundance of the land is again anticipated.

16:16–17 all your males. Presumably females were free to journey for the feast (vv. 11, 14), but it was obligatory only for males. **the place that he will choose**. See vv. 2, 6–7 and note on 12:5–6. The repeated mention of anticipated **blessing** provides incentive for Israel to enter the land.

16:18–18:22 *Leaders.* These laws mainly concern various leaders for the people of Israel: judges, priests, kings, and prophets. As in the NT, all leaders of God's people are under the authority of God's word. Leaders, like parents, exercise God's authority toward those under them, so again the sequence of the Ten Commandments is observable, as this section reflects the fifth commandment, "Honor your father and your mother" (5:16).

16:18 The appointment of **judges** in **towns** for judicial purposes recognizes the size of the population and the spread of the land (cf. 1:9–18).

16:19 You shall not pervert justice. You shall not show partiality, and you shall not accept a bribe. Justice derives from the character of God. See 1:17 and note on 1:16–17; 10:17; Ex. 23:3, 6–8.

16:21–22 tree as an Asherah . . . pillar. See note on 7:5. Canaanite worship items were to be destroyed (7:5; 12:3). This law prohibits syncretistic practices at the central place. Cf. Manasseh in 2 Kings 21:7.

17:1 sacrifice . . . blemish. See Lev. 22:17–25; Mal. 1:6–8; and note on Deut. 15:19–23. **abomination**. See note on 7:25–26.

17:2–3 does what is evil. More specifically, commits idolatry. See 4:19.

17:4–5 inquire diligently. Cf. 13:14. In 13:12–18, the city has been enticed to idolatry; here, it is a person. In 13:15 the city is put to the sword; here the person is stoned (see 13:10). Because idolatry breaks the first commandment, it is a capital offense. **out to your gates**. Capital punishment, as in the case of Jesus' crucifixion, was usually outside the walls or camp (Lev. 24:14; Num. 15:35; Heb. 13:11–13).

17:6–7 On the evidence of two witnesses or of three witnesses. The standard biblical requirement to find someone guilty of a capital offense is two witnesses (Num. 35:30; cf. 1 Kings 21:13; Heb. 10:28). In the case of **one witness**, the situation becomes one person's word against another and thus no conviction can be made. See Deut. 19:16–21 on penalties for false witnesses. Insisting that **the hand of the witnesses shall be first** to stone the guilty helps prevent false witness and adds seriousness to their testimony (cf. 13:9). **purge the evil**. See 13:5 and note.

witness. 7 [r]The hand of the witnesses shall be first against him to put him to death, and
afterward the hand of all the people. So [s]you shall purge[1] the evil[2] from your midst.

Legal Decisions by Priests and Judges

8 "If any case arises requiring decision between one kind of homicide and another, one
kind of legal right and another, or one kind of assault and another, any case within your
towns that is too difficult for you, then you shall arise and go up to [t]the place that the LORD
your God will choose. 9 [u]And you shall come to the Levitical priests and to the judge who
is in office in those days, and you shall consult them, and [v]they shall declare to you the
decision. 10 Then you shall do according to what they declare to you from that place that
the LORD will choose. And you shall be careful to do according to all that they direct you.
11 According to the instructions that they give you, and according to the decision which
they pronounce to you, you shall do. You shall not turn aside from the verdict that they
declare to you, either to the right hand or to the left. 12 The man who [w]acts presumptuously
by not obeying the priest [x]who stands to minister there before the LORD your God, or the
judge, that man shall die. So [s]you shall purge the evil from Israel. 13 And all the people
[y]shall hear and fear and not act presumptuously again.

Laws Concerning Israel's Kings

14 "When you come to the land that the LORD your God is giving you, and you possess it
and dwell in it and then say, [z]'I will set a king over me, like all the nations that are around
me,' 15 you may indeed set a king over you [a]whom the LORD your God will choose. One
[b]from among your brothers you shall set as king over you. You may not put a foreigner
over you, who is not your brother. 16 Only he must not acquire many [c]horses for himself
or cause the people [d]to return to Egypt in order to acquire many horses, since the LORD
has said to you, [e]'You shall never return that way again.' 17 And he [f]shall not acquire many
wives for himself, lest his heart turn away, [g]nor shall he acquire for himself excessive silver
and gold.

18 "And when he sits on the throne of his kingdom, [h]he shall write for himself in a book
a copy of this law, [i]approved by[3] the Levitical priests. 19 And [j]it shall be with him, and he
shall read in it all the days of his life, [k]that he may learn to fear the LORD his God by keeping all the words of this law and these statutes, and doing them, 20 that his heart may not
be lifted up above his brothers, and that he [l]may not turn aside from the commandment,
either to the right hand or to the left, [m]so that he may continue long in his kingdom, he
and his children, in Israel.

Provision for Priests and Levites

18 "The Levitical priests, all the tribe of Levi, [n]shall have no portion or inheritance with
Israel. They [o]shall eat the LORD's food offerings[4] as their[5] inheritance. 2 They shall
have no inheritance among their brothers; the LORD is their inheritance, as he promised

7 [r]ch. 13:9; [Acts 7:58] [s]ver. 12; See ch. 13:5
8 [t]See ch. 12:5
9 [u]ch. 19:17; 21:5; 2 Chr. 19:8, 10; Ps. 122:5; Jer. 18:18; Hag. 2:11; Mal. 2:7 [v]Ezek. 44:24
12 [w][ch. 18:20, 22; Ezra 10:8] [x]ch. 10:8; 18:5, 7 [s][See ver. 7 above]
13 [y]See ch. 13:11
14 [z][1 Sam. 8:5, 19, 20]
15 [a][1 Sam. 9:15; 10:24; 16:12; 1 Chr. 22:10] [b][Jer. 30:21]
16 [c][1 Kgs. 4:26; 10:26, 28; 2 Chr. 1:16; 9:28; Isa. 2:7; 31:1] [d]Isa. 31:1; Ezek. 17:15 [e]ch. 28:68; Hos. 11:5; [Ex. 13:17; 14:13; Num. 14:3, 4]; See Jer. 42:15-19
17 [f][1 Kgs. 11:3, 4; Neh. 13:26] [g][Isa. 2:7]
18 [h][2 Kgs. 11:12] [i]ch. 31:9, 26; 2 Kgs. 22:8; 2 Chr. 34:14
19 [j]Josh. 1:8 [k]ch. 4:10; 14:23
20 [l]ch. 5:32; 1 Kgs. 15:5 [m]ch. 4:40

Chapter 18

1 [n]See Num. 18:20 [o]Num. 18:8, 9; Josh. 13:14; 1 Sam. 2:28; [1 Cor. 9:13]

[1] Septuagint *drive out*; also verse 12 [2] Or *evil person*; also verse 12 [3] Hebrew *from before* [4] Or *the offerings by fire to the LORD* [5] Hebrew *his*

17:8–9 Straightforward judicial cases are dealt with in local courts. The difficult cases are to be taken to the central sanctuary. **The place that the LORD your God will choose** indicates the integration of worship with justice, deriving from the character of God as just and implying that ultimately God himself is the judge (see note on 12:5–6).

17:10–11 These verses are the emphasis of this section. The decision of the central sanctuary court is final.

17:12–13 that man shall die. To ignore or pervert justice is a capital offense, for it is a rejection of God's justice and rule. **purge the evil**. See 13:5 and note. **hear and fear and not act presumptuously again**. See 13:11 and note.

17:14–15 I will set a king over me, like all the nations. See 1 Sam. 8:5, 20. Even though it will be several centuries before Israel has a king, Deuteronomy provides legislation for that eventuality, in language that suggests time elapsing: **you possess it and dwell in it and then say**. Kings descended from Abraham were anticipated in Gen. 17:6. **whom the LORD your God will choose**. To counter the people's request to have a king like the nations, God insists that their king will be his choice. Yet God seems to allow the people some role in setting up a king. The king must be **from among your brothers**, that is, a fellow Israelite.

17:16–17 The warnings about too many **horses** and **wives** and too much wealth—which reflect the standard prerogatives of ancient kings in military, personal, and economic spheres—are precisely the pitfalls of Solomon (1 Kings 4:26; 10:14; 11:3–4). Here God is warning that governmental leaders will constantly face the temptation to abuse their power for the sake of personal gain, which is contrary to his will. Since **Egypt** was the place of slavery from which the Lord had just rescued Israel, it was prohibited for Israel to return to Egypt for help (e.g., Isa. 31:1; cf. Deut. 28:68).

17:18–20 a copy of this law. This refers probably to chs. 1–30 (see 31:9). Even the king is to be under the authority of God's word or law (see Josh. 1:7–9). Reading and obeying the word of God trains people to **fear the LORD** (see note on Deut. 6:1–2). **heart**. See notes on 4:37–39; 6:5; 6:6. **to the right hand or to the left**. See Josh. 1:7 and note on Deut. 5:32–33.

18:1–2 The Levitical priests are the adult males within **the tribe of Levi** as a whole. **shall have no portion or inheritance**. See 12:12 and note. **the LORD is their inheritance**. See Num. 18:20. This indicates the privilege

them. **3** And this shall be the priests' due from the people, from those offering a sacrifice,
whether an ox or a sheep: [p]they shall give to the priest the shoulder and the two cheeks
and the stomach. **4** [q]The firstfruits of your grain, of your wine and of your oil, and the
first fleece of your sheep, you shall give him. **5** For the LORD your God has chosen him
out of all your tribes [r]to stand and minister in the name of the LORD, him and his sons
for all time.
6 "And if a Levite comes from any of your towns out of all Israel, [s]where he lives—and
he may come when he desires[1]—[t]to the place that the LORD will choose, **7** and ministers
in the name of the LORD his God, [u]like all his fellow Levites who stand to minister there
before the LORD, **8** then he may have equal [v]portions to eat, besides what he receives from
the sale of his patrimony.[2]

Abominable Practices

9 "When you come into the land that the LORD your God is giving you, [w]you shall not
learn to follow the abominable practices of those nations. **10** There shall not be found among
you anyone [x]who burns his son or his daughter as an offering,[3] anyone who [y]practices divination or [z]tells fortunes or interprets omens, or [a]a sorcerer **11** or a charmer or [b]a medium
or a necromancer or [c]one who inquires of the dead, **12** [d]for whoever does these things is
an abomination to the LORD. And [e]because of these abominations the LORD your God is
driving them out before you. **13** You shall be blameless before the LORD your God, **14** for
these nations, which you are about to dispossess, listen to fortune-tellers and to diviners.
But as for you, the LORD your God has not allowed you to do this.

A New Prophet like Moses

15 [f]"The LORD your God will raise up for you a prophet like me from among you, from
your brothers—it is to him you shall listen— **16** just as you desired of the LORD your God
at Horeb [g]on the day of the assembly, when you said, [h]'Let me not hear again the voice of
the LORD my God or see this great fire any more, lest I die.' **17** And the LORD said to me,
[i]'They are right in what they have spoken. **18** [f]I will raise up for them a prophet like you
from among their brothers. [j]And I will put my words in his mouth, and [k]he shall speak to
them all that I command him. **19** [l]And whoever will [m]not listen to my words that he shall
speak in my name, I myself will require it of him. **20** [n]But the prophet who presumes to
speak a word in my name that I have not commanded him to speak, or[4] who speaks in
the name of other gods, that same prophet shall die.' **21** And if you say in your heart, 'How
may we know the word that the LORD has not spoken?'— **22** [o]when a prophet speaks in
the name of the LORD, if the word does not come to pass or come true, that is a word that
the LORD has not spoken; [n]the prophet has spoken it presumptuously. You need not be
afraid of him.

[1] Or *lives—if he comes enthusiastically* [2] The meaning of the Hebrew is uncertain [3] Hebrew *makes his son or his daughter pass through the fire* [4] Or *and*

3 [p]See Lev. 7:30-34
4 [q]Num. 18:12; 2 Chr. 31:5
5 [r]ch. 17:12
6 [s]Num. 35:2, 3; Judg. 17:7; 19:1 [t]See ch. 12:5
7 [u][1 Chr. 23:6; 2 Chr. 31:2]
8 [v]2 Chr. 31:4; Neh. 12:44, 47; 13:10
9 [w]ch. 12:29-31; See Lev. 18:26-30
10 [x]See Lev. 18:21 [y]2 Kgs. 17:17 [z]See Lev. 19:26 [a][Ex. 22:18]
11 [b]See Lev. 19:31 [c][1 Sam. 28:7]
12 [d]ch. 22:5; 25:16 [e]See ch. 9:4
15 [f]John 1:21, 25, 45; Cited Acts 3:22; 7:37
16 [g]See ch. 9:10 [h]See Ex. 20:19
17 [i]ch. 5:28
18 [f][See ver. 15 above] [j]Jer. 1:9; 5:14; [John 17:8] [k][John 4:25; 8:28; 12:49, 50]
19 [l][Acts 3:23] [m]Jer. 29:19; 35:13
20 [n]See ch. 13:5
22 [o][ch. 13:1-3; Jer. 28:9] [n][See ver. 20 above]

of serving the Lord in the central sanctuary, with the implied blessing of perpetual nearness to the Lord's presence.

18:3–4 Parts of the sacrifices and firstfruits are for the upkeep of the Levites. Cf. Lev. 7:28–34 and Num. 18:9–24, where the portions for the priests are slightly different.

18:5 The Levites are **chosen** by the Lord, just like the central sanctuary (e.g., 12:5), the king (17:15), and Israel itself (7:6).

18:6–8 Levites who minister in the country have the right to come from time to time to **minister** in the central sanctuary. **sale of his patrimony**. Apart from their share of offerings, Levites may also make money from their personal property.

18:9–11 the abominable practices of those nations. Cf. notes on 7:5; 12:2–3. **burns his son or his daughter as an offering**. See 12:31 and note. A thorough list is given of people and practices seeking divine help, guidance, or revelation apart from the Lord. No such practices are to be tolerated (e.g., Lev. 19:26; 1 Samuel 28; 2 Kings 17:17; Isa. 2:6; 21:6; Mic. 5:12). All are abominable (Deut. 18:9, 12). Even child sacrifice was for some pagan religions an act of seeking divine guidance or help (2 Kings 3:26–27). Deliberately juxtaposed with this section are instructions about God's prophets (Deut. 18:15–19), the avenue for true revelation.

18:12 because of these abominations the LORD your God is driving them out. The destruction of the Canaanites is not an attack on an innocent people. It is God's judgment against abominable sin (Gen. 15:16; see note on Deut. 7:2).

18:15–19 God promises a line of prophets who will speak to Israel on his behalf (cf. Jer. 1:7, 9, pertaining to Jeremiah's ministry). Moses speaks of himself as **a prophet**, the instrument of communicating God's word to Israel (cf. Deut. 18:19; Ex. 7:1). Nations listen (Deut. 18:14) to magicians, etc.; Israel is to **listen** to God's prophet (vv. 15, 19) rather than pagan means of revelation and guidance. On the **voice of the LORD**, see 5:23–28. **a prophet like you**. Now God speaks of Moses as a prophet and promises a future prophet like him for Israel. In the first century A.D., Jews expected a final prophet, whom NT writers identified as Jesus (Acts 3:22–24; 7:37; cf. John 1:21).

18:20–22 False prophets, whether speaking in God's name or the **name of other gods**, are to be put to death (13:1–5). One test of false prophecy is, if a prophet's words do not **come to pass**, then they are not the Lord's words.

Chapter 19
1[p]ch. 12:29
2[q]Ex. 21:13; Num. 35:10, 14; Josh. 20:2, 8
4[r]ch. 4:42; Num. 35:15; Josh. 20:3, 5
6[s]Num. 35:12, 19, 21, 24, 25, 27
8[t]ch. 12:20 [u]Ex. 34:24; [Ex. 23:31] [v]See Gen. 15:18-21
9[w]ver. 2; [Josh. 20:7]
11[x]ch. 27:24; Ex. 21:12, 14; See Num. 35:16-21
13[y]See ch. 7:16 [z]ch. 21:9; Num. 35:33; [1 Kgs. 2:31]
14[a]ch. 27:17; Job 24:2; Prov. 22:28; 23:10; Hos. 5:10
15[b]Cited Matt. 18:16; 2 Cor. 13:1; See Num. 35:30
16[c][Ex. 23:1; Ps. 35:11]
17[d]ch. 17:8, 9; [ch. 21:5]

Laws Concerning Cities of Refuge

19 "When [p]the LORD your God cuts off the nations whose land the LORD your God is
giving you, and you dispossess them and dwell in their cities and in their houses,
2 [q]you shall set apart three cities for yourselves in the land that the LORD your God is giving you to possess. 3 You shall measure the distances[1] and divide into three parts the area
of the land that the LORD your God gives you as a possession, so that any manslayer can
flee to them.
4 "This is the provision for [r]the manslayer, who by fleeing there may save his life. If
anyone kills his neighbor unintentionally without having hated him in the past— 5 as
when someone goes into the forest with his neighbor to cut wood, and his hand swings
the axe to cut down a tree, and the head slips from the handle and strikes his neighbor
so that he dies—he may flee to one of these cities and live, 6 lest [s]the avenger of blood in
hot anger pursue the manslayer and overtake him, because the way is long, and strike
him fatally, though the man did not deserve to die, since he had not hated his neighbor
in the past. 7 Therefore I command you, You shall set apart three cities. 8 [t]And if the LORD
your God enlarges your territory, [u]as he has sworn to your fathers, and [v]gives you all the
land that he promised to give to your fathers— 9 provided you are careful to keep all this
commandment, which I command you today, by loving the LORD your God and by walking ever in his ways—[w]then you shall add three other cities to these three, 10 lest innocent
blood be shed in your land that the LORD your God is giving you for an inheritance, and
so the guilt of bloodshed be upon you.
11 "But if anyone hates his neighbor and lies in wait for him and attacks him [x]and strikes
him fatally so that he dies, and he flees into one of these cities, 12 then the elders of his city
shall send and take him from there, and hand him over to the avenger of blood, so that he
may die. 13 [y]Your eye shall not pity him, [z]but you shall purge the guilt of innocent blood[2]
from Israel, so that it may be well with you.

Property Boundaries

14 [a]"You shall not move your neighbor's landmark, which the men of old have set, in
the inheritance that you will hold in the land that the LORD your God is giving you to
possess.

Laws Concerning Witnesses

15 "A single witness shall not suffice against a person for any crime or for any wrong in
connection with any offense that he has committed. [b]Only on the evidence of two witnesses or of three witnesses shall a charge be established. 16 If [c]a malicious witness arises
to accuse a person of wrongdoing, 17 then both parties to the dispute shall appear before
the LORD, [d]before the priests and the judges who are in office in those days. 18 The judges

[1] *Hebrew road* [2] *Or the blood of the innocent*

However, if a prophet's words *do* come to pass, that does not automatically mean that person is God's prophet (see 13:1–5 and notes).

19:1–21:14 *Protecting Life.* This section corresponds to the sixth commandment, "You shall not murder" (5:17).

19:1–13 These verses complement the setting apart of cities of refuge in Transjordan (see 4:41–43) and relate to post-conquest settlement in the land (cf. 12:29).

19:1–3 dwell in their cities and in their houses. See 6:10–11. The **three cities** of refuge are to be evenly located throughout the land to provide reasonable access. See Ex. 21:12–13 and Num. 35:9–34. Joshua 20:1–9 names these three cities as Kedesh, Shechem, and Hebron.

19:4–6 The purpose and accessibility of the cities of refuge is to ensure justice for a **manslayer** who might otherwise be vulnerable to vengeance from the **avenger of blood**, that is, someone from the victim's family. Verse 5 gives one example of manslaughter for which this provision applies. The law clearly distinguishes between manslaughter (which is unpremeditated) and murder. **did not deserve to die**. The death penalty does not apply for manslaughter.

19:8–10 The law anticipates the enlargement of Israel's land (see 12:20) and thus the need for further cities of refuge to ensure accessibility. Moses takes every opportunity to remind the people that God's promises of land obligate Israel to obedience (19:9). That these further three cities were never appointed in the OT indicates Israel's lack of obedience. **innocent blood**. A manslayer is innocent of murder.

19:11–12 Murder, unlike manslaughter, stems from hatred and is intentional (cf. v. 4). For a murderer, a city of refuge is not a permitted haven. In this case the man is handed over to the **avenger of blood** for capital punishment.

19:13 purge the guilt. Cf. 13:5 (and note), where the expression is "purge the evil."

19:14 Moving the **landmark**, or boundary stone, of a neighbor is tantamount to theft of land (see also 27:17). The law emphasizes keeping land in families, since inheritance rights are basic to Israel's life in the land. See the Jubilee laws in Lev. 25:8–34; also Prov. 23:10–11 and Hos. 5:10.

19:15 On **witnesses**, see Num. 35:30; Deut. 17:6 and note on 17:6–7. For NT application, see Matt. 18:16; 1 Tim. 5:19; cf. John 8:17; 2 Cor. 13:1.

19:16–18 In disputed legal cases, the issue is taken to the central sanctuary, **before the LORD** (17:8–9). Careful questioning is required to determine if a witness is **malicious** and **false**. Giving false testimony breaks the ninth commandment (5:20) and damages the community (cf. Ps. 27:12; Prov. 6:19; 12:17, 19; 14:5; 19:5, 9; 25:18).

shall [e]inquire diligently, and if the witness is a false witness and has accused his brother
falsely, 19 [f]then you shall do to him as he had meant to do to his brother. So you shall purge
the evil[1] from your midst. 20 And the rest [g]shall hear and fear, and shall never again commit any such evil among you. 21 [y]Your eye shall not pity. [h]It shall be life for life, eye for eye,
tooth for tooth, hand for hand, foot for foot.

Laws Concerning Warfare

20 "When you go out to war against your enemies, and see [i]horses and chariots and
an army larger than your own, you shall not be afraid of them, for the LORD your
God is [j]with you, who brought you up out of the land of Egypt. 2 And when you draw
near to the battle, [k]the priest shall come forward and speak to the people 3 and shall say
to them, 'Hear, O Israel, today you are drawing near for battle against your enemies: let
not your heart faint. Do not fear or panic or be in dread of them, 4 for the LORD your God
is he who goes with you [l]to fight for you against your enemies, to give you the victory.'
5 Then the officers shall speak to the people, saying, 'Is there any man who has built a new
house and has not dedicated it? Let him go back to his house, lest he die in the battle and
another man dedicate it. 6 And is there any man who has planted a vineyard and has not
[m]enjoyed its fruit? Let him go back to his house, lest he die in the battle and another man
enjoy its fruit. 7 [n]And is there any man who has betrothed a wife and has not taken her?
Let him go back to his house, lest he die in the battle and another man take her.' 8 And the
officers shall speak further to the people, and say, [o]'Is there any man who is fearful and
fainthearted? Let him go back to his house, lest he make the heart of his fellows melt like
his own.' 9 And when the officers have finished speaking to the people, then commanders
shall be appointed at the head of the people.
10 "When you draw near to a city to fight against it, [p]offer terms of peace to it. 11 And if
it responds to you peaceably and it opens to you, then all the people who are found in it
shall do forced labor for you and shall serve you. 12 But if it makes no peace with you, but
makes war against you, then you shall besiege it. 13 And when the LORD your God gives it
into your hand, [q]you shall put all its males to the sword, 14 [r]but the women and the little
ones, the livestock, and everything else in the city, all its spoil, you [s]shall take as plunder
for yourselves. And [t]you shall enjoy the spoil of your enemies, which the LORD your God
has given you. 15 Thus you shall do to all the cities that are very far from you, which are not
cities of the nations here. 16 But [u]in the cities of these peoples that the LORD your God is

[1] *Or evil person*

18 [e]ch. 13:14; 17:4
19 [f]Prov. 19:5, 9; [Dan. 6:24]
20 [g]See ch. 13:11
21 [y][See ver. 13 above] [h]See Ex. 21:23, 24

Chapter 20

1 [i][Josh. 17:18; Ps. 20:7; Isa. 31:1] [j]ch. 31:6, 8; 2 Chr. 13:12; 32:8
2 [k][Num. 10:8, 9; 31:6]
4 [l]ch. 1:30; 3:22; Josh. 23:10
6 [m]ch. 28:30; Lev. 19:23-25; [1 Cor. 9:7]
7 [n][ch. 24:5; 28:30]
8 [o][Judg. 7:3]
10 [p]Judg. 21:13; [ch. 2:26; 2 Sam. 20:18, 20]
13 [q]Num. 31:7
14 [r]Num. 31:9 [s]Josh. 8:2 [t]Josh. 22:8
16 [u]ch. 7:1, 2; Num. 33:52; Josh. 11:14

19:19–20 purge the evil. See 13:5 and note. Proper justice and punishment acts as a deterrent for the people. See 13:11 and note.

19:21 eye shall not pity. See 13:8. **life for life, eye for eye, tooth for tooth, hand for hand, foot for foot**. This expression expands the idea that the punishment for the false witness is to be the same as would have been imposed on the accused (19:19) and makes punishment proportionate to the crime. See Ex. 21:23–25 and Matt. 5:38. It cannot involve multiple acts of revenge (cf. Lamech, Gen. 4:24).

20:1–20 Whereas the OT usually describes war through narrative, this chapter legislates what ought to happen in warfare. This law limits the conduct of warfare and occurs in a section that could be headed "You shall not murder," devoted to ensuring no unnecessary loss of life. The concern is to minimize casualties in war. This law also distinguishes between enemy cities outside the boundaries of the Promised Land (vv. 10–15) and those within the boundaries (vv. 16–18). Even the latter case, however, need not result in total annihilation (see note on vv. 16–18). These laws on warfare (esp. vv. 16–18) create an ethical dilemma for Christians. But three things should be considered: (1) the limits and restraint of these laws; (2) their context in securing the Promised Land; and (3) the priority of offering terms of peace to cities before attacking them (see v. 10). See Gen. 15:16; and notes on Deut. 7:2; 18:12. In the NT, the Christian inheritance is a heavenly land (1 Pet. 1:4), not an earthly one, and the language of warfare is used spiritually (cf. Eph. 6:10–17).

20:1–4 The first command regarding warfare is **you shall not be afraid of them** if the enemy's army is larger than Israel's. The reason for not fearing is the presence of God (see 1:19–45). Rather, the enemy's strength highlights God's greater power in defeating them. The **priest** reinforces the command not to fear and reflects the presence of God in the midst of Israel's army.

20:5–7 Exemption from military service is extended to three groups of people. See the parallel covenant curses in 28:30. The priority is on enjoying the blessings from God in housing, crops, and marriage. The exemptions show that Israel did not need to depend on every last man fighting and that warfare was not to be an end in itself but a means to a greater end. Those who fight serve the interests of the whole community.

20:8 A fourth exemption from military service is extended to any who are **fearful and fainthearted** (cf. Gideon's army in Judg. 7:2–3). Psychologically, fearfulness could be contagious throughout the army. More significantly, fear is disobedience and God does not allow such disobedient warriors to fight.

20:10–15 The application of vv. 10–14 is limited to **cities that are very far from you** (v. 15), i.e., outside the boundaries of the Promised Land. If the city rejects the **terms of peace** and initiates war against Israel, victory over the city is assured because God **gives it into** Israel's **hand**.

20:16–18 These verses concern cities within the boundaries of the Promised Land and may presuppose that these cities have refused the invitation to surrender (see v. 10). Israel's action is much more severe in these cases, as they are to **save alive nothing that breathes** (v. 16). To **devote them to complete destruction** (v. 17) acknowledges that God is the victor and that to him belong the spoils of war (see 2:34–35; 7:2); it also is a precursor of final judgment (see Introduction to Joshua: The Destruction of the Canaanites). Such a drastic threat could encourage surrender rather than resistance. Joshua's application of these principles made room for such Gentiles to surrender and survive (e.g., Josh. 6:22–25; 9:26–27). On the nations listed

giving you for an inheritance, you shall save alive nothing that breathes, **17** but [v]you shall
devote them to complete destruction,[1] the Hittites and the Amorites, the Canaanites and
the Perizzites, the Hivites and the Jebusites, as the LORD your God has commanded, **18** that
[w]they may not teach you to do according to all their abominable practices that they have
done for their gods, and so you [x]sin against the LORD your God.

19 "When you besiege a city for a long time, making war against it in order to take it,
[y]you shall not destroy its trees by wielding an axe against them. You may eat from them,
but you shall not cut them down. Are the trees in the field human, that they should be
besieged by you? **20** Only the trees that you know are not trees for food you may destroy
and cut down, that you may build siegeworks against the city that makes war with you,
until it falls.

Atonement for Unsolved Murders

21 "If in the land that the LORD your God is giving you to possess someone is found
slain, lying in the open country, and it is not known who killed him, **2** then your
elders and your judges shall come out, and they shall measure the distance to the surrounding cities. **3** And the elders of the city that is nearest to the slain man shall take a heifer
[z]that has never been worked and that has not pulled in a yoke. **4** And the elders of that
city shall bring the heifer down to a valley with running water, which is neither plowed
nor sown, and shall break the heifer's neck there in the valley. **5** Then the priests, the sons
of Levi, shall come forward, for the LORD your God has chosen [a]them to minister to him
and to bless in the name of the LORD, and [b]by their word every dispute and every assault
shall be settled. **6** And all the elders of that city nearest to the slain man [c]shall wash their
hands over the heifer whose neck was broken in the valley, **7** and they shall testify, 'Our
hands did not shed this blood, nor did our eyes see it shed. **8** Accept atonement, O LORD,
for your people Israel, whom you have redeemed, and [d]do not set the guilt of innocent
blood in the midst of your people Israel, so that their blood guilt be atoned for.' **9** So [e]you
shall purge the guilt of innocent blood from your midst, when you do what is right in
the sight of the LORD.

Marrying Female Captives

10 "When you go out to war against your enemies, and the LORD your God gives them
into your hand and you take them captive, **11** and you see among the captives a beautiful
woman, and you desire to take her to be your wife, **12** and you bring her home to your
house, she shall shave her head and pare her nails. **13** And she shall take off the clothes in
which she was captured and shall remain in your house and [f]lament her father and her
mother a full month. After that you may go in to her and be her husband, and she shall
be your wife. **14** But if you no longer delight in her, you shall [g]let her go where she wants.
But you shall not sell her for money, nor shall you [h]treat her as a slave, since you have
humiliated her.

Inheritance Rights of the Firstborn

15 "If a man has two wives, [i]the one loved and the other unloved, and both the loved and
the unloved have borne him children, and if the firstborn son belongs to the unloved,[2]

17 [v]See ch. 7:2
18 [w]ch. 7:4; 12:30, 31; 18:9 [x]Ex. 23:33
19 [y][2 Kgs. 3:19, 25]

Chapter 21

3 [z][Num. 19:2]
5 [a]See ch. 10:8 [b]ch. 17:8, 9; 19:17
6 [c][Ps. 26:6; 73:13; Matt. 27:24]
8 [d][Jonah 1:14]
9 [e]ch. 19:13
13 [f][Ps. 45:10]
14 [g][Jer. 34:16] [h]ch. 24:7
15 [i][Gen. 29:30, 33; 1 Sam. 1:4, 5]

[1] That is, set apart (devote) as an offering to the Lord (for destruction) [2] Or *hated*; also verses 16, 17

in Deut. 20:17, cf. 7:1. Cohabiting in the Promised Land with pagan nations makes Israel vulnerable to fall into **their abominable practices**, referring to idolatry as well as immorality. See 7:2–4 and 8:9–14.

20:19–20 The law of protection of fruit trees acknowledges that Israel is to inherit trees that it did not plant (see 6:11). This law also puts a brake on human shortsightedness: the ultimate end of the land is to be a fruitful garden for God's people to enjoy.

21:1 in the land. These laws are given to keep the Promised Land free from desecration.

21:4 break the heifer's neck. This animal is not burned, as in the usual sacrifices. However, its death is a sacrifice to atone for sin committed by an unknown person.

21:9 purge the guilt. Cf. 13:5.

21:10 This law must apply for conquests of cities far away (20:10–15), otherwise the women would have been destroyed (20:17). It both ends the discussion of topics under the heading "you shall not murder" and introduces the section on "you shall not commit adultery" (5:18; see note on 21:15–23:14).

21:12–13 shave her head and pare her nails . . . take off the clothes. These actions indicate a departure from her former life, no doubt including its religious practices.

21:15–23:14 *Protecting Sexual Morality.* Many of the laws in this section address protecting the sexual integrity of God's people, corresponding to the seventh commandment, "You shall not commit adultery" (5:18).

21:15–17 This law presupposes the practice of polygamy but does not condone it. (The ethical ideal for marriage comes from Gen. 2:24; the law protects the community by setting a minimum standard of behavior that preserves

16 then on the day when [j]he assigns his possessions as an inheritance to his sons, he may
not treat the son of the loved as the firstborn in preference to the son of the unloved, who
is the firstborn, 17 but he shall acknowledge the firstborn, the son of the unloved, by giving him a double portion of all that he has, for he is [k]the firstfruits of his strength. [l]The
right of the firstborn is his.

A Rebellious Son

18 "If a man has a stubborn and rebellious son who will not obey the voice of his father
or the voice of his mother, and, though they discipline him, will not listen to them, 19 then
his father and his mother shall take hold of him and bring him out to the elders of his city
at the gate of the place where he lives, 20 and they shall say to the elders of his city, 'This our
son is stubborn and rebellious; he will not obey our voice; he is a glutton and a drunkard.'
21 [m]Then all the men of the city shall stone him to death with stones. [n]So you shall purge
the evil from your midst, [o]and all Israel shall hear, and fear.

A Man Hanged on a Tree Is Cursed

22 "And if a man has committed a crime punishable by death and he is put to death, and
you hang him on a tree, 23 [p]his body shall not remain all night on the tree, but you shall
bury him the same day, for [q]a hanged man is cursed by God. [r]You shall not defile your
land that the LORD your God is giving you for an inheritance.

Various Laws

22 "You [s]shall not see your brother's ox or his sheep going astray and ignore them. You
shall take them back to your brother. 2 And if he does not live near you and you do
not know who he is, you shall bring it home to your house, and it shall stay with you until
your brother seeks it. Then you shall restore it to him. 3 And you shall do the same with his
donkey or with his garment, or with any lost thing of your brother's, which he loses and
you find; you may not ignore it. 4 [t]You shall not see your brother's donkey or his ox fallen
down by the way and ignore them. You shall help him to lift them up again.
5 "A woman shall not wear a man's garment, nor shall a man put on a woman's cloak,
[u]for whoever does these things is an abomination to the LORD your God.
6 "If you come across a bird's nest in any tree or on the ground, with young ones or eggs
and the mother sitting on the young or on the eggs, [v]you shall not take the mother with
the young. 7 You shall let the mother go, but the young you may take for yourself, [w]that it
may go well with you, and that you may live long.
8 "When you build a new house, you shall make a parapet for your roof, that you may
not bring the guilt of blood upon your house, if anyone should fall from it.
9 [x]"You shall not sow your vineyard with two kinds of seed, lest the whole yield be forfeited,[1]
the crop that you have sown and the yield of the vineyard. 10 You shall not plow with an ox
and a donkey together. 11 You shall not wear cloth of wool and linen mixed together.
12 [y]"You shall make yourself tassels on the four corners of the garment with which you
cover yourself.

[1] Hebrew *become holy*

16 [j]1 Chr. 5:1, 2; [1 Chr. 26:10; 2 Chr. 11:19, 20, 22]
17 [k]Gen. 49:3 [l]Gen. 25:31, 33; 27:36
21 [m]ch. 13:10; See Josh. 7:25 [n]See ch. 13:5 [o]ch. 13:11; 17:13; 19:20
23 [p][Josh. 8:29; 10:26, 27; John 19:31] [q]Cited Gal. 3:13 [r]Num. 35:34

Chapter 22

1 [s]Ex. 23:4
4 [t]Ex. 23:5
5 [u][ch. 18:12; 25:16]
6 [v]Lev. 22:28
7 [w]See ch. 4:40
9 [x]Lev. 19:19
12 [y]Num. 15:38; [Matt. 23:5]

civility. On polygamy, see notes on 1 Cor. 7:2; 1 Tim. 3:2–3.) The law protects the rights of the **firstborn** even if he is the son of the **unloved** wife. **double portion**. The OT, in line with ancient Near Eastern practice, gave a double share of inheritance to the oldest son.

21:18–21 Breaking the fifth commandment (5:16) attracted the death penalty. Notice that the parents take the initiative in this penalty. **purge the evil**. See 13:5.

21:23 This law restricts the exposure of a dead criminal hanging on a tree, hence the concern to bury Jesus immediately after his death (see also Gal. 3:13).

22:1–4 Helping to protect a neighbor's property fulfills the command to love your neighbor as yourself (Lev. 19:18).

22:5 This law most likely prohibits transvestitism. The strong word **abomination** may also suggest transvestite practices associated with pagan temple prostitution. As with vv. 9–11 below, the law seeks to uphold the order and distinction in God's creation.

22:6–7 Like the treatment of trees in 20:19–20, this law preserves the means of life and seeks to prevent shortsightedness, requiring wise and respectful use of the creation.

22:8 Builders and homeowners must take adequate safety measures in building houses. Flat roofs were used for various household activities, including sleeping in hot weather.

22:9–11 These laws prohibit mixing various items, reflecting God's ordering of creation "according to its kind" (e.g., Gen. 1:25). They also reminded Israelites that God had separated them from other peoples to be distinct and holy (Deut. 14:2).

22:12 tassels. See Num. 15:38–41.

22:13–30 This group of laws deals with infringements to proper moral sexual conduct. All these laws begin with "If . . ." and deal with the response to the criminal. Behind this selection is the seventh commandment, "You shall not commit adultery" (5:18).

22:14–15 The text does not specify what constitutes **evidence of virginity**.

13[z] [2 Sam. 13:15]
19[a] [Matt. 19:8, 9; Mark 10:11; Luke 16:18]
21[b] [ch. 21:21] [c] See Gen. 34:7 [d] See ch. 13:5
22[e] Lev. 20:10; [Ezek. 16:38, 40; 23:45, 47; John 8:5] [d] [See ver. 21 above]
23[f] [Matt. 1:18, 19]
24[d] [See ver. 21 above]
28[g] Ex. 22:16, 17
30[h] See Lev. 18:8 [i] ch. 27:20; [Ruth 3:9; Ezek. 16:8]
Chapter 23
2[j] [Zech. 9:6]

Laws Concerning Sexual Immorality

13 "If any man takes a wife and [z]goes in to her and then hates her **14** and accuses her of
misconduct and brings a bad name upon her, saying, 'I took this woman, and when I came
near her, I did not find in her evidence of virginity,' **15** then the father of the young woman
and her mother shall take and bring out the evidence of her virginity to the elders of the
city in the gate. **16** And the father of the young woman shall say to the elders, 'I gave my
daughter to this man to marry, and he hates her; **17** and behold, he has accused her of misconduct, saying, "I did not find in your daughter evidence of virginity." And yet this is the
evidence of my daughter's virginity.' And they shall spread the cloak before the elders of
the city. **18** Then the elders of that city shall take the man and whip[1] him, **19** and they shall
fine him a hundred shekels[2] of silver and give them to the father of the young woman,
because he has brought a bad name upon a virgin[3] of Israel. And she shall be his wife.
[a]He may not divorce her all his days. **20** But if the thing is true, that evidence of virginity
was not found in the young woman, **21** then they shall bring out the young woman to the
door of her father's house, and [b]the men of her city shall stone her to death with stones,
because she has [c]done an outrageous thing in Israel by whoring in her father's house. [d]So
you shall purge the evil from your midst.
22 [e]"If a man is found lying with the wife of another man, both of them shall die, the man
who lay with the woman, and the woman. [d]So you shall purge the evil from Israel.
23 "If there is a [f]betrothed virgin, and a man meets her in the city and lies with her, **24** then
you shall bring them both out to the gate of that city, and you shall stone them to death with
stones, the young woman because she did not cry for help though she was in the city, and the
man because he violated his neighbor's wife. [d]So you shall purge the evil from your midst.
25 "But if in the open country a man meets a young woman who is betrothed, and the
man seizes her and lies with her, then only the man who lay with her shall die. **26** But
you shall do nothing to the young woman; she has committed no offense punishable by
death. For this case is like that of a man attacking and murdering his neighbor, **27** because
he met her in the open country, and though the betrothed young woman cried for help
there was no one to rescue her.
28 [g]"If a man meets a virgin who is not betrothed, and seizes her and lies with her, and
they are found, **29** then the man who lay with her shall give to the father of the young
woman fifty shekels of silver, and she shall be his wife, because he has violated her. He
may not divorce her all his days.
30[4] [h]"A man shall not take his father's wife, so that he does not [i]uncover his father's
nakedness.[5]

Those Excluded from the Assembly

23 "No one whose testicles are crushed or whose male organ is cut off shall enter the
assembly of the LORD.
2 [j]"No one born of a forbidden union may enter the assembly of the LORD. Even to the
tenth generation, none of his descendants may enter the assembly of the LORD.

[1] Or *discipline* [2] A *shekel* was about 2/5 ounce or 11 grams [3] Or *girl of marriageable age* [4] Ch 23:1 in Hebrew [5] Hebrew *uncover his father's skirt*

This may be a garment stained with menstrual blood (v. 17), which demonstrates that she is not pregnant, or a stain of hymenal blood, showing that the girl's first intercourse took place on her wedding night. **The gate** was where legal matters were heard and resolved.

22:19 A hundred shekels is a very hefty fine, much more than a bride-price (cf. v. 29). Workers in old Babylonian times earned half a shekel per month. Along with the rule that **he may not divorce her**, this law sought to deter men from making false allegations and pursuing easy divorce.

22:21 purge the evil. See 13:5.

22:22 Adultery was a capital offense throughout the ancient world. To be convicted, the couple must be caught in the act (**found lying**) and they were both punished equally. If the circumstances suggested that the woman had not consented, then only the man was punished (vv. 25–27).

22:23–24 betrothed . . . wife. Betrothal was much more binding than modern engagement, hence the woman is called "wife" in v. 24. **purge the evil**. See 13:5.

22:29 Fifty shekels appears to be the bride-price (see Ex. 22:16). The law seeks to protect the woman, who is less likely to be married because she has been violated.

22:30 uncover his father's nakedness. As the ESV footnote explains, this is lit., "uncover his father's skirt" (i.e., the corner of his garment). See also 27:20. It is probably an idiom meaning to bring dishonor to the father. The father's wife would presumably be a woman other than the man's mother, such as in the case of polygamy.

23:1 assembly. Generally the term is used in Deuteronomy to refer to Israel gathered at Horeb/Sinai. In this chapter it anticipates Israel gathered in the land at worship. **testicles are crushed**. This probably refers to men made eunuchs in the context of pagan worship. **cut off**. In Gal. 5:12 ("emasculate themselves") Paul uses the same verb as appears in the Greek translation of Deuteronomy, perhaps to imply that his opponents are acting like pagans; by this action the ancient Israelites would disqualify themselves from entry into the assembly.

23:2–4 Tenth generation is possibly an idiom meaning forever (see v. 6).

3 [k]"No Ammonite or Moabite may enter the assembly of the LORD. Even to the tenth
generation, none of them may enter the assembly of the LORD forever, 4 [l]because they did
not meet you with bread and with water on the way, when you came out of Egypt, and
because they [m]hired against you Balaam the son of Beor from Pethor of [n]Mesopotamia,
to curse you. 5 But the LORD your God would not listen to Balaam; instead the LORD your
God turned [o]the curse into a blessing for you, because the LORD your God loved you. 6 You
[p]shall not seek their peace or their prosperity all your days forever.
7 "You shall not abhor an Edomite, for [q]he is your brother. You shall not abhor an Egyptian,
because [r]you were a sojourner in his land. 8 Children born to them in the third generation
may enter the assembly of the LORD.

Uncleanness in the Camp

9 "When you are encamped against your enemies, then you shall keep yourself from
every evil thing.
10 "If any man among you becomes [s]unclean because of a nocturnal emission, then he
shall go outside the camp. He shall not come inside the camp, 11 but when evening comes,
he shall [t]bathe himself in water, and as the sun sets, he may come inside the camp.
12 "You shall have a place outside the camp, and you shall go out to it. 13 And you shall
have a trowel with your tools, and when you sit down outside, you shall dig a hole with
it and turn back and cover up your excrement. 14 Because [u]the LORD your God walks in
the midst of your camp, to deliver you and to give up your enemies before you, therefore
your camp must be holy, so that he may not see anything indecent among you and turn
away from you.

Miscellaneous Laws

15 [v]"You shall not give up to his master a slave[1] who has escaped from his master to you.
16 He shall dwell with you, in your midst, in the place that he shall choose within one of
your towns, wherever it suits him. You shall not wrong him.
17 "None of the [w]daughters of Israel shall be a cult prostitute, and none [x]of the sons of
Israel shall be a cult prostitute. 18 You shall not bring the fee of a prostitute or the wages
of a dog[2] into the house of the LORD your God in payment for any vow, for both of these
are an abomination to the LORD your God.
19 [y]"You shall not charge interest on loans to your brother, [z]interest on money, interest on
food, interest on anything that is lent for interest. 20 [a]You may charge a foreigner interest,
but you may not charge your brother interest, [b]that the LORD your God may bless you in
all that you undertake in the land that you are entering to take possession of it.
21 [c]"If you make a vow to the LORD your God, you shall not delay fulfilling it, for the
LORD your God will surely require it of you, and you will be guilty of sin. 22 But if you
refrain from vowing, you will not be guilty of sin. 23 You shall be careful to do what has
passed your lips, for you have voluntarily vowed to the LORD your God what you have
promised with your mouth.
24 "If you go into your neighbor's vineyard, you may eat your fill of grapes, as many as

[1] Or *servant*; the Hebrew term *'ebed* designates a range of social and economic roles (see Preface) [2] Or *male prostitute*

3 [k]Neh. 13:1, 2
4 [l][ch. 2:29] [m]Num. 22:5, 6; [2 Pet. 2:15] [n]Acts 7:2
5 [o]Num. 23:11; 24:10
6 [p][Ezra 9:12]
7 [q]Gen. 25:24-26; Num. 20:14; Obad. 10, 12 [r]ch. 10:19; Ex. 22:21; 23:9; Lev. 19:34
10 [s]Lev. 15:16
11 [t]See Lev. 15:5
14 [u]Lev. 26:12
15 [v]1 Sam. 30:15
17 [w]Lev. 19:29 [x]1 Kgs. 14:24; 15:12; 22:46; 2 Kgs. 23:7
19 [y]See Ex. 22:25 [z][Neh. 5:10]
20 [a][ch. 15:3] [b]ch. 15:10
21 [c][Ps. 66:13, 14; 76:11]; See Num. 30:2

no Ammonite or Moabite. The story of Ruth indicates that there were exceptions (see note on Ruth 1:4). **Balaam**. See Numbers 22–24.

23:7–8 You shall not abhor an Edomite. Israel's kinship with Edom is closer than that with Moab and Ammon (cf. v. 3). Edom is descended from Esau, Jacob's twin (Gen. 25:19–26). **third generation**. The possibility of foreigners becoming worshiping Israelites shows that, with God, faith is the issue more than race.

23:9–14 Israel's army fighting against the enemy was a religious gathering in the midst of which God was present. Hence laws of cleanness applied.

23:15–24:22 *Various Laws Protecting Property.* The specific stipulations conclude with an assortment of laws, many of which seem to be property offenses related to the eighth commandment, "You shall not steal" (5:19).

23:15 The refugee **slave** is most likely a foreigner, not an Israelite slave.

23:17 cult prostitute. Cultic prostitution was practiced by Canaanite religion as a fertility rite. It was strictly prohibited for ancient Israel.

23:19–20 charge interest. A distinction is made between a fellow Israelite (**brother**) and a **foreigner**. To take a loan in ancient times was an act of desperation, often caused by crop failure. Cruelly high interest rates made situations worse. The prohibition of interest among Israelites protected the poor (see Ex. 22:25). **may bless you**. Wealth comes from obedience to God, not from selfish economics.

23:21–23 Vows were voluntary but, once made, were binding (see Numbers 30; Eccles. 5:2–6; for the problem of Jephthah's vow, see note on Judg. 11:35). Vows must be kept because God keeps his promises and desires that his people imitate his moral character.

23:24–25 you may eat your fill. These laws benefit the poor and are not

25[d][Matt. 12:1; Mark 2:23; Luke 6:1]
Chapter 24
1[e]Matt. 19:7; Mark 10:4; Cited Matt. 5:31; [Isa. 50:1; Jer. 3:8]
4[f][Jer. 3:1]
5[g][ch. 20:7] [h]Prov. 5:18
7[i]Ex. 21:16; [1 Tim. 1:10] [j]ch. 21:14 [k]See ch. 13:5
8[l]See Lev. 13–14
9[m]See Num. 12:10-15 [n]ch. 25:17
13[o]See Ex. 22:26 [p]Job 29:13; 31:20 [q]Ps. 112:9; Dan. 4:27; [ch. 6:25]
14[r]Mal. 3:5; See Lev. 25:39-43
15[s]Jer. 22:13; See Lev. 19:13 [t]ch. 15:9; James 5:4

you wish, but you shall not put any in your bag. **25** If you go into your neighbor's standing grain, [d]you may pluck the ears with your hand, but you shall not put a sickle to your
neighbor's standing grain.

Laws Concerning Divorce

24 "When a man takes a wife and marries her, if then she finds no favor in his eyes
because he has found some indecency in her, and [e]he writes her a certificate of
divorce and puts it in her hand and sends her out of his house, and she departs out of
his house, **2** and if she goes and becomes another man's wife, **3** and the latter man hates
her and writes her a certificate of divorce and puts it in her hand and sends her out of his
house, or if the latter man dies, who took her to be his wife, **4** then [f]her former husband,
who sent her away, may not take her again to be his wife, after she has been defiled, for
that is an abomination before the LORD. And you shall not bring sin upon the land that
the LORD your God is giving you for an inheritance.

Miscellaneous Laws

5 [g]"When a man is newly married, he shall not go out with the army or be liable for any
other public duty. He shall be free at home one year [h]to be happy with his wife whom he
has taken.

6 "No one shall take a mill or an upper millstone in pledge, for that would be taking a
life in pledge.

7 [i]"If a man is found stealing one of his brothers of the people of Israel, and if he [j]treats
him as a slave or sells him, then that thief shall die. [k]So you shall purge the evil from
your midst.

8 "Take care, in [l]a case of leprous[1] disease, to be very careful to do according to all that
the Levitical priests shall direct you. As I commanded them, so you shall be careful to do.
9 Remember what the LORD your God did to [m]Miriam [n]on the way as you came out of
Egypt.

10 "When you make your neighbor a loan of any sort, you shall not go into his house to
collect his pledge. **11** You shall stand outside, and the man to whom you make the loan shall
bring the pledge out to you. **12** And if he is a poor man, you shall not sleep in his pledge.
13 [o]You shall restore to him the pledge as the sun sets, that he may sleep in his cloak and
[p]bless you. And [q]it shall be righteousness for you before the LORD your God.

14 "You shall not [r]oppress a hired worker who is poor and needy, whether he is one of
your brothers or one of the sojourners who are in your land within your towns. **15** [s]You
shall give him his wages on the same day, before the sun sets (for he is poor and counts on
it), [t]lest he cry against you to the LORD, and you be guilty of sin.

[1] *Leprosy* was a term for several skin diseases; see Leviticus 13

an excuse for theft. The economics of ancient Israel included generosity toward fellow Israelites (see notes on 15:4–6; 15:7–8).

24:1–4 This is a good example of "case law," where vv. 1–3 present the situation ("**When** . . .") and v. 4 is the actual law ("**then** . . ."). The law forbids the first husband taking back the wife he found **no favor** with after she is subsequently divorced or widowed. By charging his wife with **some indecency**, the first husband acquired her dowry—her father's marriage present to her—when he divorced her. Remarrying, she was given a second dowry. This example then implies that, when her second marriage ended (either through death or through more trivial grounds of divorce), she was able to keep her second dowry. The first husband is forbidden to remarry her to acquire her second dowry. This law protects the woman from exploitation by her first husband. This is the only OT law about divorce. Elsewhere divorce is presupposed (e.g., Lev. 21:7, 14; Num. 30:9). See Jesus' comments on this law in Matt. 5:31–32. In Matt. 19:7, Pharisees defend their position on divorce by appeal to this law; Jesus, however, appeals to the creation account (Gen. 1:27; 2:24) to show God's ethical ideal. This law is a concession to hardness of hearts, preserving a minimum level of civility for the theocracy.

24:5 one year. This may give the couple time to have at least one child and develop their relationship. Cf. note on 20:5–7.

24:6 mill or an upper millstone. These were basic utensils for food preparation; if taken as a pledge or security for a loan, they would deprive the poor person of the means for grinding grain.

24:7 that thief shall die. Kidnapping is regarded as theft and is the only type of theft for which the death penalty applies; these laws place a higher value on persons than on property. **purge the evil**. See 13:5.

24:8–9 leprous disease. The priests were the ones to rule on leprous diseases, as leprosy (a general term for skin diseases) made a person unclean. See Leviticus 13 and note on Lev. 13:1–59. **Miriam**, Moses' sister, suffered from leprosy (see Numbers 12).

24:10 not go into his house. The dignity of the poor person, who is forced into a loan, is preserved, and violence or theft is guarded against.

24:12 not sleep in his pledge. This forbids a person's cloak, which doubled as a blanket, to be taken to secure a loan. The basic rights of a vulnerable person are protected (see v. 13). Amos 2:8 scourges those who blatantly flout this law.

16 [u]"Fathers shall not be put to death because of their children, nor shall children be put
to death because of their fathers. Each one shall be put to death for his own sin.
17 [v]"You shall not pervert the justice due to the sojourner or to the fatherless, [w]or take a
widow's garment in pledge, 18 but [x]you shall remember that you were a slave in Egypt and
the LORD your God redeemed you from there; therefore I command you to do this.
19 [y]"When you reap your harvest in your field and forget a sheaf in the field, you shall
not go back to get it. It shall be for the sojourner, the fatherless, and the widow, [z]that the
LORD your God may bless you in all the work of your hands. 20 When you beat your olive
trees, you shall not go over them again. It shall be for the sojourner, the fatherless, and the
widow. 21 When you gather the grapes of your vineyard, you shall not strip it afterward. It
shall be for the sojourner, the fatherless, and the widow. 22 [x]You shall remember that you
were a slave in the land of Egypt; therefore I command you to do this.

25 "If there is a [a]dispute between men and they come into court and the judges decide
between them, [b]acquitting the innocent and condemning the guilty, 2 then if the
guilty man deserves to be beaten, the judge shall cause him to lie down and be beaten in
his presence with a number of stripes in proportion to his offense. 3 [c]Forty stripes may
be given him, but not more, lest, if one should go on to beat him with more stripes than
these, your brother be degraded in your sight.
4 [d]"You shall not muzzle an ox when it is treading out the grain.

Laws Concerning Levirate Marriage

5 [e]"If brothers dwell together, and one of them dies and has no son, the wife of the dead
man shall not be married outside the family to a stranger. Her [f]husband's brother shall
go in to her and take her as his wife and perform the duty of a husband's brother to her.
6 And the first son whom she bears shall succeed to the name of his dead brother, that [g]his
name may not be blotted out of Israel. 7 And if the man does not wish to take his brother's
wife, then his brother's wife shall [h]go up to the gate to the elders and say, 'My husband's
brother refuses to perpetuate his brother's name in Israel; he will not perform the duty
of a husband's brother to me.' 8 Then the elders of his city shall call him and speak to him,
and if he persists, saying, [i]'I do not wish to take her,' 9 then his brother's wife shall go up
to him in the presence of the elders and [j]pull his sandal off his foot and [k]spit in his face.
And she shall answer and say, 'So shall it be done to the man who does not [l]build up his
brother's house.' 10 And the name of his house[1] shall be called in Israel, 'The house of him
who had his sandal pulled off.'

Miscellaneous Laws

11 "When men fight with one another and the wife of the one draws near to rescue her
husband from the hand of him who is beating him and puts out her hand and seizes him
by the private parts, 12 then you shall cut off her hand. [m]Your eye shall have no pity.

[1] Hebrew *its name*

16 [u]Cited 2 Kgs. 14:6; 2 Chr. 25:4; [Jer. 31:29, 30; Ezek. 18:20]
17 [v]Ex. 22:21, 22; 23:6; [ch. 10:18; 27:19; Isa. 1:23; Jer. 5:28]; See ch. 16:19 [w][ver. 6, 13; Job 24:3]
18 [x]See ch. 5:15
19 [y]Lev. 19:9; 23:22 [z]See ch. 14:29
22 [x][See ver. 18 above]

Chapter 25

1 [a]ch. 19:17 [b][1 Kgs. 8:32; Prov. 17:15]
3 [c][2 Cor. 11:24]
4 [d]Cited 1 Cor. 9:9; 1 Tim. 5:18
5 [e]Matt. 22:24; Mark 12:19; Luke 20:28 [f][Gen. 38:8, 9; Ruth 1:12, 13; 3:9]
6 [g]Ruth 4:10
7 [h][Ruth 4:1, 2]
8 [i][Ruth 4:6]
9 [j][Ruth 4:7] [k][Num. 12:14; Job 30:10; Isa. 50:6] [l]Ruth 4:11
12 [m]See ch. 7:16

24:17–18 sojourner . . . fatherless . . . widow's garment. These three groups, as landless people, represented the most vulnerable in the land (see 10:18–19 and note). Israel's own time spent in **Egypt** as slaves was to motivate their proper treatment of landless people. See also v. 22.

24:19–22 These laws make provision for the poor. The blessings of the land are for the people as a whole to share. Cf. 23:24–25, and see Lev. 19:9–10. See also this law in practice in Ruth 2.

25:1–16 *Laws on Justice, Marriage, and Business.* The laws in this section relate to things such as the administration of justice, provision for widows, and honesty in business (cf. the ninth commandment, "You shall not bear false witness" (5:20; cf. 25:1, 13–15).

25:3 The limit of **forty stripes** was to prevent the guilty man from being degraded or abused, presumably anticipating his restoration to the community. For fear of miscounting and going beyond 40, later Jews limited flogging to 39, as in the case of Paul (2 Cor. 11:24).

25:4 Even an animal was entitled to food while it worked. Paul applied this principle to the work of evangelism and disciple-making (1 Cor. 9:9; 1 Tim. 5:18).

25:5 husband's brother. In Latin, brother-in-law is *levir*, hence the term "levirate marriage" is applied to this law. Its purpose was protection for the widow and is a case where polygamy was allowed (i.e., the brother-in-law may have already been married). See also Gen. 38:8–10. The law reflects the strong sense of obligation placed on family, as well as a desire to preserve the family line (see Deut. 25:9). Ruth 4:1–12 seems to combine this institution with redemption by the closest kinsman (see Introduction to Ruth: Key Themes). In Matt. 22:23–33 the Sadducees use this law in an effort to disprove the idea of resurrection, and Jesus reveals their faulty reasoning. It is possible that Paul's advice in 1 Cor. 7:39, allowing a widow to marry "whom she wishes," was addressed to Christians who thought this law was still applicable.

25:7 gate. See 22:15 and note on 22:14–15.

25:9 pull his sandal off his foot and spit in his face. This public event brings shame on the brother-in-law (Num. 12:14; Job 30:10). He is not, how-

13[n]Lev. 19:35, 36; [Prov. 16:11; Ezek. 45:10; Amos 8:5; Mic. 6:11]
15[o]See ch. 4:40
16[p]Prov. 11:1 [q]ch. 18:12; 22:5
17[r]Ex. 17:8 [s]ch. 24:9
18[t][Josh. 10:19]
19[u][1 Sam. 15:2, 3] [v]See Ex. 17:8-14
Chapter 26
2[w]ch. 16:10; Ex. 23:19; 34:26; Num. 15:20; 18:13; Prov. 3:9 [x]See ch. 12:5
3[y]Ex. 13:5; See ch. 1:8
5[z]Gen. 43:1, 2 [a][ch. 10:22; Gen. 46:27; Acts 7:14, 15]
6[b]Ex. 1:11, 14; Num. 20:15
7[c]Ex. 2:23-25; 3:9; Num. 20:16
8[d]Ex. 12:37, 51 [e]See ch. 4:34
9[f]See Ex. 3:8
11[g]See ch. 12:7
12[h]See Lev. 27:30 [i]ch. 14:28, 29; [Amos 4:4]

13 "You [n]shall not have in your bag two kinds of weights, a large and a small. 14 You
shall not have in your house two kinds of measures, a large and a small. 15 A full and fair[1]
weight you shall have, a full and fair measure you shall have, [o]that your days may be long
in the land that the LORD your God is giving you. 16 For [p]all who do such things, all who
act dishonestly, [q]are an abomination to the LORD your God.
17 [r]"Remember what Amalek did to you [s]on the way as you came out of Egypt, 18 how
he attacked you on the way when you were faint and weary, and [t]cut off your tail, those
who were lagging behind you, and he did not fear God. 19 Therefore [u]when the LORD your
God has given you rest from all your enemies around you, in the land that the LORD your
God is giving you for an inheritance to possess, you shall [v]blot out the memory of Amalek
from under heaven; you shall not forget.

Offerings of Firstfruits and Tithes

26 "When you come into the land that the LORD your God is giving you for an inheritance and have taken possession of it and live in it, 2 [w]you shall take some of the
first of all the fruit of the ground, which you harvest from your land that the LORD your
God is giving you, and you shall put it in a basket, and you shall [x]go to the place that the
LORD your God will choose, to make his name to dwell there. 3 And you shall go to the
priest who is in office at that time and say to him, 'I declare today to the LORD your God
that I have come into the land [y]that the LORD swore to our fathers to give us.' 4 Then the
priest shall take the basket from your hand and set it down before the altar of the LORD
your God.
5 "And you shall make response before the LORD your God, 'A [z]wandering Aramean was
my father. And he went down into Egypt and sojourned there, [a]few in number, and there
he became a nation, great, mighty, and populous. 6 And [b]the Egyptians treated us harshly
and humiliated us and laid on us hard labor. 7 Then [c]we cried to the LORD, the God of our
fathers, and the LORD heard our voice and saw our affliction, our toil, and our oppression.
8 And [d]the LORD brought us out of Egypt [e]with a mighty hand and an outstretched arm,
with great deeds of terror,[2] with signs and wonders. 9 And he brought us into this place
and gave us this land, [f]a land flowing with milk and honey. 10 And behold, now I bring
the first of the fruit of the ground, which you, O LORD, have given me.' And you shall set
it down before the LORD your God and worship before the LORD your God. 11 And [g]you
shall rejoice in all the good that the LORD your God has given to you and to your house,
you, and the Levite, and the sojourner who is among you.
12 "When you have finished paying all [h]the tithe of your produce in the third year,
which is [i]the year of tithing, giving it to the Levite, the sojourner, the fatherless, and the
widow, so that they may eat within your towns and be filled, 13 then you shall say before
the LORD your God, 'I have removed the sacred portion out of my house, and moreover,
I have given it to the Levite, the sojourner, the fatherless, and the widow, according to all

[1] Or *just*, or *righteous*; twice in this verse [2] Hebrew *with great terror*

ever, forced into taking the widow as his wife—which would have protected her from a reluctant husband.

25:13–16 two kinds of weights . . . two kinds of measures. A dishonest person could use one set of weights or measures for selling and another for buying, in order to buy more goods for the set price or to sell less produce for the price. See Lev. 19:35–36. See also Prov. 11:1; 16:11; Amos 8:5. **days may be long**. See Deut. 5:16 and note.

25:17–19 *Amalek.* See Ex. 17:8–16 for the account of the Amalekites' opposition to Israel. The Amalekites remained a thorn in Israel's side. Notably, Saul failed to destroy them (1 Sam. 15:1–9), though David later defeated them (1 Sam. 30:1–20). **rest from all your enemies**. See Deut. 3:20 and note.

26:1–19 *Firstfruits and Tithes.* The final section of specific laws deals with the offering of firstfruits and tithes in the land. This is a fitting conclusion, as it focuses on responding to God's gracious gift of the land, a key theme in the book. As God gives the land, so Israel is to give back to him in response.

26:2 first of all the fruit. This law commands a regular offering of firstfruits of the harvest, season by season. It acknowledges the goodness of the land promised by God and his faithfulness in keeping his promise (v. 3). **place that the LORD your God will choose, to make his name to dwell there.** See 12:5 and note on 12:5–6.

26:4 the priest shall take. See note on 18:3–4.

26:5–10 These verses are often regarded as an early Israelite creed, liturgically recounting God's faithfulness to his promises as the grounds of thanksgiving. **Aramean.** This refers to Jacob, who married the daughters of his uncle Laban, an Aramean (Gen. 28:5). **down into Egypt**. See Ex. 1:1–7. **treated us harshly**. See Exodus 1–2. **cried to the LORD.** See Ex. 2:23–24. **signs and wonders.** The plagues of Egypt (Ex. 7:14–12:32). **milk and honey.** See Deut. 6:3.

26:11 rejoice. See 12:7 and note. **Levite, and the sojourner.** The landless are included in the celebrations of the land (see 12:12 and note).

26:12 in the third year, which is the year of tithing. See 14:28–29 and note.

your commandment that you have commanded me. I have not transgressed any of your
commandments, [j]nor have I forgotten them. **14** [k]I have not eaten of the tithe while I was
mourning, or removed any of it while I was unclean, or offered any of it [l]to the dead. I
have obeyed the voice of the LORD my God. I have done according to all that you have
commanded me. **15** [m]Look down from your holy habitation, from heaven, and bless your
people Israel and the ground that you have given us, as you swore to our fathers, a land
flowing with milk and honey.'
16 "This day the LORD your God commands you to do these statutes and rules. You shall
therefore be careful to do them with all your heart and with all your soul. **17** [n]You have
declared today that the LORD is your God, and that you will walk in his ways, and keep
his statutes and his commandments and his rules, and will obey his voice. **18** And the LORD
has declared today that you are [o]a people for his treasured possession, as he has promised
you, and that you are to keep all his commandments, **19** and that he will set you in praise
and in fame and in honor [p]high above all nations [q]that he has made, and that you shall
be [r]a people holy to the LORD your God, as he promised."

The Altar on Mount Ebal

27 Now Moses and the elders of Israel commanded the people, saying, "Keep the whole
commandment that I command you today. **2** And on the day [s]you cross over the
Jordan to the land that the LORD your God is giving you, you shall set up large stones and
plaster them with plaster. **3** [t]And you shall write on them all the words of this law, when
you cross over to enter the land that the LORD your God is giving you, [u]a land flowing with
milk and honey, as the LORD, the God of your fathers, has promised you. **4** And when you
have crossed over the Jordan, you shall set up these stones, concerning which I command
you today, [v]on Mount Ebal, and you shall plaster them with plaster. **5** And there you shall
build an altar to the LORD your God, an altar of stones. [w]You shall wield no iron tool on
them; **6** you shall build an altar to the LORD your God of uncut[1] stones. And you shall offer
burnt offerings on it to the LORD your God, **7** and you shall sacrifice peace offerings and
[x]shall eat there, and you [x]shall rejoice before the LORD your God. **8** And [y]you shall write
on the stones all the words of this law very plainly."

Curses from Mount Ebal

9 Then Moses and the Levitical priests said to all Israel, "Keep silence and hear, O Israel:
[z]this day you have become the people of the LORD your God. **10** You shall therefore obey
the voice of the LORD your God, keeping his commandments and his statutes, which I
command you today."
11 That day Moses charged the people, saying, **12** "When you have crossed over the Jordan,
[a]these shall stand on Mount Gerizim to bless the people: Simeon, Levi, Judah, Issachar,
Joseph, and Benjamin. **13** And these shall stand on Mount Ebal for the curse: Reuben, Gad,
Asher, Zebulun, Dan, and Naphtali. **14** And [b]the Levites shall declare to all the men of Israel
in a loud voice:
15 [c]"'Cursed be the man who makes a carved or cast metal image, an abomination to
the LORD, a thing made by the hands of a craftsman, and sets it up in secret.' [d]And all the
people shall answer and say, 'Amen.'

[1] Hebrew *whole*

13 [j]Ps. 119:141, 153, 176
14 [k]Lev. 7:20; 21:1, 11; Hos. 9:4 [l][Jer. 16:7]
15 [m]Isa. 63:15; Zech. 2:13
17 [n][Ex. 24:7]
18 [o]ch. 7:6; 14:2; See Ex. 19:5
19 [p]ch. 28:1; [ch. 32:8] [q]Ps. 86:9 [r]See ch. 7:6

Chapter 27

2 [s]Josh. 4:1
3 [t]Josh. 8:32 [u]See Ex. 3:8
4 [v]ch. 11:29; Josh. 8:30
5 [w]Ex. 20:25; Josh. 8:31
7 [x]See ch. 12:7
8 [y][Hab. 2:2]
9 [z]ch. 26:18
12 [a]ch. 11:29; Josh. 8:33; [Judg. 9:7]
14 [b][ch. 33:10; Dan. 9:11]
15 [c]See Ex. 20:4; 34:17 [d][Num. 5:22; Neh. 5:13; Ps. 106:48; Jer. 11:5; 28:6; 1 Cor. 14:16]

26:14 The three disclaimers in this verse underscore the worshiper's claim to have been fully obedient. **offered any of it to the dead**. This is a pagan practice.

26:15 Look down from your holy habitation. God dwells in **heaven**, though on earth his name and presence also dwell in the central place of worship. See 4:36 and note on 12:5–6; cf. 1 Kings 8:27–30.

26:16 with all your heart and with all your soul. See 4:29; 6:5 and note.

26:18–19 treasured possession . . . holy to the LORD. See 7:6.

27:1–28:68 *Moses' Third Speech: Blessings and Curses.* A new section begins here, the laws having been completed. Along with 11:26–32, this passage brackets the laws of chs. 12–26. Ancient covenant treaties had sections of blessings (the consequences of keeping the treaty stipulations) and curses (the consequences of not keeping the covenant stipulations). Chapter 27 details a ceremony and the fact of curses for lawbreakers. Chapter 28 details the content of the blessings and curses.

27:1–8 Moses looks ahead to a covenant ceremony upon arrival in the land. Significantly, this ceremony is conducted at Shechem (see note on vv. 4–5), the place where God first made the promise of land to Abram (Gen. 12:6–7).

27:2–3 on the day. Not necessarily the precise day but simply meaning "when." **plaster them with plaster**. White plaster provides a backdrop against which the writing may be seen clearly and distinctly. **write on them**

16 [e]‘Cursed be anyone who dishonors his father or his mother.’ And all the people shall
say, ‘Amen.’
17 [f]‘Cursed be anyone who moves his neighbor’s landmark.’ And all the people shall
say, ‘Amen.’
18 [g]‘Cursed be anyone who misleads a blind man on the road.’ And all the people shall
say, ‘Amen.’
19 [h]‘Cursed be anyone who perverts the justice due to the sojourner, the fatherless, and
the widow.’ And all the people shall say, ‘Amen.’
20 [i]‘Cursed be anyone who lies with his father’s wife, because he has [j]uncovered his
father’s nakedness.’[1] And all the people shall say, ‘Amen.’
21 [k]‘Cursed be anyone who lies with any kind of animal.’ And all the people shall say,
‘Amen.’
22 [l]‘Cursed be anyone who lies with his sister, whether the daughter of his father or the
daughter of his mother.’ And all the people shall say, ‘Amen.’
23 [m]‘Cursed be anyone who lies with his mother-in-law.’ And all the people shall say,
‘Amen.’
24 [n]‘Cursed be anyone who strikes down his neighbor in secret.’ And all the people
shall say, ‘Amen.’

[1] Hebrew *uncovered his father’s skirt*

16 [e]Ex. 20:12; 21:17; Lev. 19:3; See ch. 21:18-21
17 [f]See ch. 19:14
18 [g]Lev. 19:14
19 [h]See Ex. 22:21, 22
20 [i]See Lev. 18:8 [j]See ch. 22:30
21 [k]See Lev. 18:23
22 [l]Lev. 18:9; 20:17; [Ezek. 22:11]
23 [m]Lev. 18:17; 20:14
24 [n]ch. 19:11; Ex. 21:12, 14

all the words of this law. The writing of the law is in addition to the permanent written record (31:24–26).

27:4–5 today. See note on vv. 2–3. **Mount Ebal** is on the north side of Shechem (see 11:29 and note on 27:1–8). This ceremony occurs on the mountain of curse (see v. 13) to show that the law functions as a witness against Israel because of its inevitable sin. **wield no iron tool**. Israel’s altars were to be of unhewn stone (Ex. 20:25). Excavations at Mount Ebal have uncovered a worship site with a large altar (30 x 23 feet/9.1 x 7 m) constructed of unhewn stones, accessed by a gently sloping ramp. The pottery dates to the Israelite settlement (cf. Josh. 8:30–32). This perhaps is the altar that Joshua built or is built on top of Joshua’s altar.

27:6–7 Burnt offerings were the basic sacrifices dealing with sin (Leviticus 1). The law written on the plastered stones exposes Israel’s sin, so that burnt offerings are required. After their sins are atoned for, **peace offerings** celebrate fellowship with God (Leviticus 3).

27:9 this day you have become the people of the Lord your God. Cf. Ex. 19:5–6; Deut. 7:6; 14:2. The covenant relationship is being renewed rather than initiated. The covenant of Horeb is renewed at Moab through the words of Deuteronomy, especially chs. 29–30. Then, after the conquest, it will be renewed at Shechem (Joshua 24).

27:12–13 Mount Gerizim is to the south side of Shechem, Shechem being on the shoulder of the two mountains, Gerizim and **Ebal** (see 11:29; note on 27:4–5; and map to the right). These verses describe a ceremony in which Israel hears blessings and curses concerning the law. In this chapter, however, there are only curses read by the Levites (cf. ch. 28). See Josh. 8:30–35 for the carrying out of these instructions (cf. Joshua 24). On Gerizim, see John 4:20.

27:14 Levites must refer to the Levitical priests, since the rest of the tribe of Levi are on Mount Gerizim (see v. 12).

27:15 On images, see 5:8–10. **in secret**. This list of 12 curses lifts the level of punishment for disobedience to the law from human to divine jurisdiction. The theme of secrecy (27:24) shows that even if a person’s crime may be undetected, that person remains under God’s curse. **“Amen.” All the people** express their acceptance of the justice and judgment of God.

27:16 On dishonoring **father** and **mother**, see 5:16.

27:17 On one’s **neighbor’s landmark**, see 19:14.

27:18 On misleading the **blind**, see Lev. 19:14.

27:19 On perverting **justice**, see 24:17–18.

27:20–22 On uncovering one’s **father’s nakedness**, see 22:30 and Lev. 18:8. On lying with an **animal**, see Lev. 18:23. On lying with one’s **sister**, see Lev. 18:9.

27:24 On striking down one’s **neighbor**, see 19:11.

Renewing the Covenant at Mount Ebal
c. 1406/1220 B.C.

Looking ahead to the day when the Israelites would occupy Canaan, Moses commanded the people to renew the covenant after they entered the land by placing a new copy of the terms of the covenant on Mount Ebal and reciting the blessings and curses to each other on Mount Gerizim and Mount Ebal.

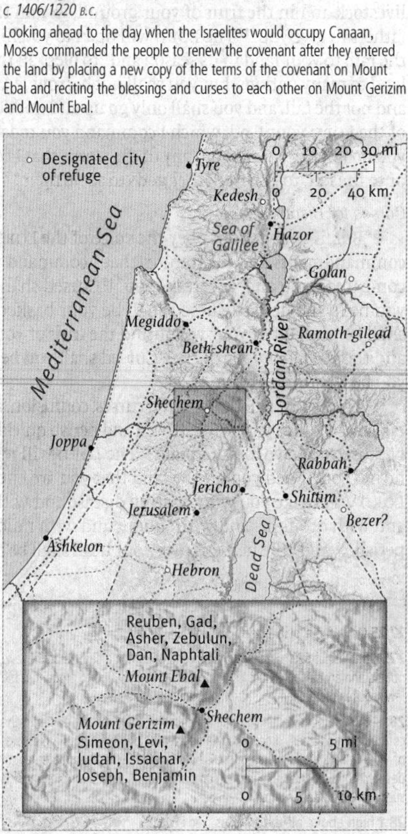

25 [o]“ ‘Cursed be anyone who takes a bribe to shed innocent blood.’ And all the people
shall say, ‘Amen.’
26 [p]“ ‘Cursed be anyone who does not confirm the words of this law by doing them.’ And
all the people shall say, ‘Amen.’

Blessings for Obedience

28 “And [q]if you faithfully obey the voice of the LORD your God, being careful to do all
his commandments that I command you today, the LORD your God will set you
[r]high above all the nations of the earth. 2 And all these blessings shall come upon you and
[s]overtake you, if you obey the voice of the LORD your God. 3 Blessed shall you be in the city,
and [t]blessed shall you be in the field. 4 Blessed shall be [u]the fruit of your womb and the
fruit of your ground and the fruit of your cattle, the increase of your herds and the young
of your flock. 5 Blessed shall be your basket and your [v]kneading bowl. 6 Blessed shall you
be [w]when you come in, and blessed shall you be when you go out.
7 “The LORD [x]will cause your enemies who rise against you to be defeated before you.
They shall come out against you one way and flee before you seven ways. 8 The LORD [y]will
command the blessing on you in your barns and [z]in all that you undertake. [a]And he will
bless you in the land that the LORD your God is giving you. 9 [b]The LORD will establish you
as a people holy to himself, as he has sworn to you, if you keep the commandments of the
LORD your God and walk in his ways. 10 And [c]all the peoples of the earth shall see that you
are [d]called by the name of the LORD, and they shall be [e]afraid of you. 11 And [f]the LORD
will make you abound in prosperity, in [u]the fruit of your womb and in the fruit of your
livestock and in the fruit of your ground, within the land that the LORD swore to your
fathers to give you. 12 The LORD will open to you his good treasury, the heavens, [g]to give
the rain to your land in its season and [h]to bless all the work of your hands. And [i]you shall
lend to many nations, but you shall not borrow. 13 And the LORD will make you [j]the head
and not the tail, and you shall only go up and not down, if you obey the commandments
of the LORD your God, which I command you today, being careful to do them, 14 [k]and if
you do not turn aside from any of the words that I command you today, to the right hand
or to the left, to go after other gods to serve them.

Curses for Disobedience

15 “But [l]if you will not obey the voice of the LORD your God or be careful to do all his
commandments and his statutes that I command you today, then all these curses shall
come upon you and [m]overtake you. 16 Cursed shall you be [n]in the city, and cursed shall
you be in the field. 17 Cursed shall be your basket and your kneading bowl. 18 Cursed
shall be the fruit of your womb and the fruit of your ground, the increase of your herds
and the young of your flock. 19 Cursed shall you be when you come in, and cursed shall
you be when you go out.
20 “The LORD [o]will send on you curses, confusion, and [p]frustration in all that you undertake to do, [q]until you are destroyed and perish quickly on account of the evil of your deeds,
because you have forsaken me. 21 The LORD will make [r]the pestilence stick to you until
he has consumed you off the land that you are entering to take possession of it. 22 [s]The
LORD will strike you with wasting disease and with fever, inflammation and fiery heat,
and with drought[1] and with [t]blight and with mildew. They shall pursue you until you
perish. 23 And [u]the heavens over your head shall be bronze, and the earth under you shall

[1] Or *sword*

25 [o]ch. 16:19; Ex. 23:7, 8; Ezek. 22:12
26 [p]ch. 28:15; Jer. 11:3; Cited Gal. 3:10

Chapter 28
1 [q][Ex. 15:26; 23:22; Lev. 26:3; Isa. 55:2] [r]ch. 26:19
2 [s]ver. 15; Zech. 1:6
3 [t][Gen. 39:5]
4 [u]ch. 7:13; 30:9; [Gen. 49:25; Ex. 23:26]
5 [v]ver. 17; [Ex. 8:3; 12:34]
6 [w]Ps. 121:8
7 [x]Ex. 23:22, 27; Lev. 26:7, 8; [ver. 25]; See 2 Sam. 22:38-41; Ps. 18:37-40
8 [y]Lev. 25:21; Ps. 133:3 [z]See ch. 12:7 [a]ch. 15:4
9 [b]ch. 7:6; 26:18, 19; 29:13; See Ex. 19:5, 6
10 [c][Isa. 61:9] [d]See Num. 6:27 [e]ch. 2:25; 11:25
11 [f]ch. 30:9 [u][See ver. 4 above]
12 [g]ch. 11:14; Lev. 26:4 [h]ch. 14:29 [i]ch. 15:6; [ver. 44; Ps. 37:26]
13 [j]Isa. 9:14, 15; 19:15
14 [k]See ch. 5:32
15 [l]Lev. 26:14; Lam. 2:17; Dan. 9:11, 13; Mal. 2:2 [m]ver. 2
16 [n][ver. 3-6]
20 [o]Mal. 2:2 [p]Ps. 80:16; Isa. 30:17; 51:20; 66:15 [q]Josh. 23:16
21 [r]See Lev. 26:25
22 [s]Lev. 26:16 [t]1 Kgs. 8:37; 2 Chr. 6:28; Amos 4:9; Hag. 2:17
23 [u]Lev. 26:19

27:25 On taking a **bribe**, see 16:19.

27:26 The list of 12 curses is not comprehensive; it is a sample of the law, not a summary of it. Cf. Paul's use of this verse in Gal. 3:10 to argue that the law requires perfect, and humanly unattainable, obedience.

28:1–68 The focus shifts from the specific sins that warrant curses to the content of the curses, preceded by a shorter list of blessings. The blessings of vv. 1–14 are the converse of the curses in vv. 15–68. The greater length devoted to the curses (54 verses compared to 14 verses for blessings) is suggestive of Israel's future.

28:1 high above all the nations. See 26:19.

28:3–6 For parallel curses, see vv. 16–19. **city . . . field . . . come in . . . go out**. The coupling of opposites implies comprehensiveness (cf. note on 6:7–9). **fruit**. The emphasis on fertility challenges the Canaanite view that Baal was the fertility god.

28:7 your enemies . . . to be defeated. Cf. v. 25.

28:9 a people holy. See 7:6 and note.

28:12 lend to many nations. Israel will be wealthy as a result of God's blessing; cf. 15:6. According to 23:20 these loans to other nations would be loans at interest (cf. note on 23:19–20). Cf. 28:44.

28:23 bronze. Unable to bring rain. **iron**. Unable to be tilled.

be iron. **24** The LORD will make the rain of your land powder. From heaven dust shall come
down on you until you are destroyed.
25 [v]"The LORD will cause you to be defeated before your enemies. You shall go out one
way against them and flee seven ways before them. And you [w]shall be a horror to all the
kingdoms of the earth. **26** And [x]your dead body shall be food for all birds of the air and for
the beasts of the earth, and [y]there shall be no one to frighten them away. **27** The LORD will
strike you [z]with the boils of Egypt, and with tumors and [a]scabs and itch, of which you
cannot be healed. **28** The LORD will strike you with [b]madness and blindness and confusion
of mind, **29** and you shall [c]grope at noonday, as the blind grope in darkness, and you shall
not prosper in your ways.[1] And you shall be only oppressed and robbed continually, and
there shall be no one to help you. **30** [d]You shall betroth a wife, but another man shall ravish
her. [e]You shall build a house, but you shall not dwell in it. [f]You shall plant a vineyard, but
you shall not enjoy its fruit. **31** Your ox shall be slaughtered before your eyes, but you shall
not eat any of it. Your donkey shall be seized before your face, but shall not be restored
to you. Your sheep shall be given to your enemies, but there shall be no one to help you.
32 [g]Your sons and your daughters shall be given to another people, while your eyes look on
and fail with longing for them all day long, [h]but you shall be helpless. **33** A nation that you
have not known shall eat up the fruit of your ground and of all your labors, and you shall
be only oppressed and crushed continually, **34** so that you are driven mad [i]by the sights that
your eyes see. **35** The LORD will strike you on the knees and on the legs [j]with grievous boils
of which you cannot be healed, from the sole of your foot to the crown of your head.
36 "The LORD will [k]bring you and your king whom you set over you to a nation that neither you [l]nor your fathers have known. And [m]there you shall serve other gods of wood and
stone. **37** And you shall become [n]a horror, a proverb, and a byword among all the peoples
where the LORD will lead you away. **38** [o]You shall carry much seed into the field and shall
gather in little, for [p]the locust shall consume it. **39** [q]You shall plant vineyards and dress
them, but you shall neither drink of the wine nor gather the grapes, for the worm shall eat
them. **40** You shall have olive trees throughout all your territory, but you [r]shall not anoint
yourself with the oil, for your olives shall drop off. **41** You shall father sons and daughters,
but they shall not be yours, for [s]they shall go into captivity. **42** [p]The cricket[2] shall possess
all your trees and the fruit of your ground. **43** [t]The sojourner who is among you shall rise
higher and higher above you, and you shall come down lower and lower. **44** [u]He shall lend
to you, and you shall not lend to him. [t]He shall be the head, and you shall be the tail.
45 [v]"All these curses shall come upon you and pursue you and overtake you till you are
destroyed, because you did not obey the voice of the LORD your God, to keep his commandments and his statutes that he commanded you. **46** They shall be [w]a sign and a wonder
against you and your offspring forever. **47** [x]Because you did not serve the LORD your God
with joyfulness and gladness of heart, because of the abundance of all things, **48** therefore
you shall serve your enemies whom the LORD will send against you, in hunger and thirst,
in nakedness, and lacking everything. And he [y]will put a yoke of iron on your neck until
he has destroyed you. **49** [z]The LORD will bring a nation against you from far away, from
the end of the earth, [a]swooping down like the eagle, a nation [b]whose language you do
not understand, **50** a hard-faced nation [c]who shall not respect the old or show mercy to
the young. **51** It shall [d]eat the offspring of your cattle and the fruit of your ground, until
you are destroyed; it also shall not leave you grain, wine, or oil, the increase of your herds
or the young of your flock, until they have caused you to perish.
52 "They shall [e]besiege you in all your towns, until your high and fortified walls, in which
you trusted, come down throughout all your land. And they shall besiege you in all your
towns throughout all your land, which the LORD your God has given you. **53** And [f]you shall

[1] *Or shall not succeed in finding your ways* [2] Identity uncertain

25 [v]ch. 32:30; Lev. 26:17, 37; Isa. 30:17; [ver. 7] [w]Ezek. 23:46
26 [x][1 Sam. 17:44, 46; Ps. 79:2; Jer. 16:4; 19:7; 34:20] [y]Jer. 7:33
27 [z][ver. 35] [a]Lev. 21:20; 22:22
28 [b][ver. 34; Zech. 12:4]
29 [c]Job 5:14; Isa. 59:10
30 [d]ch. 20:5-7; Jer. 8:10 [e]Amos 5:11; Zeph. 1:13 [f]ch. 20:6; Lev. 19:23-25; [Mic. 6:15]
32 [g][2 Chr. 29:9; Joel 3:6] [h]Neh. 5:5
34 [i]ver. 67
35 [j][ver. 27]
36 [k]2 Kgs. 17:4, 6; 24:12, 14; 25:7, 11; 2 Chr. 33:11; 36:6, 20 [l]Jer. 9:16; 16:13 [m]ver. 64; ch. 4:28
37 [n]1 Kgs. 9:7, 8; 2 Chr. 7:20; Jer. 24:9; 25:9; [Ezek. 14:8]
38 [o]Mic. 6:15; Hag. 1:6 [p]Joel 1:4; 2:25
39 [q]Zeph. 1:13
40 [r]Mic. 6:15
41 [s]Lam. 1:5
42 [p][See ver. 38 above]
43 [t][ver. 13]
44 [u][ver. 12] [t][See ver. 43 above]
45 [v]ver. 15
46 [w][Isa. 8:18]
47 [x]Neh. 9:35-37
48 [y]Jer. 28:14
49 [z][Jer. 5:15-17; 6:22, 23]; See Isa. 5:26-30 [a]Jer. 48:40; 49:22; Lam. 4:19; Hos. 8:1; Hab. 1:8; [Ezek. 17:3, 12] [b]Isa. 28:11; 33:19; Jer. 5:15
50 [c][2 Chr. 36:17; Isa. 47:6]
51 [d]ver. 33; Jer. 5:17; [Isa. 62:8, 9]
52 [e][2 Kgs. 17:5; 25:1, 2, 4]
53 [f]ver. 57; Lev. 26:29; Jer. 19:9; Ezek. 5:10; [2 Kgs. 6:28, 29; Lam. 2:20; 4:10]

28:30 betroth a wife. Cf. 24:5. **build a house . . . plant a vineyard**. Cf. 20:5–7.

28:44 lend . . . head . . . tail. Cf. vv. 12–13.

28:46 sign and a wonder. Signs and wonders usually refer to Israel's salvation (e.g., 4:34; 7:19; 26:8). Here the term is heavily ironic.

28:48 Yoke of iron suggests a return to slavery (see also v. 68) and a reversal of Israel's redemption, when God brought them out of Egypt (e.g., 5:6). See Jer. 28:14.

28:53 eat the fruit of your womb. The siege from the future enemy will be so dire that Israelites will resort to cannibalism in order to stay alive. See

eat the fruit of your womb, the flesh of your sons and daughters, whom the LORD your
God has given you, [g]in the siege and in the distress with which your enemies shall distress
you. 54 The man who is the most tender and refined among you will [h]begrudge food to his
brother, to [i]the wife he embraces,[1] and to the last of the children whom he has left, 55 so
that he will not give to any of them any of the flesh of his children whom he is eating,
because he has nothing else left, [j]in the siege and in the distress with which your enemy
shall distress you in all your towns. 56 [k]The most tender and refined woman among you,
who would not venture to set the sole of her foot on the ground because she is so delicate
and tender, will begrudge to the husband she embraces,[2] to her son and to her daughter,
57 her afterbirth that comes out from between her feet and her children whom she bears,
because lacking everything she will eat them secretly, [j]in the siege and in the distress with
which your enemy shall distress you in your towns.

58 "If you are not careful to do all the words of this law that are written in this book, that
you may fear this glorious and awesome name, [l]the LORD your God, 59 then the LORD will
bring on you and your offspring extraordinary afflictions, afflictions severe and lasting,
and sicknesses grievous and lasting. 60 And he will bring upon you again all [m]the diseases
of Egypt, of which you were afraid, and they shall cling to you. 61 Every sickness also and
every affliction that is not recorded in the book of this law, the LORD will bring upon you,
until you are destroyed. 62 Whereas [n]you were as numerous [o]as the stars of heaven, you shall
be left few in number, because you did not obey the voice of the LORD your God. 63 And as
the LORD [p]took delight in doing you good and multiplying you, so the LORD will [q]take
delight in bringing ruin upon you and destroying you. And you shall be plucked off the
land that you are entering to take possession of it.

64 "And the LORD [r]will scatter you among all peoples, from one end of the earth to the
other, and [s]there you shall serve other gods [t]of wood and stone, [u]which neither you nor
your fathers have known. 65 And [v]among these nations you shall find no respite, and there
shall be no resting place for the sole of your foot, but [w]the LORD will give you there a
trembling heart and failing eyes and [x]a languishing soul. 66 Your life shall hang in doubt
before you. Night and day you shall be in dread and have no assurance of your life. 67 [y]In
the morning you shall say, 'If only it were evening!' and at evening you shall say, 'If only it
were morning!' because of the dread that your heart shall feel, and [z]the sights that your eyes
shall see. 68 And the LORD [a]will bring you back in ships to Egypt, a journey that I promised
that [b]you should never make again; and there you shall offer yourselves for sale to your
enemies as male and female slaves, but there will be no buyer."

The Covenant Renewed in Moab

29 [3] These are the words of the covenant that the LORD commanded Moses to make
with the people of Israel [c]in the land of Moab, besides [d]the covenant that he had
made with them at Horeb.

2 [4] And Moses summoned all Israel and said to them: [e]"You have seen all that the LORD
did before your eyes in the land of Egypt, to Pharaoh and to all his servants and to all
his land, 3 the great [f]trials that your eyes saw, the signs, and those great wonders. 4 But to

[1] Hebrew *the wife of his bosom* [2] Hebrew *the husband of her bosom* [3] Ch 28:69 in Hebrew [4] Ch 29:1 in Hebrew

53 [g]ver. 55, 57
54 [h]See ch. 15:9 [i]ch. 13:6
55 [j]ver. 53
56 [k]ver. 54; Isa. 47:1
57 [j][See ver. 55 above]
58 [l]Ex. 6:3
60 [m]See ch. 7:15
62 [n]ch. 4:27; [2 Kgs. 24:14; Neh. 7:4; Jer. 42:2] [o]See ch. 10:22
63 [p]ch. 30:9; Jer. 32:41; Zeph. 3:17 [q][Prov. 1:26; Isa. 1:24; Ezek. 5:13]
64 [r]See Lev. 26:33 [s]ver. 36 [t]ch. 4:28 [u]ch. 13:6; Jer. 19:4; 44:3
65 [v][Amos 9:4] [w][Lev. 26:36] [x]Lev. 26:16
67 [y]Job 7:3, 4 [z]ver. 34
68 [a]Hos. 8:13; 9:3; [Jer. 43:7] [b]See ch. 17:16

Chapter 29

1 [c]ch. 1:5 [d]ch. 5:2, 3
2 [e]Ex. 19:4; [Josh. 23:3]
3 [f]See ch. 4:34

2 Kings 6:28–29 for the horrors of suffering siege, and Lam. 2:20 and 4:10 for what happened when Jerusalem was besieged by Babylon.

28:58 glorious and awesome name, the LORD your God. The name is *YHWH* (Yahweh), revealed to Moses at the burning bush (Ex. 3:14; see note there).

28:60 all the diseases of Egypt. See 7:15 and note on 7:13–15.

28:61 the book of this law. Similarly, v. 58. This refers to Deuteronomy 1–30. See 31:9, 24, 26.

28:62 numerous as the stars of heaven. See 1:10 and note there. This threatens a reversal or annulment of the promises to Abraham.

28:64–66 scatter. See 4:27. The curse of exile eventually comes for the northern kingdom under Assyria (2 Kings 17) and for the southern kingdom of Judah under Babylon (2 Kings 25). **serve other gods of wood and stone**. See Deut. 4:28. **no resting place**. Contrast 3:20; 12:9–10. The **dread** of Israel expressed by other nations in 2:25 and 11:25 is reversed.

29:1–30:20 *Moses' Third Speech: Final Exhortation.* These chapters have no close parallel in ancient treaties. They are the climax of the preaching of Deuteronomy, urging Israel to accept the covenant.

29:1 besides the covenant. The covenant **in the land of Moab** is a reiteration of the covenant **at Horeb** (i.e., Sinai), and the laws are the same as were given to Israel through Moses at Horeb. The Moab covenant constitutes all the spoken words of Moses in Deuteronomy.

29:2–3 You have seen . . . before your eyes . . . your eyes saw. There is a strong emphasis on having seen God's past actions, even though the addressees are the next generation. See 1:30–31 and note on 1:29–31.

29:4 not given you a heart to understand or eyes to see or ears to hear. The heart is the organ of understanding and will in the OT; Deuteronomy focuses on the heart as the center of morality. Despite the emphasis on physi-

this day [g]the LORD has not given you a heart to understand or eyes to see or ears to hear.
5 [h]I have led you forty years in the wilderness. Your clothes have not worn out on you,
and your sandals have not worn off your feet. 6 [i]You have not eaten bread, and you have
not drunk wine or strong drink, that you may know that I am the LORD your God. 7 And
when you came to this place, [j]Sihon the king of Heshbon and Og the king of Bashan
came out against us to battle, but we defeated them. 8 We took their land and [k]gave it
for an inheritance to the Reubenites, the Gadites, and the half-tribe of the Manassites.
9 [l]Therefore keep the words of this covenant and do them, that you may prosper[1] in all
that you do.

10 "You are standing today all of you before the LORD your God: the heads of your tribes,[2]
your elders, and your officers, all the men of Israel, 11 your little ones, your wives, and the
[m]sojourner who is in your camp, from [n]the one who chops your wood to the one who
draws your water, 12 so that you may enter into the [o]sworn covenant of the LORD your
God, which the LORD your God is making with you today, 13 that he may [p]establish you
today as his people, and that [q]he may be your God, as he promised you, and [r]as he swore
to your fathers, to Abraham, to Isaac, and to Jacob. 14 It is not with you alone [s]that I am
making this sworn covenant, 15 but with whoever is standing here with us today before
the LORD our God, [t]and with whoever is not here with us today.

16 "You know how we lived in the land of Egypt, and how we came through the midst of
the nations through which you passed. 17 And you have seen their detestable things, their
idols of wood and stone, of silver and gold, which were among them. 18 Beware lest there
be among you a man or woman or clan or tribe whose heart is turning away today from
the LORD our God to go and serve the gods of those nations. Beware lest there be among
you [u]a root bearing poisonous and bitter fruit, 19 one who, when he hears the words of
this sworn covenant, blesses himself in his heart, saying, 'I shall be safe, though I walk in
the stubbornness of my heart.' This will lead to the sweeping away of moist and dry alike.
20 The LORD will not be willing to forgive him, but rather [v]the anger of the LORD and [w]his
jealousy will smoke against that man, and the curses written in this book will settle upon
him, and the LORD [x]will blot out his name from under heaven. 21 And the LORD will single
him out from all the tribes of Israel for calamity, in accordance with all the curses of the
covenant written in this Book of the Law. 22 And the next generation, your children who
rise up after you, and the foreigner who comes from a far land, [y]will say, when they see the
afflictions of that land and the sicknesses with which the LORD has made it sick— 23 the
whole land burned out with brimstone and [z]salt, nothing sown and nothing growing,
where no plant can sprout, [a]an overthrow like that of Sodom and Gomorrah, [b]Admah,
and Zeboiim, which the LORD overthrew in his anger and wrath— 24 all the nations [c]will
say, [d]'Why has the LORD done thus to this land? What caused the heat of this great anger?'
25 Then people will say, 'It is because they abandoned the covenant of the LORD, the God of
their fathers, which he made with them when he brought them out of the land of Egypt,
26 and went and served other gods and worshiped them, gods whom they had not known

[1] Or *deal wisely* [2] Septuagint, Syriac; Hebrew *your heads, your tribes*

4 [g][Isa. 6:9, 10; 63:17; John 8:43; Acts 28:26, 27; Rom. 11:8, 10]
5 [h]ch. 1:3; 8:2, 4; Amos 2:10; Acts 13:18
6 [i]ch. 8:3; See Ex. 16:4
7 [j]ch. 2:24, 26, 32; 3:1; See Num. 21:21-24, 33-35
8 [k]ch. 3:12, 13; Num. 32:33
9 [l]ch. 4:6
11 [m][Ex. 12:38] [n][Josh. 9:21, 23, 27]
12 [o]Neh. 10:29
13 [p]ch. 28:9 [q]Ex. 6:7 [r]Gen. 17:7; [Gen. 50:24]
14 [s][Jer. 31:31-33; Heb. 8:8-10]
15 [t][Acts 2:39]
18 [u]Heb. 12:15
20 [v]Ps. 74:1 [w]Ps. 79:5 [x]See ch. 9:14
22 [y]ver. 24
23 [z]Judg. 9:45; Jer. 17:6; Ezek. 47:11; Zeph. 2:9 [a]Gen. 19:24, 25; Jer. 20:16; 49:18; 50:40; 2 Pet. 2:6 [b]Gen. 14:2; Hos. 11:8
24 [c]ver. 22 [d]1 Kgs. 9:8, 9; Jer. 22:8, 9

cal sight (vv. 2–3), real "sight" is with the eyes of faithful obedience. The heart must respond correctly to God (e.g., 6:5), but Israel's heart is unlikely to respond to God in the right way (e.g., 5:29; 8:17; 9:4). Israel needs God to correct its lack of right heart, eyes, and ears. See 30:6 and note. In Rom. 11:8 Paul combines this text with Isa. 29:10 to explain why many of his Jewish contemporaries do not believe in Jesus.

29:5–6 clothes . . . feet. See 8:4. **that you may know**. See 8:3.

29:7–8 Sihon . . . Og. See 2:24–3:17.

29:12–13 enter into the sworn covenant. The language of this verse has the style of a formal acceptance of the covenant and its consequences. **establish you today as his people**. See 27:9 and note.

29:15 Whoever is not here with us today refers to future generations. The covenant with God is not simply for one generation, just as the Horeb covenant was also for this current generation (5:2–3).

29:18 Beware lest. The repeated warning here shows the vulnerability of Israel's heart to go astray to idolatry. **root bearing poisonous and bitter fruit**. If one Israelite goes astray, the sin is regarded as contagious, infecting other Israelites (v. 19). Hence the need to "purge the evil" from your midst (see 13:5 and note). Cf. "root of bitterness" in Heb. 12:15, which comes from the Greek translation of this phrase.

29:19 blesses himself in his heart. An expression of pride (cf. 8:17 and note on 4:37–39).

29:20–21 jealousy. See 4:24 and note on 4:23–24. **Book of the Law**. See 28:61 and note.

29:23 The destruction of **Sodom and Gomorrah** is used several times in the Bible as the paradigmatic act of God's judgment (Gen. 19:24–25; see, e.g., Amos 4:11; Matt. 10:14; 2 Pet. 2:6). **Admah, and Zeboiim**. See Gen. 10:19 and 14:2, 8.

29:24–28 The expectation in these verses is of future idolatry (the worst sin, in Deuteronomy) and the receipt of God's curses. While ch. 28 held out blessings and curses as alternatives, it is again clear that the author of Deuteronomy expects Israel to sin because they lack correct hearts, eyes, and

and whom he had not allotted to them. 27 Therefore the anger of the LORD was kindled
against this land, [e]bringing upon it all the curses written in this book, 28 and the LORD
[f]uprooted them from their land in anger and fury and great wrath, and [g]cast them into
another land, as they are this day.'
29 "The secret things belong to the LORD our God, but the things that are revealed belong
to us and to our children forever, that we may do all the words of this law.

Repentance and Forgiveness

30 [h]"And [i]when all these things come upon you, the blessing and the curse, which I
have set before you, and [j]you call them to mind among all the nations where the
LORD your God has driven you, 2 and [k]return to the LORD your God, you and your children,
and obey his voice in all that I command you today, with all your heart and with all your
soul, 3 then the LORD your God [l]will restore your fortunes and have mercy on you, and he
will [m]gather you again from all the peoples where the LORD your God has scattered you.
4 [n]If your outcasts are in the uttermost parts of heaven, from there the LORD your God will
gather you, and from there he will take you. 5 And the LORD your God will bring you into
the land that your fathers possessed, that you may possess it. [o]And he will make you more
prosperous and numerous than your fathers. 6 And [p]the LORD your God will circumcise
your heart and the heart of your offspring, [q]so that you will love the LORD your God with
all your heart and with all your soul, that you may live. 7 And the LORD your God will put
all these curses on your foes and enemies who persecuted you. 8 And you shall again obey
the voice of the LORD and keep all his commandments that I command you today. 9 [r]The
LORD your God will make you abundantly prosperous in all the work of your hand, in
the fruit of your womb and in the fruit of your cattle and in the fruit of your ground. [s]For
the LORD will again take delight in prospering you, as he took delight in your fathers,
10 when you obey the voice of the LORD your God, to keep his commandments and his
statutes that are written in this Book of the Law, when you turn to the LORD your God
with all your heart and with all your soul.

The Choice of Life and Death

11 "For this commandment that I command you today [t]is not too hard for you, neither
is it far off. 12 [u]It is not in heaven, that you should say, 'Who will ascend to heaven for us
and bring it to us, that we may hear it and do it?' 13 Neither is it beyond the sea, that you
should say, 'Who will go over the sea for us and bring it to us, that we may hear it and
do it?' 14 But the word is very near you. It is in your mouth and in your heart, so that you
can do it.
15 "See, [v]I have set before you today life and good, death and evil. 16 If you obey the
commandments of the LORD your God[1] that I command you today, [w]by loving the LORD
your God, by walking in his ways, and by keeping his commandments and his statutes
and his rules,[2] then you shall live and multiply, and the LORD your God will bless you

[1] Septuagint; Hebrew lacks *If you obey the commandments of the LORD your God* [2] Or *his just decrees*

27 [e]See ch. 28:15-68; Lev. 26:14-39; Dan. 9:11-14
28 [f]1 Kgs. 14:15; 2 Chr. 7:20; Jer. 12:14 [g]Jer. 22:26

Chapter 30

1 [h]ch. 11:26-28; Lev. 26:40-42 [i]See ch. 28 [j]ch. 4:29-31; See 1 Kgs. 8:47-50
2 [k]Neh. 1:9; Isa. 55:7; Lam. 3:40; Joel 2:12, 13
3 [l]Ps. 126:1, 4 [m]Jer. 32:37; Ezek. 34:13; 36:24
4 [n]ch. 28:64; Neh. 1:9
5 [o]Zeph. 3:19, 20; See ch. 28:63
6 [p][Jer. 31:33; 32:39, 40; Ezek. 11:19; 36:26, 27]; See ch. 10:16 [q]ver. 16
9 [r]ch. 28:11 [s]Zeph. 3:19, 20; See ch. 28:63
11 [t][Isa. 45:19; 48:16]
12 [u][Rom. 10:6-8]
15 [v][ch. 11:26; 32:47]
16 [w]ver. 6; See ch. 6:5

ears toward God (29:4). See also 27:4 and note on 27:4–5; 30:1 and note on 30:1–2; 31:16–18.

29:29 secret things belong to the LORD our God. Not everything that is true of God has been revealed. That there are secret things anticipates the need to trust, obey, and be humble before God. What God has revealed is for the sake of obedience (see 30:11–14).

30:1–2 The context is exile, following from 29:28. The word for **mind** (Hb. *lebab*) can also be rendered "heart" (see 6:5 and note). This verse anticipates that God's words (**all these things**) will enter the exiles' hearts, leading them to **return** to God, or repent, which means to change their thinking and behavior completely. **all your heart and with all your soul.** Also 30:6, 10. See 6:5 and note.

30:3 restore your fortunes. This expression uses the Hebrew word "return." As Israel returns to God (v. 2), so he will "return" to them. **gather.** The reverse of 28:64; 29:28.

30:5 fathers. Either referring to the patriarchs—Abraham, Isaac, and Jacob (as in v. 20)—or to earlier generations living in the land.

30:6 circumcise your heart. This is a key promise in Deuteronomy, looking forward to genuine covenant participation (see Jer. 31:33; Ezek. 36:26–27; Rom. 2:25–29; Col. 2:11). See note on Deut. 10:16. **so that you will love.** God's changing of the heart enables obedience (6:5).

30:9 abundantly prosperous. Also v. 5. The blessings promised in 28:1–14 will now be realized. **fathers.** See note on 30:5.

30:11 not too hard for you. When the heart is circumcised (see note on v. 6), keeping the law is possible.

30:12–14 in your mouth and in your heart. This is the result of the circumcised heart that enables obedience (see note on v. 6). Paul quotes from these verses in Rom. 10:6–8 to show that the Jews already had the message of faith through the Scriptures.

30:15 I have set before you. See also v. 19. The climax of Moses' preaching is to seek a commitment from Israel to trust in God's grace and thus obey his commands.

in the land that you are entering to take possession of it. 17 But if [x]your heart turns away, and you will not hear, but are drawn away to worship other gods and serve them, 18 [y]I declare to you today, that you shall surely perish. You shall not live long in the land that you are going over the Jordan to enter and possess. 19 I call heaven and earth to witness against you today, that I have set before you life and death, [z]blessing and curse. Therefore choose life, that you and your offspring may live, 20 loving the LORD your God, obeying his voice [a]and holding fast to him, for [b]he is your life and length of days, that you may dwell in [c]the land that the LORD swore to your fathers, to Abraham, to Isaac, and to Jacob, to give them."

Joshua to Succeed Moses

31 So Moses continued to speak these words to all Israel. 2 And he said to them, "I am [d]120 years old today. I am no longer able to [e]go out and come in. The LORD has said to me, [f]'You shall not go over this Jordan.' 3 The LORD your God [g]himself will go over before you. He will destroy these nations before you, so that you shall dispossess them, and Joshua will go over at your head, [h]as the LORD has spoken. 4 And the LORD will do to them [i]as he did to Sihon [j]and Og, the kings of the Amorites, and to their land, when he destroyed them. 5 And the LORD will give them over to you, and you shall do to them [k]according to the whole commandment that I have commanded you. 6 [l]Be strong and courageous. Do not fear or be in dread of them, [m]for it is the LORD your God who goes with you. [n]He will not leave you or forsake you."

7 Then [o]Moses summoned Joshua and said to him in the sight of all Israel, [l]"Be strong and courageous, for you shall go with this people into the land that the LORD has sworn to their fathers to give them, and you shall put them in possession of it. 8 It is the LORD [p]who goes before you. He will be with you; [n]he will not leave you or forsake you. [q]Do not fear or be dismayed."

The Reading of the Law

9 Then Moses [r]wrote this law and gave it to the priests, the sons of Levi, [s]who carried the ark of the covenant of the LORD, and to all the elders of Israel. 10 And Moses commanded them, [t]"At the end of every seven years, at the set time in the year of release, at [u]the Feast of Booths, 11 when all Israel comes [v]to appear before the LORD your God at the place that he will choose, [w]you shall read this law before all Israel in their hearing. 12 [x]Assemble the people, men, women, and little ones, and the sojourner within your towns, that they may hear and learn to fear the LORD your God, and be careful to do all the words of this law, 13 and that their children, [y]who have not known it, [z]may hear and learn to fear the LORD your God, [a]as long as you live in the land that you are going over the Jordan to possess."

17 [x]ch. 29:18
18 [y]See ch. 4:26
19 [z]ver. 1
20 [a]See ch. 10:20 [b]Ps. 27:1; 66:9; John 11:25 [c]See ch. 1:8

Chapter 31

2 [d]ch. 34:7; [Ex. 7:7] [e]See Num. 27:17 [f]ch. 3:27; See ch. 1:37
3 [g]ch. 9:3 [h]ch. 1:38; 3:28; Num. 27:18, 21
4 [i]See ch. 2:31-35; Num. 21:21-25 [j]See ch. 3:1-7; Num. 21:33-35
5 [k]See ch. 7:2
6 [l]ver. 23; Josh. 1:6, 7; 10:25; 1 Chr. 22:13; 28:20 [m]See ch. 20:4 [n]Josh. 1:5
7 [o][ch. 3:28] [l][See ver. 6 above]
8 [p]See Ex. 13:21 [n][See ver. 6 above] [q]ch. 1:21; 7:18; Josh. 1:9; 8:1; 10:25
9 [r][ch. 17:18] [s]Num. 4:15; Josh. 3:3; 8:33; 1 Chr. 15:15
10 [t]See ch. 15:1 [u]See Lev. 23:34
11 [v]ch. 16:16; Ex. 23:14, 17; 34:23 [w]Josh. 8:34, 35; 2 Kgs. 23:2; See Neh. 8:1-3
12 [x]ch. 4:10
13 [y]ch. 11:2 [z]Ps. 78:5, 6 [a]See ch. 4:10

30:19–20 I call heaven and earth. Ancient treaties had witnesses to their ratification. Often those witnesses were the gods. In Deuteronomy, since God himself is a partner to the covenant, heaven and earth are called as witnesses. See 4:25–26 and note. Life, and living, is a key theme in ch. 30 (see vv. 6, 15, 16, 18, 19, 20). To **choose life** is to choose God himself, to trust in God's grace and circumcision of the heart. **holding fast.** See 4:4 and note on 4:3–4.

31:1–34:12 *Succession of Leadership.* The final chapters of Deuteronomy concern the succession of leadership from Moses to Joshua and the writing down of the covenant for its perpetuity and ongoing authority in Israel's life.

31:1–29 *The Commissioning of Joshua and the Writing of the Law.* It has been clear throughout Deuteronomy that Moses will die before entry into the land. Now his successor, Joshua, is commissioned.

31:2 No longer able to go out and come in refers to Moses' old age. **You shall not go over this Jordan.** Moses' exclusion from the Promised Land was due to his sin (1:37; 3:27; 4:21–22; 32:51–52; Num. 20:2–12).

31:4 Sihon and Og. See 2:24–3:11.

31:6 Be strong and courageous. This command to all Israel is also made directly to Joshua (vv. 7, 23; Josh. 1:6, 7, 9). **Do not fear.** See Deut. 1:28. **He will not leave you or forsake you.** In 1 Chron. 28:20, David applies this to Solomon; cf. Heb. 13:5.

31:7–8 Here **Moses** commissions **Joshua**, which God himself then does in v. 23.

31:9 wrote this law. The writing of Deuteronomy 1–30 by Moses indicates that God's law had ongoing validity for future generations. From now on, the mediation of God's word to Israel, given orally through Moses, will be through the written text.

31:10–11 end of every seven years, at the set time in the year of release. See 15:1. **Feast of Booths.** See 16:13–15. This passage gives one of the clearest pictures of how people were taught the law. The priests had the responsibility to **read this law** aloud to the people at the great fall festival. **at the place that he will choose.** See 12:5.

31:12 men, women, and little ones, and the sojourner. According to 16:16, only the men were required to make the pilgrimage for the feast each year. Here, that obligation is extended to everyone in the seventh year, when the law is read.

Joshua Commissioned to Lead Israel

14 And the LORD said to Moses, [b]"Behold, the days approach when you must die. Call Joshua
and present yourselves in the tent of meeting, that [c]I may commission him." And Moses and
Joshua went and presented themselves in the tent of meeting. 15 And [d]the LORD appeared in
the tent in a pillar of cloud. And the pillar of cloud stood over the entrance of the tent.
16 And the LORD said to Moses, [b]"Behold, you are about to lie down with your fathers.
Then this people will rise and [e]whore after the foreign gods among them in the land that
they are entering, and they will [f]forsake me and [g]break my covenant that I have made with
them. 17 Then my anger will be kindled against them in that day, and [h]I will forsake them
and [i]hide my face from them, and they will be devoured. And many evils and troubles will
come upon them, so that they will say in that day, [j]'Have not these evils come upon us
because [k]our God is not among us?' 18 And I will surely hide my face in that day because
of all the evil that they have done, because [l]they have turned to other gods.
19 "Now therefore write [m]this song and [n]teach it to the people of Israel. Put it in their
mouths, that this song may be [o]a witness for me against the people of Israel. 20 For when
I have brought them into the land [p]flowing with milk and honey, which I swore to give
to their fathers, and they have eaten and are full and [q]grown fat, [r]they will turn to other
gods and serve them, and [s]despise me and [g]break my covenant. 21 And when many evils
and troubles have come upon them, this song shall confront them as [t]a witness (for it will
live unforgotten in the mouths of their offspring). For [u]I know what they are inclined to
do even today, before I have brought them into the land that I swore to give." 22 So Moses
wrote this song the same day and taught it to the people of Israel.
23 [v]And the LORD[1] commissioned Joshua the son of Nun and said, [w]"Be strong and courageous, for you shall bring the people of Israel into the land that I swore to give them.
[x]I will be with you."
24 When Moses had finished [y]writing the words of this law in a book to the very end,
25 Moses commanded [z]the Levites who carried the ark of the covenant of the LORD, 26 "Take
this Book of the Law [a]and put it by the side of the ark of the covenant of the LORD your God,
that it may be there for [b]a witness against you. 27 For I know how rebellious and [c]stubborn
you are. Behold, even today while I am yet alive with you, [d]you have been rebellious against
the LORD. How much more after my death! 28 Assemble to me all the elders of your tribes
and your officers, that I may speak [e]these words in their ears and [f]call heaven and earth
to witness against them. 29 For I know that after my death [g]you will surely act corruptly
and turn aside from the way that I have commanded you. And [h]in the days to come [i]evil
will befall you, because you will do what is evil in the sight of the LORD, [j]provoking him
to anger through the work of your hands."

The Song of Moses

30 Then Moses spoke the words of this song until they were finished, in the ears of all
the assembly of Israel:

32 1 "Give ear, [k]O heavens, and I will speak,
and let [l]the earth hear the words of my mouth.
2 May [m]my teaching drop as the rain,
my speech distill as the dew,

[1] Hebrew *he*

14 [b][ch. 34:5; Num. 27:13] [c][ver. 23; Num. 27:19]
15 [d]Ex. 33:9; Num. 12:5
16 [b][See ver. 14 above] [e]Ex. 34:15, 16; Lev. 20:5; Num. 15:39 [f]ch. 32:15; Judg. 2:12; 10:6, 13 [g]Judg. 2:20
17 [h]2 Chr. 12:5; 15:2; 24:20 [i]ch. 32:20; Ps. 30:7; 104:29; Isa. 8:17; 64:7; [Isa. 59:2] [j]Judg. 6:13 [k]Num. 14:42
18 [l]ver. 20
19 [m]See ch. 32:1-43 [n][2 Sam. 1:18] [o]ver. 21, 26
20 [p]See Ex. 3:8 [q]ch. 32:15; Neh. 9:25, 26; Jer. 5:28; Hos. 13:6 [r]ver. 18 [s]Num. 14:11, 23; 16:30 [g][See ver. 16 above]
21 [t]ver. 19, 26 [u][Hos. 5:3; 13:5]
23 [v][ver. 14] [w]See ver. 6 [x]ver. 8; Josh. 1:5; 3:7
24 [y]ver. 9
25 [z]See ver. 9
26 [a][2 Kgs. 22:8] [b]ver. 19, 21
27 [c]See ch. 9:6 [d]See ch. 9:7
28 [e]See ch. 32:1-43 [f]See ch. 4:26
29 [g]Judg. 2:19; Hos. 9:9 [h]See Gen. 49:1 [i][Jer. 44:23] [j]ch. 4:25; 9:18; 32:16, 21; 1 Kgs. 16:7; 2 Kgs. 22:17

Chapter 32

1 [k]Ps. 50:4; [Josh. 24:27]; See ch. 4:26 [l]Isa. 34:1; Mic. 1:2; 6:1, 2
2 [m]Isa. 55:10, 11; [Job 29:22, 23]

31:14–15 tent of meeting. See Ex. 33:7–11 and Num. 1:1. **I may commission him**. See Deut. 31:23. **pillar of cloud**. See Ex. 33:9.

31:16–18 The clear expectation is that Israel will disobey, end up in idolatry, and become the object of God's wrath (see 30:1). **whore**. Idolatry is often described in the OT in language of whoredom and adultery (e.g., Ezekiel 16).

31:19 write this song. See v. 22 and 31:30–32:44. The anticipation is that Israel will disobey and that the song will therefore **be a witness** to Israel's disobedience (31:21).

31:21 As Deuteronomy often suggests, Israel's heart was **inclined to** faithless disobedience, not faithful obedience.

31:23 Be strong and courageous. See v. 6. **I will be with you**. The same promise was made by God to Moses in Ex. 3:12.

31:24 the words of this law in a book. See v. 9 and note there.

31:26–27 Book of the Law. I.e., chs. 1–30. See 31:9 and note there. **by the side of the ark of the covenant**. The tablets of the Ten Commandments were placed inside the ark; the Book of the Law was to be alongside the ark in the Most Holy Place of the tabernacle. One function of the law (cf. v. 19) was to **witness against** Israel, exposing its sinfulness. **stubborn**. See 9:6 and 10:16.

31:28 Heaven and earth are called **to witness against** Israel (cf. note on 30:19–20), anticipating their future faithlessness. So the three witnesses are the song (31:19), the Book of the Law (v. 26), and heaven and earth.

31:29 the work of your hands. I.e., the making of idols.

31:30–32:47 *The Song of Moses.* In addition to the writing of the law and

2 [n]Ps. 72:6; Mic. 5:7
3 [o]See ch. 3:24
4 [p]ver. 15, 18, 30, 31, 37; Ps. 18:2, 31; Isa. 30:29; Hab. 1:12; See 2 Sam. 22:2 [q][Ps. 18:30] [r]Dan. 4:37; Rev. 15:3 [s]Job 34:10
5 [t][2 Pet. 2:13] [u]Matt. 17:17; Luke 9:41; Phil. 2:15
6 [v]Isa. 63:16; 64:8 [w]Ps. 74:2 [x]ver. 15; Isa. 44:2; 51:13
7 [y][Isa. 63:11] [z]Ps. 44:1
8 [a]Acts 17:26 [b]Gen. 11:8
10 [c]ch. 8:15; Jer. 2:6; Hos. 13:5 [d]Ps. 32:10 [e]Ps. 17:8; Prov. 7:2; Zech. 2:8
11 [f]Ex. 19:4
12 [g]Ps. 78:52, 53 [h]Isa. 43:12
13 [i]Isa. 58:14; Ezek. 36:2 [j]Ps. 81:16 [k]Job 29:6 [l]ch. 8:15
14 [m]Gen. 49:11

like gentle rain upon the tender grass,
and [n]like showers upon the herb.
3 For I will proclaim the name of the LORD;
ascribe [o]greatness to our God!

4 [p]"The Rock, [q]his work is perfect,
for [r]all his ways are justice.
A God of faithfulness and [s]without iniquity,
just and upright is he.
5 They have dealt corruptly with him;
they are no longer his children [t]because they are blemished;
they are [u]a crooked and twisted generation.
6 Do you thus repay the LORD,
you foolish and senseless people?
Is not he [v]your father, who [w]created you,
who [x]made you and established you?
7 [y]Remember the days of old;
consider the years of many generations;
[z]ask your father, and he will show you,
your elders, and they will tell you.
8 When the Most High [a]gave to the nations their inheritance,
when he [b]divided mankind,
he fixed the borders[1] of the peoples
according to the number of the sons of God.[2]
9 But the LORD's portion is his people,
Jacob his allotted heritage.

10 "He found him [c]in a desert land,
and in the howling waste of the wilderness;
he [d]encircled him, he cared for him,
he [e]kept him as the apple of his eye.
11 [f]Like an eagle that stirs up its nest,
that flutters over its young,
spreading out its wings, catching them,
bearing them on its pinions,
12 [g]the LORD alone guided him,
[h]no foreign god was with him.
13 [i]He made him ride on the high places of the land,
and he ate the produce of the field,
and he suckled him with [j]honey out of the rock,
and [k]oil out of [l]the flinty rock.
14 Curds from the herd, and milk from the flock,
with fat[3] of lambs,
rams of Bashan and goats,
with the very finest[4] of the wheat—
and you drank foaming wine made from [m]the blood of the grape.

[1] Or *territories* [2] Compare Dead Sea Scroll, Septuagint; Masoretic Text *sons of Israel* [3] That is, with the best [4] Hebrew *with the kidney fat*

its recital every seven years (31:9–13), the Song of Moses also acts as a witness against Israel.

31:30 song. See vv. 19, 22.

32:4 On God as **the Rock**, see vv. 15, 18, 30–31; see also Ps. 18:2; 19:14.

32:5 no longer his children. Cf. Hos. 1:9. See note on Deut. 14:1–2. **crooked and twisted generation**. See Phil. 2:15.

32:6 your father. See v. 5. Though rare in the OT, the notion of God as father of his people is not totally new in the NT.

32:7 Remember. See 5:15 and note.

32:8–9 gave to the nations their inheritance. For example, Edom, Moab, and Ammon in 2:1–23, as well as Israel throughout the book. **According to the number of the sons of God** may suggest that certain angels ("sons of God"; see Job 1:6) are responsible for specific nations, whereas the Lord himself cares for Israel. See also the second ESV footnote on v. 8. **the LORD's portion**. A term of special affection. See notes on Deut. 4:20 and 18:1–2.

32:11 Like an eagle. See Ex. 19:4.

32:14 Bashan was a particularly fertile area, where Og had been king (3:1–11; cf. Amos 4:1).

15 "But [n]Jeshurun grew fat, and [o]kicked;
[p]you grew fat, stout, and sleek;
[q]then he forsook God [r]who made him
and scoffed at [s]the Rock of his salvation.
16 [t]They stirred him to jealousy with strange gods;
with abominations they provoked him to anger.
17 [u]They sacrificed to demons that were no gods,
to gods they had never known,
to [v]new gods that had come recently,
whom your fathers had never dreaded.
18 You were unmindful of [w]the Rock that bore[1] you,
and you [x]forgot the God who gave you birth.

19 [y]"The LORD saw it and spurned them,
because of the provocation of [z]his sons and his daughters.
20 And he said, [a]'I will hide my face from them;
I will see what their end will be,
for they are a perverse generation,
children in whom is no faithfulness.
21 [b]They have made me jealous with what is no god;
they have provoked me to anger [c]with their idols.
So [d]I will make them jealous with those who are no people;
I will provoke them to anger with [e]a foolish nation.
22 For [f]a fire is kindled by my anger,
and it burns to [g]the depths of Sheol,
devours the earth and its increase,
and sets on fire the foundations of the mountains.

23 "'And I will heap disasters upon them;
[h]I will spend my arrows on them;
24 they shall be wasted with hunger,
and devoured by plague
and poisonous pestilence;
I will send [i]the teeth of beasts against them,
with the venom of [j]things that crawl in the dust.
25 [k]Outdoors the sword shall bereave,
and indoors terror,
for young man and woman alike,
the nursing child with the man of gray hairs.
26 [l]I would have said, "I will cut them to pieces;
[m]I will wipe them from human memory,"
27 had I not feared provocation by the enemy,
lest their adversaries should misunderstand,
lest they should say, [n]"Our hand is triumphant,
it was not the LORD who did all this."'

28 "For they are a nation void of counsel,
and there is [o]no understanding in them.

[1] Or *fathered*

15 [n]ch. 33:5, 26; Isa. 44:2 [o][1 Sam. 2:29] [p]See ch. 31:20 [q]ch. 31:16 [r]ver. 6 [s]2 Sam. 22:47; Ps. 89:26; 95:1
16 [t]Ps. 78:58; See Num. 25:11
17 [u]Ps. 106:37; [1 Cor. 10:20] [v][Judg. 5:8]
18 [w]2 Sam. 22:47; Ps. 89:26; 95:1 [x]Isa. 17:10; Jer. 2:27, 32; Hos. 8:14
19 [y][Judg. 2:14] [z][Isa. 1:2]
20 [a]See ch. 31:17
21 [b]Ps. 78:58; See Num. 25:11 [c]1 Kgs. 16:13, 26; Ps. 31:6; Jonah 2:8; Acts 14:15 [d]Cited Rom. 10:19; [Hos. 1:9, 10] [e][Ps. 74:18]
22 [f]Jer. 15:14; 17:4; Lam. 4:11 [g]Ps. 86:13
23 [h]Job 6:4; Ps. 7:12, 13; 38:2; Lam. 3:12, 13; Ezek. 5:16
24 [i]Lev. 26:22; Ezek. 5:17 [j]Jer. 8:17; Mic. 7:17
25 [k]Lam. 1:20; Ezek. 7:15
26 [l]Ezek. 20:23 [m]Job 18:17; Ps. 34:16; 109:15
27 [n]Ps. 140:8; Isa. 10:13; [Num. 14:16]
28 [o]Isa. 27:11; Jer. 4:22

32:15–16 Jeshurun means the upright one, a poetic name for Israel used sarcastically here (cf. Isa. 44:2). **jealousy with strange gods**. See Deut. 4:24 and note on 4:23–24. As throughout Deuteronomy, idolatry is the key sin of and threat to Israel (see also 32:21). God, the Rock, has redeemed and provided for Israel, whereas idols or false gods have no real existence or track record (v. 17).

32:20 hide my face. Often God's punishment of sin is his withdrawal (v. 18; see also Rom. 1:24, 26, 28).

32:21 In Rom. 10:19 Paul quotes from this verse to show that Israel will need a remedy for their unbelief regarding Jesus (in Rom. 11:11, 14, Gentile faith is the remedy).

32:22 depths of Sheol. The place of the dead. See Ps. 86:13.

32:27 lest their adversaries should misunderstand. The reputation of God is the driving force behind the switch from punishment of Israel to salvation for Israel. See 9:28; also Ezek. 36:21–38.

32:29 wise. Cf. 4:6. The ideal of 4:5–8 is far from realized in this song.

29 [p]If they were wise, they would understand this;
they would [q]discern their latter end!
30 How could [r]one have chased a thousand,
and two have put ten thousand to flight,
unless their Rock [s]had sold them,
and the LORD had given them up?
31 For [t]their rock is not as our Rock;
[u]our enemies are by themselves.
32 For their vine [v]comes from the vine of Sodom
and from the fields of Gomorrah;
their grapes are grapes of [w]poison;
their clusters are bitter;
33 their wine is the poison of [x]serpents
and the cruel venom of asps.

34 "'Is not this laid up in store with me,
[y]sealed up in my treasuries?
35 [z]Vengeance is mine, and recompense,[1]
[a]for the time when their foot shall slip;
for [b]the day of their calamity is at hand,
and their doom comes swiftly.'
36 For [c]the LORD will vindicate[2] his people
[d]and have compassion on his servants,
when he sees that their power is gone
and there is none remaining, [e]bond or free.
37 Then he will say, [f]'Where are their gods,
[g]the rock in which they took refuge,
38 who ate the fat of their sacrifices
and drank the wine of their drink offering?
Let them rise up and help you;
let them be your protection!

39 "'See now that [h]I, even I, am he,
and there is no god beside me;
[i]I kill and I make alive;
[j]I wound and I heal;
and there is none that can deliver out of my hand.
40 For [k]I lift up my hand to heaven
and swear, As I live forever,
41 if I [l]sharpen my flashing sword[3]
and my hand takes hold on judgment,
I will take vengeance on my adversaries
and will repay those who hate me.
42 I will make my arrows drunk with blood,
and [m]my sword shall devour flesh—
with the blood of the slain and the captives,
from the [n]long-haired heads of the enemy.'

43 [o]"Rejoice with him, O heavens;[4]
bow down to him, all gods,[5]

29 [p]ch. 5:29; Ps. 81:13; Luke 19:42 [q]Isa. 47:7; Lam. 1:9
30 [r]See Lev. 26:8 [s]See Judg. 2:14
31 [t]1 Sam. 2:2 [u][1 Sam. 4:8]
32 [v][Isa. 1:10; Jer. 23:14; Ezek. 16:46] [w]ch. 29:18
33 [x]Job 20:14, 16; Ps. 58:4 (Heb.)
34 [y][Job 14:17; Hos. 13:12; Rom. 2:5]
35 [z]Ps. 94:1; Isa. 1:24; 59:18; Nah. 1:2; Cited Rom. 12:19; Heb. 10:30 [a][Ps. 94:18] [b][2 Pet. 2:3]
36 [c]Ps. 135:14; Cited Heb. 10:30 [d]Judg. 2:18; Ps. 106:45; [Ps. 90:13] [e]1 Kgs. 14:10; 21:21; 2 Kgs. 9:8; 14:26
37 [f]Judg. 10:14; 1 Kgs. 18:27; Jer. 2:28 [g][ver. 31]
39 [h]Isa. 41:4; 48:12 [i]1 Sam. 2:6; 2 Kgs. 5:7 [j]Job 5:18; Hos. 6:1
40 [k]See Gen. 14:22
41 [l]Ps. 7:12; Isa. 27:1; 34:5; 66:16; Ezek. 21:9, 10
42 [m]Jer. 46:10 [n]See Ps. 68:21
43 [o]Cited Rom. 15:10

[1] Septuagint *and I will repay* [2] Septuagint *judge* [3] Hebrew *the lightning of my sword* [4] Dead Sea Scroll, Septuagint; Masoretic Text *Rejoice his people, O nations* [5] Masoretic Text lacks *bow down to him, all gods*

32:30–31 Israel's **Rock** is God; the **rock** of the **enemies** refers to the so-called gods of other nations. Their gods are impotent and nothing, hence the enemies are **by themselves**. Therefore any victory over Israel must be attributed to God's giving up Israel into their hands.

32:35–36 Vengeance is mine, and recompense. Romans 12:19 and Heb. 10:30 quote the Septuagint (Gk. OT) version, "and I will repay." **For the LORD will vindicate his people**. Beyond defeat and exile, God will restore his people (Deut. 30:1–3). Cf. Heb. 10:30 and ESV footnote on Deut. 32:36.

32:39 I, even I, am he. The emphasis on "I" highlights the sovereignty of God (cf. Ex. 3:14). **no god beside me**. See Deut. 4:35; 5:7; and note on 4:35–36.

32:43 The Hebrew Masoretic text, which the ESV usually follows, presents

for he [p]avenges the blood of his children[1]
and takes vengeance on his adversaries.
He repays those who hate him[2]
and cleanses[3] his people's land."[4]

44 Moses came and recited all the words of this song in the hearing of the people, he and
[q]Joshua[5] the son of Nun. **45** And when Moses had finished speaking all these words to all
Israel, **46** he said to them, [r]"Take to heart all the words by which I am warning you today,
[s]that you may command them to your children, that they may be careful to do all the
words of this law. **47** For it is no empty word for you, [t]but your very life, and by this word
you shall live long in the land that you are going over the Jordan to possess."

Moses' Death Foretold

48 That very day the LORD spoke to Moses, **49** "Go up [u]this mountain of the Abarim, Mount
Nebo, which is in the land of Moab, opposite Jericho, and view the land of Canaan, which
I am giving to the people of Israel for a possession. **50** And die on the mountain which you
go up, and be gathered to your people, as [v]Aaron your brother died in Mount Hor and was
gathered to his people, **51** [w]because you broke faith with me in the midst of the people of
Israel at the waters of Meribah-kadesh, in the wilderness of Zin, and because you did not
treat me as holy in the midst of the people of Israel. **52** For [x]you shall see the land before
you, but you shall not go there, into the land that I am giving to the people of Israel."

Moses' Final Blessing on Israel

33 This is the blessing with which Moses [y]the man of God blessed the people of Israel
before his death. **2** He said,

[z]"The LORD came from Sinai
and dawned from Seir upon us;[6]
he shone forth from Mount Paran;
he came [a]from the ten thousands of holy ones,
with flaming fire[7] at his right hand.
3 Yes, [b]he loved his people,[8]
[c]all his holy ones were in his[9] hand;
[d]so they followed[10] in your steps,
receiving direction from you,
4 when [e]Moses commanded us a law,
as a possession for the assembly of Jacob.
5 Thus the LORD[11] [f]became king in [g]Jeshurun,
when the heads of the people were gathered,
all the tribes of Israel together.

6 [h]"Let Reuben live, and not die,
but let his men be few."

[1] Dead Sea Scroll, Septuagint; Masoretic Text *servants* [2] Dead Sea Scroll, Septuagint; Masoretic Text lacks *He repays those who hate him* [3] Or *atones for* [4] Septuagint, Vulgate; Hebrew *his land his people* [5] Septuagint, Syriac, Vulgate; Hebrew *Hoshea* [6] Septuagint, Syriac, Vulgate; Hebrew *them* [7] The meaning of the Hebrew word is uncertain [8] Septuagint; Hebrew *peoples* [9] Hebrew *your* [10] The meaning of the Hebrew word is uncertain [11] Hebrew *Thus he*

43 [p]Rev. 6:10; 19:2; [2 Kgs. 9:7; Ps. 79:10]
44 [q]Num. 13:8, 16
46 [r]ch. 11:18; See ch. 6:6 [s]See ch. 4:9
47 [t][Lev. 18:5]; See ch. 30:20
49 [u]See Num. 27:12
50 [v]Num. 20:24, 25, 28; 33:38
51 [w]Num. 20:11-13; 27:14
52 [x]ch. 3:27; 34:4

Chapter 33

1 [y]Josh. 14:6; 1 Chr. 23:14; 2 Chr. 30:16; Ezra 3:2
2 [z][Ex. 19:18, 20; Judg. 5:4, 5; Ps. 68:7, 8; Hab. 3:3] [a][Ps. 68:17; Dan. 7:10; Acts 7:53; Gal. 3:19; Heb. 2:2; Jude 14; Rev. 5:11]
3 [b]ch. 7:7, 8; 10:15; Hos. 11:1 [c][John 10:27-29; Rom. 8:35, 38, 39] [d][Luke 10:39; Acts 22:3]
4 [e]John 1:17; 7:19
5 [f]Num. 23:21; [Judg. 8:23; Isa. 33:22] [g]See ch. 32:15
6 [h][Gen. 49:3, 4]

problems in this verse. So here the Dead Sea Scrolls and Septuagint variants have been followed, as they represent an earlier stage of textual transmission (see ESV footnotes). The verse brings the song to a triumphant conclusion affirming that, despite Israel's sin and exile, God will ultimately restore them. The quotation from this verse in Rom. 15:10 uses a phrase found only in the Septuagint, "Rejoice O Gentiles, with his people," to convey the expectation that God would one day bring the light to the entire Gentile world.

32:46–47 I am warning you. The song was a witness against Israel. See 31:19 and note there. **your very life, and by this word you shall live**. Cf. 30:19–20.

32:48–33:29 *The Blessing of Moses.* Like a patriarch, Moses blesses Israel before his death. Cf. Jacob blessing his sons (Gen. 49:3–27).

32:49–51 Abarim, Mount Nebo. See 34:1. **Aaron your brother died in Mount Hor**. See 10:6 and Num. 20:24–28. **you broke faith with me**. See Num. 20:11–13. Cf. Deut. 1:37; 3:26; 4:21.

33:1–29 There is no mention of Simeon in the list of tribes, perhaps because the tribe was going to be dispersed (Gen. 49:7) and absorbed by Judah. The blessings are bracketed by statements praising God's uniqueness (Deut. 33:1–5, 26–29).

33:1 Man of God shows the high esteem in which Moses was held. See also Josh. 14:6. The term is most frequently used in the OT of Elijah and Elisha.

33:2 Sinai (in Deuteronomy, usually called Horeb) was the mountain of God, where he appeared. **Seir** is another name for Edom, in whose territory Sinai was situated (see Judg. 5:4–5). **Mount Paran** was in the same vicinity (Deut. 1:1–2). **holy ones**. Angels or heavenly beings.

33:5 The real **king** of Israel was God, despite the later development of a monarchy. **Jeshurun**. See v. 26 and 32:15. **when the heads of the people were gathered**. Refers to the covenant renewal in Moab.

33:6 Reuben was the eldest son of Jacob, and hence is listed first (as in Gen. 49:3).

7 And this he said of Judah:

"Hear, O LORD, the voice of Judah,
and bring him in to his people.
With your hands contend[1] for him,
and be a help against his adversaries."

8 And [i]of Levi he said,

"Give to Levi[2] [j]your Thummim,
and your Urim to your godly one,
[k]whom you tested at Massah,
with whom you quarreled at the waters of Meribah;
9 who said of his father and mother,
'I regard them not';
[l]he disowned his brothers
and ignored his children.
For [m]they observed your word
and kept your covenant.
10 [n]They shall teach Jacob your rules
and Israel your law;
[o]they shall put incense before you
and [p]whole burnt offerings on your altar.
11 Bless, O LORD, his substance,
and [q]accept the work of his hands;
crush the loins of his adversaries,
of those who hate him, that they rise not again."

12 [r]Of Benjamin he said,

"The beloved of the LORD dwells in safety.
The High God[3] surrounds him all day long,
and dwells between his shoulders."

13 And [s]of Joseph he said,

[t]"Blessed by the LORD be his land,
with the choicest gifts of heaven [u]above,[4]
and of the deep that crouches beneath,
14 with the choicest fruits of the sun
and the rich yield of the months,
15 with the finest produce of the ancient mountains
and the abundance of [v]the everlasting hills,
16 with the best gifts of the earth and [w]its fullness
and the favor of [x]him who dwells in the bush.
May these rest on the head of Joseph,
on the pate of him who is prince among his brothers.
17 [y]A firstborn bull[5]—he has majesty,
and his horns are the horns of a [z]wild ox;
with them [a]he shall gore the peoples,
all of them, to the ends of the earth;

8 [i][Gen. 49:5] [j]See Ex. 28:30 [k]See Ex. 17:7; Num. 20:13
9 [l]See Ex. 32:26-29 [m]Mal. 2:4-6
10 [n]ch. 17:9-11; Ezek. 44:23; See Lev. 10:11 [o]Ex. 30:7, 8; 1 Sam. 2:28 [p]Ps. 51:19; Ezek. 43:27
11 [q]Ezek. 20:40, 41; 43:27; [Amos 5:22]
12 [r][Gen. 49:27]
13 [s][Gen. 49:22] [t]Gen. 49:25 [u]ver. 28; Gen. 27:28
15 [v]Gen. 49:26; Hab. 3:6; [Ps. 90:2]
16 [w]Ps. 24:1 [x]Ex. 3:2-4; Acts 7:30, 35
17 [y][1 Chr. 5:1] [z]See Num. 23:22 [a]1 Kgs. 22:11; Ps. 44:5; Dan. 8:4

[1] Probable reading; Hebrew *With his hands he contended* [2] Dead Sea Scroll, Septuagint; Masoretic Text lacks *Give to Levi* [3] Septuagint; Hebrew *dwells in safety by him. He* [4] Two Hebrew manuscripts and Targum; Hebrew *with the dew* [5] Dead Sea Scroll, Septuagint, Samaritan; Masoretic Text *His firstborn bull*

33:8 The **Thummim** and **Urim** were possibly two flat stones, like two-sided dice, used to determine guidance (see Ex. 28:30). **Massah**. See Ex. 17:7. The blessing of **Levi** (Deut. 33:8–11) acknowledges the tribe's uprightness in the golden calf incident (Ex. 32:26–29).

33:10 The two main roles of the priestly tribe of Levi were to **teach** the **law** (31:11) and to oversee the sacrificial system.

33:12 The beloved of the LORD. Cf. Gen. 49:27.

33:13 Joseph here includes the two tribes of Manasseh and Ephraim, the sons of Joseph (see v. 17).

33:15–16 Cf. the blessing by Jacob on Joseph in Gen. 49:26. **who dwells in the bush**. See Ex. 3:1–6.

[b]they are the ten thousands of Ephraim,
and they are the thousands of Manasseh."

18 And of Zebulun he said,

[c]"Rejoice, Zebulun, in your going out,
and Issachar, in your tents.
19 They shall call peoples [d]to their mountain;
there they offer [e]right sacrifices;
for they draw from the abundance of the seas
and the hidden treasures of the sand."

20 And [f]of Gad he said,

"Blessed be he who enlarges Gad!
Gad crouches [g]like a lion;
he tears off arm and scalp.
21 [h]He chose the best of the land for himself,
for there a commander's portion was reserved;
and [i]he came with the heads of the people,
with Israel he executed the justice of the LORD,
and his judgments for Israel."

22 And [j]of Dan he said,

[k]"Dan is a lion's cub
[l]that leaps from Bashan."

23 And [m]of Naphtali he said,

"O Naphtali, sated with favor,
and full of the blessing of the LORD,
[n]possess the lake[1] and the south."

24 And [o]of Asher he said,

"Most blessed of sons be Asher;
let him be the favorite of his brothers,
and let him [p]dip his foot in oil.
25 Your bars shall be iron and bronze,
and as your days, so shall your strength be.
26 [q]"There is none like God, O [r]Jeshurun,
[s]who rides through the heavens to your help,
through the skies in his majesty.
27 The eternal God is your [t]dwelling place,[2]
and underneath are the everlasting arms.[3]
And he thrust out the enemy before you
and said, 'Destroy.'
28 So Israel lived in safety,
[u]Jacob lived [v]alone,[4]
in a land of grain and wine,
whose heavens drop down dew.
29 Happy are you, O Israel! [w]Who is like you,
a people [x]saved by the LORD,

[1] Or *west* [2] Or *a dwelling place* [3] Revocalization of verse 27 yields *He subdues the ancient gods, and shatters the forces of old* [4] Hebrew *the abode of Jacob was alone*

17[b][Gen. 48:19; Num. 1:33, 35]
18[c][Gen. 49:13-15]
19[d]Ex. 15:17; Isa. 2:3 [e]Ps. 4:5; 51:19
20[f][Gen. 49:19] [g][1 Chr. 12:8]
21[h]See Num. 32:1-5, 16-19 [i]Num. 32:31, 32; See Josh. 1:12-15; 1 Chr. 5:18-22
22[j][Gen. 49:16] [k][Gen. 49:9] [l][Josh. 19:47; Judg. 18:27]
23[m][Gen. 49:21] [n]See Josh. 19:32-39
24[o][Gen. 49:20] [p][Job 29:6]
26[q]See Ex. 15:11 [r]See ch. 32:15 [s]Ps. 68:33, 34; 104:3; Isa. 19:1; Hab. 3:8
27[t]Ps. 90:1; 91:9
28[u][Ps. 68:26; Isa. 48:1] [v]Num. 23:9
29[w][2 Sam. 7:23] [x]Isa. 45:17

33:21 chose the best of the land for himself. See Num. 32:1–5, where Gad and Reuben request land across the Jordan that is ideal for cattle.

33:22 Bashan. This blessing seems to locate **Dan** in the north of the land, predicting its migration to the north (see Judges 18).

33:23 the lake. Naphtali's land bordered the Sea of Galilee.

33:24 let him dip his foot in oil. Olive oil was a symbol of wealth.

33:26 There is none like God. Cf. 4:35. **Jeshurun**. See 32:15 and note on 32:15–16. **who rides through the heavens**. Cf. Ps. 18:10.

33:29 God promised to be a **shield** for Abram (Gen. 15:1).

29[y]Ps. 33:20; 115:9-11
Chapter 34
1[a]See Num. 27:12
2[b]See ch. 11:24
3[c]ch. 1:7 [d]Gen. 13:12; 19:17, 25, 28, 29; 2 Sam. 18:23 [e]Judg. 1:16; 3:13; 2 Chr. 28:15 [f]Gen. 14:2; 19:22
4[g]See Gen. 12:7; 50:24 [h]ch. 3:27; 32:52 [i]See ch. 1:37
6[j][Jude 9]
7[k]ch. 31:2 [l][Gen. 27:1; 48:10; Josh. 14:10, 11; 1 Sam. 3:2; 4:15]
8[m]Num. 20:29; [Gen. 50:3]
9[n]Ex. 28:3; Isa. 11:2 [o]Num. 27:18, 23 [p]Josh. 1:17
10[q][ch. 18:15, 18] [r]ch. 5:4; See Ex. 33:11
11[s]See ch. 4:34

[y]the shield of your help,
and the sword of your triumph!
Your enemies shall come fawning to you,
and you shall tread upon their backs."

The Death of Moses

34 Then Moses went up from the plains of Moab [a]to Mount Nebo, to the top of Pisgah,
which is opposite Jericho. And the LORD showed him all the land, Gilead as far as
Dan, 2 all Naphtali, the land of Ephraim and Manasseh, all the land of Judah [b]as far as the
western sea, 3 [c]the Negeb, and [d]the Plain, that is, the Valley of Jericho [e]the city of palm trees,
as far as [f]Zoar. 4 And the LORD said to him, [g]"This is the land of which I swore to Abraham,
to Isaac, and to Jacob, 'I will give it to your offspring.' [h]I have let you see it with your eyes,
but [i]you shall not go over there." 5 So Moses the servant of the LORD died there in the land
of Moab, according to the word of the LORD, 6 and he buried him in the valley in the land
of Moab opposite Beth-peor; but [j]no one knows the place of his burial to this day. 7 [k]Moses
was 120 years old when he died. [l]His eye was undimmed, and his vigor unabated. 8 And
the people of Israel [m]wept for Moses in the plains of Moab thirty days. Then the days of
weeping and mourning for Moses were ended.
9 And Joshua the son of Nun was full of [n]the spirit of wisdom, for [o]Moses had laid his
hands on him. So [p]the people of Israel obeyed him and did as the LORD had commanded
Moses. 10 And there has not [q]arisen a prophet since in Israel like Moses, [r]whom the LORD
knew face to face, 11 none like him for all [s]the signs and the wonders that the LORD sent
him to do in the land of Egypt, to Pharaoh and to all his servants and to all his land, 12 and
for all the mighty power and all the great deeds of terror that Moses did in the sight of
all Israel.

34:1–12 *The Death of Moses.* Moses dies and is buried on Mount Nebo, overlooking the Promised Land.

34:1–3 Mount Nebo, to the top of Pisgah. See 3:17, 27. **Gilead**. See 2:36 and note on 2:36–37. **Dan**. See 33:22 and note there. **western sea**. The Mediterranean. **the Negeb**. See 1:7 and note there.

34:4 the land of which I swore. See 1:7–8. Deuteronomy begins and ends with the theme of the land promised by God. **I have let you see it with your eyes, but you shall not go over there**. See 1:37 and note on 1:37–38.

34:5 servant of the LORD. Cf. Ex. 14:31; Josh. 1:1, 7, 13. This title is reserved for special leaders or others in the service of God: e.g., Abraham (Gen. 26:24), Joshua (Josh. 24:29), David (2 Sam. 3:18), Israel (Isa. 41:8–9), and a foreign king (Jer. 25:9).

34:6–7 he buried him. Unlike Joseph, whose remains were eventually buried in the land (Josh. 24:32), Moses is buried (by God himself) outside the land. **Beth-peor**. See Deut. 3:29 and note there. **vigor unabated**. Cf. 31:2.

34:9 On the commissioning of **Joshua** to succeed Moses, see 31:7–8, 14, 23. On his being **full of the spirit**, see Ex. 28:3; 31:3; 35:31; Mic. 3:8; Luke 1:15; Acts 6:3. **wisdom**. See Deut. 1:13.

34:10 there has not arisen a prophet since in Israel like Moses. See 18:15–19 for the expectation that God will raise up a prophet like Moses. Ultimately Jesus fulfills this prophecy (cf. John 1:21; Acts 3:22–24; 7:37). **face to face**. See Ex. 33:11.

Introduction to the Historical Books

The "Historical Books" of the OT, which come after the Pentateuch, tell the story of (1) Israel's entry into the Promised Land of Canaan under Joshua; (2) Israel's life in the land under the judges and the transition to kingship; (3) the division of the nation into two rival kingdoms (Israel and Judah) and life in both; (4) the downfall and exile of each kingdom; (5) life in the exile; and (6) Judah's return from exile. These books span close to 1,000 years of history, so it is not surprising that their story includes many ups and downs, twists and turns. Yet, through it all, the God who is the same yesterday, today, and forever remains the focal point of all of these books.

The date of Moses' death is calculated by working backward from 1 Kings 6:1, which states that Solomon began to build the temple 480 years after the exodus from Egypt. Comparing the information in 1 Kings with extrabiblical records indicates that the temple building began in 967 or 966 B.C. The date of the exodus, then, would be 1447 or 1446 B.C., and the date of Moses' death, 40 years later, would be 1407 or 1406. On the other hand, if one finds some symbolism in the 480-year figure (e.g., supposing it to result from 12 generations, with a generation taken to be 40 years), one may arrive at a date for the exodus of about 1260 B.C. (which some believe allows for greater agreement with Egyptian history), yielding a date around 1220 for Moses' death. See The Date of the Exodus, p. 33.

Historical Books Timeline

1406 [or 1220] B.C.	Moses' death; Israel's entry into Canaan under Joshua [See The Date of the Exodus, p. 33]
1375 [or 1210]	Joshua's death
1375–1055 [or 1210–1050/42/30]	Period of the judges
1050/42/30–1010	Saul's reign
1010–971	David's reign
971–931	Solomon's reign
931–722	Divided kingdom (Israel)—19 kings
722	Destruction of Samaria (Israel's capital) by Assyria; Israel's resettlement
931–586	Divided kingdom (Judah)—19 kings,, 1 queen
586	Destruction of Jerusalem and temple by Babylon; Judah exiled to Babylon
586–538	Judah's exile in Babylon
561	Release of King Jehoiachin from prison in Babylon
539	Cyrus II of Persia captures Babylon
538	First return of Jews to Jerusalem under Jeshua and Zerubbabel
516	Temple rebuilding completed
478	Esther and Mordecai rise in the Persian court
458	Ezra's return to Jerusalem from Babylon
445	Nehemiah's return to Jerusalem from Babylon
445–???	Walls of Jerusalem rebuilt
433	Nehemiah's visit to Babylon and return to Jerusalem

The other dates are certain with a high degree of confidence. The story of Esther and Mordecai took place in the time of Ahasuerus (Est. 1:1), who reigned over Persia 486–464 B.C.

Note that the northern kingdom of Israel lasted slightly more than 200 years (931–722 B.C.), with 19 kings. All of Israel's kings did evil in the Lord's eyes, and there were several assassinations and changes of ruling family.

In contrast, the southern kingdom of Judah lasted almost 350 years (931–586 B.C.), with the same number of kings. Thus, a greater degree of political stability existed in Judah—and, to some degree, spiritual stability, since eight kings in Judah did right in the Lord's eyes. All the kings in this lineage were descended from David, to whom God had promised there would always be a descendant of his line on the throne (2 Sam. 7:12–16).

The Babylonians attacked Jerusalem in 605 and 597 B.C., deporting the cream of Judah's society (e.g., Daniel and his friends were deported in 605) before the final destruction and deportation of 586.

From the dates above, it appears as though the exile lasted only 50 years (586–538/537 B.C.), which seems to contradict Jeremiah's prophecy about the return from exile after 70 years (Jer. 25:11; 29:10). However, the round number "70" can be calculated by one of two methods: (a) from the first deportation (605 B.C.) to the first return (538 or 537) yields 68 years; or (b) from the destruction of Jerusalem and the temple (586) to the rebuilding of the temple (516) yields 70 years. (See note on Jer. 25:11.)

Unity

In our English Bibles, there are 12 Historical Books: Joshua, Judges, Ruth, 1–2 Samuel, 1–2 Kings, 1–2 Chronicles, Ezra, Nehemiah, and Esther. In the Hebrew Bible, the books are divided differently: Joshua, Judges, 1–2 Samuel, and 1–2 Kings are part of the second section of the Bible, titled the "Former Prophets," and the rest of the Historical Books are found among the third section, titled the "Writings."

Each book evidences a different style of writing. In Joshua, for example, the accounts of Israel's entering and settling into the land of Canaan in chapters 1–11 and 22–24 are interrupted by the lists of land distributions in chapters 12–21. In Judges, we find a cyclical history spiraling downward through the regimes of successive judges. Ruth is a self-contained and beautifully told story of God's grace in the life of one family of David's ancestors. First and Second Samuel tell of the establishment of the legitimate Davidic monarchy in a richly textured account of the events; much in these books has the feel of an eyewitness account. By contrast, 1 and 2 Kings tell the story of Israel's kings after David in a much more stereotypical manner, structured around repeated formulas of the accession, main exploits, and deaths of the successive kings, all leading eventually to exile. First and Second Chronicles portray similar events to those found in 2 Samuel and 1–2 Kings. As with the composition of Kings, Chronicles enlists and shapes an array of literary and historical materials to address a new set of concerns now facing the postexilic people of God. Ezra–Nehemiah contains first-person and eyewitness accounts, lists, and correspondence about the return from Babylonian exile and postexilic life. Esther is like Ruth in being a self-contained and well-told story; it deals with life events affecting Jews in Persia in the postexilic period.

Despite the differences, all of these books present history from a God's-eye view. That is, they are not "history for history's sake," but rather, they are *theological* in nature. They tell about God's repeated in-breakings into history, whether by dramatic accounts of miracles, or by God's speaking directly to his people, or by his indirect presence, visible in the providential outworking of events. And, in the telling of all these events, the authors' perspectives are God's perspectives. So it should not surprise us that many of the books' themes echo each other and also carry forward some of the great themes of the Pentateuch.

Themes

Each historical book has its own unique themes. But many of these can be tied into larger, overarching themes that have their roots in the Pentateuch and unfold across many books. Five overarching themes pervade the Historical Books: God's sovereignty, presence, promises, kingdom, and covenant.

1. God's Sovereignty: Over Israel and the Nations

God is consistently presented in the Historical Books as sovereign over all of creation, including the elements of nature and the affairs of individuals and nations. The most spectacular way in which the writers demonstrate God's sovereignty is through various miracles. These occur throughout the OT but tend to be especially prominent in the book of Joshua (the stopping of the Jordan River and various victories over enemies) and the books of 1–2 Kings, especially in the stories of Elijah and Elisha (1 Kings 17–19; 21; 2 Kings 1–9; 13).

Also, Israel is consistently presented as under God's authority, care, and protection, and therefore obligated to return to him their love, trust, and obedience. Even the other nations were subject to God—from the small city-states and peoples in the times of Joshua, the judges, Saul, and David (e.g., the Philistines, Moabites, Canaanites), to the great empires of Assyria, Babylon, and Persia. These circumstances form the backdrop to the events of 1–2 Kings, 1–2 Chronicles, Ezra–Nehemiah, and Esther.

2. God's Presence: Near and Far

In most of the Historical Books, God is close at hand. He designated Joshua as Moses' successor, raised up the judges in response to Israel's dire straits over several centuries, and designated Saul and then David as his chosen kings. He was a source of help to the godly kings who sought him, and to bold prophets who spoke in his name (Nathan, Gad, Elijah, Micaiah, Elisha, Huldah, and others). He empowered Jeshua, Zerubbabel, Ezra, and Nehemiah to be bold leaders after the trauma of the exile. The prayers of godly kings such as David (2 Samuel 7), Solomon (1 Kings 8), Jehoshaphat (2 Chronicles 20), and others show the closeness of their relationship with God.

And yet at times God seemed more hidden. Most often, this was because of Israel's sin. Such was clearly the case in Judges (ch. 2), Samuel (1 Sam. 4:19–22), and repeatedly in 1–2 Kings and 1–2 Chronicles. Sometimes, however, God's hiddenness is not attributed to sin; it is simply a fact, and his presence must be inferred indirectly. In Ruth, for example, the author quotes the characters' references to God many times, but only mentions God in his own words twice (Ruth 1:6; 4:13). In Esther, God is not mentioned at all. In these cases (esp. Esther), it signals that sometimes Christians have to look for God's presence in very intentional ways, and that sometimes he chooses not to reveal himself as directly as at other times.

3. God's Promises: Present and Future

The Historical Books carry forward the stories of the Pentateuch, including some of its great themes. One consistent theme is God's promise to be with his people, going back to Abraham (Gen. 17:8), and continuing with Moses (Ex. 3:12), Joshua (Josh. 1:5, 9), David (2 Samuel 7), Ezra (Ezra 7:6), Nehemiah (Neh. 2:8), and many others. The important promises to Abraham—sometimes called the "Abrahamic covenant"—included the land of Canaan (Gen. 12:7; 13:15; 17:8), many descendants (Gen. 12:2; 15:5), and blessings on Abraham and, through him, on the nations (Gen. 12:1–3). The Abrahamic covenant, then, forms the foundation of much that is in the Historical Books: (1) The stage on which the books unfold is the Promised Land of Canaan. (2) Israel became a mighty nation among its immediate neighbors, with thousands upon thousands of descendants of Abraham. (3) Israel and Judah were repeatedly blessed when they followed God. Even non-Israelites were blessed when they turned to the God of Abraham (e.g., Rahab in Joshua 2 and Naaman in 2 Kings 5). God did not forsake his promises to his people.

4. God's Kingdom: Both Divine and Human

The Bible teaches that God is king over the earth (e.g., Ex. 15:18; Ps. 93:1). As noted above, the exercise of his rule can be seen in his sovereignty over all nature, people, and nations.

God also chose to exercise his rule through human kings. As far back as Abraham's day, God had promised that kings would come from Abraham's line (Gen. 17:6, 16; 35:11; 49:10). He carefully prescribed that these kings should *not* be like the kings of neighboring nations, where warfare and foreign alliances were their primary features; by contrast, Israel's kings were to be rooted in a study of God's Word, and to let God fight Israel's battles (Deut. 17:14–20; Judg. 8:22–23; 1 Sam. 8:5, 20). The king was God's representative on earth, and God's earthly kingdom was entrusted to him. We can see this clearly in texts such as 2 Chronicles 13:8, which refers to "the kingdom of the LORD in the hands of the sons of David," or 1 Chronicles

29:23, where Solomon was chosen to sit "on the throne of the LORD."

God was a father to the Davidic kings, and they were "sons" of God in perpetuity (2 Sam. 7:11–16); these promises are known as the "Davidic covenant." While most of Israel's and Judah's kings did not live up to the ideals set out in Deuteronomy 17 and 2 Samuel 7, nevertheless the model was one where the king exercised his rule in connection with God's will and in dependence upon God. The NT highlights the kingdom theme as the ultimate "Son" of God was born from the lineage of David: Jesus, the Christ (Matt. 1:1; Rom. 1:3). It is with the proclamation of the kingdom that the Messiah's ministry commences (Matt. 4:17; Mark 1:14–15; Luke 4:16–21); with his resurrection and ascension Jesus began his reign as the Davidic king (Acts 13:33; Rom. 1:4), to carry out the long-awaited work of bringing light to the Gentiles (Matt. 28:1–20; Rom. 1:5). The church, now as Christ's representative presence in the world, is called in the power of the Spirit to proclaim and live out that kingdom reign (Acts 8:12; 19:8; 20:25).

5. God's Covenant: Reward and Punishment

Life under the Abrahamic covenant required obedience to God in all realms of life. God said that Abraham had "obeyed my voice and kept my charge, my commandments, my statutes, and my laws" (Gen. 26:5). In other words, Abraham—who lived centuries before the Mosaic law was given at Mount Sinai—had lived his life in relationship with God in full accord with what later would be understood as keeping the law. The collections of Mosaic laws, and the attendant promises and obligations, have come to be known as the "Mosaic covenant," which spelled out how Israel was to shape the life of the nation under the Abrahamic covenant, which continued to be in effect through the promises of land, seed, and blessing to the nations (Gen. 12:1–3).

The book of Deuteronomy laid out most fully the rewards and punishments that would follow obedience or disobedience (Deuteronomy 27–28), and this perspective governed most of the writing of the Historical Books: when people followed the Lord, they were blessed, and when they did not, they suffered. We see this over and over again in Judges, 1–2 Samuel, 1–2 Kings, and 1–2 Chronicles. When the people turned from God, they suffered (e.g., Judges 2). The kings who sought the Lord, such as Hezekiah (2 Kings 18:7–8), were blessed, and punishment followed those who did not, such as Manasseh (2 Kings 24:3–4). In 1–2 Chronicles, especially, the author explicitly makes the connections between sin and punishment: see the accounts of Saul's death (1 Chron. 10:13) and Uzziah's leprosy (2 Chron. 26:16–23). As in Deuteronomy, the focus of these books is not so much on the individual person as on the moral condition of the people as a whole, with the king as their representative.

Distinctives

The largest single literary genre (type) in the Historical Books is prose narrative. Other genres are inserted in the narratives, including poetry (e.g., Judges 5; 1 Sam. 2:1–10; 2 Samuel 22; 1 Chron. 16:8–36), genealogies (e.g., Ruth 4:18–22; 1 Chronicles 1–9), lists (e.g., Joshua 13–21; 2 Sam. 23:8–39; 1 Kings 4:1–19; Ezra 2:1–70; 10:18–44; Nehemiah 11), letters (e.g., Ezra 4:11–22; 5:7–17; 6:2–22), and more. Prose narrative is found elsewhere in the Bible as well, not just in the Historical Books (e.g., all or parts of Genesis, Exodus, Numbers, Isaiah, Jeremiah, Ezekiel, Jonah, and Haggai, as well as the Gospels and Acts).

The historical narratives are presented as straightforward accounts of real events, and they treat miracles in the same narrative fashion as they do everyday events (e.g., the matter-of-fact mixing of the two in the Elijah and Elisha accounts). But narrative texts differ in several respects from poetic or prophetic texts. For example, as a rule, Hebrew narratives are not as selective as poetic texts (cf. the prose account of the Israelites' victory under Deborah in Judges 4 with the more sparse poetic account in Judges 5). Also, poetic texts can be much more figurative than prose texts (cf. Judg. 4:23–24 and 5:4–5, 20 on the Lord's victory; or Judg. 4:21 and 5:26–27 on the death of Sisera). In narrative, often the main story line is contained in the words of the characters, not in the prose narrative "framework" (e.g., Joshua 1 or 1 Samuel 8). Narrative texts are also usually concerned with past events, whereas prophetic texts are much more commonly present- or future-oriented.

Historical narratives are not, however, simply clusters of facts. Their authors used their God-given talents and creativity to tell the stories of real events from certain perspectives and to highlight certain facts and truths. The best way to see this is by comparing parallel accounts in 1–2 Kings and 1–2 Chronicles (in the same way in which one would compare parallel events in the Gospels); the authors of those books often relayed the same event from different, complementary perspectives, the later narrative sometimes borrowing directly from the earlier.

Notes on Critical Scholarship

Critical scholars (i.e., those whose chief concern is the origin and editorial history of the texts) in the past two centuries have provided many helpful insights into the nature, composition, and messages of the Historical Books. This should not surprise us, since all truth is God's truth. However, many critical scholars have also been profoundly skeptical of the Bible's claims, and so their results must be weighed carefully.

For example, one common theory postulates that the books of Deuteronomy through 2 Kings (minus Ruth) were editorially shaped during the exile to explain why Israel and Judah had fallen. This theory helpfully highlights many themes from Deuteronomy that are played out in the Historical Books. However, it can be used to loosen the connection of Deuteronomy with Moses (which the Bible affirms), and it is skeptical about the authorial integrity of most books as they stand today.

Many scholars today also seriously question the historical reliability of almost everything in the Historical Books. The most extreme scholars deny that any of the events described in the Historical Books took place, and they claim that all of the books were written after the exile. Other scholars are less skeptical than that but still deny that many events occurred (e.g., all the miracles, and the events before the time of Solomon). Evangelical scholars have provided helpful responses to such skeptics.

Beyond this, critical scholars have raised important issues related to specific books, which are treated in the study notes for those books. ◀

INTRODUCTION TO

JOSHUA

Author and Title

The book of Joshua is named for its leading character. (For more on Joshua, see note on 1:1.) The book's author, however, is not explicitly mentioned. The Talmud—a collection of ancient writings by rabbis on Jewish law and tradition—ascribes the book, with the exception of the account of Joshua's death, to Joshua himself (*Baba Bathra* 15a). While the book depicts Joshua writing (Josh. 8:32; 24:26), it does not claim he wrote the book. Indeed, the repeated references to something existing "to this day" (see 4:9; 5:9; 6:25; etc.) seem to suggest a significant lapse of time between the events and the book's final form. Also, the narrator in Joshua 10:13 cites what may be an earlier record of Joshua's deeds.

Date

Determining the date of the book of Joshua is difficult because, as with many other OT books, it may have been edited as it became part of the growing corpus of OT texts. Its final editing may well have taken place in the exilic period (post-587 B.C.), but its original composition was likely much earlier. A number of features point to a date of origin in the late second millennium B.C.

Theme

Joshua recounts part two of God's grandest work of redemption in the OT period. In part one (the Pentateuch), under the leadership of Moses, the Lord redeemed his people out of bondage in Egypt and formalized his covenantal love for them at Sinai. Now in part two, under the leadership of Joshua, the Lord as divine Warrior brings his people into the Land of Promise and gives them "rest."

Purpose, Occasion, and Background

From the evidence in the book itself, it appears that the purpose of the book of Joshua was to recount, from a theological perspective, the events surrounding Israel's capture and settlement of the land of Canaan—with particular emphasis on God's faithfulness in fulfilling his promise to the patriarchs, Abraham, Isaac, and Jacob. Such an account would have been relevant to ancient Israel from its earliest arrival in Canaan and to every subsequent generation of God's people to the present day.

Literary background. Joshua comes immediately after the Pentateuch and in many ways completes its story. The theme of the first five books of the Bible is the progressive fulfillment of the "patriarchal promise," made first to Abraham (Gen. 12:1–3) and reiterated to him, his son Isaac (Gen. 26:2–4), and his grandson Jacob (Gen. 28:13–15; etc.). Simply stated, the Lord promised Abraham and his descendants that they would be *blessed* and become a blessing, that they would grow to become a *great nation*, and that they would be given a *land* of their own. In addition, these blessings would be enjoyed in the context of a close *covenant relationship* with God.

By the end of the Pentateuch, Israel has been brought into the blessing of covenant relationship with the Lord and has become a great people. But they remain outside the Land of Promise, on the plains of Moab. Forty years before, the Lord had raised up Moses to lead his people out of bondage in Egypt and to bring them to the land he had promised to Abraham, Isaac, and Jacob (Ex. 3:6–8; 6:2–8). Now, after so many years of wandering, Joshua, the "new Moses" (Josh. 1:1–9), is to lead God's people into the land, take it, and divide it among them as their inheritance from the Lord.

Historical background. (See also Introduction to the Historical Books, pp. 385–387.) The dates of the exodus and the conquest of the Promised Land are interrelated, since the conquest occurred about 40 years after the exodus. Whether the exodus occurred in the fifteenth century (about 1446) or thirteenth century (about 1260) B.C. is a matter of long-standing debate among biblical scholars. (See The Date of the Exodus, p. 33.)

Were the pharaoh of the exodus explicitly named in the biblical text, this problem would be solved, but as was the custom in Egyptian records until about the tenth century B.C., he is simply called "Pharaoh." Deciding the date of the exodus and conquest does not materially affect the interpretation of the book of Joshua. Continuing archaeological work (both excavations and surface surveys) is providing helpful data, but this data requires interpretation and can often be correlated with either date of the conquest.

With regard to the manner in which Israel came to be present in Canaan, several "models" have been suggested. According to the older *conquest* model, associated with W. F. Albright, the text of Joshua describes a rapid and highly destructive conquest. Advocates of this view were convinced that the thirteenth century provided the best archaeological confirmation. Subsequent work undermined Albright's model and its archaeological support. The unfortunate result of the collapse of Albright's conquest model was that many scholars wrongly assumed that the *biblical* testimony to a conquest was also discredited. More careful reading of the biblical text, however, reveals a conquest that is protracted and not necessarily very destructive of property, except in the case of those few cities burned: Jericho, Ai, and Hazor (see note on 11:10–15). Other proposed models of Israel's emergence include the *peaceful infiltration* model (pioneered by A. Alt), the *peasant revolt* model (of G. Mendenhall), and various more recent *endogenous* models (which assume Israel to have emerged from within Canaan, rather than having entered from without).

None of the standard "models" does full justice to the biblical evidence, but each may capture an aspect of the biblical portrayal. Military conquest certainly played a part in Israel's entry into Canaan, and archaeology provides at least some interesting correlations (see notes on 6:5; 11:10–15). Further, archaeological surface surveys indicate a rapid proliferation of small settlements in the central hill country, beginning in the late thirteenth century B.C., whose inhabitants appear to have avoided eating pork. It is tempting to associate these new villages with the settling down of Israelites, perhaps after a longer or shorter period of existence as nomadic herdsmen in Canaan. Peaceful infiltration may have played some part in the settlement; Gibeon came under Israelite control without a fight (ch. 9), as did perhaps Shechem (see note on 8:30–33) and other sites. Revolt and realignment by disaffected Canaanites such as Rahab (ch. 2) almost certainly contributed to Israel's "mixed multitude" (cf. Ex. 12:38), so some degree of "endogenous" origin need not be ruled out.

For background information on the man Joshua, see note on Joshua 1:1.

The Destruction of the Canaanites

The account in Joshua presents the sensitive reader with a deep problem, namely, the apparently wholesale slaughter of the indigenous Canaanite population in order to allow the people of Israel to occupy their land. How did Israel have any right to seize that land? And how can it be God's will for them to spare none of those who resisted them in defense of their own land? Could this be a level of barbarism that God tolerated in the OT but now forbids in the NT?

Certainly people hostile to the Bible decry ancient Israel for its "ethnic cleansing," and many sensitive Christians find this deeply troubling as well. To handle the topic thoroughly would take a longer essay, but the discussion here can guide thoughts for fuller reflection.

One must begin by acknowledging that the questions are legitimate. Christians rightly condemn this kind of behavior in other circumstances, and there is no warrant today for nations to destroy other nations in order to take their land. But there are special features of the command to Israel that both make it unique (and therefore not open to be imitated) and allow it to be seen in a moral light. This command is one reason why Exodus records the call of Moses in such detail (Ex. 3:1–4:17; cf. Num. 12:1–15): Moses is God's unique choice to be the lawgiver for his people, and the commands given through Moses come from God's own mind (cf. Deut. 18:15–20). Believers accept God's appointment of Moses to speak his will. Without this command from God as delivered through Moses, Israel would have had no right to the land.

A second point to clarify is that the Pentateuch sets out laws of warfare, distinguishing between battles fought against cities outside the Promised Land (Deut. 20:10–15) and those fought against cities inside the land (Deut. 20:16–18). It is only the latter case that requires Israel to spare no one ("you shall devote them to complete destruction"); see the notes on Deuteronomy 20:1–20 and 20:16–18. The law appears to be unconditional and implacable. With these clarifications, one can now outline why this command is not an unsolvable "problem."

(1) A fundamental OT conviction is that Yahweh, the God of Israel, is the Creator of all there is, and therefore the owner of all lands. He has the right to distribute territories according to his good and holy will (cf. Ex. 19:5; Ps. 24:1). As the universal Creator, he is also the universal Judge, to whom all people everywhere are accountable: cf. Genesis 6–8 (the flood story affects all kinds of people); Genesis 11:1–9 (the Tower of Babel); Exodus 12:12 (judgment on the gods of Egypt); the prophetic oracles about the nations (see chart, p. 1264). The NT shares this basic conviction: cf. Acts 14:15–16; 17:24–31. This means that God has the ultimate rights over the land of Canaan, and that he has the right to bring the Canaanites to judgment for their moral condition and deeds.

(2) Since all people are sinners, all are rightly subject to God's judgment. The Pentateuch gives a moral rationale for the removal of the Canaanites, seeing it as divine judgment for their iniquities (see note on Gen. 15:13–16; cf. Lev. 18:24–30; Deut. 9:5). This action against these peoples, then, is an expression of God's judgment on them through the agency of Israel. This judgment therefore announces the moral nature of God to the whole world for their instruction (that announcement in all its clarity is itself part of the blessing that Israel is to bring to the whole world). In ways that are not entirely clear, the faithful will participate with God in carrying out the final judgment (1 Cor. 6:2; cf. Ps. 149:6–7), and Israel's bringing of judgment on the Canaanites foreshadows that great responsibility as well (see note on Josh. 6:17).

God's judgment allows no double standard: he did not base his choice of Israel on any merit of theirs (Deut. 7:6–9), and he calls them to embrace his love faithfully. Unfaithfulness will lead to judgment upon Israel itself, whether at the level of the individual (Ex. 22:20) or the whole people (Josh. 7:11–12; Mal. 4:6; cf. Lev. 18:28). This cannot be called "ethnic cleansing," since the treatment is just, regardless of ethnicity.

(3) Further, the Sinai covenant sets Israel up to be a "theocracy," a unique combination of what is now called "church" and "state." Membership in the people is both political and religious, and thus "citizens" are under obligation to be faithful in observing the covenant. Those who carry out egregious violations must be removed (e.g., Deut. 13:5; 17:7; etc.), and if Israel were to allow unrepentant Canaanites to remain in the land, they would drag the whole people down into idolatry, injustice, and evil (e.g., Deut. 7:4; 12:29–31), which, sadly, is just what happened. Christians are not to carry out this kind of warfare, because the people of God are no longer identified with a particular nation-state.

(4) Finally, even though the laws about destroying the Canaanites are stated in an uncompromising and unconditional way (in keeping with the rhetoric of ancient Near Eastern conquest accounts, which allows for this kind of unqualified statement), the way Israel applied those laws apparently made room for some of the Canaanites to surrender and survive, particularly if they professed faith in the one true God (see note on Josh. 2:9 for Rahab and her whole family; see note on 9:1–27 for the Gibeonites; cf. 11:19). This means that the appearance of implacability in these laws is just that, an appearance, and there is an implied allowance for exceptions. This is another point showing that, strictly speaking, the command given to Israel is nothing like "ethnic cleansing," since ethnicity itself is not the reason for the action.

These factors—God's right to allocate land and judge the world with perfect justice; the need to protect the purity of the Israelite theocracy; and the provisions for even Canaanites to be saved—all illustrate the justice that lies behind these provisions. At the same time, it is also clear that the practices known as genocide and ethnic cleansing are indeed evil, and the Israelites were not commanded to commit them. These factors were a unique part of Israel's mission; no people today have any right to use them as a warrant to support injustice.

Key Themes

The book of Joshua is fascinating not only in respect to literary and historical questions but perhaps especially in regard to several theological topics: land, leadership, the Book of the Law, covenant, Yahweh's war (Hb. *kherem*), judgment and mercy, divine sovereignty and human responsibility, promised rest, God's faithfulness and his people's response, and so forth. The theological lessons to glean from the pages of Joshua are many:

1. The Lord's abiding presence as the key to strength and courage (e.g., 1:5, 9).
2. The centrality of the Lord's instructions for succeeding in one's mission and acting with insight; land and rest as divine gifts (1:7–8).
3. The ability of the Lord to save the "outsider" (Rahab), and the danger of the "insider" falling away (Achan; see chs. 2 and 7).

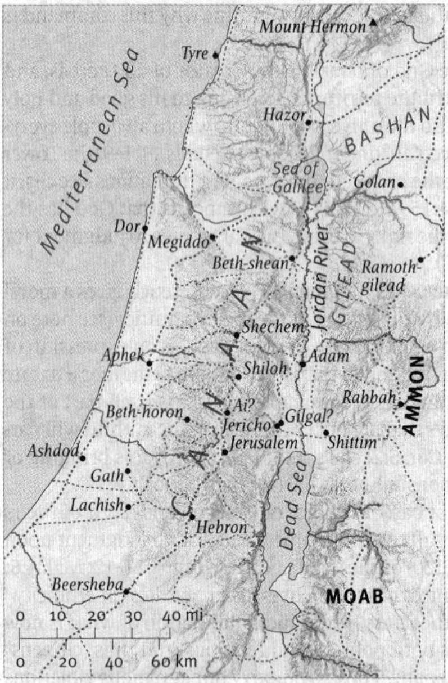

The Setting of Joshua
c. 1406/1220 B.C.

The book of Joshua recounts the Israelite conquest of the land of Canaan under the command of Joshua. The book opens at Shittim with Joshua's commission from the Lord as the leader of the Israelites, progresses through his victories over the Canaanite kings and the allotment of the land, and ends with Joshua's charge to the people to remain faithful to the Lord.

4. The Lord as divine Warrior and the reality of judgment when iniquity is full (e.g., 10:42; 11:19–20).
5. The danger of presumption and failure to inquire of the Lord (e.g., 9:14).
6. The Lord as protector of the covenant (e.g., 10:1–15, esp. v. 11).
7. The unity of the people of God (18:1–10; 22:34).
8. The sovereignty of God in giving his people place and rest (1:13; 11:23; 21:43–45).
9. The faithfulness of God in fulfilling all his good promises (1:2; 21:43–45).
10. The necessity of removing false gods and worshiping God alone (ch. 24).

The list could continue. Given the virtual identity of the names Joshua and Jesus (both are rendered "Jesus" [Gk. *'Iēsous*] in the Gk. of the Septuagint and the NT), and in light of passages such as Hebrews 4:8–11, it is not surprising that the leader Joshua has been interpreted as a "type" of Christ.

History of Salvation Summary

The story of Joshua continues on from the Pentateuch, as God uses Joshua's leadership of his people to give them what he had promised to the patriarchs. In such circumstances, there is even (in a limited way) blessing coming to Gentiles. In order to flourish and to fulfill their calling, the people of God require faithful leadership and faithful members. In Joshua, this mostly does happen (with a notable lapse, 9:14). The book closes with the people pledging continued faithfulness. The story of Israel after this time shows that their heirs did not remain faithful to this pledge, and the book warns all subsequent generations that each of them must renew this commitment. (For an explanation of the "History of Salvation," see the Overview of the Bible, pp. 23–26. See also History of Salvation in the Old Testament: Preparing the Way for Christ, pp. 2635–2661.)

Literary Features

In the Hebrew canon, the book of Joshua is included (along with Judges, 1–2 Samuel, and 1–2 Kings) in the "Former Prophets." In English Bibles, these same books are often called the "Historical Books." Both designations are apt. The book of Joshua qualifies as historiography (history writing), but it is not like the ostensibly disinterested, largely political histories that modern secular historians write. It is, rather, a didactic history written from a prophetic (that is, theological) point of view.

Multiple genres converge in the book of Joshua. The overall format is narrative or story. The specific type of story is epic—the story of a nation engaged in matters of state, including warfare. A feature of epics is the inclusion of epic catalogs (lists), and in the book of Joshua they are so extensive that the book becomes a historical chronicle in addition to an epic story.

To read the book of Joshua in keeping with its literary purpose, one needs to place oneself in the narrative world of the text. Readers need to imagine themselves present at the events, and take the literal, physical details seriously. They need to relish the suspense, the danger, and the plot conflicts that the storyteller puts forward. An *epic* presents heightened images of good and evil, and all the more so with the implied holy war motif encountered in the OT. Along with the images of good and evil, there are images of heroism to admire and emulate. Finally, the reader should look not only *at* the world of the story and its characters but *through* that world to life as it is now. Having relived the events in the story, one must ponder the recognizable human experiences and the underlying principles, especially in leadership, community, and spiritual warfare.

Outline

The book of Joshua divides logically in the middle, with the first half focusing on Israel's conquest of the land of Canaan and the second half on the distribution of the conquered territories among the Israelite tribes. Better, however, is an analysis of the book as four sections, each characterized by a key Hebrew word. The sound similarities between the Hebrew words yield the following pattern:

'abar Cross the Jordan into the land (chs. 1–5)
laqakh Take the land (chs. 6–12)
khalaq Divide the land (chs. 13–21)
'abad Serve the Lord in the land (chs. 22–24)

I. Crossing into the Land (1:1–5:15)
- A. Joshua's charge (1:1–18)
- B. Joshua, the spies, and Rahab (2:1–24)
- C. Crossing the Jordan (3:1–4:24)
- D. Ritual renewal and divine encounter (5:1–15)

II. Taking the Land (6:1–12:24)
- A. Jericho's fall: firstfruits of war (6:1–27)
- B. Israel's failure: Achan's sin; corporate guilt (7:1–26)
- C. Israel's renewal: Ai's defeat (8:1–35)
- D. Israel's Canaanite covenant: the Gibeonite ruse (9:1–27)
- E. Defense of Gibeon, conquest of the south (10:1–43)
- F. Conquest of the north and a list of defeated kings (11:1–12:24)

III. Dividing the Land (13:1–21:45)
- A. It's yours, now take it! (13:1–33)
- B. Western territories (14:1–19:51)
- C. A land of justice and worship (20:1–21:45)

IV. Serving the Lord in the Land (22:1–24:33)
- A. One nation, under God (22:1–34)
- B. Joshua's charge to Israel's leaders (23:1–16)
- C. Covenant renewal at Shechem (24:1–33)

JOSHUA

God Commissions Joshua

1 After the death of Moses the [a]servant of the LORD, the LORD said to Joshua the son
of Nun, Moses' [b]assistant, 2 "Moses my servant is dead. Now therefore arise, go over
this Jordan, you and all this people, into the land that I am giving to them, to the people
of Israel. 3 [c]Every place that the sole of your foot will tread upon I have given to you, just
as I promised to Moses. 4 [d]From the wilderness and this Lebanon as far as the great river,
the river Euphrates, all the land of the Hittites to the Great Sea toward the going down of
the sun shall be your territory. 5 [e]No man shall be able to stand before you all the days of

Chapter 1
1 [a]ver. 13, 15; Ex. 14:31; Num. 12:7; Deut. 34:5
[b]Deut. 1:38; [Ex. 24:13]
3 [c]Deut. 11:24; [ch. 14:9]
4 [d]Gen. 15:18; Ex. 23:31; See Num. 34:3-12
5 [e]Deut. 7:24

1:1–5:15 *Crossing into the Land.* The Lord speaks first in the book of Joshua. His first initiative is to pass the mantle of leadership from Moses to Joshua, who has been groomed for this very task (see Deut. 31:1–8). Joshua is to lead the people to their inheritance in the Land of Promise, but first barriers must be crossed and relationships restored.

1:1–18 *Joshua's Charge.* The first chapter of Joshua divides into three sections and consists largely of speeches. The first section (vv. 1–9) contains the Lord's words to Joshua, charging him to assume the leadership position opened up by Moses' death. The second section (vv. 10–15) recounts Joshua's initial response, charging the "officers of the people" and the Transjordanian tribes to prepare to cross the Jordan into Canaan. The final section records the people's resolve to follow Joshua as they had followed Moses (vv. 16–18).

1:1 After the death of Moses. While beginning a book with a death notice may strike a modern reader as odd, this notice effectively links the book of Joshua to the preceding "five books of Moses" (the Pentateuch), the last of which ends with a description of Moses' death (Deuteronomy 34). In similar fashion, the book of Joshua will end and the book of Judges will begin with references to the death of Joshua (Josh. 24:29; Judg. 1:1; 2:8). These notices link the books together in a continuous chain and suggest the continuity of the Lord's dealing with his people Israel through key leaders. Moreover, just as Moses is called the **servant of the LORD** here (also Josh. 1:7, 13, 15; 8:31, 33; 11:12; 12:6; 13:8; 14:7; 18:7; 22:2, 4, 5) and in the record of his death (Deut. 34:5), **Joshua** will receive the same title of honor at the end of his life (Josh. 24:29; Judg. 2:8). That the **son of Nun** was an Ephraimite is clear from Num. 13:8, but little else is known of Nun. Joshua himself is mentioned some 30 times in the Pentateuch, three times under his original name Hoshea ("salvation") and the remainder under the name Joshua ("Yahweh saves"), given him by Moses in Num. 13:16. His first appearance is as a military commander, fighting the malevolent Amalekites shortly after Israel's exodus from Egypt while Moses sat atop a nearby hill with his hands lifted toward heaven (Ex. 17:8–13). The Amalekite battle not only tested Joshua's military mettle but also underscored a fundamental principle with respect to Israel's wars—namely, that the battle is the Lord's (cf. 1 Sam. 17:47).

That the Lord should explicitly instruct Moses to record the Amalekite battle in a book and "recite it in the ears of Joshua" (Ex. 17:14) anticipates Joshua's future importance. As **Moses' assistant**, Joshua accompanied him at least partway up Mount Sinai (Ex. 24:13; 32:17), and he also assisted Moses at the tent of meeting, where the Lord would "speak to Moses face to face" (Ex. 33:11). Joshua was among the 12 men sent to explore the land of Canaan (Num. 13:8). He alone joined Caleb in exhorting the people to trust God for victory (Num. 14:6–9)—an act of faith for which only he and Caleb, among their generation, were allowed to enter the Promised Land. More than a mere assistant, Joshua was prepared by these and other experiences to become Moses' successor. Near the time of his death, when Moses requested that a successor be appointed, the Lord instructed him to commission Joshua the son of Nun, "a man in whom is the Spirit," before "all the congregation" (Num. 27:18–19). Joshua was to be the one to lead Israel into the Promised Land (Deut. 1:38; 3:28; 31:23) and to apportion it among the tribes (Num. 34:17). As the book of Joshua opens, Moses has died and the time has finally come for Joshua—"full of the spirit of wisdom, for Moses had laid his hands on him" (Deut. 34:9)—to take the lead.

1:2 the land that I am giving to them. The "patriarchal promise," first uttered to Abraham (Gen. 12:1–3), entailed three key elements: *progeny* (Abraham's descendants would become a great nation), *blessing* (Abraham's descendants would enjoy the blessings of living in covenant relationship with Yahweh—and were in turn to be a blessing to the nations), and *land* (Gen. 12:1, 5–7; 15:18). The Pentateuch ends with the first two elements beginning to be realized, but with Abraham's descendants still on the plains of Moab, east of the Jordan River, outside the Land of Promise (Num. 22:1; Deut. 34:8). The dominant theme of the book of Joshua is the Lord's faithfulness in fulfilling all his "good promises" (Josh. 21:45), especially the third element—the promise of land, which he "swore to their fathers to give them" (1:6; 21:43). Scores of references to the Lord *giving* the land appear throughout the book, eight in ch. 1 alone.

1:3 Every place that the sole of your foot will tread upon I have given to you. The fact that the Lord is sovereignly giving Israel the land does not negate their responsibility to step out in faith and take what is given (cf. vv. 9, 18).

1:4 The Land of Promise is to stretch from the **wilderness** in the south to **Lebanon** in the north, and from the **river Euphrates** in the (north) east to the **Great Sea** (the Mediterranean) in the west. This broad-brush description recalls Num. 34:1–12, where the Lord provides Moses a more detailed delineation of the boundaries of Israel's "inheritance" in the land of Canaan (see map, p. 320; cf. also Gen. 10:19; 15:18; Num. 13:17–22; Deut. 1:7).

1:5–9 Three times the Lord charges Joshua to **be strong and courageous**, words reminiscent of Joshua's earlier commissioning under Moses (see Deut. 31:6–8, 23). Joshua will need strength and courage to accept his *task* (**you shall cause this people to inherit the land**; Josh. 1:6); to obey the *Torah* (**Book of the Law** [v. 8]; most likely this would have included at least the book of Deuteronomy or portions thereof [see Deut. 31:26, "this law"]); and to resist being *terrified* (**do not be frightened, and do not be dismayed**; Josh. 1:9). Most difficult of all will be the middle responsibility—namely, to make the Lord's instructions (Hb. *Torah*) integral to who he is and what he does (v. 8a), meditating on them constantly so as to do them (v. 8b). Thus the middle exhortation is made emphatic by the addition of

your life. Just [f]as I was with Moses, so [g]I will be with you. [h]I will not leave you or forsake
you. 6 [i]Be strong and courageous, for you shall cause this people to inherit the land that
I swore to their fathers to give them. 7 Only be strong and [j]very courageous, being careful to do according to all the law [k]that Moses my servant commanded you. [l]Do not turn
from it to the right hand or to the left, that you may have good success[1] wherever you go.
8 This Book of the Law shall not depart from your mouth, but [m]you shall meditate on it
day and night, so that you may be careful to do according to all that is written in it. For
then you will make your way prosperous, and then you will have good success. 9 Have I
not commanded you? [n]Be strong and courageous. [o]Do not be frightened, and do not be
dismayed, for the LORD your God is with you wherever you go."

Joshua Assumes Command

10 And Joshua commanded the [p]officers of the people, 11 "Pass through the midst of the
camp and command the people, 'Prepare your provisions, for [q]within three days [r]you are
to pass over this Jordan to go in to take possession of the land that the LORD your God is
giving you to possess.'"

12 And to the Reubenites, the Gadites, and the half-tribe of Manasseh Joshua said,
13 "Remember the word that [s]Moses the servant of the LORD commanded you, saying,
'The LORD your God is providing you a place of rest and will give you this land.' 14 Your
wives, your little ones, and your livestock shall remain in the land that Moses gave you
beyond the Jordan, but all the men of valor among you shall pass over armed before your
brothers and shall help them, 15 [t]until the LORD gives rest to your brothers as he has to you,
and they also take possession of the land that the LORD your God is giving them. [u]Then
you shall return to the land of your possession and shall possess it, the land that Moses
the servant of the LORD gave you beyond the Jordan toward the sunrise."

16 And they answered Joshua, "All that you have commanded us we will do, and wherever
you send us we will go. 17 Just as we obeyed Moses in all things, so we will obey you. Only
may the LORD your God [v]be with you, as he was with Moses! 18 Whoever rebels against
your commandment and disobeys your words, whatever you command him, shall be put
to death. [w]Only be strong and courageous."

[1] Or *may act wisely*

5 [f]ver. 17; Ex. 3:12 [g]ver. 9, 17; ch. 3:7; 6:27; Deut. 31:8, 23 [h]Gen. 28:15; Deut. 31:6, 8; 1 Chr. 28:20; Cited Heb. 13:5
6 [i]ver. 7, 9, 18; Deut. 31:6, 7
7 [j]ch. 23:6 [k]ch. 11:15 [l]Deut. 5:32; 28:14
8 [m]Ps. 1:2; 119:15
9 [n]ver. 6, 7, 18 [o]Deut. 1:29; 7:21; 20:3; 31:6, 8
10 [p]Deut. 16:18
11 [q]ch. 3:2 [r]Deut. 9:1; 11:31
13 [s]See Num. 32:20-28
15 [t]Deut. 3:20 [u]ch. 22:4
17 [v]ver. 5
18 [w]ver. 6, 7, 9

two small words: "*only* be strong and *very* courageous." Given Joshua's leadership responsibilities, this charge to be strong and courageous would be daunting were it not for the framing promises: **I will be with you. I will not leave you or forsake you** (v. 5); and **the LORD your God is with you wherever you go** (v. 9). Fortified by these assurances of the Lord's abiding presence, Joshua is empowered to receive his commission with courage. The Hebrew terminology used in these assurances has nothing to do with worldly wealth or worldly success, but has everything to do with accomplishing one's mission and acting with keen insight in any circumstance that presents itself. Only when one fails to "ask counsel from the LORD" (9:14) is such insight lacking.

1:12 For Moses' instructions to **the Reubenites, the Gadites, and the half-tribe of Manasseh,** see Num. 32:6–7, 16–18, 28; Deut. 3:18–20. "All Israel" was to be involved in the conquest.

Joshua 1:1–9 as a "Table of Contents" for the Rest of the Book

"Table of Contents" Item:	Corresponds To:
"arise, go over this Jordan . . . into the land that I am giving . . . to the people of Israel" (1:2–5)	Israel conquers Canaan (1:10–12:24)
"you shall cause this people to inherit the land" (1:6)	Israel's inheritance distributed (chs. 13–21)
"be strong and very courageous, being careful to do according to all the law . . ." (1:7–9)	Covenant renewal (chs. 22–24)

1:13 Like the OT notion of *shalom* ("peace, well-being"), **rest** (Hb. *nuakh*) suggests freedom from threat, the enjoyment of one's inheritance, security within the borders of the land, and a state of all-around well-being. Rest is typically preceded by work, as in the creation account (Gen. 2:2–3) or in the celebration of the Sabbath (Ex. 20:8–11; Deut. 5:12–15), or even by warfare (Josh. 21:44; 23:1). The author of Hebrews weaves these OT threads together in expectation of a present spiritual and future rest (Hebrews 4) and urges his readers to "strive to enter that rest" (Heb. 4:11).

1:14 Your wives . . . shall remain in the land. Only the men were expected to participate in combat (cf. note on Jer. 50:37).

1:17 as we obeyed Moses . . . so we will obey you. In the ancient Near East, a change of leadership would typically involve a pledge of loyalty to the new leader.

Preparing to Enter Canaan

c. 1406/1220 B.C.

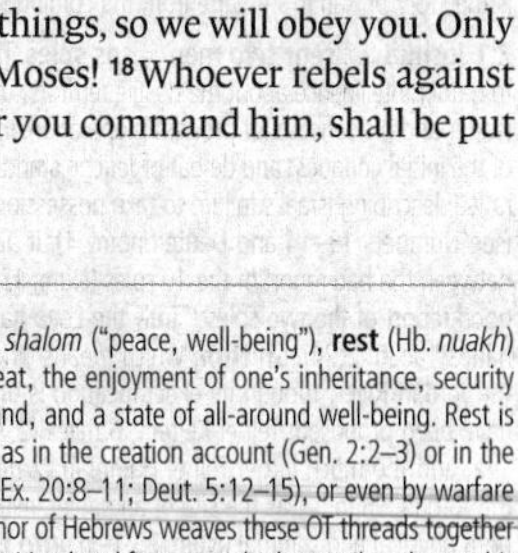

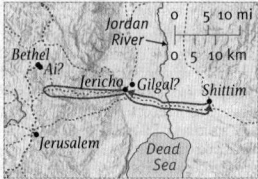

Joshua prepared to enter Canaan by sending two spies from Shittim to scout out the land and the city of Jericho. The spies spent the first night in Jericho at the house of Rahab the prostitute, who hid the men and sent away the soldiers sent by the king of Jericho to capture them. After traveling deeper into the hills and hiding for three days, the spies headed back across the Jordan River to report to Joshua at Shittim.

Rahab Hides the Spies

2 And Joshua the son of Nun [x]sent[1] two men secretly from Shittim as spies, saying, "Go,
view the land, especially Jericho." And they went and came into the house of [y]a prostitute whose name was [z]Rahab and lodged there. 2 And it was told to the king of Jericho,
"Behold, men of Israel have come here tonight to search out the land." 3 Then the king of
Jericho sent to Rahab, saying, "Bring out the men who have come to you, who entered
your house, for they have come to search out all the land." 4 But the woman had taken the
two men and hidden them. And she said, "True, the men came to me, but I did not know
where they were from. 5 And when the gate was about to be closed at dark, the men went
out. I do not know where the men went. Pursue them quickly, for you will overtake them."
6 But she had brought them up to the roof and hid them with the stalks of flax that she
had laid in order on the roof. 7 So the men pursued after them on the way to the Jordan [a]as
far as the fords. And the gate was shut as soon as the pursuers had gone out.
8 Before the men[2] lay down, she came up to them on the roof 9 and said to the men, "I
know that the LORD has given you the land, [b]and that the fear of you has fallen upon us,
and that all the inhabitants of the land [c]melt away before you. 10 For we have heard how
the LORD [d]dried up the water of the Red Sea before you when you came out of Egypt, and
[e]what you did to the two kings of the Amorites who were beyond the Jordan, to [f]Sihon and
Og, whom you devoted to destruction.[3] 11 And [g]as soon as we heard it, [h]our hearts melted,
and there was no spirit left in any man because of you, for [i]the LORD your God, he is God
in the heavens above and on the earth beneath. 12 Now then, please swear to me by the

[1] Or *had sent* [2] Hebrew *they* [3] That is, set apart (devoted) as an offering to the Lord (for destruction)

Chapter 2

1 [x]Num. 25:1 [y]Heb. 11:31; James 2:25 [z]Matt. 1:5
7 [a]Judg. 3:28; 7:24
9 [b]Ex. 15:16; 23:27 [c]ver. 11, 24; Ex. 15:15
10 [d]ch. 4:23; Ex. 14:21 [e]See Num. 21:23-26, 33-35 [f]Ps. 135:11; 136:19, 20
11 [g]Ex. 15:14, 15 [h]ver. 9; ch. 5:1; 7:5; [2 Sam. 17:10; Ps. 22:14; Isa. 13:7; Ezek. 21:7] [i]Deut. 4:39

2:1–24 *Joshua, the Spies, and Rahab.* In ch. 1, Joshua received his charge. In ch. 2, he begins to "take charge." The adventures of the spies provide the central thread around which the chapter is woven. But at least as important is the story of Rahab's escape from the coming judgment.

2:1 Joshua . . . sent two men . . . as spies. The sending of the two spies, to gather intelligence about the hostile territory, underscores Joshua's skill as a leader and his concern for prudent preparation. In the wider context, the story of the initial conquest and defeat of Jericho stands in stark contrast to the narrative describing Israel's failure to take possession of the land 40 years earlier (see Numbers 13–14 and Deuteronomy 1). It also shows the stark contrast between the bad report of the 10 spies (Num. 13:25–33) as compared to the good report of the two spies ("Truly the LORD has given all the land into our hands," Josh. 2:24). **Shittim**, which means "the Acacia trees," was east of the Jordan River, though its exact location is unknown. Two potential sites have been proposed: Tell el-Kefrein, 6 miles (9.7 km) northeast of the Dead Sea, and the much larger Tell el-Hamman, 2 miles (3.2 km) farther east of the Jordan. Shittim was the site of an earlier instance of Israelite prostitution, both physical and spiritual (Num. 25:1–3). **into the house of a prostitute**. The narrative carefully avoids any suggestion of a sexual relation between the spies and **Rahab**. The house most likely was a kind of inn or way station, which would be a logical place to stay and to gather information. Although a prostitute, Rahab was spared judgment by the mercy of God, and she is remembered as one of the ancestors of Christ (Matt. 1:5), for her faith (Heb. 11:31) and for her good works (James 2:25).

2:2 it was told to the king of Jericho. The spies' intent to remain "undercover" was singularly unsuccessful! Canaan at that time consisted of various city-states, each with a central (often walled) city surrounded by villages and farmland and each with its own "king."

2:4 I did not know. Rahab's deceptive response has been alternatively condemned as a lie or defended as justified in the context of (impending) warfare. The narrative, in fact, does not address this ethical issue, and the NT, while commending Rahab for protecting the spies, offers no explicit comment regarding her methods (Heb. 11:31; James 2:25). Similar instances of "deception" are found in Ex. 1:15–21; 1 Sam. 16:2; 1 Kings 22:19–23. Given that this is a descriptive narrative, rather than prescriptive instruction, no general ethical principles can be drawn from her actions. It is also possible, however, to say that Rahab's profession of faith (see Josh. 2:9–14) implies her new allegiance to the Lord and to his people. Thus she helps them in their warfare, and she expresses her new allegiance by protecting the spies with a ruse. (Cf. 8:5–8, where Joshua uses a ruse to win a battle.) Rahab is one of four women mentioned in the genealogy of Jesus in the first chapter of Matthew; the other three are Tamar (Matt. 1:3), Ruth the Moabitess (Matt. 1:5), and the "wife of Uriah" (Matt. 1:6).

2:6 Flax is the plant from which linen is made by a process of alternately drying and soaking the flax fibers. The flat rooftops of houses were convenient places for drying the stalks.

2:7 The **Jordan** River forms a large natural boundary between Transjordan on the east and Cisjordan on the west. As it lacked any bridges in antiquity, the Jordan was generally impassable except by swimming, or it could be waded at shallow areas (or **fords**) under appropriate water conditions. Between the Sea of Galilee in the north and the Dead Sea in the south, there were few places where the Jordan could be crossed. One such place, however, was near Jericho (on Jericho, see note on 6:1–2), and the king's men probably hoped to cut off the fleeing spies at that crossing point. (See map, p. 397.)

2:9 I know that the LORD has given you the land. Rahab shows a remarkable awareness of Israel's history and of the Lord's intention to give Israel the land of Canaan (cf. 1:2). Her confession is filled with the language and theology of the Pentateuch, especially Deuteronomy, and echoes Josh. 1:2. The narration itself does not clarify whether her confession implies spiritual conversion or simply recognition of the supreme power of Israel's God, but her later integration into Israel (6:17, 25) favors a genuine conversion.

2:10 In Genesis 15 the Lord promised Abraham that his descendants would one day inherit the land of Canaan, but not until the iniquity of the **Amorites** was full. Outside the Bible the Amorites are referred to as *Martu* (Sumerian for "westerner") and *Amurru* (Akkadian). They are attested as early as the beginning of the third millennium B.C. Migrating westward and southward into Canaan, they were at their strongest in the middle of the second millennium B.C. and faded quickly thereafter. In biblical parlance, the term "Amorite" is variously used to connote the inhabitants of Canaan generally, and the inhabitants of the hill country specifically. **Sihon and Og** are not mentioned outside the Bible (see Numbers 21; Deuteronomy 3).

2:11 as soon as we heard . . . our hearts melted. Cf. Ex. 15:14–15. On Rahab's apparent faith here, see note on Josh. 2:9.

2:12–14 we will deal kindly and faithfully with you. The response of the spies (v. 14) comes as a surprise, given that Israel was to dispossess and destroy the inhabitants of the land God had promised to Israel (see Num. 33:50–52; Deut. 7:1–2). This underscores the gracious character of the God of Israel and the fact that the boundary between Israel and Canaan was not drawn along ethnic lines but in terms of allegiance to the Lord. It also shows that there was room for exceptions in the general instruction to destroy the Canaanites, for people who came to genuine faith in the God of Israel.

12[j]ver. 18
14[k]Judg. 1:24, 25
15[l]1 Sam. 19:12; Acts 9:25; 2 Cor. 11:33
18[m]ver. 12 [n]ver. 12; ch. 6:23
19[o][Matt. 27:25]
20[p]ver. 14
23[q]ver. 7
24[r]ch. 21:44; Ex. 23:31 [s]ver. 9
Chapter 3
1[t]ch. 2:1
2[u]ch. 1:10, 11

LORD that, as I have dealt kindly with you, you also will deal kindly with my father's house, and [j]give me a sure sign 13 that you will save alive my father and mother, my brothers and sisters, and all who belong to them, and deliver our lives from death." 14 And the men said to her, "Our life for yours even to death! If you do not tell this business of ours, then when the LORD gives us the land [k]we will deal kindly and faithfully with you."

15 Then she [l]let them down by a rope through the window, for her house was built into the city wall, so that she lived in the wall. 16 And she said[1] to them, "Go into the hills, or the pursuers will encounter you, and hide there three days until the pursuers have returned. Then afterward you may go your way." 17 The men said to her, "We will be guiltless with respect to this oath of yours that you have made us swear. 18 [m]Behold, when we come into the land, you shall tie this scarlet cord in the window through which you let us down, [n]and you shall gather into your house your father and mother, your brothers, and all your father's household. 19 Then if anyone goes out of the doors of your house into the street, [o]his blood shall be on his own head, and we shall be guiltless. But if a hand is laid on anyone who is with you in the house, his blood shall be on our head. 20 But if you [p]tell this business of ours, then we shall be guiltless with respect to your oath that you have made us swear." 21 And she said, "According to your words, so be it." Then she sent them away, and they departed. And she tied the scarlet cord in the window.

22 They departed and went into the hills and remained there three days until the pursuers returned, and the pursuers searched all along the way and found nothing. 23 Then the two men returned. They came down from the hills and [q]passed over and came to Joshua the son of Nun, and they told him all that had happened to them. 24 And they said to Joshua, "Truly [r]the LORD has given all the land into our hands. And also, all the inhabitants of the land [s]melt away because of us."

Israel Crosses the Jordan

3 Then Joshua rose early in the morning and they set out [t]from Shittim. And they came to the Jordan, he and all the people of Israel, and lodged there before they passed over. 2 [u]At the end of three days the officers went through the camp 3 and commanded

[1] *Or had said*

2:15 her house was built into the city wall. This interesting architectural note explains how Rahab lowered the spies through a window to the outside of the city. Archaeological exploration at the site of Jericho (for more, see note on 6:5) suggests that the city probably enjoyed a double wall structure, with houses particularly of poorer individuals built between the inner and outer wall. Those houses abutting the outer wall may well have had a window in the wall.

2:18 scarlet cord. The instructions that Rahab should gather and retain her entire family in her house recall the procedure prescribed at the time of the first Passover (Ex. 12:22 and context). The cord's color would enable it to stand out clearly against the wall.

2:24 The spies' report echoes what Rahab herself said (v. 9).

3:1–4:24 *Crossing the Jordan.* Chapters 3 and 4 form a unit, bound together by the common theme of the Jordan crossing (see map to the right). The Hebrew verb meaning "cross (over)" (Hb. *'abar*) occurs more than 20 times in these chapters alone (more than a third of the total occurrences in the book of Joshua). References to God exalting Joshua (3:7; 4:14) also indicate that the chapters are to be read together. The apparently repetitive layout of this material relates to the literary structure: the crossing and its commemoration with memorial stones are first anticipated briefly and then described from various angles, in much the same way that a film director sometimes repeats a significant event first from one angle, then from another. In a historical narrative, even simultaneous events must be described sequentially. The actual historical sequence would have involved (1) the blockage and crossing of the Jordan and then (2) the setting up of memorial stones, taken from the river bed, at Gilgal.

3:1 Shittim. See note on 2:1.

3:2 three days. In 1:11, the officers alerted the people that they would cross over the Jordan "within three days." Now at the end of three days, the officers appear to give more specific instructions. But how does this sequence fit with the fact that the spies who were sent out in ch. 2 found it necessary to hide in the hills for "three days" (2:22) before returning to Joshua (2:24)? One possible solution is that the three-day periods mentioned in 1:11 and 3:2 are distinct, in which case the crossing of the Jordan would have taken place on the seventh day. Another solution is that Joshua had sent the spies prior to his words in 1:11 (see ESV footnote on 2:1, "had sent").

3:3 On the construction of the **ark of the covenant** and its significance as

Israel Enters Canaan

c. 1406/1220 B.C.

After crossing the Jordan River and entering Canaan, the Israelites set up camp at Gilgal. From there they continued to move westward, first destroying the imposing city of Jericho and then defeating the smaller town of Ai. Later the Gibeonites (also called Hivites) deceived the Israelites into signing a peace treaty with them.

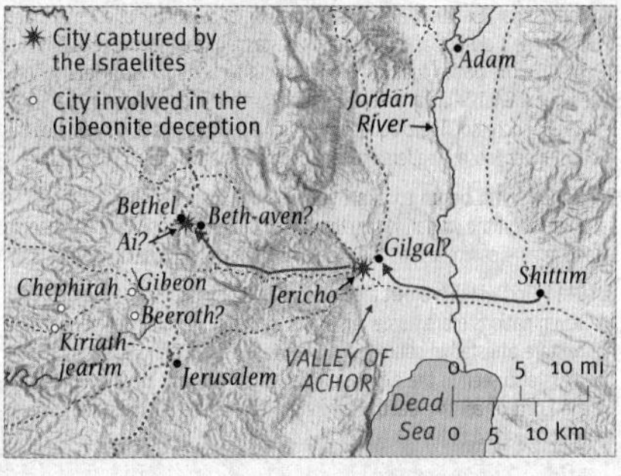

the people, "As soon as you see the ark of the covenant of the LORD your God being carried by [v]the Levitical priests, then you shall set out from your place and follow it. 4 [w]Yet
there shall be a distance between you and it, about 2,000 cubits[1] in length. Do not come
near it, in order that you may know the way you shall go, for you have not passed this
way before." 5 Then Joshua said to the people, [x]"Consecrate yourselves, for tomorrow the
LORD will do wonders among you." 6 And Joshua said to the priests, [y]"Take up the ark of
the covenant and pass on before the people." So they took up the ark of the covenant and
went before the people.

7 The LORD said to Joshua, "Today I will begin to [z]exalt you in the sight of all Israel, that
they may know that, [a]as I was with Moses, so I will be with you. 8 And as for you, command [b]the priests who bear the ark of the covenant, 'When you come to the brink of the
waters of the Jordan, [c]you shall stand still in the Jordan.'" 9 And Joshua said to the people
of Israel, "Come here and listen to the words of the LORD your God." 10 And Joshua said,
"Here is how you shall know that [d]the living God is among you and that he will without
fail [e]drive out from before you the Canaanites, the Hittites, the Hivites, the Perizzites, the
Girgashites, the Amorites, and the Jebusites. 11 Behold, the ark of the covenant of [f]the Lord
of all the earth[2] [g]is passing over before you into the Jordan. 12 Now therefore [h]take twelve
men from the tribes of Israel, [i]from each tribe a man. 13 And [j]when the soles of the feet of
the priests bearing the ark of the LORD, [f]the Lord of all the earth, shall rest in the waters of
the Jordan, the waters of the Jordan shall be cut off from flowing, and the waters coming
down from above shall [k]stand in one heap."

14 So when the people set out from their tents to pass over the Jordan with the priests
bearing [l]the ark of the covenant before the people, 15 and as soon as those bearing the ark
had come as far as the Jordan, and [m]the feet of the priests bearing the ark were dipped
in the brink of the water (now [n]the Jordan overflows all its banks [o]throughout the time
of harvest), 16 the waters coming down from above stood and rose up in a heap very far
away, at Adam, the city that is beside [p]Zarethan, and those flowing down toward the Sea
of [q]the Arabah, [r]the Salt Sea, were completely cut off. And the people passed over opposite
Jericho. 17 Now the priests bearing the ark of the covenant of the LORD stood firmly on dry
ground in the midst of the Jordan, [s]and all Israel was passing over on dry ground until all
the nation finished passing over the Jordan.

3 [v]ver. 8; Deut. 31:9, 25
4 [w][Ex. 19:12]
5 [x]ch. 7:13; Ex. 19:10, 14, 15; Lev. 20:7; Num. 11:18; 1 Sam. 16:5; Joel 2:16
6 [y]Num. 4:15
7 [z]ch. 4:14; 1 Chr. 29:25; 2 Chr. 1:1 [a]ch. 1:5
8 [b]ver. 3 [c]ver. 17
10 [d]Deut. 5:26; 1 Sam. 17:26 [e]Ex. 33:2; Deut. 7:1; Ps. 44:2; [Ex. 13:5]
11 [f]Mic. 4:13; Zech. 4:14; 6:5 [g][Deut. 9:3]
12 [h]ch. 4:2, 4 [i][Num. 13:2]
13 [j]ver. 15, 16 [f][See ver. 11 above] [k]Ps. 114:3; [Ex. 15:8; Ps. 78:13]
14 [l]Acts 7:44, 45
15 [m]ver. 13 [n]1 Chr. 12:15; Jer. 12:5; 49:19; 50:44 [o][ch. 4:18; 5:10, 12]
16 [p]1 Kgs. 4:12; 7:46 [q]See Deut. 1:1 [r]Gen. 14:3; Num. 34:3
17 [s]ch. 4:22; [Ex. 14:29]

[1] A *cubit* was about 18 inches or 45 centimeters [2] Hebrew *the ark of the covenant, the Lord of all the earth*

symbolizing and mediating the Lord's presence, see Ex. 25:10–22. When not accompanying the Israelites into battle or preceding them through the Jordan, the ark was normally kept in the Most Holy Place of the tabernacle (later the temple). As passages such as 1 Samuel 4–6 and 2 Samuel 6 dramatically demonstrate, the ark was not a magical object and was not to be trifled with.

3:4 Two thousand **cubits** is just over half a mile (0.8 km). The explicitly stated reason that the Israelites were to maintain this distance between themselves and the ark is **in order that you may know the way you shall go**. From a distance of half a mile, more people would have been able to see the ark and thus follow its path. The sacrosanct nature of the ark may also have prompted this safe distance, but this is not stated.

3:5 Consecrate yourselves. Compare the Lord's instructions through Moses at Mount Sinai (Ex. 19:10–15). Sanctifying, or "separating," oneself included washing one's clothes and temporarily abstaining from sexual relations (Ex. 19:14–15). The notice that the Lord is about to perform **wonders** (anticipated in Ex. 34:10–11) among the people further underscores Joshua's role as Moses' successor. The plagues visited on the Egyptians at the time of the exodus under Moses' leadership were described as "wonders" (Ex. 3:20).

3:7 Today I will begin to exalt you. Through Joshua's leading the people safely through the Jordan River, the Lord exalts Joshua so that the people "stood in awe of him just as they had stood in awe of Moses" (4:14).

3:10–11 God will **drive out** the seven peoples listed (described in Deut. 7:1 as "seven nations more numerous and mightier than you"; several of these nations are attested in sources outside the Bible). God's presence with his people is also seen in the expression translated **the ark of the covenant of the Lord of all the earth**. The literal Hebrew (see ESV footnote) strongly connects the Lord to his ark (cf. Josh. 3:13).

3:12 take twelve men. Anticipating the Lord's instructions in 4:2, this notice alerts the reader that the 12 chosen men will likely have an important role to play as events unfold.

3:15 At the appropriate dramatic moment, the biblical narrator notifies the reader that the Jordan **overflows all its banks**—caused by spring rains and snowmelt from the Mount Hermon region and the Jordan's headwaters—**throughout the time of harvest**, the grain harvest of March–April. The Jordan's swollen waters would have been considerably more daunting than the river at its normal 3- to 10-foot (0.9- to 3.0-m) depth and 90- to 100-foot (27- to 31-m) width. Crossing such water would be no less miraculous than crossing the Red Sea (see 4:23).

3:16 "Heap" is the same term used in the poetic celebrations of the miraculous crossing of the Red Sea (Ex. 15:8; Ps. 78:13; cf. "dry ground" in Josh. 3:17 with Ex. 14:21). It is particularly appropriate in the present passage, which adds the detail that the "heap" of water was **very far away, at Adam**. This apparently means that the water was stopped as far upriver as Adam, identified with modern Damiya, east of the Jordan and just south of the confluence with the Jabbok River (about 18 miles [29 km] north of the fords of the Jordan). It is a place where mudslides have occasionally completely blocked the Jordan's southward flow, most recently in 1927 for some 20 hours. When the text says that **the waters coming down from above stood and rose up in a heap**, the implication is a supernatural act: either the waters stopped with no visible physical obstruction holding them back, or else a mudslide blocked the river, supernaturally timed to coincide with the priests' dipping their feet in the brink of the water (Josh. 3:15).

3:17 all Israel . . . the nation. Apart from anticipations such as Ex. 19:6, "you shall be to me a kingdom of priests and a holy nation," and the promise

Chapter 4
1 [t]ch. 3:17
2 [u]ch. 3:12
3 [v]Deut. 27:2; [1 Kgs. 18:31] [w]ch. 3:13, 15 [x]ver. 8, 19, 20
6 [y]ver. 21; [Ex. 12:26; 13:14; Deut. 6:20]
7 [z]ch. 3:16 [a]Ex. 12:14; Num. 16:40
9 [b]ver. 3
12 [c]ch. 6:7, 9, 13; Num. 32:20, 21, 27
14 [d]See ch. 3:7
16 [e]Ex. 25:16, 21, 22
18 [f]ch. 3:15

Twelve Memorial Stones from the Jordan

4 When all the nation had finished passing [t]over the Jordan, the LORD said to Joshua,
2 [u]"Take twelve men from the people, from each tribe a man, 3 and command them,
saying, 'Take [v]twelve stones from here out of the midst of the Jordan, from the very place
[w]where the priests' feet stood firmly, and bring them over with you and lay them down
in [x]the place where you lodge tonight.'" 4 Then Joshua called the twelve men from the
people of Israel, whom he had appointed, a man from each tribe. 5 And Joshua said to
them, "Pass on before the ark of the LORD your God into the midst of the Jordan, and
take up each of you a stone upon his shoulder, according to the number of the tribes of
the people of Israel, 6 that this may be a sign among you. [y]When your children ask in time
to come, 'What do those stones mean to you?' 7 then you shall tell them that [z]the waters
of the Jordan were cut off before the ark of the covenant of the LORD. When it passed over
the Jordan, the waters of the Jordan were cut off. So these stones shall be to the people of
Israel [a]a memorial forever."

8 And the people of Israel did just as Joshua commanded and took up twelve stones out
of the midst of the Jordan, according to the number of the tribes of the people of Israel,
just as the LORD told Joshua. And they carried them over with them to the place where
they lodged and laid them down[1] there. 9 And Joshua set up[2] twelve stones in the midst of
the Jordan, [b]in the place where the feet of the priests bearing the ark of the covenant had
stood; and they are there to this day. 10 For the priests bearing the ark stood in the midst
of the Jordan until everything was finished that the LORD commanded Joshua to tell the
people, according to all that Moses had commanded Joshua.

The people passed over in haste. 11 And when all the people had finished passing over,
the ark of the LORD and the priests passed over before the people. 12 The sons of Reuben
and the sons of Gad and the half-tribe of Manasseh [c]passed over armed before the people
of Israel, as Moses had told them. 13 About 40,000 ready for war passed over before the
LORD for battle, to the plains of Jericho. 14 On that day the LORD [d]exalted Joshua in the
sight of all Israel, and they stood in awe of him just as they had stood in awe of Moses,
all the days of his life.

15 And the LORD said to Joshua, 16 "Command the priests bearing [e]the ark of the testimony
to come up out of the Jordan." 17 So Joshua commanded the priests, "Come up out of the
Jordan." 18 And when the priests bearing the ark of the covenant of the LORD came up from
the midst of the Jordan, and the soles of the priests' feet were lifted up on dry ground, the
waters of the Jordan returned to their place and overflowed all its banks, [f]as before.

19 The people came up out of the Jordan on the tenth day of the first month, and they

[1] Or *to rest* [2] Or *Joshua had set up*

---

to Abram that God would make him "a great nation" (Gen. 12:2), Israel is not called a "nation" until now. In Egypt and in the wilderness, Israel was a "people"; now, with their having entered the Promised Land, the term "nation" begins to apply.

4:2 The Lord's instruction that Joshua should **take twelve men . . . from each tribe a man** was apparently already anticipated by Joshua in 3:12 (cf. 4:4, "the twelve men . . . whom he had appointed"). Each of the 12 tribes is represented, which signifies the importance of the Jordan crossing for all Israel.

4:9 Joshua set up twelve stones in the midst of the Jordan. Commentators are divided over whether or not this represents a second group of stones in addition to those set up in Gilgal (vv. 8, 20). A face-value reading of the Hebrew text could suggest a second memorial, but the larger context suggests only one set of stones. Further, some read the Hebrew to the effect that Joshua had already set up 12 stones in the midst of the Jordan. **to this day**. The first occurrence of a phrase that appears frequently in the book of Joshua. The "day" in question is the day either of the biblical narrator or of his source materials (cf. 2 Chron. 5:9).

4:13 plains of Jericho. The troops passed over a broad plain between Jericho and the Jordan River, some 5 miles (8 km) east of Jericho.

4:14 exalted. Cf. 3:7.

4:19 tenth day of the first month. See note on 5:10. **Gilgal** is described as lying **on the east border of Jericho**, thus in its near vicinity. Several site identifications have been considered, but none is yet certain.

Joshua's Leadership Is Established

Transjordan tribes assent to Joshua with same response as to Moses at Sinai.	1:12–18
"The LORD said to Joshua, 'Today I will begin to exalt you in the sight of all Israel, that they may know that, as I was with Moses, so I will be with you.'"	3:7
The promise of 3:7 is fulfilled dramatically at the crossing of the Jordan River.	4:14
Joshua's encounter with the "commander of the LORD's army" was like Moses' encounter at the burning bush.	5:13–15
The Lord was with Joshua, and his fame spread throughout the land.	6:27
Joshua's obedience brings victory in battle.	11:15
"Joshua took the whole land."	11:23

encamped at [g]Gilgal on the east border of Jericho. **20** And [h]those twelve stones, which they
took out of the Jordan, Joshua set up at Gilgal. **21** And he said to the people of Israel, [i]"When
your children ask their fathers in times to come, 'What do these stones mean?' **22** then you
shall let your children know, [j]'Israel passed over this Jordan on dry ground.' **23** For the LORD
your God dried up the waters of the Jordan for you until you passed over, as the LORD your
God did to the Red Sea, [k]which he dried up for us until we passed over, **24** [l]so that all the
peoples of the earth may know that the hand of the LORD is [m]mighty, that you may [n]fear
the LORD your God forever."[1]

The New Generation Circumcised

5 As soon as all the kings of the Amorites who were beyond the Jordan to the west, and
all the kings of the Canaanites [o]who were by the sea, [p]heard that the LORD had dried
up the waters of the Jordan for the people of Israel until they had crossed over, their hearts
[q]melted and [r]there was no longer any spirit in them because of the people of Israel.
2 At that time the LORD said to Joshua, "Make [s]flint knives and circumcise the sons of
Israel a second time." **3** So Joshua made flint knives and circumcised the sons of Israel at
Gibeath-haaraloth.[2] **4** And this is the reason why Joshua circumcised them: [t]all the males
of the people who came out of Egypt, all the men of war, had died in the wilderness on
the way after they had come out of Egypt. **5** Though all the people who came out had
been circumcised, yet all the people who were born on the way in the wilderness after
they had come out of Egypt had not been circumcised. **6** For the people of Israel walked
[u]forty years in the wilderness, until all the nation, the men of war who came out of Egypt,
perished, because they did not obey the voice of the LORD; the LORD [v]swore to them that
he would not let them see the land that the LORD had sworn to their fathers to give to us,
[w]a land flowing with milk and honey. **7** So it was [x]their children, whom he raised up in
their place, that Joshua circumcised. For they were uncircumcised, because they had not
been circumcised on the way.
8 When the circumcising of the whole nation was finished, they remained in their places
in the camp until they were healed. **9** And the LORD said to Joshua, "Today I have rolled

[1] *Or all the days* [2] *Gibeath-haaraloth means the hill of the foreskins*

19 [g]ch. 5:9
20 [h]ver. 3, 9
21 [i]ver. 6
22 [j]ch. 3:17
23 [k]ch. 2:10; Ex. 14:21
24 [l]1 Kgs. 8:42, 43 [m]Deut. 3:24; Ps. 89:13 [n]Ex. 14:31; Deut. 6:2

Chapter 5

1 [o]Num. 13:29 [p]Ex. 15:14 [q]See ch. 2:11 [r]1 Kgs. 10:5
2 [s]Ex. 4:25
4 [t]Num. 14:29; 26:64, 65; Deut. 2:16; Ps. 106:26; 1 Cor. 10:5; Heb. 3:17
6 [u]Num. 14:33; Deut. 1:3; 2:7, 14; 8:4; Ps. 95:10 [v]Num. 14:23; Ps. 95:11; Heb. 3:11 [w]See Ex. 3:8
7 [x]Num. 14:31; Deut. 1:39

4:20 The **twelve stones** that **Joshua set up at Gilgal** represent the first of seven stone memorials described in Joshua (see also 7:26; 8:28–29; 8:32; 10:27; 22:34; 24:26–27). See chart, p. 428. This first one is a reminder of God's faithfulness in bringing Israel safely across the Jordan into the Promised Land.

4:21–23 The narrator so tells the account as to echo Israel's crossing of the **Red Sea**: the God who led Israel out of Egypt has brought them into Canaan and will fulfill his purpose through them (cf. Gen. 12:3). Psalm 114:3 brings together the crossings of the Red Sea and the Jordan.

4:24 The dramatic manner in which the Lord brought Israel into the land was intended to alert the **peoples of the earth** to the fact that the **hand of the LORD is mighty** and to engender true devotion—which is what **fear** of **the LORD** connotes—in the hearts of God's people **forever**, that is, through all the generations that would hear of the river passage.

5:1–15 *Ritual Renewal and Divine Encounter.* With Israel now finally in the Land of Promise, after so many years of living in the desert, the urge to begin the conquest must have been powerful. But Joshua 5 underscores matters of even greater importance. The reinstitution of the covenant sign of circumcision (vv. 2–9) and the celebration of Passover (vv. 10–12) remind God's people of their privileged covenant *relationship* with him (signified by circumcision) and of their *redemption* out of bondage by him (signified by the Passover). These two fundamentally important rites are paralleled in the NT by baptism (the sign of covenant *relationship*; Col. 2:11–12) and the Lord's Supper (celebration of *redemption* from the bondage of sin through the sacrificial death of the Lamb of God; Matt. 26:18–19). Observing circumcision and the Passover at this occasion requires that Israel act by faith: both to trust God for protection while they are vulnerable (Josh. 5:8) and to commit themselves afresh to basing their life in the land on their identity as God's people (i.e., not simply as a political entity). Fittingly, an encounter with the "commander of the army of the LORD" reminds Joshua of his *reliance* on the Lord (vv. 13–15) and, with its militaristic overtones, anticipates the commencement of the conquest in ch. 6.

5:1 Even before Israel did anything to take the land, the Lord went before and demoralized the enemy so that **there was no longer any spirit in them**. This verse is transitional: (1) it completes the account of the Jordan crossing by noting its effects on those whom the Lord would drive out of the land, and (2) it explains how it is possible for Israel to exist unopposed in enemy territory long enough for the events of ch. 5 to take place.

5:2 Make flint knives . . . circumcise . . . a second time. Circumcision was widely practiced in the ancient Near East (see Jer. 9:25–26) but not universally. The Philistines were not circumcised (1 Sam. 14:6), nor, apparently, were some inhabitants of Canaan (Gen. 34:14). Unlike its significance in Egypt, for instance, where circumcision marked a rite of passage, in Israel circumcision was a sign of the covenant instituted by Yahweh in Gen. 17:10–14 and was to be administered to all males when they were eight days old. The need to circumcise the Israelite men under Joshua's command a second time is explained in Josh. 5:4–5, 7. The use of flint knives, even in a time period when metal instruments had been developed, may attest to the antiquity of the practice (cf. Ex. 4:25), or it may have to do with the need for many instruments at one time. Flint, or obsidian, was readily available and was particularly well suited. An Egyptian text, dated to the twenty-third century B.C., speaks of 120 young men being circumcised at one time. The inscription on a similarly dated Egyptian tomb relief depicting circumcision indicates that flint knives were used.

5:6 land flowing with milk and honey. A land particularly suited to agrarian existence, Israel's new home would flow with milk (from goatherding) and honey (perhaps, in addition to naturally occurring bee's honey, also the syrup derived from boiling down figs or grapes). See Ex. 3:17; 13:5; Lev. 20:24; Num. 13:27; Deut. 6:3.

5:9 The name **Gilgal** sounds similar to a Hebrew verb meaning "to roll" (Hb. *galal*) and a noun meaning "wheel" (Hb. *galgal*), and thus is aptly associated

9[y]Gen. 34:14 [z]ch. 4:19
10[a]Ex. 12:6; Num. 9:5
12[b]Ex. 16:35
13[c]Gen. 18:2; 32:24; Acts 1:10; [Ex. 23:20, 23] [d]Num. 22:23, 31
14[e]Gen. 17:3
15[f]Ex. 3:5; Acts 7:33
Chapter 6
2[g]ch. 2:9, 24; Deut. 7:24; Neh. 9:24; [ch. 8:1]

away the [y]reproach of Egypt from you." And so the name of that place is called [z]Gilgal[1]
to this day.

First Passover in Canaan

10 While the people of Israel were encamped at Gilgal, they kept the Passover [a]on the
fourteenth day of the month in the evening on the plains of Jericho. 11 And the day after
the Passover, on that very day, they ate of the produce of the land, unleavened cakes and
parched grain. 12 And [b]the manna ceased the day after they ate of the produce of the land.
And there was no longer manna for the people of Israel, but they ate of the fruit of the
land of Canaan that year.

The Commander of the LORD's Army

13 When Joshua was by Jericho, he lifted up his eyes and looked, and behold, [c]a man
was standing before him [d]with his drawn sword in his hand. And Joshua went to him
and said to him, "Are you for us, or for our adversaries?" 14 And he said, "No; but I am the
commander of the army of the LORD. Now I have come." And Joshua [e]fell on his face to
the earth and worshiped and said to him, "What does my lord say to his servant?" 15 And
the commander of the LORD's army said to Joshua, [f]"Take off your sandals from your feet,
for the place where you are standing is holy." And Joshua did so.

The Fall of Jericho

6 Now Jericho was shut up inside and outside because of the people of Israel. None went
out, and none came in. 2 And the LORD said to Joshua, "See, [g]I have given Jericho into
your hand, with its king and mighty men of valor. 3 You shall march around the city, all

[1] *Gilgal* sounds like the Hebrew for *to roll*

with the Lord having **rolled away the reproach of Egypt**. The "reproach" may have been the aspersions the Egyptians would have cast on Israel had the Lord not succeeded in bringing them into the land (Ex. 32:12; Num. 14:13–16; Deut. 9:28), or it may refer to the reproach represented in the disobedient generation that has now died (see Josh. 5:4–6).

5:10 For the institution of the **Passover**, which celebrated Israel's deliverance from the judgment that befell the Egyptians, see Exodus 12; on the timing of the Passover, see Ex. 12:18; Lev. 23:5; etc. Preparation for the first Passover meal, shortly before Israel's departure from Egypt, took place according to Ex. 12:3 on the tenth day of the first month (Abib or Nisan, overlapping with modern March/April). The notice in Josh. 4:19 that "the people came up out of the Jordan on the tenth day of the first month" suggests a parallel; the transition from wandering in the wilderness to arrival in the land was a kind of "second exodus." In the first exodus, the Passover preceded the crossing of the Red Sea. In this "second exodus," it followed the crossing of the Jordan.

5:12 manna ceased. Cf. Ex. 16:35. Commensurate with their changed status, the people of Israel can now enjoy the **fruit of the land of Canaan**.

5:13–14 Are you for us, or for our adversaries? Joshua's question to the man with the drawn sword is best understood as, "Are you one of ours, or one of our adversaries' [soldiers]?" To this question the **commander of the army of the LORD** rightly answers "**No**," i.e., "Neither" (in other words, not in the sense that Joshua is asking the question, assuming a merely human ally or enemy). Far from suggesting a lack of commitment to his people, the Lord underscores his commitment by marshaling his hosts on their behalf. The expression **with his drawn sword in his hand** appears in Num. 22:23, 31 and 1 Chron. 21:16, where it refers to the angel of the Lord as the agent of God's zeal. The way that Josh. 5:15 (see note there) evokes Ex. 3:5 reinforces this identification and shows that the angel of the Lord is often a manifestation of the Lord himself. The "army of the LORD" is the force God commands when judging (Isa. 13:4) or protecting (1 Kings 22:19). **worshiped**. Or, "bowed down." Joshua knew he was inferior to the commander; possibly he believed he was in God's own presence. Exodus 23:20–33 relates God's promise of his angel to secure Israel's success in conquest.

5:15 Take off your sandals from your feet, for the place where you are standing is holy. Yet another indication of Joshua's status as Moses' successor: Joshua receives the same instructions Moses did at the burning bush (Ex. 3:5).

6:1–12:24 *Taking the Land.* Now that the Israelites are in the land, they must conquer it. Again, the Lord takes the initiative, his first words underscoring the fact that the land is his gift: "I have given Jericho into your hand" (6:2). Nevertheless, this does not annul the importance of God's people acting on his commands. In this section, Joshua and Israel on occasion fail in their faithfulness to the Lord. The Lord nevertheless graciously restores them and fights for them (10:42) until the land is taken.

6:1–27 *Jericho's Fall: Firstfruits of War.* As was often the case in ancient Near Eastern conquest accounts, key early conflicts are recounted in detail, while subsequent conflicts are noted more briefly. As the first city to be taken in Canaan, Jericho was to be wholly dedicated to the Lord, as a kind of symbolic "firstfruits" (cf. Lev. 23:10). The people of Israel were to take no plunder and were to leave no survivors. The chapter may be divided into three sections: the Lord's instructions to Joshua (Josh. 6:1–5); the execution of the Lord's instructions (vv. 6–21); and the aftermath of victory (vv. 22–27). Joshua was "by Jericho" in the last episode of ch. 5, and this has raised the question as to whether the early verses of ch. 6 should be regarded as the continuation of Joshua's encounter with the "commander of the army of the LORD." If this is the case, the Lord's words in vv. 2–5 were given to Joshua during this encounter. This is a possibility, but the evidence in the text does not clearly show whether this suggestion is correct or not.

6:1–2 Jericho is one of the oldest known fortified cities in the ancient Near East, as well as one of the geographically lowest, at about 750 feet (229 m) below sea level. Well supplied with spring water, Jericho was an oasis and was sometimes referred to as the "city of palms" (Judg. 1:16). Throughout its long history of occupation, the actual settled area of Jericho occasionally shifted. OT Jericho is identified with Tell es-Sultan, a mound of about 10 acres. The name "Jericho" (Hb. *yerikho*) sounds like the Hebrew word "moon" (Hb. *yareakh*), leading many to the reasonable assumption that Canaanite Jericho may have been a center of moon worship. If so, then the Lord's destruction of Jericho would have suggested victory over the false gods of Canaan (cf. his humiliation of the gods of Egypt at the time of the exodus; see Ex. 12:12; Num. 33:4). On the archaeology of Jericho, see note on Josh. 6:5.

6:3 march around the city. The remarkable instructions given to Joshua suggest a ritual aspect in the taking of Jericho, which underscores the divine agency while also recalling the divine creation in seven days.

the men of war going around the city once. Thus shall you do for six days. 4 Seven priests
shall bear seven [h]trumpets of [i]rams' horns before the ark. On the seventh day you shall
march around the city seven times, and [j]the priests shall blow the trumpets. 5 And when
they make a long blast with the ram's horn, when you hear the sound of the trumpet,
then all the people shall shout with a great shout, and the wall of the city will fall down
flat,[1] and the people shall go up, everyone straight before him." 6 So Joshua the son of
Nun called the priests and said to them, "Take up the ark of the covenant and let seven
priests bear seven trumpets of rams' horns before the ark of the LORD." 7 And he said to
the people, "Go forward. March around the city and let [k]the armed men pass on before
the ark of the LORD."

8 And just as Joshua had commanded the people, the seven priests bearing the seven
trumpets of rams' horns before the LORD went forward, blowing the trumpets, with the
ark of the covenant of the LORD following them. 9 The armed men were walking before
the priests who were blowing the trumpets, and the [l]rear guard was walking after the ark,
while the trumpets blew continually. 10 But Joshua commanded the people, "You shall not
shout or make your voice heard, neither shall any word go out of your mouth, until the day
I tell you to shout. Then you shall shout." 11 So he caused the ark of the LORD to circle the
city, going about it once. And they came into the camp and spent the night in the camp.

12 Then Joshua rose early in the morning, and [m]the priests took up the ark of the LORD.
13 And the seven priests bearing the seven trumpets of rams' horns before the ark of the

[1] Hebrew *under itself*; also verse 20

4 [h]Judg. 7:16, 22 [i]ver. 5, 6, 8, 13 [j]Num. 10:8
7 [k]ch. 4:12, 13
9 [l]ver. 13; Num. 10:25; Isa. 52:12; 58:8
12 [m]See ch. 3:6

The City of Jericho

Jericho (Tell es-Sultan) is perhaps the oldest city on earth, and it is the lowest city on the surface of the planet (c. 750 feet/229 m below sea level). Jericho has undergone massive excavation work; major digs were led by Ernst Sellin and Carl Watzinger (1907–1909, 1911), John Garstang (1930–1936), and Kathleen Kenyon (1952–1958). Many important finds have been made at the site, one of the most notable being a city wall, some 4.5 feet (1.5 m) wide, attached to a monumental round stone tower. These are some of the earliest fortifications known to mankind. The diagram below portrays some of the remains from the excavations at Jericho from various periods of her history. Thus, the outer city wall comes from the Late Middle Bronze Age (2000–1550 B.C.) whereas the inner city wall dates to the Early Bronze Age (3200–2200 B.C.). Jericho was the first city west of the Jordan captured by the Israelites under the command of Joshua (Joshua 6). Whether or not there exist archaeological remains from that destruction is a hotly debated issue among archaeologists. Following the Israelite destruction, Jericho was abandoned for centuries until a new settlement was established by Hiel the Bethelite in the ninth century B.C. (1 Kings 16:34).

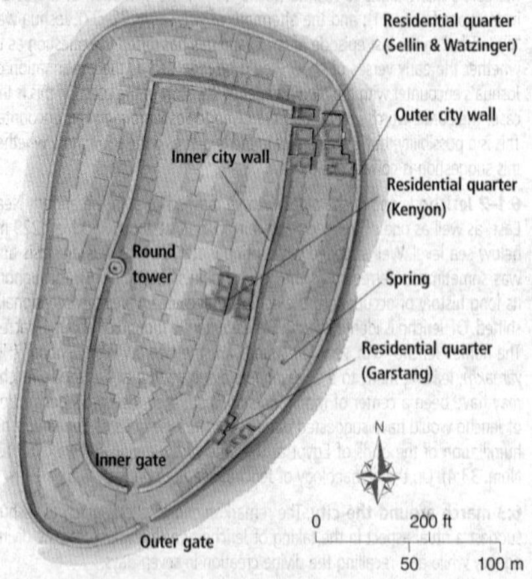

6:4 the ark. The visible symbol of the Lord's presence was at the center of the priestly and military personnel as they walked around the city of Jericho. It emphasizes that the conquest of the land of Canaan was first and foremost the Lord's doing. See also v. 8, where the ark is called the "ark of the covenant of the LORD."

6:5 and the wall of the city will fall down flat. Tell es-Sultan (OT Jericho) has had a long history of archaeological excavation. Many aspects of the site seemed to fit the biblical picture: clear evidence of fallen mud brick walls creating ramparts against the outer reinforcing wall, which could have allowed Israelite soldiers to **go up, everyone straight before him**; evidence of a rapid defeat in springtime; evidence of a lack of plundering; evidence of burning; etc. But the date seemed wrong. The question of dating the ruins of Tell es-Sultan—a site that has, in any case, experienced severe erosion—has recently been reopened. Many historians believe that the fall of Jericho occurred in the thirteenth century B.C. But some analyses of the original excavation reports, including pottery, stratigraphy, scarab data, and carbon 14 testing, have instead concluded that Jericho was destroyed at the end of the Late Bronze period (c. 1400 B.C.).

6:17 devoted to the LORD for destruction. "Devotion to destruction" (Hb. *kherem*) was not an exclusively biblical practice (cf. the Moabite Stone, where in the earliest instance of the name of Israel's God in an inscription, King Mesha speaks of devoting to destruction the city of Nebo, killing 7,000 men and women and dragging the vessels of Yahweh before Chemosh). Though such total destruction may be offensive to modern sensibilities, the Bible insists that the total destruction of Jericho was commanded by the Lord himself (Deut. 20:16–17), and it gives evidence of God's judgment on the terrible sin of the Canaanites. This order to destroy every living thing was not a license to kill indiscriminately in other warfare, because cities outside the Land of Promise were to be treated differently (Deut. 20:10–15). Rather, it was intended to punish the Canaanites (whose iniquity had become complete; cf. Gen. 15:16) and to protect the Israelites from falling into idolatry and apostasy (Deut. 7:1–6). The extermination of the Canaanites was a special case of divine judgment intruding into a period otherwise characterized by common grace; as such, it provides no pattern for general warfare (ancient or modern) but anticipates the final judgment that will befall all who persist in rebellion against God's gracious overtures. See Introduction: The Destruction of the Canaanites.

6:18 Should Israel prove unfaithful in carrying out the order for total destruction, the **camp of Israel** itself will become **a thing for destruction**. Thus, the order (see v. 17) is not an instance of ethnic cleansing but of religious purification. Canaanites such as Rahab (ch. 2) and the Gibeonites (ch. 9),

LORD walked on, and they blew the trumpets continually. And the armed men were walking
before them, and the rear guard was walking after the ark of the LORD, while the trumpets
blew continually. 14 And the second day they marched around the city once, and returned
into the camp. So they did for six days.
15 On the seventh day they rose early, at the dawn of day, and marched around the city in
the same manner seven times. It was only on that day that they marched around the city
seven times. 16 And at the seventh time, when the priests had blown the trumpets, Joshua
said to the people, "Shout, for the LORD has given you the city. 17 And the city and all that is
within it shall be [n]devoted to the LORD for destruction.[1] Only Rahab the prostitute and all
who are with her in her house shall live, because she [o]hid the messengers whom we sent.
18 But you, keep yourselves from the things devoted to destruction, lest when you have
devoted them you take any of the devoted things and make the camp of Israel [p]a thing
for destruction and [q]bring trouble upon it. 19 But all silver and gold, and every vessel of
bronze and iron, are holy to the LORD; they shall go into the treasury of the LORD." 20 So
the people shouted, and the trumpets were blown. As soon as the people heard the sound
of the trumpet, the people shouted a great shout, and [r]the wall fell down flat, so that the
people went up into the city, every man straight before him, and they captured the city.
21 Then they [s]devoted all in the city to destruction, both men and women, young and old,
oxen, sheep, and donkeys, with the edge of the sword.
22 But to the two men who had spied out the land, Joshua said, "Go into the prostitute's
house and bring out from there the woman and all who belong to her, [t]as you swore to
her." 23 So the young men who had been spies went in and brought out Rahab and [u]her
father and mother and brothers and all who belonged to her. And they brought all her
relatives and put them outside the camp of Israel. 24 And they burned the city with fire,
and everything in it. [v]Only the silver and gold, and the vessels of bronze and of iron, they
put into the treasury of the house of the LORD. 25 But Rahab the prostitute and her father's
household and all who belonged to her, Joshua saved alive. And [w]she has lived in Israel to
this day, because she hid the messengers whom Joshua sent to spy out Jericho.
26 Joshua laid an oath on them at that time, saying, [x]"Cursed before the LORD be the
man who rises up and rebuilds this city, Jericho.

"At the cost of his firstborn shall he
lay its foundation,
and at the cost of his youngest son
shall he set up its gates."

27 [y]So the LORD was with Joshua, and [z]his fame was in all the land.

Israel Defeated at Ai

7 But the people of Israel broke faith in regard to the devoted things, for [a]Achan the son
of Carmi, son of Zabdi, son of Zerah, of the tribe of Judah, took some of the devoted
things. And the anger of the LORD burned against the people of Israel.

[1] That is, set apart (devoted) as an offering to the Lord (for destruction); also verses 18, 21

17 [n]Lev. 27:28; Deut. 20:17 [o]ch. 2:4
18 [p][ch. 7:12] [q]ch. 7:25; 1 Chr. 2:7
20 [r]ver. 5; Heb. 11:30
21 [s][Deut. 7:2]
22 [t]ch. 2:14; Heb. 11:31
23 [u]ch. 2:13
24 [v]ver. 19
25 [w][Matt. 1:5]
26 [x][1 Kgs. 16:34]
27 [y]See ch. 1:5 [z]ch. 9:9

Chapter 7

1 [a]ch. 22:20; [1 Chr. 2:6, 7]

who devote themselves to the Lord, are spared, while Israelites who defy the Lord, such as Achan (ch. 7), themselves become *kherem* (i.e., devoted to destruction). Nor was sin a private affair; individual actions could jeopardize the entire camp (cf. 7:1).

6:19 Items that could not be destroyed, such as precious metals, were to **go into the treasury of the LORD**, and in that way be kept separate from common use.

6:20 So the people shouted. Hebrews 11:30 commends the people's faith, for they believed the promise of Josh. 6:2–5, showing their faith by their obedience to the instructions.

6:21 devoted . . . to destruction. See note on 6:17.

6:23 Rahab . . . and all who belonged to her are spared, in keeping with the promise in 2:14, 17–20. Their placement **outside the camp of Israel** is apparently temporary (cf. 6:25) and likely necessitated by ritual uncleanness (Lev. 13:46).

6:26 Joshua's **oath** of curse against anyone who should rebuild the city of Jericho underlines the symbolic significance of the first Canaanite city to fall. Jericho represents God's judgment on Canaan, and the continuing presence of its ruins is to serve as a warning to Israel. Any attempt to rebuild and refortify the city, therefore, will suggest defiance of the Lord's rule. For the fulfillment of Joshua's curse, see 1 Kings 16:34.

7:1–26 *Israel's Failure: Achan's Sin; Corporate Guilt.* The events of chs. 1–6 (with the possible exception of ch. 2) were initiated by divine instruction. Chapter 7 recounts how Joshua launches an attack on the city of Ai, but it makes no mention either of a divine mandate to do so or of any inquiry made to the Lord as to how Israel should proceed. Perhaps Joshua felt overconfident after the remarkable success of Israel's battle against Jericho (ch. 6), or perhaps the implication is that even an apparently easy target is not easy if the Lord is against them.

7:1 After the rousing success of Israel's first victory in Canaan, the opening summary of this chapter has an ominous ring: **But the people of Israel broke faith**. See note on 1 Chron. 2:3–8. While **Achan** is the actual perpetrator, Israel as a *covenant* community is held responsible for the presence of sin

2 Joshua sent men from Jericho to Ai, which is near [b]Beth-aven, east of Bethel, and said
to them, "Go up and spy out the land." And the men went up and spied out Ai. 3 And they
returned to Joshua and said to him, "Do not have all the people go up, but let about two
or three thousand men go up and attack Ai. Do not make the whole people toil up there,
for they are few." 4 So about three thousand men went up there from the people. And
[c]they fled before the men of Ai, 5 and the men of Ai killed about thirty-six of their men
and chased them before the gate as far as Shebarim and struck them at the descent. And
the hearts of the people [d]melted and became as water.
6 Then Joshua [e]tore his clothes and [f]fell to the earth on his face before the ark of the
LORD until the evening, he and the elders of Israel. And they put [g]dust on their heads.
7 And Joshua said, "Alas, O Lord GOD, [h]why have you brought this people over the Jordan
at all, to give us into the hands of the Amorites, to destroy us? Would that we had been
content to dwell beyond the Jordan! 8 O Lord, what can I say, when Israel has turned their
backs before their enemies! 9 For the Canaanites and all the inhabitants of the land will
hear of it and will surround us and [i]cut off our name from the earth. And what will you
do for your great name?"

The Sin of Achan

10 The LORD said to Joshua, "Get up! Why have you fallen on your face? 11 Israel has
sinned; they have [j]transgressed my covenant that I commanded them; they have taken
some of the [k]devoted things; they have stolen and lied and put them among their own
belongings. 12 [l]Therefore the people of Israel cannot stand before their enemies. They [m]turn
their backs before their enemies, because they have become [n]devoted for destruction.[1] I
will be with you no more, unless you destroy [o]the devoted things from among you. 13 Get
up! Consecrate the people and say, [p]'Consecrate yourselves for tomorrow; for thus says
the LORD, God of Israel, "There are devoted things in your midst, O Israel. You cannot
stand before your enemies until you take away the devoted things from among you." 14 In
the morning therefore you shall be brought near [q]by your tribes. And the tribe that the
LORD takes by lot shall come near by clans. And the clan that the LORD takes shall come
near by households. And the household that the LORD takes shall come near man by man.
15 [r]And he who is taken with the devoted things shall be burned with fire, he and all that

[1] That is, set apart (devoted) as an offering to the Lord (for destruction)

2 [b]ch. 18:12; 1 Sam. 13:5; 14:23; Hos. 4:15; 5:8; 10:5
4 [c]Lev. 26:17; Deut. 28:25
5 [d]ch. 2:9, 11
6 [e]Gen. 37:29, 34; Num. 14:6; 2 Sam. 1:11; 13:31 [f]Num. 14:5 [g]1 Sam. 4:12
7 [h]Ex. 5:22; 2 Kgs. 3:10
9 [i]Ps. 83:4
11 [j]ver. 15 [k]ch. 6:17, 18
12 [l]Num. 14:45; Judg. 2:14 [m]ver. 8 [n]ch. 6:18 [o]ver. 11
13 [p]ch. 3:5
14 [q]1 Sam. 10:19
15 [r]1 Sam. 14:38, 39

in its midst. Achan's abuse of the **devoted things** (on which, see notes on Josh. 6:17; 6:18; 6:19) arouses the **anger of the LORD** and leads to Israel's first defeat in the land of Canaan. Despite his fine Israelite pedigree (**of the tribe of Judah**), Achan begins the "Canaanization" of Israel.

7:2–5 For a second time (see 2:1) **Joshua sent men** to **spy out the land** (7:1). But this spying mission proves disastrous. The spies give an optimistic estimate of the challenge of taking Ai, and the cost is the lives of **thirty-six of their men** (v. 5). In a striking reversal of what had earlier been the state of Canaanite morale (2:11; 5:1), now it is the Israelites whose **hearts** have **melted** and become **as water** (7:5). The location of ancient **Ai**, whose name means "ruin," is often assumed to be at Khirbet et-Tell, in the central hill country about 13 miles (21 km) by road west of Jericho and 3,458 feet (1,054 m) higher in elevation. But the specific site identification is disputed, as the stratigraphy of et-Tell does not match important events of biblical history, such as Joshua's campaign against it. It is more likely that Ai was in the same general location but at the modern site of Khirbet el-Maqatir.

7:6–9 After tearing **his clothes** (a sign of distress and mourning; see Gen. 37:29, 34), Joshua speaks to the Lord for the first time in the chapter, raising his urgent complaint and accusing the Lord of bringing **this people over the Jordan . . . to give us into the hands of the Amorites** (Josh. 7:7). Joshua's words carry the further implication that the Lord has reversed his repeated promise (ch. 1) to give both the land and the inhabitants of Canaan into Israel's hands. Joshua's fear that **our name** will be **cut off . . . from the earth** (7:9) hints at a further reversal, namely, of the Lord's promise to Abraham to "make your name great" (Gen. 12:2). If these promises fail, Joshua insists, they will do little **for your great name** (on the issue of Israel's fate and the Lord's reputation, see Num. 14:13–16; Deut. 9:26–29). But Joshua is about to learn that his probing questions are misdirected.

7:10–12 Get up! . . . Israel has sinned. In no uncertain terms, the Lord redirects Joshua's attention to the true reason for Israel's defeat: Israel has **transgressed my covenant**. They have **taken some of the devoted things** (see notes on 6:17; 6:18; 6:19), **stolen**, **lied**, and **put them among their own belongings**—all actions explicitly forbidden in the Law of Moses (Deut. 7:25–26). Adherence to that law was insisted on in the assurances given Joshua in Josh. 1:7–8. The actual perpetrator of these crimes was Achan (7:1). But in addition to the corporate responsibility inherent in a covenant community, there was also the apparent negligence of Joshua and Israel's leaders in failing to seek divine direction for the Ai campaign (cf. 9:14's explicit reference to a similar neglect in the Gibeonite affair). No wonder, then, that **Israel cannot stand before** their **enemies** (cf. 7:13, and contrast 1:5, where the reverse was promised, on condition of Israel's faithfulness to the Lord).

7:13 Consecrate yourselves. See note on 3:5.

7:14 takes by lot. The Hebrew text reads simply "takes," and "by lot" is the likely interpretation as the means by which God indicated his choice (Urim and Thummim being the other possibility; see note on 1 Sam. 14:41–42).

7:15 The offending party, once discovered, is to be **burned with fire**, because one who takes **devoted things** commits an **outrageous** act (an

Positive and Negative Patterns of Holy War

Positive: Jericho (chs. 2–6)	Negative: Ai (7:1–8:29)
An assurance of victory (6:2)	No assurance of victory (until 8:1)
Ritual purity (3:5; 5:2, 10)	Ritual impurity (7:1, 10–26)
Unity of the assembly (6:3–5)	Disunity of the assembly (7:3; 8:1)

he has, because he has [s]transgressed the covenant of the LORD, and because he has done
[t]an outrageous thing in Israel.'"
16 So Joshua rose early in the morning and brought Israel near tribe by tribe, and the
tribe of Judah was taken. 17 And he brought near the clans of Judah, and the clan of the
[u]Zerahites was taken. And he brought near the clan of the Zerahites man by man, and
Zabdi was taken. 18 And he brought near his household man by man, and Achan the son
of Carmi, son of Zabdi, son of Zerah, of the tribe of Judah, was taken. 19 Then Joshua said
to Achan, "My son, [v]give glory to the LORD God of Israel and [w]give praise[1] to him. And
[x]tell me now what you have done; do not hide it from me." 20 And Achan answered Joshua,
"Truly [y]I have sinned against the LORD God of Israel, and this is what I did: 21 when I saw
among the spoil a beautiful cloak from Shinar, and 200 shekels of silver, and a bar of gold
weighing 50 shekels,[2] then I coveted them and took them. And see, they are hidden in the
earth inside my tent, with the silver underneath."
22 So Joshua sent messengers, and they ran to the tent; and behold, it was hidden in his
tent with the silver underneath. 23 And they took them out of the tent and brought them
to Joshua and to all the people of Israel. And they laid them down before the LORD. 24 And
Joshua and all Israel with him took Achan the son of Zerah, and the silver and the cloak
and the bar of gold, and his sons and daughters and his oxen and donkeys and sheep and
his tent and all that he had. And they brought them up to the [z]Valley of Achor. 25 And
Joshua said, "Why did you [a]bring trouble on us? The LORD brings trouble on you today."
And all Israel [b]stoned him with stones. [c]They burned them with fire and stoned them
with stones. 26 And they raised over him [d]a great heap of stones that remains to this day.
Then [e]the LORD turned from his burning anger. Therefore, to this day the name of that
place is called the Valley of Achor.[3]

The Fall of Ai

8 And the LORD said to Joshua, [f]"Do not fear and do not be dismayed. Take all the fighting men with you, and arise, go up to Ai. See, [g]I have given into your hand the king
of Ai, and his people, his city, and his land. 2 And you shall do to Ai and its king as you
did [h]to Jericho and its king. Only [i]its spoil and its livestock you shall take as plunder for
yourselves. Lay an ambush against the city, behind it."

[1] Or *and make confession* [2] A *shekel* was about 2/5 ounce or 11 grams [3] *Achor* means *trouble*

15 [s]ver. 11 [t]Gen. 34:7; Judg. 20:6
17 [u]Num. 26:20
19 [v]1 Sam. 6:5; Jer. 13:16; Mal. 2:2; John 9:24 [w]Num. 5:6, 7; 2 Chr. 30:22; Ezra 10:11; Dan. 9:4 [x]1 Sam. 14:43
20 [y]2 Sam. 12:13
24 [z]ver. 26; ch. 15:7; Isa. 65:10; Hos. 2:15
25 [a]ch. 6:18; 1 Chr. 2:7 [b]Lev. 20:2; 24:14 [c]ch. 22:20
26 [d]ch. 8:29; 2 Sam. 18:17; [Lam. 3:53] [e]Deut. 13:17

Chapter 8

1 [f]ch. 1:9; 10:25; Deut. 1:21; 7:18; 31:8 [g]ch. 2:24; 6:2
2 [h]ch. 6:21 [i]ver. 27; Deut. 20:14

act of willful, sacrilegious folly) and makes himself and **all that he has** liable to the same treatment that the "devoted things" would receive. While it is possible that Achan's family must have known of his offense and thus rightly shared his fate (v. 24), the text does not comment on this. Achan's offense is not a civil infraction (for which he alone might be held responsible; cf. Deut. 24:16), but a religious one that defiled the camp and, most especially, those closest to him.

7:19 Joshua's charge that Achan **give glory to the LORD God** and **give praise to him** is probably to be understood not so much as commanding worship as in preparing Achan to **tell me now what you have done**. The Greek words for "give glory to . . . God" appear in John 9:24, where the Jewish leaders put under oath a man whom Jesus has healed; and the word "praise" (Hb. *todah*) can connote *confession* as well as *praise*.

7:21 The allure of what Achan **saw among the spoil** was not insignificant; the five pounds of silver and a pound and a quarter of gold represent, according to some commentators, about what an average worker would have earned in a lifetime.

7:24–26 Having brought **trouble** on Israel by his covetous act, Achan is put to death and he and **all that he had** are covered under a **great heap of stones** in the **Valley of Achor** (Achor represents Hb. *'akor*, which sounds like the Hb. word for "trouble," *'akar*). The word **them** (vv. 24, 25) presumably includes Achan's children, but there is room for uncertainty here because (1) v. 15 only says "all that he has"; (2) this could be what "them" refers to; and (3) there is no mention of Achan's wife. Seven heaps or piles of stones figure in the Joshua account (see note on 4:20). The first was set up by Joshua in 4:20 as a memorial to the Lord's faithfulness in bringing Israel safely across the Jordan River. This heap of stones over Achan is a reminder of Israel's potential for unfaithfulness and of the dire consequences that result. **all Israel stoned him with stones**. This method of execution appropriately involved the entire community, as the entire community had been defiled and needed to be purified. It also freed any single individual from bearing the weight of acting as sole executioner.

8:1–35 *Israel's Renewal: Ai's Defeat.* The first attempt to defeat the city of Ai (ch. 7) apparently proceeded without divine instruction, leaving Israel in the dark regarding its compromised standing brought about by Achan's disobedience. The resulting defeat was costly, as was the remedy made necessary by Achan's/Israel's offense. The present episode recounts the successful defeat of Ai in response to explicit divine instructions, thus underscoring the importance of adherence to "the word of the LORD" (8:8, 27), followed by a special ceremony near Shechem (vv. 30–35). The passage goes into great detail for a small battle, probably to emphasize that success comes only from following the Lord's instructions.

8:1 Do not be dismayed recalls Joshua's charge in 1:9 and implies the assurance of the Lord's abiding presence. Despite breaking faith (7:1) in the preceding chapter, Israel is now restored and given a second chance.

8:2 its spoil and its livestock you shall take as plunder. God has the right to determine the nature and extent of destruction in any given instance. In Deuteronomy 20, e.g., the prescribed treatment of cities outside the land of Canaan is less severe (Deut. 20:10–15) than that of cities within the land that Israel is to occupy (Deut. 20:16–20). Compare also the total destruction of people and the taking of plunder in Deut. 2:34–35; 3:6–7. Permission to take spoil here is ironic, in view of Joshua 7: if only Achan could have waited! **ambush**. Battles were sometimes won more by deceptive military strategy than by brute military strength, as is attested not only in the Bible but also in ancient Near Eastern, Greek, and Roman sources. Unlike the earlier case of Jericho, the divine instructions for the defeat of Ai depend less, if at all, on

3 So Joshua and all the fighting men arose to go up to Ai. And Joshua chose 30,000 mighty men of valor and sent them out by night. 4 And he commanded them, "Behold, [j]you shall lie in ambush against the city, behind it. Do not go very far from the city, but all of you remain ready. 5 And I and all the people who are with me will approach the city. And when they come out against us [k]just as before, we shall flee before them. 6 And they will come out after us, until we have [l]drawn them away from the city. For they will say, 'They are fleeing from us, just as before.' So we will flee before them. 7 Then you shall rise up from the ambush and seize the city, for the LORD your God will give it into your hand. 8 And as soon as you have taken the city, you shall set the city on fire. You shall do according to the word of the LORD. [m]See, I have commanded you." 9 So Joshua sent them out. And they went to the place of ambush and lay between Bethel and Ai, to the west of Ai, but Joshua spent that night among the people.

10 Joshua arose early in the morning and mustered the people and went up, he and the elders of Israel, before the people to Ai. 11 And [n]all the fighting men who were with him went up and drew near before the city and encamped on the north side of Ai, with a ravine between them and Ai. 12 He took about 5,000 men and set them in ambush between Bethel and Ai, to the west of the city. 13 So they stationed the forces, the main encampment that was north of the city and its rear guard west of the city. But Joshua spent that night in the valley. 14 And as soon as the king of Ai saw this, he and all his people, the men of the city, hurried and went out early to the appointed place[1] toward [o]the Arabah to meet Israel in battle. [p]But he did not know that there was an ambush against him behind the city. 15 And Joshua and all Israel [q]pretended to be beaten before them and fled in the direction of the wilderness. 16 So all the people who were in the city were called together to pursue them, and as they pursued Joshua they [r]were drawn away from the city. 17 Not a man was left in Ai or Bethel who did not go out after Israel. They left the city open and pursued Israel.

18 Then the LORD said to Joshua, [s]"Stretch out the javelin that is in your hand toward Ai, for I will give it into your hand." And Joshua stretched out the javelin that was in his hand toward the city. 19 And the men in the ambush rose quickly out of their place, and as soon as he had stretched out his hand, they ran and entered the city and captured it. And they hurried to set the city on fire. 20 So when the men of Ai looked back, behold, the smoke of the city went up to heaven, and they had no power to flee this way or that, for the people who fled to the wilderness turned back against the pursuers. 21 And when Joshua and all Israel saw that the ambush had captured the city, and that the smoke of the city went up, then they turned back and struck down the men of Ai. 22 And the others came out from the city against them, so they were in the midst of Israel, some on this side, and some on that side. And Israel struck them down, until there was [t]left none that survived or escaped. 23 But the king of Ai they took alive, and brought him near to Joshua.

24 When Israel had finished killing all the inhabitants of Ai in the open wilderness where they pursued them, and all of them to the very last had fallen by the edge of the sword, all Israel returned to Ai and struck it down with the edge of the sword. 25 And all who fell that day, both men and women, were 12,000, all the people of Ai. 26 But Joshua did not draw back his hand with which he [u]stretched out the javelin until he had devoted all the inhabitants of Ai to destruction.[2] 27 Only the livestock and the spoil of that city Israel took as their plunder, according to the word of the LORD that he [v]commanded Joshua. 28 So Joshua burned Ai and made it forever a [w]heap of ruins, as it is to this day. 29 [x]And he hanged the king of Ai on a tree until evening. [y]And at sunset Joshua commanded, and they took his body down from the tree and threw it at the

4 [j]Judg. 20:29]
5 [k]ch. 7:5
6 [l]ver. 16
8 [m]2 Sam. 13:28
11 [n]ver. 5
14 [o]See Deut. 1:1 [p]Judg. 20:34
15 [q]Judg. 20:36
16 [r]ver. 6
18 [s]ver. 26
22 [t]Deut. 7:2
26 [u]ver. 18
27 [v]ver. 2
28 [w]Deut. 13:16
29 [x]ch. 10:26 [y]Deut. 21:23

[1] Hebrew *appointed time* [2] That is, set apart (devoted) as an offering to the Lord (for destruction)

miraculous intervention than on clever strategy. The key in both instances is that the Lord's instructions are to be heeded.

8:3–4 Thirty thousand **men** seems to some commentators to be a remarkably large number to **lie in ambush**. It is possible that the Hebrew word "thousand" should be understood in the alternative sense of "military unit." Further, the 30 "thousands" or "units" may not all have been involved in the ambush (see 8:12).

8:8 In contrast to the first attack on Ai, this time everything is done **according to the word of the LORD** (also v. 27).

8:12 Perhaps the **5,000 men** (or five units) set **in ambush** represent a

entrance of the gate of the city and [z]raised over it a great heap of stones, which stands
there to this day.

Joshua Renews the Covenant

30 At that time Joshua built an altar to the LORD, the God of Israel, [a]on Mount Ebal, **31** just
as Moses the servant of the LORD had commanded the people of Israel, as it is written in
the Book of the Law of Moses, "an altar of uncut stones, upon which no man has wielded
an iron tool." And they offered on it burnt offerings to the LORD and sacrificed peace offerings. **32** And there, in the presence of the people of Israel, he wrote on [b]the stones a copy of
the law of Moses, which he had written. **33** And all Israel, [c]sojourner as well as native born,
with their elders and officers and their judges, stood on opposite sides of the ark before the
Levitical priests [d]who carried the ark of the covenant of the LORD, half of them in front
of Mount Gerizim and half of them in front of Mount Ebal, [e]just as Moses the servant of
the LORD had commanded at the first, to bless the people of Israel. **34** And afterward [f]he
read all the words of the law, [g]the blessing and the curse, according to all that is written
in the Book of the Law. **35** There was not a word of all that Moses commanded that Joshua
did not read before all the assembly of Israel, [h]and the women, and the little ones, and
[i]the sojourners who lived[1] among them.

[1] Or *traveled*

29 [z]ch. 7:26
30 [a]See Ex. 20:24, 25; Deut. 27:4-6
32 [b]Deut. 27:2-4
33 [c]Deut. 31:12 [d]Deut. 31:9, 25 [e]Deut. 11:29; 27:11-13
34 [f]Deut. 31:11; Neh. 8:2, 3; 13:1 [g]Deut. 30:19; See Deut. 28:2-68
35 [h]Deut. 31:12 [i]ver. 33

subset of the force mentioned in vv. 3–4, and the other 25 thousand (or units) constitute the main attack force. If so, this may help to explain why the king of Ai falls for the ruse. Israel appears to be attempting the same direct approach of ch. 7, but with more than eight times as many troops.

8:18–20 Reminiscent of Moses' wielding the "staff of God in [his] hand" in Israel's wilderness battle against the Amalekites (Ex. 17:9) and earlier at the division of the sea (Ex. 14:16), Joshua is instructed by the Lord to **stretch out the javelin that is in your hand toward Ai**. Perhaps serving as a signal to the **men in the ambush** to arise and attack the city, this action more importantly symbolizes the Lord's giving the city into Joshua's **hand**. The stratagem succeeds, the city is set ablaze, and the soldiers of Ai have **no power** (Hb. "hands") **to flee this way or that**.

8:28–29 The defeated city of Ai is left a **heap of ruins**, and its king, after being **hanged** on a tree (see Deut. 21:22–23), is buried beneath a **great heap of stones** (see note on Josh. 4:20). Both "heaps" (different words in Hb.) remain **to this day**—that is, to the time of the text's composition. If the "great heap of stones" over Achan in 7:26 was a monument to Israel's breaking faith, the present "great heap of stones" over the king of Ai is a monument to Israel's second chance and restoration.

8:30–35 For Moses' instructions regarding the event recorded here, see Deut. 27:1–8, with which Joshua carefully complies.

8:30–33 Mount Ebal, along with its counterpart **Mount Gerizim** (see Deut. 11:29), is some 20 miles (32 km) north of Ai, near Shechem, a city with long-standing ties to the ancestors of Israel, beginning with Abraham (Gen. 12:6–7; also Jacob in Gen. 33:18–20; 34:1–31). These associations may help to explain the curious fact that Israel is able to hold a covenant renewal in Shechem, apparently without having to capture it first. Mention of **sojourner as well as native born** among those assembled at Shechem may hint that some Shechemites voluntarily joined Israel (cf. the similar case of a "mixed multitude" exiting Egypt with the Israelites in Ex. 12:38).

8:32 Joshua **wrote on the stones a copy of the law of Moses**, thereby creating a fourth stone monument in the land (see note on 4:20). This monument was to be a reminder of Israel's duty to live in obedience to the divine "Torah," or "instruction" (cf. 1:7–8).

8:34 Included in **the blessing and the curse** sections of Deuteronomy 28 are statements of the Lord's intent to set the people of Israel "high above all the nations of the earth" (or "land," Hb. *'erets*) and to "cause your enemies who rise against you to be defeated before you" (Deut. 28:1, 7). If the Canaanite kings in Joshua's day "heard" (Josh. 9:1) that these and similar words were read during the covenant renewal ceremony at Shechem, this would certainly have contributed to their alarm (see also note on 8:30–35).

The Covenant Is Renewed at Mount Ebal
c. 1406/1220 B.C.
Joshua fulfilled Moses' command to renew the covenant at Shechem by placing copies of the covenant on Mount Ebal and directing the Israelite tribes to shout the blessings and curses of the covenant to each other across the valley separating Mount Ebal and Mount Gerizim (see also Deut. 11:29–30; 27:4–13).

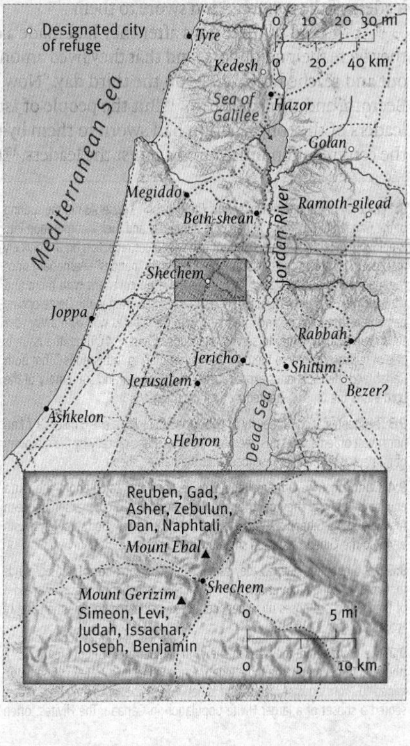

The Gibeonite Deception

9 As soon as all the kings who were beyond the Jordan [j]in the hill country and in the
lowland all along the coast [k]of the Great Sea toward Lebanon, [l]the Hittites, the Amorites,
the Canaanites, the Perizzites, the Hivites, and the Jebusites, heard of this, 2 they gathered
together as one to fight against Joshua and Israel.
3 But when the inhabitants of [m]Gibeon heard what Joshua had done [n]to Jericho and [o]to
Ai, 4 they on their part acted with cunning and went and made ready provisions and took
worn-out sacks for their donkeys, and wineskins, worn-out and torn and mended, 5 with
worn-out, patched sandals on their feet, and worn-out clothes. And all their provisions
were dry and crumbly. 6 And they went to Joshua in [p]the camp at Gilgal and said to him
and to the men of Israel, "We have come from a distant country, so now make a covenant
with us." 7 But the men of Israel said to [q]the Hivites, "Perhaps you live among us; then [r]how
can we make a covenant with you?" 8 They said to Joshua, [s]"We are your servants." And
Joshua said to them, "Who are you? And where do you come from?" 9 They said to him,
[t]"From a very distant country your servants have come, because of the name of the LORD
your God. [u]For we have heard a report of him, and all that he did in Egypt, 10 [v]and all that
he did to the two kings of the Amorites who were beyond the Jordan, to Sihon the king
of Heshbon, and to Og king of Bashan, who lived in [w]Ashtaroth. 11 So our elders and all
the inhabitants of our country said to us, 'Take provisions in your hand for the journey
and go to meet them and say to them, "We are your servants. Come now, make a covenant
with us."' 12 Here is our bread. It was still warm when we took it from our houses as our
food for the journey on the day we set out to come to you, but now, behold, it is dry and
crumbly. 13 These wineskins were new when we filled them, and behold, they have burst.
And these garments and sandals of ours are worn out from the very long journey." 14 So
the men took some of their provisions, but [x]did not ask counsel from the LORD. 15 And
Joshua [y]made peace with them and made a covenant with them, to let them live, and the
leaders of the congregation swore to them.
16 At the end of three days after they had made a covenant with them, they heard that
they were their neighbors [z]and that they lived among them. 17 And the people of Israel set
out and reached their cities on the third day. [a]Now their cities were Gibeon, Chephirah,
Beeroth, and Kiriath-jearim. 18 But the people of Israel did not attack them, because the
leaders of the congregation had sworn to them by the LORD, the God of Israel. Then all
the congregation murmured against the leaders. 19 But all the leaders said to all the con-

Chapter 9
1 [j]Deut. 1:7 [k]Num. 34:6 [l]ch. 3:10; 12:8
3 [m]ch. 10:2, 10, 12; 2 Sam. 21:1, 2; 1 Kgs. 3:4, 5; 9:2 [n]ch. 6:21, 24 [o]ch. 8:26, 28
6 [p]ch. 5:10
7 [q]ch. 11:19 [r]Ex. 23:32; Deut. 7:2; Judg. 2:2
8 [s]ver. 11
9 [t]Deut. 20:15 [u]ch. 2:10; 6:27
10 [v]See Num. 21:21-35 [w]ch. 12:4; Deut. 1:4
14 [x]Num. 27:21
15 [y]ch. 11:19
16 [z]ver. 22
17 [a][ch. 18:25-28; Ezra 2:25]

9:1–27 ***Israel's Canaanite Covenant: The Gibeonite Ruse.*** As did the sparing of the Canaanite prostitute Rahab with her family and their incorporation into Israel (2:1–21; 6:22–25), the present episode forces reflection on the divinely mandated "complete destruction" of the Canaanite "nations"—especially since the mandate explicitly states, "You shall make no covenant with them and show no mercy to them" (Deut. 7:1–2). The rationale given in the Deuteronomy passage is that to spare and intermarry with Canaanites will "turn away your sons from following me, to serve other gods" (Deut. 7:4). Thus, the issue is one of religious loyalty to the true God rather than to "other gods." That both Rahab and the Gibeonites express belief in the power and supremacy of the Lord eases the tension created by their inclusion.

9:3 The identification of the city of **Gibeon** with el-Jib, a site 6 miles (9.7 km) northwest of Jerusalem, has been confirmed archaeologically by the discovery of numerous jar handles inscribed with the name Gibeon.

9:4 Cunning (Hb. *'ormah*) implies cleverness and calculation. The extra emphasis in saying **they on their part** underscores the comparison between Joshua and the Gibeonites—that is, just as Joshua had acted shrewdly to win at Ai, so the Gibeonites acted shrewdly for the sake of their survival.

9:6 The Gibeonites claimed they came from a **distant country** as grounds for Israel's making a **covenant** with them. This deception suggests awareness of the distinction Moses drew between cities inside and outside the Land of Promise (Deut. 20:10–18).

9:7 The **Hivites** are included in the virtually identical lists of Deut. 20:17 (those to be devoted "to complete destruction") and Josh. 9:1–2 (those determined to "fight against Joshua and Israel"). The Gibeonites may have represented a subset of a larger Hivite population in Canaan. The Hivites, often identified as Hurrians, appear to have been of Indo-European origin. The comment **perhaps you live among us** indicates that the **men of Israel** were initially suspicious, but they nevertheless proceed without inquiring of the Lord (v. 14).

9:14 The notice that Israel **did not ask counsel from the LORD** represents a rare instance of explicit commentary by the narrator. While it helps explain how Israel was duped, it also constitutes a serious criticism of Israel's willingness to trust their own surface-level impressions while neglecting the insight that inquiring of the Lord could have offered. What would have happened if the Lord had revealed the Gibeonites' deception to Israel? This, of course, remains an open question—though Gibeon may have been spared on the basis of their acknowledgment of the Lord. Without directly criticizing the Gibeonites, the narrator simply notes that they "acted with cunning" (see note on v. 4) to escape God's judgment. A few verses later, however, the Gibeonites are cursed for their deception (vv. 22–23).

9:18 the leaders . . . had sworn. The right course of action in the case of wrongful or unlawful oaths involving action yet in the future (e.g., Jephthah's unwitting vow to sacrifice his daughter; Judg. 11:30–40) is to repudiate the oath and to seek forgiveness for having made it (cf. Lev. 5:4–6); however, oaths that establish a covenant relationship are of a different order and must be kept (cf. Gen. 26:26–31; 1 Sam. 20:8; 2 Sam. 21:7; Ezek. 16:59–60). The text does not state why **the congregation murmured against the leaders**, but it may have been because the covenant with the Gibeonites prevented the congregation from destroying them, or, perhaps more selfishly, from despoiling them.

20[b][Num. 1:53] [c]2 Sam. 21:2
21[d]ver. 23, 27; Deut. 29:11 [e]ver. 15
22[f]ver. 6, 9 [g]ver. 16
23[h]ver. 21, 27
24[i]Deut. 7:1, 2 [j]Ex. 15:14
27[k]ver. 21, 23; [1 Chr. 9:2; Ezra 2:43; 8:20; Neh. 7:60; 11:3] [l]Deut. 12:5
Chapter 10
1[m]ch. 8:22, 26-29 [n]See ch. 6:21, 24 [o]ch. 9:15
2[p]Deut. 11:25
4[q]ver. 1; ch. 9:15
5[r]ch. 9:2
6[s]ch. 5:10; 9:6
7[t]ch. 8:1, 3
8[u]ch. 11:6; Judg. 4:14 [v]ch. 1:5

gregation, "We have sworn to them by the LORD, the God of Israel, and now we may not
touch them. 20 This we will do to them: let them live, lest [b]wrath be upon us, [c]because of
the oath that we swore to them." 21 And the leaders said to them, "Let them live." So they
became [d]cutters of wood and drawers of water for all the congregation, just as the leaders
[e]had said of them.
22 Joshua summoned them, and he said to them, "Why did you deceive us, saying, [f]'We
are very far from you,' when [g]you dwell among us? 23 Now therefore you are cursed, and
some of you shall never be anything but servants, [h]cutters of wood and drawers of water
for the house of my God." 24 They answered Joshua, "Because it was told to your servants for
a certainty that the LORD your God had [i]commanded his servant Moses to give you all the
land and to destroy all the inhabitants of the land from before you—so [j]we feared greatly
for our lives because of you and did this thing. 25 And now, behold, we are in your hand.
Whatever seems good and right in your sight to do to us, do it." 26 So he did this to them
and delivered them out of the hand of the people of Israel, and they did not kill them. 27 But
Joshua made them that day [k]cutters of wood and drawers of water for the congregation
and for the altar of the LORD, to this day, [l]in the place that he should choose.

The Sun Stands Still

10 As soon as Adoni-zedek, king of Jerusalem, heard how Joshua had captured Ai and
had devoted it to destruction,[1] [m]doing to Ai and its king [n]as he had done to Jericho
and its king, and [o]how the inhabitants of Gibeon had made peace with Israel and were
among them, 2 [p]he[2] feared greatly, because Gibeon was a great city, like one of the royal
cities, and because it was greater than Ai, and all its men were warriors. 3 So Adoni-zedek
king of Jerusalem sent to Hoham king of Hebron, to Piram king of Jarmuth, to Japhia
king of Lachish, and to Debir king of Eglon, saying, 4 "Come up to me and help me, and
let us strike Gibeon. For [q]it has made peace with Joshua and with the people of Israel."
5 Then the five kings of the Amorites, the king of Jerusalem, the king of Hebron, the king
of Jarmuth, the king of Lachish, and the king of Eglon, [r]gathered their forces and went
up with all their armies and encamped against Gibeon and made war against it.
6 And the men of Gibeon sent to Joshua [s]at the camp in Gilgal, saying, "Do not relax your
hand from your servants. Come up to us quickly and save us and help us, for all the kings
of the Amorites who dwell in the hill country are gathered against us." 7 So Joshua went
up from Gilgal, he and [t]all the people of war with him, and all the mighty men of valor.
8 And the LORD said to Joshua, [u]"Do not fear them, for I have given them into your hands.
[v]Not a man of them shall stand before you." 9 So Joshua came upon them suddenly, having

[1] That is, set apart (devoted) as an offering to the Lord (for destruction); also verses 28, 35, 37, 39, 40 [2] One Hebrew manuscript, Vulgate (compare Syriac); most Hebrew manuscripts *they*

9:23 There is an interesting ambiguity in Joshua's words to the Gibeonite deceivers. They are pronounced **cursed**, never to be **anything but servants**. Specifically, they are to be **cutters of wood and drawers of water** (which were menial tasks in ancient societies). Yet, while v. 21 states that these duties are to be carried out "for all the congregation," Joshua assigns the Gibeonites more particularly to **the house of my God** (the summary statement in v. 27 combines both the general and the particular statements). Supplying wood and water for the extensive sacrificial system in Israel would indeed be hard work, but to be closely associated with the house of God should be construed as a blessing (Ps. 84:10).

9:27 in the place that he should choose. Cf. Deut. 12:5. Shiloh appears to have served as Israel's central sanctuary from the time of Joshua (see Josh. 18:1) until the fall of Shiloh on the eve of the monarchy (1 Sam. 4:3; cf. Ps. 78:60; Jer. 7:12). From the time of David and Solomon, Jerusalem served as the central sanctuary (2 Sam. 6:12–14; 1 Kings 9:3).

10:1–43 *Defense of Gibeon, Conquest of the South.* The end of ch. 9 finds Israel in a covenant relationship with a Canaanite city and people! The defection of an important Canaanite city causes alarm among other city leaders, and a coalition is formed. Despite Israel's presumptuousness in not inquiring of the Lord before making a covenant (9:14), once made, the covenant is defended even by the Lord himself. In ch. 10 he decisively intervenes to defend Israel's Canaanite ally. The battle is recounted first briefly in vv. 1–10, while vv. 11–15 provide additional details; vv. 16–27 add yet further details, focusing on the fates of the five kings; and, finally, vv. 28–39 recount the so-called "southern campaign" in which key southern cities are defeated. Because the events of ch. 10 are precipitated by Canaanite aggression, Israel's defeat of the south can be viewed as a defensive operation. The chapter concludes with a summary of the conquest so far (vv. 40–43).

10:1 The name **Adoni-zedek** resembles that of another king of Jerusalem, Melchizedek of Gen. 14:18. The names sound like "lord of righteousness" and "king of righteousness," respectively.

10:2–4 That the Gibeonites had submissively joined in covenant with Israel strikes fear in the heart of Adoni-zedek (and other Canaanites), for **Gibeon was a great city, like one of the royal cities** and **all its men were warriors**. A royal city would have been of sufficient importance to have its own "king" and would likely have controlled a larger district.

10:5 Amorites. See notes on 2:10 and 5:1.

10:8 I have given them into your hands. Whatever questions were raised by Israel's failure to "ask counsel from the LORD" (9:14) before making a covenant with the Gibeonites, the Lord assures Joshua that he will be with him in defending the Gibeonites against the Jerusalem coalition (see map, p. 410). The past tense "have given" is significant: God has decided on the outcome, but Israel must still do some hard fighting (cf. 1:3 and note; 2:9, 24; 6:2, 16; 8:1; 10:19).

10:9 marched up all night from Gilgal. While the precise location of

marched up all night from Gilgal. 10 [w]And the LORD threw them into a panic before Israel,
who[1] struck them with a great blow at Gibeon and chased them by the way of [x]the ascent
of Beth-horon and struck them as far as Azekah and Makkedah. 11 And as they fled before
Israel, while they were [x]going down the ascent of Beth-horon, [y]the LORD threw down large
stones from heaven on them as far as Azekah, and they died. There were more who died
because of the hailstones than the sons of Israel killed with the sword.
12 At that time Joshua spoke to the LORD in the day when the LORD gave the Amorites
over to the sons of Israel, and he said in the sight of Israel,

> [z]"Sun, stand still at Gibeon,
> and moon, in the Valley of Aijalon."
> 13 And the sun stood still, and the moon stopped,
> until the nation took vengeance on their enemies.

Is this not written in the Book of Jashar? The sun stopped in the midst of heaven and did
not hurry to set for about a whole day. 14 [a]There has been no day like it before or since,
when the LORD heeded the voice of a man, for [b]the LORD fought for Israel.
15 So [c]Joshua returned, and all Israel with him, to the camp at Gilgal.

Five Amorite Kings Executed

16 These five kings fled and hid themselves in the cave at [d]Makkedah. 17 And it was told to
Joshua, "The five kings have been found, hidden in the cave at Makkedah." 18 And Joshua
said, "Roll large stones against the mouth of the cave and set men by it to guard them,

[1] *Or and he*

10 [w]Judg. 4:15; 1 Sam. 7:10; Ps. 18:14; Isa. 28:21 [x]ch. 16:3, 5; 18:13, 14; 1 Kgs. 9:17; 1 Chr. 7:24; 2 Chr. 8:5
11 [x][See ver. 10 above] [y][Ps. 18:12-14; Isa. 30:30; Rev. 16:21]
12 [z]Hab. 3:11; [Isa. 28:21]
14 [a]Isa. 38:8; [2 Kgs. 20:11] [b]ver. 42; ch. 23:3, 10
15 [c]ver. 43
16 [d]ver. 10, 28, 29

Gilgal is not known, according to 4:19 it was "on the east border of Jericho." From the vicinity of Jericho in the Jordan Valley to Gibeon in the hill country would have been an uphill journey of 15 miles (24 km).

10:10 The Lord **threw** the Jerusalem coalition **into a panic before Israel**, and the battle spread west to **Beth-horon** and then southwestward **as far as Azekah and Makkedah**, thus covering more than 30 miles (48 km). This military action not only secured a foothold in central Canaan, controlling the major east-west corridor from the Jordan through the central hills to the coast, but also opened the way for Joshua's southern campaign (vv. 29–43).

The Conquest of Canaan: The Southern Campaign

c. 1400 B.C.

Upon hearing that the Gibeonites signed a peace treaty with the Israelites, five Amorite cities attacked Gibeon. Joshua's forces came up from Gilgal to defend the Gibeonites, and they chased the Amorites as far as Azekah and Makkedah. Joshua's forces continued their attack until they had captured Libnah, Lachish, Makkedah, Eglon, Debir, Hebron, and most likely Jarmuth.

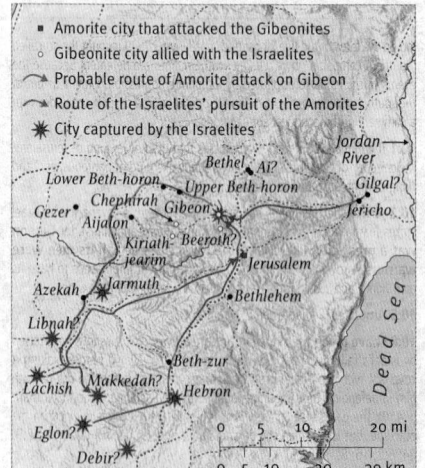

10:11 Large stones from heaven is a picturesque way of referring to the **hailstones** with which the divine Warrior decimated the fleeing Amorite troops.

10:12–14 Sun, stand still. The traditional understanding of this passage is that it refers to a miracle of cosmic proportions, in which the earth ceased rotating for a time. Since the Bible unquestionably teaches that God brought the universe into existence (Genesis 1; Ps. 33:6) and that he owns and rules it all for his own purposes (cf. Ex. 19:5; Deut. 10:14), this certainly would be possible. As alternatives to the traditional understanding, a number of possibilities have been proposed: (1) a solar eclipse (problematic, however, as the sun and moon are described in opposition, not conjunction); (2) poetic imagery (a day that seemed prolonged by virtue of how much was accomplished); (3) a day in which the sun's heat was diminished (perhaps by cloud cover), allowing Israelite troops to continue fighting; and (4) a refraction of light (causing the light to linger until the battle was completed). An additional possibility proposed more recently suggests that (5) Joshua is exploiting the Canaanites' superstitious fear of a bad omen, related to the position of the sun and the moon "standing" on the opposing horizons (the sun "at Gibeon, and the moon in the valley of Aijalon," Josh. 10:12). None of these proposals are without difficulties, however, and each fails to do justice to the claim that **there has been no day like it before or since** (v. 14). Given the miracle-working God of the Bible, the traditional understanding is certainly possible (perhaps cf. 2 Kings 20:9–11, paralleled in Isa. 38:8, where the sun's shadow moves backwards 10 steps). Although there is not enough information in the narrative to determine the precise nature of this exceptional day, the author's emphasis in any case is on the extraordinary answer that God gave to Joshua's prayer, and on the fact that **the LORD heeded the voice of a man** (Josh. 10:14). Apart from the present context, the **Book of Jashar** is mentioned only in 2 Sam. 1:18. No longer extant, the book appears to have contained poetic accounts or songs of the deeds of heroes (Hb. "Jashar" may be related to the Hb. words "sing" or "upright").

10:15 The notice that **Joshua returned . . . to the camp at Gilgal** anticipates the conclusion of the entire southern campaign (cf. v. 43 and the apparent return to the "camp at Makkedah" in the interim, v. 21). Such summary statements, followed by more detailed descriptions, are quite common in Hebrew narratives. On the logical arrangement of ch. 10, see note on vv. 1–43.

19[e][Deut. 25:18]
20[f]ch. 8:24
21[g]Ex. 11:7
25[h]ch. 1:6, 9; See Deut. 31:6-8 [i]Deut. 3:21; 7:19
26[j]ch. 8:29
27[k]Deut. 21:22, 23
28[l]ver. 10, 16, 17 [m]ch. 6:21
29[n]ch. 21:13
30[m][See ver. 28 above]
31[o]ver. 3
33[p]ch. 16:10; Judg. 1:29; See 1 Kgs. 9:15-17
34[q]ver. 3
36[r]ch. 15:13; Judg. 1:10; See ch. 14:13-15
38[s]See ch. 15:15-17; Judg. 1:11-13

19 but do not stay there yourselves. Pursue your enemies; [e]attack their rear guard. Do not
let them enter their cities, for the LORD your God has given them into your hand." **20** When
Joshua and the sons of Israel had finished striking them with a great blow [f]until they were
wiped out, and when the remnant that remained of them had entered into the fortified
cities, **21** then all the people returned safe to Joshua in the camp at Makkedah. [g]Not a man
moved his tongue against any of the people of Israel.

22 Then Joshua said, "Open the mouth of the cave and bring those five kings out to me
from the cave." **23** And they did so, and brought those five kings out to him from the cave,
the king of Jerusalem, the king of Hebron, the king of Jarmuth, the king of Lachish, and the
king of Eglon. **24** And when they brought those kings out to Joshua, Joshua summoned all
the men of Israel and said to the chiefs of the men of war who had gone with him, "Come
near; put your feet on the necks of these kings." Then they came near and put their feet
on their necks. **25** And Joshua said to them, [h]"Do not be afraid or dismayed; be strong and
courageous. [i]For thus the LORD will do to all your enemies against whom you fight." **26** And
afterward Joshua struck them and put them to death, and he hanged them on five trees.
And [j]they hung on the trees until evening. **27** But at the time of the going down of the sun,
Joshua commanded, and [k]they took them down from the trees and threw them into the
cave where they had hidden themselves, and they set large stones against the mouth of
the cave, which remain to this very day.

28 As for [l]Makkedah, Joshua captured it on that day and struck it, and its king, with the
edge of the sword. He devoted to destruction every person in it; he left none remaining.
And he did to the king of Makkedah [m]just as he had done to the king of Jericho.

Conquest of Southern Canaan

29 Then Joshua and all Israel with him passed on from Makkedah to [n]Libnah and fought
against Libnah. **30** And the LORD gave it also and its king into the hand of Israel. And he
struck it with the edge of the sword, and every person in it; he left none remaining in it.
And he did to its king [m]as he had done to the king of Jericho.

31 Then Joshua and all Israel with him passed on from Libnah to [o]Lachish and laid siege
to it and fought against it. **32** And the LORD gave Lachish into the hand of Israel, and he
captured it on the second day and struck it with the edge of the sword, and every person
in it, as he had done to Libnah.

33 Then Horam king of [p]Gezer came up to help Lachish. And Joshua struck him and his
people, until he left none remaining.

34 Then Joshua and all Israel with him passed on from Lachish to [q]Eglon. And they laid
siege to it and fought against it. **35** And they captured it on that day, and struck it with the
edge of the sword. And he devoted every person in it to destruction that day, as he had
done to Lachish.

36 Then Joshua and all Israel with him went up from Eglon to [r]Hebron. And they fought
against it **37** and captured it and struck it with the edge of the sword, and its king and its
towns, and every person in it. He left none remaining, as he had done to Eglon, and devoted
it to destruction and every person in it.

38 Then Joshua and all Israel with him turned back to [s]Debir and fought against it **39** and
he captured it with its king and all its towns. And they struck them with the edge of the
sword and devoted to destruction every person in it; he left none remaining. Just as he had
done to Hebron and to Libnah and its king, so he did to Debir and to its king.

10:21 Not a man moved his tongue. After Israel's decisive defeat of the coalition, no Canaanites dared speak a word against Israel.

10:24 In the ancient Near East, victors would often put their **feet on the necks** of defeated foes, symbolizing supremacy. This action underlies the notion of making one's enemies a footstool under one's feet (Ps. 110:1).

10:25 Joshua applies to the leaders of Israel the assurance God gave him in 1:1–9.

10:26 hanged them on five trees. A sign of curse (Deut. 21:22–23; cf. the treatment of the king of Ai in Josh. 8:28–29).

10:27 The **large stones** set **against the mouth of the cave** containing the bodies of the slain Amorite kings serve as a fifth monument in the land (see note on 4:20 and chart, p. 428). This monument recalls God's gracious action in defending Israel's covenant with a Canaanite city (even though they acted rashly in making it). **to this very day**. See note on 4:9.

10:28–39 Joshua next takes the important towns in the southern part of the land, establishing Israel's hold on it. The accounts for the various towns are similar, reflecting the uniform pattern by which God gave these enemies over to Israel. The variations probably reflect the particularities of each battle. Observe that v. 33 makes no mention of taking **Gezer** (cf. 16:10; Judg. 1:29); it finally became an Israelite possession in 1 Kings 9:15–17, when Pharaoh gave it to Solomon.

[40]So Joshua struck the whole land, the hill country and the Negeb and the lowland
[t]and the slopes, and all their kings. He left none remaining, [u]but devoted to destruction
all that breathed, just as the LORD God of Israel commanded. [41]And Joshua struck them
from [v]Kadesh-barnea as far as Gaza, and all the country of [w]Goshen, as far as Gibeon.
[42]And Joshua captured all these kings and their land at one time, [x]because the LORD God
of Israel fought for Israel. [43][y]Then Joshua returned, and all Israel with him, to the camp
at Gilgal.

Conquests in Northern Canaan

11 When Jabin, king of Hazor, heard of this, he [z]sent to Jobab king of Madon, and to
the king of Shimron, and to the king of Achshaph, [2]and to the kings who were in the
northern hill country, and in the [a]Arabah south of [b]Chinneroth, and in the lowland, and
[c]in Naphoth-dor on the [d]west, [3]to the Canaanites in the east and the west, the Amorites,
the Hittites, the Perizzites, and the [e]Jebusites in the hill country, and the [f]Hivites under
[g]Hermon in the land of [h]Mizpah. [4]And they came out with all their troops, a great horde,
in number [i]like the sand that is on the seashore, with very many horses and chariots.
[5]And all these kings joined their forces and came and encamped together at the waters
of Merom to fight against Israel.
[6]And the LORD said to Joshua, [j]"Do not be afraid of them, for tomorrow at this time I
will give over all of them, slain, to Israel. You shall [k]hamstring their horses and burn their
[l]chariots with fire." [7]So Joshua and all his warriors came [m]suddenly against them by the
waters of Merom and fell upon them. [8]And the LORD gave them into the hand of Israel,
who struck them and chased them as far as [n]Great Sidon and [o]Misrephoth-maim, and

40[t]ch. 12:8 [u]Deut. 20:16, 17
41[v]Deut. 9:23 [w]ch. 11:16
42[x]ver. 14
43[y]ver. 15

Chapter 11

1[z]ch. 10:3
2[a]ch. 3:16; Deut. 1:1 [b]ch. 12:3; 13:27; 19:35; Num. 34:11 [c]ch. 12:23 [d]ch. 17:11; Judg. 1:27
3[e]ch. 15:63 [f]Judg. 3:3 [g]See Deut. 3:8 [h]ver. 8; Gen. 31:49
4[i]Gen. 22:17; 32:12; Judg. 7:12; 1 Sam. 13:5
6[j][ch. 10:8] [k]ver. 9; 2 Sam. 8:4; 1 Chr. 18:4; [Gen. 49:6] [l]ch. 17:16-18; Deut. 20:1; Judg. 1:19; 4:3
7[m]ch. 10:9
8[n]ch. 19:28 [o]ch. 13:6

10:40–42 This interim summary of the conquest credits Joshua, in the typically hyperbolic language of ancient Near Eastern conquest accounts, with leaving **none remaining**, totally destroying **all that breathed**. (Similar language in v. 20 juxtaposes the statement that Israel's enemies were "wiped out" with the admission that a "remnant . . . remained of them.") While Joshua is credited with acting obediently by taking no prisoners, the ultimate cause of Israel's success is that **the LORD God of Israel fought for Israel** (v. 42).

10:43 Joshua's return to **the camp at Gilgal** (anticipated already in v. 15) marks the successful conclusion of the central and southern campaigns.

The Conquest of Canaan: The Northern Campaign

c. 1400 B.C.

After Joshua's forces defeated several Amorite kings in the south, the king of Hazor assembled the northern Canaanite kings to battle the Israelites. Joshua and his men defeated the Canaanites at the waters of Merom and pursued them to Great Sidon and the Valley of Mizpeh. Then Joshua turned back and captured the city of Hazor.

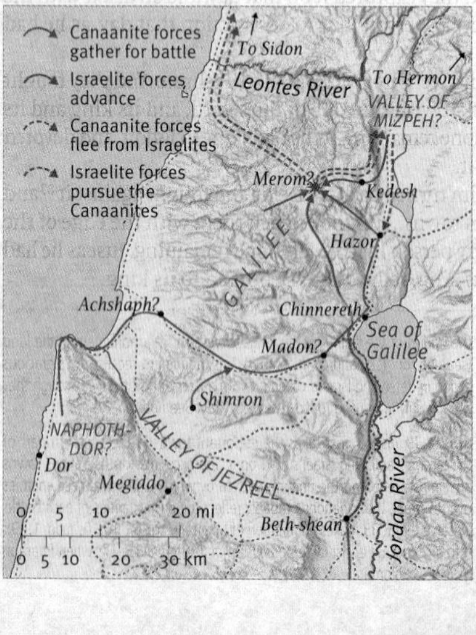

11:1–12:24 *Conquest of the North and a List of Defeated Kings.* Just as the southern campaign was a necessary sequel to Israel's defense of the Gibeonites, the northern campaign takes shape as a defensive measure against the northern kings gathered around Jabin of Hazor (see map to the left). The account gives a terse description of what must have been fierce battles, more like 10:29–43, in contrast to chs. 6 and 8 and 10:1–28. This is probably because 11:6–9 makes the main point. The idea of compliance with God's instructions given through Moses is a recurring theme (cf. 11:9, 12, 15, 20, 23), with 11:19–20 giving the narrator's theological assessment. Chapter 12 lists the kings defeated under the leadership of Moses (12:1–6) and Joshua (12:7–24), bringing the basic conquest narrative to a close.

11:1 Jabin, king of Hazor, is not to be confused with the "Jabin king of Canaan, who reigned in Hazor" during the time of Deborah and Barak (Judg. 4:2). The West Semitic name Jabin, which may mean something like "(he) builds," is attested for rulers of Hazor in the Mari texts (18th century B.C.), the Amarna texts (14th century), etc., often in compound names employing the name of a deity. Thus, "Jabin" may have been a dynastic name especially associated with Hazor. Hazor (Tell el-Qedah)—located about 10 miles (16 km) north of the Sea of Galilee and covering an area of over 200 acres—was probably the largest city in Syria-Palestine in its day. The cities **Shimron** and **Achshaph** are also attested in the Amarna texts and in the itinerary of the Egyptian pharaoh Thutmose III (15th century B.C.).

11:4 The **great horde** mustered by the northern city-kings is described colorfully as **in number like the sand that is on the seashore**. Their **chariots** were of light construction, with four-spoked wheels, and were drawn by two **horses** (contrast the "chariots of iron" of 17:16–18).

11:5 Merom may be another name for Madon (v. 1), commonly identified with Tell Qarnei Hittin, 5 miles (8 km) west of the Sea of Galilee. It is mentioned by both Thutmose III (see note on v. 1) and the Assyrian king Tiglath-pileser III (8th century B.C.).

11:6 In keeping with the biblical prohibition against amassing and placing confidence in military hardware (cf. Deut. 17:16), Joshua is to **hamstring their horses and burn their chariots**. The former would have involved cutting the horses' equivalent of the Achilles tendon, which would at the very least make the animal unfit for any military use (see also 2 Sam. 8:4).

8[p]ver. 3
9[q]ver. 6
10[r][Judg. 4:2]
11[s]ch. 10:40
12[t]Deut. 20:16, 17
15[u]Ex. 34:11, 12 [v]Deut. 7:2 [w]ch. 1:7
16[x]ch. 12:8 [y]ch. 10:41; 15:51 [z]ver. 2 [a]ver. 21
17[b]ch. 12:7 [c]ch. 12:7; 13:5 [d]See ver. 3 [e]ch. 12:7; Deut. 7:24
18[f][ch. 14:7, 10]
19[g]ch. 9:3, 7
20[h]See Ex. 4:21 [i]Deut. 20:16, 17
21[j]ch. 15:13, 14; Num. 13:22, 23; Deut. 1:28
22[k][1 Sam. 17:4]
23[l]See Num. 34:2-12 [m]See ch. 14–19; Num. 26:52-56 [n]ch. 12:7; 18:10

eastward as far as the Valley of [p]Mizpeh. And they struck them until he left none remaining. 9 And Joshua did to them [q]just as the LORD said to him: he hamstrung their horses
and burned their chariots with fire.
10 And Joshua turned back at that time and captured [r]Hazor and struck its king with
the sword, for Hazor formerly was the head of all those kingdoms. 11 And they struck
with the sword all who were in it, devoting them to destruction;[1] [s]there was none left
that breathed. And he burned Hazor with fire. 12 And all the cities of those kings, and all
their kings, Joshua captured, and struck them with the edge of the sword, devoting them
to destruction, [t]just as Moses the servant of the LORD had commanded. 13 But none of the
cities that stood on mounds did Israel burn, except Hazor alone; that Joshua burned. 14 And
all the spoil of these cities and the livestock, the people of Israel took for their plunder.
But every person they struck with the edge of the sword until they had destroyed them,
and they did not leave any who breathed. 15 [u]Just as the LORD had commanded Moses his
servant, [v]so Moses commanded Joshua, [w]and so Joshua did. He left nothing undone of all
that the LORD had commanded Moses.
16 So Joshua took all that land, [x]the hill country and all the Negeb and [y]all the land
of Goshen [z]and the lowland [z]and the Arabah [a]and the hill country of Israel and its
lowland 17 [b]from Mount Halak, which rises toward Seir, as far as [c]Baal-gad in the Valley
of Lebanon below [d]Mount Hermon. And he captured [e]all their kings and struck them
and put them to death. 18 Joshua made war [f]a long time with all those kings. 19 There
was not a city that made peace with the people of Israel except [g]the Hivites, the inhabitants of Gibeon. They took them all in battle. 20 For it was the LORD's doing [h]to harden
their hearts that they should come against Israel in battle, in order that they should be
devoted to destruction and should receive no mercy but be destroyed, [i]just as the LORD
commanded Moses.
21 And Joshua came at that time and cut off [j]the Anakim from the hill country, from
Hebron, from Debir, from Anab, and from all the hill country of Judah, and from all the
hill country of Israel. Joshua devoted them to destruction with their cities. 22 There was
none of the Anakim left in the land of the people of Israel. Only in Gaza, [k]in Gath, and
in Ashdod did some remain. 23 So Joshua took the whole land, [l]according to all that the
LORD had spoken to Moses. [m]And Joshua gave it for an inheritance to Israel [n]according to
their tribal allotments. And the land had rest from war.

[1] That is, setting apart (devoting) as an offering to the Lord (for destruction); also verses 12, 20, 21

11:10–15 That **Hazor** was **head of all those kingdoms** (v. 10) is not surprising, given its size (see note on v. 1) and prominent location beside a major north-south trade route. Having decimated the northern-coalition forces at Merom (vv. 7–9), Joshua **turned back** to Hazor, **struck its king with the sword** (v. 10) along with **all who were in it**, and finally **burned Hazor with fire** (v. 11). Joshua struck the other coalition cities as well, **devoting them to destruction** (v. 12; see Introduction: The Destruction of the Canaanites), but none of these cities was burned **except Hazor alone** (v. 13). Archaeologists looking for physical signs of Israel's conquest must keep in mind that only three sites (Jericho in 6:24, Ai in 8:28, and Hazor) are explicitly said to have been burned. The Israelites were, after all, to live in towns and houses they had not built and to enjoy vineyards and olive groves they had not cultivated (Deut. 6:10–11). The archaeology of Hazor attests several violent destructions by fire, including in c. 1400, 1300, and 1230 B.C.

11:16–20 Not unlike the brief summary of the southern campaign in 10:40–42, the summary following the successful completion of the northern campaign is cast in absolute phrases, describing how **Joshua took all that land**, from the far south to the far north. The regions that were taken are described in 11:16, and v. 17 demarcates the southern and northern boundaries of the entire conquered area. Though some mistakenly assume the conquest under Joshua to have been a blitzkrieg, in fact it took **a long time** (v. 18), perhaps about seven years. This number is calculated from information provided for Caleb, Joshua's fellow spy in Numbers 13–14. Caleb was 40 years old when Moses sent him as a spy (Josh. 14:7). From that time to the entry into the land of Canaan was another 38 years (Deut. 2:14), making Caleb 78 years old at the beginning of the conquest. Caleb receives his allotted territory at age 85 (Josh. 14:10), seven years after the start of the conquest. The political reality that **not a city . . . made peace** except **Gibeon** (11:19) is conjoined without embarrassment with the theological explanation that **it was the LORD's doing to harden their hearts** (v. 20; on the interplay of human responsibility and divine sovereignty, see the long saga of the hardening of Pharaoh's heart recounted in Exodus 4–14, beginning at 4:21).

11:21–22 That Joshua **cut off the Anakim** is highly significant. This race of giants, beside whom the spies under Moses felt like "grasshoppers" (Num. 13:33), terrified 10 of the 12 spies and prompted Israel to shrink back in fear. It is fitting to crown the account of the subjugation phase of the conquest by describing how Joshua has now largely eradicated this frightening threat (see further Josh. 14:6–15).

11:23 This verse begins the transition from the *subjugation* phase of the conquest (**Joshua took the whole land**) to the *allocation/occupation* phase (**Joshua gave it for an inheritance to Israel according to their tribal allotments**). The latter notice anticipates the events of chs. 13–19. **And the land had rest from war**. More fighting remains to be done when the Israelites attempt to occupy the conquered territories, but the Lord has proven true to the promises of 1:3–5, and the land lies subdued before them (cf. 18:1).

Kings Defeated by Moses

12 Now these are the kings of the land whom the people of Israel defeated and took
possession of their land beyond the Jordan toward the sunrise, from [o]the Valley of
the Arnon to Mount Hermon, with all [p]the Arabah eastward: **2** [q]Sihon king of the Amorites
who lived at Heshbon and ruled from Aroer, which is on the edge of the Valley of the
Arnon, and [r]from the middle of the valley as far as the [s]river Jabbok, the boundary of the
Ammonites, that is, half of Gilead, **3** and [p]the Arabah [t]to the Sea of Chinneroth eastward,
and in the direction of Beth-jeshimoth, to the Sea of the Arabah, the Salt Sea, southward
to the foot of [u]the slopes of Pisgah; **4** and [v]Og[1] king of Bashan, one of the remnant of [w]the
Rephaim, [x]who lived at Ashtaroth and at Edrei **5** and ruled over [y]Mount Hermon and [z]Salecah
and all Bashan [a]to the boundary of the Geshurites and the Maacathites, and over half of
Gilead to the boundary of Sihon king of Heshbon. **6** [b]Moses, the servant of the LORD, and
the people of Israel defeated them. And Moses the servant of the LORD [c]gave their land for
a possession to the Reubenites and the Gadites and the half-tribe of Manasseh.

Kings Defeated by Joshua

7 And these are the kings of the land whom Joshua and the people of Israel defeated
on the west side of the Jordan, from Baal-gad in the Valley of Lebanon to [d]Mount Halak,
that rises toward Seir (and Joshua gave their land to the tribes of Israel as a possession
[e]according to their allotments, **8** [f]in the hill country, in the lowland, in the Arabah, in the
slopes, in the wilderness, and in the Negeb, the land of [g]the Hittites, the Amorites, the

[1] Septuagint; Hebrew *the boundary of Og*

Chapter 12
1 [o]Num. 21:13, 24; Deut. 3:8, 9 [p]See Deut. 1:1
2 [q]Deut. 2:32, 33; 3:6, 16; See Num. 21:21-26 [r]Deut. 2:36 [s]Gen. 32:22
3 [p][See ver. 1 above] [t]ch. 11:2 [u]ch. 13:20; Deut. 3:17; 4:49
4 [v]Deut. 3:3, 10; See Num. 21:33-35 [w]ch. 13:12; 15:8; 18:16 [x]ch. 9:10; Deut. 1:4
5 [y]Deut. 3:8, 9 [z]ch. 13:11; Deut. 3:10 [a]Deut. 3:14
6 [b]See Num. 21:23, 24, 33-35 [c]ch. 13:8; Num. 32:29, 33; Deut. 3:11, 12
7 [d]ch. 11:17 [e]ch. 11:23; 18:10
8 [f]ch. 10:40; 11:16 [g]ch. 9:1

Kings Defeated by the Israelites
c. 1390 B.C.
The Israelites captured many key cities throughout Canaan, although apparently some of them were later taken back by the Canaanites (e.g., Jerusalem). Under the leadership of Moses, the Israelites captured towns east of the Jordan River, including Ashtaroth and Heshbon. Joshua led the Israelites to capture many towns west of the Jordan River (the locations of Geder and Lasharon are unknown).

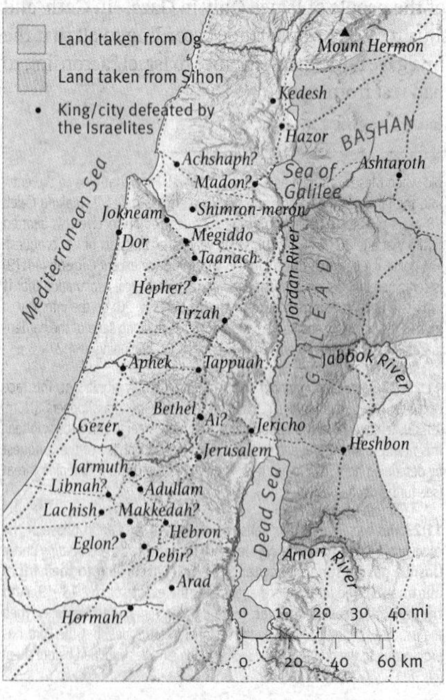

12:1–24 Now that the land has been conquered, and before it is apportioned, the full extent of the conquest is summarized. Verses 1–6 describe the land **beyond the Jordan** (from the vantage point of Israel, now west of the Jordan). This land consisted of the territories of the Transjordanian kings whom Israel had conquered under Moses' leadership (Num. 21:21–35), that Moses had allocated to the tribes of Reuben and Gad and the half-tribe of Manasseh (Num. 32:33). Joshua 12:7–24 lists the kings whom **Joshua and the people of Israel defeated on the west side of the Jordan** (v. 7), the total coming to 31 (v. 24; see note on v. 9).

12:1 took possession of their land. If the emphasis in the first half of the book of Joshua is on the Lord's faithfulness in *giving* Israel the land, it now falls to Israel to prove faithful in *taking possession*, that is, occupying the territories that will be allocated to them. The words rendered "possess" or "possession" appear with increased frequency in the second half of Joshua (in this chapter, see vv. 6–7).

12:9 The list of defeated kings (see map to the left) begins with the **king of Jericho** and generally follows the sequence of the preceding narrative: central, southern, and northern campaigns. That some kings not mentioned in the preceding narrative appear in the list reminds the reader that historical reportage can be selective; the Joshua narratives are meant to be more than a mere catalog of historical information.

12:24 This list of **thirty-one kings** suggests Israel's overall success in gaining the upper hand in Canaan and in destroying the leaders of resistance, but it does not necessarily imply the destruction of the cities formerly ruled by these kings (see note on 11:10–15).

13:1–21:45 *Dividing the Land.* As with the first two sections, this third major section in Joshua begins with a divine initiative. The Lord instructs Joshua regarding the division and allocation of the land. Packed with geographical details often lost on modern readers, the boundary descriptions and town lists that characterize this section were doubtless of great interest to ancient Israelites inheriting their allotments in the land. Over time, the *tribal allocations* presented here undoubtedly became the basis for *administrative documents*, and these would have been subject to updating as new towns or villages were founded. Despite its historical-geographical content, this lengthy section shows careful literary shaping (see Introduction: Outline, as well as the note on 14:1–19:51).

13:1–33 *It's Yours, Now Take It!* Before beginning to describe the tribal allotments west of the Jordan (ch. 14), the text stresses that, though Israel

Canaanites, the Perizzites, the Hivites, and the Jebusites): 9 [h]the king of Jericho, one; [i]the
king of Ai, which is beside Bethel, one; 10 [j]the king of Jerusalem, one; [j]the king of Hebron,
one; 11 [j]the king of Jarmuth, one; [j]the king of Lachish, one; 12 [j]the king of Eglon, one; [k]the
king of Gezer, one; 13 [l]the king of Debir, one; the king of Geder, one; 14 the king of Hormah,
one; the king of Arad, one; 15 [m]the king of Libnah, one; the king of Adullam, one; 16 [n]the
king of Makkedah, one; [o]the king of Bethel, one; 17 the king of Tappuah, one; the king of
Hepher, one; 18 the king of Aphek, one; the king of Lasharon, one; 19 [p]the king of Madon,
one; [q]the king of Hazor, one; 20 [p]the king of Shimron-meron, one; [p]the king of Achshaph,
one; 21 [r]the king of Taanach, one; [r]the king of Megiddo, one; 22 the king of Kedesh, one;
the king of Jokneam in Carmel, one; 23 [r]the king of Dor in [s]Naphath-dor, one; the king of
Goiim in Galilee,[1] one; 24 the king of Tirzah, one: in all, thirty-one kings.

Land Still to Be Conquered

13 Now Joshua [t]was old and advanced in years, and the LORD said to him, "You are
old and advanced in years, and there remains yet very much land [u]to possess.
2 [v]This is the land that yet remains: all the [w]regions of the Philistines, and all those of
the Geshurites 3 (from the [x]Shihor, which is east of Egypt, northward to the boundary of
Ekron, it is counted as Canaanite; [y]there are five rulers of the Philistines, those of Gaza,
Ashdod, Ashkelon, Gath, and Ekron), and those of [z]the Avvim, 4 in the south, all the land
of the Canaanites, and Mearah that belongs to the Sidonians, to Aphek, to the boundary
of [a]the Amorites, 5 and the land of the [b]Gebalites, and all Lebanon, toward the sunrise,
from [c]Baal-gad below Mount Hermon to [d]Lebo-hamath, 6 all the inhabitants of the hill
country from Lebanon to [e]Misrephoth-maim, even all the Sidonians. I myself will drive
[f]them out from before the people of Israel. Only [g]allot the land to Israel [h]for an inheritance,
as I have commanded you. 7 Now therefore [i]divide this land for an inheritance to the nine
tribes and half the tribe of Manasseh."

The Inheritance East of the Jordan

8 With the other half of the tribe of Manasseh[2] the Reubenites and the Gadites received
their inheritance, [j]which Moses gave them, beyond the Jordan eastward, as Moses the
servant of the LORD gave them: 9 [k]from Aroer, which is on the edge of the Valley of the
Arnon, and the city that is in the middle of the valley, and [l]all the tableland of Medeba as
far as Dibon; 10 [m]and all the cities of Sihon king of the Amorites, who reigned in Heshbon,
as far as the boundary of the Ammonites; 11 and Gilead, and the [n]region of the Geshurites
and Maacathites, and all Mount Hermon, and [n]all Bashan to Salecah; 12 [n]all the kingdom
of Og in Bashan, who reigned in Ashtaroth and in Edrei (he alone was left of [n]the remnant
of the Rephaim); [o]these Moses had struck and driven out. 13 [p]Yet the people of Israel did
not drive out the Geshurites or the Maacathites, but Geshur and Maacath dwell in the
midst of Israel to this day.

14 [q]To the tribe of Levi alone Moses gave no inheritance. The offerings by fire to the LORD
God of Israel are their inheritance, as he said to him.

[1] Septuagint; Hebrew *Gilgal* [2] Hebrew *With it*

9 [h][ch. 6:2] [i]ch. 8:29
10 [j]ch. 10:23
11 [j][See ver. 10 above]
12 [j][See ver. 10 above] [k]ch. 10:33
13 [l]ch. 10:38, 39
15 [m]ch. 10:29
16 [n]ch. 10:28 [o]ch. 8:17; Judg. 1:22
19 [p]ch. 11:1 [q]ch. 11:1, 10
20 [p][See ver. 19 above]
21 [r]ch. 17:11
23 [r][See ver. 21 above] [s]ch. 11:2

Chapter 13

1 [t]ch. 14:10; 23:1 [u]Deut. 31:3
2 [v]Judg. 3:1 [w]Joel 3:4
3 [x]1 Chr. 13:5; Jer. 2:18 [y]Judg. 3:3 [z]Deut. 2:23
4 [a]See Judg. 1:34-36
5 [b]1 Kgs. 5:18; Ps. 83:7; Ezek. 27:9 [c]ch. 11:17; 12:7 [d]Num. 34:8
6 [e]ch. 11:8 [f][ch. 23:13; Judg. 2:21-23] [g]ch. 23:4 [h]ch. 23:4; Num. 34:2
7 [i]ch. 14:1, 2
8 [j]ch. 12:6; See Num. 32:33
9 [k]Deut. 2:36 [l]ver. 16; [Num. 21:30]
10 [m]Num. 21:24, 25
11 [n]Deut. 3:14
12 [n][See ver. 11 above] [o]Num. 21:24, 35
13 [p]ver. 11
14 [q]ch. 14:3, 4; See Num. 18:20-32

has gained the upper hand, there remains much land to possess, particularly along the coast and in the far north (13:1–7). A rehearsal of what was allocated east of the Jordan under Moses (vv. 8–33) sets the stage for what follows, as does the ominous notice that the eastern tribes have failed to drive out some of their enemies, leaving them to dwell in the midst of Israel "to this day" (v. 13).

13:1 The second half of the book of Joshua begins much like the first, with both the narrator and the Lord stating the status of Israel's key leader. In 1:1 they announced that Moses was dead, and now in 13:1 they describe Joshua as **old and advanced in years** (cf. 23:1; Joshua's death is mentioned in 24:29). By this point in the narrative, the subjugation phase of the conquest is largely completed (see summaries in 10:40–43 and 11:16–23), but the territories west of the Jordan must yet be allocated and occupied (see map, p. 416). In other words, **there remains yet very much land to possess**.

13:6 I myself will drive them out. . . . Only allot the land to Israel. The boundary between the subjugation phase of the conquest and the allocation phase cannot be sharply drawn. Verses 1–7 speak of enemies whose land Israel has yet to "possess" (v. 1). The Lord pledges to continue to "drive them out" (lit., "dispossess," related to the word "possess" in v. 1) and instructs Joshua to go ahead and "allot" these lands.

13:8 It is **Moses** who first mentions the **inheritance** given to these tribes (Num. 32:33–42; Deut. 3:8–17).

13:11 Geshurites and Maacathites. Geshur and Maacah were two small kingdoms north and east of the Sea of Galilee. This Geshur is not to be confused with the Geshur mentioned in v. 2, which lay far to the south on the Philistine coast.

13:13 the people of Israel did not drive out . . . dwell in the midst of Israel to this day. See note on 15:63.

13:14 The notice that the **tribe of Levi** receives **no inheritance** (repeated in v. 33, explained in 14:3–4, and recalled in 18:7 in the midst of the allotment listings) anticipates the designation of Levitical cities in Joshua 21; cf. Deut. 10:9 and the note on Num. 18:21–24.

The Allotment of the Land

c. 1400 B.C.

During the conquest of Canaan, Joshua allotted the land to the tribes of Israel. These boundaries, however, do not necessarily reflect the land each tribe actually inhabited by the end of the conquest. Several tribes, such as Dan, were unable to drive out the Canaanites that lived in much of their allotted territory (19:47), while other tribes controlled portions of land that were not originally allotted to them (e.g., 17:11).

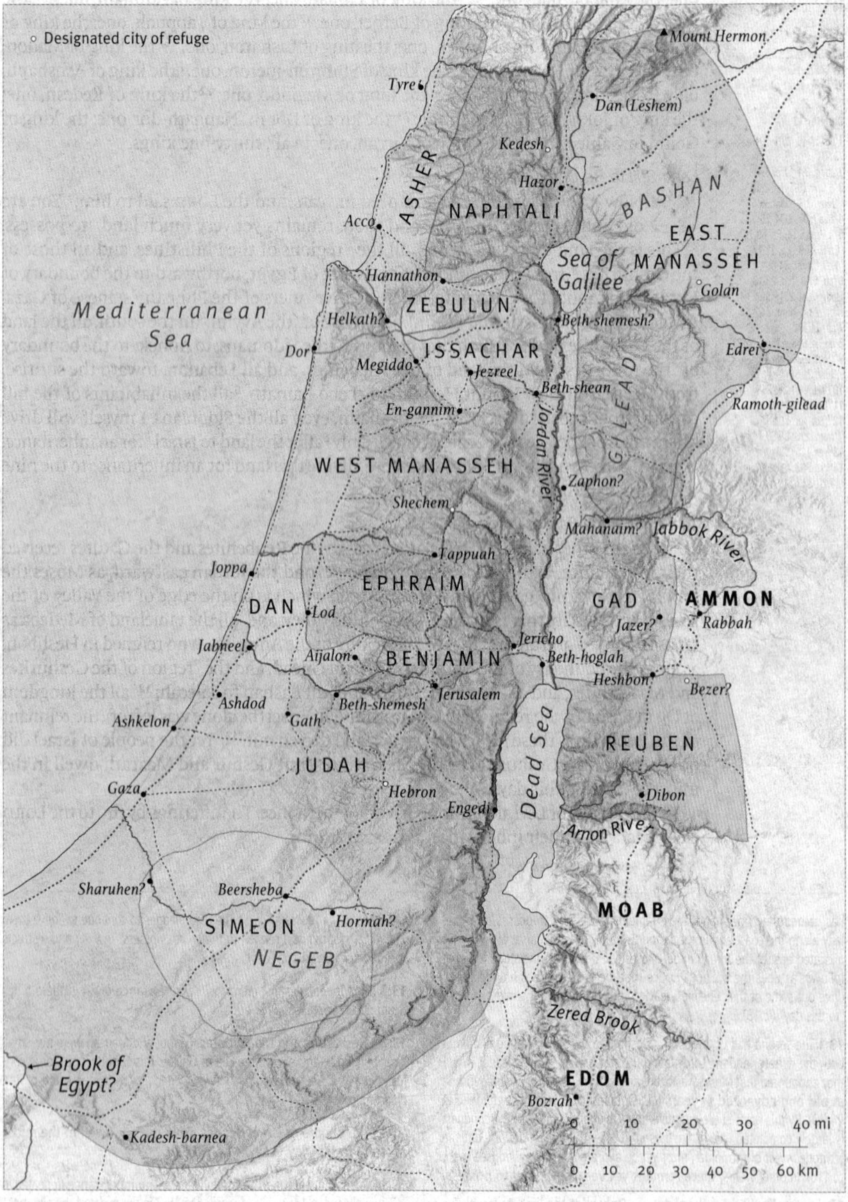

16 [r] ver. 9 [s] [Num. 21:30]
17 [s] [See ver. 16 above]
18 [t] Num. 21:23
19 [u] Num. 32:37, 38
20 [v] Deut. 4:46 [w] See ch. 12:3
21 [x] Deut. 3:10 [y] Num. 21:24 [z] Num. 31:8
22 [z] [See ver. 21 above]
25 [a] Num. 32:34-36 [b] [Deut. 3:11; 2 Sam. 11:1; 12:26]
26 [c] Gen. 32:2; 2 Sam. 2:8, 12; 17:24
27 [d] Gen. 33:17 [e] See ch. 11:2
30 [f] See ver. 26 [g] Num. 32:41; 1 Chr. 2:23; [Deut. 3:14]
31 [h] ch. 12:4 [i] ch. 17:1; Num. 32:39, 40
32 [j] Num. 22:1
33 [k] ver. 14; ch. 18:7; Num. 18:20

Chapter 14

1 [l] ch. 17:4; 21:1; Num. 34:17, 18
2 [m] Num. 26:56; 33:54; 34:13
3 [n] See ch. 13:8 [o] See ch. 13:33
4 [p] Gen. 48:5; 1 Chr. 5:1, 2
5 [q] ch. 21:2; Num. 35:1, 2

15 And Moses gave an inheritance to the tribe of the people of Reuben according to their
clans. **16** So their territory was from Aroer, [r] which is on the edge of the Valley of the Arnon,
and the city that is in the middle of the valley, and all the tableland by [s] Medeba; **17** with
Heshbon, and all its cities that are in the tableland; [s] Dibon, and Bamoth-baal, and Beth-
baal-meon, **18** [t] and Jahaz, and Kedemoth, and Mephaath, **19** and [u] Kiriathaim, and [u] Sibmah,
and Zereth-shahar on the hill of the valley, **20** and [v] Beth-peor, and [w] the slopes of Pisgah, and
[w] Beth-jeshimoth, **21** that is, [x] all the cities of the tableland, and all the kingdom of Sihon
king of the Amorites, who reigned in Heshbon, [y] whom Moses defeated with [z] the leaders
of Midian, Evi and Rekem and Zur and Hur and Reba, the princes of Sihon, who lived
in the land. **22** [z] Balaam also, the son of Beor, the one who practiced divination, was killed
with the sword by the people of Israel among the rest of their slain. **23** And the border of
the people of Reuben was the Jordan as a boundary. This was the inheritance of the people
of Reuben, according to their clans with their cities and villages.

24 Moses gave an inheritance also to the tribe of Gad, to the people of Gad, according
to their clans. **25** [a] Their territory was Jazer, and all the cities of Gilead, and half the land
of the Ammonites, to Aroer, which is east of [b] Rabbah, **26** and from Heshbon to Ramath-
mizpeh and Betonim, and from [c] Mahanaim to the territory of Debir,[1] **27** and in the valley
Beth-haram, Beth-nimrah, [d] Succoth, and Zaphon, the rest of the kingdom of Sihon king
of Heshbon, having the Jordan as a boundary, to the lower end of the Sea of [e] Chinnereth,
eastward beyond the Jordan. **28** This is the inheritance of the people of Gad according to
their clans, with their cities and villages.

29 And Moses gave an inheritance to the half-tribe of Manasseh. It was allotted to the
half-tribe of the people of Manasseh according to their clans. **30** Their region extended from
[f] Mahanaim, through all Bashan, the whole kingdom of Og king of Bashan, and all [g] the
towns of Jair, which are in Bashan, sixty cities, **31** and half Gilead, and [h] Ashtaroth, and Edrei,
the cities of the kingdom of Og in Bashan. These were allotted to the people of [i] Machir the
son of Manasseh for the half of the people of Machir according to their clans.

32 These are the inheritances that Moses distributed [j] in the plains of Moab, beyond the
Jordan east of Jericho. **33** [k] But to the tribe of Levi Moses gave no inheritance; the LORD God
of Israel is their inheritance, [k] just as he said to them.

The Inheritance West of the Jordan

14 These are the inheritances that the people of Israel received in the land of Canaan,
which [l] Eleazar the priest and Joshua the son of Nun and the heads of the fathers'
houses of the tribes of the people of Israel gave them to inherit. **2** Their inheritance was [m] by
lot, just as the LORD had commanded by the hand of Moses for the nine and one-half tribes.
3 [n] For Moses had given an inheritance to the two and one-half tribes beyond the Jordan,
[o] but to the Levites he gave no inheritance among them. **4** For [p] the people of Joseph were
two tribes, Manasseh and Ephraim. And no portion was given to the Levites in the land,
but only cities to dwell in, with their pasturelands for their livestock and their substance.
5 The people of Israel did [q] as the LORD commanded Moses; they allotted the land.

[1] Septuagint, Syriac, Vulgate; Hebrew *Lidebir*

13:22 Balaam . . . the son of Beor. His story is told in Numbers 22–24 and his death is mentioned in Num. 31:8.

14:1–19:51 *Western Territories.* This section describes the tribal allocations west of the Jordan, and it exhibits literary symmetry. It begins and ends almost identically, making reference to Eleazar the priest, Joshua, and the heads of the fathers' houses of the Israelite tribes, who distributed by lot the territories west of the Jordan (14:1–5; 19:51). Inside this outer frame are references to the inheritance of the two faithful former spies, Caleb (14:6–15) and Joshua (19:49–51). These in turn frame the major central section describing the actual allocations to the nine and a half tribes who received no inheritance east of the Jordan (15:1–19, 40–48). A crucial assembly of the whole congregation of the people of Israel at Shiloh before the "tent of meeting" (18:1–10) bisects and anchors this section, with the allotments for the major tribes of Judah and Joseph (that is, Ephraim and the half-tribe of Manasseh) preceding (15:1–17:18) and the allotments for the other seven tribes following (18:11–19:48). Thus, chs. 14–19 provide detailed *historical* information in a carefully structured *literary* form, and in so doing underscore a fundamental *theological* truth: those like Caleb or Joshua who wholly follow the Lord (14:8–9, 14) will be able to enjoy their inheritance.

14:1 Eleazar the priest was Aaron's son and successor (Num. 20:25; Deut. 10:6) and had been assigned his present task by Moses (Num. 34:17). Ten **heads** of the nine and a half **tribes** were explicitly named already in Num. 34:18–29.

14:2 That the **inheritance was by lot** guarantees divine oversight and protects Israel's leaders from any suspicion of favoritism. The Lord's progressively more detailed instructions to Moses regarding the lot-casting procedure are recorded in Num. 26:52–56; 33:50–54; 34:1–15.

14:3 Levites. See note on 13:14.

Caleb's Request and Inheritance

6 Then the people of Judah came to Joshua at Gilgal. And Caleb the son of Jephunneh
the [r]Kenizzite said to him, "You know [s]what the LORD said to Moses the man of God in
Kadesh-barnea concerning you and me. **7** I was forty years old when Moses the servant
of the LORD [t]sent me from Kadesh-barnea to spy out the land, and I brought him word
again as it was in my heart. **8** But [u]my brothers who went up with me made the heart of
the people melt; yet I wholly followed the LORD my God. **9** And Moses swore on that day,
saying, [v]'Surely the land [w]on which your foot has trodden shall be an inheritance for you
and your children forever, because you have wholly followed the LORD my God.' **10** And now,
behold, the LORD has kept me alive, [x]just as he said, these [y]forty-five years since the time
that the LORD spoke this word to Moses, while Israel walked in the wilderness. And now,
behold, I am this day [y]eighty-five years old. **11** [z]I am still as strong today as I was in the day
that Moses sent me; my strength now is as my strength was then, for war and [a]for going
and coming. **12** So now give me this hill country of which the LORD spoke on that day, for
you heard on that day how the [b]Anakim were there, with great fortified cities. It may be
that the LORD will be with me, and I shall drive them out just as the LORD said."

13 Then Joshua [c]blessed him, and he gave [d]Hebron to Caleb the son of Jephunneh for an
inheritance. **14** Therefore Hebron became the inheritance of Caleb the son of Jephunneh
the Kenizzite to this day, [e]because he wholly followed the LORD, the God of Israel. **15** [f]Now
the name of Hebron formerly was Kiriath-arba.[1] (Arba[2] was the greatest man among the
Anakim.) [g]And the land had rest from war.

The Allotment for Judah

15 The allotment for the tribe of the people of Judah according to their clans reached
southward [h]to the boundary of Edom, to [i]the wilderness of Zin at the farthest
south. **2** And their south boundary ran from the end of the [h]Salt Sea, from the bay that
faces southward. **3** It goes out southward of [j]the ascent of Akrabbim, passes along to Zin,
and goes up south of Kadesh-barnea, along by Hezron, up to Addar, turns about to Karka,
4 passes along to Azmon, goes out by [k]the Brook of Egypt, and comes to its end at the sea.
This shall be your south boundary. **5** And the east boundary is the [h]Salt Sea, to the mouth
of the Jordan. And the boundary on the north side runs from the bay of the sea at the
mouth of the Jordan. **6** And the boundary goes up to [l]Beth-hoglah and passes along north
of [m]Beth-arabah. And the boundary goes up to [n]the stone of Bohan the son of Reuben.
7 And the boundary goes up to Debir from [o]the Valley of Achor, and so northward, turning
toward Gilgal, which is opposite [p]the ascent of Adummim, which is on the south side of the
valley. And the boundary passes along to the waters of [p]En-shemesh and ends at [q]En-rogel.
8 Then the boundary goes up by [r]the Valley of the Son of Hinnom at the southern shoulder
of the Jebusite ([s]that is, Jerusalem). And the boundary goes up to the top of the mountain
that lies over against the Valley of Hinnom, on the west, at the northern end of the Valley
[t]of Rephaim. **9** Then the boundary extends from the top of the mountain [u]to the spring of
the waters of Nephtoah, and from there to the cities of Mount Ephron. Then the boundary
bends around to Baalah ([v]that is, Kiriath-jearim). **10** And the boundary circles west of Baalah

[1] *Kiriath-arba* means *the city of Arba* [2] Hebrew *He*

6 [r]ver. 13, 14; Num. 32:12; [ch. 15:17] [s]Num. 14:24, 30; Deut. 1:36, 38
7 [t]Num. 13:6, 16, 30; 14:6-9
8 [u]Deut. 1:28; See Num. 13:31-33
9 [v]Num. 14:24; Deut. 1:36 [w]ch. 1:3
10 [x]Num. 14:30 [y][ver. 7]
11 [z][Deut. 34:7] [a]Deut. 31:2
12 [b]Num. 13:28, 33
13 [c]ch. 22:6 [d]ch. 10:36, 37; 15:13, 14; 21:11, 12; Judg. 1:20; 1 Chr. 6:55, 56
14 [e]ver. 8, 9
15 [f]ver. 13; Gen. 23:2; 35:27; Judg. 1:10; See ch. 10:36 [g]See ch. 11:23

Chapter 15

1 [h]Num. 34:3 [i]Num. 33:36
2 [h][See ver. 1 above]
3 [j]Num. 34:4; Judg. 1:36
4 [k]ver. 47; Num. 34:5; [ch. 13:3]
5 [h][See ver. 1 above]
6 [l]ch. 18:19, 21 [m]ch. 18:18, 22 [n]ch. 18:17
7 [o]ch. 7:26 [p]ch. 18:17 [q]ch. 18:16; 2 Sam. 17:17; 1 Kgs. 1:9
8 [r]ch. 18:16; 2 Kgs. 23:10 [s]ver. 63; ch. 18:28; [Judg. 19:10; 1 Chr. 11:4] [t]ch. 18:16; See ch. 12:4
9 [u]ch. 18:15 [v]ver. 60; 1 Chr. 13:6

14:6–15 This section recounts Caleb's inheritance of Hebron, which **Moses swore** to give him many years before (v. 9; Deut. 1:36; cf. Num. 14:24). It is one of four narrative passages, sometimes referred to as "land-grant narratives," that are distinctive in Joshua 14–19 in that they focus on individuals. The other three are the allocation of Debir to Caleb's daughter Achsah and her husband Othniel (15:13–19; Othniel reappears in Judg. 3:7–11); the bestowal of an inheritance on the daughters of Zelophehad (Josh. 17:3–6); and the granting of Timnath-serah to Joshua (19:49–50). Despite his advanced age of **eighty-five years** (14:10), Caleb maintains that his strength is undiminished and that he will be able to drive out the formidable **Anakim**, provided that **the LORD will be with** him (v. 12). Joshua was credited with cutting off the Anakim from Hebron already in 11:21. Either the Anakim have reasserted themselves in Hebron (11:22 mentions some survivors) or, more likely, as commander-in-chief Joshua supports and receives general credit for the eventual expulsion of the Anakim by Caleb (14:12–14; 15:14). That both the summary of Joshua's defeat of the Anakim in 11:21–23 and the present account of Caleb's taking of Hebron conclude with the statement, **the land had rest from war** (14:15; cf. 11:23 and nowhere else in Joshua), suggests that both sections relate to the same events.

14:8 wholly followed the LORD. See note on 14:1–19:51. Emphasized through repetition in 14:9, 14, this commendation of Caleb sets a standard by which Israel is to be measured in the narratives that follow.

15:1–63 As the western allocations begin, pride of place goes to the important tribe of **Judah**. In keeping with the general pattern of the subsequent allotments, the tribal boundaries are first described (vv. 1–12), followed by listings of cities according to region (vv. 20–62).

15:8 Jebusite (that is, Jerusalem). Not fully conquered until the time of King David (2 Sam. 5:6–10; for other attempts, see Judg. 1:8, 21).

10 [w]1 Sam. 6:9, 12 [x]Gen. 38:12-14; Judg. 14:1
11 [y]ch. 13:3 [z]ver. 9
12 [a]ver. 47; ch. 23:4; Num. 34:6, 7; Ezek. 47:20
13 [b]ver. 54; See ch. 14:13-15
14 [c]Num. 13:22; Judg. 1:10, 20
15 [d]Judg. 1:11; [ver. 49]
17 [e]See Judg. 1:13 [f]See ch. 14:6, 13
21 [g]Gen. 35:21
24 [h]1 Sam. 23:14, 15, 19, 24; 26:1, 2
28 [i]Gen. 21:31; 26:23, 33
31 [j]1 Sam. 27:6; 30:1
33 [k][Num. 13:23]
35 [l]ch. 10:3 [m]1 Sam. 22:1 [n]1 Sam. 17:1
39 [o]ch. 10:3, 31, 32 [p]ch. 10:3, 36, 37
41 [q]ch. 10:10, 21
42 [r]ch. 10:29, 30
44 [s]1 Sam. 23:1, 2
45 [t]ch. 13:3
47 [t][See ver. 45 above] [u]See ver. 4 [v]See ver. 12
49 [w][ver. 15]
51 [x]ch. 10:41; 11:16 [y]2 Sam. 15:12
54 [z]ver. 13
55 [a]1 Sam. 23:24, 25; 25:2 [b]ver. 24
57 [c]ver. 10
60 [d]ver. 9
61 [e]ver. 6
62 [f]1 Sam. 23:29; 24:1
63 [g]See ver. 8 [h][Judg. 1:8, 21; 2 Sam. 5:6]

to Mount Seir, passes along to the northern shoulder of Mount Jearim (that is, Chesalon),
and goes down to [w]Beth-shemesh and passes along by [x]Timnah. 11 The boundary goes out
[y]to the shoulder of the hill north of Ekron, then the boundary bends around to Shikkeron
and passes along to Mount [z]Baalah and goes out to Jabneel. Then the boundary comes to
an end at the sea. 12 And the west boundary was [a]the Great Sea with its coastline. This is
the boundary around the people of Judah according to their clans.

13 According to the commandment of the LORD to Joshua, he gave to Caleb the son of
Jephunneh a portion among the people of Judah, [b]Kiriath-arba, that is, [b]Hebron (Arba was
the father of Anak). 14 And Caleb drove out from there the three sons of Anak, [c]Sheshai and
Ahiman and Talmai, the descendants of Anak. 15 And he went up from there against the
inhabitants of Debir. [d]Now the name of Debir formerly was Kiriath-sepher. 16 And Caleb
said, "Whoever strikes Kiriath-sepher and captures it, to him will I give Achsah my daughter
as wife." 17 [e]And Othniel the son of Kenaz, [f]the brother of Caleb, captured it. And he gave
him Achsah his daughter as wife. 18 When she came to him, she urged him to ask her father
for a field. And she got off her donkey, and Caleb said to her, "What do you want?" 19 She
said to him, "Give me a blessing. Since you have given me the land of the Negeb, give me
also springs of water." And he gave her the upper springs and the lower springs.

20 This is the inheritance of the tribe of the people of Judah according to their clans.
21 The cities belonging to the tribe of the people of Judah in the extreme south, toward
the boundary of Edom, were Kabzeel, [g]Eder, Jagur, 22 Kinah, Dimonah, Adadah, 23 Kedesh,
Hazor, Ithnan, 24 [h]Ziph, Telem, Bealoth, 25 Hazor-hadattah, Kerioth-hezron (that is,
Hazor), 26 Amam, Shema, Moladah, 27 Hazar-gaddah, Heshmon, Beth-pelet, 28 Hazar-
shual, [i]Beersheba, Biziothiah, 29 Baalah, Iim, Ezem, 30 Eltolad, Chesil, Hormah, 31 [j]Ziklag,
Madmannah, Sansannah, 32 Lebaoth, Shilhim, Ain, and Rimmon: in all, twenty-nine cities
with their villages.

33 And in the lowland, [k]Eshtaol, Zorah, Ashnah, 34 Zanoah, En-gannim, Tappuah, Enam,
35 [l]Jarmuth, [m]Adullam, [n]Socoh, [n]Azekah, 36 Shaaraim, Adithaim, Gederah, Gederothaim:
fourteen cities with their villages.

37 Zenan, Hadashah, Migdal-gad, 38 Dilean, Mizpeh, Joktheel, 39 [o]Lachish, Bozkath, [p]Eglon,
40 Cabbon, Lahmam, Chitlish, 41 Gederoth, Beth-dagon, Naamah, and [q]Makkedah: sixteen
cities with their villages.

42 [r]Libnah, Ether, Ashan, 43 Iphtah, Ashnah, Nezib, 44 [s]Keilah, Achzib, and Mareshah:
nine cities with their villages.

45 [t]Ekron, with its towns and its villages; 46 from Ekron to the sea, all that were by the
side of Ashdod, with their villages.

47 [t]Ashdod, its towns and its villages; [t]Gaza, its towns and its villages; to [u]the Brook of
Egypt, and [v]the Great Sea with its coastline.

48 And in the hill country, Shamir, Jattir, Socoh, 49 Dannah, Kiriath-sannah ([w]that is, Debir),
50 Anab, Eshtemoh, Anim, 51 [x]Goshen, Holon, and [y]Giloh: eleven cities with their villages.

52 Arab, Dumah, Eshan, 53 Janim, Beth-tappuah, Aphekah, 54 Humtah, [z]Kiriath-arba (that
is, [z]Hebron), and Zior: nine cities with their villages.

55 [a]Maon, [a]Carmel, [b]Ziph, Juttah, 56 Jezreel, Jokdeam, Zanoah, 57 Kain, Gibeah, and
[c]Timnah: ten cities with their villages.

58 Halhul, Beth-zur, Gedor, 59 Maarath, Beth-anoth, and Eltekon: six cities with their
villages.

60 [d]Kiriath-baal (that is, Kiriath-jearim), and Rabbah: two cities with their villages.

61 In the wilderness, [e]Beth-arabah, Middin, Secacah, 62 Nibshan, the City of Salt, and
[f]Engedi: six cities with their villages.

63 But the [g]Jebusites, the inhabitants of Jerusalem, [h]the people of Judah could not drive
out, [h]so the Jebusites dwell with the people of Judah at Jerusalem to this day.

15:13–19 he gave to Caleb . . . Caleb drove out. See note on 14:6–15. **Othniel** (15:17) reappears as a judge-deliverer in Judg. 3:7–11.

15:63 Against the backdrop of so much success, the notice that **the people of Judah could not drive out** the **Jebusites** from Jerusalem and that they

The Allotment for Ephraim and Manasseh

16 The allotment of the people of Joseph went from the Jordan by Jericho, east of the
waters of Jericho, [i]into the wilderness, going up from Jericho into the hill country
to Bethel. 2 Then [j]going from Bethel to Luz, it passes along to Ataroth, the territory of the
Archites. 3 Then it goes down westward to the territory of the Japhletites, as far as the territory of Lower [k]Beth-horon, then to [l]Gezer, and it ends at the sea.
4 [m]The people of Joseph, Manasseh and Ephraim, received their inheritance.
5 The territory of the people of Ephraim by their clans was as follows: the boundary
of their inheritance on the east was [n]Ataroth-addar as far as Upper Beth-horon, 6 and the
boundary goes from there to the sea. On the north is [o]Michmethath. Then on the east the
boundary turns around toward Taanath-shiloh and passes along beyond it on the east to
Janoah, 7 then it goes down from Janoah to Ataroth and [p]to Naarah, and touches Jericho,
ending at the Jordan. 8 From [q]Tappuah the boundary goes westward to the brook Kanah
and ends at the sea. Such is the inheritance of the tribe of the people of Ephraim by their
clans, 9 together with [q]the towns that were set apart for the people of Ephraim within the
inheritance of the Manassites, all those towns with their villages. 10 However, [r]they did not
drive out the Canaanites who lived in Gezer, so the Canaanites have lived in the midst of
Ephraim to this day but have been made [s]to do forced labor.
17 Then allotment was made to the people of Manasseh, for he was [t]the firstborn of
Joseph. To [u]Machir the firstborn of Manasseh, the father of Gilead, [v]were allotted
Gilead and Bashan, because he was a man of war. 2 And allotments were made [w]to the
rest of the people of Manasseh by their clans, Abiezer, Helek, Asriel, Shechem, Hepher,
and Shemida. These were the male descendants of Manasseh the son of Joseph, by their
clans.
3 Now [x]Zelophehad the son of Hepher, son of Gilead, son of Machir, son of Manasseh,
had no sons, but only daughters, and these are the names of his daughters: [x]Mahlah, Noah,
Hoglah, Milcah, and Tirzah. 4 They approached [y]Eleazar the priest and Joshua the son of Nun
and the leaders and said, [z]"The LORD commanded Moses to give us an inheritance along
with our brothers." So according to the mouth of the LORD he gave them an inheritance
among the brothers of their father. 5 Thus there fell to Manasseh ten portions, besides [a]the
land of Gilead and Bashan, which is on the other side of the Jordan, 6 because the daughters
of Manasseh received an inheritance along with his sons. The land of Gilead was allotted
to the rest of the people of Manasseh.
7 The territory of Manasseh reached from Asher to [b]Michmethath, which is east of
Shechem. Then the boundary goes along southward to the inhabitants of En-tappuah.
8 The land of [c]Tappuah belonged to Manasseh, but the town of Tappuah on the boundary
of Manasseh belonged to the people of Ephraim. 9 [c]Then the boundary went down to the
brook Kanah. These cities, to the south of the brook, among the cities of Manasseh, belong
to Ephraim. Then the boundary of Manasseh goes on the north side of the brook and ends
at the sea, 10 the land to the south being Ephraim's and that to the north being Manasseh's,
with the sea forming its boundary. On the north Asher is reached, and on the east Issachar.
11 Also in Issachar and in Asher [d]Manasseh had Beth-shean and its villages, and Ibleam
and its villages, and the inhabitants of [d]Dor and its villages, and the inhabitants of En-
dor and its villages, and the inhabitants of [d]Taanach and its villages, and the inhabitants

Chapter 16

1 [i]ch. 8:15; 18:12
2 [j][ch. 18:13; Gen. 28:19; Judg. 1:23, 26]
3 [k]See ch. 10:10 [l]See ch. 10:33
4 [m][ch. 17:14]
5 [n]ch. 18:13
6 [o]ch. 17:7
7 [p]1 Chr. 7:28
8 [q]ch. 17:8, 9
9 [q][See ver. 8 above]
10 [r]Judg. 1:29; 1 Kgs. 9:16 [s]ch. 17:13; Gen. 49:15

Chapter 17

1 [t]Gen. 41:51; 46:20; 48:18 [u]Gen. 50:23; Num. 26:29; 32:39, 40; 1 Chr. 7:14 [v]Deut. 3:13, 15
2 [w]See Num. 26:29-32
3 [x]Num. 26:33; 27:1; 36:2, 11
4 [y]ch. 14:1; 21:1; Num. 34:17 [z]Num. 27:6, 7; 36:2
5 [a]ver. 1; ch. 13:30, 31
7 [b]ch. 16:6
8 [c]ch. 16:8, 9
9 [c][See ver. 8 above]
11 [d]1 Chr. 7:29; [1 Kgs. 4:11, 12]

dwell with the people of Judah at Jerusalem to this day is disconcerting in at least two respects. First, it recalls Moses' repeated warnings against allowing Canaanites to survive and live among the Israelites (see notes on 6:17; 6:18). Second, it raises a theological question: how is it that the people of Judah "could not" drive out their foes? Surely the god of the Jebusites is not stronger than the God of Judah! This is not the first instance of failure to occupy (13:13), and it will not be the last. In 17:12 the Manassites are unable to occupy certain towns because "the Canaanites persisted in dwelling in that land." In 17:16 the Ephraimites cite Canaanite possession of "chariots of iron" as preventing them from taking the plains. These statements seem to be in tension with the dominant theological conviction of the book of Joshua that "the hand of the LORD is mighty" (4:24) and with the divine promise to the leader Joshua that "No man shall be able to stand before you all the days of your life. . . . You shall cause this people to inherit the land" (1:5–6). Joshua himself seems to agree with this assessment, insisting in 17:18 that "you shall drive out the Canaanites, though they have chariots of iron, and though they are strong." Perhaps statements of what Israel "could not" do are to be read as early evidence of spiritual slippage—of failure to follow the Lord "wholly" (see 14:8)—which will become increasingly evident in the book of Judges.

16:1 Chapters 16–17 describe the **allotment of the people of Joseph**, i.e., of Ephraim (16:5–10) and of Manasseh (17:1–13).

16:10 did not drive out. See note on 15:63.

17:3–6 The **daughters** of **Zelophehad** receive their inheritance, as **the LORD commanded Moses** (see Num. 27:1–11 and the qualification introduced in Num. 36:1–13). See note on Josh. 14:6–15.

of [d]Megiddo and its villages; [e]the third is Naphath.[1] 12 [f]Yet the people of Manasseh could
not take possession of those cities, but the Canaanites persisted in dwelling in that land.
13 Now when the people of Israel grew strong, they put the Canaanites [g]to forced labor,
but did not utterly drive them out.
14 Then [h]the people of Joseph spoke to Joshua, saying, "Why have you given me but [i]one
lot and one portion as an inheritance, although I am [j]a numerous people, since all along
the LORD has blessed me?" 15 And Joshua said to them, "If you are a numerous people, go
up by yourselves to the forest, and there clear ground for yourselves in the land of the
Perizzites and [k]the Rephaim, since [l]the hill country of Ephraim is too narrow for you."
16 The people of Joseph said, "The hill country is not enough for us. Yet all the Canaanites
who dwell in the plain have [m]chariots of iron, both those in Beth-shean and its villages
and those in [n]the Valley of Jezreel." 17 Then Joshua said to the house of Joseph, to Ephraim
and Manasseh, "You are a numerous people and have great power. You shall not have one
allotment only, 18 but the hill country shall be yours, for though it is a forest, you shall clear
it and possess it to its farthest borders. For you shall drive out the Canaanites, [o]though
they have chariots of iron, and though they are strong."

Allotment of the Remaining Land

18 Then the whole congregation of the people of Israel assembled at [p]Shiloh and set
up [q]the tent of meeting there. The land lay subdued before them.
2 There remained among the people of Israel seven tribes whose inheritance had not
yet been apportioned. 3 So Joshua said to the people of Israel, [r]"How long will you put
off going in to take possession of the land, which the LORD, the God of your fathers, has
given you? 4 Provide three men from each tribe, and I will send them out that they may set
out and go up and down the land. They shall write a description of it with a view to their
inheritances, and then come to me. 5 They shall divide it into seven portions. [s]Judah shall
continue in his territory on the south, [t]and the house of Joseph shall continue in their
territory on the north. 6 And you shall describe the land in seven divisions and bring the
description here to me. [u]And I will cast lots for you here before the LORD our God. 7 [v]The
Levites have no portion among you, for the priesthood of the LORD is their heritage. [w]And
Gad and Reuben and half the tribe of Manasseh have received their inheritance beyond
the Jordan eastward, which Moses the servant of the LORD gave them."
8 So the men arose and went, and Joshua charged those who went to write the description of the land, saying, "Go up and down in the land and write a description and return
to me. And I will cast lots for you here before the LORD in Shiloh." 9 So the men went and
passed up and down in the land and wrote in a book a description of it by towns in seven
divisions. Then they came to Joshua to the camp at Shiloh, 10 and Joshua [x]cast lots for

11 [d]1 Chr. 7:29; [1 Kgs. 4:11, 12] [e][ch. 11:2; 12:23]
12 [f]Judg. 1:27, 28
13 [g]ch. 16:10; Gen. 49:15
14 [h]ch. 16:4 [i][Gen. 48:22] [j]Gen. 48:19; [Num. 26:34, 37]
15 [k]See ch. 12:4 [l]ch. 24:33; Judg. 3:27
16 [m]See ch. 11:6 [n]Judg. 6:33
18 [o]Deut. 20:1; See ch. 11:6

Chapter 18

1 [p]ch. 19:51; 21:2; 22:9, 12 [q]ch. 19:51
3 [r][Judg. 18:9]
5 [s][ch. 15:1] [t][ch. 16:1, 4]
6 [u]ver. 10; ch. 14:2
7 [v]See ch. 13:33 [w]See ch. 13:8
10 [x]ver. 6

[1] The meaning of the Hebrew is uncertain

17:12 could not take possession. See note on 15:63.

17:14–15 With the influx of the Israelites into Canaan, many settlements appear in areas never before settled: the highlands and the deserts. To support this human settlement in those areas not so easily cultivable, the Israelites borrowed or developed fresh agricultural techniques. One principal development of settlers in the mountains was agricultural terracing. In addition, plastered cisterns and rock-lined silos are abundant at these sites; they are rare in earlier periods.

17:16–18 In contrast to the lighter chariots of 11:4, the **chariots of iron** of the plains-dwelling Canaanites were of heavier construction, perhaps armored with iron fittings and sporting iron-shod, six-spoked wheels (see also Judg. 1:19). Daunting as such military machinery must have been, Joshua insisted that it was no impediment to the eye of faith: **you shall drive out the Canaanites, though they have chariots of iron, and though they are strong** (see note on Josh. 15:63).

18:1–10 This section marks the structural and thematic midpoint in the account of the division of the land. Mention of **the whole congregation** of Israel calls to mind the unity of Israel as a people, even as each tribe receives its individual inheritance. That the assembly gathers before the **tent of meeting**, or tabernacle (see Ex. 27:21; 40:2), recalls Israel's history under Moses, of whom Joshua is now the successor. **Shiloh** (Khirbet Seilun), making its first biblical appearance here, serves as the central sanctuary that Israel was to establish once safely settled in the land (Deut. 12:10–11; cf. Ps. 78:60; Jer. 7:12); Shiloh was likely destroyed following the battle of Ebenezer (1 Samuel 4; Jer. 7:14; 26:6, 9) and was replaced as central sanctuary by Jerusalem in the time of King David, a fact of which the present text makes no mention. Notice that the statement, **the land lay subdued before them** (Josh. 18:1), sums up the first half of the book, while Joshua's question in v. 3, "**How long will you put off going in to take possession of the land**?" pervades the second half of the book. Mention of **the God of your fathers** evokes God's promise of land to the patriarchs (see note on 1:2), and reference to the land's having now been **given** (18:3) underscores the fulfillment of the repeated promise of ch. 1 that the Lord would "give" the land. The Lord has fulfilled all his "good promises" (21:45); how will Israel respond?

18:7 The Levites have no portion among you. See note on 13:14. Adding that **the priesthood of the LORD is their heritage**, this verse prepares for the designation in ch. 21 of Levitical cities throughout the territories.

18:9 wrote in a book. Or on a scroll, or some other writing material (the Hb. term *seper* does not specify).

them in Shiloh before the LORD. And there Joshua apportioned the land to the people of
Israel, [y]to each his portion.

The Inheritance for Benjamin

11 The lot of the tribe of the people of Benjamin according to its clans came up, and the
territory allotted to it fell between the people of Judah and the people of Joseph. 12 [z]On the
north side their boundary began at the Jordan. [a]Then the boundary goes up to the shoulder
north of Jericho, then up through the hill country westward, and it ends at the wilderness
of [b]Beth-aven. 13 From there the boundary passes along southward in the direction of Luz,
to the shoulder of [c]Luz (that is, Bethel), then the boundary goes down to [d]Ataroth-addar, on
the mountain that lies south of Lower [e]Beth-horon. 14 Then the boundary goes in another
direction, turning on the [f]western side southward from the mountain that lies to the south,
opposite Beth-horon, and it ends at Kiriath-baal ([g]that is, Kiriath-jearim), a city belonging
to the people of Judah. This forms the western side. 15 And the southern side begins at the
outskirts of Kiriath-jearim. And the boundary goes from there to Ephron,[1] [g]to the spring
of the waters of Nephtoah. 16 Then the boundary goes down to the border of the mountain
that overlooks [h]the Valley of the Son of Hinnom, which is at the north end of the Valley
of [i]Rephaim. And it then goes down the [h]Valley of Hinnom, south of the shoulder of the
Jebusites, and downward to [j]En-rogel. 17 Then it bends in a northerly direction going on to
En-shemesh, and from there goes to Geliloth, which is opposite the ascent of Adummim.
Then it goes down to [k]the stone of Bohan the son of Reuben, 18 and passing on to the north
of [l]the shoulder of Beth-arabah[2] it goes down to [l]the Arabah. 19 Then the boundary passes
on to the north of the shoulder of [k]Beth-hoglah. And the boundary ends at the northern bay
of [m]the Salt Sea, at the south end of the Jordan: this is the southern border. 20 The Jordan
forms its boundary on the eastern side. This is the inheritance of the people of Benjamin,
according to their clans, boundary by boundary all around.

21 Now the cities of the tribe of the people of Benjamin according to their clans were
[n]Jericho, Beth-hoglah, Emek-keziz, 22 Beth-arabah, Zemaraim, Bethel, 23 Avvim, Parah,
Ophrah, 24 Chephar-ammoni, Ophni, Geba—twelve cities with their villages: 25 Gibeon,
Ramah, Beeroth, 26 Mizpeh, Chephirah, Mozah, 27 Rekem, Irpeel, Taralah, 28 Zela, Haeleph,
[o]Jebus[3] (that is, Jerusalem), Gibeah[4] and Kiriath-jearim[5]—fourteen cities with their villages.
This is the inheritance of the people of Benjamin according to its clans.

The Inheritance for Simeon

19 The second lot came out for Simeon, for the tribe of the people of Simeon, according to their clans, [p]and their inheritance was in the midst of the inheritance of the
people of Judah. 2 [q]And they had for their inheritance Beersheba, Sheba, Moladah, 3 Hazar-
shual, Balah, Ezem, 4 Eltolad, Bethul, Hormah, 5 Ziklag, Beth-marcaboth, Hazar-susah,
6 Beth-lebaoth, and Sharuhen—thirteen cities with their villages; 7 Ain, Rimmon, Ether,
and Ashan—four cities with their villages, 8 together with all the villages around these
cities as far as Baalath-beer, Ramah of the Negeb. This was the inheritance of the tribe of
the people of Simeon according to their clans. 9 [r]The inheritance of the people of Simeon
formed part of the territory of the people of Judah. Because the portion of the people of
Judah was too large for them, the people of Simeon obtained an inheritance in the midst
of their inheritance.

The Inheritance for Zebulun

10 The third lot came up for the people of Zebulun, according to their clans. And the territory of their inheritance reached as far as Sarid. 11 Then their boundary goes up [s]westward

[1] See 15:9; Hebrew *westward* [2] Septuagint; Hebrew *to the shoulder over against the Arabah* [3] Septuagint, Syriac, Vulgate; Hebrew *the Jebusite* [4] Hebrew *Gibeath* [5] Septuagint; Hebrew *Kiriath*

10 [y]ch. 11:23; 12:7
12 [z][ch. 16:1] [a]ver. 21 [b]See ch. 7:2
13 [c]See ch. 16:2 [d]ch. 16:5 [e]ch. 16:3; See ch. 10:10
14 [f][ch. 19:11] [g]ch. 15:9
15 [g][See ver. 14 above]
16 [h]See ch. 15:8 [i]See ch. 12:4 [j]See ch. 15:7
17 [k]ch. 15:6
18 [l]ch. 11:2; 15:6
19 [k][See ver. 17 above] [m]ch. 15:2
21 [n]ver. 12
28 [o]See ch. 15:8

Chapter 19

1 [p]ver. 9; [Gen. 49:7]
2 [q]For ver. 2-8, see 1 Chr. 4:28-33
9 [r]ver. 1
11 [s][ch. 18:14; Gen. 49:13]

18:11 Though one of the smaller tribes, **Benjamin** was significant not only as the tribe of Israel's first king, Saul (1 Sam. 9:21), but also because it served as a buffer between the dominant tribes to the south and north; its allotted territory **fell between the people of Judah and the people of Joseph** (Ephraim and half of Manasseh).

19:1–9 That the allotment for **Simeon** fell **in the midst of the inheritance of the people of Judah** (v. 1) is explained by the fact that **the portion of the people of Judah was too large for them** (v. 9). (For a theological rationale, cf. Gen. 49:7.) Logically, no boundary description is given for Simeon, only a list of cities. Those cities that can be located stretched west to east

and on to Mareal and touches Dabbesheth, then the brook that is east of [t]Jokneam. 12 From
Sarid it goes in the other direction eastward toward the sunrise to the boundary of Chisloth-
tabor. From there it goes to Daberath, then up to Japhia. 13 From there it passes along on the
east toward the sunrise to Gath-hepher, to Eth-kazin, and going on to Rimmon it bends
toward Neah, 14 then on the north the boundary turns about to Hannathon, and it ends at
the Valley of Iphtahel; 15 and Kattath, Nahalal, [u]Shimron, Idalah, and Bethlehem—twelve
cities with their villages. 16 This is the inheritance of the people of Zebulun, according to
their clans—these cities with their villages.

The Inheritance for Issachar

17 The fourth lot came out for Issachar, for the people of Issachar, according to their clans.
18 Their territory included Jezreel, Chesulloth, [v]Shunem, 19 Hapharaim, Shion, Anaharath,
20 Rabbith, Kishion, Ebez, 21 Remeth, En-gannim, En-haddah, Beth-pazzez. 22 The boundary also touches Tabor, Shahazumah, and Beth-shemesh, and its boundary ends at the
Jordan—sixteen cities with their villages. 23 This is the inheritance of the tribe of the people
of Issachar, according to their clans—the cities with their villages.

The Inheritance for Asher

24 The fifth lot came out for the tribe of the people of Asher according to their clans.
25 Their territory included Helkath, Hali, Beten, Achshaph, 26 Allammelech, Amad, and
Mishal. On the west it touches [w]Carmel and Shihor-libnath, 27 then it turns eastward, it
goes to Beth-dagon, and touches Zebulun and the Valley of Iphtahel northward to Beth-
emek and Neiel. Then it continues in the north to [x]Cabul, 28 Ebron, Rehob, Hammon,
Kanah, as far as [y]Sidon the Great. 29 Then the boundary turns to Ramah, reaching to the
fortified city of Tyre. Then the boundary turns to Hosah, and it ends at the sea; Mahalab,[1]
Achzib, 30 Ummah, Aphek and Rehob—twenty-two cities with their villages. 31 This is
the inheritance of the tribe of the people of Asher according to their clans—these cities
with their villages.

The Inheritance for Naphtali

32 The sixth lot came out for the people of Naphtali, for the people of Naphtali, according
to their clans. 33 And their boundary ran from Heleph, from [z]the oak in Zaanannim, and
Adami-nekeb, and Jabneel, as far as Lakkum, and it ended at the Jordan. 34 Then the boundary turns [a]westward to Aznoth-tabor and goes from there to Hukkok, touching Zebulun at
the south and Asher on the west and Judah on the east at the Jordan. 35 The fortified cities
are Ziddim, Zer, Hammath, Rakkath, [b]Chinnereth, 36 Adamah, Ramah, [c]Hazor, 37 Kedesh,
Edrei, En-hazor, 38 Yiron, Migdal-el, Horem, Beth-anath, and Beth-shemesh—nineteen
cities with their villages. 39 This is the inheritance of the tribe of the people of Naphtali
according to their clans—the cities with their villages.

The Inheritance for Dan

40 The seventh lot came out for the tribe of the people of Dan, according to their clans.
41 And the territory of its inheritance included Zorah, Eshtaol, Ir-shemesh, 42 [d]Shaalabbin,
[d]Aijalon, Ithlah, 43 Elon, Timnah, Ekron, 44 Eltekeh, Gibbethon, Baalath, 45 Jehud, Bene-
berak, Gath-rimmon, 46 and Me-jarkon and Rakkon with the territory over against [e]Joppa.
47 When [f]the territory of the people of Dan was lost to them, the people of Dan went up
and fought against Leshem, and after capturing it and striking it with the sword they took
possession of it and settled in it, calling Leshem, Dan, after the name of Dan their ancestor.
48 This is the inheritance of the tribe of the people of Dan, according to their clans—these
cities with their villages.

[1] Compare Septuagint; Hebrew *Mehebel*

11 [t]ch. 12:22; 21:34
15 [u]ch. 11:1
18 [v]1 Sam. 28:4
26 [w]1 Kgs. 18:19, 20, 42; 2 Kgs. 2:25; 4:25; Song 7:5; Isa. 33:9; Jer. 50:19
27 [x][1 Kgs. 9:13]
28 [y]ch. 11:8; [Judg. 1:31]
33 [z][Judg. 4:11]
34 [a][Deut. 33:23]
35 [b]See ch. 11:2
36 [c]ch. 11:1
42 [d]Judg. 1:35
46 [e]2 Chr. 2:16; Ezra 3:7
47 [f]Judg. 1:34, 35; 18:1

along the southern reaches of Judahite territory, suggesting that Simeon may have served a protective function against enemies to the south.

19:15 Bethlehem is a northerly village not to be confused with the more famous Bethlehem in Judah (Judg. 17:7).

19:47 On how Dan's territory **was lost to them**, see Judg. 1:34. The story of how **Dan went up and fought against Leshem** is told in Judges 18, where the citizens of Laish (Leshem) are described as a people "quiet and unsuspecting" (Judg. 18:7).

The Inheritance for Joshua

49 When they had finished distributing the several territories of the land as inheritances,
the people of Israel gave an inheritance among them to Joshua the son of Nun. 50 By command of the LORD they gave him the city that he asked, [g]Timnath-serah in the hill country
of Ephraim. And he rebuilt the city and settled in it.
51 [h]These are the inheritances that Eleazar the priest and Joshua the son of Nun and
the heads of the fathers' houses of the tribes of the people of Israel distributed by lot [i]at
Shiloh before the LORD, at the entrance of the tent of meeting. So they finished dividing
the land.

The Cities of Refuge

20 Then the LORD said to Joshua, 2 "Say to the people of Israel, [j]'Appoint the cities of
refuge, of which I spoke to you through Moses, 3 that the manslayer who strikes any
person without intent or unknowingly may flee there. They shall be for you a refuge from
the avenger of blood. 4 He shall flee to one of these cities and shall stand [k]at the entrance of
the gate of the city and explain his case to the elders of that city. Then they shall take him
into the city and give him a place, and he shall remain with them. 5 And if the avenger of
blood pursues him, they shall not give up the manslayer into his hand, because he struck
his neighbor unknowingly, and did not hate him in the past. 6 And he shall remain in that
city [l]until he has stood before the congregation for judgment, until the death of him who
is high priest at the time. Then the manslayer may return to his own town and his own
home, to the town from which he fled.'"
7 So they set apart [m]Kedesh in Galilee in the hill country of Naphtali, and [n]Shechem
in the hill country of Ephraim, and [o]Kiriath-arba (that is, Hebron) [p]in the hill country of
Judah. 8 And beyond the Jordan east of Jericho, they appointed [q]Bezer in the wilderness
on the tableland, from the tribe of Reuben, and [r]Ramoth in Gilead, from the tribe of Gad,
and [s]Golan in Bashan, from the tribe of Manasseh. 9 These were the cities designated for
all the people of Israel and [t]for the stranger sojourning among them, that anyone who
killed a person without intent could flee there, so that he might not die by the hand of
the avenger of blood, till he stood before the congregation.

Cities and Pasturelands Allotted to Levi

21 Then the heads of the fathers' houses of the Levites came [u]to Eleazar the priest
and to Joshua the son of Nun and to the heads of the fathers' houses of the tribes
of the people of Israel. 2 And they said to them [v]at Shiloh in the land of Canaan, [w]"The

50 [g]ch. 24:30; Judg. 2:9
51 [h]ch. 14:1; Num. 34:17 [i]See ch. 18:1

Chapter 20

2 [j]Ex. 21:13; See Num. 35:6, 11-14; Deut. 4:41-43; 19:2-9
4 [k][Deut. 21:19; Ruth 4:1, 2; Ps. 127:5]
6 [l]Num. 35:12, 24, 25
7 [m]ch. 21:32; 1 Chr. 6:76 [n]ch. 21:21 [o]ch. 21:11, 13; See ch. 14:13-15 [p]ch. 21:11; Luke 1:39
8 [q]ch. 21:36; 1 Chr. 6:78 [r]ch. 21:38; [1 Kgs. 22:3] [s]ch. 21:27; 1 Chr. 6:71
9 [t]Num. 35:15

Chapter 21

1 [u]ch. 14:1; 17:4; 19:51; Num. 34:17, 18
2 [v]See ch. 18:1 [w]Num. 35:2

19:49–50 Like Caleb, his fellow survivor from the wilderness years, **Joshua** receives **an inheritance among them** (for Caleb, see 14:6–15). On the framing function of these two notices, see note on 14:1–19:51. **By command of the LORD**, Joshua is given **Timnath-serah** (Khirbet Tibnah; called Timnath-heres in the notice of Joshua's death in Judg. 2:6–10). The site is in southwest Ephraim, away from the more formidable cities of the period. Joshua's reception of an inheritance only after all others have received theirs speaks well of him as a leader. That his city is away from the major power centers may contain a hint that his most active leadership years are drawing to a close.

19:51 Eleazar the priest and Joshua. See note on 14:1–19:51. Everything in this concluding verse indicates that the tribal allocations have been conducted appropriately at the Lord's direction—**by lot**.

20:1–21:45 *A Land of Justice and Worship.* The designation of six cities of refuge (ch. 20) and 48 Levitical cities (21:1–42) demonstrates the Lord's concern that the land not only be duly allocated as an inheritance for the tribes (chs. 13–19) but that it be a land where justice prevails and true worship is cultivated. The section ends with yet another proclamation that the Lord has fulfilled all the good promises he made to the house of Israel (21:43–45).

20:1–2 The fullest description of how the **cities of refuge** are to function appears in Num. 35:6–34, where the Lord expands on his initial instructions to Moses in Ex. 21:12–14. They are to be six in number, chosen among the Levitical cities, with three on each side of the Jordan (Num. 35:13–14). They are to guarantee judicial due process for anyone in Israel, including "the stranger" and "the sojourner" (Num. 35:15). In Deut. 4:41–43 Moses designates by name the three cities of refuge in the newly conquered territory east of the Jordan, one each in the territories of Reuben, Gad, and eastern Manasseh. Later, in Deut. 19:1–10, he charges Israel regarding the cities to be designated west of the Jordan, though he does not name them, as the land is yet to be conquered. They are to be appropriately spaced, so that the fugitive can reach the nearest one before being overtaken by the avenger (Deut. 19:3; and see note on Josh. 20:3). Should God enlarge Israel's territory, an additional three cities can be designated (Deut. 19:8–9). That the additional three are not mentioned in Joshua may hint at the fact that Israel was not entirely successful in taking over all the land. The three cities west of the Jordan are finally named in Josh. 20:7. This overall progression is in keeping with the geographical movements of Israel and the extent of the conquest at each stage.

20:3 A **manslayer** was one who unintentionally or without premeditation took another's life. The "kinsman-redeemer" (Hb. *go'el*) was typically the nearest male relative, responsible to protect the family's lives, liberty, property, and so forth (Lev. 25:25–26). Where a life was taken, the kinsman-redeemer became the **avenger of blood**, held responsible in cases of murder to "put the murderer to death" (Num. 35:19, 21). In distinction from some of its ancient Near Eastern neighbors, Israel was to "accept no ransom for the life of the murderer" (Num. 35:31), for the Lord desired justice in respect to both guilt and innocence (Prov. 17:15).

20:6 until he has stood before the congregation . . . until the death of him who is high priest at the time. This verse compresses the fuller instructions provided in Numbers 35.

21:1–41 From the beginning of the division of the land, this section in which the **Levites** receive their inheritance has been anticipated (see note on 13:14). Mention of **Eleazar**, **Joshua**, and the **heads of the fathers' houses** (21:1),

4[x]See ver. 9-19; Ex. 6:16-19; Num. 3:17-20
5[y]See ver. 20-26
6[z]See ver. 27-33
7[a]See ver. 34-40
8[b]ver. 3 [c]Num. 35:2; See ch. 14:3-5
10[d]ver. 4
11[e]For ver. 11-19, see 1 Chr. 6:54-60 [f]See ch. 14:13-15 [g]ch. 20:7; Luke 1:39
13[h]ch. 20:7 [i]ch. 10:29
17[j]ch. 9:3
20[k]For ver. 20-26, see 1 Chr. 6:66-70
21[l]ch. 20:7, 8
27[m]For ver. 27-33, see 1 Chr. 6:71-76 [l][See ver. 21 above]
32[l][See ver. 21 above]

LORD commanded through Moses that we be given cities to dwell in, along with their
pasturelands for our livestock." 3 So by command of the LORD the people of Israel gave to
the Levites the following cities and pasturelands out of their inheritance.
4 The lot came out for the clans of the Kohathites. So those Levites who were descendants of Aaron the priest [x]received by lot from the tribes of Judah, Simeon, and Benjamin,
thirteen cities.
5 And the rest of the Kohathites received by lot [y]from the clans of the tribe of Ephraim,
from the tribe of Dan and the half-tribe of Manasseh, ten cities.
6 The [z]Gershonites received by lot from the clans of the tribe of Issachar, from the tribe
of Asher, from the tribe of Naphtali, and from the half-tribe of Manasseh in Bashan, thirteen cities.
7 The [a]Merarites according to their clans received from the tribe of Reuben, the tribe of
Gad, and the tribe of Zebulun, twelve cities.
8 These cities and their pasturelands the people of Israel [b]gave by lot to the Levites, [c]as
the LORD had commanded through Moses.
9 Out of the tribe of the people of Judah and the tribe of the people of Simeon they gave
the following cities mentioned by name, 10 which went to [d]the descendants of Aaron, one
of the clans of the Kohathites who belonged to the people of Levi; since the lot fell to them
first. 11 [e]They gave them [f]Kiriath-arba (Arba being the father of Anak), that is Hebron, [g]in
the hill country of Judah, along with the pasturelands around it. 12 But the fields of the city
and its villages had been given to Caleb the son of Jephunneh as his possession.
13 And to the descendants of Aaron the priest they gave Hebron, [h]the city of refuge for
the manslayer, with its pasturelands, [i]Libnah with its pasturelands, 14 Jattir with its pasturelands, Eshtemoa with its pasturelands, 15 Holon with its pasturelands, Debir with its
pasturelands, 16 Ain with its pasturelands, Juttah with its pasturelands, Beth-shemesh with
its pasturelands—nine cities out of these two tribes; 17 then out of the tribe of Benjamin,
[j]Gibeon with its pasturelands, Geba with its pasturelands, 18 Anathoth with its pasturelands,
and Almon with its pasturelands—four cities. 19 The cities of the descendants of Aaron,
the priests, were in all thirteen cities with their pasturelands.
20 [k]As to the rest of the Kohathites belonging to the Kohathite clans of the Levites, the
cities allotted to them were out of the tribe of Ephraim. 21 To them were given Shechem, [l]the
city of refuge for the manslayer, with its pasturelands in the hill country of Ephraim, Gezer
with its pasturelands, 22 Kibzaim with its pasturelands, Beth-horon with its pasturelands—
four cities; 23 and out of the tribe of Dan, Elteke with its pasturelands, Gibbethon with
its pasturelands, 24 Aijalon with its pasturelands, Gath-rimmon with its pasturelands—
four cities; 25 and out of the half-tribe of Manasseh, Taanach with its pasturelands, and
Gath-rimmon with its pasturelands—two cities. 26 The cities of the clans of the rest of the
Kohathites were ten in all with their pasturelands.
27 [m]And to the Gershonites, one of the clans of the Levites, were given out of the half-tribe
of Manasseh, Golan in Bashan with its pasturelands, [l]the city of refuge for the manslayer,
and Beeshterah with its pasturelands—two cities; 28 and out of the tribe of Issachar, Kishion
with its pasturelands, Daberath with its pasturelands, 29 Jarmuth with its pasturelands,
En-gannim with its pasturelands—four cities; 30 and out of the tribe of Asher, Mishal
with its pasturelands, Abdon with its pasturelands, 31 Helkath with its pasturelands, and
Rehob with its pasturelands—four cities; 32 and out of the tribe of Naphtali, Kedesh in
Galilee with its pasturelands, [l]the city of refuge for the manslayer, Hammoth-dor with its
pasturelands, and Kartan with its pasturelands—three cities. 33 The cities of the several
clans of the Gershonites were in all thirteen cities with their pasturelands.

as well as the location at **Shiloh** (v. 2), indicate that this final allocation took place at the same time and place as the general distribution of chs. 18–19. Back in Num. 35:1–8, **the LORD commanded through Moses** that 48 cities (including the six cities of refuge) be assigned to the Levites. The effect of taking cities and their pasturelands from each of the tribes would be to scatter the Levites throughout the whole of Israel (cf. Gen. 49:7). This distribution would facilitate the Levites' fulfilling their duties. Many of the cities were along borders—with the Philistines in the southwest; the Canaanites in the plains and coastlands to the north; eastern boundary regions in Transjordan; and so forth. The Levites were grouped according to their descent from one of Levi's three sons (see Gen. 46:11). The **Kohathites** (Josh. 21:4), of whom **Aaron** and his line descended (Ex. 6:16–20), received cities in the center and the south of the land, while the **Gershonites** (Josh. 21:6) and **Merarites** (v. 7) received cities in the north and east.

21:18 The priestly city of **Anathoth** (see 1 Kings 2:26) was the eventual home of the prophet Jeremiah (Jer. 1:1).

34 [n]And to the rest of the Levites, the Merarite clans, were given out of the tribe of Zebulun,
Jokneam with its pasturelands, Kartah with its pasturelands, **35** Dimnah with its pasturelands, Nahalal with its pasturelands—four cities; **36** and out of the tribe of Reuben, [o]Bezer
with its pasturelands, Jahaz with its pasturelands, **37** Kedemoth with its pasturelands, and
Mephaath with its pasturelands—four cities; **38** and out of the tribe of Gad, [o]Ramoth in
Gilead with its pasturelands, the city of refuge for the manslayer, [p]Mahanaim with its
pasturelands, **39** [p]Heshbon with its pasturelands, Jazer with its pasturelands—four cities
in all. **40** As for the cities of the several Merarite clans, that is, the remainder of the clans of
the Levites, those allotted to them were in all twelve cities.

41 [q]The cities of the Levites in the midst of the possession of the people of Israel were
in all forty-eight cities with their pasturelands. **42** These cities each had its pasturelands
around it. So it was with all these cities.

43 [r]Thus the LORD gave to Israel all the land that he swore to give to their fathers. And
they took possession of it, and they settled there. **44** [s]And the LORD gave them rest on every
side just as he had sworn to their fathers. [t]Not one of all their enemies had withstood them,
for [u]the LORD had given all their enemies into their hands. **45** [v]Not one word of all the good
promises that the LORD had made to the house of Israel had failed; all came to pass.

The Eastern Tribes Return Home

22 At that time Joshua summoned the Reubenites and the Gadites and the half-tribe
of Manasseh, **2** and said to them, "You have kept [w]all that Moses the servant of the
LORD commanded you [x]and have obeyed my voice in all that I have commanded you. **3** You
have not forsaken your brothers these many days, down to this day, but have been careful
to keep the charge of the LORD your God. **4** [y]And now the LORD your God has given rest
to your brothers, as he promised them. Therefore turn and go to your tents in the land
where your possession lies, [z]which Moses the servant of the LORD gave you on the other
side of the Jordan. **5** [a]Only be very careful to observe the commandment and the law that
Moses the servant of the LORD commanded you, [b]to love the LORD your God, and to walk
in all his ways and to keep his commandments and to cling to him and to serve him with
all your heart and with all your soul." **6** So Joshua [c]blessed them and sent them away, and
they went to their tents.

7 Now to the one half of the tribe of Manasseh Moses had given a possession in Bashan,
[d]but to the other half Joshua had given a possession beside their brothers in the land west
of the Jordan. And when Joshua sent them away to their homes and blessed them, **8** he said
to them, "Go back to your tents with much wealth and with very much livestock, with
silver, gold, bronze, and iron, and with much clothing. [e]Divide the spoil of your enemies
with your brothers." **9** So the people of Reuben and the people of Gad and the half-tribe

34 [n]For ver. 34-40, see 1 Chr. 6:77-81
36 [o]ch. 20:8
38 [o][See ver. 36 above] [p]See ch. 13:26
39 [p][See ver. 38 above]
41 [q]Num. 35:7
43 [r]Gen. 13:15; 15:18; 26:3; 28:4, 13
44 [s]See ch. 11:23 [t]ch. 10:8; 23:9 [u]ch. 2:24; Deut. 7:24
45 [v]ch. 23:14, 15

Chapter 22

2 [w]See Num. 32:20-22; Deut. 3:18-20 [x]ch. 1:16, 17
4 [y]See ch. 11:23 [z]See ch. 13:8
5 [a]Deut. 6:6, 17; 11:22 [b]ch. 23:11; Deut. 6:5; 10:12; 11:1, 13, 22
6 [c]ch. 14:13
7 [d]ch. 17:5
8 [e]Num. 31:27; 1 Sam. 30:24

21:43–45 Just as the account of the taking of the **land** drew to a close with generalizing summaries (10:40–42; 11:16–23), so the account of the dividing of the land ends with a summary section. It picks up on key motifs such as "land," "rest," and "victory" as the Lord's "gifts" (see esp. ch. 1; the word "rest" occurs also in 11:23 and 14:15, but the Hb. terminology is different). As seen later in Joshua, this section should be understood as a broad summary statement emphasizing the Lord's decisive action on behalf of Israel, rather than as a comprehensive assertion that all of Israel's enemies had been eradicated from the land. Although Israel did, in fact, take **possession** of the land and **settled there** (21:43), much work still remained to be done (see 23:5). But the key point is that the Lord has been utterly true to his **good promises**: none has failed, and **all came to pass** (21:45; the word "all" occurs six times in the Hb. text of vv. 43–45; see also 23:14).

22:1–24:33 *Serving the Lord in the Land.* Each of the preceding three major divisions of the book of Joshua receives its impetus from a *divine initiative*. The Lord instructs; Israel under Joshua's leadership responds; and the land is entered, taken, and divided. This final section lacks such a beginning. The Lord has already fulfilled all his "good promises" (21:45). Now it is Israel's turn to respond. In his old age, Joshua charges the people to be united and exclusive in "serving" the Lord alone.

22:1–34 *One Nation, Under God.* In this episode, the eastern tribes of Reuben, Gad, and eastern Manasseh are released to return to their homes, having fulfilled their duties to their fellow Israelites west of the Jordan (cf. Numbers 32). Their construction of a symbolic altar on the bank of the Jordan is at first misunderstood, and a disaster is narrowly averted. The reader does not learn the eastern tribes' motive until Josh. 22:21–29, which creates suspense. It is to the credit of the western tribes that they make a generous offer (v. 19) and then listen to the explanation and accept it (cf. Deut. 13:14). Both sides are determined to be faithful to their calling as Israel, and the account shows things working right. The key word "serve" occurs three times. Before their departure, Joshua charges the eastern tribes to serve the Lord "with all your heart and with all your soul" (Josh. 22:5). In v. 27, they insist that they "do perform the service of the LORD" (lit., "serve the service").

22:4 now the LORD your God has given rest to your brothers. See 1:12–15. The two and one-half eastern tribes are now free to go to their territories beyond the Jordan.

22:8 Divide the spoil of your enemies with your brothers. In the Bible, as generally in the ancient Near East, both victory in battle and the spoils of victory are regarded as gifts of the deity, in this case the Lord. These gifts were to be shared with allies, or covenant partners, irrespective of their actual role in the conflict (cf. Num. 31:25–31; 1 Sam. 30:24).

of Manasseh returned home, parting from the people of Israel at Shiloh, which is in the
land of Canaan, to go [f]to the land of Gilead, their own land of which they had possessed
themselves by command of the LORD through Moses.

The Eastern Tribes' Altar of Witness

10 And when they came to the region of the Jordan that is in the land of Canaan, the
people of Reuben and the people of Gad and the half-tribe of Manasseh built there an altar
by the Jordan, an altar of imposing size. 11 And the people of Israel [g]heard it said, "Behold,
the people of Reuben and the people of Gad and the half-tribe of Manasseh have built the
altar at the frontier of the land of Canaan, in the region about the Jordan, on the side that
belongs to the people of Israel." 12 And when the people of Israel heard of it, [h]the whole
assembly of the people of Israel gathered at Shiloh to make war against them.

13 Then the people of Israel sent to the people of Reuben and the people of Gad and
the half-tribe of Manasseh, in the land of Gilead, [i]Phinehas the son of Eleazar the priest,
14 and with him ten chiefs, one from each of the tribal families of Israel, [j]every one of them
the head of a family among the clans of Israel. 15 And they came to the people of Reuben,
the people of Gad, and the half-tribe of Manasseh, in the land of Gilead, and they said
to them, 16 "Thus says the whole congregation of the LORD, 'What is this breach of faith
that you have committed against the God of Israel in turning away this day from following the LORD by building yourselves an altar this day [k]in rebellion against the LORD?
17 Have we not had enough of [l]the sin at Peor from which even yet we have not cleansed
ourselves, and for which there came a plague upon the congregation of the LORD, 18 that
you too must turn away this day from following the LORD? And if [k]you too rebel against
the LORD today then tomorrow [m]he will be angry with the whole congregation of Israel.
19 But now, if the land of your possession is unclean, pass over into the LORD's land [n]where
the LORD's tabernacle stands, and take for yourselves a possession among us. [o]Only do
not rebel against the LORD or make us as rebels by building for yourselves an altar other
than the altar of the LORD our God. 20 [p]Did not Achan the son of Zerah break faith in the
matter of the devoted things, and [m]wrath fell upon all the congregation of Israel? And he
did not perish alone for his iniquity.'"

21 Then the people of Reuben, the people of Gad, and the half-tribe of Manasseh said
in answer to the heads of the families of Israel, 22 "The Mighty One, [q]God, the LORD! The
Mighty One, God, the LORD! [r]He knows; and let Israel itself know! If it was in rebellion or
in breach of faith against the LORD, do not spare us today 23 for building an altar to turn
away from following the LORD. Or if we did so to offer burnt offerings or grain offerings or
peace offerings on it, may the LORD himself [s]take vengeance. 24 No, but we did it from fear
that [t]in time to come your children might say to our children, 'What have you to do with
the LORD, the God of Israel? 25 For the LORD has made the Jordan a boundary between us
and you, you people of Reuben and people of Gad. You have no portion in the LORD.' So
your children might make our children cease to worship the LORD. 26 Therefore we said,
'Let us now build an altar, not for burnt offering, nor for sacrifice, 27 but to be [u]a witness
between us and you, and between our generations after us, that we [v]do perform the service
of the LORD in his presence with our burnt offerings and sacrifices and peace offerings,
so your children will not say to our children in time to come, "You have no portion in the
LORD."' 28 And we thought, 'If this should be said to us or to our descendants in time to
come, we should say, "Behold, the copy of the altar of the LORD, which our fathers made,

9 [f]Num. 32:1, 26, 29
11 [g]See Deut. 13:12-15
12 [h]Judg. 20:1
13 [i]Ex. 6:25; Num. 25:7; Judg. 20:28
14 [j]Num. 1:4
16 [k]ver. 18, 19; Num. 14:9; [Lev. 17:8, 9; Deut. 12:13, 14]
17 [l]Num. 25:3; Deut. 4:3; Ps. 106:28
18 [k][See ver. 16 above] [m]Num. 16:22
19 [n]ch. 18:1 [o]ver. 16, 18
20 [p]ch. 7:1, 5 [m][See ver. 18 above]
22 [q]Deut. 10:17 [r]1 Kgs. 8:39
23 [s]Deut. 18:19; 1 Sam. 20:16
24 [t]See ch. 4:6, 21
27 [u]ver. 34; ch. 24:27; Gen. 31:48 [v]Deut. 12:5, 6, 17, 18

22:10–11 altar of imposing size. Very similar Hebrew terminology is used in Ex. 3:3 to describe the burning bush as a "great sight." Apparently, the altar was built on the western shore of the Jordan, **on the side that belongs to the people of Israel**, but was conspicuous enough to be seen from either side.

22:13–20 Having misunderstood the purpose of the "imposing altar," the tribes that settled west of the Jordan send a delegation to confront the eastern tribes. That **Phinehas the son of Eleazar** heads the delegation can only strike fear in the hearts of those familiar with his history of zeal for the purity of Israel's worship (see Num. 25:1–9). For those requiring a reminder, the **sin at Peor** is explicitly mentioned in Josh. 22:17 (cf. Num. 25:3, 18), as is the case of **Achan** in Josh. 22:20, who **did not perish alone for his iniquity** (see ch. 7). Given its corporate responsibility, all Israel can suffer for the sins of a few or even just one. The delegation rightly fears that the Lord may become **angry with the whole congregation of Israel** (22:18).

22:21–31 Fearing the worst, the delegation of western tribes is relieved to hear that the altar built by the eastern tribes is but a **copy of the altar of the LORD** (v. 28). It is not intended to rival the altar at Shiloh but only to serve as a **witness between us and you** (v. 28), a visible monument refuting any suggestion (now or in the future) that the eastern tribes **have no portion in the LORD** (v. 25).

not for burnt offerings, nor for sacrifice, but to be [u]a witness between us and you.'" 29 Far be
it from us that we should [w]rebel against the LORD and turn away this day from following
the LORD [w]by building an altar for burnt offering, grain offering, or sacrifice, other than
the altar of the LORD our God that stands before his tabernacle!"
30 When [x]Phinehas the priest and the chiefs of the congregation, the heads of the families
of Israel who were with him, heard the words that the people of Reuben and the people
of Gad and the people of Manasseh spoke, [y]it was good in their eyes. 31 And Phinehas
the son of Eleazar the priest said to the people of Reuben and the people of Gad and the
people of Manasseh, "Today we know that [z]the LORD is in our midst, because you have
not committed this breach of faith against the LORD. Now you have delivered the people
of Israel from the hand of the LORD."
32 Then Phinehas the son of Eleazar the priest, and the chiefs, returned from the people
of Reuben and the people of Gad [a]in the land of Gilead to the land of Canaan, to the
people of Israel, and brought back word to them. 33 And the report [b]was good in the eyes
of the people of Israel. And the people of Israel [c]blessed God and spoke no more of making war against them to destroy the land where the people of Reuben and the people of
Gad were settled. 34 The people of Reuben and the people of Gad called the altar Witness,
"For," they said, [d]"it is a witness between us that the LORD is God."

Joshua's Charge to Israel's Leaders

23 A long time afterward, when the LORD had given [e]rest to Israel from all their
surrounding enemies, and Joshua [f]was old and well advanced in years, 2 Joshua
[g]summoned all Israel, its elders and heads, its judges and officers, and said to them, "I am
now old and well advanced in years. 3 And you have seen all that the LORD your God has
done to all these nations for your sake, [h]for it is the LORD your God who has fought for
you. 4 Behold, [i]I have allotted to you as an inheritance for your tribes those nations that
remain, along with all the nations that I have already cut off, from the Jordan to the Great
Sea in the west. 5 The LORD your God [j]will push them back before you and drive them
out of your sight. And you shall possess their land, [k]just as the LORD your God promised
you. 6 Therefore, [l]be very strong to keep and to do all that is written in the Book of the
Law of Moses, [m]turning aside from it neither to the right hand nor to the left, 7 [n]that you

28 [u][See ver. 27 above]
29 [w]See ver. 16
30 [x]ver. 13, 14 [y]ver. 33
31 [z]Lev. 26:11, 12
32 [a]ver. 10, 11, 15
33 [b]ver. 30 [c]1 Chr. 29:20; Neh. 8:6; Dan. 2:19; Luke 2:28
34 [d]ver. 27

Chapter 23

1 [e]See ch. 11:23 [f]ch. 13:1
2 [g]ch. 24:1; [Deut. 31:28; 1 Chr. 28:1]
3 [h]ch. 10:14, 42; Ex. 14:14
4 [i]See ch. 13:2-7
5 [j]ch. 13:6; Ex. 23:30; 33:2; 34:11; Deut. 11:23 [k]Num. 33:53
6 [l]ch. 1:7 [m]ch. 1:7; Deut. 5:32; 28:14
7 [n]Ex. 23:33; Deut. 7:2, 3

22:34 called the altar Witness. This sixth monument in the land (see note on 4:20) bears witness to the unity of the Transjordanian tribes with Israel west of the Jordan.

Seven Stone Memorials in the Land

4:20	Gilgal	a reminder of God's faithfulness in bringing Israel safely across the Jordan into the Promised Land
7:26	over Achan	a reminder of Israel's potential for unfaithfulness and of the dire consequences that result
8:28–29	over the king of Ai	a monument to Israel's second chance and restoration
8:30–32	Joshua engraves a copy of the law	a reminder of Israel's duty to live in obedience to the divine "Torah," or "instruction"
10:27	over Amorite kings at Gibeon	a reminder of God's gracious action in defending Israel's covenant with a Canaanite city
22:34	peace in the land of Gilead	a witness to the unity of the Transjordanian tribes with Israel west of the Jordan
24:26–27	covenant renewal at Shechem	a reminder of Israel's duty to serve the Lord, who fulfilled every promise in bringing them into the land

23:1–16 *Joshua's Charge to Israel's Leaders.* In many respects this episode mirrors the opening episode in the book of Joshua. The book began with the passing of the mantle of leadership to Joshua, after the death of Moses. Joshua, now "old and well advanced in years" (v. 1; cf. 13:1), will soon die (24:29), and so the next generation of leaders is charged in terms reminiscent of Joshua's own charge in ch. 1.

23:1 A long time afterward. Specificity is not possible, but probably more than a quarter century has elapsed since Israel first crossed the Jordan into the land—assuming that Joshua was similar in age to Caleb at the beginning of the conquest (who was nearing 80; see note on 11:16–20), and in view of Joshua's age of 110 at death (24:29). **had given rest.** The reference in Heb. 4:8 does not deny this, but rather clarifies the truth that life in the earthly Promised Land does not automatically bring one to participate in God's own "rest."

23:4–5 I have allotted . . . those nations that remain. Joshua has obeyed the mandate he received in 13:1–7 (see 23:6). With respect to these remaining peoples, Joshua reminds Israel's leaders of the Lord's promise to **drive them out** ("dispossess"; cf. 13:6) and their responsibility to **possess their land** (cf. 13:1).

23:6 Joshua charges the leaders who are to succeed him to **be very strong,** just as he had been charged three times in 1:5–9. Here he highlights only the central, key point: their greatest duty and challenge is to live and lead according to **all that is written in the Book of the Law of Moses** (cf. 1:7–8).

23:7–8 The key question facing the generation following Joshua is whom they will **serve**: the **gods** of the **nations remaining** or the true God of Israel (cf. v. 16). Allegiance to the gods of other nations continued to be the primary threat Israel faced while living among (**mix with**) the nations (cf. Ps. 106:34–36).

7 [o]Ex. 23:13; [Ps. 16:4] [p]Jer. 5:7; [Zeph. 1:5]
8 [q]ch. 22:5; Deut. 10:20; 11:22; 13:4
9 [r]ch. 13:6; Ex. 23:30; 33:2; 34:11; Deut. 11:23 [s]ch. 1:5; 10:8; 21:44
10 [t][Lev. 26:8; Deut. 32:30] [u]ver. 3; Ex. 14:14; Deut. 3:22
11 [v]ch. 22:5
12 [w]Ex. 34:16; Deut. 7:3
13 [x]Judg. 2:3, 21 [y]Ex. 23:33; Num. 33:55; Deut. 7:16; Judg. 2:3
14 [z]1 Kgs. 2:2 [a]ch. 21:45
15 [b]See Lev. 26:14-39; Deut. 28:15-68

Chapter 24

1 [c]ver. 25, 32 [d]See ch. 23:2 [e]1 Sam. 10:19
2 [f]See Gen. 11:27-32 [g][Gen. 31:30; 35:2]
3 [h]See Gen. 12:1-5; Acts 7:2-4 [i]Gen. 12:6 [j]Gen. 21:2, 3
4 [k]Gen. 25:24-26 [l]Gen. 36:8; Deut. 2:5 [m]Gen. 46:1, 6; Acts 7:15
5 [n]Ex. 3:10; 4:14 [o]See Ex. 7–12 [p]Ex. 12:37, 51
6 [p][See ver. 5 above] [q]Ex. 14:2 [r]Ex. 14:9
7 [s]Ex. 14:10 [t]Ex. 14:20 [u]Ex. 14:27, 28 [v]Deut. 4:34; 29:2 [w]See ch. 5:6

may not mix with these nations remaining among you [o]or make mention of the names
of their gods [p]or swear by them or serve them or bow down to them, **8** [q]but you shall
cling to the LORD your God just as you have done to this day. **9** [r]For the LORD has driven
out before you great and strong nations. And as for you, [s]no man has been able to stand
before you to this day. **10** [t]One man of you puts to flight a thousand, since it is the LORD
your God [u]who fights for you, just as he promised you. **11** [v]Be very careful, therefore, to
love the LORD your God. **12** For if you turn back and cling to the remnant of these nations
remaining among you [w]and make marriages with them, so that you associate with them
and they with you, **13** know for certain that [x]the LORD your God will no longer drive out
these nations before you, [y]but they shall be a snare and a trap for you, a whip on your
sides and thorns in your eyes, until you perish from off this good ground that the LORD
your God has given you.

14 "And now [z]I am about to go the way of all the earth, and you know in your hearts
and souls, all of you, that [a]not one word has failed of all the good things[1] that the LORD
your God promised concerning you. All have come to pass for you; not one of them has
failed. **15** But just as all the good things that the LORD your God promised concerning
you have been fulfilled for you, so the LORD will bring upon you [b]all the evil things,
until he has destroyed you from off this good land that the LORD your God has given
you, **16** if you transgress the covenant of the LORD your God, which he commanded you,
and go and serve other gods and bow down to them. Then the anger of the LORD will
be kindled against you, and you shall perish quickly from off the good land that he has
given to you."

The Covenant Renewal at Shechem

24 Joshua gathered all the tribes of Israel [c]to Shechem and [d]summoned the elders,
the heads, the judges, and the officers of Israel. And [e]they presented themselves
before God. **2** And Joshua said to all the people, "Thus says the LORD, the God of Israel,
'Long ago, [f]your fathers lived beyond the Euphrates,[2] Terah, the father of Abraham and
of Nahor; and [g]they served other gods. **3** [h]Then I took your father Abraham from beyond
the River and [i]led him through all the land of Canaan, and made his offspring many. [j]I
gave him Isaac. **4** And to Isaac I gave [k]Jacob and Esau. [l]And I gave Esau the hill country
of Seir to possess, [m]but Jacob and his children went down to Egypt. **5** [n]And I sent Moses
and Aaron, [o]and I plagued Egypt with what I did in the midst of it, and [p]afterward I
brought you out.

6 " 'Then [p]I brought your fathers out of Egypt, and [q]you came to the sea. [r]And the Egyptians
pursued your fathers with chariots and horsemen to the Red Sea. **7** [s]And when they cried
to the LORD, [t]he put darkness between you and the Egyptians [u]and made the sea come
upon them and cover them; [v]and your eyes saw what I did in Egypt. [w]And you lived in the

[1] Or *words*; also twice in verse 15 [2] Hebrew *the River*

23:15–16 The same God who is true to his word in keeping his promises of blessing will be true to fulfill his threats (**all the evil things**, v. 15) if Israel breaks covenant with him and decides to **serve other gods**. Key Mosaic expositions of blessings and curses are found in Lev. 26:14–46 and Deut. 28:15–68.

24:1–33 *Covenant Renewal at Shechem.* In the ancient Near East, treaties or covenants between a suzerain and his vassal(s) (i.e., a superior and his subjects) often displayed a standard format. For an outline showing how the ceremony at Shechem compared to such treaties, see chart to the right.

24:1 Shechem. See 8:30–33 and Judges 9. The archaeological record demonstrates that the city of Shechem was an important center of pagan worship in the Middle Bronze Age (2100–1550 B.C.). Extensive excavations at the mound known as Tell Balatah have revealed a large town surrounded by an elaborate fortification system. Several large and imposing "courtyard temples" have been discovered there. It is likely that the covenant renewal under Joshua took place in the excavated Fortress Temple at Shechem. It was originally constructed in the seventeenth century B.C., and it is perhaps the worship center called El-berith in Judg. 9:46.

24:2 Thus says the LORD. Joshua's utterance of these words further confirms his status as the true successor to Moses (Deut. 5:27; 18:15–19).

The Covenant Renewal Ceremony at Shechem (Josh. 24:2–27) Compared with Other Ancient Treaties

Element	Function	Verses
preamble	introduces the suzerain (i.e., the sovereign)	v. 2
historical prologue	recounts the suzerain's past gracious dealings with the vassal (i.e., the subordinate)	vv. 2–13
stipulations	outlines the vassal's consequent responsibilities in respect to the suzerain	vv. 14–24
written record	preserves the covenant agreement	v. 26
witnesses	named	vv. 26–27; cf. v. 22
blessings and curses	considered	implicit throughout, esp. in v. 20

wilderness a long time. 8 Then I brought you to the land of the Amorites, who lived on the
other side of the Jordan. [x]They fought with you, and I gave them into your hand, and you
took possession of their land, and I destroyed them before you. 9 [y]Then Balak the son of
Zippor, king of Moab, arose and fought against Israel. [z]And he sent and invited Balaam
the son of Beor to curse you, 10 [a]but I would not listen to Balaam. [a]Indeed, he blessed you.
So I delivered you out of his hand. 11 [b]And you went over the Jordan and came to Jericho,
[c]and the leaders of Jericho fought against you, and also [c]the Amorites, the Perizzites, the
Canaanites, the Hittites, the Girgashites, the Hivites, and the Jebusites. And I gave them
into your hand. 12 And I sent [d]the hornet before you, which drove them out before you, the
two kings of the Amorites; it was [e]not by your sword or by your bow. 13 I gave you a land
on which you had not labored [f]and cities that you had not built, and you dwell in them.
You eat the fruit of vineyards and olive orchards that you did not plant.'

Choose Whom You Will Serve

14 [g]"Now therefore fear the LORD and serve him in sincerity and in faithfulness. [h]Put away
the gods that your fathers served beyond the River and in Egypt, and serve the LORD. 15 [i]And
if it is evil in your eyes to serve the LORD, [j]choose this day whom you will serve, whether
[h]the gods your fathers served in the region beyond the River, or [k]the gods of the Amorites
in whose land you dwell. [l]But as for me and my house, we will serve the LORD."

16 Then the people answered, "Far be it from us that we should forsake the LORD to
serve other gods, 17 for it is the LORD our God who brought us and our fathers up from
the land of Egypt, out of the house of slavery, and who did those great signs in our sight
and preserved us in all the way that we went, and among all the peoples through whom
we passed. 18 And the LORD drove out before us all the peoples, the Amorites who lived in
the land. Therefore we also will serve the LORD, for he is our God."

19 But Joshua said to the people, "You are not able to serve the LORD, for he is [m]a holy God.
He is [n]a jealous God; [o]he will not forgive your transgressions or your sins. 20 [p]If you forsake
the LORD and serve foreign gods, then [q]he will turn and do you harm and consume you,
after having done you good." 21 And the people said to Joshua, "No, but we will serve the
LORD." 22 Then Joshua said to the people, "You are witnesses against yourselves that [r]you
have chosen the LORD, to serve him." And they said, "We are witnesses." 23 He said, "Then
[s]put away the foreign gods that are among you, and incline your heart to the LORD, the
God of Israel." 24 And the people said to Joshua, "The LORD our God we will serve, and his
voice we will obey." 25 So Joshua [t]made a covenant with the people that day, and put in place
[u]statutes and rules for them at Shechem. 26 And Joshua [v]wrote these words in the Book of

8 [x]See Num. 21:21-35
9 [y][Judg. 11:25] [z]Num. 22:5; Deut. 23:4
10 [a]Num. 23:11, 20; 24:1, 10
11 [b]ch. 3:14, 17; 4:10-13 [c]ch. 6:1; See ch. 10:1-3; 11:1-3
12 [d]Ex. 23:28; Deut. 7:20 [e]Ps. 44:3
13 [f]Deut. 6:10, 11; [ch. 11:13]
14 [g]Deut. 10:12; 1 Sam. 12:24 [h]ver. 2, 23
15 [i]1 Kgs. 18:21; Ezek. 20:39 [j]ver. 22 [h][See ver. 14 above] [k]Ex. 23:24, 32, 33; 34:15; Deut. 13:7; 29:18; Judg. 6:10 [l]Gen. 18:19
19 [m]Lev. 19:2; 1 Sam. 6:20; Ps. 99:5, 9; Isa. 5:16 [n]Ex. 20:5; Nah. 1:2 [o]Ex. 23:21
20 [p][1 Chr. 28:9; 2 Chr. 15:2; Ezra 8:22; Isa. 1:28; 65:11, 12; Jer. 17:13] [q]ch. 23:15; Isa. 63:10; [Acts 7:42]
22 [r]ver. 15
23 [s]ver. 14; Judg. 10:16; 1 Sam. 7:3
25 [t]2 Kgs. 11:17; 2 Chr. 23:16; Neh. 9:38 [u]Ex. 15:25
26 [v]Deut. 31:24

24:12 the hornet. Some interpreters understand this as a literal reference to divine intervention using insects. However, the text says "the hornet" (singular) rather than "hornets" (plural). Others take this as a reference to Egypt (the "hornet" being a symbol of Lower Egypt), but no mention of Egypt is found here or in the other related narratives. Therefore it seems best to take this as a figurative expression, with "hornet" as a metaphor for the sting of fear that the Lord inflicts on his enemies; see Ex. 23:28, where "hornet" (singular in Hb.) is paralleled in the preceding verse by "my terror" (cf. also Deut. 7:20). The focus in all three contexts where "hornet" appears is on the Lord's driving out Israel's enemies.

24:14 Against the backdrop of the Lord's faithfulness in fulfilling all his good promises, Israel is called to **fear the LORD**—a technical expression connoting not simply fear but reverence and true devotion—**and serve him in sincerity and in faithfulness**. Israel's duty to "serve" (or "worship") the Lord is the dominant theme in the final major section of the book of Joshua (chs. 22–24). The word "serve" in Hebrew (*'abad*) occurs no fewer than 16 times in ch. 24 and an additional four times in chs. 22–23.

24:15 choose this day whom you will serve. Joshua has urged the people to serve the Lord alone, and to put away the false gods (v. 14). Now he makes his admonition even sharper: **if it is evil in** their **eyes to serve the LORD** (i.e., if they prefer not to be loyal to the one true God, the Lord alone), then they must choose between two different categories of false **gods**: (1) their ancestral gods from Mesopotamia, or (2) the gods worshiped by the peoples they have dispossessed in Canaan. Joshua exercises leadership by example, committing himself and his household to serving the Lord. The people's response was to decisively reject false gods and to serve "the LORD our God" (vv. 16–17)—which Israel did "all the days of the elders who outlived Joshua" (v. 31), but which Israel failed to do in subsequent generations, as is tragically evidenced in the book of Judges.

24:19–21 You are not able to serve the LORD. Joshua's point is surely not that the people are asked to do something impossible but, rather, that serving a **holy** and **jealous God** cannot be done casually or without divine assistance. It is disconcerting that the people simply reassert their claim—**No, but we will serve the LORD** (v. 21)—rather than ask for further instruction or prayer (cf. 1 Sam. 7:8). Joshua's warning in Josh. 24:19 that **he will not forgive your transgressions or your sins** is not to suggest that God is unforgiving (quite the contrary) but that he cannot condone apostasy, the point at issue in context.

24:23 The mention of **foreign gods** makes the reader wonder how they could have been tolerated up to this point. Perhaps, as in vv. 14–15, Joshua is referring to the inner motives of their hearts.

24:24–25 The people make their promise. What sincerity and obedience will the following years reveal?

24:26–27 wrote these words in the Book of the Law of God. The title "Book of the Law of God" occurs elsewhere only at Neh. 8:18, where it is explicitly identified with the "Book of the Law of Moses" (Neh. 8:1) and "Book of the Law" (Neh. 8:3). Those same titles are also found in Joshua (see "Book of the Law" [1:8] and note on 1:5–9, and "Book of the Law of Moses" [8:31] and note on 8:32). It is likely that "the Book of the Law of God" in Joshua refers, not to additions Joshua makes to the Mosaic legislation (although Joshua is a likely source for Deuteronomy 34, the account of Moses' death), but to

the Law of God. And [w]he took a large stone and set it up there [x]under the terebinth that
was by the sanctuary of the LORD. **27** And Joshua said to all the people, "Behold, [y]this stone
shall be a witness against us, for [z]it has heard all the words of the LORD that he spoke to
us. Therefore it shall be a witness against you, lest you deal falsely with your God." **28** So
Joshua [a]sent the people away, every man to his inheritance.

Joshua's Death and Burial

29 [b]After these things Joshua the son of Nun, the servant of the LORD, died, being 110
years old. **30** And they buried him in his own inheritance at [c]Timnath-serah, which is in
the hill country of Ephraim, north of the mountain of Gaash.
31 [d]Israel served the LORD all the days of Joshua, and all the days of the elders who outlived Joshua [e]and had known all the work that the LORD did for Israel.
32 [f]As for the bones of Joseph, which the people of Israel brought up from Egypt, they
buried them at Shechem, in the piece of land [g]that Jacob bought from the sons of Hamor
the father of Shechem for a hundred pieces of money.[1] It became an inheritance of the
descendants of Joseph.
33 And Eleazar the son of Aaron died, and they buried him at Gibeah, the town of
[h]Phinehas his son, which had been given him in [i]the hill country of Ephraim.

26 [w][ch. 4:3; Gen. 28:18] [x]Gen. 35:4; Judg. 9:6
27 [y]ch. 22:27, 28, 34; Gen. 31:48, 52; Deut. 31:19, 21, 26 [z][Deut. 32:1]
28 [a]Judg. 2:6
29 [b]For ver. 29-31, see Judg. 2:7-9
30 [c][ch. 19:50]
31 [d]Judg. 2:7 [e]Deut. 11:2; 31:13
32 [f]Gen. 50:25; Ex. 13:19 [g]Gen. 33:19
33 [h]ch. 22:13 [i]ver. 30; ch. 17:15

[1] Hebrew *for a hundred qesitah*; a unit of money of unknown value

the particular covenant enacted by Joshua with the people in Josh. 24:25, in which the people reaffirm their intention to be true to the Mosaic covenant. In that case the writing has not survived, except here in the book of Joshua. **a large stone . . . a witness**. This seventh monument in the land (see note on 4:20) serves as a reminder of Israel's duty to serve the Lord, who fulfilled every promise in bringing them into the land.

24:29 Now at the end of his life, and for the first time, Joshua is called **the servant of the LORD**, an appellation Moses received at the end of his life (Deut. 34:5) and by which he is often referred to in the book of Joshua (see note on Josh. 1:1). Like Joseph before him (Gen. 50:26), Joshua is credited with a life span of **110 years**, which was considered the ideal life span in Egypt throughout its 3,000-year history from the Old Kingdom to the Hellenistic period.

24:31 The statement that **Israel served the LORD all the days of Joshua** and of the **elders** of his generation seems encouraging at first glance. But upon reflection, it is vaguely unsettling, as it allows that Israel's faithful service may be limited. What will happen in the next generation? Cf. Judg. 2:6–15.

24:32 The burial of **the bones of Joseph . . . at Shechem** brings the book of Joshua (and indeed, the patriarchal history) to a fitting close. Joseph's final wish is granted (Gen. 50:25; Ex. 13:19), and all three aspects of God's promise to the patriarchs are, at least in part, fulfilled: Israel has become a *great nation*; it stands in *blessed* relationship to the Lord; and it has a *land* of its own.

24:33 Eleazar the son of Aaron died. Given the prominence of Eleazar (see note on 14:1) both in the Pentateuch and in the book of Joshua, his death notice serves as one more sign of the passing of an era.

INTRODUCTION TO

JUDGES

Author and Title

The name of the book of Judges comes from the title given to the 12 leaders ("judges," whose temporary leadership was both civil and military) of Israel during the period between Joshua and Samuel. The book is anonymous; nowhere in Scripture is any author indicated. The book consists of various blocks of material about different judges, which conceivably could have been written by multiple authors over a period of time. Late Jewish tradition ascribes authorship to Samuel, which is certainly possible. However, in the end, the book's author is not known.

Date

Date of events. The events in Judges took place in the period between Joshua's death (either mid-14th or late-13th century B.C.) and the rise of Samuel and Saul (mid-11th century).

Date of composition. The earliest the book would have been written is after its last recorded event, in the mid-eleventh century B.C. If the phrase in 18:30, "the day of the captivity of the land," refers to the Babylonian exile, then the final form of the book does not precede the time of the exile. But most likely most of the book had been written by David's time (1010–970 B.C.), because the introductory framework in chapter 1 states that the Jebusites were living in Jerusalem "to this day" (1:21). Since David captured the city c. 1003 B.C., most Jebusites presumably did not inhabit the city after that. On the other hand, some evidence suggests they persisted in the city to some degree (e.g., 2 Sam. 24:16), so this is not a conclusive argument.

Theme

The theme of Judges is the downward spiral of Israel's national and spiritual life into chaos and apostasy, showing the need for a godly king to lead it (17:6; 21:25).

Purpose, Occasion, and Background

Purpose. The book of Judges was written to show the consequences of religious apostasy and to point the way to a king who, if righteous, would lead the people to God. In contrast to the serene way in which the book of Joshua ends—with all Israel obeying God's commands, for the most part—the book of Judges shows that, in fact, Israel began to disobey God even during the time of Joshua. This disobedience continued and grew more serious—and more debased—throughout the period of the judges. Time and again Israel turned its back on God and embraced the gods and the ways of the Canaanites, as the introductory summary in 2:16–23 indicates. Israel's history unfolded in this period in a cyclical or repetitive way: each cycle took Israel further downward in its debasement and apostasy. By the end of the book, Israel had violated its covenant with God in almost every way imaginable.

Occasion. The book of Judges arose out of the apostate conditions of the time. It was written as a justification for the monarchy, since the final verdict of the book—"In those days there was no king in Israel. Everyone did what was right in his own eyes" (21:25)—implies that things would have been different had there been a (godly) king leading the nation: they would have done right in *God's* eyes. The next book in the English Bible is Ruth, which ends with a genealogy that points to David, the godly king par excellence (Ruth 4:18–22). Following the book of Ruth, 1 and 2 Samuel relate the establishment of the legitimate Davidic monarchy

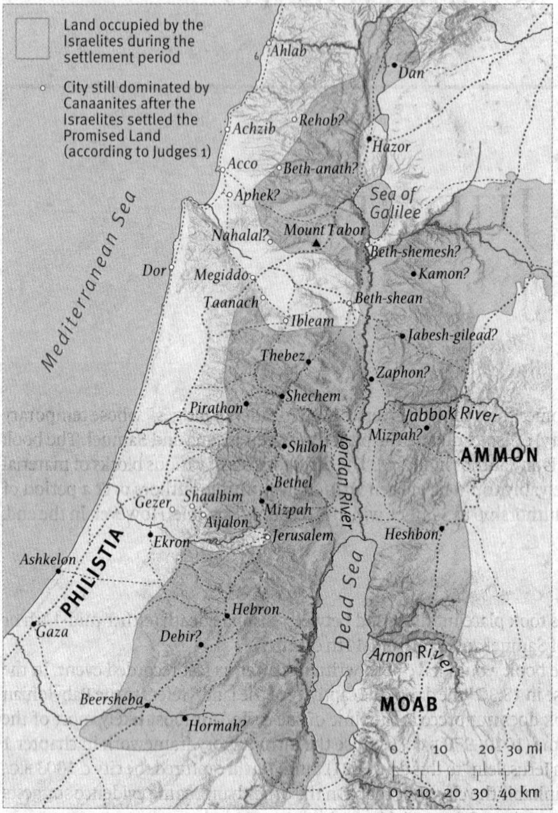

The Setting of Judges
c. 1375/1210 B.C.
The incomplete conquest of the Promised Land set the stage for the book of Judges, which recounts the exploits of various leaders raised up to deliver Israel from their oppressors.

in Israel, which God was pleased to bless (2 Samuel 7). God had planned for kings to rule in Israel from the beginning (Gen. 17:6, 16; 35:11; 49:10), and had even given instructions for their conduct (Deut. 17:14–20). These instructions were very countercultural: rather than a king "like the nations," where the prevailing model was the king as warrior, Israel's king was to focus on keeping the Mosaic law (Deut. 17:18–20). If such a king had arisen in the period of the judges, things would have been far different. As it was, Israel's apostasy pointed to the need for establishing the legitimate kingship under David.

Historical background. The period of the judges spanned a major transition in the ancient Near East, when the Late Bronze Age (c. 1550–1200 B.C.) gave way to the Early Iron Age shortly after 1200 B.C. The Late Bronze Age was a period of prosperity. In Palestine, the system of relatively small, independent city-states in the Middle Bronze Age (c. 2100–1550 B.C.) was replaced by large empires (Egyptian, Hittite, etc.) in the Late Bronze Age. However, Israelites and Canaanites were able to live there relatively undisturbed, the former in the hill country and the latter in the lowlands and coastal areas.

At the end of the Late Bronze Age, major upheavals took place throughout the Mediterranean basin. Widespread destruction is evident. Archaeological evidence shows a radical drop in population in major centers and an increase in more briefly inhabited sites in outlying areas, in the hill country, and in desert fringe areas. Imported pottery abruptly ceased. The large, visible signs of society collapsed. However, there was a continuity of culture at the grassroots level. Rough as it was, pottery did continue to be made.

The causes of the widespread destruction are not clear, but they coincide with the migrations of the "land and sea peoples" known from Egyptian texts. These peoples clashed with Egypt at the end of the thirteenth century B.C., and they were also involved in other disturbances in the eastern Mediterranean. Due to such conflicts, the Early Iron Age (c. 1200–1000 B.C.) was a "dark age" of sorts. It was not until c. 1000 B.C. that a true internationalism reasserted itself throughout the eastern Mediterranean, and houses and cities again began to rival those of the Late Bronze Age.

Canaanite religion and culture. The major problem for Israel during the period of the judges was its penchant for turning away from the Lord and toward the gods of the Canaanites. What was it about Canaanite religion and culture that proved to be such an irresistible attraction? The land of Canaan was awe-inspiring to the Israelites, as can be seen in the story of the spies who reported on its wealth and strength (Numbers 13). To a recently freed slave people, accustomed to the hardships of life in the wilderness, the cosmopolitanism and material wealth of Late-Bronze-Age Canaan, with its large urban centers, could not have failed to impress. The Canaanites were clearly superior to the Israelites on many levels: art, literature, architecture, trade, political organization, and more. It is not difficult to see how the Israelites would have been tempted by the elaborate Canaanite religious system, which ostensibly supported—and even provided—all of this.

One prominent feature of Canaanite religion was its highly sexualized orientation. The system of sacred prostitutes—"priestesses" of Baal—allowed people to combine sensual pleasures with worship of Baal. This undoubtedly was attractive to many Israelites (cf. the Israelites seduced by the Moabite women in Numbers 25).

Assessment of the Judges

Two of the most famous judges were anything but paragons of virtue. After an auspicious beginning, Gideon's badgering God for a confirmatory sign (6:36–40) may indicate a decided lack of faith (or at least fear). Later he made an ephod that became an object of worship and a snare for him, his family, and all Israel (8:24–27). Samson violated all of the main provisions of his Nazirite vow (13:7; cf. Num. 6:1–21): he drank wine at his wedding feast (Judg. 14:10: "feast" here [Hb. *mishteh*] is specifically a "drinking feast"); he had contact with the dead (e.g., 14:8–9, 19; 15:15); and he allowed his hair to be cut (16:17–19). Furthermore, he married an unbelieving Philistine (14:1–20), and he had intimate relations with at least two other Philistine women (16:1, 4).

In general, the book does not describe the judges as leading Israel in true repentance and in putting away foreign gods, certainly not in the way the reforming kings did later in the kingdom of Judah. The one judge who did the most along this line—Gideon (6:25–32)—did so only at the beginning of his "ministry"; by the end, he was leading the people in exactly the opposite direction (8:24–27).

The NT may seem to present a more idealized view of Gideon, Samson, and others than what is found in the book of Judges: Hebrews lists Gideon, Barak, Samson, and Jephthah, along with David, Samuel, and the prophets, as examples of those "who through faith conquered kingdoms, enforced justice, obtained promises, stopped the mouths of lions" (Heb. 11:32–33). However, to say that these heroes had some measure of faith is not to say that they were consistent models of faith and virtue. Undoubtedly they demonstrated faith (at times) that allowed God to "conquer kingdoms" through them, but just as surely, the book of Judges focuses more on other aspects of their character to make a point about the widespread apostasy during the period.

While the judges themselves did not always contribute to improving the spiritual conditions in the land, this was not always their fault. The people as a whole did not supply the repentance that makes a godly leader effective. But despite their flaws, the judges often acted heroically. The book of Judges does not exaggerate or romanticize their exploits. These stories are not primarily about the judges as individuals: the judges' main function is to dispense God's justice and merciful faithfulness to his people, usually by military deliverance. All servants of God's purposes for his people have their flaws; the question is whether God should choose to allow those flaws to bear their bitter fruit. Even in these circumstances, God is working out his plan; he is not thwarted, even by human failure.

Key Themes

1. Israel's existence in the land, which had been promised by God, was threatened by its continuing apostasy. Israel had not conquered the land completely (ch. 1), and its unfaithfulness was to blame (2:1–3, 20–22). Therefore, the day would come when the nation would be taken captive, away from the land (18:30).

2. The oppressions, chaos, and generally negative picture in the book are due to Israel's repeated sin. Time and again the Israelites broke the covenant, turning to the Canaanite gods and generally "doing evil" (2:3, 11–13, 17, 19; 3:6, 7, 12; 4:1; 6:1, 10; 8:24–27, 33; 10:6; 13:1; 17:6; 21:25). As a result, they repeatedly suffered the consequences.

3. God's faithfulness was the counterpoint to Israel's apostasy. Despite Israel's repeated falling away, God

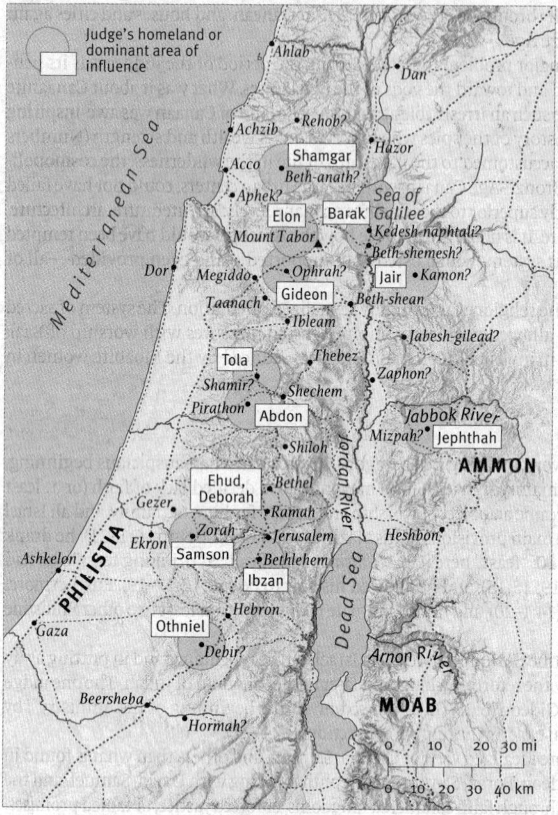

The Judges of Israel
c. 1375–1050/1210–1050 B.C.
The judges came from various tribes and regions of Israel, and they likely held varying degrees of influence over their neighboring regions and tribes.

continually delivered his people. This was due not to Israel's merits or repentance, but to God's compassion and pity (2:16, 18) and his promises to Abraham and his descendants (Deut. 6:10–11; cf. Gen. 12:7; 15:7, 18–21; 26:2–3; 35:12).

4. The judges did little to arrest the downward cycle of apostasy; if anything, they accelerated it. Major judges such as Gideon (8:24–27), Jephthah (11:30–31, 34–40), and Samson (chs. 14–16) were guilty of significant sin. The shining exception was a woman: Deborah (chs. 4–5).

5. Israel needed a godly king to lead in doing right *in the Lord's eyes* rather than a leader who "did what was right in his own eyes" (cf. 17:6; 21:25). God had promised from the beginning that there would be kings (Gen. 17:6, 16; 35:11; 49:10), and had given explicit instructions about what a godly king would look like (Deut. 17:14–20). The book of Judges shows the chaos and apostasy to which the people of Israel descended in the absence of a godly king.

History of Salvation Summary

God's people were to fulfill their calling by being faithful to the covenant in the land God had given them. The leadership of Joshua had set them up to do just this, and yet success was not automatic. The people depended on faithful leadership, which they generally lacked. Even the judges fell short of the ideal for leaders; nevertheless, God used them to preserve and chastise his people, and to teach them their need for a faithful king (a provision narrated by 1–2 Samuel). (For an explanation of the "History of Salvation," see the Overview of the Bible, pp. 23–26. See also History of Salvation in the Old Testament: Preparing the Way for Christ, pp. 2635–2661.)

The Judges

Judge	Reference	Tribe	Oppressor	Period of Oppression	Period of Rest	Total Length of Time*
Othniel	3:7–11	Judah	Mesopotamians	8 years (3:8)	40 years (3:11)	48 years
Ehud	3:12–30	Benjamin	Moabites	18 years (3:14)	80 years (3:30)	98 years
Shamgar	3:31		Philistines			
Deborah	chs. 4–5	Ephraim	Canaanites	20 years (4:3)	40 years (5:31)	60 years
Gideon	chs. 6–8	Manasseh	Midianites	7 years (6:1)	40 years (8:28)	47 years
Tola	10:1–2	Issachar			23 years (10:2)	23 years
Jair	10:3–5	Gilead-Manasseh			22 years (10:3)	22 years
Jephthah	10:6–12:7	Gilead-Manasseh	Ammonites		24 years (10:8; 12:7)	24 years
Ibzan	12:8–10	Judah or Zebulun?			7 years (12:9)	7 years
Elon	12:11–12	Zebulun			10 years (12:11)	10 years
Abdon	12:13–15	Ephraim			8 years (12:14)	8 years
Samson	chs. 13–16	Dan	Philistines	40 years (13:1)	20 years (15:20; 16:31)	60 years

* Added together, the dates in this column total about 410 years. However, many of the episodes in Judges overlap each other, unfolding in different parts of the land.

Literary Features

The format of Judges is a collection of individual "hero stories"; together, they tell the history of Israel during a specific era. Like Genesis, Judges pictures a mixture of good and bad behavior: the judges are not idealized, nor is their portrait uniformly negative. Mingled with the hero stories are brief units of historical facts about judges whose stories are not told in detail. The famous Song of Deborah (ch. 5) is poetry, while the story of Samson (chs. 13–16) meets the usual criteria of literary tragedy.

The pattern introduced in 2:11–23 shapes the plot: (1) the Israelites do what is evil in the sight of God; (2) God allows the nation to be conquered and oppressed by a neighboring nation; (3) the people cry to God; and (4) God sends a judge to deliver them (see chart, p. 448). Then the cycle repeats itself. In addition to this cycle, the book is structured on the premise of a double plot. The overall story is one of national descent into lawlessness and apostasy; but within this national narrative lies a collection of stories that celebrate the heroic exploits of judges. Even though they had severe flaws, four of these judges are mentioned among the heroes of the faith (Hebrews 11).

Realism permeates Judges, for the book refuses to overlook the sordid side of life. As the book unfolds, readers encounter shocking accounts of violence, sexual abuse, idolatry, and misuse of power. Before the book is over, gruesome scenes of bodily mutilation and dismemberment are disclosed. While Judges portrays the worst with regard to bad behavior, such realism was included to reveal something important about life and human nature apart from God.

Outline

I. The Roots of Israel's Apostasy (1:1–3:6)
  A. Prelude to apostasy: incomplete conquests (1:1–2:5)
    1. Initial battles and the seeds of apostasy (1:1–21)
    2. Incomplete conquests portending apostasy (1:22–36)
    3. The angel of the Lord and Israel's apostasy (2:1–5)
  B. The unfolding and consequences of apostasy (2:6–3:6)
    1. Joshua's death and the coming apostasy (2:6–10)
    2. The recurring pattern of Israel's apostasy, God's grace, and God's anger (2:11–23)
    3. The testing of Israel (3:1–6)

II. The Downward Spiral of Israel's Apostasy (3:7–16:31)
  A. Othniel (3:7–11)
  B. Ehud (3:12–30)

- C. Shamgar (3:31)
- D. Deborah (4:1–5:31)
  1. Victory over the Canaanites (4:1–24)
  2. Deborah and Barak's victory song (5:1–31)
- E. Gideon (6:1–8:35)
  1. Continuing apostasy (6:1–10)
  2. Gideon's call (6:11–40)
  3. Gideon's first battle (7:1–8:3)
  4. Gideon's second battle (8:4–21)
  5. Gideon's apostasy (8:22–28)
  6. Gideon, father of Abimelech (8:29–32)
  7. Continuing apostasy (8:33–35)
- F. Abimelech, apostate "king" (9:1–57)
  1. Abimelech's sordid rise (9:1–6)
  2. Indictment of Abimelech: Jotham's fable (9:7–21)
  3. Abimelech's violent reign and end (9:22–55)
  4. Final verdict on Abimelech (9:56–57)
- G. Tola (10:1–2)
- H. Jair (10:3–5)
- I. Jephthah (10:6–12:7)
  1. Apostasy and distress (10:6–18)
  2. Introduction to Jephthah (11:1–3)
  3. Jephthah's commissioning (11:4–11)
  4. Diplomatic discussions (11:12–28)
  5. Victory and Jephthah's foolish vow (11:29–40)
  6. Jephthah's conflict with Ephraim (12:1–7)
- J. Ibzan (12:8–10)
- K. Elon (12:11–12)
- L. Abdon (12:13–15)
- M. Samson (13:1–16:31)
  1. The birth of Samson (13:1–25)
  2. Samson and the Philistines, part 1 (14:1–15:20)
  3. Samson and the Philistines, part 2 (16:1–31)

III. The Depths of Israel's Apostasy (17:1–21:25)

- A. Religious corruption (17:1–18:31)
  1. Religious corruption of a household (17:1–6)
  2. Religious corruption of a Levite (17:7–13)
  3. Religious corruption of a tribe (18:1–31)
- B. Moral and social corruption (19:1–21:24)
  1. Moral outrage at Gibeah (19:1–30)
  2. Civil war (20:1–48)
  3. Chaotic aftermath (21:1–24)
- C. Final verdict (21:25)

JUDGES

Chapter 1
1[a]Num. 27:21; 1 Sam. 22:10; 2 Sam. 2:1 [b]ch. 20:18
3[c]ver. 17
7[d][Luke 16:21] [e][Lev. 24:19; 1 Sam. 15:33]
8[f][Josh. 15:63]
9[g]Josh. 9:1; 11:2, 16; 12:8
10[h]For ver. 10-15, see Josh. 15:13-19 [i]Josh. 14:15; 15:13 [j]Num. 13:22; Josh. 15:14
13[k]ch. 3:9
16[l]ch. 4:11, 17; 1 Sam. 15:6

The Continuing Conquest of Canaan

1 After the death of Joshua, the people of Israel [a]inquired of the LORD, [b]"Who shall go
up first for us against the Canaanites, to fight against them?" 2 The LORD said, "Judah
shall go up; behold, I have given the land into his hand." 3 And Judah said to Simeon his
brother, "Come up with me into the territory allotted to me, that we may fight against
the Canaanites. [c]And I likewise will go with you into the territory allotted to you." So
Simeon went with him. 4 Then Judah went up and the LORD gave the Canaanites and the
Perizzites into their hand, and they defeated 10,000 of them at Bezek. 5 They found Adoni-
bezek at Bezek and fought against him and defeated the Canaanites and the Perizzites.
6 Adoni-bezek fled, but they pursued him and caught him and cut off his thumbs and his
big toes. 7 And Adoni-bezek said, "Seventy kings with their thumbs and their big toes cut
off [d]used to pick up scraps under my table. [e]As I have done, so God has repaid me." And
they brought him to Jerusalem, and he died there.
8 [f]And the men of Judah fought against Jerusalem and captured it and struck it with the
edge of the sword and set the city on fire. 9 And afterward the men of Judah went down
to fight against the Canaanites who lived in [g]the hill country, in the Negeb, and in [g]the
lowland. 10 [h]And Judah went against the Canaanites who lived in Hebron [i](now the name of
Hebron was formerly Kiriath-arba), and they defeated [j]Sheshai and Ahiman and Talmai.
11 From there they went against the inhabitants of Debir. The name of Debir was formerly
Kiriath-sepher. 12 And Caleb said, "He who attacks Kiriath-sepher and captures it, I will give
him Achsah my daughter for a wife." 13 And Othniel the son of Kenaz, [k]Caleb's younger
brother, captured it. And he gave him Achsah his daughter for a wife. 14 When she came
to him, she urged him to ask her father for a field. And she dismounted from her donkey,
and Caleb said to her, "What do you want?" 15 She said to him, "Give me a blessing. Since
you have set me in the land of the Negeb, give me also springs of water." And Caleb gave
her the upper springs and the lower springs.
16 And the descendants of the [l]Kenite, Moses' father-in-law, went up with the people

1:1–3:6 *The Roots of Israel's Apostasy.* This introduction to the book identifies the root causes and effects of Israel's apostasy. The pattern established here is then repeated in a cyclical fashion throughout the body of the book (3:7–16:31).

1:1–2:5 *Prelude to Apostasy: Incomplete Conquests.* In the first part of the book's introduction, continuing military activity indicates that all conquests had not been completed during Joshua's day (1:1–26); several tribes achieved only incomplete conquests (1:27–36). Israel's disobedience in not completely conquering the land is confirmed in 2:1–5.

1:1–21 *Initial Battles and the Seeds of Apostasy.* The military encounters here are reminders that the peace at the end of the book of Joshua was short-lived. Judah was given a leadership role, and they allied with Simeon against the remaining Canaanites. They had some successes, but some ominous failures as well (vv. 19, 21).

1:1 After the death of Joshua a new era begins. Significantly, however, no new leader is appointed (as in Joshua 1). This foreshadows the chaotic conditions and apostasy that would prevail.

1:2–3 Judah shall go up (see note on 20:18). Judah's leadership in Israel had been anticipated as early as Jacob's blessing, when he said that kings would come from the line of Judah (Gen. 49:8–12). **Judah** and **Simeon**, the two tribes that were to lead the way into Canaan, were closely linked: both came from the same mother (Gen. 29:33, 35), and Simeon had inherited land in Judah's territory (Josh. 19:1, 9).

1:5–7 Each city and town in Canaan had its own "king," such as **Adoni-bezek**, whose name means "Lord of Bezek." **cut off his thumbs and his big toes**. This would prevent him from ever engaging in battle again. The practice of cutting off body parts of vanquished enemies is known in Mesopotamian and classical Greek sources, and was practiced by Adoni-bezek himself (v. 7).

1:8 Jerusalem was on the border between Judah and Benjamin. Neither tribe succeeded in driving out its inhabitants completely (Josh. 15:63; Judg. 1:21); that was accomplished only by David (2 Sam. 5:6–10).

1:10–15 This passage (almost identical to Josh. 15:13–19) is probably a "flashback" to the earlier capture of **Hebron** and **Debir**. Caleb offering **Achsah** as a prize to the victor is similar to Saul offering Michal to David in exchange for 100 Philistine foreskins (1 Sam. 18:25). Achsah asked for **springs of water** in addition to land, since **land** without sources of fresh water was almost worthless.

1:16 The Kenite, Moses' father-in-law was Jethro (Ex. 3:1). The Israelites and Kenites had been friendly in the wilderness (Num. 10:29–32), and the

of Judah [m]from the city of palms into the wilderness of Judah, which lies in the Negeb
near [n]Arad, [o]and they went and settled with the people. **17** [p]And Judah went with Simeon
his brother, and they defeated the Canaanites who inhabited Zephath and devoted it to
destruction. So the name of the city was called [q]Hormah.[1] **18** Judah also [r]captured Gaza
with its territory, and Ashkelon with its territory, and Ekron with its territory. **19** [p]And the
LORD was with Judah, and he took possession of the [s]hill country, but he could not drive
out the inhabitants of the plain because they had [t]chariots of iron. **20** [u]And Hebron was
given to Caleb, as Moses had said. And he drove out from it [v]the three sons of Anak. **21** But
the people of Benjamin did not drive out the Jebusites who lived in Jerusalem, [w]so the
Jebusites have lived with the people of Benjamin in Jerusalem to this day.

22 The house of Joseph also went up against Bethel, [x]and the LORD was with them. **23** And
the house of Joseph scouted out Bethel. ([y]Now the name of the city was formerly Luz.)
24 And the spies saw a man coming out of the city, and they said to him, "Please show us
the way into the city, [z]and we will deal kindly with you." **25** And he showed them the way
into the city. And they struck the city with the edge of the sword, but they let the man
and all his family go. **26** And the man went to [a]the land of the Hittites and built a city and
called its name Luz. That is its name to this day.

Failure to Complete the Conquest

27 [b]Manasseh did not drive out the inhabitants of Beth-shean and its villages, or Taanach
and its villages, or the inhabitants of Dor and its villages, or the inhabitants of Ibleam and
its villages, or the inhabitants of Megiddo and its villages, for the Canaanites persisted in
dwelling in that land. **28** When Israel grew strong, they put the Canaanites to forced labor,
but did not drive them out completely.

29 [c]And Ephraim did not drive out the Canaanites who lived in Gezer, so the Canaanites
lived in Gezer among them.

30 Zebulun did not drive out the inhabitants of Kitron, or the inhabitants of [d]Nahalol,
so the Canaanites lived among them, but became subject to forced labor.

31 [e]Asher did not drive out the inhabitants of Acco, or the inhabitants of Sidon or of
Ahlab or of Achzib or of Helbah or of Aphik or of Rehob, **32** so the Asherites lived among
the Canaanites, the inhabitants of the land, for they did not drive them out.

[1] *Hormah means utter destruction*

16 [m]Deut. 34:3 [n]Num. 21:1 [o]See Num. 10:29-32
17 [p]ver. 3 [q]Num. 21:3
18 [r][ch. 3:3; Josh. 11:22]
19 [p][See ver. 17 above] [s]See ver. 9 [t]Josh. 17:16, 18
20 [u]Num. 14:24; Deut. 1:36; Josh. 14:9, 13; 15:13, 14 [v]ver. 10
21 [w][Josh. 15:63]
22 [x]ver. 19
23 [y]Gen. 28:19; 35:6; 48:3; Josh. 18:13
24 [z]Josh. 2:12, 14
26 [a]Josh. 1:4
27 [b]For ver. 27, 28, see Josh. 17:11-13
29 [c]Josh. 16:10; 1 Kgs. 9:16
30 [d][Josh. 19:15; 21:35]
31 [e]For ver. 31, 32, see Josh. 19:24-30

cooperation here fulfills Moses' words, "we will do good to you" (Num. 10:29). **city of palms**. Another name for Jericho (Deut. 34:3; 2 Chron. 28:15).

1:18 Gaza . . . Ashkelon . . . Ekron. Judah captured three of the major Philistine cities (Josh. 13:2–3) but was not able to hold them; they later reverted to Philistine control (Judg. 14:19; 16:1; 1 Sam. 5:10).

1:19 he could not drive out the inhabitants of the plain. This seemingly innocuous notice is in fact ominous, since the Israelites' failure to drive out the Canaanites completely, as God had instructed (Josh. 6:17; 11:14), was a root cause of Israel's apostasy and troubles (Judg. 2:11–3:6). Since the three Philistine cities mentioned in 1:18 were in the plain, v. 19 must mean that the Israelites had no success beyond these three cities, and perhaps even that they lost control of them very quickly. **chariots of iron**. The Israelites did not have chariots, which were effective on the flat, coastal plains but were ineffective in the hill country of Canaan, where most of the Israelites settled.

Reasons Israel Failed to Take the Promised Land

1. The Canaanites had superior arms and fortifications	1:19
2. Israel was disposed to make alliances with the people of the land	2:1–5
3. Israel sinned and must be punished	2:20–21
4. Yahweh was testing Israel to see if they would be faithful or not	2:22–23; 3:4
5. Israel needed to be instructed in the art of war	3:1–3

1:21 Benjamin did not drive out the Jebusites. A second notice about Israelite failure (see note on v. 19) previews a series of six almost identical notices in vv. 27–36. The Israelites were apparently satisfied with a comfortable home in a productive land and were not zealous to achieve God's full purpose for their life in the land (see note on vv. 27–33).

1:22–36 *Incomplete Conquests Portending Apostasy.* The Israelites now suffered more failures in the north. After an initial success at Bethel (vv. 22–26), six tribes—Manasseh, Ephraim, Zebulun, Asher, Naphtali, and Dan—did not drive out the Canaanites from their territories (vv. 27–36). These territories fairly well spanned the northern two-thirds of the Promised Land.

1:22 The house of Joseph. There was no tribe of Joseph: his inheritance had been split between his two sons, Ephraim and Manasseh (Gen. 48:5–6; Deut. 33:17), the next two tribes mentioned (Judg. 1:27, 29). **Bethel** means "the house of God." Its honored history included Abraham's sacrifice to God (Gen. 13:3) and Jacob's revelation from God in a dream (Gen. 31:13). Joshua originally captured it (Josh. 12:16), perhaps as part of the defeat of Ai (cf. Josh. 8:17).

1:27–33 Six more tribes failed in the same way as Judah and Benjamin: Manasseh (v. 27), Ephraim (v. 29), Zebulun (v. 30), Asher (v. 31), Naphtali (v. 33), and Dan (v. 34). The effects were tragic: the Israelites turned to the Baals, the gods of those Canaanites who remained among them, and forsook the Lord. Thus, Israel's worship did not remain pure.

1:28 The Israelites subjected many of the Canaanite groups to **forced labor** (vv. 30, 33, 35; cf. Josh. 16:10; 17:13). In later times, David and Solomon also used their enemies in this way (2 Sam. 20:24; 1 Kings 9:15).

33 [f]For ver. 33, see Josh. 19:32-39
34 [g][Josh. 19:47, 48]
35 [h]Josh. 19:42
36 [i]Num. 34:4; Josh. 15:3
Chapter 2
1 [j]ver. 5 [k]Gen. 17:7; Ex. 6:4; Deut. 31:16
2 [l]Deut. 7:2 [m]Deut. 12:3
3 [n]ver. 21 [o]Num. 33:55; Josh. 23:13
7 [p]For ver. 7-9, see Josh. 24:29-31
9 [q]Josh. 19:50 [r]Josh. 24:33
11 [s]ch. 3:7; 4:1; 6:1; 10:6; 13:1
12 [t]Deut. 31:16

33 Naphtali did not drive out the inhabitants of [f]Beth-shemesh, or the inhabitants of Beth-anath, so they lived among the Canaanites, the inhabitants of the land. Nevertheless, the inhabitants of Beth-shemesh and of Beth-anath became subject to forced labor for them.

34 [g]The Amorites pressed the people of Dan back into the hill country, for they did not allow them to come down to the plain. 35 The Amorites persisted in dwelling in Mount Heres, [h]in Aijalon, and in Shaalbim, but the hand of the house of Joseph rested heavily on them, and they became subject to forced labor. 36 And the border of the Amorites ran from [i]the ascent of Akrabbim, from Sela and upward.

Israel's Disobedience

2 Now the angel of the LORD went up from Gilgal to [j]Bochim. And he said, "I brought you up from Egypt and brought you into the land that I swore to give to your fathers. I said, [k]'I will never break my covenant with you, 2 [l]and you shall make no covenant with the inhabitants of this land; [m]you shall break down their altars.' But you have not obeyed my voice. What is this you have done? 3 So now I say, [n]I will not drive them out before you, but they shall become [o]thorns in your sides, and their gods shall be a snare to you." 4 As soon as the angel of the LORD spoke these words to all the people of Israel, the people lifted up their voices and wept. 5 And they called the name of that place Bochim.[1] And they sacrificed there to the LORD.

The Death of Joshua

6 When Joshua dismissed the people, the people of Israel went each to his inheritance to take possession of the land. 7 [p]And the people served the LORD all the days of Joshua, and all the days of the elders who outlived Joshua, who had seen all the great work that the LORD had done for Israel. 8 And Joshua the son of Nun, the servant of the LORD, died at the age of 110 years. 9 And they buried him within the boundaries of [q]his inheritance in Timnath-heres, [r]in the hill country of Ephraim, north of the mountain of Gaash. 10 And all that generation also were gathered to their fathers. And there arose another generation after them who did not know the LORD or the work that he had done for Israel.

Israel's Unfaithfulness

11 [s]And the people of Israel did what was evil in the sight of the LORD and served the Baals. 12 [t]And they abandoned the LORD, the God of their fathers, who had brought them

[1] *Bochim* means *weepers*

1:34 Amorites were Canaanite peoples (cf. Josh. 3:10) living in the central hill country. They were such an obstacle to the tribe of Dan that the Danites were eventually forced to migrate northward (Josh. 19:47; Judg. 18:1).

2:1–5 *The Angel of the Lord and Israel's Apostasy.* The angel of the Lord now makes explicit that Israel's failure to drive out the Canaanites as God had instructed is the cause of his handing them over to the vicissitudes of life among their enemies. The roots of Israel's apostasy are now in full view.

2:1 The angel of the LORD was God's representative, speaking authoritatively to the people about their apostasy. He shows up suddenly elsewhere in Judges (5:23; 6:11, 12, 20–22; 13:3, 13, 15, 16, 18, 20, 21), sometimes causing fear (6:22–23), probably because of the warning about humans seeing God (Ex. 33:20; see note on Judg. 6:22). As the Lord's designated messenger (Hb. *mal'ak*), the angel speaks as the Lord himself (see note on Gen. 16:7; cf. Ex. 3:6). This angel may be the same one promised to Moses in Ex. 23:20–23, or a theophany of the Lord himself. **Gilgal** was Israel's first encampment west of the Jordan (Josh. 4:19). **I brought you up**. "You" is plural, referring to the entire nation (since those addressed here were not part of the original exodus). **I will never break my covenant**. On God's eternal covenant faithfulness, see Lev. 26:44 and Ps. 89:34.

2:2–3 God had commanded Israel to **make no covenant** with pagan nations and to tear down **their altars**. Cf. Ex. 23:32; 34:12–13; Deut. 12:3. As a consequence of Israel's disobedience, these nations would **be a snare** to them (e.g., by pagan rituals; Judg. 8:27), just as God had promised (Ex. 23:33; Num. 33:55; Josh. 23:13).

2:5 they sacrificed there. The Israelites' apparent distress at God's threats (v. 4), and their attempts to pacify God by sacrificing (v. 5), were short-lived. Verses 11–15 show their more usual pattern of apostasy.

2:6–3:6 *The Unfolding and Consequences of Apostasy.* In the second part of the book's introduction, the breakdown chronicled in ch. 1 is assumed, but the focus is less on incomplete conquests than on a theological analysis of Israel's apostasy and its consequences. The recurring downward cycle of history presented in 2:16–23 is especially captured by the statement, "whenever the judge died, they turned back and *were more corrupt* than their fathers" (2:19). The final section (3:1–6) emphasizes God's purposes in the punishments mentioned in 2:14–15, 21–23, which have to do with "testing" Israel (2:22; 3:1, 4).

2:6–10 *Joshua's Death and the Coming Apostasy.* This is a flashback to Josh. 24:28–31 and a transition to the second part of the introduction. Joshua had already died (Judg. 1:1), but the repetition of the information about Joshua introduces the apostasy to follow.

2:10 another generation . . . who did not know the LORD. The positive picture painted in Joshua (esp. Josh. 24:31) is marred by a reference to the next generation, who had forgotten **the work that** the Lord **had done for Israel** (Judg. 2:7), including the work done through Joshua.

2:11–23 *The Recurring Pattern of Israel's Apostasy, God's Grace, and God's Anger.* This section deals with the recurring patterns of Israel's apostasy and God's reaction to it. The unit might be divided into three subsections: (1) Israel's apostasy and God's anger (vv. 11–15); (2) God's grace and Israel's continuing apostasy (vv. 16–19); and (3) God's anger (vv. 20–23). The first and third sections are similar in describing Israel's apostasy and then in describing how God punished the nation, although the third section ends without reference to God's grace. The middle section presents a summary of the recurring pattern seen throughout the remainder of the book: God graciously raises up successive judges to deliver Israel, but the people fall away from him each time.

2:11 the people of Israel did what was evil in the sight of the LORD.

out of the land of Egypt. [u]They went after other gods, from among the gods of the peoples
who were around them, and [v]bowed down to them. [w]And they provoked the LORD to
anger. 13 They abandoned the LORD [x]and served the Baals and the Ashtaroth. 14 [y]So the
anger of the LORD was kindled against Israel, and he [z]gave them over to plunderers, who
plundered them. [a]And he sold them into the hand of their surrounding enemies, [b]so that
they could no longer withstand their enemies. 15 Whenever they marched out, the hand
of the LORD was against them for harm, as the LORD had warned, [c]and as the LORD had
sworn to them. And they were in terrible distress.

The LORD Raises Up Judges

16 [d]Then the LORD raised up judges, [e]who saved them out of the hand of those who
plundered them. 17 Yet they did not listen to their judges, for [f]they whored after other
gods and bowed down to them. [g]They soon turned aside from the way in which their
fathers had walked, who had obeyed the commandments of the LORD, and they did not
do so. 18 Whenever the LORD raised up judges for them, [h]the LORD was with the judge,
and he saved them from the hand of their enemies all the days of the judge. [i]For the
LORD was moved to pity by [j]their groaning because of those who afflicted and oppressed
them. 19 But [k]whenever the judge died, they turned back and were more corrupt than
their fathers, going after other gods, serving them and bowing down to them. They did
not drop any of their practices or their stubborn ways. 20 [l]So the anger of the LORD was
kindled against Israel, and he said, "Because this people [m]have transgressed my covenant
that I commanded their fathers and have not obeyed my voice, 21 [n]I will no longer drive
out before them any of the nations that Joshua left when he died, 22 in order [o]to test Israel
by them, whether they will take care to walk in the way of the LORD as their fathers did, or
not." 23 So the LORD left those nations, not driving them out quickly, and he did not give
them into the hand of Joshua.

3 [p]Now these are the nations that the LORD left, to test Israel by them, that is, all in Israel
who had not experienced all the wars in Canaan. 2 It was only in order that the generations of the people of Israel might know war, to teach war to those who had not known it
before. 3 These are the nations: [q]the five lords of the Philistines and all the Canaanites and
the Sidonians and the Hivites who lived on Mount Lebanon, from Mount Baal-hermon
as far as Lebo-hamath. 4 They were for [r]the testing of Israel, to know whether Israel would
obey the commandments of the LORD, which he commanded their fathers by the hand of

12 [u][Deut. 6:14] [v]ver. 17, 19; [Ex. 20:5] [w]Deut. 31:29
13 [x]ch. 3:7; 10:6; Ps. 106:36; [1 Sam. 7:4]
14 [y]ver. 20 [z]2 Kgs. 17:20 [a]ch. 3:8; 4:2; [Deut. 32:30; 1 Sam. 12:9] [b]Lev. 26:37; Josh. 7:12, 13
15 [c]See Lev. 26:14-46; Deut. 28:15-68
16 [d]ch. 3:9, 15; 1 Sam. 12:11; Acts 13:20 [e]ch. 3:31; 10:1, 12, 13; 12:2, 3; 13:5; [ch. 3:9; Neh. 9:27]
17 [f]ch. 8:33; Ex. 34:15 [g]Deut. 9:12
18 [h][Josh. 1:5] [i]Gen. 6:6; Deut. 32:36; Ps. 106:45; Jer. 18:8; 26:3; [Num. 23:19] [j]Ex. 2:24; 6:5
19 [k][ch. 3:12; 4:1; 6:1; 8:33]
20 [l]ver. 14 [m]Deut. 17:2; Josh. 23:16
21 [n]ver. 3; Josh. 23:13
22 [o]ch. 3:1, 4; Ex. 15:25; [Deut. 8:2, 16; 13:3]

Chapter 3

1 [p]ver. 4; ch. 2:21, 22
3 [q]See Josh. 13:2-6
4 [r]ver. 1

This clear statement of Israel's apostasy recurs throughout the book (3:7, 12; 4:1; 6:1; 10:6; 13:1), and again many times in 1–2 Kings, with reference to the kings of Israel and Judah (e.g., 1 Kings 15:26, 34; 2 Kings 21:2). Israel's tendency throughout its history was to turn away from the Lord. Only God's grace and the leadership of a few godly individuals kept Israel from complete paganism. **served the Baals**. See note on Judg. 3:7.

2:13 Ashtaroth is the plural form of Ashtoreth (Gk. *Astartē*), a goddess of fertility, love, and war who was closely associated with Baal (10:6; 1 Sam. 7:4; 12:10). Canaanite texts seldom mention Ashtoreth, but she appears in Mesopotamian texts by the name "Ishtar" and in Egyptian representations of Canaanite religion. Ashtoreth (plural Ashtaroth) should not be confused with Asherah (plural Asheroth; see notes on Judg. 3:7; 6:25–26).

2:15 as the LORD had sworn. God had threatened to deliver Israel into its enemies' hands if it forsook him (Deut. 28:25; Josh. 23:13). He also warned that these nations would be snares and traps to Israel (Ex. 23:33; Deut. 7:16; and esp. Num. 33:55), which came true with a vengeance during the period of the judges (Judg. 2:14–15, 21–23).

2:16 the LORD raised up judges. The judges' primary (though temporary) function was military; they were provided by the grace of God.

2:17 whored. The metaphor of Israel's committing adultery against God by following other gods is one of the most powerful in the OT. Ezekiel spoke against Jerusalem's adultery (Ezekiel 16; 23), and Hosea's ministry was inextricably linked with God's command to marry "a wife of whoredom" (Hosea 1–3). Israel's unfaithfulness was reprehensible to the God who had chosen, loved, and provided for his people.

2:18 moved to pity (Hb. *nakham*; cf. 1 Sam. 15:29, "have regret"; Jonah 3:10, "relented"). God graciously changed his course of action concerning the Israelites (to give them over to their enemies; Judg. 2:14–15) because of his compassion for their suffering (cf. 10:16).

2:20 this people. Literally, "this nation" (Hb. *goy*), a term normally reserved for pagans (e.g., in vv. 21, 23; 3:1). Biblical writers usually refer to Israel as a "people" (Hb. *'am*, a more intimate word). The usage of "this nation" here is freighted with contempt and reflects the disgust God feels toward his people, whom he now regards as just like the other nations.

2:21–22 I will no longer drive out . . . any of the nations. This repeats the promise (or threat) that God had made to the Israelites (Josh. 23:13), which is then carried out in Judg. 2:23. **to test Israel**. See note on 3:1.

3:1–6 *The Testing of Israel.* The final section of the introduction emphasizes God's purposes in testing Israel (vv. 1, 4; cf. 2:22). It concludes with a confirmation that Israel indeed was apostate in this period (3:5–6). The stage is now set for the accounts of the individual judges, a significant number of whom were as much part of Israel's problem as they were sources of deliverance.

3:1 to test Israel. This testing was to see if Israel would truly follow the Lord (2:22; 3:4), as when God tested Abraham (Gen. 22:1) and Hezekiah (2 Chron. 32:31). Through adversity, God tested Israel in order to refine it. Later in the book of Judges, Gideon "tested" God in a display of weak faith (Judg. 6:39).

3:3 The word **lords** here (*seren*) is Philistine, not Hebrew; the Greeks borrowed it, using it as the basis for their word *tyrannos*, "tyrant." **Philistines**

5[s]Ex. 3:8; Ps. 106:35
6[t][Ex. 34:16; Deut. 7:3; Ezra 9:12]
7[u]ch. 2:11-13 [v]ch. 6:25; Ex. 34:13
8[w]ch. 2:14 [x]Hab. 3:7
9[y]ver. 15; ch. 4:3; 6:7; 10:10 [z]ver. 15; ch. 2:16; Neh. 9:27 [a]ch. 1:13
10[b]ch. 6:34; 11:29; 13:25; 14:6, 19; 15:14
11[c][ver. 30; ch. 5:31; 8:28; Josh. 11:23]
12[d]ch. 2:19 [e]1 Sam. 12:9
13[f]ch. 6:33; Ps. 83:7 [g]ch. 1:16; Deut. 34:3
15[h]See ver. 9 [i]ch. 20:16; [1 Chr. 12:2]

Moses. **5** So the people of Israel lived [s]among the Canaanites, the Hittites, the Amorites, the
Perizzites, the Hivites, and the Jebusites. **6** [t]And their daughters they took to themselves for
wives, and their own daughters they gave to their sons, and they served their gods.

Othniel

7 [u]And the people of Israel did what was evil in the sight of the LORD. They forgot the
LORD their God and served the Baals and [v]the Asheroth. **8** Therefore the anger of the LORD
was kindled against Israel, [w]and he sold them into the hand of [x]Cushan-rishathaim king
of Mesopotamia. And the people of Israel served Cushan-rishathaim eight years. **9** But
when the people of Israel [y]cried out to the LORD, the LORD raised up a [z]deliverer for the
people of Israel, who saved them, [a]Othniel the son of Kenaz, Caleb's younger brother.
10 [b]The Spirit of the LORD was upon him, and he judged Israel. He went out to war, and
the LORD gave Cushan-rishathaim king of Mesopotamia into his hand. And his hand
prevailed over Cushan-rishathaim. **11** [c]So the land had rest forty years. Then Othniel the
son of Kenaz died.

Ehud

12 [d]And the people of Israel again did what was evil in the sight of the LORD, and the LORD
strengthened Eglon [e]the king of Moab against Israel, because they had done what was evil
in the sight of the LORD. **13** He gathered to himself the Ammonites and the [f]Amalekites,
and went and defeated Israel. And they took possession of [g]the city of palms. **14** And the
people of Israel served Eglon the king of Moab eighteen years.

15 Then the people of Israel [h]cried out to the LORD, and the LORD raised up for them
[h]a deliverer, Ehud, the son of Gera, the Benjaminite, [i]a left-handed man. The people of
Israel sent tribute by him to Eglon the king of Moab. **16** And Ehud made for himself a
sword with two edges, a cubit[1] in length, and he bound it on his right thigh under his
clothes. **17** And he presented the tribute to Eglon king of Moab. Now Eglon was a very fat
man. **18** And when Ehud had finished presenting the tribute, he sent away the people who

[1] A *cubit* was about 18 inches or 45 centimeters

were part of the mercenary sea peoples, mentioned in Egyptian texts as early as the fourteenth century B.C.

3:5–6 The book's introduction ends with a searing indictment of the Israelites' apostasy through their intermarriage and their infidelity to God.

3:7–16:31 *The Downward Spiral of Israel's Apostasy.* The body of the book of Judges includes the stories of 12 judges raised up to deliver Israel from successive crises and to "judge" Israel. Their primary function was military in nature. Most judges failed to point people convincingly to the Lord. Indeed, in some cases the judges themselves were not exemplary (e.g., Gideon, Jephthah, Samson). The recurring pattern unfolds in a downward spiral: the first judge, Othniel, was raised up by God and empowered by God's Spirit (3:9–10), whereas the next-to-last major judge, Jephthah, made a foolish vow and offered his own daughter as a "sacrifice" (whether literally or figuratively; see 11:30–40, and note on 11:39), and the last judge, Samson, was anything but a paragon of virtue (chs. 14–16).

3:7–11 *Othniel.* The Spirit of the Lord was on Othniel, the first judge (v. 10), and he delivered Israel from Cushan-rishathaim, king of Mesopotamia. The section begins by repeating much of 2:11–14. When the Israelites sinned, God gave them into foreign control for eight years (3:8). When Israel cried out for deliverance (v. 9), God provided Othniel as a deliverer.

3:7 the Baals and the Asheroth. Baal was the most powerful god of the Canaanites, and Asherah was a popular Canaanite goddess, a consort of El, the head of the Canaanite pantheon (see notes on 2:13; 6:25–26), who may have been displaced at some point by Baal. The use of the plural forms (Baals and Asheroth) shows that each was worshiped in many locales, and their local manifestations took on the character of independent gods (e.g., "Baal of Peor" [Num. 25:5], "Mount Baal-hermon" [Judg. 3:3], "Baal-gad" [Josh. 11:17], "Baal-hazor" [2 Sam. 13:23], "Baal-hamon" [Song 8:11], and Baal-berith [i.e., "the Baal of the covenant"; Judg. 8:33]). Asherah is also associated with Baal in 1 Kings 18:19 and 2 Kings 23:4.

3:9–10 Othniel of Judah had captured the city of Kiriath-sepher and become Caleb's son-in-law (see 1:13). This is the last appearance in the book of a leader from Judah, the most favored tribe. **The Spirit of the LORD was upon him**. See note on 14:6.

3:11 the land had rest forty years. Cf. 3:30; 5:31; 8:28. In 18:7, some foreigners also "lived in security" (the same Hb. word as "had rest").

3:12–30 *Ehud.* Ehud, the second judge, delivered Israel from Eglon, king of Moab (see map below). Verses 12–14 give a standard introduction, telling of the Israelites' apostasy and of God's giving them into Eglon's control for 18 years. The story that follows—of Ehud killing Eglon—is rather graphic, highlighting the rough, even grotesque nature of this period and many of its "heroes."

Ehud Defeats the Moabites

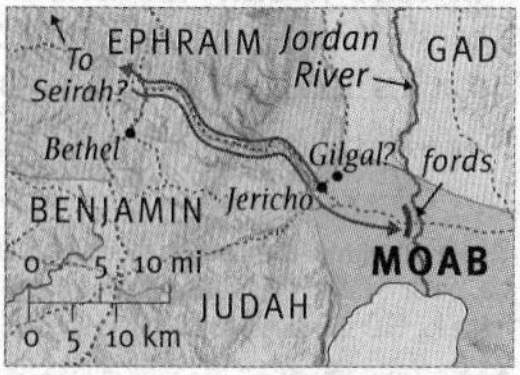

During the time of Ehud, King Eglon of Moab expanded his territory and captured the "city of palms," probably to be understood as Jericho. Ehud and the other Israelite delegates were returning from delivering their tribute to Eglon, but Ehud turned back and killed Eglon at Jericho. Then Ehud escaped to the hill country of Ephraim and mustered the warriors of Israel, who captured the fords of the Jordan River to prevent the Moabites from escaping.

carried the tribute. 19 But he himself turned back [j]at the idols near Gilgal and said, "I have
a secret message for you, O king." And he commanded, "Silence." And all his attendants
went out from his presence. 20 And Ehud came to him as he was sitting alone in his [k]cool
roof chamber. [l]And Ehud said, "I have a message from God for you." And he arose from
his seat. 21 And Ehud reached with his left hand, took the sword from his right thigh, and
thrust it into his belly. 22 And the hilt also went in after the blade, and the fat closed over
the blade, for he did not pull the sword out of his belly; and the dung came out. 23 Then
Ehud went out into the porch[1] and closed the doors of the roof chamber behind him
[m]and locked them.

24 When he had gone, the servants came, and when they saw that the doors of the roof
chamber were locked, they thought, [n]"Surely he is relieving himself in the closet of the
cool chamber." 25 And they waited till they were embarrassed. But when he still did not
open the doors of the roof chamber, they took the key and opened them, and there lay
their lord dead on the floor.

26 Ehud escaped while they delayed, and he passed beyond [o]the idols and escaped to
Seirah. 27 When he arrived, [p]he sounded the trumpet in [q]the hill country of Ephraim.
Then the people of Israel went down with him from the hill country, and he was their
leader. 28 And he said to them, "Follow after me, [r]for the LORD has given your enemies
the Moabites into your hand." So they went down after him and seized [s]the fords of the
Jordan against the Moabites and did not allow anyone to pass over. 29 And they killed at
that time about 10,000 of the Moabites, all strong, able-bodied men; not a man escaped.
30 So Moab was subdued that day under the hand of Israel. [t]And the land had rest for
eighty years.

Shamgar

31 After him was [u]Shamgar the son of Anath, who killed 600 of the Philistines [v]with an
oxgoad, and he also [w]saved Israel.

Deborah and Barak

4 [x]And the people of Israel again did what was evil in the sight of the LORD after Ehud
died. 2 And the LORD [y]sold them into the hand of [z]Jabin king of Canaan, who reigned
in [z]Hazor. The commander of his army was [a]Sisera, who lived in [b]Harosheth-hagoyim.
3 Then the people of Israel [c]cried out to the LORD for help, for he had [d]900 chariots of iron
and he oppressed the people of Israel cruelly for twenty years.

4 Now Deborah, a prophetess, the wife of Lappidoth, was judging Israel at that time. 5 She
used to sit under the palm of Deborah between Ramah and Bethel in [e]the hill country of
Ephraim, and the people of Israel came up to her for judgment. 6 She sent and summoned
[f]Barak the son of Abinoam from [g]Kedesh-naphtali and said to him, "Has not the LORD,
the God of Israel, commanded you, 'Go, gather your men at Mount [h]Tabor, taking 10,000
from the people of Naphtali and the people of Zebulun. 7 And I will draw out Sisera, the
general of Jabin's army, to meet you by [i]the river Kishon with his chariots and his troops,
[j]and I will give him into your hand'?" 8 Barak said to her, "If you will go with me, I will
go, but if you will not go with me, I will not go." 9 And she said, "I will surely go with you.
Nevertheless, the road on which you are going will not lead to your glory, for the LORD
will [k]sell Sisera into the hand of a woman." Then Deborah arose and went with Barak to
Kedesh. 10 And Barak called out [l]Zebulun and Naphtali to Kedesh. And 10,000 men went
up at his heels, and Deborah went up with him.

[1] The meaning of the Hebrew word is uncertain

19 [j]ver. 26; [Josh. 4:20]
20 [k]Amos 3:15 [l][2 Sam. 20:9, 10]
23 [m][2 Sam. 13:17, 18]
24 [n]1 Sam. 24:3
26 [o]ver. 19
27 [p]ch. 6:34; 1 Sam. 13:3 [q]See Josh. 24:33
28 [r]ch. 4:7, 14; 7:9, 15; 1 Sam. 17:47; 2 Chr. 16:8; [1 Kgs. 22:12, 15] [s]ch. 12:5; Josh. 2:7; [ch. 7:24]
30 [t]ver. 11
31 [u]ch. 5:6 [v][ch. 5:8; 1 Sam. 13:19, 22] [w]See ch. 2:16

Chapter 4

1 [x]See ch. 2:19
2 [y]ch. 2:14 [z][Josh. 11:1, 10] [a]1 Sam. 12:9; Ps. 83:9 [b]ver. 13, 16
3 [c]See ch. 3:9 [d]ver. 13; [ch. 1:19]
5 [e]See Josh. 24:33
6 [f]Heb. 11:32 [g]Josh. 19:37 [h]ch. 8:18
7 [i]ver. 13; ch. 5:21; 1 Kgs. 18:40; Ps. 83:9 [j]See ch. 3:28
9 [k]See ch. 2:14
10 [l]ch. 5:18

3:20 his cool roof chamber. In ancient cities, the coolest place in the house was on the roof (cf. the "small room on the roof" that a Shunammite couple made for Elisha, 2 Kings 4:10).

3:31 *Shamgar.* The third judge was **Shamgar**, mentioned only here and in 5:6. Shamgar's name is apparently Hurrian, not Israelite, and his designation as "son of Anath" probably refers to the Canaanite warrior goddess Anath. If so, it is ironic that God used a non-Israelite warrior to deliver Israel from its enemies. Shamgar's activity in single-handedly killing many Philistines anticipates Samson.

4:1–5:31 *Deborah.* The fourth judge was Deborah (see note on 4:4–5), whose story is the first extended account in the book (cf. Gideon in chs. 6–8; Jephthah in ch. 11; and Samson in chs. 13–16). While the pattern of apostasy continues (esp. 4:1–3), Deborah distinguishes herself as the most godly of all the judges; it is ironic that the most distinguished judge was a woman (4:8–9). She was a prophet (4:4) and "a mother in Israel" (5:7), and many sought out her judicial decisions at the "palm of Deborah" (4:5). She instructed Barak in the conduct of the battle (4:9, 14) and led in the victory song in ch. 5, where she figures prominently (5:7, 12, 15). Deborah's actions and words consis-

11[m]ch. 1:16 [n]Num. 10:29 [o]Josh. 19:33
13[p]ver. 3
14[q]ver. 7 [r]Deut. 9:3; 2 Sam. 5:24; Ps. 68:7; Isa. 52:12
15[s]ver. 23; Ps. 83:9; [Josh. 10:10]
19[t]ch. 5:25
23[u]ver. 15

11 Now Heber [m]the Kenite had separated from the Kenites, the descendants of [n]Hobab
the father-in-law of Moses, and had pitched his tent as far away as the oak in [o]Zaanannim,
which is near Kedesh.

12 When Sisera was told that Barak the son of Abinoam had gone up to Mount Tabor,
13 Sisera called out all his chariots, [p]900 chariots of iron, and all the men who were with
him, from Harosheth-hagoyim to the river Kishon. 14 And Deborah said to Barak, "Up! For
this is the day in which [q]the LORD has given Sisera into your hand. [r]Does not the LORD
go out before you?" So Barak went down from Mount Tabor with 10,000 men following
him. 15 [s]And the LORD routed Sisera and all his chariots and all his army before Barak by
the edge of the sword. And Sisera got down from his chariot and fled away on foot. 16 And
Barak pursued the chariots and the army to Harosheth-hagoyim, and all the army of Sisera
fell by the edge of the sword; not a man was left.

17 But Sisera fled away on foot to the tent of Jael, the wife of Heber the Kenite, for there
was peace between Jabin the king of Hazor and the house of Heber the Kenite. 18 And Jael
came out to meet Sisera and said to him, "Turn aside, my lord; turn aside to me; do not
be afraid." So he turned aside to her into the tent, and she covered him with a rug. 19 And
he said to her, "Please give me a little water to drink, for I am thirsty." So she opened [t]a
skin of milk and gave him a drink and covered him. 20 And he said to her, "Stand at the
opening of the tent, and if any man comes and asks you, 'Is anyone here?' say, 'No.'" 21 But
Jael the wife of Heber took a tent peg, and took a hammer in her hand. Then she went
softly to him and drove the peg into his temple until it went down into the ground while
he was lying fast asleep from weariness. So he died. 22 And behold, as Barak was pursuing
Sisera, Jael went out to meet him and said to him, "Come, and I will show you the man
whom you are seeking." So he went in to her tent, and there lay Sisera dead, with the tent
peg in his temple.

23 [u]So on that day God subdued Jabin the king of Canaan before the people of Israel.
24 And the hand of the people of Israel pressed harder and harder against Jabin the king
of Canaan, until they destroyed Jabin king of Canaan.

---

tently pointed to God, not away from him, in contrast to the poor choices of judges like Gideon, Jephthah, and Samson.

4:1–24 *Victory over the Canaanites.* This section describes Israel's remarkable victory over the more powerful Canaanites (see map to the right).

4:1–3 Israel again did . . . evil. Cf. 3:7–8, 12–14.

4:4–5 Deborah is called a **prophetess**, one of five such women in the OT (cf. Miriam [Ex. 15:20]; Huldah [2 Kings 22:14]; Isaiah's wife [Isa. 8:3]; and Noadiah [a false prophetess; Neh. 6:14]). Deborah functioned as a civil leader (Judg. 4:6–10; 5:7) and as a judge who decided cases (4:4–5). She lived in southern **Ephraim**, near Judah.

4:6–9 Has not the LORD, the God of Israel, commanded you? Deborah did not lead the army herself, but challenged Barak, a man, to do so (see also v. 14); a woman would not normally be a military leader in Israel. In response, Barak summoned the tribes of Israel and led the army (see vv. 10, 14, 15, 16, 22). At least six tribes participated in the battle: Naphtali and Zebulun (v. 6), Ephraim, Benjamin, Manasseh (Machir), and Issachar (5:14–15). This is the nearest thing to an "all-Israelite" coalition in the book. To his discredit, Barak hesitated to lead the Israelites in battle (4:8). Thus, Deborah agreed to go with him but predicted that the glory for the battle would go to a woman (see note on 5:24–27).

4:11 The introduction of **Heber**, Jael's husband, anticipates vv. 17–22. **The Kenites** were distantly related to the Israelites (see note on 1:16).

4:13 900 chariots of iron. Sisera's army was very impressive: chariots were swift, maneuverable weapons of war, the ancient equivalent of tanks (see note on 1:19). However, the chariots got mired in the **river Kishon** (see 5:19–22).

4:17–24 The story of Sisera's death by the hand of **Jael** is detailed in a slow, suspenseful manner reminiscent of the story of Ehud's killing of Eglon (3:12–30). **God** himself is credited with subduing **Jabin**, a process that took some time to complete (4:23–24).

Deborah and Barak Defeat the Canaanites

When King Jabin of Hazor began to oppress the Israelites, Deborah called upon Barak from Kedesh-naphtali to fight against him. The Israelite forces gathered at Mount Tabor, and Sisera, the commander of Jabin's army, marched his men to the Kishon River. The Israelites defeated Sisera's forces and chased them all the way back to Harosheth-hagoyim, but Sisera fled on foot to the oak at Zaanannim, where a woman named Jael killed him as he rested in her tent.

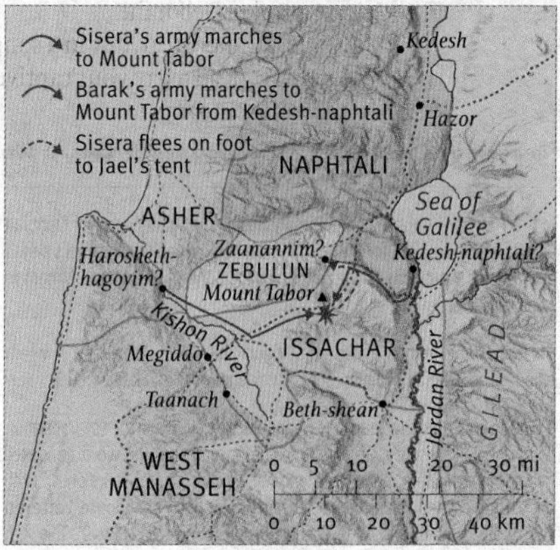

The Song of Deborah and Barak

5 [v]Then sang Deborah and Barak the son of Abinoam on that day:

2 "That the leaders took the lead in Israel,
that [w]the people offered themselves willingly,
bless the LORD!
3 "Hear, O kings; give ear, O princes;
to the LORD I will sing;
I will make melody to the LORD, the God of Israel.

4 "LORD, [x]when you went out from Seir,
when you marched from the region of Edom,
[y]the earth trembled
and the heavens dropped,
yes, the clouds dropped water.
5 The mountains [z]quaked before the LORD,
[a]even Sinai before the LORD, the God of Israel.

6 "In the days of [b]Shamgar, son of Anath,
in the days of [c]Jael, [d]the highways were abandoned,
and travelers kept to the byways.
7 The villagers ceased in Israel;
they ceased to be until I arose;
I, Deborah, arose as a mother in Israel.
8 [e]When new gods were chosen,
then war was in the gates.
[f]Was shield or spear to be seen
among forty thousand in Israel?
9 My heart goes out to the commanders of Israel
who [g]offered themselves willingly among the people.
Bless the LORD.

10 "Tell of it, [h]you who ride on white donkeys,
you who sit on rich carpets[1]
and you who walk by the way.
11 To the sound of musicians[2] at the watering places,
there they repeat the righteous triumphs of the LORD,
the righteous triumphs of his villagers in Israel.

"Then down to the gates marched the people of the LORD.

12 [i]"Awake, awake, Deborah!
Awake, awake, break out in a song!
Arise, Barak, [j]lead away your captives,
O son of Abinoam.

[1] The meaning of the Hebrew word is uncertain; it may connote *saddle blankets* [2] Or *archers*; the meaning of the Hebrew word is uncertain

Chapter 5
1 [v][Ex. 15:1]
2 [w]ver. 9; [2 Chr. 17:16]
4 [x]Deut. 33:2; [Ps. 68:7] [y]2 Sam. 22:8; Ps. 18:7; 68:8; 77:18; Nah. 1:5; Hab. 3:10
5 [z]Isa. 64:1, 3 [a][Ex. 19:18; Deut. 4:11]
6 [b]ch. 3:31 [c]ch. 4:17 [d]Lev. 26:22; Isa. 33:8; Lam. 1:4
8 [e]ch. 2:12, 17; Deut. 32:16 [f][1 Sam. 13:19, 22]
9 [g]ver. 2
10 [h][ch. 10:4; 12:14; Zech. 9:9]
12 [i]Ps. 57:8 [j]Ps. 68:18; Eph. 4:8

5:1–31 *Deborah and Barak's Victory Song.* The victory song of Deborah and Barak praises God for his triumph over the Canaanites on Israel's behalf and reviews the events of the victory (cf. the Song of Moses and Miriam in Ex. 15:1–21).

5:1 sang. This verb is a feminine singular form (i.e., "she sang"), which emphasizes Deborah's role and her prominence over Barak (cf. 4:8–9).

5:2 leaders took the lead. The Hebrew is difficult. While the ESV translation is the most likely sense, an alternative proposal is that the word translated "leaders" may literally mean, "the long-haired ones" or "the hairy ones," with the verb translated "took the lead" being "to let [hair] hang loose." **offered themselves willingly**. All the people gladly cooperated (cf. v. 9). This verb (Hb. *nadab*) is related to the noun for "freewill offerings" (Hb. *nedabah*), which were one of three types of offerings making up the "peace offerings" (Lev. 7:16; 22:23). **bless the LORD!** Cf. Judg. 5:9.

5:4–5 The Lord's marching from **Seir** and **Edom** likely refers to God's transferring his "abode" from the wilderness to Canaan (by way of the land of Edom; cf. Num. 10:12; 20:22)—from one mountain (Sinai; Judg. 5:5) to another (Zion; Ps. 2:6).

5:6–8 Before Deborah **arose** as a deliverer, life as it had been known **ceased** when Israel silently submitted to its enemies. **a mother in Israel**. A title of honor and respect. **new gods**. Cf. 10:14.

5:10–11 All classes of society were to bear witness to the mighty acts of God, from the ruling classes (those riding on **white donkeys**) to the lowest classes (those **who walk by the way**, i.e., along the road). **Watering places** were public places where the entire community gathered.

14[k]ch. 3:27; 12:15 [l][ch. 12:15] [m]Num. 32:39, 40
15[n]ch. 4:14
16[o]Gen. 49:14; Ps. 68:13; [Num. 32:1]
17[p]See Josh. 13:24-28 [q][Josh. 19:46] [r][Josh. 19:29, 31] [s]Gen. 49:13
18[t]ch. 4:10
19[u]ch. 1:27; Josh. 17:11; 1 Kgs. 4:12 [v]2 Kgs. 9:27; 23:29, 30; 2 Chr. 35:22 [w][ver. 30]
20[x]Josh. 10:11
21[y]ch. 4:7
23[z][ch. 21:9, 10]
24[a]ch. 4:17
25[b]ch. 4:19
26[c]ch. 4:21

13 Then down marched the remnant of the noble;
the people of the LORD marched down for me against the mighty.
14 From [k]Ephraim their root [l]they marched down into the valley,[1]
following you, Benjamin, with your kinsmen;
from [m]Machir marched down the commanders,
and from Zebulun those who bear the lieutenant's[2] staff;
15 the princes of Issachar came with Deborah,
and Issachar faithful to [n]Barak;
into the valley they rushed at his heels.
Among the clans of Reuben
there were great searchings of heart.
16 Why did you sit still [o]among the sheepfolds,
to hear the whistling for the flocks?
Among the clans of Reuben
there were great searchings of heart.
17 [p]Gilead stayed beyond the Jordan;
[q]and Dan, why did he stay with the ships?
[r]Asher sat still [s]at the coast of the sea,
staying by his landings.
18 [t]Zebulun is a people who risked their lives to the death;
[t]Naphtali, too, on the heights of the field.

19 "The kings came, they fought;
then fought the kings of Canaan,
at [u]Taanach, by the waters of [v]Megiddo;
[w]they got no spoils of silver.
20 [x]From heaven the stars fought,
from their courses they fought against Sisera.
21 [y]The torrent Kishon swept them away,
the ancient torrent, the torrent Kishon.
March on, my soul, with might!

22 "Then loud beat the horses' hoofs
with the galloping, galloping of his steeds.

23 "Curse Meroz, says the angel of the LORD,
curse its inhabitants thoroughly,
[z]because they did not come to the help of the LORD,
to the help of the LORD against the mighty.

24 "Most blessed of women be [a]Jael,
the wife of Heber the Kenite,
of tent-dwelling women most blessed.
25 [b]He asked for water and she gave him milk;
she brought him curds in a noble's bowl.
26 [c]She sent her hand to the tent peg

[1] Septuagint; Hebrew *in Amalek* [2] Hebrew *commander's*

5:13–18 After the call to worship (vv. 10–12), the text offers a general battle overview (v. 13) and then describes the tribes' participation (vv. 14–18). Ten of the 12 tribes are mentioned here. Five of them (and part of a sixth) are mentioned favorably because they responded to Deborah's and Barak's call to arms: **Ephraim**, **Benjamin**, western Manasseh (**Machir**) (v. 14), **Zebulun** (vv. 14, 18), **Issachar** (v. 15), and **Naphtali** (v. 18). Four tribes (and the other part of Manasseh) did not respond to the summons: **Reuben** (vv. 15–16), Gad and eastern Manasseh (**Gilead**), **Dan**, and **Asher** (v. 17). Judah and Simeon are not mentioned at all in chs. 4–5. Dan's connection with **ships** (5:17) probably reflects the tribe's original inheritance along the south-central coastal plain, with access to the sea (Josh. 19:40–46). Later, the tribe migrated northward, forced out of its territory (Josh. 19:47; Judg. 1:34; 18:1).

5:19–23 The victory proper is now described in vivid, impressionistic terms. **the stars fought . . . against Sisera** (cf. 4:15: "the LORD routed Sisera"). The imagery suggests that the forces of nature fought on God's side (and thus Canaanite deities, who supposedly ruled over these forces, were powerless to help against the true God). The frantic pounding of the **horses' hoofs** suggests the disarray caused by the waters of the **Kishon** (5:21–22; cf. 4:7).

5:24–27 Most blessed of women. **Jael** is a heroine for killing Sisera (see 4:17–22). **Between her feet he sank, he fell**. Chapter 4 tells us that Sisera already was lying down, asleep, when Jael struck him (4:21). The poem is probably speaking metaphorically, repeating graphic, emotive language to make its point, namely, that a woman triumphed over this great warrior.

and her right hand to the workmen's mallet;
she struck Sisera;
she crushed his head;
she shattered and pierced his temple.
27 Between her feet
he sank, he fell, he lay still;
between her feet
he sank, he fell;
where he sank,
there he fell—dead.

28 [d]"Out of the window she peered,
the mother of Sisera wailed through [e]the lattice:
'Why is his chariot so long in coming?
Why tarry the hoofbeats of his chariots?'
29 Her wisest princesses answer,
indeed, she answers herself,
30 'Have they not found and [f]divided the spoil?—
A womb or two for every man;
spoil of dyed materials for Sisera,
spoil of dyed materials embroidered,
two pieces of dyed work embroidered for the neck as spoil?'

31 [g]"So may all your enemies perish, O LORD!
But your friends be [h]like the sun [i]as he rises in his might."

[j]And the land had rest for forty years.

Midian Oppresses Israel

6 [k]The people of Israel did what was evil in the sight of the LORD, and the LORD gave
them into the hand of [l]Midian seven years. 2 And the hand of Midian overpowered
Israel, and because of Midian the people of Israel made for themselves the dens that are in

28[d][2 Sam. 6:16] [e][Prov. 7:6]
30[f]Ex. 15:9
31[g][Ps. 83:9, 10] [h][2 Sam. 23:4; Dan. 12:3; Matt. 13:43] [i]Ps. 19:5; 37:6 [j]See ch. 3:11

Chapter 6

1[k]See ch. 2:19 [l]Gen. 25:2; Num. 25:17, 18; Hab. 3:7

5:28–30 The mother of Sisera is a pitiable figure, but these verses highlight Jael's achievement: rather than bringing great plunder to impress his women, Sisera lay dead at another woman's feet. **A womb or two**. A crude reference to captured women.

5:31 The hymn concludes with more praise of the Lord, as many psalms do. **the land had rest for forty years**. See note on 3:11.

6:1–8:35 *Gideon.* The fifth judge was Gideon, who fought the Midianites (6:1–6) twice, first following God's instructions (7:1–8:3) and the second time on his own initiative (8:4–21). Before Gideon, Israel's apostasy had grown worse, so when the people cried out, God sent a prophet to condemn them for their covenant infidelity (6:7–10). After Gideon defeated Midian, however, he led the people of Israel into sin (8:22–28). The Israelites turned upon each other for the first time (8:16–17; cf. 9:23–54), foreshadowing later, even worse dissension (12:1–6; ch. 20). Despite God's continued intervention, and even some positive qualities in Gideon, the downward spiral in Israel's apostasy continued.

6:1–10 *Continuing Apostasy.* The familiar pattern of apostasy is resumed here (vv. 1–6). When Israel cried out for deliverance (v. 6), God sent a prophet, not a judge, who condemned Israel (vv. 7–10). God would not be confined to a mechanical "box," responding to any and all Israelite appeals regardless of circumstances.

Common Cycle for Each Judge

God's sending of judges to Israel repeatedly followed a fourfold cycle:

(1) apostasy: the Israelites do what is evil in the sight of the Lord;
(2) servitude: God allows the nation to be conquered and oppressed by a neighboring nation;
(3) supplication: the people cry out to God; and
(4) salvation: God sends a judge to deliver the Israelites.

The cycle then repeats after the judge dies.

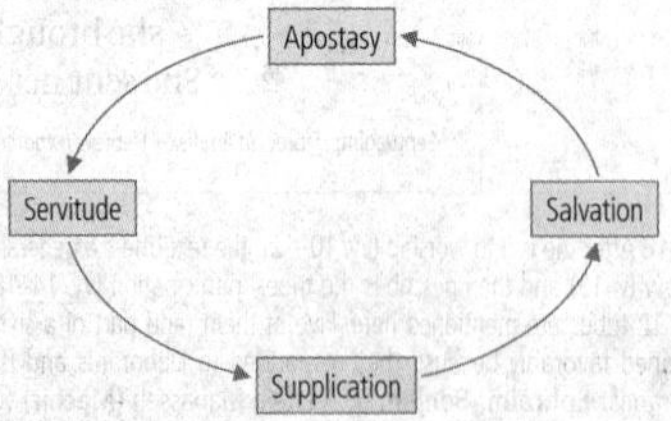

Cycles of Good and Bad under the Judges (2:11–16:31)

Pattern	Outline	Othniel	Ehud	Deborah	Gideon	Jephthah	Samson
Apostasy	2:11–13	3:7	3:12a	4:1	6:1a	10:6	13:1a
Servitude	2:14–15	3:8	3:12b–14	4:2	6:1b–6a	10:7–9	13:1b
Supplication and salvation	2:16–18	3:9–11	3:15–31	4:3–24	6:6b–8:28	11:1–33	13:24; 14:19; 15:14b–20

2 [m]1 Sam. 13:6; Heb. 11:38
3 [n]ch. 3:13 [o]ver. 33; ch. 7:12; 8:10; Gen. 29:1; 1 Kgs. 4:30; Job 1:3
4 [p][Lev. 26:16]; See Deut. 28:30-33, 51; Mic. 6:15
5 [q]ch. 7:12
6 [r]See ch. 3:9
8 [s]1 Sam. 10:18
9 [t]Ps. 44:2, 3
10 [u]Josh. 24:15; See 2 Kgs. 17:35-38
11 [v]ch. 8:2; Josh. 17:2 [w]Heb. 11:32
12 [x]ch. 13:3; Luke 1:11; [Acts 10:3] [y]Josh. 1:5
13 [z]Ps. 89:49; Isa. 63:15 [a]Ps. 44:1
14 [b]1 Sam. 12:11; [Josh. 1:9]
15 [c][Ex. 3:11] [d]1 Sam. 9:21; 18:18
16 [e]Ex. 3:12; Josh. 1:5
17 [f]Ex. 33:13 [g]2 Kgs. 20:8, 9; Isa. 7:11; [ver. 36, 37]; See Ex. 4:1-8
18 [h]ch. 13:15; Gen. 18:3-5
19 [i]Gen. 18:6-8
20 [j]ch. 13:19 [k][1 Kgs. 18:33, 34]
21 [l]Lev. 9:24; 1 Kgs. 18:38; 2 Chr. 7:1
22 [m]ch. 13:21, 22; [Gen. 32:30; Ex. 33:20; Deut. 5:26]

the mountains and [m]the caves and the strongholds. **3** For whenever the Israelites planted
crops, the Midianites and [n]the Amalekites and [o]the people of the East would come up
against them. **4** They would encamp against them [p]and devour the produce of the land,
as far as Gaza, and leave no sustenance in Israel and no sheep or ox or donkey. **5** For they
would come up with their livestock and their tents; they would come [q]like locusts in
number—both they and their camels could not be counted—so that they laid waste the
land as they came in. **6** And Israel was brought very low because of Midian. And the people
of Israel [r]cried out for help to the LORD.

7 When the people of Israel cried out to the LORD on account of the Midianites, **8** the
LORD sent a prophet to the people of Israel. And he said to them, "Thus says the LORD, the
God of Israel: [s]I led you up from Egypt and brought you out of the house of slavery. **9** And
I delivered you from the hand of the Egyptians and from the hand of all who oppressed
you, and [t]drove them out before you and gave you their land. **10** And I said to you, 'I am
the LORD your God; [u]you shall not fear the gods of the Amorites in whose land you dwell.'
But you have not obeyed my voice."

The Call of Gideon

11 Now the angel of the LORD came and sat under the terebinth at Ophrah, which belonged
to Joash [v]the Abiezrite, while his son [w]Gideon was beating out wheat in the winepress to
hide it from the Midianites. **12** And [x]the angel of the LORD appeared to him and said to
him, [y]"The LORD is with you, O mighty man of valor." **13** And Gideon said to him, "Please,
sir,[1] if the LORD is with us, why then has all this happened to us? And where are [z]all his
wonderful deeds [a]that our fathers recounted to us, saying, 'Did not the LORD bring us up
from Egypt?' But now the LORD has forsaken us and given us into the hand of Midian."
14 And the LORD[2] turned to him and said, "Go in this might of yours and save Israel from
the hand of Midian; [b]do not I send you?" **15** And he said to him, [c]"Please, Lord, how can I
save Israel? Behold, [d]my clan is the weakest in Manasseh, and I am the least in my father's
house." **16** And the LORD said to him, [e]"But I will be with you, and you shall strike the
Midianites as one man." **17** And he said to him, [f]"If now I have found favor in your eyes,
then [g]show me a sign that it is you who speak with me. **18** Please [h]do not depart from here
until I come to you and bring out my present and set it before you." And he said, "I will
stay till you return."

19 So Gideon went into his house [i]and prepared a young goat and unleavened cakes
from an ephah[3] of flour. The meat he put in a basket, and the broth he put in a pot, and
brought them to him under the terebinth and presented them. **20** And the angel of God
said to him, "Take the meat and the unleavened cakes, and put them [j]on this rock, and
[k]pour the broth over them." And he did so. **21** Then the angel of the LORD reached out the
tip of the staff that was in his hand and touched the meat and the unleavened cakes. [l]And
fire sprang up from the rock and consumed the meat and the unleavened cakes. And the
angel of the LORD vanished from his sight. **22** Then Gideon perceived that he was the angel
of the LORD. And Gideon said, [m]"Alas, O Lord GOD! For now I have seen the angel of the

[1] Or *Please, my Lord* [2] Septuagint *the angel of the LORD*; also verse 16 [3] An *ephah* was about 3/5 bushel or 22 liters

6:5 Locusts devastated land, ate crops, and darkened the skies as they were blown in by the wind (Ex. 10:13–15; cf. Joel 1:4, 15–17; 2:1–11).

6:8 The message of the unnamed **prophet** represents the first time God rebuked the people when they called upon him. The prophet reminded the Israelites of God's faithfulness and their own apostasy.

6:11–40 ***Gideon's Call.*** God's call of a reluctant Gideon is the focus of the next three accounts. First, the angel of the Lord appeared to him (vv. 11–24); then, Gideon destroyed an altar of Baal (vv. 25–35); finally, Gideon's wavering faith is on full display (vv. 36–40). Gideon's reluctance recalls that of Moses (Exodus 3–4).

6:11 the angel of the LORD. See note on 2:1. **beating out wheat in the winepress.** Grapes were normally trodden in a winepress, a square or circular pit carved into rock (cf. Isa. 16:10; Jer. 48:33), whereas wheat was usually threshed on open threshing floors, where the wind could carry away the chaff in the winnowing process (2 Sam. 24:18). Gideon's secret threshing inside a winepress—when he already had access to a true threshing floor (cf. Judg. 6:37)—shows the desperate straits because of Midianite oppression.

6:13 sir. The term is literally "my Lord" (Hb. *'Adoni*; see ESV footnote). This was a polite form of address (cf. 4:18, where Jael spoke the same words to Sisera). Gideon uses the same term to refer to God in 6:15 ("Lord"; Hb. *'Adonay*). **the LORD** (Hb. *YHWH*). This is the personal name of God (see note on Gen. 2:4).

6:15–16 I am the least. Moses and Jeremiah had similar objections when God called them (Ex. 3:11; Jer. 1:6). **I will be with you.** This promise of God's presence had also been given to Moses and Joshua (Ex. 3:12; Josh. 1:5, 9), putting Gideon in the same lineage of leaders, with the same guarantee of success. Nonetheless, Gideon had his doubts and fears (cf. Judg. 6:17 and esp. vv. 36–40).

6:22 perceived. Lit., "saw" (Hb. *ra'ah*, translated **seen** later in the verse). Gideon feared for his life because he had encountered God's angel **face to face** (cf. Gen. 32:30; Ex. 33:20).

LORD face to face." 23 But the LORD said to him, [n]"Peace be to you. Do not fear; you shall
not die." 24 Then Gideon built an altar there to the LORD and called it, [o]The LORD Is Peace.
To this day it still stands at [p]Ophrah, which belongs to the Abiezrites.
25 That night the LORD said to him, "Take your father's bull, and the second bull seven
years old, and pull down the altar of Baal that your father has, and cut down [q]the Asherah
that is beside it 26 and build an altar to the LORD your God on the top of the [r]stronghold
here, with stones laid in due order. Then take the second bull and offer it as a burnt offering with the wood of the Asherah that you shall cut down." 27 So Gideon took ten men of
his servants and did as the LORD had told him. But because he was too afraid of his family
and the men of the town to do it by day, he did it by night.

Gideon Destroys the Altar of Baal

28 When the men of the town rose early in the morning, behold, the altar of Baal was
broken down, and the Asherah beside it was cut down, and the second bull was offered on
the altar that had been built. 29 And they said to one another, "Who has done this thing?"
And after they had searched and inquired, they said, "Gideon the son of Joash has done
this thing." 30 Then the men of the town said to Joash, "Bring out your son, that he may
die, for he has broken down the altar of Baal and cut down the Asherah beside it." 31 But
Joash said to all who stood against him, "Will you contend for Baal? Or will you save
him? Whoever contends for him shall be put to death by morning. If he is a god, let him
contend for himself, because his altar has been broken down." 32 Therefore on that day

23 [n]Dan. 10:19
24 [o][Gen. 22:14; Ex. 17:15; Ezek. 48:35] [p]ver. 11; ch. 8:27, 32
25 [q]ch. 3:7
26 [r]Dan. 11:7, 10, 31 (Heb.)

Gideon Defeats the Midianites

Gideon's small army of 300 men camped by the spring of Harod while the vast Midianite army spread out in the Jezreel Valley by the hill of Moreh. When Gideon's men encircled and surprised the Midianites during the night, the Midianites fled. Gideon's men chased them to Abel-meholah and beyond, passing through Succoth and Penuel on their way to Karkor, where they captured the leaders of the Midianite army.

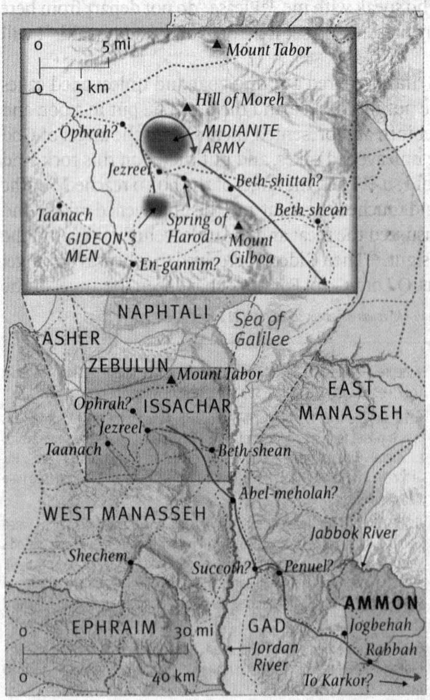

6:24 To this day. This expression is common in Joshua and Judges (e.g., Josh. 4:9; 5:9; 6:25; 7:26; Judg. 1:21, 26; 15:19). The **Abiezrites** were part of the tribe of Manasseh that settled west of the Jordan River (Num. 26:30; Josh. 17:1–2).

6:25–26 Asherah may function as both the divine name for a particular goddess or, as in these verses, refer to sacred wooden poles erected at places where she was worshiped (vv. 26, 28, 30; cf. 1 Kings 15:13; 18:19; 2 Kings 17:16). Most frequently, these sacred objects are called "Asherim" (e.g., Ex. 34:13; Deut. 7:5; 12:3; 2 Kings 17:10). **and the second bull**. There is some debate as to whether Judg. 6:25 refers to one bull or two. The word translated "and" may also be translated "namely," such that the Lord is not indicating a second animal but specifying more clearly to Gideon which bull should be used to tear down the altar and then be sacrificed. Either way, Gideon is instructed to use a bull to topple the altar of Baal, whose symbol was the bull. The need to make such an instruction explicit again shows Gideon's reluctance and slow response (cf. v. 17). **wood of the Asherah**. Ironically, Gideon's sacrifice was to be offered using the very wood of the image that he was to tear down.

6:32 Gideon's new name, **Jerubbaal**, meant "Let Baal contend," echoing Joash's mockery of those who trusted in Baal (v. 31). With this name, Gideon became a living reminder of Baal's impotence.

6:34 Spirit of the LORD clothed. See 1 Chron. 12:18; 2 Chron. 24:20. Other terms for the Spirit's activity in Judges include "was upon" (Judg. 3:10; 11:29) and "rushed upon" (14:6, 19; 15:14). See note on 14:6.

6:35 Gideon **sent messengers** to four northern tribes adjacent to each other—**Manasseh**, **Asher**, **Zebulun**, and **Naphtali**—prior to the first military encounter in 7:1–8:3.

6:36–40 Before the actual military engagement, Gideon again displays his reluctance to be a leader, for he asks for confirmatory signs from God (cf. v. 17). On the one hand, Gideon's fears are understandable: the task he is preparing to do is difficult and dangerous. On the other hand, the angel's appearance and promise (vv. 11–24) already included a confirmatory miracle (v. 21), and Gideon had already begun to obey (vv. 25–27) and to see God's protection (v. 31). In any event, God stoops to Gideon's level and grants the signs requested.

6:39 let me test. Ironically, this is the same word (Hb. *nasah*) used of God earlier, when he "tested" Israel (2:22; 3:1). Gideon's desire to test God was in direct violation of the Mosaic law, which prohibited humans from testing God (Deut. 6:16). Gideon himself was aware that he was doing something unwise, if not sinful, since he asked God not to be angry with him (Judg. 6:39). Gideon already knew God's will (cf. vv. 14–16, 36)—calling him to service on behalf of God's people—so Gideon's requests reveal his weak faith. Despite

32[s]ch. 7:1; 1 Sam. 12:11; [2 Sam. 11:21]
33[t]ver. 3 [u]Josh. 17:16
34[v]See ch. 3:10 [w]ch. 3:27
35[x]ch. 7:24
36[y]For ver. 36-40, see Ex. 4:1-7
39[z]Gen. 18:32

Chapter 7

1[a]ch. 6:32 [b][1 Sam. 29:1] [c]Gen. 12:6; Deut. 11:30
2[d]Deut. 8:17; [Isa. 10:13]
3[e]Deut. 20:8
7[f][1 Sam. 14:6; 2 Chr. 14:11]
8[g]ver. 1
9[h]Gen. 46:2, 3; 1 Kgs. 3:5 [i]See ch. 3:28

Gideon[1] was called [s]Jerubbaal, that is to say, "Let Baal contend against him," because he
broke down his altar.
33 Now [t]all the Midianites and the Amalekites and the people of the East came together,
and they crossed the Jordan and encamped in [u]the Valley of Jezreel. **34** But [v]the Spirit of
the LORD clothed Gideon, [w]and he sounded the trumpet, and the Abiezrites were called
out to follow him. **35** [x]And he sent messengers throughout all Manasseh, and they too were
called out to follow him. [x]And he sent messengers to Asher, Zebulun, and Naphtali, and
they went up to meet them.

The Sign of the Fleece

36 [y]Then Gideon said to God, "If you will save Israel by my hand, as you have said, **37** behold,
I am laying a fleece of wool on the threshing floor. If there is dew on the fleece alone, and
it is dry on all the ground, then I shall know that you will save Israel by my hand, as you
have said." **38** And it was so. When he rose early next morning and squeezed the fleece, he
wrung enough dew from the fleece to fill a bowl with water. **39** Then Gideon said to God,
[z]"Let not your anger burn against me; let me speak just once more. Please let me test just
once more with the fleece. Please let it be dry on the fleece only, and on all the ground let
there be dew." **40** And God did so that night; and it was dry on the fleece only, and on all
the ground there was dew.

Gideon's Three Hundred Men

7 Then [a]Jerubbaal (that is, Gideon) and all the people who were with him rose early and
encamped beside [b]the spring of Harod. And the camp of Midian was north of them,
[c]by the hill of Moreh, in the valley.
2 The LORD said to Gideon, "The people with you are too many for me to give the
Midianites into their hand, [d]lest Israel boast over me, saying, 'My own hand has saved
me.' **3** Now therefore proclaim in the ears of the people, saying, [e]'Whoever is fearful and
trembling, let him return home and hurry away from Mount Gilead.'" Then 22,000 of
the people returned, and 10,000 remained.
4 And the LORD said to Gideon, "The people are still too many. Take them down to the
water, and I will test them for you there, and anyone of whom I say to you, 'This one shall
go with you,' shall go with you, and anyone of whom I say to you, 'This one shall not go
with you,' shall not go." **5** So he brought the people down to the water. And the LORD said
to Gideon, "Every one who laps the water with his tongue, as a dog laps, you shall set by
himself. Likewise, every one who kneels down to drink." **6** And the number of those who
lapped, putting their hands to their mouths, was 300 men, but all the rest of the people
knelt down to drink water. **7** And the LORD said to Gideon, [f]"With the 300 men who lapped
I will save you and give the Midianites into your hand, and let all the others go every man
to his home." **8** So the people took provisions in their hands, and their trumpets. And he
sent all the rest of Israel every man to his tent, but retained the 300 men. And the camp
of Midian was below him [g]in the valley.
9 That same [h]night the LORD said to him, "Arise, go down against the camp, [i]for I have
given it into your hand. **10** But if you are afraid to go down, go down to the camp with

[1] Hebrew *he*

this lack of faith, God accommodated both of Gideon's requests (vv. 38, 40). More constructive examples of responses to God's call are Isaiah (Isa. 6:8) and Jesus' disciples (Matt. 4:20; Mark 1:18–20).

7:1–8:3 ***Gideon's First Battle.*** God clearly delivered Israel in Gideon's first military encounter (see map, p. 450). The account of Gideon's force reduction from 32,000 to 300 men (7:1–8) emphasizes that God wanted the glory for himself (esp. 7:2, 7). God's assurances of help for Israel were reinforced when Gideon overheard the Midianites speaking of God's triumph (7:9–15). The battle did not significantly involve the Israelites because God provided the victory in a special way (7:16–25). The battle's aftermath shows the resolution of the Ephraimites' misunderstanding of Gideon's intentions (8:1–3).

7:2 lest Israel boast. God made it clear from the very beginning that the glory for this victory was to be all his. This makes all the more absurd the Israelites' request after the battle that Gideon rule over them because *he* had supposedly delivered them from the Midianites (cf. 8:22).

7:3 The Mosaic laws allowed military exemptions for several classes of people, including those who were **fearful** (Deut. 20:5–8) since they might cause others also to fear.

7:4–5 Every one who laps . . . as a dog laps. The second **test** for reducing Gideon's forces involved a strange ritual: taking into account how men drank water from a brook. Neither way of drinking is singled out as the "right" way, so this may be simply a means of trimming down the number of men rather than a critique of either form of drinking.

7:10 if you are afraid. God graciously granted to Gideon, who had been reluctant and afraid previously (6:17, 23, 27, 36–40), a preview of the coming victory by allowing him to enter the Midianite camp and overhear a Midianite's dream about Israel's triumph (7:10–14).

Purah your servant. **11** [j]And you shall hear what they say, and afterward your hands shall be
strengthened to go down against the camp." [k]Then he went down with Purah his servant
to the outposts of the armed men who were in the camp. **12** And the Midianites and the
Amalekites and [l]all the people of the East lay along the valley like locusts in abundance,
and their camels were without number, [m]as the sand that is on the seashore in abundance.
13 When Gideon came, behold, a man was telling a dream to his comrade. And he said,
"Behold, I dreamed a dream, and behold, a cake of barley bread tumbled into the camp of
Midian and came to the tent and struck it so that it fell and turned it upside down, so that
the tent lay flat." **14** And his comrade answered, "This is no other than the sword of Gideon
the son of Joash, a man of Israel; God has given into his hand Midian and all the camp."
15 As soon as Gideon heard the telling of the dream and its interpretation, he worshiped.
And he returned to the camp of Israel and said, "Arise, for the LORD has given the host
of Midian into your hand." **16** And he divided the 300 men into three companies and put
trumpets into the hands of all of them and empty jars, with [n]torches inside the jars. **17** And
he said to them, "Look at me, and do likewise. When I come to the outskirts of the camp,
do as I do. **18** When I blow the trumpet, I and all who are with me, then blow the trumpets
also on every side of all the camp and shout, [o]'For the LORD and for Gideon.'"

Gideon Defeats Midian

19 So Gideon and the hundred men who were with him came to the outskirts of the camp
at the beginning of the middle watch, when they had just set the watch. And they blew
the trumpets and smashed the jars that were in their hands. **20** Then the three companies
blew the trumpets and broke the jars. They held in their left hands the torches, and in
their right hands the trumpets to blow. [o]And they cried out, "A sword for the LORD and
for Gideon!" **21** Every man stood in his place around the camp, [p]and all the army ran. They
cried out and fled. **22** [q]When they blew the 300 trumpets, [r]the LORD set [s]every man's sword
against his comrade and against all the army. And the army fled as far as Beth-shittah
toward Zererah,[1] as far as the border of Abel-meholah, by Tabbath. **23** And the men of
Israel were called out from Naphtali and from Asher and from all Manasseh, and they
pursued after Midian.
24 [t]Gideon sent messengers throughout [u]all the hill country of Ephraim, saying, "Come
down against the Midianites and capture the waters against them, as far as [v]Beth-barah,
and also the Jordan." So all the men of Ephraim were called out, and they captured the
waters as far as Beth-barah, and also the Jordan. **25** And they captured [w]the two princes of
Midian, Oreb and Zeeb. They killed Oreb [x]at the rock of Oreb, and Zeeb they killed at the
winepress of Zeeb. Then they pursued Midian, and they brought the heads of Oreb and
Zeeb to Gideon [y]across the Jordan.

Gideon Defeats Zebah and Zalmunna

8 [z]Then the men of Ephraim said to him, "What is this that you have done to us, not to
call us when you went to fight against Midian?" And they accused him fiercely. **2** And
he said to them, "What have I done now in comparison with you? Is not [a]the gleaning of
the grapes of Ephraim better than the grape harvest of Abiezer? **3** [b]God has given into your
hands the princes of Midian, Oreb and Zeeb. What have I been able to do in comparison
with you?" [c]Then their anger[2] against him subsided when he said this.

[1] Some Hebrew manuscripts *Zeredah* [2] Hebrew *their spirit*

11 [j]See ver. 13-15 [k][1 Sam. 14:9, 10]
12 [l]See ch. 6:3 [m]Josh. 11:4
16 [n]ch. 15:4; Gen. 15:17
18 [o][Ex. 14:13, 14; 2 Chr. 20:17]
20 [o][See ver. 18 above]
21 [p][2 Kgs. 7:7]
22 [q][Josh. 6:4, 16, 20] [r][Ps. 83:9; Isa. 9:4] [s]1 Sam. 14:20; [2 Chr. 20:23]
24 [t]ch. 6:35 [u]See Josh. 24:33 [v][ch. 3:28]
25 [w]ch. 8:3; Ps. 83:11 [x]Isa. 10:26 [y]ch. 8:4

Chapter 8

1 [z][ch. 12:1; 2 Sam. 19:41]
2 [a]Isa. 24:13; Jer. 49:9; Obad. 5; Mic. 7:1
3 [b]ch. 7:24, 25 [c][Prov. 15:1]

7:13–15 tumbled. This word literally means "turned itself over." The loaf in the dream, symbolizing the **sword of Gideon**, "overturned" the Midianite camp. The dream provided the confirmation that Gideon needed, in light of his earlier fear (v. 10). **he worshiped**. This indicates prostrating oneself to the ground in humble obeisance.

7:18 For the LORD and for Gideon. See note on 7:20.

7:19 middle watch. Jewish tradition speaks of three nighttime watches (*Jubilees* 49.10, 12); the "morning watch" is mentioned in Ex. 14:24 and 1 Sam. 11:11. The later division into four watches (Matt. 14:25; Mark 13:35) seems to have been influenced by Roman practice.

7:20 A sword for the LORD and for Gideon! The full war cry is now uttered in the event of battle (cf. the previews of this in vv. 14, 18). Ironically, no Israelite swords were used at all, only torches, trumpets, and jars—scarcely classic military weapons.

7:22–25 The victory was clearly God's: he turned the Midianites' swords against them (v. 22), and they fled south and east to the Jordan River and across (vv. 23–25).

8:1–3 The Ephraimites complained that they had been called out only belatedly, but Gideon's flattering response had a soothing effect on them.

8:4–21 *Gideon's Second Battle.* Following the Lord's great victory on the

4 [d]And Gideon came to the Jordan and crossed over, he and [d]the 300 men who were with
him, exhausted yet pursuing. 5 So he said to the men of [e]Succoth, "Please give loaves of
bread to the people who follow me, for they are exhausted, and I am pursuing after Zebah
and Zalmunna, the kings of Midian." 6 And the officials of Succoth said, [f]"Are the hands of
Zebah and Zalmunna already in your hand, [g]that we should give bread to your army?" 7 So
Gideon said, "Well then, when the LORD has given Zebah and Zalmunna into my hand, [h]I
will flail your flesh with the thorns of the wilderness and with briers." 8 And from there he
went up to [i]Penuel, and spoke to them in the same way, and the men of Penuel answered
him as the men of Succoth had answered. 9 And he said to the men of Penuel, [j]"When I
come again in peace, [k]I will break down this tower."

10 Now Zebah and Zalmunna were in Karkor with their army, about 15,000 men, all
who were left of all the army of [l]the people of the East, for there had fallen 120,000 men
[m]who drew the sword. 11 And Gideon went up by the way of the tent dwellers east of
[n]Nobah and Jogbehah and attacked the army, for the army felt [o]secure. 12 And Zebah and
Zalmunna fled, and he pursued them [p]and captured the two kings of Midian, Zebah
and Zalmunna, and he threw all the army into a panic.

13 Then Gideon the son of Joash returned from the battle by the ascent of Heres. 14 And
he captured a young man of Succoth and questioned him. And he wrote down for him the
officials and elders of Succoth, seventy-seven men. 15 And he came to the men of Succoth
and said, "Behold Zebah and Zalmunna, about whom you taunted me, saying, [q]'Are the
hands of Zebah and Zalmunna already in your hand, that we should give bread to your
men who are exhausted?'" 16 And he took the elders of the city, and he took thorns of the
wilderness and briers and with them taught the men of Succoth a lesson. 17 [r]And he broke
down the tower of Penuel and killed the men of the city.

18 Then he said to Zebah and Zalmunna, "Where are the men whom you killed at [s]Tabor?"
They answered, "As you are, so were they. Every one of them resembled the son of a king."
19 And he said, "They were my brothers, the sons of my mother. [t]As the LORD lives, if you
had saved them alive, I would not kill you." 20 So he said to Jether his firstborn, "Rise and
kill them!" But the young man did not draw his sword, for he was afraid, because he was
still a young man. 21 Then Zebah and Zalmunna said, "Rise yourself and fall upon us, for
as the man is, so is his strength." And Gideon arose and [u]killed Zebah and Zalmunna, and
he took [v]the crescent ornaments that were on the necks of their camels.

Gideon's Ephod

22 Then the men of Israel said to Gideon, "Rule over us, you and your son and your
grandson also, for you have saved us from the hand of Midian." 23 Gideon said to them, "I
will not rule over you, and my son will not rule over you; [w]the LORD will rule over you."
24 And Gideon said to them, "Let me make a request of you: every one of you give me the
earrings from his spoil." (For they had golden earrings, [x]because they were Ishmaelites.)
25 And they answered, "We will willingly give them." And they spread a cloak, and every
man threw in it the earrings of his spoil. 26 And the weight of the golden earrings that he

4 [d]ch. 7:6
5 [e]Gen. 33:17; Ps. 60:6
6 [f][1 Kgs. 20:11] [g][1 Sam. 25:11]
7 [h]ver. 16
8 [i]Gen. 32:30, 31; 1 Kgs. 12:25
9 [j][1 Kgs. 22:27, 28] [k]ver. 17
10 [l]See ch. 6:3 [m]ch. 20:2, 15, 17, 25, 35, 46; 2 Sam. 24:9; 2 Kgs. 3:26; 1 Chr. 21:5
11 [n]Num. 32:35, 42 [o]ch. 18:27
12 [p]Ps. 83:11
15 [q]ver. 6
17 [r][1 Kgs. 12:25]
18 [s][ch. 4:6]
19 [t]See Ruth 3:13
21 [u]Ps. 83:11 [v]ver. 26; Isa. 3:18
23 [w][1 Sam. 8:7; 10:19; 12:12, 17, 19]
24 [x][Gen. 37:25, 28, 36; 39:1]

Israelites' behalf, Gideon pursued a second military engagement. But the narrative here takes on a different tone. Whereas the Lord is prominently mentioned as the one who orchestrates the victory in the preceding chapter (ch. 7), the presence of the Lord is noticeably absent in this chapter. Even though Gideon was finishing off the action against the Midianites, the portrayal of Gideon in 8:13–21 is far from attractive (cf. his treatment of Succoth and Penuel for their obstruction of his purposes [vv. 13–17], and his reasons for slaying Zebah and Zalmunna, the Midianite kings [vv. 18–21]).

8:11–12 Gideon's active involvement in attacking and chasing the enemy contrasts sharply with his and the people's standing by while the Lord gave them the victory in the earlier encounter (see esp. 7:21).

8:16–17 Gideon's actions here fulfill his pledges in vv. 7 and 9.

8:18–21 The private nature of Gideon's feud with the Midianites is seen most clearly in this conversation, where **Zebah and Zalmunna** challenged Gideon's manhood, and Gideon responded by killing them himself. Holy war, which is to be fought at God's command for the protection of the whole people, gives no warrant for this kind of personal vengeance.

8:22–28 *Gideon's Apostasy.* Despite God's faithfulness to Gideon, he turns away from the Lord by leading the people into improper worship practices.

8:22–23 Rule over us. This request, while understandable from a human perspective, as Gideon may have begun to conduct himself like a king (v. 18), flew directly in the face of the entire narrative up to this moment: it was God (not any human being) who was to get the credit for delivering his people (see note on 7:2). **the LORD will rule over you.** The Hebrew word order might be paraphrased as, "It is *the Lord*, and no other, who shall rule over you!" While Gideon's words were theologically correct, his subsequent actions show either that he was only pretending or that he was self-deceived; he appears eventually to have been seduced by the lures of being a king (8:24–28, 31).

8:26 Despite Gideon's protest that he would not become a king (see v. 23), the ornamentation of the Midianite kings—**the crescent ornaments and the pendants and the purple garments**—was now Gideon's.

requested was 1,700 shekels[1] of gold, besides [y]the crescent ornaments and [z]the pendants
and the purple garments worn by the kings of Midian, and besides the collars that were
around the necks of their camels. 27 And Gideon [a]made an ephod of it and put it in his city,
[b]in Ophrah. And all Israel [c]whored after it there, and it became a [d]snare to Gideon and
to his family. 28 So Midian was subdued before the people of Israel, and they raised their
heads no more. [e]And the land had rest forty years in the days of Gideon.

The Death of Gideon

29 [f]Jerubbaal the son of Joash went and lived in his own house. 30 Now Gideon had [g]sev-
enty sons, his own offspring,[2] for he had many wives. 31 And his concubine [h]who was in
Shechem also bore him a son, and he called his name Abimelech. 32 And Gideon the son
of Joash died [i]in a good old age and was buried in the tomb of Joash his father, [j]at Ophrah
of the Abiezrites.

33 [k]As soon as Gideon died, the people of Israel turned again and [l]whored after the Baals
and made [m]Baal-berith their god. 34 And the people of Israel [n]did not remember the LORD
their God, who had delivered them from the hand of all their enemies on every side, 35 [o]and
they did not show steadfast love to the family of Jerubbaal (that is, Gideon) in return for
all the good that he had done to Israel.

Abimelech's Conspiracy

9 Now Abimelech the son of Jerubbaal went to Shechem to [p]his mother's relatives and said
to them and to the whole clan of his mother's family, 2 "Say in the ears of all the leaders
of Shechem, 'Which is better for you, that all [q]seventy of the sons of Jerubbaal rule over
you, or that one rule over you?' Remember also that [p]I am [r]your bone and your flesh."

3 And his mother's relatives spoke all these words on his behalf in the ears of all the
leaders of Shechem, and their hearts inclined to follow Abimelech, for they said, [s]"He is
our brother." 4 And they gave him seventy pieces of silver out of the house of [t]Baal-berith
with which Abimelech hired [u]worthless and reckless fellows, who followed him. 5 And
he went to his father's house at [v]Ophrah [w]and killed his brothers the sons of Jerubbaal,
seventy men, on one stone. But Jotham the youngest son of Jerubbaal was left, for he hid
himself. 6 And all the leaders of Shechem came together, and all [x]Beth-millo, and they went
and made Abimelech king, by the oak of the pillar at Shechem.

7 When it was told to Jotham, he went and stood on top of [y]Mount Gerizim and cried
aloud and said to them, "Listen to me, you leaders of Shechem, that God may listen to you.
8 [z]The trees once went out to anoint a king over them, and they said to the olive tree, [a]'Reign
over us.' 9 But the olive tree said to them, 'Shall I leave my abundance, by which gods and

[1] A *shekel* was about 2/5 ounce or 11 grams [2] Hebrew *who came from his own loins*

26 [y]ver. 21 [z]Isa. 3:19
27 [a]ch. 17:5; 18:14, 17; See Ex. 28:6-35 [b]ch. 6:24 [c]ver. 33; ch. 2:17; Ex. 34:15; Ps. 106:39 [d]Ex. 23:33; Deut. 7:16
28 [e][ch. 3:11; 5:31]
29 [f]ch. 6:32; 7:1
30 [g]ch. 9:2, 5
31 [h]ch. 9:1, 2
32 [i]Gen. 15:15; 25:8; Job 5:26 [j]ch. 6:24
33 [k][ch. 2:19] [l]See ver. 27 [m]ch. 9:4, 46
34 [n]Ps. 78:11, 42; 106:13, 21
35 [o]See ch. 9:16-18

Chapter 9

1 [p]ch. 8:31
2 [q]ch. 8:30 [p][See ver. 1 above] [r]Gen. 29:14
3 [s]ver. 18
4 [t]ch. 8:33; [ver. 46] [u]ch. 11:3; 2 Chr. 13:7; [Prov. 12:11; Acts 17:5]
5 [v]ch. 6:24 [w][2 Kgs. 11:1, 2]
6 [x]ver. 20; [2 Sam. 5:9]
7 [y]Deut. 11:29; 27:12; Josh. 8:33; [John 4:20]
8 [z][2 Kgs. 14:9] [a]ch. 8:22, 23

8:27 The original **ephod** was an ornate ceremonial garment worn by the high priest (Exodus 28; 39; see illustration, p. 208). It was made of choice materials ornamented with gold and onyx stones. According to the Mosaic law, there was to be only one ephod in Israel, and it was to have a "breastpiece of judgment" (Ex. 28:15–30). The ephod was used to inquire of God (cf. 1 Sam. 14:3; 23:9; 30:7). By setting up another ephod in his own city, Gideon may have been making it his own to use, at his own whim. Ultimately, **it became a snare** to Gideon and his family, echoing Judg. 2:3. **whored**. See note on 2:17.

8:29–32 *Gideon, Father of Abimelech.* This transitional unit shows that one of Gideon's most fateful contributions to Israel's future was his son **Abimelech**, whose violent story is told in ch. 9. **for he had many wives**. On polygamy, see note on Gen. 16:3 and Marriage and Sexual Morality, pp. 2543–2545. Abimelech means "my father is king." Ironically, then, Gideon, who had vigorously proclaimed that he should *not* be king (see notes on Judg. 8:22–23; 8:26), nevertheless did function as king, even to the point of giving his son such a name.

8:33–35 *Continuing Apostasy.* The steady downward cycle of Israel's apostasy continued unabated. Gideon, though he had accomplished some good things, was a significant contributing factor to this downward slide. **whored**. See note on 2:17. **Baal-berith** means "Baal of the covenant": Israel made its covenant with one of the Baals, not with its own covenant-keeping God (cf. 9:46). **Jerubbaal (that is, Gideon)**. See note on 6:32.

9:1–57 *Abimelech, Apostate "King."* This is an extended account of Abimelech's violent grab for power. The seeds of his offense are found in Israel's continuing apostasy, in its request for a warrior-king and rejection of the Lord, and in his father Gideon's misdeeds and mistakes.

9:1–6 *Abimelech's Sordid Rise.* Abimelech rose to power by ruthlessly killing his own brothers, with the help of the Shechemites. He was then "made king" at Shechem (v. 6). **Jerubbaal**. That is, Gideon (see 8:35 and note on 6:32). **worthless and reckless fellows**. Abimelech's character can be judged by the company that he kept, as can Jephthah's (cf. 11:3).

9:7–21 *Indictment of Abimelech: Jotham's Fable.* Jotham, the only brother of Abimelech who escaped his murderous rampage, provided a strong indictment of Abimelech's actions by means of a fable (vv. 7–20). The fable depicts the noble trees of the forest each in turn rejecting the call to kingship, which is finally accepted by the ignoble bramble bush (vv. 8–15). In this context, it is an indictment of the Shechemites (who have chosen the ignoble Abimelech as king), of Abimelech himself, and of the process by which this "king" was chosen (see esp. Jotham's comments in vv. 16–20). It is not an indictment of the institution of kingship in general, however, since the overall thrust of the book is that a proper king would have been good for Israel.

9:7 Mount Gerizim. When Israel had entered the land, they proclaimed the blessings of the covenant from this mountain (Josh. 8:30–35) as Moses had commanded (Deut. 11:26–32). Now Jotham utters curses from this "mountain of blessing" (see note on Judg. 9:20).

men are honored, and go hold sway over the trees?' 10 And the trees said to the fig tree,
'You come and reign over us.' 11 But the fig tree said to them, 'Shall I leave my sweetness
and my good fruit and go hold sway over the trees?' 12 And the trees said to the vine, 'You
come and reign over us.' 13 But the vine said to them, 'Shall I leave my wine that [b]cheers
God and men and go hold sway over the trees?' 14 Then all the trees said to the bramble,
'You come and reign over us.' 15 And the bramble said to the trees, 'If in good faith you are
anointing me king over you, then come and [c]take refuge in my shade, but if not, [d]let fire
come out of the bramble and devour [e]the cedars of Lebanon.'

16 "Now therefore, if you acted in good faith and integrity when you made Abimelech
king, and if you have dealt well with [f]Jerubbaal and his house and have done to him [g]as
his deeds deserved— 17 for my father fought for you and risked his life and delivered
you from the hand of Midian, 18 and you have risen up against my father's house this
day [h]and have killed his sons, seventy men on one stone, and have made [i]Abimelech,
the son of his female servant, king over the leaders of Shechem, [j]because he is your relative— 19 if you then have acted in good faith and integrity with Jerubbaal and with his
house this day, then [k]rejoice in Abimelech, and let him also rejoice in you. 20 But if not,
[l]let fire come out from Abimelech and devour the leaders of Shechem and Beth-millo;
and let fire come out from the leaders of Shechem and from Beth-millo and devour
Abimelech." 21 And Jotham ran away and fled and went to [m]Beer and lived there, because
of Abimelech his brother.

The Downfall of Abimelech

22 Abimelech ruled over Israel three years. 23 [n]And God sent an evil spirit between
Abimelech and the leaders of Shechem, and the leaders of Shechem [o]dealt treacherously
with Abimelech, 24 [p]that the violence done to the seventy sons of Jerubbaal might come,
and their blood be laid on Abimelech their brother, who killed them, and on the men of
Shechem, who strengthened his hands to kill his brothers. 25 And the leaders of Shechem
put men in ambush against him on the mountaintops, and they robbed all who passed
by them along that way. And it was told to Abimelech.

26 And Gaal the son of Ebed moved into Shechem with his relatives, and the leaders
of Shechem put confidence in him. 27 And they went out into the field and gathered the
grapes from their vineyards and trod them and held a festival; and they went into [q]the
house of their god and ate and drank and reviled Abimelech. 28 And Gaal the son of Ebed
said, [r]"Who is Abimelech, and who are we of Shechem, that we should serve him? Is he
not the son of Jerubbaal, and is not Zebul his officer? Serve the men of [s]Hamor the father
of Shechem; but why should we serve him? 29 Would that this people were under my
hand! Then I would remove Abimelech. I would say[1] to Abimelech, 'Increase your army,
and come out.'"

30 When Zebul the ruler of the city heard the words of Gaal the son of Ebed, his anger
was kindled. 31 And he sent messengers to Abimelech secretly,[2] saying, "Behold, Gaal the
son of Ebed and his relatives have come to Shechem, and they are stirring up[3] the city
against you. 32 Now therefore, go by night, you and the people who are with you, and set
an ambush in the field. 33 Then in the morning, as soon as the sun is up, rise early and rush
upon the city. And when he and the people who are with him come out against you, you
may do to them [t]as your hand finds to do."

[1] Septuagint; Hebrew *and he said* [2] Or *at Tormah* [3] Hebrew *besieging*, or *closing up*

13 [b]Ps. 104:15
15 [c]Dan. 4:12; Hos. 14:7; [Isa. 30:2] [d]ver. 20; [Num. 21:28; Ezek. 19:14] [e]1 Kgs. 4:33; 2 Kgs. 14:9; 19:23; Ps. 104:16; Isa. 2:13; 37:24
16 [f]See ch. 6:32 [g]Prov. 12:14; Isa. 3:11; [ch. 8:35]
18 [h]ver. 5, 6 [i]ch. 8:31 [j]ver. 3
19 [k][Isa. 8:6]
20 [l]ver. 15; [ver. 56, 57]
21 [m]Num. 21:16
23 [n][1 Sam. 16:14; 18:10; 19:9] [o]Isa. 33:1
24 [p]ver. 56; [1 Kgs. 2:32; Esth. 9:25; Ps. 7:16; Matt. 23:35, 36]
27 [q]ver. 4, 46
28 [r][1 Sam. 25:10] [s]Gen. 34:2, 6
33 [t]Eccles. 9:10

9:20 let fire come out. Jotham's challenge to the Shechemites and Abimelech was dramatically resolved when fire from Abimelech devoured a large number of Shechemites and a Shechemite woman killed Abimelech (vv. 49, 54).

9:22–55 *Abimelech's Violent Reign and End.* The Shechemites and Abimelech deserved each other. Abimelech, who was aided by the Shechemites, was himself now the target of their lawlessness, and discord prevailed between them (vv. 22–25)—a discord that spread into open revolt under Gaal (vv. 26–33). Abimelech was able to quell the revolt, and he razed Shechem (vv. 34–45). He also destroyed the stronghold of Shechem (its tower), burning it with fire (vv. 46–49). Abimelech himself met his end at nearby Thebez (vv. 50–55), where he also attempted to burn its tower but instead was mortally wounded by a stone dropped from it by a woman.

9:22 Ruled has the nuance "rule (as prince or commander)"; it is not the more usual word for "rule (as king)" used in 8:22–23. The ignoble **Abimelech**, who had been "made king" by the people, not by God (9:6), could only "rule" as a secondary commander, not as a true king.

9:23 an evil spirit. Cf. the "evil (or harmful) spirit" God sent to Saul (1 Sam. 16:14, 15, 16, 23a, 23b; 18:10; 19:9; see note on 1 Sam. 16:14). Here, the spirit is **between** Abimelech and the Shechemites, probably "a spirit of ill will" or "a harmful spirit" between the parties. In this way, God himself brought about the estrangement between the two sides.

34 So Abimelech and all the men who were with him rose up by night and set an ambush
against Shechem in four companies. 35 And Gaal the son of Ebed went out and stood in
the entrance of the gate of the city, and Abimelech and the people who were with him
rose from the ambush. 36 And when Gaal saw the people, he said to Zebul, "Look, people
are coming down from [u]the mountaintops!" And Zebul said to him, "You mistake[1] the
shadow of the mountains for men." 37 Gaal spoke again and said, "Look, people are coming down from the center of the land, and one company is coming from the direction
of the Diviners' Oak." 38 Then Zebul said to him, "Where is your mouth now, you who
said, [v]'Who is Abimelech, that we should serve him?' Are not these the people whom
you despised? Go out now and fight with them." 39 And Gaal went out at the head of the
leaders of Shechem and fought with Abimelech. 40 And Abimelech chased him, and he
fled before him. And many fell wounded, up to the entrance of the gate. 41 And Abimelech
lived at Arumah, and Zebul drove out Gaal and his relatives, so that they could not dwell
at Shechem.

42 On the following day, the people went out into the field, and Abimelech was told.
43 He took his people and divided them into three companies and set an ambush in the
fields. And he looked and saw the people coming out of the city. So he rose against them
and killed them. 44 Abimelech and the company that was with him [w]rushed forward and
stood at the entrance of the gate of the city, while the two companies rushed upon all
who were in the field and killed them. 45 And Abimelech fought against the city all that
day. He captured the city and killed the people who were in it, and [x]he razed the city and
[y]sowed it with salt.

46 When all the leaders of the Tower of Shechem heard of it, they entered [z]the stronghold of the house of [a]El-berith. 47 Abimelech was told that all the leaders of the Tower
of Shechem were gathered together. 48 And Abimelech went up to Mount [b]Zalmon, he
and all the people who were with him. And Abimelech took an axe in his hand and cut
down a bundle of brushwood and took it up and laid it on his shoulder. And he said to
the men who were with him, "What you have seen me do, hurry and do as I have done."
49 So every one of the people cut down his bundle and following Abimelech put it against
[c]the stronghold, and they set the stronghold on fire over them, so that all the people of
the Tower of Shechem also died, about 1,000 men and women.

50 Then Abimelech went to Thebez and encamped against Thebez and captured it. 51 But
there was a strong tower within the city, and all the men and women and all the leaders of
the city fled to it and shut themselves in, and they went up to the roof of the tower. 52 And
Abimelech came to the tower and fought against it and drew near to the door of the tower
to burn it with fire. 53 [d]And a certain woman threw an upper millstone on Abimelech's head
and crushed his skull. 54 [e]Then he called quickly to the young man his armor-bearer and
said to him, "Draw your sword and kill me, lest they say of me, 'A woman killed him.'"
And his young man thrust him through, and he died. 55 And when the men of Israel saw
that Abimelech was dead, everyone departed to his home. 56 [f]Thus God returned the evil of
Abimelech, which he committed against his father in killing his seventy brothers. 57 And
God also made all the evil of the men of Shechem return on their heads, and upon them
came [g]the curse of Jotham the son of Jerubbaal.

[1] Hebrew *You see*

36 [u]ver. 7, 25
38 [v]ver. 28, 29
44 [w]ch. 20:37
45 [x]2 Kgs. 3:25 [y]Deut. 29:23
46 [z]ver. 49 [a]ver. 4; ch. 8:33
48 [b]Ps. 68:14
49 [c]ver. 46
53 [d]2 Sam. 11:21
54 [e][1 Sam. 31:4]
56 [f][Job 31:8; Ps. 94:23; Prov. 5:22]; See ver. 24
57 [g]ver. 20

9:45 sowed it with salt. This physical yet symbolic action signified the turning of Shechem into a barren, uninhabitable desert (cf. Deut. 29:23; Job 39:6; Ps. 107:34; Jer. 17:6). It was later rebuilt by Jeroboam (1 Kings 12:25).

9:46 El-berith. "El" was the name of a well-known Canaanite god, the father of Baal. The term here is probably another way of referring to the god "Baal-berith" and would mean "El of the covenant" (see note on 8:33–35).

9:51 strong tower (cf. 8:17; 9:46–49). The foundations of a square tower (38 feet/12 m sq.) from this period were found at the site of Giloh (see Josh. 15:51; 2 Sam. 15:12). The tower was well-built, having been constructed of large, roughly hewn stones.

9:54 kill me. Being killed or bested by a woman was a disgrace to a warrior. See notes on 4:6–9; 5:24–27.

9:56–57 *Final Verdict on Abimelech.* Abimelech was not a true king; the institution of a valid monarchy in Israel would have to await a later time. God actively opposed Abimelech, in return for the evil he had done in killing his brothers. The "evil" (Hb. *ra'ah*) spirit sent by God to effect the discord (v. 23) led directly to God's repaying the "wickedness" (Hb. *ra'ah*) of Abimelech and the Shechemites (vv. 56–57). The fire that was a sign of Abimelech's poor choice (vv. 15, 20) brought the downfall of Shechem and Abimelech (vv. 49, 52), and these two devoured each other, as Jotham's fable had foretold.

Tola and Jair

10 After Abimelech there arose to [h]save Israel Tola the son of Puah, son of Dodo, a man
of Issachar, and he lived at Shamir in [i]the hill country of Ephraim. 2 And he judged
Israel twenty-three years. Then he died and was buried at Shamir.
3 After him arose Jair the Gileadite, who judged Israel twenty-two years. 4 And he had
thirty sons who [j]rode on thirty donkeys, and they had thirty cities, called Havvoth-jair to
this day, [k]which are in the land of Gilead. 5 And Jair died and was buried in Kamon.

Further Disobedience and Oppression

6 [l]The people of Israel again did what was evil in the sight of the LORD [m]and served the
Baals and the Ashtaroth, the gods of Syria, [n]the gods of Sidon, the gods of Moab, the gods
of the Ammonites, and the gods of the Philistines. And they [o]forsook the LORD and did not
serve him. 7 So the anger of the LORD was kindled against Israel, and [p]he sold them into
the hand of the Philistines and into the hand of the Ammonites, 8 and they crushed and
oppressed the people of Israel that year. For eighteen years they oppressed all the people
of Israel who were beyond the Jordan in the land of the Amorites, which is in Gilead. 9 And
the Ammonites crossed the Jordan to fight also against Judah and against Benjamin and
against the house of Ephraim, so that Israel was severely distressed.
10 And the people of Israel [q]cried out to the LORD, saying, "We have sinned against you,
because [r]we have forsaken our God and have served the Baals." 11 And the LORD said to the
people of Israel, "Did I not save you [s]from the Egyptians and [t]from the Amorites, [u]from
the Ammonites and [v]from the Philistines? 12 The Sidonians also, and [w]the Amalekites and
the Maonites oppressed you, and you cried out to me, and I [x]saved you out of their hand. 13 Yet
you have [y]forsaken me and served other gods; therefore I will save you no more. 14 Go and
cry out [z]to the gods whom you have chosen; let them save you in the time of your distress."
15 And the people of Israel said to the LORD, "We have sinned; do to us whatever seems good
to you. Only please deliver us this day." 16 So they put away the foreign gods from among
them and served the LORD, and [a]he became impatient over the misery of Israel.
17 Then the Ammonites were called to arms, and they encamped in Gilead. And the
people of Israel came together, and they encamped at [b]Mizpah. 18 And the people, the
leaders of Gilead, said one to another, "Who is the man who will begin to fight against
the Ammonites? [c]He shall be head over all the inhabitants of Gilead."

Jephthah Delivers Israel

11 Now [d]Jephthah the Gileadite was [e]a mighty warrior, but he was the son of a prostitute. Gilead was the father of Jephthah. 2 And Gilead's wife also bore him sons. And
when his wife's sons grew up, they drove Jephthah out and said to him, "You shall not
have an inheritance in our father's house, for you are the son of another woman." 3 Then
Jephthah fled from his brothers and lived in the land of [f]Tob, and [g]worthless fellows collected around Jephthah and went out with him.

Chapter 10

1 [h]ver. 12, 13; See ch. 2:16 [i]See Josh. 24:33
4 [j]ch. 5:10; 12:14 [k]Deut. 3:14
6 [l]See ch. 2:11 [m]See ch. 2:13 [n]1 Kgs. 11:5, 7, 33; 2 Kgs. 23:13 [o]ver. 10, 13; Deut. 31:16
7 [p]See ch. 2:14
10 [q]See ch. 3:9 [r]ver. 6, 13
11 [s]Ex. 14:30 [t]See Num. 21:21-32 [u][ch. 3:13] [v]ch. 3:31
12 [w][ch. 3:13; 6:3] [x]See ch. 2:16
13 [y]ver. 6, 10; [Deut. 32:15; Jer. 2:13]
14 [z]Deut. 32:37, 38
16 [a]ch. 2:18; Isa. 63:9
17 [b]ch. 11:11, 29
18 [c][ch. 11:5, 6, 8, 11]

Chapter 11

1 [d]Heb. 11:32 [e]ch. 6:12; 2 Kgs. 5:1
3 [f]2 Sam. 10:6, 8 [g]See ch. 9:4; [1 Sam. 22:2]

10:1–2 *Tola.* Tola was the sixth judge, the second "minor" judge (that is, one about whom little is recorded; Shamgar was the first), and he judged 23 years. He **arose to save** Israel (v. 1), which it needed after Abimelech's tyranny. This brief account echoes that of Deborah's early activity (cf. esp. 4:4–5; 5:7).

10:3–5 *Jair.* Jair was the seventh judge, the third minor judge, and he judged 22 years. He was rather wealthy (v. 4), and lived in Transjordan (Gilead), the same area as the next judge, Jephthah (11:1). His 30 sons (cf. 12:8–10) form a sharp contrast to Jephthah's ultimate childlessness.

10:6–12:7 *Jephthah.* Jephthah was the eighth judge, and his is the third extended account of a judge's activity (after Deborah and Gideon). Jephthah freed Israel from the Ammonite burden, but he made a foolish vow that led to a personal tragedy.

10:6–18 *Apostasy and Distress.* The introduction restates the themes in ch. 2 about Israel's apostasy and God's mercy. A new theme emerges, however, concerning the Israelites' confession and repentance (10:10, 15–16).

10:6 The references to seven groupings of foreign **gods** (cf. the seven nations in vv. 11–12) shows the wide scope of Israel's apostasy. Not only did they worship the major Canaanite deities (Baal, Asherah, Ashtoreth; see notes on 2:13; 3:7; 6:25–26), but also, apparently, the gods of any people with whom they came into contact.

10:7 Philistines . . . Ammonites. The next two major judges were God's instruments against the Ammonites (Jephthah) and the Philistines (Samson).

10:14 gods whom you have chosen. Cf. v. 6. The Israelites had also "chosen" new gods in Deborah's time (5:8).

10:16 he became impatient over the misery of Israel. Many scholars see this as a reference to God's great mercy and his capacity to be moved by Israel's misery and repentance (cf. 2:18). Another interpretation is that it is Israel's unfaithfulness, the cause of their misery, that makes God impatient. This would indicate that Israel's "repentance" here was only a superficial one.

11:1–3 *Introduction to Jephthah.* Like Jair (10:3), Jephthah was from Gilead. He was a "mighty warrior," but his illegitimacy caused his half brothers to expel him from his father's house. Like Abimelech (9:4), he attracted "worthless fellows" (11:3; cf. 2 Chron. 13:7), which did not bode well for his future; indeed, God did not "raise" him up (see note on Judg. 11:6). This is unlike the band of distressed men that David attracted, to whom he gave good leadership (see note on 1 Sam. 22:2).

4 After a time the Ammonites made war against Israel. 5 And when the Ammonites
made war against Israel, the elders of Gilead went to bring Jephthah from the land of
[f]Tob. 6 And they said to Jephthah, "Come and be our leader, that we may fight against
the Ammonites." 7 But Jephthah said to the elders of Gilead, "Did you not hate me and
drive me out of my father's house? Why have you come to me now when you are in distress?" 8 And the elders of Gilead said to Jephthah, "That is why we have turned to you
now, that you may go with us and fight against the Ammonites and [h]be our head over
all the inhabitants of Gilead." 9 Jephthah said to the elders of Gilead, "If you bring me
home again to fight against the Ammonites, and the LORD gives them over to me, I will
be your head." 10 And the elders of Gilead said to Jephthah, [i]"The LORD will be witness
between us, if we do not do as you say." 11 So Jephthah went with the elders of Gilead,
and the people [j]made him head and leader over them. And Jephthah spoke all his words
[k]before the LORD at [l]Mizpah.

12 Then Jephthah sent messengers to the king of the Ammonites and said, "What do
you have against me, that you have come to me to fight against my land?" 13 And the king
of the Ammonites answered the messengers of Jephthah, [m]"Because Israel on coming
up from Egypt took away my land, from the [n]Arnon to the [o]Jabbok and to the Jordan;
now therefore restore it peaceably." 14 Jephthah again sent messengers to the king of the
Ammonites 15 and said to him, "Thus says Jephthah: [p]Israel did not take away the land of
Moab or the land of the Ammonites, 16 but when they came up from Egypt, Israel went
through the wilderness [q]to the Red Sea and [r]came to Kadesh. 17 [s]Israel then sent messengers
to the king of Edom, saying, 'Please let us pass through your land,' [t]but the king of Edom
would not listen. And they sent also to the king of Moab, but he would not consent. So
Israel [u]remained at Kadesh.

18 "Then they journeyed through the wilderness and [v]went around the land of Edom
and the land of Moab and [w]arrived on the east side of the land of Moab and [x]camped on
the other side of the Arnon. But they did not enter the territory of Moab, for the Arnon was
the boundary of Moab. 19 [y]Israel then sent messengers to Sihon king of the Amorites, king
of Heshbon, and Israel said to him, 'Please let us pass through your land to our country,'
20 but Sihon did not trust Israel to pass through his territory, so Sihon gathered all his
people together and encamped at Jahaz and fought with Israel. 21 And the LORD, the God
of Israel, gave Sihon and all his people into the hand of Israel, and they defeated them. So
Israel took possession of all the land of the Amorites, who inhabited that country. 22 And
they took possession of all the territory of the Amorites from the Arnon to the Jabbok and
from the wilderness to the Jordan. 23 So then the LORD, the God of Israel, dispossessed the
Amorites from before his people Israel; and are you to take possession of them? 24 Will you
not possess what [z]Chemosh your god gives you to possess? [a]And all that the LORD our God
has dispossessed before us, we will possess. 25 Now are you any better than [b]Balak the son

5 [f][See ver. 3 above]
8 [h]ch. 10:18
10 [i]Jer. 42:5
11 [j]ver. 6, 8; ch. 10:18 [k]1 Sam. 10:19, 25; 11:15; 12:7; [ch. 20:1; 1 Sam. 10:17] [l]ch. 10:17
13 [m]See Num. 21:24-26 [n]Num. 21:13 [o]Gen. 32:22
15 [p]Deut. 2:9, 19
16 [q]Num. 14:25; Deut. 1:40 [r]Num. 13:26
17 [s]Num. 20:14 [t]See Num. 20:18-21 [u]Num. 20:1; Deut. 1:46
18 [v]Num. 21:4; See Deut. 2:1-8 [w]Num. 21:11 [x]Num. 21:13; 22:36
19 [y]For ver. 19-22, see Num. 21:21-26; Deut. 2:26-37
24 [z]Num. 21:29; 1 Kgs. 11:7 [a]Deut. 9:5; 18:12; Josh. 3:10
25 [b]Num. 22:2; Josh. 24:9; Mic. 6:5

11:4–11 *Jephthah's Commissioning.* After some negotiation, Jephthah was commissioned by the people—but not, apparently, by God—as "head" and "leader" (v. 11) over Israel.

11:6 Come and be our leader. God did not "raise up" Jephthah, as he had raised up previous judges (3:9, 15; 4:6; 6:14). Now, for the first time, a leader was commissioned by the people, without seeking God's approval—another sign of their increasing apostasy.

11:8 that you may go with us and fight. Cf. the language later used by the Israelites to ask Samuel for a king: "that our king may . . . go out before us and fight" (1 Sam. 8:20). In both cases, even though God acquiesced, the request was inappropriate. God, not any judge or any king, was to be Israel's prime warrior.

11:11 Jephthah spoke all his words before the LORD. Jephthah represented a strange mixture of faith and foolishness. While he acknowledged God (cf. vv. 21, 23, 27, 30–31; 12:3), overall his foolishness seemed to outstrip his faith (see note on 11:31).

11:12–28 *Diplomatic Discussions.* The negotiations between Jephthah and the Ammonites consisted largely of an impressive speech by Jephthah, answering the Ammonite charge (v. 13) that Israel had unlawfully seized the territory currently disputed. Jephthah asserted that "the LORD, the God of Israel," himself was the one who dispossessed these peoples from before Israel (vv. 21, 23, 24) and that Israel was not an aggressor (v. 15) but merely a recipient of the Lord's generosity. The Ammonites had brought this upon themselves by hindering Israel, thus prompting God's help in dispossessing them (Israel was not to take Ammonite land, since God had expressly forbidden it; Deut. 2:19). However, Sihon, king of the Amorites, had taken some of what was Moabite/Ammonite territory, and then Israel had taken this and other territory of Sihon (see Num. 21:25–26). The Ammonites, if they had indeed been involved at all, deserved what they had coming. Furthermore, the Ammonites never really had true claim to the land to begin with; rather, it was the land of the Amorites (Judg. 11:19–22). Finally, it was a little late to be challenging Israel's claim to the land in any case, since 300 years had passed since the events in question (v. 26). Jephthah ended his speech with an appeal to God to judge between the two disputants.

11:17–22 The review of the past refers to events in the **wilderness** recounted in Num. 20:14–21. **all the territory**. The limits of the Amorites' land, precisely what the Ammonites claimed was theirs in Judg. 11:13 (cf. Num. 21:24).

11:24 Chemosh was the Moabites' god (1 Kings 11:7, 33); elsewhere, the Ammonites' god was Molech (1 Kings 11:7) or Milcom (1 Kings 11:5, 33; 2 Kings 23:13). However, Ammon and Moab were closely associated (cf. Judg. 11:15; cf. Deut. 2:18–19; 23:3–5; Judg. 3:12–13), as both were

of Zippor, king of Moab? Did he ever contend against Israel, or did he ever go to war with
them? 26 While Israel lived [c]in Heshbon and its villages, and [d]in Aroer and its villages,
and in all the cities that are on the banks of the Arnon, 300 years, why did you not deliver
them within that time? 27 I therefore have not sinned against you, and you do me wrong
by making war on me. [e]The LORD, the Judge, decide this day between the people of Israel
and the people of Ammon." 28 But the king of the Ammonites did not listen to the words
of Jephthah that he sent to him.

Jephthah's Tragic Vow

29 [f]Then the Spirit of the LORD was upon Jephthah, and he passed through Gilead and
Manasseh and passed on to Mizpah of Gilead, and from Mizpah of Gilead he passed on
to the Ammonites. 30 And Jephthah [g]made a vow to the LORD and said, "If you will give
the Ammonites into my hand, 31 then whatever[1] comes out from the doors of my house
to meet me when I return in peace from the Ammonites [h]shall be the LORD's, and [i]I will
offer it[2] up for a burnt offering." 32 So Jephthah crossed over to the Ammonites to fight
against them, and the LORD gave them into his hand. 33 And he struck them from Aroer
to the neighborhood of [j]Minnith, twenty cities, and as far as Abel-keramim, with a great
blow. So the Ammonites were subdued before the people of Israel.

34 Then Jephthah came to his home at [k]Mizpah. And behold, his daughter came out to
meet him [l]with tambourines and with dances. She was his only child; besides her he had
neither son nor daughter. 35 And as soon as he saw her, he tore his clothes and said, "Alas,
my daughter! You have brought me very low, and you have become the cause of great
trouble to me. For I have opened my mouth to the LORD, [m]and I cannot take back my

26 [c]Num. 21:25 [d]Deut. 2:36
27 [e]Gen. 16:5; 18:25; 31:53; 1 Sam. 24:12, 15
29 [f]See ch. 3:10
30 [g]Gen. 28:20; 1 Sam. 1:11
31 [h][Lev. 27:2; 1 Sam. 1:28] [i]Ps. 66:13
33 [j]Ezek. 27:17
34 [k]ver. 11; ch. 10:17 [l]Ex. 15:20; 1 Sam. 18:6; Ps. 68:25; Jer. 31:4
35 [m]Num. 30:2; [Eccles. 5:4, 5]

[1] Or *whoever* [2] Or *him*

descended from Lot (Gen. 19:37, 38). The two nations likely shared cultural and religious heritages, and Chemosh may have been considered stronger than Molech/Milcom.

11:26 300 years. If the exodus took place c. 1440 B.C. (the "early date"), with the conquest of Palestine beginning about 1400, then Jephthah's speech would fall around 1106 B.C. (However, "300 years" may be a round number, giving an approximate date.) If the exodus took place c. 1260 B.C. (the "late date"), then Jephthah's number is either inaccurate or a generalization indicating simply seven or eight generations (see note on 1 Kings 6:1). See The Date of the Exodus, p. 33.

11:29–40 *Victory and Jephthah's Foolish Vow.* The conflict with the Ammonites reached its peak with their defeat by Jephthah (vv. 29, 32–33; see map to the right). However, the climax of the Jephthah narrative centers upon his rash vow (vv. 30–31, 34–40). In order to gain God's favor, he promised to sacrifice whatever came out of his house upon his victorious return. This reflected a misguided application of the principle of offering to God the best of one's treasure. Theoretically, a vow to make a burnt offering was valid: cf. Lev. 22:18–20, which also specifies what is a valid offering. The tragic result of Jephthah's vow was the sacrifice of his only child, a daughter (see note on Judg. 11:39).

11:29 the Spirit of the LORD was upon. See note on 14:6.

11:31 whatever comes out. The wording here would indicate that Jephthah intended to offer some animal as a burnt offering. However, the grammar also allows for "whoever" (see ESV footnote), in which case Jephthah would have intended to offer a human sacrifice all along. If so, what surprised him was not that he had to sacrifice a person, but that it was his daughter. Human sacrifice was strictly forbidden in Israel (Lev. 18:21; 20:2; Deut. 12:31; 18:10; Jer. 19:5; Ezek. 20:30–31; 23:37, 39). Yet, Jephthah's foolishness impelled him to make such a vow and apparently to follow through with this abomination (see note on Judg. 11:39).

11:35 I cannot take back my vow. Vows were solemn affairs, made only to God. People were not forced to take them, but, if they did, they had to be kept, under normal circumstances (Deut. 23:21–23; Ps. 15:4; Eccles. 5:4–5). But any vow that would end in sin was not binding; keeping it could not please God, and the Levitical laws provided for such instances (Lev. 5:4–6). Human sacrifice was an abomination, and Jephthah should not have followed through with killing his daughter.

Jephthah Defeats the Ammonites

Jephthah was called upon by the leaders of Gilead to fight against the Ammonites, who were oppressing the Israelites in Gilead, Ephraim, Benjamin, and Judah. After Jephthah defeated the Ammonites, the men of Ephraim became angry that they had not been called to join the battle, and they gathered to fight Jephthah at Zaphon. Jephthah's men, however, defeated the Ephraimites and killed them as they tried to return to their homes across the Jordan River.

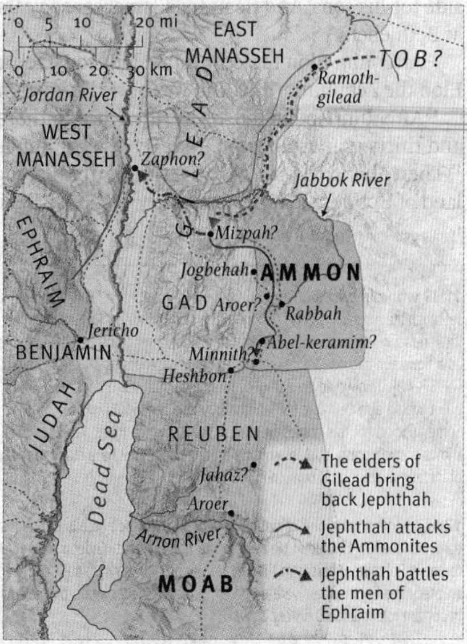

vow.” 36 And she said to him, “My father, you have opened your mouth to the LORD; do to me according to what has gone out of your mouth, now that the LORD has avenged you on your enemies, on the Ammonites.” 37 So she said to her father, “Let this thing be done for me: leave me alone two months, that I may go up and down on the mountains and weep for my virginity, I and my companions.” 38 So he said, “Go.” Then he sent her away for two months, and she departed, she and her companions, and wept for her virginity on the mountains. 39 And at the end of two months, she returned to her father, [n]who did with her according to his vow that he had made. She had never known a man, and it became a custom in Israel 40 that the daughters of Israel went year by year to lament the daughter of Jephthah the Gileadite four days in the year.

Jephthah's Conflict with Ephraim

12 [o]The men of Ephraim were called to arms, and they crossed to Zaphon and said to Jephthah, “Why did you cross over to fight against the Ammonites and did not call us to go with you? We will burn your house over you with fire.” 2 And Jephthah said to them, “I and my people had a great dispute with the Ammonites, and when I called you, you did not save me from their hand. 3 And when I saw that you would not save me, [p]I took my life in my hand and crossed over against the Ammonites, and the LORD gave them into my hand. Why then have you come up to me this day to fight against me?” 4 Then Jephthah gathered all the men of Gilead and fought with Ephraim. And the men of Gilead struck Ephraim, because they said, [q]“You are fugitives of Ephraim, you Gileadites, in the midst of Ephraim and Manasseh.” 5 And the Gileadites captured [r]the fords of the Jordan against the Ephraimites. And when any of the fugitives of Ephraim said, “Let me go over,” the men of Gilead said to him, “Are you an Ephraimite?” When he said, “No,” 6 they said to him, “Then say Shibboleth,” and he said, “Sibboleth,” for he could not pronounce it right. Then they seized him and slaughtered him at [r]the fords of the Jordan. At that time 42,000 of the Ephraimites fell.

7 Jephthah judged Israel six years. Then Jephthah the Gileadite died and was buried in his city in Gilead.[1]

Ibzan, Elon, and Abdon

8 After him Ibzan of Bethlehem judged Israel. 9 He had thirty sons, and thirty daughters he gave in marriage outside his clan, and thirty daughters he brought in from outside for his sons. And he judged Israel seven years. 10 Then Ibzan died and was buried at Bethlehem.

11 After him Elon the Zebulunite judged Israel, and he judged Israel ten years. 12 Then Elon the Zebulunite died and was buried at Aijalon in the land of Zebulun.

13 After him Abdon the son of Hillel the Pirathonite judged Israel. 14 He had forty [s]sons and thirty grandsons, who [t]rode on seventy donkeys, and he judged Israel eight years. 15 Then Abdon the son of Hillel the Pirathonite died and was buried at Pirathon in the land of Ephraim, in the hill country of the Amalekites.

[1] Septuagint; Hebrew *in the cities of Gilead*

39 [n]ver. 31
Chapter 12
1 [o]ch. 8:1
3 [p]1 Sam. 19:5; 28:21; Job 13:14; [Ps. 119:109]
4 [q][1 Sam. 25:10]
5 [r]See ch. 3:28
6 [r][See ver. 5 above]
14 [s]Job 18:19; Isa. 14:22; [1 Tim. 5:4] [t]ch. 5:10

11:39 who did with her according to his vow. Most likely this means Jephthah literally sacrificed his daughter as a burnt offering. However, another interpretation is that Jephthah dedicated his daughter to perpetual virginity, as a figurative sacrifice (cf. references to her uniqueness [v. 34] and virginity [vv. 37–40]). This would be a tragedy for her, as she would bear no children; but it would also be tragic for Jephthah, whose line would come to an end. Some support for this comes from Jephthah's speech in vv. 12–28, which shows enough grasp of Israel's history that he might well have stopped short of literally sacrificing his own child.

12:1–7 *Jephthah's Conflict with Ephraim.* This episode recalls Ephraim's earlier challenge to Gideon (8:1–3). In the first incident, Gideon was able to pacify Ephraim, whereas in the second, Jephthah did not, and a civil war erupted. The Ephraimites were defeated, and they never again played any important role in Israel's history.

12:6 Shibboleth . . . Sibboleth. The Gileadites devised a test to catch the Ephraimites using an insignificant word—it means either “a flowing stream” or “an ear of grain”—that was difficult for outsiders to pronounce correctly. In modern English usage, “Shibboleth” may refer to words, expressions, ideas, or beliefs used by “insiders” to detect “outsiders.” The terrible tragedy is that Israel is again turning upon itself in internal strife (cf. 8:17).

12:8–10 *Ibzan.* Ibzan was the ninth judge. He was distinguished for marrying his 30 sons and his 30 daughters to outsiders (v. 9). In contrast to Jephthah, left childless by his own actions, the judges who immediately preceded and followed him—Jair and Ibzan—both had 30 sons (see 10:4).

12:11–12 *Elon.* Elon was the tenth judge, but nothing of significance is reported about him other than the length of his rule (**ten years**).

12:13–15 *Abdon.* Abdon was the eleventh judge; he, like Jair and Ibzan, had many children, and he too was rather wealthy.

Chapter 13
1 [u]See ch. 2:11 [v][ch. 3:31; 10:7; 1 Sam. 12:9]
2 [w]Josh. 19:41; [Josh. 15:33] [x][1 Sam. 1:2; Luke 1:7]
3 [y]ch. 6:12; Luke 1:11, 13
4 [z]ver. 7, 14; [Num. 6:2, 3; Luke 1:15]
5 [a]ch. 16:17; 1 Sam. 1:11; [Num. 6:5] [z][See ver. 4 above] [b][1 Sam. 7:13; 2 Sam. 8:1; 1 Chr. 18:1]
6 [c]See Deut. 33:1 [d][ver. 17, 18]
7 [e]ver. 3-5
12 [f][Luke 1:66]
14 [g]ver. 4, 7

The Birth of Samson

13 And the people of Israel again [u]did what was evil in the sight of the LORD, so the
LORD gave them [v]into the hand of the Philistines for forty years.
2 There was a certain man of [w]Zorah, of the tribe of the Danites, whose name was Manoah.
[x]And his wife was barren and had no children. 3 [y]And the angel of the LORD appeared to
the woman and said to her, "Behold, you are barren and have not borne children, but you
shall conceive and bear a son. 4 Therefore be careful [z]and drink no wine or strong drink,
and eat nothing unclean, 5 for behold, you shall conceive and bear a son. [a]No razor shall
come upon his head, for the child shall be [z]a Nazirite to God from the womb, and he shall
[b]begin to save Israel from the hand of the Philistines." 6 Then the woman came and told
her husband, [c]"A man of God came to me, and his appearance was like the appearance of
the angel of God, very awesome. [d]I did not ask him where he was from, and he did not
tell me his name, 7 but he said to me, [e]'Behold, you shall conceive and bear a son. So then
drink no wine or strong drink, and eat nothing unclean, for the child shall be a Nazirite
to God from the womb to the day of his death.'"
8 Then Manoah prayed to the LORD and said, "O Lord, please let the man of God whom
you sent come again to us and teach us what we are to do with the child who will be
born." 9 And God listened to the voice of Manoah, and the angel of God came again to
the woman as she sat in the field. But Manoah her husband was not with her. 10 So the
woman ran quickly and told her husband, "Behold, the man who came to me the other
day has appeared to me." 11 And Manoah arose and went after his wife and came to the
man and said to him, "Are you the man who spoke to this woman?" And he said, "I am."
12 And Manoah said, "Now when your words come true, [f]what is to be the child's manner
of life, and what is his mission?" 13 And the angel of the LORD said to Manoah, "Of all that
I said to the woman let her be careful. 14 She may not eat of anything that comes from the
vine, [g]neither let her drink wine or strong drink, or eat any unclean thing. All that I commanded her let her observe."

13:1–16:31 *Samson.* Samson was the twelfth and last judge; he lived around the beginning of the eleventh century B.C., about 50 years before Saul became king. His strength was unparalleled. Rather than lead an army, he battled the Philistines single-handedly. He was a deeply flawed hero whose life was unduly entangled with the people against whom he fought. He violated a number of the Ten Commandments, as well as his Nazirite vow (see note on 13:5–7). Samson embodied in his own tragic-heroic life the traits that Israel exhibited during this period. While he was used of God for deliverance, and while he even called upon God on occasion to help him (15:18; 16:28, 30), his life was nevertheless one of continued unfaithfulness, just like that of the nation he judged.

13:1–25 *The Birth of Samson.* Samson's story opens with the typical statement about Israel's apostasy (v. 1; cf. 3:7, 12; 4:1; 6:1; 10:6), but the rest of ch. 13 is a lengthy and atypical introduction to Samson. It details the encounter between Samson's parents and the angel of the Lord, who announced Samson's birth and mission. Clearly, Samson was to be used by God against the Philistines (14:4), even if, in his own life, he did not follow God's instructions.

13:3 the angel of the LORD (see note on 2:1). The angel's appearance was awesome (v. 6), but his essential character was not to be revealed (vv. 6, 17–18).

13:5–7 Any man or woman could take a vow to become a **Nazirite,** to separate himself or herself to God (see Numbers 6). It was to be voluntary (Num. 6:2), for a limited time (Num. 6:5, 8, 13, 20), and involved three provisions: (1) abstinence from wine, strong drink, or anything associated with the vine (Num. 6:3–4); (2) no cutting of the hair (Num. 6:5); and (3) no contact with the dead (Num. 6:6–8). If a person became unclean, there were elaborate cleansing rituals (Num. 6:9–21). Three things are unusual concerning Samson and this vow. First, he did not take it voluntarily; it was his lot **from the womb** (Judg. 13:5, 7). Second, it was not limited in time; it was to last **to the day of his death** (vv. 5, 7; cf. 1 Sam. 1:11; Luke 1:15 for similar situations). Third, he broke every one of its stipulations: his head was sheared (Judg. 16:17, 19); he associated with the dead (14:6–9; 15:15); and he undoubtedly drank at his wedding feast (14:10–20; see note on 14:10).

13:5 begin to save Israel. Samson's successes were only for a time, since the **Philistines** were still adversaries of Israel in the days of Samuel, Saul, and David.

13:6 A man of God designates prophets elsewhere in the OT (e.g., Deut. 33:1; 1 Sam. 2:27; 1 Kings 17:18). At first, Samson's mother may have thought she was dealing with a prophet, but she quickly realized this was someone greater.

Samson's Exploits
The Philistines ruled over Israel during Samson's lifetime, and Samson was raised up by God to begin to deliver Israel from them. Samson's marriage to a Philistine woman in Timnah led to a number of encounters with the Philistines, often resulting in their harm at Samson's hand.

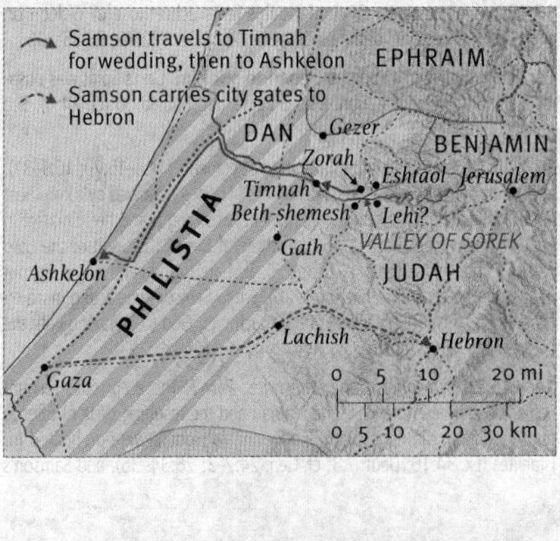

15 Manoah said to the angel of the LORD, "Please let us detain you and [h]prepare a young
goat for you." 16 And the angel of the LORD said to Manoah, "If you detain me, I will not eat
of your food. But if you prepare a burnt offering, then offer it to the LORD." (For Manoah
did not know that he was the angel of the LORD.) 17 And Manoah said to the angel of the
LORD, [i]"What is your name, so that, when your words come true, we may honor you?"
18 And the angel of the LORD said to him, [j]"Why do you ask my name, seeing [k]it is wonderful?" 19 So [l]Manoah took the young goat with the grain offering, and offered it on the rock
to the LORD, to the one who works[1] wonders, and Manoah and his wife were watching.
20 And when the flame went up toward heaven from the altar, the angel of the LORD went
up in the flame of the altar. Now Manoah and his wife were watching, [m]and they fell on
their faces to the ground.
21 The angel of the LORD appeared no more to Manoah and to his wife. [n]Then Manoah
knew that he was the angel of the LORD. 22 And Manoah said to his wife, [n]"We shall
surely die, for we have seen God." 23 But his wife said to him, "If the LORD had meant to
kill us, he would not have accepted a burnt offering and a grain offering at our hands,
or shown us all these things, or now announced to us such things as these." 24 And the
woman bore a son and called his name Samson. [o]And the young man grew, and the LORD
blessed him. 25 [p]And the Spirit of the LORD began to stir him in Mahaneh-dan, between
[q]Zorah and Eshtaol.

Samson's Marriage

14 [r]Samson went down to [s]Timnah, and at Timnah he saw one of the daughters of
the Philistines. 2 Then he came up and told his father and mother, "I saw one of the
daughters of the Philistines at Timnah. [t]Now get her for me as my wife." 3 But his father
and mother said to him, "Is there not a woman among the daughters [u]of your relatives, or
among all our people, that you must go to take a wife from the [v]uncircumcised Philistines?"
But Samson said to his father, "Get her for me, for she is right in my eyes."
4 His father and mother did not know that it was [w]from the LORD, for he was seeking an
opportunity against the Philistines. [x]At that time the Philistines ruled over Israel.
5 Then Samson went down with his father and mother to Timnah, and they came to
the vineyards of Timnah. And behold, a young lion came toward him roaring. 6 [y]Then the
Spirit of the LORD rushed upon him, and although he had nothing in his hand, he tore
the lion in pieces as one tears a young goat. But he did not tell his father or his mother
what he had done. 7 Then he went down and talked with the woman, and she was right
in Samson's eyes.
8 After some days he returned to take her. And he turned aside to see the carcass of the
lion, and behold, there was a swarm of bees in the body of the lion, and honey. 9 He scraped

[1] Septuagint, Vulgate; Hebrew *LORD, and working*

15 [h]ch. 6:19; [Gen. 18:5-8]
17 [i][ver. 6]
18 [j]Gen. 32:29 [k][Isa. 9:6]
19 [l]ch. 6:19-21
20 [m]Lev. 9:24; 1 Chr. 21:16; Ezek. 1:28
21 [n]ch. 6:22
22 [n][See ver. 21 above]
24 [o]1 Sam. 2:21; 3:19; Luke 1:80; [Luke 2:52]
25 [p]See ch. 3:10 [q]ch. 18:11; Josh. 15:33

Chapter 14

1 [r]Heb. 11:32 [s]Gen. 38:12, 13; Josh. 15:10; 19:43
2 [t][Gen. 34:4]
3 [u][Gen. 24:3, 4; 28:1, 2] [v]ch. 15:18; 1 Sam. 14:6; 17:26, 36; 31:4; 2 Sam. 1:20
4 [w]Josh. 11:20 [x]ch. 13:1; 15:11
6 [y]ver. 19; ch. 15:14; 1 Sam. 11:6; [ch. 3:10]

13:18 The angel's name was too **wonderful** to comprehend, so he does not reveal it to Samson's parents.

13:22 we have seen God. Manoah's fears echo those of Gideon on encountering the angel of the Lord (see 6:22; cf. Gen. 32:30; Ex. 33:20).

13:25 the Spirit of the LORD began to stir him. God's Spirit was pushing Samson toward the work that God wanted him to do (cf. 14:4). See note on 14:6.

14:1–16:31 Samson's exploits fall into two segments (14:1–15:20; 16:1–31), each climaxing with a mass destruction of Philistines, followed by a comment about his judging. Within these are 10 feats of strength and heroism, five in each segment (see chart, p. 463). In three of these, the Spirit of the Lord "rushed upon him" (feats 1, 2, and 5). Perhaps significantly, this did not happen in the second segment (ch. 16), when Samson was acting more on his own and increasingly falling out of touch with God (culminating with the Lord leaving him completely [v. 20]).

14:1–15:20 *Samson and the Philistines, Part 1.* These episodes recount Samson's marriage to a Philistine woman and the resulting cycle of offense and retaliation. Marriages with unbelieving foreigners were prohibited for Israelites (Ex. 34:16; Deut. 7:3; cf. Gen. 24:2–3; 26:34–35), and Samson's demand for a wife (Judg. 14:2–3) was against the tradition in which a marriage was arranged by the parents (Gen. 24:1–4; 38:6). Despite this, and despite the mostly sinful life he led, God intended to use Samson for his own purposes (Judg. 14:4).

14:1 Timnah is located at modern Tel Batash, which lies in the Shephelah (foothills) near the southern bank of the Nahal (or dry river bed) Sorek. Excavations here have uncovered a thriving Philistine city during the period of the Judges (Early Iron Age) with impressive fortifications constructed of mud-brick on stone.

14:3 uncircumcised Philistines. Cf. 15:18; 1 Sam. 14:6; 17:26, 36; 31:4; 2 Sam. 1:20; 1 Chron. 10:4. **she is right in my eyes** (cf. Judg. 14:7). This self-centered demand contrasts with being "right in the Lord's eyes" (cf. Deut. 6:18; 12:25), and foreshadows the negative conclusions concerning the entire era, that everyone did what was right in their own eyes (Judg. 17:6; 18:1; 19:1; 21:25).

14:4 it was from the LORD. Despite Israel's apostasy and Samson's unsavory life, God would use Samson for his own purposes. (Cf. 13:16; 16:20 for similar comments.)

14:5–20 At his wedding feast, Samson told his 30 companions a riddle based on a feat of strength he had displayed. When they could not solve it,

12[z]Ezek. 17:2; [1 Kgs. 10:1; Ps. 78:2; Prov. 1:6] [a]Gen. 29:27 [b]Gen. 45:22; 2 Kgs. 5:5, 22, 23
15[c]ch. 16:5 [d]ch. 15:6
16[e][ch. 16:15]
17[f][ch. 16:16]
19[g]See ver. 6 [h]ch. 1:18

it out into his hands and went on, eating as he went. And he came to his father and mother
and gave some to them, and they ate. But he did not tell them that he had scraped the
honey from the carcass of the lion.
10 His father went down to the woman, and Samson prepared a feast there, for so the
young men used to do. 11 As soon as the people saw him, they brought thirty companions
to be with him. 12 And Samson said to them, [z]"Let me now put a riddle to you. If you can
tell me what it is, within [a]the seven days of the feast, and find it out, then I will give you
thirty linen garments and thirty [b]changes of clothes, 13 but if you cannot tell me what it
is, then you shall give me thirty linen garments and thirty changes of clothes." And they
said to him, "Put your riddle, that we may hear it." 14 And he said to them,

"Out of the eater came something to eat.
Out of the strong came something sweet."

And in three days they could not solve the riddle.
15 On the fourth[1] day they said to Samson's wife, [c]"Entice your husband to tell us what
the riddle is, [d]lest we burn you and your father's house with fire. Have you invited us
here to impoverish us?" 16 And Samson's wife wept over him and said, [e]"You only hate
me; you do not love me. You have put a riddle to my people, and you have not told me
what it is." And he said to her, "Behold, I have not told my father nor my mother, and
shall I tell you?" 17 She wept before him the seven days that their feast lasted, and on
the seventh day he told her, because [f]she pressed him hard. Then she told the riddle
to her people. 18 And the men of the city said to him on the seventh day before the sun
went down,

"What is sweeter than honey?
What is stronger than a lion?"

And he said to them,

"If you had not plowed with my heifer,
you would not have found out my riddle."

19 [g]And the Spirit of the LORD rushed upon him, and he went down to [h]Ashkelon and
struck down thirty men of the town and took their spoil and gave the garments to those

[1] Septuagint, Syriac; Hebrew *seventh*

they enlisted his wife's help and she extracted the answer. In his rage at this trickery, Samson killed 30 Philistines to obtain the garments he owed his companions. In his absence, his wife was given to his best man.

14:6 the Spirit of the LORD rushed upon him. The OT speaks many times of God's Spirit acting upon individuals, usually to empower them for some service for the whole people of God. In Judges this is described by the Spirit being upon (Othniel, 3:10; Jephthah, 11:29), clothing (Gideon, 6:34), stirring (Samson, 13:25), or rushing upon someone (Samson, 14:6, 19; 15:14; cf. Saul, 1 Sam. 10:6, 10; 11:6; David, 1 Sam. 16:13). See note on 1 Sam. 10:6.

14:8–9 carcass of the lion. Samson's contact with the dead lion violated his Nazirite vow (cf. 13:5).

14:10 a feast (Hb. *mishteh*). This word denotes a feast that especially includes alcohol, another violation of Samson's Nazirite vow (cf. 13:5).

14:14 Samson's **riddle** (Hb. *khidah*) is the best example of a riddle in Scripture. Other examples include the queen of Sheba's "hard questions" (same Hebrew word, *khidah*) for Solomon (1 Kings 10:1) and Daniel's ability "to interpret dreams, explain riddles, and solve problems" (Dan. 5:12).

14:15 fourth day. The Hebrew text has "seventh day" (cf. v. 18); the ESV reading is based on Greek and Syriac versions (see ESV footnote). The difference is only one letter in Hebrew, which could easily have been miscopied by a scribe in an early manuscript. "Fourth" fits better with the immediate context (v. 14 mentions three days of futile guessing about the riddle).

14:18 If you had not plowed with my heifer. This may have been a saying in Samson's time (heifers were occasionally used for plowing; cf. Deut. 21:3). Here, it is a coarse reference to their manipulation of Samson's wife.

Samson's Ten Feats of Strength and Heroism

Part 1: Three mentions of the "Spirit of the LORD"		
1. The killing of the lion	14:5–9	"The Spirit of the LORD rushed upon him" (14:6).
2. The killing of 30 Philistines	14:19	"The Spirit of the LORD rushed upon him" (14:19).
3. The burning of the fields	15:4–6	
4. Another slaughter of the Philistines	15:7–8	
5. Escape from ropes and killing of 1,000 Philistines	15:14–17	"The Spirit of the LORD rushed upon him" (15:14).
Part 2: No mention of the "Spirit of the LORD"		
6. The Gaza-gate incident	16:3	
7. Escape from the bowstrings	16:9	
8. Escape from the new ropes	16:12	
9. Escape from the loom	16:14	
10. Final destruction of 3,000 Philistines	16:28–30	

who had told the riddle. In hot anger he went back to his father's house. 20 And Samson's
wife was given to [i]his companion, [j]who had been his best man.

Samson Defeats the Philistines

15 After some days, at the time of wheat harvest, Samson went to visit his wife with
[k]a young goat. And he said, "I will go in to my wife in the chamber." But her father
would not allow him to go in. 2 And her father said, "I really thought that you utterly
hated her, [l]so I gave her to your companion. Is not her younger sister more beautiful than
she? Please take her instead." 3 And Samson said to them, "This time I shall be innocent in
regard to the Philistines, when I do them harm." 4 So Samson went and caught 300 foxes
and took torches. And he turned them tail to tail and put a torch between each pair of tails.
5 And when he had set fire to the torches, he let the foxes go into the standing grain of
the Philistines and set fire to the stacked grain and the standing grain, as well as the olive
orchards. 6 Then the Philistines said, "Who has done this?" And they said, "Samson, the
son-in-law of the Timnite, because he has taken his wife [m]and given her to his companion."
And the Philistines came up and [n]burned her and her father with fire. 7 And Samson said
to them, "If this is what you do, I swear I will be avenged on you, and after that I will quit."
8 And he struck them hip and thigh with a great blow, and he went down and stayed in
the [o]cleft of the rock of Etam.

9 Then the Philistines came up and encamped in Judah and [p]made a raid on [q]Lehi. 10 And
the men of Judah said, "Why have you come up against us?" They said, "We have come up
to bind Samson, to do to him as he did to us." 11 Then 3,000 men of Judah went down to
the cleft of the rock of Etam, and said to Samson, "Do you not know that [r]the Philistines
are rulers over us? What then is this that you have done to us?" And he said to them, "As
they did to me, so have I done to them." 12 And they said to him, "We have come down
to bind you, that we may give you into the hands of the Philistines." And Samson said
to them, "Swear to me that you will not attack me yourselves." 13 They said to him, "No;
we will only bind you and give you into their hands. We will surely not kill you." So they
bound him with two [s]new ropes and brought him up from the rock.

14 When he came to Lehi, the Philistines came shouting to meet him. [t]Then the Spirit
of the LORD rushed upon him, and the ropes that were on his arms became as flax that
has caught fire, and his bonds melted off his hands. 15 And he found a fresh jawbone of
a donkey, and put out his hand and took it, [u]and with it he struck 1,000 men. 16 And
Samson said,

> "With the jawbone of a donkey,
>   heaps upon heaps,
> with the jawbone of a donkey
>   have I struck down a thousand men."

17 As soon as he had finished speaking, he threw away the jawbone out of his hand. And
that place [v]was called Ramath-lehi.[1]

18 And he was very thirsty, and he called upon the LORD and said, [w]"You have granted
this great salvation by the hand of your servant, and shall I now die of thirst and fall into
the hands of the uncircumcised?" 19 And God split open the hollow place that is [v]at Lehi,
and water came out from it. And when he drank, [x]his spirit returned, and he revived.

[1] *Ramath-lehi means the hill of the jawbone*

20 [i]ch. 15:2, 6 [j]John 3:29

Chapter 15

1 [k][Gen. 38:17]
2 [l]ver. 6; ch. 14:20
6 [m]ver. 2 [n]ch. 14:15
8 [o]ver. 11; Isa. 2:21; 57:5
9 [p]2 Sam. 5:18, 22 [q]ver. 14, 17, 19
11 [r]ch. 13:1; 14:4
13 [s]ch. 16:11, 12
14 [t]ch. 14:6, 19; 1 Sam. 11:6; [ch. 3:10]
15 [u]Josh. 23:10; [ch. 3:31; Lev. 26:8]
17 [v]ver. 9, 14
18 [w][Ps. 3:7]
19 [v][See ver. 17 above] [x]Gen. 45:27

15:1 a young goat. Tamar required the same gift of Judah before she would consent to sexual relations with him (Gen. 38:17).

15:4 It is possible that the animals were not **foxes** but jackals, which were more common in Palestine. The two animals look similar, and the same Hebrew word (*shu'al*) is used for both. Whereas foxes are solitary, jackals travel in packs, and thus **300** of them could be caught more easily. Both animals have long tails that could be tied together.

15:6 burned her . . . with fire. The **Philistines** retaliated by killing Samson's wife **and her father** by burning them alive. Ironically, this was the very fate she was attempting to avoid by extracting from Samson the answer to his riddle (14:15).

15:8 he struck them hip and thigh. The exact meaning of this idiom is obscure. Perhaps Samson left his enemies in a tangled jumble of legs and thighs. The expression may have originated in the art of wrestling, where brute strength like Samson's would obviously have been an advantage.

15:14–15 Spirit of the LORD. See note on 14:6. **fresh jawbone.** Presumably the advantage of this weapon was that it would not have been dry and brittle, hence there was no danger of its breaking.

15:17 Ramath-lehi. See ESV footnote; cf. Lehi in vv. 9, 14, 19.

15:18–19 uncircumcised. See note on 14:3. **to this day.** See note on 6:24.

20[y]ch. 13:1
Chapter 16
1[z]Josh. 15:47
2[a][1 Sam. 23:26; Ps. 118:10-12; Acts 9:24]
5[b]Josh. 13:3 [c]ch. 14:15 [d]ver. 19
6[d][See ver. 5 above]
7[e]ver. 11, 17
11[f]ch. 15:13, 14
15[g]ch. 14:16

Therefore the name of it was called En-hakkore;[1] it is at Lehi to this day. 20 And he judged
Israel [y]in the days of the Philistines twenty years.

Samson and Delilah

16 Samson went to [z]Gaza, and there he saw a prostitute, and he went in to her. 2 The
Gazites were told, "Samson has come here." And they [a]surrounded the place and set
an ambush for him all night at the gate of the city. They kept quiet all night, saying, "Let
us wait till the light of the morning; then we will kill him." 3 But Samson lay till midnight,
and at midnight he arose and took hold of the doors of the gate of the city and the two
posts, and pulled them up, bar and all, and put them on his shoulders and carried them
to the top of the hill that is in front of Hebron.

4 After this he loved a woman in the Valley of Sorek, whose name was Delilah. 5 And
[b]the lords of the Philistines came up to her and said to her, [c]"Seduce him, and see where
his great strength lies, and by what means we may overpower him, that we may bind
him to [d]humble him. And we will each give you 1,100 pieces of silver." 6 So Delilah said
to Samson, "Please tell me where your great strength lies, and how you might be bound,
that one could [d]subdue you."

7 Samson said to her, "If they bind me with seven fresh bowstrings that have not been dried,
[e]then I shall become weak and be like any other man." 8 Then the lords of the Philistines
brought up to her seven fresh bowstrings that had not been dried, and she bound him
with them. 9 Now she had men lying in ambush in an inner chamber. And she said to him,
"The Philistines are upon you, Samson!" But he snapped the bowstrings, as a thread of flax
snaps when it touches the fire. So the secret of his strength was not known.

10 Then Delilah said to Samson, "Behold, you have mocked me and told me lies. Please
tell me how you might be bound." 11 And he said to her, "If they bind me with [f]new ropes
that have not been used, then I shall become weak and be like any other man." 12 So Delilah
took new ropes and bound him with them and said to him, "The Philistines are upon you,
Samson!" And the men lying in ambush were in an inner chamber. But he snapped the
ropes off his arms like a thread.

13 Then Delilah said to Samson, "Until now you have mocked me and told me lies. Tell
me how you might be bound." And he said to her, "If you weave the seven locks of my head
with the web and fasten it tight with the pin, then I shall become weak and be like any
other man." 14 So while he slept, Delilah took the seven locks of his head and wove them
into the web.[2] And she made them tight with the pin and said to him, "The Philistines
are upon you, Samson!" But he awoke from his sleep and pulled away the pin, the loom,
and the web.

15 And she said to him, [g]"How can you say, 'I love you,' when your heart is not with me?

[1] *En-hakkore means the spring of him who called* [2] Compare Septuagint; Hebrew lacks *and fasten it tight . . . into the web*

15:20 Cf. 16:31. Both sections of the Samson stories (14:1–15:20; 16:1–31) end with a notice of Samson's judging Israel for **twenty years**.

16:1–31 *Samson and the Philistines, Part 2.* The second segment of the Samson stories details his fateful involvement with yet two more Philistine women—a prostitute (vv. 1–3) and Delilah (vv. 4–22)—and his final revenge on the Philistines and their god (vv. 23–31). Significantly, the Spirit of the Lord is nowhere mentioned in this chapter. Finally the Lord departs from him (v. 20), and Samson's miraculous strength is gone.

16:1 prostitute. Hebrew has two words for prostitutes. One (*qadesh*) refers to "cultic prostitutes" who served pagan gods (Gen. 38:21–22; Deut. 23:17; 1 Kings 14:24). The word here (*zonah*) signifies a second type, the common, "secular" variety (cf. Gen. 38:15).

16:2–3 at the gate. Gates from this period, the Early Iron Age, were elaborate complexes, at least two stories high, with guardrooms flanking a narrow opening. **The two posts** were set deep in the ground to support the doors. **the hill that is in front of Hebron**. The ancient route connecting Hebron and Gaza was a journey of c. 40 miles (64 km).

16:4–22 Delilah coordinated her actions with the "lords" of the Philistines to bring down Samson. She persisted and finally succeeded in persuading him to reveal the source of his amazing strength. When he broke the final Nazirite stipulation by allowing his hair to be cut, the Lord left him (v. 20) and he was captured.

16:4–5 Delilah was the third Philistine woman with whom Samson had become entangled (cf. 14:1; 16:1). **came up to her and said**. Cf. 14:15.

16:7–9 In the first test of Samson's strength, the **seven fresh bowstrings**, made of animal gut, were weaker than dried and aged strings. Samson's suggestion of these inadequate bonds shows his contempt for his adversaries, and their credulity indicates their haste to capture him. **thread of flax**. See 15:14.

16:11 new ropes. In the second test, Samson toyed with the Philistines, suggesting that they use the same bonds that the men of Judah had previously found to be worthless (see 15:13).

16:13–14 seven locks of my head. The third test, involving Samson's hair, got closer to the true source of his strength. **Made them tight with the pin** translates the same Hebrew phrase that was used when Jael drove a tent peg into Sisera's head (4:21). The exact scenario here is unclear, but Samson obviously had no trouble escaping once more. Samson, like Sisera, was unwary in the presence of a woman, naively not suspecting her of posing any danger.

You have mocked me these three times, and you have not told me where your great strength
lies." **16** And [h]when she pressed him hard with her words day after day, and urged him,
his soul was vexed to death. **17** And he told her all his heart, and said to her, [i]"A razor has
never come upon my head, for I have been a Nazirite to God from my mother's womb. If
my head is shaved, then my strength will leave me, and I shall become weak and be like
any other man."
18 When Delilah saw that he had told her all his heart, she sent and called the lords of
the Philistines, saying, "Come up again, for he has told me all his heart." Then the lords
of the Philistines came up to her and brought [j]the money in their hands. **19** She made him
sleep on her knees. And she called a man and had him shave off the seven locks of his
head. Then she began [k]to torment him, and his strength left him. **20** And she said, "The
Philistines are upon you, Samson!" And he awoke from his sleep and said, "I will go out
as at other times and shake myself free." But he did not know that [l]the LORD had left him.
21 And the Philistines seized him and gouged out his eyes and brought him down to Gaza
and bound him with bronze shackles. [m]And he ground at the mill in the prison. **22** But the
hair of his head began to grow again after it had been shaved.

The Death of Samson

23 Now the lords of the Philistines gathered to offer a great sacrifice to [n]Dagon their
god and to rejoice, and they said, "Our god has given Samson our enemy into our hand."
24 And when the people saw him, [o]they praised their god. For they said, "Our god has
given our enemy into our hand, the ravager of our country, who has killed many of us."[1]
25 And [p]when their hearts were merry, they said, "Call Samson, that he may entertain
us." So they called Samson out of the prison, and he entertained them. They made him
stand between the pillars. **26** And Samson said to the young man who held him by the
hand, "Let me feel the pillars on which the house rests, that I may lean against them."
27 Now the house was full of men and women. All the lords of the Philistines were there,
and [q]on the roof there were about 3,000 men and women, who looked on while Samson
entertained.
28 Then Samson called to the LORD and said, "O Lord GOD, [r]please remember me and
please strengthen me only this once, O God, that I may be avenged on the Philistines for
my two eyes." **29** And Samson grasped the two middle pillars on which the house rested,
and he leaned his weight against them, his right hand on the one and his left hand on the
other. **30** And Samson said, "Let me die with the Philistines." Then he bowed with all his
strength, and the house fell upon the lords and upon all the people who were in it. So the
dead whom he killed at his death were more than those whom he had killed during his
life. **31** Then his brothers and all his family came down and took him and brought him up
and buried him [s]between Zorah and Eshtaol in the tomb of Manoah his father. He had
judged Israel twenty years.

[1] *Or who has multiplied our slain*

16 [h][ch. 14:17]
17 [i][ch. 13:5]
18 [j]ver. 5
19 [k]ver. 5, 6
20 [l]1 Sam. 28:15, 16
21 [m][Ex. 11:5; Matt. 24:41]
23 [n]1 Chr. 10:10; See 1 Sam. 5:2-7
24 [o][Dan. 5:4]
25 [p]ch. 19:6; [2 Sam. 13:28]
27 [q][Deut. 22:8; 2 Sam. 11:2; Neh. 8:16; Matt. 24:17; Mark 13:15; Luke 17:31]
28 [r]Jer. 15:15
31 [s]ch. 13:25

16:16 she pressed him. Delilah did precisely what Samson's wife had done earlier (14:17). Samson's weak character shows through again: he did not learn from his previous mistake, but yielded in both cases.

16:18 told her all his heart. Delilah knew that Samson was finally telling the truth. Earlier, he had withheld his heart from her (v. 15).

16:20–21 the LORD had left him. See note on 14:4. **gouged out his eyes**. The practice of blinding an enemy and then forcing him to grind grain at a **mill** is known from ancient Near Eastern texts (e.g., the Tapikka Letters, from a 14th century B.C. Hittite administrative city). The Philistines may have adopted this practice from the Hittites.

16:22 the hair of his head began to grow again. There was no magical power in Samson's hair, for his strength came only from the Lord (14:6, 19; 15:14; 16:20). But the growth of his hair indicates that God was renewing his previous power (cf. vv. 17, 19–20). Samson may also have begun to renew his faith (cf. v. 28).

16:23–27 Despite Samson's humiliation, his life ended with vindication. His hair grew back (v. 22), and he slaughtered 3,000 Philistines (v. 27), more than he had killed previously (v. 30).

16:28–30 Samson demonstrated a measure of faith by calling upon God and believing that God could and would help him (cf. Heb. 11:32). However, Samson seems to have desired God's intervention more for personal revenge than for the protection of God's people. **two middle pillars**. A temple from the period of the judges has been unearthed at the Philistine site of Tell Qasile. It was built with two central pillars to support the roof of the entire structure, a design distinct from either Canaanite or Israelite temples.

16:31 The main body of the book of Judges now ends, with a final editorial comment about Samson's judging. Samson, the last judge, had been empowered by God's Spirit, just as the first (Othniel) had been. However, much had happened in the interim. Samson and most of his predecessors certainly were not paragons of virtue. Yet, despite the generally poor examples of the judges themselves, God had worked to deliver Israel and to protect his own name and reputation. But the book's message is not yet played out. In the following

Chapter 17
1 [t]ver. 8; ch. 18:2; See Josh. 24:33
2 [u]Ruth 3:10; 1 Sam. 15:13
3 [v][Ex. 20:4] [w][Lev. 19:4]
4 [x][Isa. 46:6]
5 [y]ch. 8:27; 18:14, 17; See Ex. 28:6-35 [z][Gen. 31:19; Hos. 3:4] [a]ver. 12; [1 Kgs. 13:33]
6 [b]ch. 18:1; 19:1; 21:25 [c][Deut. 12:8]
7 [d]ch. 19:1; Ruth 1:1, 2; Mic. 5:2; Matt. 2:1, 5, 6
8 [e]See Josh. 24:33
10 [f]ch. 18:19
11 [g][Ex. 2:21]
12 [h]ver. 5 [i][ch. 18:30]

Micah and the Levite

17 There was a man of [t]the hill country of Ephraim, whose name was Micah. **2** And he
said to his mother, "The 1,100 pieces of silver that were taken from you, about which
you uttered a curse, and also spoke it in my ears, behold, the silver is with me; I took it." And
his mother said, [u]"Blessed be my son by the LORD." **3** And he restored the 1,100 pieces of
silver to his mother. And his mother said, "I dedicate the silver to the LORD from my hand
for my son, to make [v]a carved image and [w]a metal image. Now therefore I will restore it to
you." **4** So when he restored the money to his mother, his mother [x]took 200 pieces of silver
and gave it to the silversmith, who made it into a carved image and a metal image. And it
was in the house of Micah. **5** And the man Micah had a shrine, and he made [y]an ephod and
[z]household gods, and [a]ordained[1] one of his sons, who became his priest. **6** [b]In those days
there was no king in Israel. [c]Everyone did what was right in his own eyes.
7 Now there was a young man of [d]Bethlehem in Judah, of the family of Judah, who was
a Levite, and he sojourned there. **8** And the man departed from the town of Bethlehem in
Judah to sojourn where he could find a place. And as he journeyed, he came to [e]the hill
country of Ephraim to the house of Micah. **9** And Micah said to him, "Where do you come
from?" And he said to him, "I am a Levite of Bethlehem in Judah, and I am going to sojourn
where I may find a place." **10** And Micah said to him, "Stay with me, and be to me [f]a father
and a priest, and I will give you ten pieces of silver a year and a suit of clothes and your
living." And the Levite went in. **11** And the Levite [g]was content to dwell with the man, and
the young man became to him like one of his sons. **12** And Micah [h]ordained the Levite,
and the young man [i]became his priest, and was in the house of Micah. **13** Then Micah said,
"Now I know that the LORD will prosper me, because I have a Levite as priest."

[1] Hebrew *filled the hand of*; also verse 12

chapters, the nation's apostasy sinks to even deeper levels, and the stage is set for the coming of a faithful king who will restore moral order.

17:1–21:25 *The Depths of Israel's Apostasy.* The book of Judges closes with two sections (chs. 17–18 and 19–21) characterized by the statements, "In those days there was no king in Israel" (17:6; 18:1; 19:1; 21:25) and, "everyone did what was right in his own eyes" (17:6; 21:25). Whereas chs. 2–16 describe external threats to Israel, chs. 17–21 describe internal threats to religious worship and tribal unity. The most sordid and tragic stories in the book are found here, for the ultimate depths of Israel's apostasy have now been reached. The message is that if Israel had had a godly king functioning as a king should (Deut. 17:18–20), things would have been better.

17:1–18:31 *Religious Corruption.* The first concluding section (cf. note on 17:1–21:25) depicts Micah's establishment of his own private shrine, featuring an attendant priest, and tells of the Danites' migration, during which they took Micah's priest and the symbols of his shrine away from him.

17:1–6 *Religious Corruption of a Household.* These verses depict a thieving son and an unusually forgiving mother who commit apostasy together.

17:3–4 a carved image. Such images are mentioned in the Ten Commandments (Ex. 20:4). They were normally carved from wood or chiseled out of rock but sometimes made from a mold (cf. Isa. 40:19; 44:10). **a metal image**. Cf. 2 Kings 17:16. Micah's mother approved of his making these images, showing how God's people sometimes are tempted to mix elements of true worship with practices unacceptable to God. This is another consequence of the Israelites' lack of good leadership. The **house of Micah** was a compound consisting of multiple housing units for travelers and relatives (cf. Judg. 18:2). Similar complexes, including two or more attached houses, have been uncovered by excavations at Ai and Khirbet Raddana.

17:5 a shrine. Lit., "a house of God." This was a perversion of the true sanctuary where worship was to take place (cf. "the house of God" at Shiloh in 18:31). Micah also **made an ephod** (cf. 8:27) and various **household gods** (cf. Gen. 31:19); these are later condemned as idolatry (1 Sam. 15:23). Micah further violated the Mosaic law by appointing his own son as his private **priest**, an office meant not for private but for public service. Furthermore, he was not descended from Aaron (as the priests were supposed to be), nor was he even a Levite (cf. Ex. 28:1; 40:12–15; Num. 16:39–40; 17:8).

17:6 no king in Israel. See Introduction: Purpose, Occasion, and Background (cf. 18:1; 19:1; 21:25). **right in his own eyes** (cf. 21:25). The verse is an editorial comment on the nation's apostasy. People were doing whatever they wanted, as opposed to what was right in the Lord's eyes (cf. 14:3).

17:7–13 *Religious Corruption of a Levite.* Micah meets a Levite and lures him into serving as a private priest by offering him a fine salary and a safe house.

17:9 Levite of Bethlehem. This Levite had been living as a sojourner, a resident alien, in Judah. The Levites did not have their own tribal territory, but they had 48 cities, scattered among the other tribes (Joshua 21). However, Bethlehem was not one of those cities, and this Levite was only too happy to settle in Micah's household in Ephraim and become his private priest, displacing Micah's son (Judg. 17:10–11; see note on v. 5).

Anarchy without a King: Bookends of Judges 17–21

Micah and the Danite Migration (chs. 17–18)		Gibeah's Deed and Their Punishment (chs. 19–21)	
Religious Deterioration		*Moral Deterioration*	
Beginning	"In those days there was no king in Israel. Everyone did what was right in his own eyes" (17:6).	"In those days, when there was no king in Israel . . ." (19:1).	**Beginning**
Ending	"In those days there was no king in Israel" (18:1).	"In those days there was no king in Israel. Everyone did what was right in his own eyes" (21:25).	**Ending**

Danites Take the Levite and the Idol

18 [j]In those days there was no king in Israel. And in those days [k]the tribe of the people
of Dan was seeking for itself an inheritance to dwell in, for until then no inheritance
among the tribes of Israel had fallen to them. **2** So the people of Dan sent five able men
from the whole number of their tribe, [l]from Zorah and from Eshtaol, [m]to spy out the land
and to explore it. And they said to them, "Go and explore the land." And they came [n]to the
hill country of Ephraim, to the house of Micah, and lodged there. **3** When they were by
the house of Micah, they recognized the voice of the young Levite. And they turned aside
and said to him, "Who brought you here? What are you doing in this place? What is your
business here?" **4** And he said to them, "This is how Micah dealt with me: [o]he has hired me,
and I have become his priest." **5** And they said to him, [p]"Inquire of God, please, that we may
know whether the journey on which we are setting out will succeed." **6** And the priest said
to them, [q]"Go in peace. The journey on which you go is under the eye of the LORD."
7 Then the five men departed and came to [r]Laish and saw the people who were there,
how they lived in security, after the manner of the Sidonians, [s]quiet and unsuspecting,
lacking[1] nothing that is in the earth and possessing wealth, and how [t]they were far from
the Sidonians and had no dealings with anyone. **8** And when they came to their brothers
at [u]Zorah and Eshtaol, their brothers said to them, "What do you report?" **9** They said,
[v]"Arise, and let us go up against them, for we have seen the land, and behold, it is very
good. [w]And will you do nothing? [x]Do not be slow to go, to enter in and possess the land.
10 As soon as you go, you will come to an [y]unsuspecting people. The land is spacious, for
God has given it into your hands, [z]a place where there is no lack of anything that is in
the earth."
11 So 600 men of the tribe of Dan, [a]armed with weapons of war, set out from Zorah and
Eshtaol, **12** and went up and encamped at Kiriath-jearim in Judah. On this account that
place is called [b]Mahaneh-dan[2] to this day; behold, it is west of [c]Kiriath-jearim. **13** And they
passed on from there to [d]the hill country of Ephraim, and came to the house of Micah.
14 Then the five men who had gone to scout out the country of Laish said to their brothers, "Do you know that [e]in these houses there are an ephod, household gods, a carved
image, and a metal image? Now therefore consider what you will do." **15** And they turned
aside there and came to the house of the young Levite, at the home of Micah, and [f]asked
him about his welfare. **16** Now the 600 men of the Danites, [g]armed with their weapons
of war, stood by the entrance of the gate. **17** And [h]the five men who had gone to scout
out the land went up and entered and took [i]the carved image, the ephod, the household
gods, and the metal image, while the priest stood by the entrance of the gate with the 600
men armed with weapons of war. **18** And when these went into Micah's house and took
[i]the carved image, the ephod, the household gods, and the metal image, the priest said
to them, "What are you doing?" **19** And they said to him, "Keep quiet; [j]put your hand on
your mouth and come with us and be to us [k]a father and a priest. Is it better for you to

Chapter 18
1 [j]ch. 17:6; 21:25 [k][ch. 1:34; Josh. 19:47, 48]
2 [l]ver. 8, 11; ch. 13:25 [m][Num. 13:17; Josh. 2:1] [n]ch. 17:1, 8; See Josh. 24:33
4 [o]ch. 17:10
5 [p]Num. 27:21
6 [q]1 Sam. 1:17; [1 Kgs. 22:6]
7 [r][Josh. 19:47] [s]ver. 10, 27 [t]ver. 28
8 [u]ver. 2, 11
9 [v][Num. 13:20; Josh. 2:23, 24] [w]1 Kgs. 22:3 [x][Josh. 18:3]
10 [y]ver. 7, 27 [z][ch. 19:19; Deut. 8:9]
11 [a]ver. 16
12 [b]ch. 13:25 [c]Josh. 15:60
13 [d]ver. 2
14 [e]ch. 17:4, 5
15 [f]Gen. 43:27
16 [g]ver. 11
17 [h]ver. 2, 14 [i]ver. 14; ch. 17:4, 5
18 [i][See ver. 17 above]
19 [j]Job 21:5; 29:9; 40:4; Prov. 30:32; Mic. 7:16 [k]ch. 17:10

[1] Compare 18:10; the meaning of the Hebrew word is uncertain [2] *Mahaneh-dan* means *camp of Dan*

18:1–31 *Religious Corruption of a Tribe.* A band of treacherous men from the tribe of Dan offer the Levite (see note on 17:9) more money and prestige to be their priest, so he joins them. A whole tribe now sins like Micah's family did.

18:1 no king in Israel. See Introduction: Purpose, Occasion, and Background (cf. 17:6; 19:1; 21:25). **Dan was seeking . . . an inheritance.** The Danites had been unable to settle in their allotted territory (Josh. 19:40–47), as they had failed to capture it earlier (Judg. 1:34–35).

18:2–4 Zorah . . . Eshtaol. These towns were located in the Judean lowlands approximately 15 miles (24 km) west of Jerusalem. The fact that the Danites send men who **lodged there** with Micah **to spy out the land**, recalls similar events with Rahab and the spies in Josh. 2:1.

18:5–6 Their request, regarding **whether the journey . . . will succeed**, echoes the language of Joshua, where the "prosperous way" is defined in terms of devotion to God's word (Josh. 1:8). Given the highly negative tone of Judges 17–21 and future events in this particular narrative (18:30), it is difficult to take seriously their desire to **inquire of God**. The statement, **under the eye of the LORD**, captures the ambiguity of the priest's response. The future actions of the Danites may have been seen by God, but that does not mean that they were approved by God.

18:7 Laish was located about 25 miles (40 km) north of the Sea of Galilee, making the migration of the Danites from Zorah and Eshtaol to Laish about a hundred miles. Laish was renamed Dan (v. 29; see note on 20:1–2), and it was here that Jeroboam set up one of his golden calves (1 Kings 12:29–30). The site was occupied through the Roman period.

18:12 Kiriath-jearim, a chief city of the Gibeonites (Josh. 9:17), was located approximately 8 miles (13 km) northwest of Jerusalem, though debate continues regarding its precise location.

18:14–20 ephod, household gods, a carved image, and a metal image. Micah's collection of cultic objects was quite impressive (cf. 17:3–5). Rather than offering condemnation, the Danites took the cultic objects for themselves. **a father and a priest**. The Danites' words to the Levite were the same as Micah's earlier (17:10). The Danites' offer of more money and prestige, and the Levite's acceptance, are further indications of the period's apostasy. Their plundering of another tribe (18:18, 21) fulfills Jacob's prediction that Dan would deal viciously with others, like a serpent or a viper (Gen. 49:17).

21 [l][1 Sam. 17:22; Isa. 10:28]
24 [m][Gen. 31:30]
27 [n]ver. 7, 10 [o]Josh. 19:47
28 [p]ver. 7 [q]2 Sam. 10:6; [Num. 13:21; Josh. 19:28]
29 [r]ch. 20:1; Gen. 14:14; 1 Kgs. 12:29, 30; 15:20 [s]ver. 7
30 [t]Ex. 2:22; 18:3 [u][ch. 17:12] [v]ch. 13:1; 1 Sam. 4:2, 3, 10, 11; See Ps. 78:60-64
31 [w]Josh. 18:1; 1 Sam. 1:3

Chapter 19

1 [x]ch. 17:6; 18:1; 21:25 [y]See Josh. 24:33 [z]See ch. 17:7
5 [a]ver. 8; Gen. 18:5
6 [b]ver. 9, 22; ch. 16:25; Ruth 3:7; 2 Sam. 13:28

be priest to the house of one man, or to be priest to a tribe and clan in Israel?" 20 And the
priest's heart was glad. He took the ephod and the household gods and the carved image
and went along with the people.
21 So they turned and departed, putting the little ones and the livestock and [l]the goods
in front of them. 22 When they had gone a distance from the home of Micah, the men who
were in the houses near Micah's house were called out, and they overtook the people of
Dan. 23 And they shouted to the people of Dan, who turned around and said to Micah,
"What is the matter with you, that you come with such a company?" 24 And he said,
[m]"You take my gods that I made and the priest, and go away, and what have I left? How
then do you ask me, 'What is the matter with you?'" 25 And the people of Dan said to
him, "Do not let your voice be heard among us, lest angry fellows fall upon you, and
you lose your life with the lives of your household." 26 Then the people of Dan went
their way. And when Micah saw that they were too strong for him, he turned and went
back to his home.
27 But the people of Dan took what Micah had made, and the priest who belonged to
him, and they came to Laish, to a people [n]quiet and unsuspecting, and [o]struck them with
the edge of the sword and burned the city with fire. 28 And there was no deliverer because
it was [p]far from Sidon, and they had no dealings with anyone. It was in the valley that
belongs to [q]Beth-rehob. Then they rebuilt the city and lived in it. 29 And they named the
city [r]Dan, after the name of Dan their ancestor, who was born to Israel; but [s]the name of the
city was Laish at the first. 30 And the people of Dan set up the carved image for themselves,
and Jonathan the son of Gershom, [t]son of Moses,[1] [u]and his sons were priests to the tribe
of the Danites until the day [v]of the captivity of the land. 31 So they set up Micah's carved
image that he made, [w]as long as the house of God was at Shiloh.

A Levite and His Concubine

19 In those days, [x]when there was no king in Israel, a certain Levite was sojourning in
the remote parts of [y]the hill country of Ephraim, who took to himself a concubine
from [z]Bethlehem in Judah. 2 And his concubine was unfaithful to[2] him, and she went
away from him to her father's house at Bethlehem in Judah, and was there some four
months. 3 Then her husband arose and went after her, to speak kindly to her and bring
her back. He had with him his servant and a couple of donkeys. And she brought him
into her father's house. And when the girl's father saw him, he came with joy to meet him.
4 And his father-in-law, the girl's father, made him stay, and he remained with him three
days. So they ate and drank and spent the night there. 5 And on the fourth day they arose
early in the morning, and he prepared to go, but the girl's father said to his son-in-law,
[a]"Strengthen your heart with a morsel of bread, and after that you may go." 6 So the two
of them sat and ate and drank together. And the girl's father said to the man, "Be pleased
to spend the night, and [b]let your heart be merry." 7 And when the man rose up to go, his
father-in-law pressed him, till he spent the night there again. 8 And on the fifth day he

[1] Or *Manasseh* [2] Septuagint, Old Latin *became angry with*

18:21 As the Danites fled, they placed what they had stolen **in front of them**, with the warriors behind, as protection against pursuit from Micah's household or neighbors.

18:30–31 The Levite's name is revealed for the first time (**Jonathan**), as well as his lineage—apostasy has even infected the house of **Moses**. **Captivity of the land** could refer to the Babylonian captivity (587 B.C.), or, since Dan is in the north, to the Assyrian captivity of 722 (or even earlier, when Dan passed into Assyrian control). In any case, the Danites' priest and his descendants served in that role for centuries, and only exile ended the arrangement. **Shiloh** was destroyed at the end of the period of the judges, c. 1050 B.C. (cf. Ps. 78:60; Jer. 7:12, 14; 26:6).

19:1–21:24 *Moral and Social Corruption.* This second concluding section (cf. note on 17:1–21:25) deals with outrageous actions perpetrated at Gibeah against a Levite's concubine and the aftermath of those actions. The story is similar to the assault on Lot's household in Sodom in Genesis 19, placing Gibeah on the same debased plane as Sodom (cf. Gen. 13:13; Deut. 32:32; Isa. 1:10; 3:9). This section is linked with the previous (Judges 17–18) by Levites as protagonists in both (17:7; 19:1); in the first section, a Levite from Bethlehem travels to the hill country of Ephraim, while in the second, a Levite from the hill country of Ephraim travels to Bethlehem to take a concubine. One horror seems to lead inexorably to another, apparently with no way out, as the people's unfaithfulness takes its devastating toll.

19:1–30 *Moral Outrage at Gibeah.* These verses recount one of the most sordid stories in the Bible. Rape, murder, and callous indifference lead to the death of an innocent woman and, eventually, to civil war.

19:1 no king in Israel. See Introduction: Purpose, Occasion, and Background (cf. 17:6; 18:1; 21:25). A **concubine** was a female servant or slave regarded as part of the family. Her usual function was childbearing to enlarge the family (cf. Abraham's concubine Hagar [Genesis 16]; Jacob's concubines Bilhah and Zilpah [Gen. 30:4–13]). **Bethlehem in Judah** was also the origin of Micah's priest (Judg. 17:9).

19:3–9 An elaborate and extended ritual of hospitality is played out here: the Levite stayed in the home of his concubine's father for five days, on the insistent urging of the father. Strict codes of hospitality still play a part in many tribal Near Eastern cultures. The elaborate hospitality described here stands in sharp contrast to what follows in the ensuing episodes.

arose early in the morning to depart. And the girl's father said, [c]"Strengthen your heart
and wait until the day declines." So they ate, both of them. **9** And when the man and his
concubine and his servant rose up to depart, his father-in-law, the girl's father, said to him,
"Behold, now the day has waned toward evening. Please, spend the night. Behold, the day
draws to its close. Lodge here and let your heart be merry, and tomorrow you shall arise
early in the morning for your journey, and go home."
10 But the man would not spend the night. He rose up and departed and arrived opposite [d]Jebus (that is, Jerusalem). He had with him a couple of saddled donkeys, and his
concubine was with him. **11** When they were near Jebus, the day was nearly over, and
the servant said to his master, "Come now, let us turn aside to this city of the Jebusites
and spend the night in it." **12** And his master said to him, "We will not turn aside into
the city of foreigners, who do not belong to the people of Israel, but we will pass on to
[e]Gibeah." **13** And he said to his young man, "Come and let us draw near to one of these
places and spend the night at Gibeah or at [f]Ramah." **14** So they passed on and went their
way. And the sun went down on them near Gibeah, which belongs to Benjamin, **15** and
they turned aside there, to go in and spend the night at Gibeah. And he went in and
sat down in the open square of the city, [g]for no one took them into his house to spend
the night.
16 And behold, an old man was coming from his work in the field at evening. The man
was from [h]the hill country of Ephraim, and he was sojourning in Gibeah. [i]The men of
the place were Benjaminites. **17** And he lifted up his eyes and saw the traveler in the open
square of the city. And the old man said, "Where are you going? And where do you come
from?" **18** And he said to him, "We are passing from Bethlehem in Judah to the remote
parts of the hill country of Ephraim, from which I come. I went to Bethlehem in Judah,
and I am going [j]to the house of the Lord,[1] [g]but no one has taken me into his house. **19** We
have straw and feed for our donkeys, with bread and wine for me and your female servant
and the young man with your servants. [k]There is no lack of anything." **20** And the old man
said, [l]"Peace be to you; I will care for all your wants. [m]Only, do not spend the night in the
square." **21** So he brought him into his house and gave the donkeys feed. [n]And they washed
their feet, and ate and drank.

Gibeah's Crime

22 As they were [o]making their hearts merry, behold, the men of the city, worthless fellows,
[p]surrounded the house, beating on the door. And they said to the old man, the master of
the house, "Bring out the man who came into your house, that we may know him." **23** And
the man, the master of the house, went out to them and said to them, "No, my brothers,
[q]do not act so wickedly; since this man has come into my house, [r]do not do this vile thing.
24 [s]Behold, here are my virgin daughter and his concubine. Let me bring them out now.
[t]Violate them and do with them what seems good to you, but against this man [r]do not
do this outrageous thing." **25** But the men would not listen to him. So the man seized his
concubine and made her go out to them. And they knew her and abused her all night until
the morning. And as the dawn began to break, they let her go. **26** And as morning appeared,
the woman came and fell down at the door of the man's house where her master was, until
it was light.
27 And her master rose up in the morning, and when he opened the doors of the house
and went out to go on his way, behold, there was his concubine lying at the door of the
house, with her hands on the threshold. **28** He said to her, "Get up, let us be going." [u]But
there was no answer. Then he put her on the donkey, and the man rose up and went away

[1] Septuagint *my home*; compare verse 29

8 [c]ver. 5
10 [d]See Josh. 15:8, 63
12 [e]Josh. 18:28
13 [f]Josh. 18:25
15 [g]ver. 18
16 [h]ver. 1; See Josh. 24:33 [i]ver. 14; ch. 20:4
18 [j]ch. 18:31 [g][See ver. 15 above]
19 [k][ch. 18:10]
20 [l]Gen. 43:23 [m]Gen. 19:2
21 [n]Gen. 18:4; 24:32; 43:24; [John 13:5]
22 [o]See ver. 6 [p]ch. 20:5; [Gen. 19:4]
23 [q]Gen. 19:7 [r]ch. 20:6; Gen. 34:7; Deut. 22:21; 2 Sam. 13:12; [Josh. 7:15]
24 [s][Gen. 19:8] [t]Gen. 34:2; Deut. 21:14 [r][See ver. 23 above]
28 [u][ch. 20:5]

19:10–12 Jebus (that is, Jerusalem). Jerusalem was at this time in the hands of the Jebusites and so is referred to as a **city of foreigners** (see note on 1:8). **Gibeah** was about 4 miles (6 km) north of Jerusalem. Archaeologists have discovered a massive-destruction level (c. 1100 B.C.) at the site of Gibeah, which may correspond with the destruction in chs. 19–20. The city was soon rebuilt, with an imposing rectangular fortress dating to the time of Saul (Gibeah was Saul's hometown; 1 Sam. 10:26). The Levite considered Gibeah a safer place to spend the night than Jerusalem, because it was a Benjaminite city (Judg. 19:14, 16); this, however, was a tragically fatal misjudgment.

19:16 old man . . . sojourning in Gibeah. In a striking irony—and a commentary on the degenerate state of affairs in Israel—the Levite found hospitality, not from the residents of Gibeah, but from an outsider, a sojourner. **hill country of Ephraim.** Cf. v. 1.

19:22–26 The "hospitality" offered by Gibeah was no hospitality at all; it was the "hospitality" of Sodom (cf. Genesis 19), an outrageous affront to the

29[v]ch. 20:6; [1 Sam. 11:7]
30[w][Hos. 9:9; 10:9] [x]ch. 20:7

Chapter 20
1[y]ch. 21:5; [Josh. 22:12; 1 Sam. 11:7] [z]1 Sam. 3:20; 2 Sam. 3:10; 24:2 [a][1 Sam. 7:5; 10:17]
2[b]1 Sam. 14:38 [c]ver. 15, 17, 25, 35, 46; See ch. 8:10
4[d]ch. 19:15
5[e]ch. 19:22, 25, 26
6[f]ch. 19:29 [g]See ch. 19:23
7[h]ch. 19:30

to his home. 29 And when he entered his house, he took a knife, and taking hold of his
concubine he [v]divided her, limb by limb, into twelve pieces, and sent her throughout all
the territory of Israel. 30 [w]And all who saw it said, "Such a thing has never happened or
been seen from the day that the people of Israel came up out of the land of Egypt until
this day; [x]consider it, take counsel, and speak."

Israel's War with the Tribe of Benjamin

20 Then [y]all the people of Israel came out, [z]from Dan to Beersheba, including the land
of Gilead, and the congregation assembled as one man to the LORD at [a]Mizpah.
2 And the [b]chiefs of all the people, of all the tribes of Israel, presented themselves in the
assembly of the people of God, 400,000 men on foot [c]that drew the sword. 3 (Now the people
of Benjamin heard that the people of Israel had gone up to Mizpah.) And the people of
Israel said, "Tell us, how did this evil happen?" 4 And the Levite, the husband of the woman
who was murdered, answered and said, [d]"I came to Gibeah that belongs to Benjamin, I
and my concubine, to spend the night. 5 [e]And the leaders of Gibeah rose against me and
surrounded the house against me by night. They meant to kill me, and they violated my
concubine, and she is dead. 6 [f]So I took hold of my concubine and cut her in pieces and
sent her throughout all the country of the inheritance of Israel, for they have committed
abomination and [g]outrage in Israel. 7 Behold, you people of Israel, all of you, [h]give your
advice and counsel here."
8 And all the people arose as one man, saying, "None of us will go to his tent, and none

Levite and especially to his concubine. This section closely echoes Gen. 19:4–9; indeed, it is likely that the author intentionally patterned this text after the Genesis account, as if to say, "Things are as bad now as they were in the days of Sodom and Gomorrah!"

19:22 worthless fellows. Literally, "sons of Belial." In the OT, the term "Belial" is used descriptively, speaking of perverted or worthless people (cf. 20:13; 1 Sam. 10:27; 1 Kings 21:13). In intertestamental literature, the term was used of Satan, and this is Paul's sense in 2 Cor. 6:15: "What accord has Christ with Belial?" **that we may know him**. The word "know" was the normal Hebrew euphemism for sexual relations (cf. Gen. 4:1). The same expression is found in Gen. 19:5, where the men of Sodom wanted to have homosexual relations with Lot's guests.

19:27–30 The Levite's matter-of-fact reaction to his concubine's death illustrates his callousness. His gruesome response was to cut her **into twelve pieces** and send them around to the 12 tribes to rally them against Gibeah. Saul later did the same thing with a yoke of oxen (1 Sam. 11:7); a similar practice is known from Mari, in Mesopotamia. **has never happened or been seen**. It is unclear what was being referred to here (the outrageous actions of the men of Gibeah or the cutting up of the concubine), but it is more likely the former (cf. Judg. 20:10).

20:1–48 *Civil War.* Gibeah, site of the moral outrage (ch. 19), was a Benjaminite city, and so an assembly of all Israel convened at Mizpah to unite against Benjamin (20:1–11). However, the Benjaminites, who apparently were not at the assembly (v. 3), refused to deliver the inhabitants of Gibeah to them, but rather prepared for battle (vv. 12–17). The battle was joined, Judah going first (v. 18), and the Israelites were repelled twice by the Benjaminites at Gibeah (vv. 19–28). Each time, God directed the Israelites to continue the fight (vv. 23, 28). The third time, Benjamin was routed and subjected to the complete annihilation that earlier had been reserved exclusively for the Canaanites (vv. 29–48). Readers are not told whether God approved of this; certainly he did not explicitly command it. It was a grim measure of Israel's apostasy and the attendant chaos that complete annihilation now was directed internally, against fellow Israelites.

20:1–2 from Dan to Beersheba. This phrase was commonly used to speak of the entire land of Israel, from north to south (cf. 1 Sam. 3:20; 2 Sam. 24:2; 1 Kings 4:25). **assembly**. The Hebrew word (*qahal*) denotes a specially summoned gathering, usually for a religious (Num. 16:3; 1 Chron. 28:8) or military purpose (Num. 22:4, "horde"; 1 Sam. 17:47). Here, the Israelites gathered for war against the tribe of Benjamin (see map to the right).

20:9 The tribes agreed to send a tenth of their men (v. 10), chosen **by lot**. Far from this being a matter of chance, God was always in control of the lot

Dan's Migration and Israel's War with Benjamin

The final chapters of Judges record the migration of the tribe of Dan to the north, and Israel's war with Benjamin for deeds committed against a Levite passing through Gibeah. After refusing to surrender the perpetrators to judgment, the Benjaminites were defeated by the other tribes, and the remaining Benjaminites fled to the rock of Rimmon. In order to rescue the Benjaminites from being completely wiped out, the other tribes provided wives captured from Jabesh-gilead and Shiloh.

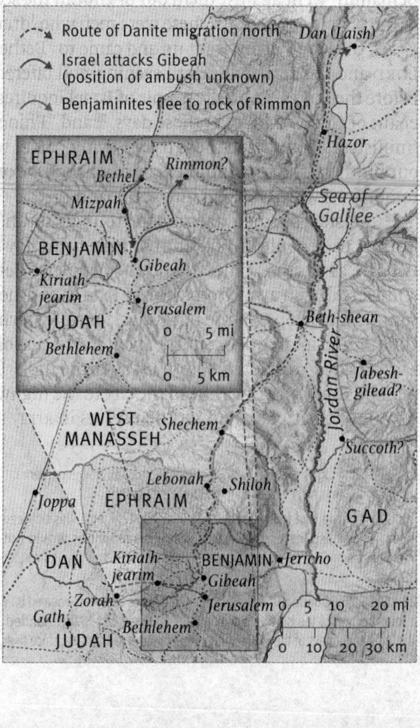

of us will return to his house. **9** But now this is what we will do to Gibeah: we will go up
against it by lot, **10** and we will take ten men of a hundred throughout all the tribes of
Israel, and a hundred of a thousand, and a thousand of ten thousand, to bring provisions
for the people, that when they come they may repay Gibeah of Benjamin, for all the outrage that they have committed in Israel." **11** So all the men of Israel gathered against the
city, united as one man.

12 [i]And the tribes of Israel sent men through all the tribe of Benjamin, saying, "What
evil is this that has taken place among you? **13** Now therefore give up the men, [j]the worthless fellows in Gibeah, that we may put them to death [k]and purge evil from Israel." But
the Benjaminites would not listen to the voice of their brothers, the people of Israel.
14 Then the people of Benjamin came together out of the cities to Gibeah to go out to
battle against the people of Israel. **15** And the people of Benjamin mustered out of their
cities on that day [l]26,000 men [m]who drew the sword, besides the inhabitants of Gibeah,
who mustered 700 chosen men. **16** Among all these were 700 chosen men who were
[n]left-handed; every one could sling a stone at a hair and not miss. **17** And the men of
Israel, apart from Benjamin, mustered [m]400,000 men who drew the sword; all these
were men of war.

18 The people of Israel arose and went up to [o]Bethel and inquired of God, [p]"Who shall
go up first for us to fight against the people of Benjamin?" And the LORD said, [p]"Judah
shall go up first."

19 Then the people of Israel rose in the morning and encamped against Gibeah. **20** And
the men of Israel went out to fight against Benjamin, and the men of Israel drew up the
battle line against them at Gibeah. **21** [q]The people of Benjamin came out of Gibeah and
destroyed on that day 22,000 men of the Israelites. **22** But the people, the men of Israel,
took courage, and again formed the battle line in the same place where they had formed
it on the first day. **23** [r]And the people of Israel went up and wept before the LORD until the
evening. And they inquired of the LORD, "Shall we again draw near to fight against our
brothers, the people of Benjamin?" And the LORD said, "Go up against them."

24 So the people of Israel came near against the people of Benjamin the second day. **25** And
Benjamin [s]went against them out of Gibeah the second day, and destroyed 18,000 men
of the people of Israel. All these were men who [t]drew the sword. **26** Then all the people of
Israel, the whole army, went up and came to [u]Bethel and wept. They sat there before the
LORD and fasted that day until evening, and offered burnt offerings and peace offerings
before the LORD. **27** And the people of Israel inquired of the LORD [v](for the ark of the covenant of God was there in those days, **28** and [w]Phinehas the son of Eleazar, son of Aaron,
[x]ministered before it in those days), saying, "Shall we go out once more to battle against
our brothers, the people of Benjamin, or shall we cease?" And the LORD said, "Go up, for
tomorrow I will give them into your hand."

29 [y]So Israel set men in ambush around Gibeah. **30** And the people of Israel went up
against the people of Benjamin on the third day and set themselves in array against
Gibeah, as at other times. **31** And the people of Benjamin went out against the people
and were drawn away from the city. And as at other times they began to strike and kill
some of the people in the highways, [z]one of which goes up to [a]Bethel and the other to
Gibeah, and in the open country, about thirty men of Israel. **32** And the people of Benjamin
said, [b]"They are routed before us, as at the first." But the people of Israel said, "Let us
flee and draw them away from the city to the highways." **33** And all the men of Israel rose
up out of their place and set themselves in array at Baal-tamar, and the men of Israel

12 [i][Deut. 13:14; Josh. 22:13, 16]
13 [j]ch. 19:22; See Deut. 13:13 [k]Deut. 13:5; 17:2
15 [l][Num. 1:37; 26:41] [m]ver. 2
16 [n]ch. 3:15; [1 Chr. 12:2]
17 [m][See ver. 15 above]
18 [o]ver. 26, 31 [p][ch. 1:1]
21 [q]ver. 25
23 [r]ver. 26-28
25 [s]ver. 21 [t]ver. 2
26 [u]ver. 18, 31
27 [v][Josh. 18:1; 1 Sam. 4:3, 4]
28 [w]Num. 25:7; 31:6; Josh. 24:33 [x]Deut. 10:8; 18:5, 7
29 [y][Josh. 8:4]
31 [z]ch. 21:19 [a]ver. 18, 26
32 [b][Josh. 8:5, 6]

(cf. Num. 26:55; Josh. 14:2; 18:6, 8, 10; Prov. 16:33). However, perhaps significantly, he is not mentioned in this instance.

20:12–14 purge evil from Israel (cf. Deut. 13:5; 17:7; etc.). This evil deed is seen as polluting the whole people. **But the Benjaminites would not listen.** Benjamin's decision to protect the evildoers sets the stage for further horrors.

20:15–16 26,000 men. The Benjaminite force, large as it was, equaled only a small fraction of the Israelite coalition (400,000 men; v. 17). **left-handed.** The left-handedness of the **700** expert slingers was an advantage, since their shots would come at an unaccustomed angle. Ironically, the name "Benjamin" means "son of the right (hand)."

20:18 Judah . . . first. As before (1:1–2), Judah took the lead. This is the tribe from which David, the greatest embodiment of the monarchy (what the Israelites most lacked at this time), would come.

20:25–26 The fasting and sacrificing of the Israelites is very rare in this period. See note on 2:5.

20:28 Phinehas. Cf. Num. 25:6–11.

34[c]ver. 41
35[d]ver. 2
37[e][Josh. 8:19]
39[f]ver. 31, 32
40[g][Josh. 8:20]
41[h]ver. 34
42[i][Josh. 8:15, 24]
45[i][See ver. 42 above] [j]ch. 21:13; Josh. 15:32
47[i][See ver. 42 above] [j][See ver. 45 above]

Chapter 21

1[k]ver. 18; ch. 20:1
2[l]ch. 20:18, 26, 31
4[m][2 Sam. 24:25]
5[n][ch. 5:23]
6[o]ver. 15
7[p]ver. 16
8[q]1 Sam. 11:1; 31:11-13

who were in ambush rushed out of their place from Maareh-geba.[1] 34 And there came against Gibeah 10,000 chosen men out of all Israel, and the battle was hard, [c]but the Benjaminites did not know that disaster was close upon them. 35 And the LORD defeated Benjamin before Israel, and the people of Israel destroyed 25,100 men of Benjamin that day. All these were men who [d]drew the sword. 36 So the people of Benjamin saw that they were defeated.

The men of Israel gave ground to Benjamin, because they trusted the men in ambush whom they had set against Gibeah. 37 [e]Then the men in ambush hurried and rushed against Gibeah; the men in ambush moved out and struck all the city with the edge of the sword. 38 Now the appointed signal between the men of Israel and the men in the main ambush was that when they made a great cloud of smoke rise up out of the city 39 the men of Israel should turn in battle. Now Benjamin had begun to strike and kill about thirty men of Israel. They said, [f]"Surely they are defeated before us, as in the first battle." 40 But when the signal began to rise out of the city in a column of smoke, the Benjaminites looked behind them, and behold, [g]the whole of the city went up in smoke to heaven. 41 Then the men of Israel turned, and the men of Benjamin were dismayed, [h]for they saw that disaster was close upon them. 42 Therefore they turned their backs before the men of Israel in [i]the direction of the wilderness, but the battle overtook them. And those who came out of the cities were destroying them in their midst. 43 Surrounding the Benjaminites, they pursued them and trod them down from Nohah[2] as far as opposite Gibeah on the east. 44 Eighteen thousand men of Benjamin fell, all of them men of valor. 45 And they turned [i]and fled toward the wilderness to the rock of [j]Rimmon. Five thousand men of them were cut down in the highways. And they were pursued hard to Gidom, and 2,000 men of them were struck down. 46 So all who fell that day of Benjamin were 25,000 men who drew the sword, all of them men of valor. 47 But 600 men turned and [i]fled toward the wilderness to the rock of [j]Rimmon and remained at the rock of Rimmon four months. 48 And the men of Israel turned back against the people of Benjamin and struck them with the edge of the sword, the city, men and beasts and all that they found. And all the towns that they found they set on fire.

Wives Provided for the Tribe of Benjamin

21 Now the men of Israel had sworn [k]at Mizpah, "No one of us shall give his daughter in marriage to Benjamin." 2 And the people came to [l]Bethel and sat there till evening before God, and they lifted up their voices and wept bitterly. 3 And they said, "O LORD, the God of Israel, why has this happened in Israel, that today there should be one tribe lacking in Israel?" 4 And the next day the people rose early and [m]built there an altar and offered burnt offerings and peace offerings. 5 And the people of Israel said, "Which of all the tribes of Israel did not come up in the assembly to the LORD?" [n]For they had taken a great oath concerning him who did not come up to the LORD to Mizpah, saying, "He shall surely be put to death." 6 And the people of Israel [o]had compassion for Benjamin their brother and said, "One tribe is cut off from Israel this day. 7 [p]What shall we do for wives for those who are left, since we have sworn by the LORD that we will not give them any of our daughters for wives?"

8 And they said, "What one is there of the tribes of Israel that did not come up to the LORD to Mizpah?" And behold, no one had come to the camp from [q]Jabesh-gilead, to the assembly. 9 For when the people were mustered, behold, not one of the inhabitants of

[1] Some Septuagint manuscripts *place west of Geba* [2] Septuagint; Hebrew *[at their] resting place*

20:35 the LORD defeated Benjamin. Despite Israel's apostasy, God still intervened in its affairs and gave victory.

20:38 ambush. Cf. the ambush set for Ai in Josh. 8:17–22.

20:47 Despite the rout, **600 men** of Benjamin survived to become the core of the renewed tribe (21:13–15).

21:1–24 *Chaotic Aftermath.* The war against Benjamin hardly solved Israel's spiritual and social problems. Chaos continued to reign. After the defeat of Benjamin, the remaining Israelites were regretful that one of the tribes might cease to exist (vv. 1–7). Thus, ch. 21 shows the provision for Benjamin's continued survival. Four hundred wives were obtained through a punitive action against Jabesh-gilead, which had not joined in the original battle (vv. 8–15). Two hundred more wives were obtained through an action at Shiloh, legitimized on more flimsy grounds (vv. 16–24). The book ends (v. 25) with one final editorial comment about the apostasy in the land.

21:1 had sworn. This oath was presumably made when the people gathered together at **Mizpah** (cf. 20:1).

21:5 great oath. A second, "greater" oath provided the justification for raiding Jabesh-gilead to provide wives for the Benjaminites. No doubt all the tribes

[q]Jabesh-gilead was there. 10 So the congregation sent 12,000 of their bravest men there
and commanded them, [r]"Go and strike the inhabitants of Jabesh-gilead with the edge
of the sword; also the women and the little ones. 11 This is what you shall do: [s]every male
and every woman that has lain with a male you shall devote to destruction." 12 And they
found among the inhabitants of Jabesh-gilead 400 young virgins who had not known a
man by lying with him, and they brought them to the camp at [t]Shiloh, which is in the
land of Canaan.

13 Then the whole congregation sent word to the people of Benjamin who were at the
[u]rock of Rimmon and [v]proclaimed peace to them. 14 And Benjamin returned at that time.
And they gave them the women whom they had saved alive of the women of Jabesh-gilead,
but they were not enough for them. 15 And the people [w]had compassion on Benjamin
because the LORD had made a breach in the tribes of Israel.

16 Then the elders of the congregation said, [x]"What shall we do for wives for those who
are left, since the women are destroyed out of Benjamin?" 17 And they said, "There must
be an inheritance for the survivors of Benjamin, that a tribe not be blotted out from Israel.
18 Yet we cannot give them wives from our daughters." [y]For the people of Israel had sworn,
"Cursed be he who gives a wife to Benjamin." 19 So they said, "Behold, there is the yearly
feast of the LORD at Shiloh, which is north of Bethel, on the east of [z]the highway that goes
up from Bethel to Shechem, and south of Lebonah." 20 And they commanded the people of
Benjamin, saying, "Go and lie in ambush in the vineyards 21 and watch. If the daughters of
Shiloh come out to [a]dance in the dances, then come out of the vineyards and snatch each
man his wife from the daughters of Shiloh, and go to the land of Benjamin. 22 And when
their fathers or their brothers come to complain to us, we will say to them, 'Grant them
graciously to us, because we did not take for each man of them his wife in battle, neither
did you give them to them, else you would now be guilty.' " 23 And the people of Benjamin
did so and took their wives, according to their number, from the dancers whom they carried
off. Then they went and returned to their inheritance [b]and rebuilt the towns and lived in
them. 24 And the people of Israel departed from there at that time, every man to his tribe
and family, and they went out from there every man to his inheritance.

25 [c]In those days there was no king in Israel. Everyone did what was right in his own
eyes.

9 [q][See ver. 8 above]
10 [r][ver. 5]
11 [s]Num. 31:17
12 [t]Josh. 18:1
13 [u]ch. 20:47 [v]Deut. 20:10
15 [w]ver. 6
16 [x]ver. 7
18 [y]ver. 1
19 [z][ch. 20:31]
21 [a]ch. 11:34; Ex. 15:20
23 [b][ch. 20:48]
25 [c]ch. 17:6; 18:1; 19:1

were expected to participate, since all 12 had been sent the gruesome remains of the Levite's concubine (19:29).

21:10–11 devote to destruction. This phrase is found throughout the book of Joshua describing the Israelites' destruction of the Canaanites (e.g., Josh. 6:17–18; 10:28, 35, 39, 40–41; 11:11, 20; see note on Deut. 20:16–18). Here, ironically, the total destruction was directed against an Israelite city, not a Canaanite one; Israel acted on its own, without God's command to take such action. The rebuilt city of **Jabesh-gilead** figures in Saul's history (1 Sam. 11:1–11; 31:11–13).

21:24 every man to his inheritance. The exact same statement is found at the end of Joshua (Josh. 24:28), but now things were far worse.

21:25 *Final Verdict.* The final editorial comment echoes earlier ones (17:6; 18:1; 19:1; see chart, p. 467). Israel's apostasy had reached the depths, and the stage was set for the coming of a godly king, David, a man after God's own heart with whom God would make an everlasting covenant (cf. Ruth 4:17; 1 Samuel 16; 2 Samuel 7; see Introduction: Purpose, Occasion, and Background). The sympathetic reader who has followed the whole narrative is left yearning for such a king.

INTRODUCTION TO

RUTH

Author and Title

The book is named for its main character, Ruth, a Moabite widow who married the Bethlehemite Boaz. She became an ancestor of King David (4:17, 22) and thus an ancestor of the Messiah (Matt. 1:1, 5–6). The author of Ruth is never named in the Bible. According to rabbinic tradition (Babylonian Talmud, *Baba Bathra* 14a–15b), Samuel is the author. This is unlikely, however, since Samuel died before David actually became king, and Ruth 4:17–22 implies that David's kingship was an established fact at the time of writing.

Date

The mention of David (4:17) and his genealogy (4:18–22) places the writing after David's accession to the throne (2 Samuel 2) in c. 1010 B.C. The narrator's explanation of a custom once current "in former times in Israel" (Ruth 4:7) distances him from the story's events, which occurred "in the days when the judges ruled" (1:1). Therefore, the book could have been written any time after 1010 B.C. by an author using accurate oral or written material as historical sources.

Theme

This book highlights how God's people experience his sovereignty, wisdom, and covenant kindness. These often come disguised in hard circumstances and are mediated through the kindness of others.

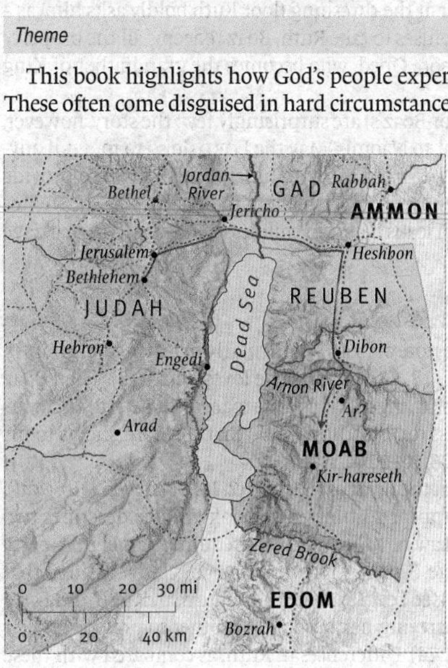

The Setting of Ruth
Set in the period of the judges, the book of Ruth records how a famine in Judah forces Naomi and her husband to leave Israel and move to Moab, where their sons marry Moabite women. When Naomi's husband and sons die, she decides to return to her home in Bethlehem in Judah, and her daughter-in-law Ruth chooses to go with her.

Family of Ruth

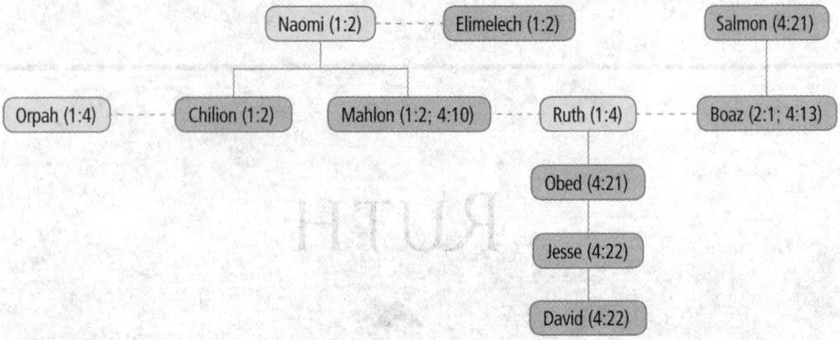

Purpose, Occasion, and Background

Given the book of Ruth's interest in all Israel (4:7, 11), it may have been written in hopes that the 12 tribes, which divided into two nations c. 930 B.C. (see 1 Kings 12:1–20), would reunite. The story itself takes place in the time of the judges (after the conquest and before c. 1050 B.C.), before a king was in place to reign over a united kingdom. This book explains the providential ancestry of David, who would become such a king.

Content

In the period of the judges, Elimelech, Naomi, and their sons leave Bethlehem because of a famine to sojourn in Moab (see map, p. 475). Naomi's husband, Elimelech, dies there. Mahlon and Chilion, the sons, marry Moabite women, Ruth and Orpah. Ten years later the sons die too, leaving no children. Naomi is bereft of family (1:1–5). Learning that the famine in Israel is over, she decides to return to Bethlehem; Orpah stays behind, but Ruth accompanies Naomi (1:6–22). At harvest time, Ruth goes to glean in a field that happens to belong to Elimelech's relative, Boaz (2:1–23). Naomi knows he is an eligible kinsman-redeemer. Following Naomi's daring plan, in a midnight encounter at the threshing floor Ruth boldly asks him, as a redeemer, to marry her (3:1–18). After a closer kinsman refuses to take Ruth, Boaz redeems all the property of the deceased and marries Ruth (4:1–12). They have a son, Obed, who becomes the grandfather of King David (4:13–22).

Ruth's words in the book (as compared with Naomi's or Boaz's) are surprisingly few; the story, however, hangs on them. Ruth expresses her lifelong commitment to Naomi, "May the LORD do so to me . . . if anything but death parts me from you" (1:17), which takes her from Moab to Judah. She resolves to provide for Naomi ("Let me go . . . and glean," 2:2), which brings her from Bethlehem to Boaz's field. She invites Boaz to "spread your wings over your servant" (3:9), which leads her from childless widowhood to marriage and motherhood (4:13).

Key Themes

1. *Kindness.* Ruth shows Naomi kindness (Hb. *hesed*, see note on 3:10), particularly in leaving her country and family to care for her mother-in-law (1:16–17; 2:11, 18, 23), because she loves her (4:15). Then Boaz shows kindness (see note on 2:20) in his welcome to Ruth, acting as a kinsman-redeemer (4:9–10) and marrying Ruth (4:13). Human kindness reflects the kindness (or "steadfast love") that the Lord shows to his people (cf. Ex. 15:13; Deut. 7:8–9; Ps. 103:4; 106:7, 10; 136:10–15).

2. *Redemption.* Redemption is bound to kindness and is at the heart of the story (2:20). "Redeem" (Hb. *ga'al*), "redeemer" (Hb. *go'el*), and "redemption" (Hb. *ge'ullah*) appear 23 times. The book of Ruth describes two legal institutions combined in one practice (which the Law of Moses does not require), namely, property redemption by a near kinsman and the "levirate" marriage. Property redemption by a relative assured that land would not remain in perpetuity outside the family (see Lev. 25:23–25). Levirate marriage (from Latin *levir*, "husband's brother") involves a childless widow marrying her husband's brother to provide an heir for the dead husband (Deut. 25:5–6; cf. note on Matt. 22:24). Differences in Ruth, as compared with these laws, reflect customs applicable to particular circumstances. Boaz, a close relative (but not the closest), redeemed the property (Ruth 4:9), married Ruth (4:10, 13), and fathered Obed (4:13, 17), who became heir to the property of the deceased.

Once redemption occurred, Ruth and Naomi's desperate conditions radically changed (4:13–17). This reversal is highlighted by contrasts: living/dead (1:8; 2:20); find/seek rest (1:9; 3:1); pleasant/bitter (1:20); full/empty (1:21; 3:17; see note on 4:15); last/first kindness (3:10). The resolution to the narrative conflict is Boaz's act of redemption (4:9–10), resulting in blessing for Ruth (in marriage, conception, and giving birth; 4:13) and for Naomi (in restored and nourished life in her old age; 4:14–15). Redemption also brought blessing to the community (4:11–12) and—through David—to the nation (4:14, 17).

History of Salvation Summary

As a foreigner and ancestor of David (4:17, 22), Ruth is a forerunner of the universal blessing that Christ's redemptive work ushered in. Many OT prophecies anticipate a new David (e.g., Jer. 33:15, 17; Ezek. 37:24; Hos. 3:5; Zech. 12:7–10) reigning over Israel and incorporating the Gentiles into his benevolent empire (e.g., Isa. 55:3–5; Amos 9:11–12). This expectation is fulfilled in David's "son," Jesus the Christ (or Messiah; cf. Matt. 1:1–6; Luke 3:31–33; Acts 13:23; Rom. 1:3–5). In him, the "gospel" preached beforehand to Abraham (Gen. 12:3; Rom. 15:8–12; Gal. 3:8), that all nations will be blessed, is fully realized (Rom. 4:9–12; Gal. 3:7–9, 14). Through Christ, David's throne is reestablished forever (Acts 15:16; Rev. 3:7; 5:5; 22:16). Christ's reign is universal (Matt. 28:18–20; Rom. 1:5; 15:8–12). In him, redeemed people of all nations, no longer strangers and aliens, become fellow citizens in God's household (Eph. 2:11–22). (For an explanation of the "History of Salvation," see the Overview of the Bible, pp. 23–26. See also History of Salvation in the Old Testament: Preparing the Way for Christ, pp. 2635–2661.)

Literary Features

In terms of compact storytelling, Ruth is a masterpiece of narrative art. It is densely packed, yet the charm of the book is evident even to the most unsophisticated reader. The book of Ruth is the classic love story of the Bible. Few stories in the Bible are told from a woman's viewpoint, but in the story of Ruth, not only is a woman the protagonist but the world of the story is a woman's world, and the writer gives attention to feminine values and feelings. Of course Boaz in his role as kinsman-redeemer cuts a striking figure as a man who embodies the Lord's own kindness. The story exalts virtuous womanhood and strong manhood.

The overall genre is story or narrative, but several further subtypes converge as well. Ruth is a love story. It is also an idyll, i.e., a brief story describing a simple, pleasant aspect of rural and domestic life. As that definition suggests, Ruth has affinities with pastoral (rural) literature, and in this case the idealized rural world provides a setting for the idealized romance of the book: even though readers know from the first verse that the story is set in tumultuous times, these do not come into view. The story is also a hero story built around the life of an exemplary heroine as well as featuring an idealized male hero. Boaz is a rarity in the Bible, a character who gets a uniformly positive portrayal; most other characters reveal their flaws. But this reflects the literary function of Boaz as the embodiment of the Lord's kindness.

The plot of the story of Ruth is a quest story in which the stated goal is to find Ruth a home (1:9 and 3:1). The plot follows the conventional U-shape of literary "comedy," with events first descending into potential tragedy and then rising to a happy ending as obstacles to fulfillment are gradually overcome.

Outline

I. Introduction: Naomi Bereft of Family (1:1–5)

II. Scene 1: Naomi Returns to Bethlehem with Ruth (1:6–22)

III. Scene 2: Ruth Gleans in Boaz's Field (2:1–23)

IV. Scene 3: Ruth, at the Threshing Floor, Asks Boaz to Marry Her (3:1–18)

V. Scene 4: Boaz Arranges Redemption at the Gate (4:1–12)

VI. Conclusion: Naomi Blessed with a New Family (4:13–17)

VII. Genealogy: Extended Blessing (4:18–22)

RUTH

Naomi Widowed

1 In the days [a]when the judges ruled there was [b]a famine in the land, and a man of
[c]Bethlehem in Judah went to sojourn in the country of Moab, he and his wife and his
two sons. 2 The name of the man was Elimelech and the name of his wife Naomi, and the
names of his two sons were Mahlon and Chilion. They were [d]Ephrathites from Bethlehem
in Judah. They went into the country of Moab and remained there. 3 But Elimelech, the
husband of Naomi, died, and she was left with her two sons. 4 These took Moabite wives;
the name of the one was Orpah and the name of the other Ruth. They lived there about
ten years, 5 and both Mahlon and Chilion died, so that the woman was left without her
two sons and her husband.

Ruth's Loyalty to Naomi

6 Then she arose with her daughters-in-law to return from the country of Moab, for she
had heard in the fields of Moab that [e]the LORD had visited his people and [f]given them food.
7 So she set out from the place where she was with her two daughters-in-law, and they went
on the way to return to the land of Judah. 8 But Naomi said to her two daughters-in-law,
"Go, return each of you to her mother's house. May the LORD [g]deal kindly with you, as you
have dealt with [h]the dead and with me. 9 The LORD grant that you may find [i]rest, each of

Chapter 1
1 [a]Judg. 2:16 [b]Gen. 12:10; 26:1; 43:1; 2 Kgs. 8:1 [c]See Judg. 17:7
2 [d]Gen. 35:19
6 [e]Ex. 3:16; 4:31; Luke 1:68 [f]Ps. 132:15
8 [g]Josh. 2:12, 14; Judg. 1:24 [h]ver. 5; ch. 2:20
9 [i]ch. 3:1

1:1–5 *Introduction: Naomi Bereft of Family.* This brief introduction presents Naomi's loss of her family. The similar phrases "a man . . . his wife and his two sons" (v. 1) and "the woman . . . two sons and her husband" (v. 5) frame the introduction.

1:1 days when the judges ruled. This period of spiritual, social, and political unrest (Judg. 2:6–3:6; 21:25b) engendered the desire for a king (Judg. 21:25) who could give rest (like that finally achieved by David; Ruth 4:17, 22; 2 Sam. 7:11; 1 Kings 5:4). A **famine** was sometimes a divine scourge (Deut. 11:14; 32:24; cf. Lev. 26:3–4), but it could also advance God's purposes, as it did for the sons of Israel in Joseph's time (Gen. 42:5; 45:5–8; Ps. 105:16–17, 23). **Bethlehem** (lit., "house of bread/food") is often associated with David in the OT (e.g., 1 Sam. 20:6) and with Jesus' birth in the NT (Matt. 2:1; Luke 2:4; John 7:42). Because of Bethlehem's location in a fertile region, Rehoboam turned it into a fortress city (2 Chron. 11:5–12). **to sojourn** (Hb. *gur*). To be a resident alien (Deut. 24:17), as in times of famine (Gen. 12:10; 26:1–3; 47:4; see also 2 Kings 8:1) or war (2 Sam. 4:3). **Moab**. A country across the Dead Sea from Judah, and one of Israel's traditional enemies (see Num. 22:1–25:9).

1:2 This verse lists the clan (**Ephrathites**), city (**Bethlehem**), and tribal territory (**Judah**) of the family of David (see note on 4:11; cf. 1 Sam. 17:12), and the family of the coming Messiah (Mic. 5:2).

1:4 Moabite wives. Ruth's husband was Mahlon (4:10). There was no formal prohibition against marrying Moabites (cf. Canaanites in Deut. 7:1–4). However, marriage to Moabites was discouraged because of their commitment to other gods (such as Molech), the Balaam debacle, Israel's debauchery with Moabite women in the wilderness, and the 10-generation Moabite male exclusion from the assembly of the Lord (Numbers 22–25; Deut. 23:3–7; Ezra 9:2, 12; 10:44; Neh. 13:25). There is a progression in the words "sojourn" (Ruth 1:1), "remained" (1:2), and **lived there**, or "settled down there" (1:4). **Ten years**, and no children, recalls the barren Sarah, who after 10 years gave Abraham her servant to have a son (Gen. 16:3; see notes on Ruth 4:11; 4:13; 4:18–22).

1:5 left without. She was the last remaining person in her family (cf. 2 Sam. 14:7); Elimelech had no immediate (living) brothers (see notes on Ruth 2:20; 3:12–13). A childless widow was in a precarious position, lacking long-term financial support. Thus she needed community help (Gen. 38:6–11; Deut. 25:5–10; 1 Kings 17:17–20; Luke 7:11–17; 1 Tim. 5:4–5).

1:6–22 *Scene 1: Naomi Returns to Bethlehem with Ruth.* This first scene relates Ruth's kindness in returning with Naomi to Bethlehem. The scene is framed by the expression "return/returned from the country of Moab" (vv. 6, 22).

1:6 The key word **return** (Hb. *shub*, also rendered in the ESV as "turn, go, or bring back") recurs 12 times in this chapter (vv. 6, 7, 8, 10, 11, 12, 15 [twice], 16, 21, 22 [twice]; see note on 4:15). **the LORD had visited**. God sent rains to water the crops; now, in the springtime, there was a long-anticipated harvest and **food**, or "bread" (Hb. *lekhem*), a play on words with Beth*lehem* (see note on 1:1).

1:7 The recurring kinship expressions **daughters-in-law** (vv. 6, 7, 8) and "my daughters" (vv. 11, 12, 13) underscore Naomi's attachment to them. **Land of Judah** likely denotes the tribal area (cf. 4:7, referring to Israel, the whole people) as opposed to the southern kingdom (e.g., 2 Kings 23:24; 25:22).

1:8–9 return each of you to her mother's house. Naomi understands the crucial role of a mother in preparing a daughter for marriage and motherhood (cf. Gen. 24:28, 67; Ruth 4:16–17; Song 3:4; 8:2; Titus 2:3–4); she hopes that both Ruth and Orpah will remarry and have children. Since Ruth's father is still alive (Ruth 2:11), Naomi thinks that Ruth can return to his house (cf. Gen. 38:11; Lev. 22:13; Judg. 19:2–3). **the LORD deal kindly with you**. Naomi's desire is fulfilled when the Lord provides a family (see notes on Ruth 2:20; 3:10) through redemption (see Introduction: Key Themes). **find rest . . . in the house of her husband**. Naomi wishes for them security and stability in raising a family (3:1; see note on 4:13).

11[j]Gen. 38:11; Deut. 25:5
13[k]Judg. 2:15; [Job 19:21; Ps. 32:4; 38:2; 39:10]
15[l]Judg. 11:24; 1 Kgs. 11:7; Jer. 48:7, 13, 46
16[m][ch. 2:11, 12]
17[n]1 Sam. 3:17; 25:22; 2 Sam. 19:13; 1 Kgs. 2:23
18[o][Acts 21:14]
19[p][Matt. 21:10]
20[q]Ex. 15:23
21[r]Job 1:21
22[s]2 Sam. 21:9; [ch. 2:23]
Chapter 2
1[t]ch. 3:2, 12 [u]ch. 4:21; Matt. 1:5
2[v][Deut. 24:19] [w]ver. 10, 13

you in the house of her husband!" Then she kissed them, and they lifted up their voices and
wept. 10 And they said to her, "No, we will return with you to your people." 11 But Naomi
said, "Turn back, my daughters; why will you go with me? Have I yet sons in my womb
[j]that they may become your husbands? 12 Turn back, my daughters; go your way, for I am
too old to have a husband. If I should say I have hope, even if I should have a husband this
night and should bear sons, 13 would you therefore wait till they were grown? Would you
therefore refrain from marrying? No, my daughters, for it is exceedingly bitter to me for
your sake that [k]the hand of the LORD has gone out against me." 14 Then they lifted up their
voices and wept again. And Orpah kissed her mother-in-law, but Ruth clung to her.
15 And she said, "See, your sister-in-law has gone back to her people and to [l]her gods;
return after your sister-in-law." 16 But Ruth said, "Do not urge me to leave you or to return
from following you. For where you go I will go, and where you lodge I will lodge. [m]Your
people shall be my people, and your God my God. 17 Where you die I will die, and there
will I be buried. [n]May the LORD do so to me and more also if anything but death parts
me from you." 18 [o]And when Naomi saw that she was determined to go with her, she said
no more.

Naomi and Ruth Return

19 So the two of them went on until they came to Bethlehem. And when they came to
Bethlehem, [p]the whole town was stirred because of them. And the women said, "Is this
Naomi?" 20 She said to them, "Do not call me Naomi;[1] call me [q]Mara,[2] for the Almighty
has dealt very bitterly with me. 21 [r]I went away full, and the LORD has brought me back
empty. Why call me Naomi, when the LORD has testified against me and the Almighty
has brought calamity upon me?"
22 So Naomi returned, and Ruth the Moabite her daughter-in-law with her, who
returned from the country of Moab. And they came to Bethlehem [s]at the beginning of
barley harvest.

Ruth Meets Boaz

2 Now Naomi had [t]a relative of her husband's, a worthy man of the clan of Elimelech,
whose name was [u]Boaz. 2 And Ruth the Moabite said to Naomi, "Let me go to the field
and [v]glean among the ears of grain after him [w]in whose sight I shall find favor." And she

[1] *Naomi* means *pleasant* [2] *Mara* means *bitter*

1:11–13 sons in my womb . . . your husbands. Naomi's question assumes that the widows should marry their dead husbands' brothers (i.e., levirate marriage, Deut. 25:5–10); but they would have to wait for such brothers to be born, and she is considered **too old** to conceive. **bitter . . . that the hand of the LORD . . . against me**. Naomi is interpreting her hard circumstances as coming from God's enmity toward her; as the rest of the book will make plain, she is mistaken (see note on Ruth 1:20–21).

1:14 Orpah kissed Naomi farewell, even though she had promised to return with her (v. 10). However, **Ruth clung** (Hb. *dabaq*) to Naomi, an expression of loyalty and devotion (cf. Gen. 2:24, "hold fast" [Hb. *dabaq*]).

1:15 Returning to **her people** meant returning to **her gods**, since gods and territory went together (Judg. 10:6). Chemosh was the main god of Moab (Num. 21:29; 1 Kings 11:7, 33; Jer. 48:7). See note on Ruth 1:4.

1:16 Ruth's decision had far-reaching spiritual implications (2:12; Mark 10:29–31). Her confession of faith, **your people . . . my God**, recalls the central covenant promise: "I will be your God and you shall be my people" (Gen. 17:7–8; Ex. 6:7; Deut. 29:13; Jer. 24:7; 31:33; Hos. 2:23; Zech. 8:8; 2 Cor. 6:16; Rev. 21:7).

1:17 May the LORD do so to me and more also. Ruth binds herself by an oath that invites punishment if she is unfaithful. She swears this oath in the name of Yahweh (cf. 1 Sam. 3:17; 1 Kings 2:23), thereby owning him as her God.

1:19 The whole town was stirred perhaps with excitement (cf. 1 Sam. 4:5, "resounded") because of Ruth, but probably in agitation (cf. Isa. 22:2, "tumultuous") because of Naomi's arrival without her husband and sons (Ruth 1:1).

1:20–21 Naomi . . . Mara. As the ESV footnotes explain, the names mean "pleasant" and "bitter" (cf. v. 13). **Almighty . . . bitterly** (cf. Job 27:2). Naomi describes her family situation before her return (as **full**) and after her return (as **empty**). **the LORD has testified against me**. He has brought **calamity** (destitution, childlessness, widowhood) **upon** her. She sees her suffering as God's testimony, i.e., as proof that God condemns her for some sin of which she is unaware (see note on Ruth 1:11–13). However, her troubles will provide the means to God's bounty, as Ruth stays with her and gleans in Boaz's field.

1:22 Ruth the Moabite. Her origins are mentioned several times (vv. 4, 22; 2:2, 6, 21; 4:5, 10; cf. 2:10). The author emphasizes how God's kindness (1:8) extends beyond, but through, the Israelites (2:20), and how it abounds to them through a foreigner (3:10; 4:13ff.). **barley harvest**. In April/May, a few weeks before the wheat harvest (see 2:23).

2:1–23 *Scene 2: Ruth Gleans in Boaz's Field.* This encounter between Ruth and Boaz in the harvest field is one of their two crucial meetings. (The other is at the threshing floor; 3:6–15.) References to Naomi (2:1; "mother-in-law" in 2:23) frame this scene.

2:1 relative . . . Boaz. The readers are told what the characters will soon discover (see note on 2:20). **Worthy** (Hb. *hayil*, lit., "of worth or excellence") connotes character, wealth, position, or strength (see note on 4:11). The same is said of Ruth (3:11).

2:2 The key word **glean** appears in this scene 12 times (vv. 2, 3, 7, 8, 15 [twice], 16, 17 [twice], 18, 19, 23). Provisions for the poor, sojourners, widows, and orphans allowed them to gather standing grain in corners or borders of fields, as well as dropped stalks and left-behind sheaves (Lev. 19:9–10; 23:22; Deut. 24:19). **in whose sight I shall find favor**. See notes on Ruth 2:10 and 2:13. Ruth recognized her dependence on the owner's permission (Gen. 34:11; Num. 32:5; 1 Sam. 25:8).

said to her, "Go, my daughter." 3 So she set out and went and gleaned in the field after the
reapers, and she happened to come to the part of the field belonging to Boaz, who was
of the clan of Elimelech. 4 And behold, Boaz came from Bethlehem. And he said to the
reapers, [x]"The LORD be with you!" And they answered, "The LORD bless you." 5 Then Boaz
said to his young man who was in charge of the reapers, "Whose young woman is this?"
6 And the servant who was in charge of the reapers answered, "She is the young Moabite
woman, [y]who came back with Naomi from the country of Moab. 7 She said, 'Please let me
glean and gather among the sheaves after the reapers.' So she came, and she has continued
from early morning until now, except for a short rest."[1]
8 Then Boaz said to Ruth, "Now, listen, my daughter, do not go to glean in another field
or leave this one, but keep close to my young women. 9 Let your eyes be on the field that
they are reaping, and go after them. Have I not charged the young men not to touch you?
And when you are thirsty, go to the vessels and drink what the young men have drawn."
10 Then [z]she fell on her face, bowing to the ground, and said to him, "Why have I found
favor in your eyes, that you should [a]take notice of me, since I am a foreigner?" 11 But Boaz
answered her, [b]"All that you have done for your mother-in-law since the death of your
husband has been fully told to me, and how you left your father and mother and your
native land and came to a people that you did not know before. 12 [c]The LORD repay you for
what you have done, and a full reward be given you by the LORD, the God of Israel, under
whose wings you have come to take refuge!" 13 Then she said, [d]"I have found favor in your
eyes, my lord, for you have comforted me and spoken kindly to your servant, though I am
not one of your servants."
14 And at mealtime Boaz said to her, "Come here and eat some bread and dip your morsel
in the wine." So she sat beside the reapers, and he passed to her roasted grain. And she
ate until [e]she was satisfied, and she had some left over. 15 When she rose to glean, Boaz
instructed his young men, saying, "Let her glean even among the sheaves, and do not
reproach her. 16 And also pull out some from the bundles for her and leave it for her to
glean, and do not rebuke her."
17 So she gleaned in the field until evening. Then she beat out what she had gleaned,
and it was about an ephah[2] of barley. 18 And she took it up and went into the city. Her
mother-in-law saw what she had gleaned. She also brought out and gave her what food
she had left over [f]after being satisfied. 19 And her mother-in-law said to her, "Where did
you glean today? And where have you worked? Blessed be the man [g]who took notice of
you." So she told her mother-in-law with whom she had worked and said, "The man's name
with whom I worked today is Boaz." 20 And Naomi said to her daughter-in-law, [h]"May he

4 [x]Ps. 129:7, 8
6 [y]ch. 1:22
10 [z][1 Sam. 25:23, 41]
[a]ver. 19
11 [b]ch. 1:14, 16, 17
12 [c][1 Sam. 24:19]
13 [d]ver. 2, 10; Gen. 33:15; 1 Sam. 1:18
14 [e]ver. 18
18 [f]ver. 14
19 [g]ver. 10
20 [h]ch. 3:10; Judg. 17:2; 1 Sam. 15:13; 23:21; 2 Sam. 2:5

[1] Compare Septuagint, Vulgate; the meaning of the Hebrew phrase is uncertain [2] An *ephah* was about 3/5 bushel or 22 liters

2:3 she happened. The narrator presents this event from the standpoint of something unknown to Ruth (see note on v. 20); since this is a story of God's mysterious providence, the words here are ironic.

2:4 The LORD be with you acknowledges the Lord's presence with the workers in the field. **The LORD bless you** recognizes that he makes their lives and work fruitful (Gen. 1:22, 28; Deut. 28:8, 11–12; see note on Ruth 2:20).

2:7 Ruth's request to **glean . . . among the sheaves** is known only through the reaper's report (cf. v. 2). **She has continued** (Hb. *'amad*; lit., "stood") may suggest that she was not yet gleaning but waiting there for the owner to grant her permission (v. 8), something that the foreman could not do. More likely (as in the ESV), she has continued to work **from early morning until now**.

2:8–9 Boaz has charged the **young men** working in his field (cf. vv. 15, 21, 22) **not to touch** Ruth, in order to ensure her safety; young men in other nearby fields might not be as trustworthy (cf. Deut. 22:25–27).

2:10 found favor. Ruth's first words to Boaz (see v. 13) convey her gratitude that he would grant her these privileges and **take notice** of her. In other words, she wonders why Boaz would act according to her need, not her social status (see note on v. 20). Ruth calls herself a **foreigner**, but by virtue of her loyalty to Naomi and to the Lord she has become a sojourner, who can enjoy many of the rights of an Israelite (see note on 1:1; Lev. 24:22; Num. 9:14; 15:14–16; Ezek. 47:22–23).

2:11 All that you have done. Boaz has learned about Ruth's kindness to Naomi and therefore knows her good intentions.

2:12 Only the **LORD** could **repay**, i.e., make restitution for Ruth's losses of husband, father, mother, and country. **Full reward** (Hb. *maskoret*) is compensation commensurate with her loss—perhaps offspring, like Abraham's "reward" (Gen. 15:1–5, Hb. *sakar*, from the same root) and Leah's "wages" (Gen. 30:18, Hb. *sakar*; cf. Ruth 4:12). On both counts Boaz himself will become the Lord's answer to Boaz's own prayer. **wings . . . refuge** (Ps. 36:7; 57:1; 91:4; Matt. 23:37). Boaz becomes the Lord's protective "wings" when he "spreads his wings" over Ruth (see note on Ruth 3:9).

2:13 found favor. This is Ruth's second reply (see note on v. 10). **comforted . . . spoken kindly**. Boaz dispels the fear and uncertainty over whether Ruth can obtain food (Gen. 50:21; Isa. 40:2). The type of **servant** (Hb. *shipkhah*) to which Ruth humbly compares herself had limited rights (cf. Gen. 16:6; Lev. 19:20).

2:15–16 even among the sheaves . . . pull out some from the bundles. Boaz's favor goes well beyond the requirements of the law (see notes on vv. 2 and 7).

2:17–18 Gleaning went from early morning (v. 7) to **evening**, i.e., before sundown. After sundown (see note on 3:2) was the time to **beat out** or winnow what was gathered. An **ephah of barley** is about 5.5 gallons (22 liters)—at least a two-week supply for the two women (see Naomi's surprise, 2:19). **food . . . left over**. See v. 14.

20[i]ch. 1:8 [j]ch. 3:9; 4:14
Chapter 3
1[k]ch. 1:9
2[l]ch. 2:1 [m]ch. 2:8
3[n]2 Sam. 12:20; 14:2
7[o]See Judg. 19:6
9[p]Ezek. 16:8; [Deut. 22:30] [q]ch. 2:20
10[r]See ch. 2:20 [s]ch. 1:8
11[t]Prov. 12:4; 31:10
12[u]ch. 4:1

be blessed by the LORD, whose kindness has not forsaken [i]the living or the dead!" Naomi
also said to her, "The man is a close relative of ours, one of [j]our redeemers." 21 And Ruth
the Moabite said, "Besides, he said to me, 'You shall keep close by my young men until
they have finished all my harvest.'" 22 And Naomi said to Ruth, her daughter-in-law, "It is
good, my daughter, that you go out with his young women, lest in another field you be
assaulted." 23 So she kept close to the young women of Boaz, gleaning until the end of the
barley and wheat harvests. And she lived with her mother-in-law.

Ruth and Boaz at the Threshing Floor

3 Then Naomi her mother-in-law said to her, "My daughter, should I not seek [k]rest for
you, that it may be well with you? 2 Is not Boaz [l]our relative, [m]with whose young women
you were? See, he is winnowing barley tonight at the threshing floor. 3 [n]Wash therefore
and anoint yourself, and put on your cloak and go down to the threshing floor, but do not
make yourself known to the man until he has finished eating and drinking. 4 But when
he lies down, observe the place where he lies. Then go and uncover his feet and lie down,
and he will tell you what to do." 5 And she replied, "All that you say I will do."
6 So she went down to the threshing floor and did just as her mother-in-law had commanded her. 7 And when Boaz had eaten and drunk, and [o]his heart was merry, he went to
lie down at the end of the heap of grain. Then she came softly and uncovered his feet and
lay down. 8 At midnight the man was startled and turned over, and behold, a woman lay
at his feet! 9 He said, "Who are you?" And she answered, "I am Ruth, your servant. [p]Spread
your wings[1] over your servant, for you are [q]a redeemer." 10 And he said, [r]"May you be blessed
by the LORD, my daughter. You have made this last kindness greater than [s]the first in that
you have not gone after young men, whether poor or rich. 11 And now, my daughter, do
not fear. I will do for you all that you ask, for all my fellow townsmen know that you are [t]a
worthy woman. 12 And now it is true that I am [u]a redeemer. Yet there is a redeemer nearer

[1] Compare 2:12; the word for *wings* can also mean *corners of a garment*

2:20 whose kindness. The referent of "whose" is ambiguous: is she speaking of the kindness of Boaz, or of the Lord? This ambiguity is probably intentional; that is, the answer is both. In this story, Boaz embodies features of God's own character, particularly his kindness. This kindness is clearly visible in vv. 8–9, 14–16, where Boaz goes well beyond any legal requirements in his generosity to Ruth. Ruth, in receiving the kindness of Boaz extended to a foreigner, is experiencing what Israel as a whole, and each faithful Israelite, receives from the Lord (cf. Deut. 7:7–9). Naomi's blessing anticipates kindness shown to the **living** in marriage (Deut. 25:5–6; Ruth 4:10a, 13) and to the **dead** (1:8) by perpetuating their name in their inheritance (4:5, 10b; Lev. 25:23, 25). **close relative . . . one of our redeemers**. Boaz is neither the closest relative to Naomi nor the only one (see note on Ruth 3:12–13). This situation combines two institutions: the redemption of family land and levirate marriage (see Introduction: Key Themes). What "happened" (2:3) is now seen to be providential.

2:21 Moabite. See note on 1:22. **close by my young men**. See notes on 2:8–9 and 2:23.

2:23 The **barley** harvest was in April/May, and the **wheat** harvest was a few weeks later (cf. 1:22). **she lived with her mother-in-law**. See 1:16.

3:1–18 *Scene 3: Ruth, at the Threshing Floor, Asks Boaz to Marry Her.* This scene depicts the second crucial encounter between Ruth and Boaz, framed by the recurrence of "my daughter" (vv. 1, 18). Several uses of "know" (Hb. *yada'* and related terms from the same root) are woven into this scene: "relative" (v. 2, lit., "one known"); "do not make yourself known" (v. 3); "observe [or, 'know'] the place where he lies" (v. 4); "my . . . townsmen know . . . you are a worthy woman" (v. 11); "until you learn [or, 'know'] how the matter turns out" (v. 18).

3:1 rest. See notes on 1:8–9 and 4:13. **be well with you**. By having children (cf. Deut. 6:3).

3:2 Is not . . . ? The rhetorical question connects **Boaz our relative** and "rest" (1:9; 3:1). **winnowing . . . tonight**. The winnowing took place during the breezes that begin after sundown (see note on 2:17–18). **threshing floor**. This was located to the east of the city so that the westerly wind carried away the chaff. (On threshing [or winnowing], see note on Ps. 1:4.) Ruth, leaving the city, goes "down to the threshing floor" (Ruth 3:3); Boaz, leaving the threshing floor, goes "up to the [city] gate" (4:1).

3:3 Wash . . . anoint . . . put on. Perhaps a sign that her mourning was over, as it was for David (2 Sam. 12:20). She must make herself attractive, like a betrothed woman (Ezek. 16:9–12), and meet Boaz at the right time: after he **finished . . . drinking** (see Ruth 3:7; Ps. 4:7; 104:15).

3:4 To **uncover his feet and lie down** there (vv. 8, 14) will demonstrate her dependence on him in view of her bold marriage proposal (v. 9). It is sometimes suggested that "his feet" (lit., "place of his feet," Hb. *margelot*) is a euphemism for sexual contact, but there is no evidence for this and it would be out of place in this story.

3:6–7 went down . . . uncovered . . . lay down. Ruth was true to her word (v. 5). **softly**. Ruth moved in stealth so as not to awaken Boaz (cf. Judg. 4:21; 1 Sam. 26:7).

3:9 Ruth, your servant. A maidservant (Hb. *'amah*), unlike a slave-servant (see note on 2:13), enjoyed the privileges of an Israelite household (e.g., Ex. 20:10) and could give birth to an heir (see Gen. 30:3–4, 9). **your wings**. Although this is an expression for "the edge of your garment" (**spread** in order to claim her in marriage; see ESV footnote), here it evokes the mention of the Lord's "wings" in Ruth 2:12 and Boaz as an embodiment of the Lord's character. **redeemer**. See note on 3:12–13.

3:10 this last kindness. That is, Ruth claiming Boaz as her redeemer (v. 9). It was a **greater** act of kindness, given the implications of redemption. The **first** act of kindness was that shown earlier to Naomi (2:11). Boaz was impressed that Ruth was not merely seeking marriage with eligible **young men**.

3:11 worthy woman. See notes on 2:1; 4:11; cf. Prov. 31:10, "excellent wife," using the same Hebrew expression, *'eshet khayil*.

3:12–13 redeemer nearer. The order of these relations is: brother, uncle, cousin, or close clan relative (Lev. 25:48–49; Num. 27:11; see Introduction: Key Themes, "Redemption"). The use of this term (Hb. *ga'al*) for "kinsman-redeemer" is separate from the way the same word is used for the Lord "redeeming" Israel (e.g., Ex. 6:6; 15:13; cf. NT usage of "redemption"). Boaz may only claim his right of redemption if the other redeemer **is not willing**

than I. 13 Remain tonight, and in the morning, if he will [v]redeem you, good; let him do
it. But if he is not willing to redeem you, then, [w]as the LORD lives, I will redeem you. Lie
down until the morning."
14 So she lay at his feet until the morning, but arose before one could recognize another.
And he said, "Let it not be known that the woman came to the threshing floor." 15 And he
said, "Bring the garment you are wearing and hold it out." So she held it, and he measured
out six measures of barley and put it on her. Then she went into the city. 16 And when she
came to her mother-in-law, she said, "How did you fare, my daughter?" Then she told her
all that the man had done for her, 17 saying, "These six measures of barley he gave to me,
for he said to me, 'You must not go back empty-handed to your mother-in-law.'" 18 She
replied, "Wait, my daughter, until you learn how the matter turns out, for the man will
not rest but will settle the matter today."

Boaz Redeems Ruth

4 Now Boaz had gone up to [x]the gate and sat down there. And behold, [y]the redeemer,
of whom Boaz had spoken, came by. So Boaz said, "Turn aside, friend; sit down here."
And he turned aside and sat down. 2 And he took ten men [z]of the elders of the city and
said, "Sit down here." So they sat down. 3 Then he said to the redeemer, "Naomi, who has
come back from the country of Moab, is selling the parcel of land that belonged to our
relative Elimelech. 4 So I thought I would tell you of it and say, [a]'Buy it in the presence of
those sitting here and in the presence of the elders of my people.' If you will redeem it,
redeem it. But if you[1] will not, tell me, that I may know, for there is no one besides you to
redeem it, and I come after you." And he said, "I will redeem it." 5 Then Boaz said, "The day
you buy the field from the hand of Naomi, you also acquire Ruth[2] the Moabite, the widow
of the dead, in order [b]to perpetuate the name of the dead in his inheritance." 6 [c]Then the
redeemer said, "I cannot redeem it for myself, lest I impair my own inheritance. Take my
right of redemption yourself, for I cannot redeem it."
7 [d]Now this was the custom in former times in Israel concerning redeeming and exchanging: to confirm a transaction, the one drew off his sandal and gave it to the other, and this
was the manner of attesting in Israel. 8 So when the redeemer said to Boaz, "Buy it for
yourself," he drew off his sandal. 9 Then Boaz said to the elders and all the people, "You
are witnesses this day that I have bought from the hand of Naomi all that belonged to
Elimelech and all that belonged to [e]Chilion and to Mahlon. 10 Also Ruth the Moabite, the
widow of Mahlon, I have bought to be my wife, [f]to perpetuate the name of the dead in his
inheritance, that the name of the dead may not be cut off from among his brothers and
from the gate of his native place. You are witnesses this day." 11 Then all the people who

[1] Hebrew *he* [2] Masoretic Text *you also buy it from Ruth*

13 [v]ch. 4:5; [Deut. 25:5] [w]Judg. 8:19; 1 Sam. 14:39; 2 Sam. 4:9; 12:5; 2 Kgs. 2:2, 6

Chapter 4

1 [x]2 Sam. 15:2; 18:4, 24, 33; 19:8; Ps. 127:5 [y]ch. 2:20
2 [z]1 Kgs. 21:8; Prov. 31:23
4 [a]Lev. 25:25; [Jer. 32:7, 8]
5 [b]ver. 10; ch. 3:13; Deut. 25:5, 6
6 [c]ch. 3:12, 13
7 [d]See Deut. 25:7-10
9 [e]ch. 1:2, 4, 5
10 [f]ver. 5

(cf. Deut. 25:7–8). **as the LORD lives**. A solemn oath (cf. Judg. 8:19; 1 Kings 2:24).

3:14 Let it not be known. Boaz is concerned for propriety and for his and Ruth's good reputation.

3:15 six measures of barley. Boaz's ample supply would also confirm his intentions to Naomi (v. 17).

3:17 not . . . empty-handed. Lit., "with nothing," as in 1:21 (cf. Deut. 15:13). Boaz functions in the story as the channel of the Lord's recompense (Ruth 2:12) and kindness (2:20) to Naomi.

4:1–12 *Scene 4: Boaz Arranges Redemption at the Gate.* This scene is framed by opening and closing at the "gate" with "elders" (vv. 1–2, 11–12). Both verb or noun forms of "redeem" occur throughout this scene (vv. 1, 3, 4, 6, 7, 8; cf. 2:20; 3:9, 12, 13; 4:14).

4:1–2 The **gate** served as a combined town hall and courthouse (2 Sam. 15:2; Job 29:7–17; Prov. 22:22; 31:23; Amos 5:10). **Elders** witnessed transactions (Ruth 4:4, 9–11; cf. Deut. 25:7) and decided cases (cf. Deut. 21:19; 22:15).

4:3 Redemption is referred to here in terms of buying and **selling** (vv. 4, 5, 8, 9, 10; Ps. 74:2; Jer. 32:7). This land, or the legal right to use it, may have been sold to buy food during the famine or before leaving for Moab. Or Naomi may still be in full possession of the land, or of its use, which she is selling out of necessity. In either case, a kinsman must redeem it.

4:4–6 The "redeemer nearer" (3:12) is given the opportunity to redeem the **field** from **Naomi**. He responds, **I will redeem it**. However, when he learns that **Ruth** will become his wife as part of the transaction, he changes his mind, **lest I impair my own inheritance**. Apparently he was concerned that any son born to him and Ruth would share the inheritance already planned for his present children. **Take my right of redemption yourself**. His decision opens the door for Boaz.

4:7–8 in former times. The practice must be explained since the audience for the book of Ruth no longer does this. **exchanging**. Transferring the right of redemption (v. 6). **sandal**. A symbol of this exchange (cf. Ps. 60:8; Amos 2:6; 8:6). Deuteronomy 25:9, however, represents a different but related custom.

4:10 Moabite (see note on 1:22). To preserve the property, Ruth was **bought** (redeemed) **to be** Boaz's **wife** (see 4:13; Deut. 25:5). **not be cut off from among his brothers**. That is, from his clan relatives (Ruth 4:3). **from the gate**. Men of this family may have held prominent positions in the gate. **His . . . place** refers to his social standing (Job 20:9; Ps. 103:16) in his home (Judg. 7:7; 1 Sam. 2:20), city (Deut. 21:19; cf. John 14:2, 3; Heb. 11:8), territory (Judg. 19:16), and country (Ex. 23:20).

4:11 Rachel and Leah. These two women were barren (as Ruth had been up to this point; see notes on 1:4; 4:13; 4:18–22), but the Lord opened their

were [g]at the gate and the elders said, "We are witnesses. May the LORD make the woman,
who is coming into your house, like Rachel and Leah, [h]who together [i]built up the house
of Israel. May you act worthily in [j]Ephrathah and [k]be renowned in Bethlehem, 12 and
may your house be like the house of Perez, [l]whom Tamar bore to Judah, because [m]of the
offspring that the LORD will give you by this young woman."

Ruth and Boaz Marry

13 So Boaz took Ruth, and she became his wife. And he went in to her, [n]and the LORD
gave her conception, and she bore a son. 14 [o]Then the women said to Naomi, "Blessed
be the LORD, who has not left you this day without [p]a redeemer, and may his name [q]be
renowned in Israel! 15 He shall be to you a restorer of life and a nourisher of your old age,
for your daughter-in-law who loves you, [r]who is more to you than seven sons, has given
birth to him." 16 Then Naomi took the child and laid him on her lap and became his nurse.
17 [s]And the women of the neighborhood gave him a name, saying, "A son has been born to
Naomi." They named him Obed. He was the father of Jesse, the father of David.

The Genealogy of David

18 Now these are the generations of Perez: [t]Perez fathered Hezron, 19 Hezron fathered
Ram, Ram fathered Amminadab, 20 [u]Amminadab fathered Nahshon, Nahshon fathered
Salmon, 21 Salmon fathered Boaz, Boaz fathered Obed, 22 Obed fathered Jesse, and Jesse
fathered David.

11 [g]See ver. 1 [h]See Gen. 29:31–30:24; 35:16-18 [i]Deut. 25:9 [j]Gen. 35:16, 19 [k]ver. 14
12 [l]Gen. 38:29; 1 Chr. 2:4; Matt. 1:3 [m]1 Sam. 2:20
13 [n]Gen. 29:31; 33:5
14 [o][Luke 1:58] [p]ch. 2:20 [q]ver. 11
15 [r]1 Sam. 1:8
17 [s]Luke 1:59
18 [t]For ver. 18-22, see 1 Chr. 2:4-15; Matt. 1:3-6
20 [u]Num. 1:7; [Ex. 6:23]

wombs (Gen. 29:31; 30:22). Leah was the mother of Judah (Gen. 35:23), ancestor of the tribe of Boaz and Naomi. Through childbearing they **built up the house of Israel**, i.e., established and perpetuated the family of Jacob (Deut. 25:9; Ps. 127:1, 3; Prov. 24:27). The people and the elders also express their blessing-wish that Boaz would **act worthily** (see notes on Ruth 2:1; 3:11). Through Boaz's offspring, David's house was built (2 Sam. 7:11, 26), which was the pride of **Ephrathah** and **Bethlehem** (see note on Ruth 1:2; cf. 1 Sam. 17:12).

4:12 Perez. Ancestor of the preeminent Judean Perezite clan (Num. 26:20–21) and of prominent leaders (1 Chron. 9:4; 27:2–3; Neh. 11:4–6; Matt. 1:12). **Tamar** and **Judah** (Tamar's father-in-law) recalls this attempted levirate marriage (Gen. 38:6–8; see note on Ruth 1:11–13). **offspring**. See 4:17; Ps. 89:4, 29.

4:13–17 *Conclusion: Naomi Blessed with a New Family.* The conclusion serves as the reversal of the introduction, showing how the Lord, through Ruth's love (v. 15), restored Naomi's life.

4:13 Ruth went from self-proclaimed slave-servant (2:13) and maidservant (3:9) to **wife** (see note on 4:10). **The LORD gave her conception** just as he did for Leah and Rachel (see note on v. 11; cf. Gen. 29:32–35; 30:23). The word **son** (Hb. *ben*) sounds like "built up" (Hb. *banah*, Ruth 4:11): the son is the one through whom the house (1:9; 4:11, 12) is built. Ruth has now found rest (see notes on 1:8–9; 3:1; cf. Ps. 113:9).

4:14 Blessed be the LORD. The **women** recognize that the Lord is the author of new life (v. 15; see notes on 2:4; 2:20) resulting from redemption. Calling the heir a **redeemer** indicates the one in whom redemption is realized.

4:15 restorer of life. Lit., "he who causes life to return [Hb. *shub*]," which reverses Naomi's complaint before the women of Bethlehem: "the LORD . . . brought me back [Hb. *shub*] empty" (1:21). **loves**. Ruth's love for Naomi has been steadfast throughout the book (cf. 1:16–17). The number **seven** expresses completion, or fullness: this is the answer to Naomi's complaint (see note on 1:20–21).

4:16 child. Cf. 1:5, 11–12. A **nurse** cares for a child as a foster mother (2 Sam. 4:4).

4:17 son . . . to Naomi. Elimelech's heir (v. 9). The Lord, through Ruth, also recompenses Naomi (2:12) and gives her rest (1:9; 3:1). The childless widow became the grandmother of **Obed**, who was the grandfather of **David**.

4:18–22 *Genealogy: Extended Blessing.* Looking backward and forward, this genealogy (cf. 1 Chron. 2:5–15) shows how the Lord repaid and rewarded Ruth, as Boaz desired (Ruth 2:12): the Lord brought about a new family line which became, through David, the greatest in all Israel. The 10 names in Ruth's new family more than fill her 10 years of childlessness (see notes on 1:4; 4:11). Noah's and Abraham's genealogies also have 10 names (Gen. 5:3–32; 11:10–26). (In a genealogy, the word "fathered" can mean fathered a later descendant; thus biblical genealogies, including this one, may skip generations when the number of names is more important than recording every single member.) The Lord made everlasting, universal covenants with Noah concerning all creation (Gen. 9:16–17), with Abraham regarding Israel and the nations (Gen. 12:2–3; 17:4, 7, 16), and with David concerning his dynasty (2 Sam. 7:16; Ps. 89:4). All three are examples of the blessing received by faith (Noah: Gen. 6:8; Heb. 11:7; Abraham: Gen. 15:6; Rom. 4:2–3, 9; Gal. 3:8–9; David: Ps. 32:1–2; Rom. 4:6). Christ is the "son" of Noah (Luke 3:36), Abraham, and David (Matt. 1:1). Jesus' genealogy includes three foreign women—Tamar, Rahab, and Ruth—all related to this genealogy (Matt. 1:3, 5; see notes on Ruth 4:12; 4:21).

4:18 Perez. See notes on v. 12 and Matt. 1:3.

4:20 Nahshon (Aaron's brother-in-law) is fifth in the list. He was a leader among the Judean clans (Ex. 6:23; Num. 1:7; 10:14; 1 Chron. 2:10).

4:21 Salmon fathered Boaz by Rahab (Matt. 1:5; see Josh. 6:25).

4:22 The Messiah, the Lion of the tribe of Judah, is the root of **Jesse** and the root and descendant of **David** (Gen. 49:9; Isa. 11:10; Rom. 15:12; Rev. 5:5; 22:16).

INTRODUCTION TO

1–2 SAMUEL

Author and Title

The Hebrew title "Samuel" refers to Samuel as the key figure in 1–2 Samuel, the one who established the monarchy in Israel by anointing first Saul and then David; Samuel was the kingmaker in the history of ancient Israel. In the Hebrew Bible, the first and second books of Samuel are counted among the "Former Prophets" (Joshua–2 Kings). The Greek translation, the Septuagint, divides Samuel and Kings into the four "Books of Kingdoms"; thus 1–2 Samuel are 1–2 Kingdoms. In the Latin Vulgate and Douay Bible they are called 1–2 Kings.

The author or authors of 1–2 Samuel are not known. First Chronicles 29:29–30 implies that Samuel (or perhaps his disciples) left written records, but because his death is mentioned in 1 Samuel 25, he could not have written most of Samuel.

Date

First and Second Samuel seem to have been composed and edited in several stages. The "Story of the Ark of God" (1 Sam. 4:1–7:1) could have originated very early—even from a pre-Davidic period, since 2 Samuel 6 is not foreshadowed in the ark narrative and the name of the town where the ark remained is different in the two narratives.

This "Story of the Ark" was embedded in a larger unit, the "Story of Samuel" (1 Sam. 1:1–7:17). It is possible that this story, and the following transitional chapter on the "Rights of the King" (1 Sam. 8:11–18), came from the earlier time of Samuel's ministry, while the "Story of Saul" (1 Samuel 9–15) originated during a later time of Samuel's era.

Sections such as the "Story of Saul and David" (1 Samuel 16–31) and the "Story of King David" (2 Samuel 1–20) must have been composed later, during King David's time, or within a generation or two after David. First Samuel 27:6 states, "Therefore Ziklag has belonged to the kings of Judah to this day." The final editing of 1–2 Samuel, except perhaps for some minor adjustments, must have been done during the late tenth century B.C., i.e., the early period of the reign of Rehoboam, king of Judah alone. Before that period the writer would have said "kings of Israel." Furthermore, the Ziklag area was captured by Egypt during Shishak's campaign in 925 B.C. The period within a generation or two after the death of the founder of a dynasty is certainly a reasonable time for an official historian to write his history. There is no reason to think that many generations must have passed before the history of David was written down.

Theme

The central theme of the books of Samuel is God's exercising of his cosmic kingship by inaugurating a Davidic dynasty ("house") in Israel (2 Samuel 7; Psalm 89), not a Saulide one (1 Sam. 13:13–14; 15:28), and by electing the holy city Zion (Jerusalem; 2 Samuel 6; Psalm 132) as the place where David's successor will establish the temple ("house") for the worship of the divine King Yahweh (see 2 Sam. 24:18). The Davidic "covenant" (2 Samuel 7; Ps. 89:3) entitled Matthew to put David at the center of the genealogical history of the divine plan of salvation (Matt. 1:1).

Purpose, Occasion, and Background

The purpose of the book of 1 Samuel is to highlight two major events: first, *the establishment of the monarchy in Israel* (chs. 8–12); and second, *the preparation of David to sit on the royal throne after Saul* (chs. 16–31). Saul was rejected by the Lord in favor of David (chs. 15–16) even though, humanly speaking, he stayed on the throne until his death at Mount Gilboa (ch. 31). Later, in 2 Samuel 7, God promises David and his house an eternal dynasty. In these two central events the role of the prophet Samuel was very important because he had anointed first Saul, then David, as king over the covenant people. The book of 1 Samuel establishes the principle that the king in Israel is to be subject to the word of God as conveyed through his prophets. In other words, obedience to the word of God is the necessary condition for a king to be acceptable to the God of Israel. This is what Jesus the Messiah-King did in his life of obedience to God the Father, even up to "death on a cross" (Phil. 2:8). First and Second Samuel deal with a transitional period in the history of ancient Israel—the transition first from the priest Eli to the judge Samuel, then from the judge Samuel to the king Saul, and then from Saul to David, who founded the dynasty that would last as long as the kingdom of Judah. The prophet Samuel thus functions as the link between the judgeship and the kingship. The kingdom of Saul was transitional in a further sense: it was more than a loose confederation that gathered together when there was a common threat, but it was not a period of strong central rule such as existed later. The story of the rise of David in the second half of 1 Samuel prepares for the full-scale kingship of David in 2 Samuel.

1 Samuel Key Themes

The themes of 1 Samuel are the kingship of God, his providential guidance, and his sovereign will and power.

1. *God's kingship.* God is the King of the universe; no human king can assume kingship except as a deputy of the divine King. God has been enthroned as King from eternity. This view is expressed in the Bible as early as Exodus 15:18: "The LORD will reign forever and ever."

The first occurrence of the word "king" in 1–2 Samuel is in the Song of Hannah (1 Sam. 2:10). Though the Lord is not explicitly described as King here, it is implied in the statement that he is the One who judges "the ends of the earth" (cf. Ps. 96:10). In this verse Hannah expresses her conviction that this King, the Lord, is the One who gives power to his human deputy (the "king") and lifts up the "power of his anointed."

According to Genesis, all human beings were created as "royal" figures in the *image of God.* Hence, humans are deputies who rule and control other creatures for the sake of the King of the universe. So when God allowed the people of Israel to have a human king (1 Sam. 8:6–9), he gave them a king only as God's earthly vice-regent or deputy, who is responsible to the Lord for his actions and subject to his commands (see esp. 1 Sam. 12:14; 2 Sam. 12:9).

The Lord's holy sovereignty is expressed also in his title "the LORD of hosts, who is enthroned on the cherubim" (1 Sam. 4:4). As in other places in the Bible, he is clearly seen as controlling events not only in Israel, the land of his covenant people, but outside Israel too, especially in Philistia (1 Sam. 4:1–6:21; 23:27; 29:4; see also Amos 9:7).

2. *God's providential guidance.* Romans 8:28 summarizes well what the author of 1 Samuel meant to convey to his readers: "And we know that for those who love God all things work together for good, for those who are called according to his purpose." God is certainly the One who providentially and individually guided the lives of chosen individuals such as Hannah, Samuel, and David; even the life of Saul was in God's providential care (see 1 Sam. 9:16). The course of life is different for each individual, but the same God, not "Fate," consistently and graciously guides one's life. Though it is often not recognized by his human agents, God's timing is always perfect (see 1 Samuel 9 and the end of 1 Samuel 23), for he is the Lord of history.

God's saving plan is fulfilled in the ongoing day-to-day lives of human beings. For example, Hannah's difficult relationship with Peninnah leads to the birth of Samuel (1 Samuel 1); Saul's donkey-searching journey leads to the encounter with the prophet Samuel (1 Samuel 9); David's chore of bringing food to his brothers enables him to see Goliath (1 Samuel 17). Ordinary situations are the most meaningful in human life, and it is in these that God "works for good."

Later, in 2 Samuel 7, God uses King David's earnest desire to build a house for the Lord to indwell as an occasion to further his plan of salvation by choosing David's line to be that of the Messiah-King who would sit on the throne of David forever. In 2 Samuel 7:16 God says to David, "And your house and your kingdom shall be made sure forever before me. Your throne shall be established forever." In other words, Yahweh, King of the universe, promises David that he will establish David's house (i.e., his dynasty) as eternal. Thus, this promise to, or "covenant" with (see Ps. 89:3), David was a turning point in the outworking of God's saving purposes.

3. *God's sovereign will and power.* As Hannah phrases it, God is the all-knowing God, "a God of knowledge" (1 Sam. 2:3b), and he chooses or rejects people according to his absolute sovereign will and purpose. From a human perspective it sometimes looks as though God has changed his mind, but God "will not lie or have regret, for he is not a man, that he should have regret" (1 Sam. 15:29). To be sure, the Lord as the sovereign deity may change his way of dealing with individuals according to his plan and purpose. But his decision is always just and right; at the same time, he is merciful and gracious to sinful human beings.

Therefore, obedience to God's word is of prime importance in human life. First and Second Samuel provide many examples of the importance of listening to the word of God. The boy Samuel listens to the word of God (1 Samuel 3), but Saul fails here, rejecting God's commandment (1 Samuel 13; 15). David fights bravely with Goliath for the honor of Yahweh's name (1 Samuel 17) but later fails to keep the commandments, committing adultery and murder (2 Samuel 11). God gives David a second chance by sending the prophet Nathan (2 Samuel 12), while Saul is finally refused a chance to repent (1 Samuel 15). Only God's grace upholds human beings, who are sinful in nature, before the holy God.

"Who is able to stand before the Lord, this holy God?" (1 Sam. 6:20)—these words of the men of Beth-shemesh well express human reality, though their understanding of God's "holiness" was not adequate (see Leviticus 19). Only the God-given way of approaching him through sacrifice can prepare sinful human beings to come closer to the holy God.

God spontaneously reveals his will in words, and his word through the prophets determines events. But not every detail is revealed to the eyes of human beings (e.g., 1 Sam. 3:1–21; 9:15–21; 16:1–13). Believers can only wait on God, who will do his will according to his own purpose.

For fighting God's battle against his enemies, Jonathan (1 Sam. 14:6) and David (1 Sam. 17:45–47) called on God's power. God uses human urges and enthusiasms for his honor—often in a way that seems to defy common sense. God is the One who works wonders and uses even his enemies (Philistine kings, Achish, etc.) to fulfill his plan and purpose. Thus, humanly impossible agendas become divinely possible, encouraging believers to put their faith in the One who is sovereign over the entire creation.

The story of 1–2 Samuel begins with Samuel and ends with David, framing the problematic figure of Saul. These three are certainly central figures in the history of the kingdom of God. Their lives illustrate many biblical themes. In God's dealings with Saul and David, one might see God's justice and his mercy, respectively; according to the NT, both qualities find their ultimate expression in the person of Jesus Christ, who died on the cross.

2 Samuel Key Themes

The themes of 1 Samuel (namely, God's kingship, providential guidance, and sovereign will and power) are related to the themes of 2 Samuel (namely, the Davidic covenant and messianic promise): the sovereign God, who has guided David's life, elects David as his deputy to represent his kingship by his eternal covenant. David thus becomes the prototype of the future Messiah, Jesus Christ.

1. *Davidic covenant.* For the Davidic covenant, see note on 2 Samuel 7:1–29.

2. *Messianic promise.* Second Samuel 7 is a turning point in the history of salvation; it clearly advances the messianic hope in the Abrahamic covenant. True, Saul was also anointed by Yahweh. David in fact called Saul "the Lord's anointed" (e.g., 1 Sam. 24:6) until the end. Yet God chose David, the youngest and forgotten son of Jesse, to establish a dynasty. David was used for God's eternal plan of salvation, not because he was perfect and ideal from a human viewpoint, but because the Lord was "with him" and David found favor in God's sight.

The idea of the eternal throne and dynasty was not a product of postexilic idealism as is sometimes claimed. Such a concept was already current in the second millennium B.C. in Canaan as *mlk ʿlm* (Ugaritic, "the king of eternity" or "king of the world") and was prominent among the Assyrians during the eighth century B.C., as can be seen in the Assyrian records. Thus, the prophecies in Isaiah 7–9 reflect the ideal of preexilic times.

Text

The Hebrew Masoretic text (MT) of 1–2 Samuel is notorious for its difficulties. Furthermore, Samuel and Jeremiah are the two OT books where the ancient Greek translations and the Hebrew are notably different in many places. Many scholars and translations too readily reject the MT in favor of the Greek,

Events of 1–2 Samuel Referenced in the Psalms

1 Samuel	Incident	Psalm
19:11	David's house surrounded	59
21:10–11	David seized by Achish	56
21:12–22:1	David escapes from Achish (called Abimelech in Psalm 34 title)	34
22:1 (possibly also 24:3)	David in cave	57; 142
22:9–19	Doeg the Edomite	52
23:14–15 (possibly)	Desert of Judah	63
23:19	David betrayed by Ziphites	54

2 Samuel	Incident	Psalm
8:1–14	Victory over Transjordan	60
chs. 11–12	Against house of Uriah	51
chs. 15–17	Absalom's revolt	3
chs. 15–17 (possibly)	Desert of Judah	63
ch. 22	Victory over all enemies	18

saying that the Greek text makes more sense and reflects the more original Hebrew text. They hold that the MT must have been corrupted into its present form through a series of scribal errors, and they try to "correct" these "corrupted" texts on the basis of the Greek texts. In fact, the Hebrew texts of Samuel from about 50 to 25 B.C. found among the Dead Sea Scrolls give support for some readings in the Greek text tradition. But the alleged similarity between the Greek texts and the Dead Sea Scrolls has been overemphasized.

One of the reasons for the difficulty of the Hebrew text of Samuel is that Samuel was written in the manner of an oral narrative—written, i.e., to be heard. Some of the repetitions are more typical of poetry than of prose. Also, at places the spelling seems to have followed the actual pronunciation instead of the "standard" Hebrew, as can be clearly seen when one compares 2 Samuel 22 and Psalm 18 in Hebrew. The MT of 1–2 Samuel is not easy. Yet if one carefully examines it with a thorough knowledge of the grammar and style of the language, in most cases the MT as it stands appears to be good, and the ESV translation has therefore followed the MT in most (but not all) places.

History of Salvation Summary

The period of the Judges shows the serious problems Israel had, both in its leadership and among the people as a whole. The books of Samuel show God's continued care for his people, in raising up for them a king whose job was to be their champion, representative, and example. Saul, by his disobedience to God's messenger, proves to be an unsuitable king. David, on the other hand, in spite of his moral failures, is God's choice to be the beginning of an enduring dynasty, from which the ultimate Ruler, who will lead Israel in bringing blessing to all the nations, will arise. (For an explanation of the "History of Salvation," see the Overview of the Bible, pp. 23–26. See also History of Salvation in the Old Testament: Preparing the Way for Christ, pp. 2635–2661.)

Literary Features

The primary genre of 1 Samuel is hero story. The author did not choose the common method of OT historians in giving coverage to a broad span of people and events but instead focused primarily on three heroic leaders whose stories are elaborated at length: Samuel, Saul, and David. Three other characters are sufficiently prominent in the narrative for their stories to be mini-hero stories: Hannah, Eli, and Jonathan. Within the species of hero story, the story of Saul is the only undisputed and fully elaborated literary tragedy in the Bible. The story of David and Goliath is the prototypical battle story in the Bible. The phase of David's life when he is the archetypal man on the run fits the narrative pattern of a fugitive story. Hannah's song of gratitude (1 Sam. 2:1–10) is a lyric poem in the specific form of a praise psalm, and Samuel's last words to the nation (1 Samuel 12) fit the genre of the farewell discourse.

The first third of 1 Samuel pits the decline of Eli and his sons against the rise of Samuel, so that readers should picture these chapters in the form of an X (Eli's decline occurring simultaneously with Samuel's ascent). The remainder of the book is likewise an extended X in which the decline of Saul is played against the rise of David. In this phase of the story, the stories of Saul and David are intertwined, as readers are kept up to date on the tragic decline of Saul and the life of the king-in-waiting as a fugitive.

First Samuel is a book of personalities, so paying close attention to characterization is important. Similarly, the book is rich in universal, recognizable human experience, with the result that building bridges between the world of the text and one's own experiences is an inviting approach to the book. Even though this book

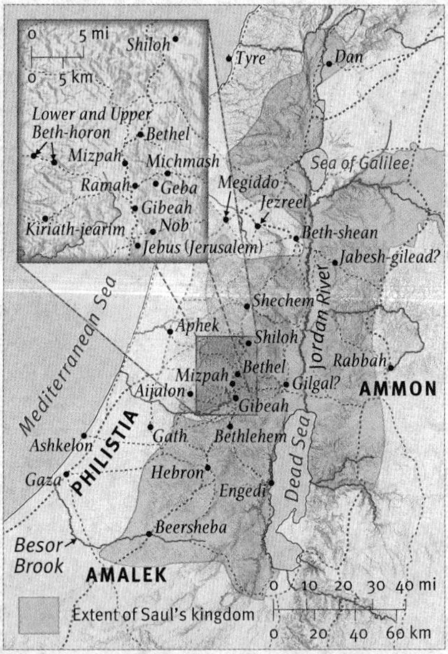

The Setting of 1 Samuel
c. 1050 B.C.
The book of 1 Samuel is set in Israel during the time of transition between the period of the judges and the period of the monarchy. It opens with Samuel's birth and then describes his role as judge over Israel. When the people ask for a king, the Lord instructs Samuel to anoint Saul as Israel's first king.

does not cover the vast spans of Israelite history that the other OT historical chronicles cover, it provides in-depth analyses of what makes for good and bad leadership. What is true for leaders, moreover, is true for all individuals in their choices for or against God. A leading literary purpose of the book is to embody universal human experience as the means of teaching moral and spiritual lessons for all people at all times.

Second Samuel is the prose epic of David, telling the story of a nation led by a heroic leader. It is at the same time a hero story in which the protagonist, while not wholly idealized, is nonetheless a largely exemplary and representative character who embodies the struggles and ideals of his society. While the story does not possess the single linear sequence of literary tragedy, nonetheless at one point it meets the essential tragic criterion of locating the source of the hero's subsequent downfall in a single tragic choice. Readers should picture David's life as portrayed in 2 Samuel as a pyramid in which the trajectory is wholly positive until the Bathsheba/Uriah debacle, after which David's life goes into comparative decline as the tragic consequences work themselves out. Two threads of action make up the story of David's heroic life: the public life of a king and the personal life of a family man.

The literary technique of realism permeates the book as the storyteller refuses to ignore either the good or the bad aspects of the characters. As with 1 Samuel, the story rings true to human experience. The dramatic impulse to present the actual words and dialogues of characters is continuous.

1 Samuel Outline

I. The Story of Samuel (1:1–7:17)
   A. Rise of Samuel as prophet (1:1–4:1a)
      1. Birth and dedication of Samuel (1:1–28)
      2. Hannah's song (2:1–10)
      3. Samuel, and Eli's two sons (2:11–36)
      4. Call of Samuel as a prophet (3:1–4:1a)
   B. Story of the ark of God (4:1b–7:1)
      1. Capture of the ark (4:1b–22)
      2. The ark in Philistia (5:1–12)
      3. Return of the ark (6:1–7:1)
   C. Judgeship of Samuel (7:2–17)

II. Transition to the Monarchy (8:1–22)

III. The Story of Saul (9:1–15:35)
- A. Saul made king (9:1–11:15)
  1. Saul's meeting with Samuel (9:1–27)
  2. Anointing of Saul and his election (10:1–27)
  3. Making Saul king (11:1–15)
- B. Samuel's address to Israel (12:1–25)
- C. Reign of Saul (13:1–15:35)
  1. Saul and the Philistines—first rejection of Saul (13:1–23)
  2. Saul and Jonathan (14:1–52)
  3. Saul and the Amalekites—second rejection of Saul (15:1–35)

IV. The Story of Saul and David (16:1–31:13)
- A. Introduction of David (16:1–23)
  1. Anointing of David (16:1–13)
  2. David at Saul's court (16:14–23)
- B. David and Goliath: battle at the Valley of Elah (17:1–54)
- C. Saul, Jonathan, and David (17:55–18:5)
- D. Saul becomes David's enemy (18:6–30)
- E. Saul's attempts to kill David (19:1–20:42)
- F. David's escapes from Saul (21:1–26:25)
  1. David's escapes (21:1–23:29)
  2. David spares Saul at Engedi (24:1–25:1)
  3. David marries Abigail (25:2–44)
  4. David spares Saul at the hill of Hachilah (26:1–25)
- G. David in Philistia (27:1–30:31)
  1. David and Achish (27:1–12)
  2. The Philistines gather for war (28:1–2)
  3. The medium of En-dor (28:3–25)
  4. The Philistine rulers reject David (29:1–11)
  5. Amalekite raid on Ziklag and David's victory (30:1–31)
- H. Deaths of Saul and Jonathan (31:1–13)

1 SAMUEL

Chapter 1
1[a][ver. 19] [b]See Josh. 24:33 [c][1 Kgs. 11:26]
3[d]ver. 21; Ex. 23:14; Deut. 16:16; [Luke 2:41] [e]See Deut. 12:5-7 [f][Josh. 18:1]
4[g]Deut. 12:17, 18; 16:11; [Neh. 8:10, 12]

The Birth of Samuel

1 There was a certain man of [a]Ramathaim-zophim of [b]the hill country of Ephraim whose
name was Elkanah the son of Jeroham, son of Elihu, son of Tohu, son of Zuph, [c]an
Ephrathite. 2 He had two wives. The name of the one was Hannah, and the name of the
other, Peninnah. And Peninnah had children, but Hannah had no children.
3 Now this man used to go up [d]year by year from his city [e]to worship and to sacrifice
to the LORD of hosts [f]at Shiloh, where the two sons of Eli, Hophni and Phinehas, were
priests of the LORD. 4 On the day when Elkanah sacrificed, [g]he would give portions to
Peninnah his wife and to all her sons and daughters. 5 But to Hannah he gave a double
portion, because he loved her, though the LORD had closed her womb.[1] 6 And her rival
used to provoke her grievously to irritate her, because the LORD had closed her womb.
7 So it went on year by year. As often as she went up to the house of the LORD, she used

[1] Syriac; the meaning of the Hebrew is uncertain. Septuagint *And, although he loved Hannah, he would give Hannah only one portion, because the LORD had closed her womb*

1:1–7:17 *The Story of Samuel.* The birth of Samuel is God's answer to the prayer of a childless woman; he is also the answer to Israel's need for a prophet who will give God's guidance to his people in their transition from the period of the judges to the period of the kings.

1:1–4:1a *Rise of Samuel as Prophet.* Like the book of Ruth, 1–2 Samuel begins with the story of an ordinary Israelite family during the period of the judges. Through one woman's grief and faith, a child is born who will be instrumental in leading Israel to the next phase of its history, the establishment of the Davidic monarchy. This section also contains the "Song of Hannah," the prototype of the Magnificat (the "Song of Mary" in Luke 1:46–55). The story of another family appears here too. The Lord is worshiped, with sacrifices, at the sanctuary of Shiloh. The priesthood is descended from Aaron. Although Eli the head priest is a good man, he has weaknesses, especially in controlling his sons. They have no interest in the demands of God, only in what they get from their position. This section alternates between passages about the growth of the boy (Hb. *na'ar*) Samuel and passages proclaiming the evil of the young men (also *na'ar*, in plural), the sons of Eli. The two themes come together when the Lord gives young Samuel his first message as a prophet, announcing judgment on the house of Eli. The section ends with the statement that Samuel was established as a prophet of the Lord before all Israel.

1:1–28 *Birth and Dedication of Samuel.* Hannah, who has been barren, gives birth to Samuel and dedicates him to serve at the sanctuary.

1:1 Ramathaim-zophim is called Ramah in v. 19 and 2:11. Samuel later lived there (7:17; 8:4; 25:1), and it is presumably the city in the land of **Zuph** (named after Samuel's ancestor Zuph) where Saul meets him (9:5).

1:2 two wives. Probably **Hannah** was Elkanah's first wife, since she is named first. Presumably he married **Peninnah** because Hannah was barren; lack of an heir was a major problem in the ancient Near East, as in many other societies. Taking a second wife was one way to try to solve the problem (Gen. 16:2), as was levirate marriage (see note on Matt. 22:24; also Gen. 38:8; Deut. 25:6). Elkanah's pedigree suggests that it would be important to him to have an heir to continue the family and also that he was prosperous enough to afford a second marriage.

1:3 year by year. This may have been an annual family or clan gathering, celebrated by all its members, including women and children, such as the one later held by David's family (20:6). **the LORD of hosts**. This is the first appearance in the Bible of the title "the LORD of hosts," to whom Elkanah sacrifices and Hannah prays (1:11) at Shiloh. The title is used in Samuel several times and very frequently in the Psalms and the Prophets. "Hosts" (Hb. *tseba'ot*) is probably the plural of an abstract noun meaning something like "plentifulness" or "numberlessness." Hence, it refers to numerous entities such as heavenly bodies (Isa. 40:26), angelic beings (Josh. 5:14, "army of the LORD"), the armies of Israel (1 Sam. 17:45), or all creatures (Gen. 2:1). The title may originally have been particularly connected with worship at the Shiloh sanctuary (see 1 Sam. 4:4), in which case "hosts" would probably have referred to angelic beings, portrayed as God's "armies." **Shiloh**, the modern Khirbet Seilun, is 20 miles (32 km) north of Jerusalem, toward the eastern border of Ephraim. The tent of meeting was set up there in Josh. 18:1. The city also appears in Judg. 21:19–24 as the place from which the Benjaminites took their brides. Its destruction, presumably at the time of the events of 1 Samuel 4, is mentioned in Ps. 78:60 and Jer. 7:12–14.

1:4 portions. Elkanah's sacrifice is a "peace offering," in which parts of the sacrificial animal are burned, parts are given to the priest, and parts are eaten by the people who brought the sacrifice (Lev. 7:11–36; see also 1 Sam. 2:12–17).

1:5 a double portion. The Hebrew is difficult here, literally "two noses as one portion," perhaps referring to two heads of sacrificed sheep. In ritual texts from the city of Emar, the head of a sacrificial animal is treated as a favored part. This probably means that Hannah was given a "double portion," possibly also of the most favored part.

1:6 her rival used to provoke her. Cf. Hagar's attitude toward Sarah after she became pregnant (Gen. 16:4).

1:7, 9 house of the LORD . . . temple of the LORD. Was this a "tent," or was it a building with solid walls? The word "house" refers to a dwelling without specifying the material. In 2 Sam. 7:2 David says that "the ark of God dwells in a tent," and in 2 Sam. 7:6 the Lord says, "I have not lived in a house . . . to this day." In 2 Samuel 7 the contrast is between a tent (i.e., a house of cloth) and a house of cedar. In 1 Sam. 2:22 there is a reference to the "tent of meeting," while "doorpost of the temple" (1:9) and "opened the doors" (3:15) suggest more of a building. Perhaps there was a more solid structure around a cloth structure. The word for "temple" (Hb. *hekal*) derives from the

to provoke her. Therefore Hannah wept and would not eat. **8** And Elkanah, her husband,
said to her, "Hannah, why do you weep? And why do you not eat? And why is your heart
sad? [h]Am I not more to you than ten sons?"
9 After they had eaten and drunk in Shiloh, Hannah rose. Now Eli the priest was sitting
on the seat beside the doorpost of [i]the temple of the LORD. **10** She was [j]deeply distressed
and prayed to the LORD and wept bitterly. **11** And she [k]vowed a vow and said, "O LORD of
hosts, if you will indeed [l]look on the affliction of your servant and [m]remember me and not
forget your servant, but will give to your servant a son, then I will give him to the LORD
all the days of his life, [n]and no razor shall touch his head."
12 As she continued praying before the LORD, Eli observed her mouth. **13** Hannah was
speaking in her heart; only her lips moved, and her voice was not heard. Therefore Eli took
her to be a drunken woman. **14** And Eli said to her, "How long will you go on being drunk?
Put your wine away from you." **15** But Hannah answered, "No, my lord, I am a woman
troubled in spirit. I have drunk neither wine nor strong drink, but [o]I have been pouring
out my soul before the LORD. **16** Do not regard your servant as [p]a worthless woman, for all
along I have been speaking out of my great anxiety and vexation." **17** Then Eli answered,
[q]"Go in peace, and the God of Israel [r]grant your petition that you have made to him." **18** And
she said, [s]"Let your servant find favor in your eyes." Then the woman [t]went her way and
ate, and her face was no longer sad.
19 They rose early in the morning and worshiped before the LORD; then they went back
to their house at [u]Ramah. And Elkanah knew Hannah his wife, and the LORD [v]remembered
her. **20** And in due time Hannah conceived and bore a son, and she called his name Samuel,
for she said, "I have asked for him from the LORD."[1]

Samuel Given to the LORD

21 The man Elkanah and all his house [w]went up to offer to the LORD the yearly sacrifice
and to pay his vow. **22** But Hannah did not go up, for she said to her husband, "As soon as
the child is weaned, I will bring him, so that he may appear in the presence of the LORD
[x]and dwell there forever." **23** [y]Elkanah her husband said to her, "Do what seems best to you;
wait until you have weaned him; [z]only, may the LORD establish his word." So the woman
remained and nursed her son until she weaned him. **24** And when she had weaned him,
[a]she took him up with her, along with a three-year-old bull,[2] an ephah[3] of flour, and a
skin of wine, and she brought him to [b]the house of the LORD at Shiloh. And the child
was young. **25** Then they slaughtered the bull, and they brought the child to Eli. **26** And
she said, "Oh, my lord! [c]As you live, my lord, I am the woman who was standing here in
your presence, praying to the LORD. **27** For this child I prayed, [d]and the LORD has granted

8 [h]Ruth 4:15
9 [i]ch. 3:3
10 [j]Job 7:11; 10:1
11 [k]Gen. 28:20; Judg. 11:30 [l]Gen. 29:32 [m]ver. 19; [Gen. 30:22] [n]Judg. 13:5; [Num. 6:5]
15 [o]Job 30:16; Ps. 42:4; Lam. 2:19; [Ps. 62:8]
16 [p]ch. 2:12; Judg. 19:22
17 [q]ch. 20:42; Judg. 18:6; 2 Kgs. 5:19; Mark 5:34 [r]Ps. 20:4, 5
18 [s]Gen. 33:15; Ruth 2:13 [t][Eccles. 9:7]
19 [u]ch. 2:11; [ver. 1] [v]ver. 11
21 [w]ver. 3
22 [x]ver. 11, 28; [ch. 2:11, 18; 3:1]
23 [y][Num. 30:7] [z]2 Sam. 7:25
24 [a]Deut. 12:5, 6, 11 [b]ver. 3, 9; [Josh. 18:1]
26 [c]ch. 17:55; 20:3; 2 Sam. 11:11; 2 Kgs. 2:2, 4, 6; 4:30
27 [d]ver. 17; [Ps. 6:9]

[1] *Samuel* sounds like the Hebrew for *heard of God* [2] Dead Sea Scroll, Septuagint, Syriac; Masoretic Text *three bulls* [3] An *ephah* was about 3/5 bushel or 22 liters

Sumerian word *egal*, meaning "big house." There are cases in Ugaritic and Mari documents where it in fact refers to a large and complex tent structure.

1:8 Elkanah is truly concerned for his wife, but the history of Israel at this point turns on Hannah's actions and the Lord's response. **Am I not more to you than ten sons?** Elkanah attempts to comfort Hannah, though he seems not to understand Hannah's deep yearning for a child.

1:9 The **seat** was a symbol of Eli's authority; normally people sat on the ground.

1:11 I will give him to the LORD all the days of his life seems to mean that Hannah will dedicate her son as a Nazirite. According to Numbers 6, people might make a special vow to separate themselves to the Lord for a time. This involved letting **no razor . . . touch** one's **head**, eating nothing from the grapevine, and not going near a dead body. Hannah mentions only the razor in the text, but that part of the vow probably stood for the whole of the regulations. According to Lev. 27:1–8, a person as young as a month old could be vowed to the Lord, apparently to work in the temple. The Leviticus passage deals with redeeming someone who has been dedicated, but Hannah does not intend to redeem her son.

1:12–19 Eli shows his piety in rebuking Hannah, whom he takes to be **drunk** (which would be an offense to the sanctuary). But Hannah explains that her visible display of emotion is genuine, due to deep anguish. Eli acknowledges his mistake and blesses Hannah—a blessing that proves effective.

1:20 The most natural meaning of the name **Samuel** is "name of God," or possibly "offspring of God." Samuel bore the name of God, who gave him to Hannah.

1:23 Elkanah has been in the background, but he supports Hannah and participates in the dedication (v. 25; 2:11).

1:24 Either a **three-year-old bull** or "three bulls" (ESV footnote). In either case Elkanah apparently was a prosperous man who was able to afford an expensive offering of a bull or bulls and large amounts of grain and **wine**. Three bulls would correspond to the priestly regulations, which specify that together with each bull sacrificed, three-tenths of an ephah of grain should be offered (Num. 15:9; 28:12, 20, 28). With three bulls, one would expect an offering of nine-tenths of an ephah, just a little less than the one ephah that Hannah offered. The **skin** (or "jar") may have held as much as 6 gallons (22 liters) of wine. The reference to the **child** anticipates references to "the boy" (the Hb. word in both cases is *na'ar*) in 1 Sam. 2:11.

28[e]Gen. 24:26, 52
Chapter 2
1[f]For ver. 1-10, see Luke 1:46-53 [g]ver. 10; Ps. 75:10; 89:17, 24; 92:10; 112:9; 148:14 [h]Ps. 9:14; 13:5; 20:5; 35:9
2[i]Ex. 15:11; Ps. 86:8; 89:6, 8 [j]Deut. 32:30, 31
4[k]Ps. 37:15; 46:9; 76:3
5[l]Ps. 113:9; Isa. 54:1 [m]Jer. 15:9
6[n]Deut. 32:39

me my petition that I made to him. **28** Therefore I have lent him to the LORD. As long as he lives, he is lent to the LORD."

[e]And he worshiped the LORD there.

Hannah's Prayer

2 And Hannah prayed and said,

[f]"My heart exults in the LORD;
[g]my horn is exalted in the LORD.
My mouth derides my enemies,
because [h]I rejoice in your salvation.
2 [i]"There is none holy like the LORD:
for there is none besides you;
there is [j]no rock like our God.
3 Talk no more so very proudly,
let not arrogance come from your mouth;
for the LORD is a God of knowledge,
and by him actions are weighed.
4 [k]The bows of the mighty are broken,
but the feeble bind on strength.
5 Those who were full have hired themselves out for bread,
but those who were hungry have ceased to hunger.
[l]The barren has borne seven,
[m]but she who has many children is forlorn.
6 [n]The LORD kills and brings to life;
he brings down to Sheol and raises up.

1:25 the bull. See note on v. 24.

1:26 As you live, or "as your soul lives," is a common form of oath (2 Sam. 11:11; 14:19), as is the phrase "as the LORD lives" (see 1 Sam. 14:39; 26:16; Jer. 16:14–15). The two were often combined (1 Sam. 20:3; 25:26; 2 Kings 2:2).

1:27 And the LORD has granted me my petition that I made to him repeats almost verbatim Eli's blessing in v. 17. Joyously, Hannah points to **this child** as the answer to her prayer. The words "petition" (here and v. 17), "asked" (v. 20), and "lent" (v. 28 twice) are all from the verbal root *sha'al*, so a wordplay may be intended.

2:1–10 *Hannah's Song.* Hannah's song fits well in the narrative and marks the end of the story of Samuel's birth. Many of Hannah's themes are found in the Magnificat of Mary (Luke 1:46–56). The reference to the "king" in 1 Sam. 2:10 also looks forward to the rest of the book. At the other end of the grand narrative of 1–2 Samuel are the songs of David in 2 Samuel 22–23. These three songs are a frame around the entire narrative of 1–2 Samuel. Hannah's song is really a song of praise, or a hymn, to the God who reverses human fortunes by his mighty power, the Creator beyond all human understanding who protects the faithful. There are many similarities to psalms and other passages of the OT, as the numerous ESV cross-references show. It is especially close to Psalm 113. It starts with Hannah's personal emotions, but it is not about gloating over Peninnah, who was presumably still living with her children in Elkanah's household. Rather, Hannah's emotions are a step toward glorifying the Lord for his guidance in human affairs. Hannah alternates between the themes of the Lord's holy sovereignty (1 Sam. 2:1b–3, 6–7, 8b–10a) and the reversal of human fortunes (vv. 4–5, 8a) and ends with the theme of kingship (v. 10b).

2:1 my horn is exalted in the LORD. The song both starts and ends with the declaration that the Lord exalts. The verb translated as "exalt" or "raise up" appears also in vv. 7, 8, and 10 and expresses the theme of the song. The Hebrew for "horn" is often used as a symbol of strength (cf. Deut. 33:17; 2 Sam. 22:3; Ps. 89:17; etc.). With the expression **my enemies**, Hannah is not making a personal attack on Peninnah (one person) but is speaking against God's enemies. His enemies are also Hannah's enemies, because his enemies attack her trust in God and his dealings with her (see Ps. 139:21–22). The climax of this verse is **because I rejoice in your salvation**.

2:2 The first and third lines of this verse are parallel: **holy** is parallel to **rock**, and **the LORD** is parallel to **God**, with different structure but similar meaning. The formula "there is no . . . like . . ." denotes incomparability. Thus, **for there is none besides you** states that there is no absolutely holy being besides the Lord; moreover, only the Lord is God, i.e., "monotheism" is true (see Deut. 4:35; 32:39; 2 Sam. 22:32). "Rock," a common OT epithet for God (e.g., Deut. 32:4, 15; 2 Sam. 22:2; 23:3), indicates God's protection and strength. In Ps. 118:22 and Isa. 8:14; 28:16; as well as in 1 Pet. 2:6–8, "rock" has a messianic significance (see note on 1 Sam. 2:10). With "**our** God," Hannah speaks as a member of the covenant community, whom she addresses in the next verse.

2:3 by him actions are weighed. The ESV follows the "spoken" (*Qere*) Hebrew tradition, and means that God's **knowledge** extends even to the motives behind human actions. The "written" (*Ketib*) tradition, "actions are not weighed," would not make sense unless one added "*his* actions are not weighed," i.e., God is not subject to human judgment.

2:5 seven. Hannah herself actually bore only six children, including Samuel (v. 21), but this is a general statement, and seven is a poetic number for perfection. **is forlorn**. The Hebrew usually means "becomes a widow," but here it means "becomes childless."

2:6–7 The Lord has total authority over life and death, including material and social life. Verses 4–5 give examples of how the Lord reverses human fortunes; vv. 6–7 state it more generally. **kills . . . brings to life**, **brings down . . . raises up**, **makes poor . . . makes rich**, **brings low . . . exalts**. These are merisms, expressions in which two words on the extreme ends of a scale are used to express everything on the whole scale. The Lord controls not only birth and death, but also the whole of life in between.

2:6 Sheol here refers to the place of the dead. In the Bible, it is usually found in idiomatic expressions such as "go down to Sheol" or "come up

7 [o]The LORD makes poor and makes rich;
[p]he brings low and he exalts.
8 [q]He raises up the poor from the dust;
he lifts the needy from the ash heap
[r]to make them sit with princes
and inherit a seat of honor.
[s]For the pillars of the earth are the LORD's,
and on them he has set the world.

9 [t]"He will guard the feet of his faithful ones,
but the wicked shall be cut off in darkness,
for not by might shall a man prevail.
10 [u]The adversaries of the LORD shall be broken to pieces;
[v]against them he will thunder in heaven.
[w]The LORD will judge the ends of the earth;
he will give strength to his king
[x]and exalt the horn of his anointed."

11 Then Elkanah went home [y]to Ramah. [z]And the boy[1] was ministering to the LORD in the presence of Eli the priest.

Eli's Worthless Sons

12 Now the sons of Eli were [a]worthless men. [b]They did not know the LORD. 13 The custom of the priests with the people was that when any man offered sacrifice, the priest's servant would come, while the meat was boiling, with a three-pronged fork in his hand, 14 and he would thrust it into the pan or kettle or cauldron or pot. All that the fork brought up

[1] Hebrew *na'ar* can be rendered *boy* (2:11, 18, 21, 26, 3:1, 8), *servant* (2:13, 15), or *young man* (2:17), depending on the context

7[o][Job 1:21] [p]Job 5:11; Ps. 75:7
8[q]Ps. 113:7, 8; [Dan. 4:17; Luke 1:52] [r]Job 36:7 [s][Job 38:4-6; Ps. 24:2; 102:25; 104:5]
9[t]Ps. 121:3; Prov. 3:26; [Ps. 91:11]
10[u]Ps. 2:9 [v]ch. 7:10; Ps. 18:13; [2 Sam. 22:14] [w]Ps. 96:10, 13; 98:9 [x]ver. 1; [Ps. 89:24]
11[y]ch. 1:19 [z]ver. 18; ch. 3:1
12[a]See ch. 1:16 [b]Judg. 2:10

from Sheol." God is also the One who **raises up** a soul from Sheol (e.g., Ps. 30:3), so he has authority over the dead as well as the living. He is the One who holds the key to Job's question: "If a man dies, shall he live again?" (Job 14:14). Job remains confident: "For I know that my Redeemer lives, and at the last he will stand upon the earth" (Job 19:25). Hannah affirms that same confidence.

2:8 The Lord is sovereign over life, for he created and owns the **world**. The exact meaning of the word **pillars** (Hb. *metsuqe*) is not known, but there are similar expressions using the ordinary word for "pillars" (Hb. *'ammudim*; Job 9:6; Ps. 75:3) or "foundations" (2 Sam. 22:16). The reference to the foundation or support ("pillars") of the earth is meaningful here, for the Lord upholds both the place where his people live as well as the moral order of this world; he protects his faithful, while he destroys the wicked (1 Sam. 2:9).

2:9 Darkness functions here as a metaphor for the silence brought upon the wicked in death (Ps. 35:6–8).

2:10 For the kingship of the Lord and his role as **judge**, see Ps. 96:10. **The ends of the earth** almost always appears in the context of describing the Lord's uniqueness, majesty, and dominion (e.g., Ps. 67:7; 98:3; Prov. 30:4; Isa. 52:10; Mic. 5:4; Zech. 9:10). Since there was as yet no **king** in Israel, it is possible that the last two lines are a comment by the narrator rather than part of Hannah's prayer. The law made provision for a king, however, and the institution was well known in Israel even before it was practiced (Judg. 8:22; 9:6; 1 Samuel 8), so there is no reason to think that these are not Hannah's words. **His anointed**, or "his messiah," appears here for the first time in the Bible (though Hb. *mashiakh*, "anointed," is used of priests, e.g., Lev. 4:3). In the OT, priests and prophets are also referred to as "anointed," but in Samuel most references are royal. Though the anointing of kings is known from various places in the ancient Near East, "messiah" as a royal title is attested only in the Bible. The song concludes with a twofold plea for the Lord to raise the king of Israel to a position of prominence (**exalt the horn**) worthy of the great God who appointed him.

The Rise of Samuel, Israel's Last Judge

Decline of Eli's Sons	Rise of Samuel
Wickedness of Eli's sons (1 Sam. 2:12–17)	Samuel approved by Eli (1 Sam. 2:18–21)
Eli reproves his sons (1 Sam. 2:22–25)	Samuel grows in favor (1 Sam. 2:26)
Prophecy against Eli and sons (1 Sam. 2:27–36; cf. 4:11–18)	Samuel called and given prophetic word (1 Sam. 3:1–4:1a)
The Philistines; the ark and Eli's house [defeat/capture/covenant defiled] (1 Sam. 4:1b–22)	The Philistines; the ark and Samuel [return/victory/covenant renewed] (1 Sam. 7:2–17)

2:11–36 *Samuel, and Eli's Two Sons.* At the same time that the boy Samuel is ministering to the Lord at Shiloh (vv. 11, 18; 3:1), Eli's own two sons are hindering the worship there.

2:12–17 The **priest's servant** (vv. 13, 15) was probably one of the **worthless . . . sons of Eli** (v. 12; cf. "young man" [Hb. *na'ar*; vv. 13, 15, ESV footnote] with "young men" [Hb. *ne'arim*, plural of *na'ar*, v. 17]), rather than merely a servant. Some interpret vv. 13–14 as being the accepted, though degenerate, custom, and vv. 15–16 as representing the perversion of this custom. Another interpretation is that the author condemns both practices. This latter view is supported by the use of the word **moreover** (Hb. *gam*) at the beginning of v. 15. Thus in this passage there are two general statements about the sons (vv. 12, 17) framing descriptions of two of their wicked practices.

2:12–13 Custom (Hb. *mishpat*) usually means an expected standard (e.g., Deut. 18:3, "this shall be the priest's due [*mishpat*] from the people, from those offering a sacrifice"); it can also mean "justice" (cf. 1 Sam. 8:3). Although it is hardly likely that the young men were ignorant of the regulations, their lack of real knowledge of the Lord or even concern for his honor (**They did not know the LORD**) meant that they completely ignored his commands.

2:13–14 The priests were to be supported by portions of the sacrifices of the people. In various parts of the Mosaic law the portion to be given to the priests is specified for various sacrifices, e.g., Deut. 18:3 (shoulder,

the priest would take for himself. This is what they did at Shiloh to all the Israelites who
came there. **15** Moreover, [c]before the fat was burned, the priest's servant would come and
say to the man who was sacrificing, "Give meat for the priest to roast, for he will not accept
boiled meat from you but only raw." **16** And if the man said to him, "Let them burn the fat
first, and then take as much as you wish," he would say, "No, you must give it now, and if
not, I will take it by force." **17** Thus the sin of the young men was very great [d]in the sight
of the LORD, [e]for the men treated the offering of the LORD with contempt.

18 [f]Samuel was ministering before the LORD, a boy [g]clothed with a linen ephod. **19** And
his mother used to make for him a little robe and take it to him each year [h]when she went
up with her husband to offer the yearly sacrifice. **20** Then Eli would bless Elkanah and his
wife, and say, "May the LORD give you children by this woman [i]for the petition she asked
of the LORD." So then they would return to their home.

21 [j]Indeed the LORD visited Hannah, and she conceived and bore three sons and two
daughters. [k]And the boy Samuel grew in the presence of the LORD.

Eli Rebukes His Sons

22 Now Eli was very old, and he kept hearing all that his sons were doing to all Israel,
and how they lay with the women who [l]were serving at the entrance to the tent of meeting. **23** And he said to them, "Why do you do such things? For I hear of your evil dealings
from all these people. **24** No, my sons; it is no good report that I hear the people of the
LORD spreading abroad. **25** If someone sins against a man, God will mediate for him, but
if someone sins against the LORD, who can intercede for him?" But they would not listen
to the voice of their father, [m]for it was the will of the LORD to put them to death.

26 Now the boy Samuel [n]continued to grow both in stature and in favor with the LORD
and also with man.

The LORD Rejects Eli's Household

27 And there came [o]a man of God to Eli and said to him, "Thus says the LORD, [p]'Did I
indeed reveal myself to the house of your father when they were in Egypt subject to the
house of Pharaoh? **28** [q]Did I choose him out of all the tribes of Israel to be my priest, to

15 [c]Lev. 3:5, 16; 7:23, 25, 31
17 [d][Gen. 6:11] [e][Mal. 2:8]
18 [f]ver. 11; ch. 3:1 [g]Ex. 28:4; 2 Sam. 6:14; 1 Chr. 15:27
19 [h]ch. 1:3
20 [i]ch. 1:28
21 [j]Gen. 21:1 [k]ver. 26; ch. 3:19; [Judg. 13:24; Luke 1:80; 2:40]
22 [l]Ex. 38:8
25 [m][Josh. 11:20]
26 [n]Luke 2:52
27 [o]1 Kgs. 13:1 [p][Ex. 3–12]
28 [q]Ex. 28:1; Num. 18:1, 7

cheeks, and stomach) and Lev. 7:31–32 (breast and right thigh). But the practice in 1 Sam. 2:13–14 has little in common with the regulations on priestly rights.

2:15–16 This is an extraordinary situation: the **priest**, who was supposed to know the rules of sacrifice, was engaging in behavior that shocked even the ordinary worshiper. The **fat** was normally removed from certain internal organs and offered as a burnt offering to God (see Ex. 29:13; Lev. 3:3–5). Also, the priest would normally take his share right after killing the animal, before giving it to the worshiper.

2:17 It was because the sons of Eli did not know the Lord (v. 12) that they could treat **with contempt** his holy sacrifices that he had commanded for worship.

2:18–21 The story returns to another *na'ar* ("young man, boy"), **Samuel** (cf. note on vv. 12–17, "young man"). Before, Samuel was **ministering** "in the presence of Eli the priest" (v. 11), but now he is ministering simply **before the LORD**, in the garment of a priest. The **linen ephod** was probably a simple tunic or apron worn by priests (22:18) or sometimes by others, as by David as he brought the ark to Jerusalem (2 Sam. 6:14).

2:22–23 The **women** were not Canaanite cult prostitutes, as is sometimes speculated. Lying with them was considered among the sons' **evil dealings**.

2:25 if someone sins against the LORD, who can intercede for him? This shows the need for a mediator between man and God. Because of Eli's sons' willful rejection of him, **it was the will of the LORD to put them to death**. When God is determined to destroy, no human intercession is effective. For the writers of the Bible, the fact that divine providence and human character mingle means that destinies are regarded as ultimately the result of the divine will. The most obvious example is Pharaoh in Ex. 7:13, 22, etc. But this does not mean that people are not accountable; Hophni and Phinehas had rejected God, even ignoring their father's warning.

2:26 Similar language is used in Luke 2:52 to describe the physical and spiritual growth of the boy Jesus.

2:27–28 Did I indeed reveal . . . ? Did I choose him . . . ? These are rhetorical questions, expecting "Yes, indeed!" as an answer. **The house of your father** in vv. 27, 28, 30 is a technical term referring to Eli's extended family. "Your father" probably refers specifically to Ithamar, son of Aaron, who was made a priest of the Lord at Mount Sinai along with his father and brothers (Ex. 28:1; cf. 1 Chron. 24:3). Eli was a descendant of this house, according to 1 Chron. 24:3, where it is stated that his great-great-great-grandson Ahimelech was "of the sons of Ithamar." The descent from Eli to this Ahimelech is as follows: Eli—Phinehas—Ahitub (1 Sam. 14:3)—Ahimelech—Abiathar (22:20)—Ahimelech (2 Sam. 8:17; 1 Chron. 24:6). The duties of the priest were **to go up to** the Lord's **altar**, i.e., (1) to burn offerings on the altar (e.g., Lev. 1:9), which was connected with the privilege of being sustained from portions of the sacrifices, a privilege that Eli's sons were abusing (1 Sam. 2:12–17); (2) to **burn incense** on the altar of incense (Ex. 30:1; see Luke 1:9); and (3) to **wear an ephod before** God. This ephod was probably not the linen garment of 1 Sam. 2:18, but the jeweled breastplate described in Exodus 28 that symbolized the people of Israel, with pockets for the sacred lots (for priests casting lots, see Lev. 16:8, etc.). According to 1 Sam. 21:9, that ephod was later kept in the sanctuary of Nob, and Abiathar took it with him when he escaped to David (23:6). **I gave to the house of your father all my offerings by fire**. Except for the case of burnt offerings, which were wholly burned, when an offering was made, part was burned as a "memorial portion," but the rest of the grain offerings, sin offerings, and guilt offerings and a part of the peace offerings were normally eaten by the priests (Lev. 6:14–18; 7:1–38).

2:27 A **man of God** is a synonym for "prophet" (e.g., 9:6; 2 Kings 1:9). **Thus the LORD has said** is the regular prophetic "messenger formula." In Samuel this formula appears also in 1 Sam. 10:18; 15:2; 2 Sam. 7:5, 8;

go up to my altar, to burn incense, [r]to wear an ephod before me? [s]I gave to the house of
your father all my offerings by fire from the people of Israel. **29** Why then do you [t]scorn[1]
my sacrifices and my offerings that I commanded for my dwelling, and honor your sons
above me by fattening yourselves on the choicest parts of every offering of my people
Israel?' **30** Therefore the LORD, the God of Israel, declares: [v]'I promised that your house
and the house of your father should go in and out before me forever,' [w]but now the LORD
declares: 'Far be it from me, for those who honor me I will honor, and those who despise
me shall be lightly esteemed. **31** Behold, [x]the days are coming when I will cut off your
strength and the strength of your father's house, so that there will not be an old man in
your house. **32** Then [y]in distress you will look with envious eye on all the prosperity that
shall be bestowed on Israel, [z]and there shall not be an old man in your house forever.
33 The only one of you whom I shall not cut off from my altar shall be spared to weep
his[2] eyes out to grieve his heart, and all the descendants[3] of your house shall die by the
sword of men.[4] **34** [a]And this that shall come upon your two sons, Hophni and Phinehas,
shall be the sign to you: both of them shall die [b]on the same day. **35** [c]And I will raise up
for myself a faithful priest, who shall do according to what is in my heart and in my
mind. [d]And I will build him a sure house, and he shall go in and out before [e]my anointed
forever. **36** And everyone who is left in your house shall come to implore him for a piece
of silver or a loaf of bread and shall say, "Please put me in one of the priests' places, that
I may eat a morsel of bread."'"

The LORD Calls Samuel

3 [f]Now the boy Samuel was ministering to the LORD in the presence of Eli. [g]And the
word of the LORD was rare in those days; there was no frequent vision.
2 At that time Eli, [h]whose eyesight had begun to grow dim so that he could not see, was
lying down in his own place. **3** [i]The lamp of God had not yet gone out, and Samuel was
lying down [j]in the temple of the LORD, where the ark of God was.
4 Then the LORD called Samuel, and he said, "Here I am!" **5** and ran to Eli and said, "Here
I am, for you called me." But he said, "I did not call; lie down again." So he went and lay
down.
6 And the LORD called again, "Samuel!" and Samuel arose and went to Eli and said,
"Here I am, for you called me." But he said, "I did not call, my son; lie down again." **7** Now

[1] Hebrew *kick at* [2] Septuagint; Hebrew *your;* twice in this verse [3] Hebrew *increase* [4] Septuagint; Hebrew *die as men*

28 [r][ch. 14:3; 22:18] [s]Lev. 2:3, 10; 6:16; 7:7, 8, 34; 10:14, 15; Num. 5:9, 10; See Num. 18:8-19
29 [t]Deut. 32:15
30 [v]Ex. 27:21; 29:9 [w][Jer. 18:9, 10]
31 [x]1 Kgs. 2:27; [ch. 4:11, 18, 20; 22:18, 19]
32 [y]ch. 4:11; [Judg. 18:30]; See Ps. 78:59-64 [z][Zech. 8:4]
34 [a]1 Kgs. 13:3 [b]ch. 4:11
35 [c]1 Kgs. 2:35; 1 Chr. 29:22 [d]ch. 25:28; 1 Kgs. 11:38; [2 Sam. 7:11, 27] [e]2 Sam. 22:51; Ps. 18:50; [Ps. 89:20]

Chapter 3

1 [f]ch. 2:11, 18 [g][ver. 21; Ps. 74:9; Amos 8:11]
2 [h]ch. 4:15; Gen. 27:1; 48:10; [Deut. 34:7]
3 [i]Ex. 27:20, 21; Lev. 24:2, 3; 2 Chr. 13:11 [j]ch. 1:9

12:7, 11; 24:12. In the ancient world, messengers were supposed to recite their messages verbatim, so the messenger would begin with "[The sender] has spoken thus" and use the first person in the body of the message (e.g., Gen. 45:9).

2:29 You is plural here. The form of the verb **scorn** indicates a habitual action. By scorning the offerings, Eli is scorning the Lord and honoring his sons, while the Lord honors those who honor him and lightly esteems those who despise him (v. 30).

2:30 Though the Lord **promised**, he can revoke his promise for willful disregard of the terms of the promise. **Far be it from me** is a statement of strong denial of the previous statement (e.g., Gen. 44:7; 1 Sam. 12:23; 2 Sam. 20:20; cf. also 1 Sam. 20:9).

2:31–34 This is a curse for breaking the Lord's covenant, with punishment given in words of curses similar to the curses in the covenant. **Behold, the days are coming** is an eschatological formula often found in the Prophets. The **only one** who **shall be spared** is Abiathar, who escaped when the priests of Nob were killed (22:20). Solomon later banished him to Anathoth; see 1 Kings 2:26–27, where it is stated that the banishment was a fulfillment of the prophecy against Eli. Jeremiah was probably descended from this house (Jer. 1:1). **All the descendants** is a general statement, because there are references to those who were left (see the previous clause in 1 Sam. 2:33, as well as v. 36). Eli will not live to experience the punishment, but the death of his two sons **on the same day** will be a **sign** to him that the prophecy is true.

2:35 The **faithful priest** with a **sure house** is probably Zadok, priest under David and a descendant of Ithamar's brother Eleazar, son of Aaron (2 Sam. 8:17; 1 Chron. 24:3; see also Judg. 20:28). The Hebrew word "faithful" is the same as "sure" later in the sentence: the *ne'eman* priest will have a *ne'eman* house. The **anointed** is the king. The wording here is similar to that in 2 Samuel 7, where David is promised a "sure" house (2 Sam. 7:16).

3:1–4:1a *Call of Samuel as a Prophet.* This passage tells how the Lord called Samuel to be a prophet—the prophet who will anoint the first two legitimate kings of Israel. As a true prophet, he must speak the words of God and never hide them; Israel is to respond by believing these words and obeying them. God repeats his judgment on the house of Eli (2:27–36), foreshadowing his rejection of the house of Saul. The passage begins with a situation ("the word of the LORD was rare," 3:1), which God then relieves (3:19–4:1a). The Lord calls Samuel three times, each call increasing in intensity; but Samuel thinks it is only his foster father Eli who is calling. Finally the elderly Eli perceives who is calling, and Samuel receives his first communication from the Lord. The events of 4:1b–7:1 probably take place while Samuel is growing up, before he is established as a prophet. He reappears in 7:3.

3:1 The word of the LORD was rare in those days, but that is about to change.

3:3 The **lamp of God** was placed in the tent of meeting, outside the veil before the Most Holy Place, where the ark was, and burned every day from evening to morning (Ex. 27:20–21; Lev. 24:1–3). It **had not yet gone out**, so the time was probably just before dawn. The **ark of God** had probably been placed in Shiloh when the tent of meeting was set up there in Josh. 18:1. In Judg. 20:26–27 the ark is said to have been in Bethel, but it was apparently moved back to Shiloh.

3:7 Samuel did not yet know the LORD in a personal relationship, though of course he knew *about* him.

11 [k]2 Kgs. 21:12; Jer. 19:3
12 [l]See ch. 2:30-36
13 [l][See ver. 12 above] [m]ch. 2:12, 17, 22 [n]ch. 2:23-25
14 [o][Isa. 22:14]
17 [p][Ruth 1:17]
18 [q][2 Sam. 10:12; Job 1:21; 2:10; Ps. 39:9; Isa. 39:8]
19 [r]See ch. 2:21 [s][ch. 9:6]
20 [t]See 2 Sam. 3:10
21 [u][Josh. 18:1] [v]ver. 1, 4
Chapter 4
1 [w][ch. 5:1; 7:12] [x]ch. 29:1; Josh. 12:18

Samuel did not yet know the LORD, and the word of the LORD had not yet been revealed
to him.
8 And the LORD called Samuel again the third time. And he arose and went to Eli and
said, "Here I am, for you called me." Then Eli perceived that the LORD was calling the boy.
9 Therefore Eli said to Samuel, "Go, lie down, and if he calls you, you shall say, 'Speak, LORD,
for your servant hears.'" So Samuel went and lay down in his place.
10 And the LORD came and stood, calling as at other times, "Samuel! Samuel!" And Samuel
said, "Speak, for your servant hears." 11 Then the LORD said to Samuel, "Behold, I am about
to do a thing in Israel [k]at which the two ears of everyone who hears it will tingle. 12 On that
day I will fulfill against Eli [l]all that I have spoken concerning his house, from beginning
to end. 13 [l]And I declare to him that I am about to punish his house forever, for the iniquity
that he knew, [m]because his sons were blaspheming God,[1] [n]and he did not restrain them.
14 Therefore I swear to the house of Eli [o]that the iniquity of Eli's house shall not be atoned
for by sacrifice or offering forever."
15 Samuel lay until morning; then he opened the doors of the house of the LORD. And
Samuel was afraid to tell the vision to Eli. 16 But Eli called Samuel and said, "Samuel, my
son." And he said, "Here I am." 17 And Eli said, "What was it that he told you? Do not hide
it from me. [p]May God do so to you and more also if you hide anything from me of all that
he told you." 18 So Samuel told him everything and hid nothing from him. And he said,
[q]"It is the LORD. Let him do what seems good to him."
19 [r]And Samuel grew, and the LORD was with him [s]and let none of his words fall to the
ground. 20 And all Israel [t]from Dan to Beersheba knew that Samuel was established as a
prophet of the LORD. 21 And the LORD appeared again at Shiloh, for the LORD revealed
himself to Samuel [u]at Shiloh [v]by the word of the LORD.

The Philistines Capture the Ark

4 And the word of Samuel came to all Israel.
Now Israel went out to battle against the Philistines. They encamped at [w]Ebenezer, and
the Philistines encamped at [x]Aphek. 2 The Philistines drew up in line against Israel, and
when the battle spread, Israel was defeated before the Philistines, who killed about four

[1] *Or blaspheming for themselves*

3:10 Samuel! Samuel! The Lord called other people twice by name at a crucial point in their lives; e.g., Abraham (Gen. 22:11), Jacob (Gen. 46:2), and Moses (Ex. 3:4).

3:11 This is the Lord's first word to Samuel as a prophet. It is often difficult for the recipient to receive the Lord's initial revelation; cf. Moses (Ex. 4:13) and Isaiah (Isa. 6:9).

3:12 all that I have spoken. Cf. 2:27–36.

3:13 The MT reads "blaspheming for themselves" (see ESV footnote). In Hebrew the phrases **blaspheming God** and "blaspheming for themselves" differ by just one consonant. That consonant was left out by pious scribes so that in copying they would not even need to write the offensive phrase "blaspheming God." Cf. Ex. 22:28; Lev. 24:15.

3:14 Eli's house has despised God's sacrifices and offerings (2:29), and hence these things will have no efficacy on their behalf. Though normal or inadvertent sins of priests could be **atoned for** by **offering** (Lev. 4:3–12), Eli's sons sinned defiantly, and their guilt could not be removed (Num. 15:30; see also Heb. 10:26), as Eli himself recognizes (1 Sam. 2:25).

3:17 May God do so to you and more also if is a form of solemn appeal to the Lord, a kind of oath. Cf. Ruth 1:17; 1 Sam. 14:44; 25:22; 2 Sam. 3:9; 19:13; 1 Kings 19:2.

3:18 It is the LORD. Eli accepts the judgment humbly.

3:19 the LORD . . . let none of his words fall to the ground. I.e., all that Samuel spoke was fulfilled, and thus he could be known as a prophet (Deut. 18:21–22). On the relationship between the prophet and the word of the Lord, see Jer. 20:8–9; Amos 3:8.

3:20 From Dan to Beersheba is the traditional limits of Israel to the north and south (Judg. 20:1; 2 Sam. 17:11).

4:1b–7:1 *Story of the Ark of God.* The ark of the covenant was the visible sign of the presence and power of God. Previously housed in the Shiloh sanctuary, it now takes center stage. After a disastrous defeat by the Philistines, the elders of Israel realize that the defeat was the work of the Lord, but there is no indication that they seek to know how they have sinned. Instead, they decide that their own action of bringing the ark to the battlefield will save them, almost as if they were forcing the Lord to do their will. But the ark is not a charm. Israel is defeated, the ark is captured by the Philistines, and Eli and his sons die. Probably Shiloh itself is destroyed soon after, since Eli's descendants go to Nob (21:1–9; 22:6–23). God, however, cannot let the enemy think that they have defeated him. For seven months he causes plagues and disturbances wherever the ark is taken, until the Philistines give up and send the ark back to Israel with a tribute of gold. It remains in Kiriath-jearim until David takes it to Jerusalem (2 Samuel 6). Samuel is completely absent from this story (reappearing in 1 Sam. 7:3), which indicates that these events took place while he was growing up. The Philistines, who appear in both Judges and Samuel, were one of the "Sea Peoples" who migrated from across the Aegean and settled on the coastal plain of southern Palestine about 1200 B.C., establishing a league of city-states. (The Philistines of Genesis were probably from an earlier wave of immigrants from across the Aegean.) They seem to have adopted the Canaanite language and proper names and gods soon after they arrived (see notes on 1 Sam. 5:2; 31:10). They were skilled in pottery and also in metallurgy (13:20).

4:1b–22 *Capture of the Ark.* After suffering defeat in battle at the hands of the Philistines, the people of Israel try to use the ark of the covenant to ensure victory; instead, the Philistines defeat them again, killing Eli's two sons and taking the ark into exile. When Eli hears of it, he suddenly dies. For reflections on these events cf. Ps. 78:58–66 and Jer. 7:8–15.

4:1b The **Philistines** make their first appearance in 1–2 Samuel. **Aphek** was 8 miles (13 km) east of Tel Aviv, north of the Philistia plain, and just to the west of the hill country of Ephraim. The Shillo River, which goes through the center of Ephraim, comes out of the mountains nearby. The

thousand men on the field of battle. 3 And when the people came to the camp, the elders
of Israel said, "Why has the LORD defeated us today before the Philistines? Let us bring the
ark of the covenant of the LORD here [y]from Shiloh, that it[1] may come among us and save
us from the power of our enemies." 4 So the people sent to Shiloh and brought from there
the ark of the covenant of the LORD of hosts, [z]who is enthroned on the cherubim. And the
two sons of Eli, Hophni and Phinehas, were there with the ark of the covenant of God.
5 As soon as the ark of the covenant of the LORD came into the camp, all Israel [a]gave a
mighty shout, so that the earth resounded. 6 And when the Philistines heard the noise of

[1] *Or he*

3[y] Josh. 18:1
4[z] Ex. 25:22; 2 Sam. 6:2; Ps. 80:1; 99:1; [Num. 7:89]
5[a] Josh. 6:5, 20

location of **Ebenezer** is uncertain, but it may have been a site 2 miles (3.2 km) farther east. The Philistines were interested in expanding their control to the north.

4:3–4 from Shiloh. The **ark of the covenant** had been "in the temple of the LORD" in Shiloh (3:3). (On the details of the ark, cf. Ex. 25:10–22; 37:1–9; and illustration to the right.) Moses was commanded by the Lord to put the tablets of the covenant, or the "testimony," into the ark (Ex. 25:16; Deut. 10:5; cf. 1 Kings 8:9). **Cherubim** often appear in the iconography of the ancient Near East as hybrid figures, with animal and human characteristics. **enthroned**. The ark was the visible sign of the holy presence of the Lord, whose real throne is on high, above the heavens. But it was more than just a sign, for the ark was also the focal point of God's actual presence among his people (Ex. 25:22 says, "There I will meet with you, and from above the mercy seat, from between the two cherubim that are on the ark of the testimony, I will speak with you . . ."; cf. Num. 7:89; also Ex. 29:42–43; 30:6, 36; 37:1–9; 40:34–38; Lev. 16:2; Num. 17:4). The conception of the ark as a visible sign of the Lord's presence gave a military importance to the ark (as can be seen in Num. 10:33–36 and Joshua 3–4; 6); it functioned as a battle safeguard and showed that the Lord was present and fighting for Israel. This understanding was certainly behind the actions of the elders in the present story. They may have thought that the Lord smote them because they had not trusted in the ark and had neglected it. Or perhaps they just thought that it would perform a miracle if used magically. That the ark would inevitably grant victory was a persistent idea that even the present story was not able to dispel. For the phrase **the LORD of hosts**, see note on 1 Sam. 1:3; cf. chart, p. 1775. **Let us bring the ark of the covenant of the LORD . . . that it may come among us**. The Hebrew might also mean "that he [the LORD] may come" (see ESV footnote), but in either case, the elders are treating the Lord as a thing. By saying "bring," the narrator is probably conveying the idea that the people treated this sacred object disrespectfully as an instrument through which victory might be attained. Surely, the covenant people had lost the sense of awe toward God's holy presence. They **brought from there the ark**. The verb is literally "carried" (Hb. *nasa'*); to "carry" the ark by its poles was the proper way to move it (Ex. 25:14); see also 2 Sam. 6:13; cf. 2 Sam. 6:3, where "carried" is literally "made to ride" (Hb. *rakab*). That **Hophni and Phinehas** (cf. 1 Sam. 2:12–17, 27–36) were there suggests that they supported the move, at least to some extent. Eli, however, seems to have had reservations (4:13).

The Journey of the Ark of the Covenant in 1–2 Samuel

1 Sam. 3:3	The Lord calls to Samuel who is sleeping in the tent of meeting, "where the ark of God was"
1 Samuel 4	Philistines capture the ark (for seven months: 1 Sam. 6:1)
1 Sam. 5:1–7	Philistines bring the ark to Ashdod, setting it up next to the idol Dagon
1 Sam. 5:8–9	Philistines bring the ark to Gath
1 Sam. 5:10–12	Philistines send the ark to Ekron
1 Sam. 6:10–15	Philistines return the ark with guilt offering to Beth-shemesh
1 Sam. 6:19–21	The Lord strikes 70 men for looking upon the ark
1 Sam. 7:1–2	Men of Kiriath-jearim take the ark to the house of Abinadab (where it stays for 20 years)
1 Sam. 14:18	Saul commands Ahijah to bring the ark to the war camp
2 Sam. 6:2–5	David begins to move the ark to Jerusalem on a cart
2 Sam. 6:6–7	The Lord strikes Uzzah dead for holding on to the ark
2 Sam. 6:10–11	David takes the ark to the house of Obed-edom, where it stays for three months
2 Sam. 6:12–17	David brings the ark to Jerusalem, and places it inside the tent he pitched for it
2 Sam. 15:24–25	Zadok brings the ark to David, who commands him to carry it back to Jerusalem
2 Sam. 15:29	Zadok and Abiathar carry the ark back to Jerusalem

4:3 The **elders of Israel** appear throughout the history of Israel. They were a group of senior tribal leaders entrusted with important decisions. They are mentioned from the time of the sojourn in Egypt through to the NT (e.g., Ex. 3:16; Num. 11:16; Josh. 24:31; 1 Kings 20:7; Ezra 5:5; Matt. 16:21; Acts 22:5). Other nations also had them (Num. 22:7). Cities also were governed by elders (e.g., Deut. 19:12; 1 Sam. 11:3; 16:4; 1 Kings 21:8). In Samuel the elders of Israel are instrumental in establishing a king. They ask Samuel for a king (1 Sam. 8:4); Saul is concerned with their opinion (15:30); they are leaders in choosing a king after Saul's death (2 Sam. 3:17; 5:3); and they are in Absalom's council (2 Sam. 17:4).

4:5 a mighty shout. The Israelites are confident in the ark, but the rest of the story will show that they have failed to approach God's presence in faith and obedience.

4:6 In Samuel, the term **Hebrews** is usually used by the Philistines as a designation for the Israelites (14:11; 29:3). The term apparently derives from the name Eber (Gen. 10:21–25). So in the biblical tradition, "Hebrew" is an

The Ark of the Covenant

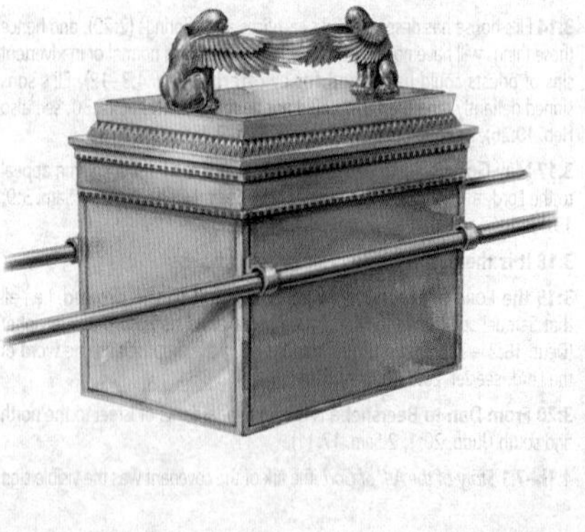

9 [b][2 Sam. 10:12; 1 Cor. 16:13] [c]Judg. 13:1
10 [d]ver. 2; Ps. 78:62; [Lev. 26:17; Deut. 28:25] [e]2 Sam. 18:17; 19:8; 2 Kgs. 14:12; 2 Chr. 25:22
11 [f][ch. 2:32; Ps. 78:60, 61] [g]ch. 2:34; Ps. 78:64
12 [h]See Josh. 7:6
13 [i]ver. 18; ch. 1:9
15 [j]1 Kgs. 14:4; [ch. 3:2]
16 [k]2 Sam. 1:4
18 [l]ver. 13
20 [m]Gen. 35:17

the shouting, they said, "What does this great shouting in the camp of the Hebrews mean?"
And when they learned that the ark of the LORD had come to the camp, 7 the Philistines
were afraid, for they said, "A god has come into the camp." And they said, "Woe to us! For
nothing like this has happened before. 8 Woe to us! Who can deliver us from the power of
these mighty gods? These are the gods who struck the Egyptians with every sort of plague
in the wilderness. 9 [b]Take courage, and be men, O Philistines, lest you become slaves to the
Hebrews [c]as they have been to you; be men and fight."
10 So the Philistines fought, [d]and Israel was defeated, [e]and they fled, every man to his
home. And there was a very great slaughter, for thirty thousand foot soldiers of Israel
fell. 11 [f]And the ark of God was captured, [g]and the two sons of Eli, Hophni and Phinehas,
died.

The Death of Eli

12 A man of Benjamin ran from the battle line and came to Shiloh the same day, [h]with
his clothes torn and with dirt on his head. 13 When he arrived, [i]Eli was sitting on his seat by
the road watching, for his heart trembled for the ark of God. And when the man came into
the city and told the news, all the city cried out. 14 When Eli heard the sound of the outcry,
he said, "What is this uproar?" Then the man hurried and came and told Eli. 15 Now Eli was
ninety-eight years old [j]and his eyes were set so that he could not see. 16 And the man said to
Eli, "I am he who has come from the battle; I fled from the battle today." And he said, [k]"How
did it go, my son?" 17 He who brought the news answered and said, "Israel has fled before the
Philistines, and there has also been a great defeat among the people. Your two sons also, Hophni
and Phinehas, are dead, and the ark of God has been captured." 18 As soon as he mentioned
the ark of God, Eli fell over backward [l]from his seat by the side of the gate, and his neck was
broken and he died, for the man was old and heavy. He had judged Israel forty years.
19 Now his daughter-in-law, the wife of Phinehas, was pregnant, about to give birth.
And when she heard the news that the ark of God was captured, and that her father-
in-law and her husband were dead, she bowed and gave birth, for her pains came upon
her. 20 And about the time of her death the women attending her said to her, [m]"Do not
be afraid, for you have borne a son." But she did not answer or pay attention. 21 And she

ethnic term (see Gen. 14:13) distinct from religio-political designations such as "Israel," "sons of Israel," etc.

4:7–8 A god . . . the gods. The Hebrew word for "god(s)" in both cases is *'elohim*, the plural of *'eloah* ("god"). *Elohim* is the usual word to refer to the God of Israel (e.g., Gen. 1:1); the plural form is used to express majesty, but it is always used with a singular verb. In 1 Sam. 4:7, the Philistines think that the ark is a god (or God) that has come (singular); in v. 8, they use the plural form for "struck." The narrator seems to be mocking their misunderstanding of the one God of Israel. Exodus 7–12 describes how God "struck the Egyptians with every sort of plague." **Struck the Egyptians . . . in the wilderness** probably reflects the Philistines' ignorance about the exact course of events during Israel's wilderness wanderings.

4:10 Israel was defeated. In view of v. 3, one cannot suppose that the Philistines on their own were the cause. **every man to his home**. Literally, "every man to his tent." This is a common cliché for disbanding an army, either by decision (Judg. 20:8; 1 Sam. 13:2; 2 Sam. 20:1, 22; 1 Kings 12:16) or because of defeat (2 Sam. 18:17; 19:8; 2 Chron. 25:22).

4:12 The messenger **ran** a distance of nearly 22 miles (35 km). Tearing one's **clothes**, often along with putting **dirt** on one's **head**, was the normal reaction to grief or horror in the OT (e.g., 2 Sam. 1:2, 11; 3:31; 13:19, 31; 15:32; Job 2:12).

4:13 Eli was **sitting** beside the gate (v. 18) **watching** the road. But he could not see the messenger when he entered. Presumably the people of the city brought the messenger to Eli to tell him the news in person.

4:17 Your two sons . . . are dead is the sign that Eli had been told to expect as a forewarning of the near demise of his house (2:34), but it seems that he is even more concerned about the **ark**.

4:19 Bowed is literally "crouched," the position for giving birth. It was probably a premature delivery brought on by shock.

4:21–22 Like Eli, Phinehas's wife seems more concerned with the **ark** than with her husband. **Ichabod** means "where is the glory?" She mourns for Israel without the presence of God. **Departed** (Hb. *galah*) does not mean just to "go

The Ark's Travels in 1 Samuel 3–7

After suffering losses in battle against the Philistines at Ebenezer, the Israelite forces called for the ark of the covenant to be brought to the battle from Shiloh. But the Israelites were defeated again, and the Philistines captured the ark. The ark's presence in each Philistine city caused the people to suffer terrible tumors, so it was sent away to another city. Eventually the ark was returned to Israel at Beth-shemesh, and then it was brought to Kiriath-jearim, where it remained for some 20 years.

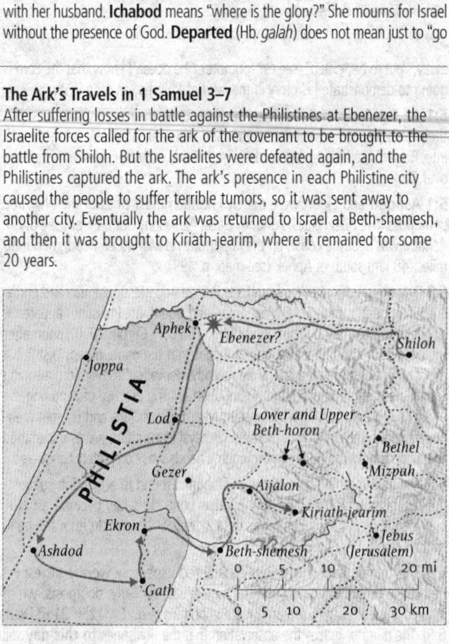

named the child [n]Ichabod, saying, [o]"The glory has departed[1] from Israel!" because [p]the
ark of God had been captured and because of her father-in-law and her husband. 22 And
she said, "The glory has departed from Israel, [p]for the ark of God has been captured."

The Philistines and the Ark

5 When the Philistines captured the ark of God, they brought it from [q]Ebenezer to
[r]Ashdod. 2 Then the Philistines took the ark of God and brought it into the house
of Dagon and set it up beside [s]Dagon. 3 And when the people of Ashdod rose early the
next day, behold, [t]Dagon had fallen face downward on the ground before the ark of the
LORD. So they took Dagon and put him back in his place. 4 But when they rose early on
the next morning, behold, Dagon had fallen face downward on the ground before the
ark of the LORD, [u]and the head of Dagon and both his hands were lying cut off on the
threshold. Only the trunk of Dagon was left to him. 5 This is why the priests of Dagon
and all who enter the house of Dagon [v]do not tread on the threshold of Dagon in Ashdod
to this day.

6 [w]The hand of the LORD was heavy against the people of Ashdod, and he terrified and
afflicted them with [x]tumors, both Ashdod and its territory. 7 And when the men of Ashdod
saw how things were, they said, "The ark of the God of Israel must not remain with us,
for his hand is hard against us and against Dagon our god." 8 So they sent and gathered
together all [y]the lords of the Philistines and said, "What shall we do with the ark of the God
of Israel?" They answered, "Let the ark of the God of Israel be brought around to Gath."
So they brought the ark of the God of Israel there. 9 But after they had brought it around,
[z]the hand of the LORD was against the city, causing a very great panic, and he afflicted the
men of the city, both young and old, so that [x]tumors broke out on them. 10 So they sent
the ark of God to Ekron. But as soon as the ark of God came to Ekron, the people of Ekron
cried out, "They have brought around to us the ark of the God of Israel to kill us and our
people." 11 [y]They sent therefore and gathered together all the lords of the Philistines and
said, "Send away the ark of the God of Israel, and let it return to its own place, that it may
not kill us and our people." For there was a deathly panic throughout the whole city. [w]The
hand of God was very heavy there. 12 The men who did not die were struck with [x]tumors,
and the cry of the city went up to heaven.

[1] Or *gone into exile*; also verse 22

21 [n]ch. 14:3 [o]Ps. 78:61; [Ps. 26:8] [p]ver. 11
22 [p][See ver. 21 above]
Chapter 5
1 [q]ch. 4:1; 7:12 [r]Josh. 13:3
2 [s]Judg. 16:23
3 [t][Isa. 46:1, 2]
4 [u][Jer. 50:2; Ezek. 6:4, 6; Mic. 1:7]
5 [v][Zeph. 1:9]
6 [w][Ex. 9:3; Ps. 32:4; Acts 13:11] [x]ch. 6:5
8 [y]Josh. 13:3
9 [z]ch. 7:13; 12:15; Deut. 2:15 [x][See ver. 6 above]
11 [y][See ver. 8 above] [w][See ver. 6 above]
12 [x][See ver. 6 above]

away," but to be "exiled" (see ESV footnote). She doesn't know that the Lord is going to demonstrate his glory in the land of Philistia, as seen in ch. 5.

5:1–12 *The Ark in Philistia.* The Philistines think their victory indicates that their god, Dagon, is superior to the God of Israel, and they bring the ark into Dagon's temple to honor their god. God, however, shows his power over Dagon.

5:1 Ashdod and Ekron were the two northernmost cities of the Philistine pentapolis (five ruling cities: Ashdod, Gaza, Ashkelon, Gath, Ekron; see 6:17). Ashdod was near the coast, on the important Via Maris (Sea Road), about 30 miles (48 km) south of Aphek (see map, p. 499).

5:2 Dagon is a deity known from Early Bronze Age Mesopotamian and northern Syrian cities such as Ebla, Mari, Emar, and Ugarit. The Philistines apparently adopted him as their principal god (Judg. 16:23; 1 Chron. 10:10) soon after their arrival in Canaan. It was once thought that the name meant "fish," but this view is no longer accepted. More recently, derivation from a word meaning "grain" has been proposed, but it is not certain. The practice of capturing the enemy's gods was common in ancient Near East warfare and is often mentioned in documents such as the Assyrian royal inscriptions. It was understood that a people whose gods were in enemy hands was completely conquered.

5:3 The next morning, the statue of Dagon is found in a position suggesting submission **before the ark of the LORD**. This has become a battle between deities. Dagon cannot protect himself or his people from the hand of the Lord (v. 6).

5:5 The temple **threshold** was considered especially worthy of respect because it separated sacred and common areas; similarly, doorposts, which marked the entrance to a home, were important (e.g., Ex. 12:7; 21:6; Deut. 6:9). The narrator makes the observation that the Philistines **to this day** still bear witness to the humiliation of their god. This custom is said to have survived in Gaza into the first centuries A.D.

5:6 The **tumors**, together with an apparently abnormal number of mice in the area (6:5), have led most commentators to identify the disease as bubonic plague. Yet 5:12 has no reference to the mice at all. See note on 6:4.

5:8 The five (6:4, 16) **lords** were the rulers of the five ruling Philistine cities (i.e., the Philistine pentapolis; see 6:17). **Gath** was the city of Goliath (17:4), Achish (21:10; 27:2), and Ittai and the 600 Gittites (2 Sam. 15:18–19). Gath is probably Tel ets-Tsafi, about 12 miles (19 km) east of Ashdod and 5 miles (8 km) south of Ekron (1 Sam. 5:10), at the foot of the Judean hills.

5:10 Ekron is another city of the Philistine pentapolis, most probably Tel Miqne, 22 miles (35 km) west of Jerusalem, on the western border between Philistia and Judah. This journey of the ark, taken from city to city by its panicky "captors," is almost a parody of a triumph march. Ekron has been discovered and excavated by archaeologists. A monumental inscription, belonging to the early seventh century B.C., has been found in what appears to be a temple complex. It is a plea to a goddess to protect Achish, the ruler of Ekron, and to bless him with long life, and to bless his land.

5:11 a deathly panic. I.e., one that causes death.

6:1–7:1 *Return of the Ark.* The Philistines test whether their troubles come from Israel's God, which leads to the ark's return to the territory of Israel.

6:2 The **Philistines** reluctantly admit defeat and consult with their **priests** and **diviners** on how to **send** the ark back.

6:3 While a **guilt offering** as described in Lev. 5:14–17 did not exist for the Philistines, the ancient Near East shared the concept of misappropriating holy

The Ark Returned to Israel

6 The ark of the LORD was in the country of the Philistines seven months. 2 And the
Philistines called for the priests and [a]the diviners and said, "What shall we do with
the ark of the LORD? Tell us with what we shall send it to its place." 3 They said, "If you
send away the ark of the God of Israel, do not send it empty, but by all means return him
[b]a guilt offering. Then you will be healed, and it will be known to you why [c]his hand
does not turn away from you." 4 And they said, "What is the guilt offering that we shall
return to him?" They answered, "Five golden [d]tumors and five golden mice, [e]according
to the number of the lords of the Philistines, for the same plague was on all of you and
on your lords. 5 So you must make images of your [d]tumors and images of your mice that
ravage the land, [f]and give glory to the God of Israel. Perhaps [g]he will lighten his hand
from off you [h]and your gods and your land. 6 Why should you harden your hearts as [i]the
Egyptians and [j]Pharaoh hardened their hearts? After he had dealt severely with them,
[k]did they not send the people away, and they departed? 7 Now then, take and prepare [l]a
new cart and two milk cows [m]on which there has never come a yoke, and yoke the cows
to the cart, but take their calves home, away from them. 8 And take the ark of the LORD
and place it on the cart and put in a box at its side [n]the figures of gold, which you are
returning to him as [b]a guilt offering. Then send it off and let it go its way 9 and watch. If
it goes up on the way to its own land, to [o]Beth-shemesh, then it is he who has done us
this great harm, but if not, then we shall know that it is not [p]his hand that struck us; it
happened to us by coincidence."

10 The men did so, and took two milk cows and yoked them to the cart and shut up
their calves at home. 11 And they put the ark of the LORD on the cart and the box with the
golden mice and the images of their tumors. 12 And the cows went straight in the direction of [q]Beth-shemesh along [r]one highway, lowing as they went. They turned neither
to the right nor to the left, and the lords of the Philistines went after them as far as the
border of [q]Beth-shemesh. 13 Now the people of [q]Beth-shemesh were reaping their wheat
harvest in the valley. And when they lifted up their eyes and saw the ark, they rejoiced
to see it. 14 The cart came into the field of Joshua of Beth-shemesh and stopped there. [s]A
great stone was there. And they split up the wood of the cart and offered the cows as a
burnt offering to the LORD. 15 And the Levites took down the ark of the LORD and the
box that was beside it, in which were the golden figures, and set them upon [s]the great
stone. And the men of [q]Beth-shemesh offered burnt offerings and sacrificed sacrifices on
that day to the LORD. 16 And when [t]the five lords of the Philistines saw it, they returned
that day to Ekron.

17 These are the golden tumors that the Philistines returned as a [u]guilt offering to the
LORD: one for Ashdod, one for Gaza, one for Ashkelon, one for Gath, one for Ekron, 18 and
the golden mice, according to the number of all the cities of the Philistines belonging

Chapter 6
2 [a]Deut. 18:10; [Gen. 41:8; Ex. 7:11; Dan. 2:2; 5:7]
3 [b][Lev. 5:15, 16] [c]ver. 9
4 [d]ch. 5:6, 9, 12 [e]ver. 17, 18; Josh. 13:3; Judg. 3:3
5 [d][See ver. 4 above] [f][Josh. 7:19] [g][ch. 5:6, 9, 11] [h]ch. 5:3, 4, 7
6 [i][Ex. 14:17] [j]Ex. 8:15, 32; [Ex. 7:13; 9:7, 35; 10:1] [k]Ex. 12:31
7 [l][2 Sam. 6:3] [m][Num. 19:2]
8 [n]ver. 4, 5 [b][See ver. 3 above]
9 [o]Josh. 15:10 [p]ver. 3
12 [q]Josh. 21:16 [r]Num. 20:19
13 [q][See ver. 12 above]
14 [s]ver. 18
15 [s][See ver. 14 above] [q][See ver. 12 above]
16 [t]See ver. 4
17 [u]ver. 3, 8

things or places for profane use. Thus the Philistines viewed their current plight as God's "heavy hand" (1 Sam. 5:11) upon them for their desecration of the sacred ark; this desecration required a sacrifice as some kind of recompense to the God of the ark.

6:4 Five golden tumors and five golden mice. The exact relationship between the tumors and the mice is difficult to determine, but from the list in vv. 17–18 one possibility is that only five golden objects are involved and that the "and" should be taken here as "namely," as is not uncommon in Hebrew, yielding "five golden tumors, namely, five golden mice" (see also v. 11). While that reading is grammatically possible, most interpreters understand 10 items set forth here: five golden tumors as well as five golden mice.

6:5 Even the pagan Philistines must eventually **give glory to the God of Israel**.

6:6 as the Egyptians. The Philistine religious professionals knew all about the events of the exodus (see esp. Ex. 10:1–2).

6:7–9 This is an experiment to discover whether the cause of the Philistines' troubles was a natural event (**coincidence**, v. 9) or a supernatural one (**it is he who has done us this great harm**, v. 9). Untrained **milk cows** could not pull a **cart** together well, and if they went anywhere, it would be **home** to their **calves**. Therefore, if they pulled the cart uphill toward Israel, it must be the work of the Lord (v. 9).

6:11 The golden mice and the images of their tumors refers either to 10 items or to five (see note on v. 4). If the latter, then the images would be "mouse-shaped" gold items made to symbolize their tumors.

6:12 Beth-shemesh was partway up the Sorek Valley, a valley connecting Israel and Philistia, the scene of many of Samson's exploits. Zorah, Eshtaol, Timnah, and Delilah's home were all in that valley (Judg. 13:25; 14:1; 16:4). Ekron was near the place where the valley opens up into the plain.

6:15 Beth-shemesh is listed among the Levitical cities in Josh. 21:16.

6:17–18 This is a formal list with a heading, details (lit., "for Ashdod one; for Gaza one; for Ashkelon one; for Gath one; for Ekron one"), and summary. Many similar lists have been discovered all over the ancient Near East. In these, the summary always encapsulates the details. This structure suggests that the gold tumors in the heading and details may be the same as the gold mice in the summary (v. 18; see also the lists in 30:26–31 and 2 Sam. 23:8–39; but see notes on 1 Sam. 6:4; 6:11). The summary is: "**and** [or, namely] **the golden mice, according to the number of all the cities of the Philistines belonging to the five lords**," i.e., both walled forts and their surrounding unwalled villages. This phraseology was probably chosen

to the five lords, [v]both fortified cities and unwalled villages. [w]The great stone beside
which they set down the ark of the LORD is a witness to this day in the field of Joshua
of Beth-shemesh.
19 [x]And he struck some of the men of Beth-shemesh, because they looked upon the ark
of the LORD. He struck seventy men of them,[1] and the people mourned because the LORD
had struck the people with a great blow. **20** Then the men of Beth-shemesh said, [y]"Who is
able to stand before the LORD, this holy God? And to whom shall he go up away from us?"
21 So they sent messengers to the inhabitants of [z]Kiriath-jearim, saying, "The Philistines
have returned the ark of the LORD. Come down and take it up to you."

7 And the men of Kiriath-jearim came and took up the ark of the LORD and brought
it to the house of [a]Abinadab on the hill. And they consecrated his son Eleazar to
have charge of the ark of the LORD. **2** From the day that the ark was lodged at Kiriath-
jearim, a long time passed, some twenty years, and all the house of Israel lamented
after the LORD.

Samuel Judges Israel

3 And Samuel said to all the house of Israel, [b]"If you are returning to the LORD with
all your heart, then [c]put away the foreign gods and the [d]Ashtaroth from among you and
[e]direct your heart to the LORD [f]and serve him only, and he will deliver you out of the hand
of the Philistines." **4** So the people of Israel put away the Baals and the Ashtaroth, and they
served the LORD only.
5 Then Samuel said, "Gather all Israel at [g]Mizpah, and I will pray to the LORD for you."
6 So they gathered at [g]Mizpah [h]and drew water and poured it out before the LORD [i]and
fasted on that day and said there, [j]"We have sinned against the LORD." And Samuel judged
the people of Israel at Mizpah. **7** Now when the Philistines heard that the people of Israel
had gathered at Mizpah, the lords of the Philistines went up against Israel. And when the
people of Israel heard of it, they were afraid of the Philistines. **8** And the people of Israel
said to Samuel, "Do not cease to cry out to the LORD our God for us, that he may save us
from the hand of the Philistines." **9** So Samuel took a nursing lamb and offered it as a
whole burnt offering to the LORD. And [k]Samuel cried out to the LORD for Israel, and the
LORD answered him. **10** As Samuel was offering up the burnt offering, the Philistines drew
near to attack Israel. [l]But the LORD thundered with a mighty sound that day against the

[1] Most Hebrew manuscripts *struck of the people seventy men, fifty thousand men*

18 [v][Deut. 3:5] [w]ver. 14, 15
19 [x][Ex. 19:21; Num. 4:15, 20; 2 Sam. 6:7]
20 [y][2 Sam. 6:9]
21 [z]1 Chr. 13:5, 6; [Josh. 9:17; 18:14]

Chapter 7

1 [a]2 Sam. 6:3
3 [b]1 Kgs. 8:48; Isa. 55:7; Hos. 6:1; Joel 2:12; See Deut. 30:2-10 [c]Gen. 35:2; Josh. 24:14, 23; [Judg. 10:16] [d]Judg. 2:13 [e][2 Chr. 19:3; 30:19; Ezra 7:10] [f]Deut. 6:13; 10:20; 13:4; Cited Matt. 4:10; Luke 4:8
5 [g][Judg. 20:1]
6 [g][See ver. 5 above] [h][2 Sam. 14:14] [i]ch. 31:13; Neh. 9:1 [j]Judg. 10:10
9 [k]Ps. 99:6; Jer. 15:1
10 [l]ch. 2:10; [2 Sam. 22:14, 15; Ps. 18:13]

to ensure that no part of the Philistine territory was left out. The five cities named in v. 17 would include "all the cities of the Philistines belonging to the five lords," since each of the five Philistine cities would have unwalled villages associated with it. (Note "Ashdod and its territory" in 5:6; a similar phrase refers to a political unit in Assyrian annals. In 27:5–6, Ziklag is a "country town" belonging to the "royal city" of Gath.) This list may have been put into the box with the gold items.

6:19 The Hebrew expression **looked upon** indicates staring, and perhaps gloating; this irreverence explains why God **struck some of the men**. The puzzling Hebrew text "seventy men, fifty thousand men" (ESV footnote) may possibly mean "seventy men, i.e., five people out of every thousand" (or "every clan"). If this is the correct meaning, then the population of the city would have been 14,000 people (or 14 clans).

6:20 The people of **Beth-shemesh** sound like the people of Ashdod (5:7–8).

6:21 Kiriath-jearim was about 10 miles (16 km) farther up the Sorek Valley toward Jerusalem. It was a strategic location, situated on a hill at the juncture of the boundaries of Judah, Dan, and Benjamin.

7:1 Eleazar is also the name of Aaron's son (e.g., Ex. 6:23, 25; Num. 3:2); the name Eleazar was probably common in the Levitical families. In fact, it may be that Eleazar was descended from Aaron and that was why the people of Beth-shemesh asked Kiriath-jearim to take the ark.

7:2–17 *Judgeship of Samuel.* Nothing has been heard of Samuel for 20 years (since 4:1), but then he calls the people to repent and put aside idolatry, and the people respond. Samuel is not a military figure, but through his prayer and worship the Lord works, and Israel is at peace with its neighbors. He is clearly the leader of "all . . . Israel" (8:4). Samuel is also a judge in the more modern sense of the word.

7:3–4 Returning here is the act of repentance, i.e., a change of direction back to the Lord. Samuel gives three commands: (1) turn away from idolatry; (2) direct the **heart to the LORD**; and (3) **serve him** alone (see Deut. 6:4–15; Josh. 24:14–28; Judg. 10:6–16). **Foreign gods and the Ashtaroth** refers to the totality of idols. **The Baals and the Ashtaroth** has the same meaning.

7:5–6 Mizpah is probably the modern Tel en-Natsbeh, about 7 miles (11 km) north of Jerusalem, near an important north-south road. It was a place of assembly for all Israel, as in Judges 20–21 and 1 Sam. 10:17–27, where Saul was proclaimed king. It was on Samuel's circuit for judging (7:16). **I will pray to the LORD for you**. Samuel was known as an intercessor (v. 8; 12:23; Jer. 15:1). They **drew water and poured it out before the LORD and fasted**. Like fasting, pouring out the water was an act of self-denial as part of Israel's confession. **We have sinned against the LORD**. The people's action was also an act of offering with similarities to the whole burnt offering in 1 Sam. 7:9—it was given completely to the Lord.

7:9 nursing lamb. An animal could be sacrificed once it was eight days old (Ex. 22:30; Lev. 22:27). A basic purpose of the **whole burnt offering** was to make atonement (Lev. 1:4).

7:10 The term for **confusion** (Hb. *hamam*) occurs first in Ex. 14:24, where the Lord threw the Egyptian army into "panic" (see also Ex. 23:27; Josh. 10:10). See especially 2 Sam. 22:15 (cf. Ps. 18:14), where the Lord's lightning routs (same Hb. word, *hamam*) the enemy.

7:13 did not again enter the territory of Israel. The victory is here

Philistines and threw them into confusion, and they were defeated before Israel. 11 And
the men of Israel went out from Mizpah and pursued the Philistines and struck them,
as far as below Beth-car.
12 Then Samuel [m]took a stone and set it up between Mizpah and Shen[1] and called its
name Ebenezer;[2] for he said, "Till now the LORD has helped us." 13 [n]So the Philistines
were subdued and did not again enter the territory of Israel. And the hand of the LORD
was against the Philistines all the days of Samuel. 14 The cities that the Philistines had
taken from Israel were restored to Israel, from Ekron to Gath, and Israel delivered their
territory from the hand of the Philistines. There was peace also between Israel and the
Amorites.
15 [o]Samuel judged Israel all the days of his life. 16 And he went on a circuit year by year
to Bethel, Gilgal, and Mizpah. And he judged Israel in all these places. 17 Then he would
return to [p]Ramah, for his home was there, and there also he judged Israel. [q]And he built
there an altar to the LORD.

Israel Demands a King

8 When Samuel became old, [r]he made his sons judges over Israel. 2 The name of his firstborn son was Joel, and the name of his second, Abijah; they were judges in Beersheba.
3 Yet his sons did not walk in his ways [s]but turned aside after gain. [t]They took bribes and
perverted justice.
4 Then all the elders of Israel gathered together and came to Samuel at [p]Ramah 5 and
said to him, "Behold, you are old and your sons do not walk in your ways. [u]Now appoint

12 [m]Gen. 28:18; 31:45; 35:14; Josh. 4:9; 24:26
13 [n][Judg. 13:1]
15 [o]ver. 6; ch. 12:11; [Judg. 2:16]
17 [p]ch. 1:19 [q][ch. 14:35; Judg. 21:4]

Chapter 8

1 [r]Deut. 16:18
3 [s][Ex. 18:21] [t][Ex. 23:8; Deut. 16:19; Ps. 15:5]
4 [p][See ch. 7:17 above]
5 [u]ver. 19, 20; [Deut. 17:14; Hos. 13:10; Acts 13:21]

[1] Hebrew; Septuagint, Syriac *Jeshanah* [2] *Ebenezer* means *stone of help*

described as a decisive turning point, although Philistine garrisons appear in 10:5; 13:3. Perhaps this refers only to a temporary condition, such as during **all the days of Samuel**.

7:14 from Ekron to Gath. Ekron and Gath were the easternmost cities of the Philistine pentapolis (see note on 5:1). This verse probably means that the cities and territories that had come under the control of those two ruling cities were freed from their control. The **Amorites**, broadly speaking, were the pre-Israelite Canaanites (see 2 Sam. 21:2). Thus Israel was not bothered by enemies from inside or from outside.

7:15 Samuel judged (see v. 6) **Israel all the days of his life**. This is a summary of Samuel's activities as judge; from his hometown of Ramah, he visited the cities of Bethel, Gilgal, and Mizpah, which are all in or around the district of the Benjaminite clans.

7:16 Bethel was one of the most important sacred sites, being associated with the patriarchs (see Gen. 35:15). The ark was there at one time (Judg. 20:26–27). Joshua 18:21–22 lists it as a Benjaminite city, but during most of history it was a part of Ephraim. It was in Bethel, as well as in Dan, that Jeroboam established a sanctuary for worshiping a golden calf as a rival to Jerusalem (1 Kings 12:28–29). The modern site is Beitin, 10 miles (16 km) north of Jerusalem, at the intersection of two major highways—the mountain ridge road and the main road leading from Jericho to the coastal plain. The site of **Gilgal** has not yet been identified. It was the place on "the east border of Jericho" where Joshua and the Israelites camped after crossing the Jordan River (Josh. 4:19, etc.). This ancient city was a place of worship and sacrifice in the Benjaminite district. Gilgal was important in the kingship of Saul: he was ordered to go there and wait on God after his private anointing (1 Sam. 10:1); there the people made him king (11:15); and there his perpetual (i.e., dynastic) kingship was rejected (13:8–15) and finally negated (15:23). Later, in the eighth century, Amos (Amos 4:4; 5:5) and Hosea (Hos. 4:15; 9:15; 12:11) denounced Gilgal, along with Bethel, as an active but illegitimate place of worship. Thus, the narrator summarizes Samuel's era: Israel was secure and stable both externally and internally under the judgeship of Samuel, for the hand of the Lord was against the Philistines and there was peace between the Israelites and the Amorites. Samuel's annual visits from his hometown of Ramah gave the people confidence and trust in God and in Samuel's leadership. In the next episode, however, the people of Israel senselessly request a new institution (kingship) rather than a new judge, despite Samuel's opposition.

8:1–22 *Transition to the Monarchy.* Chapter 8 is a turning point in OT history, marking the transition from judgeship to kingship. The people want a change: up until now they had depended on the Lord to raise up judges to lead them as needed, but now they want a monarchy, "like all the nations" (v. 5). Why did they want a king? Of course, Samuel's sons were causing problems, but instead of rejecting hereditary judges and demanding that Samuel's sons be removed, they ask for a hereditary kingship. Probably they were feeling the threat of the Philistines and Ammonites (v. 20; 9:16; 10:5; 12:12), but the phrase "like all the nations" seems to be a key. Rather than following God's way for them, they preferred to follow the ways of the world around them. It was ultimately a rejection of the kingship of God (8:7).

8:1 he made his sons judges. Samuel himself may have contributed to the problem (see note on vv. 1–22) by appointing his sons as judges. There had not been hereditary judges before; Gideon had rejected the idea (Judg. 8:22–23).

8:2 Beersheba was the extreme south of Israel in traditional descriptions (cf. 3:20). It appears in stories of the patriarchs (Gen. 21:31; 22:19; 26:33; 46:1), and Amos denounced it, together with Bethel and Gilgal (Amos 5:5). A fortress has been discovered at Beersheba (Stratum VII) that belongs to the period of the judges. Its length is about 164 feet (50 m), and it is surrounded by a double fortification wall. It was destroyed in the second half of the eleventh century B.C. The remains indicate that Beersheba was an important administrative center at this time.

8:3 turned aside after gain . . . took bribes and perverted justice. When leaders use their office for self-enrichment, and as a result distort their decisions, they betray the fundamental purpose of judges and are a danger in all societies. Such practices are denounced over and over in the Bible (cf. Deut. 16:19; Ps. 26:10; Prov. 15:27; 17:23; Isa. 33:15; Ezek. 22:12; Amos 5:12; Hab. 1:2–4).

8:4–5 appoint for us a king . . . like all the nations. Samuel had appointed judges. The elders, recognizing his authority, ask for a king. (**To judge** can also carry the nuance "to govern.") They want to exchange their unique glory as the people of the incomparable God (2:2), who had brought

for us a king to judge us like all the nations." 6 But the thing displeased Samuel when
they said, "Give us a king to judge us." And Samuel prayed to the LORD. 7 And the LORD
said to Samuel, "Obey the voice of the people in all that they say to you, [v]for they have not
rejected you, [w]but they have rejected me from being king over them. 8 According to all
the deeds that they have done, from the day I brought them up out of Egypt even to this
day, forsaking me and serving other gods, so they are also doing to you. 9 Now then, obey
their voice; only you shall solemnly warn them [x]and show them the ways of the king who
shall reign over them."

Samuel's Warning Against Kings

10 So Samuel told all the words of the LORD to the people who were asking for a king
from him. 11 He said, [y]"These will be the ways of the king who will reign over you: [z]he
will take your sons and appoint them to his chariots and to be his horsemen and to run
before his chariots. 12 And he will appoint for himself commanders of thousands and commanders of fifties, and some [a]to plow his ground and to reap his harvest, and to make his
implements of war and the equipment of his chariots. 13 He will take your daughters to be
perfumers and cooks and bakers. 14 [b]He will take the best of your fields and vineyards and
olive orchards and give them to his servants. 15 He will take the tenth of your grain and
of your vineyards and give it to his officers and to his servants. 16 He will take your male
servants and female servants and the best of your young men[1] and your donkeys, and put
them to his work. 17 He will take the tenth of your flocks, and you shall be his slaves. 18 And
in that day you will cry out because of your king, whom you have chosen for yourselves,
[c]but the LORD will not answer you in that day."

The LORD Grants Israel's Request

19 But the people refused to obey the voice of Samuel. And they said, "No! But there
shall be a king over us, 20 [d]that we also may be like all the nations, and that our king may
judge us and go out before us and fight our battles." 21 And when Samuel had heard all
the words of the people, he repeated them in the ears of the LORD. 22 And the LORD said to
Samuel, [e]"Obey their voice and make them a king." Samuel then said to the men of Israel,
"Go every man to his city."

[1] Septuagint *cattle*

7 [v][Ex. 16:8] [w]ch. 10:19
9 [x]See ver. 11-18
11 [y]ch. 10:25; See Deut. 17:16-20 [z]ch. 14:52
12 [a]See Gen. 45:6
14 [b]1 Kgs. 21:7; [Ezek. 46:18]
18 [c]Prov. 1:28; Isa. 1:15; Mic. 3:4
20 [d]ver. 5
22 [e]ver. 7; [Hos. 13:11]

them out of Egypt (8:8) and was even now protecting them (10:19), for status in the world, in order to be "like all the nations." The law had given permission, but not a requirement, to appoint a king (Deut. 17:14–20).

8:6 the thing displeased Samuel. Lit., "the thing was evil in Samuel's eyes." It was more than just a personal sense of rejection.

8:9–18 Solemnly warn them is a legal expression that implies giving someone full knowledge of an action. **the ways of the king**. The word translated "ways" (Hb. *mishpat*, "judgment, decision, rule, justice, custom") appears frequently in Samuel. In 2:13 it referred to the "customs" or "rights" of the priest (see note on 2:12–13; also Deut. 18:3, "this shall be the priest's due from the people"). In 1 Sam. 8:3, Samuel's sons "perverted *mishpat*." In 10:25, Samuel writes the *mishpat* of the king in a book. Here one might paraphrase it as "normal kingly ways." Some of these things were the normal cost of a central, standing administration, but others indicate a predictable abuse of power (see note on 8:14–15). There is no reason to think this passage comes from a later writer disillusioned with the Israelite monarchy.

8:11 Chariots had long been known in Canaan as instruments of war (Judg. 4:13 and Ugaritic texts). Later, David experimented with them, and Solomon used them regularly (2 Sam. 8:4; 1 Kings 4:26). Having men **run before his chariots** was a status symbol—both Absalom and Adonijah had a chariot and horses and horsemen and 50 runners to run before them (2 Sam. 15:1; 1 Kings 1:5).

8:12–13 The **commanders of thousands and commanders of fifties** were probably permanent officers over conscripted units—presumably military commanders were required due to the demand for a king to "fight our battles" (v. 20). To support this army, they need professionals to make weapons, provide food, and manufacture at least some comforts (**perfumers and cooks and bakers**; cf. "one of the perfumers," Neh. 3:8).

8:14–15 The best of your fields and vineyards and olive orchards goes beyond what is needed for the administration of a government and predicts the corrupting influence of a king's power. Rather than serving the people without seeking self-enrichment (as Samuel did, 12:3–5), the king would use his power to "take" the best for himself (8:11–13) and those around him (vv. 14–15). **Servants** refers to high-ranking officials, as can be seen by seals that have been found inscribed with "servant of [King] X." As 22:7 shows, Saul would indeed make his "servants" commanders and give them agricultural properties.

8:17 you shall be his slaves. The climax of Samuel's solemn warning. The Israelites and all their possessions are subject to the king's use. Conscripted labor (cf. 1 Kings 5:13–16; 12:4, 18) would probably be the most onerous form of this "slavery."

8:19–21 "We," "us," and "our" appear frequently in this short speech. The king's functions are (1) to give influence and status **like all the nations**; (2) to **judge us**—the fundamental function (2 Sam. 14:4; 15:2–4; 1 Kings 3:16–28; Psalm 72); and (3) to **go out before us and fight our battles**—i.e., be a war leader (e.g., 1 Sam. 11:1–11; 14:47–48; 23:27–28; 2 Sam. 5:19).

8:22 make them a king. The Lord acquiesces to the people's demands, even though it means that they have rejected him (v. 7). By raising up David's dynasty, God will bring good out of their errant desire.

Chapter 9
1 [f]ch. 14:51; 1 Chr. 8:33; 9:39
2 [g][ch. 8:16] [h]ch. 10:23
4 [i]See Josh. 24:33 [j]2 Kgs. 4:42
5 [k]ch. 10:2
6 [l]Deut. 33:1; Judg. 13:6; 1 Kgs. 13:1 [m]ch. 3:19
7 [n][1 Kgs. 14:3; 2 Kgs. 4:42; 8:8]
9 [o]Gen. 25:22
11 [p]Gen. 24:11
12 [q]ch. 16:2; 20:29; Gen. 31:54 [r]ch. 10:5; 1 Kgs. 3:2-4

Saul Chosen to Be King

9 There was a man of Benjamin whose name was [f]Kish, the son of Abiel, son of Zeror,
son of Becorath, son of Aphiah, a Benjaminite, a man of wealth. 2 And he had a son
whose name was Saul, [g]a handsome young man. There was not a man among the people
of Israel more handsome than he. [h]From his shoulders upward he was taller than any of
the people.
3 Now the donkeys of Kish, Saul's father, were lost. So Kish said to Saul his son, "Take
one of the young men with you, and arise, go and look for the donkeys." 4 And he passed
through [i]the hill country of Ephraim and passed through the land of [j]Shalishah, but they
did not find them. And they passed through the land of Shaalim, but they were not there.
Then they passed through the land of Benjamin, but did not find them.
5 When they came to the land of Zuph, Saul said to his servant[1] who was with him,
"Come, let us go back, [k]lest my father cease to care about the donkeys and become anxious
about us." 6 But he said to him, "Behold, there is [l]a man of God in this city, and he is a man
who is held in honor; [m]all that he says comes true. So now let us go there. Perhaps he can
tell us the way we should go." 7 Then Saul said to his servant, "But if we go, [n]what can we
bring the man? For the bread in our sacks is gone, and there is no present to bring to the
man of God. What do we have?" 8 The servant answered Saul again, "Here, I have with
me a quarter of a shekel[2] of silver, and I will give it to the man of God to tell us our way."
9 (Formerly in Israel, when a man [o]went to inquire of God, he said, "Come, let us go to the
seer," for today's "prophet" was formerly called a seer.) 10 And Saul said to his servant, "Well
said; come, let us go." So they went to the city where the man of God was.
11 As they went up the hill to the city, [p]they met young women coming out to draw water
and said to them, "Is the seer here?" 12 They answered, "He is; behold, he is just ahead of
you. Hurry. He has come just now to the city, because the people [q]have a sacrifice today on
[r]the high place. 13 As soon as you enter the city you will find him, before he goes up to the
high place to eat. For the people will not eat till he comes, since he must bless the sacrifice;
afterward those who are invited will eat. Now go up, for you will meet him immediately."
14 So they went up to the city. As they were entering the city, they saw Samuel coming out
toward them on his way up to the high place.

[1] Hebrew *young man*; also verses 7, 8, 10, 27 [2] A *shekel* was about 2/5 ounce or 11 grams

9:1–15:35 *The Story of Saul.* Saul, the first king over all Israel, rises from obscurity and starts out well, but proves himself unsuited to the role because he will not listen obediently to the word of God that comes through Samuel.

9:1–11:15 *Saul Made King.* This section starts with an ordinary family engaged in ordinary activities (similar to ch. 1), but it is soon clear that the Lord is working through these events. Here the story centers on Saul, who is told by Samuel that the Lord has chosen him to be the king to save his people. Saul is anointed, and the Spirit of the Lord comes upon him. Soon after, Saul is publicly chosen by lot. When Jabesh-gilead is threatened, Saul shows his leadership and saves the city. With this he is fully accepted as king, and there is a formal coronation ceremony at Gilgal.

9:1–27 *Saul's Meeting with Samuel.* God uses circumstances to bring Saul to Samuel, and he informs Samuel of his plans to anoint Saul.

9:1 The scene suddenly switches from Ramah (8:4) to a seemingly unrelated story, that of a young man looking for some donkeys, who just happens to come to a certain city on a certain day.

9:2 handsome young man. Saul seems to be the ideal person, with excellent potential, particularly as a leader whom others would admire and follow. His physical appearance helps Saul to make a good impression on the people. **From his shoulders upward he was taller than any of the people** (cf. 10:23). This probably means that the heads of most people reached only to his shoulders.

9:3 one of the young men. This could also mean "the first of the servants" (i.e., the head servant). The Hebrew (*na'ar*, lit., "young man") does not necessarily refer to someone who is young: Ziba, Saul's steward, was a *na'ar* who had 15 sons and 20 servants (2 Sam. 9:10).

9:4–5 The text states that Saul and his servant went **through the hill country of Ephraim** and then gives the names of three places in Ephraim where they did not find the donkeys—**the land of Shalishah, the land of Shaalim**, and **the land of Benjamin**—and then states that they came to **the land of Zuph**, apparently the land of Samuel's ancestor Zuph in the hill country of Ephraim (1:1).

9:6–8 Just as Saul is about to give up, God intervenes through the words of Saul's servant and through the fact that the servant just happens to have some **silver**. It was customary to take a **present** when seeking the help of a seer (see 1 Kings 14:3; 2 Kings 5:5; 8:8). Gifts were an integral part of social dealings in the ancient world.

9:9 Inquire is a general verb used of legitimate inquiries of the Lord, either through a prophet or by lots (cf. 1 Sam. 10:22; 22:10; 23:2; 2 Kings 22:13; Jer. 21:2), though it could also refer to inquiring of pagan gods (2 Kings 1:2). **Seer, prophet**, and "man of God" (1 Sam. 9:6) are used almost indistinguishably in the OT.

9:12 Samuel was **just ahead of** Saul, apparently returning to Ramah from his circuit (7:17), because there was **a sacrifice today**. Again, God's guidance is emphasized. Though later "high places," even those where the Lord was worshiped, were considered places for apostasy (2 Kings 23:15), worshiping the Lord at a **high place** was considered legitimate before the time of the temple (1 Kings 3:2, 4).

9:14 they saw Samuel coming out toward them on his way up to the high place. The full name of Samuel's city, Ramathaim (1:1), means "two hills." Presumably the city was on one hill and the high place was on another.

15 Now the day before Saul came, [s]the LORD had [t]revealed to Samuel: 16 "Tomorrow about
this time I will send to you a man from the land of Benjamin, [u]and you shall anoint him to
be prince[1] over my people Israel. He shall save my people from the hand of the Philistines.
[v]For I have seen[2] my people, because their cry has come to me." 17 When Samuel saw Saul,
the LORD told him, [w]"Here is the man of whom I spoke to you! He it is who shall restrain
my people." 18 Then Saul approached Samuel in the gate and said, "Tell me where is the
house of the seer?" 19 Samuel answered Saul, "I am the seer. Go up before me to the high
place, for today you shall eat with me, and in the morning I will let you go and will tell
you all that is on your mind. 20 [x]As for your donkeys that were lost three days ago, do not
set your mind on them, for they have been found. And for whom is all that is desirable
in Israel? Is it not for you and for all your father's house?" 21 Saul answered, "Am I not a
Benjaminite, [y]from the least of the tribes of Israel? [z]And is not my clan the humblest of all
the clans of the tribe of Benjamin? Why then have you spoken to me in this way?"

22 Then Samuel took Saul and his young man and brought them into the hall and gave
them a place at the head of those who had been invited, who were about thirty persons.
23 And Samuel said to the cook, "Bring the portion I gave you, of which I said to you, 'Put
it aside.'" 24 So the cook took up [a]the leg and what was on it and set them before Saul. And
Samuel said, "See, what was kept is set before you. Eat, because it was kept for you until
the hour appointed, that you might eat with the guests."[3]

So Saul ate with Samuel that day. 25 And when they came down from the high place into
the city, a bed was spread for Saul[4] [b]on the roof, and he lay down to sleep. 26 Then at the
break of dawn[5] Samuel called to Saul on the roof, "Up, that I may send you on your way."
So Saul arose, and both he and Samuel went out into the street.

27 As they were going down to the outskirts of the city, Samuel said to Saul, "Tell the
servant to pass on before us, and when he has passed on, stop here yourself for a while,
that I may make known to you the word of God."

Saul Anointed King

10 [c]Then Samuel took a flask of oil and poured it on his head [d]and kissed him and
said, "Has not the LORD anointed you to be prince[6] over [e]his people Israel? And you
shall reign over the people of the LORD and you will save them from the hand of their
surrounding enemies. And this shall be the sign to you that the LORD has anointed you
to be prince[7] over his heritage. 2 When you depart from me today, you will meet two men
by [f]Rachel's tomb in the territory of Benjamin at Zelzah, and they will say to you, [g]'The
donkeys that you went to seek are found, and now [h]your father has ceased to care about
the donkeys and is anxious about you, saying, "What shall I do about my son?"' 3 Then
you shall go on from there farther and come to the [i]oak of Tabor. Three men [j]going up
[k]to God at Bethel will meet you there, one carrying three young goats, another carrying
three loaves of bread, and another carrying a skin of wine. 4 And they will greet you and

15 [s]ch. 15:1; [Acts 13:21] [t]Ruth 4:4
16 [u]ch. 10:1 [v]Ex. 2:25; 3:7, 9
17 [w][ch. 16:12]
20 [x]ver. 3
21 [y][Judg. 20:46; 21:6; Ps. 68:27] [z]ch. 15:17; [Judg. 6:15]
24 [a]Ex. 29:22, 27; Lev. 7:32, 33; [Ezek. 24:4]
25 [b][Deut. 22:8; 2 Sam. 11:2; 16:22; Neh. 8:16; Matt. 24:17; Acts 10:9]

Chapter 10

1 [c]ch. 9:16; 16:13; 2 Sam. 2:4; 1 Kgs. 1:34, 39; 2 Kgs. 9:1, 3, 6 [d][Ps. 2:12] [e]Deut. 32:9; Ps. 78:71
2 [f]Gen. 35:19, 20 [g]ch. 9:3, 4 [h]ch. 9:5
3 [i]Gen. 13:18 [j][Judg. 20:31] [k]Gen. 28:22; 35:1, 3, 7

[1] Or *leader* [2] Septuagint adds *the affliction of* [3] Hebrew *appointed, saying, 'I have invited the people'* [4] Septuagint; Hebrew *and he spoke with Saul* [5] Septuagint; Hebrew *And they arose early and at the break of dawn* [6] Or *leader* [7] Septuagint; Hebrew lacks *over his people Israel? And you shall. . . . to be prince*

9:16 you shall anoint him. Various objects or persons were set aside for a divinely chosen task and anointed, such as the altar (Ex. 29:36), the tent (Ex. 30:26), the high priest (Ex. 28:41), or the king (Judg. 9:8; 1 Sam. 15:1; 2 Sam. 2:4; 1 Kings 1:34). The king was "the anointed one" or "messiah" of the Lord.

9:20–21 for whom is all that is desirable in Israel? As king, who would receive the choicest things of the land (see 8:11–17), why should Saul concern himself with donkeys? However, Samuel's question may be an implicit condemnation since it may also be translated, "For whom is all the desire of Israel?" In Saul, Israel gets what it desires (ch. 8). **Am I not . . . from the least . . . the humblest of all the clans**? Saul's surprise at the sudden elevation of his importance by Samuel indicates that he understands this question in the former, positive sense.

9:24 the cook took up the leg. The leg was the priest's portion (Ex. 29:27). Saul is told in 1 Sam. 10:4 to accept bread that probably was originally intended as an offering and would have been eaten by the priests (cf. Num. 18:8). These are indications of the sacredness of his kingship.

9:27 Samuel made clear to Saul in vv. 20 and 23 that he had been given special knowledge, so now Saul would have no doubts that what he was to hear was truly the **word of God**.

10:1–27 *Anointing of Saul and His Election.* Samuel anoints Saul privately, and then the whole nation discovers by means of lots that Saul is God's choice.

10:1 the LORD has anointed you. This is a private anointing. Later Samuel will demonstrate publicly by lots that Saul has been chosen by the Lord, not just by Samuel (see vv. 17–27). **his heritage**. Or, "his inheritance." The Hebrew term *nakhalah* appears six times in Samuel and can refer either to the Lord's land or to his people Israel, and sometimes to both. Here, it seems that "the people" is meant (see 9:16).

10:4 The **two loaves of bread** were probably intended for the sacrificial meal, because the men were "going up to God at Bethel" (v. 3). See note on 9:24. Thus Saul's new position and authority as divinely anointed king is acknowledged.

5[l]ver. 10 [m]ch. 13:3, 4 [n][ch. 9:12]
6[o]ver. 10; ch. 11:6; 16:13; [Num. 11:25; Judg. 3:10; 14:6, 19] [p]ver. 10; ch. 19:23, 24
7[q]Ex. 4:8; Judg. 6:17; Luke 2:12 [r]Josh. 1:5; Judg. 6:12
8[s]ch. 11:14, 15; 13:4 [t]ch. 11:15 [u]ch. 13:8
10[v]ver. 5 [o][See ver. 6 above]
11[w]ch. 19:24; [Matt. 13:54, 55; John 7:15]
12[x][Isa. 54:13; John 6:45] [w][See ver. 11 above]
14[y]ch. 14:50 [z]See ch. 9:4-6
16[a]ch. 9:20
17[b][ch. 11:15] [c]ch. 7:5, 6
18[d]Judg. 6:8, 9; [ch. 12:8]
19[e]ch. 8:7, 19; 12:12

give you two loaves of bread, which you shall accept from their hand. 5 After that you shall
come to [l]Gibeath-elohim,[1] [m]where there is a garrison of the Philistines. And there, as soon
as you come to the city, you will meet a group of prophets coming down [n]from the high
place with harp, tambourine, flute, and lyre before them, prophesying. 6 [o]Then the Spirit
of the LORD will rush upon you, [p]and you will prophesy with them and be turned into
another man. 7 Now when [q]these signs meet you, do what your hand finds to do, [r]for God
is with you. 8 Then go down before me [s]to Gilgal. And behold, I am coming down to you
to offer burnt offerings and [t]to sacrifice peace offerings. [u]Seven days you shall wait, until
I come to you and show you what you shall do."

9 When he turned his back to leave Samuel, God gave him another heart. And all these
signs came to pass that day. 10 When they came to [v]Gibeah,[2] behold, a group of prophets
met him, [o]and the Spirit of God rushed upon him, and he prophesied among them. 11 And
when all who knew him previously saw how he prophesied with the prophets, the people
said to one another, "What has come over the son of Kish? [w]Is Saul also among the prophets?" 12 And a man of the place answered, [x]"And who is their father?" Therefore it became
a proverb, [w]"Is Saul also among the prophets?" 13 When he had finished prophesying, he
came to the high place.

14 [y]Saul's uncle said to him and to his servant, "Where did you go?" And he said, [z]"To
seek the donkeys. And when we saw they were not to be found, we went to Samuel." 15 And
Saul's uncle said, "Please tell me what Samuel said to you." 16 And Saul said to his uncle, [a]"He
told us plainly that the donkeys had been found." But about the matter of the kingdom,
of which Samuel had spoken, he did not tell him anything.

Saul Proclaimed King

17 Now Samuel called the people together [b]to the LORD [c]at Mizpah. 18 And he said to the
people of Israel, [d]"Thus says the LORD, the God of Israel, 'I brought up Israel out of Egypt,
and I delivered you from the hand of the Egyptians and from the hand of all the kingdoms
that were oppressing you.' 19 [e]But today you have rejected your God, who saves you from

[1] *Gibeath-elohim means the hill of God* [2] *Gibeah means the hill*

10:5 group of prophets . . . with harp, tambourine, flute . . . prophesying. Though music may have been used in pagan worship to induce trances, these prophets were still able to walk and play instruments while prophesying. No practices such as self-flagellation or laceration are mentioned here, and the music was probably used to focus attention on the Lord. These same four instruments are mentioned as providing music for feasting in Isa. 5:12. The "harp" was similar to today's concert harp. The "tambourine" was similar to the modern tambourine, but without the small cymbals. The precise nature of the "flute" is unknown. Various types of wind instruments are known from pictures. Most depict pipes being played vertically, more like a recorder than today's concert flute. Examples of metal and bone flutes have been found; wood and reed were probably also common. The **lyre** was basically a sound box, with arms in a U-shape supporting a bar across the top. Depictions of musicians playing the lyre in the ancient Near East are common, and some specimens of the instrument itself have been excavated. The lyre seems to have been considered the premier instrument. In 1 Sam. 16:16, Saul's servants suggest seeking out a lyre player.

10:6 In 1–2 Samuel, the phrase "the Spirit of the LORD" appears only in connection with his anointed ones, i.e., Saul and David (1 Sam. 16:13–14; 2 Sam. 23:2). The expression **the Spirit of the LORD will rush upon** (someone) appears only in Judges and 1 Samuel, ending with David (Judg. 14:6, 19; 15:14; 1 Sam. 10:10; 11:6; 16:13). It always speaks of God's Spirit coming suddenly on someone to equip and empower that person to serve the interests of God's people. The onrush of the Spirit of the Lord upon Saul is predicted, but not manipulated as in Canaanite practices; it is necessary in order to dispel any doubts Saul might have about his choice and as a public demonstration that he is now the "prince" (10:1). It is related to his election as king, and does not mean that he is becoming a prophet (cf. v. 11). **be turned into another man**. Not by losing self, but rather by being equipped with power to play a new role (see Judg. 6:34; 11:29). Cf. "another heart" (1 Sam. 10:9).

10:8 Samuel instructs Saul to **go down before** him to the worship center at **Gilgal**, and to **wait** for him there for **seven days**. The events at Gilgal described in 11:15 and 13:8 were probably other occasions.

10:9–10 In fulfillment of Samuel's prior predictions (vv. 2–7), Saul is given **another heart** and he prophesies, an action linked with the fact that the **Spirit of God rushed upon him** (cf. v. 6; 11:6). This might not be a permanent spiritual renewal or conversion, but Saul is confirmed as the one to deliver Israel (see 10:7, "do what your hand finds to do"; cf. 9:16) and is reminded of God's presence by means of this visible sign (cf. Judg. 14:6, 19; 15:14). Later the Spirit of the Lord "departed from Saul" (1 Sam. 16:14; 18:12).

10:11–12 What has come over the son of Kish? The fact that Saul is now "another man" (v. 6) with "another heart" (v. 9) is externally evident to **all who knew him previously**. A second question, **Is Saul also among the prophets?** (also 19:24), became proverbial and was applied to situations where the participation or alliance of one person or group in the activities of another was unexpected. Saul's inclusion among the prophets was shocking.

10:12 who is their father? The question may simply be about leadership, since "father" is elsewhere synonymous with the prophetic "leader" (2 Kings 2:12; 6:21; 13:14). If this is so, the implication may be either that no good leader would permit someone like Saul to join or that Saul is, in fact, the new leader of the prophets. There is some evidence that prophets were not always viewed positively, and so another possibility is that Saul's presence with such "madmen" (cf. 2 Kings 9:11) is suspicious. Finally, if Samuel is their leader then it is an ironic statement, since Saul will ultimately oppose Samuel's authority (see note on 1 Sam. 19:23–24).

10:14–16 Saul's uncle, probably Abner (see 14:50), asks where he had been and **what Samuel said** to him. Saul's fate would be of great concern to Abner, since he was possibly next in line after Kish and Saul to inherit Abiel's estate (see 9:1).

10:17–27 This event is to show that the choice of Saul as king is not just Samuel's, but God's.

all your calamities and your distresses, and you have said to him, 'Set a king over us.' Now
therefore [f]present yourselves before the LORD by your tribes and by your thousands."
20 Then Samuel [g]brought all the tribes of Israel near, and the tribe of Benjamin was taken
by lot. 21 He brought the tribe of Benjamin near by its clans, and the clan of the Matrites
was taken by lot;[1] and Saul the son of Kish was taken by lot. But when they sought him, he
could not be found. 22 [h]So they inquired again of the LORD, "Is there a man still to come?"
and the LORD said, "Behold, he has hidden himself among the baggage." 23 Then they ran
and took him from there. And when he stood among the people, [i]he was taller than any
of the people from his shoulders upward. 24 And Samuel said to all the people, "Do you
see him [j]whom the LORD has chosen? There is none like him among all the people." And
all the people shouted, [k]"Long live the king!"
25 Then Samuel told the people [l]the rights and duties of the kingship, and he wrote them
in a book and laid it up before the LORD. Then Samuel sent all the people away, each one
to his home. 26 Saul also went to his home [m]at Gibeah, and with him went men of valor
whose hearts God had touched. 27 But some [n]worthless fellows said, "How can this man
save us?" And they despised him and brought him no present. But he held his peace.

Saul Defeats the Ammonites

11 [o]Then Nahash the Ammonite went up and besieged [p]Jabesh-gilead, and all the
men of Jabesh said to Nahash, [q]"Make a treaty with us, and we will serve you." 2 But
Nahash the Ammonite said to them, "On this condition I will make a treaty with you,
[r]that I gouge out all your right eyes, and thus [s]bring disgrace on all Israel." 3 The elders of

[1] Septuagint adds *finally he brought the family of the Matrites near, man by man*

19 [f]Josh. 24:1
20 [g]Josh. 7:14, 16, 17
22 [h]See ch. 22:10
23 [i]ch. 9:2
24 [j]2 Sam. 21:6 [k]2 Sam. 16:16; 1 Kgs. 1:25, 39; 2 Kgs. 11:12; 2 Chr. 23:11
25 [l]See ch. 8:11-18; Deut. 17:14-20
26 [m]ch. 11:4
27 [n]ch. 2:12; Deut. 13:13

Chapter 11

1 [o]ch. 12:12 [p]Judg. 21:8 [q]Gen. 26:28; 1 Kgs. 20:34; Ezek. 17:13; [Ex. 23:32; 34:12, 15; Deut. 7:2]
2 [r][Num. 16:14] [s]ch. 17:26; Gen. 34:14

10:20–21 Lots are also used for identifying a person in Josh. 7:14–18 and 1 Sam. 14:41–42, and for dividing the land in Josh. 14:2; 18:1–19:51; 21:1–45. See note on Acts 1:26.

Saul Rescues Jabesh-gilead

c. 1050 B.C.

Soon after Saul was anointed king of Israel, the people of Jabesh-gilead were attacked by the Ammonites. When Saul heard the news at Gibeah, he quickly mustered the Israelite forces at Bezek and defeated the Ammonites in battle. Samuel then called upon the people to confirm Saul's kingship at Gilgal.

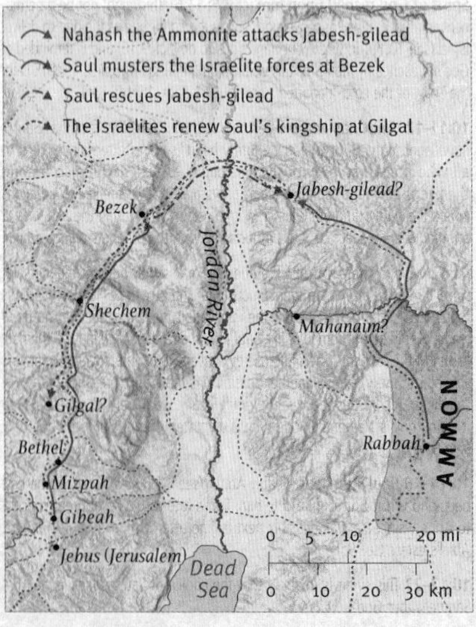

10:22 Saul had **hidden himself**, perhaps for fear of accepting his new responsibilities.

10:24 At last Saul is publicly and officially presented and accepted by the people as the **king**. Samuel emphasizes the divine decision in Saul's choice. Here he says that **the LORD has chosen**, while in 12:13 he says to the people, "you have chosen."

10:25 The rights and duties of the kingship is lit., "the rule [Hb. *mishpat*] of the kingship," i.e., the relationship between the king and the people, about which both the newly enthroned king and the people must have legal agreement. Legal agreements were usually written down and confirmed by the seals of the witnesses. Here **Samuel** was the intermediary and witness. He also **laid** the document **before the LORD**, i.e., deposited it in a sanctuary (cf. putting the Book of the Law or the covenant into or beside the ark; Ex. 25:16; 40:20; Deut. 31:26).

10:26 Gibeah ("hill"), Saul's home, was about 3 miles (4.8 km) north of Jerusalem, with a panoramic view and a north-south road nearby. This is probably the same as "Gibeath-elohim, where there is a garrison of the Philistines" (v. 5). A fortress with casemate walls and corner towers has been excavated there, but it is not certain whether it was built by the Philistines or the Israelites.

11:1–15 *Making Saul King.* This episode shows how Saul becomes the *de facto* king and is accepted by all Israel because of his victory over the Ammonites. The Dead Sea Scroll of Samuel, 4QSam[a], has an otherwise unknown paragraph about the background of an oppression by "Nahash, king of the Ammonites." It says that Nahash had been gouging out the eyes of the Transjordan Gadites and Reubenites and that 7,000 men had fled to Jabesh-gilead. But because 1 Sam. 11:1–2 says "Nahash the Ammonite," not "Nahash, king of the Ammonites," it seems unlikely that the paragraph in question was lost from the text in the course of transmission. More likely, it is a later addition. It is possible that the person who added this paragraph was following a true tradition, but one that was not part of 1 Samuel. The demand for a king in ch. 8 may have been made in the midst of such Ammonite oppression. Even if the biblical author knew about it, however, he may not have included it because he was more concerned with the deliverance of the Transjordan Israelites by Saul than with their oppression by Nahash.

11:1 Jabesh-gilead was probably east of the Jordan River near the western edge of the Gilead mountains (see map to the left).

11:2 To **make a treaty** is literally "to cut a treaty," which usually involved sacrificial animals. But Nahash demands to cut the treaty with the men's eyes.

Jabesh said to him, "Give us seven days' respite that we may send messengers through all
the territory of Israel. Then, if there is no one to save us, we will give ourselves up to you."
4 When the messengers came to [t]Gibeah of Saul, they reported the matter in the ears of
the people, [u]and all the people wept aloud.
5 Now, behold, Saul was coming from the field behind the oxen. And Saul said, "What
is wrong with the people, that they are weeping?" So they told him the news of the men
of Jabesh. **6** [v]And the Spirit of God rushed upon Saul when he heard these words, and his
anger was greatly kindled. **7** He took a yoke of oxen [w]and cut them in pieces and sent them
throughout all the territory of Israel by the hand of the messengers, saying, [x]"Whoever does
not come out after Saul and Samuel, so shall it be done to his oxen!" Then the dread of the
LORD fell upon the people, and they came out [y]as one man. **8** When he mustered them at
[z]Bezek, [a]the people of Israel were three hundred thousand, and the men of Judah thirty
thousand. **9** And they said to the messengers who had come, "Thus shall you say to the
men of Jabesh-gilead: 'Tomorrow, by the time the sun is hot, you shall have [b]salvation.'"
When the messengers came and told the men of Jabesh, they were glad. **10** Therefore the
men of Jabesh said, [c]"Tomorrow we will give ourselves up to you, and you may do to us
whatever seems good to you." **11** [d]And the next day Saul put the people [e]in three companies.
And they came into the midst of the camp in the morning watch and struck down the
Ammonites until the heat of the day. And those who survived were scattered, so that no
two of them were left together.

The Kingdom Is Renewed

12 Then the people said to Samuel, [f]"Who is it that said, 'Shall Saul reign over us?' [g]Bring
the men, that we may put them to death." **13** But Saul said, [h]"Not a man shall be put
to death this day, for today [i]the LORD has worked [j]salvation in Israel." **14** Then Samuel
said to the people, "Come, let us go to Gilgal and there renew the kingdom." **15** So all the
people went to [k]Gilgal, and there they made Saul king [l]before the LORD in Gilgal. There
[m]they sacrificed peace offerings before the LORD, and there Saul and all the men of Israel
rejoiced greatly.

Samuel's Farewell Address

12 And Samuel said to all Israel, "Behold, I have obeyed [n]your voice in all that you
have said to me [o]and have made a king over you. **2** And now, behold, the king
[p]walks before you, [q]and I am old and gray; and behold, my sons are with you. I have
walked before you from my youth until this day. **3** Here I am; testify against me before
the LORD and before [r]his anointed. [s]Whose ox have I taken? Or whose donkey have I
taken? Or whom have I defrauded? Whom have I oppressed? Or from whose hand have
I taken a bribe to blind my eyes with it? Testify against me[1] and I will restore it to you."
4 They said, "You have not defrauded us or oppressed us or taken anything from any

[1] Septuagint; Hebrew lacks *Testify against me*

4 [t]ch. 10:26 [u]Judg. 2:4; 21:2
6 [v]See ch. 10:6, 10
7 [w][Judg. 19:29] [x]Judg. 21:5, 8, 10 [y]Judg. 20:1
8 [z]Judg. 1:5 [a][Judg. 20:15-17; 2 Sam. 24:9]
9 [b]ver. 13
10 [c]ver. 3
11 [d][ch. 31:11] [e]Judg. 7:16
12 [f]ch. 10:27 [g][Luke 19:27]
13 [h]2 Sam. 19:22 [i][ch. 19:5; Ex. 14:13] [j]ver. 9
15 [k]ch. 10:8 [l]ch. 15:33; [ch. 10:17; Judg. 11:11] [m]ch. 10:8

Chapter 12

1 [n]ch. 8:5, 19, 20 [o]ch. 10:24; 11:14, 15
2 [p][ch. 8:20; Num. 27:17] [q]ch. 8:1, 5
3 [r]ch. 24:6; 26:9, 11, 16; 2 Sam. 1:14, 16; [ch. 10:1] [s][Ex. 20:17; Num. 16:15]

11:3 For **elders**, see note on 4:3.

11:4 There were probably strong blood ties between Jabesh-gilead and **Gibeah** (see Judg. 21:12). The 42-mile (68-km) journey from Jabesh to Gibeah may have taken two days.

11:6–7 As in 10:6 (see note there), **the Spirit of God rushed upon Saul**, but here he is filled with power like one of the judges (Judg. 3:10; 6:34; 11:29; 14:6, 19; 15:14). He apparently did not need to identify himself to his fellow Israelites other than as "Saul"; the message itself seems to presuppose some degree of authority, though he also invokes Samuel's authority. Saul issues a conditional curse (**Whoever does not come out**), symbolized by his dismembering of the oxen (cf. Judg. 19:29–30).

11:8 **Bezek** was probably on the opposite side of the Jordan from Jabesh.

11:10 **Give ourselves up to you** can also mean "march out to you." The speech of the men is deliberately ambiguous.

11:11 Saul uses the tactic of dividing the forces into **three companies** (cf. Judg. 7:16; 9:43; 2 Sam. 18:2; Job 1:17).

11:12–15 After Saul's victory, the people are enthusiastic about him. Note that Samuel still plays the crucial role in establishing and promoting kingship in Israel (see v. 7). This ceremony at the worship center of **Gilgal** seems to be a religious coronation rather than the event of political recognition in 10:17–25.

12:1–25 *Samuel's Address to Israel.* The setting of this address is not clear. The sentence structure at the end of ch. 11 suggests a complete end of a section and therefore that ch. 12 begins a new section. The address was probably given on an occasion different from that in ch. 11. From now on, Samuel is no longer the judge of all Israel: the age of kingship has begun. But this is neither a retirement ceremony for Samuel nor his last public address; his authority as the prophet who gives the word of God to the king and people of Israel remains powerful (see 12:18), and he has one more king to anoint (ch. 16).

12:2 **And now** contrasts Saul as the king and Samuel as the judge. **behold, the king walks before you**. Saul has been ruling over the people for some time.

12:3–6 Samuel asks the people to **testify** to the integrity of his life as a judge, in contrast with that of his sons (see 8:3). It is a case between him and the people, argued with the Lord as witness. He is not asking for judgment on his life as a prophet, a matter between him and God. **Whose ox have I taken?** Samuel has not used his power or office as a means of personal enrichment (cf. notes on 8:3; 8:14–15).

man's hand." **5** And he said to them, "The LORD is witness against you, and [r]his anointed
is witness this day, that you have not found anything [t]in my hand." And they said, "He
is witness."
6 And Samuel said to the people, [u]"The LORD is witness,[1] who appointed Moses and
Aaron and brought your fathers up out of the land of Egypt. **7** Now therefore stand still
that I may plead with you before the LORD concerning all the righteous deeds of the
LORD that he performed for you and for your fathers. **8** [v]When Jacob went into Egypt,
and the Egyptians oppressed them,[2] [w]then your fathers cried out to the LORD and [x]the
LORD sent Moses and Aaron, [y]who brought your fathers out of Egypt and made them
dwell in this place. **9** But [z]they forgot the LORD their God. [a]And he sold them into the
hand of Sisera, commander of the army of Hazor,[3] [b]and into the hand of the Philistines,
[c]and into the hand of the king of Moab. And they fought against them. **10** [d]And they
cried out to the LORD and said, 'We have sinned, because we have forsaken the LORD
[e]and have served the Baals and the Ashtaroth. But now [f]deliver us out of the hand of
our enemies, that we may serve you.' **11** And the LORD sent [g]Jerubbaal [h]and Barak[4] [i]and
Jephthah and [j]Samuel and delivered you out of the hand of your enemies on every side,
and you lived in safety. **12** And when you saw that [k]Nahash the king of the Ammonites
came against you, [l]you said to me, 'No, but a king shall reign over us,' [m]when the LORD
your God was your king. **13** And now [n]behold the king whom you have chosen, for whom
you have asked; behold, [o]the LORD has set a king over you. **14** If you will [p]fear the LORD
and serve him and obey his voice and not rebel against the commandment of the LORD,
and if both you and the king who reigns over you will follow the LORD your God, it
will be well. **15** But [q]if you will not obey the voice of the LORD, but rebel against the
commandment of the LORD, then [r]the hand of the LORD will be against you and [s]your
king.[5] **16** Now therefore [t]stand still and see this great thing that the LORD will do before
your eyes. **17** [u]Is it not wheat harvest today? [v]I will call upon the LORD, that he may send
thunder and rain. And you shall know and see that [w]your wickedness is great, which
you have done in the sight of the LORD, in asking for yourselves a king." **18** So Samuel
called upon the LORD, and the LORD sent thunder and rain that day, [x]and all the people
greatly feared the LORD and Samuel.
19 And all the people said to Samuel, [y]"Pray for your servants to the LORD your God,
that we may not die, for we have added to all our sins this evil, to ask for ourselves a king."
20 And Samuel said to the people, "Do not be afraid; you have done all this evil. Yet [z]do not
turn aside from following the LORD, but serve the LORD with all your heart. **21** And [z]do
not turn aside after [a]empty things that cannot profit or deliver, for they are empty. **22** [b]For
the LORD will not forsake his people, [c]for his great name's sake, because [d]it has pleased
the LORD to make you a people for himself. **23** Moreover, as for me, far be it from me that
I should sin against the LORD by ceasing [e]to pray for you, [f]and I will instruct you in the
good and the right way. **24** [g]Only fear the LORD and serve him faithfully with all your heart.
For consider [h]what great things he has done for you. **25** But if you still do wickedly, [i]you
shall be swept away, [j]both you and your king."

5 [r][See ver. 3 above] [t]Ex. 21:16; 22:4
6 [u][Mic. 6:4]
8 [v]Gen. 46:5, 6 [w]Ex. 2:23 [x]Ex. 3:10; 4:14-16 [y][ch. 10:18]
9 [z]Judg. 3:7 [a]Judg. 4:2 [b]Judg. 10:7; 13:1; [Judg. 3:31] [c]Judg. 3:12
10 [d]Judg. 10:10; [Judg. 3:9] [e]Judg. 2:13 [f]Judg. 10:15
11 [g]Judg. 6:14, 32 [h]Judg. 4:6, 8, 10 [i]Judg. 11:1 [j]See ch. 7:10-13
12 [k]ch. 11:1 [l]ch. 8:5, 19 [m][ch. 8:7; 10:19; Judg. 8:23]
13 [n]ch. 10:24 [o]ch. 9:16, 17; [Hos. 13:11]
14 [p]ver. 24; Deut. 6:2; Josh. 24:14
15 [q]Lev. 26:14, 15; Deut. 28:15; Josh. 24:20 [r]ch. 5:9 [s][ver. 9]
16 [t]Ex. 14:13
17 [u][Prov. 26:1] [v]ch. 7:9, 10; [James 5:16-18] [w]ch. 8:7
18 [x]Ex. 14:31; [Ezra 10:9]
19 [y]ver. 23; [Ex. 9:28; 10:17; Jer. 15:1]
20 [z]Deut. 11:16
21 [z][See ver. 20 above] [a]Jer. 16:19; Hab. 2:18; [1 Cor. 8:4]
22 [b]1 Kgs. 6:13; Ps. 94:14; [1 Kgs. 8:57] [c]Josh. 7:9; Ps. 106:8; Jer. 14:21; Ezek. 20:9, 14, 22 [d]Deut. 7:7, 8; 14:2; [1 Pet. 2:9]
23 [e]See ver. 19 [f]1 Kgs. 8:36; 2 Chr. 6:27; Ps. 27:11; [Prov. 4:11; Jer. 6:16]
24 [g]ver. 14; [Eccles. 12:13] [h]Deut. 10:21; Ps. 126:2, 3
25 [i]Josh. 24:20; [Num. 16:26] [j][Deut. 28:36]

[1] Septuagint; Hebrew lacks *is witness* [2] Septuagint; Hebrew lacks *and the Egyptians oppressed them* [3] Septuagint *the army of Jabin king of Hazor* [4] Septuagint, Syriac; Hebrew *Bedan* [5] Septuagint; Hebrew *fathers*

12:7–12 Samuel turns to the relationship between the Lord and the people. His speech is similar to speeches by Joshua (Joshua 23–24) and Solomon (1 Kings 8:12–61).

12:10 the Baals and the Ashtaroth. I.e., the foreign gods and goddesses; see note on 7:3–4.

12:14–15 Samuel concludes his official speech by summarizing his admonitions to the covenant people. Not only the people but also the **king** should be obedient to the Lord; no king in Israel is exempt from obeying the Lord's commandments.

12:21 Empty things (Hb. *tohu*) refers here to vain idols. An idol is "nothing"—a vacuous entity that gives the one who trusts in it only vanity or emptiness in return.

12:22 The Lord will not deal with his chosen people according to their wicked deeds (v. 25), but will treat them mercifully **for his great name's sake**. This is the biblical principle of divine saving grace or favor.

12:23 Praying (intercession) and instruction are two of Samuel's major roles as the prophet of the Lord, even after the inauguration of kingship.

12:25 Both the people and the king are obliged to obey the word of the Lord; otherwise both will **be swept away** (as in Saul's case; see ch. 13).

13:1–15:35 *Reign of Saul.* Saul, though chosen directly by God and initially zealous for the Lord, is easily moved by circumstances. He is successful against the Philistines and Amalekites, but he also does things in his own way or—even worse—in the people's way, against the word of the Lord. As a result, Samuel tells Saul that his kingdom (13:14) and even his own kingship (15:23) will be taken away. This difficult relationship between Saul and Samuel continues even after Samuel's death (see ch. 28). The two incidents of Saul's dis-

Chapter 13
2[k]ver. 5, 11, 16, 23; ch. 14:31 [l]ver. 15; ch. 10:26
3[m]ch. 10:5 [n]ver. 16; ch. 14:5 [o][Judg. 3:27]
5[p]Josh. 11:4 [q]ch. 14:23
6[r]Judg. 6:2; Heb. 11:38
8[s]ch. 10:8
13[t]2 Sam. 24:10; 1 Chr. 21:8; 2 Chr. 16:9 [u]ch. 15:11

Saul Fights the Philistines

13 Saul lived for one year and then became king, and when he had reigned for two
years over Israel,[1] **2** Saul chose three thousand men of Israel. Two thousand were with
Saul in [k]Michmash and the hill country of Bethel, and a thousand were with Jonathan in
[l]Gibeah of Benjamin. The rest of the people he sent home, every man to his tent. **3** Jonathan
defeated [m]the garrison of the Philistines that was [n]at Geba, and the Philistines heard of
it. And Saul [o]blew the trumpet throughout all the land, saying, "Let the Hebrews hear."
4 And all Israel heard it said that Saul had defeated the garrison of the Philistines, and
also that Israel had become a stench to the Philistines. And the people were called out to
join Saul at Gilgal.
5 And the Philistines mustered to fight with Israel, thirty thousand chariots and six
thousand horsemen and troops [p]like the sand on the seashore in multitude. They came
up and encamped in Michmash, to the east of [q]Beth-aven. **6** When the men of Israel saw
that they were in trouble (for the people were hard pressed), the people hid themselves [r]in
caves and in holes and in rocks and in tombs and in cisterns, **7** and some Hebrews crossed
the fords of the Jordan to the land of Gad and Gilead. Saul was still at Gilgal, and all the
people followed him trembling.

Saul's Unlawful Sacrifice

8 [s]He waited seven days, the time appointed by Samuel. But Samuel did not come to
Gilgal, and the people were scattering from him. **9** So Saul said, "Bring the burnt offering
here to me, and the peace offerings." And he offered the burnt offering. **10** As soon as he had
finished offering the burnt offering, behold, Samuel came. And Saul went out to meet him
and greet him. **11** Samuel said, "What have you done?" And Saul said, "When I saw that the
people were scattering from me, and that you did not come within the days appointed,
and that the Philistines had mustered at Michmash, **12** I said, 'Now the Philistines will
come down against me at Gilgal, and I have not sought the favor of the LORD.' So I forced
myself, and offered the burnt offering." **13** And Samuel said to Saul, [t]"You have done foolishly. [u]You have not kept the command of the LORD your God, with which he commanded

[1] Hebrew *Saul was one year old when he became king, and he reigned two years over Israel* (see 1 Samuel 10:6); some Greek manuscripts give Saul's age when he began to reign as thirty years

obedience frame the great victory against the Philistines at Michmash (ch. 14). Even in the midst of victory, however, Saul almost manages to destroy his own house by cursing his son, through whom the battle was won. Chapters 13–15 are a buildup toward David's being chosen as king (ch. 16).

13:1–23 *Saul and the Philistines—First Rejection of Saul.* In preparing for battle, Saul disobeys God's commands given through Samuel; God cannot endure such a king over Israel.

13:1 The Hebrew text of this verse is difficult, and various solutions have been proposed. One possibility (see ESV footnote) is that some numbers, giving Saul's age and length of reign, were lost from the text at a very early point in its transmission. (Most Septuagint manuscripts lack this verse completely.) Acts 13:21 says that Saul reigned for "forty years." This has led some translations to say that Saul reigned "forty years" or else "forty-two years" (taking Acts 13:21 as a round number). Josephus, *Jewish Antiquities* 6.378, also has Saul reigning for 40 years, but the Latin text of that passage has 20 years, as does Josephus in *Jewish Antiquities* 10.143. The ESV text attempts to make sense of the Hebrew as it stands, indicating the time gaps between the events. Another possibility is that the author is making a comment about the immature Saul (as if he were only a year old, after becoming "another man," 10:6) and his ineffective reign (as if it were only two years), although this is only a speculative possibility.

13:2 In ch. 9 Saul is described as a "young man," but here he has a son who can command troops, and thus a number of years may have passed. **Michmash** is about 7 miles (11 km) northeast of Jerusalem and 3 or 4 miles (4.8 or 6.4 km) south of Bethel. These **three thousand men** were his standing army.

13:3 defeated the garrison. The word translated as "garrison" here and in v. 4 is singular, while in 10:5 it is plural. ("Garrison" in 13:23 is a different word.) The **trumpet** also signals a revolt in Judg. 3:27 and 2 Sam. 15:10. For **Hebrews**, see note on 1 Sam. 4:6.

13:5 Thirty thousand chariots seems very high, and perhaps the Syriac translation (and one tradition of the Septuagint) preserves the true reading, "three thousand." **Beth-aven** is probably the Beth-aven near Ai (Josh. 7:2).

13:7 land of Gad and Gilead. Or "land of Gad, that is, Gilead" (cf. note on 6:4).

13:8–15 Saul had summoned the army to meet at Gilgal, the place where he had "waited" (10:8) and been crowned (11:15). Again, "waiting" at Gilgal seems to have a special religious meaning. After this period of time, however, Saul offers sacrifices and breaks the commandment of the Lord (13:13). Some interpreters take this to mean that he did not obey the Lord's word through Samuel recorded in 10:8, to the effect that Saul should wait seven days for Samuel to come and offer burnt offerings and show Saul what to do. Others think the statement in 10:8 occurred several years earlier, and that Saul violates another (unrecorded) command from Samuel, or the command that only a priest should offer sacrifices (Num. 18:7), or the general principle that he should have waited to learn God's will through the prophet. In any case, Saul knows he has done wrong, for he starts making excuses (1 Sam. 13:11–12). Apparently he had been told not to make any move until Samuel gave him the word of the Lord. Here Saul shows his tendency to be moved by circumstances and to rely on religious ritual to gain God's favor (see 14:24 and the incident in 4:3) rather than to trust and obey the word of the Lord.

13:13–14 Saul's disobedience brings a serious result—the cessation of his **kingdom**—for in Israel the kingship itself is under the authority of the word of God (see 12:20–25). Saul fails to acknowledge the prophet's higher role as the divine messenger and to listen to the word of God (cf. 15:11, 13, 19, 22–23).

you. For then the LORD would have established your kingdom over Israel forever. **14** But
now [v]your kingdom shall not continue. The LORD has sought out a man [w]after his own
heart, and the LORD has commanded him to be prince[1] over his people, because you have
not kept what the LORD commanded you." **15** And Samuel arose and went up from Gilgal.
The rest of the people went up after Saul to meet the army; they went up from Gilgal[2] to
[x]Gibeah of Benjamin.

And Saul numbered the people who were present with him, [y]about six hundred men.
16 And Saul and Jonathan his son and the people who were present with them stayed
in [z]Geba of Benjamin, but the Philistines encamped in Michmash. **17** And [a]raiders came
out of the camp of the Philistines in three companies. One company turned toward
Ophrah, to the land of Shual; **18** another company turned toward [b]Beth-horon; and
another company turned toward the border that looks down on the Valley of [c]Zeboim
toward the wilderness.

19 [d]Now there was no blacksmith to be found throughout all the land of Israel, for the
Philistines said, "Lest the Hebrews make themselves swords or spears." **20** But every one of
the Israelites went down to the Philistines to sharpen his plowshare, his mattock, his axe,
or his sickle,[3] **21** and the charge was two-thirds of a shekel[4] for the plowshares and for the
mattocks, and a third of a shekel[5] for sharpening the axes and for setting the goads.[6] **22** So
on the day of the battle [e]there was neither sword nor spear found in the hand of any of
the people with Saul and Jonathan, but Saul and Jonathan his son had them. **23** And [f]the
garrison of the Philistines went out to the [g]pass of [h]Michmash.

[1] Or *leader* [2] Septuagint; Hebrew lacks *The rest of the people . . . from Gilgal* [3] Septuagint; Hebrew *plowshare* [4] Hebrew *was a pim* [5] A *shekel* was about 2/5 ounce or 11 grams [6] The meaning of the Hebrew verse is uncertain

14 [v]ch. 15:28 [w]Cited Acts 13:22
15 [x]ver. 2 [y]ch. 14:2
16 [z]ver. 3; ch. 14:5
17 [a]ch. 14:15
18 [b]See Josh. 10:10 [c]Neh. 11:34
19 [d][2 Kgs. 24:14]
22 [e][Judg. 5:8]
23 [f]ch. 14:1, 4, 6, 11; 2 Sam. 23:14 [g]ch. 14:4, 5; Isa. 10:28, 29 [h]Isa. 10:28

The Battle at Michmash
As the Philistines strengthened their grip on the central hill country of Israel, they placed troops at Michmash and sent raiding parties into the countryside. After Saul's son Jonathan captured the town of Geba, Saul mustered more Israelite forces at Gilgal and joined Jonathan. A daring raid by Jonathan across the ravine separating Michmash and Geba led to an Israelite victory over the Philistines, and the Israelites drove them from the hill country.

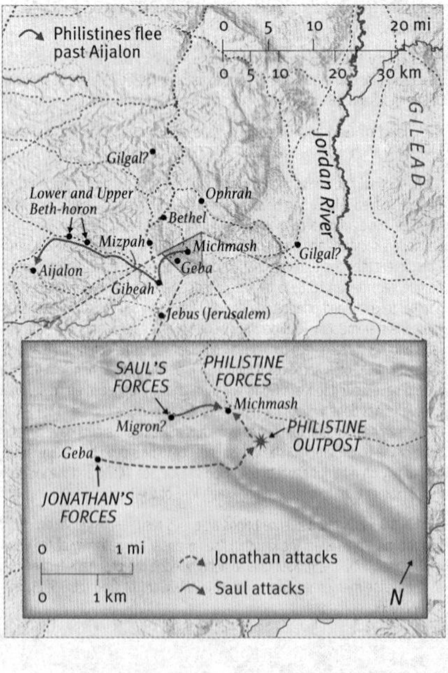

13:16 Geba is only a mile or two from **Michmash**, separated from it by a deep ravine, which is an important pass from the Jordan Valley into the Ephraimite hills (see map to the left). The Philistines were stationed at the hilltop that overlooks the ravine from the north, while Saul's army was encamped to the south. See ch. 14.

13:17–18 The raiders' division into **three companies**, going in different directions, recalls Saul's own earlier tactics (see note on 11:11).

13:19–22 no blacksmith (in) **Israel**. The Philistines apparently had been able to monopolize the production of the kind of metal (probably iron) needed for **swords** and **spears**, putting the Israelites at a great disadvantage. Thus the Israelite victory at Michmash (ch. 14) was indeed the Lord's doing. (Iron plow points have been found, however, in Israelite contexts as early as the 11th century B.C. at the site of Gibeah.) As the ESV footnote explains, the Hebrew text refers to a weight called a "pim" (taken to be **two-thirds of a shekel**). A number of weights marked "pim" have been found.

14:1–52 *Saul and Jonathan.* Jonathan's act of trust in this chapter is sandwiched between two instances of Saul's disobedience in chs. 13 and 15. The narrator thus clearly contrasts Saul and Jonathan before dealing with Saul and David (chs. 16ff.).

14:2–3 The **outskirts of Gibeah** may mean "the edge of the hill." **Migron** may mean "threshing floor." Court was often held under a tree (22:6; Judg. 4:5) or on threshing floors (1 Kings 22:10). For **ephod,** see note on 1 Sam. 2:27–28.

14:4 Bozez means "the gleaming one," and **Seneh** means "the thorny one."

14:6 Jonathan's trust contrasts with Saul's concern about numbers (13:11, 15). **Uncircumcised** was a customary derogatory epithet used of the Philistines (cf. Judg. 14:3; 15:18; 1 Sam. 17:26; 31:4; 2 Sam. 1:20).

14:10 if they say, "Come up to us." This would give Jonathan and the armor-bearer the opportunity to get into the Philistine camp at what was probably its most thinly protected point, without raising an alarm. The guards' words in v. 12 suggest that an attack by these two lone men was the last thing on their mind.

14:14 The Hebrew "yoke" (ESV footnote) was a unit for measuring area.

14:15 A very great panic is literally "a panic of God" (see ESV footnote), suggesting divine intervention.

14:16 Though Saul was in Gibeah, about 4 miles (6.4 km) from Michmash, his **watchmen** were probably stationed nearer, watching Michmash.

Chapter 14
2[h][See ch. 13:23 above] [i]ch. 13:15
3[j]ch. 22:9, 11, 20 [k]ch. 4:21 [l]See Josh. 18:1 [m]ch. 2:28
4[n]ch. 13:23
5[o]ch. 13:3, 16
6[p]ch. 17:26; Judg. 14:3 [q][Judg. 7:4, 7; 2 Chr. 14:11]
11[r]ch. 13:6
15[s]ch. 13:17
16[t]Josh. 2:9
19[u]Num. 27:21
20[v][Judg. 7:22; 2 Chr. 20:23]
21[w][ch. 29:4]
22[x]ver. 11; ch. 13:6 [y]See Josh. 24:33
23[z]Ex. 14:30 [a]ch. 13:5
24[b][Josh. 6:26]

Jonathan Defeats the Philistines

14 One day Jonathan the son of Saul said to the young man who carried his armor,
"Come, let us go over to the Philistine garrison on the other side." But he did not
tell his father. 2 Saul was staying in the outskirts of Gibeah in the pomegranate cave[1] at
[h]Migron. The people who were with him were about [i]six hundred men, 3 including [j]Ahijah
the son of Ahitub, [k]Ichabod's brother, son of Phinehas, son of Eli, the priest of the LORD
[l]in Shiloh, [m]wearing an ephod. And the people did not know that Jonathan had gone.
4 Within [n]the passes, by which Jonathan sought to go over to the Philistine garrison, there
was a rocky crag on the one side and a rocky crag on the other side. The name of the one
was Bozez, and the name of the other Seneh. 5 The one crag rose on the north in front of
Michmash, and the other on the south in front of [o]Geba.

6 Jonathan said to the young man who carried his armor, "Come, let us go over to the
garrison of these [p]uncircumcised. It may be that the LORD will work for us, [q]for nothing can hinder the LORD from saving by many or by few." 7 And his armor-bearer said to
him, "Do all that is in your heart. Do as you wish.[2] Behold, I am with you heart and soul."
8 Then Jonathan said, "Behold, we will cross over to the men, and we will show ourselves
to them. 9 If they say to us, 'Wait until we come to you,' then we will stand still in our
place, and we will not go up to them. 10 But if they say, 'Come up to us,' then we will go
up, for the LORD has given them into our hand. And this shall be the sign to us." 11 So
both of them showed themselves to the garrison of the Philistines. And the Philistines
said, "Look, Hebrews are coming [r]out of the holes where they have hidden themselves."
12 And the men of the garrison hailed Jonathan and his armor-bearer and said, "Come up
to us, and we will show you a thing." And Jonathan said to his armor-bearer, "Come up
after me, for the LORD has given them into the hand of Israel." 13 Then Jonathan climbed
up on his hands and feet, and his armor-bearer after him. And they fell before Jonathan,
and his armor-bearer killed them after him. 14 And that first strike, which Jonathan and
his armor-bearer made, killed about twenty men within as it were half a furrow's length
in an acre[3] of land. 15 And there was a panic in the camp, in the field, and among all the
people. The garrison and even [s]the raiders trembled, the earth quaked, and it became a
very great panic.[4]

16 And the watchmen of Saul in Gibeah of Benjamin looked, and behold, the multitude
[t]was dispersing here and there.[5] 17 Then Saul said to the people who were with him, "Count
and see who has gone from us." And when they had counted, behold, Jonathan and his
armor-bearer were not there. 18 So Saul said to Ahijah, "Bring the ark of God here." For the
ark of God went at that time with the people[6] of Israel. 19 Now [u]while Saul was talking
to the priest, the tumult in the camp of the Philistines increased more and more. So Saul
said to the priest, "Withdraw your hand." 20 Then Saul and all the people who were with
him rallied and went into the battle. And behold, [v]every Philistine's sword was against his
fellow, and there was very great confusion. 21 Now the Hebrews who had been with the
Philistines before that time and who had gone up with them into the camp, [w]even they
also turned to be with the Israelites who were with Saul and Jonathan. 22 Likewise, when
all the men of Israel [x]who had hidden themselves [y]in the hill country of Ephraim heard
that the Philistines were fleeing, they too followed hard after them in the battle. 23 [z]So the
LORD saved Israel that day. And the battle passed beyond [a]Beth-aven.

Saul's Rash Vow

24 And the men of Israel had been hard pressed that day, [b]so Saul had laid an oath on the
people, saying, "Cursed be the man who eats food until it is evening and I am avenged on

[1] Or *under the pomegranate* [tree] [2] Septuagint *Do all that your mind inclines to* [3] Hebrew *a yoke* [4] Or *became a panic from God* [5] Septuagint; Hebrew *they went here and there* [6] Hebrew; Septuagint *"Bring the ephod." For at that time he wore the ephod before the people*

14:18 The **ark** had apparently been brought from Kiriath-jearim to be with the army for some special reason, and Saul wanted **Ahijah**, who carried the sacred lots in the ephod, to cast the lots before the ark.

14:21–22 These verses describe several groups who earlier distanced themselves from Israel. Some people called **Hebrews** had previously defected to the Philistines (cf. 29:3) while others **had hidden themselves** during this time of war. Now that the conflict goes favorably, both groups commit to fighting for Israel.

14:23 beyond Beth-aven. This battle seems to have driven the Philistines from the central mountain areas.

14:24 so Saul had laid an oath. Jonathan, of course, had not been present at the time.

my enemies." So none of the people had tasted food. **25** Now when all the people[1] came to
the forest, behold, there was honey on the ground. **26** And when the people entered the forest, behold, the honey was dropping, but no one put his hand to his mouth, for the people
feared the oath. **27** But Jonathan had not heard his father charge the people with the oath,
[c]so he put out the tip of the staff that was in his hand and dipped it in the honeycomb
and put his hand to his mouth, and his eyes became bright. **28** Then one of the people said,
"Your father strictly charged the people with an oath, saying, 'Cursed be the man who eats
food this day.'" And the people were [d]faint. **29** Then Jonathan said, "My father has troubled
the land. See how my eyes have become bright because I tasted a little of this honey. **30** How
much better if the people had eaten freely today of the spoil of their enemies that they
found. For now the defeat among the Philistines has not been great."
31 They struck down the Philistines that day from [e]Michmash to [f]Aijalon. And the people
were very [d]faint. **32** The people [g]pounced on the spoil and took sheep and oxen and calves
and slaughtered them on the ground. And the people ate them [h]with the blood. **33** Then
they told Saul, "Behold, the people are sinning against the LORD by eating [h]with the blood."
And he said, "You have dealt treacherously; roll a great stone to me here."[2] **34** And Saul
said, "Disperse yourselves among the people and say to them, 'Let every man bring his ox
or his sheep and slaughter them here and eat, and do not sin against the LORD by eating
with the blood.'" So every one of the people brought his ox with him that night and they
slaughtered them there. **35** And Saul [i]built an altar to the LORD; it was the first altar that
he built to the LORD.
36 Then Saul said, "Let us go down after the Philistines by night and plunder them until
the morning light; let us not leave a man of them." And they said, "Do whatever seems
good to you." But [j]the priest said, "Let us draw near to God here." **37** And Saul inquired of
God, "Shall I go down after the Philistines? Will you give them into the hand of Israel?"
[k]But he did not answer him that day. **38** And Saul said, "Come here, all you leaders of the
people, and know and see how this sin has arisen today. **39** For [l]as the LORD lives who saves
Israel, [m]though it be in Jonathan my son, he shall surely die." But there was not a man
among all the people who answered him. **40** Then he said to all Israel, "You shall be on one
side, and I and Jonathan my son will be on the other side." And the people said to Saul,
"Do what seems good to you." **41** Therefore Saul said, "O LORD God of Israel, why have you
not answered your servant this day? If this guilt is in me or in Jonathan my son, O LORD,
God of Israel, give Urim. But if this guilt is in your people Israel, give Thummim."[3] [n]And
Jonathan and Saul were taken, but the people escaped. **42** Then Saul said, [n]"Cast the lot
between me and my son Jonathan." And Jonathan was taken.
43 Then Saul said to Jonathan, [o]"Tell me what you have done." And Jonathan told him,
[p]"I tasted a little honey with the tip of the staff that was in my hand. Here I am; I will
die." **44** And Saul said, [q]"God do so to me and more also; [r]you shall surely die, Jonathan."
45 Then the people said to Saul, "Shall Jonathan die, who has worked this great salvation
in Israel? Far from it! [l]As the LORD lives, [s]there shall not one hair of his head fall to the
ground, for he has worked with God this day." So the people ransomed Jonathan, so that
he did not die. **46** Then Saul went up from pursuing the Philistines, and the Philistines
went to their own place.

[1] Hebrew *land* [2] Septuagint; Hebrew *this day* [3] Vulgate and Septuagint; Hebrew *Therefore Saul said to the LORD, the God of Israel, "Give Thummim."*

27 [c]ver. 43
28 [d]Judg. 8:4, 5
31 [e]ch. 13:2 [f]Josh. 10:12 [d][See ver. 28 above]
32 [g]ch. 15:19 [h][Lev. 3:17]
33 [h][See ver. 32 above]
35 [i][ch. 7:12, 17]
36 [j]ver. 3, 18, 19
37 [k]ch. 28:6
39 [l]See Ruth 3:13 [m]ver. 44
41 [n][ch. 10:20, 21; Josh. 7:16-18; Acts 1:24-26]
42 [n][See ver. 41 above]
43 [o][Josh. 7:19] [p]ver. 27
44 [q]See Ruth 1:17 [r]ver. 39
45 [l][See ver. 39 above] [s]2 Sam. 14:11; 1 Kgs. 1:52; Luke 21:18; Acts 27:34; [Matt. 10:30; Luke 12:7]

14:27 His eyes became bright suggests renewed vitality (cf. Ezra 9:8; Ps. 13:3; 19:8; 38:10; Prov. 29:13).

14:28 this day. See v. 24 ("until it is evening"). The day began at sunset.

14:32–33 When evening comes (v. 34) and the people are once again free to eat (cf. v. 24), they are in such a hurry that they do not put the animals they kill on a stone in order to drain the **blood** properly from them (v. 33). Eating meat with blood is strictly prohibited in the law (Gen. 9:4; Lev. 7:26; 17:10–14; Deut. 12:16).

14:39 he shall surely die. Saul assumes that the Lord's silence regarding Saul's prior question (v. 37) is due to some unknown sin (v. 38). Just as it was Saul's own willful (and faulty) decision to impose the ban on eating (v. 24), it is also his decision to kill the person, whoever it is, whose guilt has prevented the Lord from answering him.

14:41–42 give Urim. . . . give Thummim. . . . Cast the lot. The Urim and Thummim (or just Urim) are mentioned also in Ex. 28:30; Num. 27:21; Deut. 33:8; 1 Sam. 28:6; and Ezra 2:63. They may have been two stones of two different colors—a bright color and a dark color, perhaps—one representing a positive and the other a negative answer, that were kept in the "breastpiece of judgment" of the priest's ephod (see Ex. 28:30; Lev. 8:8). They were the only legitimate means of directly seeking a "yes" or "no" answer from the Lord, apart from God's speaking directly to people.

14:45 Shall Jonathan die . . . ? . . . As the LORD lives . . . The people use the same oath that Saul used in v. 39. They obviously think God spoke much more clearly in Jonathan's victory than in Saul's rash oath (v. 24).

Saul Fights Israel's Enemies

47 When Saul had taken the kingship over Israel, he fought against all his enemies on every side, against Moab, [t]against the Ammonites, against Edom, against the kings of [u]Zobah, and against the Philistines. Wherever he turned he routed them. **48** And he did valiantly [v]and struck the Amalekites and delivered Israel out of the hands of those who plundered them.

49 [w]Now the sons of Saul were Jonathan, Ishvi, and Malchi-shua. And the names of his two daughters were these: the name of the firstborn was [x]Merab, and the name of the younger Michal. **50** And the name of Saul's wife was Ahinoam the daughter of Ahimaaz. [y]And the name of the commander of his army was Abner the son of Ner, [z]Saul's uncle. **51** [a]Kish was the father of Saul, and Ner the father of Abner was the son of [a]Abiel.

52 There was hard fighting against the Philistines all the days of Saul. And when Saul saw any strong man, or any valiant man, [b]he attached him to himself.

The Lord Rejects Saul

15 And Samuel said to Saul, [c]"The LORD sent me to anoint you king over his people Israel; now therefore listen to the words of the LORD. **2** Thus says the LORD of hosts, 'I have noted what Amalek did to Israel [d]in opposing them on the way when they came up out of Egypt. **3** Now go and strike Amalek and [e]devote to destruction[1] all that they have. Do not spare them, [f]but kill both man and woman, child and infant, ox and sheep, camel and donkey.'"

4 So Saul summoned the people and numbered them in Telaim, two hundred thousand men on foot, and ten thousand men of Judah. **5** And Saul came to the city of Amalek and lay in wait in the valley. **6** Then Saul said to [g]the Kenites, "Go, depart; go down from among the Amalekites, lest I destroy you with them. [h]For you showed kindness to all the people of Israel when they came up out of Egypt." So the Kenites departed from among the Amalekites. **7** [i]And Saul defeated the Amalekites from [j]Havilah as far as [k]Shur, which is east of Egypt. **8** And he took Agag the king of the Amalekites alive [l]and devoted to destruction all the people with the edge of the sword. **9** [m]But Saul and the people spared Agag and the best of the sheep and of the oxen and of the fattened calves[2] and the lambs, and all that was good, and would not utterly destroy them. All that was despised and worthless they devoted to destruction.

10 The word of the LORD came to Samuel: **11** [n]"I regret[3] that I have made Saul king, for he has turned back from following me and [o]has not performed my commandments." And Samuel was angry, and he cried to the LORD all night. **12** And Samuel rose early to meet

[1] That is, set apart (devote) as an offering to the Lord (for destruction); also verses 8, 9, 15, 18, 20, 21 [2] The meaning of the Hebrew term is uncertain
[3] See also verses 29, 35

47 [t]ch. 11:11 [u]2 Sam. 8:3; 10:6
48 [v]ch. 15:3, 7
49 [w][ch. 31:2; 2 Sam. 2:8-10; 1 Chr. 8:33; 9:39] [x]ch. 18:17, 19
50 [y]2 Sam. 2:8 [z][ch. 10:14]
51 [a]ch. 9:1
52 [b]ch. 8:11
Chapter 15
1 [c]ch. 9:16
2 [d]See Ex. 17:8-16; Deut. 25:17-19
3 [e]Lev. 27:28, 29; Josh. 6:17, 21 [f][ch. 22:19]
6 [g]ch. 27:10; Judg. 1:16 [h][Ex. 18:10, 19; Num. 10:29, 32]
7 [i]ch. 14:48 [j]Gen. 2:11; 25:18 [k]ch. 27:8; [Gen. 16:7; Ex. 15:22]
8 [l][ch. 27:8, 9; 30:1]
9 [m]ver. 15, 21; [ch. 28:18]
11 [n]See Gen. 6:6 [o]ver. 3, 9; [ch. 13:13]

14:47–48 These countries are mentioned in 2 Sam. 8:12 as having been subdued by David.

14:49 It is possible, but not certain, that **Ishvi** is a variation of the name Ish-bosheth (2 Sam. 2:8; he is called "Eshbaal" in 1 Chron. 8:33).

14:50–51 Abner's father was Ner, his brother was Kish, and his nephew (Kish's son) was Saul. When 9:1 says that Kish was the "son of Abiel," it probably means "grandson of Abiel (Jeiel)" (cf. 1 Chron. 9:35).

15:1–35 *Saul and the Amalekites—Second Rejection of Saul.* Here, finally, Saul is rejected completely.

15:2 Thus says the LORD. See note on 2:27. **what Amalek did to Israel**. The Amalekites, a nomadic tribe that inhabited the desert south of Judah (Num. 13:29), are the archetypal plunderers in biblical tradition. They attacked Israel at Rephidim (Ex. 17:8), and the Lord declared war on them (Ex. 17:14–16; Deut. 25:17–19). They joined other groups against Israel in Num. 14:41–45; Judg. 3:13; 6:3; 10:12. They attacked David's city of Ziklag (1 Samuel 30), and David subdued them in 2 Sam. 8:12.

15:3 devote to destruction. This practice, known also as "imposing the ban," denotes setting aside something as the Lord's share. Usually such a ban meant that all living things—men, women, children, and livestock—were to be killed (cf. Deut. 20:16–17; Josh. 6:17, 21; see also 1 Sam. 22:19, where Saul unjustly carries this out on the priestly town of Nob). One purpose of such total destruction was to stop the spread of the "abominable practices" of paganism (Deut. 20:16–18). The ban against **Amalek** is based on Deut. 25:19.

15:4 Although the army of **Judah** is mentioned separately (as also in 11:8), it seems that Judahites in general considered themselves part of the nation. This is suggested by David (a Judahite) going to serve Saul (16:14–23), the presence of David's brothers in Saul's army (ch. 17), and Saul's search for David in the Judahite region of Ziph (23:14–29; 26:1–4). It is not surprising that Judah was heavily involved in the battle against Amalek, since the territory of Judah was near the Amalekites and therefore must have been particularly subject to their raids (30:14).

15:6 Kenites. Moses' father-in-law Jethro was a Kenite (Judg. 1:16), and he and his son had been helpful to the Israelites (Exodus 18; Num. 10:29–32). **depart; . . . lest I destroy you with them**. The Kenites had settled among the Amalekites. David likewise spared them during his time in Ziklag (1 Sam. 27:8–10; 30:29). Saul's action in this situation is commendable.

15:9 Spared is in sharp contrast to Samuel's instructions ("Do not spare," v. 3). **Saul and the people** places most of the responsibility for this disobedience on Saul himself.

15:11 I regret (also vv. 29, 35). Here, as in Gen. 6:6, the Lord "regrets" a decision. This means that God feels genuine sorrow when contemplating Saul's sin. But it does not mean that God thinks his decision to make Saul king was a mistake in the overall course of his plans for history (cf. Isa. 46:9–10). For more on divine regret, see note on 1 Sam. 15:29.

15:12 Carmel here is a town in Judah about 7 miles (11 km) south of

Saul in the morning. And it was told Samuel, "Saul came to [p]Carmel, and behold, he set
up a monument for himself and turned and passed on and went down to Gilgal." 13 And
Samuel came to Saul, and Saul said to him, [q]"Blessed be you to the LORD. I have performed
the commandment of the LORD." 14 And Samuel said, "What then is this bleating of the
sheep in my ears and the lowing of the oxen that I hear?" 15 Saul said, "They have brought
them from the Amalekites, [r]for the people spared the best of the sheep and of the oxen
to sacrifice to the LORD your God, and the rest we have devoted to destruction." 16 Then
Samuel said to Saul, "Stop! I will tell you what the LORD said to me this night." And he
said to him, "Speak."

17 And Samuel said, [s]"Though you are little in your own eyes, are you not the head of
the tribes of Israel? The LORD anointed you king over Israel. 18 And the LORD sent you
on a mission and said, 'Go, devote to destruction the sinners, the Amalekites, and fight
against them until they are consumed.' 19 Why then did you not obey the voice of the LORD?
[t]Why did you pounce on the spoil and do what was evil in the sight of the LORD?" 20 And
Saul said to Samuel, [u]"I have obeyed the voice of the LORD. I have gone on the mission
on which the LORD sent me. I have brought Agag the king of Amalek, and I have devoted
the Amalekites to destruction. 21 [v]But the people took of the spoil, sheep and oxen, the
best of the things devoted to destruction, to sacrifice to the LORD your God in Gilgal."
22 And Samuel said,

[w]"Has the LORD as great delight in burnt offerings and sacrifices,
as in obeying the voice of the LORD?
Behold, [x]to obey is better than sacrifice,
and to listen than the fat of rams.
23 For rebellion is as the sin of divination,
and presumption is as iniquity and [y]idolatry.
Because [z]you have rejected the word of the LORD,
[a]he has also rejected you from being king."

24 Saul said to Samuel, [b]"I have sinned, for I have transgressed the commandment of the
LORD and your words, because I feared the people and obeyed their voice. 25 Now therefore,
please pardon my sin and [c]return with me that I may bow before the LORD." 26 And Samuel
said to Saul, "I will not return with you. [d]For you have rejected the word of the LORD, [e]and
the LORD has rejected you from being king over Israel." 27 [f]As Samuel turned to go away,
Saul seized the skirt of his robe, and it tore. 28 And Samuel said to him, [g]"The LORD has
torn the kingdom of Israel from you this day and has given it to a neighbor of yours, who
is better than you. 29 And also the Glory of Israel [h]will not lie or have regret, for he is not a

12 [p]Josh. 15:55
13 [q]See Ruth 2:20
15 [r]ver. 9, 21
17 [s][ch. 9:21]
19 [t]ch. 14:32
20 [u]ver. 13
21 [v]ver. 15
22 [w]Ps. 40:6-8; 50:8, 9; Prov. 21:3; Isa. 1:11-13, 16, 17; Jer. 7:22, 23; Mic. 6:6-8; Heb. 10:6-9 [x]Eccles. 5:1; Hos. 6:6; Matt. 9:13; 12:7; Mark 12:33
23 [y]See Gen. 31:19, 34 [z]ver. 26 [a]ch. 13:14
24 [b][2 Sam. 12:13]
25 [c]ver. 30
26 [d]ver. 23 [e]ch. 16:1
27 [f][1 Kgs. 11:30, 31]
28 [g]ch. 28:17, 18
29 [h]Num. 23:19; [Ezek. 24:14]

Hebron. It is the setting for ch. 25. That Saul has gone there to **set up a monument for himself** raises further suspicions about his character.

15:15 Saul's excuse for his disobedience (**the people spared**) contrasts with the facts ("Saul and the people spared," v. 9). **to sacrifice to the LORD your God**. They probably did intend to sacrifice the animals, or there would have been no reason to go to Gilgal. But they were probably also planning to share in eating the sacrifices, contrary to the decree of destruction (see note on v. 3).

15:17 Samuel reminds Saul here again (see v. 1) that **the LORD anointed you king over Israel**. Why should Saul, as God's anointed, yield to the people's opinion over God's? He became king because the people asked for a king; now he is rejected because he listened to them (cf. Prov. 29:25) rather than leading them to obey God.

15:20–21 I have obeyed . . . but the people. Cf. note on v. 15.

15:22 The Lord himself does not need **sacrifices** like gods in other religions. Rather, the people need to bring sacrifices in order to approach the holy God (see Leviticus 1–5). Even the best **sacrifice** without obedience gains nothing.

15:23 Rebellion (cf. 12:15) and **presumption** mean rejecting the Lord, equivalent to apostasy. The Hebrew word *terapim*, here translated **idolatry**, refers to either "household gods" (Gen. 31:19; Judg. 17:5; 1 Sam. 19:13) or "ancestor figurines" used as aids to divination (Ezek. 21:21; Hos. 3:4; Zech. 10:2). Saul is **rejected** as **king** here and also in 1 Sam. 15:26 (see 13:13–14).

15:24–26 Saul confesses, "**I have sinned**." At least he admits the basic issue in v. 24 (**I feared the people**); but instead of being struck with the awfulness of his sin, the guilt of which can be taken away by God alone, Saul is more concerned with his standing with the people and the elders (v. 30). **the LORD has rejected you from being king**. In 13:13 Saul's dynasty was rejected, while here he himself is rejected as king.

15:27 Saul seizes the **skirt of** Samuel's **robe** as a final, deferential plea for mercy.

15:28 The term **this day** is used in a legal sense: the rejection is final and has already taken effect (see Ruth 4:9–10; Ps. 2:7). In God's sight, God has already **torn** and **given** (past tense), though the actual realization is yet to come.

15:29 The term "regret" poses a difficulty, since vv. 11 and 35 say that God *did* regret making Saul king, while here Samuel denies that God will ever **lie or have regret** (cf. Num. 23:19). The term for "have regret" (Hb. *nakham*) can be translated "relent" or "change one's mind" (e.g., Ex. 32:12, 14; Num. 23:19; 1 Sam. 24:16 [1 Chron. 21:15]; Ps. 106:45; Jer. 15:6; 18:8, 10; 26:3, 13, 19; 42:10; Ezek. 24:14; Joel 2:13–14; Amos 7:3, 6; Jonah 3:9–10; 4:2) or "have pity or compassion" (Deut. 32:36; Judg. 2:18; Ps. 90:13; 135:14) as well as "be sorry" or "have regret" (cf. Gen. 6:6–7). Thus the term as used in 1 Sam. 15:11, 35 describes God's own feeling of sorrow or regret that Saul had turned out as he did (and does not even address the question whether God knew of it beforehand), while in v. 29 God will not regret or change his mind concerning a decision once he has made it. For further discussion

30 [i][John 5:44; 12:43] [j]ver. 25
33 [k][Judg. 1:7] [l]ver. 12, 21
34 [m][ch. 1:19] [n]ch. 11:4
35 [o][ch. 19:24] [p]ch. 16:1 [q]ver. 11

Chapter 16

1 [r]ch. 15:35 [s]ch. 15:23, 26 [t]See ch. 10:1 [u]Ps. 78:70; 89:19, 20; Acts 13:22
2 [v][ch. 9:12; 20:29]
3 [w]ch. 9:16
4 [x]ch. 21:1 [y]1 Kgs. 2:13; [2 Kgs. 9:22]
5 [z]Josh. 3:5
6 [a]ch. 17:13
7 [b]Ps. 147:10, 11

man, that he should have regret." **30** Then he said, "I have sinned; yet [i]honor me now before
the elders of my people and before Israel, [j]and return with me, that I may bow before the
LORD your God." **31** So Samuel turned back after Saul, and Saul bowed before the LORD.
32 Then Samuel said, "Bring here to me Agag the king of the Amalekites." And Agag
came to him cheerfully.[1] Agag said, "Surely the bitterness of death is past." **33** And Samuel
said, [k]"As your sword has made women childless, so shall your mother be childless among
women." And Samuel hacked Agag to pieces before the LORD [l]in Gilgal.
34 Then Samuel went [m]to Ramah, and Saul went up to his house in [n]Gibeah of Saul.
35 [o]And Samuel did not see Saul again until the day of his death, [p]but Samuel grieved over
Saul. [q]And the LORD regretted that he had made Saul king over Israel.

David Anointed King

16 The LORD said to Samuel, [r]"How long will you grieve over Saul, since [s]I have rejected
him from being king over Israel? [t]Fill your horn with oil, and go. I will send you
to Jesse the Bethlehemite, [u]for I have provided for myself a king among his sons." **2** And
Samuel said, "How can I go? If Saul hears it, he will kill me." And the LORD said, "Take
a heifer with you and say, [v]'I have come to sacrifice to the LORD.' **3** And invite Jesse to the
sacrifice, and I will show you what you shall do. [w]And you shall anoint for me him whom
I declare to you." **4** Samuel did what the LORD commanded and came to Bethlehem. The
elders of the city [x]came to meet him trembling and said, [y]"Do you come peaceably?" **5** And
he said, "Peaceably; I have come to sacrifice to the LORD. [z]Consecrate yourselves, and come
with me to the sacrifice." And he consecrated Jesse and his sons and invited them to the
sacrifice.
6 When they came, he looked on [a]Eliab and thought, "Surely the LORD's anointed is before
him." **7** But the LORD said to Samuel, [b]"Do not look on his appearance or on the height of
his stature, because I have rejected him. For the LORD sees not as man sees: man looks on

[1] Or *haltingly* (compare Septuagint); the Hebrew is uncertain

of God's "relenting" from sending good or disaster on a people, see note on Jonah 3:10.

15:30 honor me now. What Saul wants most is now clearly seen (cf. vv. 24–25).

15:31 Samuel, who is a man (cf. "is not a man," v. 29), changes his mind and stays with Saul, whether out of concern for Saul personally (v. 35) or for the peace of the nation.

15:32–33 Bring here to me Agag. Samuel himself takes on the task that Saul failed to finish. **Hacked . . . to pieces** was not the normal means of putting to death. Usually slaying **before the LORD** involves sacrificing an animal (cf. Ex. 29:11; Lev. 1:5), but in this case Agag himself is the sacrifice, justly put to death for his own sin (see note on 1 Sam. 15:3).

15:34 Ramah is only 2 miles (3.2 km) from **Gibeah**.

15:35 Formerly angry, Samuel now **grieved over Saul**. On **the LORD regretted**, see notes on vv. 11 and 29.

16:1–31:13 *The Story of Saul and David.* Now that Saul has been completely disqualified as king, David is introduced as his successor, and God trains David, through suffering, to lead his people.

16:1–23 *Introduction of David.* In chs. 13 and 15, Saul was told that he and his dynasty had been rejected and that the kingdom had been given to a neighbor, a man after the Lord's heart (cf. 13:14; 15:28). It is now revealed that this neighbor is a son of Jesse of Bethlehem—but his name is not stated until the middle of ch. 16. In the second half of the chapter, the Lord uses the words of one of Saul's attendants to bring David to court. The Lord is with David, while his Spirit has left Saul and has been replaced by a spirit that does harm and turns him against David.

16:1–13 *Anointing of David.* God indicates to Samuel that of all the sons of Jesse, David, the least likely, is his choice. After David's anointing (which is done with a limited audience), the Spirit of God empowers him for service.

16:1 Jesse was a descendant of Perez, son of Judah and Tamar (Gen. 38:29), and a grandson of Ruth and Boaz (Ruth 4:18–22). Bethlehem is in Judah, about 10 miles (16 km) from Ramah.

16:2 and say, "I have come to sacrifice to the LORD." This was a true but incomplete statement of the reasons for Samuel to come to Bethlehem (see v. 1), and yet the Lord told him to say it, so it should not be considered morally wrong. It seems that telling part of what one knows to be true, in order to conceal other information, is morally right in some situations, particularly adversarial situations such as this one. Moreover, the Lord had the right to hide his intentions from Saul, who had proved himself faithless.

16:5 Consecrate yourselves. They would probably wash themselves and perhaps also wash their clothes (Ex. 19:10; Num. 8:21; 11:18). As in 1 Sam. 9:22, the feast seems to have a selective guest list.

16:7 man looks on the outward appearance, but the LORD looks on the heart. Outward appearance cannot predict whether someone will faithfully obey the Lord, for a person's actions flow from his heart (cf. 2 Chron. 16:9; Ps. 51:10; Prov. 4:23; Mark 7:21–23; Luke 6:45; 1 Thess. 2:4). The "heart" in Scripture refers to a person's inward moral and spiritual life, including the emotions, will, and reason.

The Fall of Saul and the Rise of David in 1 Samuel

Saul	David
Holy Spirit removed; evil spirit given (16:14–23)	Anointed with Holy Spirit (16:1–13)
Jealous and treacherous (ch. 18)	Faithful friend (ch. 20)
Attempts to kill David (ch. 19)	Protects Saul's life (chs. 24; 26)
Failed holy warrior (ch. 15)	Mighty holy warrior (ch. 17)
Kingdom torn away (13:13–14; 15:11, 26)	Kingdom promised forever (2 Sam. 7:1–17)

the outward appearance, [c]but the LORD looks on the heart." 8 Then Jesse called [d]Abinadab
and made him pass before Samuel. And he said, "Neither has the LORD chosen this one."
9 Then Jesse made [d]Shammah pass by. And he said, "Neither has the LORD chosen this one."
10 And Jesse made seven of his sons pass before Samuel. And Samuel said to Jesse, "The
LORD has not chosen these." 11 Then Samuel said to Jesse, "Are all your sons here?" And he
said, [e]"There remains yet the youngest,[1] but behold, he is keeping the sheep." And Samuel
said to Jesse, [f]"Send and get him, for we will not sit down till he comes here." 12 And he
sent and brought him in. Now he was [g]ruddy and had beautiful eyes and was handsome.
And the LORD said, [h]"Arise, anoint him, for this is he." 13 Then Samuel took [i]the horn of oil
[j]and anointed him in the midst of his brothers. [k]And the Spirit of the LORD rushed upon
David from that day forward. And Samuel rose up and went to Ramah.

David in Saul's Service

14 [l]Now the Spirit of the LORD departed from Saul, [m]and a harmful spirit from the LORD
tormented him. 15 And Saul's servants said to him, "Behold now, a harmful spirit from God
is tormenting you. 16 Let our lord now command your servants [n]who are before you to
seek out a man who is skillful in playing the lyre, and when the harmful spirit from God
is upon you, he will [o]play it, and you will be well." 17 So Saul said to his servants, "Provide
for me a man who can play well and bring him to me." 18 One of the young men answered,
"Behold, I have seen a son of Jesse the Bethlehemite, who is skillful in playing, [p]a man
of valor, a man of war, prudent in speech, and a man of good presence, [q]and the LORD is
with him." 19 Therefore Saul sent messengers to Jesse and said, "Send me David your son,
[r]who is with the sheep." 20 [s]And Jesse took a donkey laden with bread and a skin of wine
and a young goat and sent them by David his son to Saul. 21 And David came to Saul [t]and
entered his service. And Saul loved him greatly, and he became his armor-bearer. 22 And
Saul sent to Jesse, saying, "Let David remain in my service, for he has found favor in my
sight." 23 And [u]whenever the harmful spirit from God was upon Saul, David took the lyre
[o]and played it with his hand. So Saul was refreshed and was well, and the harmful spirit
departed from him.

David and Goliath

17 Now the Philistines [v]gathered their armies for battle. And they were gathered
at [w]Socoh, which belongs to Judah, and encamped between Socoh and [x]Azekah,
in [y]Ephes-dammim. 2 And Saul and the men of Israel were gathered, and encamped
in [z]the Valley of Elah, and drew up in line of battle against the Philistines. 3 And the

[1] *Or smallest*

7 [c]1 Kgs. 8:39; 1 Chr. 28:9; Ps. 7:9; Jer. 11:20; 17:10; 20:12; [Acts 1:24]
8 [d]ch. 17:13
9 [d][See ver. 8 above]
11 [e]ch. 17:13; [2 Sam. 13:3; 1 Chr. 2:13] [f][2 Sam. 7:8; Ps. 78:70, 71]
12 [g]ch. 17:42 [h][ch. 9:17]
13 [i]ver. 1 [j][ch. 10:1; Ps. 89:20] [k]ch. 10:6, 10; 11:6; See Judg. 3:10
14 [l]ch. 18:12; 28:15, 16; [Judg. 16:20] [m]ch. 18:10; 19:9; [Judg. 9:23]
16 [n]ver. 21, 22; 1 Kgs. 10:8 [o]ch. 18:10; 19:9; [2 Kgs. 3:15]
18 [p]See ch. 17:32, 34-36 [q]ch. 3:19; 18:12, 14
19 [r]ver. 11; ch. 17:15, 34
20 [s][ch. 17:18]
21 [t]See ver. 16
23 [u]ver. 14, 16 [o][See ver. 16 above]

Chapter 17

1 [v]ch. 13:5 [w]Josh. 15:35 [x]Josh. 10:10; Neh. 11:30 [y][1 Chr. 11:13]
2 [z]ver. 19; ch. 21:9

16:8–9 And he said. It is not clear whether the Lord is speaking to Samuel or Samuel is speaking to Jesse.

16:10 seven of his sons. Was David the seventh son or the eighth? David is listed as "seventh" in 1 Chron. 2:15, but this may represent a "telescoping" of a genealogy to give David the number of perfection (see notes on 1 Chron. 2:9–17; Matt. 1:17). Other interpreters suggest that David may have had an additional brother who died childless and was omitted from the genealogy in 1 Chronicles 2 (1 Sam. 17:12 also says that Jesse had eight sons).

16:13 David's name is mentioned here for the first time. **the Spirit of the LORD rushed upon David from that day forward.** See note on 10:6. The narrator does not say who among those present knew what the anointing was for.

16:14–23 *David at Saul's Court.* Saul and David become acquainted when David begins serving Saul. As the story develops, David will become Saul's most successful servant.

16:14 The Spirit of the LORD departed from Saul as soon as the Lord's Spirit came upon David to anoint him for kingship (see v. 13). This statement is not relevant to the issue of whether people can lose their salvation; it is not describing the Holy Spirit's role in individual regeneration in a NT sense. Rather, in light of v. 13, it should be seen as being about gaining or losing the Spirit's empowering for the role of king (see 10:1, 6, 10; 11:6; 16:13; and perhaps Ps. 51:11). From this point to the end of his life, Saul will continually make futile attempts to govern without the empowering of the Holy Spirit. A **harmful spirit** sent by the Lord **tormented** Saul as a form of judgment for his sin of turning against the Lord (1 Sam. 15:22–29). Though God himself never does evil, he sometimes sends evil agents to accomplish his purposes (such as the Babylonians coming to punish Israel, cf. Jer. 20:4–6; or sinful people crucifying Christ, cf. notes on Gen. 50:18–21; Mark 14:21; Acts 2:23; 4:27; 4:28; see also 1 Kings 22:20–23).

16:16–18 David was already **skillful in playing the lyre**, but **a man of valor, a man of war** probably refers to his ability and not his experience (cf. 17:13, 33); perhaps some knew of how he single-handedly defeated both lions and bears (cf. 17:36). **The LORD is with him** is a continual theme in David's story (17:37; 18:12; 20:13; 2 Sam. 5:10; 7:3, 9; see also Gen. 21:22; 26:3; 28:15; 31:3; 39:2; Ex. 3:12).

16:20 donkey laden. Some scholars think this was a specific amount, similar to the Assyrian unit "donkey," which was about 80–160 liters, or 2 1/2 to 5 bushels.

16:21 An **armor-bearer** was a close personal attendant. Both Jonathan's armor-bearer (14:1) and Saul's (31:4–5) had a close relationship with their masters.

16:22 As was his custom (see 14:52), Saul attached the valiant David to himself.

16:23 and the harmful spirit departed from him. David is referred to as "the sweet psalmist of Israel" (2 Sam. 23:1) and as the author of several

4[a][2 Sam. 21:19; 1 Chr. 20:4] [b]ch. 21:10; Josh. 11:22; 13:3
6[c]ver. 45
7[d]ver. 41
8[e]ch. 8:17
9[f][ch. 11:1]
10[g]ver. 25, 26, 36, 45; [2 Sam. 21:21]
12[h]ver. 58; ch. 16:1, 18; Ruth 4:22 [i]Gen. 35:19 [j]ver. 58; ch. 16:1, 18 [k]ch. 16:10, 11; [1 Chr. 2:13-15]
13[l]ch. 16:6, 8, 9; [1 Chr. 2:13]
14[m]ch. 16:11

Philistines stood on the mountain on the one side, and Israel stood on the mountain
on the other side, with a valley between them. **4** And there came out from the camp of
the Philistines a champion named [a]Goliath of [b]Gath, whose height was six[1] cubits[2] and
a span. **5** He had a helmet of bronze on his head, and he was armed with a coat of mail,
and the weight of the coat was five thousand shekels[3] of bronze. **6** And he had bronze
armor on his legs, and a [c]javelin of bronze slung between his shoulders. **7** The shaft of
his spear was like a weaver's beam, and his spear's head weighed six hundred shekels
of iron. [d]And his shield-bearer went before him. **8** He stood and shouted to the ranks of
Israel, "Why have you come out to draw up for battle? Am I not a Philistine, and [e]are
you not servants of Saul? Choose a man for yourselves, and let him come down to me.
9 If he is able to fight with me and kill me, then we will be your servants. But if I prevail against him and kill him, then you shall be our servants [f]and serve us." **10** And the
Philistine said, [g]"I defy the ranks of Israel this day. Give me a man, that we may fight
together." **11** When Saul and all Israel heard these words of the Philistine, they were
dismayed and greatly afraid.

12 Now David was [h]the son of an [i]Ephrathite of Bethlehem in Judah, [j]named Jesse, [k]who
had eight sons. In the days of Saul the man was already old and advanced in years.[4] **13** The
three oldest sons of Jesse had followed Saul to the battle. And [l]the names of his three sons
who went to the battle were Eliab the firstborn, and next to him Abinadab, and the third
Shammah. **14** [m]David was the youngest. The three eldest followed Saul, **15** but David went

[1] Hebrew; Septuagint, Dead Sea Scroll and Josephus *four* [2] A *cubit* was about 18 inches or 45 centimeters [3] A *shekel* was about 2/5 ounce or 11 grams
[4] Septuagint, Syriac; Hebrew *advanced among men*

songs (2 Sam. 1:17–27; 22:1–51; 1 Chron. 16:7–36; see also Amos 6:5) and many psalms. He is also credited with establishing the temple musicians (1 Chron. 6:31). The music that David habitually played in Saul's presence was not merely beautiful, but music of worship to the Lord, causing Saul to be refreshed and the harmful spirit to flee (cf. 2 Chron. 5:13–14).

17:1–54 *David and Goliath: Battle at the Valley of Elah.* The story of David and Goliath, one of the best-known in the Bible, tells how David trusted God and God delivered David and his people. It is the means by which young David, already chosen and anointed privately and taken up by Saul as a court musician, comes onto the public stage. David's victory leads to Saul's jealousy, which drives the plot of the rest of the book. David shows himself better qualified than Saul to serve as the king of Israel, who should be the "champion" (v. 4) of God's people in battle and in the life of faith.

17:1–2 The **Valley of Elah** runs westward from Bethlehem, from the hill country of Judah, toward Gath and Ekron (see v. 52; and map to the right). It is immediately south of and parallel to the Sorek Valley (see note on 6:12). Control of this valley would give the **Philistines** entry into the hill country of Judah. **Socoh** is about 14 miles (22 km) west of Bethlehem toward the Philistine territory. **Azekah**, about 2–3 miles (3.2–4.8 km) northwest of Socoh, controlled the main road across the Valley of Elah.

17:4–11 A **champion** in biblical, ancient Near Eastern, and Homeric literature is a man who steps out to fight between the two battle lines. Here Goliath offers to fight, on behalf of his side, against any champion that Israel will put forward; the victor's side then, would partake of his victory (vv. 8–10). Goliath's armament was the best that the highly skilled Philistines could obtain, either by manufacture or by trade. The **shield** (Hb. *tsinnah*) was a large standing shield that covered the whole body. Most of his armament was **bronze**, except his **spear's head** of **iron**—this was just the beginning of the Iron Age. It weighed 600 shekels (about 15 lb. or 6.6 kg). His **coat of mail** weighed 5,000 shekels (about 125 lb. or 55 kg). It is not surprising that the Israelites were dismayed. **Six cubits and a span** is about 9 feet 9 inches (3 m). At the site of Gath (Tel es-Safi), an early Philistine inscription has been found that dates to the tenth or early ninth century B.C. It is an ostracon, i.e., an inscription scratched on a piece of pottery. It seems that the name "Goliath" is written on the shard. Whether this is the Goliath of the biblical account is uncertain.

17:11 It was Saul's job to accept the challenge on behalf of Israel; instead he was **greatly afraid** (cf. 15:24) along with everyone else.

17:12 An **Ephrathite** refers to a man from the Judean Ephrathah, around **Bethlehem** (cf. Ruth 1:2; 4:11; Mic. 5:2).

The Battle at Elah

Sometime after being anointed as the next king of Israel, David was sent from Bethlehem by his father to take food to his brothers serving in the Israelite army near Socoh and Azekah. When David arrived, he learned of the Philistines' challenge to the Israelites to send a champion to fight their warrior Goliath from Gath. David took up the challenge and killed Goliath, leading the Israelites to rout the Philistines and chase them all the way to Gath and Ekron.

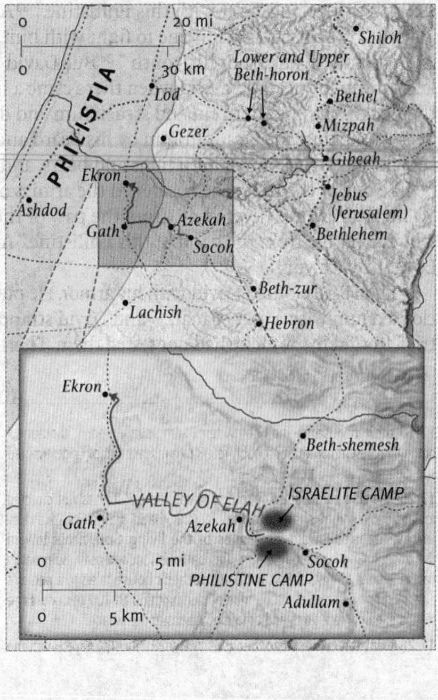

back and forth from Saul [n]to feed his father's sheep at Bethlehem. 16 For forty days the
Philistine came forward and took his stand, morning and evening.
17 And Jesse said to David his son, "Take for your brothers an ephah[1] of this parched
grain, and these ten loaves, and carry them quickly to the camp to your brothers. 18 [o]Also
take these ten cheeses to the commander of their thousand. [p]See if your brothers are well,
and bring some token from them."
19 Now Saul and they and all the men of Israel were in the Valley of Elah, fighting with
the Philistines. 20 And David rose early in the morning and left the sheep with a keeper
and took the provisions and went, as Jesse had commanded him. And he came to [q]the
encampment as the host was going out to the battle line, shouting the war cry. 21 And Israel
and the Philistines drew up for battle, army against army. 22 And David left the [r]things in
charge of the keeper of the [r]baggage and ran to the ranks and went and greeted his brothers. 23 As he talked with them, behold, [s]the champion, the Philistine of Gath, Goliath by
name, came up out of the ranks of the Philistines and spoke [t]the same words as before.
And David heard him.
24 All the men of Israel, when they saw the man, fled from him and were much afraid.
25 And the men of Israel said, "Have you seen this man who has come up? Surely he has
come up to [u]defy Israel. And the king will enrich the man who kills him with great riches
[v]and will give him his daughter and make his father's house free in Israel." 26 And David
said to the men who stood by him, "What shall be done for the man who kills this Philistine
and takes away [w]the reproach from Israel? For who is this [x]uncircumcised Philistine, that
he should [u]defy the armies of [y]the living God?" 27 And the people answered him in the
same way, [z]"So shall it be done to the man who kills him."
28 Now Eliab his eldest brother heard when he spoke to the men. And Eliab's anger
was kindled against David, and he said, "Why have you come down? And with whom
have you left those few sheep in the wilderness? I know your presumption and the evil
of your heart, for you have come down to see the battle." 29 And David said, "What have I
done now? Was it not but a word?" 30 And he turned away from him toward another, and
spoke [b]in the same way, and the people answered him again as before.
31 When the words that David spoke were heard, they repeated them before Saul, and
he sent for him. 32 And David said to Saul, [c]"Let no man's heart fail because of him. [d]Your
servant will go and fight with this Philistine." 33 And Saul said to David, "You are not
able to go against this Philistine to fight with him, for you are but a youth, and he has
been a man of war from his youth." 34 But David said to Saul, "Your servant used to
keep sheep for his father. And when there came a lion, or a bear, and took a lamb from
the flock, 35 I went after him and struck him and delivered it out of his mouth. And if
he arose against me, I caught him by his beard and struck him and killed him. 36 Your
servant has struck down both lions and bears, and this uncircumcised Philistine shall
be like one of them, [e]for he has defied the armies of the living God." 37 And David said,
[f]"The LORD who delivered me from the paw of the lion and from the paw of the bear
will deliver me from the hand of this Philistine." And Saul said to David, "Go, [g]and the
LORD be with you!"
38 Then Saul clothed David with his armor. He put a helmet of bronze on his head and
clothed him with a coat of mail, 39 and David strapped his sword over his armor. And he
tried in vain to go, for he had not tested them. Then David said to Saul, "I cannot go with

[1] An *ephah* was about 3/5 bushel or 22 liters

15 [n]ch. 16:19
18 [o][ch. 16:20] [p][Gen. 37:14]
20 [q]ch. 26:5, 7
22 [r][Isa. 10:28; Acts 21:15]
23 [s]ver. 4 [t]ver. 8
25 [u]ver. 10, 36, 45 [v][Josh. 15:16]
26 [w]ch. 11:2 [x]See Judg. 14:3 [u][See ver. 25 above] [y]Deut. 5:26; Josh. 3:10
27 [z]ver. 25
30 [b]ver. 26, 27
32 [c][Deut. 20:3] [d][ch. 16:18]
36 [e]ver. 10, 26
37 [f][2 Tim. 4:17] [g][ch. 20:13; 1 Chr. 22:11, 16]

17:18 their thousand. The Hebrew term *'elep* usually means "thousand," but in the present context it probably refers to a military unit of undetermined size. See note on 1 Chron. 12:23–37.

17:25–26 Have you seen? "You" is plural; the question is not directed toward David. **What shall be done**? By faith, David grasps Goliath's challenge as directed toward the **armies of the living God**, hence toward the unseen God himself. To David, this battle is fundamentally spiritual in nature (see vv. 45–47; cf. Eph. 6:12). **His father's house** refers to a person's extended family, smaller than a tribe or clan, with 50 to 100 persons. **Free** means exempt from taxes and other obligations to the palace.

17:28 Eliab the **eldest brother** (see v. 12; 20:29) is annoyed with the conduct of his youngest brother at this crucial time. David seemed to him to be just a show-off.

17:34 a lion, or a bear. Both lions and bears were common in the Palestine of the Israelite period.

17:36 for he has defied the armies of the living God. See note on vv. 25–26. David is confident that God will defend his own honor and defeat Goliath.

17:37–39 The LORD . . . will deliver me. Because of his faith in God, David shows more willingness to do battle on behalf of God's people, and to defend God's honor, than the seasoned warrior Saul.

these, for I have not tested them." So David put them off. **40** Then he took his staff in his
hand and chose five smooth stones from the brook and put them in his shepherd's pouch.
His sling was in his hand, and he approached the Philistine.
41 And the Philistine moved forward and came near to David, [h]with his shield-bearer in
front of him. **42** And when the Philistine looked and saw David, he disdained him, for he
was but a youth, [i]ruddy and handsome in appearance. **43** And the Philistine said to David,
"Am I [j]a dog, that you come to me with sticks?" And the Philistine cursed David by his
gods. **44** The Philistine said to David, "Come to me, and I will give your flesh [k]to the birds
of the air and to the beasts of the field." **45** Then David said to the Philistine, "You come
to me with a sword and with a spear and with [l]a javelin, but I come to you in the name
of the LORD of hosts, the God of the armies of Israel, [e]whom you have defied. **46** This day
the LORD will deliver you into my hand, and I will strike you down and cut off your head.
[m]And I will give the dead bodies of the host of the Philistines this day [n]to the birds of the
air and to the wild beasts of the earth, [o]that all the earth may know that there is a God in
Israel, **47** and that all this assembly may know that [p]the LORD saves not with sword and
spear. [q]For the battle is the LORD's, and he will give you into our hand."
48 When the Philistine arose and came and drew near to meet David, David ran quickly
toward the battle line to meet the Philistine. **49** And David put his hand in his bag and took
out a stone and slung it and struck the Philistine on his forehead. The stone sank into his
forehead, and he fell on his face to the ground.
50 So David prevailed over the Philistine with a sling and with a stone, and struck the
Philistine and killed him. There was no sword in the hand of David. **51** Then David ran and
stood over the Philistine [r]and took his sword and drew it out of its sheath and killed him
and cut off his head with it. When the Philistines saw that their champion was dead, [s]they
fled. **52** And the men of Israel and Judah rose with a shout and pursued the Philistines as
far as Gath[1] and the gates of [t]Ekron, so that the wounded Philistines fell on the way from
[u]Shaaraim as far as [v]Gath and Ekron. **53** And the people of Israel came back from chasing the
Philistines, and they plundered their camp. **54** And David took [w]the head of the Philistine
[x]and brought it to Jerusalem, but he put his armor in his tent.
55 As soon as Saul saw David go out against the Philistine, he said to Abner, [y]the commander of the army, "Abner, [z]whose son is this youth?" And Abner said, [a]"As your soul
lives, O king, I do not know." **56** And the king said, "Inquire whose son the boy is." **57** And
as soon as David returned from the striking down of the Philistine, Abner took him, and
brought him before Saul [b]with the head of the Philistine in his hand. **58** And Saul said
to him, "Whose son are you, young man?" And David answered, [c]"I am the son of your
servant Jesse the Bethlehemite."

David and Jonathan's Friendship

18 As soon as he had finished speaking to Saul, the soul of Jonathan was knit to the
soul of David, and Jonathan [d]loved him as his own soul. **2** And Saul took him that
day [e]and would not let him return to his father's house. **3** Then Jonathan made a covenant
with David, because [d]he loved him as his own soul. **4** And Jonathan stripped himself of

[1] Septuagint; Hebrew *Gai*

41 [h]ver. 7
42 [i]ch. 16:12
43 [j]ch. 24:14; 2 Sam. 3:8; 9:8; 16:9; 2 Kgs. 8:13
44 [k]ver. 46
45 [l]ver. 6 [e][See ver. 36 above]
46 [m]Deut. 28:26 [n]ver. 44 [o]1 Kgs. 18:36; [Josh. 4:24]
47 [p]Hos. 1:7; [Ps. 44:6, 7; Zech. 4:6] [q]2 Chr. 20:15
51 [r]ch. 21:9; [2 Sam. 23:21] [s][Heb. 11:34]
52 [t]Josh. 15:11 [u]Josh. 15:36 [v]See ver. 4
54 [w]ver. 57 [x][2 Sam. 5:6, 7]
55 [y]2 Sam. 2:8 [z][ch. 16:21, 22] [a]See ch. 1:26
57 [b]ver. 54
58 [c]ver. 12

Chapter 18

1 [d]ch. 20:17; Deut. 13:6; [ch. 19:2; 2 Sam. 1:26]
2 [e][ch. 17:15]
3 [d][See ver. 1 above]

17:43 sticks. Goliath sees David's staff (v. 40) but not the true weapon, the sling. Slings were known as weapons in Egypt from at least the beginning of the second millennium B.C., and slingers are pictured on the reliefs at Nineveh. See also Judg. 20:16. Goliath's **gods** are probably Dagon (1 Sam. 5:2) and Ashtaroth (31:10).

17:44, 46 In Israel, being deprived of burial and exposed to **birds** and **beasts** was considered worse than death itself (see 31:8–13; 2 Samuel 21; Ps. 79:2–3; Jer. 7:33; 8:1–2).

17:52 men of Israel and Judah. There were divisions between Judah and the rest of Israel from the earliest time of the Davidic monarchy (see 11:8; 15:4; 2 Sam. 19:41–43). "Gai" (ESV footnote) seems to refer to the valley that leads to Gath. For **Ekron**, see 1 Sam. 5:10.

17:54 Jerusalem refers to a suburb in the area around Jerusalem, not the Jebusite walled city that David captured later (see 2 Sam. 5:6–9).

17:55–18:5 *Saul, Jonathan, and David.* At first everyone loves David. Saul takes him into his service; all of Saul's officials (his potential rivals) love him; even members of Saul's own family love him. Jonathan, who had relied on the Lord in his own victory at Michmash, has an especially close relationship with David, despite realizing at some point that David will supplant him as king.

17:55–58 whose son is this youth? Even though Saul knew David from before, he would not remember the name of David's father. Saul is asking about David's background—his family and hence his social status or pedigree—so that he may ask his father to let him keep David permanently (see 18:2).

18:2 Saul took him—according to "the ways of the king" (8:11). **His father's house** refers to David's extended family (see 17:25–26).

18:3–4 he loved him as his own soul. Jonathan would eventually give up any claim to the throne for David's sake (23:17) and even risk his life (20:30–33) for David; see note on 2 Sam. 1:26. **Jonathan . . . gave it to**

the robe that was on him and gave it to David, and his armor, and even his sword and his
bow and his belt. 5 And David went out [f]and was successful wherever Saul sent him, so
that Saul set him over the men of war. And this was good in the sight of all the people and
also in the sight of Saul's servants.

Saul's Jealousy of David

6 As they were coming home, when David returned from striking down the Philistine,
[g]the women came out of all the cities of Israel, singing and dancing, to meet King Saul,
with tambourines, with songs of joy, and with musical instruments.[1] 7 And the women
[h]sang to one another as they celebrated,

> [i]"Saul has struck down his thousands,
> and David his ten thousands."

8 And Saul was very angry, and this saying displeased him. He said, "They have ascribed
to David ten thousands, and to me they have ascribed thousands, and what more can he
have but [j]the kingdom?" 9 And Saul eyed David from that day on.

10 The next day [k]a harmful spirit from God rushed upon Saul, and [l]he raved within
his house while David was [m]playing the lyre, as he did day by day. [n]Saul had his spear in
his hand. 11 And Saul [o]hurled the spear, for he thought, "I will pin David to the wall." But
David evaded him twice.

12 [p]Saul was afraid of David because [q]the LORD was with him [r]but had departed from
Saul. 13 So Saul removed him from his presence and made him a commander of a thousand. [s]And he went out and came in before the people. 14 And David [t]had success in all
his undertakings, [q]for the LORD was with him. 15 And when Saul saw that [t]he had great
success, he stood in fearful awe of him. 16 [u]But all Israel and Judah loved David, for he went
out and came in before them.

David Marries Michal

17 Then Saul said to David, "Here is [v]my elder daughter Merab. [w]I will give her to you
for a wife. Only be valiant for me [x]and fight the LORD's battles." For Saul thought, "Let not
my hand be against him, [y]but let the hand of the Philistines be against him." 18 And David
said to Saul, [z]"Who am I, and who are my relatives, my father's clan in Israel, that I should
be son-in-law to the king?" 19 But at the time when Merab, Saul's daughter, should have
been given to David, she was given to [a]Adriel the [b]Meholathite for a wife.

20 Now [v]Saul's daughter Michal [c]loved David. And they told Saul, and the thing pleased
him. 21 Saul thought, "Let me give her to him, that she may [d]be a snare for him [e]and that
the hand of the Philistines may be against him." Therefore Saul said to David a second
time,[2] [f]"You shall now be my son-in-law." 22 And Saul commanded his servants, "Speak
to David in private and say, 'Behold, the king has delight in you, and all his servants love

[1] *Or triangles, or three-stringed instruments* [2] *Hebrew by two*

5 [f]ver. 14, 15, 30
6 [g]Ex. 15:20; Judg. 11:34
7 [h][Ex. 15:21] [i]ch. 21:11; 29:5
8 [j]ch. 15:28
10 [k]ch. 16:14; [Judg. 9:23] [l]ch. 19:23, 24; [1 Kgs. 18:29; Acts 16:16] [m]See ch. 16:16 [n]ch. 19:9
11 [o]ch. 19:10; 20:33
12 [p]ver. 15, 29 [q]ver. 28; ch. 16:18 [r]ch. 16:14; 28:15
13 [s]ver. 16; [Num. 27:17; 2 Sam. 5:2]
14 [t]ver. 5 [q][See ver. 12 above]
15 [t][See ver. 14 above]
16 [u][ver. 5]
17 [v]ch. 14:49 [w]ch. 17:25 [x]ch. 25:28 [y]ver. 21, 25
18 [z]ver. 23; 2 Sam. 7:18
19 [a][2 Sam. 21:8] [b]Judg. 7:22
20 [v][See ver. 17 above] [c]ver. 28
21 [d]Ex. 10:7 [e]ver. 17 [f][ver. 26]

David. Primogeniture, whereby the firstborn son received the primary leadership role and a double portion of the family inheritance, was a tradition but not an absolute rule. Nevertheless, as the popular eldest son, Jonathan would have been accepted as Saul's heir (1 Sam. 20:31; 23:17; 2 Sam. 1:4). Since to all appearances the dynasty had just begun, however, David was considered even more of a threat to Jonathan than to Saul. No one seems to have viewed Jonathan's gifts to David as a sign of abdication, but Jonathan's actions (perhaps unwittingly) foreshadowed the transfer of the kingship to David. It is not recorded at what point Jonathan realized that David was God's chosen.

18:6–30 *Saul Becomes David's Enemy.* As David's success increases, Saul's jealousy also increases.

18:6 Women in Israel celebrated a victory with **singing and dancing** and instruments, especially with **tambourines** (Ex. 15:20; Judg. 11:34; see note on 1 Sam. 10:5). Many clay figurines or plaques depicting women playing tambourines have been discovered in Israel, Phoenicia, and Transjordan. They may have had a connection with prayers or praises for victory.

18:7–9 sang to one another. I.e., antiphonally or responsively. Because **thousands/ten thousands** is a common parallelism, the general meaning of the song is, "Saul and David have killed many thousands." Yet naming two distinct people in a number parallelism is unusual, and Saul interpreted it in the worst possible light. Hearing David even mentioned together with him in the same song, Saul begins to grow suspicious of David. The rest of the book is a description of Saul's attempts, more and more openly, to get rid of David.

18:12 Saul was afraid of David because the LORD was with him. Cf. v. 14 and 16:18. Saul's primary concern was not the Lord's honor or the people's welfare but himself.

18:17 fight the LORD's battles. See 17:47. Saul tried to make ill use of David's zeal for God, hoping that very zeal would lead to his death by the hand of the Philistines. Saul's plotting shows little faith in the Lord, for he thought the Philistines could defeat David even though "the LORD was with him" (18:12).

18:18–19 Who am I? Saul used David's humble reply as an excuse to give Merab to another man. For Merab's children, see 2 Sam. 21:8.

18:20–21 that she may be a snare for him. Saul again tries to make ill use of someone's love (cf. v. 17)—this time, his daughter's—to destroy David.

you. Now then become the king's son-in-law.'" 23 And Saul's servants spoke those words in
the ears of David. And David said, [g]"Does it seem to you a little thing to become the king's
son-in-law, since I am a poor man and have no reputation?" 24 And the servants of Saul told
him, "Thus and so did David speak." 25 Then Saul said, "Thus shall you say to David, 'The
king desires no [h]bride-price except a hundred foreskins of the Philistines, [i]that he may be
avenged of the king's enemies.'" [j]Now Saul thought to make David fall by the hand of the
Philistines. 26 And when his servants told David these words, it pleased David well to be
the king's son-in-law. [k]Before the time had expired, 27 David arose and went, [l]along with
his men, and killed two hundred of the Philistines. [m]And David brought their foreskins,
which were given in full number to the king, that he might become the king's son-in-law.
And Saul gave him his daughter Michal for a wife. 28 But when Saul saw and knew that
[n]the LORD was with David, [o]and that Michal, Saul's daughter, loved him, 29 Saul was even
more afraid of David. So Saul was David's enemy continually.

30 [p]Then the commanders of the Philistines came out to battle, and as often as they
came out [q]David had more success than all the servants of Saul, so that his name was
highly esteemed.

Saul Tries to Kill David

19 And Saul spoke to Jonathan his son and to all his servants, that they should kill
David. [r]But Jonathan, Saul's son, delighted much in David. 2 And Jonathan told
David, "Saul my father seeks to kill you. Therefore be on your guard in the morning. Stay
in a secret place and hide yourself. 3 And I will go out and stand beside my father in the
field where you are, and I will speak to my father about you. And if I learn anything I will
tell you." 4 And Jonathan spoke well of David to Saul his father and said to him, "Let not the
king [s]sin against his servant David, because he has not sinned against you, and because his
deeds have brought good to you. 5 For [t]he took his life in his hand [u]and he struck down the
Philistine, [v]and the LORD worked a great salvation for all Israel. You saw it, and rejoiced.
Why then will you sin against [w]innocent blood by killing David without cause?" 6 And
Saul listened to the voice of Jonathan. Saul swore, [x]"As the LORD lives, he shall not be put
to death." 7 And Jonathan called David, and Jonathan reported to him all these things. And
Jonathan brought David to Saul, and he was in his presence [y]as before.

8 And there was war again. And David went out and fought with the Philistines and
struck them with a great blow, so that they fled before him. 9 [z]Then a harmful spirit
from the LORD came upon Saul, as he sat in his house with his spear in his hand. [a]And
David was playing the lyre. 10 [b]And Saul sought to pin David to the wall with the spear,
but he eluded Saul, so that he struck the spear into the wall. And David fled and escaped
that night.

11 [c]Saul sent messengers to David's house to watch him, that he might kill him in the
morning. But Michal, David's wife, told him, "If you do not escape with your life tonight,
tomorrow you will be killed." 12 [d]So Michal let David down through the window, and he
fled away and escaped. 13 Michal took [e]an image[1] and laid it on the bed and put a pillow
of goats' hair at its head and covered it with the clothes. 14 And when Saul sent messengers
to take David, she said, "He is sick." 15 Then Saul sent the messengers to see David, saying,
"Bring him up to me in the bed, that I may kill him." 16 And when the messengers came
in, behold, [e]the image was in the bed, with the pillow of goats' hair at its head. 17 Saul said

[1] Or *a household god*

23 [g][Num. 16:9]
25 [h]Gen. 34:12; Ex. 22:17 [i]ch. 14:24 [j]ver. 17, 21
26 [k][ver. 21]
27 [l]ver. 13 [m]2 Sam. 3:14
28 [n]ver. 12 [o]ver. 20
30 [p]ch. 19:8; [2 Sam. 11:1] [q]ver. 5

Chapter 19

1 [r]ch. 18:1
4 [s][Gen. 42:22]
5 [t]ch. 28:21; Judg. 12:3; [Judg. 9:17] [u]ch. 17:49, 50 [v][ch. 11:13; 1 Chr. 11:14] [w]Matt. 27:4
6 [x]See Ruth 3:13
7 [y]ch. 16:21; 18:2, 13
9 [z]See ch. 16:14 [a]See ch. 16:16
10 [b]ch. 18:11; 20:33
11 [c]See Ps. 59
12 [d][Josh. 2:15; Acts 9:24, 25]; 2 Cor. 11:33
13 [e]See Gen. 31:19
16 [e][See ver. 13 above]

18:25 The **bride-price** was normally money, but since David could not afford what was due a king's daughter, the king graciously let him display his valor instead. The Philistines had **foreskins** because they were "uncircumcised" (see 14:6 and note).

19:1–20:42 *Saul's Attempts to Kill David.* Saul moves from trying to use the Philistines to kill David to actually ordering him killed. Jonathan brings about one reconciliation (and there may have been another one after ch. 19), but David finally flees the court permanently.

19:4 Jonathan appeals to Saul the **king** on the basis of a king's obligation to do justice (see 25:31).

19:5 took his life in his hand. I.e., risked his life (see also 28:21; Judg. 12:3).

19:9 harmful spirit from the LORD. See note on 16:14.

19:10 he struck the spear into the wall. David came close to losing his life, but "the LORD was with him" (see 18:12). **David fled and escaped** also in 19:12, 18. See note on Acts 9:25.

19:13 The **image** (Hb. *terapim*) here was of human size and shape; contrast Laban's smaller household gods in Gen. 31:19, 34–35.

19:14 He is sick was apparently a lie, since David had fled. The biblical historians often record such actions without any explicit moral evaluation.

to Michal, "Why have you deceived me thus and let my enemy go, so that he has escaped?"
And Michal answered Saul, "He said to me, 'Let me go. [f]Why should I kill you?'"
18 Now David fled and escaped, and he came to Samuel at [g]Ramah and told him all that
Saul had done to him. And he and Samuel went and lived at Naioth. 19 And it was told Saul,
"Behold, David is at Naioth in Ramah." 20 Then Saul sent messengers to take David, and
when they saw the company of the prophets prophesying, and Samuel standing as head
over them, [h]the Spirit of God came upon the messengers of Saul, [i]and they also prophesied.
21 When it was told Saul, he sent other messengers, [i]and they also prophesied. And Saul
sent messengers again the third time, [i]and they also prophesied. 22 Then he himself went
to Ramah and came to the great well that is in Secu. And he asked, "Where are Samuel
and David?" And one said, "Behold, they are at Naioth in [g]Ramah." 23 And he went there
to Naioth in Ramah. [j]And the Spirit of God came upon him also, and as he went he prophesied until he came to Naioth in Ramah. 24 [k]And he too stripped off his clothes, and he too
prophesied before Samuel and lay naked all that day and all that night. Thus it is said, [l]"Is
Saul also among the prophets?"

17 [f][2 Sam. 2:22]
18 [g]ch. 1:19
20 [h][ch. 10:5, 6, 10] [i][Num. 11:25; Joel 2:28]
21 [i][See ver. 20 above]
22 [g][See ver. 18 above]
23 [j][ch. 18:10]
24 [k]Isa. 20:2; Mic. 1:8; [2 Sam. 6:20] [l]ch. 10:11, 12

19:18 Naioth may refer to a shepherds' camp. The prophetic fraternities of Israel lived in such settlements.

19:20–21 They also prophesied (twice in these verses) probably implies that Saul's messengers uttered words of prayer and praise to God as well as admonition and rebuke to each other, under the influence of the **Spirit of God**. Their aggressive intent was humbled before the Lord's anointed king. See also 2 Kings 1:9–15, where another king sends messengers three times in vain. Some interpreters also see parallels in 1 Kings 8:10–11 and 2 Chron. 5:14.

19:23–24 he too prophesied before Samuel. The earlier question of 10:12, "Who is their father?" is answered by Samuel's presence as "head" over the prophets (cf. 19:20). As three groups of messengers sent by Saul to take David succumb to prophesying (vv. 20–21), the **Spirit of God** came on Saul to take away his self-control and turn his hostility to prophetic praise. Even the will of the king is subject to the Lord's will. **And he too stripped off his clothes**. The aggressive, angry king is humbled, even comically humiliated, before the power of the Lord, against whom he vainly strives. For the second time, background is provided for the old proverb (see note on 10:11–12), **"Is Saul also among the prophets?"** In the earlier context (10:11–12) Saul was being established as king. In ch. 19, he openly seeks to kill the Lord's anointed (v. 1), and the throne, like his clothes, is beginning to be stripped from him.

20:1 It seems that before Saul had arrived in Naioth, David had come there. After that David **fled from Naioth** and went back to Gibeah, and things settled down. Then he **came . . . before Jonathan**. Hence, it could be

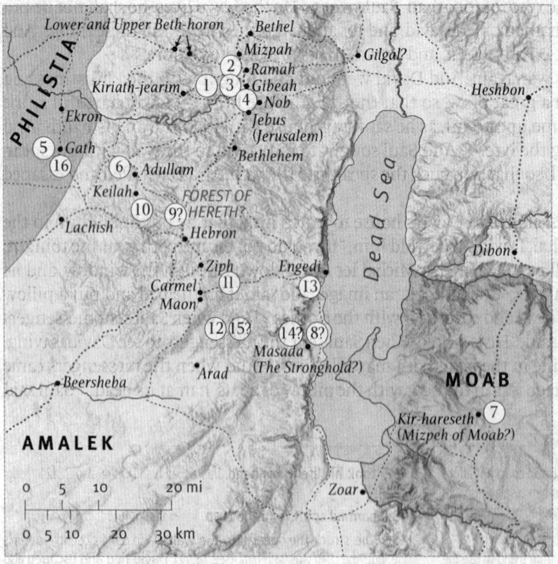

David Flees from Saul

David's growing reputation among the people as a warrior and leader incited Saul's jealousy, and Saul began trying to kill David. David fled from Saul in Gibeah (1) and went to Samuel at Naioth in Ramah (2), but soon Saul sought him there, and David fled back to Jonathan in Gibeah (3). After Jonathan warned David of Saul's determination to kill him, David fled to Ahimelech the priest at Nob (4), where he collected food and Goliath's sword. David briefly sought refuge in the Philistine city of Gath (5) and then set up his headquarters at the cave of Adullam (6), where the ranks of his army swelled to 400 men. In order to protect his parents from harm, David left them in the care of the king of Moab at Mizpeh (7) and went to live in "the stronghold" (8). After some time, David went to the forest of Hereth (9) and then left to rescue nearby Keilah (10) from some Philistine raiding parties. When David heard that Saul was coming to Keilah, he and his growing army of 600 men relocated to the wilderness of Ziph (11). After the men of Ziph betrayed David to Saul, David and his men went to live in the wilderness of Maon (12) and narrowly escaped capture there by Saul. Fleeing the strongholds of Engedi (13), David again evaded capture by Saul and refused an opportunity to take Saul's life. David returned to "the stronghold" (14) and then to the wilderness of Paran (15). While he was there, David was again betrayed to Saul by the men of Ziph and refused another opportunity to take Saul's life. Finally, David and his men sought refuge with Achish, the king of Gath (16).

Chapter 20
1 [m]ch. 1:19
3 [n]See Gen. 33:15 [o]ch. 25:26; 2 Kgs. 2:2, 4, 6; 4:30; See Ruth 3:13 [p]ch. 1:26
5 [q]ver. 18; Num. 10:10; 28:11 [r]ch. 19:2, 3
6 [s]ver. 18 [t]ch. 16:4 [u][ch. 9:12]
7 [v]ch. 25:17; Esth. 7:7; [ver. 33]
8 [w]ver. 16, 42; ch. 18:3; 23:18; [2 Sam. 21:7] [x]2 Sam. 14:32
9 [v][See ver. 7 above]
13 [y][Ruth 1:17] [z]Josh. 1:5, 17; 1 Kgs. 1:37; 1 Chr. 22:11, 16; [ch. 17:37]
15 [a]2 Sam. 9:1, 3, 7; 21:7
16 [b][ch. 25:22; Josh. 22:23]
17 [c]ch. 18:1, 3
18 [d]ver. 5 [e]ver. 6 [f]ver. 25, 27
21 [g]ver. 3; See Ruth 3:13
22 [h]ver. 37
23 [i]ver. 14, 15 [j]ver. 42

Jonathan Warns David

20 Then David fled from Naioth [m]in Ramah and came and said before Jonathan,
"What have I done? What is my guilt? And what is my sin before your father, that
he seeks my life?" **2** And he said to him, "Far from it! You shall not die. Behold, my father
does nothing either great or small without disclosing it to me. And why should my father
hide this from me? It is not so." **3** But David vowed again, saying, "Your father knows well
that [n]I have found favor in your eyes, and he thinks, 'Do not let Jonathan know this, lest
he be grieved.' But truly, [o]as the LORD lives and [p]as your soul lives, there is but a step
between me and death." **4** Then Jonathan said to David, "Whatever you say, I will do for
you." **5** David said to Jonathan, "Behold, tomorrow is [q]the new moon, and I should not fail
to sit at table with the king. But let me go, [r]that I may hide myself in the field till the third
day at evening. **6** [s]If your father misses me at all, then say, 'David earnestly asked leave of
me to run [t]to Bethlehem his city, for there is a yearly [u]sacrifice there for all the clan.' **7** If
he says, 'Good!' it will be well with your servant, but if he is angry, then know that [v]harm
is determined by him. **8** Therefore deal kindly with your servant, [w]for you have brought
your servant into a covenant of the LORD with you. [x]But if there is guilt in me, kill me
yourself, for why should you bring me to your father?" **9** And Jonathan said, "Far be it from
you! If I knew that [v]it was determined by my father that harm should come to you, would
I not tell you?" **10** Then David said to Jonathan, "Who will tell me if your father answers
you roughly?" **11** And Jonathan said to David, "Come, let us go out into the field." So they
both went out into the field.

12 And Jonathan said to David, "The LORD, the God of Israel, be witness![1] When I have
sounded out my father, about this time tomorrow, or the third day, behold, if he is well
disposed toward David, shall I not then send and disclose it to you? **13** But should it please
my father to do you harm, [y]the LORD do so to Jonathan and more also if I do not disclose
it to you and send you away, that you may go in safety. [z]May the LORD be with you, as he
has been with my father. **14** If I am still alive, show me the steadfast love of the LORD, that
I may not die; **15** [a]and do not cut off[2] your steadfast love from my house forever, when the
LORD cuts off every one of the enemies of David from the face of the earth." **16** And Jonathan
made a covenant with the house of David, saying, [b]"May[3] the LORD take vengeance on
David's enemies." **17** And Jonathan made David swear again by his love for him, [c]for he
loved him as he loved his own soul.

18 Then Jonathan said to him, [d]"Tomorrow is the new moon, and [e]you will be missed,
because [f]your seat will be empty. **19** On the third day go down quickly to the place where
you hid yourself when the matter was in hand, and remain beside the stone heap.[4] **20** And
I will shoot three arrows to the side of it, as though I shot at a mark. **21** And behold, I will
send the boy, saying, 'Go, find the arrows.' If I say to the boy, 'Look, the arrows are on this
side of you, take them,' then you are to come, for, [g]as the LORD lives, it is safe for you and
there is no danger. **22** But if I say to the youth, [h]'Look, the arrows are beyond you,' then go,
for the LORD has sent you away. **23** [i]And as for the matter of which you and I have spoken,
behold, [j]the LORD is between you and me forever."

24 So David hid himself in the field. And when the new moon came, the king sat down

[1] Hebrew lacks *be witness* [2] Or *but if I die, do not cut off* [3] Septuagint *earth,* [16]*let not the name of Jonathan be cut off from the house of David. And may*
[4] Septuagint; Hebrew *the stone Ezel*

interpreted: "Now David had fled from Naioth in Ramah. He came before Jonathan and said. . . ."

20:3 David vowed again. Perhaps a reference to v. 1, since the triplet of rhetorical questions in v. 1 ("What . . . ? What . . . ? What . . . ?") may resemble an oath. Another possibility is that David's earlier oath is unrecorded.

20:5 The **new moon** was the day of the new appearance of the crescent moon in the western sky at sunset, marking the beginning of the month in the lunar calendar. It was one of the principal festivals (see Num. 10:10; 1 Chron. 23:31; Isa. 1:14; Ezek. 46:3; etc.). It seems that the king, as head of the clan, presided over his household's celebration of the festival. It was often impossible to predict the exact day when the new moon would become visible, so it may be that the feast was held on the first possible day, and if the moon did not appear on that day, the feast was held on the second day as well (1 Sam. 20:27). Hence, David proposed meeting on the "third day."

20:13 The LORD do so to Jonathan and more also is an oath formula (see note on 3:17). **as he has been with my father**. The past tense may show that Jonathan recognizes that the Lord has left Saul.

20:15 my house. I.e., "my offspring"; see v. 42 and 2 Samuel 9, where David fulfills his "kindness" to Jonathan's son Mephibosheth.

20:22 if I say to the youth, "Look, the arrows are beyond you." To any other observer, Jonathan would appear to be shouting to the young man who had run to retrieve the arrows. But David, in hiding, would also hear the words and know they had another meaning, a warning to flee from Saul.

to eat food. 25 The king sat on his seat, as at other times, on the seat by the wall. Jonathan
sat opposite,[1] and Abner sat by Saul's side, [k]but David's place was empty.
26 Yet Saul did not say anything that day, for he thought, "Something has happened to
him. [l]He is not clean; surely he is not clean." 27 But on [m]the second day, the day after the
new moon, [k]David's place was empty. And Saul said to Jonathan his son, "Why has not
the son of Jesse come to the meal, either yesterday or today?" 28 Jonathan answered Saul,
[n]"David earnestly asked leave of me to go to Bethlehem. 29 He said, 'Let me go, for our clan
holds a sacrifice in the city, and my brother has commanded me to be there. So now, if I
have found favor in your eyes, let me get away and see my brothers.' For this reason he
has not come to the king's table."
30 Then Saul's anger was kindled against Jonathan, and he said to him, "You son of a
perverse, rebellious woman, do I not know that you have chosen the son of Jesse to your
own shame, and to the shame of your mother's nakedness? 31 For as long as the son of Jesse
lives on the earth, neither you nor your kingdom shall be established. Therefore send
and bring him to me, for he shall surely die." 32 Then Jonathan answered Saul his father,
[o]"Why should he be put to death? What has he done?" 33 [p]But Saul hurled his spear at him
to strike him. So Jonathan knew [q]that his father was determined to put David to death.
34 And Jonathan rose from the table in fierce anger and ate no food the second day of the
month, for he was grieved for David, because his father had disgraced him.
35 In the morning Jonathan went out into the field to the appointment with David, and
with him a little boy. 36 And he said to his boy, "Run and find the arrows that I shoot." As the
boy ran, he shot an arrow beyond him. 37 And when the boy came to the place of the arrow
that Jonathan had shot, Jonathan called after the boy and said, [r]"Is not the arrow beyond
you?" 38 And Jonathan called after the boy, "Hurry! Be quick! Do not stay!" So Jonathan's
boy gathered up the arrows and came to his master. 39 But the boy knew nothing. Only
Jonathan and David knew the matter. 40 And Jonathan gave his weapons to his boy and said
to him, "Go and carry them to the city." 41 And as soon as the boy had gone, David rose from
beside the stone heap[2] and fell on his face to the ground and bowed three times. And they
kissed one another and wept with one another, David weeping the most. 42 Then Jonathan
said to David, [s]"Go in peace, because we have sworn both of us in the name of the LORD,
saying, [t]'The LORD shall be between me and you, [u]and between my offspring and your
offspring, forever.'" And he rose and departed, and Jonathan went into the city.[3]

David and the Holy Bread

21 [4] Then David came to [v]Nob to [w]Ahimelech the priest. And Ahimelech [x]came to meet
David trembling and said to him, "Why are you alone, and no one with you?" 2 And
David said to Ahimelech the priest, "The king has charged me with a matter and said to
me, 'Let no one know anything of the matter about which I send you, and with which I

[1] Compare Septuagint; Hebrew *stood up* [2] Septuagint; Hebrew *from beside the south* [3] This sentence is 21:1 in Hebrew [4] Ch 21:2 in Hebrew

25 [k]ver. 18
26 [l]Lev. 7:21; See Lev. 11:24-28; 15:1-4
27 [m][ver. 34] [k][See ver. 25 above]
28 [n]ver. 6
32 [o]ch. 19:5
33 [p]ch. 18:11; 19:10 [q]ver. 7
37 [r]ver. 22
42 [s]ver. 13; ch. 1:17 [t]ver. 23 [u]ver. 15

Chapter 21

1 [v]ch. 22:9, 11, 19; Neh. 11:32; Isa. 10:32 [w][ch. 14:3; Mark 2:26] [x][ch. 16:4]

20:26 Because the feast involved sacrifices, one had to be **clean** in order to participate.

20:29 My brother presumably refers to David's eldest brother, Eliab (17:28). It reflects a system of family leadership passing to the eldest son; his father Jesse had already retired (see 17:12; cf. Laban's role in Gen. 24:50).

20:30 to the shame of your mother's nakedness. The emphasis is on the disgrace or shame that Saul thinks Jonathan has brought to himself and his family.

20:31 neither you nor your kingdom shall be established. This was true, but Jonathan had already come to terms with it (vv. 14–15). Saul took for granted that kingship was hereditary, though there was no divine justification for his doing so.

20:37–38 Is not the arrow beyond you? See note on v. 22. **Hurry! Be quick!** Jonathan seeks to indicate to David the urgency of his warning.

20:40–41 as soon as the boy had gone. Jonathan had presumably arranged the signal of the arrow (vv. 20–22) so that David would not be seen, but now he seems to decide that it was safe enough to risk the farewell meeting he longed to have.

21:1–26:25 ***David's Escape from Saul.*** David begins his life as a fugitive. He moves around from place to place, gathering a group of 400 men, which later increases to 600, sometimes acting as a protector, sometimes fleeing Saul. Saul, on the other hand, is single-minded in his determination to kill David. He destroys the priests of Nob for innocently aiding David, and whenever he gets some firm news of David, he pursues him with his whole army. David continues to respect Saul as king and does not kill him, even when he apparently has God-sent opportunities to do so.

21:1–23:29 ***David's Escapes.*** Chapter 21 tells of David's visit to the shrine at Nob, and ch. 22 tells of the disastrous consequences of that visit. Interspersed throughout these chapters are various other stories of David's flight from Saul.

21:1 Nob, a city between Jerusalem and Gibeah, apparently became the priestly city after the destruction of Shiloh. **Ahimelech** was the great-grandson of Eli (see note on 2:27–28). Jesus refers to this incident as being "in the time of Abiathar the high priest" (Mark 2:26). Though Ahimelech's son Abiathar was not yet high priest at that time, the phrase identified him for Jesus' audience by the title he later held. (See note on Mark 2:25–26.)

21:2 The king has charged me. David deceived Ahimelech the priest by implying that he (David) was on official business for the king. David's deception, however, resulted in the deaths of Ahimelech and the priests at Nob

4[y]Ex. 25:30; Lev. 24:5; Matt. 12:3, 4; Mark 2:25, 26; Luke 6:3, 4 [z]Ex. 19:15
6[y][See ver. 4 above] [a]Lev. 24:8, 9
7[b]ch. 22:9; See Ps. 52
9[c]ch. 17:51 [d]ch. 17:2
10[e]See Ps. 34
11[f]ch. 18:7; 29:5
12[g][Luke 2:19]

Chapter 22

1[h]See Ps. 57; 142 [i]2 Sam. 23:13; 1 Chr. 11:15
2[j][Judg. 9:4; 11:3] [k][ch. 23:13; 25:13]

have charged you.' I have made an appointment with the young men for such and such a
place. 3 Now then, what do you have on hand? Give me five loaves of bread, or whatever is
here." 4 And the priest answered David, "I have no common bread on hand, but there is [y]holy
bread—[z]if the young men have kept themselves from women." 5 And David answered the
priest, "Truly women have been kept from us as always when I go on an expedition. The
vessels of the young men are holy even when it is an ordinary journey. How much more
today will their vessels be holy?" 6 So the priest gave him [y]the holy bread, for there was no
bread there but the bread of the Presence, [a]which is removed from before the LORD, to be
replaced by hot bread on the day it is taken away.

7 Now a certain man of the servants of Saul was there that day, detained before the LORD.
His name was [b]Doeg the Edomite, the chief of Saul's herdsmen.

8 Then David said to Ahimelech, "Then have you not here a spear or a sword at hand?
For I have brought neither my sword nor my weapons with me, because the king's business required haste." 9 And the priest said, [c]"The sword of Goliath the Philistine, whom
you struck down in [d]the Valley of Elah, behold, it is here wrapped in a cloth behind the
ephod. If you will take that, take it, for there is none but that here." And David said, "There
is none like that; give it to me."

David Flees to Gath

10 And David rose and fled that day from Saul and went to [e]Achish the king of Gath.
11 And the servants of Achish said to him, "Is not this David the king of the land? [f]Did they
not sing to one another of him in dances,

> 'Saul has struck down his thousands,
> and David his ten thousands'?"

12 And David [g]took these words to heart and was much afraid of Achish the king of Gath.
13 So he changed his behavior before them and pretended to be insane in their hands and
made marks on the doors of the gate and let his spittle run down his beard. 14 Then Achish
said to his servants, "Behold, you see the man is mad. Why then have you brought him
to me? 15 Do I lack madmen, that you have brought this fellow to behave as a madman in
my presence? Shall this fellow come into my house?"

David at the Cave of Adullam

22 David departed from there and escaped to [h]the cave of [i]Adullam. And when his
brothers and all his father's house heard it, they went down there to him. 2 [j]And
everyone who was in distress, and everyone who was in debt, and everyone who was bitter
in soul,[1] gathered to him. And he became commander over them. And there were with
him [k]about four hundred men.

3 And David went from there to Mizpeh of Moab. And he said to the king of Moab,
"Please let my father and my mother stay[2] with you, till I know what God will do for
me." 4 And he left them with the king of Moab, and they stayed with him all the time that

[1] Or *discontented* [2] Syriac, Vulgate; Hebrew *go out*

(22:9–19; cf. 22:22). Though David normally acted as an upright man, the Bible does not hesitate to record honestly his instances of wrongdoing.

21:4–5 Common bread, which might be eaten by anyone, is distinguished from **holy bread**, which, like sacrifices, could be eaten only by the clean (e.g., Lev. 10:10). Sexual contact was one source of uncleanness (Ex. 19:15; Lev. 15:18), especially on a military expedition (see 2 Sam. 11:9–11). The "holy bread" was the bread of the Presence of Ex. 25:30; Lev. 24:5–9; etc. Ahimelech was bending the rules, since only priests were allowed to eat the bread, and only in a holy place. However, Jesus endorsed Ahimelech's judgment in putting mercy before ceremonial law.

21:7 Doeg. Cf. 22:9–19.

21:9 ephod. See note on 2:27–28.

21:10–15 David apparently had the idea of serving **Achish** (**into my house**, v. 15) as an anonymous mercenary, but he was recognized. It is not clear why they called David "king." They may be speaking ironically, mocking David. Or perhaps the Philistines used the word in a somewhat different sense from the Hebrew term; thus here Achish is called "king," though Gath is just a city, not a nation. "Achish" may have been a title or a common name for a Philistine ruler, like "Pharaoh" for an Egyptian king (see 27:2). Psalms 34 and 56 were in response to this occasion.

21:14 you see the man is mad. God's protection of David continues, as Achish is convinced by David's pretended insanity.

22:1–4 Adullam is halfway between Gath and Bethlehem, and the cave is probably nearby. David's family is in danger from Saul, so they join him. But because life in the wilderness would be too difficult for David's aged parents, he takes them to **Moab**, where Jesse's grandmother Ruth had come from. It must have been a very difficult journey, presumably involving a descent of about 3,000 feet (914 m) to the Dead Sea, followed by a similar ascent back up to the plateau of Moab.

22:2 everyone who was in distress. David was gathering the outcasts of Israel, but under his leadership they became an effective fighting force (cf. 23:5; 27:8), for "the LORD was with him" (18:12).

David was in the stronghold. 5 Then the prophet [l]Gad said to David, "Do not remain in
the stronghold; depart, and go into the land of Judah." So David departed and went into
the forest of Hereth.

Saul Kills the Priests at Nob

6 Now Saul heard that David was discovered, and the men who were with him. Saul was
sitting at Gibeah under [m]the tamarisk tree on the height with his spear in his hand, and
all his servants were standing about him. 7 And Saul said to his servants who stood about
him, "Hear now, people of Benjamin; will the son of Jesse [n]give every one of you fields and
vineyards, will he make you all commanders of thousands and commanders of hundreds,
8 that all of you have conspired against me? No one discloses to me [o]when my son makes
a covenant with the son of Jesse. None of you [p]is sorry for me or discloses to me that my
son has stirred up my servant against me, [q]to lie in wait, as at this day." 9 Then answered
[r]Doeg the Edomite, who stood by the servants of Saul, "I saw the son of Jesse [s]coming to
Nob, to [t]Ahimelech the son of Ahitub, 10 [u]and he inquired of the LORD for him and [v]gave
him provisions and gave him the sword of Goliath the Philistine."

11 Then the king sent to summon Ahimelech the priest, the son of Ahitub, and all his
father's house, the priests who were at Nob, and all of them came to the king. 12 And Saul
said, "Hear now, son of Ahitub." And he answered, "Here I am, my lord." 13 And Saul said to
him, "Why have you conspired against me, you and the son of Jesse, in that you have given
him bread and a sword and [u]have inquired of God for him, so that he has risen against me,
[w]to lie in wait, as at this day?" 14 Then Ahimelech answered the king, "And who among all
your servants is so faithful as David, who is the king's son-in-law, and captain over[1] your
bodyguard, and honored in your house? 15 Is today the first time [u]that I have inquired of
God for him? No! Let not the king impute anything to his servant or to all the house of
my father, for your servant has known nothing of all this, [x]much or little." 16 And the king
said, "You shall surely die, Ahimelech, you and all your father's house." 17 And the king
said to [y]the guard who stood about him, "Turn and kill the priests of the LORD, because
their hand also is with David, and they knew that he fled and did not disclose it to me."
But the servants of the king would not put out their hand to strike the priests of the LORD.
18 Then the king said to Doeg, "You turn and strike the priests." And Doeg the Edomite
turned and struck down the priests, [z]and he killed on that day eighty-five persons who
wore the linen ephod. 19 And Nob, the city of the priests, he put to the sword; [a]both man
and woman, child and infant, ox, donkey and sheep, he put to the sword.

20 But one of the sons of Ahimelech the son of Ahitub, named [b]Abiathar, escaped and
fled after David. 21 And Abiathar told David that Saul had killed the priests of the LORD.
22 And David said to Abiathar, "I knew on that day, [c]when Doeg the Edomite was there,
that he would surely tell Saul. I have occasioned the death of all the persons of your father's

[1] Septuagint, Targum; Hebrew *and has turned aside to*

5 [l]2 Sam. 24:11, 18, 19; 1 Chr. 21:9, 11, 13, 18, 19; 29:29; 2 Chr. 29:25
6 [m][ch. 31:13; Gen. 21:33]
7 [n][ch. 8:14]
8 [o]ch. 18:3 [p][ch. 23:21] [q]ver. 13
9 [r]ch. 21:7; See Ps. 52 [s]ch. 21:1 [t][ch. 14:3]
10 [u]ch. 23:2, 4; 30:8; 2 Sam. 5:19, 23; [Num. 27:21] [v]ch. 21:6, 9
13 [u][See ver. 10 above] [w]ver. 8
15 [u][See ver. 10 above] [x]ch. 25:36
17 [y][2 Kgs. 10:25; 11:4, 6; 2 Chr. 12:10]
18 [z][ch. 2:31]
19 [a][ch. 15:3]
20 [b]ch. 23:6, 9
22 [c]ch. 21:7

22:5 The **stronghold** was probably not in Judah, since Gad told David to **go into the land of Judah**. It may have been Masada, the mesa on the western shore of the Dead Sea, which would be the last holdout of the Jews in A.D. 73. The location of **Hereth** is unknown. It took faith to go back to Judah despite the danger (23:3).

22:6–23 This episode must have occurred soon after 21:1–9, since Ahimelech knows nothing about the break between Saul and David.

22:6 Saul was sitting at Gibeah under the tamarisk tree. See note on 14:2–3.

22:7–8 David apparently retains his popularity even with Saul's **servants** (i.e., officials; see 18:5, 22), who, though they remain with Saul, make no attempt to help him against David. As Samuel had predicted (8:12–14), Saul made men commanders and gave them fields and vineyards.

22:8 Despite Saul's claims, there is no evidence that Jonathan, who had tried to calm things down, had **stirred up** David, or that David was lying **in wait** for Saul. **all of you have conspired against me**. Saul does not trust in the Lord, and now he trusts no one else either, fearing even his own servants. Saul's jealousy has distorted his vision. Trying to rule without help from the Holy Spirit (see note on 16:14), he is alone.

22:9 Doeg's presence in Nob was mentioned in 21:7. He is called **the Edomite** three times in this episode (22:9, 18, 22; also 21:7), probably to point out that it was a foreigner who betrayed David and killed the priests, something that Saul's Israelite servants refused to do.

22:10 In 21:1–9 there is no reference to Ahimelech's consulting the Lord; hence Doeg may be lying here. Saul's suspicions were inflamed by the fact that Doeg referred to an inquiry (often used in military situations), called the bread **provisions**, and mentioned Goliath's **sword**. Whom but Saul could David be planning to fight?

22:19 Saul treats **Nob** like some enemy city that has been "devoted to destruction" (cf. 15:3). Thus, Saul completely destroys the priests' city, though he failed to carry out the ban against the Amalekites (ch. 15). He is destroying part of his own kingdom.

22:20 Abiathar, the one priest who escaped the massacre at Nob, will bring the ephod (see note on 21:9) with him when he comes to David (23:6). Thus the true priesthood and priestly counsel move from Saul to David. Abiathar will remain with David as his priest until David's death (2 Sam. 20:25), helping him against Absalom (2 Sam. 15:27–29; 17:15; 19:11). Solomon will eventually banish him (1 Sam. 2:33; 1 Kings 2:26–27).

23[d][1 Kgs. 2:26]
Chapter 23
1[e]Josh. 15:44
2[f]See ch. 22:10
4[f][See ver. 2 above] [g]ver. 14; Josh. 24:11; Judg. 7:7; 20:28
6[h]ch. 22:20
9[i]ch. 30:7; [Num. 27:21]
12[j]ver. 20
13[k]ch. 25:13; 27:2; [ch. 22:2; 30:9, 10] [l][2 Sam. 15:20]
14[m]See Ps. 63 [n]Josh. 15:24
17[o]ch. 24:20; [ch. 20:31]
18[p]ch. 18:3; 20:8, 16, 42; [2 Sam. 21:7]
19[q]ch. 26:1; See Ps. 54 [r]Num. 21:20
20[s]ver. 12

house. **23** [d]Stay with me; do not be afraid, for he who seeks my life seeks your life. With me
you shall be in safekeeping."

David Saves the City of Keilah

23 Now they told David, "Behold, the Philistines are fighting against [e]Keilah and are
robbing the threshing floors." **2** Therefore David [f]inquired of the LORD, "Shall I go
and attack these Philistines?" And the LORD said to David, "Go and attack the Philistines
and save Keilah." **3** But David's men said to him, "Behold, we are afraid here in Judah; how
much more then if we go to Keilah against the armies of the Philistines?" **4** Then David
[f]inquired of the LORD again. And the LORD answered him, "Arise, go down to Keilah, [g]for
I will give the Philistines into your hand." **5** And David and his men went to Keilah and
fought with the Philistines and brought away their livestock and struck them with a great
blow. So David saved the inhabitants of Keilah.
6 [h]When Abiathar the son of Ahimelech had fled to David to Keilah, he had come down
with an ephod in his hand. **7** Now it was told Saul that David had come to Keilah. And
Saul said, "God has given him into my hand, for he has shut himself in by entering a
town that has gates and bars." **8** And Saul summoned all the people to war, to go down to
Keilah, to besiege David and his men. **9** David knew that Saul was plotting harm against
him. And he said to Abiathar the priest, [i]"Bring the ephod here." **10** Then David said, "O
LORD, the God of Israel, your servant has surely heard that Saul seeks to come to Keilah,
to destroy the city on my account. **11** Will the men of Keilah surrender me into his hand?
Will Saul come down, as your servant has heard? O LORD, the God of Israel, please tell
your servant." And the LORD said, "He will come down." **12** Then David said, "Will the men
of Keilah surrender me and my men into the hand of Saul?" And the LORD said, [j]"They
will surrender you." **13** Then David and his men, [k]who were about six hundred, arose and
departed from Keilah, and they went [l]wherever they could go. When Saul was told that
David had escaped from Keilah, he gave up the expedition. **14** And David remained in the
strongholds in the wilderness, in the hill country [m]of the wilderness of [n]Ziph. And Saul
sought him every day, but God did not give him into his hand.

Saul Pursues David

15 David saw that Saul had come out to seek his life. David was in the wilderness of Ziph
at Horesh. **16** And Jonathan, Saul's son, rose and went to David at Horesh, and strengthened
his hand in God. **17** And he said to him, "Do not fear, for the hand of Saul my father shall
not find you. You shall be king over Israel, and I shall be next to you. [o]Saul my father also
knows this." **18** [p]And the two of them made a covenant before the LORD. David remained
at Horesh, and Jonathan went home.
19 [q]Then the Ziphites went up to Saul at Gibeah, saying, "Is not David hiding among
us in the strongholds at Horesh, on the hill of Hachilah, which is south of [r]Jeshimon?
20 Now come down, O king, according to all your heart's desire to come down, [s]and our

23:1 Keilah was probably a site 3 miles (4.8 km) south of Adullam and east of Gath, and was apparently closer to Philistine territory than Hereth was.

23:2 It is not clear how David **inquired of the LORD**, since Abiathar did not come until David was already in Keilah (v. 6). Perhaps he inquired through the prophet Gad (cf. 22:5), or directly in prayer.

23:5 Perhaps the Philistines brought **their livestock** to forage on the "threshing floors" at Keilah.

23:7 God has given him into my hand. Saul apparently still believes that the Lord is on his side instead of seriously considering whether he himself is on the Lord's side. A **town that has gates and bars** could be a protection, but it could also be a trap (see Judg. 16:2).

23:12–13 Will the men of Keilah surrender me? Saul had destroyed Nob on a lesser pretext, so he was certainly willing and presumably able to destroy Keilah. From the standpoint of the men of Keilah, David had brought more trouble than relief for them. The Philistines, after all, had gone after only grain. See the similar situation in 2 Sam. 20:14–22. **They will surrender you**. Accepting the answer from God, David acted accordingly. **Arose and departed** suggests immediate action. They **went wherever they could go**, trusting in divine guidance each step of the way.

23:14–15 Ziph was about 5 miles (8 km) southeast of Hebron, near where the land starts going down toward the Dead Sea. **Horesh** was probably a grove of trees nearby. **God did not give him into his hand**. Saul's greater authority and army cannot triumph over God's protection of David.

23:16–18 Jonathan visits David during this difficult time. **You shall be king over Israel**. Though David's position is much worse than in ch. 20, Jonathan sees even more clearly than before that David will be king. Jonathan's trust in the Lord makes him able to accept anything the Lord has in store for him, so he can encourage David **in God**. They again make a covenant **before the LORD** (see 20:8, 16). **Next to you** is second in rank, but not an heir, as with Mordecai (Est. 10:3), or Elkanah, "the next in authority to the king" (2 Chron. 28:7).

23:19 The **Ziphites** were Judahites, but they apparently were not happy to have David and his men in the area. Psalm 54 was in response to this occasion.

part shall be to surrender him into the king's hand." 21 And Saul said, [t]"May you be blessed
by the LORD, [u]for you have had compassion on me. 22 Go, make yet more sure. Know and
see the place where his foot is, and who has seen him there, for it is told me that he is very
cunning. 23 See therefore and take note of all the lurking places where he hides, and come
back to me with sure information. Then I will go with you. And if he is in the land, I will
search him out among all the thousands of Judah." 24 And they arose and went to Ziph
ahead of Saul.
Now David and his men were [v]in the wilderness of Maon, [w]in the Arabah to the south
of [r]Jeshimon. 25 And Saul and his men went to seek him. And David was told, so he went
down to the rock and lived in the wilderness of Maon. And when Saul heard that, he
pursued after David in the wilderness of Maon. 26 Saul went on one side of the mountain,
and David and his men on the other side of the mountain. And David was hurrying to
get away from Saul. As Saul and his men were closing in on David and his men to capture
them, 27 a messenger came to Saul, saying, "Hurry and come, for the Philistines have made
a raid against the land." 28 So Saul returned from pursuing after David and went against
the Philistines. Therefore that place was called the Rock of Escape.[1] 29[2] And David went
up from there and lived in the strongholds of [x]Engedi.

David Spares Saul's Life

24 [3] [y]When Saul returned from following the Philistines, he was told, "Behold, David
is in the wilderness of Engedi." 2 Then Saul took [z]three thousand chosen men out
of all Israel and went to seek David and his men in front of the Wildgoats' Rocks. 3 And
he came to the sheepfolds by the way, where there was a cave, and Saul went in [a]to relieve
himself.[4] Now David and his men were sitting in the innermost parts [b]of the cave. 4 And
the men of David said to him, [c]"Here is the day of which the LORD said to you, 'Behold,
I will give your enemy into your hand, and you shall do to him as it shall seem good
to you.'" Then David arose and stealthily cut off a corner of Saul's robe. 5 And afterward
[d]David's heart struck him, because he had cut off a corner of Saul's robe. 6 He said to his
men, [e]"The LORD forbid that I should do this thing to my lord, the LORD's anointed, to
put out my hand against him, seeing he is [f]the LORD's anointed." 7 So David persuaded
his men with these words [g]and did not permit them to attack Saul. And Saul rose up and
left the cave and went on his way.
8 Afterward David also arose and went out of the cave, and called after Saul, "My lord
the king!" And when Saul looked behind him, David bowed with his face to the earth and
paid homage. 9 And David said to Saul, "Why do you listen to the words of men who say,
'Behold, David seeks your harm'? 10 Behold, this day your eyes have seen how the LORD
gave you today into my hand in the cave. [h]And some told me to kill you, but I spared you.[5]
I said, 'I will not put out my hand against my lord, [f]for he is the LORD's anointed.' 11 See,
my father, see the corner of your robe in my hand. For by the fact that I cut off the corner

[1] Or *Rock of Divisions* [2] Ch 24:1 in Hebrew [3] Ch 24:2 in Hebrew [4] Hebrew *cover his feet* [5] Septuagint, Syriac, Targum; Hebrew *it* [my eye] *spared you*

21 [t]See Ruth 2:20 [u][ch. 22:8]
24 [v]ch. 25:2; Josh. 15:55 [w]See Deut. 1:1 [r][See ver. 19 above]
29 [x]Josh. 15:62; 2 Chr. 20:2; Song 1:14; Ezek. 47:10

Chapter 24

1 [y]ch. 23:28
2 [z]ch. 26:2
3 [a]Judg. 3:24 [b]See Ps. 57; 142
4 [c]ver. 7; [ch. 26:8]
5 [d]2 Sam. 24:10
6 [e]ch. 26:11 [f]See ch. 12:3
7 [g][Ps. 7:4]
10 [h]ver. 4 [f][See ver. 6 above]

23:21 for you have had compassion on me. Saul's only interest continues to be himself (see note on 18:12).

23:24–28 Maon was about 5 miles (8 km) south of Ziph. The mountain was probably the one now called Mount Kholed. Apparently David was on the eastern slope trying to escape toward the Dead Sea, while Saul on the other slope divided his force into two flanks and sent them around the mountain to the north and south to encircle David. Since the land to the east was open country, he could easily have captured him.

23:27 the Philistines have made a raid. The raid was undoubtedly caused by the Lord in order to save David at the last minute, when Saul and his men "were closing in on David and his men" (v. 26).

23:29 Engedi is an oasis on the western shore of the Dead Sea, due east of Ziph.

24:1–26:25 The three episodes in the next three chapters all have the same theme: David, who as a warrior has already killed many of the Lord's enemies, should not kill for his own advantage but let the Lord act for him. He has already thought through the matter regarding Saul, but in ch. 25 the same issue comes up unexpectedly, and he is about to act in a purely natural way when God sends Abigail to save him.

24:1–25:1 *David Spares Saul at Engedi.* David has an opportunity to kill Saul, but shows his respect for God's appointment of Saul and his patience to wait for God's timing.

24:2 Three thousand chosen men is five times as many as David's men (23:13) and suggests Saul's paranoia.

24:4 The **corner of Saul's robe** proves that David could have killed Saul if he had so chosen (see v. 11). The robe was symbolic of royal authority (cf. 18:4).

24:6 David respects Saul as **the LORD's anointed** because Saul is still on the royal throne as king over Israel, even though the Spirit of the Lord has already left him. The Lord had previously anointed Saul as king (10:1), and in David's eyes Saul still retains that status. The anointed of the Lord should not be killed or even cursed (cf. 26:9; Ex. 22:28; 2 Sam. 1:14; 19:21).

of your robe and did not kill you, you may know and see that [i]there is no wrong or treason
in my hands. I have not sinned against you, though [j]you hunt my life to take it. 12 [k]May
the LORD judge between me and you, may the LORD avenge me against you, but my hand
shall not be against you. 13 As the proverb of the ancients says, 'Out of the wicked comes
wickedness.' But my hand shall not be against you. 14 After whom has the king of Israel
come out? After whom do you pursue? [l]After a dead dog! [m]After a flea! 15 [k]May the LORD
therefore be judge and give sentence between me and you, and see to it and [n]plead my
cause and deliver me from your hand."
16 As soon as David had finished speaking these words to Saul, Saul said, [o]"Is this your
voice, my son David?" And Saul lifted up his voice and wept. 17 He said to David, "You are
more righteous than I, [p]for you have repaid me good, whereas I have repaid you evil. 18 And
you have declared this day how you have dealt well with me, in that you did not kill me
when the LORD put me into your hands. 19 For if a man finds his enemy, will he let him
go away safe? So may the LORD reward you with good for what you have done to me this
day. 20 And now, behold, [q]I know that you shall surely be king, and that the kingdom of
Israel shall be established in your hand. 21 [r]Swear to me therefore by the LORD that you
will not cut off my offspring after me, and [s]that you will not destroy my name out of my
father's house." 22 And David swore this to Saul. Then Saul went home, but David and his
men went up [t]to the stronghold.

The Death of Samuel

25 [u]Now Samuel died. And all Israel assembled [v]and mourned for him, and they buried
him [w]in his house at [x]Ramah.

David and Abigail

Then David rose and went down to [y]the wilderness of Paran. 2 And there was a man in
[z]Maon whose business was in [a]Carmel. The man was very rich; he had three thousand
sheep and a thousand goats. [b]He was shearing his sheep in Carmel. 3 Now the name of
the man was Nabal, and the name of his wife Abigail. The woman was discerning and
beautiful, but the man was harsh and badly behaved; [c]he was a Calebite. 4 David heard in
the wilderness that Nabal [b]was shearing his sheep. 5 So David sent ten young men. And
David said to the young men, "Go up to Carmel, and go to Nabal and greet him in my
name. 6 And thus you shall greet him: [d]'Peace be to you, and peace be to your house, and
peace be to all that you have. 7 I hear that you have shearers. Now your shepherds have
been with us, and we did them no harm, [e]and they missed nothing all the time they were
in Carmel. 8 Ask your young men, and they will tell you. Therefore let my young men find

11 [i]Ps. 7:3 [j]ch. 26:20
12 [k]Gen. 16:5; Judg. 11:27
14 [l]See ch. 17:43 [m]ch. 26:20
15 [k][See ver. 12 above] [n]ch. 25:39; Ps. 35:1; 43:1; 119:154
16 [o]ch. 26:17
17 [p][ch. 26:21]
20 [q]ch. 23:17
21 [r][Gen. 21:23] [s][2 Sam. 21:7]
22 [t]ch. 23:29

Chapter 25

1 [u]ch. 28:3 [v]Gen. 50:10; [Num. 20:29; Deut. 34:8] [w][1 Kgs. 2:34] [x]ch. 1:19 [y]Num. 10:12
2 [z]ch. 23:24 [a]Josh. 15:55 [b][Gen. 38:13; 2 Sam. 13:23]
3 [c][ch. 30:14]
4 [b][See ver. 2 above]
6 [d][1 Chr. 12:18; Matt. 10:13; Luke 10:5]
7 [e]ver. 15, 21

24:12 May the LORD judge. David believes that Saul should be punished for his wrongdoing, but he is willing to let the Lord avenge him (cf. Deut. 32:35).

24:13 Out of the wicked comes wickedness. That is, if David were indeed as wicked as Saul believed him to be, he would certainly have killed Saul.

24:18 you have dealt well with me. Saul's only concern continues to be himself (cf. v. 21; also 23:21; and note on 18:12).

24:20 I know that you shall surely be king. Saul acknowledges that David is right, but as with the reconciliation in 19:7, his calming down will only be temporary.

24:22 but David and his men went up to the stronghold. Despite Saul's acknowledgment in v. 20, David does not trust him.

25:1 When Samuel died, **all Israel assembled and mourned for him**. Scripture nowhere suggests that one should not mourn (see note on 1 Thess. 4:13). **in his house**. Burial in a house was common in some cultures of that day, though it was unusual in Israel. Perhaps David went to **Paran** because he feared that Samuel's death might turn Saul against him again.

25:2–44 *David Marries Abigail.* Although Nabal's rudeness provokes David to anger, Nabal's wife Abigail manages to persuade David not to take vengeance. After Nabal dies, David takes Abigail as his wife.

25:2–3 "The wilderness of Paran" (v. 1) usually refers to the northeast part of the Sinai peninsula (Num. 10:12). If the "stronghold" of 1 Sam. 24:22 is Masada (see note on 22:5), it would not have been very distant. Apparently David came back soon to the wilderness of Maon, south of Ziph, where he had been previously (23:24). **Carmel** is not the mountain in the north of Israel but a Judahite town between Ziph and Maon (cf. 15:12).

25:3 The name **Nabal** means "foolish" or "boorish" (see v. 25). It appears to be his real name, but since it is unlikely that someone would be given a name with that meaning, its origin may have been another Hebrew word that is now unknown. **Calebite** may mean a descendant of Caleb, one of the scouts who was willing to enter Canaan (Num. 14:6–7) and who was given the land around Hebron (Josh. 14:6–14). Thus it would mean that Nabal was prominent both by wealth and by descent. Nabal's wife **Abigail** is a different woman from David's sister Abigail (1 Chron. 2:16–17), who married a different man, Ithra (Jether) the Ishmaelite (2 Sam. 17:25; 1 Chron. 2:17). David will later marry Nabal's wife Abigail (1 Sam. 25:42).

25:4–8 Sheepshearing was a time of festivity (v. 8) as well as work. David addresses Nabal very politely and respectfully. David's sending **ten young men** suggests that he was asking for a substantial handout, but hardly enough to feed 600 men. David's claim that his men had caused Nabal no problem (v. 7) is backed up by Nabal's servant in vv. 15–16, who even adds that they were helpful. It may be that David is hoping to develop this spontaneous helpfulness into a regular relationship.

favor in your eyes, for we come [f]on a feast day. Please give whatever you have at hand to
your servants and to your son David.'"
9 When David's young men came, they said all this to Nabal in the name of David, and
then they waited. 10 And Nabal answered David's servants, [g]"Who is David? Who is the son
of Jesse? [h]There are many servants these days who are breaking away from their masters.
11 Shall I take [i]my bread and my water and my meat that I have killed for my shearers and
give it to [j]men who come from I do not know where?" 12 So David's young men turned
away and came back and told him all this. 13 And David said to his men, "Every man strap
on his sword!" And every man of them strapped on his sword. David also strapped on his
sword. And [k]about four hundred men went up after David, [k]while two hundred [l]remained
with the baggage.
14 But one of the young men told Abigail, Nabal's wife, "Behold, David sent messengers
out of the wilderness to greet our master, and he railed at them. 15 Yet the men were very
good to us, and we suffered no harm, [n]and we did not miss anything when we were in
the fields, as long as we went with them. 16 They were [o]a wall to us both by night and by
day, all the while we were with them keeping the sheep. 17 Now therefore know this and
consider what you should do, [p]for harm is determined against our master and against all
his house, and he is such [q]a worthless man that one cannot speak to him."
18 Then Abigail made haste and took two hundred loaves and two skins of wine and five
sheep already prepared and five seahs[1] of parched grain and a hundred clusters of raisins
and two hundred cakes of figs, and laid them on donkeys. 19 And she said to her young
men, "Go on before me; behold, I come after you." But she did not tell her husband Nabal.
20 And as she rode on the donkey and came down under cover of the mountain, behold,
David and his men came down toward her, and she met them. 21 Now David had said,
"Surely in vain have I guarded all that this fellow has in the wilderness, [r]so that nothing
was missed of all that belonged to him, and he has [s]returned me evil for good. 22 [t]God do
so to the enemies of David[2] and more also, if by morning I leave so much as one male of
all who belong to him."
23 When Abigail saw David, she hurried [u]and got down from the donkey [v]and fell before
David on her face and bowed to the ground. 24 She fell at his feet and said, [w]"On me alone,
my lord, be the guilt. Please let your servant speak in your ears, and hear the words of
your servant. 25 Let not my lord regard [q]this worthless fellow, Nabal, for as his name is, so
is he. Nabal[3] is his name, and folly is with him. But I your servant did not see the young
men of my lord, whom you sent. 26 Now then, my lord, [x]as the LORD lives, and as your
soul lives, because [y]the LORD has restrained you from bloodguilt and from [z]saving with
your own hand, now then [a]let your enemies and those who seek to do evil to my lord be
as Nabal. 27 And now let this [b]present that your servant has brought to my lord be given to
the young men who follow my lord. 28 Please forgive the trespass of your servant. For the
LORD will certainly make my lord [c]a sure house, because my lord [d]is fighting the battles of
the LORD, and evil shall not be found in you so long as you live. 29 If men rise up to pursue
you and to seek your life, the life of my lord shall be bound in the bundle of the living in
the care of the LORD your God. And the lives of your enemies [e]he shall sling out as from
the hollow of a sling. 30 And when the LORD has done to my lord according to all the good

[1] A *seah* was about 7 quarts or 7.3 liters [2] Septuagint *to David* [3] *Nabal* means *fool*

8 [f]Esth. 8:17; 9:19, 22
10 [g][Judg. 9:28] [h][Judg. 12:4]
11 [i][Judg. 8:6] [j][ch. 22:2]
13 [k]ch. 23:13; 27:2; [ch. 22:2] [l]ch. 30:24
15 [n]ver. 7, 21
16 [o][Job 1:10]
17 [p][ch. 20:7] [q]Deut. 13:13
21 [r]ver. 7, 15 [s]Ps. 109:5; [Prov. 17:13]
22 [t]See Ruth 1:17
23 [u]Josh. 15:18; Judg. 1:14; [Gen. 24:64] [v]ver. 41; Ruth 2:10
24 [w][2 Sam. 14:9]
25 [q][See ver. 17 above]
26 [x]See ch. 20:3 [y][Gen. 20:6] [z][Rom. 12:19; Heb. 10:30] [a][2 Sam. 18:32]
27 [b]ch. 30:26; Gen. 33:11; [2 Kgs. 5:15]
28 [c]1 Kgs. 11:38; [ch. 2:35; 2 Sam. 7:11, 27; 1 Kgs. 9:5; 1 Chr. 17:10, 25] [d]ch. 18:17
29 [e]Jer. 10:18

25:10 Nabal answers David's polite request not just with refusal (which might have been justifiable) but with contempt. Like Saul and Doeg (20:27, 30; 22:8, 9, 13), Nabal seems to use **the son of Jesse** as a belittling term.

25:18 The list of Abigail's gifts resembles (in items and quantity) a list of the food supplied to an Egyptian expeditionary force to Palestine during the reign of Ramses II.

25:22 God do so to the enemies of David and more also is a common conditional curse formula (as in 3:17 and 14:44). **Male** (lit., "one who urinates at a wall") is a stereotyped formula that always refers to the killing of all males of a group (see 1 Kings 14:10; 16:11; 21:21; 2 Kings 9:8).

25:23–31 Abigail first calms David's anger. She says, **On me alone . . . be the guilt**, i.e., "If you kill anybody, kill me," but then explains why he should not kill her: he can hardly kill a woman traveling alone who humbly presents him with provisions! Then she reasons with him, assuming that he has already agreed with her (**the LORD has restrained you**; v. 26). In this speech **your servant** is feminine, i.e., "your maidservant, Abigail." The concern about **bloodguilt** (v. 26) also appears in vv. 31 (**shed blood**) and 33, as well as 2 Sam. 16:7–8 and 21:1. The avoidance of bloodguilt should have been of supreme importance even to Saul as the ruler of Israel (see 1 Sam. 19:5), and this was the key issue to David in his relationship with Saul. Whether David spares or kills Nabal has a symbolic aspect, since David is preparing for his future kingship. **The bundle of the living** (25:29), or "the document of the living," is probably equivalent to "the book of the living" in Ps. 69:28. Like David's men (1 Sam. 24:4), Abigail in 25:30 seems to refer to a promise made by the Lord to David, though there is no explicit reference to it, so it is unknown when or to what audience it was made. There are also suggestions of it in 2 Sam. 3:9–10 and 5:2.

31[z][See ver. 26 above]
32[f]Gen. 24:27; Ps. 41:13; 72:18; Luke 1:68
33[y][See ver. 26 above] [z][See ver. 26 above]
34[g]See Ruth 3:13 [y][See ver. 26 above]
35[h]See ch. 1:17
36[i][2 Sam. 13:23] [j][2 Sam. 13:28; 1 Kgs. 21:7] [k]ch. 22:15
38[l]ch. 26:10
39[f][See ver. 32 above] [m]See ch. 24:15 [n]ver. 26, 33, 34 [o]1 Kgs. 2:44; [Ps. 7:16; Ezek. 17:19] [p][Song 8:8]
41[q][Ruth 2:10]
43[r]Josh. 15:56 [s]ch. 27:3; 30:5; 2 Sam. 2:2; 3:2, 3; 1 Chr. 3:1

Chapter 26

1[t]ch. 23:19; See Ps. 54
2[u]ch. 23:14 [v]ch. 24:2
5[w]ch. 14:50; 17:55; 2 Sam. 2:8 [x]ch. 17:20
6[y]2 Sam. 2:18; 3:39; 16:10; 19:22; 1 Chr. 2:16

that he has spoken concerning you and has appointed you prince[1] over Israel, **31** my lord shall have no cause of grief or pangs of conscience for having shed blood without cause or for my lord [z]working salvation himself. And when the LORD has dealt well with my lord, then remember your servant."

32 And David said to Abigail, [f]"Blessed be the LORD, the God of Israel, who sent you this day to meet me! **33** Blessed be your discretion, and blessed be you, [y]who have kept me this day from bloodguilt [z]and from working salvation with my own hand! **34** For as surely [g]as the LORD, the God of Israel, lives, [y]who has restrained me from hurting you, unless you had hurried and come to meet me, truly by morning there had not been left to Nabal so much as one male." **35** Then David received from her hand what she had brought him. And he said to her, [h]"Go up in peace to your house. See, I have obeyed your voice, and I have granted your petition."

36 And Abigail came to Nabal, and behold, [i]he was holding a feast in his house, like the feast of a king. And Nabal's heart [j]was merry within him, for he was very drunk. So she told him nothing [k]at all until the morning light. **37** In the morning, when the wine had gone out of Nabal, his wife told him these things, and his heart died within him, and he became as a stone. **38** And about ten days later [l]the LORD struck Nabal, and he died.

39 When David heard that Nabal was dead, he said, [f]"Blessed be the LORD who has [m]avenged the insult I received at the hand of Nabal, [n]and has kept back his servant from wrongdoing. [o]The LORD has returned the evil of Nabal on his own head." Then David sent and [p]spoke to Abigail, to take her as his wife. **40** When the servants of David came to Abigail at Carmel, they said to her, "David has sent us to you to take you to him as his wife." **41** And she rose [q]and bowed with her face to the ground and said, "Behold, your handmaid is a servant to wash the feet of the servants of my lord." **42** And Abigail hurried and rose and mounted a donkey, and her five young women attended her. She followed the messengers of David and became his wife.

43 David also took Ahinoam of [r]Jezreel, [s]and both of them became his wives. **44** Saul had given Michal his daughter, David's wife, to Palti the son of Laish, who was of Gallim.

David Spares Saul Again

26 [t]Then the Ziphites came to Saul at Gibeah, saying, "Is not David hiding himself on the hill of Hachilah, which is on the east of Jeshimon?" **2** So Saul arose and went down to [u]the wilderness of Ziph with [v]three thousand chosen men of Israel to seek David in the wilderness of Ziph. **3** And Saul encamped on the hill of Hachilah, which is beside the road on the east of Jeshimon. But David remained in the wilderness. When he saw that Saul came after him into the wilderness, **4** David sent out spies and learned that Saul had indeed come. **5** Then David rose and came to the place where Saul had encamped. And David saw the place where Saul lay, with [w]Abner the son of Ner, the commander of his army. Saul was lying within [x]the encampment, while the army was encamped around him.

6 Then David said to Ahimelech the Hittite, and to Joab's brother [y]Abishai the son

[1] Or *leader*

25:32–35 David, having calmed down, agrees with Abigail completely and thanks the Lord and her. In his restraint about shedding the blood of fellow Israelites, David shows himself more qualified than Saul to be king. Giving up vengeance meant breaking the vow made in v. 22. If one vows to sin, however, it is better in the eyes of the Lord to break the vow than to commit the sin vowed, a principle that Jephthah (Judg. 11:29–40) and Herod the tetrarch (Matt. 14:7–9) should have heeded. (Of course, making a rash oath in the first place was a sin that needed to be compensated for, as Lev. 5:4–6 requires.)

25:35 Go up in peace to your house. This is more than just a conventional greeting. David is telling Abigail that her household is safe.

25:37–38 and his heart died within him. Abigail's words had a devastating effect on Nabal. Whether he had a heart attack or a stroke (**he became as a stone**), **ten days later the LORD struck Nabal, and he died.**

25:43 Ahinoam is from **Jezreel** in Judah, near Maon, Ziph, and Carmel. Because she is always mentioned first, David probably married her before he married Abigail. Ahinoam was the mother of David's eldest son, Amnon (2 Sam. 3:2; 13:1–13), and Abigail became the mother of David's little-known second son Chileab (2 Sam. 3:3), also known as Daniel (1 Chron. 3:1). Since no mention is made of him in the later squabbles, he probably died young. These marriages were undoubtedly important in helping David become king at Hebron.

25:44 David had probably not seen his first wife, **Michal**, since she helped him escape from Saul in 19:11–17, but he apparently still wanted her as his wife, and perhaps still loved her (cf. 2 Sam. 3:14–16).

26:1–25 *David Spares Saul at the Hill of Hachilah.* This chapter resembles ch. 24, but there are too many differences to say that they are different versions of the same event. The location is different, and it is difficult to see how an encampment in the open air could be the same as one that occurred in a cave.

26:1 The **Ziphites** are no happier to have David among them now than they were in 23:19.

26:6 Ahimelech the Hittite is mentioned nowhere else in Scripture; he may have been a hired warrior. **Joab's brother Abishai the son of Zeruiah.** Zeruiah was David's sister (1 Chron. 2:16–17), so Joab and Abishai were David's nephews. For the family background, see note on 2 Sam. 2:13.

of Zeruiah, [z]"Who will go down with me into the camp to Saul?" And Abishai said, "I
will go down with you." 7 So David and Abishai went to the army by night. And there
lay Saul sleeping within [x]the encampment, with his spear stuck in the ground [a]at his
head, and Abner and the army lay around him. 8 Then Abishai said to David, [b]"God has
given your enemy into your hand this day. Now please let me pin him to the earth with
one stroke of the spear, and I will not strike him twice." 9 But David said to Abishai,
"Do not destroy him, for who can put out his hand [c]against the LORD's anointed and
be guiltless?" 10 And David said, [d]"As the LORD lives, [e]the LORD will strike him, or [f]his
day will come to die, [g]or he will go down into battle and perish. 11 [h]The LORD forbid
that I should put out my hand against the LORD's anointed. But take now the spear
that is [i]at his head and the jar of water, and let us go." 12 So David took the spear and
the jar of water from Saul's head, and they went away. No man saw it or knew it, nor
did any awake, for they were all asleep, because [j]a deep sleep from the LORD had fallen
upon them.

13 Then David went over to the other side and stood far off on the top of the hill, with
a great space between them. 14 And David called to the army, and to Abner the son of Ner,
saying, "Will you not answer, Abner?" Then Abner answered, "Who are you who calls to
the king?" 15 And David said to Abner, "Are you not a man? Who is like you in Israel? Why
then have you not kept watch over your lord the king? For one of the people came in to
destroy the king your lord. 16 This thing that you have done is not good. [k]As the LORD lives,
you deserve to die, because you have not kept watch over your lord, the LORD's anointed.
And now see where the king's spear is and the jar of water that was [l]at his head."

17 Saul recognized David's voice and said, [m]"Is this your voice, my son David?" And David
said, "It is my voice, my lord, O king." 18 And he said, [n]"Why does my lord pursue after his
servant? For what have I done? What evil is on my hands? 19 Now therefore let my lord the
king hear the words of his servant. If it is the LORD who has stirred you up against me,
may he accept an offering, but if it is men, may they be cursed before the LORD, [o]for they
have driven me out this day that I should have no share in [p]the heritage of the LORD, saying, 'Go, serve other gods.' 20 Now therefore, let not my blood fall to the earth away from
the presence of the LORD, for the king of Israel has come out to seek [q]a single flea like one
who hunts a partridge in the mountains."

21 Then Saul said, [r]"I have sinned. Return, my son David, for I will no more do you
harm, because my life was precious in your eyes this day. Behold, I have acted foolishly,
and have made a great mistake." 22 And David answered and said, "Here is the spear, O
king! Let one of the young men come over and take it. 23 [s]The LORD rewards every man
for his righteousness and his faithfulness, for the LORD gave you into my hand today,
and I would not put out my hand against the LORD's anointed. 24 Behold, as your life was
precious this day in my sight, so may my life be precious in the sight of the LORD, and
may he deliver me out of all tribulation." 25 Then Saul said to David, "Blessed be you, my
son David! You will do many things and will [t]succeed in them." So David went his way,
and Saul returned to his place.

6 [z][Judg. 7:9-11]
7 [x][See ver. 5 above] [a]ver. 11, 16
8 [b][ch. 24:4, 18]
9 [c]ver. 11, 16, 23; ch. 24:6, 10; [2 Sam. 1:16]
10 [d][Ruth 3:13] [e][ch. 25:38] [f][Gen. 47:29; Deut. 31:14] [g]ch. 31:6
11 [h]ch. 24:6 [i]ver. 7, 16
12 [j]Gen. 2:21; 15:12
16 [k][Ruth 3:13] [l]ver. 7, 11
17 [m]ch. 24:16
18 [n]ch. 24:9, 11
19 [o][Ps. 120:5] [p]2 Sam. 14:16; 20:19; 21:3
20 [q]ch. 24:14
21 [r]ch. 15:24; [ch. 24:17, 18]
23 [s][Ps. 7:8; 18:20]
25 [t][Gen. 32:28]

26:8–9 God has given your enemy into your hand. Abishai uses the same arguments as David's men in 24:4, and David again refuses, adding that God will surely strike Saul instead, a lesson he perhaps learned from the death of Nabal (25:39).

26:11–12 "take now the spear. . . ." So David took the spear. The narrator can say that David took the spear because he was the one who ordered it to be taken. Similarly, Abiathar told David that Saul had killed the priests (22:21), although Doeg did the actual killing.

26:16 you deserve to die, because you have not kept watch over your lord. The "you's" are all plural here in Hebrew—David is accusing Saul's men collectively.

26:19–20 As in 10:1, **heritage** seems to refer both to Israel as the inherited land and to the people as the covenant community (see also 2 Sam. 14:16; 20:19; 21:3). Chasing David away from the Lord's heritage so that he may have no **share** of it and trying to force him to **serve other gods** is a capital offense against the Lord of Israel, who owns the land of Israel and rules his people Israel through his representative, the king. Those who commit this sin should be **cursed before the LORD**. This is what David is conveying to Saul, **the king of Israel** (1 Sam. 26:20). David seems to be near the end of his endurance. "Serve other gods" reflects the common Near Eastern idea that a god could be worshiped only on its own soil (2 Kings 5:17) and also perhaps the idea that one worships the god of the people among whom one lives. This is not David's own view, but his report of the views of others who were **saying** this. First and Second Samuel do not envisage a limitation to the power of the Lord. Certainly God is portrayed as being able to work in Philistia (1 Samuel 4–6), and God even seems to be directing the moves of the Philistine rulers (23:27; 29:4). When David is actually in Philistia, he does in fact worship the Lord (30:6–8; see also note on 29:6). **Partridge** is literally a "calling [bird]." Abner had asked who was "calling" the king (26:14), so David wryly compares himself to "the caller."

27:1–30:31 *David in Philistia.* David and his men finally gain some stability by going to Philistia and serving Achish of Gath, though they manage to avoid attacking Israel. Yet when the Philistines mobilize for a massive attack on Saul's army in the Jezreel Valley, it seems that David must become an enemy

David Flees to the Philistines

27 Then David said in his heart, "Now I shall perish one day by the hand of Saul. There
is nothing better for me than that I should escape to the land of the Philistines.
Then Saul will despair of seeking me any longer within the borders of Israel, and I shall
escape out of his hand." 2 So David arose and went over, he and [u]the six hundred men who
were with him, [v]to Achish the son of Maoch, king of Gath. 3 And David lived with Achish
at Gath, he and his men, every man with his household, and David with [w]his two wives,
Ahinoam of Jezreel, and Abigail of Carmel, Nabal's widow. 4 And when it was told Saul
that David had fled to Gath, he no longer sought him.
5 Then David said to Achish, "If [x]I have found favor in your eyes, let a place be given me
in one of the country towns, that I may dwell there. For why should your servant dwell
in the royal city with you?" 6 So that day Achish gave him [y]Ziklag. Therefore Ziklag has
belonged to the kings of Judah to this day. 7 [z]And the number of the days that David lived
in the country of the Philistines was a year and four months.
8 Now David [a]and his men went up and made raids against [b]the Geshurites, [c]the Girzites,
and [d]the Amalekites, for these were the inhabitants of the land from of old, [e]as far as Shur,
to the land of Egypt. 9 And David would strike the land and would leave neither man nor
woman alive, but would take away the sheep, the oxen, the donkeys, the camels, and the
garments, and come back to Achish. 10 When Achish asked, "Where have you [f]made a raid
today?" David would say, "Against the Negeb of Judah," or, "Against the Negeb of [g]the
Jerahmeelites," or, "Against the Negeb of [h]the Kenites." 11 And David would leave neither
man nor woman alive to bring news to Gath, thinking, "lest they should tell about us and
say, 'So David has done.'" Such was his custom all the while he lived in the country of the
Philistines. 12 And Achish trusted David, thinking, "He has made himself an utter stench
to his people Israel; therefore he shall always be my servant."

Saul and the Medium of En-dor

28 In those days [i]the Philistines gathered their forces for war, to fight against Israel.
And Achish said to David, "Understand that you and your men are to go out with
me in the army." 2 David said to Achish, "Very well, you shall know what your servant can
do." And Achish said to David, "Very well, I will make you my bodyguard for life."
3 Now [j]Samuel had died, and all Israel had mourned for him and buried him [k]in Ramah,

Chapter 27
2 [u]ch. 23:13; [2 Sam. 15:18] [v]ch. 21:10; [1 Kgs. 2:39]
3 [w]See ch. 25:43
5 [x]See Gen. 33:15
6 [y]Josh. 15:31
7 [z][ch. 29:3]
8 [a]See 1 Chr. 12 [b]Josh. 13:2 [c][Josh. 16:10; Judg. 1:29] [d][ch. 15:7, 8] [e]See ch. 15:7
10 [f][ch. 23:27] [g]ch. 30:29 [h]See Judg. 1:16
Chapter 28
1 [i][ch. 29:1]
3 [j]ch. 25:1 [k]ch. 1:19

of his own people. The Philistine lords do not trust him in battle, however, so he and his men go back to their city of Ziklag (30:1), only to find that it has been destroyed by the Amalekites. David manages to pursue and destroy the raiders and gain much spoil, which he shares with the cities of Judah. Chapter 28, the story of Saul and the medium of En-dor, tells how Saul, faced with the Philistine invasion, seeks advice from Samuel through divination but receives only a prophecy of his own death.

27:1–12 *David and Achish.* Here, as in 21:10, David goes to Gath as a mercenary. Whereas before he went anonymously and alone, here he goes in his own name, accompanied by his 600 men and their families, presumably having first negotiated their status with Achish. As he said in 26:19, he has finally concluded that he can no longer stay in Israel. The difficulties experienced by the families of the men (27:3) are also probably an important reason for his move. Whether this Achish is the Achish of 21:10 is not certain; "Achish" may have been a title. But if it is the same person, he is probably more impressed by David's resourcefulness than angry at the previous deception. While David stayed with the technically advanced Philistines, he may have learned some useful things (such as the military system). Though he is the rightful king, he must remain a while longer in exile from Israel.

27:5 David does not mean a specific location with the term **a place**. Asking a lord for land was not an unusual practice. The feudal practice of giving land to the servants of the king was widespread in Israel (22:7) as well as among the Philistines. David probably pointed out to Achish that he and his men were uncultured Israelites; as fugitives, they were used to rough conditions and thus unsuited to life in the sophisticated and probably crowded capital. His real motive, however, was probably to get away from Gath so that he could act freely, without interference.

27:6 The exact location of **Ziklag**, part of the Negeb (Josh. 15:31), is unknown (see note on 1 Sam. 30:9). The Negeb was comparatively distant from Gath, but the nearer cities probably belonged to other vassals of Achish, a fact that David must have been well aware of when he made his request. **to this day**. See Introduction: Date.

27:8 The **Geshurites** are those mentioned as living near the Philistines (Josh. 13:2), not the Geshurites living near Bashan (Josh. 13:11). The **Girzites** are not mentioned elsewhere in the Bible. The **Amalekites** of 1 Samuel 15 and 30 were located to the south, toward the Egyptian border.

27:10 The **Negeb** corresponds to today's northern Negev, i.e., the district east and west of Beersheba and north of Kadesh-barnea. David would tell Achish that he attacked Judahite, Jerahmeelite, or Kenite settlements in the area. The **Jerahmeelites** and **Kenites** are mentioned in 30:29 and seem to have been friendly to Israel. For the Kenites, see note on 15:6.

27:12 always be my servant. Lit., "be my eternal servant," meaning a permanent servant or vassal. Cf. Deut. 15:17; Job 41:4.

28:1–2 *The Philistines Gather for War.* After David has been with Achish for over a year, the Philistines decide on a major attack on Israel involving the forces of all five of their cities. The aim is apparently to gain control over the northern Jezreel Valley, a wide, agriculturally rich plain that goes as far east as the Jordan River. **you and your men are to go out with me**. David, as a vassal of Achish, is naturally expected to participate in the attack. **Bodyguard** is a specific position, while "my servant" (27:12) refers to David's status as the king's subject. The story of the Philistine attack on Israel resumes at 29:1.

28:3–25 *The Medium of En-dor.* Saul faces overwhelming odds in the impending Philistine invasion. In his extremity he apparently decides that the only one who can guide him is the prophet who told him that he had been chosen by God as king to save Israel from its enemies (10:1). Contact with the dead was forbidden by the Lord (see note on 28:3–4), as Saul well knows (v. 3), but he goes ahead anyway. This passage should not be used as an

his own city. And Saul had put [l]the mediums and the necromancers out of the land. **4** The
Philistines assembled and came and encamped [m]at Shunem. And Saul gathered all Israel,
and they encamped [n]at Gilboa. **5** When Saul saw the army of the Philistines, he was afraid,
and his heart trembled greatly. **6** And when Saul inquired of the LORD, [o]the LORD did not
answer him, either [p]by dreams, or [q]by Urim, or by prophets. **7** Then Saul said to his servants,
[r]"Seek out for me a woman who is a medium, that I may go to her and inquire of her." And
his servants said to him, "Behold, there is a medium at [s]En-dor."
8 So Saul [t]disguised himself and put on other garments and went, he and two men with
him. And they came to the woman by night. And he said, [u]"Divine for me by a spirit and
bring up for me whomever I shall name to you." **9** The woman said to him, "Surely you
know what Saul has done, [l]how he has cut off the mediums and the necromancers from
the land. Why then are you laying a trap for my life to bring about my death?" **10** But Saul
swore to her by the LORD, [v]"As the LORD lives, no punishment shall come upon you for
this thing." **11** Then the woman said, "Whom shall I bring up for you?" He said, "Bring up
Samuel for me." **12** When the woman saw Samuel, she cried out with a loud voice. And the
woman said to Saul, "Why have you deceived me? You are Saul." **13** The king said to her,
"Do not be afraid. What do you see?" And the woman said to Saul, "I see a god coming up
out of the earth." **14** He said to her, "What is his appearance?" And she said, "An old man
is coming up, and he is wrapped [w]in a robe." And Saul knew that it was Samuel, and he
bowed with his face to the ground and paid homage.
15 Then Samuel said to Saul, "Why have you disturbed me by bringing me up?" Saul
answered, "I am in great distress, for the Philistines are warring against me, and [x]God has
turned away from me and [y]answers me no more, either by prophets or by dreams. Therefore
I have summoned you to tell me what I shall do." **16** And Samuel said, "Why then do you
ask me, since the LORD has turned from you and become your enemy? **17** The LORD has
done to you as he spoke by me, for [z]the LORD has torn the kingdom out of your hand and
given it to your neighbor, David. **18** [a]Because you did not obey the voice of the LORD and

3 [l][Ex. 22:18; Lev. 19:31; 20:27; Deut. 18:10, 11]
4 [m]Josh. 19:18 [n]ch. 31:1
6 [o]ver. 15; ch. 14:37 [p]Num. 12:6 [q][Ex. 28:30; Num. 27:21; Deut. 33:8]
7 [r][1 Chr. 10:13] [s]Josh. 17:11; Ps. 83:10
8 [t]1 Kgs. 20:38; 22:30; 2 Chr. 18:29; 35:22 [u][Deut. 18:10]
9 [l][See ver. 3 above]
10 [v]See Ruth 3:13
14 [w]ch. 15:27
15 [x]ch. 16:14; 18:12 [y]ver. 6
17 [z]ch. 15:28
18 [a]ch. 15:9

argument for having séances. Though it suggests that in some circumstances a medium may be able to contact the dead, it stresses the wrongness of the practice. Furthermore, the only message from the dead Samuel, besides a repetition of the message of Saul's rejection, was that Saul and his sons would die. The Chronicler specifically mentions this incident as one reason for Saul's death: "So Saul died for his breach of faith . . . in that he did not keep the command of the LORD, and also consulted a medium, seeking guidance. He did not seek guidance from the LORD" (1 Chron. 10:13–14).

28:3–4 Verse 3 gives the information necessary to understand the rest of this chapter, reminding the reader that Samuel was dead (cf. 25:1) and stating that Saul had driven out mediums (cf. 28:9). Verse 4 jumps chronologically to a point following ch. 29; here, the Philistines are already at Shunem, a city on the opposite (north) side of the Jezreel Valley from Mount Gilboa. The Mosaic laws forbade as abominations **mediums** and **necromancers**, who consult the spirits of the dead, as well as other forms of divination (Lev. 19:31; 20:6, 27; Deut. 18:10–12; see also 1 Sam. 15:23). Necromancy and other forms of divination were common throughout the ancient Near East, and many divination texts have been discovered; biblical religion is the only one known to forbid it. Such religious practices were widespread in ancient Canaan (Deut. 18:10–12), and they continued to be a problem throughout the Israelite monarchy (e.g., 2 Kings 21:6; 23:24; Isa. 8:19). By driving out the mediums, Saul was certainly trying to be faithful to the Lord, in his own way. The Hebrew word rendered "medium" in 1 Sam. 28:3, 9 (*'ob*) can mean (1) "the spirit of a dead person" in general (as in v. 8); (2) "necromancy," i.e., divining by an *'ob*; or (3) "a medium," i.e., one who practices necromancy. In v. 7, "a woman who is a medium" is literally "a woman who has an *'ob*." The term "necromancers" (*yidde 'oni*), which always appears with "mediums," is literally "(all-) knowing"; it refers to the practice of necromancy or to its practitioner, but not to the spirit of the dead.

28:6 By dreams, or by Urim, or by prophets were the allowable means of determining the will of the Lord. **The LORD did not answer** because he had rejected Saul from being king (15:23).

28:7 En-dor was 4.5 miles (7.2 km) northeast of Shunem, where the Philistines were encamped, so it was on the other side of the enemy from Saul.

28:8 Night was the appropriate time for consulting the spirits of the dead. Saul's fasting (v. 20) may also have been in preparation for the ceremony.

28:11 There is no description of the wording used to call up Samuel from the dead. Perhaps the writer did not even want to mention the actual deed.

28:12 she cried out with a loud voice. Perhaps Samuel's appearance surprised the woman and she thought something was happening outside her control. Another possibility is that her previous activities had called up only deceptive demonic imitations of a dead person's spirit, but this time she suddenly realized that something much more real was happening. Readers are not told how the woman realized who **Saul** was. Perhaps the spirit called his name as he came up.

28:13–14 A god is literally "gods" with a plural verbal form, so not "God," which is a plural noun but takes a singular verb. This term is used of the spirits of the dead in ancient Near Eastern texts. The Moabite "gods" may also have been the spirits of the dead (see Num. 25:2; Ps. 106:28). Saul, however, is interested in Samuel as a person and asks about **his** (singular) **appearance**. The **robe** was Samuel's characteristic garment (1 Sam. 15:27).

28:15–19 Then Samuel said to Saul. The character of this event has long been debated—whether the spirit was really Samuel, or how the medium could command the spirit of a holy prophet. As far as the narrator is concerned, this really is the spirit of the dead prophet Samuel. He is called "Samuel" in vv. 15–16. He speaks much as he had spoken to Saul during his lifetime (cf. vv. 16–18 with 15:18, 26–28: in both places, Samuel describes David as Saul's "neighbor"). He uses the name of **the LORD** seven times, and adds the true prophecy that Saul and his **sons** will die. It is hard to think that the narrator thought this was a deceptive illusion performed by the woman or some demonic spirit deceiving Saul. An evil spirit would not deliver a true prophecy or true words to Saul, as Samuel does in 28:16–19. That the woman's actions brought Samuel up is implied by v. 15, **Why have you disturbed me**? So whatever the limits on a medium's power normally were, in this case the Lord let her rouse the spirit of Samuel himself.

28:19 Be with me may simply mean that Saul will die, but some think it implies more, that Saul's spirit will join Samuel's in the place of the dead (perhaps even among those whose sins are forgiven). In 2 Sam. 12:23, David

19[b]ch. 31:2
21[c]See Judg. 12:3

Chapter 29

1[d]ch. 28:1 [e]ch. 4:1; Josh. 12:18 [f]Judg. 7:1 [g]Josh. 17:16
2[h]Josh. 13:3 [i]ch. 28:1, 2
3[j][ch. 27:7] [k][Dan. 6:5]
4[h][See ver. 2 above] [l]ch. 27:6; 30:1 [m][ch. 14:21]

did not carry out his fierce wrath against Amalek, therefore the LORD has done this thing
to you this day. 19 Moreover, the LORD will give Israel also with you into the hand of the
Philistines, and tomorrow you [b]and your sons shall be with me. The LORD will give the
army of Israel also into the hand of the Philistines."
20 Then Saul fell at once full length on the ground, filled with fear because of the words
of Samuel. And there was no strength in him, for he had eaten nothing all day and all
night. 21 And the woman came to Saul, and when she saw that he was terrified, she said
to him, "Behold, your servant has obeyed you. [c]I have taken my life in my hand and have
listened to what you have said to me. 22 Now therefore, you also obey your servant. Let me
set a morsel of bread before you; and eat, that you may have strength when you go on your
way." 23 He refused and said, "I will not eat." But his servants, together with the woman,
urged him, and he listened to their words. So he arose from the earth and sat on the bed.
24 Now the woman had a fattened calf in the house, and she quickly killed it, and she took
flour and kneaded it and baked unleavened bread of it, 25 and she put it before Saul and
his servants, and they ate. Then they rose and went away that night.

The Philistines Reject David

29 [d]Now the Philistines had gathered all their forces at [e]Aphek. And the Israelites were
encamped by [f]the spring that is in [g]Jezreel. 2 As [h]the lords of the Philistines were
passing on by hundreds and by thousands, and David and his men were passing on in
the rear [i]with Achish, 3 the commanders of the Philistines said, "What are these Hebrews
doing here?" And Achish said to the commanders of the Philistines, "Is this not David, the
servant of Saul, king of Israel, who has been with me [j]now for days and years, and since
he deserted to me [k]I have found no fault in him to this day." 4 But [h]the commanders of
the Philistines were angry with him. And the commanders of the Philistines said to him,
"Send the man back, that he may return [l]to the place to which you have assigned him. He
shall not go down with us to battle, [m]lest in the battle he become an adversary to us. For

says he will eventually go to his dead son. Sometimes the term "Sheol" refers to the place of the dead, which was pictured as being below the earth (the spirit of Samuel is "brought up"; cf. 1 Sam. 28:8, 13, 15). In such cases, no distinction is made between the pious and the wicked. In other cases, a distinction is crucial (see note on Ps. 49:15).

28:24 A **fattened calf** is a stall-fed calf that was being prepared for eating, rather than a pasture-fed calf.

28:25 Saul **went away**, back to Gilboa. Saul apparently accepted that his death was the unalterable word of the Lord; he does not try to escape the battle on the next day.

29:1–11 *The Philistine Rulers Reject David.* Although Achish of Gath trusts David, the other Philistine commanders suspect that he would betray them, and they insist that he be sent home. In God's providence, David is thus spared the occasion to shed Israelite blood.

29:1 The story backtracks to right after 28:2, partially repeating 28:1. Here the Philistines are still at their gathering point in **Aphek**, while in 28:4 they had already advanced to Shunem. Aphek was also where the Philistines had camped in 4:1 (see maps, p. 499 and to the right). Because it was at the northernmost point in the Philistine coastal plain, it was a strategic place to gather for a general attack on the Jezreel Valley. The **spring** is probably the spring of Harod, southeast of the city of Jezreel at the foot of Mount Gilboa; here Gideon encamped against the Midianites (Judg. 7:1).

29:2–3 The **lords of the Philistines** are the rulers of the five Philistine cities (see 6:4, 16–18). These *seranim* (Hb.) in 29:2, 6, and 7 seem to be the same as the **commanders**, or "rulers" (Hb. *sarim*; plural of *sar*), in vv. 3, 4, and 9. An inscription from Ekron gives evidence that *sar* was the title of the ruler of a Philistine city.

29:4 Unlike Achish, the other Philistine **commanders** mistrusted David, fearing that he would seek to regain the favor of Saul (**his lord**) by presenting to him **the heads of the men here** (probably meaning "our heads"). One can see the hand of the Lord working even through the Philistine commanders to keep David from fighting the Lord's people, which he had managed to avoid doing so far. That would probably have shut him off from being accepted by Israel as king (27:8–12) and would have been a terrible evil (see note on 25:32–35).

David Recovers Plunder from the Amalekites

As David and his men sought refuge in Philistia, the Philistines gathered their forces at Aphek to attack the Israelites. The Philistine commanders, skeptical of David's loyalty in battle against his fellow Israelites, sent him to his home in Ziklag. When David arrived, he discovered that the Amalekites had raided the Negeb and burned Ziklag to the ground, carrying away many captives and belongings. David and his men pursued them, crossing the Besor Brook and attacking the Amalekites. He recovered all that had been taken, returned to Ziklag, and sent a portion of the spoils to the leaders of towns in the region (the locations of Bethel, Siphmoth, Racal, and Athach are unknown).

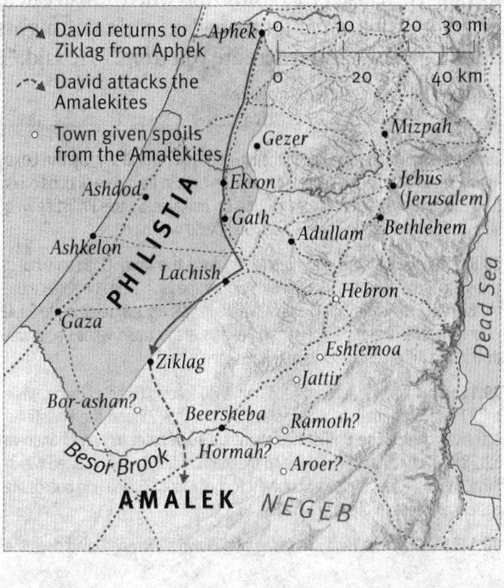

how could this fellow reconcile himself to his lord? Would it not be with the heads of the
men here? 5 Is not this David, of whom they sing to one another in dances,

[n]"Saul has struck down his thousands,
and David his ten thousands'?"

6 Then Achish called David and said to him, [o]"As the LORD lives, you have been honest, and
to me it seems right that [p]you should march out and in with me in the campaign. For I have
found nothing wrong in you from the day of your coming to me to this day. Nevertheless, the
lords do not approve of you. 7 So go back now; and go peaceably, that you may not displease
the lords of the Philistines." 8 And David said to Achish, "But what have I done? What have
you found in your servant from the day I entered your service until now, that I may not go
and fight against the enemies of my lord the king?" 9 And Achish answered David and said,
"I know that you are as blameless in my sight [q]as an angel of God. Nevertheless, [r]the commanders of the Philistines have said, 'He shall not go up with us to the battle.' 10 Now then rise
early in the morning [s]with the servants of your lord who came with you, and start early in the
morning, and depart as soon as you have light." 11 So David set out with his men early in the
morning to return to the land of the Philistines. But the Philistines went up to [t]Jezreel.

David's Wives Are Captured

30 Now when David and his men came to [u]Ziklag on the third day, [v]the Amalekites had
[w]made a raid against the Negeb and against Ziklag. They had overcome Ziklag and
burned it with fire 2 and taken captive the women and all[1] who were in it, both small and
great. They killed no one, but carried them off and went their way. 3 And when David and his
men came to the city, they found it burned with fire, and their wives and sons and daughters
taken captive. 4 Then David and the people who were with him raised their voices and wept
until they had no more strength to weep. 5 David's [x]two wives also had been taken captive,
Ahinoam of Jezreel and Abigail the widow of Nabal of Carmel. 6 And David was greatly
distressed, for the people spoke [y]of stoning him, because all the people were bitter in soul,[2]
each for his sons and daughters. But David strengthened himself in the LORD his God.
7 [z]And David said to Abiathar the priest, the son of Ahimelech, "Bring me the ephod." So
Abiathar brought the ephod to David. 8 [a]And David inquired of the LORD, "Shall I pursue
after this [b]band? Shall I overtake them?" He answered him, "Pursue, for you shall surely
overtake [c]and shall surely rescue." 9 So David set out, and [d]the six hundred men who were
with him, and they came to the brook Besor, where those who were left behind stayed.
10 But David pursued, he and four hundred men. [e]Two hundred stayed behind, who were
too exhausted to cross the brook Besor.
11 They found an Egyptian in the open country and brought him to David. And they gave
him bread and he ate. They gave him water to drink, 12 and they gave him a piece of a cake of
figs and two clusters of raisins. And when he had eaten, [f]his spirit revived, for he had not eaten
bread or drunk water for three days and three nights. 13 And David said to him, "To whom
do you belong? And where are you from?" He said, "I am a young man of Egypt, servant to

[1] Septuagint; Hebrew lacks *and all* [2] Compare 22:2

5 [n]ch. 18:7; 21:11
6 [o]See ch. 20:3 [p]2 Sam. 3:25; 2 Kgs. 19:27; Ps. 121:8; Isa. 37:28
9 [q]2 Sam. 14:17, 20; 19:27 [r]Josh. 13:3
10 [s][1 Chr. 12:19, 22]
11 [t]Josh. 17:16

Chapter 30

1 [u]ch. 29:4, 11 [v]ch. 27:8; [ch. 15:3, 7] [w]ver. 14
5 [x]See ch. 25:42, 43
6 [y][Ex. 17:4; Num. 14:10]
7 [z]ch. 23:6, 9
8 [a]See ch. 22:10 [b][1 Chr. 12:21] [c]ver. 18
9 [d]See ch. 23:13
10 [e]ver. 21
12 [f]Judg. 15:19; [ch. 14:27]

29:6 It seems strange that Achish the Philistine ruler would say "**as the LORD lives.**" Yet to polytheistic people, to make an oath in the name of gods other than the gods they normally serve is not unthinkable. So this Philistine king may well have sworn to David by the God David worshiped.

29:8 fight against the enemies of my lord the king. One can suspect ambiguity here as to the identity of "my lord the king." On the surface the phrase refers to Achish, but it is possible David was actually referring to Saul, whose enemies were the Philistines. Readers are not told what David was thinking, but the commanders may have been wise.

29:11 From here, the action splits. Chapter 30 follows David's actions, while ch. 31 is a continuation of Saul's actions in 28:5–25 and the Philistines' actions in ch. 29. **The Philistines went up to Jezreel** by way of Shunem (cf. 28:4, then ch. 31). Saul's visit to the medium (28:5–25) occurred within this location. Jezreel is at the northwest foot of Mount Gilboa and guards the eastern entrance to the Jezreel Valley.

30:1–31 *Amalekite Raid on Ziklag and David's Victory.* David does the kingly work of delivering the people of Ziklag from their Amalekite captors, and of leading his own followers in dividing the spoil generously.

30:1 the third day. It was about 50 miles (81 km) from Aphek to Ziklag. The Amalekites surely knew that the bulk of the armies of Philistia and Judah (v. 14) had gone to the battle in the north, and they took advantage of that fact.

30:6 But David strengthened himself in the LORD his God, and God comforts and strengthens him. Rather than despairing, David turns to God in prayer and worship (cf. Ps. 56:3–4).

30:7 As in 23:9–10, David has **Abiathar** inquire of the Lord, using the sacred lots kept in the ephod. The Lord is still guiding David (30:8).

30:9 If the hypothesis is correct that Ziklag was Tel esh-Sheriah and the **brook Besor** was Wadi Ghazzeh, this takes place about 12 miles (19 km) southwest of Ziklag.

30:11–12 Bread here may refer simply to bread, or it may be a general term for food, so that what they specifically gave the Egyptian is stated in the next sentence. The sugar of the dried fruit would have had an immediate effect.

an Amalekite, and my master left me behind because I fell sick three days ago. 14 [g]We had
made a raid against the Negeb of [h]the Cherethites and against that which belongs to Judah
and against the Negeb of Caleb, and we burned Ziklag with fire." 15 And David said to him,
"Will you take me down to this band?" And he said, "Swear to me by God that you will not
kill me or deliver me into the hands of my master, and I will take you down to this [i]band."

David Defeats the Amalekites

16 And when he had taken him down, behold, they were spread abroad over all the
land, eating and drinking and dancing, because of all the great spoil they had taken from
the land of the Philistines and from the land of Judah. 17 And David struck them down
from twilight until the evening of the next day, and not a man of them escaped, except
four hundred young men, who mounted camels and fled. 18 [j]David recovered all that the
Amalekites had taken, and David rescued his two wives. 19 Nothing was missing, whether
small or great, sons or daughters, spoil or anything that had been taken. [j]David brought
back all. 20 David also captured all the flocks and herds, and the people drove the livestock
before him,[1] and said, "This is David's spoil."

21 Then David came to [k]the two hundred men who had been too exhausted to follow
David, and who had been left [k]at the brook Besor. And they went out to meet David and to
meet the people who were with him. And when David came near to the people he greeted
them. 22 Then all the wicked and worthless fellows among the men who had gone with
David said, "Because they did not go with us, we will not give them any of the spoil that
we have recovered, except that each man may lead away his wife and children, and depart."
23 But David said, "You shall not do so, my brothers, with what the LORD has given us. He
has preserved us and given into our hand the band that came against us. 24 Who would
listen to you in this matter? [l]For as his share is who goes down into the battle, so shall his
share be who stays by the baggage. They shall share alike." 25 And he made it a statute and
a rule for Israel from that day forward to this day.

26 When David came to Ziklag, he sent part of the spoil to his friends, the elders of Judah,
saying, "Here is a present for you from the spoil of the enemies of the LORD." 27 It was for those
in [m]Bethel, in Ramoth of the Negeb, in [n]Jattir, 28 in [o]Aroer, in Siphmoth, in [p]Eshtemoa, 29 in
Racal, in the cities of [q]the Jerahmeelites, in the cities of [r]the Kenites, 30 in [s]Hormah, in Bor-
ashan, in Athach, 31 in [t]Hebron, for all the places where David and his men had roamed.

The Death of Saul

31 [u]Now the Philistines were fighting against Israel, and the men of Israel fled before
the Philistines and fell slain [v]on Mount Gilboa. 2 And the Philistines overtook Saul
and his sons, and the Philistines struck down [w]Jonathan and [x]Abinadab and Malchi-shua,
the sons of Saul. 3 [y]The battle pressed hard against Saul, and the archers found him, and he

[1] The meaning of the Hebrew clause is uncertain

14 [g]ver. 1 [h]2 Sam. 8:18; 15:18; 20:7, 23; 1 Kgs. 1:38, 44; 1 Chr. 18:17; [Ezek. 25:16; Zeph. 2:5]
15 [i][ch. 25:3]
18 [j]ver. 8
19 [j][See ver. 18 above]
21 [k]ver. 10
24 [l][Num. 31:27; Josh. 22:8]
27 [m]Gen. 28:19; See Judg. 1:22-26 [n]Josh. 15:48
28 [o]Deut. 2:36; Josh. 13:16 [p]Josh. 15:50
29 [q]ch. 27:10 [r]See Judg. 1:16
30 [s]Judg. 1:17
31 [t]Josh. 14:13-15; Judg. 1:10; 2 Sam. 2:1-4

Chapter 31

1 [u]For ver. 1-13, see 1 Chr. 10:1-12 [v]ch. 28:4; [2 Sam. 1:6, 21; 21:12]
2 [w]1 Chr. 8:33 [x][ch. 14:49]
3 [y][2 Sam. 1:6]

30:14 "Cherethites" seems to be a synonym for "Philistines" in Ezek. 25:16 and Zeph. 2:5. Since the Philistines are known to be of Aegean origin, the word probably derived from "Cretan." So the **Negeb of the Cherethites** is probably southern Philistia. The **Negeb of Caleb** is the area south of Hebron.

30:17 The word translated **twilight** usually means "dusk" but occasionally it can also mean "dawn," and the sense here is disputed. If it means "dawn," David and his men probably waited until morning to attack in order to avoid killing their own people or letting the Amalekites escape, and the battle continued during the daylight hours until sunset, which would be considered the start of the next day (see note on 14:28). The singular subject **David** in 30:17–20 stresses that this was David's personal victory.

30:19 Nothing was missing. Under God's direction (vv. 8, 23), David, who would soon be king, rescued every one of the people who had sided with him, and for whom he was responsible.

30:22 Worthless is also used variously to describe a supposedly drunken woman (1:16), Eli's sons (2:12), the men who opposed Saul (10:27), Nabal (25:25), David as described by Shimei (2 Sam. 16:7), and the rebel Sheba (2 Sam. 20:1).

30:24 They shall share alike. David, who will rule as a righteous king, generously distributes the spoils of victory to all who sided with him, and even gives gifts to others (vv. 26–31) who will soon be his subjects.

30:25 Rule (Hb. *mishpat*) is translated elsewhere as "custom" (2:13), "ways" (8:11), and "rights and duties" (10:25).

30:26–31 See note on v. 24. **Hebron** was the major city in the area. **Bethel** is not the famous Bethel (7:16; 10:3; 13:2) but an otherwise unknown city in Judah. **Jattir** and **Eshtemoa** are Levitical cities in the Judean hills (Josh. 15:48, 50; 21:14); **Bor-ashan** is probably Ashan in the Shephelah (Josh. 19:7). The locations of the other places are uncertain. The position of Hebron at the end of the list points toward David's going to Hebron and being made king (2 Sam. 2:4).

31:1–13 *Deaths of Saul and Jonathan.* The army of Israel is completely defeated, Saul's sons are killed, Saul kills himself to avoid capture, and the Philistines take over the region. But the men of Jabesh-gilead, the city that Saul saved at the beginning of his reign, bravely rescue the bodies of Saul and his sons from dishonor.

31:1 The events of this chapter directly follow those of chs. 28 and 29. The Philistines have left their camp at Shunem and are attacking the Israelite army on Mount Gilboa (cf. 28:4; see map, p. 540).

was badly wounded by the archers. 4 [z]Then Saul said to his armor-bearer, "Draw your sword,
and thrust me through with it, lest these [a]uncircumcised come and thrust me through,
and mistreat me." But his armor-bearer would not, [b]for he feared greatly. Therefore Saul
took his own sword [c]and fell upon it. 5 And when his armor-bearer saw that Saul was dead,
he also fell upon his sword and died with him. 6 Thus Saul died, and his three sons, and
his armor-bearer, and all his men, on the same day together. 7 And when the men of Israel
who were on the other side of the valley and those beyond the Jordan saw that the men
of Israel had fled and that Saul and his sons were dead, they abandoned their cities and
fled. And the Philistines came and lived in them.

8 The next day, when the Philistines came to strip the slain, they found Saul and his three
sons fallen on Mount Gilboa. 9 So they cut off his head and stripped off his armor and sent
messengers throughout the land of the Philistines, [d]to carry the good news [e]to the house
of their idols and to the people. 10 [f]They put his armor in the temple of [g]Ashtaroth, and
they fastened his body to the wall of [h]Beth-shan. 11 [i]But when the inhabitants of Jabesh-
gilead heard what the Philistines had done to Saul, 12 [j]all the valiant men arose and went
all night and took the body of Saul and the bodies of his sons from the wall of Beth-shan,
and they came to Jabesh [k]and burned them there. 13 And they took their bones [l]and buried
them under [m]the tamarisk tree in Jabesh and [n]fasted seven days.

4 [z][Judg. 9:54] [a]See Judg. 14:3 [b][2 Sam. 1:14] [c][2 Sam. 1:10]
9 [d][2 Sam. 1:20] [e][Judg. 16:23, 24]
10 [f][ch. 21:9] [g]See Judg. 2:13 [h]Josh. 17:11
11 [i]2 Sam. 21:10; See ch. 11:1-11
12 [j]2 Sam. 2:4-7 [k][2 Chr. 16:14; 21:19; Jer. 34:5]
13 [l]2 Sam. 21:12, 14 [m][ch. 22:6] [n][Gen. 50:10]

The Battle at Mount Gilboa

c. 1010 B.C.

Philistine forces advanced to Shunem from Aphek and prepared to attack the Israelites near their camp in Jezreel. Saul, fearing the great army that faced him, slipped away during the night to consult a medium at En-dor in order to seek the counsel of the deceased Samuel. When the Philistines attacked the next morning, the Israelites retreated up the slopes of Mount Gilboa. Saul and three of his sons were killed, and the Philistines mocked Israel by hanging their bodies on the wall of Beth-shean. Later, men from Jabesh-gilead traveled through the night and recovered the bodies.

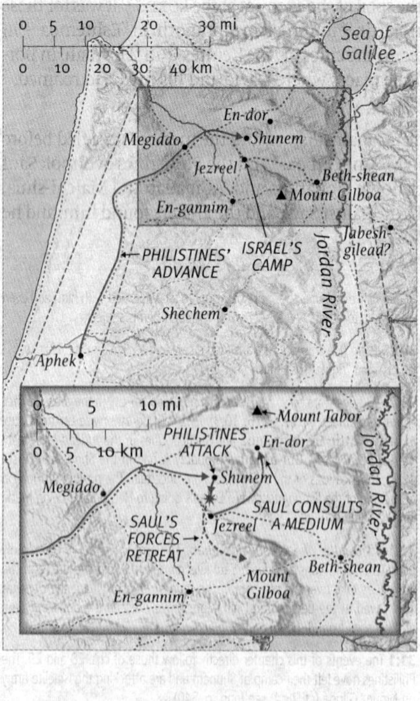

31:4 Saul took his own sword and fell upon it. See note on 2 Sam. 1:6–10 for the claim that Saul did not commit suicide but rather was killed by an Amalekite.

31:6 As Samuel's spirit had said (cf. 28:19), the Lord gave Israel into the hands of the Philistines, and Saul and his sons joined the dead. Truly, "Your glory, O Israel, is slain on your high places!" (2 Sam. 1:19).

31:7 The **other side of the valley** is the north side of the Jezreel Valley.

31:10 Beth-shan is at the junction of the north-south road along the Jordan Valley and the road from Gilead to the Jezreel Valley. It was occupied almost continuously until the early Arab period. A temple of the eleventh century B.C. to the fertility goddess Anit has been discovered there. This may have been the **temple** referred to here, because **Ashtaroth** can refer to goddesses in general (see note on 7:3–4). During the Iron Age, Beth-shan was occupied by the Philistines. Excavations at the site have confirmed this settlement by the recovery of vast amounts of Philistine pottery, weapons, tools, and jewelry dating to the Iron I and II periods (1200–586 B.C.).

31:11–13 Saul had saved **Jabesh-gilead** at the beginning of his reign (ch. 11), a fact that the men of the city remembered. They cross the Jordan and go about 10 miles (16 km) to Beth-shan. The burning of bodies was usually considered desecration, but here the purpose may have been to keep them from further dishonor. **bones**. Even after lengthy burning, large bones would remain. David later reburied the bones (2 Sam. 21:12–14).

INTRODUCTION TO

2 SAMUEL

See Introduction to 1–2 Samuel, pp. 485–490.

Outline

- I. Story of King David (1:1–20:26)
  - A. David and the death of Saul (1:1–27)
  - B. David becomes king (2:1–5:5)
  - C. Jerusalem, the city of David (5:6–25)
  - D. Zion, the place of worship (6:1–23)
  - E. Davidic covenant: eternal throne (7:1–29)
  - F. Catalog of David's military activities (8:1–18)
  - G. Mephibosheth (9:1–13)
  - H. Israel-Ammon war (10:1–12:31)
    1. Beginning of Israel-Ammon war (10:1–19)
    2. David and Bathsheba (11:1–12:25)
    3. End of Israel-Ammon war (12:26–31)
  - I. Absalom's banishment and reinstatement (13:1–14:33)
  - J. Absalom's rebellion (15:1–19:43)
    1. Absalom's conspiracy (15:1–12)
    2. David's escape from Absalom (15:13–16:14)
    3. Ahithophel and Hushai (16:15–17:23)
    4. David arrives at Mahanaim (17:24–29)
    5. Death of Absalom (18:1–19:8a)
    6. David's return to Jerusalem (19:8b–43)
  - K. Sheba's rebellion (20:1–26)
- II. Epilogue (21:1–24:25)
  - A. Famine and the death of Saul's sons (21:1–14)
  - B. Philistine wars (21:15–22)
  - C. Song of David (22:1–51)
  - D. Last words of David (23:1–7)
  - E. David's heroes (23:8–39)
  - F. The census and the threshing floor (24:1–25)

2 SAMUEL

David Hears of Saul's Death

1 After the death of Saul, when David had returned [a]from striking down the Amalekites,
David remained two days in Ziklag. **2** And on the third day, behold, [b]a man came from
Saul's camp, [c]with his clothes torn and dirt on his head. And when he came to David, [d]he
fell to the ground and paid homage. **3** David said to him, "Where do you come from?"
And he said to him, "I have escaped from the camp of Israel." **4** And David said to him,
[e]"How did it go? Tell me." And he answered, "The people fled from the battle, and also
many of the people have fallen and are dead, and Saul and his son Jonathan are also
dead." **5** Then David said to the young man who told him, "How do you know that Saul
and his son Jonathan are dead?" **6** And the young man who told him said, [f]"By chance I
happened to be on Mount Gilboa, and there was Saul leaning on his spear, and behold,
the chariots and the horsemen were close upon him. **7** And when he looked behind him,
he saw me, and called to me. And I answered, 'Here I am.' **8** And he said to me, 'Who are
you?' I answered him, 'I am an Amalekite.' **9** And he said to me, [g]'Stand beside me and
kill me, for anguish has seized me, and yet my life still lingers.' **10** So I stood beside him
and killed him, because I was sure that he could not live after he had fallen. [h]And I took
the crown that was on his head and the armlet that was on his arm, and I have brought
them here to my lord."

11 Then David took hold of his clothes and [i]tore them, and so did all the men who were
with him. **12** And they mourned and wept [j]and fasted until evening for Saul and for Jonathan
his son and for the people of the LORD and for the house of Israel, because they had fallen
by the sword. **13** And David said to the young man who told him, "Where do you come
from?" And he answered, "I am the son of a sojourner, an Amalekite." **14** David said to him,
"How is it you were not [k]afraid to put out your hand to destroy [l]the LORD's anointed?"
15 Then [m]David called one of the young men and said, "Go, execute him." And he struck
him down so that he died. **16** And David said to him, [n]"Your blood be on your head, for your
own mouth has testified against you, saying, 'I have killed [o]the LORD's anointed.'"

Chapter 1
1 [a]See 1 Sam. 30:17-20
2 [b]ch. 4:10 [c]See Josh. 7:6 [d]ch. 14:4
4 [e][1 Sam. 4:16]
6 [f]For ver. 6-10, see 1 Sam. 31:1-4; 1 Chr. 10:1-6
9 [g][Judg. 9:54]
10 [h][2 Kgs. 11:12]
11 [i]ch. 13:31; [ch. 3:31]; See Josh. 7:6
12 [j][ch. 3:35]
14 [k][1 Sam. 24:6, 10; 26:9; 31:4] [l]See 1 Sam. 12:3
15 [m]ch. 4:10
16 [n][ch. 3:29; Josh. 2:19; 1 Kgs. 2:32, 37; Matt. 27:25] [o]See 1 Sam. 12:3

1:1–20:26 *Story of King David.* Most of 2 Samuel recounts the rise of David's kingship, first over Judah and then over all Israel, and the major challenge to David's rule resulting from David's own sins.

1:1–27 *David and the Death of Saul.* The earliest history of the Israelite monarchy now moves into its second stage, the era of King David. The narrator first looks back to the end of Saul's life (the death of Saul and his sons at Mount Gilboa; 1 Samuel 31). David, who is in Ziklag, hears of the death of Saul. But instead of rejoicing, he mourns Saul's death and executes the man who claims to have killed Saul. His elegy shows his deep personal grief over the deaths of Saul and Jonathan in battle. David was not a vengeful rebel against Saul, and thus can receive the kingship in good conscience.

1:1–2 Verse 1 follows the events of 1 Samuel 30; in 2 Sam. 1:2 an Amalekite man (cf. v. 8) arrives to report the events of 1 Samuel 31. Saul probably died at about the same time that David returned to **Ziklag**, since the Amalekite arrived on the **third day** after David's return. The torn **clothes** and **dirt** are signs of mourning (see note on 1 Sam. 4:12).

1:6–10 So I stood beside him and killed him (v. 10). The narrator (whom readers should believe) in 1 Samuel 31 says that Saul killed himself. Having already read that, readers know that this man is lying to gain favor with the person who was most likely to replace Saul as king. Saul had destroyed most of the Amalekites (1 Samuel 15), but since this man was the son of a sojourner (2 Sam. 1:13), his presence in Israel is no surprise. The **crown** and the **armlet** are the royal insignia; the crown was given to the king at the time of his investiture (2 Kings 11:12); "armlet" appears elsewhere only in Num. 31:50, where it is an ornament worn by Midianites.

1:12 David and his men **fasted** as a sign of mourning (as in 1 Sam. 31:13; 2 Sam. 3:35). After this summary statement, the story resumes the actual dialogue between David and the young man who brought this news of Saul's death.

1:14 How is it you were not afraid . . . to destroy the LORD's anointed? See note on 1 Sam. 24:6. As a sojourner who was subject to the laws of Israel (Lev. 24:22), the Amalekite should have recognized the sanctity of Saul as his king (contrast Saul's armor-bearer; 1 Sam. 31:4–5). David himself had refrained from killing Saul (1 Samuel 24; 26). Clearly, David did not ascend to the throne through violence or disloyalty (cf. note on 2 Sam. 1:1–27).

1:15 Go, execute him. David believed the Amalekite's story (but see note on vv. 6–10), and on that basis had him put to death. David's action provides

17 [p][ch. 3:33; 2 Chr. 35:25]
18 [q]Josh. 10:13
19 [r]ver. 25, 27
20 [s]Mic. 1:10 [t][1 Sam. 31:9; Amos 3:9] [u][Ex. 15:20; Judg. 11:34] [v]See Judg. 14:3
21 [w]1 Sam. 31:1 [x][1 Sam. 10:1]

David's Lament for Saul and Jonathan

17 And David [p]lamented with this lamentation over Saul and Jonathan his son, **18** and
he said it[1] should be taught to the people of Judah; behold, it is written in [q]the Book of
Jashar.[2] He said:

19 "Your glory, O Israel, is slain on your high places!
[r]How the mighty have fallen!
20 [s]Tell it not in Gath,
[t]publish it not in the streets of Ashkelon,
[u]lest the daughters of the Philistines rejoice,
lest the daughters of [v]the uncircumcised exult.

21 [w]"You mountains of Gilboa,
let there be no dew or rain upon you,
nor fields of offerings![3]
For there the shield of the mighty was defiled,
the shield of Saul, not [x]anointed with oil.

22 "From the blood of the slain,
from the fat of the mighty,

[1] Septuagint; Hebrew *the Bow*, which may be the name of the lament's tune [2] Or *of the upright* [3] Septuagint *firstfruits*

clear evidence that he had no complicity in Saul's death. Though the Amalekite intended to win David's favor, David made it clear that his action constituted the murder of "the LORD's anointed" (v. 14), for which the just punishment would be execution.

1:16 Your blood be on your head means that the Amalekite (not David) is responsible for his own death (see Josh. 2:19; 1 Kings 2:32, 37; Ezek. 33:4).

1:17–27 And David lamented. David's lament is a profound expression of public and personal grief. As part of the historical records of David's reign, the lament provides lasting evidence of David's innocent ascent to the throne (cf. notes on vv. 1–27 and 14). Though grievously wronged by Saul, David nonetheless chose to remember Saul in a generous way, setting an example of graciously emphasizing the good that someone has done after that person dies. The recurring theme of **how the mighty have fallen** (vv. 19, 25, 27) provides the structure of David's lament, which exhorts Israel first to mourn **Saul** (v. 23) and then to mourn **my brother Jonathan** (v. 26), then closes with the repetition of the haunting refrain, "How the mighty have fallen" (v. 27).

1:18 The ESV text, saying **it should be taught**, refers to the lament that follows. The Hebrew text (see ESV footnote) is "the Bow should be taught to the people of Judah." This may be a heading, meaning, "In order to give the men of Judah military training (with the bow and other weapons)." Compare the heading of Psalm 60, "A Miktam of David; for instruction." Or, "the Bow" may be the name of the melody for this lament. The **Book of Jashar** is a non-biblical written source which also included Josh. 10:12–13 and, according to the Septuagint text, Solomon's poem in 1 Kings 8:12–13.

1:19 How the mighty have fallen! This is the theme line of David's lament for Saul and Jonathan, repeated in v. 25 and at the end in v. 27. Verses 19 and 25 form a literary "envelope" (or *inclusio*) that constitutes an inverted distant parallelism. That is, v. 19a (**Your glory . . . is slain on your high places**) is parallel to v. 25b ("Jonathan lies slain on your high places"), while v. 19b ("How the mighty have fallen") is repeated in v. 25a.

1:20 Gath and **Ashkelon** are Philistine cities. David cannot bear to think about the Philistine victory celebrations (cf. the Israelite women rejoicing in 1 Sam. 18:6–7).

1:21 let there be no dew or rain . . . nor fields of offerings! David wishes for lack of blessing on the place where Saul and Jonathan died. The line **the shield of the mighty was defiled** is paralleled by the next line, **the shield of Saul, not anointed with oil** (i.e., "not in proper condition," since leather shields were treated with oil).

1:22 Blood and **fat** are often used as a word pair to refer to the whole of a sacrifice. For **bow of Jonathan**, see 1 Sam. 20:20.

The Setting of 2 Samuel

c. 1000 B.C.

The book of 2 Samuel recounts David's reign over Israel and his battles to establish Israel as the dominant power in Syria and Palestine. David expanded Israel's borders from Saul's fledgling territory until, by the end of his reign, he controlled all of Israel, Edom, Moab, Ammon, Syria, and Zobah. Other kingdoms, such as Tyre and Hamath, established treaties with him.

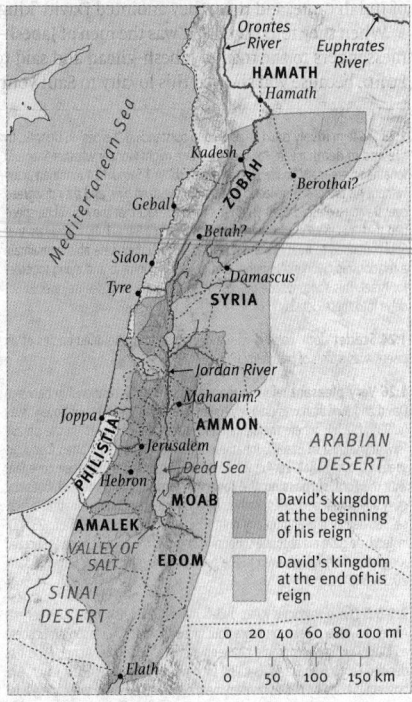

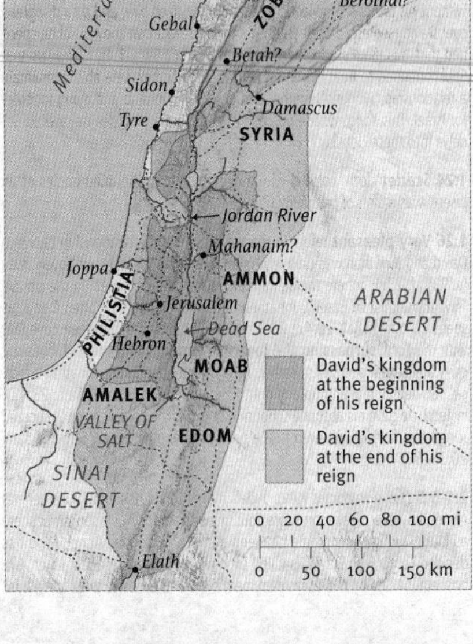

[y]the bow of Jonathan turned not back,
and the sword of Saul returned not empty.

23 "Saul and Jonathan, beloved and lovely!
In life and in death they were not divided;
they were [z]swifter than eagles;
they were [a]stronger than lions.

24 "You daughters of Israel, weep over Saul,
who clothed you luxuriously in scarlet,
[b]who put ornaments of gold on your apparel.

25 [c]"How the mighty have fallen
in the midst of the battle!

"Jonathan lies slain on your high places.
26 I am distressed for you, my brother Jonathan;
very pleasant have you been to me;
[d]your love to me was extraordinary,
surpassing the love of women.

27 [c]"How the mighty have fallen,
and the weapons of war perished!"

David Anointed King of Judah

2 After this David [e]inquired of the LORD, "Shall I go up into any of the cities of Judah?"
And the LORD said to him, "Go up." David said, "To which shall I go up?" And he said,
"To [f]Hebron." 2 So David went up there, and [g]his two wives also, Ahinoam of Jezreel and
Abigail the widow of Nabal of Carmel. 3 And David brought up [h]his men who were with
him, everyone with his household, and they lived in the towns of Hebron. 4 And the men
of Judah came, and there they anointed David [i]king over the house of Judah.
When they told David, [j]"It was the men of Jabesh-gilead who buried Saul," 5 David sent
messengers to the men of Jabesh-gilead and said to them, [k]"May you be blessed by the
LORD, because you showed this loyalty to Saul your lord and buried him. 6 Now may the

22[y][1 Sam. 18:4]
23[z][Jer. 4:13; Hab. 1:8] [a][Judg. 14:18]
24[b][Ezek. 16:11]
25[c]ver. 19
26[d]See 1 Sam. 18:1, 3
27[c][See ver. 25 above]

Chapter 2

1[e]See 1 Sam. 22:10 [f]See Josh. 14:13
2[g]See 1 Sam. 25:42, 43
3[h]1 Sam. 27:2, 3; 30:1; See 1 Chr. 12:1-22
4[i]ch. 5:5 [j]1 Sam. 31:11-13
5[k]See Ruth 2:20

1:23 The term **lovely** could be applied to outstanding "heroes" in Ugaritic. **In life and in death** means "all the time." One might wonder whether Saul and Jonathan were really "in life . . . **not divided**." In 1 Samuel 14 Jonathan acted without his father's knowledge and readily criticized him, and they disagreed over David (see esp. 1 Sam. 22:8). Yet from the fact that the Amalekite specified that "his [Saul's] son Jonathan" was dead (2 Sam. 1:4), it appears that Saul continued to treat him as his heir. Apparently they were able to maintain a relationship, working together and eventually fighting and dying together for Israel. This song, whose purpose is to celebrate and idealize, would not delve into these details.

1:24 Scarlet cloth, colored with a dye made from the dried bodies of an insect, was a sign of prosperity (Prov. 31:21).

1:26 Very pleasant refers to the way in which the relationship between David and Jonathan was uniquely "good," i.e., in a "pleasant" or "lovely" way (v. 23; cf. 23:1, where the same word is translated "sweet" in the phrase "sweet psalmist of Israel"). Jonathan deeply loved and supported David (as seen in 1 Sam. 18:1–20:42; 23:16–18), in accordance with their covenant with the Lord. **surpassing the love of women**. David's remark does not carry any sexual overtones. Rather, he is calling attention to Jonathan's radical self-denial in giving up any right to the throne of Israel (1 Sam. 23:17); instead, he gave his absolute support to David as the Lord's choice to succeed Jonathan's father Saul, even to the point of risking his life for David (1 Sam. 20:30–33).

2:1–5:5 *David Becomes King.* Judah makes David its king. Saul's general Abner, however, seeks to restore Saul's kingdom with Saul's son Ish-bosheth as king. During the struggle between the two kingdoms, Abner, who has decided to go with David, is killed by David's commander Joab. Later, Ish-bosheth is killed by two of his own men, but David executes them for murder. With no candidate for king in the house of Saul, all of Israel unites to anoint the hero David as king. There are many cases of Israelites' shedding the blood of fellow Israelites, and this is tragic; but the narrator holds David innocent in each case, and thus he is qualified to be king over all Israel.

2:1–3 With Saul no longer pursuing him and Ziklag burned, David, after inquiring of the Lord (as in 1 Sam. 23:2), moves to the **Hebron** area with his family and men. His **wives** were from the region, and he had sent parts of the spoil from his battle with the Amalekites to the elders of the area (1 Sam. 30:26–31). Hebron was the most important city of southern Judah and not far from Bethlehem. It was associated with Abraham (Gen. 13:18; 23:2; 25:10) and was a Levitical city (Josh. 21:13).

2:4 Judah has apparently decided that having a king is a good thing; but rather than seeking out a relative of Saul (who was from the tribe of Benjamin, 1 Sam. 9:1), the people choose one of their own as king, the hero David, who was chosen by the Lord (1 Sam. 16:1–23; 25:30). Even in Saul's time, Judah formed a separate part of the army (1 Sam. 11:8; 15:4), and now it was prepared to act independently from the rest of Israel.

2:4b–7 See 1 Sam. 31:11–13. David seems to be presenting himself as Saul's successor and suggesting that **Jabesh-gilead** should enter into a treaty relationship with Judah; Gilead, however, soon becomes part of Ish-bosheth's kingdom (2 Sam. 2:8–9). David is not motivated by mere politics when he sends **messengers** to Jabesh-gilead. He is moved by their faithfulness toward their mutual sovereign and wants to reward them with blessings from the Lord and with his own work on their behalf.

2:8–9 Abner tries to continue Saul's kingdom, even on a reduced scale. (For Abner, see note on 1 Sam. 14:50–51.) Saul's son **Ish-bosheth** appears as Eshbaal in the genealogies in 1 Chron. 8:33; 9:39. It is uncertain whether he is the Ishvi of 1 Sam. 14:49. (For his name, see note on 2 Sam. 4:4.)

7 [l][See ver. 4 above]
8 [l]1 Sam. 14:50 [m]See Josh. 13:26
11 [n]ch. 5:5; 1 Kgs. 2:11 [l][See ver. 4 above]
13 [o][Jer. 41:12]

LORD show steadfast love and faithfulness to you. And I will do good to you because you
have done this thing. 7 Now therefore let your hands be strong, and be valiant, for Saul
your lord is dead, and [l]the house of Judah has anointed me king over them."

Ish-bosheth Made King of Israel

8 But [l]Abner the son of Ner, commander of Saul's army, took Ish-bosheth the son of
Saul and brought him over to [m]Mahanaim, 9 and he made him king over Gilead and the
Ashurites and Jezreel and Ephraim and Benjamin and all Israel. 10 Ish-bosheth, Saul's son,
was forty years old when he began to reign over Israel, and he reigned two years. But the
house of Judah followed David. 11 [n]And the time that David was king in Hebron over [l]the
house of Judah was seven years and six months.

The Battle of Gibeon

12 Abner the son of Ner, and the servants of Ish-bosheth the son of Saul, went out from
Mahanaim to Gibeon. 13 And Joab the son of Zeruiah and the servants of David went out
and met them at [o]the pool of Gibeon. And they sat down, the one on the one side of the
pool, and the other on the other side of the pool. 14 And Abner said to Joab, "Let the young
men arise and compete before us." And Joab said, "Let them arise." 15 Then they arose and
passed over by number, twelve for Benjamin and Ish-bosheth the son of Saul, and twelve
of the servants of David. 16 And each caught his opponent by the head and thrust his
sword in his opponent's side, so they fell down together. Therefore that place was called

From these verses and 3:9, it appears that Ish-bosheth was little more than a puppet for Abner. **Mahanaim**, a city on the Jabbok River, was apparently the capital of Gilead. The fact that the capital had to be in Transjordan suggests the precariousness of Ish-bosheth's reign. **Gilead and the Ashurites and Jezreel** refers to the northern and Transjordanian part of the country, **Ephraim and Benjamin** to the central and main part. Ish-bosheth did not necessarily have real control over all this area, especially since the Philistines apparently were in the Jezreel Valley (1 Sam. 31:7). **All Israel** is a summary description of the area just mentioned.

2:10–11 For a time, there are two kings in the land of Israel. David has apparently decided that his allegiance to Saul as God's anointed king does not extend to Saul's descendants, as succeeding events will show. For example, in 4:11 he refers to Ish-bosheth just as a "righteous man," not as a king or an anointed one. Ish-bosheth **reigned two years**, but David's reign as king at Hebron in Judah lasted seven and a half years. It probably took some time after Ish-bosheth's death for Israel to recognize David (5:1); the period when David was king in Hebron over all Israel before capturing Jerusalem (5:5) may also be included in the **seven years and six months**.

2:12 Gibeon is about 6 miles (9.7 km) north-northwest of Jerusalem. The "pool" (v. 13) is probably the huge round cistern cut into the rock on the north side of the site of Gibeon. Excavations at Gibeon have uncovered an elaborate water system. One part of the system is a large, circular shaft (37 feet [11 m] in diameter), which was cut into bedrock to a depth of 82 feet (25 m). At the bottom was the water table that formed a pool. The pool was reached by a staircase also cut into the limestone. This is probably the pool mentioned in the present text (cf. Jer. 41:12).

2:13 This marks the first appearance of **Joab the son of Zeruiah**, though Abishai was referred to as his brother in 1 Sam. 26:6. Joab was commander over the army (2 Sam. 8:16) and appears frequently in 2 Samuel, often as a mover of events. Since Abner knows him and his brothers well (2:20–22), Joab probably came to Saul's court soon after David's rise to prominence. He was one of the three sons (Joab, Abishai, and Asahel) of David's sister Zeruiah, and thus was David's nephew (v. 18). Joab's father probably died young, since he had a grave in Bethlehem (v. 32) and it was unusual for a man to be known by his mother's name. Zeruiah is not identified in Samuel, but according to 1 Chron. 2:16, she and Abigail, the mother of Amasa (2 Sam. 17:25), were sisters of David and his brothers. Abigail is identified in 2 Sam. 17:25 as "the daughter of Nahash, sister of Zeruiah." Therefore, it appears that Abigail and probably Zeruiah were maternal half sisters of David by an earlier marriage of their mother. (David's sister Abigail is a different Abigail from Nabal's wife, who later became David's wife; see note on 1 Sam. 25:3.)

David's Struggle for Power

c. 1010 B.C.

Immediately after Saul's death, a struggle for power ensued between David and Ish-bosheth (or Eshbaal), Saul's youngest and only surviving son. David ruled over his native tribe of Judah from Hebron, while Ish-bosheth ruled over the rest of Israel from Mahanaim across the Jordan River, and they fought against each other for seven years. David's power continued to grow, and eventually Ish-bosheth and his commander Abner were assassinated, leaving David as the sole ruler of all Israel.

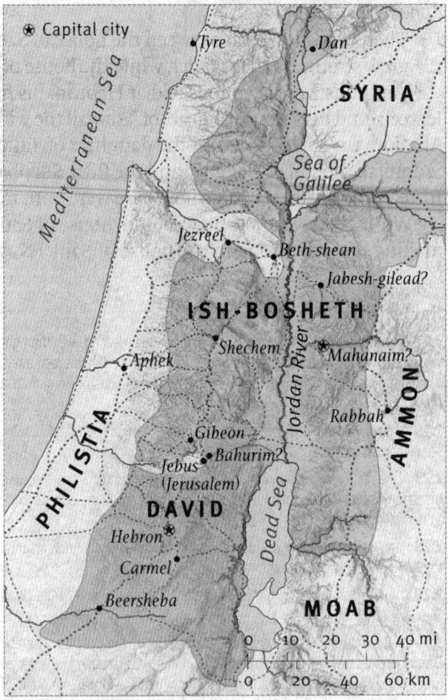

Helkath-hazzurim,[1] which is at Gibeon. **17** And the battle was very fierce that day. And
Abner and the men of Israel were beaten before the servants of David.
18 And the [p]three sons of Zeruiah were there, Joab, Abishai, and Asahel. Now Asahel
was [q]as swift of foot as a wild gazelle. **19** And Asahel pursued Abner, and as he went, he
turned neither to the right hand nor to the left from following Abner. **20** Then Abner looked
behind him and said, "Is it you, Asahel?" And he answered, "It is I." **21** Abner said to him,
"Turn aside to your right hand or to your left, and seize one of the young men and take
his spoil." But Asahel would not turn aside from following him. **22** And Abner said again
to Asahel, "Turn aside from following me. Why should I strike you to the ground? How
then could I lift up my face to your brother Joab?" **23** But he refused to turn aside. Therefore
Abner struck him [r]in the stomach with the butt of his spear, so that the spear came out at
his back. And he fell there and died where he was. And all who came to the place where
Asahel had fallen and died, stood still.
24 But Joab and Abishai pursued Abner. And as the sun was going down they came to the
hill of Ammah, which lies before Giah on the way to the wilderness of Gibeon. **25** And the
people of Benjamin gathered themselves together behind Abner and became one group
and took their stand on the top of a hill. **26** Then Abner called to Joab, "Shall the sword
devour forever? Do you not know that the end will be bitter? How long will it be before
you tell your people to turn from the pursuit of their brothers?" **27** And Joab said, "As God
lives, if [s]you had not spoken, surely the men would not have given up the pursuit of their
brothers until the morning." **28** So Joab blew the trumpet, and all the men stopped and
pursued Israel no more, nor did they fight anymore.
29 And Abner and his men went all that night through [t]the Arabah. They crossed the
Jordan, and marching the whole morning, they came to [u]Mahanaim. **30** Joab returned
from the pursuit of Abner. And when he had gathered all the people together, there were
missing from David's servants nineteen men besides Asahel. **31** But the servants of David
had struck down of Benjamin 360 of Abner's men. **32** And they took up Asahel and buried
him in the tomb of his father, which was at Bethlehem. And Joab and his men marched
all night, and the day broke upon them at Hebron.

Abner Joins David

3 There was a long war between the house of Saul and the house of David. And David
grew stronger and stronger, while the house of Saul became weaker and weaker.
2 [v]And sons were born to David at Hebron: his firstborn was Amnon, of [w]Ahinoam of
Jezreel; **3** and his second, Chileab, of [w]Abigail the widow of Nabal of Carmel; and the third,
Absalom the son of Maacah [x]the daughter of Talmai king of [y]Geshur; **4** and the fourth,
[z]Adonijah the son of Haggith; and the fifth, Shephatiah the son of Abital; **5** and the sixth,
Ithream, of Eglah, David's wife. These were born to David in Hebron.
6 While there was war between the house of Saul and the house of David, Abner was
making himself strong in the house of Saul. **7** Now Saul had a concubine whose name

[1] *Helkath-hazzurim means the field of sword-edges*

18 [p]1 Chr. 2:16; [1 Sam. 26:6] [q][ch. 22:34; 1 Chr. 12:8; Ps. 18:33; Song 2:17; 8:14; Hab. 3:19]
23 [r]ch. 3:27; 4:6; 20:10
27 [s]ver. 14; [Prov. 17:14]
29 [t]See Deut. 1:1 [u]ver. 8; See Josh. 13:26

Chapter 3

2 [v]For ver. 2-5, see 1 Chr. 3:1-4 [w]1 Sam. 25:42, 43
3 [w][See ver. 2 above] [x]ch. 13:37, 38 [y]ch. 14:32; 15:8; [1 Sam. 27:8]
4 [z]1 Kgs. 1:5

2:17 This transitional verse connects the first episode, dealing with the fight at Gibeon, and the second episode, where the death of Asahel is recounted. After this episode, the enmity between the surviving sons of Zeruiah and Abner, the killer of Asahel, will be a major factor.

2:19 Asahel was one of David's mighty warriors, "one of the thirty" (23:24; see also 1 Chron. 11:26; 27:7).

2:23 Abner, an experienced warrior, apparently stopped suddenly, thrusting **his spear** backward so forcefully that it went right through Asahel's body as he ran into it.

2:28 Here, as in 18:16 and 20:22, Joab uses a **trumpet** to summon an army to mark the end of fighting after a victory.

2:29 The **Arabah** is part of the Jordan Valley rift that is south of the Dead Sea.

3:1–4:12 Chapters 3–4 describe the slow steps of the process whereby **David grew stronger and stronger** (3:1) and thus became king over all Israel. A major concern of the author is to show that David was not guilty of involvement in the death of Abner or Ish-bosheth.

3:2–5 A list of David's sons born in Hebron. David's sons **Amnon** and **Absalom** come to the fore in chs. 13–18, and the struggle for the succession between **Adonijah** and Solomon is described in 1 Kings 1–2. The other sons are not mentioned in the narratives of Samuel–Kings. It is assumed that **Chileab** (called Daniel in 1 Chron. 3:1) died young, since he is not mentioned as a possible successor in 1 Kings 1. After the deaths of Amnon (2 Sam. 13:28–29) and Absalom (18:15), Adonijah is apparently the eldest surviving son of David. **Geshur** was north of the area controlled by Saul's house, so David's marriage with the daughter of its king was one of the steps in strengthening him against Ish-bosheth (3:1). Absalom apparently named a daughter after his mother **Maacah** (1 Kings 15:2; 2 Chron. 11:20–22).

3:6–39 Abner, after a quarrel with Ish-bosheth, convinces the elders of Israel that they should go with David. But Abner is killed by Joab. The author repeatedly stresses that David had not consented to this (vv. 21, 26, 28, 37); indeed, since Abner was plotting to make David king of Israel, it would seem that David would have had nothing to gain and something to lose from Abner's death.

3:7 Saul's concubine **Rizpah** had borne him two sons. She would later

7[a]ch. 21:8-10 [b][ch. 16:21]
8[c]See 1 Sam. 17:43
9[d]ver. 35; See Ruth 1:17 [e]1 Sam. 15:28; 16:1, 12; 28:17; 1 Chr. 12:23
10[f]ch. 17:11; 24:2, 15; Judg. 20:1; 1 Sam. 3:20; 1 Kgs. 4:25
13[g][Gen. 43:3] [h]1 Sam. 14:49
14[i]1 Sam. 18:25, 27
16[j]ch. 16:5; 17:18; 19:16; 1 Kgs. 2:8
18[k]See ver. 9
19[l][1 Chr. 12:29]
21[m]ver. 12 [n]1 Kgs. 11:37
25[o]See 1 Sam. 29:6

was [a]Rizpah, the daughter of Aiah. And Ish-bosheth said to Abner, [b]"Why have you gone
in to my father's concubine?" 8 Then Abner was very angry over the words of Ish-bosheth
and said, "Am I [c]a dog's head of Judah? To this day I keep showing steadfast love to the
house of Saul your father, to his brothers, and to his friends, and have not given you into
the hand of David. And yet you charge me today with a fault concerning a woman. 9 [d]God
do so to Abner and more also, if I do not accomplish for David [e]what the LORD has sworn
to him, 10 to transfer the kingdom from the house of Saul and set up the throne of David
over Israel and over Judah, [f]from Dan to Beersheba." 11 And Ish-bosheth could not answer
Abner another word, because he feared him.

12 And Abner sent messengers to David on his behalf,[1] saying, "To whom does the land
belong? Make your covenant with me, and behold, my hand shall be with you to bring
over all Israel to you." 13 And he said, "Good; I will make a covenant with you. But one thing
I require of you; that is, [g]you shall not see my face unless you first bring [h]Michal, Saul's
daughter, when you come to see my face." 14 Then David sent messengers to Ish-bosheth,
Saul's son, saying, "Give me my wife Michal, [i]for whom I paid the bridal price of a hundred foreskins of the Philistines." 15 And Ish-bosheth sent and took her from her husband
Paltiel the son of Laish. 16 But her husband went with her, weeping after her all the way to
[j]Bahurim. Then Abner said to him, "Go, return." And he returned.

17 And Abner conferred with the elders of Israel, saying, "For some time past you have
been seeking David as king over you. 18 Now then bring it about, [k]for the LORD has promised David, saying, 'By the hand of my servant David I will save my people Israel from
the hand of the Philistines, and from the hand of all their enemies.'" 19 Abner also spoke
to [l]Benjamin. And then Abner went to tell David at Hebron all that Israel and the whole
house of Benjamin thought good to do.

20 When Abner came with twenty men to David at Hebron, David made a feast for Abner
and the men who were with him. 21 And Abner said to David, "I will arise and go and [m]will
gather all Israel to my lord the king, that they may make a covenant with you, and that
you may [n]reign over all that your heart desires." So David sent Abner away, and he went
in peace.

22 Just then the servants of David arrived with Joab from a raid, bringing much spoil
with them. But Abner was not with David at Hebron, for he had sent him away, and he
had gone in peace. 23 When Joab and all the army that was with him came, it was told
Joab, "Abner the son of Ner came to the king, and he has let him go, and he has gone in
peace." 24 Then Joab went to the king and said, "What have you done? Behold, Abner came
to you. Why is it that you have sent him away, so that he is gone? 25 You know that Abner
the son of Ner came to deceive you and to know [o]your going out and your coming in, and
to know all that you are doing."

Joab Murders Abner

26 When Joab came out from David's presence, he sent messengers after Abner, and they
brought him back from the cistern of Sirah. But David did not know about it. 27 And when

[1] Or *where he was*; Septuagint *at Hebron*

protect their bodies after their deaths (ch. 21). Taking a king's wives seems to have been considered a prerogative of the throne (see 12:8; 16:21–22; 1 Kings 2:22), though that is not necessarily what Abner had in mind, even if the accusation about his relationship with Rizpah was true.

3:9–10 As Saul's general, Abner must have known about Saul's recognition of David as his successor (1 Sam. 24:20). People in general also seem to have had knowledge about a promise of God to David (2 Sam. 3:18; see also 1 Sam. 24:4; 25:30).

3:12–15 David clearly does not mind taking the Israelite kingdom from Ish-bosheth, and he stresses his closeness to Saul as Saul's son-in-law. In 1 Sam. 18:25–27, David gave Saul 200 Philistine foreskins though Saul had demanded only 100 as a bride-price, so the extra hundred was in essence a gift. David here just states that he has legally paid the bride-price. Apparently because David never divorced Michal even though her father Saul had given her to another man (1 Sam. 25:44), he still describes her as his wife. David presumably expects Abner to support David's argument when the matter is discussed in Ish-bosheth's court.

3:17–19 The Israelites, even the members of Saul's own tribe of Benjamin, seem to think they are getting nowhere with Ish-bosheth as king.

3:22–30 Here, as in 18:14 and 20:10, the motive for Joab's actions in killing Abner can be seen either as concern for David's position (3:25), concern for his own position (esp. since David had not told him what was going on, v. 23), personal revenge (v. 30), or a mixture. The readers are not told exactly what part Abishai (v. 30) plays, but he seems to have been a loyal supporter of his brother Joab (see 10:9–12; 18:2; 20:6–10; see also note on 8:13–14).

3:25 Know your going out and your coming in mainly refers to military actions (as in 1 Sam. 18:13). In other words, Joab claims that Abner came as a spy.

3:26 Sirah is about 2.5 miles (4 km) north of Hebron.

Abner returned to Hebron, Joab took him aside into the midst of the gate to speak with
him privately, [p]and there he struck him [q]in the stomach, so that he died, for the blood
of Asahel his brother. **28** Afterward, when David heard of it, he said, "I and my kingdom
are forever guiltless before the LORD for the blood of Abner the son of Ner. **29** [r]May it fall
upon the head of Joab and upon all his father's house, and may the house of Joab never be
without [s]one who has a discharge or who is [t]leprous or who holds a spindle or who falls
by the sword or who lacks bread!" **30** So Joab and Abishai his brother killed Abner, because
[u]he had put their brother Asahel to death in the battle at Gibeon.

David Mourns Abner

31 Then David said to Joab and to all the people who were with him, [v]"Tear your clothes
and [w]put on sackcloth and mourn before Abner." And King David followed the bier. **32** They
buried Abner at Hebron. And the king lifted up his voice and wept at the grave of Abner,
and all the people wept. **33** And the king [x]lamented for Abner, saying,

[y]"Should Abner die [z]as a fool dies?
34 Your hands were not bound;
your feet were not fettered;
as one falls before the wicked
you have fallen."

And all the people wept again over him. **35** Then all the people came [a]to persuade David to
eat bread while it was yet day. But David swore, saying, [b]"God do so to me and more also,
if I taste bread or anything else [c]till the sun goes down!" **36** And all the people took notice
of it, and it pleased them, as everything that the king did pleased all the people. **37** So all
the people and all Israel understood that day that it had not been the king's will to put
to death Abner the son of Ner. **38** And the king said to his servants, "Do you not know that
a prince and a great man has fallen this day in Israel? **39** And I was gentle today, though
anointed king. [d]These men, the sons of Zeruiah, are more severe than I. [e]The LORD repay
the evildoer according to his wickedness!"

Ish-bosheth Murdered

4 When Ish-bosheth, Saul's son, heard that Abner had died at Hebron, [f]his courage failed,
and all Israel was dismayed. **2** Now Saul's son had two men who were captains of raiding bands; the name of the one was Baanah, and the name of the other Rechab, sons of
Rimmon a man of Benjamin from Beeroth ([g]for Beeroth also is counted part of Benjamin;
3 [h]the Beerothites fled [i]to Gittaim and have been sojourners there to this day).
4 [j]Jonathan, the son of Saul, had a son who was crippled in his feet. He was five years
old when the news about Saul and Jonathan [k]came from Jezreel, and his nurse took him
up and fled, and as she fled in her haste, he fell and became lame. And his name was
Mephibosheth.
5 Now the sons of Rimmon the Beerothite, Rechab and Baanah, set out, and about the
heat of the day they came to the house of Ish-bosheth as he was taking his noonday rest.

27 [p]1 Kgs. 2:5, 32; [ch. 20:9, 10] [q]See ch. 2:23
29 [r]See ch. 1:16 [s]Lev. 15:2 [t]Lev. 14:2
30 [u]ch. 2:23
31 [v]See Josh. 7:6 [w]Gen. 37:34; 1 Kgs. 20:31
33 [x][ch. 1:17; 2 Chr. 35:25] [y][Eccles. 2:16] [z]ch. 13:12, 13
35 [a]ch. 12:17 [b]See Ruth 1:17 [c][ch. 1:12]
39 [d][ch. 16:10; 19:22] [e][Ps. 28:4; 2 Tim. 4:14]

Chapter 4

1 [f]Ezra 4:4; Isa. 13:7; Jer. 6:24
2 [g]Josh. 18:25
3 [h][1 Sam. 31:7] [i]Neh. 11:33
4 [j]ch. 9:3, 6 [k]1 Sam. 29:1, 11

3:27 into the midst of the gate. City gates were elaborate structures.

3:28–39 Joab is apparently too important and useful for David to punish him for killing Abner, so he does the best he can by cursing him, having a funeral for Abner, and publicly mourning and chanting a lament for him. This is the only funeral described in detail in the OT. As elsewhere, tearing clothes, wearing **sackcloth**, and fasting are features of mourning. **All Israel** refers to Abner's own countrymen. It was important for David and his future kingdom that "all Israel" know it was not the king's will to put to death Abner son of Ner (see note on 1 Sam. 14:50–51).

3:29 One who **holds a spindle** is one forced to do the work of spinning, i.e., in that culture, a woman.

3:36 everything that the king did pleased all the people. The remarkable result of God's blessing on these initial days of David's reign.

4:1–12 Chapter 4 relates the death of Saul's son, the rival king Ish-bosheth.

4:2–3 Beeroth is about 2 miles south of Gibeon and is one of the cities, led by Gibeon, that tricked Joshua into making a treaty with them (Josh. 9:17). The Beerothites had probably **fled to Gittaim** (which according to Neh. 11:33 was a city in Benjamin) at the time Saul put the Gibeonites to death (see 2 Sam. 21:1). Apparently after that the Benjaminites, including **Rimmon** and his family, came to live there. If this is correct, it suggests that the incident of the Gibeonites occurred early in Saul's reign, since Rimmon, the father of **Baanah** and **Rechab**, is described as being "from Beeroth." This passage stresses that those who killed Ish-bosheth were not partisans of David but were from Saul's own tribe.

4:4 The information about **Mephibosheth** is probably put here to show why there was no move to make him king after Ish-bosheth's death—he was still a child, and he was **crippled**. He is further mentioned in 9:1–13; 16:1–4; 19:24–29; and 21:7. (The Mephibosheth in 21:8 is a different person, the son of Saul and Rizpah.) Apparently his real name was "Merib-baal" (1 Chron. 8:34; 9:40). Because "baal" could mean "lord" in general, the name probably referred to the Lord of Israel (as in 2 Sam. 5:20), but at some point, in order to avoid using the name of the god Baal, it was euphemistically changed in Samuel to "Mephibosheth," *boshet* meaning "shame." Similarly, Saul's son Ish-bosheth is called "Eshbaal" in 1 Chron. 8:33 and 9:39, but "Ish-bosheth"

6 [l] See ch. 2:23
7 [m] ch. 2:29; See Deut. 1:1
8 [n] 1 Sam. 19:10, 11; 23:15
9 [o] See Ruth 3:13 [p] 1 Kgs. 1:29
10 [q] See ch. 1:4-10 [r] ch. 1:15
11 [s] [Gen. 9:5, 6]
12 [t] ch. 3:32

Chapter 5

1 [u] For ver. 1-3, see 1 Chr. 11:1-3 [v] See Gen. 29:14
2 [w] [1 Sam. 18:13] [x] ch. 7:7; 1 Chr. 17:6; Ps. 78:71, 72; [Matt. 2:6]
3 [y] ch. 3:12, 13, 21; [2 Kgs. 11:17] [z] Judg. 11:11; 1 Sam. 23:18
4 [a] 1 Kgs. 2:11; 1 Chr. 3:4; 29:27
5 [a] [See ver. 4 above] [b] ch. 2:11
6 [c] For ver. 6-10, see 1 Chr. 11:4-9 [d] Judg. 19:11; [Josh. 15:63; Judg. 1:21]

6 And they came into the midst of the house as if to get wheat, and they stabbed him [l] in the
stomach. Then Rechab and Baanah his brother escaped.[1] **7** When they came into the house,
as he lay on his bed in his bedroom, they struck him and put him to death and beheaded
him. They took his head and went by the way of [m] the Arabah all night, **8** and brought the
head of Ish-bosheth to David at Hebron. And they said to the king, "Here is the head of Ish-
bosheth, the son of Saul, your enemy, [n] who sought your life. The LORD has avenged my lord
the king this day on Saul and on his offspring." **9** But David answered Rechab and Baanah
his brother, the sons of Rimmon the Beerothite, [o] "As the LORD lives, [p] who has redeemed
my life out of every adversity, **10** [q] when one told me, 'Behold, Saul is dead,' and thought he
was bringing good news, [r] I seized him and killed him at Ziklag, which was the reward I
gave him for his news. **11** How much more, when wicked men have killed a righteous man
in his own house on his bed, shall I not now [s] require his blood at your hand and destroy
you from the earth?" **12** And David commanded his young men, and they killed them and
cut off their hands and feet and hanged them beside the pool at Hebron. But they took
the head of Ish-bosheth and buried it [t] in the tomb of Abner at Hebron.

David Anointed King of Israel

5 Then all the tribes of Israel [u] came to David at Hebron and said, "Behold, [v] we are your
bone and flesh. **2** In times past, when Saul was king over us, [w] it was you who led out
and brought in Israel. And the LORD said to you, [x] 'You shall be shepherd of my people
Israel, and you shall be prince[2] over Israel.'" **3** So all the elders of Israel came to the king at
Hebron, [y] and King David made a covenant with them at Hebron [z] before the LORD, and they
anointed David king over Israel. **4** David was thirty years old when he began to reign, and
[a] he reigned forty years. **5** [a] At Hebron he reigned over Judah [b] seven years and six months,
and at Jerusalem he reigned over all Israel and Judah thirty-three years.[3]
6 [c] And the king and his men went to Jerusalem [d] against the Jebusites, the inhabitants

[1] Septuagint *And behold, the doorkeeper of the house had been cleaning wheat, but she grew drowsy and slept. So Rechab and Baanah his brother slipped in*
[2] Or *leader* [3] Dead Sea Scroll lacks verses 4–5

in Samuel; and Jerubbaal (Judg. 9:1, 57) is called "Jerubbesheth" in 2 Sam. 11:21.

4:7 This verse is an expansion of the previous verse.

4:8 Saul, your enemy, who sought your life. It is true that Saul had sought David's life. Nevertheless, David had already rejected killing Saul (1 Sam. 24:4–6; 26:8–9), and furthermore, that did not provide an excuse to kill a "righteous man" (2 Sam. 4:11).

4:10–11 This refers to the incident in 1:13–16. The Amalekite had at least given the excuse that Saul had requested his own death, but Ish-bosheth's death was outright murder. Yet David says nothing here about Ish-bosheth as the Lord's anointed.

4:12 Unlike the case of Joab, there is no problem with executing the killers of Ish-bosheth. For hanging a body after death, see 21:6 and Josh. 10:26.

5:1–25 It is not clear how soon the events of ch. 5 followed those of ch. 4 (see note on 2:10–11). Presumably the deaths of Abner and Ish-bosheth caused a shock among David's supporters in the north (3:19) and caused them to put off accepting David as king. Some of the shock seems to have remained at the time this account was written. David apparently just bided his time, waiting for the elders of Israel to decide that they wanted him as king.

5:1–5 At last, David is accepted and anointed as king over the entire house of Israel. First, messengers from **all the tribes** come and ask him to become king; then the **elders of Israel** come themselves. David makes a **covenant** with them as representatives of the nation (cf. 1 Sam. 10:25), and they anoint him **king over Israel** (cf. 1 Sam. 11:15). David is one of them (see Deut. 17:15), he is a proven military leader, and he is the chosen of the Lord. Many critical scholars argue that the Bible contains little historically reliable information regarding David and his rule. Some believe it is mere fabrication. But no persuasive evidence contradicting the biblical account has been found. In 1993, an inscription was found at Tell Dan that mentions the "house of David," and it dates to the ninth century B.C. The term "house of David" may also appear on the Moabite stone that comes from the same century.

5:1 we are your bone and flesh. Even though there is a distinct division between Judah and the rest of Israel, they still recognize each other as kin (cf. "brothers," 2:26–27).

5:6–25 *Jerusalem, the City of David.* David captures the Jebusite city of Jerusalem to serve as the capital of his united Israel. He builds a palace in his royal city and continues to have children there. He also defeats the Philistines.

5:6–13 The account of David's kingship over Israel starts with the capture of **Jerusalem**, on the boundary between Judah and Benjamin. It had not been controlled by any tribe, and thus it was both symbolically and geographically better suited to be the capital of all Israel than Hebron (in central Judah). Jerusalem was the "Salem" of Melchizedek (Gen. 14:18). It has been fortified since the Middle Bronze Age, i.e., the first half of the second millennium B.C. In the second half of the millennium it was one of the city-states of Canaan that was under the influence of Egypt. Several letters from the king of Jerusalem to the pharaoh exist among the fourteenth-century Amarna letters. The Jebusites are listed among the Canaanites in Gen. 10:16 and, broadly speaking, were considered to be among the Amorites (Josh. 10:5). The city was too strong to be conquered at the time of Joshua (Josh. 15:63; Judg. 1:21). The Jebusite city, **the stronghold of Zion**, was located on the western slope of the Kidron Valley above the city's water source, the spring of Gihon. An extensive network of water tunnels has been excavated, one of which was probably the **water shaft** through which David's men entered the city. This water shaft is often identified with "Warren's Shaft," which is directly over the water channel near the spring, though recent archaeological finds have challenged this. According to 1 Chron. 11:6, Joab led the attack and was therefore made David's chief commander.

5:6–8 the blind and the lame will ward you off. The Jebusites probably meant that the fortifications were so strong that the city needed no able-bodied defenders. David quotes their words in ordering the attack, referring to the Jebusite defenders as "the blind and the lame." **The blind and the lame shall not come into the house** may mean that the Jebusites were not allowed at David's court.

5:6 The Canaanite or Jebusite city of **Jerusalem** was located on a hill known as "Ophel." It is located in the southeastern part of the modern city. The Ophel was inhabited as far back as the Chalcolithic period (3rd millennium B.C.). The city is mentioned in Egyptian texts from the twentieth century B.C.

JERUSALEM IN THE TIME OF DAVID (C. 1010–970 B.C.)

About four millennia ago, Melchizedek was king of Jerusalem, which was then called Salem (Gen. 14:18). This was an unwalled city, which was taken over in c. 1850 B.C. by the Jebusites, who built a city wall around it and called it Jebus (cf. 1 Chron. 11:4).

King David captured this city after having ruled for seven years in Hebron (2 Sam. 5:5). The city was strongly fortified, especially the area around the Gihon Spring, where massive towers dating from this period have been excavated. The Jebusites were so confident of their fortifications that they taunted David, saying that even the blind and the lame would prevent him from capturing their city (2 Sam. 5:6).

However, Joab, David's commander-in-chief, managed to secretly enter the city through its water system and open the gates for David to take control (1 Chron. 11:6). The Jebusite Citadel was destroyed and replaced by the "stronghold of Zion, that is, the city of David" (2 Sam. 5:7).

Later on in his life, David built an altar on the threshing floor of Araunah the Jebusite, which stopped a plague sent by God upon Israel from reaching Jerusalem (2 Sam. 24:18–25).

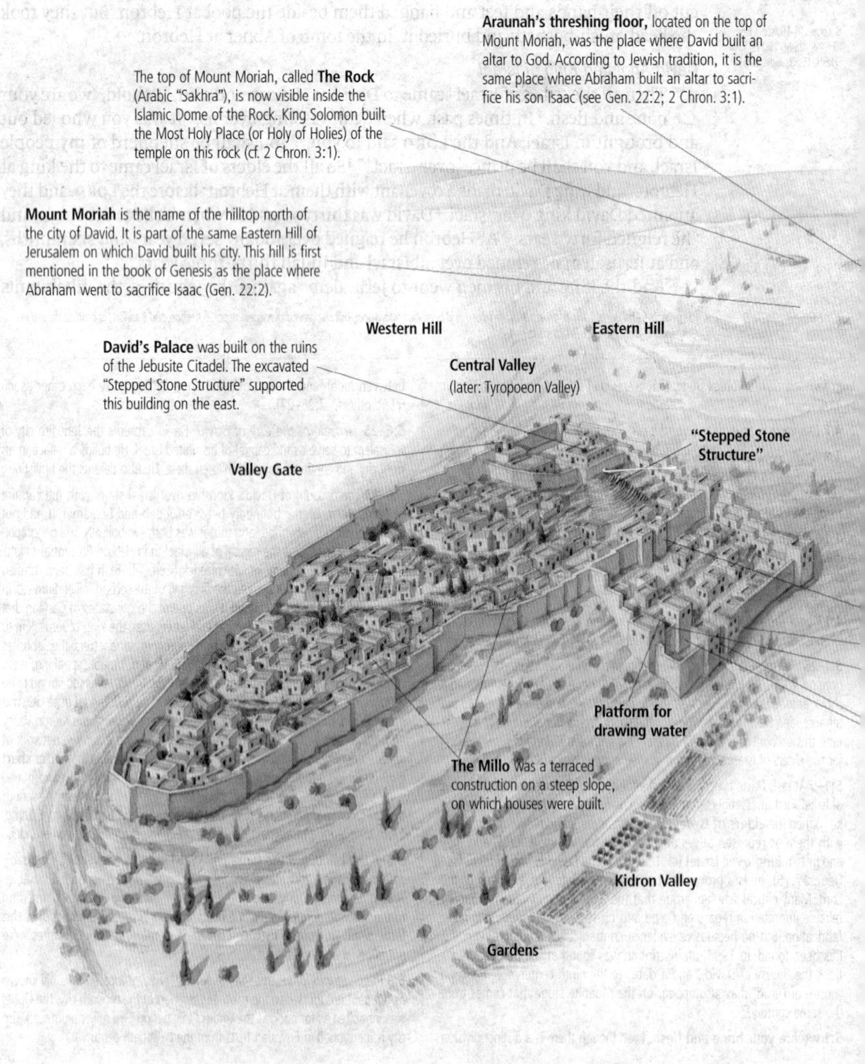

Araunah's threshing floor, located on the top of Mount Moriah, was the place where David built an altar to God. According to Jewish tradition, it is the same place where Abraham built an altar to sacrifice his son Isaac (see Gen. 22:2; 2 Chron. 3:1).
The top of Mount Moriah, called **The Rock** (Arabic "Sakhra"), is now visible inside the Islamic Dome of the Rock. King Solomon built the Most Holy Place (or Holy of Holies) of the temple on this rock (cf. 2 Chron. 3:1).
Mount Moriah is the name of the hilltop north of the city of David. It is part of the same Eastern Hill of Jerusalem on which David built his city. This hill is first mentioned in the book of Genesis as the place where Abraham went to sacrifice Isaac (Gen. 22:2).
Western Hill
Eastern Hill
David's Palace was built on the ruins of the Jebusite Citadel. The excavated "Stepped Stone Structure" supported this building on the east.
Central Valley
(later: Tyropoeon Valley)
"Stepped Stone Structure"
Valley Gate
Platform for drawing water
The Millo was a terraced construction on a steep slope, on which houses were built.
Kidron Valley
Gardens

7[e]ch. 6:12, 16
9[e][See ver. 7 above]
[f]1 Kgs. 9:15, 24; 11:27; 2 Kgs. 12:20; 2 Chr. 32:5
11[g]For ver. 11-25, see 1 Chr. 14:1-16 [h]1 Kgs. 5; 6
13[i][1 Chr. 3:9]
14[j][1 Chr. 3:5-8]
17[k]ch. 23:14; 1 Sam. 22:4, 5

of the land, who said to David, "You will not come in here, but the blind and the lame
will ward you off"—thinking, "David cannot come in here." 7 Nevertheless, David took
the stronghold of Zion, [e]that is, the city of David. 8 And David said on that day, "Whoever
would strike the Jebusites, let him get up the water shaft to attack 'the lame and the blind,'
who are hated by David's soul." Therefore it is said, "The blind and the lame shall not come
into the house." 9 And David lived in the stronghold and called it [e]the city of David. And
David built the city all around from the [f]Millo inward. 10 And David became greater and
greater, for the LORD, the God of hosts, was with him.

11 [g]And [h]Hiram king of Tyre sent messengers to David, and cedar trees, also carpenters
and masons who built David a house. 12 And David knew that the LORD had established him
king over Israel, and that he had exalted his kingdom for the sake of his people Israel.

13 And David took more [i]concubines and wives from Jerusalem, after he came from
Hebron, and more sons and daughters were born to David. 14 [j]And these are the names of
those who were born to him in Jerusalem: Shammua, Shobab, Nathan, Solomon, 15 Ibhar,
Elishua, Nepheg, Japhia, 16 Elishama, Eliada, and Eliphelet.

David Defeats the Philistines

17 When the Philistines heard that David had been anointed king over Israel, all the
Philistines went up to search for David. But David heard of it and went down [k]to the

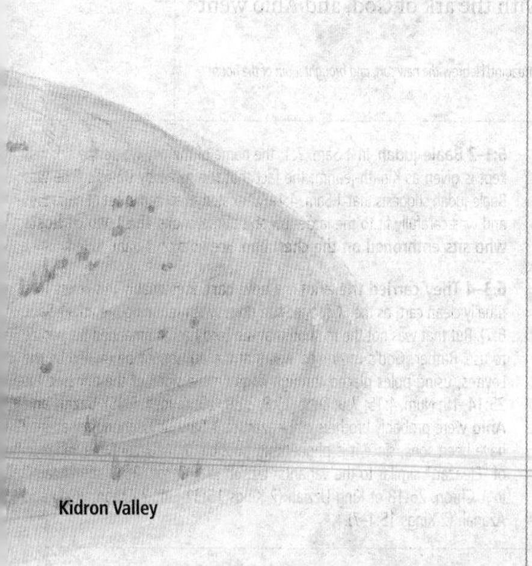

The excavated **Spring and Pool Towers** protected the abundant water supply of the Gihon Spring. Water from the pool would presumably have been drawn from a wooden platform.

5:8 water shaft. See note on vv. 6–13.

5:9 the Millo. Cf. 1 Kings 9:15, 24; 11:27; 1 Chron. 11:8; 2 Chron. 32:5. The Hebrew word means "the fill." It was a series of terrace walls, built on a steep slope, supporting the fill behind it in order to create level areas. Houses were then built on these artificial platforms, which were connected by narrow staircases. It was apparently the king's duty to look after this construction. During heavy rainfalls, the fill became heavy and increased the pressure on the terrace walls, thus requiring regular maintenance of these walls. When this construction was neglected, the houses would fall down the steep slope and the city would disintegrate. Remains of these supporting walls have been found on the eastern slope of the city of David.

5:10 For the LORD, the God of hosts, was with him, as he was when David was first anointed in 1 Sam. 16:18.

5:11 Hiram king of Tyre is mentioned in 1 Kings 5:1–18 as a friend of Solomon who provides the cedars to build the temple, just as here he provides David with cedars to build his house. Tyre was a trading empire, and it was in its interest to keep the inland trade routes, especially those through Israel to Egypt, open to its merchants. According to Josephus, however, Hiram did not begin to reign until near the end of David's own reign. If that is correct, either this construction should be dated toward the end of David's reign or the Hiram in 1 Kings is the successor (probably son) of the Hiram here, who continued his father's good relationship with David. The cedars of Lebanon (which have now all but disappeared) were famous throughout the Near East. There are Assyrian reliefs of men cutting them down and transporting them to Nineveh.

5:13–14 This is a summary statement about David's kingship in Jerusalem (cf. 3:2–5); it does not mean that these sons were all born before 5:17. The birth of **Solomon** is mentioned in 12:24. None of the other sons play a major role in the Samuel–Kings narratives. The parallel passages 1 Chron. 3:5–8 and 14:4–7 list two more sons in addition, and comparison with a Dead Sea Scroll suggests that the two names might have been omitted in the Masoretic text of Samuel. **Nathan** (2 Sam. 5:14) was an ancestor of Jesus (Luke 3:31; see note on Luke 3:23–38), as was Solomon (Matt. 1:6–7).

5:17–21 Until now the **Philistines** may have considered that David was to some extent still their vassal (1 Samuel 27); at least they must have been happy about his struggle with Ish-bosheth. But when David becomes **king over Israel** (i.e., both Israel and Judah) and even captures Jerusalem, they realize that he is a threat. **went down to the stronghold**. This is probably a stronghold toward the Philistine country. The **Valley of Rephaim** is the valley leading toward Jerusalem from the southwest. The incident in 2 Sam. 23:13–17 may have happened at this time. **David inquired of the LORD** as he did in 1 Sam. 23:2, 11; 30:8; and 2 Sam. 2:1. **like a breaking flood**. Throughout the ancient Near East writings, battles are described in terms of floods. "Baal" in **Baal-perazim** is here a common noun meaning "lord" (see note on 4:4). **The Philistines left their idols there** (5:21) is a reversal of

stronghold. 18 Now the Philistines had come and spread out in [l]the Valley of Rephaim.
19 And David [m]inquired of the LORD, "Shall I go up against the Philistines? Will you give
them into my hand?" And the LORD said to David, "Go up, for I will certainly give the
Philistines into your hand." 20 And David came to Baal-perazim, and David defeated them
there. And he said, "The LORD has broken through my enemies before me like a breaking
flood." [n]Therefore the name of that place is called Baal-perazim.[1] 21 And the Philistines left
their idols there, and David and his men carried them away.

22 And the Philistines came up yet again [o]and spread out in the Valley of Rephaim. 23 [p]And
when David inquired of the LORD, he said, "You shall not go up; go around to their rear,
and come against them opposite the balsam trees. 24 And [q]when you hear the sound of
marching in the tops of the balsam trees, then rouse yourself, [r]for then the LORD has gone
out before you to strike down the army of the Philistines." 25 And David did as the LORD
commanded him, and struck down the Philistines from Geba [s]to Gezer.

The Ark Brought to Jerusalem

6 [t]David again gathered all the chosen men of Israel, thirty thousand. 2 And David
arose and went with all the people who were with him from [u]Baale-judah [v]to bring
up from there the ark of God, which is called by the name of the LORD of hosts [w]who
sits enthroned on the cherubim. 3 And they carried the ark of God [x]on a new cart and
brought it [y]out of the house of Abinadab, which was on the hill. And Uzzah and Ahio,[2]
the sons of Abinadab, were driving the new cart,[3] 4 with the ark of God, and Ahio went
before the ark.

[1] *Baal-perazim* means *lord of bursting through* [2] Or *and his brother*; also verse 4 [3] Compare Septuagint; Hebrew *the new cart, and brought it out of the house of Abinadab, which was on the hill*

18 [l]ver. 22; ch. 23:13; Josh. 15:8; 18:16; [Josh. 17:15]
19 [m]See ch. 2:1
20 [n]Isa. 28:21
22 [o]ver. 18
23 [p]See 1 Sam. 22:10
24 [q][2 Kgs. 7:6] [r][Judg. 4:14]
25 [s]Josh. 10:33
Chapter 6
1 [t]For ver. 1-11, see 1 Chr. 13:6-14
2 [u]Josh. 15:9, 60 [v]2 Chr. 1:4 [w]Ex. 25:22; 1 Sam. 4:4; Ps. 80:1
3 [x][1 Sam. 6:7] [y][1 Sam. 7:1]

1 Samuel 4, where the Philistines carried off the ark of the covenant. According to 1 Chron. 14:12, David had the idols burned.

5:22–25 It may be that the **sound of marching** was a distinct sound caused by the Lord that frightened the Philistines (as in 2 Kings 7:6). Another possibility is that the Philistines knew the sound was the sound of **trees**, so David was able to use the sound as cover for his attack. By this victory, David drove the Philistines out of the central hill country.

6:1–23 *Zion, the Place of Worship.* Jerusalem was not only to be the political capital of a united Israel, it was to be the religious center also. David brought the ark of the Lord of hosts from Baale-judah, where it had been most of the time ever since the Philistines returned it in 1 Samuel 6. Psalm 132 refers to this occasion.

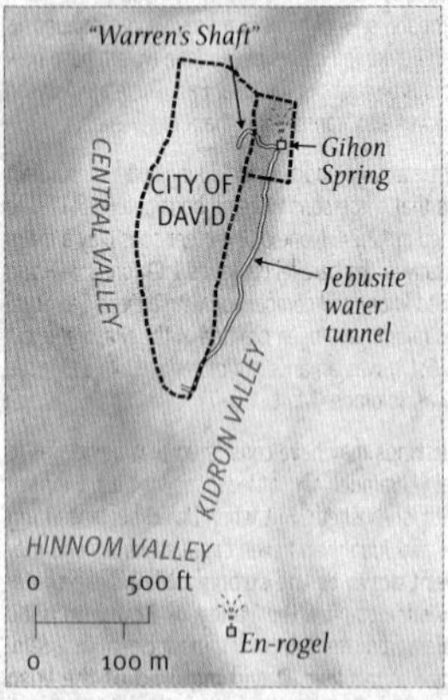

David Captures the Stronghold of Zion
c. 1005 B.C.
After securing his reign over all Israel, David moved his capital from Hebron, a southern city of Judah, to a more central and tribally neutral location at Jerusalem. At the time, Jerusalem (called "the stronghold of Zion") was held by the Jebusites, and its terraced defensive walls and nearby steep hills and valleys made it seem impenetrable. But David sent men up a water shaft (believed by some to be Warren's Shaft) to capture the stronghold, and he renamed it the city of David.

6:1–2 Baale-judah. In 1 Sam. 7:1, the name of the city where the ark was kept is given as Kiriath-jearim; the fact that the name by David's time was Baale-judah suggests that 1 Sam. 4:1–7:2 existed as an earlier set of narratives and was carefully fit to the larger context of the books. **the LORD of hosts who sits enthroned on the cherubim**. See note on 1 Sam. 4:3–4.

6:3–4 They carried the ark on a **new cart**. Presumably this refers to a ritually clean cart, as the Philistines had done when returning the ark (1 Sam. 6:7). But that was not the method that the Lord had commanded his people to use. Rather, God's command was that the ark should be carried by the Levites, using poles placed through rings on the sides of the ark (see Ex. 25:14–15; Num. 4:15; 7:9; Deut. 10:8; 31:9, 25; cf. Josh. 3:15). **Uzzah and Ahio** were probably brothers of Eleazar (cf. 1 Sam. 7:1), though they may have been sons, since it is phonetically possible that "Uzzah" is a variation of "Eleazar," similar to the variants "Uzziel" in 1 Chron. 25:4 and "Azarel" in 1 Chron. 25:18 or King Uzziah (2 Kings 15:32–34; 2 Chron. 26:1) and Azariah (2 Kings 15:1–7).

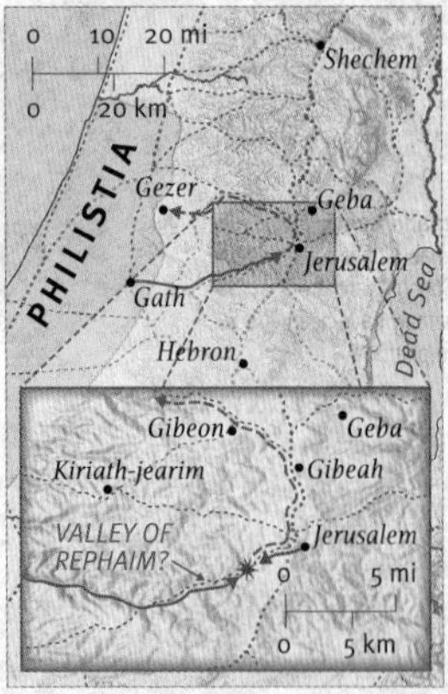

David Defeats the Philistines
c. 1000 B.C.
Soon after David moved his capital to Jerusalem, the Philistines prepared to attack David's forces at the nearby Valley of Rephaim. David defeated them, but they regrouped and prepared for a second attack. This time David attacked them from the rear and struck them down from Geba (or perhaps Gibeon) to Gezer.

5[z][1 Chr. 13:8]; See Ps. 150:3-5
6[a][1 Chr. 13:9] [b][Num. 4:15; 1 Chr. 15:2]
7[c][1 Sam. 6:19]
10[d][1 Chr. 15:25]
11[e]1 Chr. 26:5
12[f]For ver. 12-19, see 1 Chr. 15:25–16:3 [g][1 Kgs. 8:1]
13[h][Num. 4:15; 7:9; Josh. 3:3; 1 Chr. 15:2, 15] [i][1 Kgs. 8:5]
14[j][Ex. 15:20; Ps. 30:11; 150:4] [k]1 Sam. 2:18
17[l][1 Chr. 15:1; 2 Chr. 1:4; Ps. 132:8] [m][1 Kgs. 8:5, 62, 63]
18[n][1 Kgs. 8:14, 55]
19[o]1 Chr. 16:43

Uzzah and the Ark

5 And David and all the house of Israel were celebrating before the LORD, with [z]songs[1]
and lyres and harps and tambourines and castanets and cymbals. **6** And when they came
to the threshing floor of [a]Nacon, Uzzah [b]put out his hand to the ark of God and took hold
of it, for the oxen stumbled. **7** And the anger of the LORD was kindled against Uzzah, and
[c]God struck him down there because of his error, and he died there beside the ark of God.
8 And David was angry because the LORD had broken out against Uzzah. And that place is
called Perez-uzzah[2] to this day. **9** And David was afraid of the LORD that day, and he said,
"How can the ark of the LORD come to me?" **10** So David was not willing to take the ark of
the LORD into the city of David. But David took it aside [d]to the house of Obed-edom the
Gittite. **11** And the ark of the LORD remained in the house of Obed-edom the Gittite three
months, [e]and the LORD blessed Obed-edom and all his household.
12 And it was told King David, "The LORD has blessed the household of Obed-edom
and all that belongs to him, because of the ark of God." [f]So David went and brought up
the ark of God from the house of Obed-edom [g]to the city of David with rejoicing. **13** And
when [h]those who bore the ark of the LORD had gone six steps, [i]he sacrificed an ox and a
fattened animal. **14** And David [j]danced before the LORD with all his might. And David was
[k]wearing a linen ephod. **15** So David and all the house of Israel brought up the ark of the
LORD with shouting and with the sound of the horn.

David and Michal

16 As the ark of the LORD came into the city of David, Michal the daughter of Saul looked
out of the window and saw King David leaping and dancing before the LORD, and she
despised him in her heart. **17** And they brought in the ark of the LORD and set it [l]in its place,
inside the tent that David had pitched for it. [m]And David offered burnt offerings and peace
offerings before the LORD. **18** And when David had finished offering the burnt offerings
and the peace offerings, [n]he blessed the people in the name of the LORD of hosts **19** and
distributed among all the people, the whole multitude of Israel, both men and women,
a cake of bread, a portion of meat,[3] and a cake of raisins to each one. [o]Then all the people
departed, each to his house.

[1] Septuagint, 1 Chronicles 13:8; Hebrew *fir trees* [2] *Perez-uzzah* means *the breaking out against Uzzah* [3] Vulgate; the meaning of the Hebrew term is uncertain

6:5 Before the LORD, as in Ex. 28:29, means that the Lord himself was present above the ark (see note on 1 Sam. 4:3–4). Both this passage and 1 Sam. 4:1–7:2 show that the ark was not just an arbitrary symbol of God's presence, but God himself manifested his presence in a special way where the ark was, so the ark should not be treated lightly. **with songs and lyres**. Music is part of worship in most societies, and it was an important part of Israelite worship. The prophets in 1 Sam. 10:5 were accompanied by harp, tambourine, flute, and lyre. David sings God's praises in 2 Sam. 22:50, and in his old age he organized musicians to praise the Lord in the temple (1 Chron. 15:16; 23:1–5). The Psalms contain many references to using music in worship, as in Psalms 32; 71; 92; 149; and 150. For descriptions of lyres, **harps**, and **tambourines**, see note on 1 Sam. 10:5. The word translated **castanets** appears only here in the Bible. Since it means "shaking," "castanets" is a reasonable guess. It might also be a "sistrum," an instrument consisting of metal rings or disks shaken on rods. There were various types of **cymbals** in the ancient Near East; some were several inches in diameter. Some were held upright while playing, like the modern orchestral cymbal; in other cases, the two cymbals of the pair were held horizontally with rods, one above the other. If one follows the alternative translation in the ESV footnote (reading "fir trees" for "songs") the meaning may be "branches of fir trees" (cf. Matt. 21:8), or "instruments made of fir wood."

6:6–11 and God struck him down (v. 7). The death of Uzzah resembles the outbreak against Beth-shemesh in 1 Sam. 6:19. Touching the ark was a direct violation of God's law (Num. 4:15). Even though Uzzah's motive was clearly to prevent desecration, his fault was occasioned by the earlier mistake in the mode of transporting the ark (see note on 2 Sam. 6:3–4). **afraid of the LORD**. This incident was a dramatic reminder to David of God's holiness and of the necessity of approaching God only according to his revealed instruction, so much so that David was afraid even to bring the ark back to Jerusalem.

6:11 and the LORD blessed Obed-edom. The presence of the Lord brings much blessing to the household where the Lord is honored.

6:12–15 those who bore the ark. This time the ark is carried, as is proper (v. 13; 1 Chron. 15:12–15; see also 2 Sam. 15:24). The text may indicate that only one sacrifice was offered at the beginning of the journey, when they **had gone six steps**. But some interpreters think it means that David sacrificed every six steps. There are other references to repeated sacrifices in relation to processions in Near Eastern literature. Solomon also sacrificed a huge number of animals when he dedicated the temple (1 Kings 8:63). **he sacrificed**. Here and in 2 Sam. 6:17 it is doubtful that David himself killed all the animals, but it was done at his direction, and this emphasizes that he was the central figure in the retrieval of the ark. David's **ephod** was the simple linen robe worn by priests (cf. 1 Sam. 2:18). The ram's **horn** was an instrument used especially for signaling. **with rejoicing**. David is filled with joy because the ark coming to Jerusalem means that God himself is bringing the blessing of his presence to David and his kingdom.

6:14 David danced before the LORD. The term for "dancing" in vv. 14 and 16 does not appear elsewhere in Scripture and seems to describe a whirling dance. Dancing expresses joy (cf. Ex. 15:20–21; Ps. 30:11) and can be a part of jubilant worship (cf. Ps. 149:3; 150:4).

6:16–19 Michal . . . despised him in her heart. Michal is identified not as David's wife but as the **daughter of Saul**, and she shares in Saul's lack of spiritual discernment. She should have been rejoicing with David "and all the house of Israel" (v. 5) at this great occasion, for the Lord himself was coming to dwell in the midst of his people in Jerusalem. The motif of a royal woman looking out a palace **window** is common in the Bible (see Judg. 5:28; 2 Kings 9:30), as well as on ivories discovered in Syria, Phoenicia, and Israel. The **tent** corresponds to the tabernacle of Exodus 26. These gift items are mentioned in a list formula, as in 1 Sam. 6:17 and 25:18.

20 And David returned to bless his household. But Michal the daughter of Saul came
out to meet David and said, "How the king of Israel honored himself today, [p]uncovering
himself today before the eyes of his servants' female servants, as one of the [q]vulgar fellows
shamelessly uncovers himself!" 21 And David said to Michal, "It was before the LORD, [r]who
chose me above your father and above all his house, to appoint me as prince[1] over Israel,
the people of the LORD—and I will celebrate before the LORD. 22 I will make myself yet
more contemptible than this, and I will be abased in your[2] eyes. But by the female servants
of whom you have spoken, by them I shall be held in honor." 23 And Michal the daughter
of Saul had no child to the day of her death.

The LORD's Covenant with David

7 [s]Now when the king lived in his house and the LORD [t]had given him rest from all his
surrounding enemies, 2 the king said to [u]Nathan the prophet, "See now, I dwell [v]in a
house of cedar, but the ark of God dwells [w]in a tent." 3 And Nathan said to the king, [x]"Go,
do all that is in your heart, for the LORD is with you."
4 But that same night the word of the LORD came to Nathan, 5 "Go and tell my servant
David, 'Thus says the LORD: [y]Would you build me a house to dwell in? 6 I have not lived
in a house [z]since the day I brought up the people of Israel from Egypt to this day, but I
have been moving about [a]in a tent for my dwelling. 7 In all places where [b]I have moved
with all the people of Israel, did I speak a word with [c]any of the judges[3] of Israel, whom I
commanded [d]to shepherd my people Israel, saying, "Why have you not built me a house
of cedar?"' 8 Now, therefore, thus you shall say to my servant David, 'Thus says the LORD of
hosts, [e]I took you from the pasture, from following the sheep, that you should be prince[4]
over my people Israel. 9 [f]And I have been with you wherever you went and have cut off
all your enemies from before you. And I will make for you a great name, like the name
of the great ones of the earth. 10 And I will appoint a place for my people Israel [g]and will
plant them, so that they may dwell in their own place [h]and be disturbed no more. [i]And
violent men shall afflict them no more, as formerly, 11 [j]from the time that I appointed
judges over my people Israel. And [k]I will give you rest from all your enemies. Moreover,
the LORD declares to you that [l]the LORD will make you a house. 12 [m]When your days are
fulfilled and [n]you lie down with your fathers, [o]I will raise up your offspring after you, who

[1] Or *leader* [2] Septuagint; Hebrew *my* [3] Compare 1 Chronicles 17:6; Hebrew *tribes* [4] Or *leader*

20 [p]ver. 14, 16; [1 Sam. 19:24] [q]Judg. 9:4
21 [r]1 Sam. 13:14; 15:28

Chapter 7

1 [s]For ver. 1-29, see 1 Chr. 17:1-27 [t]See Josh. 11:23
2 [u]ver. 17; ch. 12:1 [v]ch. 5:11 [w]Ex. 26:1
3 [x]1 Kgs. 8:17, 18; 1 Chr. 22:7; 28:2; [Acts 7:46]
5 [y]1 Kgs. 5:3; 8:19; 1 Chr. 22:8; 28:3
6 [z]1 Kgs. 8:16 [a]Ex. 40:18, 19, 34
7 [b]Lev. 26:11, 12; Deut. 23:14 [c][1 Chr. 17:6] [d]See ch. 5:2
8 [e]1 Sam. 16:11; Ps. 78:70
9 [f]ch. 5:10; 8:6, 14; 1 Sam. 18:14
10 [g]Ps. 44:2; 80:8; Jer. 24:6; Amos 9:15 [h]2 Kgs. 21:8 [i][Ps. 89:22]
11 [j]See Judg. 2:14-16; 1 Sam. 12:9-11 [k]ver. 1; See Josh. 11:23 [l]ver. 27; 1 Kgs. 11:38; [Ex. 1:21; 1 Sam. 2:35]
12 [m][1 Kgs. 2:1] [n]1 Kgs. 1:21; 2:10; Acts 13:36; [Deut. 31:16] [o]1 Kgs. 8:20; Ps. 132:11

6:20–23 Although David returns to the members of his household for the purpose of blessing them, he is greeted by his wife Michal's sarcastic comment, "**How the king of Israel honored himself today**." No doubt she felt he should have worn his royal robes as would befit a king, but David stresses that he was dressed simply **before the LORD**. Michal accuses David of **uncovering himself**, which seems to be a reflection more of Michal's bitterness and contempt for David than a true statement of fact. The "linen ephod" worn by David (v. 14) was a simple white garment worn by priests in the fulfillment of their duties (1 Sam. 22:18). **had no child**. The text does not say what caused her childlessness, leaving the reader to reflect on whether it was a natural result of the rift between Michal and David, or whether it was due to God's judgment of Michal (as would seem to be the case) for her contempt toward David in his divinely appointed role as king of Israel.

7:1–29 *Davidic Covenant: Eternal Throne.* This chapter, with its messianic promise, is a key passage in the history of salvation. The Lord promises to make one family, that of David, the representative of his people forever. Verses 8–17 are often described as the "Davidic covenant," even though the term "covenant" does not appear there. But in Ps. 89:3 this promise is described using the words, "I have made a covenant with my chosen one." David expresses his desire to build a house for the Lord. But the Lord does not approve, and instead states on his own initiative that he will establish David's house (i.e., dynasty) eternally, promising him an eternal throne: "And your house and your kingdom shall be made sure forever before me. Your throne shall be established forever" (2 Sam. 7:16). This is not, however, a guarantee that every occupant of the throne of David will himself enjoy the blessings without regard for his own piety (v. 14). Psalm 132:11 says that on this occasion the Lord swore to David with "a sure oath," from which he would not turn back, that "one of the sons of your body I will set on your throne" (cf. 2 Sam. 7:12). This points to Solomon, who would "sit on the throne of Israel" and build "the house for the name of the LORD" (1 Kings 8:20), and eventually to Jesus, the Messiah who would sit on the throne eternally, thus establishing David's throne forever (2 Sam. 7:16; Luke 1:32–33). See 2 Chron. 13:5; 21:7; Ps. 89:20–38; Isa. 55:3; Jer. 33:17, 20–22; etc.

7:1–3 David contrasts his own **cedar** house (5:11) with the **tent** that houses the **ark** (6:17). It was common in the ancient Near East for a king to build a temple to honor his god. **the LORD is with you**. Nathan probably means these words as a general comment on David and gives his own opinion as David's counselor. That night, however, he receives a specific revelation from God, which he delivers to David as a prophet, the messenger of God.

7:6–7 I have not lived in a house. Nothing in the regulations about the ark in Exodus suggests that it was placed in a building; rather, it needed carrying poles (Ex. 25:10–16). The shrine at Shiloh did have a door and was called a "house" or "temple" (1 Sam. 1:9; 3:3, 15; see note on 1 Sam. 1:7, 9), but even a tent could be called a "house," and since there is also a reference to the "entrance of the tent of meeting," it may be that some kind of structure was built around the tent at Shiloh. The ark had also been in the house of Abinadab (2 Sam. 6:3) for several decades, but that was considered a temporary expedient.

7:8–17 God will not let David build him a house; rather, he will build David a house, i.e., a ruling dynasty (see note on 1 Chron. 17:10b–14). According to 1 Kings 5:3, Solomon said David was not able to build the temple "because of the warfare with which his enemies surrounded him," and in 1 Chron. 22:8 David says the Lord said he could not do so because "you have shed much blood and have waged great wars. You shall not build a house to my name, because you have shed so much blood before me on the earth" (see note on 1 Chron. 22:6–16).

7:12 Your offspring after you refers to Solomon.

shall come from your body, and I will establish his kingdom. **13** [p]He shall build a house
for my name, and [q]I will establish the throne of his kingdom forever. **14** [r]I will be to him
a father, and he shall be to me a son. When he commits iniquity, [s]I will discipline him
with the rod of men, with the stripes of the sons of men, **15** [s]but my steadfast love will
not depart from him, [t]as I took it from Saul, whom I put away from before you. **16** [u]And
your house and your kingdom shall be made sure forever before me.[1] [u]Your throne shall
be established forever.'" **17** In accordance with all these words, and in accordance with all
this vision, Nathan spoke to David.

David's Prayer of Gratitude

18 Then King David went in and sat before the LORD and said, [v]"Who am I, O Lord GOD,
and what is my house, that you have brought me thus far? **19** And yet this was a small thing
in your eyes, O Lord GOD. [w]You have spoken also of your servant's house for a great while
to come, and this is instruction for mankind, O Lord GOD! **20** And what more can David say
to you? [x]For you know your servant, O Lord GOD! **21** Because of your promise, and according to your own heart, you have brought about all this greatness, to make your servant
know it. **22** [y]Therefore you are great, O LORD God. [z]For there is none like you, and there is
no God besides you, according to all that we have heard with our ears. **23** [a]And who is like
your people Israel, the one nation on earth whom God went to redeem to be his people,
making himself a name [b]and doing for them[2] great and awesome things by driving out[3]
before your people, whom [c]you redeemed for yourself from Egypt, a nation and its gods?
24 [d]And you established for yourself your people Israel to be your people forever. And you,
O LORD, became their God. **25** And now, O LORD God, confirm forever the word that you
have spoken concerning your servant and concerning his house, and do as you have spoken. **26** And your name will be magnified forever, saying, 'The LORD of hosts is God over
Israel,' and the house of your servant David will be established before you. **27** For you, O
LORD of hosts, the God of Israel, have made this revelation to your servant, saying, 'I will
build you a house.' Therefore your servant has found courage to pray this prayer to you.
28 And now, O Lord GOD, you are God, and [e]your words are true, and you have promised
this good thing to your servant. **29** Now therefore may it please you to bless the house of
your servant, so that it may continue forever before you. For you, O Lord GOD, have spoken,
[f]and with your blessing shall the house of your servant be blessed forever."

David's Victories

8 [g]After this David defeated the Philistines and subdued them, and David took [h]Metheg-
ammah out of the hand of the Philistines.

2 [i]And he defeated Moab and he measured them with a line, making them lie down on
the ground. Two lines he measured to be put to death, and one full line to be spared. And
the Moabites [j]became servants to David and [k]brought tribute.

3 David also defeated [l]Hadadezer the son of Rehob, king of [m]Zobah, as he went to restore

[1] Septuagint; Hebrew *you* [2] With a few Targums, Vulgate, Syriac; Hebrew *you* [3] Septuagint (compare 1 Chronicles 17:21); Hebrew *for your land*

13 [p]1 Kgs. 5:5; 6:12; 8:19; 1 Chr. 22:10; 28:6 [q]ver. 16; Ps. 89:4, 29, 36, 37
14 [r]Ps. 89:26, 27; Cited Heb. 1:5 [s]Ps. 89:32, 33
15 [s][See ver. 14 above] [t]1 Sam. 15:23, 28; [1 Kgs. 11:13, 34]
16 [u]ver. 13; Ps. 89:36, 37; [Luke 1:33]
18 [v][Gen. 32:10]
19 [w]ver. 12, 13; 1 Chr. 17:17
20 [x]See Ps. 139:1-4
22 [y]1 Chr. 16:25; 2 Chr. 2:5 [z]Ex. 15:11; Deut. 3:24; Ps. 86:8; 89:6, 8; Isa. 45:5; Jer. 10:6
23 [a]Deut. 4:7, 34; 33:29; Ps. 147:20 [b]Deut. 10:21 [c]Deut. 9:26; Neh. 1:10
24 [d]ver. 13, 16, 26; Deut. 26:18
28 [e]John 17:17
29 [f]ch. 22:51; Ps. 89:28, 29

Chapter 8

1 [g]For ver. 1-18, see 1 Chr. 18:1-17; Ps. 60 [h][1 Chr. 18:1]
2 [i]Num. 24:17 [j]ver. 6, 14; [Ps. 60:8] [k][1 Sam. 10:27; 2 Kgs. 17:3; Ps. 72:10]
3 [l][ch. 10:16, 19; 1 Chr. 18:3] [m]ch. 10:6; 1 Sam. 14:47; 1 Kgs. 11:23

7:14 Hebrews 1:5 applies the words **I will be to him a father, and he shall be to me a son** to Christ because, as Messiah, Jesus inherits David's role as representative of God's people (his "son," Ex. 4:22–23; cf. Ps. 89:26–27).

7:18–29 In this moving prayer, David uses the phrase **O Lord GOD** (or "O LORD God") eight times, expressing his close intimacy with his God. **This is instruction for mankind** (v. 19) means that all people can learn about God's faithfulness and grace from his promises to David. The phrase could also be translated, "Is this your custom for mankind?" i.e., "You do not usually do this for humans." **there is none like you, and there is no God besides you** (v. 22). This is an explicit statement of monotheism (cf. 1 Sam. 2:2). Then follows the expression **who is like your people Israel**, which describes the incomparability (hence the uniqueness) of Israel, God's people, whom he has redeemed from Egypt and established for himself forever.

7:18 Who am I, O Lord . . . , that you have brought me thus far? In spite of dramatic military success and the popular acclaim of the whole nation, David humbly considers himself unworthy of all the Lord's blessings, attributing his success instead to the Lord (cf. Prov. 3:34; James 4:6; 1 Pet. 5:5). He understands rightly that the covenant (2 Sam. 7:8–17) expresses God's faithfulness to his promises to his people (vv. 21–29).

8:1–18 *Catalog of David's Military Activities.* Chapter 8 is a catalog of David's military victories, from the old enemies, the Philistines, to the Transjordan nations of Moab and Ammon, through the Syrian countries, and all the way to "the River" (the Euphrates), ending with a statement about his administration. The varied events of this chapter are not necessarily chronological with the rest of the book. The Ammon war of chs. 10–12 may have been the prelude to David's defeat of the important kingdom of Zobah in this chapter. Chapter 8 has ties with the title to Psalm 60: "when he strove with Aram-naharaim and with Aram-zobah [cf. 2 Sam. 8:3], and when Joab on his return struck down twelve thousand of Edom in the Valley of Salt [cf. v. 13]." The older empires in Egypt and Mesopotamia were at a low point, which allowed David to take advantage of the international situation.

8:1 Metheg-ammah is otherwise unknown—perhaps it refers to a type of land. After the time of David, there are no references to battles with the **Philistines** until the time of Hezekiah (2 Kings 18:8).

8:3–12 The events of chs. 10–12 may have been the prelude to 8:3, as

his power at the river Euphrates. 4 [n]And David took from him 1,700 horsemen, and 20,000
foot soldiers. And David [o]hamstrung all the chariot horses but left enough for 100 chariots.
5 [p]And when the [q]Syrians of Damascus came to help [l]Hadadezer king of [m]Zobah, David
struck down 22,000 men of the Syrians. 6 Then David put garrisons in Aram of Damascus,
and the Syrians [r]became servants to David and brought tribute. [s]And the LORD gave victory to David wherever he went. 7 And David took [t]the shields of gold that were carried
by the servants of Hadadezer and brought them to Jerusalem. 8 And from Betah and from
Berothai, cities of Hadadezer, King David took very much bronze.
9 When Toi king of [u]Hamath heard that David had defeated the whole army of Hadadezer,
10 Toi sent his son Joram to King David, to ask about his health and to bless him because
he had fought against Hadadezer and defeated him, for Hadadezer had often been at war
with Toi. And Joram brought with him articles of silver, of gold, and of bronze. 11 [v]These
also King David dedicated to the LORD, together with the silver and gold that he dedicated
from all the nations he subdued, 12 from Edom, [w]Moab, [x]the Ammonites, [y]the Philistines,
[z]Amalek, and from the spoil of Hadadezer the son of Rehob, king of [m]Zobah.
13 And David made a name for himself when he returned from striking down 18,000
Edomites in [a]the Valley of Salt. 14 Then he put garrisons in Edom; throughout all Edom he
put garrisons, [b]and all the Edomites became David's servants. And the LORD gave victory
to David wherever he went.

David's Officials

15 So David reigned over all Israel. And David administered justice and equity to all
his people. 16 [c]Joab the son of Zeruiah was over the army, and [d]Jehoshaphat the son of
Ahilud was recorder, 17 and [e]Zadok the son of Ahitub and Ahimelech the son of Abiathar
were priests, and [f]Seraiah was secretary, 18 and [g]Benaiah the son of Jehoiada was over[1] the
[h]Cherethites and the Pelethites, and David's sons were priests.

[1] Compare 20:23, 1 Chronicles 18:17, Syriac, Targum, Vulgate; Hebrew lacks *was over*

4 [n][1 Chr. 18:4] [o]See Josh. 11:6
5 [p][1 Kgs. 11:23-25] [q]See Josh. 11:6 [l][See ver. 3 above] [m][See ver. 3 above]
6 [r]ver. 2, 14 [s]ver. 14
7 [t][2 Kgs. 11:10; 2 Chr. 23:9; Song 4:4]
9 [u]1 Kgs. 8:65; 2 Kgs. 18:34
11 [v]1 Kgs. 7:51; 1 Chr. 26:26
12 [w]ver. 2 [x]ch. 10:14; 12:30 [y]See ch. 5:17-25 [z]1 Sam. 30:20 [m][See ver. 3 above]
13 [a]2 Kgs. 14:7; [Josh. 15:62]
14 [b]Gen. 25:23; 27:29, 37, 40; Num. 24:18
16 [c]For ver. 16-18, see ch. 20:23-26 [d]1 Kgs. 4:3
17 [e]1 Chr. 24:3, 6 [f][1 Chr. 18:16]
18 [g]1 Kgs. 4:4; [ch. 23:20-23] [h]ch. 15:18; 20:7; 1 Sam. 30:14; 1 Kgs. 1:38

suggested by the references in ch. 10 to Zobah and Hadadezer (10:6, 16). If so, Hadadezer—after the disastrous defeat by David and the defection of his vassals (10:19) and the defeat of Ammon (12:31)—went to the Euphrates to try to restore his power over his vassals but was attacked on the way by David. **Zobah** and **Damascus** were both in Syria (Hb. *'Aram*). Zobah was in the northern part of the Lebanon Valley (see Josh. 11:17; 12:7), in what is now called the Bekaa Valley. Hadadezer's name does not appear outside the Bible, but there are similarities to an unnamed Syrian king of David's time mentioned in Assyrian annals. Having captured chariot horses, David apparently decided to experiment with a small chariot force. It is not clear why he would hamstring the other horses (2 Sam. 8:4). It was probably to keep them from being used again by enemy soldiers, but it also may have been in response to the warning in Deut. 17:16 that the king must not acquire many horses for himself (cf. Josh. 11:6–9). The hamstrung horses supposedly could have been used as farm or pack horses. **Hamath** was on the middle Orontes River; it bordered Zobah on the north. The treasures (2 Sam. 8:11) later became part of Solomon's treasure, used either to build the temple or were placed in the temple treasury (1 Kings 7:51; 1 Chron. 18:8).

8:4 While the verse says that **David took from him 1,700 horsemen**, 1 Chron. 18:4 says that he "took from him 1,000 chariots" and "7,000 horsemen." The Septuagint agrees with Chronicles. Although there is not enough information available to account for this difference, one possible explanation is that someone miscopied the text of Samuel, and the Septuagint (along with Chronicles) retains the true reading.

8:6 And the LORD gave victory to David wherever he went. The narrator continues to point to God's blessing, not David's skill, as the reason for David's victories (cf. v. 14; 1 Sam. 18:12).

8:13–14 The **Valley of Salt** must have been in the Edomite territory south and east of the Dead Sea. First Chronicles 18:12 states that Abishai killed the **Edomites**. The deeds of David's generals were ascribed to David, just as the deeds of Abishai's men were ascribed to Abishai. Joab seems to have led the campaign; it was at this time that Hadad, of the royal house of Edom, escaped to Egypt (1 Kings 11:14–22; title of Psalm 60).

8:15–18 This is a list of David's officials (for similar lists, cf. 20:23–26; 1 Kings 4:1–6). Like the list in Kings, this one starts with the office of the king. It was the task of the king to establish **justice and equity** (see 1 Kings 10:9). **Jehoshaphat the son of Ahilud** appears as **recorder** in all three lists. The offices of "recorder" and "secretary" (2 Sam. 8:17) were common in surrounding countries. Jerusalem, like other city-states of the time, had a long history of civil administration, which David could take over and use.

8:17 Zadok helped David during Absalom's rebellion (15:27–28; 17:15; 19:11) and later supported Solomon (1 Kings 1:8). His father **Ahitub** was probably a different person from Ahitub the father of Ahimelech, priest at Nob (1 Sam. 22:9). **Abiathar** appeared in 1 Samuel accompanying David (1 Sam. 22:20; 23:6; 30:7) and worked with Zadok during Absalom's rebellion. Abiathar apparently named his son **Ahimelech** after his father (1 Sam. 22:20), a common practice. For Abiathar's genealogy, see note on 1 Sam. 2:27–28. Other passages such as the account of Absalom's rebellion and the lists of officials in 2 Sam. 20:25 and 1 Kings 4:4 refer to the priests as "Zadok and Abiathar." It is often suggested that "Ahimelech the son of Abiathar" is a scribal error for "Abiathar son of Ahimelech." Another possibility is that Abiathar retired his position as one of the chief priests in favor of a son, as Zadok later did (1 Kings 4:2), and then perhaps the son later died or had some other problem, so Abiathar resumed the position. The secretary **Seraiah** might be the same as the "Sheva" (2 Sam. 20:25) and "Shisha" (1 Kings 4:3) mentioned in the other two lists, but this is not established. It may be that it was a foreign name, which would be especially liable to variant spellings.

8:18 Benaiah was in charge of David's personal force of **Cherethites and . . . Pelethites**. He was one of David's "mighty men" (23:20–22). Like Zadok, he supported Solomon against Adonijah and became commander of the whole army under Solomon (1 Kings 1:1–2:46; 4:1–6). The Cherethites and Pelethites were foreigners who made up the king's bodyguard (cf. 1 Sam. 28:2). **David's sons were priests**. It is not known what their duties were, but obviously their duties were not important compared to those of the Levitical priests Zadok, Abiathar, and Ahimelech, who were concerned with the ark (2 Sam. 15:24); the other lists do not mention David's sons in this capacity. They may have been just chaplains for the rituals carried out in the royal family. The priestly line and the royal line were essentially separate.

Chapter 9
1 [i]1 Sam. 18:3; 20:14, 15, 42
2 [j]ch. 16:1-4; 19:17, 29
3 [k]1 Sam. 20:14 [l]ch. 4:4
4 [m]ch. 17:27
6 [n]ch. 16:4; 19:24, 25, 30; 21:7; [1 Chr. 8:34; 9:40]
7 [i][See ver. 1 above] [o]ch. 19:28; 1 Kgs. 2:7; [2 Kgs. 25:29]
8 [p]ch. 16:9; 1 Sam. 24:14
10 [o][See ver. 7 above] [q]ch. 19:17
11 [o][See ver. 7 above]
12 [r]1 Chr. 8:34
13 [o][See ver. 7 above] [l][See ver. 3 above]
Chapter 10
1 [s]For ver. 1-19, see 1 Chr. 19:1-19
2 [t]1 Sam. 11:1
4 [u][Isa. 20:4]

David's Kindness to Mephibosheth

9 And David said, "Is there still anyone left of the house of Saul, that I may [i]show him
kindness for Jonathan's sake?" **2** Now there was a servant of the house of Saul whose
name was [j]Ziba, and they called him to David. And the king said to him, "Are you Ziba?"
And he said, "I am your servant." **3** And the king said, "Is there not still someone of the
house of Saul, that I may show [k]the kindness of God to him?" Ziba said to the king, "There
is still a son of [l]Jonathan; he is crippled in his feet." **4** The king said to him, "Where is he?"
And Ziba said to the king, "He is in the house of [m]Machir the son of Ammiel, at Lo-debar."
5 Then King David sent and brought him from the house of Machir the son of Ammiel, at
Lo-debar. **6** And [n]Mephibosheth the son of Jonathan, son of Saul, came to David and fell on
his face and paid homage. And David said, "Mephibosheth!" And he answered, "Behold, I
am your servant." **7** And David said to him, "Do not fear, [i]for I will show you kindness for the
sake of your father Jonathan, and I will restore to you all the land of Saul your father, and
[o]you shall eat at my table always." **8** And he paid homage and said, "What is your servant,
that you should show regard for [p]a dead dog such as I?"
9 Then the king called Ziba, Saul's servant, and said to him, "All that belonged to Saul
and to all his house I have given to your master's grandson. **10** And you and your sons and
your servants shall till the land for him and shall bring in the produce, that your master's grandson may have bread to eat. But Mephibosheth your master's grandson [o]shall
always eat at my table." Now Ziba had [q]fifteen sons and twenty servants. **11** Then Ziba said
to the king, "According to all that my lord the king commands his servant, so will your
servant do." So Mephibosheth [o]ate at David's[1] table, like one of the king's sons. **12** And
Mephibosheth had a young son, [r]whose name was Mica. And all who lived in Ziba's house
became Mephibosheth's servants. **13** So Mephibosheth lived in Jerusalem, for [o]he ate always
at the king's table. Now [l]he was lame in both his feet.

David Defeats Ammon and Syria

10 [s]After this the king of the Ammonites died, and Hanun his son reigned in his
place. **2** And David said, "I will deal loyally[2] with Hanun the son of [t]Nahash, as his
father dealt loyally with me." So David sent by his servants to console him concerning
his father. And David's servants came into the land of the Ammonites. **3** But the princes
of the Ammonites said to Hanun their lord, "Do you think, because David has sent comforters to you, that he is honoring your father? Has not David sent his servants to you to
search the city and to spy it out and to overthrow it?" **4** So Hanun took David's servants
and shaved off half the beard of each and cut off their garments in the middle, [u]at their

[1] Septuagint; Hebrew *my* [2] Or *kindly*; twice in this verse

9:1–13 *Mephibosheth.* David keeps his promise to Jonathan and Saul that he would not destroy their descendants (1 Sam. 20:14–17, 42; 24:21–22) as often happened in changes of dynasty (cf. 2 Kings 10; 11; etc.).

9:2–4 For **Ziba**, the **servant** (here the Hb. word is *'ebed*) of Saul's house, see note on v. 9. The exact location of **Lo-debar** is unknown, but it seems to have been in northern Transjordan (17:27). Mephibosheth had probably been taken to Transjordan soon after Saul's death (4:4), during the time his uncle Ish-bosheth ruled from the Transjordanian city of Mahanaim (2:8).

9:6–8 For the name **Mephibosheth**, see note on 4:4. Note that the word **father** (Hb. *'ab*) in 9:7 means "father" in one sentence and "grandfather" in the next. This phenomenon can also be seen in some of the genealogies (e.g., probably 1 Sam. 9:1). In 2 Sam. 9:9–10, the "grandson" is literally "son" (Hb. *ben*), as can be seen in the translation of the same Hebrew phrase in 16:3. **Dead dog** is a term of self-abasement here and in 1 Sam. 24:14; in 2 Sam. 16:9 it is used for contempt.

9:9 Ziba is here referred to as a **servant** (Hb. *na'ar*, "young man, servant"), but because Ziba had 15 sons (v. 10), it was probably the more specific "steward of an estate." Ziba had probably continued to be the steward in charge of the land after Saul's death, but had paid the benefits of the estate to David or to someone to whom David had assigned the land. But from now on he is required to pay the benefits to Mephibosheth.

9:11 Mephibosheth ate at David's table, like one of the king's sons. The arrangement David sets up for Mephibosheth is similar to that of at least David's older sons. Though the king's sons "ate at David's table," some of them lived in their own houses in Jerusalem (13:7, 20) and had fields and agricultural lands of their own to support them (13:23; 14:30).

9:12 Mica (or "Micah") had many descendants, through whom the house of Saul and Jonathan was preserved (1 Chron. 8:35–40; 9:41–44).

10:1–12:31 *Israel-Ammon War.* The Ammonite war is the background of the next three chapters. As far as David's empire went, it led to his domination of the Syrian kingdoms (see 8:3–12; 10:15–19). More importantly to the biblical writer, however, it was the setting for David's great sin (11:1–12:25).

10:1–19 *Beginning of Israel-Ammon War.* The war began because the Ammonites disgraced David's ambassadors; it did not result from any wrongdoing by David.

10:1–5 Nahash was presumably the Nahash of 1 Samuel 11. David wants to **deal loyally** with Hanun because of his father Nahash, who showed "loyalty" to David in accordance with their treaty. While his loyalty, or "kindness" (Hb. *hesed*), toward Mephibosheth (2 Samuel 9) was "for Jonathan's sake," this "kindness" is for diplomatic reasons: David wants to keep the Ammonites as peaceful neighbors. It may be that the **princes of the Ammonites** (10:3) are alarmed by the representatives of David, who had conquered Moab (8:2), the country directly south of them. Humiliating the official envoys (10:4) certainly means breaking off diplomatic relations. David allows his messengers to **remain at Jericho** so that they would not have to display their humiliation in court.

hips, and sent them away. 5 When it was told David, he sent to meet them, for the men
were greatly ashamed. And the king said, "Remain at Jericho until your beards have grown
and then return."
6 When the Ammonites saw that they had become a stench to David, the Ammonites sent
and hired the Syrians of [v]Beth-rehob, and [w]the Syrians of Zobah, 20,000 foot soldiers, and
the king of [x]Maacah with 1,000 men, and the men of [y]Tob, 12,000 men. 7 And when David
heard of it, he sent Joab and all the host of [z]the mighty men. 8 And the Ammonites came
out and drew up in battle array at the entrance of the gate, and [w]the Syrians of Zobah and
of Rehob and [y]the men of Tob and Maacah were by themselves in the open country.
9 When Joab saw that the battle was set against him both in front and in the rear, he
chose some of the best men of Israel and arrayed them against the Syrians. 10 The rest
of his men he put in the charge of Abishai his brother, and he arrayed them against the
Ammonites. 11 And he said, "If the Syrians are too strong for me, then you shall help me,
but if the Ammonites are too strong for you, then I will come and help you. 12 [a]Be of good
courage, and [b]let us be courageous for our people, and for the cities of our God, and [c]may
the LORD do what seems good to him." 13 So Joab and the people who were with him drew
near to battle against the Syrians, and they fled before him. 14 And when the Ammonites
saw that the Syrians fled, they likewise fled before Abishai and entered the city. Then Joab
returned from fighting against the Ammonites and came to Jerusalem.
15 But when the Syrians saw that they had been defeated by Israel, they gathered them-

6 [v]Judg. 18:28 [w]ch. 8:3, 5 [x][Josh. 13:11, 13] [y]Judg. 11:3, 5
7 [z]ch. 23:8
8 [w][See ver. 6 above] [y][See ver. 6 above]
12 [a]See Deut. 31:6 [b]1 Sam. 4:9; [1 Cor. 16:13] [c]1 Sam. 3:18

David Defeats the Ammonites and the Syrians
c. 995 B.C.
After purposely humiliating ambassadors sent by David, the Ammonites prepared for David's response by calling for help from the king of Maacah, the men of Tob, and the Syrians living in Beth-rehob and Zobah. When David's commander Joab defeated these forces, the Syrians called for more troops from beyond the Euphrates River and attacked David at Helam. David's forces defeated them again, and the Syrians became subject to Israel.

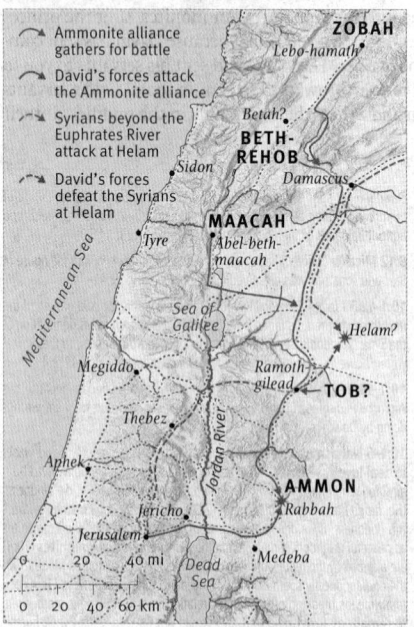

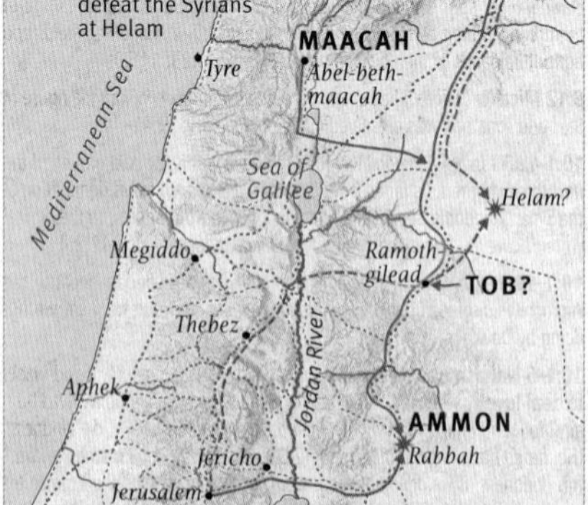

10:6–8 Beth-rehob, Zobah, Maacah, and **Tob** were Syrian kingdoms in the northern Transjordan and Lebanon Valley. For the relationship of this passage with 8:3–4, see note on 8:3–12. Hiring armies was not uncommon (2 Kings 7:6). The numbers of troops are mentioned according to the usual list formula (see note on 1 Sam. 6:17–18). **Syrians** can also be translated "Aram" or "Arameans," the normal term for Syria or the Syrians. "Aramaic," the later common language (cf. 2 Kings 18:26), was the language of Syria. The **gate** (2 Sam. 10:8) is that of the city of Rabbah (11:1), the capital of Ammon, near present-day Amman, Jordan.

10:9–19 David's army under Joab is trapped between the Syrians and the Ammonites, but they defeat the Syrians and force them to leave. **Hadadezer** of Zobah (see 8:5) attacks again at **Helam**, apparently a city in northern Transjordan, but is again defeated.

10:12 let us be courageous . . . and may the LORD do what seems good to him. Joab expresses both faith in God and a resolve to fight with all his strength. Faith and human effort are not incompatible with each other. Joab is a complicated figure: as here, he can express sturdy piety (e.g., 24:3), and he can also display a chilling ruthlessness in preserving David's and his own position (e.g., 18:14–15; 20:9–10, 20–22). It is not surprising that David does not trust him to treat Solomon well after Joab supported Adonijah (1 Kings 1:7, 19; 2:5–6).

11:1–12:25 *David and Bathsheba.* The story of the Ammonite war continues up through 11:1 and is concluded in 12:26–31. In between comes the account of David and Bathsheba (11:2–12:25). The story of the war thus is a "frame" around the story of David and Bathsheba: "Joab/Rabbah" and "David/Jerusalem" in 11:1 correspond to "Joab/Rabbah" in 12:26 and "David/Jerusalem" in 12:31.

11:1 With the defeat of the Syrians, David is free to concentrate on besieging Rabbah (10:14). **the time when kings go out to battle. . . . But David remained at Jerusalem.** The connection of these two phrases hints that something is wrong: the kings go out to battle, but this king does not. And **all Israel** went out to battle, but Israel's leader did not. Readers can see a contrast between the king who is at leisure (11:2) and the soldiers on the field (v. 11).

11:2 The **woman bathing** is probably "purifying herself from her uncleanness" (v. 4) after her menstrual period (Lev. 15:19–24). Clearly, then, the child who would be conceived in 2 Sam. 11:5 was not Uriah's. **Beautiful** is literally "very good in appearance." Compared with the usual Hebrew adjective *yapah* for "beautiful" (as in 1 Sam. 25:3, where it is used of Abigail), the emphasis here is more distinctly on the woman's appearance. A terraced structure, first built in the fourteenth or thirteenth century B.C., has been found

16[d][ch. 8:3] [e][1 Chr. 19:16]
18[f][1 Chr. 19:18]
19[g]ch. 8:6
Chapter 11
1[h]1 Chr. 20:1 [i]1 Kgs. 20:22, 26; 2 Chr. 36:10 [j]ch. 12:26; Deut. 3:11
2[k]See 1 Sam. 9:25
3[l][1 Chr. 3:5] [m]ch. 23:39
4[n]Lev. 15:19, 28; 18:19
8[o]See Gen. 18:4
11[p]ch. 7:2, 6 [q]ch. 20:6; 1 Kgs. 1:33 [r]See 1 Sam. 1:26
13[s][Gen. 19:33, 35] [q][See ver. 11 above]

selves together. 16 And Hadadezer sent and brought out the Syrians who were beyond [d]the
Euphrates.[1] They came to Helam, with [e]Shobach the commander of the army of Hadadezer
at their head. 17 And when it was told David, he gathered all Israel together and crossed
the Jordan and came to Helam. The Syrians arrayed themselves against David and fought
with him. 18 And the Syrians fled before Israel, and David killed of the Syrians the men
of 700 chariots, and 40,000 horsemen, and wounded [f]Shobach the commander of their
army, so that he died there. 19 And when all the kings who were servants of Hadadezer saw
that they had been defeated by Israel, they made peace with Israel [g]and became subject to
them. So the Syrians were afraid to save the Ammonites anymore.

David and Bathsheba

11 [h, i]In the spring of the year, the time when kings go out to battle, David sent Joab,
and his servants with him, and all Israel. And they ravaged the Ammonites and
besieged [j]Rabbah. But David remained at Jerusalem.
2 It happened, late one afternoon, when David arose from his couch and was walking on
[k]the roof of the king's house, that he saw from the roof a woman bathing; and the woman
was very beautiful. 3 And David sent and inquired about the woman. And one said, "Is not
this [l]Bathsheba, the daughter of Eliam, the wife of [m]Uriah the Hittite?" 4 So David sent
messengers and took her, and she came to him, and he lay with her. ([n]Now she had been
purifying herself from her uncleanness.) Then she returned to her house. 5 And the woman
conceived, and she sent and told David, "I am pregnant."
6 So David sent word to Joab, "Send me Uriah the Hittite." And Joab sent Uriah to David.
7 When Uriah came to him, David asked how Joab was doing and how the people were
doing and how the war was going. 8 Then David said to Uriah, "Go down to your house
and [o]wash your feet." And Uriah went out of the king's house, and there followed him a
present from the king. 9 But Uriah slept at the door of the king's house with all the servants
of his lord, and did not go down to his house. 10 When they told David, "Uriah did not go
down to his house," David said to Uriah, "Have you not come from a journey? Why did
you not go down to your house?" 11 Uriah said to David, [p]"The ark and Israel and Judah
dwell in booths, and my lord Joab and [q]the servants of my lord are camping in the open
field. Shall I then go to my house, to eat and to drink and to lie with my wife? As you live,
and [r]as your soul lives, I will not do this thing." 12 Then David said to Uriah, "Remain here
today also, and tomorrow I will send you back." So Uriah remained in Jerusalem that day
and the next. 13 And David invited him, and he ate in his presence and drank, [s]so that he
made him drunk. And in the evening he went out to lie on his couch with [q]the servants
of his lord, but he did not go down to his house.

[1] Hebrew *the River*

in Jerusalem as part of the city of King David. Over 50 feet (15 m) in height, it may have served as the foundation for a large base that held the highest buildings of Jerusalem. David's palace perhaps sat there, overlooking the entire city (see illustration, p. 550).

11:3 Uriah the Hittite is listed among David's top warriors, the "thirty," in 23:39.

11:4 Given the elaborate attempt David makes (vv. 6–13) to cover up the initial act of his adultery, it is hardly likely that he makes his intention clear when he summons Bathsheba. Probably David makes inquiry about the welfare of the family of his trusted general during Uriah's absence and gives Uriah's wife the honor of a private interview, even sending **messengers** (plural) to invite Bathsheba; after Uriah's death, David takes Uriah's widow under his protection as his own wife (v. 27).

11:6–13 The king had certain rights, but clearly adultery was not one of them. Instead of repenting and trying to settle the matter openly, David tries to cover it up by making it appear that his child by Bathsheba is Uriah's.

11:9 Sexual intercourse was a source of ritual impurity (Ex. 19:15; Lev. 15:18), and so it was avoided during a military campaign, as is mentioned in 1 Sam. 21:5. (See Deut. 23:9. "Evil" in that passage refers to something "unseemly" or "improper," rather than morally evil. Certainly "excrement" [Deut. 23:13] is not morally evil, but like intercourse it does make one unclean.) Uriah considered himself still on duty, in contrast to David.

11:14–15 It is ironic that Uriah should unknowingly take with him the **letter** that orders him killed. David is hopelessly overwhelmed by the need to cover

The Rise and Failure of David in 1 and 2 Samuel

David's Rise (1 Samuel 16–2 Samuel 10)	David's Failures (2 Samuel 11–20)
Eager holy warrior	Remains in palace
Marries honorably	Adultery with Bathsheba
Protects Saul's life	Plots Uriah's death
Decisive	Indecisive
Prayers effective	Prayers ineffective
Fearless when outnumbered	Fearfully takes census
Attracts thousands of followers	Loses thousands of followers

14 In the morning David [t]wrote a letter to Joab and sent it by the hand of Uriah. 15 In the
letter he wrote, "Set Uriah in the forefront of the hardest fighting, and then draw back
from him, [u]that he may be struck down, and die." 16 And as Joab was besieging the city, he
assigned Uriah to the place where he knew there were valiant men. 17 And the men of the
city came out and fought with Joab, and some of the servants of David among the people
fell. Uriah the Hittite also died. 18 Then Joab sent and told David all the news about the
fighting. 19 And he instructed the messenger, "When you have finished telling all the news
about the fighting to the king, 20 then, if the king's anger rises, and if he says to you, 'Why
did you go so near the city to fight? Did you not know that they would shoot from the
wall? 21 [v]Who killed Abimelech the son of Jerubbesheth? Did not a woman cast an upper
millstone on him from the wall, so that he died at Thebez? Why did you go so near the
wall?' then you shall say, 'Your servant Uriah the Hittite is dead also.'"
22 So the messenger went and came and told David all that Joab had sent him to tell. 23 The
messenger said to David, "The men gained an advantage over us and came out against us
in the field, but we drove them back to the entrance of the gate. 24 Then the archers shot at
your servants from the wall. Some of the king's servants are dead, and your servant Uriah
the Hittite is dead also." 25 David said to the messenger, "Thus shall you say to Joab, 'Do not
let this matter displease you, for the sword devours now one and now another. Strengthen
your attack against the city and overthrow it.' And encourage him."
26 When the wife of Uriah heard that Uriah her husband was dead, she lamented over
her husband. 27 And when the mourning was over, David sent and brought her to his
house, and [w]she became his wife and bore him a son. But the thing that David had done
displeased the LORD.

Nathan Rebukes David

12 And the LORD sent [x]Nathan to David. He came to him and said to him, [y]"There were
two men in a certain city, the one rich and the other poor. 2 The rich man had very
many flocks and herds, 3 but the poor man had nothing but one little ewe lamb, which he
had bought. And he brought it up, and it grew up with him and with his children. It used
to eat of his morsel and drink from his cup and lie in his arms,[1] and it was like a daughter
to him. 4 Now there came a traveler to the rich man, and he was unwilling to take one of
his own flock or herd to prepare for the guest who had come to him, but he took the poor
man's lamb and prepared it for the man who had come to him." 5 Then David's anger was
greatly kindled against the man, and he said to Nathan, [z]"As the LORD lives, the man who
has done this deserves to die, 6 and he shall restore the lamb [a]fourfold, because he did this
thing, and because he had no pity."
7 Nathan said to David, "You are the man! Thus says the LORD, the God of Israel, [b]'I

[1] Hebrew *bosom*; also verse 8

14 [t]1 Kgs. 21:8, 9
15 [u]ch. 12:9
21 [v]Judg. 9:53
27 [w]ch. 12:9

Chapter 12

1 [x]ver. 7, 13, 15, 25; ch. 7:2, 4, 17; 1 Kgs. 1:10, 22, 34; 4:5; 1 Chr. 29:29; 2 Chr. 9:29 [y][ch. 14:5-7; Judg. 9:8-15]; 1 Kgs. 20:35-41
5 [z]See Ruth 3:13
6 [a][Ex. 22:1; Luke 19:8]
7 [b]1 Sam. 16:13

up his wrongdoings, even if it means taking another person's life—and even more, the life of a faithful soldier.

11:21 Abimelech was a son of Gideon, who was also known as Jerubbaal (Judg. 8:29–9:57). Here, the element "baal" in a name is changed to "bosheth" ("shame"), so it becomes **son of Jerubbesheth**, as can be seen elsewhere in Samuel with the names Ish-bosheth and Mephibosheth (see note on 2 Sam. 4:4). **Did not a woman**. Abimelech had told his armor-bearer to kill him "lest they say of me, 'a woman killed him'" (Judg. 9:54), but this was said of him anyway.

11:25 Do not let this matter displease you. David probably knows that Joab would not have been happy about killing a good commander. David is saying, "He might have been killed anyway."

11:26–27 The **mourning** period was probably seven days (Gen. 50:10; 1 Sam. 31:13).

11:27 But the thing that David had done displeased the LORD is literally, "The matter that David did was evil in the eyes of the LORD"; see 12:9 and Ps. 51:4. This contrasts with David's words to Joab two verses earlier, "Do not let this matter displease you."

12:1–31 David started by breaking the tenth commandment (coveting, Ex. 20:17), then the seventh (adultery, Ex. 20:14), and then the sixth (murder, Ex. 20:13), while the Lord silently watched his behavior. Here at last the Lord calls him to account for standing above the law. Psalm 51 was composed in response to this occasion. **Nathan** apparently asks David to intervene in a legal matter. The "parable" (2 Sam. 12:1–4) is similar to the plea of the wise woman of Tekoa in ch. 14 and that of the prophet in 1 Kings 20:35–43. In all these cases, it is pointed out to the king that his own actions do not match his judgments.

12:4 That the Lord has special concern for the poor is a major theme in the Bible, and as his representative, the king and other judges were supposed to protect against abuse by the powerful (Ex. 23:6; Lev. 19:15; Prov. 31:9; Isa. 3:14; etc.). The rich man **took the poor man's lamb**, just as David "took" Bathsheba (see 2 Sam. 11:4).

12:5–6 David has a true concern for justice when he is not blinded by his own passion (cf. his ready acceptance of Abigail's words in 1 Sam. 25:32–33). For **fourfold**, see Ex. 22:1.

12:7–13 This passage has similarities with Nathan's prophecy in ch. 7. In both, the Lord looks back on what he has done by grace for David. But while in ch. 7 the Lord graciously promised him an enduring house, here he announces that David by his own deeds will experience misery in his house. David has **despised** the Lord and his word.

9[c]Num. 15:31 [d]1 Sam. 15:19 [e]ch. 11:15, 17 [f]ch. 11:27
12[g]ch. 16:22
13[h][1 Sam. 15:24] [i]ch. 24:10; Ps. 32:5; 51:4 [j]Ps. 32:1; Mic. 7:18; Zech. 3:4
14[k]Isa. 52:5; [Ezek. 36:20, 23; Rom. 2:24]
16[l][1 Kgs. 21:27] [m]ch. 13:31
20[n]Ruth 3:3 [o]Job 1:20
22[p][Jonah 3:9]
23[q]Job 7:8-10
24[r]Matt. 1:6 [s]1 Chr. 22:9

anointed you king over Israel, and I delivered you out of the hand of Saul. **8** And I gave
you your master's house and your master's wives into your arms and gave you the house
of Israel and of Judah. And if this were too little, I would add to you as much more.
9 [c]Why have you despised the word of the LORD, [d]to do what is evil in his sight? [e]You
have struck down Uriah the Hittite with the sword and [f]have taken his wife to be your
wife and have killed him with the sword of the Ammonites. **10** Now therefore the sword
shall never depart from your house, because you have despised me and have taken the
wife of Uriah the Hittite to be your wife.' **11** Thus says the LORD, 'Behold, I will raise up
evil against you out of your own house. And I will take your wives before your eyes and
give them to your neighbor, and he shall lie with your wives in the sight of this sun.
12 For you did it secretly, [g]but I will do this thing before all Israel and before the sun.'"
13 [h]David said to Nathan, [i]"I have sinned against the LORD." And Nathan said to David,
[j]"The LORD also has put away your sin; you shall not die. **14** Nevertheless, because by this
deed you have utterly [k]scorned the LORD,[1] the child who is born to you shall die." **15** Then
Nathan went to his house.

David's Child Dies

And the LORD afflicted the child that Uriah's wife bore to David, and he became sick.
16 David therefore sought God on behalf of the child. And David [l]fasted and went in [m]and
lay all night on the ground. **17** And the elders of his house stood beside him, to raise him
from the ground, but he would not, nor did he eat food with them. **18** On the seventh day
the child died. And the servants of David were afraid to tell him that the child was dead,
for they said, "Behold, while the child was yet alive, we spoke to him, and he did not listen
to us. How then can we say to him the child is dead? He may do himself some harm." **19** But
when David saw that his servants were whispering together, David understood that the
child was dead. And David said to his servants, "Is the child dead?" They said, "He is dead."
20 Then David arose from the earth [n]and washed and anointed himself and changed his
clothes. And he went into the house of the LORD [o]and worshiped. He then went to his own
house. And when he asked, they set food before him, and he ate. **21** Then his servants said
to him, "What is this thing that you have done? You fasted and wept for the child while
he was alive; but when the child died, you arose and ate food." **22** He said, "While the child
was still alive, I fasted and wept, for I said, [p]'Who knows whether the LORD will be gracious to me, that the child may live?' **23** But now he is dead. Why should I fast? Can I bring
him back again? I shall go to him, [q]but he will not return to me."

Solomon's Birth

24 Then David comforted his wife, Bathsheba, and went in to her and lay with her, and
[r]she bore a son, and he called his name [s]Solomon. And the LORD loved him **25** and sent a
message by Nathan the prophet. So he called his name Jedidiah,[2] because of the LORD.

[1] Masoretic Text *the enemies of the LORD*; Dead Sea Scroll *the word of the LORD* [2] *Jedidiah* means *beloved of the LORD*

12:8 gave you . . . your master's wives. There is no other record of David marrying Saul's wives, but he was certainly in a position to do so.

12:9 This sin was against the Lord, as David should have known through the **word of the LORD** (cf. Ps. 51:4). **With the sword** is a general term for causing violent death, as in 2 Sam. 11:25, not necessarily a reference to the specific mode of death (see 11:24).

12:10–11 the sword shall never depart from your house. David's sons Amnon (13:29), Absalom (18:15), and Adonijah (1 Kings 2:25) all will die by the sword. **he shall lie with your wives in the sight of this sun**. Absalom will rebel against David and publicly lie with David's concubines on a rooftop (2 Sam. 16:22).

12:13–14 David confesses and appears to have genuine repentance. Yet the results of his actions remain. As the ESV footnote explains, for **scorned the LORD** the Masoretic text has "scorned the enemies of the LORD," but this may not be the original wording. Modern scholars conclude that the word "enemies" was inserted (either by the author himself, or by a copyist) as a euphemism to avoid directly saying the words "scorn the LORD."

12:15–23 When the child falls ill, David still hopes that the Lord might change his mind and so petitions him with fasting (as in Judg. 20:26; Ezra 8:23; Est. 4:16; Ps. 35:13; etc.). **washed and anointed himself . . . ate**. Because fasting and refraining from anointing were also part of ordinary mourning (1 Sam. 31:13; 2 Sam. 3:35; 14:2), David's actions puzzle his servants, who seem to have thought he had been mourning.

12:20 The **house** is presumably the tent where the ark of the covenant was housed (6:17). "House" can also refer to a tent, as it may in Ugaritic and Akkadian.

12:23 I shall go to him. Some interpreters understand David to be saying simply that he, like the child, will someday die. But "shall go *to him*" seems to indicate the expectation of future personal reunion.

12:24–25 First Chronicles 3:5 suggests that **Solomon** was the fourth son of David by Bathsheba. This verse may skip over a number of years to introduce the most important child of the union. **And the LORD loved him** hints at Solomon's future role as king; God's grace has triumphed over David's terrible sin. The line promised to David will continue through this son of David and Bathsheba, and from this line the Messiah will eventually come (Matt. 1:6).

Rabbah Is Captured

26 [t]Now Joab [u]fought against [v]Rabbah of the Ammonites and took the royal city. 27 And
Joab sent messengers to David and said, "I have fought against Rabbah; moreover, I have
taken the city of waters. 28 Now then gather the rest of the people together and encamp
against the city and take it, lest I take the city and it be called by my name." 29 So David
gathered all the people together and went to Rabbah and fought against it and took it.
30 And he took the crown of their king from his head. The weight of it was a talent[1] of
gold, and in it was a precious stone, and it was placed on David's head. And he brought
out the spoil of the city, a very great amount. 31 And he brought out the people who were
in it and set them to labor with saws and iron picks and iron axes and made them toil at[2]
the brick kilns. And thus he did to all the cities of the Ammonites. Then David and all the
people returned to Jerusalem.

Amnon and Tamar

13 Now [w]Absalom, David's son, had a beautiful sister, whose name was [x]Tamar. And
after a time Amnon, David's son, loved her. 2 And Amnon was so tormented that he
made himself ill because of his sister Tamar, for she was a virgin, and it seemed impossible
to Amnon to do anything to her. 3 But Amnon had a friend, whose name was Jonadab, the
son of [y]Shimeah, David's brother. And Jonadab was a very crafty man. 4 And he said to him,
"O son of the king, why are you so haggard morning after morning? Will you not tell me?"
Amnon said to him, "I love Tamar, my brother Absalom's sister." 5 Jonadab said to him, "Lie
down on your bed and pretend to be ill. And when your father comes to see you, say to
him, 'Let my sister Tamar come and give me bread to eat, and prepare the food in my sight,
that I may see it and eat it from her hand.'" 6 So Amnon lay down and pretended to be ill.
And when the king came to see him, Amnon said to the king, "Please let my sister Tamar
come and [z]make a couple of cakes in my sight, that I may eat from her hand."
7 Then David sent home to Tamar, saying, "Go to your brother Amnon's house and prepare
food for him." 8 So Tamar went to her brother Amnon's house, where he was lying down.
And she took dough and kneaded it and made cakes in his sight and baked the cakes.
9 And she took the pan and emptied it out before him, but he refused to eat. And Amnon
said, [a]"Send out everyone from me." So everyone went out from him. 10 Then Amnon said
to Tamar, "Bring the food into the chamber, that I may eat from your hand." And Tamar
took the cakes she had made and brought them into the chamber to Amnon her brother.
11 But when she brought them near him to eat, he took hold of her and said to her, "Come,
lie with me, my sister." 12 She answered him, "No, my brother, do not violate[3] me, for [b]such
a thing is not done in Israel; do not do this [c]outrageous thing. 13 As for me, where could
I carry my shame? And as for you, you would be as one of [d]the outrageous fools in Israel.
Now therefore, please speak to the king, for he will not withhold me from you." 14 But he
would not listen to her, and being stronger than she, he violated her and lay with her.

[1] A *talent* was about 75 pounds or 34 kilograms [2] Hebrew *pass through* [3] Or *humiliate*; also verses 14, 22, 32

26 [t]For ver. 26-31, see 1 Chr. 20:1-3 [u]ch. 11:1 [v]Deut. 3:11

Chapter 13

1 [w]ch. 3:2, 3; 1 Chr. 3:2 [x]1 Chr. 3:9
3 [y]1 Chr. 2:13; [1 Sam. 16:9; 17:13]
6 [z]Gen. 18:6
9 [a][Gen. 45:1]
12 [b]Lev. 18:9, 11; 20:17 [c]Gen. 34:7; Judg. 19:23; 20:6
13 [d][ch. 3:33]

12:26–31 *End of Israel-Ammon War.* Having recorded the birth of Solomon, the author returns to the siege of Rabbah, last mentioned in 11:25. The "city of waters" was probably that section of the city that controlled the water supply. With no water, the surrender of the city itself would follow shortly. Therefore, Joab calls David to come to the front so that the king can get credit for its capture.

13:1–14:33 *Absalom's Banishment and Reinstatement.* Chapters 13–20 show the "evil . . . out of your own house" that Nathan warned David of in 12:11, namely, the rebellion of his son Absalom. Absalom kills his half brother Amnon to avenge the rape of his sister, but is eventually pardoned by David. Absalom then forms a conspiracy and declares himself king, but the rebellion is put down and Absalom is killed. In the aftermath there is an attempt by a group of Benjaminites to withdraw from Israel, but the attempt is thwarted. Often in this section the narrator has to follow several simultaneous story lines. Several times he backtracks and picks up a line by repeating the last statement in that line with expansion or variation (see 13:34a and 37; 15:37 and 16:15; 18:17b and 19:8b; 18:33 and 19:4; 19:24a and 25). The writer of 1–2 Kings uses this same technique to keep track of reigns in Judah and Israel.

13:1–22 After a time suggests that some time has passed since the end of ch. 12. This is an account of both rape and incest—the brother-sister relationship between Tamar and Amnon is referred to a dozen times. This rape was an **outrageous thing** (see Gen. 34:7; Deut. 22:21; Judg. 20:6; Jer. 29:23) that was **not done in Israel** (2 Sam. 13:12). Since it occurred in the royal family, it had implications for the whole nation.

13:1–2 Tamar was Absalom's full sister and the half sister of Amnon, David's eldest son. **he made himself ill**. Amnon's "love" could better be described as "lust."

13:3 The term **crafty** (Hb. *khakam*) is normally translated as "wise" or "skillful." Here, however, it is used in a negative sense.

13:6–8 The word for **cakes** (Hb. *lebibah*) is used only here in Scripture. It is related to the word "heart" (Hb. *lebab*), so it may have been thought of as a food for the sick. The word translated **baked** (v. 8) usually means "boiled" (see 1 Sam. 2:13), so it may be a type of dumpling. It apparently never occurred to David to be suspicious, and Tamar, of course, would obey her father.

13:12–13 such a thing is not done in Israel. Intercourse between brother and sister, even half brother and half sister, was forbidden in Lev. 18:9, and

18[e]Gen. 37:3; Judg. 5:30; Ps. 45:14
19[f]See Josh. 7:6 [g]See ch. 1:11 [h]Jer. 2:37
22[i]Gen. 24:50; 31:24
23[j]Gen. 31:19; 38:12, 13; 1 Sam. 25:4

15 Then Amnon hated her with very great hatred, so that the hatred with which he
hated her was greater than the love with which he had loved her. And Amnon said to her,
"Get up! Go!" 16 But she said to him, "No, my brother, for this wrong in sending me away
is greater than the other that you did to me."[1] But he would not listen to her. 17 He called
the young man who served him and said, "Put this woman out of my presence and bolt
the door after her." 18 Now she was wearing [e]a long robe[2] with sleeves, for thus were the
virgin daughters of the king dressed. So his servant put her out and bolted the door after
her. 19 And Tamar [f]put ashes on her head and [g]tore the long robe that she wore. And [h]she
laid her hand on her head and went away, crying aloud as she went.

20 And her brother Absalom said to her, "Has Amnon your brother been with you? Now
hold your peace, my sister. He is your brother; do not take this to heart." So Tamar lived,
a desolate woman, in her brother Absalom's house. 21 When King David heard of all these
things, he was very angry.[3] 22 But Absalom spoke to Amnon [i]neither good nor bad, for
Absalom hated Amnon, because he had violated his sister Tamar.

Absalom Murders Amnon

23 After two full years Absalom had [j]sheepshearers at Baal-hazor, which is near Ephraim,
and Absalom invited all the king's sons. 24 And Absalom came to the king and said, "Behold,
your servant has sheepshearers. Please let the king and his servants go with your servant."
25 But the king said to Absalom, "No, my son, let us not all go, lest we be burdensome to

[1] Compare Septuagint, Vulgate; the meaning of the Hebrew is uncertain [2] Or *a robe of many colors* (compare Genesis 37:3); also verse 19 [3] Dead Sea Scroll, Septuagint add *But he would not punish his son Amnon, because he loved him, since he was his firstborn*

the stress on the outrageousness makes it seem likely that this prohibition was accepted at the time of David. **he will not withhold me from you**. Perhaps Tamar is saying that David would be willing to bend the rules, or perhaps she is just trying to escape.

13:15–17 While Amnon's response to Tamar may be an archetypal example of a "blame the victim" mentality, it is particularly striking in the context of sexual lust. **wrong in sending me away**. Tamar's appeal is based on the fact that within this ancient Near Eastern cultural setting Amnon's actions required marriage (Deut. 22:28–29). **Put this woman out**. Amnon's hatred and contempt of his sister is expressed by his final refusal to heed her wishes or even use her name.

13:16 this wrong . . . is greater than the other. If a man seduced an unmarried (or unbetrothed) woman, he had to marry her, unless her father refused; if he raped her, he was not permitted to divorce her (Ex. 22:16; Deut. 22:28–29). Having ruined her life, he had a responsibility toward her.

13:18 The only other place this kind of **robe** appears in the Bible is in the Joseph story (Gen. 37:3, as the ESV footnote explains).

13:19 Putting **ashes** (or dirt) on one's head and tearing one's clothes were expressions of grief or humiliation (see note on 1 Sam. 4:12), as was covering the head with the hand(s) or a garment (2 Sam. 15:30; Est. 6:12; Jer. 2:37).

13:20 Do not take this to heart, perhaps because it would be easier to remain quiet, or perhaps because Absalom was determined to take vengeance in his own time. Absalom himself did take it to heart (cf. vv. 23–29).

13:21 David was **very angry**, but he did not do anything. He showed favoritism toward his eldest son (see ESV footnote; cf. 3:2), which was the source of many of the later problems in David's family (cf. 1 Kings 1:6). Heads of households have to deal justly with members of their household, but because of his sin with Bathsheba, David had lost his moral courage and clarity of judgment.

13:22 Spoke . . . neither good nor bad may mean "do nothing against" (see Gen. 31:24, 29).

13:23 As seen in 1 Samuel 25, sheepshearing was a time of feasting. Absalom **invited all the king's sons**, and the next four verses explain how he gives the invitation. Absalom invited David, probably guessing that he would decline, in order to lend an aura of importance to the occasion and to mask his true intentions. If he had started out by inviting Amnon, it could have seemed suspicious.

13:29 The king's sons seem to have normally ridden mules. Absalom even rides one into battle (18:9).

David and Absalom

c. 985 B.C.

In retaliation for the incestuous rape of his sister, Absalom killed his brother Amnon at Baal-hazor and fled to Geshur. After three years, arrangements were made for Absalom to return to Jerusalem, and later he and David were reconciled. Soon after this, however, Absalom led a coup against David in Hebron, and David fled to Mahanaim. When Absalom attacked David's forces in the forest of Ephraim, Absalom was defeated and killed, allowing David to return to Jerusalem.

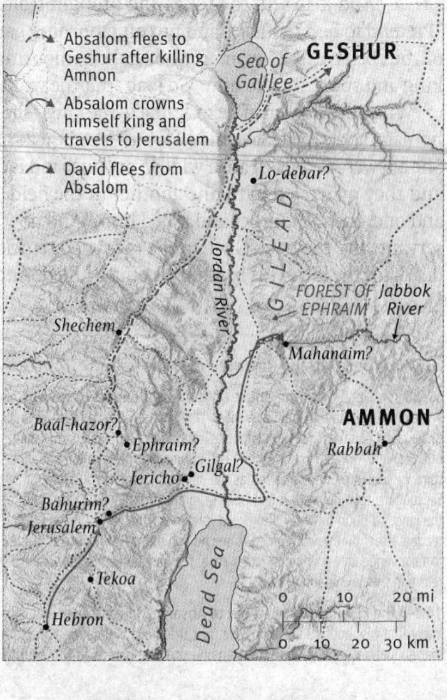

you." He pressed him, but he would not go but gave him his blessing. 26 Then Absalom said,
"If not, please let my brother Amnon go with us." And the king said to him, "Why should
he go with you?" 27 But Absalom pressed him until he let Amnon and all the king's sons
go with him. 28 Then Absalom commanded his servants, "Mark when Amnon's [k]heart is
merry with wine, and when I say to you, 'Strike Amnon,' then kill him. Do not fear; have
I not commanded you? Be courageous and be valiant." 29 So the servants of Absalom did
to Amnon as Absalom had commanded. Then all the king's sons arose, and each mounted
his mule and fled.

30 While they were on the way, news came to David, "Absalom has struck down all the
king's sons, and not one of them is left." 31 Then the king arose and [l]tore his garments and
[m]lay on the earth. And all his servants who were standing by tore their garments. 32 But
[n]Jonadab the son of Shimeah, David's brother, said, "Let not my lord suppose that they have
killed all the young men, the king's sons, for Amnon alone is dead. For by the command
of Absalom this has been determined from the day he violated his sister Tamar. 33 Now
therefore let not my lord the king so [o]take it to heart as to suppose that all the king's sons
are dead, for Amnon alone is dead."

Absalom Flees to Geshur

34 [p]But Absalom fled. And the young man who kept the watch lifted up his eyes and
looked, and behold, many people were coming from the road behind him[1] by the side
of the mountain. 35 And Jonadab said to the king, "Behold, the king's sons have come;
as your servant said, so it has come about." 36 And as soon as he had finished speaking,
behold, the king's sons came and lifted up their voice and wept. And the king also and all
his servants wept very bitterly.

37 [q]But Absalom fled and went to [r]Talmai the son of Ammihud, king of [s]Geshur. And
David mourned for his son day after day. 38 [q]So Absalom fled and went to Geshur, and was
there three years. 39 And the spirit of the king[2] longed to go out[3] to Absalom, because [t]he
was comforted about Amnon, since he was dead.

Absalom Returns to Jerusalem

14 Now Joab the son of Zeruiah knew [u]that the king's heart went out to Absalom.
2 And Joab sent to [v]Tekoa and brought from there a wise woman and said to her,
"Pretend to be a mourner and put on mourning garments. [w]Do not anoint yourself with
oil, but behave like a woman who has been mourning many days for the dead. 3 Go to the
king and speak thus to him." So Joab [x]put the words in her mouth.

4 When the woman of Tekoa came to the king, [y]she fell on her face to the ground and paid
homage and said, [z]"Save me, O king." 5 And the king said to her, "What is your trouble?"
She answered, [a]"Alas, I am a widow; my husband is dead. 6 And your servant had two sons,
and they quarreled with one another in the field. There was no one to separate them,
and one struck the other and killed him. 7 And now the whole clan has risen against your
servant, and they say, 'Give up the man who struck his brother, that we may put him to
death for the life of his brother whom he killed.' And so they would [b]destroy the heir also.

[1] Septuagint *the Horonaim Road* [2] Dead Sea Scroll, Septuagint; Hebrew *David* [3] Compare Vulgate *ceased to go out*

28 [k]See Judg. 19:6
31 [l]See ch. 1:11 [m]ch. 12:16
32 [n]ver. 3
33 [o]ch. 19:19
34 [p]ver. 37, 38
37 [q]ver. 34 [r]ch. 3:3; 1 Chr. 3:2 [s]ch. 14:23, 32; 15:8
38 [q][See ver. 37 above]
39 [t]Gen. 24:67; 38:12; [Gen. 37:35]

Chapter 14

1 [u]ch. 13:39
2 [v]2 Chr. 11:6; 20:20; Amos 1:1 [w][ch. 12:20; Ruth 3:3]
3 [x]ver. 19; [Ex. 4:15]
4 [y]ch. 1:2 [z]2 Kgs. 6:26
5 [a]See ch. 12:1
7 [b][Matt. 21:38; Mark 12:7; Luke 20:14]

13:37 Talmai was Absalom's maternal grandfather (3:3).

13:39 The Hebrew for **the spirit of the king longed to go out to Absalom** is difficult. It could also mean "the spirit of the king ceased to go out against Absalom" (cf. ESV footnote). The Hebrew lacks the word "spirit," but the verb "longed" or "ceased" is feminine and thus implies that the spirit or soul is properly inferred as the subject. (Some manuscripts of the Septuagint, together with a text from Qumran, explicitly have "the spirit of the king," though this may also be an inference.) The author is thus telling readers either that David yearned to see his son or that he no longer wanted to take vengeance on him; in either case, readers are set up for Absalom's return in the next chapter.

14:1–3 the king's heart went out to Absalom. This does not necessarily imply that his thoughts were positive, just that he was thinking about the matter. Joab recruited a **wise woman** and **put the words in her mouth** in an effort to push the king toward reconciliation with Absalom. (Later, however, Joab certainly does not seem to favor Absalom; cf. 18:10–18.) **Tekoa**, hometown of Amos (Amos 1:1), is in the Judean hills about 10 miles (16 km) south of Jerusalem, near Bethlehem.

14:4–7 The woman, using a "parable" as Nathan did (cf. 12:1–7), appeals to the king to set aside the ordinary laws demanding the death of a murderer (e.g., Num. 35:31), not because of any extenuating circumstances in the killing but for the good of the family. David must have first associated the woman's account with the story of Cain and Abel, and then soon realized that it would apply to Absalom's murder of Amnon.

14:7 heir. Apparently Absalom was now considered the heir, at least in popular sentiment. The idea of a smoldering **coal** is an image of "hope for the family." **Neither name nor remnant** means "no remaining posterity."

Thus they would quench my coal that is left and leave to my husband neither name nor
[c]remnant on the face of the earth."

8 Then the king said to the woman, "Go to your house, and I will give orders concerning you." **9** And the woman of Tekoa said to the king, [d]"On me be the guilt, my lord the
king, and on my father's house; let the king and his throne be guiltless." **10** The king said,
"If anyone says anything to you, bring him to me, and he shall never touch you again."
11 Then she said, "Please let the king invoke the LORD your God, that [e]the avenger of blood
kill no more, and my son be not destroyed." He said, [f]"As the LORD lives, [g]not one hair of
your son shall fall to the ground."

12 Then the woman said, "Please let your servant speak a word to my lord the king." He
said, "Speak." **13** And the woman said, "Why then have you planned such a thing against
[h]the people of God? For in giving this decision the king convicts himself, inasmuch as the
king does not bring [i]his banished one home again. **14** We must all die; we are [j]like water
spilled on the ground, which cannot be gathered up again. But God will not take away
life, and he devises means [k]so that the banished one will not remain an outcast. **15** Now I
have come to say this to my lord the king because the people have made me afraid, and
your servant thought, 'I will speak to the king; it may be that the king will perform the
request of his servant. **16** For the king will hear and deliver his servant from the hand of the
man who would destroy me and my son together from [l]the heritage of God.' **17** And your
servant thought, 'The word of my lord the king will set me at rest,' for my lord the king is
[m]like the angel of God to discern good and evil. The LORD your God be with you!"

18 Then the king answered the woman, "Do not hide from me anything I ask you." And
the woman said, "Let my lord the king speak." **19** The king said, "Is the hand of Joab with
you in all this?" The woman answered and said, [n]"As surely as you live, my lord the king,
one cannot turn to the right hand or to the left from anything that my lord the king has
said. It was your servant Joab who commanded me; [o]it was he who put all these words
in the mouth of your servant. **20** In order to change the course of things your servant Joab
did this. But my lord has wisdom like the wisdom of [m]the angel of God to know all things
that are on the earth."

21 Then the king said to Joab, "Behold now, I grant this; go, bring back the young man
Absalom." **22** And Joab fell on his face to the ground and paid homage [p]and blessed the
king. And Joab said, "Today your servant knows that I have found favor in your sight, my
lord the king, in that the king has granted the request of his servant." **23** So Joab arose and
went to [q]Geshur and brought Absalom to Jerusalem. **24** And the king said, "Let him dwell
apart in his own house; he is not to come into my presence." So Absalom lived apart in his
own house and did not come into the king's presence.

25 Now in all Israel there was no one so much to be praised for his handsome appearance as Absalom. [r]From the sole of his foot to the crown of his head there was no blemish
in him. **26** And when he cut the hair of his head (for at the end of every year he used to cut
it; when it was heavy on him, he [s]cut it), he weighed the hair of his head, two hundred
shekels[1] by the king's weight. **27** There were born [t]to Absalom three sons, and one daughter
whose name was Tamar. She was a beautiful woman.

[1] A *shekel* was about 2/5 ounce or 11 grams

7 [c][Gen. 45:7]
9 [d]1 Sam. 25:24
11 [e]Num. 35:19, 21; Deut. 19:12 [f]See Ruth 3:13 [g]1 Sam. 14:45; Acts 27:34
13 [h]Judg. 20:2 [i][ch. 13:37, 38]
14 [j][1 Sam. 7:6] [k]Num. 35:15, 25, 28
16 [l]See 1 Sam. 26:19
17 [m]ch. 19:27; 1 Sam. 29:9
19 [n]1 Sam. 1:26 [o]ver. 3
20 [m][See ver. 17 above]
22 [p]1 Kgs. 8:66
23 [q]ch. 13:38
25 [r]Deut. 28:35; Job 2:7; Isa. 1:6
26 [s]Ezek. 44:20
27 [t][ch. 18:18]

14:8–17 Perhaps David already suspects that Joab is involved in the woman's coming to him, so he deliberately uses the vague word "anyone" (**If anyone says anything to you**) in v. 10. The woman, however, sticks to her own story by referring to **my son**, while she uses a very sensitive term, **avenger of blood** (v. 11), which would apply to the king himself, who has been thinking about his own son (v. 1). She asks for an immediate ruling on her own (bogus) case so that she can comment on it (cf. vv. 13–14). By his words in v. 11b, David indirectly expresses his determination (**As the LORD lives**) to bring back his own lost son. The woman says what Joab has sent her to say (vv. 13–14) and then goes back to her made-up story (vv. 15–17). **This** in v. 15 would refer both to her real message in vv. 13–14 and to her "family problem" in vv. 5–7. This woman wisely finishes her dialogue with King David by mentioning her own problem, thus placing herself on the side of the needy and helpless, not in the position of an accuser of the king.

14:18–20 David suspects the woman's real purpose (cf. vv. 1–17). Having patiently heard her out, he now asks her straightforwardly if Joab was involved in her coming to him with her story.

14:24 he is not to come into my presence. David's forgiveness is incomplete, as Absalom complains in v. 32. David is confused: he is unwilling to punish, but also unwilling to forgive fully, so the situation festers.

14:25–27 These verses prepare readers for what is told later about Absalom, especially how he "stole the hearts of the men of Israel" (15:6) by his personal charms. The reference to his abundant **hair** looks ahead to his manner of death, i.e., by being caught by his head in a tree (see 18:9). **The king's weight** indicates that there was a royal standard at the Israelite court.

14:27 Since the **three sons** are unnamed and Absalom says he had no sons (18:18), these sons probably died young. His **daughter**, **Tamar**, was probably named for his sister (see note on 13:1–2).

28 So Absalom lived two full years in Jerusalem, without coming into the king's presence.
29 Then Absalom sent for Joab, to send him to the king, but Joab would not come to him.
And he sent a second time, but Joab would not come. 30 Then he said to his servants, "See,
Joab's field is next to mine, and he has barley there; go and set it on fire." So Absalom's
servants set the field on fire.[1] 31 Then Joab arose and went to Absalom at his house and said
to him, "Why have your servants set my field on fire?" 32 Absalom answered Joab, "Behold,
I sent word to you, 'Come here, that I may send you to the king, to ask, "Why have I come
from [q]Geshur? It would be better for me to be there still." Now therefore let me go into the
presence of the king, [u]and if there is guilt in me, let him put me to death.'" 33 Then Joab
went to the king and told him, and he summoned Absalom. So he came to the king and
bowed himself on his face to the ground before the king, and the king kissed Absalom.

Absalom's Conspiracy

15 After this Absalom [v]got himself a chariot and horses, and fifty men to run before
him. 2 And Absalom used to rise early and stand beside [w]the way of the gate. And
when any man had a dispute to come before the king for judgment, Absalom would call
to him and say, "From what city are you?" And when he said, "Your servant is of such and
such a tribe in Israel," 3 Absalom would say to him, "See, your claims are good and right, but
there is no man designated by the king to hear you." 4 Then Absalom would say, [x]"Oh that
I were judge in the land! Then every man with a dispute or cause might come to me, and I
would give him justice." 5 And whenever a man came near to pay homage to him, he would
put out his hand and take hold of him and kiss him. 6 Thus Absalom did to all of Israel who
came to the king for judgment. So Absalom stole the hearts of the men of Israel.
7 And at the end of four[2] years Absalom said to the king, "Please let me go and pay my
vow, which I have vowed to the LORD, in Hebron. 8 For your servant [z]vowed a vow [a]while I
lived at Geshur in Aram, saying, 'If the LORD will indeed bring me back to Jerusalem, then
I will offer worship to[3] the LORD.'" 9 The king said to him, [b]"Go in peace." So he arose and
went to Hebron. 10 But Absalom sent secret messengers throughout all the tribes of Israel,
saying, "As soon as you hear the sound of the trumpet, then say, 'Absalom is king at Hebron!'"
11 With Absalom went two hundred men from Jerusalem [c]who were invited guests, and
they went in their innocence and knew nothing. 12 And while Absalom was offering the
sacrifices, he sent for[4] [d]Ahithophel the Gilonite, [e]David's counselor, from his city [f]Giloh.
And the conspiracy grew strong, and the people with Absalom [g]kept increasing.

[1] Septuagint, Dead Sea Scroll add *So Joab's servants came to him with their clothes torn, and they said to him, "The servants of Absalom have set your field on fire."* [2] Septuagint, Syriac; Hebrew *forty* [3] Or *will serve* [4] Or *sent*

32 [q][See ver. 23 above] [u]1 Sam. 20:8

Chapter 15

1 [v]1 Kgs. 1:5
2 [w]See Ruth 4:1
4 [x]Judg. 9:29
8 [z]Gen. 28:20, 21; 1 Sam. 1:11 [a]ch. 13:38
9 [b]1 Sam. 1:17
11 [c][1 Sam. 9:13; 16:3, 5]
12 [d]ver. 31; ch. 16:20; 17:1, 14, 23 [e]1 Chr. 27:33; [Ps. 41:9; 55:12-14] [f]Josh. 15:51 [g]Ps. 3:1

14:28–32 Believing that **Joab** could orchestrate a long-awaited audience with the king, **Absalom** compels Joab's attention by setting his **field on fire**. He finds his current status unsatisfactory and wants either restoration to the royal household or, if guilty, execution (v. 32).

14:33 the king kissed Absalom. The kiss points to Absalom's restoration and closes the section consisting of chs. 13–14, which is a prologue to the revolt of Absalom in chs. 15–19. Clearly the king's kiss was less than full restoration since Absalom himself will soon "kiss away" the hearts of Israel (15:5–6).

15:1–19:43 *Absalom's Rebellion.* This long section of 2 Samuel is divided into six parts: (1) Absalom's conspiracy and proclaiming himself king (15:1–12); (2) David's escape from Absalom, and the people he met on the way (15:13–16:14); (3) the war council where the competition between Ahithophel and Hushai determines David's fate (16:15–17:23); (4) David's favorable reception at Mahanaim (17:24–29); (5) the battle and the death of Absalom (18:1–19:8a); and (6) David's return to Jerusalem (19:8b–43).

15:1–12 *Absalom's Conspiracy.* Absalom plans his conspiracy and proclaims himself king.

15:1 a chariot and horses, and fifty men to run before him. Absalom's self-exalting pride stands in contrast to David's humility (1 Sam. 26:9–11; 2 Sam. 7:18; 15:25–26). Later Adonijah behaves similarly, exalting himself, "saying 'I will be king'" (1 Kings 1:5). See also 1 Sam. 8:11.

15:3 there is no man designated by the king to hear you. Absalom's statement must be somewhat of an exaggeration, for the widow of Tekoa got a hearing, and if it were known that there was no chance of a hearing, people would not have come.

15:4 Oh that I were judge in the land! Absalom is appealing to the tradition of the king as "judge" (cf. Prov. 31:9; Isa. 11:3–5), which is closely bound to the concept of the Lord as judge (Ps. 96:10; Isa. 33:22), not to the judgeships of the previous era (as seen in the book of Judges). Thus Absalom is saying, "Oh that I were king!" (see 1 Sam. 8:5). This is in line with his chariot and runners (2 Sam. 15:1). Since Absalom's conduct was public ("beside the way of the gate," v. 2), news of what he was doing must have quickly reached David, but he did nothing to stop it (see notes on 13:21; 14:24).

15:7 Hebron, the chief city of Judah, was where David ruled as king of Judah (2:4) and where Absalom was born (3:2–3).

15:10 The phrase **the tribes of Israel** sometimes refers to all of Israel, and at other times refers to Israel as opposed to Judah. Here, it refers to all of Israel, including Judah. It is clear that Judah participated in the rebellion. Absalom raises his revolt in Hebron, and his named associates—Ahithophel of Giloh (15:12; see Josh. 15:51) and Amasa, David's nephew (2 Sam. 17:25)—are both from Judah. Furthermore, in 19:11 David asks why the elders of Judah are reluctant to bring him back. In chs. 15–18, "Israel" usually means "Absalom's side," while David's side is referred to as "David's servants" or "the army."

15:12 These **sacrifices** were apparently part of a coronation ceremony (see 1 Sam. 11:14–15; 1 Kings 1:9–11) formally asserting Absalom's kingship (2 Sam. 15:10; 16:16).

David Flees Jerusalem

13 And a messenger came to David, saying, [h]"The hearts of the men of Israel have gone
after Absalom." **14** Then David said to all his servants who were with him at Jerusalem,
"Arise, and let us [i]flee, or else there will be no escape for us from Absalom. Go quickly, lest
he overtake us quickly and bring down ruin on us and strike the city with the edge of the
sword." **15** And the king's servants said to the king, "Behold, your servants are ready to do
whatever my lord the king decides." **16** So the king went out, and all his household after
him. And the king left [j]ten concubines to keep the house. **17** And the king went out, and
all the people after him. And they halted at the last house.

18 And [k]all his servants passed by him, and all the Cherethites, and all the Pelethites,
and all the six hundred Gittites who had followed him from [l]Gath, passed on before the
king. **19** Then the king said to [m]Ittai the Gittite, "Why do you also go with us? Go back and
stay with the king, for you are a foreigner and also an exile from your home. **20** You came
only yesterday, and shall I today make you wander about with us, since I go [n]I know not
where? Go back and take your brothers with you, and may the LORD show[1] steadfast love
and faithfulness to you." **21** But Ittai answered the king, [o]"As the LORD lives, and as my lord
the king lives, [p]wherever my lord the king shall be, whether for death or for life, there
also will your servant be." **22** And David said to Ittai, "Go then, pass on." So Ittai the Gittite
passed on with all his men and all the little ones who were with him. **23** And all the land
wept aloud as all the people passed by, and the king crossed [q]the brook [r]Kidron, and all
the people passed on toward [s]the wilderness.

24 And [t]Abiathar came up, and behold, [u]Zadok came also with all the Levites, [v]bearing
the ark of the covenant of God. And they set down the ark of God until the people had
all passed out of the city. **25** Then the king said to Zadok, "Carry the ark of God back into
the city. If I find favor in the eyes of the LORD, he will [w]bring me back and let me see both
it and his [x]dwelling place. **26** But if he says, 'I have no [y]pleasure in you,' behold, here I am,
[z]let him do to me what seems good to him." **27** The king also said to Zadok the priest, "Are
you not a [a]seer? Go back[2] to the city in peace, with [b]your two sons, Ahimaaz your son, and
Jonathan the son of Abiathar. **28** See, I will wait at [c]the fords of [s]the wilderness until word
comes from you to inform me." **29** So Zadok and Abiathar carried the ark of God back to
Jerusalem, and they remained there.

30 But David went up the ascent of the Mount of Olives, weeping as he went, [d]barefoot
and [e]with his head covered. And all the people who were with him covered their heads,
and they went up, [f]weeping as they went. **31** And it was told David, "Ahithophel is among
the conspirators with Absalom." And David said, "O LORD, please [g]turn the counsel of
Ahithophel into foolishness."

13 [h]Judg. 9:3
14 [i]ch. 19:9
16 [j]ch. 16:21, 22; 20:3
18 [k]See ch. 8:18 [l]1 Sam. 27:2
19 [m]ch. 18:2
20 [n][1 Sam. 23:13]
21 [o]See Ruth 3:13 [p][Ruth 1:16, 17]
23 [q]1 Kgs. 2:37; 15:13; 2 Kgs. 23:4, 6, 12 [r][John 18:1] [s]ch. 16:2; 17:16, 29
24 [t]Num. 4:15 [u]1 Sam. 22:20 [v]ch. 8:17; 20:25
25 [w]Ps. 43:3 [x]Ex. 15:13; Jer. 25:30
26 [y]ch. 22:20; Num. 14:8; 1 Kgs. 10:9; 2 Chr. 9:8; Ps. 18:19; 22:8; Isa. 62:4 [z]1 Sam. 3:18
27 [a]See 1 Sam. 9:9 [b]ch. 17:17
28 [c]ch. 17:16 [s][See ver. 23 above]
30 [d]Isa. 20:2-4 [e]ch. 19:4; Esth. 6:12; Jer. 14:3, 4 [f]Ps. 126:6
31 [g]ch. 16:23; 17:14, 23

[1] Septuagint; Hebrew lacks *may the LORD show* [2] Septuagint *The king also said to Zadok the priest, "Look, go back*

15:13–16:14 *David's Escape from Absalom.* This section describes David's flight from Jerusalem to the Jordan River. Psalm 3 is said to have been composed in response to this occasion. David flees Jerusalem, lest the city be destroyed. On the way he meets a loyal band of foreigners, the priests Abiathar and Zadok, his friend Hushai, Mephibosheth's servant Ziba, and the Benjaminite Shimei.

15:18–20 The **Cherethites** and the **Pelethites** are David's bodyguard (8:18). The **Gittites** (i.e., men from Gath) are not likely David's own 600 men who had gone with him from Israel to Ziklag (1 Sam. 27:2), since they had come **yesterday** (2 Sam. 15:20), that is, recently, and could **go back** to their homes.

15:23 The **brook Kidron** runs just east of Jerusalem; the Mount of Olives (v. 30) is to the east of the brook.

15:24–37 Though David leaves the city, by the providence of God he is able to set up a messenger system—Hushai, to Zadok and Abiathar, to their sons (via a maid, 17:17), to David (15:36).

15:25–26 Carry the ark of God back into the city. David does not try to use the ark as some sort of "good luck charm," in contrast to the attitude of the elders in 1 Sam. 4:3. Perhaps he realizes that Absalom's rebellion is partly the result of his own sins (2 Sam. 12:10), and he does not know how far the Lord intends to punish him (**let him do to me what seems good to him**). His symbols of mourning and penitence and acceptance of malice (15:30; 16:10) are probably related to this. Since he also considers the rebellion wrong, however, he is willing to use prayer and the human opportunities God gives him (15:28, 31, 34; see Neh. 4:9).

15:27 Are you not a seer? Perhaps David is implying that Zadok does not know precisely what God will do about David (see note on vv. 25–26); or maybe he is indicating that Zadok, because the people hold him in honor as a seer, will be allowed to pass safely into the city, where he will be most useful to David.

15:28 The **fords of the wilderness** were at the west bank of the Jordan River.

15:30 Going **barefoot and with his head covered** were signs of mourning (cf. Est. 6:12; Isa. 20:2). **weeping as he went**. David had many reasons to weep: his own misfortunes and the dangers he now faced; the troubles now facing Israel and his own family, for which he was partly responsible; and the dishonor that would surely come to God as a result of all this.

15:31–32 Ahithophel was David's trusted counselor (v. 12; cf. 16:23), but now he was **among the conspirators**. This led David to pray, **"O LORD, please turn the counsel of Ahithophel into foolishness."** His prayer was answered in the very next verse by the arrival of Hushai, who would prove invaluable to him (see 16:15–17:23 and notes).

32 While David was coming to the summit, where God was worshiped, behold, Hushai
[h]the Archite came to meet him [i]with his coat torn and [i]dirt on his head. 33 David said to
him, "If you go on with me, you will be [j]a burden to me. 34 But if you return to the city and
say to Absalom, [k]'I will be your servant, O king; as I have been your father's servant in time
past, so now I will be your servant,' then you will defeat for me the counsel of Ahithophel.
35 Are not Zadok and Abiathar the priests with you there? So whatever you hear from the
king's house, [l]tell it to Zadok and Abiathar the priests. 36 Behold, [m]their two sons are with
them there, Ahimaaz, Zadok's son, and Jonathan, Abiathar's son, [m]and by them you shall
send to me everything you hear." 37 So Hushai, [n]David's friend, came into the city, [o]just as
Absalom was entering Jerusalem.

David and Ziba

16 When David had passed a little beyond [p]the summit, [q]Ziba the servant of
Mephibosheth met him, with a couple of donkeys saddled, bearing two hundred
loaves of bread, [r]a hundred bunches of raisins, a hundred of summer fruits, and a skin of
wine. 2 And the king said to Ziba, "Why have you brought these?" Ziba answered, [s]"The
donkeys are for the king's household to ride on, the bread and summer fruit for the young
men to eat, and the wine for those who [t]faint in the wilderness to drink." 3 And the king said,
"And where is your master's son?" [u]Ziba said to the king, "Behold, he remains in Jerusalem,
for he said, 'Today the house of Israel will give me back the kingdom of my father.'" 4 Then
the king said to Ziba, "Behold, all that belonged to Mephibosheth is now yours." And Ziba
said, "I pay homage; let me ever find favor in your sight, my lord the king."

Shimei Curses David

5 When King David came to [v]Bahurim, there came out a man of the family of the house
of Saul, whose name was [w]Shimei, the son of Gera, and as he came [x]he cursed continually.
6 And he threw stones at David and at all the servants of King David, and all the people
and all the mighty men were on his right hand and on his left. 7 And Shimei said as he
[x]cursed, "Get out, get out, you man of blood, you worthless man! 8 The LORD [y]has avenged
on you all [z]the blood of the house of Saul, in whose place you have reigned, and the LORD
has given the kingdom into the hand of your son Absalom. See, your evil is on you, for
you are a man of blood."

9 Then Abishai the son of Zeruiah said to the king, "Why should this [a]dead dog [b]curse
my lord the king? Let me go over and take off his head." 10 But the king said, [c]"What have
I to do with you, [d]you sons of Zeruiah? If he is cursing because the LORD has said to him,
'Curse David,' who then shall say, 'Why have you done so?'" 11 And David said to Abishai
and to all his servants, "Behold, [e]my own son seeks my life; how much more now may this
Benjaminite! Leave him alone, and let him curse, for the LORD has told him to. 12 It may

32 [h]Josh. 16:2 [i]See Josh. 7:6
33 [j]ch. 19:35
34 [k]ch. 16:19
35 [l]ch. 17:15, 16
36 [m]ch. 17:17
37 [n]ch. 16:16; 1 Chr. 27:33 [o]ch. 16:15

Chapter 16

1 [p]ch. 15:30, 32 [q]See ch. 9:2-13 [r][1 Sam. 25:18]
2 [s][Judg. 5:10; 10:4] [t]ver. 14; ch. 17:29
3 [u]ch. 19:26, 27
5 [v]See ch. 3:16 [w]ch. 19:16; See 1 Kgs. 2:8, 36-46 [x]ch. 19:21
7 [x][See ver. 5 above]
8 [y]Judg. 9:24, 56, 57; 1 Kgs. 2:32, 33 [z]See ch. 1:16
9 [a]ch. 9:8; 1 Sam. 24:14; [ch. 3:8] [b][Ex. 22:28]
10 [c]ch. 19:22 [d]See 1 Sam. 26:6
11 [e]ch. 12:11

15:33–36 whatever you hear . . . tell. Although earlier David may have questioned Zadok's "seeing" (v. 27), it is clear that what Zadok and Abiathar "hear" from the undercover work of Hushai in Jerusalem (v. 34) will benefit David and his followers (vv. 35–36; cf. 17:15–16, 22).

15:37 David's friend. "Friend" may be a title because it is not the normal word for "friend" and it seems to be one kind of royal official described in 1 Kings 4:5. David is called the friend of Hushai in 2 Sam. 16:17, however, so it also expresses a relationship.

16:1–4 Ziba, the **servant of Mephibosheth** (the disabled grandson of Saul, whom David had taken into his care; see ch. 9), arrives with provisions for David and his people. Ziba implies that the gifts are entirely his idea, and that Mephibosheth himself sees David's plight as an opportunity to reclaim the kingdom (**Today the house of Israel will give me back the kingdom of my father**). Mephibosheth will later present a somewhat different version of the situation (19:24–29). As the next section and ch. 20 show, some Benjaminites still felt animosity toward David, so David may have been very unsure about Mephibosheth's loyalty. **Behold, all that belonged to Mephibosheth is now yours**. David judged too quickly, without opportunity to hear a defense from the accused Mephibosheth. Cf. notes on 13:21 and 14:24. The list of food items in 16:1 is similar to the list in 1 Sam. 25:18.

16:5 Shimei is apparently a prominent man (19:16). **Bahurim** is a Benjaminite town on the north side of the Mount of Olives, though it did have inhabitants who supported David (17:18). Shimei will act very differently the next time he meets David (19:16).

16:8 Shimei was probably blaming David for the deaths of Abner (3:26–30) and Ish-bosheth (ch. 4), and possibly for the deaths of Saul's sons and grandsons (21:1–9) or even that of Saul himself, though he is not necessarily accusing David of actual complicity in the deaths. Since the writer of Samuel goes to great lengths to absolve David from complicity, one can surmise that some people harbored ill will toward David because of the house of Saul, even at the time 1–2 Samuel was written.

16:9 As always, Abishai is ready to act (cf. 1 Sam. 26:8). Cursing a ruler is forbidden in Ex. 22:28.

16:10 What have I to do with you? David's point is that he and Abishai do not see things the same way, and it would be disastrous for him to take Abishai's advice.

16:11 let him curse, for the LORD has told him to. David expresses his trust in God's providence (cf. 15:25–26; 16:12). He still wonders whether all this opposition is the Lord's just punishment for his sin, and he humbly endures the abuse.

16:12 It may be . . . that the LORD will repay me with good for his cursing today. Cf. the opposite perspective in Prov. 24:17–18: "Do not rejoice when your enemy falls . . . lest the LORD see it and be displeased, and turn away his anger from him" (cf. Prov. 26:2; also 1 Pet. 2:19–23; 3:9).

be that the LORD will look on the wrong done to me,[1] and that the LORD will repay me
with good for his cursing today." **13** So David and his men went on the road, while Shimei
went along on the hillside opposite him and [f]cursed as he went and threw stones at him
and flung dust. **14** And the king, and all the people who were with him, [g]arrived weary at
the Jordan.[2] And there he refreshed himself.

Absalom Enters Jerusalem

15 [h]Now Absalom and all the people, the men of Israel, came to Jerusalem, and Ahithophel
with him. **16** And when Hushai the Archite, [h]David's friend, came to Absalom, Hushai said
to Absalom, [i]"Long live the king! Long live the king!" **17** And Absalom said to Hushai, "Is
this your loyalty to your friend? [j]Why did you not go with your friend?" **18** And Hushai
said to Absalom, "No, for whom the LORD and this people and all the men of Israel have
chosen, his I will be, and with him I will remain. **19** And again, [k]whom should I serve?
Should it not be his son? As I have served your father, so I will serve you."

20 Then Absalom said to Ahithophel, "Give your counsel. What shall we do?" **21** Ahithophel
said to Absalom, "Go in to [l]your father's concubines, whom he has left to keep the house,
and all Israel will hear that you have made yourself a stench to your father, and [m]the hands
of all who are with you will be strengthened." **22** So they pitched a tent for Absalom [n]on the
roof. And Absalom went in to his father's concubines [o]in the sight of all Israel. **23** Now in
those days the counsel that Ahithophel gave was as if one consulted the word of God; so
was all the counsel of Ahithophel esteemed, [p]both by David and by Absalom.

Hushai Saves David

17 Moreover, Ahithophel said to Absalom, "Let me choose twelve thousand men, and I
will arise and pursue David tonight. **2** I will come upon him while he is [q]weary and
discouraged and throw him into a panic, and all the people who are with him will flee. [r]I
will strike down only the king, **3** and I will bring all the people back to you as a bride comes
home to her husband. You seek the life of only one man,[3] and all the people will be at peace."
4 And the advice seemed right in the eyes of Absalom and all the elders of Israel.

5 Then Absalom said, "Call [s]Hushai the Archite also, and let us hear what he has to say."
6 And when Hushai came to Absalom, Absalom said to him, "Thus has Ahithophel spoken;
shall we do as he says? If not, you speak." **7** Then Hushai said to Absalom, "This time the

[1] Septuagint, Vulgate *will look upon my affliction* [2] Septuagint; Hebrew lacks *at the Jordan* [3] Septuagint; Hebrew *back to you. Like the return of the whole is the man whom you seek*

13 [f]ch. 19:21
14 [g]ver. 2
15 [h]ch. 15:37
16 [h][See ver. 15 above] [i]1 Sam. 10:24; 1 Kgs. 1:25, 39; 2 Kgs. 11:12
17 [j][ch. 19:25]
19 [k]ch. 15:34
21 [l]ch. 15:16; 20:3 [m]ch. 2:7; Zech. 8:9, 13
22 [n]See 1 Sam. 9:25 [o]ch. 12:11, 12
23 [p]ch. 15:12

Chapter 17

2 [q]ch. 16:14; [Deut. 25:18] [r][1 Kgs. 22:31]
5 [s]ch. 16:16-18

16:14 arrived weary at the Jordan. The journey was 21 miles (36 km) from Jerusalem to the Jordan, and the road descended about 3,500 feet (1,067 m).

16:15–17:23 *Ahithophel and Hushai.* The writer resumes his account from 15:37. For "Israel," see note on 15:10.

16:15–17 As the rebellious **Absalom** arrives in Jerusalem, **Ahithophel**, who has deserted to him from David (see note on 15:31–32), comes with him. Soon **Hushai**, a **friend** of David (see notes on 15:31–32; 15:37), arrives as well, proclaiming **"Long live the king!" Why did you not go with your friend?** (i.e., David; cf. 15:37). Understandably, Absalom questions the sincerity of Hushai's greeting.

16:18–19 No . . . I will serve you. Hushai probably knows it will be hard to convince Absalom that he has forsaken David and is now supporting Absalom.

16:21–22 Following Ahithophel's advice, Absalom publicly had sexual relations with several of David's **concubines** who had been left behind to "keep the house" (15:16). Such an outrageous action would indeed have **strengthened . . . the hands** of Absalom's followers, as he made it clear that he was claiming the throne. Nathan had prophesied such an event (cf. **in the sight of all Israel** with "in the sight of this sun," 12:11), and the rooftop of 16:22 may have been the very rooftop from which David had seen Bathsheba (11:2).

16:23 The high estimation of Ahithophel's advice suggests that Hushai has a difficult task before him, in which he can succeed only with the help of the Lord.

17:1–23 This chapter presents the crucial contest between Ahithophel and Hushai before Absalom and the elders of Israel (vv. 4, 14). Ahithophel makes the very sound proposal to attack and kill David immediately. With no one else to turn to, he says, the whole country would embrace Absalom. If this "good counsel" (v. 14) had been followed, it is likely that David, whose large group was indeed **weary and discouraged** (v. 2; see 16:14), would have been defeated. Absalom, however, decides to hear the opinion of Hushai. He trusts him enough to hear him but, sensibly, not enough to invite him to take part in the deliberations of the war council (**Call Hushai**, 17:5). Hushai gives a vivid, time-consuming speech full of similes, making a proposal that is flattering to Absalom as leader of **all Israel** (v. 11), but that will let David regroup and choose his own time and place of battle with his experienced, trained force. Hushai apparently then withdraws while the council considers the proposals. Hushai knows that if Ahithophel's advice is accepted, there will be no time to lose, so even before he hears the results of the deliberations he sends word to David that he should at least cross the Jordan River (vv. 15–16). The council rejects Ahithophel's good counsel in favor of Hushai's deceptive and wrong counsel. The writer specifically says that this rejection was the work of the Lord: **for the LORD had ordained to defeat the good counsel of Ahithophel** (v. 14). The poor decision seals Absalom's doom. When Absalom finally gathers his army and goes after David (v. 24), David is already in Mahanaim in Gilead, with the forest of Ephraim (18:6) between him and Absalom.

17:1 Ahithophel suggests that he himself lead the force against David.

17:7–13 my counsel is that all Israel be gathered to you . . . and that you go to battle in person (v. 11). Hushai appeals to Absalom's pride and suggests that Absalom, not Ahithophel, should gather even more support and then personally lead the forces against David (v. 11). Hushai also stresses the undisputed facts of the bravery of David and his men and David's reputation as a soldier among all Israel.

counsel that Ahithophel has given is not good." 8 Hushai said, "You know that your father
and his men are mighty men, and that they are enraged,[1] [t]like a bear robbed of her cubs in
the field. Besides, your father is expert in war; he will not spend the night with the people.
9 Behold, even now he has hidden himself in one of the pits or in some other place. And
as soon as some of the people fall[2] at the first attack, whoever hears it will say, 'There has
been a slaughter among the people who follow Absalom.' 10 Then even the valiant man,
whose heart is like the heart of a lion, will utterly [u]melt with fear, for all Israel knows that
your father is a mighty man, and that those who are with him are valiant men. 11 But my
counsel is that all Israel be gathered to you, [v]from Dan to Beersheba, [w]as the sand by the
sea for multitude, and that you go to battle in person. 12 So we shall come upon him in
some place where he is to be found, and we shall light upon him as the dew falls on the
ground, and of him and all the men with him not one will be left. 13 If he withdraws into
a city, then all Israel will bring ropes to that city, and we shall drag it into the valley, until
not even a pebble is to be found there." 14 And Absalom and all the men of Israel said, "The
counsel of Hushai the Archite is better than the counsel of Ahithophel." [x]For the LORD
had ordained[3] to defeat the good counsel of Ahithophel, so that the LORD might bring
harm upon Absalom.

15 [y]Then Hushai said to Zadok and Abiathar the priests, "Thus and so did Ahithophel
counsel Absalom and the elders of Israel, and thus and so have I counseled. 16 Now therefore send quickly and tell David, 'Do not stay tonight at [z]the fords of the wilderness, but
by all means pass over, lest the king and all the people who are with him be [a]swallowed
up.'" 17 Now [b]Jonathan and Ahimaaz were waiting at [c]En-rogel. A female servant was to
go and tell them, and they were to go and tell King David, for they were not to be seen
entering the city. 18 But a young man saw them and told Absalom. So both of them went
away quickly and came to the house of a man at [d]Bahurim, who had a well in his courtyard. And they went down into it. 19 [e]And the woman took and spread a covering over the
well's mouth and scattered grain on it, and nothing was known of it. 20 When Absalom's
servants came to the woman at the house, they said, "Where are Ahimaaz and Jonathan?"
And the woman said to them, "They have gone over the brook[4] of water." And when they
had sought and could not find them, they returned to Jerusalem.

21 After they had gone, the men came up out of the well, and went and told King David.
They said to David, [f]"Arise, and go quickly over the water, for thus and so has Ahithophel
counseled against you." 22 Then David arose, and all the people who were with him, and
they crossed the Jordan. By daybreak not one was left who had not crossed the Jordan.

23 When Ahithophel saw that his counsel was not followed, he saddled his donkey and
went off home to [g]his own city. He [h]set his house in order and [i]hanged himself, and he
died and was buried in the tomb of his father.

24 Then David came to [j]Mahanaim. And Absalom crossed the Jordan with all the men of
Israel. 25 Now Absalom had set [k]Amasa over the army instead of Joab. Amasa was the son of a
man named Ithra the Ishmaelite,[5] who had married Abigal the daughter of [l]Nahash, sister
of Zeruiah, Joab's mother. 26 And Israel and Absalom encamped in the land of Gilead.

27 When David came to Mahanaim, [m]Shobi the son of Nahash from [n]Rabbah of the

8 [t]Prov. 17:12; Hos. 13:8
10 [u]See Josh. 2:11
11 [v]See ch. 3:10 [w]See Gen. 22:17
14 [x]ch. 15:31, 34
15 [y]ch. 15:35, 36
16 [z]ch. 15:28 [a]ch. 20:19
17 [b]ch. 15:27, 36 [c]Josh. 15:7; 18:16
18 [d]See ch. 3:16
19 [e][Josh. 2:6]
21 [f]ver. 15, 16
23 [g]ch. 15:12 [h][2 Kgs. 20:1] [i][Matt. 27:5]
24 [j]See Josh. 13:26
25 [k]ch. 19:13; 20:9, 12; 1 Kgs. 2:5, 32 [l][1 Chr. 2:13, 16]
27 [m][ch. 10:1, 2] [n]ch. 12:26, 29

[1] Hebrew *bitter of soul* [2] Or *And as he falls on them* [3] Hebrew *commanded* [4] The meaning of the Hebrew word is uncertain [5] Compare 1 Chronicles 2:17; Hebrew *Israelite*

17:13 Cities were often attacked by pulling down the walls by means of **ropes** attached to grappling hooks. Since cities were usually built on high places, they were hard to rebuild once the stones of their walls had been dragged **into the valley**. For attacking an entire **city** in order to get one person who had fled there, cf. 1 Sam. 23:7–13; 2 Sam. 20:14–22.

17:17 En-rogel, now known as "Job's Well," is just south of where the Kidron Valley joins the Hinnom Valley, on the boundary between Judah and Benjamin (Josh. 15:7; 18:16). It would have been dangerous for the priests' sons, apparently known supporters of David (2 Sam. 17:18), to be seen in Jerusalem. Therefore, a necessary link in the chain from Hushai to David is the **female servant**, probably a maid in the household of one of the priests whose normal duties took her to the water.

17:23 He set his house in order and hanged himself. Ahithophel is wise enough to realize that the rejection of his advice means the defeat of Absalom and his own ruin, for God is with David, not Absalom.

17:24–29 ***David Arrives at Mahanaim.*** From the place where he crossed the Jordan River (see 16:14), David had traveled another 37 miles (59 km) north.

17:24 As Hushai suggested (v. 11), Absalom gathers **all the men of Israel** and goes after David.

17:25 For Absalom's cousin **Amasa**, see note on 2:13.

17:27 Mahanaim, a city in the deep canyon of the Jabbok River, is where Ish-bosheth had his capital. **Shobi the son of Nahash from Rabbah of the Ammonites** apparently was the brother of Hanun, the king of Ammon (10:2). David had probably set him on the throne in place of his brother (12:30). It is remarkable that he did not try to revolt at this time. **Machir** had sheltered Mephibosheth in his childhood (9:4). **Barzillai** later accompanies David on

27 [o]ch. 9:4 [p]ch. 19:31, 32; 1 Kgs. 2:7; [Ezra 2:61]
29 [q]ch. 16:2 [r]ch. 15:23
Chapter 18
2 [s]ch. 15:19
3 [t]ch. 21:17
5 [u]ver. 12
6 [v]ver. 17; [Josh. 17:15, 18]
9 [w][ch. 14:26]
12 [x]ver. 5
17 [y]Josh. 7:26; 8:29 [z]ch. 19:8; 20:1, 22; 1 Sam. 4:10; 2 Kgs. 8:21
18 [a]Gen. 28:18 [b][Gen. 14:17] [c]ch. 14:27

Ammonites, and [o]Machir the son of Ammiel from Lo-debar, and [p]Barzillai the Gileadite
from Rogelim, **28** brought beds, basins, and earthen vessels, wheat, barley, flour, parched
grain, beans and lentils,[1] **29** honey and curds and sheep and cheese from the herd, for David
and the people with him to eat, for they said, "The people are hungry and [q]weary and
thirsty [r]in the wilderness."

Absalom Killed

18 Then David mustered the men who were with him and set over them commanders
of thousands and commanders of hundreds. **2** And David sent out the army, one
third under the command of Joab, one third under the command of Abishai the son of
Zeruiah, Joab's brother, and one third under the command of [s]Ittai the Gittite. And the
king said to the men, "I myself will also go out with you." **3** [t]But the men said, "You shall
not go out. For if we flee, they will not care about us. If half of us die, they will not care
about us. But you are worth ten thousand of us. Therefore it is better that you send us
help from the city." **4** The king said to them, "Whatever seems best to you I will do." So the
king stood at the side of the gate, while all the army marched out by hundreds and by
thousands. **5** And the king ordered Joab and Abishai and Ittai, "Deal gently for my sake
with the young man Absalom." [u]And all the people heard when the king gave orders to
all the commanders about Absalom.
6 So the army went out into the field against Israel, and the battle was fought in the [v]forest
of Ephraim. **7** And the men of Israel were defeated there by the servants of David, and the
loss there was great on that day, twenty thousand men. **8** The battle spread over the face of
all the country, and the forest devoured more people that day than the sword.
9 And Absalom happened to meet the servants of David. Absalom was riding on his mule,
and the mule went under the thick branches of a great oak,[2] [w]and his head caught fast in
the oak, and he was suspended between heaven and earth, while the mule that was under
him went on. **10** And a certain man saw it and told Joab, "Behold, I saw Absalom hanging
in an oak." **11** Joab said to the man who told him, "What, you saw him! Why then did you
not strike him there to the ground? I would have been glad to give you ten pieces of silver
and a belt." **12** But the man said to Joab, "Even if I felt in my hand the weight of a thousand
pieces of silver, I would not reach out my hand against the king's son, for [x]in our hearing
the king commanded you and Abishai and Ittai, 'For my sake protect the young man
Absalom.' **13** On the other hand, if I had dealt treacherously against his life[3] (and there is
nothing hidden from the king), then you yourself would have stood aloof." **14** Joab said, "I
will not waste time like this with you." And he took three javelins in his hand and thrust
them into the heart of Absalom while he was still alive in the oak. **15** And ten young men,
Joab's armor-bearers, surrounded Absalom and struck him and killed him.
16 Then Joab blew the trumpet, and the troops came back from pursuing Israel, for Joab
restrained them. **17** And they took Absalom and threw him into a great pit in the forest and
raised over him [y]a very great heap of stones. And all Israel [z]fled every one to his own home.
18 Now Absalom in his lifetime had taken and set up for himself [a]the pillar that is in [b]the
King's Valley, for he said, [c]"I have no son to keep my name in remembrance." He called the
pillar after his own name, and it is called Absalom's monument[4] to this day.

[1] Hebrew adds *and parched grain* [2] Or *terebinth; also verses 10, 14* [3] Or *at the risk of my life* [4] Or *Absalom's hand*

his trip back to Jerusalem (19:31–39). The fact that these people came from a distance suggests that David had real support in the area of Gilead.

18:1–19:8a *Death of Absalom.* After a brief description of the battle, the author focuses on how Absalom died and on David's grief over his son's death.

18:2–3 Ittai was mentioned in 15:19. David's men believe that the success or failure of the rebellion depends on whether Absalom can kill David, an opinion that was also expressed by Ahithophel (17:3).

18:5 Deal gently . . . with . . . Absalom. Why did David make this request? Was it out of pure fatherly love, or also a feeling of guilt toward Absalom?

18:6–8 The **forest of Ephraim** was actually not in Ephraim, but east of the Jordan in Gilead. Gilead was apparently known for its forests (Jer. 22:6). Here David's experienced army could effectively attack a much larger force, most of whom were apparently unable to move around effectively in a forest (**the forest devoured more people . . . than the sword**).

18:9 Mules were the normal mounts of the king's sons (13:29). **his head caught fast in the oak.** Most take this to mean that the specific part of Absalom's head that got tangled in the tree was his hair (cf. 14:26). In God's providence, the source of his pride became the cause of his downfall.

18:14 The narrator stresses repeatedly (vv. 5, 12) that David had ordered all the troops to spare Absalom. **Joab** probably worries that Absalom, who had risen from disgrace once before, even using Joab himself (14:1–24), might be able to cause problems again.

18:17 every one to his own home. See note on 1 Sam. 4:10.

18:18 I have no son. See note on 14:27. The author contrasts the memorial pillar with Absalom's actual tomb, a big pile of rocks (18:17; cf. Josh. 7:26;

David Hears of Absalom's Death

19 Then Ahimaaz the son of Zadok said, [d]"Let me run and carry news to the king that
[e]the LORD has delivered him from the hand of his enemies." 20 And Joab said to him, "You
are not to carry news today. You may carry news another day, but today you shall carry no
news, because the king's son is dead." 21 Then Joab said to the Cushite, "Go, tell the king
what you have seen." The Cushite bowed before Joab, and ran. 22 Then Ahimaaz the son
of Zadok said again to Joab, "Come what may, let me also run after the Cushite." And
Joab said, "Why will you run, my son, seeing that you will have no reward for the news?"
23 "Come what may," he said, "I will run." So he said to him, "Run." Then Ahimaaz ran by
the way of [f]the plain, and outran the Cushite.

24 Now David [g]was sitting between the two gates, and [h]the watchman went up to the
roof of the gate by the wall, and when he lifted up his eyes and looked, he saw a man
running alone. 25 The watchman called out and told the king. And the king said, "If he is
alone, there is news in his mouth." And he drew nearer and nearer. 26 The watchman saw
another man running. And the watchman called to the gate and said, "See, another man
running alone!" The king said, "He also brings news." 27 The watchman said, "I think the
running of the first is [i]like the running of Ahimaaz the son of Zadok." And the king said,
[j]"He is a good man and comes with good news."

28 Then Ahimaaz cried out to the king, "All is well." And he bowed before the king with
his face to the earth and said, [k]"Blessed be the LORD your God, who has delivered up the
men who raised their hand against my lord the king." 29 And the king said, [l]"Is it well with
the young man Absalom?" Ahimaaz answered, "When Joab sent the king's servant, your
servant, I saw a great commotion, but I do not know what it was." 30 And the king said,
"Turn aside and stand here." So he turned aside and stood still.

David's Grief

31 And behold, the Cushite came, and the Cushite said, "Good news for my lord the
king! For [m]the LORD has delivered you this day from the hand of all who rose up against
you." 32 The king said to the Cushite, [l]"Is it well with the young man Absalom?" And the
Cushite answered, [n]"May the enemies of my lord the king and all who rise up against you
for evil be like that young man." 33 [1] And the king was deeply moved and went up [g]to the
chamber over the gate and wept. And as he went, he said, [o]"O my son Absalom, my son,
my son Absalom! Would I had died instead of you, O Absalom, my son, my son!"

Joab Rebukes David

19 It was told Joab, "Behold, the king is weeping and mourning for Absalom." 2 So
the victory that day was turned into mourning for all the people, for the people
heard that day, "The king is grieving for his son." 3 And the people stole into the city that
day as people steal in who are ashamed when they flee in battle. 4 The king [p]covered his

[1] Ch 19:1 in Hebrew

19 [d]ch. 15:36 [e]ver. 31
23 [f][Deut. 34:3]
24 [g]ch. 19:8 [h][ch. 13:34; 2 Kgs. 9:17]
27 [i][2 Kgs. 9:20] [j][1 Kgs. 1:42]
28 [k]See Gen. 14:20
29 [l]ch. 20:9
31 [m]ver. 19
32 [l][See ver. 29 above] [n]1 Sam. 25:26
33 [g][See ver. 24 above] [o]ch. 19:4

Chapter 19

4 [p]ch. 15:30

8:29). The "Absalom's Tomb" now seen in the Kidron Valley in Jerusalem is a Hellenistic or Roman-period structure.

18:19–23 today you shall carry no news, because the king's son is dead. Joab does not seem to be trying to hide anything from David (**Go, tell the king what you have seen**). But he apparently wants to protect **Ahimaaz, son of Zadok** the priest, from having to deliver the bad news to David. **Then Ahimaaz . . . outran the Cushite.** It may be that the Cushite took a direct road over the mountains, while Ahimaaz took the longer but easier way along the plain.

18:24 The **two gates** are the outer gate and the inner gate of the gate complex.

18:25 A man running **alone** would be a messenger; a group would probably be men fleeing.

18:29 a great commotion. Ahimaaz may have been trying to break the news gently. He must have known Absalom was dead, or else he would have just said he did not know anything.

18:33 O Absalom, my son, my son! David is overcome with grief. He has lost another son whom he loved. First he lost Absalom's love and loyalty, and now he has lost Absalom's life and all hope of reconciliation. It is possible that David is beginning to see how God's punishment for his sin with Bathsheba (prophesied by Nathan in 12:10–11) has tragically come to pass; but his grief is clouding his sight of his duties toward his loyal troops (19:1–8).

19:2 So the victory that day was turned into mourning. David lets his own grief overcome not just his kingly responsibilities but even his gratitude to God for saving the nation.

19:4–6 Because David has **covered his face** with grief, he has **covered with shame the faces** of his loyal **servants. you love those who hate you and hate those who love you.** The words for "love" and "hate" here can mean "be loyal" and "be disloyal."

19:8 David makes peace with his men, behaving as king and **sitting in the gate.** Kings and elders are often described as sitting at the gate (Deut. 25:7; Ruth 4:11; 1 Kings 22:10; Jer. 39:3); at the excavations at Dan, what appears to be a canopy base has been found within the Iron Age gate. In the wake of Absalom's failed rebellion, David will have to work at reuniting the nation.

19:8b–43 ***David's Return to Jerusalem.*** Although David can return to Jerusalem in triumph, there are still occasions for division. As Nathan had

face, and the king cried with a loud voice, [q]"O my son Absalom, O Absalom, my son, my
son!" 5 Then Joab came into the house to the king and said, "You have today covered with
shame the faces of all your servants, who have this day saved your life and the lives of your
sons and your daughters and the lives of your wives and your concubines, 6 because you
love those who hate you and hate those who love you. For you have made it clear today
that commanders and servants are nothing to you, for today I know that if Absalom were
alive and all of us were dead today, then you would be pleased. 7 Now therefore arise, go
out and speak [r]kindly to your servants, for I swear by the LORD, if you do not go, not a
man will stay with you this night, and this will be worse for you than all the evil that has
come upon you from your youth until now." 8 Then the king arose and took his [s]seat in
the gate. And the people were all told, "Behold, the king is sitting in the gate." And all the
people came before the king.

David Returns to Jerusalem

Now Israel had [t]fled every man to his own home. 9 And all the people were arguing
throughout all the tribes of Israel, saying, [u]"The king delivered us from the hand of our
enemies and [v]saved us from the hand of the Philistines, and now [w]he has fled out of the
land from Absalom. 10 But Absalom, whom we anointed over us, is dead in battle. Now
therefore why do you say nothing about bringing the king back?"

11 And King David sent this message to [x]Zadok and Abiathar the priests: "Say to the elders
of Judah, 'Why should you be the last to bring the king back to his house, when the word
of all Israel has come to the king?[1] 12 You are my brothers; [y]you are my bone and my flesh.
Why then should you be the last to bring back the king?' 13 And say to Amasa, [z]'Are you not
my bone and my flesh? [a]God do so to me and more also, if you are not [b]commander of my
army from now on in place of Joab.'" 14 And he swayed the heart of all the men of Judah
[c]as one man, so that they sent word to the king, "Return, both you and all your servants."
15 So the king came back to the Jordan, and Judah came to Gilgal to meet the king and to
bring the king over the Jordan.

David Pardons His Enemies

16 And [d]Shimei the son of Gera, the Benjaminite, from Bahurim, hurried to come down
with the men of Judah to meet King David. 17 And with him were a thousand men from
Benjamin. And [e]Ziba the servant of the house of Saul, with his fifteen sons and his twenty
servants, rushed down to the Jordan before the king, 18 and they crossed the ford to bring
over the king's household and to do his pleasure. And Shimei the son of Gera fell down
before the king, as he was about to cross the Jordan, 19 and said to the king, [f]"Let not my
lord hold me guilty or remember how your servant [g]did wrong on the day my lord the
king left Jerusalem. Do not let the king take it to heart. 20 For your servant knows that I
have sinned. Therefore, behold, I have come this day, the first [h]of all the house of Joseph
to come down to meet my lord the king." 21 Abishai the son of Zeruiah answered, "Shall
not Shimei be put to death for this, because [i]he cursed the LORD's anointed?" 22 But David
said, [j]"What have I to do with you, you sons of Zeruiah, that you should this day be as an

[1] Septuagint; Hebrew *to the king, to his house*

4 [q]ch. 18:33
7 [r]Gen. 34:3 (Heb.)
8 [s]ch. 18:4, 24, 33; See Ruth 4:1 [t]See ch. 18:17
9 [u]See ch. 8:1-14 [v]ch. 5:20; 8:1 [w]ch. 15:14
11 [x]ch. 15:29
12 [y]ch. 5:1; [Gen. 29:14]
13 [z]ch. 17:25 [a]See Ruth 1:17 [b]ch. 8:16
14 [c][Judg. 20:1]
16 [d]ch. 16:5; 1 Kgs. 2:8
17 [e]ch. 9:2, 10; See ch. 16:1-4
19 [f][1 Sam. 22:15] [g]See ch. 16:5-13
20 [h][ch. 16:5]
21 [i][Ex. 22:28]
22 [j]ch. 16:10

prophesied, because of David's sin, the "sword [would] never depart" from his house (12:10).

19:8b–15 The whole country finally agrees to bring David back, but even this creates problems as it shows the division between **Judah** and the rest of **Israel**. Israel (in this chapter referring to the northern tribes) had spoken with David about coming back to Jerusalem, but David has to make a special appeal to Judah. So a Judean contingent accompanies David back, apparently without consultation with the other tribes. However, Israel and Judah argue over the ceremony of David's triumphal return to his capital (vv. 41–43).

19:10–11 why do you say nothing? The question highlights the factions that developed within both Israel and Judah concerning the validity of David's return to the throne. David uses the support he is getting from Israel to motivate Judah to action.

19:13 commander of my army. It seems shocking to demote the victorious loyal general Joab in favor of the soundly defeated rebel general **Amasa** (17:25). Perhaps David pointed out that Joab had disobeyed his specific order about Absalom (18:5). He probably could have added that, if Joab claimed it had been necessary to kill Absalom, he (David) was also doing what was necessary to reunite the nation.

19:15 Gilgal was an important religious center near Jericho and the Jordan River (Josh. 4:19; 5:10; 1 Sam. 10:8; 11:14; 13:12; 15:21), but its location is uncertain.

19:16–23 At the Jordan (see v. 15), David meets various people he had encountered during his flight from Jerusalem. The first of these is Shimei, who had cursed him as he fled (16:5–13). Now that the Lord has repaid David with good for his patience under Shimei's cursing (16:12), **Abishai** thinks **Shimei** should be put to death as he deserves. But David wants this to be a day of rejoicing, not retribution. However he apparently did not fully forgive Shimei (cf. 1 Kings 2:8–9, 36–46).

adversary to me? [k]Shall anyone be put to death in Israel this day? For do I not know that
I am this day king over Israel?" 23 [l]And the king said to Shimei, "You shall not die." And
the king gave him his oath.
24 And [m]Mephibosheth the son of Saul came down to meet the king. He had neither
taken care of his feet nor trimmed his beard nor washed his clothes, from the day the
king departed until the day he came back in safety. 25 And when he came to Jerusalem
to meet the king, the king said to him, [n]"Why did you not go with me, Mephibosheth?"
26 He answered, "My lord, O king, my servant deceived me, for your servant said to him,
'I will saddle a donkey for myself,[1] that I may ride on it and go with the king.' For [o]your
servant is lame. 27 [p]He has slandered your servant to my lord the king. But my lord the
king is [q]like the angel of God; do therefore what seems good to you. 28 For all my father's
house were but men doomed to death before my lord the king, but [r]you set your servant
among those who eat at your table. What further right have I, then, to cry to the king?"
29 And the king said to him, "Why speak any more of your affairs? I have decided: you and
Ziba shall divide the land." 30 And Mephibosheth said to the king, "Oh, let him take it all,
since my lord the king has come safely home."
31 Now [s]Barzillai the Gileadite had come down from Rogelim, and he went on with the
king to the Jordan, to escort him over the Jordan. 32 Barzillai was a very aged man, eighty
years old. [t]He had provided the king with food while he stayed at Mahanaim, for he was a
very wealthy man. 33 And the king said to Barzillai, "Come over with me, and I will provide
for you with me in Jerusalem." 34 But Barzillai said to the king, [u]"How many years have I
still to live, that I should go up with the king to Jerusalem? 35 I am this day [v]eighty years
old. Can I discern what is pleasant and what is not? Can your servant taste what he eats
or what he drinks? Can I still listen to the voice of singing men and singing women? Why
then should your servant be [w]an added burden to my lord the king? 36 Your servant will
go a little way over the Jordan with the king. Why should the king repay me with such a
reward? 37 Please let your servant return, that I may die in my own city near the grave of
my father and my mother. But here is your servant [x]Chimham. Let him go over with my
lord the king, and do for him whatever seems good to you." 38 And the king answered,
"Chimham shall go over with me, and I will do for him whatever seems good to you, and
all that you desire of me I will do for you." 39 Then all the people went over the Jordan, and
the king went over. And [y]the king kissed Barzillai and blessed him, and he returned to his
own home. 40 The king went on to Gilgal, and Chimham went on with him. All the people
of Judah, and also half the people of Israel, brought the king on his way.
41 Then all the men of Israel came to the king and said to the king, "Why have our
brothers the men of Judah stolen you away and [z]brought the king and his household over
the Jordan, and all David's men with him?" 42 All the men of Judah answered the men of
Israel, "Because the king is [a]our close relative. Why then are you angry over this matter?
Have we eaten at all at the king's expense? Or has he given us any gift?" 43 And the men
of Israel answered the men of Judah, "We have [b]ten shares in the king, and in David also
we have more than you. Why then did you despise us? Were we not the first to speak of

[1] Septuagint, Syriac, Vulgate *Saddle a donkey for me*

22 [k][1 Sam. 11:13]
23 [l][1 Kgs. 2:8, 9, 37, 46]
24 [m]ch. 9:6
25 [n][ch. 16:17]
26 [o]ch. 9:3
27 [p]ch. 16:3 [q]ch. 14:17, 20; 1 Sam. 29:9
28 [r]ch. 9:7, 10, 13
31 [s]1 Kgs. 2:7
32 [t]ch. 17:27-29
34 [u]Gen. 47:8
35 [v][Ps. 90:10] [w]ch. 15:33
37 [x]1 Kgs. 2:7; Jer. 41:17
39 [y]See ch. 14:33
41 [z]ver. 15
42 [a]ver. 12
43 [b][1 Kgs. 11:30, 31]

19:24–30 David also met **Mephibosheth the son of Saul**. Mephibosheth was actually Jonathan's son (4:4) and Saul's grandson. But here the narrator emphasizes that Saul's rightful heir (9:1–3) is submitting to David. Mephibosheth tells David that Ziba was lying when he said Mephibosheth had chosen to stay in Jerusalem (16:3). The narrator does not directly state which one is telling the truth—after all, he may not have had direct information—but the sorrow evidenced in 19:24 suggests that he believes Mephibosheth, and Mephibosheth's gracious humility in v. 30 also supports this view. In a city facing invasion, when even the king's household was grateful for two donkeys (16:1), it is not surprising that Mephibosheth, who was **lame** (19:26), was stuck when his own donkey was taken by Ziba.

19:25 To Jerusalem implies that Mephibosheth "came down" (v. 24) from his home and arrived in Jerusalem **to meet the king**, and that this event occurred later, after David had come to Jerusalem.

19:31–40 As he crossed the Jordan (see v. 15), David also met **Barzillai**, who had helped him in Mahanaim (v. 32; cf. 17:27). **I will provide for you with me in Jerusalem**. David wanted to repay Barzillai's kindness, but Barzillai, who was **eighty years old**, preferred to return home, **that I may die in my own city**. David never forgot Barzillai's help (1 Kings 2:7).

19:41–43 Apparently David left Mahanaim and came to the Jordan without allowing time for all the northern tribes to come and accompany him. They resent this, being the larger group and considering themselves more loyal to David (vv. 9–11) than Judah, which they accuse of "privatizing" the king. The men of Judah retort that David did not favor his own tribe with grants (unlike Saul in 1 Sam. 22:7). In making Jerusalem his capital and bringing the ark there, David seems to have made an effort to be an Israelite king, not a Judahite king ruling Israel. But he was not able to overcome the division. **We**, **our**, and **us** in 2 Sam. 19:42–43 are singular—"I," "my," and "me"—in the Hebrew, suggesting the acrimony of the debate.

43 [c]Isa. 9:21; 11:13
Chapter 20
1 [d]See Deut. 13:13 [e][ch. 19:43] [f]ver. 22; 1 Kgs. 12:16; 2 Chr. 10:16
3 [g]ch. 15:16; 16:21, 22
4 [h]ch. 17:25; 19:13
6 [i]ch. 11:11; 1 Kgs. 1:33
7 [j]ver. 23; See ch. 8:18
9 [k][Matt. 26:49; Mark 14:45; Luke 22:47]
10 [l]1 Kgs. 2:5 [m]See ch. 2:23
14 [n][2 Kgs. 15:29] [o]Num. 21:16

bringing back our king?" [c]But the words of the men of Judah were fiercer than the words
of the men of Israel.

The Rebellion of Sheba

20 Now there happened to be there [d]a worthless man, whose name was Sheba, the
son of Bichri, a Benjaminite. And he blew the trumpet and said,

[e]"We have no portion in David,
and we have no inheritance in the son of Jesse;
[f]every man to his tents, O Israel!"

2 So all the men of Israel withdrew from David and followed Sheba the son of Bichri. But
the men of Judah followed their king steadfastly from the Jordan to Jerusalem.
3 And David came to his house at Jerusalem. And the king took [g]the ten concubines
whom he had left to care for the house and put them in a house under guard and provided
for them, but did not go in to them. So they were shut up until the day of their death,
living as if in widowhood.
4 Then the king said to [h]Amasa, "Call the men of Judah together to me within three days,
and be here yourself." 5 So Amasa went to summon Judah, but he delayed beyond the set
time that had been appointed him. 6 And David said to Abishai, "Now Sheba the son of
Bichri will do us more harm than Absalom. Take [i]your lord's servants and pursue him, lest
he get himself to fortified cities and escape from us."[1] 7 And there went out after him Joab's
men and the [j]Cherethites and the Pelethites, and all the mighty men. They went out from
Jerusalem to pursue Sheba the son of Bichri. 8 When they were at the great stone that is in
Gibeon, Amasa came to meet them. Now Joab was wearing a soldier's garment, and over it
was a belt with a sword in its sheath fastened on his thigh, and as he went forward it fell
out. 9 And Joab said to Amasa, "Is it well with you, my brother?" And Joab took Amasa by
the beard with his right hand [k]to kiss him. 10 But Amasa did not observe the sword that
was in Joab's hand. [l]So Joab struck him with it [m]in the stomach and spilled his entrails to
the ground without striking a second blow, and he died.
Then Joab and Abishai his brother pursued Sheba the son of Bichri. 11 And one of Joab's
young men took his stand by Amasa and said, "Whoever favors Joab, and whoever is for
David, let him follow Joab." 12 And Amasa lay wallowing in his blood in the highway. And
anyone who came by, seeing him, stopped. And when the man saw that all the people
stopped, he carried Amasa out of the highway into the field and threw a garment over
him. 13 When he was taken out of the highway, all the people went on after Joab to pursue
Sheba the son of Bichri.
14 And Sheba passed through all the tribes of Israel to [n]Abel of [n]Beth-maacah,[2] and all
[o]the Bichrites[3] assembled and followed him in. 15 And all the men who were with Joab came

[1] Hebrew *and snatch away our eyes* [2] Compare 20:15; Hebrew *and Beth-maacah* [3] Hebrew *Berites*

20:1–26 *Sheba's Rebellion.* Sheba's rebellion is directly connected with the split within the nation seen in 19:41–43. It does not seem to have gained support outside of his own clan (20:14), but the feeling that the king was not treating them well seems to have lingered among the northern tribes, then increased under Solomon (who did not require Judah to supply him with food in the list in 1 Kings 4:7–19), and finally caused the nation to split in two (1 Kings 12).

20:1 Seeming to say, "If we do not have 10 shares, we have none," Sheba revolts. His rallying cry will later be used by Jeroboam (1 Kings 12:16). Saul (1 Sam. 13:3) and Absalom (2 Sam. 15:10) also announced their rebellions by a **trumpet**.

20:3 The **ten concubines** are those whom Absalom had claimed in 16:22.

20:4–5 David had made **Amasa** commander in 19:13, replacing Joab. **Three days** is a rather short time if he is supposed to gather men from all over Judah, and indeed he failed to gather an army in **the set time that had been appointed him**.

20:6 When Amasa failed to produce an armed force on schedule (v. 5), David turned to **Abishai**, brother of Joab, David's former general whom he had passed over in favor of Amasa (see note on 19:13). Abishai and Joab had often worked together in battle (3:30; 10:9–10; 18:2; also 1 Kings 11:15; 1 Chron. 18:12), so David probably should not have been too surprised at what soon transpired (2 Sam. 20:10). **Sheba . . . will do us more harm than Absalom**. David seems to have overestimated Sheba's strength. Though "all the men of Israel" had initially followed him, apparently only the members of Sheba's own Bichrite clan were truly committed to his cause (v. 14). **Your lord's servants** refers to David's standing army, as does "the servants of David" in 18:7.

20:8–10 Readers are not told why **Amasa** was in **Gibeon** instead of Judah. The **sword** conspicuously falls out of Joab's **belt**, but when he takes Amasa's **beard** with his **right hand**, with his left hand he either picks it up again or gets out a hidden sword (cf. the story of Ehud in Judg. 3:15–23). Compare Joab's similar murder of Abner in 2 Sam. 3:27 and his execution of Absalom in 18:14. **brother**. Joab and Amasa were first cousins.

20:11–13 The **people** who are addressed in v. 11 and who **stopped** at the sight of **Amasa** were probably the "men of Judah" of v. 4 who had come from Judah to Gibeon with Amasa.

20:14 Sheba and his men go to **Abel**, in the north of Israel, just west of Dan.

20:15 The **mound** is a ramp built against the wall to get near its top.

and besieged him in [n]Abel of Beth-maacah. [p]They cast up a mound against the city, and
it stood against the rampart, and they were battering the wall to throw it down. 16 Then
a wise woman called from the city, "Listen! Listen! Tell Joab, 'Come here, that I may speak
to you.'" 17 And he came near her, and the woman said, "Are you Joab?" He answered, "I
am." Then she said to him, "Listen to the words of your servant." And he answered, "I am
listening." 18 Then she said, "They used to say in former times, 'Let them but ask counsel
at [n]Abel,' and so they settled a matter. 19 I am one of those who are peaceable and faithful
in Israel. You seek to destroy a city that is a mother in Israel. Why will you [q]swallow up
[r]the heritage of the LORD?" 20 Joab answered, "Far be it from me, far be it, that I should
[q]swallow up or destroy! 21 That is not true. But a man of [s]the hill country of Ephraim,
called Sheba the son of Bichri, has lifted up his hand against King David. Give up him
alone, and I will withdraw from the city." And the woman said to Joab, "Behold, his head
shall be thrown to you over the wall." 22 Then the woman went to all the people [t]in her
wisdom. And they cut off the head of Sheba the son of Bichri and threw it out to Joab. So
he blew the trumpet, and they dispersed from the city, [u]every man to his home. And Joab
returned to Jerusalem to the king.

23 [v]Now Joab was in command of all the army of Israel; and Benaiah the son of Jehoiada
was in command of the Cherethites and the Pelethites; 24 and [w]Adoram was in charge of the
forced labor; and Jehoshaphat the son of Ahilud was the recorder; 25 and Sheva was secretary;
and [x]Zadok and Abiathar were priests; 26 and [y]Ira the Jairite was also David's priest.

David Avenges the Gibeonites

21 Now there was a famine in the days of David for three years, year after year. And
David [z]sought the face of the LORD. And the LORD said, "There is bloodguilt on
Saul and on his house, because he put the Gibeonites to death." 2 So the king called the
Gibeonites and spoke to them. Now the Gibeonites were not of the people of Israel but
[a]of the remnant of the Amorites. Although the people of Israel had sworn to spare them,
Saul had sought to strike them down in his zeal for the people of Israel and Judah. 3 And

15 [n][See ver. 14 above] [p]2 Kgs. 19:32; Isa. 37:33; Jer. 6:6; Ezek. 4:2; 26:8
18 [n][See ver. 14 above]
19 [q]ch. 17:16 [r]See 1 Sam. 26:19
20 [q][See ver. 19 above]
21 [s]See Josh. 24:33
22 [t]ver. 16; [Eccles. 9:14, 15] [u]See 1 Sam. 4:10
23 [v]For ver. 23-26, see ch. 8:16-18; 1 Kgs. 4:3-6
24 [w][1 Kgs. 12:18]
25 [x]ch. 15:24; 19:11
26 [y][ch. 23:38]

Chapter 21

1 [z][Num. 27:21]
2 [a]See Josh. 9:3-17

battering the wall. This might mean that Joab's men were undermining the walls or, more generally, attacking the walls, as by battering rams.

20:16–22 The **woman** is **wise** (v. 16), i.e., skilled in choosing means for an end (in this case, to avert destruction) and in persuasive speech. In this narrative, "wisdom" is not necessarily morally positive. **A mother in Israel** (v. 19) describes a main city with associated (daughter) villages (cf. Judg. 1:27). Israel is the **heritage of the LORD**. Joab denies (2 Sam. 20:20) that he has any desire to **swallow up or destroy** (the woman's words): he will be content if Sheba is handed over to him. The woman goes one better, persuading the townspeople to **cut off the head of Sheba** to end the siege decisively. The **hill country of Ephraim** (v. 21) includes Benjaminite territory.

20:22 Joab returned to Jerusalem to the king. Apparently David did not punish Joab for the murder of Amasa (since Joab was still commander at the end of David's reign; 1 Kings 1:19), but he did not forgive him either (1 Kings 2:5).

20:23–26 This list is very similar to the lists in 8:15–18 and 1 Kings 4:1–6. The posts and officials overlap to a large degree, but the order is different, and unlike the others, this one does not start out with the king. For **Benaiah** (2 Sam. 20:23), see note on 8:18. An official **in charge of the forced labor** (20:24) is not mentioned in ch. 8, so it is possible that this list is dated toward the end of David's reign. The office is probably listed after the bodyguards as a military office because it involved mostly captured peoples, at least at first. **Adoram** was eventually stoned to death by the northern tribes at the time of Rehoboam (1 Kings 12:18). He is probably the same person as Adoniram in 1 Kings 4:6. The office of overseeing the forced labor is not mentioned again in the Bible, but a seventh-century seal bearing a similar title has been found. For the offices of **recorder** (2 Sam. 20:24) and **secretary**, and **Zadok and Abiathar** (v. 25), see notes on 8:15–18 and 8:17. **David's priest** (20:26) may have been similar to a private chaplain or adviser, probably the same office as Solomon's "priest and king's friend" (1 Kings 4:5).

21:1–24:25 *Epilogue.* These last four chapters form an epilogue. There are six sections arranged concentrically. The first section deals with a drought, the last with a plague. The second and fifth talk about David's heroes, and the middle two are psalms of David. They are not placed in chronological order with the rest of the book (note the vague expression "in the days of David" in 21:1). The last section is climactic, describing the events leading to the purchase of the land on which Solomon would build the temple.

21:1–14 *Famine and the Death of Saul's Sons.* When told by the Lord that a famine is the result of Saul's misdeed against the Gibeonites, David has Saul's sons slain to make atonement.

21:1–2 Joshua 9 tells how the **Gibeonites** tricked the Israelites into guaranteeing their safety with an oath (Josh. 9:15). Because of his **zeal**, Saul had broken that oath and killed some Gibeonites. This incident is not recorded elsewhere, but Saul's ability to act ruthlessly (though hardly out of zeal for Israel) is also shown in 1 Sam. 22:16–19.

21:3–6 Asked how Saul's misdeeds against them could be atoned, the Gibeonites requested that **seven of his sons** be given to them to be put to death. This apparently ignores the command in Deut. 24:16: "nor shall children be put to death because of their fathers." Various explanations have been offered as to why God allowed this to happen: (1) These seven were accomplices in Saul's acts. Yet the text in no way suggests this; furthermore, even Merab's oldest son could scarcely have been more than 10 when Saul died, because David must have been at least in his late teens when Merab married (1 Sam. 18:19) and was no more than 30 when Saul died (2 Sam. 5:4). See also note on 4:2–3. (2) A more plausible suggestion is that God still exacted punishment from Saul's house for some of the evil that Saul had done; this is consistent with a pattern elsewhere in which serious sins, especially of a king, result in punishment on the sinner's descendants as well (cf. Ex. 20:5; 1 Sam. 2:33–34; 3:13–14; 1 Kings 14:10–11; 2 Kings 9:7–9). (3) A third suggestion is that the execution of seven men was excessive punishment, because although the Lord told David that Saul's actions had caused the famine (2 Sam. 21:1), he did not tell David to put anyone to death. In that case, the solution proposed by the Gibeonites was excessively vindictive, while the text hints that a monetary payment (see v. 4) and the restoration of land (see v. 5) may have been sufficient. In any case, the narrator never tells readers

David said to the Gibeonites, "What shall I do for you? And how shall I make atonement,
that you may bless [b]the heritage of the LORD?" 4 The Gibeonites said to him, "It is not a
matter of silver or gold between us and Saul or his house; neither is it for us to put any
man to death in Israel." And he said, "What do you say that I shall do for you?" 5 They said
to the king, "The man who consumed us and planned to destroy us, so that we should
have no place in all the territory of Israel, 6 let seven of his sons be given to us, so that we
may hang them before the LORD at [c]Gibeah of Saul, [d]the chosen of the LORD." And the
king said, "I will give them."

7 But the king spared Mephibosheth, the son of Saul's son Jonathan, because of [e]the oath
of the LORD that was between them, between David and Jonathan the son of Saul. 8 The
king took the two sons of [f]Rizpah the daughter of Aiah, whom she bore to Saul, Armoni
and Mephibosheth; and the five sons of Merab[1] the daughter of Saul, whom [g]she bore
to [h]Adriel the son of Barzillai the Meholathite; 9 and he gave them into the hands of the
Gibeonites, and they hanged them on the mountain before the LORD, and the seven of
them perished together. They were put to death in the first days of harvest, [i]at the beginning of barley harvest.

10 [j]Then Rizpah the daughter of Aiah took sackcloth and spread it for herself on the
rock, from the beginning of harvest until rain fell upon them from the heavens. And she
did not allow the birds of the air to come upon them by day, or the beasts of the field by
night. 11 When David was told what Rizpah the daughter of Aiah, the concubine of Saul, had
done, 12 David went and took the bones of Saul and the bones of his son Jonathan from the
men of Jabesh-gilead, [k]who had stolen them from the public square of [l]Beth-shan, where
the Philistines had hanged them, on the day the Philistines killed Saul on Gilboa. 13 And
he brought up from there the bones of Saul and the bones of his son Jonathan; and they
gathered the bones of those who were hanged. 14 And they buried the bones of Saul and his
son Jonathan in the land of Benjamin in [m]Zela, in the tomb of Kish his father. And they did
all that the king commanded. And after that [n]God responded to the plea for the land.

War with the Philistines

15 There was war again between the Philistines and Israel, and David went down together
with his servants, and they fought against the Philistines. And David grew weary. 16 And
Ishbi-benob, one of the descendants [o]of the giants, whose spear weighed three hundred
shekels[2] of bronze, and who was armed with a new sword, thought to kill David. 17 But
Abishai the son of Zeruiah came to his aid and attacked the Philistine and killed him.
Then David's men swore to him, [p]"You shall no longer go out with us to battle, lest you
quench [q]the lamp of Israel."

18 [r]After this there was again war with the Philistines at Gob. Then [s]Sibbecai [t]the
Hushathite struck down Saph, who was one of the descendants [u]of the giants. 19 And

3 [b]See 1 Sam. 26:19
6 [c]1 Sam. 10:26; 11:4 [d]1 Sam. 10:24
7 [e]1 Sam. 20:8, 42; 23:18
8 [f]ch. 3:7 [g][Gen. 50:23] [h][1 Sam. 18:19]
9 [i]Ruth 1:22
10 [j][Deut. 21:23]
12 [k]1 Sam. 31:10-13; [ch. 2:4] [l]Josh. 17:11
14 [m]Josh. 18:28 [n]ch. 24:25
16 [o]ver. 18, 20, 22
17 [p][ch. 18:3] [q]ch. 22:29; 1 Kgs. 11:36; 15:4; 2 Kgs. 8:19; 2 Chr. 21:7; Ps. 132:17
18 [r]For ver. 18-22, see 1 Chr. 20:4-8 [s]1 Chr. 11:29; 27:11 [t]ch. 23:27 [u]ver. 16, 20, 22

[1] Two Hebrew manuscripts, Septuagint; most Hebrew manuscripts *Michal* [2] A *shekel* was about 2/5 ounce or 11 grams

that God approved of David's action here; thus David may simply be acting according to widespread beliefs or the Gibeonite demands rather than divine command (see notes on 13:21; 16:1–4). The relief from the famine (21:14) does show that the payment was enough (and indeed more than enough), but it is also a response to David's decency with the bones of these victims, as well as those of Saul and Jonathan.

21:7–8 The writer lists the sons of Saul who were handed over to the Gibeonites. **Mephibosheth** the son of **Rizpah** (Saul's concubine; see 3:7) is different from **Mephibosheth** son of Jonathan, who was spared. Likewise Barzillai, grandfather of five of the hanged men, is not the Barzillai of 19:31–40. For Merab's marriage to Adriel, see 1 Sam. 18:19.

21:9 The **beginning of barley harvest** was April.

21:10–14 Rizpah, mother of two of the men hanged by the Gibeonites, sheltered their bodies from the birds and wild animals (cf. 1 Sam. 17:44, 46; Ps. 79:2). According to Deut. 21:22–23, the bodies of those who are hanged should be buried that same day (see Josh. 8:29). **Until rain fell upon them** may mean "until the rain should have fallen upon them." It may have been decided that the men would not be buried until the rains fell and the famine stopped. This suggests that, when David heard what Rizpah was doing, he buried them earlier than planned, and then God responded (2 Sam. 21:14), probably by sending rain. David also **took the bones of Saul and . . . his son Jonathan** (see 1 Sam. 31:12–13) and, presumably, buried them alongside the seven others of Saul's family who had just been killed. Saul was apparently from Gibeah (1 Sam. 11:4), but his family could have originally come from the Benjaminite town of **Zela** (Josh. 18:28).

21:15–22 *Philistine Wars.* This section recounts four fights of David's men with Philistine giants. "There was war again" suggests that this is an excerpt from some writing about David's wars.

21:16 The **giants** (Hb. *rapah*) are usually understood as referring to the Rephaim, the ancient, pre-Israelite inhabitants of Canaan (e.g., Gen. 14:5; 15:20; Deut. 2:10–11, 20–21; 3:11; Josh. 12:4; 13:12; 17:15).

21:19 Elhanan . . . struck down Goliath the Gittite. Since in 1 Samuel 17 David killed Goliath of Gath ("Gittite" means someone from Gath), this statement has caused endless controversy. (1) Some say that the deed of Elhanan was later attributed to David, or that the name "Goliath" only later became attached to David's victim, but these interpretations would deny the truthfulness of 1 Samuel 17, and other solutions are preferable. (2) Based on the parallel passage in 1 Chron. 20:5, some think that "Lahmi the brother of" has been deleted from the text before "Goliath" in this verse, and given some of the challenges encountered in establishing the

there was again war with the Philistines at Gob, and [v]Elhanan the son of Jaare-oregim,
the Bethlehemite, struck down Goliath the Gittite, [w]the shaft of whose spear was like a
weaver's beam.[1] 20 And there was again war at Gath, where there was a man of great stature,
who had six fingers on each hand, and six toes on each foot, twenty-four in number, and he
also was descended [x]from the giants. 21 And when [y]he taunted Israel, Jonathan the son of
Shimei, David's brother, struck him down. 22 These four were descended [x]from the giants
in Gath, and they fell by the hand of David and by the hand of his servants.

David's Song of Deliverance

22 And David spoke [z]to the LORD the words of this song on the day when the LORD
delivered him from the hand of all his enemies, and from the hand of Saul.
2 [a]He said,

[b]"The LORD is my rock and my fortress and my deliverer,
3 [c]my[2] God, my rock, [d]in whom I take refuge,
[e]my shield, and [f]the horn of my salvation,
[g]my stronghold and [h]my refuge,
my savior; you save me from violence.
4 I call upon the LORD, who is [i]worthy to be praised,
and I am saved from my enemies.

5 [j]"For the waves of death encompassed me,
the torrents of destruction assailed me;[3]
6 [k]the cords of Sheol entangled me;
the snares of death confronted me.
7 [l]"In my distress I called upon the LORD;
to my God I called.
From his temple he heard my voice,
and my cry [m]came to his ears.

8 "Then [n]the earth reeled and rocked;
[o]the foundations of the heavens trembled
and quaked, because he was angry.
9 Smoke went up from his nostrils,[4]
and devouring fire from his mouth;
[p]glowing coals flamed forth from him.

[1] Contrast 1 Chronicles 20:5, which may preserve the original reading [2] Septuagint (compare Psalm 18:2); Hebrew lacks *my* [3] Or *terrified me* [4] Or *in his wrath*

19 [v][ch. 23:24] [w]1 Sam. 17:7; 1 Chr. 20:5
20 [x]ver. 16, 18
21 [y]1 Sam. 17:10, 25, 26, 36, 45
22 [x][See ver. 20 above]

Chapter 22

1 [z][Ex. 15:1; Judg. 5:1; 1 Chr. 16:7]
2 [a]For ver. 1-51, see Ps. 18:2-50 [b]Deut. 32:4; Ps. 31:3; 71:3; 91:2; 144:2
3 [c]ver. 32, 47 [d][Heb. 2:13] [e]ver. 31; Gen. 15:1 [f]Luke 1:69 [g]Ps. 9:9; 59:9, 16, 17; 62:2, 6; [Prov. 18:10] [h]Ps. 14:6; 46:7, 11; 71:7; Jer. 16:19
4 [i]1 Chr. 16:25; Ps. 48:1; 96:4
5 [j][Ps. 42:7; 93:4; Jonah 2:3]
6 [k]Ps. 116:3
7 [l]Ps. 116:4; 120:1; Jonah 2:2 [m]Ps. 18:6
8 [n]Judg. 5:4; Ps. 77:18; 97:4 [o][Job 26:11]
9 [p]ver. 13

original text of 1–2 Samuel (see Introduction to 1–2 Samuel: Text), this is a distinct possibility. (3) Another suggestion is that the passages refer to two different men named Goliath. Because there are so many duplicate names in the OT, this is also a possibility. (4) A final suggestion, similar to the third solution, is that "Goliath" was a common noun for a giant, just as "Achish" (1 Sam. 21:10; 27:2) may have been a title or common noun for a Philistine ruler (just as "Pharaoh" is a title of the king of Egypt, not a name). There is therefore no conflict in saying that both David and Elhanan killed [a] "Goliath." The name "Goliath" is traceable back to the non-Semitic Anatolian name *Walwatta*, and the name has been found in an early Philistine inscription.

21:21 Jonathan may be the Jonathan listed as one of David's 30 mighty men (23:32). **Shimei** was David's third eldest brother. His name is given in various forms in 1 Sam. 16:9; 17:13; 2 Sam. 13:3; and 1 Chron. 2:13.

22:1–51 *Song of David.* David's song is almost identical with Psalm 18. There are many differences in spelling, etc., in the Hebrew text of the two passages, but few of the differences come across in a translation. Most of these differences can be understood when one realizes that, while the book of Psalms, regularly used in worship, uses "standard" Hebrew spelling, the spelling in the Samuel passage is much more phonetic in character because as a narrative it was written as it was meant to be heard. In other words, David's personal song of 2 Samuel 22 has been adapted to serve as a public hymn in Psalm 18 (see note). Such phonetic spelling is common throughout the books of Samuel (see Introduction to 1–2 Samuel: Text).

22:1 The heading to David's song does not refer to one particular incident, but to David's deliverance from **the hand of all his enemies**. Similar elaborate descriptions, followed by "He said" (v. 2), can be found in the headings of second-millennium Egyptian songs.

22:5–6 The name **Sheol** can refer to the place of the dead; here it is used as a synonym for "death." All four lines say in prose, "I was facing death."

22:7 Having described his situation, David now describes the Lord's response. **Heard** (Hb. *shama'*) does not simply mean a passive "hearing"; it implies an attentive listening and, usually, a positive response. **Temple** probably refers to the heavenly temple of God, from which he came down (v. 10; see Ps. 11:4; Mic. 1:2–3).

22:8–16 The Lord's sudden appearance to help David is described in vivid metaphor. The natural phenomenon that would cover most of the description is a volcano, which causes earthquake, **smoke**, **fire**, fiery **coals**, and ash clouds. Earthquake imagery is often associated with the Lord (Ps. 77:18; Isa. 5:25; 24:18). Earthquakes, if not volcanoes, were well known in that region; see Amos 1:1. Judges 5:4–5 reads, "LORD, when you went out from Seir . . . the earth trembled and the heavens dropped, yes, the clouds dropped water. The mountains quaked before the LORD." Many of the references can also be taken as storm images; describing battle in terms of a storm is common both in the Bible and in other ancient Near Eastern literature. In this song, the Lord is depicted as a mighty warrior riding in a chariot drawn by the wind or a cherub. David is probably thinking mainly of

10[q]Ps. 144:5 [r]Isa. 64:1 [s][Ex. 20:21; 1 Kgs. 8:12; Ps. 97:2]
11[t]Ps. 104:3
12[s][See ver. 10 above] [u]Job 36:29
13[v]ver. 9
14[w]Job 37:4; Ps. 29:3
15[x]Deut. 32:23; Ps. 7:13; 77:17; 144:6; Hab. 3:11
16[y]Ex. 15:8
17[z]Ps. 144:7
20[a]Ps. 31:8; 118:5 [b]See ch. 15:26
21[c]1 Sam. 26:23; 1 Kgs. 8:32; Ps. 7:8 [d][Ps. 24:4]
22[e]Gen. 18:19; Prov. 8:32
23[f]Ps. 119:30, 102
24[g][Gen. 6:9; 17:1; Job 1:1]
25[d][See ver. 21 above]
26[h][Matt. 5:7] [g][See ver. 24 above]
28[i][Ps. 72:12, 13] [j][Isa. 2:11, 12, 17; Luke 1:51]
29[k]Job 29:3; Ps. 27:1; [ch. 21:17]
31[l]Deut. 32:4; Matt. 5:48

10 [q]He bowed the heavens and [r]came down;
[s]thick darkness was under his feet.
11 He rode on a cherub and flew;
he was seen on [t]the wings of the wind.
12 He made [s]darkness around him [u]his canopy,
thick clouds, a gathering of water.
13 Out of the brightness before him
[v]coals of fire flamed forth.
14 [w]The LORD thundered from heaven,
and the Most High uttered his voice.
15 And he sent out [x]arrows and scattered them;
lightning, and routed them.
16 Then the channels of the sea were seen;
the foundations of the world were laid bare,
at the rebuke of the LORD,
at the [y]blast of the breath of his nostrils.

17 [z]"He sent from on high, he took me;
he drew me out of many waters.
18 He rescued me from my strong enemy,
from those who hated me,
for they were too mighty for me.
19 They confronted me in the day of my calamity,
but the LORD was my support.
20 [a]He brought me out into a broad place;
he rescued me, because [b]he delighted in me.

21 "The LORD [c]dealt with me according to my righteousness;
according to the [d]cleanness of my hands he rewarded me.
22 [e]For I have kept the ways of the LORD
and have not wickedly departed from my God.
23 [f]For all his rules were before me,
and from his statutes I did not turn aside.
24 I was [g]blameless before him,
and I kept myself from guilt.
25 [d]And the LORD has rewarded me according to my righteousness,
according to my cleanness in his sight.

26 [h]"With the merciful you show yourself merciful;
with the [g]blameless man you show yourself blameless;
27 with the purified you deal purely,
and with the crooked you make yourself seem tortuous.
28 [i]You save a humble people,
[j]but your eyes are on the haughty to bring them down.
29 [k]For you are my lamp, O LORD,
and my God lightens my darkness.
30 For by you I can run against a troop,
and by my God I can leap over a wall.
31 This God—[l]his way is perfect;

actual fighting, though he may have also been thinking of some instances of spiritual battle.

22:10 The Lord **bowed** (or "spread open" or "parted"; Hb. *natah*) **the heavens**.

22:15 Them refers to David's enemies.

22:17 many waters. Cf. v. 5, where "waves" and "torrents" of trouble were overwhelming David.

22:20 The Hebrew for **broad place** is the opposite of an expression for being "greatly distressed" (lit., "the matter is narrow for") in 1 Sam. 30:6; 2 Sam. 13:2; etc.

22:26–27 In Hebrew these are four lines, all of the form "With the X [person] you show yourself X." To the **crooked**, i.e., to deceptive, dishonest people, God shows himself **tortuous**, i.e., he makes simple truths seem confusing and impossible to understand.

22:28 This verse restates the theme of Hannah's song at the beginning of Samuel (1 Sam. 2:7–8): God controls human destiny, humbling the proud but raising the humble.

the [m]word of the LORD proves true;
he is [n]a shield for all those who take refuge in him.

32 "For who is God, but the LORD?
[o]And who is a rock, except our God?
33 This God is my [p]strong refuge
and has made my[1] way blameless.[2]
34 [q]He made my feet like the feet of a deer
and set me secure [r]on the heights.
35 [s]He trains my hands for war,
so that my arms can bend a bow of bronze.
36 You have given me the shield of your salvation,
and your gentleness made me great.
37 [t]You gave a wide place for my steps under me,
and my feet[3] did not slip;
38 I pursued my enemies and destroyed them,
and did not turn back until they were consumed.
39 I consumed them; I thrust them through, so that they did not rise;
they fell [u]under my feet.
40 For you equipped me with strength for the battle;
you made [v]those who rise against me sink under me.
41 You [w]made my enemies turn their backs to me,[4]
those who hated me, and I destroyed them.
42 They looked, but there was none to save;
they cried to the LORD, but [x]he did not answer them.
43 I beat them fine [y]as the dust of the earth;
I crushed them and stamped them down [z]like the mire of the streets.

44 "You delivered me from strife with my people;[5]
you kept me as the head of [a]the nations;
[b]people whom I had not known served me.
45 Foreigners came cringing to me;
as soon as they heard of me, they obeyed me.
46 Foreigners lost heart
and came trembling[6] [c]out of their fortresses.

47 "The LORD lives, and blessed be my rock,
and exalted be [d]my God, [e]the rock of my salvation,
48 the God who gave me vengeance
and [f]brought down peoples under me,
49 who brought me out from my enemies;
you exalted me above [v]those who rose against me;
you delivered me from [g]men of violence.

50 [h]"For this I will praise you, O LORD, among the nations,
and sing praises to your name.
51 [i]Great salvation he brings[7] to his king,

31 [m]Prov. 30:5 [n]ver. 3; Ps. 5:12; 33:20; 59:11; 84:9
32 [o]See ver. 2
33 [p]ver. 2; Ps. 28:8; 31:3, 4
34 [q]See ch. 2:18 [r]Deut. 32:13; 33:29; Isa. 58:14
35 [s]Ps. 144:1
37 [t]Prov. 4:12
39 [u][Mal. 4:3]
40 [v]Ps. 44:5; 59:1
41 [w]Ex. 23:27
42 [x]1 Sam. 28:6; Prov. 1:28; [Isa. 1:15; Mic. 3:4]
43 [y]2 Kgs. 13:7 [z]Isa. 10:6; Mic. 7:10; Zech. 10:5
44 [a]See ch. 8:1-14 [b]Isa. 55:5
46 [c]Mic. 7:17
47 [d]ver. 3, 32 [e]Deut. 32:15; Ps. 89:26; 95:1
48 [f]Ps. 144:2
49 [v][See ver. 40 above] [g]Ps. 140:1
50 [h]Cited Rom. 15:9
51 [i][Ps. 144:10]

[1] Or *his*; also verse 34 [2] Compare Psalm 18:32; Hebrew *he has blamelessly set my way free*, or *he has made my way spring up blamelessly* [3] Hebrew *ankles*
[4] Or *You gave me my enemies' necks* [5] Septuagint *with the peoples* [6] Compare Psalm 18:45; Hebrew *equipped themselves* [7] Or *He is a tower of salvation*

22:32–33 This also (cf. note on v. 28) is similar to 1 Sam. 2:2 (in Hannah's song), extolling the Lord as a **rock** and the one and only God. It also reflects back to the beginning of David's song (2 Sam. 22:2–3), calling God a **refuge**. The first part of the song (vv. 2–31) has described the fight in terms of the actions of the Lord; this next section (vv. 32–49) covers the fight with enemies in terms of what David did, thanks to the Lord, who equipped him for battle (v. 40).

22:35 A **bow of bronze** is probably a bow reinforced with bronze, which would be difficult to draw but powerful. Note that "bronze" is a symbol of strength in Job 6:12; 40:18; Jer. 1:18; etc. God gave David skill and strength to conduct warfare and defeat his enemies.

22:47–49 These verses end the second half of David's song, summarizing what the Lord has done and repeating the key word **rock**.

22:50–51 This is the conclusion of the whole of David's song, with a reference to ch. 7 and to the last verse of the Song of Hannah (1 Sam. 2:10).

51 l[1 Sam. 16:12, 13; Ps. 89:20] kch. 7:12, 13; Ps. 89:29
Chapter 23
1 i[ch. 7:8, 9; Ps. 78:70, 71] j[See ch. 22:51 above]
2 m[2 Pet. 1:21]
3 n See ch. 22:2, 3, 32, 47 oEx. 18:21; 2 Chr. 19:7, 9
4 p[Judg. 5:31; Prov. 4:18; Hos. 6:5]
5 qch. 7:15, 16; Ps. 89:29; Isa. 55:3
8 rFor ver. 8-39, see 1 Chr. 11:11-47 s[1 Chr. 27:2, 3]
9 t1 Chr. 27:4 uver. 28

and shows steadfast love to [l]his anointed,
to David and his offspring [k]forever."

The Last Words of David

23 Now these are the last words of David:

The oracle of David, the son of Jesse,
the oracle of [i]the man who was raised on high,
[j]the anointed of the God of Jacob,
the sweet psalmist of Israel:[1]

2 [m]"The Spirit of the LORD speaks by me;
his word is on my tongue.
3 The God of Israel has spoken;
[n]the Rock of Israel has said to me:
When one rules justly over men,
ruling [o]in the fear of God,
4 he [p]dawns on them like the morning light,
like the sun shining forth on a cloudless morning,
like rain[2] that makes grass to sprout from the earth.

5 "For does not my house stand so with God?
[q]For he has made with me an everlasting covenant,
ordered in all things and secure.
For will he not cause to prosper
all my help and my desire?
6 But worthless men[3] are all like thorns that are thrown away,
for they cannot be taken with the hand;
7 but the man who touches them
arms himself with iron and the shaft of a spear,
and they are utterly consumed with fire."[4]

David's Mighty Men

8 [r]These are the names of the mighty men whom David had: [s]Josheb-basshebeth a
Tahchemonite; he was chief of the three.[5] He wielded his spear[6] against eight hundred
whom he killed at one time.
9 And next to him among the three mighty men was Eleazar the son of [t]Dodo, son of
[u]Ahohi. He was with David when they defied the Philistines who were gathered there for

[1] Or *the favorite of the songs of Israel* [2] Hebrew *from rain* [3] Hebrew *worthlessness* [4] Hebrew *consumed with fire in the sitting* [5] Or *of the captains* [6] Compare 1 Chronicles 11:11; the meaning of the Hebrew expression is uncertain

23:1–7 *Last Words of David.* The "last words of David" are a song praising God for establishing his house as the ruler; the song reflects back to God's promise in 7:8–19. Like the wisdom psalms, it also contrasts the just ruler and worthless men. This psalm uses two different metaphors. One compares the righteous ruler to the morning light at sunrise and the shafts of sunshine on the grass after rain; the other compares worthless men to uprooted thorns.

23:1 This long title section is similar to some Egyptian poems with a title. The formula **the oracle of . . . the oracle of the man** also appears in Num. 24:3, 15 (see also Prov. 30:1). The man **who was raised on high** refers to David's kingly position. **the sweet psalmist of Israel.** Many psalms declare David as their author; cf. David's musical gifts in 1 Sam. 16:18; 2 Sam. 1:17–18; Amos 6:5.

23:2 The Spirit of the LORD speaks by me shows that David represents himself as a prophet, whose songs and wise sayings come from God (cf. Matt. 22:43; Acts 1:16; 2:30; 4:25; Heb. 4:7).

23:3 The king who **rules justly over men** is one who rules **in the fear of God**, according to the divine statutes.

23:4 Like the morning light, like the sun . . . like rain are images for bringing health and life. **He** in this verse is the just ruler of the previous verse, not God.

23:5 This verse refers to the covenant God made with David in ch. 7 (see also Ps. 89:29; 132:12). **Ordered in all things and secure** is probably legal terminology, stressing the validity of the covenant.

23:7 The Hebrew for **consumed with fire** may be rendered "consumed with fire in the sitting" (see ESV footnote), which perhaps suggests "consumed with fire on the spot." For fire as an instrument of God's judgment, cf. Isa. 9:18; 10:17.

23:8–39 *David's Heroes.* This list of David's mighty men begins formally with "These are the names of" and ends with the total number, "thirty-seven in all" (v. 39). (For lists, see note on 1 Sam. 6:17–18.) The list is divided into two groups: "the three," i.e., Josheb-basshebeth, Eleazar, and Shammah (2 Sam. 23:8–12), and "the thirty" (23:18–39). Thirty-four names are listed among "the thirty": this could mean that (1) "thirty" is a round number, or (2) the group began with 30 members and continued to be called "the thirty" when others were added; or (3) the group remained at 30, but when some died they were replaced by other names on this list (the parallel list in 1 Chron. 11:10–47 has 16 additional names in 1 Chron. 11:41–47, probably for this reason). These 34 names plus "the three" make up the "thirty-seven" of 2 Sam. 23:39.

battle, and the men of Israel withdrew. **10** He rose and struck down the Philistines until his
hand was weary, and his hand clung to the sword. And the LORD brought about a great
victory that day, and the men returned after him only to strip the slain.
11 And next to him was Shammah, the son of Agee the [v]Hararite. The Philistines gathered
together at Lehi, where there was a plot of ground full of lentils, and the men fled from
the Philistines. **12** But he took his stand in the midst of the plot and defended it and struck
down the Philistines, and the LORD worked a great victory.
13 And three of the thirty chief men went down and came about harvest time to David
at the [w]cave of Adullam, when a band of Philistines was encamped [x]in the Valley of
Rephaim. **14** David was then [y]in the stronghold, and [z]the garrison of the Philistines was
then at Bethlehem. **15** And David said longingly, "Oh, that someone would give me water
to drink from the well of Bethlehem that is by the gate!" **16** Then the three mighty men
broke through the camp of the Philistines and drew water out of the well of Bethlehem
that was by the gate and carried and brought it to David. But he would not drink of it.
He poured it out to the LORD **17** and said, "Far be it from me, O LORD, that I should do
this. Shall I drink [a]the blood of the men who went at the risk of their lives?" Therefore he
would not drink it. These things the three mighty men did.
18 Now Abishai, the brother of Joab, the son of Zeruiah, was chief of the thirty.[1] And he
wielded his spear against three hundred men[2] and killed them and won a name beside
the three. **19** He was the most renowned of the thirty[3] and became their commander, but
he did not attain to [b]the three.
20 And [c]Benaiah the son of Jehoiada was a valiant man[4] of [d]Kabzeel, a doer of great
deeds. He struck down two ariels[5] of Moab. He also went down and struck down a lion
in a pit on a day when snow had fallen. **21** And he struck down an Egyptian, a handsome
man. The Egyptian had a spear in his hand, but Benaiah went down to him with a staff
and snatched the spear out of the Egyptian's hand and killed him with his own spear.
22 These things did Benaiah the son of Jehoiada, and won a name beside the three mighty
men. **23** He was renowned among the thirty, but he did not attain to the three. And David
set him over his bodyguard.
24 [e]Asahel the brother of Joab was one of the thirty; Elhanan the son of Dodo of Bethlehem,
25 [f]Shammah of Harod, Elika of Harod, **26** Helez the Paltite, Ira the son of Ikkesh [g]of Tekoa,
27 Abiezer [h]of Anathoth, Mebunnai [i]the Hushathite, **28** Zalmon [j]the Ahohite, Maharai [k]of
Netophah, **29** Heleb the son of Baanah [k]of Netophah, Ittai the son of Ribai of [l]Gibeah of the
people of Benjamin, **30** Benaiah [m]of Pirathon, Hiddai of the brooks of [n]Gaash, **31** Abi-albon the
Arbathite, Azmaveth of [o]Bahurim, **32** Eliahba the Shaalbonite, the sons of Jashen, Jonathan,
33 [p]Shammah the Hararite, Ahiam the son of Sharar the Hararite, **34** Eliphelet the son of
Ahasbai [q]of Maacah, [r]Eliam the son of [s]Ahithophel of Gilo, **35** Hezro[6] [t]of Carmel, Paarai
the Arbite, **36** Igal the son of Nathan [u]of Zobah, Bani the Gadite, **37** Zelek the Ammonite,
Naharai [v]of Beeroth, the armor-bearer of Joab the son of Zeruiah, **38** [w]Ira the [x]Ithrite, Gareb
the Ithrite, **39** [y]Uriah the Hittite: thirty-seven in all.

David's Census

24 [z,a]Again the anger of the LORD was kindled against Israel, and he incited David
against them, saying, [b]"Go, number Israel and Judah." **2** So the king said to Joab,
the commander of the army,[7] who was with him, "Go through all the tribes of Israel, [c]from

[1] Two Hebrew manuscripts, Syriac; most Hebrew manuscripts *three* [2] Or *slain ones* [3] Compare 1 Chronicles 11:25; Hebrew *Was he the most renowned of the three?* [4] Or *the son of Ishhai* [5] The meaning of the word *ariel* is unknown [6] Or *Hezrai* [7] Septuagint *to Joab and the commanders of the army*

11 [v]ver. 33
13 [w]See 1 Sam. 22:1 [x]See ch. 5:18
14 [y]1 Sam. 22:4, 5 [z][1 Sam. 13:23]
17 [a][Lev. 17:10]
19 [b]1 Chr. 11:21
20 [c]ch. 8:18; 20:23 [d]Josh. 15:21
24 [e]ch. 2:18; 1 Chr. 27:7
25 [f][1 Chr. 11:27; 27:8]
26 [g]See ch. 14:2
27 [h]Josh. 21:18 [i]ch. 21:18
28 [j]ver. 9 [k]2 Kgs. 25:23
29 [k][See ver. 28 above] [l]Josh. 18:28; Judg. 19:14
30 [m]Judg. 12:13, 15; 1 Chr. 27:14 [n]Josh. 24:30; Judg. 2:9
31 [o][ch. 3:16]
33 [p]ver. 11
34 [q]ch. 10:6, 8 [r]ch. 11:3 [s]ch. 15:12
35 [t]Josh. 15:55
36 [u]ch. 8:3
37 [v]ch. 4:2
38 [w][ch. 20:26] [x]1 Chr. 2:53
39 [y]ch. 11:3, 6

Chapter 24

1 [z]For ver. 1-25, see 1 Chr. 21:1-28 [a][1 Chr. 21:1] [b][1 Chr. 27:23, 24]
2 [c]ver. 15; See ch. 3:10

23:11–12 Shammah was defending the **plot**, or rather the **lentils** in it, against theft. Compare the Philistines' robbing the threshing floors in 1 Sam. 23:1.

23:13–17 These **three** men were apparently not the above "three," but rather members of the "thirty." This episode may have occurred while David was fleeing Saul, or possibly during one of the Philistine attacks in 5:17–25. **Oh, that someone would give me water . . . from the well of Bethlehem**. The taste of the water differs from place to place, and of course the water that one grew up drinking tastes best. David's words are not a command; it probably did not occur to him that someone might actually act on his words. This episode shows the love that his men had for their leader and his regard for them.

23:16–17 He poured it out to the LORD. This may at first seem wasteful of David, and ungrateful, but it is a gesture showing great value. He likens the water to the **blood** of his men, and for David to drink the water obtained at the risk of their lives would have been to take their blood lightly. But to pour it out before the Lord was a way of saying that he was not worthy of it, and he was offering it to the Lord instead. Such "drink offerings" were often poured out before the Lord: see Gen. 35:14; Num. 15:7–10; 28:7–15; etc.

23:18–39 This is the list of David's "thirty men." They are **Abishai**,

3[d]Deut. 1:11
5[e]Deut. 2:36; Josh. 13:9, 16 [f][Num. 13:23] [g]Num. 21:32; 32:1, 3
6[h]Josh. 19:28; Judg. 18:28
7[i]Josh. 11:3; Judg. 3:3
9[j]Judg. 8:10
10[k]1 Sam. 24:5 [l]ch. 12:13 [m]See 1 Sam. 13:13

Dan to Beersheba, and number the people, that I may know the number of the people."
3 But Joab said to the king, [d]"May the LORD your God add to the people a hundred times
as many as they are, while the eyes of my lord the king still see it, but why does my lord
the king delight in this thing?" 4 But the king's word prevailed against Joab and the commanders of the army. So Joab and the commanders of the army went out from the presence of the king to number the people of Israel. 5 They crossed the Jordan and began from
[e]Aroer,[1] and from the city that is in the middle of the [f]valley, toward Gad and on to [g]Jazer.
6 Then they came to Gilead, and to Kadesh in the land of the Hittites;[2] and they came to
Dan, and from Dan[3] they went around to [h]Sidon, 7 and came to the fortress of Tyre and to
all the cities of the [i]Hivites and [i]Canaanites; and they went out to the Negeb of Judah at
Beersheba. 8 So when they had gone through all the land, they came to Jerusalem at the
end of nine months and twenty days. 9 And Joab gave the sum of the numbering of the
people to the king: in Israel there were 800,000 valiant men [j]who drew the sword, and
the men of Judah were 500,000.

The LORD's Judgment of David's Sin

10 But [k]David's heart struck him after he had numbered the people. And David said to
the LORD, [l]"I have sinned greatly in what I have done. But now, O LORD, please take away
the iniquity of your servant, for I have done [m]very foolishly." 11 And when David arose in

[1] Septuagint; Hebrew *encamped in Aroer* [2] Septuagint; Hebrew *to the land of Tahtim-hodshi* [3] Septuagint; Hebrew *they came to Dan-jaan and*

Benaiah, and the men listed in vv. 24–39. Most of the first dozen and a large part of the remainder are Judahites, so the group was probably formed early in David's career. The list has 34 names, probably representing 35 men (see note on v. 32). Probably those of "the thirty" who died in battle, such as Asahel (v. 24; 2:18–23) and Uriah (11:17; 23:39), were replaced by others. Some of the names appear as officers in 1 Chronicles 27, and most appear in the list in 1 Chron. 11:20–47, which is an expansion of this but is not labeled as being a list of "the thirty" (cf. 2 Sam. 23:24 and 1 Chron. 11:26).

23:32 The **sons of Jashen** probably refers to two men, possibly twins. In the list of names, however, they seem to be counted as one item. The translation of vv. 32–33 given here is the most natural, but it should be noted that those verses have been translated a number of ways (see also 1 Chron. 11:34–35).

24:1–25 *The Census and the Threshing Floor.* The Lord's anger and David's sin lead to a plague, but also to the purchase of a site in Jerusalem to offer burnt offerings to the Lord.

24:1 Here the text says, **the LORD . . . incited David**, while 1 Chron. 21:1 reads, "Satan . . . incited David." The Lord allowed Satan to incite David. God himself never does evil, but sometimes he uses evil moral agents (demons and sinful human beings) to accomplish his purposes. For more on how to reconcile the two accounts, see note on 1 Chron. 21:1; see also notes on Gen. 50:18–21; 1 Sam. 16:14; Mark 14:21; Acts 2:23; 4:28; 18:9–11; 27:30; 2 Tim. 2:10.

24:3 By numbering the people for military purposes (v. 9), David apparently showed lack of trust in the Lord to supply the necessary men when needed, and wrongful pride in the hundreds of thousands of forces at his command (see v. 10). **Joab** knew it was wrong. Exodus 30:12 has a reference to the need for a "ransom" after the counting. Cf. note on 1 Chron. 21:5–6.

24:5–8 The details of the census trip are not certain, but it seems that the men began at **Aroer**, a city on the Arnon River on the border with Moab, went north through **Gilead** and Bashan, and then went north-northwest to **Dan**. From there they went to the coast (the **fortress of Tyre** is probably not the city of Tyre, but an Israelite fortress), then south to **Beersheba**, and then back to **Jerusalem**.

24:9 The numbering yields **800,000 valiant men** in Israel and **500,000** in Judah. For the discrepancy in these numbers and those cited in 1 Chron. 21:5–6, see note there.

24:10 David's heart struck him. His conscience convicted him that his census was sin (see v. 17; and note on v. 3). **I have sinned**. The text does not specify why it was sin, but such an action could have been motivated by pride, trust in self, and lack of trust in the Lord.

David's Census
c. 975 B.C.

David ordered his commander Joab to take a census of all the people in the regions in which he exercised direct control. The reason for this census was probably to assess David's military capacity (see 2 Sam. 24:9; 1 Chron. 21:5). Joab's men left Jerusalem and began the census at Aroer, on the edge of the Arnon River. They progressed to Jazer near Rabbah, to Gilead, and on to Dan. After turning toward Sidon and the fortress of Tyre, they headed to Beersheba in the Negeb of Judah, and then they returned to Jerusalem.

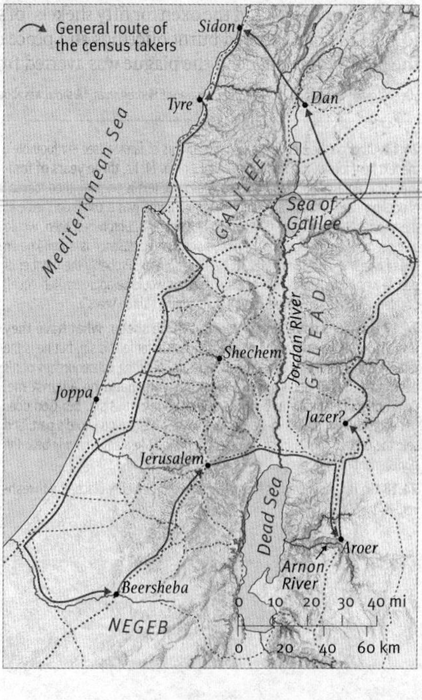

the morning, the word of the LORD came to [n]the prophet Gad, David's [o]seer, saying, **12** "Go
and say to David, 'Thus says the LORD, Three things I offer[1] you. Choose one of them, that
I may do it to you.'" **13** So Gad came to David and told him, and said to him, "Shall [p]three[2]
years of famine come to you in your land? Or will you flee three months before your foes
while they pursue you? Or shall there be three days' pestilence in your land? Now consider,
and decide what answer I shall return to him who sent me." **14** Then David said to Gad, "I
am in great distress. Let us fall into the hand of the LORD, [q]for his mercy is great; but let
me not fall into the hand of man."

15 [r]So the LORD sent a pestilence on Israel from the morning until the appointed time.
And there died of the people from [s]Dan to Beersheba 70,000 men. **16** And when [t]the angel
stretched out his hand toward Jerusalem [u]to destroy it, [v]the LORD relented from the calamity and said to the angel [u]who was working destruction among the people, "It is enough;
now stay your hand." And [t]the angel of the LORD was by the threshing floor of [w]Araunah
the Jebusite. **17** Then David spoke to the LORD when he saw the angel who was striking the
people, and said, "Behold, I have sinned, and I have done wickedly. But these sheep, what
have they done? Please let your hand be against me and against my father's house."

David Builds an Altar

18 And Gad came that day to David and said to him, "Go up, raise an altar to the LORD
on the threshing floor of [x]Araunah the Jebusite." **19** So David went up at Gad's word, as the
LORD commanded. **20** And when Araunah looked down, he saw the king and his servants
coming on toward him. And Araunah went out and paid homage to the king with his
face to the ground. **21** And Araunah said, "Why has my lord the king come to his servant?"
David said, "To buy the threshing floor from you, in order to build an altar to the LORD,
that the plague [y]may be averted from the people." **22** Then Araunah said to David, "Let my
lord the king take and offer up what seems good to him. Here are the oxen for the burnt
offering and the [z]threshing sledges and the yokes of the oxen for the wood. **23** All this, O
king, Araunah gives to the king." And Araunah said to the king, "May the LORD your God
[a]accept you." **24** But the king said to Araunah, "No, but I will buy it from you for a price. I
will not offer burnt offerings to the LORD my God that cost me nothing." So David bought
the threshing floor and the oxen for fifty shekels[3] of silver. **25** And David built there an altar
to the LORD and offered burnt offerings and peace offerings. [b]So the LORD responded to
the plea for the land, and the plague was averted from Israel.

[1] Or *hold over* [2] Compare 1 Chronicles 21:12, Septuagint; Hebrew *seven* [3] A *shekel* was about 2/5 ounce or 11 grams

11 [n]See 1 Sam. 22:5 [o]See 1 Sam. 9:9
13 [p][1 Chr. 21:12]
14 [q]Ps. 119:156
15 [r]1 Chr. 27:24 [s]ver. 2
16 [t]2 Kgs. 19:35; 2 Chr. 32:21; Isa. 37:36; Acts 12:23 [u]Ex. 12:13, 23 [v]Gen. 6:6; 1 Sam. 15:11; Joel 2:13, 14; Jonah 3:10 [w][2 Chr. 3:1]
18 [x][2 Chr. 3:1]
21 [y]Num. 16:48, 50
22 [z]1 Kgs. 19:21
23 [a]Deut. 33:11; [Ps. 20:3]
25 [b]ch. 21:14

24:13 Although the Hebrew reads "*seven* years of famine"(see ESV footnote), the text here follows the Septuagint and 1 Chron. 21:12, **three years of famine**, which makes good sense. If the Masoretic text is original, then "seven" is possibly used symbolically, since that time frame was a common theme in the ancient Near East (see Gen. 41:30; 2 Kings 8:1). Chronicles, then, would give the nonfigurative period. Famine, sword, and pestilence is a well-known trio of disasters (Jer. 14:12; 18:21; Ezek. 5:17; etc.). Probably the number of people who would die in each of these disasters would be approximately equal; pestilence kills faster (**three days'**) than famine ("three years").

24:17 Behold, I have sinned. . . . But these sheep, what have they done? David pleads that the people may not suffer for his sin, but he is the representative of God's people, and thus they bear the consequences of his behavior, whether good or evil. **Please let your hand be against me.** David offers personally to bear the punishment for this sin, but God does not accept the offer. This is, however, a worthy gesture on David's part, and sets the pattern for his ultimate descendant, the Messiah, who will bear the punishment due his people.

24:18 Go up. From David's home there was a yet higher place, the **threshing floor of Araunah the Jebusite**. The Jebusites were the previous inhabitants of Jerusalem (see 5:6), some of whom still lived there.

24:20 Araunah looked down. Threshing floors were usually on a high place so that the wind could blow the chaff away. This location would later become the site of the temple (see note on v. 25). It is on the top of the hill to the north of the city of David, about 450 yards (412 m) from it. (See illustration, p. 550.)

24:23–24 David feels that because he is the one who sinned, and because it is for the sake of the nation, he should pay for the sacrifice. He pays **fifty shekels of silver** for the **threshing floor and the oxen**. First Chronicles 21:25 says that he paid "600 shekels of gold by weight for the site"; probably the "site" mentioned there is the larger piece of land on Mount Moriah.

24:25 God accepted David's **burnt offerings**, and through the **peace offerings** David enjoyed the presence of the Lord. Thus God **responded to the plea for the land**. But this site will become much more significant in the future, for as the parallel account (in 1 Chron. 22:1) states, this threshing floor is the site on which Solomon would build the temple to the Lord—making this a fitting end to the story of David.

INTRODUCTION TO

1–2 KINGS

Author and Title

As the titles of the books indicate, 1–2 Kings describe the period of the monarchy in ancient Israel (970–586 B.C.), excluding most of the reigns of King Saul and King David (which are mainly described in 1–2 Samuel, with the conclusion to David's reign appearing in 1 Kings 1:1–2:11). Ancient Jewish tradition attributes this account to the prophet Jeremiah, although the books themselves do not specify the author. Internal evidence, however, does establish that the author or authors were deeply influenced by the book of Deuteronomy and sought to provide Israel with an explanation of its past in terms of the theological program outlined in that book. This is clearly signaled, for example, in the opening section of David's parting speech to Solomon (1 Kings 2:1–4), where the language closely parallels the following phrases from Deuteronomy: "keep the charge of the LORD your God" (Deut. 11:1); "walking in his ways" (Deut. 8:6); "keeping all his statutes and his commandments" (Deut. 6:2); "that you may prosper in all you do" (Deut. 29:9); "that he may confirm the word that the LORD swore to your fathers" (Deut. 9:5); "with all your heart and with all your soul" (Deut. 4:29). "Deuteronomic" language such as this appears again and again in 1–2 Kings, as first Solomon himself (1 Kings 11), and then almost all the succeeding kings of Israel and Judah, are weighed in relation to the Mosaic law code and found wanting (e.g., Jeroboam, 1 Kings 12:25–33; 14:1–16; Ahaz, 2 Kings 16:1–4). For this reason, the authors of 1–2 Kings have often been referred to in recent biblical scholarship as "Deuteronomists." Beyond this one fact, however, nothing can be said for sure about the authorship of these books. Some have speculated that these "Deuteronomists" were Levites or priests; others, that they were prophets; and still others, that they were the wise men of the Jerusalem court. No one can really know.

Date

In their present form, 1–2 Kings could not have been written before the sixth century B.C., since 2 Kings 25:27–30 describes the release of King Jehoiachin from prison in Babylon in 561 and the books must therefore date from some time after that. It is possible (and some scholars certainly believe) that this late exilic or postexilic version of Kings builds on earlier editions dating from before the exile of many Judeans to Babylon in 586 B.C., or from the period of the exile itself. There is also evidence that at least some editing of the text took place in the Persian period (539–c. 330 B.C.). Notice, for example, the intriguing references to "the kings of the west" and "the governors of the land" (1 Kings 10:15). These seem best understood as representing a Persian perspective on the region west of the Euphrates, which was administered on behalf of the Persian emperor by governors (cf. Ezra 8:36; Neh. 2:7, 9).

Theme

These two books set out to provide for their readers an explanation of Israel's later monarchic period in terms of the theological vision outlined in the book of Deuteronomy, so that these readers can move forward in their present times with a solidly grounded faith in the one God who controls both nature and history. The books maintain that it is this good and all-powerful God who oversaw the destruction of his chosen city and temple, and the exile to Babylon, in 586 B.C. because of Israel's great sinfulness (2 Kings 17:7–23; 24:1–4). Yet there remains hope because God's chosen royal line has not come to an end (2 Kings 25:27–30), and God remains ready to forgive those who are repentant (1 Kings 8:22–61).

Purpose, Occasion, and Background

In the year 609 B.C. the pharaoh of Egypt, Neco II, marched north to support his allies the Assyrians in their conflict with the Babylonians and their allies the Medes. On the way, Neco was opposed by King Josiah of Judah at the city of Megiddo, who was perhaps hoping to establish his independence from an increasingly powerful Egypt or hoping to benefit from being seen to take the Babylonians' side. Josiah was killed in the ensuing battle, and Judah's independence was lost. The new king, Jehoahaz, found himself imprisoned in Egypt while his brother Eliakim reigned in Judah as a vassal of Egypt under the name of Jehoiakim.

Around 604 B.C., however, Jehoiakim switched his allegiance to Babylon. Then, a few years later, he rebelled against the Babylonian king. Consequently, at the end of the year 598 B.C., when the Babylonian army was before the gates of Jerusalem, Egyptian forces were not on hand to help. The city surrendered to the Babylonians in 597 B.C., and the new king, Jehoiachin, was deported to Babylon along with many other leading citizens and much plunder. Nebuchadnezzar, king of Babylon, then placed Jehoiachin's uncle Mattaniah on the throne and gave him the new name of Zedekiah. From early in his reign Zedekiah was involved in discussions with neighboring peoples about the possibility of revolt, and eventually revolt occurred. A new siege of Jerusalem by the Babylonians ensued. It was temporarily lifted when the new pharaoh, Apries, sent an army into Palestine, but resumed when the Egyptian army withdrew. After two years of siege, with all supplies of food exhausted, the city eventually fell in 587 or 586 B.C.

The fall of Jerusalem and the events that immediately followed it came as a devastating blow to the people of Judah. Jerusalem lay in ruins; both ordinary houses and the royal palace had been destroyed, and the city's defenses had been pulled down. Most seriously of all, the temple—the great symbol of Yahweh's presence with Israel—had been dismantled. Many had been killed, and many others had been deported to Babylon to work in the fields as well as in administration. Among the deportees were the leaders of the Judean community, who joined King Jehoiachin and the others deported there earlier. The people left in Judah were only the "poorest of the land" (2 Kings 25:12; see Jer. 39:10; 52:16), watched over by a garrison of troops in Jerusalem and initially by a native (non-Davidic) Judean leader named Gedaliah, who based himself in the city of Mizpah, about 7.5 miles (12 km) from the former capital. The pain and grief of the time is well expressed in Lamentations 1:1: "How lonely sits the city that was full of people! How like a widow has she become, she who was great among the nations! She who was a princess among the provinces has become a slave." What did it all mean? Was Israel's God not in fact in control of nature and history, as Mosaic religion claimed? Were there other, more powerful gods in Babylon who had engineered the Babylonian victory over Israel? If the God of Moses *did* exist, and *was* good and all-powerful, how was it that God's chosen city and temple had been destroyed, and how was it that God's chosen royal line (the line of David) had all but come to its end?

The books of Kings must be understood against this background. They represent a sustained response to such questions, and are designed to provide their readers a true interpretation of what happened to Israel in 586 B.C. Israel's God is indeed in control of nature and history; there are no other, more powerful gods anywhere. It is in fact this good and all-powerful God who has himself overseen the destruction of his chosen city and his temple, and the exile to Babylon. The reason for these actions lies in Israel's great sinfulness. Israel has not obeyed God or heeded his word through the prophets, from the reign of Solomon onward.

Solomon turned away from the true God to worship other gods (1 Kings 2:12–11:43). Jeroboam son of Nebat led northern Israel into independence from Solomon's son Rehoboam and Judah (1 Kings 12:1–24) and into institutionalized idolatry, with gods manufactured by Jeroboam (1 Kings 12:25–33) or introduced from elsewhere (1 Kings 16:29–2 Kings 10:31), and this ultimately led to exile in Assyria for the northern tribes (2 Kings 17). Although the religious situation in Judah was initially no better than that in Israel (1 Kings 14:22–24; 15:3–5), Judah's story afterward was not one of continuous apostasy. Relatively good kings did rule in the gaps between the wicked kings (1 Kings 15:9–22:50; 2 Kings 12:1–15:38); and toward the end of the monarchy ruled two of the best kings ever (Hezekiah, 2 Kings 18:1–20:21; Josiah, 2 Kings 22:1–23:30). Sin gradually accumulated, nevertheless, resulting in exile also for the kingdom of Judah. Yet it is implied that hope remains, for God's chosen royal line has not in fact come to an utter end (2 Kings 25:27–30), and God remains God, ever ready to forgive those who repent. The fact that God is "one" thus represents both the ultimate reason for the events of 586 B.C. and the ultimate ground for Israel's hope of restoration; for if there is only one God, nothing and no one can frustrate his purposes.

Key Themes

1. *Yahweh is the only true God.* There is only one living God, and he is the Lord (1 Kings 18:15; 2 Kings 5:15). This Lord is not to be confused with the various so-called gods worshiped in Israel and other nations, for these are simply human creations (1 Kings 12:25–30; 2 Kings 17:16; 19:14–19). They are part of the created order, like the people who worship them; and they are powerless, futile entities (1 Kings 16:13; 18:22–40; 2 Kings 17:15; 18:33–35). The Lord, by contrast, is the incomparable Creator of heaven and earth (1 Kings 8:23; 2 Kings 19:15). He is utterly distinct from the world that he has created (cf. 1 Kings 8:9, 14–21, 27–30, where he is neither truly "in" the ark nor "in" the temple; and 18:26–38, where the antics of the Baal priests apparently imply belief in an intrinsic connection between their actions and divine action, while Elijah's behavior implies quite the reverse). At the same time, the Lord is powerfully active within his world. It is he, and no one else, who controls nature (1 Kings 17–19; 2 Kings 1:2–17; 4:8–37; 5:1–18; 6:1–7, 27).

2. *Yahweh controls history.* The Lord, and neither an idol god, nor king, nor prophet, controls history (1 Kings 11:14, 23; 14:1–18; 22:1–38; 2 Kings 5:1–18; 10:32–33; 18:17–19:37). This is perhaps illustrated most clearly in the way in which prophets function within 1–2 Kings, describing the future before God brings it about (1 Kings 11:29–39; 13:1–32; 16:1–4; 20:13–34; 2 Kings 19:6–7, 20–34). Nothing can hinder the fulfillment of this prophetic word, although God himself, in his freedom, can override its fulfillment for his own purposes (cf. 1 Kings 21:17–29; 2 Kings 3:15–27, where the ending to the story is somewhat unexpected).

3. *Yahweh demands exclusive worship.* As the only God there is, the Lord demands exclusive worship. He will not take his place alongside the gods, nor is he willing to be displaced by them. He refuses to be confused with any part of the created order. He alone will be worshiped, by Israelite and foreigner alike (1 Kings 8:41–43, 60; 2 Kings 5:15–18; 17:24–41).

4. *The content and place of true worship.* Much of 1–2 Kings is therefore concerned to describe what is illegitimate in terms of worship. The main interest is in the *content* of this worship, which must neither involve idols or images nor reflect any aspect of the fertility and other cults of "the nations" (1 Kings 11:1–40; 12:25–13:34; 14:22–24; 16:29–33; 2 Kings 16:1–4; 17:7–23; 21:1–9). There is a subsidiary concern about the *place* of worship, which is ideally the Jerusalem temple, and not the local "high places" (1 Kings 3:2; 5:1–9:9; 15:14; 22:43; 2 Kings 18:4; 23:1–20).

5. *The consequences of false worship.* The books of 1–2 Kings also describe the moral wrongs that inevitably accompany false worship. They claim that true worship of God is always bound up with obedience to the law of God, and that the worship of something *other than God* inevitably leads to some kind of mistreatment of fellow mortals in the *eyes of God*; see 1 Kings 21, where the kind of abandonment of God envisaged in Exodus 20 leads to wholesale breach of the other commandments described there (2 Kings 16:1–4, esp. v. 3; 2 Kings 21:1–16, esp. vv. 6, 16). By the same token, true wisdom is defined in 1–2 Kings in terms of true worship and wholehearted obedience. It cannot be divorced from either (see 1 Kings 1–11, where much can be learned about the nature of true wisdom).

6. *Yahweh as just and gracious Lawgiver.* As the Giver of the law, which defines true worship and right thinking and behavior generally, the Lord is also the one who executes justice on wrongdoers. The world of 1–2 Kings is a moral world in which wrongdoing is punished, whether the sinner be king (Solomon in 1 Kings 11:9–13; Jeroboam in 1 Kings 14:1–18), or prophet (the unnamed Judean in 1 Kings 13:7–25; the disobedient man in 1 Kings 20:35–43), or ordinary Israelite (Gehazi in 2 Kings 5:19–27; the Israelite officer in 2 Kings 7:17–20). It is not a vending-machine world, however, in which every coin of sin that is inserted results in individually packaged retribution. There is no neat correlation between sin and judgment in Kings, even though people are told that they must obey God if they are to be blessed by him (e.g., Solomon in 1 Kings 2:1–4; Jeroboam in 1 Kings 11:38). This is largely because of the compassionate character of the Judge, who does not desire final judgment to fall on his creatures (2 Kings 13:23; 14:27) and who often delays or mitigates such judgment (1 Kings 21:25–29; 2 Kings 22:15–20). God's grace is to be found everywhere in 1–2 Kings (1 Kings 11:9–13; 15:1–5; 2 Kings 8:19), confounding expectations that the reader might have formed on the basis of an oversimplified understanding of law. Sin can, nevertheless, accumulate to such an extent that judgment falls, not only on individuals but on whole cultures, sweeping the relatively innocent away with the guilty (2 Kings 17:1–23; 23:29–25:26).

7. *Yahweh as promise-giver.* Israel's God is not only a lawgiver, however, but also a promise-giver. In 1–2 Kings it is a promise usually to be found at the heart of the Lord's gracious behavior toward his people. The two most important divine promises referred to are those given to the patriarchs on the one hand, and to David on the other.

The *patriarchal promise to Abraham, Isaac, and Jacob*—descendants and everlasting possession of the land of

Canaan—clearly influences God's treatment of his people at various points in the story (2 Kings 13:23, and implicitly in 1 Kings 4:20–21, 24; 18:36). That promise also lies in the background of Solomon's prayer in 1 Kings 8:22–53, as Solomon looks forward to the possibility of forgiveness after judgment. The future-oriented aspect of the promise in this passage is interesting because it is a promise in clear tension with the story's ending in 2 Kings 25, where disobedience has led to expulsion from the land and exile in a foreign empire. It seems that the true fulfillment of the promise is thought still to be in the future, even though it has also played its part in the past.

The *promise given to David*, that he should have an eternal dynasty, shares in the same kind of tension, and indeed appears in 1–2 Kings in a curiously paradoxical form. In much of the narrative it provides an explanation for why the Davidic dynasty survives when other dynasties do not, *in spite of* the disobedience of David's successors (1 Kings 11:36; 15:4; 2 Kings 8:19). It is viewed, in other words, as unconditional in one aspect. Judah's fate is not to be the same as Israel's and Jerusalem's fate is to be different from Samaria's, because God has promised David a "lamp," a descendant who will always sit on his throne. So when Solomon sins, the Davidic line does not lose the throne entirely, but retains "one tribe" (1 Kings 11:36) in the meantime, with the prospect of restoring its dominion at some time in the future (1 Kings 11:39). When Abijam sins, likewise, his son still retains the Judean throne (1 Kings 15:4).

The background here is the promise to David recorded in 2 Samuel 7, where the sins of David's descendants are to be punished by the "rod of men" rather than by the kind of divine rejection Saul experienced (2 Sam. 7:14–16). This promise makes the ultimate difference between Davidic kings and those of other royal houses throughout much of the books of Kings, and makes the Judean dynasty unshakable even while the dynasties of the northern kingdom are like reeds "shaken in the water" (1 Kings 14:15). This dynasty survives *in spite of* the *disobedience* of David's successors. At other times, however, the continuance of the dynasty is made *dependent on* the *obedience* of David's successors (1 Kings 2:4; 8:25; 9:4–5). The promise is treated as conditional. As the books progress, it seems that this latter view prevails, as accumulating sin puts the promise in its unconditional aspect under great stress and in the end brings down God's judgment on Judah just as severely as on Israel (2 Kings 16:1–4; 21:1–15; 23:31–25:26).

Yet Jehoiachin lives (2 Kings 25:27–30). The authors of Kings did not need to record this fact. They could have allowed Jehoiachin to dwell in obscurity with Zedekiah (2 Kings 24:18–25:7), who effectively ends up as the eunuch in Babylon that the prophet Isaiah had foreseen (2 Kings 20:18)—a mutilated man deprived of the heirs who might later claim the throne. The significance of this postscript on Jehoiachin appears clearer in an earlier section of 2 Kings. After the reign of two relatively righteous kings (Asa and Jehoshaphat), Judah found herself with two kings who share with King Ahab's children both their names (Jehoram, Ahaziah) and their attraction to idolatry (2 Kings 8:16–29). Yet God had promised David an ever-burning "lamp" in Jerusalem (2 Kings 8:19; cf. 1 Kings 11:36; 15:4), an everlasting dynasty. Therefore, although Ahab's dynasty comes to an end in 2 Kings 9–10, David's dynasty does not. Although Ahaziah dies and his mother Athaliah tries to wipe out the entire royal family (2 Kings 11:1), one royal prince remains to carry on the family line (2 Kings 11:2). Against all the odds, Joash survives six years of his grandmother's rule to emerge once again as king in a land purified of the worship of foreign gods (2 Kings 11:3–20).

Later, Jehoiachin reappears in the narrative of 1–2 Kings in a manner strikingly reminiscent of this reappearance of Joash after that earlier destruction of "all the royal family" (2 Kings 11:1). Like Joash, he unexpectedly survives in the midst of carnage; and like Joash during Athaliah's reign, he represents the potential for the continuation of the Davidic line at a later time. All is not yet necessarily lost. The destruction of the family of the last king of Judah (Zedekiah) does not mean that no Davidic descendant is left. Second Kings 25:27–30 hints that the unconditional aspects of the Davidic promise may still, even after awful judgment has fallen, remain in force. Similarly, the prayer of Solomon in 1 Kings 8:22–53 looks beyond the disaster of exile, grounding its hope for the restoration of Israel to its land in God's gracious and unconditional election of Abraham, Isaac, and Jacob (see also 1 Kings 18:36–37; 2 Kings 13:23; 14:27). Solomon's prayer had also refused to accept that God's words about the rejection of people, city, and temple (e.g., 2 Kings 21:14; 23:27) were his final words. The words in 2 Kings 25:27–30 express the hope that God may indeed be found to be, in the end as in the beginning, a God of grace and not only of commandment, and that a Son of David will one day appear to introduce his righteous rule on the earth.

History of Salvation Summary

God's purpose in establishing Israel had been to bring blessing to the world through the people's covenant faithfulness. He instituted the Davidic dynasty to lead the people in their faithfulness. The history of Israel, as told by 1–2 Kings, is full of tragedies: the rupture of the kingdom so that the north was in rebellion against David's house; the failures of so many kings, north and south, to live faithfully and to lead wisely; and the deportations of the north and then of the south. And yet God will not fail in his purpose: Kings ends with kindness shown to David's heir (2 Kings 25:27–30), which leaves the hope that the Davidic line will continue, leading to the ultimate heir, the Messiah, and the hope that a chastened Israel may itself be restored and may fulfill its calling for the world. (For an explanation of the "History of Salvation," see the Overview of the Bible, pp. 23–26. See also History of Salvation in the Old Testament: Preparing the Way for Christ, pp. 2635–2661.)

Literary Features

First and Second Kings are written in the form of historical narrative—specifically, a record of monarchical succession. The main rhetorical format of this court history is the summary of individual kings' careers, consisting of the name of each king, what kingdom he ruled (Israel or Judah), the date of his accession to the throne, the length of his reign, his religious and other policies, the details of his death, and the name of his successor. Yet the authors are as much theologians as historians. It is not their intention to provide every historical detail, and on occasion they direct readers who want more information to consult other sources. The authors' main intention is to interpret the history of Israel along theological lines, showing what happens when political and spiritual leaders foolishly choose to worship false gods instead of wisely choosing to worship the one true God.

Solomon is the dominant character in the first half of 1 Kings, and the prophet Elijah in the second half. These two "close-ups" are balanced by a host of brief vignettes, chiefly of kings. The book is also unified by the choice that each king (along with the nation itself) must make between following God and worshiping idols. The general movement of the book is from wisdom to folly, as Solomon's downfall is recapitulated in the choices of his sons and grandsons. The archetype of the evil king dominates the book, with the figure of King David repeatedly invoked as the royal standard by which his successors are measured and found wanting. Subgenres that appear intermittently in 1 Kings are the farewell address, the list of government officials, the building description, the dedicatory prayer, the inventory, the curse, the miracle story, the bet, and the taunt.

Like 1 Kings, 2 Kings is encyclopedic in its scope, summarizing the careers of nearly 30 kings. The extensive portrait of the life of the prophet Elisha is an exception to this "broadstroke" format. The general shape of 2 Kings is tragic, depicting how a great nation falls into ruin. Some of the episodes in the book are narratives in their own right, and they fall into a number of subgenres, including confrontation story, medical case, ascension story, succession story, recovery story, battle story, hero story, miracle story, resurrection narrative, murder story, revenge narrative, prayer, prophecy, reformation story, and captivity narrative. Far from simply giving the facts, the historian tells what happened with a reporter's eye for the significant detail, a storyteller's flair for the dramatic, and a pastor's heart for teaching people the difference between right and wrong. The principle of organization is chiefly chronological, covering some 300 years of royal history. Despite the abundance of kings whose careers are summarized, a repeated cycle unifies the book, consisting of reformation, deformation, and decline.

1 Kings Outline

I. The Reign of King Solomon (1:1–11:43)
   A. Solomon becomes king (1:1–2:46)
   B. More on Solomon and wisdom (3:1–28)
   C. Solomon's rule over Israel (4:1–20)
   D. Solomon and the nations (4:21–34)
   E. Preparations for building the temple (5:1–18)
   F. Solomon builds the temple and his palace (6:1–7:51)
   G. The ark brought to the temple (8:1–21)
   H. Solomon's prayer (8:22–53)
   I. The temple narrative ended (8:54–9:9)
   J. Glory under a cloud (9:10–10:29)
   K. Solomon's apostasy, opponents, and death (11:1–43)

II. The Kingdom Is Divided (12:1–14:31)
   A. The kingdom torn away (12:1–33)
   B. The man of God from Judah (13:1–34)
   C. The end of Jeroboam (14:1–20)
   D. The end of Rehoboam (14:21–31)

III. Abijam and Asa (15:1–24)

IV. From Nadab to Ahab (15:25–16:34)

V. Elijah and Ahab (17:1–22:40)
   A. Elijah and the drought (17:1–24)
   B. Elijah and the prophets of Baal (18:1–46)
   C. Elijah and the Lord (19:1–21)
   D. Ahab's war against Syria (20:1–43)
   E. Naboth's vineyard (21:1–29)
   F. Ahab killed in battle (22:1–40)

VI. Jehoshaphat and Ahaziah (22:41–53)

1 Kings

Chapter 1
3[a]Josh. 19:18
5[b]2 Sam. 3:4 [c]2 Sam. 15:1
6[d]2 Sam. 3:3, 4; 1 Chr. 3:2
7[e]2 Sam. 2:13, 18
[f]2 Sam. 20:25
8[f][See ver. 7 above]
[g]2 Sam. 8:18 [h]2 Sam. 12:1 [i]ch. 4:18 [j]See 2 Sam. 23:8-39
9[k]Josh. 15:7; 2 Sam. 17:17
10[l]2 Sam. 12:24

David in His Old Age

1 Now King David was old and advanced in years. And although they covered him with
clothes, he could not get warm. 2 Therefore his servants said to him, "Let a young woman
be sought for my lord the king, and let her wait on the king and be in his service. Let her lie
in your arms,[1] that my lord the king may be warm." 3 So they sought for a beautiful young
woman throughout all the territory of Israel, and found Abishag the [a]Shunammite, and
brought her to the king. 4 The young woman was very beautiful, and she was of service to
the king and attended to him, but the king knew her not.

Adonijah Sets Himself Up as King

5 Now [b]Adonijah the son of Haggith exalted himself, saying, "I will be king." [c]And he
prepared for himself chariots and horsemen, and fifty men to run before him. 6 His father
had never at any time displeased him by asking, "Why have you done thus and so?" He was
also a very handsome man, [d]and he was born next after Absalom. 7 He conferred with [e]Joab
the son of Zeruiah and with [f]Abiathar the priest. And they followed Adonijah and helped
him. 8 But [f]Zadok the priest and [g]Benaiah the son of Jehoiada and [h]Nathan the prophet
and [i]Shimei and Rei and [j]David's mighty men were not with Adonijah.
9 Adonijah sacrificed sheep, oxen, and fattened cattle by the Serpent's Stone, which is
beside [k]En-rogel, and he invited all his brothers, the king's sons, and all the royal officials
of Judah, 10 but he did not invite Nathan the prophet or Benaiah or the mighty men or
[l]Solomon his brother.

[1] Or *in your bosom*

1:1–11:43 *The Reign of King Solomon.* The first 11 chapters of 1 Kings are an extensive description of the reign of David's son Solomon, a king who was great when he obeyed God and depended on God for wisdom but whose reign ended in tragedy as he departed from God's ways and worshiped other gods.

1:1–2:46 *Solomon Becomes King.* The beginning of the Solomon story is also the end of the David story, specifically the section of David's story that begins in 2 Samuel 7–12, where Nathan and Bathsheba, who play such important roles in 1 Kings 1–2, are first prominent. Nathan had promised David that God would raise up one of his sons and establish his kingdom forever (2 Sam. 7:12–13). How would this promise be fulfilled, in view of Nathan's later word of judgment to David in 2 Samuel 12 and the awful story that follows in 2 Samuel 13–24? The first two chapters of Kings set out to resolve this question.

1:2–4 let her wait on the king and be in his service. . . . lie in your arms. The Hebrew expression for "wait" appears in Lev. 18:23 (as "give herself"), where it refers to availability for sexual intercourse; "be in his service" leaves the precise nature of the service unstated; and "in your arms" has sexual overtones in Gen. 16:5 ("your embrace"); 2 Sam. 12:8; and Mic. 7:5. This **beautiful** young woman, **Abishag**, is no doubt intended to interest David sexually; and his impotence (**the king knew her not**) is all the encouragement that Adonijah needs to foment rebellion ("I will be king," 1 Kings 1:5).

1:5–6 Adonijah was the fourth of David's sons born in Hebron (2 Sam. 3:2–5), and the eldest surviving. The first, Amnon, and third, Absalom, have died by this point in the story (2 Samuel 13–18), and the second, Chileab, is presumably also dead (unmentioned after 2 Samuel 3). **exalted himself**. This implies that Adonijah is usurping David's (and God's) right to designate a successor (cf. the same term in Num. 16:3); this contrasts with David, who waited patiently for God to raise him to office, even refusing to take Saul's life (1 Samuel 16–31). Here, however, the authors recall Absalom in their reference to **chariots and horsemen** (or horses) and **men** (cf. 2 Sam. 15:1); and by their reference to the fact that Adonijah was a **very handsome man** (cf. 2 Sam. 14:25–26), they already hint that he too is heading for disaster. **His father had never** asked, **"Why have you done thus and so?"** Adonijah, like Absalom, was in part the product of parental negligence and indulgence; David never held him accountable for his actions (cf. notes on 2 Sam. 13:21; 14:24; 15:4).

1:7–9 The events of chs. 1–2 are to be understood in light of the Judah/Israel tensions already evident in the books of Samuel and soon to reappear in 1 Kings 12 (cf. 2 Sam. 20:1; 1 Kings 12:16). **Joab** and **Abiathar** were men with deep roots in David's Judean past (e.g., 1 Sam. 22:20–23; 2 Samuel 2–3). By contrast, only **Benaiah** and **David's mighty men** (special guard) in the opposing group had such a long-standing association with David (see 2 Sam. 23:8–39). Note that it was the **royal officials of Judah** who were invited to Adonijah's feast, not those of Israel. **Shimei** was an antagonist of David from the house of Saul (2 Sam. 16:5–14), while neither **Nathan** nor **Zadok** appear in the narrative before 2 Sam. 7:2 and 8:17, respectively (i.e., after David's move from Hebron to Jerusalem in 2 Sam. 5:6–10). **En-rogel**. The spring En-rogel was south of Jerusalem, at the juncture of the Hinnom and Kidron Valleys, and provided the city with a source of water additional to the important Gihon Spring (see 1 Kings 1:33) about half a mile to the north.

Nathan and Bathsheba Before David

11 Then Nathan said to Bathsheba the mother of Solomon, "Have you not heard that
[b]Adonijah the son of Haggith has become king and David our lord does not know it?
12 Now therefore come, let me give you advice, that you may save your own life and the life
of your son Solomon. 13 Go in at once to King David, and say to him, 'Did you not, my lord
the king, swear to your servant, saying, [m]"Solomon your son shall reign after me, and he
shall sit on my throne"? Why then is Adonijah king?' 14 Then while you are still speaking
with the king, I also will come in after you and confirm[1] your words."
15 So Bathsheba went to the king in his chamber (now the king was very old, and Abishag
the Shunammite was attending to the king). 16 Bathsheba bowed and paid homage to the
king, and the king said, "What do you desire?" 17 She said to him, "My lord, you swore to
your servant by the LORD your God, saying, [m]'Solomon your son shall reign after me, and
he shall sit on my throne.' 18 And now, behold, Adonijah is king, although you, my lord the
king, do not know it. 19 [n]He has sacrificed oxen, fattened cattle, and sheep in abundance,
and has invited all the sons of the king, [f]Abiathar the priest, and Joab the commander of
the army, but [l]Solomon your servant he has not invited. 20 And now, my lord the king, the
eyes of all Israel are on you, to tell them who shall sit on the throne of my lord the king
after him. 21 Otherwise it will come to pass, when my lord the king [o]sleeps with his fathers,
that I and my son Solomon will be counted offenders."
22 While she was still speaking with the king, Nathan the prophet came in. 23 And they
told the king, "Here is Nathan the prophet." And when he came in before the king, he
bowed before the king, with his face to the ground. 24 And Nathan said, "My lord the king,
have you said, 'Adonijah shall reign after me, and he shall sit on my throne'? 25 For he has
gone down this day and [n]has sacrificed oxen, fattened cattle, and sheep in abundance, and
has invited all the king's sons, the commanders[2] of the army, and Abiathar the priest. And
behold, they are eating and drinking before him, and saying, [p]'Long live King Adonijah!'
26 [q]But me, your servant, and Zadok the priest, and Benaiah the son of Jehoiada, and your
servant Solomon he has not invited. 27 Has this thing been brought about by my lord the
king and you have not told your servants who should sit on the throne of my lord the
king after him?"

Solomon Anointed King

28 Then King David answered, "Call Bathsheba to me." So she came into the king's presence and stood before the king. 29 And the king swore, saying, [r]"As the LORD lives, who
has redeemed my soul out of every adversity, 30 [s]as I swore to you by the LORD, the God of
Israel, saying, 'Solomon your son shall reign after me, and he shall sit on my throne in my
place,' even so will I do this day." 31 Then Bathsheba bowed with her face to the ground and
paid homage to the king and said, [t]"May my lord King David live forever!"
32 King David said, "Call to me Zadok the priest, Nathan the prophet, and Benaiah the
son of Jehoiada." So they came before the king. 33 And the king said to them, "Take with
you [u]the servants of your lord and have Solomon my son ride on my own mule, and bring
him down to [v]Gihon. 34 And let Zadok the priest and Nathan the prophet there [w]anoint him
king over Israel. [x]Then blow the trumpet and say, [y]'Long live King Solomon!' 35 You shall

[1] Or *expand on* [2] Hebrew; Septuagint *Joab the commander*

11 [b][See ver. 5 above]
13 [m]ver. 30; [1 Chr. 22:9]
17 [m][See ver. 13 above]
19 [n]ver. 9 [f][See ver. 7 above] [l][See ver. 10 above]
21 [o]ch. 2:10; 2 Sam. 7:12; [Deut. 31:16]
25 [n][See ver. 19 above] [p]See 1 Sam. 10:24
26 [q]ver. 8, 10, 32
29 [r]See Ruth 3:13
30 [s]ver. 13, 17
31 [t]Neh. 2:3; Dan. 2:4; 3:9; 5:10; 6:6, 21
33 [u]2 Sam. 11:11; 20:6 [v]2 Chr. 32:30; 33:14
34 [w]See 1 Sam. 10:1 [x]2 Sam. 15:10; 2 Kgs. 9:13; 11:14 [y][ver. 25]; See 1 Sam. 10:24

1:13 Did you not . . . swear? This oath is not mentioned anywhere in 2 Samuel, and Nathan himself does not mention it to David when he confronts him in 1 Kings 1:24–27. Perhaps it was a private assurance from David to Bathsheba that was not public knowledge.

1:18 you . . . do not know it. The play on the idea of "knowing" in ch. 1 underlines the extent of David's loss of power in his old age. He was not able to "know" Abishag sexually (v. 4) as he had once known Bathsheba, and now he does not know about Adonijah, even though he had previously had the reputation of possessing "wisdom like the wisdom of the angel of God to know all things that are on the earth" (2 Sam. 14:20).

1:20–21 Bathsheba is concerned that if David does not appoint Solomon as the next monarch prior to his death (**sleeps with his fathers**), she and her son will be treated as rivals for the throne (**counted offenders**) and their lives will be at risk.

1:22–27 Long live King Adonijah! While Adonijah's attempts to consolidate power and succeed David as king are evident (vv. 5–9), Nathan emphasizes the alarming purpose of the events to motivate David to quickly resolve the problem of royal succession.

1:31 May my lord King David live forever! As is clear from the context, Bathsheba uses the conventional form of speech that one would normally use in addressing a king (cf. Dan. 3:9; 6:21). The use of this convention, however, does not imply that Bathsheba is insincere, but that she is reaffirming her loyalty to David.

1:33 my own mule. Solomon's ride on David's mule marks him as David's

then come up after him, and he shall come and sit on my throne, for he shall be king in my
place. And I have appointed him to be ruler over Israel and over Judah." 36 And Benaiah the
son of Jehoiada answered the king, "Amen! May the LORD, the God of my lord the king,
say so. 37 [z]As the LORD has been with my lord the king, even so may he be with Solomon,
[a]and make his throne greater than the throne of my lord King David."
38 So Zadok the priest, Nathan the prophet, and Benaiah the son of Jehoiada, [b]and the
Cherethites and the Pelethites went down and had Solomon ride on King David's mule
and brought him to Gihon. 39 There Zadok the priest took the horn of [c]oil from the tent
and [d]anointed Solomon. [x]Then they blew the trumpet, and all the people said, [y]"Long live
King Solomon!" 40 And all the people went up after him, playing on pipes, and rejoicing
with great joy, so that the earth was split by their noise.
41 Adonijah and all the guests who were with him heard it as they finished feasting. And
when Joab heard the sound of the trumpet, he said, "What does this uproar in the city
mean?" 42 While he was still speaking, behold, [e]Jonathan the son of Abiathar the priest
came. And Adonijah said, "Come in, [f]for you are a worthy man and bring good news."
43 Jonathan answered Adonijah, "No, for our lord King David has made Solomon king,
44 and the king has sent with him Zadok the priest, Nathan the prophet, and Benaiah the
son of Jehoiada, and the [b]Cherethites and the Pelethites. And they had him ride on the
king's mule. 45 And Zadok the priest and Nathan the prophet have anointed him king at
[v]Gihon, and they have gone up from there rejoicing, so that the city is in an uproar. This
is the noise that you have heard. 46 [g]Solomon sits on the royal throne. 47 Moreover, the
king's servants came to congratulate our lord King David, saying, [h]'May your God make
the name of Solomon more famous than yours, and make his throne greater than your
throne.' And the king [i]bowed himself on the bed. 48 And the king also said, 'Blessed be
the LORD, the God of Israel, [j]who has granted someone[1] to sit on my throne this day, my
own eyes seeing it.'"
49 Then all the guests of Adonijah trembled and rose, and each went his own way. 50 And
Adonijah feared Solomon. So he arose and went [k]and took hold of [l]the horns of the altar.
51 Then it was told Solomon, "Behold, Adonijah fears King Solomon, for behold, he has
laid hold of the horns of the altar, saying, 'Let King Solomon swear to me first that he
will not put his servant to death with the sword.'" 52 And Solomon said, "If he will show
himself a worthy man, [m]not one of his hairs shall fall to the earth, but if wickedness is
found in him, he shall die." 53 So King Solomon sent, and they brought him down from
the altar. And he came and paid homage to King Solomon, and Solomon said to him, "Go
to your house."

David's Instructions to Solomon

2 [n]When David's time to die drew near, he commanded Solomon his son, saying, 2 [o]"I
am about to go the way of all the earth. [p]Be strong, and show yourself a man, 3 and
keep the charge of the LORD your God, walking in his ways and keeping his statutes, his
commandments, his rules, and his testimonies, as it is written in the Law of Moses, [q]that

[1] Septuagint *one of my offspring*

37 [z]See 1 Sam. 20:13 [a]ver. 47
38 [b]See 2 Sam. 8:18
39 [c][Ps. 89:20]; See Ex. 30:23-32 [d]1 Chr. 29:22 [x][See ver. 34 above] [y][See ver. 34 above]
42 [e]2 Sam. 15:27, 36; 17:17 [f]2 Sam. 18:27
44 [b][See ver. 38 above]
45 [v][See ver. 33 above]
46 [g]1 Chr. 29:23
47 [h]ver. 37 [i][Gen. 47:31]
48 [j]ch. 3:6; [Ps. 132:11, 12]
50 [k]ch. 2:28 [l]Ex. 27:2
52 [m]See 1 Sam. 14:45

Chapter 2

1 [n][Gen. 47:29]
2 [o]Josh. 23:14 [p]See Josh. 1:6, 7
3 [q]Deut. 29:9; 1 Chr. 22:12, 13

favored son. More than this, the mule itself may also have been regarded as a symbol of kingship (see Zech. 9:9; Matt. 21:1–11).

1:38 Cherethites and . . . Pelethites. These are probably the "servants" of v. 33, apparently David's own personal troops (cf. 2 Sam. 8:18; 15:18; 20:7, 23). They were probably mercenaries drawn from among the non-Israelite population of Canaan, most likely (as the names imply) of Cretan and Philistine origin.

1:39 the tent. The most natural assumption might be that this is "the tent of the LORD" that appears also in 2:28–30, i.e., the tabernacle. The Chronicler, however (2 Chron. 1:1–6), differentiates David's tent in Jerusalem (the temporary location of the ark of the covenant) from the tabernacle in Gibeon, so the reference is in fact unclear.

1:41–49 guests . . . heard it. The location of Adonijah's party at En-rogel (v. 9), just south of Jerusalem in the Kidron Valley, prevented direct observation of Solomon's anointing (vv. 38–40), but they could hear the subsequent celebration. Adonijah's guests **trembled and rose** (v. 49), knowing that alignment with him may mean being designated rebels. Notice how carefully Jonathan the son of Abiathar expresses his personal loyalties to **our lord King David** (vv. 43, 47).

1:50 horns of the altar. Adonijah believes that the altar, as a holy place, protects him from Solomon's vengeance. This reflects a common ancient Near Eastern custom with regard to asylum at shrines (cf. Ex. 21:12–14).

2:2–3 Be strong, and show yourself a man. David's parting words to Solomon echo God's words to Joshua upon his "succession" to the leadership of Israel after Moses' death (Josh. 1:6–9). This injunction begins by using the language of warriorship before moving on immediately to define the framework within which this strength must be exercised (obedience to God, in accordance with the **Law of Moses**). Particularly in view here (as in Joshua) is the law code of Deuteronomy, as the language of 1 Kings 2:3–4 indicates (cf. Deut. 4:29; 6:2; 8:6; 9:5; 11:1; 29:9). "Show yourself a man" seems to be an idiom that refers primarily to conducting oneself bravely (cf. 1 Sam. 4:9; 1 Cor. 16:13), as defined specifically here within the framework of faithful

you may prosper in all that you do and wherever you turn, 4 that the LORD may [r]establish
his word that he spoke concerning me, saying, [s]'If your sons pay close attention to their
way, [t]to walk before me in faithfulness with all their heart and with all their soul, [u]you
shall not lack[1] a man on the throne of Israel.'

5 "Moreover, you also know what Joab the son of Zeruiah [v]did to me, how he dealt with
the two commanders of the armies of Israel, [w]Abner the son of Ner, [x]and Amasa the son of
Jether, whom he killed, avenging[2] in time of peace for blood that had been shed in war,
and putting the blood of war[3] on the belt around his[4] waist and on the sandals on his feet.
6 Act therefore [y]according to your wisdom, but do not let his gray head go down to Sheol in
peace. 7 But deal loyally with the sons of [z]Barzillai the Gileadite, and let them be [a]among
those who eat at your table, [b]for with such loyalty[5] they met me when I fled from Absalom
your brother. 8 And there is also with you [c]Shimei the son of Gera, the Benjaminite from
Bahurim, who cursed me with a grievous curse on the day [d]when I went to Mahanaim.
[e]But when he came down to meet me at the Jordan, I swore to him by the LORD, saying, 'I
will not put you to death with the sword.' 9 Now therefore do not hold him guiltless, [f]for
you are a wise man. You will know what you ought to do to him, and you shall [g]bring his
gray head down with blood to Sheol."

The Death of David

10 [h]Then David slept with his fathers and was buried in [i]the city of David. 11 And the
time that David reigned over Israel was [j]forty years. He reigned seven years in Hebron
and thirty-three years in Jerusalem. 12 [k]So Solomon sat on the throne of David his father,
and his kingdom was firmly established.

4 [r]2 Sam. 7:25 [s]Ps. 132:12 [t][ch. 3:6; 9:4; 2 Kgs. 20:3] [u]ch. 8:25; 9:5; 2 Sam. 7:12, 13
5 [v]2 Sam. 18:5, 12, 14; [2 Sam. 3:39] [w]ver. 32; 2 Sam. 3:27 [x]2 Sam. 20:10
6 [y][ver. 9]
7 [z]See 2 Sam. 19:31-38 [a]2 Sam. 9:7, 10 [b]2 Sam. 17:27-29
8 [c]2 Sam. 16:5 [d]2 Sam. 17:24 [e]2 Sam. 19:18
9 [f][ver. 6] [g][Gen. 42:38; 44:31]
10 [h]ch. 1:21; Acts 2:29; 13:36 [i]ch. 3:1; 9:24
11 [j]2 Sam. 5:4, 5; 1 Chr. 29:26, 27
12 [k]1 Chr. 29:23; 2 Chr. 1:1

[1] Hebrew *there shall not be cut off for you* [2] Septuagint; Hebrew *placing* [3] Septuagint *innocent blood* [4] Septuagint *my;* twice in this verse [5] Or *steadfast love*

adherence to the Mosaic law; it will take bravery for Solomon to lead the people faithfully.

2:4 his word that he spoke concerning me. The reference is apparently to 2 Sam. 7:11b–16, although that passage does not explicitly mention any conditions attached to the promise (**If your sons pay close attention to their way**). It is in fact plainly stated (2 Sam. 7:14–15) that wrongdoing on the part of David's successors will not lead to the end of the dynasty, and this is reflected also in 1–2 Kings (cf. 1 Kings 11:36; 15:4; 2 Kings 8:19). Kings thus carries a degree of tension as to the precise implications of the Davidic promise, a tension that remains even by the end of 2 Kings 25.

2:5 what Joab the son of Zeruiah did to me. Joab is to be killed so as to clear David's house of "the guilt for the blood" that he "shed without cause" (v. 31). It is curious, however, that David himself had apparently not been sufficiently concerned about this bloodguilt to take action against someone who had been so useful to him (e.g., 2 Sam. 11:15; 14:1–33; 19:1–8). Perhaps beneath David's words is more of a political than a religious concern. Joab is too dangerous to be allowed to live in Solomon's united kingdom once David is gone because he is too much a man of the Judean past (as Shimei is too much a man of the Israelite past, 1 Kings 2:8–9). Between these disruptive elements from Judah and Israel, elements that are hostile to harmony, stands Barzillai (v. 7; cf. 2 Sam. 17:27–29; 19:31–39) from Gilead in Transjordan. He is a model of dutiful service to his king, which is rewarded in peaceful fellowship for his sons around the king's table.

2:6 according to your wisdom. Solomon must not act rashly, but must find some clever justification for removing Joab from the scene (see also v. 9 in reference to Shimei) so that he does not die a peaceful and natural death in old age (**do not let his gray head go down to Sheol in peace**). For "Sheol," see note on 1 Sam. 2:6. Solomon's wisdom (Hb. *khokhmah*) will be highlighted in the following chapters (1 Kings 3:1–28; 4:29–34; 10:1–13), but it will never again be used to such ruthless effect.

2:10 David slept with his fathers. The metaphor of sleep hints at the expectation of awakening sometime in the future, and "with his fathers" hints that previous generations also join in this hope, and that David is somehow now with them. This phrase will be repeated many times in Kings and Chronicles.

2:11 David **reigned over Israel** for **forty years**, and died in 970 B.C.

2:12 his kingdom was firmly established. The Hebrew *kun* ("established") is strategically positioned at the beginning, in the middle, and at the end of vv. 12–46 (vv. 12, 24, 45–46), recalling 2 Sam. 7:11b–16, where it appears on three occasions (2 Sam. 7:12, 13, 16) in relation to God's action in ensuring for David an everlasting dynasty. God has done for Solomon what he had done earlier for David (2 Sam. 5:12), in accordance with his promise to David (1 Kings 2:24).

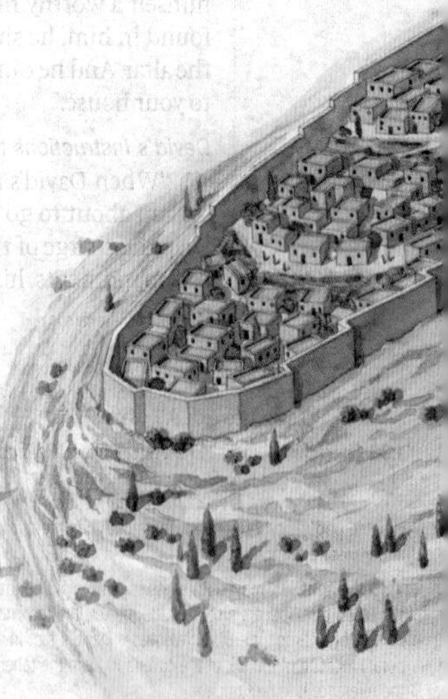

JERUSALEM IN THE TIME OF SOLOMON (C. 970–930 B.C.)

David commanded his son Solomon to build a new temple. This work took seven years, followed by 13 years of building an adjacent royal complex (1 Kings 6:38; 7:1). As this quarter was located outside and north of the original city of David, new city walls must have been built to connect the two areas.

Built atop Mount Moriah (2 Chron. 3:1), Solomon's temple was Israel's first permanent sanctuary. The royal complex immediately to the south of the temple (see also Solomon's Temple and Palace Complex, p. 607) consisted of Solomon's own palace and a smaller house for his Egyptian wife (1 Kings 7:8), an armory called the "House of the Forest of Lebanon" (vv. 2–5), a Hall of Pillars (v. 6), and a Hall of the Throne (v. 7). A special "Ascent" connected this complex with the temple.

The area between the temple complex and the city of David was called the Ophel.

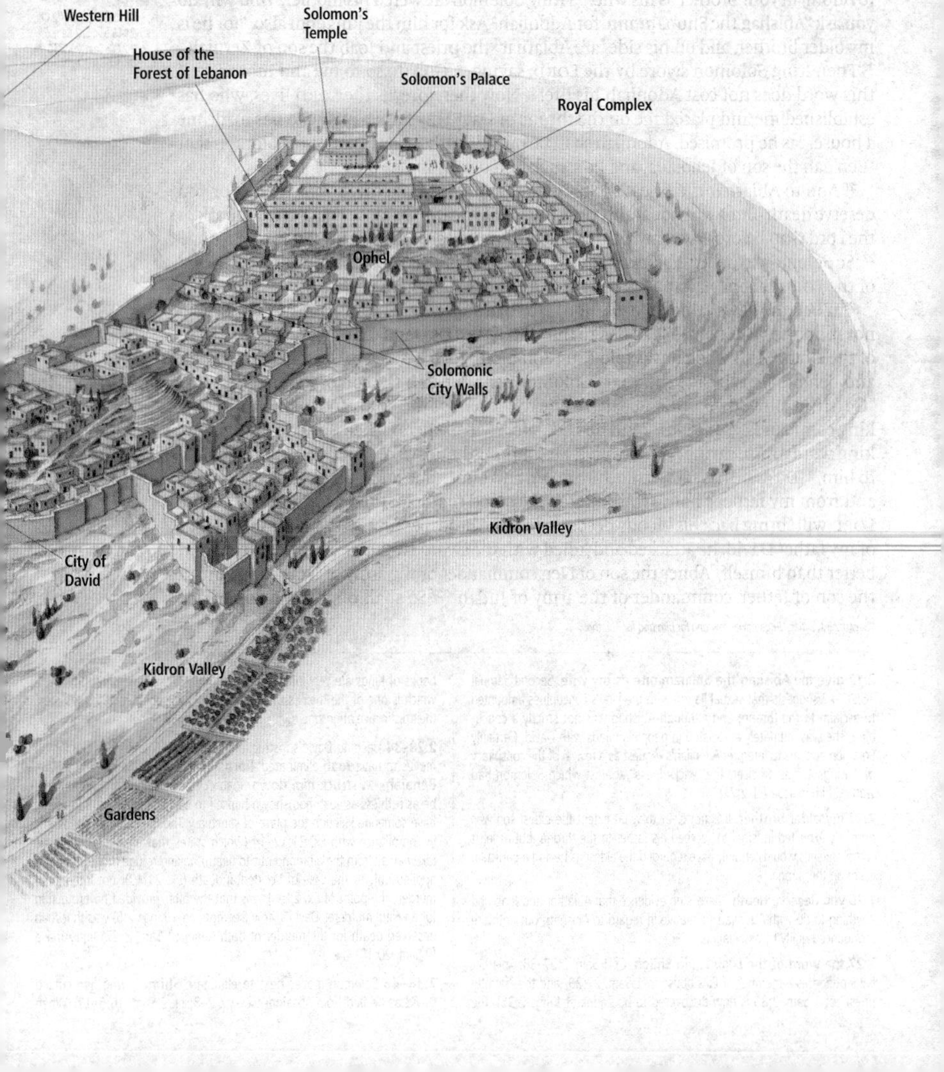

Solomon's Reign Established

13 Then Adonijah the son of Haggith came to Bathsheba the mother of Solomon. And she
said, [l]"Do you come peacefully?" He said, "Peacefully." 14 Then he said, "I have something to
say to you." She said, "Speak." 15 He said, "You know that [m]the kingdom was mine, and that
all Israel fully expected me to reign. However, the kingdom has turned about and become
my brother's, [n]for it was his from the LORD. 16 And now I have one request to make of you;
do not refuse me." She said to him, "Speak." 17 And he said, "Please ask King Solomon—he
will not refuse you—to give me [o]Abishag the Shunammite as my wife." 18 Bathsheba said,
"Very well; I will speak for you to the king."

19 So Bathsheba went to King Solomon to speak to him on behalf of Adonijah. And the
king rose to meet her and bowed down to her. Then he sat on his throne and had a seat
brought for the king's mother, [p]and she sat on his right. 20 Then she said, "I have one small
request to make of you; do not refuse me." And the king said to her, "Make your request,
my mother, for I will not refuse you." 21 She said, "Let [o]Abishag the Shunammite be given
to Adonijah your brother as his wife." 22 King Solomon answered his mother, "And why do
you ask [o]Abishag the Shunammite for Adonijah? Ask for him the kingdom also, [q]for he is
my older brother, and on his side [r]are Abiathar[1] the priest and Joab the son of Zeruiah."
23 Then King Solomon swore by the LORD, saying, [s]"God do so to me and more also if
this word does not cost Adonijah his life! 24 Now therefore [t]as the LORD lives, who has
established me and placed me on the throne of David my father, and who has made me
a house, [u]as he promised, Adonijah shall be put to death today." 25 So King Solomon sent
[v]Benaiah the son of Jehoiada, and he struck him down, and he died.

26 And to Abiathar the priest the king said, "Go to [w]Anathoth, to your estate, for you
deserve death. But I will not at this time put you to death, [x]because you carried the ark of
the Lord GOD before David my father, [y]and because you shared in all my father's affliction."
27 [z]So Solomon expelled Abiathar from being priest to the LORD, thus fulfilling [a]the word
of the LORD that he had spoken concerning the house of Eli in Shiloh.

28 When the news came to Joab—for Joab [b]had supported Adonijah although [c]he had
not supported Absalom—Joab fled to the tent of the LORD and caught hold of the [d]horns
of the altar. 29 And when it was told King Solomon, "Joab has fled to the tent of the LORD,
and behold, he is beside the altar," Solomon sent Benaiah the son of Jehoiada, saying,
"Go, strike him down." 30 So Benaiah came to the tent of the LORD and said to him, "The
king commands, 'Come out.'" But he said, "No, I will die here." Then Benaiah brought the
king word again, saying, "Thus said Joab, and thus he answered me." 31 The king replied
to him, [e]"Do as he has said, strike him down and bury him, [f]and thus take away from me
and from my father's house the guilt for the blood that Joab shed without cause. 32 The
LORD will [g]bring back his bloody deeds on his own head, because, without the knowledge
of my father David, he attacked and killed with the sword two men [h]more righteous and
better than himself, [i]Abner the son of Ner, commander of the army of Israel, and [j]Amasa
the son of Jether, commander of the army of Judah. 33 [g]So shall their blood come back

[1] Septuagint, Syriac, Vulgate; Hebrew *and for him and for Abiathar*

13 [l]1 Sam. 16:4
15 [m][ch. 1:5, 25] [n]1 Chr. 22:9, 10; 28:5-7
17 [o]ch. 1:3, 4
19 [p][Ps. 45:9]
21 [o][See ver. 17 above]
22 [o][See ver. 17 above] [q]ch. 1:6; 1 Chr. 3:2, 5 [r]ch. 1:7
23 [s]See Ruth 1:17
24 [t]See Ruth 3:13 [u]2 Sam. 7:11, 13; 1 Chr. 22:10
25 [v]2 Sam. 8:18
26 [w]Josh. 21:18 [x]1 Sam. 23:6; 2 Sam. 15:24, 29 [y]See 1 Sam. 22:20-23
27 [z][ver. 35] [a]See 1 Sam. 2:27-36
28 [b]ch. 1:7 [c]2 Sam. 17:25; 18:2 [d]ch. 1:50
31 [e][Ex. 21:14] [f]Num. 35:33; Deut. 19:13; 21:8, 9
32 [g]See Judg. 9:24 [h]2 Chr. 21:13 [i]ver. 5; 2 Sam. 3:27 [j]2 Sam. 20:9, 10
33 [g][See ver. 32 above]

2:17 give me Abishag the Shunammite as my wife. Second Samuel 16:20–22 suggests that sexual liaison with the king's concubines amounted to a claim to the throne; and although Abishag was not strictly a concubine, she was intimately associated in people's minds with David. Certainly Solomon appears to interpret Adonijah's request as a revival of the conspiracy of 1 Kings 1—as precisely the "wickedness" against which Solomon had warned him in 1:52 (cf. 2:22).

2:22 my older brother. It is not clear to what extent the eldest son was normally expected in Israel to succeed his father to the throne, but at least some Israelites would certainly have regarded the eldest as having a particular claim on the throne.

2:26 you deserve death. There is no evidence that Abiathar and Joab had anything to do with Adonijah's initiative in regard to Abishag, but both are pronounced guilty by association.

2:27 the word of the LORD . . . in Shiloh. Cf. 1 Sam. 2:27–36. Abiathar is identified as a member of Eli's house in 1 Sam. 22:20, and the "faithful priest" of 1 Sam. 2:35 is now discovered to be Zadok (1 Kings 2:35). The books of Kings are very interested in this idea of prophecy and fulfillment, which is one of the themes that binds the books together and gives them their distinctive atmosphere.

2:28–34 Heeding David's instructions (see vv. 5–6 and notes), Solomon moves to have **Joab** eliminated. **horns of the altar**. See note on 1:50. **Benaiah . . . struck him down**. Joab does not think that Solomon will be as ruthless as Joab had shown himself to be, that is, prepared even to have someone killed in the place of sanctuary. Though this was not strictly in compliance with Ex. 21:12–14 (which states that a murderer is to be *taken away* from the altar and put to death), taking refuge in the sanctuary applied only to the case of accidental death (Ex. 21:13), not intentional murder; the point of Ex. 21:14 was that the altar provided no protection for a willful murderer. David's view (see note on 1 Kings 2:5) was that Joab deserved death for the murder of both Abner (2 Sam. 3:27) and Amasa (2 Sam. 20:10).

2:36–46 Solomon moves next to eliminate **Shimei**, who had cursed David as he fled from Absalom (see vv. 7–8; cf. 2 Sam. 16:5–13). When

on the head of Joab and on the head of his descendants forever. But for David and for
his descendants and for his house and for his throne there shall be peace from the LORD
forevermore." 34 Then Benaiah the son of Jehoiada went up and struck him down and
put him to death. And he was buried in his own house in the wilderness. 35 [k]The king put
Benaiah the son of Jehoiada over the army in place of Joab, and the king put [l]Zadok the
priest [m]in the place of Abiathar.

36 Then the king sent and summoned [n]Shimei and said to him, "Build yourself a house
in Jerusalem and dwell there, and do not go out from there to any place whatever. 37 For
on the day you go out and cross [o]the brook Kidron, know for certain that you shall die.
[p]Your blood shall be on your own head." 38 And Shimei said to the king, "What you say is
good; as my lord the king has said, so will your servant do." So Shimei lived in Jerusalem
many days.

39 But it happened at the end of three years that two of Shimei's servants ran away to
[q]Achish, son of Maacah, king of Gath. And when it was told Shimei, "Behold, your servants
are in Gath," 40 Shimei arose and saddled a donkey and went to Gath to Achish to seek
his servants. Shimei went and brought his servants from Gath. 41 And when Solomon
was told that Shimei had gone from Jerusalem to Gath and returned, 42 the king sent
and summoned Shimei and said to him, "Did I not make you swear by the LORD and
solemnly warn you, saying, 'Know for certain that on the day you go out and go to any
place whatever, you shall die'? And you said to me, 'What you say is good; I will obey.'
43 Why then have you not kept your oath to the LORD and the commandment with which
I commanded you?" 44 The king also said to Shimei, "You know in your own heart [r]all
the harm that you did to David my father. So the LORD will [s]bring back your harm on
your own head. 45 But King Solomon shall be blessed, [t]and the throne of David shall be
established before the LORD forever." 46 Then the king commanded Benaiah the son of
Jehoiada, and he went out and struck him down, and he died.

[u]So the kingdom was established in the hand of Solomon.

Solomon's Prayer for Wisdom

3 [v]Solomon made a marriage alliance with Pharaoh king of Egypt. He took Pharaoh's
daughter and brought her into [w]the city of David until he had finished [x]building his
own house [y]and the house of the LORD [z]and the wall around Jerusalem. 2 [a]The people
were sacrificing at the high places, however, because no house had yet been built for the
name of the LORD.

3 Solomon [b]loved the LORD, [c]walking in the statutes of David his father, only he sacrificed
and made offerings at the high places. 4 And the king went to Gibeon to sacrifice there,

35 [k]ch. 4:4 [l]1 Chr. 29:22 [m]ver. 27
36 [n]ver. 8
37 [o]2 Sam. 15:23 [p]See 2 Sam. 1:16
39 [q][1 Sam. 27:2]
44 [r]See 2 Sam. 16:5-14 [s]See 1 Sam. 25:39
45 [t][Prov. 25:5]
46 [u]ver. 12; [2 Chr. 1:1]

Chapter 3

1 [v]ch. 7:8; 9:16, 24; 2 Chr. 8:11 [w]See ch. 2:10 [x]ch. 7:1 [y]See ch. 6 [z]ch. 9:15
2 [a]ch. 22:43; [Deut. 12:2, 3]
3 [b]Deut. 6:5; 30:16, 20; [Ps. 31:23] [c]ver. 6, 14

Shimei ignores Solomon's order not to go from Jerusalem to any other place (1 Kings 2:36, cf. v. 42), Solomon orders his execution (v. 46). He thus proves himself to be a "wise" king (vv. 6, 9), but it is a dubious kind of wisdom.

3:1–28 *More on Solomon and Wisdom.* Although a kind of wisdom has already guided Solomon in his treatment of those who were a threat to him (2:6, 9), ch. 3 confirms that in fact he still lacks a truly "wise and discerning mind" (v. 12). The new gift of wisdom that he now receives from God allows him to govern more justly, as the story in vv. 16–28 illustrates.

3:1 marriage alliance with Pharaoh. This is another dubious act to add to those in ch. 2. Deuteronomy warns against a "return to Egypt" (Deut. 17:16) in terms of too-close relations with that nation. The Hebrew verb (*khatan*), translated "made a marriage alliance" in 1 Kings 3:1, is translated "intermarry" in Deut. 7:3, where the command not to marry foreigners is explicitly tied to a warning that such marriages will lead the people to serve other gods (Deut. 7:4). This becomes all too real for Solomon (1 Kings 11:3–4). Even though Solomon "loved the LORD" (3:3), he is a king with a divided heart, failing to keep the Law of Moses wholeheartedly as David had instructed (2:1–4).

3:2 the high places. This is the standard translation of the Hebrew *bamot*, but it is not clear that height (whether natural or artificial) was an intrinsic feature of these worship sites. The idea is simply that of publicly accessible structures (including unenclosed altars and temples with altars) within which or on which offerings were made to God or the gods. The continuation and proliferation of these local places of worship (as opposed to the one place of worship described in Deuteronomy 12) is one of the main concerns of the authors of 1–2 Kings (1 Kings 22:43; 2 Kings 12:3; 14:4; 15:4, 35). Solomon begins by tolerating worship of the Lord at these places and ends up being drawn into full-blown apostasy (1 Kings 11:7–8), as also later do Israel and Judah (e.g., 12:28–31; 2 Kings 21:3–9). See also note on 2 Kings 16:1–4.

Solomon's Tainted Glory in 1 Kings

Positives	Negatives
David's chosen heir (ch. 1)	Gained power in bloody coup (ch. 2)
Nathan's early support (ch. 1)	Prophetic voice disappears
Prayer for wisdom to rule righteously (chs. 3–4)	Rules with forced labor; accumulates wealth unjustly (9:15–22; 10:26–29)
Completion and dedication of temple (chs. 5–8)	Foreign wives lead him to idolatry (11:1–8)
The Lord supports Solomon (9:1–9)	The Lord rejects Solomon (11:9–12)

[d]for that was the great high place. Solomon used to offer a thousand burnt offerings on
that altar. 5 [e]At Gibeon [f]the LORD appeared to Solomon [g]in a dream by night, and God
said, "Ask what I shall give you." 6 And Solomon said, "You have shown great and steadfast
love to your servant David my father, because [h]he walked before you in faithfulness, in
righteousness, and in uprightness of heart toward you. And you have kept for him this
great and steadfast love and [i]have given him a son to sit on his throne this day. 7 And now,
O LORD my God, [j]you have made your servant king in place of David my father, [k]although
I am but a little child. I do not know [l]how to go out or come in. 8 [m]And your servant is in
the midst of your people whom you have chosen, a great people, [n]too many to be numbered or counted for multitude. 9 [o]Give your servant therefore an understanding mind [p]to
govern your people, that I may [q]discern between good and evil, for who is able to govern
this your great people?"

10 It pleased the Lord that Solomon had asked this. 11 And God said to him, "Because
you have asked this, and have not asked for yourself long life or riches or the life of your
enemies, but have asked for yourself understanding to discern what is right, 12 behold, [r]I
now do according to your word. Behold, [s]I give you a wise and discerning mind, so that
none like you has been before you and none like you shall arise after you. 13 [t]I give you
also what you have not asked, [u]both riches and honor, so that no other king shall compare
with you, all your days. 14 And if you will walk in my ways, keeping my statutes and my
commandments, [v]as your father David walked, then [w]I will lengthen your days."

15 And Solomon [x]awoke, and behold, it was a dream. Then he came to Jerusalem and
stood before the ark of the covenant of the Lord, and offered up burnt offerings and peace
offerings, and made a feast for all his servants.

Solomon's Wisdom

16 Then two prostitutes came to the king [y]and stood before him. 17 The one woman said,
"Oh, my lord, this woman and I live in the same house, and I gave birth to a child while she
was in the house. 18 Then on the third day after I gave birth, this woman also gave birth.
And we were alone. There was no one else with us in the house; only we two were in the
house. 19 And this woman's son died in the night, because she lay on him. 20 And she arose
at midnight and took my son from beside me, while your servant slept, and laid him at
her breast, and laid her dead son at my breast. 21 When I rose in the morning to nurse my
child, behold, he was dead. But when I looked at him closely in the morning, behold, he
was not the child that I had borne." 22 But the other woman said, "No, the living child is
mine, and the dead child is yours." The first said, "No, the dead child is yours, and the
living child is mine." Thus they spoke before the king.

23 Then the king said, "The one says, 'This is my son that is alive, and your son is dead';
and the other says, 'No; but your son is dead, and my son is the living one.'" 24 And the

4 [d]2 Chr. 1:3, 6, 13; [1 Chr. 16:39; 21:29]
5 [e]For ver. 5-14, see 2 Chr. 1:7-12 [f]ch. 9:2; 11:9 [g][Num. 12:6; Matt. 1:20; 2:13, 19]
6 [h]ch. 2:4; 9:4; [Ps. 15:2] [i]ch. 1:48
7 [j][1 Chr. 28:5] [k][1 Chr. 29:1] [l]Num. 27:17
8 [m]Deut. 7:6 [n]Gen. 13:16; 15:5
9 [o][Prov. 2:6, 9; James 1:5] [p]Ps. 72:1, 2 [q][2 Sam. 14:17; Isa. 7:15; Heb. 5:14]
12 [r][1 John 5:14, 15] [s]ch. 4:29-31; 5:12; 10:23, 24; Eccles. 1:16
13 [t][Matt. 6:33] [u]ch. 4:21-24; 10:23, 27; [Prov. 3:16]
14 [v]ver. 6; ch. 15:5 [w][Ps. 91:16; Prov. 3:2]
15 [x]Gen. 41:7
16 [y]Num. 27:2

3:7–9 I am but a little child. Solomon feels inadequate in view of the great task that confronts him. Although he has used wisdom before in dealing with affairs of state, now he confesses basic ignorance: **I do not know how to go out or come in**. He needs an **understanding mind to govern your people, that** he **may discern between good and evil**.

3:11–14 Since Solomon did **not** ask for **long life or riches or the life of** his **enemies**, God gave him **what** he did **not** ask for, **both riches and honor,** and promised to **lengthen** his days. Significantly, there is no mention of enemies, confirming that Solomon's "wisdom" in ch. 2 was of an unenlightened, self-serving kind, which must now be replaced with something higher if he is to rule justly and well over his subjects. It is the fear of the Lord that is the true beginning of wisdom (Job 28:28; Ps. 111:10; Prov. 15:33). **I give you a wise and discerning mind**. This wisdom is a supernatural gift from God. It is not innate (as it is implicitly in 1 Kings 2:6–9); and it is not acquired by patient hard work, utilizing careful observation and self-discipline (as it is explicitly in much of Proverbs and in 1 Kings 4:29–34). In the possession of such wisdom Solomon was unparalleled in Israelite history (**none like you has been before you and none like you shall arise after you**), as Hezekiah was unparalleled in trust (2 Kings 18:5) and Josiah in obedience to the Law of Moses (2 Kings 23:25).

3:16 two prostitutes. Prostitutes appear in Proverbs 1–9 as one category of women that men do well to avoid. Men should set their hearts instead on a relationship with Lady Wisdom, who will help them see through seductive and misleading words (e.g., Prov. 6:20–29). Solomon, the possessor of wisdom, likewise has no difficulty seeing through the words spoken by the two women here. They **stood before him** because, in the absence of a second witness to corroborate their testimony (Deut. 19:15), the normal legal procedures could not be followed. The Israelite king represented the highest court of appeal and was the foundation of all administration and justice (cf. 1 Kings 3:28).

3:24 Bring me a sword. Solomon's old "wisdom" had led previously to the use of the **sword**, but only for arguably unjust executions. His new wisdom leads him in more constructive ways: the sword functions in the service not of the ruthless self but of the kingdom as a whole (cf. Ps. 45:2–4).

3:27–28 This legal case reveals that the Lord had granted Solomon's prior request for wisdom (vv. 9, 12); through Solomon's understanding of human nature, the identity of the true mother is rightly ascertained, and Israel realizes that **the wisdom of God was in him**.

4:1–20 *Solomon's Rule over Israel.* The Hebrew text treats vv. 1–20 as a single unit. Verse 1 indicates that the following verses will concern the king's rule over all Israel, and v. 20 provides a fitting climax to this initial description of his reign by telling what the consequences of his organizing abilities were

26[z]Gen. 43:30; Jer. 31:20; [Isa. 49:15]
28[a]ver. 9, 11, 12; [Ezra 7:25]
Chapter 4
2[b]1 Chr. 6:10
3[c]2 Sam. 8:16; 20:24
4[d]ch. 2:35 [e]2 Sam. 20:25; [ch. 2:27, 35]
5[f]ver. 7 [g][2 Sam. 15:37; 16:16; 1 Chr. 27:33]
6[h]ch. 5:14; [ch. 12:18; 2 Sam. 20:24; 2 Chr. 10:18] [i][ch. 9:15]
8[j]See Josh. 24:33
11[k]Josh. 11:2

king said, "Bring me a sword." So a sword was brought before the king. **25** And the king
said, "Divide the living child in two, and give half to the one and half to the other." **26** Then
the woman whose son was alive said to the king, because [z]her heart yearned for her son,
"Oh, my lord, give her the living child, and by no means put him to death." But the other
said, "He shall be neither mine nor yours; divide him." **27** Then the king answered and
said, "Give the living child to the first woman, and by no means put him to death; she is
his mother." **28** And all Israel heard of the judgment that the king had rendered, and they
stood in awe of the king, because they perceived that [a]the wisdom of God was in him to
do justice.

Solomon's Officials

4 King Solomon was king over all Israel, **2** and these were his high officials: Azariah the
son of Zadok was [b]the priest; **3** Elihoreph and Ahijah the sons of Shisha were secretaries; [c]Jehoshaphat the son of Ahilud was recorder; **4** [d]Benaiah the son of Jehoiada was in
command of the army; [e]Zadok and Abiathar were priests; **5** Azariah the son of Nathan was
over [f]the officers; Zabud the son of Nathan was priest and [g]king's friend; **6** Ahishar was in
charge of the palace; and [h]Adoniram the son of Abda was in charge of [i]the forced labor.
7 Solomon had twelve officers over all Israel, who provided food for the king and his
household. Each man had to make provision for one month in the year. **8** These were their
names: Ben-hur, in [j]the hill country of Ephraim; **9** Ben-deker, in Makaz, Shaalbim, Beth-
shemesh, and Elonbeth-hanan; **10** Ben-hesed, in Arubboth (to him belonged Socoh and all
the land of Hepher); **11** Ben-abinadab, in all [k]Naphath-dor (he had Taphath the daughter

("Judah and Israel . . . were happy"). This is the kingdom that results from wise King Solomon's just rule (cf. Psalm 72, a psalm "Of Solomon").

4:2 Among the **high officials** of the kingdom first described is the (chief) **priest**, who is surprisingly named not as Zadok (2:35) but as **Azariah the son of Zadok**. For some undisclosed reason Zadok himself is now in a lesser position, along with an apparently reinstated Abiathar (4:4; cf. 2:26–27). The new order, designed in God-given wisdom, is different from the old order, in which Zadok had replaced the (unjustly?) banished Abiathar.

4:3 The **secretaries** may have had general managerial responsibilities, or more specific tasks such as recording history or writing letters, while the **recorder** may in fact have been a herald or even the state prosecutor.

4:5 Azariah was in charge of the 12 **officers** over all Israel mentioned in vv. 7–19, while **Zabud** held the office of **king's friend** (i.e., personal adviser; cf. Hushai in 2 Sam. 15:37; 16:16; 17:5–16).

4:6 Ahishar was the royal steward (cf. 16:9; 18:3), while **Adoniram . . . was in charge of the forced labor** (cf. 5:13–18; 9:15–22).

4:7–19 twelve officers. The task of Solomon's representatives in the various regions of Israel was to provide **for the king and his household** on an annual rotation, each region being responsible for one month in each year. These officers may have been tax supervisors, whose job was to ensure that local government paid its dues to central government. Although the number "twelve" is the traditional number of the Israelite tribes, and some of the regions mentioned in vv. 7–19 may have been based on tribal areas (e.g., **Naphtali**, **Issachar**, and **Benjamin**), what is described here is not strictly a tribal system of support for central government (e.g., the **hill country of Ephraim** in v. 8 is not to be understood as corresponding to the tribal area "Ephraim"). Solomon's arrangements move beyond the tribal system, while having points of contact with it. The **one governor who was over the land** was most likely Azariah (v. 5), to whom the 12 district officers were responsible. This system apparently continued after the death of the king. Evidence for it is perhaps to be found at the excavations of Eshtemoa in the hill country of Judah. There five jars have been discovered, filled with over 60 pounds (27 kg) of silver. The pottery dates to the ninth or eighth century B.C. On two of the jars the word "fifth" appears; this probably refers to a tax that would equal 20 percent.

4:9 A double-sided board game has been found at the site of **Beth-shemesh** from the tenth century B.C. Carved into one side of the board is a man's name, "Hanan." That name also appears on an ostracon from Beth-shemesh dating to the twelfth century B.C. and on a tenth-century bowl found at nearby Tel Batash. The Bible lists the site of **Elonbeth-hanan** immediately after Beth-shemesh as part of Solomon's second economic district.

The Extent of Solomon's Kingdom
c. 971–931 B.C.

Solomon's reign marked the zenith of Israel's power and wealth in biblical times. His father, David, had bestowed upon him a kingdom that included Edom, Moab, Ammon, Syria, and Zobah. Solomon would later bring the kingdom of Hamath under his dominion as well, and his marriage to Pharaoh's daughter sealed an alliance with Egypt. His expansive kingdom controlled important trade routes between several major world powers, including Egypt, Arabia, Mesopotamia, and Anatolia (Asia Minor).

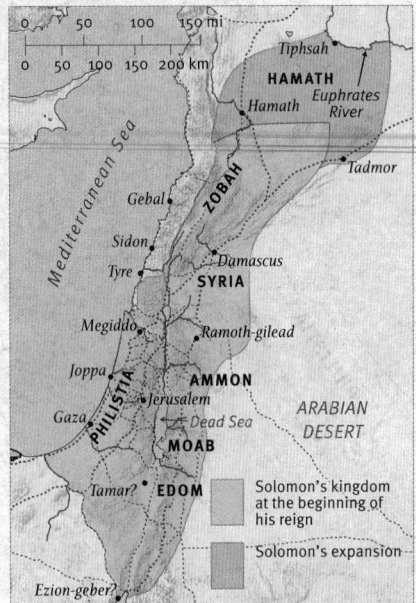

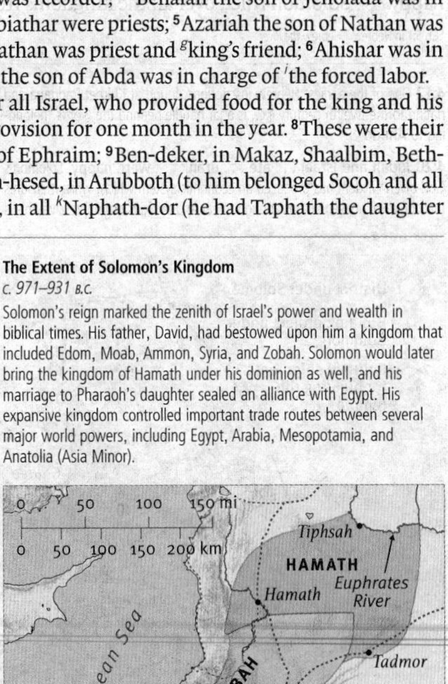

of Solomon as his wife); 12 Baana the son of Ahilud, in [l]Taanach, Megiddo, and all [l]Beth-
shean that is beside Zarethan below Jezreel, and from Beth-shean to Abel-meholah, as
far as the other side of Jokmeam; 13 Ben-geber, [m]in Ramoth-gilead (he had [n]the villages
of Jair the son of Manasseh, which are in Gilead, and he had [o]the region of Argob, which
is in Bashan, sixty great cities with walls and bronze bars); 14 Ahinadab the son of Iddo,
in Mahanaim; 15 Ahimaaz, in Naphtali (he had taken Basemath the daughter of Solomon
as his wife); 16 Baana the son of Hushai, in Asher and Bealoth; 17 Jehoshaphat the son of
Paruah, in Issachar; 18 [p]Shimei the son of Ela, in Benjamin; 19 Geber the son of Uri, in the
land of Gilead, [q]the country of Sihon king of the Amorites and of Og king of Bashan. And
there was one governor who was over the land.

Solomon's Wealth and Wisdom

20 Judah and Israel were as many [r]as the sand by the sea. They ate and drank and were
happy. 21 [1] [s]Solomon ruled over all the kingdoms from the [t]Euphrates[2] to the land of the

[1] Ch 5:1 in Hebrew [2] Hebrew *the River*

12 [l][Josh. 17:11]
13 [m][ch. 22:3] [n]Num. 32:41 [o]Deut. 3:4
18 [p]ch. 1:8
19 [q]Deut. 3:8-10
20 [r]Gen. 22:17; [ch. 3:8; 2 Chr. 1:9]
21 [s]2 Chr. 9:26 [t]Gen. 15:18; Ex. 23:31; Josh. 1:4; Ps. 72:8

4:12 One of the earliest Hebrew inscriptions, found at Khirbet Raddana and dating to the twelfth century B.C., is a jar handle bearing the words "belonging to **Ahilud**."

4:20 Judah and Israel . . . ate . . . drank . . . were happy. Solomon's God-given wisdom has produced an economic system which, while it ensures that the royal household has enough to eat and drink, is not oppressive. This is true even though the people are **as many as the sand by the sea** (cf. Gen. 22:17; and note Solomon's concern in 1 Kings 3:8–9 that he would not be able to govern so many people). This is government by the righteous person under the blessing of God: when their leader thrives, the people rejoice (Prov. 29:2).

4:21–34 *Solomon and the Nations.* Israel's peace and prosperity is based in part on Solomon's dominion over the surrounding kingdoms (they contribute

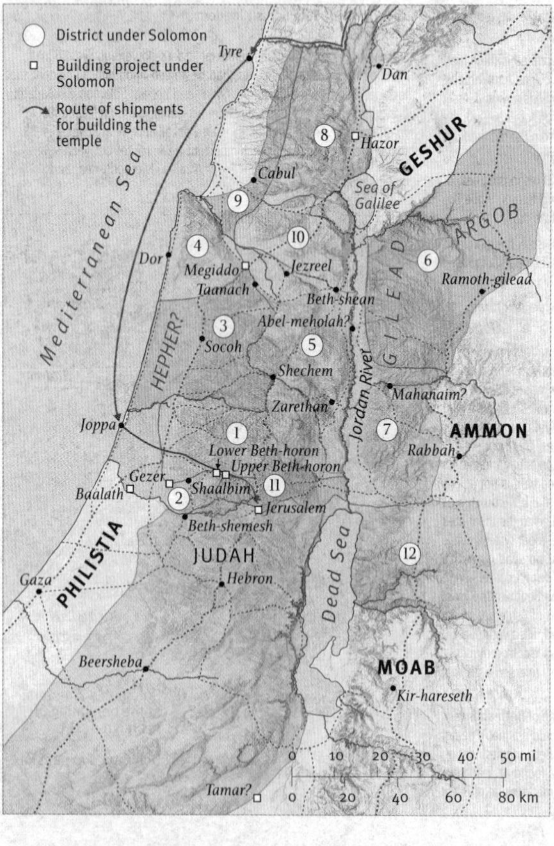

Solomon's Administrative Districts
c. 950 B.C.
Solomon reorganized the Israelite territory of his kingdom into 12 districts, each of which was responsible to supply the immense provisions for the king for one month out of the year. It appears that Judah, Solomon's tribe, was exempted from this burden. Solomon also fortified key towns throughout his kingdom and built store cities for his economic enterprises. Among his most significant building projects were the temple and his royal palace in Jerusalem, built largely with cedar supplied by King Hiram of Tyre.

Philistines and to the border of Egypt. [u]They brought tribute and served Solomon all the
days of his life.
22 Solomon's provision for one day was thirty cors[1] of fine flour and sixty cors of meal, 23 ten
fat oxen, and twenty pasture-fed cattle, a hundred sheep, besides deer, gazelles, roebucks,
and fattened fowl. 24 For he had dominion over all the region west of the Euphrates[2] from
Tiphsah to [v]Gaza, over all the kings west of the Euphrates. [w]And he had peace on all sides
around him. 25 And Judah and Israel [x]lived in safety, [y]from Dan even to Beersheba, [z]every
man under his vine and under his fig tree, all the days of Solomon. 26 [a]Solomon also had
40,000[3] stalls of horses for his chariots, and 12,000 horsemen. 27 And those officers supplied
provisions for King Solomon, and for all who came to King Solomon's table, each one in
his month. They let nothing be lacking. 28 Barley also and straw for the horses and [b]swift
steeds they brought to the place where it was required, each according to his duty.
29 [c]And God gave Solomon wisdom and understanding beyond measure, and breadth of
mind [d]like the sand on the seashore, 30 so that Solomon's wisdom surpassed the wisdom of
all [e]the people of the east [f]and all the wisdom of Egypt. 31 For he was [c]wiser than all other
men, wiser than Ethan the Ezrahite, and Heman, Calcol, and Darda, the sons of Mahol,
and his fame was in all the surrounding nations. 32 [g]He also spoke 3,000 proverbs, [h]and
his songs were 1,005. 33 He spoke of trees, from the cedar that is in Lebanon to the hyssop
that grows out of the wall. He spoke also of beasts, and of birds, and of reptiles, and of
fish. 34 And people of all nations came to hear the wisdom of Solomon, and from [i]all the
kings of the earth, who had heard of his wisdom.

Preparations for Building the Temple

5 [4] Now [j]Hiram king of Tyre sent his servants to Solomon when he heard that they had
anointed him king in place of his father, [k]for Hiram always loved David. 2 And Solomon
sent word to Hiram, 3 [l]"You know that David my father could not build a house for the

[1] A *cor* was about 6 bushels or 220 liters [2] Hebrew *the River;* twice in this verse [3] Hebrew; one Hebrew manuscript (see 2 Chron. 9:25 and Septuagint of 1 Kings 10:26) *4,000* [4] Ch 5:15 in Hebrew

21 [u]Ps. 68:29; 72:10, 11
24 [v]Gen. 10:19 [w]1 Chr. 22:9
25 [x]Jer. 23:6; 32:37; Ezek. 28:26 [y]See 2 Sam. 3:10 [z]Mic. 4:4; Zech. 3:10; [2 Kgs. 18:31; Isa. 36:16]
26 [a][ch. 10:26; 2 Chr. 1:14; 9:25]
28 [b]Esth. 8:10, 14; Mic. 1:13
29 [c]ch. 3:12 [d][ver. 20]
30 [e]Judg. 6:3 [f]Acts 7:22; [Isa. 19:11]
31 [c][See ver. 29 above]
32 [g]Prov. 1:1; Eccles. 12:9 [h]Song 1:1
34 [i]2 Chr. 9:23; [ch. 10:1]

Chapter 5

1 [j][2 Chr. 2:3] [k]2 Sam. 5:11; 1 Chr. 14:1
3 [l]For ver. 3-11, see 2 Chr. 2:3-16

to the prosperity and represent no threat to the peace, vv. 21–28). Solomon's wisdom is admired throughout the world (vv. 29–34).

4:21–24 Solomon exerted a dominating influence **over all the kingdoms from the Euphrates to the land of the Philistines and to the border of Egypt**, an area further defined as extending from **Tiphsah** (an important city on the Euphrates, about 75 miles [121 km] south of Carchemish on the main trade route connecting Mesopotamia with Syria) to **Gaza** (on the western coast of Palestine, in the far south of Philistia). It is a large area, corresponding to the ideal extent of Israel's dominion as promised to Abraham in Gen. 15:18.

4:25 And Judah and Israel lived in safety . . . every man under his vine and under his fig tree. The people lived under God's blessing (cf. Joel 2:22; contrast Ps. 105:33; Jer. 5:17), having a degree of economic independence—somewhat akin to living in the kingdom of the "last days" foreseen by the prophet Micah, when swords will be beaten into plowshares and every man will have a stake in the land (Mic. 4:1–4).

4:26 40,000 stalls of horses. Based on the available OT source documents, the number of stalls is uncertain. Although most Hebrew manuscripts place the number at 40,000, a Greek Septuagint manuscript and one Hebrew manuscript place the number at 4,000, which is also the number indicated in 2 Chron. 9:25; hence the number here could possibly be a copying error. See ESV footnote. (Cf. the 1,400 chariots in 1 Kings 10:26, which would suggest fewer than 40,000 horse stalls.) In either case, such a large number of stalls (even 4,000) would violate the prohibition in Deut. 17:16 that the king "must not acquire many horses for himself." Tripartite pillared buildings have been unearthed at numerous Iron Age sites—Megiddo, Hazor, Beth-shemesh, and elsewhere. Each unit has a central hall flanked by two parallel aisles, separated by rows of pillars. These buildings have been identified by numerous scholars as "stalls" or stables (although some argue they are storehouses, army barracks, or bazaars) and, indeed, some of them date to the time of Solomon.

4:28 horses and swift steeds. The darker side of Solomon is once again hinted at (see also v. 26), even in the midst of the glories of the early part of his reign. Deuteronomy 17:16 forbids the king from acquiring "many horses for himself" and forbids him further from making the people "return to Egypt in order to acquire many horses" (Deut. 17:16; cf. 1 Kings 10:26–29).

4:30–31 the wisdom of all the people of the east . . . of Egypt. Solomon's wisdom exceeded that of people from places renowned for their wisdom, including "all the people of the east" (cf. Matt. 2:1–12). Egypt specifically provides many examples of wisdom literature (e.g., "The Wisdom of Amen-em-ope," which many OT scholars believe influenced Prov. 22:17–23:12). Solomon's wisdom was also greater than that of the named individuals famous for their wisdom.

4:33 He spoke of trees . . . beasts . . . birds . . . reptiles, and of fish. Careful observation of the natural world and how it works is one of the "normal" ways in which people gain wisdom (e.g., Job 38–41; Prov. 30:15–31; Matt. 6:25–34). Solomon was concerned with the natural world, from the largest tree (the proverbially high **cedar that is in Lebanon**) to the smallest plant (e.g., **hyssop**), and including all sorts of fauna. Wisdom "from below" (as here) and wisdom "from above" (as received by Solomon in 1 Kings 3) are thus combined in this one person, the wisest of all Israel's kings.

5:1–18 *Preparations for Building the Temple.* In the Hebrew text, these 18 verses form part of the same unit as the material on Solomon's rule over the surrounding kingdoms and his immense wisdom. The preparation for the building of the temple is thus part of the discourse about Solomon and the nations, and Hiram king of Tyre is simply one of those who "served Solomon all the days of his life" (4:21; cf. 9:19, where Lebanon is part of "all the land of his dominion").

5:1–6 At the site of 'Ain Dara in northern Syria, a temple has been found that dates to the thirteenth to eighth centuries B.C. It closely parallels the date, design, and size of Solomon's temple built in the tenth century B.C. This find helps corroborate the date of Solomon's temple in the early first millennium B.C. Cf. note on 7:1–12.

5:3–4 could not build a house. Solomon's response to Hiram's greeting takes Hiram back to that important moment in David's life (2 Sam. 7:1–17) when David was addressed by God, not only about the succession (which has just happened) but also about the temple (which has not yet been built). God has given Solomon the **rest on every side** that he had promised to David (2 Sam. 7:11), so much so that **there is neither adversary nor misfortune**. This picture reflects God's intended result when the people of

name of the LORD his God [m]because of the warfare with which his enemies surrounded
him, until the LORD put them under the soles of his feet. **4** [n]But now the LORD my God has
given me rest on every side. There is neither adversary nor misfortune. **5** And so I intend
to build a house for the name of the LORD my God, [o]as the LORD said to David my father,
'Your son, whom I will set on your throne in your place, shall build the house for my name.'
6 Now therefore command that cedars of Lebanon be cut for me. And my servants will join
your servants, and I will pay you for your servants such wages as you set, for you know that
there is no one among us who knows how to cut timber like the Sidonians."

7 As soon as Hiram heard the words of Solomon, he rejoiced greatly and said, "Blessed
be the LORD this day, who has given to David a wise son to be over this great people."
8 And Hiram sent to Solomon, saying, "I have heard the message that you have sent to me.
I am ready to do all you desire in the matter of cedar and cypress timber. **9** My servants
shall bring it down to the sea from Lebanon, and I will make it into rafts to go by sea to
the place you direct. And I will have them broken up there, and you shall receive it. And
you shall meet my wishes [p]by providing food for my household." **10** So Hiram supplied
Solomon with all the timber of cedar and cypress that he desired, **11** while Solomon gave
Hiram 20,000 cors[1] of wheat as food for his household, and 20,000[2] cors of beaten oil.
Solomon gave this to Hiram year by year. **12** And the LORD gave Solomon wisdom, [q]as he
promised him. And there was peace between Hiram and Solomon, and the two of them
made a treaty.

13 King Solomon drafted [r]forced labor out of all Israel, and the draft numbered 30,000
men. **14** And he sent them to Lebanon, 10,000 a month in shifts. They would be a month
in Lebanon and two months at home. [s]Adoniram was in charge of the draft. **15** Solomon
also [t]had 70,000 burden-bearers and 80,000 stonecutters in the hill country, **16** besides
Solomon's 3,300 [u]chief officers who were over the work, [v]who had charge of the people
who carried on the work. **17** At the king's command [w]they quarried out great, costly stones
in order to lay the foundation of the house with dressed stones. **18** So Solomon's builders
and Hiram's builders and [x]the men of Gebal did the cutting and prepared the timber and
the stone to build the house.

Solomon Builds the Temple

6 [y]In the four hundred and eightieth year after the people of Israel came out of the land
of Egypt, in the fourth year of Solomon's reign over Israel, in the month of Ziv, which
is the second month, [z]he began to build the house of the LORD. **2** [a]The house that King
Solomon built for the LORD was sixty cubits[3] long, twenty cubits wide, and thirty cubits
high. **3** The vestibule in front of the nave of the house was twenty cubits long, equal to

[1] A *cor* was about 6 bushels or 220 liters [2] Septuagint; Hebrew *twenty* [3] A *cubit* was about 18 inches or 45 centimeters

3 [m]1 Chr. 22:8; 28:3
4 [n][ch. 4:24; 1 Chr. 22:9]
5 [o]2 Sam. 7:13; 1 Chr. 17:12; 22:10; 28:6
9 [p][Ezra 3:7; Ezek. 27:17; Acts 12:20]
12 [q]ch. 3:12
13 [r]ch. 4:6; 9:15
14 [s]See ch. 4:6
15 [t]2 Chr. 2:18; [ch. 9:20-22]
16 [u]ch. 4:5 [v]ch. 9:23
17 [w][ch. 6:7; 1 Chr. 22:2]
18 [x]Josh. 13:5; Ezek. 27:9

Chapter 6

1 [y]2 Chr. 3:1, 2 [z]Acts 7:47
2 [a]2 Chr. 3:3, 4; See Ezek. 40–42

Israel have a wise ruler and they walk in obedience to God's commandments. Given this situation, the time is right for the temple-building project, divinely ordained as the task for David's successor (2 Sam. 7:12–13).

5:5 build the house for my name. Cf. 2 Sam. 7:13.

5:6 Sidonians is a general term for the Phoenicians, famous for their expertise in **timber**. Sidon, like Tyre, was on the Phoenician coast, south of what is now Beirut. **my servants will join your servants . . . such wages as you set.** Solomon suggests to Hiram a cooperative venture and, possibly (although the Hb. is ambiguous), that Hiram should set the wages to be paid to his men.

5:7–8 Blessed be the LORD. A Gentile recognizes God's blessing on his **great people**, Israel.

5:9–12 My servants shall bring it down. Hiram responds with proposals of his own—that his own men alone should deal with cutting the wood and transporting it down the coast to Israel, and that Solomon's men should be involved only after this has been done. The wages, moreover, are to be paid not to his laborers, but in the form of supplies of **food for his** royal **household**. Solomon thus gets what he desires (Hb. *khepets*, vv. 8, 10), in the materials for the temple, but Hiram, too, has his **wishes** (Hb. *khepets*, v. 9) for provisions fulfilled. It is apparently a happy arrangement, sealed by a **treaty**—an arrangement that is testimony to the **wisdom** that God has given to Solomon. Yet nothing has been said about Hiram's *first* counterproposal to Solomon concerning work methods (v. 9); the narrative proceeds as if he had not spoken, as a task force from Israel is dispatched to Lebanon "in shifts" to help with the timber (v. 14). Although he is happy to negotiate with Hiram to a certain extent, Solomon is also prepared to ignore terms that do not suit him. This clearly implies that Solomon has the upper hand in the relationship, something that becomes even more apparent in 9:10–10:29.

5:13 Solomon drafted forced labor out of all Israel. First Kings 9:15–23 makes it clear that Solomon did not conscript *Israelites* to work abroad, but only workers from the *Canaanite* population of Israel. Two quite distinct groups are intended in 5:13–18 and 9:15–23. The first comprises **30,000** Canaanites and is supervised by 550 officials; the other comprises 150,000 Israelites and is supervised by 3,300 foremen.

5:14 at home. The Hebrew *bebeto*, "in his house," likely refers to Solomon's house or palace, the construction of which will be described in ch. 7. Even at this stage, the authors hint, Solomon is spending twice as much time on his palace ("house") as on the temple (cf. 6:38–7:1), while appearing to press quickly ahead with the temple.

5:17–18 Dressed stones probably describes ashlar masonry, a prominent feature of royal Israelite architecture. Fine examples of ashlar masonry may be seen at Megiddo (10th–9th centuries B.C.), Gezer (10th century), Tel Dan, Ramet Rahel, and elsewhere. The actual quarries for ashlar blocks have been found at Megiddo and Samaria.

4 [b]Ezek. 40:16; 41:16, 26
5 [c]Ezek. 41:6 [d]ver. 16, 19, 20, 23, 31; ch. 7:49; 8:6, 8; 2 Chr. 4:20; 5:7, 9; Ps. 28:2 [e]Ezek. 41:5, 6
7 [f]ch. 5:18; Deut. 27:5, 6
9 [g]ver. 14, 38
12 [h]ch. 9:4; [ch. 2:4] [i]2 Sam. 7:13; 1 Chr. 22:10
13 [j]Ex. 25:8 [k]Deut. 31:6, 8; Josh. 1:5

the width of the house, and ten cubits deep in front of the house. 4 And [b]he made for the
house windows with recessed frames.[1] 5 [c]He also built a structure[2] against the wall of the
house, running around the walls of the house, both the nave and [d]the inner sanctuary. And
he made [e]side chambers all around. 6 The lowest story[3] was five cubits broad, the middle
one was six cubits broad, and the third was seven cubits broad. For around the outside of
the house he made offsets on the wall in order that the supporting beams should not be
inserted into the walls of the house.

7 When the house was built, [f]it was with stone prepared at the quarry, so that neither
hammer nor axe nor any tool of iron was heard in the house while it was being built.

8 The entrance for the lowest[4] story was on the south side of the house, and one went
up by stairs to the middle story, and from the middle story to the third. 9 [g]So he built the
house and finished it, and he made the ceiling of the house of beams and planks of cedar.
10 He built the structure against the whole house, five cubits high, and it was joined to the
house with timbers of cedar.

11 Now the word of the LORD came to Solomon, 12 "Concerning this house that you are
building, [h]if you will walk in my statutes and obey my rules and keep all my commandments and walk in them, then I will establish my word with you, [i]which I spoke to David
your father. 13 And [j]I will dwell among the children of Israel [k]and will not forsake my
people Israel."

[1] Or *blocked lattice windows* [2] Or *platform*; also verse 10 [3] Septuagint; Hebrew *structure*, or *platform* [4] Septuagint, Targum; Hebrew *middle*

5:18 The **men of Gebal** are workers from Byblos, a coastal city north of Tyre.

6:1–7:51 *Solomon Builds the Temple and His Palace.* With preparation for the temple building complete, the narrative moves on to a detailed description of the building itself and its furnishings, interrupted in 7:1–12 by a description of the building of the royal palace complex. The authors seem to suggest that Solomon's concern for his own house delayed the completion of the temple.

6:1–10 he began to build the house of the LORD. After a note about the dates involved (v. 1), the description of the temple begins with its external structure. The authors describe its overall proportions and its basic form (vv. 2–3); its **windows** (v. 4); and the strange structure around it with its **side chambers** (vv. 5–6, 8, 10). The work was carried out with reverence, avoiding the use of iron tools at the temple site: **neither hammer nor axe nor any tool of iron** (see Ex. 20:25 and Deut. 27:5–6 for the prohibitions that appear to be in mind here). The dimensions of the temple in common cubits were 90 feet (27 m) long, 30 feet (9 m) wide, and 45 feet (14 m) high (see illustration, pp. 604–605).

6:1 The **four hundred and eightieth year** after Israel's release from slavery and the **fourth year of Solomon's reign** over Israel was around the year 966 B.C. This text is important in relation to the date of Israel's exodus from Egypt. Taken at face value, the figure of 480 years would support the traditional "early" date for the exodus, c. 1446 B.C. On the other hand, if one allows for some symbolism in understanding the 480-year figure (e.g., supposing it to result from 12 generations, with a generation taken symbolically to be 40 years, although it is actually about 25), one would arrive at a "late" date for the exodus of about 1260 B.C. (which some feel allows for greater agreement with Egyptian history). For further discussion concerning the date of the exodus, see The Date of the Exodus, p. 33.

6:12–13 Concerning this house that you are building. The temple is placed firmly in its proper theological context. God will certainly **dwell among** his people once the temple is built (v. 13), but this "dwelling" will be on the same basis as before: the people's obedience to the law (cf. Lev. 26:11–12). The temple itself, for all its splendor, does not change anything about the nature of the divine-human relationship. This was something that the Israelites were apt to forget after the temple had been built and had become a centrally important aspect of national life (cf. Jer. 7:1–34). God is not as impressed with structures as he is with obedience, a point made later by Stephen in his speech to the Sanhedrin in Acts 7; and the beauty of temples is never any guarantee that God will not leave them or bring judgment on them (cf. Luke 21:5–6).

Jerusalem at the Time of Solomon
c. 950 B.C.

Through various building projects Solomon began to transform the small military stronghold of the city of David into a full-scale city that would be the geographical center of Israelite religion. He built the temple of the Lord and the royal palace complex on the hill to the north of the stronghold and encircled it with a wall. Ironically, Solomon also allowed his many foreign wives to establish pagan shrines on the hill to the east of the city, which would later be called the Mount of Corruption.

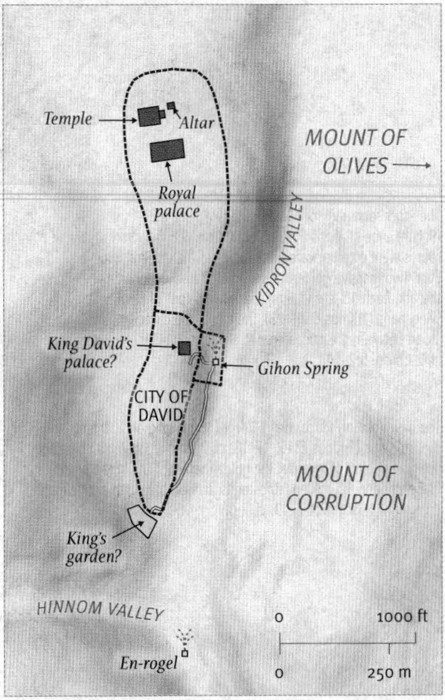

A structure with three levels was built around the walls of the temple. The lower chamber was 7.5 feet (2.3 m) wide, the middle chamber was 9 feet (2.7 m) wide, and the upper chamber was 10.5 feet (3.2 m) wide (1 Kings 6:5–6, 8, 10).
Two ornate wooden doors, overlaid with gold, separated the inner sanctuary from the nave (1 Kings 6:31–32).
The nave had clerestory windows with recessed frames (1 Kings 6:4).
The inner sanctuary (or Most Holy Place) was a 30-foot (9.1-m) cube (1 Kings 6:15–29; 2 Chron. 3:8–14). Such rooms were often elevated in temples of the ancient Near East. Two massive golden cherubim stood on either side of the ark, each 15 feet (4.6 m) tall with 15-foot (4.6-m) wingspans (1 Kings 6:23–28). The ark of the covenant stood between the two cherubim (1 Kings 8:1–11; cf. 2 Chron. 5:2–14).
The nave (or Holy Place) was 60 feet (18 m) long and 30 feet (9.1 m) wide (1 Kings 6:15, 17–18; cf. 2 Chron. 3:5–7). It contained the golden altar of incense; the golden table for the bread of the Presence; and 10 golden lampstands, five on the north and five on the south (1 Kings 7:48–49; cf. 2 Chron. 4:7).
Ten bronze wheeled stands, each holding a large basin, contained water for rinsing off the animal parts that were used for the burnt offerings (1 Kings 7:27–38; cf. 2 Chron. 4:6).

The vestibule was 30 feet (9.1 m) wide and 15 feet (4.6 m) deep (1 Kings 6:3; cf. 2 Chron. 3:4).
Temple Architectural Plan
N
0 10 20 30 40 ft
0 5 10 m
The hollow bronze pillar on the north was called "Boaz," and the one on the south was called "Jachin" (1 Kings 7:21; cf. 2 Chron. 3:17).
The bronze altar for burnt offerings was 15 feet (4.6 m) high and 30 feet (9.1 m) long and wide (cf. 2 Chron. 4:1).
Two ornate wooden, folding doors, overlaid with gold, separated the nave from the vestibule (1 Kings 6:33–35).
The "sea" was a metal basin 7.5 feet (2.3 m) high and 15 feet (4.6 m) in diameter. It held 12,000 gallons (44,000 liters) of water for the priests to wash in. It was supported by 12 bronze oxen in sets of three, facing in each direction (1 Kings 7:23–26; cf. 2 Chron. 4:2–5).

SOLOMON'S TEMPLE

Solomon began to build "the house of the LORD" in Jerusalem on Mount Moriah in the spring of 967 or 966 B.C. (1 Kings 6:1; 2 Chron. 3:1–2) and completed it seven years later, in the fall of 960 or 959 (1 Kings 6:38). The temple itself, not including the surrounding chambers on three sides, was 90 feet (27 m) long, 30 feet (9 m) wide, and 45 feet (14 m) high. It stood in the middle of a court with boundary walls.

14 [l]So Solomon built the house and finished it. 15 He lined the walls of the house on
the inside with boards of cedar. From the floor of the house to the walls of the ceiling,
he covered them on the inside with wood, [m]and he covered the floor of the house with
boards of cypress. 16 [n]He built twenty cubits of the rear of the house with boards of cedar
from the floor to the walls, and he built this within as an inner sanctuary, as [o]the Most
Holy Place. 17 The house, that is, the nave in front of the inner sanctuary, was forty cubits
long. 18 The cedar within the house was carved in the form of [p]gourds and open flowers.
All was cedar; no stone was seen. 19 The inner sanctuary he prepared in the innermost
part of the house, to set there the ark of the covenant of the LORD. 20 The inner sanctuary[1]
was twenty cubits long, twenty cubits wide, and twenty cubits high, and he overlaid it
with pure gold. He also overlaid[2] an altar of cedar. 21 And Solomon overlaid the inside
of the house with pure gold, and he drew chains of gold across, in front of the inner
sanctuary, and overlaid it with gold. 22 And he overlaid the whole house with gold, until
all the house was finished. [q]Also the whole altar that belonged to the inner sanctuary he
overlaid with gold.

23 [r]In the inner sanctuary [s]he made two cherubim of olivewood, each ten cubits high.
24 Five cubits was the length of one wing of the cherub, and five cubits the length of the
other wing of the cherub; it was ten cubits from the tip of one wing to the tip of the other.
25 The other cherub also measured ten cubits; both cherubim had the same measure and
the same form. 26 The height of one cherub was ten cubits, and so was that of the other
cherub. 27 He put the cherubim in the innermost part of the house. [t]And the wings of the
cherubim were spread out so that a wing of one touched the one wall, and a wing of the
other cherub touched the other wall; their other wings touched each other in the middle
of the house. 28 And he overlaid the cherubim with gold.

29 Around all the walls of the house he carved engraved figures of cherubim and palm
trees and open flowers, in the inner and outer rooms. 30 The floor of the house he overlaid
with gold in the inner and outer rooms.

31 For the entrance to the inner sanctuary he made doors of olivewood; the lintel and
the doorposts were five-sided.[3] 32 He covered the two doors of olivewood with carvings of
cherubim, palm trees, and open flowers. He overlaid them with gold and spread gold on
the cherubim and on the palm trees.

33 So also he made for the entrance to the nave doorposts of olivewood, in the form of
a square, 34 and two doors of cypress wood. [u]The two leaves of the one door were folding, and the two leaves of the other door were folding. 35 On them he carved cherubim
and palm trees and open flowers, and he overlaid them with gold evenly applied on the
carved work. 36 [v]He built the inner court with three courses of cut stone and one course
of cedar beams.

37 [w]In the fourth year the foundation of the house of the LORD was laid, in the month
of Ziv. 38 And in the eleventh year, in the month of Bul, which is the eighth month, the
house was finished in all its parts, and according to all its specifications. He was seven
years in building it.

Solomon Builds His Palace

7 Solomon was [x]building his own house thirteen years, and he finished his entire
house.

2 He built [y]the House of the Forest of Lebanon. Its length was a hundred cubits[4] and
its breadth fifty cubits and its height thirty cubits, and it was built on four[5] rows of cedar
pillars, with cedar beams on the pillars. 3 And it was covered with cedar above the chambers
that were on the forty-five pillars, fifteen in each row. 4 There were window frames in three
rows, and window opposite window in three tiers. 5 All the doorways and windows[6] had
square frames, and window was opposite window in three tiers.

6 And he made [z]the Hall of Pillars; its length was fifty cubits, and its breadth thirty cubits.
There was a porch in front with pillars, and [a]a canopy in front of them.

[1] Vulgate; Hebrew *and before the inner sanctuary* [2] Septuagint *made* [3] The meaning of the Hebrew phrase is uncertain [4] A *cubit* was about 18 inches or 45 centimeters [5] Septuagint *three* [6] Septuagint; Hebrew *posts*

14 [l]ver. 9, 38
15 [m][ch. 7:7]
16 [n]2 Chr. 3:8 [o]ch. 7:50; 8:6; Ex. 26:33, 34; 2 Chr. 3:8; Ezek. 45:3; Heb. 9:3
18 [p]ch. 7:24
22 [q]Ex. 30:1, 3, 6
23 [r]For ver. 23-27, see 2 Chr. 3:10-12 [s]Ex. 37:7-9
27 [t]ch. 8:7; Ex. 25:20; 37:9; 2 Chr. 5:8
34 [u][Ezek. 41:24]
36 [v]ch. 7:12
37 [w]ver. 1

Chapter 7

1 [x]ch. 3:1; 9:10; 2 Chr. 8:1
2 [y]ch. 10:17, 21
6 [z][ver. 12] [a]Ezek. 41:25, 26

7[b]ch. 6:15, 16
8[c]ch. 3:1; 2 Chr. 8:11
12[d]ch. 6:36 [e][ver. 6]

7 And he made the Hall of the Throne where he was to pronounce judgment, even the
Hall of Judgment. [b]It was finished with cedar from floor to rafters.[1]
8 His own house where he was to dwell, in the other court back of the hall, was of like
workmanship. Solomon also made a house like this hall for Pharaoh's daughter [c]whom
he had taken in marriage.
9 All these were made of costly stones, cut according to measure, sawed with saws, back
and front, even from the foundation to the coping, and from the outside to the great court.
10 The foundation was of costly stones, huge stones, stones of eight and ten cubits. 11 And
above were costly stones, cut according to measurement, and cedar. 12 [d]The great court had
three courses of cut stone all around, and a course of cedar beams; so had the inner court
of the house of the LORD and [e]the vestibule of the house.

[1] Syriac, Vulgate; Hebrew *floor*

6:14–35 Solomon built the house and finished it. The repetition of v. 9a in v. 14 indicates a resumption of the main story line of vv. 1–10 after the digression of vv. 11–13, and also a change of focus. Now the *inside* of the temple is described. Most attention is paid to the **inner sanctuary** (vv. 16, 19–32), which is not surprising since it was the **Most Holy Place** (or "Holy of Holies") where the **ark of the covenant** was to be placed (v. 19). Compared to this place, the other parts of the temple were less significant, and they receive only the limited attention due them—although there is much interest in the splendor of the decoration. It was within the inner sanctuary that the Lord sat, enthroned on the **cherubim** (v. 23; see 1 Sam. 4:4; Ps. 80:1; 99:1). These were strange, winged creatures that could take various specific forms, combining features of different known earthly creatures, somewhat akin to the multifaceted beasts of Assyrian art. Cherubim thrones are well attested in Syria-Palestine. These particular Jerusalem **cherubim** dominated the sanctuary, reaching halfway to its ceiling and all the way across from wall to wall.

6:14–22 An inscribed ivory pomegranate has been found that was thought to have come from Solomon's temple in Jerusalem. The inscription reads, "Belonging to the temple of Yahweh, holy to the priests." However, the pomegranate is unprovenanced and first came to the attention of scholars after being found in an antiquities shop in Jerusalem. At the time of writing, scholars are undecided whether or not it is a forgery. The authenticity of the ivory pomegranate is not in doubt, but that of the inscription has yet to be determined.

6:36 Having toured the interior of the temple, the reader is again outside in the **inner court** that stands before it.

6:38–7:1 the house was finished. The Hebrew is "he completed [*kalah*] the temple [*bayit*]," and it is followed by: "he spent seven years building it [*banah*]. But his own house [*bayit*] Solomon spent thirteen years building [*banah*]; and he completed [*kalah*] the whole of his house [*kol* + *bayit*]." Two "houses" are in view here, and an emphatic contrast is being made between them. Solomon spent much more time building his own house or palace complex than he did building God's house, another indication of his divided heart. The likely emphasis of 7:1 is in fact as follows: "But his *own* house Solomon spent thirteen years building; and he completed the *whole* of *his* house." The temple is not really "complete" until all the work on its interior is complete and it is being worshiped in; and this is not the case until 7:51.

7:1–12 The only evidence for Solomon's palace complex (see illustration to the right) comes from the Bible. It appears to have been built according to the plan of a neo-Hittite palace type called a *bit hilani* (Hb.). This type of palace has been found in northern Syria at the sites of Tell Ta'yinat and Zinjirli. Cf. note on 5:1–6.

7:2–5 The House of the Forest of Lebanon, just the first of the several buildings of the palace complex, was much bigger than the temple (cf. 6:2). The temple had quite a bit of **cedar** of Lebanon in it (6:9–10, 15–16, 18, 20, 36); this building, however, had so much cedar (7:2–3, 7, 11, 12) that it could be named after the forest from which the cedar came—even though it was apparently designed only as a treasury or armory (cf. 10:17, 21; Isa. 22:8). This confirms that the king was much more concerned about his palace than about the Lord's temple.

7:6–12 the Hall of Pillars. The remaining buildings that formed part of the complex are described. Besides "the Hall of Pillars," which was almost

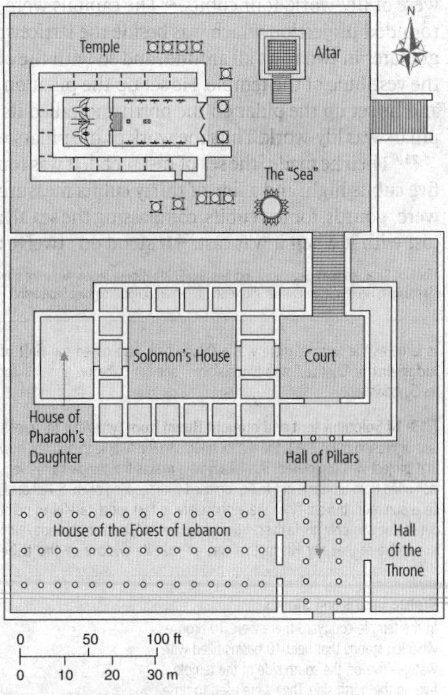

Solomon's Temple and Palace Complex

To get to the new quarter that Solomon built from the old city of David, one had to pass through the gate in the northern Davidic city wall. Going in a northerly direction, the new complex consisted of an entrance hall, the so-called Hall of Pillars (1 Kings 7:6); the House of the Forest of Lebanon (7:2–5); the porch (7:6b); the king's house (7:8a); and the house of his wife, Pharaoh's daughter (7:8b).

The House of the Forest of Lebanon, shown here to the west of the Hall of Pillars, served as an armory. The main hall had rows of cedar pillars, and gold shields and targets hung on its walls (10:16–17). To the east of the Hall of Pillars was the porch, or Hall of the Throne, Solomon's place of judgment. Beyond the Hall of Pillars lay Solomon's palace. Here is the setting which so impressed the Queen of Sheba on her visit to King Solomon (1 Kings 10).

There are parallels between this palace complex and the contemporary palaces of northern Syria, with the order of the parts of the building in 1 Kings 7 corresponding to the order of the units in these palaces.

The Temple Furnishings

13 And King Solomon sent and brought [f]Hiram from Tyre. 14 He was the son of a widow
of the tribe of Naphtali, and his father was a man of Tyre, a worker in bronze. And [g]he
was full of wisdom, understanding, and skill for making any work in bronze. He came to
King Solomon and did all his work.

15 [h]He cast [i]two pillars of bronze. [j]Eighteen cubits was the height of one pillar, and a
line of twelve cubits measured its circumference. It was hollow, and its thickness was four
fingers. The second pillar was the same.[1] 16 He also made two capitals of cast bronze to set
on the tops of the pillars. The height of the one capital was five cubits, and [j]the height of
the other capital was five cubits. 17 There were lattices of checker work with wreaths of
chain work for the capitals on the tops of the pillars, a lattice[2] for the one capital and a
lattice for the other capital. 18 Likewise he made pomegranates[3] in two rows around the one
latticework to cover the capital that was on the top of the pillar, and he did the same with
the other capital. 19 Now the capitals that were on the tops of the pillars in the vestibule
were of lily-work, four cubits. 20 The capitals were on the two pillars and also above the
rounded projection which was beside the latticework. There were [k]two hundred pomegranates in two rows all around, and so with the other capital. 21 [l]He set up the pillars at
the vestibule of the temple. He set up the pillar on the south and called its name Jachin,
and he set up the pillar on the north and called its name Boaz. 22 And on the tops of the
pillars was lily-work. Thus the work of the pillars was finished.

23 [m]Then he made [n]the sea of cast metal. It was round, ten cubits from brim to brim, and
five cubits high, and a line of thirty cubits measured its circumference. 24 Under its brim
were [o]gourds, for ten cubits, compassing the sea all around. The gourds were in two rows,
cast with it when it was cast. 25 It stood on [p]twelve oxen, three facing north, three facing

[1] Targum, Syriac (compare Septuagint and Jeremiah 52:21); Hebrew *fingers. And a line of twelve cubits measured the circumference of the second pillar*
[2] Septuagint; Hebrew *seven*; twice in this verse [3] Two manuscripts (compare Septuagint); Hebrew *pillars*

13 [f][2 Chr. 2:14]
14 [g][Ex. 31:3-5; 35:31]
15 [h]For ver. 15-21, see 2 Chr. 3:15-17 [i]2 Kgs. 25:17; 1 Chr. 18:8; 2 Chr. 4:12; Jer. 52:21-23 [j]ver. 41
16 [j][See ver. 15 above]
20 [k][ver. 42; 2 Chr. 3:16; 4:13; Jer. 52:23]
21 [l]2 Chr. 3:17
23 [m]For ver. 23-26, see 2 Chr. 4:2-5 [n]2 Kgs. 16:17; 25:13; 1 Chr. 18:8; Jer. 52:17; [Ex. 30:18]
24 [o][ch. 6:18]
25 [p]Jer. 52:20

as large as the temple, there was a throne hall, also called the **Hall of Judgment** or "Justice," and two palaces, one for Solomon and one for his Egyptian wife.

7:13–14 Solomon sent and brought Hiram from Tyre. After the important digression of vv. 1–12, the author returns to the temple to describe how that project was completed. This Hiram who makes the temple furnishings fashioned from bronze is not to be confused with the king of ch. 5. Although he is summoned from Tyre, the authors are in fact most careful to point out that it was only his **father**, from whom he had learned his trade, who is a native of that city. His mother was an Israelite **widow of the tribe of Naphtali** in the far north of the country, near the Phoenician coast. Therefore, Hiram, who had one Jewish parent, was not simply a Gentile with no Israelite roots. He is described in a way reminiscent of a famous Israelite with a similar job to do, Bezalel son of Uri, the chief craftsman involved in the construction of the tabernacle (Ex. 31:1–11; 35:30–35). Both men are said to be **full of wisdom, understanding, and skill** with regard to **work in bronze**.

7:15–21 two pillars of bronze. Two massive pillars, called **Jachin** and **Boaz** (v. 21), were positioned at the temple entrance, and along with their **capitals** stood 27 cubits (40 feet/12 m), almost as high as the temple itself

Bronze Basins and Stands

In the temple courtyard there were 10 bronze wheeled stands that held 10 basins filled with water—five on the south side of the temple, five on the north side. They were used to rinse off the animal parts that were used for the burnt offerings (1 Kings 7:27–38; 2 Chron. 4:6). Each stand was 6 feet (1.8 m) long, 6 feet (1.8 m) wide, and 4.5 feet (1.4 m) high. Each basin was 4.5 feet (1.4 m) in diameter and held 240 gallons (909 l) of water.

27[q] 2 Kgs. 25:13; 2 Chr. 4:14; Jer. 52:17
37[q] [See ver. 27 above]
38[r] 2 Chr. 4:6; [Ex. 30:18]
40[s] For ver. 40-51, see 2 Chr. 4:11–5:1 [t] Ex. 27:3; 38:3
41[u] ver. 17, 18
42[v] [ver. 20]
44[w] ver. 23, 25
45[x] Ex. 27:3; 38:3
46[y] Josh. 13:27 [z] Josh. 3:16
47[a] [1 Chr. 22:3, 14]
48[b] See Ex. 37:25-29

west, three facing south, and three facing east. The sea was set on them, and all their rear
parts were inward. **26** Its thickness was a handbreadth,[1] and its brim was made like the
brim of a cup, like the flower of a lily. It held two thousand baths.[2]

27 He also made the [q]ten stands of bronze. Each stand was four cubits long, four cubits
wide, and three cubits high. **28** This was the construction of the stands: they had panels,
and the panels were set in the frames, **29** and on the panels that were set in the frames were
lions, oxen, and cherubim. On the frames, both above and below the lions and oxen, there
were wreaths of beveled work. **30** Moreover, each stand had four bronze wheels and axles
of bronze, and at the four corners were supports for a basin. The supports were cast with
wreaths at the side of each. **31** Its opening was within a crown that projected upward one
cubit. Its opening was round, as a pedestal is made, a cubit and a half deep. At its opening
there were carvings, and its panels were square, not round. **32** And the four wheels were
underneath the panels. The axles of the wheels were of one piece with the stands, and the
height of a wheel was a cubit and a half. **33** The wheels were made like a chariot wheel; their
axles, their rims, their spokes, and their hubs were all cast. **34** There were four supports at
the four corners of each stand. The supports were of one piece with the stands. **35** And on
the top of the stand there was a round band half a cubit high; and on the top of the stand
its stays and its panels were of one piece with it. **36** And on the surfaces of its stays and on
its panels, he carved cherubim, lions, and palm trees, according to the space of each, with
wreaths all around. **37** After this manner he made [q]the ten stands. All of them were cast
alike, of the same measure and the same form.

38 And he made [r]ten basins of bronze. Each basin held forty baths, each basin measured
four cubits, and there was a basin for each of the ten stands. **39** And he set the stands, five
on the south side of the house, and five on the north side of the house. And he set the sea
at the southeast corner of the house.

40 [s]Hiram also made [t]the pots, the shovels, and the basins. So Hiram finished all the work
that he did for King Solomon on the house of the LORD: **41** the two pillars, the two bowls
of the capitals that were on the tops of the pillars, and the two [u]latticeworks to cover the
two bowls of the capitals that were on the tops of the pillars; **42** and the [v]four hundred
pomegranates for the two latticeworks, two rows of pomegranates for each latticework,
to cover the two bowls of the capitals that were on the pillars; **43** the ten stands, and the ten
basins on the stands; **44** and [w]the one sea, and the twelve oxen underneath the sea.

45 Now [x]the pots, the shovels, and the basins, all these vessels in the house of the LORD,
which Hiram made for King Solomon, were of burnished bronze. **46** In the plain of the
Jordan the king cast them, in the clay ground between [y]Succoth and [z]Zarethan. **47** And
Solomon left all the vessels unweighed, because there were so many of them; [a]the weight
of the bronze was not ascertained.

48 So Solomon made all the vessels that were in the house of the LORD: [b]the golden altar,

[1] A *handbreadth* was about 3 inches or 7.5 centimeters [2] A *bath* was about 6 gallons or 22 liters

(30 cubits [45 feet/14 m], according to 6:2). They may have been freestanding, though some temples from the ancient world had pillars supporting the roof of the porch. The pillars probably had double capitals: one with **latticework, five cubits** (7.5 feet/2.3 m) high (7:16; cf. 2 Chron. 3:15; Jer. 52:22), and the other with **lily-work, four cubits** (6 feet/1.8 m) high (1 Kings 7:19). When the temple was destroyed (2 Kings 25:17), however, there seems to have been only one 3-cubit (4.5-foot/1.4-m) capital of latticework, possibly from the renovations under Jehoash (2 Kings 12:6–16) or Josiah (2 Kings 22:3–7). Cf. note on 2 Chron. 3:15–17.

7:23–47 Cf. note on 2 Chron. 4:2–6. The **sea of cast metal** was a large metal basin designed to contain water, representing the forces of chaos subdued and brought to order by the Lord, who is Creator of the world (cf. Gen. 1:1–2:3; Ps. 74:12–17; 89:5–12; 93:1–5). Associated with the sea are **ten stands of bronze** (1 Kings 7:27), decorated with **lions, oxen, and cherubim** (v. 29), each designed to hold a **basin** smaller than the sea (vv. 30, 38). **Five** stands with their basins were placed **on the south side** of the temple along with the sea, and **five on the north** (v. 39). The **basins** of v. 40 are not those of vv. 38–39, but different utensils used in cleaning out the altar (cf. Ex. 27:3); the **pots** and **shovels** would also have been used for this purpose.

7:23 ten cubits from brim to brim . . . thirty cubits (in) **circumference**. The simplest explanation for these figures is that they are given in whole numbers, and are accurate to the degree of detail implied in such numbers. The authors were not trying to give a precise equivalent for pi (which for the ten-cubit diameter would yield a circumference of 31.46 cubits, or less if the diameter were a bit less than 10 cubits).

7:25 At Nimrud in Assyria was found a tiny ivory bull used to support a dish or tray on its top. It may have been an object of trade from Syria, and it was manufactured there in the eighth century B.C. It is reminiscent of the "sea of cast metal" that sat on 12 monumental metal oxen at the front of Solomon's temple.

7:48–51 Solomon made all the vessels. Hiram takes responsibility only for the work in bronze, while Solomon has charge of the work in **gold**. Hiram may himself have been "full of wisdom, understanding, and skill" (v. 14) and a worthy successor, to some extent, to Bezalel; but the authors are eager to portray Solomon as the one who preeminently embodies these qualities (cf. 3:4–15; 4:29).

[c]the golden table for [d]the bread of the Presence, **49** [e]the lampstands of pure gold, five on
the south side and five on the north, before the inner sanctuary; [f]the flowers, the lamps,
and the tongs, of gold; **50** the cups, snuffers, basins, dishes for incense, and [g]fire pans, of
pure gold; and the sockets of gold, for the doors of the innermost part of the house, [h]the
Most Holy Place, and for the doors of the nave of the temple.
51 Thus all the work that King Solomon did on the house of the LORD was finished. And
Solomon brought in [i]the things that David his father had dedicated, the silver, the gold,
and the vessels, and stored them in the treasuries of the house of the LORD.

The Ark Brought into the Temple

8 [j]Then Solomon assembled the elders of Israel and all the heads of the tribes, [k]the leaders of the fathers' houses of the people of Israel, before King Solomon in Jerusalem, [l]to
bring up the ark of the covenant of the LORD out of [m]the city of David, which is Zion. **2** And
all the men of Israel assembled to King Solomon at [n]the feast in the month Ethanim, which
is the seventh month. **3** And all the elders of Israel came, and [o]the priests took up the ark.
4 And they brought up the ark of the LORD, [p]the tent of meeting, and all the holy vessels
that were in the tent; the priests and the Levites brought them up. **5** And King Solomon
and all the congregation of Israel, who had assembled before him, were with him before
the ark, [q]sacrificing so many sheep and oxen that they could not be counted or numbered.
6 [r]Then the priests brought the ark of the covenant of the LORD [s]to its place in [t]the inner
sanctuary of the house, in the Most Holy Place, underneath the wings of the cherubim.
7 For the cherubim spread out their wings over the place of the ark, so that the cherubim
overshadowed the ark and its poles. **8** [u]And the poles were so long that the ends of the poles
were seen from the Holy Place before [t]the inner sanctuary; but they could not be seen from
outside. And they are there to this day. **9** There was nothing in the ark except [v]the two tablets
of stone that Moses put there at Horeb, where [w]the LORD made a covenant with the people
of Israel, when they came out of the land of Egypt. **10** And when the priests came out of the
Holy Place, [x]a cloud filled the house of the LORD, **11** so that the priests could not stand to
minister because of the cloud, for the glory of the LORD filled the house of the LORD.

Solomon Blesses the LORD

12 [y]Then Solomon said, "The LORD[1] has said that he would dwell [z]in thick darkness.
13 [a]I have indeed built you an exalted house, [b]a place for you to dwell in forever." **14** Then
the king turned around and [c]blessed all the assembly of Israel, while all the assembly of
Israel stood. **15** And he said, [d]"Blessed be the LORD, the God of Israel, who with his hand
has fulfilled [e]what he promised with his mouth to David my father, saying, **16** [f]'Since the
day that I brought my people Israel out of Egypt, I chose no city out of all the tribes of

[1] Septuagint *The LORD has set the sun in the heavens, but*

48 [c][2 Chr. 4:8]; See Ex. 37:10-16 [d]Ex. 25:30; See Lev. 24:5-8
49 [e]2 Chr. 4:7 [f]See Ex. 25:31-38
50 [g]Ex. 27:3 [h]See ch. 6:16
51 [i]2 Sam. 8:11

Chapter 8

1 [j]For ver. 1-9, see 2 Chr. 5:2-10 [k]Num. 1:16 [l][2 Sam. 6:17] [m]See 2 Sam. 5:7
2 [n]ver. 65; Lev. 23:34; See 2 Chr. 7:8-10
3 [o][Num. 4:15; Deut. 31:9; Josh. 3:3, 6; 1 Chr. 15:14, 15]
4 [p][ch. 3:4; 2 Chr. 1:3]
5 [q][2 Sam. 6:13]
6 [r]2 Sam. 6:17 [s]Ex. 26:33, 34 [t]See ch. 6:5
8 [u]Ex. 25:13-15 [t][See ver. 6 above]
9 [v]Ex. 25:21; 40:20; Deut. 10:2, 5; Heb. 9:4 [w]Ex. 34:27, 28; Deut. 4:13
10 [x]Ex. 40:34, 35; 2 Chr. 5:13, 14; 7:1, 2; [Ezek. 10:3, 4]
12 [y]For ver. 12-50, see 2 Chr. 6:1-39 [z]Ps. 18:11; 97:2; [Lev. 16:2]
13 [a]2 Sam. 7:13 [b]Ex. 15:17; [Ps. 132:14]
14 [c]ver. 55; 2 Sam. 6:18
15 [d]Luke 1:68 [e]ch. 6:12
16 [f]See 2 Sam. 7:4-16, 25

8:1–21 *The Ark Brought to the Temple.* The ark of the covenant of God, the great symbol of the Lord's presence with his people and the place where the tablets of the law were kept (Ex. 25:10–22; Deut. 10:1–5; Joshua 3–6), had hitherto remained in a tent sanctuary somewhere in the old city of David (2 Sam. 6:16–17; 7:2; 1 Kings 3:15), apart from the brief trip described in 2 Sam. 15:24–29. The temple was now ready to receive it.

8:2 the feast in . . . the seventh month is the Feast of Booths (cf. vv. 65–66; Lev. 23:33–43), during which the Israelites had been instructed to live in temporary shelters as a reminder of the exodus. It was observed in September/October.

8:3–4 the priests took up the ark. Not even the **elders of Israel** are safe in the immediate proximity of the ark (cf. Josh. 3:1–4; 2 Sam. 6:1–7), and only priests could have taken it right into the inner sanctuary (1 Kings 8:6) of the temple. The moving of the ark, along with the **tent of meeting** (i.e., the tabernacle), symbolized the moving of the "name" of the God of the exodus from a temporary to a more permanent dwelling (cf. 2 Sam. 7:6).

8:8 to this day. This phrase appears a number of times in 1–2 Kings when connections are being made between past and present (1 Kings 9:13, 21; 10:12; 12:19; 2 Kings 2:22; 8:22; 14:7; 16:6; 17:23, 34, 41; cf. also 2 Kings 10:27). Since the ark of the covenant had disappeared long before the period in which the books of Kings reached their final form, however, the phrase represents here a survival either from the source documents used when the books were put together or from an earlier (preexilic) version that was later expanded.

8:9 Though the ark had once contained the jar of manna and Aaron's rod (Heb. 9:4; see Ex. 16:32–34; Num. 17:10–11), there was now **nothing in the ark except the two tablets of stone** on which were written the Ten Commandments. "Nothing in the ark" may also anticipate the later observation that nothing on earth can "contain" the Lord (1 Kings 8:27). The ark was simply a witness to God's covenant and a symbol of his real presence; it could not contain him.

8:10 A **cloud** was often associated with God's appearing in the OT (e.g., Ex. 13:21–22; 16:10; 19:9), and a cloud also covered the tabernacle upon its completion in Ex. 40:34–38.

8:11 the priests could not stand to minister. The presence of the Lord was so powerful that the priests lost even the strength to stand. Cf. Ex. 40:35; Rev. 15:8.

8:12–13 The coming of the ark to the temple and the appearance of the cloud of God's glory are sure signs that the new worship arrangements have the divine blessing (notice the connection to the **thick darkness** in Ex. 20:21; Deut. 4:11; 5:22). The God of the exodus and Sinai has come **to dwell** in his temple.

Israel in which to build a house, [g]that my name might be there. [h]But I chose David to be
over my people Israel.' **17** [i]Now it was in the heart of David my father to build a house for
the name of the LORD, the God of Israel. **18** But the LORD said to David my father, 'Whereas
it was in your heart to build a house for my name, you did well that it was in your heart.
19 [j]Nevertheless, you shall not build the house, but your son who shall be born to you shall
build the house for my name.' **20** Now the LORD has fulfilled his promise that he made. For
I have risen in the place of David my father, and sit on the throne of Israel, [k]as the LORD
promised, and I have built the house for the name of the LORD, the God of Israel. **21** And
there I have provided a place for the ark, [l]in which is the covenant of the LORD that he
made with our fathers, when he brought them out of the land of Egypt."

Solomon's Prayer of Dedication

22 Then Solomon [m]stood before the altar of the LORD in the presence of all the assembly
of Israel and [n]spread out his hands toward heaven, **23** and said, "O LORD, God of Israel,
[o]there is no God like you, in heaven above or on earth beneath, [p]keeping covenant and
showing steadfast love to your servants who walk before you with all their heart; **24** you
have kept with your servant David my father what you declared to him. [e]You spoke with
your mouth, and with your hand have fulfilled it this day. **25** Now therefore, O LORD, God
of Israel, keep for your servant David my father what you have promised him, saying,
[q]'You shall not lack a man to sit before me on the throne of Israel, if only your sons pay
close attention to their way, to walk before me as you have walked before me.' **26** [r]Now
therefore, O God of Israel, let your word be confirmed, which you have spoken to your
servant David my father.

27 "But will God indeed dwell on the earth? Behold, [s]heaven and the highest heaven
cannot contain you; how much less this house that I have built! **28** Yet have regard to the
prayer of your servant and to his plea, O LORD my God, listening to the cry and to the
prayer that your servant prays before you this day, **29** [t]that your eyes may be open night
and day toward this house, the place of which you have said, [u]'My name shall be there,'
that you may listen to the prayer that your servant offers toward this place. **30** And listen
to the plea of your servant and of your people Israel, when they pray toward this place.
And listen in heaven your dwelling place, and when you hear, forgive.

31 "If a man sins against his neighbor and is made to take [v]an oath and comes and swears
his oath before your altar in this house, **32** then hear in heaven and act and judge your servants, [w]condemning the guilty by bringing his conduct on his own head, and vindicating
the righteous by rewarding him according to his righteousness.

33 [x]"When your people Israel are defeated before the enemy because they have sinned
against you, and [y]if they turn again to you and acknowledge your name and pray and plead

16 [g]ver. 29; Deut. 12:11 [h]1 Sam. 16:1; 2 Sam. 7:8; 1 Chr. 28:4
17 [i]2 Sam. 7:2, 3; 1 Chr. 17:1, 2
19 [j]ch. 5:3, 5; 2 Sam. 7:5, 12, 13
20 [k]1 Chr. 28:5, 6
21 [l]ver. 9; Deut. 31:26
22 [m]ver. 54; 2 Chr. 6:12, 13 [n][Ex. 9:33; Ezra 9:5; Isa. 1:15]
23 [o]Ex. 15:11; 2 Sam. 7:22 [p]See Deut. 7:9
24 [e][See ver. 15 above]
25 [q]See ch. 2:4
26 [r]2 Sam. 7:25
27 [s]2 Chr. 2:6; [Isa. 66:1; Jer. 23:24; Acts 7:49; 17:24]
29 [t]ver. 52; [2 Chr. 7:15; Neh. 1:6] [u]ver. 16; ch. 9:3; Deut. 12:11
31 [v][Ex. 22:11]
32 [w]Deut. 25:1
33 [x]Lev. 26:17; Deut. 28:45 [y]Lev. 26:40; [Neh. 1:9]

8:17 the name of the LORD. In Solomon's speech (vv. 16–20) and also in the prayer that follows (vv. 22–53), the word "name" is used to avoid saying that God himself actually dwells in the temple (cf. also 3:2; 5:3, 5). God's presence in the temple was real (for God's "name" represents all that he is; see note on Acts 10:48), and the people would get his attention by calling his name, but he was not to be thought of as "living" in the temple (as was imagined of the false gods of other nations) in any sense that would detract from the reality of his transcendence.

8:22–53 *Solomon's Prayer.* The ark of the covenant has arrived in the temple (vv. 1–13), and Solomon has addressed the people about the meaning of the event (vv. 14–21). He now turns to address God, reflecting on the nature of God's "dwelling" in the temple and offering a sevenfold petitionary prayer (each section involving a plea that God should "hear from heaven"; vv. 32, 34, 36, 39, 43, 45, 49) for those who will approach him in the temple. The prayer is important for understanding the books of Kings as a whole, for it places both the temple and the law in wider perspective. The temple is an important building, but God is not confined by a building and is certainly not dependent on it. He will survive even its destruction, and will hear his people's prayers when they go into exile. Likewise, obedience to the law is very important, but Solomon holds out hope for restoration, even when the people fail to obey.

8:24 In bringing the temple to completion, the Lord has **kept** the promise he **declared to** his **servant David**. Cf. 2 Sam. 7:13.

8:27–30 will God indeed dwell on the earth? Though God will dwell in the temple (vv. 10, 13; cf. note on 1 Sam. 4:3–4), it is not to be thought of as the only place where God is, but as a special place where his **name** is, a place toward which his **eyes** are **open** (1 Kings 8:29; cf. Isa. 66:1–3). The hearing of prayer is done **in heaven** (1 Kings 8:30), which is (if anywhere is) the **dwelling place** of God. Even then, however, God cannot be limited to any one place; he cannot, strictly speaking, dwell in even the **highest heaven** (v. 27). He cannot be confined by space.

8:31–32 If a man sins against his neighbor. This is the first of seven specific petitions. It concerns a legal case in which difficulties over evidence or witnesses make it impossible to resolve the case in any normal way (cf. 3:16–28). A priestly ritual is involved here (cf. Num. 5:11–31): God himself is invoked as judge to condemn the **guilty** and clear the **righteous** individual.

8:33–40 When your people Israel are defeated. The second, third, and fourth petitions concern defeat in battle, and subsequent exile from the **land** (vv. 33–34), drought (vv. 35–36), and assorted perils such as **famine**, **pestilence**, and siege (vv. 37–40). In each case the cause of the problem is sin, and the main requirement of the situation is forgiveness, although divine instruction is also requested (v. 36).

with you in this house, 34 then hear in heaven and forgive the sin of your people Israel and
bring them again to the land that you gave to their fathers.
35 [z]"When heaven is shut up and there is no rain because they have sinned against you,
if they pray toward this place and acknowledge your name and turn from their sin, when
you afflict them, 36 then hear in heaven and forgive the sin of your servants, your people
Israel, when [a]you teach them [b]the good way in which they should walk, and grant rain
upon your land, which you have given to your people as an inheritance.
37 [c]"If there is famine in the land, if there is pestilence or blight or mildew or locust
or caterpillar, if their enemy besieges them in the land at their gates,[1] whatever plague,
whatever sickness there is, 38 whatever prayer, whatever plea is made by any man or by all
your people Israel, each knowing the affliction of his own heart and stretching out his
hands toward this house, 39 then hear in heaven your dwelling place and forgive and act
and render to each whose heart you know, according to all his ways ([d]for you, you only,
know the hearts of all the children of mankind), 40 that they may fear you [e]all the days that
they live in the land that you gave to our fathers.
41 "Likewise, when a foreigner, who is not of your people Israel, comes from a far country
for your name's sake 42 (for they shall hear of your great name [f]and your mighty hand, and
of your outstretched arm), when he comes and prays toward this house, 43 hear in heaven
your dwelling place and do according to all for which the foreigner calls to you, in order
[g]that all the peoples of the earth may know your name and [h]fear you, as do your people
Israel, and that they may know that this house that I have built is called by your name.
44 "If your people go out to battle against their enemy, by whatever way you shall send
them, and they pray to the LORD [i]toward the city that you have chosen and the house
that I have built for your name, 45 then hear in heaven their prayer and their plea, and
maintain their cause.
46 "If they sin against you—[j]for there is no one who does not sin—and you are angry with
them and give them to an enemy, so that they are carried away captive [k]to the land of the
enemy, far off or near, 47 yet [l]if they turn their heart in the land to which they have been carried
captive, and repent and plead with you in the land of their captors, saying, [m]'We have sinned
and have acted perversely and wickedly,' 48 [n]if they repent with all their mind and with all
their heart in the land of their enemies, who carried them captive, and pray to you [o]toward
their land, which you gave to their fathers, the city that you have chosen, and the house that
I have built for your name, 49 then hear in heaven your dwelling place their prayer and their
plea, and maintain their cause 50 and forgive your people who have sinned against you, and all
their transgressions that they have committed against you, and [p]grant them compassion in
the sight of those who carried them captive, that they may have compassion on them 51 ([q]for
they are your people, and your heritage, which you brought out of Egypt, [r]from the midst
of the iron furnace). 52 [s]Let your eyes be open to the plea of your servant and to the plea of
your people Israel, giving ear to them whenever they call to you. 53 For you separated them
from among all the peoples of the earth to be your heritage, [t]as you declared through Moses
your servant, when you brought our fathers out of Egypt, O Lord GOD."

Solomon's Benediction

54 [u]Now as Solomon finished offering all this prayer and plea to the LORD, he arose
from before the altar of the LORD, where he had [v]knelt with hands outstretched toward

[1] Septuagint, Syriac *in any of their cities*

35 [z]Deut. 11:17; Luke 4:25; [Lev. 26:17; Deut. 28:25]
36 [a][Ps. 25:4; 27:11; 86:11] [b]1 Sam. 12:23
37 [c][Lev. 26:16, 25, 26; Deut. 28:21, 22, 37, 38, 42, 52; 2 Chr. 20:9]
39 [d]1 Chr. 28:9; Acts 1:24; [1 Sam. 16:7; Jer. 17:10]
40 [e]Deut. 12:1
42 [f]Deut. 3:24; 2 Chr. 6:32
43 [g]ver. 60; [Josh. 4:24] [h]Ps. 102:15
44 [i][ver. 48]
46 [j]Prov. 20:9; Eccles. 7:20; Rom. 3:23; James 3:2; 1 John 1:8, 10 [k]Lev. 26:34, 44; Deut. 28:36, 64
47 [l]Lev. 26:40 [m]Neh. 1:6; Ps. 106:6; Dan. 9:5
48 [n]1 Sam. 7:3; Jer. 29:12-14 [o]Dan. 6:10; [ver. 44; Ps. 5:7; Jonah 2:4]
50 [p]Ps. 106:46
51 [q]Deut. 9:29; [Neh. 1:10] [r]Deut. 4:20; Jer. 11:4
52 [s][ver. 29]
53 [t]Ex. 19:5, 6; Deut. 9:26, 29; 14:2
54 [u]2 Chr. 7:1 [v][2 Chr. 6:13]

8:41–43 The fifth petition turns from Israelites to the **foreigner** who has heard of the Lord's **great name**, **mighty hand**, and **outstretched arm** (Deut. 4:34; 5:15) and prays toward the temple. Solomon desires that this person, too, would know answered prayer and that **all the peoples of the earth** should **know** God's **name and fear** him (cf. Isa. 2:1–5; 56:6–8; Luke 7:1–10).

8:44–45 If your people go out to battle. The sixth petition, like the second, is concerned with war, but this time the focus is not on defeat as a result of sin but on victory in God's cause (**whatever way you shall send them**). The army is envisaged as fighting to bring God's justice to the earth.

8:46–51 carried away captive. The seventh petition returns to the question of defeat and exile, the major concern of the prayer. If exile should take place, and if the people should **repent** and pray toward **land**, **city**, and temple (v. 48; cf. Dan. 6:10 for the practice), then God is asked to regard them once more as his people and **maintain their cause** (1 Kings 8:49; cf. v. 45). They are the Lord's **heritage** or inheritance, the people **brought out of Egypt** (v. 51; cf. Deut. 4:20); Solomon implicitly looks for a "second exodus," from a different land, to match the first one.

8:54–9:9 *The Temple Narrative Ended.* The authors now tell of Solomon's second address to the people (8:54–61), of the conclusion of the festivities associated with the temple's dedication (8:62–66), and of God's second

heaven. **55** And he stood and [w]blessed all the assembly of Israel with a loud voice, saying,
56 "Blessed be the LORD who has given rest to his people Israel, according to all that he
promised. [x]Not one word has failed of all his good promise, which he spoke by Moses
his servant. **57** The LORD our God be with us, as he was with our fathers. [y]May he not
leave us or forsake us, **58** that he may [z]incline our hearts to him, to walk in all his ways
and to keep his commandments, his statutes, and his rules, which he commanded our
fathers. **59** Let these words of mine, with which I have pleaded before the LORD, be near
to the LORD our God day and night, and may he maintain the cause of his servant and
the cause of his people Israel, as each day requires, **60** that [a]all the peoples of the earth
may know that [b]the LORD is God; there is no other. **61** [c]Let your heart therefore be wholly
true to the LORD our God, walking in his statutes and keeping his commandments, as
at this day."

Solomon's Sacrifices

62 [d]Then [e]the king, and all Israel with him, offered sacrifice before the LORD. **63** Solomon
offered as peace offerings to the LORD 22,000 oxen and 120,000 sheep. So the king and all
the people of Israel dedicated the house of the LORD. **64** The same day the king consecrated
the middle of the court that was before the house of the LORD, for there he offered the
burnt offering and the grain offering and the fat pieces of the peace offerings, because
[f]the bronze altar that was before the LORD was too small to receive the burnt offering and
the grain offering and the fat pieces of the peace offerings.

65 So Solomon held [g]the feast at that time, and all Israel with him, a great assembly,
from [h]Lebo-hamath to [i]the Brook of Egypt, before the LORD our God, seven days.[1] **66** On
the eighth day he sent the people away, and they blessed the king and went to their homes
joyful and glad of heart for all the goodness that the LORD had shown to David his servant
and to Israel his people.

The LORD Appears to Solomon

9 [j]As soon as Solomon had finished building the house of the LORD [k]and the king's house
and [l]all that Solomon desired to build, **2** [m]the LORD appeared to Solomon a second
time, as he had appeared to him at Gibeon. **3** And the LORD said to him, "I have heard your
prayer and your plea, which you have made before me. I have consecrated this house that
you have built, [n]by putting my name there forever. [o]My eyes and my heart will be there
for all time. **4** And as for you, if you will [p]walk before me, [q]as David your father walked,
with integrity of heart and uprightness, doing according to all that I have commanded
you, and keeping my statutes and my rules, **5** [r]then I will establish your royal throne over
Israel forever, as I promised David your father, saying, 'You shall not lack a man on the
throne of Israel.' **6** [s]But if you turn aside from following me, you or your children, and do
not keep my commandments and my statutes that I have set before you, but go and serve

[1] Septuagint; Hebrew *seven days and seven days, fourteen days*

55 [w]ver. 14
56 [x]Josh. 21:45; 23:14
57 [y][Deut. 31:6; Josh. 1:5; 1 Sam. 12:22]
58 [z]Ps. 119:36
60 [a]ver. 43 [b]Deut. 4:35, 39; [ch. 18:39]
61 [c]2 Kgs. 20:3; [ch. 11:4; 15:3, 14]
62 [d]For ver. 62-66, see 2 Chr. 7:4-10 [e][Ezra 6:16, 17]
64 [f]See 2 Chr. 4:1
65 [g]ver. 2; Lev. 23:34 [h]Num. 13:21; 34:8 [i]Num. 34:5; 2 Kgs. 24:7

Chapter 9

1 [j]For ver. 1-9, see 2 Chr. 7:11-22 [k]ch. 7:1; 2 Chr. 8:1 [l]ver. 19; 2 Chr. 8:6
2 [m]ch. 3:5; 11:9
3 [n]ch. 8:16, 29 [o]Deut. 11:12
4 [p][Gen. 17:1] [q]ch. 11:4, 6, 38; 14:8; 15:5
5 [r]ch. 6:12; 1 Chr. 22:10; See ch. 2:4
6 [s][2 Sam. 7:14; Ps. 89:30, 32]

appearance to Solomon, in which he responds to Solomon's prayer with some solemn words about dynasty and temple, people and land (9:1–9).

8:54–61 rest to his people Israel. Solomon once again celebrates the fulfillment of God's promises, though this time more broadly than in vv. 15–21. He refers here to the promises given through **Moses**, alluding in the word "rest" to the establishment of Israel within the land of Canaan. The ultimate purpose of Israel's walking in God's ways is that **all the peoples of the earth may know that the LORD is God; there is no other** (cf. Deut. 4:35). This idea of Israel's role in the world (cf. 1 Kings 8:41–43) goes all the way back to Gen. 12:1–3 and is found also in passages such as Ex. 19:6, where Israel is to be a "kingdom of priests," mediating from God to his world. Israel's calling is to be a light for the Gentiles (Isa. 49:6), bringing God's salvation to the ends of the earth.

8:62–64 offered sacrifice. Chapter 8 closes with an account of the sacrifices offered in the course of the dedication of the temple—so many that the **bronze altar** outside the temple was not sufficient for the task. Part of the courtyard in front of the temple had to be **consecrated** for use as well.

8:65–66 from Lebo-hamath to the Brook of Egypt. This phrase designates the whole Solomonic empire and is analogous to similar phrases in 4:21, 24 ("from the Euphrates to the land of the Philistines and to the border of Egypt"; and "from Tiphsah to Gaza"). Presumably Lebo-hamath ("entrance to Hamath") therefore lay to the north of Hamath itself, which lay in central Syria on the river Orontes. This picture of a happy, unified kingdom stretching from Egypt to the Euphrates (they **went to their homes joyful and glad of heart**) very much corresponds to the picture in ch. 4.

9:2 a second time. The first occasion on which God appeared to Solomon (3:4–15) marked the beginning of his rise to greatness. This second appearance marks the end point of his upward mobility, and points ahead to disaster.

9:4–5 You shall not lack a man on the throne of Israel. Cf. note on 2 Chron. 7:17–18.

9:6 if you turn aside from following me, you or your children. Although the place of the temple as a focal point for prayer has been assured by God, as Solomon had asked (v. 3; cf. 8:27–53), and there was also a favorable response to his request about the future of the dynasty (9:4–5; cf. 8:25–26), the future of the temple and the dynasty depends on the obedience of Solomon and of future generations of Israelites. The particular focus here is on the issue of idolatry: the people must not **go and serve other gods and worship them**.

other gods and worship them, 7 [t]then I will cut off Israel from the land that I have given
them, [u]and the house that I have consecrated for my name I will cast out of my sight,
[v]and Israel will become a proverb and a byword among all peoples. 8 And this house will
become a heap of ruins.[1] Everyone passing by it will be astonished and will hiss, and they
will say, [w]'Why has the LORD done thus to this land and to this house?' 9 Then they will say,
'Because [x]they abandoned the LORD their God who brought their fathers out of the land
of Egypt and laid hold on other gods and worshiped them and served them. Therefore
the LORD has brought all this disaster on them.'"

Solomon's Other Acts

10 [y]At the end of [z]twenty years, in which Solomon had built the two houses, the house
of the LORD and the king's house, 11 and Hiram king of Tyre had supplied Solomon with
cedar and cypress timber and gold, as much as he desired, King Solomon gave to Hiram
twenty cities in the land of Galilee. 12 But when Hiram came from Tyre to see the cities
that Solomon had given him, they did not please him. 13 Therefore he said, "What kind of
cities are these that you have given me, my brother?" So they are called the land of [a]Cabul
to this day. 14 Hiram had sent to the king 120 talents[2] of gold.

15 And this is the account of [b]the forced labor that King Solomon drafted to build the
house of the LORD and his own house and [c]the Millo and the wall of Jerusalem and [d]Hazor
and [e]Megiddo and Gezer 16 (Pharaoh king of Egypt had gone up and captured Gezer and
burned it with fire, and had killed [f]the Canaanites who lived in the city, and had given it
as dowry to [g]his daughter, Solomon's wife; 17 so Solomon rebuilt Gezer) and [h]Lower Beth-
horon 18 and Baalath and Tamar in the wilderness, in the land of Judah,[3] 19 and all the store
cities that Solomon had, and [i]the cities for his chariots, and the cities for [j]his horsemen,
and whatever Solomon [k]desired to build in Jerusalem, in Lebanon, and in all the land of

[1] Syriac, Old Latin; Hebrew *will become high* [2] A *talent* was about 75 pounds or 34 kilograms [3] Hebrew lacks *of Judah*

7 [t]Deut. 4:26; 2 Kgs. 17:23; 25:21 [u]Jer. 7:14 [v]Deut. 28:37; [Ps. 44:14]
8 [w]Deut. 29:24-26; Jer. 22:8, 9
9 [x]ch. 18:18
10 [y]For ver. 10-28, see 2 Chr. 8:1-18 [z][ch. 6:37, 38; 7:1]
13 [a][Josh. 19:27]
15 [b]ch. 5:13 [c]ver. 24; See 2 Sam. 5:9 [d]Josh. 11:1 [e]Josh. 17:11
16 [f]Josh. 16:10 [g]ch. 3:1; 7:8
17 [h]See Josh. 10:10
19 [i]ch. 10:26; 2 Chr. 1:14; 9:25 [j]ch. 4:26 [k]ver. 1

9:7–8 Disobedience will lead to loss of the Promised Land, and the magnificent temple will become a **heap of ruins** to be scoffed at by those passing by (cf. Deut. 29:22–28; Lam. 1:12; 2:15). Israel will be in fact transformed from a nation proverbial for its wisdom (1 Kings 4:21–34) into a nation that is itself **a proverb and a byword**. This word pair comes directly from the list of covenant curses in Deuteronomy 28 (v. 37), a chapter that lies behind so much of the prayer of 1 Kings 8:22–53. This prayer has assumed the inevitability of sin (esp. 8:46), making it clear that the "if" in 9:6 cannot be anything other than a "when" in reality (8:46); obedience will inevitably give way to apostasy. A dark cloud now looms over the Solomonic empire.

9:10–10:29 *Glory under a Cloud.* Solomon's rule over the surrounding kingdoms, combined with his status in the world in general (4:21–34), put him in a position to build and dedicate the temple (5:1–8:66). First Kings 9:10–10:29 now considers the glory of this Solomonic empire in the light of 8:22–53 and 9:1–9. Earlier themes are picked up again (Solomon's dealings with Hiram; his use of forced labor; foreigners coming to listen to his great wisdom), but they are repeated in a way that hints not of wisdom but of foolishness. The glory of the Solomonic empire is glory under a cloud, destined to fade away.

9:10–13 twenty cities in the land of Galilee. The fortress at Rosh Zayit lay in the border area between Israel and Phoenicia at this time. Excavations there have found that spaces between walls have been filled in with wood from the cedars of Lebanon. The site perhaps represents a fortress built by Israel with Phoenician materials and then given to Hiram of Tyre along with 19 other cities (v. 11).

9:10 At the end of twenty years would be c. 946 B.C.

9:11 Hiram king of Tyre was first encountered in 5:1–18, where Solomon's wise dealings with him were described. In one sense 9:10–14 simply confirms the impression gained there, that Hiram is the "junior partner" in his relationship with Solomon. The **gold** mentioned in v. 11 was not referenced in the agreement struck between the two kings in 5:1–18, but Hiram nevertheless supplied Solomon with **as much as he desired**. Solomon in turn "rewards" him with **twenty cities** of dubious worth.

9:13 land of Cabul. The name probably comes from Hebrew *kabal*, from which is derived the noun *kebel* ("fetters") that is found in Ps. 149:8, a psalm that celebrates the supremacy of Israel over the nations. Hiram calls the land "fettered" because this word reflects the nature of his relationship with Solomon, as can be seen in his continuing willingness, even though he is displeased, to send men to sea to bring back more treasures for the Israelite king (1 Kings 9:26–28; 10:11–12, 22).

9:14 The references to **gold** in this Hiram story are only the first of many mentions of this metal in the current section of 1 Kings (cf. v. 28; 10:2, 10–11, 14, 16–18, 21–22, 25). Solomon accumulates gold in extraordinarily large and increasing amounts (**120 talents** in 9:14; 420 in 9:28; 666 in 10:14; 10:10 is the exception). The gold is indeed collected from more and more exotic places (9:28; 10:22). This emphasis on gold throughout 9:10–10:29 is striking when this section of Kings is compared with the description of Solomon's glory in chs. 4–5. There prosperity is described in terms of food rather than precious metals, and the emphasis lies not on luxury at the royal court but on the way that prosperity was shared with the king's subjects. It is also striking that 9:6–9 has just warned about "turning away from God," and biblical texts associate the accumulation of wealth with apostasy (e.g., Deut. 17:17; Prov. 30:8). God may well have given Solomon riches, but will they lead him astray?

9:15–25 the account of the forced labor. This is another section that refers the reader back to 5:1–18. Here it is clarified that Solomon did not use his task force of 30,000 only for the temple but also for his other building operations, and that it did not include his Israelite subjects (who had other jobs to do), but only Canaanite laborers. The significance of this delayed clarification becomes clear in the authors' associating these **Canaanites** with **Pharaoh's daughter** (9:24). She was first introduced (waiting for her palace) in 3:1, using language reminiscent of the Deuteronomic warnings about intermarriage with foreigners (Deut. 7:1–6; precisely those **Amorites**, **Hittites**, **Perizzites**, **Hivites**, and **Jebusites** mentioned in 1 Kings 9:20) because of the danger of apostasy. Their appearance here along with Pharaoh's daughter serves to prepare the reader for Solomon's apostasy. He will be seduced by the other gods (11:2), even though he is for the moment an orthodox worshiper in the temple (9:25).

9:15 Excavations at **Hazor**, **Megiddo**, and **Gezer** have revealed extensive building for fortification and government from the Solomonic period. All three sites include four entry gates that are connected to an outer casemate wall

21 [l][Judg. 1:21, 27, 29; 3:1] [m][Josh. 15:63; 17:12] [n]Judg. 1:28 [o]Ezra 2:55-58; Neh. 7:57-60; 11:3
22 [p]Lev. 25:39
23 [q][2 Chr. 8:10] [r]ch. 5:16
24 [g][See ver. 16 above] [s]ch. 7:8 [t]ch. 11:27; [2 Sam. 5:9; 2 Chr. 32:5] [u]See ver. 15
26 [v]ch. 22:48; Num. 33:35; Deut. 2:8

his dominion. 20 All the people who were left of the Amorites, the Hittites, the Perizzites,
the Hivites, and the Jebusites, who were not of the people of Israel— 21 [l]their descendants
who were left after them in the land, [m]whom the people of Israel were unable to devote
to destruction[1]—[n]these Solomon drafted to be [o]slaves, and so they are to this day. 22 But
[p]of the people of Israel Solomon made no slaves. They were the soldiers, they were his
officials, his commanders, his captains, his chariot commanders and his horsemen.
23 These were the chief officers who were over Solomon's work: [q]550 [r]who had charge
of the people who carried on the work.
24 But [g]Pharaoh's daughter went up from the city of David to [s]her own house that Solomon
had built for her. [t]Then he built [u]the Millo.
25 Three times a year Solomon used to offer up burnt offerings and peace offerings on
the altar that he built to the LORD, making offerings with it[2] before the LORD. So he finished the house.
26 King Solomon built a fleet of ships at [v]Ezion-geber, which is near Eloth on the shore

[1] That is, set apart (devote) as an offering to the Lord (for destruction) [2] Septuagint lacks *with it*

system. Megiddo in particular, with its palaces and stables/storehouses, provides a good picture of a Solomonic royal city. **the Millo**. See note on 2 Sam. 5:9.

9:17–19 A series of fortresses have been discovered in the central Negev, which appear to have been part of a defensive network built during the time of Solomon in the tenth century B.C. Their purpose was to provide a solid line of defense against invasion from the south, particularly from Egypt. The fortresses were occupied for only a short time (50 years at the most).

9:26–28 Many scholars have tried to identify **Ezion-geber** with the modern Tell el-Kheleifeh, but this site was not settled until the eighth century B.C., at least 200 years after Solomon's time.

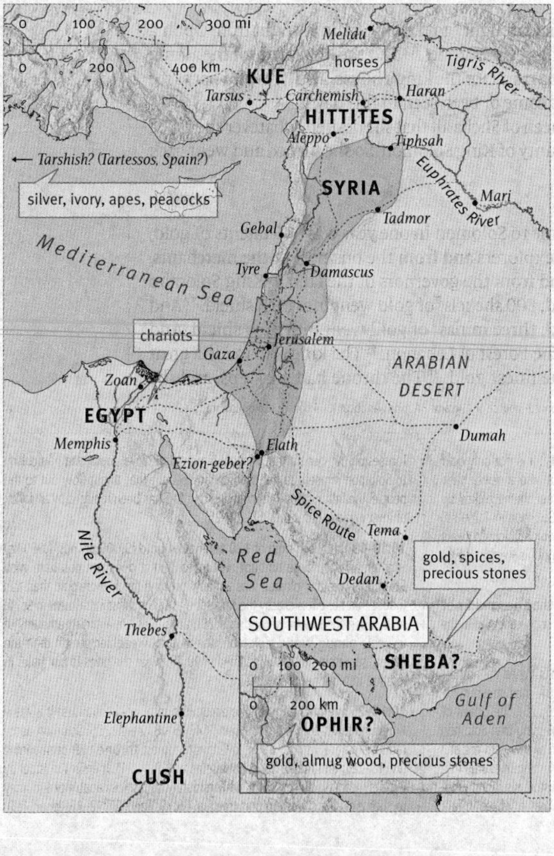

Solomon's International Ventures
c. 950 B.C.

Solomon's firm control of important trade routes linking Egypt, Arabia, Mesopotamia, and Anatolia (Asia Minor) provided him with incalculable wealth. Partnering with King Hiram of Tyre, Solomon also launched his own trading expeditions to Ophir to acquire valuable and exotic goods. The queen of Sheba's visit to Solomon attests to his great fame throughout the ancient world. Solomon further augmented his wealth by buying horses from Kue and chariots from Egypt and selling them to the kings of Syria and the Hittites.

of the Red Sea, in the land of Edom. 27 And Hiram sent [w]with the fleet his servants, seamen
who were familiar with the sea, together with the servants of Solomon. 28 And they went to
[x]Ophir and brought from there gold, 420 talents, and they brought it to King Solomon.

The Queen of Sheba

10 [y]Now when [z]the queen of [a]Sheba heard of the fame of Solomon concerning the name
of the LORD, she came [b]to test him with hard questions. 2 She came to Jerusalem with
a very great retinue, with camels [c]bearing spices and very much gold and precious stones.
And when she came to Solomon, she told him all that was on her mind. 3 And Solomon
answered all her questions; there was nothing hidden from the king that he could not
explain to her. 4 And when the queen of Sheba had seen all the wisdom of Solomon, the
house that he had built, 5 the food of his table, the seating of his officials, and the attendance
of his servants, their clothing, his cupbearers, and his burnt offerings that he offered at
the house of the LORD, there was no more breath in her.

6 And she said to the king, "The report was true that I heard in my own land of your
words and of your wisdom, 7 but I did not believe the reports until I came and my own
eyes had seen it. And behold, the half was not told me. Your wisdom and prosperity surpass the report that I heard. 8 [e]Happy are your men! Happy are your servants, who continually stand before you and hear your wisdom! 9 [f]Blessed be the LORD your God, who
has delighted in you and set you on the throne of Israel! [g]Because the LORD loved Israel
forever, he has made you king, [h]that you may execute justice and righteousness." 10 [i]Then
she gave the king 120 talents[1] of gold, and a very great quantity of spices and precious
stones. Never again came such an abundance of spices as these that the queen of Sheba
gave to King Solomon.

11 Moreover, [j]the fleet of Hiram, which brought [k]gold from Ophir, brought from Ophir a
very great amount of almug wood and precious stones. 12 And the king made of the almug
wood supports for the house of the LORD and for the king's house, also lyres and harps for
the singers. No such almug wood has come or been seen to this day.

13 And King Solomon gave to the queen of Sheba all that she desired, whatever she asked
besides what was given her by the bounty of King Solomon. So she turned and went back
to her own land with her servants.

Solomon's Great Wealth

14 [l]Now the weight of gold that came to Solomon in one year was 666 talents of gold,
15 besides that which came from the explorers and from the business of the merchants,
and from all the kings of the west and from the governors of the land. 16 King Solomon
made 200 large shields of beaten gold; 600 shekels[2] of gold went into each shield. 17 And
he made 300 [m]shields of beaten gold; three minas[3] of gold went into each shield. And
the king put them in [n]the House of the Forest of Lebanon. 18 The king also made a great
ivory throne and overlaid it with the finest gold. 19 The throne had six steps, and the

[1] A *talent* was about 75 pounds or 34 kilograms [2] A *shekel* was about 2/5 ounce or 11 grams [3] A *mina* was about 1 1/4 pounds or 0.6 kilogram

27 [w]ch. 10:11
28 [x]ch. 10:11; 22:48; 1 Chr. 29:4; Job 22:24; 28:16; Ps. 45:9; Isa. 13:12

Chapter 10

1 [y]For ver. 1-13, see 2 Chr. 9:1-12 [z][Matt. 12:42; Luke 11:31] [a]Ps. 72:10, 15; Isa. 60:6; Jer. 6:20; Ezek. 27:22, 23; 38:13; Joel 3:8 [b]See Judg. 14:12
2 [c]ver. 10
8 [e][Prov. 8:34]
9 [f]ch. 5:7 [g]2 Chr. 2:11 [h]2 Sam. 8:15; [Ps. 72:2]
10 [i]ver. 2
11 [j]ch. 9:27 [k]See ch. 9:28
14 [l]For ver. 14-28, see 2 Chr. 9:13-28
17 [m]ch. 14:26 [n]ch. 7:2

10:1 queen of Sheba. Cf. note on 2 Chron. 9:1–9, 12. It is not only gold that arrives from Arabia ("Ophir" in 1 Kings 9:28) but also a queen who comes **to test** Solomon **with hard questions**, another theme picked up from earlier in the narrative (cf. the worldwide fame of Solomon in 4:29–34, which attracts foreigners to his court). The ease with which Solomon deals with her questions, combined with her own observation of his wealth, leaves her breathless (10:5).

10:3 there was nothing hidden from the king that he could not explain to her. Solomon's wisdom, given by God, was unprecedented in the entire world, and it amazes this foreign queen (v. 4).

10:8 Happy are your men! Happy are your servants. When the authors of 1–2 Kings described the joyful kingdom back in ch. 4, they stressed the benefits of Solomon's wisdom for all his subjects (4:20, 25). The queen of Sheba, however, refers much more specifically to the blessing that Solomon must be to his court officials. While Solomon's wisdom and wealth are still remarkable, and are still evidence of God's abundant blessing, it seems that his great wisdom, wealth, and power have begun to distort his moral judgment in the proper use of these blessings. Chapter 10 as a whole in fact focuses on this benefit that wisdom brings to the royal court, and particularly to Solomon himself, rather than on any benefit that might flow out to the people. The influx of food described in chs. 4–5 has been replaced by an influx of luxury goods (10:2, 10–12, 22, 25).

10:10–13 The queen's gift of **120 talents of gold** (9,000 pounds/4,080 kg) is a remarkably large amount, yet in context it does not compare with Solomon's wealth. Solomon was already receiving much more gold than this (notice that her gift is exactly the same size as Hiram's *first installment* in 9:14, now superseded by his second in 9:28), as well as unparalleled amounts of valuable **almug wood**. Solomon was a vastly wealthier person than the queen, something that is underlined in 10:13. What she gives to him pales in relation to what he gives to her.

10:14–25 weight of gold. The accumulation of gold continues; it is mentioned no fewer than 11 times in vv. 14, 16–18, 21–22, 25. Solomon decorates his palace with it (v. 16); overlays the finest **throne** ever seen with it (vv. 18–20); and makes household items with it (v. 21). It arrives in Israel by various means, including **ships of Tarshish** (v. 22), ships capable of a journey to such a far-flung western port (see Isa. 66:19; Ezek. 27:12–15; Jonah 1:3).

throne had a round top,[1] and on each side of the seat were armrests and two lions standing beside the armrests, 20 while twelve lions stood there, one on each end of a step on
the six steps. The like of it was never made in any kingdom. 21 All King Solomon's drinking vessels were of gold, and all the vessels of [n]the House of the Forest of Lebanon were
of pure gold. None were of silver; silver was not considered as anything in the days of
Solomon. 22 For the king had [o]a fleet of ships of Tarshish at sea with the fleet of Hiram.
Once every three years the fleet of ships of Tarshish used to come bringing gold, silver,
ivory, apes, and peacocks.[2]

23 [p]Thus King Solomon excelled all the kings of the earth in riches and in wisdom. 24 And
the whole earth sought the presence of Solomon to hear his wisdom, which God had put
into his mind. 25 Every one of them brought his present, articles of silver and gold, garments, myrrh, spices, horses, and mules, so much year by year.

26 [q]And Solomon gathered together [r]chariots and horsemen. He had 1,400 chariots and
12,000 horsemen, whom he stationed in the [s]chariot cities and with the king in Jerusalem.
27 And the king made silver as common in Jerusalem as stone, and he made cedar as plentiful
as [t]the sycamore of the Shephelah. 28 And Solomon's [u]import of horses was from Egypt and
Kue, and the king's traders received them from Kue at a price. 29 A chariot could be imported
from Egypt for 600 shekels of silver and a horse for 150, and so through the king's traders
they were exported to all the kings of [v]the Hittites and the kings of Syria.

Solomon Turns from the Lord

11 Now [w]King Solomon loved many foreign women, along with the daughter of
Pharaoh: Moabite, Ammonite, Edomite, Sidonian, and Hittite women, 2 from the
nations concerning which the LORD had said to the people of Israel, [x]"You shall not enter
into marriage with them, neither shall they with you, for surely they will turn away your
heart after their gods." Solomon clung to these in love. 3 He had 700 wives, who were princesses, and 300 concubines. And his wives turned away his heart. 4 For when Solomon was
old his wives turned away his heart after other gods, and [y]his heart was not wholly true
to the LORD his God, [z]as was the heart of David his father. 5 For Solomon went after [a]Ash-
toreth the goddess of the Sidonians, and after [b]Milcom the abomination of the Ammonites.
6 So Solomon did what was evil in the sight of the LORD and did not wholly follow the
LORD, as David his father had done. 7 Then Solomon built a high place for [c]Chemosh
the abomination of Moab, and for [d]Molech the abomination of the Ammonites, on the
mountain east of Jerusalem. 8 And so he did for all his foreign wives, who made offerings
and sacrificed to their gods.

[1] *Or and at the back of the throne was a calf's head* [2] *Or baboons*

21 [n][See ver. 17 above]
22 [o]ch. 22:48; Gen. 10:4; 1 Chr. 1:7; 2 Chr. 20:36, 37; Ps. 48:7; 72:10
23 [p][ch. 3:12, 13; 4:30]
26 [q]For ver. 26-29, see 2 Chr. 1:14-17 [r][ch. 4:26; 2 Chr. 9:25] [s]ch. 9:19
27 [t]1 Chr. 27:28
28 [u]2 Chr. 9:28; [Deut. 17:16]
29 [v]Judg. 1:26

Chapter 11

1 [w]Neh. 13:26; [Deut. 17:17]
2 [x]See Ex. 34:16
4 [y][ch. 8:61] [z]ch. 9:4
5 [a]ver. 33; Judg. 2:13; 2 Kgs. 23:13 [b][ver. 7]
7 [c]Num. 21:29; 2 Kgs. 23:13 [d]Lev. 18:21; 20:2-4; 2 Kgs. 23:10; Acts 7:43; [ver. 5]

These ships are said to have sailed to lands so distant that it took **three years** to return with their extraordinary cargo.

10:26–29 chariots and horsemen . . . silver. The accumulation of silver and horses, as well as gold, is forbidden by Deut. 17:16–17 (see note on 1 Kings 4:28). The significant addition to the theme here is the detail that **Solomon's import of horses was from Egypt** (10:28). All but one of the instructions about kingship in Deut. 17:16–17 have thus far been violated by Solomon. That remaining one (he must not take many wives) will be taken up in 1 Kings 11.

11:1–43 ***Solomon's Apostasy, Opponents, and Death.*** Throughout chs. 1–10 the reader has received hints that all is not well with Solomon's heart: 3:1–3 juxtaposed his love for God with suggestions of divided loyalties revealed in his choice of marriage partner; 4:26 and 4:28 told of his accumulation of horses; 6:38–7:1 pursued the question of building project priorities; and 10:26–29 did the same with regard to horses, in a context in which the topic of Solomon's great wealth was introduced and the marriage question again briefly addressed. Since the prayer of 8:22–53 and God's response to it in 9:1–9 have made clear both the importance of keeping the law and the consequences of disobedience, 9:10–10:29 sounded ominous; and now the authors reveal the inevitable consequences of all that has gone before. Solomon's sins have led him to apostasy.

11:1–4 Solomon loved many foreign women . . . clung to these in love. Solomon loved (Hb. *'ahab*, 3:3) the Lord, but he also loved (Hb. *'ahab*) the **daughter of Pharaoh** and many other women, and he clung (Hb. *dabaq*) to them (11:2). Both verbs appear in Deuteronomy (Deut. 6:5; 10:12, 20; 11:1, 22; 13:4; 30:20), where they speak of unswerving human loyalty to God. Solomon's **heart**, however, was divided (1 Kings 11:4); and in spite of his pious hope that God would always turn Israelite hearts to himself (8:58), the king's wives, in his old age, **turned away his heart** in the opposite direction, **after other gods**.

11:5 At ancient Ugarit in Syria the sun was worshiped as Shapash, the moon as Yarikh, and Venus as Astarte. **Ashtoreth** is the biblical name for Astarte (a deliberate distortion of the original using the vowels of the Hb. word *boshet*, "shame"). **Milcom** was a god of the underworld.

11:6 Individual kings are characteristically assessed in 1–2 Kings in terms of whether on the whole they "did what was right" or **what was evil** in the eyes of the Lord (e.g., 1 Kings 15:11, 26, 34); Judean kings are additionally said to be like **David** or not (e.g., 15:3, 11).

11:7–8 The worship of other **gods** at high places lies at the very heart of the authors' concern in 1–2 Kings (e.g., 1 Kings 12:25–33; 14:23; 16:31–33). **Chemosh** was the chief god of the Moabites, already known in ancient Ebla in Syria as Kamish and probably to be identified with the Mesopotamian deity Nergal, an underworld god associated with famine, drought, plague, and death. **Molech** is possibly, but not certainly, to be identified with Milcom in 11:5. The biblical authors associate Molech with child sacrifice, which was a prominent feature of at least some of the

The Lord Raises Adversaries

9 And the LORD was angry with Solomon, because [e]his heart had turned away from the
LORD, the God of Israel, [f]who had appeared to him twice 10 and [g]had commanded him
concerning this thing, that he should not go after other gods. But he did not keep what
the LORD commanded. 11 Therefore the LORD said to Solomon, "Since this has been your
practice and you have not kept my covenant and my statutes that I have commanded
you, [h]I will surely tear the kingdom from you and will give it to your servant. 12 Yet for
the sake of David your father I will not do it in your days, but I will tear it out of the
hand of your son. 13 However, [i]I will not tear away all the kingdom, but [j]I will give one
tribe to your son, for the sake of David my servant and for the sake of Jerusalem [k]that
I have chosen."

14 And the LORD raised up an adversary against Solomon, Hadad the Edomite. He was
of the royal house in Edom. 15 For [l]when David was in Edom, and Joab the commander
of the army went up to bury the slain, he struck down every male in Edom 16 (for Joab
and all Israel remained there six months, until he had cut off every male in Edom). 17 But
Hadad fled to Egypt, together with certain Edomites of his father's servants, Hadad still
being a little child. 18 They set out from Midian and came to [m]Paran and took men with
them from Paran and came to Egypt, to Pharaoh king of Egypt, who gave him a house
and assigned him an allowance of food and gave him land. 19 And Hadad found great
favor in the sight of Pharaoh, so that he gave him in marriage the sister of his own wife,
the sister of Tahpenes the queen. 20 And the sister of Tahpenes bore him Genubath his
son, whom Tahpenes weaned in Pharaoh's house. And Genubath was in Pharaoh's house
among the sons of Pharaoh. 21 But when Hadad heard in Egypt [n]that David slept with his
fathers and that Joab the commander of the army was dead, Hadad said to Pharaoh, "Let
me depart, that I may go to my own country." 22 But Pharaoh said to him, "What have you
lacked with me that you are now seeking to go to your own country?" And he said to him,
"Only let me depart."

23 God also raised up as an adversary to him, Rezon the son of Eliada, who had fled
from his master [o]Hadadezer king of Zobah. 24 And he gathered men about him and
became leader of a marauding band, [p]after the killing by David. And they went to
Damascus and lived there and made him king in Damascus. 25 He was an adversary of
Israel all the days of Solomon, doing harm as Hadad did. And he loathed Israel and
reigned over Syria.

26 [q]Jeroboam the son of Nebat, [r]an Ephraimite of Zeredah, a servant of Solomon, whose
mother's name was Zeruah, a widow, also [s]lifted up his hand against the king. 27 And
this was the reason why he lifted up his hand against the king. [t]Solomon built the Millo,
and closed up the breach of the city of David his father. 28 The man Jeroboam was very
able, and when Solomon saw that the young man was industrious he gave him charge
over all the forced labor of the house of Joseph. 29 And at that time, when Jeroboam
went out of Jerusalem, the prophet [u]Ahijah the Shilonite found him on the road. Now
Ahijah had dressed himself in a new garment, and the two of them were alone in the
open country. 30 Then Ahijah laid hold of the new garment that was on him, [v]and tore
it into twelve pieces. 31 And he said to Jeroboam, "Take for yourself ten pieces, for thus
says the LORD, the God of Israel, 'Behold, [w]I am about to tear the kingdom from the
hand of Solomon and will give you ten tribes 32 (but [x]he shall have one tribe, for the
sake of my servant David and for the sake of Jerusalem, [y]the city that I have chosen out
of all the tribes of Israel), 33 because they have[1] forsaken me [z]and worshiped Ashtoreth

[1] Septuagint, Syriac, Vulgate *he has*; twice in this verse

9 [e]ver. 2, 4 [f]ch. 3:5; 9:2
10 [g]ch. 6:12; 9:6
11 [h]ver. 31; [ch. 12:15, 16]
13 [i][2 Sam. 7:15; Ps. 89:33] [j]ver. 32, 36; [ch. 12:20] [k]Deut. 12:5, 11
15 [l]2 Sam. 8:14; 1 Chr. 18:12, 13
18 [m]Num. 10:12; Deut. 33:2
21 [n]ch. 2:10
23 [o][2 Sam. 10:16]
24 [p]2 Sam. 8:3; 10:8, 18
26 [q]ch. 12:2; 2 Chr. 13:6 [r]1 Sam. 1:1 [s]2 Sam. 20:21
27 [t]ch. 9:24; [2 Sam. 5:9]
29 [u]ch. 12:15; 14:2; 15:29; 2 Chr. 9:29
30 [v][1 Sam. 15:27]
31 [w]ver. 11-13
32 [x]ver. 13; ch. 12:21 [y]ch. 14:21; See Deut. 12:5
33 [z]ver. 5, 7

polytheistic Canaanite religion practiced in ancient times in Syria-Palestine. This sacrificing involved the burning of the victim (e.g., Lev. 18:21; 2 Kings 16:3; 21:6; Jer. 32:35).

11:9–13 the LORD was angry with Solomon . . . I will surely tear the kingdom from you. This is what 2:4; 8:25; and 9:4–5 have led the reader to expect. Yet the punishment is unexpectedly mitigated: **I will not do it in your days** (11:12). . . . **I will not tear away all the kingdom** (v. 13). **One tribe** remains out of grace, **for the sake of David my servant and for the sake of Jerusalem that I have chosen**.

11:14–25 In 5:4, Solomon told Hiram, in the midst of God's blessing, that he had peace on every side (no **adversary**). Now the blessing has departed and the peace is fractured. Two men who had hitherto not caused Solomon

the goddess of the Sidonians, Chemosh the god of Moab, and Milcom the god of the
Ammonites, and they have not walked in my ways, doing what is right in my sight
and keeping my statutes and my rules, as David his father did. 34 Nevertheless, I will
not take the whole kingdom out of his hand, but I will make him ruler all the days of
his life, for the sake of David my servant whom I chose, who kept my commandments
and my statutes. 35 [a]But I will take the kingdom out of his son's hand and will give it to
you, ten tribes. 36 Yet to his son [x]I will give one tribe, that David my servant may always
have [b]a lamp before me in Jerusalem, [y]the city where I have chosen to put my name.
37 And I will take you, and you shall reign over all that your soul desires, and you shall
be king over Israel. 38 And if you will listen to all that I command you, and will walk in
my ways, and do what is right in my eyes by keeping my statutes and my commandments, as David my servant did, [c]I will be with you and [d]will build you a sure house,
as I built for David, and I will give Israel to you. 39 And I will afflict the offspring of
David because of this, but not forever.'" 40 Solomon sought therefore to kill Jeroboam.
But Jeroboam arose and fled into Egypt, to [e]Shishak king of Egypt, and was in Egypt
until the death of Solomon.

41 [f]Now the rest of the acts of Solomon, and all that he did, and his wisdom, are they
not written in the Book of the Acts of Solomon? 42 And the time that Solomon reigned in
Jerusalem over all Israel was forty years. 43 And Solomon [g]slept with his fathers and was
buried in the city of David his father. And [h]Rehoboam his son reigned in his place.

35 [a]ver. 12; ch. 12:16, 17
36 [x][See ver. 32 above] [b]ch. 15:4; 2 Sam. 21:17; 2 Kgs. 8:19; 2 Chr. 21:7 [y][See ver. 32 above]
38 [c]Josh. 1:5 [d]1 Sam. 2:35; 2 Sam. 7:11, 27
40 [e]ch. 14:25; 2 Chr. 12:2, 5, 7, 9
41 [f]For ver. 41-43, see 2 Chr. 9:29-31
43 [g]ch. 2:10; 14:20 [h]Matt. 1:7

significant problems are now **raised up** by God to oppose the apostate king in his old age. The first is **Hadad**, a victim of David's wars (2 Sam. 8:13–14); the second is **Rezon**, who had apparently either escaped from the battle described in 2 Sam. 8:3–4 or **fled** from **Hadadezer** later, unwilling to submit to imperial rule from Jerusalem. **Damascus**, from ancient times a major site on the main caravan route from Africa to Mesopotamia, now becomes the capital of the Aramean kingdom of **Syria**, which will rise to become a significant power in the region during the divided monarchy in Israel. Syria will often be in conflict with Israel and Judah but will sometimes ally with them against common foes. The kingdom will ultimately be absorbed into the Assyrian Empire as a result of the campaigns of Tiglath-pileser III in 733–732 B.C. Rezon opposes Solomon from the north, Hadad from the south; and where the king once had peace on all sides, he now finds enemies.

11:26–33 Solomon's most important enemy, **Jeroboam the son of Nebat**, was to be found right on his doorstep. He was the former superintendent of the **forced labor of the house of Joseph**, those who had been helping with the construction work in Jerusalem (vv. 27–28). He was approached outside the city by the **prophet Ahijah** (v. 29) with a prophecy concerning the kingship. The scene is reminiscent of the rejection of Saul in 1 Samuel 15; in both passages an outer garment is torn as a symbol of the fact that God is tearing the kingdom away from the reigning king (cf. 1 Sam. 15:27–28; 1 Kings 11:11). The **garment** here is divided into 12 pieces, of which **ten**, symbolizing 10 northern tribes, are given to Jeroboam (vv. 30–31). **One tribe** is to remain for the sake of **David** and **Jerusalem** (i.e., Judah). Benjamin is not included in the math here (cf. 12:21), perhaps because this tribe was regarded simply as Jerusalem's own territory, on the analogy of the Canaanite city-state; this territory came with the city, and needed no special mention.

11:34–39 a lamp before me in Jerusalem. The mitigation of vv. 13–14 is repeated, although in a slightly different way. Solomon will lose no tribes during his lifetime; and his son is to have one tribe, so that the Davidic flame will always burn. In fact, although Jeroboam has been promised that he can also have a dynasty like David's if he is obedient (v. 38), this promise already conceals within it the expectation of failure; the division of the kingdom in v. 39 is **not forever**.

11:43 The oft-repeated "he **slept with his fathers**" (see note on 2:10) reflected the reality that almost all Israelite burials were in multichambered, rock-hewn tombs carved into hillsides. They were probably used as family tombs, so that even in death family ties were underscored.

Solomon's Enemies

c. 950 B.C.

Though Solomon held a firm grip on his kingdom throughout his lifetime, there were still those who worked to subvert his rule. Hadad was a member of the royal family of Edom who fled to Egypt to escape David's purge of all Edomite males. He would later return to Edom to oppose Solomon. Rezon was originally an outlaw in Zobah who gathered a bandit army and established himself as king in Damascus. Jeroboam originally oversaw one of Solomon's forced labor units, but Ahijah's prophecy foretelling Jeroboam's eventual rule over 10 Israelite tribes caused Solomon to seek to kill him, so he fled to Egypt.

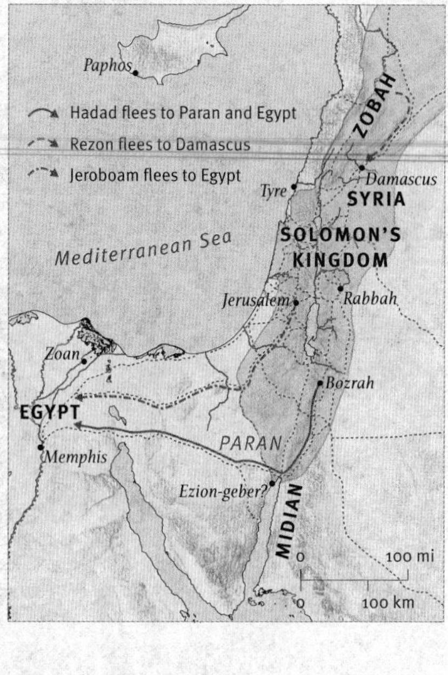

Rehoboam's Folly

12 [i]Rehoboam went to [j]Shechem, for all Israel had come to Shechem to make him
king. 2 And as soon as [k]Jeroboam the son of Nebat heard of it (for [l]he was still in
Egypt, where he had fled from King Solomon), then Jeroboam returned from[1] Egypt. 3 And
they sent and called him, and Jeroboam and all the assembly of Israel came and said to
Rehoboam, 4 [m]"Your father made our yoke heavy. Now therefore lighten the hard service
of your father and his heavy yoke on us, and we will serve you." 5 He said to them, [n]"Go
away for three days, then come again to me." So the people went away.
6 Then King Rehoboam took counsel with the old men, who had stood before Solomon
his father while he was yet alive, saying, "How do you advise me to answer this people?"
7 And they said to him, "If you will be a servant to this people today and serve them, and
speak good words to them when you answer them, then they will be your servants forever."
8 But he abandoned the counsel that the old men gave him and took counsel with the young
men who had grown up with him and stood before him. 9 And he said to them, "What do
you advise that we answer this people who have said to me, 'Lighten the yoke that your

[1] Septuagint, Vulgate (compare 2 Chronicles 10:2); Hebrew *lived in*

Chapter 12

1 [i]For ver. 1-19, see 2 Chr. 10:1-19 [j]Judg. 9:6]
2 [k]ch. 11:26 [l]ch. 11:40
4 [m]ch. 4:7, 22; 9:15; See 1 Sam. 8:11-18
5 [n]ver. 12

The Kingdom Divides
931 B.C.
When Solomon's son Rehoboam arrived at Shechem for his coronation after his father's death, he refused to lighten his father's heavy tax burden on the people, and the 10 northern tribes revolted and set up Jeroboam as their king. The northern kingdom would now be known as Israel and the southern kingdom as Judah. Five years later, Shishak (also called Sheshonq) king of Egypt invaded Judah and Israel and captured a number of towns. Rehoboam avoided Jerusalem's destruction by paying off Shishak with many of the treasures Solomon had placed in the temple.

11 [m][See ver. 4 above]
12 [o]ver. 5
14 [m][See ver. 4 above]
15 [p]ver. 24 [q]ch. 11:11, 31
16 [r]See 2 Sam. 20:1
17 [s]ch. 11:13, 36
18 [t]ch. 4:6; 5:14
19 [u]2 Kgs. 17:21
20 [v]ch. 11:13, 32, 36
21 [w]For ver. 21-24, see 2 Chr. 11:1-4
22 [x]2 Chr. 12:5, 7, 15
23 [y][ver. 17]
24 [z]ver. 15

father put on us'?" 10 And the young men who had grown up with him said to him, "Thus
shall you speak to this people who said to you, 'Your father made our yoke heavy, but you
lighten it for us,' thus shall you say to them, 'My little finger is thicker than my father's
thighs. 11 And now, whereas [m]my father laid on you a heavy yoke, I will add to your yoke.
My father disciplined you with whips, but I will discipline you with scorpions.' "
12 So Jeroboam and all the people came to Rehoboam the third day, as the king said,
[o]"Come to me again the third day." 13 And the king answered the people harshly, and forsaking the counsel that the old men had given him, 14 he spoke to them according to the
counsel of the young men, saying, [m]"My father made your yoke heavy, but I will add to
your yoke. My father disciplined you with whips, but I will discipline you with scorpions."
15 So the king did not listen to the people, for [p]it was a turn of affairs brought about by
the LORD that he might fulfill his word, which [q]the LORD spoke by Ahijah the Shilonite
to Jeroboam the son of Nebat.

The Kingdom Divided

16 And when all Israel saw that the king did not listen to them, the people answered the
king, "What portion do we have in David? We have no inheritance in the son of Jesse. [r]To
your tents, O Israel! Look now to your own house, David." So Israel went to their tents.
17 But Rehoboam reigned over [s]the people of Israel who lived in the cities of Judah. 18 Then
King Rehoboam sent [t]Adoram, who was taskmaster over the forced labor, and all Israel
stoned him to death with stones. And King Rehoboam hurried to mount his chariot to
flee to Jerusalem. 19 [u]So Israel has been in rebellion against the house of David to this day.
20 And when all Israel heard that Jeroboam had returned, they sent and called him to the
assembly and made him king over all Israel. There was none that followed the house of
David but [v]the tribe of Judah only.
21 [w]When Rehoboam came to Jerusalem, he assembled all the house of Judah and the
tribe of Benjamin, 180,000 chosen warriors, to fight against the house of Israel, to restore
the kingdom to Rehoboam the son of Solomon. 22 But the word of God came to [x]Shemaiah
the man of God: 23 "Say to Rehoboam the son of Solomon, king of Judah, and to all the
house of Judah and Benjamin, and to the [y]rest of the people, 24 'Thus says the LORD, You
shall not go up or fight against your relatives the people of Israel. Every man return to
his home, [z]for this thing is from me.' " So they listened to the word of the LORD and went
home again, according to the word of the LORD.

12:1–14:31 *The Kingdom Is Divided.* The kingdom is now torn away, as threatened in ch. 11. Two kingdoms emerge: Judah and Israel, ruled by Rehoboam and Jeroboam respectively.

12:1–33 *The Kingdom Torn Away.* As Moses once led his people out from slavery under the Egyptian pharaoh, so Jeroboam now leads Israel out from "slavery" under the house of David; but "Jeroboam as Moses" is soon transformed into "Jeroboam as Aaron" as he fashions golden calves for Israel to worship. Such idolatrous worship will eventually result in disaster for Israel.

12:1 Shechem is a place of covenant renewal (Josh. 24:1–27), and the place also where kingship first briefly intruded itself into the tribal life of Israel (Judges 9). It is the ideal place for a prospective king to be invited and confronted with the question of how he is going to exercise his kingship.

12:4 Your father made our yoke heavy. Solomon's regime in the latter years has been unduly harsh. The Israelites are no longer a people living in freedom in the Promised Land; they have become once more a people under **hard service**, as they were in Egypt (Ex. 1:14; 2:23). They toil as oxen would under a **heavy yoke**.

12:10–11 My little finger is thicker than my father's thighs. The foolish advice of the younger men to Rehoboam is literally in Hebrew "my little one is thicker than my father's thighs," most likely a reference to his sexual organ rather than a literal finger. Power and sexual potency were very much connected in the ancient Near East (see ch. 1). The equally obscure **scorpions** (12:11) is probably a reference to a particularly vicious form of whip.

12:14 I will add to your yoke. In reacting in this way, Rehoboam is behaving exactly as Pharaoh had behaved before him, responding to the words of Moses by increasing the oppression (cf. Ex. 5:1–21).

12:15 a turn of affairs brought about by the LORD. Amid all the human decisions, God's decision is being carried through, as was the case with the hardening of Pharaoh's heart (Ex. 4:21; 7:3–4, 13).

12:16 What portion do we have in David? Kingship cannot be imposed on the people but must have their consent, so they take upon their lips a cry that is similar to that of Sheba in 2 Sam. 20:1, and they leave for **their tents**.

12:18 Adoram. It is not clear whether this is the person mentioned in 4:6 and 5:14. He comes not to reimpose conditions of **forced labor** on Israel (since Israel has not yet been under such conditions; 9:15–23), but to initiate them. If the Israelites think their experience under Solomon was the "hard service" of Egypt, they are to discover now that this was as nothing compared to life under the proposed new regime. This regime will regard them as if they were Canaanites.

12:24 they listened to the word of the LORD and went home. At least for now a war is averted, but this peace does not last long. The reader will later learn of continual war between north and south throughout the period after the division of the kingdoms (14:30; 15:6, 16), until the two sides see that they are indeed **relatives** (12:24; cf. ch. 22, esp. v. 44) and should accept the status quo.

The Divided Kingdom: Kings of Judah (all dates B.C.)

King	Years of Reign	Total Years	Accession Year*	Possible Co-Reigns	References in 1–2 Kings**	Notes
Rehoboam	931/930–915/914	17			1 Kings 12:1–24; 14:21–31	
Abijah/Abijam	915/914–912/911	3	18 of Jeroboam I		1 Kings 15:1–8	
Asa	912/911–871/870	41	20 of Jeroboam I		1 Kings 15:9–24	
Jehoshaphat	871/870–849/848	25	4 of Ahab	with Asa from 873	1 Kings 22:41–50	
Jehoram/Joram	849/848–842	7 (8)	5 of Joram	with Jehoshaphat from 853	2 Kings 8:16–24	Married Athaliah, a daughter of Ahab (Israel)
Ahaziah	842–841	1 (2)	11 of Joram		2 Kings 8:25–29; 9:21–28	Killed by Jehu (Israel) in 841
Athaliah (Q.)	841–835	6			2 Kings 11:1–20	Killed by Jehoiada the priest
Joash/Jehoash	835–796/795	39 (40)	7 of Jehu		2 Kings 12:1–21	Hidden from Athaliah for 6 years (841–835) by Jehosheba, the sister of Ahaziah; protected by Jehoiada the priest
Amaziah	796/795–767	29	2 of Joash/ Jehoash		2 Kings 14:1–22	
Uzziah/Azariah	767–740/739	52	27 of Jeroboam II	with Amaziah from 791	2 Kings 15:1–7	
Jotham	750–735/730	16 (20)	2 of Pekah	Uzziah is alive in 750 but inactive in rule (cf. 2 Kings 15:5)	2 Kings 15:32–38	
Ahaz	735/730–715	16 (20)	17 of Pekah		2 Kings 16:1–20	
Hezekiah	715–687/686	29	3 of Hoshea	with Ahaz from 728	2 Kings 18:1–20:21	
Manasseh	687/686–642	55	No further accession dates after fall of Israel in 722	with Hezekiah from 697/696	2 Kings 21:1–18	
Amon	642–640	2			2 Kings 21:19–26	
Josiah	640–609	31			2 Kings 22:1–23:30	Killed by Pharaoh Neco of Egypt
Jehoahaz	609	3 months			2 Kings 23:31–34	Taken by Pharaoh Neco to Egypt
Jehoiakim	609–598	11			2 Kings 23:35–24:7	Set on the throne by Pharaoh Neco of Egypt
Jehoiachin/ Jeconiah	598–597	3 months			2 Kings 24:8–17; 25:27–30	Exiled to Babylon by Nebuchadnezzar in 597; released and honored by Evil-merodach of Babylon in 562
Zedekiah	597–586	11			2 Kings 24:18–20	Zedekiah is Jehoiachin's uncle; Jerusalem and Judah fall to Babylon in 586

**This chart follows the dating method found in both Kings and Chronicles: For Judah, accession to the throne is marked by a year within the reign of a king of Israel. Parentheses—e.g., 39 (40)—indicate non-accession year dating (year of accession is counted in the totals of both the predecessor and the new king). The actual number of years in a reign can be determined by subtracting 1 from the number given (40 – 1 = 39 actual years).*

***The verses cited in 1–2 Kings do not include the initial mention of a ruler, which occurs in reference to the death of his father (e.g., Abijam in 1 Kings 14:31).*

The Divided Kingdom: Kings of Israel (all dates B.C.)

King	Years of Reign	Total Years	Accession Year*	Possible Co-Reigns	References in 1–2 Kings**	Notes
Jeroboam I	931/930–911/910	21 (22)			1 Kings 11:26–40; 12:1–14:20	
Nadab	911/910–910/909	1 (2)	2 of Asa		1 Kings 15:25–32	Killed by Baasha
Baasha	910/909–887/886	23 (24)	3 of Asa		1 Kings 15:27–16:7	
Elah	887/886–886/885	1 (2)	26 of Asa		1 Kings 16:8–14	Killed by Zimri
Zimri	886/885	7 days	26 of Asa		1 Kings 16:9–20	Killed himself by burning the king's house down while he was in it
Omri	886/885–875/874	11 (12)	31 of Asa	Tibni reigns after Zimri for 5 years as rival to Omri	1 Kings 16:16–17, 21–28	
Ahab	875/874–853	21 (22)	38 of Asa		1 Kings 16:29–17:1; 18:1–19:3; 20:1–22:40	
Ahaziah	853–852	1 (2)	17 of Jehoshaphat		1 Kings 22:51–53; 2 Kings 1:1–18	
Joram/Jehoram	852–841	11 (12)	18 of Jehoshaphat		2 Kings 3:1–27; ("king of Israel" in 6:8–7:20); 9:14–26	Killed by Jehu in 841
Jehu	841–814/813	27 (28)			2 Kings 9:1–10:36	
Jehoahaz	814/813–798/797	16 (17)	23 of Joash/ Jehoash		2 Kings 13:1–9	
Joash/Jehoash	798/797–782/781	15 (16)	37 of Joash/ Jehoash		2 Kings 13:10–25; 14:8–16	
Jeroboam II	782/781–753	41	15 of Amaziah	with Joash/ Jehoash from 793/792	2 Kings 14:23–29	
Zechariah	753–752	6 months	38 of Uzziah		2 Kings 15:8–12	Killed by Shallum
Shallum	752	1 month	39 of Uzziah		2 Kings 15:10, 13–16	Killed by Menahem
Menahem	752–742/741	10	39 of Uzziah		2 Kings 15:14–22	
Pekahiah	742/741–740/739	2	50 of Uzziah		2 Kings 15:23–26	Killed by Pekah
Pekah	740/739–732/731	20***	52 of Uzziah	20 years counted from 752 to include the reigns of rivals Menahem and Pekahiah	2 Kings 15:25, 27–31	Killed by Hoshea
Hoshea	732/731–722	9	12 of Ahaz		2 Kings 15:30; 17:1–6	Samaria and Israel fall to Assyria in 722

** This chart follows the dating method found in both Kings and Chronicles: For Israel, accession to the throne is marked by a year within the reign of a king of Judah. Parentheses—e.g., 21 (22)—indicate non-accession year dating (year of accession is counted in the totals of both the predecessor and the new king). The actual number of years in a reign can be determined by subtracting 1 from the number given (22 – 1 = 21 actual years).*

***The verses cited in 1–2 Kings do not include the initial mention of a ruler when it occurs in reference to the death of his father (e.g., Nadab in 1 Kings 14:20).*

****See note on 2 Kings 15:27–31.*

Jeroboam's Golden Calves

25 Then Jeroboam [a]built Shechem in the hill country of Ephraim and lived there. And
he went out from there and [b]built Penuel. 26 And Jeroboam said in his heart, "Now the
kingdom will turn back to the house of David. 27 If this people [c]go up to offer sacrifices
in the temple of the LORD at Jerusalem, then the heart of this people will turn again to
their lord, to Rehoboam king of Judah, and they will kill me and return to Rehoboam
king of Judah." 28 So the king took counsel and [d]made two calves of gold. And he said to
the people, "You have gone up to Jerusalem long enough. [e]Behold your gods, O Israel,
who brought you up out of the land of Egypt." 29 And he set one in Bethel, and the other
he put in Dan. 30 Then [f]this thing became a sin, for the people went as far as Dan to be
before one.[1] 31 He also made [g]temples on high places and [h]appointed priests from among
all the people, who were not of the Levites. 32 And Jeroboam appointed a feast on the fifteenth day of the eighth month like [i]the feast that was in Judah, and he offered sacrifices
on the altar. So he did in Bethel, sacrificing to the calves that he made. And he placed in
Bethel [j]the priests of the high places that he had made. 33 He went up to the altar that he
had made in Bethel on the fifteenth day in the eighth month, in the month that he had
devised from his own heart. And he instituted a feast for the people of Israel and went up
to the altar [k]to make offerings.

A Man of God Confronts Jeroboam

13 And behold, [l]a man of God came out of Judah by the word of the LORD to Bethel.
Jeroboam was standing by the altar [m]to make offerings. 2 [n]And the man cried against
the altar by the word of the LORD and said, "O altar, altar, thus says the LORD: 'Behold, a
son shall be born to the house of David, [o]Josiah by name, and he shall sacrifice on you the
priests of the high places who make offerings on you, and human bones shall be burned
on you.'" 3 And he gave [p]a sign the same day, saying, "This is the sign that the LORD has
spoken: 'Behold, the altar shall be torn down, and the ashes that are on it shall be poured
out.'" 4 And when the king heard the saying of the man of God, which he cried against
the altar at Bethel, Jeroboam stretched out his hand from the altar, saying, "Seize him."

[1] Septuagint *went to the one at Bethel and to the other as far as Dan*

25 [a][Judg. 9:45] [b][Judg. 8:17]
27 [c]Deut. 12:5, 6
28 [d]2 Kgs. 10:29; 17:16; 2 Chr. 11:15; 13:8; Hos. 8:5, 6; 10:5; 13:2; [ch. 14:9] [e][Ex. 32:4, 8]
30 [f]ch. 13:34; 2 Kgs. 17:21
31 [g]ch. 13:32 [h]ch. 13:33; 2 Kgs. 17:32; 2 Chr. 11:14, 15; 13:9
32 [i]Lev. 23:33, 34; Num. 29:12 [j]ch. 13:2; [Amos 7:13]
33 [k]ch. 13:1

Chapter 13

1 [l]2 Kgs. 23:17 [m]ch. 12:33
2 [n]ver. 32 [o]2 Kgs. 23:15, 16
3 [p]See Judg. 6:17

12:25–33 A ritual complex from the ninth century B.C. has been discovered at Tell Dan. It consists of a square enclosure with a raised platform inside, perhaps as a base for a temple, and a sacrificial altar. This sacred center is possibly what remains of what Jeroboam erected at the site of Dan.

12:25 Jeroboam built Shechem . . . Penuel. The first task undertaken by Jeroboam was the obvious one of defense. He fortified (built up) two major cities.

12:27–28 two calves of gold. Fear that the presence of the **temple of the LORD at Jerusalem** will lead northern Israel to return to Rehoboam leads Jeroboam to invent his own worship system, central to which are these calves. His words to the people about them—**Behold your gods, O Israel, who brought you up out of the land of Egypt**—are almost exactly the words with which the people greeted the construction of the calf by Aaron (Ex. 32:4). These bull icons were unacceptable as representations of the Lord, since Mosaic religion requires a clear distinction between the Creator and the created. The worship of bull icons as representations of *other* gods was more unacceptable still. It blurs the distinction between the Lord and other gods, a blurring already in evidence in 1 Kings 14:15 (see note). The high god of the Canaanite pantheon, El, is frequently called "the bull" in ancient texts from Ugarit in Syria, and his son Baal-hadad (the biblical Baal) is himself also represented as a bull. The bull is further associated in Sumerian and Akkadian texts with the worship of the moon god Sin, and in Egyptian texts with the high god Amon-Re. A cult site from c. 1200 B.C. has been found on a hill in northern Samaria. Among the remains was a bull figurine with well-defined genitalia, representing fertility and potency. Baal worship was probably occurring at this high place. Judges 6:25 reveals that a rogue Baal cult was in practice among Israelites.

12:29–33 Jeroboam builds centers of worship within his own territory to rival Jerusalem—one in the far north (**Dan**) and one in the far south (**Bethel**). This represents the proliferation of "high places" about which the authors of 1–2 Kings are so deeply concerned (see 1 Kings 3:2). The sanctuary at Bethel is the more important of the two for these authors, for it is here that Jeroboam invests the major part of his effort to set up his new worship arrangements. He builds a temple at this high place, appoints **priests** to service it who had not been set apart by God for such service, and invents a central **feast** to celebrate in it—a version of the Feast of Booths (or Tabernacles), celebrated in Jerusalem in the seventh month (cf. 8:2; Lev. 23:33–43), but now in northern Israel in the **eighth month**. Aaron, too, having made his golden calf, built an altar and announced a festival on a date **devised from his own heart** (cf. Ex. 32:5); and on that occasion, too, the **Levites** were not involved in the celebrations (Ex. 32:26). It is false worship, and Jeroboam's action in leading the people into it will constantly be referred to in the rest of 1–2 Kings (e.g., 1 Kings 15:26, 34; 16:26). This worship is Israel's characteristic sin that eventually leads the people to exile in a foreign land (2 Kings 17:20–23).

13:1–34 *The Man of God from Judah.* Jeroboam stands at the altar of his new temple in Bethel as Solomon had stood at his altar in Jerusalem (8:22), ready to dedicate it to his gods; but since this temple has no legitimacy, he does not get a chance to speak.

13:2 The prophetic words about the future king **Josiah** point forward to a time when all the northern Israelite dynasties have come to an end, and only the **house of David** remains to take action against Bethel (2 Kings 22:1–23:30).

13:3–5 Since Josiah's reign is still a long way off, a **sign** is also described and then enacted, indicating that the prophecy is true: **the altar . . . was torn down, and the ashes poured out from the altar**. This demonstration of God's power strikingly illustrates the truth that God is not under Jeroboam's control just because he has invented a new worship system, any more than God's prophet is under royal control when the king's **hand** stretches out to capture him, and the king experiences an immediate judgment from God: **he could not draw it back to himself**.

6[q]Ex. 8:8; 9:28; 10:17; Num. 21:7; Acts 8:24
7[r][1 Sam. 9:7; 2 Kgs. 5:15]
8[s]Num. 22:18; 24:13 [t]ver. 16, 17
11[u]ver. 25; [2 Kgs. 23:18]
16[v]ver. 8, 9
17[w]ch. 20:35; 1 Thess. 4:15
24[x]ch. 20:36
25[y]ver. 11

And his hand, which he stretched out against him, dried up, so that he could not draw it
back to himself. 5 The altar also was torn down, and the ashes poured out from the altar,
according to the sign that the man of God had given by the word of the LORD. 6 And the
king said to the man of God, [q]"Entreat now the favor of the LORD your God, and pray for
me, that my hand may be restored to me." And the man of God entreated the LORD, and
the king's hand was restored to him and became as it was before. 7 And the king said to the
man of God, "Come home with me, and refresh yourself, and [r]I will give you a reward."
8 And the man of God said to the king, [s]"If you give me half your house, [t]I will not go in
with you. And I will not eat bread or drink water in this place, 9 for so was it commanded
me by the word of the LORD, saying, 'You shall neither eat bread nor drink water nor
return by the way that you came.'" 10 So he went another way and did not return by the
way that he came to Bethel.

The Prophet's Disobedience

11 Now [u]an old prophet lived in Bethel. And his sons[1] came and told him all that the
man of God had done that day in Bethel. They also told to their father the words that he
had spoken to the king. 12 And their father said to them, "Which way did he go?" And his
sons showed him the way that the man of God who came from Judah had gone. 13 And
he said to his sons, "Saddle the donkey for me." So they saddled the donkey for him and
he mounted it. 14 And he went after the man of God and found him sitting under an oak.
And he said to him, "Are you the man of God who came from Judah?" And he said, "I am."
15 Then he said to him, "Come home with me and eat bread." 16 And he said, [v]"I may not
return with you, or go in with you, neither will I eat bread nor drink water with you in
this place, 17 for it was said to me [w]by the word of the LORD, 'You shall neither eat bread
nor drink water there, nor return by the way that you came.'" 18 And he said to him, "I also
am a prophet as you are, and an angel spoke to me by the word of the LORD, saying, 'Bring
him back with you into your house that he may eat bread and drink water.'" But he lied to
him. 19 So he went back with him and ate bread in his house and drank water.

20 And as they sat at the table, the word of the LORD came to the prophet who had brought
him back. 21 And he cried to the man of God who came from Judah, "Thus says the LORD,
'Because you have disobeyed the word of the LORD and have not kept the command that
the LORD your God commanded you, 22 but have come back and have eaten bread and
drunk water in the place of which he said to you, "Eat no bread and drink no water," your
body shall not come to the tomb of your fathers.'" 23 And after he had eaten bread and
drunk, he saddled the donkey for the prophet whom he had brought back. 24 And as he
went away [x]a lion met him on the road and killed him. And his body was thrown in the
road, and the donkey stood beside it; the lion also stood beside the body. 25 And behold,
men passed by and saw the body thrown in the road and the lion standing by the body.
And they came and told it in the city where [y]the old prophet lived.

26 And when the prophet who had brought him back from the way heard of it, he said,
"It is the man of God who disobeyed the word of the LORD; therefore the LORD has given
him to the lion, which has torn him and killed him, according to the word that the LORD
spoke to him." 27 And he said to his sons, "Saddle the donkey for me." And they saddled
it. 28 And he went and found his body thrown in the road, and the donkey and the lion
standing beside the body. The lion had not eaten the body or torn the donkey. 29 And the
prophet took up the body of the man of God and laid it on the donkey and brought it

[1] Septuagint, Syriac, Vulgate; Hebrew *son*

13:7–32 Jeroboam's invitation to the **man of God** to dine and receive a **reward** is best understood as an attempt to buy his loyalty, perhaps hoping for the curse on the altar to be reversed. The invitation from the **old prophet** living **in Bethel** is best understood in the same way (v. 15), as an attempt to stave off the destruction of Bethel (and the desecration of his own tomb that he knows must follow the Judean's words of v. 2; see v. 32). No doubt concern about the possibility of such a corruption of the man of God lay behind the detailed instructions given to him about his journey (vv. 9, 17)—that he should go directly to Bethel and come directly back, not even stopping to **eat** and **drink**; and that he should vary his route so that he could not be easily found and prevented from completing his mission (he should not **return by the way that** he **came**). Disobedience leads him to an unfortunate end: a **lion** meets him on the road and kills him (vv. 23–25)—a lion ordained by God and behaving quite out of character (**the lion had not eaten the body or torn the donkey**, v. 28). True prophecy will bring forth the judgment it promises. Even prophets cannot escape if they are disobedient. **Bethel** will indeed be destroyed (v. 32), and by extension all the other **houses of the high places** in **Samaria**, for which Bethel provides the focal point. The name "Samaria" is used here by extension for the territory of which the city of Samaria became the capital under Omri, the father of Ahab (16:24).

back to the city[1] to mourn and to bury him. **30** And he laid the body in his own grave. And
they mourned over him, saying, [z]"Alas, my brother!" **31** And after he had buried him, he
said to his sons, "When I die, bury me in the grave in which the man of God is buried; [a]lay
my bones beside his bones. **32** [b]For the saying that he called out by the word of the LORD
against the altar in Bethel and against [c]all the houses of the high places that are in the
cities of [d]Samaria shall surely come to pass."
33 After this thing Jeroboam did not turn from his evil way, but made priests for the
high places again from among all the people. Any who would, he ordained to be priests
of the high places. **34** [e]And this thing became sin to the house of Jeroboam, [f]so as to cut it
off and to destroy it from the face of the earth.

Prophecy Against Jeroboam

14 At that time Abijah the son of Jeroboam fell sick. **2** And Jeroboam said to his wife,
"Arise, and disguise yourself, that it not be known that you are the wife of Jeroboam,
and go to [g]Shiloh. Behold, Ahijah the prophet is there, [h]who said of me that I should be
king over this people. **3** [i]Take with you ten loaves, some cakes, and a jar of honey, and go
to him. He will tell you what shall happen to the child."
4 Jeroboam's wife did so. She arose and went to [g]Shiloh and came to the house of [j]Ahijah.
Now [j]Ahijah could not see, for his eyes were dim because of his age. **5** And the LORD said
to [j]Ahijah, "Behold, the wife of Jeroboam is coming to inquire of you concerning her son,
for he is sick. Thus and thus shall you say to her."
When she came, she pretended to be another woman. **6** But when [j]Ahijah heard the
sound of her feet, as she came in at the door, he said, "Come in, wife of Jeroboam. Why
do you pretend to be another? For I am charged with unbearable news for you. **7** Go, tell
Jeroboam, 'Thus says the LORD, the God of Israel: [k]"Because I exalted you from among the
people and made you leader over my people Israel **8** and [l]tore the kingdom away from the
house of David and gave it to you, and yet you have not been [m]like my servant David, who
kept my commandments and followed me with all his heart, doing only that which was
right in my eyes, **9** but you have done evil above all who were before you and have gone and
[n]made for yourself other gods and [o]metal images, provoking me to anger, and [p]have cast
me behind your back, **10** therefore behold, I will bring harm upon the house of Jeroboam
and [q]will cut off from Jeroboam every male, [r]both bond and free in Israel, and [s]will burn
up the house of Jeroboam, as a man burns up dung until it is all gone. **11** [t]Anyone belonging to Jeroboam who dies in the city the dogs shall eat, and anyone who dies in the open
country the birds of the heavens shall eat, for the LORD has spoken it."' **12** Arise therefore,

[1] Septuagint; Hebrew *he came to the city of the old prophet*

30 [z][Jer. 22:18]
31 [a][2 Kgs. 23:17, 18]
32 [b]ver. 2; See 2 Kgs. 23:16-19 [c]ch. 12:31 [d][ch. 16:24]
34 [e]ch. 12:30; 2 Kgs. 17:21 [f]ch. 14:10; [ch. 15:29, 30]

Chapter 14

2 [g]See Josh. 18:1 [h]See ch. 11:29-31
3 [i][1 Sam. 9:7, 8]
4 [g][See ver. 2 above] [j]ch. 11:29
5 [j][See ver. 4 above]
6 [j][See ver. 4 above]
7 [k]ch. 16:2; [2 Sam. 12:7, 8]
8 [l]ch. 11:31 [m]ch. 11:33, 38; 15:5; [ch. 9:4]
9 [n]ch. 12:28; 2 Chr. 11:15 [o][Ex. 34:17] [p]Ezek. 23:35; [Neh. 9:26; Ps. 50:17]
10 [q]ch. 21:21; 2 Kgs. 9:8 [r]Deut. 32:36; 2 Kgs. 14:26 [s]ch. 16:3
11 [t]ch. 16:4; 21:24

13:33–34 did not turn from his evil way, but made priests . . . again. The Hebrew is literally "did not return from his evil way, but returned and made priests," playing on the verb *shub* ("to return") earlier in the story (vv. 16, 18, 19, 20, 22, 23, 26, 29) and particularly on the phrase "return by the way" in vv. 9, 10, 17. The man of God was told not to retrace his steps at any point on his journey, but he did so in order to return to the prophet's house (vv. 19, 22). Because he allowed himself to be brought back alive ("returned") by this prophet (vv. 18, 20, 23, 26), he was eventually brought back dead (v. 29), as God's judgment fell upon him. In spite of this, Jeroboam also "retraces his steps," and this too will bring downfall and destruction (v. 34).

14:1–20 *The End of Jeroboam.* Jeroboam had been promised a dynasty ("house") just like David's (11:38). His desire also to have a temple ("house") just like David's, however, led him into disobedience, and ch. 13 has just revealed what happens to the disobedient. First Kings 14:1–20 now describes what happened as a result of Jeroboam's desire to have the two "houses" he wanted instead of the one he was promised.

14:2 disguise yourself. In spite of the events of ch. 13, Jeroboam still thinks he can control his world, using religion to his own advantage. He apparently believes that he can fool the old prophet **Ahijah** into giving him a positive message about his son. The theme of royal disguise appears in other places in the OT where the point is made that God, not the king, will determine the course of events (e.g., 1 Samuel 28; 1 Kings 20:35–43; 22:29–38; 2 Chron. 35:20–27).

14:6 I am charged with unbearable news. Jeroboam's wife has been sent to **Ahijah** to find out about her sick child; she discovers when she arrives at the prophet's house that *he* has also been sent to *her* with a message about the kingship.

14:10 Since Jeroboam has failed to be like David (v. 8) and has worshiped other gods as Solomon did (v. 9), his dynasty will come to an end for lack of **male** descendants. The Hebrew behind **"every** male" is literally "he who urinates against a wall" (see also 1 Sam. 25:22, 34; 1 Kings 16:11; 21:21; 2 Kings 9:8), and the imagery is thus connected to that of God's judgment (**as a man burns up dung** or excrement **until it is all gone**). God is going to clean up Jeroboam's house. The Hebrew behind **bond and free** appears on four other occasions in the OT (Deut. 32:36; 1 Kings 21:21; 2 Kings 9:8; and, in a slightly different form, 2 Kings 14:26). It is a difficult phrase to interpret, but probably is an idiom for the ability of the males of the royal house to be of strong help to the king; neither those who are important to Jeroboam in this regard nor those who are not will be able to assist him. A contrast with David's dynasty is seen here: David "shall not lack" (lit., "there shall not be cut off for David") a descendant on the throne (1 Kings 2:4; 8:25; 9:5), but Jeroboam's descendants will be **cut off**.

14:11 Jeroboam's dynasty will come to a dishonorable end, since the bodies mentioned will not be buried but will be eaten by **dogs** and **birds** (cf. 1 Sam. 31:8–13 for the importance of proper burial in Israel). Only Jeroboam's son Abijah will escape this fate (1 Kings 14:13).

14:15 the LORD will strike Israel. Ahijah turns from the immediate situation to what will happen in the distant future. In the absence of a strong

12[u]ver. 17
13[v]2 Chr. 12:12; 19:3
14[w]See ch. 15:27-29
15[x]Deut. 29:28; Ps. 52:5; Prov. 2:22 [y]Josh. 23:15, 16 [z][2 Kgs. 15:29] [a]Ex. 34:13; Deut. 12:3
17[b]ch. 15:21, 33; 16:6, 8, 15, 23 [c]ver. 12
18[d]ver. 13
19[e]See 2 Chr. 13:2-20
21[f]2 Chr. 12:13 [g]ch. 11:32, 36 [h]2 Chr. 12:13
22[i][2 Chr. 12:1, 14] [j]See Num. 25:11
23[k]See Deut. 12:2 [l]See Ex. 23:24 [m]ver. 15 [n]Deut. 12:2; 2 Kgs. 16:4; Isa. 57:5; Jer. 2:20
24[o]See Deut. 23:17
25[p]2 Chr. 12:2, 9-11
26[q][ch. 15:18] [r]ch. 10:17

go to your house. [u]When your feet enter the city, the child shall die. **13** And all Israel shall
mourn for him and bury him, for he only of Jeroboam shall come to the grave, because
in him [v]there is found something pleasing to the LORD, the God of Israel, in the house
of Jeroboam. **14** [w]Moreover, the LORD will raise up for himself a king over Israel who shall
cut off the house of Jeroboam today. And henceforth, **15** the LORD will strike Israel as a
reed is shaken in the water, and [x]root up Israel out of [y]this good land that he gave to their
fathers and scatter them [z]beyond the Euphrates,[1] because they have made their [a]Asherim,
provoking the LORD to anger. **16** And he will give Israel up because of the sins of Jeroboam,
which he sinned and made Israel to sin."

17 Then Jeroboam's wife arose and departed and came to [b]Tirzah. And [c]as she came to the
threshold of the house, the child died. **18** And all Israel buried him and mourned for him,
[d]according to the word of the LORD, which he spoke by his servant Ahijah the prophet.

The Death of Jeroboam

19 Now the rest of the acts of Jeroboam, [e]how he warred and how he reigned, behold,
they are written in the Book of the Chronicles of the Kings of Israel. **20** And the time that
Jeroboam reigned was twenty-two years. And he slept with his fathers, and Nadab his son
reigned in his place.

Rehoboam Reigns in Judah

21 [f]Now Rehoboam the son of Solomon reigned in Judah. Rehoboam was forty-one years
old when he began to reign, and he reigned seventeen years in Jerusalem, [g]the city that the
LORD had chosen out of all the tribes of Israel, to put his name there. [h]His mother's name
was Naamah the Ammonite. **22** [i]And Judah did what was evil in the sight of the LORD, and
they [j]provoked him to jealousy with their sins that they committed, more than all that
their fathers had done. **23** For they also built for themselves [k]high places [l]and pillars and
[m]Asherim on every high hill and [n]under every green tree, **24** and there were also [o]male cult
prostitutes in the land. They did according to all the abominations of the nations that the
LORD drove out before the people of Israel.

25 [p]In the fifth year of King Rehoboam, Shishak king of Egypt came up against Jerusalem.
26 He took away the treasures of the house of the LORD and the treasures of the king's house.
[q]He took away everything. He also took away all the shields of gold [r]that Solomon had

[1] Hebrew *the River*

dynasty to rule Israel, this nation is destined to know only the instability of a **reed . . . shaken** (or "swaying") **in the water**. Eventually the Israelites will suffer exile from the **good land that he gave to their fathers** to a land **beyond the Euphrates** River. The political instability of which Ahijah speaks is well described in the following account of the northern kingdom; the land beyond the Euphrates, it will turn out, is Assyria (2 Kings 17:1–6, 21–23). The idolatrous worship that lies at the root of Israel's problem is here summed up in terms of the making of **Asherim**, or Asherah poles. The goddess Asherah is known from Ugaritic texts under the name Athirat, the wife of the chief god El and the mother of the gods. In syncretistic Israelite circles she inevitably appears as the wife of the Lord. The Asherim were cult symbols connected with the worship of this goddess, probably wooden artifacts representing a tree (cf. Deut. 16:21, which suggests that sometimes an "Asherah" could actually *be* a tree; Hos. 4:12).

14:17 Jeroboam has apparently moved his royal court to **Tirzah**, although this was not previously mentioned in the narrative.

14:19 the Book of the Chronicles of the Kings of Israel. The authors of Kings specifically claim to have had access to written sources of information about the monarchic period, both for Israel and for Judah (v. 29; 15:7, 23, 31; 16:5, 14, 20, 27; 22:39, 45; 2 Kings 1:18; 8:23; 10:34; 12:19; 13:8, 12; 14:15, 18, 28; 15:6, 11, 15, 21, 26, 31, 36; 16:19; 20:20; 21:17, 25; 23:28; 24:5). The reference here is to Israelite royal annals, preserved in palace archives and temple libraries or archives along with foreign annals and inscriptions of various kinds. No copy of any of these chronicles remains today; they are not found in the Bible, and they are different from the books of 1 and 2 Chronicles. By the end of the second millennium B.C. and the beginning of the first, literacy was widespread in and around Palestine, and writing was being employed in legal, business, literary, and religious texts. In Iron Age Israel itself, from 1200 B.C. all the way to the fall of Judah in 587–586, writing was a pervasive phenomenon.

14:21–31 *The End of Rehoboam.* The story of Rehoboam's reign, begun in ch. 12, has been delayed as the authors have followed Jeroboam through rebellion to idolatry and judgment, and on to death. They now return to what has been happening in Judah in the meantime.

14:22–24 Judah did what was evil. It is a marked feature of 1–2 Kings that each king mentioned is evaluated in terms of his commitment to the Lord, or lack of it, as evidenced by his religious policies (see note on 1 Kings 11:6; and chart, p. 628). Here, however, the emphasis falls on the nation as a whole rather than simply on the king himself; the whole nation has become involved in idolatrous worship. The text thus looks ahead to the end of Judah, just as was the case with Israel (14:15). God will drive Judah out of the Promised Land just as he "drove out" the various peoples that lived there before because of their **abominations**.

14:23 High places and **Asherim** (see notes on 3:2; 14:15) as aspects of the idolatrous worship of Judah are mentioned alongside **pillars** (Hb. *matstsebot*), which Deut. 12:3 lists among the Canaanite cult objects that the people must destroy upon entry to the land. These pillars were upright standing stones of various sizes, dedicated to particular deities and sometimes bearing the image and inscription of a deity.

14:24 male cult prostitutes. One aspect of the syncretistic worship of Judah under Rehoboam was religiously legitimized prostitution within the sanctuary. It is possible that the sexual intercourse envisaged had a specifically ritual character, designed to persuade the gods and goddesses to act in a similar way and deliver, through their intercourse, fertility to the land and to the community (cf. Hos. 4:1–19).

14:25–26 Shishak king of Egypt has often been identified with the

made, 27 and King Rehoboam made in their place shields of bronze, and committed them
to the hands of the officers of the guard, who kept the door of the king's house. 28 And as
often as the king went into the house of the LORD, the guard carried them and brought
them back to the guardroom.
29 [s]Now the rest of the acts of Rehoboam and all that he did, are they not written in the
Book of the Chronicles of the Kings of Judah? 30 [t]And there was war between Rehoboam
and Jeroboam continually. 31 And Rehoboam slept with his fathers and was buried with
his fathers in the city of David. [u]His mother's name was Naamah the Ammonite. And
[v]Abijam his son reigned in his place.

Abijam Reigns in Judah

15 [w]Now in the eighteenth year of King Jeroboam the son of Nebat, Abijam began
to reign over Judah. 2 He reigned for three years in Jerusalem. His mother's name
was Maacah the daughter of Abishalom. 3 And he walked in all the sins that his father did
before him, and [x]his heart was not wholly true to the LORD his God, as the heart of David
his father. 4 Nevertheless, for David's sake the LORD his God gave him [y]a lamp in Jerusalem,
setting up his son after him, and establishing Jerusalem, 5 because [z]David did what was
right in the eyes of the LORD and did not turn aside from anything that he commanded
him all the days of his life, [a]except in the matter of Uriah the Hittite. 6 [b]Now there was war
between Rehoboam and Jeroboam all the days of his life. 7 [c]The rest of the acts of Abijam
and all that he did, are they not written in the Book of the Chronicles of the Kings of Judah?
[d]And there was war between Abijam and Jeroboam. 8 [e]And Abijam slept with his fathers,
and they buried him in the city of David. And Asa his son reigned in his place.

29 [s]For ver. 29-31, see 2 Chr. 12:15, 16
30 [t]ch. 15:6; [ch. 12:21-24]
31 [u]2 Chr. 12:13 [v][Matt. 1:7]

Chapter 15
1 [w]2 Chr. 13:1, 2
3 [x]ch. 11:4; [ver. 14; ch. 8:61]
4 [y]See ch. 11:36
5 [z]ch. 9:4; 14:8 [a]2 Sam. 11:4, 15; 12:9
6 [b]ch. 14:30
7 [c][2 Chr. 13:22] [d]See 2 Chr. 13:2-20
8 [e]2 Chr. 14:1

Evaluating Kings of Israel and Judah in 1–2 Kings

Good / Bad / Mixture of good and bad

Kings of Israel	Kings of Judah
Jeroboam (1 Kings 12:25–33)	Rehoboam (1 Kings 14:21–31)
Nadab (1 Kings 15:25–31)	Abijam (1 Kings 15:1–8)
Baasha (1 Kings 15:33–16:7)	Asa (1 Kings 15:9–24)
Elah (1 Kings 16:8–14)	Jehoshaphat (1 Kings 22:41–50)
Zimri (1 Kings 16:15–20)	Jehoram (2 Kings 8:16–24)
Omri (1 Kings 16:21–27)	Ahaziah (2 Kings 8:25–29; 9:29)
Ahab (1 Kings 16:29–33)	Athaliah (2 Kings 11) queen
Ahaziah (1 Kings 22:51–53; 2 Kings 1)	Joash (2 Kings 12)
Joram (Jehoram) (2 Kings 1:17; 3:1–3)	Amaziah (2 Kings 14:1–22)
Jehu (2 Kings 9:30–10:36)	Azariah (Uzziah) (2 Kings 15:1–7)
Jehoahaz (2 Kings 13:1–9)	Jotham (2 Kings 15:32–38)
Jehoash (2 Kings 13:10–25)	Ahaz (2 Kings 16)
Jeroboam II (2 Kings 14:23–29)	Hezekiah (2 Kings 18–20)
Zechariah (2 Kings 15:8–12)	Manasseh (2 Kings 21:1–18)
Shallum (2 Kings 15:13–16)	Amon (2 Kings 21:19–26)
Menahem (2 Kings 15:17–22)	Josiah (2 Kings 22:1–23:30)
Pekahiah (2 Kings 15:23–26)	Jehoahaz (Shallum) (2 Kings 23:31–35)
Pekah (2 Kings 15:27–31)	Jehoiakim (2 Kings 23:36–24:7)
Hoshea (2 Kings 17)	Jehoiachin (2 Kings 24:8–17; 25:27–30)
	Zedekiah (2 Kings 24:18–25:26)

pharaoh Sheshonq I (945–924 B.C.), founder of the Twenty-second Dynasty in Egypt, whose army apparently passed through Judah on its way to fight in northern Israel. If Shishak *is* Sheshonq, one must imagine that he did not attack Jerusalem on his way north precisely because Rehoboam bought him off with the **treasures of the house of the LORD and the treasures of the king's house**. This is the first of a series of notices in 1–2 Kings about the loss of treasure from the temple and the palace (1 Kings 15:18; 2 Kings 14:14; 16:8; 18:15–16; 24:13), the culmination of which will come in 2 Kings 25. A monumental relief on the Bubastite Portal of the main temple of Amon at Karnak (near Luxor, in Egypt) catalogs, town by town, Shishak's military incursion into Israel and Judah. The Karnak relief provides striking verification of the biblical account.

14:29 the Book of the Chronicles of the Kings of Judah. See note on 14:19.

15:1–24 *Abijam and Asa.* The authors continue to tell about the kings of Judah before returning to pick up the threads of the history of Israel with Nadab, son of Jeroboam. Abijam (vv. 1–8) is a characteristically bad Judean king, indulging in the idolatry of Solomon in his later days and of Rehoboam; Asa (vv. 9–24) is a characteristically good Judean king, behaving relatively faithfully like David and the earlier Solomon. These two set the pattern for all the Judean kings who follow, who are measured in terms of whether they have been "like David" or not.

15:2–3 If **Abishalom** (v. 2) is the same as David's son Absalom, one should remember that the Hebrew terms **daughter** and **father** (as well as "mother," v. 10) do not necessarily refer to first-generation descent, and can mean "granddaughter" and "forefather" (and "grandmother").

15:4 a lamp in Jerusalem. See note on 11:34–39.

15:5 David was basically committed to God, although even he had sinned **in the matter of Uriah the Hittite** (with Uriah's wife, Bathsheba, 1 Samuel 11).

15:6–7 there was war between Rehoboam and Jeroboam . . . between Abijam and Jeroboam. This puzzling juxtaposition is presumably designed to emphasize the continuity between the two wars; the feud between the houses of Rehoboam and Jeroboam that began with the events of ch. 12 is still rumbling on. On the **Chronicles of the Kings**, see note on 14:19.

Asa Reigns in Judah

9 In the twentieth year of Jeroboam king of Israel, Asa began to reign over Judah, 10 and
he reigned forty-one years in Jerusalem. His mother's name was Maacah the daughter of
Abishalom. 11 [f]And Asa did what was right in the eyes of the LORD, as David his father had
done. 12 He put away the [g]male cult prostitutes out of the land and removed [h]all the idols
that his fathers had made. 13 [i]He also removed Maacah his mother from being queen mother
because she had made an abominable image for Asherah. And Asa cut down her image and
[j]burned it at the brook Kidron. 14 [k]But the high places were not taken away. Nevertheless, [l]the
heart of Asa was wholly true to the LORD all his days. 15 And [m]he brought into the house of the
LORD the sacred gifts of his father and his own sacred gifts, silver, and gold, and vessels.
16 [n]And there was war between Asa and Baasha king of Israel all their days. 17 [o]Baasha
king of Israel went up against Judah and [p]built Ramah, [q]that he might permit no one to
go out or come in to Asa king of Judah. 18 Then Asa took all the silver and the gold [r]that
were left in the treasures of the house of the LORD and the treasures of the king's house
and gave them into the hands of his servants. [s]And King Asa sent them to Ben-hadad the
son of Tabrimmon, the son of Hezion, king of Syria, [t]who lived in Damascus, saying,
19 "Let there be [u]a covenant[1] between me and you, as there was between my father and your
father. Behold, I am sending to you a present of silver and gold. Go, break your covenant
with Baasha king of Israel, that he may withdraw from me." 20 And Ben-hadad listened to
King Asa and sent the commanders of his armies against the cities of Israel and conquered
[v]Ijon, [w]Dan, [x]Abel-beth-maacah, and all [y]Chinneroth, with all the land of Naphtali. 21 And
when Baasha heard of it, [z]he stopped building Ramah, and he lived in [a]Tirzah. 22 Then
King Asa made a proclamation to all Judah, none was exempt, and they carried away the
stones of Ramah and its timber, with which Baasha had been building, and with them
King Asa built [b]Geba of Benjamin and [c]Mizpah. 23 [d]Now the rest of all the acts of Asa,
all his might, and all that he did, and the cities that he built, are they not written in the
Book of the Chronicles of the Kings of Judah? But in his old age he was diseased in his
feet. 24 And Asa slept with his fathers and was buried with his fathers in the city of David
his father, and [e]Jehoshaphat his son reigned in his place.

Nadab Reigns in Israel

25 [f]Nadab the son of Jeroboam began to reign over Israel in the second year of Asa king
of Judah, and he reigned over Israel two years. 26 He did what was evil in the sight of the
LORD [g]and walked in the way of his father, and in his sin [h]which he made Israel to sin.
27 [i]Baasha the son of Ahijah, of the house of Issachar, conspired against him. And Baasha
struck him down at [j]Gibbethon, which belonged to the Philistines, for Nadab and all Israel
were laying siege to Gibbethon. 28 So Baasha killed him in the third year of Asa king of
Judah and reigned in his place. 29 And as soon as he was king, he killed all the house of

[1] Or *treaty;* twice in this verse

11 [f]2 Chr. 14:2
12 [g]See ch. 14:24 [h][2 Chr. 15:8]
13 [i]For ver. 13-15, see 2 Chr. 15:16-18 [j][Ex. 32:20]
14 [k]ch. 22:43; [2 Kgs. 12:3; 14:4] [l][ver. 3]
15 [m][ch. 7:51]
16 [n]ver. 32
17 [o]For ver. 17-22, see 2 Chr. 16:1-6 [p]ver. 21, 22 [q][ch. 12:27]
18 [r]ch. 14:26 [s][2 Kgs. 12:18] [t]ch. 11:24
19 [u][2 Chr. 16:7]
20 [v]2 Kgs. 15:29 [w]Judg. 18:29 [x]2 Sam. 20:14; 2 Kgs. 15:29 [y]See Josh. 11:2
21 [z]ver. 17 [a]ch. 14:17; 16:6, 9
22 [b]Josh. 21:17 [c]Josh. 18:26
23 [d]For ver. 23, 24, see 2 Chr. 16:11-14
24 [e]2 Chr. 17:1; [Matt. 1:8]
25 [f]ch. 14:20
26 [g][ver. 34] [h]ver. 30; ch. 12:30; 14:16
27 [i]ch. 14:14 [j]ch. 16:15; Josh. 19:44; 21:23

15:10–11 Asa **reigned forty-one years**, from 910 to 869 B.C. On the generations depicted by mother, **daughter**, and **father**, see note on vv. 2–3.

15:12 He put away the male cult prostitutes. See note on 14:24.

15:13 The **queen mother** played an important role within the family politics of the court, as an adviser of the king and as teacher of the royal children. **abominable image for Asherah**. This is another object associated with the worship of the goddess Asherah to go alongside the Asherim mentioned in 14:15, 23. On the **brook Kidron**, see note on 2 Chron. 15:16.

15:14–15 the high places were not taken away. By removing the high places Asa could have focused his reforms upon worship in Jerusalem, but otherwise he was commended for his religious policy; he was faithful enough to bring **into the house of the LORD the sacred gifts of his father and his own sacred gifts**. When 2 Chron. 14:3 says that Asa removed the high places, this should be taken as meaning some but not all of them (cf. 2 Chron. 15:17).

15:17 Baasha king of Israel. Asa's reign in Judah was a long one, and he saw five Israelite kings rise and fall before the infamous Ahab began his rule (16:29). Baasha is the second of these (15:33–16:7), and he finds Asa's military position so precarious that he is able to push into Benjamin and fortify (build up) **Ramah**, only a few miles north of Jerusalem.

15:18–19 Asa took all the silver and the gold. Asa was forced to send a substantial bribe to **Damascus** to try to buy a new friend, reviving the treaty between his father Abijah and the previous Syrian king **Tabrimmon** (cf. note on 2 Chron. 16:2–5). A marker dedicated to the god Baal Melqart has been found at Aleppo in northern Syria. It bears an Aramaic inscription that mentions Barhada, son of Tabrimmon, son of **Hezion**.

15:23 Chronicles of the Kings. See note on 14:19.

15:25–16:34 *From Nadab to Ahab.* The fulfillment of the prophecy against the house of Jeroboam has been delayed until it has been made clear how differently God treats the house of David, whose wicked kings do not bring the downfall of the dynasty "because for David's sake the LORD his God gave him a lamp in Jerusalem" (15:4). Now, however, everything turns out as Ahijah had prophesied in ch. 14.

15:29 He left to the house of Jeroboam not one that breathed. Baasha fulfills the prophecy of 14:10–11.

Jeroboam. He left to the house of Jeroboam not one that breathed, until he had destroyed
it, [k]according to the word of the LORD that he spoke by his servant Ahijah the Shilonite. 30 It
was for the sins of Jeroboam that he sinned and [h]that he made Israel to sin, and because
of the anger to which he provoked the LORD, the God of Israel.
31 Now the rest of the acts of Nadab and all that he did, are they not written in the Book
of the Chronicles of the Kings of Israel? 32 [l]And there was war between Asa and Baasha
king of Israel all their days.

Baasha Reigns in Israel

33 In the third year of Asa king of Judah, Baasha the son of Ahijah began to reign over all
Israel at Tirzah, and he reigned twenty-four years. 34 He did what was evil in the sight of the
LORD [m]and walked in the way of Jeroboam and in his sin which he made Israel to sin.

16 And the word of the LORD came to [n]Jehu the son of [o]Hanani against Baasha, saying, 2 "Since I [p]exalted you out of the dust and made you leader over my people
Israel, and [q]you have walked in the way of Jeroboam and have made my people Israel to
sin, provoking me to anger with their sins, 3 behold, I will utterly [r]sweep away [s]Baasha
and his house, and I will make your house [t]like the house of Jeroboam the son of Nebat.
4 [u]Anyone belonging to Baasha who dies in the city the dogs shall eat, and anyone of his
who dies in the field the birds of the heavens shall eat."
5 Now the rest of the acts of Baasha and what he did, and his might, are they not written
in the Book of the Chronicles of the Kings of Israel? 6 And Baasha slept with his fathers

29 [k]ch. 14:10, 14
30 [h][See ver. 26 above]
32 [l]ver. 16
34 [m][ver. 26]

Chapter 16

1 [n]2 Chr. 19:2; 20:34 [o]2 Chr. 16:7
2 [p][ch. 14:7] [q]ch. 15:34
3 [r][ch. 14:10; 21:21] [s]ver. 11 [t][ch. 15:29]
4 [u][ch. 14:11; 21:24]

War between Israel and Judah

As Israel and Judah battled each other to determine their permanent border, King Baasha of Israel attempted to restrict access to Judah by moving the border down to Ramah. Rather than fight with Baasha himself, King Asa of Judah bribed Ben-hadad of Syria to attack the northern border of Israel and force Baasha to withdraw from Ramah. Once Baasha withdrew, Asa carried away the building supplies of Ramah and used them to fortify Mizpah (further north) and Geba (near the pass at Michmash).

15:31 Chronicles of the Kings (also 16:5). See note on 14:19.

16:1–7 God's judgment would come upon **Baasha and his house** (v. 3; cf. v. 11) both because of his **being like the house of Jeroboam** and **because he destroyed** Jeroboam's house (v. 7; cf. 15:29). The fact that God had ordained that Jeroboam's house be destroyed did not absolve Baasha of moral responsibility for his actions. Similar revulsion to bloodshed is expressed in Hos. 1:4, even though that bloodshed was also God-ordained, according to 1 Kings 21:21–24 (cf. 2 Kings 9:14–10:17).

16:11 he struck down all the house of Baasha. Zimri in turn fulfills the word of the prophet Jehu (v. 7), although he then reigns for only seven days (v. 15)—just before the civil war described in vv. 21–22, from which Omri emerges as king.

16:14 Chronicles of the Kings (also vv. 20, 27). See note on 14:19.

16:17 Omri attacked Zimri at **Tirzah**. This site is probably to be identified with modern Tell el-Farah that was excavated in the 1940s. The first Iron Age level at the site is covered by an ash layer, which indicates a destruction, perhaps Omri's capture of the city.

16:24 The only recorded events of Omri's reign are the purchase of the **hill of Samaria** and the building of a new northern capital on it. The authors of 1–2 Kings did not consider anything else of any great importance, even though Omri's house held the throne for over 100 years and the northern kingdom in due course became so identified with this dynasty that even after the Omride period it could be referred to in Assyrian records as "the land of Omri." This suggests that Omri was a more substantial international figure than could be deduced simply from 1 Kings. Archaeologists have determined that the city of Samaria was inhabited from the time of Omri (c. 886–875 B.C.) till it was destroyed by the Assyrians in 722.

16:31–33 went and served Baal and worshiped him . . . made an Asherah. The last and worst of the Israelite kings who ruled during the reign of Asa in Judah (see note on 15:17) was **Ahab** son of Omri. He added to the **sins of Jeroboam the son of Nebat** a marriage to a foreign woman, **Jezebel**, who inevitably led him into the worship of a foreign god, Baal. Baal is not strictly a name but a title (meaning "lord") for the ancient Semitic god Hadad—"Lord Hadad" (Baal-hadad)—first known from the ancient city of Ebla in northwestern Syria and from Egypt, but most thoroughly understood through the Ugaritic texts from Ras Shamra on the Syrian coast. These texts depict Baal (Hadad) as a storm god; the fertility of the land depends on his sending rain. He is son of the high god El and husband of the goddess Anat; his enemies are Yam ("Sea") and Mot ("Death"); his weapons are thunder and lightning; and his symbolic representation is the bull. Baal worship presented an attractive alternative or supplement to the worship of the Lord (Yahweh)

and was buried at [v]Tirzah, and Elah his son reigned in his place. 7 Moreover, the word of
the LORD came by the prophet [n]Jehu the son of Hanani against Baasha and his house,
both because of all the evil that he did in the sight of the LORD, provoking him to anger
with the work of his hands, in being like the house of Jeroboam, and also because [w]he
destroyed it.

Elah Reigns in Israel

8 In the twenty-sixth year of Asa king of Judah, Elah the son of Baasha began to reign
over Israel in Tirzah, and he reigned two years. 9 But his servant [x]Zimri, commander of
half his chariots, conspired against him. When he was at Tirzah, drinking himself drunk
in the house of Arza, [y]who was over the household in Tirzah, 10 Zimri came in and struck
him down and killed him, in the twenty-seventh year of Asa king of Judah, and reigned
in his place.

11 When he began to reign, as soon as he had seated himself on his throne, he struck down
[z]all the house of Baasha. He [a]did not leave him a single male of his relatives or his friends.
12 Thus Zimri destroyed all the house of Baasha, [b]according to the word of the LORD, which
he spoke against Baasha by [n]Jehu the prophet, 13 for all the sins of Baasha and the sins of
Elah his son, which they sinned and which they made Israel to sin, [c]provoking the LORD
God of Israel to anger with their idols. 14 Now the rest of the acts of Elah and all that he
did, are they not written in the Book of the Chronicles of the Kings of Israel?

Zimri Reigns in Israel

15 In the twenty-seventh year of Asa king of Judah, Zimri reigned seven days in Tirzah.
Now the troops were encamped against [d]Gibbethon, which belonged to the Philistines,
16 and the troops who were encamped heard it said, "Zimri has conspired, and he has
killed the king." Therefore all Israel made Omri, the commander of the army, king over
Israel that day in the camp. 17 So Omri went up from Gibbethon, and all Israel with him,
and they besieged Tirzah. 18 And when Zimri saw that the city was taken, he went into
the citadel of the king's house and burned the king's house over him with fire and died,
19 because of his sins that he committed, doing evil in the sight of the LORD, [e]walking in
the way of Jeroboam, and for his sin which he committed, making Israel to sin. 20 Now
the rest of the acts of Zimri, and the conspiracy that he made, are they not written in the
Book of the Chronicles of the Kings of Israel?

Omri Reigns in Israel

21 Then the people of Israel were divided into two parts. Half of the people followed
Tibni the son of Ginath, to make him king, and half followed Omri. 22 But the people
who followed Omri overcame the people who followed Tibni the son of Ginath. So Tibni
died, and Omri became king. 23 In the thirty-first year of Asa king of Judah, Omri began
to reign over Israel, and he reigned for twelve years; six years he reigned in Tirzah. 24 He
bought the hill of [f]Samaria from Shemer for two talents[1] of silver, and he fortified the
hill and called the name of the city that he built [g]Samaria, after the name of Shemer, the
owner of the hill.

25 [h]Omri did what was evil in the sight of the LORD, and did more evil [i]than all who were
before him. 26 For [e]he walked in all the way of Jeroboam the son of Nebat, and in the sins
that he made Israel to sin, [j]provoking the LORD, the God of Israel, to anger by their idols.
27 Now the rest of the acts of Omri that he did, and the might that he showed, are they not
written in the Book of the Chronicles of the Kings of Israel? 28 And Omri slept with his
fathers and was buried in Samaria, and Ahab his son reigned in his place.

Ahab Reigns in Israel

29 In the thirty-eighth year of Asa king of Judah, Ahab the son of Omri began to reign over
Israel, and Ahab the son of Omri reigned over Israel in Samaria twenty-two years. 30 And
Ahab the son of Omri did evil in the sight of the LORD, [k]more than all who were before
him. 31 And as if it had been a light thing for him to walk in the sins of Jeroboam the son of
Nebat, [l]he took for his wife Jezebel the daughter of Ethbaal king of the [m]Sidonians, [n]and

[1] A *talent* was about 75 pounds or 34 kilograms

6 [v]ch. 14:17; 15:21
7 [n][See ver. 1 above] [w]ch. 15:27, 29; [Hos. 1:4]
9 [x]2 Kgs. 9:31 [y][ch. 18:3]
11 [z][ver. 3] [a][1 Sam. 25:22]
12 [b]ver. 3 [n][See ver. 1 above]
13 [c]ver. 26; Deut. 32:21
15 [d]ch. 15:27
19 [e][ch. 15:26, 34]
24 [f][ch. 13:32] [g]ver. 28, 29, 32
25 [h]Mic. 6:16 [i]ver. 30
26 [e][See ver. 19 above] [j]ver. 13
30 [k]ch. 21:25; [ver. 25]
31 [l][Ex. 34:16; Deut. 7:3] [m]Judg. 18:7 [n]ch. 21:25, 26; [2 Kgs. 3:2; 10:18; 17:16]

went and served Baal and worshiped him. **32** He erected an altar for Baal in [o]the house of
Baal, which he built in Samaria. **33** And Ahab made an [p]Asherah. Ahab did more to provoke
the LORD, the God of Israel, to anger [k]than all the kings of Israel who were before him.
34 [q]In his days Hiel of Bethel built [r]Jericho. He laid its foundation at the cost of Abiram his
firstborn, and set up its gates at the cost of his youngest son Segub, according to the word
of the LORD, which he spoke by Joshua the son of Nun.

Elijah Predicts a Drought

17 Now Elijah the Tishbite, of [s]Tishbe[1] in Gilead, said to Ahab, [t]"As the LORD, the God
of Israel, lives, [u]before whom I stand, [v]there shall be neither dew nor rain these years,
except by my word." **2** And the word of the LORD came to him: **3** "Depart from here and
turn eastward and hide yourself by the brook Cherith, which is east of the Jordan. **4** You
shall drink from the brook, and I have commanded the ravens to feed you there." **5** So he
went and did according to the word of the LORD. He went and lived by the brook Cherith
that is east of the Jordan. **6** And the ravens brought him bread and meat in the morning,

[1] Septuagint; Hebrew *of the settlers*

32 [o]2 Kgs. 10:21, 26, 27
33 [p]ch. 18:19; 2 Kgs. 13:6; 17:10; 21:3; 2 Chr. 14:3; [Ex. 34:13; Jer. 17:2] [k][See ver. 30 above]
34 [q][Josh. 6:26] [r]See 2 Kgs. 2:4, 18-22

Chapter 17

1 [s][Judg. 12:4] [t]ch. 18:10, 15; 22:14; 2 Kgs. 3:14; 5:16; See Ruth 3:13 [u]ch. 18:15; [Deut. 10:8] [v]Luke 4:25; James 5:17; [ch. 18:1]

for many Israelites throughout their time in Canaan, no doubt partly because that land was so utterly dependent on rain for its fertility. On "Asherah," see note on 14:15.

16:34 Hiel . . . built Jericho. . . . at the cost of Abiram his firstborn, and . . . his youngest son Segub. Joshua had pronounced a curse on anyone who might rebuild Jericho (Josh. 6:26), and the authors of 1–2 Kings understand this curse as the prophetic **word of the LORD**. Although the text does not say specifically how the two sons of Hiel died, it is possible that he offered them in sacrifice, or that they died as a special judgment from God, in fulfillment of Joshua's curse. Child sacrifice was a prominent feature among the polytheistic Canaanite religions of the day. Israel's Scriptures, however, were steadfastly opposed to any such practice. Solomon's altars for Chemosh and Molech (1 Kings 11:7) could have been the point of entry of this pagan abomination into Israel, and the Phoenician Jezebel would have encouraged it. If the sons of Hiel died by sacrifice, this would be evidence of the difference between Israel's past under Joshua and its present under an apostate monarchy; Israelites no longer conquer the Canaanites at Jericho but rather embrace their religion there.

Elijah and Elisha

c. 875–797 B.C.

Elijah and his successor Elisha figure prominently in 1 and 2 Kings as they prophesied against the wickedness of Ahab and Joram (also called Jehoram) of Israel. Elijah's opposition to pagan worship also put him at odds with Jezebel, Ahab's Phoenician wife, who supported hundreds of prophets of Baal and Asherah. Eventually Elisha sent someone to anoint Jehu, one of Joram's commanders, to be the next king and to execute judgment on the entire family of Ahab.

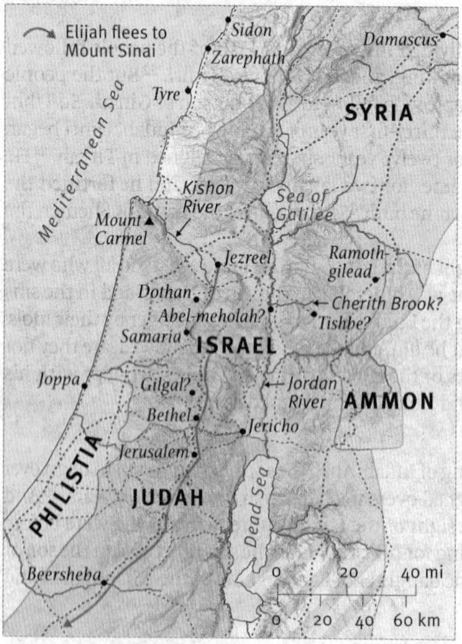

17:1–22:40 *Elijah and Ahab.* Before this time no prophet addressed the house of Omri as Israel's earlier royal houses had been addressed (cf. 14:7–13; 16:1–4), but now Elijah is introduced. His announcement of doom on the house of Omri will be delayed, however, until 21:21–24. His first task is to tackle the problem of the Baal worship that Ahab has introduced into Israel in 16:31–32, and to demonstrate beyond all doubt that Baal is no more a god in any real sense than are Jeroboam's bull calves.

17:1–24 *Elijah and the Drought.* Chapter 17 provides the context—a divinely ordained drought—in which the climactic demonstration of the truth about God and the "gods" will take place (18:16–40). This passage teaches that it is the Lord, not Baal or any other "god," who controls both life and death, both fertility and infertility.

17:1 neither dew nor rain these years, except by my word. In Canaanite religion, Baal had authority over rain and fertility. The absence of rain meant the absence of Baal, who must periodically submit to the god of death Mot (during the dry season), only to be revived at a later date and once again water the earth (during the rainy season). This cyclical and polytheistic view of reality is the focus of Elijah's challenges. Elijah worships a single God who **lives** and yet, while *living*, can deny both dew and rain to the land. The Lord, not Baal, brings fertility; and the Lord's presence in judgment, not his absence in death, leads to infertility.

17:5 east of the Jordan. Elijah hides in an inhospitable area where there is no normal food supply. God is nevertheless able to provide for him, for God controls not just the rain but the whole natural order, including the ravens (v. 6).

17:6 bread and meat in the morning . . . in the evening. As the Israelites had once been the beneficiaries of God's provision of bread and meat in the wilderness (Exodus 16, esp. vv. 8, 12–13), now Elijah eats even more generous amounts (twice daily) of the same.

17:9 Zarephath, which belongs to Sidon. The heartland of Baal worship in Sidon might have been thought by many to be a region over which Israel's God could have no authority. Yet one discovers as the story unfolds that it is nevertheless an area also badly affected by the drought announced

9[w]Obad. 20; Luke 4:26
10[w][See ver. 9 above] [x]Num. 15:32, 33
12[t][See ver. 1 above]
18[y][Luke 4:34; 5:8] [z]See Deut. 33:1
21[a]2 Kgs. 4:34, 35; Acts 20:10
22[b][Heb. 11:35]
24[c][John 3:2]
Chapter 18
1[d]See ch. 17:1
3[e]ch. 16:9
4[f]ver. 13

and bread and meat in the evening, and he drank from the brook. 7 And after a while the
brook dried up, because there was no rain in the land.

The Widow of Zarephath

8 Then the word of the LORD came to him, 9 "Arise, go to [w]Zarephath, which belongs to
Sidon, and dwell there. Behold, I have commanded a widow there to feed you." 10 So he
arose and went to [w]Zarephath. And when he came to the gate of the city, behold, a widow
was there [x]gathering sticks. And he called to her and said, "Bring me a little water in a
vessel, that I may drink." 11 And as she was going to bring it, he called to her and said,
"Bring me a morsel of bread in your hand." 12 And she said, [t]"As the LORD your God lives,
I have nothing baked, only a handful of flour in a jar and a little oil in a jug. And now I
am gathering a couple of sticks that I may go in and prepare it for myself and my son, that
we may eat it and die." 13 And Elijah said to her, "Do not fear; go and do as you have said.
But first make me a little cake of it and bring it to me, and afterward make something for
yourself and your son. 14 For thus says the LORD, the God of Israel, 'The jar of flour shall not
be spent, and the jug of oil shall not be empty, until the day that the LORD sends rain upon
the earth.'" 15 And she went and did as Elijah said. And she and he and her household ate
for many days. 16 The jar of flour was not spent, neither did the jug of oil become empty,
according to the word of the LORD that he spoke by Elijah.

Elijah Raises the Widow's Son

17 After this the son of the woman, the mistress of the house, became ill. And his illness was so severe that there was no breath left in him. 18 And she said to Elijah, [y]"What
have you against me, O [z]man of God? You have come to me to bring my sin to remembrance and to cause the death of my son!" 19 And he said to her, "Give me your son."
And he took him from her arms and carried him up into the upper chamber where he
lodged, and laid him on his own bed. 20 And he cried to the LORD, "O LORD my God,
have you brought calamity even upon the widow with whom I sojourn, by killing her
son?" 21 [a]Then he stretched himself upon the child three times and cried to the LORD,
"O LORD my God, let this child's life[1] come into him again." 22 And the LORD listened to
the voice of Elijah. And the life of the child came into him again, and [b]he revived. 23 And
Elijah took the child and brought him down from the upper chamber into the house
and delivered him to his mother. And Elijah said, "See, your son lives." 24 And the woman
said to Elijah, [c]"Now I know that you are a man of God, and that the word of the LORD
in your mouth is truth."

Elijah Confronts Ahab

18 [d]After many days the word of the LORD came to Elijah, in the third year, saying, "Go,
show yourself to Ahab, and I will send rain upon the earth." 2 So Elijah went to show
himself to Ahab. Now the famine was severe in Samaria. 3 And Ahab called Obadiah, who
was [e]over the household. (Now Obadiah feared the LORD greatly, 4 and [f]when Jezebel cut
off the prophets of the LORD, Obadiah took a hundred prophets and hid them by fifties in

[1] Or *soul*; also verse 22

in v. 1 (cf. v. 12). The Lord is God of all lands and can bring drought to all lands. He can even "command" a **widow** in this northern region to feed Elijah—although since the widow herself shows no awareness of having been directly **commanded** by God, it may be best to understand the verb here and in v. 4 in a more indirect way (i.e., "I have ordained that . . .").

17:13 first make me a little cake. Against all parental instinct, the woman is asked to give Elijah something to eat first, before feeding herself and her **son**. This is to ask for a great step of faith.

17:15 she and he and her household ate for many days. God looks after people not only in Israel but also on the Phoenician coast.

17:18–20 You have come to me to bring my sin to remembrance and to cause the death of my son! The widow appears to have been convinced of the truth of Elijah's religion by the demonstration of God's power in vv. 8–16. When death does eventually catch up with the family, she knows that it must be the Lord's doing; she blames God's prophet for reminding God of her sin. **Elijah** concurs with her view about who is the ultimate cause (**have you brought calamity . . . by killing her son?**), but in his prayer he makes no comment on whether the widow's sin was the human cause. In a world where there is only one true God, everything must in the end lie in his power.

17:21 he stretched himself upon the child three times. The purpose of this action is not made clear. Biblical prophets are often found "acting out" as well as speaking (e.g., Ezekiel 4), and Elijah's actions here appear to be part of his prayer that the **child's life** should **come into him again**. This is the final illustration that the Lord is the only true God because it demonstrates that when faced with the "god of death," the Lord, unlike Baal, does not need to submit to him. He can cross the border from Israel to Sidon to bring life out of death. The Lord cannot be barred even from a place such as the underworld (Ps. 139:7–12).

18:1–46 *Elijah and the Prophets of Baal.* In ch. 17 Elijah has lived privately, first in the Transjordanian wilderness and then in a Sidonian home. Now he reappears in public. The drought is to end, but it must become clear beforehand, not only to the widow of Zarephath but also to all Israel, who is God.

a cave and fed them with bread and water.) 5 And Ahab said to Obadiah, "Go through the
land to all the springs of water and to all the valleys. Perhaps we may find grass and save
the horses and mules alive, and not lose some of the animals." 6 So they divided the land
between them to pass through it. Ahab went in one direction by himself, and Obadiah
went in another direction by himself.
7 And as Obadiah was on the way, behold, Elijah met him. And Obadiah recognized him
and fell on his face and said, "Is it you, my lord Elijah?" 8 And he answered him, "It is I. Go,
tell your lord, 'Behold, Elijah is here.'" 9 And he said, "How have I sinned, that you would
give your servant into the hand of Ahab, to kill me? 10 [g]As the LORD your God lives, there
is no nation or kingdom where my lord has not sent to seek you. And when they would
say, 'He is not here,' he would take an oath of the kingdom or nation, that they had not
found you. 11 And now you say, 'Go, tell your lord, "Behold, Elijah is here."' 12 And as soon
as I have gone from you, [h]the Spirit of the LORD will carry you I know not where. And
so, when I come and tell Ahab and he cannot find you, he will kill me, although I your
servant have feared the LORD from my youth. 13 Has it not been told my lord what I did
[i]when Jezebel killed the prophets of the LORD, how I hid a hundred men of the LORD's
prophets by fifties in a cave and fed them with bread and water? 14 And now you say, 'Go,
tell your lord, "Behold, Elijah is here"'; and he will kill me." 15 And Elijah said, [g]"As the
LORD of hosts lives, before whom I stand, I will surely show myself to him today." 16 So
Obadiah went to meet Ahab, and told him. And Ahab went to meet Elijah.
17 When Ahab saw Elijah, Ahab said to him, [j]"Is it you, you [k]troubler of Israel?" 18 And
he answered, "I have not troubled Israel, but you have, and your father's house, because
you have [l]abandoned the commandments of the LORD and [m]followed the Baals. 19 Now
therefore send and gather all Israel to me at Mount [n]Carmel, and the [o]450 prophets of
Baal and [p]the 400 prophets of Asherah, [q]who eat at Jezebel's table."

The Prophets of Baal Defeated

20 So Ahab sent to all the people of Israel and gathered the prophets together at Mount
Carmel. 21 And Elijah came near to all the people and said, "How long [r]will you go limping between two different opinions? [s]If the LORD is God, follow him; but if Baal, then
follow him." And the people did not answer him a word. 22 Then Elijah said to the people,
[t]"I, even I only, am left a prophet of the LORD, but Baal's prophets are [u]450 men. 23 Let two
bulls be given to us, and let them choose one bull for themselves and cut it in pieces and
lay it on the wood, but put no fire to it. And I will prepare the other bull and lay it on the
wood and put no fire to it. 24 And you call upon the name of your god, and I will call upon
the name of the LORD, and the God who [v]answers by fire, he is God." And all the people
answered, "It is well spoken." 25 Then Elijah said to the prophets of Baal, "Choose for yourselves one bull and prepare it first, for you are many, and call upon the name of your god,

10 [g]See ch. 17:1
12 [h]2 Kgs. 2:16; Ezek. 3:12, 14; 8:3; Acts 8:39
13 [i]ver. 4
15 [g][See ver. 10 above]
17 [j][ch. 21:20] [k][Josh. 7:25]
18 [l]ch. 9:9; 2 Chr. 15:2; 24:20 [m]ch. 16:31
19 [n]See Josh. 19:26 [o]ver. 22 [p]See ch. 16:33 [q][2 Kgs. 3:13]
21 [r][2 Kgs. 17:41] [s]Josh. 24:15; [Matt. 6:24]
22 [t]ch. 19:10, 14 [u]ver. 19
24 [v]See ver. 38

18:1–16 Even though Elijah has been living only a few miles from Jezebel's hometown (Sidon), he has remained hidden from Ahab. **Obadiah**, like the widow of Zarephath (17:18), connects the prophet's presence with imminent punishment for his own sin. Yet as genuine as his piety is, Obadiah has misunderstood the situation. Elijah assures him of this with a solemn oath.

18:17–18 you troubler of Israel. Ahab sees Elijah, the prophet who has pronounced God's judgment, as the cause of the nation's trouble. But Elijah rightly answers that Ahab, who has turned to other gods, is the true troubler of Israel. The relatively rare Hebrew verb *'akar*, "to trouble," is also found in 1 Sam. 14:24–46, where there is also a dispute about who is really the troubler of Israel. Is it Saul, who has bound the people under a foolish oath, as Jonathan claims (1 Sam. 14:29; cf. Judg. 11:29–40), or is it Jonathan himself? On a previous occasion Israel had found and killed a man who was bringing "trouble" on them, and had thus escaped God's curse (Joshua 6–7; esp. notice the use of *'akar* in Josh. 6:18 and 7:25). These other stories make it clear that much is at stake in this debate about who has truly **troubled Israel**. Elijah's claim is that the trouble has religious roots: the abandonment of the **commandments of the LORD** and the embrace of the **Baals** (various local manifestations of the god Baal-hadad; see note on 1 Kings 16:31–33). Ahab, not Elijah, is the "Achan" of this particular narrative.

18:20 all the people of Israel. The identity of the true "troubler of Israel" in Joshua 7 had been settled in public before all Israel; similarly, all Israel is now gathered on **Mount Carmel**—a hill situated on a headland by modern Haifa that forms the northwestern end of a range of hills 13 miles (21 km) long, commonly referred to as the Carmel range. As a notable landmark, it is mentioned in early Egyptian and Mesopotamian texts.

18:21 limping. The rare Hebrew verb *pasakh* occurs again in v. 26, where the prophets of Baal "limped around the altar." The irregular steps of their ritual dance portray an inability to move properly. The worship of the people is no better than the worship of these prophets, as they refuse to choose between the Lord and Baal but look to retain both options.

18:22 I, even I only, am left. Although other prophets of the Lord still existed in Israel at this time (cf. vv. 4, 13; 20:35–43; 22:1–28), Elijah's emphasis here is on his belief that he is the only one willing to take a public stand against the prophets of Baal. Further, it is part of Elijah's general strategy to underscore the overwhelming odds against his success, as seen in the numerical imbalance (18:25) and in his allowing the Baal prophets first choice of bull and first opportunity at evoking a divine reaction.

18:24 the God who answers by fire, he is God. The Lord's association with fire is well attested in the OT (e.g., Lev. 9:24; 10:2; Num. 16:35). Similarly, extrabiblical sources give evidence that Baal was thought of as a god who controls fire and lightning. The question here is, which of these claims about control over fire is true?

28 [w][Lev. 19:28; Deut. 14:1]
29 [x][Ex. 29:39, 41]
30 [y]ch. 19:10, 14
31 [z]Gen. 32:28; 35:10; 2 Kgs. 17:34
33 [a]Gen. 22:9; Lev. 1:7 [b][Judg. 6:20]
36 [c]ver. 29 [d]See Ex. 3:6 [e]Josh. 4:24; 1 Sam. 17:46 [f][Num. 16:28]
38 [g]ver. 24; See Lev. 9:24
39 [h]ver. 24
40 [i]Judg. 4:7 [j][2 Kgs. 10:25]
42 [k][James 5:17, 18]
44 [l][Luke 12:54]

but put no fire to it." **26** And they took the bull that was given them, and they prepared it
and called upon the name of Baal from morning until noon, saying, "O Baal, answer us!"
But there was no voice, and no one answered. And they limped around the altar that they
had made. **27** And at noon Elijah mocked them, saying, "Cry aloud, for he is a god. Either
he is musing, or he is relieving himself, or he is on a journey, or perhaps he is asleep and
must be awakened." **28** And they cried aloud and [w]cut themselves after their custom with
swords and lances, until the blood gushed out upon them. **29** And as midday passed, they
raved on until the time of [x]the offering of the oblation, but there was no voice. No one
answered; no one paid attention.

30 Then Elijah said to all the people, "Come near to me." And all the people came near
to him. And he repaired the altar of the LORD that had been [y]thrown down. **31** Elijah took
twelve stones, according to the number of the tribes of the sons of Jacob, to whom the word
of the LORD came, saying, [z]"Israel shall be your name," **32** and with the stones he built an
altar in the name of the LORD. And he made a trench about the altar, as great as would
contain two seahs[1] of seed. **33** [a]And he put the wood in order and cut the bull in pieces
and laid it on the wood. And he said, "Fill four jars with water and [b]pour it on the burnt
offering and on the wood." **34** And he said, "Do it a second time." And they did it a second
time. And he said, "Do it a third time." And they did it a third time. **35** And the water ran
around the altar and filled the trench also with water.

36 And at the time of [c]the offering of the oblation, Elijah the prophet came near and
said, "O LORD, [d]God of Abraham, Isaac, and Israel, let it be known this day that [e]you are
God in Israel, and that I am your servant, and that [f]I have done all these things at your
word. **37** Answer me, O LORD, answer me, that this people may know that you, O LORD,
are God, and that you have turned their hearts back." **38** [g]Then the fire of the LORD fell and
consumed the burnt offering and the wood and the stones and the dust, and licked up the
water that was in the trench. **39** And when all the people saw it, they fell on their faces and
said, [h]"The LORD, he is God; the LORD, he is God." **40** And Elijah said to them, "Seize the
prophets of Baal; let not one of them escape." And they seized them. And Elijah brought
them down to [i]the brook Kishon and [j]slaughtered them there.

The LORD Sends Rain

41 And Elijah said to Ahab, "Go up, eat and drink, for there is a sound of the rushing
of rain." **42** So Ahab went up to eat and to drink. And Elijah went up to the top of Mount
Carmel. [k]And he bowed himself down on the earth and put his face between his knees.
43 And he said to his servant, "Go up now, look toward the sea." And he went up and looked
and said, "There is nothing." And he said, "Go again," seven times. **44** And at the seventh
time he said, "Behold, [l]a little cloud like a man's hand is rising from the sea." And he said,
"Go up, say to Ahab, 'Prepare your chariot and go down, lest the rain stop you.'" **45** And
in a little while the heavens grew black with clouds and wind, and there was a great rain.

[1] A *seah* was about 7 quarts or 7.3 liters

18:26 O Baal, answer us! The Hebrew verb "answer" is a key word throughout this story; cf. "No one answered" (v. 29) and "Answer me, O LORD" (v. 37).

18:27 musing . . . relieving himself . . . on a journey . . . asleep and must be awakened. After several hours Elijah begins to taunt the prophets of Baal with some disrespectful suggestions as to why they are receiving no answer. A real god would not be limited in such ways.

18:28–29 cut themselves. The attempt to manipulate Baal into action involves self-mutilation. The kind of condition in view here as these prophets **raved on** is also well attested outside Palestine (e.g., in the account of an Egyptian traveler, Wen-Amon, c. 1100 B.C., about a violent prophetic frenzy amid a temple ritual in Byblos, on the Phoenician coast north of Jezebel's hometown of Sidon).

18:30 he repaired the altar of the LORD. The authors of 1–2 Kings are generally opposed to worship at such "high places" (see note on 1 Kings 3:2), but they are even more opposed to idolatry, and they do not criticize Elijah for this action. The Lord himself removes the altar after it has served its purpose (18:38).

18:35 the water ran around the altar. The whole area is saturated with water so that there is no possibility of natural combustion. If this offering is consumed in fire, it must be the Lord's doing.

18:36–37 Answer me, O LORD, answer me. Elijah's public prayer gives evidence of great faith and confidence that God will answer.

18:38–39 The **fire of the LORD** consumes not only the **burnt offering and the wood** but also the inflammable **stones** and the saturated **dust**, as well as the **water that was in the trench**. This cannot be the result of any natural phenomenon, since even lightning would not consume the stones. As **all the people** realize, this fire can only be a special work of God.

18:42 Elijah **bowed himself down on the earth and put his face between his knees.** The significance of this prophetic action, like that in 17:21, is not made clear. He could be praying for rain, or he might simply be exhausted.

18:45–46 Jezreel. As the rains began, **Ahab . . . went to Jezreel**, where he had a palace (21:1) and where Jezebel was staying (19:1–2). The fact that Elijah also went to Jezreel suggests that he thought his war with Baal worship was over, which turned out to be a misjudgment.

And Ahab rode and went to [m]Jezreel. **46** [n]And the hand of the LORD was on Elijah, [o]and he
gathered up his garment and ran before Ahab to the entrance of [p]Jezreel.

Elijah Flees Jezebel

19 Ahab told Jezebel all that Elijah had done, and how [q]he had killed all the prophets
with the sword. **2** Then Jezebel sent a messenger to Elijah, saying, [r]"So may the gods
do to me and more also, if I do not make your life as the life of one of them by this time
tomorrow." **3** Then he was afraid, and he arose and ran for his life and came to [s]Beersheba,
which belongs to Judah, and left his servant there.

4 But he himself went a day's journey into the wilderness and came and sat down under a
broom tree. [t]And he asked that he might die, saying, "It is enough; now, O LORD, take away
my life, for I am no better than my fathers." **5** And he lay down and slept under a broom
tree. And behold, an angel touched him and said to him, "Arise and eat." **6** And he looked,
and behold, there was at his head a cake baked on hot stones and a jar of water. And he ate
and drank and lay down again. **7** And the angel of the LORD came again a second time and
touched him and said, "Arise and eat, for the journey is too great for you." **8** And he arose
and ate and drank, and went in the strength of that food [u]forty days and forty nights to
[v]Horeb, the mount of God.

The LORD Speaks to Elijah

9 There he came to a cave and lodged in it. And behold, [w]the word of the LORD came to
him, and he said to him, "What are you doing here, Elijah?" **10** He said, "I have been very
[x]jealous for the LORD, the God of hosts. For the people of Israel have forsaken your covenant,
[y]thrown down your altars, and [z]killed your prophets with the sword, [a]and I, even I only,
am left, and they seek my life, to take it away." **11** And he said, "Go out and [b]stand on the
mount before the LORD." And behold, the LORD passed by, and [c]a great and strong wind
tore the mountains and broke in pieces the rocks before the LORD, but the LORD was not
in the wind. And after the wind [d]an earthquake, but the LORD was not in the earthquake.
12 And after the earthquake a fire, but the LORD was not in the fire. And after the fire the
sound of a low whisper.[1] **13** And when Elijah heard it, [e]he wrapped his face in his cloak and
went out and stood at the entrance of the cave. And behold, [f]there came a voice to him and

[1] *Or a sound, a thin silence*

45 [m]Josh. 17:16
46 [n]2 Kgs. 3:15; Ezek. 1:3; 3:14 [o]Ex. 12:11; 2 Kgs. 4:29; 9:1; Jer. 1:17 [p]Josh. 17:16

Chapter 19

1 [q]ch. 18:40
2 [r][ch. 20:10]; See Ruth 1:17
3 [s]See Gen. 21:31
4 [t][Num. 11:15; Jonah 4:3, 8]
8 [u]Ex. 24:18; 34:28; Deut. 9:9, 18; Matt. 4:2; Mark 1:13; Luke 4:2 [v]Ex. 3:1
9 [w]ver. 13
10 [x]Num. 25:11, 13 [y]ch. 18:30; Cited Rom. 11:3 [z]ch. 18:4 [a]ch. 18:22
11 [b]Ex. 24:12; 34:2 [c]Ezek. 1:4
11 [d]Ezek. 37:7
13 [e][Ex. 3:6] [f]ver. 9

19:1–21 *Elijah and the Lord.* Elijah has won a mighty battle on the mountain, but a still more formidable opponent than Ahab awaits him in the form of Queen Jezebel. Victory now becomes defeat as Elijah retreats, both physically and mentally, and ultimately arrives not at Mount Carmel but at another mountain to confront not Baal but the Lord himself, whom Elijah serves but whose ways he only partly understands and accepts.

19:1–2 Jezebel sent a messenger. Jezebel has a consistent track record of disposing of the Lord's prophets (cf. 18:4, 13) and is to be taken seriously when she threatens to take Elijah's **life**.

19:3 he was afraid, and he arose and ran for his life. Elijah has shown himself to be a man of faith and courage who trusts God for miracles and, above all, moves to locations only in response to God's commands (cf. 17:2–5, 8–10; 18:1–2). But the "word of the LORD" is absent in 19:3 and does not reappear until v. 9, when it takes the form of a question, clarifying that Elijah's journey on this occasion was not divinely initiated. The shock of Jezebel's resistance after Mount Carmel has led Elijah to forget to think theologically, so he flees from Jezreel in the north to **Beersheba** in the far south of the Promised Land—as far away from Jezebel as he can get. The distance from the top of Mount Carmel to Beersheba was about 120 miles (193 km), which would have taken an ordinary single traveler around six days, but less if he ran part of the way.

19:5 The **broom tree** is a bush with many branches and twigs, small leaves, and clusters of flowers. **an angel touched him**. Elijah has been responding so far only to Jezebel's "messenger" (Hb. *mal'ak*, v. 2). Now it is God's turn to take the initiative with an "angel" or messenger of his own (also Hb. *mal'ak*). It is God's first move in leading Elijah back onto the path of faith from which he has strayed.

19:7 the journey is too great. Elijah thought his journey was over; he has had "enough" (Hb. *rab*, v. 4). But now he is to fortify himself for a further journey, which will otherwise be "too great" (also Hb. *rab*). Food is God's response to Elijah both when he cries "enough" and when he needs "enough."

19:8 he arose . . . and went . . . to Horeb, the mount of God. Horeb is another name for Mount Sinai, where God first spoke the Ten Commandments to the people of Israel (Exodus 19–20). The **forty days and forty nights** of Elijah's travels recall Israel's own wandering in the wilderness (Num. 14:33–34) and Moses' first sojourn on this same mountain (Ex. 24:18; see also Ex. 3:1; 19:3). Will Elijah, like Moses, see God (Ex. 33:12–23); and if so, will it make any difference to his current attitude? This journey from near Beersheba to Mount Horeb was about 250 miles (400 km), unless Elijah went by a more circuitous route. The last part of the journey would have been much longer than the air distance because of rugged terrain.

19:10 I, even I only, am left. Elijah seems to have partially forgotten his past: miraculous provision, the raising of a dead child, mighty acts of God on mountaintops. He mentions none of these, but talks only of Israelite apostasy and prophetic casualties. The resistance of one person (Jezebel) has turned massive victory into overwhelming defeat, in Elijah's mind. He is certainly not the only one left, but that is how he feels.

19:11–12 not in the wind . . . not in the earthquake . . . not in the fire. The emphasis on Mount Carmel had been on God's spectacular ways, particularly his use of fire. The emphasis here is on God's quiet ways. He is not to be found in the spectacular elements of the storm outside the cave but instead in a **low whisper**. The Hebrew is literally (see ESV footnote) "a voice/sound, a thin silence" (*qol demamah daqqah*), i.e., the same "voice" (Hb. *qol*) that speaks to Elijah in v. 13. On this occasion (but not always; cf. Isa. 30:27; Nah. 1:3–5) God reveals himself in quietness.

19:13–14 What are you doing here, Elijah? The point of the demonstration on the mountain was presumably that Elijah would answer this question differently on the second occasion of its asking (cf. v. 9). His answer is, how-

said, "What are you doing here, Elijah?" 14 He said, [x]"I have been very jealous for the LORD,
the God of hosts. For the people of Israel have forsaken your covenant, [y]thrown down your
altars, and killed your prophets with the sword, and I, even I only, am left, and they seek
my life, to take it away." 15 And the LORD said to him, "Go, return on your way to the wilderness of Damascus. And when you arrive, you shall anoint Hazael to be king over Syria.
16 [g]And Jehu the son of Nimshi you shall anoint to be king over Israel, and [h]Elisha the son of
Shaphat of Abel-meholah you shall anoint to be prophet in your place. 17 And the one who
escapes from [i]the sword of Hazael [j]shall Jehu put to death, and the one who escapes from
the sword of Jehu [k]shall Elisha put to death. 18 [l]Yet I will leave seven thousand in Israel, all
the knees that have not bowed to Baal, and every mouth that has not [m]kissed him."

The Call of Elisha

19 So he departed from there and found Elisha the son of Shaphat, who was plowing with
twelve yoke of oxen in front of him, and he was with the twelfth. Elijah passed by him and
cast [n]his cloak upon him. 20 And he left the oxen and ran after Elijah and said, [o]"Let me kiss
my father and my mother, and then I will follow you." And he said to him, "Go back again,
for what have I done to you?" 21 And he returned from following him and took the yoke of
oxen and sacrificed them and boiled their flesh [p]with the yokes of the oxen and gave it to
the people, and they ate. Then he arose and went after Elijah and assisted him.

Ahab's Wars with Syria

20 [q]Ben-hadad the king of Syria gathered all his army together. [r]Thirty-two kings
were with him, and horses and chariots. And he went up and closed in on [s]Samaria
and fought against it. 2 And he sent messengers into the city to Ahab king of Israel and
said to him, "Thus says Ben-hadad: 3 'Your silver and your gold are mine; your best wives
and children also are mine.'" 4 And the king of Israel answered, "As you say, my lord, O
king, I am yours, and all that I have." 5 The messengers came again and said, "Thus says
Ben-hadad: 'I sent to you, saying, "Deliver to me your silver and your gold, your wives
and your children." 6 Nevertheless I will send my servants to you tomorrow about this
time, and they shall search your house and the houses of your servants and lay hands on
whatever pleases you and take it away.'"

14 [x][See ver. 10 above] [y][See ver. 10 above]
16 [g]See 2 Kgs. 9:1-6 [h][ver. 19-21; 2 Kgs. 2:9, 15]
17 [i]2 Kgs. 8:12; 13:3, 22 [j]See 2 Kgs. 9–10 [k][Hos. 6:5]
18 [l]Cited Rom. 11:4 [m][Hos. 13:2]
19 [n]2 Kgs. 2:8
20 [o][Matt. 8:21, 22; Luke 9:61, 62]
21 [p][2 Sam. 24:22]

Chapter 20

1 [q]2 Kgs. 6:24; 8:7; [ch. 15:18] [r]ch. 22:31 [s]ch. 16:24

ever, exactly the same as before (**I have been very jealous for the LORD**; cf. vv. 10, 14); the entire point of the demonstration seems to have passed him by. There is in fact a suggestion in the text that he does not particularly *wish* to understand what God is saying through these events. He has always claimed to "stand before the LORD" (Hb. *'amad lipne YHWH*; 17:1; 18:15); but here on Mount Horeb, in spite of the command of 19:11 ("Go out and stand . . . before the LORD," Hb. *'amad lipne YHWH*), he apparently stays in the cave until the storm is over and he hears the "whisper" (v. 12). When he does go out, it is with his **cloak** over his **face**, which makes it difficult for him to "see."

19:15–18 Go, return on your way to the wilderness of Damascus. These words indicate the real point of the "low whisper" (v. 12). God gives Elijah new instructions: whereas he has run south in despair to the desert of Beersheba, he must now return to the very north of Syria-Palestine in obedience and **anoint Hazael**, **Jehu**, and **Elisha**. A new political and religious order is to succeed the old, and this order will bring about the final victory over Baal worship. Total victory will come as a result of an ordinary political process (a "whisper"), as God removes certain kings and sets up others; it will not come only as a result of obviously spectacular demonstrations of divine power (wind, earthquake, and fire) as at Carmel (18:20–40). And it will arrive not as a result of Elijah's efforts but as a result of the efforts of others. Elijah's role is now to prepare the way for these "others," who are only a few of many servants of God who **have not bowed to Baal** or **kissed him**. God has ways of working other than the spectacular (though he is always free to work in supernatural ways).

19:19 he departed from there and found Elisha. Is Elijah back on track as a result of his trip to Mount Horeb? The closing verses of ch. 19 suggest not. There is no mention here or in the upcoming chapters of Elijah's ever meeting (or trying to meet) Hazael and Jehu (see vv. 15–16). One never reads of Hazael's being anointed, while it falls to Elisha to arrange the anointing of Jehu (2 Kings 9:1–13). Even Elijah's response to God's command about Elisha seems less than wholehearted. There is no mention of his "anointing" of Elisha as his prophetic successor; he merely enlists him as his assistant (1 Kings 19:21). Yet the names of the two prophets indicate the way that God's plan is nevertheless unfolding. Elijah has all but had his day—the day when it was established that "the LORD, he is God" (18:39), which is what the name "Elijah" means. The new era of salvation belongs to Elisha, whose name means "God saves."

19:20–21 Let me kiss my father and my mother. Elijah's apparent lack of enthusiasm for God's plan stands in sharp contrast to Elisha's reaction. He immediately leaves his normal employment to follow his new mentor, pausing only briefly to cut his ties with his old life. He kisses his parents goodbye and destroys his old means of sustenance (the 12 **yoke of oxen and . . . the yokes of the oxen** that control them). The Hebrew verb "to kiss" occurs in 1–2 Kings only here and in 1 Kings 19:18 ("every mouth that has not kissed him"). What the kisses have in common is that they both say something about allegiance. The worshipers of Baal kiss him, symbolizing that they have abandoned (Hb. *'azab* in 18:18; 19:10, 14) the Lord. Elisha wants to kiss his parents, symbolizing that he has abandoned home and livelihood *for* the Lord (cf. Hb. *'azab* in v. 20, where Elisha **left the oxen**).

20:1–43 *Ahab's War against Syria.* After Elijah's recruitment of Elisha, one expects to read of his anointing of Hazael as king over Syria and of Jehu as king over Israel (cf. 19:15–18). Instead, one finds a story in which a different prophet appears and in which a different king of Syria (Ben-hadad) loses a war with Ahab. The message of ch. 19 is thus underlined: Elijah is not the only servant of God left, in spite of what he has claimed (19:10, 14); and the quiet ways of God must take their course for a while before the events spoken of in 19:17 come to pass.

20:2–9 Your silver and your gold are mine (v. 3). The king of Syria seeks to reduce Israel to vassal status. His terms are at first accepted by Ahab (v. 4), only to be later rejected (vv. 5–9) after a revision in v. 6 that apparently makes them more extensive (**whatever pleases you**), intrusive (**search your house**), and immediate (**tomorrow**).

7 Then the king of Israel called all the [t]elders of the land and said, [u]"Mark, now, and see
how this man is seeking trouble, for he sent to me for my wives and my children, and for
my silver and my gold, and I did not refuse him." 8 And all the elders and all the people
said to him, "Do not listen or consent." 9 So he said to the messengers of Ben-hadad, "Tell
my lord the king, 'All that you first demanded of your servant I will do, but this thing I
cannot do.'" And the messengers departed and brought him word again. 10 Ben-hadad sent
to him and said, [v]"The gods do so to me and more also, if the dust of Samaria shall suffice
for handfuls for all the people [w]who follow me." 11 And the king of Israel answered, "Tell
him, 'Let not him who straps on his armor boast himself as he who takes it off.'" 12 When
Ben-hadad heard this message as [x]he was drinking with the kings in the booths, he said
to his men, "Take your positions." And they took their positions against the city.

Ahab Defeats Ben-hadad

13 And behold, a prophet came near to Ahab king of Israel and said, "Thus says the LORD,
Have you seen all this great multitude? Behold, [y]I will give it into your hand this day,
[z]and you shall know that I am the LORD." 14 And Ahab said, "By whom?" He said, "Thus
says the LORD, By the servants of the governors of the districts." Then he said, "Who shall
begin the battle?" He answered, "You." 15 Then he mustered the servants of the governors
of the districts, and they were 232. And after them he mustered all the people of Israel,
seven thousand.

16 And they went out at noon, while Ben-hadad [x]was drinking himself drunk in the
booths, he and the thirty-two kings who helped him. 17 The servants of the governors of
the districts went out first. And Ben-hadad sent out scouts, and they reported to him, "Men
are coming out from Samaria." 18 He said, "If they have come out for peace, take them alive.
Or if they have come out for war, take them alive."

7 [t]ch. 21:8, 11 [u][2 Kgs. 5:7]
10 [v]ch. 19:2 [w][Ex. 11:8]
12 [x][ch. 16:9]
13 [y]ver. 28 [z][ch. 18:36]
16 [x][See ver. 12 above]

Ahab's Wars with Syria

Ahab's reign was marked by repeated conflict with Ben-hadad of Syria. Ben-hadad's poor military organization accounted for his failed siege of Samaria, and Ahab defeated him again the next spring at Aphek. Ahab lost his life, however, attempting to retake Ramoth-gilead from Ben-hadad at the eastern edge of his kingdom.

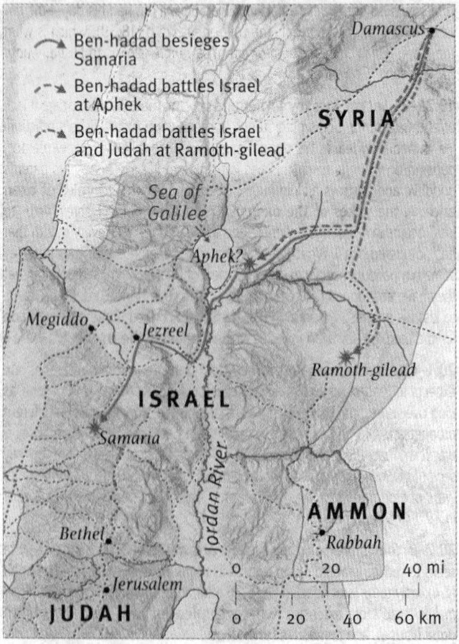

20:11 Let not him who straps on his armor boast himself as he who takes it off. It is unwise to boast about one's exploits before the battle has even begun; there is time enough for boasting when the battle is won.

20:14–18 Israel is to fight according to a divine battle plan that does not make much human sense (as in the case of Gideon in Judges 7). The **servants** (plural of Hb. *na'ar*) are to initiate the battle—young men unschooled in military matters, like the young and untrained David, who is also called a *na'ar* in 1 Sam. 17:33 (a "youth," in contrast to the warrior Goliath). The plan benefits from the fact that Ben-hadad is **drunk** as the Israelites approach (1 Kings 20:12, 16) and seemingly incapable of uttering coherent or sensible instructions (v. 18).

20:22–25 strengthen yourself. Both sides prepare for a continuation of warfare in the following **spring**, a characteristic time for kings to go to war (cf. 2 Sam. 11:1). The Syrian preparations involve a reorganization of the empire (1 Kings 20:24)—the replacement of the vassal **kings** with **commanders** directly accountable to Ben-hadad. The royal advisers seek greater military cohesion through a greater degree of political control. The Syrians also raise a new army to replace the one destroyed in v. 21, planning next time to **fight** the Israelites **in the plain** (v. 23), where **horse** and **chariot** will give them an advantage that is all too easily lost in the **hills** (cf. Judg. 1:19). But the theological reasoning that underlies their military strategy is faulty. The Lord is the only real God there is, and he is active both in the hills (1 Kings 18) and anywhere else he chooses (ch. 17).

20:26 Aphek. The second battle is considerably farther north (see Josh. 19:30; Judg. 1:31) than the first, which took place near Samaria (1 Kings 20:1). In another incident, Ahab and Ben-hadad II conspired together against the Assyrian threat from the east. A text from the Assyrian king Shalmaneser III (ruled 859 to 824 B.C.) describes a battle he fought at Qarqar on the Orontes River in 853. A coalition was apparently able to halt any Assyrian advance. According to the text, "Ahab the Israelite" provided "2,000 chariots and 10,000 men" to the coalition, which included Ben-hadad II and others. The authors of Kings have not even mentioned this battle, however, because it is not relevant to their theme.

20:28 god of the hills . . . not a god of the valleys. God intends to refute the Syrians' false notions about him.

20:31 Sackcloth signifies penitence (cf. 21:27), and **ropes** signify submissiveness (prisoners may be led by them).

22 [a]ver. 13 [b]2 Sam. 11:1
26 [b][See ver. 22 above] [c]2 Kgs. 13:17
28 [d]ch. 17:18 [e]ver. 23 [f]ver. 13
30 [c][See ver. 26 above] [g]ch. 22:25; 2 Kgs. 9:2; 2 Chr. 18:24
31 [h]See 2 Sam. 3:31
32 [h][See ver. 31 above]
34 [i]ch. 15:20 [j][ch. 11:24]
35 [k]2 Kgs. 2:3, 5, 7, 15 [l]ch. 13:17, 18
36 [m][ch. 13:24]

19 So these went out of the city, the servants of the governors of the districts and the
army that followed them. 20 And each struck down his man. The Syrians fled, and Israel
pursued them, but Ben-hadad king of Syria escaped on a horse with horsemen. 21 And the
king of Israel went out and struck the horses and chariots, and struck the Syrians with a
great blow.
22 Then [a]the prophet came near to the king of Israel and said to him, "Come, strengthen
yourself, and consider well what you have to do, for [b]in the spring the king of Syria will
come up against you."
23 And the servants of the king of Syria said to him, "Their gods are gods of the hills,
and so they were stronger than we. But let us fight against them in the plain, and surely
we shall be stronger than they. 24 And do this: remove the kings, each from his post, and
put commanders in their places, 25 and muster an army like the army that you have lost,
horse for horse, and chariot for chariot. Then we will fight against them in the plain, and
surely we shall be stronger than they." And he listened to their voice and did so.

Ahab Defeats Ben-hadad Again

26 [b]In the spring, Ben-hadad mustered the Syrians and went up to [c]Aphek to fight against
Israel. 27 And the people of Israel were mustered and were provisioned and went against
them. The people of Israel encamped before them like two little flocks of goats, but the
Syrians filled the country. 28 And a [d]man of God came near and said to the king of Israel,
"Thus says the LORD, 'Because the Syrians have said, [e]"The LORD is a god of the hills but
he is not a god of the valleys," therefore [f]I will give all this great multitude into your hand,
and you shall know that I am the LORD.'" 29 And they encamped opposite one another
seven days. Then on the seventh day the battle was joined. And the people of Israel struck
down of the Syrians 100,000 foot soldiers in one day. 30 And the rest fled into the city of
[c]Aphek, and the wall fell upon 27,000 men who were left.
Ben-hadad also fled and entered [g]an inner chamber in the city. 31 And his servants said to
him, "Behold now, we have heard that the kings of the house of Israel are merciful kings.
Let us [h]put sackcloth around our waists and ropes on our heads and go out to the king of
Israel. Perhaps he will spare your life." 32 So they [h]tied sackcloth around their waists and
put ropes on their heads and went to the king of Israel and said, "Your servant Ben-hadad
says, 'Please, let me live.'" And he said, "Does he still live? He is my brother." 33 Now the
men were watching for a sign, and they quickly took it up from him and said, "Yes, your
brother Ben-hadad." Then he said, "Go and bring him." Then Ben-hadad came out to him,
and he caused him to come up into the chariot. 34 And Ben-hadad said to him, [i]"The cities that my father took from your father I will restore, and you may establish bazaars for
yourself in [j]Damascus, as my father did in Samaria." And Ahab said, "I will let you go on
these terms." So he made a covenant with him and let him go.

A Prophet Condemns Ben-hadad's Release

35 And a certain man of [k]the sons of the prophets said to his fellow [l]at the command of
the LORD, "Strike me, please." But the man refused to strike him. 36 Then he said to him,
"Because you have not obeyed the voice of the LORD, behold, as soon as you have gone from
me, a lion shall strike you down." And as soon as he had departed from him, [m]a lion met
him and struck him down. 37 Then he found another man and said, "Strike me, please."
And the man struck him—struck him and wounded him. 38 So the prophet departed and

20:34 cities . . . bazaars. The Israelite cities taken by the Syrians in an earlier period are returned, and Ahab is given trading privileges in Damascus.

20:35 sons of the prophets. A reference to members of prophetic communities (see note on 2 Kings 2:3; also 2 Kings 4:1; 6:1).

20:36 a lion shall strike you down. The scene is reminiscent of ch. 13, where the same point is made (even prophets must obey the divine word) and the same punishment is pronounced. The implication is also clear in both passages: if disobedient prophets cannot escape God's judgment, then disobedient kings certainly will not.

20:39–42 Your servant went out into the midst of the battle. In a scene reminiscent of 2 Sam. 12:1–4, the prophet tricks the king into pronouncing judgment on himself, albeit with a disguise whose purpose is obscure. (Did Ahab know this man, or did prophets have distinctive facial garb?) He tells a story that implies that because he failed in his guard duties, he is liable to pay a fine of a **talent of silver** (an impossible amount for an ordinary soldier to raise) or suffer death. Ahab agrees on the justice of the death sentence and thus provides the prophet with the opportunity to declare *Ahab's* **life** forfeit because Ahab has released an enemy king whom God **had devoted to destruction** (cf. 1 Sam. 15:17–24). Ahab's death is in fact strangely prefigured in the very manner in which God's word about it comes to him. A prophet has disguised himself as a soldier fresh from fighting the Syrians, in order to catch the king. In 1 Kings 22:29–40 *Ahab* will disguise himself as a soldier when going out to fight the Syrians, in order to trap a prophet (and his God). His strategy will fail as spectacularly as this prophet's has succeeded.

waited for the king by the way, [n]disguising himself with a bandage over his eyes. **39** And
as the king passed, he cried to the king and said, "Your servant went out into the midst
of the battle, and behold, a soldier turned and brought a man to me and said, 'Guard this
man; if by any means he is missing, [o]your life shall be for his life, or else you shall pay a
talent[1] of silver.' **40** And as your servant was busy here and there, he was gone." The king
of Israel said to him, "So shall your judgment be; you yourself have decided it." **41** Then he
hurried to take the bandage away from his eyes, and the king of Israel recognized him as
one of the prophets. **42** And he said to him, "Thus says the LORD, 'Because you have let go
out of your hand the man whom I had devoted to destruction,[2] therefore [o]your life shall
be for his life, and your people for his people.'" **43** And the king of Israel [p]went to his house
vexed and sullen and came to Samaria.

Naboth's Vineyard

21 Now Naboth the Jezreelite had a vineyard in [q]Jezreel, beside the palace of Ahab king
of Samaria. **2** And after this Ahab said to Naboth, [r]"Give me your vineyard, that I
may have it for a vegetable garden, because it is near my house, and I will give you a better
vineyard for it; or, if it seems good to you, I will give you its value in money." **3** But Naboth
said to Ahab, "The LORD forbid [s]that I should give you the inheritance of my fathers." **4** And
Ahab [t]went into his house vexed and sullen because of what Naboth the Jezreelite had
said to him, for he had said, "I will not give you the inheritance of my fathers." And he lay
down on his bed and turned away his face and would eat no food.
5 But Jezebel his wife came to him and said to him, "Why is your spirit so vexed that
you eat no food?" **6** And he said to her, "Because I spoke to Naboth the Jezreelite and said
to him, 'Give me your vineyard for money, or else, if it please you, I will give you another
vineyard for it.' And he answered, 'I will not give you my vineyard.'" **7** And Jezebel his wife
said to him, "Do you now govern Israel? Arise and eat bread and let your heart be cheerful;
I will give you the vineyard of Naboth the Jezreelite."
8 [u]So she wrote letters in Ahab's name and sealed them with his seal, and she sent the letters to [v]the elders and the leaders who lived with Naboth in his city. **9** And she wrote in the
letters, "Proclaim a fast, and set Naboth at the head of the people. **10** And set two [w]worthless
men opposite him, and let them bring a charge against him, saying, [x]'You have cursed[3] God
and the king.' Then take him out and stone him to death." **11** And the men of his city, [v]the
elders and the leaders who lived in his city, did as Jezebel had sent word to them. As it was
written in the letters that she had sent to them, **12** [y]they proclaimed a fast and set Naboth
at the head of the people. **13** And the two worthless men came in and sat opposite him. And
the worthless men brought a charge against Naboth in the presence of the people, saying,
"Naboth cursed God and the king." So they took him outside the city and stoned him to death
with stones. **14** Then they sent to Jezebel, saying, "Naboth has been stoned; he is dead."
15 As soon as Jezebel heard that Naboth had been stoned and was dead, Jezebel said to

[1] A *talent* was about 75 pounds or 34 kilograms [2] That is, set apart (devoted) as an offering to the Lord (for destruction) [3] Hebrew *blessed*; also verse 13

38 [n]1 Sam. 28:8
39 [o][2 Kgs. 10:24]
42 [o][See ver. 39 above]
43 [p]ch. 21:4

Chapter 21

1 [q]ch. 18:45, 46
2 [r][1 Sam. 8:14]
3 [s]Lev. 25:23; Num. 36:7; Ezek. 46:18
4 [t]ch. 20:43
8 [u][Esth. 3:12] [v]ch. 20:7; Ruth 4:2
10 [w]See Deut. 13:13 [x]Ex. 22:28; Lev. 24:16; [Acts 6:11; 23:5]
11 [v][See ver. 8 above]
12 [y][Isa. 58:4]

21:1–29 *Naboth's Vineyard.* An apparently reinvigorated Elijah appears again in Jezreel to denounce a new and heinous crime and to foretell the destruction of Ahab's family for all its sins.

21:1 Excavations at Tel **Jezreel** have unearthed a fortified acropolis from the ninth century B.C. The construction at the site is large and elaborate, with the dressed masonry typical of royal palaces of that era. The archaeologist at this site concluded that it was built by either Omri or Ahab, and that it was the auxiliary residence for the king of Israel.

21:2 The Hebrew for **vegetable garden** occurs elsewhere in the OT only in Deut. 11:10, where a contrast is offered between Egypt (a vegetable garden requiring human care) and the Promised Land (which the Lord cares for). Israel is also sometimes portrayed in the OT as a vine under God's special care (e.g., Isa. 3:13–15). With these wider observations in mind, Ahab's desire to replace a **vineyard** with a vegetable garden may express (albeit unconsciously) a deeper desire to make Israel "like Egypt"—to blur Israel's special identity as God's people.

21:3 the inheritance of my fathers. The land of Israel belonged not to the families who technically "owned" it but to God, who had brought the Israelites into the land in fulfillment of the Abrahamic promise and had, through Joshua, allocated its various parts to the tribes as their inheritance (e.g., Gen. 17:8; Lev. 25:23; Josh. 13:1–7). Individual Israelites could not sell land in perpetuity, and a complex set of laws kept land in the family and prevented its accumulation in the hands of a few (e.g., Deut. 25:5–10). Ahab's offer is therefore evidence of his disregard for Israelite law.

21:7 Do you now govern Israel? Jezebel wrongly assumes that a king should use government power for personal gain. As this narrative shows, the real driving force in the kingdom of Israel is **Jezebel** (cf. 19:1–2), not the passive Ahab, and she is contemptuous of her husband's unwillingness to behave as a despotic king.

21:8–10 Proclaim a fast. Jezebel's plan to have Naboth executed on false charges requires a public setting, **elders** and **leaders** who take lightly their responsibility to be the guardians of justice (cf. Deut. 19:11–13; 21:1–9), and **two worthless men** who are prepared to function as the two witnesses required by OT law (cf. Deut. 19:15–21).

21:15 take possession of the vineyard. The implication appears to be that the king may confiscate the property of an executed criminal, a custom

Ahab, "Arise, take possession of the vineyard of Naboth the Jezreelite, which he refused
to give you for money, for Naboth is not alive, but dead." 16 And as soon as Ahab heard
that Naboth was dead, Ahab arose to go down to the vineyard of Naboth the Jezreelite,
to take possession of it.

The LORD Condemns Ahab

17 [z]Then the word of the LORD came to Elijah the Tishbite, saying, 18 "Arise, go down to
meet Ahab king of Israel, who is in [a]Samaria; behold, he is in the vineyard of Naboth, where
he has gone to take possession. 19 And you shall say to him, 'Thus says the LORD, "Have you
killed and also taken possession?"' And you shall say to him, 'Thus says the LORD: [b]"In the
place where dogs licked up the blood of Naboth shall dogs lick your own blood."'"
20 Ahab said to Elijah, [c]"Have you found me, O my enemy?" He answered, "I have found
you, because [d]you have sold yourself to do what is evil in the sight of the LORD. 21 Behold, I
will bring disaster upon you. I will utterly burn you up, and [e]will cut off from Ahab every
male, bond or free, in Israel. 22 And I will make your house like [f]the house of Jeroboam the
son of Nebat, and like [g]the house of Baasha the son of Ahijah, for the anger to which you
have provoked me, and because you [h]have made Israel to sin. 23 And of Jezebel the LORD
also said, [i]'The dogs shall eat Jezebel within [j]the walls of Jezreel.' 24 [k]Anyone belonging
to Ahab who dies in the city the dogs shall eat, and anyone of his who dies in the open
country the birds of the heavens shall eat."

Ahab's Repentance

25 ([l]There was none who sold himself to do what was evil in the sight of the LORD like
Ahab, whom Jezebel his wife incited. 26 He acted very abominably in going after [m]idols, as
[n]the Amorites had done, whom the LORD cast out before the people of Israel.)
27 And when Ahab heard those words, he [o]tore his clothes and [p]put sackcloth on his flesh
and [q]fasted and lay in sackcloth and went about dejectedly. 28 And the word of the LORD
came to Elijah the Tishbite, saying, 29 "Have you seen how Ahab has humbled himself
before me? Because he has humbled himself before me, I will not bring the disaster in his
days; [r]but in his son's days I will bring the disaster upon his house."

Ahab and the False Prophets

22 For three years Syria and Israel continued without war. 2 [s]But in the third year
[t]Jehoshaphat the king of Judah came down to the king of Israel. 3 And the king of
Israel said to his servants, "Do you know that [u]Ramoth-gilead belongs to us, and we keep
quiet and do not take it out of the hand of the king of Syria?" 4 And he said to Jehoshaphat,
"Will you go with me to battle at Ramoth-gilead?" And Jehoshaphat said to the king of
Israel, [v]"I am as you are, my people as your people, my horses as your horses."
5 And Jehoshaphat said to the king of Israel, "Inquire first for the word of the LORD."

17 [z][Ps. 9:12]
18 [a]ch. 16:24
19 [b]ch. 22:38; 2 Kgs. 9:26
20 [c][ch. 18:17] [d]ver. 25; 2 Kgs. 17:17; Rom. 7:14
21 [e]2 Kgs. 9:8; [ch. 14:10]
22 [f]ch. 15:29 [g]ch. 16:3, 11 [h]ch. 14:16
23 [i]2 Kgs. 9:36 [j][2 Sam. 20:15]
24 [k][ch. 14:11; 16:4]
25 [l]See ch. 16:30-33
26 [m][ch. 15:12; 2 Kgs. 17:12; 21:11] [n]Gen. 15:16
27 [o]2 Kgs. 6:30 [p]See 2 Sam. 3:31 [q]2 Sam. 12:16
29 [r]2 Kgs. 9:25

Chapter 22

2 [s]For ver. 1-35, see 2 Chr. 18:2-34 [t]ch. 15:24
3 [u]Deut. 4:43; Josh. 21:38; 2 Kgs. 8:28; 9:1, 14; 2 Chr. 22:5
4 [v]2 Kgs. 3:7

that is known from non-Israelite texts but for which there is no provision in Israelite law. This serves to emphasize the extent to which Ahab and Jezebel are moving outside the sphere of Israelite law and custom and introducing foreign ideas.

21:19 In the place where dogs licked up the blood of Naboth shall dogs lick your own blood. Ahab died in battle and was buried in Samaria (22:34–37), not outside Jezreel "in the place" where Naboth was stoned (21:19; cf. v. 13); and yet, when dogs in Samaria lick up his blood washed from his chariot, the authors declare that to be according to these words (22:38). There are two main ways to explain how the prophecy and its fulfillment are related: (1) the prophecy was fulfilled in stages, first by Ahab's death and then by the death of his son Joram, whose body was in fact thrown into Naboth's vineyard (2 Kings 9:25–26, which also is "according to the word of the LORD"); or (2) the Hebrew words translated "in the place where dogs licked up" could be taken as "in place of dogs licking up," i.e., Ahab will suffer a similar fate to Naboth. Either solution is possible, although the first seems to account better for the way the text draws attention to the prophecy, and for the delay of punishment due to Ahab's repentance (1 Kings 21:29).

21:23–24 The dogs shall eat . . . the birds of the heavens shall eat. It was considered a terrible thing in Israel not to be afforded a proper burial; Deut. 28:25–26 and Jer. 16:4 capture the horror well.

21:29 Because he has humbled himself. Ahab was the worst of kings (vv. 25–26), adding to Jeroboam's sin the worship of Baal (16:30–33). But the great sinner demonstrates penitence at this point, and avoids God's judgment on his house in his lifetime.

22:1–40 *Ahab Killed in Battle*. Although the house of Ahab stands under a prophetic curse, the full outworking of God's wrath will be delayed until the reign of Ahab's son (see 21:27–29). Ahab's own death, however, has now been foretold by two different prophets, with apparently no delay in sight (20:41–42; 21:19); the appearance of a third prophet now brings the reader to that event.

22:1–5 The peace that followed the battle of Aphek (20:26–34) lasted **three years**. Even after such a crushing defeat, the **king of Syria** was able to hold on to the strategically important city of **Ramoth-gilead** in Transjordan, which was situated on a major trade route running from the Red Sea to Damascus. More about **Jehoshaphat**, king of Judah, will be revealed shortly (22:41–50), but from these verses two things are already apparent: he is at peace with Ahab (cf. v. 44) after the long war described in 14:30; 15:6–7, 16–22; and he is a devout man (cf. 22:43, 46), happy to go with Ahab **to battle at Ramoth-gilead**, but first wishing to **inquire . . . for the word of the LORD**.

6 Then the king of Israel [w]gathered the prophets together, about four hundred men, and
said to them, "Shall I go to battle against Ramoth-gilead, or shall I refrain?" And they said,
"Go up, for the Lord will give it into the hand of the king." 7 But [x]Jehoshaphat said, "Is
there not here another prophet of the LORD of whom we may inquire?" 8 And the king of
Israel said to Jehoshaphat, "There is yet one man by whom we may inquire of the LORD,
Micaiah the son of Imlah, but I hate him, for he never prophesies good concerning me, but
evil." And Jehoshaphat said, "Let not the king say so." 9 Then the king of Israel summoned
an officer and said, "Bring quickly Micaiah the son of Imlah." 10 Now the king of Israel
and Jehoshaphat the king of Judah were sitting on their thrones, arrayed in their robes,
at the threshing floor [y]at the entrance of the gate of Samaria, and all the prophets were
prophesying before them. 11 And Zedekiah the son of Chenaanah made for himself [z]horns
of iron and said, "Thus says the LORD, 'With these [a]you shall push the Syrians until they
are destroyed.'" 12 And all the prophets prophesied so and said, "Go up to Ramoth-gilead
and triumph; the LORD will give it into the hand of the king."

Micaiah Prophesies Against Ahab

13 And the messenger who went to summon Micaiah said to him, "Behold, the words of
the prophets with one accord are favorable to the king. Let your word be like the word of
one of them, and speak favorably." 14 But Micaiah said, [b]"As the LORD lives, [c]what the LORD
says to me, that I will speak." 15 And when he had come to the king, the king said to him,
"Micaiah, shall we go to Ramoth-gilead to battle, or shall we refrain?" And he answered
him, "Go up and triumph; the LORD will give it into the hand of the king." 16 But the
king said to him, "How many times shall I make you swear that you speak to me nothing
but the truth in the name of the LORD?" 17 And he said, "I saw all Israel scattered on the
mountains, [d]as sheep that have no shepherd. And the LORD said, 'These have no master;
let each return to his home in peace.'" 18 And the king of Israel said to Jehoshaphat, [e]"Did
I not tell you that he would not prophesy good concerning me, but evil?" 19 And Micaiah
said, "Therefore hear the word of the LORD: [f]I saw the LORD sitting on his throne, [g]and
all the host of heaven standing beside him on his right hand and on his left; 20 and the
LORD said, 'Who will entice Ahab, that he may go up and fall at Ramoth-gilead?' And one
said one thing, and another said another. 21 Then a spirit came forward and stood before
the LORD, saying, 'I will entice him.' 22 And the LORD said to him, 'By what means?' And
he said, 'I will go out, and will be [h]a lying spirit in the mouth of all his prophets.' And he
said, 'You are to entice him, and you shall succeed; go out and do so.' 23 Now therefore
behold, the LORD has put a lying spirit in the mouth of all these your prophets; the LORD
has declared disaster for you."
24 Then Zedekiah the son of Chenaanah came near [i]and struck Micaiah on the cheek and

6 [w]ch. 18:19
7 [x]2 Kgs. 3:11
10 [y]See Ruth 4:1
11 [z][Zech. 1:18, 19] [a][Deut. 33:17]
14 [b]See ch. 17:1 [c]Num. 22:18; 24:13
17 [d]Num. 27:17; Matt. 9:36
18 [e]ver. 8
19 [f]Isa. 6:1; Dan. 7:9; Rev. 4:2 [g][Deut. 33:2; Job 1:6; 2:1; Ps. 103:21; Dan. 7:10; Heb. 12:22]
22 [h][Judg. 9:23; Ezek. 14:9; 2 Thess. 2:11]
24 [i][Lam. 3:30; Mic. 5:1; Matt. 5:39; Acts 23:2]

22:6–7 gathered the prophets together. The Hebrew expression occurs in the OT only here (with its parallel in 2 Chron. 18:5) and in 1 Kings 18:20, where Ahab had previously gathered prophets together in response to Elijah's demand for the attendance of "the 450 prophets of Baal and the 400 prophets of Asherah" (18:19) on Mount Carmel. As things turned out, only the 450 prophets of Baal actually turned up on that occasion (18:22, 25), leaving the 400 prophets of Asherah—precisely the number of **men** mentioned here in 22:6—unaccounted for. It is already implied, therefore, that these prophets are not truly prophets of the **Lord**, but in fact prophets committed to the religion of Jezebel. This is probably further implied in Jehoshaphat's response to their advice, which indicates his suspicion of these prophets: **Is there not here another prophet of the LORD**? Jehoshaphat has been seeking "the word of the LORD." Ahab summons just the prophets, and Jehoshaphat then subtly asks whether there is not a (genuine) prophet of the Lord who might now be consulted. (Cf. also note on 2 Chron. 18:4–14.)

22:8 Let not the king say so. A prophet of the Lord should not be marginalized simply because of what has happened in the past (**he never prophesies good concerning me**).

22:10–12 The harvesting of cereal crops in Israel was followed by a threshing (beating) and winnowing process, in which the threshed material was thrown into the air with a fork or a shovel to allow the breeze to separate the grain, the straw, and the chaff. The grain would then be cleaned and stored in jars, grain pits, or storage houses. The location of this activity was the **threshing floor**, an open area sufficiently large for the task, sometimes situated (as in this case) at the city **gate**, and useful for large gatherings of people. It is here that **all the prophets were prophesying before** the kings, and here that **Zedekiah** acted out his play with **horns**, a reminder once again of the worship of Baal and Asherah (see notes on 12:27–28; 16:31–33).

22:15–16 Go up and triumph. Surprisingly, Micaiah's first words to Ahab are exactly those of the other prophets (cf. vv. 12, 15), but Ahab sees that his words are a mere mocking imitation of these court prophets who tell him only what he wants to hear.

22:21 a spirit came forward. The imagery is that of a council of war, with the heavenly king sitting on his throne surrounded by his army, making plans to defeat Ahab in battle.

22:23 put a lying spirit in the mouth of all these . . . prophets. Though God himself does not do evil, he sometimes uses evil agents to accomplish his purposes (see notes on 1 Sam. 16:14; 2 Chron. 18:15–22).

22:24 How did the Spirit of the LORD go from me to speak to you? Micaiah's claim in v. 23 was that Zedekiah and his colleagues had a lying spirit. Zedekiah's response is that he himself has been influenced by "the Spirit of the LORD," who cannot have been speaking to both him and Micaiah.

25[j]ch. 20:30
27[k][2 Chr. 16:10] [l][Judg. 8:9]
28[m][Num. 16:29; Deut. 18:22] [n]Mic. 1:2
30[o]2 Chr. 35:22
31[p][ch. 20:1, 16, 24]
34[q][2 Chr. 35:23]
38[r]ch. 21:19
39[s][Amos 3:15]
41[t]For ver. 41-43, see 2 Chr. 20:31-33 [u]ver. 51
43[v][2 Chr. 17:3]

said, "How did the Spirit of the LORD go from me to speak to you?" 25 And Micaiah said,
"Behold, you shall see on that day when you go [j]into an inner chamber to hide yourself."
26 And the king of Israel said, "Seize Micaiah, and take him back to Amon the governor
of the city and to Joash the king's son, 27 and say, 'Thus says the king, [k]"Put this fellow in
prison and feed him meager rations of bread and water, [l]until I come in peace."'" 28 And
Micaiah said, "If you return in peace, [m]the LORD has not spoken by me." And he said,
[n]"Hear, all you peoples!"

Ahab Killed in Battle

29 So the king of Israel and Jehoshaphat the king of Judah went up to Ramoth-gilead.
30 And the king of Israel said to Jehoshaphat, [o]"I will disguise myself and go into battle,
but you wear your robes." And the king of Israel disguised himself and went into battle.
31 Now the king of Syria had commanded [p]the thirty-two captains of his chariots, "Fight
with neither small nor great, but only with the king of Israel." 32 And when the captains
of the chariots saw Jehoshaphat, they said, "It is surely the king of Israel." So they turned
to fight against him. And Jehoshaphat cried out. 33 And when the captains of the chariots
saw that it was not the king of Israel, they turned back from pursuing him. 34 But a certain
man drew his bow at random[1] and struck the king of Israel between the scale armor and
the breastplate. Therefore he said to the driver of his chariot, "Turn around and carry me
out of the battle, [q]for I am wounded." 35 And the battle continued that day, and the king
was propped up in his chariot facing the Syrians, until at evening he died. And the blood of
the wound flowed into the bottom of the chariot. 36 And about sunset a cry went through
the army, "Every man to his city, and every man to his country!"
37 So the king died, and was brought to Samaria. And they buried the king in Samaria.
38 And they washed the chariot by the pool of Samaria, and the dogs licked up his blood,
and the prostitutes washed themselves in it, [r]according to the word of the LORD that he
had spoken. 39 Now the rest of the acts of Ahab and all that he did, and [s]the ivory house that
he built and all the cities that he built, are they not written in the Book of the Chronicles
of the Kings of Israel? 40 So Ahab slept with his fathers, and Ahaziah his son reigned in
his place.

Jehoshaphat Reigns in Judah

41 [t]Jehoshaphat the son of [u]Asa began to reign over Judah in the fourth year of Ahab
king of Israel. 42 Jehoshaphat was thirty-five years old when he began to reign, and he
reigned twenty-five years in Jerusalem. His mother's name was Azubah the daughter of
Shilhi. 43 [v]He walked in all the way of Asa his father. He did not turn aside from it, doing

[1] Hebrew *in his innocence*

22:25 All will become clear, Micaiah claims, when the disaster that he is predicting eventually falls and Zedekiah is forced to **hide** away in the city inside someone's home (the **inner chamber** was also Ben-hadad's hiding place after the disaster at Aphek, 20:30).

22:26 Amon is evidently one of Ahab's high officials, entrusted with control of city affairs in Samaria, while **Joash the king's son** is responsible for the confinement of prisoners (see also Jer. 36:26; 38:6). It is not clear whether this office requires that its holder literally be the son of the king.

22:30 the king of Israel disguised himself. Ahab's disguise is evidence of unclear thinking, for if Micaiah has truly been lying, there is no danger, and if he has been telling the truth, Ahab will die, whatever he does. The disguise is also a harbinger of disaster; it recalls the actions of both Saul and Jeroboam just before their deaths (cf. 1 Sam. 28:8; 1 Kings 14:1–18). It is foolish to think that a mere disguise will hide someone from the Lord's purposes.

22:32–33 Jehoshaphat cried out. And when the captains . . . saw that it was not the king of Israel. Although Jehoshaphat alone is wearing royal robes, he is saved from death because his Judean shout (either its form or its content) reveals that he is not the man whom Ben-hadad is determined to kill (v. 31).

22:34 between the scale armor and the breastplate. The arrow shot **at random** flies unerringly to one of the few undefended spots on Ahab's body, and thus fulfills what Micaiah had warned of in vv. 20–23.

22:35 propped up in his chariot. The king stays on the battlefield all day long, presumably to encourage his troops; but at sunset he dies.

22:38 according to the word of the LORD. See 21:19, although that verse does not mention **prostitutes**, but only **dogs**. There is already a close association between the two, however, in Deut. 23:17–18, which enjoins the Israelite never to become a cult prostitute (Hb. *qedeshah* for a woman or *qadesh* for a man) or to bring into the temple the earnings of a female prostitute (Hb. *zonah*) or a male prostitute (Hb. *keleb*, lit., "dog"; see ESV footnote on Deut. 23:18). This association reminds the reader of the idolatrous career that has brought Ahab to this ignominious end.

22:39 Chronicles of the Kings (also v. 45). See note on 14:19. Archaeologists have uncovered a palace reminiscent of Ahab's **ivory house** at Samaria. Numerous costly ivory articles were found in the debris of the building.

22:41–53 *Jehoshaphat and Ahaziah.* Both Jehoshaphat and Ahaziah have already entered the narrative of 1 Kings as characters in Ahab's story—comrade-in-arms and successor, respectively (vv. 2–4, 40). Now they are given a place of their own.

22:43–46 He walked in all the way of Asa his father. Jehoshaphat's religious policy is the same as Asa's. He does what is **right in the sight of the LORD** (cf. 15:11), and he will have nothing to do with **cult prostitutes**

what was right in the sight of the LORD. Yet [w]the high places were not taken away, and the
people still sacrificed and made offerings on the high places. 44 [x]Jehoshaphat also made
peace with the king of Israel.
45 Now the rest of the acts of Jehoshaphat, and his might that he showed, and how he
warred, are they not written [y]in the Book of the Chronicles of the Kings of Judah? 46 And
from the land he exterminated the remnant [z]of the male cult prostitutes who remained
in the days of his father Asa.
47 [a]There was no king in Edom; a deputy was king. 48 Jehoshaphat made [b]ships of Tarshish
to go to [c]Ophir for gold, but they did not go, for the ships were wrecked at [d]Ezion-geber.
49 Then Ahaziah the son of Ahab said to Jehoshaphat, "Let my servants go with your servants in the ships," but Jehoshaphat was not willing. 50 [e]And Jehoshaphat slept with his
fathers and was buried with his fathers in the city of David his father, and Jehoram his
son reigned in his place.

Ahaziah Reigns in Israel

51 Ahaziah the son of Ahab [f]began to reign over Israel in Samaria in the seventeenth
year of Jehoshaphat king of Judah, and he reigned two years over Israel. 52 He did what
was evil in the sight of the LORD [g]and walked in the way of his father and in the way of
his mother and in the way of Jeroboam the son of Nebat, who made Israel to sin. 53 [h]He
served Baal and worshiped him and provoked the LORD, the God of Israel, to anger [i]in
every way that his father had done.

43 [w][ch. 15:14; 2 Kgs. 12:3]
44 [x][2 Chr. 18:1; 20:35, 36]
45 [y][2 Chr. 20:34]
46 [z]ch. 14:24; 15:12
47 [a][2 Sam. 8:14; 2 Kgs. 3:9; 8:20]
48 [b]See ch. 10:22 [c]See ch. 9:28 [d]See ch. 9:26
50 [e]2 Chr. 21:1
51 [f]ver. 40
52 [g][ch. 15:26]
53 [h]ch. 16:30 [i][ch. 16:31, 32]

(15:12), even if the **high places** have still not been **taken away** (15:14). Jehoshaphat is a good king, and he is even at **peace with the king of Israel**, which Asa was not (15:16, 32).

22:47 There was no king in Edom; a deputy was king. The Hebrew for "deputy" is otherwise used in 1–2 Kings only of Solomon's various officials (1 Kings 4:5, 27; 5:16; 9:23); Jehoshaphat controls Edom as Solomon had controlled his various districts, which is why the "king" of Edom turns up in alliance with Judah in 2 Kings 3 in a noticeably supporting role. Judah's control of Edom was not challenged until the reign of Jehoshaphat's son Jehoram (2 Kings 8:20–22).

22:48 the ships were wrecked at Ezion-geber. Because Jehoshaphat rules over Edom, just as Solomon had, he is able like Solomon to build a fleet of ships at Ezion-geber (near Elath in Edom; cf. 9:26–28), but he does not benefit from them. These turn out to be not days of glory for the house of David but days of humbling (cf. 11:39).

22:49 Jehoshaphat was not willing. Solomon's Israel was truly unified, but the current peace between Israel and Judah (v. 44) is little more than the absence of hostility. Whereas Solomon took Sidonians on board his ships (9:27), Jehoshaphat refuses even to have Israelites along. (As 2 Chron. 20:35 tells it, Jehoshaphat was originally willing to cooperate with Ahaziah to build the merchant ships. But after Eliezer prophesied against Jehoshaphat's alliance with Ahaziah [2 Chron. 20:37], Jehoshaphat changed his mind, which is the situation described here in 1 Kings.)

22:50 slept with his fathers (see note on 2:10). Jehoshaphat will reappear in 2 Kings 3, in what must be regarded as a "flashback" to the earlier part (i.e., the first seven years) of Jehoram of Israel's reign, when Jehoshaphat was still on the throne of Judah (cf. 1 Kings 22:42; 2 Kings 3:1).

INTRODUCTION TO

2 KINGS

See Introduction to 1–2 Kings, pp. 585–590.

Outline

I. The Death of Ahaziah (1:1–18)

II. Elisha and Israel (2:1–10:36)
- A. Elijah gives way to Elisha (2:1–25)
- B. Elisha and the conquest of Moab (3:1–27)
- C. Elisha's miracles (4:1–44)
- D. A Syrian is healed (5:1–27)
- E. Elisha and Syria (6:1–23)
- F. The siege of Samaria (6:24–7:20)
- G. The Shunammite's land restored (8:1–6)
- H. Hazael murders Ben-hadad (8:7–15)
- I. Jehoram and Ahaziah (8:16–29)
- J. The end of Ahab's house (9:1–10:17)
- K. Jehu destroys Baal worship (10:18–36)

III. Joash (11:1–12:21)

IV. Jehoahaz and Jehoash (13:1–25)

V. Amaziah, Jeroboam II, and Azariah (14:1–15:7)

VI. Israel's Last Days (15:8–31)

VII. Jotham and Ahaz (15:32–16:20)

VIII. The End of Israel (17:1–41)

IX. Hezekiah (18:1–20:21)

X. Manasseh and Amon (21:1–26)

XI. Josiah (22:1–23:30)

XII. The End of Judah (23:31–25:30)

2 KINGS

Elijah Denounces Ahaziah

1 [a]After the death of Ahab, Moab [b]rebelled against Israel.
2 Now Ahaziah fell through the lattice in his upper chamber in Samaria, and lay sick; so
he sent messengers, telling them, "Go, inquire of [c]Baal-zebub, the god of Ekron, [d]whether
I shall recover from this sickness." 3 But the angel of the LORD said to Elijah [e]the Tishbite,
"Arise, go up to meet the messengers of the king of Samaria, and say to them, 'Is it because
there is no God in Israel that you are going to inquire of [c]Baal-zebub, the god of Ekron?
4 Now therefore thus says the LORD, [f]You shall not come down from the bed to which you
have gone up, but you shall surely die.'" So Elijah went.
5 The messengers returned to the king, and he said to them, "Why have you returned?"
6 And they said to him, "There came a man to meet us, and said to us, 'Go back to the king
who sent you, and say to him, Thus says the LORD, Is it because there is no God in Israel
that you are sending to inquire of [c]Baal-zebub, the god of Ekron? Therefore you shall not
come down from the bed to which you have gone up, but you shall surely die.'" 7 He said
to them, "What kind of man was he who came to meet you and told you these things?"
8 They answered him, [g]"He wore a garment of hair, with a belt of leather about his waist."
And he said, "It is Elijah the Tishbite."
9 Then the king sent to him a captain of fifty men with his fifty. He went up to Elijah,
who was sitting on the top of a hill, and said to him, [h]"O man of God, the king says, 'Come
down.'" 10 But Elijah answered the captain of fifty, "If I am a man of God, [i]let fire come
down from heaven and consume you and your fifty." Then fire came down from heaven
and consumed him and his fifty.
11 Again the king sent to him another captain of fifty men with his fifty. And he answered

Chapter 1

1 [a]ch. 3:5 [b][2 Sam. 8:2]
2 [c][Matt. 10:25; 12:24, 27; Mark 3:22; Luke 11:15, 18, 19] [d][ch. 8:8]
3 [e]1 Kgs. 17:1; 21:17 [c][See ver. 2 above]
4 [f]ver. 6, 16
6 [c][See ver. 2 above]
8 [g][Zech. 13:4; Matt. 3:4; Mark 1:6]
9 [h]Deut. 33:1; Judg. 13:6; 1 Sam. 2:27; 9:6
10 [i]Luke 9:54

1:1–18 *The Death of Ahaziah.* Like his father Ahab, Ahaziah is destined to meet Elijah. The occasion for their confrontation is an injury sustained by the king when falling out the window of his upper chamber in Samaria.

1:1 After the death of Ahab, Moab rebelled. More on this rebellion will be related in ch. 3. It is mentioned here to make the point that, whereas the relatively righteous Jehoshaphat maintained his control of other nations (Edom, 1 Kings 22:47), Ahab's Baal-worshiping son did not. An inscribed stone monument of King Mesha of Moab (commonly known as the "Mesha Inscription" or "Moabite Stone") probably refers to this same Moabite rebellion (see note on 2 Kings 3:4–27).

1:2 Samaria was the capital of the northern kingdom of Israel from the time of Omri (1 Kings 16:24) until the fall of the northern kingdom under Hoshea (2 Kings 17). **Ekron** was an important Philistine city about 25 miles (40 km) west of Jerusalem. **Baal-zebub** means "lord of the flies" and is probably a deliberate Hebrew corruption of "Baal-zebul" ("Baal the exalted" or "Baal/master of the height" or possibly "Baal/master of the dwelling"; cf. note on Matt. 10:25), intended to express the authors' scorn of or hostility toward this "deity." Ahaziah looks for help from this local manifestation of the god Baal (see 1 Kings 16:31–33), perhaps regarding the Ekronite version of the deity as especially powerful.

1:3–4 In a scene reminiscent of the opening verses of 1 Kings 19, the Lord sends an **angel** (Hb. *mal'ak*) in response to other people's sending **messengers** (also Hb. *mal'ak*, 2 Kings 1:2).

1:8 He wore a garment of hair. The Hebrew is lit., "He was a man who was a lord/owner of hair"—possibly a play on words with "lord of the flies" in v. 2. The "hair" could be either animal or human, which is why translations of the Hebrew have varied between "garment of hair" and "hairy" (i.e., long-haired, bearded).

1:9–12 the king sent to him a captain of fifty men. The odds would seem good for 50 soldiers to be able to bring back one man, but the Lord is on Elijah's side. This is not the first time a negative oracle addressed to a king elicits an attempt to capture the prophet who delivered it (cf. 1 Kings 13:1–7; 17:1–4; 18:9–10; also 1 Sam. 19:19–24). The prophetic word, however, cannot be brought under human control, and the God of Mount Carmel sends **fire** from **heaven** to underline this fact (cf. 1 Kings 18:38). Two "lords" vie for worship throughout the Elijah story (Baal and Yahweh), both of them identified with fire—and Ahaziah has chosen the wrong one. Here 100 soldiers die as a result of Ahaziah's choice to turn from God, again showing that the sins of leaders often lead to tragic consequences for those whom they lead (see note on 2 Sam. 24:17).

1:13–18 third captain. This man shows Elijah the respect he is due as a prophet of the Lord and escapes with his life. On the other hand, Ahaziah has his desired meeting with Elijah, and it changes nothing; the king dies. His brother **Jehoram** succeeds him (v. 17; cf. 3:1). On the **Chronicles of the Kings**, see note on 1 Kings 14:19.

12[j]Job 1:16
13[k][1 Sam. 26:21; Ps. 72:14]
16[c][See ver. 2 above]
17[l][ch. 3:1; 8:16]

Chapter 2

1[m][Gen. 5:24] [n]See 1 Kgs. 19:19-21 [o]ch. 4:38; [Josh. 5:9]
2[p][Ruth 1:15, 16] [q]See Ruth 3:13

and said to him, "O man of God, this is the king's order, 'Come down quickly!'" 12 But
Elijah answered them, "If I am a man of God, [j]let fire come down from heaven and consume you and your fifty." Then the fire of God came down from heaven and consumed
him and his fifty.
13 Again the king sent the captain of a third fifty with his fifty. And the third captain of
fifty went up and came and fell on his knees before Elijah and entreated him, "O man of
God, please let my life, and the life of these fifty servants of yours, [k]be precious in your
sight. 14 Behold, fire came down from heaven and consumed the two former captains of
fifty men with their fifties, but now let my life be precious in your sight." 15 Then the angel
of the LORD said to Elijah, "Go down with him; do not be afraid of him." So he arose and
went down with him to the king 16 and said to him, "Thus says the LORD, 'Because you
have sent messengers to inquire of [c]Baal-zebub, the god of Ekron—is it because there is
no God in Israel to inquire of his word?—therefore you shall not come down from the
bed to which you have gone up, but you shall surely die.'"
17 So he died according to the word of the LORD that Elijah had spoken. Jehoram became
king in his place [l]in the second year of Jehoram the son of Jehoshaphat, king of Judah,
because Ahaziah had no son. 18 Now the rest of the acts of Ahaziah that he did, are they
not written in the Book of the Chronicles of the Kings of Israel?

Elijah Taken to Heaven

2 Now when the LORD was about to [m]take Elijah up to heaven by a whirlwind, Elijah
and [n]Elisha were on their way from [o]Gilgal. 2 And Elijah said to Elisha, [p]"Please stay
here, for the LORD has sent me as far as Bethel." But Elisha said, [q]"As the LORD lives, and

2:1–10:36 *Elisha and Israel.* Elijah's days have been numbered since 1 Kings 19:15–18, and particularly God's instructions there about Elisha. The end of the war with Baal worship will not come about until Elisha has succeeded Elijah, and Hazael and Jehu have appeared. This section of 1–2 Kings now tells of these events.

2:1–25 *Elijah Gives Way to Elisha.* The prophetic mantle passes from Elijah to Elisha. As Elijah has called fire *down from* heaven in ch. 1, so he now will be lifted in fire *up to* heaven, and Elisha will be authenticated as his successor.

2:1 The idea of going **up to heaven** at the end of an earthly life was not common in ancient Israel. The OT more characteristically speaks of the deceased's "going down" to Sheol, the world of the dead (e.g., Job 7:9; Isa. 57:9; see note on 1 Sam. 2:6). It was the fate even of mighty heroes of the Hebrew tradition to be "gathered to their people" in this way (e.g., Gen. 25:7–8; 1 Kings 2:10). Elijah represents a remarkable exception to this way of speaking (see also Enoch in Gen. 5:24; cf. Heb. 11:5). This does not mean that the OT faithful had no fellowship with God after they died, but only that this idea is seldom made explicit in the OT (but see indications of hope for continuing fellowship with God after death in Ps. 16:10–11; 17:15; 23:6; 115:17–18; Eccles. 12:7; and certainly here in 2 Kings 2:11). In the NT, Jesus implied that Abraham, Isaac, and Jacob were alive and in God's presence (Matt. 22:32); Moses and Elijah appeared talking with Jesus in Matt. 17:3; and the parable of the rich man and Lazarus implied fellowship in Abraham's presence immediately after death (Luke 16:22–25). Extrabiblical texts underline the unusual nature, in the ancient Near Eastern context, of any idea that mortals can enter and remain in heaven. The best known of these is the Akkadian myth of Adapa, the son of Ea, who visits heaven and almost obtains eternal life, but is compelled in the end to return to earth. It is not clear whether the Lord has any reason for sending Elijah from **Gilgal** to Bethel, and then on to Jericho (2 Kings 2:2–4); but all three cities appear in 2 Kings as locations of prophetic communities ("sons of the prophets"; see note on v. 3; also v. 5; 4:38), and Elijah is probably their leader (as Elisha is later).

2:2 Bethel is identified with Jeroboam's apostasy in 1 Kings 12–13. **Please stay here.** It is never made clear why Elijah, in the course of his roundabout journey, keeps trying to get Elisha to remain behind on the very day that the prophetic succession is to take place ("today the LORD will take away your master"), but it is probably a testing of Elisha's mettle as the professed disciple and designated successor to Elijah. This may provide further evidence

Israel and Judah in 2 Kings
c. 853 B.C.
The book of 2 Kings recounts events in Israel and Judah from the death of Ahab to the exile of Israel and Judah. The complex and shifting political setting for the book involves Israel, Judah, Syria, Ammon, Moab, Edom, and Philistia, as well as Egypt, Assyria, Babylonia, and other kingdoms far beyond Israel's borders.

as you yourself live, I will not leave you." So they went down to Bethel. 3 And [r]the sons of
the prophets who were in Bethel came out to Elisha and said to him, "Do you know that
today the LORD will take away your master from over you?" And he said, "Yes, I know it;
keep quiet."
4 Elijah said to him, "Elisha, [p]please stay here, for the LORD has sent me to [t]Jericho." But
he said, [q]"As the LORD lives, and as you yourself live, I will not leave you." So they came
to Jericho. 5 [r]The sons of the prophets who were at Jericho drew near to Elisha and said to
him, "Do you know that today the LORD will take away your master from over you?" And
he answered, "Yes, I know it; keep quiet."
6 Then Elijah said to him, [p]"Please stay here, for the LORD has sent me to the Jordan."
But he said, "As the LORD lives, and as you yourself live, I will not leave you." So the two
of them went on. 7 Fifty men of [r]the sons of the prophets also went and stood at some
distance from them, as they both were standing by the Jordan. 8 Then Elijah [u]took his
cloak and rolled it up and struck the water, [v]and the water was parted to the one side and
to the other, till the two of them could go over on dry ground.
9 When they had crossed, Elijah said to Elisha, "Ask what I shall do for you, before I am
taken from you." And Elisha said, "Please let there be a double portion of your spirit on
me." 10 And he said, "You have asked a hard thing; yet, if you see me as I am being taken
from you, it shall be so for you, but if you do not see me, it shall not be so." 11 And as they
still went on and talked, behold, [w]chariots of fire and horses of fire separated the two of
them. And Elijah went up by a whirlwind into heaven. 12 And Elisha saw it and he cried, "My
father, my father! [x]The chariots of Israel and its horsemen!" And he saw him no more.
Then he took hold of his own clothes [y]and tore them in two pieces. 13 And he took up
the cloak of Elijah that had fallen from him and went back and stood on the bank of the
Jordan. 14 Then he took the cloak of Elijah that had fallen from him and struck the water,
saying, "Where is the LORD, the God of Elijah?" And when he had struck the water, [v]the
water was parted to the one side and to the other, and Elisha went over.

Elisha Succeeds Elijah

15 Now when [r]the sons of the prophets who were at Jericho saw him opposite them, they
said, "The spirit of Elijah rests on Elisha." And they came to meet him and bowed to the

3 [r]ch. 4:1, 38; 5:22; 6:1; 9:1; 1 Kgs. 20:35
4 [p][See ver. 2 above] [t][Josh. 6:26; 1 Kgs. 16:34] [q][See ver. 2 above]
5 [r][See ver. 3 above]
6 [p][See ver. 2 above]
7 [r][See ver. 3 above]
8 [u][1 Kgs. 19:19] [v][Ex. 14:21; Josh. 3:16]
11 [w]See ch. 6:17
12 [x]ch. 13:14 [y][1 Kgs. 11:30]
14 [v][See ver. 8 above]
15 [r][See ver. 3 above]

of Elijah's reluctance to fully embrace God's plans for the future (see 1 Kings 19:13–21). Elijah affirms a little later that Elisha can receive Elijah's spiritual power only if he sees him when he is taken away by God (2 Kings 2:9–10). The prophets in the meantime are to "keep quiet"; it is disrespectful to speak of Elijah's passing while he is still around.

2:3 The **sons of the prophets** are not their physical descendants but groups of prophets usually affiliated with a more prominent prophet (cf. 1 Sam. 10:5; 19:20; 1 Kings 18:4; 2 Kings 4:1, 38; 6:1; 9:1). (The phrase "sons of" can mean "members of a guild of"; cf. "the sons of the gatekeepers" in Ezra 2:42.) Though groups of false prophets also exist (e.g., 1 Kings 22:6), the prophetic groups associated with true prophets such as Samuel and Elijah are never viewed as false prophets but as servants of God, and therefore they must have received special revelations from God (which is the requirement for a true prophet: Deut. 18:18, 20; Jer. 14:14; Ezek. 13:1–3), though none of their prophecies are recorded in Scripture. In this text God has revealed to them that **today the LORD will take away** Elijah.

2:4–5 Jericho was in the Jordan Valley about 10 miles (16 km) to the northwest of the Dead Sea and is best known as the city that the Israelites first conquered in Canaan.

2:6–8 The **Jordan** River runs along a short stretch of a geological fault that starts in the north in Syria and extends southward into Africa. This scene of the crossing of the Jordan is reminiscent of Moses at the Red Sea, where the people also **go over** on dry land (Ex. 14:15–31, esp. vv. 21–22). Later in the chapter, Elisha proves that he is Joshua to Elijah's Moses by recrossing the river (see note on 2 Kings 2:14).

2:9 Elisha requests of Elijah what an eldest son would expect of a father in Israel: a **double portion** of the inheritance (see Deut. 21:15–17). In this case, however, the inheritance is not land but spiritual power: Elisha has already left behind him normal life and the normal rules of inheritance (cf. 1 Kings 19:19–21).

2:10 You have asked a hard thing. It is not clear how Elisha's request can be hard, given that Elisha is ordained by God to succeed Elijah as a Spirit-empowered prophet. Is Elijah simply looking for difficulties? But cf. note on v. 2.

2:11–13 chariots of fire and horses of fire. The divine army, last encountered waging war on Ahab (1 Kings 22:1–38), has come for Elijah; Elisha sees it, as he will see it again in 2 Kings 6:8–23. In biblical tradition, both chariotry and fire have strong associations with God's self-disclosure. Both images come together in the most common natural form of divine appearing ("theophany") in the OT: the thunderstorm—the storm cloud representing the divine chariot or throne (Ezekiel 1; Hab. 3:8) and the fiery lightning bolts representing the divine weapons (Ps. 18:14; Hab. 3:11). In response to this particular theophany, Elisha **took hold of his own clothes and tore them in two pieces**. This is perhaps part of a mourning ritual (cf. Gen. 37:34; 2 Sam. 13:31; Isa. 37:1), but it is also suggestive of leaving his old life behind, as he picks up instead the **cloak of Elijah** (used in 1 Kings 19:19–21 to symbolize Elisha's prophetic call).

2:14 the water was parted . . . and Elisha went over. The Spirit who empowered Elijah has now come upon Elisha, and miracles immediately follow. As Elijah's true successor, Elisha is able to repeat Elijah's action in parting the waters (v. 8). There is also a kind of parallel in the life of Joshua, for Joshua also crossed the Jordan in Joshua 3 and entered the land of Israel near Jericho, "repeating" Moses' action in parting the waters (Exodus 14).

2:15 they came to meet him and bowed. The roots of the Jericho community's allegiance to Elisha lie in their conviction that he is Elijah's bona fide successor (**The spirit of Elijah rests on Elisha**).

ground before him. 16 And they said to him, "Behold now, there are with your servants fifty
strong men. Please let them go and seek your master. It may be that [z]the Spirit of the LORD
has caught him up and cast him upon some mountain or into some valley." And he said,
"You shall not send." 17 But when they urged him [a]till he was ashamed, he said, "Send."
They sent therefore fifty men. And for three days they sought him but did not find him.
18 And they came back to him while he was staying at Jericho, and he said to them, "Did I
not say to you, 'Do not go'?"
19 Now the men of the city said to Elisha, "Behold, the situation of this city is pleasant,
as my lord sees, but the water is bad, and the land is unfruitful." 20 He said, "Bring me a
new bowl, and put salt in it." So they brought it to him. 21 Then he went to the spring of
water and [b]threw salt in it and said, "Thus says the LORD, I have healed this water; from
now on neither death nor miscarriage shall come from it." 22 So the water has been healed
to this day, according to the word that Elisha spoke.
23 He went up from there to Bethel, and while he was going up on the way, some small
boys came out of the city and jeered at him, saying, "Go up, you baldhead! Go up, you baldhead!" 24 And he turned around, and when he saw them, [c]he cursed them in the name of
the LORD. And two she-bears came out of the woods and tore forty-two of the boys. 25 From
there he went on to [d]Mount Carmel, and from there he returned [e]to Samaria.

Moab Rebels Against Israel

3 [f]In the eighteenth year of Jehoshaphat king of Judah, Jehoram the son of Ahab became
king over Israel in Samaria, and he reigned twelve years. 2 He did what was evil in the
sight of the LORD, though not like his father and mother, for he put away the [g]pillar of Baal
[h]that his father had made. 3 Nevertheless, he clung to [i]the sin of Jeroboam the son of Nebat,
[j]which he made Israel to sin; he did not depart from it.
4 Now Mesha king of Moab was a sheep breeder, [k]and he had to deliver to the king
of Israel 100,000 lambs and the wool of 100,000 rams. 5 But [l]when Ahab died, the king
of Moab rebelled against the king of Israel. 6 So King Jehoram marched out of Samaria at
that time and mustered all Israel. 7 And he went and sent word to Jehoshaphat king of

16 [z]See 1 Kgs. 18:12
17 [a]ch. 8:11
21 [b][ch. 4:41; Ex. 15:25]
24 [c][Neh. 13:25]
25 [d]Josh. 19:26; 1 Kgs. 18:19, 20 [e][ch. 3:11]

Chapter 3

1 [f][ch. 1:17]
2 [g][ch. 10:26, 27; Ex. 23:24] [h]1 Kgs. 16:31, 32
3 [i]1 Kgs. 12:28, 31, 32 [j]See 1 Kgs. 14:16
4 [k][Isa. 16:1, 2]
5 [l]ch. 1:1

2:16 Please let them go and seek your master. The sons of the prophets seem to understand that the prophetic succession has taken place, but do not fully understand what has happened. Standing at a distance (v. 7), they have seen the fire and the whirlwind (v. 11), but they have not perceived what was happening in the storm's midst. They wonder, therefore, whether the **Spirit of the LORD** has not simply **caught** Elijah **up and cast him upon some mountain or into some valley;** and they at least want to retrieve Elijah's body for burial (cf. 1 Sam. 31:11–13).

2:19–22 the water is bad, and the land is unfruitful. This is the first of two stories that further authenticate Elisha as Elijah's prophetic successor, a man able both to bless and to curse in the Lord's name (cf. Moses in Deuteronomy 28). Jericho was in an area ideal for settlement because of the presence of the perennial spring 'Ain es-Sultan, which irrigated the fertile land around it. This story, however, tells of contamination of the water supply (the rebuilding of the city having taken place under the shadow of Joshua's curse; Josh. 6:26; 1 Kings 16:34). The remedy offered by the new Joshua (Elisha), who has just crossed the Jordan, involves a **new bowl** and **salt**. New items, being uncontaminated, were customarily employed in rituals in the ancient Near East (e.g., Judg. 16:11; 1 Kings 11:29). Elsewhere in the OT, **salt** is associated with the covenant and is included as part of offerings made to the Lord (see "salt of the covenant" in Lev. 2:13; cf. Num. 18:19), as well as being used in other specific rituals (Judg. 9:45; Ezek. 16:4). The use of salt here is likewise symbolic, for by itself a tiny bowl of salt would have no effect on a constantly flowing spring. The healing of the water was therefore accomplished by supernatural means: **Thus says the LORD, I have healed this water.**

2:23–24 jeered at him. The focal point for Israel's apostasy was **Bethel** (see 1 Kings 12:25–13:34). Therefore, it is no surprise to find young people from this city adopting a disrespectful attitude toward a prophet of the Lord, and to treat a prophet with disrespect is to treat God himself with disrespect. The reference to the **baldhead** is not clear, but Elisha might have already been so bald by nature that to youthful eyes he looked grotesque; or perhaps some prophets, like later Christian monks, shaved their heads as a mark of their vocation. **he cursed them. . . . And two she-bears . . . tore forty-two of the boys.** Though this judgment may at first seem harsh, the group must have included over 50 boys old enough to be out running in a pack, and so they constituted something of a physical threat to Elisha. The authors of Kings regularly show that contempt toward divinely called prophets is disastrous for God's people.

2:25 The succession narrative now complete, Elisha ends his journey with a visit to **Mount Carmel**—the scene of Elijah's great victory—and a return to **Samaria** to continue the war against Baal worship.

3:1–27 *Elisha and the Conquest of Moab.* One expects that Elisha, as Elijah's successor, will also be involved in politics, and in this story he is consulted about a military campaign. The narrative noticeably echoes 1 Kings 22:1–28.

3:2 not like his father and mother. As one of a number of surprises in ch. 3, Jehoram son of Ahab is distanced from the rest of his family by the way in which his reign is described. The implication is that while he tolerated the Baal cult (cf. v. 13; 9:22; 10:18–28), he did not himself worship **Baal** (he removed Baal's **pillar** from the temple; see 1 Kings 14:23).

3:4–27 The Moabite Stone (currently in the Louvre Museum in Paris) is a stele set up by Mesha, king of Moab, to commemorate his achievements. Mesha makes his version of a war fought with Israel in 850 B.C. prominent; the Israelite account appears in this chapter. The two accounts differ: Mesha emphasizes his victories over Israel, and the biblical writer emphasizes Israel's successful counterattacks.

3:4–5 Mesha was a ninth-century **king of Moab**, the successor of his father Chemosh-yatti according to the Moabite Stone (see notes on 1:1; 3:4–27). He began his reign under the dominion of the Israelite house of Omri, and was required to pay his overlord "tribute" (i.e., taxation) in the form of a percentage of his agricultural produce (**lambs** and **wool**), which is understandable given the importance of sheep in the economy of ancient Palestine. After the death of Ahab, Mesha took advantage of the new situation and rebelled, inciting Ahab's son Jehoram to launch the military campaign described in this chapter (see map, p. 650).

3:7–9 he went and sent word to Jehoshaphat. Like his father before him, Jehoram seeks help from his southern neighbor Jehoshaphat, whose

Judah, "The king of Moab has rebelled against me. Will you go with me to battle against
Moab?" And he said, "I will go. [m]I am as you are, my people as your people, my horses as
your horses." 8 Then he said, "By which way shall we march?" Jehoram answered, "By the
way of the wilderness of Edom."
9 So the king of Israel went with the king of Judah and [n]the king of Edom. And when
they had made a circuitous march of seven days, there was no water for the army or for
the animals that followed them. 10 Then the king of Israel said, "Alas! [o]The LORD has
called these three kings to give them into the hand of Moab." 11 [p]And Jehoshaphat said,
"Is there no prophet of the LORD here, through whom we may inquire of the LORD?"
Then one of the king of Israel's servants answered, [q]"Elisha the son of Shaphat is here,
[r]who poured water on the hands of Elijah." 12 And Jehoshaphat said, "The word of the
LORD is with him." So the king of Israel and Jehoshaphat and the king of Edom went
down to him.
13 And Elisha said to the king of Israel, [s]"What have I to do with you? Go to [t]the prophets
of your father and to [u]the prophets of your mother." But the king of Israel said to him,
"No; it is [o]the LORD who has called these three kings to give them into the hand of Moab."
14 And Elisha said, [v]"As the LORD of hosts lives, before whom I stand, were it not that I
have regard for Jehoshaphat the king of Judah, I would neither look at you nor see you.
15 But now [w]bring me a musician." And when the musician played, [x]the hand of the LORD
came upon him. 16 And he said, "Thus says the LORD, 'I will make this dry streambed full
of pools.' 17 For thus says the LORD, 'You shall not see wind or rain, but that streambed
shall be filled with water, so that you shall drink, you, your livestock, and your animals.'
18 This is a light thing in the sight of the LORD. He will also give the Moabites into your

7 [m]1 Kgs. 22:4
9 [n][1 Kgs. 22:47]
10 [o][Josh. 7:7]
11 [p]1 Kgs. 22:7 [q][ch. 2:25] [r][1 Kgs. 19:21; John 13:4, 5]
13 [s][Ezek. 14:3] [t]1 Kgs. 22:6 [u]1 Kgs. 18:19 [o][See ver. 10 above]
14 [v]ch. 5:16; 1 Kgs. 17:1
15 [w][1 Sam. 10:5; 1 Chr. 25:1] [x]1 Kgs. 18:46; Ezek. 1:3; 3:14, 22; 8:1; 37:1; 40:1

Moab, Edom, and Libnah Revolt
853, 848 B.C.
When King Ahab of Israel died, King Mesha of Moab seized the opportunity to throw off the yoke of tribute imposed on his people by David. Israel, Judah, and Edom (which still belonged to Judah) joined forces to attack Moab, but their efforts failed to re-subdue the nation. Perhaps emboldened by Moab's success, Edom later revolted against the rule of King Jehoram (also called Joram) of Judah. At the same time, the western town of Libnah also revolted against Judah.

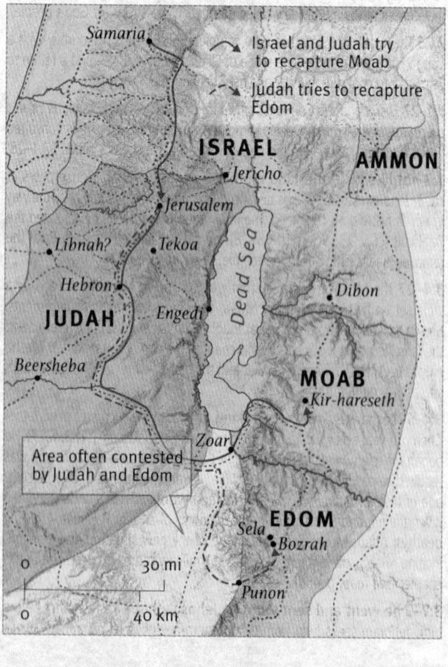

initial response is recognizable from 1 Kings 22:4: **I am as you are, my people as your people, my horses as your horses**. Missing on this occasion, however, is any desire on Jehoshaphat's part to discover the counsel of the Lord before going off to war (contrast 1 Kings 22:5); here he moves directly from agreement to tactics (2 Kings 3:8), and from tactics to action (v. 9). This is surprising. The *tactics* involve attacking Moab from the south, through the **wilderness of Edom**, rather than from the north. This is possible because Edom is under Judean rule (1 Kings 22:47) and her king is Jehoshaphat's deputy rather than an independent monarch. The *action* involves a march in which the combined armies get lost, caught in a **circuitous march**. Unsurprisingly, a military venture undertaken without prophetic advice faces disaster.

3:11–14 Is there no prophet of the LORD here? Jehoshaphat's memory suddenly returns, and he asks the right question (cf. 1 Kings 22:7). Elisha, the one **who poured water on the hands of Elijah** (probably a reference to Elisha's role as Elijah's servant), is found to be in their midst. Unimpressed as he is with Jehoram's piety, Elisha agrees to help because of righteous (albeit forgetful) Jehoshaphat's presence in the alliance.

3:15–19 bring me a musician. Music plays a part in Elisha's attainment of the prophetic state in which he utters his prophecy (cf. 1 Sam. 10:5–11; note on 1 Sam. 10:5). The immediate crisis (no water, 2 Kings 3:9) is to be dealt with by miracle, as the nearby **streambed shall be filled with water** from an unspecified and unexpected source (neither **wind** nor **rain**). God will further grant the alliance a comprehensive victory over Moab. They will **attack every fortified city and every choice city** (or perhaps "major town"), devastating the land as they move through it. Deuteronomy 20:19–20 prohibits this kind of destruction in normal cases, but here it appears that Elisha portrays the Moabites as a nation to be given over to desolation (like the cities of Canaan in Deut. 20:16–18), rather than simply subjugated.

3:20–24 Events begin to unfold in line with Elisha's prophecy. Water mysteriously flows **from the direction of Edom** (Hb. *'Edom*), fooling the Moabites into thinking the allies have slaughtered each other because in the morning sunlight the water appears **red** (Hb. *'adummim*) **as blood** (Hb. *dam*); notice the play on words with *'Edom*. Their reckless advance on the Israelite camp is met with force.

3:25 The combined armies act out Elisha's words (cf. v. 19) point by point, attacking all the Moabite cities including **Kir-hareseth**, strategically situated on a rocky hill overlooking the Dead Sea about 17 miles (27 km) south of the Arnon Gorge and 11 miles (18 km) east of the Dead Sea.

3:27 Facing defeat by Israel, Mesha offered his son as **burnt offering on**

hand, **19** and you shall attack every fortified city and every choice city, and shall fell every
good tree and stop up all springs of water [y] and ruin every good piece of land with stones."
20 The next morning, about the time of [z] offering the sacrifice, behold, water came from
the direction of Edom, till the country was filled with water.
21 When all the Moabites heard that the kings had come up to fight against them, all
who were able to put on armor, from the youngest to the oldest, were called out and were
drawn up at the border. **22** And when they rose early in the morning and the sun shone
on the water, the Moabites saw the water opposite them as red as blood. **23** And they said,
"This is blood; the kings have surely fought together and struck one another down. Now
then, Moab, to the spoil!" **24** But when they came to the camp of Israel, the Israelites rose
and struck the Moabites, till they fled before them. And they went forward, striking the
Moabites as they went.[1] **25** And they overthrew the cities, and [a] on every good piece of land
every man threw a stone until it was covered. They stopped every spring of water and
felled all the good trees, till only its stones were left in [b] Kir-hareseth, and the slingers surrounded and attacked it. **26** When the king of Moab saw that the battle was going against
him, he took with him 700 [c] swordsmen to break through, opposite the king of Edom, but
they could not. **27** Then he took his oldest son who was to reign in his place [d] and offered
him for a burnt offering on the wall. And there came great wrath against Israel. And they
withdrew from him and returned to their own land.

Elisha and the Widow's Oil

4 Now the wife of one of the [e] sons of the prophets cried to Elisha, "Your servant my
husband is dead, and you know that your servant feared the LORD, [f] but the creditor
has come to take my two children to be his slaves." **2** And Elisha said to her, "What shall I
do for you? Tell me; what have you in the house?" And she said, "Your servant has nothing
in the house except a jar of oil." **3** Then he said, "Go outside, borrow vessels from all your
neighbors, empty vessels and not too few. **4** Then go in and shut the door behind yourself
and your sons and pour into all these vessels. And when one is full, set it aside." **5** So she
went from him and shut the door behind herself and her sons. And as she poured they
brought the vessels to her. **6** When the vessels were full, she said to her son, "Bring me
another vessel." And he said to her, "There is not another." Then the oil stopped flowing.
7 She came and told the [g] man of God, and he said, "Go, sell the oil and pay your debts, and
you and your sons can live on the rest."

Elisha and the Shunammite Woman

8 One day Elisha went on to [h] Shunem, where a [i] wealthy woman lived, who urged him
to eat some food. So whenever he passed that way, he would turn in there to eat food.
9 And she said to her husband, "Behold now, I know that this is a holy [g] man of God who
is continually passing our way. **10** Let us make a small room on the roof with walls and
put there for him a bed, a table, a chair, and a lamp, so that whenever he comes to us, he
can go in there."
11 One day he came there, and he turned into the chamber and rested there. **12** And he
said to [j] Gehazi his servant, "Call this Shunammite." When he had called her, she stood

[1] Septuagint; the meaning of the Hebrew is uncertain

19 [y] [ver. 25; Isa. 25:2]
20 [z] [Ex. 29:39, 40]
25 [a] [ver. 19] [b] Isa. 16:7; [Isa. 15:1; 16:11; Jer. 48:31, 36]
26 [c] [Judg. 20:2]
27 [d] Amos 2:1; [Mic. 6:7]

Chapter 4

1 [e] See ch. 2:3 [f] [Lev. 25:39-41; 1 Sam. 22:2; Neh. 5:5; Matt. 18:25]
7 [g] See Deut. 33:1
8 [h] Josh. 19:18 [i] [1 Sam. 25:2; 2 Sam. 19:32]
9 [g] [See ver. 7 above]
12 [j] ch. 5:20, 21, 25; 8:4, 5

the wall. As a consequence, **there came great wrath** (Hb. *qetsep*) **against Israel.** This is not to be understood as *divine* anger, because on the one hand the biblical authors did not regard the Moabite god Chemosh as a real god (1 Kings 11:7), and on the other hand Israel's God would surely not have acted on Moab's behalf as a result of a ritual practice that was abhorrent to him (cf. 2 Kings 16:3; 17:17; 21:6). It seems, instead, that this "great wrath" is human wrath (as on both other occasions in Kings when *qetsep* appears, 5:11; 13:19): Mesha's troops respond to his desperate act with an anger that carries them to victory against the odds.

4:1–44 *Elisha's Miracles.* Both Elijah and Elisha are now associated with the God who provides water at will (cf. 1 Kings 18), whether by ordinary means (wind and rain, 1 Kings 18:45) or not (neither wind nor rain, 2 Kings 3:17). A number of further miracles serve in the same way as a reminder of Elijah.

4:1–7 the creditor has come to take my two children to be his slaves. Indebtedness was a common problem throughout the ancient Near East and could lead to the loss of property, home, fields, and ultimately the freedom of the debtor (cf. Neh. 5:4–5; Isa. 50:1; Amos 2:6; 8:6). Persons and property ending up in the hands of creditors could often be redeemed (cf. Ruth 4:1–12; Jer. 32:6–15), and among the responsibilities of the "kinsman-redeemer" in an extended Israelite family was the maintenance or redemption of the person or dependents of a kinsman in debt (Lev. 25:35–55). In the apparent absence of a true kinsman for the widow in this story, Elisha as the leader of the prophetic communities effectively takes on this kind of role for her. The proceeds from the sale of the multiplied **oil** (cf. 1 Kings 17:7–16) will leave her and her **sons** sufficient money to live on even after she has paid off her **debts**.

4:10 a small room on the roof. Roofs in ancient Israel were typically flat and served as important areas in the life of the family (cf. Josh. 2:6–8; 2 Sam. 11:2; 2 Kings 23:12; Jer. 19:13), providing among other things temporary guest accommodations (cf. 1 Sam. 9:26; 2 Sam. 16:22; 1 Kings 17:17–24). The structure in question here, however, is more permanent (it has **walls**).

before him. 13 And he said to him, "Say now to her, 'See, you have taken all this trouble
for us; what is to be done for you? Would you have a word spoken on your behalf to the
king or to [k]the commander of the army?'" She answered, "I dwell among my own people."
14 And he said, "What then is to be done for her?" Gehazi answered, "Well, she has no son,
and her husband is old." 15 He said, "Call her." And when he had called her, she stood in
the doorway. 16 And he said, "At this season, [l]about this time next year, you shall embrace
a son." And she said, "No, my lord, [g]O man of God; [m]do not lie to your servant." 17 But the
woman conceived, and she bore a son about that time [l]the following spring, as Elisha
had said to her.

Elisha Raises the Shunammite's Son

18 When the child had grown, he went out one day to his father among the reapers.
19 And he said to his father, "Oh, [n]my head, my head!" The father said to his servant, "Carry
him to his mother." 20 And when he had lifted him and brought him to his mother, the
child sat on her lap till noon, and then he died. 21 And she went up [o]and laid him on
the bed of the [g]man of God and shut the door behind him and went out. 22 Then she
called to her husband and said, "Send me one of the servants and one of the donkeys,
that I may quickly go to [g]the man of God and come back again." 23 And he said, "Why
will you go to him today? It is neither [p]new moon nor Sabbath." She said, "All is well."
24 Then she saddled the donkey, and she said to her servant, "Urge the animal on; do not
slacken the pace for me unless I tell you." 25 So she set out and came to the man of God
[q]at Mount Carmel.

When the man of God saw her coming, he said to Gehazi his servant, "Look, there is the
Shunammite. 26 Run at once to meet her and say to her, 'Is all well with you? Is all well with
your husband? Is all well with the child?'" And she answered, "All is well." 27 And when she
came [r]to the mountain to the man of God, she caught hold of his feet. And Gehazi came
to push her away. But the man of God said, "Leave her alone, for she is in bitter distress,
and the LORD has hidden it from me and has not told me." 28 Then she said, "Did I ask
my lord for a son? [s]Did I not say, 'Do not deceive me?'" 29 He said to Gehazi, [t]"Tie up your
garment and [u]take my staff in your hand and go. If you meet anyone, [v]do not greet him,
and if anyone greets you, do not reply. And [u]lay my staff on the face of the child." 30 Then
the mother of the child said, [w]"As the LORD lives and as you yourself live, I will not leave
you." So he arose and followed her. 31 Gehazi went on ahead and laid the staff on the face
of the child, but there was no sound or sign of life. Therefore he returned to meet him
and told him, "The child [x]has not awakened."

32 When Elisha came into the house, he saw the child lying dead on his bed. 33 So he
went in and [y]shut the door behind the two of them [z]and prayed to the LORD. 34 Then he
went up and lay on the child, putting his mouth on his mouth, his eyes on his eyes, and
his hands on his hands. And as [a]he stretched himself upon him, the flesh of the child
became warm. 35 Then he got up again and walked once back and forth in the house, and
went up [a]and stretched himself upon him. The child sneezed seven times, and the child
opened his eyes. 36 Then he summoned Gehazi and said, "Call this Shunammite." So he
called her. And when she came to him, he said, "Pick up your son." 37 She came and fell at
his feet, bowing to the ground. [b]Then she picked up her son and went out.

13 [k]2 Sam. 19:13; [ch. 5:1]
16 [l]Gen. 18:14; [Gen. 17:21] [g][See ver. 7 above] [m]ver. 28
17 [l][See ver. 16 above]
19 [n][Ps. 121:6]
21 [o]ver. 32 [g][See ver. 7 above]
22 [g][See ver. 7 above]
23 [p][Num. 28:11]
25 [q]ch. 2:25
27 [r]ver. 25
28 [s]ver. 16
29 [t]See 1 Kgs. 18:46 [u][Ex. 7:19; 14:16; Acts 19:12] [v]Luke 10:4
30 [w]See Ruth 3:13
31 [x][John 11:11]
33 [y]ver. 4; Matt. 6:6; [Matt. 9:25; Mark 5:37, 40; Luke 8:51] [z]1 Kgs. 17:20
34 [a]1 Kgs. 17:21; [Acts 20:10]
35 [a][See ver. 34 above]
37 [b]1 Kgs. 17:23; Heb. 11:35; [ch. 8:1, 5]

4:13 a word spoken on your behalf. Elisha offers the Shunammite woman benefits, through his patronage, from the king or the commander of the army—two of the most powerful people in the land. She has no need of their help, however, because she is wealthy (v. 8) and, living among her own kinfolk (**my own people**), has their support and protection. She is not vulnerable like the widow in vv. 1–7.

4:23 The implication to be drawn from the husband's response is that it was customary in Israel to consult prophets only on particular rest days—the **new moon**, marking the beginning of each month, and the **Sabbath** (cf. 1 Sam. 20:5–34; Hos. 2:11; Amos 8:5). The practice of celebrating on the first of the month had ancient roots; the new moon was already one of the principal lunar festivals in Old Babylonian times. This woman's business, however, will not wait. **All is** not really **well**, but she does not want either her husband or Gehazi (2 Kings 4:26) getting in her way as she seeks Elisha's help.

4:27 the LORD has hidden it from me. Elisha had not foreseen this happening. Prophets are not omniscient, but depend always on God's revelation.

4:29 Tie up your garment. As the woman had arrived at Carmel in great haste (v. 24), so Elisha sends Gehazi back to Shunem in similar haste, his garment hitched up so that he can run (cf. 1 Kings 18:46).

4:30–31 I will not leave you. The woman is not willing to accept Elisha's plan to resurrect the boy from a distance by means of his **staff**; she wants his personal attention, which in the end does in fact prove crucial. Only his own prayer and mysterious actions succeed in bringing the boy back to life (cf. 1 Kings 17:19–23).

4:34 Elisha's actions vividly picture God restoring breath to the child (**putting his mouth on his mouth**), as well as sight (**his eyes**) and strength (**his hands**). As Elisha **stretched himself upon him**, it portrayed the Spirit of God who, through Elisha, was being imparted to the child to give him life.

38[c]ch. 2:1 [d]ch. 8:1 [e]See ch. 2:3 [f]Deut. 33:3; Luke 10:39; Acts 22:3; [ch. 2:3, 5] [g]Ezek. 24:3
41[h][ch. 2:21; Ex. 15:25]
42[i][1 Sam. 9:4] [j][1 Sam. 9:7] [k]See Matt. 14:16-21; 15:32-38; Mark 6:37-44; 8:4-9; Luke 9:13-17; John 6:5-13

Chapter 5
1[l]Luke 4:27 [m][ch. 4:13]
2[n]ch. 6:23
5[o][ch. 4:42; 8:8, 9; 1 Sam. 9:7] [p]ver. 22, 23; [Judg. 14:12]
7[q]See Gen. 44:13 [r][Gen. 30:2; Deut. 32:39; 1 Sam. 2:6] [s][1 Kgs. 20:7]
8[t]See Deut. 33:1

Elisha Purifies the Deadly Stew

38 And Elisha came again to [c]Gilgal when [d]there was a famine in the land. And as [e]the
sons of the prophets [f]were sitting before him, he said to his servant, [g]"Set on the large pot,
and boil stew for the sons of the prophets." 39 One of them went out into the field to gather
herbs, and found a wild vine and gathered from it his lap full of wild gourds, and came
and cut them up into the pot of stew, not knowing what they were. 40 And they poured
out some for the men to eat. But while they were eating of the stew, they cried out, "O
man of God, there is death in the pot!" And they could not eat it. 41 He said, "Then bring
flour." [h]And he threw it into the pot and said, "Pour some out for the men, that they may
eat." And there was no harm in the pot.

42 A man came from [i]Baal-shalishah, [j]bringing the man of God bread of the firstfruits,
twenty loaves of barley and fresh ears of grain in his sack. And Elisha said, [k]"Give to the
men, that they may eat." 43 But his servant said, "How can I set this before a hundred men?"
So he repeated, "Give them to the men, that they may eat, for thus says the LORD, 'They
shall eat and have some left.'" 44 So he set it before them. And they ate and had some left,
according to the word of the LORD.

Naaman Healed of Leprosy

5 [l]Naaman, [m]commander of the army of the king of Syria, was a great man with his
master and in high favor, because by him the LORD had given victory to Syria. He was
a mighty man of valor, but he was a leper.[1] 2 Now the Syrians on [n]one of their raids had
carried off a little girl from the land of Israel, and she worked in the service of Naaman's
wife. 3 She said to her mistress, "Would that my lord were with the prophet who is in
Samaria! He would cure him of his leprosy." 4 So Naaman went in and told his lord, "Thus
and so spoke the girl from the land of Israel." 5 And the king of Syria said, "Go now, and I
will send a letter to the king of Israel."

So he went, [o]taking with him ten talents of silver, six thousand shekels[2] of gold, and ten
[p]changes of clothing. 6 And he brought the letter to the king of Israel, which read, "When
this letter reaches you, know that I have sent to you Naaman my servant, that you may
cure him of his leprosy." 7 And when the king of Israel read the letter, [q]he tore his clothes
and said, [r]"Am I God, to kill and to make alive, that this man sends word to me to cure a
man of his leprosy? Only [s]consider, and see how he is seeking a quarrel with me."

8 But when Elisha the [t]man of God heard that the king of Israel had torn his clothes,
he sent to the king, saying, "Why have you torn your clothes? Let him come now to me,
that he may know that there is a prophet in Israel." 9 So Naaman came with his horses and

[1] *Leprosy* was a term for several skin diseases; see Leviticus 13 [2] A *talent* was about 75 pounds or 34 kilograms; a *shekel* was about 2/5 ounce or 11 grams

4:38 famine in the land. Elisha's third miracle (see note on vv. 1–44) is reminiscent of the healing of the water of Jericho (2:19–22). Famine is the context in which the whole succeeding narrative up to ch. 8 takes place (see 8:1), although a general state of famine does not imply an absolute absence of food (see, e.g., 4:42–44).

4:40–41 death in the pot. As with the salt thrown into the water at Jericho (2:21), the flour used by Elisha is a visible sign of the Lord's power working through Elisha.

4:42–44 bread of the firstfruits. The final miracle of the chapter (see note on vv. 1–44) also concerns provision for the people who depend on Elisha. A limited amount of food is once again multiplied (cf. vv. 1–7), in face of the incomprehension of the **servant**, so that it not only provides immediate needs but also produces a surplus. It is the final demonstration in the chapter that the God of Elisha heals, provides, and brings life from death.

5:1–27 *A Syrian Is Healed.* The account of Elisha's miracles continues with the story that again picks up themes from the Elijah story: the Lord is seen to be God, not only of Israelites, but also of foreigners (1 Kings 17:17–24), and is in fact acknowledged as the only real God there is (1 Kings 18:20–40).

5:1 the LORD had given victory to Syria. It was common throughout the ancient Near East for peoples to claim that their gods had given them victory in battle, but the claim here is of a distinctively monotheistic kind; here (as always in the Bible) Israel's God is responsible for victory or defeat in battles, no matter which gods may be worshiped by the victorious or defeated peoples (cf. Dan. 1:1–2). The vanquished here are not specified but may have included Israel, which was defeated at Ramoth-gilead in 1 Kings 22:29–36. The general by whom God had given the Syrians victory on this occasion was himself a **leper** (Hb. *metsora'*); he suffered from some kind of disfigurement of the skin (but not necessarily what is known by modern people as "leprosy"; see note on Luke 5:12), rendering him ritually unclean from an Israelite point of view (cf. Leviticus 13–14; Num. 12:1–15; 2 Sam. 3:28–29).

5:5–7 a letter to the king of Israel. An uneasy truce appears to be in force between Syria and Israel. There is sufficient tension, however, for the king of Israel to be concerned that the king of Syria is **seeking a quarrel** in asking him to perform a task (**cure him of his leprosy**) that only divinity can accomplish—akin to the raising of someone from the dead (**to kill and to make alive**). The tearing of **clothes**, as well as indicating sorrow (see note on 2:11–13), could also signify consternation (cf. 22:11–13). There is sufficient quiet, on the other hand, for **Naaman** to travel safely to Israel with his **letter** and his various gifts. **Ten talents of silver** represents about 750 pounds (341 kg) of this metal, compared with 150 pounds (68 kg; **six thousand shekels**) **of gold**, reflecting the much greater value of the gold (which here is equivalent to the combined annual wages of 600 common laborers).

5:9–12 stood at the door. Naaman clearly expects personal and immediate attention from Elisha, but Elisha addresses him only through a **messenger** and sends him to **wash in the Jordan**; moreover, Naaman was looking for a **cure**, and Elisha apparently offers only ritual cleansing (**wash . . . be clean**; cf. the cleansing ritual of Leviticus 13–14 with its use of the same Hb. verbs

chariots and stood at the door of Elisha's house. 10 And Elisha sent a messenger to him,
saying, [u]"Go and wash in the Jordan seven times, and your flesh shall be restored, and you
shall be clean." 11 But Naaman was angry and went away, saying, "Behold, I thought that
he would surely come out to me and stand and call upon the name of the LORD his God,
and wave his hand over the place and cure the leper. 12 Are not Abana[1] and Pharpar, the
rivers of [v]Damascus, better than all the waters of Israel? Could I not wash in them and be
clean?" So he turned and went away in a rage. 13 But his servants came near and said to him,
[w]"My father, it is a great word the prophet has spoken to you; will you not do it? Has he
actually said to you, 'Wash, and be clean'?" 14 So he went down and dipped himself seven
times in the Jordan, according to the word of the man of God, [x]and his flesh was restored
like the flesh of a little child, [y]and he was clean.

Gehazi's Greed and Punishment

15 Then he returned to the man of God, he and all his company, and he came and stood
before him. And he said, "Behold, I know that [z]there is no God in all the earth but in Israel;
so [a]accept now a present from your servant." 16 But he said, [b]"As the LORD lives, before
whom I stand, [c]I will receive none." And he urged him to take it, but he refused. 17 Then
Naaman said, "If not, please let there be given to your servant two mule loads of earth,
for from now on your servant will not offer burnt offering or sacrifice to any god but the
LORD. 18 In this matter may the LORD pardon your servant: when my master goes into the
house of [d]Rimmon to worship there, [e]leaning on my arm, and I bow myself in the house
of Rimmon, when I bow myself in the house of Rimmon, the LORD pardon your servant
in this matter." 19 He said to him, [f]"Go in peace."

But when Naaman had gone from him a short distance, 20 [g]Gehazi, the servant of Elisha
the man of God, said, "See, my master has spared this Naaman the Syrian, in not accepting
from his hand what he brought. [h]As the LORD lives, I will run after him and get something
from him." 21 So Gehazi followed Naaman. And when Naaman saw someone running after
him, he got down from the chariot to meet him and said, [i]"Is all well?" 22 And he said,
"All is well. My master has sent me to say, 'There have just now come to me from [j]the hill
country of Ephraim two young men of the sons of the prophets. Please give them a talent of silver and [k]two changes of clothing.' " 23 And Naaman said, [l]"Be pleased to accept
two talents." And he urged him and tied up two talents of silver in two bags, with two
changes of clothing, and laid them on two of his servants. And they carried them before
Gehazi. 24 And when he came to the hill, he took them from their hand and put them in
the house, and he sent the men away, and they departed. 25 He went in and stood before
his master, and Elisha said to him, "Where have you been, Gehazi?" And he said, "Your
servant went nowhere." 26 But he said to him, "Did not my heart go when the man turned
from his chariot to meet you? Was it a time to accept money and garments, olive orchards

[1] Or *Amana*

10 [u][John 9:7]
12 [v][1 Kgs. 11:24]
13 [w][ch. 6:21; 8:9; Judg. 17:10]
14 [x]ver. 10; [Job 33:25] [y]Luke 4:27
15 [z][Dan. 2:47; 3:29; 6:26, 27] [a][Gen. 33:11]
16 [b]ch. 3:14; 1 Kgs. 17:1 [c][Gen. 14:23]
18 [d][1 Kgs. 15:18; Zech. 12:11] [e]ch. 7:2, 17
19 [f]1 Sam. 1:17
20 [g]ch. 4:12 [h]See Ruth 3:13
21 [i]ch. 9:11
22 [j]See Josh. 24:33 [k]ver. 5
23 [l]ch. 6:3

[Lev. 14:8–9 and in 13:7, 35; 14:2, 23, 32]). This he could have had at home, by bathing in the **rivers of Damascus**.

5:13 Has he actually said . . . ? Naaman's **servants** have been listening more attentively, for Elisha did not speak only of ritual cleansing but of healing ("your flesh shall be restored," v. 10). They urge Naaman to consider Elisha's actual words and act on them.

5:14–15 a little child. The Hebrew is *na'ar qaton*, and there is evidently a play on the phrase *na'arah qetannah* ("little girl") in v. 2. The "great man" (v. 1) had a problem, to which the "little girl" had the solution; but the solution involved Naaman's becoming, like her, "a little child"—someone under prophetic authority, humbly acknowledging his new faith (**I know that there is no God in all the earth but in Israel**). He had looked to the prophet himself for a cure, in line with the words of his Israelite informant (v. 3); but the way in which the cure has been wrought has made it clear to him that Elisha's God is a living person, not simply a convenient metaphor for unnatural prophetic powers.

5:16 I will receive none. For Elisha to accept a gift is to risk the impression that he is personally responsible for what has happened.

5:17 two mule loads of earth. The earth is to be used in the construction of a mud-brick altar (cf. Ex. 20:24–25) for Naaman's worship of the Lord.

5:18 May the LORD pardon is reminiscent of Solomon's prayer in 1 Kings 8:22–53, with its frequent requests to forgive (1 Kings 8:30, 34, 36, 39, 50) and its consideration of the foreigner who prays toward the temple (1 Kings 8:41–43). Naaman's dilemma is that he will still be required in the course of his official duties to attend the temple of **Rimmon**—a reference to the storm god Baal-hadad under a name that has not been previously encountered (see note on 1 Kings 16:31–33; cf. Zech. 12:11).

5:20–22 I will run . . . and get something from him. Gehazi either has not grasped the meaning of what has happened or does not care; he tries to "cash in" on an act of God (cf. Joshua 7; Acts 8:18–24) by means of a story designed to explain a change of heart on Elisha's part (he has **two** new arrivals to provide for).

5:26 Was it a time to accept . . . ? Gehazi's aspirations to wealth and status have led him to forget the Lord (cf. Deut. 6:10–12; also compare the list of items here with the catalog of royal wealth in 1 Sam. 8:14–17). Just as kings can misuse their power for self-enrichment, so can the servants of prophets.

27 [m] Ex. 4:6; Num. 12:10; [ch. 15:5]

Chapter 6

1 [n] See ch. 2:3
6 [o] [ch. 2:21]
13 [p] Gen. 37:17
16 [q] 2 Chr. 32:7; [Ps. 55:18; Rom. 8:31]
17 [r] ver. 20 [s] ch. 2:11; [Ps. 34:7; 68:17]; See Zech. 1:8-10; 6:1-7
18 [t] [Gen. 19:11]
20 [r] [See ver. 17 above]

and vineyards, sheep and oxen, male servants and female servants? 27 Therefore the leprosy
of Naaman shall cling to you and to your descendants forever." So he went out from his
presence [m]a leper, like snow.

The Axe Head Recovered

6 Now [n]the sons of the prophets said to Elisha, "See, the place where we dwell under
your charge is too small for us. 2 Let us go to the Jordan and each of us get there a log,
and let us make a place for us to dwell there." And he answered, "Go." 3 Then one of them
said, "Be pleased to go with your servants." And he answered, "I will go." 4 So he went with
them. And when they came to the Jordan, they cut down trees. 5 But as one was felling a
log, his axe head fell into the water, and he cried out, "Alas, my master! It was borrowed."
6 Then the man of God said, "Where did it fall?" When he showed him the place, [o]he cut
off a stick and threw it in there and made the iron float. 7 And he said, "Take it up." So he
reached out his hand and took it.

Horses and Chariots of Fire

8 Once when the king of Syria was warring against Israel, he took counsel with his servants,
saying, "At such and such a place shall be my camp." 9 But the man of God sent word to
the king of Israel, "Beware that you do not pass this place, for the Syrians are going down
there." 10 And the king of Israel sent to the place about which the man of God told him.
Thus he used to warn him, so that he saved himself there more than once or twice.
11 And the mind of the king of Syria was greatly troubled because of this thing, and he
called his servants and said to them, "Will you not show me who of us is for the king of
Israel?" 12 And one of his servants said, "None, my lord, O king; but Elisha, the prophet
who is in Israel, tells the king of Israel the words that you speak in your bedroom." 13 And
he said, "Go and see where he is, that I may send and seize him." It was told him, "Behold,
he is in [p]Dothan." 14 So he sent there horses and chariots and a great army, and they came
by night and surrounded the city.
15 When the servant of the man of God rose early in the morning and went out, behold,
an army with horses and chariots was all around the city. And the servant said, "Alas, my
master! What shall we do?" 16 He said, "Do not be afraid, [q]for those who are with us are
more than those who are with them." 17 Then Elisha prayed and said, "O LORD, please
[r]open his eyes that he may see." So the LORD opened the eyes of the young man, and he
saw, and behold, the mountain was full of [s]horses and chariots of fire all around Elisha.
18 And when the Syrians came down against him, Elisha prayed to the LORD and said,
"Please strike this people with blindness." [t]So he struck them with blindness in accordance with the prayer of Elisha. 19 And Elisha said to them, "This is not the way, and this
is not the city. Follow me, and I will bring you to the man whom you seek." And he led
them to Samaria.
20 As soon as they entered Samaria, Elisha said, "O LORD, [r]open the eyes of these men,

6:1–23 *Elisha and Syria.* With the healing of Naaman, Elisha has involved himself with Syria for the first time. That involvement now occupies most of the attention of the authors for the next two chapters, as they prepare the reader for the bloody events of chs. 8–10.

6:1–7 While one of the prophetic communities is building a new place to meet, a member of the group loses a borrowed **axe head**. Elisha has past experience of manipulating the waters of the Jordan by the Lord's power (2:14), and here he is miraculously able to make the **iron float** like the piece of wood he has thrown in beside it.

6:8 the king of Syria was warring against Israel. Relations between Syria and Israel have deteriorated since ch. 5.

6:9 the man of God sent word. Elisha intervenes to help Jehoram, not because anything has changed in his behavior (3:2–3, 13) but simply because the time has not yet arrived for final judgment on this royal house (cf. chs. 9–10). Prophetic oracles apparently were often sought or offered in the ancient Near East in relation to military campaigns (see note on 3:11–14).

6:13 Dothan is only 10 miles (16 km) north of the capital city of Samaria, illustrating the extent of Syrian penetration into Israel at this time. But the Syrian king is deluded in his belief that he can **send and seize** Elisha (cf. 1 Kings 13:1–6; 18:9–14; 2 Kings 1:2–17).

6:16 those who are with us. Elisha knows that the Lord has sent an army of angels to protect him, and apparently he can see them but the servant cannot. They are more than a match for the Syrian army (cf. Ps. 91:11; Heb. 1:14).

6:17 the LORD opened the eyes of the young man. The angelic armies have been there all along, but they are invisible to Elisha's servant until the Lord enables him to see them (cf. 2:11; also Num. 22:31; Luke 2:13; Col. 1:16). **the mountain was full**. Syrian troops may surround (Hb. *sabab*) the city (2 Kings 6:15), but Elisha himself is supported **all around** (Hb. *sabib*) by the army of the Lord.

6:18 blindness. Probably not a loss of physical sight (since the Syrians would not doubt their location just because they could no longer physically see it), but rather a dazed mental condition in which they are open to suggestion and manipulation but still able to follow the prophet to Samaria. The Syrians are "bedazzled" and do not "see" things clearly, whereas Elisha's servant has been given perfect clarity of "sight" about reality.

6:19 I will bring you to the man whom you seek. The statement is somewhat puzzling, but rather than leaving the Syrians, Elisha did in fact bring them face to face with the man they were looking for.

that they may see." So the LORD opened their eyes and they saw, and behold, they were
in the midst of Samaria. 21 As soon as the king of Israel saw them, he said to Elisha, [u]"My
father, shall I strike them down? Shall I strike them down?" 22 He answered, "You shall
not strike them down. Would you strike down those whom you have taken captive [v]with
your sword and with your bow? [w]Set bread and water before them, that they may eat and
drink and go to their master." 23 So he prepared for them a great feast, and when they had
eaten and drunk, he sent them away, and they went to their master. And the Syrians did
not come again [x]on raids into the land of Israel.

Ben-hadad's Siege of Samaria

24 Afterward [y]Ben-hadad king of Syria mustered his entire army and went up and besieged
Samaria. 25 And there was a great famine in Samaria, as they besieged it, until a donkey's
head was sold for eighty shekels of silver, and the fourth part of a kab[1] of dove's dung for
five shekels of silver. 26 Now as the king of Israel was passing by on the wall, a woman cried
out to him, saying, "Help, my lord, O king!" 27 And he said, "If the LORD will not help you,
how shall I help you? From the threshing floor, or from the winepress?" 28 And the king
asked her, "What is your trouble?" She answered, "This woman said to me, 'Give your
son, that we may eat him today, and we will eat my son tomorrow.' 29 [z]So we boiled my
son and ate him. And on the next day I said to her, 'Give your son, that we may eat him.'
But she has hidden her son." 30 When the king heard the words of the woman, [a]he tore his
clothes—now he was passing by on the wall—and the people looked, and behold, [a]he had
sackcloth beneath on his body— 31 and he said, [b]"May God do so to me and more also, if
the head of Elisha the son of Shaphat remains on his shoulders today."

32 Elisha was sitting in his house, [c]and the elders were sitting with him. Now the king
had dispatched a man from his presence, but before the messenger arrived Elisha said to
the elders, "Do you see how this [d]murderer has sent to take off my head? Look, when the
messenger comes, shut the door and hold the door fast against him. Is not the sound of his
master's feet behind him?" 33 And while he was still speaking with them, the messenger
came down to him and said, "This trouble is from the LORD! [e]Why should I wait for the
LORD any longer?"

Elisha Promises Food

7 But Elisha said, "Hear the word of the LORD: thus says the LORD, [f]Tomorrow about
this time a seah[2] of fine flour shall be sold for a shekel,[3] and two seahs of barley for a
shekel, at the gate of Samaria." 2 Then [g]the captain on whose hand the king leaned said to

[1] A *shekel* was about 2/5 ounce or 11 grams; a *kab* was about 1 quart or 1 liter [2] A *seah* was about 7 quarts or 7.3 liters [3] A *shekel* was about 2/5 ounce or 11 grams

21 [u]ch. 5:13; 8:9; Judg. 17:10
22 [v]Gen. 48:22 [w]Rom. 12:20
23 [x]ver. 8, 9; ch. 5:2; 24:2
24 [y]1 Kgs. 20:1
29 [z][Lev. 26:29; Deut. 28:53, 57; Ezek. 5:10]
30 [a]1 Kgs. 21:27
31 [b][1 Kgs. 19:2]; See Ruth 1:17
32 [c]Ezek. 8:1; 14:1; 20:1 [d][1 Kgs. 18:4; 21:13]
33 [e][Job 2:9]

Chapter 7

1 [f]ver. 18
2 [g]ver. 17, 19; [ch. 5:18]

6:22 You shall not strike them down. Jehoram would not kill men **taken captive with your sword and with your bow**, and these are not even men like that. They are to be treated as guests.

6:24–7:20 *The Siege of Samaria.* The uneasy peace of ch. 5 gave way in 6:8–23 to sporadic fighting involving Syrian raids into Israelite territory, curtailed because of what has just happened to the last of the raiding parties (6:23), but now comes a full-blown invasion.

6:25 donkey's head . . . dove's dung. Donkeys were commonly found among the domestic animals in Syria-Palestine, and various OT laws identify them as significant possessions (e.g., Ex. 13:13; 20:17; 22:4). So severe was the siege that the inhabitants of Samaria were reduced not only to slaughtering and eating valuable animals, but also to consuming body parts that would not normally be consumed, and purchasing them for exorbitant prices (the cost of a live *horse* in 1 Kings 10:29 is only 150 shekels of silver, and here a donkey's head costs **eighty**). During this crisis even half a liter (**the fourth part of a kab**) of dove's dung cost what the average worker could make in six months (**five shekels of silver**).

6:26–27 Help, my lord, O king. The plea is directed to the king as the ultimate court of human justice, as in 1 Kings 3:16–28, but Israel has strayed a long way from that glorious era when a wise king could ensure justice. The normal food supply is exhausted; nothing comes from the **threshing floor** (see note on 1 Kings 22:10–12) or **winepress** (a flat, hard surface on which grapes could be trodden, with the juice running off into a reservoir and then being poured into large jars for fermentation).

6:28–29 Give your son. The Assyrian king Ashurbanipal also reports that, during his two-year siege of Babylon (which ended in 648 B.C.), "famine seized them; for their hunger they ate the flesh of their sons and daughters"; the Bible itself reports other instances of cannibalism arising from a long siege (e.g., Lam. 2:20; 4:10; Ezek. 5:10).

6:30–31 he tore his clothes. See notes on 2:11–13; 5:5–7; **sackcloth** is also symbolic of mourning and distress. Jehoram appears to believe that removing Elisha will remove the problems he is facing.

6:32 the elders were sitting with him. As the "sons of the prophets" seem to have gathered to listen to the prophet (ch. 4), so here the elders of Samaria are gathered together in Elisha's house (cf. the similar scenario in Ezek. 8:1; 20:1).

7:1 a seah of fine flour . . . two seahs of barley. A seah is about 7 quarts (7.7 liters). The king will have to wait no longer: salvation is imminent, and normal business **at the gate of Samaria** will be resumed on the following day (the prices are much lower here than in 6:25). The open area inside city gates served various important social purposes in ancient times. Among other things, agricultural activities took place and business was transacted there (e.g., Gen. 23:10; 34:20).

7:2 windows in heaven. It is impossible for this officer to imagine how such an economic recovery could happen overnight, in the aftermath of such

2[h]Mal. 3:10; [Gen. 7:11]
3[i][Lev. 13:46]
6[j][ch. 6:17; 2 Sam. 5:24; Job 15:21] [k][1 Kgs. 10:29]
7[l][Ps. 48:4-6; Prov. 28:1]
16[m]ver. 1
17[n]ver. 2 [o]ch. 6:32
19[n][See ver. 17 above] [p]ver. 2

the man of God, [h]"If the LORD himself should make windows in heaven, could this thing
be?" But he said, "You shall see it with your own eyes, but you shall not eat of it."

The Syrians Flee

3 Now there were four men who were lepers[1] [i]at the entrance to the gate. And they said
to one another, "Why are we sitting here until we die? 4 If we say, 'Let us enter the city,' the
famine is in the city, and we shall die there. And if we sit here, we die also. So now come,
let us go over to the camp of the Syrians. If they spare our lives we shall live, and if they
kill us we shall but die." 5 So they arose at twilight to go to the camp of the Syrians. But
when they came to the edge of the camp of the Syrians, behold, there was no one there.
6 For the Lord had made the army of the Syrians [j]hear the sound of chariots and of horses,
the sound of a great army, so that they said to one another, "Behold, the king of Israel has
hired against us [k]the kings of the Hittites and the kings of Egypt to come against us." 7 [l]So
they fled away in the twilight and abandoned their tents, their horses, and their donkeys,
leaving the camp as it was, and fled for their lives. 8 And when these lepers came to the edge
of the camp, they went into a tent and ate and drank, and they carried off silver and gold
and clothing and went and hid them. Then they came back and entered another tent and
carried off things from it and went and hid them.

9 Then they said to one another, "We are not doing right. This day is a day of good
news. If we are silent and wait until the morning light, punishment will overtake us.
Now therefore come; let us go and tell the king's household." 10 So they came and called
to the gatekeepers of the city and told them, "We came to the camp of the Syrians, and
behold, there was no one to be seen or heard there, nothing but the horses tied and
the donkeys tied and the tents as they were." 11 Then the gatekeepers called out, and it
was told within the king's household. 12 And the king rose in the night and said to his
servants, "I will tell you what the Syrians have done to us. They know that we are hungry. Therefore they have gone out of the camp to hide themselves in the open country,
thinking, 'When they come out of the city, we shall take them alive and get into the
city.'" 13 And one of his servants said, "Let some men take five of the remaining horses,
seeing that those who are left here will fare like the whole multitude of Israel who have
already perished. Let us send and see." 14 So they took two horsemen, and the king sent
them after the army of the Syrians, saying, "Go and see." 15 So they went after them as
far as the Jordan, and behold, all the way was littered with garments and equipment
that the Syrians had thrown away in their haste. And the messengers returned and
told the king.

16 Then the people went out and plundered the camp of the Syrians. So a seah of fine
flour was sold for a shekel, and two seahs of barley for a shekel, [m]according to the word
of the LORD. 17 Now the king had appointed [n]the captain on whose hand he leaned to
have charge of the gate. And the people trampled him in the gate, so that he died, as
the man of God had said [o]when the king came down to him. 18 For when the man of
God had said to the king, "Two seahs of barley shall be sold for a shekel, and a seah of
fine flour for a shekel, about this time tomorrow in the gate of Samaria," 19 [n]the captain
had answered the man of God, "If the LORD himself should make windows in heaven,
could such a thing be?" And he had said, [p]"You shall see it with your own eyes, but you
shall not eat of it." 20 And so it happened to him, for the people trampled him in the
gate and he died.

[1] *Leprosy* was a term for several skin diseases; see Leviticus 13

a terrible siege. Will God hand out unexpected material blessings through the windows of his heavenly storehouse (cf. Ps. 78:23; Mal. 3:10)? To mock the prophetic word is to mock the Lord himself, however, so he **shall see it . . . but . . . not eat**.

7:3–4 four men who were lepers. A leper had first brought the Syrians to Samaria during Jehoram's reign (5:1–7), and four men with a similar ailment now drive them away. Faced with certain death if they **enter the city** or **sit** where they are, they instead choose possible death in the **camp of the Syrians**.

7:6 kings of Egypt. Perhaps the four lepers (Hb. *metsora'im*), seen in the twilight (v. 5), are mistaken for a mercenary army drawn from northern Syria and from Egypt (Hb. *Mitsrayim*); otherwise, the delusion came from another source.

7:13–14 five of the remaining horses. Only **two horsemen** are sent. Perhaps they take with them three spare horses, or one spare horse (if the horsemen took two chariots, each having two horses).

7:20 the people trampled him. The skeptical officer of v. 2, ironically

The Shunammite's Land Restored

8 Now Elisha had said to the woman [q]whose son he had restored to life, "Arise, and
depart with your household, and sojourn wherever you can, for the LORD [r]has called
for a famine, and it will come upon the land for [s]seven years." 2 So the woman arose and
did according to the word of the man of God. She went with her household and sojourned
in the land of the Philistines seven years. 3 And at the end of the seven years, when the
woman returned from the land of the Philistines, she went to appeal to the king for her
house and her land. 4 Now the king was talking with [t]Gehazi the servant of the man of
God, saying, "Tell me all the great things that Elisha has done." 5 And while he was telling
the king how [q]Elisha had restored the dead to life, behold, the woman whose son he had
restored to life appealed to the king for her house and her land. And Gehazi said, "My
lord, O king, here is the woman, and here is her son whom Elisha restored to life." 6 And
when the king asked the woman, she told him. So the king appointed an official for her,
saying, "Restore all that was hers, together with all the produce of the fields from the day
that she left the land until now."

Hazael Murders Ben-hadad

7 Now Elisha came to [u]Damascus. [v]Ben-hadad the king of Syria was sick. And when it
was told him, "The man of God has come here," 8 the king said to [w]Hazael, [x]"Take a present
with you and go to meet the man of God, [y]and inquire of the LORD through him, saying,
'Shall I recover from this sickness?'" 9 So Hazael went to meet him, and took a present
with him, all kinds of goods of Damascus, forty camels' loads. When he came and stood
before him, he said, [z]"Your son Ben-hadad king of Syria has sent me to you, saying, 'Shall I
recover from this sickness?'" 10 And Elisha said to him, [a]"Go, say to him, 'You shall certainly
recover,' but[1] the LORD has shown me that [b]he shall certainly die." 11 And he fixed his gaze
and stared at him, [c]until he was embarrassed. And the man of God wept. 12 And Hazael
said, "Why does my lord weep?" He answered, "Because I know [d]the evil that you will do to
the people of Israel. You will set on fire their fortresses, and you will kill their young men

[1] *Some manuscripts say, 'You shall certainly not recover,' for*

Chapter 8
1 [q]ch. 4:35 [r]Ps. 105:16; Hag. 1:11 [s][Gen. 41:27]
4 [t]See ch. 4:12
5 [q][See ver. 1 above]
7 [u][1 Kgs. 11:24] [v]ch. 6:24; 1 Kgs. 20:1
8 [w]1 Kgs. 19:15, 17 [x]See 1 Sam. 9:7 [y][ch. 1:2]
9 [z][ch. 5:13]
10 [a]ver. 14 [b]ver. 15
11 [c]ch. 2:17
12 [d]ch. 10:32; 12:17; 13:3, 7, 22; Amos 1:3, 4

stationed at the very **gate** at which he had anticipated seeing no trade, is trampled in the scramble to acquire goods, fulfilling Elisha's prophecy.

8:1–6 *The Shunammite's Land Restored.* After the long narrative about the siege of Samaria, the Shunammite woman of 4:8–37 reappears. The key to understanding this new story is found in 4:13, where the woman declines Elisha's offer of help because she has a home among her own people. In 8:1–6, however, she no longer has such a home, for she has followed Elisha's advice and avoided famine by sojourning in Philistia.

8:1 Elisha had said. The prophecy had been delivered around the same time that Elisha restored the woman's son to life, and the **famine** had followed shortly thereafter (cf. 4:38). This general state of famine is to be distinguished from the even more severe famine in the city of Samaria described in 6:24–7:20, which is specifically the result of siege.

8:2 The **land of the Philistines** was a natural place for the Shunammite woman to seek refuge during a time of famine in Israel (the patriarch Isaac himself moved into this region in similar circumstances; Gen. 26:1), not least because of its proximity to Egypt, the breadbasket of the ancient world and the common destination throughout the biblical period of people escaping times of hardship (e.g., Gen. 12:10; 41:53–42:5; 47:4).

8:3 her house and her land. Someone has taken the woman's property in her absence—perhaps Jehoram himself, showing the same land-grabbing tendencies as his parents (cf. 1 Kings 21). The **king** was now the recipient of her appeal, as the person with primary responsibility under God for the establishment and maintenance of order and justice throughout the kingdom (cf. Psalm 72). In Israel the end of the seventh year was a proper time for restoration of property and cancellation of debt (Ex. 21:2–3; Deut. 15:1).

8:6 all the produce. The king goes farther than restoring everything that belonged to the woman; he also provides her with all the income from her land that she would have received had she stayed in the country.

8:7–15 *Hazael Murders Ben-hadad.* The house of Omri has now held the throne of Israel since 1 Kings 16:23, and in spite of Elijah's prophecy in 1 Kings 21:21–24 about its end, one now reads of Ahab's second apostate son holding on to his kingdom with the help of Elijah's successor (e.g., 2 Kings 3:1–27; 6:9–10). Has Elijah sabotaged God's plan by failing to anoint Hazael and Jehu (1 Kings 19:15–18)? It turns out that the answer is no. Hazael is now introduced, to be followed shortly by Jehu.

8:8–9 meet the man of God. Ben-hadad II consults Israel's God about his future in much the same way that King Ahaziah of Israel earlier consulted Baal-zebub of Ekron (see note on 1:2). It appears to have been customary when consulting prophets to offer some payment, in this case an extravagant gift of **forty camels' loads** of **goods** (cf. 1 Sam. 9:1–9; 1 Kings 14:1–4; 2 Kings 5:1–6). The messenger **Hazael** enters the narrative mysteriously. Readers are not told his lineage, nor even his role (servant? officer?). He comes from nowhere—a mere "dog," as he puts it in 8:13. A fragmentary Assyrian text on a basalt statue of King Shalmaneser III refers to him similarly as the "son of nobody," doubtless reflecting lowly, nonroyal origins.

8:10 say to him, "You shall certainly recover." This is what the Hebrew text says. But the word translated "to him" (Hb. *lo*) is sometimes to be read as the negative word "not" (the Hb. word *lo'* has virtually the same sound as the almost identical Hb. word *lo*). If this is the case, then Hazael is to say to Ben-hadad, "You will certainly *not* recover" (see ESV footnote), and Hazael would have lied to the king (v. 14). But if the Hebrew of Elisha's statement does indeed mean "You shall certainly recover," it could have been a truthful prediction about the course of Ben-hadad's sickness that was still negated when Hazael murdered him—i.e., Ben-hadad could have recovered had Hazael not murdered him. Alternatively, some have suggested that Elisha's statement was in fact deceptive, to lull the king into a false sense of security, so that he would be unprepared for Hazael's attack.

8:11 he fixed his gaze. The text does not identify "he" and "him" in this verse. Most interpreters understand the first "he" to be Elisha, who "fixed his gaze" on Hazael, staring at him but also seeing with prophetic vision what Hazael would do in the future. Hazael does not know how to respond and is **embarrassed**, and then Elisha weeps. An alternative interpretation is that Hazael remains dazed by what he has heard and so he stares at Elisha, until Elisha's weeping breaks into his reverie.

12[e]Isa. 13:16; Hos. 13:16; Nah. 3:10; [Ps. 137:9; Hos. 10:14]
13[f]See 1 Sam. 17:43 [g][1 Kgs. 19:15]
14[h]ver. 10
16[i][ch. 1:17; 3:1]
17[j]For ver. 17-24, see 2 Chr. 21:5-10
18[k][ver. 26]
19[l]2 Sam. 7:12, 13; Ps. 132:11 [m]1 Kgs. 11:36; 15:4; [2 Sam. 21:17]
20[n]ch. 3:9; [1 Kgs. 22:47]
21[o]See 2 Sam. 18:17
22[p][Gen. 27:40] [q]Josh. 10:29, 30
24[r][2 Chr. 21:20] [s][2 Chr. 21:17; 22:6; 25:23]
25[t]For ver. 25-29, see 2 Chr. 22:1-6 [u][ch. 9:29]
26[v][2 Chr. 22:2] [w][1 Kgs. 15:10]
28[x]ver. 15

with the sword [e]and dash in pieces their little ones and rip open their pregnant women."
13 And Hazael said, "What is your servant, [f]who is but a dog, that he should do this great
thing?" Elisha answered, [g]"The LORD has shown me that you are to be king over Syria."
14 Then he departed from Elisha and came to his master, who said to him, "What did Elisha
say to you?" And he answered, "He told me [h]that you would certainly recover." 15 But the
next day he took the bed cloth[1] and dipped it in water and spread it over his face, till he
died. And Hazael became king in his place.

Jehoram Reigns in Judah

16 In the fifth year of [i]Joram the son of Ahab, king of Israel, when Jehoshaphat was king
of Judah,[2] Jehoram the son of Jehoshaphat, king of Judah, began to reign. 17 He was [j]thirty-
two years old when he became king, and he reigned eight years in Jerusalem. 18 And he
walked in the way of the kings of Israel, as the house of Ahab had done, for [k]the daughter
of Ahab was his wife. And he did what was evil in the sight of the LORD. 19 Yet the LORD
was not willing to destroy Judah, for the sake of David his servant, [l]since he promised to
give [m]a lamp to him and to his sons forever.

20 In his days Edom revolted from the rule of Judah and set up [n]a king of their own.
21 Then Joram[3] passed over to Zair with all his chariots and rose by night, and he and his
chariot commanders struck the Edomites who had surrounded him, but his army [o]fled
home. 22 [p]So Edom revolted from the rule of Judah to this day. Then [q]Libnah revolted at the
same time. 23 Now the rest of the acts of Joram, and all that he did, are they not written in
the Book of the Chronicles of the Kings of Judah? 24 So Joram slept with his fathers and was
buried [r]with his fathers in the city of David, and [s]Ahaziah his son reigned in his place.

Ahaziah Reigns in Judah

25 [t]In the [u]twelfth year of Joram the son of Ahab, king of Israel, Ahaziah the son of
Jehoram, king of Judah, began to reign. 26 Ahaziah was [v]twenty-two years old when he
began to reign, and he reigned one year in Jerusalem. His mother's name was Athaliah;
she was [w]a granddaughter of Omri king of Israel. 27 He also walked in the way of the house
of Ahab and did what was evil in the sight of the LORD, as the house of Ahab had done,
for he was son-in-law to the house of Ahab.

28 He went with Joram the son of Ahab to make war against [x]Hazael king of Syria at

[1] The meaning of the Hebrew is uncertain [2] Septuagint, Syriac lack *when Jehoshaphat was king of Judah* [3] *Joram* is an alternate spelling of *Jehoram* (the son of Jehoshaphat) as in verse 16; also verses 23, 24

8:15 Hazael became king. Hazael came to power in Syria at some point between the Assyrian Shalmaneser III's campaign in the west in his fourteenth year (845 B.C.), when it is known that Ben-hadad (a throne name; his personal name was Adad-idri) was still on the throne, and the campaign of Shalmaneser's eighteenth year (841), which records Hazael as king. He reigned for about 40 years as one of Israel's most bitter enemies.

8:16–29 ***Jehoram and Ahaziah.*** Judah was last mentioned in ch. 3, when Jehoshaphat was king of Judah. Another Judean king has come and gone in the meantime, however, and the reader must be told about him and be introduced to his successor in order to understand chs. 9–10.

8:16 Jehoram the son of Jehoshaphat. First introduced briefly in 1 Kings 22:50, this king is mentioned again in 2 Kings 1:17. In 8:21, 23–24, his name appears as "Joram," which is also the name of the king of *Israel* in this period (v. 16). This Israelite king is himself called "Jehoram" in such verses as 1:17 and 3:1. At precisely the point when the southern monarchy has come to resemble the northern monarchy most closely in its worship (see note on 8:18), their kings are called by the same name, and one must work hard to distinguish their actions in the text.

8:18 Jehoram **walked in the way of the kings of Israel**. His father, Jehoshaphat, had made peace with the king of Israel in the aftermath of the struggles that arose out of the division of the kingdoms under Jeroboam and Rehoboam (1 Kings 22:44). From Jehoshaphat's reign onward, the fortunes of the house of Omri and the house of David were closely interconnected. There was intermarriage between the two families (Jehoram had married the **daughter of Ahab**), and the two kingdoms followed a similar religious policy (**as the house of Ahab had done**).

8:19 he promised to give a lamp to him. See 1 Kings 11:36; 15:4. Sins in David's family are to be punished not with the destruction of his dynasty but with the "rod of men" (2 Sam. 7:14–16)—divine discipline, characterized in 1–2 Kings as "affliction" (see 1 Kings 11:39). So it is that **the LORD was not willing to destroy Judah, for the sake of David his servant**.

8:20–22 In his days Edom revolted. The "affliction" on David's house in this case (cf. note on v. 19) comes in Jehoram's failure to subdue a rebellion by Edom, a country hitherto ruled by a **king** appointed by Judah (1 Kings 22:47; see note on 2 Kings 3:7–9), and in unrest even within Judah itself: **Libnah** was a Judean city to the southwest of Jerusalem and 5 miles (8 km) to the northeast of Lachish, with which it is associated in 19:8. Chronicles adds to this picture of a weak king by telling of attacks from the Philistines and Arabs who had given tribute to Jehoram's father (2 Chron. 21:16–17).

8:23 Chronicles of the Kings. See note on 1 Kings 14:19.

8:25–27 Ahaziah the son of Jehoram. This Judean king, too, has habits of religion to match those of the family to whom he is related by marriage (**He also walked in the way of the house of Ahab**). The fact that he **reigned** for only **one year**, combined with the fact that he began his reign in the **twelfth year of Joram . . . king of Israel** (i.e., Joram's last year, 3:1), is the first hint of moving toward the end of the house of Omri.

8:28–29 war against Hazael king of Syria. The context in which the house of Omri comes to its end is now provided. Another joint battle against the Syrians at **Ramoth-gilead** (cf. 1 Kings 22:1–4) is followed by withdrawal to the Omride stronghold of **Jezreel**, so that the Israelite king can recover from his wounds. Ramoth-gilead is apparently back in Israelite hands by this point in the narrative (2 Kings 9:14), perhaps abandoned in the course of the general Syrian retreat in 7:3–7.

[y]Ramoth-gilead, and the Syrians wounded Joram. 29 [z]And King Joram returned to be healed
in Jezreel of the wounds that the Syrians had given him at [a]Ramah, when he fought against
Hazael king of Syria. And [b]Ahaziah the son of Jehoram king of Judah went down to see
Joram the son of Ahab in Jezreel, because he was sick.

Jehu Anointed King of Israel

9 Then Elisha the prophet called one of [c]the sons of the prophets and said to him, [d]"Tie
up your garments, and take this [e]flask of oil in your hand, and go to [f]Ramoth-gilead.
2 And when you arrive, look there for Jehu [g]the son of Jehoshaphat, son of Nimshi. And go
in and have him rise from among [h]his fellows, and lead him to an inner chamber. 3 Then
take the flask of oil and pour it on his head and say, 'Thus says the LORD, [i]I anoint you
king over Israel.' Then open the door and flee; do not linger."
4 So the young man, the servant of the prophet, went to Ramoth-gilead. 5 And when
he came, behold, the commanders of the army were in council. And he said, "I have a
word for you, O commander." And Jehu said, "To which of us all?" And he said, "To you,
O commander." 6 So he arose and went into the house. And the young man poured the
oil on his head, saying to him, "Thus says the LORD, the God of Israel, [i]I anoint you king
over the people of the LORD, over Israel. 7 And you shall strike down the house of Ahab
your master, so that I may avenge [j]on Jezebel the blood of my servants the prophets, and
the blood of all the servants of the LORD. 8 For the whole house of Ahab shall perish, [k]and
I will cut off from Ahab [l]every male, [m]bond or free, in Israel. 9 And I will make the house
of Ahab like [n]the house of Jeroboam the son of Nebat, and like [o]the house of Baasha the
son of Ahijah. 10 [p]And the dogs shall eat Jezebel in the territory of Jezreel, and none shall
bury her." Then he opened the door and fled.
11 When Jehu came out to the servants of his master, they said to him, [q]"Is all well? Why
did [r]this mad fellow come to you?" And he said to them, "You know the fellow and his
talk." 12 And they said, "That is not true; tell us now." And he said, "Thus and so he spoke
to me, saying, 'Thus says the LORD, I anoint you king over Israel.'" 13 Then in haste [s]every
man of them took his garment and put it under him on the bare[1] steps, and they blew the
trumpet and proclaimed, [t]"Jehu is king."

Jehu Assassinates Joram and Ahaziah

14 Thus Jehu the son of Jehoshaphat the son of Nimshi conspired against Joram. ([u]Now
Joram with all Israel had been on guard at Ramoth-gilead against [v]Hazael king of Syria,
15 [w]but King Joram had returned to be healed in Jezreel of the wounds that the Syrians
had given him, when he fought with Hazael king of Syria.) So Jehu said, "If this is your
decision, then let no one slip out of the city to go and tell the news in Jezreel." 16 Then Jehu
mounted his chariot and went to Jezreel, for Joram lay there. And Ahaziah king of Judah
had come down to visit Joram.
17 Now the watchman was standing on the tower in Jezreel, and he saw the company of
Jehu as he came and said, "I see a company." And Joram said, "Take a horseman and send to
meet them, and let him say, 'Is it peace?'" 18 So a man on horseback went to meet him and

[1] The meaning of the Hebrew word is uncertain

28 [y][1 Kgs. 22:3]
29 [z]ch. 9:15 [a]2 Chr. 22:6; [ver. 28; 2 Chr. 22:5] [b]ch. 9:16

Chapter 9

1 [c]See ch. 2:3 [d]See 1 Kgs. 18:46 [e]1 Sam. 10:1 [f]ch. 8:28; [1 Kgs. 22:3]
2 [g]ver. 14; [ver. 20; 1 Kgs. 19:16] [h][ver. 5, 11]
3 [i][1 Kgs. 19:16; 2 Chr. 22:7]
6 [i][See ver. 3 above]
7 [j][1 Kgs. 18:4]; See 1 Kgs. 21:5-15
8 [k]ch. 10:17; 1 Kgs. 21:21; [1 Kgs. 14:10] [l]See 1 Sam. 25:22 [m]Deut. 32:36
9 [n]1 Kgs. 14:10; 15:29; 21:22 [o]1 Kgs. 16:3, 11; 21:22
10 [p]ver. 35, 36; 1 Kgs. 21:23
11 [q]ch. 5:21 [r]Jer. 29:26; Hos. 9:7; [John 10:20; Acts 26:24]
13 [s][Matt. 21:8; Mark 11:8] [t][1 Kgs. 1:34]
14 [u][ch. 8:28] [v][1 Kgs. 19:17]
15 [w]ch. 8:29

9:1–10:17 *The End of Ahab's House.* Of the players in the last act of Ahab's drama who were mentioned in 1 Kings 19:15–18, only Jehu has remained out of the picture. His story is now told.

9:1 Tie up your garments. See 1 Kings 18:46 and 2 Kings 4:29; speed will be important for this messenger from among the **sons of the prophets** (the prophetic communities over which Elisha presides; see note on 2:3). The army is still at **Ramoth-gilead**, even though the king has withdrawn to Jezreel (8:29).

9:2 Jehu the son of Jehoshaphat, son of Nimshi. Jehu was described in 1 Kings 19:16 only as "son of Nimshi" (cf. also 2 Kings 9:20), but Nimshi now turns out in fact to have been his grandfather rather than his father (who shares his name with a Judean king, Jehoshaphat). This use of Hebrew *ben* to mean "grandson" rather than "son" certainly occurs in the OT (e.g., Gen. 29:5; 31:28), but it is unusual for the grandfather to be referred to in citations of this particular kind; perhaps Nimshi was a particularly well-known person.

9:3 flask of oil. Elijah had been commanded to **anoint** Jehu **king over Israel** (1 Kings 19:16), but had failed to do so. It is left to Elisha now to fulfill his mission. Anointing with oil was a common practice in the ancient Near East to mark various rites of passage, and in Israel it was closely associated with the enthronement of kings (see 1 Sam. 16:13). It appears to be bound up with the king's legitimacy and right to rule; to be the "anointed of the Lord" is to be a person inviolable and sacrosanct (1 Sam. 24:6–7; 2 Sam. 19:21–22). The secret anointing that takes place here (in an "inner chamber"; 2 Kings 9:2) is particularly reminiscent of Samuel's anointing of Saul (cf. 1 Sam. 9:27–10:1). The reasons for Elisha's advice to the messenger to **open the door and flee** are not provided, but the reference to Jehu's reckless chariot driving in 2 Kings 9:20 perhaps suggests that he has a reputation for rash behavior and could be dangerous to the messenger.

9:7 you shall strike down the house of Ahab. The oracle actually delivered by the messenger is much longer than the one pronounced by Elisha

20[x][2 Sam. 18:27] [y]1 Kgs. 19:17; [ver. 2, 14]
21[z]1 Kgs. 18:44 [a]2 Chr. 22:7 [b]1 Kgs. 21:1; [ver. 26]
22[c][2 Chr. 21:13]
25[d][ch. 7:2] [b][See ver. 21 above] [e]1 Kgs. 21:19, 29 [f]See Isa. 13:1

said, "Thus says the king, 'Is it peace?'" And Jehu said, "What do you have to do with peace?
Turn around and ride behind me." And the watchman reported, saying, "The messenger
reached them, but he is not coming back." **19** Then he sent out a second horseman, who
came to them and said, "Thus the king has said, 'Is it peace?'" And Jehu answered, "What
do you have to do with peace? Turn around and ride behind me." **20** Again the watchman
reported, "He reached them, but he is not coming back. And the driving [x]is like the driving
of Jehu [y]the son of Nimshi, for he drives furiously."

21 Joram said, [z]"Make ready." And they made ready his chariot. [a]Then Joram king of
Israel and Ahaziah king of Judah set out, each in his chariot, and went to meet Jehu,
and met him [b]at the property of Naboth the Jezreelite. **22** And when Joram saw Jehu,
he said, "Is it peace, Jehu?" He answered, "What peace can there be, so long as [c]the
whorings and the sorceries of your mother Jezebel are so many?" **23** Then Joram reined
about and fled, saying to Ahaziah, "Treachery, O Ahaziah!" **24** And Jehu drew his bow
with his full strength, and shot Joram between the shoulders, so that the arrow pierced
his heart, and he sank in his chariot. **25** Jehu said to Bidkar [d]his aide, "Take him up and
throw him [b]on the plot of ground belonging to Naboth the Jezreelite. For remember,
when you and I rode side by side behind Ahab his father, how [e]the LORD made this
[f]pronouncement against him: **26** 'As surely as I saw yesterday the blood of Naboth and
the blood of his sons—declares the LORD—I will repay you on this plot of ground.'
Now therefore take him up and throw him on the plot of ground, in accordance with
the word of the LORD."

in v. 3. The essence of the message is given there, with its fuller form being delayed until later, presumably so that repetition should not unnecessarily hold up the narrative. For the same reason, only the essence of the message is later communicated by Jehu to his fellow officers (v. 12), the details being subsumed under "Thus and so he spoke to me." **the blood of my servants the prophets**. Elijah did not explicitly state to Ahab in 1 Kings 21:21–24 that the Lord's action against Ahab's house would be partly a matter of vengeance for the blood of the prophets. This is *implicit* in 1 Kings 19:14–18, however, where God's response to Elijah's complaint about the murder of the prophets (1 Kings 18:4, 13) is precisely to send him to anoint Jehu (among others).

9:10 none shall bury her. Similarly, this is not explicitly stated in 1 Kings 21:23, nor indeed is it said that Jezebel's body would be like "dung on the face of the field . . . so that no one can say, 'This is Jezebel'" (2 Kings 9:37); but these things are implicit in the statement that **dogs shall eat Jezebel** (1 Kings 21:23). It was considered a terrible thing in Israel not to be afforded a proper burial (cf. Deut. 28:25–26; Jer. 16:4).

9:13 they blew the trumpet and proclaimed, "Jehu is king." The people's eagerness to do this suggests that there was already unrest in the army because of Jehoram's lack of success in his military ventures.

9:17–20 I see a company. As Jehu approaches with his army, it is not at first clear to those within the city what is happening. The **watchman** initially sees only a **company** (lit., "a multitude"). Later, after the two messengers sent out to elicit information have failed to return, he deduces from the manner in which the lead chariot is being driven that **Jehu** is involved: **he drives furiously**.

9:22 Is it peace, Jehu? It seems improbable that Jehoram and Ahaziah would have left the safety of Jezreel to meet Jehu if there had been any doubt in their minds about his intentions. The Hebrew *hashalom* has the sense, "Is all well?" (cf. 4:26; 5:21; 9:11). Jehoram has sent messengers, and has now gone out himself, to discover what brings Jehu to Jezreel: has disaster overtaken Ramoth-gilead, and is this company all that remains of his army? Jehu's response is to ask how things can be well in a kingdom dominated by the Baal religion and the **whorings** of Joram's **mother Jezebel**. "Whorings" (Hb. *zenunim*), also linked with **sorceries** (Hb. *keshapim*) in Nah. 3:4, is a term associated with fertility religion in Hosea (Hos. 1:2; 2:2, 4; 4:12; 5:4). It is derived from the Hebrew verb *zanah* (cf. 1 Kings 3:16; 22:38).

9:25–26 plot of ground belonging to Naboth the Jezreelite. See the prophecy of Elijah to Ahab in 1 Kings 21:17–24, which precipitated that king's death (1 Kings 22, esp. v. 38; see also note on 1 Kings 21:19) in circumstances similar to those of his son Jehoram (death by arrow, 1 Kings 22:34).

Jehu Executes Judgment

841 B.C.

Elisha fulfilled the Lord's prophecy to Elijah by sending someone to Ramoth-gilead to anoint Jehu, one of Joram's commanders, as king of Israel. Jehu promptly headed for Jezreel, where King Joram (also called Jehoram) of Israel was recovering from some battle wounds. When Joram and King Ahaziah of Judah went out in their chariots to meet Jehu, Jehu mortally wounded Joram with an arrow and chased Ahaziah to Beth-haggan, where he wounded him as well. It appears that Ahaziah then fled to Megiddo, where he died (see also 2 Chron. 22:9).

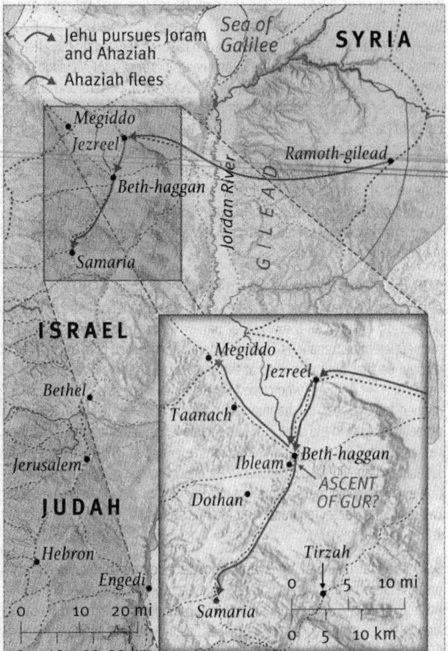

27 [g]When Ahaziah the king of Judah saw this, he fled in the direction of Beth-haggan.
And Jehu pursued him and said, "Shoot him also." And they shot him[1] in the chariot at
the ascent of Gur, which is by [h]Ibleam. And he fled to [h]Megiddo and died there. 28 [i]His
servants carried him in a chariot to Jerusalem, and buried him in his tomb with his fathers
in the city of David.
29 In the [j]eleventh year of Joram the son of Ahab, Ahaziah began to reign over Judah.

Jehu Executes Jezebel

30 When Jehu came to Jezreel, Jezebel heard of it. And [k]she painted her eyes and adorned
her head and looked out of the window. 31 And as Jehu entered the gate, she said, [l]"Is it
peace, you Zimri, murderer of your master?" 32 And he lifted up his face to the window
and said, "Who is on my side? Who?" Two or three eunuchs looked out at him. 33 He said,
"Throw her down." So they threw her down. And some of her blood spattered on the wall
and on the horses, and they trampled on her. 34 Then he went in and ate and drank. And
he said, "See now to this cursed woman and bury her, [m]for she is a king's daughter." 35 But
when they went to bury her, they found no more of her than the skull and the feet and
the palms of her hands. 36 When they came back and told him, he said, "This is the word
of the LORD, which he spoke by his servant Elijah the Tishbite: [n]'In the territory of Jezreel
the dogs shall eat the flesh of Jezebel, 37 and the corpse of Jezebel shall be [o]as dung on the
face of the field in the territory of Jezreel, so that no one can say, This is Jezebel.'"

Jehu Slaughters Ahab's Descendants

10 Now Ahab had seventy sons in [p]Samaria. So Jehu wrote letters and sent them to
Samaria, to the rulers of the city,[2] to the elders, and to [q]the guardians of the sons[3]
of Ahab, saying, 2 "Now then, as soon as this letter comes to you, seeing your master's
sons are with you, and there are with you chariots and horses, fortified cities also, and
weapons, 3 select the best and fittest of your master's sons and set him on his father's

[1] Syriac, Vulgate (compare Septuagint); Hebrew lacks *and they shot him* [2] Septuagint, Vulgate; Hebrew *rulers of Jezreel* [3] Hebrew lacks *of the sons*

27 [g][2 Chr. 22:9] [h]Josh. 17:11
28 [i]ch. 23:30; 2 Chr. 35:24]
29 [j]ch. 8:25]
30 [k]Jer. 4:30; Ezek. 23:40]
31 [l]See 1 Kgs. 16:9-20
34 [m]1 Kgs. 16:31
36 [n]1 Kgs. 21:23
37 [o][Ps. 83:10; Jer. 8:2; 9:22; 16:4; 25:33]

Chapter 10

1 [p]1 Kgs. 16:24 [q][Esth. 2:7]

9:27–28 he fled to Megiddo and died there. Linked with Ahab in marriage and at one with him in religion, **Ahaziah** also shares in his fate. He is **shot . . . in the chariot**, later to be transported dead to his capital city for burial (cf. 1 Kings 22:34–37). The shooting takes place near **Ibleam**, one of the cities that guarded access to and from the southern end of the Jezreel Valley, as Ahaziah flees south from Jezreel back toward Samaria; but after the attack he abruptly changes direction and heads northwest for Megiddo in the western part of the Jezreel Valley. Megiddo was an important and strategic city in ancient times, controlling the main international highway running from Egypt to Damascus as it entered the valley. Israelite remains at Megiddo from the period of the divided monarchy are numerous. An imposing water tunnel, probably cut during Ahab's reign (9th century B.C.), was discovered here. A large vertical shaft (115 feet/35 m) was cut into bedrock, and then a 200-foot (61-m) horizontal shaft was dug to reach a spring outside the city. A series of buildings was discovered that probably served as either storehouses or stables in the time of Ahab.

9:29 the eleventh year of Joram the son of Ahab. In 8:25 one reads of "the twelfth year." Accession dates could be reckoned in different ways, particularly in terms of the way that part-years were handled, resulting in such apparent discrepancies. The new information is given here to clarify how it could be that both men died at the same time if Jehoram reigned for 12 years (3:1) yet Ahaziah, who came to the throne in Jehoram's "twelfth year," reigned for one year. The fragmentary ninth-century B.C. Tell Dan inscription probably alludes to the deaths of these same kings, although the Syrian king responsible for the inscription there claims *responsibility* for the deaths of the Judean and Israelite kings mentioned—a good example of the oversimplification and hyperbole that is typical of victory monuments in the ancient Near East. Perhaps Hazael regarded Jehu as a vassal, and felt justified in claiming Jehu's feats as his own.

9:30 she painted her eyes and adorned her head. This could mean only that Jezebel met her end proudly, dressed up as a queen should be. Her posture, however, echoes the "woman in the window" motif found on carved ivory plaques from various ancient Near Eastern sites (see note on 2 Sam. 6:16–19), which may represent the goddess Astarte, one of the wives of Baal; so perhaps Jezebel is being represented as the very incarnation of the religion that she brought into Israel from Sidon.

9:31 Is it peace, you Zimri? "Is it peace?" is a question intricately tied to the demise of Ahab and his dynasty (see note on v. 22; cf. vv. 18–19; 1 Kings 22:28). Jezebel asks, sarcastically, whether "all is well" (knowing that all is far from well) and she taunts Jehu as one who is unlikely to survive his own revolution (Zimri's reign was a "seven-day wonder"; see 1 Kings 16:8–20).

9:32 It was common practice in the ancient world for the king to have a harem (cf. 1 Kings 11:3), and for the harem to be provided with guards. These guards were typically **eunuchs** (castrated males), so that the king could be sure that the males close to his women were not capable of sexual relations with them. Eunuchs also performed an important role in the official hierarchy of the ancient Near East more generally. In neo-Assyrian sources, e.g., they are attested at the royal court, in the army, in the bureaucracy, and in the provincial administration. They functioned, among many other roles, as the king's personal attendants, cooks, palace guards, scribes, and ambassadors.

9:36 the word of the LORD, which he spoke by his servant Elijah. Using the language of covenant curses, Elijah earlier prophesied the "cutting off" of all the males of Ahab's house (1 Kings 21:21–22; 2 Kings 9:8–9) as well as the gruesome death of Jezebel (1 Kings 21:23; 2 Kings 9:10). **dogs shall eat**. The exposure of Jezebel's corpse to devouring dogs meant disgrace since burial was now impossible. Now that Jezebel is dead, Jehu turns his attention to Ahab's sons (see note on 10:1).

10:1 Now Ahab had seventy sons in Samaria. Elijah had prophesied that the Lord would consume Ahab's descendants and cut off from him every last male in Israel (1 Kings 21:21; cf. the previous prophecies against Jeroboam and Baasha in 1 Kings 14:10; 16:3). Jehu now looks to fulfill this prophecy. The **guardians of the sons of Ahab** are probably those *in general* who were loyal to Ahab and to his house, as distinct from the **rulers** and the **elders** with their specific roles.

10:3 fight for your master's house. By writing letters to the leading citizens and challenging them to place one of Ahab's potential heirs **on his father's throne**, Jehu forces them to choose sides.

5[r]Josh. 9:8, 11
6[q][See ver. 1 above]
7[s][1 Kgs. 21:21]
9[t]ch. 9:14, 24
10[u][1 Sam. 3:19] [v]1 Kgs. 21:19, 21, 29
13[w][ch. 8:29; 9:16; 2 Chr. 22:8]
15[x]See Jer. 35:6-10, 14, 16, 18 [y]1 Chr. 2:55 [z]Ezra 10:19; Ezek. 17:18
16[a][1 Kgs. 19:10]
17[b]ch. 9:8; 2 Chr. 22:8 [v][See ver. 10 above]

throne and fight for your master's house." **4** But they were exceedingly afraid and said,
"Behold, the two kings could not stand before him. How then can we stand?" **5** So he
who was over the palace, and he who was over the city, together with the elders and the
guardians, sent to Jehu, saying, [r]"We are your servants, and we will do all that you tell
us. We will not make anyone king. Do whatever is good in your eyes." **6** Then he wrote
to them a second letter, saying, "If you are on my side, and if you are ready to obey me,
take the heads of your master's sons and come to me at Jezreel tomorrow at this time."
Now the king's sons, seventy persons, were with the great men of the city, [q]who were
bringing them up. **7** And as soon as the letter came to them, they took the king's sons
[s]and slaughtered them, seventy persons, and put their heads in baskets and sent them to
him at Jezreel. **8** When the messenger came and told him, "They have brought the heads
of the king's sons," he said, "Lay them in two heaps at the entrance of the gate until the
morning." **9** Then in the morning, when he went out, he stood and said to all the people,
"You are innocent. [t]It was I who conspired against my master and killed him, but who
struck down all these? **10** Know then that there shall [u]fall to the earth nothing of the
word of the LORD, which the LORD spoke concerning the house of Ahab, for the LORD
has done [v]what he said by his servant Elijah." **11** So Jehu struck down all who remained
of the house of Ahab in Jezreel, all his great men and his close friends and his priests,
until he left him none remaining.

12 Then he set out and went to Samaria. On the way, when he was at Beth-eked of the
Shepherds, **13** Jehu met [w]the relatives of Ahaziah king of Judah, and he said, "Who are
you?" And they answered, "We are the relatives of Ahaziah, and we came down to visit
the royal princes and the sons of the queen mother." **14** He said, "Take them alive." And
they took them alive and slaughtered them at the pit of Beth-eked, forty-two persons,
and he spared none of them.

15 And when he departed from there, he met [x]Jehonadab the son of [y]Rechab coming
to meet him. And he greeted him and said to him, "Is your heart true to my heart as
mine is to yours?" And Jehonadab answered, "It is." Jehu said,[1] "If it is, [z]give me your
hand." So he gave him his hand. And Jehu took him up with him into the chariot.
16 And he said, "Come with me, and see [a]my zeal for the LORD." So he[2] had him ride
in his chariot. **17** And when he came to Samaria, [b]he struck down all who remained to
Ahab in Samaria, till he had wiped them out, according to the word of the LORD [v]that
he spoke to Elijah.

[1] Septuagint; Hebrew lacks *Jehu said* [2] Septuagint, Syriac, Targum; Hebrew *they*

10:5 he who was over the palace . . . he who was over the city. These are the "rulers of the city" mentioned in v. 1. The position of palace administrator was an important one (cf. 15:5; 18:18, 37; 19:2), and his power at least in Judah is indicated in Isa. 22:22. Both the title ("he who was over the palace") and sometimes the names of its holders are found in extrabiblical inscriptions. The joint reply of these two officials along with the **elders** and the other former Ahab loyalists (the "guardians") reveals that they are no longer Ahab's or Jehoram's, but are now Jehu's **servants**.

10:7 they took the king's sons and slaughtered them. This fulfills the word of the Lord in 9:7–9 and is similar to other instances in which entire groups of people are put to death (e.g., Dan. 6:24, which likewise does not commend the action; cf. note on 2 Sam. 21:3–6). This kind of drastic action against a royal household was not at all uncommon in the ancient world, as the present incumbents of thrones tried to ensure a future free of retaliation. For example, the Aramaic Panammuwa Inscription (c. 733–727 B.C.) records that Panammuwa of Sam'al was the survivor of a palace coup in which a brother killed his father Barsur, along with 70 brothers of his father. This text and the biblical text in Judg. 9:5, where Abimelech kills 70 of his brothers before being crowned king, may suggest that the number **seventy** in such contexts is a round number, or a matter of literary convention, rather than an exact number. In any case, the number of sons of such a monarch could be quite large.

10:8–10 two heaps at the entrance of the gate. The Assyrian king Ashurnasirpal II records in an inscription that during his siege of the city of Damdammusa he cut off the heads of 600 of his enemy's troops and, in an act of intimidation, "built a pile of heads before his gate." Jehu's aim is similar: to convince the people that resistance is futile. He knows **who struck down all these**, but the people do not; and he invites them to believe that the **heads** mean that the revolution is bigger than he is, involving mysterious powers more lethal than his (he **killed** only his **master**); it is truly **the LORD** who is at work in overthrowing the house of Ahab. As fair-minded (implied by **innocent**) people, they should be able to arrive at the correct interpretation of the evidence.

10:13–14 His work in Jezreel complete, Jehu leaves for Samaria. On the way, he encounters some **relatives of Ahaziah king of Judah**. The Judean royal family keeps being drawn into the events, even though there was no prophetic forewarning. Cf. 9:27 for the death of Ahaziah. **they took them alive and slaughtered them**. This new king is thorough in exterminating all traces of the past, and the consequences for Judah will be dire (11:1).

10:15 Is your heart true to my heart as mine is to yours? The Hebrew vocabulary of *yashar* ("right," "true") and *lebab* ("heart") appears in other places in 1–2 Kings (e.g., 1 Kings 14:8), including 2 Kings 10:30 in relation to Jehu himself: "you have done well in carrying out what is right in my eyes, and have done to the house of Ahab according to all that was in my heart." The wording here underlines that the theme throughout the chapter is "who is on the Lord's side; who is in the right?" **Jehonadab**, who is on the right side, reappears in Jeremiah 35 ("Jonadab") as the founder of a purist religious group committed to Israel's older ways.

Jehu Strikes Down the Prophets of Baal

18 Then Jehu assembled all the people and said to them, [c]"Ahab served Baal a little, but
Jehu will serve him much. **19** Now therefore call to me all the [d]prophets of Baal, all his
worshipers and all his priests. Let none be missing, for I have a great sacrifice to offer to
Baal. Whoever is missing shall not live." But Jehu did it with cunning in order to destroy
the worshipers of Baal. **20** And Jehu ordered, [e]"Sanctify [f]a solemn assembly for Baal." So
[g]they proclaimed it. **21** And Jehu sent throughout all Israel, and all the worshipers of Baal
came, so that there was not a man left who did not come. And they entered [h]the house
of Baal, and the house of Baal was filled from one end to the other. **22** He said to him who
was in charge of the wardrobe, "Bring out the vestments for all the worshipers of Baal."
So he brought out the vestments for them. **23** Then Jehu went into the house of Baal with
Jehonadab the son of Rechab, and he said to the worshipers of Baal, "Search, and see that
there is no servant of the LORD here among you, but only the worshipers of Baal." **24** Then
they[1] went in to offer sacrifices and burnt offerings.

Now Jehu had stationed eighty men outside and said, "The man who allows any of
those whom I give into your hands to escape [i]shall forfeit his life." **25** So as soon as he had
made an end of offering the burnt offering, Jehu said to the guard and to the officers, [j]"Go
in and strike them down; let not a man escape." So when they put them to the sword, the
guard and the officers cast them out and went into the inner room of the house of Baal,
26 and they brought out the [k]pillar that was in [h]the house of Baal and burned it. **27** And
they demolished the [k]pillar of Baal, and demolished the house of Baal, and made it [l]a
latrine to this day.

Jehu Reigns in Israel

28 Thus Jehu wiped out Baal from Israel. **29** But Jehu did not turn aside from [m]the sins of
Jeroboam the son of Nebat, [n]which he made Israel to sin—that is, the golden calves that
were in Bethel and in Dan. **30** And the LORD said to Jehu, "Because you have done well in
carrying out what is right in my eyes, and have done to the house of Ahab according to all
that was in my heart, [o]your sons of the fourth generation shall sit on the throne of Israel."

[1] Septuagint *he* (compare verse 25)

18 [c]1 Kgs. 16:31, 32
19 [d]1 Kgs. 18:19; 22:6
20 [e][Joel 1:14] [f][Lev. 23:36] [g][Ex. 32:5]
21 [h]ch. 11:18; 1 Kgs. 16:32
24 [i][1 Kgs. 20:39, 42]
25 [j][1 Kgs. 18:40]
26 [k]ch. 3:2; 1 Kgs. 14:23 [h][See ver. 21 above]
27 [k][See ver. 26 above] [l][Ezra 6:11; Dan. 2:5; 3:29]
29 [m]See 1 Kgs. 12:28-31 [n]See 1 Kgs. 14:16
30 [o]ch. 15:12; [ver. 35; ch. 13:1, 10; 14:23; 15:8]

10:18–36 *Jehu Destroys Baal Worship.* It is no surprise to find Jehu now taking decisive action against the worship of Baal, for 1 Kings 19:15–18 had pointed toward final victory over Baal worship in naming Jehu (along with Hazael, 2 Kings 10:32–33) as the Lord's instrument of judgment.

10:18–19 Jehu assembled all the people. Samaria had been the focal point for the Baal cult (cf. 1 Kings 16:32–33), to which Jehu now gives his attention. His strategy is to feign enthusiasm while preparing for destruction; he tells the people that although the dynasty has changed, the religious policy will remain the same (**Ahab served Baal a little, but Jehu will serve him much**).

10:20 Sanctify a solemn assembly. This phrase is unparalleled in Hebrew, but a Ugaritic text concerned with gaining protection for the royal ancestors of King Ammurapi of Ugarit suggests that it represents genuine Canaanite religious terminology.

10:25 inner room. The Hebrew is *'ir*, which normally means "city." In this context it presumably refers to some "city-like" aspect of the temple, behind its own walls—perhaps an inner room or a walled courtyard.

10:27 the pillar of Baal . . . the house of Baal. See 1 Kings 16:32–33 and 2 Kings 3:2. Baal worship in Israel is officially at an end. It has neither royal patronage nor royal tolerance.

10:29 did not turn aside from the sins of Jeroboam. The worship of Baal was only a particularly bad form of the idolatry practiced in Israel. Jehu has dealt with Baal worship, but he does nothing at all about the **golden calves . . . in Bethel and in Dan** that Jeroboam installed after leading Israel in revolt against the house of David (1 Kings 12:25–30). The symbolism of these calves encouraged a blurring of the distinction between Mosaic and Canaanite religion; the high god of the Canaanite pantheon, El, is frequently called "the bull" in Ugaritic materials (signifying his strength and fertility), and Baal himself is also represented as a bull. Archaeologists have discovered bull icons at numerous sites in Syria-Palestine, including Byblos, Ugarit, and Hazor.

10:30 Since Jehu does not abolish the golden calves in Bethel and Dan (v. 29; cf. v. 31), it is surprising to find him addressed as someone who has carried out **what is right** (Hb. *yashar*) in the **eyes** of the Lord. In other places, the authors of Kings use *yashar* only positively, with regard to David (1 Kings 15:5) and the relatively good (i.e., non-idolatrous) kings of Judah (1 Kings 15:11; 22:43; 2 Kings 12:2; 14:3; 15:3, 34; 18:3; 22:2). It is even more surprising to find Jehu receiving a David-like dynastic promise. His descendants will **sit on the throne of Israel** to the **fourth generation**. This is not the same thing as a promise of *eternal* dynasty, but it is nevertheless extraordinary; Jeroboam was promised a dynasty like David's if he did "what was right" in the Lord's eyes (1 Kings 11:38), but then he failed and lost this opportunity (1 Kings 14:8). Evidently what Jehu has done that is right (eradication of Baal worship) far outweighs what he continues to do that is wrong.

10:32–33 the LORD began to cut off parts of Israel. First Kings 19:15–18 pointed to a time when God's judgment would fall on Israel because of Baal worship. Jehu would deal with those who escaped Hazael, and Elisha with those who escaped Jehu. Implicit in such an ordering was that Hazael would turn out to be the greatest destroyer of the three—something to which 2 Kings 8:12 also pointed, with its emphasis on Hazael's brutality. It is no surprise, therefore, to find now an account of Hazael's aggression against Israel. He is said to have conquered Transjordan as far south as the **Valley of the Arnon**, the southern limit of Israelite Transjordanian territory (cf. Josh. 12:2). This military success occurred during the lull in Assyrian aggression against Syria-Palestine between the campaign of Shalmaneser III's twenty-first year (838 B.C.), when he captured four of Hazael's cities and accepted tribute from the peoples of the Phoenician coast, and the campaign of the fifth year of Adad-nirari III (806). This respite enabled Damascus to turn its full attention toward Israel and Judah and to subject these kingdoms to prolonged pressure in the last decades of the ninth century. More of Hazael's conquests will be reported later (2 Kings 12:17–18; 13:3–7, 22–23).

10:34 the rest of the acts of Jehu. Jehu appears in Assyrian records describ-

31[p]ver. 29
32[q][ch. 13:25; 14:25] [r][ch. 8:12; 1 Kgs. 19:17]
33[s]Deut. 2:36 [t][Amos 1:3, 4]

Chapter 11

1[u]For ver. 1-3, see 2 Chr. 22:10-12 [v]ch. 8:26
2[w][ver. 21; ch. 12:1]
4[x]For ver. 4-20, see 2 Chr. 23:1-21 [y]ver. 9 [z]ver. 19

31 But Jehu was not careful to walk in the law of the LORD, the God of Israel, with all his
heart. [p]He did not turn from the sins of Jeroboam, which he made Israel to sin.
32 In those days the LORD [q]began to cut off parts of Israel. [r]Hazael defeated them throughout the territory of Israel: 33 from the Jordan eastward, all the land of Gilead, the Gadites,
and the Reubenites, and the Manassites, from [s]Aroer, which is by the Valley of the Arnon,
that is, [t]Gilead and Bashan. 34 Now the rest of the acts of Jehu and all that he did, and all
his might, are they not written in the Book of the Chronicles of the Kings of Israel? 35 So
Jehu slept with his fathers, and they buried him in Samaria. And Jehoahaz his son reigned
in his place. 36 The time that Jehu reigned over Israel in Samaria was twenty-eight years.

Athaliah Reigns in Judah

11 [u]Now when [v]Athaliah the mother of Ahaziah saw that her son was dead, she arose
and destroyed all the royal family. 2 But Jehosheba, the daughter of King Joram, sister
of Ahaziah, took [w]Joash the son of Ahaziah and stole him away from among the king's
sons who were being put to death, and she put[1] him and his nurse in a bedroom. Thus
they[2] hid him from Athaliah, so that he was not put to death. 3 And he remained with her
six years, hidden in the house of the LORD, while Athaliah reigned over the land.

Joash Anointed King in Judah

4 [x]But in the seventh year [y]Jehoiada sent and brought the captains of [z]the Carites and of
the guards, and had them come to him in the house of the LORD. And he made a covenant
with them and put them under oath in the house of the LORD, and he showed them the

[1] Compare 2 Chronicles 22:11; Hebrew lacks *and she put* [2] Septuagint, Syriac, Vulgate (compare 2 Chronicles 22:11) *she*

ing an event that must have taken place shortly after his accession to the throne, during the western campaign of Shalmaneser III's eighteenth year (841 B.C.). During that campaign King Shalmaneser besieged Damascus, marched on to the Hauran Mountains in southern Syria, then through Gilead to the south of the Sea of Galilee and through Jezreel to Ba'li-ra'si (perhaps Mount Carmel) near Tyre. Hosea 10:14 may preserve a memory of this march through northern Palestine, since "Shalman" there is probably an abbreviated form of Shalmaneser's name. At this time, Shalmaneser collected tribute from "Jehu the Israelite" as well as from Tyre and Sidon. The Black Obelisk of Shalmaneser III (859–824 B.C.), found at the site of Nimrud, depicts the Israelite king Jehu giving tribute. Jehu, or perhaps his emissary, lies prostrate before the king while other Israelites present tribute that includes gold and silver objects. If the figure is Jehu, then it is the only extant pictorial representation of an Israelite king from antiquity. Shalmaneser III, after having received tribute from Jehu, also plundered Tyre and Sidon in Phoenicia. In commemoration of this successful campaign, Shalmaneser had his portrait carved on the cliffs of the Dog River, north of Beirut.

11:1–12:21 *Joash.* The destruction of the house of Ahab has greatly affected the house of David: Ahaziah (of Judah) has been killed, just like Jehoram (of Israel), and a number of his relatives have suffered the same fate as Ahab's relatives (10:12–14). Have the two houses become so identified in intermarriage (8:18, 27) that a distinction no longer exists between them? Chapters 11–12 clarify that in fact the distinction remains, for David's house survives even the assault of wicked Queen Athaliah, a Judean "Jezebel."

11:1–3 Athaliah the mother of Ahaziah. Possibly a daughter of Jezebel (8:26), Athaliah certainly displays the same ruthless streak. Her attack on the **royal family** is stemmed only by the resourceful **Jehosheba**, who hides the young **Joash** and **his nurse** in the Jerusalem temple. The nurse's willingness to share danger with the child in her care contrasts sharply with the spineless leading men of Samaria in 10:1–7. Cf. note on 2 Chron. 22:10–12.

11:4 Jehoiada . . . the Carites and . . . the guards. It is subsequently clarified that Jehoiada is the chief priest (vv. 9, 15). Jerusalem's guards and their duties around the palace and the temple have been described in 1 Kings 14:27–28. The Carites appear in the consonantal Hebrew text of 2 Sam. 20:23 as part of the elite royal bodyguard alongside the Pelethites. They may well be the same body as (or at least the regiment may be descended from the regiment of) the Cherethites, with whom the Pelethites normally appear in the OT (2 Sam. 8:18; 15:18; 20:7, 23; 1 Kings 1:38, 44); see note on 1 Kings 1:38.

Syria Captures Gilead
c. 825–798 B.C.

The Syrians under Hazael continued to plague Israel during Jehu's reign, eventually capturing all of Gilead from Aroer on the Arnon River to Bashan in the north. Later during the reign of Jehoash (also called Joash), Hazael attacked Gath on the western border of Judah, and Jehoash sent Hazael treasures from the temple of the Lord to persuade him to withdraw from attacking Jerusalem.

king's son. 5 And he commanded them, "This is the thing that you shall do: one third of
you, [a]those who come off duty on the Sabbath and guard the king's house 6 ([b]another third
being at the gate Sur and a third at the gate behind the guards) shall guard the palace.[1]
7 And the two divisions of you, which come on duty in force on the Sabbath and guard the
house of the LORD on behalf of the king, 8 shall surround the king, each with his weapons
in his hand. And whoever approaches the ranks is to be put to death. Be with the king
[c]when he goes out and when he comes in."
9 The captains did according to all that Jehoiada the priest commanded, and they each
brought his men who were to go off duty on the Sabbath, with those who were to come on
duty on the Sabbath, and came to Jehoiada the priest. 10 And the priest gave to the captains
the spears and [d]shields that had been King David's, which were in the house of the LORD.
11 And the guards stood, every man with his weapons in his hand, from the south side
of the house to the north side of the house, around the altar and the house on behalf of
the king. 12 Then he brought out the king's son and put [e]the crown on him and gave him
[f]the testimony. And they proclaimed him king and anointed him, and they clapped their
hands and said, [g]"Long live the king!"
13 When Athaliah heard the noise of the guard and of the people, she went into the house
of the LORD to the people. 14 And when she looked, there was the king standing [h]by the
pillar, according to the custom, and the captains and the trumpeters beside the king, and
all the people of the land rejoicing and [i]blowing trumpets. And Athaliah [j]tore her clothes
and cried, "Treason! Treason!" 15 Then Jehoiada the priest commanded the captains who
were set over the army, "Bring her out between the ranks, and put to death with the sword
anyone who follows her." For the priest said, "Let her not be put to death in the house of
the LORD." 16 So they laid hands on her; and she went through the horses' entrance to the
king's house, and there she was put to death.
17 And Jehoiada [k]made a covenant between the LORD and the king and people, that
they should be the LORD's people, and also [l]between the king and the people. 18 Then all
the people of the land went to [m]the house of Baal and tore it down; [n]his altars and his
images they broke in pieces, and they killed Mattan the priest of Baal before the altars.
And the priest posted watchmen over the house of the LORD. 19 And he took the captains,
[o]the Carites, the guards, and all the people of the land, and they brought the king down
from the house of the LORD, marching through [p]the gate of the guards to the king's
house. And he took his seat on the throne of the kings. 20 So all the people of the land
rejoiced, and the city was quiet after Athaliah had been put to death with the sword at
the king's house.

[1] The meaning of the Hebrew word is uncertain

5 [a][1 Chr. 9:25]
6 [b][2 Chr. 23:5]
8 [c][Num. 27:17]
10 [d]2 Sam. 8:7; 1 Chr. 18:7
12 [e][2 Sam. 1:10] [f]Ex. 25:16; 31:18; See Deut. 17:18-20 [g]1 Sam. 10:24; 2 Sam. 16:16; 1 Kgs. 1:39
14 [h]ch. 23:3; [2 Chr. 34:31] [i]1 Kgs. 1:34 [j]See Gen. 44:13
17 [k][Josh. 24:25] [l]2 Sam. 5:3
18 [m]ch. 10:21, 23, 26 [n][Deut. 12:3]
19 [o]ver. 4 [p]ver. 6; [2 Chr. 23:20]

11:5–8 This is the thing that you shall do. The normal duties of the troops mentioned here are reasonably clear: the guarding of **the king's house** (the royal palace) and **the house of the LORD** (the temple), along with two important gates. The **gate Sur** was a gate in the walled enclosure that surrounded the temple precincts and the royal residences in Jerusalem, probably to be identified with the gate of Shallecheth of 1 Chron. 26:16 (called the "Gate of the Foundation" in 2 Chron. 23:5). From this gate a road ascended to the Fish Gate at the northwest corner of the city's outer defensive wall. The **gate behind the guards** was apparently located in a wall separating the temple and palace complexes (2 Kings 11:19) and is called the "upper gate" in 2 Chron. 23:20 (cf. 2 Kings 15:35). The interpretation of the troops' reassignments, however, is more difficult. It does not seem likely that the troops in 11:5–6 are being assigned to guard the king's **palace** (v. 6), for the terminology used to specify the building at the end of v. 6 (Hb. *habbayit massakh*, perhaps "house named destruction"?) is not the same as the terminology used of the royal palace in v. 5 ("the king's house," Hb. *bet-hammelek*). Furthermore, Athaliah leaves the royal palace unhindered in v. 13, with no guards in sight. Most likely, then, it is the temple ("palace") of Baal that is to be guarded in v. 6—the building destined for destruction in v. 18. Troops are sent to both temples: the "house named destruction" (vv. 5–6) and the "house of the LORD" (v. 7). They are sent to the first in order to discourage interference by the worshipers of Baal and to detain the priest Mattan. The overall concern is that sufficient security be provided for the coronation ceremony to take place within the temple precincts.

11:10 spears and shields. Since it is not likely that the soldiers needed to be armed by the chief priest, it is probably the symbolism that is important here. The commanders are making it clear that they have allied themselves with David's cause, and at the same time they are receiving articles to be given to the new king as symbols of his royal power (the spear is a prominent royal weapon in the books of Samuel; e.g., 1 Sam. 18:10–11; 22:6).

11:12 the testimony. Joash is presented with a list of divinely ordained laws (Hb. *'edut*). For kings ruling under divine law, see Deut. 17:18–20; 1 Kings 2:3; 2 Kings 23:3.

11:14 pillar. In 1–2 Kings the Hebrew *'ammud* has appeared thus far only in 1 Kings 7, referring to the pillars of the Solomonic palace (1 Kings 7:2–3, 6) and temple (1 Kings 7:15–22, 41–42). Either Jachin or Boaz is probably in view here (1 Kings 7:21); "Jachin" may mean "the establisher," and would thus provide a fitting location for a coronation. The emphasis on **custom** is important in a context where the authors are trying to stress the legitimacy of Joash's claim to the throne; the coronation takes place in line with law and custom, and in full view of the **people of the land**.

11:17 Jehoiada made a covenant. The **king and people** once more identify themselves as **the LORD's people** through a covenant-renewal ceremony (cf. Josh. 24:1–27; 2 Kings 23:1–3). At the same time, a covenant is made between the king and the people (cf. 2 Sam. 5:1–3), redefining kingship in distinctively Israelite terms after a period in which foreign ideas have dominated.

21 [q]For ch. 11:21–12:15, see 2 Chr. 24:1-14

Chapter 12

3 [r]ch. 14:4; 15:35; 1 Kgs. 15:14; 22:43
4 [s]ch. 22:4 [t][Ex. 35:5; 1 Chr. 29:9]
9 [u][Mark 12:41; Luke 21:1]
10 [v][ch. 22:4]
12 [w][ch. 22:5, 6]
13 [x][2 Chr. 24:14] [y]1 Kgs. 7:50
15 [z]ch. 22:7
16 [a]Lev. 5:15, 18 [b]Lev. 4:24, 29 [c]Lev. 7:7; Num. 18:19
17 [d]ch. 8:12; [1 Kgs. 19:17]

Jehoash Reigns in Judah

21 [1] [q]Jehoash[2] was seven years old when he began to reign.
12 In the seventh year of Jehu, Jehoash[3] began to reign, and he reigned forty years in
Jerusalem. His mother's name was Zibiah of Beersheba. **2** And Jehoash did what
was right in the eyes of the LORD all his days, because Jehoiada the priest instructed him.
3 Nevertheless, [r]the high places were not taken away; the people continued to sacrifice and
make offerings on the high places.

Jehoash Repairs the Temple

4 Jehoash said to the priests, "All the money of the holy things [s]that is brought into
the house of the LORD, the money for which each man is assessed—the money from the
assessment of persons—and [t]the money that a man's heart prompts him to bring into the
house of the LORD, **5** let the priests take, each from his donor, and let them repair the house
wherever any need of repairs is discovered." **6** But by the twenty-third year of King Jehoash,
the priests had made no repairs on the house. **7** Therefore King Jehoash summoned Jehoiada
the priest and the other priests and said to them, "Why are you not repairing the house?
Now therefore take no more money from your donors, but hand it over for the repair of
the house." **8** So the priests agreed that they should take no more money from the people,
and that they should not repair the house.
9 Then Jehoiada the priest took [u]a chest and bored a hole in the lid of it and set it beside
the altar on the right side as one entered the house of the LORD. And the priests who
guarded the threshold put in it all the money that was brought into the house of the LORD.
10 And whenever they saw that there was much money in the chest, the king's secretary
and the high priest came up and they bagged and counted [v]the money that was found in
the house of the LORD. **11** Then they would give the money that was weighed out into the
hands of the workmen who had the oversight of the house of the LORD. And they paid it
out to the carpenters and the builders who worked on the house of the LORD, **12** and [w]to
the masons and the stonecutters, as well as to buy timber and quarried stone for making
repairs on the house of the LORD, and for any outlay for the repairs of the house. **13** [x]But
there were not made for the house of the LORD [y]basins of silver, snuffers, bowls, trumpets,
or any vessels of gold, or of silver, from the money that was brought into the house of the
LORD, **14** for that was given to the workmen who were repairing the house of the LORD
with it. **15** And [z]they did not ask for an accounting from the men into whose hand they
delivered the money to pay out to the workmen, for they dealt honestly. **16** The money
from [a]the guilt offerings and the money from the [b]sin offerings was not brought into the
house of the LORD; [c]it belonged to the priests.
17 At that time [d]Hazael king of Syria went up and fought against Gath and took it. But

[1] Ch 12:1 in Hebrew [2] *Jehoash* is an alternate spelling of *Joash* (son of Ahaziah) as in verse 2 [3] *Jehoash* is an alternate spelling of *Joash* (son of Ahaziah) as in 11:2; also verses 2, 4, 6, 7, 18

11:21 Joash, introduced by that name in v. 2, will be called **Jehoash** throughout most of ch. 12, to be called Joash again only in 12:19, where his death is reported. See also note on 13:9.

12:2–3 Jehoash (i.e., Joash; see note on 11:21) **did what was right**. He was a relatively good king who rejected idolatrous worship (contrast the verdict on the idolaters Jehoram and Ahaziah in 8:18, 27), but the **high places were not taken away** (see note on 1 Kings 3:2; cf. also 1 Kings 15:14; 22:43).

12:4–5 repair the house. The temple of the Lord had suffered neglect during the years in which the worship of Baal was encouraged, and to neglect a temple in the ancient world was to neglect its deity and to risk his or her disapproval and the possible undermining of a king's legitimate authority to rule (which is why a king such as Esarhaddon of Assyria had servants traveling around his realm and sending him reports about the state of its temples). Three sources of income are specified as the repair project gets underway here. Two of these represent regular temple income: payments made in relation to the periodic census of male Israelites (**money for which each man is assessed**; Ex. 30:11–16), and monetary equivalents for things dedicated to God (**money from the assessment of persons**; Lev. 27:1–25). **Money that a man's heart prompts him to bring** refers to a special fund-raising campaign similar to that initiated by Moses, at God's command, in Exodus 35 (where people also give from the heart; Ex. 35:5, 21–22, 26, 29).

12:7–12 hand it over. Joash's initial plan was to leave the matter to the **priests** themselves (vv. 4–5). But this plan fails because, it is implied, the priests are not eager to spend good money on mere buildings, even though they are well provided for through the normal sacrificial system (v. 16; cf. Num. 5:5–10). Joash himself therefore takes control of the project, ensuring that the income goes directly to the **workmen** appointed to supervise the work.

12:13 But there were not made . . . any vessels of gold, or of silver. Joash's achievements, after all his efforts, are somewhat disappointing: only a very humble restoration of the temple has taken place, and it stands as a poor reflection of its former glory (cf. 1 Kings 7:50). Once again the reader is reminded of the "affliction of the house of David" theme (1 Kings 11:39) that has surfaced in the description of even the best of the post-Solomonic Judean kings.

12:17–18 took all the sacred gifts. The theme of affliction continues: Judah, too, is oppressed by **Hazael king of Syria** (cf. 10:32–33 for his assault on Israel), as he turns east from the Philistine city of **Gath** to attack **Jerusalem**. This presupposes that Hazael could move at will through Israelite territory to the north, so that the campaign is best dated during the reign of

when Hazael set his face [e]to go up against Jerusalem, [18]Jehoash king of Judah [f]took all the
sacred gifts that Jehoshaphat and Jehoram and Ahaziah his fathers, the kings of Judah,
had dedicated, [g]and his own sacred gifts, and all the gold that was found in the treasuries
of the house of the LORD and of the king's house, and sent these to Hazael king of Syria.
Then Hazael went away from Jerusalem.

The Death of Joash

[19]Now the rest of the acts of Joash and all that he did, are they not written in the Book
of the Chronicles of the Kings of Judah? [20] [h]His servants arose and made a conspiracy [i]and
struck down Joash in the house of [j]Millo, on the way that goes down to Silla. [21]It was
[k]Jozacar the son of Shimeath and Jehozabad the son of [k]Shomer, his servants, who struck
him down, so that he died. And they buried him with his fathers in the city of David, [l]and
Amaziah his son reigned in his place.

Jehoahaz Reigns in Israel

13 In the twenty-third year of Joash the son of Ahaziah, king of Judah, Jehoahaz the
son of Jehu began to reign over Israel in Samaria, and he reigned seventeen years.
[2]He did what was evil in the sight of the LORD and followed the sins of Jeroboam the son of
Nebat, [m]which he made Israel to sin; he did not depart from them. [3] [n]And the anger of the
LORD was kindled against Israel, and he gave them continually into the hand of [o]Hazael
king of Syria and into the hand of [p]Ben-hadad the son of Hazael. [4]Then Jehoahaz [q]sought
the favor of the LORD, and the LORD listened to him, [r]for he saw the oppression of Israel,
how the king of Syria oppressed them. [5](Therefore the LORD gave Israel [s]a savior, so that
they escaped from the hand of the Syrians, and the people of Israel lived in [t]their homes
as formerly. [6]Nevertheless, they did not depart from the sins of the house of Jeroboam,
[m]which he made Israel to sin, but walked[1] in them; and [u]the Asherah also remained in
Samaria.) [7]For there was not left to Jehoahaz an army of more than fifty horsemen and
ten chariots and ten thousand footmen, for the king of Syria had destroyed them and
made them like the dust [v]at threshing. [8]Now the rest of the acts of Jehoahaz and all that
he did, and his might, are they not written in the Book of the Chronicles of the Kings of
Israel? [9]So Jehoahaz slept with his fathers, and they buried him in Samaria, and Joash his
son reigned in his place.

Jehoash Reigns in Israel

[10]In the thirty-seventh year of Joash king of Judah, Jehoash[2] the son of Jehoahaz began
to reign over Israel in Samaria, and he reigned sixteen years. [11]He also did what was evil in

[1] Septuagint, Syriac, Targum, Vulgate; Hebrew *he walked* [2] *Jehoash* is an alternate spelling of *Joash* (son of Jehoahaz) as in verses 9, 12–14; also verse 25

17 [e][2 Chr. 24:23, 24]
18 [f]ch. 16:8; 18:15, 16; 1 Kgs. 15:18; [ch. 14:14; 1 Kgs. 14:26] [g]ver. 4
20 [h]For ver. 20, 21, see 2 Chr. 24:25-27 [i]ch. 14:5 [j][2 Sam. 5:9]
21 [k][2 Chr. 24:26] [l]ch. 14:1

Chapter 13

2 [m]See 1 Kgs. 14:16
3 [n][Judg. 2:14] [o]ch. 8:12; [1 Kgs. 19:17] [p]ver. 24, 25
4 [q]Ex. 32:11; [Ps. 78:34] [r]ch. 14:26; Ex. 3:7, 9
5 [s][Judg. 3:9; Neh. 9:27] [t]See 2 Sam. 18:17
6 [m][See ver. 2 above] [u]1 Kgs. 16:33
7 [v][Amos 1:3]

Jehu's son Jehoahaz (c. 815–799 B.C.), who fared even worse than his father at the hands of Syria (13:1–7, 22–23). Like Asa, Joash knows no Solomonic peace during his rule, and tribute flows north from Israel to Syria, instead of south from Syria to Israel (cf. 1 Kings 15:18–24). Both Asa and Joash in fact empty the **treasuries of the house of the LORD and of the king's house**. Long past are those days when the king of Israel had "rest on every side" (1 Kings 5:4). Much later, Hag. 2:7–8 (see notes there) foretold that one day the nations would bring their wealth to the temple.

12:19 Chronicles of the Kings. See note on 1 Kings 14:19.

12:20 Silla was probably a neighborhood of Jerusalem below "the Millo" (see note on 2 Sam. 5:9), and the **house of Millo** was perhaps a prominent building in the Millo.

13:1–25 *Jehoahaz and Jehoash.* The reader is now updated on what has been happening in Israel during the reigns of those two kings whose accessions took place within Joash of Judah's lifetime.

13:1–5 the anger of the LORD was kindled against Israel. Under normal circumstances, one might expect the appearance of a prophet to announce the end of Jehu's house because of its sins (v. 2; cf. 1 Kings 14:6–16). The divine promise to Jehu, however, is functioning like the earlier promise to David (2 Sam. 7:1–17; 2 Kings 10:30), and the Israelite royal house is for the moment being treated like the Judean royal house. The anger of the Lord is thus expressed only in the form of Syrian oppression.

13:4–5 Jehoahaz sought the favor of the LORD. The language throughout vv. 3–5 is reminiscent of the book of Judges, where Israel's recurring idolatry was followed by divine anger, expressing itself in oppression by foreigners. When Israel cried out under this oppression, God sent a **savior** (2 Kings 13:5; cf. Judg. 3:9, 15) to rescue them. It seems likely that the "savior" in question here is Assyria, whose interest in Syria-Palestine was rekindled in the closing years of the ninth century B.C., resulting in a measure of relief for Israel as the attention of Damascus necessarily turned to the north.

13:6 the Asherah . . . remained in Samaria. On Asherim, see note on 1 Kings 14:15. The English translation here implies that this is the same Asherah that Ahab made earlier (mentioned in 1 Kings 16:33), which in that case must have survived Jehu's reformation. But it could also be translated "an Asherah (once again) stood in Samaria."

13:7–8 dust at threshing. See note on 1 Kings 22:10–12. God's punishment is so severe that it reduces the **army** of Jehoahaz to little more than a remnant, as insubstantial as chaff in the breeze. On the **Chronicles of the Kings** (also in 2 Kings 13:12), see note on 1 Kings 14:19.

13:9 The next king of Israel, introduced here as **Joash**, is referred to as both Joash (e.g., v. 14) and Jehoash (v. 25) throughout the rest of this chapter and in ch. 14 (e.g., 14:8–9). He is not to be confused with Joash of Judah; see note on 11:21.

11[m][See ver. 2 above]
12[w]ch. 14:15 [x]See ver. 14-19, 25 [y]See ch. 14:8-14
14[z]ch. 2:12
17[a]1 Kgs. 20:26
19[b]See Deut. 33:1 [c]ver. 25
20[d]ch. 1:1; 3:7; 24:2
22[e]ch. 8:12
23[f]ch. 14:27 [g][Ex. 2:24, 25] [h]Ex. 32:13
25[i][ch. 10:32; 14:25] [j]ver. 18, 19; [Amos 1:4]
Chapter 14
1[k]For ver. 1-6, see 2 Chr. 25:1-4 [l][ch. 13:10] [m]ch. 12:21

the sight of the LORD. He did not depart from all the sins of Jeroboam the son of Nebat,
[m]which he made Israel to sin, but he walked in them. 12 [w]Now the rest of the acts of Joash
[x]and all that he did, [y]and the might with which he fought against Amaziah king of Judah,
are they not written in the Book of the Chronicles of the Kings of Israel? 13 So Joash slept
with his fathers, and Jeroboam sat on his throne. And Joash was buried in Samaria with
the kings of Israel.

The Death of Elisha

14 Now when Elisha had fallen sick with the illness of which he was to die, Joash king of
Israel went down to him and wept before him, crying, [z]"My father, my father! The chariots
of Israel and its horsemen!" 15 And Elisha said to him, "Take a bow and arrows." So he took
a bow and arrows. 16 Then he said to the king of Israel, "Draw the bow," and he drew it. And
Elisha laid his hands on the king's hands. 17 And he said, "Open the window eastward,"
and he opened it. Then Elisha said, "Shoot," and he shot. And he said, "The LORD's arrow
of victory, the arrow of victory over Syria! For you shall fight the Syrians in [a]Aphek until
you have made an end of them." 18 And he said, "Take the arrows," and he took them. And
he said to the king of Israel, "Strike the ground with them." And he struck three times and
stopped. 19 Then [b]the man of God was angry with him and said, "You should have struck
five or six times; then you would have struck down Syria until you had made an end of it,
but now you will strike down Syria only [c]three times."
20 So Elisha died, and they buried him. Now bands of [d]Moabites used to invade the land
in the spring of the year. 21 And as a man was being buried, behold, a marauding band was
seen and the man was thrown into the grave of Elisha, and as soon as the man touched
the bones of Elisha, he revived and stood on his feet.
22 [e]Now Hazael king of Syria oppressed Israel all the days of Jehoahaz. 23 [f]But the LORD
was gracious to them and had compassion on them, [g]and he turned toward them, [h]because
of his covenant with Abraham, Isaac, and Jacob, and would not destroy them, nor has he
cast them from his presence until now.
24 When Hazael king of Syria died, Ben-hadad his son became king in his place. 25 Then
Jehoash the son of Jehoahaz took again from Ben-hadad the son of Hazael the cities [i]that
he had taken from Jehoahaz his father in war. [j]Three times Joash defeated him and recovered the cities of Israel.

Amaziah Reigns in Judah

14 [k]In the [l]second year of Joash the son of Joahaz, king of Israel, [m]Amaziah the son
of Joash, king of Judah, began to reign. 2 He was twenty-five years old when he
began to reign, and he reigned twenty-nine years in Jerusalem. His mother's name was

13:14–19 Joash (Jehoash of Israel) weeps because he thinks he is on the verge of defeat, having inherited depleted resources in **chariots** and **horsemen** from his father (v. 7). Elisha, who knows of other chariots and horsemen of Israel who are not of flesh and blood (2:11–12; 6:8–17), is able to promise the king a series of victories (**three times**, 13:19). The victories would have been greater in number had the king, in response to prophetic commands, been more enthusiastically obedient (**"You should have struck five or six times"**) to the words of the prophet (cf. 1 Kings 13:1–32). **Aphek** lay **eastward** of the main Israelite territory in Transjordan, the direction in which Jehoash shoots the **arrow** and from which the Syrian threat to Israel typically came.

13:20–21 grave of Elisha. Tombs in ancient Israel were often dug out of soft rock, or located in caves (e.g., Genesis 23), and they were not difficult to access. It is probably important to know at this point that Elisha's powers to resurrect live on (cf. 2 Kings 4:8–37), because as this **man was thrown** (Hb. *shalak*) into the grave of Elisha, so God will soon "throw" (or "cast") Israel into exile in Assyria (17:20, same verb, *shalak*). The Israelites need to maintain contact with the great prophets of the past through obedience to their teachings if this "death" in exile is also to be followed by an unexpected resurrection (cf. Ezek. 37:1–14).

13:23–25 his covenant with Abraham, Isaac, and Jacob. Here is a deeper reason than the one given in 10:30 for Israel's survival during Jehoahaz's reign. Long before he made promises to Jehu about kingship and a covenant with David, God was dealing with Israel's ancestors (e.g., Gen. 15:1–21; 17:1–27). That is why he kept the Syrians at bay during the reign of Jehoahaz, in spite of Israel's sin; and that is why the equally sinful Jehoash was later able to lead Israel to something of a recovery (in a period when Hazael's successor Ben-hadad III was preoccupied with the Assyrian threat to his north). Even **until now** (2 Kings 13:23), in the time that the authors are writing (after Israel's exile), Israel remains in God's **presence**.

13:25 Three times Joash (i.e., Jehoash; see note on v. 9) **defeated him**, fulfilling the prophecy of Elisha (v. 19).

14:1–15:7 *Amaziah, Jeroboam II, and Azariah.* The impetus of the recovery in the closing verses of ch. 13 continues into ch. 14, as the house of Jehu brings Israel relief, not only from Syria but also from a hostile Judah.

14:1–6 Amaziah was a relatively good (i.e., non-idolatrous) king of Judah (**he did what was right in the eyes of the LORD**), basically keeping the **Law of Moses** (Deut. 24:16) while failing like others before him to remove the **high places** (see note on 1 Kings 3:2; also 1 Kings 15:11; 22:43; 2 Kings 12:2). Yet in ways not further defined here, the kings throughout the period from Joash to Jotham are regarded by the authors of Kings as **not like David** (contrast 1 Kings 3:3; 15:11; 22:43 with 2 Kings 12:2; 14:3; 15:3, 34 in terms of what is and is not said); there is some doubt in the authors' minds about the wholeheartedness of these kings' commitment to the Lord.

Jehoaddin of Jerusalem. 3 And he did what was right in the eyes of the LORD, yet not like
David his father. He did in all things as Joash his father had done. 4 [n]But the high places
were not removed; [o]the people still sacrificed and made offerings on the high places.
5 And as soon as the royal power was [p]firmly in his hand, he struck down his servants
[q]who had struck down the king his father. 6 But he did not put to death the children
of the murderers, according to what is written in the Book of the Law of Moses, where
the LORD commanded, [r]"Fathers shall not be put to death because of their children,
nor shall children be put to death because of their fathers. But each one shall die for
his own sin."

7 [s]He struck down ten thousand Edomites in [t]the Valley of Salt and took [u]Sela by storm,
and called it [v]Joktheel, which is its name to this day.

8 [w]Then Amaziah sent messengers to Jehoash[1] the son of Jehoahaz, son of Jehu, king
of Israel, saying, "Come, [x]let us look one another in the face." 9 And Jehoash king of Israel
sent word to Amaziah king of Judah, [y]"A thistle on Lebanon sent to a cedar on Lebanon,
saying, 'Give your daughter to my son for a wife,' and a wild beast of Lebanon passed by
and trampled down the thistle. 10 You have indeed [z]struck down Edom, [a]and your heart has
lifted you up. Be content with your glory, and stay at home, for why should you provoke
trouble so that you fall, you and Judah with you?"

11 But Amaziah would not listen. So Jehoash king of Israel went up, and he and Amaziah
king of Judah [x]faced one another in battle at [b]Beth-shemesh, which belongs to Judah. 12 And
Judah was defeated by Israel, [c]and every man fled to his home. 13 And Jehoash king of Israel
captured Amaziah king of Judah, the son of Jehoash, son of Ahaziah, at Beth-shemesh,
and came to Jerusalem and broke down the wall of Jerusalem for four hundred cubits,[2]
from [d]the Ephraim Gate to [e]the Corner Gate. 14 And he seized [f]all the gold and silver, and
all the vessels that were found in the house of the LORD and in the treasuries of the king's
house, also hostages, and he returned to Samaria.

15 [g]Now the rest of the acts of Jehoash that he did, and his might, and how he fought
with Amaziah king of Judah, are they not written in the Book of the Chronicles of the
Kings of Israel? 16 And Jehoash slept with his fathers and was buried in Samaria with the
kings of Israel, and Jeroboam his son reigned in his place.

17 [h]Amaziah the son of Joash, king of Judah, lived fifteen years after the death of Jehoash

[1] *Jehoash* is an alternate spelling of *Joash* (son of Jehoahaz) as in 13:9, 12–14; also verses 9, 11–16 [2] A *cubit* was about 18 inches or 45 centimeters

4 [n]See ch. 12:3 [o][ch. 16:4]
5 [p][ch. 15:19] [q]ch. 12:20
6 [r]Deut. 24:16; [Jer. 31:30; Ezek. 18:4, 20]
7 [s]2 Chr. 25:11 [t]2 Sam. 8:13; 1 Chr. 18:12; See Ps. 60 [u]Isa. 16:1 [v][Josh. 15:38]
8 [w]For ver. 8-14, see 2 Chr. 25:17-24 [x][ch. 23:29]
9 [y][Judg. 9:8-15]
10 [z]ver. 7 [a]Deut. 8:14; 2 Chr. 26:16; 32:25; Ezek. 28:2, 5, 17
11 [x][See ver. 8 above] [b]Josh. 15:10
12 [c]See 1 Sam. 4:10
13 [d]Neh. 8:16; 12:39 [e]2 Chr. 25:23; 26:9; Jer. 31:38; Zech. 14:10
14 [f]ch. 12:18; 1 Kgs. 7:51
15 [g]ch. 13:12, 13
17 [h]For ver. 17-22, see 2 Chr. 25:25–26:2

14:7 Valley of Salt . . . Sela. Edom had revolted against Judean rule during the reign of Jehoram (8:20–22). Amaziah does not reestablish Judean control over Edom, but this important victory does ultimately have implications for Judah's ability to trade (see note on 14:22).

14:9–10 A thistle . . . sent to a cedar. Emboldened by the success of his Edomite campaign, Amaziah has decided for unstated reasons to confront the more powerful Jehoash of Israel, so Jehoash sends him this insult and warning. The point of Jehoash's parable is that a puny thistle (i.e., Amaziah), easily trampled by any **wild beast**, should not make the mistake of comparing itself in might to the immovable cedar **on Lebanon** (Jehoash). **Be content with your glory, and stay at home**. Jehoash is not seeking conflict with Amaziah.

14:11–14 Beth-shemesh. This important town on the northwest border of Judah, about 20 miles (32 km) by road from Jerusalem, guarded an important pass from the Philistine plain. Defeat here inevitably led to an assault on Jerusalem itself and the destruction of about 600 feet (183 m) of city **wall** on the northern side between the **Ephraim Gate** (the main gate in the center of the northern wall) and the **Corner Gate** (probably at the northwestern corner of the city).

14:15–17 the rest of the acts of Jehoash. . . . Amaziah . . . lived fifteen years. The surprising repetition of this information concerning Jehoash in the context of Amaziah's reign (cf. 13:12–13) may be intended to contrast the two kings in their deaths: Jehoash, who did not seek conflict with fellow Israelites, came to a natural and peaceful end, while Amaziah, the aggressor who acted as Rehoboam had been forbidden to act, met a violent death (14:19–20; cf. 1 Kings 12:22–24). It is also possible, however, that Jehoash is highlighted here because he was the effective ruler of Judah in this period, as was his son Jeroboam after him; Amaziah is not said to have "ruled" in Judah after Jehoash's death, but only to have "lived" there. On the **Chronicles of the Kings** (also 2 Kings 14:18, 28), see note on 1 Kings 14:19.

14:19 they made a conspiracy against him. Nothing is said of any reprisals by Amaziah's son against the conspirators (15:1–7; contrast 14:5–6), perhaps implying that Azariah was himself one of the mysterious "they." Amaziah was bound to be unpopular, given the consequences for the city of Jerusalem from his military folly. The city of **Lachish** where he died was the most important fortified city in Judah after Jerusalem, defending one of the east-west valleys that gave access to the Judean Plateau and Jerusalem from the coastal plains.

14:22 after the king slept with his fathers. The immediate context might lead the reader to think of Amaziah, but in fact it is Jehoash who has just been described as sleeping with his fathers (cf. v. 16). If the reference is indeed to Jehoash, this is further evidence that he was the one exercising power in Judah after the battle of Beth-shemesh (see note on vv. 15–17). It was only after his death and with the decline of Syria (see note on v. 25) that Azariah was able to consolidate Amaziah's gains in Edom by claiming the port of **Elath** at the north end of the Gulf of Aqaba (the Red Sea). This town, closely associated with Ezion-geber and the trade of the Solomonic era with the wider world (1 Kings 9:26), stood at the southern end of the great King's Highway that ran all the way north through Transjordan to Damascus and facilitated trade connections especially with southern Arabia. Presumably it was lost to Judah when Edom revolted during Jehoram's reign (2 Kings 8:20–22).

19[i]See Josh. 10:3
22[j]ch. 16:6; Deut. 2:8; [2 Chr. 8:17; 26:2]

son of Jehoahaz, king of Israel. 18 Now the rest of the deeds of Amaziah, are they not written in the Book of the Chronicles of the Kings of Judah? 19 And they made a conspiracy against him in Jerusalem, and he fled to [i]Lachish. But they sent after him to Lachish and put him to death there. 20 And they brought him on horses; and he was buried in Jerusalem with his fathers in the city of David. 21 And all the people of Judah took Azariah, who was sixteen years old, and made him king instead of his father Amaziah. 22 He built [j]Elath and restored it to Judah, after the king slept with his fathers.

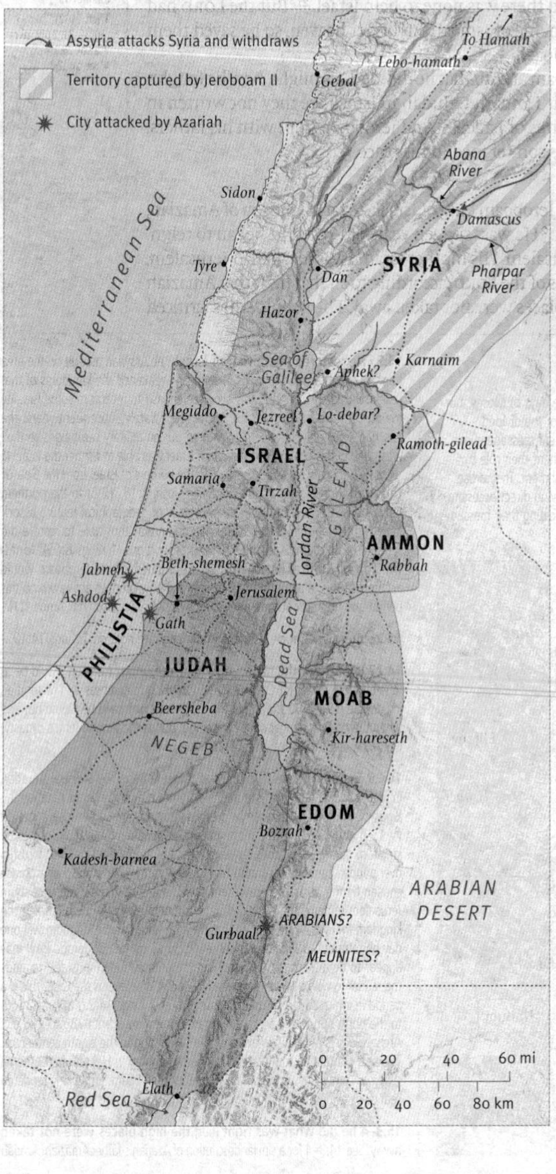

Resurgence during the Time of Azariah and Jeroboam II

c. 767–753 B.C.

A power vacuum created by Assyria's attack and withdrawal from Syria allowed Jeroboam II of Israel and Azariah (also called Uzziah) of Judah to recover land that had once belonged to their kingdoms. Jeroboam recovered much of Gilead, and Azariah recovered Elath on the Red Sea. Jeroboam also subdued much of Syria's territory for a time, and Azariah captured some Philistine towns and fought against the Arabians at Gurbaal and the Meunites.

Jeroboam II Reigns in Israel

23 In the fifteenth year of Amaziah the son of Joash, king of Judah, Jeroboam the son of
Joash, king of Israel, began to reign in Samaria, and he reigned forty-one years. 24 And he
did what was evil in the sight of the LORD. He did not depart from all the sins of Jeroboam
the son of Nebat, [k]which he made Israel to sin. 25 [l]He restored the border of Israel [m]from
Lebo-hamath as far as the Sea of [n]the Arabah, according to the word of the LORD, the God
of Israel, which he spoke by his servant [o]Jonah the son of Amittai, the prophet, who was
from [p]Gath-hepher. 26 For the LORD [q]saw that the affliction of Israel was very bitter, [r]for
there was none left, bond or free, and there was none to help Israel. 27 [s]But the LORD had
not said that he would blot out the name of Israel from under heaven, so he saved them
by the hand of Jeroboam the son of Joash.
28 Now the rest of the acts of Jeroboam and all that he did, and his might, how he fought,
and how he restored [t]Damascus and [u]Hamath to Judah in Israel, are they not written in
the Book of the Chronicles of the Kings of Israel? 29 And Jeroboam slept with his fathers,
the kings of Israel, and Zechariah his son reigned in his place.

Azariah Reigns in Judah

15 [v]In the twenty-seventh year of Jeroboam king of Israel, [w]Azariah the son of Amaziah,
king of Judah, began to reign. 2 He was [x]sixteen years old when he began to reign,
and he reigned fifty-two years in Jerusalem. His mother's name was Jecoliah of Jerusalem.
3 And he did what was right in the eyes of the LORD, according to all that his father Amaziah
had done. 4 [y]Nevertheless, the high places were not taken away. The people still sacrificed

24 [k]See 1 Kgs. 14:16
25 [l][ch. 10:32; 13:25] [m]See 1 Kgs. 8:65 [n]See Deut. 3:17 [o]Jonah 1:1; [Matt. 12:39, 40] [p]Josh. 19:13
26 [q]Ex. 3:7; [ch. 13:4] [r]See Deut. 32:36
27 [s][ch. 13:5, 23]
28 [t][2 Sam. 8:6; 1 Kgs. 11:24; 1 Chr. 18:5, 6] [u]2 Chr. 8:3

Chapter 15

1 [v][ch. 14:17] [w][ver. 13, 30, 32, 34; 2 Chr. 26:1]
2 [x]2 Chr. 26:3, 4
4 [y]See ch. 12:3

Prophets of Israel and Judah

c. 875–430 B.C.

Prophets had been a part of Israelite society since the days of Moses, but the complex political, religious, and social situations of the divided monarchy made their role of communicating God's clear message even more pronounced. Unlike priests, prophets did not inherit their role by birth and often were not part of the religious establishment. They arose from various parts of Israel and Judah, with some having direct access to the king (e.g., Elijah and Elisha) and others communicating their messages directly to the people (e.g., Amos and Nahum).

14:25 He restored the border of Israel. The Assyrian assault on the area north of Israel (alluded to in 13:5) seriously weakened the kingdoms of that region, including Syria, and this allowed Jehoash to recapture some Israelite towns from the Syrians (13:25). In the immediately subsequent years, the Assyrian kings only infrequently ventured out on military campaigns to their west, and in this context Jeroboam II of Israel was able to further the Israelite recovery begun by his father, extending the borders of Israel from the **Sea of the Arabah** in the south (the Dead Sea, Josh. 3:16; 12:3) to the northern **Lebo-hamath** ("entrance to Hamath," a city or geographical feature associated with Hamath in central Syria). Jeroboam was thus able to restore the territory of northern Israel to Solomonic proportions (1 Kings 8:65). **Jonah the son of Amittai** (cf. Jonah 1:1) had prophesied that Jeroboam would accomplish this, although Jonah was not the only prophet active during this period and his was not the only message for Israel (cf. Hos. 1:1; Amos 1:1).

14:26 there was none left, bond or free. See note on 1 Kings 14:10.

14:27 To **blot out the name of Israel from under heaven** would be to destroy Israel utterly (cf. Deut. 9:14–19), making forgiveness and restoration impossible (cf. Deut. 29:20). This **the LORD had not said** he would do; and when there was a danger of its happening, during the time of Jehu's dynasty, God took steps to deliver Israel from her enemies.

14:28 Judah in Israel. This unusual phrase reflects the unusual situation in Judah and Israel during the reigns of Jehoash and Jeroboam II, when the kings of Israel were apparently in effective control of Judah (see notes on vv. 15–17, 19, 22). It is perhaps an Israelite designation for the whole restored kingdom during Jeroboam's reign, representing Jeroboam's claim to lordship over a Judah currently integrated into **Israel**. Alternatively, it could be a phrase chosen by the authors to represent their view that the Davidic dynasty in Jerusalem remains the chosen dynasty, that Judah is the heartland of the kingdom that rightly belongs to that dynasty, and that the kingdom will one day be returned to Judah in its entirety (cf. 1 Kings 11:39). Jeroboam II may appear to be a "second Solomon," but the phrase "Judah in Israel" reminds the reader to whom this territory really belongs. Whatever is the case, this is a period in which territory is being **restored** (cf. 2 Kings 14:22) to Israel, both to the north and to the south. Jeroboam II ruled Israel from 786 to 746 B.C. Archaeologists at Megiddo discovered a seal dating to the eighth century B.C. The seal contains a roaring lion; above the animal in Hebrew is the name "Shema," and below is the phrase "Servant of Jeroboam." The finely rendered seal gives evidence of a high level of craftsmanship at this time.

15:3–4 he did what was right [but] **the high places were not taken away**. See 14:3–4 for a similar description of Azariah's father Amaziah. Azariah

5[z]For ver. 5-7, see 2 Chr. 26:21-23 [a]See Lev. 13:46
7[b][2 Chr. 26:23]
9[c]See 1 Kgs. 14:16
10[d][Amos 7:9]
12[e]ch. 10:30
13[f][ver. 1] [g]1 Kgs. 16:24
14[h]1 Kgs. 14:17
16[i]See ch. 8:12
19[j]1 Chr. 5:26 [k][ch. 14:5]

and made offerings on the high places. **5** [z]And the LORD touched the king, so that he was
a leper[1] to the day of his death, [a]and he lived in a separate house.[2] And Jotham the king's
son was over the household, governing the people of the land. **6** Now the rest of the acts
of Azariah, and all that he did, are they not written in the Book of the Chronicles of the
Kings of Judah? **7** And Azariah slept with his fathers, and they buried him with his fathers
[b]in the city of David, and Jotham his son reigned in his place.

Zechariah Reigns in Israel

8 In the thirty-eighth year of Azariah king of Judah, Zechariah the son of Jeroboam
reigned over Israel in Samaria six months. **9** And he did what was evil in the sight of the
LORD, as his fathers had done. He did not depart from the sins of Jeroboam the son of
Nebat, [c]which he made Israel to sin. **10** Shallum the son of Jabesh conspired against him
and [d]struck him down at Ibleam and put him to death and reigned in his place. **11** Now the
rest of the deeds of Zechariah, behold, they are written in the Book of the Chronicles of
the Kings of Israel. **12** (This was [e]the promise of the LORD that he gave to Jehu, "Your sons
shall sit on the throne of Israel to the fourth generation." And so it came to pass.)

Shallum Reigns in Israel

13 Shallum the son of Jabesh began to reign in the thirty-ninth year of [f]Uzziah[3] king of
Judah, and he reigned one month in [g]Samaria. **14** Then Menahem the son of Gadi came
up from [h]Tirzah and came to Samaria, and he struck down Shallum the son of Jabesh in
Samaria and put him to death and reigned in his place. **15** Now the rest of the deeds of
Shallum, and the conspiracy that he made, behold, they are written in the Book of the
Chronicles of the Kings of Israel. **16** At that time Menahem sacked Tiphsah and all who
were in it and its territory from Tirzah on, because they did not open it to him. Therefore
he sacked it, [i]and he ripped open all the women in it who were pregnant.

Menahem Reigns in Israel

17 In the thirty-ninth year of Azariah king of Judah, Menahem the son of Gadi began
to reign over Israel, and he reigned ten years in Samaria. **18** And he did what was evil in
the sight of the LORD. He did not depart all his days from all the sins of Jeroboam the
son of Nebat, which he made Israel to sin. **19** [j]Pul[4] the king of Assyria came against the
land, and Menahem gave [j]Pul a thousand talents[5] of silver, that he might help him [k]to
confirm his hold on the royal power. **20** Menahem exacted the money from Israel, that is,
from all the wealthy men, fifty shekels[6] of silver from every man, to give to the king of
Assyria. So the king of Assyria turned back and did not stay there in the land. **21** Now the

[1] *Leprosy* was a term for several skin diseases; see Leviticus 13 [2] The meaning of the Hebrew word is uncertain [3] Another name for *Azariah* [4] Another name for *Tiglath-pileser III* (compare verse 29) [5] A *talent* was about 75 pounds or 34 kilograms [6] A *shekel* was about 2/5 ounce or 11 grams

is also called Uzziah in various places (cf. 15:13, 30, 32, 34). Azariah's (Uzziah's) reign saw the beginning of Isaiah's prophetic ministry (Isa. 1:1; 6:1).

15:5 a leper to the day of his death. At some point during his reign, Azariah became a leper (see note on 5:1) and was unable to govern, occupying a **separate house**—lit. in Hebrew "the house of freedom" (*bet hakhopshit*), which is probably a metaphor for being relieved of responsibility in government more than a description of his living conditions. The king was seriously incapacitated and was regarded as effectively dead (cf. the related Hb. word *khopshi* in connection with the world of the dead in Job 3:19, "free," and Ps. 88:5, "set loose"). Cf. also note on 2 Chron. 26:21–23. His son **Jotham** therefore exercised effective governmental power in Judah.

15:6 On the **Chronicles of the Kings** (also vv. 11, 15, 21, 26, 31, 36), see note on 1 Kings 14:19.

15:8–31 *Israel's Last Days.* Israel's respite from foreign oppression is as temporary as her domination of Judah. With the passing of Jeroboam II, the nation has reached the "fourth generation" of the divine promise to Jehu (10:30) and has returned to the unstable government of the northern kingdom implied by 1 Kings 14:15 and illustrated in 1 Kings 14–16 (before the houses of Omri and Jehu were established). Reign now follows reign in quick succession, as the reader moves toward the end of Israel's story.

15:8–12 After the glorious reign of Jeroboam II, the reign of his son **Zechariah** marks the end of the dynasty of Jehu, as foretold in 10:30.

15:16–22 Menahem sacked Tiphsah. This attack on an important city on the Euphrates River is the last, brutal action of an Israelite king claiming control of a Solomon-like empire (cf. 1 Kings 4:24). Such a campaign would probably have taken place early in his reign, either before the campaigns of **Pul the king of Assyria** in 743–740 B.C. began, or during these years as part of the anti-Assyrian struggle in the region. "Pul" is the Hebrew version of the Akkadian "Pulu," a short name for Tiglath-pileser III, known from the Babylonian king lists. Tiglath-pileser's goal was apparently to establish an Assyrian trading center on the border with Egypt, and he required control of the intervening regions to accomplish this and to ensure safe passage for trade between Philistia and Assyria. Menahem's tributary payment of **a thousand talents of silver** makes him Assyria's friend for the time being, and is mentioned in Assyrian records relating to Tiglath-pileser's successful campaign of 738 B.C. against Syria and Phoenicia.

15:20 Menahem exacted the money from Israel. Sixty-three ostraca were found at Samaria that record tax payments dated by years of the king. These may in fact have been the additional tax payments that Menahem imposed on Israel to pay off the Assyrian king Pul in 738 B.C.

rest of the deeds of Menahem and all that he did, are they not written in the Book of the
Chronicles of the Kings of Israel? 22 And Menahem slept with his fathers, and Pekahiah
his son reigned in his place.

Pekahiah Reigns in Israel

23 In the fiftieth year of Azariah king of Judah, Pekahiah the son of Menahem began
to reign over Israel in Samaria, and he reigned two years. 24 And he did what was evil in
the sight of the LORD. He did not turn away from the sins of Jeroboam the son of Nebat,
[c]which he made Israel to sin. 25 And Pekah the son of Remaliah, his captain, conspired
against him with fifty men of the people of Gilead, and struck him down in Samaria, in
the citadel of the king's house with Argob and Arieh; he put him to death and reigned
in his place. 26 Now the rest of the deeds of Pekahiah and all that he did, behold, they are
written in the Book of the Chronicles of the Kings of Israel.

Pekah Reigns in Israel

27 In the fifty-second year of Azariah king of Judah, Pekah the son of Remaliah began
to reign over Israel in Samaria, and he reigned twenty years. 28 And he did what was evil
in the sight of the LORD. He did not depart from the sins of Jeroboam the son of Nebat,
[l]which he made Israel to sin.

29 In the days of Pekah king of Israel, [m]Tiglath-pileser king of Assyria came and captured
[n]Ijon, [o]Abel-beth-maacah, Janoah, [p]Kedesh, [q]Hazor, Gilead, and [r]Galilee, all the land of
Naphtali, and he carried the people captive to Assyria. 30 Then Hoshea the son of Elah

24 [c][See ver. 9 above]
28 [l]See 1 Kgs. 14:16
29 [m]ch. 16:7; [1 Chr. 5:6, 26; 2 Chr. 28:20] [n]1 Kgs. 15:20 [o]2 Sam. 20:14, 15 [p]Josh. 19:37 [q]Josh. 11:1; Judg. 4:2; 1 Kgs. 9:15 [r]Isa. 9:1

15:27–31 Pekah is the last of the Israelite kings to rule during the long reign of **Azariah** in Judah. Pekah's **twenty years** in power appear to be counted from before the period when he **began to reign over Israel in Samaria** and governed only part of the Israelite territory mentioned in v. 29; for if Menahem was king of Israel in 738 B.C. (see note on vv. 16–22) and Pekah was succeeded by Hoshea around 732 (see note on 17:1–2), Pekah could not have reigned for 20 years over **Israel** as a whole. The end of the period in which he did reign over *all* Israel saw **Tiglath-pileser king of Assyria** annex much of Israel's northern and eastern territory during his campaigns of 733–732 B.C. (see notes on 15:37; 16:7–9). This list of conquered towns to the west of the Jordan, however, is not exhaustive but representative (moving from **Ijon**, at the northern end of the Huleh Valley and guarding the main highway leading from Palestine to Syria, to **Hazor**, the largest site in Upper Galilee and occupying the most strategic position in the region). The Assyrians also deported a significant percentage of Israel's population, which was a major feature of Tiglath-pileser's imperial policy, designed to increase the Assyrian labor force and reduce the possibility of further opposition among subjugated peoples.

15:32–16:20 *Jotham and Ahaz.* The house of David has seen three of its last four kings assassinated, and the fourth set aside his power because of illness. Things are not about to improve, as Jotham and his apostate son Ahaz are introduced.

15:34–35 the high places were not removed. See note on 1 Kings 3:2. Jotham was a relatively good (i.e., non-idolatrous) king. Nevertheless, he is described as being like **his father** rather than like David (see note on 2 Kings 14:1–6), and he failed to centralize worship of the Lord in Jerusalem, allowing people to continue worshiping at the "high places." The **upper gate** is the "gate behind the guards" mentioned in 11:6, presumably damaged in the course of Jehoash's incursion into Jerusalem in 14:13–14. Jotham's reign saw the beginning of Micah's prophetic ministry (Mic. 1:1).

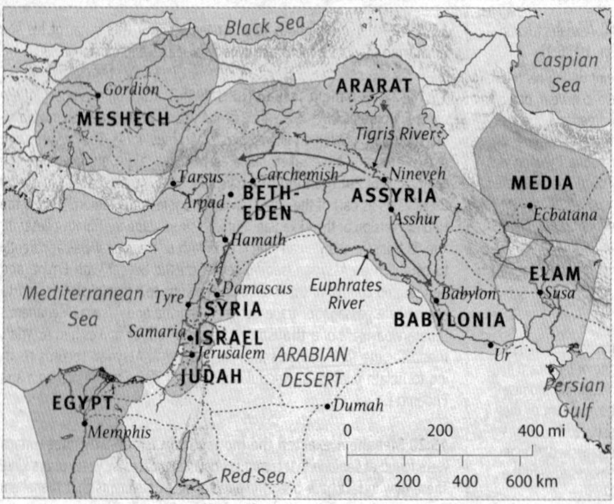

The Resurgence of Assyrian Influence
c. 740 B.C.

Looming over most of the latter history of the divided monarchy is the growing power and influence of Assyria. The resurgence of this ancient empire dominated much of the politics of the ancient Near East from the time of Jeroboam and Azariah until the empire's demise at the end of the seventh century B.C. Israel bore the brunt of Assyria's forays into Palestine, though Judah experienced its share of attacks as well. Assyria would eventually engulf nearly the entire Near East from Ur to Ararat to Egypt.

30[s][ch. 17:1]
33[t]For ver. 33, 34, see 2 Chr. 27:1, 2
34[u]ver. 3; [2 Chr. 27:6]
35[v]See ch. 12:3

made a conspiracy against Pekah the son of Remaliah and struck him down and put him to
death and reigned in his place, [s]in the twentieth year of Jotham the son of Uzziah. **31** Now
the rest of the acts of Pekah and all that he did, behold, they are written in the Book of the
Chronicles of the Kings of Israel.

Jotham Reigns in Judah

32 In the second year of Pekah the son of Remaliah, king of Israel, Jotham the son of
Uzziah, king of Judah, began to reign. **33** He was [t]twenty-five years old when he began
to reign, and he reigned sixteen years in Jerusalem. His mother's name was Jerusha the
daughter of Zadok. **34** And he did what was right in the eyes of the LORD, [u]according to
all that his father Uzziah had done. **35** [v]Nevertheless, the high places were not removed.

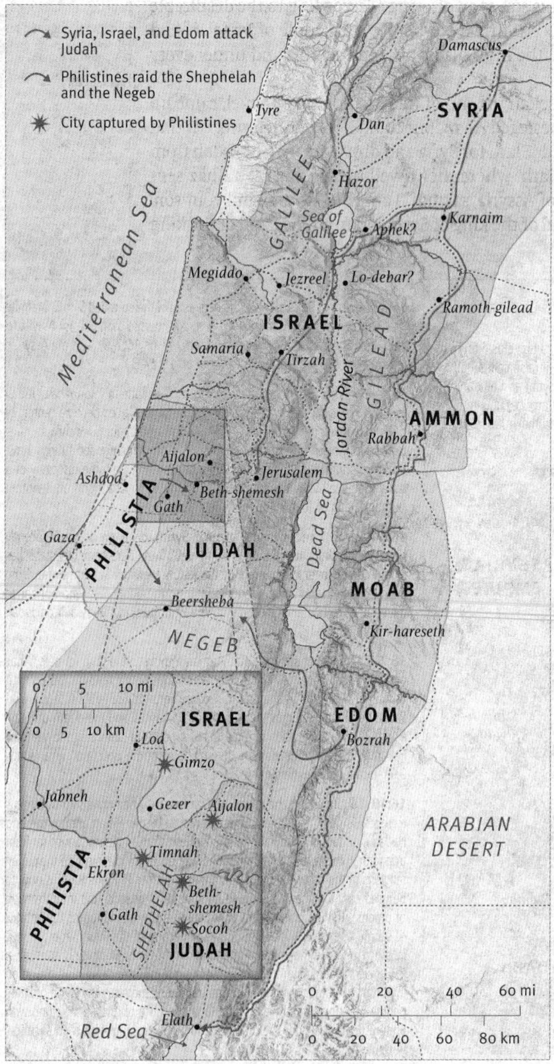

Syria and Israel Attack Judah
c. 740–732 B.C.

As the Assyrian Empire expanded westward, Syria and Israel sought to compel Judah and the other nearby states to form an anti-Assyrian alliance. Judah refused, leading Syria and Israel to attack Jerusalem. Syria also wrested Elath from Judah and gave it to the Edomites. The Edomites may have also raided Judah and taken captives at this time (see 2 Chron. 28:17). The Philistines, who may have been part of the anti-Assyrian alliance, attacked Judah as well, capturing several cities in the Shephelah and the Negeb (see 2 Chron. 28:18).

The people still sacrificed and made offerings on the high places. He built [w]the upper
gate of the house of the LORD. 36 Now the rest of the acts of Jotham and all that he did,
are they not written in the Book of the Chronicles of the Kings of Judah? 37 In those days
the LORD began to send [x]Rezin the king of Syria and [x]Pekah the son of Remaliah against
Judah. 38 Jotham slept with his fathers and was buried with his fathers in the city of David
his father, and Ahaz his son reigned in his place.

Ahaz Reigns in Judah

16 In the seventeenth year of Pekah the son of Remaliah, Ahaz the son of Jotham,
king of Judah, began to reign. 2 Ahaz was [y]twenty years old when he began to
reign, and he reigned sixteen years in Jerusalem. And he did not do what was right in
the eyes of the LORD his God, as his father David had done, 3 but he walked in the way of
the kings of Israel. [z]He even burned his son as an offering,[1] [a]according to the despicable
practices of the nations whom the LORD drove out before the people of Israel. 4 [b]And
he sacrificed and made offerings [c]on the high places and on the hills and under every
green tree.

5 [d]Then Rezin king of Syria and [d]Pekah the son of Remaliah, king of Israel, came up
to wage war on Jerusalem, and they besieged Ahaz [e]but could not conquer him. 6 At that
time Rezin the king of Syria recovered [f]Elath for Syria and drove the men of Judah from
[f]Elath, and the Edomites came to Elath, where they dwell to this day. 7 [g]So Ahaz sent
messengers to [h]Tiglath-pileser king of Assyria, saying, "I am your servant and your son.
Come up and rescue me from the hand of the king of Syria and from the hand of the king

[1] *Or made his son pass through the fire*

35 [w]2 Chr. 23:20; 27:3
37 [x]ch. 16:5; Isa. 7:1

Chapter 16

2 [y]For ver. 2-4, see 2 Chr. 28:1-4
3 [z][Ps. 106:37, 38]; See Lev. 18:21 [a]ch. 21:2; [Deut. 12:31; 18:9]
4 [b][ch. 14:4] [c]Deut. 12:2; 1 Kgs. 14:23
5 [d]ch. 15:37 [e][2 Chr. 28:5, 6]
6 [f]See ch. 14:22
7 [g]See 2 Chr. 28:16 [h]See ch. 15:29

Assyria Captures Northern Israel

733 B.C.

King Ahaz of Judah, suffering attacks on all sides due to his refusal to join an alliance against Assyria, called upon Tiglath-pileser III (also called Pul) of Assyria for help. The Assyrians captured Damascus (Syria) and all of Galilee and Gilead from Israel. Ahaz's petition came at a price, however, for he was required to pay a large tribute to Assyria and make Judah a vassal kingdom of the empire.

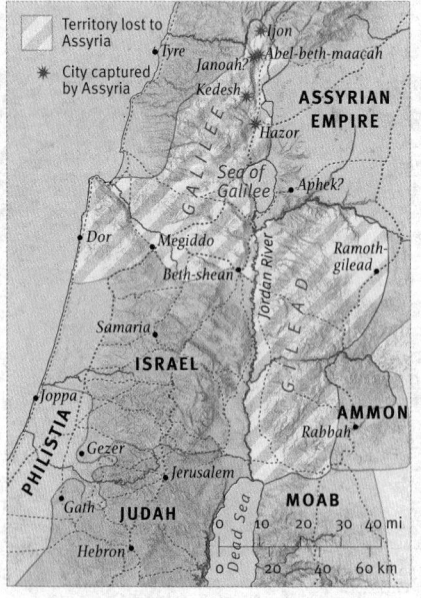

15:37 Rezin . . . Pekah. This is the beginning of the so-called Syro-Ephraimite War seen so prominently in Isaiah 7–9. In due course Judah will ask Assyria to help fight off Israel and Syria (see note on 2 Kings 16:7–9), and the Assyrian response is reflected already in the note on 15:27–31.

16:1–4 he did not do what was right. With Jotham's son **Ahaz**, Judah returns to officially sanctioned idolatry as the **high places** become centers of Canaanite religion (cf. 1 Kings 14:23–24). This religion includes child sacrifice to the god Molech (Ahaz **burned his son as an offering**; see 1 Kings 11:7; 16:34). Confirmation for the rule of Ahaz has come from the discovery of a bulla (clay seal) with the inscription, "Belonging to Ahaz [son of] Yehotam [Jotham], king of Judah" (see note on 2 Kings 18:1).

16:6 Rezin . . . recovered Elath for Syria. This town had only recently been won back for Judah by Azariah (14:22). Rezin here briefly reestablishes Syrian control over the entirety of the King's Highway in Transjordan from Damascus to Elath, and surrenders Elath to the Edomites, who appear to have taken part as allies, along with the Philistines, in the assault on Judah (2 Chron. 28:17–18).

16:7–9 I am your servant. Rather than turning to the Lord for help, Ahaz accepts vassal status to Assyria and requests his new overlord's help, which arrives in the form of the Assyrian campaigns of 733–732 B.C. in Syria-Palestine. This resulted in the capture of Damascus and the death of Rezin as well as the annexation of large parts of northern Israel and the death of Pekah (15:29–30). **Kir** was the original home of the people of Syria (Amos 9:7), located somewhere in Mesopotamia.

16:10–16 the altar that was at Damascus. Ahaz travels to Damascus to meet his new overlord and is so impressed by this Syrian altar to the god Hadad that he has a copy of it installed in Jerusalem. Ahaz has strayed far from true faith in the Lord, and his religion is full-fledged syncretism with the pagan religions of the other nations. The old **bronze altar** (1 Kings 8:64) is now to be used only for Ahaz **to inquire by**, i.e., for divination (the interpretation of omens). This probably refers to extispicy, the examination of the entrails of sacrificial animals, focusing on the inspection of the liver (hepatoscopy), in order to divine the will and intentions of the gods. Extispicy is attested in the ancient Near East from early in the second millennium B.C. and played an important role not only at royal courts but also in the everyday life of ordinary people. The god Hadad was central to the practice of divination, along with Shamash the sun god. The practice is forbidden, along with child sacrifice, in Deut. 18:10.

8[i]See ch. 12:18
9[j][2 Chr. 28:21] [k][Amos 1:5] [l]Isa. 22:6; Amos 1:5; 9:7
10[m]See ch. 15:29 [n]Isa. 8:2
12[o]See 2 Chr. 26:16-19
14[p]2 Chr. 4:1 [q][Ex. 40:6, 29] [r]ver. 11
15[s]Ex. 29:39-41 [t]ver. 14
17[u]1 Kgs. 7:23, 25
19[v][2 Chr. 28:26]
20[w][2 Chr. 28:27]

Chapter 17

1[x][ch. 15:30]
3[y]For ver. 3-7, see ch. 18:9-12 [z][Hos. 10:14]

of Israel, who are attacking me." **8** Ahaz also [i]took the silver and gold that was found in
the house of the LORD and in the treasures of the king's house and sent a present to the
king of Assyria. **9** [j]And the king of Assyria listened to him. The king of Assyria marched up
against Damascus [k]and took it, carrying its people captive to [l]Kir, and he killed Rezin.
10 When King Ahaz went to Damascus to meet [m]Tiglath-pileser king of Assyria, he
saw the altar that was at Damascus. And King Ahaz sent to [n]Uriah the priest a model of
the altar, and its pattern, exact in all its details. **11** And Uriah the priest built the altar; in
accordance with all that King Ahaz had sent from Damascus, so Uriah the priest made
it, before King Ahaz arrived from Damascus. **12** And when the king came from Damascus,
the king viewed the altar. [o]Then the king drew near to the altar and went up on it **13** and
burned his burnt offering and his grain offering and poured his drink offering and threw
the blood of his peace offerings on the altar. **14** And [p]the bronze altar that was before the
LORD he removed [q]from the front of the house, from the place between [r]his altar and
the house of the LORD, and put it on the north side of [r]his altar. **15** And King Ahaz commanded Uriah the priest, saying, "On the great altar burn [s]the morning burnt offering
and the evening grain offering and the king's burnt offering and his grain offering, with
the burnt offering of all the people of the land, and their grain offering and their drink
offering. And throw on it all the blood of the burnt offering and all the blood of the sacrifice, but [t]the bronze altar shall be for me to inquire by." **16** Uriah the priest did all this,
as King Ahaz commanded.
17 And King Ahaz cut off the frames of the stands and removed the basin from them,
and he took down [u]the sea[1] from off the bronze oxen that were under it and put it on
a stone pedestal. **18** And the covered way for the Sabbath that had been built inside the
house and the outer entrance for the king he caused to go around the house of the LORD,
because of the king of Assyria. **19** Now the rest of the acts of Ahaz that he did, are they
not written [v]in the Book of the Chronicles of the Kings of Judah? **20** And Ahaz slept with
his fathers and [w]was buried with his fathers in the city of David, and Hezekiah his son
reigned in his place.

Hoshea Reigns in Israel

17 In the twelfth year of Ahaz king of Judah, [x]Hoshea the son of Elah began to reign
in Samaria over Israel, and he reigned nine years. **2** And he did what was evil in the
sight of the LORD, yet not as the kings of Israel who were before him. **3** [y]Against him came
up [z]Shalmaneser king of Assyria. And Hoshea became his vassal and paid him tribute.
4 But the king of Assyria found treachery in Hoshea, for he had sent messengers to So,
king of Egypt, and offered no tribute to the king of Assyria, as he had done year by year.
Therefore the king of Assyria shut him up and bound him in prison. **5** Then the king of
Assyria invaded all the land and came to Samaria, and for three years he besieged it.

[1] Compare 1 Kings 7:23

16:17–18 cut off the frames . . . took down the sea. See 1 Kings 7:23–36. The architectural details that follow the information about the frames and the sea, and what Ahaz does about these, are unfortunately obscure. All that seems clear is that his actions are motivated by a desire not to offend the **king of Assyria**. In doing these things, Ahaz desecrates the furnishings of the temple of the Lord. Obedience to the Lord is gone, the Lord's blessing and protection are gone, and now the beauty of the Lord's temple is gradually being removed.

16:19 Chronicles of the Kings. See note on 1 Kings 14:19.

17:1–41 *The End of Israel.* The authors now describe the uprooting and scattering of Israel, long foretold (1 Kings 14:15) but delayed because of God's promises and God's character (2 Kings 10:30; 13:1–25; 14:23–29).

17:1–5 Hoshea was the last ruler of the northern kingdom of Israel (732–722 B.C.). A seal from this time has been found that reads, "Belonging to Abdi servant of Hoshea." It is one of the final artifacts from Israel before it was destroyed at the hands of the Assyrians.

17:1–2 evil . . . , yet not as the kings of Israel who were before him. As with the kings of Judah who were "not like David" (14:3; see 12:2; 15:3, 34), the reader is left to surmise what exactly this means. Perhaps **Hoshea** was not wholly unrestrained in his pursuit of Jeroboam's sins, as he ruled over what remained of northern Israel after the Assyrian assault of 732 B.C. (15:27–31). His succession to the throne as an Assyrian vassal is recorded not only in 15:30 and 17:1 but also in an inscription of Tiglath-pileser III himself, who claims that he "placed Hoshea as king over them."

17:3–4 he had sent messengers to So, king of Egypt. Hoshea had reestablished his **vassal** status with Tiglath-pileser's successor Shalmaneser V (727–722 B.C.) but later reneged on this agreement and courted Egypt instead, bringing down upon himself the wrath of the Assyrian king. The identity of "So, king of Egypt" is a matter of debate. The pharaoh in question might have been Osorkon IV, the last pharaoh of the twenty-second dynasty (730–715 B.C.), or Tefnakht, founder of the overlapping and rising twenty-fourth dynasty (727–720). Some scholars have proposed an Egyptian military commander named Sib'e, but he is unknown in any other texts. Alternatively, "So" may not be a personal name but may be based on the name of the town, "Sais," the capital of King Tefnakht.

The Fall of Israel

6 In the ninth year of Hoshea, the king of Assyria [a]captured Samaria, [b]and he carried
the Israelites away to Assyria [c]and placed them in Halah, and on the Habor, the river of
[d]Gozan, and in the cities of [e]the Medes.

Exile Because of Idolatry

7 And this occurred because the people of Israel had sinned against the LORD their God,
[f]who had brought them up out of the land of Egypt from under the hand of Pharaoh king
of Egypt, and had feared other gods 8 [g]and walked in the customs of the nations whom the
LORD drove out before the people of Israel, [h]and in the customs that the kings of Israel had
practiced. 9 And the people of Israel did secretly against the LORD their God things that
were not right. They built for themselves high places in all their towns, [i]from watchtower
to fortified city. 10 They set up for themselves [j]pillars and Asherim on every high hill and
under every green tree, 11 and there they made offerings on all the high places, as the nations
did whom the LORD carried away before them. And they did wicked things, provoking
the LORD to anger, 12 and they served idols, [k]of which the LORD had said to them, "You
shall not do this." 13 Yet the LORD [l]warned Israel and Judah [m]by every prophet [n]and every
seer, saying, [o]"Turn from your evil ways and keep my commandments and my statutes,

6 [a][Hos. 13:16] [b][Lev. 26:32, 33; Deut. 28:36, 64; 29:27, 28] [c]ch. 18:11; [1 Chr. 5:26] [d]Isa. 37:12 [e]Ezra 6:2; Isa. 13:17; 21:2; Jer. 51:11, 28
7 [f]ver. 36; Lev. 25:38; See Ex. 20:2
8 [g]Lev. 18:3; Deut. 18:9 [h]ver. 19; ch. 16:3
9 [i]ch. 18:8
10 [j]See Ex. 23:24
12 [k]See Ex. 20:4
13 [l]Neh. 9:30 [m]ver. 23 [n]See 1 Sam. 9:9 [o]Jer. 18:11; 25:5; 35:15

17:6 the king of Assyria captured Samaria. Shalmaneser is identified here as the conqueror of Samaria, c. 722 B.C., after a three-year siege (see also 18:9–10); this agrees with the Babylonian Chronicle. But Shalmaneser's successor Sargon II (722–705 B.C.) takes this honor for himself in his inscriptions, perhaps in order to claim more success for himself than he actually achieved and also to give himself legitimacy (as a usurper of the Assyrian throne) by connecting himself with the previous reign. The places of exile mentioned in this verse (**Halah, the Habor, the river of Gozan, the cities of the Medes**) are scattered widely over the Assyrian Empire, from the western to the eastern borders. An Aramaic inscription from the tenth century B.C. mentions the city of "Gozan." The inscription has 23 lines, and it appears on a life-size statue of King Haddayishi, the ruler of Sikanu and Gozan. It was found in a field near Tell Fakhariyah in northeastern Syria.

17:7–23 this occurred because the people of Israel had sinned (v. 7). Of the different explanations that might have been given for the way in which the northern kingdom came to its end, the authors of 1–2 Kings are interested only in this most fundamental explanation; the remainder of 2 Kings 17:7–23 catalogs the details. The **people of Israel** worshiped false gods **from watchtower to fortified city** (i.e., from the smallest to the largest place where people lived) at their **high places** (see 1 Kings 3:2), building themselves **pillars and Asherim** and **two calves** (see 1 Kings 12:28; 14:15, 23), and worshiping **Baal** (see 1 Kings 16:31–33). All of this was done in flagrant disregard for God's **Law** and **covenant** and in defiance of his **prophets**. Interestingly, however, some of the sins listed are not those of Israel only but also of **Judah**, which is drawn into the condemnation. Only in the account of Ahaz's reign have the authors mentioned child sacrifice (2 Kings 17:17; cf. 16:3) and **divination** (cf. 16:15); and only when they reach Manasseh's reign will the authors tell of **omens** (cf. 21:6) and worship of the **host of heaven** (17:16; cf. 21:3), i.e., the sun, the moon, the planets, and the stars. In the ancient Near East these astral bodies were identified with specific gods and goddesses and worshiped as such, and their movements were carefully studied for astrological reasons. Israel encountered worship of this kind as soon as it entered Canaan, as indicated by Judg. 2:13: "they . . . served the Baals and the Ashtaroth" ("Ashtoreth" [2 Kings 23:13] is the biblical name for Astarte or Venus, and the plural forms of the names of these gods here refer to various local manifestations of Hadad and Astarte). Astral worship is forbidden to Israelites in Deut. 4:19–20, as indeed divination and omens (along with fire sacrifice) are prohibited in Deut. 18:10.

17:7 The authors describe the disobedience as sin against God's love and faithfulness, thus clarifying its seriousness.

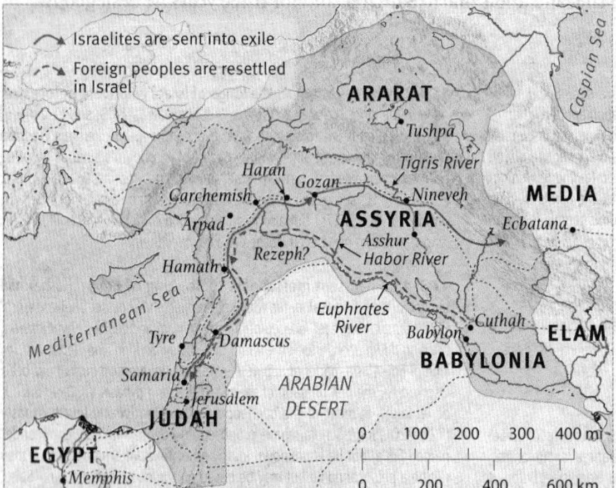

The Fall of Samaria and Deportation of Israelites
722 B.C.

During the reign of Hoshea of Israel, Shalmaneser of Assyria attacked Israel and made it a vassal kingdom. Later, however, Hoshea conspired against Assyria, refusing to pay the tribute and appealing to Egypt for help, so the Assyrians came and besieged Samaria until it fell. Many Israelites were exiled far from Israel to the area near Gozan and the cities of the Medes, and foreign peoples from other parts of the empire were relocated to Israel in an effort to prevent revolt. This signaled the end of the northern kingdom of Israel.

in accordance with all the Law that I commanded your fathers, and that I sent to you by my servants the prophets."

14 But they would not listen, [p]but were stubborn, as their fathers had been, who did not believe in the LORD their God. 15 They despised his statutes [q]and his covenant that he made with their fathers and the warnings that he gave them. They went after [r]false idols [s]and became false, and they followed the nations that were around them, concerning whom the [t]LORD had commanded them that they should not do like them. 16 And they abandoned all the commandments of the LORD their God, and made for themselves metal images of [u]two calves; and they [v]made an Asherah and [w]worshiped all the host of heaven and served [x]Baal. 17 [y]And they burned their sons and their daughters as offerings[1] and used [z]divination and [a]omens and [b]sold themselves to do evil in the sight of the LORD, provoking him to anger. 18 Therefore the LORD was very angry with Israel and removed them out of his sight. None was left but [c]the tribe of Judah only.

19 [d]Judah also did not keep the commandments of the LORD their God, but walked in the customs that Israel had introduced. 20 And the LORD rejected all the descendants of Israel and afflicted them [e]and gave them into the hand of plunderers, until he had cast them out of his sight.

21 [f]When he had torn Israel from the house of David, [g]they made Jeroboam the son of Nebat king. And Jeroboam drove Israel from following the LORD [h]and made them commit great sin. 22 The people of Israel walked in all the sins that Jeroboam did. They did not depart from them, 23 until the LORD removed Israel out of his sight, [i]as he had spoken by all his servants the prophets. [j]So Israel was exiled from their own land to Assyria until this day.

Assyria Resettles Samaria

24 [k]And the king of Assyria brought people from [l]Babylon, Cuthah, [m]Avva, [n]Hamath, and [o]Sepharvaim, and placed them in the cities of Samaria instead of the people of Israel. And they took possession of Samaria and lived in its cities. 25 And at the beginning of their dwelling there, they did not fear the LORD. Therefore the LORD sent lions among them, which killed some of them. 26 So the king of Assyria was told, "The nations that you have carried away and placed in the cities of Samaria do not know the law of the god of the land. Therefore he has sent lions among them, and behold, they are killing them, because they do not know the law of the god of the land." 27 Then the king of Assyria commanded, "Send there one of the priests whom you carried away from there, and let him[2] go and dwell there and teach them the law of the god of the land." 28 So one of the priests whom they had carried away from Samaria came and lived in [p]Bethel and taught them how they should fear the LORD.

29 But every nation still made gods of its own and put them [q]in the shrines of the high places that the Samaritans had made, every nation in the cities in which they lived. 30 The men of [r]Babylon made Succoth-benoth, the men of Cuth made Nergal, the men of Hamath made Ashima, 31 and the Avvites made Nibhaz and Tartak; and the Sepharvites [s]burned their children in the fire to [t]Adrammelech and Anammelech, the gods of [u]Sepharvaim. 32 [v]They also feared the LORD [w]and appointed from among themselves all sorts of people as priests of the high places, who sacrificed for them in the shrines of [x]the high places. 33 So they feared the LORD but also served their own gods, after the manner of the nations from among whom they had been carried away.

34 To this day they do according to the former manner. They do not fear the LORD, and they do not follow the statutes or the rules or the law or the commandment that the LORD commanded the children of Jacob, [y]whom he named Israel. 35 The LORD made a covenant

[1] *Or made their sons and their daughters pass through the fire* [2] Syriac, Vulgate; Hebrew *them*

14 [p]Deut. 9:6; 2 Chr. 30:8; [Deut. 31:27; Acts 7:51]
15 [q]Deut. 29:25 [r]Deut. 32:21; [1 Kgs. 16:13] [s]Jer. 2:5; Rom. 1:21 [t]Deut. 12:30, 31
16 [u]See 1 Kgs. 12:28 [v]1 Kgs. 14:15, 23; 15:13; 16:33 [w]ch. 21:3; 23:5; [Deut. 4:19] [x]ch. 11:18; 1 Kgs. 16:31; 22:53
17 [y]ch. 16:3; [Lev. 18:21; Ezek. 23:37] [z][Deut. 18:10] [a][Lev. 19:26] [b]See 1 Kgs. 21:20
18 [c][1 Kgs. 11:13, 32; 12:20]
19 [d][Jer. 3:8]
20 [e]Judg. 2:14; [ch. 13:3; 15:29]
21 [f]1 Kgs. 11:11, 31 [g]1 Kgs. 12:20 [h]See 1 Kgs. 14:16
23 [i]ver. 13 [j]ver. 6
24 [k]Ezra 4:2, 10 [l]ver. 30 [m][ch. 18:34] [n]See 1 Kgs. 8:65 [o]ver. 31; ch. 18:34; 19:13
28 [p]1 Kgs. 12:29
29 [q]1 Kgs. 12:31; 13:32
30 [r]ver. 24
31 [s]See ver. 17 [t][ch. 19:37] [u]ver. 24
32 [v][Zeph. 1:5] [w]See 1 Kgs. 12:31 [x]ver. 29
34 [y]Gen. 32:28; 35:10; 1 Kgs. 18:31

17:24–41 the king of Assyria brought people . . . and placed them in the cities of Samaria. The land of Israel is not left empty; people from places both close at hand (e.g., **Hamath**) and farther away (e.g., **Babylon**) are settled there. Their religion is the subject of interest in this last section of the chapter. It was a religion that involved them in what they thought of as fearing the God of Israel while also serving **their own gods** (v. 33), but that the authors regarded as not fearing the Lord at all (v. 34). As the only God who truly exists, the Lord claims exclusive worship; a broad pantheon of gods is not acceptable. The deities in question include **Succoth-benoth** (the goddess Banitu and possibly also Sakkut/Ninurta); the Mesopotamian underworld god **Nergal** (associated with famine, drought, plague, and death); and the West Semitic god **Ashima**. **Nibhaz** and **Tartak** may be Elamite deities, while **Adrammelech** and **Anammelech** may be Phoenician and Emarite gods respectively.

with them and commanded them, [z]"You shall not fear other gods [a]or bow yourselves to
them or serve them or sacrifice to them, 36 but [b]you shall fear the LORD, [c]who brought you
out of the land of Egypt with great power and [d]with an outstretched arm. You shall bow
yourselves to him, and to him you shall sacrifice. 37 And the statutes and the rules and the
law and the commandment that he wrote for you, [e]you shall always be careful to do. [z]You
shall not fear other gods, 38 and [f]you shall not forget the covenant that I have made with
you. [z]You shall not fear other gods, 39 but [b]you shall fear the LORD your God, and he will
deliver you out of the hand of all your enemies." 40 However, they would not listen, but
they did according to their former manner.

41 [g]So these nations feared the LORD and also served their carved images. Their children
did likewise, and their children's children—as their fathers did, so they do to this day.

Hezekiah Reigns in Judah

18 [h]In the third year of Hoshea son of Elah, king of Israel, [i]Hezekiah the son of Ahaz,
king of Judah, began to reign. 2 He was [j]twenty-five years old when he began to reign,
and he reigned twenty-nine years in Jerusalem. His mother's name was [k]Abi the daughter
of Zechariah. 3 [l]And he did what was right in the eyes of the LORD, according to all that
David his father had done. 4 [m]He removed the high places and broke the [n]pillars and cut
down [o]the Asherah. And he broke in pieces [p]the bronze serpent that Moses had made, for
until those days the people of Israel had made offerings to it (it was called Nehushtan).[1]
5 [q]He trusted in the LORD, the God of Israel, [r]so that there was none like him among all the
kings of Judah after him, nor among those who were before him. 6 [s]For he held fast to the
LORD. He did not depart from following him, but kept the commandments that the LORD
commanded Moses. 7 [t]And the LORD was with him; wherever he went out, [u]he prospered.
He rebelled against the king of Assyria and would not serve him. 8 [v]He struck down the
Philistines as far as Gaza and its territory, [w]from watchtower to fortified city.

9 In the fourth year of King Hezekiah, which was the seventh year of Hoshea son of
Elah, king of Israel, [x]Shalmaneser king of Assyria came up against Samaria and besieged
it, 10 and at the end of three years he took it. In the sixth year of Hezekiah, which was the
ninth year of Hoshea king of Israel, Samaria was taken. 11 The king of Assyria carried the
Israelites away to Assyria and put them in [y]Halah, and on the [y]Habor, [y]the river of Gozan,
and in the cities of the Medes, 12 because they did not obey the voice of the LORD their God
but transgressed his covenant, even all that Moses the servant of the LORD commanded.
They neither listened nor obeyed.

[1] *Nehushtan* sounds like the Hebrew for both *bronze* and *serpent*

35 [z]Judg. 6:10 [a]See Ex. 20:5
36 [b]Deut. 6:13 [c]ver. 7 [d]Ex. 6:6; Deut. 4:34
37 [e]Deut. 5:32 [z][See ver. 35 above]
38 [f]Deut. 4:23 [z][See ver. 35 above]
39 [b][See ver. 36 above]
41 [g][Zeph. 1:5]

Chapter 18

1 [h][ch. 16:2; 17:1] [i]2 Chr. 28:27; Matt. 1:9
2 [j]For ver. 2, 3, see 2 Chr. 29:1, 2 [k][2 Chr. 29:1]
3 [l]ch. 20:3; 2 Chr. 31:20
4 [m]ver. 22; 2 Chr. 31:1 [n]ch. 17:10; See Ex. 23:24 [o]ch. 17:16; See Deut. 16:21 [p]Num. 21:8, 9
5 [q]ch. 19:10 [r]ch. 23:25
6 [s][Deut. 10:20; Josh. 23:8]
7 [t]2 Chr. 15:2 [u][ch. 16:7]
8 [v][Isa. 14:29] [w]ch. 17:9
9 [x]For ver. 9-12, see ch. 17:3-7
11 [y]ch. 17:6; 1 Chr. 5:26

18:1–20:21 *Hezekiah.* A king is now presented who is not merely similar to David, like Asa and Jehoshaphat (1 Kings 15:11; 22:43), but resembles him more closely than any other Davidic king so far. It is this king who reforms Judean worship, making it what it should be, and whose trust in God is vindicated, as the Assyrians fail to take Jerusalem as they have taken Samaria.

18:1 Extrabiblical evidence for the reign of **Hezekiah** comes from a bulla (clay seal) bearing his name. It reads, "Belonging to Hezekiah [son of Ahaz], king of Judah." The only other Judahite king whose seal impression has been found is Ahaz (see note on 16:1–4).

18:4 He removed the high places. This is a significant accomplishment because even the most righteous of Judean kings prior to Hezekiah in 1–2 Kings failed to do this (e.g., 1 Kings 3:2; 15:14; 22:43). Hezekiah also destroys the **pillars** and the **Asherah** (see notes on 1 Kings 14:15; 14:23), perhaps a particular Asherah that Hezekiah's father Ahaz placed in the Jerusalem temple (as Manasseh will later do, 2 Kings 21:3; 23:12). Hezekiah takes further action against the **bronze serpent** named **Nehushtan**, which Moses had made in the wilderness (Num. 21:4–9) and which had recently itself become an object of worship (no doubt because of the close association of serpents with the goddess Asherah). At the site of Beersheba, archaeologists discovered a horned altar. The altar, from the late eighth century B.C., was built of hewn stones and had a serpent carved into one of its blocks. Obviously, this altar was used at the site in an aberrant cultic worship. It was probably destroyed during King Hezekiah's religious reforms.

18:5–6 He trusted in the LORD. Hezekiah's trust was unparalleled in Judean history (**there was none like him among all the kings of Judah**), and was evidenced in the way that he **held fast** to God (Hb. *dabaq*) throughout his life (cf. Deut. 10:20; 11:22; 13:4; 30:20), in contrast to Solomon, who in his old age "held fast" (Hb. *dabaq*; see 1 Kings 11:2, "clung") to foreign wives and broke the Law of **Moses**.

18:7–8 The consequence of Hezekiah's religious faithfulness was that his military exploits paralleled David's in a unique way: **the LORD was with him** (cf. 1 Sam. 16:18; 18:12, 14; 2 Sam. 5:10); he **prospered** in war (cf. 1 Sam. 18:5, 14, 15); and he **struck down the Philistines** (cf. 1 Sam. 18:27; 19:8). He was quite unlike his father Ahaz, for he **rebelled against the king of Assyria and would not serve him** (cf. 2 Kings 16:7). His rebellious acts may have begun as early as 720 B.C., when one of the inscriptions of the Assyrian king Sargon II describes the Assyrian as "the subduer of the country Judah which lies far away"; but the authors mainly have in mind the events following Sargon's unexpected death on the battlefield in 705, when widespread revolt broke out in Syria-Palestine, leading to an Assyrian invasion of Palestine in 701 (see note on 18:13). Hezekiah's attack on the Philistines was in fact a preemptive strike against Assyrian allies in advance of this invasion.

18:9–12 Shalmaneser king of Assyria came up against Samaria. The fate of the northern kingdom at the hands of the king of Assyria is reiterated

13[z]For ver. 13-37, see 2 Chr. 32:1-20; Isa. 36:1-22
14[a][ch. 23:33]
15[b][ch. 12:18; 16:8]
17[c]Isa. 20:1 [d]Isa. 7:3; [ch. 20:20]
18[e]Isa. 22:20 [f]Isa. 22:15

Sennacherib Attacks Judah

13 [z]In the fourteenth year of King Hezekiah, Sennacherib king of Assyria came up against
all the fortified cities of Judah and took them. 14 And Hezekiah king of Judah sent to the
king of Assyria at Lachish, saying, "I have done wrong; withdraw from me. Whatever you
impose on me I will bear." [a]And the king of Assyria required of Hezekiah king of Judah
three hundred talents[1] of silver and thirty talents of gold. 15 And Hezekiah [b]gave him all
the silver that was found in the house of the LORD and in the treasuries of the king's house.
16 At that time Hezekiah stripped the gold from the doors of the temple of the LORD and
from the doorposts that Hezekiah king of Judah had overlaid and gave it to the king of
Assyria. 17 And the king of Assyria sent the [c]Tartan, the Rab-saris, and the Rabshakeh with
a great army from Lachish to King Hezekiah at Jerusalem. And they went up and came
to Jerusalem. When they arrived, they came and stood by [d]the conduit of the upper pool,
which is on the highway to the Washer's Field. 18 And when they called for the king, there
came out to them [e]Eliakim the son of Hilkiah, who was over the household, and [f]Shebnah
the secretary, and Joah the son of Asaph, the recorder.

[1] A *talent* was about 75 pounds or 34 kilograms

here (cf. 17:1–6) to remind readers of the context in which Hezekiah pursued his bold policy of rebellion. Israel's rebellion met with a devastating response.

18:13–19:37 A six-sided prism has been found that contains the annals of Sennacherib, king of Assyria (704–681 B.C.). It dates to 689 B.C. and recounts eight military campaigns. One of these describes Sennacherib's siege of Jerusalem in the following way (referring to Hezekiah): "Himself I made a prisoner in Jerusalem, his royal residence like a bird in a cage." Although this is Sennacherib's account of the siege, it is noteworthy that no Assyrian record mentions any capture of Jerusalem, so these sources are not in conflict with the record of Sennacherib's departure and death in 19:36–37.

18:13–14 In 701 B.C. **Sennacherib**, king of Assyria, launched a major assault against Judah. Archaeology sheds significant light on this event. The Sennacherib Relief found at Nineveh depicts the Assyrian attack on the Judean city of **Lachish**. Sennacherib built a siege ramp on the southwestern corner of the city and destroyed its defenses by using archers, infantry, and siege machines. The Judeans responded by erecting a countersiege ramp to bolster their defenses. It was to no avail: Sennacherib conquered Lachish. Both of the actual ramps have been uncovered.

18:13 Sennacherib king of Assyria came up against all the fortified cities of Judah. After Sargon II's death, the new Assyrian king Sennacherib (704–681 B.C.) first campaigned in southern Mesopotamia (703–702) against the king of Babylon, Marduk-apla-iddina II (see 20:12), before turning his attention to Syria-Palestine in 701. (See map to the right.) The rebellion there quickly collapsed, and Hezekiah found himself without effective allies and without fortresses. Sennacherib's own account of the campaign is found in its earliest form on the Rassam Cylinder, which dates from immediately after the events (700 B.C.).

18:14–16 I have done wrong. Hezekiah's first response to the crisis is to bargain—a disappointing prologue to what will eventually turn out to be his finest hour. On **Lachish**, see notes on 14:19 and 18:13–14. As one of Judah's most important cities, Lachish received particular attention from Sennacherib during this campaign, and after a siege it was eventually captured and burned to the ground. When Sennacherib later constructed his royal palace at Nineveh, he commissioned a set of stone reliefs to commemorate his famous conquest of the city. The choice of the assault on Lachish for this impressive artistic representation is interesting, in that it serves to underline (without intending to do so) that Sennacherib did not capture Jerusalem.

18:17 Still besieging Lachish, Sennacherib decides after all not to accept Hezekiah's attempt to persuade him to withdraw (no doubt because Hezekiah was one of the moving forces in the revolt), and he sends an army to Jerusalem to pressure Hezekiah to surrender. The **Tartan** (Assyrian *turtanu*) was one of two persons in the Assyrian army with this title who often led campaigns on behalf of the emperor, and the **Rab-saris** was himself often dispatched on campaigns at the head of Assyrian forces. The **Rabshakeh**, or "chief cupbearer," would have accompanied the emperor as a personal attendant. His presence in this delegation is no doubt to be explained in terms of his linguistic abilities (vv. 19, 26). The **conduit of the upper pool** is of uncertain location, but was just outside the city wall; it is the place where Isaiah had earlier called on Ahaz to exercise faith in the midst of war (Isa. 7:1–9). The **Washer's Field** may plausibly be associated with the spring En-rogel to the south of Jerusalem at the juncture of the Hinnom and the Kidron Valleys—a natural place, because of its water supply, for the Assyrian army to encamp.

18:18 over the household . . . the secretary . . . the recorder. Three of the most important of the Judean officials go out to negotiate with the three Assyrian officials (see also 1 Kings 4:1–6).

Assyria Attacks Judah
701 B.C.

During the reign of Hezekiah of Judah, Sennacherib of Assyria attacked cities along the western edge of Judah, and he sent officials to besiege Jerusalem and convince Hezekiah to surrender. The Cushite king Tirhakah advanced from Egypt to support Hezekiah but apparently failed. The siege of Jerusalem was broken when the angel of the LORD killed 185,000 Assyrians in a single night. Sennacherib withdrew and returned to Nineveh in Assyria, where his own sons killed him.

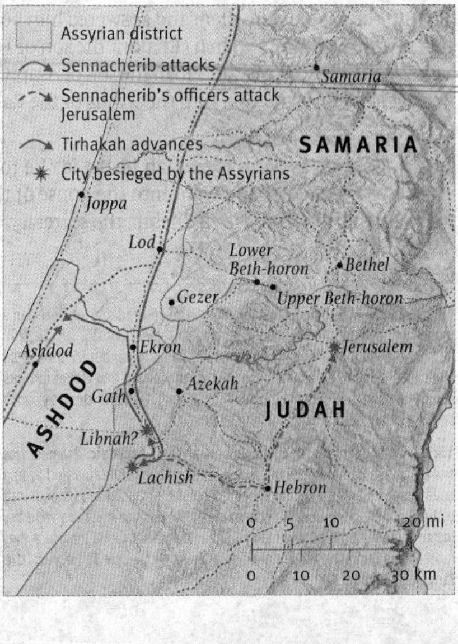

19 And the Rabshakeh said to them, "Say to Hezekiah, 'Thus says the great king, the king
of Assyria: On what do you rest this trust of yours? 20 Do you think that mere words are
strategy and power for war? In whom do you now trust, that you have rebelled against me?
21 Behold, you are trusting now in Egypt, that broken reed of [g]a staff, which will pierce the
hand of any man who leans on it. Such is Pharaoh king of Egypt to all who trust in him.
22 But if you say to me, "We trust in the LORD our God," is it not he [h]whose high places
and altars Hezekiah has removed, saying to Judah and to Jerusalem, "You shall worship
before this altar in Jerusalem"? 23 Come now, make a wager with my master the king of
Assyria: I will give you two thousand horses, if you are able on your part to set riders on
them. 24 How then can you repulse a single captain among the least of my master's servants, when you trust in Egypt for chariots and for horsemen? 25 Moreover, is it without
the LORD that I have come up against this place to destroy it? The LORD said to me, Go up
against this land, and destroy it.'"

26 Then [e]Eliakim the son of Hilkiah, and [f]Shebnah, and Joah, said to the Rabshakeh,
"Please speak to your servants in [i]Aramaic, for we understand it. Do not speak to us in
the language of Judah within the hearing of the people who are on the wall." 27 But the
Rabshakeh said to them, "Has my master sent me to speak these words to your master
and to you, and not to the men sitting on the wall, who are doomed with you to eat their
own dung and to drink their own urine?"

28 Then the Rabshakeh stood and called out in a loud voice in the language of Judah:
"Hear the word of the great king, the king of Assyria! 29 Thus says the king: 'Do not let
Hezekiah deceive you, for he will not be able to deliver you out of my[1] hand. 30 Do not
let Hezekiah make you trust in the LORD by saying, The LORD will surely deliver us, and
this city will not be given into the hand of the king of Assyria.' 31 Do not listen to Hezekiah,
for thus says the king of Assyria: 'Make your peace with me[2] and come out to me. Then
[j]each one of you will eat of his own vine, and each one of his own fig tree, and each one of
you will drink the water of his own cistern, 32 until I come and take you away to a land like
your own land, [k]a land of grain and wine, a land of bread and vineyards, a land of olive
trees and [l]honey, that you may live, and not die. And do not listen to Hezekiah when he
misleads you by saying, "The LORD will deliver us." 33 [m]Has any of the gods of the nations
ever delivered his land out of the hand of the king of Assyria? 34 [n]Where are the gods of
[o]Hamath and [p]Arpad? Where are the gods of Sepharvaim, Hena, and [q]Ivvah? Have they
delivered Samaria out of my hand? 35 Who among all the gods of the lands have delivered
their lands out of my hand, [r]that the LORD should deliver Jerusalem out of my hand?'"

36 But the people were silent and answered him not a word, for the king's command was,
"Do not answer him." 37 Then [s]Eliakim the son of Hilkiah, who was over the household,
and Shebna the secretary, and Joah the son of Asaph, the recorder, came to Hezekiah [t]with
their clothes torn and told him the words of the Rabshakeh.

Isaiah Reassures Hezekiah

19 [u]As soon as King Hezekiah heard it, [t]he tore his clothes and [v]covered himself
with sackcloth and went into the house of the LORD. 2 And he sent Eliakim, who
was over the household, and Shebna the secretary, and the senior priests, [v]covered with

[1] Hebrew *his* [2] Hebrew *Make a blessing with me*

21 [g][Ezek. 29:6, 7]; See Isa. 30:2, 3, 7
22 [h][ver. 4; 2 Chr. 31:1]
26 [e][See ver. 18 above] [f][See ver. 18 above] [i][Ezra 4:7; Dan. 2:4]
31 [j][1 Kgs. 4:25]
32 [k]Deut. 8:7, 8 [l]See Ex. 3:8
33 [m]ch. 19:12; [Isa. 10:10, 11]
34 [n][ch. 19:13] [o]See 1 Kgs. 8:65 [p]Isa. 10:9 [q][ch. 17:24]
35 [r][Dan. 3:15]
37 [s]ver. 18, 26; ch. 19:2 [t]See Josh. 7:6

Chapter 19

1 [u]For ver. 1-37, see 2 Chr. 32:20-22; Isa. 37:1-38 [t][See ch. 18:37 above] [v]See 2 Sam. 3:31
2 [v][See ver. 1 above]

18:19–25 On what do you rest this trust? The matter of Hezekiah's **trust** (cf. v. 5) lies at the heart of this speech (see also vv. 20, 21, 22, 24). Sennacherib reasons that trust in **Egypt** would be futile, but so also would **trust in the LORD**, for it is his **high places and altars** that **Hezekiah has removed**, and indeed it is the Lord who has sent Assyria to **destroy** Judah because of this sacrilege!

18:26–28 Please speak to your servants in Aramaic. Aramaic was the language of the Assyrian Empire west of the Euphrates and would have been understood by the educated Judean royal officials, though not by the ordinary **people** on the city **wall**. However, the Assyrians were trying to appeal to the people over the heads of their rulers, therefore they ignored the request and continued to address the people in Hebrew (**the language of Judah**).

18:29–30 The Rabshakeh equates trust in the Lord with deception; the reader is prepared to see God vindicate that trust.

18:31–35 eat of his own vine . . . his own fig tree . . . drink the water of his own cistern. The Assyrian king is presented as a powerful god who is able to provide for his worshipers, in contrast to the allegedly weak God of Israel who is unable to **deliver**. The language of the false promise recalls Deut. 8:7–9.

19:1–2 he tore his clothes. On the tearing of clothes as a sign of deep emotion, see note on 5:5–7. The contrast between the wicked Jehoram (6:30–31) and the pious Hezekiah is particularly interesting. The besieged Jehoram is unwilling to wait for God and looks instead to remove the head of God's prophet, while Hezekiah humbly sends a message **to the prophet Isaiah** to request prayer to God (19:4).

4[w][2 Sam. 16:12] [x]ver. 16 [y][Isa. 1:9]
6[z]ch. 18:17 [a]See ch. 18:22-25, 30-35
7[b]ver. 9 [c]ver. 37
8[d]Josh. 10:29 [e]ch. 18:14; Josh. 10:31
9[f][1 Sam. 23:27]
10[g]ch. 18:5 [h]ch. 18:30
12[i]ch. 18:33 [j]ch. 17:6 [k]Gen. 11:31; Ezek. 27:23 [l]Ezek. 27:23; Amos 1:5
13[m]ch. 18:34
14[n][2 Chr. 32:17]
15[o]See Ex. 25:22 [p]1 Kgs. 18:39; Neh. 9:6; Ps. 86:10; Isa. 37:16, 20; 44:6; Jer. 10:10, 12
16[q]Ps. 31:2; 71:2; Dan. 9:18 [r]2 Chr. 6:40; Dan. 9:18 [s]ver. 4
18[t]2 Chr. 32:19; Ps. 115:4
19[u]Josh. 4:24; Ps. 83:18 [p][See ver. 15 above]

sackcloth, to the prophet Isaiah the son of Amoz. 3 They said to him, "Thus says Hezekiah,
This day is a day of distress, of rebuke, and of disgrace; children have come to the point
of birth, and there is no strength to bring them forth. 4 [w]It may be that the LORD your
God heard all the words of the Rabshakeh, whom his master the king of Assyria has
sent [x]to mock the living God, and will rebuke the words that the LORD your God has
heard; therefore lift up your prayer for [y]the remnant that is left." 5 When the servants
of King Hezekiah came to Isaiah, 6 Isaiah said to them, "Say to your master, 'Thus says
the LORD: Do not be afraid because of the words that you have heard, with which [z]the
servants of the king of Assyria have [a]reviled me. 7 Behold, I will put a spirit in him, so
that [b]he shall hear a rumor and return to his own land, and I will make him [c]fall by the
sword in his own land.' "

Sennacherib Defies the LORD

8 The Rabshakeh returned, and found the king of Assyria fighting against [d]Libnah,
for he heard that the king had left [e]Lachish. 9 [f]Now the king heard concerning Tirhakah
king of Cush, "Behold, he has set out to fight against you." So he sent messengers again
to Hezekiah, saying, 10 "Thus shall you speak to Hezekiah king of Judah: 'Do not let your
God [g]in whom you trust deceive you by promising that [h]Jerusalem will not be given
into the hand of the king of Assyria. 11 Behold, you have heard what the kings of Assyria
have done to all lands, devoting them to destruction. And shall you be delivered? 12 [i]Have
the gods of the nations delivered them, the nations that my fathers destroyed, [j]Gozan,
[k]Haran, Rezeph, and the people of [l]Eden who were in Telassar? 13 [m]Where is the king of
Hamath, the king of Arpad, the king of the city of Sepharvaim, the king of Hena, or the
king of Ivvah?' "

Hezekiah's Prayer

14 Hezekiah received [n]the letter from the hand of the messengers and read it; and
Hezekiah went up to the house of the LORD and spread it before the LORD. 15 And Hezekiah
prayed before the LORD and said: "O LORD, the God of Israel, [o]enthroned above the
cherubim, [p]you are the God, you alone, of all the kingdoms of the earth; you have made
heaven and earth. 16 [q]Incline your ear, O LORD, and hear; [r]open your eyes, O LORD, and
see; and hear the words of Sennacherib, which he has sent [s]to mock the living God.
17 Truly, O LORD, the kings of Assyria have laid waste the nations and their lands 18 and
have cast their gods into the fire, for they were not gods, [t]but the work of men's hands,
wood and stone. Therefore they were destroyed. 19 So now, O LORD our God, save us,
please, from his hand, [u]that all the kingdoms of the earth may know that [p]you, O LORD,
are God alone."

19:3–4 there is no strength. It is a day of great humiliation and powerlessness. The **remnant**, in this context, likely comprises those from the northern kingdom (Israel) who sought refuge in Judah, and specifically in Jerusalem, in the face of prior Assyrian aggression, along with those of the southern kingdom (Judah) who survive Sennacherib's siege (see Introduction to Micah: Key Themes). The only hope for this remnant is that the Lord, who is truly **the living God** and not simply one false god among many, will act to defend his name (see 2 Kings 19:30–31).

19:7–9 I will put a spirit in him. According to the prophet Isaiah (cf. vv. 2, 5–6), the Lord will so influence Sennacherib's thinking that several events will occur. Sennacherib will **hear** (Hb. *shama'*) a certain **rumor**, abandon his campaign, and **return** (Hb. *shub*) **to his own land**, where he will meet his death (v. 7). However, the timing of this is not clear. Repetition of the pair of Hebrew verbs ("hear" and "return"), found again in vv. 8–9, encourages the hope that Sennacherib's doom is imminent: in v. 8, **Rabshakeh . . . heard** (Hb. *shama'*) **that the king had left Lachish** and he **returned** to him (Hb. *shub*); in v. 9, the **king heard** (Hb. *shama'*) **concerning Tirhakah king of Cush** and **sent messengers again** (lit., "he returned [Hb. *shub*] and sent") **to Hezekiah**. The ultimate fulfillment of the prophecy does not in fact occur until vv. 35–37. "Tirhakah king of Cush" commanded an Egyptian army that marched into Palestine in 701 B.C. to aid the rebels. He would later be a pharaoh of Egypt (690–664). Sennacherib defeated this Egyptian force at Eltekeh, about 12 miles (19 km) east of the Mediterranean on the eastern border of the coastal plain.

19:10–13 Do not let your God in whom you trust deceive you. The argument is subtly different on this second speech by the Assyrians. In 18:19–35 the Rabshakeh claimed that Hezekiah was deceiving the people about what would happen if they trusted the Lord (18:29–30); here he claims that Hezekiah is the one deceived by the God in whom he trusts. This is a God, according to Sennacherib, who is not only weak but duplicitous; and he invites Hezekiah to turn his back on this deity and save himself from the fate of all those other kings who went to their doom clinging to their idols.

19:15–19 Hezekiah prayed before the LORD. Hezekiah's response on this occasion is not to send messengers to Isaiah, asking the prophet to pray (v. 4), but rather to pray himself to God, who is here envisaged as dwelling in a special way in the Jerusalem temple and as being invisibly enthroned in the Most Holy Place on two enormous **cherubim** (see note on 1 Sam. 4:3–4; cf. also 1 Kings 8:6–7). This God is God **alone**, creator of **heaven and earth**, and therefore **God . . . of all the kingdoms of the earth**. He is not to be confused with the gods of the nations against whom the Assyrians have known admittedly great success—"gods" who are in fact mere cult images made of **wood** and overlaid with metal and precious stones. Hezekiah now asks that Jerusalem be delivered for the glory of God himself: **that all the kingdoms of the earth may know that you, O LORD, are God alone**.

Isaiah Prophesies Sennacherib's Fall

20 Then Isaiah the son of Amoz sent to Hezekiah, saying, "Thus says the LORD, the God
of Israel: Your prayer to me about Sennacherib king of Assyria [v]I have heard. 21 This is the
word that the LORD has spoken concerning him:

"She despises you, she scorns you—
[w]the virgin daughter of Zion;
she [x]wags her head behind you—
the daughter of Jerusalem.

22 "Whom have you [y]mocked and [z]reviled?
Against whom have you raised your voice
and lifted your eyes to the heights?
Against [a]the Holy One of Israel!
23 [b]By your messengers you have mocked the Lord,
and you have said, [c]'With my many chariots
I have gone up the heights of the mountains,
to the far recesses of [d]Lebanon;
I felled its tallest cedars,
its choicest cypresses;
I entered its farthest lodging place,
its most [e]fruitful forest.
24 I dug wells
and drank foreign waters,
and I dried up with the sole of my foot
all the streams [f]of Egypt.'

25 "Have you not heard
that [g]I determined it long ago?
I planned from days of old
what [h]now I bring to pass,
that you should turn fortified cities
into heaps of ruins,
26 while their inhabitants, shorn of strength,
are dismayed and confounded,
and have become [i]like plants of the field
and like tender grass,
like grass on the housetops,
blighted before it is grown.

27 "But I know your sitting down
[j]and your going out and coming in,
and your raging against me.
28 Because you have raged against me
and your complacency has come into my ears,
I will [k]put my hook in your nose
and my bit in your mouth,
and [l]I will turn you back on the way
by which you came.

20 [v][ch. 20:5]
21 [w]Lam. 2:13 [x]Job 16:4; Ps. 22:7; 109:25; Lam. 2:15
22 [y]ver. 4 [z]ver. 6 [a]Ps. 71:22; Isa. 5:24; 60:9; Jer. 51:5
23 [b]ch. 18:17 [c]Ps. 20:7 [d]See Judg. 9:15 [e]2 Chr. 26:10; [Isa. 10:18]
24 [f]Isa. 19:6
25 [g][Isa. 45:7] [h][Isa. 10:5]
26 [i]Ps. 129:6
27 [j][1 Sam. 29:6]
28 [k]Ezek. 29:4; 38:4; [Job 41:2; Isa. 30:28; Amos 4:2] [l]ver. 33, 36

19:20–28 A second prophecy from **Isaiah** (cf. vv. 6–7), in three parts, brings God's response to Hezekiah's prayer. This first part concerns Sennacherib's blasphemy, pride, and ultimate downfall. He thinks of himself as a god, claiming to have brought judgment (as only the Lord can do) on the mighty **cedars** of **Lebanon** and on **Egypt** (cf. Ps. 29:5; Isa. 2:12–13; 19:1–15; Amos 2:9; Zech. 11:1–3); he has allegedly ascended the **heights** so that he can look God straight in the face (cf. Ps. 73:8; 75:4–5; Isa. 14:13–15); and he boasts that he has both brought and withheld fertility on the earth, creating water supplies and drying up rivers (cf. Ps. 36:8–9; Jer. 2:13; 17:13; 51:36; Ezekiel 31; Hos. 13:15). His great mistake has been to imagine that what he has accomplished in his military campaigns has been achieved in his own strength. In reality, it was the Lord who **determined it long ago**. It was God who **planned from days of old** that Sennacherib would **turn fortified cities into heaps of ruins** (2 Kings 19:25), so his pride in his mighty accomplishments is foolishness. In fact, Assyria is merely the rod of God's anger (cf. Isa. 10:5–11). Likewise, the Lord will bring an end to his campaigns, causing Sennacherib to **turn . . . back on the way by which** he **came**, led like an animal by a **hook** in the **nose** and a **bit** in the **mouth** (2 Kings 19:28).

19:21 Daughter of Zion (or **daughter of Jerusalem**) is frequently used in the OT as a personification of the city of Jerusalem and its inhabitants.

29 “And this shall be [m]the sign for you: this year eat what grows of itself, and in the second
year what springs of the same. Then in the third year sow and reap and plant vineyards,
and eat their fruit. 30 [n]And the surviving remnant of the house of Judah shall again take
root downward and bear fruit upward. 31 For out of Jerusalem shall go a remnant, and out
of Mount Zion [o]a band of survivors. [p]The zeal of the LORD will do this.
32 “Therefore thus says the LORD concerning the king of Assyria: He shall not come into
this city or shoot an arrow there, or come before it with a shield or [q]cast up a siege mound
against it. 33 [r]By the way that he came, by the same he shall return, and he shall not come
into this city, declares the LORD. 34 [s]For I will defend this city to save it, for my own sake
[t]and for the sake of my servant David.”
35 And that night [u]the angel of the LORD went out and struck down 185,000 in the
camp of the Assyrians. And when people arose early in the morning, behold, these were
all dead bodies. 36 Then Sennacherib king of Assyria departed and went home and lived at
[v]Nineveh. 37 And as he was worshiping in the house of Nisroch his god, [w]Adrammelech and
Sharezer, his sons, struck him down with the sword and escaped into the land of Ararat.
And Esarhaddon his son reigned in his place.

Hezekiah's Illness and Recovery

20 [x]In those days [y]Hezekiah became sick and was at the point of death. And Isaiah the
prophet the son of Amoz came to him and said to him, “Thus says the LORD, [z]‘Set
your house in order, for you shall die; you shall not recover.’ ” 2 Then Hezekiah turned his
face to the wall and prayed to the LORD, saying, 3 “Now, O LORD, [a]please remember how
I have walked before you in faithfulness and [b]with a whole heart, [c]and have done what is
good in your sight.” [d]And Hezekiah wept bitterly. 4 And before Isaiah had gone out of the
middle court, the word of the LORD came to him: 5 “Turn back, and say to Hezekiah [e]the
leader of my people, Thus says the LORD, the God of David your father: [f]I have heard your
prayer; [g]I have seen your tears. Behold, I will heal you. On the third day you shall go up to
the house of the LORD, 6 and I will add fifteen years to your life. I will deliver you and this
city out of the hand of the king of Assyria, [h]and I will defend this city for my own sake
and for my servant David's sake.” 7 And Isaiah said, “Bring a cake of figs. And let them take
and lay it on the boil, that he may recover.”

29 [m]ch. 20:8, 9; 1 Sam. 2:34; Isa. 7:11, 14
30 [n][2 Chr. 32:22, 23]
31 [o][Isa. 10:20] [p]Isa. 9:7
32 [q]2 Sam. 20:15
33 [r]ver. 28
34 [s]ch. 20:6; [Isa. 31:5] [t]1 Kgs. 11:13
35 [u][Ex. 12:23; 2 Sam. 24:16]
36 [v]Gen. 10:11; Jonah 1:2
37 [w][ch. 17:31]

Chapter 20

1 [x]For ver. 1-11, see Isa. 38:1-22 [y]2 Chr. 32:24 [z][2 Sam. 17:23]
3 [a][Neh. 5:19; 13:14, 22, 31] [b]See 1 Kgs. 8:61 [c]ch. 18:3 [d][Ps. 39:12, 13]
5 [e]1 Sam. 9:16; 10:1 [f]ch. 19:20; [Ps. 65:2] [g]Ps. 39:12; 56:8
6 [h]ch. 19:34

Jerusalem is as defenseless as a virgin daughter, but because of the Lord's protection she will not be violated by mighty Sennacherib; in fact, she **wags her head** at him, scoffing at his pride.

19:29–31 this shall be the sign for you. The second part of Isaiah's prophecy looks beyond the withdrawal of the Assyrians from Judah. The sign that Judah will recover from the Assyrian assault is to be found in the way that the survivors will be provided for in the short term: initially they will be able to survive only because of the crops that spring up from what is already in the ground, but **in the third year** they will resume normal agricultural practice, able to **bear fruit**.

19:32–34 concerning the king of Assyria. The third part of Isaiah's prophecy makes explicit the circumstances in which Sennacherib will **return** home **by the way that he came** (vv. 28, 33). He will return home before the army encamped outside the city of Jerusalem takes military action against it—**for the sake of** God's **servant David** (cf. 1 Kings 11:13, 32; 2 Kings 8:19).

19:35–36 Sennacherib king of Assyria departed and went home. The event precipitating Sennacherib's “return” to Nineveh when he “heard” about it (see note on vv. 7–9) involved enormous casualties suffered by his army outside Jerusalem, with **185,000** struck down in one night by the **angel of the LORD**. Here is God's remarkable answer to Hezekiah's prayer, “O LORD our God, save us, please, from his hand” (v. 19), and the fulfillment of God's promise in vv. 32–34.

19:37 Sennacherib, who had “mocked and reviled” the Lord, is killed by **his sons**, and all his proud boasting (18:22, 32–35; 19:10–13) ends in nothing. Though he was **worshiping in the house of Nisroch his god**, this false god could not protect the king. The name “Nisroch” is not attested in Assyrian sources, and readers are left to guess at the deity intended (perhaps it is Ashur, the chief god of Assyria). Sennacherib's assassins flee to **Ararat**, known to the Assyrians as Urartu, a kingdom of eastern Asia Minor that flourished from the ninth to the sixth centuries B.C. **Esarhaddon** ruled Assyria from 681 to 669 B.C. In his own records he describes the events surrounding his accession to the throne, referring to his “elder brothers who . . . went out of their senses . . . and butted each other—like kids—to take over the kingship,” and of the “flight of the usurpers . . . to an unknown country.” One of his letters identifies one of the assassins as Arad-Mullissu, probably the **Adrammelech** of the biblical text.

20:1 In those days. Verses 1–19 represent a “flashback” to the period around 713–712 B.C., some 12 years before Sennacherib's invasion and some 15 years before Hezekiah's death (cf. v. 6).

20:2 Hezekiah turned his face to the wall. Hezekiah is in distress and wishes to be left alone, although for different reasons from Ahab in 1 Kings 21:4.

20:3 please remember. The prayer is somewhat more self-centered than the one in 19:15–19, stressing the king's own righteousness. This is the first hint in this passage that Hezekiah has an attitude problem.

20:4 The middle court was the area between the temple and the palace (see Solomon's Temple and Palace Complex, p. 607); Isaiah is on the way back to the temple. The **word of the LORD** comes to him suddenly and unexpectedly.

20:5 On the third day. A detail not included in Isaiah's parallel account (Isa. 38:5). **you shall go up.** God's response to Hezekiah's prayer (2 Kings 20:3) shows that many prophecies, though stated in unconditional terms (v. 1), have implied conditions.

20:7 Figs had long been cultivated in Palestine. They could be eaten fresh or dried, made into cakes, or fermented and made into wine. Here a **cake of figs**, serving as a compress, is applied to what may have been an abscess. The belief that figs had medicinal qualities is also attested earlier at Ugarit and

8 And Hezekiah said to Isaiah, "What shall be the sign that the LORD will heal me, and
that I shall go up to the house of the LORD on the third day?" 9 And Isaiah said, "This shall
be [i]the sign to you from the LORD, that the LORD will do the thing that he has promised:
shall the shadow go forward ten steps, or go back ten steps?" 10 And Hezekiah answered,
"It is an easy thing for the shadow [j]to lengthen ten steps. Rather let the shadow go back
ten steps." 11 And Isaiah the prophet called to the LORD, [k]and he brought the shadow back
ten steps, by which it had gone down on the steps of Ahaz.

Hezekiah and the Babylonian Envoys

12 [l]At that time [m]Merodach-baladan the son of Baladan, king of Babylon, [n]sent envoys
with letters and a present to Hezekiah, for he heard that Hezekiah had been sick. 13 And
Hezekiah welcomed them, and he showed them [o]all his treasure house, the silver, the
gold, the spices, the precious oil, his armory, all that was found in his storehouses. There
was nothing in his house or in all his realm that Hezekiah did not show them. 14 Then
Isaiah the prophet came to King Hezekiah, and said to him, "What did these men say?
And from where did they come to you?" And Hezekiah said, "They have come from a far
country, from Babylon." 15 He said, "What have they seen in your house?" And Hezekiah
answered, "They have seen all that is in my house; there is nothing in my storehouses
that I did not show them."

16 Then Isaiah said to Hezekiah, "Hear the word of the LORD: 17 Behold, the days are
coming, when [p]all that is in your house, and that which your fathers have stored up till
this day, shall be carried to Babylon. Nothing shall be left, says the LORD. 18 [q]And some of
your own sons, who shall be born to you, shall be taken away, [r]and they shall be eunuchs
in the palace of the king of Babylon." 19 Then Hezekiah said to Isaiah, [s]"The word of the
LORD that you have spoken is good." For he thought, "Why not, if there will be peace and
security in my days?"

20 [t]The rest of the deeds of Hezekiah and all his might and how he made [u]the pool
and the conduit [v]and brought water into the city, are they not written in the Book of the
Chronicles of the Kings of Judah? 21 [w]And Hezekiah slept with his fathers, and Manasseh
his son reigned in his place.

Manasseh Reigns in Judah

21 [x]Manasseh was twelve years old when he began to reign, and he reigned fifty-
five years in Jerusalem. His mother's name was Hephzibah. 2 And he did what
was evil in the sight of the LORD, [y]according to the despicable practices of the nations

9 [i]See ch. 19:29
10 [j]Ps. 102:11
11 [k][Josh. 10:12, 13]
12 [l]For ver. 12-19, see Isa. 39:1-8 [m][Isa. 39:1] [n][2 Chr. 32:31]
13 [o][2 Chr. 32:27]
17 [p]ch. 24:13; Jer. 20:5; [ch. 25:13]; See Jer. 27:19-22
18 [q]ch. 24:12; 2 Chr. 33:11 [r][Dan. 1:3]
19 [s]1 Sam. 3:18; [2 Chr. 32:25, 26]
20 [t][2 Chr. 32:32] [u]ch. 18:17; Neh. 2:14; 3:16 [v]2 Chr. 32:30; [Isa. 22:9, 11]
21 [w]2 Chr. 32:33

Chapter 21

1 [x]For ver. 1-9, see 2 Chr. 33:1-9
2 [y][ch. 16:3]

later in Rome. But the healing of such a serious illness (v. 1) probably included a supernatural work of God as well.

20:8–11 What shall be the sign that the LORD will heal me? The king is unwilling to believe the promise of healing without a **sign**, which is provided in the unnatural movement of a **shadow** on some **steps** associated with **Ahaz** (it moves **back**, even though the sun has already caused it to go **down** the **steps**). The text offers no explanation of the details of this miracle; in the biblical worldview, nothing is beyond the power of the Maker of heaven and earth. Hezekiah, too, is sinking down toward death, but he will miraculously recover and **go up** to the temple.

20:12 When Sargon II ascended the Assyrian throne in 722 B.C., **Merodach-baladan** (the Hb. name for Marduk-apla-iddina II) had himself crowned king in Babylon, and the ensuing conflict in Mesopotamia lasted intermittently until Esarhaddon's reign in Assyria (see notes on 17:24–41; 19:37). This visit of Merodach-baladan's envoys to Jerusalem is best set during his first spell of kingship in Babylon (722–710 B.C.), before Sargon II reconquered Babylonia after 710 and drove him into exile.

20:13–18 he showed them all his treasure house. Hezekiah is evidently proud of his wealth, but pride comes before a fall (cf. Prov. 11:2), when **nothing shall be left** and even some of the king's **sons** (descendants) will be taken away into exile in **Babylon**. On **eunuchs**, see note on 2 Kings 9:32, although here the term may be intended metaphorically rather than literally (the "sons" will be powerless servants of the **king of Babylon**).

20:19 Why not? Hezekiah is surprisingly unmoved by Isaiah's prophecy, and again displays self-centeredness. All he cares about is **peace and security in** his **days**. Even this "king like David" has his dark side.

20:20 the pool and the conduit. The Gihon Spring in the Kidron Valley was Jerusalem's crucial water resource, and a large quarter-mile-long conduit (often known as the Siloam Channel) brought water from there to a reservoir at the southern end of the city of David. Since this water supply lay outside the city's walls and was vulnerable in time of siege, a subsidiary tunnel leading from the Siloam conduit allowed residents to access its water from inside the city walls. In preparation for the Assyrian attack, Hezekiah had an additional tunnel cut that diverted water from the Gihon Spring directly underground to the Pool of Siloam, which now lay within the city walls, whereupon the old water system was apparently abandoned. An inscription cut into the conduit wall and known as the Siloam Tunnel Inscription commemorates this accomplishment. On the **Chronicles of the Kings**, see note on 1 Kings 14:19.

21:1–26 *Manasseh and Amon.* The Lord has kept faith with the house of David even through the bad times because of his promise to David, but hints abound throughout chs. 16–20 that Judah will ultimately share Israel's fate and go into exile. With Manasseh, these hints of disaster give way to explicit prophetic announcements of judgment.

21:1–9 Manasseh is the very worst of the Judean kings, indulging in all that has been most reprehensible in the religion of Israel (both north and south) in the preceding chapters of 1–2 Kings, and adding to it (**despicable practices**

3 [z]ch. 18:4 [a]See Deut. 16:21 [b]1 Kgs. 16:32, 33 [c]ch. 17:16; 23:5; [Deut. 4:19]
4 [d]Jer. 7:30; 32:34 [e]ver. 7; ch. 23:27; 2 Sam. 7:13; 1 Kgs. 8:29; 9:3; [Deut. 12:11]
5 [c][See ver. 3 above] [f]ch. 23:12; 1 Kgs. 6:36; 7:12
6 [g]See Lev. 18:21 [h]See Lev. 19:26 [i]ch. 17:17 [j]ch. 23:24; See Lev. 19:31
7 [a][See ver. 3 above] [e][See ver. 4 above]
8 [k][2 Sam. 7:19]
11 [l]ver. 2; ch. 23:26; 24:3, 4; Jer. 15:4 [m]1 Kgs. 21:26 [n]ver. 16 [o]ver. 21
12 [p]1 Sam. 3:11; Jer. 19:3
13 [q]Isa. 34:11; [Isa. 28:17; Lam. 2:8; Amos 7:7, 8]
16 [r]ch. 24:4 [s]ver. 11
17 [t]See 2 Chr. 33:11-19
18 [u]For ver. 18-24, see 2 Chr. 33:20-25 [v]ver. 26

whom the LORD drove out before the people of Israel. **3** For he rebuilt the high places
[z]that Hezekiah his father had destroyed, and he erected altars for Baal and made [a]an
Asherah, [b]as Ahab king of Israel had done, [c]and worshiped all the host of heaven and
served them. **4** [d]And he built altars in the house of the LORD, of which the LORD had said,
[e]"In Jerusalem will I put my name." **5** And he built altars [c]for all the host of heaven in
[f]the two courts of the house of the LORD. **6** [g]And he burned his son as an offering[1] and
[h]used fortune-telling and [i]omens and dealt [j]with mediums and with necromancers. He
did much evil in the sight of the LORD, provoking him to anger. **7** And the carved image
of [a]Asherah that he had made he set in the house of which the LORD said to David and
to Solomon his son, "In this house, [e]and in Jerusalem, which I have chosen out of all
the tribes of Israel, I will put my name forever. **8** [k]And I will not cause the feet of Israel to
wander anymore out of the land that I gave to their fathers, if only they will be careful
to do according to all that I have commanded them, and according to all the Law that
my servant Moses commanded them." **9** But they did not listen, and Manasseh led them
astray to do more evil than the nations had done whom the LORD destroyed before the
people of Israel.

Manasseh's Idolatry Denounced

10 And the LORD said by his servants the prophets, **11** [l]"Because Manasseh king of Judah has
committed these abominations and has done things [m]more evil than all that the Amorites
did, who were before him, [n]and has made Judah also to sin [o]with his idols, **12** therefore thus
says the LORD, the God of Israel: Behold, I am bringing upon Jerusalem and Judah such
disaster[2] that the ears of everyone who hears of it [p]will tingle. **13** [q]And I will stretch over
Jerusalem the measuring line of Samaria, and the plumb line of the house of Ahab, and
I will wipe Jerusalem as one wipes a dish, wiping it and turning it upside down. **14** And
I will forsake the remnant of my heritage and give them into the hand of their enemies,
and they shall become a prey and a spoil to all their enemies, **15** because they have done
what is evil in my sight and have provoked me to anger, since the day their fathers came
out of Egypt, even to this day."

16 [r]Moreover, Manasseh shed very much innocent blood, till he had filled Jerusalem
from one end to another, besides the sin [s]that he made Judah to sin so that they did what
was evil in the sight of the LORD.

17 [t]Now the rest of the acts of Manasseh and all that he did, and the sin that he committed, are they not written in the Book of the Chronicles of the Kings of Judah? **18** [u]And
Manasseh slept with his fathers and was buried in the garden of his house, [v]in the garden
of Uzza, and Amon his son reigned in his place.

[1] Hebrew *made his son pass through the fire* [2] Or *evil*

of the nations). His father's reforms are reversed as the **high places** are **rebuilt** (v. 3) so that idolatry can resume there, and a new **Asherah** (v. 3) replaces the one that Hezekiah removed (see 18:4). Manasseh built **altars for all the host of heaven** (21:5; see 17:7–23) **in the two courts** of the temple (both in the inner court described in 1 Kings 6:36 and in the "middle court" described in 2 Kings 20:4). His grandfather Ahaz is his role model, as he sacrifices his own **son** in the fire (21:6) and uses **fortune-telling and omens** (v. 6; see 16:3, 17:7–23; also Deut. 18:10). **Ahab** (cf. 2 Kings 21:3) stands behind Ahaz; and King Saul's reign is also echoed in the reference to **mediums** and **necromancers** (v. 6; 1 Sam. 28:3–25), divination by inquiring of the dead. The Lord *of* hosts (1 Kings 18:15; 19:10; etc.) has become to Manasseh merely a god *among* hosts, with a consort goddess for company (**Asherah**) and open to manipulation by occult means. If the Lord previously **drove out before the people of Israel** the **nations** that did these things (2 Kings 21:2, 9), what will happen now to Judah?

21:7 A decorative pitcher found at the site of Lachish dates to the thirteenth century B.C. On the shoulder of the vessel is a stylized tree, representing the Canaanite goddess **Asherah**. An inscription above the tree refers to an offering to Elat, another name for the goddess. Israel is told not to worship trees as an Asherah (cf. Deut. 16:21; Judg. 6:25–30; 1 Kings 14:15; 15:13; 2 Kings 18:4; Mic. 5:13–15).

21:8 For the **feet of Israel to wander . . . out of the land** would be for the people to go into exile; the biblical authors make it clear that the exile of Judah was due to moral reasons (Judah's unfaithfulness) rather than to any weakness in God.

21:12 the ears of everyone who hears of it will tingle. The **disaster** now to befall **Jerusalem and Judah** will cause a reaction in people who hear of it—perhaps a sensation in the ears, or more likely a shaking in terror as the news enters the body through the ears (cf. Ex. 15:14; Deut. 2:25; Isa. 32:11; 64:2).

21:13 the measuring line . . . the plumb line. The city will be assessed by the divine architect (cf. the use of the measuring line in Isa. 34:11; Lam. 2:8) and, like a dangerous building, will be condemned.

21:17–18 Manasseh's burial site lay outside the "city of David" (i.e., the original settled area of Jerusalem on the southern hill) that is noted as the resting place of preceding kings (e.g., Ahaz in 16:20). The **garden of Uzza** was perhaps an enclosure on the Temple Mount dedicated to the Arabian goddess al-Uzza, who was identified with Venus (notice Manasseh's worship of astral deities in 21:3), or an enclosure at the southern end of the Kidron Valley, just outside the city walls, where there was a "king's garden" (25:4; Neh. 3:15). Already in Solomon's day, the eastern slopes of the Kidron Valley were associated with idolatrous worship (1 Kings 11:7). On the **Chronicles of the Kings** (also 2 Kings 21:25), see note on 1 Kings 14:19.

Amon Reigns in Judah

19 Amon was twenty-two years old when he began to reign, and he reigned two years
in Jerusalem. His mother's name was Meshullemeth the daughter of Haruz of Jotbah.
20 And he did what was evil in the sight of the LORD, [w]as Manasseh his father had done.
21 He walked in all the way in which his father walked and served [x]the idols that his father
served and worshiped them. 22 [y]He abandoned the LORD, the God of his fathers, and did
not walk in the way of the LORD. 23 And the servants of Amon conspired against him and
put the king to death in his house. 24 But the people of the land struck down all those who
had conspired against King Amon, and the people of the land made Josiah his son king in
his place. 25 Now the rest of the acts of Amon that he did, are they not written in the Book
of the Chronicles of the Kings of Judah? 26 And he was buried in his tomb [z]in the garden
of Uzza, and Josiah his son reigned in his place.

Josiah Reigns in Judah

22 [a]Josiah was eight years old when he began to reign, and he reigned thirty-one years
in Jerusalem. His mother's name was Jedidah the daughter of Adaiah of [b]Bozkath.
2 And he did what was right in the eyes of the LORD and walked in all the way of David his
father, [c]and he did not turn aside to the right or to the left.

Josiah Repairs the Temple

3 In the eighteenth year of King Josiah, the king sent Shaphan the son of Azaliah, son
of Meshullam, the secretary, to the house of the LORD, saying, 4 "Go up to [d]Hilkiah the

20 [w]See ver. 2-6, 11
21 [x]ver. 11
22 [y]ch. 22:17; [1 Kgs. 11:33]
26 [z]ver. 18

Chapter 22

1 [a]See 2 Chr. 34:1, 2 [b]Josh. 15:39
2 [c]See Deut. 5:32
4 [d][ch. 12:10]

21:19–26 Amon. See note on 2 Chron. 33:21–25.

22:1–23:30 *Josiah.* Josiah is a long-awaited king (cf. 1 Kings 13:2) and the doer of many significant deeds, but he comes too late to make any difference to Judah's fate.

22:2 Josiah is the ideal king of Deut. 17:20, who does not **turn** from the Mosaic law **to the right or to the left**. He transcends even **David** and Hezekiah in his faithfulness to God (2 Kings 23:21–25).

22:3–7 the king sent Shaphan. Josiah's initial concern is simply to repair the temple, like Joash in 12:1–16, not to reform its worship. In fact, the reforms introduced by Joash some 200 years previously are still

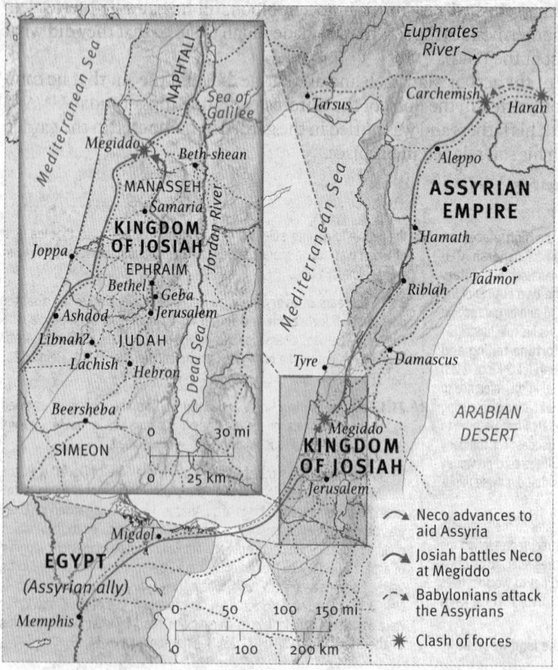

Josiah's Reforms and His Battle with Neco
628–609 B.C.
Early in his reign, King Josiah of Judah launched a massive effort to abolish pagan worship throughout Judah and the land of Israel and to refurbish the temple of the LORD in Jerusalem. At the same time, the waning power of the Assyrians allowed him to add much of the land of Israel to his kingdom. Josiah met his demise at Megiddo, however, as he sought to prevent Pharaoh Neco II of Egypt from reaching Carchemish to assist the Assyrians, who were being attacked by forces from the rising Babylonian Empire.

high priest, that he may count the money [e]that has been brought into the house of the
LORD, which [f]the keepers of the threshold have collected from the people. 5 [g]And let
it be given into the hand of the workmen who have the oversight of the house of the
LORD, and let them give it to the workmen who are at the house of the LORD, repairing
the house 6 (that is, to the carpenters, and to the builders, and to the masons), and let
them use it for buying timber and quarried stone to repair the house. 7 But [h]no accounting shall be asked from them for the money that is delivered into their hand, for they
deal honestly."

Hilkiah Finds the Book of the Law

8 And Hilkiah the high priest said to Shaphan the secretary, "I have found [i]the Book of
the Law in the house of the LORD." And Hilkiah gave the book to Shaphan, and he read
it. 9 And Shaphan the secretary came to the king, and reported to the king, "Your servants
have emptied out the money that was found in the house and have delivered it into the
hand of the workmen who have the oversight of the house of the LORD." 10 Then Shaphan
the secretary told the king, "Hilkiah the priest has given me a book." And Shaphan read
it before the king.
11 When the king heard the words of the Book of the Law, [j]he tore his clothes. 12 And the
king commanded Hilkiah the priest, and [k]Ahikam the son of Shaphan, and [l]Achbor the
son of [l]Micaiah, and Shaphan the secretary, and Asaiah the king's servant, saying, 13 "Go,
inquire of the LORD for me, and for the people, and for all Judah, concerning the words of
this book that has been found. For great is [m]the wrath of the LORD that is kindled against
us, because our fathers have not obeyed the words of this book, to do according to all that
is written concerning us."
14 So Hilkiah the priest, and Ahikam, and Achbor, and Shaphan, and Asaiah went to
Huldah the prophetess, the wife of Shallum the son of [n]Tikvah, son of [n]Harhas, keeper of
the wardrobe (now she lived in Jerusalem in [o]the Second Quarter), and they talked with
her. 15 And she said to them, "Thus says the LORD, the God of Israel: 'Tell the man who sent
you to me, 16 Thus says the LORD, Behold, I will bring disaster upon this place and upon
its inhabitants, all the words of the book that the king of Judah has read. 17 [p]Because they
have forsaken me and have made offerings to other gods, that they might provoke me to
anger with all the work of their hands, therefore [m]my wrath will be kindled against this
place, and it will not be quenched. 18 But to the king of Judah, who sent you to inquire
of the LORD, thus shall you say to him, Thus says the LORD, the God of Israel: Regarding
the words that you have heard, 19 [q]because your heart was penitent, and you [r]humbled
yourself before the LORD, when you heard how I spoke against this place and against its
inhabitants, that they should become [s]a desolation and [t]a curse, and you [u]have torn your
clothes and wept before me, I also have heard you, declares the LORD. 20 Therefore, behold,
I will gather you to your fathers, and [v]you shall be gathered to your grave in peace, and
your eyes shall not see all the disaster that I will bring upon this place.'" And they brought
back word to the king.

4 [e]ch. 12:4 [f]ch. 12:9
5 [g]ch. 12:11, 12, 14
7 [h]ch. 12:15
8 [i]Deut. 31:24-26; 2 Chr. 34:14
11 [j]See Josh. 7:6
12 [k]ch. 25:22; Jer. 26:24; 39:14; 40:5 [l][2 Chr. 34:20]
13 [m]Deut. 29:27
14 [n][2 Chr. 34:22] [o]Zeph. 1:10
17 [p]ch. 21:22; Deut. 29:25, 26 [m][See ver. 13 above]
19 [q][Ps. 51:17; Isa. 57:15] [r]1 Kgs. 21:29 [s]Lev. 26:31, 32; 2 Chr. 30:7; Jer. 25:18; 44:22; Mic. 6:16 [t]Jer. 24:9; 26:6; 44:22 [u]ver. 11
20 [v]Ps. 37:37; Isa. 57:1, 2

in place: it is still the task of the doorkeepers to collect the **money** for temple repairs, and it is the task of the **secretary** to oversee, with the high priest, the counting and distribution of the money to the men in charge of the work.

22:8 I have found the Book of the Law. The phrase "Book of the Law" is used in the Pentateuch only in reference to Deuteronomy (e.g., Deut. 28:61; 29:21), which was read to the king and provided the basis for his actions. Available to the kings of Israel and Judah in previous years (cf. 1 Kings 2:3; 2 Kings 10:31; 14:6; 18:6), it was evidently lost or concealed during the long reign of the apostate Manasseh, who systematically infringed its laws.

22:11–13 Although it is not until the eighteenth year of his reign (v. 3) that the new king begins to take action concerning the apostate condition of worship in Judah, the authors of 1–2 Kings do not blame him. Brought up in a royal court that had been apostate for 57 years and that subjected all opposition to a reign of terror, Josiah was not aware of the Lord's demands. As soon as he became aware, **he tore his clothes** in grief and despair (cf. 1 Kings 21:27; 2 Kings 5:7–8; 6:30; 11:14; 19:1–2) and sent officials to **inquire of the LORD**.

22:14–16 Huldah. It was not Jeremiah or Zephaniah (Jer. 1:2; Zeph. 1:1) who was consulted, but an obscure **prophetess** who was the wife of a court official or perhaps of one of the temple personnel (it is not clear whether **Shallum** was in charge of the **wardrobe** of the *king* or of the *priests*). Huldah lived in the **Second Quarter** of Jerusalem, probably a residential area on the western hill. Her words confirm what is already known from the unnamed prophets of 2 Kings 21: the Lord is going to **bring disaster** on Jerusalem and its people.

22:20 you shall be gathered to your grave in peace. Because Josiah has humbled himself before the Lord, he will not personally **see all the disaster** that is to fall on Jerusalem. He will die before the terrible events prophesied in 21:12–14 and 22:15–17 come to pass.

Josiah's Reforms

23 [w]Then the king sent, and all the elders of Judah and Jerusalem were gathered to him. 2 And the king went up to the house of the LORD, and with him all the men of Judah and all the inhabitants of Jerusalem and the priests and the prophets, all the people, both small and great. And [x]he read in their hearing all the words of the Book of the Covenant [y]that had been found in the house of the LORD. 3 And the king stood [z]by the pillar and [a]made a covenant before the LORD, [b]to walk after the LORD and to keep his commandments and his testimonies and his statutes with all his heart and all his soul, to perform the words of this covenant that were written in this book. And all the people joined in the covenant.

4 And the king commanded Hilkiah the high priest and the priests [c]of the second order and the keepers of the threshold to bring out of the temple of the LORD all the vessels made for [d]Baal, for [e]Asherah, and for all the host of heaven. [f]He burned them outside Jerusalem in the fields of the Kidron and carried their ashes to Bethel. 5 And he deposed the priests whom the kings of Judah had ordained to make offerings in the high places at the cities of Judah and around Jerusalem; those also who burned incense to Baal, to the sun and the moon and the constellations [g]and all the host of the heavens. 6 And he brought out [h]the Asherah from the house of the LORD, outside Jerusalem, to the brook Kidron, [i]and burned it at the brook Kidron [j]and beat it to dust and cast the dust of it upon the graves [k]of the common people. 7 And he broke down the houses of [l]the male cult prostitutes who were in the house of the LORD, [m]where the women wove hangings for [h]the Asherah. 8 And he brought all the priests out of the cities of Judah, and defiled the high places where the priests had made offerings, from [n]Geba to Beersheba. And he broke down the high places of the gates that were at the entrance of the gate of Joshua the governor of the city, which were on one's left at the gate of the city. 9 [o]However, the priests of the high places did not come up to the altar of the LORD in Jerusalem, but they ate unleavened bread among their brothers. 10 And he defiled [p]Topheth, which is [q]in the Valley of the Son of Hinnom, [r]that no one might burn his son or his daughter as an offering to [s]Molech.[1] 11 And he removed the horses that the kings of Judah had dedicated to the sun, at the entrance to the house of the LORD, by the chamber of Nathan-melech the chamberlain, which was in the precincts.[2] And he burned the chariots of the sun with fire. 12 And the altars [t]on the roof of the upper chamber of Ahaz, which the kings of Judah had made, and the altars [u]that Manasseh had made in the two courts of the house of the LORD, he pulled down and broke in pieces[3] and cast the dust of them [v]into the brook Kidron. 13 And the king defiled the high places

[1] Hebrew *might cause his son or daughter to pass through the fire for Molech* [2] The meaning of the Hebrew word is uncertain [3] Hebrew *pieces from there*

Chapter 23
1 [w]For ver. 1-3, see 2 Chr. 34:29-32
2 [x]See Deut. 31:11 [y]ch. 22:8
3 [z]ch. 11:14 [a][ch. 11:17] [b]Deut. 13:4
4 [c][ch. 25:18; Jer. 52:24] [d]ch. 21:3 [e]See Deut. 16:21 [f]ver. 15
5 [g]ch. 21:3
6 [h]See Deut. 16:21 [i]ver. 15 [j]ver. 15; [2 Chr. 15:16] [k][2 Chr. 34:4]
7 [l]1 Kgs. 14:24; 15:12; See Deut. 23:17 [m][Ezek. 16:16] [h][See ver. 6 above]
8 [n]1 Kgs. 15:22
9 [o]See Ezek. 44:10-14
10 [p]Isa. 30:33; Jer. 7:31, 32; 19:6, 11-14 [q]See Josh. 15:8 [r]See Lev. 18:21 [s]See 1 Kgs. 11:7
12 [t][Jer. 19:13; 32:29; Zeph. 1:5] [u]ch. 21:5 [v]ver. 4, 6

23:2–3 the king went up to the house of the LORD. Since Josiah is a pious king, Huldah's oracle about the future does not deflect him from the path of religious reform; reformation in the light of the **Book of the Covenant** is still the right thing to do. His first move is to organize a covenant-renewal ceremony (cf. 11:12–14, when the king also **stood by the pillar**).

23:4–9 all the vessels made for Baal, for Asherah. Everything to do with Baal and Asherah and the worship of the **host of heaven** is subject to radical treatment (see 1 Kings 14:15; 16:31–33; 2 Kings 17:7–23). The **Kidron** Valley, whose eastern slopes had been associated with idolatry since the time of Solomon (1 Kings 11:7), was a convenient place to destroy their cult objects, thereby removing them from Jerusalem and desecrating the valley itself as a religious site. On **male cult prostitutes** (2 Kings 23:7), see note on 1 Kings 14:24. The **hangings for the Asherah** (2 Kings 23:7) are probably ritual garments used in the worship of this goddess (cf. 10:22). Among the **high places** destroyed (see note on 1 Kings 3:2) were some at a particular **gate** (2 Kings 23:8) of the city (otherwise unknown).

23:8 defiled the high places where the priests had made offerings. These were local places of worship in various cities (see note on 1 Kings 3:2). One example is probably an Israelite temple found at the site of Arad. It was built in the tenth century B.C., and has many similarities to the Solomonic Jerusalem temple: e.g., a sacrificial altar in the courtyard of the Arad complex measured exactly the same as the temple altar described in Ex. 27:1. The Arad complex was not a legitimate Israelite shrine and was therefore abolished in the seventh century B.C., through the reforms of either Josiah or Hezekiah.

23:10 The **Valley of the Son of Hinnom** ran along the western and southern sides of ancient Jerusalem until it met the Kidron Valley running from north to south. It is here associated with the worship of **Molech** (see note on 1 Kings 11:7–8), and **Topheth** is the site where this worship was practiced. Sacred sites of this kind, containing urns holding ashes and bone remains of children and animals, have been found at Carthage and other Phoenician colonies of the western Mediterranean. "Hinnom Valley" is the short form of the name, which was transliterated into Greek as "Gehenna" (see note on Matt. 23:15).

23:11 horses that the kings of Judah had dedicated to the sun. The practice of dedicating horses to the sun appears to have been distinctively Assyrian (by way of the Hurrian peoples of Mitanni in northern Mesopotamia and Syria in the second half of the second millennium B.C.). In an excavation in Jerusalem, dating from the eighth to seventh centuries B.C., hundreds of religious vessels were found. Among these were animal figurines, many of them horses. Some of the horses had a disk between their ears, perhaps representing the sun. They could have been miniatures of the horses described here, placed **at the entrance to the house of the LORD**.

23:12 altars on the roof. A Ugarit text (describing the ritual for the annual celebration of the grape harvest at the temple of Baal in that city) mentions a king sacrificing on a roof (in the context of the worship of Shaphash, the female sun deity at Ugarit). The roof is a natural location for worship of the starry host (see 16:1–4).

23:13 Because of its hosting of idolatrous altars, the Mount of Olives, the

that were east of Jerusalem, to the south of [w]the mount of corruption, which Solomon the
king of Israel had built for [x]Ashtoreth the abomination of the Sidonians, and for [y]Chemosh
the abomination of Moab, and for [z]Milcom the abomination of the Ammonites. 14 And
he broke in pieces the [a]pillars and cut down the Asherim and filled their places with the
bones of men.
15 Moreover, the altar at Bethel, the high place erected [b]by Jeroboam the son of Nebat,
[c]who made Israel to sin, [d]that altar with the high place he pulled down and burned,[1] reducing it to dust. He also burned the Asherah. 16 And as Josiah turned, he saw the tombs there
on the mount. And he sent and took the bones out of the tombs and burned them on the
altar and defiled it, [e]according to the word of the LORD that the man of God proclaimed,
who had predicted these things. 17 Then he said, "What is that monument that I see?" And
the men of the city told him, [f]"It is the tomb of the man of God who came from Judah
and predicted[2] these things that you have done against the altar at Bethel." 18 And he said,
"Let him be; let no man move his bones." So they let his bones alone, with the bones [g]of
the prophet who came out of Samaria. 19 And Josiah removed all the shrines also of the
high places that were [h]in the cities of Samaria, which kings of Israel had made, provoking the LORD to anger. He did to them according to all that he had done at Bethel. 20 And
[i]he sacrificed all the priests of the high places who were there, on the altars, [j]and burned
human bones on them. Then he returned to Jerusalem.

Josiah Restores the Passover

21 And the king commanded all the people, [k]"Keep the Passover to the LORD your God,
[l]as it is written in this Book of the Covenant." 22 [m]For no such Passover had been kept since
the days of the judges who judged Israel, or during all the days of the kings of Israel or
of the kings of Judah. 23 But in the eighteenth year of King Josiah this Passover was kept
to the LORD in Jerusalem.
24 Moreover, Josiah put away [n]the mediums and the necromancers and [o]the household
gods and [p]the idols and all the abominations that were seen in the land of Judah and in
Jerusalem, that he might establish [q]the words of the law that were written in the book
[r]that Hilkiah the priest found in the house of the LORD. 25 [s]Before him there was no king
like him, who turned to the LORD with all his heart and with all his soul and with all his
might, according to all the Law of Moses, nor did any like him arise after him.
26 Still the LORD did not turn from the burning of his great wrath, by which his anger
was kindled against Judah, [t]because of all the provocations with which Manasseh had
provoked him. 27 And the LORD said, "I will remove Judah also out of my sight, [u]as I have

[1] Septuagint *broke in pieces its stones* [2] Hebrew *called*

13 [w][1 Kgs. 11:7] [x]See 1 Kgs. 11:5 [y][Num. 21:29] [z][1 Kgs. 11:5]
14 [a]See Ex. 23:24
15 [b]1 Kgs. 12:28, 29, 33 [c]See 1 Kgs. 14:16 [d]ver. 6
16 [e]1 Kgs. 13:2
17 [f]1 Kgs. 13:1, 30
18 [g]1 Kgs. 13:11, 31
19 [h][2 Chr. 34:6, 7]
20 [i][ch. 11:18; Ex. 22:20; 1 Kgs. 18:40] [j]2 Chr. 34:5
21 [k]See 2 Chr. 35:1-17 [l]See Ex. 12:3-11; Lev. 23:5, 8; Num. 9:2-4; Deut. 16:2-8
22 [m]2 Chr. 35:18, 19
24 [n]ch. 21:6; See Lev. 19:31 [o]See Gen. 31:19 [p]ch. 21:11, 21 [q]Lev. 19:31; 20:27; Deut. 18:11 [r]ch. 22:8
25 [s][ch. 18:5]
26 [t]ch. 21:11; 24:3, 4; Jer. 15:4
27 [u]ch. 17:18, 20; 18:11; 21:13

central summit on a ridge of three running to the east of Jerusalem and the Kidron Valley, is here called the **mount of corruption**. On **Ashtoreth** (Astarte), see note on 17:7–23; on **Chemosh** and **Milcom**, see notes on 1 Kings 11:5; 11:7–8.

23:14 he broke in pieces the pillars. Josiah is destroying all the buildings associated with idol worship. Excavations at 'En Hatzeva, 20 miles (32 km) southwest of the Dead Sea, have uncovered a huge cache of religious objects from the seventh to sixth centuries B.C. These objects were used in a nearby shrine. The shrine and the objects appear to be Edomite. The temple was suddenly destroyed, perhaps during Josiah's reforms.

23:15–20 altar at Bethel. A marked feature of Josiah's reforms is that he not only destroys but also defiles (vv. 8, 10, 13), particularly by placing pagan religious objects in proximity with graves and human bones (vv. 6, 14). It has already been hinted in v. 4 that this procedure was extended to **Bethel**, and now that narrative is picked up. Josiah takes action against this cult, which survives in the activities of the new settlers in the land of Israel (17:24–41), in fulfillment of the prophecy of 1 Kings 13:2 (see also 1 Kings 13:11–32 for the background to 2 Kings 23:17–18). Josiah's opportunity to act in this way in Assyrian territory arose from King Ashurbanipal's death around 630 B.C. and the consequent civil war and general strife in Assyria; Assyria was not capable of exercising effective control in Syria-Palestine during this period.

23:22 A **Passover** like this had not been observed **since the days of the judges who judged Israel** (see Josh. 5:10–12 for the last mention of Passover in the narrative; also Deut. 16:1–8 for the stipulations, esp. v. 6). In celebrating this festival Josiah outstrips not only Hezekiah in faithfulness to God, but even David.

23:24 On **mediums** and **necromancers**, see note on 21:1–9. The **household gods** were images of deities (see note on 19:15–19) that could be either life-size (1 Sam. 19:13–16) or figurine-size (Gen. 31:19–35). They could be used in divination in general (Ezek. 21:21; Zech. 10:2), and perhaps necromancy in particular. Some extrabiblical texts suggest that the worship of such family deities in the ancient Near East was closely linked with the care and worship of dead ancestors, and rituals in Mesopotamia certainly involved such figurines that often represented a dead person, who was believed to speak through the representation.

23:25 In spite of several generations of idolatry and rebellion against the Lord, somehow Josiah arose as a righteous king who not only appeared outwardly to be righteous but **turned to the LORD with all his heart and with all his soul and with all his might, according to all the Law of Moses**.

23:26 Though Josiah was himself righteous (v. 25), it was not enough to turn away God's wrath from the nation that had done such evil: **Still the LORD did not turn from the burning of his great wrath**. The righteousness of this one king could not change the overall situation. **because of all the provocations with which Manasseh had provoked him**. God must purge his people of deeply rooted unfaithfulness, and only exile would accomplish this.

removed Israel, and I will cast off this city that I have chosen, Jerusalem, [v]and the house
of which I said, My name shall be there."

Josiah's Death in Battle

28 Now the rest of the acts of Josiah and all that he did, are they not written in the
Book of the Chronicles of the Kings of Judah? 29 [w]In his days [x]Pharaoh Neco king of Egypt
went up to the king of Assyria to the river Euphrates. King Josiah went to meet him, and
Pharaoh Neco killed him at [y]Megiddo, as soon as he saw him. 30 [z]And his servants carried
him dead in a chariot from [y]Megiddo and brought him to Jerusalem and buried him in
his own tomb. [a]And the people of the land took Jehoahaz the son of Josiah, and anointed
him, and made him king in his father's place.

Jehoahaz's Reign and Captivity

31 [b]Jehoahaz was twenty-three years old when he began to reign, and he reigned three
months in Jerusalem. His mother's name was [c]Hamutal the daughter of Jeremiah of Libnah.
32 And he did what was evil in the sight of the LORD, [d]according to all that his fathers had
done. 33 And [x]Pharaoh Neco put him in bonds at [e]Riblah in the land of [f]Hamath, that he
might not reign in Jerusalem, and laid on the land a tribute of a hundred talents[1] of silver
and a talent of gold. 34 And [x]Pharaoh Neco made Eliakim the son of Josiah king in the place
of Josiah his father, and [g]changed his name to Jehoiakim. But he took Jehoahaz away,
[h]and he came to Egypt and died there. 35 And Jehoiakim [i]gave the silver and the gold to
Pharaoh, but he taxed the land to give the money according to the command of Pharaoh.
He exacted the silver and the gold of the people of the land, from everyone according to
his assessment, to give it to Pharaoh Neco.

Jehoiakim Reigns in Judah

36 [j]Jehoiakim was twenty-five years old when he began to reign, and he reigned eleven years
in Jerusalem. His mother's name was Zebidah the daughter of Pedaiah of Rumah. 37 And he
did what was evil in the sight of the LORD, [d]according to all that his fathers had done.

24 [k]In his days, Nebuchadnezzar king of Babylon came up, and Jehoiakim became his
servant for three years. Then he turned and rebelled against him. 2 And the LORD
sent against him bands of the [l]Chaldeans and [m]bands of the Syrians and bands of the
Moabites and bands of the Ammonites, and sent them against Judah to destroy it, [n]accord-
ing to the word of the LORD that he spoke by his servants the prophets. 3 Surely this came
upon Judah at the command of the LORD, to remove them out of his sight, [o]for the sins
of Manasseh, according to all that he had done, 4 and also [p]for the innocent blood that he
had shed. For he filled Jerusalem with innocent blood, and the LORD would not pardon.
5 [q]Now the rest of the deeds of Jehoiakim and all that he did, are they not written in the
Book of the Chronicles of the Kings of Judah? 6 So Jehoiakim [r]slept with his fathers, and
Jehoiachin his son reigned in his place. 7 [s]And the king of Egypt did not come again out of
his land, [t]for the king of Babylon had taken all that belonged to the king of Egypt [u]from
the Brook of Egypt to the river Euphrates.

Jehoiachin Reigns in Judah

8 [v]Jehoiachin was [w]eighteen years old when he became king, and he reigned three months
in Jerusalem. His mother's name was Nehushta the daughter of Elnathan of Jerusalem. 9 And
he did what was evil in the sight of the LORD, [x]according to all that his father had done.

Jerusalem Captured

10 At that time the servants of [y]Nebuchadnezzar king of Babylon came up to Jerusalem,
and the city was besieged. 11 And [y]Nebuchadnezzar king of Babylon came to the city while
his servants were besieging it, 12 [z]and Jehoiachin the king of Judah gave himself up to the
king of Babylon, himself and his mother and his servants and his officials and his palace

[1] A *talent* was about 75 pounds or 34 kilograms

27 [v]See ch. 21:4
29 [w]For ver. 29, 30, see 2 Chr. 35:20-24 [x]Jer. 46:2 [y][Judg. 5:19; Zech. 12:11]
30 [z][ch. 9:28] [y][See ver. 29 above] [a]For ver. 30-34, see 2 Chr. 36:1-4
31 [b][1 Chr. 3:15; Jer. 22:11] [c]ch. 24:18
32 [d][ch. 24:9, 19]
33 [x][See ver. 29 above] [e]ch. 25:6, 20, 21; Jer. 39:5, 6; 52:9, 10, 26, 27 [f]See 1 Kgs. 8:65
34 [x][See ver. 29 above] [g][ch. 24:17; Dan. 1:7] [h]Jer. 22:11, 12; [Ezek. 19:3, 4]
35 [i]ver. 33
36 [j]2 Chr. 36:5
37 [d][See ver. 32 above]

Chapter 24

1 [k]2 Chr. 36:6; Jer. 25:1, 9; Dan. 1:1
2 [l]ch. 25:4; Jer. 32:28, 29; 35:11; [Ezek. 19:8] [m]Jer. 35:11 [n]ch. 20:17; 21:12-14; 23:27
3 [o]ch. 21:11; 23:26
4 [p]ch. 21:16
5 [q]2 Chr. 36:8
6 [r][2 Chr. 36:6; Jer. 22:18, 19; 36:30]
7 [s]Jer. 37:5-7 [t][Jer. 46:2, 20, 24, 26] [u]See Num. 34:5
8 [v][1 Chr. 3:16; Esth. 2:6; Jer. 22:24, 28; 24:1; 37:1] [w][2 Chr. 36:9]
9 [x]ch. 23:37
10 [y]Dan. 1:1
11 [y][See ver. 10 above]
12 [z][Jer. 24:1; 29:1, 2; Ezek. 17:12]

23:28–30 Pharaoh Neco killed him at Megiddo. After the death of the Assyrian king Ashurbanipal around 630 B.C., Egypt gradually emerged as the major power in Syria-Palestine and as the ally of Assyria in its struggle with Babylon, sending troops northward, at least from 616 onward, to join with the Assyrians in battle. The battle mentioned here took place in 609 B.C. as Pharaoh Neco II marched north for what was apparently the last joint Assyrian-Egyptian engagement with the Babylonians (and their allies, the Medes). Megiddo controlled the main international highway running from

12[a][2 Chr. 36:10] [b][ch. 25:27]
13[c]ch. 20:17; Isa. 39:6 [d]2 Chr. 36:7; Ezra 1:7; Dan. 1:2; 5:2, 3 [e]See 1 Kgs. 7:48-50 [f]Jer. 20:5
14[g]Jer. 24:1 [h][ver. 16; Jer. 52:28] [i]Jer. 24:1; 29:2; [1 Sam. 13:19, 22] [j]ch. 25:12
15[k]2 Chr. 36:10; Esth. 2:6; [Jer. 22:24-26]
16[l][ver. 14]
17[m]For ver. 17-20, see 2 Chr. 36:10-13 [n][Jer. 37:1] [o][1 Chr. 3:15] [p][ch. 23:34; 2 Chr. 36:4]
18[q]For ch. 24:18–25:21, see Jer. 52:1-27 [r]ch. 23:31

officials. [a]The king of Babylon took him prisoner [b]in the eighth year of his reign **13** and
carried off all the treasures of the house of the LORD [c]and the treasures of the king's house,
[d]and cut in pieces all the vessels of gold in the temple of the LORD, [e]which Solomon king
of Israel had made, [f]as the LORD had foretold. **14** [g]He carried away all Jerusalem and all the
officials and all the mighty men of valor, [h]10,000 captives, [i]and all the craftsmen and the
smiths. None remained, [j]except the poorest people of the land. **15** [k]And he carried away
Jehoiachin to Babylon. The king's mother, the king's wives, his officials, and the chief men
of the land he took into captivity from Jerusalem to Babylon. **16** And the king of Babylon
brought captive to Babylon all the men of valor, [l]7,000, and the craftsmen and the metal
workers, 1,000, all of them strong and fit for war. **17** [m]And the king of Babylon [n]made
Mattaniah, [o]Jehoiachin's uncle, king in his place, [p]and changed his name to Zedekiah.

Zedekiah Reigns in Judah

18 [q]Zedekiah was twenty-one years old when he became king, and he reigned eleven
years in Jerusalem. His mother's name was [r]Hamutal the daughter of Jeremiah of Libnah.

Egypt to Damascus as it entered the Jezreel Valley (see note on 9:27–28). Josiah's decision to confront the Egyptian army there implies that he had captured Megiddo from either the Egyptians or the Assyrians before the battle, and was perhaps hoping to benefit from being seen to take the Babylonians' side. But Josiah died in the battle. On the **Chronicles of the Kings**, see note on 1 Kings 14:19. The Babylonian Chronicle recounts the expeditions of Pharaoh Neco II of Egypt to aid the Assyrians. Josiah sought to prevent Egypt's reinforcing of Assyria. Evidence of the battle at Megiddo can be seen at the site.

23:31–25:30 *The End of Judah.* The story of 1–2 Kings now comes to its end as imperial power passes to Babylon, temple and palace are destroyed, and Jerusalem's treasures are carried off to a foreign land. It is left to Josiah's grandson Jehoiachin to offer such hope as can be found for the future of the Davidic "lamp" (1 Kings 11:36).

23:31–35 Jehoahaz. The new king of Judah is summoned to Pharaoh Neco's temporary headquarters at **Riblah** on the eastern bank of the Orontes River, as the Egyptians return from the unsuccessful siege of Haran (609 B.C.). Jehoahaz is removed from power and subsequently imprisoned in **Egypt**. (See note on 2 Chron. 36:1–4.)

23:36–24:7 Jehoahaz's replacement is his brother **Jehoiakim**, who is confronted by the armies of **Babylon** that have just dismantled the Assyrian Empire and now invade Palestine in pursuit of complete victory over Egypt. Their ruler is **Nebuchadnezzar**, who was never able to defeat Egypt completely but did enough to ensure that the **king of Egypt did not come again out of his land**. Jehoiakim first switched his allegiance from Egypt to Babylon (604 B.C.), but after Nebuchadnezzar's failed attempt to invade Egypt in 601 (i.e., after **three years**), he rebelled against Babylon and looked once again to Egypt for help (cf. Jer. 46:14–28).

24:2 and the LORD sent against him bands. Cf. 23:26–27.

24:5 Chronicles of the Kings. See note on 1 Kings 14:19.

24:8–17 Jehoiachin. The Babylonian withdrawal from Palestine in 601 B.C. turned out to be only temporary, and Jehoiakim's rebellion brought the Babylonian army to the gates of **Jerusalem** at the end of the year 598. The city surrendered to the Babylonians on the fifteenth or sixteenth of March 597 B.C., by which time Jehoiachin was king. Significant deportations followed; on deportation as an imperial tactic, see note on 15:27–31. Although 1–2 Kings does not mention this, the prophet Ezekiel was among the exiles; his prophetic ministry began a few years later in Babylon (Ezek. 1:2–3).

24:10–17 This first capture of Jerusalem occurred in 597 B.C., the seventh year of the reign of Nebuchadnezzar. The Babylonian Chronicle tells of the king's army laying siege to Jerusalem, capturing it, and appointing his own king over it. He then took tribute from Judah.

24:18–25:7 Jehoiachin's uncle Mattaniah ruled next, under the name of **Zedekiah**, as a Babylonian vassal. Jeremiah 27–29 suggests that from early in his reign (Jer. 27:1; 28:1) he was plotting revolt, and eventually he **rebelled**. A two-year siege of Jerusalem followed, and the city eventually fell in 587 or 586 B.C. As the city wall was being breached on the northern side, Zedekiah managed to escape **by night** with his troops through an exit in the southeastern wall that is probably to be identified with the Fountain Gate of Neh. 3:15. He was captured while fleeing to the **Arabah** by way of the Wadi Kelt in the vicinity of **Jericho** (see also note on 2 Chron. 36:11–16).

Babylon Attacks Judah
597, 586 B.C.

The final years of the kingdom of Judah were marked by a power struggle between the Egyptians and the Babylonians, the rising power that had overtaken the Assyrian Empire. King Nebuchadnezzar of Babylon eventually won out and seized control of the Mediterranean coastal lands. When Zedekiah, who had been placed on the throne of Judah by the Babylonians, rebelled, Nebuchadnezzar besieged Jerusalem and captured the city. Zedekiah fled toward the east but was captured near Jericho and sent to Riblah to be judged.

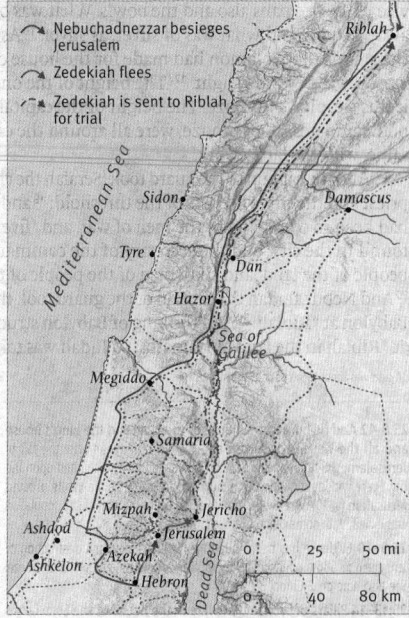

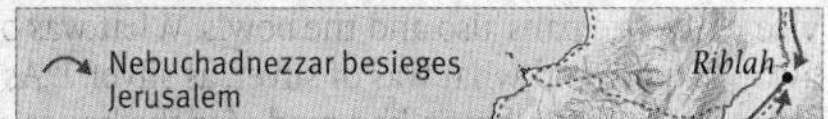

19 And he did what was evil in the sight of the LORD, [s]according to all that Jehoiakim had
done. 20 For because of the anger of the LORD it came to the point in Jerusalem and Judah
that he cast them out from his presence.
[t]And Zedekiah rebelled against the king of Babylon.

Fall and Captivity of Judah

25 [u]And in the ninth year of his reign, in the tenth month, on the tenth day of the
month, [v]Nebuchadnezzar king of Babylon came with all his army against Jerusalem
and laid siege to it. [w]And they built siegeworks all around it. 2 So the city was besieged till
the eleventh year of King Zedekiah. 3 On the ninth day of the fourth month [x]the famine
was so severe in the city that there was no food for the people of the land. 4 Then a breach
was made in the city, and all the men of war fled by night by the way of the gate between
the two walls, by [y]the king's garden, and [z]the Chaldeans were around the city. And they
went in the direction of the [a]Arabah. 5 But the army of the Chaldeans pursued the king
and overtook him in the plains of Jericho, and all his army was scattered from him. 6 Then
they captured the king [b]and brought him up to the king of Babylon at [c]Riblah, and they
passed sentence on him. 7 They slaughtered the sons of Zedekiah before his eyes, [d]and put
out the eyes of Zedekiah and bound him in chains and took him to Babylon.
8 [e]In the fifth month, on [f]the seventh day of the month—that was the nineteenth year
of King Nebuchadnezzar, king of Babylon—Nebuzaradan, the captain of the bodyguard,
a servant of the king of Babylon, came to Jerusalem. 9 [g]And he burned the house of the
LORD [h]and the king's house and all the houses of Jerusalem; every great house he burned
down. 10 And all the army of the Chaldeans, who were with the captain of the guard, [i]broke
down the walls around Jerusalem. 11 [j]And the rest of the people who were left in the city
and the deserters who had deserted to the king of Babylon, together with the rest of the
multitude, Nebuzaradan the captain of the guard carried into exile. 12 But the captain of
the guard left [k]some of the poorest of the land to be vinedressers and plowmen.
13 [l]And the pillars [m]of bronze that were in the house of the LORD, and [n]the stands and
[o]the bronze sea that were in the house of the LORD, the Chaldeans broke in pieces and
carried the bronze to Babylon. 14 [p]And they took away the pots and the shovels and the
snuffers and the dishes for incense and all the vessels of bronze used in the temple service, 15 the fire pans also and the bowls. What was of gold the captain of the guard took
away as gold, and what was of silver, as silver. 16 As for the two pillars, the one sea, and
the stands that Solomon had made for the house of the LORD, [q]the bronze of all these
vessels was beyond weight. 17 [r]The height of the one pillar was eighteen cubits,[1] and on
it was a capital of bronze. The height of the capital was three cubits. A latticework and
pomegranates, all of bronze, were all around the capital. And the second pillar had the
same, with the latticework.
18 [s]And the captain of the guard took [t]Seraiah the chief priest and [u]Zephaniah the second
priest and the three keepers of the threshold; 19 and from the city he took an officer who
had been in command of the men of war, and [v]five men of the king's council who were
found in the city; and the secretary of the commander of the army, who mustered the
people of the land; and sixty men of the people of the land, who were found in the city.
20 And Nebuzaradan the captain of the guard took them and brought them to the king of
Babylon at [w]Riblah. 21 And the king of Babylon struck them down and put them to death
at [w]Riblah in the land of Hamath. [x]So Judah was taken into exile out of its land.

[1] A *cubit* was about 18 inches or 45 centimeters

19 [s]ch. 23:37
20 [t][Ezek. 17:18]

Chapter 25

1 [u]For ver. 1-7, see 2 Chr. 36:17-20; Jer. 39:1-7; 52:4-11 [v]Jer. 34:1, 2; 39:1, 2; Ezek. 24:2 [w][Ezek. 21:22; 26:8]
3 [x][Lam. 4:9, 10]
4 [y]Neh. 3:15 [z]See ch. 24:2 [a]See Deut. 1:1
6 [b]Jer. 32:4 [c][ch. 23:33]
7 [d][Ezek. 12:13]
8 [e]For ver. 8-12, see Jer. 39:8-12; 52:12-16 [f][Jer. 52:12]
9 [g]2 Chr. 36:19; Ps. 79:1 [h][Hos. 8:14; Amos 2:5]
10 [i]Neh. 1:3
11 [j]2 Chr. 36:20
12 [k]ch. 24:14; Jer. 40:7
13 [l][Jer. 27:19, 22]; For ver. 13-17, see 2 Chr. 36:18-20; Jer. 52:17-23 [m]1 Kgs. 7:15 [n]1 Kgs. 7:27 [o]1 Kgs. 7:23
14 [p]Ex. 27:3; 1 Kgs. 7:45, 50
16 [q]1 Kgs. 7:47
17 [r][1 Kgs. 7:15-18; 2 Chr. 3:15]
18 [s]For ver. 18-21, see Jer. 52:24-27 [t]1 Chr. 6:14; Ezra 7:1 [u]Jer. 21:1; 29:25; 37:3
19 [v]Esth. 1:14; [Jer. 52:25]
20 [w]ch. 23:33
21 [w][See ver. 20 above] [x][ch. 23:27; Lev. 26:33; Deut. 28:64]

25:8–12 And he burned the house of the LORD and the king's house and all the houses of Jerusalem (v. 9). A few weeks after the fall of **Jerusalem**, the full vengeance of the Babylonian king was visited upon the city. Every important building was **burned down** (v. 9); the **walls around Jerusalem** (v. 10) were broken down; and a further section of the population was exiled, with some being executed.

25:9–10 Evidence has been found for Nebuchadnezzar's destruction of Jerusalem in 586 B.C., including Babylonian arrowheads of iron and bronze. See also note on 2 Chron. 36:17–21.

25:13–14 Pillars of bronze that were in the house of the LORD begins a detailed list of temple furnishings (vv. 13–17) carried off by the Babylonians for the value of their metal. **The pots and the shovels and the snuffers and the dishes for incense** and all the rest were beautiful instruments used to worship the Lord of heaven and earth (see notes on 1 Kings 7:15–21; 7:23–47). But the Lord has abandoned this temple, so its outward beauty has become a deceptive illusion of his presence. Its destruction is a fitting end to the nation. No mention is made of the ark of the covenant; presumably that also was taken (cf. Jer. 3:16). "How lonely sits the city that was full of people!" (Lam. 1:1).

25:21 Almost all hope is gone in the summary statement, **So Judah was**

22[y]Jer. 39:14; 40:5 [z]ch. 22:12
23[a]For ver. 23, 24, see Jer. 40:7-9 [b]Josh. 18:26
25[c]Jer. 41:1, 2 [d]Jer. 40:14, 15
26[e]See Jer. 43:4-7
27[f]For ver. 27-30, see Jer. 52:31-34 [g]ch. 24:12, 15 [h]Gen. 40:13, 20
29[i]2 Sam. 9:7, 13

Gedaliah Made Governor of Judah

22 And over the people who remained in the land of Judah, whom Nebuchadnezzar king
of Babylon had left, he appointed [y]Gedaliah the son of [z]Ahikam, son of Shaphan, governor.
23 [a]Now when all the captains and their men heard that the king of Babylon had appointed
Gedaliah governor, they came with their men to Gedaliah at [b]Mizpah, namely, Ishmael
the son of Nethaniah, and Johanan the son of Kareah, and Seraiah the son of Tanhumeth
the Netophathite, and Jaazaniah the son of the Maacathite. 24 And Gedaliah swore to them
and their men, saying, "Do not be afraid because of the Chaldean officials. Live in the land
and serve the king of Babylon, and it shall be well with you." 25 [c]But in the seventh month,
[d]Ishmael the son of Nethaniah, son of Elishama, of the royal family, came with ten men and
struck down Gedaliah and put him to death along with the Jews and the Chaldeans who
were with him at Mizpah. 26 [e]Then all the people, both small and great, and the captains
of the forces arose and went to Egypt, for they were afraid of the Chaldeans.

Jehoiachin Released from Prison

27 [f]And in the thirty-seventh year of [g]the exile of Jehoiachin king of Judah, in the twelfth
month, on the twenty-seventh day of the month, Evil-merodach king of Babylon, in the
year that he began to reign, graciously [h]freed[1] Jehoiachin king of Judah from prison. 28 And
he spoke kindly to him and gave him a seat above the seats of the kings who were with
him in Babylon. 29 So Jehoiachin put off his prison garments. And every day of his life [i]he
dined regularly at the king's table, 30 and for his allowance, a regular allowance was given
him by the king, according to his daily needs, as long as he lived.

[1] Hebrew *reign, lifted up the head of*

taken into exile out of its land. (See map below.) But the land is still "its land," holding out the promise of a future return.

25:22–26 Gedaliah, the new **governor** of the territory, was the grandson of King Josiah's secretary **Shaphan**. His subsequent assassination precipitated a general flight to **Egypt**.

25:27–30 Evil-merodach king of Babylon . . . freed Jehoiachin. Evil-merodach (in Akkadian, Amel-Marduk) was Nebuchadnezzar's son and successor, ruling 562–560 B.C. His release of the Judean king **from prison** in 561 B.C. gives the reader some hope that there is still a future for the Davidic line—that the words of 2 Sam. 7:15–16 are still true: "my steadfast love will not depart from him. . . . your kingdom shall be made sure forever." Cuneiform texts found in the excavations of Babylon throw light on the treatment of the Judahite king Jehoiachin after he went into captivity in 597 B.C. The texts are ration receipts, probably of an officer in charge of delivering supplies to prisoners or foreigners in Babylon. Jehoiachin is mentioned by name as receiving oil (cf. 2 Kings 25:30).

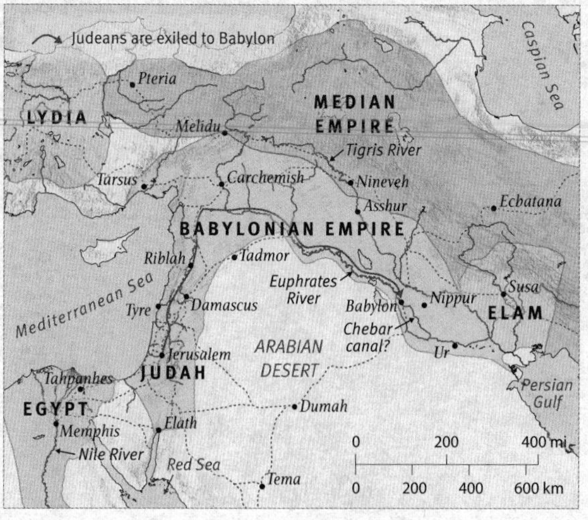

Exile to Babylon

597, 586, 582 B.C.

It appears that three separate deportations of Judeans to Babylon took place under the rule of Nebuchadnezzar (see also Jer. 52:28–30). The first came during the reign of Jehoiachin, when Nebuchadnezzar besieged Jerusalem and carried away many of the treasures of the temple and the royal palace. The second occurred after the fall of Jerusalem in 586 B.C., when the walls of the city were leveled and the temple was completely destroyed. The third appears to have occurred around 582 B.C. while King Nebuchadnezzar was reasserting his control over the general region of Palestine (see note on Jer. 52:28–30).

INTRODUCTION TO

1–2 CHRONICLES

Author and Title

The text nowhere directly identifies its author (traditionally designated "the Chronicler"). Jewish tradition assigned the work to Ezra the scribe, who lived in the fifth century B.C., and some modern scholarship has supported this view. But the question of authorship is closely linked to the view one takes of the original form of the Chronicler's work and its relationship to Ezra–Nehemiah (see the sections on the Date and the Purpose, Occasion, and Background). In any case, the internal evidence indicates that the author was a priest or Levite with scribal training who was employed in the service of the temple during the Persian period (539–332 B.C.) and had access to the temple records.

The Hebrew title of the work, *Dibre Hayyamim*, is derived from 1 Chronicles 27:24 and may be translated "the events of the years" or "annals." In the Septuagint (Greek translation), it is known as *Paraleipomena* or "the things omitted," indicating that it was considered a supplement to the books of Samuel and Kings. The English title derives from a suggestion by Jerome, the translator of the Vulgate (a Latin translation), that a more suitable title would be "the chronicle of the whole sacred history." Martin Luther adopted this proposal, titling his translation of the books *Die Chronika*, and versions ever since the Reformation have followed his practice.

Date

Until the latter half of the twentieth century it was widely held that Chronicles and Ezra–Nehemiah were originally a single work recounting Israel's history from Adam to the time of Nehemiah, c. 430 B.C. (see Neh. 5:14). However, most scholars now consider them separate works from the same temple circles of priests and scribes. The inclusion in Chronicles of modified passages from Ezra–Nehemiah (1 Chron. 9:2–34 = Neh. 11:3–19; 2 Chron. 36:22–23 = Ezra 1:1–3) points to Chronicles being a somewhat later work. The list of the postexilic Davidic descendants in 1 Chronicles 3:17–24 suggests a date of c. 400 B.C., or possibly some decades later.

Theme

The central theme of Chronicles is *the significance of the Davidic covenant as the enduring basis of Israel's life and hope*. The Davidic covenant is expressed in the two institutions that derive directly from it: the monarchy and the temple. These institutions are mutually related (1 Chron. 17:10b–14), and together they represent God's kingdom in Israel (2 Chron. 13:5, 8). The Davidic covenant does not replace the Mosaic covenant but builds on it for the new age of the monarchy and the temple. Further dimensions of the Davidic covenant are discussed below under Key Themes.

Purpose, Occasion, and Background

The Babylonian campaign against Judah, which began in 605 B.C. under Nebuchadnezzar, climaxed in the destruction of Jerusalem and its temple in 586 and the deportation of many of its leading people to settlements near Babylon. The conquest meant the overthrow of the Davidic monarchy and the end of Judah as a nation-state. Babylon, in turn, fell in 538 B.C. to the Persians under Cyrus II. The Persians followed a more benign policy of permitting the exiled people groups to return to their lands (now provinces in the

Basic Chronology of 1–2 Chronicles

Events	Dates	Passages
Foundation of the Davidic monarchy	c. 1010–931 B.C.	1 Chronicles 10–2 Chronicles 9
History of Judah from the division of the kingdom until its fall	931–586	2 Chron. 10:1–36:21
Babylonian captivity	586–538	2 Chron. 36:17–21
Cyrus's decree	538	2 Chron. 36:22–23

Persian Empire) to rebuild their cities and reestablish their religious practices. Groups of exiles from Judah, including priests and civil leaders, returned in 538 B.C., but the temple was not completely rebuilt until 516. This initial restoration was followed by those who returned in 458 B.C. with Ezra, who came to reestablish the Law of Moses as the rule for the community's life, and Nehemiah, who arrived as governor in 445 to rebuild the walls of Jerusalem.

Chronicles was most probably composed in this period, or some years afterward. Judah, as the historical heir of Israel, had been reconstituted in the land, with the temple rebuilt and functioning in Jerusalem. Yet it was a community much reduced in strength and numbers, occupying only a small portion of the land compared to the preexilic kingdom. The people of Judah were subject to foreign overlords, living in the midst of a mixed, and sometimes antagonistic, population. In many ways their conditions in the land were still characterized by exile rather than restoration (see Ezra 9:6–15; Neh. 9:32–36). The questions of Israel's place in God's purposes and the meaning of his ancient promises to David were pressing ones.

With such questions in mind, the Chronicler wrote to commend a positive prescription for the spiritual and social renewal of his community. He presented an interpretation of Israel's past, drawing mainly on the books of Samuel and Kings. He recast and supplemented those books in many ways, not only to show how the nation's unfaithfulness to God had led it into disaster but also to point out how its faithful kings and people had experienced God's blessing. These episodes were evidently intended to encourage a similar response in the hearer. The exhortative character of Chronicles is pronounced, especially in the speeches of the kings and prophets. Those recorded speeches rhetorically address the people and priests of the Chronicler's present, the historical heirs of preexilic Israel.

The Chronicler's narrative method is clear and explicit. He recounts the history of Israel and the Davidic monarchy down to the exile primarily as a matter of "seeking God" or "forsaking him," and sets out the consequences that flow from that choice for the king and people. To *seek God* means to orient one's life toward him in active faith and obedience, to be diligent in fulfilling the commands of the Mosaic law, to oppose idolatry, and especially to support and participate in the authorized worship of the temple (see 1 Chron. 10:13; 13:3; 15:13; 16:10; 22:19; 28:9; 2 Chron. 1:5; 12:14; 14:4, 7; 15:2, 4; 16:12; 17:4; 18:4; 19:3; 20:4; 22:9; 26:5; 30:19; 31:21; 34:3). Those who seek God experience his blessing, typically in the form of large families (1 Chron. 14:3–7; 2 Chron. 11:19–21; 13:21; 24:3), building projects (1 Chron. 14:1; 2 Chron. 8:1–6; 11:5–12; 14:6–7; 17:12; 26:2, 6; 27:3–4; 32:5, 29–30; 33:14), riches and honor (1 Chron. 14:2, 17; 29:2–5; 2 Chron. 9:13–14, 22; 26:8, 15), military strength and success (1 Chron. 5:20–22; 14:8–16; 18:1–20:8; 2 Chron. 8:3; 13:13–18; 14:9–15; 20:20–26; 25:11–13; 26:4–8; 27:5–7; 32:20–22), and peace for the land (1 Chron. 22:18; 23:25; 2 Chron. 14:4–7; 15:15, 19; 17:10).

The converse is to *forsake God,* which includes apostasy and idolatry, the neglect and abuse of the temple and its institutions, despising the word of prophets, and egregious violence (see 1 Chron. 28:9; 2 Chron. 12:1, 5; 13:10; 21:10; 24:18). God's punishment for forsaking him and his law includes defeat and despoiling by foreign enemies (1 Chron. 10:1–7; 2 Chron. 12:2–4; 21:8–11, 16–17; 24:23–24; 25:17–24; 28:5–8, 16–21; 33:10–11; 35:20–24; 36:5–19), sickness and death for disobedient individuals (1 Chron. 2:3; 10:13–14; 2 Chron. 16:12; 21:12–15, 18–19; 22:7–9; 23:14–15; 24:25; 25:27; 26:16–21; 33:24; 35:23–24), and, finally, forfeiture of the land and exile for the people (1 Chron. 5:26; 9:1; 2 Chron. 36:18, 20). The basic concepts represented by "seeking God" or "forsaking" him are, of course, also expressed by a broader range of phrases ("to serve God with a whole heart"; "to do what is right [*or* evil] in the eyes of the LORD"; and esp. "to be unfaithful"; see note on 1 Chron. 2:3–8).

Just as important as the exhortation to faithful seeking, if not more so, is *the message of forgiveness and restoration to God through sacrifices of atonement and humble prayer*. The Chronicler is insistent that from beginning (1 Chron. 2:3, 7) to end (2 Chron. 36:14), Israel is a sinful people that fails to reverence God in his holiness as they should. That sinfulness extends even to David (1 Chron. 21:1), who best exemplifies for the Chronicler what it means to seek God. Yet God in his mercy provides the way back to himself. The temple stands where David repented and offered sacrifice. It is designated by God as the instrument of his forgiveness and the point at which the consequences of sin may be reversed (2 Chron. 7:12–16). This emphasis on repentance explains one of the notable differences in presentation and purpose between Chronicles and Kings. The Chronicler would certainly agree with the writer(s) of Kings that figures such as Rehoboam and Manasseh were notorious sinners whose disobedience divided the kingdom and led to its fall. But the Chronicler also uses them as examples of repentance and personal recipients of God's grace.

The destruction of the kingdom of Judah and the exile of its people are duly explained as the consequence of Israel's persistent unfaithfulness and its rejection of the prophetic summons to repentance (2 Chron. 36:16). But the ending of Chronicles—Cyrus's decree to return and rebuild the temple (2 Chron. 36:22–23)—takes the reader full circle to the beginning: a representative core of God's people has once again been gathered to the land and to the temple in Jerusalem, their daily round of worship standing in continuity with the preexilic days (1 Chron. 9:2–34). The Chronicler has shown how Israel's fall occurred, how such a disaster may be avoided in the future, and how all who belong to Israel may be gathered and consolidated as God's people. At the center stands the temple, the symbol of Yahweh's constant will to forgive and restore his penitent people who "seek his face" in prayer (2 Chron. 7:14). The restored temple testifies to the permanent continuance of God's covenant promises to David. Holding fast to those promises, and supporting the temple institutions that testify to them, is Israel's road to greater blessing and restoration.

A key question in discerning the Chronicler's purpose has to do with the promise to David of a permanent dynasty (1 Chron. 17:12–14; 2 Chron. 6:16–17; 13:5) in an age when the Davidic monarchy had long since ceased to function. Some commentators believe that the Chronicler envisioned a return to something like the preexilic kingdom, with a descendant of David once more enthroned in Jerusalem. Yet nothing in the book allows it to be tied so directly to the political circumstances of postexilic Judah. Alternatively, it has been argued that the Chronicler saw the temple and its priestly institutions as the heir to these promises, replacing the defunct monarchy in the theocratic rule of the religious community. Against this is the fact that the Chronicler goes to great lengths to show that the monarchy and the temple are separate pillars of God's rule in Israel, and that the Davidic house has been preserved through great danger (see 2 Chronicles 21–23, esp. 23:3) and down into the Chronicler's day (1 Chron. 3:17–24). Moreover, the Davidic dynasty is connected with God's own throne and eternal kingdom as the instrument of God's rule over Israel (1 Chron. 28:5; 2 Chron. 9:8) and therefore has a transcendent character compared to "the kingdoms of the countries" (1 Chron. 29:30). For these reasons, it seems clear that the Chronicler understood the Davidic line to be a focus of hope for the future, although he has not specified what this hope entails. This can be called an *implicit messianism*, a hope that will bear fruit in the appearance of Christ. The Chronicler's eye, however, is directed more to what his own community may become in the interim: he envisions "all Israel" (not only Judah but all the tribes) as once more possessing the land, living according to the Law of Moses, and worshiping at the temple.

History of Salvation Summary

God chose Israel to be his people, through whom he would bless all peoples, especially by raising up the ultimate heir of David to rule them. He gave his people the privilege of worshiping and obeying him, but sadly, they were unfaithful, and he disciplined them severely. For all that, the exile was not the end of Israel's story. Members of the restoration community were the heirs of Israel, both of its mission and of its privileges. May they be faithful this time! (For an explanation of the "History of Salvation," see the Overview of the Bible, pp. 23–26. See also History of Salvation in the Old Testament: Preparing the Way for Christ, pp. 2635–2661.)

Literary Features

First and Second Chronicles are both court histories, but within that genre they are very different books; 1 Chronicles also focuses strongly on the heroic figure of King David. Specific forms of documentary writing include genealogies, inventories, and summaries of events such as lists of David's victories. There are also speeches or orations, prayers, and a psalm of praise (1 Chron. 16:8–36). The story of David is placed within the encompassing story of God's dealings with his covenant nation Israel, whose identity assumes a corporate character (repeatedly called "all Israel"). Smaller groups of people round out the cast of characters, including the Levites, the priests, others who assisted in worship at the temple, and military and civil officials. Because the writer gives readers a largely idealized picture of David's reign, especially regarding the religious life of the nation, a picture emerges of a good society ruled by an ideal ruler under God's providential control.

Second Chronicles is expansive in its scope, tracing the history of a nation as embodied in its kings over a span of 400 years. Because the focus is so thoroughly on individual kings, the book has the feel of an anthology of brief biographies and hero stories. The stories of many of the kings and their disappointing downfalls have affinities with literary tragedy, and the pictures of national life under the good kings are brief utopian visions of a good society. The format of 2 Chronicles has more in common with the flow of a story than a history book. Stories are based on a principle of back-and-forth rhythm, and 2 Chronicles obeys this rule of narrative construction. As the narrative progresses, the pendulum swings back and forth between good and bad rulers, and between God's blessing and punishment. The reader also moves back and forth between religious events and more "secular" political or military events (with some of the material resembling what one might encounter in *any* book of ancient history). Just as readers remember a story partly as a gallery of memorable characters, so 2 Chronicles likewise remains in the reader's memory as a collection of imposing kings with impressive-sounding names. Finally, the author alternates between relatively brief accounts of evil kings and more extended accounts of good kings. In 2 Chronicles 11–36, kings are presented as characters to emulate for their faith or shun for their impiety.

Key Themes

1. *The Davidic covenant.* God's promissory covenant with David (1 Chron. 17:10b–14, 23–27; 2 Chron. 6:10, 15–17, 42; 7:17–18; 13:8; 23:3) is the source of the Davidic dynasty and Solomon's temple. God's commitment to "build a house" for David is fulfilled in the accession of Solomon and the line of his descendants, while the temple is completed as God promised (2 Chron. 6:10). The covenant has its origin in God's purpose and initiative in electing David to be his king (1 Chron. 28:4) and Solomon to be his temple builder (1 Chron. 22:9–10; 28:5).

God is committed to maintaining his covenant in preserving the Davidic house even through apostasy (2 Chron. 21:13) and exile (1 Chron. 3:17–24). The covenant continues "forever" because of God's gracious love for Israel, a point frequently celebrated in worship (see 1 Chron. 16:41; 2 Chron. 5:13; 20:21); nevertheless, there are conditions of obedience to God's commands if the king and his people are to experience the blessings of the covenant (1 Chron. 28:9; 2 Chron. 7:17–18; 15:2, 7).

While the Davidic covenant plays a preeminent role in the work, it does not displace the Mosaic covenant as the foundation for Israel's existence in the exodus (see 1 Chron. 17:5; 2 Chron. 5:10; 6:5; 7:22; 20:7) and the way in which the nation must live its life before God. The Law of Moses remains the standard of authority and the mark of obedience to God's will, according to which David and his successors are judged (1 Chron. 15:15; 22:13; 2 Chron. 7:17; 12:2; 14:4; 19:10; 24:9; 25:4; 35:6). David instituted a number of reforms in the organization of worship and the duties of the Levites (1 Chron. 16:4, 37–40; 23:1–26:32), but these changes did not alter the fundamental status of the Mosaic law. The reforming kings (including Jehoshaphat, 2 Chron. 17:7–9; and Josiah, 2 Chronicles 34–35) took care to ensure that their measures would bring Judah's life into closer conformity with the Law of Moses.

2. *The temple.* Solomon's temple looms very large in Chronicles, all the more so in comparison to the books of Samuel and Kings. Much of the presentation of David's reign is taken up with his preparations for the temple, including the ark narrative (1 Chronicles 13, 15–16), which is really a harbinger of the building that will house the symbol of God's presence (1 Chron. 17:1; 2 Chron. 5:4–5; 6:41). Moreover, David's wars (1 Chronicles 18–20) have their primary meaning for the Chronicler in securing "rest" for the land as the condition for temple building (1 Chron. 22:17–19). The portrayal of Solomon's reign is also taken up almost entirely with describing the construction and dedication of the temple (2 Chron. 2:1–8:16). In post-Solomonic history, the temple plays a central role in the reigns of Hezekiah (2 Chronicles 29–30) and Josiah (2 Chronicles 34–35).

The temple's great significance for the Chronicler is as the manifestation of the Davidic covenant alongside the dynasty. The temple and the Davidic house have a mutually supportive relationship. Just as David provided for the construction of the building (1 Chron. 22:2–16; 29:2–5) and organized its personnel (1 Chronicles 23–26), his faithful successors should take pains to ensure that its round of worship is maintained (see 2 Chron. 13:10–12), and the building is kept in repair (see 2 Chron. 24:4–14) or purified after defilement (2 Chron. 29:3–19; 34:8–13). Conversely, it is the temple personnel who should come to the aid of the Davidic dynasty in its time of crisis (2 Chron. 23:10–16).

Above all, the Chronicler's interest in the temple lies with its personnel, especially the Levites. Considerable attention is given to their activities of offering praise in song and music (1 Chron. 6:31–47; 9:33; 15:19; 16:4–6, 37–38; 25:1–31; 2 Chron. 5:12–13; 7:6; 8:14–15; 20:21–22; 30:21; 35:15), uttering prophecy and encouragement (1 Chron. 25:1; 2 Chron. 20:14–17), supporting the Aaronic priests in administering the sacrifices (2 Chron. 29:34; 35:11–14), safeguarding the holiness of the temple (1 Chron. 9:17–27; 26:1–19; 2 Chron. 23:18), and other kinds of administration and teaching (1 Chron. 9:28–29, 31–32; 26:20–32; 2 Chron. 17:8–9; 24:4–5, 8–11; 29:3–19; 31:11–19; 34:9–13). In short, the Levites played an essential role in maintaining the whole apparatus of worship, and in many ways may be seen as the forerunners of the Christian ministry (see Rom. 15:16). Their principal service is to offer the praise that accompanies the regular sacrifices, declaring God's eternal covenant love to Israel (1 Chron. 16:34; 2 Chron. 5:13) and assisting the people in their own offering of praise (2 Chron. 7:3). Worship for the Chronicler is a means of transformation into covenant obedience and the kindling of faith and hope.

3. *The people of Israel.* The Chronicler sought to address some urgent questions in his day concerning the identity of Israel and to instill fresh confidence in the people. The genealogies of Israel that begin the work (1 Chronicles 1–9) start by tracing the people's ancestry back to Adam, a striking reminder that Israel lay at the center of God's purpose from the very beginning of creation. Although only a "remnant" and a provincial outpost in a great empire, Israel must remember that its security and destiny rest with Yahweh, "who rule[s] over all the kingdoms of the nations" and has given the land to Abraham's descendants "forever" (2 Chron. 20:6–7).

Second, the continuation of the genealogies makes it clear that Israel in its broadest extent embraces all 12 tribes that were descended from Jacob/Israel's sons (1 Chron. 2:1). While 2 Chronicles 11–36 is mainly the narrative of Judah and Benjamin, the northern tribes never forfeited their status as members of Israel, even in their rebellion against the rightful Davidic king (2 Chron. 13:5). Judah and Benjamin formed the core of the preexilic southern kingdom as well as being the majority of the restoration community, but they did so as the representative center, to which all who belonged by ancestry to Israel might join themselves. The Chronicler shows how this might be done, first of all by presenting the ideal picture of "all Israel" united in their support of David and Solomon at the foundation of the Davidic monarchy and the dedication of the temple (see 1 Chron. 11:1–12:40; 13:2, 5; 15:3; 28:1; 29:6; 2 Chron. 1:2; 5:2; 6:3; 7:8–10). The division of the kingdom under Rehoboam led to a centuries-long schism in the people, and the northern tribes lapsed into apostasy (2 Chron. 13:8–9). With the fall of the northern kingdom, however, Hezekiah made brotherly overtures to the north to heal these divisions through participation in temple worship (see 2 Chron. 30:6–9) as one people under the Davidic king, as they had been in Solomon's day (2 Chron. 30:23–27). The participation of northerners in Josiah's Passover (2 Chron. 35:17) and the membership of people from Ephraim and Manasseh in the postexilic community in Jerusalem (1 Chron. 9:3) demonstrated the same desire to include "all Israel" once more, with the temple (a visible symbol of the Davidic covenant) as the focus of unity.

Chronicles might also be called a genuinely populist work. Although its concern with kings and the priesthood might seem hierarchical, it demonstrates a striking interest in the broad participation of the people in the life of the nation. Compared to the presentation in the books of Samuel and Kings, the Chronicler consistently highlights the role of the people at large in laying the religious foundations of the nation (see 1 Chron. 11:4; 13:2; 15:25; 2 Chron. 1:2–3), no doubt as a way of affirming that "all Israel" (both north and south, the laity as well as the priesthood) has a share in these institutions. The Chronicler also shows the people responding generously to appeals to support the temple (1 Chron. 29:5–9; 2 Chron. 31:4–10) and participating in the numerous acts of religious reform and covenant renewal (see 2 Chron. 15:8–17; 17:7–9; 23:16–21; 31:1; 34:29–32). All these portrayals show the covenant people at their best, responding to the call to "seek God" and entering into his blessing. This was evidently an outlook that the Chronicler desired the people of his own day to emulate.

Comparison of 1–2 Chronicles with 2 Samuel and 1–2 Kings

	1 Chronicles	2 Samuel
Genealogies	1:1–9:44	
Death of Saul and sons	10:1–14	1 Sam. 31:1–2 Sam. 1:16
Lament for Saul		2 Sam. 1:17–27
David king of Judah		2:1–7
War between house of Saul and David; Ish-bosheth made king		2:8–3:1
David's sons in Hebron		3:2–5
Abner helps David		3:6–21
Joab kills Abner		3:22–39
Ish-bosheth killed		4:1–12
David king of Judah and Israel	11:1–3	5:1–5
Conquest of Jerusalem	11:4–9	5:6–10
David's mighty men	11:10–47	23:8–39
David's men at Ziklag	12:1–22	
Celebration at Hebron	12:23–40	
Attempted return of ark; death of Uzzah	13:1–14	6:1–11
David's house built	14:1–2	5:11–12
David's children in Jerusalem	14:3–7	5:13–16
David defeats Philistines	14:8–17	5:17–25
Spiritual preparation for the ark's return	15:1–24	
Ark brought to Jerusalem	15:25–16:6	6:12–19
David and Michal		6:20–23
David's psalm of praise	16:7–43	
David's desire to build the temple	17:1–2	7:1–3
Davidic covenant	17:3–15	7:4–17
David's prayer of praise	17:16–27	7:18–29
David's victories	18:1–13	8:1–14
David's officials	18:14–17	8:15–18
David helps Mephibosheth		9:1–13
Ammonites defeated	19:1–15	10:1–14
Syrians defeated	19:16–19	10:15–19
Ammonites defeated	20:1–3	11:1; 12:26–31
David and Bathsheba		11:2–12:25
Amnon, Tamar, and Absalom		13:1–14:33
Absalom's rebellion		15:1–19:43
Sheba's rebellion		20:1–26
Famine; death of Saul's sons		21:1–14
War with Philistines; the Philistine giants	20:4–8	21:15–22
David's psalm of deliverance		22:1–51
David's last words		23:1–7
David's census	21:1–27	24:1–25
David plans for the temple	21:28–22:5	
David's charge to Solomon and the leaders	22:6–19	
David organizes temple personnel	23:1–26:32	
Israel's military	27:1–15	
Israel's leaders	27:16–34	
David's charge to Israel; affirmation of Solomon	28:1–10	
Pattern for the temple	28:11–21	
Offerings for the temple	29:1–9	
David's prayer of thanks for the temple	29:10–19	
		1 Kings
David and Abishag		1:1–4
Adonijah claims the throne		1:5–27
Solomon's coronation	29:20–25	1:28–40
David instructs Solomon		2:1–9
Death of David	29:26–30	2:10–11
Solomon establishes his kingdom		2:12–46
	2 Chronicles	
Solomon marries Pharaoh's daughter		3:1–3
Solomon at Gibeon	1:1–6	3:4
God gives Solomon wisdom	1:7–12	3:5–14
Solomon's wise judgment		3:16–28
Solomon's prosperity	1:14–17	4:20–34
Preparations for the temple	2:1–18	5:1–18
Temple built	3:1–5:1	6:1–38; 7:13–51
Solomon's palace		7:1–12
Ark brought to temple	5:2–12	8:1–9
God's glory fills the temple	5:13–14	8:10–11
Solomon blesses the people	6:1–11	8:12–21
Solomon consecrates the temple	6:12–42	8:22–61
Fire from the LORD consumes the sacrifices	7:1–3	
Solomon and the people offer sacrifices	7:4–7	8:62–64
Feast of Tabernacles	7:8–10	8:65–66
The covenant confirmed	7:11–22	9:1–9
Solomon's territory increases	8:1–6	9:10–19
Solomon's enemies defeated	8:7–10	9:20–23
Solomon's religious practices	8:11–16	9:24–25
Solomon's economic operations	8:17–18	9:26–28
Queen of Sheba visits	9:1–12	10:1–13
Solomon's wealth	9:13–28	10:14–29
Solomon's apostasy and adversaries		11:1–40
Death of Solomon	9:29–31	11:41–43
Division of the kingdom	10:1–11:23	12:1–33
Man of God from Judah warns Jeroboam (Israel)		13:1–34
Ahijah's prophecy against Jeroboam		14:1–18
Death of Jeroboam		14:19–20
Shishak invades Judah	12:1–12	14:25–28
Reign of Rehoboam (Judah)	12:13–16	14:21–24, 29–31
War between Judah and Israel	13:1–22	15:1–8
Evaluation of Asa (Judah)	14:1–8	15:9–12
Ethiopians defeated	14:9–15	

Azariah the prophet	15:1–7	
Asa's reforms	15:8–19	15:13–15
Asa defeats Syria	16:1–10	15:16–22
Death of Asa	16:11–14	15:23–24
Reigns of Nadab, Baasha, Elah, Zimri, Omri (Israel)		15:25–16:28
Ahab becomes king (Israel)		16:29–34
Elijah		17:1–19:18; 21:17–29
Call of Elisha		19:19–21
Ahab conquers Syria, acquires Naboth's vineyard		20:1–21:29
Evaluation of Jehoshaphat (Judah)	17:1–9	
Expansion of Judah	17:10–19	
Jehoshaphat's alliance with Ahab; death of Ahab	18:1–34	22:1–40
Jehoshaphat's reforms, crisis, and deliverance	19:1–20:30	
Reign of Jehoshaphat	20:31–37	22:41–50
Reign of Ahaziah (Israel)		22:51–53
		2 Kings
Death of Ahaziah; Elijah's prophecy		1:1–18
Elijah and Elisha		2:1–25
Evaluation of Jehoram (Israel)		3:1–3
Moab rebels		3:4–27
The widow's oil		4:1–7
The Shunammite woman		4:8–37
Miracles for the prophets		4:38–44
Naaman healed		5:1–27
The axe-head recovered		6:1–7
Chariots of fire		6:8–23
Siege of Samaria		6:24–7:20
Shunammite's land restored		8:1–6
Hazael kills Ben-hadad		8:7–15
Evaluation of Jehoram (Judah)	21:1–7	8:16–19
Edom and Libnah rebel	21:8–11	8:20–22
Warning of Elijah	21:12–15	
Invasion of Philistia and Arabia	21:16–17	
Death of Jehoram	21:18–20	8:23–24
Reign of Ahaziah (Judah)	22:1–9	8:25–29; 9:15–16, 27–28; 10:12–14
Reign of Jehu (Israel)	22:7–9	9:1–10:36
Reign of Athaliah (Judah)	22:10–23:15	11:1–16
Jehoiada's reforms (Judah)	23:16–21	11:17–20
Evaluation of Joash (Judah)	24:1–3	11:21–12:3
Joash repairs the temple	24:4–14	12:4–16
Death of Jehoiada	24:15–16	
Jehoiada's son killed	24:17–22	
Syria invades Judah	24:23–24	12:17–18
Death of Joash	24:25–27	12:19–21
Reign of Jehoahaz (Israel)		13:1–9
Reign of Jehoash (Israel)		13:10–13
Elisha's final prophecy and death		13:14–25
Reign of Amaziah (Judah)	25:1–16	14:1–20
Israel defeats Judah	25:17–24	14:8–14
Death of Amaziah	25:25–28	14:17–20
Evaluation of Uzziah (Judah)	26:1–5	14:21–22; 15:1–5
Reign of Jeroboam II (Israel)		14:23–29
Victories of Uzziah	26:6–15	
Sinful offering of Uzziah	26:16–21	
Death of Uzziah	26:22–23	15:6–7
Reign of Zechariah (Israel)		15:8–12
Reign of Shallum (Israel)		15:13–16
Reign of Menahem (Israel)		15:17–22
Reign of Pekahiah (Israel)		15:23–26
Reign of Pekah (Israel)		15:27–31
Reign of Jotham (Judah)	27:1–9	15:32–38
Evaluation of Ahaz (Judah)	28:1–4	16:1–4
Israel defeats Judah	28:5–21	16:5–9
Ahaz's idolatry and death	28:22–27	16:10–12
Fall of Israel		17:1–23
Resettlement of Israel		17:24–41
Evaluation of Hezekiah (Judah)	29:1–2	18:1–8
Hezekiah cleanses the temple	29:3–19	
Hezekiah restores temple worship	29:20–36	
Hezekiah restores Passover	30:1–27	
Hezekiah destroys idols, organizes priests	31:1–21	
Fall of Israel (restated)		18:9–12
Assyria invades Judah	32:1–23	18:13–19:37
Hezekiah's illness and restoration	32:24–26	20:1–11
Hezekiah's wealth and foolish pride	32:27–31	20:12–19
Death of Hezekiah	32:32–33	20:20–21
Reign of Manasseh (Judah)	33:1–9	21:1–18
Manasseh's repentance	33:10–20	
Reign of Amon (Judah)	33:21–25	21:19–26
Evaluation of Josiah (Judah)	34:1–2	22:1–2
Josiah's early reforms	34:3–7	
Josiah repairs temple	34:8–13	22:3–7
Book of Law discovered; Josiah's reforms	34:14–33	22:8–23:20
Passover celebrated	35:1–19	23:21–27
Death of Josiah	35:20–27	23:28–30
Reign of Jehoahaz (Judah)	36:1–3	23:31–33
Reign of Jehoiakim (Judah)	36:4–8	23:34–24:7
Reign of Jehoiachin (Judah); Babylonian captivity	36:9–10	24:8–17
Evaluation of Zedekiah (Judah)	36:11–12	24:18–20
Destruction of Jerusalem	36:13–21	25:1–21
Remnant flees to Egypt		25:22–26
Jehoiachin released		25:27–30
Proclamation by Cyrus	36:22–23	

Outline for 1–2 Chronicles

Chronicles is a carefully constructed work with a clearly directed narrative. Its material falls into three major sections that overlap their present division into two books. Each of these sections has in turn a number of more or less discrete units. In greater detail, these units are as follows:

I. A Genealogical Presentation of the Tribes of Israel (1 Chron. 1:1–9:44)

- A. Adam to Esau (1:1–54)
- B. The sons of Israel (2:1–2)
- C. The tribe of Judah (2:3–4:23)
- D. The tribe of Simeon (4:24–43)
- E. The Transjordanian tribes (5:1–26)
- F. The tribe of Levi (6:1–81)
- G. Other northern tribes (7:1–40)
- H. The tribe of Benjamin (8:1–40)
- I. The resettlement of Jerusalem (9:1–34)
- J. The genealogy of Saul (9:35–44)

II. The United Kingdom of David and Solomon (1 Chron. 10:1–2 Chron. 9:31)

- A. David's rise to power over Israel (1 Chron. 10:1–12:40)
- B. David's transfer of the ark of the covenant to Jerusalem (13:1–16:43)
- C. The dynastic promise to David (17:1–27)
- D. David's wars (18:1–20:8)
- E. David's census and preparation for the temple (21:1–29:30)
- F. Solomon's temple preparations (2 Chron. 1:1–2:18)
- G. Solomon's building of the temple (3:1–5:1)
- H. The dedication of the temple (5:2–7:22)
- I. Solomon's other accomplishments (8:1–16)
- J. Solomon's international relations and renown (8:17–9:31)

III. The Kingdom of Judah down to the Exile (2 Chron. 10:1–36:23)

- A. Rehoboam (10:1–12:16)
- B. Abijah (13:1–14:1)
- C. Asa (14:2–16:14)
- D. Jehoshaphat (17:1–21:1)
- E. Jehoram and Ahaziah (21:2–22:12)
- F. Joash (23:1–24:27)
- G. Amaziah (25:1–28)
- H. Uzziah (26:1–23)
- I. Jotham (27:1–9)
- J. Ahaz (28:1–27)
- K. Hezekiah (29:1–32:33)
- L. Manasseh (33:1–20)
- M. Amon (33:21–25)
- N. Josiah (34:1–35:27)
- O. The last four kings (36:1–21)
- P. Restoration (36:22–23)

1 Chronicles

Chapter 1
1[a]Gen. 4:25, 26; 5:3, 6
2[b]For ver. 2-4, see Gen. 5:9-32
4[c]Gen. 6:10; 9:18
5[d]For ver. 5-7, see Gen. 10:2-4
8[e]For ver. 8-10, see Gen. 10:6-8
11[f]For ver. 11-16, see Gen. 10:10-18
17[g]For ver. 17-23, see Gen. 10:22-29

From Adam to Abraham

1 [1] [a]Adam, Seth, Enosh; 2 [b]Kenan, Mahalalel, Jared; 3 Enoch, Methuselah, Lamech; 4 Noah,
[c]Shem, Ham, and Japheth.
5 [d]The sons of Japheth: Gomer, Magog, Madai, Javan, Tubal, Meshech, and Tiras. 6 The
sons of Gomer: Ashkenaz, Riphath,[2] and Togarmah. 7 The sons of Javan: Elishah, Tarshish,
Kittim, and Rodanim.
8 [e]The sons of Ham: Cush, Egypt, Put, and Canaan. 9 The sons of Cush: Seba, Havilah,
Sabta, Raama, and Sabteca. The sons of Raamah: Sheba and Dedan. 10 Cush fathered Nimrod.
He was the first on earth to be a mighty man.[3]
11 [f]Egypt fathered Ludim, Anamim, Lehabim, Naphtuhim, 12 Pathrusim, Casluhim (from
whom the Philistines came), and Caphtorim.
13 Canaan fathered Sidon his firstborn and Heth, 14 and the Jebusites, the Amorites, the
Girgashites, 15 the Hivites, the Arkites, the Sinites, 16 the Arvadites, the Zemarites, and the
Hamathites.
17 [g]The sons of Shem: Elam, Asshur, Arpachshad, Lud, and Aram. And the sons of Aram:[4]
Uz, Hul, Gether, and Meshech. 18 Arpachshad fathered Shelah, and Shelah fathered Eber.
19 To Eber were born two sons: the name of the one was Peleg[5] (for in his days the earth
was divided), and his brother's name was Joktan. 20 Joktan fathered Almodad, Sheleph,
Hazarmaveth, Jerah, 21 Hadoram, Uzal, Diklah, 22 Obal,[6] Abimael, Sheba, 23 Ophir, Havilah,
and Jobab; all these were the sons of Joktan.

[1] Many names in these genealogies are spelled differently in other biblical books [2] Septuagint; Hebrew *Diphath* [3] Or *He began to be a mighty man on the earth* [4] Septuagint; Hebrew lacks *And the sons of Aram* [5] *Peleg* means *division* [6] Septuagint, Syriac (compare Genesis 10:28); Hebrew *Ebal*

1:1–9:44 *A Genealogical Presentation of the Tribes of Israel.* The genealogies of chs. 1–9 are intended to show the Chronicler's own generation, now existing as the small province of Yehud (Judah) in the Persian Empire, that they are still God's people Israel and retain their central place in God's purposes for humanity. The identity and legitimacy of this people are traced in a line beginning with Adam (1:1) and extending through the tribes of Israel (chs. 2–8) down to the community of Judean exiles restored from captivity in Babylon (9:2–34). This community is depicted not as the sum total of the people but as the representative nucleus or focus to which "all Israel" may join in God's work of restoration. The tribal genealogies have been carefully structured to show how the Chronicler conceived of Israel:

- Judah (2:3–4:23)
- Simeon (4:24–43)
- The Transjordanian tribes (5:1–26)
- Levi (6:1–81)
- The northern tribes (7:1–40)
- Benjamin (8:1–40)

The greatest amount of detail is devoted to Judah, Levi, and Benjamin. Judah and Benjamin bracket the lists, while Levi is placed at the center. The significance of this arrangement is discussed in greater detail below; briefly, it indicates that Judah and Benjamin (the core of the old southern kingdom, along with Simeon, whose territory was merged with Judah's) enclose or enfold Israel, while the Levites provide its spiritual heart.

This section also announces in advance some of the book's key themes: Israel's history of unfaithfulness (Hb. *ma'al*), leading to exile (5:25–26; 9:1); the persistence of the Davidic line after the exile as the bearer of God's promise to his people (3:17–24); and the central role of the Levites and the Aaronic priests in offering worship and making atonement for Israel (6:1–81).

The opening chapter, drawn almost wholly from Genesis, traces the descent of Israel (as Jacob is consistently known in the book) from Adam and depicts the place of his descendants among the nations. The line of divine election runs from Adam through 10 generations to Noah, then through Shem in 10 generations to Abraham and on to Israel. The author highlights this theme by presenting first the secondary lines of descent before dealing, last of all, with the figures who form the ancestral link between Adam and Israel. The descendants of Japheth and Ham (1 Chron. 1:5–16) are listed before the Shemites, leading to Abraham (1:17–27). Next, the descendants of Abraham's concubines Hagar and Keturah are given (1:29–33) before Isaac (1:34); then Esau's line (1:35–54) before Israel's sons (2:1).

1:1–54 *Adam to Esau.* This first genealogy takes the story from Adam, the first human, through Abraham and Isaac; then it focuses on Isaac's son Esau and the kings who descended from him.

1:1–4 From Genesis 5. Israel's direct ancestral link with **Adam** means that Israel is the focus of God's purpose from creation. The line of **Noah** marks a fresh start for humanity after the flood.

1:5–27 From Gen. 10:1–29; 11:10–32. Israel is located within the nations of the world, which are similarly God's creation and part of his purpose for Israel. The line of election is continued through **Abraham**, who is also recalled as the recipient of covenantal promises in 1 Chron. 16:16 and 2 Chron. 20:7.

24 [h]Shem, Arpachshad, Shelah; 25 Eber, Peleg, Reu; 26 Serug, Nahor, Terah; 27 Abram, that
is, Abraham.

From Abraham to Jacob

28 The sons of Abraham: [i]Isaac and [j]Ishmael. 29 [k]These are their genealogies: the firstborn
of Ishmael, Nebaioth, and Kedar, Adbeel, Mibsam, 30 Mishma, Dumah, Massa, Hadad, Tema,
31 Jetur, Naphish, and Kedemah. These are the sons of Ishmael. 32 [l]The sons of Keturah,
Abraham's concubine: she bore Zimran, Jokshan, Medan, Midian, Ishbak, and Shuah. The
sons of Jokshan: Sheba and Dedan. 33 The sons of Midian: Ephah, Epher, Hanoch, Abida,
and Eldaah. All these were the descendants of Keturah.

34 Abraham fathered [i]Isaac. The sons of Isaac: [m]Esau and [n]Israel. 35 [o]The sons of Esau:
Eliphaz, Reuel, Jeush, Jalam, and Korah. 36 The sons of Eliphaz: Teman, Omar, Zepho,
Gatam, Kenaz, and of Timna,[1] Amalek. 37 The sons of Reuel: Nahath, Zerah, Shammah,
and Mizzah.

38 [p]The sons of Seir: Lotan, Shobal, Zibeon, Anah, Dishon, Ezer, and Dishan. 39 The sons
of Lotan: Hori and Hemam;[2] and Lotan's sister was Timna. 40 The sons of Shobal: Alvan,[3]
Manahath, Ebal, Shepho,[4] and Onam. The sons of Zibeon: Aiah and Anah. 41 The son[5] of
Anah: Dishon. The sons of Dishon: Hemdan,[6] Eshban, Ithran, and Cheran. 42 The sons of
Ezer: Bilhan, Zaavan, and Akan.[7] The sons of Dishan: Uz and Aran.

43 [q]These are the kings who reigned in the land of Edom before any king reigned over
the people of Israel: Bela the son of Beor, the name of his city being Dinhabah. 44 Bela died,
and Jobab the son of Zerah of [r]Bozrah reigned in his place. 45 Jobab died, and Husham of
the land of the [s]Temanites reigned in his place. 46 Husham died, and Hadad the son of
Bedad, who defeated Midian in the country of Moab, reigned in his place, the name of his
city being Avith. 47 Hadad died, and Samlah of Masrekah reigned in his place. 48 Samlah
died, and Shaul of Rehoboth on the Euphrates[8] reigned in his place. 49 Shaul died, and Baal-
hanan, the son of Achbor, reigned in his place. 50 Baal-hanan died, and Hadad reigned in
his place, the name of his city being Pai; and his wife's name was Mehetabel, the daughter
of Matred, the daughter of Mezahab. 51 And Hadad died.

The chiefs of Edom were: chiefs Timna, Alvah, Jetheth, 52 Oholibamah, Elah, Pinon,
53 Kenaz, Teman, Mibzar, 54 Magdiel, and Iram; these are the chiefs of Edom.

A Genealogy of David

2 These are the sons of [t]Israel: [u]Reuben, Simeon, Levi, Judah, [v]Issachar, Zebulun, 2 [w]Dan,
[x]Joseph, [y]Benjamin, [z]Naphtali, [a]Gad, and Asher. 3 [b]The sons of Judah: [c]Er, Onan and
Shelah; these three Bath-shua the Canaanite bore to him. Now Er, Judah's firstborn, was

[1] Septuagint (compare Genesis 36:12); Hebrew lacks *and of* [2] Septuagint (compare Genesis 36:22); Hebrew *Homam* [3] Septuagint (compare Genesis 36:23); Hebrew *Alian* [4] Septuagint (compare Genesis 36:23); Hebrew *Shephi* [5] Hebrew *sons* [6] Septuagint (compare Genesis 36:26); Hebrew *Hamran* [7] Septuagint (compare Genesis 36:27); Hebrew *Jaakan* [8] Or *the River*

24 [h]For ver. 24, 27, see Gen. 11:10-26; Luke 3:34-36
28 [i]Gen. 21:2, 3 [j]Gen. 16:11, 15
29 [k]For ver. 29-31, see Gen. 25:13-16
32 [l]For ver. 32, 33, see Gen. 25:1-4
34 [i][See ver. 28 above] [m]Gen. 25:25, 26 [n]Gen. 32:28
35 [o]For ver. 35-37, see Gen. 36:4, 5, 9-13
38 [p]For ver. 38-42, see Gen. 36:20-28
43 [q]For ver. 43-54, see Gen. 36:31-43
44 [r]Isa. 34:6; 63:1
45 [s]Gen. 36:11; Job 2:11; Jer. 49:7, 20; Ezek. 25:13

Chapter 2

1 [t]ch. 1:34 [u]Gen. 29:32-35 [v]Gen. 30:18-20
2 [w]Gen. 30:6 [x]Gen. 30:22-24 [y]Gen. 35:18 [z]Gen. 30:8 [a]Gen. 30:10-13
3 [b]Gen. 38:2-5; 46:12 [c]Gen. 38:7

1:28–34 The details of Abraham's descendants are drawn from Gen. 25:1–4, 12–16. The **concubine** (1 Chron. 1:32) was an auxiliary wife; cf. Gen. 25:6, which speaks of Keturah in this way.

1:35–54 From Gen. 36:10–14, 20–28, 31–43. The descendants of **Esau** and the **sons of Seir** (the Edomites) are considered together here, as both inhabited the neighboring territory of Edom, and the latter would often have conflicting relations with Judah (2 Chron. 20:10; 21:8; 25:5–13; 28:17). **And of Timna, Amalek** (1 Chron. 1:36) is literally "and Timna and Amalek." The names have been added here in an abbreviated note from Gen. 36:12, which here, as elsewhere in this chapter (e.g., 1 Chron. 1:4), omits kinship details.

2:1–2 *The Sons of Israel.* The line of divine election culminates in the sons of Israel, the subject of the following genealogies. But the Chronicler does not consider them in the traditional order of these verses (drawn apparently from Gen. 35:22–26). Further, his actual listing of the 12 tribes differs because it includes the half-tribes of Manasseh in Transjordan (1 Chron. 5:23–26) and west of the Jordan (7:14–19) and omits mention of Zebulun and Dan.

2:3–4:23 *The Tribe of Judah.* The first and most extensive place is given to Judah. This material is of diverse origin and much of it is fragmentary, but the author has arranged it as follows into an artistic whole according to the principles of a large-scale *inclusio* (or concentric-ring structure in which the last elements repeat the first):

2:3	Shelah, the oldest surviving son of Judah
2:4–8	Perez and Zerah, Judah's sons by Tamar
2:9–3:24	Hezron, ancestor of David and his line
4:1–20	Perez's other descendants
4:21–23	Shelah's descendants

As is common in such literary arrangements, the central unit (2:9–3:24) is the focus of chief interest because it leads to David, the central human character in Chronicles. This unit has its own complex arrangement of materials (see below).

2:3–8 In the Chronicler's presentation, **Judah** is preeminent in Israel as a matter of divine choice, both as "leader" of the other tribes and as the source of David and his line, who are the bearers of divine promises of good for Israel (see 28:4). Judah's five sons demonstrate both Yahweh's judgment on disobedience (**Er**, **Onan**, **Shelah**) and his electing grace in continuing the lines of **Perez** and **Zerah**, the twins born from Judah's illicit union with **Tamar** (Genesis 38). **Achan** is *'Akar* ("trouble") in the Hebrew text, an example of wordplay on the **troubler** (Hb. *'oker*) **of Israel** (see Josh. 7:24–26). His breach of faith (**broke faith**, Hb. *ma'al*) is the first instance of a key term in the book that denotes Israel's failure to reverence Yahweh and render to him his due in obedience and worship (see Lev. 26:40). The Chronicler sees this as the archetypal sin of Israel that punctuates its history from beginning

evil in the sight of the LORD, and he put him to death. **4** His daughter-in-law [d]Tamar also
bore him Perez and Zerah. Judah had five sons in all.
5 The [e]sons of Perez: Hezron and Hamul. **6** The sons of Zerah: Zimri, Ethan, Heman,
Calcol, and Dara, five in all. **7** The son[1] of Carmi: Achan, the troubler of Israel, who [f]broke
faith in the matter of the devoted thing; **8** and Ethan's son was Azariah.
9 The sons of Hezron that were born to him: Jerahmeel, [g]Ram, and [h]Chelubai. **10** [g]Ram
fathered Amminadab, and [i]Amminadab fathered [j]Nahshon, prince of the sons of Judah.
11 Nahshon fathered [k]Salmon,[2] Salmon fathered [l]Boaz, **12** Boaz fathered Obed, [l]Obed
fathered Jesse. **13** [m]Jesse fathered Eliab his firstborn, Abinadab the second, [n]Shimea the
third, **14** Nethanel the fourth, Raddai the fifth, **15** Ozem the sixth, [o]David the seventh. **16** And
their sisters were Zeruiah and Abigail. [p]The sons of Zeruiah: Abishai, Joab, and Asahel,
three. **17** [q]Abigail bore Amasa, and the father of Amasa was [q]Jether the Ishmaelite.
18 [r]Caleb the son of Hezron fathered children by his wife Azubah, and by Jerioth; and
these were her sons: Jesher, Shobab, and Ardon. **19** When Azubah died, [r]Caleb married
[s]Ephrath, who bore him [t]Hur. **20** Hur fathered Uri, and Uri fathered [u]Bezalel.
21 Afterward Hezron went in to the daughter of [v]Machir the father of Gilead, whom he
married when he was sixty years old, and she bore him Segub. **22** And Segub fathered Jair,
who had twenty-three cities in the land of Gilead. **23** [w]But Geshur and Aram took from them
Havvoth-jair, Kenath, and its villages, sixty towns. All these were descendants of Machir,
the father of Gilead. **24** After the death of Hezron, [x]Caleb went in to Ephrathah,[3] the wife
of Hezron his father, and she bore him [y]Ashhur, the father of Tekoa.
25 The sons of [z]Jerahmeel, the firstborn of Hezron: Ram, his firstborn, Bunah, Oren,
Ozem, and Ahijah. **26** Jerahmeel also had another wife, whose name was Atarah; she was
the mother of Onam. **27** The sons of Ram, the firstborn of Jerahmeel: Maaz, Jamin, and
Eker. **28** The sons of Onam: Shammai and Jada. The sons of Shammai: Nadab and Abishur.
29 The name of Abishur's wife was Abihail, and she bore him Ahban and Molid. **30** The sons
of Nadab: Seled and Appaim; and Seled died childless. **31** The son[4] of Appaim: Ishi. [a]The
son of Ishi: Sheshan. The son of Sheshan: Ahlai. **32** The sons of Jada, Shammai's brother:
Jether and Jonathan; and Jether died childless. **33** The sons of Jonathan: Peleth and Zaza.
These were the descendants of Jerahmeel. **34** Now Sheshan had no sons, only daughters, but
Sheshan had an Egyptian slave whose name was Jarha. **35** So Sheshan gave his daughter in
marriage to Jarha his slave, and she bore him Attai. **36** Attai fathered Nathan, and Nathan
fathered [b]Zabad. **37** [b]Zabad fathered Ephlal, and Ephlal fathered [c]Obed. **38** Obed fathered
Jehu, and Jehu fathered Azariah. **39** Azariah fathered Helez, and Helez fathered Eleasah.
40 Eleasah fathered Sismai, and Sismai fathered Shallum. **41** Shallum fathered Jekamiah,
and Jekamiah fathered [d]Elishama.
42 The sons of [e]Caleb the brother of Jerahmeel: Mareshah[5] his firstborn, who fathered
Ziph. The son[6] of Mareshah: [f]Hebron.[7] **43** The sons of Hebron: Korah, Tappuah, Rekem and

[1] Hebrew *sons* [2] Septuagint (compare Ruth 4:21); Hebrew *Salma* [3] Septuagint, Vulgate; Hebrew *in Caleb Ephrathah* [4] Hebrew *sons*; three times in this verse [5] Septuagint; Hebrew *Mesha* [6] Hebrew *sons* [7] Hebrew *the father of Hebron*

4 [d]Gen. 38:11, 14, 29, 30; Ruth 4:12; Matt. 1:3
5 [e]Gen. 46:12; Ruth 4:18
7 [f]Josh. 6:18; 7:1
9 [g]Ruth 4:19; Matt. 1:3, 4 [h][ver. 13, 42]
10 [g][See ver. 9 above] [i]Ruth 4:19; Matt. 1:4 [j]Num. 1:7; 2:3
11 [k][Ruth 4:20, 21; Matt. 1:4] [l]Ruth 4:21, 22; Matt. 1:5, 6
12 [l][See ver. 11 above]
13 [m]1 Sam. 16:6, 8; 17:13 [n][1 Sam. 16:9; 17:13]
15 [o][1 Sam. 16:10; 17:12, 14]
16 [p]2 Sam. 2:18
17 [q][2 Sam. 17:25]
18 [r][ver. 9]
19 [r][See ver. 18 above] [s][ver. 50] [t]Ex. 17:10, 12; 24:14
20 [u]Ex. 31:2
21 [v]Num. 27:1
23 [w][Num. 32:41, 42; Deut. 3:14; Josh. 13:30]
24 [x]ver. 19, 50 [y]ch. 4:5
25 [z]ver. 9
31 [a][ver. 34, 35]
36 [b]ch. 11:41
37 [b][See ver. 36 above] [c][2 Chr. 23:1]
41 [d]2 Kgs. 25:25
42 [e]ver. 9 [f]See Josh. 14:13

to end (see 1 Chron. 5:25; 9:1; 10:13; 2 Chron. 12:2; 26:16, 18; 28:19; 29:6, 19; 30:7; 36:14). The terrible consequences of *ma'al* include the loss of the Promised Land and the pain of exile; nevertheless, the Chronicler will show that these penalties can be reversed by heartfelt repentance and faithful obedience. Such a response is expressed above all in true worship according to the Law of Moses. The election of David, whose ancestry is given next, is concerned primarily with the establishment of such worship in Israel.

2:9–17 Verses 10–12 are drawn mainly from Ruth 4:19–22. In the Chronicler's presentation, only the line of **David** (1 Chron. 2:15) is derived from **Ram**, and the rest of Judah is considered under the rubric of Hezron's other sons, Jerahmeel and Caleb (**Chelubai** is a variant of "Caleb"). The genealogy of Ram down to David (vv. 10–17) and David's own descendants (3:1–24) form an *inclusio* (or literary "bookends") around the Calebites (2:18–24, 42–55) and Jerahmeelites (vv. 25–41). Although 1 Sam. 16:10–13 indicates that David was the eighth son of **Jesse**, the Chronicler presents him as the seventh, perhaps to indicate his favored place in God's purpose. Telescoping (the omission of names) is a common feature of these genealogies, and often carries theological significance. (See note on 1 Sam. 16:10.)

2:18–24 Caleb the son of Hezron is to be distinguished from the later contemporary of Joshua (see 4:15). He was a forefather of **Bezalel** (2:20), the principal craftsman for the tabernacle (Ex. 31:2; 2 Chron. 1:5). By placing a reference to Bezalel directly after the genealogy of David, the author indicates the very close connection between the Davidic monarchy and the temple, one of the central themes of his historical narrative.

2:25–41 Two lists (vv. 25–33 and 34–41) have been joined together here, probably from material preserved by this clan, the descendants of **Jerahmeel, the firstborn of Hezron**. The Jerahmeelites lived in the Negeb, on Judah's southern frontier, in David's day (1 Sam. 27:10). If this record of 23 generations is complete, **Elishama** may have been a contemporary of David, and the Chronicler would be drawing on ancient records from the early monarchy.

2:42–55 An addition to vv. 18–24, comprising early lists of the descendants of Caleb (vv. 42–50a) and his son Hur (vv. 50b–55). Personal and place names are found together in this section (**Hebron**, **Beth-zur**, **Kiriath-jearim**, **Bethlehem**), so "father" here sometimes denotes the "founder" or "leader" of a city.

Shema. 44 Shema fathered Raham, the father of Jorkeam; and Rekem fathered Shammai.
45 The son of Shammai: Maon; and Maon fathered Beth-zur. 46 Ephah also, Caleb's concubine, bore Haran, Moza, and Gazez; and Haran fathered Gazez. 47 The sons of Jahdai:
Regem, Jotham, Geshan, Pelet, Ephah, and Shaaph. 48 Maacah, Caleb's concubine, bore
Sheber and Tirhanah. 49 She also bore Shaaph the father of Madmannah, Sheva the father
of Machbenah and the father of Gibea; and the [g]daughter of Caleb was Achsah. 50 These
were the descendants of Caleb.

The sons[1] of Hur the firstborn of [h]Ephrathah: Shobal the father of Kiriath-jearim,
51 [i]Salma, the father of Bethlehem, and Hareph the father of Beth-gader. 52 Shobal the father
of Kiriath-jearim had other sons: [j]Haroeh, half of the Menuhoth. 53 And the clans of Kiriath-
jearim: the Ithrites, the Puthites, the Shumathites, and the Mishraites; from these came
the [k]Zorathites and the Eshtaolites. 54 The sons of Salma: Bethlehem, the Netophathites,
Atroth-beth-joab and half of the Manahathites, the Zorites. 55 The clans also of the scribes
who lived at Jabez: the Tirathites, the Shimeathites and the Sucathites. These are the [l]Kenites
who came from Hammath, the father of [m]the house of Rechab.

Descendants of David

3 [n]These are the sons of David who were born to him in Hebron: the firstborn, Amnon,
by Ahinoam the Jezreelite; the second, [o]Daniel, by Abigail the Carmelite, 2 the third,
Absalom, whose mother was Maacah, the daughter of Talmai, king of Geshur; the fourth,
Adonijah, whose mother was Haggith; 3 the fifth, Shephatiah, by Abital; the sixth, Ithream,
by his wife Eglah; 4 six were born to him in Hebron, [p]where he reigned for seven years and
six months. [q]And he reigned thirty-three years in Jerusalem. 5 [r]These were born to him in
Jerusalem: [s]Shimea, Shobab, Nathan and [t]Solomon, four by [u]Bath-shua, the daughter of
[u]Ammiel; 6 then Ibhar, [v]Elishama, Eliphelet, 7 Nogah, Nepheg, Japhia, 8 Elishama, [w]Eliada,
and Eliphelet, nine. 9 All these were David's sons, besides the sons of the concubines, [x]and
Tamar was their sister.

10 The son of Solomon was [y]Rehoboam, [z]Abijah his son, [a]Asa his son, [b]Jehoshaphat his
son, 11 [c]Joram his son, [d]Ahaziah his son, [e]Joash his son, 12 [f]Amaziah his son, [g]Azariah his son,
[h]Jotham his son, 13 [i]Ahaz his son, [j]Hezekiah his son, [k]Manasseh his son, 14 [l]Amon his son,
[m]Josiah his son. 15 The sons of Josiah: [n]Johanan the firstborn, the second [o]Jehoiakim, the third
[p]Zedekiah, the fourth Shallum. 16 The descendants of [q]Jehoiakim: [r]Jeconiah his son, [s]Zedekiah
his son; 17 and the sons of Jeconiah, the [t]captive: [u]Shealtiel his son, 18 Malchiram, Pedaiah,
Shenazzar, Jekamiah, Hoshama and Nedabiah; 19 and the sons of Pedaiah: [v]Zerubbabel and
Shimei; and the sons of [v]Zerubbabel: Meshullam and Hananiah, and Shelomith was their
sister; 20 and Hashubah, Ohel, Berechiah, Hasadiah, and Jushab-hesed, five. 21 The sons of
Hananiah: Pelatiah and Jeshaiah, his son[2] Rephaiah, his son Arnan, his son Obadiah, his
son Shecaniah. 22 The son[3] of Shecaniah: [w]Shemaiah. And the sons of Shemaiah: [x]Hattush,

[1] Septuagint, Vulgate; Hebrew *son* [2] Septuagint (compare Syriac, Vulgate); Hebrew *sons of*; four times in this verse [3] Hebrew *sons*

49 [g][Josh. 15:17; Judg. 1:13]
50 [h]ch. 4:4; [ver. 19]
51 [i][ch. 4:4]
52 [j][ch. 4:2]
53 [k]ch. 4:2
55 [l]Judg. 1:16 [m]2 Kgs. 10:15; Jer. 35:2

Chapter 3

1 [n]For ver. 1-4, see 2 Sam. 3:2-5 [o][2 Sam. 3:3]
4 [p]2 Sam. 2:11 [q]2 Sam. 5:5
5 [r]For ver. 5-8, see ch. 14:4-7; 2 Sam. 5:14-16 [s][ch. 14:4; 2 Sam. 5:14] [t]2 Sam. 12:24 [u][2 Sam. 11:3]
6 [v][ch. 14:5; 2 Sam. 5:15]
8 [w][ch. 14:7]
9 [x]2 Sam. 13:1
10 [y]1 Kgs. 11:43 [z][1 Kgs. 14:31; 15:1] [a]1 Kgs. 15:8 [b]1 Kgs. 15:24
11 [c]2 Kgs. 8:16 [d]2 Kgs. 8:24; [2 Chr. 21:17; 22:6] [e]2 Kgs. 11:2
12 [f]2 Kgs. 12:21 [g][2 Kgs. 15:30] [h]2 Kgs. 15:7
13 [i]2 Kgs. 15:38 [j]2 Kgs. 16:20 [k]2 Kgs. 20:21
14 [l]2 Kgs. 21:18 [m]2 Kgs. 21:26
15 [n][2 Kgs. 23:30] [o][2 Kgs. 23:34] [p][2 Kgs. 24:17]
16 [q][Matt. 1:11] [r][2 Kgs. 24:6; Jer. 22:24] [s][2 Kgs. 24:17]
17 [t]2 Kgs. 24:15 [u]Ezra 3:2; 5:2; Hag. 1:1, 12, 14; 2:2, 23; Matt. 1:12; Luke 3:27
19 [v]Ezra 2:2; Hag. 1:1, 12, 14; Zech. 4:6
22 [w]Neh. 3:29 [x]Ezra 8:2

3:1–24 The genealogy of Ram (2:10–17) is resumed in this composite list of David's descendants, recounted in three distinct sections: David's children (3:1–9); **Solomon** and the kings of Judah (vv. 10–16); and the postexilic generations (vv. 17–24). The literary arrangement of this material is an important indicator of the author's message: just as Judah heads the genealogies of Israel (though Reuben was in fact the firstborn), the line of David's descendants is placed in the center of the genealogy of Judah as the focus of hope and expectation.

3:1–9 Drawn mainly from 2 Sam. 3:2–5 and 5:14–16 (see notes there), with a few textual variations (**Daniel** for "Chileab," and the addition of **Eliphelet**, 1 Chron. 3:6, and **Nogah**, v. 7). The Chronicler's narrative omits discussion of the troubles that beset David's family in later years (2 Samuel 13–19; 1 Kings 1), but mention here of **Amnon**, **Absalom**, **Adonijah**, and **Tamar** implies that the reader is expected to be familiar with these accounts.

3:10–16 The complete Davidic line down to the exile is given here, following the spelling used in Kings (**Azariah** is a variant of "Uzziah," 2 Chronicles 26). The pattern is altered in 1 Chron. 3:15–16 because **Josiah** was succeeded by three of his sons, but not according to their birth order: **Shallum** (throne name: Jehoahaz), replaced by **Jehoiakim** (succeeded by his own son, **Jeconiah** [a variant of "Jehoiachin"]), then **Zedekiah**, the last king of Judah.

3:17–24 Although the monarchy ceased to function as a political fact with the fall of Jerusalem (586 B.C.), the continuation of David's line after the exile still testified to God's promise of an enduring "house" for him, through which God's kingdom would be eternally established (17:10b, 14). **Zerubbabel** played a central role in the restoration of the temple (Ezra 5:2; Hag. 1:12–15). Possibly Ezra 3:2, which calls Zerubbabel the son of Shealtiel, implies an adoption or levirate marriage (see note on Matt. 22:24). It is unclear from 1 Chron. 3:21 whether this list runs for six generations or more into the postexilic period, but in either case it appears to extend down to, or close to, the Chronicler's own day. The preservation of the Davidic line in the family of **Elioenai** (v. 24) should inspire trust among the postexilic community in God's ancient promises, although no particular individual is identified here as David's successor. The Chronicler holds to the ancient messianic hope focused on the house of David, but does not specify how or through whom it will be fulfilled.

3:19 sons of Zerubbabel. Matthew 1:13 and Luke 3:27 both trace Jesus' descent from David through other sons of Zerubbabel than those mentioned

Chapter 4
1[y][Gen. 46:12] [z]Gen. 38:29 [a]ch. 2:7
2[b][ch. 2:52] [c]ch. 2:53
4[d][ver. 18] [e]ver. 18, 39 [f][Gen. 35:19; ch. 2:50, 51]
5[g]ch. 2:24
9[h][Gen. 34:19]
13[i]Josh. 15:17 [j]Judg. 1:13; 3:9, 11
15[k]Num. 13:6
18[l][ver. 4]
21[m]ch. 2:3; Gen. 38:1, 5; 46:12; Num. 26:20
24[n]Num. 26:12

Igal, Bariah, Neariah, and Shaphat, six. **23** The sons of Neariah: Elioenai, Hizkiah, and Azrikam, three. **24** The sons of Elioenai: Hodaviah, Eliashib, Pelaiah, Akkub, Johanan, Delaiah, and Anani, seven.

Descendants of Judah

4 [y]The sons of Judah: [z]Perez, Hezron, [a]Carmi, Hur, and Shobal. **2** [b]Reaiah the son of Shobal fathered Jahath, and Jahath fathered Ahumai and Lahad. These were the clans of the [c]Zorathites. **3** These were the sons[1] of Etam: Jezreel, Ishma, and Idbash; and the name of their sister was Hazzelelponi, **4** and [d]Penuel fathered [e]Gedor, and Ezer fathered Hushah. These were the sons of Hur, the firstborn of [f]Ephrathah, the father of Bethlehem. **5** [g]Ashhur, the father of Tekoa, had two wives, Helah and Naarah; **6** Naarah bore him Ahuzzam, Hepher, Temeni, and Haahashtari. These were the sons of Naarah. **7** The sons of Helah: Zereth, Izhar, and Ethnan. **8** Koz fathered Anub, Zobebah, and the clans of Aharhel, the son of Harum. **9** Jabez was [h]more honorable than his brothers; and his mother called his name Jabez, saying, "Because I bore him in pain."[2] **10** Jabez called upon the God of Israel, saying, "Oh that you would bless me and enlarge my border, and that your hand might be with me, and that you would keep me from harm[3] so that it might not bring me pain!" And God granted what he asked. **11** Chelub, the brother of Shuhah, fathered Mehir, who fathered Eshton. **12** Eshton fathered Beth-rapha, Paseah, and Tehinnah, the father of Ir-nahash. These are the men of Recah. **13** The sons of [i]Kenaz: [j]Othniel and Seraiah; and the sons of Othniel: Hathath and Meonothai.[4] **14** Meonothai fathered Ophrah; and Seraiah fathered Joab, the father of Ge-harashim,[5] so-called because they were craftsmen. **15** The sons of [k]Caleb the son of Jephunneh: Iru, Elah, and Naam; and the son[6] of Elah: Kenaz. **16** The sons of Jehallelel: Ziph, Ziphah, Tiria, and Asarel. **17** The sons of Ezrah: Jether, Mered, Epher, and Jalon. These are the sons of Bithiah, the daughter of Pharaoh, whom Mered married;[7] and she conceived and bore[8] Miriam, Shammai, and Ishbah, the father of Eshtemoa. **18** And his Judahite wife bore [l]Jered the father of Gedor, Heber the father of Soco, and Jekuthiel the father of Zanoah. **19** The sons of the wife of Hodiah, the sister of Naham, were the fathers of Keilah the Garmite and Eshtemoa the Maacathite. **20** The sons of Shimon: Amnon, Rinnah, Ben-hanan, and Tilon. The sons of Ishi: Zoheth and Ben-zoheth. **21** The sons of [m]Shelah the son of Judah: Er the father of Lecah, Laadah the father of Mareshah, and the clans of the house of linen workers at Beth-ashbea; **22** and Jokim, and the men of Cozeba, and Joash, and Saraph, who ruled in Moab and returned to Lehem[9] (now the records[10] are ancient). **23** These were the potters who were inhabitants of Netaim and Gederah. They lived there in the king's service.

Descendants of Simeon

24 [n]The sons of Simeon: Nemuel, Jamin, Jarib, Zerah, Shaul; **25** Shallum was his son, Mibsam his son, Mishma his son. **26** The sons of Mishma: Hammuel his son, Zaccur his

[1] Septuagint (compare Vulgate); Hebrew *father* [2] *Jabez* sounds like the Hebrew for *pain* [3] Or *evil* [4] Septuagint, Vulgate; Hebrew lacks *Meonothai* [5] *Ge-harashim* means *valley of craftsmen* [6] Hebrew *sons* [7] The clause *These are . . . married* is transposed from verse 18 [8] Hebrew lacks *and bore* [9] Vulgate (compare Septuagint); Hebrew *and Jashubi-lahem* [10] Or *matters*

here. Apparently they were using other historical records than those preserved in 1 Chronicles.

4:1–23 Information about other **clans** rounds off the genealogy of Judah and completes the literary *inclusio* (see note on 2:3–4:23) into which all this fragmentary and diverse material has been arranged: vv. 1–20 of ch. 4 supply additional details of the descendants of **Perez** (2:4–8), while 4:21–23 fill out the lineage of Judah's third son, **Shelah** (2:3), the first to have children after the "false starts" with Er and Onan.

4:1 "Caleb" would be expected here, rather than **Carmi**, which may reflect early scribal confusion (see Gen. 46:9) or textual corruption of "Chelubai" (1 Chron. 2:9).

4:9–10 Jabez prays that his name (Hb. *ya'bets*), which contains the same three consonants (*'-b-ts*) as the Hebrew for "pain" (*'otseb*), will not be an ill omen, but rather that he will live under God's blessing and protection (with land equating to livelihood). That God answers heartfelt prayer is a prominent theme of the narrative. On the gift of territorial expansion and divine protection in response to prayer, see 5:20–22 and 2 Chron. 20:6–12.

4:13–15 The Kenizzites appear to have been a southern tribe that was absorbed into Judah. **Othniel** was the first major judge of Israel (Judg. 3:7–11) and a nephew of **Caleb** (Josh. 15:17).

4:21–23 linen workers . . . potters. These records from preexilic times (vv. 22–23) indicate that certain Israelite clans, at least, acted as guilds, specializing in particular trades or crafts such as linen work or pottery; see 2:55 on scribes. **Lehem** may be Bethlehem. Royal seal impressions from jar handles dating from the Iron II period (1000–586 B.C.) have been found throughout Israel. The impressions contain two-line inscriptions: the upper line reads "belonging to the king"; the lower line contains names of cities. The towns mentioned in 4:23 may have supplied such goods.

4:24–43 *The Tribe of Simeon.* The tribe of **Simeon** is considered next because its allotted territory lay within Judah's borders and was taken from that tribe (vv. 28–33; see Josh. 19:1–9), though by David's time (1 Chron. 4:31) Simeon had been largely absorbed back into Judah. Nevertheless, some Simeonite clans maintained their tribal identity through genealogical records (vv. 34–38), which would have included the historical notes of two military expansions undertaken to relieve the pressures of overpopulation (v. 38): one westward into Philistine territory in the **days of Hezekiah** in the eighth century B.C.

son, Shimei his son. 27 Shimei had sixteen sons and six daughters; but his brothers did
not have many children, [o]nor did all their clan multiply [p]like the men of Judah. 28 [q]They
lived in Beersheba, Moladah, Hazar-shual, 29 [r]Bilhah, Ezem, [s]Tolad, 30 [s]Bethuel, Hormah,
Ziklag, 31 Beth-marcaboth, [t]Hazar-susim, [t]Beth-biri, and [t]Shaaraim. These were their cities
until David reigned. 32 And their villages were Etam, Ain, Rimmon, Tochen, and Ashan,
five cities, 33 along with all their villages that were around these cities as far as [u]Baal. These
were their settlements, and they kept a genealogical record.
34 Meshobab, Jamlech, Joshah the son of Amaziah, 35 Joel, Jehu the son of Joshibiah, son
of Seraiah, son of Asiel, 36 Elioenai, Jaakobah, Jeshohaiah, Asaiah, Adiel, Jesimiel, Benaiah,
37 Ziza the son of Shiphi, son of Allon, son of Jedaiah, son of Shimri, son of Shemaiah—
38 these mentioned by name were princes in their clans, [v]and their fathers' houses increased
greatly. 39 They journeyed to the entrance of [w]Gedor, to the east side of the valley, to seek
pasture for their flocks, 40 where they found rich, good pasture, and the land was very
broad, [x]quiet, and peaceful, for the former inhabitants there belonged to Ham. 41 [y]These,
registered by name, came in the days of Hezekiah, king of Judah, and destroyed their tents
and the Meunites who were found there, and marked them for destruction to this day,
[z]and settled in their place, because there was pasture there for their flocks. 42 And some of
them, five hundred men of the Simeonites, went to [a]Mount Seir, having as their leaders
Pelatiah, Neariah, Rephaiah, and Uzziel, the sons of Ishi. 43 And they defeated [b]the remnant
of the Amalekites who had escaped, and they have lived there to this day.

Descendants of Reuben

5 The sons of Reuben the firstborn of Israel ([c]for he was the firstborn, but because [d]he
defiled his father's couch, [e]his birthright was given to the sons of Joseph the son of
Israel, so that he could not be enrolled as the oldest son; 2 [f]though Judah became strong
among his brothers and a [g]chief came from him, yet the birthright belonged to Joseph),
3 the [h]sons of Reuben, the firstborn of Israel: Hanoch, Pallu, Hezron, and Carmi. 4 The sons
of Joel: Shemaiah his son, Gog his son, Shimei his son, 5 Micah his son, Reaiah his son, Baal
his son, 6 Beerah his son, whom [i]Tiglath-pileser[1] king of Assyria carried away into exile;
he was a chief of the Reubenites. 7 And his kinsmen by their clans, [j]when the genealogy of
their generations was recorded: the chief, Jeiel, and Zechariah, 8 and Bela the son of Azaz,
son of [k]Shema, son of Joel, who lived in [l]Aroer, as far as [m]Nebo and [n]Baal-meon. 9 He also
lived to the east as far as the entrance of the desert this side of the Euphrates, because their
livestock had multiplied [o]in the land of Gilead. 10 And in the days of Saul they waged war
against the [p]Hagrites, who fell into their hand. And they lived in their tents throughout
all the region east of Gilead.

Descendants of Gad

11 The sons of Gad lived over against them in the land of Bashan as far as [q]Salecah:
12 Joel the chief, Shapham the second, Janai, and Shaphat in Bashan. 13 And their kinsmen
according to their fathers' houses: Michael, Meshullam, Sheba, Jorai, Jacan, Zia and Eber,
seven. 14 These were the sons of Abihail the son of Huri, son of Jaroah, son of Gilead, son of
Michael, son of Jeshishai, son of Jahdo, son of Buz. 15 Ahi the son of Abdiel, son of Guni, was

[1] Hebrew *Tilgath-pilneser*; also verse 26

27 [o][ver. 38] [p][Num. 2:4, 13; 26:14, 22]
28 [q]For ver. 28-33, see Josh. 19:2-8
29 [r][Josh. 19:3] [s][Josh. 19:4]
30 [s][See ver. 29 above]
31 [t][Josh. 19:5, 6]
33 [u][Josh. 19:8]
38 [v][ver. 27]
39 [w]ver. 4, 18
40 [x][Judg. 18:7, 27]
41 [y]See ver. 34-38 [z][ch. 5:22]
42 [a]Gen. 36:8
43 [b][1 Sam. 15:8; 30:17]

Chapter 5

1 [c]Gen. 29:32; 49:3 [d]Gen. 35:22; 49:4 [e]See Gen. 48:15-22
2 [f]See Gen. 49:8-10 [g]Mic. 5:2; Matt. 2:6
3 [h]Gen. 46:9; Ex. 6:14; Num. 26:5, 6
6 [i]2 Chr. 28:20
7 [j]ver. 17
8 [k][ver. 4] [l]Deut. 2:36; Josh. 13:16 [m]Num. 32:3 [n]Num. 32:38
9 [o]Josh. 22:9
10 [p]ver. 19, 20; ch. 11:38; 27:30
11 [q]Josh. 12:5; 13:11

(vv. 39–41), and another into the southern part of the Negeb (vv. 42–43). The westward campaign to **Gedor** (probably "Gerar") is depicted in the language of the conquest under Joshua: **marked . . . for destruction** (v. 41) signifies the religious *kherem* (Hb.) or "ban," in which a pagan people and their goods were "devoted" or wholly destroyed (see note on 1 Sam. 15:3).

5:1–26 *The Transjordanian Tribes.* The Transjordanian tribe of Reuben (vv. 1–10), tribe of Gad (vv. 11–17), and half-tribe of Manasseh (vv. 23–26) are considered next, although by the Chronicler's time these tribes had largely lost their own identities as a consequence of the Assyrian invasions in the eighth century B.C. Nonetheless, the Chronicler still included within his conception of "all Israel" whatever remnants of the northern tribes still existed (see 2 Chron. 30:10–20).

5:1–2 On account of Reuben's grave sin against his father, he forfeited **his birthright** as Israel/Jacob's **firstborn** to Joseph's sons Ephraim and Manasseh (see Gen. 35:22; 49:3–4), while leadership passed to **Judah**, from whose tribe David (**a chief**) arose. Yet the Chronicler expresses a receptive openness to the non-Judahite Israelites by stressing that **the birthright belonged to Joseph**, whose descendants formed the core of the former northern kingdom.

5:3–6 This is a fragmentary genealogy of Reuben's line, extending down to their exile by the Assyrian king **Tiglath-pileser** III, in his conquest of Gilead (Transjordanian Israel) in 733 B.C. See also 2 Chron. 28:19–21.

5:7–10 These verses recount an earlier expansion of the Reubenites into **Gilead**, a land later recaptured by the Moabites (in the 9th century B.C.). The **Hagrites** were linked with the Moabites (Ps. 83:6) and were understood to be descendants of Hagar (Genesis 16).

5:11–17 The Chronicler's information about the descendants of **Gad** in **Bashan** (roughly, to the northeast of the Sea of Galilee) is taken from records

chief in their fathers' houses, 16 and they lived in Gilead, in Bashan and in its towns, and in
all the pasturelands of [r]Sharon to their limits. 17 All of these were recorded in genealogies
in the days of [s]Jotham king of Judah, and in the days of [t]Jeroboam king of Israel.

18 The Reubenites, the Gadites, and the half-tribe of Manasseh had valiant men who
carried shield and sword, and drew the bow, [u]expert in war, 44,760, able to go to war.
19 They waged war against the [v]Hagrites, [w]Jetur, Naphish, and Nodab. 20 And when they
prevailed[1] over them, the Hagrites and all who were with them were given into their hands,
[x]for they cried out to God in the battle, and he granted their urgent plea [y]because they
trusted in him. 21 They carried off their livestock: 50,000 of their camels, 250,000 sheep,
2,000 donkeys, and 100,000 men alive. 22 For many fell, because the war was of God. And
they lived [z]in their place until [a]the exile.

The Half-Tribe of Manasseh

23 The members of the half-tribe of Manasseh lived in the land. They were very numerous from Bashan to Baal-hermon, [b]Senir, and Mount Hermon. 24 These were the heads of
their fathers' houses: Epher,[2] Ishi, Eliel, Azriel, Jeremiah, Hodaviah, and Jahdiel, mighty
warriors, famous men, heads of their fathers' houses. 25 But they broke faith with the God
of their fathers, and [c]whored [d]after the gods of the peoples of the land, whom God had
destroyed before them. 26 So the God of Israel stirred up the spirit of [e]Pul king of Assyria,
the spirit of [f]Tiglath-pileser king of Assyria, and he took them into exile, namely, the
Reubenites, the Gadites, and the half-tribe of Manasseh, and brought them [g]to Halah,
[g]Habor, Hara, and [g]the river Gozan, to this day.

Descendants of Levi

6 [3] [h]The sons of Levi: Gershon, Kohath, and Merari. 2 [i]The sons of Kohath: Amram, Izhar,
Hebron, and Uzziel. 3 [j]The children of Amram: Aaron, Moses, and Miriam. [k]The sons
of Aaron: Nadab, Abihu, Eleazar, and Ithamar. 4 [l], [m]Eleazar fathered [n]Phinehas, Phinehas
fathered Abishua, 5 Abishua fathered Bukki, Bukki fathered Uzzi, 6 Uzzi fathered Zerahiah,

[1] Or *they were helped to prevail* [2] Septuagint, Vulgate; Hebrew *and Epher* [3] Ch 5:27 in Hebrew

16 [r]ch. 27:29
17 [s]2 Kgs. 15:5, 32 [t]2 Kgs. 14:16, 28
18 [u]Num. 1:3
19 [v]See ver. 10 [w]ch. 1:31; [Gen. 25:15]
20 [x][2 Chr. 14:11; 18:31] [y]Ps. 22:4, 5
22 [z]ch. 4:41 [a]ver. 6; 2 Kgs. 15:29; 17:6
23 [b]Deut. 3:9; Ezek. 27:5
25 [c]See Ex. 34:15 [d]2 Kgs. 17:7
26 [e]2 Kgs. 15:19 [f]See ver. 6 [g]2 Kgs. 17:6; 18:11

Chapter 6

1 [h]ch. 23:6; Gen. 46:11; Ex. 6:16; Num. 26:57
2 [i]Ex. 6:18; [ver. 22]
3 [j]Ex. 6:20; 15:20 [k]Lev. 10:1, 12
4 [l]For ver. 4-6, 11-14, see Ezra 7:1-5 [m]For ver. 4-8, see ver. 50-53 [n]See Ex. 6:25

(possibly a military census; see v. 18) dating from the eighth century B.C. reigns of **Jotham king of Judah** and **Jeroboam king of Israel** (v. 17).

5:18–22 for they cried out to God (v. 20). The Chronicler has reworked a military census and battle report (v. 18) concerning the two and a half tribes to express one of his characteristic theological ideas: that God answers his people and grants them victory when they cry out to him in trusting prayer (see 2 Chron. 13:13–16; 14:9–15; 20:5–12, 22–23). **They prevailed over them** (1 Chron. 5:20) may be (see ESV footnote), "they were helped to prevail over them," an allusion to divine aid in battle. For examples of "help" as a theological concept, see 12:18; 2 Chron. 25:8; 32:8.

5:22 because the war was of God. See also 2 Chron. 20:15 and 32:8 for the idea that God fights for his people.

5:23–24 The **half-tribe of Manasseh** lived east of the Jordan between the boundary of Gad's territory (**Bashan**) and **Mount Hermon** in Lebanon. These details are probably drawn from old military records. Their large numbers and their extensive lands indicate divine blessing.

5:25–26 Nevertheless, the **half-tribe of Manasseh** was defeated and exiled, along with the **Reubenites** and **Gadites**, into Assyrian lands by **Tiglath-pileser** (known as "Pulu" in the Babylonian Chronicle; see note on 2 Kings 15:16–22). However this may have looked from the perspective of worldly politics, the Chronicler attributes the defeat and exile to God's initiative in human affairs: **the God of Israel stirred up the spirit of Pul** (see also 2 Chron. 21:16; 36:22). The writer's brief account is based on 2 Kings 17:7–23, along with particular details from 2 Kings 15:29; 17:6; 18:11, to which he has added his own characteristic emphasis, that because these idolatrous Israelites **broke faith** (Hb. *ma'al*), they were punished by suffering foreign invasion and exile. Exactly the same fate will befall Judah for the same reasons (1 Chron. 9:1; 2 Chron. 36:14–20). Just as 1 Chron. 5:20–22 portrays the result of faithfulness to God, vv. 25–26 depict the consequences of the opposite attitude. This basic contrast will be reflected throughout the narrative. The fate of these Transjordanian tribes is representative of the other northern tribes' fate as well. The Chronicler does not, however, describe their invasion and deportation by the Assyrians, but only alludes to these events in 2 Chron. 30:6–7.

6:1–81 *The Tribe of Levi.* The significance of Levi is shown both by the amount of space devoted to this tribe and by its central position within this section of the book. Just as Judah (2:3–4:23) heads the genealogies of Israel (because of the leadership provided by the Davidic monarchy), and Benjamin (8:1–40) concludes them (because of its close association with the preexilic kingdom of Judah and the restoration community), Levi is placed in the literary and spiritual center of the Chronicler's ideal conception of Israel. The Chronicler will show that the Davidic monarchy and the Jerusalem temple (which is served in every respect by the Levites) together constitute the institutional foundations of Israel's existence, and in fact have a mutually supportive relationship. Primacy among the Levites belongs to the Aaronic high priests (6:1–15), who offered sacrifices of atonement for a guilty nation (v. 49)—one of the principal themes of the book (see 2 Chron. 7:12–14; 29:24). Other Levites were charged with the ministry of worship in Gibeon and Jerusalem (1 Chron. 6:31–48), another matter to which the Chronicler will frequently draw attention (see 16:7, 37; 23:1–27:34; 2 Chron. 29:27–28). At the same time, the Levites, who possessed no tribal territory themselves, are distributed throughout the cities of Israel (1 Chron. 6:54–81).

6:1–15 Drawing from Ex. 6:16–25 for 1 Chron. 6:1–4a, this genealogy focuses on the line of **Eleazar** descended through **Kohath** from **Levi**, as the origin of the high-priestly line down to the exiled **Jehozadak**. The list of high priests is incomplete, omitting several mentioned in other parts of this book (Jehoiada, 2 Chron. 22:11; two other Azariahs, 2 Chron. 26:20, 31:10) and elsewhere in the OT (Eli and his descendants, 1 Sam. 14:3; Uriah, 2 Kings 16:10). The concluding note on the deportation of Jehozadak is a sober reminder that sin and its consequences touched even the most sacred person among the people (see 2 Chron. 36:14). Nevertheless, Jehozadak's line was preserved into the postexilic period (see Ezra 5:2, where he is called Jozadak), just as David's line was (1 Chron. 3:17–24), as indications of God's continuing commitment to his people. One of the insistent themes of Chronicles is that God's grace is not nullified by human disobedience, but that rather God creates fresh opportunities for each generation to trust and obey.

Zerahiah fathered [o]Meraioth, **7** Meraioth fathered Amariah, Amariah fathered Ahitub,
8 [p]Ahitub fathered [q]Zadok, Zadok fathered Ahimaaz, **9** Ahimaaz fathered Azariah, Azariah
fathered Johanan, **10** and Johanan fathered Azariah ([r]it was he who served as priest [s]in the
house that Solomon built in Jerusalem). **11** [l]Azariah fathered [t]Amariah, Amariah fathered
Ahitub, **12** Ahitub fathered Zadok, Zadok fathered [u]Shallum, **13** Shallum fathered [v]Hilkiah,
Hilkiah fathered Azariah, **14** Azariah fathered [w]Seraiah, Seraiah fathered Jehozadak; **15** and
[x]Jehozadak went into exile when the LORD sent Judah and Jerusalem into exile [y]by the
hand of Nebuchadnezzar.

16[1] The [z]sons of Levi: Gershom, Kohath, and Merari. **17** And these are the names of the
sons of Gershom: [a]Libni and Shimei. **18** [b]The sons of Kohath: Amram, Izhar, Hebron and
Uzziel. **19** [c]The sons of Merari: Mahli and Mushi. These are the clans of the Levites according to their fathers. **20** [d]Of Gershom: Libni his son, [e]Jahath his son, Zimmah his son, **21** Joah
his son, Iddo his son, Zerah his son, Jeatherai his son. **22** [f]The sons of Kohath: Amminadab
his son, Korah his son, Assir his son, **23** Elkanah his son, Ebiasaph his son, Assir his son,
24 Tahath his son, Uriel his son, Uzziah his son, and Shaul his son. **25** The sons of Elkanah:
Amasai and Ahimoth, **26** Elkanah his son, Zophai his son, Nahath his son, **27** Eliab his son,
Jeroham his son, Elkanah his son. **28** The sons of Samuel: Joel[2] his firstborn, the second
Abijah.[3] **29** [g]The sons of Merari: Mahli, Libni his son, Shimei his son, Uzzah his son, **30** Shimea
his son, Haggiah his son, and Asaiah his son.

31 These are the men [h]whom David put in charge of the service of song in the house of
the LORD [i]after the ark rested there. **32** They ministered with song before the tabernacle
of the tent of meeting until Solomon built the house of the LORD in Jerusalem, and they
performed their service according to their order. **33** These are the men who served and their
sons. Of the sons of the Kohathites: Heman the singer the son of Joel, son of [j]Samuel, **34** son
of Elkanah, son of Jeroham, son of Eliel, son of Toah, **35** son of Zuph, son of Elkanah, son of
Mahath, son of Amasai, **36** son of Elkanah, son of Joel, son of Azariah, son of Zephaniah, **37** son
of Tahath, son of Assir, son of Ebiasaph, son of Korah, **38** son of Izhar, son of Kohath, son of
Levi, son of Israel; **39** and his brother [k]Asaph, who stood on his right hand, namely, Asaph
the son of Berechiah, son of Shimea, **40** son of Michael, son of Baaseiah, son of Malchijah,
41 son of Ethni, son of Zerah, son of Adaiah, **42** son of Ethan, son of Zimmah, son of Shimei,
43 son of Jahath, son of Gershom, son of Levi. **44** On the left hand were their brothers, the sons
of Merari: Ethan the son of Kishi, son of Abdi, son of Malluch, **45** son of Hashabiah, son of
Amaziah, son of Hilkiah, **46** son of Amzi, son of Bani, son of Shemer, **47** son of Mahli, son of
Mushi, son of Merari, son of Levi. **48** And their brothers the Levites were appointed for all
the service of the tabernacle of the house of God.

49 But Aaron and his sons made offerings [l]on the altar of burnt offering and on [m]the
altar of incense for all the work of the Most Holy Place, and [n]to make atonement for Israel,
according to all that Moses the servant of God had commanded. **50** [o]These are the sons of
Aaron: Eleazar his son, Phinehas his son, Abishua his son, **51** Bukki his son, Uzzi his son,

[1] Ch 6:1 in Hebrew [2] Septuagint, Syriac (compare verse 33 and 1 Samuel 8:2); Hebrew lacks *Joel* [3] Hebrew *and Abijah*

6 [o][ch. 9:11; Neh. 11:11]
8 [p]2 Sam. 8:17 [q]2 Sam. 15:27
10 [r]2 Chr. 26:17, 18 [s]See 1 Kgs. 6; 2 Chr. 3
11 [l][See ver. 4 above] [t]2 Chr. 19:11; Ezra 7:3
12 [u][Neh. 11:11]
13 [v]2 Kgs. 22:4; Ezra 7:1
14 [w]2 Kgs. 25:18
15 [x][Ezra 3:2] [y]See 2 Kgs. 25:8-21
16 [z]For ver. 16-19, see Ex. 6:16-19
17 [a][ch. 23:7]
18 [b]ch. 23:12
19 [c]ch. 23:21; [ver. 44, 47]
20 [d]For ver. 20, 21, see ver. 41-43 [e]ver. 43
22 [f]For ver. 22-28, see ver. 33-38
29 [g][ver. 19, 44-47]
31 [h]See ch. 16:4-6 [i]See ch. 15:25–16:1; 2 Sam. 6:12-17
33 [j][ver. 28]
39 [k]ch. 15:17, 19; 2 Chr. 5:12; Ezra 2:41; Neh. 7:44
49 [l]Lev. 1:7, 9 [m]Ex. 30:7 [n]Ex. 30:10; Lev. 4:20
50 [o]For ver. 50-53, see ver. 4-8

6:10 Azariah. See note on 1 Kings 4:2.

6:16–30 This section details the three main divisions or clans of the Levites, descended from **Gershom** (the Chronicler's usual spelling for "Gershon"), **Kohath**, and **Merari**. Verses 16–19a are based on Num. 3:17–20. Seven generations are given for the descendants of Gershom and Merari, probably taking them down to the time of David, who reorganized the duties of the Levites (on **Asaiah**, 1 Chron. 6:30, see 15:6).

6:22–27 The Kohathite line is a little more difficult to follow. **Amminadab** may be an alternative name for Izhar (see v. 38) or Amram (v. 18). Verses 22–27 present the vertical line of descent from Korah, also giving seven generations, from Kohath through **Assir** to **Shaul**. Combined with this are horizontal lines of the family tree (**Elkanah** and **Ebiasaph**, v. 23, are Assir's brothers).

6:28 The genealogy of the prophet **Samuel** identifies him as a Kohathite. First Samuel 1:1 states that his father Elkanah was from an "Ephraimite" family, but this may indicate the locality in which they lived as part of a Kohathite clan (see Josh. 21:20–21) rather than their tribal identity. A clear genealogical link with the Kohathite singer Heman is established in 1 Chron. 6:33–38 (basically the same as vv. 22–28, with the names arranged in a single vertical line).

6:31–48 Genealogical details are provided of the Levites whom David **put in charge of the service of song** (v. 31) before the ark in Jerusalem and the tabernacle in Gibeon (explained in detail in 16:4–6, 41–42). Their leaders were appointed from each of the Levitical clans: **Heman**, from the Kohathites (6:33–38); **Asaph**, from the Gershomites (vv. 39–43); and **Ethan**, from the Merarites (vv. 44–47). Each line is traced back vertically to Levi.

6:49–53 The work of the Aaronic priests in making **atonement for Israel** will be a recurrent theme in the narrative as the means of restoring and maintaining Israel's relationship with God (see 2 Chron. 13:10–11; 29:21). Verses 50–53 of 1 Chronicles 6 repeat vv. 4–8 to enclose the Levitical genealogies within the line of Aaronides down to **Zadok** and **Ahimaaz**, who were contemporaries of Solomon. Aaron's first two sons, Nadab and Abihu, who died for their disobedience, are not mentioned here (cf. v. 3; 24:1–2; also Ex. 6:23; 24:9; Lev. 10:1–7; Num. 3:2–4; 26:60–61).

54 [p]Gen. 25:16; Num. 31:10 [q]Josh. 21:4, 10
56 [r][Josh. 14:13; 15:13]
57 [s]For ver. 57-60, see Josh. 21:13-19
61 [t][ver. 66-70; Josh. 21:5]
63 [u]Josh. 21:7
64 [v]Josh. 21:3
65 [w]See ver. 57-60
66 [x]For ver. 66-70, see Josh. 21:20-26
68 [y]Josh. 12:22; 1 Kgs. 4:12
71 [z]For ver. 71-76, see Josh. 21:27-33 [a]Josh. 9:10
77 [b]For ver. 77-81, see Josh. 21:34-39 [c][Josh. 19:12, 13]
78 [d]Josh. 13:32
80 [e]1 Kgs. 22:3, 4; 2 Kgs. 9:1, 14 [f]See Gen. 32:2
81 [g]Josh. 13:17; 21:39 [h]Num. 21:32; Josh. 21:39

Chapter 7

1 [i][Num. 26:23] [j][Gen. 46:13]
2 [k]2 Sam. 24:1, 2, 9

Zerahiah his son, 52 Meraioth his son, Amariah his son, Ahitub his son, 53 Zadok his son,
Ahimaaz his son.
54 These are their dwelling places according to their [p]settlements within their borders:
to the sons of Aaron of the [q]clans of Kohathites, for theirs was the first lot, 55 to them they
gave Hebron in the land of Judah and its surrounding pasturelands, 56 [r]but the fields of the
city and its villages they gave to Caleb the son of Jephunneh. 57 [s]To the sons of Aaron they
gave the cities of refuge: Hebron, Libnah with its pasturelands, Jattir, Eshtemoa with its
pasturelands, 58 Hilen with its pasturelands, Debir with its pasturelands, 59 Ashan with its
pasturelands, and Beth-shemesh with its pasturelands; 60 and from the tribe of Benjamin,
Gibeon,[1] Geba with its pasturelands, Alemeth with its pasturelands, and Anathoth with
its pasturelands. All their cities throughout their clans were thirteen.
61 [t]To the rest of the Kohathites were given by lot out of the clan of the tribe, out of the
half-tribe, the half of Manasseh, ten cities. 62 To the Gershomites according to their clans
were allotted thirteen cities out of the tribes of Issachar, Asher, Naphtali and Manasseh
in Bashan. 63 [u]To the Merarites according to their clans were allotted twelve cities out of
the tribes of Reuben, Gad, and Zebulun. 64 [v]So the people of Israel gave the Levites the
cities with their pasturelands. 65 They gave by lot out of the tribes of Judah, Simeon, and
Benjamin [w]these cities that are mentioned by name.
66 [x]And some of the clans of the sons of Kohath had cities of their territory out of the tribe
of Ephraim. 67 They were given the cities of refuge: Shechem with its pasturelands in the
hill country of Ephraim, Gezer with its pasturelands, 68 [y]Jokmeam with its pasturelands,
Beth-horon with its pasturelands, 69 Aijalon with its pasturelands, Gath-rimmon with its
pasturelands, 70 and out of the half-tribe of Manasseh, Aner with its pasturelands, and
Bileam with its pasturelands, for the rest of the clans of the Kohathites.
71 [z]To the Gershomites were given out of the clan of the half-tribe of Manasseh: Golan
in Bashan with its pasturelands and [a]Ashtaroth with its pasturelands; 72 and out of the
tribe of Issachar: Kedesh with its pasturelands, Daberath with its pasturelands, 73 Ramoth
with its pasturelands, and Anem with its pasturelands; 74 out of the tribe of Asher: Mashal
with its pasturelands, Abdon with its pasturelands, 75 Hukok with its pasturelands, and
Rehob with its pasturelands; 76 and out of the tribe of Naphtali: Kedesh in Galilee with
its pasturelands, Hammon with its pasturelands, and Kiriathaim with its pasturelands.
77 [b]To the rest of the Merarites were allotted out of the tribe of Zebulun: [c]Rimmono
with its pasturelands, [c]Tabor with its pasturelands, 78 and [d]beyond the Jordan at Jericho,
on the east side of the Jordan, out of the tribe of Reuben: Bezer in the wilderness with
its pasturelands, Jahzah with its pasturelands, 79 Kedemoth with its pasturelands, and
Mephaath with its pasturelands; 80 and out of the tribe of Gad: [e]Ramoth in Gilead with
its pasturelands, [f]Mahanaim with its pasturelands, 81 [g]Heshbon with its pasturelands,
and [h]Jazer with its pasturelands.

Descendants of Issachar

7 The sons[2] of Issachar: Tola, [i]Puah, [j]Jashub, and Shimron, four. 2 The sons of Tola: Uzzi,
Rephaiah, Jeriel, Jahmai, Ibsam, and Shemuel, heads of their fathers' houses, namely
of Tola, mighty warriors of their generations, their number [k]in the days of David being
22,600. 3 The son[3] of Uzzi: Izrahiah. And the sons of Izrahiah: Michael, Obadiah, Joel,
and Isshiah, all five of them were chief men. 4 And along with them, by their generations,
according to their fathers' houses, were units of the army for war, 36,000, for they had
many wives and sons. 5 Their kinsmen belonging to all the clans of Issachar were in all
87,000 mighty warriors, enrolled by genealogy.

[1] Septuagint, Syriac (compare Joshua 21:17); Hebrew lacks *Gibeon* [2] Syriac (compare Vulgate); Hebrew *And to the sons* [3] Hebrew *sons*; also verses 10, 12, 17

6:54–81 Summarized from Joshua 21 with some small omissions and variations of order. As a sign of their central role in the nation's life and well-being, it was intended that the Levites, with no allocated tribal land of their own, should reside throughout the tribal territory of Israel as spiritual representatives and leaders of the people.

7:1–40 *Other Northern Tribes.* This chapter contains briefer details of those tribes, including part of Benjamin, that belonged to the old northern kingdom of Israel. They are enclosed within the genealogies as part of the Chronicler's ideal conception of "all Israel" as a unity that existed in David's time (v. 2), even though their lands were no longer under Israelite control at the time of the Chronicler's writing.

7:1–5 The list of the descendants of **Issachar** is composed from Gen. 46:13, Num. 26:23–25, and a military census from David's reign (1 Chron. 7:2–5; see ch. 21).

Descendants of Benjamin

6 [l]The sons of Benjamin: Bela, Becher, and Jediael, three. 7 The sons of Bela: Ezbon,
Uzzi, Uzziel, Jerimoth, and Iri, five, heads of fathers' houses, mighty warriors. And their
enrollment by genealogies was 22,034. 8 The sons of Becher: Zemirah, Joash, Eliezer,
Elioenai, Omri, Jeremoth, Abijah, [m]Anathoth, and Alemeth. All these were the sons of
Becher. 9 And their enrollment by genealogies, according to their generations, as heads
of their fathers' houses, mighty warriors, was 20,200. 10 The son of Jediael: Bilhan. And
the sons of Bilhan: Jeush, Benjamin, Ehud, Chenaanah, Zethan, Tarshish, and Ahishahar.
11 All these were the sons of Jediael according to the heads of their fathers' houses, mighty
warriors, 17,200, able to go to war. 12 And Shuppim and Huppim were the sons of Ir,
Hushim the son of [n]Aher.

Descendants of Naphtali

13 [o]The sons of Naphtali: [p]Jahziel, Guni, Jezer and [q]Shallum, the descendants of
Bilhah.

Descendants of Manasseh

14 [r]The sons of Manasseh: Asriel, whom his Aramean concubine bore; she bore [s]Machir
the father of Gilead. 15 And Machir took a wife for Huppim and for Shuppim. The name of
his sister was Maacah. And the name of the second was Zelophehad, and [t]Zelophehad had
daughters. 16 And Maacah the wife of Machir bore a son, and she called his name Peresh;
and the name of his brother was Sheresh; and his sons were Ulam and Rakem. 17 The son
of Ulam: [u]Bedan. These were the sons of Gilead the son of Machir, son of Manasseh. 18 And
his sister Hammolecheth bore Ishhod, Abiezer and Mahlah. 19 The sons of Shemida were
Ahian, Shechem, Likhi, and Aniam.

Descendants of Ephraim

20 The [v]sons of Ephraim: Shuthelah, and Bered his son, Tahath his son, Eleadah his son,
Tahath his son, 21 Zabad his son, Shuthelah his son, and Ezer and Elead, whom the men
of Gath who were born in the land killed, because they came down to raid their livestock.
22 And Ephraim their father mourned many days, and his brothers came to comfort him.
23 And Ephraim went in to his wife, and she conceived and bore a son. And he called his
name Beriah, because disaster had befallen his house.[1] 24 His daughter was Sheerah, who
built both Lower and Upper [w]Beth-horon, and Uzzen-sheerah. 25 Rephah was his son,
Resheph his son, Telah his son, Tahan his son, 26 Ladan his son, Ammihud his son, [x]Elishama
his son, 27 Nun[2] his son, [y]Joshua his son. 28 [z]Their possessions and settlements were Bethel
and its towns, and to the east Naaran, and to the west [a]Gezer and its towns, Shechem and
its towns, and Ayyah and its towns; 29 [b]also in possession of the Manassites, [c]Beth-shean
and its towns, Taanach and its towns, Megiddo and its towns, Dor and its towns. In these
lived the sons of Joseph the son of Israel.

Descendants of Asher

30 [d]The sons of Asher: Imnah, Ishvah, Ishvi, Beriah, and their sister Serah. 31 The sons
of Beriah: Heber, and Malchiel, who fathered Birzaith. 32 Heber fathered Japhlet, Shomer,

[1] *Beriah* sounds like the Hebrew for *disaster* [2] Hebrew *Non*

6 [l]Gen. 46:21; Num. 26:38; See ch. 8:1-40
8 [m][ch. 6:60]
12 [n][ch. 8:1]
13 [o]Num. 26:48-50 [p][Num. 26:48] [q][Num. 26:49]
14 [r]For ver. 14-19, see Num. 26:29-33 [s]See Josh. 17:1
15 [t]Num. 27:1; 36:11; Josh. 17:3
17 [u]1 Sam. 12:11
20 [v]Num. 26:35
24 [w]See Josh. 10:10, 11
26 [x]Num. 1:10; 7:48
27 [y]Num. 13:8, 16
28 [z]Josh. 16:2, 3 [a]Josh. 16:3
29 [b]Josh. 17:7 [c]Josh. 17:11
30 [d]Gen. 46:17; Num. 26:44

7:6–12 These details of **Benjamin** differ from other lists (Gen. 46:21; Num. 26:38–39; 1 Chron. 8:1–3) and originate mainly in military registers (7:7, 9, 11), probably the same as for Issachar. A second Benjaminite genealogy is given in ch. 8, though for a different purpose.

7:13 Drawn from Gen. 46:24 and Num. 26:48–49. The extreme brevity may reflect the limitations in the Chronicler's sources. Details for Dan and Zebulun are also missing, probably because of the fragmentary nature of records from the early monarchy.

7:14–19 This section concerns the half of **Manasseh** that lived west of the Jordan. Details are drawn from Num. 26:29–33 and Josh. 17:1–3. This genealogy is of a different character from the preceding ones, with a particular emphasis on women (**Maacah**, **Zelophehad**, **Hammolecheth**), suggesting an origin in the domestic social world. Maacah is called the **sister** of **Machir** in 1 Chron. 7:15, then his **wife** in v. 16; but "sister/brother" often has the sense of "relative" in the OT.

7:15 and Zelophehad had daughters. See Num. 26:33; 27:1–11.

7:20–29 The vertical genealogy of **Joshua**, the most famous Ephraimite, is given in vv. 20–27 (from Num. 26:35). Into this list a historical note (1 Chron. 7:21b–24) has been inserted that probably refers to the postconquest period: the building of Lower and Upper Beth-horon fits better with the time of tribal settlement. In this case, **Ephraim** (v. 22) would refer not to the patriarch but to a later descendant of the same name. **Gath** may be Gittaim, on the Ephraimite border. Verses 28–29 draw on Joshua 16–17 for details of the settlements of Ephraim and Manasseh, since both tribes descended from Joseph.

7:30–40 Genesis 46:17, Num. 26:44–46, and details from a military register (1 Chron. 7:40) provide the information for **Asher**. The total of fighting men for Asher (**26,000**, v. 40) is significantly less than that in Moses' day (Num. 26:47).

Hotham, and their sister Shua. 33 The sons of Japhlet: Pasach, Bimhal, and Ashvath. These
are the sons of Japhlet. 34 The sons of Shemer his brother: Rohgah, Jehubbah, and Aram.
35 The sons of Helem his brother: Zophah, Imna, Shelesh, and Amal. 36 The sons of Zophah:
Suah, Harnepher, Shual, Beri, Imrah. 37 Bezer, Hod, Shamma, Shilshah, Ithran, and Beera.
38 The sons of Jether: Jephunneh, Pispa, and Ara. 39 The sons of Ulla: Arah, Hanniel, and
Rizia. 40 All of these were men of Asher, heads of fathers' houses, approved, mighty warriors, chiefs of the princes. Their number enrolled by genealogies, for service in war, was
26,000 men.

A Genealogy of Saul

8 [e]Benjamin fathered Bela his firstborn, Ashbel the second, [f]Aharah the third, 2 Nohah
the fourth, and Rapha the fifth. 3 And Bela had sons: Addar, Gera, Abihud, 4 Abishua,
[g]Naaman, Ahoah, 5 Gera, [h]Shephuphan, and Huram. 6 These are the sons of Ehud (they
were heads of fathers' houses of the inhabitants of Geba, and they were carried into exile
to [i]Manahath): 7 Naaman,[1] Ahijah, and Gera, that is, Heglam,[2] who fathered Uzza and
Ahihud. 8 And Shaharaim fathered sons in the country of Moab after he had sent away
Hushim and Baara his wives. 9 He fathered sons by Hodesh his wife: Jobab, Zibia, Mesha,
Malcam, 10 Jeuz, Sachia, and Mirmah. These were his sons, heads of fathers' houses. 11 He
also fathered sons by Hushim: Abitub and Elpaal. 12 The sons of Elpaal: Eber, Misham,
and Shemed, who built [j]Ono and [k]Lod with its towns, 13 and Beriah and [l]Shema (they
were heads of fathers' houses of the inhabitants of [m]Aijalon, who caused the inhabitants
of Gath to flee); 14 and Ahio, Shashak, and Jeremoth. 15 Zebadiah, Arad, Eder, 16 Michael,
Ishpah, and Joha were sons of Beriah. 17 Zebadiah, Meshullam, Hizki, Heber, 18 Ishmerai,
Izliah, and Jobab were the sons of Elpaal. 19 Jakim, Zichri, Zabdi, 20 Elienai, Zillethai, Eliel,
21 Adaiah, Beraiah, and Shimrath were the sons of Shimei. 22 Ishpan, Eber, Eliel, 23 Abdon,
Zichri, Hanan, 24 Hananiah, Elam, Anthothijah, 25 Iphdeiah, and Penuel were the sons of
Shashak. 26 Shamsherai, Shehariah, Athaliah, 27 Jaareshiah, Elijah, and Zichri were the sons
of Jeroham. 28 These were the heads of fathers' houses, according to their generations, chief
men. These lived in Jerusalem.

29 [n, o]Jeiel[3] the father of Gibeon lived in Gibeon, and the name of his wife was Maacah.
30 His firstborn son: Abdon, then Zur, Kish, Baal, Nadab, 31 Gedor, Ahio, Zecher, 32 and Mikloth
(he fathered Shimeah). Now these also lived opposite their kinsmen in Jerusalem, with
their kinsmen. 33 [p]Ner was the father of Kish, Kish of Saul, Saul of [q]Jonathan, Malchi-shua,
Abinadab and Eshbaal; 34 and the son of Jonathan was Merib-baal; and Merib-baal was the
father of [r]Micah. 35 The sons of Micah: Pithon, Melech, Tarea, and Ahaz. 36 Ahaz fathered
Jehoaddah, and Jehoaddah fathered Alemeth, Azmaveth, and Zimri. Zimri fathered Moza.
37 Moza fathered Binea; Raphah was his son, Eleasah his son, Azel his son. 38 Azel had six sons,
and these are their names: Azrikam, Bocheru, Ishmael, Sheariah, Obadiah, and Hanan. All
these were the sons of Azel. 39 The sons of Eshek his brother: Ulam his firstborn, Jeush the

Chapter 8
1 [e][ch. 7:6; Gen. 46:21; Num. 26:38] [f][ch. 7:12]
4 [g]Num. 26:40
5 [h][ch. 7:12]
6 [i][ch. 2:52, 54]
12 [j]Ezra 2:33; Neh. 6:2; 7:37; 11:35 [k][Acts 9:32, 35, 38]
13 [l][ver. 21] [m]Josh. 10:12
29 [n][ch. 9:35] [o]For ver. 29-32, see ch. 9:35-38
33 [p]For ver. 33-38, see ch. 9:39-44; [1 Sam. 9:1; 14:51] [q]ch. 10:2; 1 Sam. 31:2
34 [r]2 Sam. 9:12

[1] Hebrew *and Naaman* [2] Or *he carried them into exile* [3] Compare 9:35; Hebrew lacks *Jeiel*

8:1–40 *The Tribe of Benjamin.* Although Benjamin has already been considered (7:6–12), a second, more detailed genealogy of this tribe is given here that has little in common with the earlier list and serves a different function. The structure of Judah-Levi-Benjamin is completed here. The other tribes are enclosed within an ideal conception of Israel as a nation led by the royal tribe of Judah in partnership with its neighbor Benjamin, with Levi at the center to remind the people of their spiritual vocation. Although most of Benjamin sided with the north in the disruption of the kingdom under Rehoboam, the Benjaminite area around Jerusalem as far as Bethel remained loyal to the Davidic king (see 1 Kings 12:21). Judah (including Simeon) and Benjamin formed the southern kingdom, and they are regularly mentioned together in this book (2 Chron. 11:1–3, 10; 14:8; 15:2, 9; 31:1). Together they were the legitimate heirs of Israel as it existed under the united monarchy. Judah and Benjamin also formed the core of the postexilic community in Jerusalem and Judah (cf. Ezra 1:5; Neh. 11:4–9). Verses 1–28 of 1 Chronicles 8 are especially concerned with the location of the Benjaminite settlements in Jerusalem and further afield (vv. 6, 12, 13, 28, 29, 32). Most of the details in this section are probably from preexilic sources. They would have reminded the Chronicler's readers of their identity and ancient claim to the land, founded on God's promise and gift (16:17–18; 2 Chron. 20:7).

8:1–7 The descendants of the famous judge **Ehud** (Judg. 3:15), who settled in the Benjaminite city of **Geba** (see 1 Kings 15:22) before their removal to **Manahath** (probably in Judah).

8:8–27 These are the descendants of **Elpaal**, who led a westward expansion into the coastal plain (vv. 12–13) and settled in Jerusalem (v. 28).

8:29–40 This is the genealogy of the most famous Benjaminite family, detailing the ancestry of **Saul** and his descendants through 15 generations. (Ner, in 1 Sam. 14:50, has the same name as Saul's ancestor.) The first section of the list is probably of early preexilic origin, since it contains names that would have been unacceptable in later times because of possible pagan connotations (**Baal**, 1 Chron. 8:30; **Eshbaal**, v. 33, is known elsewhere as Ishbosheth, 2 Sam. 2:8; and **Merib-baal**, 1 Chron. 8:34, is known as Mephibosheth, 2 Sam. 4:4). First Chronicles 8:35–38 extends the family line into the late preexilic time. These details are not known from other earlier sources, and were preserved among those families that prized the memory of their descent from Israel's first king.

second, and Eliphelet the third. 40 The sons of Ulam were men who were mighty warriors,
bowmen, having many sons and grandsons, 150. All these were Benjaminites.

A Genealogy of the Returned Exiles

9 So all Israel was recorded in genealogies, and these are written in the Book of the
Kings of Israel. And [s]Judah was taken into exile in Babylon because of their breach
of faith. 2 [t]Now the first to [u]dwell again in their possessions in their cities were Israel, the
priests, the Levites, and the [v]temple servants. 3 And some of the people of Judah, Benjamin,
Ephraim, and Manasseh lived in Jerusalem: 4 Uthai the son of Ammihud, son of Omri,
son of Imri, son of Bani, from the sons of [w]Perez the son of Judah. 5 And of the Shilonites:
Asaiah the firstborn, and his sons. 6 Of the sons of Zerah: Jeuel and their kinsmen, 690.
7 Of the Benjaminites: Sallu the son of Meshullam, son of Hodaviah, son of Hassenuah,
8 Ibneiah the son of Jeroham, Elah the son of Uzzi, son of Michri, and Meshullam the son
of Shephatiah, son of Reuel, son of Ibnijah; 9 and their kinsmen according to their generations, [x]956. All these were heads of fathers' houses according [y]to their fathers' houses.

10 [z]Of the priests: Jedaiah, Jehoiarib, Jachin, 11 and Azariah the son of Hilkiah, son of
Meshullam, son of Zadok, son of Meraioth, son of Ahitub, the [a]chief officer of the house
of God; 12 and Adaiah the son of Jeroham, son of Pashhur, son of Malchijah, and Maasai
the son of Adiel, son of Jahzerah, son of Meshullam, son of Meshillemith, son of Immer;
13 besides their kinsmen, heads of their fathers' houses, 1,760, mighty men for the work
of the service of the house of God.

14 [b]Of the Levites: Shemaiah the son of Hasshub, son of Azrikam, son of Hashabiah, of
the sons of Merari; 15 and Bakbakkar, Heresh, Galal and Mattaniah the son of Mica, son of

Chapter 9
1 [s]ch. 5:25, 26
2 [t]For ver. 2-22, see Neh. 11:3-22 [u]Ezra 2:70; Neh. 7:73 [v]Ezra 2:43, 58; 7:7; 8:17, 20; Neh. 3:26; 7:60, 73; 10:28; 11:3, 21; [Josh. 9:27]
4 [w][ch. 2:5, 6]
9 [x][Neh. 11:8] [y][2 Chr. 35:4, 5]
10 [z]For ver. 10-13, see Neh. 11:10-14
11 [a][Jer. 20:1; Acts 4:1]
14 [b]For ver. 14-17, see Neh. 11:15-19

9:1–34 *The Resettlement of Jerusalem.* The Chronicler focuses on the worship personnel who return to inhabit Jerusalem.

9:1 The summarizing conclusion to the tribal **genealogies** of **all Israel** in chs. 2–8. Judah's exile to Babylon for **breach of faith** (Hb. *ma'al*) parallels the fate of the northern tribes (see 5:25–26) and represents the culmination of the narrative of the post-Solomonic dynasty in 2 Chron. 10–36 (see esp. 2 Chron. 36:14–20). **the Book of the Kings of Israel**. See note on 1 Kings 14:19.

9:2–34 The resettlement of **Jerusalem** and Judah after the exile indicates that a new chapter has opened in Israel's existence. The punishment of exile is past (2 Chron. 36:22–23), so the people should respond to God's grace by ordering their lives in the right way, in the hope of a fuller restoration than their present experience. Their obedient response includes repopulating Jerusalem (1 Chron. 9:2–17; for an account of how this was encouraged by Nehemiah see Neh. 11:1–19, which is closely related to this passage), and a renewed commitment to supporting the temple and its services, signified here by its personnel (1 Chron. 9:10–33).

9:3–9 The repopulated Jerusalem includes people from **Ephraim** and **Manasseh**, as well as **Judah** and **Benjamin**, as a representative nucleus of all Israel. The Judahites are listed as descendants of the patriarch's sons **Perez**, Shelah (assuming the word **Shilonites** should have the vowels for "Shelanites"; see Num. 26:20), and **Zerah**.

9:10–13 The **priests** in postexilic Jerusalem are commended for their ability and commitment to the temple ministry (v. 13). Their numbers (**1,760**) have grown significantly since earlier days (1,192 in Neh. 11:12–14).

9:14–16 The Levitical singers and musicians include descendants of **Asaph** and **Jeduthun**, choir leaders in David's day (6:39; 25:1). Other singers **lived in the villages of the Netophathites**, near Bethlehem (Neh. 12:28).

9:17–32 The Chronicler gives special attention to the Levitical gatekeepers, tracing their authority to their service under **Phinehas** (v. 20; see Num. 25:6–11) and their appointment by **David** (1 Chron. 9:22; 26:1–32). Along with their primary duty of safeguarding the sanctity and security of the temple (which entailed regular shifts by Levites from the villages near Jerusalem, 9:22–25), the gatekeepers were also responsible for the **utensils** and supplies used in the daily sacrifices (vv. 28–32).

9:31 and Mattithiah . . . was entrusted with making the flat cakes. The responsibilities of vv. 28–31 may strike the modern reader as obscure and dull. Perhaps they seemed so to the ancient reader as well. Nevertheless, the whole work of the sanctuary depended on the faithfulness of these men; and all of God's people may take comfort from this reminder that God both notices and remembers those who faithfully perform routine tasks in service to him. The mention of these servants was probably a source of pride to their later descendants.

9:35–44 *The Genealogy of Saul.* Saul's genealogy is repeated from 8:29–38. Its main purpose here is to introduce the Chronicler's account of Saul's reign (ch. 10). While his dynasty ended with his death (10:6), nevertheless his family line continued for many generations as a part of Israel (9:40–44).

9:40 Merib-baal. See note on 8:29–40.

1 Chron. 10:1–2 Chron. 9:31 *The United Kingdom of David and Solomon.* The second major section of 1–2 Chronicles concerns the reigns of David and Solomon over the whole people and land of Israel, and overlaps the division of Chronicles into two scrolls. The rule of these two kings is presented as a unity, in that David makes the essential preparations for what Solomon completes. David is the dominant personality and human subject of interest from 1 Chronicles 11 to the end of the first book. With regard to his own rule and contributions to the kingdom, four achievements stand out in particular: (1) David conquers Jerusalem and brings the ark of the covenant there, as a precursor to the temple that Solomon will build (chs. 11; 15); (2) he secures peace for the land so that Solomon may complete his task (chs. 18–20); (3) he provides Solomon with the plans for the temple and the wealth to build it (chs. 22; 28–29); and (4) he organizes the personnel for the future temple and the kingdom that Solomon will inherit (chs. 23–27). The two kings are bound together as well in the establishment of an enduring dynasty in the line of David, in which both the temple and the kingship will testify to God's unending covenant with David (17:11–14). Chapters 10–12 recount the establishment of David's kingship over Israel in two episodes: the death of Saul and the end of his dynasty (10:1–14), and the transfer of power over the nation to David (11:1–12:40). The Chronicler presents these events in a strikingly different way from 1–2 Samuel. Presupposing his readers' familiarity with the earlier accounts, he omits most of the subsidiary episodes and details to concentrate on his central theme: David's entry into kingship inaugurated a permanent change for good in Israel's relationship with

Zichri, son of Asaph; 16 and Obadiah the son of Shemaiah, son of Galal, son of Jeduthun, and
Berechiah the son of Asa, son of Elkanah, who lived in the villages of the Netophathites.
17 The gatekeepers were Shallum, Akkub, Talmon, Ahiman, and their kinsmen (Shallum
was the chief); 18 until then they were [c]in the king's gate on the east side as the gatekeepers
of the camps of the Levites. 19 Shallum the son of Kore, son of [d]Ebiasaph, son of Korah, and
his kinsmen of his fathers' house, the [e]Korahites, were in charge of the work of the service,
keepers of the thresholds of the tent, as their fathers had been in charge of the camp of
the LORD, keepers of the entrance. 20 And [f]Phinehas the son of Eleazar was the chief officer
over them in time past; the LORD was with him. 21 [g]Zechariah the son of Meshelemiah was
gatekeeper at the entrance of the tent of meeting. 22 All these, who were chosen as gatekeepers at the thresholds, were 212. They were enrolled by genealogies in their villages.
[h]David and Samuel [i]the seer established them in their office of trust. 23 So they and their
sons were in charge of the gates of the house of the LORD, that is, the house of the tent,
as guards. 24 The gatekeepers were on the four sides, east, west, north, and south. 25 And
their kinsmen who were [j]in their villages were obligated to come [k]in every seven days, in
turn, to be with these, 26 for the four chief gatekeepers, who were Levites, were entrusted
to be over [l]the chambers and the treasures of the house of God. 27 And they lodged around
the house of God, for on them lay the duty of watching, and [m]they had charge of opening
it every morning.
28 Some of them had charge of the utensils of service, for they were required to count
them when they were brought in and taken out. 29 Others of them were appointed over
the furniture and over all the holy utensils, also over the [n]fine flour, the wine, the oil, the
incense, and the spices. 30 Others, of the sons of the priests, [o]prepared the mixing of the
spices, 31 and Mattithiah, one of the Levites, the firstborn of [p]Shallum the [e]Korahite, was
entrusted with [q]making the flat cakes. 32 Also some of their kinsmen of the Kohathites
had [r]charge of the showbread, to prepare it every Sabbath.
33 Now these, the [s]singers, the heads of fathers' houses of the Levites, were in the chambers of the temple free from other service, for they were on duty day and night. 34 These
were heads of fathers' houses of the Levites, according to their generations, leaders. These
lived in Jerusalem.

Saul's Genealogy Repeated

35 [t]In Gibeon lived the father of Gibeon, Jeiel, and the name of his wife was Maacah, 36 and
his firstborn son Abdon, then Zur, Kish, Baal, Ner, Nadab, 37 Gedor, Ahio, Zechariah, and
Mikloth; 38 and Mikloth was the father of Shimeam; and these also lived opposite their
kinsmen in Jerusalem, with their kinsmen. 39 [u]Ner fathered Kish, Kish fathered Saul, Saul
fathered Jonathan, Malchi-shua, Abinadab, and Eshbaal. 40 And the son of Jonathan was
[v]Merib-baal, and Merib-baal fathered Micah. 41 The sons of Micah: Pithon, Melech, Tahrea,
and [w]Ahaz.[1] 42 And Ahaz fathered [x]Jarah, and Jarah fathered Alemeth, Azmaveth, and Zimri.
And Zimri fathered Moza. 43 Moza fathered Binea, and [y]Rephaiah was his son, Eleasah
his son, Azel his son. 44 Azel had six sons and these are their names: Azrikam, Bocheru,
Ishmael, Sheariah, Obadiah, and Hanan; these were the sons of Azel.

The Death of Saul and His Sons

10 [z]Now the Philistines fought against Israel, and the men of Israel fled before the
Philistines and fell slain on Mount Gilboa. 2 And the Philistines overtook Saul and
his sons, and the Philistines struck down Jonathan and Abinadab and Malchi-shua, the

[1] Compare 8:35; Hebrew lacks *and Ahaz*

18 [c]Ezek. 46:1, 2
19 [d][ch. 26:1] [e]ch. 12:6; Num. 26:58; 2 Chr. 20:19
20 [f][Num. 25:11-13]
21 [g]ch. 26:2
22 [h][ch. 26:1, 2] [i]See 1 Sam. 9:9
25 [j]ver. 16 [k][2 Kgs. 11:5]
26 [l][1 Kgs. 6:5, 8]
27 [m]See Num. 1:53
29 [n]ch. 23:29; Lev. 6:20, 21
30 [o]See Ex. 30:23-25
31 [p]ver. 19 [e][See ver. 19 above] [q]ch. 23:29
32 [r]See Lev. 24:5-8
33 [s]ch. 6:31; 25:1
35 [t]For ver. 35-38, see ch. 8:29-32
39 [u]For ver. 39-44, see ch. 8:33-38
40 [v][2 Sam. 4:4; 9:6, 10]
41 [w]ch. 8:35
42 [x][ch. 8:36]
43 [y][ch. 8:37]

Chapter 10

1 [z]For ver. 1-12, see 1 Sam. 31:1-13

God. In short, David's rule was the instrument of God's own kingship in Israel, and he was raised to that office by the prophetic word for the salvation of the people.

10:1–12:40 *David's Rise to Power over Israel.* After the death of Saul, David rises to be king over all Israel. The Chronicler focuses on the unity of Israel as it acclaims David as its king, passing over most of the conflict with Saul and Ishbosheth that 2 Samuel describes.

10:1–12 Taken mainly from 1 Sam. 31:1–13. Saul's reign is significant for the Chronicler only as a failure. It ends in disaster for Israel at the hands of the **Philistines** (1 Chron. 10:7), against whom Saul had originally been raised up as a military savior (1 Sam. 9:16). Saul's death, together with three of his sons, also marks the end of his royal house (1 Chron. 10:6): none of his descendants (see 8:33–40) will rule in his place over Israel. **temple of Dagon** (10:10). Saul's humiliation after his death contrasts with the triumph of the ark over Dagon in 1 Sam. 5:1–4.

sons of Saul. 3 The battle pressed hard against Saul, and the archers found him, and he was
wounded by the archers. 4 Then Saul said to his armor-bearer, "Draw your sword and thrust
me through with it, lest these uncircumcised come and mistreat me." But his armor-bearer
would not, for he feared greatly. Therefore Saul took his own sword and fell upon it. 5 And
when his armor-bearer saw that Saul was dead, he also fell upon his sword and died. 6 Thus
Saul died; he and his three sons and all his house died together. 7 And when all the men of
Israel who were in the valley saw that the army[1] had fled and that Saul and his sons were
dead, they abandoned their cities and fled, and the Philistines came and lived in them.
8 The next day, when the Philistines came to strip the slain, they found Saul and his sons
fallen on Mount Gilboa. 9 And they stripped him and took his head and his armor, and sent
messengers throughout the land of the Philistines to carry the good news to their idols
and to the people. 10 And they put his armor in the temple of their gods and fastened his
head in the temple of Dagon. 11 But when all Jabesh-gilead heard all that the Philistines
had done to Saul, 12 all the valiant men arose and took away the body of Saul and the bodies of his sons, and brought them to Jabesh. And they buried their bones under the oak
in Jabesh and fasted seven days.
13 So Saul died [a]for his breach of faith. He broke faith with the LORD in that he did not
keep the command of the LORD, and also [b]consulted a medium, seeking guidance. 14 He
[c]did not seek guidance from the LORD. Therefore the LORD put him to death and [d]turned
the kingdom over to David the son of Jesse.

[1] Hebrew *they*

13[a]1 Sam. 13:13, 14; 15:23 [b]1 Sam. 28:7
14[c][1 Sam. 28:6] [d]ch. 12:23; 1 Sam. 15:28; 2 Sam. 3:9, 10

Saul Dies on Mount Gilboa
c. 1010 B.C.
Philistine forces advanced to Shunem from Aphek and prepared to attack the Israelites near their camp in Jezreel. When the Philistines attacked the next morning, the Israelites retreated up the slopes of Mount Gilboa. Saul and three of his sons were killed, and the Philistines triumphantly put their bodies on display in the temple of Dagon at Beth-shean. Later, men from Jabesh-gilead traveled through the night and recovered the bodies.

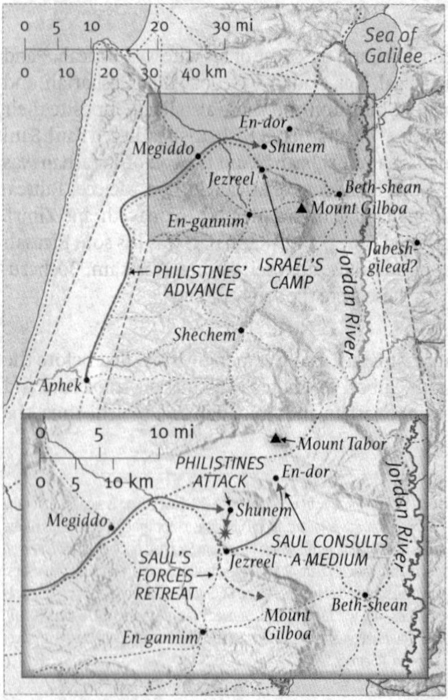

10:4 Saul took his own sword and fell upon it. See note on 2 Sam. 1:6–10 for the claim that Saul did not commit suicide but rather was killed by an Amalekite.

10:6 all his house died together. See note on 1 Sam. 31:6.

10:11–12 Saul had saved **Jabesh-gilead** at the beginning of his reign (1 Samuel 11), a fact that the men of the city remembered, giving a proper burial to Saul and his sons. However, David later reburied their bones "in the land of Benjamin in Zela, in the tomb of Kish his father" (2 Sam. 21:14).

10:13–14 the LORD put him to death. This is the Chronicler's theological explanation for the death of Saul, caused by **his breach of faith** (Hb. *ma'al*; see 2:7; 5:25; 9:1), and expressed especially in failing to **keep the command of the LORD** (see 1 Sam. 13:13), consulting the medium of En-dor (1 Samuel 28), and failing to **seek** the Lord, which here denotes not the search for a prophetic oracle (which Saul had sought; see 1 Sam. 28:6) but rather the deficiency of his basic spiritual condition (see 1 Chron. 28:9). **Therefore the LORD . . . turned the kingdom over to David** (10:14). This is the main point of this chapter. A second decisive turning point from God in the history of the kingdom occurs in 2 Chron. 10:15, when Rehoboam "did not listen to the people."

11:1–12:40 David's accession to the kingship is presented as a sequence of growing recognition, power, and popular support from "all Israel" (11:1, 4, 10; 12:38). This section is organized as an *inclusio* (literary "bookends"), beginning and ending with David's anointing as king at Hebron (11:1–3; 12:38–40) and incorporating material illustrating this theme from different periods of David's rise to power and his actual rule.

11:1–3 From 2 Sam. 5:1–3 (see note on 2 Sam. 5:1–5), omitting reference here to the war with Ishbosheth and David's seven-year reign in Hebron as king of Judah (2 Sam. 2:1–4:12; 5:4–5; contrast 1 Chron. 3:4; 29:27). David is recognized as king by **all Israel** and anointed as such **according to the word of the LORD by Samuel** (see 1 Sam. 13:14; 15:28).

11:1 your bone and flesh. Even though there was a distinct division between Judah and the rest of Israel, they still recognized each other as kin (similarly, "brothers" in 2 Sam. 2:26–27).

11:4–9 From 2 Sam. 5:6–10. The conquest of **Jerusalem** (see note on 2 Sam. 5:6) by **David and all Israel** (cf. 2 Sam. 5:6, "the king and his men") is presented as the first act of his reign, providing him with a capital and **stronghold**, and the tribes with a focus of national unity. With an eye to his own postexilic community, the Chronicler presents Jerusalem as the possession not just of Judah, but of "all Israel," from the beginning.

11:8 the Millo (lit., "the fill"). See note on 2 Sam. 5:9.

Chapter 11
1 [e]For ver. 1-9, see 2 Sam. 5:1-3, 6-10
2 [f]Ezek. 34:23
3 [g]ver. 10; ch. 12:23; 1 Sam. 16:1, 3, 12, 13
4 [h]See Josh. 15:8 [i]Judg. 1:21
6 [j]2 Sam. 8:16
9 [k]Esth. 9:4
10 [l]For ver. 10-41, see 2 Sam. 23:8-39 [m]ver. 3
11 [n][2 Sam. 23:8] [o][ch. 12:18]
12 [p][ch. 27:4]

David Anointed King

11 [e]Then all Israel gathered together to David at Hebron and said, "Behold, we are
your bone and flesh. 2 In times past, even when Saul was king, it was you who led
out and brought in Israel. And the LORD your God said to you, [f]'You shall be shepherd
of my people Israel, and you shall be prince over my people Israel.'" 3 So all the elders
of Israel came to the king at Hebron, and David made a covenant with them at Hebron
before the LORD. And they anointed David king over Israel, [g]according to the word of the
LORD by Samuel.

David Takes Jerusalem

4 And David and all Israel went to Jerusalem, [h]that is, Jebus, where the Jebusites were,
[i]the inhabitants of the land. 5 The inhabitants of Jebus said to David, "You will not come
in here." Nevertheless, David took the stronghold of Zion, that is, the city of David. 6 David
said, "Whoever strikes the Jebusites first [j]shall be chief and commander." And Joab the son
of Zeruiah went up first, so he became chief. 7 And David lived in the stronghold; therefore
it was called the city of David. 8 And he built the city all around from the Millo in complete
circuit, and Joab repaired the rest of the city. 9 And David [k]became greater and greater, for
the LORD of hosts was with him.

David's Mighty Men

10 [l]Now these are the chiefs of David's mighty men, who gave him strong support in his
kingdom, together with all Israel, to make him king, [m]according to the word of the LORD
concerning Israel. 11 This is an account of David's mighty men: [n]Jashobeam, a [n]Hachmonite,
was [o]chief of the three.[1] He wielded his spear against 300 whom he killed at one time.
12 And next to him among the three mighty men was Eleazar the son of [p]Dodo, the

[1] Compare 2 Samuel 23:8; Hebrew *thirty*, or *captains*

11:9 for the LORD of hosts was with him. A similar theme is seen in 1 Samuel, where David's successes are due not to him but to God's favor and presence in his life.

11:10–47 From 2 Sam. 23:8–39, with additional material (1 Chron. 11:41b–47). These details of David's mighty men illustrate the kind of support David received both at the beginning and at later periods of his reign. Such support is not simply of human origin but is divinely ordained (v. 10).

11:12–13 For some reason the material about Shammah from 2 Sam. 23:9–11

The Chronicler's Presentation of the Reigns of David and Solomon

In contrast to 1–2 Samuel and 1–2 Kings, the Chronicler focuses overwhelmingly on the religious significance of the united reign of David and Solomon, principally their joint role in establishing the Davidic covenant and the Jerusalem temple. Little attention is paid to the personal and political dimensions of their rule. This difference of focus largely explains why and how the Chronicler has recast his sources, adding or omitting material, and sometimes reordering the narrative.

The Presentation of David's Reign in 1 Chronicles 11–29	Chronicles passes over David's sins against Uriah and Bathsheba, along with his ensuing family and political troubles.	Cf. 2 Samuel 11–24
	The Chronicler's additions and expansions focus on David's activity for the temple. David's wars acquire materials for the temple. Additions to the census account (2 Samuel 24) explain the choice of the temple site in 1 Chronicles 21.	1 Chron. 18:8, 11; 21:27–22:1
	Extensive additions focus on David's preparations for the temple and its personnel. David, as much as Solomon, shaped Israel's traditions of worship in the temple.	1 Chronicles 22–29
The Presentation of Solomon's Reign in 2 Chronicles 1–9	Chronicles omits the account of Solomon's forceful rise to power over his enemies (but cf. 1 Kings 2:46; 2 Chron. 1:1).	Cf. 1 Kings 1–2
	Chronicles omits reference to Solomon's delay of temple construction in order to build his palace, as well as details of that building.	Cf. 1 Kings 7:1–12
	Chronicles omits reference to Solomon's foreign wives and his culpability for the division of the kingdom.	Cf. 1 Kings 11
	Chronicles moves the account of Solomon's Egyptian wife, placing it after the temple's dedication.	Cf. 1 Kings 3; 2 Chronicles 8
	Chronicles omits many of the details of the temple's construction and furnishings found in 1 Kings 7:13–51, concentrating instead on the temple as the place of God's earthly presence, and focusing on the act of dedication.	2 Chronicles 3–7
	Solomon's prayer of dedication sets a pattern for all other royal prayers. The additions in 2 Chron. 7:12–16 highlight the temple as the place of repentance.	Cf. 1 Kings 8; 2 Chronicles 6–7

Ahohite. 13 He was with David at Pas-dammim [q]when the Philistines were gathered there
for battle. There was a plot of ground full of barley, and the men fled from the Philistines.
14 But he took his[1] stand in the midst of the plot and defended it and killed the Philistines.
And the LORD saved them by a great victory.
15 Three of the thirty chief men went down to the rock to David at the cave of Adullam,
when the army of Philistines was encamped in the [r]Valley of Rephaim. 16 David was then
in the stronghold, and the [s]garrison of the Philistines was then at Bethlehem. 17 And David
said longingly, "Oh that someone would give me water to drink from the well of Bethlehem
that is by the gate!" 18 Then the three mighty men broke through the camp of the Philistines
and drew water out of the well of Bethlehem that was by the gate and took it and brought
it to David. But David would not drink it. He poured it out to the LORD 19 and said, "Far be
it from me before my God that I should do this. Shall I drink the lifeblood of these men?
For at the risk of their lives they brought it." Therefore he would not drink it. These things
did the three mighty men.
20 Now Abishai, the brother of Joab, was chief of the thirty.[2] And he wielded his spear against
300 men and killed them and won a name beside the three. 21 He was the most renowned[3]
of the thirty[4] and became their commander, but he did not attain to the three.
22 And Benaiah the son of Jehoiada was a valiant man[5] of Kabzeel, a doer of great deeds.
He struck down two heroes of Moab. He also went down and struck down a lion in a pit
on a day when snow had fallen. 23 And he struck down an Egyptian, a man of great stature,
five cubits[6] tall. The Egyptian had in his hand a spear [t]like a weaver's beam, but Benaiah
went down to him with a staff and snatched the spear out of the Egyptian's hand and
killed him with his own spear. 24 These things did Benaiah the son of Jehoiada and won a
name beside the three mighty men. 25 He was renowned among the thirty, but he did not
attain to the three. And David set him over his bodyguard.
26 The mighty men were [u]Asahel the brother of Joab, Elhanan the son of Dodo of
Bethlehem, 27 Shammoth of Harod,[7] Helez the Pelonite, 28 Ira the son of Ikkesh of Tekoa,
Abiezer of Anathoth, 29 Sibbecai the Hushathite, Ilai the Ahohite, 30 Maharai of Netophah,
Heled the son of Baanah of Netophah, 31 Ithai the son of Ribai of Gibeah of the people
of Benjamin, Benaiah of Pirathon, 32 Hurai of the brooks of Gaash, Abiel the Arbathite,
33 Azmaveth of Baharum, Eliahba the Shaalbonite, 34 Hashem[8] the Gizonite, Jonathan the
son of Shagee the Hararite, 35 Ahiam the son of Sachar the Hararite, Eliphal the son of Ur,
36 Hepher the Mecherathite, Ahijah the Pelonite, 37 Hezro of Carmel, Naarai the son of Ezbai,
38 Joel the brother of Nathan, Mibhar the son of [v]Hagri, 39 Zelek the Ammonite, Naharai of
Beeroth, the armor-bearer of Joab the son of Zeruiah, 40 Ira the Ithrite, Gareb the Ithrite,
41 Uriah the Hittite, [w]Zabad the son of Ahlai, 42 Adina the son of Shiza the Reubenite, a
leader of the Reubenites, and thirty with him, 43 Hanan the son of Maacah, and Joshaphat
the Mithnite, 44 Uzzia the Ashterathite, Shama and Jeiel the sons of Hotham the Aroerite,
45 Jediael the son of Shimri, and Joha his brother, the Tizite, 46 Eliel the Mahavite, and
Jeribai, and Joshaviah, the sons of Elnaam, and Ithmah the Moabite, 47 Eliel, and Obed,
and Jaasiel the Mezobaite.

The Mighty Men Join David

12 [x]Now these are the men who came to David at Ziklag, while he could not move
about freely because of Saul the son of Kish. And they were among the mighty men
who helped him in war. 2 They [y]were bowmen and could shoot arrows and sling stones

[1] Compare 2 Samuel 23:12; Hebrew *they . . . their* [2] Syriac; Hebrew *three* [3] Compare 2 Samuel 23:19; Hebrew *more renowned among the two* [4] Syriac; Hebrew *three* [5] Syriac; Hebrew *the son of a valiant man* [6] A *cubit* was about 18 inches or 45 centimeters [7] Compare 2 Samuel 23:25; Hebrew *the Harorite* [8] Compare Septuagint and 2 Samuel 23:32; Hebrew *the sons of Hashem*

13 [q][2 Sam. 23:11, 12]
15 [r]ch. 14:8
16 [s][1 Sam. 10:5]
23 [t]1 Sam. 17:7
26 [u]ch. 27:7
38 [v][ch. 5:10]
41 [w][ch. 2:36]

Chapter 12

1 [x]See 1 Sam. 27:2-6
2 [y]2 Chr. 17:17; Ps. 78:9

is not included here. The Chronicler may have skipped over this material intentionally, in which case the plurals "they . . . their" in 1 Chron. 11:14 (see ESV footnote) indicate that others (possibly including **David**) were with **Eleazar** in this battle **at Pas-dammim**, a location not mentioned in 2 Samuel. Other interpreters, however, think the material in 2 Sam. 23:9b–11a was omitted from 1 Chron. 11:13 because of a later copyist's error.

11:15–19 The identity of these **three mighty men** is not known.

11:18 He poured it out to the LORD. David poured out the water as an offering to Yahweh and in deference to his loyal men, who risked their lives on his behalf; see note on 2 Sam. 23:16–17.

11:25–47 The original list of the **thirty** (vv. 26–40b = 2 Sam. 23:24–39) has been supplemented with material from a different source (1 Chron. 11:41b–47; see note on 2 Sam. 23:8–39). The places associated with these names that can be identified are all in Transjordan (1 Chron. 11:42, 44, 46), indicating a preexilic origin to this list.

12:1–22 Before his reign in Hebron, David took refuge from Saul in various strongholds in the Judean desert, then in Ziklag for 16 months, under the

2[z][Judg. 3:15; 20:16] [a]ver. 29
3[b]Josh. 18:28 [c]ch. 11:28; 27:12
4[d]Josh. 9:3
6[e]ch. 9:19
8[f]2 Sam. 2:18
14[g][Lev. 26:8]
15[h]See Josh. 3:15
18[i]See Judg. 3:10 [j][2 Sam. 17:25] [k][1 Sam. 25:6]
19[l]See 1 Sam. 29:2-9 [m][1 Sam. 29:4]
21[n]1 Sam. 30:1
23[o]ch. 11:1; 2 Sam. 2:3, 4; 5:1

with either the right or the [z]left hand; they were Benjaminites, [a]Saul's kinsmen. **3** The chief
was Ahiezer, then Joash, both sons of Shemaah of [b]Gibeah; also Jeziel and Pelet, the sons
of Azmaveth; Beracah, Jehu of [c]Anathoth, **4** Ishmaiah of [d]Gibeon, a mighty man among
the thirty and a leader over the thirty; Jeremiah,[1] Jahaziel, Johanan, Jozabad of Gederah,
5 Eluzai,[2] Jerimoth, Bealiah, Shemariah, Shephatiah the Haruphite; **6** Elkanah, Isshiah,
Azarel, Joezer, and Jashobeam, the [e]Korahites; **7** And Joelah and Zebadiah, the sons of
Jeroham of Gedor.

8 From the Gadites there went over to David at the stronghold in the wilderness mighty
and experienced warriors, expert with shield and spear, whose faces were like the faces of
lions and who were [f]swift as gazelles upon the mountains: **9** Ezer the chief, Obadiah second,
Eliab third, **10** Mishmannah fourth, Jeremiah fifth, **11** Attai sixth, Eliel seventh, **12** Johanan
eighth, Elzabad ninth, **13** Jeremiah tenth, Machbannai eleventh. **14** These Gadites were officers of the army; the least was a [g]match for a hundred men and the greatest for a thousand.
15 These are the men who crossed the Jordan in the first month, when it was [h]overflowing
all its banks, and put to flight all those in the valleys, to the east and to the west.

16 And some of the men of Benjamin and Judah came to the stronghold to David. **17** David
went out to meet them and said to them, "If you have come to me in friendship to help
me, my heart will be joined to you; but if to betray me to my adversaries, although there
is no wrong in my hands, then may the God of our fathers see and rebuke you." **18** Then
[i]the Spirit clothed [j]Amasai, chief of the thirty, and he said,

> "We are yours, O David,
> and with you, O son of Jesse!
> [k]Peace, peace to you,
> and peace to your helpers!
> For your God helps you."

Then David received them and made them officers of his troops.

19 Some of the men of Manasseh deserted to David [l]when he came with the Philistines
for the battle against Saul. (Yet he did not help them, for the rulers of the Philistines took
counsel and sent him away, saying, [m]"At peril to our heads he will desert to his master
Saul.") **20** As he went to Ziklag, these men of Manasseh deserted to him: Adnah, Jozabad,
Jediael, Michael, Jozabad, Elihu, and Zillethai, chiefs of thousands in Manasseh. **21** They
helped David against [n]the band of raiders, for they were all mighty men of valor and were
commanders in the army. **22** For from day to day men came to David to help him, until
there was a great army, like an army of God.

23 These are the numbers of the divisions of the armed troops [o]who came to David

[1] Hebrew verse 5 [2] Hebrew verse 6

protection of the Philistine king Achish (1 Sam. 27:6). This section provides a literary flashback to those days and places, which are grouped within the larger unit of 1 Chron. 11:1–12:40 under the theme of growing support for David from every tribe of Israel. The catchword "help" connects this section, denoting personal commitment to and partnership with David in his task (vv. 1, 17, 18, 19, 21, 22). More specifically, "help" here signifies military support and originates in God's own support for David (v. 18).

12:1–7 These verses describe the growing support for David from Saul's own tribe of Benjamin, during his stay in **Ziklag**, just before Saul's death on Mount Gilboa.

12:8–15 These verses detail the support that David received from the **Gadites** from Transjordan, during an earlier period, possibly at Adullam (1 Sam. 22:1) or Engedi, on the shore of the Dead Sea (1 Sam. 23:29).

12:8 mighty and experienced warriors, expert with shield and spear. A frequent theme here (see vv. 2, 14, 21–22) is that the most skillful and heroic warriors in Israel are pledging allegiance to David, confirming that he is the Lord's anointed and that God's favor is on him.

12:16–18 These verses reflect the same period, when David's life is threatened by Saul, and the loyalty of those who come to him in his stronghold cannot be assumed. The prophecy by **Amasai** affirms and encourages loyalty to David, declaring that he enjoys God's support. **Peace** does not imply absence of battle but victory and "success" that attains a full and lasting peace and well-being (see note on John 14:27). **The Spirit clothed** is the Chronicler's characteristic idiom for prophetic inspiration (2 Chron. 15:1; 20:14; 24:20; see Judg. 6:34). David united the fractious tribes around his kingship, but that unity was shattered by his intemperate grandson Rehoboam. The northern tribes rejected Rehoboam's rule in words that ironically echoed Amasai's declaration of support: "What portion have we in David? We have no inheritance in the son of Jesse" (2 Chron. 10:16).

12:19–21 On the Philistines' relations with David, see 1 Samuel 29.

12:22 from day to day men came to David to help him. A summarizing comment on the whole chapter: from small beginnings (1 Sam. 27:2), a great army was progressively gathered to David, up to his anointing as king in Hebron. **like an army of God**. David did not have to seek these warriors: God was strengthening him.

12:23–37 These verses list military contingents from every tribe that defected to David in Hebron, corresponding to the elders of every tribe, who anointed him (11:3). **To turn the kingdom of Saul over to him** refers back to 10:14 and summarizes the overall theme of chs. 10–12. **according to the word of the LORD**. The tribes, like their elders (11:3), act in obedience to the prophetic word declaring David to be king. Some interpreters understand these to be the actual numbers of soldiers, since elsewhere the "tens" and "hundreds" and "thousands" add up correctly (see Num. 1:46). Others conclude that the total number of troops seems overly high for such a gathering. One possibility is

in Hebron [p]to turn the kingdom of Saul over to him, [q]according to the word of the
LORD. 24 The men of Judah bearing shield and spear were 6,800 armed troops. 25 Of the
Simeonites, mighty men of valor for war, 7,100. 26 Of the Levites 4,600. 27 The prince
Jehoiada, of the house of Aaron, and with him 3,700. 28 [r]Zadok, a young man mighty in
valor, and twenty-two commanders from his own fathers' house. 29 Of the Benjaminites,
[s]the kinsmen of Saul, 3,000, of whom the [t]majority had to that point kept their allegiance
to the house of Saul. 30 Of the Ephraimites 20,800, mighty men of valor, famous men
in their fathers' houses. 31 Of the half-tribe of Manasseh 18,000, who were [u]expressly
named to come and make David king. 32 Of Issachar, men who [v]had understanding of the
times, to know what Israel ought to do, 200 chiefs, and all their kinsmen under their command. 33 Of Zebulun 50,000 seasoned troops, [w]equipped for battle with all the weapons
of war, to help David[1] with [x]singleness of purpose. 34 Of Naphtali 1,000 commanders
with whom were 37,000 men armed with shield and spear. 35 Of the Danites 28,600
men equipped for battle. 36 Of [y]Asher 40,000 [z]seasoned troops [z]ready for battle. 37 Of the
Reubenites and Gadites and the half-tribe of Manasseh from beyond the Jordan, 120,000
men armed with all the weapons of war.

38 All these, men of war, arrayed in battle order, came to Hebron with [a]a whole heart to
make David king over all Israel. Likewise, all the rest of Israel were of a [b]single mind to
make David king. 39 And they were there with David for three days, eating and drinking,
for their brothers had made preparation for them. 40 And also their relatives, from as far as
Issachar and Zebulun and Naphtali, came bringing food on donkeys and on camels and
on mules and on oxen, abundant provisions of flour, [c]cakes of figs, clusters of raisins, and
wine and oil, oxen and sheep, for there was joy in Israel.

The Ark Brought from Kiriath-Jearim

13 David consulted with the commanders of thousands and of hundreds, with every
leader. 2 And David said to all the assembly of Israel, "If it seems good to you and
from the LORD our God, let us send abroad to our brothers [d]who remain in all the lands
of Israel, as well as to the priests and Levites in the cities that have pasturelands, that they
may be gathered to us. 3 Then let us bring again the ark of our God to us, [e]for we did not
seek it[2] in the days of Saul." 4 All the assembly agreed to do so, for the thing was right in
the eyes of all the people.

Uzzah and the Ark

5 [f]So David assembled all Israel [g]from the [h]Nile[3] of Egypt to Lebo-hamath, to bring the
ark of God [i]from Kiriath-jearim. 6 [j]And David and all Israel went up to [k]Baalah, that is, to

[1] Septuagint; Hebrew lacks *David* [2] Or *him* [3] Hebrew *Shihor*

23 [p]ch. 10:14 [q]ch. 11:3, 10; 1 Sam. 16:1, 3
28 [r]ch. 6:8; 2 Sam. 8:17
29 [s]ver. 2 [t][2 Sam. 2:8, 9]
31 [u]See Num. 1:17
32 [v][Esth. 1:13]
33 [w]ver. 36, 38 [x][Ps. 12:2]
36 [y][2 Sam. 2:9] [z]ver. 33
38 [a][1 Kgs. 8:61] [b][ver. 33]
40 [c][1 Sam. 25:18; 30:12]

Chapter 13

2 [d][1 Sam. 31:1]
3 [e][1 Sam. 7:1, 2]
5 [f]ch. 15:3; 2 Sam. 6:1 [g][1 Kgs. 8:65] [h]See Num. 34:5 [i][1 Sam. 6:21; 7:1]
6 [j]For ver. 6-14, see 2 Sam. 6:2-11 [k]Josh. 15:9, 60

that the word for "thousand" (Hb. *'elep*) in a military census denotes a "unit" (of undetermined size); cf. note on Num. 1:20–46. It is also possible that the word originally had the vowels of the word for "chief" (Hb. *'allup*). By this second possibility, the **6,800** in 1 Chron. 12:24 would reveal that Judah supplied 800 armed troops under six commanders. The contributions from Judah and Levi (vv. 26–28) may seem surprisingly low compared to the northern and Transjordanian tribes (vv. 30–37), but these numbers may indicate those who rallied to David at a later stage than others from their tribes (since David had already been king in Hebron for several years).

12:38–40 for there was joy in Israel. The three-day festival celebrated the covenant made "before the LORD" between David and the elders of Israel (11:1–3). Religious celebrations in Chronicles are regularly characterized by joy (15:25; 29:22; 2 Chron. 7:8–10; 30:23–27). Under David's leadership, God had given the nation peace, unity, prosperity, and joy.

13:1–16:43 *David's Transfer of the Ark of the Covenant to Jerusalem.* The ark signified the Mosaic covenant and was the symbol and location of God's presence on earth. But it had been neglected throughout Saul's reign, being laid up in the village of Kiriath-jearim (13:3, 5). David's concern for the ark is a sign of his commitment to God and his faithful regard for Israel's religious foundation from the time of Moses. His acting on this concern leads directly to the establishment of God's covenant with him (ch. 17), and the Davidic covenant in turn becomes the new, enlarged basis of Israel's existence. The Mosaic covenant, however, always remains the foundation. The Chronicler departs from the order of his source (2 Samuel 5–6) to present David's first attempt to retrieve the ark (1 Chron. 13:5–14 = 2 Sam. 6:1–11) *before* the establishment of his home and family in Jerusalem and his defeat of the Philistines (1 Chron. 14:1–17 = 2 Sam. 5:11–25). The point of this repositioning of material is to show where David's true priorities lie.

13:1–4 David's consultation of the leaders and the **assembly of Israel** shows a concern with national unity and popular participation in issues touching the nation's life. The decision to retrieve the **ark** is jointly taken, rather than being purely David's concern. **we did not seek it**. Cf. "seek my face," 2 Chron. 7:14. To "seek" the ark would mean caring for it rightly as the focus of worship. "Seeking God" will emerge as a major theme of the narrative. David's reign will mark a decisive change from the **days of Saul** in the people's commitment to God and to the divinely authorized emblems of Israelite faith.

13:5–6 As with the decision to retrieve the **ark**, the mission itself involves **all Israel** (vv. 5–6), and not simply David's soldiers (cf. 2 Sam. 6:1). Verse 5b of 1 Chronicles 13 describes the broadest possible participation of Israelites: **from the Nile of Egypt to Lebo-hamath** in the far northeast. For a comparable conception of the boundaries of the Promised Land, see Gen. 15:18. On the **ark of God . . . who sits enthroned above the cherubim**, see note on 1 Sam. 4:3–4.

Kiriath-jearim that belongs to Judah, to bring up from there the ark of God, which is called
by the name of the LORD who [l]sits enthroned above the cherubim. 7 And they carried the
ark of God on a new cart, from the house of [m]Abinadab, and Uzzah and Ahio[1] were driving
the cart. 8 And David and all Israel were celebrating before God with all their might, with
song and [n]lyres and harps and tambourines and cymbals and trumpets.
9 And when they came to the threshing floor of [o]Chidon, Uzzah put out his hand to take
hold of the ark, for the oxen stumbled. 10 And the anger of the LORD was kindled against
Uzzah, and he struck him down [p]because he put out his hand to the ark, and [q]he died there
before God. 11 And David was angry because the LORD had broken out against Uzzah. And
that place is called Perez-uzza[2] to this day. 12 And David was afraid of God that day, and he
said, "How can I bring the ark of God home to me?" 13 So David did not take the ark home
into the city of David, but took it aside to the house [r]of Obed-edom the Gittite. 14 And the
ark of God remained with the household of Obed-edom in his house three months. [s]And
the LORD blessed the household of Obed-edom and all that he had.

David's Wives and Children

14 [t]And Hiram king of Tyre sent messengers to David, and cedar trees, also masons
and carpenters to build a house for him. 2 And David knew that the LORD had established him as king over Israel, and that his kingdom was highly exalted for the sake of
his people Israel.
3 And David took more wives in Jerusalem, and David fathered more sons and daughters. 4 [u]These are the names of the children born to him in Jerusalem: [v]Shammua, Shobab,
Nathan, Solomon, 5 Ibhar, Elishua, Elpelet, 6 Nogah, Nepheg, Japhia, 7 Elishama, [w]Beeliada
and [x]Eliphelet.

Philistines Defeated

8 When the Philistines heard that David had been anointed king over all Israel, all the
Philistines went up to search for David. But David heard of it and went out against them.
9 Now the Philistines had come and [y]made a raid in the [z]Valley of Rephaim. 10 And David
inquired of God, "Shall I go up against the Philistines? Will you give them into my hand?"
And the LORD said to him, "Go up, and I will give them into your hand." 11 And he went
up to Baal-perazim, and David struck them down there. And David said, "God has broken

[1] *Or and his brother* [2] *Perez-uzza means the breaking out against Uzzah*

6 [l]See 1 Sam. 4:4
7 [m][1 Sam. 7:1]
8 [n][ch. 15:16]
9 [o][2 Sam. 6:6]
10 [p][ch. 15:13, 15; Num. 4:15] [q]Lev. 10:2
13 [r][2 Chr. 25:24]
14 [s][ch. 26:4, 5]

Chapter 14

1 [t]For ver. 1-16, see 2 Sam. 5:11-25
4 [u]For ver. 4-7, see ch. 3:5-8 [v][ch. 3:5]
7 [w][ch. 3:8] [x]2 Sam. 5:16
9 [y]ver. 13 [z]ch. 11:15

13:7–12 Despite their zeal, David and his companions on this occasion fail to respect the sanctity of the ark. Treatment of the ark is tantamount to treatment of God himself. Transporting it by **cart** (v. 7), as the Philistines had done (1 Samuel 6), rather than by the Levites bearing it on poles (Ex. 25:12–15; cf. note on 2 Sam. 6:3–4), demonstrated a lack of reverence for the sacred object of God's presence and for the Law of Moses. Uzzah's action was well-intentioned, but in taking hold of the ark as a layman, he similarly transgressed against its awesome holiness (see Num. 4:15; also note on 2 Sam. 6:6–11). The outburst of divine punishment **against Uzzah** both angers and frightens David, causing him to temporarily abandon the mission that had begun in such high spirits (1 Chron. 13:8). David and Israel must learn that God's holiness is a dangerous thing and should not be treated lightly.

13:8 On **David . . . celebrating before God** with various instruments, see note on 2 Sam. 6:5.

13:13–14 Leaving the ark with **Obed-edom** may have been a case of David's foisting his dangerous burden on the first convenient foreigner, particularly if **Gittite** (a resident of Gath) denotes a Philistine. Even so, **the LORD blessed the household of Obed-edom**, indicating his approval of the mission itself (and Obed-edom's care of the ark), though not the way the mission was conducted. God's blessing on Obed-edom's household is recalled in 26:4–5, where Obed-edom is ranked among the Levitical gatekeepers; cf. 15:18, 24.

14:1–17 Some of the events described here actually preceded the first mission to collect the ark (see 2 Sam. 5:11–25), but as with 1 Chronicles 11–12, the writer is not offering an alternative chronology to his source in 2 Samuel. The events in question (esp. 1 Chron. 14:1, 3–5) were evidently not confined to the three months that the ark was in the house of Obed-edom (13:14). Rather, these materials have been repositioned here as illustrations of the Chronicler's message that blessings accrued to David because he gave priority to seeking God (see 13:3), and that his reign was the antithesis of Saul's. Although David had not gone about the mission in quite the correct way, his basic intentions were right. The blessings that come to David include a palace, a growing family, military success, and the acclaim and fear of the surrounding nations. Each of these will serve as typical blessings on righteous kings in the subsequent narrative. A subsidiary theme of this chapter is the consolidation of David's power in and around Jerusalem.

14:1–2 Hiram king of Tyre. See note on 2 Sam. 5:11. Hiram's assistance in building David's **house** (palace) in Jerusalem signifies a Gentile ruler's recognition of David's kingship over Israel. Hiram will later help Solomon build another "house," the temple (2 Chron. 2:11–16).

14:3–7 See 3:5–8. **Nathan** (14:4) was an ancestor of Jesus (Luke 3:31; see note on Luke 3:23–38). **Beeliada** was also known as Eliada (2 Sam. 5:16; 1 Chron. 3:8). The Chronicler omits a reference to Hebron in his source to concentrate on Jerusalem, the seat of David's dynastic house (signified by **Solomon**, 14:4). David's family flourishes, in contrast to Saul's (10:6).

14:8–16 The first battle between David and the **Philistines** (vv. 8–12) may be a flashback to the time before David had conquered Jerusalem (2 Sam. 5:17, the source of 1 Chron. 14:8, refers to "the stronghold," possibly in Adullam, 1 Sam. 22:4). The time of the second battle is uncertain. In their present context, both battle reports illustrate the threats that existed to the ark's progress to Jerusalem. David's success against the Philistines cleared the way for the mission to be resumed unimpeded.

14:10 David inquired of God. See note on 1 Sam. 23:2.

through[1] my enemies by my hand, like a bursting flood." Therefore the name of that place
is called Baal-perazim. 12 And they left their gods there, and David gave command, and
they were burned.
13 And the Philistines yet again [a]made a raid in the valley. 14 And when David again
inquired of God, [b]God said to him, "You shall not go up after them; go around and come
against them opposite the balsam trees. 15 And when you hear the sound of marching in
the tops of the balsam trees, then go out to battle, for God has gone out before you to strike
down the army of the Philistines." 16 And David did as God commanded him, and they
struck down the Philistine army from Gibeon to Gezer. 17 And the fame of David went out
into all lands, and the LORD brought the [c]fear of him upon all nations.

The Ark Brought to Jerusalem

15 David[2] built houses for himself in the city of David. And he prepared a place for the
ark of God and [d]pitched a tent for it. 2 Then David said that no one but the Levites
may carry [e]the ark of God, for the LORD had chosen them to carry the ark of the LORD and
to minister to him forever. 3 [f]And David assembled all Israel at Jerusalem to bring up the
ark of the LORD [g]to its place, which he had prepared for it. 4 And David gathered together
the sons of Aaron and [h]the Levites: 5 of the sons of Kohath, Uriel the chief, with 120 of his
brothers; 6 of the sons of Merari, Asaiah the chief, with 220 of his brothers; 7 of the sons
of Gershom, Joel the chief, with 130 of his brothers; 8 of the sons of Elizaphan, Shemaiah
the chief, with 200 of his brothers; 9 of the sons of Hebron, Eliel the chief, with 80 of his
brothers; 10 of the sons of Uzziel, Amminadab the chief, with 112 of his brothers. 11 Then
David summoned the priests [i]Zadok and [j]Abiathar, and the Levites Uriel, Asaiah, Joel,
Shemaiah, Eliel, and Amminadab, 12 and said to them, "You are the heads of the fathers'
houses of the Levites. [k]Consecrate yourselves, you and your brothers, so that you may
bring up the ark of the LORD, the God of Israel, [l]to the place that I have prepared for it.
13 [m]Because you did not carry it the first time, the LORD our God broke out against us,

[1] *Baal-perazim* means *Lord of breaking through* [2] Hebrew *He*

13 [a]ver. 9
14 [b]ver. 16
17 [c][Deut. 2:25]

Chapter 15

1 [d]ch. 16:1
2 [e]ver. 15, 26; Num. 4:2, 15
3 [f]ch. 13:5; [1 Kgs. 8:1] [g]ver. 1, 12; 2 Sam. 6:17
4 [h]See ch. 6:16-30
11 [i]ch. 6:8; 16:39 [j]1 Sam. 22:20; 1 Kgs. 2:26
12 [k]2 Chr. 35:6 [l]ver. 1, 3
13 [m]ch. 13:7; 2 Sam. 6:3

14:15 sound of marching. See note on 2 Sam. 5:22–25.

14:17 The Chronicler offers a summarizing comment, with another implicit contrast between David and Saul: victory leading to security for Israel and **fame** for David, as opposed to defeat leading to occupation of Israel's land by foreigners and ignominy for Saul (10:7, 13–14). **The LORD brought the fear of him upon all nations**. Such fear will keep them from attacking Israel. See also 2 Chron. 14:14; 17:10; 20:29 for other examples of a fear sent by God on neighboring peoples.

15:1–29 David's second attempt to bring the ark to Jerusalem is successful because, as well as preparing a suitable place to receive the holy object, this time he instructs and organizes the Levites and priests in the right way of transporting it (see note on 13:7–12). The relatively brief account of the second mission in 2 Sam. 6:12–19 has been expanded here to show it as the climax of a carefully planned religious procession. Into the account of these preparations the Chronicler has inserted lists of the Levites involved and descriptions of their musical duties (1 Chron. 15:4–10, 16–24). David emerges as the decisive figure in determining the new role of the Levites as the leaders of music and worship, once the ark has come to its permanent rest in Jerusalem and would no longer be borne about by them. Just as Moses set out the duties of the Levites for the wilderness days (see Num. 3:5–9; 4:4–33), so David does the same for the more settled period of his kingdom. At the same time, he is very solicitous about the Law of Moses as the foundation for his own innovations in worship (see 1 Chron. 15:2, 13, 15).

David Defeats the Philistines

c. 1000 B.C.

Soon after David was established as king over all Israel, the Philistines prepared to attack David's forces at the nearby Valley of Rephaim. David defeated them, but they regrouped and prepared for a second attack. This time David attacked them from the rear and struck them down from Gibeon (or perhaps Geba) to Gezer.

15:1–3 David uses the three-month interval that the ark is in the house of Obed-edom (13:14) to make the necessary preparations in procedures and personnel that were lacking in the first mission that ended in debacle. The **tent** is not the Mosaic "tent of meeting," which was in Gibeon at the time (16:39), but a temporary lodging for the ark (see 17:1). David now understands that violation of the law governing the correct handling of the ark had scuttled the earlier attempt; hence his words here about the **Levites** (see Deut. 10:8; 18:5).

15:4–10 David's authority is expressed in summoning the priests and Levites together for their sacred task. The three main divisions of the Levites (**Kohath, Merari, Gershom**) are named. The Kohathites were responsible for carrying the ark (see Num. 7:9). The final three groups mentioned (1 Chron. 15:8–10) are also Kohathite families (see 6:18).

15:11–15 David's instruction to the priests and Levites to **consecrate** themselves denotes not only ritual actions and abstinences (see Ex. 19:14–15) but also the internal attitude that should accompany the handling of holy things. "Seeking" God **according to the rule** is not legalism but devout regard for the **word of the LORD** and a safeguard against the kind of disaster that occurred in Perez-uzza (1 Chron. 15:13; cf. 13:5–11).

because we did not seek him according to the rule." 14 So the priests and the Levites consecrated themselves to bring up the ark of the LORD, the God of Israel. 15 And the Levites
carried the ark of God on their shoulders [n]with the poles, [o]as Moses had commanded
according to the word of the LORD.
16 David also commanded the chiefs of the Levites to appoint their brothers as the singers who should play loudly on [p]musical instruments, on harps and lyres and cymbals,
to raise sounds of joy. 17 So the Levites appointed [q]Heman the son of Joel; and of his
brothers [r]Asaph the son of Berechiah; and of the sons of Merari, their brothers, [s]Ethan
the son of Kushaiah; 18 and with them their brothers of the second order, Zechariah,
Jaaziel, Shemiramoth, Jehiel, Unni, Eliab, Benaiah, Maaseiah, Mattithiah, Eliphelehu,
and Mikneiah, and the gatekeepers Obed-edom and Jeiel. 19 The singers, Heman, Asaph,
and Ethan, were to sound bronze cymbals; 20 Zechariah, [t]Aziel, Shemiramoth, Jehiel, Unni,
Eliab, Maaseiah, and Benaiah were to play harps according to [u]Alamoth; 21 but Mattithiah,
Eliphelehu, Mikneiah, [v]Obed-edom, Jeiel, and Azaziah were to lead with lyres according to [w]the Sheminith. 22 Chenaniah, leader of the Levites in music, should direct the
music, for he understood it. 23 Berechiah and Elkanah were to be gatekeepers for the ark.
24 Shebaniah, Joshaphat, Nethanel, Amasai, Zechariah, Benaiah, and Eliezer, the priests,
should [x]blow the trumpets before the ark of God. [v]Obed-edom and Jehiah were to be
gatekeepers for the ark.
25 [y]So David and the elders of Israel and the commanders of thousands went to bring up
the ark of the covenant of the LORD from the house of [v]Obed-edom with rejoicing. 26 And
because God helped the Levites who were carrying the ark of the covenant of the LORD,
they sacrificed [z]seven bulls and seven rams. 27 David was clothed with a robe of fine linen,
as also were all the Levites who were carrying the ark, and the singers and Chenaniah the
leader of the music of the singers. And David wore a linen ephod. 28 So all Israel brought
up the ark of the covenant of the LORD with shouting, to the sound of the horn, [a]trumpets,
and cymbals, and made loud music on [b]harps and lyres.
29 And as the ark of the covenant of the LORD came to the city of David, Michal the
daughter of Saul looked out of the window and saw King David dancing and celebrating,
and she despised him in her heart.

The Ark Placed in a Tent

16 And they brought in the ark of God and set it inside [c]the tent that David had pitched
for it, and they offered burnt offerings and peace offerings before God. 2 And when
David had finished offering the burnt offerings and the peace offerings, he blessed the
people in the name of the LORD 3 and distributed to all Israel, both men and women, to
each a loaf of bread, a portion of meat,[1] and a cake of raisins.

[1] Compare Septuagint, Syriac, Vulgate; the meaning of the Hebrew is uncertain

15 [n]Ex. 25:14 [o]Num. 4:15; 7:9
16 [p][ch. 13:8; 16:5, 42]
17 [q]ch. 6:33 [r]ch. 6:39 [s]ch. 6:44
20 [t][ver. 18] [u]See Ps. 46, title
21 [v]ch. 26:4 [w]See Ps. 6, title
24 [x]ver. 28; ch. 16:6; Num. 10:8 [v][See ver. 21 above]
25 [y]For ver. 25-28, see 2 Sam. 6:12-15 [v][See ver. 21 above]
26 [z]Num. 23:1; Job 42:8
28 [a][ver. 24] [b]ver. 16

Chapter 16

1 [c]ch. 15:1

15:16 This marks a turning point in the history of Israel's worship: the **Levites** are appointed, under David, to a new ministry of music and praise, which will be conducted in the presence of the ark (on the significance of their leadership of worship for Israel, see 16:4–7 and note). Solomon will follow in David's footsteps in the organization of the Levites for the temple worship (2 Chron. 8:14).

15:17–24 The Levites respond to David's instructions. In contrast to the free exuberance of the earlier expedition (13:8), only Levites duly consecrated for the task may lead the procession. **Obed-edom** (15:18, 24; see note on 13:13–14) may have been included among the Levitical **gatekeepers**, despite his probable Philistine origin, on account of his care for the ark. If so, "Levite" may have been a functional description (denoting one doing a particular task) as well as a genealogical one in the early monarchy. The postexilic community took a much stricter line on genealogical descent (see Ezra 2:61–63).

15:25–29 This section supplements 2 Sam. 6:12–16 (which focuses overwhelmingly on David) to emphasize the participation of **all Israel** (1 Chron. 15:28) in the second mission to bring back the ark. References to David's own activity are muted (e.g., his **dancing**, 2 Sam. 6:14), while particular details about the Levites and God's help for them are added (1 Chron. 15:26–28). The ark is consistently called the **ark of the covenant of the LORD** (vv. 25, 26, 28, 29), perhaps to stress the true focus of this chapter and the joyful solemnity of the occasion. As the **daughter of Saul**, David's estranged wife **Michal** shows herself to be hostile to David's concern for the ark (see 13:3). See also note on 2 Sam. 6:16–19.

16:1–43 The brief account in 2 Sam. 6:17–20 of the ark's arrival in Jerusalem and the festivities that followed is greatly expanded by details of David's provisions for worship (1 Chron. 16:4–7, 37–42) and a psalm of praise (vv. 8–36). Worship before the ark as the primary symbol of God's presence and power (see v. 11 and Num. 10:35) is the principal theme of this chapter. The implicit message for the Chronicler's own audience is that such worship, diligently undertaken, will transform and embolden them as they call upon God's strength. This chapter also leads up to the first high point of Chronicles, the dynastic promise to David (1 Chron. 17:10–14). A reciprocal relationship of divine blessing and human obedience can be seen in this arrangement:

(chs. 11–12) God raises David to kingship over Israel
  (ch. 13) David's first attempt to retrieve the ark
    (ch. 14) God exalts David in Jerusalem and over the Philistines
  (chs. 15–16) David's second (successful) attempt to retrieve the ark
(ch. 17) God promises David a perpetual dynasty

16:1–3 Just as Moses **blessed the people** after their completion of the

4 Then he appointed some of the Levites as ministers before the ark of the LORD, to
invoke, to thank, and to praise the LORD, the God of Israel. 5 [d]Asaph was the chief, and
second to him were Zechariah, Jeiel, Shemiramoth, Jehiel, Mattithiah, Eliab, Benaiah,
Obed-edom, and Jeiel, who were to play harps and lyres; Asaph was to sound the cymbals,
6 and Benaiah and Jahaziel the priests were to blow trumpets regularly before the ark of
the covenant of God. 7 Then on that day [e]David first appointed that thanksgiving be sung
to the LORD by Asaph and his brothers.

David's Song of Thanks

8 [f]Oh give thanks to the LORD; [g]call upon his name;
[h]make known his deeds among the peoples!
9 Sing to him, sing praises to him;
tell of all his wondrous works!
10 Glory in his holy name;
let the hearts of those who seek the LORD rejoice!
11 [i]Seek the LORD and his strength;
seek his presence continually!
12 [j]Remember the wondrous works that he has done,
[k]his miracles and the judgments he uttered,
13 O offspring of Israel his servant,
children of Jacob, his chosen ones!

14 He is the LORD our God;
[l]his judgments are in all the earth.
15 Remember his covenant forever,
the word that he commanded, for a thousand generations,
16 the covenant [m]that he made with Abraham,
his sworn promise to Isaac,
17 which [n]he confirmed to Jacob as a statute,
to Israel as an everlasting covenant,
18 saying, [o]"To you I will give the land of Canaan,
as your portion for an inheritance."

19 When you were [p]few in number,
of little account, and [q]sojourners in it,
20 wandering from nation to nation,
from one kingdom to another people,
21 he allowed no one to oppress them;
he [r]rebuked kings on their account,
22 saying, "Touch not my anointed ones,
do my [s]prophets no harm!"

23 [t]Sing to the LORD, all the earth!
Tell of his salvation from day to day.
24 Declare his glory among the nations,
his marvelous works among all the peoples!

5 [d]ch. 6:39
7 [e][2 Sam. 22:1; 23:1]
8 [f]For ver. 8-22, see Ps. 105:1-15 [g]Isa. 12:4 [h][Ps. 145:11, 12]
11 [i]Ps. 24:6; 27:8
12 [j][Ps. 77:11; 143:5] [k]Ps. 78:43
14 [l]Isa. 26:9
16 [m]Gen. 17:2; 22:16; 26:3; 28:13; [Luke 1:73]
17 [n]Gen. 35:11, 12
18 [o]Gen. 13:15; 15:18-21
19 [p]Deut. 7:7; 26:5 [q]Heb. 11:9
21 [r][Gen. 12:17; 20:3]
22 [s][Gen. 20:7]
23 [t]For ver. 23-33, see Ps. 96:1-13

tabernacle (Ex. 39:43), so too does David upon fulfillment of this task. Solomon will do likewise at the dedication of the temple (2 Chron. 6:3).

16:4–7 David institutionalizes what he initiated in 15:16 for the procession: a permanent, daily ministry of worship by the Levites before the ark (16:6, 37), as well as in connection with the sacrifices, held at that time in Gibeon (vv. 39–42). The musicians who took part in the procession (15:17–21) are assigned to this duty or to Gibeon (16:39, 41). Their task is **to invoke, to thank, and to praise the LORD**. This is a comprehensive description of worship through prayer and song, expressed above all in the Psalms.

16:8–36 This psalm of praise is a composite from Ps. 105:1–15 (= 1 Chron. 16:8–22), Ps. 96:1–13 (= 1 Chron. 16:23–33), and Ps. 106:1, 47–48 (= 1 Chron. 16:34–36) that the Chronicler has carefully woven together and modified slightly at various points for his purposes. It can be seen as expressing the thoughts of praise and gratitude evoked by the successful transfer of the ark to Jerusalem, while also addressing some lively concerns of the Chronicler's own postexilic community.

16:8–22 The summons to **seek the LORD and his strength; seek his presence continually** (v. 11) is especially appropriate before the ark, and a characteristic thought for the writer (see 22:19a). Worship for the Chronicler means transformative engagement with God. The repeated instruction to Israel to **remember** God's miracles in the past, and his promises of the land and

25 For [u]great is the LORD, and greatly to be praised,
and he is to be feared [v]above all gods.
26 For all the gods of the peoples are worthless idols,
[w]but the LORD made the heavens.
27 Splendor and majesty are before him;
strength and joy are in his place.

28 Ascribe to the LORD, O families of the peoples,
[x]ascribe to the LORD glory and strength!
29 Ascribe to the LORD the glory due his name;
bring an offering and come before him!
[y]Worship the LORD in the splendor of holiness;[1]
30 tremble before him, all the earth;
yes, the world is established; it shall never be moved.
31 [z]Let the heavens be glad, and let the earth rejoice,
and let them say among the nations, [a]"The LORD reigns!"
32 [b]Let the sea roar, and all that fills it;
let the field exult, and everything in it!
33 Then shall the trees of the forest sing for joy
before the LORD, for he comes to judge the earth.
34 Oh give thanks to the LORD, for he is good;
for his steadfast love endures forever!

35 [c]Say also:

"Save us, O God of our salvation,
and gather and deliver us from among the nations,
that we may give thanks to your holy name
and glory in your praise.
36 [d]Blessed be the LORD, the God of Israel,
from everlasting to everlasting!"

[e]Then all the people said, "Amen!" and praised the LORD.

Worship Before the Ark

37 So David left Asaph and his brothers there [f]before the ark of the covenant of the
LORD to minister regularly before the ark [g]as each day required, 38 and also [h]Obed-edom
and his[2] sixty-eight brothers, while [h]Obed-edom, the son of Jeduthun, and [i]Hosah were
to be gatekeepers. 39 And he left [j]Zadok the priest and his brothers the priests before the
tabernacle of the LORD [k]in the high place that was at Gibeon 40 to offer burnt offerings to
the LORD [l]on the altar of burnt offering [m]regularly morning and evening, to do all that is
written in the Law of the LORD that he commanded Israel. 41 With them were [n]Heman and
Jeduthun [o]and the rest of those chosen and [p]expressly named to give thanks to the LORD,
[q]for his steadfast love endures forever. 42 Heman and Jeduthun had trumpets and cymbals
for the music and instruments [r]for sacred song. The sons of Jeduthun were appointed to
the gate.
43 [s]Then all the people departed each to his house, and David went home to bless his
household.

[1] Or *in holy attire* [2] Hebrew *their*

25 [u]Ps. 145:3 [v][Ps. 95:3]
26 [w][Ps. 115:15; Isa. 42:5; 44:24; Jer. 10:11, 12]
28 [x][Ps. 29:1]
29 [y][Ps. 110:3]
31 [z][Isa. 49:13] [a]Ps. 93:1; 97:1; 99:1; [Isa. 52:7; Rev. 11:15, 17; 19:6]
32 [b]Ps. 98:7
35 [c]For ver. 35, 36, see Ps. 106:47, 48
36 [d]Ps. 41:13; [1 Kgs. 8:15] [e][Deut. 27:15; Ps. 106:48]
37 [f]ver. 4, 5 [g]2 Chr. 31:16
38 [h]ch. 26:4 [i]ch. 26:10, 16
39 [j]ch. 15:11 [k]See 1 Kgs. 3:4
40 [l]Ex. 27:1 [m]See Ex. 29:38-41; Num. 28:3-8
41 [n]See ch. 6:33 [o][ch. 25:1, 3, 6] [p]Num. 1:17 [q]2 Chr. 5:13; 7:3, 6; 20:21; Ezra 3:11; Jer. 33:11; See ver. 34
42 [r][ch. 25:7; 2 Chr. 29:27]
43 [s]2 Sam. 6:19, 20

protection to **Abraham** and **Israel** (16:18–22), would resonate with the small and vulnerable postexilic community, whose hold on the land could seem tenuous and under threat (see Nehemiah 4; 6).

16:23–33 The celebration in worship of God's kingship over all the earth is fitting before his ark-throne (13:6) and should evoke a similar faith and hope in Israel. The psalm declares that **the gods of the peoples are worthless idols**, whereas Israel's God reigns and **comes to judge the earth**.

16:34–36 This thought leads naturally to the petition for deliverance and salvation **from among the nations** as the climax of the psalm. At this point, the prayer speaks more to the Chronicler's generation than to David's, and expresses the longing for a greater restoration and consolidation of a scattered people to be gathered in worship before God.

16:37–43 Besides ministering before the ark, the Levites are also appointed to assist at the Mosaic tabernacle at Gibeon by offering praise at the times of sacrifice. Solomon will move the tabernacle into the temple at the time of its dedication (2 Chron. 5:5).

The LORD's Covenant with David

17 [t]Now when David lived in his house, David said to Nathan the prophet, "Behold, I
dwell in a house of cedar, but the ark of the covenant of the LORD is under a tent."
2 And Nathan said to David, "Do all that is in your heart, for God is with you."
3 But that same night the word of the LORD came to Nathan, 4 "Go and tell my servant
David, 'Thus says the LORD: [u]It is not you who will build me a house to dwell in. 5 For I
have not lived in a house since the day I brought up Israel to this day, [v]but I have gone
from tent to tent and from dwelling to dwelling. 6 In all places where I have moved with
all Israel, did I speak a word with any of the judges of Israel, whom I commanded to shepherd my people, saying, "Why have you not built me a house of cedar?"' 7 Now, therefore,
thus shall you say to my servant David, 'Thus says the LORD of hosts, I took you from the
pasture, from following the sheep, to be prince over my people Israel, 8 and I have been
with you wherever you have gone and have cut off all your enemies from before you.
And I will make for you a name, like the name of the great ones of the earth. 9 And I will
appoint a place for my people Israel and will plant them, that they may dwell in their own
place and be disturbed no more. And violent men shall waste them no more, as formerly,
10 from the time that I appointed judges over my people Israel. And I [w]will subdue all your
enemies. Moreover, I declare to you that the LORD will build you a house. 11 When your
days are fulfilled to walk with your fathers, I will raise up your offspring after you, one
of your own sons, and I will establish his kingdom. 12 He shall build a house for me, and
I will establish his throne forever. 13 [x]I will be to him a father, and he shall be to me a son.
I will not take my steadfast love from him, [y]as I took it from him who was before you,
14 but I will confirm him in my house and in my kingdom forever, and his throne shall
be established forever.'" 15 In accordance with all these words, and in accordance with all
this vision, Nathan spoke to David.

David's Prayer

16 Then King David went in and sat before the LORD and said, "Who am I, O LORD
God, and what is my house, that you have brought me thus far? 17 And this was a small
thing in your eyes, O God. You have also spoken of your servant's house for a great while
to come, and have shown me future generations,[1] O LORD God! 18 And what more can
David say to you for honoring your servant? For you know your servant. 19 [z]For your servant's sake, O LORD, and according to your own heart, you have done all this greatness,
in making known all these great things. 20 There is none like you, O LORD, and there is
no God besides you, according to all that we have heard with our ears. 21 And who is like
your people Israel, the one[2] nation on earth whom God went to redeem to be his people,
making for yourself a name for great and awesome things, in driving out nations before
your people whom you redeemed from Egypt? 22 And you made your people Israel to be
your people forever, and you, O LORD, became their God. 23 And now, O LORD, let the word
that you have spoken concerning your servant and concerning his house be established

[1] The meaning of the Hebrew is uncertain [2] Septuagint, Vulgate *other*

Chapter 17
1 [t]For ver. 1-27, see 2 Sam. 7:1-29
4 [u]ch. 28:3
5 [v][2 Sam. 7:6]
10 [w][2 Sam. 7:11]
13 [x]Cited Heb. 1:5 [y][1 Sam. 15:23, 28]
19 [z][2 Sam. 7:21]

17:1–27 *The Dynastic Promise to David.* See 2 Sam. 7:1–29 and note. David's wish to build a house or temple for Yahweh meets with refusal, but God promises that he will build a perpetual house or dynasty for David and that one of David's sons will build a temple for Yahweh. The promise to David has the nature of a covenant and is central to the message of Chronicles. The twofold manifestation of this covenant will be the *Davidic dynasty* and *Solomon's temple*, and henceforth the Chronicler will show that Israel's identity as God's people will be expressed through these two institutions. The promise to David is similarly the seedbed of the OT's messianic hope, which the NT will show is fulfilled in Jesus as the descendant of David (Rom. 1:3). The Chronicler's immediate interest, however, is more focused on Solomon as the chosen heir and temple builder (1 Chron. 17:11–14).

17:1–2 David's desire to build a temple to house the ark appears as his own initiative, which **Nathan the prophet** supports until he is overruled by God (cf. note on 2 Sam. 7:1–3). The Chronicler omits 2 Sam. 7:1b ("the LORD had given him rest from all his surrounding enemies") primarily in order to contrast David's reign as the time of subduing Israel's enemies (see 1 Chronicles 18–20) and Solomon's as the era of peace and temple building (22:9).

17:3–10a A temple does feature in God's plans for Israel, but it is not given to David to build it (see note on 2 Sam. 7:8–17). The initiative lies with God, who chose David for leadership and will give him great renown in the world (1 Chron. 17:8) and will give his people Israel a secure livelihood in the land (v. 9).

17:10b–14 Rather than David building Yahweh a house, God **will build . . . a house** for David, in the form of a sure and perpetual dynasty. **Your offspring after you** refers to Solomon. As for the "son" who succeeds to the throne, God **will establish his kingdom**. The declaration **he shall build a house for me, and I will establish his throne forever** suggests that building the temple is the act of obedience that will confirm or ratify the promise. God's **steadfast love** (Hb. *hesed*) will never be withdrawn from him as it was from Saul, not because David's successor will be without sin (2 Sam. 7:14b, omitted by the Chronicler, reads: "When he commits iniquity, I will discipline him with the rod of men"), but because God's love for David's house and his commitment to it will surpass its failings. In fact God says of

Chapter 18
1[a]For ver. 1-17, see 2 Sam. 8:1-18
3[b][2 Sam. 8:3] [c]See 1 Kgs. 8:65
4[d][2 Sam. 8:4]
5[e]ch. 19:6

forever, and do as you have spoken, **24** and your name will be established and magnified
forever, saying, 'The LORD of hosts, the God of Israel, is Israel's God,' and the house of your
servant David will be established before you. **25** For you, my God, have revealed to your
servant that you will build a house for him. Therefore your servant has found courage
to pray before you. **26** And now, O LORD, you are God, and you have promised this good
thing to your servant. **27** Now you have been pleased to bless the house of your servant,
that it may continue forever before you, for it is you, O LORD, who have blessed, and it
is blessed forever."

David Defeats His Enemies

18 [a]After this David defeated the Philistines and subdued them, and he took Gath and
its villages out of the hand of the Philistines.

2 And he defeated Moab, and the Moabites became servants to David and brought
tribute.

3 David also defeated [b]Hadadezer king of [c]Zobah-Hamath, as he went to set up his
monument[1] at the river Euphrates. **4** And David took from him 1,000 chariots, [d]7,000
horsemen, and 20,000 foot soldiers. And David hamstrung all the chariot horses, but left
enough for 100 chariots. **5** And when the Syrians of Damascus came to help Hadadezer
king [e]of Zobah, David struck down 22,000 men of the Syrians. **6** Then David put garrisons[2]

[1] Hebrew *hand* [2] Septuagint, Vulgate, 2 Samuel 8:6 (compare Syriac); Hebrew lacks *garrisons*

the Davidic house and kingdom that it is **my house and . . . my kingdom**: in other words, God's eternal, heavenly kingdom (see Ps. 103:19; 145:11–13) will be actually present in and expressed through the Davidic kingdom (see 1 Chron. 28:5; 2 Chron. 13:8). Hebrews 1:5 applies the words **I will be to him a father, and he shall be to me a son** to Christ, because as Messiah he inherits the role of David as representative of God's people (his "son," Ex. 4:22–23; cf. Ps. 89:26–27).

17:16–27 David's prayer of wondering praise (vv. 16–22; see note on 2 Sam. 7:18–29) leads into a petition that God will confirm his covenantal promise so that David's house will **be established forever**. The enduring character of the Davidic covenant in the Chronicler's own (kingless) day should inspire confidence and hope in the promises to which it testifies.

18:1–20:8 *David's Wars.* First Chronicles 18–20 deals with David's wars and the extension of his power over the surrounding nations. The Chronicler has drawn very selectively from 2 Samuel 8–21, passing over a mass of material relating to David's personal life, most notably the Bathsheba affair (2 Sam. 11:2–12:25) and the troubles that engulfed his family and throne (2 Samuel 13–20). The writer has omitted this material not in order to "whitewash" David's reputation (since other matters that reflect positively on him, e.g., his kindness to Mephibosheth, 2 Samuel 9, are also passed over), but to show how God's promises to David (esp. 1 Chron. 17:8–10b) are being fulfilled and how David as a warrior and king contributed to the preparations for building the temple. As elsewhere in Chronicles (see above on chs. 11–12; 14), the materials do not always follow a strict chronology, but are used as illustrations from traditional sources.

18:1–13 From 2 Sam. 8:1–14. David's victories—over the **Philistines** in the southwest, the **Moabites** to the east of the Dead Sea, the **Edomites** in the southeast, and **Hadadezer** of Zobah in the distant northeast—brought security to Israel (see 1 Chron. 17:9) and extended its boundaries, or at least its zones of influence, to their farthest point in history (cf. note on 2 Sam. 8:3–12). The divine promise "I will subdue all your enemies" (1 Chron. 17:10; contrast 2 Sam. 7:11, "I will give you rest from all your enemies") is expressly recalled in 1 Chron. 18:1, and the victories are ascribed to Yahweh (vv. 6, 13). David **dedicated** the gifts he received and the spoils of war to Yahweh, that is, for the provisioning and upkeep of the temple (see 26:27; 2 Chron. 5:1). The Chronicler's addition to his source in 1 Chron. 18:8b (**With it Solomon made the bronze sea and the pillars and the vessels of bronze**) amplifies this point and stresses that the temple, as well as the people, benefited from David's wars.

18:4 On **1,000 chariots, 7,000 horsemen**, see note on 2 Sam. 8:4.

18:6 Gave victory is sometimes the nuance of the verb "save" (see ESV footnote); cf. 11:14; 18:13.

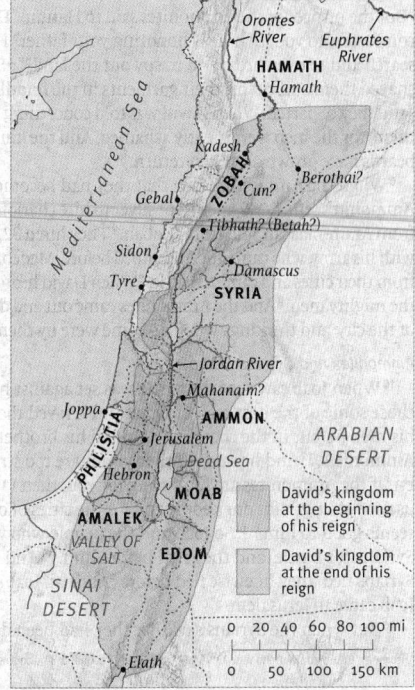

The Extent of David's Kingdom
1010–971 B.C.

David's many battles eventually established Israel as the dominant power in Syria and Palestine. David expanded Israel's borders from Saul's fledgling territory until, by the end of his reign, he controlled all of Israel, Edom, Moab, Ammon, Syria, and Zobah. Other kingdoms, such as Tyre and Hamath, established treaties with him.

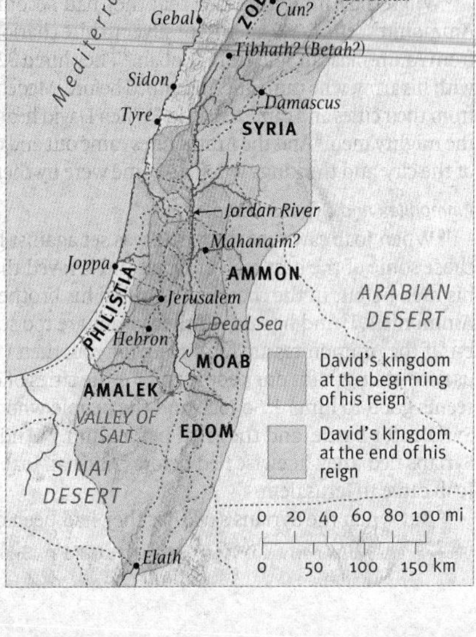

in Syria of Damascus, and the Syrians became servants to David and brought tribute. And
the LORD gave victory to David[1] wherever he went. 7 And David took the shields of gold
that were carried by the servants of Hadadezer and brought them to Jerusalem. 8 And from
[f]Tibhath and from Cun, cities of Hadadezer, David took a large amount of bronze. [g]With
it Solomon made the bronze sea and the pillars and the vessels of bronze.
9 When [h]Tou king of Hamath heard that David had defeated the whole army of Hadadezer,
king [e]of Zobah, 10 he sent his son [i]Hadoram to King David, to ask about his health and to
bless him because he had fought against [b]Hadadezer and defeated him; for [b]Hadadezer
had often been at war with Tou. And he sent all sorts of articles of gold, of silver, and
of bronze. 11 These also King David dedicated to the LORD, together with the silver and
gold that he had carried off from all the nations, from [j]Edom, Moab, the Ammonites, the
Philistines, and Amalek.
12 And [k]Abishai, the son of Zeruiah, killed 18,000 Edomites in the Valley of Salt. 13 Then
he put garrisons in Edom, and all the Edomites became David's servants. And the LORD
gave victory to David wherever he went.

David's Administration

14 So David reigned over all Israel, and he administered justice and equity to all his
people. 15 And [l]Joab the son of Zeruiah was over the army; and Jehoshaphat the son of
Ahilud was recorder; 16 [m]and Zadok the son of Ahitub and [n]Ahimelech the son of Abiathar
were priests; and [o]Shavsha was secretary; 17 and Benaiah the son of Jehoiada was over the
Cherethites and the Pelethites; and David's sons were the [p]chief officials in the service
of the king.

The Ammonites Disgrace David's Men

19 [q]Now after this Nahash the king of the Ammonites died, and his son reigned in
his place. 2 And David said, "I will deal kindly with Hanun the son of Nahash, for
his father dealt kindly with me." So David sent messengers to console him concerning his
father. And David's servants came to the land of the Ammonites to Hanun to console him.
3 But the princes of the Ammonites said to Hanun, "Do you think, because David has sent
comforters to you, that he is honoring your father? Have not his servants come to you to
search and to overthrow and to spy out the land?" 4 So Hanun took David's servants and
shaved them and cut off their garments in the middle, at their hips, and sent them away;
5 and they departed. When David was told concerning the men, he sent messengers to meet
them, for the men were greatly ashamed. And the king said, "Remain at Jericho until your
beards have grown and then return."
6 When the Ammonites saw that they had become a stench to David, Hanun and the
Ammonites sent 1,000 talents[2] of silver to hire chariots and horsemen [r]from Mesopotamia,
from Aram-maacah, and from [s]Zobah. 7 They hired 32,000 chariots and the king of Maacah
with his army, who came and encamped before [t]Medeba. And the Ammonites were mustered
from their cities and came to battle. 8 When David heard of it, he sent Joab and all the army of
the mighty men. 9 And the Ammonites came out and drew up in battle array at the entrance
of the city, and the kings who had come were by themselves in the open country.

Ammonites and Syrians Defeated

10 When Joab saw that the battle was set against him both in front and in the rear, he
chose some of the best men of Israel and arrayed them against the Syrians. 11 The rest of
his men he put in the charge of [u]Abishai his brother, and they were arrayed against the
Ammonites. 12 And he said, "If the Syrians are too strong for me, then you shall help me,
but if the Ammonites are too strong for you, then I will help you. 13 Be strong, and let us
use our strength for our people and for the cities of our God, and may the LORD do what
seems good to him." 14 So Joab and the people who were with him drew near before the
Syrians for battle, and they fled before him. 15 And when the Ammonites saw that the
Syrians fled, they likewise fled before [u]Abishai, Joab's brother, and entered the city. Then
Joab came to Jerusalem.
16 But when the Syrians saw that they had been defeated by Israel, they sent messen-

[1] Hebrew *the LORD saved David*; also verse 13 [2] A *talent* was about 75 pounds or 34 kilograms

8 [f][2 Sam. 8:8] [g]1 Kgs. 7:15, 23; 2 Chr. 4:12, 15, 16
9 [h][2 Sam. 8:9] [e][See ver. 5 above]
10 [i][2 Sam. 8:10] [b][See ver. 3 above]
11 [j][2 Sam. 8:12]
12 [k]1 Sam. 26:6; [2 Sam. 8:13]
15 [l][ch. 11:6]
16 [m][2 Sam. 8:17; 20:25] [n][ch. 24:3, 6] [o][2 Sam. 8:17; 1 Kgs. 4:3]
17 [p][2 Sam. 8:18]

Chapter 19

1 [q]For ver. 1-19, see 2 Sam. 10:1-19
6 [r][2 Sam. 10:6] [s]ch. 18:5, 9
7 [t]Num. 21:30; Josh. 13:9, 16
11 [u]ch. 18:12
15 [u][See ver. 11 above]

16[v][2 Sam. 10:16, 18] [w]2 Sam. 10:16
18[x][2 Sam. 10:18] [v][See ver. 16 above]
19[w][See ver. 16 above]
Chapter 20
1[y]2 Sam. 11:1 [z]2 Sam. 12:26
2[a]For ver. 2, 3, see 2 Sam. 12:30, 31
3[b][2 Sam. 12:31]

gers and brought out the Syrians who were beyond the Euphrates,[1] with [v]Shophach the
commander of the army of [w]Hadadezer at their head. 17 And when it was told to David,
he gathered all Israel together and crossed the Jordan and came to them and drew up his
forces against them. And when David set the battle in array against the Syrians, they fought
with him. 18 And the Syrians fled before Israel, and David killed of the Syrians the men of
[x]7,000 chariots and 40,000 [x]foot soldiers, and put to death also [v]Shophach the commander
of their army. 19 And when the servants of [w]Hadadezer saw that they had been defeated by
Israel, they made peace with David and became subject to him. So the Syrians were not
willing to save the Ammonites anymore.

The Capture of Rabbah

20 [y]In the spring of the year, the time when kings go out to battle, Joab led out the
army and ravaged the country of the Ammonites and came and besieged Rabbah.
But David remained at Jerusalem. And [z]Joab struck down Rabbah and overthrew it.
2 [a]And David took the crown of their king from his head. He found that it weighed a
talent[2] of gold, and in it was a precious stone. And it was placed on David's head. And he
brought out the spoil of the city, a very great amount. 3 And he brought out the people
who were in it and set them to labor[3] [b]with saws and iron picks and axes.[4] And thus
David did to all the cities of the Ammonites. Then David and all the people returned
to Jerusalem.

[1] Hebrew *the River* [2] A *talent* was about 75 pounds or 34 kilograms [3] Compare 2 Samuel 12:31; Hebrew *he sawed* [4] Compare 2 Samuel 12:31; Hebrew *saws*

18:12 On the **Valley of Salt**, see note on 2 Sam. 8:13–14.

18:14–17 From 2 Sam. 8:15–18 (cf. note there). As David's empire expanded, his government was organized, apparently on the model of contemporary Egyptian practice, to oversee the major spheres of national life: army, court, and official worship.

18:15–17 On **Jehoshaphat**, **Ahilud**, **Zadok**, **Ahitub**, **Ahimelech**, **Abiathar**, and **Benaiah**, see notes on 2 Sam. 8:17; 8:18.

19:1–20:3 From 2 Sam. 10:1–19; 11:1; 12:26, 30–31. The chief difference is the Chronicler's omission of the sin with Bathsheba from 1 Chron. 20:1. The Chronicler is not hiding David's sin, since it was well known, but is probably focusing on the victorious outcome of this warfare. The Ammonites lived east of Gad and had troubled Israel in Saul's day (1 Sam. 11:1–11). David had a friendship treaty with Nahash, but Hanun, suspecting David's motives, provoked a diplomatic incident. The Aramean states (1 Chron. 19:6), from which Hanun sought help, were situated farther north, from around Damascus to beyond the Euphrates. The passage moves from the fate of David's mission of consolation (19:1–5), to the mustering of the armies and the first battle (19:6–15), to the comprehensive war against the Syrians (19:16–19), to the final conquest of Ammon (20:1–3). The battles described in 19:1–15 seem to have preceded the decisive campaign in 18:5–8. David receives the crown of Ammon for his own house (20:2); this contributes to the implicit messianism of the book, since the line of David will produce One who will rule the Gentiles.

19:2 On **Hanun the son of Nahash**, see note on 2 Sam. 10:1–5.

19:6–7 On **Zobah** and **Maacah**, see note on 2 Sam. 10:6–8.

19:18 For the number **7,000** here, 2 Sam. 10:18 has "700." The difference is probably due not to a discrepancy in the original manuscripts but to a scribal error in the later transmission of the text of either book.

20:1–3 The climax of these wars is Joab's destruction of the Ammonite capital, Rabbah, and David's coronation with the crown of the Ammonites' king (see 17:8). The Chronicler omits 2 Sam. 12:27–29, Joab's summons to David to come to Rabbah.

20:1 the time when kings go out to battle. . . . But David remained at Jerusalem. See note on 2 Sam. 11:1; the Chronicler omits any mention of David's sin with Bathsheba (see note on 1 Chron. 18:1–20:8). **Joab struck down Rabbah and overthrew it**. Cf. note on 2 Sam. 12:26–31.

David Defeats the Ammonites and the Syrians
c. 995 B.C.
After purposely humiliating ambassadors sent by David, the Ammonites prepared for David's response by calling for help from the king of Maacah and from Syrians living in Zobah and other regions north of Israel. When David's commander Joab defeated these forces, the Syrians called for more troops from beyond the Euphrates River and attacked David at Helam. David's forces defeated them again, and the Syrians became subject to Israel.

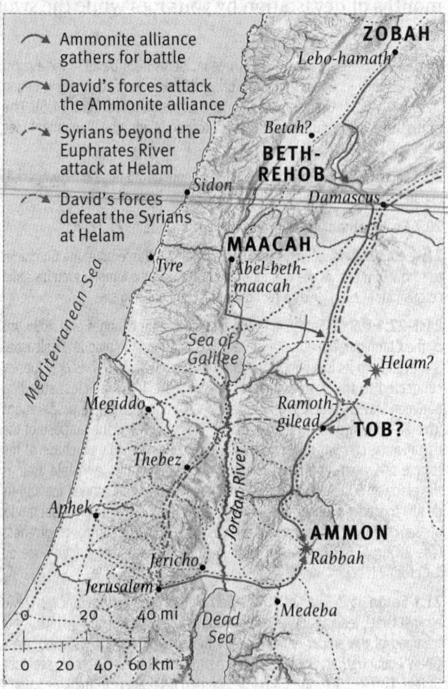

Philistine Giants Killed

4 [c]And after this there arose war with the Philistines at Gezer. Then Sibbecai the Hushathite
struck down Sippai, who was one of the descendants of the giants, and the Philistines were
subdued. 5 And there was again war with the Philistines, and Elhanan the son of [d]Jair
struck down Lahmi [d]the brother of Goliath the Gittite, the shaft of whose spear was like a
weaver's beam. 6 And there was again war at Gath, where there was a man of great stature,
who had six fingers on each hand and six toes on each foot, twenty-four in number, and
he also was descended from the giants. 7 And when he taunted Israel, Jonathan the son
of [e]Shimea, David's brother, struck him down. 8 These were descended from the giants in
Gath, and they fell by the hand of David and by the hand of his servants.

David's Census Brings Pestilence

21 [f]Then [g]Satan stood against Israel and incited David to number Israel. 2 So David
said to Joab and the commanders of the army, "Go, number Israel, from Beersheba
to Dan, and bring me a report, that I may know their number." 3 But Joab said, "May the
LORD add to his people a hundred times as many as they are! Are they not, my lord the
king, all of them my lord's servants? Why then should my lord require this? Why should
it be a cause of guilt for Israel?" 4 But the king's word prevailed against Joab. So Joab
departed and went throughout all Israel and came back to Jerusalem. 5 And Joab gave
the sum of the numbering of the people to David. In all Israel there were [h]1,100,000
men who drew the sword, and in Judah [h]470,000 who drew the sword. 6 [i]But he did not
include Levi and Benjamin in the numbering, for the king's command was abhorrent
to Joab.

7 But God was displeased with this thing, and he struck Israel. 8 And David said to
God, "I have sinned greatly in that I have done this thing. But now, please [j]take away the
iniquity of your servant, for I have acted very foolishly." 9 And the LORD spoke to Gad,
David's [k]seer, saying, 10 "Go and say to David, 'Thus says the LORD, Three things I offer
you; choose one of them, that I may do it to you.'" 11 So Gad came to David and said to
him, "Thus says the LORD, 'Choose what you will: 12 either [l]three years of famine, or three
months of devastation by your foes while the sword of your enemies overtakes you, or

4 [c]For ver. 4-8, see 2 Sam. 21:18-22
5 [d][2 Sam. 21:19]
7 [e]ch. 2:13; 2 Sam. 13:3; [1 Sam. 16:9; 17:13]

Chapter 21
1 [f]For ver. 1-28, see 2 Sam. 24:1-25 [g]Zech. 3:1, 2; [2 Sam. 24:1]; See Job 1:6-12; 2:1-7
5 [h][2 Sam. 24:9]
6 [i]ch. 27:24
8 [j][2 Sam. 12:13]
9 [k]ch. 29:29; See 1 Sam. 9:9
12 [l][2 Sam. 24:13]

20:4–8 From 2 Sam. 21:18–22. Three incidents from David's war against the Philistines in Gezer and Gath bring this unit back to where it began (1 Chron. 18:1). **the giants**: lit., "the Rephaim" (see Gen. 14:5). **The Philistines were subdued** is the Chronicler's additional comment (see 1 Chron. 17:10).

20:5 Lahmi the brother of Goliath. See note on 2 Sam. 21:19, which has apparently suffered textual corruption.

20:7 On **Jonathan** and **Shimea**, see note on 2 Sam. 21:21.

21:1–29:30 *David's Census and Preparation for the Temple.* The Chronicler tells how David paves the way for Solomon to build the temple; even his sinful census (21:1–22:1) yields a plot of land for the building site.

21:1–22:1 From 2 Sam. 24:1–25, with significant changes and additions by the Chronicler. The account of David's census and the plague it unleashes is moved from its location at the end of 2 Samuel (where it is only loosely connected to the narrative) to a pivotal place in Chronicles, standing between David's wars (1 Chronicles 18–20) and his temple preparations (chs. 22–29), into which it immediately leads (22:1–2). The purpose of the narrative here is not only to recount and explain David's purchase of the temple site, but especially to expound the meaning of the temple itself as the place of God's mercy and forgiveness, where sin is atoned for and its deadly consequences removed. Significantly, it is David, the principal model of "seeking God" in this work, who exemplifies the need for forgiveness (see 2 Chron. 6:36), as well as being the model penitent (see note on 1 Chron. 21:17).

21:1 Satan. In 2 Sam. 24:1, it is God himself who in anger incites David against Israel, leading to the census. God's angelic "adversary" (which is the meaning of the proper name; see ESV footnote on Job 1:6) is in no sense God's equal (rather, Satan's counterpart in the Bible is Michael; see Jude 9; Rev. 12:7–9). Still, the Chronicler wanted his readers to think of Satan's malice as God's means of carrying out his will (see note on 2 Sam. 24:1). Nevertheless, David himself sinned in giving in to Satan's enticement and ordering the census. This census was sinful probably because it arose from David's presumptuous military ambitions (see 1 Chron. 21:5) and pride, rather than from Yahweh's express command. In addition, David neglected to levy the poll tax for a census required by Ex. 30:12, an act of disobedience that could bring plague on the people.

21:3 guilt (Hb. *'ashmah*; see Lev. 6:7). A key term in the Chronicler's theology (see 2 Chron. 24:18; 28:13; 33:23). This addition to 2 Sam. 24:3 emphasizes David's culpability.

21:5–6 The Chronicler adds that **Joab** found the king's command **abhorrent** (again emphasizing David's sinfulness), for which reason Joab excluded the priestly tribe of Levi from the count (perhaps in deference to Num. 1:47–49), as well as Benjamin, whose territory included Jerusalem (the site of the ark) and Gibeon (the site of the tabernacle). **In all Israel there were 1,100,000 men**. The parallel passage in 2 Sam. 24:9 records 800,000 men in Israel and 500,000 men in Judah, which adds up to 1,300,000. It will not do to call this apparent discrepancy a "disagreement," since the Chronicler respected and drew on Samuel and Kings (see Introduction: Purpose, Occasion, and Background); but arriving at the exact explanation is a challenge. One possible solution begins by taking the **470,000** men in Judah as part of the total of "all Israel" (in Chronicles "all Israel" often includes Judah: e.g., 1 Chron. 13:6; 28:4; 2 Chron. 11:3; 24:5; 31:1), and proceeds to notice that in 1 Chron. 21:6 the Chronicler says that Joab's figures here were incomplete, for he **did not include Levi and Benjamin in the numbering**. Therefore, the census was unfinished, leaving the actual number of God's people uncertain (see v. 3 and 27:23–24, where the text again emphasizes that the numbers were incomplete).

21:7–13 David's confession of guilt leads him to appeal to God's **mercy**, which **is very great** (the Chronicler adds "very" to his source to underscore this point). **sword**. A prominent image in the choice of punishments (v. 12;

15[m]See Gen. 6:6
16[n]1 Kgs. 20:31; See 2 Sam. 3:31
18[o][2 Chr. 3:1]
25[p][2 Sam. 24:24]
26[q]See Lev. 9:24
29[r]ch. 16:39; 2 Chr. 1:3; [1 Kgs. 3:4]
Chapter 22
1[s]ch. 21:18, 19, 26, 28; 2 Chr. 3:1; [Deut. 12:5]

else three days of the sword of the LORD, pestilence on the land, with the angel of the
LORD destroying throughout all the territory of Israel.' Now decide what answer I shall
return to him who sent me." 13 Then David said to Gad, "I am in great distress. Let me
fall into the hand of the LORD, for his mercy is very great, but do not let me fall into the
hand of man."
14 So the LORD sent a pestilence on Israel, and 70,000 men of Israel fell. 15 And God sent
the angel to Jerusalem to destroy it, but as he was about to destroy it, the LORD saw, and
he [m]relented from the calamity. And he said to the angel who was working destruction, "It
is enough; now stay your hand." And the angel of the LORD was standing by the threshing floor of Ornan the Jebusite. 16 And David lifted his eyes and saw the angel of the LORD
standing between earth and heaven, and in his hand a drawn sword stretched out over
Jerusalem. Then David and the elders, [n]clothed in sackcloth, fell upon their faces. 17 And
David said to God, "Was it not I who gave command to number the people? It is I who
have sinned and done great evil. But these sheep, what have they done? Please let your
hand, O LORD my God, be against me and against my father's house. But do not let the
plague be on your people."

David Builds an Altar

18 Now [o]the angel of the LORD had commanded Gad to say to David that David should
go up and raise an altar to the LORD on the threshing floor of Ornan the Jebusite. 19 So
David went up at Gad's word, which he had spoken in the name of the LORD. 20 Now
Ornan was threshing wheat. He turned and saw the angel, and his four sons who were
with him hid themselves. 21 As David came to Ornan, Ornan looked and saw David and
went out from the threshing floor and paid homage to David with his face to the ground.
22 And David said to Ornan, "Give me the site of the threshing floor that I may build on
it an altar to the LORD—give it to me at its full price—that the plague may be averted
from the people." 23 Then Ornan said to David, "Take it, and let my lord the king do what
seems good to him. See, I give the oxen for burnt offerings and the threshing sledges for
the wood and the wheat for a grain offering; I give it all." 24 But King David said to Ornan,
"No, but I will buy them for the full price. I will not take for the LORD what is yours, nor
offer burnt offerings that cost me nothing." 25 So David paid Ornan [p]600 shekels[1] of gold
by weight for the site. 26 And David built there an altar to the LORD and presented burnt
offerings and peace offerings and called on the LORD, and the LORD[2] [q]answered him
with fire from heaven upon the altar of burnt offering. 27 Then the LORD commanded
the angel, and he put his sword back into its sheath.
28 At that time, when David saw that the LORD had answered him at the threshing floor
of Ornan the Jebusite, he sacrificed there. 29 For the tabernacle of the LORD, which Moses
had made in the wilderness, and the altar of burnt offering [r]were at that time in the high
place at Gibeon, 30 but David could not go before it to inquire of God, for he was afraid of
the sword of the angel of the LORD.

22 Then David said, [s]"Here shall be the house of the LORD God and here the altar of
burnt offering for Israel."

[1] A *shekel* was about 2/5 ounce or 11 grams [2] Hebrew *he*

see also vv. 16, 27, 30) and perhaps an ironic comment on David's attempt to muster a great army of men "who drew the sword" (v. 5).

21:12 three years of famine. Cf. note on 2 Sam. 24:13.

21:14–16 On **relented** (v. 15), see notes on 1 Sam. 15:11–29 and Jonah 3:10. The Chronicler does not tell readers what **the LORD saw**; probably it is the impending **calamity**. The angel with the drawn sword over Jerusalem evokes the image of Abraham with his knife over Isaac in "the land of Moriah" (Gen. 22:2, 9–10). Uniquely in the Bible, the Chronicler will in fact identify the future temple site as Mount Moriah (2 Chron. 3:1). In both cases, the covenantal promises (Gen. 17:3–8; 1 Chron. 17:8–14) seem threatened with destruction were it not for God's merciful reversal of his command and provision of an alternative sacrifice (21:26; cf. Gen. 22:13).

21:17 Compared to 2 Sam. 24:17 (see note there), David here makes a fuller and more emphatic confession of his personal responsibility and guilt in calling the census, and asks for the plague to be taken from the people.

21:18–27 the angel of the LORD . . . commanded Gad. The altar is God's initiative and provision for atonement. David's purchase of the threshing floor of Ornan for the **full price** (vv. 22, 24; cf. note on 2 Sam. 24:23–24) echoes Abraham's purchase of the cave of Machpelah (Gen. 23:9) and continues the Abraham-David typology.

21:25 600 shekels. See note on 2 Sam. 24:23–24.

21:26 David built there an altar. See note on 2 Sam. 24:25. **The LORD answered him with fire from heaven**, signifying God's approval of the site (see Lev. 9:24; 2 Chron. 7:1).

21:28–22:1 This material is not found in 2 Samuel 24. It explains why David did not go to Gibeon to offer a sacrifice and why he concluded that God had authorized the transfer of that sanctuary to the new site in Jerusalem (see 2 Chron. 1:3–6; 5:5).

David Prepares for Temple Building

2 David commanded to gather together the [t]resident aliens who were in the land of
Israel, and he [u]set stonecutters to prepare dressed stones for building the house of God.
3 David also provided great quantities of iron for nails for the doors of the gates and for
clamps, [v]as well as bronze in quantities beyond weighing, 4 and cedar timbers without
number, [w]for the Sidonians and Tyrians brought great quantities of cedar to David. 5 For
David said, [x]"Solomon my son is young and inexperienced, and the house that is to be built
for the LORD must be exceedingly magnificent, of fame and glory throughout all lands.
I will therefore make preparation for it." So David provided materials in great quantity
before his death.

Solomon Charged to Build the Temple

6 Then he called for Solomon his son and charged him to build a house for the LORD,
the God of Israel. 7 David said to Solomon, "My son, [y]I had it in my heart to build a house
to the name of the LORD my God. 8 But the word of the LORD came to me, saying, [z]'You
have shed much blood and have waged great wars. You shall not build a house to my
name, because you have shed so much blood before me on the earth. 9 Behold, a son shall
be born to you who shall be a man of rest. [a]I will give him rest from all his surrounding
enemies. [b]For his name shall be Solomon, and I will give peace and quiet to Israel in his
days. 10 [c]He shall build a house for my name. [d]He shall be my son, and I will be his father,
and I will establish his royal throne in Israel forever.'
11 "Now, my son, [e]the LORD be with you, so that you may succeed in building the house
of the LORD your God, as he has spoken concerning you. 12 [f]Only, may the LORD grant you
discretion and understanding, that when he gives you charge over Israel you may keep
the law of the LORD your God. 13 [g]Then you will prosper if you are careful to observe the
statutes and the rules that the LORD commanded Moses for Israel. [h]Be strong and courageous. Fear not; do not be dismayed. 14 With great pains I have provided for the house of
the LORD [i]100,000 talents[1] of gold, a million talents of silver, and [j]bronze and iron beyond
weighing, for there is so much of it; timber and stone, too, I have provided. To these you
must add. 15 You have an abundance of workmen: stonecutters, masons, carpenters, and
all kinds of craftsmen without number, skilled in working 16 gold, silver, bronze, and iron.
Arise and work! [k]The LORD be with you!"
17 David also commanded [l]all the leaders of Israel to help Solomon his son, saying, 18 "Is
not the LORD your God with you? And [m]has he not given you peace on every side? For he
has delivered the inhabitants of the land into my hand, and the land is subdued before the
LORD and his people. 19 Now [n]set your mind and heart to seek the LORD your God. Arise
and build the sanctuary of the LORD God, [o]so that the ark of the covenant of the LORD and
the holy vessels of God may be brought into a house built [p]for the name of the LORD."

[1] A *talent* was about 75 pounds or 34 kilograms

2[t][1 Kgs. 9:20, 21; 2 Chr. 2:17] [u][1 Kgs. 5:17]
3[v]ver. 14; 1 Kgs. 7:47
4[w][1 Kgs. 5:6]
5[x]ch. 29:1; [1 Kgs. 3:7; Prov. 4:3]
7[y]ch. 17:1, 2; 28:2; 2 Sam. 7:2, 3; 1 Kgs. 8:17; See Ps. 132:1-5
8[z]ch. 28:3; [1 Kgs. 5:3]
9[a]1 Kgs. 5:4; [ver. 18; 1 Kgs. 4:25] [b]2 Sam. 12:24
10[c]See 2 Sam. 7:13 [d]ch. 28:6; 2 Sam. 7:14; Heb. 1:5
11[e]ver. 16; [1 Sam. 20:13]
12[f][1 Kgs. 3:9, 12; Ps. 72:1]
13[g]ch. 28:7 [h]ch. 28:20; [Deut. 31:6, 7; Josh. 1:6, 7, 9]
14[i][ch. 29:4] [j]ver. 3
16[k]ver. 11
17[l]See ch. 28:1-6
18[m]ch. 23:25; [Deut. 12:10; Josh. 21:44; 23:1; 2 Sam. 7:1]; See ver. 9
19[n][2 Chr. 20:3] [o]1 Kgs. 8:6, 21; 2 Chr. 5:7; 6:11 [p]ver. 7; 1 Kgs. 5:3

22:2–19 David's designation of the temple site (v. 1) leads directly into the next major unit of the work (chs. 22–29), which describes David's preparation for building the temple. Although David was prevented from taking part in the actual construction, he stands alongside Solomon in this chapter as the one who provided the materials, personnel, and conditions essential for the task. Chapter 22 has the form of a private commissioning of Solomon, while chs. 28–29 include a public commissioning "in the sight of all Israel" (28:8). Their reigns are presented as a complementary unit, both being essential for the fulfillment of the task: what David begins, Solomon completes. The presentation of events is modeled in part on the transfer of leadership from Moses to Joshua (see esp. Deut. 31:6–8, 23; Josh. 1:5, 7–9).

22:2–5 David's preparation of the temple workforce included the imposition of forced labor on **resident aliens** (see 2 Sam. 20:24; cf. notes on 2 Chron. 2:2; 8:7–10). War booty provided some of the material (see 1 Chron. 18:8). These events belong to the last years of David's life, when Solomon was still **young and inexperienced** (22:5)—hence David's solicitous care.

22:6–16 David's private commission to his son is intended to prepare him in mind and heart for his demanding duty. David refers back to the dynastic promise (17:7–14), amplifying some of its statements. His disqualification by Yahweh from temple building (22:8) arises chiefly from the character of his reign, a time of warfare and subduing enemies (chs. 18–20), in contrast to Solomon's reign, the promised time of **peace and quiet** for Israel (see also Deut. 12:10–11). The wordplay on Solomon's name (Hb. *Shelomoh*) and "peace" (Hb. *shalom*) underlines this point.

22:11–13 Along with fulfilling his commission to build, David emphasizes Solomon's need to keep the Law of Moses in the ruling of his kingdom. **Be strong and courageous. Fear not**. See Deut. 31:7–8 and Josh. 1:9.

22:14 David's provision for the temple preparation is distinct from the donation of 3,000 talents of gold and 7,000 talents of silver that he gave out of his own treasure (29:3–4).

22:17–19 David's exhortation to the leaders of Israel to **seek the LORD** entails active obedience to the divine command: **Arise and build the sanctuary of the LORD God**. Solomon must already have been appointed to a co-regency with David by this time (see 1 Kings 1:28–2:12) in order for David to command Israel's leaders to assist Solomon in his task. As elsewhere in the book, the order of 1 Chronicles 22–29 is dictated more by thematic considerations than by strict chronology.

David Organizes the Levites

23 [q]When David was old and full of days, [r]he made Solomon his son king over
Israel.
2 David[1] assembled all the leaders of Israel and the priests and the Levites. 3 The Levites,
[s]thirty years old and upward, were numbered, and [t]the total was [u]38,000 men. 4 "Twenty-
four thousand of these," David said,[2] [v]"shall have charge of the work in the house of the
LORD, 6,000 shall be [w]officers and judges, 5 4,000 gatekeepers, and 4,000 shall offer praises
to the LORD with the instruments [x]that I have made for praise." 6 [y]And David organized
them in divisions [z]corresponding to the sons of Levi: Gershon, Kohath, and Merari.
7 [a]The sons of Gershon[3] were Ladan and Shimei. 8 The sons of Ladan: [b]Jehiel the chief,
and Zetham, and Joel, three. 9 The sons of Shimei: Shelomoth, Haziel, and Haran, three.
These were the heads of the fathers' houses of Ladan. 10 And the sons of Shimei: Jahath,
Zina, and Jeush and Beriah. These four were the sons of Shimei. 11 Jahath was the chief, and
Zizah the second; but Jeush and Beriah did not have many sons, therefore they became
counted as a single father's house.
12 [c]The sons of Kohath: Amram, Izhar, Hebron, and Uzziel, four. 13 [d]The sons of Amram:
Aaron and Moses. [e]Aaron was set apart to dedicate the most holy things, that he and
his sons forever should [f]make offerings before the LORD and [g]minister to him and
[h]pronounce blessings in his name forever. 14 But the sons of Moses the [i]man of God were
named among the [j]tribe of Levi. 15 The [k]sons of Moses: Gershom and Eliezer. 16 The sons
of Gershom: [l]Shebuel the chief. 17 The sons of Eliezer: Rehabiah the chief. Eliezer had
no other sons, but the sons of Rehabiah were very many. 18 The sons of Izhar: Shelomith
the chief. 19 The [m]sons of Hebron: Jeriah the chief, Amariah the second, Jahaziel the
third, and Jekameam the fourth. 20 [n]The sons of Uzziel: Micah the chief and Isshiah
the second.
21 [o]The sons of Merari: Mahli and Mushi. The sons of Mahli: Eleazar and [p]Kish. 22 Eleazar
died [q]having no sons, but only daughters; their [r]kinsmen, the sons of Kish, married them.
23 [s]The sons of Mushi: Mahli, Eder, and Jeremoth, three.
24 [t]These were the sons of Levi by their fathers' houses, the heads of fathers' houses [u]as
they were listed according to the number of the names of the individuals from [v]twenty
years old and upward who were to do the work for the service of the house of the LORD.
25 For David said, "The LORD, the God of Israel, [w]has given rest to his people, and he dwells
in Jerusalem forever. 26 And so the Levites no longer need [x]to carry the tabernacle or any
of the things for its service." 27 For by the last words of David the sons of Levi were numbered from [v]twenty years old and upward. 28 For their duty was to assist the sons of Aaron
for the service of the house of the LORD, having the care of the courts and the chambers,
the cleansing of all that is holy, and any work for the service of the house of God. 29 Their
duty was also to assist with the [y]showbread, the [z]flour for the grain offering, the wafers
of unleavened bread, the [a]baked offering, the [b]offering mixed with oil, and all [c]measures
of quantity or size. 30 And they were to stand every morning, thanking and praising the
LORD, and likewise at evening, 31 and whenever burnt offerings were offered to the LORD
[d]on Sabbaths, [e]new moons, and feast days, [f]according to the number required of them,
regularly before the LORD. 32 Thus [g]they were to keep charge of the tent of meeting and

[1] Hebrew *He* [2] Hebrew lacks *David said* [3] Vulgate (compare Septuagint, Syriac); Hebrew *to the Gershonite*

Chapter 23
1 [q]ch. 29:28 [r][ch. 28:5; 29:22, 28]; See 1 Kgs. 1:33-39
3 [s]Num. 4:3, 47 [t]ver. 24; Num. 1:2 [u][Num. 4:47, 48]
4 [v][2 Chr. 2:2, 18; 34:12; Ezra 3:8, 9] [w]ch. 26:29; [Deut. 16:18; 2 Chr. 19:8]
5 [x]2 Chr. 29:25, 26; Neh. 12:36; Amos 6:5
6 [y][2 Chr. 8:14; 23:18; 35:4; Ezra 6:18] [z]ch. 6:1, 16; Ex. 6:16; Num. 26:57
7 [a]ch. 26:21
8 [b]ch. 15:18; 29:8; [ch. 26:21]
12 [c]ch. 6:18; 26:23; Ex. 6:18; Num. 3:19
13 [d]Ex. 6:20 [e]Ex. 28:1; [Heb. 5:4] [f]Ex. 30:7; Num. 16:40; 1 Sam. 2:28 [g]Deut. 21:5 [h]Num. 6:23
14 [i][ch. 26:23-25] [j]Deut. 33:1
15 [k]Ex. 2:22; 18:3, 4
16 [l]ch. 26:24
19 [m]ch. 24:23; [ch. 26:31]
20 [n]ch. 24:24, 25
21 [o]ch. 6:19, 29; 24:26; Ex. 6:19; [Num. 26:58] [p]ch. 24:29
22 [q]ch. 24:28 [r][Num. 36:6, 8]
23 [s]ch. 24:30
24 [t][Num. 10:17, 21] [u]ver. 3 [v]2 Chr. 31:17; Ezra 3:8; [ver. 3; Num. 4:3; 8:24]
25 [w]See ch. 22:18
26 [x]See Num. 4:5-15
27 [v][See ver. 24 above]
29 [y]See Lev. 24:5-8 [z]ch. 9:29; Lev. 6:20, 21 [a]ch. 9:31 [b]Lev. 6:21; 7:12 [c][Lev. 19:35]
31 [d]Isa. 1:13 [e]See Num. 28:11 [f]See Lev. 23:2, 4
32 [g]Num. 1:53

23:1–27:34 Chapters 23–27 detail David's further preparations for Solomon's rule, in the provision of religious, military, and political leadership. These chapters consist mainly of lists of temple personnel and royal officials, interspersed with narrative and descriptive notes. The primary interest lies in David's organization of the Levites (23:3–32; 24:20–26:28) and the Aaronic priests (24:1–19) for temple worship and administration. David's reorganization of the Levites' work was a necessary consequence of the construction of the temple and the central place it would have in the nation's life. The structures of the temple ritual are shown to rest on royal authority.

23:3 A legitimate census of the Levites, as in Num. 4:1–3. The age of commencing service (**thirty . . . and upward**) was later lowered to 20 (1 Chron. 23:24, 27). **38,000**. The Hebrew word here for "thousand" may denote "groups" or "units" of indeterminate size (see note on 12:23–37).

23:6–23 David organizes the Levites according to their traditional clans: the Gershonites (vv. 7–11), the Kohathites (vv. 12–20), and the Merarites (vv. 21–23).

23:13b This summarizes the specific duties of the priesthood.

23:24–32 David appears as the successor to Moses (see Numbers 4) in redefining the Levites' duties for the new age of the temple. As assistants of the priests, the Levites have responsibility for the temple precincts and vessels, preparing food for the offerings, and the service of music and praise that accompanies the times of sacrifice.

the sanctuary, and to attend the sons of Aaron, their brothers, for the [h]service of the house
of the LORD.

David Organizes the Priests

24 The divisions of the sons of Aaron were these. The sons of [i]Aaron: Nadab, Abihu,
Eleazar, and Ithamar. 2 [j]But Nadab and Abihu died before their father and had no
children, so Eleazar and Ithamar became the priests. 3 With the help of [k]Zadok of the sons
of Eleazar, and Ahimelech of the sons of Ithamar, David organized them according to the
appointed duties in their service. 4 Since more chief men were found among the sons of
Eleazar than among the sons of Ithamar, they organized them under sixteen heads of
fathers' houses of the sons of Eleazar, and eight of the sons of Ithamar. 5 They divided
them [l]by lot, all alike, for there were sacred officers and officers of God among both the
sons of Eleazar and the sons of Ithamar. 6 And the scribe Shemaiah, the son of Nethanel, a
Levite, recorded them in the presence of the king and the princes and Zadok the priest and
[m]Ahimelech the son of Abiathar and the heads of the fathers' houses of the priests and of
the Levites, one father's house being chosen for Eleazar and one chosen for Ithamar.

7 The first lot fell to Jehoiarib, the second to Jedaiah, 8 the third to Harim, the fourth to
Seorim, 9 the fifth to Malchijah, the sixth to Mijamin, 10 the seventh to Hakkoz, the eighth
to [n]Abijah, 11 the ninth to Jeshua, the tenth to Shecaniah, 12 the eleventh to Eliashib, the
twelfth to Jakim, 13 the thirteenth to Huppah, the fourteenth to Jeshebeab, 14 the fifteenth
to Bilgah, the sixteenth to Immer, 15 the seventeenth to Hezir, the eighteenth to Happizzez,
16 the nineteenth to Pethahiah, the twentieth to Jehezkel, 17 the twenty-first to Jachin, the
twenty-second to Gamul, 18 the twenty-third to Delaiah, the twenty-fourth to Maaziah.
19 These had as their appointed duty in their service [o]to come into the house of the LORD
according to the procedure established for them by Aaron their father, as the LORD God
of Israel had commanded him.

20 And of the rest of the sons of Levi: [p]of the sons of Amram, Shubael; of the sons of
Shubael, Jehdeiah. 21 [q]Of Rehabiah: of the sons of Rehabiah, Isshiah the chief. 22 Of the
Izharites, Shelomoth; of the sons of Shelomoth, Jahath. 23 [r]The sons of Hebron:[1] Jeriah
the chief,[2] Amariah the second, Jahaziel the third, Jekameam the fourth. 24 [s]The sons of
Uzziel, Micah; of the sons of Micah, Shamir. 25 The brother of Micah, Isshiah; of the sons
of Isshiah, Zechariah. 26 [t]The sons of Merari: Mahli and Mushi. The sons of Jaaziah: Beno.[3]
27 The sons of Merari: of Jaaziah, Beno, Shoham, Zaccur, and Ibri. 28 Of Mahli: Eleazar, [u]who
had no sons. 29 Of Kish, the sons of Kish: Jerahmeel. 30 [v]The sons of Mushi: Mahli, Eder, and
Jerimoth. These were the sons of the Levites according to their fathers' houses. 31 These
also, the head of each father's house and his younger brother alike, [w]cast lots, just as their
brothers the sons of Aaron, in the presence of King David, [x]Zadok, Ahimelech, and the
heads of fathers' houses of the priests and of the Levites.

David Organizes the Musicians

25 David and the chiefs of the service also set apart for the service the sons of [y]Asaph,
and of [z]Heman, and of [a]Jeduthun, who [b]prophesied with lyres, with [c]harps, and
with cymbals. The list of those who did the work and of their duties was: 2 Of the sons

[1] Compare 23:19; Hebrew lacks *Hebron* [2] Compare 23:19; Hebrew lacks *the chief* [3] Or *his son*; also verse 27

32 [h]See Num. 3:6-9

Chapter 24

1 [i]Lev. 10:1, 6; Num. 26:60
2 [j]Lev. 10:2; Num. 26:61
3 [k]ver. 31; 2 Sam. 8:17
5 [l]ver. 31
6 [m]2 Sam. 8:17; [ch. 18:16; 1 Sam. 22:20; 23:6]
10 [n]Luke 1:5
19 [o]ch. 9:25
20 [p]ch. 23:13
21 [q]ch. 23:17
23 [r]ch. 23:19
24 [s]ch. 23:20
26 [t]ch. 23:21
28 [u]ch. 23:22
30 [v]ch. 23:23
31 [w]ver. 5; ch. 25:8; 26:13, 14; Neh. 11:1 [x]ver. 6

Chapter 25

1 [y]See ch. 6:39 [z]See ch. 6:33 [a]ch. 16:41 [b][Ex. 15:20; 2 Kgs. 3:15] [c]ch. 15:16; Neh. 12:27

24:1–19 David's provision for the temple services included organizing the priests into 24 divisions selected by lot. A duty roster of 24 divisions provided for two weeks of service by each division, based on a lunar calendar of 48 weeks.

24:2 Nadab and Abihu died. See Lev. 10:1–3. The priesthood was hereditary, and descended through the lines of **Eleazar** and **Ithamar**.

24:3 Zadok. See 1 Kings 1:8; 2:35. **Ahimelech**. The son of Abiathar (2 Sam. 8:17), with whom Zadok is usually paired (2 Sam. 15:35; 1 Kings 4:4).

24:5–6 While David appointed the priestly divisions, duties were allocated impartially by the drawing of lots. The lots were drawn alternately between the families of Eleazar and of Ithamar for the first 16 lots; then the remaining eight assignments to duty fell automatically to the families of Eleazar.

24:7 Jehoiarib appears as the ancestor of Mattathias in *1 Macc.* 2:1.

24:10 Hakkoz. See Ezra 2:61–63. **Abijah**. An ancestor of John the Baptist (Luke 1:5).

24:20–31 The list of Levites in 23:6–23 is updated to include another generation in six of the Levitical families. Like the Aaronic priestly families, the Levites also cast lots without distinction for their duties.

25:1–31 See 23:4b. David's organization of the Levitical musicians (initiated in chs. 15–16) was to prepare them for leading worship in the temple. Like the priests, the musicians were arranged into 24 divisions for their duties, according to the number of sons of the three main family groups. Their service accompanied the regular offerings of the priests. The Chronicler was probably seeking to encourage a similar ministry among the Levitical singers of the second temple, whose service, authorized by David, would also connect the community of their day with the preexilic Davidic kingdom.

25:1–8 David and the leaders of the Levites divided the musicians into the

2[b][See ver. 1 above]
3[b][See ver. 1 above]
5[d][2 Sam. 24:11]
6[c][See ver. 1 above]
7[e][ch. 23:5]
8[f]ch. 26:13
Chapter 26
2[g]ch. 9:21
4[h]ch. 15:18, 24; 16:38
5[i]ch. 13:14; 2 Sam. 6:11

of Asaph: Zaccur, Joseph, Nethaniah, and Asharelah, sons of Asaph, under the direction
of Asaph, who [b]prophesied under the direction of the king. 3 Of Jeduthun, the sons of
Jeduthun: Gedaliah, Zeri, Jeshaiah, Shimei,[1] Hashabiah, and Mattithiah, six, under the
direction of their father Jeduthun, [b]who prophesied with the lyre in thanksgiving and
praise to the LORD. 4 Of Heman, the sons of Heman: Bukkiah, Mattaniah, Uzziel, Shebuel
and Jerimoth, Hananiah, Hanani, Eliathah, Giddalti, and Romamti-ezer, Joshbekashah,
Mallothi, Hothir, Mahazioth. 5 All these were the sons of Heman [d]the king's seer, according
to the promise of God to exalt him, for God had given Heman fourteen sons and three
daughters. 6 They were all under the direction of their father in the music in the house
of the LORD with cymbals, [c]harps, and lyres for the service of the house of God. Asaph,
Jeduthun, and Heman were under the order of the king. 7 The number of them along with
their brothers, who were trained in singing to the LORD, all who were skillful, was [e]288.
8 And they cast lots for their duties, [f]small and great, teacher and pupil alike.

9 The first lot fell for Asaph to Joseph; the second to Gedaliah, to him and his brothers and
his sons, twelve; 10 the third to Zaccur, his sons and his brothers, twelve; 11 the fourth to Izri,
his sons and his brothers, twelve; 12 the fifth to Nethaniah, his sons and his brothers, twelve;
13 the sixth to Bukkiah, his sons and his brothers, twelve; 14 the seventh to Jesharelah, his
sons and his brothers, twelve; 15 the eighth to Jeshaiah, his sons and his brothers, twelve;
16 the ninth to Mattaniah, his sons and his brothers, twelve; 17 the tenth to Shimei, his sons
and his brothers, twelve; 18 the eleventh to Azarel, his sons and his brothers, twelve; 19 the
twelfth to Hashabiah, his sons and his brothers, twelve; 20 to the thirteenth, Shubael, his
sons and his brothers, twelve; 21 to the fourteenth, Mattithiah, his sons and his brothers,
twelve; 22 to the fifteenth, to Jeremoth, his sons and his brothers, twelve; 23 to the sixteenth,
to Hananiah, his sons and his brothers, twelve; 24 to the seventeenth, to Joshbekashah, his
sons and his brothers, twelve; 25 to the eighteenth, to Hanani, his sons and his brothers,
twelve; 26 to the nineteenth, to Mallothi, his sons and his brothers, twelve; 27 to the twentieth, to Eliathah, his sons and his brothers, twelve; 28 to the twenty-first, to Hothir, his sons
and his brothers, twelve; 29 to the twenty-second, to Giddalti, his sons and his brothers,
twelve; 30 to the twenty-third, to Mahazioth, his sons and his brothers, twelve; 31 to the
twenty-fourth, to Romamti-ezer, his sons and his brothers, twelve.

Divisions of the Gatekeepers

26 As for the divisions of the gatekeepers: of the Korahites, Meshelemiah the son of
Kore, of the sons of Asaph. 2 And Meshelemiah had sons: [g]Zechariah the firstborn,
Jediael the second, Zebadiah the third, Jathniel the fourth, 3 Elam the fifth, Jehohanan
the sixth, Eliehoenai the seventh. 4 And [h]Obed-edom had sons: Shemaiah the firstborn,
Jehozabad the second, Joah the third, Sachar the fourth, Nethanel the fifth, 5 Ammiel the
sixth, Issachar the seventh, Peullethai the eighth, [i]for God blessed him. 6 Also to his son
Shemaiah were sons born who were rulers in their fathers' houses, for they were men of
great ability. 7 The sons of Shemaiah: Othni, Rephael, Obed and Elzabad, whose brothers
were able men, Elihu and Semachiah. 8 All these were of the sons of Obed-edom with

[1] One Hebrew manuscript, Septuagint; most Hebrew manuscripts lack *Shimei*

three family groups of Asaph, Jeduthun, and Heman (see 6:31–47), **who prophesied with** musical instruments, i.e., wrote songs. In some cases, their songs seem to have become part of OT Scripture, for **Asaph** is named in the titles of Psalms 50 and 73–83, and **Jeduthun** in the titles of Psalms 39, 62, and 77. In addition, **Heman** here may be the same person as Heman the Ezrahite named in the title of Psalm 88 (cf. also 1 Chron. 6:33). The verb "to prophesy" (Hb. *naba'*) indicates that their songs were prompted or guided by the Spirit of God. This shows that "prophecy" is not always a direct announcement of God's plans; it indicates that the person is operating as God's authorized spokesman, here providing the right way for God's people to sing to him (they **prophesied . . . in thanksgiving and praise to the LORD**, 25:3).

25:4 The last nine names of Heman's sons have unusual Hebrew forms, and some have suggested that they are based on the first lines of various psalms, possibly applied as nicknames to these families.

25:7–31 The 24 divisions of 12 members each were assigned their duties impartially by lot, as were the priests (24:5). Each group varied in age and contained both teachers and pupils (25:8).

26:1–32 See 9:17–27 and 23:4a. The primary duty of the Levitical gatekeepers was to safeguard the sanctuary from trespass by unauthorized persons and from defilement by idolatrous practices (see 2 Chron. 29:3–7). They were also responsible for the temple treasuries and the maintenance of the building and its equipment (see 1 Chron. 9:22–32). The gatekeepers played a vital role in aiding the high priest Jehoiada in opposing Athaliah (2 Chron. 23:4–8, 19), and in the reforms by Hezekiah (2 Chron. 31:14) and Josiah (2 Chron. 34:9).

26:1–11 The gatekeepers included the families of **Meshelemiah** (vv. 1–3, 9), **Obed-edom** (vv. 4–8), and **Hosah** (vv. 10–11; see 16:38). Obed-edom is probably to be identified with the Philistine caretaker of the ark in 13:14. The inclusion within this company of one who was not an Israelite by birth suggests a certain fluidity in the early monarchy over who might count as a "Levite." The postexilic period took a much stricter line over Levitical genealogy (see Ezra 2:61–63). **Asaph**. A shortened form of Ebiasaph (1 Chron. 9:19).

their sons and brothers, able men qualified for the service; sixty-two of Obed-edom. 9 And
Meshelemiah had sons and brothers, able men, eighteen. 10 And [j]Hosah, of the sons of
Merari, had sons: Shimri the chief (for though he was not the firstborn, his father made
him chief), 11 Hilkiah the second, Tebaliah the third, Zechariah the fourth: all the sons and
brothers of Hosah were thirteen.

12 These divisions of the gatekeepers, corresponding to their chief men, had duties, just
as their brothers did, ministering in the house of the LORD. 13 And they cast lots by fathers'
houses, [k]small and great alike, for their gates. 14 The lot for the east fell to Shelemiah. They
cast lots also for his son Zechariah, a shrewd counselor, and his lot came out for the north.
15 Obed-edom's came out for the south, and to his sons was allotted [l]the gatehouse. 16 For
Shuppim and [j]Hosah it came out for the west, at the gate of Shallecheth on the road that
goes up. Watch corresponded to watch. 17 On the east there were six each day,[1] on the north
four each day, on the south four each day, as well as two and two at the gatehouse. 18 And for
the [n]colonnade[2] on the west there were four at the road and two at the colonnade. 19 These
were the divisions of the gatekeepers among the Korahites and the sons of Merari.

Treasurers and Other Officials

20 And of the Levites, Ahijah had charge of [o]the treasuries of the house of God and the
treasuries of the dedicated gifts. 21 The sons of Ladan, the sons of the Gershonites belonging
to Ladan, the heads of the fathers' houses belonging to Ladan the Gershonite: [p]Jehieli.[3]

22 [q]The sons of Jehieli, Zetham, and Joel his brother, were in charge of the treasuries
of the house of the LORD. 23 [r]Of the Amramites, the Izharites, the Hebronites, and the
Uzzielites— 24 and [s]Shebuel the son of Gershom, son of Moses, was chief officer in charge
of the treasuries. 25 His brothers: from [t]Eliezer were his son Rehabiah, and his son [u]Jeshaiah,
and his son Joram, and his son Zichri, and his son [v]Shelomoth. 26 This Shelomoth and his
brothers were in charge of all the treasuries of the dedicated gifts that David the king and
the heads of the fathers' houses and the officers of the thousands and the hundreds and the
commanders of the army [w]had dedicated. 27 From spoil won in battles they dedicated gifts
for the maintenance of the house of the LORD. 28 Also all that [x]Samuel the seer and Saul
the son of Kish and Abner the son of Ner and Joab the son of Zeruiah had dedicated—all
dedicated gifts were in the care of [v]Shelomoth[4] and his brothers.

29 Of the Izharites, Chenaniah and his sons were appointed to [y]external duties for Israel,
[z]as officers and judges. 30 Of the Hebronites, [a]Hashabiah and his brothers, 1,700 men of
ability, had the oversight of Israel westward of the Jordan for all the work of the LORD
and for the service of the king. 31 Of the Hebronites, [b]Jerijah was chief of the Hebronites
of whatever genealogy or fathers' houses. (In the fortieth year of David's reign search was
made and men of great ability among them were found at [c]Jazer in Gilead.) 32 King David
appointed him and his brothers, 2,700 men of ability, heads of fathers' houses, to have the
oversight of the Reubenites, the Gadites and the half-tribe of the Manassites for everything
pertaining to God and for [d]the affairs of the king.

Military Divisions

27 This is the number of the people of Israel, the heads of fathers' houses, the commanders of thousands and hundreds, and their officers who served the king in all
matters concerning the divisions that came and went, month after month throughout
the year, each division numbering 24,000:

10 [j]ch. 16:38
13 [k]ch. 25:8
15 [l]Neh. 12:25; [2 Chr. 25:24]
16 [j][See ver. 10 above]
18 [n]2 Kgs. 23:11
20 [o]ver. 22, 24, 26; ch. 28:12; Ezra 2:69; Neh. 10:38
21 [p][ch. 29:8]
22 [q][ch. 23:8]
23 [r]ch. 23:12
24 [s]ch. 23:16; [ch. 24:20]
25 [t][ch. 23:17] [u][ch. 24:21] [v][ch. 23:18]
26 [w]2 Sam. 8:11
28 [x]ch. 29:29; See 1 Sam. 9:9 [v][See ver. 25 above]
29 [y]Neh. 11:16 [z]ch. 23:4; See Deut. 16:18
30 [a]ch. 27:17
31 [b]ch. 24:23; [ch. 23:19] [c]ch. 6:81; Num. 21:32; Josh. 21:39
32 [d]2 Chr. 19:11

[1] Septuagint; Hebrew *six Levites* [2] Or *court*; Hebrew *parbar* (meaning unknown); twice in this verse [3] The Hebrew of verse 21 is uncertain [4] Hebrew *Shelomith*

26:12–19 The assignment of duties by lot. The **east** gate (v. 14) was the position of greatest responsibility, requiring six gatekeepers, because it would lead directly to the temple entrance. It was known as "the king's gate" in postexilic times (9:18).

26:20–28 Certain Kohathite families, the Ladanites and Amramites, had duties as treasurers. The two **treasuries** were located near the gates (see 9:26): one for the **house of God** (presumably to store the regular tithes and offerings), and another for the **dedicated gifts**, i.e., the spoils of war (see 18:11) and other special gifts.

26:29–32 See 23:4b. Two other groups of Levites, the **Izharites** and the **Hebronites**, were assigned to serve outside Jerusalem **as officers and judges** among the Israelite tribes both west and east of the Jordan. The Hebronites were appointed **for all the work of the LORD and for the service of the king**. Possibly this signifies responsibilities for religious and civil taxation and administration. These arrangements were made in the last year of David's rule (c. 970 B.C.; 26:31; see 29:27).

27:1–34 The Chronicler concludes this section on David's provision of leader-

2 [e]Jashobeam the son of Zabdiel was in charge of the first division in the first month;
in his division were 24,000. 3 He was a [f]descendant of Perez and was chief of all the commanders. He served for the first month. 4 [g]Dodai the Ahohite[1] was in charge of the division
of the second month; in his division were 24,000. 5 The third commander, for the third
month, was [h]Benaiah, the son of Jehoiada the chief priest; in his division were 24,000.
6 This is the Benaiah [i]who was a mighty man of the thirty and in command of the thirty;
Ammizabad his son was in charge of his division.[2] 7 [j]Asahel the brother of Joab was fourth,
for the fourth month, and his son Zebadiah after him; in his division were 24,000. 8 The
fifth commander, for the fifth month, was [k]Shamhuth the Izrahite; in his division were
24,000. 9 Sixth, for the sixth month, was [l]Ira, the son of Ikkesh the Tekoite; in his division
were 24,000. 10 Seventh, for the seventh month, was [m]Helez the Pelonite, of the sons of
Ephraim; in his division were 24,000. 11 Eighth, for the eighth month, was [n]Sibbecai the
Hushathite, of the Zerahites; in his division were 24,000. 12 Ninth, for the ninth month,
was [o]Abiezer of Anathoth, a Benjaminite; in his division were 24,000. 13 Tenth, for the
tenth month, was [p]Maharai of Netophah, of the Zerahites; in his division were 24,000.
14 Eleventh, for the eleventh month, was [q]Benaiah of Pirathon, of the sons of Ephraim; in
his division were 24,000. 15 Twelfth, for the twelfth month, was [r]Heldai the Netophathite,
of [s]Othniel; in his division were 24,000.

Leaders of Tribes

16 Over the tribes of Israel, for the Reubenites, Eliezer the son of Zichri was chief officer; for the Simeonites, Shephatiah the son of Maacah; 17 for Levi, [t]Hashabiah the son of
Kemuel; for Aaron, [u]Zadok; 18 for Judah, Elihu, one of David's brothers; for Issachar, Omri
the son of Michael; 19 for Zebulun, Ishmaiah the son of Obadiah; for Naphtali, Jeremoth
the son of Azriel; 20 for the Ephraimites, Hoshea the son of Azaziah; for the half-tribe of
Manasseh, Joel the son of Pedaiah; 21 for the half-tribe of Manasseh in Gilead, Iddo the son
of Zechariah; for Benjamin, Jaasiel the son of Abner; 22 for Dan, Azarel the son of Jeroham.
These were the [v]leaders of the tribes of Israel. 23 David did not count those below twenty
years of age, for the [w]LORD had promised to make Israel as many as the stars of heaven.
24 Joab the son of Zeruiah began to count, but [x]did not finish. Yet [y]wrath came upon Israel
for this, and the number was not entered in the chronicles of King David.

25 Over the king's treasuries was [z]Azmaveth the son of Adiel; and over the treasuries
in the country, in the cities, in the villages, and in the towers, was Jonathan the son of
Uzziah; 26 and over those who did the work of the field for tilling the soil was Ezri the son
of Chelub; 27 and over the vineyards was Shimei the Ramathite; and over the produce of
the vineyards for the wine cellars was Zabdi the Shiphmite. 28 Over the olive and [a]sycamore
trees in the Shephelah was Baal-hanan the Gederite; and over the stores of oil was Joash.
29 Over the herds that pastured in [b]Sharon was Shitrai the Sharonite; over the herds in the
valleys was Shaphat the son of Adlai. 30 Over the camels was Obil the Ishmaelite; and over
the donkeys was Jehdeiah the Meronothite. Over the flocks was Jaziz the [c]Hagrite. 31 All
these were stewards of King David's property.

32 Jonathan, David's uncle, was a counselor, being a man of understanding and a scribe.
He and Jehiel the son of Hachmoni attended the king's sons. 33 [d]Ahithophel was the [e]king's

[1] Septuagint; Hebrew *Ahohite and his division and Mikloth the chief officer* [2] Septuagint, Vulgate; Hebrew *was his division*

Chapter 27
2 [e]ch. 11:11; [2 Sam. 23:8]
3 [f]Num. 26:20
4 [g]2 Sam. 23:9; [ch. 11:12]
5 [h]2 Sam. 8:18
6 [i]ch. 11:24, 25; 2 Sam. 23:20-28
7 [j]ch. 11:26; 2 Sam. 23:24
8 [k][ch. 11:27; 2 Sam. 23:25]
9 [l]ch. 11:28
10 [m]ch. 11:27
11 [n]ch. 11:29; 20:4; 2 Sam. 21:18
12 [o]ch. 11:28
13 [p]ch. 11:30
14 [q]ch. 11:31
15 [r][2 Sam. 23:29] [s]ch. 4:13; Judg. 1:13; 3:9
17 [t]ch. 26:30 [u]ch. 24:3
22 [v]ch. 28:1
23 [w]See Gen. 15:5
24 [x][ch. 21:5, 6] [y]ch. 21:7; 2 Sam. 24:12-15
25 [z]ch. 11:33; 2 Sam. 23:31
28 [a]1 Kgs. 10:27; 2 Chr. 1:15; 9:27
29 [b]ch. 5:16
30 [c]See ch. 5:10
33 [d]See 2 Sam. 15:12 [e]See 2 Sam. 15:37

ship for Solomon with details (derived from four lists) of the non-Levitical military and political officials serving the kingdom.

27:1–15 The 12 military commanders are listed among David's "mighty men" (11:11–47) and included among the leaders of Israel who were directly involved in the temple preparations (28:1). The army depicted here is not David's more permanent force (see 2 Sam. 15:18; 23:8–39), but a citizen militia of 12 divisions, each doing a month's duty on rotation. **24,000**. Probably either an ideal number or "24 units" (see note on 1 Chron. 12:23–37).

27:16–22 These **leaders of the tribes** are probably David's appointees. Their actual role in his administration is unknown. This section may indicate that the centralization of power, together with a move away from the old tribal system of eldership during Solomon's reign (1 Kings 4:7–19), had already begun in the latter part of David's reign. The order and enumeration of the tribes differs here from 1 Chronicles 2, counting Aaron as a tribe and omitting Gad and Asher.

27:23–24 Joab's failure to complete the unauthorized census (21:6) stemmed from his recognition that David's presumptuous act ran counter to God's promise of innumerable descendants to Abraham (see Gen. 15:5).

27:25–31 A list of 12 administrators of the royal **property** (v. 31b). David is presented as one blessed with wealth. His estates included storehouses in Jerusalem and the provinces, lands for various crops, and livestock. The incomes from these sources would have met some of the expenses of his bureaucracy.

27:32–34 An additional list of royal counselors (see 18:14–17). This **Jonathan, David's uncle**, is not otherwise known. **Ahithophel** is mentioned frequently in 2 Sam. 15:12–17:23.

counselor, and Hushai the Archite was the king's friend. 34 Ahithophel was succeeded by
Jehoiada the son of [f]Benaiah, and [g]Abiathar. Joab was [h]commander of the king's army.

David's Charge to Israel

28 [i]David assembled at Jerusalem all the officials of Israel, the [j]officials of the tribes,
the officers of the divisions that served the king, the [k]commanders of thousands,
the commanders of hundreds, the [l]stewards of all the property and livestock of the king
and his sons, together with the palace officials, the [m]mighty men and all the seasoned warriors. 2 Then King David rose to his feet and said: "Hear me, my brothers and my people.
[n]I had it in my heart to build a house of rest for the ark of the covenant of the LORD and
for the [o]footstool of our God, and I made preparations for building. 3 But God said to me,
[p]'You may not build a house for my name, for you are a man of war and have shed blood.'
4 Yet the LORD God of Israel [q]chose me from all my father's house to be king over Israel
[r]forever. [s]For he chose Judah as leader, and in the house of Judah my father's [t]house, and
among my father's sons he took pleasure in me to make me king over all Israel. 5 And of
[u]all my sons (for the LORD has given me many sons) he [v]has chosen Solomon my son to
sit on the throne of the kingdom of the LORD over Israel. 6 He said to me, 'It is [w]Solomon
your son who shall build my house and my courts, for I have chosen him to be my son,
and I will be his father. 7 I will establish his kingdom [r]forever [x]if he continues strong in
keeping my commandments and my rules, as he is today.' 8 Now therefore in the sight of
all Israel, the assembly of the LORD, and in the hearing of our God, observe and seek out
all the commandments of the LORD your God, that you may possess this good land and
leave it for an inheritance to your children after you forever.

David's Charge to Solomon

9 "And you, Solomon my son, know the God of your father and serve him with a [y]whole
heart and with a willing mind, [z]for the LORD searches all hearts and understands every
plan and thought. [a]If you seek him, he will be found by you, but if you forsake him, he
will cast you off forever. 10 Be careful now, for the LORD has chosen you to build a house
for the sanctuary; [b]be strong and do it."

11 Then David gave Solomon his son the [c]plan of the [d]vestibule of the temple,[1] and of
its houses, its treasuries, its upper rooms, and its inner chambers, and of the room for the
[e]mercy seat; 12 and the plan of all that he had in mind for the courts of the house of the
LORD, all the surrounding chambers, [f]the treasuries of the house of God, and the treasuries
for dedicated gifts; 13 for the [g]divisions of the priests and of the [h]Levites, and all the work
of the service in the house of the LORD; for all the vessels for the service in the house of the
LORD, 14 the weight of gold for all golden vessels for each service, the weight of silver vessels
for each service, 15 the weight of the golden [i]lampstands and their lamps, the weight of
gold for each lampstand and its lamps, the weight of silver for a lampstand and its lamps,
according to the use of each lampstand in the service, 16 the weight of gold for each table
for the showbread, the silver for the silver tables, 17 and pure gold for the forks, the basins
and the cups; for the golden bowls and the weight of each; for the silver bowls and the

[1] Hebrew lacks *of the temple*

34 [f][ver. 5] [g]1 Kgs. 1:7; [ch. 24:6] [h][ch. 11:6]

Chapter 28

1 [i]ch. 23:2 [j]See ch. 27:16-22 [k]See ch. 27:1-15 [l]See ch. 27:25-31 [m]See ch. 11:10-47
2 [n]See ch. 22:7 [o]Ps. 99:5; 132:7; Isa. 66:1; Lam. 2:1; [Ps. 110:1]
3 [p]See 2 Sam. 7:5, 13
4 [q]1 Sam. 16:12, 13 [r]ch. 17:23, 27 [s]ch. 5:2; Gen. 49:8; Ps. 78:68 [t]1 Sam. 16:1
5 [u]See ch. 3:1-9; 14:3-7 [v]ch. 22:9; 23:1
6 [w]See 2 Sam. 7:13, 14
7 [r][See ver. 4 above] [x][ch. 22:13]
9 [y][1 Kgs. 8:61] [z]See 1 Sam. 16:7 [a]See 2 Chr. 15:2
10 [b]ver. 20; Ezra 10:4; Hag. 2:4
11 [c]ver. 19; See Ex. 25:40 [d]1 Kgs. 6:3; 2 Chr. 3:4 [e]Ex. 25:17
12 [f]See ch. 26:20
13 [g]ch. 24:1 [h]ch. 23:6
15 [i]See Ex. 25:31-37

28:1–21 This section resumes in a public setting the charge and exhortation given in private by David in ch. 22. The audience (28:1) consists of the military and tribal leaders and the royal overseers listed in ch. 27, along with David's leading soldiers (see 11:10–12:40).

28:2–3 David explains that his failure to build a temple was due to Yahweh's disqualification of him from that task on account of his preoccupation in warfare (v. 3; see 22:8–9). David's description of the temple as a **house of rest for the ark of the covenant . . . for the footstool of our God** (see Ps. 132:7, 8, 14) indicates that the temple will signify not only the land at rest (and thus a fitting project for the "man of rest"; 1 Chron. 22:9), but also God's own rest among his people, and thus the completion of his work (cf. Gen. 2:1–3).

28:4–5 The project of temple building is a matter of God's choice, not David's. After David, **Solomon** is the only king in the OT said to be **chosen** by God (another factor that unifies the reign of these two kings in the Chronicler's presentation). Solomon is chosen to sit on Yahweh's **throne** (v. 5), to be his adopted son (v. 6), and to build God's temple (v. 10).

28:6 Solomon . . . shall build my house. Cf. 17:11–14; 22:9–10.

28:7, 9 The establishment of Solomon's kingdom is dependent on his obedience to Yahweh's commands. Solomon will prove obedient in the task of temple building, but will fail to serve God **with a whole heart** throughout his reign (see 1 Kings 11:4).

28:11–19 David passes on to Solomon the temple **plan** that he received as a revelation from God (v. 19), just as Moses received the plan ("pattern," Ex. 25:9, 40) for the tabernacle from God. The gold and silver temple **vessels** (1 Chron. 28:14–17), which Solomon's craftsmen fashioned (2 Chron. 4:6–22), were removed by the Babylonians at the fall of Jerusalem (2 Chron. 36:18) then returned by the Persians at the restoration after the exile (Ezra 1:7–11). They signified the continuity of the Chronicler's generation with the preexilic temple worship, and God's covenant faithfulness to his people.

18 [j]See Ex. 30:1 [k]See Ex. 25:18-22; 1 Kgs. 6:23-28
19 [l]ver. 11, 12; Ex. 25:40
20 [m]See ch. 22:13; Josh. 1:5
21 [n]ver. 13; See ch. 24-26 [o][Ex. 35:25, 26; 36:1, 2]
Chapter 29
1 [p]ch. 22:5; [1 Kgs. 3:7] [q]ver. 19
2 [r][Isa. 54:11, 12; Rev. 21:19-21]
4 [s][ch. 22:14] [t]See 1 Kgs. 9:28
6 [u]ch. 27:1; 28:1 [v]See ch. 27:25-31
7 [w]Ezra 2:69; 8:27; Neh. 7:70-72
8 [x]ch. 23:8; [ch. 26:21]
9 [y][2 Kgs. 12:4; 2 Cor. 9:7]
10 [z]Luke 1:68
11 [a][1 Tim. 1:17; Rev. 5:13]

weight of each; 18 for the [j]altar of incense made of refined gold, and its weight; also his
plan for the golden chariot of the [k]cherubim that spread their wings and covered the ark
of the covenant of the LORD. 19 "All this he made clear to me in writing from the hand of
the LORD, [l]all the work to be done according to the plan."
20 Then David said to Solomon his son, [m]"Be strong and courageous and do it. Do not
be afraid and do not be dismayed, for the LORD God, even my God, is with you. He will
not leave you or forsake you, until all the work for the service of the house of the LORD is
finished. 21 And behold the [n]divisions of the priests and the Levites for all the service of the
house of God; and with you in all the work will be [o]every willing man who has skill for
any kind of service; also the officers and all the people will be wholly at your command."

Offerings for the Temple

29 And David the king said to all the assembly, "Solomon my son, whom alone God has
chosen, is [p]young and inexperienced, and the work is great, for [q]the palace will not
be for man but for the LORD God. 2 So I have provided for the house of my God, so far as I
was able, the gold for the things of gold, the silver for the things of silver, and the bronze
for the things of bronze, the iron for the things of iron, and wood for the things of wood,
besides great quantities of [r]onyx and stones for setting, antimony, colored stones, all sorts
of precious stones and marble. 3 Moreover, in addition to all that I have provided for the
holy house, I have a treasure of my own of gold and silver, and because of my devotion to
the house of my God I give it to the house of my God: 4 [s]3,000 talents[1] of gold, of the gold
of [t]Ophir, and 7,000 talents of refined silver, for overlaying the walls of the house,[2] 5 and for
all the work to be done by craftsmen, gold for the things of gold and silver for the things
of silver. Who then will offer willingly, consecrating himself[3] today to the LORD?"
6 Then [u]the leaders of fathers' houses made their freewill offerings, as did also the leaders of the tribes, the commanders of thousands and of hundreds, and [v]the officers over
the king's work. 7 They gave for the service of the house of God 5,000 talents and 10,000
[w]darics[4] of gold, 10,000 talents of silver, 18,000 talents of bronze and 100,000 talents of
iron. 8 And whoever had precious stones gave them to the treasury of the house of the
LORD, in the care of [x]Jehiel the Gershonite. 9 Then the people rejoiced because they had
given willingly, for with a [y]whole heart they had offered freely to the LORD. David the
king also rejoiced greatly.

David Prays in the Assembly

10 Therefore David blessed the LORD in the presence of all the assembly. And David said:
[z]"Blessed are you, O LORD, the God of Israel our father, forever and ever. 11 [a]Yours, O LORD,
is the greatness and the power and the glory and the victory and the majesty, for all that is

[1] A *talent* was about 75 pounds or 34 kilograms [2] Septuagint; Hebrew *houses* [3] Or *ordaining himself*; Hebrew *filling his hand* [4] A *daric* was a coin weighing about 1/4 ounce or 8.5 grams

28:19 in writing from the hand of the LORD. One interpretation is that David is claiming prophetic inspiration for his writing of the temple plans he has just described (cf. 2 Chron. 29:25, where "from the LORD" is lit., "by the hand of the LORD"), and thus divine authorization for the plans. It is possible, however, that David is making a stronger claim, namely, that the temple plans were given to him in written form by God (cf. Ex. 24:12; 31:18; 32:16).

28:20–21 David commissions Solomon in public, just as he had previously done in private (22:11–13).

29:1–9 David exhorts all of the assembly to support Solomon in his task by contributing to the temple fund, just as he has himself given generously from his own personal property. The temple is designated a **palace**, indicating that it is God's kingly residence among his people. The freewill offerings of the people that David calls for signify that they are **consecrating** themselves to Yahweh (cf. v. 5, ESV footnote: it is the same expression used of the ordination of priests; Ex. 28:41). The people's response calls to mind the gifts made by the Israelites for the tabernacle in Moses' day (Ex. 35:20–29). The writer stresses their wholehearted and joyful devotion to the task.

29:7 darics. The daric was a Persian coin first minted under Darius I (522–486 B.C.). The Chronicler uses this contemporary loanword to convey to his readers the value of what was given, and to indicate a sense of the leaders' generosity. The example of the people in David's day was intended to speak to the Chronicler's own generation, encouraging them in their commitment to the upkeep of the temple, its services, and its personnel. See also 2 Chron. 31:4–10.

29:10–19 David's great prayer of praise and supplication marks the climax of his reign. Israel's king praises God for his universal **kingdom** and recognizes him as the source of all wealth and **strength** (vv. 10–13). Indeed, even the generosity of David and the people in providing for the temple comes from God himself (vv. 14, 16). They depend entirely on God for their security and well-being, and even in the Promised Land they are **strangers** and **sojourners** before God (v. 15). David then reflects that God examines the human heart for **uprightness** or integrity (v. 17), a further indication that the Chronicler cares above all for the inner reality of faith. David concludes by praying that God will keep the people in the same purpose and mind as they have shown this day, and will give to Solomon a **whole heart** in obedience to God's commandments (vv. 18–19).

29:22b they made Solomon the son of David king the second time. Solomon had been rather hurriedly anointed and installed as king in response to Adonijah's attempted coup (1 Kings 1:28–40, not mentioned in Chronicles). This second ceremony occurred when his succession was secure and widely acknowledged (1 Chron. 29:24). David himself had been anointed king on

in the heavens and in the earth is yours. Yours is the kingdom, O LORD, and you are exalted
as head above all. 12 [b]Both riches and honor come from you, and you rule over all. [c]In your
hand are power and might, and in your hand it is to make great and to give strength to
all. 13 And now we thank you, our God, and praise your glorious name.
14 "But who am I, and what is my people, that we should be able thus to offer willingly?
For all things come from you, and of your own have we given you. 15 [d]For we are strangers
before you and sojourners, as all our fathers were. Our days on the earth are [e]like a shadow,
and there is no abiding.[1] 16 O LORD our God, all this abundance that we have provided for
building you a house for your holy name comes from your hand and is all your own. 17 I
know, my God, [f]that you test the heart and [g]have pleasure in uprightness. In the uprightness of my heart I have freely offered all these things, and now I have seen your people,
who are present here, offering freely and joyously to you. 18 O LORD, the God of Abraham,
Isaac, and Israel, our fathers, keep forever such purposes and thoughts in the hearts of your
people, and direct their hearts toward you. 19 [h]Grant to Solomon my son a whole heart that
he may keep your commandments, your testimonies, and your statutes, performing all,
and that he may [i]build the palace [j]for which I have made provision."
20 Then David said to all the assembly, [k]"Bless the LORD your God." And all the assembly
blessed the LORD, the God of their fathers, [l]and bowed their heads and paid homage to
the LORD and to the king. 21 And they offered sacrifices to the LORD, and on the next day
offered burnt offerings to the LORD, 1,000 bulls, 1,000 rams, and 1,000 lambs, with their
[m]drink offerings, and sacrifices in abundance for all Israel. 22 And they ate and drank before
the LORD on that day with great gladness.

Solomon Anointed King

And they made Solomon the son of David king [n]the second time, and they [o]anointed
him as prince for the LORD, and [p]Zadok as priest.
23 [q]Then Solomon sat on the [r]throne of the LORD as king in place of David his father. And
he prospered, and all Israel obeyed him. 24 All the leaders and the mighty men, and also all
the sons of King David, pledged their allegiance to King Solomon. 25 And the LORD made
Solomon very [s]great in the sight of all Israel and [t]bestowed on him such royal majesty as
had not been on any king before him in Israel.

The Death of David

26 Thus David the son of Jesse reigned over all Israel. 27 The [u]time that he reigned over
Israel was forty years. He reigned seven years in Hebron and thirty-three years in Jerusalem.
28 Then he died [v]at a good age, [w]full of days, riches, and honor. And Solomon his son reigned
in his place. 29 Now the acts of King David, from first to last, are written in the Chronicles
[x]of Samuel the seer, and in the Chronicles of [y]Nathan the prophet, and in the Chronicles of
[z]Gad the seer, 30 with accounts of all his rule and his might and of the circumstances [a]that
came upon him and upon Israel and upon all the kingdoms of the countries.

[1] Septuagint, Vulgate; Hebrew *hope*, or *prospect*

12 [b][1 Kgs. 3:13; 2 Chr. 1:12; Rom. 11:36] [c]2 Chr. 20:6
15 [d]See Lev. 25:23 [e]Job 14:2; Ps. 102:11; 144:4
17 [f]ch. 28:9; Prov. 17:3; [1 Sam. 16:7] [g][Prov. 11:20]
19 [h][Ps. 72:1] [i]ver. 1, 2 [j]ch. 22:14
20 [k]See Josh. 22:33 [l]See Ex. 4:31
21 [m]Gen. 35:14
22 [n][ch. 23:1] [o]See 1 Kgs. 1:38, 39 [p]1 Kgs. 2:35
23 [q]1 Kgs. 2:12 [r]ch. 28:5; [2 Chr. 9:8]
25 [s]2 Chr. 1:1; [Josh. 3:7] [t]1 Kgs. 3:13; 2 Chr. 1:12; [Eccles. 2:9]
27 [u]2 Sam. 5:4, 5; 1 Kgs. 2:11
28 [v][Gen. 15:15; 25:8] [w]ch. 23:1
29 [x]ch. 26:28; [1 Sam. 9:9] [y]See 2 Sam. 12:1 [z]See 1 Sam. 22:5
30 [a][Dan. 4:23, 25]

three occasions: privately before his family (1 Sam. 16:13), and twice in Hebron (2 Sam. 2:4; 5:3).

29:23 The Lord has done for **Solomon** what he had earlier done for **David** (14:2), in accordance with his promise to David (1 Kings 2:24).

29:26–30 See 1 Kings 2:10–11. The various **Chronicles** mentioned in 1 Chron. 29:29 probably contained much of the material that is included in the books of Samuel and Kings, but may have included additional records as well (see note on 1 Kings 14:19). **Samuel**, **Nathan**, and **Gad** all played roles in the life of David (see 1 Chron. 9:22; 17:1–15; 21:9–13). **The kingdoms of the countries** most likely refers to the surrounding nations that David had subjugated.

INTRODUCTION TO

2 CHRONICLES

See Introduction to 1–2 Chronicles, pp. 697–704.

For an outline for 2 Chronicles, see Outline for 1–2 Chronicles, p. 704.

The beginning of what is today called 2 Chronicles comes midway in the second major section of Chronicles, on the united kingdom of David and Solomon (1 Chronicles 10–2 Chronicles 9). The Solomonic narrative (2 Chronicles 1–9) marks the successful completion of what David began (1 Chronicles 10–29). God declares the meaning of the temple as the place of repentance and restoration, and as the charter for the future of the kingdom (2 Chron. 7:11–22). The third major section (chs. 10–36) recounts the history of the kingdom from its division until the fall of Judah and the exile, ending in the invitation for the exiles to return to Judea and rebuild (36:22–23).

The Chronicler's account of Solomon's reign is basically a continuation of his narrative about David, as both father and son rule over all the land and all the people; what David begins, Solomon completes. After David, Solomon's reign (chs. 1–9) is given the most extensive treatment in Chronicles, yet there is less interest in the king himself than in the abiding achievement of his reign: the successful construction of the temple and the inauguration of its regular services. Solomon's obedience here marks the fulfillment of the Davidic covenant. The Chronicler omits many of the personal details of Solomon's life found in 1 Kings 1–11, both negative and positive, to concentrate on this theme.

2 CHRONICLES

Solomon Worships at Gibeon

1 [a]Solomon the son of David established himself in his kingdom, [b]and the LORD his
God was with him and made him exceedingly great.
2 Solomon spoke to all Israel, to the [c]commanders of thousands and of hundreds, to
the judges, and to all the leaders in all Israel, the heads of fathers' houses. **3** And Solomon,
and all the assembly with him, went to [d]the high place that was at Gibeon, [e]for [f]the tent
of meeting of God, which Moses the servant of the LORD had made in the wilderness,
was there. **4** [g](But David had brought up the ark of God from Kiriath-jearim to the place
that David had prepared for it, for he had pitched a tent for it in Jerusalem.) **5** Moreover,
[h]the bronze altar that [i]Bezalel the son of Uri, son of Hur, had made, was there before the
tabernacle of the LORD. And Solomon and the assembly [j]sought it[1] out. **6** And Solomon
went up there to the bronze altar before the LORD, which was at the tent of meeting, [k]and
offered a thousand burnt offerings on it.

Solomon Prays for Wisdom

7 [l]In that night God appeared to Solomon, and said to him, "Ask what I shall give you."
8 And Solomon said to God, "You have shown great and steadfast love to David my father,
[m]and have made me king in his place. **9** O LORD God, [n]let your word to David my father be
now fulfilled, for you have made me king over a people as numerous [o]as the dust of the
earth. **10** Give me now wisdom and knowledge to [p]go out and come in before this people,
for who can govern this people of yours, which is so great?" **11** God answered Solomon,
"Because this was in your heart, and you have not asked for [q]possessions, wealth, honor,
or the life of those who hate you, and have not even asked for long life, but have asked for
wisdom and knowledge for yourself that you may govern my people over whom I have
made you king, **12** wisdom and knowledge are granted to you. I will also give you [q]riches,
possessions, and honor, [r]such as none of the kings had who were before you, and none
after you shall have the like." **13** So Solomon came from[2] the [s]high place at Gibeon, from
before [t]the tent of meeting, to Jerusalem. And he reigned over Israel.

Solomon Given Wealth

14 [u]Solomon gathered together chariots and horsemen. [v]He had 1,400 chariots and 12,000
horsemen, whom he stationed [w]in the chariot cities and with the king in Jerusalem. **15** And
the king made silver and gold as common in Jerusalem as stone, and he made cedar as plen-

[1] Or *him* [2] Septuagint, Vulgate; Hebrew *to*

Chapter 1
1 [a]1 Kgs. 2:46 [b]1 Chr. 29:25
2 [c]1 Chr. 27:1
3 [d]See 1 Kgs. 3:4 [e]1 Chr. 16:39; 21:29 [f]Ex. 29:10; Lev. 10:7; Num. 14:10
4 [g]See 2 Sam. 6:2-17; 1 Chr. 15:25–16:1
5 [h]Ex. 27:1, 2; 38:1, 2 [i]Ex. 31:2 [j][1 Chr. 13:3]
6 [k]1 Kgs. 3:4
7 [l]For ver. 7-12, see 1 Kgs. 3:5-14
8 [m]1 Chr. 28:5
9 [n]ch. 6:17; 1 Kgs. 8:26 [o]Gen. 13:16
10 [p][Num. 27:17; Deut. 31:2]
11 [q]Eccles. 5:19; 6:2
12 [q][See ver. 11 above] [r]ch. 9:22; [1 Chr. 29:25]
13 [s]See 1 Kgs. 3:4 [t]ver. 3
14 [u]For ver. 14-17, see ch. 9:25-28; 1 Kgs. 10:26-29 [v][1 Kgs. 4:26] [w][1 Kgs. 9:19]

1:1–2:18 *Solomon's Temple Preparations.* God provides Solomon with the wealth, material, and workers to build the temple.

1:1–6 Solomon's journey to the Mosaic tabernacle and altar at **Gibeon**, like David's mission to retrieve the ark (1 Chron. 13:1–16:43), is presented as a public enterprise that involves **all Israel** (cf. 1 Kings 2:4). Like David, Solomon maintains continuity with the Mosaic covenant as the foundation of his own reign. **Sought it out** (cf. ESV footnote, "him," i.e., Yahweh) continues the parallel with David (see 1 Chron. 13:3). Solomon begins his reign as David instructed him (1 Chron. 22:19), by worshiping God and seeking guidance. **Bezalel** is the master craftsman of the tabernacle, assisted by Oholiab (see Ex. 31:1–11). See note on 2 Chron. 2:11–16.

1:7–13 Solomon's faithful seeking leads to a nighttime appearance of God (in a dream, according to 1 Kings 3:5), in which God invites Solomon to **ask** in prayer for whatever he desires (cf. John 15:7). Solomon's request that God will fulfill his promise to David (see 1 Chron. 17:23) looks forward to the completion of the temple (2 Chron. 6:17), while his request for **wisdom and knowledge** is focused not on selfish ambition but on the need to **govern** God's **people** wisely (see note on 1 Kings 3:11–14). God grants Solomon's request and also promises him **riches, possessions, and honor** that he did not request. This theme is taken up again at the end of the Solomon narrative (2 Chron. 8:1–9:28). **numerous as the dust of the earth.** God's covenant promise to Abraham (Gen. 13:16) was being fulfilled in Solomon's day.

1:14–17 From 1 Kings 10:27–29, and repeated with some modifications at 2 Chron. 9:25–28. This section demonstrates the fulfillment of God's promise of wealth (1:12; see note on 1 Kings 10:26–29).

tiful as the sycamore of the Shephelah. **16** And Solomon's import of horses was from Egypt
and Kue, and the king's traders would buy them from Kue for a price. **17** They imported a
chariot from Egypt for 600 shekels[1] of silver, and a horse for 150. Likewise through them
these were exported to all the kings of the Hittites and the kings of Syria.

Preparing to Build the Temple

2 [2] [x]Now Solomon purposed to build a temple for the name of the LORD, and a royal
palace for himself. **2** [3] [y]And Solomon assigned 70,000 men to bear burdens and 80,000
to quarry in the hill country, and [z]3,600 to oversee them. **3** [a]And Solomon sent word to
Hiram the king of Tyre: [b]"As you dealt with David my father and sent him cedar to build
himself a house to dwell in, so deal with me. **4** Behold, I am about to build a house for the
name of the LORD my God and dedicate it to him for the burning of [c]incense of sweet
spices before him, and for [d]the regular arrangement of the showbread, and for [e]burnt
offerings morning and evening, [f]on the Sabbaths and the new moons and the appointed
feasts of the LORD our God, as ordained forever for Israel. **5** The house that I am to build
will be great, [g]for our God is greater than all gods. **6** [h]But who is able to build him a house,
since [h]heaven, even highest heaven, cannot contain him? Who am I to build a house for
him, except as a place to make offerings before him? **7** So now [i]send me a man skilled to
work in gold, silver, bronze, and iron, and in purple, crimson, and blue fabrics, trained
also in engraving, to be with the skilled workers who are with me in Judah and Jerusalem,
[j]whom David my father provided. **8** Send me also cedar, cypress, and algum timber from
Lebanon, for I know that [k]your servants know how to cut timber in Lebanon. And my
servants will be with your servants, **9** to prepare timber for me in abundance, for the house
I am to build will be great and wonderful. **10** [l]I will give for your servants, the woodsmen
who cut timber, 20,000 cors[4] of crushed wheat, 20,000 cors of barley, 20,000 baths[5] of
wine, and 20,000 baths of oil."

11 Then Hiram the king of Tyre answered in a letter that he sent to Solomon, [m]"Because
the LORD loves his people, he has made you king over them." **12** Hiram also said, "Blessed
be the LORD God of Israel, [n]who made heaven and earth, who has given King David a wise
son, who has discretion and understanding, [o]who will build a temple for the LORD and
a royal palace for himself.

13 "Now I have sent a skilled man, who has understanding, Huram-abi, **14** [p]the son of a
woman of the daughters of Dan, and his father was a man of Tyre. He is [q]trained to work
in gold, silver, bronze, iron, stone, and wood, and in purple, blue, and crimson fabrics and
fine linen, and to do all sorts of engraving and execute any design that may be assigned
him, with your craftsmen, the craftsmen of my lord, David your father. **15** Now therefore
the wheat and barley, oil and wine, [r]of which my lord has spoken, let him send to his
servants. **16** [s]And we will cut whatever timber you need from Lebanon and bring it to you
in rafts by sea to [t]Joppa, so that you may take it up to Jerusalem."

[1] A *shekel* was about 2/5 ounce or 11 grams [2] Ch 1:18 in Hebrew [3] Ch 2:1 in Hebrew [4] A *cor* was about 6 bushels or 220 liters [5] A *bath* was about 6 gallons or 22 liters

Chapter 2
1 [x]1 Kgs. 5:5
2 [y]ver. 18; 1 Kgs. 5:15, 16; [ch. 8:7, 8; 1 Kgs. 9:20, 21] [z][1 Kgs. 5:16]
3 [a]For ver. 3-16, see 1 Kgs. 5:2-11 [b]1 Chr. 14:1
4 [c]See Ex. 30:7 [d]See Lev. 24:5-8 [e]See Num. 28:3-8 [f]ch. 8:13; Num. 28:9, 11, 19, 26
5 [g]Ps. 135:5; [Ex. 15:11; 1 Chr. 16:25; Ps. 86:8]
6 [h]ch. 6:18; 1 Kgs. 8:27; Isa. 66:1; Acts 7:49
7 [i]ver. 13, 14 [j]1 Chr. 22:15
8 [k]ch. 9:10, 11
10 [l][1 Kgs. 5:11]
11 [m]ch. 9:8; 1 Kgs. 10:9
12 [n]See Gen. 1:1 [o][ver. 1]
14 [p]1 Kgs. 7:14 [q][ver. 7]
15 [r]ver. 10
16 [s][1 Kgs. 5:9] [t]See Josh. 19:46

2:1 a temple for the name of the LORD. See Deut. 12:5. God's "name" in association with a place signifies his actual presence there among his people, where God may be met and petitioned. Yet in no sense is God contained or limited by his localized presence: see 2 Chron. 2:6. The Chronicler's temple theology embraces both the actual or real presence of God and his majestic transcendence. It is a forerunner to the doctrine of the incarnation of God in Christ (see John 2:21). **royal palace.** Linked here with the temple, perhaps to indicate the close connection between the two "houses" of the Davidic covenant (see 1 Chron. 17:14). While the Chronicler mentions Solomon's palace a number of times (2 Chron. 2:12; 7:11; 8:1; 9:3–4, 11), he passes over the account of its construction (1 Kings 7:1–12).

2:2 Solomon used the forced labor of Canaanites living in the land (see vv. 17–18; cf. notes on 8:7–10; 1 Chron. 22:2–5) for the construction work. Subject peoples were often conscripted to such work in the ancient world.

2:3–10 Solomon's letter to **Hiram, king of Tyre** (who had earlier assisted David; 1 Chron. 14:1), is considerably expanded from 1 Kings 5:3–6 to describe the purpose of the temple for regular and seasonal worship according to the Law of Moses, to express the supremacy and transcendence of Israel's God (2 Chron. 2:5–6), and to request a skilled craftsman (v. 7), along with different kinds of timber (v. 8). The Hebrew for **skilled** (*khakam*) also means "wise." Its use here consciously echoes Solomon's request for wisdom (1:10) and the wisdom and knowledge Solomon needs for building the temple (2:5–6). The skills called for here recall Oholiab's work on the tabernacle, under the direction of Bezalel (Ex. 31:1–11).

2:6 heaven, even highest heaven, cannot contain him. See note on 1 Kings 8:27–30.

2:11–16 Hiram's letter of reply includes a Gentile's acknowledgment of Yahweh as Creator, and of God's gift of wisdom to Solomon (v. 12), which is especially focused on the task of temple building (cf. note on 1 Kings 5:9–12). **Huram-abi** is likened to Oholiab (the mothers of both men are said to be descended from **Dan**; see Ex. 31:6; cf. note on 1 Kings 7:13–14), while Solomon the temple builder is implicitly compared to Bezalel, who directed the building of the tabernacle (see 2 Chron. 1:5). The reference in 2:16 to **Joppa** (not mentioned in 1 Kings 5:9) may reflect Ezra 3:7. Timber from Lebanon for the second temple was floated to that port.

17 Then Solomon counted all the resident aliens who were in the land of Israel, [u]after the census of them that David his father had taken, and there were found 153,600. 18 [v]Seventy thousand of them he assigned to bear burdens, 80,000 to quarry in the hill country, and 3,600 as overseers to make the people work.

Solomon Builds the Temple

3 [w]Then Solomon began to build the house of the LORD in Jerusalem [x]on Mount Moriah, where the LORD[1] had appeared to David his father, at the place that David had appointed, [y]on the threshing floor of Ornan the Jebusite. 2 He began to build in the second month of the fourth year of his reign. 3 These are Solomon's [z]measurements[2] for building the house of God: [a]the length, in cubits[3] of the old standard, was sixty cubits, and the breadth twenty cubits. 4 The vestibule in front of the nave of the house was twenty cubits long, equal to the width of the house,[4] and its height was 120 cubits. He overlaid it on the inside with pure gold. 5 [b]The nave he lined with cypress and covered it with fine gold [c]and made palms and chains on it. 6 He adorned the house with settings of precious stones. The gold was gold of Parvaim. 7 So he lined the house with gold—its beams, its thresholds, its walls, and its doors—[c]and he carved cherubim on the walls.

8 [d]And he made the Most Holy Place. Its length, corresponding to the breadth of the house, was twenty cubits, and its breadth was twenty cubits. He overlaid it with 600 talents[5] of fine gold. 9 The weight of gold for the nails was fifty shekels.[6] And he overlaid [e]the upper chambers with gold.

10 [f]In the Most Holy Place he made two cherubim of wood[7] and overlaid[8] them with gold. 11 The wings of the cherubim together extended twenty cubits: one wing of the one, of five cubits, touched the wall of the house, and its other wing, of five cubits, touched the wing of the other cherub; 12 and of this cherub, one wing, of five cubits, touched the wall of the house, and the other wing, also of five cubits, was joined to the wing of the first cherub. 13 The wings of these cherubim extended twenty cubits. The cherubim[9] stood on their feet, [g]facing the nave. 14 [h]And he made the veil of blue and purple and crimson fabrics and fine linen, and he worked cherubim on it.

15 [i]In front of the house he made two pillars thirty-five cubits high, with a capital of five cubits on the top of each. 16 He made chains like a necklace[10] and put them on the tops of the pillars, and he made a hundred pomegranates and put them on the chains. 17 [j]He set up the pillars in front of the temple, one on the south, the other on the north; that on the south he called Jachin, and that on the north Boaz.

[1] Septuagint; Hebrew lacks *the LORD* [2] Syriac; Hebrew *foundations* [3] A *cubit* was about 18 inches or 45 centimeters [4] Compare 1 Kings 6:3; the meaning of the Hebrew is uncertain [5] A *talent* was about 75 pounds or 34 kilograms [6] A *shekel* was about 2/5 ounce or 11 grams [7] Septuagint; the meaning of the Hebrew is uncertain [8] Hebrew *they overlaid* [9] Hebrew *they* [10] Hebrew *chains in the inner sanctuary*

17 [u][1 Chr. 22:2]
18 [v]See ver. 2

Chapter 3

1 [w]For ver. 1, 2, see 1 Kgs. 6:1 [x]Gen. 22:2, 14 [y][1 Chr. 21:15, 18, 28]
3 [z][Ezra 3:11] [a]For ver. 3, 4, see 1 Kgs. 6:2, 3
5 [b]1 Kgs. 6:17 [c]1 Kgs. 6:29, 32
7 [c][See ver. 5 above]
8 [d][1 Kgs. 6:16]
9 [e]1 Chr. 28:11
10 [f]For ver. 10-13, see 1 Kgs. 6:23-28
13 [g][Ezek. 40:9]
14 [h]See Ex. 26:31
15 [i]For ver. 15, 16, see 1 Kgs. 7:15-20; [1 Kgs. 7:15; 2 Kgs. 25:17; Jer. 52:21]
17 [j]1 Kgs. 7:21

3:1–5:1 *Solomon's Building of the Temple.* The temple is to be a fit place for God to dwell among his people.

3:1–17 The Chronicler's actual account of the construction of the temple is much briefer than his source (1 Kings 6). The architectural details of 1 Kings 6:4–20a are passed over, as are the descriptions of the intricate carvings or stonework in 1 Kings 6:29–36. Instead, the Chronicler leads his readers in their imagination through the vestibule (2 Chron. 3:4) into the ornate nave or Holy Place (vv. 5–7), then on to the Most Holy Place (vv. 8–13), partitioned off by the veil (v. 14). The numerous references to gold (vv. 4–10) and cherubim (vv. 7, 10–14) highlight the splendor of the temple as the heavenly King's earthly palace. As its structure and furnishings indicate, it stood in continuity with the Mosaic tabernacle, at the same time exceeding it in beauty and opulence. The temple measured about 90 feet by 30 feet (27 m by 9.1 m; v. 3), so it was not particularly large compared to many modern church buildings, and it did not function as a place of congregational worship. Only priests would have been admitted to the temple itself, and only the high priest could enter the Most Holy Place, and only on the Day of Atonement.

3:1 Mount Zion is identified here with **Mount Moriah**, where Abraham was commanded to offer Isaac (Gen. 22:2).

3:2 See 1 Kings 6:1. Depending on which chronology is followed, this may have been in either 966 or 959 B.C.

3:4 120 cubits. The Septuagint and other ancient versions of the OT suggest that the **vestibule** was actually 20 cubits (30 feet/9.1 m) high. The Hebrew text lacks the word "cubits," so precise identification of the height is uncertain.

3:6 Parvaim. Possibly a place in northeastern Arabia.

3:8–13 The **Most Holy Place** was the secret, cube-shaped room in which the ark of the covenant would be finally deposited (5:7). The **cherubim** were angelic beings that combined human and animal features (cf. Ezek. 10:14; 41:18–19) and served as throne-guards to the ark. On the construction of the temple, see note on 1 Kings 6:14–35.

3:14 The Most Holy Place was separated from the rest of the sanctuary by a **veil** as well as by doors (4:22). The inclusion of the veil signified the continuity of the temple with the Mosaic tabernacle (Ex. 26:31–35). Herod's temple was similarly arranged (Matt. 27:51); the tearing of the veil at the death of Christ indicated that the "shadow" of the Mosaic institutions had now given way to the final sacrifice of Christ, with all its benefits (see Heb. 9:11–12; 10:1).

3:15–17 thirty-five cubits high. Probably the combined heights of the pillars (see note on 1 Kings 7:15–21; cf. 1 Kings 7:15; 2 Kings 25:17). **Jachin**

Chapter 4
1[k]ch. 7:7; 8:12; [ch. 15:8; 1 Kgs. 8:64; 2 Kgs. 16:14]; See Ezek. 43:13-17
2[l]For ver. 2-5, see 1 Kgs. 7:23-26
5[m][1 Kgs. 7:26]
6[n]1 Kgs. 7:38, 39
7[o]ver. 20; 1 Kgs. 7:49; See Ex. 25:31-39; 27:20, 21
8[p]ver. 19; [1 Kgs. 7:48]
9[q]1 Kgs. 6:36 [r][ch. 6:13; 2 Kgs. 21:5]
10[s]1 Kgs. 7:39
11[t]For ch. 4:11–5:1, see 1 Kgs. 7:40-51 [u][1 Kgs. 7:13, 14]
12[v]1 Kgs. 7:41
13[w][1 Kgs. 7:20]
14[n][See ver. 6 above]
16[x]1 Chr. 28:17 [t][See ver. 11 above] [y]ch. 2:13; [1 Kgs. 7:14]
18[z]1 Kgs. 7:47
19[a]ver. 8
20[b]ver. 7

The Temple's Furnishings

4 He made [k]an altar of bronze, twenty cubits[1] long and twenty cubits wide and ten cubits high. 2 [l]Then he made the sea of cast metal. It was round, ten cubits from brim to brim, and five cubits high, and a line of thirty cubits measured its circumference. 3 Under it were figures of gourds,[2] for ten cubits, compassing the sea all around. The gourds were in two rows, cast with it when it was cast. 4 It stood on twelve oxen, three facing north, three facing west, three facing south, and three facing east. The sea was set on them, and all their rear parts were inward. 5 Its thickness was a handbreadth.[3] And its brim was made like the brim of a cup, like the flower of a lily. [m]It held 3,000 baths.[4] 6 [n]He also made ten basins in which to wash, and set five on the south side, and five on the north side. In these they were to rinse off what was used for the burnt offering, and the sea was for the priests to wash in.

7 And he made ten golden lampstands [o]as prescribed, and set them in the temple, five on the south side and five on the north. 8 [p]He also made ten tables and placed them in the temple, five on the south side and five on the north. And he made a hundred basins of gold. 9 He made [q]the court of the priests [r]and the great court and doors for the court and overlaid their doors with bronze. 10 [s]And he set the sea at the southeast corner of the house.

11 [t, u]Hiram also made the pots, the shovels, and the basins. [u]So Hiram finished the work that he did for King Solomon on the house of God: 12 the two pillars, [v]the bowls, and the two capitals on the top of the pillars; and the two latticeworks to cover the two bowls of the capitals that were on the top of the pillars; 13 [w]and the 400 pomegranates for the two latticeworks, two rows of pomegranates for each latticework, to cover the two bowls of the capitals that were on the pillars. 14 [n]He made the stands also, and the basins on the stands, 15 and the one sea, and the twelve oxen underneath it. 16 The pots, the shovels, [x]the forks, and all the equipment for these [t, y]Huram-abi made of burnished bronze for King Solomon for the house of the LORD. 17 In the plain of the Jordan the king cast them, in the clay ground between Succoth and Zeredah.[5] 18 [z]Solomon made all these things in great quantities, for the weight of the bronze was not sought.

19 So Solomon made all the vessels that were in the house of God: the golden altar, [a]the tables for the bread of the Presence, 20 the lampstands and their lamps of pure gold [b]to burn before the inner sanctuary, as prescribed; 21 the flowers, the lamps, and the tongs, of purest gold; 22 the snuffers, basins, dishes for incense, and fire pans, of pure gold, and the sockets[6] of the temple, for the inner doors to the Most Holy Place and for the doors of the nave of the temple were of gold.

[1] A *cubit* was about 18 inches or 45 centimeters [2] Compare 1 Kings 7:24; Hebrew *oxen*; twice in this verse [3] A *handbreadth* was about 3 inches or 7.5 centimeters [4] A *bath* was about 6 gallons or 22 liters [5] Spelled *Zarethan* in 1 Kings 7:46 [6] Compare 1 Kings 7:50; Hebrew *the entrance of the house*

("he establishes"); **Boaz** ("in him is strength"). The names may signify that Yahweh establishes his covenant through the temple.

4:1–5:1 The temple's furnishings communicated the same message as that signified by the structure of the building: the presence of the holy God in the midst of his people, and his gracious provision of atonement and forgiveness. For the Chronicler's own generation, the fact that these vessels had been returned from their Babylonian captivity (Ezra 1:3–11; 6:5) was a sign as well that they were still God's covenant people and the heirs of his promises to David and Solomon.

4:1 Solomon's **altar** stood outside the temple. Perhaps it stood in front of the temple entrance, just as Moses' altar had stood before the entrance of the tabernacle (Ex. 40:6), though it may have stood in the northeast corner, opposite the bronze sea basin in the southeast corner.

4:2–6 On various details of the temple, cf. notes on 1 Kings 7:23–47. The **sea** was a large, circular water tank, located outside the southeast corner of the temple (2 Chron. 4:10) and used by the priests for their ceremonial cleansing before they entered the temple (v. 6). It corresponded to the bronze basin that had stood between the entrance to the tabernacle and the Mosaic altar (Ex. 30:18–21). **3,000 baths**. First Kings 7:26 reads "two thousand baths." The difference may be due to a copyist's error. The **twelve oxen** probably signified the tribes of Israel, especially as they were encamped around the four sides of the tabernacle in the wilderness (see Num. 2:1–31).

4:2 ten cubits . . . thirty cubits. See note on 1 Kings 7:23.

4:7–8 In contrast to the tabernacle, with its one seven-branched lampstand and table (Ex. 25:31–36), Solomon's temple had **ten** of each (but cf. 1 Kings 7:48, which mentions only one table). The **tables** were apparently for the "bread of the Presence" (2 Chron. 4:19; see 1 Chron. 9:32), a perpetual bread offering to Yahweh, through which Israel consecrated itself to God (Ex. 25:30).

4:9 the court of the priests. A feature that also corresponds to the tabernacle; see Ex. 27:9–19.

4:11b–22 The **bronze** vessels and furnishings were located in the temple entrance and court, while those in the interior (the place of greater holiness) were made of **gold**. The **golden altar** was for the burning of incense (see Ex. 30:1–10; 1 Chron. 28:18). The **Most Holy Place** was separated from the nave (the Holy Place) by **inner doors . . . of gold** as well as the veil (2 Chron. 3:14).

4:19 Solomon made all the vessels. See note on 1 Kings 7:48–51.

5 [c]Thus all the work that Solomon did for the house of the LORD was finished. And
Solomon brought in the things that David his father had dedicated, and stored the
silver, the gold, and all the vessels in the treasuries of the house of God.

The Ark Brought to the Temple

2 Then Solomon assembled the elders of Israel and all the heads of the tribes, the
leaders of the fathers' houses of the people of Israel, in Jerusalem, to bring up the ark
of the covenant of the LORD out of [d]the city of David, which is Zion. 3 And all the men
of Israel assembled before the king at the feast that is in the seventh month. 4 And all
the elders of Israel came, [e]and the Levites took up the ark. 5 And they brought up the
ark, the tent of meeting, and all the holy vessels that were in the tent; [f]the Levitical
priests brought them up. 6 And King Solomon and all the congregation of Israel, who
had assembled before him, were before the ark, sacrificing so many sheep and oxen
that they could not be counted or numbered. 7 Then the priests brought the ark of the
covenant of the LORD to its place, in the inner sanctuary of the house, in the Most Holy
Place, underneath the wings of the cherubim. 8 The cherubim spread out their wings
over the place of the ark, so that the cherubim made a covering above the ark and its
poles. 9 And the poles were so long that the ends of the poles were seen [g]from the Holy
Place before the inner sanctuary, but they could not be seen from outside. And they
are[1] there to this day. 10 There was nothing in the ark except the two tablets [h]that Moses
put there at Horeb, where the LORD made a covenant with the people of Israel, when
they came out of Egypt. 11 And when the priests came out of the Holy Place (for all the
priests who were present had consecrated themselves, without regard to [i]their divisions,
12 and all the Levitical [j]singers, [k]Asaph, [l]Heman, and Jeduthun, their sons and kinsmen,
arrayed in fine linen, with [m]cymbals, harps, and lyres, stood east of the altar with 120
[n]priests who were trumpeters; 13 and it was the duty of the trumpeters and singers to
make themselves heard in unison in praise and thanksgiving to the LORD), and when
the song was raised, [o]with trumpets and cymbals and other musical instruments, in
praise to the LORD,

> [p]"For he is good,
>   for his steadfast love endures forever,"

the house, the house of the LORD, was filled with a cloud, 14 so that the priests could not stand
to minister because of the cloud, [q]for the glory of the LORD filled the house of God.

[1] Hebrew *it is*

Chapter 5
1 [c]For ver. 1-10, see 1 Kgs. 7:51–8:9
2 [d]2 Sam. 6:12
4 [e][ver. 7; 1 Kgs. 8:3]
5 [f]ch. 23:18; 30:27
9 [g][1 Kgs. 8:8]
10 [h]Deut. 10:2, 5; [ch. 6:11]
11 [i]1 Chr. 24:1, 5; [Luke 1:5]
12 [j]See 1 Chr. 25:1-4 [k]See 1 Chr. 6:39 [l]See 1 Chr. 6:33 [m]1 Chr. 15:16; Ps. 150:3-5 [n]ch. 7:6; 1 Chr. 15:24
13 [o]1 Chr. 16:42 [p]See 1 Chr. 16:34
14 [q]ch. 7:2; 1 Kgs. 8:11; [Ex. 40:35; Ezek. 10:3, 4]

5:1 A summary statement, again recalling that the temple was the joint enterprise of **Solomon** and **David** (see 1 Chron. 17:8; 22:2–16).

5:2–7:22 *The Dedication of the Temple.* The Chronicler's account of the dedication of the temple is notably longer than his description of the building work (77 verses compared to 40), since he is more concerned with the meaning of the temple than with its physical structure. This interest is conveyed through the two theophanies (5:14; 7:1–3), Solomon's great prayer of dedication (6:14–42), and God's message to Solomon (7:12–22).

5:2–3 Just as David had summoned all the leaders of Israel to retrieve the **ark** from Kiriath-jearim (1 Chronicles 13; 15), Solomon also assembled them for the ark's final journey from its tent in the **city of David** (see 1 Chron. 16:1). **the feast that is in the seventh month.** The Feast of Booths (see Lev. 23:33–43). The temple was completed in the eighth month of Solomon's eleventh year (see 1 Kings 6:38 = 959 or 952 B.C.), and the dedication took place 11 months later. The Israelites had been instructed to live in temporary shelters during this feast, to commemorate the exodus. It was observed annually in the seventh month of the Jewish calendar (September–October).

5:5 Moses' **tent of meeting** and its **holy vessels** were brought up from Gibeon (1:3) to join the **ark**. Similarly, the **Levitical priests** Asaph, Heman, and Jeduthun (5:12; see 1 Chron. 16:37, 42) were united for this ceremony. Henceforth, all of Israel's worship would be focused on the Jerusalem temple.

5:7–9 The **priests** completed the transfer of the ark, since only they could enter the **Most Holy Place. And they are there to this day.** A comment from an early author, whose work was used by the author of Kings (see note on 1 Kings 8:8) and the Chronicler. The ark was apparently destroyed along with the first temple and was never replaced.

5:10 The ark had once contained the jar of manna and Aaron's rod (Heb. 9:4; see Ex. 16:32–34; Num. 17:10–11), but now held only the **two tablets** inscribed with the Ten Commandments.

5:11–14 The Chronicler inserts a lengthy sentence (vv. 11b–13) into his source (1 Kings 8:10) to describe a highly festive scene, suggesting that the cloud of God's glory (see Ex. 13:21–22) that filled the temple came in response to the Levites' and priests' worship. The Chronicler's own generation should draw a similar lesson, that God will surely be present when his people offer praise and thanksgiving. The appearance of the cloud and the inability of the priests even to **stand to minister** in God's presence signified that God in his majesty was taking up residence in his temple. There is an evident parallel here, and in 2 Chron. 7:3, with the appearance of the glory cloud in the tabernacle and over the tent of meeting (cf. Ex. 40:34–35). The visible manifestation of God's glory and presence was known in later Judaism as the "Shekinah," and it provides the background to John's comment about the incarnate Son: "we have seen his glory" (John 1:14). The praise of 2 Chron. 5:13b appears again in 20:21b. God's **steadfast love** (Hb. *hesed*) in particular denotes his covenant commitment to David (1 Chron. 17:13), which has finally resulted in this temple.

Chapter 6
1[r]For ver. 1-39, see 1 Kgs. 8:12-50; [Ex. 20:21; Heb. 12:18]
2[s][Ps. 135:21]
6[t]ch. 12:13; Ps. 78:68 [u]1 Chr. 28:4; See 1 Sam. 16:11-13
7[v]2 Sam. 7:2; 1 Chr. 17:1; 28:2
8[v][See ver. 7 above]
11[w][ch. 5:10]
13[x][2 Kgs. 11:14; 23:3] [y][1 Kgs. 8:54]
14[z]See Ex. 15:11 [a]See Deut. 7:9
15[b]1 Chr. 22:9, 10
16[c]ch. 7:18; See 1 Kgs. 2:4 [d]Ps. 132:12
18[e]See ch. 2:6
20[f][ver. 40]

Solomon Blesses the People

6 [r]Then Solomon said, "The LORD has said that he would dwell in thick darkness. 2 But
I have built you [s]an exalted house, a place for you to dwell in forever." 3 Then the king
turned around and blessed all the assembly of Israel, while all the assembly of Israel stood.
4 And he said, "Blessed be the LORD, the God of Israel, who with his hand has fulfilled what
he promised with his mouth to David my father, saying, 5 'Since the day that I brought my
people out of the land of Egypt, I chose no city out of all the tribes of Israel in which to build
a house, that my name might be there, and I chose no man as prince over my people Israel;
6 [t]but I have chosen Jerusalem that my name may be there, [u]and I have chosen David to be
over my people Israel.' 7 [v]Now it was in the heart of David my father to build a house for
the name of the LORD, the God of Israel. 8 But the LORD said to David my father, 'Whereas
[v]it was in your heart to build a house for my name, you did well that it was in your heart.
9 Nevertheless, it is not you who shall build the house, but your son who shall be born to
you shall build the house for my name.' 10 Now the LORD has fulfilled his promise that
he made. For I have risen in the place of David my father and sit on the throne of Israel,
as the LORD promised, and I have built the house for the name of the LORD, the God of
Israel. 11 And there I have set the ark, [w]in which is the covenant of the LORD that he made
with the people of Israel."

Solomon's Prayer of Dedication

12 Then Solomon stood before the altar of the LORD in the presence of all the assembly of Israel and spread out his hands. 13 [x]Solomon had made a bronze platform five
cubits[1] long, five cubits wide, and three cubits high, and had set it in the court, and he
stood on it. [y]Then he knelt on his knees in the presence of all the assembly of Israel,
and spread out his hands toward heaven, 14 and said, "O LORD, God of Israel, [z]there
is no God like you, in heaven or on earth, [a]keeping covenant and showing steadfast
love to your servants who walk before you with all their heart, 15 [b]who have kept with
your servant David my father what you declared to him. You spoke with your mouth,
and with your hand have fulfilled it this day. 16 Now therefore, O LORD, God of Israel,
keep for your servant David my father what you have promised him, saying, [c]'You
shall not lack a man to sit before me on the throne of Israel, [d]if only your sons pay
close attention to their way, to walk in my law as you have walked before me.' 17 Now
therefore, O LORD, God of Israel, let your word be confirmed, which you have spoken
to your servant David.

18 "But will God indeed dwell with man on the earth? Behold, [e]heaven and the highest
heaven cannot contain you, how much less this house that I have built! 19 Yet have regard
to the prayer of your servant and to his plea, O LORD my God, listening to the cry and to
the prayer that your servant prays before you, 20 [f]that your eyes may be open day and night
toward this house, the place where you have promised to set your name, that you may
listen to the prayer that your servant offers toward this place. 21 And listen to the pleas of

[1] A *cubit* was about 18 inches or 45 centimeters

6:1–42 The Chronicler follows his source quite closely in his presentation of Solomon's prayer of dedication for the temple (see 1 Kings 8:12–50a). Yet whereas the earlier version finishes with an appeal to the exodus under Moses as the basis of God's relationship with Israel (1 Kings 8:50b–53), the Chronicler focuses instead on the Davidic covenant (2 Chron. 6:41–42, from Ps. 132:8–10). For the Chronicler's own postexilic generation, the temple signified God's promise to David of an enduring kingdom, however restricted Israel's present circumstances might seem. As the focal point of God's presence on earth, the temple also stood as a constant visible encouragement to prayer, as indicated by the different circumstances of need envisioned by Solomon in his prayer (2 Chron. 6:12–42).

6:1–2 God was present in the **thick darkness** of the cloud on Mount Sinai (see Ex. 20:21), and has now graciously come to **dwell** in the Most Holy Place of the temple.

6:3–11 Solomon's accession to the throne, the completion of the temple, and the placing of the ark are all due to God's fulfilling his promise to David (see 1 Chron. 17:23–24). Human obedience to God's commands is the means of ratifying or accepting God's promises, as well as a condition for experiencing the reality of the promises in the present (see 2 Chron. 6:14–17), yet God himself provides the grace for his people to obey.

6:7 On the **name of the LORD**, see notes on 1 Kings 8:17 and Acts 10:48.

6:12–13 The prayer of dedication is offered from a specially constructed platform **before the altar** of burnt offerings, in front of the temple entrance.

6:15 On God's promises to David, cf. 1 Chron. 17:11–14 and 22:9–10.

6:18–21 The infinite God cannot be contained within space (**heaven and the highest heaven**), let alone any man-made structure, yet he has made the temple the point of contact and immediate communication with his people. Prayer in or toward the temple will come before God in his heavenly **dwelling place** because his **name** is on the temple (vv. 20, 34, 38), which signifies both his spiritual presence in that place and his ownership of it and is thus an invitation to pray there in confident faith. (See note on 2:1.) The NT equivalent is prayer offered in Jesus' name (see John 14:13–14).

your servant and of your people Israel, when they pray toward this place. And listen from
heaven your dwelling place, [g]and when you hear, forgive.
22 "If a man sins against his neighbor and is made to take an oath and comes and swears
his oath before your altar in this house, 23 then hear from heaven and act and judge your
servants, repaying the guilty by bringing his conduct on his own head, and vindicating
the righteous by rewarding him according to his righteousness.
24 "If your people Israel are defeated before the enemy because they have sinned against
you, and they turn again and acknowledge your name and pray and plead with you in
this house, 25 [g]then hear from heaven and forgive the sin of your people Israel and bring
them again to the land that you gave to them and to their fathers.
26 [h]"When heaven is shut up and there is no rain because they have sinned against you,
if they pray toward this place and acknowledge your name and turn from their sin, when
you afflict[1] them, 27 [g]then hear in heaven and forgive the sin of your servants, your people
Israel, when you teach them the good way[2] in which they should walk, and grant rain
upon your land, which you have given to your people as an inheritance.
28 [i]"If there is famine in the land, if there is pestilence or blight or mildew or locust or
caterpillar, if their enemies besiege them in the land at their gates, whatever plague, whatever sickness there is, 29 whatever prayer, whatever plea is made by any man or by all your
people Israel, each knowing his own affliction and his own sorrow and stretching out his
hands toward this house, 30 [g]then hear from heaven your dwelling place and forgive and
render to each whose heart you know, according to all his ways, [j]for you, you only, know
the hearts of the children of mankind, 31 that they may fear you and walk in your ways all
the days that they live in the land that you gave to our fathers.
32 "Likewise, when a foreigner, who is not of your people Israel, comes from a far country
for the sake of your great name and your mighty hand and your outstretched arm, when
he comes and prays toward this house, 33 hear from heaven your dwelling place and do
according to all for which the foreigner calls to you, in order that all the peoples of the
earth may know your name and fear you, as do your people Israel, and that they may know
that this house [k]that I have built is called by your name.
34 "If your people go out to battle against their enemies, by whatever way you shall
send them, and they pray to you toward this city that you have chosen and the house
that I have built for your name, 35 then hear from heaven their prayer and their plea, and
maintain their cause.
36 "If they sin against you—[l]for there is no one who does not sin—and you are angry
with them and give them to an enemy, so that they are carried away captive to a land far
or near, 37 yet if they turn their heart in the land to which they have been carried captive,
and repent and plead with you in the land of their captivity, saying, 'We have sinned and
have acted perversely and wickedly,' 38 if they repent with all their mind and with all their
heart in the land of their captivity to which they were carried captive, and pray toward
their land, which you gave to their fathers, the city that you have chosen and the house
that I have built for your name, 39 then hear from heaven your dwelling place their prayer

21[g][Dan. 9:19]
25[g][See ver. 21 above]
26[h]ch. 7:13; [1 Kgs. 17:1]
27[g][See ver. 21 above]
28[i][ch. 20:9]
30[g][See ver. 21 above]
[j]See 1 Sam. 16:7
33[k]ch. 7:14; [James 2:7]
36[l]Eccles. 7:20; James 3:2; 1 John 1:8

[1] Septuagint, Vulgate; Hebrew *answer* [2] Septuagint, Syriac, Vulgate (compare 1 Kings 8:36); Hebrew *toward the good way*

6:22–40 Solomon offers some representative situations in which Israelites and even foreigners (v. 32) should offer prayer at or toward the temple, seeking forgiveness, vindication, and divine help.

6:22–23 See Ex. 22:7–12; Num. 5:11–31; and note on 1 Kings 8:31–32. The Law of Moses provided for oaths to be taken in the sanctuary to determine guilt or innocence if there were no witnesses to an offense.

6:24–25 See Lev. 26:17; Deut. 28:25; and note on 1 Kings 8:33–40. National defeat is included among the curses for covenant breaking. Exile is one possible punishment.

6:26–27 heaven is shut up . . . no rain. See Lev. 26:19; Deut. 28:23–24; 2 Chron. 7:13; and note on 1 Kings 8:33–40.

6:28–31 See Deut. 28:21 and note on 1 Kings 8:33–40. The emphasis is on God's intimate knowledge of and concern for each individual among his people.

6:32–33 See note on 1 Kings 8:41–43. **Your mighty hand and your outstretched arm** calls to mind God's deliverance in the exodus (Ex. 3:19–20). Solomon envisions Gentiles making pilgrimage to pray at the temple because of what they have heard about this event. On the temple as a place of prayer for all nations, see also Isa. 2:2–4 and Zech. 8:20–23.

6:34–35 God's help in answer to prayer made in time of war is depicted in 13:14–15; 14:11; 18:31; 20:5–23; 32:20–22. See note on 1 Kings 8:44–45.

6:36–39 See note on 1 Kings 8:46–51. Exile from the Promised Land is presented as the climax of punishments on account of sin (see 2 Chron. 36:15–20). **there is no one who does not sin.** Cf. Prov. 20:9; Eccles. 7:20; Rom. 3:23. Solomon prays that Yahweh will respond to the heartfelt repentance of his people in exile and their intercession **toward** the **house that I have built for your name**. Bodily posture was a part of prayer, especially for exiles like Daniel, who consciously prayed in the direction of Jerusalem (Dan. 6:10).

40[m]Neh. 1:6, 11; [ver. 20; ch. 7:15] [n]Ps. 130:2
41[o]Ps. 132:8, 9; [1 Chr. 28:2] [p][Isa. 61:10] [q][ch. 7:10; Neh. 9:25]
42[r]Ps. 132:10 [s][Ps. 132:1]
Chapter 7
1[t]1 Kgs. 8:54 [u]Lev. 9:24; 1 Kgs. 18:38; 1 Chr. 21:26 [v]See ch. 5:13
3[w]See ch. 5:13
4[x]1 Kgs. 8:62, 63
6[y][1 Chr. 15:16] [w][See ver. 3 above] [z]ch. 5:12
7[a]For ver. 7-10, see 1 Kgs. 8:64-66
8[b]See Num. 34:8 [c]See Num. 34:5

and their pleas, and maintain their cause and forgive your people who have sinned against
you. **40** Now, O my God, [m]let your eyes be open [n]and your ears attentive to the prayer of
this place.

41 "And now arise, O LORD God, and go to your [o]resting place,
you and the ark of your might.
Let your priests, O LORD God, be [p]clothed with salvation,
and let your saints [q]rejoice in your goodness.
42 O LORD God, [r]do not turn away the face of your anointed one!
[s]Remember your steadfast love for David your servant."

Fire from Heaven

7 [t]As soon as Solomon finished his prayer, [u]fire came down from heaven and consumed
the burnt offering and the sacrifices, [v]and the glory of the LORD filled the temple. **2** And
the priests could not enter the house of the LORD, because the glory of the LORD filled the
LORD's house. **3** When all the people of Israel saw the fire come down and the glory of the
LORD on the temple, they bowed down with their faces to the ground on the pavement
and worshiped and gave thanks to the LORD, saying, "For he is good, [w]for his steadfast
love endures forever."

The Dedication of the Temple

4 [x]Then the king and all the people offered sacrifice before the LORD. **5** King Solomon
offered as a sacrifice 22,000 oxen and 120,000 sheep. So the king and all the people dedicated
the house of God. **6** The priests stood at their posts; [y]the Levites also, with the instruments
for music to the LORD that King David had made for giving thanks to the LORD—[w]for
his steadfast love endures forever—whenever David offered praises by their ministry;[1]
[z]opposite them the priests sounded trumpets, and all Israel stood.

7 [a]And Solomon consecrated the middle of the court that was before the house of the
LORD, for there he offered the burnt offering and the fat of the peace offerings, because
the bronze altar Solomon had made could not hold the burnt offering and the grain offering and the fat.

8 At that time Solomon held the feast for seven days, and all Israel with him, a very great
assembly, from [b]Lebo-hamath to the [c]Brook of Egypt. **9** And on the eighth day they held
a solemn assembly, for they had kept the dedication of the altar seven days and the feast
seven days. **10** On the twenty-third day of the seventh month he sent the people away to
their homes, joyful and glad of heart for the prosperity that the LORD had granted to David
and to Solomon and to Israel his people.

[1] Hebrew *by their hand*

6:41–42 In place of the ending to this prayer in 1 Kings 8:50b–53 (an appeal to God's mercy shown in the exodus), the Chronicler inserts a version of Ps. 132:8–10, which concerns the transfer of the ark into the temple. It functions here as a prayer that God will once again come in power and grace for the Chronicler's generation and their temple, as he had done for the people and temple of Solomon's day. Verse 42 of 2 Chronicles 6 is a prayer for the Davidic descendants, the recipients of God's covenant promise of **steadfast love for David**. For the Chronicler, this enduring covenant is now the basis of the relationship between God and his people.

7:1–22 God's twofold answer to Solomon's prayer (through the appearance of the glory of the Lord in vv. 1–3 and the words from God in vv. 12–22) takes readers to the heart of the Chronicler's message of repentance and restoration. The Chronicler is acutely aware of Israel's sinfulness (6:36), knowing that this will result in exile; but against this bleak fact he highlights Yahweh's undeserved restorative mercy and forgiveness toward his people, for which the temple is the visible symbol. The assurance that the temple is indeed the divinely sanctioned place of atonement and prayer should encourage the Chronicler's own postexilic generation to respond accordingly, confident that God will grant a greater measure of restoration and blessing. Ultimately, salvation will come not through a material building but through the One whom the temple foreshadows (John 2:19–21).

7:1b–3 An addition to 1 Kings 8. A parallel with David (see 1 Chron. 21:26) and Moses is intended here: just as a divine fire consumed the burnt offering in the newly erected Mosaic tabernacle, and "the glory of the LORD" was visible to the people (see Lev. 9:23–24), the **fire . . . from heaven** that consumed the sacrifice signaled acceptance of the temple and the priests' ministry there, while the **glory of the LORD** appeared on the **temple**, and the people worshiped. **For he is good, for his steadfast love endures forever**. Variations on this refrain from Psalm 136 occur several times in the book (see 1 Chron. 16:34; 2 Chron. 5:13; 7:6; 20:21) and may indicate a link between the author and the temple singers.

7:4–10 The dedication of the temple at the Feast of Tabernacles (see 5:3) entailed vast numbers of sacrifices (7:5) and involved the whole nation in its broadest extent (v. 8). Unity, joy, and gratitude to God are the keynotes of this festival.

7:8 Lebo-hamath to the Brook of Egypt designates the whole of Solomon's empire (see note on 1 Kings 8:65–66).

7:11–22 God's reply to Solomon's prayer is presented immediately after the account of the dedication, although in fact 13 years had elapsed, in which time the palace was also completed (v. 11; see 1 Kings 7:1; 9:10). Yahweh's appearance at night (2 Chron. 7:12) corresponds to his first appearance to Solomon at Gibeon, at the beginning of his reign (1:7).

7:12b–16 The Chronicler's addition to 1 Kings 9:3–4 provides a succinct summary of the central message of the book: the meaning of the temple and the response that God looks for in his people.

If My People Pray

11 [d]Thus Solomon finished the house of the LORD and the king's house. All that Solomon
had planned to do in the house of the LORD and in his own house he successfully accomplished. 12 Then the LORD appeared to Solomon in the night and said to him: "I have
heard your prayer [e]and have chosen this place for myself as a house of sacrifice. 13 [f]When
I shut up the heavens so that there is no rain, or command the locust to devour the land,
or send pestilence among my people, 14 if my people who are called by my name [g]humble
themselves, and pray and seek my face and turn from their wicked ways, then I will hear
from heaven and will forgive their sin and heal their land. 15 [h]Now my eyes will be open
and my ears attentive to the prayer that is made in this place. 16 [e]For now I have chosen and
consecrated this house that my name may be there forever. My eyes and my heart will be
there for all time. 17 And as for you, if you will walk before me as David your father walked,
doing according to all that I have commanded you and keeping my statutes and my rules,
18 then I will establish your royal throne, as I covenanted with David your father, saying,
[i]'You shall not lack a man to rule Israel.'

19 [j]"But if you[1] turn aside and forsake my statutes and my commandments that I have
set before you, and go and serve other gods and worship them, 20 [k]then I will pluck you[2]
up from my land that I have given you, and this house that I have consecrated for my
name, I will cast out of my sight, and I will make it [l]a proverb and a byword among all
peoples. 21 And at this house, which was exalted, everyone passing by will be astonished
and say, [m]'Why has the LORD done thus to this land and to this house?' 22 Then they will

[1] The Hebrew for *you* is plural here [2] Hebrew *them*; twice in this verse

11 [d]For ver. 11-22, see 1 Kgs. 9:1-9
12 [e]See Deut. 12:5
13 [f][ch. 6:26, 28]
14 [g][ch. 12:7]
15 [h]See ch. 6:40
16 [e][See ver. 12 above]
18 [i]1 Kgs. 8:25; See ch. 6:16
19 [j][Lev. 26:14; Deut. 28:15]
20 [k][Deut. 29:28] [l]See Deut. 28:37
21 [m]Deut. 29:24; Jer. 22:8, 9

The Extent of Solomon's Kingdom
c. 971–931 B.C.

Solomon's reign marked the zenith of Israel's power and wealth in biblical times. His father David had bestowed upon him a kingdom that included Edom, Moab, Ammon, Syria, and Zobah. Solomon would later bring the kingdom of Hamath-zobah under his dominion as well, and his marriage to Pharaoh's daughter sealed an alliance with Egypt. His expansive kingdom controlled important trade routes between several major world powers, including Egypt, Arabia, Mesopotamia, and Anatolia (Asia Minor).

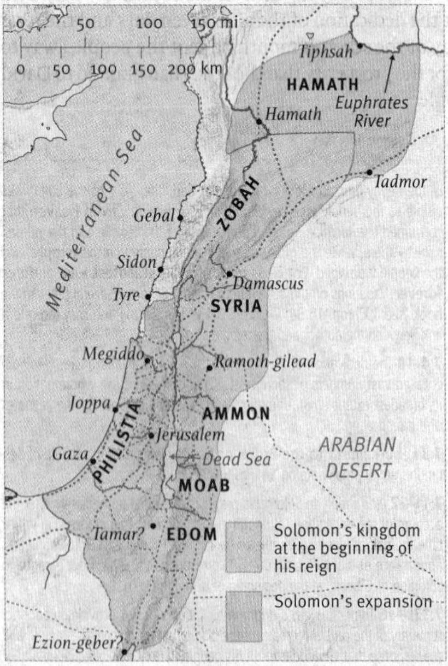

7:12b The temple is for **sacrifice** as well as prayer. The OT understanding of worship regularly joins sacrifices (of atonement, dedication, or thanksgiving) with prayer as the material expression of the worshiper's inner disposition.

7:13 A summary reference to the divine punishments mentioned in Solomon's prayer (6:26, 28).

7:14 if my people. God's purpose above all is to forgive his penitent people and **heal their land**. The specific vocabulary of this verse (**humble themselves, pray, seek, turn**) describes different aspects of heartfelt repentance and will recur throughout chs. 10–36. "Heal their land" includes deliverance from drought and pestilence as well as the return of exiles to their rightful home (6:38). For the Chronicler, this includes the restoration of the people to their right relationship with God. Cf. Jer. 25:5; 26:3.

7:15–16 The invitation to prayer and repentance (v. 14) is sealed with the strong assurance of God's presence and attention in the temple.

7:17–18 A summons to Solomon to be obedient to the Law of Moses as the grounds for establishing his throne. **a man to rule Israel**. See Mic. 5:2. Messianic hopes for the continuation of the Davidic line continued to be affirmed in the Chronicler's time, even though the last Davidic king had been deposed in 586 B.C.

7:19–22 The statement **if you turn aside and forsake my statutes** is addressed to the people ("you" in v. 19 is plural; see notes on 1 Kings 9:6; 9:7–8). While the temple signified God's will to forgive and restore, the stubborn rejection of his statutes and **commandments** would lead to God's rejection of both people and temple (see Deut. 29:24–28). The decisive factor, as shown throughout the rest of the book, is whether the call to repentance is heeded.

8:1–18 This section generally follows 1 Kings 9:10–28, with a significant variation and addition (see 2 Chron. 8:2–4, 12–16).

8:1–16 *Solomon's Other Accomplishments.* Solomon's further conquests and building projects are revealed, as well as his attention to matters of worship, both for himself and for the people. The success of Solomon's various building projects are seen as blessings that follow his obedience in building the temple (which, along with his palace, took **twenty years** to complete).

8:2 According to 1 Kings 9:11–14, Solomon had actually given these **cities** to **Hiram**, perhaps as collateral for a loan (1 Kings 9:14; cf. notes on 1 Kings 9:10–13; 9:10; 9:11). The Chronicler would then be describing their subsequent reversion to Israelite control.

say, 'Because they abandoned the LORD, the God of their fathers who brought them out
of the land of Egypt, and laid hold on other gods and worshiped them and served them.
Therefore he has brought all this disaster on them.'"

Solomon's Accomplishments

8 [n]At the end of twenty years, in which Solomon had built the house of the LORD and
his own house, 2 Solomon rebuilt the cities that Hiram had given to him, and settled
the people of Israel in them.
3 And Solomon went to Hamath-zobah and took it. 4 He built Tadmor in the wilderness
and all the store cities that he built in Hamath. 5 He also built [o]Upper Beth-horon and Lower
Beth-horon, [p]fortified cities [p]with walls, gates, and bars, 6 and Baalath, and all the store
cities that Solomon had and all the cities for his chariots and the cities for his horsemen,
and whatever Solomon desired to build in Jerusalem, in Lebanon, and in all the land of
his dominion. 7 [q]All the people who were left of the Hittites, the Amorites, the Perizzites,
the Hivites, and the Jebusites, who were not of Israel, 8 from their descendants who were
left after them in the land, whom the people of Israel had not destroyed—these Solomon
drafted [r]as forced labor, and so they are to this day. 9 But of the people of Israel Solomon
made no slaves for his work; they were soldiers, and his officers, the commanders of his
chariots, and his horsemen. 10 And these were the chief officers of King Solomon, 250, who
exercised authority over the people.
11 [s]Solomon brought Pharaoh's daughter up from the city of David to the house that he
had built for her, for he said, "My wife shall not live in the house of David king of Israel,
for the places to which the ark of the LORD has come are holy."
12 Then Solomon offered up burnt offerings to the LORD on the altar of the LORD
[t]that he had built before the vestibule, 13 [u]as the duty of each day required, offering
[v]according to the commandment of Moses for the Sabbaths, the new moons, and the
[w]three annual feasts—the Feast of Unleavened Bread, the Feast of Weeks, and the Feast
of Booths. 14 According to the ruling of David his father, he appointed [x]the divisions of
the priests for their service, [y]and the Levites for their offices of praise and [z]ministry before
the priests [u]as the duty of each day required, and [a]the gatekeepers in their divisions at
each gate, for so David [b]the man of God had commanded. 15 And they did not turn aside
from what the king had commanded the priests and Levites concerning any matter and
concerning the treasuries.
16 Thus was accomplished all the work of Solomon from[1] the day the foundation
of the house of the LORD was laid until it was finished. So the house of the LORD was
completed.
17 Then Solomon went to [c]Ezion-geber and [d]Eloth on the shore of the sea, in the land
of Edom. 18 And Hiram sent to him by the hand of his servants ships and servants familiar

[1] Septuagint, Syriac, Vulgate; Hebrew *to*

Chapter 8
1 [n]For ver. 1-18, see 1 Kgs. 9:10-28
5 [o]See Josh. 16:3, 5 [p]ch. 14:7; Deut. 3:5
7 [q]See Gen. 15:18-21
8 [r]ch. 10:18; 1 Kgs. 4:6; 9:21; 12:18; [Josh. 16:10]
11 [s]1 Kgs. 3:1; 7:8; 9:24
12 [t]ch. 4:1; 15:8
13 [u][Ex. 29:38] [v]Num. 28:3, 9, 11, 26; 29:2 [w]Ex. 23:14; Deut. 16:16
14 [x]See 1 Chr. 24 [y]See 1 Chr. 25 [z]ch. 7:6 [u][See ver. 13 above] [a]See 1 Chr. 9:17-23; 26 [b]Neh. 12:24, 36
17 [c]1 Kgs. 9:26 [d][Deut. 2:8; 2 Kgs. 14:22]

8:3–4 Hamath-zobah lay about 120 miles (193 km) north of Damascus (see 1 Chron. 18:3), while **Tadmor** lay about 125 miles (201 km) to the northeast. Control over these commercial cities represented the farthest extent of Solomon's power. First Kings does not mention these campaigns.

8:5 Upper Beth-horon and Lower Beth-horon were located on a ridge above the Valley of Aijalon northwest of Jerusalem. They were crucial to the security of the city and provided access to the international coastal highway (see also note on 1 Kings 9:17–19).

8:7–10 In keeping with an ancient practice of controlling enemies, Solomon **drafted** the descendants of the Canaanites into **forced labor** for his construction projects throughout the nation. According to 1 Kings 5:13–18, Solomon imposed a less rigorous demand on the Israelites.

8:11 Solomon's Egyptian wife, **Pharaoh's daughter**, was kept in a separate house and away from the ark, probably on account of her paganism (see 1 Kings 11:7–8). See Solomon's Temple and Palace Complex, p. 607.

8:12–15 The Chronicler expands the brief note in 1 Kings 9:25, detailing the pattern of daily, weekly, monthly, and annual sacrifices and feasts instituted in the temple by Solomon, along with his organization of the temple personnel. Solomon's fidelity to the instructions of **Moses** (2 Chron. 8:13) and **David** (vv. 14–15) is emphasized.

8:16 So the house of the LORD was completed. The completion of the temple did not come with its building or dedication but with the institution of its regular services. Solomon proved himself faithful in his commission, and the subsequent details of his reign (8:17–9:28) represent God's blessing on his obedience (see 1:12).

8:17–9:31 *Solomon's International Relations and Renown.* Solomon's reputation and influence extend beyond the borders of Israel.

8:17–18; 9:10–11 Ezion-geber. See note on 1 Kings 9:26–28. Israel forms the land bridge (and the trade routes) connecting the Mediterranean lands with the kingdoms on the Red Sea and beyond, into Asia. Solomon profited from his control of these routes, and from his maritime partnership with **Hiram**, the king of Tyre. The Tyreans (a people of Phoenician stock) were renowned for their seamanship. **Ophir** was probably in southwest Arabia or the Horn of Africa.

with the sea, and they went to Ophir together with the servants of Solomon and brought
from there [e]450 talents[1] of gold and brought it to King Solomon.

The Queen of Sheba

9 [f]Now when [g]the queen of Sheba heard of the fame of Solomon, she came to Jerusalem
to test him with hard questions, having a very great retinue and camels bearing spices
and very much gold and precious stones. And when she came to Solomon, she told him
all that was on her mind. 2 And Solomon answered all her questions. There was nothing
hidden from Solomon that he could not explain to her. 3 And when [g]the queen of Sheba
had seen the wisdom of Solomon, the house that he had built, 4 the food of his table, the
seating of his officials, and the attendance of his servants, and their clothing, his cupbearers, and their clothing, and his burnt offerings that he offered at the house of the LORD,
there was no more breath in her.

[1] A *talent* was about 75 pounds or 34 kilograms

18 [e]ch. 9:10; [1 Kgs. 9:28]

Chapter 9

1 [f]For ver. 1-12, see 1 Kgs. 10:1-13 [g][Matt. 12:42; Luke 11:31]

3 [g][See ver. 1 above]

9:1–9, 12 This section closely follows 1 Kings 10:1–13. **Sheba**, or Saba, corresponds roughly to modern Yemen and was a mercantile kingdom that traded in luxury goods from East Africa and India. The queen's visit may have had commercial trade purposes (see 2 Chron. 9:1, 9) prompted by Solomon's naval activities in the south of the Red Sea, but her visit is presented primarily as a quest for **wisdom** (vv. 1, 6). Solomon is acknowledged as excelling in both wisdom and wealth (see 1:12). The Gentile **queen** recognizes that Solomon's greatness is from Yahweh (9:8; see 2:12) and that Solomon sits on God's **throne** as his **king** (cf. 1 Kings 10:9, "the throne of Israel"). For the Chronicler, the Davidic kingdom is the earthly expression of God's eternal kingdom (see 1 Chron. 17:14; 28:5; 2 Chron. 13:8). Recognition (esp. from a Gentile monarch) that God was the actual King of Israel could only encourage the postexilic community, when no descendant of David was on the throne.

9:7 Happy are these your servants. See note on 1 Kings 10:8.

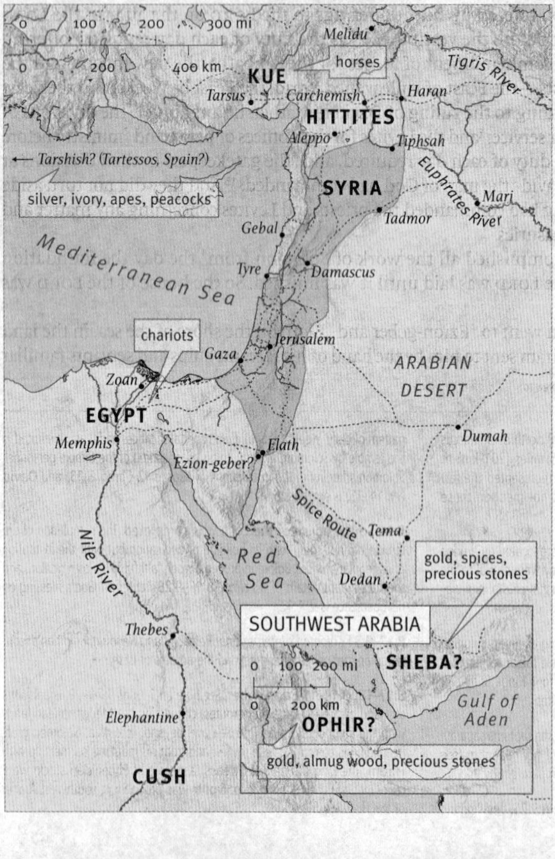

Solomon's International Ventures
c. 950 B.C.

Solomon's firm control of important trade routes linking Egypt, Arabia, Mesopotamia, and Anatolia (Asia Minor) provided him with incalculable wealth. Partnering with King Hiram of Tyre, Solomon also launched his own trading expeditions to Ophir to acquire valuable and exotic goods. The queen of Sheba's visit to Solomon attests to his great fame throughout the ancient world. Solomon further augmented his wealth by buying horses from Kue and chariots from Egypt and selling them to the kings of Syria and the Hittites.

8[h]1 Chr. 29:23 [i]ch. 2:11
10[j]ch. 8:18
11[k][1 Kgs. 10:12]
12[l][1 Kgs. 10:13]
13[m]For ver. 13-28, see 1 Kgs. 10:14-28
14[n]Ps. 68:29; 72:10
16[o][1 Kgs. 10:17]
21[p]ch. 20:36, 37
22[q]1 Kgs. 3:13
25[r][ch. 1:14; 1 Kgs. 4:26; 10:26]
26[s]1 Kgs. 4:21 [t]Gen. 15:18; Ex. 23:31; Ps. 72:8
27[u]ch. 1:15
28[v]ch. 1:16

5 And she said to the king, "The report was true that I heard in my own land of your
words and of your wisdom, 6 but I did not believe the[1] reports until I came and my own
eyes had seen it. And behold, half the greatness of your wisdom was not told me; you surpass the report that I heard. 7 Happy are your wives![2] Happy are these your servants, who
continually stand before you and hear your wisdom! 8 Blessed be the LORD your God, who
has delighted in you [h]and set you on his throne as king for the LORD your God! [i]Because
your God loved Israel and would establish them forever, he has made you king over them,
that you may execute justice and righteousness." 9 Then she gave the king 120 talents[3] of
gold, and a very great quantity of spices, and precious stones. There were no spices such
as those that the queen of Sheba gave to King Solomon.

10 Moreover, the servants of Hiram and the servants of Solomon, [j]who brought gold from
Ophir, brought algum wood and precious stones. 11 And the king made from the algum
wood [k]supports for the house of the LORD and for the king's house, lyres also and harps
for the singers. There never was seen the like of them before in the land of Judah.

12 And King Solomon gave to the queen of Sheba all that she desired, whatever she asked
[l]besides what she had brought to the king. So she turned and went back to her own land
with her servants.

Solomon's Wealth

13 [m]Now the weight of gold that came to Solomon in one year was 666 talents of gold,
14 besides that which the explorers and merchants brought. [n]And all the kings of Arabia
and the governors of the land brought gold and silver to Solomon. 15 King Solomon
made 200 large shields of beaten gold; 600 shekels[4] of beaten gold went into each shield.
16 And he made 300 shields of beaten gold; [o]300 shekels of gold went into each shield;
and the king put them in the House of the Forest of Lebanon. 17 The king also made
a great ivory throne and overlaid it with pure gold. 18 The throne had six steps and a
footstool of gold, which were attached to the throne, and on each side of the seat were
armrests and two lions standing beside the armrests, 19 while twelve lions stood there,
one on each end of a step on the six steps. Nothing like it was ever made for any kingdom.
20 All King Solomon's drinking vessels were of gold, and all the vessels of the House of
the Forest of Lebanon were of pure gold. Silver was not considered as anything in the
days of Solomon. 21 For the king's ships went to [p]Tarshish with the servants of Hiram.
Once every three years the ships of Tarshish used to come bringing gold, silver, ivory,
apes, and peacocks.[5]

22 Thus King Solomon [q]excelled all the kings of the earth in riches and in wisdom.
23 And all the kings of the earth sought the presence of Solomon to hear his wisdom,
which God had put into his mind. 24 Every one of them brought his present, articles of
silver and of gold, garments, myrrh, spices, horses, and mules, so much year by year.
25 And Solomon had [r]4,000 stalls for horses and chariots, and 12,000 horsemen, whom
he stationed in the chariot cities and with the king in Jerusalem. 26 [s]And he ruled over all
the kings [t]from the Euphrates[6] to the land of the Philistines and to the border of Egypt.
27 [u]And the king made silver as common in Jerusalem as stone, and he made cedar as
plentiful as the sycamore of the Shephelah. 28 [v]And horses were imported for Solomon
from Egypt and from all lands.

[1] Hebrew *their* [2] Septuagint (compare 1 Kings 10:8); Hebrew *men* [3] A *talent* was about 75 pounds or 34 kilograms [4] A *shekel* was about 2/5 ounce or 11 grams [5] Or *baboons* [6] Hebrew *the River*

9:9–12 On the queen's gift of **120 talents of gold**, see note on 1 Kings 10:10–13.

9:13–28 This section closely follows 1 Kings 10:14–28. The Chronicler's presentation of Solomon concludes with a description of the king at the zenith of his wealth and international renown (a far cry from the difficult conditions of the postexilic days; see Ezra 9:7; Neh. 9:36–37).

9:13–14 Solomon's annual revenues in gold (equal to about 22 tons) would have been derived from both tribute and trade (see note on 1 Kings 10:14–25).

9:15–16 The House of the Forest of Lebanon was Solomon's palace, which contained great quantities of cedar (see 1 Kings 7:2). The gold shields were lost as booty to Pharaoh Shishak by Solomon's son Rehoboam (2 Chron. 12:9).

9:21 Tarshish is usually identified with Tartessus in Spain, but here the Chronicler seems to use it more generically, in the sense of "the ends of the earth" (cf. Ps. 72:10).

9:22–28 Solomon is presented as supreme over **all the kings of the earth**, in keeping with the promises made at the beginning of his reign (1:12). Verses 25–28 of ch. 9 are a partial repetition of 1:14–17, and thus form an *inclusio* (literary "bookends") around the Chronicler's portrayal of Solomon (cf. note on 1 Kings 10:26–29).

Solomon's Death
29 [w]Now the rest of the acts of Solomon, from [x]first to last, are they not written in the
history of [y]Nathan the prophet, and in the prophecy of [z]Ahijah the Shilonite, and in the
visions of [a]Iddo [b]the seer concerning Jeroboam the son of Nebat? 30 Solomon reigned in
Jerusalem over all Israel forty years. 31 And Solomon slept with his fathers and was buried
in [c]the city of David his father, and Rehoboam his son reigned in his place.

The Revolt Against Rehoboam
10 [d]Rehoboam went to Shechem, for all Israel had come to Shechem to make him
king. 2 And as soon as Jeroboam the son of Nebat heard of it (for he was in Egypt,
[e]where he had fled from King Solomon), then Jeroboam returned from Egypt. 3 And they

29 [w]For ver. 29-31, see 1 Kgs. 11:41-43 [x]1 Chr. 29:29 [y]2 Sam. 12:1 [z]1 Kgs. 11:29 [a]ch. 12:15; 13:22 [b]2 Sam. 24:11; See 1 Sam. 9:9
31 [c][1 Kgs. 2:10]
Chapter 10
1 [d]For ver. 1-19, see 1 Kgs. 12:1-20
2 [e]1 Kgs. 11:40

9:29–31 This is from 1 Kings 11:41–43, but with additional reference to **Ahijah the Shilonite** (see 1 Kings 11:29–40) and **Iddo the seer** (traditionally identified with the unknown prophet in 1 Kings 13). Although the Chronicler omits the accounts of Solomon's apostasy and the rebellions he faced in his declining years (1 Kings 11), the allusion to the words of these prophets directs the reader to the account in Kings, where a more critical portrayal of Solomon is preserved. As with his presentation of David, the Chronicler's focus here is on the positive achievement of Solomon's reign and its abiding significance for his community. **Solomon slept with his fathers.** See notes on 1 Kings 2:10 and 11:43.

10:1–36:23 *The Kingdom of Judah down to the Exile.* The post-Solomonic narrative in Chronicles deals almost exclusively with the kingdom of Judah, following the division of the kingdom under Rehoboam. In

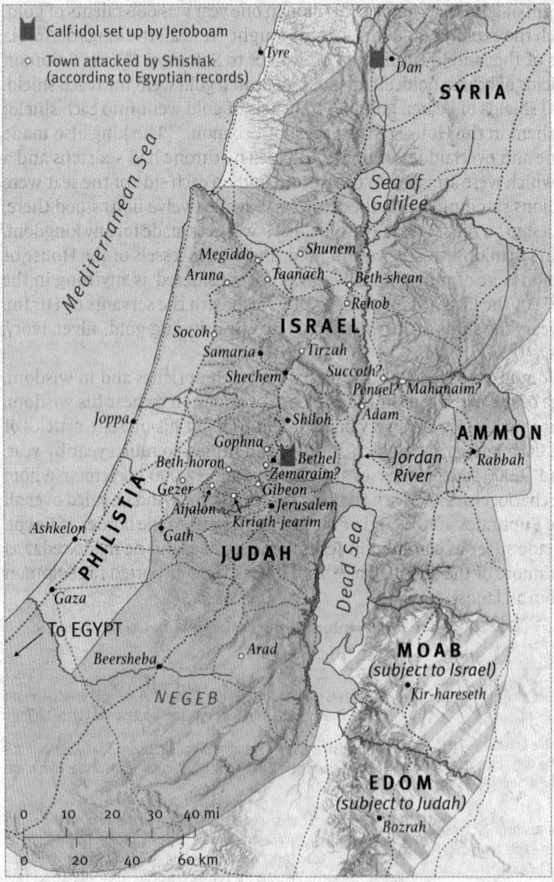

The Kingdom Divides
931 B.C.
When Solomon's son Rehoboam arrived at Shechem for his coronation after his father's death, he refused to lighten his father's heavy tax burden on the people, and the 10 northern tribes revolted and set up Jeroboam as their king. The northern kingdom would now be known as Israel and the southern kingdom as Judah. Five years later, Shishak (also called Sheshonq) king of Egypt invaded Judah and Israel and captured a number of towns. Rehoboam avoided Jerusalem's destruction by paying off Shishak with many of the treasures Solomon had placed in the temple.

4 [f][1 Kgs. 5:15]
7 [g][1 Kgs. 12:7]
15 [h]See 1 Kgs. 11:29-39
16 [i]See 2 Sam. 20:1
18 [j][1 Kgs. 4:6; 5:14]

sent and called him. And Jeroboam and all Israel came and said to Rehoboam, 4 [f]"Your father made our yoke heavy. Now therefore lighten the hard service of your father and his heavy yoke on us, and we will serve you." 5 He said to them, "Come to me again in three days." So the people went away.

6 Then King Rehoboam took counsel with the old men,[1] who had stood before Solomon his father while he was yet alive, saying, "How do you advise me to answer this people?" 7 And they said to him, [g]"If you will be good to this people and please them and speak good words to them, then they will be your servants forever." 8 But he abandoned the counsel that the old men gave him, and took counsel with the young men who had grown up with him and stood before him. 9 And he said to them, "What do you advise that we answer this people who have said to me, 'Lighten the yoke that your father put on us'?" 10 And the young men who had grown up with him said to him, "Thus shall you speak to the people who said to you, 'Your father made our yoke heavy, but you lighten it for us'; thus shall you say to them, 'My little finger is thicker than my father's thighs. 11 And now, whereas my father laid on you a heavy yoke, I will add to your yoke. My father disciplined you with whips, but I will discipline you with scorpions.'"

12 So Jeroboam and all the people came to Rehoboam the third day, as the king said, "Come to me again the third day." 13 And the king answered them harshly; and forsaking the counsel of the old men, 14 King Rehoboam spoke to them according to the counsel of the young men, saying, "My father made your yoke heavy, but I will add to it. My father disciplined you with whips, but I will discipline you with scorpions." 15 So the king did not listen to the people, for it was a turn of affairs brought about by God that the LORD might fulfill his word, [h]which he spoke by Ahijah the Shilonite to Jeroboam the son of Nebat.

16 And when all Israel saw that the king did not listen to them, the people answered the king, "What portion have we in David? We have no inheritance in the son of Jesse. [i]Each of you to your tents, O Israel! Look now to your own house, David." So all Israel went to their tents. 17 But Rehoboam reigned over the people of Israel who lived in the cities of Judah. 18 Then King Rehoboam sent [j]Hadoram,[2] who was taskmaster over the forced labor, and the people of Israel stoned him to death with stones. And King Rehoboam quickly mounted his chariot to flee to Jerusalem. 19 So Israel has been in rebellion against the house of David to this day.

[1] Or *the elders*; also verses 8, 13 [2] Spelled *Adoram* in 1 Kings 12:18

contrast to 1–2 Kings, the history of the northern kingdom is considered by the Chronicler only as it touches upon that of Judah, such as in war (e.g., 2 Chronicles 13; 16; 18) or in moves toward unity (chs. 29–30). The Chronicler never disputed that the northern tribes belonged to Israel but insisted that legitimacy and leadership lay with the Davidic monarchy and the tribe of Judah.

10:1–12:16 *Rehoboam.* The reign of Rehoboam (931–915 B.C.) is dominated by the division of the kingdom and the consequences thereof. While Rehoboam is judged negatively for his failures as a leader, the Chronicler also uses his example to show how repentance and obedience may lead to the restoration of blessing.

10:1–19 From 1 Kings 12:1–19. The division of the kingdom was a complex matter, to which Solomon (2 Chron. 10:4, 10, 11) and Jeroboam (13:6–7) both contributed through their disobedience, but here the focus is on Rehoboam's folly in alienating the northerners. At the same time, the author notes that this was a **turn of affairs brought about by God** (10:15), indicating that God remained in control of his kingdom and that the northerners' rebellion was understandable; it was, in fact, in accordance with the prophetic word (v. 15, which presupposes the reader's knowledge of 1 Kings 11:29–39). It was the northerners' later idolatry that made their continuing rebellion reprehensible (2 Chron. 13:8–10).

10:1–5 Rather than simply make **Rehoboam** king (as he no doubt expected), the tribal leaders wished to negotiate the terms of his kingship, including relief from the forced labor imposed by Solomon.

10:1 Shechem. See note on 1 Kings 12:1.

10:2 Jeroboam. See 1 Kings 11:26–40.

10:4 Your father made our yoke heavy. See note on 1 Kings 12:4.

10:7 Speak good words appears to be a technical term meaning "make an agreement" (see 2 Kings 25:28–29).

10:10 My little finger. See note on 1 Kings 12:10–11.

10:14–15 I will discipline you with scorpions. The attempt to browbeat the people with threats backfired, not least because the course of events was determined by God's will and the prophetic word (cf. notes on 1 Kings 12:14; 12:15).

10:16 This poetic fragment announcing rejection of the house of David contrasts pointedly with the poetic declaration of loyalty in 1 Chron. 12:18. It was apparently the rallying cry of the northern tribes against Judah (see 2 Sam. 20:1).

10:18 Hadoram was Solomon's taskmaster, also called "Adoram" (see note on 1 Kings 12:18) or "Adoniram" (1 Kings 4:6; 5:14).

Rehoboam Secures His Kingdom

11 [k]When Rehoboam came to Jerusalem, he assembled the house of Judah and Benjamin,
180,000 chosen warriors, to fight against Israel, to restore the kingdom to Rehoboam.
2 But the word of the LORD came to [l]Shemaiah the man of God: 3 "Say to Rehoboam the
son of Solomon, king of Judah, and to all Israel in Judah and Benjamin, 4 'Thus says the
LORD, You shall not go up or fight against [m]your relatives. Return every man to his home,
for this thing is from me.' " So they listened to the word of the LORD and returned and
did not go against Jeroboam.
5 Rehoboam lived in Jerusalem, and he built [n]cities for defense in Judah. 6 He built
Bethlehem, Etam, Tekoa, 7 Beth-zur, Soco, Adullam, 8 Gath, [o]Mareshah, Ziph, 9 Adoraim,
Lachish, Azekah, 10 Zorah, Aijalon, and Hebron, fortified cities that are in Judah and in
Benjamin. 11 He made the fortresses strong, and put commanders in them, and stores of
food, oil, and wine. 12 And he put shields and spears in all the cities and made them very
strong. So he held Judah and Benjamin.

Priests and Levites Come to Jerusalem

13 And the priests and the Levites who were in all Israel presented themselves to him
from all places where they lived. 14 For the Levites left [p]their common lands and their
holdings and came to Judah and Jerusalem, [q]because Jeroboam and his sons cast them
out from serving as priests of the LORD, 15 and he appointed his own [r]priests for the high
places and for the goat idols and for [s]the calves that he had made. 16 [t]And those who had
set their hearts to seek the LORD God of Israel came after them from all the tribes of Israel
to Jerusalem to sacrifice to the LORD, the God of their fathers. 17 [u]They strengthened the
kingdom of Judah, and for three years they made Rehoboam the son of Solomon secure,
for they walked for three years in the way of David and Solomon.

Rehoboam's Family

18 Rehoboam took as wife Mahalath the daughter of Jerimoth the son of David, and of
Abihail the daughter of [v]Eliab the son of Jesse, 19 and she bore him sons, Jeush, Shemariah,
and Zaham. 20 After her he took [w]Maacah the daughter of Absalom, who bore him [x]Abijah,
Attai, Ziza, and Shelomith. 21 Rehoboam loved Maacah the daughter of Absalom above
all his wives and concubines (he took eighteen wives and sixty concubines, and fathered
twenty-eight sons and sixty daughters). 22 [y]And Rehoboam appointed [x]Abijah the son of
Maacah as chief prince among his brothers, for he intended to make him king. 23 And
he dealt wisely and distributed some of his sons through all the districts of Judah and

Chapter 11
1 [k]For ver. 1-4, see 1 Kgs. 12:21-24
2 [l]ch. 12:5, 15
4 [m]ch. 28:8, 11
5 [n]ver. 23; ch. 8:5; 12:4; 14:6; 17:2, 19; 21:3
8 [o]ch. 14:9
14 [p]Num. 35:2 [q]ch. 13:9
15 [r]1 Kgs. 12:31; 13:33 [s]See 1 Kgs. 12:28
16 [t]ch. 15:9
17 [u][ch. 12:1]
18 [v]1 Sam. 16:6; 17:13, 28; [1 Chr. 27:18]
20 [w]1 Kgs. 15:2 [x][1 Kgs. 14:31]
22 [y][Deut. 21:15-17] [x][See ver. 20 above]

11:1–12:16 The Chronicler's account of Rehoboam's rule over the southern kingdom is much longer and more complex than that given in Kings (1 Kings 14:21–31). As the first king of Judah after the division of the kingdom, Rehoboam serves to illustrate several of the key themes that will recur throughout the subsequent history of the Davidic monarchy: the blessings that flow from repentance and obedience to the prophetic word; conversely, the punishment that follows disobedience to God's law; the function of the faithful Levites in strengthening the kingdom; and the constant presence of the prophetic word to guide and rebuke. Rehoboam's reign shows how the principles and promises of judgment and restoration in 2 Chron. 7:13–14 are being enacted in the life of the kingdom, even when the king falls short of the ideal compared to his people (12:14).

11:1–4 This is from 1 Kings 12:21–24. Rehoboam's attempt to reunite the kingdom by force is averted by the prophet **Shemaiah** (see 2 Chron. 12:5, 7), who informs him that the division is from God (11:4; see 10:15).

11:4 your relatives. Despite their rebellion (for which they had good reason at this point), the northern tribes did not cease to be part of "all Israel." **they listened to the word of the LORD**. See note on 1 Kings 12:24.

11:5–23 This information has no parallel in Kings but is derived from another source or sources (see note on 12:15–16). It illustrates the blessings that come to Judah following Rehoboam's and the people's obedience to the word of Yahweh (11:4), while Jeroboam leads the northerners into apostasy.

11:5–12 The **fortified cities** covered the eastern, southern, and western approaches to Judah, and were thus probably intended as a defense against Egypt, Jeroboam's ally. Yet they did not prove effective against Shishak (12:4).

11:13–17 Jeroboam instituted his own syncretistic cult in Bethel and Dan to deter his people from going to sacrifice in Jerusalem and possibly defecting to Rehoboam (1 Kings 12:26–33). The Chronicler condemns him for his **goat idols** as well as golden **calves** (2 Chron. 11:15; see Lev. 17:7), and for driving out the legitimate priesthood (2 Chron. 11:14; 13:9). The exemplary attitude is shown by those Levites who took the costly step of abandoning their lands to move to Judah, and those laypeople who followed them to Jerusalem to offer sacrifice (11:16). Israel's true unity was centered on the temple worship (see 15:9). The theme of the Levites' "strengthening the kingdom" is frequent in Chronicles (see 19:8–11; 20:14–17; 29:25–30), and the task remained equally relevant in the Chronicler's own day (1 Chron. 9:2).

11:17 Rehoboam's and Judah's commitment to faithful worship and obedience to God's law lasted only **three years** (12:1).

11:18–23 The growth of Rehoboam's family is a sign of God's blessing on him, although these details must refer to the whole of his 17-year reign, and not just the three-year period of faithfulness to God's law. His family is of strong Davidic lineage: the father of **Mahalath** was **Jerimoth**, presumably the son of one of David's concubines (1 Chron. 3:9), while **Maacah** was probably the granddaughter of David's son **Absalom**, through his daughter Tamar (2 Sam. 14:27).

12:1 After a faithful beginning, Rehoboam seems to have descended into

Benjamin, in all the fortified cities, and he gave them abundant provisions and procured
wives for them.[1]

Egypt Plunders Jerusalem

12 [z]When the rule of Rehoboam was established [a]and he was strong, [b]he abandoned
the law of the LORD, and all Israel with him. **2** [c]In the fifth year of King Rehoboam,
because they had been unfaithful to the LORD, [d]Shishak king of Egypt came up against
Jerusalem **3** with 1,200 chariots and 60,000 horsemen. And the people were without number
who came with him from Egypt—[e]Libyans, Sukkiim, and Ethiopians. **4** And he took [f]the
fortified cities of Judah and came as far as Jerusalem. **5** Then [g]Shemaiah the prophet came to
Rehoboam and to the princes of Judah, who had gathered at Jerusalem because of Shishak,
and said to them, "Thus says the LORD, [h]'You abandoned me, so I have abandoned you to
the hand of Shishak.'" **6** Then the princes of [i]Israel and the king humbled themselves and
said, [j]"The LORD is righteous." **7** When the LORD saw that they humbled themselves, the
word of the LORD came to Shemaiah: [k]"They have humbled themselves. I will not destroy
them, but I will grant them some deliverance, [l]and my wrath shall not be poured out on
Jerusalem by the hand of Shishak. **8** Nevertheless, they shall be servants to him, [m]that they
may know my service and the service of the kingdoms of the countries."
9 [n]So Shishak king of Egypt came up against Jerusalem. He took away the treasures of
the house of the LORD and the treasures of the king's house. He took away everything.
He also took away [o]the shields of gold that Solomon had made, **10** and King Rehoboam
made in their place shields of bronze and committed them to the hands of the officers
of the guard, who kept the door of the king's house. **11** And as often as the king went
into the house of the LORD, the guard came and carried them and brought them back
to the guardroom. **12** And when [p]he humbled himself the wrath of the LORD turned
from him, so as not to make a complete destruction. Moreover, [q]conditions were good[2]
in Judah.
13 [r]So King Rehoboam grew strong in Jerusalem and reigned. Rehoboam was forty-one
years old when he began to reign, and he reigned seventeen years in Jerusalem, the city
that the LORD had chosen out of all the tribes of Israel to put his name there. His mother's
name was Naamah the Ammonite. **14** And he did evil, [s]for he did not set his heart to seek
the LORD.
15 [t]Now the acts of Rehoboam, [u]from first to last, are they not written in the chronicles
of [v]Shemaiah the prophet and of [w]Iddo [x]the seer?[3] There were continual wars between
Rehoboam and Jeroboam. **16** And Rehoboam slept with his fathers and was buried in the
city of David, and [y]Abijah[4] his son reigned in his place.

Chapter 12
1 [z]ch. 11:17 [a]ch. 26:16 [b]See 1 Kgs. 14:22-24
2 [c]1 Kgs. 14:25 [d]1 Kgs. 11:40
3 [e]ch. 16:8; Nah. 3:9; [Dan. 11:43]
4 [f]See ch. 11:5-12
5 [g]ch. 11:2; 1 Kgs. 12:22 [h][ch. 15:2]
6 [i][ch. 21:2] [j]Ex. 9:27
7 [k][ch. 7:14; 1 Kgs. 21:29; James 4:10] [l][ch. 34:25]
8 [m][Deut. 28:47, 48; Isa. 26:13]
9 [n]For ver. 9-11, see 1 Kgs. 14:26-28 [o]ch. 9:15, 16; 1 Kgs. 10:16, 17
12 [p][ch. 7:14; 1 Kgs. 21:29; James 4:10] [q][ch. 19:3]
13 [r]1 Kgs. 14:21
14 [s][ch. 19:3]
15 [t][1 Kgs. 14:29] [u]ch. 9:29; 1 Chr. 29:29 [v]ver. 5; 1 Kgs. 12:22 [w]ch. 9:29; 13:22 [x]See 1 Sam. 9:9
16 [y][1 Kgs. 14:31]

[1] Hebrew *and sought a multitude of wives* [2] Hebrew *good things were found* [3] After *seer*, Hebrew adds *according to genealogy* [4] Spelled *Abijam* in 1 Kings 14:31

pride and a reliance on his own strength instead of dependence on God. That he and his people **abandoned the law of the LORD** is equated with abandoning God himself (v. 5): there is no effective relationship with God without obedience to his revealed will. The NT makes the same point positively when Jesus equates love for him with obedience to his commandments (John 14:21).

12:2 unfaithful (Hb. *ma'al*). A key term for the Chronicler. See note on 1 Chron. 2:3–8. The Egyptian invasion follows hard on the heels of national apostasy and is explicitly identified by the writer as God's punishment for sin; but not every instance of distress or suffering in Chronicles is understood this way (e.g., 2 Chron. 20:1–12; 32:1, where Judah suffers foreign invasion after its kings have acted faithfully; similarly 13:8). **Shishak** is Sheshonq I, who ruled from 945–924 B.C. His campaign through Judah and Israel is commemorated in inscriptions on the temple at Karnak. **fifth year**. 925 B.C. (see note on 1 Kings 14:25–26).

12:3 Sukkiim. Soldiers probably of Libyan origin, mentioned in Egyptian records of the thirteenth and twelfth centuries B.C.

12:5 You abandoned me, so I have abandoned you. See 1 Chron. 28:9; 2 Chron. 15:2.

12:6–8 humbled themselves. See 7:14. The partial **deliverance** that Judah experienced was intended to teach its people a fuller devotion to God. For the Chronicler's own generation, it would have called to mind their own circumstances: subject to the Persian kings, yet free to worship Yahweh in his temple (see Ezra 9:8–9).

12:9–11 Resumes the account from 1 Kings 14:26–28 (see note on 1 Kings 14:25–26). The **treasures** of the temple and palace were surrendered as tribute to avert an attack on the city.

12:12 when he humbled himself the wrath of the LORD turned from him. This is the key point concerning Rehoboam's reign that the Chronicler wishes to make for his readers.

12:14 The writer's overall estimate of Rehoboam is negative: whereas 1 Kings 14:22 (see note there) blames the people for "doing evil," the Chronicler makes this charge against Rehoboam and adds that **he did not set his heart to seek the LORD** (cf. 2 Chron. 11:16).

12:15–16 These verses generally follow 1 Kings 14:29–31 but specify that historical records from **Shemaiah** and **Iddo** contributed to the Chronicler's sources (see note on 1 Kings 14:19). The Chronicler's use of such sources accounts for much of the material in his work that is additional to 1–2 Kings.

Abijah Reigns in Judah

13 [z]In the eighteenth year of King Jeroboam, [y]Abijah began to reign over Judah. 2 He
reigned for three years in Jerusalem. His mother's name was [a]Micaiah[1] the daughter
of Uriel of Gibeah.
[b]Now there was war between Abijah and Jeroboam. 3 Abijah went out to battle, having
an army of valiant men of war, 400,000 chosen men. And Jeroboam [c]drew up his line of
battle against him with 800,000 chosen mighty warriors. 4 Then Abijah stood up on Mount
[d]Zemaraim that is in [e]the hill country of Ephraim and said, "Hear me, O Jeroboam and all
Israel! 5 Ought you not to know that the LORD God of Israel [f]gave the kingship over Israel
forever to David and his sons by [g]a covenant of salt? 6 Yet Jeroboam the son of Nebat, a
servant of Solomon the son of David, rose up [h]and rebelled against his lord, 7 and certain
[i]worthless scoundrels gathered about him and defied Rehoboam the son of Solomon,
when Rehoboam was [j]young and irresolute[2] and could not withstand them.
8 "And now you think to withstand the kingdom of the LORD in the hand of the sons
of David, because you are a great multitude and have with you [k]the golden calves that
Jeroboam made you for gods. 9 [l]Have you not driven out the priests of the LORD, the sons
of Aaron, and the Levites, and made priests for yourselves like the peoples of other lands?
Whoever comes [m]for ordination[3] with a young bull or seven rams becomes a priest of
what are [n]no gods. 10 But as for us, the LORD is our God, and we have not forsaken him. We
have priests ministering to the LORD who are sons of Aaron, and Levites for their service.
11 They offer to the LORD [o]every morning and every evening burnt offerings and incense
of sweet spices, set out [p]the showbread on the table of pure gold, [q]and care for the golden
lampstand that its lamps may [r]burn every evening. For we [s]keep the charge of the LORD
our God, but you have forsaken him. 12 Behold, God is with us at our head, and his priests
[t]with their battle trumpets to sound the call to battle against you. O sons of Israel, [u]do not
fight against the LORD, the God of your fathers, for you cannot succeed."
13 Jeroboam had sent [v]an ambush around to come upon them from behind. Thus his
troops[4] were in front of Judah, and the ambush was behind them. 14 And when Judah
looked, behold, the battle was in front of and behind them. [w]And they cried to the LORD,
and the priests [t]blew the trumpets. 15 Then the men of Judah raised the battle shout. And
when the men of Judah shouted, [x]God defeated Jeroboam and all Israel before Abijah
and Judah. 16 The men of Israel fled before Judah, [y]and God gave them into their hand.
17 Abijah and his people struck them with great force, so there fell slain of Israel 500,000
chosen men. 18 Thus the men of Israel were subdued at that time, and the men of Judah
prevailed, [z]because they relied on the LORD, the God of their fathers. 19 And Abijah pursued

[1] Spelled *Maacah* in 1 Kings 15:2 [2] Hebrew *soft of heart* [3] Hebrew *to fill his hand* [4] Hebrew *they*

Chapter 13
1 [z]1 Kgs. 15:1, 2 [y][See ch. 12:16 above]
2 [a][ch. 11:20] [b]1 Kgs. 15:7
3 [c]ch. 14:10; Judg. 20:22; 1 Sam. 17:2
4 [d]Josh. 18:22 [e]See Josh. 24:33
5 [f]2 Sam. 7:12, 13, 16 [g]Num. 18:19
6 [h]1 Kgs. 11:26; 12:19, 20
7 [i]See Judg. 9:4 [j][ch. 12:13; 1 Kgs. 14:21]
8 [k]See 1 Kgs. 12:28
9 [l]ch. 11:14, 15 [m]ch. 29:31 [n]Jer. 5:7
11 [o]ch. 2:4 [p]See Lev. 24:5-9 [q]See Ex. 25:31-39 [r]Ex. 27:20, 21; Lev. 24:2-4 [s]Num. 1:53
12 [t]Num. 10:9 [u][Acts 5:39]
13 [v][Josh. 8:9]
14 [w]ch. 14:11 [t][See ver. 12 above]
15 [x]ch. 14:12
16 [y]ch. 16:8
18 [z][ch. 14:11; 16:7, 8]

13:1–14:1 *Abijah.* The Chronicler's account of Abijah's reign is much longer than that given in 1 Kings 15:1–8 (where he is called Abijam). It is, in fact, mainly the development of the statement in 1 Kings 15:7 that "there was war between Abijam and Jeroboam" through the detailed record of one incident, a battle between these kings in the hill country of Ephraim. In the estimation of 1 Kings 15:3, Abijah, like his father Rehoboam, "was not wholly true to the LORD." The Chronicler would probably agree (since it appears from 2 Chron. 14:3–5; 15:8, 16 that idolatrous worship was practiced throughout Judah during Abijah's reign), but he refrains from explicit comment on the king's own piety to concentrate instead on what God accomplished through his reign. The Chronicler notes that in contrast to Jeroboam's kingdom and cult, the Davidic monarchy is the object of God's enduring promise (13:5, 8); the Jerusalem priesthood is legitimate and faithful (13:10–11); and the men of Judah trust in God (13:13, 18). It is for these reasons that the southern kingdom enjoys God's protection and blessing, even if Abijah himself (like his father) falls somewhat short of the ideal.

13:2 three years. 915–912 B.C. **Micaiah**. Also spelled Maacah. See 11:20.

13:3 To judge from Abijah's words in v. 8, Jeroboam probably instigated this war, seeking to reunite the kingdom by force, as Rehoboam had tried to do (11:1–4). On the size of the armies, see note on 1 Chron. 12:23–37. However the numbers should be understood, Judah is outnumbered two to one by Israel.

13:4 Mount Zemaraim. Probably on the northern border of Benjamin, on the frontier between the two kingdoms; see Josh. 18:22. Abijah's speech is one of several royal addresses in Chronicles that serve to convey the author's concerns—in this case, his condemnation of the northern kingdom for its apostasy and continuing rebellion.

13:5–8a Abijah condemns Jeroboam and the northerners for opposing God's grant of perpetual **kingship over Israel** to **David and his sons**. The term **covenant of salt** denotes a permanent provision; see Num. 18:19. Jeroboam's kingship is dismissed as rebellion against his master, Solomon, while the Davidic kingdom is nothing less than the **kingdom of the LORD** (see 2 Chron. 9:8).

13:8b–12 Abijah condemns the northerners for their religious unfaithfulness in making calf idols (see Hos. 8:6) and driving out the Aaronic priests and Levites in favor of their own appointees. Judah, by contrast, has the legitimate priesthood and temple worship, so Israel should not **fight against the LORD**. For the Chronicler's own audience, Abijah's speech may have functioned as a sermonic appeal to the different tribes to be united around the temple, under the leadership of the Davidic family.

13:13–19 This battle report echoes older OT narratives in which God fights for and with his people (cf. v. 14 with Josh. 6:20). Judah's reliance on God (2 Chron. 13:14, 18) is the key factor in its success.

13:19 Bethel was one of the locations of Jeroboam's calf cult (see v. 8 and 1 Kings 12:28–29).

19[a][ch. 15:8; 17:2] [b][Josh. 15:9]
20[c]1 Sam. 25:38 [d]1 Kgs. 14:20
22[e]ch. 24:27 [f]ch. 9:29; 12:15

Chapter 14
1[g][1 Kgs. 15:8]
3[h][ch. 15:17; 1 Kgs. 15:14] [i]See Ex. 23:24 [j]Ex. 34:13
5[h][See ver. 3 above] [k]ch. 34:4, 7; Lev. 26:30; Isa. 17:8; 27:9; Ezek. 6:4, 6
6[l]See ch. 11:5 [m]ch. 15:15; 20:30
7[n]ch. 8:5 [m][See ver. 6 above]
8[o][ch. 13:3]
9[p]ch. 12:3; 16:8 [q]ch. 11:8; Josh. 15:44
10[r]ch. 13:3 [q][See ver. 9 above]
11[s]ch. 13:14; Ex. 14:10

Jeroboam [a]and took cities from him, Bethel with its villages and Jeshanah with its villages
and [b]Ephron[1] with its villages. 20 Jeroboam did not recover his power in the days of Abijah.
[c]And the LORD struck him down, [d]and he died. 21 But Abijah grew mighty. And he took
fourteen wives and had twenty-two sons and sixteen daughters. 22 The rest of the acts of
Abijah, his ways and his sayings, are written in the [e]story of the prophet [f]Iddo.

Asa Reigns in Judah

14 [2] [g]Abijah slept with his fathers, and they buried him in the city of David. And Asa
his son reigned in his place. In his days the land had rest for ten years. 2 [3] And Asa
did what was good and right in the eyes of the LORD his God. 3 He took away the foreign
altars [h]and the high places and broke down [i]the pillars and cut down the [j]Asherim 4 and
commanded Judah to seek the LORD, the God of their fathers, and to keep the law and
the commandment. 5 He also took out of all the cities of Judah [h]the high places and the
[k]incense altars. And the kingdom had rest under him. 6 He built [l]fortified cities in Judah,
for the land had rest. He had no war in those years, [m]for the LORD gave him peace. 7 And he
said to Judah, "Let us build these cities and surround them with [n]walls and towers, gates
and bars. The land is still ours, because we have sought the LORD our God. We have sought
him, [m]and he has given us peace on every side." So they built and prospered. 8 And Asa had
an army of [o]300,000 from Judah, armed with large shields and spears, and 280,000 men
from Benjamin that carried shields and drew bows. All these were mighty men of valor.
9 Zerah [p]the Ethiopian came out against them with an army of a million men and 300
chariots, and came as far as [q]Mareshah. 10 And Asa went out to meet him, and [r]they drew
up their lines of battle in the Valley of Zephathah at [q]Mareshah. 11 And Asa [s]cried to the

[1] Or *Ephrain* [2] Ch 13:23 in Hebrew [3] Ch 14:1 in Hebrew

13:21 Large families are a conventional sign in Chronicles of God's blessing on those who rely on him (see 1 Chron. 28:5; 2 Chron. 11:18–21).

13:22 the story of the prophet Iddo. Cf. notes on 12:15–16 and 1 Kings 14:19.

14:2–16:14 *Asa.* The Chronicler's account of Asa's reign (910–869 B.C.) is also much longer and more complex than that given in the earlier history (1 Kings 15:9–24). It describes a reign that begins well but ends badly, as trust in God and obedience to the prophetic word give way to a dependence on human alliances and the rejection of the prophetic word.

14:2–8 Asa begins his reign in an exemplary way by rooting out idolatry and commanding Judah **to seek the LORD** (see 1 Chron. 22:19). **High places** were local sites usually associated with pagan worship (see Deut. 12:2–3). **Asherim**. Poles representing the fertility goddess Asherah. The subsequent building projects, large army, and peace are typical blessings for faithfulness and obedience in Chronicles (see 2 Chron. 11:5–12; 13:3; 17:10).

14:9 Zerah the Ethiopian. Lit., "the Cushite," from modern Sudan (see 12:3; 16:8). Not otherwise known, but possibly a general in the service of Pharaoh Osorkon I, son of Shoshenq I (12:2). **A million men** is literally "a thousand thousands" and represents an enormous number. An alternative way to understand this is "a thousand units" (see note on 1 Chron. 12:23–37). This is more than double the army following Asa (2 Chron. 14:8). **Mareshah**. One of Rehoboam's fortified cities on Judah's southwestern border (11:8).

14:11–15 Asa's prayer reflects the situation envisioned in 6:34–35. Many of the motifs of sacred warfare found in ch. 13 are expressed here as well and will recur in ch. 20: a prayer (or speech) is made by the king before battle,

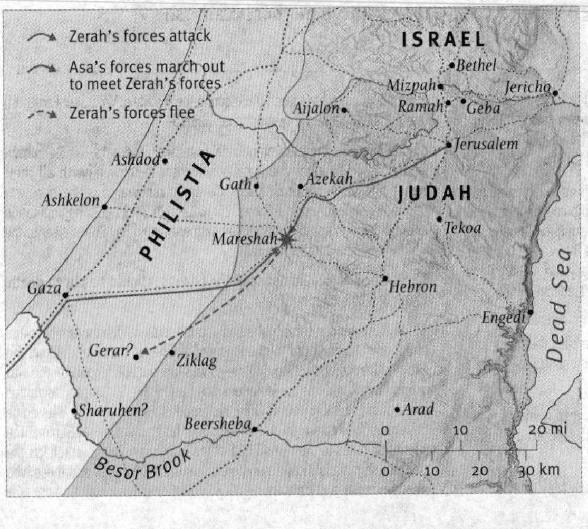

Zerah Attacks Judah
898 B.C.
At some point during Asa's long and prosperous reign over Judah, Zerah the Ethiopian led a vast army from the south to attack Judah at a valley near Mareshah. Asa's army routed Zerah's forces and pursued them to Gerar until none of them remained. Perhaps as punishment for Philistia allowing Zerah's army to pass through their nation, Asa's men then plundered many towns in the region around Gerar before returning to Jerusalem.

LORD his God, "O LORD, there is none like you to help, between the mighty and the weak.
Help us, O LORD our God, [t]for we rely on you, [u]and in your name we have come against
this multitude. O LORD, you are our God; let not man prevail against you." 12 [v]So the LORD
defeated the Ethiopians before Asa and before Judah, and the Ethiopians fled. 13 Asa and
the people who were with him pursued them as far as [w]Gerar, and the Ethiopians fell
until none remained alive, for they were broken before the LORD and his army. The men
of Judah[1] carried away very much spoil. 14 And they attacked all the cities around [w]Gerar,
[x]for the fear of the LORD was upon them. They plundered all the cities, for there was much
plunder in them. 15 And they struck down the tents of those who had livestock and carried
away sheep in abundance and camels. Then they returned to Jerusalem.

Asa's Religious Reforms

15 [y]The Spirit of God came upon Azariah the son of Oded, 2 and he went out to meet
Asa and said to him, "Hear me, Asa, and all Judah and Benjamin: [z]The LORD is with
you while you are with him. [a]If you seek him, he will be found by you, [b]but if you forsake
him, he will forsake you. 3 [c]For a long time Israel was without the true God, and without
a teaching priest and without law, 4 [d]but when in their distress they turned to the LORD,
the God of Israel, and sought him, he was found by them. 5 In those times there was no
peace [e]to him who went out or to him who came in, for great disturbances afflicted all the
inhabitants of the lands. 6 They were broken in pieces. Nation was crushed by nation and
city by city, for God troubled them with every sort of distress. 7 [f]But you, take courage! Do
not let your hands be weak, [g]for your work shall be rewarded."
8 As soon as Asa heard these words, [h]the prophecy of Azariah the son of Oded, he took
courage and put away the detestable idols from all the land of Judah and Benjamin and
from [i]the cities that he had taken in [j]the hill country of Ephraim, and he repaired the
altar of the LORD [k]that was in front of the vestibule of the house of the LORD.[2] 9 And he
gathered all Judah and Benjamin, [l]and those from Ephraim, Manasseh, and Simeon who
were residing with them, for great numbers had deserted to him from Israel when they
saw that the LORD his God was with him. 10 They were gathered at Jerusalem in the third
month of the fifteenth year of the reign of Asa. 11 They sacrificed to the LORD on that day
[m]from the spoil that they had brought 700 oxen and 7,000 sheep. 12 [n]And they entered
into a covenant to seek the LORD, the God of their fathers, with all their heart and with all
their soul, 13 but that whoever would not seek the LORD, the God of Israel, [o]should be put
to death, whether young or old, man or woman. 14 They swore an oath to the LORD with a
loud voice and with shouting and with trumpets and with horns. 15 And all Judah rejoiced
over the oath, for they had sworn with all their heart and had sought him with their whole
desire, and he was found by them, [p]and the LORD gave them rest all around.
16 [q]Even Maacah, [r]his mother, King Asa removed from being queen mother because she

[1] Hebrew *They* [2] Hebrew *the vestibule of the LORD*

11 [t]ch. 13:18 [u][1 Sam. 17:45]
12 [v]ch. 13:15
13 [w]Gen. 10:19; 20:1; 26:1, 6
14 [w][See ver. 13 above] [x]ch. 17:10; 20:29; [Gen. 35:5]

Chapter 15
1 [y]ch. 20:14; 24:20; Num. 24:2; Judg. 3:10; [ver. 8]
2 [z]ch. 20:17 [a]1 Chr. 28:9; Isa. 55:6; Jer. 29:13 [b]ch. 12:5; 24:20
3 [c][Hos. 3:4]
4 [d]Deut. 4:30, 31
5 [e]Judg. 5:6
7 [f]Josh. 1:6, 7, 9 [g]Gen. 15:1; [Ps. 62:12]
8 [h][ver. 1] [i]ch. 17:2; [ch. 13:19] [j]See Josh. 24:33 [k]ch. 8:12
9 [l]ch. 11:16
11 [m]See ch. 14:13-15
12 [n]ch. 29:10; 34:31; 2 Kgs. 23:3; Neh. 10:29
13 [o]See Deut. 13:6-9
15 [p]ch. 14:7; 20:30
16 [q]For ver. 16-18, see 1 Kgs. 15:13-15 [r][1 Kgs. 15:2, 10]

expressing trust in God (see 13:4–12; 20:5–12); Judah faces overwhelming odds (see 13:3; 20:2); and Yahweh strikes the enemy (see 13:15–16; 20:22–23). **The fear of the LORD** was upon them (see 1 Chron. 14:17; 2 Chron. 20:29). The **plunder** was used for sacrifices (15:11).

15:1–7 Azariah is not otherwise known. His speech is intended to encourage Asa to continue his reforms and lead the people into covenant renewal. **If you seek him**. See 1 Chron. 28:9. The theme of "seeking the LORD" recurs throughout 2 Chronicles 15 (vv. 4, 12, 13, 15). Verses 3–6 call to mind the unstable time of the judges, marked by cycles of apostasy and return to God (see Judges 3), and the absence of effective spiritual leadership (see Judg. 17:5–6).

15:8 Cities that he had taken in . . . Ephraim implies that there had been conflict between Judah and Israel prior to the thirty-sixth year of Asa's reign (16:1; c. 875 B.C.).

15:9 The Chronicler highlights a number of occasions when northerners are reunited with their fellow Israelites in Judah, always in the context of worship and seeking God (cf. 11:16; 30:11, 18, 25; 35:18).

15:10 the third month of the fifteenth year. Probably May/June 895 B.C. The assembly may have taken place during the Festival of Weeks (or Pentecost) (see Ex. 23:16 ["Feast of Harvest"]; Lev. 23:15–21).

15:12 Effectively a renewal of the Sinai covenant (Exodus 19–20; 24), allowing the people to affirm their total commitment to Yahweh (**with all their heart and with all their soul**). Covenant renewal in connection with reform is also featured in 2 Chron. 23:16; 29:10; 34:31–32. The implication of these popular acts of religious commitment would have been clear to the Chronicler's own community.

15:13 whoever would not seek the LORD . . . should be put to death. See Deut. 13:6–10 and 17:2–7.

15:16 The **queen mother** played an important role within the family politics of the court as an adviser of the king and teacher of the royal children. The **brook Kidron**, or the "Kidron Valley," was just outside Jerusalem and was used as a refuse dump for idolatrous objects (29:16; 30:14). An inscription found at the site of Khirbet El-Qom, near modern Hebron, reads: "Blessed be Uriyahu by Yahweh and by his Asherah; from his enemies he saved him!" The inscription dates to the second half of the eighth century B.C. It reflects the constant struggle in Judah between true servants of Yahweh and those who were syncretists and idolaters.

16[s]Ex. 34:13 [t][ch. 30:14; 2 Kgs. 23:6, 15]
17[u][ch. 14:3, 5]

Chapter 16

1[v]For ver. 1-6, see 1 Kgs. 15:17-22 [w][1 Kgs. 16:8] [x][ch. 15:9]
4[y][Ex. 1:11]
7[z]ch. 19:2; 1 Kgs. 16:1 [a]See 1 Sam. 9:9 [b][Isa. 31:1; Jer. 17:5]

had made a detestable image [s]for Asherah. Asa cut down her image, [t]crushed it, and burned
it at the brook Kidron. **17** [u]But the high places were not taken out of Israel. Nevertheless,
the heart of Asa was wholly true all his days. **18** And he brought into the house of God the
sacred gifts of his father and his own sacred gifts, silver, and gold, and vessels. **19** And there
was no more war until the thirty-fifth year of the reign of Asa.

Asa's Last Years

16 [v]In the [w]thirty-sixth year of the reign of Asa, Baasha king of Israel went up against
Judah and built Ramah, [x]that he might permit no one to go out or come in to Asa
king of Judah. **2** Then Asa took silver and gold from the treasures of the house of the LORD
and the king's house and sent them to Ben-hadad king of Syria, who lived in Damascus,
saying, **3** "There is a covenant[1] between me and you, as there was between my father and
your father. Behold, I am sending to you silver and gold. Go, break your covenant with
Baasha king of Israel, that he may withdraw from me." **4** And Ben-hadad listened to King
Asa and sent the commanders of his armies against the cities of Israel, and they conquered
Ijon, Dan, Abel-maim, and all the [y]store cities of Naphtali. **5** And when Baasha heard of it,
he stopped building Ramah and let his work cease. **6** Then King Asa took all Judah, and
they carried away the stones of Ramah and its timber, with which Baasha had been building, and with them he built Geba and Mizpah.
7 At that time [z]Hanani [a]the seer came to Asa king of Judah and said to him, [b]"Because

[1] Or *treaty*; twice in this verse

15:17 The high places were not taken out of Israel probably refers to those cities that had previously belonged to the northern kingdom and were then under Asa's control ("out of Israel" is the Chronicler's addition to 1 Kings 15:14a); in Judah, by contrast, Asa's reforms had been much more successful (2 Chron. 14:3, 5). **the heart of Asa was wholly true all his days** (cf. 1 Kings 15:14). This is the overall assessment of his reign, despite the decline of his last years (see note on 2 Chron. 16:13–14).

16:1–14 Asa's last five years are marked by spiritual and physical decline, stemming from his unfaithful response to a military threat from the northern kingdom. He reverses the pattern of his earlier life: a covenant or treaty with Ben-hadad of Syria or Aram (vv. 2–6), in contrast to his covenant with Yahweh (15:12); he rejects the words of Hanani and mistreats him (16:7–10), in contrast to his response to Azariah (15:1–8); he fails to "seek the LORD" in his illness (16:12–13), in contrast to 14:4, 7 and 15:15.

16:1 The thirty-sixth year of the reign of Asa would be c. 876 or 875 B.C. As it stands, the text raises a problem, since **Baasha** had already been dead 10 years by this time (see 1 Kings 15:33; 16:8; and note on 1 Kings 15:17). One possible explanation is that the text here has suffered from a copying error. Letters from the Hebrew alphabet were originally used to denote numbers, and here (and in 2 Chron. 15:19) a scribe might have confused two similar-looking letters (י or *yod* for 10 and ל or *lamedh* for 30, letters that looked more alike in early handwritten Hebrew script than they do in modern typography). If so, then perhaps the original said that this was the "sixteenth year of the reign of Asa"—i.e., 896 or 895 B.C. **Ramah** lay about 5 miles (8 km) north of Jerusalem, and commanded the main road to and from the city.

16:2–5 silver and gold. See note on 1 Kings 15:18–19. **There is** (or "Let there be") **a covenant**. By entering into an alliance with Ben-hadad (at the expense of the temple and his palace), Asa countered the threat from Baasha, but his action reflected a lack of faith in Yahweh, who had delivered him from a greater threat (2 Chron. 16:8). Foreign alliances are condemned in 19:2; 20:35–37; 22:5; 28:16–21.

16:7–9 The rebuke by **Hanani** contrasts with Azariah's exhortation (15:2–7). Asa, who had once **relied** on Yahweh (14:11; 16:8), has **relied** instead **on the king of Syria** and will now face future **wars** (v. 9; contrast 15:15, 19). Hanani implies that Asa could have defeated Syria as well as Israel (16:7), had he trusted in God. During the reign of Asa's son Jehoshaphat, Judah will in fact be at war with Syria (18:30). **the eyes of the LORD run to and fro throughout the whole earth**. God continuously watches and evaluates everyone's inner thoughts, attitudes, and convictions (**heart**). Similar wording appears in Zech. 4:10.

War between Israel and Judah

As Israel and Judah battled each other to determine their permanent border, King Baasha of Israel attempted to restrict access to Judah by moving the border down to Ramah. Rather than fight with Baasha himself, King Asa of Judah bribed Ben-hadad of Syria to attack the northern border of Israel and force Baasha to withdraw from Ramah. Once Baasha withdrew, Asa carried away the building supplies of Ramah and used them to fortify Mizpah (further north) and Geba (near the pass at Michmash).

you relied on the king of Syria, and did not rely on the LORD your God, the army of the
king of Syria has escaped you. 8 Were not [c]the Ethiopians and [d]the Libyans a huge army
with very many chariots and horsemen? Yet [e]because you relied on the LORD, he gave
them into your hand. 9 [f]For the eyes of the LORD run to and fro throughout the whole
earth, to give strong support to those [g]whose heart is blameless[1] toward him. [h]You have
done foolishly in this, for from now on [i]you will have wars." 10 Then Asa was angry with
the seer and put him [j]in the stocks in prison, for he was in a rage with him because of this.
And Asa inflicted cruelties upon some of the people at the same time.
11 [k]The acts of Asa, from first to last, are written in the Book of the Kings of Judah and
Israel. 12 In the thirty-ninth year of his reign Asa was diseased in his feet, and his disease
became severe. Yet even in his disease he did not seek the LORD, but sought help from
physicians. 13 And Asa slept with his fathers, dying in the forty-first year of his reign. 14 They
buried him in the tomb that he had cut for himself in the city of David. They laid him on
a bier [l]that had been filled with various kinds of spices prepared by the perfumer's art,
[m]and they made a very great fire in his honor.

Jehoshaphat Reigns in Judah

17 Jehoshaphat his son reigned in his place and strengthened himself against Israel.
2 He placed forces in all the [n]fortified cities of Judah and set garrisons in the land of
Judah, and in the cities of Ephraim [o]that Asa his father had captured. 3 The LORD was with
Jehoshaphat, because he walked in the earlier ways of his father David. He did not seek
the Baals, 4 but sought the God of his father and walked in his commandments, [p]and not
according to the practices of Israel. 5 Therefore the LORD established the kingdom in his
hand. And all Judah [q]brought tribute to Jehoshaphat, [r]and he had great riches and honor.
6 His heart was courageous in the ways of the LORD. And furthermore, [s]he took the high
places and the Asherim out of Judah.
7 In the third year of his reign he sent his officials, Ben-hail, Obadiah, Zechariah,
Nethanel, and Micaiah, [t]to teach in the cities of Judah; 8 [u]and with them the Levites,
Shemaiah, Nethaniah, Zebadiah, Asahel, Shemiramoth, Jehonathan, Adonijah, Tobijah,
and Tobadonijah; and with these Levites, the priests Elishama and Jehoram. 9 And [t]they

[1] *Or whole*

8 [c]ch. 14:9 [d]ch. 12:3 [e][ch. 13:16, 18]
9 [f]Zech. 4:10; [Prov. 15:3] [g][1 Kgs. 8:61] [h]1 Sam. 13:13 [i]1 Kgs. 15:16, 32
10 [j][ch. 18:26]
11 [k]For ver. 11-14, see 1 Kgs. 15:23, 24
14 [l][Gen. 50:2; Mark 16:1; John 19:39, 40] [m][ch. 21:19; Jer. 34:5]

Chapter 17

2 [n]See ch. 11:5 [o]ch. 15:8
4 [p][1 Kgs. 12:28]
5 [q][ch. 32:23] [r]ch. 18:1
6 [s][ch. 15:17; 20:33; 1 Kgs. 22:43]
7 [t]See ch. 35:3
8 [u]ch. 19:8
9 [t][See ver. 7 above]

16:10 Asa was angry with the seer. Asa's response is the first act of persecution of a prophet by a king recorded in the OT (see 18:26; 24:21; 25:16; 36:16). **Put him in the stocks** calls to mind the persecution of Jeremiah (Jer. 20:2).

16:11–12 the Book of the Kings of Judah and Israel. See 12:15; 13:22; and note on 1 Kings 14:19. The Chronicler does not specify whether Asa's foot disease is divine punishment for his lack of faith and his abuse of Hanani, though this may be implied. (An explicit connection between sickness and divine punishment is made in 2 Chron. 21:16–20; 26:16–23.) The primary concern here is Asa's response: **he did not seek the LORD** (cf. 14:4, 7; 15:12). He is not criticized so much for seeking **help from physicians** (or "healers"), but for doing so apart from "the LORD, [his] healer" (Ex. 15:26), and his promises of "healing" in 2 Chron. 7:14 (see 30:20).

16:13–14 forty-first year. Asa ruled 912–871 B.C. Funeral reports in Chronicles are often used to pass a theological judgment on a reign. **a very great fire.** See 21:19; Jer. 34:5. The **honor** shown Asa at his funeral indicates that he was held in high esteem by the people. The Chronicler also seems to have taken a generally positive view of his reign, despite the decline of his last five years (or his last 25 years; see note on 2 Chron. 16:1).

17:1–21:1 ***Jehoshaphat.*** Jehoshaphat's reign (871–849 B.C.) probably included three years as co-regent with Asa during his illness (see 20:31; 2 Kings 3:1; 8:16). The Chronicler's account of his reign is much longer than that given in Kings, where Jehoshaphat plays a subordinate role to the northern kings Ahab (1 Kings 22:4–5, 29–33) and Jehoram (2 Kings 3:4–27). The Chronicler passes over the Jehoram narrative and assigns Jehoshaphat a central significance in his own right, as one who strengthens his kingdom spiritually and militarily (2 Chron. 17:1–19), organizes its system of courts (19:1–11), and demonstrates exemplary faith and leadership in the face of a terrible military threat (20:1–29). At the same time, Jehoshaphat is criticized for his alliances with the apostate northern kingdom (19:1–3; 20:37). Like his predecessors, Jehoshaphat is thus a mixture of good and bad qualities, with a preponderance of good.

17:1–6 Jehoshaphat's actions at the start of his reign are directed toward reforming the nation's religious life and strengthening its military capabilities, no doubt in view of the border conflicts with the northern kingdom that marked the previous reigns. As long as he continues in this attitude of faith in God and loyalty to the ways of David (vv. 3–6), his kingdom will enjoy security and prosperity. On later occasions, however, Jehoshaphat will be drawn into alliances through marriage or military and commercial arrangements with the northern kingdom, and all of these will lead to potentially disastrous consequences.

17:3–4 The Chronicler's characteristic theme of "seeking God" is accompanied by obedience to God's **commandments.** This is the first mention of the **Baals** in Chronicles. Under Ahab and his Tyrean wife Jezebel (contemporaries of Jehoshaphat), the northern kingdom adopted Canaanite Baal worship (1 Kings 16:31), leading to conflict with Elijah (1 Kings 19).

17:5 The LORD established the kingdom in his hand, continuing the promise made to David (see 1 Chron. 17:11). God acts in and through his people's obedience to fulfill his word.

17:6 Reform of worship is characteristic of faithful kings in Chronicles (see 14:3, 5; 15:8; 34:4).

17:7–9 In the third year of his reign. Probably the first year of his reign alone (870 B.C.), following a three-year co-regency with his father (see 16:12; 20:31). Jehoshaphat's reforms were not limited to worship but also included a mission by his officials, along with a number of Levites and priests, to instruct the nation in the Law of Moses. It was God's intention from Israel's beginning that his people be thoroughly conversant with the law (see Deut. 6:6–9). Besides administering sacrifices, it was the duty of priests in particular to instruct the people in the law (see Lev. 10:11; Deut. 33:10; Jer. 18:18; Mal. 2:7). On the role of the Levites in teaching the law, see Neh. 8:7–9.

10[V]ch. 14:14; 20:29
11[W][ch. 26:8; 2 Sam. 8:2]
16[X]Judg. 5:2, 9; Neh. 11:2
17[Y][1 Chr. 12:2]
19[Z]ver. 2

Chapter 18

1[a]ch. 17:5 [b]ch. 21:6; 2 Kgs. 8:18
2[c]For ver. 2-34, see 1 Kgs. 22:2-35

taught in Judah, having the Book of the Law of the LORD with them. They went about
through all the cities of Judah and taught among the people.
10 [V]And the fear of the LORD fell upon all the kingdoms of the lands that were around
Judah, and they made no war against Jehoshaphat. 11 Some of the Philistines [W]brought
Jehoshaphat presents and silver for tribute, and the Arabians also brought him 7,700
rams and 7,700 goats. 12 And Jehoshaphat grew steadily greater. He built in Judah fortresses and store cities, 13 and he had large supplies in the cities of Judah. He had soldiers,
mighty men of valor, in Jerusalem. 14 This was the muster of them by fathers' houses: Of
Judah, the commanders of thousands: Adnah the commander, with 300,000 mighty men
of valor; 15 and next to him Jehohanan the commander, with 280,000; 16 and next to him
Amasiah the son of Zichri, [X]a volunteer for the service of the LORD, with 200,000 mighty
men of valor. 17 Of Benjamin: Eliada, a mighty man of valor, with 200,000 men [Y]armed
with bow and shield; 18 and next to him Jehozabad with 180,000 armed for war. 19 These
were in the service of the king, besides [Z]those whom the king had placed in the fortified
cities throughout all Judah.

Jehoshaphat Allies with Ahab

18 Now Jehoshaphat [a]had great riches and honor, [b]and he made a marriage alliance
with Ahab. 2 [c]After some years he went down to Ahab in Samaria. And Ahab killed
an abundance of sheep and oxen for him and for the people who were with him, and
induced him to go up against Ramoth-gilead. 3 Ahab king of Israel said to Jehoshaphat
king of Judah, "Will you go with me to Ramoth-gilead?" He answered him, "I am as you
are, my people as your people. We will be with you in the war."
4 And Jehoshaphat said to the king of Israel, "Inquire first for the word of the LORD."
5 Then the king of Israel gathered the prophets together, four hundred men, and said to
them, "Shall we go to battle against Ramoth-gilead, or shall I refrain?" And they said, "Go
up, for God will give it into the hand of the king." 6 But Jehoshaphat said, "Is there not here
another prophet of the LORD of whom we may inquire?" 7 And the king of Israel said to
Jehoshaphat, "There is yet one man by whom we may inquire of the LORD, Micaiah the
son of Imlah; but I hate him, for he never prophesies good concerning me, but always
evil." And Jehoshaphat said, "Let not the king say so." 8 Then the king of Israel summoned
an officer and said, "Bring quickly Micaiah the son of Imlah." 9 Now the king of Israel and

17:10–11 See 1 Chron. 14:17 and 2 Chron. 14:14. The blessings of peace with the neighboring nations, and tribute from them, are presented as a consequence of the people's faithfulness to the law. The significance of this for the Chronicler's own relatively weak and impoverished community is clear. **Arabians** probably refers to tribes living to the south and southwest of Judah, close to the Philistines (see 21:16–17; 26:6–7).

17:12–19 The description of Jehoshaphat's military forces looks forward to the account of his alliance with Ahab in ch. 18. Large armies are regularly a sign of God's blessing in Chronicles, but the author will show that they are no certain defense if priorities are wrong and faith is misplaced (cf. Ps. 33:16–19). The details seem to be drawn from a military census list. **thousands**. These may be actual numbers, or they may indicate military units (actual size uncertain); see note on 1 Chron. 12:23–37.

18:1–27 The account of Jehoshaphat's alliance with Ahab is taken with few changes from 1 Kings 22:1–40, but the additional comments in 2 Chron. 18:1–2 and in 19:1–3 give it an altogether different significance. Jehoshaphat, rather than Ahab (and the divine punishment he received for spurning the prophetic word), is the focus here. The Chronicler is concerned to show that Jehoshaphat is equally subject to the prophetic word, but that by repentance and a conscientious return to God's way, he may escape divine wrath. As with his father Asa (see 16:3), Jehoshaphat seeks an alliance with the northern kingdom that is based not on righteous grounds but on political expediency that may draw Judah into destruction. In his account of Hezekiah's reign (chs. 29–30), the Chronicler will indicate how a true and beneficial unity among the tribes of Israel can be achieved.

18:1–2 The Chronicler's introduction alludes to the **marriage** of Jehoshaphat's son Jehoram to Ahab's daughter Athaliah (see 21:6), some years before the battle Ahab initiated against Syria to recapture Ramoth-gilead. The statement that **Jehoshaphat had great riches and honor** is an indication of divine blessing on his reign and casts his alliance with Ahab into a yet more reprehensible light. The marriage between the royal houses was intended to seal peace between the kingdoms after 50 years of hostilities. Such an alliance, however, would require Jehoshaphat to "help the wicked and love those who hate the LORD" (19:2). Ahab's great feast for Jehoshaphat and his persuasive words **induced** (Hb. *sut*) or enticed him to take part in the battle (see also 1 Chron. 21:1; 2 Chron. 32:11, 15). The same Hebrew word is found in 18:31 ("God *drew them away* from him") as the positive counterbalance to the evil into which Ahab draws Jehoshaphat.

18:3 Ramoth-gilead was southeast of the Sea of Galilee (probably Tell Ramith, near the modern Jordanian city of Ramtha; see Deut. 4:43). The Syrians captured it during the reign of Ben-hadad (c. 860–843 B.C.). Jehoshaphat's words indicate his commitment to the treaty with Ahab.

18:4–14 Jehoshaphat (in contrast to Ahab) is at least concerned to seek the **word of the LORD** concerning the advisability of the mission (vv. 4, 6, 7). Ahab's **four hundred men** were called **prophets** (cf. also note on 1 Kings 22:6–7), but they were also government officials, probably connected with the Baal and Asherah worship that Jezebel had introduced into the northern kingdom (see 1 Kings 18:19). Their words (2 Chron. 18:5, 11) and symbolic actions (v. 10; see Jer. 27:2–7) are unequivocal and exactly what Ahab wants to hear. Jehoshaphat, however, does not recognize them as prophets of Yahweh and so persists in his request (2 Chron. 18:6). **Micaiah the son of Imlah** is one of the authentic prophets of Yahweh (in a kingdom where they had recently been persecuted; see 1 Kings 18:4). His initial words to Ahab (2 Chron. 18:14) were apparently spoken in an ironic tone, as Ahab's reaction (v. 15) suggests.

18:9–11 sitting at the threshing floor. See note on 1 Kings 22:10–12.

Jehoshaphat the king of Judah were sitting on their thrones, arrayed in their robes. And
they were sitting at the threshing floor [d]at the entrance of the gate of Samaria, and all the
prophets were prophesying before them. 10 And Zedekiah the son of Chenaanah made
for himself horns of iron and said, "Thus says the LORD, 'With these you shall push the
Syrians until they are destroyed.'" 11 And all the prophets prophesied so and said, "Go up
to Ramoth-gilead and triumph. The LORD will give it into the hand of the king."
12 And the messenger who went to summon Micaiah said to him, "Behold, the words
of the prophets with one accord are favorable to the king. Let your word be like the word
of one of them, and speak favorably." 13 But Micaiah said, [e]"As the LORD lives, [f]what my
God says, that I will speak." 14 And when he had come to the king, the king said to him,
"Micaiah, shall we go to Ramoth-gilead to battle, or shall I refrain?" And he answered, "Go
up and triumph; they will be given into your hand." 15 But the king said to him, "How many
times shall I make you swear that you speak to me nothing but the truth in the name of
the LORD?" 16 And he said, "I saw all Israel scattered on the mountains, [g]as sheep that have
no shepherd. And the LORD said, 'These have no master; let each return to his home in
peace.'" 17 And the king of Israel said to Jehoshaphat, "Did I not tell you that he would not
prophesy good concerning me, but evil?" 18 And Micaiah said, "Therefore hear the word
of the LORD: [h]I saw the LORD sitting on his throne, and all the host of heaven standing
on his right hand and on his left. 19 And the LORD said, 'Who will entice Ahab the king of
Israel, that he may go up and fall at Ramoth-gilead?' And one said one thing, and another
said another. 20 Then a spirit came forward and stood before the LORD, saying, 'I will entice
him.' And the LORD said to him, 'By what means?' 21 And he said, 'I will go out, and will be
[i]a lying spirit in the mouth of all his prophets.' And he said, 'You are to entice him, and you
shall succeed; go out and do so.' 22 Now therefore behold, the LORD has put a lying spirit in
the mouth of these your prophets. The LORD has declared disaster concerning you."
23 Then Zedekiah the son of Chenaanah came near [j]and struck Micaiah on the cheek
and said, "Which way did the Spirit of the LORD go from me to speak to you?" 24 And
Micaiah said, "Behold, you shall see on that day when you go into an inner chamber to
hide yourself." 25 And the king of Israel said, "Seize Micaiah and take him back to Amon
[k]the governor of the city and to Joash the king's son, 26 and say, 'Thus says the king, [l]Put
this fellow in prison and feed him with meager rations of bread and water until I return
in peace.'" 27 And Micaiah said, "If you return in peace, the LORD has not spoken by me."
And he said, [m]"Hear, all you peoples!"

The Defeat and Death of Ahab

28 So the king of Israel and Jehoshaphat the king of Judah went up to Ramoth-gilead.
29 And the king of Israel said to Jehoshaphat, "I will disguise myself and go into battle,
but you wear your robes." And the king of Israel disguised himself, and they went into
battle. 30 Now the king of Syria had commanded the captains of his chariots, "Fight with
neither small nor great, but only with the king of Israel." 31 As soon as the captains of the
chariots saw Jehoshaphat, they said, "It is the king of Israel." So they turned to fight against
him. And Jehoshaphat cried out, and the LORD helped him; God drew them away from
him. 32 For as soon as the captains of the chariots saw that it was not the king of Israel,

9 [d]See Ruth 4:1
13 [e]1 Kgs. 17:1 [f]Num. 22:18; 24:13
16 [g]Num. 27:17; Matt. 9:36
18 [h]See 1 Kgs. 22:19
21 [i]See 1 Kgs. 22:22
23 [j]See 1 Kgs. 22:24
25 [k]ch. 34:8
26 [l]See ch. 16:10
27 [m]Mic. 1:2

18:14 Go up and triumph. See note on 1 Kings 22:15–16.

18:15–22 Ahab's insistence on hearing what Micaiah had really received from Yahweh is answered with a report of two visions. The first concerns the outcome of the battle (v. 16), while the second makes the remarkable claim that God put a **lying spirit in the mouth of** Ahab's **prophets** (vv. 18–22); see notes on 1 Sam. 16:14 and 1 Kings 22:24. The sense here is that, as a follower of false gods (see 1 Kings 16:30–33), Ahab is fittingly deceived by their spokesmen, his prophets. God's action has the nature of a test. The irony of the situation is that Ahab is told the truth (2 Chron. 18:16, 18–22) but does not recognize it as such, even though he had insisted that Micaiah tell him the truth (v. 15). His repudiation of Micaiah's message and his treatment of the prophet (v. 26) indicate his contempt for the truth.

18:23–27 Zedekiah . . . struck Micaiah on the cheek. Zedekiah had claimed to speak in the name of Yahweh (v. 10), but he shows by his violent and contemptuous conduct his scant concern for the truth. Ahab's treatment of Micaiah foreshadows Jeremiah's suffering (Jer. 37:14–16).

18:24 you shall see . . . inner chamber. See note on 1 Kings 22:25.

18:25 Amon . . . Joash. See note on 1 Kings 22:26.

18:28–34 Ahab is enticed into battle, as the spirit had promised (v. 20). His decision to **disguise** himself, while rather cynically directing Jehoshaphat to wear his royal **robes**, indicates his dominant role in the alliance and perhaps also represents a contrived attempt to evade Micaiah's word of doom. But events turn out the opposite of what Ahab intended: Jehoshaphat is delivered in battle as a consequence of his desperate prayer (v. 31b, **and the LORD helped him; God drew them away from him** is the Chronicler's own addition to the text; see note on vv. 1–2), while Ahab dies from an apparently **random** arrow (v. 33), clear evidence of God's sovereign direction of events.

18:29 I will disguise myself. See note on 1 Kings 22:30.

they turned back from pursuing him. 33 But a certain man drew his bow at random[1] and
struck the king of Israel between the scale armor and the breastplate. Therefore he said to
the driver of his chariot, "Turn around and carry me out of the battle, for I am wounded."
34 And the battle continued that day, and the king of Israel was propped up in his chariot
facing the Syrians until evening. Then at sunset he died.

Jehoshaphat's Reforms

19 Jehoshaphat the king of Judah returned in safety to his house in Jerusalem. 2 But [n]Jehu
the son of [o]Hanani [p]the seer went out to meet him and said to King Jehoshaphat,
"Should you [q]help the wicked and love those who hate the LORD? Because of this, [r]wrath
has gone out against you from the LORD. 3 Nevertheless, [s]some good is found in you, for
[t]you destroyed the Asheroth out of the land, and have [u]set your heart to seek God."
4 Jehoshaphat lived at Jerusalem. And he went out again among the people, from
Beersheba to [v]the hill country of Ephraim, and brought them back to the LORD, the God
of their fathers. 5 He appointed [w]judges in the land in all [x]the fortified cities of Judah, city
by city, 6 and said to the judges, "Consider what you do, [y]for you judge not for man but
for the LORD. He is with you in giving judgment. 7 Now then, let the fear of the LORD be
upon you. Be careful what you do, for [z]there is no injustice with the LORD our God, [a]or
partiality or taking bribes."
8 Moreover, in Jerusalem Jehoshaphat [b]appointed certain Levites and priests and heads
of families of Israel, [y]to give judgment for the LORD and to decide disputed cases. They had
their seat at Jerusalem. 9 And he charged them: [c]"Thus you shall do in the fear of the LORD, in
faithfulness, [d]and with your whole heart: 10 [e]whenever a case comes to you from your brothers who live in their cities, concerning bloodshed, law or commandment, statutes or rules,
then you shall warn them, that they may not incur guilt before the LORD and [f]wrath may
not come upon you and your brothers. Thus you shall do, and you will not incur guilt. 11 And
behold, Amariah the chief priest is over you [g]in all matters of the LORD; and Zebadiah the
son of Ishmael, the governor of the house of Judah, in all the king's matters, and the Levites
will serve you as officers. [h]Deal courageously, and may the LORD be with the upright!"[2]

Jehoshaphat's Prayer

20 After this [i]the Moabites and Ammonites, and with them some of the Meunites,[3]
came against Jehoshaphat for battle. 2 Some men came and told Jehoshaphat, "A
great multitude is coming against you from Edom,[4] from beyond the sea; and, behold, they

[1] Hebrew *in his innocence* [2] Hebrew *the good* [3] Compare 26:7; Hebrew *Ammonites* [4] One Hebrew manuscript; most Hebrew manuscripts *Aram* (Syria)

Chapter 19

2 [n]ch. 20:34; 1 Kgs. 16:1 [o]ch. 16:7 [p]See 1 Sam. 9:9 [q][ch. 18:1; 20:37; Ps. 139:21] [r]ver. 10; ch. 24:18; 32:25
3 [s]ch. 12:12; 1 Kgs. 14:13 [t]ch. 17:6 [u]ch. 30:19; Ezra 7:10
4 [v]See Josh. 24:33
5 [w][Deut. 16:18] [x]See ch. 11:5
6 [y]Deut. 1:17
7 [z]Deut. 32:4; Job 8:3; 34:10; [Gen. 18:25; Rom. 9:14] [a]See Deut. 10:17
8 [b]ch. 17:8, 9 [y][See ver. 6 above]
9 [c]2 Sam. 23:3 [d]1 Kgs. 8:61
10 [e]See Deut. 17:8 [f]ver. 2
11 [g]1 Chr. 26:30, 32 [h]1 Chr. 28:10; [Ezra 10:4]

Chapter 20

1 [i]2 Kgs. 1:1; 3:4, 7

19:1–3 This is the Chronicler's own addition to 1 Kings 22. **Jehu the son of Hanani** had ministered in the days of Baasha, king of Israel (1 Kings 16:1–3). His denunciation of Jehoshaphat for his alliance with the ungodly Ahab echoes his criticism of the wicked Baasha (1 Kings 16:7). **Love** here denotes not emotion but the commitment to support a treaty. God's **wrath** is a matter of immense seriousness, yet may be averted or mitigated by repentance (see 2 Chron. 12:7; 32:25–26). Jehu's acknowledgment that **some good is found** in Jehoshaphat recognizes his basic commitment to **seek God** and looks forward to his subsequent actions of repentance and reform (19:4–11).

19:4–11 Jehoshaphat (whose name means "Yahweh judges") institutes a judicial reform that embraces both religious and civil matters. Jehoshaphat's primary concern is to appoint judges of integrity and impartiality, who are exhorted to perform their office in the **fear of the LORD** (vv. 7, 9).

19:4 he went out again. A continuation of the religious teaching mission described in 17:7–9, this time involving the king himself. **From Beersheba to the hill country of Ephraim** describes the limits of Judah from south to north.

19:5–7 Jehoshaphat's action in appointing **judges** in the **fortified cities of Judah** and his words of admonition to them are inspired by the instructions in Deut. 16:18–17:13. Israel's judges must act out of a sense of sacred duty (**you judge not for man but for the LORD**) and must reflect Yahweh's concern for justice and impartiality.

19:8–11 These are legal reforms for Jerusalem involving certain priests, Levites, and heads of families as judges. The Jerusalem court would have supplemented the existing local courts in the land and probably dealt with the more difficult **disputed cases**. The presiding justices **Amariah the chief priest** and **Zebadiah . . . the governor** are responsible for the interests of the temple and the crown, respectively. The Chronicler is careful to show through Jehoshaphat's reforms that, along with inculcating personal faith and obedience to Yahweh (v. 4), the judicial system has a vital role in ensuring that the nation's life is righteous and just, so that the people do not incur **guilt** and **wrath**.

20:1–30 This is the Chronicler's own material, describing a victory over Judah's enemies in which the sovereign God alone acts for his people. In contrast to earlier battles (chs. 13; 14), Judah's part is simply to pray for God's help, trust in his word, worship him (20:18–22), and then watch thankfully while the Divine Warrior destroys the enemy. The narrative draws together a wide range of religious themes and practices, especially those centered on the temple, and also alludes to many earlier scriptural texts and themes. Jehoshaphat's faith is presented here in the most positive light (although the Chronicler will go on to show a further lapse in vv. 35–37), and the rest of the nation (conceived here as a sacred assembly) similarly acts in an exemplary way. The significance of the narrative for the Chronicler's own postexilic community seems clear: although Judah was a small and oppressed outpost of the Persian Empire, recourse to the temple in prayer and trust in the prophetic word (v. 20) was its sure defense in the most testing circumstances, including the dangers posed by its hostile neighbors (cf. Ezra 4; Nehemiah 4).

20:1–2 After this. The invasion followed Jehoshaphat's religious and judicial reforms (ch. 19), and so was not an instance of divine punishment (cf. 12:2) but rather an opportunity to exercise faith (see 32:1). The **Moabites** and **Ammonites** lived east of the Dead Sea. The **Meunites** are equated with the people of Mount Seir (20:10, 22, 23), on the southern border of Judah

are in [j]Hazazon-tamar" (that is, [k]Engedi). 3 Then Jehoshaphat was afraid and set his face
[l]to seek the LORD, and [m]proclaimed a fast throughout all Judah. 4 And Judah assembled to
seek help from the LORD; from all the cities of Judah they came to seek the LORD.
5 And Jehoshaphat stood in the assembly of Judah and Jerusalem, in the house of the
LORD, before the new court, 6 and said, "O LORD, God of our fathers, are you not [n]God in
heaven? You [o]rule over all the kingdoms of the nations. [p]In your hand are power and might,
so that none is able to withstand you. 7 Did you not, our God, [q]drive out the inhabitants
of this land before your people Israel, and give it forever to the descendants of [r]Abraham

2 [j]Gen. 14:7 [k]See 1 Sam. 23:29
3 [l]ch. 19:3; [1 Chr. 22:19] [m]Ezra 8:21; Jer. 36:9; Jonah 3:5; [Joel 1:14; 2:15]
6 [n]See Deut. 4:39 [o][Dan. 4:17, 25, 32] [p]1 Chr. 29:12
7 [q]Ps. 44:2 [r]Isa. 41:8; James 2:23

(see Deut. 2:1; 2 Chron. 26:7). **Engedi** lies on the midpoint of the Dead Sea's western shore. **great multitude**. See 13:8; 14:9; 32:7. Judah was apparently outnumbered by the coalition of enemy nations.

20:3–4 to seek the LORD. See 1 Chron. 22:19. "Seeking the LORD" was characteristic of Jehoshaphat at his best (see 2 Chron. 17:4; 18:4; 19:3). The **fast** was an expression of the special intensity of the people's prayer (see Judg. 20:26; Ezra 8:21–23).

20:5–12 Jehoshaphat's prayer **in the house of the LORD** begins by calling to mind God's universal sovereignty (v. 6), his gift of the land to Abraham's descendants (v. 7), and the **sanctuary** that testifies to God's promise to **hear** his people's prayers and **save** them (v. 9, a clear allusion to the circumstances envisioned in Solomon's dedicatory prayer in 6:14–42). In the juridical style of the so-called psalms of lament (see Psalms 44; 74), Jehoshaphat then complains to God against the injustice of the invaders, acknowledging that Judah is **powerless against** them, but steadfastly trusting God to **execute judgment on them**.

20:14–19 The prophecy of **Jahaziel**, given by the **Spirit of the LORD** in answer to Jehoshaphat's prayer, exhorts the people not to be afraid (see v. 3)

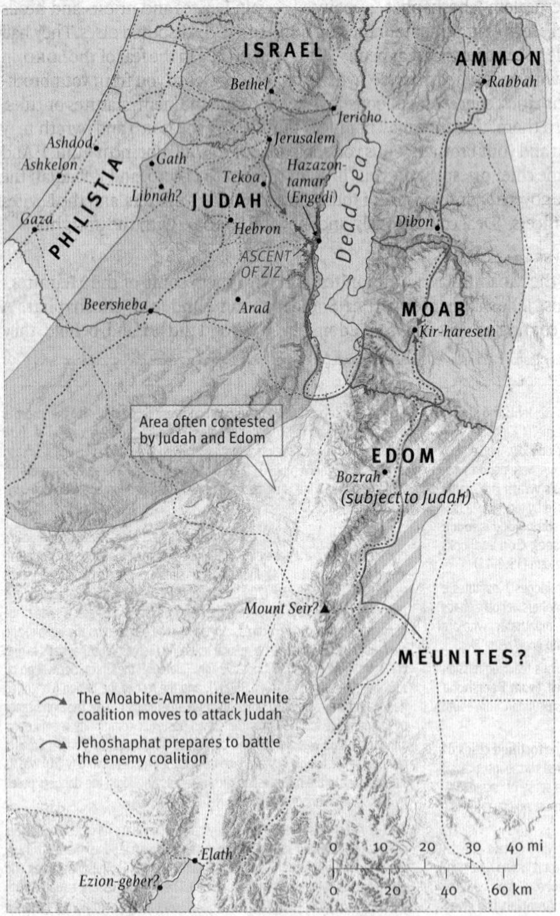

The Moabite Alliance Attacks Judah

Early in Jehoshaphat's reign over Judah, the Moabites rebelled and gained independence from Israel. Soon after this they formed a coalition with the Ammonites and the Meunites to attack Judah. When they had crossed the Dead Sea and were making their way up the ascent of Ziz at Hazazon-tamar (Engedi), Jehoshaphat's army prepared to meet them in battle. Before the battle could begin, however, the Lord caused the Moabites and the Ammonites to turn and attack the Meunites, and the coalition was routed.

your friend? **8** And they have lived in it and have built for you in it a sanctuary for your
name, saying, **9** [s]'If disaster comes upon us, the sword, judgment,[1] or pestilence, or famine,
[t]we will stand before this house and before you—[u]for your name is in this house—and
cry out to you in our affliction, and you will hear and save.' **10** And now behold, the men of
[v]Ammon and Moab and [w]Mount Seir, whom [x]you would not let Israel invade when they
came from the land of Egypt, [y]and whom they avoided and did not destroy— **11** behold,
they reward us [z]by coming to drive us out of your possession, which you have given us
to inherit. **12** O our God, will you not [a]execute judgment on them? For we are powerless
against this great horde that is coming against us. We do not know what to do, but [b]our
eyes are on you."

13 Meanwhile all Judah stood before the LORD, with their little ones, their wives, and
their children. **14** And [c]the Spirit of the LORD came upon Jahaziel the son of Zechariah,
son of Benaiah, son of Jeiel, son of Mattaniah, a Levite of the sons of Asaph, in the midst
of the assembly. **15** And he said, "Listen, all Judah and inhabitants of Jerusalem and King
Jehoshaphat: Thus says the LORD to you, [d]'Do not be afraid and do not be dismayed at
this great horde, [e]for the battle is not yours but God's. **16** Tomorrow go down against them.
Behold, they will come up by the ascent of Ziz. You will find them at the end of [f]the valley,
east of the wilderness of Jeruel. **17** [g]You will not need to fight in this battle. Stand firm, hold
your position, and see the salvation of the LORD on your behalf, O Judah and Jerusalem.'
[d]Do not be afraid and do not be dismayed. Tomorrow go out against them, [h]and the LORD
will be with you."

18 Then Jehoshaphat [i]bowed his head with his face to the ground, and all Judah and
the inhabitants of Jerusalem fell down before the LORD, worshiping the LORD. **19** And
the Levites, of the [j]Kohathites and the [k]Korahites, stood up to praise the LORD, the God
of Israel, with a very loud voice.

20 And they rose early in the morning and went out into [l]the wilderness of Tekoa. And
when they went out, Jehoshaphat stood and said, "Hear me, Judah and inhabitants of
Jerusalem! [m]Believe in the LORD your God, and you will be established; believe his prophets,
and you will succeed." **21** And when he had taken counsel with the people, he appointed
those who were to sing to the LORD and praise him [n]in holy attire, as they went before
the army, and say,

> [o]"Give thanks to the LORD,
> for his steadfast love endures forever."

22 And when they began to sing and praise, the LORD set [p]an ambush against the men of
[q]Ammon, Moab, and Mount Seir, who had come against Judah, so that they were routed.
23 For the men of Ammon and Moab rose against the inhabitants of Mount Seir, devoting
them to destruction, and when they had made an end of the inhabitants of Seir, [r]they all
helped to destroy one another.

The LORD Delivers Judah

24 When Judah came to the watchtower of the wilderness, they looked toward the horde,
and behold, there[2] were dead bodies lying on the ground; none had escaped. **25** When

[1] Or *the sword of judgment* [2] Hebrew *they*

9 [s]ch. 6:28-30; 1 Kgs. 8:33, 37; [Ezek. 14:21] [t][Ezra 10:1] [u]ch. 6:20
10 [v]ver. 1, 22, 23 [w]ch. 25:11, 14; Gen. 32:3; 36:8 [x]Deut. 2:4, 5, 9, 19 [y]Num. 20:21
11 [z]Ps. 83:6, 7, 12
12 [a][1 Sam. 3:13] [b]Ps. 25:15; 123:1, 2; 141:8
14 [c]See ch. 15:1
15 [d]ch. 32:7; [Deut. 1:29, 30; 31:6, 8] [e]1 Sam. 17:47
16 [f]Num. 13:23
17 [g][Ex. 14:13, 14] [d][See ver. 15 above] [h]ch. 15:2; 32:8; [Num. 14:9]
18 [i]ch. 29:29, 30; Ex. 4:31; Neh. 8:6
19 [j]Ex. 6:16, 18 [k]See 1 Chr. 9:19
20 [l][2 Sam. 14:2] [m]Isa. 7:9
21 [n]See 1 Chr. 16:29 [o]See 1 Chr. 16:34
22 [p][ch. 13:13] [q]ver. 10
23 [r][Judg. 7:22; 1 Sam. 14:20]

and informs them that God and not Judah will do the fighting. The people must confront the enemy, but as prayerful spectators, not combatants. Verse 17 is based very closely on Ex. 14:13–14 ("Fear not, stand firm, and see the salvation of the LORD. . . . The LORD will fight for you, and you only have to be silent"), pointing to a fundamental similarity between these two miraculous deliverances. Judah's response must not be mere passivity: **Tomorrow go down against them** is "fighting talk," but Judah's part in this instance is not to take up arms but to exercise faith and to offer prayer and praise (see Eph. 6:10–18). The Levites' ministry of leading praise appropriately concludes the great gathering for prayer.

20:20–23 The **wilderness of Tekoa** lies about 12 miles (19 km) south of Jerusalem. Jehoshaphat's call to faith is based on Isa. 7:9. **Believe** here means the active and obedient trust that God rewards (see Heb. 11:6), acting on the revealed word of **his prophets**, including Jahaziel. The singers whom Jehoshaphat appointed to go out **before the army** were evidently Levites (**in holy attire**; see 1 Chron. 16:29), declaring words from Psalm 136 as their battle song (see 1 Chron. 16:34; 2 Chron. 5:13). Their song of **praise** invokes God to move against their enemies (20:22; see 1 Chron. 16:35). **Ambush** may denote either angelic agents (see 2 Chron. 32:21) or men (see Judg. 9:25), in which case there were mutual suspicions among the coalition forces, leading to panic and their own destruction (2 Chron. 20:23; see Judg. 7:22; 1 Sam. 14:20).

20:24–30 Verse 24 calls to mind Israel's sight of the dead Egyptians in Ex. 14:30 (see note on 2 Chron. 20:14–19). **Valley of Beracah**. "Beracah" means "blessing." There may be a recollection of this event in the prophecy in Joel 3:2, 12 ("the Valley of Jehoshaphat"). The return to Jerusalem takes the form of a triumphal procession, which ends appropriately in the temple, where the people had first sought God's deliverance (2 Chron. 20:5). **the fear of**

Jehoshaphat and his people came to take their spoil, they found among them, in great
numbers, goods, clothing, and precious things, which they took for themselves until
they could carry no more. They were three days in taking the spoil, it was so much. 26 On
the fourth day they assembled in the Valley of Beracah,[1] for there they blessed the LORD.
Therefore the name of that place has been called the Valley of Beracah to this day. 27 Then
they returned, every man of Judah and Jerusalem, and Jehoshaphat at their head, returning to Jerusalem with joy, [s]for the LORD had made them rejoice over their enemies. 28 They
came to Jerusalem with harps and lyres and trumpets, to the house of the LORD. 29 [t]And
the fear of God came on all the kingdoms of the countries when they heard that the LORD
had fought against the enemies of Israel. 30 So the realm of Jehoshaphat was quiet, [u]for his
God gave him rest all around.

31 [v]Thus Jehoshaphat reigned over Judah. He was thirty-five years old when he began to
reign, and he reigned twenty-five years in Jerusalem. His mother's name was Azubah the
daughter of Shilhi. 32 He walked in the way of Asa his father and did not turn aside from
it, doing what was right in the sight of the LORD. 33 [w]The high places, however, were not
taken away; [x]the people had not yet set their hearts upon the God of their fathers.

34 Now the rest of the acts of Jehoshaphat, from first to last, are written in the chronicles
of [y]Jehu the son of Hanani, [z]which are recorded in the Book of the Kings of Israel.

The End of Jehoshaphat's Reign

35 [a]After this Jehoshaphat king of Judah joined with Ahaziah king of Israel, who acted
wickedly. 36 He joined him in building ships to go to [b]Tarshish, and they built the ships
in Ezion-geber. 37 Then Eliezer the son of Dodavahu of Mareshah prophesied against
Jehoshaphat, saying, [c]"Because you have joined with Ahaziah, the LORD will destroy what
you have made." And the ships were wrecked and were not able to go to Tarshish.

Jehoram Reigns in Judah

21 [d]Jehoshaphat slept with his fathers and was buried with his fathers in the city of
David, and Jehoram his son reigned in his place. 2 He had brothers, the sons of
Jehoshaphat: Azariah, Jehiel, Zechariah, Azariah, Michael, and Shephatiah; all these were
the sons of Jehoshaphat king of [e]Israel.[2] 3 Their father gave them great gifts of silver, gold,
and valuable possessions, together with [f]fortified cities in Judah, but he gave the kingdom
to Jehoram, because he was the firstborn. 4 When Jehoram had ascended the throne of
his father and was established, he killed all his brothers with the sword, and also some
of the princes of [e]Israel. 5 [g]Jehoram was [h]thirty-two years old when he became king, and
he reigned eight years in Jerusalem. 6 [i]And he walked in the way of the kings of Israel, as
the house of Ahab had done, for [j]the daughter of Ahab was his wife. And he did what was
evil in the sight of the LORD. 7 Yet the LORD was not willing to destroy the house of David,
because of the covenant that he had made with David, and since he had promised to give
[k]a lamp to him and to his sons forever.

8 In his days Edom revolted from the [l]rule of Judah and set up a king of their own. 9 Then
Jehoram passed over with his commanders and all his chariots, and he rose by night and

[1] *Beracah* means *blessing* [2] That is, Judah

27 [s]Neh. 12:43
29 [t]ch. 14:14; 17:10
30 [u][ch. 14:6, 7; 15:15]
31 [v]For ver. 31-33, see 1 Kgs. 22:41-43
33 [w][ch. 17:6] [x]ch. 12:14
34 [y]ch. 19:2 [z]1 Kgs. 16:1, 7
35 [a]1 Kgs. 22:48, 49
36 [b]ch. 9:21
37 [c][ch. 19:2]

Chapter 21

1 [d]1 Kgs. 22:50
2 [e][ch. 24:5]
3 [f]See ch. 11:5
4 [e][See ver. 2 above]
5 [g]For ver. 5-10, see 2 Kgs. 8:17-22 [h][ver. 20]
6 [i]See 1 Kgs. 12:28-30; 16:31-33 [j]ch. 18:1; 2 Kgs. 8:18
7 [k]See 1 Kgs. 11:36; [2 Sam. 21:17]
8 [l]ver. 10

God. See 1 Chron. 14:17; 2 Chron. 14:14; 17:10; also note on Acts 9:31. **God gave him rest all around**. See 1 Chron. 22:9 and 2 Chron. 14:6.

20:31–34 Adapted from 1 Kings 22:41–45 (cf. note on 1 Kings 22:43–46). Some have claimed that 2 Chron. 20:33 is inconsistent with 17:6, which says that Jehoshaphat "took the high places . . . out of Judah," but both statements can be true if 17:6 refers to Jehoshaphat's official actions and 20:33 indicates that the people's commitment to Jehoshaphat's reforms was not wholehearted in every place (cf. 1 Kings 22:43). The Chronicler explains why: **the people had not yet set their hearts upon the God of their fathers** (2 Chron. 20:33).

20:35–37 Adapted and expanded from 1 Kings 22:48–49. Jehoshaphat repeats his error of making an alliance (this time, a commercial one) with the northern king, Ahab's son **Ahaziah**. The Chronicler has added the prophetic denunciation by **Eliezer**.

21:1–20 The Chronicler's account of Jehoram's reign is considerably expanded over the description given in 2 Kings 8:16–24. The dominant concern here, and in the accounts of his successor Ahaziah (2 Chron. 22:1–9) and the usurper Athaliah (22:10–23:21), is the disastrous influence of the house of Ahab on the Davidic dynasty and Judah. While the Chronicler's portrayal of Jehoram is unremittingly negative, he highlights God's promise to David (21:7) as the grounds for hope in the most troubled days. Again, the Chronicler's own community may take this example from history and apply it to their own circumstances.

21:1 Jehoshaphat slept with his fathers. See notes on 1 Kings 2:10 and 11:43; cf. 1 Kings 22:50.

21:2–22:12 *Jehoram and Ahaziah.* God demonstrates his faithfulness to his promise to preserve David's house, even when the spirit of Ahab is manifested in specific Davidic kings.

21:2–6 Jehoram reigned c. 849–842 B.C., including a co-regency with his father from 853 (see 2 Kings 1:17 and note on 2 Kings 8:16). His marriage

10[m] ver. 8
11[n] Ex. 34:16; Lev. 17:7; 20:5
12[o] ch. 17:3 [p] ch. 14:2-5
13[l] [See ver. 6 above] [n] [See ver. 11 above] [q] See 1 Kgs. 16:31-33 [r] ver. 4
15[s] ver. 18, 19
16[t] [1 Kgs. 11:14, 23] [u] ch. 17:11; 22:1; 26:7
17[v] ch. 25:23; [ch. 22:6]
18[w] ver. 15
19[x] ch. 16:14
20[y] [ver. 5]

struck the Edomites who had surrounded him and his chariot commanders. 10 So Edom
revolted from [m]the rule of Judah to this day. At that time Libnah also revolted from his
rule, because he had forsaken the LORD, the God of his fathers.
11 Moreover, he made high places in the hill country of Judah and led the inhabitants
of Jerusalem [n]into whoredom and made Judah go astray. 12 And a letter came to him from
Elijah the prophet, saying, "Thus says the LORD, the God of David your father, [o]'Because
you have not walked in the ways of Jehoshaphat your father, or [p]in the ways of Asa king
of Judah, 13 [l]but have walked in the way of the kings of Israel and have enticed Judah
and the inhabitants of Jerusalem [n]into whoredom, [q]as the house of Ahab led Israel into
whoredom, and also you [r]have killed your brothers, of your father's house, who were
better than you, 14 behold, the LORD will bring a great plague on your people, your children, your wives, and all your possessions, 15 and you yourself will have a severe sickness
[s]with a disease of your bowels, until your bowels come out because of the disease, day
by day.'"
16 [t]And the LORD stirred up against Jehoram the anger[1] of the Philistines and of [u]the
Arabians who are near the Ethiopians. 17 And they came up against Judah and invaded
it and carried away all the possessions they found that belonged to the king's house,
and also his sons and his wives, so that no son was left to him except [v]Jehoahaz, his
youngest son.
18 And after all this the LORD struck him [w]in his bowels with an incurable disease. 19 In
the course of time, at the end of two years, his bowels came out because of the disease,
and he died in great agony. His people made no fire in his honor, [x]like the fires made for
his fathers. 20 [y]He was thirty-two years old when he began to reign, and he reigned eight

[1] Hebrew *spirit*

to Athaliah, the **daughter of Ahab**, implicated him in the **evil** ways of that kingdom. Once in sole possession of the throne, Jehoram demonstrated his true character through the murder of his brothers and other possible rivals (a policy that Athaliah would later repeat; see 2 Chron. 22:10). Alliance with the ungodly would bring the dynasty to the brink of destruction.

21:6 he walked in the way of the kings of Israel. See note on 2 Kings 8:18.

21:7 Because of the covenant that he had made with David is the Chronicler's comment added to his source (see 1 Chron. 17:14). **a lamp to him and to his sons forever**. A metaphor of persistence and permanence in the darkest times, perhaps suggested by the constantly burning temple lamps (2 Chron. 13:11). As the subsequent narrative shows, the Davidic line will be brought perilously close to extinction through murder and war (21:4, 17; 22:10), until it hangs by the slenderest thread. Against all odds, the dynasty will be preserved in God's grace, but Jehoram must still bear the punishment of his own wickedness (21:10–20; cf. notes on 2 Kings 8:19; 8:20–22).

21:8–10 This is taken from 2 Kings 8:20–22, with the additional comment that the revolts happened **because** Jehoram **had forsaken the LORD, the God of his fathers** (see 1 Chron. 28:9). **Libnah** was a Judahite city on the border with Philistia.

21:11–20 This is the Chronicler's own material. In contrast to his father Jehoshaphat, who sought to suppress the heathenish **high places** (17:6), Jehoram actually promotes their construction, probably as a consequence of his marriage alliance with the northern kingdom. **Whoredom** was a traditional term among the prophets for apostasy into idolatry (see Ezek. 16:16; Hos. 4:17–18). As always in Chronicles, the errant king is subject to prophetic rebuke; here, it takes the singular form of a **letter . . . from Elijah the prophet**. The last years of Elijah's ministry overlapped with the beginning of Jehoram's reign (2 Kings 1:17). As he had opposed Ahab (1 Kings 17–18), Elijah now condemns Ahab's spiritual successor (2 Chron. 21:6, 13) for leading Judah into idolatry and for murdering his own brothers. The destruction of Jehoram's own family is decreed, to be fulfilled at the hands **of the Philistines and of the Arabians**, while Jehoram himself is condemned to a fatal bowel **disease**. On disease as divine punishment, see 16:12; 26:19–21; and note on John 9:2. Jehoram's exclusion from burial **in the tombs of the kings** is a final indication that he belonged to the ways of Ahab rather than David.

Edom and Libnah Revolt
848 B.C.
Perhaps emboldened by Moab's rebellion from Israel a few years earlier, Edom revolted against the rule of King Jehoram (also called Joram) of Judah. Jehoram led his army to Edom to put down the rebellion, but his efforts failed. At the same time, the western priestly town of Libnah revolted against Judah, apparently because of Jehoram's idolatrous practices. Philistines and Arabians also attacked Judah and plundered the royal palace, carrying away all its possessions and many of Jehoram's wives and sons.

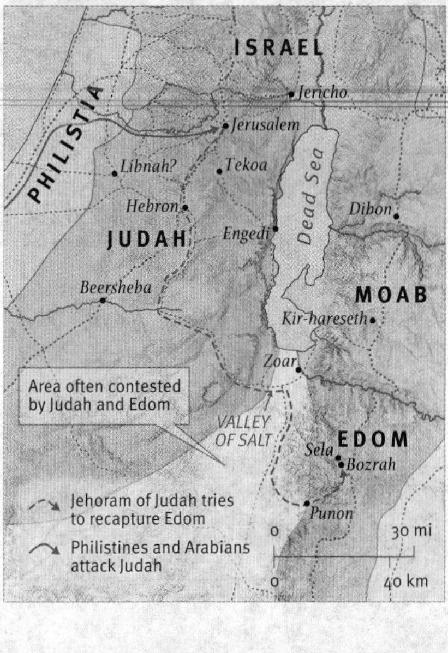

years in Jerusalem. And he departed [z]with no one's regret. [a]They buried him in the city of
David, but not in the tombs of the kings.

Ahaziah Reigns in Judah

22 [b]And the inhabitants of Jerusalem made Ahaziah, his youngest son, king in his
place, for the band of men that came with [c]the Arabians to the camp had killed
all the older sons. So Ahaziah the son of Jehoram king of Judah reigned. 2 Ahaziah was
twenty-two[1] years old when he began to reign, and he reigned one year in Jerusalem. His
mother's name was Athaliah, [d]the granddaughter of Omri. 3 He also walked in the ways
of the house of Ahab, for his mother was his counselor in doing wickedly. 4 He did what
was evil in the sight of the LORD, as the house of Ahab had done. For after the death of
his father they were his counselors, to his undoing. 5 He even followed their counsel and
went with Jehoram the son of Ahab king of Israel to make war against Hazael king of
Syria at Ramoth-gilead. And the Syrians wounded Joram, 6 and he returned to be healed
in Jezreel of the wounds that he had received at Ramah, when he fought against Hazael
king of Syria. And Ahaziah the son of Jehoram king of Judah went down to see Joram the
son of Ahab in Jezreel, because he was wounded.

7 But it was ordained by God that the downfall of Ahaziah should come about through
his going to visit Joram. For when he came there, [e]he went out with Jehoram to meet
Jehu the son of Nimshi, [f]whom the LORD had anointed to destroy the house of Ahab.

[1] See 2 Kings 8:26; Hebrew *forty-two*; Septuagint *twenty*

20 [z][Jer. 22:18] [a][ch. 24:25; 28:27]

Chapter 22

1 [b]For ver. 1-6, see 2 Kgs. 8:24-29 [c]See ch. 21:16
2 [d][ch. 21:6]
7 [e]2 Kgs. 9:21 [f]2 Kgs. 9:6, 7

Jehu Executes Judgment

841 B.C.

During a battle with Syria at Ramoth-gilead, King Joram (also called Jehoram) of Israel was wounded and went to Jezreel to recover. While he was there, Jehu, one of Joram's commanders, came from Ramoth-gilead to carry out the Lord's judgment on Joram's family. When Joram and King Ahaziah of Judah went out in their chariots to meet Jehu, Jehu mortally wounded Joram with an arrow and chased Ahaziah to Beth-haggan, where he wounded him as well. It appears that Ahaziah then fled to Megiddo, where he died (2 Kings 9:27).

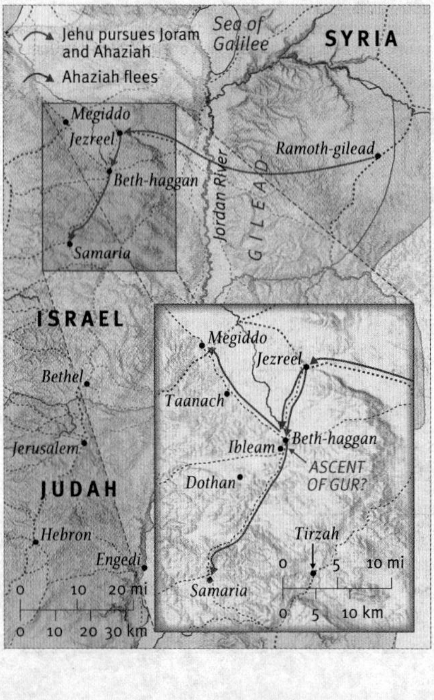

22:1–9 The Chronicler's account of **Ahaziah**'s brief reign (842–841 B.C.) is adapted from 2 Kings 8:24–29; 9:21, 28; 10:13–14. The main interest lies with the malignant influence of the **house of Ahab** over the young and ineffectual king. Ahaziah's mother **Athaliah** is a daughter of Ahab (see 2 Chron. 18:1; 22:2) and **his counselor in doing wickedly** (the Chronicler's addition to the text). As queen mother, she held an official position in the court as a royal adviser. Her role was supplemented by other officials from the house of Ahab, who were Ahaziah's **counselors, to his undoing** (v. 4b, the Chronicler's addition).

22:5–9 Ahaziah's decision to join **Jehoram** (a variant spelling of Joram), king of Israel, in his bid to recapture **Ramoth-gilead** from **Hazael**, king of Syria, comes at the behest of his "Ahabite" counselors. Some years previously, Jehoshaphat had allied himself with Joram's father Ahab in an identical mission, ending in Ahab's death (ch. 18). Joram was wounded at Ramoth-gilead, and withdrew to **Jezreel** to recuperate. Ahaziah came to visit his ally there, only to fall into the hands of **Jehu**, Joram's commander, whom God had chosen **to destroy the house of Ahab** (see 1 Kings 19:15–17). Jehu's violent coup is described in detail in 2 Kings 9:1–28. The Chronicler assumes his readers' acquaintance with this narrative and focuses instead on Ahaziah's fate, which he remarks was **ordained by God** (see 2 Chron. 10:15; 24:20). Ahaziah falls under the same judgment as the house of Ahab, insofar as he followed the ways of that apostate dynasty.

22:9 In contrast to Joram, whose body was left exposed on Naboth's field (2 Kings 9:26), Ahaziah is granted a decent burial out of respect for his grandfather Jehoshaphat.

22:10–12 Athaliah is nothing more than a violent usurper who attempts to secure the throne for herself by massacring rivals from the **royal family**, including her own relatives. Like Jehoram (21:4), she brings the Davidic dynasty to the brink of destruction. But while she rules the land for six years (probably 841–835 B.C.), she does so without legitimacy: no statements at the beginning or end of her rule make her reign official. The contrasting figure to her is Ahaziah's sister **Jehoshabeath**, who courageously conceals the infant heir **Joash** throughout those years. The Chronicler adds the comment that Jehoshabeath is also the **wife of Jehoiada the high priest**, which helps explain how the child could be concealed in the temple buildings throughout Athaliah's rule. Mention of Jehoiada here also prepares the way for the following account of Athaliah's overthrow by the high priest.

23:1–24:27 *Joash.* Joash's rule marks not only the restoration of the throne to the rightful Davidic king but also Judah's return to its covenant commitment to be the Lord's people (23:16). Thanks largely to Jehoiada and his

8 [g]And when Jehu was [h]executing judgment on the house of Ahab, he met the princes
of Judah and the sons of Ahaziah's brothers, who attended Ahaziah, and he killed them.
9 [i]He searched for Ahaziah, and he was captured while hiding in Samaria, and he was
brought to Jehu and put to death. [j]They buried him, for they said, "He is the grandson
of Jehoshaphat, [k]who sought the LORD with all his heart." And the house of Ahaziah had
no one able to rule the kingdom.

Athaliah Reigns in Judah

10 [l]Now when Athaliah the mother of Ahaziah saw that her son was dead, she arose and
destroyed all the royal family of the house of Judah. 11 But Jehoshabeath,[1] the daughter of
the king, took Joash the son of Ahaziah and stole him away from among the king's sons
who were about to be put to death, and she put him and his nurse in a bedroom. Thus
Jehoshabeath, the daughter of King Jehoram and wife of Jehoiada the priest, because she
was a sister of Ahaziah, hid him[2] from Athaliah, so that she did not put him to death. 12 And
he remained with them six years, hidden in the house of God, while Athaliah reigned
over the land.

Joash Made King

23 [m]But in the seventh year Jehoiada took courage and entered into a covenant with
the commanders of hundreds, Azariah the son of Jeroham, Ishmael the son of
Jehohanan, Azariah the son of Obed, Maaseiah the son of Adaiah, and Elishaphat the
son of Zichri. 2 And they went about through [n]Judah and gathered the Levites from all
the cities of Judah, and the heads of fathers' houses of Israel, and they came to Jerusalem.
3 And all the assembly made a covenant with the king in the house of God. And Jehoiada[3]
said to them, "Behold, the king's son! Let him reign, [o]as the LORD spoke concerning the
sons of David. 4 This is the thing that you shall do: [p]of you priests and Levites who come
off duty on the Sabbath, one third shall be gatekeepers, 5 and one third shall be at the
king's house and one third at the Gate of the Foundation. And all the people shall be in
the courts of the house of the LORD. 6 Let no one enter the house of the LORD except the
priests [q]and ministering Levites. They may enter, for they are holy, but all the people shall
keep the charge of the LORD. 7 The Levites shall surround the king, each with his weapons
in his hand. And whoever enters the house shall be put to death. Be with the king when
he comes in and when he goes out."

8 The Levites and all Judah did according to all that Jehoiada the priest commanded,
and they each brought his men, who were to go off duty on the Sabbath, with those who
were to come on duty on the Sabbath, for Jehoiada the priest did not dismiss [r]the divisions. 9 And Jehoiada the priest gave to the captains the spears and the large and small
shields that had been King David's, which were in the house of God. 10 And he set all the
people as a guard for the king, every man with his weapon in his hand, from the south
side of the house to the north side of the house, around the altar and the house. 11 Then
they brought out the king's son and put the crown on him and gave him [s]the testimony.

[1] Spelled *Jehosheba* in 2 Kings 11:2 [2] That is, Joash [3] Hebrew *he*

8 [g]See 2 Kgs. 10:11-14 [h][ch. 24:24]
9 [i][2 Kgs. 9:27] [j]2 Kgs. 9:28 [k]ch. 17:4
10 [l]For ver. 10-12, see 2 Kgs. 11:1-3

Chapter 23

1 [m]For ver. 1-21, see 2 Kgs. 11:4-20
2 [n]See ch. 21:2
3 [o]See ch. 6:16
4 [p][1 Chr. 9:25; 24:4]
6 [q]See 1 Chr. 23:27-29
8 [r]See 1 Chr. 24
11 [s]Deut. 17:18, 19

watchful concern for the nation's life, these reforms are successful for a while, but things go awry once the old high priest has died. Joash is the first in a sequence of three kings (followed by Amaziah and Uzziah) whose reigns begin on a relatively positive note but end in failure or ignominy because they reject godly counsel.

23:1–21 This is drawn mainly from 2 Kings 11:4–20, with numerous changes to reflect the Chronicler's particular concerns.

23:1b–2 This is the Chronicler's addition, mentioning the role of the **Levites** and the **heads of fathers' houses**, as well as military figures, in the uprising (cf. note on 2 Kings 11:4). Other references to the Levites in their key role of defending the king and the sanctity of the temple have been added in 2 Chron. 23:5–8.

23:3 The assembly was the representative body of leaders of the people. Wise kings sought the advice and support of this body in their undertakings (see 1 Chron. 13:2; 29:1; 2 Chron. 30:2). The **covenant with the king** probably included the arrangements under which Joash would rule, including Jehoiada's supervisory regency until Joash reached adulthood (see 24:4). **Let him reign, as the LORD spoke concerning the sons of David**. The Chronicler's addition affirms that the coup was in keeping with God's promise to preserve David's line (see 1 Chron. 17:14; 2 Chron. 6:10; 21:7).

23:4 This is the thing that you shall do. See note on 2 Kings 11:5–8.

23:5–6 The Chronicler adds that **all the people** participated in the coup, though he is careful to note that they remained **in the courts** and did not enter the temple.

23:8 The coup was timed for the changing of the temple and palace guards on the Sabbath, to bring the maximum number of armed men into the temple precincts without arousing suspicion.

23:9 the spears and . . . shields. See note on 2 Kings 11:10.

23:11 Along with his coronation and anointing, Joash is presented with the **testimony**, which several interpreters understand to be the terms of his covenant with the assembly (v. 3), while others think it is a copy of the laws of

And they proclaimed him king, and Jehoiada and his sons anointed him, and they said,
[t]"Long live the king."

Athaliah Executed

12 When Athaliah heard the noise of the people running and praising the king, she
went into the house of the LORD to the people. 13 And when she looked, there was the king
standing by his pillar at the entrance, and the captains and the trumpeters beside the king,
and all the people of the land rejoicing and blowing trumpets, and the singers with their
musical instruments leading in the celebration. And Athaliah tore her clothes and cried,
"Treason! Treason!" 14 Then Jehoiada the priest brought out the captains who were set over
the army, saying to them, "Bring her out between the ranks, and anyone who follows her
is to be put to death with the sword." For the priest said, "Do not put her to death in the
house of the LORD." 15 So they laid hands on her,[1] and she went into the entrance of [u]the
horse gate of the king's house, and they put her to death there.

Jehoiada's Reforms

16 And Jehoiada made a covenant between himself and all the people and the king that
they should be the LORD's people. 17 Then all the people went to the house of Baal and
tore it down; his altars and his images they broke in pieces, [v]and they killed Mattan the
priest of Baal before the altars. 18 And Jehoiada posted watchmen for the house of the LORD
under the direction of [w]the Levitical priests and the Levites [x]whom David had organized
to be in charge of the house of the LORD, to offer burnt offerings to the LORD, [y]as it is
written in the Law of Moses, with rejoicing and with singing, [z]according to the order of
David. 19 He stationed [a]the gatekeepers at the gates of the house of the LORD so that no
one should enter who was in any way unclean. 20 And he took the captains, the nobles, the
governors of the people, and all the people of the land, and they brought the king down
from the house of the LORD, marching [b]through the upper gate to the king's house. And
they set the king on the royal throne. 21 So all the people of the land rejoiced, and the city
was quiet after Athaliah had been put to death with the sword.

Joash Repairs the Temple

24 [c]Joash[2] was seven years old when he began to reign, and he reigned forty years in
Jerusalem. His mother's name was Zibiah of Beersheba. 2 [d]And Joash did what was
right in the eyes of the LORD all the days of Jehoiada the priest. 3 Jehoiada got for him two
wives, and he had sons and daughters.

4 After this Joash [e]decided to [f]restore the house of the LORD. 5 And he gathered the priests
and the Levites and said to them, "Go out to the cities of [g]Judah and gather from all Israel

[1] Or *they made a passage for her* [2] Spelled *Jehoash* in 2 Kings 12:1

11 [t]See 1 Sam. 10:24
15 [u]Neh. 3:28; Jer. 31:40; [2 Kgs. 11:16]
17 [v]Deut. 13:9
18 [w]ch. 5:5; 30:27 [x]1 Chr. 23:6, 30, 31; 24:1 [y]Num. 28:2 [z][1 Chr. 25:2]
19 [a]See 1 Chr. 26:1-19
20 [b][2 Kgs. 11:19; 15:35]

Chapter 24

1 [c]For ver. 1-14, see 2 Kgs. 11:21–12:15
2 [d][ch. 26:5]
4 [e][1 Chr. 22:7] [f]ver. 12
5 [g]See ch. 21:2

God (perhaps the book of Deuteronomy) as specified in Deut. 17:18 (see note on 2 Kings 11:12).

23:13–15 The **pillar** is probably either Boaz or Jachin, the pillars at the temple entrance (3:17; see note on 2 Kings 11:14). The Chronicler has added the reference to the **singers with their musical instruments leading in the celebration**, who are evidently Levites (see 1 Chron. 23:5; 25:6). Athaliah's cry of **Treason!** shows that, as well as being blind to her own position as a violent usurper, she had no inkling that any of the house of David had survived. Jehoiada's instruction to remove her from the temple precincts for execution is in order to avoid defiling the sacred site any more; yet ironically, his own son will not be spared this fate (2 Chron. 24:21–22).

23:16–21 The climax of these dramatic events is the ceremony of covenant renewal led by Jehoiada, in which the high priest, king, and people commit themselves afresh to **be the LORD's people** (cf. note on 2 Kings 11:17). Effectively, this meant the reaffirmation of the Law of Moses as the rule for the kingdom and the removal of pagan practices and cultic personnel. The temple of **Baal** in Jerusalem may have been built for Athaliah as part of the marriage alliance with the northern kingdom, much as Solomon had provided shrines for his foreign wives (1 Kings 11:7–8). Verses 18b–19 of 2 Chronicles 23 are the Chronicler's addition, affirming that, as part of the covenant renewal, temple worship was also brought into proper conformity with the stipulations of **Moses** and **David**.

24:1–27 Loosely adapted from 2 Kings 11:21–12:21, this is supplemented with the Chronicler's own material (see 2 Chron. 24:27). Joash's reign (835–796 B.C.) falls into two parts: a faithful period, while Jehoiada the priest was alive (vv. 1–16), followed by apostasy ending in judgment (vv. 17–27). Throughout 2 Chronicles, the religious character of a king can be readily gauged by his attitude toward the temple, and this is most evident in the case of Joash: in his faithful period, he is devoted to the restoration of the temple (vv. 4, 5, 12), but in his apostasy, he abandons it for idolatry (v. 18).

24:2 Joash did what was right. See note on 2 Kings 12:2–3.

24:3 The Chronicler's addition. **got for him two wives**. Jehoiada acts to ensure that the Davidic line will continue after its near destruction.

24:4 restore. Literally, "to renew." The temple had been despoiled by Athaliah and her family (v. 7) and probably neglected before that time.

24:5–6, 9 repair the house of your God. See note on 2 Kings 12:4–5. Kings refers to three sources of revenue (cf. 2 Kings 12:4), but the Chronicler specifies instead only the census tax imposed by Moses for the construction and maintenance of the tabernacle (see Ex. 30:16). The typological correspondence and continuity between the Mosaic tabernacle and the temple is one of the Chronicler's characteristic themes (see notes on 2 Chronicles 3–4). Verses 5–6 of ch. 24 offer a rare note of criticism of the priests and Levites for failing to perform their task.

6 [h]See Ex. 30:12-16 [i]See Num. 17:7, 8
7 [j][ch. 21:17] [k][1 Kgs. 15:15]
9 [l][Ezra 1:1] [h][See ver. 6 above]
14 [m][2 Kgs. 12:13]
18 [o]See Deut. 16:21 [p]ch. 19:2, 10; 28:11, 13; 29:8; 32:25
19 [q]Jer. 25:4; [Matt. 23:34; Luke 11:49]; See ch. 36:15 [r]Neh. 13:15, 21
20 [s]ch. 15:1; 20:14 [t][Matt. 23:35] [u][Num. 14:41] [v]ch. 15:2
21 [w][Neh. 9:26] [x]Matt. 23:35; Luke 11:51
22 [y][Gen. 9:5]
23 [z][2 Kgs. 12:17, 18]

money to repair the house of your God from year to year, and see that you act quickly."
But the Levites did not act quickly. 6 So the king summoned Jehoiada the chief and said to
him, "Why have you not required the Levites to bring in from Judah and Jerusalem [h]the
tax levied by Moses, the servant of the LORD, and the congregation of Israel for [i]the tent of
testimony?" 7 For [j]the sons of Athaliah, that wicked woman, had broken into the house of
God, and had also used all [k]the dedicated things of the house of the LORD for the Baals.

8 So the king commanded, and they made a chest and set it outside the gate of the house
of the LORD. 9 And [l]proclamation was made throughout Judah and Jerusalem to bring in
for the LORD [h]the tax that Moses the servant of God laid on Israel in the wilderness. 10 And
all the princes and all the people rejoiced and brought their tax and dropped it into the
chest until they had finished.[1] 11 And whenever the chest was brought to the king's officers
by the Levites, when they saw that there was much money in it, the king's secretary and
the officer of the chief priest would come and empty the chest and take it and return it
to its place. Thus they did day after day, and collected money in abundance. 12 And the
king and Jehoiada gave it to those who had charge of the work of the house of the LORD,
and they hired masons and carpenters to restore the house of the LORD, and also workers in iron and bronze to repair the house of the LORD. 13 So those who were engaged in
the work labored, and the repairing went forward in their hands, and they restored the
house of God to its proper condition and strengthened it. 14 And when they had finished,
they brought the rest of the money before the king and Jehoiada, and with it [m]were made
utensils for the house of the LORD, both for the service and for the burnt offerings, and
dishes for incense and vessels of gold and silver. And they offered burnt offerings in the
house of the LORD regularly all the days of Jehoiada.

15 But Jehoiada grew old and full of days, and died. He was 130 years old at his death.
16 And they buried him in the city of David among the kings, because he had done good
in Israel, and toward God and his house.

17 Now after the death of Jehoiada the princes of Judah came and paid homage to the
king. Then the king listened to them. 18 And they abandoned the house of the LORD, the
God of their fathers, and served [o]the Asherim and the idols. And [p]wrath came upon Judah
and Jerusalem for this guilt of theirs. 19 [q]Yet he sent prophets among them to bring them
back to the LORD. [r]These testified against them, but they would not pay attention.

Joash's Treachery

20 [s]Then the Spirit of God clothed Zechariah [t]the son of Jehoiada the priest, and he stood
above the people, and said to them, "Thus says God, [u]'Why do you break the commandments of the LORD, so that you cannot prosper? [v]Because you have forsaken the LORD, he
has forsaken you.'" 21 But [w]they conspired against him, [x]and by command of the king they
stoned him with stones in the court of the house of the LORD. 22 Thus Joash the king did
not remember the kindness that Jehoiada, Zechariah's father, had shown him, but killed
his son. And when he was dying, he said, "May the LORD see [y]and avenge!"[2]

Joash Assassinated

23 At the end of the year [z]the army of the Syrians came up against Joash. They came to
Judah and Jerusalem and destroyed all the princes of the people from among the people

[1] Or *until it was full* [2] Hebrew *and seek*

24:8–11 Joash's initiative allowed the people to bring their tax directly to the temple. **all the people rejoiced and brought their tax**. See 1 Chron. 29:6–9. The Chronicler wants his readers to see the temple not as a burden but as a joyful duty (see Ex. 36:4–7).

24:13–14 The repairs were made according to the original design, and the surplus funds were used for the temple vessels (see 2 Kings 12:13–14). **vessels of gold and silver**. Second Kings 12:13 says that vessels of gold and silver were not made while the temple was being repaired, while 2 Chron. 24:14 specifies that **when they had finished** those repairs, they used **the rest of the money** to make these vessels. The Chronicler specifies that Joash's revival of temple worship lasted **all the days of Jehoiada**, and did not extend into his later years of apostasy following Jehoiada's death (see note on vv. 1–27).

24:15–22 This section is found only in Chronicles. Jehoiada's age at death, **130**, exceeds that of Aaron (123, Num. 33:39) and Moses (120, Deut. 34:7). His burial **among the kings** is unique for a high priest. **the king listened to them.** Without Jehoiada's influence, Joash succumbs to the evil counsel of certain leaders who identified with the old ways of the house of Ahab. As always in Chronicles, God's punishment for apostasy is not immediate but is preceded by the prophetic summons to repentance (see 2 Chron. 36:15). The speech by **Zechariah** is characteristic of the Chronicler's vocabulary and theology (cf. 1 Chron. 28:9; 2 Chron. 7:19, 22; 15:2). His dying words are an appeal for divine justice. Jesus may have used this incident as an illustration of the judgment coming on his own violent and unbelieving generation (see note on Matt. 23:35).

24:23–27 This follows the outline of 2 Kings 12:17–21 (see notes on 2 Kings

and sent all their spoil to the king of Damascus. 24 Though the army of the Syrians had come
with few men, [a]the LORD delivered into their hand a very great army, [v]because Judah[1] had
forsaken the LORD, the God of their fathers. Thus they [b]executed judgment on Joash.
25 When they had departed from him, leaving him [c]severely wounded, [d]his servants
conspired against him because of the blood of [e]the son[2] of Jehoiada the priest, and killed
him on his bed. So he died, and they buried him in the city of David, [f]but they did not bury
him in the tombs of the kings. 26 Those who conspired against him were Zabad the son
of Shimeath the Ammonite, and Jehozabad the son of Shimrith the Moabite. 27 Accounts
of his sons and of the many oracles against him and of [g]the rebuilding[3] of the house of
God are written in the [h]Story of the Book of the Kings. And Amaziah his son reigned in
his place.

Amaziah Reigns in Judah

25 [i]Amaziah was twenty-five years old when he began to reign, and he reigned twenty-
nine years in Jerusalem. His mother's name was Jehoaddan of Jerusalem. 2 And he
did what was right in the eyes of the LORD, [j]yet not with a whole heart. 3 And as soon as
the royal power was firmly his, he killed his servants who had struck down the king his
father. 4 But he did not put their children to death, according to what is written in the
Law, in the Book of Moses, where the LORD commanded, [k]"Fathers shall not die because
of their children, nor children die because of their fathers, but each one shall die for his
own sin."

Amaziah's Victories

5 Then Amaziah assembled the men of Judah and set them by fathers' houses under
commanders of thousands and of hundreds for all Judah and Benjamin. He mustered
those [l]twenty years old and upward, and found that they were [m]300,000 choice men,
fit for war, [n]able to handle spear and shield. 6 He hired also 100,000 mighty men of
valor from Israel for 100 talents[4] of silver. 7 But [o]a man of God came to him and said,
"O king, do not let the army of Israel go with you, for the LORD is not with Israel, with
all these Ephraimites. 8 But go, act, be strong for the battle. Why should you suppose
that God will cast you down before the enemy? [p]For God has power to help or to cast
down." 9 And Amaziah said to the man of God, "But what shall we do about the hundred
talents that I have given to the army of Israel?" The man of God answered, "The LORD
is able to give you much more than this." 10 Then Amaziah discharged the army that
had come to him from Ephraim to go home again. And they became very angry with
Judah and returned home in fierce anger. 11 But Amaziah took courage and led out his
people and went to the [q]Valley of Salt and struck down [r]10,000 men of Seir. 12 The men
of Judah captured another 10,000 alive and took them to the top of a rock and threw
them down from the top of the rock, and they were all dashed to pieces. 13 But the men
of the army whom Amaziah sent back, not letting them go with him to battle, raided
the cities of Judah, [s]from Samaria to Beth-horon, and struck down 3,000 people in them
and took much spoil.

[1] Hebrew *they* [2] Septuagint, Vulgate; Hebrew *sons* [3] Hebrew *founding* [4] A *talent* was about 75 pounds or 34 kilograms

24 [a]Isa. 30:17; [Lev. 26:8, 36, 37] [v][See ver. 20 above] [b][ch. 22:8]
25 [c][Deut. 28:35] [d]For ver. 25-27, see 2 Kgs. 12:20, 21 [e][ver. 21, 22] [f][ch. 21:20; 28:27]
27 [g]ver. 12 [h]ch. 13:22

Chapter 25

1 [i]For ver. 1-4, see 2 Kgs. 14:1-6
2 [j][ver. 14]
4 [k]Deut. 24:16; [Jer. 31:30; Ezek. 18:20]
5 [l]Num. 1:3 [m][ch. 11:1; 13:3; 17:14-18; 26:13] [n]1 Chr. 12:8
7 [o]Deut. 33:1
8 [p][ch. 20:6]
11 [q]2 Kgs. 14:7 [r]ch. 20:10
13 [s][ch. 15:8; 19:4]

12:17–18; 12:20), but is mainly the Chronicler's own material. Defeat by the smaller Syrian army is a reversal of Judah's earlier experience (see 2 Chron. 14:8–9) and a sign of divine judgment. Joash's fate is a case of "measure for measure." As Joash had supported those who **conspired** to kill Zechariah (24:21), now his own officials **conspired** to do the same to him in revenge for Zechariah's death. His exclusion from the **tombs of the kings** is in pointed contrast with Jehoiada (v. 16).

25:1–28 *Amaziah.* This section is drawn mainly from 2 Kings 14:2–20, with a long interpolation (2 Chron. 25:5–16) accounting for Amaziah's defeat by Israel. His reign (796–767 B.C.) is divided into a period of relative obedience and blessing, followed by outright apostasy and judgment. Yet throughout his reign, Amaziah is basically halfhearted and divided in his loyalty to God, so his final failure is one of steady degeneration rather than radical reversal. Amaziah's reign included a long co-regency (792–767 B.C.) with his son Uzziah as a result of his capture by the Israelite (northern) king Joash (v. 23).

25:2 yet not with a whole heart. Second Kings 14:4 mentions Amaziah's failure to remove the high places.

25:5–16 This provides the background and aftermath to the comment in 2 Kings 14:7 on the war against Edom. Amaziah's decision to hire mercenaries from the northern kingdom (2 Chron. 25:6) is denounced by an unnamed prophet because **the LORD is not with Israel** (on account of its continuing idolatry; see 2 Kings 13:11), and because a king should trust in God rather than his army (2 Chron. 25:8). Encouraged by the thought of material gain, Amaziah heeds the prophet's call to dismiss the mercenaries and proceeds to a bloodthirsty victory against the **men of Seir** (an alternative name for Edom, Gen. 32:3). Amaziah's worship of the captured Edomite gods (perhaps to placate their presumed displeasure) only provokes Yahweh's anger. Again, the possibility of repentance is offered by God's prophet (see 2 Chron. 25:19), but Amaziah seals his fate by silencing godly **counsel** in favor of his own advisers (v. 17).

25:11 Valley of Salt. See note on 2 Kings 14:7.

14[t][ch. 28:23] [r][See ver. 11 above]
15[u][ver. 11]
16[v][Josh. 11:20]
17[w]For ver. 17-24, see 2 Kgs. 14:8-14
18[x][Judg. 9:8]
19[y]See ch. 26:16
20[z]ver. 14, 15
23[a]ch. 21:17 [b]Neh. 8:16
24[c]1 Chr. 26:15
25[d]For ch. 25:25–26:2, see 2 Kgs. 14:17-22

Chapter 26

3[e]For ver. 3, 4, see 2 Kgs. 15:2, 3

Amaziah's Idolatry

14 After Amaziah came from striking down the Edomites, [t]he brought the gods [r]of the
men of Seir and set them up as his gods and worshiped them, making offerings to them.
15 Therefore the LORD was angry with Amaziah and sent to him a prophet, who said to
him, "Why have you sought the gods of a people [u]who did not deliver their own people
from your hand?" 16 But as he was speaking, the king said to him, "Have we made you a
royal counselor? Stop! Why should you be struck down?" So the prophet stopped, but
said, "I know that [v]God has determined to destroy you, because you have done this and
have not listened to my counsel."

Israel Defeats Amaziah

17 [w]Then Amaziah king of Judah took counsel and sent to Joash the son of Jehoahaz, son
of Jehu, king of Israel, saying, "Come, let us look one another in the face." 18 And Joash the
king of Israel sent word to Amaziah king of Judah, [x]"A thistle on Lebanon sent to a cedar
on Lebanon, saying, 'Give your daughter to my son for a wife,' and a wild beast of Lebanon
passed by and trampled down the thistle. 19 You say, 'See, I[1] have struck down Edom,' and
[y]your heart has lifted you up in boastfulness. But now stay at home. Why should you
provoke trouble so that you fall, you and Judah with you?"

20 But Amaziah would not listen, for it was of God, in order that he might give them
into the hand of their enemies, [z]because they had sought the gods of Edom. 21 So Joash
king of Israel went up, and he and Amaziah king of Judah faced one another in battle at
Beth-shemesh, which belongs to Judah. 22 And Judah was defeated by Israel, and every
man fled to his home. 23 And Joash king of Israel captured Amaziah king of Judah, the
son of Joash, son of [a]Ahaziah, at Beth-shemesh, and brought him to Jerusalem and broke
down the wall of Jerusalem for 400 cubits,[2] from [b]the Ephraim Gate to the Corner Gate.
24 And he seized all the gold and silver, and all the vessels that were found in the house
of God, in the care of [c]Obed-edom. He seized also the treasuries of the king's house, also
hostages, and he returned to Samaria.

25 [d]Amaziah the son of Joash, king of Judah, lived fifteen years after the death of Joash the
son of Jehoahaz, king of Israel. 26 Now the rest of the deeds of Amaziah, from first to last,
are they not written in the Book of the Kings of Judah and Israel? 27 From the time when
he turned away from the LORD they made a conspiracy against him in Jerusalem, and he
fled to Lachish. But they sent after him to Lachish and put him to death there. 28 And they
brought him upon horses, and he was buried with his fathers in the city of David.[3]

Uzziah Reigns in Judah

26 And all the people of Judah took Uzziah, who was sixteen years old, and made him
king instead of his father Amaziah. 2 He built Eloth and restored it to Judah, after
the king slept with his fathers. 3 Uzziah was [e]sixteen years old when he began to reign, and

[1] Hebrew *you* [2] A *cubit* was about 18 inches or 45 centimeters [3] Hebrew *of Judah*

25:17–24 wild beast . . . trampled down the thistle. See note on 2 Kings 14:9–10. Israelite (northern) king Joash interprets Amaziah's invitation as a veiled challenge to battle, perhaps in order to avenge the rampage of the Israelite mercenaries against the towns of Judah (2 Chron. 25:13). The Chronicler's added comment in v. 20 that Amaziah's refusal to heed Joash's blunt advice **was of God** points to God's sovereign control over human decisions as much as actions (see 10:15; 22:7). Amaziah is sorely rewarded for his pride (25:19; see Prov. 16:18) as well as his idolatry. **Obed-edom**. See 1 Chron. 13:14 and 26:15.

25:25–28 The Chronicler adds that the conspiracy against Amaziah (see note on 2 Kings 14:19) began **when he turned away from the LORD**, which may be a reference to his apostasy in 2 Chron. 25:14 and 20. Perhaps an alliance of priests and military leaders, similar to the one that overthrew Athaliah for Joash (ch. 23), collaborated to repay Amaziah for despoiling the temple and for his defeat by Israel.

26:1–23 *Uzziah.* See 2 Kings 15:2–7. The Chronicler reproduces most of this section of 2 Kings, but splices it with a lengthy passage of his own material (2 Chron. 26:5–20a) illustrating God's blessing on Uzziah's reign (792–740 B.C.) and recounting the cause of his downfall. As with his presentation of Joash and Amaziah, the Chronicler has divided Uzziah's reign into two parts: a period of faithfulness and blessing, followed by sin and punishment. The language ("to seek God," "prosper," "God helped him," "fame") and the motifs of blessing (military success, building projects, armed forces) are all characteristic of the Chronicler's style and thought, and they carry a sober message. The chapter is essentially a sermon on the dangers of pride: Uzziah's God-given success leads him into presumption, seeking an office of spiritual leadership that could never be rightly his.

26:1 Uzziah is also called by the variant form "Azariah" in 2 Kings 15:1, 6–7; 1 Chron. 3:12 (but cf. 2 Kings 15:13, 30, 32, 34, where he is called Uzziah). The Chronicler's preference for "Uzziah" may be in order to avoid confusion with the chief priest Azariah in 2 Chron. 26:17–20.

26:2 the king slept with his fathers. See notes on 1 Kings 2:10 and 2 Kings 14:22.

26:3 The reign of **Uzziah** included co-regencies with his father Amaziah (796–767 B.C.) and his son Jotham (750–733). Uzziah's reign saw the beginning of Isaiah's prophetic ministry (Isa. 1:1; 6:1).

he reigned fifty-two years in Jerusalem. His mother's name was Jecoliah of Jerusalem. 4 And
he did what was right in the eyes of the LORD, according to all that his father Amaziah
had done. 5 He set himself to seek God [f]in the days of Zechariah, [g]who instructed him in
the fear of God, and as long as he sought the LORD, God made him prosper.
6 He went out and [h]made war against the Philistines and broke through the wall of
Gath and the wall of Jabneh and the wall of Ashdod, and he built cities in the territory of
Ashdod and elsewhere among the Philistines. 7 God helped him [i]against the Philistines
and against the Arabians who lived in Gurbaal and against the [j]Meunites. 8 The Ammonites
[k]paid tribute to Uzziah, and his fame spread even to the border of Egypt, for he became
very strong. 9 Moreover, Uzziah built towers in Jerusalem at [l]the Corner Gate and at [m]the
Valley Gate and at [n]the Angle, and fortified them. 10 And he built towers in the wilderness and [o]cut out many cisterns, for he had large herds, both in the Shephelah and in the
plain, and he had farmers and vinedressers in the hills and in the fertile lands, for he loved
the soil. 11 Moreover, Uzziah had an army of soldiers, fit for war, in divisions according to
the numbers in the muster made by Jeiel the secretary and Maaseiah the officer, under the
direction of Hananiah, one of the king's commanders. 12 The whole number of the heads
of fathers' houses of mighty men of valor was 2,600. 13 Under their command was an army
of [p]307,500, who could make war with mighty power, to help the king against the enemy.
14 And Uzziah prepared for all the army shields, spears, helmets, [q]coats of mail, bows, and
stones for slinging. 15 In Jerusalem he made machines, invented by skillful men, to be on

5 [f][ch. 24:2] [g][Dan. 1:17; 10:1]
6 [h][Isa. 14:29]
7 [i]ch. 21:16 [j][ch. 20:1]
8 [k][ch. 17:11; 2 Sam. 8:2]
9 [l]See 2 Kgs. 14:13 [m]Neh. 2:13, 15; 3:13 [n]Neh. 3:19
10 [o]Deut. 6:11; Neh. 9:25
13 [p][ch. 25:5]
14 [q]Neh. 4:16

Judah's Resurgence during Uzziah's Reign

c. 767–740 B.C.

A power vacuum created by Assyria's attack and withdrawal from Syria allowed King Azariah (also called Uzziah) of Judah to recover land that had once belonged to Judah. Azariah recovered Elath on the Red Sea, captured some Philistine towns, and fought against the Arabians at Gurbaal and against the Meunites.

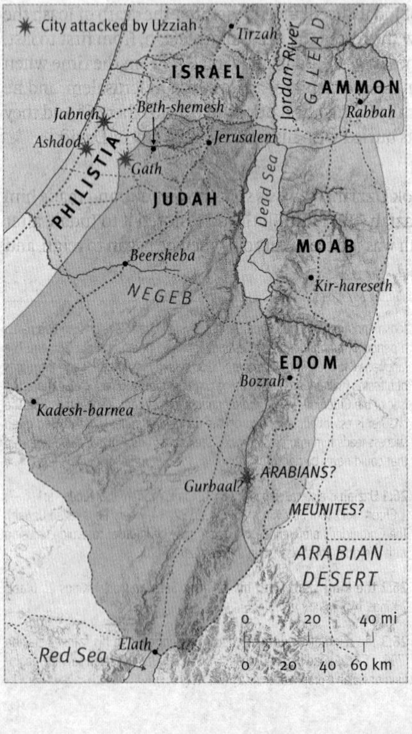

26:5 Zechariah acted as a religious adviser to Uzziah, as Jehoiada had done for Joash (24:2). Nothing else is known about this Zechariah. He is not the same as the Zechariah of 24:20–21 or the author of the canonical book Zechariah, who began his ministry in 520 B.C.

26:6–8 Uzziah's victories over the **Philistines** in the west and southwest were reinforced by building settlements in these conquered territories. The **Arabians** (or "Arabs") and **Meunites** (see 20:1) were nomadic groups in the south.

26:9–10 Corner Gate. See 25:23. Uzziah stands out as an enthusiastic promoter of farming throughout the **wilderness** of Judah and the Negeb, the foothills of the **Shephelah** (west of Jerusalem), and the coastal **plain**.

26:11–15 On the roles of armies as a mark of blessing on righteous kings, see 1 Chron. 12:23–40; 2 Chron. 13:3–4; 14:8; 17:12–19. Verse 13 of ch. 26 could be interpreted as "300 units (or commanders) with 7,500 men" (see note on 1 Chron. 12:23–37). **Machines** or "inventions" are implements of war from which men hurled projectiles in defense of the city. Murals from the siege of Lachish (701 B.C.) show defenders on the city walls shooting arrows and hurling stones from behind wooden frames on which shields have been hung.

26:16–20 Unfaithful translates Hebrew *ma'al* (see note on 1 Chron. 2:3–8). It carries the sense of affronting God's holiness (as in a violated oath; see Lev. 6:1–7) or failing to accord him his due in worship. Uzziah impugned God's holiness by trespassing on the temple, which was for the priests and Levites only, and by seeking to offer **incense**, a duty reserved for the **priests** alone (see Ex. 30:1–10; Num. 16:40). In his pride, he wished to have spiritual as well as political authority over the people. Uzziah's presumptuous act recalls Korah's rebellion (Num. 16:1–40). Azariah's rebuke still offers Uzziah the chance to repent and leave, and it is only in the course of his **angry**, impenitent outburst against the priests that the king is struck with a skin disease.

26:21–23 Because he **was a leper to the day of his death** (cf. note on 2 Kings 15:5), King Uzziah was not buried in the normal royal tombs of Jerusalem but in a **field**. A stone plaque was found in Jerusalem, on the Mount of Olives, from the Second Temple period that bears the inscription, "Here were brought the bones of Uzziah, king of Judah. Do not open!" It may be that the king's bones were moved to the Mount of Olives many centuries after his death.

26:21 Because of his leprosy, Uzziah had to withdraw from his royal duties (see Lev. 13:46; Num. 5:1–4), and **Jotham** became co-regent.

26:22 Isaiah the prophet . . . wrote. Not the canonical book bearing his name, but another work by this prophet, who received his call in the year of Uzziah's death (Isa. 6:1); see note on 2 Chron. 32:32–33.

the towers and the corners, to shoot arrows and great stones. And his fame spread far, for
he was marvelously helped, till he was strong.

Uzziah's Pride and Punishment

16 But when [r]he was strong, [s]he grew proud, to his destruction. For he was unfaithful to
the LORD his God and entered the temple of the LORD to burn incense on the altar of incense.
17 But [t]Azariah the priest went in after him, with eighty priests of the LORD who were men
of valor, 18 and they withstood King Uzziah and said to him, [u]"It is not for you, Uzziah, to
burn incense to the LORD, [v]but for the priests, the sons of Aaron, who are consecrated to
burn incense. Go out of the sanctuary, for you have done wrong, and it will bring you no
honor from the LORD God." 19 Then Uzziah was angry. Now he had a censer in his hand to
burn incense, and when he became angry with the priests, [w]leprosy[1] broke out on his forehead in the presence of the priests in the house of the LORD, by the altar of incense. 20 And
Azariah the chief priest and all the priests looked at him, and behold, he was leprous in his
forehead! And they rushed him out quickly, and he himself hurried to go out, because the
LORD had struck him. 21 [x]And King Uzziah was a leper to the day of his death, and being
a leper lived [y]in a separate house, for he was excluded from the house of the LORD. And
Jotham his son was over the king's household, governing the people of the land.
22 Now the rest of the acts of Uzziah, from first to last, [z]Isaiah the prophet the son of
Amoz wrote. 23 And Uzziah slept with his fathers, and they buried him with his fathers
in the burial field that belonged to the kings, for they said, "He is a leper." And Jotham
his son reigned in his place.

Jotham Reigns in Judah

27 [a]Jotham was twenty-five years old when he began to reign, and he reigned sixteen
years in Jerusalem. His mother's name was Jerushah the daughter of Zadok. 2 And
he did what was right in the eyes of the LORD according to all that his father Uzziah had
done, [b]except he did not enter the temple of the LORD. But the people still followed corrupt practices. 3 He built the upper gate of the house of the LORD and did much building
on the wall of [c]Ophel. 4 Moreover, he built cities in the hill country of Judah, and forts
and towers on the wooded hills. 5 He fought with the king of the Ammonites and prevailed against them. And the Ammonites gave him that year 100 talents[2] of silver, and
10,000 cors[3] of wheat and 10,000 of barley. The Ammonites paid him the same amount
in the second and the third years. 6 So Jotham became mighty, because he ordered his
ways before the LORD his God. 7 [d]Now the rest of the acts of Jotham, and all his wars and
his ways, behold, they are written in the Book of the Kings of Israel and Judah. 8 He was
[e]twenty-five years old when he began to reign, and he reigned sixteen years in Jerusalem.
9 And Jotham slept with his fathers, and they buried him in the city of David, and Ahaz
his son reigned in his place.

Ahaz Reigns in Judah

28 [f]Ahaz was twenty years old when he began to reign, and he reigned sixteen years in
Jerusalem. And he did not do what was right in the eyes of the LORD, as his father
David had done, 2 but he walked in the ways of the kings of Israel. He even made [g]metal

[1] *Leprosy* was a term for several skin diseases; see Leviticus 13 [2] A *talent* was about 75 pounds or 34 kilograms [3] A *cor* was about 6 bushels or 220 liters

16 [r][ch. 12:1; Deut. 32:15] [s]ch. 32:25; Ezek. 28:2, 5, 17; [ch. 25:19; Deut. 8:14; 2 Kgs. 14:10]
17 [t]1 Chr. 6:10
18 [u]Num. 16:40; 18:7 [v]Ex. 30:7, 8
19 [w][Ex. 4:6; Num. 12:10; 2 Kgs. 5:27]
21 [x]For ver. 21-23, see 2 Kgs. 15:5-7 [y][Lev. 13:46; Num. 5:2]
22 [z]Isa. 1:1; 6:1

Chapter 27

1 [a]For ver. 1-3, see 2 Kgs. 15:33-35
2 [b][ch. 26:16]
3 [c]ch. 33:14; Neh. 3:26, 27; 11:21
7 [d][2 Kgs. 15:36]
8 [e]ver. 1

Chapter 28

1 [f]For ver. 1-4, see 2 Kgs. 16:2-4
2 [g][Ex. 34:17]

27:1–9 *Jotham.* The account of Jotham's reign (750–735 B.C., including 10 years as co-regent with Uzziah) is expanded from 2 Kings 15:33–38 to show that his military success and power were due to his faithfulness to God (2 Chron. 27:6). Jotham is presented in a wholly positive way, in contrast to his father Uzziah (v. 2b) and his son Ahaz (ch. 28), of whom the Chronicler has nothing good to say.

27:2 Corrupt practices probably refers to worship at the high places (see note on 2 Kings 15:34–35).

27:3b–6 This is the Chronicler's addition. **Ophel**. The higher part of the area in between the Temple Mount and the city of David (33:14; Neh. 3:26). **Ammonites**. See 2 Chron. 26:8. The cessation of tribute after three years may reflect the rising power of Syria (Aram) in the lands across the Jordan. **Jotham became mighty**. The same Hebrew verb is used of Uzziah (26:16), but unlike his father, Jotham does not succumb to pride.

27:7 His wars may include the initial stages of confrontation with the Syro-Ephraimite coalition (see 2 Kings 15:37).

28:1–27 *Ahaz.* The Chronicler's account of Ahaz's reign (735–715 B.C.) incorporates the introduction and conclusion from 2 Kings 16, and follows the same topics, but otherwise the details are different. The Chronicler amplifies the negative assessment of Ahaz in 2 Kings, showing how his apostasy led Judah astray and brought it to ruin. The charge that Ahaz was "very unfaithful" (Hb. *ma'ol ma'al*, 2 Chron. 28:19; see v. 21) exceeds even that made against Saul (1 Chron. 10:13). Yet the dark picture of Judah's decline is mitigated somewhat by the action of its northern kinsmen, who show a measure of repentance and responsiveness to the prophetic word (2 Chron. 28:8–15).

28:1 he did not do what was right. See note on 2 Kings 16:1–4.

28:2 metal images for the Baals. The Chronicler's addition (see 24:7). Baal worship was especially associated with Ahab's dynasty (1 Kings 16:31).

images for [h]the Baals, 3 and [i]he made offerings in the [j]Valley of the Son of Hinnom and
[k]burned his sons as an offering,[1] according to [l]the abominations of the nations whom the
LORD drove out before the people of Israel. 4 And he sacrificed and [i]made offerings on the
high places and on the hills and under every green tree.

Judah Defeated

5 [m]Therefore the LORD his God gave him into the hand of the king of Syria, who defeated
him and took captive a great number of his people and brought them to Damascus. He
was also given into the hand of the king of Israel, who struck him with great force. 6 For
[n]Pekah the son of Remaliah killed 120,000 from Judah in one day, all of them men of valor,

[1] Hebrew *made his sons pass through the fire*

2 [h]Judg. 2:11
3 [i]ver. 25 [j]See Josh. 15:8
[k]ch. 33:6; [Lev. 18:21]
[l]ch. 33:2; Deut. 18:9
4 [i][See ver. 3 above]
5 [m]Isa. 7:1; [2 Kgs. 16:5, 6]
6 [n]2 Kgs. 15:27; 16:5

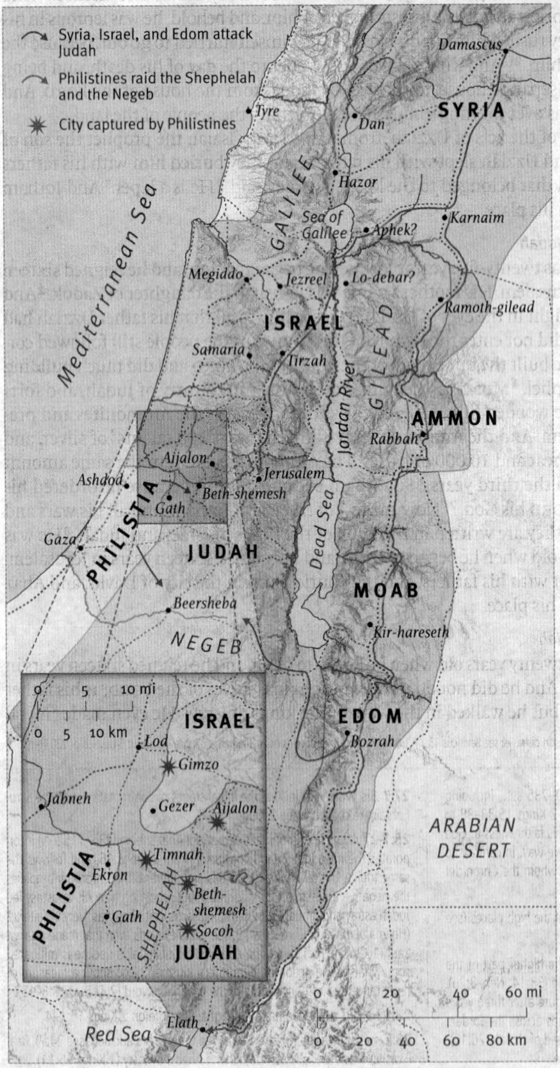

Syria and Israel Attack Judah

c. 740–732 B.C.

As the Assyrian Empire expanded westward, Syria and Israel sought to compel Judah and the other nearby states to form an anti-Assyrian alliance. Judah refused, leading Syria and Israel to attack Jerusalem. Syria also wrested Elath from Judah and gave it to the Edomites. The Edomites may have also raided Judah and taken captives at this time (see 28:17). The Philistines, who may have been part of the anti-Assyrian alliance, attacked Judah as well, capturing several cities in the Shephelah and the Negeb (see 28:18).

because they had forsaken the LORD, the God of their fathers. 7 And Zichri, a mighty man
of Ephraim, killed Maaseiah the king's son and Azrikam the commander of the palace
and Elkanah the next in authority to the king.

8 The men of Israel took captive 200,000 [o]of their relatives, women, sons, and daughters.
They also took much spoil from them and brought the spoil to Samaria. 9 But a prophet
of the LORD was there, whose name was Oded, and he went out to meet the army that
came to Samaria and said to them, "Behold, because the LORD, the God of your fathers,
[p]was angry with Judah, he gave them into your hand, but you have killed them in a rage
[q]that has reached up to heaven. 10 And now you intend to subjugate the people of Judah
and Jerusalem, male and female, as your slaves. Have you not sins of your own against the
LORD your God? 11 Now hear me, and send back the captives [o]from your relatives whom
you have taken, for the fierce wrath of the LORD is upon you."

12 Certain chiefs also of the men of Ephraim, Azariah the son of Johanan, Berechiah the
son of Meshillemoth, Jehizkiah the son of Shallum, and Amasa the son of Hadlai, stood
up against those who were coming from the war 13 and said to them, "You shall not bring
the captives in here, for you propose to bring upon us guilt against the LORD in addition
to our present sins and guilt. For our guilt is already great, and there is fierce wrath against
Israel." 14 So the armed men left the captives and the spoil before the princes and all the
assembly. 15 And [r]the men who have been mentioned by name rose and took the captives,
and with the spoil they clothed all who were naked among them. They clothed them, gave
them sandals, [s]provided them with food and drink, and anointed them, and carrying all
the feeble among them on donkeys, they brought them to their kinsfolk at Jericho, [t]the
city of palm trees. Then they returned to Samaria.

16 [u]At that time King Ahaz sent to the king[1] of Assyria for help. 17 For the Edomites had
again invaded and defeated Judah and carried away captives. 18 [v]And the Philistines had
made raids on [w]the cities in the Shephelah and the Negeb of Judah, and had taken Beth-
shemesh, Aijalon, Gederoth, Soco [x]with its villages, Timnah with its villages, and Gimzo
with its villages. And they settled there. 19 For the LORD humbled Judah because of Ahaz
king of Israel, for he had made [y]Judah act sinfully[2] and had been very unfaithful to the
LORD. 20 So [z]Tiglath-pileser[3] king of Assyria came against him and afflicted him instead
of strengthening him. 21 [a]For Ahaz took a portion from the house of the LORD and the
house of the king and of the princes, and gave tribute to the king of Assyria, but it did
not help him.

Ahaz's Idolatry

22 In the time of his distress he became yet more faithless to the LORD—this same King
Ahaz. 23 For [b]he sacrificed to the gods of Damascus that had defeated him and said, [c]"Because
the gods of the kings of Syria helped them, I will sacrifice to them that they may help

8 [o]ch. 11:4
9 [p]Isa. 47:6; Ezek. 25:12, 15; 26:2 [q]Ezra 9:6; Rev. 18:5
11 [o][See ver. 8 above]
15 [r]ver. 12; [ch. 31:19; Num. 1:17] [s]2 Kgs. 6:22; Prov. 25:21, 22; Rom. 12:20 [t]Deut. 34:3; Judg. 1:16
16 [u][2 Kgs. 16:7, 8]
18 [v][Ezek. 16:27, 57] [w]See Josh. 15:33-36 [x][Num. 21:25]
19 [y]See ch. 21:2
20 [z][2 Kgs. 15:29; 16:7]
21 [a]2 Kgs. 16:8, 9
23 [b][ch. 25:14] [c][Jer. 44:17, 18]

[1] Septuagint, Syriac, Vulgate (compare 2 Kings 16:7); Hebrew *kings* [2] Or *wildly* [3] Hebrew *Tilgath-pilneser*

28:3 Valley of the Son of Hinnom. See 33:6 and Jer. 7:31. The Canaanite practice of child sacrifice is condemned in the strongest of terms in Lev. 20:1–5.

28:5–7 See 2 Kings 16:5–7 and Isa. 7:1–6. The Chronicler spells out that the attacks by **Syria** and **Israel** were acts of divine judgment because Ahaz and the people **had forsaken the LORD**. Although the coalition failed to capture Jerusalem, they evidently overran the countryside around the city, and the captives taken to **Damascus** were a harbinger of the exile to come (2 Chron. 36:20). On the numbers, see note on 1 Chron. 12:23–37.

28:8–15 Just as Syria has done (v. 5), Israel removes its captives with the intention of enslaving them. The intervention by **Oded** indicates that the northern tribes still belong to "the Israel of God," even though they are "in rebellion against the house of David" (10:19). The northern and southern tribes are **relatives** (lit., "brothers"), and both divisions of the people have aroused God to anger by their unfaithfulness (28:9, 11). The way back for both sides lies through repentance, which the leaders of Ephraim demonstrate in their response to Oded's words. Their admission of **guilt** (v. 13) refers primarily to the charges of rebellion made by Abijah in 13:4–12.

28:16–21 Ahaz's appeal here to Tiglath-pileser III of **Assyria** for **help** against the **Edomites** and **Philistines** encroaching on Judah's southern borders (see 2 Kings 16:6–7a) misfired. Although Judah received relief from its enemies (including the Syro-Ephraimite coalition, 2 Kings 16:9), it would end up as vassal to Assyria for 30 years (see Isa. 7:17; 8:7–8). Ahaz's misstep was in seeking help from the ungodly, rather than from God (see 1 Chron. 5:20; 12:18; 2 Chron. 25:8).

28:22–27 See 2 Kings 16:10–18. Judah reaches its lowest point before the exile through Ahaz's desecration of the temple and his suppression of worship according to the Law of Moses (2 Chron. 28:24; see 29:7, 18–19) in favor of pagan practices. The blasphemous worship of false gods is now officially promoted by a Davidic king. Although this will be reversed somewhat by the reforming kings Hezekiah (chs. 29–32) and Josiah (chs. 34–35), Judah is set on a course that will culminate in destruction and exile (see 28:5). Ahaz is denied burial in the royal **tombs** as a mark of God's judgment on his wickedness (see 21:20; 24:25; 26:23).

me." But they were the ruin of him and of all Israel. 24 And Ahaz gathered together the
vessels of the house of God and [d]cut in pieces the vessels of the house of God, and he shut
up the doors of the house of the LORD, and he made himself [e]altars in every corner of
Jerusalem. 25 In every city of Judah he made high places to [f]make offerings to other gods,
provoking to anger the LORD, the God of his fathers. 26 [g]Now the rest of his acts and all
his ways, from first to last, behold, they are written in the Book of the Kings of Judah and
Israel. 27 And Ahaz slept with his fathers, and they buried him in the city, in Jerusalem,
for [h]they did not bring him into the tombs of the kings of Israel. And Hezekiah his son
reigned in his place.

Hezekiah Reigns in Judah

29 [i]Hezekiah began to reign when he was twenty-five years old, and he reigned twenty-
nine years in Jerusalem. His mother's name was Abijah[1] the daughter of [k]Zechariah.
2 And he did what was right in the eyes of the LORD, according to all that David his father
had done.

Hezekiah Cleanses the Temple

3 In the first year of his reign, in the first month, he [l]opened the doors of the house of
the LORD and repaired them. 4 He brought in the priests and the Levites and assembled

[1] Spelled *Abi* in 2 Kings 18:2

24[d][2 Kgs. 16:17] [e][ch. 30:14]
25[f]ver. 3
26[g]For ver. 26, 27, see 2 Kgs. 16:19, 20
27[h][ch. 21:20; 24:25]
Chapter 29
1[i]For ver. 1, 2, see 2 Kgs. 18:1-3 [k][ch. 26:5]
3[l][ver. 7; ch. 28:24]

28:26 On the **Book of the Kings of Judah and Israel**, see note on 1 Kings 14:19.

29:1–32:33 *Hezekiah.* The Chronicler devotes more attention to Hezekiah's reign (715–687 B.C.) than to that of any other king since David and Solomon. His account has little in common with 2 Kings 18–20, which concentrates mainly on Hezekiah's role in the Assyrian crisis of 701 B.C. The Chronicler, by contrast, is primarily interested in presenting Hezekiah as a restorer and reformer of Judah's worship. Most of his account is devoted to describing the cleansing of the temple and the restoration of worship after Ahaz's apostasy, followed by a national celebration of Passover (2 Chronicles 29–31). For the Chronicler, Hezekiah's successful resistance to Sennacherib and the prosperity of his kingdom (ch. 32) are a consequence of his religious reforms. The Chronicler's presentation of Hezekiah combines traits of both David and Solomon, especially in organizing the priests and Levites for their work and worship, and in presiding over the great rededication of the temple.

29:3 Hezekiah **opened the doors of the house of the LORD**, reversing his father's action (28:24).

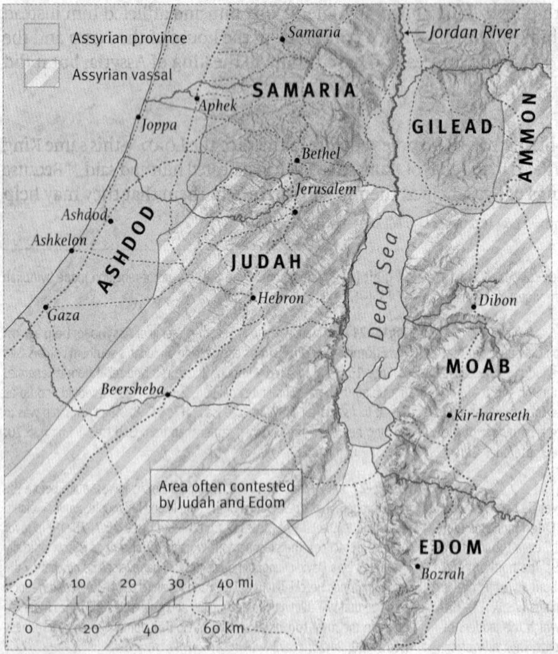

Judah after the Fall of Israel
c. 722 B.C.
During the reign of King Ahaz of Judah, both Israel and Judah had become vassals (semi-independent subjects) of Assyria. Later, however, King Hoshea of Israel rebelled, causing the Assyrians to completely annex Israel as a province of the empire. Philistia was annexed into the empire as well, leaving Judah, Ammon, Moab, and Edom as the remaining vassals in the region.

them in the square on the east **5** and said to them, "Hear me, Levites! Now [m]consecrate yourselves, and consecrate the house of the LORD, the God of your fathers, and carry out the filth from the Holy Place. **6** For our fathers have been unfaithful and have done what was evil in the sight of the LORD our God. They have forsaken him and [n]have turned away their faces from the habitation of the LORD and turned their backs. **7** They also [o]shut the doors of the vestibule and put out the lamps and have not burned incense or offered burnt offerings in the Holy Place to the God of Israel. **8** Therefore [p]the wrath of the LORD came on Judah and Jerusalem, and he has made them [q]an object of horror, of astonishment, [r]and of hissing, as you see with your own eyes. **9** For behold, [s]our fathers have fallen by the sword, and our sons and our daughters and our wives are in captivity for this. **10** Now [t]it is in my heart [u]to make a covenant with the LORD, the God of Israel, in order that his fierce anger may turn away from us. **11** My sons, do not now be negligent, [v]for the LORD has chosen you to stand in his presence, to minister to him and to be his ministers and make offerings to him."

12 Then the Levites arose, [w]Mahath the son of Amasai, and Joel the son of Azariah, of the sons of [x]the Kohathites; and of the sons of [x]Merari, Kish the son of Abdi, and Azariah the son of Jehallelel; and of the [x]Gershonites, Joah the son of Zimmah, and Eden the son of Joah; **13** and of the sons of [y]Elizaphan, Shimri and Jeuel; and of the sons of [z]Asaph, Zechariah and Mattaniah; **14** and of the sons of [a]Heman, Jehuel and Shimei; and of the sons of [b]Jeduthun, Shemaiah and Uzziel. **15** They gathered their brothers and [c]consecrated themselves and went in as the king had commanded, [d]by the words of the LORD, [e]to cleanse the house of the LORD. **16** The priests went into the inner part of the house of the LORD to cleanse it, and they brought out all the uncleanness that they found in the temple of the LORD into the court of the house of the LORD. And the Levites took it and carried it out to [f]the brook Kidron. **17** They began to consecrate [g]on the first day of the first month, and on the eighth day of the month they came to the vestibule of the LORD. Then for eight days they consecrated the house of the LORD, and on the sixteenth day of the first month they finished. **18** Then they went in to Hezekiah the king and said, "We have cleansed all the house of the LORD, the altar of burnt offering and all its utensils, and the table for the showbread and all its utensils. **19** All the utensils [h]that King Ahaz discarded in his reign when he was faithless, we have made ready and consecrated, and behold, they are before the altar of the LORD."

Hezekiah Restores Temple Worship

20 Then Hezekiah the king rose early and gathered the officials of the city and went up to the house of the LORD. **21** And they brought seven bulls, seven rams, seven lambs, and seven male goats [i]for a sin offering for the kingdom and for the sanctuary and for Judah. And he commanded the priests, the sons of Aaron, to offer them on the altar of the LORD. **22** So they slaughtered the bulls, and the priests received the blood [j]and threw it against the altar. And they slaughtered the rams, and their blood was thrown against the altar. And they slaughtered the lambs, and their blood was thrown against the altar. **23** Then the goats for the sin offering were brought to the king and the assembly, [k]and they laid their

5 [m]ver. 15, 34; ch. 35:6; 1 Chr. 15:12; Ezra 6:20
6 [n]Jer. 2:27; Ezek. 8:16
7 [o]ch. 28:24
8 [p]See ch. 24:18 [q]Deut. 28:25 [r]Jer. 19:8; 25:9, 18; 29:18; Mic. 6:16
9 [s]ch. 28:5, 6, 8, 17
10 [t]See 1 Chr. 22:7 [u]See ch. 15:12
11 [v]Num. 3:6; 8:14; 18:2, 6
12 [w]ch. 31:13 [x]Num. 3:17
13 [y]1 Chr. 15:8 [z]1 Chr. 6:39
14 [a]1 Chr. 6:33 [b]1 Chr. 9:16
15 [c]See ver. 5 [d]ch. 30:12 [e][Neh. 13:9]
16 [f]See 2 Sam. 15:23
17 [g]ver. 3
19 [h][ch. 28:24]
21 [i][Lev. 4:14]
22 [j]Lev. 8:15, 19, 24; Heb. 9:21; [ch. 35:11]
23 [k]Lev. 4:15

29:4–5 The appeal to the Levites to **consecrate** themselves recalls David's summons to the priests and Levites in the sacred mission to retrieve the ark (1 Chron. 15:11–15). The **filth** denotes pagan cult objects that had been installed in the sanctuary, which were to be removed and burned in the Kidron Valley (2 Chron. 29:16).

29:6 Unfaithful (Hb. *ma'al*) and **forsaken** are key terms in the Chronicler's theological vocabulary, accounting for punishment and exile.

29:8 an object of horror, of astonishment, and of hissing. See Jer. 29:18.

29:9–10 Hezekiah recalls the terrible consequences of Ahaz's apostasy and announces his intention to **make a covenant with the LORD** to avert **his fierce anger**. No ceremony of covenant renewal is described (see 15:12; 23:16), but it is clear by their response that the people took this appeal to heart.

29:12–14 The list of Levites who lead the work of purification closely parallels the list in 1 Chron. 15:5–10, except that representatives of the Levitical singers (**Asaph**, **Heman**, and **Jeduthun**) have replaced Hebron and Uzziel.

29:16–17 the brook Kidron. See 15:16; 30:14. The work of cleansing the temple took two weeks, until the **sixteenth day of the first month**, two days past the proper date of Passover (see Num. 9:1–11 and note on 2 Chron. 30:2–4).

29:18–19 All the utensils that King Ahaz discarded in his reign . . . we have made ready and consecrated. See note on 1 Chron. 28:11–19.

29:20–22 The restoration of worship following the cleansing of the temple begins with a sin offering for all Israel as the appointed means in the Law of Moses for removing every kind of evil and defilement from the people (see Lev. 4:1–5:13).

29:23 Laid their hands on them calls to mind the scapegoat ritual of the Day of Atonement (Lev. 16:20–22).

hands on them, 24 and the priests slaughtered them and made a sin offering with their
blood on the altar, [l]to make atonement for all Israel. For the king commanded that the
burnt offering and the sin offering should be made for all Israel.
25 [m]And he stationed the Levites in the house of the LORD with cymbals, harps, and lyres,
[n]according to the commandment of David and of Gad [o]the king's seer and of [p]Nathan the
prophet, for the commandment was from the LORD through his prophets. 26 The Levites
stood with [q]the instruments of David, [r]and the priests with the trumpets. 27 Then Hezekiah
commanded that the burnt offering be offered on the altar. And when the burnt offering
began, [s]the song to the LORD began also, and the trumpets, accompanied by the instruments of David king of Israel. 28 The whole assembly worshiped, and the singers sang, and
the trumpeters sounded. All this continued until the burnt offering was finished. 29 When
the offering was finished, [t]the king and all who were present with him bowed themselves
and worshiped. 30 And Hezekiah the king and the officials commanded the Levites to sing
praises to the LORD with the words of David and of Asaph the seer. And they sang praises
with gladness, and they bowed down and worshiped.
31 Then Hezekiah said, [u]"You have now consecrated yourselves to[1] the LORD. Come near;
bring sacrifices and thank offerings to the house of the LORD." And the assembly brought
sacrifices and thank offerings, and all who were [v]of a willing heart brought burnt offerings.
32 The number of the burnt offerings that the assembly brought was 70 bulls, 100 rams,
and 200 lambs; all these were for a burnt offering to the LORD. 33 And the consecrated
offerings were 600 bulls and 3,000 sheep. 34 But the priests were too few and could not flay
all the burnt offerings, so until other priests had consecrated themselves, [w]their brothers
the Levites helped them, until the work was finished—[x]for the Levites were more upright
in heart than the priests in consecrating themselves. 35 Besides the great number of burnt
offerings, there was [y]the fat of the peace offerings, and there were [z]the drink offerings
for the burnt offerings. Thus the service of the house of the LORD was restored. 36 And
Hezekiah and all the people rejoiced because God had provided for the people, for the
thing came about suddenly.

Passover Celebrated

30 Hezekiah sent to all Israel and Judah, and wrote letters also to Ephraim and
Manasseh, that they should come to the house of the LORD at Jerusalem to keep the
Passover to the LORD, the God of Israel. 2 For the king and his princes and all the assembly
in Jerusalem had taken counsel to keep the Passover [a]in the second month— 3 for they
could not keep it [b]at that time [c]because the priests had not consecrated themselves in sufficient number, nor had the people assembled in Jerusalem— 4 and the plan seemed right
to the king and all the assembly. 5 So they decreed to make a proclamation throughout all
Israel, [d]from Beersheba to Dan, that the people should come and keep the Passover to the
LORD, the God of Israel, at Jerusalem, for they had not kept it as often as prescribed. 6 [e]So
couriers went throughout all Israel and Judah with letters from the king and his princes,
as the king had commanded, saying, "O people of Israel, [f]return to the LORD, the God of

[1] Hebrew *filled your hand for*

24 [l]Lev. 4:26
25 [m]1 Chr. 16:4; 25:6; [1 Chr. 15:16] [n]ch. 8:14; 1 Chr. 23:5; 25:1 [o]See 1 Sam. 9:9 [p]2 Sam. 12:1
26 [q]1 Chr. 23:5; [Amos 6:5] [r]See 1 Chr. 15:24
27 [s][ch. 23:18]
29 [t][ch. 20:18]
31 [u]ch. 13:9; [Ex. 28:41] [v]Ex. 35:5, 22
34 [w][ch. 35:11] [x][ch. 30:3]
35 [y]Lev. 3:1, 16 [z]Num. 15:5, 7, 10

Chapter 30

2 [a]ver. 13, 15; Num. 9:10, 11
3 [b][ch. 29:17; Ex. 12:6, 18] [c]ch. 29:34; [ver. 24]
5 [d]See 2 Sam. 3:10
6 [e][Esth. 3:13, 15; 8:10, 14; Jer. 51:31] [f]Jer. 4:1; Joel 2:12, 13

29:25–30 The **burnt offering** that is accompanied by the Levites' singing and music signifies the people's act of consecrating themselves afresh to Yahweh (v. 31). **the song to the LORD**. See 1 Chron. 16:7.

29:31–36 The **sacrifices and thank offerings** that the people bring to the temple are individual (rather than regular, communal) expressions of worship and thanksgiving.

30:1–27 The account of Hezekiah's Passover is not mentioned in 2 Kings. Hezekiah demonstrates his commitment to the Law of Moses by pressing on to this celebration immediately after the reconsecration of the temple. At the same time, the ceremony is unorthodox in its date (cf. note on 2 Chron. 30:2–4) and in the participation of the ceremonially unclean (vv. 18–20). The Passover is also the occasion in which people from the north and south are reunited (at least in principle) in true worship at the temple, in contrast to earlier attempts to secure a false unity through force of arms (see 11:1–4; 13:8) or ungodly alliances (see 18:1; 19:2; 20:35).

30:1 all Israel and Judah. The destruction of the northern kingdom in 725–722 B.C. by Assyria and the deportation of much of its population (2 Kings 17:5–6) allowed Hezekiah to make this invitation at the beginning of his reign (715 B.C.).

30:2–4 The **Passover** was delayed until the **second month**, in an application of the principle in Num. 9:9–13 providing for those who were ceremonially unclean or absent on a journey. This is an early example of the Law of Moses' being interpreted to cover new situations. Hezekiah's consultation of the **assembly** in decision making aligns him with David (1 Chron. 13:1–5) and Solomon (2 Chron. 1:2–5).

30:6–9 The **letters** of invitation are similar in content and language to Hezekiah's speech to the priests and Levites (29:5–11). More than an invitation to participate in a festival (30:8b), they are really a summons to repentance (**return to the LORD**), so that God will avert his **anger** and the captives of the Assyrians will be returned (v. 9).

Abraham, Isaac, and Israel, that he may turn again to the remnant of you who have escaped
from the hand of [g]the kings of Assyria. 7 [h]Do not be like your fathers and your brothers,
who were faithless to the LORD God of their fathers, so that he made them a desolation,
as you see. 8 [i]Do not now be stiff-necked as your fathers were, but yield yourselves to the
LORD and come to his sanctuary, which he has consecrated forever, and serve the LORD
your God, [j]that his fierce anger may turn away from you. 9 For [f]if you return to the LORD,
your brothers and your children [k]will find compassion with their captors and return to
this land. For [l]the LORD your God is gracious and merciful and will not turn away his face
from you, [m]if you return to him."

10 [e]So the couriers went from city to city through the country of [n]Ephraim and Manasseh,
and as far as Zebulun, but [o]they laughed them to scorn and mocked them. 11 However, [p]some
men of Asher, of Manasseh, and of Zebulun humbled themselves and came to Jerusalem.
12 The hand of God was also on Judah to give them one heart to do what the king and the
princes commanded [q]by the word of the LORD.

13 And many people came together in Jerusalem to keep the Feast of Unleavened Bread
[r]in the second month, a very great assembly. 14 They set to work and removed [s]the altars
that were in Jerusalem, and all the altars for burning incense they took away [t]and threw
into the brook Kidron. 15 [u]And they slaughtered the Passover lamb on the fourteenth day
of the second month. [v]And the priests and the Levites were ashamed, [w]so that they consecrated themselves and brought burnt offerings into the house of the LORD. 16 [x]They took
their accustomed posts according to the Law of Moses [y]the man of God. The priests threw
the blood that they received from the hand of the Levites. 17 For there were many in the
assembly who had not consecrated themselves. Therefore the Levites had to slaughter
the Passover lamb for everyone who was not clean, to consecrate it to the LORD. 18 For a
majority of the people, [z]many of them from Ephraim, Manasseh, Issachar, and Zebulun,
had not cleansed themselves, yet they ate the Passover otherwise [a]than as prescribed. For
Hezekiah had prayed for them, saying, "May the good LORD pardon everyone 19 [b]who sets
his heart to seek God, the LORD, the God of his fathers, even though not according to the
sanctuary's rules of cleanness."[1] 20 And the LORD heard Hezekiah and healed the people.
21 And the people of Israel who were present at Jerusalem kept [c]the Feast of Unleavened
Bread seven days with great gladness, and the Levites and the priests praised the LORD day
by day, singing with all their might[2] to the LORD. 22 And Hezekiah spoke [d]encouragingly
to all the Levites who showed good skill in the service of the LORD. So they ate the food
of the festival for seven days, sacrificing [e]peace offerings and giving thanks to the LORD,
the God of their fathers.

23 Then the whole assembly agreed together to keep the feast [f]for another seven days.
So they kept it for another seven days with gladness. 24 For Hezekiah king of Judah [g]gave
the assembly 1,000 bulls and 7,000 sheep for offerings, and the princes gave the assembly
1,000 bulls and 10,000 sheep. And the priests [h]consecrated themselves in great numbers.
25 The whole assembly of Judah, and the priests and the Levites, [i]and the whole assembly
that came out of Israel, and the sojourners who came out of the land of Israel, and the
sojourners who lived in Judah, rejoiced. 26 So there was great joy in Jerusalem, for [j]since
the time of Solomon the son of David king of Israel there had been nothing like this in
Jerusalem. 27 Then [k]the priests and the Levites arose and [l]blessed the people, and their
voice was heard, and their prayer came to [m]his holy habitation in heaven.

[1] Hebrew *not according to the cleanness of holiness* [2] Compare 1 Chronicles 13:8; Hebrew *with instruments of might*

6 [g]2 Kgs. 15:19, 29
7 [h][Ezek. 20:18]
8 [i]Ex. 32:9; Deut. 9:6; 10:16; 2 Kgs. 17:14; Neh. 9:16, 29; Jer. 7:26; 17:23; [Acts 7:51] [j]ch. 29:10
9 [f][See ver. 6 above] [k][Ps. 106:46] [l]Ex. 34:6; Dan. 9:9 [m]See 1 Sam. 7:3
10 [e][See ver. 6 above] [n]ver. 1 [o][ch. 36:16]
11 [p]ver. 18, 21, 25
12 [q][ch. 29:15]
13 [r]ver. 2
14 [s]ch. 28:24 [t][ch. 15:16; 2 Kgs. 23:6]
15 [u]ch. 35:11 [v][ch. 29:34] [w][Ezra 6:20]
16 [x]ch. 35:10 [y]Deut. 33:1
18 [z]ver. 11, 25 [a]See Ex. 12:43-49
19 [b]ch. 19:3
21 [c]Ex. 12:15; 13:6; Ezra 6:22
22 [d]ch. 32:6; Isa. 40:2 [e][Lev. 5]
23 [f][1 Kgs. 8:65]
24 [g][ch. 35:7-9] [h]ver. 3; ch. 29:34
25 [i]ver. 11, 18
26 [j]See ch. 7:8-10
27 [k]ch. 5:5; 23:18 [l]See Num. 6:23-27 [m]Deut. 26:15; Ps. 68:5

30:11 humbled themselves. See 7:14.

30:14 the brook Kidron. See 29:16–17.

30:17 the Levites had to slaughter the Passover lamb for everyone. A new, permanent change in their duties (see 35:5–6). It had previously been the responsibility of the elders to slaughter the Passover lamb (Ex. 12:21).

30:18–20 Although the northerners who ate the Passover were ceremonially unclean and thus deficient according to the letter of the law, their genuine repentance and Hezekiah's intercession were enough to override this deficiency. **And the LORD heard Hezekiah and healed the people** in fulfillment of the promise in 7:14. "Healing" here is probably a metaphor for forgiveness and spiritual cleansing so that the people could come before God in keeping with Hezekiah's prayer (see Ps. 41:4; Jer. 30:17).

30:23–27 The **feast** was extended for another week, just as the temple dedication had been, and the **great joy** of this occasion recalls the time of Solomon (7:9–10).

Hezekiah Organizes the Priests

31 Now when all this was finished, all Israel who were present went out to the cities
of Judah and [n]broke in pieces the [o]pillars and cut down [p]the Asherim and broke
down the high places and the altars throughout all Judah and Benjamin, and in Ephraim
and Manasseh, until they had destroyed them all. Then all the people of Israel returned
to their cities, every man to his possession.
2 And Hezekiah appointed [q]the divisions of the priests and of the Levites, division by
division, each according to his service, the priests and the Levites, [r]for burnt offerings
and peace offerings, to minister in the gates of the camp of the LORD and to give thanks
and praise. 3 [s]The contribution of the king from his own possessions was for the burnt
offerings: the burnt offerings of morning and evening, and the burnt offerings for the
Sabbaths, the new moons, and the appointed feasts, [t]as it is written in the Law of the
LORD. 4 And he commanded the people who lived in Jerusalem to give [u]the portion due
to the priests and the Levites, that they might give themselves to the Law of the LORD.
5 As soon as the command was spread abroad, the people of Israel gave in abundance the
firstfruits of grain, wine, oil, honey, and of all the produce of the field. And they brought
in abundantly [v]the tithe of everything. 6 And the people of Israel and Judah who lived
in the cities of Judah also brought in the tithe of cattle and sheep, and [w]the tithe of the
dedicated things that had been dedicated to the LORD their God, and laid them in heaps.
7 In the third month they began to pile up the heaps, and finished them in the seventh
month. 8 When Hezekiah and the princes came and saw the heaps, they blessed the LORD
and his people Israel. 9 And Hezekiah questioned the priests and the Levites about the
heaps. 10 Azariah the chief priest, who was [x]of the house of Zadok, answered him, "Since
they began to bring the contributions into the house of the LORD, we have eaten and had
enough and have plenty left, [y]for the LORD has blessed his people, so that we have this
large amount left."
11 Then Hezekiah commanded them to prepare [z]chambers in the house of the LORD,
and they prepared them. 12 And they faithfully brought in the contributions, the tithes,
and the dedicated things. The chief officer [a]in charge of them was Conaniah the Levite,
with [b]Shimei his brother as second, 13 [b]while Jehiel, Azaziah, Nahath, Asahel, Jerimoth,
Jozabad, Eliel, Ismachiah, [b]Mahath, and Benaiah were overseers assisting Conaniah and
Shimei his brother, by the appointment of Hezekiah the king and [x]Azariah the chief officer
of the house of God. 14 And Kore the son of Imnah the Levite, keeper of the east gate, was
over the freewill offerings to God, to apportion the contribution reserved for the LORD and
the most holy offerings. 15 [b]Eden, Miniamin, Jeshua, Shemaiah, Amariah, and Shecaniah
were faithfully assisting him in [d]the cities of the priests, to distribute the portions to their
brothers, old and young alike, by divisions, 16 except those enrolled by genealogy, males
from three years old and upward—all who entered the house of the LORD [e]as the duty
of each day required—for their service according to their offices, by their divisions. 17 The
enrollment of the priests was according to their fathers' houses; that of the Levites [f]from
twenty years old and upward was according to their offices, by their divisions. 18 They were

Chapter 31
1 [n]2 Kgs. 18:4 [o]See Deut. 16:22 [p]See Deut. 16:21
2 [q]1 Chr. 23:6; 24:1 [r]1 Chr. 23:30, 31
3 [s][ch. 35:7] [t]See Num. 28:3–29:40
4 [u][Neh. 13:10]; See Num. 18:8-24
5 [v]Neh. 13:12
6 [w]Lev. 27:30; Deut. 14:28
10 [x]1 Chr. 6:8 [y][Mal. 3:10]
11 [z]1 Chr. 9:26, 33; [2 Kgs. 23:11; Neh. 10:39]
12 [a][ch. 35:9; Neh. 13:13] [b][ch. 29:12, 14]
13 [b][See ver. 12 above] [x][See ver. 10 above]
15 [b][See ver. 12 above] [d]See Josh. 21:9-19
16 [e]1 Kgs. 8:59; Ezra 3:4; Neh. 11:23; 12:47
17 [f]1 Chr. 23:24, 27

31:1 all Israel. The festival united the Israelites of the north and south and sparked a popular movement to eradicate pagan worship from **Ephraim** and **Manasseh**, as well as **Judah** and **Benjamin**.

31:2–21 The final stage in Hezekiah's reforms is the restoration of the temple services, which had evidently lapsed when Ahaz closed the temple (28:24). This requires the reorganization of the priests and Levites for the offering of sacrifices and praise (31:2) and the reinstatement of tithes and offerings to support the temple personnel (vv. 4–19). The Chronicler is at pains to demonstrate that the people support the temple generously (v. 5) and that Hezekiah makes effective provisions for the faithful collection and distribution of the gifts (vv. 11–19). The consequence of Hezekiah's faithful leadership is blessing on the people and his own reign (vv. 10, 21). The account stands as an evident example and encouragement to the Chronicler's own community (see Neh. 10:35–39).

31:3 Hezekiah leads with the example of his own generosity, as David had done before (1 Chron. 29:2–5).

31:5–6 The **firstfruits** were for the priests (Num. 18:12–13) and the tithes were for the Levites (Num. 18:21, 24).

31:7 The amassing of food lasts from the grain harvest **in the third month** (May–June, the Feast of Weeks or Pentecost) until the fruit and vine harvest **in the seventh month** (September–October, the Feast of Ingathering or Tabernacles). On these occasions and at Passover, all Israelite men were to come to the temple (Ex. 23:16–17).

31:11–15 Hezekiah's provision of storerooms and appointing of Levites to be in charge of them recalls David's arrangements (1 Chron. 23:28; 28:12). **Conaniah** and **Shimei**, with their 10 assistants, are responsible for the storerooms, while **Kore** and his six assistants arrange for distribution in the priests' cities (see 1 Chron. 6:54–60).

31:16–18 Distribution was made to **priests** and their families, including provision for **males from three years old**, i.e., the age by which all of them had been weaned.

enrolled with all their little children, their wives, their sons, and their daughters, the whole
assembly, for they were faithful in keeping themselves holy. [19] And for the sons of Aaron,
the priests, who were in the fields of common land belonging to their cities, there were
men in the several cities who were [g]designated by name to distribute portions to every
male among the priests and to everyone among the Levites who was enrolled.
[20] Thus Hezekiah did throughout all Judah, [h]and he did what was good and right and
faithful before the LORD his God. [21] And every work that he undertook in the service of
the house of God and in accordance with the law and the commandments, seeking his
God, he did with all his heart, and prospered.

Sennacherib Invades Judah

32 [i]After these things and these acts of faithfulness, Sennacherib king of Assyria came
and invaded Judah and encamped against the fortified cities, thinking to win them
for himself. [2] And when Hezekiah saw that Sennacherib had come and intended to fight
against Jerusalem, [3] he planned with his officers and his mighty men to stop the water of
the springs that were outside the city; and they helped him. [4] A great many people were
gathered, and they stopped all the springs and [j]the brook that flowed through the land,
saying, "Why should the kings of Assyria come and find much water?" [5] He set to work
resolutely and built up [k]all the wall that was broken down and raised towers upon it,[1]
and outside it he built another wall, and he strengthened the [l]Millo in the city of David.
He also made weapons and shields in abundance. [6] And he set combat commanders over
the people and gathered them together to him in the square at the gate of the city and
spoke [m]encouragingly to them, saying, [7] [n]"Be strong and courageous. [o]Do not be afraid
or dismayed before the king of Assyria and all the horde that is with him, [p]for there are
more with us than with him. [8] With him is [q]an arm of flesh, [r]but with us is the LORD our
God, to help us and to fight our battles." And the people took confidence from the words
of Hezekiah king of Judah.

Sennacherib Blasphemes

[9] After this, Sennacherib king of Assyria, who was besieging Lachish with all his forces,
sent his servants to Jerusalem to Hezekiah king of Judah and to all the people of Judah
who were in Jerusalem, saying, [10] "Thus says Sennacherib king of Assyria, 'On what are
you trusting, that you endure the siege in Jerusalem? [11] Is not Hezekiah misleading you,
that he may give you over to die by famine and by thirst, when he tells you, "The LORD our
God will deliver us from the hand of the king of Assyria"? [12] [s]Has not this same Hezekiah
taken away his high places and his altars and commanded Judah and Jerusalem, "Before

[1] Vulgate; Hebrew *and raised upon the towers*

19 [g][ch. 28:15; Num. 1:17]; See ver. 12-15
20 [h]2 Kgs. 18:3; 20:3

Chapter 32

1 [i]For ver. 1-22, see 2 Kgs. 18:13–19:37; Isa. 36:1–37:38
4 [j]ver. 30
5 [k]ch. 25:23; [Isa. 22:9, 10] [l]See 2 Sam. 5:9
6 [m]ch. 30:22; Isa. 40:2
7 [n]See Deut. 31:6 [o]ch. 20:15 [p]2 Kgs. 6:16
8 [q]Jer. 17:5 [r]ch. 15:2; 20:17
12 [s][ch. 31:1]

31:20–21 The summarizing evaluation of Hezekiah echoes the praise of the king in 2 Kings 18:3, 5–7a but reflects the Chronicler's characteristic vocabulary and concept of the exemplary king: **seeking his God**, **with all his heart**, and **prospered**. This recalls David's exhortation of Solomon (see 1 Chron. 22:13, 19; 28:9).

32:1–23 The Chronicler's account of Sennacherib's invasion (701 B.C.) greatly condenses and simplifies the record given in 2 Kings 18–19 (see note on 2 Kings 18:13). That earlier account depicts a rather more ambivalent (but still fundamentally positive) portrait of Hezekiah (see 2 Kings 18:14–16, 21, 23). The Chronicler omits these details to present Hezekiah at his faithful best, but his principal concern is to highlight the uniqueness and supremacy of Israel's God, and his ability to **deliver** his people from their enemies (note Sennacherib's constant taunting use of this verb in 2 Chron. 32:11, 13, 14, 15, 17).

32:1–8 After these things. Like Jehoshaphat (20:1), Hezekiah's faithful acts are followed by an aggressive invasion, an event that becomes an occasion for testing the king's faith and resourcefulness. Hezekiah's response includes taking practical measures for the defense of Jerusalem (32:2–6a) and encouraging the people not to fear the strength of men (**arm of flesh**; see Jer. 17:5) but to have confidence in God's **help** (see 2 Chron. 14:11). **Be strong and courageous. Do not be afraid** echoes David's charge to Solomon (1 Chron. 22:13), based in turn on Moses' words to Joshua (Deut. 31:6; Josh. 1:9).

32:1–4, 30 Toward the end of the eighth century B.C., Hezekiah built a new **water** system for Jerusalem, which incorporated part of the earlier system. A tunnel was constructed that brought water directly from the Gihon Spring to the Pool of Siloam. Two teams cut toward each other, one from the spring and one from the pool. The Siloam Inscription, which was discovered in the tunnel in 1880, describes the final moments of the meeting of the two teams.

32:5 he built another wall. In the 1970 excavation of Jerusalem in the Jewish Quarter of the Old City, archaeologist Nahman Avigad discovered a wall 21 feet (6.4 m) thick from the eighth to seventh centuries B.C. It was probably erected by Hezekiah to protect the city against the invading Assyrians. The city wall was also extended to accommodate the growth in population caused by the influx of refugees from the north. **the Millo**. See note on 2 Sam. 5:9.

32:9–16 Sennacherib . . . was besieging Lachish. See note on 2 Kings 18:17. See 2 Kings 18:19–25, 27–35; 19:9–13 (and notes), which the address of Sennacherib's **servants** summarizes. The speech follows the familiar pattern of psychological warfare, attempting to separate a people from their leader and to intimidate them into submission. Moreover, the people are constantly challenged on their confidence in the Lord, whom the Assyrians consider no more **able to deliver** than the gods of the lands they had conquered. The blasphemy and hubris of Sennacherib and his officers (2 Chron. 32:17, 19) are an affront to Yahweh's honor and invite his reply.

JERUSALEM IN THE TIME OF HEZEKIAH (C. 725–686 B.C.)

During the reign of King Hezekiah, the city of Jerusalem expanded more than ever before. Many refugees from the Assyrian invasion settled on the Western Hill, as the ancient city built by King Solomon on the Eastern Hill was not able to absorb them. New city walls encircled both hills, and thus Jerusalem became a city that was "bound firmly together" (Ps. 122:3).

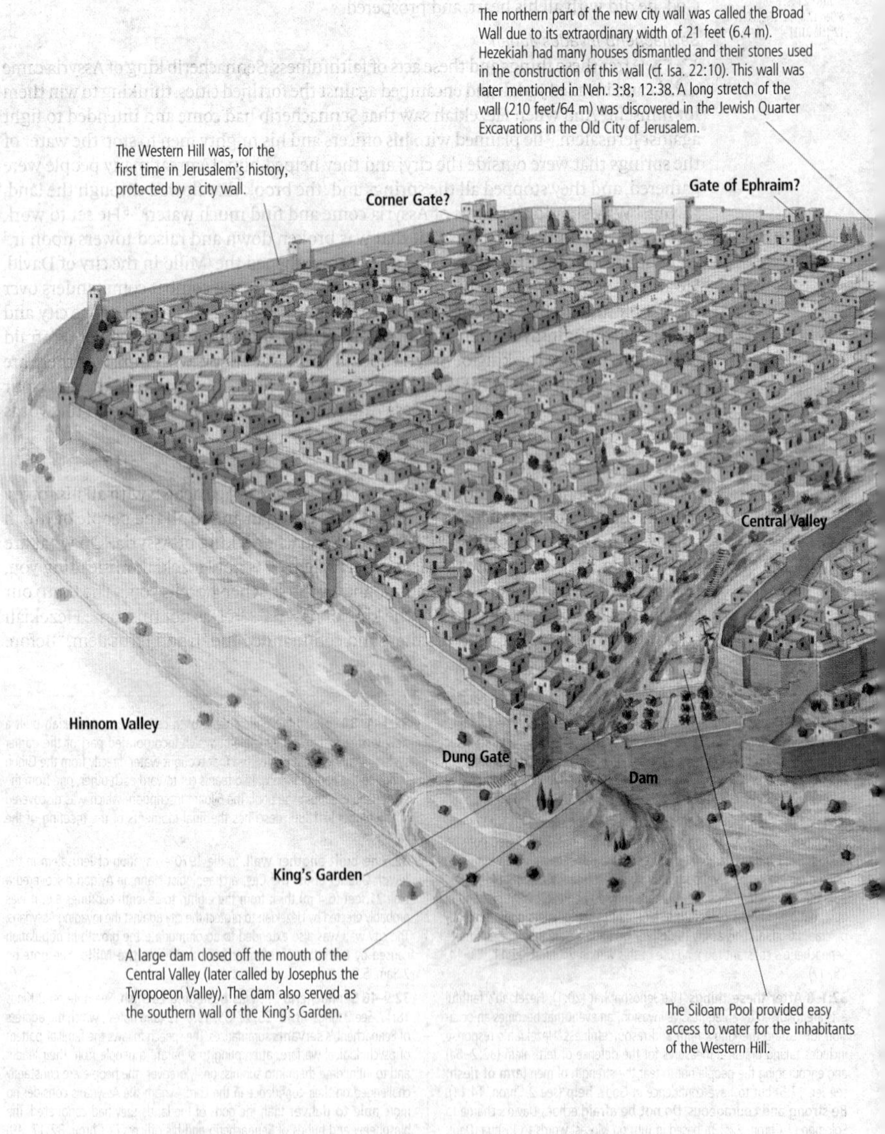

The northern part of the new city wall was called the Broad Wall due to its extraordinary width of 21 feet (6.4 m). Hezekiah had many houses dismantled and their stones used in the construction of this wall (cf. Isa. 22:10). This wall was later mentioned in Neh. 3:8; 12:38. A long stretch of the wall (210 feet/64 m) was discovered in the Jewish Quarter Excavations in the Old City of Jerusalem.
The Western Hill was, for the first time in Jerusalem's history, protected by a city wall.
Corner Gate?
Gate of Ephraim?
Central Valley
Hinnom Valley
Dung Gate
Dam
King's Garden
A large dam closed off the mouth of the Central Valley (later called by Josephus the Tyropoeon Valley). The dam also served as the southern wall of the King's Garden.
The Siloam Pool provided easy access to water for the inhabitants of the Western Hill.

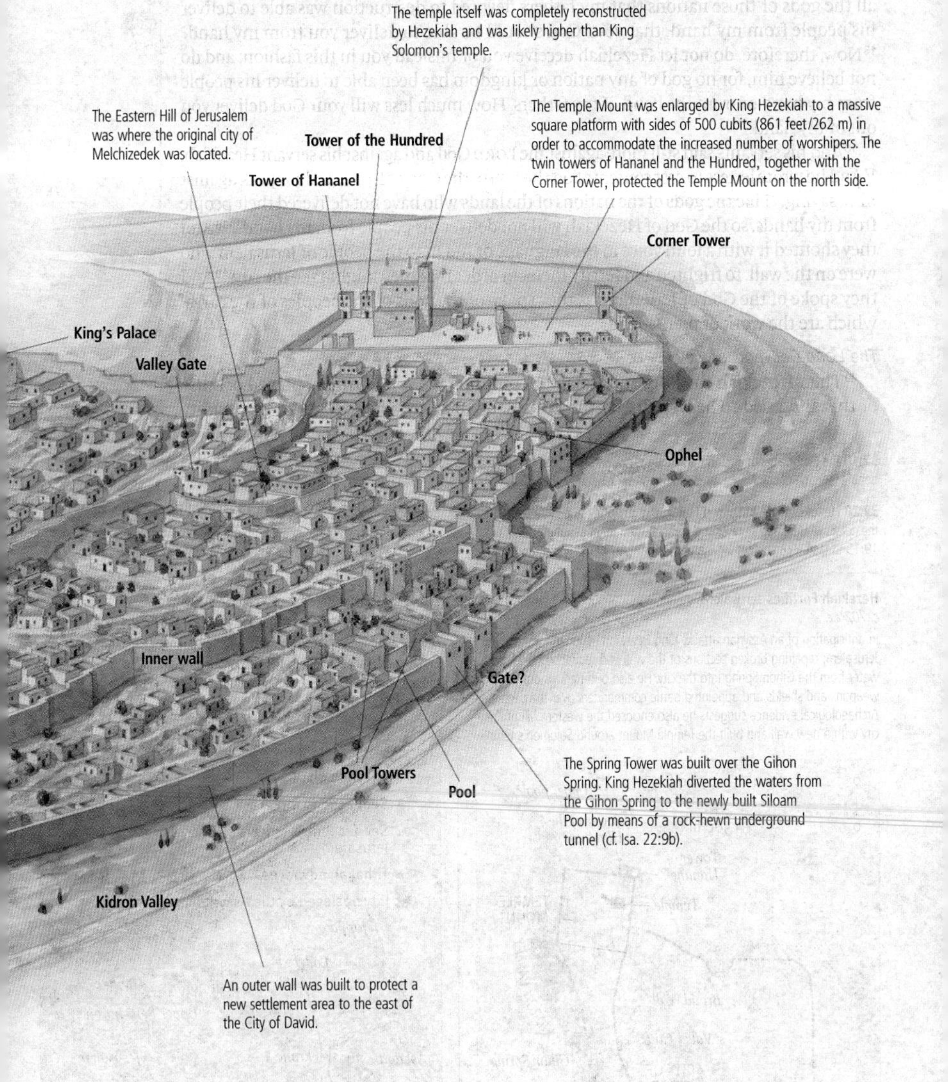

The temple itself was completely reconstructed by Hezekiah and was likely higher than King Solomon's temple.
The Eastern Hill of Jerusalem was where the original city of Melchizedek was located.
Tower of the Hundred
Tower of Hananel
The Temple Mount was enlarged by King Hezekiah to a massive square platform with sides of 500 cubits (861 feet/262 m) in order to accommodate the increased number of worshipers. The twin towers of Hananel and the Hundred, together with the Corner Tower, protected the Temple Mount on the north side.
Corner Tower
King's Palace
Valley Gate
Ophel
Inner wall
Gate?
Pool Towers
Pool
The Spring Tower was built over the Gihon Spring. King Hezekiah diverted the waters from the Gihon Spring to the newly built Siloam Pool by means of a rock-hewn underground tunnel (cf. Isa. 22:9b).
Kidron Valley
An outer wall was built to protect a new settlement area to the east of the City of David.

one altar you shall worship, and on it you shall burn your sacrifices"? 13 Do you not know
what I and my fathers have done to all the peoples of other lands? Were the gods of the
nations of those lands at all able to deliver their lands out of my hand? 14 Who among
all the gods of those nations that my fathers devoted to destruction was able to deliver
his people from my hand, that your God should be able to deliver you from my hand?
15 Now, therefore, do not let Hezekiah deceive you or mislead you in this fashion, and do
not believe him, for no god of any nation or kingdom has been able to deliver his people
from my hand or from the hand of my fathers. How much less will your God deliver you
out of my hand!'"

16 And his servants said still more against the LORD God and against his servant Hezekiah.
17 And he wrote letters to cast contempt on the LORD, the God of Israel, and to speak against
him, saying, "Like the gods of the nations of the lands who have not delivered their people
from my hands, so the God of Hezekiah will not deliver his people from my hand." 18 And
they shouted it with a loud voice in the language of Judah to the people of Jerusalem who
were on the wall, to frighten and terrify them, in order that they might take the city. 19 And
they spoke of the God of Jerusalem as they spoke of the gods of the peoples of the earth,
which are the work of men's hands.

The LORD Delivers Jerusalem

20 Then Hezekiah the king and Isaiah the prophet, the son of Amoz, prayed because
of this and cried to heaven. 21 And the LORD sent an angel, who cut off all the mighty

32:18 The **language of Judah** was Hebrew; Aramaic was then the international language of the Near East (see 2 Kings 18:26–35).

32:20 Hezekiah the king and Isaiah the prophet. The Chronicler omits the details of Hezekiah's prayer and Isaiah's prophecy of salvation (see 2 Kings 19:15–34) to focus on his familiar point that God has promised to hear his people's prayer in times of distress (cf. 2 Chron. 6:24–25). **cried to heaven**. Cf. note on 2 Kings 19:1–2.

32:21 See 2 Kings 19:35–37. **with shame of face**. The Chronicler's addi-

Hezekiah Fortifies Jerusalem

c. 702 B.C.

In anticipation of an Assyrian attack, King Hezekiah of Judah fortified Jerusalem, repairing broken sections of the wall and redirecting the flow of water from the Gihon Spring into the city. He also outfitted his army with weapons and shields and appointed battle commanders over the people. Archaeological evidence suggests he also enclosed the western hill of the city with a new wall and built the Temple Mount around Solomon's temple.

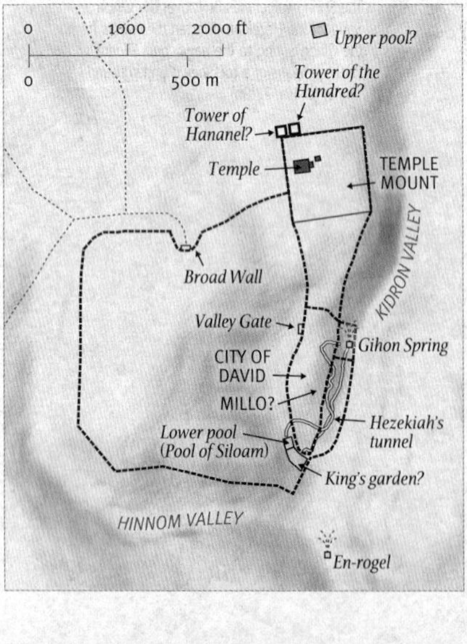

Assyria Attacks Judah

701 B.C.

During the reign of Hezekiah of Judah, Sennacherib of Assyria came and attacked cities along the western edge of Judah, and he sent officials to besiege Jerusalem and convince Hezekiah to surrender. The Cushite king Tirhakah advanced from Egypt to support Hezekiah (2 Kings 19:9; Isa. 37:9) but apparently failed. The siege of Jerusalem was broken when the angel of the Lord killed 185,000 Assyrians in a single night. Sennacherib withdrew and returned to Nineveh in Assyria, where his own sons killed him.

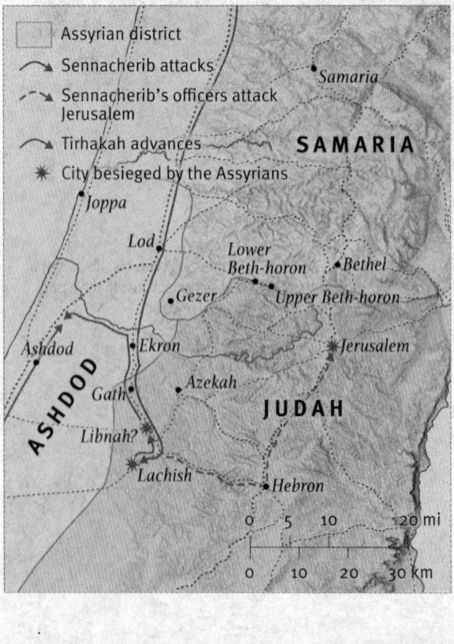

21 [t][Ps. 44:15; Jer. 7:19]
23 [u][ch. 17:5]
24 [v]See 2 Kgs. 20:1-11; Isa. 38:1-8
25 [w][Ps. 116:12] [x]See ch. 26:16 [y]ch. 19:2; 24:18
26 [z]Jer. 26:18, 19; [ch. 33:12]
27 [a]ch. 36:10
30 [b]2 Kgs. 20:20; [Isa. 22:9, 11] [c]1 Kgs. 1:33
31 [d]2 Kgs. 20:12; Isa. 39:1 [e]ver. 24 [f]Deut. 8:2
32 [g]See Isa. 36–39 [h]See 2 Kgs. 18–20
33 [i][2 Sam. 15:30]

Chapter 33

1 [j]For ver. 1-9, see 2 Kgs. 21:1-9
2 [k]ch. 28:3

warriors and commanders and officers in the camp of the king of Assyria. So he returned
with [t]shame of face to his own land. And when he came into the house of his god, some of
his own sons struck him down there with the sword. 22 So the LORD saved Hezekiah and
the inhabitants of Jerusalem from the hand of Sennacherib king of Assyria and from the
hand of all his enemies, and he provided for them on every side. 23 And many [u]brought
gifts to the LORD to Jerusalem and precious things to Hezekiah king of Judah, so that he
was exalted in the sight of all nations from that time onward.

Hezekiah's Pride and Achievements

24 [v]In those days Hezekiah became sick and was at the point of death, and he prayed
to the LORD, and he answered him and gave him a sign. 25 But Hezekiah [w]did not make
return according to the benefit done to him, for [x]his heart was proud. Therefore [y]wrath
came upon him and Judah and Jerusalem. 26 But Hezekiah [z]humbled himself for the pride
of his heart, both he and the inhabitants of Jerusalem, so that the wrath of the LORD did
not come upon them in the days of Hezekiah.

27 And Hezekiah had very great riches and honor, and he made for himself treasuries
for silver, for gold, for precious stones, for spices, for shields, and for all kinds of [a]costly
vessels; 28 storehouses also for the yield of grain, wine, and oil; and stalls for all kinds of
cattle, and sheepfolds. 29 He likewise provided cities for himself, and flocks and herds in
abundance, for God had given him very great possessions. 30 This same Hezekiah [b]closed
the upper outlet of the waters of [c]Gihon and directed them down to the west side of the
city of David. And Hezekiah prospered in all his works. 31 And so in the matter of the
envoys of the princes of Babylon, [d]who had been sent to him to inquire about [e]the sign
that had been done in the land, God left him to himself, [f]in order to test him and to know
all that was in his heart.

32 Now the rest of the acts of Hezekiah and his good deeds, behold, they are written [g]in
the vision of Isaiah the prophet the son of Amoz, [h]in the Book of the Kings of Judah and
Israel. 33 And Hezekiah slept with his fathers, and they buried him in the [i]upper part of
the tombs of the sons of David, and all Judah and the inhabitants of Jerusalem did him
honor at his death. And Manasseh his son reigned in his place.

Manasseh Reigns in Judah

33 [j]Manasseh was twelve years old when he began to reign, and he reigned fifty-five
years in Jerusalem. 2 And he did what was evil in the sight of the LORD, according to [k]the abominations of the nations whom the LORD drove out before the people of

tion, highlighting the element of confrontation between the arrogant Assyrian king and God himself (see Ps. 34:4–7; 35:4–5). Although Sennacherib's army withdrew shortly afterward, his murder did not occur until 20 years later, in 681 B.C. (see notes on 2 Kings 19:35–36; 19:37).

32:23 Hezekiah recalls Solomon in the esteem and **gifts** he receives from foreigners (9:23–24).

32:24–33 The conclusion to the Chronicler's account of Hezekiah's reign mentions his other achievements and his prayers, as well as his lapse into sinful pride.

32:24–26, 31 See 2 Kings 20:1–19. These events preceded Sennacherib's invasion by a few years. The **sign** was the miraculous backward movement of the shadow, signifying the extension of Hezekiah's life in answer to prayer. Related to this incident was the king's proud display of his wealth before the Babylonian envoys. This incurred God's **wrath**, but Hezekiah and the people's humble repentance (see 2 Chron. 7:14) is said to have spared Jerusalem **in the days of Hezekiah** (see 2 Kings 20:16–18). Even a good king such as Hezekiah could contribute to Judah's fate; like Josiah (2 Chron. 34:28), however, he was spared from seeing it in his days.

32:24 In those days. See note on 2 Kings 20:1.

32:27–30a Riches and honor are standard signs of divine blessing on faithful reigns (see 1 Chron. 29:28; 2 Chron. 1:11; 17:5). Hezekiah's tunnel with the renowned Siloam Inscription (discovered in 1880) was part of the engineering work referred to in 32:30a (see vv. 3–4).

32:31 the envoys of the princes of Babylon. See note on 2 Kings 20:12.

32:32–33 the acts of Hezekiah and his good deeds. See note on 2 Kings 20:20. **the vision of Isaiah the prophet . . . in the Book of the Kings of Judah and Israel**. Not the canonical book of Isaiah's prophecy but a historical work now lost (see notes on 1 Kings 14:19; 2 Chron. 26:22).

33:1–20 *Manasseh.* See 2 Kings 21:1–10, 17–18. Chronicles differs most markedly from Kings by including a section describing Manasseh's imprisonment in Babylon and his religious reforms (2 Chron. 33:11–17), and by omitting 2 Kings 21:11–15, where Manasseh is condemned as a primary cause of the exile (but see note on 2 Chron. 33:10). The reason for the difference lies in their respective aims: Kings presents Manasseh as the worst of Judah's kings whose sins make the exile inevitable, while Chronicles uses him to illustrate the possibility of forgiveness and restoration, even for "the foremost of sinners" (see 1 Tim. 1:15). Both accounts are highly selective in their treatment of the longest reign in Judah's history, and the additional material in Chronicles should not be considered fictional. The Chronicler would certainly agree with 2 Kings that Manasseh's sins contributed to the final outcome of exile, just as the king's own punishment (2 Chron. 33:11) anticipates what will happen to the people. Manasseh's repentance and reforms may also explain why the exile did not come in his day: they had the effect of postponing, but not entirely removing, the consequences of Israel's unfaithfulness, on which God had pronounced judgment (v. 10).

33:1 fifty-five years. 697–642 B.C., including probably a co-regency of 10 years with Hezekiah.

33:2–9 These verses largely reproduce 2 Kings 21:2–9 (see notes). Manasseh sets about reversing all the reforms his father had instituted,

Israel. 3 For he rebuilt the high places [l]that his father Hezekiah had broken down, and he
erected altars to the Baals, and made [m]Asheroth, and worshiped all the host of heaven and
served them. 4 And he built altars in the house of the LORD, of which the LORD had said,
[n]"In Jerusalem shall my name be forever." 5 And he built altars for all the host of heaven
in [o]the two courts of the house of the LORD. 6 [p]And he burned his sons as an offering [q]in
the Valley of the Son of Hinnom, and [r]used fortune-telling and omens and sorcery, and
dealt with [s]mediums and with necromancers. He did much evil in the sight of the LORD,
provoking him to anger. 7 And [t]the carved image of the idol that he had made he set in the
house of God, of which God said to David and to Solomon his son, "In this house, and in
Jerusalem, which I have chosen out of all the tribes of Israel, [n]I will put my name forever,
8 and I will no more remove the foot of Israel from the land [u]that I appointed for your
fathers, if only they will be careful to do all that I have commanded them, all the law, the
statutes, and the rules given through Moses." 9 Manasseh led Judah and the inhabitants
of Jerusalem astray, to do more evil than the nations whom the LORD destroyed before
the people of Israel.

Manasseh's Repentance

10 The LORD spoke to Manasseh and to his people, but they paid no attention. 11 [v]Therefore
the LORD brought upon them the commanders of the army of the king of Assyria, who
captured Manasseh with hooks and [w]bound him with chains of bronze and brought him
to Babylon. 12 And when he was in distress, he entreated the favor of the LORD his God
[x]and humbled himself greatly before the God of his fathers. 13 He prayed to him, and [y]God
was moved by his entreaty and heard his plea and brought him again to Jerusalem into
his kingdom. [z]Then Manasseh knew that the LORD was God.

14 Afterward he built an outer wall for the city of David west of [a]Gihon, in the valley,
and for the entrance into [b]the Fish Gate, and carried it around [c]Ophel, and raised it to a
very great height. He also put commanders of the army in all the fortified cities in Judah.
15 And [d]he took away the foreign gods and the idol from the house of the LORD, and all
the altars that he had built on the mountain of the house of the LORD and in Jerusalem,
and he threw them outside of the city. 16 He also restored the altar of the LORD and offered
on it sacrifices of peace offerings and of thanksgiving, and he commanded Judah to serve
the LORD, the God of Israel. 17 [e]Nevertheless, the people still sacrificed at the high places,
but only to the LORD their God.

18 Now the rest of the acts of Manasseh, and [f]his prayer to his God, and the words of
[g]the seers who spoke to him in the name of the LORD, the God of Israel, behold, they are
in the [h]Chronicles of the Kings of Israel. 19 And his prayer, and how [y]God was moved by
his entreaty, and all his sin and his faithlessness, and the sites [i]on which he built high
places and set up the [l]Asherim and the images, before [x]he humbled himself, behold, they
are written in the Chronicles of the Seers.[1] 20 So Manasseh slept with his fathers, and they
buried him in his house, and Amon his son reigned in his place.

[1] One Hebrew manuscript, Septuagint; most Hebrew manuscripts *of Hozai*

3 [l]ch. 30:14; 31:1; 2 Kgs. 18:4 [m]See Deut. 16:21; [Deut. 17:3]
4 [n]ch. 6:6
5 [o]ch. 4:9
6 [p]ch. 28:3 [q]See Josh. 15:8 [r]Deut. 18:10 [s]See 1 Sam. 28:3
7 [t]ver. 15 [n][See ver. 4 above]
8 [u]2 Sam. 7:10
11 [v][Deut. 28:36] [w][ch. 36:6; Judg. 16:21]
12 [x][ch. 32:26]
13 [y]1 Chr. 5:20; Ezra 8:23 [z][Dan. 4:25]
14 [a]1 Kgs. 1:33 [b]Neh. 3:3; 12:39; Zeph. 1:10 [c]ch. 27:3
15 [d]ver. 3, 5, 7
17 [e][ch. 32:12]
18 [f]ver. 13, 19 [g]See 1 Sam. 9:9 [h][2 Kgs. 21:17]
19 [y][See ver. 13 above] [i]ver. 3 [x][See ver. 12 above]

promoting idolatry and succumbing to the depravity of child sacrifice and sorcery.

33:10 The LORD spoke to Manasseh and to his people alludes to 2 Kings 21:10 and is intended as a summary of the prophecy of judgment in 2 Kings 21:11–15. **But they paid no attention** is based on 2 Kings 21:9a. In their rejection of God's word, Manasseh and his people prefigure the last generation of the kingdom (2 Chron. 36:15–16).

33:11 Manasseh's imprisonment in **Babylon** is not attested to outside the Bible. But this account is often associated with the widespread rebellion in 652–648 B.C. by Shamash-shum-ukin, king of Babylon, against his younger brother and overlord Ashurbanipal, king of **Assyria**. Once he had taken Babylon, Ashurbanipal turned his attention to the western part of his empire and its vassal states, which included Judah. Manasseh may have joined in the rebellion, or at least have been suspected of supporting it.

33:12–13 The description of Manasseh's prayer and God's response is strongly influenced by the thought and vocabulary of 7:14. **Knew that the LORD was God** is similar to a very common expression by Ezekiel, the prophet of the exile: "you/they will know that I am the LORD" (e.g., Ezek. 5:13; 7:27; 13:21).

33:14 Manasseh's building projects and military measures can be understood in light of Assyria's need for a buffer-state in the southwest against Egypt, following the suppression of Shamash-shum-ukin's rebellion. Building projects and armies are regular marks of blessing on faithful kings (see 11:5–12; 14:6–8; 17:12–19; 26:9–15).

33:15–16 Manasseh's religious reform was directed at removing his earlier pagan innovations (vv. 3, 7). The reform centered on the temple, and little if any of it extended beyond Jerusalem. Verse 17 makes it clear that the people continued in their familiar ways. Manasseh removed the idols (v. 15), but it is not stated that he destroyed them, as Josiah did (34:4–7). Amon would later put them back to use.

33:18–20 The Chronicler has considerably expanded the concluding formula in 2 Kings 21:17–18 to emphasize that Manasseh's prayer and his humble repentance constitute the chief significance of his reign. **Faithlessness** is the key Hebrew theological term *ma'al* (see note on 1 Chron. 2:3–8).

21[j] For ver. 21-25, see 2 Kgs. 21:19-24
22[k] ver. 7; [ch. 34:3, 4]
23[l] ver. 12

Chapter 34

1[m] For ver. 1, 2, see 2 Kgs. 22:1, 2
3[n] See ch. 14:3
4[o] [2 Kgs. 23:6] [n] [See ver. 3 above]
5[p] 2 Kgs. 23:20; [1 Kgs. 13:2]
6[q] 2 Kgs. 23:15, 19
7[n] [See ver. 3 above] [r] [Deut. 9:21]
8[s] For ver. 8-28, see 2 Kgs. 22:3-20 [t] ch. 18:25 [u] 2 Sam. 8:16
9[v] ch. 35:8 [q] [See ver. 6 above]
11[w] Neh. 2:8

Amon's Reign and Death

21 [j]Amon was twenty-two years old when he began to reign, and he reigned two years
in Jerusalem. **22** And he did what was evil in the sight of the LORD, as Manasseh his father
had done. Amon sacrificed to all the images [k]that Manasseh his father had made, and
served them. **23** And he did not humble himself before the LORD, [l]as Manasseh his father
had humbled himself, but this Amon incurred guilt more and more. **24** And his servants
conspired against him and put him to death in his house. **25** But the people of the land
struck down all those who had conspired against King Amon. And the people of the land
made Josiah his son king in his place.

Josiah Reigns in Judah

34 [m]Josiah was eight years old when he began to reign, and he reigned thirty-one years
in Jerusalem. **2** And he did what was right in the eyes of the LORD, and walked in the
ways of David his father; and he did not turn aside to the right hand or to the left. **3** For in
the eighth year of his reign, while he was yet a boy, he began to seek the God of David his
father, and in the twelfth year he began to purge Judah and Jerusalem of the high places,
the [n]Asherim, and the carved and the metal images. **4** And they chopped down the altars
of the Baals in his presence, and he cut down the [o]incense altars that stood above them.
And he broke in pieces the [n]Asherim and the carved and the metal images, and he made
dust of them and [o]scattered it over the graves of those who had sacrificed to them. **5** [p]He
also burned the bones of the priests on their altars and cleansed Judah and Jerusalem.
6 And in the [q]cities of Manasseh, Ephraim, and Simeon, and as far as Naphtali, in their
ruins[1] all around, **7** he broke down the altars and beat the [n]Asherim and the images [r]into
powder and cut down all the incense altars throughout all the land of Israel. Then he
returned to Jerusalem.

The Book of the Law Found

8 [s]Now in the eighteenth year of his reign, when he had cleansed the land and the house,
he sent Shaphan the son of Azaliah, and Maaseiah the [t]governor of the city, and Joah
the son of Joahaz, [u]the recorder, to repair the house of the LORD his God. **9** They came to
[v]Hilkiah the high priest and gave him the money that had been brought into the house
of God, which the Levites, the keepers of the threshold, had collected from [q]Manasseh
and Ephraim and from all the remnant of Israel and from all Judah and Benjamin and
from the inhabitants of Jerusalem. **10** And they gave it to the workmen who were working in the house of the LORD. And the workmen who were working in the house of the
LORD gave it for repairing and restoring the house. **11** They gave it to the carpenters and
the builders to buy quarried stone, and timber for binders and [w]beams for the buildings
that the kings of Judah had let go to ruin. **12** And the men did the work faithfully. Over

[1] The meaning of the Hebrew is uncertain

33:21–25 *Amon.* See 2 Kings 21:19–24. The Chronicler has added to the account of Amon's brief reign (642–640 B.C.) the charge that, in contrast to his father, Amon **did not humble himself**, but rather **incurred guilt more and more**. His revival of Manasseh's idolatry (2 Chron. 33:22) contributed to God's wrath against Judah (see 19:10; 24:18; 28:25; 36:16), as well as serving as a prelude to Josiah's reform (ch. 34).

34:1–35:27 *Josiah.* See 2 Kings 22:1–23:30a. The considerable space that the Chronicler devotes to Josiah's reign (640–609 B.C.) is a mark of his importance as an example of godly leadership. From his youth (2 Chron. 34:3), Josiah demonstrates faithfulness to God. Like the other great kings before him, he promotes reform according to the Law of Moses and instructions of David, eliminating idolatry and restoring the temple (34:3–13, 33). Although the inexorable shadow of exile hangs over his reign (34:23–28), Josiah persists in leading his people into a renewal of their relationship with God and in reestablishing the Law of Moses as the basis of the nation's future life (34:29–32). The climax of his reformation (as it was for Hezekiah) is the celebration of a Passover unexcelled in its inclusive breadth and faithfulness (35:18). Josiah is evidently a model for faithful living for the Chronicler's own restoration community, centered on the temple and governed by the same law (see Neh. 8:1–8).

34:2 did not turn aside to the right hand or to the left. See note on 2 Kings 22:2.

34:3–7 Josiah's decisive move against pagan worship is made as soon as he has come of age by turning 20 (see Num. 1:3). The reform includes both Judah and the territories of the former northern kingdom, where the decline of Assyrian power after the death of Ashurbanipal in 627 B.C. allowed Josiah to pursue his religious and political concerns.

34:6–7 A fortress at Mesad Havashyahu on the Mediterranean Sea has been discovered that dates to the last third of the seventh century B.C. Several Hebrew ostraca found there indicate that the site was under Judean control. Josiah's control thus extended not only to the north, as far as Naphtali, but also westward to the coast.

34:8–13 When he had cleansed (v. 8) or "in order to cleanse." The repair of the temple in 622 B.C. was part of the continuing process of reform that Josiah had initiated. **he sent Shaphan**. See note on 2 Kings 22:3–7. The Chronicler adds that contributions came **from Manasseh and Ephraim and from all the remnant of Israel**, as well as **Judah**, pointing to the unity that now existed among the people and their shared interest in the temple (see 1 Chron. 9:3). The Chronicler further states that the repair work was done under Levitical supervision (see 2 Chron. 24:8–12; 29:12–19).

them were set Jahath and Obadiah the Levites, of the sons of Merari, and Zechariah and
Meshullam, of the sons of the Kohathites, to have oversight. [x]The Levites, all who were
skillful with instruments of music, 13 were over [y]the burden-bearers and directed all who
did work in every kind of service, and some of the Levites were scribes and officials and
gatekeepers.
14 While they were bringing out the money that had been brought into the house of the
LORD, [v]Hilkiah the priest found the Book of the Law of the LORD given through Moses.
15 Then Hilkiah answered and said to Shaphan the secretary, "I have found the Book of
the Law in the house of the LORD." And Hilkiah gave the book to Shaphan. 16 Shaphan
brought the book to the king, and further reported to the king, "All that was committed
to your servants they are doing. 17 They have emptied out the money that was found in
the house of the LORD and have given it into the hand of the overseers and the workmen."
18 Then Shaphan the secretary told the king, "Hilkiah the priest has given me a book." And
Shaphan read from it before the king.
19 And when the king heard the words of the Law, [z]he tore his clothes. 20 And the king
commanded Hilkiah, Ahikam the son of Shaphan, Abdon the son of Micah, Shaphan the
secretary, and Asaiah the king's servant, saying, 21 "Go, inquire of the LORD for me and for
those who are left in Israel and in Judah, concerning the words of the book that has been
found. For great is [a]the wrath of the LORD that is poured out on us, because our fathers
have not kept the word of the LORD, to do according to all that is written in this book."

Huldah Prophesies Disaster

22 So Hilkiah and those whom the king had sent[1] went to Huldah the prophetess, the
wife of Shallum the son of Tokhath, son of Hasrah, keeper of the wardrobe (now she lived
in Jerusalem in the Second Quarter) and spoke to her to that effect. 23 And she said to them,
"Thus says the LORD, the God of Israel: 'Tell the man who sent you to me, 24 Thus says the
LORD, Behold, I will bring disaster upon this place and upon its inhabitants, all the curses
that are written in the book that was read before the king of Judah. 25 Because they have
forsaken me and [b]have made offerings to other gods, that they might provoke me to anger
with all the works of their hands, therefore [a]my wrath will be poured out on this place and
will not be quenched. 26 But to the king of Judah, who sent you to inquire of the LORD,
thus shall you say to him, Thus says the LORD, the God of Israel: Regarding the words that
you have heard, 27 because your heart was tender and you humbled yourself before God
when you heard his words against this place and its inhabitants, and you have humbled
yourself before me and have torn your clothes and wept before me, I also have heard you,
declares the LORD. 28 Behold, I will gather you to your fathers, and you shall be gathered
to your grave in peace, and your eyes shall not see all the disaster that I will bring upon
this place and its inhabitants.'" And they brought back word to the king.
29 [c]Then the king sent and gathered together all the elders of Judah and Jerusalem. 30 And
the king went up to the house of the LORD, with all the men of Judah and the inhabitants
of Jerusalem and the priests and the Levites, all the people both great and small. And he
read in their hearing all the words of the Book of the Covenant that had been found in
the house of the LORD. 31 And the king [d]stood in his place [e]and made a covenant before
the LORD, to walk after the LORD and to keep his commandments and his testimonies
and his statutes, with all his heart and all his soul, to perform the words of the covenant
that were written in this book. 32 Then he made all who were present in Jerusalem and in

12 [x]1 Chr. 23:5
13 [y]ch. 2:2, 18; Neh. 4:10
14 [v][See ver. 9 above]
19 [z]See Josh. 7:6
21 [a]ch. 12:7
25 [b]ch. 28:3, 4, 25 [a][See ver. 21 above]
29 [c]For ver. 29-32, see 2 Kgs. 23:1-3
31 [d]ch. 6:13; 2 Kgs. 11:14; [ch. 30:16] [e]See ch. 15:12

[1] Syriac, Vulgate; Hebrew lacks *had sent*

34:14 the Book of the Law. This is usually understood to be a scroll of Deuteronomy or a portion of it. Its discovery in the course of temple repair is itself a reward for faithfulness because it becomes the springboard of further reform (2 Chron. 34:29–33; cf. note on 2 Kings 22:8).

34:19–21 those who are left in Israel and in Judah. Another added reference to the northern kingdom to stress the unity of Israel (see v. 9). **great is the wrath of the LORD . . . because our fathers have not kept the word of the LORD**. See note on 2 Kings 22:11–13.

34:22–24 Huldah. See note on 2 Kings 22:14–16. **all the curses**. An allusion to the covenant curses in Deuteronomy 27–29 (cf. 2 Kings 22:16, "all the words").

34:27 humbled yourself before me. This is the Chronicler's addition, alluding to 7:14, emphasizing Josiah's exemplary spiritual character (see 34:1–3).

34:28 gathered to your grave in peace. The promise is not negated by Josiah's death in battle; Huldah's prophecy means that the destruction and exile will not occur during Josiah's lifetime (cf. note on 2 Kings 22:20).

34:30–31 the king went up to the house of the LORD. See note on 2 Kings 23:2–3.

33[f]ch. 28:3; 33:2
Chapter 35
1[g]2 Kgs. 23:21-23 [h]Ex. 12:6; Ezra 6:19
2[i]ch. 29:11
3[j]ch. 17:9; Neh. 8:7, 9; [ch. 15:3; 30:22; Lev. 10:11; Deut. 33:10; Ezra 7:10; Mal. 2:7]
4[k]1 Chr. 9:9 [l]See 1 Chr. 23–26 [m]ch. 8:14
5[n]Ps. 134:1 [o][Ezra 6:18]
6[p]See ch. 29:5
7[q][ch. 31:3]
8[r]ch. 34:9, 14
10[s]ch. 30:16 [t]Ezra 6:18
11[u]ch. 30:15; Ezra 6:20 [v]See ch. 29:22 [w][ch. 29:34]
13[x]Ex. 12:8, 9; Deut. 16:7 [y][1 Sam. 2:13-15]
15[z]See 1 Chr. 25 [a]See 1 Sam. 9:9 [b]See 1 Chr. 9:17-29; 26:1-19
17[c]See ch. 30:21
18[d]2 Kgs. 23:22, 23

Benjamin join in it. And the inhabitants of Jerusalem did according to the covenant of
God, the God of their fathers. 33 And Josiah took away [f]all the abominations from all the
territory that belonged to the people of Israel and made all who were present in Israel
serve the LORD their God. All his days they did not turn away from following the LORD,
the God of their fathers.

Josiah Keeps the Passover

35 [g]Josiah kept a Passover to the LORD in Jerusalem. And they slaughtered the Passover
lamb [h]on the fourteenth day of the first month. 2 He appointed the priests to their
offices [i]and encouraged them in the service of the house of the LORD. 3 And he said to the
Levites [j]who taught all Israel and who were holy to the LORD, "Put the holy ark in the house
that Solomon the son of David, king of Israel, built. You need not carry it on your shoulders. Now serve the LORD your God and his people Israel. 4 Prepare yourselves [k]according
to your fathers' houses by your divisions, [l]as prescribed in the writing of David king of
Israel [m]and the document of Solomon his son. 5 And [n]stand in the Holy Place [o]according
to the groupings of the fathers' houses of your brothers the lay people, and according to
the division of the Levites by fathers' household. 6 And slaughter the Passover lamb, and
[p]consecrate yourselves, and prepare for your brothers, to do according to the word of the
LORD by Moses."

7 Then Josiah contributed to the lay people, as Passover offerings for all who were present,
lambs and young goats from the flock to the number of 30,000, and 3,000 bulls; [q]these
were from the king's possessions. 8 And his officials contributed willingly to the people,
to the priests, and to the Levites. [r]Hilkiah, Zechariah, and Jehiel, the chief officers of the
house of God, gave to the priests for the Passover offerings 2,600 Passover lambs and 300
bulls. 9 Conaniah also, and Shemaiah and Nethanel his brothers, and Hashabiah and Jeiel
and Jozabad, the chiefs of the Levites, gave to the Levites for the Passover offerings 5,000
lambs and young goats and 500 bulls.

10 When the service had been prepared for, the priests [s]stood in their place, [t]and the
Levites in their divisions according to the king's command. 11 [u]And they slaughtered the
Passover lamb, and the priests [v]threw the blood that they received from them [w]while
the Levites flayed the sacrifices. 12 And they set aside the burnt offerings that they might
distribute them according to the groupings of the fathers' houses of the lay people, to offer
to the LORD, as it is written in the Book of Moses. And so they did with the bulls. 13 [x]And
they roasted the Passover lamb with fire according to the rule; and they [y]boiled the holy
offerings in pots, in cauldrons, and in pans, and carried them quickly to all the lay people.
14 And afterward they prepared for themselves and for the priests, because the priests, the
sons of Aaron, were offering the burnt offerings and the fat parts until night; so the Levites
prepared for themselves and for the priests, the sons of Aaron. 15 The singers, the sons of
Asaph, were in their place [z]according to the command of David, and Asaph, and Heman,
and Jeduthun the king's [a]seer; [b]and the gatekeepers were at each gate. They did not need
to depart from their service, for their brothers the Levites prepared for them.

16 So all the service of the LORD was prepared that day, to keep the Passover and to offer
burnt offerings on the altar of the LORD, according to the command of King Josiah. 17 And
the people of Israel who were present kept the Passover at that time, [c]and the Feast of
Unleavened Bread seven days. 18 [d]No Passover like it had been kept in Israel since the days

---

34:32–33 Josiah imposes on the people a pledge of obedience to the Mosaic covenant, which they maintain in **all the territory . . . of Israel** (i.e., in both the north and south)—but only while Josiah lives (**all his days they did not turn away**). When Josiah dies, so too does the people's commitment to their covenant (see notes on ch. 36).

35:1–19 See 2 Kings 23:21–23. Just as Josiah encouraged and instructed the priests and Levites "in the service of the house of the LORD," the detailed account of his Passover serves as an encouragement and model to the Chronicler's own generation in their use of the temple for worship and spiritual renewal. The Passover was the most significant pilgrimage festival in the postexilic community for reaffirming their identity and vocation as Yahweh's people (see Ezra 6:19–22; cf. note on 2 Kings 23:22).

35:1 the first month. The regular month for celebration (Num. 28:16), in contrast to Hezekiah's delayed observance (2 Chron. 30:2).

35:3–6 Put the holy ark in the house that Solomon . . . built (v. 3). The ark may have been removed during the reigns of Manasseh and Amon, or in the course of Josiah's renovation works. Josiah directs the Levites in their new duties of slaughtering and skinning the Passover lambs (see v. 11).

35:7–9 Josiah and his officials emulate David (1 Chron. 29:2–5) and Solomon (2 Chron. 7:5) in their generosity.

35:18 No Passover like it. Josiah's Passover surpassed all other centralized celebrations (including Hezekiah's unorthodox Passover; 30:2–4, 18–20) in its faithful commitment to worship as authorized by Moses and David, and in its broad inclusion of **all Judah and Israel** (cf. note on 2 Kings 23:22).

of Samuel the prophet. None of the kings of Israel had kept such a Passover as was kept
by Josiah, and the priests and the Levites, and all Judah and Israel who were present, and
the inhabitants of Jerusalem. 19 In the eighteenth year of the reign of Josiah this Passover
was kept.

Josiah Killed in Battle

20 [e]After all this, when Josiah had prepared the temple, Neco king of Egypt went up
to fight at [f]Carchemish on the Euphrates, and Josiah went out to meet him. 21 But he
sent envoys to him, saying, "What have we to do with each other, king of Judah? I am
not coming against you this day, but against the house with which I am at war. And
God has commanded me to hurry. Cease opposing God, who is with me, lest he destroy
you." 22 Nevertheless, Josiah did not turn away from him, but [g]disguised himself in
order to fight with him. He did not listen to the words of Neco from the mouth of
God, but came to fight in the plain of [h]Megiddo. 23 And the archers shot King Josiah.
And the king said to his servants, [i]"Take me away, for I am badly wounded." 24 So his
servants took him out of the chariot and carried him in his second chariot and brought
him to Jerusalem. And he died and was buried in the tombs of his fathers. [j]All Judah
and Jerusalem mourned for Josiah. 25 [k]Jeremiah also uttered a lament for Josiah; and
all [l]the singing men and singing women have spoken of Josiah in their laments to this
day. They made these a rule in Israel; behold, they are written in the Laments. 26 Now

20 [e]2 Kgs. 23:29, 30 [f][Jer. 46:2]
22 [g][1 Kgs. 22:30] [h]Judg. 5:19
23 [i][1 Kgs. 22:34]
24 [j][Zech. 12:11]
25 [k]Lam. 4:20; [2 Sam. 1:17] [l]2 Sam. 19:35; Ezra 2:65; Neh. 7:67; [Matt. 9:23]

35:20–27 Josiah's death occurred in the course of confronting Pharaoh **Neco** II at Megiddo in 609 B.C., when the Egyptian king was bringing his army north to help the Assyrians against Babylon. Apparently Josiah decided to seek favor with Babylon by opposing the Egyptians (see note on 2 Kings 23:28–30), but this indicated a turning away from trust in the Lord. Josiah's failure to **listen to the words of Neco from the mouth of God** (2 Chron. 35:22) contrasts with his attention to God's words from the Book of the Law and from Huldah the prophetess (34:19, 26–27). Here God spoke even through an Egyptian king, warning Josiah against meddling in a war between Babylon and Egypt (cf. Prov. 26:17). The manner of his death is also uncomfortably like Ahab's (2 Chron. 18:29–34). Nevertheless, Josiah's reign is judged very positively, as his burial and the mourning for him attest. **the Laments**. Not the biblical book of Lamentations.

36:1–21 *The Last Four Kings.* See 2 Kings 23:31–25:21. The Chronicler

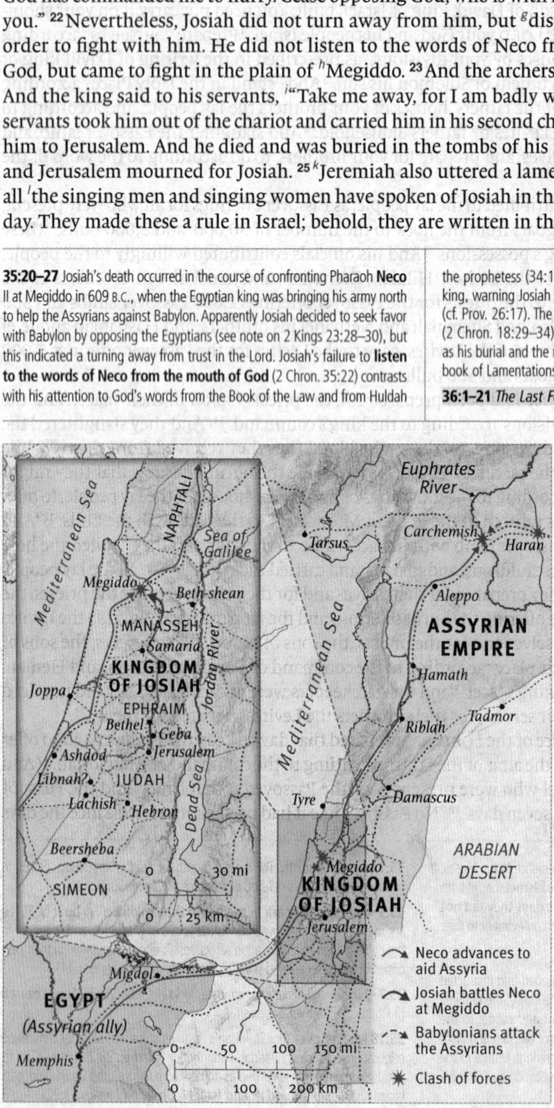

Josiah's Reforms and His Battle with Neco
628–609 B.C.
Early in his reign, King Josiah of Judah launched a massive effort to abolish pagan worship throughout Judah and the land of Israel and to refurbish the temple of the Lord in Jerusalem. At the same time, the waning power of the Assyrians allowed him to add much of the land of Israel to his kingdom. Josiah met his demise at Megiddo, however, as he sought to prevent Pharaoh Neco II of Egypt from reaching Carchemish to assist the Assyrians, who were being attacked by forces from the rising Babylonian Empire.

Chapter 36
1 *m*For ver. 1-4, see 2 Kgs. 23:30-34
3 *n*Deut. 22:19
5 *o*2 Kgs. 23:36, 37
6 *p*2 Kgs. 24:1 *q*[ch. 33:11] *r*[2 Kgs. 24:6; Jer. 22:18, 19; 36:30]
7 *s*2 Kgs. 24:13; Ezra 1:7; Dan. 1:1, 2; 5:2; [ver. 10, 18]
8 *t*2 Kgs. 24:5, 6

the rest of the acts of Josiah, and his good deeds according to what is written in the
Law of the LORD, 27 and his acts, first and last, behold, they are written in the Book of
the Kings of Israel and Judah.

Judah's Decline

36 *m*The people of the land took Jehoahaz the son of Josiah and made him king in his
father's place in Jerusalem. 2 Jehoahaz was twenty-three years old when he began to
reign, and he reigned three months in Jerusalem. 3 Then the king of Egypt deposed him
in Jerusalem and *n*laid on the land a tribute of a hundred talents of silver and a talent[1] of
gold. 4 And the king of Egypt made Eliakim his brother king over Judah and Jerusalem,
and changed his name to Jehoiakim. But Neco took Jehoahaz his brother and carried him
to Egypt.
5 *o*Jehoiakim was twenty-five years old when he began to reign, and he reigned eleven years
in Jerusalem. He did what was evil in the sight of the LORD his God. 6 *p*Against him came
up Nebuchadnezzar king of Babylon *q*and bound him in chains *r*to take him to Babylon.
7 *s*Nebuchadnezzar also carried part of the vessels of the house of the LORD to Babylon
and put them in his palace in Babylon. 8 *t*Now the rest of the acts of Jehoiakim, and the

[1] A *talent* was about 75 pounds or 34 kilograms

presents the reigns of the last four kings of Judah quite summarily, as the history of the nation accelerates toward an outcome that has been inevitable since Manasseh's reign. With Josiah's death, the covenant is abandoned by king and people alike. The Chronicler treats the last four reigns essentially as a unit: he omits the names of the queen mothers and the customary death notices, so that there is no strict separation between each of the reigns, and the common fate of these kings is exile, as it will be for the people. Another common theme is the temple vessels (2 Chron. 36:7, 10, 18; see note on 1 Chron. 28:11–19). As well as the kings (2 Chron. 36:5, 9, 11–12), the whole nation from its leaders down shares in the mounting collective guilt (v. 14) that finally overwhelms it in destruction. Yet the exile is a positive time of purification, and the book concludes on a surprising upswing in a new act of God's grace declared through a pagan king (vv. 22–23).

36:1–4 Pharaoh Neco II asserted control over Judah after Josiah's death. The "people of the land" who made **Jehoahaz** king (see 23:13; 26:1; 33:25) probably hoped he would continue Josiah's opposition to Egypt. Neco preempted this risk by deposing him in favor of **Eliakim**, whom he renamed **Jehoiakim** as a mark of his authority over him. The **tribute** that Neco imposed **on the land** was a tax exacted from those who had supported Jehoahaz (2 Kings 23:35). Inscription 88 of the Arad Ostraca, dating to c. 600 B.C., is fragmentary but appears to be a letter from a king who has just been enthroned. The king is apparently warning the military commander of Arad of a possible military encounter with Egypt. Arad at this time guarded the southern end of Judah. The excavator identified the king who wrote this letter as Jehoahaz, who ruled Judah for three months in 609 B.C. (Cf. note on 2 Kings 23:31–35.)

36:5–8 Jehoiakim's reign (609–598 B.C.) was marked by a return to idolatry (Jer. 25:1–7) and the king's persecution of the prophets (Jer. 26:20–24; 36:20–31). **Nebuchadnezzar**, following his defeat of Neco at Carchemish (605 B.C.), besieged Jerusalem (2 Kings 24:1) and carried off some of its citizens and some of the temple **vessels** to Babylon (2 Chron. 36:7; Dan. 1:1–2). This may have been the occasion when Nebuchadnezzar **bound him in chains to take him to Babylon**, making Jehoiakim into his vassal. Jehoiakim later rebelled against the Babylonians, and in 598 B.C. Nebuchadnezzar again besieged Jerusalem, just after Jehoiakim's death.

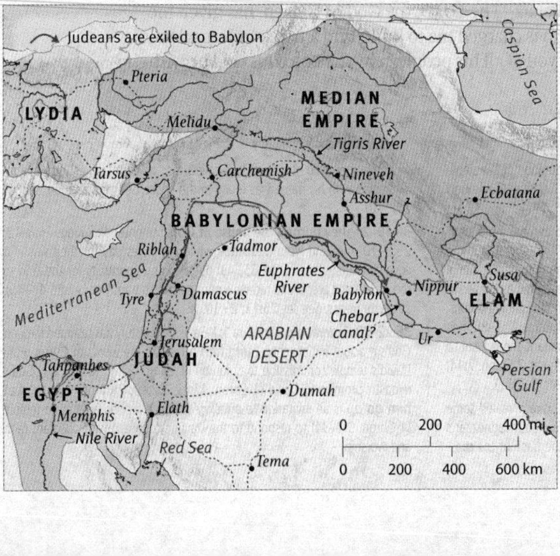

Exile to Babylon
597, 586, 582 B.C.
It appears that there were three separate deportations of Judeans to Babylon under the rule of Nebuchadnezzar (see also Jer. 52:28–30). The first came in 597 B.C. during the reign of Jehoiachin, when Nebuchadnezzar besieged Jerusalem and carried away many of the treasures of the temple and the royal palace. The second occurred after the fall of Jerusalem in 586 B.C., when the walls of the city were leveled and the temple was completely destroyed. The third appears to have occurred around 582 B.C. while King Nebuchadnezzar was reasserting his control over the general region of Palestine (see note on Jer. 52:28–30).

abominations that he did, and what was found against him, behold, they are written in
the Book of the Kings of Israel and Judah. And Jehoiachin his son reigned in his place.
9 [u]Jehoiachin was eighteen[1] years old when he became king, and he reigned three months
and ten days in Jerusalem. He did what was evil in the sight of the LORD. 10 In [v]the spring
of the year King Nebuchadnezzar sent and brought him to Babylon, [w]with the precious
vessels of the house of the LORD, and made his brother [x]Zedekiah king over Judah and
Jerusalem.
11 [y]Zedekiah was twenty-one years old when he began to reign, and he reigned eleven
years in Jerusalem. 12 He did what was evil in the sight of the LORD his God. He did not
humble himself before [z]Jeremiah the prophet, who spoke from the mouth of the LORD.
13 [a]He also rebelled against King Nebuchadnezzar, who had made him swear by God. [b]He
stiffened his neck and hardened his heart against turning to the LORD, the God of Israel.
14 All the officers of the priests and the people likewise were exceedingly unfaithful, following all the abominations of the nations. And they polluted the house of the LORD that
he had made holy in Jerusalem.
15 The LORD, the God of their fathers, [c]sent persistently to them by his messengers,
because he had compassion on his people and on his dwelling place. 16 [d]But they kept
mocking the messengers of God, [e]despising his words and scoffing at his prophets, [f]until
the wrath of the LORD rose against his people, until there was no remedy.

Jerusalem Captured and Burned

17 [g]Therefore he brought up against them the king of the Chaldeans, who killed their
young men with the sword in the house of their sanctuary and had no compassion on
young man or virgin, old man or aged. He gave them all into his hand. 18 [h]And all the vessels of the house of God, great and small, and the treasures of the house of the LORD, and
the treasures of the king and of his princes, all these he brought to Babylon. 19 [i]And they
burned the house of God and broke down the wall of Jerusalem and burned all its palaces
with fire and destroyed all its precious vessels. 20 He [j]took into exile in Babylon those who
had escaped from the sword, [k]and they became servants to him and to his sons until the
establishment of the kingdom of Persia, 21 to fulfill the word of the LORD by the mouth
of Jeremiah, until the land had [l]enjoyed its Sabbaths. All the days that it lay desolate [m]it
kept Sabbath, to fulfill seventy years.

The Proclamation of Cyrus

22 [n]Now in the first year of Cyrus king of Persia, [o]that the word of the LORD by the
mouth of Jeremiah might be fulfilled, [p]the LORD stirred up the spirit of Cyrus king of
Persia, so that he made a proclamation throughout all his kingdom and also put it in
writing: 23 "Thus says Cyrus king of Persia, 'The LORD, the God of heaven, has given me
all the kingdoms of the earth, and he has charged me to build him a house at Jerusalem,
which is in Judah. Whoever is among you of all his people, may the LORD his God be with
him. Let him go up.'"

[1] Septuagint (compare 2 Kings 24:8); most Hebrew manuscripts *eight*

9 [u]For ver. 9, 10, see 2 Kgs. 24:8-17
10 [v]2 Sam. 11:1 [w][ver. 7, 18] [x]Jer. 37:1; [2 Kgs. 24:17]
11 [y]For ver. 11-13, see 2 Kgs. 24:18-20; Jer. 52:1, 2
12 [z]See Jer. 21:3-7; 27:12-22; 32:1-5; 37:6-10; 38:17-26
13 [a]Jer. 52:3; Ezek. 17:15, 18 [b]See ch. 30:8
15 [c]Jer. 7:13, 25; 25:3, 4; 26:5; 29:19; 35:15; 44:4; [Jer. 11:7; 32:33]
16 [d][Jer. 5:12, 13] [e][Prov. 1:25, 30] [f][Ezra 5:12]
17 [g]For ver. 17-20, see 2 Kgs. 25:1-7; [Deut. 28:49; Ezra 9:7]
18 [h]2 Kgs. 25:13-15; [ver. 7, 10]
19 [i]2 Kgs. 25:9
20 [j]2 Kgs. 25:11 [k]Jer. 27:7
21 [l]Lev. 26:34, 35, 43; [Dan. 9:2] [m][Lev. 25:4, 5]
22 [n]For ver. 22, 23, see Ezra 1:1-3 [o]Jer. 25:12, 13; 29:10; 33:10, 11, 14 [p]Isa. 44:28

36:9–10 The reign of **Jehoiachin** lasted only for the duration of the siege, before he was exiled to Babylon. **Brother** here denotes "relative" (**Zedekiah** was Jehoiachin's uncle).

36:11–16 Zedekiah's reign (597–586 B.C.) culminated in rebellion, a siege of almost two years, the destruction of Jerusalem and the temple, and the deportation of its leading citizens (see Jer. 52:28–30 and note for additional information about Jerusalem's final days). This reign is presented as the zenith of disobedience to God, with the king leading the way and the people becoming **exceedingly unfaithful** (Hb. *ma'al*; see note on 1 Chron. 2:3–8). Their **mocking** rejection of the **prophets** (see Jer. 25:4) meant the refusal to repent, so now there was **no remedy** (lit., "no healing"; see 2 Chron. 7:14) against God's **wrath** (see 34:25 and note on 2 Kings 24:18–25:7).

36:17–21 Excavations on the Ophel hill in Jerusalem have revealed some domestic structures belonging to Judeans just before Nebuchadnezzar's destruction in 586 B.C. One four-room house sits at the base of the massive stone-stepped structure. It is called the "house of Ahiel" because an inscription with his name was found in the house. See also note on 2 Kings 25:9–10.

36:19–21 they burned the house of God. See notes on 2 Kings 25:8–12; 25:9–10. The land lying **desolate** while the exiles pay for their sins is a covenant curse (Lev. 26:34–35, 43) but also an opportunity for the land to recuperate and prepare to receive a purified people back (see Lev. 26:44–45). **seventy years**. See Jer. 25:11; 29:10.

36:22–23 *Restoration.* From Ezra 1:1–3a. Israel's history has resumed through God's gracious initiative. **to build him a house**. The words of **Cyrus** recall David's temple commission to Solomon (1 Chron. 22:6, 18–19) and God's dynastic promise to David (1 Chron. 17:12; 22:10; 2 Chron. 6:9–10). **Let him go up** is an invitation to a restored people around a restored temple (1 Chron. 9:2–34) to respond to the Davidic covenant with obedient faith and worship.

INTRODUCTION TO

EZRA

Author and Title

Ezra 1–6 recounts events long before Ezra's time, and the book does not state who wrote this section. Ezra is the main figure in chapters 7–10; part of this section clearly comes from his own hand, since it is written in the first person. This part is often called the Ezra Memoir (7:27–9:15). The final author of the whole book is unknown. Some scholars think it was written by the same person who wrote 1–2 Chronicles (also unknown) because its narrative continues directly from the end of 2 Chronicles and because they have common themes. It is also widely thought that the author of Ezra (whether the Chronicler or not) wrote the book of Nehemiah as well. In ancient times, the two books were counted as one, as is known from the earliest Jewish references to them. As is the case with a number of other books in the OT canon, the author had various sources at his disposal. Besides the "Ezra Memoir," parts of Nehemiah are written in the first person, implying a record left by him. The narrative refers to letters and other documents to which (or to copies of which) the author must have had access.

Relationship of Ezra–Nehemiah to 1–2 Chronicles

1–2 Chronicles	Ezra–Nehemiah
Chronicles ends with the Cyrus Edict.	Ezra begins with the Cyrus Edict.
Chronicles emphasizes Jerusalem and the temple.	Ezra–Nehemiah emphasizes Jerusalem and the temple.
Chronicles has a priestly focus.	Ezra is more focused on the law itself.
Chronicles is more focused on Davidic leadership, suggesting composition around the time of Zerubbabel; cf. Zechariah 4 (520–515 B.C.).	
Chronicles omits Solomon's downfall due to intermarriage.	Nehemiah appeals to Solomon as a negative example (Neh. 13:26).
	Ezra–Nehemiah contains unique first-person memoirs.

Date

The events narrated in Ezra cover almost a century. Jews had been taken into exile in Babylon by King Nebuchadnezzar in 586 B.C., but in 539 King Cyrus of Persia overthrew the Babylonian king, Nabonidus. By doing so, he took control of a vast empire, including the territory of the former kingdoms of Israel and Judah. In 538 B.C., Cyrus issued a decree that the Jewish exiles were free to return to their ancestral home. Ezra 1–6 covers the return of the first wave of exiles, who came with their leaders, Zerubbabel and the priest Jeshua (see map, p. 802, for the route), in 538–535 B.C. (the preparations plus the journey itself would have taken many months, perhaps more than a year; cf. 7:9). These chapters continue the narrative up to the time when they rebuilt the temple at Jerusalem (516 B.C.), where Solomon's temple had stood until it was destroyed by Nebuchadnezzar. Chapters 7–10 cover a time more than half a century later, beginning with Ezra's arrival in Jerusalem in 458 B.C. The book provides little information about the intervening period.

Chronology of Ezra–Nehemiah

Ezra 1–6	537–515 B.C.
Ezra 7–Nehemiah 13	458–433 B.C.

These dates do not reveal when the book was actually written. As already noted, it belongs closely with Nehemiah. Thus, it must be dated after the latest events in that book, or between 433 and 424 B.C. at the earliest (see note on Neh. 13:6).

Theme

The theme of Ezra is faithfulness to the Lord, both in worship (hence the importance of building the new temple) and in keeping the Torah, the Mosaic law (7:6).

Purpose, Occasion, and Background

The Jewish community was struggling to maintain its identity as the people of the Lord, as it faced internal and external pressures. The community was located in Jerusalem and in towns and villages in the territory of the former kingdom of Judah. Its position was somewhat insecure for at least two reasons. First, the community was composed of those who had been away in exile for a long period—70 years according to Jeremiah (Jer. 25:11). (This may be reckoned, as a round number, either from the first wave of exiles in 605 B.C. to the return in 538–535, or from the destruction of the temple in 586 to the building of the new one in 516; see notes on Jer. 25:11; Dan. 9:2; Zech. 1:12.) They returned as strangers to a land that had a population consisting of Jews who had not been taken into exile, along with persons of other ethnic origins who had begun to settle there. In addition, leaders in Samaria (the old northern capital) who now held power in the Persian province Beyond the River (see note on Ezra 4:1–2) resented the resurgence of Jerusalem as a separate administrative and political center. The returnees therefore had to press their claim to ancient entitlements in the land against local opposition. They were able to do so by virtue of providential help from a succession of Persian kings, though this support was variable. The persistence of opposition from enemies is clear in Ezra 4 and Nehemiah 4; 6.

Second, the Jewish community was insecure because of the severe moral and religious challenge presented by the need to remain a distinctive people faithful to the Lord. The time that elapses in the narrative of Ezra and Nehemiah allows this challenge to appear. When Ezra arrives in Jerusalem, he finds the people intermarrying with non-Jews (Ezra 9–10), which poses a threat to the community because it implies a loosening of the covenantal bond between the Lord and his people. This explains the strong emphasis in both books on keeping strictly separate from the so-called peoples of the land, who, because they do not hold to the religion of the Lord, are morally identified with the old inhabitants of the land whom Israel was long ago commanded to drive out (9:1; see also Deut. 7:1–5). Ezra is often blamed for exclusivism in his attitude toward the mixed marriages. But the issue is essentially religious, and also a matter of survival. It has to be balanced by the openness of the community to non-Jews, who were welcome to adopt the religion of the Lord (Ezra 6:21). In this respect Ezra is no different from the book of Ruth. Marriages to such converts, and to their children, were not part of Ezra's concern in chapters 9–10, but only marriages that were leading to apostasy (as is clear in Neh. 13:23–24). The problem was acute, however. Under Ezra's leadership the people agree to face up to this danger, but the same issue reemerges late in Nehemiah's time (Neh. 13:23–29), about 15 years after Ezra's arrival, when Ezra is apparently no longer on the scene. Finally, another challenge to faithfulness came from economic pressures, which emerge clearly when Nehemiah requires sustained manpower to complete the city wall (Nehemiah 5).

Several issues occasioned the writing of both books. Zerubbabel and Jeshua rebuilt the temple, since this is the first and indispensable mark that the Lord is once again the center of worship in Jerusalem, the ancient Davidic capital. The prophets Haggai and Zechariah also helped to bring this project to fruition (Ezra 5:1). Ezra, "a scribe skilled in the Law of Moses" (7:6), called the community back to covenant loyalty and thus to obedience to the Mosaic law contained in the Pentateuch. Nehemiah rebuilt the city walls so that the community could enjoy security against possible outright attack by enemies who might take advantage of any weakening in the imperial protection of Judah.

These separate missions were closely associated. Ezra, though responsible for the law, is also charged by the Persian authorities with gifts for the temple, so that he continues the provision for the temple originally made by King Cyrus through Zerubbabel. The books also make it clear that the work of Ezra and Nehemiah overlapped, since Nehemiah 8 indicates that Ezra leads the great covenant-renewal ceremony that followed the completion of the city walls. Again, at the dedication of the wall, each plays a part in the ceremony (Neh. 12:33, 38). And most importantly, this ceremony concludes in the temple, so that the projects of the temple and the securing of the city are finally seen to be one.

The author of Ezra and Nehemiah balances these various concerns. There is a note of thankfulness to

God for his faithfulness in restoring the community despite enormous odds. Indeed, this repopulation of the ancient Promised Land after exile was nothing less than a fulfillment of prophecy (see Isa. 40:1–11; Jer. 25:11). But there is also regret that the community is prone to failure in its vocation as a faithful people. The author records a number of great gatherings of the people for the purpose of celebration (Ezra 3:1–13; 6:19; Nehemiah 8), or of communal repentance (Ezra 10; Nehemiah 9). The pervasive concern is the need for the community to remain absolutely faithful to the Lord, because of the conviction that its very life depends on it. The knowledge that the Lord has already judged his people with a great exile is very present in the author's mind.

A telling insight into the purpose of the two books is given by the prayers of Ezra in Ezra 9:8–9 and in Nehemiah 9:32–37 (the latter may or may not be Ezra's). The second prayer, besides expressing thanksgiving and confession, acknowledges that the members of the community are still suffering because of their sins, and are slaves even in their own land. While the author of Ezra–Nehemiah sees God's providential hand in the benign attitude of the Persian kings, he also knows that the community's situation is as yet far short of full deliverance. This combination of confession and petition is at the heart of his message. The book aims not only to encourage the community to persevere in hope but also to bring them again to repentance, so that the ancient promises of freedom in service to the Lord alone might be more fully realized among them.

Chronology of Ezra

Event	Year	Reference
Cyrus king of Persia captures Babylon	539 B.C.	Dan. 5:30–31
First year of King Cyrus; issues proclamation freeing Jewish exiles to return	538–537	Ezra 1:1–4
Jewish exiles, led by Sheshbazzar, return from Babylon to Jerusalem	537?	Ezra 1:11
Altar rebuilt	537	Ezra 3:1–2
Temple rebuilding begins	536	Ezra 3:8
Adversaries oppose the rebuilding	536–530	Ezra 4:1–5
Temple rebuilding ceases	530–520	Ezra 4:24
Temple rebuilding resumes (2nd year of Darius)	520	Ezra 5:2; cf. Hag. 1:14
Temple construction completed (6th year of Darius)	516	Ezra 6:15
Ezra departs from Babylon to Jerusalem (arrives in 7th year of Artaxerxes)	458	Ezra 7:6–9
Men of Judah and Benjamin assemble at Jerusalem	458	Ezra 10:9
Officials conduct three-month investigation	458–457	Ezra 10:16–17

Key Themes

1. The Lord is faithful to his promises, and his mercy exceeds his anger (9:13).
2. The Lord works providentially by all means, especially through powerful rulers, to bring about his greater purposes (e.g., 6:22).
3. The exiles—being the remnant of Israel, or the "holy race" (9:2, 8)—are bound by covenant to guard their identity and character as the people of the Lord by obeying his law.
4. Belonging to the people of the Lord, however, is not essentially by membership in a "race" but by willing acceptance of his covenant, and thus it is open to people of any nation (6:21).
5. Allegiance to the Lord is demonstrated by due attention to worship. In Ezra, this is shown especially in the building of the temple and in the proper ordering of its work, as evidenced in the institution of priests, Levites, gatekeepers, musicians, and other temple servants in their duties (2:36–58; 3:10–11).
6. The keynote of worship is joy (6:22).

History of Salvation Summary

The exile was not the end of the story for God's ancient people, nor of their calling to bring light to the world. Ezra stresses God's providence and mercy in moving imperial rulers to favor his people, and in raising up new shepherds to serve them (Jer. 23:3–4), especially Ezra and other priests and Levites. Nevertheless, not all the promises of the prophets have come to pass (Ezra 9:8–9); God will do still more through them.

The Persian Empire at the Time of Ezra
c. 458 B.C.
During the time of Ezra the Persian Empire had reached its greatest extent, engulfing nearly the entire Near East. In 539 B.C. the Persians under Cyrus the Great defeated the Babylonians and absorbed their territory into the empire, including the lands of Israel and Judah (known as Beyond the River). The next year Cyrus allowed the people of Judah to return home under the leadership of Zerubbabel and rebuild the temple of the Lord. Later, around 458 B.C., another group of Judean exiles returned under Ezra's leadership.

The people really have a new chance to live as God's distinctive people. (For an explanation of the "History of Salvation," see the Overview of the Bible, pp. 23–26. See also History of Salvation in the Old Testament: Preparing the Way for Christ, pp. 2635–2661.)

Literary Features

The author's primary impulse is to record the historical facts surrounding the two returns to Palestine—sometimes in the form of lists and inventories, sometimes in the form of narrative or story. But this documentary aim is combined with a religious impulse to choose events from the era that teach religious lessons about God's covenant faithfulness and the need for his people to maintain high standards of holiness in their communal and personal lives.

The primary form of Ezra is historical narrative, specifically a story that narrates the return of groups of people to their homeland after exile. But the flow of the story is interrupted by a variety of documentary material—lists of people and supplies, transcripts of official documents, the genealogy of Ezra, royal and other official letters, memoirs, and prayer. Sometimes the material tells a story; at other times it resembles a daily newspaper or modern archived material.

Ezra is the central character in this story of starting over. He is a decisive character whose arrival with the second wave of returnees causes sparks to fly. Characters of secondary importance include three Persian kings (Cyrus, Darius, and Artaxerxes), Zerubbabel (who leads the first return and the rebuilding of the temple), the workers who rebuild the temple, and the Israelites who marry foreign women with pagan worship practices.

Outline

I. Cyrus's Decree and the Return of Exiles from Babylon (1:1–2:70)
   - A. The decree (1:1–4)
   - B. The exiles respond to the decree (1:5–11)
   - C. The exiles live again in their ancestral homes (2:1–70)

II. The Returned Exiles Rebuild the Temple on Its Original Site (3:1–6:22)
   A. The foundations of the temple are laid (3:1–13)
   B. Enemies stall the project by conspiring against it (4:1–24)
   C. The work is resumed, and local officials seek confirmation of Cyrus's decree (5:1–17)
   D. King Darius discovers and reaffirms Cyrus's decree, and the work is completed (6:1–22)

III. Ezra the Priest Comes to Jerusalem to Establish the Law of Moses (7:1–8:36)
   A. King Artaxerxes gives Ezra authority to establish the Mosaic law (7:1–28)
   B. Ezra journeys to Jerusalem with a new wave of returnees, bearing royal gifts for the temple (8:1–36)

IV. Ezra Discovers and Confronts the Problem of Intermarriage (9:1–10:44)
   A. Ezra discovers the problem of marriage to idolaters, and prays (9:1–15)
   B. The people agree to dissolve the marriages (10:1–17)
   C. List of those who were implicated (10:18–44)

EZRA

The Proclamation of Cyrus

1 [a]In the first year of Cyrus king of Persia, [b]that the word of the LORD by the mouth of
Jeremiah might be fulfilled, the LORD stirred up the spirit of Cyrus king of Persia, so
[c]that he made a proclamation throughout all his kingdom and also put it in writing:
2 "Thus says Cyrus king of Persia: The LORD, the God of heaven, has given me all the
kingdoms of the earth, and [d]he has charged me to build him a house at Jerusalem, which
is in Judah. 3 Whoever is among you of all his people, may his God be with him, and let
him go up to Jerusalem, which is in Judah, and rebuild the house of the LORD, the God
of Israel—[e]he is the God who is in Jerusalem. 4 And let each survivor, in whatever place
he sojourns, be assisted by the men of his place with silver and gold, with goods and with
beasts, besides freewill offerings for the house of God that is in Jerusalem."
5 Then rose up the heads of the fathers' houses of Judah and Benjamin, and the priests
and the Levites, [f]everyone whose spirit [g]God had stirred to go up to rebuild the house of
the LORD that is in Jerusalem. 6 And all who were about them [h]aided them with vessels
of silver, with gold, with goods, with beasts, and with costly wares, besides all that was
freely offered. 7 [i]Cyrus the king also brought out the vessels of the house of the LORD that
[j]Nebuchadnezzar had carried away from Jerusalem and placed in the house of his gods.
8 Cyrus king of Persia brought these out in the charge of [k]Mithredath the treasurer, who
counted them out to [l]Sheshbazzar the prince of Judah. 9 And this was the number of them:
[m]30 basins of gold, 1,000 basins of silver, 29 censers, 10 30 bowls of gold, 410 bowls of sil-

Chapter 1

1 [a]For ver. 1-3, see 2 Chr. 36:22, 23 [b]Jer. 25:12, 13; 29:10 [c]ch. 5:13
2 [d]Isa. 44:28; [Isa. 45:1, 13]
3 [e]Dan. 6:26
5 [f][Phil. 2:13] [g]ver. 1
6 [h][ch. 4:4]; Jer. 38:4
7 [i]ch. 5:14; 6:5 [j]2 Kgs. 24:13; 2 Chr. 36:7
8 [k]ch. 4:7 [l]ch. 5:14
9 [m][ch. 8:27; 1 Chr. 28:17]

1:1–2:70 *Cyrus's Decree and the Return of Exiles from Babylon.* With the eye of faith, Ezra describes monumental political changes in the world as God's special favor for his people.

1:1–11 King Cyrus of Persia decrees that Jewish exiles may return to Jerusalem and rebuild the ruined temple.

1:1–4 *The Decree.* In the famous Cyrus Cylinder, the king boasts that those "of the holy cities beyond the Tigris whose sanctuaries had been in ruins over a long period . . . I returned to their places." Ezra 1 reflects that proclamation as it affected the Jews.

1:1 the first year of Cyrus. The narrative of Ezra continues from Chronicles (see 2 Chron. 36:22–23). The year of the decree is 538 B.C. (for more on the date and occasion, see Introduction: Date). **that the word of the LORD by the mouth of Jeremiah might be fulfilled.** See Jer. 25:11–14; 32:36–38. The whole book of Ezra is the story of God's work to fulfill his promises by bringing his people back from exile and establishing them once again in their land. The prophet Jeremiah had foretold an exile lasting 70 years, after which time Babylon would be punished and Judah restored. **the LORD stirred up the spirit of Cyrus king of Persia.** This acknowledgment of God's hand behind the events of the book is the perspective through which all those events are to be viewed (cf. Ezra 1:5; 3:11; 5:5; 6:22; 7:6, 9; 8:18, 22; 10:14). On Cyrus's role, see also Isa. 44:28; 45:1. Cyrus's proclamation is only the beginning of a series of events that will fulfill the prophecy. It is first made orally, and carried through the vast Persian Empire (see map, p. 802; also Est. 1:22), and then set down in writing, giving it the status of a solemn decree.

1:2 The name **God of heaven** is used elsewhere for the Lord when Jews relate to non-Jews (see 5:12). Cyrus uses diplomatic language typical of the time, yet what he says corresponds to the message of the book of Ezra.

1:3–4 he is the God who is in Jerusalem. No doubt this is Cyrus's real view, although he is not necessarily claiming that there is only one God; he may be allowing for other gods (cf. the statement of Darius the king in 6:12). **go up to Jerusalem.** The phrase implies worship (cf. Ps. 122:1). The focus of the decree is the rebuilding of the temple more than the returning of the exiles in itself. Cyrus both urges Jews to return and obliges the people of his kingdom to supply them with what they need for the temple and its worship. See also Ex. 12:35–36.

1:5–11 *The Exiles Respond to the Decree.* The exiles' leaders gather money and materials for the temple. Cyrus brings the items taken from the temple in 586 B.C. for the people to take back to Jerusalem.

1:5 Those exiles **whose spirit God had stirred** (as he had stirred up Cyrus, v. 1) respond to the decree. The response is spearheaded by the leadership of the people, namely, the **heads of the fathers' houses** (extended families) and priests. It is not haphazard, but an action of the exiled community as a whole. The three tribes—**Judah**, **Benjamin**, and the **Levites** (Levi)—are those that had constituted the former kingdom of Judah, and had thus been taken off to Babylon in 586 B.C. No mention is made here or elsewhere of any large-scale return of the other tribes, though a few people from other tribes are sometimes mentioned or implied (see 1 Chron. 9:3; 2 Chron. 11:16; cf. Luke 2:36). The OT gives no further information on the fate of the other "lost tribes."

1:6–11 People help the exiles as commanded by their king, and Cyrus gives back the **vessels of the house of the LORD** (v. 7), once stolen from the temple (2 Kings 25:13–17). These are handed over to **Sheshbazzar** (Ezra 1:8), one of the early leaders of the returning exiles. The title **prince of Judah** (v. 8) simply means that he was a leading member of the exiled community. In 5:14–16 the initiation of the temple's reconstruction is attributed to Sheshbazzar, and there he is called "governor."

1:9 And this was the number of them: 30 basins of gold, 1,000 basins of silver, 29 censers. This detailed catalog of vessels used in the temple in Jerusalem is a testimony to God's faithfulness in preserving not only

Chapter 2
1 [n]For ver. 1-70, see Neh. 7:6-73 [o]2 Kgs. 24:14-16; 25:11; 2 Chr. 36:20
2 [p]Esth. 2:5, 6

ver, and 1,000 other vessels; 11 all the vessels of gold and of silver were 5,400. All these did
Sheshbazzar bring up, when the exiles were brought up from Babylonia to Jerusalem.

The Exiles Return

2 [n]Now these were the people of the province who came up out of the captivity of those
exiles [o]whom Nebuchadnezzar the king of Babylon had carried captive to Babylonia. They
returned to Jerusalem and Judah, each to his own town. 2 They came with Zerubbabel, Jeshua,
Nehemiah, Seraiah, Reelaiah, [p]Mordecai, Bilshan, Mispar, Bigvai, Rehum, and Baanah.

a remnant of the people but also the materials they would need to reinstate temple worship in Jerusalem. God had not forgotten his promises.

2:1–70 *The Exiles Live Again in Their Ancestral Homes.* This long chapter documents the exiles' return from Babylon to resettle in their former homes in Jerusalem and Judah. (The information from ch. 2 is given again in Neh. 7:6–73 in connection with a covenant renewal under Nehemiah.) It shows that the exiled Judeans responded to Cyrus's decree and took it as a fulfillment of prophecy. The return is not just the end of the exile but also a reoccupation of the ancient homeland.

2:2a The leaders of the community are named, with **Zerubbabel**, the main figure, and **Jeshua**, the priest, given pride of place (see also Hag. 1:12–14; Zech. 3:1–10; 4:7–10). Zerubbabel descended from King Jehoiachin (cf. 1 Chron. 3:16–19, where he is called Jeconiah), who was exiled in 597 B.C. and later given a place of honor in the Babylonian court (2 Kings 24:15; 25:27–30). Haggai recalls his royal lineage (Hag. 2:23; cf. Jer. 22:24). The other names in Ezra 2:2 are mostly unknown. (The **Nehemiah** who later rebuilt the walls of Jerusalem came almost a century after these first returnees; the **Mordecai** of the book of Esther was also much later, and did not return to Jerusalem. **Rehum** may be the same as in 4:8.) Some exiles may have taken Babylonian names, as occurs in the book of Daniel (e.g., Shadrach, Meshach, and Abednego; see Dan. 1:7).

2:2b–70 Those who returned are divided into ordinary Israelites (vv. 2b–35) and servants of the temple, including priests and Levites (vv. 36–58). (The same division recurs in vv. 59–63, regarding legitimacy.) The balance shows a clear interest in the temple and its staffing. This return is about reestablishing the worship of Yahweh there.

2:2b–35 The laity is described partly according to kinship divisions (vv. 2b–19) and partly according to place (vv. 20–35), without a real distinction in the

Judea under Persian Rule
538–332 B.C.
Under Persian rule, the lands of Israel (now called Samaria) and Judah (now called Judea) were minor provinces within the satrapy called Beyond the River. It appears that Edomites encroached upon Judea's southern border after the fall of Jerusalem to the Babylonians, and this territory was now called Idumea. These regional boundaries remained more or less the same throughout the Persian period. Returning Judeans settled mostly in the province of Judea, but a few settled in the plain of Ono and Idumea as well.

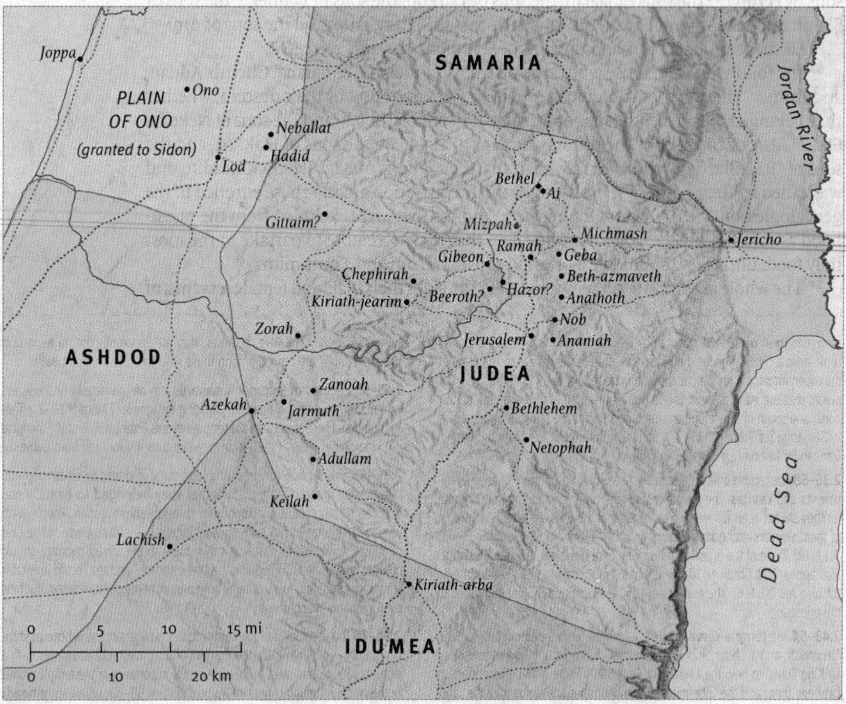

The number of the men of the people of Israel: 3 [q]the sons of Parosh, 2,172. 4 The sons
of Shephatiah, 372. 5 The sons of Arah, 775. 6 The sons of Pahath-moab, namely the sons
of Jeshua and Joab, 2,812. 7 The sons of Elam, 1,254. 8 The sons of Zattu, 945. 9 The sons of
Zaccai, 760. 10 The sons of Bani, 642. 11 The sons of Bebai, 623. 12 The sons of Azgad, 1,222.
13 The sons of Adonikam, 666. 14 The sons of Bigvai, 2,056. 15 The sons of Adin, 454. 16 The
sons of Ater, namely of Hezekiah, 98. 17 The sons of Bezai, 323. 18 The sons of Jorah, 112.
19 The sons of Hashum, 223. 20 The sons of Gibbar, 95. 21 The sons of Bethlehem, 123. 22 The
men of Netophah, 56. 23 The men of Anathoth, 128. 24 The sons of Azmaveth, 42. 25 The sons
of Kiriath-arim, Chephirah, and Beeroth, 743. 26 The sons of Ramah and Geba, 621. 27 The
men of Michmas, 122. 28 The men of Bethel and Ai, 223. 29 The sons of Nebo, 52. 30 The sons
of Magbish, 156. 31 The sons of [r]the other Elam, 1,254. 32 The sons of Harim, 320. 33 The sons
of Lod, Hadid, and Ono, 725. 34 The sons of Jericho, 345. 35 The sons of Senaah, 3,630.
36 The priests: the [s]sons of Jedaiah, of the house of Jeshua, 973. 37 The sons of Immer,
1,052. 38 The [t]sons of Pashhur, 1,247. 39 The sons of Harim, 1,017.
40 The Levites: the sons of [u]Jeshua and Kadmiel, of the sons of Hodaviah, 74. 41 The singers:
the sons of [v]Asaph, 128. 42 The sons of the [w]gatekeepers: the sons of Shallum, the sons of Ater, the
sons of Talmon, the sons of Akkub, the sons of Hatita, and the sons of Shobai, in all 139.
43 [x]The temple servants: the sons of Ziha, the sons of Hasupha, the sons of Tabbaoth,
44 the sons of Keros, the sons of Siaha, the sons of Padon, 45 the sons of Lebanah, the sons of
Hagabah, the sons of Akkub, 46 the sons of Hagab, the sons of Shamlai, the sons of Hanan,
47 the sons of Giddel, the sons of Gahar, the sons of Reaiah, 48 the sons of Rezin, the sons
of Nekoda, the sons of Gazzam, 49 the sons of Uzza, the sons of Paseah, the sons of Besai,
50 the sons of Asnah, the sons of Meunim, the sons of Nephisim, 51 the sons of Bakbuk,
the sons of Hakupha, the sons of Harhur, 52 the sons of Bazluth, the sons of Mehida, the
sons of Harsha, 53 the sons of Barkos, the sons of Sisera, the sons of Temah, 54 the sons of
Neziah, and the sons of Hatipha.
55 [y]The sons of Solomon's servants: the sons of Sotai, the sons of Hassophereth, the
sons of Peruda, 56 the sons of Jaalah, the sons of Darkon, the sons of Giddel, 57 the sons of
Shephatiah, the sons of Hattil, the sons of Pochereth-hazzebaim, and the sons of Ami.
58 All the temple servants and the sons of Solomon's servants were 392.
59 The following were those who came up from Tel-melah, Tel-harsha, Cherub, Addan,
and Immer, [z]though they could not prove their fathers' houses or their descent, whether
they belonged to Israel: 60 the sons of Delaiah, the sons of Tobiah, and the sons of Nekoda,
652. 61 Also, of the sons of the priests: the sons of Habaiah, the sons of Hakkoz, and the
sons of [a]Barzillai (who had taken a wife from the daughters of Barzillai the Gileadite, and
was called by their name). 62 These sought their registration among those enrolled in the
genealogies, but they were not found there, and [b]so they were excluded from the priesthood as unclean. 63 The [c]governor told them that they were not [d]to partake of the most
holy food, until there should be a priest to consult [e]Urim and Thummim.
64 [f]The whole assembly together was 42,360, 65 besides their male and female servants, of

3 [q]ch. 8:3; 10:25
31 [r][ver. 7]
36 [s]For ver. 36-39, see 1 Chr. 24:7-18
38 [t]1 Chr. 9:12
40 [u][Neh. 10:9]
41 [v]See 1 Chr. 6:39
42 [w]1 Chr. 9:17, 18
43 [x]1 Chr. 9:2; Neh. 11:3
55 [y]Neh. 11:3; [1 Kgs. 9:21]
59 [z][1 Chr. 9:1]
61 [a]2 Sam. 17:27
62 [b][Num. 3:10]
63 [c]Neh. 8:9 [d]Lev. 22:2, 10, 15, 16 [e]See Ex. 28:30
64 [f]Neh. 7:66, 67

form (**the men of** and **the sons of** seem interchangeable). The numbers may come from a census. The list shows an interest in the legitimate membership of the covenant people, as well as the legitimate reclaiming of ancestral land. The places that are named are in the territories of Judah and Benjamin (cf. 1:5), north and south of Jerusalem; a large proportion of the territories are actually in Benjamin (cf. Josh. 18:21–27). Some of them recall the first conquest of Canaan by Joshua (e.g., Bethel and Ai).

2:36–58 The temple officials are divided according to function, headed by the **priests** and **Levites**. The priests (vv. 36–39) are the most important group, for they are set apart for worship at the altar; the Levites are attendants, some of them **singers** and **gatekeepers** (vv. 40–42; see also 1 Chron. 6:33–43; 9:17–18). Three of the priestly names given here (**Jedaiah**, **Immer**, **Pashhur**) also appear in 1 Chron. 9:10–13 in that list of those who returned from exile (cf. also Jer. 20:1–6). The number of Levites is surprisingly low compared to the priests.

2:43–54 The **temple servants** (Hb. *netinim*, a term appearing only in Ezra, Nehemiah, and 1 Chron. 9:2) were a further, lower class of officials appointed by King David to help the Levites (cf. Ezra 8:20). There may be a connection between them and the Gibeonites, whom Joshua made servants of the sanctuary (Josh. 9:23, 27). Here, however, they are apparently not slaves, and in Neh. 10:28 they are named among those who take the covenant oath.

2:55–58 The **sons of Solomon's servants** may be connected with foreigners whom Solomon originally drafted for building the temple (1 Kings 9:20–21). They are numbered here along with the temple servants (Ezra 2:43), and like them are not regarded as slaves. Presumably they all returned voluntarily from Babylon.

2:59–63 This section considers the legitimacy of claims to citizenship and membership in the priesthood. **whether they belonged to Israel**. It was important in this returning community to establish credentials. People were coming back after a long exile to claim inheritance and property. In the case of priests, it was paramount that only those with the correct pedigree should officiate at the altar. Such claims needed evidence, and the record inevitably contained gaps. The claims entered here are not permanently refused, but held over, pending further inquiry.

2:64–70 The conclusion of the chapter gives numbers of the **whole assembly** (vv. 64–66), then gives the number of their livestock, and closes with a picture of full resettlement (v. 70). The crucial importance of the temple project to the whole returning enterprise is signaled in vv. 68–69, where some **heads**

whom there were 7,337, and they had 200 male and female [g]singers. 66 Their horses were
736, their mules were 245, 67 their camels were 435, and their donkeys were 6,720.
68 [h]Some of the heads of families, when they came to the house of the LORD that is in
Jerusalem, made freewill offerings for the house of God, to erect it on its site. 69 According
to their ability they gave to [i]the treasury of the work 61,000 darics[1] of gold, 5,000 minas[2]
of silver, and 100 priests' garments.
70 [j]Now the priests, the Levites, some of the people, the singers, the gatekeepers, and the
temple servants lived in their towns, and all the rest of Israel[3] in their towns.

Rebuilding the Altar

3 [k]When the seventh month came, and the children of Israel were in the towns, the people
gathered as one man to Jerusalem. 2 Then arose Jeshua the son of Jozadak, with his fellow priests, and [l]Zerubbabel the son of [m]Shealtiel with his kinsmen, and they built the altar
of the God of Israel, to offer burnt offerings on it, [n]as it is written in the Law of Moses the
[o]man of God. 3 They set the altar in its place, [p]for fear was on them because of the peoples of
the lands, and [q]they offered burnt offerings on it to the LORD, burnt offerings morning and
evening. 4 [r]And they kept the Feast of Booths, [s]as it is written, [t]and offered the daily burnt
offerings by number according to the rule, as each day required, 5 and after that the regular
burnt [u]offerings, the offerings at the new moon [v]and at all the appointed feasts of the LORD,
and the offerings of everyone who made a freewill offering to the LORD. 6 From the first day of
the seventh month they began to offer burnt offerings to the LORD. But the foundation of the
temple of the LORD was not yet laid. 7 So they gave money to the masons and the carpenters,
[w]and food, drink, and oil to the Sidonians and the Tyrians [x]to bring cedar trees from Lebanon
to the sea, to Joppa, [y]according to the grant that they had from Cyrus king of Persia.

Rebuilding the Temple

8 Now in the second year after their coming to the house of God at Jerusalem, in the
second month, [z]Zerubbabel the son of Shealtiel and [z]Jeshua the son of Jozadak made a
beginning, together with the rest of their kinsmen, the priests and the Levites and all who
had come to Jerusalem from the captivity. They [a]appointed the Levites, from twenty years
old and upward, to [b]supervise the work of the house of the LORD. 9 And [z]Jeshua with his

[1] A *daric* was a coin weighing about 1/4 ounce or 8.5 grams [2] A *mina* was about 1 1/4 pounds or 0.6 kilogram [3] Hebrew *all Israel*

65 [g]See 2 Chr. 35:25
68 [h]Neh. 7:70-72
69 [i][1 Chr. 26:20]
70 [j]Neh. 7:73
Chapter 3
1 [k]Neh. 7:73; 8:1
2 [l]Matt. 1:12; Luke 3:27 [m]1 Chr. 3:17; Matt. 1:12; Luke 3:27 [n]Deut. 12:5, 6 [o]See Deut. 33:1
3 [p][ch. 4:4] [q]Ex. 29:38; Num. 28:3, 4
4 [r]Zech. 14:16; See Neh. 8:14-17 [s]Ex. 23:16; Lev. 23:34 [t]See Num. 29:12-38
5 [u]See Num. 28:11-15 [v]Num. 29:39
7 [w]1 Kgs. 5:6, 9; 2 Chr. 2:10 [x]2 Chr. 2:16 [y]ch. 1:3, 4; 6:3
8 [z]ch. 2:2; 4:3 [a]1 Chr. 23:24 [b]1 Chr. 23:4
9 [z][See ver. 8 above]

of families, i.e., key people in the community, give of their own substance to initiate the rebuilding (cf. Ex. 36:2–7). The location of the former temple is regarded as a holy place, such that it can already be called **the house of the LORD that is in Jerusalem**.

2:69 darics. A daric was a gold coin used throughout the Persian Empire. Introduced by Darius I at the end of the sixth century B.C., it weighed about 0.3 ounces (8.5 grams). Beginning in the second half of the fifth century B.C., these coins with Hebrew letters on them appear in Judah. Several of them bear the name of the Persian province Yehud (i.e., Judah), which probably indicates that the province had some freedom to mint its own coins.

3:1–6:22 ***The Returned Exiles Rebuild the Temple on Its Original Site.*** The book of Ezra spans several generations, as the returnees rebuild and encounter resistance, and finally receive renewed imperial authorization for their efforts.

3:1–13 ***The Foundations of the Temple Are Laid.*** In this section the altar is rebuilt on its former site, and foundations are laid for the new temple.

3:1 According to Israel's calendar of pilgrimage feasts, the **seventh month**, Tishri (roughly September), was the month of the great Day of Atonement (Lev. 23:26–32), followed by the Feast of Booths (or Tabernacles; Lev. 23:33–43), which celebrated the exodus from Egypt. Thus in the first year of the return, the people make their first pilgrimage to Jerusalem.

3:2 built the altar. On this occasion, the broken altar had first to be repaired so that sacrifices could once again be made. The leading roles of **Jeshua** and **Zerubbabel** are again emphasized, with some stress on the role of the priests.

3:3 in its place. There may have been visible remains of the original altar (as perhaps implied by Jer. 41:4–5); in any case, its exact location was evidently known. The altar has absolute priority, as it had at the first entry into the land, many years before (Deut. 27:1–8). The haste to erect it is perhaps heightened by the fear of **the peoples of the lands**. This phrase refers to residents of Judah, and perhaps neighboring areas, who were not part of the group returning from exile. Some may have had Jewish origins, but they present themselves as a distinct group, and they would soon oppose the work. The exiles' **fear** is another echo of their first occupation of the land, when fear had at first overwhelmed the Israelites (Num. 14:1–3). On this occasion, despite their fear, they are resolute. **Burnt offerings** were to be offered daily on the altar, morning and evening, as Moses commanded in Ex. 29:38–42.

3:4–7 The people keep the **Feast of Booths**, with its proper sacrifices (see Num. 29:12–38).

3:6 they began to offer. The perspective shifts to the regular sacrificial worship (see 2 Chron. 2:4), since the particular acts of worship in the seventh month are essentially portrayed as a renewal and a beginning. The next task is to rebuild the temple, and the preparations recall those made by King Solomon half a millennium earlier (Ezra 3:7; cf. 1 Kings 5:13–18; 1 Chron. 22:4, 15; 2 Chronicles 2).

3:8 Work begins on the temple itself, with the laying of its foundation in the **second year** of the return (c. 537 B.C.). The **second month**, Ziv (1 Kings 6:1)—the same time of year when Solomon had begun his temple (2 Chron. 3:2)—is in the spring. The time of the return from exile is dated with the formula **after their coming to the house of God at Jerusalem**. Even though the temple still lies in ruins, the place could be called "the house of God" because of its consecration for worship (see Jer. 41:5). The narrator stresses that it is those who have come **from the captivity** who do this. The priests and Levites are emphasized, and the qualifying age for Levitical service is mentioned (cf. 1 Chron. 23:24).

3:9 The names are those of "Levites," as specified in v. 8. Thus **Jeshua** is not the high priest of that name, nor are these Levite **sons of Judah** members of the tribe of Judah; this "Judah" is probably another form of "Hodaviah," named along with **Kadmiel** in 2:40.

sons and his brothers, and Kadmiel and his sons, the sons of Judah, together [b]supervised
the workmen in the house of God, along with the [c]sons of Henadad and the Levites, their
sons and brothers.
10 And when the builders laid the foundation of the temple of the LORD, the priests in
their vestments came forward with trumpets, and the Levites, the sons of Asaph, with
cymbals, to praise the LORD, [d]according to the directions of David king of Israel. 11 And
they sang responsively, praising and giving thanks to the LORD,

> [e]"For he is good,
> for his steadfast love endures forever toward Israel."

And all the people shouted with a great shout when they praised the LORD, because the
foundation of the house of the LORD was laid. 12 But many of the priests and Levites and heads
of fathers' houses, [f]old men who had seen the first house, wept with a loud voice when they
saw the foundation of this house being laid, though many shouted aloud for joy, 13 so that the
people could not distinguish the sound of the joyful shout from the sound of the people's
weeping, for the people shouted with a great shout, and the sound was heard far away.

9[b][See ver. 8 above] [c]Neh. 10:9, 10
10[d]1 Chr. 6:31; 16:4-6; 25:1, 2
11[e]See 1 Chr. 16:34, 41
12[f]Hag. 2:3

3:10–11 all the people shouted with a great shout. The laying of the foundations occasions praise, which echoes the celebrations of King David when he prepared for the building of Solomon's temple (cf. 1 Chronicles 16, esp. vv. 7, 34, 37).

3:12–13 But many . . . wept with a loud voice. Sadness is mixed with this rejoicing, for some of the very old remembered the former temple and believed that this new one would not match the former temple's glory. The picture of mitigated celebration is a small symbol of the whole event of the return, which was in itself a triumph yet fell far short of the great hopes the people might have had (cf. Hag. 2:2–9).

4:1–24 ***Enemies Stall the Project by Conspiring against It.*** The rebuilding project encounters opposition from other groups in the region, and the work ceases.

4:1–2 the adversaries of Judah and Benjamin. The **returned exiles** found themselves in a Persian province, called Beyond the River (v. 11; i.e., beyond the Euphrates from the perspective of the Persian power centers). Its administrative center was in Samaria, the capital of the former northern kingdom of Israel. Its population was composed largely of the descendants of peoples settled there by **Esarhaddon king of Assyria** (reigned c. 681–669 B.C.) in c. 671–670 (see 2 Kings 17:24–33; Isa. 7:8), long after Assyria conquered the northern kingdom in 722 and began to resettle the land with exiles from other lands. Apparently Samaria was a hotbed of unrest for decades. **Let us build with you, for we worship your God as you do.** Indeed, these peoples' ancestors had been taught the religion of Yahweh by a priest sent for that purpose (2 Kings 17:24–28), though the same account tells that they worshiped other gods as well (2 Kings 17:29–41), and they are identified as "adversaries" (Ezra 4:1).

4:3 Zerubbabel, Jeshua, and the rest of the heads of fathers' houses

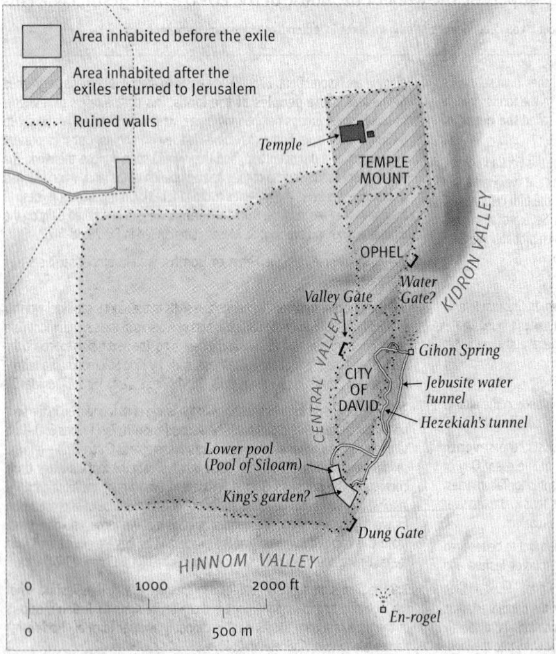

Jerusalem at the Time of Zerubbabel
538–515 B.C.

Among the first tasks undertaken upon the exiles' return was the rebuilding of the altar and the temple. Almost immediately the altar was set up, and regular burnt offerings were resumed. About a year later the foundations of the temple were laid, but opposition from other local governors halted the completion of the temple for over 20 years. Finally, in 515 B.C. (during the reign of Darius) the temple was completed. The city walls, however, would not be rebuilt until about 70 years later under the leadership of Nehemiah.

Chapter 4
1[g]See ver. 7-10
2[h]2 Kgs. 17:24, 32, 33
[i]2 Kgs. 19:37 [j][ver. 10]
3[k]Neh. 2:20 [l]ch. 1:1-3
4[m]ch. 3:3
6[n]Esth. 1:1; Dan. 9:1
7[o]ch. 1:8 [p][2 Kgs. 18:26]
9[q][2 Kgs. 17:24, 30, 31]
[r][ch. 5:6; 6:6]

Adversaries Oppose the Rebuilding

4 Now when [g]the adversaries of Judah and Benjamin heard that the returned exiles were
building a temple to the LORD, the God of Israel, 2 they approached Zerubbabel and
the heads of fathers' houses and said to them, "Let us build with you, for we worship your
God as you do, and we have been sacrificing to him ever [h]since the days of [i]Esarhaddon
king of Assyria [j]who brought us here." 3 But Zerubbabel, Jeshua, and the rest of the heads
of fathers' houses in Israel said to them, [k]"You have nothing to do with us in building a
house to our God; but we alone will build to the LORD, the God of Israel, [l]as King Cyrus
the king of Persia has commanded us."
4 Then [m]the people of the land discouraged the people of Judah and made them afraid
to build 5 and bribed counselors against them to frustrate their purpose, all the days of
Cyrus king of Persia, even until the reign of Darius king of Persia.
6 And in the reign of [n]Ahasuerus, in the beginning of his reign, they wrote an accusation
against the inhabitants of Judah and Jerusalem.

The Letter to King Artaxerxes

7 In the days of Artaxerxes, Bishlam and [o]Mithredath and Tabeel and the rest of their associates wrote to Artaxerxes king of Persia. The letter was written [p]in Aramaic and translated.[1]
8 Rehum the commander and Shimshai the scribe wrote a letter against Jerusalem to
Artaxerxes the king as follows: 9 Rehum the commander, Shimshai the scribe, and the
rest of their associates, the [q]judges, the [r]governors, the officials, the Persians, the men of

[1] Hebrew *written in Aramaic and translated in Aramaic*, indicating that 4:8–6:18 is in Aramaic; another interpretation is *The letter was written in the Aramaic script and set forth in the Aramaic language*

present a united answer declining the offer of help (vv. 1–2): **we alone will build to the LORD**. Their stated ground for declining the help is that the decree of Cyrus applied only to the returning exiles. No doubt they understood that the actual intent behind the request was to frustrate the project.

4:4–5 The real attitude of these residents, now called **the people of the land**, emerges. They showed their determined opposition **all the days of Cyrus** (from the time the opposition began in 538 or 537 B.C.; Cyrus died in 530) **even until the reign of Darius** (reigned 522–486). Therefore, the opposition continued over a period of about 20 years, up to the completion of the temple in 516 B.C. The discouragement apparently involved turning local officials against the project. Even though the project actually had the full authority of King Cyrus behind it, local enemies would exploit the distance of Jerusalem from the imperial center to their own advantage.

4:6–23 This section interrupts the historical narrative (1:1–4:5) and mentions two later examples of hostility from the people of the land (4:6 and 4:7–23), showing that persistent and recurring hostility to the returning Jews occurred for a century or more after Cyrus's decree. The narrative resumes at v. 24. The technique employed was familiar practice in ancient history writing. Its purpose here is to show that the problems faced by the new community were not isolated but were deeply rooted in its situation.

4:6 This verse jumps forward to later events during the reign of **Ahasuerus** (reigned 486–464 B.C.), otherwise known as Xerxes, who appears in the book of Esther (cf. Est. 1:1).

4:7–23 While the author is on the topic of the opposition by the people of the land, he jumps forward yet further to another hostile episode, when a formal letter of complaint was sent by leaders in the province to King Artaxerxes I (reigned 464–423 B.C.).

4:7–8 The **letter** form follows known practice in the Persian period: formal address, greetings, information, and request. The precise occasion of this action against the community is not known, but it presupposed that the people had made an attempt to rebuild the city walls sometime before the mission of Nehemiah, who arrived in 445 B.C. (still in the reign of Artaxerxes) and completed the rebuilding of the walls despite strenuous attempts to stop the work at that time too (Nehemiah 4; 6). The present letter was written **in Aramaic**, which had been the official imperial language under the Babylonians and was still used in diplomacy. The letter might have been **translated** into Persian (for the benefit of the king), or into Hebrew (therefore implying that the author knew of a Hebrew copy). But when the letter is introduced in the book of Ezra (Ezra 4:7b), the language changes from Hebrew to Aramaic, and continues in Aramaic until 6:18, returning to Hebrew from 6:19 to the end. Citing the letters in Aramaic gives authenticity to Ezra's account (cf. also 7:12–26); it is not entirely clear, however, why Ezra's own narrative in this section also uses Aramaic (e.g., 4:23–5:5; 6:13–18). Perhaps it was natural, given that the letters were in Aramaic. In any case, the reader comes away confident that the author was fluent enough in Aramaic to understand the royal letters.

4:9 The officials give their credentials as leaders and also stress that their rights in the land have imperial warrant because of the older Assyrian resettlements.

Adversaries Hinder Work

Ezra 4:5	The people of the land hired counselors to work against the Israelites from the reigns of Cyrus (539–530 B.C.) to Darius (522–486)
Ezra 4:6	Accusations arose during the reign of Xerxes (Ahasuerus) (486–464)
Ezra 4:7–23	Accusations arose during the reign of Artaxerxes (464–423):
	• First threat: they will withhold money (v. 13)
	• Second threat: the king is dishonored (v. 14)
	• Third threat: they have rebelled before (v. 15)
	• Fourth threat: they will take over the whole area (v. 16)
Ezra 4:24–6:12	Work on the temple stopped from 536–520; Darius finally gives order to rebuild it

Erech, the Babylonians, the men of Susa, that is, the [s]Elamites, 10 and the rest of the nations
whom the great and noble [t]Osnappar deported and settled in the cities of Samaria and
in the rest of the province Beyond the River. 11 (This is a copy of the letter that they sent.)
"To Artaxerxes the king: Your servants, the men of the province Beyond the River, send
greeting. And now 12 be it known to the king that the Jews who came up from you to us
have gone to Jerusalem. They are rebuilding that rebellious and wicked city. They are
[v]finishing the walls and repairing the foundations. 13 Now be it known to the king that if
this city is rebuilt and the walls finished, they will not pay [w]tribute, custom, or toll, and
the royal revenue will be impaired. 14 Now because we eat the salt of the palace and it is
not fitting for us to witness the king's dishonor, therefore we send and inform the king,
15 in order that search may be made in the book of the records of your fathers. You will find
in the book of the records and learn that this city is a rebellious city, hurtful to kings and
provinces, and that sedition was stirred up in it from of old. That was why this city was
laid waste. 16 We make known to the king that if this city is rebuilt and its walls finished,
you will then have no possession in the province Beyond the River."

The King Orders the Work to Cease

17 The king sent an answer: "To Rehum the commander and Shimshai the scribe and the
rest of their associates who live in Samaria and in the rest of the province Beyond the River,
greeting. And now 18 the letter that you sent to us has been [x]plainly read before me. 19 And
I made a decree, and search has been made, and it has been found that this city from of old
has risen against kings, and that rebellion and sedition have been made in it. 20 And mighty
kings have been over Jerusalem, [y]who ruled over the whole province Beyond the River, to
whom [z]tribute, custom, and toll were paid. 21 Therefore make a decree that these men be
made to cease, and that this city be not rebuilt, until a decree is made by me. 22 And take
care not to be slack in this matter. Why should damage grow to the hurt of the king?"

23 Then, when the copy of King Artaxerxes' letter was read before Rehum and Shimshai
the scribe and their associates, they went in haste to the Jews at Jerusalem and by force
and power made them cease. 24 Then the work on the house of God that is in Jerusalem
stopped, and it ceased until the second year of the reign of Darius king of Persia.

Rebuilding Begins Anew

5 Now the prophets, [a]Haggai and [b]Zechariah the son of Iddo, prophesied to the Jews
who were in Judah and Jerusalem, in the name of the God of Israel who was over
them. 2 [c]Then Zerubbabel the son of Shealtiel and [d]Jeshua the son of Jozadak arose and
began to rebuild the house of God that is in Jerusalem, and the prophets of God were
[e]with them, supporting them.

3 At the same time [f]Tattenai the governor of the province Beyond the River and Shethar-

9 [s]Isa. 11:11
10 [t][ver. 2]
12 [v]ch. 5:3, 9
13 [w]ver. 20; ch. 7:24
18 [x][Neh. 8:8]
20 [y]1 Kgs. 4:21; Ps. 72:8; [Gen. 15:18; Josh. 1:4] [z]ver. 13; [ch. 7:24]

Chapter 5

1 [a]Hag. 1:1 [b]Zech. 1:1
2 [c]ch. 3:2 [d]See ch. 3:2 [e][ch. 6:14]
3 [f]ch. 6:6, 13

4:10 The Assyrian king **Osnappar** is probably Ashurbanipal (668–627 B.C.); he continued the resettlement of Israel, which his predecessors began (see vv. 1–2).

4:11 Beyond the River. The name of the Persian province, which apparently included Jerusalem, until the decree of Cyrus returned the land to the Jews.

4:12 that rebellious and wicked city. Jerusalem had in fact often been more acquiescent to the empire than the biblical writers thought proper (note the highly critical view of the kings Ahaz and Manasseh in 2 Kings 16–21), though there had been some switching of loyalties during the last days of the kingdom (2 Kings 18:7; 24:1, 20). The letter plays on the empire's ready suspicions of rebellion. **They are finishing the walls and repairing the foundations**. By the time of this letter, considerable repair work had already been done on the wall around Jerusalem.

4:13–16 The threat of an independence movement in Jerusalem is exaggerated. The imperial **records** would include those of Assyria and Babylon, empires to which the Persians regarded themselves legitimate successors.

4:20 mighty kings. A possible reference to the relatively powerful united monarchy under David and Solomon. The king's response (vv. 17–22) gave license to the enemies of the exiles to stop the work by force, an action that might underlie the news later heard by Nehemiah that the walls of Jerusalem lay in ruins (Neh. 1:3).

4:24 The word **then** picks up the story from v. 5, before the long interlude of vv. 6–23, bringing the narrative back to the period principally in view (soon after the first return). The story now records the outcome of the mission to prevent the building of the temple. It is implied that the work had ceased soon after it began, i.e., within about two years after c. 537 B.C. (see 3:8). It resumed in the **second year of the reign of Darius king of Persia**, which is 520 B.C. The period of inactivity therefore lasted around 15 years.

5:1–17 *The Work Is Resumed, and Local Officials Seek Confirmation of Cyrus's Decree.* After a period of inactivity, the leaders resume work on rebuilding the temple, and provincial officials inquire into its legitimacy.

5:1–2 The **prophets, Haggai and Zechariah**, are also known from their books, which contain prophecies made in the second year of King Darius, 520 B.C. (Hag. 1:1; 2:1; Zech. 1:1, 7; cf. note on Ezra 4:24; cf. also 6:14). Haggai proclaims that the people were in trouble because they had lost sight of their top priority of rebuilding the temple (Hag. 1:4–6). Verses 1–2 of Ezra 5 bring out the connection between the prophetic work and the renewed action, following the discouragement recorded in 4:4–5, 24. In beginning again, **Zerubbabel** and **Jeshua** are simply reimplementing Cyrus's decree, recognizing it as the will and purpose of God.

5:3–5 The officials **Tattenai** and **Shethar-bozenai** are much more neutral than the officials named in 4:8–10. Clearly they have no knowledge of Cyrus's decree, no doubt because the work had long stopped, and they presumably

3[g]ch. 4:12
5[h]Ps. 33:18; [ch. 7:6, 28]
6[f][See ver. 3 above] [i][ch. 4:9]
9[g][See ver. 3 above]
11[j]1 Kgs. 6:1 [k]ch. 4:12
12[l]2 Chr. 36:16, 17 [m]2 Kgs. 24:2; See 2 Kgs. 25:8-11
13[n]ch. 1:1
14[o]ch. 1:7, 8; 6:5 [p]ch. 1:8
16[p][See ver. 14 above] [q]ch. 3:8, 10 [r][ch. 6:15]
17[s]ch. 6:1, 2

bozenai and their associates came to them and spoke to them thus: [g]"Who gave you a decree
to build this house and to finish this structure?" **4** They[1] also asked them this: "What are
the names of the men who are building this building?" **5** But [h]the eye of their God was on
the elders of the Jews, and they did not stop them until the report should reach Darius
and then an answer be returned by letter concerning it.

Tattenai's Letter to King Darius

6 This is a copy of the letter that [f]Tattenai the governor of the province Beyond the
River and Shethar-bozenai and his associates, the [i]governors who were in the province
Beyond the River, sent to Darius the king. **7** They sent him a report, in which was written as follows: "To Darius the king, all peace. **8** Be it known to the king that we went to
the province of Judah, to the house of the great God. It is being built with huge stones,
and timber is laid in the walls. This work goes on diligently and prospers in their hands.
9 Then we asked those elders and spoke to them thus: [g]'Who gave you a decree to build
this house and to finish this structure?' **10** We also asked them their names, for your
information, that we might write down the names of their leaders.[2] **11** And this was their
reply to us: 'We are the servants of the God of heaven and earth, and we are rebuilding
the house that was built many years ago, [j]which a great king of Israel built and [k]finished.
12 [l]But because our fathers had angered the God of heaven, he [m]gave them into the hand
of Nebuchadnezzar king of Babylon, the Chaldean, who destroyed this house and carried
away the people to Babylonia. **13** [n]However, in the first year of Cyrus king of Babylon,
Cyrus the king made a decree that this house of God should be rebuilt. **14** [o]And the gold
and silver vessels of the house of God, which Nebuchadnezzar had taken out of the
temple that was in Jerusalem and brought into the temple of Babylon, these Cyrus the
king took out of the temple of Babylon, and they were delivered to one whose name was
[p]Sheshbazzar, whom he had made governor; **15** and he said to him, "Take these vessels,
go and put them in the temple that is in Jerusalem, and let the house of God be rebuilt
on its site." **16** Then this [p]Sheshbazzar came and [q]laid the foundations of the house of
God that is in Jerusalem, and from that time until now it has been in building, and it
is [r]not yet finished.' **17** Therefore, if it seems good to the king, [s]let search be made in the
royal archives there in Babylon, to see whether a decree was issued by Cyrus the king for
the rebuilding of this house of God in Jerusalem. And let the king send us his pleasure
in this matter."

[1] Septuagint, Syriac; Aramaic *We* [2] Aramaic *of the men at their heads*

came to power only after the exiles first arrived. They are interested only in the proper authorization of this important thing that was happening under their jurisdiction, and they do not actually interfere with the work's progress. The author knows that a higher authority, **the eye of . . . God** (5:5), was watching over the builders' activity and that God was protecting them (cf. Ps. 33:18).

5:6 The **copy of the letter** has a formal opening similar to the one in 4:7–16.

5:8 The **province of Judah** lay within the Persian province Beyond the River, of which Tattenai was governor in Samaria. (Texts from the reign of Darius I dating 520–519 B.C. name the local governor of the province "Beyond the River" as Tattanu [cf. Tattenai; vv. 3, 6; 6:6, 13].) The expression **the house of the great God** is a diplomatic way of referring to the temple and the God of Israel, and does not imply that the writers of the letter believe in him. The use of **huge stones** and **timber** recalls the building of the first temple (1 Kings 6:36; 7:12) and was a common practice in the ancient Near East.

5:9–10 The officials' concern for administrative propriety is reflected in their inquiries about both the original authorization and the names of those who are to be held responsible for the action being undertaken.

5:11–17 The letter now reports the reply of the Jewish leaders. (Quotation was also a feature of known formal Persian letters.)

5:11 The letter writers probably got their information from the returned exiles themselves, since it reflects their understanding of the situation. **We are the servants of the God of heaven and earth.** They do not hesitate to say that they are serving not a local deity but the one true God of the whole world. They give this answer instead of giving their individual names when asked (v. 10). The **great king of Israel** is Solomon.

5:12 This verse sums up the message of 1–2 Kings.

5:13–15 These verses essentially repeat information found in 1:2–4. The report stops short of claiming that Cyrus had also commanded that the building be funded by donations from Babylon (1:4). This was perhaps more than Tattenai (or even the exiles) wished to urge at this point.

5:13 Cyrus the king made a decree. See 1:1–4.

5:14 Sheshbazzar was introduced as "the prince of Judah" in 1:8, being the one who had received directly from King Cyrus the charge to rebuild the temple. Here he is called **governor**, a name applied to Tattenai himself in 5:3; it seems that the term could be used somewhat loosely, since Judah would not have had a "governor" on a par with the governor of the entire province Beyond the River (v. 6, etc.). Darius's reply also refers to a "governor of the Jews" (6:7), a name given to Zerubbabel in Hag. 1:1.

5:16–17 it has been in building. The period when building had ceased was irrelevant both to the information Tattenai was giving and to the request he was making. The author therefore omits here the specific work of Zerubbabel, Jeshua, Haggai, and Zechariah (though their names were no doubt among those asked for by the governor, and sent with the letter; see v. 10). Tattenai, following the Jews' own account, wants to make a link between the original authorization and the present building activity, and so portrays Sheshbazzar as having laid the foundations of the temple, since it was done under his authority, though that achievement is attributed to the work initiated by Zerubbabel and Jeshua in 3:8–10.

The Decree of Darius

6 Then Darius the king made a decree, and [t]search was made in Babylonia, in the house
of the archives where the documents were stored. 2 And in Ecbatana, the citadel that
is [u]in the province of Media, a scroll was found on which this was written: "A record. 3 In
the first year of Cyrus the king, Cyrus the king issued a decree: Concerning the house of
God at Jerusalem, let the house be rebuilt, the place where sacrifices were offered, and let
its foundations be retained. Its height shall be sixty cubits[1] and its breadth sixty cubits,
4 [v]with three layers of great stones and one layer of timber. Let the cost be paid from
the royal treasury. 5 And also [w]let the gold and silver vessels of the house of God, which
Nebuchadnezzar took out of the temple that is in Jerusalem and brought to Babylon, be
restored and brought back to the temple that is in Jerusalem, each to its place. You shall
put them in the house of God."

6 "Now therefore, [x]Tattenai, governor of the province Beyond the River, Shethar-bozenai,
[y]and your[2] associates the governors who are in the province Beyond the River, keep away.
7 Let the work on this house of God alone. Let the governor of the Jews and the elders of
the Jews rebuild this house of God on its site. 8 Moreover, [z]I make a decree regarding what
you shall do for these elders of the Jews for the rebuilding of this house of God. The cost
is to be paid to these men in full and without delay from the royal revenue, the tribute of
the province from Beyond the River. 9 And whatever is needed—bulls, rams, or sheep for
burnt offerings to the God of heaven, wheat, salt, wine, or oil, as the priests at Jerusalem
require—let that be given to them day by day without fail, 10 that they may offer pleasing
sacrifices to the God of heaven [a]and pray for the life of the king and his sons. 11 Also I make
a decree that if anyone alters this edict, a beam shall be pulled out of his house, and he
shall be impaled on it, and [b]his house shall be made a dunghill. 12 May the God [c]who has
caused his name to dwell there overthrow any king or people who shall put out a hand
to alter this, or to destroy this house of God that is in Jerusalem. I Darius make a decree;
let it be done with all diligence."

The Temple Finished and Dedicated

13 Then, according to the word sent by Darius the king, [x]Tattenai, the governor of the
province Beyond the River, Shethar-bozenai, and their associates did with all diligence what
Darius the king had ordered. 14 [d]And the elders of the Jews built and prospered through

[1] A *cubit* was about 18 inches or 45 centimeters [2] Aramaic *their*

Chapter 6
1 [t]ch. 5:17
2 [u][2 Kgs. 17:6]
4 [v]1 Kgs. 6:36
5 [w]ch. 1:7, 8; 5:14
6 [x]ch. 5:3, 6 [y]ch. 5:6
8 [z]ch. 7:13, 21
10 [a]Jer. 29:7; [1 Tim. 2:2]
11 [b]Dan. 2:5; 3:29
12 [c]1 Kgs. 9:3
13 [x][See ver. 6 above]
14 [d]ch. 5:1, 2

6:1–22 *King Darius Discovers and Reaffirms Cyrus's Decree, and the Work Is Completed.* A record of Cyrus's decree is discovered, and King Darius confirms that the Jews are to be allowed to continue the work.

6:1–2 The **search** for Cyrus's decree is **made** first **in Babylonia**, where Cyrus had declared himself king in 539 B.C. and where many exiled Jews lived. But the scroll containing the record of the decree was found in **Ecbatana** (v. 2), a summer residence of the Persian kings, where Cyrus may have gone soon after his triumph over Babylon. The **province of Media** (v. 2) was formerly the seat of an empire itself, but Cyrus had made it part of the Persian realm. Leather scrolls are known to have been used in Persia for official documents in Aramaic. The document now discovered is called a **record** (v. 2) and is apparently a memorandum concerning the decree rather than the decree itself (which would probably have been written on a clay tablet).

6:3–5 This record is not identical with the **decree** as recorded in 1:2–4. It makes new stipulations about the building, its location, its size, and its materials. This may be because a copy of the original decree had been found (see note on 6:1–2), and additional instructions may have been added to it for a particular recipient or destination. Moreover, different copies of Cyrus's original decree may have been made, varying in wording according to the purpose for each copy (the one in 1:2–4 included wording for public proclamation, while this version in 6:3–5 was an official version for royal archives). The size of the temple might be specified in order to limit it, since public funds were being used to pay for it. The absence of a length dimension is odd, and the greater breadth than Solomon's temple is unexpected (1 Kings 6:2), especially in view of Ezra 3:12.

6:4 The prescription of **three layers of great stones and one layer of timber** exactly follows the construction of the older temple (1 Kings 6:36; 7:12), which was modeled after temples in other lands (cf. 1 Kings 5:1–12). While the original decree had required people in Babylon to support the cost of the exiles' project (Ezra 1:4), this record requires that the **cost** be met from the **royal treasury**.

6:6–12 Darius now instructs Tattenai and his fellow officials to allow the work to continue.

6:7 Governor of the Jews refers to Zerubbabel (Hag. 1:1). Nothing is known of what became of the first governor, Sheshbazzar.

6:8–10 Darius not only confirms Cyrus's decree but also provides for costs to be met from taxes raised in Beyond the River itself (v. 8). He also provides for materials for sacrifice in perpetuity (v. 9), with the political stipulation that the Jews **pray for the life of the king and his sons** (v. 10)—showing that Darius's generosity was part of his policy to sustain Persian power.

6:11–12 Darius makes in effect a further **decree**, backed up with a typical threatened sanction (v. 11). The final warning borrows language from the Jews' own way of speaking about God's presence in Jerusalem (**the God who has caused his name to dwell there**, v. 12; cf. Deut. 12:5); Darius strikingly acknowledges the efficacy of the God of Jerusalem in his own place (although, like Cyrus in Ezra 1:3, he might not be claiming that there is only one true God).

6:13–22 Darius's decree is implemented, the temple is completed and dedicated, and Passover is kept.

6:13 Tattenai and his fellow officials respond quickly to Darius's decree.

6:14 the elders of the Jews built and prospered. That is, they were successful in their building. Their success came **through the prophesying of Haggai the prophet and Zechariah the son of Iddo**. This passage

the prophesying of Haggai the prophet and Zechariah the son of Iddo. They finished their
building by decree of the God of Israel and [e]by decree of Cyrus and [f]Darius and [g]Artaxerxes
king of Persia; 15 and this house was finished on the third day of the [h]month of Adar, in
the sixth year of the reign of Darius the king.

16 And the people of Israel, the priests and the Levites, and the rest of the returned exiles,
celebrated the [i]dedication of this house of God with joy. 17 They offered at the dedication
of this house of God 100 bulls, 200 rams, 400 lambs, and as a sin offering for all Israel [j]12
male goats, according to the number of the tribes of Israel. 18 And they set the priests [k]in
their divisions and the Levites [l]in their divisions, for the service of God at Jerusalem, [m]as
it is written in the Book of Moses.

Passover Celebrated

19 [n]On the fourteenth day of the first month, the returned exiles kept the Passover. 20 [o]For
the priests and the Levites had purified themselves together; all of them were clean. [p]So
they slaughtered the Passover lamb for all the returned exiles, for their fellow priests, and

14 [e]ver. 3; ch. 1:1; 5:13 [f]ver. 12; [ch. 4:24] [g]ch. 7:1
15 [h]Esth. 3:7
16 [i]1 Kgs. 8:63; 2 Chr. 7:5
17 [j][ch. 8:35]
18 [k]1 Chr. 24:1; 2 Chr. 35:5 [l]1 Chr. 23:6 [m]Num. 3:6; 8:9
19 [n]Ex. 12:6
20 [o]2 Chr. 30:15 [p]2 Chr. 35:11

emphasizes that God—here represented as speaking through his prophets—is the real influence behind events. **The God of Israel** has also given a **decree** that the work should proceed. But the actions of the kings of Persia on the Jews' behalf, in the **decree of Cyrus and Darius and Artaxerxes king of Persia**, are also acknowledged. The inclusion here of Artaxerxes, who ruled after the events of this chapter, anticipates his decree in support of Ezra's mission (7:11–26).

6:15 The **month of Adar** (February/March) was the last month of the year, and the dedication of the temple falls fittingly in it, just before the celebrations of the new year that would follow. The **sixth year of the reign of Darius** was 515 B.C., almost exactly 70 years after the destruction of the first temple (586), thus fulfilling the prophecy of 70 years of exile (one way of reading Jer. 25:11–12; 29:10; see Introduction: Purpose, Occasion, and Background, and note on Jer. 25:11).

6:16–17 the people of Israel. Even though the returned exiles consisted of only three tribes (see note on 1:5), they are taken to represent all 12 tribes, **the number of the tribes of Israel** (6:17). The other divisions, **the priests and the Levites** and the laity, are a typical way of describing the whole community in Ezra. **with joy**. See note on vv. 19–22. The **dedication** (Hb. *hanukkah*) **of this house** (v. 17) follows its completion, and is celebrated with lavish sacrifices, as Solomon's temple had been (see 1 Kings 8:62–64). (The later Jewish holiday of Hanukkah, however, was based not on this dedication but on the rededication of the temple under the Maccabees in 164 B.C.; see Intertestamental Events Timeline, pp. 1788–1789.) The **sin offering for all Israel** (Ezra 6:17) recalls the sin offering prescribed for the Day of Atonement (Lev. 16:15–16) and is appropriate at this rededication following God's former judgment on his people. Here again the symbolic unity of Israel is emphasized.

6:18 The **priests** and **Levites** are set **in their divisions**, i.e., according to the roster for duty in the temple, as King David had once done (1 Chronicles 23–27). The phrase **as it is written in the Book of Moses** applies to the general assignment of the priests and Levites to their respective duties (Numbers 3; 8) rather than to the system of divisions outlined in Chronicles.

6:19–22 (The narrative returns to Hebrew in v. 19; see note on 4:7–8.) The **Passover** is **kept** on its appointed date, followed immediately by the **Feast of Unleavened Bread** (6:22), which lasts for **seven days** (Lev. 23:5–6). The priests and Levites **had purified themselves** and **were clean** (Ezra 6:20); i.e., they had made the necessary ritual preparations. The participants are the **people of Israel**, the **returned** exiles again representing the whole, and the people of the land **who had joined them** (see note on v. 21). **the Lord had made them joyful** (v. 22). He had fulfilled his prophecies and answered his people's prayers. There is spontaneous joy when God's people see evidence that he is working in the world. The reference to the **king of Assyria** (v. 22) at first seems odd because kings of Persia have supported the Jews in Ezra. The reference here, however, is based on the continuity of the various empires. The king of Persia now ruled over the territorial empire of the Assyrians, and thus he could be called "king of Assyria" (cf. Herodotus, *History* 1.178, in a discussion of Cyrus's conquests, where Babylon is called the strongest city "in Assyria"). This wording emphasizes the turn in fortunes,

Kings of Persia Mentioned in Ezra–Nehemiah

Cyrus	539–530 B.C.
Darius I	522–486
Xerxes (Ahasuerus)	485–464
Artaxerxes I	464–423

Zerubbabel's Temple

The rebuilding of Jerusalem's temple was done in stages (c. 536–516 B.C.). First, the altar was built, so that sacrifices could again be made (Ezra 3:2–3). The second phase was the laying of the foundation of the temple. This elicited mixed reactions from the people. Some rejoiced that the foundation was laid, while others, especially the elder priests, were sad, presumably because the quality of construction was inferior to that of the previous temple. Due to the opposition of the local population and the lack of motivation among the Jews, it took 20 years to complete the construction of the temple building.

The only information given in the biblical record about the architecture of the temple is the dimensions, which were sixty cubits (90 feet/27 m) high and wide (Ezra 6:3). As there is no mention of the length of the building, these dimensions must refer to the facade of the temple, i.e., the Porch.

for themselves. 21 It was eaten by the people of Israel who had returned from exile, and
[q]also by every one who had joined them and separated himself [r]from the uncleanness of
the peoples of the land to worship the LORD, the God of Israel. 22 And they kept the Feast
of Unleavened Bread [s]seven days with joy, for the LORD had made them joyful [t]and had
turned the heart of [u]the king of Assyria to them, so that he aided them in the work of the
house of God, the God of Israel.

Ezra Sent to Teach the People

7 Now after this, [v]in the reign of [v]Artaxerxes king of Persia, [w]Ezra the son of Seraiah,
son of Azariah, son of Hilkiah, 2 son of Shallum, son of Zadok, son of Ahitub, 3 son of
Amariah, son of Azariah, son of Meraioth, 4 son of Zerahiah, son of Uzzi, son of Bukki,
5 son of Abishua, son of Phinehas, son of Eleazar, son of Aaron the chief priest— 6 this Ezra
went up from Babylonia. He was a scribe [x]skilled in the Law of Moses that the LORD, the
God of Israel, had given, and the king granted him all that he asked, [y]for the hand of the
LORD his God was on him.

7 And there went up also to Jerusalem, in the seventh year of Artaxerxes the king, some
of the people of Israel, and [z]some of the priests and [a]Levites, the singers and gatekeepers,
and the temple [b]servants. 8 And Ezra[1] came to Jerusalem in the fifth month, which was
in the seventh year of the king. 9 For on the first day of the first month he began to go up
from Babylonia, and on the first day of the fifth month he came to Jerusalem, [c]for the good
hand of his God was on him. 10 For Ezra had set his heart to study the Law of the LORD,
and to do it [d]and to [e]teach his statutes and rules in Israel.

11 This is a copy of the letter that King Artaxerxes gave to Ezra the priest, the scribe, a

[1] Aramaic *he*

21 [q]Neh. 9:2; 10:28; [ch. 9:1] [r]ch. 9:11
22 [s]Ex. 12:15; 13:6; 2 Chr. 30:21; 35:17 [t]ch. 7:27; [Prov. 21:1] [u][Neh. 13:6]

Chapter 7

1 [v]Neh. 2:1 [w]For ver. 1-5, see 1 Chr. 6:4-14
6 [x]ver. 11, 12, 21; Neh. 8:1-3, 13; 12:26, 36 [y]ver. 9, 28; ch. 8:18, 22, 31; Neh. 2:8, 18; [ch. 5:5]
7 [z]See ch. 8:1-14 [a]ch. 8:15-19 [b]ch. 8:17, 20; [ch. 2:43]
9 [c]See ver. 6
10 [d]ver. 25; [Deut. 33:10] [e][2 Chr. 17:7; Mal. 2:7; Matt. 23:2, 3]; See Neh. 8:1-8

under God, since the Assyrians had been used as God's agent of punishment centuries before (Neh. 9:32; Isa. 10:5–11).

6:21 Remarkably, the returning Jews are joined by **every one who had . . . separated himself from the uncleanness of the peoples of the land to worship the LORD.** This shows that the community was essentially religious, rather than based merely on physical birth and lineage, and that outsiders could convert into it.

7:1–8:36 *Ezra the Priest Comes to Jerusalem to Establish the Law of Moses.* The narrative now skips to a time 57 years later (see note on 7:1–7), when Ezra the scribe is commissioned by King Artaxerxes to establish the Torah of Moses in the Jerusalem community. This section recounts Ezra's commission, his journey, and his companions.

7:1–28 *King Artaxerxes Gives Ezra Authority to Establish the Mosaic Law.* This section describes how Artaxerxes gave Ezra the authority to establish the Mosaic law in the province of Yehud (i.e., Judah), to appoint magistrates to administer that law, and to provide for the further adornment of the temple.

7:1–7 Ezra is introduced first as a priest, his lineage going back to **Aaron the chief priest** (v. 5), the brother of Moses (cf. Ex. 4:14; 28:1–2). He comes **in the reign of Artaxerxes** (Ezra 7:1), in the **seventh year** (v. 7), i.e., 458 B.C.—57 years after the temple dedication.

7:6–7 Ezra is also **a scribe skilled in the Law of Moses**. No doubt God raised up a scribe with expert knowledge of the law because, after 70 years of exile, the people badly need instruction in how to live according to the Law of Moses. Ezra has apparently asked the king for permission and resources to go **to Jerusalem** (v. 7). **Artaxerxes** is supportive, again at the prompting of God, who gives favor to Ezra: **and the king granted him all that he asked, for the hand of the LORD his God was on him** (see notes on 1:1; 6:14). He comes with a new wave of migrants, **priests**, laity, and **Levites**, including **singers** and **gatekeepers** (7:7; see note on 2:36–58). The return of exiles did not happen all at once.

7:9 the first month . . . the fifth month. The journey from Babylon to Jerusalem had taken nearly four months. It was about 900 miles (1,448 km). This was a slow pace, probably because the caravan included children and elderly people. (And 8:31 indicates that there was an 11-day delay before departure.)

7:10 Ezra's mission was to teach God's **statutes and rules,** i.e., the extensive laws of God given to Moses in addition to the Ten Commandments (see Deut. 4:1; 5:1), under the general rubric of **the Law** (Hb. *torah*) **of the LORD.** These are contained throughout Exodus to Deuteronomy, especially in Exodus 20–23, Leviticus, and Deuteronomy 12–26. Readers are told nothing of how this mission came to be in Ezra's heart. The terms **study**, **do**, and **teach** (indeed, the whole account of Ezra 7–10) present Ezra as the ideal priest in Israel, whose task is to lead God's people in worship and holiness of life (see Deut. 33:10): his ministry stems from a faithful life (cf. Mal. 2:1–9; 1 Tim. 4:6–16).

7:11–28 This section tells how Artaxerxes supports Ezra by commissioning

The Hand of God in Ezra and Nehemiah

Ezra 7:6	The king granted Ezra all that he asked	for the hand of the Lord his God was on him
Ezra 7:9	Ezra began to go up from Babylon and came to Jerusalem	for the good hand of his God was on him
Ezra 7:28	Ezra took courage before the king and his men, and gathered leading men from Israel to go with him	for the hand of the Lord his God was on him
Ezra 8:18	Ezra is sent ministers for the house of God	by the good hand of their God on them
Ezra 8:22	On all who seek God	the hand of their God is for good
Ezra 8:31	God delivered them from the hand of the enemy and from ambushes by the way	[for] the hand of their God was on them
Neh. 2:8	King Artaxerxes granted what Nehemiah asked	for the good hand of his God was upon him

12[f]Ezek. 26:7; Dan. 2:37 [g]See ver. 6 [h]ch. 4:11, 17
13[i]ch. 6:8
14[j]ver. 15, 28; ch. 8:25; [Esth. 1:14]
15[j][See ver. 14 above] [k]2 Chr. 6:2; [Ps. 135:21]
16[l]ch. 8:25 [m]1 Chr. 29:6, 9
17[n]Deut. 12:5, 11
24[o]ch. 4:13, 20
25[p]Ex. 18:21, 22; Deut. 16:18 [q]See ver. 10
27[r]1 Chr. 29:10 [s]ch. 6:22
28[t]ch. 9:9

man learned in matters of the commandments of the LORD and his statutes for Israel:
12"Artaxerxes, [f]king of kings, to Ezra the priest, the [g]scribe of the Law of the God of heaven.
Peace.[1] [h]And now **13** [i]I make a decree that anyone of the people of Israel or their priests
or Levites in my kingdom, who freely offers to go to Jerusalem, may go with you. **14** For
you are sent by the king [j]and his seven counselors to make inquiries about Judah and
Jerusalem according to the Law of your God, which is in your hand, **15** and also to carry
the silver and gold that the king [j]and his counselors have freely offered to the God of
Israel, [k]whose dwelling is in Jerusalem, **16** [l]with all the silver and gold that you shall find
in the whole province of Babylonia, and [m]with the freewill offerings of the people and the
priests, vowed willingly for the house of their God that is in Jerusalem. **17** With this money,
then, you shall with all diligence buy bulls, rams, and lambs, with their grain offerings
and their drink offerings, and [n]you shall offer them on the altar of the house of your God
that is in Jerusalem. **18** Whatever seems good to you and your brothers to do with the rest
of the silver and gold, you may do, according to the will of your God. **19** The vessels that
have been given you for the service of the house of your God, you shall deliver before the
God of Jerusalem. **20** And whatever else is required for the house of your God, which it falls
to you to provide, you may provide it out of the king's treasury.

21 "And I, Artaxerxes the king, make a decree to all the treasurers in the province Beyond
the River: Whatever Ezra the priest, the scribe of the Law of the God of heaven, requires of
you, let it be done with all diligence, **22** up to 100 talents[2] of silver, 100 cors[3] of wheat, 100
baths[4] of wine, 100 baths of oil, and salt without prescribing how much. **23** Whatever is
decreed by the God of heaven, let it be done in full for the house of the God of heaven, lest
his wrath be against the realm of the king and his sons. **24** We also notify you that it shall
not be lawful to impose [o]tribute, custom, or toll on anyone of the priests, the Levites, the
singers, the doorkeepers, the temple servants, or other servants of this house of God.

25 "And you, Ezra, according to the wisdom of your God that is in your hand, [p]appoint
magistrates and judges who may judge all the people in the province Beyond the River,
all such as know the laws of your God. [q]And those who do not know them, you shall teach.
26 Whoever will not obey the law of your God and the law of the king, let judgment be
strictly executed on him, whether for death or for banishment or for confiscation of his
goods or for imprisonment."

27 [r]Blessed be the LORD, the God of our fathers, [s]who put such a thing as this into the
heart of the king, to beautify the house of the LORD that is in Jerusalem, **28** [t]and who
extended to me his steadfast love before the king and his counselors, and before all the

[1] Aramaic *Perfect* (probably a greeting) [2] A *talent* was about 75 pounds or 34 kilograms [3] A *cor* was about 6 bushels or 220 liters [4] A *bath* was about 6 gallons or 22 liters

him and providing further for the temple. The text of the letter (vv. 12–26) is in Aramaic (see note on 4:7–8).

7:11 The king's decree is in the form of a **letter** addressed to **Ezra**, which could be used to enforce the king's command.

7:12 The title **king of kings** was used by kings of Persia and expresses their sovereignty over many subject peoples. Ezra is called **the scribe of the Law of the God of heaven**, which possibly refers to a kind of responsibility for Jewish affairs that he already held in Babylon.

7:13 The **decree** echoes that of Cyrus in authorizing any Jews who wish **to go to Jerusalem** (see 1:3).

7:14 The commission to **make inquiries about Judah and Jerusalem according to the Law of your God** no doubt reflects Ezra's own priority, and perhaps his belief that the law is not being properly kept.

7:15–20 Artaxerxes turns to the needs of the temple, perhaps showing his own perception of Ezra's task, in accordance with Cyrus's original decree in 538 B.C., 80 years earlier (see note on 1:1).

7:15–16 The **king and his counselors** give money for the temple and permit Ezra to gather further resources in the **whole province of Babylonia**, perhaps from non-Jews as well as Jews.

7:17–18 The provision specifies the temple worship but also leaves extensive discretion to Ezra in his expenditure.

7:19–20 vessels . . . for the service of the house of your God. Artaxerxes adds these to the temple treasures originally returned by Cyrus, apparently as his own gift, and, finally, allows Ezra to take whatever he needs from the **king's treasury** (v. 20), i.e., from public funds.

7:21 The **decree** now specifically addresses the royal treasury officials in **Beyond the River**, compelling them to make provision for Ezra up to specified limits.

7:22 The talent was 75 pounds (34 kg), and the amount of **silver** specified has been estimated at between a quarter and a third of all the annual taxation raised in "Beyond the River." The **wheat**, **wine**, and **oil** would have been used for cereal offerings, for drink offerings, and for the lamp kept lit in the temple (Ex. 27:20; 29:2). With a "cor" at 6 bushels (220 liters) and a "bath" at 6 gallons (23 liters), the quantities would have supplied the temple's needs for perhaps two years. **Salt**, supplied without limit, was for preservation and seasoning (Ex. 30:35; Lev. 2:13).

7:23 In making these provisions (v. 22), the king may actually intend to ward off the **wrath** of God against the **king and his sons**, i.e., his own kingdom, present and future (see also 6:10).

7:27 Blessed be the LORD . . . who put such a thing as this into the heart of the king. See note on 1:1. **to beautify the house of the LORD**. The author uses the same terms as Isa. 60:7 (see note), indicating that he sees this event as fulfillment of Isaiah's prophecy.

king's mighty officers. I took courage, for the hand of the LORD my God was on me, and
I gathered leading men from Israel to go up with me.

Genealogy of Those Who Returned with Ezra

8 These are the heads of their fathers' houses, and this is the genealogy of those who
went up with me from Babylonia, in the reign of Artaxerxes the king: 2 Of the sons
of Phinehas, Gershom. Of the sons of [u]Ithamar, Daniel. Of the sons of David, [v]Hattush.
3 Of the sons of Shecaniah, who was of the sons of [w]Parosh, Zechariah, with whom were
registered 150 men. 4 [x]Of the sons of Pahath-moab, Eliehoenai the son of Zerahiah, and
with him 200 men. 5 Of the sons of Zattu,[1] Shecaniah the son of Jahaziel, and with him
300 men. 6 Of the sons of Adin, Ebed the son of Jonathan, and with him 50 men. 7 Of
the sons of Elam, Jeshaiah the son of Athaliah, and with him 70 men. 8 Of the sons of
Shephatiah, Zebadiah the son of Michael, and with him 80 men. 9 Of the sons of Joab,
Obadiah the son of Jehiel, and with him 218 men. 10 Of the sons of Bani,[2] Shelomith the
son of Josiphiah, and with him 160 men. 11 [y]Of the sons of Bebai, Zechariah, the son of
Bebai, and with him 28 men. 12 Of the sons of Azgad, Johanan the son of Hakkatan, and
with him 110 men. 13 Of the sons of Adonikam, those who came later, their names being
Eliphelet, Jeuel, and Shemaiah, and with them 60 men. 14 Of the sons of Bigvai, Uthai and
Zaccur, and with them 70 men.

Ezra Sends for Levites

15 I gathered them to the river that runs to [z]Ahava, and there we camped three days. As I
reviewed the people and the priests, I found there [a]none of the sons of Levi. 16 Then I sent for
Eliezer, Ariel, Shemaiah, Elnathan, Jarib, Elnathan, Nathan, Zechariah, and [b]Meshullam,
leading men, and for Joiarib and Elnathan, who were men of insight, 17 and sent them
to Iddo, the leading man at the place Casiphia, telling them what to say to Iddo and his
brothers and[3] the temple servants at the place Casiphia, namely, to send us ministers for
the house of our God. 18 And [c]by the good hand of our God on us, they brought us a man
of discretion, of the sons of [d]Mahli the son of Levi, son of Israel, namely Sherebiah with
his sons and kinsmen, 18; 19 also [e]Hashabiah, and with him Jeshaiah of [f]the sons of Merari,
with his kinsmen and their sons, 20; 20 [g]besides 220 of the temple servants, whom David
and his officials had set apart to attend the Levites. These were all [h]mentioned by name.

Fasting and Prayer for Protection

21 [i]Then I proclaimed a fast there, at the river [j]Ahava, that we might humble ourselves
before our God, [k]to seek from him a safe journey for ourselves, our children, and all our
goods. 22 For I was ashamed to ask the king for a band of soldiers and horsemen to protect
us against the enemy on our way, since we had told the king, [l]"The hand of our God is for

[1] Septuagint; Hebrew lacks *of Zattu* [2] Septuagint; Hebrew lacks *Bani* [3] Hebrew lacks *and*

Chapter 8
2 [u]1 Chr. 24:3, 4 [v][1 Chr. 3:22]
3 [w]For ver. 3, see ch. 2:3-15
4 [x]ch. 10:30
11 [y]ch. 10:28
15 [z]ver. 21, 31 [a][ch. 7:7]
16 [b]ch. 10:15
18 [c]See ch. 7:6 [d]1 Chr. 6:19
19 [e]Neh. 12:24 [f]1 Chr. 6:1, 16
20 [g]ch. 2:43; 7:7 [h]Num. 1:17
21 [i]See 2 Chr. 20:3 [j]ver. 15, 31 [k][Ps. 5:8]
22 [l]See ch. 7:6

8:1–36 *Ezra Journeys to Jerusalem with a New Wave of Returnees, Bearing Royal Gifts for the Temple.* This section gives a more extended account of Ezra's return to Jerusalem. Readers learn of those who returned with Ezra (vv. 1–14), of how he recruited additional priests (vv. 15–20), of their prayer for the journey (vv. 21–23), and of Ezra's provision for the temple (vv. 24–36).

8:1–14 The party that returned with Ezra was a considerable addition to the community in Judah. It is numbered here according to the **heads of their fathers' houses**, i.e., heads of families (v. 1). Their **genealogy** refers to their formal registration in the list of those returning (as in v. 3, **registered**, which translates the same Hb. word). There are two priestly divisions, namely, **Phinehas** (v. 2; son of Eleazar, Num. 25:7) and **Ithamar** (Ezra 8:2; see Ex. 28:1). These were the remaining sons of Aaron following the judgment on Nadab and Abihu (Lev. 10:1–7). Ezra himself was of the line of Phinehas (Ezra 7:5). **Daniel** (8:2) is otherwise unknown, and is not the Daniel who was carried off to Babylon in 605 B.C. (see Dan. 1:1, 6; also note on Dan. 1:1–2), for this is now 458 (see note on Ezra 7:1–7). A third division is a line of **David** (8:2; for **Hattush**, see 1 Chron. 3:22). Ezra's party therefore aims to replenish the priesthood, and perhaps also to renew the claims of the Davidic house to rule in Judah.

8:15 The party camps outside Babylon at the **river that runs to Ahava**, no doubt one of the network of canals extending from the Euphrates. Ezra discovers that, though he had priests with him, there were **none of the sons of Levi**, i.e., the lower order of clergy, the Levites (see 2:40).

8:17 Nothing is known of **Iddo** or of **Casiphia**, to which Ezra's delegation (v. 16) is sent. But it was apparently a place where Levites and **temple servants** (see 2:43–54; 1 Chron. 9:2) might be expected to be found, and perhaps where they continued to be trained for the day when there would be a temple again in Jerusalem.

8:18–19 Mahli and **Merari** belong to the same Levitical family, Merari being a **son of Levi** (Num. 3:33).

8:20 The number of those who respond to Ezra's call is small, but symbolically important for the nation's future.

8:21 a fast. The custom of fasting grew in importance in the exile as part of a spirit of penitence (see Neh. 9:1; Est. 4:3). **humble ourselves**. This implied a deliberate penitential attitude, as in the Day of Atonement (Lev. 16:31). Yet the prayer (Ezra 8:22–23) chiefly expresses the people's trust in God as they sought to demonstrate his reality to the Persian king. The king's ongoing support, they know, may depend on his belief in the reality and power of the God of Israel.

8:22 On **the power of his wrath**, see 6:10 and 7:23. Contrast Ezra's policy in 8:22 with Nehemiah's (Neh. 2:9).

22[m][2 Chr. 15:2]
24[e][See ver. 19 above]
25[n]ch. 7:15, 16 [o]See ch. 7:14
26[p][ch. 1:9-11]
28[q]Lev. 21:6 [r]Lev. 22:2, 3
29[s][ch. 10:6]
30[p][See ver. 26 above]
31[t][ch. 7:9] [u]See ch. 7:6
32[v]Neh. 2:11
33[w][ch. 1:9-11] [x]Neh. 3:4, 21 [y]Neh. 11:16 [z]Neh. 3:24
35[a]ch. 2:1 [b][ch. 6:17]
36[c]ch. 7:21 [d]Esth. 3:12; 8:9; 9:3; Dan. 3:2, 3, 27; 6:2, 3
Chapter 9
1[e][ch. 6:21; Neh. 9:2] [f]Deut. 12:30, 31 [g]See Ex. 13:5

good on [m]all who seek him, and the power of his wrath is against all who forsake him."
23 So we fasted and implored our God for this, and he listened to our entreaty.

Priests to Guard Offerings

24 Then I set apart twelve of the leading priests: [e]Sherebiah, [e]Hashabiah, and ten of
their kinsmen with them. 25 And I weighed out to them the [n]silver and the gold and the
vessels, the offering for the house of our God that the king and his [o]counselors and his
lords and all Israel there present had offered. 26 [p]I weighed out into their hand 650 talents[1]
of silver, and silver vessels worth 200 talents,[2] and 100 talents of gold, 27 20 bowls of gold
worth 1,000 darics,[3] and two vessels of fine bright bronze as precious as gold. 28 And I said
to them, [q]"You are holy to the LORD, and [r]the vessels are holy, and the silver and the gold
are a freewill offering to the LORD, the God of your fathers. 29 Guard them and keep them
until you weigh them before the chief priests and the Levites and the heads of fathers'
houses in Israel at Jerusalem, [s]within the chambers of the house of the LORD." 30 So the
priests and the Levites [p]took over the weight of the silver and the gold and the vessels, to
bring them to Jerusalem, to the house of our God.
31 Then we departed from the river Ahava [t]on the twelfth day of the first month, to go
to Jerusalem. [u]The hand of our God was on us, and he delivered us from the hand of the
enemy and from ambushes by the way. 32 [v]We came to Jerusalem, and there we remained
three days. 33 On the fourth day, within the house of our God, the silver and the gold and
the vessels were [w]weighed into the hands of [x]Meremoth the priest, son of Uriah, and with
him was Eleazar the son of Phinehas, and with them were the Levites, [y]Jozabad the son of
Jeshua and Noadiah the son of [z]Binnui. 34 The whole was counted and weighed, and the
weight of everything was recorded.
35 At that time [a]those who had come from captivity, the returned exiles, offered burnt
offerings to the God of Israel, [b]twelve bulls for all Israel, ninety-six rams, seventy-seven
lambs, and as a sin offering twelve male goats. All this was a burnt offering to the LORD.
36 [c]They also delivered the king's commissions to the king's [d]satraps[4] and to the governors
of the province Beyond the River, and they aided the people and the house of God.

Ezra Prays About Intermarriage

9 After these things had been done, the officials approached me and said, "The people of
Israel and the priests and the [e]Levites have not separated themselves from the peoples
of the lands [f]with their abominations, from the [g]Canaanites, the Hittites, the Perizzites,

[1] A *talent* was about 75 pounds or 34 kilograms [2] Revocalization; the number is missing in the Masoretic Text [3] A *daric* was a coin weighing about 1/4 ounce or 8.5 grams [4] A *satrap* was a Persian official

8:23 and he listened to our entreaty. God's oversight of the events of history is the background against which this entire book is written (cf. v. 31; also note on 1:1).

8:24–36 Ezra entrusts the offerings that he has gathered for the temple to the priests who are with him (see 7:15–16, 22).

8:26 The amounts of **silver** and **gold** are extraordinarily large, the silver weighing around 25 tons (22 metric tons) and the gold 3.75 tons (3.4 metric tons).

8:28 The priests themselves are **holy to the LORD** (Ex. 29:1), namely, set aside for his service, and the precious metals and **vessels** have been donated into the holy sphere, and so they are also **holy** (see Ex. 30:26–29 for consecrated utensils).

8:29–30 The holy **vessels** are rightly entrusted to the **priests**; they remain in priestly possession until handed over to their counterparts in the temple itself.

8:31 The group sets out **on the twelfth day of the first month** (Nisan, March/April); the plan to leave on the first day (7:9) had been delayed by the need to send for more Levites. **he delivered us from the hand of the enemy.** Whether there were actual attacks on the group is not said, but God's protection on the journey makes this departure from Babylon resemble the ancient exodus of Israel from Egypt (e.g., Ex. 17:8–13; cf. notes on Ezra 1:1; 8:21; 8:22; 8:23).

8:32 We came to Jerusalem. This was on the first day of the fifth month (Ab, July/August; cf. 7:9), so the journey of roughly 900 miles (1,448 km) lasted nearly four months (see note on 7:9).

8:33–34 After a three-day rest, the treasures for the temple are handed over to the priests as planned (vv. 28–30).

8:35 For these **exiles** it is a first chance to see and worship at the rebuilt temple, and their sacrifices resemble those made at its first dedication (see 6:16–17). **twelve bulls.** See note on 6:16–17.

8:36 to the king's satraps and to the governors. A "satrap" was a governor of a "satrapy" (province), such as Beyond the River. The double expression here (satraps, governors) is a loose way of referring to the governing officials in general, who continue to have good relations with the community in Judah.

9:1–10:44 *Ezra Discovers and Confronts the Problem of Intermarriage.* Ezra discovers that the Jewish community has mixed with idolatrous non-Jewish groups in religion and in marriage, and he leads the community in an act of repentance and in a systematic separation from the foreign women and their children.

9:1–15 *Ezra Discovers the Problem of Marriage to Idolaters, and Prays.* Ezra hears the news of the marriages to adherents of other religions, and he prays for the people.

9:1–2 For **the peoples of the lands**, see note on 3:3. They are further identified as idolatrous nations, for **the Canaanites, the Hittites, the Perizzites, the Jebusites, . . . and the Amorites** are among the seven nations that Israel was commanded by Moses to drive out of the land (see

the Jebusites, the Ammonites, the Moabites, the Egyptians, and the Amorites. 2 [h]For they
have taken some of their daughters to be wives for themselves and for their sons, so that
the [i]holy race[1] has [j]mixed itself with the peoples of the lands. And in this faithlessness the
hand of the officials and chief men has been foremost." 3 As soon as I heard this, I [k]tore my
garment and my cloak and pulled hair from my head and beard and [l]sat appalled. 4 Then
all who [m]trembled at the words of the God of Israel, because of the faithlessness of the
returned exiles, gathered around me while I sat [n]appalled until the evening sacrifice. 5 And
at the [n]evening sacrifice I rose from my fasting, with my garment [k]and my cloak torn, and
fell upon my knees [o]and spread out my hands to the LORD my God, 6 saying:

"O my God, I am ashamed and blush to lift my face to you, my God, for our iniquities
[p]have risen higher than our heads, and our [q]guilt has [r]mounted up to the heavens. 7 [s]From
the days of our fathers to this day we have been in great [q]guilt. And for our iniquities we,
our kings, and our priests have been given into the hand of the kings of the lands, to the
sword, to captivity, to plundering, [t]and to utter shame, as it is today. 8 But now for a brief
moment favor has been shown by the LORD our God, to leave us a [u]remnant and to give
us a [v]secure hold[2] within his holy place, that our God may [w]brighten our eyes and grant
us a little reviving in our slavery. 9 [x]For we are slaves. Yet our God has not forsaken us in
our slavery, [y]but has extended to us his steadfast love before the kings of Persia, to grant
us some reviving to set up the house of our God, to repair its ruins, and to give us protection[3] in Judea and Jerusalem.

10 "And now, O our God, what shall we say after this? For we have forsaken your commandments, 11 which you commanded by your servants the prophets, saying, 'The land
that you are entering, to take possession of it, is a land impure with the impurity of the
peoples of the lands, with their abominations that have filled it from end to end with
[z]their uncleanness. 12 [a]Therefore do not give your daughters to their sons, neither take
their daughters for your sons, and never seek their peace or prosperity, that you may be
strong and eat the good of the land [b]and leave it for an inheritance to your children forever.'

[1] Hebrew *offspring* [2] Hebrew *nail, or tent-pin* [3] Hebrew *a wall*

2 [h]ch. 10:2; Neh. 13:23, 27; [Ex. 34:16; Deut. 7:3; Neh. 10:30] [i]See Deut. 7:6 [j]Ps. 106:35; [2 Cor. 6:14]
3 [k]See Josh. 7:6 [l][Neh. 1:4]
4 [m]ch. 10:3; Isa. 66:2, 5 [n]Ex. 29:39, 41
5 [n][See ver. 4 above] [k][See ver. 3 above] [o]1 Kgs. 8:22
6 [p][Ps. 38:4] [q]ver. 7, 13, 15; ch. 10:10, 19; 2 Chr. 24:18 [r][2 Chr. 28:9; Rev. 18:5]
7 [s]Ps. 106:6; Dan. 9:5, 6 [q][See ver. 6 above] [t]Dan. 9:7, 8
8 [u]ver. 13, 14, 15 [v]Isa. 22:23 [w]Ps. 13:3
9 [x][Neh. 9:36] [y]ch. 7:28
11 [z]ch. 6:21
12 [a]See ver. 2 [b][Prov. 13:22]

Deut. 7:1–5). The **Ammonites** and **Moabites** were nations east of the river Jordan, outside the Promised Land, who were regarded as especially hostile to Israel (Deut. 23:3–4). And in Lev. 18:3, Egypt is regarded as morally equal to Canaan. The peoples of the land who keep themselves distinct from the returned temple-community are thus portrayed as the same in principle and in character as these ancient enemies. These are specifically **wives** (Ezra 9:2) of foreign nations who had not abandoned their worship of other gods, for 6:21 makes it clear that such people could join the people of Israel if they were willing to follow the Lord God alone (see note on 6:21). **Their abominations** (9:1) refers to these peoples' worship of other gods and the associated practices that Yahweh, God of Israel, regarded as particularly wicked (Deut. 12:31). It is implied that the foreigners' religions in Ezra's day were just as idolatrous as in ancient times, and thus it is clear that the issue is not ethnic purity (cf. Ezra 6:21). Intermarriage with the indigenous population carried the danger of religious apostasy, and therefore was expressly forbidden by the law (Deut. 7:3). The **holy race** (Ezra 9:2) is literally "holy seed/offspring" and alludes to the "offspring" of Abraham, who bore the ancient promise of covenant and land (Gen. 12:1–3; 15:5; 17:7–8). The "holy seed" was also seen in prophecy as the surviving remnant that would be brought to life again after the terrible judgment of the exile (Isa. 6:13). The involvement of all classes of the community—the **priests**, the **Levites**, and the **people of Israel** (Ezra 9:1), as well as the **officials and chief men** (v. 2)—shows that the problem included all the people. The term **faithlessness** (Hb. *ma'al*, v. 2) is an extremely strong expression for abandonment of the faith, especially by leaders (see 1 Chron. 10:13, where it is translated "breach of faith").

9:3 Ezra expresses his deep dismay by performing ritual acts of mourning. His severe reaction results from the fact that the "holy race" has compromised its newly won salvation by returning to the sins that had brought judgment in the first place.

9:4 trembled at the words of the God of Israel. An expression for pious eagerness to obey God, and respect for his holiness (cf. Isa. 66:2).

9:6–7 Ezra confesses sin on behalf of the covenant community, beginning with the historic sins of Israel that had led to the Babylonian exile.

9:6 our iniquities . . . our guilt. These two strong terms (Hb. *'awon*, "iniquity," and *'ashmah*, "guilt") are each repeated twice here. Ezra recognizes the justice of the punishment of exile.

9:7 the days of our fathers. That is, the time before the exile (see Zech. 1:4). The terms **sword**, **captivity**, **plundering**, and **shame** sum up the disasters experienced by the people because they failed to keep the covenant, and bring to mind the covenantal consequences for disobedience noted in Lev. 26:14–39 and Deut. 28:15–68 (cf. 2 Kings 17:20; Jer. 24:9–10).

9:8 for a brief moment favor. Ezra refers to the time since Cyrus's edict. This was nearly a century, but was short in the sweep of Israel's history. The idea of a **remnant** could be attached to notions of God's judgment, for it can refer to a small remnant left afterward, or to the subject of renewed punishment (see Isa. 6:13a; 10:22; Jer. 24:8). But prophets also spoke positively of a remnant of Israel who would repent and be restored after the purifying judgment of exile, and who would continue to bear the identity and destiny of Israel (see Isa. 10:20–21; Jer. 24:4–7 also has the idea, though not the term). Ezra applies the term to the returned exiles (as does Nehemiah [Neh. 1:2]). **his holy place.** This refers narrowly to the temple and more broadly to the land of Judah.

9:9 we are slaves . . . in our slavery. The idea that the exiles remain slaves is unexpected after their restoration to the land, but acknowledges that they are still under the foreign authority of **Persia** (see Neh. 9:36–37). Therefore, the favorable view of Persia thus far does not prevent the exiles' aspiration to complete freedom. Even so, though they are under this foreign authority, God has shown **steadfast love**, the special quality of faithful love that characterizes his attachment to Israel in the covenant, and that he expects in return (Hos. 6:6).

9:10–12 Ezra alludes to Deut. 7:1–5 and the present community's breach of its prohibition of intermarriage.

9:11 impure . . . impurity . . . uncleanness. Ezra uses language from the "holiness" vocabulary to stress the incompatibility of the indigenous people's way of life and worship with that mandated by the holy God of Israel.

13[c]ver. 6, 7 [d]Job 11:6; Ps. 103:10 [e]ver. 8
14[f]See ver. 2 [g][Deut. 9:8] [e][See ver. 13 above]
15[e][See ver. 13 above] [h]Neh. 9:33; Ps. 119:137; Jer. 12:1; Dan. 9:14 [i]Ps. 130:3

Chapter 10

1[j]Neh. 1:4, 5 [k]Neh. 1:6; Dan. 9:20 [l]Deut. 9:18 [m][2 Chr. 20:9]
2[n]See ch. 9:2
3[o]2 Chr. 34:31 [p][ver. 44] [q]ch. 9:4 [r]Deut. 7:2, 3
4[s]1 Chr. 28:10; [2 Chr. 19:11]
5[t]Neh. 5:12; 13:25
6[u]ver. 1 [v]ch. 8:29 [w]Neh. 12:22, 23 [x]Neh. 3:1 [y]Deut. 9:18

13 And after all that has come upon us for our evil deeds and for [c]our great guilt, seeing
that you, our [d]God, have punished us less than our iniquities deserved and have given us
such a [e]remnant as this, 14 shall we break your commandments again and [f]intermarry with
the peoples who practice these abominations? Would you not be angry with us [g]until you
consumed us, so that there should be no [e]remnant, nor any to escape? 15 O LORD, the God
of Israel, you are just, for we are left a [e]remnant that has escaped, as it is today. Behold, we
are before you in our [h]guilt, [i]for none can stand before you because of this."

The People Confess Their Sin

10 [j]While Ezra prayed and [k]made confession, weeping and [l]casting himself down
[m]before the house of God, a very great assembly of men, women, and children,
gathered to him out of Israel, for the people wept bitterly. 2 And Shecaniah the son of
Jehiel, of the sons of Elam, addressed Ezra: [n]"We have broken faith with our God and
have married foreign women from the peoples of the land, but even now there is hope
for Israel in spite of this. 3 Therefore [o]let us make a covenant with our God to put away all
these wives and [p]their children, according to the counsel of my lord[1] and of [q]those who
tremble at the commandment of our God, and let it be done [r]according to the Law. 4 Arise,
for it is your task, and we are with you; [s]be strong and do it." 5 Then Ezra arose and made
the leading priests and Levites and all Israel [t]take an oath that they would do as had been
said. So they took the oath.

6 Then Ezra withdrew [u]from before the house of God and went to the [v]chamber of
[w]Jehohanan the son of [x]Eliashib, where he spent the night,[2] neither [y]eating bread nor
drinking water, for he was mourning over the faithlessness of the exiles. 7 And a proclamation was made throughout Judah and Jerusalem to all the returned exiles that they should
assemble at Jerusalem, 8 and that if anyone did not come within three days, by order of the
officials and the elders all his property should be forfeited, and he himself banned from
the congregation of the exiles.

9 Then all the men of Judah and Benjamin assembled at Jerusalem within the three days.
It was the ninth month, on the twentieth day of the month. And all the people sat in the
open square before the house of God, trembling because of this matter and because of the

[1] Or *of the Lord* [2] Probable reading; Hebrew *where he went*

9:15 Ezra knows that God is both **just** and merciful. (For God as "just," or "righteous," see also Deut. 32:4; Ps. 119:137.) The very existence of the postexilic **remnant** proves his mercy; yet equally God would be justified in bringing renewed judgment on the sinful people. The prayer serves as a petition for mercy, and it prompts Ezra and his close associates to turn the people from their sin.

10:1–17 *The People Agree to Dissolve the Marriages.* Ezra prays, and the people confess their sin (vv. 1–2). They agree to do God's will (vv. 3–5). Ezra seeks an answer (vv. 6–8), which is for them to separate from their wives (vv. 9–12), and the people obey (vv. 13–17).

10:1 Ezra's own report of the events (7:27–9:15) now gives way to a different narrative voice, though the account continues without a break. **a very great assembly**. Under God, Ezra's public prayer and demonstration of grief bring a large number of people to repentance, as shown by the statement that they **wept bitterly**. The term "assembly" is used for a formal gathering of Israel as a religious community.

10:2 Shecaniah speaks for the whole gathering, perhaps by prearrangement. **Jehiel**. See also v. 26; Shecaniah's own father may have had a mixed marriage. **broken faith**. See note on 9:1–2 concerning "faithlessness." The word translated **married** is not the usual one, but means literally "we have given a home"; Shecaniah's words may imply that these illicit relationships were not marriages in the full sense.

10:3 Shecaniah's belief that "there is hope for Israel" (v. 2) is dependent on making a **covenant** with **God**, meaning in this instance a solemn and binding promise to **put away** the foreign **wives and their children**. As with the term for "marriage," this is not the usual expression for "divorce," and may also imply that these were not proper marriages. The word means simply "bring out." In effect, this meant excommunicating them from the community of returned exiles. The text does not make clear any other details concerning matters of ongoing support and protection for these wives and their children (cf. v. 44), or concerning what happened to them (but see note on vv. 18–44). Because this represents a different situation in a different context as compared to 1 Cor. 7:12–14 (where Paul tells Christians not to divorce their unbelieving spouses), and because this example was recorded here in Ezra for descriptive rather than normative reasons, there would be no justification for anyone to take similar actions today. In Ezra's context, members of God's people had defied God's law in taking these wives, while Paul gives his instructions to people who probably converted after their marriage. **the counsel of my lord** (i.e., Ezra). Ezra may have already outlined a plan for taking care of the foreign wives and their children, even though it is not recorded here. **according to the Law**. That is, Deut. 7:1–5 (see note on Ezra 9:1–2). **those who tremble**. See note on 9:4.

10:4 be strong and do it. This is like the charge to Joshua at the first entry of Israel into the land (Josh. 1:6–7), and relates both to overcoming enemies and to keeping the law.

10:5 The **oath** is in effect the same as the covenant (v. 3). All three main sections of the community take this oath.

10:6 Jehohanan the son of Eliashib. Both names are common and appear in several lists in Ezra and Nehemiah (see Ezra 10:24, 27, 36; Neh. 12:10, 13). It is not always possible to know whether the same name refers to the same person. This family evidently had a caretaking role in the temple (see Neh. 13:4).

10:7 assemble at Jerusalem. Such assemblies normally occurred during the three regular pilgrimage feasts (Passover, Pentecost, Tabernacles); this was a special gathering, since the survival of the community was at stake.

10:8 banned from the congregation. Anyone who refused to participate in the plan to renounce the foreign wives and children would share their excommunication.

10:9 The **ninth month**, Chislev, is roughly December, the time of the so-called early rains. The people are **trembling** partly for fear of God (as in 9:4), and partly because they are cold and wet in the **heavy rain**.

[z]heavy rain. 10 And Ezra the priest stood up and said to them, "You have broken faith and
married foreign women, and so increased the guilt of Israel. 11 Now then [a]make confession
to the LORD, the God of your fathers and do his will. [b]Separate yourselves from the peoples
of the land and from the foreign wives." 12 Then all the assembly answered with a loud
voice, "It is so; we must do as you have said. 13 But the people are many, and it is a time of
heavy rain; we cannot stand in the open. Nor is this a task for one day or for two, for we
have greatly transgressed in this matter. 14 Let our officials stand for the whole assembly.
Let all in our cities who have taken foreign wives come [c]at appointed times, and with them
the elders and judges of every city, [d]until the fierce wrath of our God over this matter is
turned away from us." 15 Only Jonathan the son of Asahel and Jahzeiah the son of Tikvah
opposed this, and [e]Meshullam and [f]Shabbethai the Levite supported them.
16 Then the returned exiles did so. Ezra the priest selected men,[1] heads of fathers' houses,
according to their fathers' houses, each of them designated by name. On the first day of
the tenth month they sat down to examine the matter; 17 and by the first day of the first
month they had come to the end of all the men who had married foreign women.

Those Guilty of Intermarriage

18 Now there were found some of the sons of the priests who had married foreign women:
Maaseiah, Eliezer, Jarib, and Gedaliah, some of the sons of [g]Jeshua the son of Jozadak and
his brothers. 19 They [h]pledged themselves to put away their wives, and their guilt offering
was [i]a ram of the flock for their guilt.[2] 20 [j]Of the sons of Immer: Hanani and Zebadiah.
21 [k]Of the sons of Harim: Maaseiah, Elijah, Shemaiah, Jehiel, and Uzziah. 22 Of the sons of
Pashhur: Elioenai, Maaseiah, Ishmael, Nethanel, Jozabad, and Elasah.
23 Of the Levites: Jozabad, Shimei, Kelaiah (that is, Kelita), Pethahiah, Judah, and Eliezer.
24 Of the singers: Eliashib. Of the gatekeepers: Shallum, Telem, and Uri.
25 And of Israel: of the sons of Parosh: Ramiah, Izziah, Malchijah, Mijamin, Eleazar,
Hashabiah,[3] and Benaiah. 26 Of the sons of Elam: Mattaniah, Zechariah, Jehiel, Abdi,
Jeremoth, and Elijah. 27 Of the sons of Zattu: Elioenai, Eliashib, Mattaniah, Jeremoth,
Zabad, and Aziza. 28 Of the sons of Bebai were Jehohanan, Hananiah, Zabbai, and Athlai.
29 Of the sons of Bani were Meshullam, Malluch, Adaiah, Jashub, Sheal, and Jeremoth. 30 Of
the sons of Pahath-moab: Adna, Chelal, Benaiah, Maaseiah, Mattaniah, Bezalel, Binnui,
and Manasseh. 31 Of the [l]sons of Harim: Eliezer, Isshijah, Malchijah, Shemaiah, Shimeon,
32 Benjamin, Malluch, and Shemariah. 33 Of the sons of Hashum: Mattenai, Mattattah,
Zabad, Eliphelet, Jeremai, Manasseh, and Shimei. 34 Of the sons of [m]Bani: Maadai, Amram,
Uel, 35 Benaiah, Bedeiah, Cheluhi, 36 Vaniah, Meremoth, Eliashib, 37 Mattaniah, Mattenai,
Jaasu. 38 Of the sons of Binnui:[4] Shimei, 39 Shelemiah, Nathan, Adaiah, 40 Machnadebai,
Shashai, Sharai, 41 Azarel, Shelemiah, Shemariah, 42 Shallum, Amariah, and Joseph. 43 Of
the sons of Nebo: Jeiel, Mattithiah, Zabad, Zebina, Jaddai, Joel, and Benaiah. 44 All these
had married foreign women, and some of the women [n]had even borne children.[5]

[1] Syriac; Hebrew *And there were selected Ezra* . . . [2] Or *as their reparation* [3] Septuagint; Hebrew *Malchijah* [4] Septuagint; Hebrew *Bani, Binnui* [5] Or *and they put them away with their children*

9 [z][1 Sam. 12:18]
11 [a][Josh. 7:19] [b]ver. 3
14 [c]Neh. 13:31 [d]2 Chr. 29:10; 30:8; [Num. 25:4]
15 [e]ch. 8:16 [f]Neh. 11:16
18 [g]ch. 3:2
19 [h]See 2 Kgs. 10:15 [i]Lev. 6:6
20 [j]For ver. 20-43, see ch. 2:3-42
21 [k][ver. 31]
31 [l]ver. 21
34 [m][ver. 29]
44 [n][ver. 3]

10:10 The terms of Ezra's accusation have appeared already in 9:1–2, 4, 6–7; 10:2. **increased the guilt of Israel**. The return from exile had signified that all of Israel's past sins had been forgiven (Isa. 40:1–2). Ezra now points to renewed sin, beyond that which had previously been forgiven, and thus the possibility of the renewed wrath of God.

10:11 Make confession is based on Hebrew words that could also be translated in other contexts as "give thanks or praise" (Hb. *natan* + *todah*; cf. Josh. 7:19 and ESV footnote). Some overlap of these meanings is not surprising because rightful confession is itself a kind of worship of God.

10:12–15 The people as a whole respond with a solemn admission of their guilt and with resolution to act to address the problem, as in the making of a covenant (see also Ex. 19:8; 24:3, 7). They then propose a practical means of conducting the procedure.

10:14 wrath of our God. See note on v. 10.

10:15 opposed this. This probably means that these men opposed the entire resolution to put away the foreign wives. But the verse contains some ambiguity in Hebrew, and some interpreters think these men opposed the proposed means of proceeding because they wished to act more swiftly.

10:16–17 This summary account of the proceedings shows that it was undertaken by duly appointed authorities in the community, and thus it was not merely Ezra's doing. **examine the matter** (v. 16). The need for rigorous inquiry was an established part of the duties of judges (see Deut. 17:4). The whole inquiry took three months.

10:18–44 *List of Those Who Were Implicated.* The list of around a hundred names is surprisingly short, and may suggest a more limited problem than one might have expected. Either the list has been abbreviated or in fact those involved were few. In the latter case, the severe reaction of Ezra and the community recognizes the extreme danger that the whole community could face by the actions of only a few in this fundamental area of its covenantal life (compare the notion of purging "the evil from your midst," Deut. 17:7). The list is divided, typically for Ezra, into **priests** (Ezra 10:18), **Levites** (v. 23), and **Israel** (vv. 25–43). The **guilt offering** (v. 19) was presumably to be brought by each person in the list. The extensive inquiry must have considered each case separately. In some cases, a wife and her children might actually have adopted the religion of Israel, as anticipated and permitted in 6:21. The inquiry might have come down to an examination of such people's beliefs. Those who were turned away probably returned to their non-Jewish families.

INTRODUCTION TO

NEHEMIAH

Author and Title

Nehemiah is the central figure in the book, and it contains some of his own records, but he is not the author of the whole book. The author is probably the same as the author of Ezra (see Introduction to Ezra).

Date

For the key background dates to the book of Nehemiah, see Introduction to Ezra. Nehemiah arrived in Jerusalem in 445 B.C., 13 years after Ezra arrived. He returned for a further visit sometime between 433 and 423 B.C. He may have made several journeys between Persian capitals and Jerusalem in this period of 20 years.

Theme

The theme of Nehemiah is the Lord's protection of his people and the need for their faithfulness in keeping the Torah (the Mosaic law) and their faithfulness in worship.

Purpose, Occasion, and Background

The purpose and background of Nehemiah are the same as that for Ezra (see Introduction to Ezra).

Key Themes

1. The Lord hears prayer (1:4–6).
2. The Lord works providentially, especially through powerful rulers, to bring about his greater purposes (e.g., 2:8).
3. The Lord protects his people; therefore, they do not need to be afraid (4:14).
4. The Lord is merciful and faithful to his promises despite his people's persistence in sin (9:32–35).
5. Worship is at the center of the life of God's people, and it includes the willing, joyful giving of their resources (10:32–39).
6. God's people need to be on their guard against their own moral weakness (ch. 13).

Chronology of Nehemiah

Event	Month/Day	Year	Reference
Hanani brings Nehemiah a report from Jerusalem (20th year of Artaxerxes I)		445–444 B.C.	1:1
Nehemiah before King Artaxerxes	1	445	2:1
Nehemiah arrives to inspect Jerusalem walls		445	2:11
Wall is finished	6/25	445	6:15
People of Israel gather	7	445	7:73–8:1
People of Israel celebrate Feast of Booths	7/15–22	445	8:14
People of Israel fast and confess sins	7/24	445	9:1
Nehemiah returns to Susa (32nd year of Artaxerxes I)		433–432	5:14; 13:6

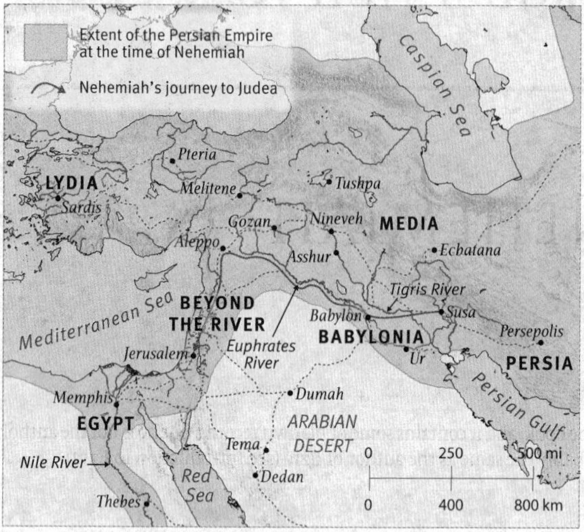

The Persian Empire at the Time of Nehemiah
c. 450 B.C.
During the time of Nehemiah, the Persian Empire had reached its greatest extent, engulfing nearly the entire Near East. In 539 B.C. the Persians under Cyrus the Great defeated the Babylonians and absorbed the lands of Israel and Judah (known as Beyond the River) into his empire. The next year he allowed the people of Judah (now called Jews) to return home and rebuild the temple of the Lord. Several waves of returning Jews continued to resettle in Judea, and Nehemiah was granted permission to rebuild Jerusalem's ruined walls around 445 B.C.

History of Salvation Summary

After the exile, God is renewing his people in the land, in order to carry out what he promised to Abraham. God's people must renew their commitment to covenant faithfulness, laying hold of God's forgiveness and seeking to practice purity in their corporate and private lives. God in his mercy raised up Ezra the priest and teacher, and Nehemiah the governor, to lead his people in the hard work that this renewal requires. The public ceremonies of chapters 8–10 enact this renewal, confessing past unfaithfulness and recognizing that everything—including the fulfilling of Israel's mission to bring light to the world—depends on God's grace and steadfast commitment to his promises (9:32–38). (For an explanation of the "History of Salvation," see the Overview of the Bible, pp. 23–26. See also History of Salvation in the Old Testament: Preparing the Way for Christ, pp. 2635–2661.)

Literary Features

Nehemiah is a sequel to Ezra. Two main actions occur: the rebuilding of the wall of Jerusalem and the recommitment of the returned exiles to fulfill their covenant obligations. There is something for virtually everyone—a general's diary, a governor's report, a civil record, a management handbook, and a memoir—all in one short book. The events covered span approximately 13 years. Part of the liveliness of the book stems from the striking character of Nehemiah, who emerges from the pages as a godly and decisive leader.

The book of Nehemiah displays the same mixture of narrative and documentary material (lists, inventories, genealogies) as Ezra, but it possesses a stronger narrative flair. The rebuilding of the city wall becomes a full-fledged conflict story, replete with suspense and heroism. The covenant-renewal ceremony (chs. 8–9) is one of the grand dramas in the Bible. The title character, Nehemiah, is such a commanding figure that the overall story is also a hero story. But documentary material continually interrupts the flow of the narrative, showing the historical impulse of the author. Since much of the book is cast in first-person narrative, the book also has the flavor of a memoir.

Outline

I. Nehemiah Returns to Jerusalem to Rebuild Its Walls (1:1–2:20)
   A. Nehemiah learns of Jerusalem's dilapidation (1:1–11)
   B. Nehemiah gains permission to return and inspects Jerusalem's walls (2:1–16)
   C. First signs of opposition (2:17–20)

II. The Wall Is Built, Despite Difficulties (3:1–7:4)
  A. The people work systematically on the walls (3:1–32)
  B. Opposition intensifies, but the people continue watchfully (4:1–23)
  C. Nehemiah deals with injustices in the community; Nehemiah's personal contribution to the project (5:1–19)
  D. A conspiracy against Nehemiah, but the wall is finished (6:1–7:4)

III. A Record of Those Who Returned from Exile (7:5–73)

IV. The Reading of the Law, and Covenant Renewal (8:1–10:39)
  A. The law is read (8:1–8)
  B. The people are to be joyful (8:9–12)
  C. The people keep the Feast of Booths (8:13–18)
  D. A prayer of confession, penitence, and covenant commitment (9:1–38)
  E. Signatories and specific commitments (10:1–39)

V. The Population of Jerusalem and the Villages; Priests and Levites (11:1–12:43)
  A. Those who lived in Jerusalem and the villages of Judah (11:1–36)
  B. High priests and leading Levites since the time of Zerubbabel (12:1–26)
  C. Dedication of the walls (12:27–43)

VI. Nehemiah Deals with Problems in the Community (12:44–13:31)
  A. The administration of offerings for the temple (12:44–47)
  B. Ejection of Tobiah the Ammonite from the temple (13:1–9)
  C. Dealing with neglect of the offerings (13:10–14)
  D. Dealing with Sabbath breaking (13:15–22)
  E. The problem of intermarriage again (13:23–29)
  F. Summary of Nehemiah's temple reforms (13:30–31)

NEHEMIAH

Report from Jerusalem

1 The words of [a]Nehemiah the son of Hacaliah.
Now it happened in the month of [b]Chislev, [c]in the twentieth year, as I was in [d]Susa
the citadel, 2 that [e]Hanani, one of my brothers, came with certain men from Judah. And I
asked them concerning the Jews who escaped, who had survived the exile, and concerning
Jerusalem. 3 And they said to me, "The remnant there in the province who had survived
the exile is in great trouble and [f]shame. [g]The wall of Jerusalem is broken down, [h]and its
gates are destroyed by fire."

Nehemiah's Prayer

4 As soon as I heard these words I [i]sat down and wept and mourned for days, and I
continued fasting and praying before the [j]God of heaven. 5 And I said, "O LORD God of
heaven, [k]the great and awesome God who keeps covenant and steadfast love with those
who love him and keep his commandments, 6 [l]let your ear be attentive and your eyes open,
to hear the prayer of your servant that I now pray before you day and night for the people
of Israel your servants, [m]confessing the sins of the people of Israel, which we have sinned
against you. Even [n]I and my father's house have sinned. 7 [o]We have acted very corruptly
against you and have not kept the commandments, the statutes, and the rules [p]that you
commanded your servant Moses. 8 Remember the word that you commanded your servant

Chapter 1
1 [a]ch. 10:1 [b]Zech. 7:1 [c]ch. 2:1 [d]Esth. 1:2, 5; 2:3, 5
2 [e]ch. 7:2
3 [f]ch. 2:17 [g]ch. 2:13; 2 Kgs. 25:10 [h]ch. 2:3, 13, 17
4 [i][Ezra 9:3] [j]ch. 2:4
5 [k]ch. 9:32; Dan. 9:4; [Deut. 7:21]
6 [l]Dan. 9:18; [1 Kgs. 8:29; 2 Chr. 6:40] [m]Ezra 10:1; Dan. 9:20 [n][Ps. 106:6]
7 [o]Dan. 9:5 [p]Deut. 28:15

1:1–2:20 *Nehemiah Returns to Jerusalem to Rebuild Its Walls.* This section recounts Nehemiah's burden for and first efforts in rebuilding Jerusalem. He learns of Jerusalem's decrepit condition (1:1–11), gains permission to rebuild the city, inspects its walls (2:1–16), and endures the first wave of opposition (2:17–20).

1:1–11 *Nehemiah Learns of Jerusalem's Dilapidation.* Nehemiah hears of the distress of Jerusalem and Judah (vv. 1–3) and prays for God's favor toward them (vv. 4–11).

1:1 Nehemiah the son of Hacaliah. Nehemiah's name means "Yahweh has comforted." **The twentieth year** is that of Artaxerxes' reign, 445 B.C., 13 years after Ezra's arrival in Jerusalem (see Ezra 7:7). **Chislev** is the ninth month (November/December), in the winter (see Ezra 10:9). **Susa the citadel**, or "fortress," was one of the royal seats. Ecbatana (Ezra 6:2) was a royal summer home, and Susa was a winter residence.

1:2–3 Hanani, one of my brothers. See also 7:2. **came with certain men.** It is not known whether these men were residents of Jerusalem or of Persia, nor is the nature of their mission known. **the Jews who escaped, who had survived the exile.** This, along with **the remnant**, refers to the returned exiles living in Jerusalem and Judah (see note on Ezra 9:8). The report about the **wall of Jerusalem** might mean that the wall had never been successfully rebuilt since the first return of exiles, or that an attempt to rebuild it had been thwarted, perhaps by command of the reigning king, Artaxerxes (see note on Ezra 4:20).

1:4 wept and mourned. Compare the reaction of Ezra when he discovered sin in the community (Ezra 9:4–5; 10:1). **God of heaven** was a way of referring to God in international contexts (cf. Ezra 1:2; 5:12).

1:5 O LORD God of heaven. This combination of names means that the God of Israel (Ex. 3:13–15) is the only God. **keeps covenant and steadfast love with those who love him and keep his commandments.** Cf. Deut. 7:9. Steadfast love is the quality of God's faithfulness to Israel in his covenant with them. Such covenant faithfulness requires Israel's love in return (see also Deut. 6:5). This love also includes faithfulness, and is made evident in keeping God's law as given to Moses; obedience is the proper response to God's love, not the precondition of it.

1:6 Nehemiah's **prayer** begins with a confession recalling all the past **sins** of **Israel**, as well as those of Nehemiah himself and of his family. Such confession is generally the right beginning in prayer, but Nehemiah especially acknowledges that Israel's sin has led to the present deplorable situation in Jerusalem. Israel has not responded to God's gracious covenant in the way outlined in v. 5. Nehemiah's prayer also recalls Solomon's when he dedicated the first temple (1 Kings 8:28–30). His use of the term "servant" for himself (**your servant**) and Israel (**your servants**) is significant since he is also a servant of King Artaxerxes. Ezra used a form of the same word (Hb. *'ebed*) to speak of "slavery" to Persia (Ezra 9:9). Nehemiah's prayer raises the question of who is the real Lord of Israel.

1:7 the commandments, the statutes, and the rules. See note on Ezra 7:10.

1:8–9 Remember. Moses also called on God to remember his promises when Israel was suffering his judgment because of sin (Ex. 32:13; Deut. 9:27). Nehemiah now recalls God's words about the essential choice placed before Israel in the covenant, in which disobedience would lead to scattering, or exile, **among the peoples** (Lev. 26:27–33; Deut. 4:25–27; 28:64), while obedience would bring blessing (Lev. 26:3–13; Deut. 28:1–14). **if you return to me.** In Nehemiah's perspective, however, the threatened exile did indeed happen; so he now appeals to God's old promise that even then, if Israel repented, he would restore them to the land and prosperity (Lev. 26:40–42; Deut. 4:29–31; 30:1–6). The restoration has happened in one sense, for many of God's people have returned from exile, but it remains incomplete because the land is not yet secure. **the place that I have chosen, to make my name dwell there.** Again, the reference is to the old promise to bring Israel

8 [q]Lev. 26:33; Deut. 28:64; See Deut. 4:25-27
9 [r]Lev. 26:39-42; Deut. 4:29-31; 30:2, 3 [s]Deut. 30:4 [t]Deut. 12:5
10 [u]Deut. 9:29
11 [See ver. 6 above] [v]ch. 2:1]

Chapter 2

1 [w]ch. 1:1; 5:14 [x]Ezra 7:1 [y][ch. 1:11]
2 [z]Prov. 15:13
3 [a]1 Kgs. 1:31; Dan. 2:4; 5:10; 6:21 [b]ver. 13, 17; ch. 1:3
4 [c]ver. 20; ch. 1:4, 5; Ezra 5:12; Dan. 2:18
6 [d][Ps. 45:9] [e][ch. 5:14; 13:6]
7 [f]Ezra 8:36
8 [g]ch. 7:2 [h]ver. 18; See Ezra 7:6

Moses, saying, 'If you are unfaithful, [q]I will scatter you among the peoples, 9 [r]but if you
return to me and keep my commandments and do them, [s]though your outcasts are in the
uttermost parts of heaven, from there I will gather them and bring them [t]to the place that
I have chosen, to make my name dwell there.' 10 [u]They are your servants and your people,
whom you have redeemed by your great power and by your strong hand. 11 O Lord, [l]let
your ear be attentive to the prayer of your servant, and to the prayer of your servants who
delight to fear your name, and give success to your servant today, and grant him mercy
in the sight of this man."

Now I was [v]cupbearer to the king.

Nehemiah Sent to Judah

2 In the month of Nisan, [w]in the twentieth year of King [x]Artaxerxes, when wine was
before him, [y]I took up the wine and gave it to the king. Now I had not been sad in his
presence. 2 And the king said to me, "Why is your face sad, seeing you are not sick? This
is nothing but [z]sadness of the heart." Then I was very much afraid. 3 I said to the king,
[a]"Let the king live forever! Why should not my face be sad, [b]when the city, the place of
my fathers' graves, lies in ruins, and its gates have been destroyed by fire?" 4 Then the king
said to me, "What are you requesting?" So I prayed [c]to the God of heaven. 5 And I said to
the king, "If it pleases the king, and if your servant has found favor in your sight, that
you send me to Judah, to the city of my fathers' graves, that I may rebuild it." 6 And the
king said to me ([d]the queen sitting beside him), "How long will you be gone, and when
will you return?" So it pleased the king to send me [e]when I had given him a time. 7 And
I said to the king, "If it pleases the king, let letters be given me [f]to the governors of the
province Beyond the River, that they may let me pass through until I come to Judah, 8 and
a letter to Asaph, the keeper of the king's forest, that he may give me timber to make
beams for the gates of [g]the fortress of the temple, and for the wall of the city, and for the
house that I shall occupy." And the king granted me what I asked, [h]for the good hand of
my God was upon me.

into its land (Deut. 12:5). The "place" in question was primarily the city where the Lord's sanctuary would be, which was finally Jerusalem (2 Kings 21:4). The dwelling of the "name" meant the Lord's claiming of the place as his own, in contrast to the claims of other gods or rulers.

1:10 redeemed by your great power and by your strong hand. The reference, both here and in Deut. 4:34, is to (1) the deliverance of Israel from slavery in Egypt, (2) the miraculous signs in the afflictions of Egypt, and (3) the defeat of Egypt in the Red Sea (Exodus 7–15).

1:11 fear your name. On fearing God, see note on Prov. 1:7 and other verses mentioned there. To "fear God's name" is essentially the same as fearing God himself, since the "name" of God here represents God's character and all that he is (cf. Deut. 10:20; 28:58). **mercy in the sight of this man** (i.e., Artaxerxes). Nehemiah knows that God can move powerful people to act in ways that accord with his own plans, and in favor of his people (see Ezra 6:22). But he may also know that Artaxerxes has already decreed that work on rebuilding Jerusalem should stop (see note on Neh. 1:2–3; see also Ezra 4:23). Therefore, Nehemiah's petition may bring danger to him. The position of **cupbearer to the king** was a high office and involved regular access to the king.

2:1–16 *Nehemiah Gains Permission to Return and Inspects Jerusalem's Walls.* Nehemiah makes his petition to the king and is allowed to go to Jerusalem (vv. 1–8). He surveys the walls, finding them in very poor condition (vv. 9–16).

2:1 The date, **Nisan, in the twentieth year** (i.e., March/April of 445 B.C.), is surprising because Nisan is the first month, and yet the earlier events of ch. 1 took place in Chislev, the ninth month (December). Of various proposed solutions, the best is perhaps that the author counts the years of Artaxerxes' reign from the actual month of his accession (which is not precisely known), so that his "twentieth year" might span two calendar years (446–445 B.C.). In that case, this incident in the month of Nisan would be four months after the news about Jerusalem came to Nehemiah.

2:2 Nehemiah's expression of sadness is the prelude to his request. Nehemiah did not show his grief immediately (i.e., during the four months since 1:1), perhaps because it was part of his duty to be positive and encouraging. But now he has decided to speak. The king's diagnosis of **sadness of the heart** perceives some discontentment as the cause. Nehemiah was **very much afraid** because he was about to say something that the king might take as disloyalty.

2:3 Let the king live forever! Nehemiah first shows his loyalty and explains the reason for his grief, without yet making his request. **my fathers' graves.** He may think that this way of speaking about Jerusalem will make the king sympathetic.

2:4 The king then invites a request. **So I prayed.** Nehemiah had prayed a great deal, of course (see 1:4), but here he quickly speaks to God (probably silently) before he answers the king.

2:5–6 Continuing in great deference, Nehemiah makes his request (v. 5). The king agrees without deliberation, apart perhaps from a glance at **the queen sitting beside him**, and demands only that Nehemiah commit to a date when he will return to Susa.

2:7–8 Nehemiah, emboldened, now asks for specific authority to show letters to the **governors of the province Beyond the River**, who no doubt included the very people who had previously persuaded Artaxerxes to halt the rebuilding of the city (Ezra 4:7–9). He goes further, however, requesting timber from the **king's forest** for specific projects. The location of this forest is unknown. It might refer to Lebanon, or to some area nearer Jerusalem. At that time the land in general was more forested than in modern times. The name **Asaph** suggests that he was a Jewish royal official. The **fortress of the temple** was a special defense of the temple, probably on the northern, most vulnerable side, where later the Roman Antonia Fortress stood. It may have included the towers mentioned in Neh. 3:1. For the **wall of the city** the wood would have been needed mainly for the gates. Finally Nehemiah asks for wood to repair his own house, possibly an existing house passed down in his own family. Artaxerxes agrees, following his own previous generosity to the project in Jerusalem (Ezra 7:21–24), and also that of his predecessors, Cyrus (Ezra 1:4) and Darius (Ezra 6:8–12).

2:8 for the good hand of my God was upon me. See note on v. 18.

Nehemiah Inspects Jerusalem's Walls

9 Then I came to [i]the governors of the province Beyond the River and gave them the
king's letters. Now the king had sent with me officers of the army and horsemen. 10 But
when [j]Sanballat the Horonite and [k]Tobiah the Ammonite servant heard this, it displeased
them greatly that someone had come to seek the welfare of the people of Israel.
11 [l]So I went to Jerusalem and was there three days. 12 Then I arose in the night, I and a few
men with me. And I told no one what my God had put into my heart to do for Jerusalem.
There was no animal with me but the one on which I rode. 13 I went out by night by [m]the
Valley Gate to the Dragon Spring and to [n]the Dung Gate, and I inspected the walls of
Jerusalem [o]that were broken down [p]and its gates that had been destroyed by fire. 14 Then I
went on to [q]the Fountain Gate and to [r]the King's Pool, but there was no room for the animal
that was under me to pass. 15 Then I went up in the night [s]by the valley and inspected the
wall, and I turned back and entered by the Valley Gate, and so returned. 16 And the officials
did not know where I had gone or what I was doing, and I had not yet told the Jews, the
priests, the nobles, the officials, and the rest who were to do the work.
17 Then I said to them, "You see the trouble we are in, [t]how Jerusalem lies in ruins with
its gates burned. Come, let us build the wall of Jerusalem, that we may no longer [u]suffer
derision." 18 And I told them [v]of the hand of my God that had been upon me for good, and
also of the words that the king had spoken to me. And they said, "Let us rise up and build."
[w]So they strengthened their hands for the good work. 19 But when Sanballat the Horonite
and Tobiah the Ammonite servant and [x]Geshem the Arab heard of it, [y]they jeered at us and
despised us and said, "What is this thing that you are doing? [z]Are you rebelling against the
king?" 20 Then I replied to them, [a]"The God of heaven will make us prosper, and we his
servants will arise and build, but you have no portion or right or claim[1] in Jerusalem."

[1] Or *memorial*

9 [i]Ezra 8:36
10 [j]ver. 19; ch. 4:1, 7; 6:1, 2, 5, 12, 14; 13:28 [k]ch. 13:4
11 [l]Ezra 8:32
13 [m]ch. 3:13; 2 Chr. 26:9 [n]ch. 3:13, 14; 12:31 [o]ch. 1:3 [p]ver. 3, 17
14 [q]ch. 3:15; 12:37 [r]2 Kgs. 20:20; [ch. 3:16; 2 Chr. 32:3, 30]
15 [s]2 Sam. 15:23
17 [t]ver. 3, 13; ch. 1:3 [u]ch. 1:3; Ps. 44:13; 79:4; Jer. 24:9; Ezek. 5:14, 15; 22:4
18 [v]ver. 8 [w][2 Sam. 2:7]
19 [x][ch. 6:6] [y]ch. 4:1; Ps. 44:13 [z]ch. 6:6
20 [a]ver. 4

2:9 Nehemiah's imperial authority is visible in the **officers** and **horsemen** sent with him.

2:10 Sanballat the Horonite is known from other sources to have been governor of Samaria at a later time, and may be so already. His Babylonian name does not necessarily mean that he was Babylonian; he probably came from Upper or Lower Beth-horon near Jerusalem (Josh. 16:3, 5). **Tobiah** is a Jewish name, yet as an **Ammonite** he belongs to a people that was one of Israel's historic enemies (2 Sam. 10:1–11). The term **servant** here may mean that he is an official, also from Samaria. These Samarians apparently wanted to assert their authority in Judah.

2:11–12 three days. Ezra 8:32 speaks of a similar length of time. **in the night**. Nehemiah aims to keep his mission secret from potential enemies as long as possible, but also from his own people till his plans are fully formed (see also Neh. 2:16).

2:13–15 Nehemiah surveys the **walls** chiefly on the southern and eastern sides, i.e., the so-called city of David and the Kidron Valley. The **Valley Gate** was probably on the southwestern side of the city of David, and the **Dung Gate**, leading to the city dump, at its southern tip. The **Dragon Spring, Fountain Gate**, and **King's Pool** are unidentified, but were no doubt on the east where the Kidron Valley's water sources were. The **valley** is the Kidron Valley, to which Nehemiah has had to descend because he cannot pass close to the walls higher up, since the rubble from their destruction has made passage impossible. He returns by the Valley Gate, having apparently made only a partial circuit.

2:17–20 *First Signs of Opposition.* Nehemiah now exhorts his countrymen. They are willing to work, but opposition quickly emerges, as vv. 9–10 have already hinted.

2:17 Come, let us build the wall of Jerusalem. His own heart having been stirred up for the Lord's work, Nehemiah calls on others to join him. **suffer derision**. A direct reference to the shame brought upon Jerusalem by God's former judgment on it (Jer. 24:9).

2:18 the hand of my God. See also 1:10; 2:8; Ezra 7:6, 9, 28; 8:18, 22, 31, and chart, p. 814. This recurring expression recognizes that God was orchestrating blessing for his people. The people had to see that their bad situation was not irreversible because God could change things.

2:19 The opponents of the people allege that they are **rebelling against the king**, an extremely serious charge, one that Artaxerxes had previously believed (Ezra 4:12–13, 19–22). The opponents now include **Geshem the Arab**, perhaps from Kedar in Arabia; Kedarites had settled close to Judah, east and south (see Isa. 21:16–17; Jer. 49:28–33).

2:20 Nehemiah knows that the king is on his side, but he attributes his authority to **the God of heaven. but you have no portion or right or claim in Jerusalem**. Nehemiah clearly distinguishes between God's people and the enemies of God who oppose the work. Once he is convinced that they are opposing the work of the Lord, he makes no effort to include them or even to pursue further discussions with them. A "portion" is an allocated share, as given to the tribes by Joshua (Josh. 18:5–6; 19:9); it is also used metaphorically of belonging (2 Sam. 20:1). "Right" is entitlement, and "claim" is literally "memorial," i.e., a claim based in ancient tradition, and possibly referring to the right to worship in Jerusalem.

3:1–7:4 *The Wall Is Built, Despite Difficulties.* This section records the building and repairing of the walls by all the people of Judah, despite the efforts of certain groups to stop them. Excavations on the Ophel hill of Jerusalem have uncovered remains of Nehemiah's wall system. This wall system apparently incorporated walls from previous ages. It was not strongly built, and it reflects Jerusalem's diminutive size at the time (see illustration, pp. 828–829).

3:1–32 *The People Work Systematically on the Walls.* The building work is described, and the workers are named, section by section. The point of this account is to show that the people as a whole responded to Nehemiah's challenge and believed that God would give them success. The description of the work demonstrates the concerted effort of the people.

3:1–2 Eliashib the high priest was the grandson of Jeshua, the priest in Zerubbabel's time (see 12:10; Ezra 5:2). **with his brothers**. The work was allocated to groups within the community, identified mainly by family and sometimes by where they lived. It began and ended at the **Sheep Gate**, on the northern side of the city (Neh. 3:32; see map, p. 827). This was near the temple, and possibly was so named because sheep were brought through it for sacrifice (see also John 5:2). It may also be why the priests worked here, and why they **consecrated** the gate. The direction of the work on the wall was counterclockwise. **Tower of the Hundred**. See note on Neh. 2:7–8.

Rebuilding the Wall

3 Then [b]Eliashib the high priest rose up with his brothers the priests, and they built
[c]the Sheep Gate. They consecrated it and [d]set its doors. They consecrated it as far as
the Tower of the Hundred, as far as the [e]Tower of Hananel. 2 And next to him [f]the men of
Jericho built. And next to them[1] Zaccur the son of Imri built.
3 The sons of Hassenaah built [g]the Fish Gate. [h]They laid its beams and [d]set its doors, its
bolts, and its bars. 4 And next to them [i]Meremoth the son of Uriah, son of Hakkoz repaired.
And next to them [j]Meshullam the son of Berechiah, son of Meshezabel repaired. And next
to them Zadok the son of Baana repaired. 5 And next to them [k]the Tekoites repaired, but
their nobles would not stoop to serve their Lord.[2]
6 Joiada the son of Paseah and Meshullam the son of Besodeiah [l]repaired the Gate of
Yeshanah.[3] [h]They laid its beams and [d]set its doors, its bolts, and its bars. 7 And next to
them repaired Melatiah the Gibeonite and Jadon the Meronothite, the men of Gibeon
and of Mizpah, the seat of [m]the governor of the province Beyond the River. 8 Next to
them Uzziel the son of Harhaiah, goldsmiths, repaired. Next to him Hananiah, one of
the perfumers, repaired, and they restored Jerusalem as far as [n]the Broad Wall. 9 Next to

[1] Hebrew *him* [2] Or *lords* [3] Or *of the old city*

Chapter 3
1 [b]ver. 20, 21; ch. 13:4, 7, 28 [c]ver. 32; ch. 12:39; John 5:2 [d]ch. 6:1; 7:1 [e]Jer. 31:38; Zech. 14:10
2 [f]Ezra 2:34
3 [g]ch. 12:39; 2 Chr. 33:14; Zeph. 1:10 [h][ch. 2:8] [d][See ver. 1 above]
4 [i]ver. 21; Ezra 8:33 [j]ver. 30; Ezra 8:16
5 [k]ver. 27; [2 Sam. 14:2]
6 [l]ch. 12:39 [h][See ver. 3 above] [d][See ver. 1 above]
7 [m]ch. 2:7, 9
8 [n]ch. 12:38

The precise line of the walls followed by Nehemiah cannot be completely reconstructed. Regarding many of the features mentioned, little is known.

3:3 The **Fish Gate** may have been at the northwest corner.

3:4 repaired. The work is sometimes "building" and sometimes "repairing," suggesting that the parts of the walls were in various states of dilapidation.

3:5 the Tekoites . . . their nobles. The leading people of Tekoa, not far south of Jerusalem, may have resented Nehemiah's leadership. The Hebrew translated **their Lord** has the form of a plural (see ESV footnote), but the plural form is often used to express respect to a single master: for this construction in relation to God, see 8:10; 10:29; cf. Deut. 10:17 ("*Lord* of lords"); Ps. 8:1; 135:5; 136:3; in relation to a man, see Gen. 42:33; Judg. 3:25. In view of the use in Nehemiah, this probably refers to God; but perhaps the form, which could refer to Nehemiah, is used to convey the notion that one properly serves God by obeying Nehemiah.

3:7 Mizpah was an important administrative center after the fall of Jerusalem (Jer. 41:1). Apparently the Samarian governor of **Beyond the River** continued to hold sessions there.

3:8 goldsmiths . . . perfumers. Many workers in the community were organized in guilds. The **Broad Wall** enclosed part of the western city (some of which has been excavated).

3:9 ruler of half the district of Jerusalem. Similar expressions occur

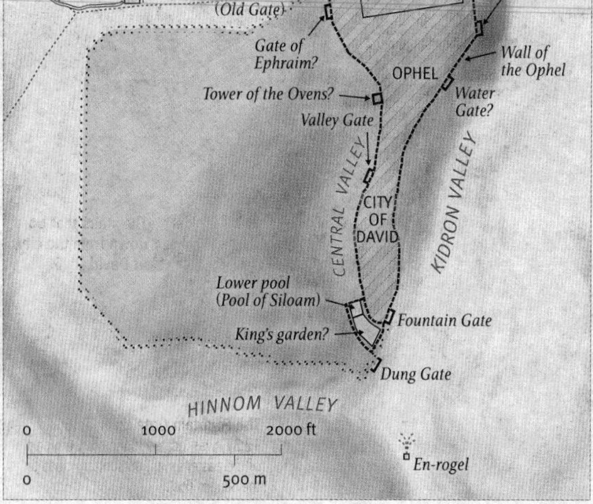

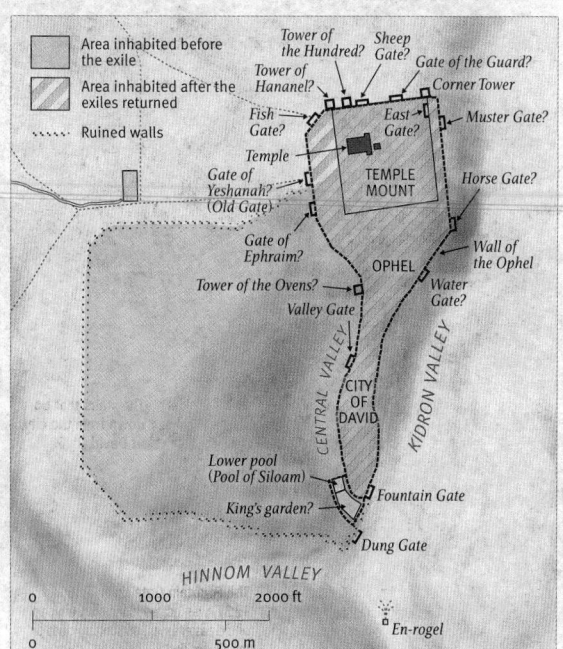

Jerusalem at the Time of Nehemiah
c. 445 B.C.
Though Nehemiah gives a careful listing of the sections of Jerusalem's walls that were rebuilt, it is difficult to be certain exactly which walls and gates he was referring to. The city had extended beyond the city of David and the Temple Mount by the time of Hezekiah, but it appears that only the Temple Mount and the city of David were enclosed within Nehemiah's walls. An ambitious project nonetheless, it was completed in only 52 days, providing Jerusalem with some measure of protection from its enemies.

JERUSALEM IN THE TIME OF NEHEMIAH (C. 444–420? B.C.)

Jerusalem was destroyed by the Babylonians in 586 B.C. Upon their return from exile in 536 B.C., the Jews, under the leadership of Zerubbabel and Jeshua, first restored the altar and then laid the foundation of the temple. Twenty years later, in 516 B.C., the temple was rebuilt. This time period is referred to as the Second Temple period.
Later on, and under very difficult circumstances, Nehemiah restored the city wall. This is described in great detail in ch. 3. There is ample archaeological evidence, both positive and negative, to show that only the Eastern Hill of Jerusalem was fortified at that time and that the eastern wall of the city was built higher up the slope than the previous wall, so that the city was smaller than that of Solomon.

The Valley Gate (2:13, 15; 3:13), the remains of which were excavated in 1924, was part of the western city wall. The other gates and the Tower of the Ovens, mentioned in chs. 3 and 12, are unattested to in the archaeological record, but are placed in the drawing in the order in which Nehemiah records them.

The Western Hill was not occupied at this time. However, the ruins of the Broad Wall (3:8; 12:38), the Middle Gate (cf. Jer. 39:3), and the destroyed houses remained part of the landscape of Jerusalem. This area was not rebuilt until the middle of the second century B.C.

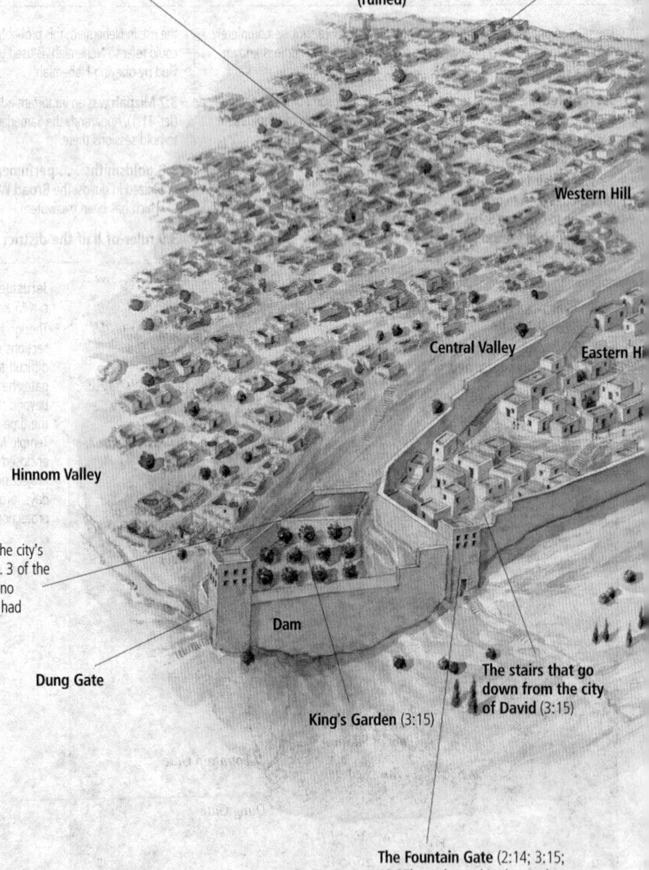

The Siloam Pool was again used as the city's water source. There is no mention in ch. 3 of the Gihon Spring, probably because it was no longer accessible after the Babylonians had destroyed its protective towers.

The Fountain Gate (2:14; 3:15; 12:37) was located in the southern part of the eastern wall, presumably close to the Siloam Pool.

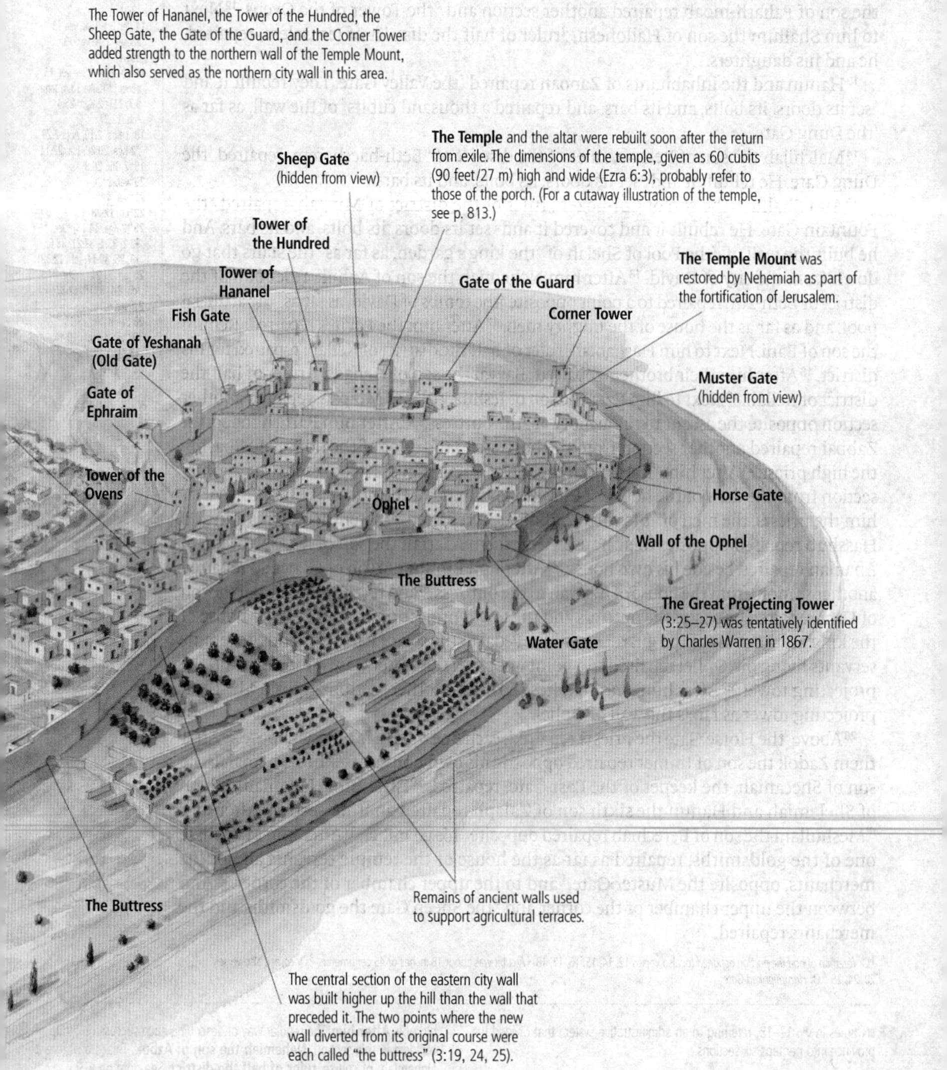
The Tower of Hananel, the Tower of the Hundred, the Sheep Gate, the Gate of the Guard, and the Corner Tower added strength to the northern wall of the Temple Mount, which also served as the northern city wall in this area.
The Temple and the altar were rebuilt soon after the return from exile. The dimensions of the temple, given as 60 cubits (90 feet/27 m) high and wide (Ezra 6:3), probably refer to those of the porch. (For a cutaway illustration of the temple, see p. 813.)
Sheep Gate (hidden from view)
Tower of the Hundred
Tower of Hananel
Gate of the Guard
The Temple Mount was restored by Nehemiah as part of the fortification of Jerusalem.
Fish Gate
Corner Tower
Gate of Yeshanah (Old Gate)
Muster Gate (hidden from view)
Gate of Ephraim
Tower of the Ovens
Ophel
Horse Gate
Wall of the Ophel
The Buttress
The Great Projecting Tower (3:25–27) was tentatively identified by Charles Warren in 1867.
Water Gate
The Buttress
Remains of ancient walls used to support agricultural terraces.
The central section of the eastern city wall was built higher up the hill than the wall that preceded it. The two points where the new wall diverted from its original course were each called "the buttress" (3:19, 24, 25).

them Rephaiah the son of Hur, [o]ruler of half the district of[1] Jerusalem, repaired. **10** Next
to them Jedaiah the son of Harumaph repaired opposite his house. And next to him
Hattush the son of Hashabneiah repaired. **11** Malchijah the son of Harim and Hasshub
the son of Pahath-moab repaired another section and [p]the Tower of the Ovens. **12** Next
to him Shallum the son of Hallohesh, [q]ruler of half the district of Jerusalem, repaired,
he and his daughters.

13 Hanun and the inhabitants of Zanoah repaired [r]the Valley Gate. They rebuilt it and
[s]set its doors, its bolts, and its bars, and repaired a thousand cubits[2] of the wall, as far as
[t]the Dung Gate.

14 Malchijah the son of Rechab, ruler of the district of [u]Beth-haccherem, repaired [t]the
Dung Gate. He rebuilt it and [s]set its doors, its bolts, and its bars.

15 And Shallum the son of Col-hozeh, ruler of the district of Mizpah, repaired [v]the
Fountain Gate. He rebuilt it and covered it and [s]set its doors, its bolts, and its bars. And
he built the wall of [w]the Pool of Shelah of [x]the king's garden, as far as [y]the stairs that go
down from the city of David. **16** After him Nehemiah the son of Azbuk, ruler of half the
district of Beth-zur, repaired to a point opposite [z]the tombs of David, as far as [a]the artificial
pool, and as far as the house of the mighty men. **17** After him the Levites repaired: Rehum
the son of Bani. Next to him Hashabiah, ruler of half the district of Keilah, repaired for his
district. **18** After him their brothers repaired: Bavvai the son of Henadad, ruler of half the
district of Keilah. **19** Next to him Ezer the son of Jeshua, ruler of Mizpah, repaired another
section opposite the ascent to the armory at [b]the buttress.[3] **20** After him Baruch the son of
Zabbai repaired another section from the buttress to the door of the house of [c]Eliashib
the high priest. **21** After him [d]Meremoth the son of Uriah, son of Hakkoz repaired another
section from the door of the house of Eliashib to the end of the house of Eliashib. **22** After
him the priests, the men of [e]the surrounding area, repaired. **23** After them Benjamin and
Hasshub repaired opposite their house. After them Azariah the son of Maaseiah, son of
Ananiah repaired beside his own house. **24** After him Binnui the son of Henadad repaired
another section, from the house of Azariah to the buttress **25** and to [f]the corner. Palal the son
of Uzai repaired opposite the buttress and the tower projecting from the upper house of
the king at [g]the court of the guard. After him Pedaiah the son of Parosh **26** [h]and the temple
servants living on [i]Ophel repaired to a point opposite [j]the Water Gate on the east and the
projecting tower. **27** After him [k]the Tekoites repaired another section opposite the great
projecting tower as far as the wall of Ophel.

28 Above [l]the Horse Gate the priests repaired, each one opposite his own house. **29** After
them Zadok the son of Immer repaired opposite his own house. After him Shemaiah the
son of Shecaniah, the keeper of the East Gate, repaired. **30** After him Hananiah the son
of Shelemiah and Hanun the sixth son of Zalaph repaired another section. After him
[m]Meshullam the son of Berechiah repaired opposite [n]his chamber. **31** After him Malchijah,
one of the goldsmiths, repaired as far as the house of the temple servants and of the
merchants, opposite the Muster Gate,[4] and to the upper chamber of the corner. **32** And
between the upper chamber of the corner and [o]the Sheep Gate the goldsmiths and the
merchants repaired.

[1] Or *foreman of half the portion assigned to;* also verses 12, 14, 15, 16, 17, 18 [2] A *cubit* was about 18 inches or 45 centimeters [3] Or *corner;* also verses 20, 24, 25 [4] Or *Hammiphkad Gate*

9 [o]ver. 12
11 [p]ch. 12:38
12 [q]ver. 9
13 [r]ch. 2:13, 15; 2 Chr. 26:9 [s]See ver. 1 [t]ch. 2:13; 12:31
14 [u]Jer. 6:1 [t][See ver. 13 above] [s][See ver. 13 above]
15 [v]ch. 2:14 [s][See ver. 13 above] [w][Luke 13:4; John 9:7, 11] [x]2 Kgs. 25:4 [y]ch. 12:37
16 [z]1 Kgs. 2:10; Acts 2:29 [a]2 Kgs. 20:20; Isa. 22:11
19 [b]2 Chr. 26:9
20 [c]ver. 1
21 [d]ver. 4
22 [e]ch. 12:28
25 [f][2 Kgs. 14:13] [g]Jer. 32:2; 33:1; 37:21; 38:6, 13, 28; 39:14; [ch. 12:39]
26 [h]ch. 11:21 [i]2 Chr. 27:3 [j]ch. 8:1, 3, 16; 12:37
27 [k]ver. 5
28 [l]See 2 Chr. 23:15
30 [m]ver. 4 [n][ch. 12:44; 13:7]
32 [o]See ver. 1

six times in vv. 12–18, referring to an administrative system that divided the province into perhaps six sections.

3:13 Valley Gate . . . Dung Gate. See note on 2:13–15; and map, p. 827. **a thousand cubits**. About 500 yards (457 m).

3:15 Fountain Gate. See note on 2:13–15. **city of David**. The part of the city originally occupied by David, extending south of what is now the Temple Mount.

3:16 On the eastern side of the city, Nehemiah has to build a new line of wall, rather than simply repair the old one, because the preexilic wall was so badly destroyed here. The line of the new wall is now described in relation to a variety of features of the city, most of which can no longer be certainly located. It is positioned higher up the slope of the Kidron Valley than the old one. **After him**. The regular way of describing each successive group of builders in this section. **Nehemiah the son of Azbuk**. This is a different Nehemiah, of course. **ruler of half the district**. See note on v. 9.

3:23 opposite their house. This shows one factor in deciding who would build each section (see also vv. 28–29).

3:26 temple servants. See note on Ezra 2:43–54. **Ophel**. A name for the whole southeastern hill. The **Water Gate**, in the old wall, had probably opened onto the Gihon Spring, the main water source outside the city wall.

3:29 The **East Gate** may have been a gate into the temple rather than a gate in the wall.

3:32 Sheep Gate. See note on vv. 1–2.

Chapter 4
1[q]ver. 7; ch. 2:10, 19
2[r]1 Kgs. 16:24
3[q][See ver. 1 above]
[s][Lam. 5:18]
4[t]Ps. 123:3, 4 [u]Ps. 79:12
5[v]Ps. 69:27, 28; 109:14, 15; Jer. 18:23
7[q][See ver. 1 above]
8[w]See Ps. 83:3-5
14[x][Num. 14:9]; Deut. 1:29
[y]Deut. 7:21; 10:17
[z]2 Sam. 10:12
15[a][Job 5:12]

Opposition to the Work

4 [1] Now when [q]Sanballat heard that we were building the wall, he was angry and greatly
enraged, and he jeered at the Jews. **2** And he said in the presence of his brothers and
of the army of [r]Samaria, "What are these feeble Jews doing? Will they restore it for themselves?[2] Will they sacrifice? Will they finish up in a day? Will they revive the stones out of
the heaps of rubbish, and burned ones at that?" **3** [q]Tobiah the Ammonite was beside him,
and he said, "Yes, what they are building—[s]if a fox goes up on it he will break down their
stone wall!" **4** [t]Hear, O our God, for we are despised. [u]Turn back their taunt on their own
heads and give them up to be plundered in a land where they are captives. **5** [v]Do not cover
their guilt, and let not their sin be blotted out from your sight, for they have provoked
you to anger in the presence of the builders.

6 So we built the wall. And all the wall was joined together to half its height, for the
people had a mind to work.

7 [3] But when [q]Sanballat and Tobiah and the Arabs and the Ammonites and the Ashdodites
heard that the repairing of the walls of Jerusalem was going forward and that the breaches
were beginning to be closed, they were very angry. **8** [w]And they all plotted together to come
and fight against Jerusalem and to cause confusion in it. **9** And we prayed to our God and
set a guard as a protection against them day and night.

10 In Judah it was said,[4] "The strength of those who bear the burdens is failing. There is
too much rubble. By ourselves we will not be able to rebuild the wall." **11** And our enemies
said, "They will not know or see till we come among them and kill them and stop the work."
12 At that time the Jews who lived near them came from all directions and said to us ten
times, "You must return to us."[5] **13** So in the lowest parts of the space behind the wall, in
open places, I stationed the people by their clans, with their swords, their spears, and their
bows. **14** And I looked and arose and said to the nobles and to the officials and to the rest of
the people, [x]"Do not be afraid of them. Remember the Lord, [y]who is great and awesome,
[z]and fight for your brothers, your sons, your daughters, your wives, and your homes."

The Work Resumes

15 When our enemies heard that it was known to us [a]and that God had frustrated their
plan, we all returned to the wall, each to his work. **16** From that day on, half of my servants

[1] Ch 3:33 in Hebrew [2] Or *Will they commit themselves to God?* [3] Ch 4:1 in Hebrew [4] Hebrew *Judah said* [5] The meaning of the Hebrew is uncertain

4:1–23 *Opposition Intensifies, but the People Continue Watchfully.* While the building continues, Sanballat and his allies resort to direct action in order to stop it, but their plot is foiled.

4:1–2 Sanballat. See 2:9–10. (The name of a later Sanballat appears on a 4th-century-B.C. papyrus from Wadi edh-Dhaliyeh, where fragmentary scrolls were found in a cave in the highlands near Samaria. In one of these scrolls a certain Sanballat administers the country.) Sanballat was **angry and greatly enraged** because of the challenge to his authority. **he jeered** (4:1). He is clearly worried by the Jews' action, but expresses it in mockery, no doubt to encourage his **brothers** (or allies) to join him in resisting. **army of Samaria**. It is not clear whether Sanballat really had the authority to command an army. **Will they restore it for themselves?** Ironically, the answer to this and Sanballat's subsequent mocking questions will be yes.

4:4–5 Nehemiah interjects in his own voice a prayer similar to certain prayers for deliverance from enemies in the Psalms (e.g., Psalm 74; 79). He prays that what his enemies wish for him would return **on their own heads**; indeed, he prays that they would suffer captivity such as the Jews had recently experienced. The motive is not mere revenge but rather the honor of God, who is the real object of the enemies' insults and whose purposes they do not understand.

4:6 half its height. At this point, the project could still be thwarted. Yet the commitment of the people is a sign of likely success, since it is based on faith in God. **for the people had a mind to work**. One aspect of God's blessing on this project was that he gave the people a deep desire to do the work, and he sustained that desire throughout the time that the wall was being built.

4:7 Arabs . . . Ammonites . . . Ashdodites. Geshem was an Arab, and Tobiah an Ammonite (2:19; see also note on 2:10). It looks as though they belonged to certain groups in Judah who were strongly opposed to the project. Ashdod was formerly a Philistine city on the west (Mediterranean) coast, but it became the name of the entire province, first under Assyria, then under Persia. The people groups named here suggest that the Jewish community is surrounded on three sides—east, west, and south. This plot runs counter to the clear authorization that Nehemiah received from the Persian king, so it is hard to judge how successful it could hope to be. Yet surely it was intimidating, since Susa was about 1,100 miles (1,770 km) away, a journey of approximately 55 days (averaging 20 miles or 32 km per day). **they were very angry**. Probably because their own plans were failing.

4:9 And we prayed to our God and set a guard. Nehemiah has prayed before in a threatening situation (2:4). Along with his prayers, he takes prudent action.

4:10–12 These verses tell of the same action described in v. 9 but spell it out at greater length and focus on the danger to the project. The task itself is massive and discouraging (v. 10); the enemies have terrified the people with the threat of a deadly night attack (v. 11); and the friends and families of people who have come in from the villages to work on the walls try to persuade them to come home because of the danger (v. 12).

4:13 Nehemiah again sets a guard (see v. 9).

4:14 Do not be afraid is both a command and an exhortation, rooted in the call to believe that God can overcome his enemies (see also Deut. 1:21, 29; Josh. 1:9), as he has in the past (in the exodus from Egypt and the capture of Canaan).

4:15 God had frustrated their plan. From now on the immediate threat is apparently over, but the work continues with half the people's attention given to defense.

4:16 my servants. A group that was especially close to Nehemiah, and perhaps specially trained.

worked on construction, and half held the spears, shields, bows, and [b]coats of mail. And the
leaders stood behind the whole house of Judah, 17 who were building on the wall. Those who
carried burdens were loaded in such a way that each labored on the work with one hand
and held his weapon with the other. 18 And each of the builders had his sword strapped at
his side while he built. The man who sounded the trumpet was beside me. 19 And I said to
[c]the nobles and to the officials and to the rest of the people, "The work is great and widely
spread, and we are separated on the wall, far from one another. 20 In the place where you
hear the sound of the trumpet, rally to us there. [d]Our God will fight for us."

21 So we labored at the work, and half of them held the spears from the break of dawn
until the stars came out. 22 I also said to the people at that time, "Let every man and his
servant pass the night within Jerusalem, that they may be a guard for us by night and may
labor by day." 23 So neither I nor my brothers nor my servants nor the men of the guard who
followed me, none of us took off our clothes; [e]each kept his weapon at his right hand.[1]

Nehemiah Stops Oppression of the Poor

5 Now there arose [f]a great outcry of the people and of their wives [g]against their Jewish
brothers. 2 For there were those who said, "With our sons and our daughters, we are
many. So let us get grain, that we may eat and keep alive." 3 There were also those who
said, "We are mortgaging our fields, our vineyards, and our houses to get grain because
of the famine." 4 And there were those who said, "We have borrowed money for [h]the king's
tax on our fields and our vineyards. 5 Now [i]our flesh is as the flesh of our brothers, our
children are as their children. Yet [j]we are forcing our sons and our daughters to be slaves,
and some of our daughters have already been enslaved, but it is not in our power to help
it, for other men have our fields and our vineyards."

6 I was very angry when I heard [f]their outcry and these words. 7 I took counsel with
myself, and I brought charges against the nobles and the officials. I said to them, [k]"You are
exacting interest, each from his brother." And I held a great assembly against them 8 and
said to them, "We, as far as we are able, [l]have bought back our Jewish brothers who have
been sold to the nations, but you even sell your brothers that they may be sold to us!" They
were silent and could not find a word to say. 9 So I said, "The thing that you are doing is not

[1] Probable reading; Hebrew *each his weapon the water*

16 [b]2 Chr. 26:14
19 [c]ver. 14
20 [d]Ex. 14:14, 25; Deut. 1:30; 3:22; 20:4; Josh. 23:10
23 [e]ver. 17

Chapter 5

1 [f][Ex. 3:9; Isa. 5:7] [g]Lev. 25:35, 37; Deut. 15:7
4 [h]Ezra 4:13, 20; 7:24
5 [i]Isa. 58:7; [Gen. 29:14] [j][Ex. 21:7; Lev. 25:39; 2 Kgs. 4:1]
6 [f][See ver. 1 above]
7 [k][Ex. 22:25; Lev. 25:36; Ps. 15:5; Ezek. 22:12]
8 [l]Lev. 25:48, 49

4:17 each labored on the work with one hand and held his weapon with the other. Though Nehemiah and the people prayed and trusted God for protection (see vv. 4, 9, 14, 20), they also kept their weapons close at hand (see vv. 16, 18, 23), ready to defend themselves from attack; God often accomplishes his purposes through ordinary human means.

4:20 With the people spread out all around the wall, they were potentially vulnerable at every point (v. 19). Nehemiah addresses this problem by his plan to let the **sound of the trumpet** be heard, a well-established call to arms (cf. Judg. 3:27; 1 Sam. 13:3). **Our God will fight for us.** Cf. Ex. 14:14; Deut. 1:30.

4:21–22 A final picture of watchfulness, both day and night. Nehemiah may have feared losing some of his workforce at night, so he kept them in the city (**Jerusalem**; v. 22).

4:23 my servants. Nehemiah's immediate associates (see v. 16). In not taking **off** their **clothes**, they remained prepared for engagement with the enemy, if need be.

5:1–19 *Nehemiah Deals with Injustices in the Community; Nehemiah's Personal Contribution to the Project.* Nehemiah takes measures to end the exploitation of the weak in the community by its powerful members, who are ignoring God's commandments.

5:1 Nehemiah's story of the restoration is not triumphalistic, for it tells of serious shortcomings in the community. **great outcry**. This is typical language of protest under oppression (see Ex. 2:23). **The people** are the rank and file of the Jews. **And of their wives** adds to the picture of families made desperate by hunger. **Jewish brothers** shows the strong bond among all Israelites, such that, by Mosaic law, none should permanently enslave or exploit another (see Deut. 15:1–18).

5:2 Several kinds of complaints emerge in vv. 2–5, each concerning some cause of hardship, all made worse by the preoccupation with the walls, and apparently by a bad harvest. **let us get grain**. This cry, perhaps coming especially from the women, probably arises because the men who are fully engaged on the building project are not able to do their usual work and are therefore unable to feed their families.

5:3–4 We are mortgaging, that is, raising money by temporarily forfeiting the use and fruit of their property, which means that they also risk becoming insolvent. Some are borrowing to pay the heavy tax on produce levied by the Persians.

5:5 our flesh . . . our brothers. The complaint emphasizes the close relationship among Israelites (see note on v. 1). **forcing our sons and our daughters to be slaves**. Temporary debt-slavery (but not permanent chattel-slavery) was permitted in Mosaic law among Israelites, and was often the only way a debt could be paid, either after six years (Deut. 15:12) or at the Year of Jubilee (Lev. 25:39–40). But even this practice might hit families hard in the current situation; there is also a suggestion that those taken into debt-slavery are not being treated properly.

5:7 The nobles and the officials within the Jewish community are accused of oppressing their own people, showing that the danger to the community comes not only from outside but also from within. Oppression of the weak by the strong had been one of the reasons for God's anger that had brought about the exile (see Isa. 5:7, 8–10; Amos 2:6–8). **exacting interest**. While property might be taken in pledge, pending repayment of a loan, taking interest from a fellow Israelite who borrowed out of poverty and need was forbidden (Deut. 23:19–20).

5:8 our Jewish brothers. See vv. 1, 5. Nehemiah stresses this kinship in order to drive home the people's neglect of this great principle underlying the law. **sold . . . sell . . . sold**. In his anger, Nehemiah brings out the irony of the Jews being redeemed from exile only to be sold into slavery by their own brothers.

good. Ought you not to walk [m]in the fear of our God [n]to prevent the taunts of the nations
our enemies? **10** Moreover, I and my brothers and my servants are lending them money and
grain. Let us abandon this exacting of interest. **11** Return to them this very day their fields,
their vineyards, their olive orchards, and their houses, and the percentage of money, grain,
wine, and oil that you have been exacting from them." **12** Then they said, "We will restore
these and [o]require nothing from them. We will do as you say." And I called the priests and
[p]made them swear [q]to do as they had promised. **13** [r]I also shook out the fold[1] of my garment
and said, "So may God shake out every man from his house and from his labor who does
not keep this promise. So may he be shaken out and emptied." [s]And all the assembly said
"Amen" and praised the LORD. And the people did as they had promised.

Nehemiah's Generosity

14 Moreover, from the time that I was appointed to be their governor in the land of
Judah, from [t]the twentieth year to [u]the thirty-second year of Artaxerxes the king, twelve
years, [v]neither I nor my brothers ate the food allowance of the governor. **15** The former
governors who were before me laid heavy burdens on the people and took from them for
their daily ration[2] forty shekels[3] of silver. Even their servants lorded it over the people.
But I did not do so, [w]because of the fear of God. **16** I also persevered in the work on this
wall, and we acquired no land, and all my servants were gathered there for the work.
17 Moreover, there were [x]at my table 150 men, Jews and officials, besides those who came
to us from the nations that were around us. **18** [y]Now what was prepared at my expense[4]
for each day was one ox and six choice sheep and birds, and every ten days all kinds of
wine in abundance. Yet for all this [v]I did not demand the food allowance of the governor,
because the service was too heavy on this people. **19** [z]Remember for my good, O my God,
all that I have done for this people.

Conspiracy Against Nehemiah

6 Now when [a]Sanballat and Tobiah and [b]Geshem the Arab and the rest of our enemies
heard that I had built the wall and that there was no breach left in it ([c]although up to
that time I had not set up the doors in the gates), **2** Sanballat and Geshem sent to me, saying,
"Come and let us meet together at Hakkephirim in the plain of [d]Ono." But they intended
to do me harm. **3** And I sent messengers to them, saying, "I am doing a great work and I
cannot come down. Why should the work stop while I leave it and come down to you?"

9 [m]Lev. 25:36 [n]ch. 4:4; [2 Sam. 12:14]
12 [o][ch. 10:31] [p]Ezra 10:5 [q][Jer. 34:8, 9]
13 [r][Acts 18:6] [s]ch. 8:6; [Deut. 27:15]; 1 Chr. 16:36; Ps. 106:48
14 [t]ch. 2:1 [u]ch. 13:6 [v][2 Thess. 3:8]
15 [w]ver. 9
17 [x][2 Sam. 9:7, 10]; 1 Kgs. 18:19
18 [y][1 Kgs. 4:22, 23] [v][See ver. 14 above]
19 [z]ch. 13:14, 22, 31

Chapter 6

1 [a]ch. 2:10, 19; 4:1, 7 [b][ver. 6] [c][ch. 3:1, 3]
2 [d]1 Chr. 8:12

[1] Hebrew *bosom* [2] Compare Vulgate; Hebrew *took from them with food and wine afterward* [3] A *shekel* was about 2/5 ounce or 11 grams [4] Or *prepared for me*

5:9 fear of our God. See note on 1:11. **taunts**. See 4:1–4.

5:10 Nehemiah admits that he and his closest associates are implicated in the injustice and therefore presents his moral challenge as something to which he himself must respond.

5:11–12 Return . . . their fields. This appeal not only commands a return of the interest that was illegitimately seized, but is apparently a general amnesty, occasioned by the crisis and going beyond the provisions for debt-release (Deut. 15:1–11) or jubilee (Leviticus 25), since it is to be done without delay. The people agree, and solemnly undertake to keep their word.

5:13 shook out the fold. A symbolic action matching the words of the curse that follow. **So may God shake out**. This type of curse-formula was a solemn, conventional way of compelling commitment to a course of action. By saying **Amen**, the whole assembly took upon itself the terms of Nehemiah's curse.

5:14 governor. This is the first indication that Nehemiah held this official post in the province of Yehud (i.e., Judea), within the larger province of Beyond the River, and indeed that others had done so before him. **twentieth . . . thirty-second year**. 445 to 433 B.C. **food allowance of the governor**. Governors apparently had the right to raise taxes for their own use, but Nehemiah has not taken this due.

5:15 former governors. Nehemiah's predecessors, however, had used the people for the enrichment of themselves and their **servants**. **fear of God**. Nehemiah might mean that he respects God's law requiring all Jews to regard themselves as "brothers" (see vv. 1, 5, 8).

5:16 I also persevered. Nehemiah has put himself on a par with his fellow Jews, laboring with them and not using his position for gain.

5:17 at my table. This seems to refer to obligations that fell to Nehemiah by virtue of his position as governor. Those **who came . . . from the nations** may have been diplomatic visitors.

5:18 This heavy burden (v. 17) makes Nehemiah's self-sacrifice concerning the **food allowance** all the more remarkable. He does not wish to live comfortably while his people are in need.

5:19 Remember. See note on 1:8–9. This is the first of Nehemiah's prayers for God to remember: asking God to remember Nehemiah and his deeds, cf. 13:14, 22, 31; and to remember his opponents, cf. 6:14; 13:29. These prayers reflect the awareness that a merely human judgment might not achieve full justice. Nehemiah's deeds demonstrate his sincere faith, while the schemes of the opponents demonstrate their opposition to the well-being of God's people.

6:1–7:4 ***A Conspiracy against Nehemiah, but the Wall Is Finished.*** Nehemiah's enemies try to scare him into ceasing the work, but he is not deterred and the wall is finished.

6:1 With the wall almost complete, **Sanballat**, **Tobiah**, **Geshem**, and the **rest of our enemies** (see 2:10, 19) turn in desperation to trickery, knowing that they cannot overcome the Jews by direct assault.

6:2 Hakkephirim in the plain of Ono. This unknown place is presumably near the town of Ono (see Ezra 2:33), north of Jerusalem, perhaps serving as a kind of neutral ground. Nehemiah sees it as a conspiracy against him, since he knows they want to frustrate his work.

6:3 I am doing a great work and I cannot come down. Nehemiah would not divert time and effort from the Lord's work for discussions with his enemies that he knew would be fruitless at best and probably dangerous to him as well.

4 And they sent to me four times in this way, and I answered them in the same manner.
5 In the same way Sanballat for the fifth time sent his servant to me with an open letter in
his hand. 6 In it was written, "It is reported among the nations, and Geshem[1] also says it,
that you and [e]the Jews intend to rebel; that is why you are building the wall. And according to these reports you wish to become their king. 7 And you have also set up prophets to
proclaim concerning you in Jerusalem, 'There is a king in Judah.' And now the king will
hear of these reports. So now come and let us take counsel together." 8 Then I sent to him,
saying, "No such things as you say have been done, for you are inventing them out of your
own mind." 9 For they all wanted to frighten us, thinking, "Their hands will drop from the
work, and it will not be done." But now, O God,[2] strengthen my hands.

10 Now when I went into the house of Shemaiah the son of Delaiah, son of Mehetabel,
who was [f]confined to his home, he said, "Let us meet together in the house of God, within
the temple. Let us close the doors of the temple, for they are coming to kill you. They are
coming to kill you by night." 11 But I said, "Should such a man as I run away? And what
man such as I could go into the temple and live?[3] I will not go in." 12 And I understood
and saw that God had not sent him, [g]but he had pronounced the prophecy against me
because Tobiah and Sanballat had hired him. 13 For this purpose he was hired, that I should
be afraid and act in this way and sin, and so they could give me a bad name in order to
taunt me. 14 [h]Remember Tobiah and Sanballat, O my God, according to these things that
they did, and also [i]the prophetess Noadiah and the rest of the prophets who wanted to
make me afraid.

The Wall Is Finished

15 So the wall was finished on the twenty-fifth day of the month Elul, in fifty-two days.
16 And [j]when all our enemies heard of it, all the nations around us were afraid and fell
greatly in their own esteem, [k]for they perceived that this work had been accomplished
with the help of our God. 17 Moreover, in those days the nobles of Judah sent many letters

[1] Hebrew *Gashmu* [2] Hebrew lacks *O God* [3] *Or would go into the temple to save his life*

6 [e]ch. 2:19
10 [f][Jer. 36:5]
12 [g][Ezek. 13:17, 22]
14 [h]ch. 13:29 [i][Ezek. 13:17]
16 [j]ch. 2:10; 4:1, 7 [k][Ps. 126:2]

6:4 Nehemiah follows diplomatic protocol in the exchange of letters. Sanballat was, after all, the governor of Samaria, and relations with him would ultimately be important.

6:5–7 Sanballat's **fifth** attempt was an **open letter** (v. 5), its public nature intended to exert extra pressure on Nehemiah, perhaps by creating fear within his own community that his actions could lead to disaster. In the letter, Sanballat takes up the old allegation of rebellion against Persia (see Ezra 4:12–13) and claims to have testimony to it **among the nations** (Neh. 6:6), i.e., in the surrounding Persian provinces. **you wish to become their king. . . . There is a king in Judah** (vv. 6–7). If this charge were true, it would certainly inflame the Persians. And there was truth, of course, in the Jewish expectation of a coming Davidic king, based on prophetic promises (see Isa. 9:6–7; Jer. 23:5–6). A century earlier, Zerubbabel may have excited messianic expectations (see note on Ezra 2:2a). Sanballat portrays himself as loyal to Persia and also as the Jews' friend, offering to defuse the danger posed by these alleged rumors. **the** (Persian) **king will hear** (Neh. 6:7). This is, of course, a veiled threat.

6:6 you and the Jews intend to rebel; that is why you are building the wall. . . . you wish to become their king. These are lies and false accusations.

6:8 Nehemiah flatly denies the accusations (vv. 6–7). While he may have held long-term messianic hopes, as many no doubt did, he remained a loyal servant of Artaxerxes. Nehemiah had no aspirations to kingship—nor indeed a claim to it, since there is no reason to think he was of the Davidic line.

6:9 they all wanted to frighten us. Nehemiah sees the real intention of Sanballat's maneuvering and expresses the issue at stake: the work cannot be prevented by the schemes of enemies—that had been settled from the start, because the favor of the king himself had been secured by God's providence. Nehemiah acknowledges this fact by another prayer interjected into his narrative (see 2:4; 4:4–5; cf. note on 5:19).

6:10 Shemaiah is not otherwise known, but may have been a priest, which explains his proposal for a meeting in the temple (perhaps a second meeting from the one mentioned here). **confined to his home**. This possible translation of a difficult Hebrew word tries to explain why Nehemiah went to this man's house. It is not clear why he had been confined to his home: perhaps it was meant as a prophetic symbolic act suggesting that Jerusalem was surrounded by enemies. **within the temple . . . for they are coming to kill you**. This "warning" suggests a plot by Sanballat and other enemies. Shemaiah proposes that Nehemiah simply take refuge in the temple.

6:11 Nehemiah responds that such an act would be cowardly, and possibly sacrilegious.

6:12 God had not sent him. Shemaiah was pretending to speak with prophetic authority, but Nehemiah sees that his **prophecy** was false.

6:13 To **be afraid** would be in this case the opposite of having faith, and hence **sin** (see Deut. 1:28–33, also notes on Ezra 3:3; Neh. 4:14). This sort of unbelief would enable his enemies **to taunt** Nehemiah (see 5:9) and thus undermine his authority.

6:14 Nehemiah thinks again of prayer, calling on God to **remember** those who had tried to turn him (and therefore also his fellow Jews) from faith (cf. Matt. 18:6). This "remember" is typical of Nehemiah's prayers (Neh. 1:8; see note on 5:19), which always seek God's justice, whether for blessing or for judgment. **Tobiah** is placed first again here, but the circle of Nehemiah's enemies, including **the prophetess Noadiah** and other **prophets**, must have been considerable. Perhaps there were many incidents such as the one recorded here.

6:15–16 Elul was the sixth **month** (August–September), so it has been less than six months since Nehemiah spoke to the king. No doubt the speed of the building work itself contributed to the fear now felt by the enemies. Those enemies among **the nations around us** surely include Sanballat, Tobiah, and Geshem, and their peoples (see 4:7). **they perceived that this work had been accomplished with the help of our God**. If God had helped the people of Judah so remarkably in this way, the nations feared that this same God would turn Judah into a powerful nation that would be a threat to them.

6:17 The complicity of the **nobles of Judah** with **Tobiah** now strongly emerges; it is an alliance based on the marriages of Tobiah, an "Ammonite" (2:10), and his son into families of the Jewish nobility. It is ironic that Tobiah is

18 [l]Ezra 2:5 [m]Ezra 8:16
Chapter 7
1 [n][ch. 6:1]
2 [o]ch. 1:2 [p]ch. 2:8 [q][ch. 13:13]
5 [r]Ezra 1:11
6 [s]For ver. 6-73, see Ezra 2:1-70
7 [t][Ezra 2:2]
10 [u][Ezra 2:5]
12 [v][ver. 34]
15 [w][Ezra 2:10]
23 [x][Ezra 2:17]
25 [y][Ezra 2:20]
28 [z][Ezra 2:24]
29 [a][Ezra 2:25]
34 [b][ver. 12]
39 [c]1 Chr. 9:10; 24:7
40 [d]1 Chr. 9:12; 24:14
41 [e]1 Chr. 9:12
42 [f]1 Chr. 24:8

to Tobiah, and Tobiah's letters came to them. 18 For many in Judah were bound by oath to
him, because he was the son-in-law of Shecaniah the son of [l]Arah: and his son Jehohanan
had taken the daughter of [m]Meshullam the son of Berechiah as his wife. 19 Also they spoke
of his good deeds in my presence and reported my words to him. And Tobiah sent letters
to make me afraid.

7 Now when the wall had been built [n]and I had set up the doors, and the gatekeepers,
the singers, and the Levites had been appointed, 2 I gave [o]my brother Hanani and
Hananiah the governor of [p]the castle charge over Jerusalem, for he was [q]a more faithful
and God-fearing man than many. 3 And I said to them, "Let not the gates of Jerusalem be
opened until the sun is hot. And while they are still standing guard, let them shut and
bar the doors. Appoint guards from among the inhabitants of Jerusalem, some at their
guard posts and some in front of their own homes." 4 The city was wide and large, but the
people within it were few, and no houses had been rebuilt.

Lists of Returned Exiles

5 Then my God put it into my heart to assemble the nobles and the officials and the
people to be enrolled by genealogy. And I found the book of the genealogy of [r]those who
came up at the first, and I found written in it:

6 [s]These were the people of the province who came up out of the captivity of those
exiles whom Nebuchadnezzar the king of Babylon had carried into exile. They returned
to Jerusalem and Judah, each to his town. 7 They came with Zerubbabel, Jeshua, Nehemiah,
[t]Azariah, Raamiah, Nahamani, Mordecai, Bilshan, Mispereth, Bigvai, Nehum, Baanah.

The number of the men of the people of Israel: 8 the sons of Parosh, 2,172. 9 The sons of
Shephatiah, 372. 10 The sons of Arah, [u]652. 11 The sons of Pahath-moab, namely the sons of
Jeshua and Joab, 2,818. 12 The sons of [v]Elam, 1,254. 13 The sons of Zattu, 845. 14 The sons
of Zaccai, 760. 15 The sons of [w]Binnui, 648. 16 The sons of Bebai, 628. 17 The sons of Azgad,
2,322. 18 The sons of Adonikam, 667. 19 The sons of Bigvai, 2,067. 20 The sons of Adin, 655.
21 The sons of Ater, namely of Hezekiah, 98. 22 The sons of Hashum, 328. 23 The sons of
[x]Bezai, 324. 24 The sons of Hariph, 112. 25 The sons of [y]Gibeon, 95. 26 The men of Bethlehem
and Netophah, 188. 27 The men of Anathoth, 128. 28 The men [z]of Beth-azmaveth, 42. 29 The
men of [a]Kiriath-jearim, Chephirah, and Beeroth, 743. 30 The men of Ramah and Geba, 621.
31 The men of Michmas, 122. 32 The men of Bethel and Ai, 123. 33 The men of the other
Nebo, 52. 34 The sons of [b]the other Elam, 1,254. 35 The sons of Harim, 320. 36 The sons of
Jericho, 345. 37 The sons of Lod, Hadid, and Ono, 721. 38 The sons of Senaah, 3,930.

39 The priests: the sons of [c]Jedaiah, namely the house of Jeshua, 973. 40 The sons of [d]Immer,
1,052. 41 The sons of [e]Pashhur, 1,247. 42 The sons of [f]Harim, 1,017.

so highly regarded among the Israelites, in view of the measures Ezra had taken against intermarriage (Ezra 9–10). This perhaps explains Tobiah's hostility to Nehemiah's work, which was seen as being in continuity with Ezra's work.

6:18 bound by oath to him. It is not clear in what way they were bound. But there was clearly a powerful lobby in Jerusalem committed to Tobiah and opposed to Nehemiah.

7:1 Gatekeepers, singers, Levites is a typical grouping of worship officials (see Ezra 2:40–42), so it is surprising to find them in connection with guarding the walls. Yet the guarding of the city was ultimately related to establishing the worship of Yahweh in his temple.

7:2 On **Hanani**, see 1:2. He and **Hananiah** (7:2) may possibly replace the "rulers" named in 3:9, 12.

7:3 Caution is still necessary. The guards are appointed from among those who live in the city and thus are most committed to it.

7:4 Apparently the people are relatively **few** in number. The building of **houses** has taken second place to reconstructing the walls.

7:5–73 *A Record of Those Who Returned from Exile.* Nehemiah lists the returned exiles from the time of Zerubbabel.

7:5 my God put it into my heart. Cf. 2:12. Nehemiah maintains a close relationship with God, as evidenced by his frequent prayers and his clear convictions about God's guidance. He now decides to make a census of the people, and is helped by the discovery of the **book of the genealogy** of the **first** returnees.

7:6–73 This list is virtually identical to the one in Ezra 2 (see notes there). Therefore, its purpose is not to give new information but to highlight Nehemiah's next concern after completing the walls, namely, to repopulate Jerusalem (see Neh. 7:4). He may have had in mind such prophecies as Isaiah 62. Regarding the discrepancies in exact numbers between the list of returning exiles in Ezra 2:1–67 and Neh. 7:6–66, various solutions have been proposed, and several factors may have contributed to the differences. Since Nehemiah was reading from a copy of an older list (either the list in Ezra or an official list that both of them consulted), the list may have been updated and corrected to allow for a number of births and deaths that occurred shortly after the exiles returned, and perhaps in some cases people were counted or grouped differently or in different categories. Either or both lists may also have been corrected and supplemented by a number of relatives who had been delayed on the journey by illness or for other reasons, and were added later. Some of the differences may also be due to copying errors.

7:73b This half of the verse is an addition to Ezra 2:70. It brings the perspective of the narrative back to Nehemiah's time. The reference to the **seventh month** (September/October)—a festival month including the Day of Atonement—leads into the covenant renewal that follows.

43 The Levites: the sons of Jeshua, namely of Kadmiel of the sons of [g]Hodevah, 74. 44 The
singers: the sons of Asaph, 148. 45 The gatekeepers: the sons of Shallum, the sons of Ater,
the sons of Talmon, the sons of Akkub, the sons of Hatita, the sons of Shobai, 138.
46 The temple servants: the sons of Ziha, the sons of Hasupha, the sons of Tabbaoth,
47 the sons of Keros, the sons of [h]Sia, the sons of Padon, 48 the sons of Lebana, the sons of
[i]Hagaba, the sons of [i]Shalmai, 49 the sons of Hanan, the sons of Giddel, the sons of Gahar,
50 the sons of Reaiah, the sons of Rezin, the sons of Nekoda, 51 the sons of Gazzam, the
sons of Uzza, the sons of Paseah, 52 the sons of Besai, the sons of Meunim, the sons of
[j]Nephushesim, 53 the sons of Bakbuk, the sons of Hakupha, the sons of Harhur, 54 the
sons of [k]Bazlith, the sons of Mehida, the sons of Harsha, 55 the sons of Barkos, the sons
of Sisera, the sons of Temah, 56 the sons of Neziah, the sons of Hatipha.
57 The sons of Solomon's servants: the sons of Sotai, the sons of Sophereth, the sons of
[l]Perida, 58 the sons of Jaala, the sons of Darkon, the sons of Giddel, 59 the sons of Shephatiah,
the sons of Hattil, the sons of Pochereth-hazzebaim, the sons of [m]Amon.
60 All the temple servants and the sons of Solomon's servants were 392.
61 [n]The following were those who came up from Tel-melah, Tel-harsha, Cherub, [o]Ad-
don, and Immer, but they could not prove their fathers' houses nor their descent, whether
they belonged to Israel: 62 the sons of Delaiah, the sons of Tobiah, the sons of Nekoda, 642.
63 Also, of the priests: the sons of Hobaiah, the sons of Hakkoz, the sons of Barzillai (who
had taken a wife of the daughters of Barzillai the Gileadite and was called by their name).
64 These sought their registration among those enrolled in the genealogies, but it was not
found there, so they were excluded from the priesthood as unclean. 65 [p]The [q]governor told
them that they were not to partake of the most holy food until a priest with Urim and
Thummim should arise.

Totals of People and Gifts

66 The whole assembly together was 42,360, 67 besides their male and female servants, of
whom there were 7,337. And they had 245 singers, male and female. 68 Their horses were
736, their mules 245,[1] 69 their camels 435, and their donkeys 6,720.
70 Now some of the heads of fathers' houses gave to the work. The [q]governor gave to the
treasury 1,000 darics[2] of gold, 50 basins, 30 priests' garments and 500 minas[3] of silver.[4]
71 And some of the heads of fathers' houses gave into the treasury of the work 20,000 darics
of gold and 2,200 minas of silver. 72 [r]And what the rest of the people gave was 20,000 darics
of gold, 2,000 minas of silver, and 67 priests' garments.
73 So the priests, the Levites, the gatekeepers, the singers, some of the people, the temple
servants, and all Israel, lived in their towns.
[s]And when the seventh month had come, the people of Israel were in their towns.

Ezra Reads the Law

8 And all the people gathered as one man into the square before [t]the Water Gate. And
they told [u]Ezra the scribe to bring the Book of the Law of Moses that the LORD had
commanded Israel. 2 So Ezra the priest [v]brought the Law before the assembly, both men

[1] Compare Ezra 2:66 and the margins of some Hebrew manuscripts; Hebrew lacks *Their horses . . . 245* [2] A *daric* was a coin weighing about 1/4 ounce or 8.5 grams [3] A *mina* was about 1 1/4 pounds or 0.6 kilogram [4] Probable reading; Hebrew lacks *minas of silver*

43 [g][Ezra 2:40; 3:9]
47 [h][Ezra 2:44]
48 [i][Ezra 2:46]
52 [j][Ezra 2:50]
54 [k][Ezra 2:52]
57 [l][Ezra 2:55]
59 [m][Ezra 2:57]
61 [n]Ezra 2:59 [o][Ezra 2:59]
65 [p]Ezra 2:63 [q]ch. 8:9; 10:1
70 [q][See ver. 65 above]
72 [r][Ezra 2:69]
73 [s]Ezra 3:1

Chapter 8

1 [t]ch. 3:26 [u]See Ezra 7:6
2 [v]See Deut. 31:11

8:1–10:39 *The Reading of the Law and Covenant Renewal.* In this long section, the Book of the Law is solemnly read, the Feast of Booths is kept, and a great act of covenant renewal is performed. For the first time in this book, Ezra enters the narrative. This section shows the unity of his and Nehemiah's projects. With the walls securely in place, the centrality of the Mosaic law is once again made prominent, since it is not security alone that is essential to the life of the community, nor even the temple, but trust in God and obedience to God's Word as revealed through Moses. The whole passage has Leviticus 23 especially in mind.

8:1–8 *The Law Is Read.* Ezra reads the Book of the Law to all the people, and the Levites ensure that everyone has understood it.

8:1 The **Water Gate**. See note on 3:26. The people could have gathered either inside or outside the gate. **the Book of the Law of Moses**. The phrase presumably refers here to all or most of what is known as the Pentateuch, though in Deuteronomy similar expressions apparently refer to that book in particular (Deut. 28:58, 61; 31:9; see also 2 Kings 22:8).

8:2 priest. Ezra had authorization from Artaxerxes (Ezra 7:25–26), but more importantly, from the Mosaic law itself (Deut. 33:10). **the assembly**. The people of Israel gathered for worship. The inclusion of both **men and women** is stressed, since the strict keeping of the great Jerusalem feasts was expected of men only (Deut. 16:16–17). **all who could understand**. "Understanding" is a key theme in this chapter, since it was vital that all should be able to know and learn God's ways as revealed to Israel. The reading and teaching of the law may have been neglected in the generations since the first return from Babylon. The **first day of the seventh month** was a day of "solemn rest," like a Sabbath, in the month in which the Day of Atonement was kept and the Feast of Booths was celebrated (see Lev. 23:24–25, 27, 34). Remarkably,

2 [w]Lev. 23:24
3 [x]See ch. 13:1
6 [y]See ch. 5:13 [z]Ps. 134:2; Lam. 3:41; [1 Tim. 2:8] [a]See 2 Chr. 20:18
7 [b][ch. 9:4] [c]See 2 Chr. 35:3 [d]ch. 9:3
9 [e]ch. 7:65, 70; 10:1; Ezra 2:63 [f]ch. 12:26 [g]ver. 2; Lev. 23:24; Num. 29:1 [h][Eccles. 3:4]
10 [i]Esth. 9:19, 22
12 [j]ver. 7, 8
14 [k]Lev. 23:34, 40, 42
15 [l]Lev. 23:4 [m]Deut. 16:16 [n][Lev. 23:40]
16 [o]See 1 Sam. 9:25 [p]ver. 1, 3; ch. 3:26 [q]ch. 12:39; 2 Kgs. 14:13; 2 Chr. 25:23

and women and all who could understand what they heard, [w]on the first day of the seventh month. 3 [x]And he read from it facing the square before the Water Gate from early
morning until midday, in the presence of the men and the women and those who could
understand. And the ears of all the people were attentive to the Book of the Law. 4 And Ezra
the scribe stood on a wooden platform that they had made for the purpose. And beside
him stood Mattithiah, Shema, Anaiah, Uriah, Hilkiah, and Maaseiah on his right hand,
and Pedaiah, Mishael, Malchijah, Hashum, Hashbaddanah, Zechariah, and Meshullam on
his left hand. 5 And Ezra opened the book in the sight of all the people, for he was above
all the people, and as he opened it all the people stood. 6 And Ezra blessed the LORD, the
great God, and all the people answered, [y]"Amen, Amen," [z]lifting up their hands. [a]And they
bowed their heads and worshiped the LORD with their faces to the ground. 7 [b]Also Jeshua,
Bani, Sherebiah, Jamin, Akkub, Shabbethai, Hodiah, Maaseiah, Kelita, Azariah, Jozabad,
Hanan, Pelaiah, the Levites,[1] [c]helped the people to understand the Law, [d]while the people
remained in their places. 8 They read from the book, from the Law of God, clearly,[2] and
they gave the sense, so that the people understood the reading.

This Day Is Holy

9 And Nehemiah, who was [e]the governor, and Ezra [f]the priest and scribe, and the Levites
who taught the people said to all the people, [g]"This day is holy to the LORD your God; [h]do
not mourn or weep." For all the people wept as they heard the words of the Law. 10 Then he
said to them, "Go your way. Eat the fat and drink sweet wine and [i]send portions to anyone
who has nothing ready, for this day is holy to our Lord. And do not be grieved, for the joy
of the LORD is your strength." 11 So the Levites calmed all the people, saying, "Be quiet, for
this day is holy; do not be grieved." 12 And all the people went their way to eat and drink
and to send portions and to make great rejoicing, because [j]they had understood the words
that were declared to them.

Feast of Booths Celebrated

13 On the second day the heads of fathers' houses of all the people, with the priests and
the Levites, came together to Ezra the scribe in order to study the words of the Law. 14 And
they found it written in the Law that the LORD had commanded by Moses [k]that the people
of Israel should dwell in booths[3] during the feast of the seventh month, 15 and that they
should proclaim it and [l]publish it in all their towns and [m]in Jerusalem, "Go out to the
hills and bring [n]branches of olive, wild olive, myrtle, palm, and other leafy trees to make
booths, as it is written." 16 So the people went out and brought them and made booths for
themselves, each [o]on his roof, and in their courts and in the courts of the house of God,
and in the square at [p]the Water Gate and in the square at [q]the Gate of Ephraim. 17 And all

[1] Vulgate; Hebrew *and the Levites* [2] Or *with interpretation*, or *paragraph by paragraph* [3] Or *temporary shelters*

the Day of Atonement is apparently not observed on this occasion, or at least its observance is not recorded.

8:3 from early morning until midday. The book was lengthy, and there may have been frequent pauses for explanation of the text (see note on v. 7).

8:4 The **platform**, together with the group of leading men standing with Ezra, emphasized the solemnity of the reading, and allowed all the people to see and hear Ezra.

8:5 opened the book. The act of reading, in this carefully organized setting, is also a corporate act of worship.

8:7 The **Levites** presumably moved among the crowd, ensuring that all could **understand** what was being read. Such interpretation was one of their special tasks (see also Deut. 33:10; 2 Chron. 17:7–9). In order to facilitate this teaching, the law may have been read in manageable sections. The kind of understanding meant is primarily spiritual, though there could also have been problems with basic concepts and even language and audibility.

8:8 They read. The verse sums up vv. 3–7 and combines the reading and interpreting, though the primary reading was done by Ezra.

8:9–12 *The People Are to Be Joyful.* Though sorrow for sin was a positive response, joy at renewed relationship with God was the teaching's ultimate purpose.

8:9 Nehemiah and Ezra together decide that this **holy** day (Lev. 23:24) should be one of joy, though the reading has led many to sense the need to repent of their sins.

8:10 the joy of the LORD is your strength. As the people rejoiced in God and delighted in his presence, he would show himself strong to help them and defend them. "Joy" was a keynote because God had saved Israel, in both the remote and the recent past, and this story of salvation would have been told again in the reading of the Book of the Law.

8:12 eat . . . drink . . . send portions. These are important themes of worship in Deuteronomy, where worship was associated with God's rich gifts and the privilege of sharing them (Deut. 12:12; 14:23, 26, 27–29).

8:13–18 *The People Keep the Feast of Booths.* This family-oriented festival highlighted God's protection of Israel in the desert before the conquest.

8:13–14 The following **day**, the leaders of the community, taking up their responsibility for studying the **Law**, realize that they are in the month of the Feast of Booths, or the **feast of the seventh month** (Lev. 23:33–43).

8:15 The people kept this feast by living in temporary dwellings made from **branches** to commemorate how they had lived in **booths** in the wilderness after God had brought them out of Egypt (Lev. 23:43).

8:17 from the days of Jeshua the son of Nun. "Jeshua" is another form of "Joshua." **had not done so**. Although the Feast of Booths had been celebrated on occasion (cf. 1 Kings 8:65; 2 Chron. 7:9; Ezra 3:4), it had

the assembly of those who had returned from the captivity made booths and lived in the
booths, for from the days of Jeshua the son of Nun to that day [r]the people of Israel had
not done so. And there was [s]very great rejoicing. 18 And day by day, from the first day to
the last day, [t]he read from the Book of the Law of God. They kept the feast seven days, and
[u]on the eighth day there was a solemn assembly, according to the rule.

The People of Israel Confess Their Sin

9 Now on the twenty-fourth day of [v]this month the people of Israel were assembled
[w]with fasting [x]and in sackcloth, [y]and with earth on their heads. 2 [z]And the Israelites[1]
separated themselves from all foreigners and stood and confessed their sins and the iniquities of their fathers. 3 [a]And they stood up in their place and read from the Book of the
Law of the LORD their God for a quarter of the day; for another quarter of it they made
confession and worshiped the LORD their God. 4 On the stairs of the Levites stood [b]Jeshua,
Bani, Kadmiel, Shebaniah, Bunni, Sherebiah, Bani, and Chenani; and they cried with a
loud voice to the LORD their God. 5 Then the Levites, Jeshua, Kadmiel, Bani, Hashabneiah,
Sherebiah, Hodiah, Shebaniah, and Pethahiah, said, "Stand up and bless the LORD your
God from everlasting to everlasting. [c]Blessed be your glorious name, which is exalted
above all blessing and praise.
6 [2] [d]"You are the LORD, you alone. [e]You have made heaven, [f]the heaven of heavens, [g]with all
their host, [e]the earth and all that is on it, the seas and all that is in them; [h]and you preserve
all of them; and the host of heaven worships you. 7 You are the LORD, the God [i]who chose
Abram and brought him out of [j]Ur of the Chaldeans [k]and gave him the name Abraham.
8 [l]You found his heart faithful before you, [m]and made with him the covenant to give to his
offspring [n]the land of the Canaanite, the Hittite, the Amorite, the Perizzite, the Jebusite,
and the Girgashite. [o]And you have kept your promise, for you are righteous.
9 [p]"And you saw the affliction of our fathers in Egypt and heard [q]their cry at the Red
Sea, 10 [r]and performed signs and wonders against Pharaoh and all his servants and all the
people of his land, for you knew that [s]they acted arrogantly against our fathers. And [t]you
made a name for yourself, as it is to this day. 11 [u]And you divided the sea before them, so
that they went through the midst of the sea on dry land, and you cast their pursuers into
the depths, [v]as a stone into mighty waters. 12 By [w]a pillar of cloud you led them in the day,
and by a pillar of fire in the night to light for them the way in which they should go. 13 [x]You
came down on Mount Sinai [y]and spoke with them from heaven and gave them [z]right rules

[1] Hebrew *the offspring of Israel* [2] Septuagint adds *And Ezra said*

17 [r][1 Kgs. 8:2; 2 Chr. 7:9; 8:13; Ezra 3:4] [s][2 Chr. 30:21]
18 [t]Deut. 31:10, 11 [u]Lev. 23:36; Num. 29:35

Chapter 9

1 [v][ch. 8:2] [w][1 Sam. 7:6] [x]See 2 Sam. 3:31 [y]See Josh. 7:6
2 [z]ch. 10:28; 13:3, 30; [Ezra 6:21; 10:11]
3 [a]ch. 8:7, 8
4 [b][ch. 8:7]
5 [c][1 Chr. 29:13]
6 [d]See 2 Kgs. 19:15 [e]See Gen. 1:1 [f]See Deut. 10:14 [g]See Gen. 2:1 [h][Ps. 36:6]
7 [i]See Gen. 11:31 [j]Gen. 11:31 [k]Gen. 17:5
8 [l]Gen. 15:6 [m]Gen. 12:7; 15:18; 17:7-9 [n]See Ex. 13:5 [o][Josh. 23:14]
9 [p]Ex. 3:7 [q]Ex. 14:10
10 [r]See Ex. 7–14 [s]Ex. 18:11 [t]Isa. 63:12, 14; Jer. 32:20; Dan. 9:15; [Ex. 9:16]
11 [u]Ex. 14:21, 22, 27, 28; Ps. 78:13 [v]Ex. 15:5, 10
12 [w]ver. 19; Ex. 13:21, 22; Num. 14:14; 1 Cor. 10:1
13 [x]Ex. 19:20 [y]See Ex. 20:1-17 [z]Ps. 19:8, 9; [Rom. 7:12]; See Ps. 119

apparently not been celebrated in this way (with such overwhelming joy, or in such unsettled conditions, or with all the people participating).

8:18 seven days. See Lev. 23:34. For the reading of the law at the Feast of Booths (every seven years), see Deut. 31:10–11.

9:1–38 *A Prayer of Confession, Penitence, and Covenant Commitment.* The next phase in the great act of covenant renewal is a prayer of praise, confession, and petition.

9:1 the twenty-fourth day. It is still the seventh **month**, after the seven days of the Feast of Booths and an eighth day of solemn assembly (8:18).

9:2 separated themselves from all foreigners. This is in line with the measures described in Ezra 9–10. Here it refers not just to marriage but to the integrity of the community in general. **iniquities of their fathers.** That is, of all previous generations, as in the prayer that follows (Neh. 9:6–37).

9:3 Book of the Law. See note on 8:1.

9:4–5 Some of these leading **Levites** were among those who interpreted the law while Ezra read it (8:7–8). They now lead in prayer. Ezra himself has fallen into the background. Yet some translations have "And Ezra said" at the beginning of 9:6, following the ancient Greek text (see ESV footnote), not the Hebrew.

9:6–37 The prayer resembles in part Ezra's prayer of confession upon his discovery of the problem of mixed marriages (Ezra 9:6–15). It has even more in common with certain psalms of confession (such as Psalm 78; 105–106), which interweave confession with memories of God's grace, and notes of petition. The prayer follows the biblical story as told in Genesis–Kings.

9:6–8 The Levites' prayer begins with Genesis: the universal God of creation **chose Abram** and brought his descendants into the land he promised to them.

9:6 You are the LORD, you alone. The uniqueness of Israel's God was proclaimed in the story of creation. **heaven . . . the earth.** Together these sum up the whole creation (see Gen. 1:1; Ex. 20:11). **All their host** could refer to either angels or stars.

9:7 Ur of the Chaldeans is in southern Mesopotamia (see Gen. 11:31). **the name Abraham.** See Gen. 17:5.

9:8 the covenant. God promised Abraham both descendants and land when he made a covenant with him. This was essentially a covenant of **promise** (Gen. 15:18–21; 17:4–8). The promise to drive out other nations has particular overtones in this period of restoration to the land. **you are righteous.** This is one of God's essential characteristics (Deut. 32:4; Ps. 119:137), shown here in his faithfulness to his promises.

9:9–15 The prayer now recalls God's deliverance of Israel in the exodus from Egypt, as told in the book of Exodus.

9:9–11 heard their cry at the Red Sea. This telescopes the whole story from Exodus 2–15 (see Ex. 2:23–25; 14:1–15:27). **signs and wonders . . . divided the sea.** This phrase refers to the miracles done against Pharaoh to compel him to release the Israelites (Exodus 7–15).

9:12 The **pillar of cloud** and the **pillar of fire** provided God's guidance (see Ex. 13:21–22).

9:13–14 Mount Sinai is the place of the Mosaic covenant, where God gave the Ten Commandments and other **rules, laws, statutes,** and **commandments,** i.e., detailed instructions applying the force of the

and true laws, good statutes and commandments, 14 [a]and you made known to them your
holy Sabbath and commanded them commandments and statutes and a law by Moses
your servant. 15 [b]You gave them bread from heaven for their hunger and [c]brought water
for them out of the rock for their thirst, and you [d]told them to go in to possess the land
that you had sworn to give them.

16 "But they and our fathers [e]acted presumptuously and stiffened their neck and did not
obey your commandments. 17 They refused to obey [f]and were not mindful of the wonders
that you performed among them, but they stiffened their neck and appointed a leader to
return to their slavery in Egypt. But you are a God ready to forgive, [g]gracious and merciful,
slow to anger and abounding in steadfast love, and did not forsake them. 18 Even [h]when
they had made for themselves a golden[1] calf and said, 'This is your God who brought you
up out of Egypt,' [i]and had committed great blasphemies, 19 you [j]in your great mercies
did not forsake them in the wilderness. [k]The pillar of cloud to lead them in the way did
not depart from them by day, [k]nor the pillar of fire by night to light for them the way by
which they should go. 20 [l]You gave your good Spirit to instruct them [m]and did not withhold your manna from their mouth and gave them water for their thirst. 21 [n]Forty years
you sustained them in the wilderness, and they lacked nothing. Their clothes did not wear
out and their feet did not swell.

22 "And you gave them kingdoms and peoples and allotted to them every corner. [o]So they
took possession of the land of Sihon king of Heshbon [p]and the land of Og king of Bashan.
23 You multiplied their children [q]as the stars of heaven, and you brought them into the
land that you had told their fathers to enter and possess. 24 [r]So the descendants went in
and possessed the land, [s]and you subdued before them the inhabitants of the land, the
Canaanites, and gave them into their hand, with their kings and the peoples of the land,
that they might do with them as they would. 25 And they captured [t]fortified cities and [u]a
rich land, and took possession of [v]houses full of all good things, cisterns already hewn,
vineyards, olive orchards and fruit trees in abundance. So they ate and were filled [w]and
became fat and delighted themselves in [x]your great goodness.

26 [y]"Nevertheless, they were disobedient and rebelled against you [z]and cast your law
behind their back [a]and killed your prophets, who [b]had warned them in order to turn them
back to you, [c]and they committed great blasphemies. 27 [d]Therefore you gave them into the
hand of their enemies, who made them suffer. [e]And in the time of their suffering they cried
out to you and you heard them from heaven, and according to your great mercies you gave
them [f]saviors who saved them from the hand of their enemies. 28 [g]But after they had rest
they did evil again before you, and you abandoned them to the hand of their enemies,
so that they had dominion over them. Yet when they turned and cried to you, you heard
from heaven, [h]and many times you delivered them according to your mercies. 29 [b]And you
warned them in order to turn them back to your law. Yet [i]they acted presumptuously and
did not obey your commandments, but sinned against your rules, [j]which if a person does
them, he shall live by them, [k]and they turned a stubborn shoulder [l]and stiffened their neck

14 [a]Ex. 16:23; 20:8-11; [Gen. 2:2, 3; Ezek. 20:12, 20]
15 [b][Ex. 16:14, 15; Ps. 78:25; 105:40; 1 Cor. 10:3]; Cited John 6:31 [c]Ex. 17:6; Num. 20:10; Ps. 78:15-17; 105:41; 1 Cor. 10:4 [d]Deut. 1:8
16 [e]Ex. 18:11
17 [f]Ps. 78:11, 42, 43 [g]ver. 31; Ex. 34:6; Num. 14:18; Ps. 86:5, 15; Joel 2:13
18 [h]Ex. 32:4; Ps. 106:19, 20; Acts 7:41 [i]ver. 26; Ps. 78:41, 58; [Heb. 3:15]
19 [j]ver. 27, 31; Ps. 106:45 [k]See ver. 12
20 [l]Isa. 63:11; [Num. 11:17] [m][Ex. 16:35]; See ver. 15
21 [n]Deut. 2:7
22 [o]See Num. 21:21-31 [p]See Num. 21:33-35
23 [q]Gen. 15:5; 22:17
24 [r]See Josh. 1–12 [s]Ps. 44:2, 3
25 [t]Deut. 3:5; 9:1; Josh. 10:20; 14:12 [u]ver. 35; [Num. 13:20, 27; Deut. 8:7, 8; Ezek. 20:6] [v]Deut. 6:11 [w]Deut. 32:15 [x]ver. 35; Hos. 3:5
26 [y]Judg. 2:11, 12; Ezek. 20:21 [z]Ps. 50:17; [1 Kgs. 14:9] [a]1 Kgs. 18:4; 19:10; 2 Chr. 24:20, 21; Matt. 23:37; Acts 7:52 [b]See ver. 30 [c]See ver. 18
27 [d]Judg. 2:14; Ps. 106:41, 42 [e]Ps. 106:44, 45 [f]Judg. 2:16; 3:9
28 [g]Judg. 3:11, 12, 30; 4:1; 5:31; 6:1 [h]Ps. 106:43
29 [b][See ver. 26 above] [i]ver. 10, 16 [j]See Lev. 18:5 [k]Zech. 7:11 [l]See ver. 16

[1] Hebrew *metal*

Ten Commandments to many cases in life. Law codes are found in Ex. 20:22–23:19; Leviticus; Deuteronomy 12–26.

9:15 bread from heaven . . . water. Cf. Ex. 16:14–15; 17:6.

9:16–18 Israel has often rebelled against God and must rely on his grace (see Deut. 9:4–6). **appointed a leader**. See Num. 14:4. The people must have gone ahead and chosen a different leader, though Numbers 14 contains no record of the actual appointment. **Golden calf** refers to the apostasy committed while the covenant was still being made at Sinai (Exodus 32; Deut. 9:7–21). Yet God was **ready to forgive, gracious and merciful** (Neh. 9:17). See Ex. 34:6–7. God immediately made a new covenant and promised his continued presence, despite Israel's sin.

9:19–21 The Levites' confession continues to recount God's goodness in the wilderness.

9:21 Forty years. See Deut. 2:7. **Their clothes did not wear out and their feet did not swell**. From Deut. 8:4, recounting God's extraordinary preservation.

9:22–25 At this point the prayer retells in brief the story of the occupation of the land. It covers the events of the book of Joshua, using the language of Deuteronomy. **Sihon . . . Og**. See Deut. 2:26–3:11. **stars of heaven**. See Deut. 1:10.

9:25 a rich land. See Deut. 6:10–11; 8:7–10. The prospect of a plentiful land was accompanied in Deuteronomy by warnings that wealth could lead to abandonment of God (Deut. 6:12–15; 8:11–20). This is precisely what happened.

9:26–28 This pattern of sin, judgment, repentance, and deliverance is typical of the book of Judges. **killed your prophets**. Cf. Matt. 23:31; Acts 7:52.

9:29–31 The idea of God's long patience with the Israelites' sin, calling them back by the prophets but ending finally in judgment, is the story of 1–2 Kings (see 2 Kings 17).

and would not obey. 30 Many years [m]you bore with them [n]and warned them [o]by your Spirit
through your prophets. [p]Yet they would not give ear. [q]Therefore you gave them into the
hand of the peoples of the lands. 31 Nevertheless, [r]in your great mercies [s]you did not make
an end of them or forsake them, [t]for you are a gracious and merciful God.
32 "Now, therefore, our God, [u]the great, the mighty, and the awesome God, who keeps
covenant and steadfast love, let not all the hardship seem little to you that has come upon
us, upon our kings, our princes, our priests, our prophets, our fathers, and all your people,
[v]since the time of the kings of Assyria until this day. 33 [w]Yet you have been righteous in all
that has come upon us, for you have dealt faithfully [x]and we have acted wickedly. 34 Our
kings, our princes, our priests, and our fathers have not kept your law or paid attention to
your commandments and your warnings that you gave them. 35 Even in their own kingdom,
[y]and amid your great goodness that you gave them, and in the large and [y]rich land that
you set before them, [z]they did not serve you or turn from their wicked works. 36 Behold,
[a]we are slaves this day; in the land that you gave to our fathers to enjoy its fruit and its
good gifts, behold, we are slaves. 37 [b]And its rich yield goes to the kings whom you have
set over us because of our sins. They rule over our bodies and over our livestock as they
please, and we are in great distress.
38 [1] "Because of all this [c]we make a firm covenant in writing; on [d]the sealed document
are the names of [2] our princes, our Levites, and our priests.

The People Who Sealed the Covenant

10 [3] [e]"On the seals are the names of [4] Nehemiah [f]the governor, [g]the son of Hacaliah,
Zedekiah, 2 [h]Seraiah, Azariah, Jeremiah, 3 Pashhur, Amariah, Malchijah, 4 [i]Hattush,
Shebaniah, Malluch, 5 Harim, Meremoth, Obadiah, 6 Daniel, Ginnethon, Baruch,
7 Meshullam, Abijah, Mijamin, 8 Maaziah, Bilgai, Shemaiah; these are the priests. 9 And the
Levites: [j]Jeshua the son of Azaniah, Binnui of the sons of [k]Henadad, Kadmiel; 10 and their
brothers, Shebaniah, Hodiah, Kelita, Pelaiah, Hanan, 11 Mica, Rehob, Hashabiah, 12 Zaccur,
Sherebiah, Shebaniah, 13 Hodiah, Bani, Beninu. 14 The chiefs of the people: [l]Parosh, Pahath-
moab, Elam, Zattu, Bani, 15 Bunni, Azgad, Bebai, 16 Adonijah, Bigvai, Adin, 17 Ater, Hezekiah,
Azzur, 18 Hodiah, Hashum, Bezai, 19 Hariph, Anathoth, Nebai, 20 Magpiash, Meshullam,
Hezir, 21 Meshezabel, Zadok, Jaddua, 22 Pelatiah, Hanan, Anaiah, 23 Hoshea, Hananiah,
Hasshub, 24 Hallohesh, Pilha, Shobek, 25 Rehum, Hashabnah, Maaseiah, 26 Ahiah, Hanan,
Anan, 27 Malluch, Harim, Baanah.

The Obligations of the Covenant

28 [m]"The rest of the people, the priests, the Levites, the gatekeepers, the singers, the
temple servants, [n]and all who have separated themselves from the peoples of the lands
to the Law of God, their wives, their sons, their daughters, all who have knowledge and
understanding, 29 join with their brothers, their nobles, [o]and enter into a curse and an oath
[p]to walk in God's Law that was given by Moses the servant of God, and to observe and do

[1] Ch 10:1 in Hebrew [2] Hebrew lacks *the names of* [3] Ch 10:2 in Hebrew [4] Hebrew lacks *the names of*

30 [m][Acts 13:18] [n]ver. 26, 29, 34; 2 Kgs. 17:13 [o]1 Pet. 1:10, 11; 2 Pet. 1:21 [p]Acts 7:51 [q]Ezra 9:7; [Isa. 42:24]
31 [r]ver. 19, 27 [s]Jer. 4:27; 5:10, 18 [t]ver. 17
32 [u]ch. 1:5; Deut. 7:21 [v]2 Kgs. 17:3
33 [w]See Ezra 9:15 [x]Ps. 106:6; Dan. 9:5
35 [y]ver. 25 [z]Deut. 28:47
36 [a]Ezra 9:9
37 [b]Deut. 28:33, 51
38 [c]2 Kgs. 23:3; 2 Chr. 29:10; 34:31; Ezra 10:3; [ch. 10:29]; ch. 10:1 [d][ch. 10:1]

Chapter 10
1 [e]ch. 9:38 [f]See ch. 8:9 [g]ch. 1:1
2 [h]For ver. 2-27, see ch. 12:2-21
4 [i]Ezra 8:2
9 [j]Ezra 2:40 [k]Ezra 3:9
14 [l]See ch. 7:8-42; Ezra 2:3-35
28 [m]See Ezra 2:36-54 [n]See ch. 9:2
29 [o]ch. 5:12, 13; Deut. 29:12, 14; [Ps. 119:106] [p][2 Kgs. 23:3; 2 Chr. 34:31]

9:30 into the hand of the peoples. For the northern kingdom this meant Assyria (2 Kings 17), while for Judah it meant Babylon (2 Kings 24–25).

9:31 you did not make an end of them. Second Chronicles 36:22–23 and the books of Ezra and Nehemiah demonstrate this.

9:32–33 All the hardship refers to the sufferings of both exiles (Assyrian and Babylonian). The people have suffered greatly, yet God has been **righteous** (v. 33) in his judgment (see note on v. 8).

9:34–35 The prayer acknowledges again that the people sinned amid God's blessing.

9:36–37 we are slaves. This sinfulness explains why the people are not yet entirely free and why the blessings of the land are not yet fully enjoyed under Persian rule, even though that rule is somewhat gentler than was the rule of Assyria and Babylon.

9:38 To mend the situation, the people will now enter a solemn **covenant** (Hb. *'amanah*). The word used is not the usual word for "covenant," which is *berit*, but a rarer one that emphasizes faithfulness; the people pledge to keep faithfully what they now undertake.

10:1–39 *Signatories and Specific Commitments.* Many of the people agree to the covenant, and they accept the responsibility of funding the temple's activities.

10:1–27 The long list of those who put their names to the covenant is designed to show that the entire community—priests, Levites, and lay leaders—was wholeheartedly behind it. These are prominent people in the community; many of their names have appeared before in Nehemiah (esp. in vv. 20–27; see also ch. 3).

10:28–39 The people essentially undertake to keep the entire Mosaic law. The enumeration of laws is selective, however, highlighting major issues of their day.

10:28–29 The range of those who solemnly agreed to the covenant is now widened to include all groups in the community.

10:29 a curse and an oath. The two expressions convey together the people's serious intention to keep their commitment. The "curse" refers to some terrible penalty, perhaps performed as a ritual, that they accept as their due if they fail (see 1 Kings 19:2; Jer. 34:18). **commandments . . . rules . . . statutes.** See note on Neh. 9:13–14.

all the commandments of the LORD our Lord and his rules and his statutes. 30 [q]We will not
give our daughters to the peoples of the land or take their daughters for our sons. 31 [r]And
if the peoples of the land bring in goods or any grain on the Sabbath day to sell, we will
not buy from them on the Sabbath or on a holy day. And we will forego the crops of the
[s]seventh year and the [t]exaction of every debt.
32 "We also take on ourselves the obligation to give yearly [u]a third part of a shekel[1] for
the service of the house of our God: 33 [v]for the showbread, [w]the regular grain offering, [w]the
regular burnt offering, the Sabbaths, the new moons, the appointed feasts, the holy things,
and the sin offerings to make atonement for Israel, and for all the work of the house of our
God. 34 [x]We, the priests, the Levites, and the people, have likewise cast lots [y]for the wood
offering, to bring it into the house of our God, according to our fathers' houses, at times
appointed, year by year, to burn on the altar of the LORD our God, [z]as it is written in the
Law. 35 We obligate ourselves [a]to bring the firstfruits of our ground and the firstfruits of
all fruit of every tree, year by year, to the house of the LORD; 36 also to bring to the house of
our God, to the priests who minister in the house of our God, the firstborn of our sons and
of our cattle, [b]as it is written in the Law, and the firstborn of our herds and of our flocks;
37 [c]and to bring the first of our dough, and our contributions, the fruit of every tree, the
wine and the oil, to the priests, [d]to the chambers of the house of our God; and to bring to
the Levites the tithes from our ground, for it is the Levites who collect the tithes in all our
towns where we labor. 38 And the priest, the son of Aaron, shall be with the Levites when
the Levites receive the tithes. And the Levites shall bring up the tithe of the tithes to the
house of our God, to the chambers of [e]the storehouse. 39 For the people of Israel and the
sons of Levi [f]shall bring the contribution of grain, wine, and oil to the chambers, where
the vessels of the sanctuary are, as well as the priests who minister, and the gatekeepers
and the singers. [g]We will not neglect the house of our God."

The Leaders in Jerusalem

11 Now the leaders of the people [h]lived in Jerusalem. And the rest of the people [i]cast
lots to bring one out of ten to live in Jerusalem [j]the holy city, while nine out of ten[2]
remained in the other towns. 2 And the people blessed all the men [k]who willingly offered
to live in Jerusalem.

[1] A *shekel* was about 2/5 ounce or 11 grams [2] Hebrew *nine hands*

30 [q]Ex. 34:16; Deut. 7:3; Ezra 9:12, 14
31 [r]Ex. 20:10; Lev. 23:3; Deut. 5:12; See ch. 13:15-22 [s]Ex. 23:10, 11; Lev. 25:4 [t]Deut. 15:1, 2; [ch. 5:12]
32 [u][Matt. 17:24]
33 [v]2 Chr. 2:4; [1 Chr. 9:32]; See Lev. 24:5-9 [w]See Num. 28; 29
34 [x][ch. 11:1] [y]ch. 13:31; [Isa. 40:16] [z]Lev. 6:12
35 [a]Ex. 23:19; 34:26; Lev. 19:23, 24; Num. 18:12; Deut. 26:2
36 [b]Ex. 13:2, 12, 13; Lev. 27:26, 27; Num. 18:15, 16
37 [c]Lev. 23:17; Num. 15:20, 21; 18:12; Deut. 18:4 [d]1 Chr. 9:26; 2 Chr. 31:11
38 [e]1 Chr. 26:20
39 [f][ch. 13:12; Deut. 12:6, 11; 2 Chr. 31:12] [g][ch. 13:11]

Chapter 11

1 [h][1 Chr. 9:3] [i]ch. 10:34 [j]ver. 18; Isa. 48:2; 52:1; Matt. 4:5; 27:53
2 [k][Judg. 5:9; 2 Chr. 17:16]

10:30 The Mosaic prohibition of intermarriage with the **peoples of the land** (as worshipers of other gods) is in the forefront because it was such a problem in the recent past (Ezra 9–10).

10:31 The **Sabbath** commandment (Ex. 20:8–11; Deut. 5:12–15) was no doubt important as a key marker of Israel's identity compared with the surrounding groups of people who did not acknowledge Yahweh as their God. Trading with these people on the Sabbath must have been a temptation (see Neh. 13:16–22). **crops of the seventh year**. The Sabbath idea extended to the seventh year, when the normal work of cultivation was prohibited (Lev. 25:2–7).

10:32 third part of a shekel. No Pentateuchal law requires this tax, so it is a new commitment. (See, however, Moses' particular levy in Ex. 30:11–16.) The purpose is to support **the service of the house of our God**; God's people must be true to their calling as a worshiping community.

10:33 This is intended as a comprehensive list of the offerings and occasions of temple worship. **showbread**. See Lev. 24:5–9.

10:34 wood offering. Again, no specific law requires this tax, but the need for it is implied in Lev. 6:12–13; for this reason it is said, **it is written in the Law**.

10:35–37 These verses summarize the agricultural offerings made to supply the temple personnel, as specified in various Pentateuchal laws (e.g., Ex. 23:19; 34:26; Num. 18:12–13; Deut. 26:1–11). These offerings were not always paid (see Neh. 13:10).

10:36 firstborn of our sons. In fact, these were "redeemed" by sacrifice (Ex. 13:13; 34:20). **herds . . . flocks**. See Num. 18:15–18 and Deut. 15:19–23.

10:37 first of our dough. See Num. 15:20–21 and Deut. 18:4. **Tithes** are due to the Levites according to Num. 18:21–24, though the laity participates in a celebration of the tithe at the sanctuary in Deut. 14:22–27.

10:38 the Levites shall bring up the tithe of the tithes to the house of our God. This refers to the Levites' offering of part of the tithe to the priests (Num. 18:25–32). Even those who serve in the temple were responsible to give to God from what they received.

10:39 not neglect the house of our God. To maintain the temple personnel is at the same time to care for the temple and to honor God, and thus to foster covenant faithfulness.

11:1–12:43 *The Population of Jerusalem and the Villages; Priests and Levites.* These chapters depict the people's efforts to populate Jerusalem.

11:1–36 *Those Who Lived in Jerusalem and the Villages of Judah.* This chapter addresses the need to maintain a proportion of the population in Jerusalem, and records the names of leaders who lived there. Populated villages of Judah are also named.

11:1 The **leaders** of the community are concentrated in **Jerusalem**, but the picture of an underpopulated city is reinforced here (see also 7:4). The people in the provincial towns **cast lots** to decide who should relocate to the capital. **one out of ten**. It is not said how the people decided on this plan.

11:2 the men who willingly offered. Perhaps this implies that there were not enough of them to make up the required one in 10 (v. 1), but another interpretation is that this is simply another way of describing those who were chosen to go to Jerusalem.

3 [l]These are the chiefs of the province who lived in Jerusalem; but in the towns of Judah
[m]everyone lived on his property in their towns: Israel, the priests, the Levites, [n]the temple
servants, [o]and the descendants of Solomon's servants. **4** And in Jerusalem lived certain of
the sons of Judah and of the sons of Benjamin. Of the sons of Judah: Athaiah the son of
Uzziah, son of Zechariah, son of Amariah, son of Shephatiah, son of Mahalalel, of the
sons of [p]Perez; **5** and Maaseiah the son of Baruch, son of Col-hozeh, son of Hazaiah, son
of Adaiah, son of Joiarib, son of Zechariah, son of the Shilonite. **6** All the sons of Perez who
lived in Jerusalem were 468 valiant men.

7 And these are the sons of Benjamin: Sallu the son of Meshullam, son of Joed, son of
Pedaiah, son of Kolaiah, son of Maaseiah, son of Ithiel, son of Jeshaiah, **8** and his broth-
ers, men of valor, 928.[1] **9** Joel the son of Zichri was their overseer; and Judah the son of
Hassenuah was second over the city.

10 Of the priests: Jedaiah the son of Joiarib, Jachin, **11** Seraiah the son of Hilkiah, son
of Meshullam, son of Zadok, son of Meraioth, son of Ahitub, ruler of the house of God,
12 and their brothers who did the work of the house, 822; and Adaiah the son of Jeroham,
son of Pelaliah, son of Amzi, son of Zechariah, son of Pashhur, son of Malchijah, **13** and
his brothers, heads of fathers' houses, 242; and Amashsai, the son of Azarel, son of Ahzai,
son of Meshillemoth, son of Immer, **14** and their brothers, mighty men of valor, 128; their
overseer was Zabdiel the son of Haggedolim.

15 And of the Levites: Shemaiah the son of Hasshub, son of Azrikam, son of Hashabiah,
son of Bunni; **16** and Shabbethai and [q]Jozabad, of the chiefs of the Levites, who were over
[r]the outside work of the house of God; **17** and [s]Mattaniah the son of Mica, son of Zabdi, son
of Asaph, who was the leader of the praise,[2] who gave thanks, and Bakbukiah, the second
among his brothers; and Abda the son of Shammua, son of Galal, son of Jeduthun. **18** All
the Levites in [t]the holy city were 284.

19 The gatekeepers, Akkub, Talmon and their brothers, who kept watch at the gates,
were 172. **20** And the rest of Israel, and of the priests and the Levites, were in all the towns
of Judah, [u]every one in his inheritance. **21** [v]But the temple servants lived on Ophel; and
Ziha and Gishpa were over the temple servants.

22 The overseer of the Levites in Jerusalem was Uzzi the son of Bani, son of Hashabiah,
son of Mattaniah, son of Mica, of the sons of Asaph, the singers, over the work of the
house of God. **23** [w]For there was a command from the king concerning them, and a fixed
provision for the singers, [x]as every day required. **24** And Pethahiah the son of Meshezabel,
of the sons of Zerah the son of Judah, was at the king's side[3] in all matters concerning
the people.

Villages Outside Jerusalem

25 And as for the villages, with their fields, some of the people of Judah lived in [y]Kiriath-
arba and its villages, and in Dibon and its villages, and in Jekabzeel and its villages, **26** and
in Jeshua and in Moladah and Beth-pelet, **27** in Hazar-shual, in Beersheba and its villages,
28 in Ziklag, in Meconah and its villages, **29** in En-rimmon, in Zorah, in Jarmuth, **30** Zanoah,

[1] Compare Septuagint; Hebrew *Jeshaiah, and after him Gabbai, Sallai, 928* [2] Compare Septuagint, Vulgate; Hebrew *beginning* [3] Hebrew *hand*

3 [l]For ver. 3-19, see 1 Chr. 9:2-34 [m]ver. 20 [n]Ezra 2:43 [o]Ezra 2:55
4 [p][Gen. 38:29]
16 [q]Ezra 8:33 [r]1 Chr. 26:29
17 [s]ch. 12:8, 24
18 [t]See ver. 1
20 [u]ver. 3
21 [v]ch. 3:26
23 [w]Ezra 6:8, 9; 7:20 [x]ch. 12:47; 2 Chr. 31:16
25 [y]Josh. 14:15; 21:11

11:3 The **temple servants**, along with gatekeepers and singers (vv. 19, 21–22), were classes of Levites (see Ezra 2:40–43). **the descendants of Solomon's servants**. See note on Ezra 2:55–58.

11:4 sons of Judah . . . sons of Benjamin. These were the two tribes of the southern kingdom (see 1 Kings 12:21–23) that had composed the exiles in Babylon, and now compose the community that has been restored.

11:9 second over the city. See also 3:9, 12. It is not made clear how these offices relate.

11:11 The **ruler of the house of God** is the high priest.

11:12 of the house. This probably means inside the temple; contrast v. 16.

11:16 the outside work of the house of God. This is a lesser role than that of the priests in v. 12, befitting the Levites' lower rank.

11:20–21 the rest of Israel. That is, after a tenth of the population had been resettled in Jerusalem (v. 1). **His inheritance** refers to one's ancestral property (see note on Ezra 2:59–63). **Ophel**. See note on Neh. 3:26.

11:23–24 command from the king. This must mean the Persian king (rather than King David, who had originally organized the Levitical singers; 1 Chronicles 25), since the note about **Pethahiah** as being **at the king's side** must mean that this person was responsible for Jewish affairs at the royal court. He may have taken over in this role from Ezra for reasons unknown.

11:25–36 This list of villages is prompted by the allusion to the population in the province as opposed to Jerusalem (see v. 1). A number of the place-names in Judah occur also in Josh. 15:20–63. For the villages of Benjamin, see also Ezra 2:26–33. See map, p. 843.

11:30 from Beersheba to the Valley of Hinnom. The people of Judah lived in the area south of Jerusalem. Beersheba was in the far south of the territory, and the Valley of Hinnom was on the southern edge of Jerusalem.

30[z]See Josh. 15:8
35[a]ch. 6:2; 1 Chr. 8:12
Chapter 12
1[b]Ezra 2:1, 2 [c]ver. 47; See 1 Chr. 3:19 [d]See Ezra 3:2 [e]For ver. 1-7, see ver. 12-21; ch. 10:2-8
8[f]ver. 24; ch. 11:17; [2 Chr. 5:13]

Adullam, and their villages, Lachish and its fields, and Azekah and its villages. So they
encamped from Beersheba to [z]the Valley of Hinnom. 31 The people of Benjamin also lived
from Geba onward, at Michmash, Aija, Bethel and its villages, 32 Anathoth, Nob, Ananiah,
33 Hazor, Ramah, Gittaim, 34 Hadid, Zeboim, Neballat, 35 Lod, and [a]Ono, the valley of craftsmen. 36 And certain divisions of the Levites in Judah were assigned to Benjamin.

Priests and Levites

12 These are [b]the priests and the Levites who came up with [c]Zerubbabel the son of
Shealtiel, and [d]Jeshua: [e]Seraiah, Jeremiah, Ezra, 2 Amariah, Malluch, Hattush,
3 Shecaniah, Rehum, Meremoth, 4 Iddo, Ginnethoi, Abijah, 5 Mijamin, Maadiah, Bilgah,
6 Shemaiah, Joiarib, Jedaiah, 7 Sallu, Amok, Hilkiah, Jedaiah. These were the chiefs of the
priests and of their brothers in the days of Jeshua.
8 And the Levites: Jeshua, Binnui, Kadmiel, Sherebiah, Judah, and Mattaniah, who with
his brothers was [f]in charge of the songs of thanksgiving. 9 And Bakbukiah and Unni and

11:31–35 The villages of Benjamin lie mainly to the north and west of Jerusalem.

11:36 The **Levites** were in effect a third tribe in the restored community, for they originally had settlements throughout the land (see Joshua 21). This verse simply records that since the restored community did not consist of Judah alone, the Levites did not relate only to that tribe.

12:1–26 *High Priests and Leading Levites since the Time of Zerubbabel.* This section records the priests and Levites from the time of Zerubbabel (c. 538–535 B.C.) to Nehemiah. The aim is to show that the Levitical service was sustained during a very difficult era in Israel's history.

12:1a Zerubbabel . . . and Jeshua. Zerubbabel was the first leader of the exiles who returned to Judah following the decree of King Cyrus in 538 B.C., and Jeshua was the high priest who returned with him. This was about a century before Nehemiah (see note on Ezra 2:2a).

12:1b–9 A list of priests in the time of Zerubbabel is listed, followed by a list of Levites from the same time.

Judea under Persian Rule
538–332 B.C.
Under Persian rule, the lands of Israel (now called Samaria) and Judah (now called Judea) were minor provinces within the satrapy called Beyond the River. Returning Judeans settled mostly in the province of Judea, but a few settled in the plain of Ono and Idumea as well. The fact that the plain of Ono lay outside the jurisdiction of Judea may explain why Nehemiah suspected that the other local governors intended to do him harm there.

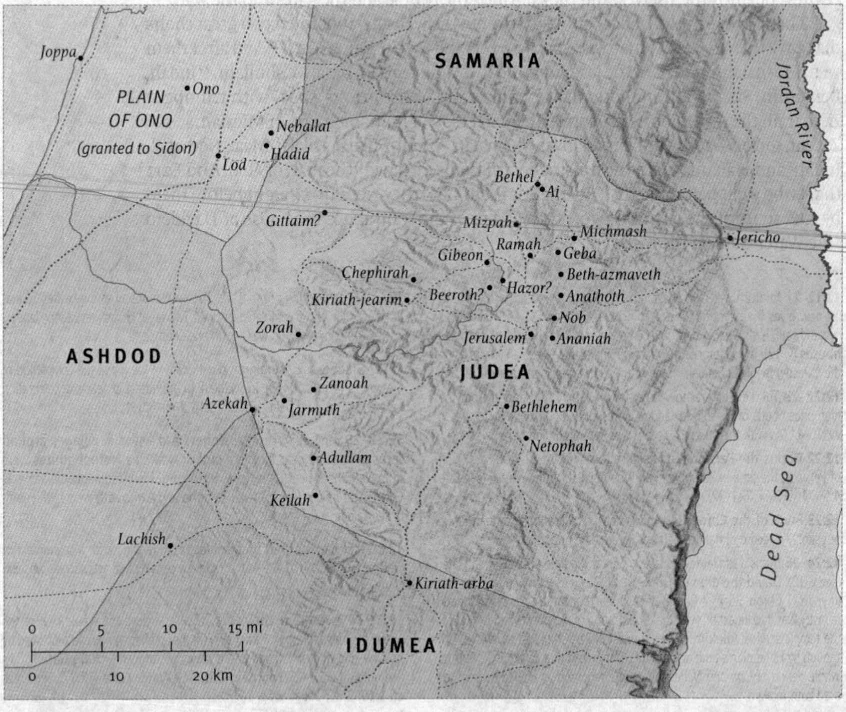

their brothers stood opposite them [g]in the service. 10 And Jeshua was the father of Joiakim,
Joiakim the father of Eliashib, Eliashib the father of Joiada, 11 Joiada the father of Jonathan,
and Jonathan the father of Jaddua.
12 [h]And in the days of Joiakim were priests, heads of fathers' houses: of Seraiah, Meraiah; of
Jeremiah, Hananiah; 13 of Ezra, Meshullam; of Amariah, Jehohanan; 14 of Malluchi, Jonathan;
of Shebaniah, Joseph; 15 of Harim, Adna; of Meraioth, Helkai; 16 of Iddo, Zechariah; of
Ginnethon, Meshullam; 17 of Abijah, Zichri; of Miniamin, of Moadiah, Piltai; 18 of Bilgah,
Shammua; of Shemaiah, Jehonathan; 19 of Joiarib, Mattenai; of Jedaiah, Uzzi; 20 of Sallai,
Kallai; of Amok, Eber; 21 of Hilkiah, Hashabiah; of Jedaiah, Nethanel.
22 In the days of Eliashib, Joiada, Johanan, and Jaddua, the Levites were recorded as
heads of fathers' houses; so too were the priests in the reign of Darius the Persian. 23 As for
the sons of Levi, their heads of fathers' houses [i]were written in the Book of the Chronicles
until the days of Johanan the son of Eliashib. 24 And the chiefs of the Levites: Hashabiah,
Sherebiah, and [j]Jeshua the son of Kadmiel, with their brothers who stood opposite them,
[k]to praise and to give thanks, [l]according to the commandment of David [m]the man of God,
[n]watch by watch. 25 Mattaniah, Bakbukiah, Obadiah, Meshullam, Talmon, and Akkub were
gatekeepers standing guard at [o]the storehouses of the gates. 26 These were in the days of
Joiakim the son of Jeshua son of Jozadak, and in the days of [p]Nehemiah the governor and
of [p]Ezra, the priest and scribe.

Dedication of the Wall

27 And at [q]the dedication of the wall of Jerusalem they sought the Levites in all their
places, to bring them to Jerusalem to celebrate the dedication with gladness, with thanksgivings and with singing, [r]with cymbals, harps, and lyres. 28 And the sons of the singers
gathered together from the district surrounding Jerusalem and from the villages of the
Netophathites; 29 also from Beth-gilgal and from the region of Geba and Azmaveth, for
the singers had built for themselves villages around Jerusalem. 30 And the priests and the
Levites [s]purified themselves, and they purified the people and the gates and the wall.
31 Then I brought the leaders of Judah up onto the wall and appointed two great choirs
that gave thanks. [t]One went to the south on the wall to [u]the Dung Gate. 32 And after them
went Hoshaiah and half of the leaders of Judah, 33 and Azariah, Ezra, Meshullam, 34 Judah,
Benjamin, Shemaiah, and Jeremiah, 35 and certain of the priests' sons [v]with trumpets:
Zechariah the son of Jonathan, son of Shemaiah, son of Mattaniah, son of Micaiah, son of
Zaccur, son of Asaph; 36 and his relatives, Shemaiah, Azarel, Milalai, Gilalai, Maai, Nethanel,
Judah, and Hanani, [w]with the musical instruments of David [x]the man of God. And Ezra
the scribe went before them. 37 At [y]the Fountain Gate they went up straight before them
by [z]the stairs of the city of David, at the ascent of the wall, above the house of David, to
[a]the Water Gate on the east.

9 [g][ver. 24]
12 [h]ver. 26
23 [i]See 1 Chr. 9:14-16
24 [j]ch. 10:9; Ezra 2:40 [k]ch. 11:17; [2 Chr. 5:13] [l]See 1 Chr. 25 [m]ver. 36 [n][ver. 9; Ezra 3:11]
25 [o][1 Chr. 26:15]
26 [p]ch. 8:9
27 [q]See Num. 7:10 [r]See 1 Chr. 15:16
30 [s]ch. 13:22, 30
31 [t][ver. 38] [u]ch. 2:13; 3:13
35 [v]See 1 Chr. 15:24
36 [w]1 Chr. 23:5 [x]ver. 24
37 [y]ch. 2:14; 3:15 [z]ch. 3:15 [a]ch. 3:26; 8:1, 3, 16

12:12–21 Joiakim was high priest in succession to Jeshua (cf. v. 10), so this list now gives the priests in his day. It includes **Ezra** (v. 13), so Joiakim was evidently still high priest when Ezra came to Jerusalem. **heads of fathers' houses** (v. 12). The list proceeds by family names: thus, Meraiah was priest in the (priestly) family of Seraiah. Some of the family names occur in vv. 1–7.

12:22–23 The Levites are now recorded by family. The period from the high priesthoods of Eliashib to Jaddua corresponds approximately to that in vv. 10–11. As with the priests, a record was kept according to families.

12:22 Darius the Persian is a reference to Darius I (522–486 B.C.), king of Persia at the time of Zerubbabel and the building of the temple (see Ezra 4:5, 24; 5:1–17; 6:1–22).

12:23 Book of the Chronicles. This is not the biblical book of that name, but simply a record of names, perhaps kept by the priests.

12:24–26 This is a similar record (see v. 23) for the time of Joiakim and later (see v. 10). **David the man of God.** That is, David as a prophet as recorded in v. 36; 1 Chron. 25:2; 2 Chron. 8:14. In each of these texts his prophetic ministry was in connection with the organization of the priests and Levites for the temple service. **Joiakim** was high priest in Ezra's time (see Neh. 12:12), though by Nehemiah's time apparently Eliashib held that office (3:1). But the whole period of Ezra and Nehemiah is here regarded as unified and associated with Joiakim.

12:27–43 *Dedication of the Walls.* This section describes the Levites' role at the dedication of the completed city wall. Two great choirs precede the leaders in two companies on the wall, north and south.

12:27 Gladness . . . singing is reminiscent of the joy at the completion of the temple (Ezra 3:10–13). Joy is the right attitude at all feasts of celebration before the Lord (see Deut. 12:18; 16:14; Neh. 8:9–12).

12:28–29 Families of Levitical **singers** had settled in **villages around Jerusalem** to be near the place of their work. The **Netophathites** were from Netophah, near Bethlehem. **Beth-gilgal** is presumably the same as Gilgal, near Jericho (see Josh. 4:19). **Geba** and **Azmaveth** were to the north of Jerusalem.

12:30 They had **purified themselves**, as in readiness for a solemn act of worship (see Ex. 19:10, 14–15), perhaps by certain ritual acts such as washing clothes (Num. 8:5–7).

12:31–37 Two great choirs symbolically enclose the whole city for the purpose of the dedication. Ezra goes with the southern group, accompanied by half the leaders of Judah and priests playing instruments. **Dung Gate** (v. 31). See note on 2:13–15. **Fountain Gate . . . Water Gate** (12:37). See notes on 3:15; 3:26; and map, p. 827.

38[b][ver. 31] [c]ch. 3:11 [d]ch. 3:8
39[e]See ch. 8:16 [f]ch. 3:6 [g]See ch. 3:3 [h]ch. 3:1 [i]See ch. 3:1 [j]See ch. 3:25
41[k]See 1 Chr. 15:24
44[l]ch. 13:5, 12, 13; [2 Chr. 31:11, 12]
45[m]See 1 Chr. 25; 26
46[n]1 Chr. 25:1; 2 Chr. 29:30
47[o]ch. 11:23; 2 Chr. 31:16 [p]Num. 18:21, 24 [q]See Num. 18:26-28

Chapter 13

1[r]ch. 8:3, 8, 9, 18; 9:3; [Deut. 31:11, 12; 2 Kgs. 23:2] [s]See Deut. 23:3-5
3[t]See ch. 9:2 [u][Ex. 12:38; Num. 11:4]
4[v]ver. 28; ch. 3:1 [w][ch. 12:44] [x]ch. 2:10
5[y]Num. 18:21, 24

38 [b]The other choir of those who gave thanks went to the north, and I followed them
with half of the people, on the wall, above [c]the Tower of the Ovens, to [d]the Broad Wall,
39 and above [e]the Gate of Ephraim, and by [f]the Gate of Yeshanah,[1] and by [g]the Fish Gate and
[h]the Tower of Hananel and [h]the Tower of the Hundred, to [i]the Sheep Gate; and they came
to a halt at [j]the Gate of the Guard. **40** So both choirs of those who gave thanks stood in the
house of God, and I and half of the officials with me; **41** and the priests Eliakim, Maaseiah,
Miniamin, Micaiah, Elioenai, Zechariah, and Hananiah, [k]with trumpets; **42** and Maaseiah,
Shemaiah, Eleazar, Uzzi, Jehohanan, Malchijah, Elam, and Ezer. And the singers sang with
Jezrahiah as their leader. **43** And they offered great sacrifices that day and rejoiced, for God
had made them rejoice with great joy; the women and children also rejoiced. And the joy
of Jerusalem was heard far away.

Service at the Temple

44 [l]On that day men were appointed over the storerooms, the contributions, the firstfruits,
and the tithes, to gather into them the portions required by the Law for the priests and for
the Levites according to the fields of the towns, for Judah rejoiced over the priests and the
Levites who ministered. **45** And they performed the service of their God and the service of
purification, as did the singers and the gatekeepers, [m]according to the command of David
and his son Solomon. **46** For long ago in the days of David and [n]Asaph there were directors
of the singers, and there were songs[2] of praise and thanksgiving to God. **47** And all Israel
in the days of Zerubbabel and in the days of Nehemiah gave the [o]daily portions for the
singers and the gatekeepers; [p]and they set apart that which was for the Levites; [q]and the
Levites set apart that which was for the sons of Aaron.

Nehemiah's Final Reforms

13 On that day [r]they read from the Book of Moses in the hearing of the people. And in
it was found written [s]that no Ammonite or Moabite should ever enter the assembly
of God, **2** for they did not meet the people of Israel with bread and water, but hired Balaam
against them to curse them—yet our God turned the curse into a blessing. **3** As soon as the
people heard the law, [t]they separated from Israel all [u]those of foreign descent.
4 Now before this, [v]Eliashib the priest, who [w]was appointed over the chambers of the house
of our God, and who was related to [x]Tobiah, **5** prepared for Tobiah a large chamber where they
had previously put the grain offering, the frankincense, the vessels, and the tithes of grain,
wine, and oil, [y]which were given by commandment to the Levites, singers, and gatekeepers,
and the contributions for the priests. **6** While this was taking place, I was not in Jerusalem,

[1] *Or of the old city* [2] *Or leaders*

12:38–43 Nehemiah goes with the group on the northern wall. The pattern is the same as for the southern wall.

12:38–39 For the topographical details, see 2:11–16 and 3:1–32.

12:40 Both processions continue into the temple area, where they meet for the culmination of the ceremony.

12:43 joy of Jerusalem. See note on v. 27.

12:44–13:31 *Nehemiah Deals with Problems in the Community.* This section records problems that arose in the administration and practice of storing contributions for the temple and its personnel. It also describes Nehemiah's ongoing problems with his people and his opponents.

12:44–47 *The Administration of Offerings for the Temple.* The purpose of this section is to recall that the work of the priests and Levites had been put in place from ancient times, and that since the days of Zerubbabel (a century before Nehemiah) they had been duly provided for.

12:44 On that day. Arrangements for overseeing the proper collection of tithes and other offerings are made afresh at the time of the dedication of the wall. For the offerings themselves, see notes on 10:35–37; 10:38; 10:39. **portions required by the Law**. The Pentateuchal requirement (Lev. 7:33) applied only to the priests, but here it is widened to include all the Levites (an adaptation to the needs of the postexilic community; 2 Chron. 31:19 probably records a similar adaptation).

12:45–46 The roles of the various branches of Levites are recapitulated. **command of David**. See v. 24.

13:1–9 *Ejection of Tobiah the Ammonite from the Temple.* Nehemiah's opponents were as resilient as he was. His absences led to setbacks. Still in connection with the ceremony of dedication, a new resolution is made in respect to protecting the community from foreign religion.

13:1–2 On that day. See 12:44. **no Ammonite or Moabite**. This text closely follows Deut. 23:3–5, which expressly excluded Moabites and Ammonites from the religious assembly of Israel (for several generations) because of their historical enmity against Israel and their infectious idolatry (see Numbers 22–25).

13:3 separated . . . foreign descent. This resembles the measures taken by Ezra a decade or so earlier (Ezra 9–10), but there is no sign here of compulsory divorce. Note Ezra 6:21, which allowed foreigners to join Israel if they embraced the Jewish religion, as in the book of Ruth (who was a Moabite).

13:4–9 The connection of these verses with vv. 1–3 lies in the fact that **Tobiah**, already known to be an enemy of the community (2:10; 4:7–8), was an Ammonite. Eliashib's offense is also related to the theme of the proper administration of tithes and offerings (12:44), because Tobiah has been given a room in the temple reserved for these.

13:4 Now before this. The time is unspecified.

13:6 I was not in Jerusalem. When Nehemiah was given leave of absence, the king had required him to name a time for his return (2:6). It is not clear whether he had traveled more than once between Jerusalem

for [z]in the thirty-second year of Artaxerxes [a]king of Babylon I went to the king. And after
some time I asked leave of the king 7 and came to Jerusalem, and I then discovered the evil
that Eliashib had done for Tobiah, [b]preparing for him a chamber in the courts of the house
of God. 8 And I was very angry, and I threw all the household furniture of Tobiah out of the
chamber. 9 Then I gave orders, and they [c]cleansed the chambers, and I brought back there
the vessels of the house of God, with the grain offering and the frankincense.
10 I also found out that [d]the portions of the Levites had not been given to them, so that
the Levites and the singers, who did the work, had fled each [e]to his field. 11 [f]So I confronted
the officials and said, [g]"Why is the house of God forsaken?" And I gathered them together
and set them in their stations. 12 Then all Judah brought [h]the tithe of the grain, wine, and
oil into the storehouses. 13 And [i]I appointed as treasurers over the storehouses Shelemiah
the priest, Zadok the scribe, and Pedaiah of the Levites, and as their assistant Hanan the
son of Zaccur, son of Mattaniah, [j]for they were considered reliable, and their duty was to
distribute to their brothers. 14 [k]Remember me, O my God, concerning this, and do not wipe
out my good deeds that I have done for the house of my God and for his service.
15 In those days I saw in Judah people treading winepresses [l]on the Sabbath, and bringing in heaps of grain and loading them on donkeys, and also wine, grapes, figs, and all
kinds of loads, [m]which they brought into Jerusalem on the Sabbath day. And [n]I warned
them on the day when they sold food. 16 Tyrians also, who lived in the city, brought in fish
and all kinds of goods and sold them on the Sabbath to the people of Judah, in Jerusalem
itself! 17 [o]Then I confronted the nobles of Judah and said to them, "What is this evil thing
that you are doing, [p]profaning the Sabbath day? 18 [q]Did not your fathers act in this way,
and did not our God bring all this disaster[1] on us and on this city? Now you are bringing
more wrath on Israel by profaning the Sabbath."
19 As soon as it [r]began to grow dark at the gates of Jerusalem before the Sabbath, I commanded that the doors should be shut and gave orders that they should not be opened
until after the Sabbath. And I stationed some of my servants at the gates, that no load
might be brought in on the Sabbath day. 20 Then the merchants and sellers of all kinds of
wares lodged outside Jerusalem once or twice. 21 [s]But I warned them and said to them,
"Why do you lodge outside the wall? If you do so again, I will lay hands on you." From
that time on they did not come on the Sabbath. 22 Then I commanded the Levites [t]that
they should purify themselves and come and guard the gates, to keep the Sabbath day
holy. [u]Remember this also in my favor, O my God, and spare me according to the greatness
of your steadfast love.
23 In those days also I saw the Jews [v]who had married women [w]of Ashdod, [x]Ammon, and

[1] The Hebrew word can mean *evil*, *harm*, or *disaster*, depending on the context

6 [z]ch. 5:14 [a]Ezra 6:22
7 [b]ver. 5
9 [c]2 Chr. 29:15, 16, 18
10 [d]2 Chr. 31:4; [Mal. 3:8] [e]ch. 12:28, 29
11 [f]ver. 17, 25 [g][ch. 10:39]
12 [h][ch. 10:38, 39; 12:44]
13 [i][2 Chr. 31:12, 13] [j]ch. 7:2; [1 Cor. 4:2]
14 [k]ver. 22, 31; ch. 5:19
15 [l][Ex. 20:10] [m]See ch. 10:31 [n]ver. 21
17 [o]ver. 11 [p][Matt. 12:5]
18 [q]See Jer. 17:19-23
19 [r]Lev. 23:32
21 [s]ver. 15
22 [t]ch. 12:30 [u][ver. 14, 31]
23 [v]Ezra 9:2; 10:10 [w][ch. 4:7] [x][ver. 1; Ezra 9:1]

and the royal court. In any case, he is now called back in the **thirty-second year** (433 B.C.; cf. 1:1) for an unspecified time. The journey to Susa took about 55 days to travel the 1,100 miles (1,770 km), and another 55 days to return (averaging 20 miles or 32 km per day). Eliashib (see 12:10) may have been opposed to Nehemiah's policy of strict separation from the community's neighbors, and thus may have taken advantage of his perhaps lengthy absence. **king of Babylon**. An unexpected name for the Persian Artaxerxes; but see Ezra 5:13 and 6:22, where Persian kings are called king of Babylon and Assyria, respectively. This is because the successive empires in some sense took on the identity of their predecessors. In addition, Artaxerxes might actually have been holding court in Babylon at the time. Nehemiah's return to Jerusalem must have been before Artaxerxes' death in 423 B.C.

13:9 Cleansed, that is, purified in a ritual sense. Nehemiah sees the misuse of the temple as a desecration. He restores the polluted area to its proper use.

13:10–14 *Dealing with Neglect of the Offerings.* The incident in the temple was not isolated, for the provision for the clergy had effectively lapsed, and as a result the worship itself had suffered because the clergy had to leave Jerusalem, which was disastrous for the community. Contrast the commitments made by the people in 10:32–39. Nehemiah once again puts the administration of the offerings on a firm footing, so that the restored community can actually live out its covenant privilege.

13:11 I confronted the officials. Note Nehemiah's fearless action (see also v. 17).

13:14 Remember me. This prayer, asking in typical idiom (see 1:8; 5:19; 6:14) that God should take note of his faithful actions, somewhat resembles certain psalms, in which the psalmist pleads his righteousness in the context of praise (e.g., Psalm 7; 17; see also Neh. 13:22, 29–30).

13:15–22 *Dealing with Sabbath Breaking.* The community once again sins, this time by breaking the Sabbath, which leads Nehemiah to rebuke the people.

13:15–16 The people of Judah break the **Sabbath** by trading. **Tyrians**. Foreigners would not be bound by the Sabbath law, of course, but they find a ready market among the Jews.

13:18 Did not your fathers act in this way . . . ? Sabbath breach was a telling aspect of previous generations' lax attitude toward the Torah (see Jer. 17:19–27; Amos 8:4–6). Here the exile is attributed to it.

13:19–22 Nehemiah still has enough personal authority and resources to enforce his reforms (though it is not clear whether he is still governor at this point).

13:22 the Levites . . . purify themselves. Implicitly, through negligence, the gatekeeper Levites had been failing in their duties and needed to be ritually purified again for their task.

13:23–29 *The Problem of Intermarriage Again.* Ignoring commitments (like

23[x][ver. 1; Ezra 9:1]
25[o][See ver. 17 above] [y]Ezra 10:5; [ch. 10:29, 30]
26[z]See 1 Kgs. 11:1-8 [a]1 Kgs. 3:13; 2 Chr. 1:12 [b][2 Sam. 12:24]
27[c]Ezra 10:2
28[d]ch. 12:10, 11, 22 [e]ver. 4, 7; ch. 3:1 [f]ch. 2:10, 19
29[g][ch. 6:14] [h]Mal. 2:4
30[i]ch. 10:30
31[j]ch. 10:34 [k]Ezra 10:14 [l]ver. 14, 22

[x]Moab. **24** And half of their children spoke the language of Ashdod, and they could not
speak the language of Judah, but only the language of each people. **25** [o]And I confronted
them and cursed them and beat some of them and pulled out their hair. [y]And I made them
take an oath in the name of God, saying, "You shall not give your daughters to their sons,
or take their daughters for your sons or for yourselves. **26** [z]Did not Solomon king of Israel
sin on account of such women? [a]Among the many nations there was no king like him, and
he was [b]beloved by his God, and God made him king over all Israel. Nevertheless, foreign
women made even him to sin. **27** Shall we then listen to you and do all this great evil and
[c]act treacherously against our God by marrying foreign women?"

28 And one of the sons of [d]Jehoiada, the son of [e]Eliashib the high priest, was the son-in-
law of [f]Sanballat the Horonite. Therefore I chased him from me. **29** [g]Remember them, O
my God, because they have desecrated the priesthood [h]and the covenant of the priesthood
and the Levites.

30 [i]Thus I cleansed them from everything foreign, and I established the duties of the
priests and Levites, each in his work; **31** and I provided [j]for the wood offering [k]at appointed
times, and for the firstfruits.

[l]Remember me, O my God, for good.

Sabbath keeping) that should have sustained Israelite identity had led to intermarriage with persons of other religions.

13:23–27 Ezra's measures (Ezra 9–10) apparently had little lasting effect. The real problem of mixed marriages is illustrated vividly here, as the children of these unions, in losing the **language of Judah** (Neh. 13:24), were in effect losing their entire religious heritage.

13:25–27 In his violent but symbolically powerful reaction, Nehemiah calls the people back to the Mosaic law (Deut. 7:1–5) and points to the example of **Solomon**, who was turned from faithfulness to the Lord by his foreign wives (1 Kings 11).

13:28 The spiritual adulteration through intermarriage has even affected the family of the high priest Eliashib, who once more appears on the side of religious laxity.

13:29 Remember them. See also 6:14. **covenant of the priesthood**. A reference to the special obligations laid on the priests and Levites, for the sake of the whole people (cf. 1 Sam. 2:27–36; Mal. 2:4–9).

13:30–31 *Summary of Nehemiah's Temple Reforms.* These verses highlight all that Nehemiah has done to ensure pure worship in the temple and to establish proper support for the priests.

13:31 wood offering. See 10:34. **Remember me**. See 13:14. This prayer stands alone, and may be taken as a general prayer that God should keep in view all of Nehemiah's work, from start to finish.

INTRODUCTION TO

ESTHER

Author and Title

Like many OT books, Esther is an anonymous work. The only hints of its origin are the references it contains to some of the key events of the story being committed to writing in either official court records (2:23; 6:1) or edicts issued by the king or his representatives (3:12–15; 8:8–14). It is possible that the author was someone like Mordecai, who had access to such material and a keen interest in Jewish affairs. His familiarity with Persian customs of the time suggests that he lived not long after the events described.

However, certain features of the book have troubled both Jewish and Christian readers: it does not mention God, it promotes a festival not prescribed in the Law of Moses, and it has an apparently vindictive spirit that some have found offensive. As late as the Reformation, Martin Luther criticized it on the grounds that it was too aggressively Jewish and had no gospel content. Nevertheless, it was recognized as Scripture by the Jews well before the time of Christ—a long tradition clearly evident in Jewish writings just after the NT. For example, Josephus says that the Jewish Scriptures were written from the time of Moses "until Artaxerxes" (*Against Apion* 1.40–41), and elsewhere he identifies this Artaxerxes as "Ahasuerus" in the book of Esther (*Jewish Antiquities* 11.184). Therefore he apparently counts Esther as the last book to be written in the Jewish canon. And the Mishnah has an entire tractate (*Megillah*) that discusses the time and manner of reading Esther publicly on the Feast of Purim. The Jewish scholar Aquila included Esther in his translation of the Hebrew Bible into Greek around A.D. 130. In the Christian church, Esther was listed among the books of the OT canon at the Council of Carthage in A.D. 397 but was widely and perhaps universally accepted in the Western church before that time (though doubts about its canonicity had persisted among some in the Eastern church).

Date

Since the book of Esther is anonymous, it cannot be dated by the years of its author. However, it matches well the time period in which it is set (the reign of Ahasuerus, 486–464 B.C.); hence it is probably from this time or soon thereafter.

Theme

The book of Esther tells how a Jewish girl became the queen of Persia and saved her people from a plot to destroy them. She is assisted in this by Mordecai, her cousin and guardian. It also explains how a special festival, called Purim, was established to recall and celebrate the deliverance that the Jews had experienced.

Purpose, Occasion, and Background

As its content makes clear, Esther was written to explain the origin of the Feast of Purim and to ensure that it would be observed by all future generations of the Jewish people (9:28). It is also clear that it has achieved this purpose, since Jews have continued to observe Purim to the present day, with the book of Esther being read as part of the festivities.

The word *Purim* is derived from the Persian word *pur* ("lot") and recalls how Haman, the enemy of the Jews, cast lots to determine the best day to carry out his plan to exterminate them (3:7). Of all the Jewish festivals, Purim is the most secular in flavor, and one of the most joyful. These days it is normally celebrated

The Persian Empire at the Time of Esther

c. 479 B.C.

Long before Esther's time, the people of Israel and Judah (later called Jews) had been dispersed throughout the Near East by the Assyrians and the Babylonians. Eventually the Persians absorbed nearly all of these lands into their empire, which reached its greatest extent during the time of Esther. Thus Haman's plot to exterminate all Jews throughout the Persian Empire would have annihilated virtually all of the Jewish people, and Esther's daring actions saved them from complete destruction.

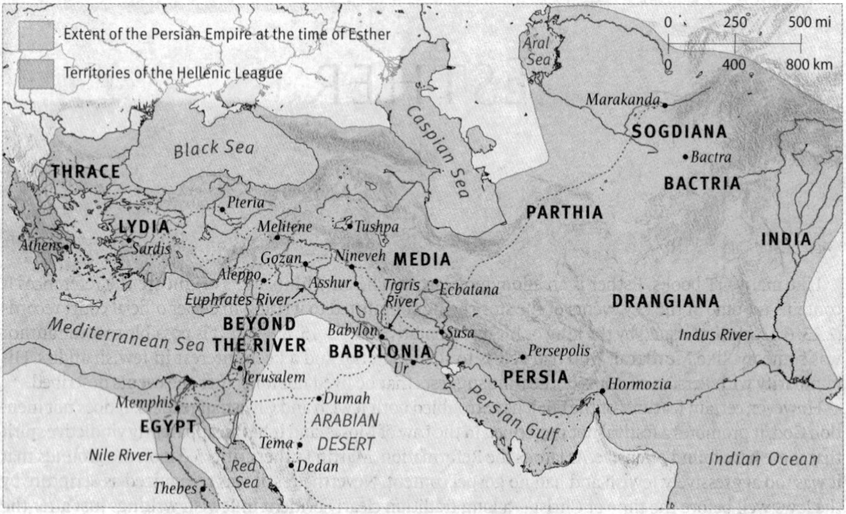

on only one day, the fourteenth of Adar (in February/March), preceded by a day of fasting. Children are given *gragers* (rattles) so that, when the story of Esther is read, they can make a loud noise to drown out the name of the wicked Haman whenever it occurs. Other festivities include exchanging presents, giving food parcels to the poor, performing Purim plays, and wearing costumes. In Israel, a Purim carnival is held. It has become a celebration, not just of the deliverance experienced in the days of Esther and Mordecai, but of the amazing survival of the Jewish people for thousands of years in spite of persecution and hardship.

In terms of biblical history, Esther belongs to the period after the Babylonian exile, when Persia had replaced Babylon as the ruling power. The story is set in Susa, the Persian capital, during the reign of King Ahasuerus, better known by his Greek name, Xerxes I (486–464 B.C.). Some Jews had returned to Jerusalem, where they enjoyed a reasonable amount of control over their own affairs as described in the books of Ezra and Nehemiah. Others, like Esther and Mordecai, were still in exile. As a minority group, the Jews were viewed with suspicion and sometimes faced threats to their existence from people in a position to harm them. In this respect Esther and Mordecai's situation was similar to that of Daniel and his friends a century or so earlier.

Apart from the book of Esther itself, the main sources of information about Persia in the relevant period are the writings of the Greek historian Herodotus (c. 485–425 B.C.) and a limited amount of relevant archaeological evidence from Susa and elsewhere. Esther herself is not mentioned in these sources, and Herodotus gives the name of Xerxes' wife as Amestris. However, Xerxes may have had more than one wife, and it was Esther who was of special interest to the biblical author. In other respects the details of the book agree with what is known of the period from other sources (e.g., see notes on 1:1; 1:2–3; 1:4; 2:5; 2:6; 2:7; 2:15; 2:16; 2:18).

Key Themes

Esther does much more than explain the origin of Purim. It is a most entertaining story, and it communicates some important truths about *how* and *why* the Jews survived such an overwhelming threat. This message can be summarized under three headings:

1. *Divine providence.* While God is never mentioned in the book, there are many hints of his presence. The downfall of Vashti (1:10–22), the decision to hold an elaborate "beauty contest" as a way of replacing her

(2:1–18), and Mordecai's overhearing of a plot against the king (2:19–23) all conspire to move Esther and Mordecai into positions of power before the threat posed by Haman emerges (3:1–3). Once it does, the perfect timing of apparently fortuitous events again and again tips the balance in favor of the Jews and against their enemies. The king's insomnia on the night before Mordecai's execution (6:1–3), Haman's entry at the moment Ahasuerus is wondering how to reward Mordecai (6:6), and the king's return just when Haman is falling on Esther's couch (7:8) all significantly affect the eventual outcome, but none is knowingly caused by any of the human characters. Moreover, the characters themselves seem to be aware that something more than chance is shaping events. Mordecai is sure the Jews will be delivered in some way or other and suspects that Esther has "come to the kingdom for such a time as this" (4:14). Even Haman's wife knows that if Mordecai is a Jew, then Haman is destined to fall before him (6:13), and Esther's calling of a fast before approaching the king can hardly be anything other than an appeal for divine help (4:16).

The deliverance experienced here in Esther is very different from the exodus from Egypt in the time of Moses. There are no signs and wonders, no special revelations, no prophet like Moses—and no one even mentions God! Yet the way the story is told makes it clear that, even when God is most hidden, he is still present and working to protect and deliver his chosen people.

2. *Human responsibility*. Although the story shows that the outcome is a divine gift rather than a human achievement, Esther and Mordecai do show great initiative and courage, and their actions are obviously significant. A little over a century earlier, the prophet Jeremiah had written to the exiles in Babylon about the responsibilities and benefits of good citizenship, especially under foreign rule: "Thus says the LORD . . . seek the welfare of the city where I have sent you into exile, and pray to the LORD on its behalf, for in its welfare you will find your welfare" (Jer. 29:4–7).

Esther and Mordecai are not unambiguously noble in the way that Daniel and his friends were. Nevertheless, Mordecai's action when he discovers a plot to harm the king (Est. 2:19–23) is a good example of someone behaving as Jeremiah had advised, and it shows the benefits that this can bring. Furthermore, Esther's careful planning, along with her willingness to put her own life at risk to save her people, is especially heroic (4:16). Esther and Mordecai both illustrate the fact that divine providence does not negate the responsibility of people to act with courage and resolve when circumstances require it.

3. *The absurdity of wickedness*. Ahasuerus and Haman were important people who wielded considerable power. But the story of Esther again and again evokes laughter at their expense. Ahasuerus rules over 127 provinces but cannot control his wife (Queen Vashti), and his so-called "wise men" are no better (1:12–13). But the most telling humor is at the expense of Haman. The reader is clearly meant to laugh at the way his vanity traps him into having to publicly honor the very man he intended to kill (6:6–11), and his death on the gallows he had prepared for Mordecai (7:8–10) is a classic case of a villain falling into his own pit (cf. Ps. 7:15). This is all obviously meant to teach that the arrogant of this world are not nearly as powerful as they think they are, and that when they oppose God's people (and therefore God himself) they only succeed in bringing about their own destruction. God laughs at such people (Ps. 2:4), and the story of Esther invites us to laugh with him.

Relevance for Christians Today

Esther is part of a much larger story that runs all the way from Abraham to Christ and, through him, to the church. If Haman had succeeded, the Jewish people as a whole would have been destroyed, and the story of God's saving work in and through Abraham's descendants would have come to an end. There would have been no fulfillment in Christ, and therefore no gospel and no Christian church. Nothing less than that was at stake. That is why Christians should read the book of Esther, not just as a story about the Jews but as part of their own heritage. It is because of this fundamental connection between God's purposes in the OT and NT that Christians are to value and learn from the whole Bible as the Word of God (see 1 Cor. 10:11). This side of the cross, Jews and Gentiles have been made one new people in Christ (Eph. 2:11–16). Christians are not obliged to observe the Feast of Purim, but they are to take to heart the truth that God providentially watches over his own, and that no power leveled against them can ultimately prevail (Rom. 8:28).

Sadly, the evil of anti-Semitism still exists, and it would be foolish to think that Christians are immune from it. The history of the church indicates otherwise, and, as part of the Christian Canon, the book of Esther still warns against it. But the only real solution to it is the gospel, and the transformation God brings about in the hearts of those who believe it. That is a beginning, however, not an end, and Christians are called to live in a world with some striking resemblances to the one Esther and Mordecai lived in. Governing authorities are often indifferent and sometimes even hostile to the faith of believers, and especially in the West, events often take their normal course with little or no evidence of the miraculous. But the book of

Esther, like the NT, teaches how to live in that world with courage and integrity, carrying out responsibilities to the best of one's ability and trusting God in his providence to protect and provide.

History of Salvation Summary

For each following generation of Jews, the book of Esther answers the question, "How is it that we are still here?" by pointing to God's often hidden purpose. In the larger story of the Canon, it shows how God has preserved the offspring of Abraham for his purpose of bringing blessing to the whole world through them by raising up the Messiah and by including Gentile believers in his people. Thus Gentile Christians own this as their story too. (For an explanation of the "History of Salvation," see the Overview of the Bible, pp. 23–26. See also History of Salvation in the Old Testament: Preparing the Way for Christ, pp. 2635–2661.)

Literary Features

The book of Esther is a story par excellence. It has virtually all the ingredients that people through the ages have most loved in a story—a beautiful and courageous heroine, a romantic love thread, a dire threat to the good characters, a thoroughly evil villain, suspense, dramatic irony, evocative descriptions of exotic places, sudden reversal of action, poetic justice, and a happy ending.

The specific type of story represented by the book of Esther is hero story, as the action is constructed around the engaging central figure of a heroine whose Persian name Esther means "star." But the story is also a patriotic story of national history—a rescue story in which a whole nation is delivered from destruction. The U-shaped descent into potential tragedy and ascent to a happy ending is a plot pattern known as comedy.

The heroine Esther is a developing character, not a character who displays admirable qualities right from the start. In her early days in the harem, she fits right in with the pagan lifestyle that prevails among the young women who spend a whole year beautifying themselves in a spa. People in the harem do not even know that Esther is a religious person. She has two names, hinting at the identity crisis that she undergoes when she rises to the highest level of Persian society. But Esther becomes heroic when she is transformed by the ordeal of needing to save her nation.

There is satire (the exposure of vice or folly) in the book, focused especially on the character of Haman, who is both narcissistic and vengeful.

Outline

I. Introduction (1:1–2:23)
   A. Queen Vashti's downfall (1:1–22)
   B. Esther's rise to the throne (2:1–18)
   C. Mordecai's success in foiling a plot against the king (2:19–23)

II. Main Action (3:1–9:19)
   A. Haman plots to kill the Jews (3:1–15)
   B. Mordecai and Esther plan to save their people (4:1–17)
   C. Esther is favorably received by the king and prepares to expose Haman (5:1–8)
   D. Haman prepares to hang Mordecai (5:9–14)
   E. Mordecai is honored and Haman is humiliated (6:1–13)
   F. Esther brings about Haman's destruction (6:14–7:10)
   G. Esther wins the right of the Jews to defend themselves (8:1–17)
   H. The Jews completely destroy their enemies (9:1–19)

III. Conclusion (9:20–10:3)
   A. The establishment of the Feast of Purim (9:20–32)
   B. Mordecai's high rank and beneficent rule (10:1–3)

ESTHER

The King's Banquets

1 Now in the days of Ahasuerus, the Ahasuerus who reigned [a]from India to Ethiopia
over [b]127 provinces, 2 in those days when King Ahasuerus [c]sat on his royal throne in
[d]Susa, the citadel, 3 in the third year of his reign [e]he gave a feast for all his officials and
servants. The army of Persia and Media and the nobles and governors of the provinces
were before him, 4 while he showed the riches of his royal glory and the splendor and
pomp of his greatness for many days, 180 days. 5 And when these days were completed,
the king gave for all the people present in Susa the citadel, both great and small, a feast
lasting for seven days in the court of [f]the garden of the king's palace. 6 There were white
cotton curtains and violet hangings fastened with cords of fine linen and purple to silver
rods[1] and marble pillars, and also [g]couches of gold and silver on a mosaic pavement of
porphyry, marble, mother-of-pearl and precious stones. 7 Drinks were served in golden
vessels, vessels of different kinds, and the royal wine was lavished according to the bounty
of the king. 8 And drinking was according to this edict: "There is no compulsion." For the
king had given orders to all the staff of his palace to do as each man desired. 9 Queen Vashti
also gave a feast for the women in the palace that belonged to King Ahasuerus.

Queen Vashti's Refusal

10 On the seventh day, [h]when the heart of the king was merry with wine, he commanded
Mehuman, Biztha, [i]Harbona, [j]Bigtha and Abagtha, Zethar and Carkas, the seven eunuchs
who served in the presence of King Ahasuerus, 11 to bring Queen Vashti before the king
with [k]her royal crown,[2] in order to show the peoples and the princes her beauty, for she
was lovely to look at. 12 But Queen Vashti refused to come at the king's command delivered
by the eunuchs. At this the king became enraged, and his anger burned within him.
13 Then the king said to [l]the wise men [m]who knew the times (for this was the king's

[1] *Or rings* [2] *Or headdress*

Chapter 1
1 [a]ch. 8:9 [b]ch. 8:9; 9:30; [Dan. 6:1]
2 [c]1 Kgs. 1:46 [d]See Neh. 1:1
3 [e]ch. 2:18; [Gen. 40:20; 1 Kgs. 3:15; Mark 6:21]
5 [f]ch. 7:7, 8
6 [g][Ezek. 23:41; Amos 6:4]
10 [h][2 Sam. 13:28] [i]ch. 7:9 [j][ch. 2:21; 6:2]
11 [k]ch. 2:17; 6:8
13 [l]Jer. 10:7; Dan. 2:12, 13; Matt. 2:1 [m]1 Chr. 12:32

1:1–2:23 *Introduction.* In this opening section the author sets the scene by describing Queen Vashti's downfall (1:1–22), her replacement by Esther (2:1–18), and how Mordecai foils a plot against the king (2:19–23). This situates Esther and Mordecai for the roles they will play in the main action that follows.

1:1–22 *Queen Vashti's Downfall.* This is a mini-story in its own right. The scene is set by a description of two banquets, hosted by the king and queen respectively (vv. 1–8, 9). Vashti's defiance of the king and its consequences follow.

1:1 Ahasuerus, better known by his Greek name, Xerxes I, was king of Persia from 486–464 B.C. **India**. The land around the Indus Valley (now Pakistan). **Ethiopia**. The land just south of Egypt (now northern Sudan).

1:2–3 Susa, in western **Persia** (the city is now called Shush, in the southwestern part of modern Iran), was one of Persia's four capital cities (see Neh. 1:1; Dan. 8:2). **Media**. Northwestern Persia, near the Caspian Sea. Once a separate nation, it was conquered c. 550 B.C. by Cyrus the Great, who founded the Persian Empire. The time (483 B.C., **the third year of** Xerxes' **reign**), and the presence of the **army**, suggest that Xerxes may have been building support for his invasion of Greece (preparations c. 483–480; the Battle of Thermopylae took place in 480).

1:4 The **180 days** were presumably not spent in continuous feasting but in festivities punctuated by sumptuous meals.

1:5 Susa the citadel refers to the fortified palace complex. The **feast lasting for seven days** was probably the climax of the 180 days of festivities (v. 4). **court of the garden**. An enclosed courtyard for entertaining in the summer months (see 7:7).

1:6–8 no compulsion. King Ahasuerus set aside the custom that everyone had to drink whenever the king drank.

1:9 A separate **feast for the women** was another departure from normal Persian practice (cf. v. 8; 5:5–6), perhaps because of the large number of guests.

1:10 eunuchs. Castrated men who, among other duties, **served** in the royal harem.

1:12 The author does not explain why **Vashti refused to come**, probably because the reasons were irrelevant: even the queen was expected to obey the king absolutely.

1:13 wise men. Official advisers to the king (cf. Gen. 41:8; Ex. 7:11; Jer. 50:35; Dan. 2:48). **the times**. The most favorable times for particular actions (see Est. 3:7). **versed in law and judgment**. Trained to make decisions in accordance with the law (see Dan. 1:3–4; Acts 7:22).

procedure toward all who were versed in law and judgment, **14** the men next to him being
Carshena, Shethar, Admatha, Tarshish, Meres, Marsena, and [n]Memucan, [o]the seven princes
of Persia and Media, [p]who saw the king's face, and sat first in the kingdom): **15** "According to
the law, what is to be done to Queen Vashti, because she has not performed the command
of King Ahasuerus delivered by the eunuchs?" **16** Then Memucan said in the presence of the
king and the officials, "Not only against the king has Queen Vashti done wrong, but also
against all the officials and all the peoples who are in all the provinces of King Ahasuerus.
17 For the queen's behavior will be made known to all women, causing them to look at
their husbands with contempt, since they will say, 'King Ahasuerus commanded Queen
Vashti to be brought before him, and she did not come.' **18** This very day the noble women
of Persia and Media who have heard of the queen's behavior will say the same to all the
king's officials, and there will be contempt and wrath in plenty. **19** If it please the king, let
a royal order go out from him, and let it be written among the laws of the Persians and
the Medes so [q]that it may not be repealed, that Vashti is never again to come before King
Ahasuerus. And let the king give her royal position to another who is better than she.
20 So when the decree made by the king is proclaimed throughout all his kingdom, for it
is vast, [r]all women will give honor to their husbands, high and low alike." **21** This advice
pleased the king and the princes, and the king did as Memucan proposed. **22** He sent letters to all the royal provinces, [s]to every province in its own script and to every people in
its own language, that every man be master in his own household and speak according
to the language of his people.

Esther Chosen Queen

2 After these things, [t]when the anger of King Ahasuerus had abated, he remembered
Vashti [u]and what she had done and what had been decreed against her. **2** Then the
king's young men who attended him said, "Let beautiful young virgins be sought out for
the king. **3** And let the king appoint officers in all the provinces of his kingdom to gather
all the beautiful young virgins to the harem in Susa the citadel, under custody of [v]Hegai,
the king's eunuch, who is in charge of the women. [w]Let their cosmetics be given them.
4 And let the young woman who pleases the king be queen instead of Vashti." This pleased
the king, and he did so.

5 Now there was a Jew in Susa the citadel whose name was [x]Mordecai, the son of Jair, son
of Shimei, son of Kish, a Benjaminite, **6** [y]who had been carried away from Jerusalem among
the captives carried away with Jeconiah king of Judah, whom Nebuchadnezzar king of
Babylon had carried away. **7** He was bringing up Hadassah, that is Esther, [z]the daughter
of his uncle, for she had neither father nor mother. The young woman had a beautiful

14 [n]ver. 16, 21 [o]Ezra 7:14 [p]2 Kgs. 25:19
19 [q]ch. 8:8; Dan. 6:8, 12, 15
20 [r][Eph. 5:22, 24, 33; Col. 3:18; 1 Tim. 2:12; 1 Pet. 3:1]
22 [s]ch. 3:12; 8:9

Chapter 2

1 [t][ch. 7:10] [u]ch. 1:19, 20
3 [v]ver. 8, 15 [w]ver. 9, 12
5 [x][Ezra 2:2]
6 [y]2 Kgs. 24:14, 15; 2 Chr. 36:10, 20; Jer. 24:1; 29:1, 2
7 [z]ver. 15

1:14 the seven princes. The inner circle of the king's advisers. **Media**. See note on vv. 2–3.

1:15–18 officials. Senior male civil servants appointed by the king. **noble women**. Wives of the officials. **Memucan** predicts that these women will show **contempt** for their husbands, and that the men, like the king, will be full of **wrath** toward their wives. Moreover, this will not be limited to one stratum of society. Memucan repeatedly uses **all** to impress on the king the danger of a total breakdown of proper domestic order.

1:19–20 The absolute authority of the Persian king is expressed in laws which, once **written**, **may not be repealed** (see Dan. 6:8). This legal convention will give rise to a difficult situation later in the story: what if the king changes his mind? (See Est. 8:5–8; cf. Dan. 6:14–18.) Paradoxically, Vashti is to be punished by being forbidden to do what she has already refused to do: **come** to the king. But **never again** implies divorce and the end of her queenship.

1:21–22 The way in which the wise men resort to law to try to control their wives suggests that they must already have thought this was a widespread domestic problem—a problem, however, that would certainly not have been easily rectified simply by issuing a legal edict. The command that local **household** leaders should each **speak according to the language of his people** is probably intended to ensure that the substance of the edict is understood by all family members everywhere.

2:1–18 *Esther's Rise to the Throne.* Esther finds favor with the king and is chosen to replace Vashti.

2:1–4 In a more sober mood, the king apparently regrets dismissing his beautiful queen. But a solution is at hand. In contrast to the wise men of ch. 1, the **young men** were probably the king's personal household servants (see 6:3). Their suggestion that **beautiful young virgins** should be gathered for the king's appraisal immediately attracts his interest and approval, creating the opportunity for Esther to make her appearance. In line with normal practice, a **eunuch** (see 1:10–11) is in charge of the king's **women** (his harem). **Hegai** may be the same officer of Xerxes (Ahasuerus) that Herodotus refers to in Greek as "Hegias."

2:5 The name **Mordecai** occurs in Persian treasury records of the period as the name of a government official, but whether he was *this* Mordecai is not known. The Mordecai of the book of Esther has a genealogy that links him to King Saul, who lived 500 years earlier. He belongs to the same tribe (**a Benjaminite**), and his great-grandfather, **Kish**, has the same name as Saul's father (1 Sam. 9:1–2). For the significance of this, see note on Est. 3:1.

2:6 Jeconiah, also known as Jehoiachin, was the second-to-last king of Judah. He was deported to Babylon in 597 B.C. (2 Kings 24:10–15), 114 years before the present events. So the clause **who had been carried away from Jerusalem** cannot refer to Mordecai himself (it would make him about 120 years old) but to Kish, his great-grandfather, mentioned in Est. 2:5.

2:7 Hadassah ("myrtle") is the Hebrew name of Mordecai's cousin; **Esther**

8[a]ver. 3 [b]ver. 3
9[c]ver. 3, 12
10[d]ver. 20
15[e]ver. 7; ch. 9:29
[f]ver. 3, 8
17[g]ch. 1:11; 6:8

figure and was lovely to look at, and when her father and her mother died, Mordecai
took her as his own daughter. 8 So when the king's order and his edict were proclaimed,
and [a]when many young women were gathered in Susa the citadel in custody of [b]Hegai,
Esther also was taken into the king's palace and put in custody of Hegai, who had charge
of the women. 9 And the young woman pleased him and won his favor. And he quickly
provided her [c]with her cosmetics and her portion of food, and with seven chosen young
women from the king's palace, and advanced her and her young women to the best place
in the harem. 10 [d]Esther had not made known her people or kindred, for Mordecai had
commanded her not to make it known. 11 And every day Mordecai walked in front of the
court of the harem to learn how Esther was and what was happening to her.

12 Now when the turn came for each young woman to go in to King Ahasuerus, after
being twelve months under the regulations for the women, since this was the regular
period of their beautifying, six months with oil of myrrh and six months with spices
and ointments for women— 13 when the young woman went in to the king in this way,
she was given whatever she desired to take with her from the harem to the king's palace.
14 In the evening she would go in, and in the morning she would return to the second
harem in custody of Shaashgaz, the king's eunuch, who was in charge of the concubines.
She would not go in to the king again, unless the king delighted in her and she was summoned by name.

15 When the turn came for Esther [e]the daughter of Abihail the uncle of Mordecai, who
had taken her as his own daughter, to go in to the king, she asked for nothing except what
[f]Hegai the king's eunuch, who had charge of the women, advised. Now Esther was winning
favor in the eyes of all who saw her. 16 And when Esther was taken to King Ahasuerus, into
his royal palace, in the tenth month, which is the month of Tebeth, in the seventh year of
his reign, 17 the king loved Esther more than all the women, and she won grace and favor
in his sight more than all the virgins, so that he set [g]the royal crown[1] on her head and

[1] *Or headdress*

("star") is her Persian name. The reference to her great beauty prepares the reader for what follows.

2:8–9 It was presumably an honor to be chosen for the harem, though it is unclear from the word **taken** whether she went willingly or unwillingly. Given **the king's order**, she presumably had no choice in the matter. Once there, however, she appears to have been fully compliant, quickly winning the **favor** of Hegai, who provided her with the finest of everything and promoted her to the **best place in the harem**. The **seven chosen young women**, her personal maids-in-waiting, already hint at her royal bearing and destiny.

2:10–11 Mordecai's instruction to Esther not to reveal **her people or kindred** is the first hint of the anti-Semitism that will surface in ch. 3. See note on 3:15.

2:12–14 Both the time involved and the cosmetics used indicate the elaborate nature of the beauty treatment the chosen women received. **the regulations for the women**. This further indication of the strict regimen of the Persian court shows how difficult, and potentially costly, it was for women like Vashti and Esther to assert their independence. **myrrh**. An expensive perfume obtained from trees native to Africa and southern Asia (cf. Prov. 7:17; Song 1:13; Matt. 2:11; John 19:39). **Concubines**, women officially recognized as the king's mistresses, were housed separately (in the **second harem**), having a lower status than his wife or wives. **Shaashgaz** corresponds to Hegai, who was in charge of the *first* harem (see note on Est. 2:1–4). Each woman's first night with the king was her initiation as a concubine. For some, there would be no other such night.

2:15 Abihail. The **uncle** referred to in v. 7. By taking **nothing except what Hegai . . . advised**, Esther shows her trust in his experience and goodwill toward her. The fact that Esther **was winning favor in the eyes of all who saw her** bodes well for her success on this, her night of nights.

2:16 Tebeth, in midwinter, was the **tenth month** of the Jewish religious calendar. **seventh year**. Four years after the events recounted in ch. 1 (see 1:3; and chart below).

Chronology in Esther

The events of Esther unfold over a period of 10 years.

Reference	Event	Month	Day	Year of Ahasuerus's Reign	Year
1:3	Ahasuerus holds his banquets			3	483 B.C.
2:16	Esther goes to Ahasuerus	10		7	479
3:7	Haman casts his lots	1		12	474
3:12	Haman issues his decree	1	13	12	474
3:13	Date planned for annihilation of the Jews	12	13	13	473
8:9	Mordecai issues his decree	3	23	13	473
8:12; 9:1	Day upon which Jews could defend themselves from attack	12	13	13	473
9:6–10, 20–22	Ten sons of Haman executed; Feast of Purim celebrated	12	14, 15	13	473

made her queen instead of Vashti. **18** Then the king [h]gave a great feast for all his officials
and servants; it was Esther's feast. He also granted a remission of taxes to the provinces
and gave gifts with royal generosity.

Mordecai Discovers a Plot

19 Now when the virgins were gathered together [i]the second time, Mordecai was sitting
[j]at the king's gate. **20** [k]Esther had not made known her kindred or her people, as Mordecai
had commanded her, for Esther obeyed Mordecai just [l]as when she was brought up by
him. **21** In those days, as Mordecai was sitting at the king's gate, [m]Bigthan and [n]Teresh,
two of the king's eunuchs, who guarded the threshold, became angry and sought to lay
hands on King Ahasuerus. **22** And this came to the knowledge of Mordecai, [o]and he told
it to Queen Esther, and Esther told the king in the name of Mordecai. **23** When the affair
was investigated and found to be so, the men were both hanged on the gallows.[1] And it
was recorded in [p]the book of the chronicles in the presence of the king.

Haman Plots Against the Jews

3 After these things King Ahasuerus [q]promoted Haman [r]the Agagite, the son of
Hammedatha, [s]and advanced him and set his throne above all the officials who were
with him. **2** And all the king's servants who were at the king's gate bowed down and paid
homage to Haman, for the king had so commanded concerning him. [t]But Mordecai did
not bow down or pay homage. **3** Then the king's servants who were [u]at the king's gate
said to Mordecai, "Why do you transgress [v]the king's command?" **4** And when they spoke
to him day after day and he would not listen to them, they told Haman, in order to see
whether Mordecai's words would stand, for he had told them that he was a Jew. **5** And
when Haman saw that [t]Mordecai did not bow down or pay homage to him, Haman was
[w]filled with fury. **6** But he disdained to lay hands on Mordecai alone. So, as they had made
known to him the people of Mordecai, Haman sought to destroy all the Jews, the people
of Mordecai, throughout the whole kingdom of Ahasuerus.

7 In the first month, which is the month of Nisan, in the twelfth year of King Ahasuerus,
[x]they cast Pur (that is, they cast lots) before Haman day after day; and they cast it month
after month till the twelfth month, which is [y]the month of Adar. **8** Then Haman said to

18 [h]See ch. 1:3
19 [i]ver. 3, 4 [j]ver. 21; ch. 3:2, 3; 5:9, 13; 6:10, 12
20 [k]ver. 10 [l]ver. 7
21 [m][ch. 1:10; 6:2] [n]ch. 6:2
22 [o]ch. 6:2; [ch. 7:9]
23 [p]ch. 6:1; 10:2

Chapter 3

1 [q]ch. 5:11 [r]ver. 10; ch. 8:3, 5; 9:24 [s]ch. 5:11
2 [t]ch. 5:9
3 [u]See ch. 2:19 [v]ver. 2
5 [t][See ver. 2 above] [w]Dan. 3:19
7 [x]ch. 9:24, 26 [y]Ezra 6:15

[1] *Or suspended on a stake*

2:18 Esther's feast. A feast in her honor as the new queen (cf. 1:3, 5, 9). **remission of taxes**. A customary form of celebration referred to by Herodotus in his history of the Persian Empire. **gifts with royal generosity**. Probably in the form of food given to the poor, so that all could share in the celebrations (see 9:22; Jer. 40:5).

2:19–23 *Mordecai's Success in Foiling a Plot against the King.* Mordecai, entirely without intent, is in the right place at the right time to serve King Ahasuerus. This is one of many examples where readers are meant to recognize God's hidden direction of events, though God is never explicitly named (see Introduction: Key Themes).

2:19 the second time. The meaning of this is uncertain. It possibly refers to a second gathering of all the virgins of v. 2 for a ceremonial parade to complete the celebration of Esther's coronation. **the king's gate**. A place where justice was dispensed by officials appointed by the king (2 Sam. 15:2–6; cf. Ruth 4:1–11).

2:21 Mordecai was sitting. Probably as an official, because of Esther's new influence with the king. **the threshold**. The door to the king's private quarters.

2:22–23 hanged on the gallows. A practice known from ancient records. Cf. Ezra 6:11. **the chronicles**. A record of significant events in the king's reign (e.g., 1 Kings 14:29).

3:1–9:19 *Main Action.* This is the heart of the story, where the main events take place. A plot to destroy the Jews (3:1–15) is foiled by a series of courageous actions by Esther and Mordecai (4:1–8:17), culminating in complete victory for the Jews (9:1–19).

3:1–15 *Haman Plots to Kill the Jews.* This complication sets the key events of the story in motion.

3:1 the Agagite. A descendant of Agag, king of the Amalekites, the ancient enemies of Israel (Ex. 17:8–16). Agag was defeated by King Saul and killed by the prophet Samuel (1 Sam. 15:1–33). The conflict between **Haman** and Mordecai mirrors the earlier conflict between their ancestors, Saul and Agag (see note on Est. 2:5).

3:2–4 bowed down and paid homage. According to Herodotus, bowing to superiors was a normal part of Persian court etiquette rather than an act of worship (cf. Gen. 23:7; 1 Kings 1:16). **Mordecai did not bow** because "he was a Jew." The text does not give any more reason for Mordecai's refusal to bow, but given Haman's ancestry and animosity to the Jews, Mordecai apparently felt he could not bow to him without compromising his identity as a Jew. It is also possible that Haman was claiming some kind of divine status and Mordecai refused to give him that kind of honor. **he had told them that he was a Jew**. Mordecai did the very thing he had told Esther not to do in her situation (Est. 2:10, 20).

3:5–6 Haman . . . disdained to lay hands on Mordecai alone. Mordecai's refusal to bow gave Haman the opportunity to reveal his hatred of the Jews by setting out to destroy them all. **the whole kingdom of Ahasuerus**. This included Jerusalem and the surrounding area with its mainly Jewish population (see 1:1; cf. Neh. 1:1–3).

3:7 Nisan. The first month of the Jewish religious calendar, which began in spring with the Passover (Ex. 12:1–2). While the Jews prepared to celebrate their deliverance from Egypt, Haman plotted their destruction. **the twelfth year**. Cf. Est. 2:16; Haman has been biding his time for five years. **Pur**. The Persian word for "lot," from which the term *purim* ("lots") is derived (9:26). **cast lots**. A traditional way of seeking divine guidance (Josh. 18:6; Prov. 16:33) or, as here, finding the most opportune time to do something.

King Ahasuerus, "There is a certain people scattered abroad and dispersed among the
peoples in all the provinces of your kingdom. [z]Their laws are different from those of every
other people, and they do not keep the king's laws, so that it is not to the king's profit to
tolerate them. 9 If it please the king, let it be decreed that they be destroyed, and I will pay
10,000 talents[1] of silver into the hands of those who have charge of the king's business,
that they may put it into the king's treasuries." 10 [a]So the king took his signet ring from
his hand and gave it to Haman [b]the Agagite, the son of Hammedatha, [c]the enemy of the
Jews. 11 And the king said to Haman, "The money is given to you, the people also, to do
with them as it seems good to you."

12 [d]Then the king's scribes were summoned on the thirteenth day of the first month,
and an edict, according to all that Haman commanded, was written to the king's [e]satraps
and to the governors over all the provinces and to the officials of all the peoples, [f]to every
province in its own script and every people in its own language. It was written [g]in the name
of King Ahasuerus [h]and sealed with the king's signet ring. 13 Letters were sent [i]by couriers
to all the king's provinces with instruction [j]to destroy, to kill, and to annihilate all Jews,
young and old, women and children, [k]in one day, the thirteenth day of the twelfth month,
which is the month of Adar, [l]and to plunder their goods. 14 [m]A copy of the document was
to be issued as a decree in every province by proclamation to all the peoples to be ready
for that day. 15 [i]The couriers went out hurriedly by order of the king, and the decree was
issued in Susa the citadel. And the king and Haman sat down to drink, [n]but the city of
Susa was thrown into confusion.

Esther Agrees to Help the Jews

4 When Mordecai learned all that had been done, Mordecai tore his clothes [o]and put on
sackcloth and ashes, and went out into the midst of the city, and he cried out with a
loud and bitter cry. 2 He went up to the entrance of the king's gate, for no one was allowed
to enter the king's gate clothed in sackcloth. 3 And in every province, wherever the king's
command and his decree reached, there was great mourning among the Jews, [p]with fasting
and weeping and lamenting, and many of them [q]lay in sackcloth and ashes.

4 When Esther's young women and her eunuchs came and told her, the queen was deeply
distressed. She sent garments to clothe Mordecai, so that he might take off his sackcloth,
but he would not accept them. 5 Then Esther called for Hathach, one of the king's eunuchs,
who had been appointed to attend her, and ordered him to go to Mordecai to learn what
this was and why it was. 6 Hathach went out to Mordecai in the open square of the city in
front of the king's gate, 7 and Mordecai told him all that had happened to him, [r]and the
exact sum of money that Haman had promised to pay into the king's treasuries for the
destruction of the Jews. 8 Mordecai also gave him [s]a copy of the written decree issued in Susa
for their destruction, that he might show it to Esther and explain it to her and command
her to go to the king to beg his favor and plead with him on behalf of her people. 9 And
Hathach went and told Esther what Mordecai had said. 10 Then Esther spoke to Hathach
and commanded him to go to Mordecai and say, 11 "All the king's servants and the people

8 [z][Ezra 4:12, 13; Acts 16:20, 21]
10 [a]ch. 8:2; Gen. 41:42 [b]ver. 1 [c]ch. 7:6; 8:1; 9:10, 24
12 [d]ch. 8:9 [e]See Ezra 8:36 [f]ch. 1:22; 8:9 [g]ch. 8:8, 10; [1 Kgs. 21:8] [h]ch. 8:8, 10
13 [i]ch. 8:10; [2 Chr. 30:6] [j]ch. 7:4; 8:11 [k]ch. 8:12; [ch. 9:1] [l]ch. 8:11
14 [m]ch. 8:13, 14
15 [i][See ver. 13 above] [n][ch. 8:15]

Chapter 4

1 [o]See 2 Sam. 3:31
3 [p]ver. 16; ch. 9:31 [q]Dan. 9:3; [Isa. 58:5]
7 [r]ch. 3:9
8 [s]ch. 3:14; 8:13

[1] A *talent* was about 75 pounds or 34 kilograms

3:8 they do not keep the king's laws. An allusion to Mordecai's refusal to bow (v. 2), with the (false) implication that all Jews behave similarly. **not to the king's profit**. A clever tactic by Haman. The remission of taxes (2:18) and the unsuccessful war with Greece (see note on 1:2–3) may have left the royal treasury low on funds.

3:9 Haman offers to pay **10,000 talents of silver**, a huge sum (on the order of 12 million ounces; see ESV footnote).

3:10 signet ring. A ring used to seal official documents (Jer. 22:24). Haman is empowered to act with royal authority.

3:11 The money is given to you. Ahasuerus authorizes Haman to use as much of the 10,000 talents of silver as he needs to implement his plan.

3:12 the first month. Presumably of the following (13th) year of Ahasuerus's reign (see v. 7).

3:13 the twelfth month. Because of the extent of the empire, it took almost 12 months to notify and prepare all of those responsible for putting the edict into effect.

3:15 sat down to drink. Haman and the king callously celebrate the forthcoming massacre. **but . . . Susa was thrown into confusion**. Reassuring evidence that many of Susa's citizens did not share Haman's intense hatred of the Jews.

4:1–17 *Mordecai and Esther Plan to Save Their People.* Esther and Mordecai respond to Haman's plan with a counterplan of their own.

4:1–3 sackcloth and ashes . . . fasting and weeping. Traditional ways of expressing grief in the ancient Near East, including Israel (Gen. 37:34; 2 Sam. 1:11; Job 1:20; Isa. 15:1–3; Jonah 3:6). The ban on such behavior in **the king's gate** (see note on Est. 2:19) is understandable, given its unseemly character and the strict court etiquette reflected elsewhere in the book (see 1:8; 3:12; 4:11; cf. Neh. 2:1).

4:4 garments to clothe Mordecai. Given the ban of v. 2, Esther probably feared for Mordecai's safety.

4:11 one law. The law in this matter was absolute, without any qualifications or exceptions. The strict court etiquette shows the king's total power over the

of the king's provinces know that if any man or woman goes to the king inside [t]the inner
court without being called, [u]there is but one law—to be put to death, except the one [v]to
whom the king holds out the golden scepter so that he may live. But as for me, I have not
been called to come in to the king these thirty days."
12 And they told Mordecai what Esther had said. 13 Then Mordecai told them to reply to
Esther, "Do not think to yourself that in the king's palace you will escape any more than
all the other Jews. 14 For if you keep silent at this time, relief and deliverance will rise for
the Jews from another place, but you and your father's house will perish. And who knows
whether you have not come to the kingdom for such a time as this?" 15 Then Esther told
them to reply to Mordecai, 16 "Go, gather all the Jews to be found in Susa, and hold a fast on
my behalf, and do not eat or drink for [w]three days, night or day. I and my young women will
also fast as you do. Then I will go to the king, though it is against the law, [x]and if I perish,
I perish." 17 Mordecai then went away and did everything as Esther had ordered him.

Esther Prepares a Banquet

5 [y]On the third day Esther put on her royal robes and stood in [z]the inner court of the
king's palace, in front of the king's quarters, while the king was sitting on his royal
throne inside the throne room opposite the entrance to the palace. 2 And when the king
saw Queen Esther standing in the court, [a]she won favor in his sight, [b]and he held out to
Esther the golden scepter that was in his hand. Then Esther approached and touched
the tip of the scepter. 3 And the king said to her, "What is it, Queen Esther? What is your
request? It shall be given you, even [c]to the half of my kingdom." 4 And Esther said, "If it
please the king, let the king and Haman come today to a feast that I have prepared for
the king." 5 Then the king said, "Bring Haman quickly, so that we may do as Esther has
asked." So the king and Haman came to the feast that Esther had prepared. 6 [d]And as they
were drinking wine after the feast, the king said to Esther, [e]"What is your wish? It shall
be granted you. And what is your request? [c]Even to the half of my kingdom, it shall be
fulfilled." 7 Then Esther answered, "My wish and my request is: 8 [f]If I have found favor in
the sight of the king, and if it please the king to grant my wish and fulfill my request, let
the king and Haman come to [g]the feast that I will prepare for them, and tomorrow I will
do as the king has said."

Haman Plans to Hang Mordecai

9 And Haman went out that day [h]joyful and glad of heart. But when Haman saw Mordecai
[i]in the king's gate, [j]that he neither rose nor trembled before him, he was filled with wrath
against Mordecai. 10 Nevertheless, Haman restrained himself and went home, and he sent
and brought his friends and [k]his wife Zeresh. 11 And Haman recounted to them the splendor

11 [t]ch. 5:1; [ch. 6:4] [u]Dan. 2:9 [v]ch. 5:2; 8:4
16 [w][ch. 5:1] [x][Gen. 43:14]

Chapter 5

1 [y][ch. 4:16] [z]ch. 4:11; [ch. 6:4]
2 [a][ch. 2:9] [b]ch. 4:11; 8:4
3 [c]ch. 7:2; [Mark 6:23]
6 [d]ch. 7:2 [e]ver. 3; ch. 7:2; 9:12 [c][See ver. 3 above]
8 [f]ch. 7:3; 8:5 [g]ch. 6:14
9 [h]1 Kgs. 8:66 [i]See ch. 2:19 [j]ch. 3:5
10 [k]ch. 6:13

lives of his subjects (cf. v. 2). **not been called . . . these thirty days**. An indication that the king's love for Esther may have begun to wane, making Esther's task even more difficult (see 2:14, 17).

4:14 deliverance will rise. Despite his emotional turmoil (v. 4), deep down Mordecai is sure that the Jews will survive. This reflects his faith that God will protect his people, though the text does not make this explicit. **from another place**. Mordecai does not seem to know what other source of help would appear, but he expresses confidence that God will somehow rescue his people. **your father's house**. Esther's family on her father's side. Since Mordecai is sure the Jews will be delivered, his statement that Esther and her family **will perish** presumably means that they will be punished for Esther's refusal to act. God is apparently the one who will punish them, though again, this is not explicitly said. **you have . . . come . . . for such a time as this**. The strongest hint yet of Mordecai's belief in divine providence.

4:16 hold a fast. This is not a spontaneous outpouring of grief as in v. 3, but an organized activity aimed at increasing Esther's chances of success, through earnest prayer—the strongest indication yet of Esther's (and Mordecai's) faith in God (cf. Ezra 9:5; Neh. 1:4). **if I perish, I perish**. Esther realizes that God cannot be manipulated, even by fasting (cf. Dan. 3:17–18).

5:1–8 *Esther Is Favorably Received by the King and Prepares to Expose Haman.* Esther takes advantage of her renewed influence with the king to begin to implement her own plan to defeat Haman's plot.

5:1–2 the third day. At the end of the three days of fasting (4:16). **the inner court**. Esther stands where Ahasuerus can see her and waits for him either to reject or receive her. This is a very tense moment, for she is risking her life. **the golden scepter**. See 4:11.

5:3 even . . . half of my kingdom. The Greek historian Herodotus describes Xerxes (Ahasuerus) as making such an offer, though on a different occasion. Esther rightly understands it as a traditional, grand gesture rather than one the king expects to be taken seriously (cf. Mark 6:23, where Herod makes a similar offer).

5:4 a feast that I have prepared. Esther had carefully planned what she would do if she was received favorably. By inviting Haman too, she flatters him and sets him up for a colossal fall.

5:8 the feast that I will prepare. Another feast, on the following day. Esther bides her time, as Haman had done. She puts Haman further off guard and makes sure the king is in the best possible mood before revealing what she wants.

5:9–14 *Haman Prepares to Hang Mordecai.* A dangerous development. Events may be moving too swiftly for Mordecai to be saved.

5:9–13 joyful . . . filled with wrath. Haman is elated at how he has been treated by the king and queen, but again becomes incensed by Mordecai's refusal to bow to him. He won't be able to enjoy the (second) feast until he has dealt with Mordecai.

11 [l]See ch. 9:7-10 [m]ch. 3:1
13 [i][See ver. 9 above]
14 [k][See ver. 10 above]
[n]ch. 6:4; 7:9, 10; [ch. 8:7; 9:13, 25]

Chapter 6

1 [o]ch. 2:23; 10:2
2 [p]ch. 2:22 [q][ch. 1:10; 2:21] [r]ch. 2:21
4 [s][ch. 4:11; 5:1] [t]ch. 5:14
6 [u]ver. 7, 9, 11
8 [v][1 Kgs. 1:33] [w]ch. 1:11; 2:17
9 [x][Gen. 41:43]
10 [y]See ch. 2:19
12 [z]See 2 Sam. 15:30
13 [a]ch. 5:10, 14

of his riches, [l]the number of his sons, all the promotions with which [m]the king had honored
him, and how he had advanced him above the officials and the servants of the king. 12 Then
Haman said, "Even Queen Esther let no one but me come with the king to the feast she
prepared. And tomorrow also I am invited by her together with the king. 13 Yet all this is
worth nothing to me, so long as I see Mordecai the Jew sitting [i]at the king's gate." 14 Then
[k]his wife Zeresh and all his friends said to him, [n]"Let a gallows[1] fifty cubits[2] high be made,
and in the morning tell the king to have Mordecai hanged upon it. Then go joyfully with
the king to the feast." This idea pleased Haman, and he had the gallows made.

The King Honors Mordecai

6 On that night the king could not sleep. And he gave orders to bring [o]the book of
memorable deeds, the chronicles, and they were read before the king. 2 And it was
found written how [p]Mordecai had told about [q]Bigthana[3] and [r]Teresh, two of the king's
eunuchs, who guarded the threshold, and who had sought to lay hands on King Ahasuerus.
3 And the king said, "What honor or distinction has been bestowed on Mordecai for this?"
The king's young men who attended him said, "Nothing has been done for him." 4 And
the king said, "Who is in the court?" Now Haman had just entered [s]the outer court of the
king's palace to speak to the king about having Mordecai hanged on [t]the gallows[4] that
he had prepared for him. 5 And the king's young men told him, "Haman is there, standing in the court." And the king said, "Let him come in." 6 So Haman came in, and the king
said to him, "What should be done to the man [u]whom the king delights to honor?" And
Haman said to himself, "Whom would the king delight to honor more than me?" 7 And
Haman said to the king, "For the man whom the king delights to honor, 8 let royal robes be
brought, which the king has worn, [v]and the horse that the king has ridden, and on whose
head [w]a royal crown[5] is set. 9 And let the robes and the horse be handed over to one of the
king's most noble officials. Let them dress the man whom the king delights to honor, and
let them lead him on the horse through the square of the city, [x]proclaiming before him:
'Thus shall it be done to the man whom the king delights to honor.'" 10 Then the king said
to Haman, "Hurry; take the robes and the horse, as you have said, and do so to Mordecai
the Jew, who sits [y]at the king's gate. Leave out nothing that you have mentioned." 11 So
Haman took the robes and the horse, and he dressed Mordecai and led him through the
square of the city, proclaiming before him, "Thus shall it be done to the man whom the
king delights to honor."

12 Then Mordecai returned to the king's gate. But Haman hurried to his house, mourning [z]and with his head covered. 13 And Haman told [a]his wife Zeresh and all his friends
everything that had happened to him. Then his wise men and his wife Zeresh said to him,
"If Mordecai, before whom you have begun to fall, is of the Jewish people, you will not
overcome him but will surely fall before him."

[1] Or *stake;* twice in this verse [2] A *cubit* was about 18 inches or 45 centimeters [3] *Bigthana* is an alternate spelling of *Bigthan* (see 2:21) [4] Or *suspended on a stake* [5] Or *headdress*

5:14 a gallows. There was a gallows in 2:23, but this is another gallows, to be erected especially for hanging Mordecai. Its enormous height (75 feet/23 m) reflects Haman's "towering" rage; it is probably intended to make a public spectacle of Mordecai. **tell the king**. Zeresh assumes that Haman's influence is now so great that he can virtually order the king to hang Mordecai. Mordecai's fate now seems to depend on whose influence over Ahasuerus will prevail—Haman's or Esther's. **This idea pleased Haman, and he had the gallows made**. Haman, who is just as much under the influence of his wife and friends as Ahasuerus is under the influence of Haman and Esther, unwittingly builds the means for his own demise.

6:1–13 *Mordecai Is Honored and Haman Is Humiliated.* Events now move so tellingly in favor of Esther and Mordecai that a presumption of God's providential involvement becomes unavoidable.

6:1 that night the king could not sleep. The timing of this episode of royal insomnia is exquisite—another strong indication that something more than chance is involved (cf. Dan. 6:18). **the book of memorable deeds, the chronicles**. See note on Est. 2:22–23. Again, the request for this book and the reading of the passage about Mordecai can hardly be mere good luck.

6:5 Haman is there. Haman now waits as Esther had done in 5:1. Again, the timing is perfect. Invisibly, and without explicit comment in the text, God is at work to protect his people.

6:6 What should be done to the man . . . the king delights to honor? Neither Ahasuerus nor Haman is aware of the heavy irony involved in the question. The events now unfolding are completely out of their control.

6:7–9 Haman's response shows both the extent of his vanity and his total unawareness of the trap he is walking into. **the horse that the king has ridden . . . a royal crown**. Even greater honors than those bestowed on Joseph (Gen. 41:42–43).

6:10–11 do so to Mordecai the Jew. Haman belatedly realizes the fate he has brought on himself.

6:12–13 mourning and with his head covered. See 4:1–3. Now it is Haman's turn to do as his intended victims had done when the decree of destruction was first published. **wise men**. These are normally associated with kings (see note on 1:13) and therefore serve as a subtle reminder of the heights from which Haman has begun to fall. **If Mordecai . . . , is of the Jewish people, you . . . will surely fall before him**. Even Haman's wife and advisers sense that an irresistible power or person protects the Jewish people.

Esther Reveals Haman's Plot

14 While they were yet talking with him, the king's eunuchs arrived and hurried to bring
Haman [b]to the feast that Esther had prepared.

7 So the king and Haman went in to feast with Queen Esther. 2 And on the second day, as
they were drinking wine after the feast, the king again said to Esther, [c]"What is your
wish, Queen Esther? It shall be granted you. And what is your request? [d]Even to the half of
my kingdom, it shall be fulfilled." 3 Then Queen Esther answered, [e]"If I have found favor
in your sight, O king, and if it please the king, let my life be granted me for my wish, and
my people for my request. 4 [f]For we have been sold, I and my people, [g]to be destroyed, to
be killed, and to be annihilated. If we had been sold merely as slaves, men and women, I
would have been silent, for our affliction is not to be compared with the loss to the king."
5 Then King Ahasuerus said to Queen Esther, "Who is he, and where is he, who has dared[1]
to do this?" 6 And Esther said, [h]"A foe and enemy! This wicked Haman!" Then Haman was
terrified before the king and the queen.

Haman Is Hanged

7 And the king arose in his wrath from the wine-drinking and went into [i]the palace
garden, but Haman stayed to beg for his life from Queen Esther, for he saw that harm was
determined against him by the king. 8 And the king returned from [i]the palace garden to
the place where they were drinking wine, as Haman was falling on [j]the couch where Esther
was. And the king said, "Will he even assault the queen in my presence, in my own house?"
As the word left the mouth of the king, they covered Haman's face. 9 Then [k]Harbona, one
of the eunuchs in attendance on the king, said, "Moreover, [l]the gallows[2] that Haman has
prepared for Mordecai, [m]whose word saved the king, is standing at Haman's house, fifty
cubits[3] high." 10 And the king said, "Hang him on that." [n]So they hanged Haman on the
gallows that he had prepared for Mordecai. [o]Then the wrath of the king abated.

Esther Saves the Jews

8 On that day King Ahasuerus gave to Queen Esther the house of Haman, [h]the enemy
of the Jews. And Mordecai came before the king, for Esther had told [p]what he was to
her. 2 [q]And the king took off his signet ring, which he had taken from Haman, and gave it
to Mordecai. And Esther set Mordecai over the house of Haman.
3 Then Esther spoke again to the king. She fell at his feet and wept and pleaded with him
to avert the evil plan of Haman [r]the Agagite and the plot that he had devised against the
Jews. 4 [s]When the king held out the golden scepter to Esther, 5 Esther rose and stood before
the king. And she said, "If it please the king, [t]and if I have found favor in his sight, and if
the thing seems right before the king, and I am pleasing in his eyes, let an order be written
to revoke [u]the letters devised by Haman [r]the Agagite, the son of Hammedatha, which he
wrote to destroy the Jews who are in all the provinces of the king. 6 For how can I bear [v]to
see the calamity that is coming to my people? Or how can I bear to see the destruction of my
kindred?" 7 Then King Ahasuerus said to Queen Esther and to Mordecai the Jew, "Behold, [w]I

14 [b]ch. 5:8
Chapter 7
2 [c]ch. 5:6; 9:12 [d]ch. 5:3
3 [e]ch. 5:8
4 [f]ch. 3:9; 4:7 [g]ch. 3:13; 8:11
6 [h]See ch. 3:10
7 [i]ch. 1:5
8 [i][See ver. 7 above] [j][ch. 1:6]
9 [k]ch. 1:10 [l]See ch. 5:14 [m][ch. 2:22]
10 [n][Ps. 7:16; Prov. 11:5, 6; Dan. 6:24] [o][ch. 2:1]
Chapter 8
1 [h][See ch. 7:6 above] [p][ch. 2:7, 15]
2 [q]ch. 3:10
3 [r]ch. 3:1; 9:24
4 [s]ch. 4:11; 5:2
5 [t]ch. 5:8; 7:3 [u][ch. 3:13] [r][See ver. 3 above]
6 [v][ch. 7:4]
7 [w]ver. 1

[1] Hebrew *whose heart has filled him* [2] Or *stake*; also verse 10 [3] A *cubit* was about 18 inches or 45 centimeters

6:14–7:10 *Esther Brings About Haman's Destruction.* This is the dramatic heart of the story, where Esther risks all to save her people.

7:2 Even . . . half of my kingdom. See note on 5:3.

7:4 I and my people. Esther reveals that she is a Jew and that Ahasuerus has been tricked into ordering the death of the queen he loves. **we have been sold**. Haman had "bought" the king's agreement to his plan (3:9). **our affliction is not to be compared with the loss to the king**. With this exaggerated comparison, Esther, like Haman, appeals to the king's self-interest. If he reduced the Jews to slavery, he would at least have the benefit of their free labor. By killing them, he will lose a valuable asset.

7:7 the palace garden. See 1:5. Ahasuerus withdraws briefly to compose himself.

7:8 falling on the couch. Haman was probably kneeling, perhaps with his hands or arms on the couch (probably to seek mercy from Esther), but the king's perception is distorted by his anger (taking Haman's move as an **assault** on Esther). **they covered Haman's face**. Covering the head of a condemned prisoner is a custom well known in both ancient and modern times.

7:10 Hang him on that. A gruesome piece of poetic justice that completes the "fall" Haman's wife had predicted (see 5:13; 6:13).

8:1–17 *Esther Wins the Right of the Jews to Defend Themselves.* In this section Esther solves the apparently unsolvable problem: how can something unchangeable (the king's edict) be changed?

8:1–2 Ahasuerus gave . . . Esther the house of Haman. The property of condemned criminals was forfeited to the crown. **Esther . . . told what he** (Mordecai) **was to her**. Previously Esther had revealed only that she was a Jew. **his signet ring**. See note on 3:10.

8:3–8 Haman was dead, but the edict of destruction he had issued with the king's authority was still in force, for **an edict . . . cannot be revoked** (v. 8; cf. Dan. 6:8). Given this state of affairs, the only way a decree could be countered was by issuing another one that made it difficult or impossible to implement the first.

have given Esther the house of Haman, and they have hanged him on the gallows,[1] because
he intended to lay hands on the Jews. **8** But you may write as you please with regard to the
Jews, in the name of the king, [x]and seal it with the king's ring, for an edict written in the
name of the king and sealed with the king's ring [y]cannot be revoked."
9 [z]The king's scribes were summoned at that time, in the third month, which is the month
of Sivan, on the twenty-third day. And an edict was written, according to all that Mordecai
commanded concerning the Jews, to [a]the satraps and the governors and the officials of the
provinces [b]from India to Ethiopia, [b]127 provinces, [c]to each province in its own script and
to each people in its own language, and also to the Jews in their script and their language.
10 [d]And he wrote in the name of King Ahasuerus [e]and sealed it with the king's signet ring.
Then he sent the letters by mounted couriers riding on [f]swift horses that were used in
the king's service, bred from the royal stud, **11** saying that the king allowed the Jews who
were in every city [g]to gather and defend their lives, [h]to destroy, to kill, and to annihilate
any armed force of any people or province that might attack them, children and women
included, [i]and to plunder their goods, **12** [j]on one day throughout all the provinces of King
Ahasuerus, on the thirteenth day of the twelfth month, which is the month of Adar. **13** [k]A
copy of what was written was to be issued as a decree in every province, being publicly
displayed to all peoples, and the Jews were to be ready on that day to take vengeance on
their enemies. **14** So the couriers, mounted on their [f]swift horses that were used in the king's
service, rode out hurriedly, urged by the king's command. And the decree was issued in
Susa the citadel.
15 Then Mordecai went out from the presence of the king [l]in royal robes of blue and
white, with a great golden crown[2] and [m]a robe of fine linen and purple, [n]and the city of
Susa shouted and rejoiced. **16** The Jews had [o]light and gladness and joy and honor. **17** And in
every province and in every city, wherever the king's command and his edict reached, there
was gladness and joy among the Jews, a feast and [p]a holiday. [q]And many from the peoples
of the country declared themselves Jews, [r]for fear of the Jews had fallen on them.

The Jews Destroy Their Enemies

9 [s]Now in the twelfth month, which is the month of Adar, [t]on the thirteenth day of
the same, [u]when the king's command and edict were about to be carried out, [j]on the
very day when the enemies of the Jews hoped to gain the mastery over them, the reverse
occurred: the Jews gained mastery over those who hated them. **2** [v]The Jews gathered in their
cities throughout all the provinces of King Ahasuerus to lay hands on those who sought
their harm. And no one could stand against them, [w]for the fear of them had fallen on all
peoples. **3** All the officials of the provinces and [x]the satraps and the governors and the royal
agents also helped the Jews, for the fear of Mordecai had fallen on them. **4** For Mordecai
was great in the king's house, and his fame spread throughout all the provinces, for the
man Mordecai grew [y]more and more powerful. **5** The Jews struck all their enemies with the
sword, killing and destroying them, and did as they pleased to those who hated them. **6** In
Susa the citadel itself the Jews killed and destroyed 500 men, **7** and also killed Parshandatha

[1] Or *stake* [2] Or *headdress*

8 [x]ver. 10; ch. 3:12 [y][ch. 1:19; Dan. 6:8, 12, 15]
9 [z]ch. 3:12 [a]See Ezra 8:36 [b]ch. 1:1 [c]ch. 1:22; 3:12
10 [d]ch. 3:12, 13 [e]ch. 3:12 [f]1 Kgs. 4:28
11 [g]ch. 9:2, 15, 16, 18 [h]ch. 3:13; 7:4 [i][ch. 9:10, 15, 16]
12 [j]ch. 3:13; 9:1
13 [k]ch. 3:14; 4:8
14 [f][See ver. 10 above]
15 [l][Gen. 41:42; Dan. 5:29] [m][1 Chr. 15:27] [n][ch. 3:15]
16 [o][Ps. 97:11]
17 [p]ch. 9:19, 22; 1 Sam. 25:8 [q]ch. 9:27 [r]ch. 9:2

Chapter 9

1 [s]ch. 8:12 [t]ver. 17 [u]ch. 3:13 [j][See ch. 8:12 above]
2 [v]ver. 15, 16, 18; ch. 8:11 [w]ch. 8:17
3 [x]See Ezra 8:36
4 [y][2 Sam. 3:1]; 1 Chr. 11:9

8:9 Sivan. The third month of the Jewish religious calendar, in late spring (around May–June).

8:11 any armed force. The Jews are only permitted to defend themselves by destroying armed enemies who **attack them.** (It is possible, but not certain, that the wording of 9:5 is broader, indicating that they also attacked known enemies who would have done them harm but who simply refrained from attacking them on that day.) **children and women included.** Any children and women who participated in the attack upon them.

8:12 the thirteenth day of . . . Adar. See 3:13.

8:13 take vengeance on their enemies. Defend themselves by killing all who tried to kill them (see note on v. 11).

8:15 Susa . . . rejoiced (cf. 3:15). This is further evidence that Haman's attitude to the Jews was not typical.

8:16 The Jews had . . . honor. Probably because people saw that the king himself now favored them.

8:17 joy among the Jews. They rightly saw that they were already as good as saved because their enemies would now be afraid to attack them. **many . . . declared themselves Jews.** Tried to pass themselves off as Jews. **fear of the Jews.** Because of the power now wielded by Mordecai (v. 15; 9:3–4).

9:1–19 *The Jews Completely Destroy Their Enemies.* This is the climax of the story, where the tables are completely turned and the enemies of the Jews get what they deserve.

9:1–10 The Jews . . . did as they pleased (v. 5). In context, this cannot mean that they cast off all restraint, but that they gave full vent to their (understandable) desire to destroy their attackers, as they were allowed to do (see notes on 8:11; 9:11–15). **laid no hand on the plunder** (also in vv. 15–16). They were allowed to take plunder (8:11), but they did only what was necessary to defend themselves.

and Dalphon and Aspatha 8 and Poratha and Adalia and Aridatha 9 and Parmashta and Arisai and Aridai and Vaizatha, 10 [z]the ten sons of Haman the son of Hammedatha, [a]the enemy of the Jews, [b]but they laid no hand on the plunder.

11 That very day the number of those killed in Susa the citadel was reported to the king. 12 And the king said to Queen Esther, "In Susa the citadel the Jews have killed and destroyed 500 men and also the ten sons of Haman. What then have they done in the rest of the king's provinces! [c]Now what is your wish? It shall be granted you. And what further is your request? It shall be fulfilled." 13 And Esther said, "If it please the king, let the Jews who are in Susa be allowed [d]tomorrow also to do according to this day's edict. And let the ten sons of Haman be hanged on the gallows."[1] 14 So the king commanded this to be done. A decree was issued in Susa, and the ten sons of Haman were hanged. 15 The Jews who were in Susa gathered also on the fourteenth day of the month of Adar and they killed 300 men in Susa, but they laid no hands on the plunder.

16 [e]Now the rest of the Jews who were in the king's provinces also [f]gathered to defend their lives, and got relief from their enemies and killed 75,000 of those who hated them, but they laid no hands on the plunder. 17 This was [g]on the thirteenth day of the month of Adar, and on the fourteenth day they rested and made that a day of feasting and gladness. 18 But the Jews who were in Susa gathered [g]on the thirteenth day and on the fourteenth, and rested [h]on the fifteenth day, making that a day of feasting and gladness. 19 Therefore the Jews of the villages, who live in [i]the rural towns, hold the fourteenth day of the month of Adar as a day for gladness and feasting, as [j]a holiday, and [k]as a day on which they send gifts of food to one another.

The Feast of Purim Inaugurated

20 And Mordecai recorded these things and sent letters to all the Jews who were in all the provinces of King Ahasuerus, both near and far, 21 obliging them to keep the fourteenth day of the month Adar and also the fifteenth day of the same, year by year, 22 as the days on which the Jews got relief from their enemies, and as the month that had been turned for them from sorrow into gladness and from mourning into [j]a holiday; that they should make them days of feasting and gladness, days for sending gifts of food to one another and gifts to the poor.

23 So the Jews accepted what they had started to do, and what Mordecai had written to them. 24 For Haman the Agagite, the son of Hammedatha, [l]the enemy of all the Jews, [m]had plotted against the Jews to destroy them, and [n]had cast Pur (that is, cast lots), to crush and to destroy them. 25 But when it came before the king, he gave orders in writing [o]that his evil plan that he had devised against the Jews [p]should return on his own head, and that he and his sons should be hanged on the gallows.[2] 26 Therefore they called these days Purim, after the term [n]Pur. Therefore, because of all that was written in [q]this letter, and of what they had faced in this matter, and of what had happened to them, 27 the Jews firmly obligated

[1] *Or stake* [2] *Or suspended on a stake*

10 [z]ver. 13, 14; [ch. 5:11] [a]See ch. 3:10 [b][ch. 8:11]
12 [c]ch. 5:6; 7:2
13 [d]ver. 15; ch. 8:11
16 [e]ver. 2 [f]ver. 2; [ch. 8:11]
17 [g]ver. 1
18 [g][See ver. 17 above] [h]ver. 21
19 [i]Deut. 3:5; Ezek. 38:11; Zech. 2:4 [j]ch. 8:17 [k]Neh. 8:10, 12
22 [j][See ver. 19 above]
24 [l]See ch. 3:10 [m]ch. 3:6 [n]ch. 3:7
25 [o]ch. 7:9, 10; 8:3, 7 [p][Ps. 7:16]
26 [n][See ver. 24 above] [q]ver. 20

9:11–15 tomorrow also. Probably because there were still armed men in Susa committed to carrying out the first edict. **the ten sons of Haman were hanged**. In keeping with Persian royal practice, the king wipes out the conspirator's family publicly, to deter other would-be plotters against himself and the Jews.

9:16–19 These verses explain why two different dates arose for celebrating the deliverance of the Jews. In rural areas the fighting was completed on the **thirteenth** day of Adar, so they celebrated on the **fourteenth**. But in Susa it did not finish until the fourteenth, so they celebrated on the **fifteenth**—as they were still doing when Esther was written (v. 19).

9:20–10:3 *Conclusion.* The story ends by showing what came about as a result of the deliverance the Jews experienced.

9:20–32 *The Establishment of the Feast of Purim.* These verses show how the spontaneous celebrations of vv. 16–19 gave way to a properly organized, annual festival.

9:20–22 the fourteenth . . . and also the fifteenth. The days on which the rural and the urban Jews (respectively) had spontaneously begun to celebrate their deliverance (see note on vv. 16–19). Mordecai avoids any difficulties this might cause by ordering that both days be observed. **gifts of food**. This would enable all alike to share in the feasting, including the **poor** (cf. Deut. 16:11; Neh. 8:10, 12; note on Est. 2:18).

9:23–32 Purim. This is the Hebrew plural of **Pur** (see note on 3:7). Jews still keep the Feast of Purim today. **This second letter** suggests that the differences between rural and urban Jews, referred to in 9:9–16, had persisted to some extent in spite of the first letter (vv. 20–22). Both were distributed in the form of *many* **letters**, carried by many messengers but with the same basic content. **words of peace and truth**. A conventional, formal opening for Jewish letters (even today), but with added significance here. The intention of this letter was to bring peace between different Jewish communities by establishing the one true (correct) manner of observing the festival. **as . . . with regard to their fasts and their lamenting**. The Jews were to take their obligation to observe the joyful Feast of Purim just as seriously as they had already accepted their obligation to observe days of fasting and weeping (Lev. 16:29–31; Zech. 7:3; 8:19).

27 [t] [Isa. 56:3, 6; Zech. 2:11] [s] ver. 21
29 [t] ch. 2:15 [u] ver. 20; ch. 8:10
30 [v] ch. 1:1; 8:9
31 [w] ch. 4:3
32 [x] ver. 26
Chapter 10
1 [y] Isa. 11:11; 24:15
2 [z] ch. 8:15; 9:4 [a] ch. 2:23; 6:1
3 [b] 2 Chr. 28:7; [Gen. 41:40] [c] [Neh. 2:10; Ps. 122:8, 9]

themselves and their offspring and [t]all who joined them, that without fail they would
keep [s]these two days according to what was written and at the time appointed every year,
28 that these days should be remembered and kept throughout every generation, in every
clan, province, and city, and that these days of Purim should never fall into disuse among
the Jews, nor should the commemoration of these days cease among their descendants.
29 Then Queen Esther, [t]the daughter of Abihail, and Mordecai the Jew gave full written
authority, confirming [u]this second letter about Purim. **30** Letters were sent to all the Jews,
[v]to the 127 provinces of the kingdom of Ahasuerus, in words of peace and truth, **31** that
these days of Purim should be observed at their appointed seasons, as Mordecai the Jew
and Queen Esther obligated them, and as they had obligated themselves and their offspring, with regard to [w]their fasts and their lamenting. **32** The command of Queen Esther
confirmed these practices of [x]Purim, and it was recorded in writing.

The Greatness of Mordecai

10 King Ahasuerus imposed tax on the land and on [y]the coastlands of the sea. **2** And all
the acts of his power and might, and the full account of the high honor of Mordecai,
[z]to which the king advanced him, are they not written in [a]the Book of the Chronicles of the
kings of Media and Persia? **3** For Mordecai the Jew was [b]second in rank to King Ahasuerus,
and he was great among the Jews and popular with the multitude of his brothers, for he
[c]sought the welfare of his people and spoke peace to all his people.

10:1–3 *Mordecai's High Rank and Beneficent Rule.* After all the turmoil of the preceding chapters, the story at last arrives at a state of peace.

10:1 imposed tax. Reversing the (temporary) remission of 2:18. If the **coastlands of the sea** are remote parts of Ahasuerus's empire (bordering the eastern Mediterranean), taxing them shows the impressive extent of his power (1:1; 10:2).

10:2 the Chronicles. See note on 2:22–23. **Media and Persia**. See note on 1:2–3.

10:3 second in rank to King Ahasuerus. Cf. Joseph (Gen. 41:40). **brothers**. Fellow Jews. **welfare, peace**. Under Mordecai as the king's chief officer, the Jews experienced exactly the opposite of what they had experienced under Haman.

Introduction to the Poetic and Wisdom Literature

Poetry is pervasive in the Hebrew Bible—the only books in the OT without any poetry are Leviticus, Ruth, Esther, Haggai, and Malachi (although 1 Kings and Nehemiah could perhaps be added to this list). In order to be a competent reader of Scripture, one must have some understanding of the nature and conventions of OT poetry: What is it? How does it work? Who wrote it?

Even in English it is not always a simple matter to distinguish poetry from prose. Often the reader is simply guided by the layout of the text: in poetry, each line of poetry has its own line of text; in prose, there are no special line breaks. No such convention can be seen in our oldest biblical Hebrew manuscripts, and only with the work of the medieval Jewish scribes were biblical texts presented in a manner that distinguishes prose and poetry.

"Poets" in Ancient Israel?

If the boundary between prose and poetry is sometimes difficult to discern, so too are the traces of poets in the archaeological record of ancient Israel. While the nations of Israel and Judah had functioning bureaucracies and civil servants as well as a temple complex that required administration and accounts, little explicit evidence remains for the education of the people who filled these positions or for the milieu in which they would have matured and flourished. There is enough to know there was a literate scribal class, but not enough to say how they became such.

In biblical literature, the concerns of poetry and scribes come together. In addition to the Psalms, the biblical Wisdom Books are also books of poetry, and the poets and sages who were responsible for them belonged to that scribal class (e.g., see Prov. 25:1). Even if the extrabiblical record of their activity is minimal, their contribution to the writings that became the Scripture of Israel is immense. Wherever poetry is found in the Bible, one finds literary reflection in the service of worship and godly living.

What Is Hebrew "Poetry"?

Poetry is commonly recognized by lines exhibiting rhythm and rhyme, readily exemplified by nursery rhymes: even the simple "One, two, buckle my shoe" demonstrates both aspects. This brief snippet exhibits rhythm (*óne, twó,* [pause] *búckle my shóe*), terseness, assonance (the resemblance of the vowel sounds in "one" and "buckle", and "two" and "shoe"), and rhyme—and this sort of wordcraft can also be seen in the work of the ancient Hebrew poets. Apart from rhyme, conventions such as terse expression, freedom in word order, and an absence of typical prose particles also distinguish biblical Hebrew poetry from prose.

One prominent feature of biblical poetry not found in English poems is that of the "seconding sequence"; that is, a line of Hebrew poetry generally has two parts. The poet's art allows the relationship between those parts to be crafted in manifold ways. Here is Psalm 19:1:

> The heavens declare the glory of God,
> and the sky above proclaims his handiwork.
>
> *Hashamayim mesapperim kebod 'El*
> *Uma'aseh yadaw maggid haraqia'*

In the opening of Psalm 19, *the heavens* in the first part finds an echo in *the sky above* in the second part; likewise, *declare* parallels *proclaims*, and *the glory of God* partners *his handiwork*. With nearly one-to-one correspondence, it is obvious why such poetic parallelism has often been called "synonymous"—one of three such categories, the others being "antithetical," where the second part provides the opposite to the first part (e.g., "A wise son makes a glad father, but a foolish son is a sorrow to his mother," Prov. 10:1), and "synthetic," where the two parts of the line do not display either of these kinds of semantic relationship.

Assigning a line of poetry to one of these simple categories represents only a first small step in discerning the poet's art. This "parallel" structure offers the poet a surprisingly rich framework for artistic development: the poet is not simply saying the same thing twice in slightly different terms. The parallel line structure provided Hebrew poets with a means of exploiting similarity and difference on the levels of *sound, syntax,* and *semantics* to achieve an artistically compelling expression of their vision. Unfortunately, of these three elements, the first two (sound and syntax) usually do not survive translation. In the Hebrew of Psalm 19:1, both parts of the line are roughly 11/12 syllables, with three stresses in the first part, and four in the second. Syntactically, they form a very neat "envelope" structure, of the a-b-c/c′-b′-a′ pattern: subject-verb-object/object-verb-subject. Such symmetry already begins to express the totality of the poet's vision.

However, semantics—the meanings of words—are observable in translation. Of course, complete overlap of the meanings of words cannot be sustained across languages, so there is still an advantage to those who can enjoy the poetry in its original setting. While the simple matches across the parts of this first line of Psalm 19 were noted above, there is yet more to be observed. The a:a′ pair ("heavens" and "sky above") are not precise synonyms. "Heavens" is the more generic term, and occurs well over 400 times in the OT; by contrast, "sky above" (Hb. *raqia'*) occurs only 17 times, and nine of those are in the creation account of Genesis 1. Even in this apparently simple development, which exploits the seconding pattern of the parallel line structure, the poet moves from the more generic assertion in the first part to the more specific in the second to display God's glory in his creative acts ("handiwork"). (Confirmation of this allusion to creation comes in Ps. 19:4, which partners "earth" and "world" so that Ps. 19:1 and Ps. 19:4

together allude to the "heavens and earth" of Gen. 1:1.) Something similar could be noted of the verbs: "declare" (Hb. *mesapperim*) refers to the simple act of rehearsal or recounting; "proclaim" (Hb. *maggid*) on the other hand brings the nuance of announcement, of revelation, of *news*. This invitation to savor the wonder of creation's wordless confession of the glories of God (Ps. 19:1–4a), then, forms a profound counterpart to the famous reflection on the verbal expressions of the will of the Lord found in the law (Ps. 19:7–11).

Many lines of Hebrew verse do not offer *this* kind of parallel correspondence, however. Sometimes simple grammatical dependency binds the parts together (e.g., Ps. 19:3), or the first part asks a question that the second part answers (Ps. 19:12). Sometimes there is a narrative development (Ps. 19:5, 13), sometimes an escalation or intensification of terms (Ps. 19:1, 10). These few examples are drawn from a single psalm with fairly regular features; surveying the entire poetic corpus would add a myriad of possibilities. Consistently, however, the art and craft of the Bible's poems offers an invitation to read slowly, to have one's vision broadened, one's perception deepened—or, as it was put above, to see literary reflection in the service of worship and godly living.

Where Is Poetry Found in the OT?

Poetry is pervasive throughout the OT, in spite of the fact there is no word in biblical Hebrew for "poem." The medieval Jewish scholars responsible for the accentuation of the Hebrew text of the Bible used a distinct notation for Psalms, Job, and Proverbs (their order in the Hebrew Bible) that marked these books as "poetic." However, as the chart below shows, Hebrew terms may refer to a particular kind of poem, and thus illustrate their wide diffusion. As this simple (and partial) list demonstrates, poetry is at home in every part of Israelite life.

Songs and prayers of praise and lament most naturally cluster in the book of Psalms, although they can be found elsewhere in the OT as well (e.g., 2 Samuel 22 [and Psalm 18]; 1 Chronicles 16; Habakkuk 3). There is considerable overlap here, with some of the "epic poetry" found in the Pentateuch (e.g., Genesis 49; Exodus 15; Deuteronomy 32; 33) and beyond (Judges 5). Wisdom and "song" often come together (e.g., Ps. 49:4), and the parallel structure of the Hebrew poetic line was a perfect vehicle for proverbial sayings (Proverbs 10–31). Likewise, the dialogues of the book of Job (Job 3–41) are formed entirely in poetry. The book of Lamentations contains a collection of *qinah* poems, whose acrostic structure also forges a connection to a "wisdom" form of composition (see further that book's introduction). The term *massa'* points to a connection with the Hebrew prophets, whose oracles were normally delivered in verse form. The greater part of Isaiah–Malachi is written in poetry: while definitions of a "prophet" may vary, the writing prophets at any rate may at least be said to be poets.

Hebrew Terms for Types of Poems

Category	Hebrew Term	Meaning
general	*shir*	song
	tehillah	prayer, song of praise
	zamir/zimrah	song
	qinah	lament, dirge, with a grieving content
wisdom sayings	*mashal*	proverb
	khidah	riddle
prophetic poetry	*massa'*	oracular utterance, "burden"

What Is Hebrew "Wisdom"?

Hebrew "wisdom" is readily recognized but difficult to define. Some choose simply to define "wisdom" by the literature that best represents it, so that it becomes a list of books. Since wisdom concerns are scattered widely throughout the Bible, this approach is unhelpfully restrictive. Others choose to define "wisdom" as an outlook, almost a philosophy of life. But different "wisdom" writers have differing emphases, so this approach seems too fragmentary. Further, the wisdom writings are of varied character themselves: there is the instructional or proverbial wisdom of Proverbs (basic instructions in how to live), the contemplative wisdom of Job and Ecclesiastes (pondering the perplexing side of life), and the lyric wisdom of the Song of Solomon (a story celebrating one of God's best gifts). What the books and outlooks have in common, however, is a keen interest in the way the world works, humanity's place within it, and how all this operates under God's creative, sovereign care. Biblical "wisdom," then, might be defined as *skill in the art of godly living*, or more fully, *that orientation which allows one to live in harmonious accord with God's ordering of the world*. And "Wisdom Literature" consists of those writings that reflect on or inform that orientation.

Unlike psalmody, wisdom does not have an exclusive relationship with poetry. There are wisdom strands throughout the OT. The "court" stories of Joseph, Esther, and Daniel, e.g., all might be said to be "embodied" wisdom. The special connection with the court of Solomon (see esp. 1 Kings 3:1–28; 4:29–34) is well known, and Solomon may be seen as the "patron" of wisdom in the OT (see Prov. 1:1; 10:1; 25:1; Song 1:1; and by implication Eccles. 1:1). Unlike Job and Proverbs, Ecclesiastes' unique content is communicated in a distinctive style that often defies a simple prose/poetry categorization. By contrast, the lyrical lines of the Song of Solomon's expressions of love are clearly poetic, but its content stands slightly apart from that typical of the "wisdom" books. Some psalms are devoted to "wisdom" themes (e.g., Psalms 37; 49; 73) and show how keeping the law in joyful response to God's goodness (e.g., Psalms 1; 19; 119) is the epitome of wise living.

Contexts for Wisdom and Poetry

Given the preceding discussion, the social setting of wisdom writing would by definition be among those of the literate class, and this in turn suggests a setting within the social elite. It is no surprise, then, that wisdom literature finds a strong connection to the royal court, or that the hymnic poetry of the Psalms (associated with David, Jerusalem, and the temple) likewise has pronounced royal overtones. On the other hand, many of the proverbs do not require high-status origins; rather, they more naturally can be thought of as "folk wisdom," which places their social milieu within the home or clan. It is helpful to distinguish here between wisdom *writing*, which requires scribal education, and wisdom more generally, which could be found at any level of society.

Poetic conventions and wisdom reflections were not unique to Israel in the ancient Near East. The discovery of the Ugaritic texts, found at modern Ras Shamra on the coast of Syria in 1929 and fully deciphered by the end of 1930, revealed a poetic literature dating to the second half of the second millennium B.C. whose diction shared much with the poetry of the Hebrew Bible. Their discovery stimulated renewed study of biblical Hebrew poetry. The literary remains of Israel's neighbors have also provided striking parallels to the wisdom literature. Egyptian "instruction" literature evokes strong resonances with Proverbs, the best-known being that of *The Instruction of Amenemope* (c. 13th century B.C.), which has marked similarities to Proverbs 22:17–24:22. Cuneiform texts from Mesopotamia stretching back into the third millennium B.C. wrestle with the problem of the "righteous sufferer" in a manner comparable to the book of Job. There are also points of contact with Aramaic wisdom literature, and parallels may even be drawn with later Greek writings. Some students of the Scriptures are bothered by the parallels with extrabiblical literature. What sense does it make to speak in terms of "inspiration," when much of Psalm 104, e.g., seems to be shared with Egyptian hymnody? Or when the struggles of Job are paralleled in part by Mesopotamian "righteous sufferer" stories? Here it must be remembered that inspiration is not simply a matter of forms, motifs, or structures, but of *content* that uses various existing forms in a way that accurately reveals the true and living God and his will for his people.

Two advantages in particular are gained by noting such extrabiblical parallels. (1) They demonstrate that the Bible's inspired authors both *inhabit* and *challenge* their contemporary cultural milieu. The questions of ancient Israelites about life were not so very different from the questions of ancient Egyptians, or Sumerians, or Syrians. To that extent, these cross-connections illustrate the degree to which ancient Israel participated in the wider culture of the ancient Near East. Israel and Judah are sometimes portrayed as if they were a "backwater," tucked away in a corner of their world, but such literary parallels show their high level of cultural integration. (2) On the other hand, the writers of biblical wisdom were no mere imitators, producing derivative echoes of their cosmopolitan neighbors. In terms of *scope, originality,* and *profundity,* the biblical writings remain unrivaled. Indeed, one of the small mysteries about them—Job, Psalms, and Proverbs in particular—is just why they are written on such a grand scale. In terms of range and depth of vision, they far transcend their nonbiblical parallels, their outlook reflecting the greatness of the God who informs and indeed shapes them. Awareness of the distinctive contours of biblical poetry and wisdom sharpens our understanding of the insights and concerns of Israel's poets and sages.

Poetic and wisdom literature tends to resist a straightforward chronological setting. Rightly understanding the Bible's histories and prophetic literature depends to an extent on taking their historical context into account; such is not normally the case for Israel's hymns and wisdom. Evidence from the ancient Near East demonstrates that hymnic and wisdom writings are among the most ancient of literary deposits, and likewise some of the Bible's poetic compositions may be among its oldest. But it is also clear that throughout the histories of Israel and Judah, Hebrew poets and sages were at work—from earliest days, on past the canonical compositions, up through the Hellenistic period in the post-canonical books of *Sirach* and *Wisdom of Solomon* and beyond. Their writings often defy a precise historical setting. To take one example at random, a saying like "Whoever plans to do evil will be called a schemer" (Prov. 24:8) requires no precise historical context, nor do we have the evidence to give it one. While particular poems and prayers (e.g., Psalm 137; see notes) may be tied to a given historical circumstance, such cases remain the exception.

Unifying Themes

Each of the books included in this overarching introduction has distinctive content. Still, in these poetic strands of the Bible, whether inclined toward wisdom or hymnody, there are a number of themes that surface repeatedly. Only a few of the most prominent are discussed here. (For more, see the Key Themes sections in the individual books.)

The *fear of the Lord* provides a pervasive orientation throughout the Psalms and Wisdom Books. The phrase, or one like it, appears about 60 times in these books, but its significance goes beyond its simple frequency. It also sets the framework in which wise living takes place. So in the book of Job it becomes the leading question of the outer frame of the book (Job 1:9). It nearly brackets the entire collection of the Psalms: the first injunction in the Psalms directs rulers to "serve the LORD with fear" (Ps. 2:11); while to fear the Lord gives one pleasure (Ps. 145:19). Proverbs is permeated with this outlook: not only is "the fear of the LORD . . . the beginning of knowledge" (Prov. 1:7), but so too it is "a fountain of life" (Prov. 14:27). Even the apparently skeptical Ecclesiastes joins in, since whatever else may happen, "God is the one you must fear" (Eccles. 5:7; cf. 8:12; 12:13).

The *limits of human wisdom* form the natural counterpart to the fear of God. To be sure, there is something about "wisdom" that implies a depth of understanding, in particular of how God has ordered the world and how to live in accord with that divine ordering. The characterization of Solomon's wisdom as being that of a proto-natural scientist (1 Kings 4:33) points in this direction and sheds light on the nature lesson the Lord gave Job (esp. in Job 38–39). This already implies limits to human wisdom, however, and the two strands (fear of God; human limitations) come together powerfully in Job 28. Again this outlook also informs Ecclesiastes. The several "who knows?" texts point in this direction (e.g., Eccles. 3:21; 6:12), as does the reflection on oath taking (Eccles. 5:2). Contrary to modern secular humanist claims, this is no denigration of human dignity: it is rather to recognize the context in which human freedom is most fully realized (cf. Psalm 8; also Ps. 16:1–11; 108:1–6; etc.).

This literature reflects on *the righteous and the wicked in relation to God*. This is an ancient problem (cf. Gen. 18:23), and lies at the heart of the first psalm's evocative portrait of the nature and prospects of the "righteous" contrasting with the fate of the "wicked" (Ps. 1:5–6), a contrast worked out in a sustained way in Psalms 37 and 73. The bulk of the dialogues of Job turn on rightly assessing Job's character and how this places him in relationship to God. Many proverbs observe the behavior of the righteous and wicked, and the outcomes their actions bring; such reflections are especially dense in Proverbs 10–12, as the collection of axioms gets under way following the book's extended introduction. As the psalmist of Psalm 73 and the "Preacher" (*Qoheleth* in Ecclesiastes) noted, the simple correlation of God's rewarding the righteous and punishing the wicked does not always seem to hold (cf. Eccles. 7:15), and so a question of justice is raised, and with it the problem of evil—one of the deepest mysteries faced by people of faith.

This leads in turn to the way in which these books *grapple with suffering*. Naturally, interest here gravitates to the book of Job. Interpreters differ over just what solution the book offers (see the notes on Job for details), but there can be little doubt that a resolution is achieved in the presence of the Creator, the only place where the meaning of human suffering can be understood. But beyond this, many psalms voice a lament ("lament" providing the largest single category of psalm "type") that gives voice to this crisis before God (e.g., Psalms 3; 4; 6; 10; 13). Even the only subliminally theological Song of Solomon expresses not only the delights of love satisfied but the agonies of love unfulfilled (e.g., Song 5:6–8; cf. 8:6–7).

Given that the thread of life before God is woven through each of these books, a further common theme is *the nature of true piety*. The interest of the book of Job in this question was already seen above: is it possible to worship God with integrity (cf. Satan's question in Job 1:9)? One of the designs of the narrative is to answer this question in the affirmative. Again, virtually the whole of the Psalter quite naturally sings of worship with integrity (e.g., Psalms 25; 26; 31; 84). ◂

INTRODUCTION TO

JOB

Author

While Job is one of the most profound books of the Bible, its anonymous author can be known only through reading between its lines. Certainly he can be numbered among "the wise" (cf. Prov. 24:23), given his fondness for proverbs, which he quotes to develop a point: "those who plow iniquity and sow trouble reap the same" (Job 4:8); "man is born to trouble as the sparks fly upward" (5:7); "a stupid man will get understanding when a wild donkey's colt is born a man!" (11:12).

Though the story of Job has its setting outside Israel to the east and south (Uz is related to Edom, which may be the setting of the book, cf. 2:11; 6:19; Lam. 4:21), the author of Job is a Hebrew, thoroughly immersed in the Hebrew Scriptures (see below).

The author of Job was a well-traveled individual who could draw on a wealth of knowledge and experience. He knew the constellations (Job 9:9; 38:31), could discuss meteorology (38:22–38) or describe a sophisticated mining operation (28:1–11). He could refer to skiffs of papyrus reed plying the waters (9:26), or the plants that grew in the marshes (8:11–19). He had observed ostriches, eagles, mountain goats, hippopotamuses, crocodiles, and war horses (chs. 39–41). As was true of all the wise, he made extensive use of nature analogies to explain and defend moral truths.

Etymologically the name Job could be related to the Hebrew word for "enemy," with reference to either Job's attitude to God or his response to suffering. The name might also be a contracted form of "Where is my father?" But it is difficult to know, because its actual meaning was already lost to the earliest rabbinic commentators. However, the name is known outside the Bible. It is the name of the prince of Ashtaroth in Bashan in the Amarna tablets (c. 1350 B.C.), and the name of a Palestinian chief in an Egyptian text (c. 2000 B.C.). At Ugarit a version of the name appears in a list of palace personnel.

Date

There are no historical allusions in the book to determine its time or circumstances. From ancient times there has been much discussion about the occasion for writing Job. The Babylonian Talmud records a variety of opinions as to the author of the book, ranging from someone in the time of the patriarchs, to Moses, to one of those who returned from the Babylonian captivity (*Baba Bathra* 15a). The hero of the book is given a patriarchal setting, authentic in detail and coloring, which has led some interpreters to suggest an early date, perhaps as early as the time of Abraham.

The earliest reference to Job outside the book itself is in Ezekiel. The prophet names three paragons of virtue: Noah, Daniel, and Job (Ezek. 14:14, 20). It is not certain whether Ezekiel knew of these men from the biblical narrative or from other traditions; this is particularly true for Daniel, a book that could not have been complete in Ezekiel's day. If Ezekiel knew of Job through the biblical book, then it would be preexilic.

Attempts have been made to date Job on the basis of theological development within the Scriptures. Job has been viewed as an elaborate *midrash* (type of commentary) on Deuteronomy 28, or as an effort to apply a discussion of the problem of suffering for the nation (such as that depicted in Isaiah) to the individual. Arguments based on "theological development," however, are difficult to sustain, because they presuppose that one can actually describe how such themes developed over time.

The author of Job makes direct allusion to the Hebrew Scriptures (e.g., Ps. 8:4; cf. Job 7:17–18), and at times quotes lines directly (e.g., Ps. 107:40; cf. Job 12:21, 24). Such precise repetition of phrases and reapplication of biblical thought indicates that the poet had access to these writings, though again it cannot be certain in what form they existed.

Some have suggested, therefore, that the theological questions addressed in Job, and the use of Scripture in the book, indicate a time for the composition approximating Ezekiel's, but confidence in such a conclusion is hard to come by. The author uses a lot of vocabulary with meanings known in later Hebrew. This does not confirm a more precise dating but may favor a date that is exilic (587 to 538 B.C.) or postexilic (after 538).

Theological Themes

The book of Job concerns itself with the question of faith in a sovereign God. Can God be trusted? Is he good and just in his rule of the world? Job will declare outright that God has wronged him (19:6–7). At the same time, Job is certain that his "enemy" is actually his advocate and will vindicate him.

The book sets out from the beginning to show that the reasons for human suffering often remain a secret to human beings. Indeed, Job's sufferings come upon him because Satan accused him in the heavenly courts, and the reader never learns whether these reasons were explained to Job. Probably they were not. There is irony in the book of Job, due to the fact that God seems both too close and too far away. On the one hand, Job complains that God is watching him every moment so that he cannot even swallow his spit (7:19). On the other hand, Job finds God elusive, feeling that he cannot be found (9:11). Though God is intensely concerned about humans, he does not always answer their most agonizing questions.

At the same time, Job's friends offer no real help. They come to "comfort" him (2:11), but Job ends up declaring them "miserable comforters" who would "comfort" him "with empty nothings" (21:34). These friends represent an oversimplified "orthodoxy," based on a misreading of the wisdom tradition to the effect that all troubles are punishments for wrongdoing. Their "comfort" consists largely of applying this message to Job, urging him to identify his sin and repent of it. In so doing, these friends serve as a mirror for all readers who might be inclined to say similar things to people in distress.

Astonishingly, the Lord does not take Job to task over his words, instead calling them "right" (42:7). The book as a whole illustrates that a full understanding of God's reasons for events is not a prerequisite for faithfulness amid terrible suffering. Further, Job's deep perplexity and questioning are not a provocation to God.

Purpose, Occasion, and Background

The book of Job addresses a universal problem for all people of all faith perspectives, even for those who believe that the world is the result of impersonal forces operating in a predetermined manner. The author of Job specifically addresses those who believe in a personal Creator, known by the name Yahweh (the LORD), according to his self-revelation. His work is simply about God and man; it was written to those who struggle with the justice of a sovereign God in a world filled with suffering.

The author does not provide a theodicy in the sense of defending the justice of God. Job's friends serve as a foil to that end. Their wisdom is a human effort to resolve this dilemma, but as far as the author is concerned, these efforts fail. God also declares that the friends are in the wrong (42:8). Elihu's intervention probes further, but neither is he the intermediary whom Job seeks. The author is concerned about the triumph of faith in a time of suffering. To this end his hero succeeds. Job can triumphantly declare, "I know that my Redeemer lives" (19:25). Job's resolve to love and trust the one who seems to attack him as an enemy is evident throughout.

The problem of suffering is timeless, whether national or individual. It is therefore not helpful to infer specific national settings that might have inspired the book of Job, whatever proposed relationships may be observed to books such as Deuteronomy and Isaiah. The author is careful not to allow his reflections to be limited by a particular set of circumstances.

The wisdom writers of Israel worked within their own context of thought and worldview. Though they did use sayings and works from other cultures, particularly Egypt, they wrote to articulate their own faith for their people, who were the primary readers. At the same time, they considered their thoughts applicable to all people of all times: "Hear this, all peoples! Give ear, all inhabitants of the world, both low and high, rich and poor together! My mouth shall speak wisdom; the meditation of my heart shall be understanding" (Ps. 49:1–3). A universal and timeless perspective is deliberately conveyed by the selection of a non-Israelite hero, the intentional avoidance of the Israelite name for God in the poetic section (from ch. 3 on) until God speaks (except for the reference to Isa. 41:20 in Job 12:9), and the relative absence of any specific historical allusions.

Job and His Setting

As already indicated, the Israelite author presents Job as a person living in Uz, which is outside the borders of Israel itself. His piety (1:1) exemplifies the ideal in Israelite wisdom, and he invokes the name of Yahweh (1:21). At the same time, his relationship to Abraham's offspring remains a mystery. The events of the book seem to be set in the times of the patriarchs, Abraham, Isaac, and Jacob. The way Ezekiel 14:14, 20 (see note there) refer to Job along with two others apparently from ancient times enhances this impression. So do the favorite names for the deity, "God" (Hb. *'Eloah*, the singular of *'Elohim*) and "the Almighty" (Hb. *Shadday*), which seem more suited to the days before Exodus 3:14; 6:3 (the name Yahweh, the LORD, appears only in Job 1–2, and 38–42, with one lone exception in the middle of the book, 12:9).

The prophet Ezekiel mentions Job along with Noah and Daniel, and this seems to imply that he took Job as a real person. This is also the implication of James 5:11: "Behold, we consider those blessed who remained steadfast. You have heard of the steadfastness of Job, and you have seen the purpose of the Lord, how the Lord is compassionate and merciful." At the same time, the author has supplied many details for the sake of his literary presentation: the question of whether Job and his friends actually spoke exalted poetry to each other is not important to the author's purposes.

History of Salvation Summary

In the history of God's dealings with his people, the question of the apparently undeserved suffering of faithful individuals recurs again and again. The book of Job reminds God's people that they have an enemy who will denounce them (Satan), and, through the ignorance of Job's friends, it helps the faithful to remember at all times how small a part of any situation is the fragment that they see. This equips believers to trust and obey amid life's perplexities, and it enables the faithful to support and encourage one another in a spirit of tenderness and humility (Rom. 12:15). The death and resurrection of Jesus have not removed this perplexity. They have, however, given a firm foundation to Job's hope in his "Redeemer" (Job 19:25–27). (For an explanation of the "History of Salvation," see the Overview of the Bible, pp. 23–26. See also History of Salvation in the Old Testament: Preparing the Way for Christ, pp. 2635–2661.)

Literary Features

A prose account of the fall and restoration of the pious Job frames the book as a whole (1:1–2:13; 42:7–17). Here readers meet a blameless man, whose peace and prosperity are tragically disrupted when—unknown to him—God points him out to Satan (see note on 1:6). The question posed in 1:9, "Does Job fear God for no reason?" appears to be the leading concern of the prose, and it receives a full and satisfactory answer by the book's conclusion.

Within those prose bookends, though, a dramatic poetic dialogue unfolds as readers listen to the main protagonists in the story. Job's soliloquies (chs. 3; 28; 29–31) bracket three rounds of impassioned debate (chs. 4–14; 15–21; 22–27) with his "friends"—Eliphaz, Bildad, and Zophar (cf. 2:11). Their dialogue descends from intuitive integrity in Job (cf. 3:23–25; 6:4) and sympathy from his friends (4:2–5) at the beginning, to embittered self-justification in Job (ch. 27) and outrageous accusation from his friends (ch. 22) at the end. Throughout, the main concern seems to be a question Eliphaz voiced: "Can mortal man be in the right before God? Can a man be pure before his Maker?" (4:17; cf. Job at 9:2; 31:6; Bildad at 25:4). Consequently, Job himself comes under increasing scrutiny as he mounts an increasingly bold defense of his innocence in the face of the simplistic ethical onslaught of his friends.

Job longs for divine vindication, and for an intermediary who can bring this about (cf. 9:33; 16:19–21; 19:25–27). The reader, who has had a privileged glimpse into the heavenly mysteries behind Job's suffering, is prepared by the end of the dialogues for God to declare to the disputants their errors and relieve Job of his misery. It is not to be, however—at least not yet.

Instead, a new character makes an entrance, one who alone in the book bears a Hebrew name: Elihu ("he is God" or possibly "Yahweh is God") son of Barachel ("may God bless" or "God has blessed"; cf. 32:6). Through five uninterrupted chapters (chs. 32–37) he rebukes both Job and his friends—but how are readers to understand his intervention? Commentators vary dramatically in their assessments. From the text itself, certain factors stand out. (1) Elihu provides in small measure the "intermediary" for whom Job hoped. Elihu himself is not the answer to Job's quest, but he does point in the right direction. (2) The dialogues to this point appeal to tradition and observation; Elihu introduces the notion of inspiration (32:8, 18–20). Some see here an overtly prophetic response to the wisdom discussion. (3) Elihu cites and finds wanting both sides of the debate (33:1; 34:2). Again, Elihu anticipates the stance that God himself will take (chs. 38–42). (4) Perhaps most important, Elihu reorients the entire debate. The focus slowly but surely swings away from Job and the problem of human morality, urging attention to God alone as the grounds of certainty and hope (cf. 36:22–23; 37:14–24).

At the same time, Elihu may be overestimating his own contribution (32:6–10). He knows no more of the actual reasons for the events (chs. 1–2) than the three friends do, and some of his arguments overlap theirs. Further, when the Lord finally speaks (38:1), he seems to ignore Elihu entirely (cf. also 42:7). Elihu may be asserting some true things at the core of his argument, but how he applies these things and the conclusions he draws about Job contrast significantly with the Lord's speech to Job. On a literary level, Elihu's speech builds suspense by delaying the final outcome.

Finally, the Lord appears in the whirlwind (38:1; 40:6)—as Job had suspected he might (cf. 9:17a). The "Yahweh speeches" (chs. 38–41) do not directly engage Job's questions but point rather to the reality of the God behind, and now clearly within, his suffering.

The reader's insight into the "true" state of affairs comes by the prose introduction (chs. 1–2), which helps both to nuance the content of the dialogues and to explain the outcomes in the book's conclusion. While Job's assertions of innocence have some justification, his character develops throughout the speeches. On the other hand, the friends may claim some kernel of truth, but despite their "orthodoxy," the reader can make an informed judgment about how their accusations apply to Job. Thus, the Lord's commendation of Job and instruction to the friends to beg Job's intercession on their behalf (42:7–9) is in part explained by the context set in the opening two chapters.

The most important key word in the book is the term "comfort"; the book shows where true comfort is to be found. In 2:11 Job's three friends come to comfort him; in 6:10 Job takes comfort in not having denied the words of the Holy One; in 7:13 Job claims that God will not allow his bed to comfort him. In 15:11 Eliphaz claims to be offering the comforts of God, while in 16:2 Job calls his friends miserable comforters, and in 21:34 he declares they are trying to comfort him with empty nothings. In 21:2 Job sarcastically offers to his friends the "comfort" of hearing him out. The key comes in 42:6 (if the reading of the ESV footnote is followed; see note there): now that God has spoken, Job can say that he is "comforted in dust and ashes." When Job's relatives and friends come to comfort him in 42:11, this is probably ironic: Job found the comfort he needed in the vision of God's unsearchable wisdom.

Outline

I. Prologue: Job's Character and the Circumstances of His Test (1:1–2:13)
  A. The integrity of Job (1:1–5)
  B. The first test (1:6–22)
    1. The challenge in heaven (1:6–12)
    2. The loss of family and possessions (1:13–19)
    3. Job's confession and confidence (1:20–22)
  C. The second test (2:1–10)
    1. The challenge in heaven (2:1–6)
    2. Job's affliction and confession (2:7–10)
  D. Job's comforters (2:11–13)

II. Dialogue: Job, His Suffering, and His Standing before God (3:1–42:6)
  A. Job: despair for the day of his birth (3:1–26)
    1. Introduction (3:1–2)
    2. Job curses his birth (3:3–10)
    3. Job longs for rest (3:11–19)
    4. Job laments his suffering (3:20–26)
  B. The friends and Job: can Job be right before God? (4:1–25:6)
    1. First cycle (4:1–14:22)
      a. Eliphaz: can mortal man be in the right before God? (4:1–5:27)
      b. Job: life is futile (6:1–7:21)
      c. Bildad: the wisdom of the sages (8:1–22)
      d. Job: how can a mortal be just before God? (9:1–10:22)
      e. Zophar: repent (11:1–20)
      f. Job: a challenge to the "wisdom" of his friends (12:1–14:22)

2. Second cycle (15:1–21:34)
   a. Eliphaz: Job's words condemn him (15:1–35)
   b. Job: hope for a sufferer (16:1–17:16)
   c. Bildad: punishment for the wicked (18:1–21)
   d. Job: my Redeemer lives (19:1–29)
   e. Zophar: the wicked will die (20:1–29)
   f. Job: the wicked prosper (21:1–34)
3. Third cycle (22:1–25:6)
   a. Eliphaz: Job is guilty (22:1–30)
   b. Job: God is hidden (23:1–24:25)
   c. Bildad: an unanswered question (25:1–6)

C. Job: the power of God, place of wisdom, and path of integrity (26:1–31:40)
   1. The mystery and majesty of God's ways (26:1–14)
   2. A claim to integrity and a wish for vindication (27:1–23)
   3. Where is wisdom found? (28:1–28)
   4. The path of Job's life (29:1–31:40)

D. Elihu: suffering as a discipline (32:1–37:24)
   1. Introduction: Elihu and his anger (32:1–5)
   2. The voice of youth (32:6–22)
   3. An arbiter for Job (33:1–33)
   4. An appeal to the wise (34:1–37)
   5. What right does Job have before God? (35:1–16)
   6. The mercy and majesty of God (36:1–37:24)

E. Challenge: the Lord answers Job (38:1–42:6)
   1. The first challenge: understanding the universe (38:1–40:2)
   2. Job's response: silence (40:3–5)
   3. The second challenge: understanding justice and power (40:6–41:34)
   4. Job's response: submission (42:1–6)

III. Epilogue: The Vindication, Intercession, and Restoration of Job (42:7–17)

A. The Lord rebukes the three friends (42:7–9)
B. The Lord restores Job (42:10–17)

JOB

Job's Character and Wealth

1 There was a man in the land of [a]Uz whose name was [b]Job, and that man was [c]blameless
and upright, one who [d]feared God and [e]turned away from evil. 2 There were born to
him [f]seven sons and three daughters. 3 He possessed 7,000 sheep, 3,000 camels, 500 yoke of
oxen, and 500 female donkeys, and very many servants, so that this man was the greatest
of all [g]the people of the east. 4 His sons used to go and hold a feast in the house of each one
on his day, and they would send and invite their three sisters to eat and drink with them.
5 And when the days of the feast had run their course, Job would send and [h]consecrate
them, and he would rise early in the morning and [i]offer burnt offerings according to the
number of them all. For Job said, "It may be that my children have sinned, and [j]cursed[1]
God in their hearts." Thus Job did continually.

Satan Allowed to Test Job

6 Now there was a day when [k]the sons of God came to present themselves before the
LORD, and [l]Satan[2] also came among them. 7 The LORD said to Satan, "From where have

[1] The Hebrew word *bless* is used euphemistically for *curse* in 1:5, 11; 2:5, 9 [2] Hebrew *the Accuser* or *the Adversary*; so throughout chapters 1–2

Chapter 1

1 [a]Jer. 25:20; Lam. 4:21 [b]Ezek. 14:14, 20; James 5:11 [c]ver. 8; ch. 2:3; [ch. 9:20; Gen. 6:9; 17:1] [d]ch. 4:6; Prov. 16:6 [e][ch. 28:28; Ps. 34:14]
2 [f]ch. 42:13
3 [g]See Judg. 6:3
5 [h]1 Sam. 16:5 [i]ch. 42:8; Gen. 8:20 [j]ch. 2:5; [Ps. 10:3]
6 [k]ch. 2:1; 38:7; Gen. 6:2, 4 [l][1 Chr. 21:1; Zech. 3:1; Rev. 12:9, 10]

1:1–2:13 *Prologue: Job's Character and the Circumstances of His Test.* The prologue opens by introducing Job as a man who was blameless and upright in character, blessed in family and possessions, and whose life embodied the fear of God both for himself and on behalf of his family (1:1–5). The second section details the heavenly conversations and earthly actions related to Satan's two-stage request to test Job's character by afflicting him (1:6–2:10). The final section describes how Job's three friends hear of his suffering and come to offer sympathy and comfort, which creates the context for the rest of the book (2:11–13). The narration of the prologue is integrally important for the interpretation of the book as a whole because it describes for the hearer/reader something that the three friends will continually address: *To what extent do the circumstances of Job's life on earth reveal what is true about him before God?* The three friends (as well as Elihu, in his own way) assume that Job's circumstances reveal some hidden sin or wayward path in Job's character that has provoked God's displeasure, correction, or judgment. Job's friends will continually argue that his circumstances necessarily represent a choice that he has to make: either repent and agree with God, or continue as you are and receive the full punishment signified in your suffering. In responding to his friends, Job insists both that he is right before God and that it is ultimately God who has brought about his circumstances. Throughout the dialogue, Job tries to maintain that he is in the right while also arguing God's character back to him in lament about why his righteousness and justice do not appear to be borne out in events on earth. In the end, God will reprove Job for the extent of his conclusions about what circumstances on earth might mean for God's governance and justice (38:1–41:34). However, God will also vindicate Job before his friends, judge them with respect to their words, and call Job to intercede on their behalf (42:7–17).

1:1–5 *The Integrity of Job.* The prologue opens with a brief description of Job's character and circumstances, which become the context for the subsequent tests.

1:1 the land of Uz. The location of this land to the east is unknown, but it may be related to Aram in the north (Gen. 10:22–23), where Abraham's nephew and family lived (Gen. 22:21), or to a descendant of Seir who lived alongside the sons of Esau in the land also referred to as Edom (Gen. 36:28). The faithfulness of Job is stated at the outset (and affirmed again in Job 1:8; 2:3): he is **blameless and upright** (a phrase also used in reference to Noah in Gen. 6:9 and to Abraham in Gen. 17:1) and **one who feared God and turned away from evil** (which echoes the characteristics of one who is "wise" in Proverbs; see Prov. 3:7; 14:16; 16:6). This description represents a gap between what the reader has been told and what the three friends come to assume about Job.

1:2–4 The large numbers of children, livestock, and **servants**, together with the feasting, suggest the enormous prosperity of Job's life at this point. **on his day**. Cf. 18:20.

1:5 cursed God in their hearts. The Hebrew reads literally "blessed God in their hearts" (see ESV footnote), but the context indicates that the opposite sense "to curse" is intended (the same verb is also used with this inferred sense in 1:11; 2:5, 9; 1 Kings 21:10, 13). This construction is undoubtedly a euphemism (i.e., using inference rather than explicit vocabulary to refer to someone "cursing God"). This play on the word "bless" in the description and dialogues of the prologue creates irony with the conclusion of the epilogue (Job 42:7–17), where Job's three friends are instructed that they are the ones in need of Job's intercessory prayer because they had spoken foolishly about God (see 42:7–8).

1:6–22 *The First Test.* This section presents the occasion, dialogue, and events of Job's first test.

1:6–12 *The Challenge in Heaven.* With Job now introduced, the scene switches to the heavenly court. The Lord draws Satan's attention to Job, thus initiating the chain of events that occupy the rest of the book. The earthly protagonists remain oblivious to these heavenly deliberations.

1:6 Sons of God refers to heavenly beings gathered before God like a council before a king (see 15:8; Ps. 29:1; Isa. 6:1–8). The Hebrew idiom "sons of" can be used of a group that is led by a figure referred to as their "father" (e.g., the "father" of a band of prophets in 1 Sam. 10:12). **Satan**. The Hebrew noun *satan* is commonly used to refer to someone generally as an adversary (e.g., 1 Sam. 29:4; 1 Kings 11:14) but here refers to a specific individual ("the Accuser" or the "Adversary," ESV footnote) who does not appear to be one of

you come?" Satan answered the LORD and said, "From [m]going to and fro on the earth, and
from walking up and down on it." 8 And the LORD said to Satan, "Have you [n]considered
my [o]servant Job, that there is none like him on the earth, [p]a blameless and upright man,
who fears God and turns away from evil?" 9 Then Satan answered the LORD and said, "Does
Job fear God for no reason? 10 Have you not put [q]a hedge around him and his house and
all that he has, on every side? You have [r]blessed the work of his hands, and his possessions
have increased in the land. 11 But [s]stretch out your hand and [t]touch all that he has, and he
will [u]curse you [v]to your face." 12 And the LORD said to Satan, "Behold, all that he has is in
your hand. Only against him do not stretch out your hand." So Satan went out from the
presence of the LORD.

Satan Takes Job's Property and Children

13 Now there was a day when his sons and daughters were eating and drinking wine
in their oldest brother's house, 14 and there came a messenger to Job and said, "The oxen
were plowing and the donkeys feeding beside them, 15 and [w]the Sabeans fell upon them
and took them and struck down the servants[1] with the edge of the sword, and I alone have
escaped to tell you." 16 While he was yet speaking, there came another and said, [x]"The fire
of God fell from heaven and burned up the sheep and the servants and consumed them,
and I alone have escaped to tell you." 17 While he was yet speaking, there came another
and said, [y]"The Chaldeans formed [z]three groups and made a raid on the camels and took
them and struck down the servants with the edge of the sword, and I alone have escaped
to tell you." 18 While he was yet speaking, there came another and said, [a]"Your sons and
daughters were eating and drinking wine in their oldest brother's house, 19 and behold,
a great wind came across [b]the wilderness and struck the four corners of the house, and it
fell upon the young people, and they are dead, and I alone have escaped to tell you."
20 Then Job arose and [c]tore his [d]robe and [e]shaved his head [f]and fell on the ground and worshiped. 21 And he said, [g]"Naked I came from my mother's womb, and naked shall I [h]return.
The LORD [i]gave, and the LORD has taken away; [j]blessed be the name of the LORD."
22 [k]In all this Job did not sin or charge God with [l]wrong.

Satan Attacks Job's Health

2 Again [m]there was a day when the sons of God came to present themselves before the
LORD, and Satan also came among them to present himself before the LORD. 2 And
the LORD said to Satan, "From where have you come?" Satan answered the LORD and said,
"From going to and fro on the earth, and from walking up and down on it." 3 And the
LORD said to Satan, "Have you considered my servant Job, that there is none like him on
the earth, a blameless and upright man, who fears God and turns away from evil? He still
[n]holds fast his integrity, although you incited me against him to destroy him [o]without

[1] Hebrew *the young men*; also verses 16, 17

7 [m]ch. 2:2; [1 Pet. 5:8]
8 [n]ch. 2:3 [o]Num. 12:7; 2 Sam. 7:5; Isa. 20:3 [p]ver. 1
10 [q][Ps. 3:3; 34:7] [r][Ps. 128:1, 2]
11 [s]ch. 2:5 [t]ch. 19:21; Isa. 53:4 (Heb.) [u]ver. 5 [v]Isa. 65:3
15 [w]ch. 6:19; See 1 Kgs. 10:1
16 [x]2 Kgs. 1:12
17 [y]Gen. 11:28; 2 Kgs. 24:2 [z][Judg. 7:16; 1 Sam. 11:11]
18 [a]ver. 4, 13
19 [b]Isa. 21:1; Jer. 4:11; Hos. 13:15
20 [c]See Gen. 37:29 [d]Ezra 9:3 [e]Jer. 7:29 [f][1 Pet. 5:6]
21 [g]Eccles. 5:15; [Ps. 49:17; 1 Tim. 6:7] [h][Gen. 3:19; Ps. 90:3; Eccles. 12:7] [i][Eccles. 5:19; James 1:17] [j]Ps. 113:2; Dan. 2:20; [Eph. 5:20; 1 Thess. 5:18]
22 [k]ch. 2:10 [l]ch. 24:12

Chapter 2

1 [m]ch. 1:6
3 [n]ver. 9; [ch. 27:5, 6] [o]ch. 9:17

the company but who **also came among them**. The dialogue that follows reveals the character of this figure to be consistent with that of the serpent in Genesis 3, a character who is also referred to by the use of this noun as the proper name, "Satan" (e.g., 1 Chron. 21:1; see also Rev. 12:9).

1:9–11 Satan suggests that the elements of prosperity in Job's life cast doubt on the sincerity of his fear of God; he contends that if God will only remove the protection of these things, Job will **curse** (lit., "bless"; see note on v. 5) him outright.

1:12 The fact that Satan has to ask permission to test Job (see also 2:6) indicates that the extent of his authority falls ultimately under the sovereign governance of God—something that Job also refers to, but without knowledge of or reference to the heavenly dialogue and its relation to his troubles (1:21; 2:10).

1:13–19 *The Loss of Family and Possessions.* Job's troubles are described as coming from multiple directions. The **Sabeans** come from the south (v. 15), the **fire** from heaven (v. 16), the **Chaldeans** from the north (v. 17), and the sirocco **wind** from the east (v. 19). The narrative presents each of the tragedies in rapid succession, giving the reader a feeling described well by Job's later words, "he will not let me get my breath" (9:18).

1:20–22 *Job's Confession and Confidence.* Distraught with grief at the calamities that have crushed the household (introduced in vv. 2–4), Job turns to God in lament-laden worship.

1:20 In the wake of his loss, Job embodies both grief (**Job . . . tore his robe and shaved his head**) and trust in the Lord (**and fell on the ground and worshiped**).

1:21 In contrast to what Satan suggests will happen (vv. 9–11), Job cries out from a posture of grief and worship, "**blessed be the name of the LORD.**"

2:1–10 *The Second Test.* This section presents the setting, dialogue, and events relating to Job's second test, which parallel the description and extend the sphere of the first test (1:6–22).

2:1–6 *The Challenge in Heaven.* The second glimpse of the heavenly court (**Again**, v. 1) deliberately echoes the first (cf. 1:6–12). Taking ultimate responsibility for Job's calamities, the Lord again fixes Satan's attention on Job's **blameless** and God-honoring character (2:3). Satan responds by seeking permission to attack Job himself, urging that this will reveal the insincerity of Job's devotion to God (vv. 4–5; cf. 1:9).

2:3 The Lord points out to Satan that even after all that has happened to him, Job **still holds fast his integrity**, a description referring to the whole of his grief, worship, and profession in 1:20–21 as a faithful response.

reason." 4 Then Satan answered the LORD and said, "Skin for skin! All that a man has he
will give for his life. 5 But [p]stretch out your hand and touch his bone and his flesh, and he
will [q]curse you to your face." 6 And the LORD said to Satan, "Behold, he is in your hand;
only spare his life."
7 So Satan went out from the presence of the LORD and struck Job with loathsome [r]sores
from [s]the sole of his foot to the crown of his head. 8 And he took [t]a piece of broken pottery
with which to scrape himself while he sat in [u]the ashes.
9 Then his wife said to him, "Do you still [v]hold fast your integrity? [q]Curse God and die."
10 But he said to her, "You speak as one of the [w]foolish women would speak. [x]Shall we receive
good from God, and shall we not receive evil?"[1] [y]In all this Job did not [z]sin with his lips.

Job's Three Friends

11 Now when Job's three [a]friends heard of all this evil that had come upon him, they
came each from his own place, Eliphaz [b]the Temanite, Bildad [c]the Shuhite, and Zophar
the Naamathite. They made an appointment together to come to [d]show him sympathy
and comfort him. 12 And when they saw him from a distance, they did not recognize him.
And they raised their voices and wept, and they [e]tore their robes and sprinkled [f]dust on
their heads toward heaven. 13 And they sat with him on the ground [g]seven days and seven
nights, and no one spoke a word to him, for they saw that his suffering was very great.

Job Laments His Birth

3 After this Job [h]opened his mouth and cursed the day of his birth. 2 And Job said:

3 [i]"Let the day perish on which I was born,
and the night that said,
'A man is conceived.'

[1] Or *disaster*; also verse 11

5 [p]ch. 1:11 [q]ch. 1:5
7 [r]Ex. 9:9; Lev. 13:18; [Deut. 28:27] [s]Deut. 28:35; Isa. 1:6
8 [t]ch. 41:30 [u]ch. 42:6; Ezek. 27:30; Jonah 3:6; Matt. 11:21
9 [v]ver. 3 [q][See ver. 5 above]
10 [w][Ps. 74:18, 22] [x][James 5:10, 11] [y]ch. 1:22 [z][Ps. 39:1]
11 [a][Prov. 17:17] [b]See 1 Chr. 1:45 [c]Gen. 25:2; 1 Chr. 1:32 [d]ch. 42:11; [Rom. 12:15]
12 [e]See Gen. 37:29 [f]See Josh. 7:6; Neh. 9:1; Lam. 2:10; Ezek. 27:30
13 [g]Ezek. 3:15; [Gen. 50:10]

Chapter 3

1 [h]ch. 33:2; Ps. 78:2
3 [i][ch. 10:18, 19]; See Jer. 20:14-18

2:4–5 Skin for skin! It is possible that the metaphor refers to the further test Satan is about to request, namely, the permission to afflict Job's own body. However, the structure of vv. 4–5 suggests that it and the following phrase (**All that a man has he will give for his life**) are referring primarily to what has already happened. Satan is crassly suggesting that Job maintained his integrity because it cost him only the "skin" of his livestock and family, which he was happy to trade for his own. The next phrase begins with an explicit adversative in Hebrew (**But**), which contains Satan's final plea: afflict Job in **his bone and his flesh** and then he will surely **curse** God outright.

2:6 only spare his life. The sparing of Job's life is not a mercy, and not merely a concession necessary to the test, but is integral to the test. The most difficult of life's sorrows are sometimes found when even the mercy of death is denied (cf. 3:20–23; 6:9). This was the ultimate test of faith.

2:7–10 *Job's Affliction and Confession.* Already in a physical and emotional posture of grief (see 1:20), Job is struck with sores (2:7) and his wife's question (v. 9), to which he responds further in grief (v. 8) and trust in God (v. 10).

2:9 Although the reference to Job's wife is very brief, the content of her speech is significant for how it relates to the heavenly dialogue and for what this connection reveals about the nature of her comments. Her rhetorical question doubts the sensibility of the very thing God finds commendable about Job (**Do you still hold fast your integrity?** see v. 3), and her suggested response advises Job to take the action Satan was looking to provoke (**Curse God and die**; see 1:11; 2:4).

2:10 Job responds to his wife with a measured rebuke: he does not presume to know her heart fully, but warns her against speaking like **one of the foolish women**.

2:11–13 *Job's Comforters.* After hearing about his troubles, Job's three friends come together to show him sympathy and to mourn with him.

2:11 The **three friends** of Job all have southern origins known in the OT. **Eliphaz** is from Teman, an important city in Edom (Gen. 36:11, 15; Ezek. 25:13; Amos 1:11–12), which was apparently known for its wisdom (Jer. 49:7). **Bildad** is from Shuah, a name of one of the sons of Abraham from his marriage to Keturah, whose brother was Midian and whose nephews were Sheba and Dedan (Gen. 25:2; 1 Chron. 1:32), the latter being the name of a place in Edom or Arabia. **Zophar** is from Naamah, which is the name of a woman listed in the genealogy of Cain (Gen. 4:22), from whom the Kenites were descendants (Gen. 4:22). The Kenites are also mentioned in connection with the Midianites in the Sinai and Arabian deserts (Num. 10:29; Judg. 4:11). **comfort**. On this key word in Job, see Introduction: Literary Features.

2:12 It is likely that Job's friends **did not recognize him** because, in addition to his sores, Job bore the external effects of both the emotional weight and physical manifestations of his grief (see 1:20; 2:7–8).

2:13 The silence over a period of **seven days and seven nights** signifies a complete time of mourning in response to the suffering of Job. Ezekiel exhibited a similar response upon meeting the exiles in Babylon (see Ezek. 3:15).

3:1–42:6 *Dialogue: Job, His Suffering, and His Standing before God.* Between the brief narrative sections of the prologue (1:1–2:13) and epilogue (42:7–17), the large central section of the book consists of dialogue in poetic form (except for the narrative introduction of Elihu in 32:1–5) that focuses on the question of what Job's suffering reveals both about him and about God's governing of the world. This section progresses in five main parts: Job's opening lament (3:1–26), a lengthy section of interchanges between the three friends and Job (4:1–25:6), Job's closing monologue (26:1–31:40), Elihu's response (32:1–37:24), and the Lord's appearance to and interaction with Job (38:1–42:6).

3:1–26 *Job: Despair for the Day of His Birth.* After the prose introduction (vv. 1–2), Job curses the day of his birth (vv. 3–10), expanding on this theme with two sequences of "why?" questions: the first expresses longing for rest (vv. 11–19); the second laments his anxious suffering (vv. 20–26). Job's opening lament plays off the vocabulary of light and darkness in relation to both questions of the section: "Why did I not die at birth?" (v. 11) and "Why is light given to a man whose way is hidden, whom God has hedged in?" (v. 23). Job is mystified by his current circumstances, and here he wonders whether he would have been better off in the darkness of never being born at all rather than having the light of life result in such suffering and grief. The vocabulary of Job's lament is the beginning of a theme throughout the dialogue with his friends in which darkness and light will be used to refer to both death and life as well as to what is hidden and what is revealed.

5[j]ch. 10:21, 22; 12:22; 24:17; 28:3; 34:22; 38:17; Ps. 23:4; Isa. 9:2; Matt. 4:16
8[k]ch. 41:1
9[l]ch. 41:18
11[m]ch. 10:18, 19
12[n]Gen. 30:3; 50:23; Isa. 66:12
14[o][Isa. 58:12]
16[p]Ps. 58:8; Eccles. 6:3; [1 Cor. 15:8]
17[q]ch. 17:16
18[r]Ex. 3:7
20[s]Prov. 31:6
21[t]Rev. 9:6 [u]Prov. 2:4

4 Let that day be darkness!
May God above not seek it,
nor light shine upon it.
5 Let gloom and [j]deep darkness claim it.
Let clouds dwell upon it;
let the blackness of the day terrify it.
6 That night—let thick darkness seize it!
Let it not rejoice among the days of the year;
let it not come into the number of the months.
7 Behold, let that night be barren;
let no joyful cry enter it.
8 Let those curse it who curse the day,
who are ready to rouse up [k]Leviathan.
9 Let the stars of its dawn be dark;
let it hope for light, but have none,
nor see [l]the eyelids of the morning,
10 because it did not shut the doors of my mother's womb,
nor hide trouble from my eyes.

11 "Why [m]did I not die at birth,
come out from the womb and expire?
12 Why did [n]the knees receive me?
Or why the breasts, that I should nurse?
13 For then I would have lain down and been quiet;
I would have slept; then I would have been at rest,
14 with kings and counselors of the earth
who [o]rebuilt ruins for themselves,
15 or with princes who had gold,
who filled their houses with silver.
16 Or why was I not as a hidden [p]stillborn child,
as infants who never see the light?
17 There the wicked cease from troubling,
and there the weary are at [q]rest.
18 There the prisoners are at ease together;
they hear not the voice of [r]the taskmaster.
19 The small and the great are there,
and the slave is free from his master.

20 "Why is light given to him who is in misery,
and life to [s]the bitter in soul,
21 who [t]long for death, but it comes not,
and dig for it more than for [u]hidden treasures,

3:1–2 *Introduction.* Job **cursed the day of his birth** because it represented the path of his entire life, which had led to his present distress.

3:3–10 *Job Curses His Birth.* In skillfully crafted poetry, Job rues the *moment* of his birth—in distinction from the birth itself: he will continue to see life as a divine gift (see note on 10:8–13), and he does not ever appear to be suicidal. Rather, he wishes that reality had been different, and that he would not have seen the light of day.

3:8 Aspects of ancient myth are sometimes referenced metaphorically in Scripture, often in images of God's power or authority (cf. 26:12). By referring here to those who set a **curse** upon a **day** by calling upon **Leviathan** (see note on Ps. 74:14), Job calls for their incantations as one more piece of his lament against the day of his birth.

3:11–19 *Job Longs for Rest.* Job's futile curses progress from the day of his birth to the first moments of life. Just as he wishes the day was darkness and time erased, so too he wishes that life had been death (vv. 11–12, 16), for at least that would have brought peace in the company of the dead (vv. 13–15, 17–19).

3:13–19 Job describes death as rest from the toil of life by picturing its effect on persons both high and low in society, and wishes he had joined all who were already in this state of rest rather than being born. In vv. 13–15 Job refers to the **kings** and **princes** who labored to obtain wealth and build cities but now lay without them in death. In vv. 16–19 Job focuses on the way death removes the constraints of social position, focusing attention particularly on **the small** and **the slave**, and those who have been **weary** or **prisoners**.

3:20–26 *Job Laments His Suffering.* The final sequence of "why" questions reflects Job's current miserable state, carrying forward the themes of **light** (vv. 20, 23) and **death** (vv. 21–22). Musing on those who **dig** for **treasures** (v. 21b), Job anticipates the terms in which some of his puzzles will be solved in the poem on "wisdom" (see ch. 28).

22 who rejoice exceedingly
and are glad when they find the grave?
23 Why is light given to a man whose [v]way is hidden,
whom God has [w]hedged in?
24 For my sighing comes [x]instead of[1] my bread,
and my [y]groanings are poured out like water.
25 [z]For the thing that I fear comes upon me,
and what I dread befalls me.
26 I am not at ease, nor am I quiet;
I have no rest, but trouble comes."

Eliphaz Speaks: The Innocent Prosper

4 Then Eliphaz the Temanite answered and said:

2 " If one ventures a word with you, will you be impatient?
Yet who can keep from speaking?
3 Behold, you have instructed many,
and you have [a]strengthened the weak hands.
4 Your words have upheld him who was stumbling,
and you have [a]made firm the feeble knees.
5 But now it has come to you, and you are impatient;
it touches you, and you are dismayed.
6 [b]Is not your fear of God[2] your [c]confidence,
and the integrity of your ways your hope?

7 "Remember: [d]who that was innocent ever perished?
Or where were the upright cut off?
8 As I have seen, those who [e]plow iniquity
and sow trouble reap the same.
9 By [f]the breath of God they perish,
and by [g]the blast of his anger they are consumed.
10 The roar of the lion, the voice of the fierce lion,
[h]the teeth of the young lions are broken.
11 The strong lion perishes for lack of prey,
and the cubs of the lioness are scattered.

[1] Or *like;* Hebrew *before* [2] Hebrew lacks *of God*

23[v]Isa. 40:27 [w][ch. 1:10]; See ch. 19:8
24[x][Ps. 42:3; 80:5; 102:9] [y]Ps. 22:1; 38:8
25[z][Prov. 10:24]

Chapter 4

3[a]Isa. 35:3; [Heb. 12:12]
4[a][See ver. 3 above]
6[b]ch. 1:1 [c]ch. 31:24; Prov. 3:26
7[d][Ps. 37:25]
8[e]Hos. 10:13; [Ps. 7:14; Prov. 22:8; Gal. 6:7, 8]
9[f]Isa. 30:33 [g]ch. 15:30; Ex. 15:8; Ps. 18:15; [Isa. 11:4; 2 Thess. 2:8]
10[h]Ps. 58:6; [ch. 29:17; Ps. 3:7]

3:23 In his accusation, Satan argued that Job was upright only because God had put a "hedge" of blessing around him (1:10). Here in the opening lament of the dialogues, Job refers to his sustained life amid inscrutable circumstances of suffering as rendering him one **whom God has hedged in**. Satan's contention is disproved through Job's continued faithfulness. Job's overall lament of his situation is something which God both reproves (see chs. 38–41) and commends (42:7).

4:1–25:6 *The Friends and Job: Can Job Be Right before God?* The main section of the book contains the dialogue between Job and the three friends that opens with Job's initial lament (3:1–16) and then alternates between speeches by each friend (Eliphaz, Bildad, Zophar) and responses by Job. The dialogue consists of two full cycles containing a speech by each friend and response by Job (4:1–14:22; 15:1–21:34). Job appears to cut off Bildad in the midst of his third speech (22:1–25:6), which is followed by a lengthy section of Job's final argument (26:1–31:40). In his opening response, Eliphaz initiates what will become a recurring question and theme for the speeches of the friends: "Can mortal man be in the right before God?" (4:17; see also 9:2; 15:14; 25:4). The friends assume that both Job's circumstances and his response to them are indications that he is in the wrong before God and needs to acknowledge and repent of his sin. However, Job will insist not only that he is not guilty of some hidden iniquity but that it is God who ultimately has allowed and governed his circumstances.

4:1–14:22 *First Cycle.* Although Eliphaz begins this round of dialogues with a fairly gentle tone (4:3–4), sympathy for Job rapidly fades. The character of Job is consistently probed under the assumption that his moral failures account for his present plight (by Eliphaz in chs. 4–5, Bildad in ch. 8, and Zophar in ch. 11). Job responds in kind: bewildered by his suffering, he angrily argues (chs. 6–7), legally disputes (chs. 9–10), and resolutely rejects (chs. 12–14) the counsel of his friends.

4:1–5:27 *Eliphaz: Can Mortal Man Be in the Right before God?* Eliphaz opens his first response with a brief affirmation of Job's character (4:2–4) before asserting what he knows to be true about how God works (4:7–5:16) and articulating the core of the friends' argument: in light of Job's circumstance, he cannot be in the right before God (see 4:17). In light of his confidence that his description and inferences are correct, Eliphaz suggests that Job accept his circumstance as God's reproof in order that he might be delivered (5:17–27). When the dialogue with the three friends is finished, Elihu will suggest something quite similar to Eliphaz, even if he takes a slightly different approach (see 32:1–37:24; and 36:7–21 in particular).

4:8 those who plow iniquity and sow trouble reap the same. At the opening of his speech, Eliphaz states the dictum that the friends will relentlessly defend throughout the dialogue. For them this proverb is unequivocal—it is true in all circumstances in the same way. Character can be judged by circumstances.

4:10–11 Typical of wisdom exponents, Eliphaz turns to nature to demonstrate

12 [j]ch. 26:14
13 [j]ch. 20:2 [k]ch. 33:15; Gen. 2:21; 15:12; 1 Sam. 26:12; Isa. 29:10
16 [l]Num. 12:8 [m][1 Kgs. 19:12]
17 [n]ch. 9:2; 10:4; 25:4; 32:2
18 [o]ch. 15:15
19 [p]ch. 10:9; 13:12; 33:6; Isa. 64:8; 2 Cor. 4:7; 5:1 [q]Gen. 2:7; 3:19; 18:27 [r][ch. 13:28]
20 [s][Ps. 90:5, 6; Isa. 38:12] [t][Isa. 42:25; 57:1]
21 [u]ch. 36:12; Prov. 5:23; 10:21; [Hos. 4:6]

Chapter 5

1 [v]ch. 15:15; Ps. 89:5, 7; Zech. 14:5
3 [w]Jer. 12:2, 3; [Ps. 37:35, 36; 73:18–20]
4 [x][Ps. 119:155] [y]ch. 29:7; Ps. 127:5; Prov. 22:22; [Josh. 20:4; Amos 5:12]; See Ruth 4:1

12 "Now a word was brought to me stealthily;
my ear received [j]the whisper of it.
13 Amid [j]thoughts from [k]visions of the night,
when [k]deep sleep falls on men,
14 dread came upon me, and trembling,
which made all my bones shake.
15 A spirit glided past my face;
the hair of my flesh stood up.
16 It stood still,
but I could not discern its appearance.
[l]A form was before my eyes;
there was silence, then I heard [m]a voice:
17 [n]'Can mortal man be in the right before[1] God?
Can a man be pure before his Maker?
18 Even in his servants [o]he puts no trust,
and his angels he charges with error;
19 how much more those who dwell in houses of [p]clay,
whose foundation is in [q]the dust,
who are crushed like [r]the moth.
20 Between [s]morning and evening they are beaten to pieces;
they perish forever [t]without anyone regarding it.
21 Is not their tent-cord plucked up within them,
[u]do they not die, and that without wisdom?'

5

1 "Call now; is there anyone who will answer you?
To which of [v]the holy ones will you turn?
2 Surely vexation kills the fool,
and jealousy slays the simple.
3 [w]I have seen the fool taking root,
but suddenly I cursed his dwelling.
4 His children are [x]far from safety;
they are crushed in [y]the gate,
and there is no one to deliver them.

[1] Or *more than*; twice in this verse

his truth. Even an animal as mighty as the lion is incapable of altering the operation of natural law to protect its own young. A man like Job cannot alter the function of moral law any more than the lion can alter natural law.

4:12–21 In his first speech, Eliphaz describes the event (vv. 12–16) and content (vv. 17–21) of a vision. The implied heavenly source of the vision is meant to grant authority to the message, which centers on the opening question: "Can mortal man be in the right before God?" While the vision has been typically read as belonging to Eliphaz, some interpreters have argued that it should be understood as a vision originally reported by Job, which is then quoted by Eliphaz. The primary impetus for interpreting the vision as a quotation is the argument that the recurring question of v. 17 (see 9:2; 15:14; 25:4) is in tension with the theology of Eliphaz and the friends (i.e., they are arguing precisely that a righteous person can be in the right before God). While interpreting the vision as a quotation offers a solution if there is in fact a conflict, it lacks the support of the typical features found in Job that would mark a quotation in the text (e.g., there is no attribution of the speech to Job, nor has Job said anything like this up to this point) and creates other interpretative difficulties. Nevertheless, this view is set out here to present both interpretative options for readers of Job.

4:17–18 The opening questions of v. 17 present an interpretative difficulty: what do they mean and what is their function in the dialogue? Are they Eliphaz's way of reminding Job that all creation has been affected by sin? Are they Job's questions (see note on vv. 12–21) asking whether it is possible to live in such a manner as to receive only good things from God? Neither of these possibilities appears fully satisfying: the first because Eliphaz would then be arguing that what has happened to Job is a consequence that should be expected by all people, including himself; the second because it is not the purpose of Job's lament to ask whether it would have been possible so to live as to avoid his circumstances. A literary key for answering the question is found in the function of the prologue. The content of the heavenly dialogues (1:8; 2:3) and the comments of the narrator (1:1–5, 22; 2:10) place *the evaluation of Job's character* at the forefront for interpreting the book as a whole. In the dialogue of chs. 3–31, the friends are seeking to judge the nature of the very thing to which the reader has been made privy: God's evaluation of Job. The tension of the dialogue begins with Eliphaz's vision, which functions as a response to Job's initial lament (3:1–26): How can you presume that you are in the right? Eliphaz argues that if even angels are found at fault before God, then the fact of compounded and devastating suffering should lead Job, a mortal man, to seek God for help rather than presuming the right to protest against him (see 5:8).

4:19–21 Eliphaz follows the opening question to Job with an extended description to illustrate his greater-to-lesser argument. If angels are held guilty (see v. 18), then how much more so are mortals **who dwell in houses of clay** (v. 19), who **perish forever without anyone regarding it** (v. 20), and who **die . . . without wisdom** (v. 21)?

5:1 After Eliphaz presents what he regards as the weight of his vision (see 4:17–21), he asks rhetorically if there are any creatures left on earth (**anyone**) or in heaven (**the holy ones**) to whom Job can presume to appeal.

5 The hungry eat his harvest,
and he takes it even out of thorns,[1]
and the thirsty pant[2] after his[3] wealth.
6 For affliction does not come from the dust,
nor does trouble sprout from the ground,
7 but man is [z]born to trouble
as the sparks fly upward.

8 "As for me, I would seek God,
and to God would I commit my cause,
9 who [a]does great things and [b]unsearchable,
[c]marvelous things without number:
10 he gives [d]rain on the earth
and sends waters on the fields;
11 he [e]sets on high those who are lowly,
and those who mourn are lifted to safety.
12 He [f]frustrates the devices of the crafty,
so that their hands achieve no success.
13 He [g]catches the wise in their own craftiness,
and the schemes of the wily are brought to a quick end.
14 They meet with darkness in the daytime
and [h]grope at noonday as in the night.
15 But he [i]saves the needy from the sword of their mouth
and from the hand of the mighty.
16 So the poor have hope,
and [j]injustice shuts her mouth.

17 "Behold, [k]blessed is the one whom God reproves;
therefore [l]despise not the discipline of the [m]Almighty.
18 For he wounds, but he [n]binds up;
he [o]shatters, but his hands heal.
19 He will [p]deliver you from six troubles;
in seven no [q]evil[4] shall touch you.
20 [r]In famine he will redeem you from death,
and in war from the power of the sword.
21 You shall be [s]hidden from the lash of the tongue,
and shall not fear destruction when it comes.
22 At destruction and famine you shall laugh,
and shall not fear [t]the beasts of the earth.
23 For you shall be in league with the stones of the field,
and the beasts of the field shall be at peace with you.
24 You shall know that your [u]tent is at peace,
and you shall inspect your fold and miss nothing.
25 You shall know also that your [v]offspring shall be many,
and your descendants as [w]the grass of the earth.
26 You shall come to your grave in [x]ripe old age,
like a sheaf gathered up in its season.
27 Behold, this we have [y]searched out; it is true.
Hear, and know it for your good."[5]

7[z]ch. 14:1; Gen. 3:17-19; Eccles. 2:23
9[a]ch. 9:10; [ch. 37:5; Ps. 40:5; 72:18; Rom. 11:33; Rev. 15:3] [b]ch. 9:10; 11:7; 34:24 [c][ch. 10:16]
10[d]Ps. 65:9, 10; 147:8; Jer. 5:24; 14:22; Acts 14:17; [Ps. 104:10, 13; Matt. 5:45]
11[e]1 Sam. 2:7; [Ps. 113:7]
12[f][Neh. 4:15; Ps. 33:10; Isa. 8:10]
13[g]Cited 1 Cor. 3:19; [Ps. 9:15, 16]
14[h]ch. 12:25; Deut. 28:29; [Isa. 59:10]
15[i]Ps. 35:10
16[j]Ps. 107:42; [Ps. 63:11]
17[k]Ps. 94:12; [James 1:12] [l]Prov. 3:11; Heb. 12:5; Rev. 3:19 [m]Gen. 17:1
18[n]Isa. 30:26; 61:1; Hos. 6:1 [o][Deut. 32:39]
19[p]Ps. 34:19; 91:3; 1 Cor. 10:13 [q]Ps. 91:10
20[r]Ps. 33:19; 37:19
21[s][Ps. 31:20]
22[t][Isa. 11:8, 9; 35:9; 65:25; Ezek. 34:25; Hos. 2:18]
24[u][ch. 21:9]
25[v]ch. 21:8; Ps. 112:2 [w]Ps. 72:16
26[x][Gen. 15:15; 25:8; 35:29; Prov. 9:11; 10:27]
27[y][Ps. 111:2]

[1] The meaning of the Hebrew is uncertain [2] Aquila, Symmachus, Syriac, Vulgate; Hebrew could be read as *and the snare pants* [3] Hebrew *their* [4] Or *disaster*
[5] Hebrew *for yourself*

5:6–7 Eliphaz reinforces his previous point (see 4:8) by returning to the language of agriculture: **affliction** and **trouble** do not grow out of the **dust** or **ground**, but out of what is sown from the day a person is **born**.

5:16 The wicked sit in stunned silence at the reversal of their fortune. As is the case in several places in the dialogues, the second line of the verse (**injustice shuts her mouth**) is similar to a line from the Psalms (see Ps. 107:42, "the wickedness shuts its mouth"). Eliphaz implies in this section (Job 5:8–16) that Job should reconsider the reversal of his circumstances as representing God's just purposes (see v. 17).

5:21 The reference to the **lash of the tongue** is included in a list of troubles

Chapter 6
3[z][Prov. 27:3]
4[a]Ps. 38:2
9[b]1 Kgs. 19:4; [Num. 11:15]
10[c][Isa. 30:14] [d]Lev. 19:2; Isa. 57:15; Hos. 11:9
14[e][Prov. 11:24] [f][Prov. 17:17]
15[g][Ps. 38:11; 41:9] [h][1 Sam. 14:33] [i][Jer. 15:18]
18[j][Gen. 1:2; Jer. 4:23]

Job Replies: My Complaint Is Just

6 Then Job answered and said:

2 "Oh that my vexation were weighed,
and all my calamity laid in the balances!
3 For then it would be heavier than [z]the sand of the sea;
therefore my words have been rash.
4 For [a]the arrows of the Almighty are in me;
my spirit drinks their poison;
the terrors of God are arrayed against me.
5 Does the wild donkey bray when he has grass,
or the ox low over his fodder?
6 Can that which is tasteless be eaten without salt,
or is there any taste in the juice of the mallow?[1]
7 My appetite refuses to touch them;
they are as food that is loathsome to me.[2]

8 "Oh that I might have my request,
and that God would fulfill my hope,
9 that it would [b]please God to crush me,
that he would let loose his hand and cut me off!
10 This would be my comfort;
I would even exult[3] in pain [c]unsparing,
for I have not denied the words of [d]the Holy One.
11 What is my strength, that I should wait?
And what is my end, that I should be patient?
12 Is my strength the strength of stones, or is my flesh bronze?
13 Have I any help in me,
when resource is driven from me?

14 "He who [e]withholds[4] kindness from a [f]friend
forsakes the fear of the Almighty.
15 My [g]brothers are [h]treacherous as a torrent-bed,
as torrential [i]streams that pass away,
16 which are dark with ice,
and where the snow hides itself.
17 When they melt, they disappear;
when it is hot, they vanish from their place.
18 The caravans turn aside from their course;
they go up into [j]the waste and perish.

[1] The meaning of the Hebrew word is uncertain [2] The meaning of the Hebrew is uncertain [3] The meaning of the Hebrew word is uncertain [4] Syriac, Vulgate (compare Targum); the meaning of the Hebrew word is uncertain

that threaten a person's life (vv. 19–26) along with famine, war, danger of wild beasts, and anything that might endanger the peace of flocks, family, or person (e.g., disease, disaster, etc.). Eliphaz uses the numerical saying ("from six . . . in seven") to draw particular attention to the final element: if Job will accept his situation as God's discipline, he will be spared from his trouble and brought to "a ripe old age" (v. 26).

6:1–7:21 *Job: Life Is Futile.* In his first response, Job longs that his life would be cut off (6:9) so that he could rest from his suffering, knowing that he had not denied God (6:10). Job found his life unbearable on account of the empty comfort offered by his friends (6:14–30) and what he describes as the continued watchfulness of God (7:11–21). The speech as a whole shows a remarkable progression. Job moves from first-person soliloquy in 6:2–13 (continuing his introspective mode from ch. 3), shifting to second-person (plural) address to speak directly to the friends (for the first time) so as to question the nature of their "comfort" (6:14–30). Then Job relapses into first-person reflection on the futility of his life (7:1–6), before a transitional movement (7:7–10) now in second person singular (to Eliphaz himself). Finally, the pivotal 7:11 introduces Job's first direct address to God (7:12–21).

6:8–9 Although Job lamented his birth (in ch. 3), only now does he express a hope for death (at God's hand, not his own) to alleviate his suffering.

6:10 When Job says, **"I have not denied the words of the Holy One,"** he is referring, at least in part, to the fact that he has not concealed something that is out of accord with what God desires of his servants—something that Eliphaz had implied in his first response (see 5:17).

6:14 After Eliphaz suggests that Job should consider his suffering as an indication that he has been a fool (see 5:3ff.), Job argues that one **who withholds kindness from a friend** is himself acting out of accord with wisdom (i.e., **forsakes the fear of the Almighty**).

6:15 A **torrent-bed** is a wadi, a depression or rift in the rocks that gathers water from cloudbursts or melting ice, which races down the slope. Desert

19 The caravans of [k]Tema look,
the travelers of [l]Sheba hope.
20 They are [m]ashamed because they were confident;
they come there and are [m]disappointed.
21 For you have now become nothing;
you see my calamity and are afraid.
22 Have I said, 'Make me a gift'?
Or, 'From your wealth offer a bribe for me'?
23 Or, 'Deliver me from the adversary's hand'?
Or, 'Redeem me from the hand of [n]the ruthless'?

24 "Teach me, and I will be silent;
make me understand how I have gone astray.
25 How forceful are upright words!
But what does reproof from you reprove?
26 Do you think that you can reprove words,
when the speech of a despairing man is [o]wind?
27 You would even [p]cast lots over the fatherless,
and bargain over your friend.

28 "But now, be pleased to look at me,
for I will not lie to your face.
29 [q]Please turn; let no injustice be done.
Turn now; my vindication is at stake.
30 Is there any injustice on my tongue?
Cannot my palate discern the cause of calamity?

Job Continues: My Life Has No Hope

7 1 "Has not man [r]a hard service on earth,
and are not his [s]days like the days of a hired hand?
2 Like a slave who longs for [t]the shadow,
and like [u]a hired hand who looks for his [v]wages,
3 so I am allotted months of [w]emptiness,
[x]and nights of misery are apportioned to me.
4 [y]When I lie down I say, 'When shall I arise?'
But the night is long,
and I am full of tossing till the dawn.
5 My flesh is clothed with [z]worms and [a]dirt;
my skin hardens, then [b]breaks out afresh.
6 My days are [c]swifter than [d]a weaver's shuttle
and come to their end without hope.

7 "Remember that my life is a [e]breath;
my eye will never again see good.
8 [f]The eye of him who sees me will behold me no more;
while your eyes are on me, [g]I shall be gone.
9 As [h]the cloud fades and vanishes,
so he who [i]goes down to Sheol does not come up;
10 he [j]returns no more to his house,
nor does his [k]place know him anymore.

19 [k]Gen. 25:15; 1 Chr. 1:30; Isa. 21:14; Jer. 25:23 [l]See 1 Kgs. 10:1
20 [m]Isa. 1:29; Jer. 14:3
23 [n]ch. 15:20; 27:13
26 [o]ch. 7:7; Isa. 41:29
27 [p]Joel 3:3; Nah. 3:10
29 [q]ch. 17:10

Chapter 7

1 [r]ch. 14:14; Isa. 40:2 [s]ch. 14:5; Ps. 39:4
2 [t]Song 2:17; 4:6; Jer. 6:4 [u]ch. 14:6 [v]Lev. 19:13
3 [w]ver. 16 [x][ch. 30:17]
4 [y]Deut. 28:67
5 [z]Isa. 14:11 [a][ch. 2:8] [b][ch. 2:7]
6 [c]ch. 9:25 [d][Isa. 38:12]
7 [e]ch. 6:26; Ps. 78:39
8 [f]ch. 20:9; [ch. 8:18; Ps. 37:36] [g][ver. 2]
9 [h]ch. 30:15 [i]See ch. 21:13
10 [j]ch. 10:21; 2 Sam. 12:23 [k]ch. 20:9; Ps. 103:16; [ch. 8:18]

travelers could not carry sufficient water; they depended on rains or melting snow, which quickly dried up in the hot sun.

6:19 Both **Tema** and **Sheba** continue the southeastern setting of the book (cf. 2:11).

6:25–26 If **upright words** are used properly, they can function to **reprove** a person, discouraging him from taking a foolish path (v. 25). However, Job argues that as a **despairing man** he is pouring out his complaint before God and that his friends assume wrongly that his **words** (v. 26) reveal something in need of their rebuke. As the dialogue progresses, Job will increasingly argue that the aim of his friends' rebuke misses him entirely. Bildad will echo Job's reference to his own speech as **wind** in the opening lines of the response that follows (see 8:2).

6:28–30 For the first time, Job directly asserts before God his innocence, which requires his **vindication**. Although this claim is directed to the friends, Job will soon repeat it to God—by implication in 7:20, and then throughout

11 [l]Ps. 40:9 [m]ch. 21:4; Ps. 77:3 [n]ch. 10:1; 21:25; 1 Sam. 1:10; Isa. 38:15; [ch. 3:20]
12 [o]Gen. 1:21
13 [p][ch. 9:27]
15 [q][ch. 19:20; 30:17]
16 [r][ch. 9:21; 10:1] [s]ch. 10:20; 14:6; Ex. 14:12; [Ps. 39:13] [t]ver. 3
17 [u]Ps. 8:4; 144:3; Heb. 2:6
18 [v]Ps. 17:3 [w]Ps. 11:4, 5
19 [x]ch. 14:6
20 [y]ch. 16:12; Lam. 3:12
21 [z]Dan. 12:2 [a][ch. 8:5; 24:5; Prov. 1:28] [b][ver. 8]

Chapter 8

1 [c]ch. 2:11
2 [d]1 Kgs. 19:11; [ch. 15:2]
3 [e]ch. 34:12; [Gen. 18:25; Deut. 32:4; 2 Chr. 19:7; Ezra 9:15; Dan. 9:14; Rom. 3:5]
4 [f]ch. 1:5, 18, 19

11 "Therefore I will not [l]restrain my mouth;
I will speak in the anguish of my spirit;
I will [m]complain in [n]the bitterness of my soul.
12 Am I the sea, or [o]a sea monster,
that you set a guard over me?
13 [p]When I say, 'My bed will comfort me,
my couch will ease my complaint,'
14 then you scare me with dreams
and terrify me with visions,
15 so that I would choose strangling
and death rather than my [q]bones.
16 I [r]loathe my life; I would not live forever.
[s]Leave me alone, for my days are [t]a breath.
17 [u]What is man, that you make so much of him,
and that you set your heart on him,
18 [v]visit him every morning
and [w]test him every moment?
19 How long will you not [x]look away from me,
nor leave me alone till I swallow my spit?
20 If I sin, what do I do to you, you watcher of mankind?
Why have you made me [y]your mark?
Why have I become a burden to you?
21 Why do you not pardon my transgression
and take away my iniquity?
For now I shall lie in [z]the earth;
you will [a]seek me, [b]but I shall not be."

Bildad Speaks: Job Should Repent

8 Then [c]Bildad the Shuhite answered and said:

2 "How long will you say these things,
and the words of your mouth be a [d]great wind?
3 [e]Does God pervert justice?
Or does the Almighty pervert the right?
4 If your [f]children have sinned against him,
he has delivered them into the hand of their transgression.

his speeches with ever-increasing insistence (cf. 10:5–7; 13:16–18; 27:1–6; 29:1–25; 31:1–40).

7:11 In the initial response to each friend, Job primarily addresses his friends first (6:1–7:10) before turning to offer further lament and complaint to God (vv. 12–21). The three parallel statements of this verse (**I will . . .**) mark the transition from Job's response to Eliphaz to his response to God. That transition is also represented by the change in reference to God from the third person (e.g., "he" in 6:9) to the second (e.g., "you" in 7:12). Similar statements mark the major transition in Job's initial responses to Bildad (10:1–2) and Zophar (13:13–17).

7:12 Job asks whether God considers him to be something as large or powerful as the **sea** or a **sea monster** because he feels his suffering is disproportionate to the weight of his being. In the literature of the ancient Near East, the sea is often described or personified as a threat to the created order that needs to be contained or conquered (see 26:12; 38:8–11). "Sea" (*Yam*) and "sea monster" (*Tannin*) are both known figures from Canaanite religion: *Yam* as the power contesting supremacy with Baal, and *Tannin* as one of the chaos monsters (cf. Ps. 74:13; Isa. 51:9).

7:16 I loathe my life. Job will declare his rejection of his life again with the same verb in 9:21. When Job is fully confronted with the mystery of God, he will reject his words using the same verb ("I despise myself," 42:6). The verb is repeated across these verses to contrast Job's changed attitude as he comes to recognize that he had given up on understanding what his own life and circumstances meant in a manner that assumed more than he could possibly see or know.

7:17–18 The opening line of v. 17 (**What is man, that you make so much of him**) echoes the thought of Ps. 8:4 ("what is man that you are mindful of him"). However, where Psalm 8 marvels at how humanity has been crowned with glory by God, Job laments what he describes as the burdensome weight of God's watchful presence crushing him as a mortal being (Job 7:20).

8:1–22 *Bildad: The Wisdom of the Sages.* Bildad immediately begins with a stern rebuke: Job's words are a tempestuous wind (see 6:26), and whatever has come upon his children or upon Job himself has to be right, because God does not pervert justice (8:1–7). If Job will simply listen to the wisdom to which Bildad is pointing him, he will remember that the wicked do not endure (vv. 8–19), and that God will surely restore Job if he is truly blameless (vv. 20–22).

8:4–6 After the rhetorical questions of v. 3, Bildad presents two conditional statements to Job that are meant to represent the necessary consequences of God's justice. The first (v. 4), though set as a conditional, assumes that Job's children have suffered because of their sin. The second is then meant to call Job to remember that if he will repent (v. 5) and if he is blameless (v. 6), then God will spare him from the end that his children have suffered.

5 If you will seek God
and [g]plead with the Almighty for mercy,
6 if you are pure and upright,
surely then he will [h]rouse himself for you
and [i]restore your rightful habitation.
7 And though your beginning was small,
[j]your latter days will be very great.

8 "For [k]inquire, please, of bygone ages,
and consider what [l]the fathers have searched out.
9 For we are but of yesterday and know nothing,
for our days on earth are [m]a shadow.
10 Will they not teach you and tell you
and utter words out of their understanding?

11 "Can papyrus grow where there is no marsh?
Can reeds flourish where there is no water?
12 While yet in flower and not cut down,
they [n]wither before any other plant.
13 Such are the paths of all who [o]forget God;
[p]the hope of [q]the godless shall perish.
14 His confidence is severed,
and his trust is [r]a spider's web.[1]
15 He leans against his [s]house, but it does not stand;
he lays hold of it, but it does not endure.
16 He is a lush plant before the sun,
and his [t]shoots spread over his garden.
17 His roots entwine the stone heap;
he looks upon a house of stones.
18 If he is destroyed from his [u]place,
then it will deny him, saying, 'I have never [v]seen you.'
19 Behold, this is the joy of his way,
and out of [w]the soil others will spring.

20 "Behold, God will not reject a blameless man,
nor take the hand of evildoers.
21 He will yet [x]fill your mouth with laughter,
and your lips with shouting.
22 Those who hate you will be [y]clothed with shame,
and the tent of the wicked will be no more."

Job Replies: There Is No Arbiter

9 Then Job answered and said:

2 "Truly I know that it is so:
But how can a man be [z]in the right before God?

[1] Hebrew *house*

5[g]ch. 9:15
6[h]See Ps. 7:6 [i][Prov. 3:33]
7[j][ch. 42:12; James 5:11]
8[k]Deut. 4:32; 32:7; [ch. 15:18] [l]ch. 15:18
9[m]ch. 14:2; 17:7; 1 Chr. 29:15; Ps. 102:11; 109:23; 144:4; Eccles. 6:12
12[n][Ps. 37:2; 129:6]
13[o]See Ps. 9:17 [p]Prov. 10:28; 11:7 [q]ch. 13:16; 15:34; 27:8
14[r][Isa. 59:5, 6]
15[s]ch. 27:18
16[t]Ps. 80:11
18[u]See ch. 7:10 [v]ch. 7:8
19[w][1 Sam. 2:7, 8; Ps. 103:16; 113:7]
21[x]Ps. 126:2
22[y]Ps. 35:26; 132:18; [Ps. 109:29]

Chapter 9

2[z]ch. 4:17

8:8–10 If Eliphaz based his counsel on the night vision (see note on 4:12–21), here Bildad appeals instead to the tradition of the **fathers**.

8:11–19 Typical of wisdom literature, Bildad uses an analogy from nature to illustrate his point regarding the vulnerability of the wicked. **Papyrus** and **reeds** grow quickly in the wetlands to a height of 15 feet (4.6 m) or more, but are also the most vulnerable of plants, dependent on a constant supply of water. Other plants are deeply rooted in rocky soil, but they can be uprooted, leaving no trace of their presence. The way of the wicked is precarious and futile.

8:20–22 In his conclusion, Bildad asserts two things: if Job were a **blameless man** God would not have rejected him (v. 20); and the **tent of the wicked** will not stand for long (v. 22). Job will question the truth of each assertion: If a man were blameless, how could he show himself to be right before the God of justice (see 9:2)? And if **shame** and disaster are the fate of the wicked, how is it that the wicked so often appear to prosper in relative safety (see 12:6; 21:7)?

9:1–10:22 *Job: How Can a Mortal Be Just before God?* Job accepts the truth of both God's justice and his promises to the upright (9:2), but in light of his friends' suggested accusations, he feels caught. Job wonders how he could plead his case before God when there is no one who would be able to arbitrate the case (9:3–35). Here Job's speech is relentlessly legal: ch. 9 is framed by the term **contend** (Hb. *rib*, 9:3; 10:2), and legal terms are liberally sprinkled throughout the chapter (e.g., 9:2, 3, 14, 19, 20, 32, 33). Thus Job laments before God the weight of suffering in his life (10:1–22).

9:1–2 When Job says, **"I know that it is so"** (v. 2), he is most likely affirming that he also believes what is at the core of Bildad's response: God is just, and he will not reject the upright (8:3, 20). However, given these truths and how

3 If one wished to [a]contend with him,
one could not answer him once in a thousand times.
4 He is [b]wise in heart and mighty in strength
—who has [c]hardened himself against him, and succeeded?—
5 he who removes mountains, and they know it not,
when he overturns them in his anger,
6 who [d]shakes the earth out of its place,
and [e]its pillars tremble;
7 who commands the sun, and it does not rise;
who seals up the stars;
8 who alone [f]stretched out the heavens
and trampled the waves of the sea;
9 who [g]made [h]the Bear and [i]Orion,
the Pleiades [j]and the chambers of the south;
10 who does [k]great things beyond searching out,
and marvelous things beyond number.
11 Behold, he passes by me, and I [l]see him not;
he moves on, but I do not perceive him.
12 Behold, he snatches away; [m]who can turn him back?
[n]Who will say to him, 'What are you doing?'

13 "God will not turn back his anger;
beneath him bowed the helpers of [o]Rahab.
14 [p]How then can I [q]answer him,
choosing my words with him?
15 [r]Though I am in the right, I cannot answer him;
I must [s]appeal for mercy to my accuser.[1]
16 If I summoned him and he answered me,
I would not believe that he was listening to my voice.
17 For he crushes me with a tempest
and multiplies my wounds [t]without cause;
18 he will not let me get my breath,
but fills me with bitterness.
19 If it is a contest of [u]strength, behold, he is mighty!
If it is a matter of justice, who can [v]summon him?[2]
20 Though I am in the right, [w]my own mouth would condemn me;
though I am blameless, he would prove me perverse.
21 I am [x]blameless; I regard not myself;
I [y]loathe my life.

3[a][ch. 10:2; Ps. 143:2; Rom. 3:20]
4[b][ch. 12:13; 36:5] [c][Ex. 7:13; 32:9]
6[d]Isa. 2:19, 21; 13:13; Hag. 2:6, 21; Heb. 12:26 [e]ch. 26:11; Ps. 75:3
8[f]ch. 26:7; Ps. 104:2; Jer. 10:12; 51:15; Zech. 12:1
9[g]Gen. 1:16 [h]ch. 38:32 [i]ch. 38:31; Amos 5:8 [j]ch. 37:9
10[k]See ch. 5:9
11[l]ch. 23:8, 9
12[m]ch. 11:10; 23:13 [n]Isa. 45:9; [Jer. 18:6; Rom. 9:20]
13[o]ch. 26:12; Ps. 87:4; 89:10; Isa. 30:7; 51:9
14[p]ch. 15:16 [q]ver. 3
15[r]ch. 10:15 [s]ch. 8:5
17[t]ch. 2:3; [ch. 34:6]
19[u][ver. 4] [v]Jer. 49:19; 50:44
20[w]ch. 15:6
21[x]ch. 1:1 [y]ch. 7:16 (Heb.); [ch. 10:1]

[1] Or *to my judge* [2] Compare Septuagint; Hebrew *me*

the friends have interpreted his circumstances, Job slightly modifies the original question of Eliphaz's dream and asks, **But how can a man be in the right before God?** If God is just and Job is in fact innocent of the foolishness or wickedness his friends suggest, how can he go about arguing his case?

9:3–10 Job does not respond further to the specifics of Bildad's argument but instead describes the difficulty of anyone arguing a case before God (vv. 3–4), given his power and strength (vv. 5–10). The form of the Hebrew verse is significant: it is a "participial hymn." The name of such poems derives from the Hebrew verb form used in vv. 5–10; they typically offer praise to God for his mighty acts in creation (e.g., Psalm 136; Jer. 10:12–13; Amos 4:13; 5:8–9; 9:5–6). Here, however, like the inversion of Psalm 8 in Job 7:11, Job uses the form to declare what he perceives as God's *un*creative power (see also 12:13–25). Verse 10 of ch. 9 repeats yet another line from Eliphaz (see 5:9), but Job uses it to reinforce the seeming futility of attempting to **contend** with God.

9:13 Rahab, like Leviathan (see 3:8; cf. 7:12), is the name of a beast from the myths of the non-Israelite peoples. Here the name seems to represent specifically the forces of chaos (see note on Isa. 30:6–7). Earlier Job had asked that those ready to demolish Leviathan would remove his day from the universe (cf. Job 3:8). Only God is able to vanquish such powers, as Job here confesses. Job cannot hope to contest God, however just Job may judge his case to be.

9:15 Though I am in the right, I cannot answer him. Job states here (and again in v. 20) his contention that his friends have applied their theology to him and his circumstances in a way that traps him. Job's friends have argued that God is just, that he does not reject the blameless, and that Job's circumstances indicate he is hiding something for which he ought to repent. Job agrees that God is just, but feels there is no room for him to make the case that he is innocent of what his friends presume.

9:20 The form of the verb translated **would prove me perverse** makes it possible for the subject to be either **he** (referring to God) or "it" (referring to Job's mouth). For either possibility, the point is the same. If his mouth would prove him to be in the wrong, it is because Job thinks that God would find his words wanting. When Job says, **"I am blameless"** (also in v. 21), he unknowingly echoes God's description of him in the prologue (1:8; 2:3).

9:21 I regard not myself. Job seems to be saying that he does not care whether he lives or dies. He is prepared to risk his life to find justice (13:14).

22 It is all one; therefore I say,
'He [z]destroys both the blameless and the wicked.'
23 When [a]disaster brings sudden death,
he mocks at the calamity[1] of the innocent.
24 [b]The earth is given into the hand of the wicked;
he [c]covers the faces of its judges—
[d]if it is not he, who then is it?

25 "My [e]days are swifter than [f]a runner;
they flee away; they see no good.
26 They go by like [g]skiffs of reed,
like [h]an eagle swooping on the prey.
27 If I say, [i]'I will forget my complaint,
I will put off my sad face, and [j]be of good cheer,'
28 I become [k]afraid of all my suffering,
for I know you will not [l]hold me innocent.
29 I shall be [m]condemned;
why then do I labor in vain?
30 If I wash myself with snow
and [n]cleanse my hands with lye,
31 yet you will plunge me into a pit,
and my own clothes will [o]abhor me.
32 For he is not a man, as I am, that I might answer him,
that we should [p]come to trial together.
33 [q]There is no[2] arbiter between us,
who might lay his hand on us both.
34 [r]Let him take his [s]rod away from me,
and let [t]not dread of him terrify me.
35 Then I would speak without fear of him,
for I am not so in myself.

Job Continues: A Plea to God

10 1 "I [u]loathe my life;
I will give free utterance to my [v]complaint;
I will speak in [w]the bitterness of my soul.
2 I will say to God, Do not [x]condemn me;
let me know why you [y]contend against me.
3 [z]Does it seem good to you to oppress,
to despise [a]the work of your hands
[b]and favor the designs of the wicked?
4 Have you [c]eyes of flesh?
[d]Do you see as man sees?
5 Are your days as the days of man,
or your [e]years as a man's years,
6 that you [f]seek out my iniquity
and search for my sin,
7 although you [g]know that I am not guilty,
and there is [h]none to deliver out of your hand?

[1] The meaning of the Hebrew word is uncertain [2] Or *Would that there were an*

22 [z]Eccles. 9:2, 3; Ezek. 21:3
23 [a]Isa. 10:26
24 [b][ch. 10:3] [c]See ch. 12:17 [d][ch. 24:25]
25 [e]ch. 7:6 [f][2 Chr. 30:6; Jer. 51:31]
26 [g][Isa. 18:2] [h]Hab. 1:8
27 [i][ch. 7:13] [j]Ps. 39:13
28 [k][Ps. 119:120] [l]ch. 10:14
29 [m][ch. 10:2]
30 [n]Isa. 1:25; Jer. 2:22; See ch. 22:30
31 [o]ch. 19:19; 30:10
32 [p]Eccles. 6:10; Rom. 9:20
33 [q]ver. 19; 1 Sam. 2:25; [ch. 16:21]
34 [r][Ps. 39:10] [s]ch. 21:9; Ps. 89:32; Isa. 10:24 [t][ch. 13:21; 33:7]

Chapter 10

1 [u][ch. 7:16; 9:21; Num. 11:15; 1 Kgs. 19:4] [v]ch. 21:4; 23:2 [w]See ch. 7:11
2 [x]ch. 9:29 [y]ch. 9:3
3 [z]ch. 13:9; Ps. 89:38 [a]ch. 14:15; Ps. 138:8; Isa. 64:8 [b][ch. 9:24]
4 [c][John 8:15] [d]1 Sam. 16:7
5 [e]ch. 36:26; Ps. 77:10; [Ps. 90:4; 2 Pet. 3:8]
6 [f][ch. 14:16]
7 [g][ch. 2:3, 9] [h]Deut. 32:39; Isa. 43:13

9:22–24 While Job's friends have assumed that his suffering is evidence of some hidden wickedness, Job argues that from what is observable, **both the blameless and the wicked** are destroyed (v. 22), fall prey to **disaster** (v. 23), and suffer from the perversion of justice (v. 24)—and that all of these things are governed, ultimately, by God (**if it is not he, who then is it?**).

9:32–35 When Job says, "**there is no arbiter**" in v. 33 (or wishes that there were one, see ESV footnote), his words are partially an indictment against his friends, who have not served him well as comforters (while upholding both the character of God and the integrity of Job). In light of his friends' failure, Job longs for someone who could hear his case impartially, and for the removal of the threat of further suffering (v. 34), so that he could **speak** freely (v. 35).

10:1–2 As in 7:11, Job explicitly announces his turn to address his Creator directly.

10:3 Job's awareness that he is **the work of** God's **hands** provides the theme for the verses that follow.

8[i]Ps. 119:73
9[j]See ch. 4:17 [k]ch. 34:15; Gen. 2:7; 3:19; Ps. 146:4; Eccles. 12:7
13[l]ch. 23:14; 27:11
14[m]ch. 13:27; 33:11; Ps. 130:3 [n]ch. 9:28
15[o]Isa. 3:11 [p]ch. 9:15 [q][Ps. 25:18]
16[r]ch. 28:8; Hos. 5:14; 13:7; [Isa. 38:13] [s][ch. 5:9]
17[t][ch. 16:8; Ruth 1:21] [u][ch. 19:12]
18[v]ch. 3:11; [ch. 3:3]
19[w]Obad. 16
20[x]See ch. 14:1 [y]See ch. 7:16 [z]ch. 9:27; Ps. 39:13
21[a][ch. 16:22; 2 Sam. 12:23] [b]ch. 30:26; Ps. 88:12 [c]See ch. 3:5

Chapter 11
1[d]ch. 2:11
2[e]Prov. 10:19; Eccles. 5:3

8 [i]Your hands fashioned and made me,
and now you have destroyed me altogether.
9 Remember that you have made me like [j]clay;
and will you return me to the [k]dust?
10 Did you not pour me out like milk
and curdle me like cheese?
11 You clothed me with skin and flesh,
and knit me together with bones and sinews.
12 You have granted me life and steadfast love,
and your care has preserved my spirit.
13 Yet these things you hid in your heart;
I know that [l]this was your purpose.
14 If I sin, you [m]watch me
and do not [n]acquit me of my iniquity.
15 [o]If I am guilty, woe to me!
If I am [p]in the right, I cannot lift up my head,
for I am filled with disgrace
and [q]look on my affliction.
16 And were my head lifted up,[1] you would hunt me like [r]a lion
and again work [s]wonders against me.
17 You renew your [t]witnesses against me
and increase your vexation toward me;
you [u]bring fresh troops against me.

18 [v]"Why did you bring me out from the womb?
Would that I had died before any eye had seen me
19 [w]and were as though I had not been,
carried from the womb to the grave.
20 [x]Are not my days few?
[y]Then cease, and leave me alone, [z]that I may find a little cheer
21 before I go—and [a]I shall not return—
to the land of [b]darkness and [c]deep shadow,
22 the land of gloom like thick darkness,
like deep shadow without any order,
where light is as thick darkness."

Zophar Speaks: You Deserve Worse

11 Then [d]Zophar the Naamathite answered and said:

2 "Should [e]a multitude of words go unanswered,
and a man full of talk be judged right?
3 Should your babble silence men,
and when you mock, shall no one shame you?

[1] Hebrew lacks *my head*

10:8–13 Through a sequence of vivid metaphors, Job describes his own conception and gestation as an act of God's creation. Job shares the wonder of the psalmist (Ps. 139:14) and the insight given to the prophet (Jer. 1:5a), but he employs it here to press his claim of innocence before God.

10:15–17 Job states both sides of the dilemma he faces: if he is **guilty** of what his friends have inferred, it will not be good for him (v. 15, **woe to me!**); if he is in the **right** (v. 15; see also 9:15, 20), he feels he has no strength to walk upright because of the weight of his suffering (10:15) and the threat of further affliction (vv. 16–17).

10:18–19 Why did you bring me out from the womb? Job caps the argument begun in v. 3 and returns to his earlier sentiments. He should have been stillborn (3:10); if he had to be born, he should have been left alone and allowed to die in peace (7:16–17). Why should God make so much of humans that he would continually watch over them in such misery?

10:21–22 The repetition of the terms **darkness** and **shadow** and the adjectives used to modify them (**thick**, **deep**) in Job's description of death underscore his plea for a reprieve from suffering while he still has days left in the light of life.

11:1–20 *Zophar: Repent.* Like Bildad (see 8:1–22), Zophar responds with a sharp challenge to what he sees as empty words and presumption in Job (11:2–12). He then calls Job to prayer and repentance, promising that God will transform Job's circumstances if he will simply step back from his pride (vv. 13–20). Zophar's indignant speech makes an implicit connection between moral standing and knowledge of God: since Job's situation marks him out as morally corrupt (cf. vv. 5–6, 11, 14), he cannot know God rightly.

4 For [f]you say, 'My [g]doctrine is pure,
and I am clean in God's[1] eyes.'
5 But oh, that God would speak
and open his lips to you,
6 and that he would tell you the secrets of wisdom!
For he is manifold in [h]understanding.[2]
Know then that God [i]exacts of you less than your guilt deserves.

7 [j]"Can you find out the deep things of God?
Can you find out the limit of the Almighty?
8 It is [k]higher than heaven[3]—what can you do?
Deeper than Sheol—what can you know?
9 Its measure is longer than the earth
and broader than the sea.
10 If he [l]passes through and [m]imprisons
and summons the court, who can [n]turn him back?
11 For he knows [o]worthless men;
when he sees iniquity, will he not consider it?
12 But a stupid man will get understanding
when [p]a wild donkey's colt is [q]born a man!

13 "If you [r]prepare your heart,
you will [s]stretch out your hands toward him.
14 If iniquity is in your hand, put it far away,
and let not injustice dwell in your tents.
15 Surely then you will [t]lift up your face without [u]blemish;
you will be secure and will not fear.
16 You will [v]forget your misery;
you will remember it as waters that have passed away.
17 And your life will be [w]brighter than the noonday;
its darkness will be like the morning.
18 And you will feel secure, because there is hope;
you will look around and [x]take your rest in security.
19 You will [x]lie down, and none will make you afraid;
many will [y]court your favor.
20 But [z]the eyes of the wicked will fail;
all way of escape will be lost to them,
and their hope is [a]to breathe their last."

Job Replies: The LORD Has Done This

12 Then Job answered and said:

2 "No doubt you are the people,
and wisdom will die with you.

[1] Hebrew *your* [2] The meaning of the Hebrew is uncertain [3] Hebrew *The heights of heaven*

4 [f]ch. 10:7 [g]Deut. 32:2; Prov. 4:2; Isa. 29:24
6 [h]ch. 5:12 (Heb.) [i][Ezra 9:13]
7 [j]ch. 5:9; Eccles. 3:11; 8:17; [Ps. 145:3; Rom. 11:33]
8 [k][ch. 22:12; Ps. 139:8]
10 [l]See ch. 9:11-16 [m]See ch. 12:14 [n]ch. 9:12; 23:13
11 [o]Ps. 26:4
12 [p]See ch. 39:5-8 [q][Ps. 73:22; Eccles. 3:18]
13 [r]Ps. 78:8; See 1 Sam. 7:3 [s]Ps. 44:20; 88:9; 143:6
15 [t]ch. 22:26; [Gen. 4:5; Ps. 119:6; 1 John 3:21] [u]ch. 31:7; 2 Pet. 3:14
16 [v][Isa. 65:16]
17 [w][Ps. 37:6; Isa. 58:8, 10]
18 [x]Lev. 26:5, 6; Ps. 4:8; Prov. 3:24; Isa. 17:2; Zeph. 3:13
19 [x][See ver. 18 above] [y]Ps. 45:12
20 [z]ch. 17:5; 31:16 [a]Jer. 15:9

11:5–6 Zophar shares Job's longing that Job might have a direct audience with God, but for exactly the opposite purpose. Job longs for vindication; Zophar is certain that Job would be condemned.

11:7 There is irony in this verse that will be revealed to Zophar only in the events of the epilogue (see 42:7–9). Although he accusingly asks Job whether he is able to discover the depth and extent of God's work, it is Zophar who presumes that God's purposes in Job's suffering are transparent enough to rebuke Job and call him to repent.

11:12 Although there is a question about how the second line of this proverb relates to the first (i.e., whether the first line is being compared to the impossibility in the second of a **wild donkey** giving birth either to a **man** or to a domesticated **colt**), the function of the proverb in Zophar's speech is clear. He is calling Job to stop insisting on foolishness, because, like the path of the **stupid man**, it will never lead to **understanding**. Zophar calls Job instead to turn away from the insistence that he is in the right and to seek God in prayer and repentance (vv. 13–20).

11:20 Zophar's final statement about the fate of the **wicked** stands in stark contrast to what he describes in vv. 13–19 as the benefits God will bestow on Job if he will only repent. Zophar's statement is meant to warn Job against continuing in his current path (see v. 18 and the contrast relating to **hope**).

12:1–14:22 *Job: A Challenge to the "Wisdom" of His Friends.* In the longest response of the dialogues with the three friends, Job shows his growing frustration with their claims to wisdom (even though he agrees with them about God's supreme power; 12:1–13:2) and with the conclusions they have drawn (13:3–19); then, once again, he addresses his lamentation directly to God (13:20–14:22).

12:2–3 Job reveals his frustration through sarcasm. In what may be a rejoinder to Zophar's wish that God would tell Job "the secrets of wisdom" (see

3 But I have [b]understanding as well as you;
I am not inferior to you.
Who does not know [c]such things as these?
4 I am [d]a laughingstock to my friends;
I, who [e]called to God and he answered me,
a just and blameless man, am a laughingstock.
5 In the thought of one who is [f]at ease there is contempt for misfortune;
it is ready for those whose feet slip.
6 [g]The tents of robbers are at peace,
and those who provoke God are secure,
who bring their god in their hand.[1]

7 "But ask the beasts, and they will teach you;
the birds of the heavens, and they will tell you;
8 or the bushes of the earth,[2] and they will teach you;
and the fish of the sea will declare to you.
9 Who among all these does not know
that [h]the hand of the LORD has done this?
10 In [i]his hand is the life of every living thing
and the breath of all mankind.
11 Does not [j]the ear test words
as the palate tastes food?
12 Wisdom is with [k]the aged,
and understanding in length of days.

13 [l]"With God[3] are wisdom and might;
he has counsel and understanding.
14 If he tears down, none can rebuild;
if he [m]shuts a man in, none can open.
15 If he [n]withholds the waters, they dry up;
if he [o]sends them out, they overwhelm the land.
16 With him are strength and [p]sound wisdom;
the deceived and the deceiver are his.
17 He leads [q]counselors away stripped,
and [r]judges he makes fools.
18 He [s]looses the bonds of kings
and binds a waistcloth on their hips.
19 He leads priests away stripped
and overthrows the mighty.
20 He deprives of speech those who are trusted
[t]and takes away the discernment of the elders.

[1] The meaning of the Hebrew is uncertain [2] Or *speak to the earth* [3] Hebrew *him*

Chapter 12
3[b][ch. 13:2; 15:9] [c]ch. 16:2
4[d]ch. 16:10; 17:2, 6; 21:3; 30:1 [e]Ps. 91:15
5[f]ch. 3:18
6[g]See ch. 21:7
9[h]Isa. 41:20; [ch. 1:21]
10[i]Num. 16:22; Dan. 5:23; Acts 17:28
11[j]ch. 34:3
12[k]ch. 32:7; [Ps. 119:100]
13[l][ch. 9:4; 36:5]
14[m]ch. 11:10; [Isa. 22:22; Rev. 3:7]
15[n][Deut. 11:17; 1 Kgs. 8:35; 17:1] [o][Gen. 7:11-24; Ps. 147:18; Amos 9:6]
16[p][ch. 5:12]
17[q][2 Sam. 17:23] [r]ch. 9:24; Isa. 40:23; [Isa. 29:14; 44:25; 1 Cor. 1:19]
18[s]Ps. 116:16
20[t][ch. 32:9]

11:5–6), he states, "**wisdom will die with you**" to make the point that his friends speak as though they alone were wise (12:2). However, says Job, "**I am not inferior to you**" (v. 3; 13:2), and he sets out to illustrate the lack of depth and breadth in their approach (12:4–25).

12:4–6 Job reproves his friends by pointing out that their approach to wisdom seems to ignore the realities of both the suffering of the righteous (like his own, v. 4) and the safety of the wicked (v. 6). Furthermore, his friends have not acted as true wisdom requires, but have instead expressed **contempt** rather than comfort from their place of being **at ease** (v. 5; see also 6:14).

12:6 The tents of robbers are at peace. With the reference to the image of the "tents" of the wicked, Job may have intended a counterpoint to one or more of his friends' earlier assertions (see 5:24; 8:22; 11:14).

12:7–9 As further reproof, Job suggests that his friends ought to inquire of the animals and plants of creation, which all **know** that it is ultimately **the LORD** who governs all of life.

12:9 the hand of the LORD has done this? This line is the only occurrence of the name of God (Hb. *YHWH*) in Job outside of the prologue and chs. 38–42 and is identical to a line in the book of Isaiah (Isa. 41:20).

12:13–25 In this section, Job asserts that the scope of God's providential governing of the world is much more extensive than what his friends assume by their responses. Again as in 9:3–10, Job employs the distinctive form of the "participial hymn" (see note on 9:3–10) in an ironic fashion. Here Job asserts God's sovereign control over nature and its destructive powers before employing the participial form to survey God's supreme prerogative over human rulers (12:17–24).

12:17–21 The whole of social order and any sphere of leadership within it are subject to God and his purposes: counselors, judges, kings, priests, advisers, elders, princes, and soldiers.

12:18 He looses the bonds of kings, i.e., kings lose their thrones. The bond may be thought of as the royal sash or belt, which is replaced by that of an ordinary robe.

21 He [u]pours contempt on princes
and loosens the belt of the strong.
22 He [v]uncovers the deeps out of darkness
and brings [w]deep darkness to light.
23 He [x]makes nations great, and he destroys them;
he enlarges nations, and [y]leads them away.
24 He takes away understanding from the chiefs of the people of the earth
and [z]makes them wander in a trackless waste.
25 They [a]grope in the dark without light,
and he makes them [b]stagger like a drunken man.

Job Continues: Still I Will Hope in God

13 1 "Behold, my eye has seen all this,
my ear has heard and understood it.
2 [c]What you know, I also know;
I am not inferior to you.
3 [d]But I would speak to the Almighty,
and I desire to [e]argue my case with God.
4 As for you, [f]you whitewash with lies;
[g]worthless physicians are you all.
5 Oh that you would [h]keep silent,
and it would be your wisdom!
6 Hear now my argument
and listen to the pleadings of my lips.
7 Will you [i]speak falsely for God
and speak [i]deceitfully for him?
8 Will you show partiality toward him?
Will you [j]plead the case for God?
9 Will it be well with you when he [k]searches you out?
Or [l]can you deceive him, as one deceives a man?
10 He will surely rebuke you
if in secret you show partiality.
11 Will not his [m]majesty terrify you,
and the dread of him fall upon you?
12 Your maxims are proverbs of [n]ashes;
your defenses are defenses of clay.
13 "Let me have silence, and I will speak,
and let come on me what may.
14 Why should I take my flesh in my teeth
and [o]put my life in my hand?
15 [p]Though he slay me, I will [q]hope in him;[1]
yet I will [r]argue my ways to his face.

21 [u]Ps. 107:40
22 [v]Dan. 2:22; 1 Cor. 4:5 [w]See ch. 3:5
23 [x]Isa. 9:3; 26:15 [y][2 Kgs. 18:11]
24 [z]Ps. 107:40; [ch. 6:18]
25 [a]See ch. 5:14 [b]Ps. 107:27; Isa. 19:14

Chapter 13

2 [c][ch. 12:3; 15:9]
3 [d]ch. 23:4; 31:35 [e][ver. 15, 18]
4 [f]Ps. 119:69 [g][ch. 16:2]
5 [h]Prov. 17:28
7 [i]ch. 27:4
8 [j][Judg. 6:31]
9 [k]Prov. 28:11 [l]Gal. 6:7
11 [m]ch. 31:23
12 [n]Isa. 44:20
14 [o]See Judg. 12:3
15 [p][Prov. 14:32] [q]ch. 14:14 [r][ver. 3; ch. 27:5]

[1] Or *Behold, he will slay me; I have no hope*

12:21–24 He pours contempt on princes (v. 21a) and **makes them wander in a trackless waste** (v. 24b) are identical to the two lines of Ps. 107:40. The psalm speaks of judgment against oppressive rulers; in Job these phrases serve as a part of the description of God's sovereign governing over all social order. **Loosens the belt** is a common metaphor for disarming a soldier.

12:23 he enlarges nations. This may have the negative sense of "disperse" or "scatter," making the second line antithetical to the first. Sometimes God makes nations great and then destroys them, while other times he first scatters a nation and then gives it peace or leads it in an orderly way.

13:3–19 Before he turns to God in lament, Job argues that his friends have both misdiagnosed him (he calls his friends "worthless physicians" in v. 4) and misrepresented God (see vv. 7–10).

13:4 you whitewash with lies. The image of applying "whitewash" is not itself negative, but refers to the process of repairing something that is cracked or broken (e.g., a pot) by smearing it with a material that would both bond the pieces and seal the cracks. Job's contention with his friends is that they have sought to "whitewash" the situation with what they ought to know is not true about either Job or God.

13:6–10 Job uses law and present court language to make his case—he is stating his arguments. The friends are denigrating Job in their arguments and showing favoritism to his divine opponent in making their **case** for him (v. 8). In the end God does rebuke the friends, exactly as Job had warned (42:7–8).

13:11 Will not his majesty terrify you? Job questions whether his friends have taken seriously the glory and power of God in how easily and lightly they have spoken on his behalf. In a later response, Job speaks of his own fear at the thought of facing the majesty of God (31:23).

13:15 Job is aware of the force of his own argument in 12:17–25, yet cannot

17[s]ch. 21:2
18[t]See ch. 33:5
19[u]Isa. 50:8, 9
20[v][Gen. 3:8]
21[w]ch. 9:34; Ps. 39:10 [x]ch. 9:34; 33:7
22[y]ch. 14:15
23[z][Ps. 19:12]
24[a]Deut. 32:20 [b]ch. 19:11; 33:10; [Lam. 2:5]
25[c]Lev. 26:36 [d]ch. 21:18; Ps. 83:13
26[e][Ps. 149:9] [f]Ps. 25:7
27[g][ch. 33:11] [h]See ch. 10:14
28[i]Prov. 12:4; 14:30; Hab. 3:16 [j]ch. 4:19

Chapter 14

1[k]ch. 15:14; 25:4; Matt. 11:11 [l]ch. 10:20; 16:22; Gen. 47:9; Ps. 39:5; 89:47 [m]See ch. 5:7
2[n]Ps. 103:15; Isa. 40:6, 7; James 1:10; 1 Pet. 1:24 [o]Ps. 37:2; 90:6 [p]See ch. 8:9; 17:7; Ps. 109:23
3[q][Ps. 8:4; 144:3] [r]ch. 22:4; Ps. 143:2
4[s]ch. 15:14; [Ps. 51:5; John 3:6]
5[t][ch. 7:1; Ps. 39:4] [u]ch. 21:21
6[v]ch. 7:19 [w]ch. 7:1

16 This will be my salvation,
that the godless shall not come before him.
17 [s]Keep listening to my words,
and let my declaration be in your ears.
18 Behold, I have [t]prepared my case;
I know that I shall be in the right.
19 [u]Who is there who will contend with me?
For then I would be silent and die.
20 Only grant me two things,
then I will not [v]hide myself from your face:
21 [w]withdraw your hand far from me,
and let not [x]dread of you terrify me.
22 [y]Then call, and I will answer;
or let me speak, and you reply to me.
23 How many are my iniquities and my sins?
[z]Make me know my transgression and my sin.
24 Why [a]do you hide your face
and [b]count me as your enemy?
25 Will you frighten [c]a driven leaf
and pursue dry [d]chaff?
26 For you [e]write bitter things against me
and make me inherit [f]the iniquities of my youth.
27 You put my feet in [g]the stocks
and [h]watch all my paths;
you set a limit for[1] the soles of my feet.
28 Man[2] wastes away like [i]a rotten thing,
like a garment that is [j]moth-eaten.

Job Continues: Death Comes Soon to All

14 1 "Man who is [k]born of a woman
is [l]few of days and [m]full of trouble.
2 He comes out like [n]a flower and [o]withers;
he flees like [p]a shadow and continues not.
3 And do you [q]open your eyes on such a one
and [r]bring me into judgment with you?
4 Who can bring [s]a clean thing out of an unclean?
There is not one.
5 Since his [t]days are determined,
and [u]the number of his months is with you,
and you have appointed his limits that he cannot pass,
6 [v]look away from him and leave him alone,[3]
that he may enjoy, like [w]a hired hand, his day.

[1] Or *you marked* [2] Hebrew *He* [3] Probable reading; Hebrew *look away from him, that he may cease*

avoid taking the risk that God will **slay** him. **I will hope in him.** "Hope" is to wait for something; waiting may or may not be patient, and it may or may not be with a positive expectation. Job is impatient and expects his life will end shortly. Job will not wait; he is willing to risk his life to make his case against God (but cf. 14:19).

13:16 the godless shall not come before him. The **salvation** Job hopes for is that he will yet be able to make the case for his innocence before God. He anticipates that God will yet be his redeemer (see 19:25).

13:20 Only grant me two things. Job abruptly shifts from warning his friends to pleading his case with God.

13:26 you write bitter things against me. Job is referring to God's accusations against him, not to an indictment to punish him with suffering.

13:27 you set a limit for the soles of my feet. The metaphor refers either to confinement ("set a limit for") or to a tracing of movement ("marked"; see ESV footnote). Both concepts are present: Job's feet are in the stocks, and God watches everywhere he goes. Both cannot be true at the same time, but both express God's vigilant pursuit of Job.

13:28–14:22 In this section of lament before God, Job moves from referring primarily to his own situation (13:20–27) to focus on the nature of life for any mortal.

13:28 Man wastes away. The speech takes another abrupt turn. Job's thoughts on mortality are introduced with a proverb, which uses a pronoun as a generic reference to the human race (see ESV footnote).

14:4 Who can bring a clean thing out of an unclean? Job describes human life as hard and short, a theme already declared to the friends in 7:1–10, and uses this question and answer to point out that no mortal is able to work outside of the limits that God has set (see also 14:5).

7 “For there is hope for a tree,
if it be cut down, that it will sprout again,
and that its shoots will not cease.
8 Though its root grow old in the earth,
and [x]its stump die in the soil,
9 yet at the scent of water it will bud
and put out [y]branches like a young plant.
10 But a man dies and is laid low;
man breathes his last, and [z]where is he?
11 [a]As waters fail from a lake
and a river wastes away and dries up,
12 so a man lies down and rises not again;
till [b]the heavens are no more he will not awake
or be [c]roused out of his sleep.
13 Oh that you would [d]hide me in [e]Sheol,
that you would [d]conceal me [f]until your wrath be past,
that you would appoint me a set time, and remember me!
14 If a man dies, shall he live again?
All the days of my [g]service I would [h]wait,
till my renewal[1] should come.
15 You would [i]call, and I would answer you;
you would long for the [j]work of your hands.
16 For then you would [k]number my steps;
you would not keep [l]watch over my sin;
17 my transgression would be [m]sealed up in a bag,
and you would cover over my iniquity.

18 “But the mountain falls and [n]crumbles away,
and [o]the rock is removed from its place;
19 the waters wear away the stones;
the torrents wash away the soil of the earth;
so you destroy the hope of man.
20 You prevail forever against him, and he passes;
you change his countenance, and send him away.
21 His sons come to honor, and he [p]does not know it;
they are brought low, and he perceives it not.
22 He feels only the pain of his own body,
and he mourns only for himself.”

Eliphaz Accuses: Job Does Not Fear God

15 Then [q]Eliphaz the Temanite answered and said:

2 “Should [r]a wise man answer with [s]windy knowledge,
and fill his [t]belly with [u]the east wind?

[1] *Or relief*

8[x]Isa. 11:1
9[y][ch. 29:19]
10[z]ch. 29:7
11[a]Isa. 19:5
12[b]Deut. 11:21; Ps. 89:29; [Ps. 72:5; Matt. 5:18] [c][John 11:11]
13[d][Ps. 27:5; 31:20] [e]See ch. 21:13 [f][Isa. 26:20]
14[g]ch. 7:1 [h]ch. 13:15
15[i]ch. 13:22 [j]See ch. 10:3
16[k]ch. 31:4; 34:21 [l][ch. 10:6]
17[m]Deut. 32:34; [Hos. 13:12]
18[n]Isa. 34:4 [o]ch. 18:4
21[p][Eccles. 9:5]

Chapter 15

1[q]ch. 2:11
2[r][ch. 12:3] [s]ch. 16:3 [t]ver. 35 [u]ch. 6:26; 8:2; Hos. 12:1

14:7–14 Job laments the limits of mortality by contrasting the consequences of cutting down a **tree** (vv. 7–9) and the death of a **man** (vv. 10–14). There is **hope** (v. 7) for a tree that even if **root** and **stump** decay (v. 8), it may still grow again (v. 9). However, when a man dies, his life on earth is finished (see vv. 10, 12, 14). Thus, Job says that though a tree may **sprout again** (v. 7), he must look for **renewal** (v. 14) within the days of his life on earth (the Hb. words translated as “sprout again” and “renewal” are related).

14:10 where is he? Since the focus of this section is mortal life, Job’s question does not specifically pertain to his thoughts on life after death (which he possibly alludes to in v. 12) but to the fact that there is no chance for vindication through restored life on earth after suffering and death.

14:15–22 Although Job longs for renewal in which God would secure his path and forgive his sin (vv. 15–17), he concludes that just as the elements wash away rock and soil, so God will wear down a man over the course of his life (vv. 18–22).

14:19 Here Job evokes the language of his earlier description: although a tree may have “hope” of renewal (v. 7), God can remove **the hope of man** through the persistent eroding effect of suffering and difficulty.

15:1–21:34 *Second Cycle.* The positions established by each participant harden in the second round of speeches. Once again Eliphaz (ch. 15), Bildad (ch. 18), and Zophar (ch. 20) align Job’s suffering with the punishment due to the wicked. Job’s responses (chs. 16–17; 19; 21) typically show his refusal to accept responsibility for his situation (e.g., 19:2–6) and characterize the wicked not as sufferers but as those who prosper despite their careless godlessness (e.g., 21:7–16).

15:1–35 *Eliphaz: Job’s Words Condemn Him.* In his second response, which

3 Should he argue in unprofitable talk,
or in words with which he can do no good?
4 But you are doing away with the fear of God[1]
and hindering meditation before God.
5 For your iniquity teaches your mouth,
and you choose the tongue of the crafty.
6 Your [v]own mouth condemns you, and not I;
[w]your own lips testify against you.

7 [x]"Are you the first man who was born?
Or [y]were you brought forth [z]before the hills?
8 Have you listened in [a]the council of God?
And do you limit wisdom to yourself?
9 [b]What do you know that we do not know?
What do you understand that is not clear to us?
10 [c]Both the gray-haired and the aged are among us,
older than your father.
11 Are the comforts of God too small for you,
or the word that deals gently with you?
12 Why does your heart carry you away,
and why do your eyes flash,
13 that you turn your [d]spirit against God
and bring such words out of your mouth?
14 [e]What is man, [f]that he can be pure?
Or he who is [g]born of a woman, that he can be righteous?
15 Behold, God[2] [h]puts no trust in his [i]holy ones,
and the heavens are not pure in his sight;
16 [j]how much less one who is abominable and [k]corrupt,
a man who [l]drinks injustice like water!

17 "I will show you; hear me,
and what I have seen I will declare
18 (what wise men have told,
without hiding it [m]from their fathers,
19 to whom alone the land was given,
and no [n]stranger passed among them).
20 The wicked man writhes in pain all his days,
through all the [o]years that are laid up for [p]the ruthless.
21 [q]Dreadful sounds are in his ears;
in [r]prosperity the destroyer will come upon him.
22 He does not believe that he will return out of darkness,
and he is marked for the sword.

[1] Hebrew lacks *of God* [2] Hebrew *he*

6 [v]ch. 9:20; Luke 19:22 [w]2 Sam. 1:16
7 [x][ch. 38:21] [y]Prov. 8:25 [z]Ps. 90:2
8 [a]ch. 29:4; Jer. 23:18; [Gen. 1:26; 3:22]
9 [b]ch. 12:3; 13:2
10 [c][ch. 12:12; 32:6, 7]
13 [d][ch. 21:4]
14 [e]For ver. 14-16, see ch. 25:4-6 [f][ch. 14:4; Ps. 14:3; Prov. 20:9; Eccles. 7:20; 1 John 1:8, 10] [g]See ch. 14:1
15 [h]ch. 4:18 [i]See ch. 5:1
16 [j]ch. 9:14 [k][Ps. 14:3; 53:1] [l]ch. 34:7; [Prov. 19:28; 26:6]
18 [m][ch. 8:8]; See Ps. 44:1
19 [n]Joel 3:17
20 [o][ch. 21:19; 24:1] [p]ch. 6:23; 27:13
21 [q]See ch. 18:11 [r][1 Thess. 5:3]

initiates the second round of dialogues, Eliphaz dispenses with his earlier commendation of Job's character (see 4:3–6) and opens by accusing him of speaking out of iniquity rather than wisdom (15:2–16). The second half of the response is a more aggressive assertion of the content of Eliphaz's first speech: the consequence of wickedness is suffering, and thus suffering indicates that a person is wicked and should not protest innocence (vv. 17–35).

15:2 Should a wise man answer with windy knowledge . . . ? It is possible that Eliphaz is asking whether he as a wise man should respond to Job, but the contents of vv. 3–6 indicate that the function of this question is to dispute Job's claim to be wise (see 12:3; 13:2). Eliphaz argues that Job's words reveal someone who is full of wind rather than wisdom.

15:4 fear of God. As the ESV footnote says, the Hebrew lacks the words "of God." However, the reference to God in the second half of the verse and the thrust of vv. 2–6 underscore that this is precisely what Eliphaz is inferring: Job has become careless in his complaint to God and is **doing away with** the very thing that will bring him relief (namely, repentance and humility before God) and thus is **hindering** his **meditation** from being heard.

15:8 Have you listened in the council of God? The question ought to appear ironic to the reader, who has been made privy to the conversations represented in the prologue (1:7–12; 2:2–6). Eliphaz is himself guilty of the very sort of presumption for which he criticizes Job: he has concluded wrongly that Job's suffering is a transparent indicator of God's judgment.

15:14–16 Eliphaz revisits the central questions of his first response (see 4:17–21): if God does not trust fully even his heavenly servants (15:15), how can Job, as a mere man (v. 14), continue to protest his innocence (v. 16)?

15:20–35 In a section intended to function like the description of the foolish man in his first response (see 5:2–5), Eliphaz portrays the **wicked man** to implicate Job. Central to the portrayal are the images of one who is terrified as judgment comes to him amid his seeming prosperity (see 15:21, 24, 27, 32–33). Eliphaz is hoping that Job will see himself in the images and turn from defending himself to repentance.

23 He [s]wanders abroad for bread, saying, 'Where is it?'
He knows that a day of darkness is ready at his hand;
24 distress and anguish terrify him;
they [t]prevail against him, like a king ready for battle.
25 Because he has stretched out his hand against God
and defies the Almighty,
26 [u]running [v]stubbornly against him
with a thickly bossed shield;
27 because he has [w]covered his face with his fat
and gathered fat upon his waist
28 and has lived in desolate cities,
in houses that none should inhabit,
which were ready to become heaps of ruins;
29 he will not be rich, and his wealth will not endure,
nor will his possessions spread over the earth;[1]
30 he will not depart from darkness;
the flame will dry up his shoots,
and by [x]the breath of his mouth he will depart.
31 Let him not [y]trust in emptiness, deceiving himself,
for emptiness will be his payment.
32 It will be paid in full [z]before his time,
and his branch will not be green.
33 He will shake off his unripe grape like the vine,
and cast off his blossom like the olive tree.
34 For [a]the company of the godless is barren,
and [b]fire consumes the tents of bribery.
35 They [c]conceive trouble and give birth to evil,
and their [d]womb prepares deceit."

Job Replies: Miserable Comforters Are You

16 Then Job answered and said:

2 " I have heard [e]many such things;
[f]miserable comforters are you all.
3 Shall [g]windy words have an end?
Or what provokes you that you answer?
4 I also could speak as you do,
if you were in my place;
I could join words together against you
and [h]shake my head at you.
5 I could strengthen you with my mouth,
and the solace of my lips would assuage your pain.

23 [s]Ps. 59:15; 109:10
24 [t]ch. 14:20
26 [u][ch. 16:14; Dan. 8:6] [v]Ps. 75:5
27 [w]See Ps. 17:10
30 [x]ch. 4:9
31 [y][Isa. 59:4]
32 [z]ch. 22:16; Eccles. 7:17; [Ps. 55:23; 102:24]
34 [a]ch. 16:7 [b][ch. 20:26]
35 [c]Ps. 7:14; Isa. 59:4; [Hos. 10:13] [d]See ver. 2

Chapter 16

2 [e][ch. 12:3] [f][ch. 13:4]
3 [g][ch. 15:2]
4 [h]2 Kgs. 19:21; Ps. 22:7; 109:25; Isa. 37:22; Jer. 18:16; Lam. 2:15; Matt. 27:39; Mark 15:29

[1] *Or nor will his produce bend down to the earth*

15:27 The doubled use of **fat** invokes a well-known image for proud, complacent disregard of God (see Ps. 73:7; 119:70; cf. Job 16:8 and note).

15:31–35 These verses contain an example of Job's claim that his friends are "withholding kindness" from him (see 6:14; 12:5). With the presumption that his perspective is clear and right, Eliphaz mercilessly chooses vocabulary that focuses on the loss of Job's offspring as indication of God's judgment: **emptiness** (15:31), **his branch will not be green** (v. 32), the early loss of **grape** or **blossom** (v. 33), his **company** is **barren** (v. 34), and **conceive**, **give birth**, and **womb** (v. 35). Given what the reader knows about Job, this section ought to instill humility on the part of any person who seeks to pursue another with rebuke—and compassion for Job as one who endured not only the loss of his children but also the presumptuous, compounded, and condemning "comfort" of his friends.

16:1–17:16 *Job: Hope for a Sufferer.* Job begins by pointing out that his friends have failed as comforters (16:2–5), even though comfort was their original purpose for coming to him (see 2:11). He then describes the seeming paradox of his situation: God is the one who has brought these things upon him, and although others take this as a sign of his judgment, Job trusts that God can testify on his behalf (16:6–17:9). In the final section Job presents his friends with the consequential dilemma of their words: their condemnation leaves death as Job's only hope, but to long for death is to give up on any possibility of vindication and is no hope at all (17:10–16).

16:4–5 Job is not suggesting that he would act like his friends if the roles were reversed. He is trying to get his friends to put themselves in his place so that they will see how little comfort they are offering.

7[i][ch. 15:34]; See ch. 1:15-19
8[j]ch. 10:17; [Ruth 1:21] [k][Ps. 109:24]
9[l]ch. 18:4; Hos. 6:1; Amos 1:11 [m]ch. 30:21 [n]Ps. 35:16; 37:12; 112:10; Lam. 2:16; Acts 7:54
10[o]Ps. 22:13 [p]Ps. 3:7; Isa. 50:6; Lam. 3:30; Mic. 5:1; [1 Kgs. 22:24; Acts 23:2] [q]Ps. 35:15
12[r]Lam. 3:12; [ch. 7:20]
13[s]Jer. 50:29 [t]ch. 27:22 [u]ch. 20:25; [Lam. 2:11]
14[v]ch. 30:14 [w]ch. 15:26
15[x]See 2 Sam. 3:31 [y][Ps. 75:10] [z][Ps. 7:5]
16[a]See ch. 3:5
17[b]Isa. 53:9
18[c]Isa. 26:21; Ezek. 24:7 [d][Gen. 4:10]
19[e]Ps. 89:37; Rom. 1:9 [f][Ps. 148:1]
20[g][ch. 12:5]
21[h][ch. 31:35]
22[i]See ch. 10:21

Chapter 17

1[j][ch. 18:5, 6] [k][Ps. 88:3, 4]
2[l]1 Sam. 1:6, 7; [ch. 12:6]

6 "If I speak, my pain is not assuaged,
and if I forbear, how much of it leaves me?
7 Surely now God has worn me out;
[i]he has[1] made desolate all my company.
8 And he has shriveled me up,
which is [j]a witness against me,
and my [k]leanness has risen up against me;
it testifies to my face.
9 He has [l]torn me in his wrath [m]and hated me;
he has [n]gnashed his teeth at me;
my adversary sharpens his eyes against me.
10 Men have [o]gaped at me with their mouth;
they have [p]struck me insolently on the cheek;
they [q]mass themselves together against me.
11 God gives me up to the ungodly
and casts me into the hands of the wicked.
12 I was at ease, and he broke me apart;
he seized me by the neck and dashed me to pieces;
he set me up as his [r]target;
13 his [s]archers surround me.
He slashes open my kidneys [t]and does not spare;
he [u]pours out my gall on the ground.
14 He breaks me with [v]breach upon breach;
he [w]runs upon me like a warrior.
15 I have sewed [x]sackcloth upon my skin
and have laid [y]my strength [z]in the dust.
16 My face is red with weeping,
and on my eyelids is [a]deep darkness,
17 although there is no [b]violence in my hands,
and my prayer is pure.

18 "O earth, [c]cover not my blood,
and let my [d]cry find no resting place.
19 Even now, behold, my [e]witness is in heaven,
and he who testifies for me is [f]on high.
20 My friends [g]scorn me;
my eye pours out tears to God,
21 that he would [h]argue the case of a man with God,
as[2] a son of man does with his neighbor.
22 For when a few years have come
I shall go the way [i]from which I shall not return.

Job Continues: Where Then Is My Hope?

17
1 "My spirit is broken; my days are [j]extinct;
[k]the graveyard is ready for me.
2 Surely there are mockers about me,
and my eye dwells on their [l]provocation.

[1] Hebrew *you have*; also verse 8 [2] Hebrew *and*

16:8 To counter Eliphaz's description of the "fat" wicked person (15:27), Job points to his own **shriveled** and emaciated state. It **testifies** that God's hand is against him (cf. Ps. 6:2; 22:17; also linking the motif of hostile stares; see Job 16:10), but not that he is guilty (v. 17).

16:12–14 Job uses the imagery of warfare, and what happens to a city and its inhabitants when it is attacked or breached, to express how he feels broken open by God.

16:15 sewed sackcloth upon my skin. Job's constant grief is like a coarse cloth stitched to his skin, a reality of acute and unending pain. **laid my strength in the dust**. Lit., "buried my horn in the ground." The horn of an animal represents strength, power, and nobility. Every semblance of dignity and worth has been taken from Job.

16:16 deep darkness. Lit., "shadow of death." Job's gaunt eyes are those of a dying man.

16:19 Who is Job's **witness . . . in heaven** who **testifies** on his behalf? One of the "holy ones," derided by Eliphaz (5:1)? Job's tentative plea for an "arbiter" (9:33) grows in confidence here with the knowledge that God alone is the source of his suffering. So too will his realization grow that God alone is his

3 "Lay down a pledge for me with you;
who is there who will put up [m]security for me?
4 Since you have closed their hearts to understanding,
therefore you will not let them triumph.
5 He who informs against his friends to get a share of their property—
the [n]eyes of his children will fail.

6 "He has made me [o]a byword of the peoples,
and I am one before whom men spit.
7 My [p]eye has grown dim from vexation,
and all my members are like [q]a shadow.
8 The upright are [r]appalled at this,
and the innocent stirs himself up against the godless.
9 Yet the righteous holds to his way,
and he who has [s]clean hands grows stronger and stronger.
10 But you, [t]come on again, all of you,
and I shall not find a wise man among you.
11 My [u]days are past; my plans are broken off,
the desires of my heart.
12 They [v]make night into day:
'The light,' they say, 'is near to the darkness.'[1]
13 If I hope for [w]Sheol as [x]my house,
if I make my bed in darkness,
14 if I say to the pit, 'You are my father,'
and to the worm, 'My mother,' or 'My sister,'
15 where then is my hope?
Who will see my hope?
16 Will it go down to the bars of [w]Sheol?
Shall we [y]descend together [z]into the dust?"

Bildad Speaks: God Punishes the Wicked

18 Then [a]Bildad the Shuhite answered and said:

2 " How long will you [b]hunt for words?
Consider, and then we will speak.
3 Why are we counted as [c]cattle?
Why are we stupid in your sight?
4 You who [d]tear yourself in your anger,
shall the earth be forsaken for you,
or [e]the rock be removed out of its place?

5 "Indeed, [f]the light of the wicked is put out,
and the flame of his fire does not shine.

[1] The meaning of the Hebrew is uncertain

3[m]Ps. 119:122; Isa. 38:14; Heb. 7:22
5[n][ch. 11:20; 31:16]
6[o]ch. 30:9; Deut. 28:37; [Ps. 44:14; 69:11]
7[p][Ps. 6:7; 31:9] [q]See ch. 14:2
8[r]Isa. 52:14
9[s]See ch. 22:30
10[t]ch. 6:29
11[u]ch. 7:6; 9:25
12[v][ch. 11:17]
13[w]See ch. 21:13 [x][Eccles. 12:5]
16[w][See ver. 13 above] [y][ch. 3:17-19] [z]ch. 21:26; 40:13

Chapter 18

1[a]ch. 2:11; 8:1
2[b][Matt. 22:15; Mark 12:13; Luke 20:20]
3[c]Ps. 73:22
4[d]ch. 16:9 [e]ch. 14:18
5[f]ch. 21:17; Prov. 13:9; 20:20; 24:20; See Ps. 18:28

hope for vindication. This may not be clear to Job yet (thus 16:21 distinguishes the "witness" from God), but it will be so eventually; cf. 19:25.

17:5 Since vv. 1–4 are likely addressed to God (vv. 3–4 directly), in v. 5 Job may be asking God to remember what his friends have done, warning the friends of the consequences of such actions, or both. Many interpreters think that v. 5 quotes a proverb of the day, which if true bears a message similar to other warnings in the OT against being a false witness (see Deut. 19:18–19; Prov. 19:5, 9).

17:7 all my members. Job's entire body is exhausted from grief and pain; this summarizes his theme from 16:7–16.

17:10–16 In both lines of v. 12, Job appears to refer to the perspective of his friends: they argue that if he will simply repent, God will restore him and turn his **night into day** (see 5:17–27; 8:5–7; 11:13–20). However, Job argues that simply accepting the perspective of his friends would be to make his **bed in darkness** (17:13) because it would be a response void of the faith that trusts that God is both sovereign and just (and thus knows the truth) and of the **hope** (v. 15) that he will be vindicated by God. Throughout the dialogue in chs. 3–31, Job is essentially arguing God's character back to God from the belief that he is just. In so doing, Job the sufferer is structuring his lament as ultimately a posture of hope.

18:1–21 *Bildad: Punishment for the Wicked.* Like Eliphaz, Bildad omits any of the appeals to Job in his first response (see 8:5–7) and opens by venting his frustration (18:2–4): Who is Job to maintain his position and criticize the words of his friends? The remainder of Bildad's response is an unyielding description of the end of the wicked (vv. 5–21) that appears to be motivated as much by his reactive irritation as by any further desire to correct Job.

18:5–6 Bildad is likely responding to Job with the repeated images of the **light of the wicked** (**flame, lamp**) going **dark** (**put out, does not shine**)

6[g]ch. 10:22
7[h][ch. 5:13]
9[i]Ps. 140:5
11[j]ch. 15:21; 20:25; 27:20; 30:15; Jer. 6:25; 46:5; 49:29
12[k]Ps. 38:17
13[l]Isa. 14:30
14[m][Rev. 9:11]
15[n]See Ps. 11:6; Ezek. 38:22
16[o]ch. 29:19; Hos. 9:16 [p]ch. 14:2
17[q]Ps. 34:16; Prov. 10:7; [Ps. 109:13, 15]
18[r]ch. 10:21, 22
19[s]Isa. 14:22
20[t]Ps. 37:13; Jer. 50:27; Ezek. 21:25, 29; Obad. 12; [1 Sam. 26:10] [u][ch. 21:6]
21[v]Judg. 2:10; Jer. 9:3; 10:25; 1 Thess. 4:8; 2 Thess. 1:8

Chapter 19

3[w]Gen. 31:7

6 The light is [g]dark in his tent,
and his lamp above him is put out.
7 His strong steps are shortened,
and his [h]own schemes throw him down.
8 For he is cast into a net by his own feet,
and he walks on its mesh.
9 [i]A trap seizes him by the heel;
a snare lays hold of him.
10 A rope is hidden for him in the ground,
a trap for him in the path.
11 [j]Terrors frighten him on every side,
and chase him at his heels.
12 His strength is famished,
and calamity is [k]ready for his stumbling.
13 It consumes the parts of his skin;
[l]the firstborn of death consumes his limbs.
14 He is torn from the tent in which he trusted
and is brought to [m]the king of terrors.
15 In his tent dwells that which is none of his;
[n]sulfur is scattered over his habitation.
16 His [o]roots dry up beneath,
and his branches [p]wither above.
17 His [q]memory perishes from the earth,
and he has no name in the street.
18 [r]He is thrust from light into darkness,
and driven out of the world.
19 He has no [s]posterity or progeny among his people,
and no survivor where he used to live.
20 They of the west are appalled at his [t]day,
and [u]horror seizes them of the east.
21 Surely such are the dwellings of the unrighteous,
such is the place of him who [v]knows not God."

Job Replies: My Redeemer Lives

19 Then Job answered and said:

2 "How long will you torment me
and break me in pieces with words?
3 These [w]ten times you have cast reproach upon me;
are you not ashamed to wrong me?

to make the point that Job ought to take the "darkness" (see 17:12–13) as precisely such a warning (see also 18:18).

18:7–10 Bildad uses the vocabulary of a **trap** (**net**, **snare**, **rope**) in these verses to argue that what Job describes as God breaking him apart (see 16:7–14) is better described as Job suffering the consequences of his own sin (**his own schemes throw him down**, 18:7).

18:11–14 The vocabulary of these verses has led some interpreters to explain the references to the **firstborn of death** and the **king of terrors** as allusions to figures in either Babylonian or Ugaritic mythology. While it is difficult to discern whether such an allusion is intended, it is clear that Bildad is personifying the process and finality of death: calamity is wearing the wicked person (i.e., Job) down, which will lead ultimately to the finality of death itself (v. 14). When Bildad uses the phrase "the firstborn of death," he may be intentionally picking up the familial references from Job's response and turning them against him (see 17:14).

18:14–21 Bildad refers throughout this section to the destruction of both the house (e.g., **tent**, vv. 14–15; **habitation**, v. 15; **dwellings**, **place**, v. 21) and the household (**memory**, **name**, v. 17; **posterity**, **progeny**, and **survivor**, v. 19) of the wicked in order to assert that Job's circumstances show he is one **who knows not God** (v. 21).

19:1–29 *Job: My Redeemer Lives.* Job begins by asking his friends how long they will persist in accusing him and why they feel no shame for the manner in which they have done so. Even if he has done wrong, Job maintains that it is God who has brought about his circumstances (vv. 2–6). Job laments that although he cries out for justice, his continued suffering has brought only isolation and indifference from his family and friends (vv. 7–22). Job concludes with the wish that his belief in God's vindication of him would be inscribed in rock as a permanent witness (vv. 23–27) and with a warning to his friends against continuing to pursue him with such anger and certainty that they are right, lest they fall under the very sort of judgment they assume has fallen on Job (vv. 28–29).

19:2 How long . . . ? Job opens by echoing the question from the first line of each of Bildad's speeches (see 8:2; 18:2) to draw attention to how relentless his friends have been in condemning him.

19:3 Job uses the phrase **ten times** as a figure of speech indicating a full measure rather than 10 actual interchanges (see also Gen. 31:7, 41; Num. 14:22).

4 And even if it be true that I have erred,
my error remains with myself.
5 If indeed you [x]magnify yourselves against me
and make my disgrace an argument against me,
6 know then that God has [y]put me in the wrong
and closed his net about me.
7 Behold, I [z]cry out, 'Violence!' but I am not answered;
I call for help, but there is no justice.
8 He has [a]walled up my way, so that I cannot pass,
and he has set darkness upon my paths.
9 He has [b]stripped from me my glory
and taken the [c]crown from my head.
10 He breaks me down on every side, and I [d]am gone,
and my hope has he pulled up like a tree.
11 He has kindled his wrath against me
and [e]counts me as his adversary.
12 His [f]troops come on together;
they have [g]cast up their siege ramp[1] against me
and encamp around my tent.

13 "He has put my [h]brothers far from me,
and [i]those who knew me are wholly estranged from me.
14 My relatives [j]have failed me,
my close [k]friends have forgotten me.
15 The guests [l]in my house and my maidservants count me as a stranger;
I have become a foreigner in their eyes.
16 I call to my servant, but he gives me no answer;
I must plead with him with my mouth for mercy.
17 My breath is strange to my [m]wife,
and I am a stench to the children of [n]my own mother.
18 Even young [o]children despise me;
when I rise they talk against me.
19 All my [p]intimate friends abhor me,
and those whom I loved have turned against me.
20 My [q]bones stick to my skin and to my flesh,
and I have escaped by the skin of my teeth.
21 Have mercy on me, have mercy on me, O you my friends,
for the hand of God has [r]touched me!
22 Why do you, like God, [s]pursue me?
Why are you not satisfied with my flesh?

[1] Hebrew *their way*

5[x]Ps. 35:26; 38:16; 55:12
6[y][ch. 8:3; 34:12; Lam. 3:36]
7[z]ch. 24:12; Hab. 1:2; [Lam. 3:8]
8[a]Lam. 3:7, 9; Hos. 2:6; [ch. 3:23; 13:27]
9[b]Ps. 89:44 [c]Ps. 89:39; Lam. 5:16; [ch. 29:14]
10[d]ch. 27:21; [ch. 10:21; 14:20]
11[e]See ch. 13:24
12[f][ch. 10:17; 25:2] [g]ch. 30:12
13[h]Ps. 69:8; [ch. 6:15] [i][Ps. 31:11; 88:8, 18]
14[j]Ps. 38:11 [k]Ps. 55:13
15[l][Gen. 17:27; Matt. 10:36]
17[m]ch. 2:9 [n]ch. 3:10
18[o][2 Kgs. 2:23]
19[p][Ps. 41:9; 55:13, 14]
20[q]Ps. 102:5; [Lam. 4:8]
21[r]ch. 1:11; Isa. 53:4
22[s][Ps. 69:26]

19:6 The verb translated **put me in the wrong** is the same verb that Bildad used in 8:3 (translated as "to pervert"). Job uses this verb to make his point clear: even in the very protesting of his innocence, Job is affirming his belief that God is just, but he also continues to affirm that his suffering is not because of his sin and that God is the one who has ultimately allowed or brought it about.

19:7 I cry out, "Violence!" The prophet Habakkuk opens his oracle with a similar statement and complaint before God (see Hab. 1:2–4).

19:8 He has walled up my way. God's fence had at first kept trouble away from Job (1:10), but now it was a wall that gave Job no way of escape (cf. 3:23). The very scale of his suffering is, for Job, a sign of its divine origin.

19:13–19 Viewed apart from Job's suffering, these verses are a remarkable register of the social world of the ancient Israelite patriarch. Within Job's anguished state, he takes a complete inventory of his social isolation. An explicit link is also forged between the poetic dialogue and the story told in the prose frame; cf. v. 14 and 42:11.

19:20 Although **by the skin of my teeth** has become an idiomatic expression in English for just barely accomplishing or avoiding something, the intended referent of the Hebrew phrase is not so clear (i.e., what is meant by the "skin" of the teeth is difficult to determine). However, the general sense of the English phrase, which has typically been explained as having its origins from this verse in Job, fits the context well: Job's body bears the effects of both his emotional and physical suffering and gives witness to the fact that he has narrowly **escaped** his own death.

19:22 Why are you not satisfied with my flesh? If his friends were so convinced that Job had sinned and that his obvious physical suffering represented God's judgment, he asks them why they continue their relentless pursuit of him. From Job's perspective, his friends have chosen to use whatever

23[t]Isa. 30:8
24[u]Jer. 17:1
25[v]ch. 30:23 [w]Isa. 43:14; 44:6, 24; 49:7; [Gen. 48:16; Ps. 19:14; 103:4; 1 Thess. 1:10] [x]ch. 41:33
26[y]Ps. 17:15; 1 Cor. 13:12; 1 John 3:2
27[z][Prov. 27:2] [a][Ps. 73:26]
28[s][See ver. 22 above]
29[b]Eccles. 12:14; See Ps. 58:11

Chapter 20

1[c]ch. 2:11
2[d]ch. 4:13
4[e][Deut. 4:32]
5[f]Ps. 37:35, 36
6[g][Isa. 14:13, 14; Obad. 3, 4]

23 "Oh that my words were written!
Oh that they were [t]inscribed in a book!
24 Oh that with an iron [u]pen and lead
they were engraved in the rock forever!
25 For I [v]know that my [w]Redeemer lives,
and at the last he will stand upon the [x]earth.[1]
26 And after my skin has been thus destroyed,
yet in[2] my flesh I shall [y]see God,
27 whom I shall see for myself,
and my eyes shall behold, and not [z]another.
My heart [a]faints within me!
28 If you say, 'How we will [s]pursue him!'
and, 'The root of the matter is found in him,'
29 be afraid of the sword,
for wrath brings the punishment of the sword,
that you may know there is [b]a judgment."

Zophar Speaks: The Wicked Will Suffer

20 Then [c]Zophar the Naamathite answered and said:

2 "Therefore my [d]thoughts answer me,
because of my haste within me.
3 I hear censure that insults me,
and out of my understanding a spirit answers me.
4 Do you not know this from of old,
[e]since man was placed on earth,
5 [f]that the exulting of the wicked is short,
and the joy of the godless but for a moment?
6 [g]Though his height mount up to the heavens,
and his head reach to the clouds,

[1] Hebrew *dust* [2] Or *without*

he has left as means to torment him (see v. 2), and he is pleading that they might show him mercy (see v. 21).

19:23–24 Job wishes that his **words** could be recorded as a witness that would remain when he is dead. He refers to two methods of recording that were common in the ancient Near East. **inscribed in a book**. This process could refer either to writing in a scroll or book or to an inscription on a clay tablet, all of which represent writing materials that would have been more or less portable. **engraved in the rock**. Job also wishes that his words could be inscribed in a more public and permanent fashion. An example of this type of monument is preserved in the inscription of Darius I at Behistun (modern Bisitun, in western Iran), on which the cuneiform signs were inlaid with **lead** in order to facilitate the reading of the inscription from the road below. Although it is not commented on explicitly in the book itself, the writing of the book of Job is in many respects a fulfillment of his wish in a way that both includes and extends beyond the purposes Job had in mind.

19:25–27 For. Job is stating here the grounds for wishing that his words would be recorded (vv. 23–24). **I know that my Redeemer lives** (v. 25). The Hebrew noun (*go'el*) translated "Redeemer" is the same word used frequently in the OT to refer to a "kinsman-redeemer," who had both rights and responsibilities for vindicating a family member (see Ruth 4:1–6). In the OT, God says that he will "redeem" his people from slavery (Ex. 6:6) and is thus later referred to as "the Redeemer of Israel" (Isa. 43:14; 44:6). For God as an individual's "Redeemer," see Gen. 48:16; Ps. 19:14 (and see note on Ps. 25:22). Job's description of his "Redeemer" as one who "lives" (Job 19:25) and his following reference to "God" (v. 26) indicate he believes that God is the one who ultimately will vindicate him. **yet in my flesh I shall see God** (v. 26), **whom I shall see for myself** (v. 27). Because of the content of Job's earlier laments and the difficulty of the Hebrew in v. 26, interpreters have questioned the likelihood that Job is expressing in these verses a belief that God will redeem him after death. However, while the focus of Job's dialogue and lament is the desire that what he believes to be true "in heaven" (i.e., before God) would also be shown to be true on earth, such a desire makes sense only if it is grounded in a belief that God is his Redeemer and that he will vindicate Job even in death.

19:28–29 Job tells his friends their certainty that **the root of the matter is found in him** has led them to pursue him in **wrath**. Job uses the image of the **sword** to refer to passing **judgment** and to warn the friends against their presumption that they can understand, and actually wield, the sword of judgment that belongs to God alone. In calling his friends to be careful how they judge him lest they fall under the punishment of the very sword they presume to wield, Job suggests something similar to what Jesus will teach explicitly in the Sermon on the Mount (see Matt. 7:1–5).

19:29 wrath brings the punishment of the sword. The wrath of the friends is a "crime of the sword," a sin deserving of punishment (cf. 31:11, 28). False testimony demands the same penalty that would have been given the accused (Deut. 19:16–19); the accusations of the friends were worthy of death. **know there is a judgment**. The Hebrew for this line is elliptical; it seems to mean either that there is a judge or that there is a judgment, as the ESV renders. The appearance of the Redeemer, says Job, would be bad news for his friends.

20:1–29 *Zophar: The Wicked Will Die.* In his second response, Zophar opens with a brief expression of frustration (vv. 2–3), presumably in response to Job's insistence that God has brought about his circumstances and Job's belief that God will yet vindicate him. The remainder of the response is one long description of the short and insufferable life of the wicked, by which Zophar intends to implicate and rebuke Job (vv. 4–29).

20:3 censure that insults me. Zophar may be referring to Job's response to his last speech, in which Job sarcastically criticized his friends and claimed that he was not their inferior (see 12:2–3).

20:6–7 Zophar warns Job that whatever **height** a wicked man may have achieved will not change the fact that, when his end comes, it will be

7 he will perish forever like his own [h]dung;
those who have seen him will say, [i]'Where is he?'
8 He will fly away like [j]a dream and not be found;
he will be chased away like a vision of the night.
9 [k]The eye that saw him will see him no more,
nor will his place any more behold him.
10 His children will seek the favor of the poor,
and his hands will [l]give back his wealth.
11 His bones are full of his [m]youthful vigor,
but it will lie [n]down with him in the dust.

12 "Though evil is sweet in his mouth,
though he hides it [o]under his tongue,
13 though he is loath to let it go
and holds it in his mouth,
14 yet his food is turned in his stomach;
it is the venom of [p]cobras within him.
15 He swallows down riches and vomits them up again;
God casts them out of his belly.
16 He will suck the poison of cobras;
[q]the tongue of a viper will kill him.
17 He will not look upon [r]the rivers,
the streams flowing with [s]honey and [t]curds.
18 He will [u]give back the fruit of his toil
and will not [v]swallow it down;
from the profit of his trading
he will get no enjoyment.
19 For he has crushed and abandoned the poor;
he has seized a house that he did not build.

20 "Because he [w]knew no [x]contentment in his belly,
[y]he will not let anything in which he delights escape him.
21 There was nothing left after he had eaten;
therefore his prosperity will not endure.
22 In the fullness of his sufficiency he will be in distress;
the hand of everyone in misery will come against him.
23 To fill his belly to the full,
God[1] will send his burning anger against him
and rain it upon him [z]into his body.
24 [a]He will flee from an iron weapon;
[b]a bronze arrow will strike [c]him through.
25 It [d]is drawn forth and comes out of his body;
[e]the glittering point comes out of his [f]gallbladder;
[g]terrors come upon him.
26 Utter darkness is laid up for his treasures;
[h]a fire not fanned will devour him;
what is left in his tent will be consumed.

[1] Hebrew *he*

7 [h]Ps. 83:10; Zeph. 1:17; [1 Kgs. 14:10; 2 Kgs. 9:37] [i]ch. 14:10
8 [j]Ps. 73:20; 90:5; Isa. 29:7, 8
9 [k]See ch. 7:8, 10
10 [l]ver. 18
11 [m][ch. 13:26; Ps. 25:7] [n]ch. 21:26
12 [o]Ps. 10:7
14 [p]Deut. 32:33; Ps. 140:3
16 [q]Isa. 59:5; [Prov. 23:32]
17 [r][Ps. 36:8; Jer. 17:6] [s][Deut. 32:13, 14] [t][ch. 29:6]
18 [u]ver. 10 [v]ver. 15
20 [w]Isa. 59:8 [x]Prov. 17:1 [y][Eccles. 5:13, 14]
23 [z][Num. 11:33; Ps. 78:30, 31]
24 [a][Isa. 24:18; Jer. 48:44; Amos 5:19] [b]2 Sam. 22:35 [c]Judg. 5:26
25 [d]Judg. 3:22 [e]Deut. 32:41 [f]ch. 16:13 [g]See ch. 18:11
26 [h][ch. 15:34; Ps. 21:9]

quick and complete. **"Where is he?"** Zophar may be recasting the question Job asked in 14:10 as what could well be ironically and justifiably spoken about Job if he does not pull back from his insistence that he is innocent.

20:10–21 Zophar argues that neither the wicked man (vv. 12–19) nor his offspring (v. 10) will enjoy the benefits of what he has acquired, because he has gained it through the oppression of others (vv. 19–21). Instead, his **children** will be forced to beg from the **poor** (v. 10), who were some of the very people their father oppressed to gain his wealth (v. 19). The description also includes several images that describe the way of the wicked as something like gluttony: their hunger for **evil** is unrestrained and insatiable (vv. 12, 13, 20, 21), which leads to whatever has been gained instead rotting them from the inside out (vv. 14–16).

20:23–25 Although Job had referred to his circumstances as equivalent to God attacking and breaking him open (see 16:12–14), Zophar uses similar imagery of sword and **arrow** to assert that it is God who will indeed strike the wicked with the wrath of his judgment. Zophar is likely hinting that Job ought to take his own description of feeling "broken open" as an indication of God's impending judgment rather than of any injustice from God.

27 [i]The heavens will reveal his iniquity,
and the earth will rise up against him.
28 The possessions of his house will be carried away,
dragged off in the day of God's[1] wrath.
29 [j]This is the wicked man's portion from God,
[j] the heritage decreed for him by God."

Job Replies: The Wicked Do Prosper

21 Then Job answered and said:

2 [k]"Keep listening to my words,
and let this be your comfort.
3 Bear with me, and I will speak,
and after I have spoken, [l]mock on.
4 As for me, is my [m]complaint against man?
Why should I not be impatient?
5 Look at me and be appalled,
and [n]lay your hand over your mouth.
6 When I remember, I am dismayed,
and shuddering seizes my flesh.
7 [o]Why do the wicked live,
reach old age, and grow mighty in power?
8 Their [p]offspring are established in their presence,
and their descendants before their eyes.
9 Their houses are [q]safe from fear,
and [r]no rod of God is upon them.
10 Their bull breeds without fail;
their cow calves and [s]does not miscarry.
11 They send out their [t]little boys like a flock,
and their children dance.
12 They sing to [u]the tambourine and [v]the lyre
and rejoice to the sound of [v]the pipe.
13 They [w]spend their days in prosperity,
and in [x]peace they go down to [y]Sheol.
14 They say to God, [z]'Depart from us!
We do not desire the knowledge of your ways.
15 [a]What is the Almighty, that we should serve him?
And what [b]profit do we get if we pray to him?'
16 Behold, is not their prosperity in their hand?
[c]The counsel of the wicked is far from me.

17 "How often is it that [d]the lamp of the wicked is put out?
That their calamity comes upon them?
That God[2] distributes pains in his anger?

[1] Hebrew *his* [2] Hebrew *he*

27 [i][ch. 16:18, 19]
29 [j]ch. 27:13; [ch. 18:21; 31:2, 3]

Chapter 21
2 [k]ch. 13:17
3 [l][ch. 16:10, 20; 17:2]
4 [m]ch. 10:1; 23:2
5 [n]ch. 29:9; 40:4; Judg. 18:19
7 [o]ch. 12:6; Ps. 17:14; 37:1, 35; 73:3, 5; 92:7; Eccles. 8:14; Jer. 12:1, 2; Hab. 1:13, 16; Mal. 3:14, 15
8 [p][ch. 5:25]
9 [q][ch. 5:24] [r]See ch. 9:34
10 [s]Ex. 23:26
11 [t][Ps. 17:14]
12 [u]Ex. 15:20 [v]ch. 30:31; Gen. 4:21
13 [w]ch. 36:11 [x]ch. 34:20; [ch. 24:19] [y]ch. 7:9; 14:13; 17:13; See Ps. 16:10
14 [z]ch. 22:17
15 [a][Ex. 5:2] [b]See ch. 34:9
16 [c]ch. 22:18; [Ps. 1:1]
17 [d]See ch. 18:5, 6

20:27 The heavens . . . and the earth. Although it is not his purpose, Zophar hints here at the central tension of the book: what is the relationship between what is true before God and what takes place on earth? The friends wrongly assume that Job's circumstances on earth are a transparent indicator of his guilt before God in heaven. Job has governed his life by a belief that God is indeed just, and his lament reflects his desire that God's justice would be manifested more than it is in his present life on earth. In the end, Zophar will realize that what the heavens **will reveal** is his own error, not Job's **iniquity** (see 42:7–9).

21:1–34 *Job: The Wicked Prosper.* Job's response closes the second cycle of the dialogue with his friends by focusing directly on the assertion that *the wicked suffer immediate and lasting grief*, which is at the heart of the argument of each of his friends and is the thrust of Zophar's most recent response (see ch. 20). Job argues that the wicked do not self-destruct in their greed but rather live in grand style, and are respected and honored in death (21:7–21, 27–34). In the midst of his response, Job questions whether his friends truly understand life on earth; he does this in a manner that makes it seem as if God needs to be instructed (vv. 22–26).

21:7–16 Job argues not only that the **wicked** prosper and their **offspring** flourish (vv. 7–8), but also that their lives often appear unhindered by any of the signs of judgment that the friends so confidently describe (vv. 9–13)—a perspective that shares much with Psalm 73. Furthermore, Job points out that the evidence for what he is claiming is not even concealed by the wicked themselves, who choose to follow their pursuits with open indifference to and even proclaimed defiance against the Lord (Job 21:14–16).

21:17–21 Job challenges Bildad's earlier assertion that **the lamp of the wicked is put out** (see 18:5–6) by asking how often this is true (21:17–18). Furthermore, Job's friends have argued that God's judgment of the wicked

18 That they are like [e]straw before the wind,
and like [f]chaff that the storm carries away?
19 You say, 'God [g]stores up their iniquity for their [h]children.'
Let him pay it out to them, that they may [i]know it.
20 Let their own eyes see their destruction,
and let them [j]drink of the wrath of the Almighty.
21 For what do they care for their houses after them,
when [k]the number of their months is cut off?
22 [l]Will any teach God knowledge,
seeing that he [m]judges those who are on high?
23 One dies in his full vigor,
being wholly at ease and secure,
24 his pails[1] full of milk
and [n]the marrow of his bones moist.
25 Another dies in [o]bitterness of soul,
never having tasted of prosperity.
26 They [p]lie down alike in the dust,
and [q]the worms cover them.

27 "Behold, I know your thoughts
and your schemes to wrong me.
28 For you say, [r]'Where is the house of the prince?
Where is [s]the tent in which the wicked lived?'
29 Have you not asked those who travel the roads,
and do you not accept their testimony
30 that [t]the evil man is spared in the day of calamity,
that he is rescued in the day of wrath?
31 Who declares his way [u]to his face,
and who [v]repays him for what he has done?
32 When he is [w]carried to the grave,
watch is kept over his tomb.
33 [x]The clods of the valley are sweet to him;
[y]all mankind follows after him,
and those who go before him are innumerable.
34 How then will you comfort me with empty nothings?
There is nothing left of your answers but falsehood."

Eliphaz Speaks: Job's Wickedness Is Great

22 Then [z]Eliphaz the Temanite answered and said:

2 [a]"Can a man be profitable to God?
Surely he who is wise is profitable to himself.

[1] The meaning of the Hebrew word is uncertain

18 [e]ch. 13:25; Ps. 83:13 [f]Ps. 1:4; 35:5; Isa. 17:13; 29:5
19 [g]ch. 15:20 [h]Ex. 20:5 [i]Isa. 9:9; Ezek. 25:14; Hos. 9:7
20 [j]Ps. 60:3; 75:8; Isa. 51:17, 22; Jer. 25:15; Obad. 16; Rev. 14:10
21 [k]ch. 14:5
22 [l]Isa. 40:14; Rom. 11:34; 1 Cor. 2:16 [m][ch. 4:18; 15:15]
24 [n]Prov. 3:8; [Isa. 58:11; 66:14]
25 [o]See ch. 7:11
26 [p]ch. 20:11; [Eccles. 9:2] [q]Isa. 14:11
28 [r][ch. 20:6, 7] [s][ch. 8:22; 15:34]
30 [t][Prov. 16:4; 2 Pet. 2:9]
31 [u]Deut. 7:10; Hos. 5:5; Gal. 2:11 [v]Deut. 7:10
32 [w]ch. 10:19
33 [x]ch. 38:38 [y][ch. 30:23; Heb. 9:27]

Chapter 22

1 [z]ch. 2:11
2 [a]See ch. 35:7

falls also on the **children** of the wicked (cf. 20:10), but Job replies that, if the wicked person does not **see**, **drink**, and **know** his own punishment, it has little effect as judgment, because he is dead and without care for what happens after him (21:19–21).

21:22 In previous speeches, Eliphaz had asked how Job could presume to be in the right when God judges even the heavenly beings (see 4:18; 15:15). Here Job recasts the truth of Eliphaz's assertion so as to question the approach of his friends: their presuming to discern events on earth as transparent indicators of judgment contradicts the facts of experience in such a way as to suggest that **God** needs to be reminded or instructed in their **knowledge**. However, since God is the judge of **those who are on high** and unseen, the friends should be all the more cautious of presuming to discern exhaustively what God's purposes are simply based upon what they see on earth.

21:33 all mankind follows after him. In addition to the argument that a person's circumstances are not necessarily a transparent indicator of blessing or judgment, there is an additional warning embedded in Job's description: many people are fooled by the external circumstances of the evil man (who is the subject of this description, see v. 30ff.) into following him in life and honoring him in death.

22:1–25:6 *Third Cycle.* The consistent pattern of the first two cycles unravels in this last dialogue. Eliphaz begins by depicting Job's life as a constant stream of wicked activity (ch. 22), in contrast to the perception Job offered in his first speech (cf. 4:6–7). Job's reply (chs. 23–24) strongly implies that the divine power that has touched him is typically capricious and destructive. Bildad offers the beginning of a reply (ch. 25, only six verses), before Job interrupts with a further assertion of the impenetrable mystery of divine power (ch. 26, beginning Job's final reply to his friends). No room appears in this cycle for a contribution from Zophar. If there was any comfort in the friends' attending to Job, it has entirely evaporated. The two parties have argued themselves increasingly apart, revising earlier judgments as they do so.

22:1–30 *Eliphaz: Job Is Guilty.* In his final speech, launching the uniquely shaped third cycle, Eliphaz revisits earlier themes with renewed fervor and final-

3 Is it any pleasure to the Almighty if you are in the right,
or is it gain to him if you [b]make your ways blameless?
4 Is it for your fear of him that he reproves you
and [c]enters into judgment with you?
5 Is not your evil abundant?
There is no end to your iniquities.
6 For you have [d]exacted pledges of your brothers for nothing
[e]and stripped the naked of their clothing.
7 You have given no water to the weary to drink,
and you have [f]withheld bread from the hungry.
8 [g]The man with power possessed the land,
and [h]the favored man lived in it.
9 You have [i]sent widows away empty,
and [j]the arms of [k]the fatherless were crushed.
10 Therefore [l]snares are all around you,
and sudden terror overwhelms you,
11 or [m]darkness, so that you cannot see,
and a [n]flood of [o]water covers you.

12 "Is not God high in the heavens?
See [p]the highest stars, how lofty they are!
13 But you say, [q]'What does God know?
Can he judge through [r]the deep darkness?
14 [s]Thick clouds veil him, so that he does not see,
and he walks on the vault of heaven.'
15 Will you keep to the old way
that wicked men have trod?
16 They were snatched away [t]before their time;
their foundation was washed away.
17 They said to God, [u]'Depart from us,'
and [v]'What can the Almighty do to us?'[1]
18 Yet he filled their houses with good things—
but [w]the counsel of the wicked is far from me.
19 [x]The righteous see it and are glad;
the innocent one [y]mocks at them,
20 saying, 'Surely our adversaries are cut off,
and what they left [z]the fire has consumed.'

3 [b]See Ps. 18:32
4 [c]ch. 14:3; [Ps. 143:2]
6 [d]ch. 24:3, 9; Ex. 22:26; Deut. 24:6, 17; Ezek. 18:12, 16 [e][ch. 31:16]
7 [f][ch. 31:17; Isa. 58:7; Ezek. 18:7, 16; Matt. 25:42]
8 [g][ch. 35:9] [h]2 Kgs. 5:1; Isa. 9:15
9 [i][Luke 1:53] [j][ch. 38:15] [k]ch. 31:21; Isa. 10:2; Ezek. 22:7
10 [l]ch. 18:8-10
11 [m][Ex. 10:22, 23] [n]ch. 38:34 [o][ch. 27:20; Ps. 69:1, 2, 14, 15; 124:5; Lam. 3:54; Jonah 2:3, 5]
12 [p][ch. 11:8]
13 [q]Ps. 73:11; [Ps. 10:11; 59:7; 64:5; 94:7; Isa. 29:15; Ezek. 8:12; 9:9] [r]ch. 38:9
14 [s][Ps. 139:11, 12]; [Prov. 8:27; Isa. 40:22]
16 [t]See ch. 15:32
17 [u]ch. 21:14 [v][Ps. 4:6]
18 [w]ch. 21:16
19 [x]Ps. 52:6; 58:10; 107:42; [Ps. 64:10] [y]Ps. 2:4
20 [z]ch. 1:16

[1] Hebrew *them*

ity: he questions whether Job has any basis to lament before God (vv. 2–4), asserts again that Job's circumstances reveal his abundant evil (vv. 4–11), compares Job's words to those of the wicked (vv. 12–20), and calls him once more to repent so that he might find his ways established by God (vv. 21–30).

22:2–4 Eliphaz opens his response with three rhetorical questions that ask Job whether it makes any sense that God would bring suffering on one who is **wise** (v. 2), **blameless** (v. 3), or who fears him (v. 4). Eliphaz argues that, since wisdom is **profitable** for the person and not somehow profitable for God (vv. 2–3), there could be no purpose for suffering other than to indicate judgment and a need to repent (v. 4). In framing his response this way, Eliphaz inverts Job's own earlier reasoning that any sin of his could be of no consequence to so great a God (7:20). He also continues to assert that Job's circumstances on earth are transparent and exhaustive indicators that can and ought to be read only as signs of God's judgment.

22:5–11 Eliphaz assumes that Job's circumstances reveal significant **evil** in his life, and thus he feels justified in describing the likely ways that Job has sinned.

22:6 Eliphaz's first accusation evokes the law that a person should not take someone else's life necessities to secure a debt—like a cloak (see Ex. 22:26; Deut. 24:17–18) or a mill or millstone used to grind grain for food (see Deut. 24:6).

22:9 In his description of Job's presumed mistreatment of **widows** and **the fatherless**, Eliphaz speaks in terms similar to the warnings in the law against such practices (see Ex. 22:22; Deut. 24:17) and to prophetic oracles of judgment (see Isa. 1:17; Jer. 22:3; Ezek. 22:7).

22:13 In response to Job's continued insistence that the wicked prosper on earth and that his circumstances are not the consequences of sin, Eliphaz asserts that Job is guilty of implying that God is so high that he is unable to "know" or **judge** life on earth. A question similar to the one that Eliphaz puts in Job's mouth here (**What does God know?**) is used of the wicked in Ps. 73:11, but it comes amid a lament over their prosperity and safety that is itself similar to Job's complaint (see Ps. 73:1–17). Eliphaz wrongly equates Job's attitude toward God with that of the wicked.

22:17–18 In these verses Eliphaz essentially quotes some of Job's words from 21:14–16. However, where Job was arguing that the wicked prosper in spite of open rebellion, Eliphaz is asserting that their prosperity and rebellion are momentary and that the wicked are "snatched away before their time" (22:16). Thus, when Job said, "the counsel of the wicked is far from me" (21:16b) in order to distance himself from the rebellion and practices of which his friends accused him, Eliphaz uses the same words to cast Job's position on these matters as itself **the counsel of the wicked** (22:18).

21 [a]"Agree with God, and [b]be at peace;
thereby good will come to you.
22 Receive instruction from [c]his mouth,
and [d]lay up his words in your heart.
23 If you [e]return to the Almighty you will be [f]built up;
if you [g]remove injustice far from your tents,
24 if you lay gold in [h]the dust,
and gold of [i]Ophir among the stones of the torrent-bed,
25 then the Almighty will be your gold
and your precious silver.
26 For then you [j]will delight yourself in the Almighty
and [k]lift up your face to God.
27 You will [l]make your prayer to him, and he will hear you,
and you will [m]pay your vows.
28 You will decide on a matter, and it will be established for you,
and [n]light will shine on your ways.
29 For when they are humbled you say, 'It is because of pride';[1]
but he saves [o]the lowly.
30 He [p]delivers even the one who is not innocent,
who will be delivered through [q]the cleanness of your hands."

Job Replies: Where Is God?

23

Then Job answered and said:

2 "Today also my [r]complaint is bitter;[2]
my [s]hand is heavy on account of my groaning.
3 Oh, [t]that I knew where I might find him,
that I might come even to his [u]seat!
4 I would [v]lay my case before him
and fill my mouth with arguments.
5 I would know what he would answer me
and understand what he would say to me.
6 Would he [w]contend with me in the greatness of his power?
No; he would pay attention to me.
7 There an upright man could argue with him,
and I would be acquitted forever by my judge.

8 "Behold, [x]I go forward, but he is not there,
and backward, but I do not perceive him;
9 on the left hand when he is working, I do not behold him;
he turns to the right hand, but I do not see him.

[1] *Or you say, 'It is exaltation'* [2] *Or defiant*

21 [a]See Ps. 119:45 [b][Prov. 3:2]
22 [c]Prov. 2:6; [Mal. 2:7] [d]Ps. 119:11
23 [e][ch. 8:5, 6; 11:13, 14; Mal. 3:7] [f]Jer. 24:6; 33:7 [g]ch. 11:14
24 [h]ch. 20:11; 21:26 [i]See 1 Kgs. 9:28
26 [j]ch. 27:10; Ps. 37:4; Isa. 58:14 [k]See ch. 11:15
27 [l]ch. 33:26; Ps. 50:14, 15; Isa. 58:9 [m]Ps. 50:14
28 [n]Prov. 4:18
29 [o]Ps. 138:6; Prov. 3:34; 29:23; Matt. 23:12; Luke 1:52; James 4:6; 1 Pet. 5:5
30 [p][Gen. 18:26] [q]ch. 17:9; Ps. 18:20, 24; 24:4; 26:6; [ch. 9:30]

Chapter 23

2 [r]ch. 10:1; 21:4 [s][Ps. 32:4]
3 [t][ch. 13:3; 16:21] [u][Ps. 9:7, 8; Isa. 57:15, 16]
4 [v]See ch. 33:5
6 [w][ch. 9:34; 13:21]
8 [x]ch. 9:11; 35:14

22:21 Implicit in the plea for Job to "**Agree with God**" is Eliphaz's presumption that his interpretation of Job's circumstances is equivalent to God's. In particular, it seems Eliphaz thinks his argument in vv. 17–18 should be a compelling enough reason for Job to relent and finally agree that his suffering is rooted in his wickedness.

22:30 This verse is another instance of unintended irony in the words of the friends. Eliphaz is suggesting that Job's repentance would lead to his being able to intercede and bring deliverance even for **one who is not innocent**. What Eliphaz does not know is that he stands in need of the very deliverance he describes and that it will in fact come through Job's intercession on his behalf (see 42:7–9).

23:1–24:25 *Job: God Is Hidden.* Job is tired of arguing his case before his friends, which is revealed in part by the way he largely ignores the content of Eliphaz's most recent response. Instead, he expresses his longing to be able to come before God directly, because Job trusts that his ways are truly known and would be vindicated by God (23:1–17). In the second part of the speech, Job laments that judgment does not appear to come more evidently on those who oppress the needy for their own gain (24:1–25).

23:2 The opening phrase of Job's response is probably directed at his friends more than at God. When he begins with "**Today also . . .**" Job is implying that after all of the dialogue with his friends they have neither attended to him well nor persuaded him of his guilt. **my hand is heavy**. Although it is not typically stated in this manner, the images of the hand "being strengthened" (e.g., Isa. 35:3) or "falling" (e.g., Jer. 6:24) are used in the OT to refer respectively to a person being either encouraged or discouraged.

23:3–7 The last time Job used this kind of legal language, he was convinced that God would both ignore and condemn him (cf. 9:3, 16, 19). Here, his convictions are just the opposite: if Job were granted an audience, God would **pay attention** (23:6), and Job would be **acquitted** (v. 7).

23:10–12 In his wish to present a case before God, Job refers to the manner of his life in vocabulary typical of the wisdom literature. He trusts that God

10 But he [y]knows [z]the way that I [a]take;
when he has [b]tried me, I shall come out as gold.
11 My foot [c]has held fast to his steps;
I have kept his way and have [d]not turned aside.
12 I have not departed from the commandment of his lips;
I have [e]treasured the words of his mouth more than my [f]portion of food.
13 But he is unchangeable,[1] and [g]who can turn him back?
What he [h]desires, that he does.
14 For he will complete what he [i]appoints for me,
and many such things are [j]in his mind.
15 Therefore I am terrified at his presence;
when I consider, I am in dread of him.
16 God has made my [k]heart faint;
the Almighty has terrified me;
17 yet I am not silenced because of the darkness,
nor because thick darkness covers my face.

24

1 "Why are [l]not times of judgment [m]kept by the Almighty,
and why do those who know him never see his [n]days?
2 Some move [o]landmarks;
they seize flocks and pasture them.
3 They drive away the donkey of the fatherless;
they [p]take the widow's ox for a pledge.
4 They [q]thrust the poor off the road;
the poor of the earth [r]all hide themselves.
5 Behold, like wild donkeys in the desert
the poor[2] [s]go out to their toil, [t]seeking game;
the wasteland yields food for their children.
6 They gather their[3] fodder in the field,
and they glean the vineyard of the wicked man.
7 They [u]lie all night naked, without clothing,
and have no covering in the cold.
8 They are wet with the rain of the mountains
and [v]cling to the rock for lack of shelter.
9 (There are those who snatch the fatherless child from the breast,
and they take a pledge against the poor.)

10 [y]Ps. 139:1-3 [z]Ps. 139:24 [a][ch. 9:35] [b]Ps. 17:3; 26:2; 66:10; 139:23; Zech. 13:9; Mal. 3:3; 1 Pet. 1:7; Rev. 3:18; [James 1:12]
11 [c]Ps. 17:5; 44:18 [d]Ps. 125:5
12 [e][Ps. 119:11] [f][Ps. 119:103; John 4:32, 34]
13 [g][ch. 9:12; 12:14] [h]Ps. 115:3
14 [i][1 Thess. 3:3] [j][ch. 10:13; 27:11]
16 [k]Deut. 20:3; [Ps. 22:14]

Chapter 24

1 [l]Eccles. 9:12; Isa. 13:22; Jer. 27:7; Ezek. 22:3; 30:3 [m]ch. 15:20 [n]Isa. 2:12; 13:6, 9; Joel 1:15; 2:1; Amos 5:18; See ch. 18:20
2 [o]See Deut. 19:14
3 [p]See ch. 22:6
4 [q]Amos 2:7; 5:12; Mal. 3:5 [r]Prov. 28:28; [ch. 30:5, 6]
5 [s]Ps. 104:23 [t]Ps. 104:21
7 [u][Ex. 22:26, 27; Deut. 24:12, 13]
8 [v]Lam. 4:5

[1] Or *one* [2] Hebrew *they* [3] Hebrew *his*

knows the way that he has walked (v. 10): Job has persevered in God's **steps**, he has **not turned aside** from **his way** (v. 11), and he has valued God's **commandment** and **the words of his mouth** more than provision for his own physical well-being (v. 12).

23:13–17 Although he has carefully considered his way (vv. 10–12), Job believes it is ultimately God who will bring about his purposes through what he **appoints** (vv. 13–14; for similar statements, see Prov. 16:1, 9; 20:24; Jer. 10:23). Consequently, Job confesses that he is **terrified** at the thought of God's **presence** (Job 23:15–16). Still, even in the **darkness** of not being able to understand his path or God's purposes fully, he is compelled to continue his lament: **yet I am not silenced** (v. 17).

24:1–25 Job has persisted in arguing against his friends' assertion that the wicked are judged transparently and immediately on earth, but he also clings to his belief in the justice of God as the ground for his lament and hope for vindication. In this part of his speech, Job wishes that God's governing of the world would be more apparent (v. 1). He offers a further description of the acts of the wicked (vv. 2–4, 9, 13–17, 21), the consequences on their victims (vv. 5–12), the seeming blindness of his friends to this reality (vv. 18–20), and the lack of any apparent judgment (vv. 22–25). Job does not address God in this response, nor does he seem necessarily to be responding directly to his friends as much as he is speaking exhaustedly in their presence.

24:1 Job asks a question that represents two perspectives: **Why** is it that the wicked do not seem to experience **times of judgment** and that the righteous **never see his days?** "The day of the Lord" is a common phrase in the OT that refers to the coming judgment of the Lord on the nations (see Joel 2:1ff.; cf. note on Amos 5:18–20), but also represents the full revealing of God's glory and the restored beauty of his people. A "day of the Lord" is an occasion on which God the Almighty shows his hand.

24:2–12 Job's description of the injustices of the wicked (vv. 2–4) and the effects on their victims (vv. 5–12) appears to emphasize the severity and visibility of these things, which ought to be evident to observers on earth as well as to God. The conclusion in v. 12, that God ignores these evils, is precisely opposite the conclusion drawn in a passage with similar concerns, Lam. 3:31–36.

24:9 Some interpreters have suggested that the Hebrew word translated "**against**" in the second line (*'al*) should be understood instead as "child" (*'ul*), with the sense "they take the child of the poor as a pledge," because it would be more consistent with the focus on the **fatherless child** in the first line. However, the translation "against" does not exclude the possibility that the second line may refer to a child being taken as a pledge, neither does it require it as the sole referent. Still, v. 3 and vv. 10–12 seem to suggest that what was taken in pledge was the means by which the poor family could

10 They go about naked, without clothing;
hungry, they [w]carry the sheaves;
11 among the olive rows of the wicked[1] they make oil;
they tread the winepresses, but suffer thirst.
12 From out of the city the dying groan,
and the soul of [x]the wounded cries for help;
yet God charges no one with [y]wrong.

13 "There are those who rebel [z]against the light,
who are not acquainted with its ways,
and do not stay in its paths.
14 The murderer rises before it is light,
that he [a]may kill the poor and needy,
and in the night he is like a thief.
15 The eye of the adulterer also waits for [b]the twilight,
saying, 'No [c]eye will see me';
and he veils his face.
16 In the dark they [d]dig through houses;
by day they shut themselves up;
they do not know the light.
17 For [e]deep darkness is morning to all of them;
for they are friends with the terrors of deep darkness.

18 "You say, [f]'Swift are they on the face of the waters;
their portion is cursed in the land;
no treader turns toward their vineyards.
19 Drought and heat snatch away the snow waters;
so does [g]Sheol those who have sinned.
20 The womb forgets them;
the worm finds them sweet;
they are [h]no longer remembered,
so wickedness is broken like [i]a tree.'

21 "They wrong the barren, childless woman,
and do no good to the widow.
22 Yet God[2] prolongs the life of the mighty by his power;
they rise up when they despair of life.

[1] Hebrew *their olive rows* [2] Hebrew *he*

10[w][2 Tim. 2:6; James 5:4]
12[x]Jer. 51:52; Ezek. 30:24 [y]ch. 1:22
13[z]John 3:19, 20
14[a][Ps. 10:8]
15[b]Prov. 7:9 [c]Ps. 10:11
16[d]Ex. 22:2; Matt. 6:20; [ch. 31:9]
17[e]See ch. 3:5
18[f][ch. 9:26; Hos. 10:7]
19[g]See ch. 21:13
20[h][Prov. 10:7] [i][ch. 18:16]

have been clothed and fed (which, of course, would be equivalent in its effects to taking a child from a nursing mother).

24:13–17 These verses are linked together by a play on the senses of the word "light" and its related vocabulary. Job begins by describing **those who rebel against the light** as those who oppose wisdom and righteousness—not knowing **its ways** or walking in **its paths** (v. 13). Job then describes how this manner of life is revealed in the light of day and the dark of night: the **murderer** gets up **before it is light** to pursue injustice and continues to prowl around at **night** (v. 14); the **adulterer** assumes that in the **twilight** his actions will go unseen (v. 15); thus they each bring ruinous effects on other households at night, while seeking to guard themselves during the **day** (v. 16). Job implies that their reversal of the typical times of sleep and labor (**deep darkness** has become **morning**) is itself a manifestation of the fact that they **do not know the light** and instead have chosen foolishly to become **friends with the terrors of deep darkness** (vv. 16–17).

24:18–20 The function of these three verses in Job's speech is difficult to determine. The statements seem to be more consistent with the viewpoint of the friends than of Job. It is for this reason that v. 18 begins with **"You say,"** which is not explicit in the Hebrew but is inferred from the content and possible purpose of these verses. If this is Job's purpose, then he is once again restating the type of assertions that his friends have made. He does so to show that such statements seem to willfully ignore the actual state of affairs on earth (for another example, see 21:28, where "For you say" is explicit in the Hb.). Another possible interpretation is to take the statements following 24:18a as Job's description of what he wishes would come to pass: e.g., "let their portion be cursed in the land" (v. 18b). If Job's intention is to express the wish that judgment would be more apparent, then he is possibly taking up the theme of the questions that opened the section (see v. 1).

24:18 "Swift are they on the face of the waters" may represent a saying or idiom from the time of the writing, but the referent and meaning of the phrase are not clear. It may be that "swift" refers to the fleeting life of the wicked either described by the friends or desired by Job (see note on vv. 18–20).

24:21 Job focuses on the **barren, childless woman** and **the widow** to recast once again the truth embedded within his friends' accusations (see 22:9). The care of widows, orphans, and sojourners is a central theme in the instruction of the law (see Ex. 22:21–27; Deut. 24:17–22). Such care is to be both a priority of faithfulness on the part of God's people, and, if injustice in these areas went unaddressed, an indicator that Israel had forgotten her own history. Even though justice in these areas is supposed to be what God desires, the obvious existence of injustice seems unhindered by any sign of judgment. If what Job's friends assert to be true has any merit, judgment ought to be evident on those who exploit widows to their own gain.

23[j]See Ps. 11:4; Prov. 15:3
24[k]Ps. 37:10 [l][ch. 27:19] [m]ch. 14:2
25[n][ch. 9:24]
Chapter 25
1[o]ch. 2:11
3[p]ch. 19:12; Ps. 103:21 [q]Matt. 5:45; James 1:17
4[r]ch. 4:17-19; 9:2; 15:14-16; Ps. 130:3; 143:2 [s]See ch. 14:1 [t]ch. 14:4
6[u]ch. 9:14; 15:16 [v]Ps. 22:6; Isa. 41:14 [w]ch. 35:8
Chapter 26
2[x]Isa. 40:29 [y]Gen. 49:24; Hos. 7:15
3[z]Ps. 73:24; James 1:5
4[a]Gen. 2:7

23 He gives them security, and they are supported,
and his [j]eyes are upon their ways.
24 They are exalted [k]a little while, and then [l]are gone;
they are brought low and gathered up like all others;
they are [m]cut off like the heads of grain.
25 If it is [n]not so, who will prove me a liar
and show that there is nothing in what I say?"

Bildad Speaks: Man Cannot Be Righteous

25 Then [o]Bildad the Shuhite answered and said:

2 "Dominion and fear are with God;[1]
he makes peace in his high heaven.
3 Is there any number to his [p]armies?
Upon whom does his [q]light not arise?
4 How then can man be [r]in the right before God?
How can he who is [s]born of woman be [t]pure?
5 Behold, even the moon is not bright,
and the stars are not pure in his eyes;
6 [u]how much less man, who is [v]a maggot,
and [w]the son of man, who is a worm!"

Job Replies: God's Majesty Is Unsearchable

26 Then Job answered and said:

2 "How you have [x]helped him who has no power!
How you have saved [y]the arm that has no strength!
3 How you have [z]counseled him who has no wisdom,
and plentifully declared sound knowledge!
4 With whose help have you uttered words,
and whose breath [a]has come out from you?

[1] Hebrew *him*

25:1–6 *Bildad: An Unanswered Question.* Bildad's words represent the final speech of the three friends. By returning to the central question from Eliphaz's initial response (v. 4; see 4:17–19), Bildad reveals the dilemma within which the friends have constrained themselves and the posture they have embodied toward God and Job as a result. Since the friends have argued their theological understanding and application as representing God's perspective, they have consistently thought of the choice before them as being that either God or Job must be in the wrong. On account of Job's suffering and their own confidence about being able to interpret it, the friends have never really brought their own viewpoint under scrutiny or given thought to the possibility that they may be wrong in both their defense of God and their pursuit of Job.

25:4 How then can man be in the right before God? This question is repeated several times throughout the dialogue between Job and his friends in slightly different forms: it is asked originally by Eliphaz (4:17), recast and used by Job in his second speech (9:2), repeated and reinforced by Eliphaz (15:14), and returned to again here by Bildad in the final speech of the friends.

26:1–31:40 *Job: The Power of God, Place of Wisdom, and Path of Integrity.* The dialogue between Job and his three friends has a pattern in which each speech by Job is followed by responses from the friends in a particular order: Eliphaz, Bildad, and then Zophar. After two full cycles of the dialogue, it appears that Job is tired of the repetitive and relentless nature of his friends' responses. He signals the end of the dialogue by cutting Bildad's third response short (i.e., it is only six verses long) and precluding any third speech from Zophar. Job concludes with a lengthy monologue in which he takes up several subjects related particularly to the theme of what is hidden and what is revealed. The friends' presumed knowledge does not necessarily promote justice nor take into consideration the extent of the mystery of God's ways (26:1–14). Job cannot agree that his suffering reveals wickedness, and he wishes that those who oppose him would be like the wicked when they are finally cut off (27:1–23). Job describes the value, mystery, and place of wisdom (28:1–28). Job also longs for the past (29:1–25), laments the present (30:1–31), and finishes with a plea that the character of his life would be revealed for what it is and judged accordingly (31:1–40). Given the perceived tensions with Job's earlier statements on the wicked in ch. 27, and the apparently independent status of the wisdom "hymn" in ch. 28, some argue that voices other than Job's should be heard speaking these passages. On the other hand, it is possible to follow the text as it is. After all, 31:40 says, "The words of Job are ended," which seems to clearly attribute these speeches to Job. These questions are taken up in context below.

26:1–14 *The Mystery and Majesty of God's Ways.* Job criticizes his friends for what is likely an unintentional but still unacceptable consequence of their approach (vv. 1–4). He questions their certitude by alluding to how much is hidden from human perspective simply in the existence and divine government of the created world (vv. 5–14).

26:2–3 How you have helped . . . saved . . . counseled . . . ! With these three statements Job is suggesting that the presumed theological orthodoxy of Bildad (and the other two friends) rings hollow due to its lack of any actual protection for him or reflection on the justice they pronounce. In their defense of God, the friends have neither actively helped the poor and needy (since all they have done is wrongly accuse Job who has been their protector), nor have they bothered to discern the potentially disastrous consequences of their approach (judging the circumstance of those in need to be the result of their own sin).

26:4 In light of the implied negative answer to the statements of vv. 2–3, Job asks his friends to examine **whose help** and **whose breath** has been behind

5 The [b]dead tremble
under the waters and their inhabitants.
6 Sheol is [c]naked before God,[1]
and [d]Abaddon has no covering.
7 He [e]stretches out the north over [f]the void
and hangs the earth on nothing.
8 He [g]binds up the waters in his thick clouds,
and the cloud is not split open under them.
9 He covers the face of the full moon[2]
and [h]spreads over it his cloud.
10 He has inscribed [i]a circle on the face of the waters
at the boundary between light and darkness.
11 [j]The pillars of heaven tremble
and are astounded at his [k]rebuke.
12 By his power he [l]stilled the sea;
by his understanding he shattered [m]Rahab.
13 [n]By his wind the heavens were made fair;
his hand pierced [o]the fleeing serpent.
14 Behold, these are but the outskirts of his [p]ways,
and how small [q]a whisper do we hear of him!
But the thunder of his power who can understand?"

Job Continues: I Will Maintain My Integrity

27 And Job again [r]took up his discourse, and said:

2 "As God lives, who has [s]taken away my right,
and the Almighty, who has [t]made my soul bitter,
3 as long as my breath is in me,
and [u]the spirit of God is in my nostrils,
4 my lips will not speak [v]falsehood,
and my tongue will not utter [v]deceit.
5 Far be it from me to say that you are right;
till I die I will not put away my [w]integrity from me.
6 I [x]hold fast my righteousness and will not let it go;
my heart does not [y]reproach me for any of my days.

5 [b]Ps. 88:10
6 [c]Ps. 139:8; Prov. 15:11 [d]Rev. 9:11
7 [e]See ch. 9:8 [f][Gen. 1:2]
8 [g]Prov. 30:4
9 [h][ch. 36:29]
10 [i]Prov. 8:29; [ch. 38:8-11; Ps. 33:7; Jer. 5:22]
11 [j]ch. 9:6; Ps. 75:3 [k]Ps. 104:7
12 [l]Isa. 51:15; Jer. 31:35 [m]See ch. 9:13
13 [n][Ps. 33:6] [o]Isa. 27:1
14 [p]ch. 40:19 [q]ch. 4:12

Chapter 27

1 [r]ch. 29:1; See Num. 23:7
2 [s]ch. 34:5 [t][Ruth 1:20; 2 Kgs. 4:27]
3 [u]ch. 33:4; [Gen. 2:7]
4 [v]ch. 13:7
5 [w]ch. 2:3, 9; [ch. 13:15]
6 [x]ch. 2:3 [y][Acts 23:1; 24:16; 1 Cor. 4:4]

[1] Hebrew *him* [2] Or *his throne*

their words, lest they assume resolutely but wrongly that they have spoken on God's behalf.

26:5–14 Job alludes to some obvious areas of knowledge that are open before God but concealed from human perspective, in order to warn his friends against their continued presumption that they know God's purposes in Job's disastrous circumstances.

26:5–10 Job uses the repeated vocabulary of this section to emphasize things that are clearly known to God but are hidden from human cognizance. The state or realm of the **dead** is not visible to humanity (**under the waters**, **Sheol**, and **Abaddon**), but it is **naked** and **has no covering** before God (vv. 5–6). Likewise, the description of the creation or existence of the natural world implies that other things may be hidden: the heavens appear perched **over the void**, and the **earth** appears to hang **on nothing** (v. 7); a **cloud** often **binds up**, **covers**, and **spreads over** another element of the heavens and itself **is not split open** (vv. 8–9); and it is God who has set the limits for all of these divine artifacts (v. 10).

26:9 The Hebrew word for "**full moon**" (cf. Ps. 81:3) is a homonym (same sound and spelling but different meaning) with the word for "throne" (see ESV footnote). If either the latter sense is intended or the author is employing intentional ambiguity in using the word, then the image may refer to the heavens as concealing God in the place of his rule.

26:11–14 The images in these verses all focus on God's power and echo a similar description in Job's first response to Bildad (see 9:5–13). The created world reveals not only that some things are hidden (26:5–10) but also the vast implications of God's power as the one who created and governs everything. **Rahab** (v. 12) and the **fleeing serpent** (v. 13) refer to the same being and make the point that God is and will be sovereign over any powerful figure opposed to him (note that in Isaiah, God uses "Rahab" as another name for Egypt, see Isa. 30:7). If it is by God's **power** and **understanding** that he rules creation (Job 26:12), Job concludes by asking how it is that, as one who merely hears the **thunder of his power**, any person could presume to **understand** it (v. 14).

27:1–23 *A Claim to Integrity and a Wish for Vindication.* Job refuses to agree that his friends are right, and he maintains that his circumstances are not an indication of undisclosed sin (vv. 1–6). In images similar to those his friends have used against him, Job wishes that his adversaries would be considered as the wicked are before God (vv. 7–23).

27:1 The first part of Job's long response is marked with the heading typical of the dialogues, "Then Job answered and said" (see 26:1 and the verse that introduces each response from 4:1ff.). The heading here and in 29:1 (**And Job again took up his discourse**) helps to bind together the entirety of chs. 26–31 as Job's final speech of the dialogue, which functions as a closing statement as well as a direct response to his friends.

27:5 you. The Hebrew is plural; Job is addressing his friends collectively.

27:6 By asserting that he will **hold fast** to his integrity, Job echoes the Lord's description of him in the prologue (see 2:3).

7 “Let my enemy be as the wicked,
and let him who rises up against me be as the unrighteous.
8 [z]For what is the hope of the godless [a]when God cuts him off,
when God takes away his life?
9 [b]Will God hear his cry
when distress comes upon him?
10 Will he [c]take delight in the Almighty?
Will he call upon God at all times?
11 I will teach you concerning the hand of God;
[d]what is with the Almighty I will not conceal.
12 Behold, all of you have seen it yourselves;
why then have you become altogether vain?

13 [e]“This is the portion of a wicked man with God,
and the heritage that [f]oppressors receive from the Almighty:
14 If his [g]children are multiplied, it is for [h]the sword,
and his descendants have not enough bread.
15 Those who survive him the pestilence buries,
and his [i]widows do not weep.
16 Though he [j]heap up silver like dust,
and pile up clothing like clay,
17 he may pile it up, but the righteous will wear it,
and [k]the innocent will divide the silver.
18 He builds his [l]house like a moth’s,
like [m]a booth that [n]a watchman makes.
19 He goes to bed rich, but will [o]do so no more;
he opens his eyes, and [p]his wealth is gone.
20 [q]Terrors overtake him like [r]a flood;
in the night a whirlwind [s]carries him off.
21 [t]The east wind lifts him up and he is gone;
it [u]sweeps him out of his place.
22 It[1] hurls at him [v]without pity;
he flees from its[2] power in headlong flight.
23 It [w]claps its hands at him
and [x]hisses at him from its place.

Job Continues: Where Is Wisdom?

28

1 “Surely there is a mine for silver,
and a place for gold that they [y]refine.
2 Iron is taken out of the earth,
and copper is smelted from the ore.

[1] Or *He* (that is, God); also verse 23 [2] Or *his*; also verse 23

8[z]See ch. 8:13 [a]Matt. 16:26; [Luke 12:20]
9[b]Ps. 18:41; Prov. 1:28; 15:29; Isa. 1:15; Jer. 11:11; 14:12; Ezek. 8:18; Mic. 3:4; Zech. 7:13; [ch. 35:12, 13]; See Ps. 66:18
10[c]See ch. 22:26
11[d]ch. 10:13; 23:14
13[e]ch. 20:29; [ch. 18:21; 31:2] [f]ch. 6:23; 15:20
14[g]Deut. 28:41; Hos. 9:13, 16 [h]Jer. 15:2
15[i]Ps. 78:64
16[j]Zech. 9:3
17[k][Prov. 13:22; Eccles. 2:26]
18[l]ch. 8:14, 15 [m]Isa. 1:8 [n]Song 1:6; 8:11, 12
19[o]Jer. 8:2; Ezek. 29:5 [p]ch. 24:24
20[q]See ch. 18:11 [r]See ch. 22:11 [s]ch. 34:20, 25; 36:20
21[t][ch. 30:22] [u]ch. 8:18
22[v]ch. 16:13
23[w]Lam. 2:15; Ezek. 25:6; Nah. 3:19 [x][2 Chr. 29:8; Jer. 49:17; Lam. 2:15; Ezek. 27:36; Zeph. 2:15]

Chapter 28

1[y][Mal. 3:3]

27:7–23 Because these verses seem more consistent with the speeches of Job’s friends, it has been suggested that they may be misplaced and ought to be interpreted as belonging to Bildad’s speech in ch. 25. However, the similarity to the speeches of the friends can also be understood to be part of Job’s purpose. Unlike his three friends, Job is not referring solely to what the wicked receive on earth, but wishes that his “enemy” would be like the wicked “when God cuts him off” and “takes away his life” (27:8). If Job is actually blameless before God, then those who have been his adversaries ought to consider how God weighs their own actions in light of the judgment they have described.

27:7–8 Job declares that if he is right to maintain his integrity (see vv. 2–6), then he also wishes that his adversaries would be considered **as the wicked** and **unrighteous** (v. 7). However, unlike his friends, who assume that judgment on the wicked is generally experienced in life on earth and is transparent to observers, Job says there is no **hope** for the wicked **when God cuts him off** and **takes away his life** (v. 8).

27:11 concerning the hand of God. Hand (Hb. *yad*) is often a metaphor for power, but justice is the question that concerns Job and his friends. Eliphaz claimed to speak for God in correcting Job (cf. 22:26–27). Job in turn has declared that he received revelation from God that he could not deny (6:10); he **will not conceal** what is with God (27:11), i.e., the thoughts of the Almighty.

27:13 The Hebrew phrase translated **“with God”** is often explained as being better interpreted “from God,” because it would provide a parallel with the second line of the verse. The proposed change is minimal and consists of one letter in the Hebrew text being understood as accidentally appended to this phrase from the word that precedes it. However, since v. 11 has the similar phrase “with the Almighty,” the sense of v. 13 in context does not require the change. The two phrases also appear central to Job’s point: if his integrity is actually what is true “with God,” then Job’s friends ought to consider whether they are the ones who stand in danger of the judgment that they have described.

28:1–28 *Where Is Wisdom Found?* In a magnificent poem that plays on the theme of the dialogues regarding what is hidden and what is revealed,

3 Man puts an end to darkness
and searches out to the farthest limit
the ore in [z]gloom and [a]deep darkness.
4 He opens shafts in a valley away from where anyone lives;
they are forgotten by travelers;
they hang in the air, far away from mankind; they swing to and fro.
5 As for the earth, [b]out of it comes bread,
but underneath it is turned up as by fire.
6 Its stones are the place of [c]sapphires,[1]
and it has dust of gold.

7 "That path no bird of prey knows,
and the falcon's eye has not seen it.
8 [d]The proud beasts have not trodden it;
[e]the lion has not passed over it.

9 "Man puts his hand to [f]the flinty rock
and overturns mountains by the roots.
10 He cuts out channels in the rocks,
and his eye sees every precious thing.
11 He dams up the streams so that they do not trickle,
and the thing that is hidden he brings out to light.

12 [g]"But where shall wisdom be found?
And where is the place of understanding?
13 Man does not know its worth,
and it is not found in [h]the land of the living.
14 [i]The deep says, 'It is not in me,'
and the sea says, 'It is not with me.'
15 It [j]cannot be bought for gold,
and silver cannot be weighed as its price.

[1] Or *lapis lazuli*; also verse 16

3 [z]ch. 10:22 [a]See ch. 3:5
5 [b]Ps. 104:14
6 [c]Ex. 24:10
8 [d]ch. 41:34 [e]ch. 10:16
9 [f]Deut. 8:15; 32:13; Ps. 114:8
12 [g][Prov. 16:16; Eccles. 7:24]
13 [h]See Ps. 27:13
14 [i]Gen. 49:25
15 [j]Prov. 3:14; 8:10, 11, 19; 16:16

Job reflects on the value, mystery, and place of wisdom. The poem is structured around a question that is repeated with slight variation: **"But where shall wisdom be found? And where is the place of understanding?"** (vv. 12, 20). Although man has shown great skill in mining the earth for its hidden and valuable resources (vv. 1–11), where is he to look for wisdom, which is beyond measure in its value and outside of the sphere of mere discovery (vv. 12–22)? God is the one who knows its place and by whom wisdom is both given and governed (vv. 23–28). Interpreters have questioned whether ch. 28 is actually Job's speech, since it might appear to dampen the weight of God's response in chs. 38–41. However, even though the poem appears to be self-contained, the description of wisdom in the chapter is consistent with the grounds for Job's lament. It represents what will be shown to be true of him in the end: Job is not reproved because he has promoted folly (unlike his friends) but rather because the inferences he has drawn from wisdom have not properly reflected what he is able to know in light of what he believes to be true.

28:1–11 The structure of the Hebrew phrases brings the **earth** (v. 5) and its valuable treasures into focus in this section. Although it takes considerable effort (indicated by the multifaceted references to **darkness** in v. 3, **far away** locations in v. 4, and **rock** in vv. 9–10), human industry has developed ways to mine the earth for its precious elements (**silver**, **gold**, **iron**, **copper**, **sapphires**) or cultivate it (grain for **bread**). In these realms, whatever is **hidden** is brought **out to light** (v. 11).

28:3 Job has used the phrase **deep darkness** in various images throughout the dialogue with his friends (see 3:5; 12:22; 16:16; 24:17; and also 10:22). Here the phrase describes the success of human industry. As the remainder of the chapter makes clear, Job uses the description to question, if not implicitly rebuke, his friends for presuming they have been similarly successful either in discovering wisdom's place in the world or discerning its presence or absence in the heart of another.

28:4 Mining practices in the ancient Near East have been neither fully discovered nor studied enough to determine precisely what is being pictured in this verse. The word translated **"shafts"** is typically used to refer to the gully of an intermittent stream (just as the word translated "channels" in v. 10 is typically used to refer to either a "river" or as the proper name "the Nile"). Archaeologists have discovered horizontal mining shafts, some examples of which are also intersected by vertical shafts that were likely used to vent mining operations. Whether it is these vertical shafts that **hang in the air** or not, the purpose of the images is clear: the threefold description of the remote location of the mine (**away from where anyone lives**, **forgotten by travelers**, and **away from mankind**) further indicates the difficulty and effort involved in humanity's pursuit of precious materials.

28:7–8 Neither the birds of the sky (represented by the **falcon's eye**) nor the animals of the earth (represented by the **lion**) have any knowledge of endeavors like mining. It is a uniquely human accomplishment and application of skill.

28:11 Job's description of human industry in vv. 1–11 is summed up well in the second line of this verse: **the thing that is hidden he brings out to light**.

28:12–22 The questions of vv. 12 and 20 frame this section, which describes the value of **wisdom** and the place of **understanding** as unknown to mankind. The fact that they are unknown is emphasized by the number of negative statements in vv. 13–19: e.g., **not know, not found, not in . . . with me, cannot be bought . . . weighed . . . valued, cannot equal it** (twice), **nor can it be exchanged . . . valued**.

28:15–19 These verses contain multiple references to **gold** and to other precious stones such as blue **sapphire** (lapis lazuli), black or white **onyx**, opaque

16[k]Ps. 45:9; Isa. 13:12 [l]See 1 Kgs. 9:28 [m]Gen. 2:12 [n]Ex. 24:10
18[o]Ezek. 27:16 [p]Prov. 3:15; 8:11; 20:15; 31:10; Lam. 4:7
19[q]Ex. 28:17; 39:10; Ezek. 28:13
21[r]ch. 12:10; 30:23
22[s]See ch. 26:6
23[t]For ver. 23-28, see Prov. 8:22-31
24[u][Prov. 15:3; Zech. 4:10]
25[v][Ps. 135:7]
26[w]ch. 38:25
28[x]Deut. 4:6; Ps. 111:10; Prov. 1:7; [Eccles. 12:13] [y]Prov. 3:7; 14:16; 16:6

Chapter 29

1[z]ch. 27:1; See Num. 23:7
3[a]ch. 18:6; 2 Sam. 21:17; Ps. 18:28
4[b]Ps. 25:14; Prov. 3:32; See ch. 15:8

16 It cannot be valued in [k]the gold of [l]Ophir,
in precious [m]onyx or [n]sapphire.
17 Gold and glass cannot equal it,
nor can it be exchanged for jewels of fine gold.
18 No mention shall be made of [o]coral or of crystal;
the price of wisdom is above [o, p]pearls.
19 [q]The topaz of Ethiopia cannot equal it,
nor can it be valued in pure gold.

20 "From where, then, does wisdom come?
And where is the place of understanding?
21 It is hidden from the eyes of [r]all living
and concealed from the birds of the air.
22 [s]Abaddon and Death say,
'We have heard a rumor of it with our ears.'

23 [t]"God understands the way to it,
and he knows its place.
24 For he [u]looks to the ends of the earth
and sees everything under the heavens.
25 When he [v]gave to the wind its weight
and apportioned the waters by measure,
26 when he made a decree for the rain
and [w]a way for the lightning of the thunder,
27 then he saw it and declared it;
he established it, and searched it out.
28 And he said to man,
'Behold, [x]the fear of the Lord, that is wisdom,
and to [y]turn away from evil is understanding.'"

Job's Summary Defense

29 And Job again [z]took up his discourse, and said:

2 "Oh, that I were as in the months of old,
as in the days when God watched over me,
3 when his [a]lamp shone upon my head,
and by his light I walked through darkness,
4 as I was in my prime,[1]
when the [b]friendship of God was upon my tent,

[1] Hebrew *my autumn days*

shiny **crystal**, bright **coral**, and yellow chrysolite (**topaz**). All are expensive and difficult to obtain, yet none are comparable to the value of wisdom.

28:21 In contrast to the earlier description about "the paths" of mining and industry (see vv. 7–8), the place of wisdom is hidden **from the eyes of all living** creatures on the earth, including humans, as well as from **the birds of the air**.

28:22 The reference to **Abaddon and Death** here is likely playing off Job's earlier description of them as a realm that is also hidden from human observation (see 26:5–6). These two names may be simple personifications, or they may use ideas from pagan myths (e.g., with Death [Hb. *mawet*] corresponding to the Canaanite deity Mot) to show that these other powers cannot find wisdom.

28:23–28 The closing section of the chapter makes it clear that only **God understands** and **knows** wisdom and how it is acquired (v. 23). He is the only one before whom both **the earth** and **the heavens** (v. 24) are fully revealed because he is the one who created them (vv. 25–27). Wisdom is thus given by God (it came through his speaking) and defined in relation to him (v. 28): **the fear of the Lord, that is wisdom** (see Prov. 1:7; 9:10) and **to turn away from evil is understanding** (see Prov. 3:7; 16:6). Job may be rebuking his friends for their treatment of him, implying that they have not acted in a way consistent with the fear of the Lord (cf. the way that the book characterizes Job himself, Job 1:1).

29:1–31:40 *The Path of Job's Life.* Job reflects on his life in the past (29:1–25), the present (30:1–31), and what he wishes would be revealed and vindicated in the future (31:1–40). Much as Job's soliloquy in ch. 3 launched the dialogues with his somber reflection on his origins, so too chs. 29–31 conclude the dialogues with Job's reflections on his current and future state.

29:1–25 Job laments the loss of the past, when he felt that he had the presence and protection of God (vv. 1–6) as well as the respect of all those among whom he lived (vv. 7–25), which matched the way he lived his life in pursuit of righteousness and justice (see vv. 12–17).

29:1 And Job again took up his discourse. See note on 27:1.

29:2–6 Job refers to days in which he felt the presence of God guarding (**when God watched over me**, v. 2) and guiding him (**when his lamp shone upon my head, and by his light I walked**, v. 3). Job felt that it was a time when he was in his **prime** (or with the ESV footnote, autumn days, which would be the season of harvest) because the **friendship of God** (v. 4) was evident on his household (v. 5) as well as his flocks and fields (v. 6).

5 when the Almighty was yet with me,
when my [c]children were all around me,
6 when my steps were [d]washed with [e]butter,
and [f]the rock poured out for me streams of [g]oil!
7 When I went out to [h]the gate of the city,
when I prepared my seat in the square,
8 the young men saw me and withdrew,
and the aged rose and stood;
9 the princes refrained from talking
and [i]laid their hand on their mouth;
10 the voice of the nobles was hushed,
and their [j]tongue stuck to the roof of their mouth.
11 When the ear heard, it called me blessed,
and when the eye saw, it approved,
12 because I [k]delivered the poor who cried for help,
and the fatherless who had none to help him.
13 [l]The blessing of him who was [m]about to perish came upon me,
and I caused [n]the widow's heart to sing for joy.
14 I [o]put on righteousness, and it clothed me;
my justice was like a robe and [p]a turban.
15 I was [q]eyes to the blind
and feet to the lame.
16 I was a father to the needy,
and I searched out [r]the cause of him whom I did not know.
17 I [s]broke [t]the fangs of the unrighteous
and made him drop his prey from his teeth.
18 [u]Then I thought, 'I shall die in my [v]nest,
and I shall multiply my days as [w]the sand,
19 my [x]roots spread out to [y]the waters,
with the dew all night on my [z]branches,
20 my glory fresh with me,
and my [a]bow ever [b]new in my hand.'

21 "Men listened to me and waited
and kept silence for my counsel.
22 After I spoke they did not speak again,
and my word [c]dropped upon them.
23 They waited for me as for the rain,
and they [d]opened their mouths as for the [e]spring rain.
24 I smiled on them when they had no confidence,
and [f]the light of my [g]face they did not cast down.

5 [c]ch. 1:2; [Ps. 128:3]
6 [d][Gen. 49:11] [e]ch. 20:17 [f]Deut. 32:13, 14; Ps. 81:16 [g][Deut. 33:24]
7 [h]See ch. 5:4
9 [i]See ch. 21:5
10 [j]Ps. 22:15; 137:6; Lam. 4:4; Ezek. 3:26
12 [k]Ps. 72:12
13 [l]ch. 31:20 [m]Prov. 31:6; Isa. 27:13 [n][Ruth 2:20]
14 [o]Ps. 132:9; Isa. 59:17; 61:10; [Isa. 11:5; Eph. 6:14; 1 Thess. 5:8] [p]Isa. 62:3; Zech. 3:5; [ch. 19:9]
15 [q]Num. 10:31
16 [r][Prov. 29:7]
17 [s]Ps. 3:7 [t]Ps. 58:6; Prov. 30:14
18 [u][Ps. 30:6] [v]Num. 24:21; See ch. 39:27 [w]Gen. 22:17
19 [x]ch. 18:16 [y]See Ps. 1:3 [z][ch. 14:9]
20 [a]Gen. 49:24 [b][Isa. 40:31; 41:1]
22 [c][Deut. 32:2; 33:28]
23 [d]Ps. 119:131; [Isa. 5:14] [e]Prov. 16:15; Jer. 3:3; Zech. 10:1; [Deut. 11:14]
24 [f]Prov. 16:15 [g]Gen. 4:5

29:6 washed with butter. Job was renowned for his herds of cattle and his olive groves that produced riches from the earth.

29:7–25 Job opens and closes this section with a description of the honor that he once received from people in every sphere of influence (vv. 7–10, 21–25). Job's wish is not simply that he would regain his honor but that the grounds for this respect would be remembered (beginning with **because** in v. 12): he not only spoke in wisdom but also embodied what it required by caring for the **poor** and **fatherless** (v. 12), for the one about to **perish**, and for the widow (v. 13), and by protecting and preserving the **needy** (vv. 14–17). When Job looks back on what he thought the course of his life would be, he uses several images, including that of a well-rooted tree that would continue to bear fruit, benefiting himself and others (vv. 18–20; for similar images of the benefits of a faithful life, see Ps. 1:3; Prov. 3:18; Jer. 17:7–8).

29:11–13 The **blessing** that Job received from others (v. 13; see also v. 11) signified the blessing he had been to those who had no one to **help** them and needed to be **delivered** (v. 12). In the next section, Job will lament his need for someone to deliver him, now that he is the one crying for help (see 30:20, 28; also 30:24).

29:14–16 Job had been a person of significant means (see v. 6) who used his possessions and influence as if he were **clothed** with **righteousness** and **justice** (v. 14) to provide what the **blind**, **lame** (v. 15), **needy**, and those he **did not know** (v. 16) could not do for themselves. Job's actions contrast with how he is treated now that he is in need (see 30:10–15).

29:16 searched out the cause. Job took up legal cases even when there could be no possible benefit for him.

29:17 The wicked are pictured here as if they hunt for victims like a predator. Job describes his actions on behalf of the needy as equivalent to breaking **the fangs of the unrighteous**, presumably because he exposed and unraveled the means by which they had snared the poor as their **prey**.

29:20 Job is likely referring to the internal strength (**my glory**) and the external vigor (**my bow**) that were the mutual signs of the benefits of a life lived in wisdom.

29:24 As one who utilized his means for righteousness and justice (vv. 12–17), the smile and **light** of Job's face encouraged those without hope and reflected the character and presence of God (see "lamp" and "light" in v. 3).

25 [h] ch. 15:24
Chapter 30
1 [i] See ch. 12:4 [j] ch. 32:6; [ch. 32:4]
2 [k] For ver. 2-8, see ch. 24:4-8 [l] [ch. 5:26]
3 [m] [ver. 17] [n] Jer. 2:6 [o] ch. 38:27; Zeph. 1:15
5 [p] [1 Sam. 26:19]
6 [q] 1 Sam. 13:6; Jer. 4:29
7 [r] ch. 6:5 [s] Prov. 24:31; Zeph. 2:9
9 [t] Ps. 69:12; Lam. 3:14, 63 [u] See ch. 17:6
10 [v] Ps. 88:8; [ch. 17:6] [w] Num. 12:14; Isa. 50:6; Matt. 26:67; 27:30
12 [x] Ps. 109:6 [y] ch. 19:12
13 [z] ch. 6:2
14 [a] ch. 16:14

25 I chose their way and sat as chief,
and I lived like [h] a king among his troops,
like one who comforts mourners.

30

1 "But now they [i] laugh at me,
men who are [j] younger than I,
whose fathers I would have disdained
to set with the dogs of my flock.
2 What could I gain from the strength of their hands,
[k] men whose [l] vigor is gone?
3 Through want and hard hunger
they [m] gnaw [n] the dry ground by night in [o] waste and desolation;
4 they pick saltwort and the leaves of bushes,
and the roots of the broom tree for their food.[1]
5 [p] They are driven out from human company;
they shout after them as after a thief.
6 In the gullies of the torrents they must dwell,
in holes of the earth and of [q] the rocks.
7 Among the bushes they [r] bray;
under [s] the nettles they huddle together.
8 A senseless, a nameless brood,
they have been whipped out of the land.

9 "And now I have become their [t] song;
I am [u] a byword to them.
10 They [v] abhor me; they keep aloof from me;
they do not hesitate to [w] spit at the sight of me.
11 Because God has loosed my cord and humbled me,
they have cast off restraint[2] in my presence.
12 On my [x] right hand the rabble rise;
they push away my feet;
they [y] cast up against me their ways of destruction.
13 They break up my path;
they promote my [z] calamity;
they need no one to help them.
14 As through a wide [a] breach they come;
amid the crash they roll on.

[1] Or *warmth* [2] Hebrew *the bridle*

29:25 It is with some irony that Job refers to the past, when some listened for his words and did not speak afterward (vv. 21–22), and also to the way that he formerly lived **like one who comforts mourners**. His friends originally set out to comfort him (see 2:11) but instead became agitated with his words and ended up acting as his accusers.

30:1–31 Job contrasts the honor of his past (29:1–25) with his present circumstances by describing the men who taunt him (30:1–8), their actions against him (vv. 9–15), and his own internal affliction (vv. 16–23) before a concluding section that references both his past acts of compassion and his present lack of hope or help (vv. 24–31).

30:1–8 Job describes just how much of a reversal his current situation represents: although he had delivered the truly needy from the oppression of the unrighteous (29:11–17), those who presume to mock him as if he has received the judgment of the unrighteous are themselves needy, because of their own actions and foolishness (see 30:8).

30:4 The plants mentioned here represent the food of desperation: **saltwort** is a low, struggling bush with thick, sour-tasting leaves; the **broom tree** is a shrub with long, straight branches, small leaves, and poisonous **roots**. Because the broom tree's roots are both poisonous and known for their heat when burned (see Ps. 120:4), an alternate vocalization of the Hebrew is sometimes followed with the sense "for their warmth" (see ESV footnote). However, the known quality of the broom tree's roots may be used here simply to highlight the dire situation of these men.

30:8 senseless. The Hebrew is lit., "sons of a fool" and infers further that the men being described are in some way morally responsible for their circumstances (see 2:10; cf. the description of the foolish in Prov. 1:7, 29–32; etc.).

30:9–15 Although Job had restrained the unrighteous (see 29:12, 17), he describes those who now presume to deride him, casting off any restraint, as if they are taking advantage of an easy military conquest in which they sing and spit at his downfall (30:9–11) while building siege ramps against him, breaching his defenses, and looting him (vv. 12–15).

30:11 In contrast to the past, God has **loosed** the **cord** that secured Job's tent (cf. 29:4), and men of low esteem have taken the opportunity to unbridle their tongues (see ESV footnote) and embolden their posture in his **presence** (cf. 30:9–10 with 29:7–11).

30:14 amid the crash. The rabble storm upon Job, like a troop of soldiers pouring through a wide breach in a fortification. They continue uninhibited in their plunder.

15 [b]Terrors are turned upon me;
my honor is pursued as by the wind,
and my prosperity has passed away like [c]a cloud.

16 "And now my soul is [d]poured out within me;
days of affliction have taken hold of me.
17 [e]The night [f]racks my bones,
and the pain that [g]gnaws me takes no rest.
18 With great force my garment is [h]disfigured;
it binds me about like the collar of my tunic.
19 God[1] has cast me into the mire,
and I have become like [i]dust and ashes.
20 I cry to you for help and you do not answer me;
I stand, and you only look at me.
21 You have [j]turned cruel to me;
with the might of your hand you [k]persecute me.
22 [l]You lift me up on the wind; you make me ride on it,
and you toss me about in the roar of the storm.
23 [m]For I know that you will bring me to death
and to the house appointed for [n]all living.

24 "Yet does not one in a [o]heap of ruins stretch out his hand,
and in his disaster cry for help?[2]
25 Did not I [p]weep for him whose day was hard?
Was not my soul grieved for the needy?
26 But [q]when I hoped for good, evil came,
and when I waited for light, [r]darkness came.
27 My inward parts are in turmoil and never still;
days of affliction [s]come to meet me.
28 I [t]go about darkened, but not by the sun;
I stand up in [u]the assembly and cry for help.
29 I am a brother of [v]jackals
and a companion of [w]ostriches.
30 My [x]skin turns black and falls from me,
and my [y]bones burn with heat.
31 My [z]lyre is [a]turned to mourning,
and my [z]pipe to the voice of those who weep.

Job's Final Appeal

31
1 "I have made a covenant with my [b]eyes;
how then could I gaze at a virgin?
2 What would be [c]my portion from God above
and [c]my heritage from the Almighty on high?

[1] Hebrew *He* [2] The meaning of the Hebrew is uncertain

15[b]See ch. 18:11 [c]ch. 7:9; Isa. 44:22
16[d]1 Sam. 1:15; [ch. 10:1]
17[e][ch. 7:3] [f]ch. 33:19 [g]ver. 3
18[h][1 Sam. 28:8; 1 Kgs. 20:38]
19[i]ch. 42:6; [Gen. 18:27]
21[j]Lam. 4:3; [Isa. 63:10] [k]ch. 16:9
22[l][ch. 27:21]
23[m]ch. 19:25 [n]ch. 28:21
24[o]Ps. 79:1; Jer. 26:18; Mic. 1:6; 3:12
25[p]Ps. 35:13, 14; Rom. 12:15
26[q]Jer. 8:15; 14:19 [r]ch. 10:21, 22
27[s]2 Sam. 22:6; Ps. 18:5
28[t]Ps. 38:6; 42:9; 43:2 [u]Prov. 26:26
29[v]Mic. 1:8 [w]Isa. 13:21; 34:13; Jer. 50:39; Mic. 1:8
30[x][Ps. 119:83; Lam. 4:8; 5:10] [y]Ps. 102:3
31[z]ch. 21:12 [a]Lam. 5:15

Chapter 31

1[b][Isa. 33:15; Matt. 5:28]
2[c]See ch. 20:29

30:16–23 Job laments the isolation in which he now pours out his soul (v. 16) as one who wastes away without help (vv. 17–22) and waits for death (v. 23).

30:16 my soul is poured out. An idiom for grief; cf. the psalmist in his longing for worship at the temple (Ps. 42:4).

30:18 The description of Job's solitary grief and **disfigured** clothes contrasts with his earlier image of being clothed with righteousness and justice for the sake of delivering those in need (see 29:14).

30:20 Job feels that his present **cry** for **help** from God (also v. 28) is unanswered, which contrasts with the descriptions of Job's earlier actions on behalf of others (see 29:12).

30:24–31 Job concludes the section by picturing himself as being like one of those whose cries for **help** he used to answer (vv. 24–25) but who in his own distress has found **evil** where he hoped for **good** (v. 26), and isolation and mourning (vv. 27, 29–31) when he has called for **help** (v. 28).

31:1–40 After contrasting the honor of his past (29:1–25) with the disdain he receives because of his circumstances in the present (ch. 30), Job confesses one last time that he has lived his life in the pursuit of righteousness because he believes that is how it should be lived before God, that turning from God's way is without benefit, and that further curses should come on him if these things are not true. Job begins by affirming his commitment to fidelity and questions how he could break it (31:1–4). Sections that follow each open with a conditional statement implying that his life has not been patterned by what is described: stealing or coveting (vv. 5–8, 9–12), neglecting the needs of those both within his household and without (vv. 13–15, 16–18, 19–23, 31–32), trust in or worship of anything other than God (vv. 24–28), concealing hatred or sin (vv. 29–30, 33–34), or improper oversight of his land (vv. 38–40). Embedded in the end of this section is a final wish that the charges would be presented to him so that he could give an account (vv. 35–37).

31:1–4 Job believes that his life is lived before and governed by **the Almighty**

4[d]ch. 14:16; 34:21; 2 Chr. 16:9; Prov. 5:21; 15:3; Jer. 16:17; 32:19; Zech. 4:10 [e]ch. 14:16
6[f]Dan. 5:27
7[g]Num. 15:39; Eccles. 11:9 [h][ch. 11:15]
8[i]Lev. 26:16; Deut. 28:30, 38; [John 4:37]
9[j][ch. 24:15]
10[k][Ex. 11:5; Isa. 47:2] [l][2 Sam. 12:11; Jer. 8:10]
11[m]ver. 28; [Lev. 20:10; Deut. 22:22]
12[n]See Prov. 6:27-29
14[o]Ps. 17:3
15[p]ch. 34:19; Prov. 14:31; 22:2; [Eph. 6:9]
16[q][ch. 22:7] [r]ch. 11:20; 17:5
19[s]ch. 29:13 [t]ch. 24:7, 10
20[u]ch. 29:13; Deut. 24:13

3 Is not calamity for the unrighteous,
and disaster for the workers of iniquity?
4 [d]Does not he see my ways
and [e]number all my steps?

5 "If I have walked with falsehood
and my foot has hastened to deceit;
6 (Let me be [f]weighed in a just balance,
and let God know my integrity!)
7 if my step has turned aside from the way
and [g]my heart has gone after my eyes,
and if any [h]spot has stuck to my hands,
8 then let me [i]sow, and another eat,
and let what grows for me[1] be rooted out.

9 "If my heart has been enticed toward a woman,
and I have [j]lain in wait at my neighbor's door,
10 then let my wife [k]grind for another,
and let others [l]bow down on her.
11 For that would be a heinous crime;
that would be an iniquity [m]to be punished by the judges;
12 for that would be a fire [n]that consumes as far as Abaddon,
and it would burn to the root all my increase.

13 "If I have rejected the cause of my manservant or my maidservant,
when they brought a complaint against me,
14 what then shall I do when God rises up?
When he [o]makes inquiry, what shall I answer him?
15 Did [p]not he who made me in the womb make him?
And did not one fashion us in the womb?

16 "If I have [q]withheld anything that the poor desired,
or have [r]caused the eyes of the widow to fail,
17 or have eaten my morsel alone,
and the fatherless has not eaten of it
18 (for from my youth the fatherless[2] grew up with me as with a father,
and from my mother's womb I guided the widow[3]),
19 if I have seen anyone [s]perish for [t]lack of clothing,
or the needy without [t]covering,
20 if his body has not [u]blessed me,[4]
and if he was not warmed with the fleece of my sheep,

[1] Or *let my descendants* [2] Hebrew *he* [3] Hebrew *her* [4] Hebrew *if his loins have not blessed me*

(v. 2), who does **number all my steps** (v. 4). His confidence in this fact is the grounds upon which he uses the same vocabulary to make his final wish that "the Almighty" might answer him (v. 35) and that he could give him "an account of all my steps" (v. 37).

31:1 In affirming his moral purity, Job recalls a personal commitment he had made regarding what he would and would not gaze at, what he calls **a covenant with my eyes**. In particular, he professes purity in avoiding sexual lust: **how then could I gaze at a virgin?** The faithful reader would recognize the soundness of such a commitment, and Jesus teaches about such purity of desires (Matt. 5:28).

31:5–7 Job's references to the way he has **walked** (v. 5), to where his **heart** has led him (v. 7), and to whether he has **turned aside from the way** (v. 7) describe his life in images that evoke the profile of wisdom (e.g., see Prov. 4:10–19, 23–27).

31:11–12 Job grounds his own caution against adultery (v. 9) in the warnings of its consequences—both in being **punished by the judges** (see also v. 28) and in its having ruinous and far-reaching effects like **fire** (see also Prov. 6:27–29). The reference to **Abaddon** (Job 31:12) signifies Job's presumption that the way he has walked has consequences beyond the mere extent of all his earthly **increase** (see Prov. 7:21–27).

31:13–15 Job did not reject the needs of his servants (v. 13) lest they should have a **complaint** against him (v. 14) for which he would have no **answer** for God (v. 15). Job will use this vocabulary again in his final plea that he would receive an answer from his "adversary" (v. 35; the Hb. term is related to the noun translated "complaint" in v. 14).

31:16–23 Care for the **poor**, **widow** (v. 16), **fatherless** (v. 17), **needy** (v. 19), and sojourner (see vv. 31–32) is prescribed in the Pentateuch (see Ex. 22:21–27; Lev. 19:33; Deut. 24:17–18). Such action shows that someone understands that he or she lives with others before God and is called to fear him alone (Job 31:23). Job lived this way because he believed God weighed his actions, and he understood that **calamity** was the consequence for the unrighteous (see vv. 2–4).

21 if I have raised my hand against [v]the fatherless,
because I saw my help in [w]the gate,
22 then let my shoulder blade fall from my shoulder,
and let my arm be broken from its socket.
23 For I was [x]in terror of calamity from God,
and I could not have faced his [x]majesty.

24 [y]"If I have made gold my [z]trust
or called [a]fine gold my confidence,
25 if I have [b]rejoiced because my wealth was abundant
or because [c]my hand had found much,
26 [d]if I have looked at the sun[1] when it shone,
or [e]the moon moving in splendor,
27 and my heart has been secretly enticed,
and my mouth has kissed my hand,
28 this also would be [f]an iniquity to be punished by the judges,
for I would have been false to God above.

29 "If I have [g]rejoiced at the ruin of him who hated me,
or exulted when evil overtook him
30 ([h]I have not let my mouth sin
by asking for his life with a curse),
31 if the men of my tent have not said,
'Who is there that has not been filled with his [i]meat?'
32 ([j]the sojourner has not lodged in the street;
I have opened my doors to the traveler),
33 if I [k]have concealed my transgressions [l]as others do[2]
by hiding my iniquity in my heart,
34 because I stood in great fear of [m]the multitude,
and the contempt of families terrified me,
so that I kept silence, and did not go out of doors—
35 Oh, that I had one to hear me!
(Here is my signature! Let the Almighty [n]answer me!)
Oh, that I had [o]the indictment written by my adversary!
36 Surely I would carry it on my [p]shoulder;
I would [q]bind it on me as [r]a crown;
37 I would give him an account of all my steps;
like a prince I would approach him.

38 "If my land has cried out against me
and its furrows have wept together,
39 [s]if I have eaten its yield without payment
and made its owners [t]breathe their last,
40 let [u]thorns grow instead of wheat,
and foul weeds instead of barley."

The words of Job are ended.

[1] Hebrew *the light* [2] Or *as Adam did*

21 [v]ch. 22:9 [w]See ch. 5:4
23 [x]ch. 13:11
24 [y]Mark 10:24, 25 [z]ch. 4:6 [a]ch. 28:16
25 [b]Ps. 62:10 [c]Deut. 8:17
26 [d]Deut. 4:19; [Deut. 17:3; 2 Kgs. 23:5, 11; Ezek. 8:16] [e]See Jer. 44:17-19
28 [f]ver. 11
29 [g]Prov. 17:5
30 [h][Matt. 5:44; Rom. 12:14]
31 [i]Ex. 16:12; 1 Sam. 25:11
32 [j][Gen. 19:2, 3; Judg. 19:20, 21; Matt. 25:35; Heb. 13:2]
33 [k]Prov. 28:13 [l]Gen. 3:8, 12
34 [m][Ex. 23:2]
35 [n]ch. 13:22 [o][ch. 19:23]
36 [p]Isa. 9:6; 22:22 [q]Prov. 6:21 [r]Zech. 6:11
39 [s][ch. 22:6-9; Luke 10:7; 2 Tim. 2:6; James 5:4] [t][1 Kgs. 21:16, 19]
40 [u]Gen. 3:18

31:24–28 Job has guarded against both the idolatry of trusting the wealth that God has provided rather than trusting God (vv. 24–25), and the idolatry of worshiping what God has created (vv. 26–27). Job's faithfulness in this matter is grounded in the fact that idolatry is to be **punished by the judges** as an action that is **false to God above** (see v. 12), as is adultery. This is the emphasis of Job's final appeal: he has consciously lived his life as if it were open before and in service to the God of heaven and earth.

31:31 "Who is there that has not been filled with his meat?" The question obviously calls for a negative response; those of Job's household were always well fed. Offering food and lodging was of critical importance to secure strangers from the dangers of the streets at night.

31:33 as others do. There may be an allusion here to the Genesis story, where Adam tried to conceal his sin from God (see ESV footnote).

31:35–37 Job wishes once again for an answer regarding his offenses (v. 35; see vv. 13–15), so that he might give **an account of all my steps** (v. 37) to the One who numbers them (see v. 4; the Hb. for "numbers" and "account" are related).

32:1–37:24 *Elihu: Suffering as a Discipline.* The opening verses of this sec-

Chapter 32
1[v]See ch. 33:9
2[w]Gen. 22:21; Jer. 25:23 [x]ch. 4:17; [ch. 34:5; 35:2; 40:8]
3[y]ch. 8:6; 22:5
6[z]ch. 15:10
8[a]ch. 33:4; 34:14 [b]ch. 33:4; Gen. 2:7 [c]ch. 35:11; 38:36; 39:17; 1 Kgs. 3:12; 4:29; Prov. 2:6; Eccles. 2:26; Dan. 1:17; 2:21; James 1:5
9[d]1 Cor. 1:26; [ch. 12:20; Matt. 11:25]
13[e]Jer. 9:23

Elihu Rebukes Job's Three Friends

32 So these three men ceased to answer Job, because he was [v]righteous in his own eyes.
2 Then Elihu the son of Barachel [w]the Buzite, of the family of Ram, burned with
anger. He burned with anger at Job because he justified himself [x]rather than God. 3 He
burned with anger also at Job's three friends because they had found no answer, although
they had [y]declared Job to be in the wrong. 4 Now Elihu had waited to speak to Job because
they were older than he. 5 And when Elihu saw that there was no answer in the mouth of
these three men, he burned with anger.
6 And Elihu the son of Barachel the Buzite answered and said:

"I am young in years,
and you are [z]aged;
therefore I was timid and afraid
to declare my opinion to you.
7 I said, 'Let days speak,
and many years teach wisdom.'
8 But it is [a]the spirit in man,
[b]the breath of the Almighty, that makes him [c]understand.
9 [d]It is not the old[1] who are wise,
nor the aged who understand what is right.
10 Therefore I say, 'Listen to me;
let me also declare my opinion.'

11 "Behold, I waited for your words,
I listened for your wise sayings,
while you searched out what to say.
12 I gave you my attention,
and, behold, there was none among you who refuted Job
or who answered his words.
13 Beware [e]lest you say, 'We have found wisdom;
God may vanquish him, not a man.'
14 He has not directed his words against me,
and I will not answer him with your speeches.

15 "They are dismayed; they answer no more;
they have not a word to say.
16 And shall I wait, because they do not speak,
because they stand there, and answer no more?

[1] Hebrew *many* [in years]

tion introduce the person and perspective of Elihu (32:1–5) and are followed by an uninterrupted section of his speeches. These include an announcement of his intention to speak (32:6–22) and an initial challenge to Job (ch. 33), a general dispute against what Job has asserted (ch. 34), a description of Job's place before God (35:1–16), and a lengthy section that describes and defends God's majesty (36:1–37:24). Elihu is not addressed in the Lord's speeches that follow immediately after his own (see 38:1–40:2; 40:6–41:34), nor is he referred to in the description either of the prologue (1:1–2:13) or the epilogue (42:7–17). Interpreters have differed on how to understand the function of Elihu's speeches in light of this lack of explicit reference or evaluation. While the Lord's response to Job will include some vocabulary and references that are similar to portions of Elihu's speeches, he does not commend either Elihu's suggested reasons for Job's suffering or his anger against Job (see note on 32:2). See also the discussion of Elihu in the Introduction: Literary Features.

32:1–5 *Introduction: Elihu and His Anger.* The brief narrative section preceding Elihu's speeches indicates that Job's three friends have nothing more to say to Job (v. 1), introduces Elihu (v. 2a), and describes his perspective on what has transpired (vv. 2b–5). The section contains repeated statements that indicate the manner in which Elihu takes up his speech: he "burned with anger" (vv. 2, 3, 5) because no **answer** had been given to Job (vv. 1, 3, 5).

32:2 Elihu's introduction includes a reference to his father and family that is more explicit than that of any of the three friends (see 2:11; and 4:1; 8:1; 11:1). The reference may be included for the way it signifies Elihu's understanding of his role (e.g., **Barachel** may mean either "may God bless" or "God has blessed") or possibly his need for further introduction in light of his youth.

32:3 Although Elihu **burned with anger** against both Job and his friends (vv. 2–3), when the same phrase is used of the Lord in the epilogue, his anger burns only against the three friends because they had not affirmed what was right about the Lord, as Job had done (see 42:7).

32:6–22 *The Voice of Youth.* Elihu's opening speech is a repetitive declaration of what the opening narrative section has described (see vv. 1–5): Elihu has waited to speak because he is younger than the three friends, but now that it is clear to him that they do not have an answer for Job, he feels compelled to speak. Elihu directs this section primarily at the friends and emphasizes his right and intention to "declare my opinion" (32:6, 10, 11).

32:8 Elihu plays on the words **spirit** and **breath** in his early speeches (see also 33:4; 34:14) in the way most likely to evoke Job's earlier plea (see 27:2–3) as he asserts his own right to speak.

17 I also will answer with my share;
I also will declare my opinion.
18 For I am full of words;
the spirit within me constrains me.
19 Behold, my belly is like wine that has no vent;
like new [f]wineskins ready to burst.
20 [g]I must speak, that I may find [h]relief;
I must open my lips and answer.
21 I will not [i]show partiality to any man
or use flattery toward any person.
22 For I do not know how to flatter,
else my Maker would soon take me away.

Elihu Rebukes Job

33 1 "But now, hear my speech, O Job,
and listen to all my words.
2 Behold, I [j]open my mouth;
the tongue in my mouth speaks.
3 My words declare the uprightness of my heart,
and what my lips know they speak sincerely.
4 [k]The Spirit of God has made me,
and [l]the breath of the Almighty gives me life.
5 [m]Answer me, if you can;
[n]set your words in order before me; take your stand.
6 Behold, I am toward God as you are;
I too was pinched off from a piece of [o]clay.
7 Behold, no [p]fear of me need terrify you;
my [q]pressure will not be heavy upon you.

8 "Surely you have spoken in my ears,
and I have heard the sound of your words.
9 You say, 'I am [r]pure, without [s]transgression;
I am clean, and there is no iniquity in me.
10 Behold, he finds occasions against me,
he [t]counts me as his enemy,
11 he [u]puts my feet in the stocks
and [v]watches all my paths.'

12 "Behold, in this you are not right. I will answer you,
for God is greater than man.
13 Why do you [w]contend against him,
saying, 'He [x]will answer none of man's[1] words'?[2]
14 For God [y]speaks in one way,
[z]and in two, though man [a]does not perceive it.

[1] Hebrew *his* [2] Or *He will not answer for any of his own words*

19 [f]Matt. 9:17; [Josh. 9:4]
20 [g][Ps. 39:3] [h]1 Sam. 16:23
21 [i]Lev. 19:15

Chapter 33

2 [j]ch. 3:1
4 [k]ch. 27:3 [l]ch. 32:8; Gen. 2:7; [Ezek. 37:9; Acts 17:25]
5 [m]ver. 32 [n]ch. 13:18; 23:4; [Ps. 5:3]
6 [o]See ch. 4:19
7 [p]ch. 9:34, 35; 13:21 [q][ch. 23:2]
9 [r]ch. 9:21; 10:7; 11:4; 12:4; 13:18; 16:17; 23:10, 11; 27:5; 29:14; 32:1; 34:5 [s]ch. 34:6
10 [t]See ch. 13:24
11 [u]ch. 13:27 [v]ch. 10:14; 14:16; 31:4
13 [w]ch. 13:3; 16:21; 31:35; 40:2 [x]See ch. 9:12
14 [y][ch. 40:5; Ps. 62:11] [z]ver. 29 [a][1 Sam. 3:4, 6]

32:18–20 As in v. 8, Elihu claims he is not speaking by choice but by necessity. Elihu may be thinking he is like a prophet, but the reader must judge whether he is right. (On the difficulty of assessing Elihu, see the discussion in the Introduction: Literary Features.)

33:1–33 *An Arbiter for Job.* Elihu opens and closes this section with a call for Job to listen to his words and answer if he is able (vv. 1–7, 31–33). He then presents a summary of Job's contentions regarding himself, his circumstances, and God's seeming silence (vv. 8–13) before suggesting ways that God speaks in order to turn a person from the way that leads to death (vv. 14–30).

33:1 Elihu frames his rebuke with a call for Job to **listen** to his words (also vv. 31, 33), which he likely sees as serving to fill the silence left by Job's friends as well as to explain how God may be speaking on the very points where Job has claimed he is silent.

33:2–4 Elihu appears to be evoking Job's earlier statement where he declared that, as long as he had breath, his lips could not speak falsely by agreeing that his friends were right (see 27:2–6). Elihu plays on Job's words (see also 32:8) to assert that what he has to say is equally an upright and sincere declaration.

33:9 Elihu summarizes Job's statements as if Job had argued that he was **pure** and **without transgression**. However, it is clear from Job's regular practice of making burnt offerings that this was not his claim (see 1:5), which was focused instead on denying the suggestion that some hidden sin was at the root of his suffering. By mischaracterizing Job's plea, Elihu ends up offering a similar argument to that of the three friends: God is greater than man (33:12) and thus he must have intended to warn or rebuke Job (vv. 14–30).

33:11 puts my feet in the stocks. Elihu quotes Job verbatim (cf. 13:27). God had made Job his enemy, pursuing him like a leaf driven in the wind (13:24–25).

33:14 For God speaks . . . though man does not perceive it. Elihu is

15[b]See Num. 12:6 [c]ch. 4:13 [d]Ps. 17:3
16[e]ch. 36:10, 15; Ps. 40:6; Isa. 50:5
17[f]ch. 36:9
18[g]ch. 36:12
19[h]ch. 30:17
20[i]Ps. 107:18 [j]Prov. 23:3
21[k][Ps. 22:17]
22[l]ver. 24, 28 [m]2 Sam. 24:16, 17; Ps. 78:49
23[n]Gen. 16:7; 22:11; 48:16; Ps. 34:7; Isa. 63:9; [Mal. 3:1] [o]Gen. 42:23; Isa. 43:27 [p]Eccles. 7:28; [Song 5:10] [q][Prov. 14:2; Ezek. 18:21, 22]
24[r]ch. 36:18; Ps. 49:7
25[s]2 Kgs. 5:14; [Heb. 9:12]
26[t]See ch. 22:27 [u]Ps. 17:15 [v][2 Sam. 12:13; Prov. 28:13; Luke 15:21-24; 1 John 1:9]
27[w]Ps. 106:6; [Rom. 6:21]
28[x]Isa. 38:17 [y]ver. 22, 24 [z][ch. 3:9]
29[a]ver. 14
30[b]Ps. 56:13
32[c]ver. 5 [d]ch. 34:33
33[e]Ps. 34:11

15 In [b]a dream, in [c]a vision of [d]the night,
when [c]deep sleep falls on men,
while they slumber on their beds,
16 then he [e]opens the ears of men
and terrifies them with warnings,
17 that he may turn man aside from his [f]deed
and conceal pride from a man;
18 he keeps back his soul from the pit,
his life from [g]perishing by the sword.

19 "Man is also rebuked with pain on his bed
and with continual strife in his [h]bones,
20 so that his [i]life loathes bread,
and his appetite [j]the choicest food.
21 His flesh is so wasted away that it cannot be seen,
and his bones that were not seen [k]stick out.
22 His soul draws near [l]the pit,
and his life to [m]those who bring death.
23 If there be for him [n]an angel,
[o]a mediator, [p]one of the thousand,
to declare to man what is [q]right for him,
24 and he is merciful to him, and says,
'Deliver him from going down into the pit;
I have found [r]a ransom;
25 let his flesh [s]become fresh with youth;
let him return to the days of his youthful vigor';
26 then man[1] [t]prays to God, and he accepts him;
he [u]sees his face with a shout of joy,
and he [v]restores to man his righteousness.
27 He sings before men and says:
'I [w]sinned and perverted what was right,
and it was not repaid to me.
28 He has redeemed my [x]soul from going down [y]into the pit,
and my life shall [z]look upon the light.'

29 "Behold, God does all these things,
twice, [a]three times, with a man,
30 to bring back his soul from the pit,
that he may be lighted with [b]the light of life.
31 Pay attention, O Job, listen to me;
be silent, and I will speak.
32 If you have any words, [c]answer me;
[d]speak, for I desire to justify you.
33 If not, [e]listen to me;
be silent, and I will teach you wisdom."

[1] Hebrew *he*

suggesting that Job has not recognized and maybe even has ignored the ways in which God has spoken to him.

33:18 Elihu repeatedly states that the purpose of God's speaking to a person in the way he describes is to keep **his soul from the pit** (also vv. 22, 24, 28, 30). Thus he implies that Job's suffering may be a corrective of his overall path rather than simply punishment for some hidden sin. However, given the Lord's description of Job in the prologue (see 1:8; 2:3), Elihu's suggestion seems very similar to, if not an even more severe condemnation than, the one offered by the three friends.

33:19–22 The images that Elihu employs in this section are surely aimed at encouraging Job to see his similar physical state as signifying that God has spoken mercifully through his circumstances, to keep him from the path he was on (see v. 18).

33:23–28 Elihu poses a hypothetical situation in which an **angel** or **mediator** might act on behalf of a person to deliver him (vv. 23–25), and he suggests that the appropriate response would be repentance and rejoicing (vv. 26–28). When Elihu tells Job that he should not fail to accept the correction because of the "greatness of the ransom" (36:18), he implies that the loss of all of Job's possessions and family might be such a **ransom** for his deliverance (33:24).

Elihu Asserts God's Justice

34 Then Elihu answered and said:

2 "Hear my words, you wise men,
and give ear to me, you who know;
3 for [g]the ear tests words
as the palate tastes food.
4 Let us choose [h]what is right;
let us know among ourselves what is good.
5 For Job has said, 'I am [i]in the right,
and [j]God has taken away my right;
6 in spite of my right I am counted a liar;
my wound is incurable, though I am [k]without transgression.'
7 What man is like Job,
who [l]drinks up scoffing like water,
8 who travels in company with evildoers
and walks [m]with wicked men?
9 For [n]he has said, 'It profits a man nothing
that he should take delight in God.'

10 "Therefore, hear me, you men of understanding:
far be it from God that he should [o]do wickedness,
and from the Almighty that he should do wrong.
11 For according to [p]the work of a man he will repay him,
and [q]according to his ways he will make it befall him.
12 Of a truth, God will not do wickedly,
and [r]the Almighty will not pervert justice.
13 Who gave him charge over the earth,
and who [s]laid on him[1] the whole world?
14 If he should [t]set his heart to it
and [u]gather to himself his [v]spirit and his breath,
15 all flesh would perish together,
and man would [w]return to dust.

16 "If you have understanding, hear this;
listen to what I say.
17 [x]Shall one who hates justice govern?
Will you condemn him who is righteous and mighty,

[1] Hebrew lacks *on him*

Chapter 34
3[g]ch. 12:11
4[h]1 Thess. 5:21, 22
5[i]See ch. 33:9 [j]ch. 27:2
6[k]ch. 33:9
7[l]See ch. 15:16
8[m][Ps. 1:1]
9[n]ch. 9:22, 23, 30, 31; 21:7, 15; 24:1; [ch. 35:3; Mal. 3:14]
10[o]ch. 36:23; Gen. 18:25; Deut. 32:4; 2 Chr. 19:7; Ps. 92:15; Rom. 9:14
11[p]Ps. 62:12; Prov. 24:12; Matt. 16:27; Rom. 2:6; 2 Cor. 5:10; 1 Pet. 1:17; Rev. 22:12 [q]Jer. 17:10; 32:19; Ezek. 33:20
12[r]See ch. 8:3
13[s]See ch. 38:4-7
14[t][ch. 2:3] [u]Ps. 104:29; [Ps. 146:4] [v]ch. 32:8
15[w]See ch. 10:9
17[x][Gen. 18:25]

34:1–37 *An Appeal to the Wise.* Elihu sets out to dispute Job in a speech structured by its general statements of address. He is calling "wise men" to hear Job's contention that he is in the right (vv. 2–9) and "men of understanding" to hear Elihu's disputation of this claim (vv. 10–34), with both groups bracketed together as those who will agree with Elihu against Job (vv. 35–37).

34:1–9 Elihu calls those who are wise to weigh Job's claim that he is right and that God has taken away what he was entitled to (vv. 1–6); he prefigures his conclusion when he says that Job "walks with wicked men" (vv. 7–9; see v. 36).

34:3 palate tastes food. Truth is discerned through hearing, just as the quality of food is discerned through tasting. Job used this same proverb earlier to challenge the wisdom of his friends (12:11). Elihu repeats the proverb to challenge his listeners to weigh Job's words.

34:4–6 With the repeated reference to **right** in these verses, Elihu seems to be playing particularly off Job's statements in 27:2–6, where he lamented that God had taken his right away and he refused to agree that his friends were right about him.

34:8 Elihu describes Job as one who **walks** with **evildoers** and **wicked men**, which is a path that the wise are called to avoid (see Ps. 1:1). He will ground this description in what he feels Job's assertion about himself and God (Job 34:5) necessarily means (see vv. 11–13).

34:9 Although Job had stated that the wicked and the righteous seem to suffer the same fate, in order to argue against his friends' suggestion that the wicked are always punished, he did not state precisely what Elihu presents here. Job had governed his life by **delight in God** and his words (see 23:10–12), and he had argued that it was the wicked who live, often in prosperity, as if service to the Almighty **profits a man nothing** (see 21:15).

34:10–37 Although Elihu has already indicated his conclusion about Job (vv. 7–9), he sets out to prove that Job should be condemned for his claims.

34:10–12 These verses represent the grounds for Elihu's argument against Job: since God **will repay** a man in accord with his **work** and **ways** (v. 11), Job's claim that he is right and that God has taken away his right (see v. 5) would be the same as saying that God has acted in **wickedness** (v. 10) so as to **pervert justice** (v. 12). Although it takes a slightly different shape, Elihu's argument results in the same dilemma that resulted from the arguments of the three friends: either Job is in the right or God is in the right, but it cannot be both (see 8:2–7).

18 who [y]says to a king, 'Worthless one,'
and to nobles, 'Wicked man,'
19 who [z]shows no partiality to princes,
nor regards the rich [a]more than the poor,
for [b]they are all the work of his hands?
20 In a moment [c]they die;
at [d]midnight the people are shaken and pass away,
and the mighty are taken away by [e]no human hand.

21 "For his eyes are on [f]the ways of a man,
and he sees all his [f]steps.
22 There is no [g]gloom or [h]deep darkness
where evildoers may hide themselves.
23 For God[1] has no need to consider a man further,
that he should go before God in [i]judgment.
24 He [j]shatters the mighty without investigation
and sets [l]others in their place.
25 Thus, knowing their works,
he [m]overturns them in the night, and they are crushed.
26 He strikes them for their wickedness
in a place for all to see,
27 because they turned aside from [n]following him
and had no regard for any of his ways,
28 so that they [o]caused the cry of the poor to come to him,
and he [p]heard the cry of the afflicted—
29 When he is quiet, who can condemn?
When he hides his face, who can behold him,
whether it be a nation or a man?—
30 that a godless man should not reign,
that he should not ensnare the people.

31 "For has anyone said to God,
'I have borne punishment; I will not offend any more;
32 [r]teach me what I do not see;
if I have done iniquity, I will do it no more'?
33 Will he then make repayment to suit you,
because you reject it?
For you must choose, and not I;
therefore [s]declare what you know.[2]
34 Men of understanding will say to me,
and the wise man who hears me will say:
35 'Job [t]speaks without knowledge;
his words are without insight.'
36 Would that Job were tried to the end,
because he answers like wicked men.

[1] Hebrew *he* [2] The meaning of the Hebrew in verses 29–33 is uncertain

18 [y]Ex. 22:28
19 [z]Deut. 10:17; 2 Chr. 19:7; Acts 10:34; Rom. 2:11; Gal. 2:6; Eph. 6:9; Col. 3:25; 1 Pet. 1:17 [a][James 2:5] [b]See ch. 31:15
20 [c]ch. 21:13 [d]Ex. 11:4; [ch. 27:20; 36:20] [e]Dan. 8:25; [Lam. 4:6]
21 [f]ch. 14:16; See ch. 31:4
22 [g][Ps. 139:12; Amos 9:2, 3; Heb. 4:13] [h]See ch. 3:5
23 [i]ch. 14:3
24 [j]Ps. 2:9 [l]See ch. 8:19
25 [m]Prov. 12:7
27 [n]1 Sam. 15:11; Ps. 28:5; Isa. 5:12
28 [o]ch. 35:9; James 5:4; [Gen. 18:20, 21] [p]Ex. 3:7; 22:23; Isa. 32:17
32 [r]ch. 35:11; 36:22; Ps. 19:12; 86:11
33 [s]ch. 33:32
35 [t]See ch. 35:16

34:23 God has no need to consider a man further. The subject of this sentence is "he" in Hebrew (see ESV footnote), and just whom that refers to must be inferred from the context. Some interpreters suggest that it refers to "man," with the sense that a person does not set his own times for judgment, which would require a slight emendation of the Hebrew text. However, understanding God as the subject makes sense in the context of Elihu's dispute: Job has been calling for some opportunity to present his case before either God or an arbitrator, but Elihu is suggesting that God has already acted and does not need to give further consideration to Job's or any other person's case.

34:26–28 Although Elihu does not apply the images directly to Job, his description suggests something very similar to what the three friends had already argued (see 22:5–11): Job has been struck **for all to see** (34:26) because he must have **turned aside** from following the Lord's **ways** (v. 27) by mistreating the **poor** and **afflicted** (v. 28).

34:34–37 Elihu concludes with the presumption that any who are truly **men of understanding** or **wise** would agree with him (v. 34; see vv. 2, 10) that Job speaks like a fool who is **without knowledge** or **insight** (v. 35). Furthermore, Elihu wishes boldly that the judgment signified in Job's suffering would be taken to its logical end (v. 36), because in addition to whatever **sin** he is ultimately being punished for, Job's words also express **rebellion** and arrogance against God (v. 37).

37 For he adds rebellion to his sin;
he [u]claps his hands among us
and multiplies his words against God."

Elihu Condemns Job

35 And Elihu answered and said:

2 "Do you think this to be just?
Do you say, [v]'It is my right before God,'
3 that you ask, [w]'What advantage have I?
How am I better off than if I had sinned?'
4 I will answer you
and [x]your friends with you.
5 [y]Look at the heavens, and see;
and behold the clouds, which are higher than you.
6 If you have sinned, [z]what do you accomplish against him?
And if your transgressions are multiplied, what do you do to him?
7 [a]If you are righteous, what do you give to him?
Or what does he receive from your hand?
8 Your wickedness concerns a man like yourself,
and your righteousness [b]a son of man.

9 "Because of the multitude of [c]oppressions people [d]cry out;
they call for help because of the arm of [e]the mighty.[1]
10 But none says, 'Where is God my [f]Maker,
who gives [g]songs in the night,
11 who teaches us [h]more than the beasts of the earth
and makes us wiser than the birds of the heavens?'
12 There they [i]cry out, but he does not answer,
because of the pride of evil men.
13 Surely God does not hear an empty cry,
nor does the Almighty regard it.
14 How much less when you say that you [j]do not see him,
that the case is before him, and you are [k]waiting for him!
15 And now, because [l]his anger does not punish,
and he does not take much note of transgression,[2]
16 Job opens his mouth in empty talk;
he [m]multiplies words [n]without knowledge."

[1] Or *the many* [2] Theodotion, Symmachus (compare Vulgate); the meaning of the Hebrew word is uncertain

37[u]See ch. 27:23
Chapter 35
2[v]See ch. 32:2
3[w]See ch. 34:9
4[x]ch. 34:8, 36
5[y][ch. 22:12]
6[z]Prov. 8:36; Jer. 7:19
7[a]ch. 22:2, 3; Prov. 9:12; Luke 17:10; [ch. 41:11; Rom. 11:35]
8[b]ch. 25:6
9[c]Amos 3:9 [d]Ex. 2:23; [ch. 34:28] [e][ch. 22:8]
10[f]ch. 4:17; Deut. 32:6 [g]Ps. 42:8; 77:6; 149:5; [Acts 16:25]
11[h]ch. 36:22; Ps. 94:12; Isa. 28:26
12[i]See ch. 27:9
14[j]ch. 9:11; 23:8, 9 [k][ch. 13:15]
15[l]Num. 16:29; Ps. 89:32
16[m]ch. 34:37 [n]ch. 34:35; 36:12; 38:2; 42:3

35:1–16 ***What Right Does Job Have Before God?*** Elihu argues against what he sees as Job's presumption before God. Where Job said that the wicked and the righteous appear to suffer indiscriminately, Elihu argues that Job is acting as if his righteousness grants him some expectation of favor before God, when neither faithfulness nor wickedness accomplishes anything with or against God (vv. 1–8). Furthermore, where Job had maintained that the oppressed cry out and the wicked are not punished, Elihu argues that they often cry out in pride rather than in prayer to God, and thus God does not regard their cries, much less Job's vain request and foolish words (vv. 9–16).

35:2 my right before God. Job was declaring himself right before God. He asserted that God had wronged him (19:6), which in the view of Elihu amounted to claiming that *he* was right rather than God (32:2).

35:6–8 Elihu repeats an aspect of Eliphaz's final argument against Job—that God does not profit from Job's righteousness (see 22:2–3). (However, where Elihu merely mentions **wickedness** within his comparison [35:8], Eliphaz detailed the likely specifics of Job's evil [see 22:5–9].) Neither Eliphaz nor Elihu understand that the whole impetus for Job's complaint is his desire to see God vindicated on earth in and through the lives of those who are faithful to him.

35:12–13 When Elihu says that God does not heed the cry of the oppressed **because of the pride of evil men** (v. 12b), he does not explicitly indicate whether he is referring to those who cry out or to their oppressors. However, Elihu's repeated emphasis that God does not **answer** (v. 12a), listen (**hear**), or **regard** an **empty cry** (v. 13) indicates that he is most likely referring to the pride of the oppressed.

35:14–16 Elihu argues that if God does not regard the cries of the proud oppressed (vv. 9–13), how can Job expect an answer (v. 14) to what Elihu assumes is the even more obstinate stance of one who takes his own lack of punishment as reason to speak foolishly (vv. 15–16). This is extraordinarily insensitive, considering Job's actual situation. Elihu is revealing a high view of his own importance.

36:1–37:24 ***The Mercy and Majesty of God.*** Elihu concludes with a lengthy speech that he introduces as being "on God's behalf" (36:2–4). He begins by inferring that Job's situation is an example of God using affliction to deliver the righteous from their sin if they are willing to accept his correction (36:5–21).

Elihu Extols God's Greatness

36 And Elihu continued, and said:

2 "Bear with me a little, and I will show you,
for I have yet something to say on God's behalf.
3 I will get my knowledge from [o]afar
and ascribe [p]righteousness to my [q]Maker.
4 For truly my words are not false;
one who is [r]perfect in knowledge is with you.

5 "Behold, God is mighty, and [s]does not despise any;
he is [t]mighty in strength of understanding.
6 He does not keep the wicked alive,
but gives [u]the afflicted their right.
7 He does not withdraw his [v]eyes from the righteous,
but with [w]kings on the throne
he sets them forever, and they are [x]exalted.
8 And if they are [y]bound in chains
and caught in the cords of affliction,
9 then he declares to them their work
and their transgressions, that they are [z]behaving arrogantly.
10 He [a]opens their ears to instruction
and commands that they [b]return from iniquity.
11 [c]If they listen and serve him,
they [d]complete their days in prosperity,
and their years in pleasantness.
12 But if they do not listen, they [e]perish by the sword
and die [f]without knowledge.

13 "The [g]godless in heart cherish anger;
they do not cry for help when he [h]binds them.
14 They [i]die in youth,
and their life ends among the cult prostitutes.
15 He delivers [j]the afflicted by their affliction
and [k]opens their ear by adversity.
16 He also allured you out of distress
into [l]a broad place where there was no cramping,
and what was set on your [m]table was full of [n]fatness.

Chapter 36
3 [o][Ps. 78:2] [p][Rev. 15:3, 4; 16:5, 7; 19:1, 2] [q]ch. 35:10
4 [r]ch. 37:16
5 [s]ch. 8:20 (Heb.); [Ps. 138:6] [t]ch. 9:4; 12:13, 16
6 [u]ver. 15; ch. 34:28
7 [v][Ps. 33:18; 34:15] [w]Ps. 132:12; [Ps. 113:8] [x]Ps. 75:10
8 [y]ver. 13; Ps. 107:10
9 [z]ch. 15:25
10 [a]ch. 33:16 [b]Jer. 18:11
11 [c]For ver. 11, 12, see Isa. 1:19, 20 [d]ch. 21:13
12 [e]ch. 33:18 [f][ch. 4:21]; See ch. 35:16
13 [g]ch. 15:34 [h]ver. 8
14 [i]ch. 15:32; 22:16; Ps. 55:23
15 [j]ver. 6; See ch. 33:15-28 [k]ver. 10; [Ps. 119:67, 71]
16 [l][ch. 37:10; Ps. 4:1; 18:19; 31:8; 118:5] [m]Ps. 23:5 [n]Ps. 36:8

Elihu then describes God's power and majesty as manifested audibly and visibly in storms, through which God accomplishes whatever purpose he has in mind (36:22–37:13). Finally, he calls Job to consider whether he knows how God does any of these things (37:14–20), to remind him of God's majesty and power (37:21–23)—the reason both that men fear God and that he does not regard those who do not fear him (37:24).

36:2–4 Elihu presents his final speech as something offered **on God's behalf** (v. 2), emphasizing that, unlike Job (see 34:35), he has understanding that comes from outside himself (36:3) and that he is **perfect in knowledge** (v. 4), something he will later ascribe also to God (see 37:16). Again, he seems more arrogant than he realizes, as young men sometimes do.

36:5–21 Elihu begins by describing God's power and wisdom (v. 5) and asserts that he governs justly over the lives of both the **wicked** (v. 6) and the **righteous** (v. 7). The section is focused on **affliction** (v. 8; also vv. 6, 15, 21), which God uses to deliver the righteous from their sin unless they reject his correction and show themselves to be like the godless (vv. 8–15). Elihu appeals to Job to consider his own circumstances as an example of this choice, and encourages him to embrace the mercy of his affliction rather than his iniquity (vv. 16–21).

36:6–7 The statement that God **gives the afflicted their right** (v. 6b) comes directly between the mention of the **wicked** (v. 6a) and the **righteous** (v. 7), expressing the heart of Elihu's argument: the afflicted (see vv. 8, 15, 21) are treated justly by God and reveal the state of their heart by how they respond to affliction.

36:8–15 Elihu describes **affliction** using the language of captivity: people are **bound in chains and caught in the cords** (v. 8) because God **binds them** (v. 13). He argues that God uses this captivity of affliction to speak to people about their sin (v. 9) and **opens their ears** to his correction (vv. 10, 15). Those who **listen** (v. 11) will be delivered by God (v. 15); those who **do not listen** (v. 12) will be judged even in the circumstances of their death (vv. 13–14).

36:10 When he states that God **opens** the **ears** (also v. 15), Elihu is continuing his point from an earlier speech, suggesting ways that God has been speaking and that Job may be failing to listen (see 33:14, 16).

36:13–14 Elihu describes those who hold onto their **anger** rather than crying out when God **binds** them through affliction (see v. 8). He does so now to warn that Job's continued complaint could lead him to a state and end like that of the **godless in heart**.

36:16–21 Elihu addresses Job more directly by describing the change in his circumstances (vv. 16–20) and warns him against choosing his **iniquity** rather than embracing the purpose of his **affliction** (v. 21; see vv. 8–15).

17 "But you are full of the judgment on the wicked;
judgment and justice seize you.
18 Beware lest wrath entice you into scoffing,
and let not the greatness of [o]the ransom turn you aside.
19 Will your [p]cry for help avail to keep you from distress,
or all the force of your strength?
20 Do not long for [q]the night,
when peoples vanish [r]in their place.
21 Take care; [s]do not turn to iniquity,
for this you have chosen rather than affliction.
22 Behold, God is exalted in his power;
who is [t]a teacher like him?
23 Who has [u]prescribed for him his way,
or who can say, [v]'You have done wrong'?

24 "Remember to [w]extol his work,
of which men have [x]sung.
25 All mankind has looked on it;
man beholds it from afar.
26 Behold, God is great, and we [y]know him not;
the number of his [z]years is unsearchable.
27 For he draws up the drops of water;
they distill his [a]mist in [b]rain,
28 which [c]the skies pour down
and drop on mankind abundantly.
29 Can anyone understand [d]the spreading of the clouds,
the thunderings of his [e]pavilion?
30 Behold, he scatters his lightning about him
and covers the roots of the sea.
31 For by these he [f]judges peoples;
he gives [g]food in abundance.
32 He covers his [h]hands with the lightning
and commands it to strike the mark.
33 Its crashing declares his presence;[1]
the cattle also declare that he rises.

Elihu Proclaims God's Majesty

37

1 "At this also my heart trembles
and leaps out of its place.
2 Keep listening to the thunder of his voice
and the rumbling that comes from his mouth.

[1] Hebrew *declares concerning him*

18 [o]ch. 33:24
19 [p]Prov. 11:4
20 [q]ch. 27:20; 34:20, 25 [r]ch. 40:12
21 [s]Ps. 66:18
22 [t]ch. 34:32; 35:11
23 [u]ch. 34:13; [Isa. 40:13, 14; Rom. 11:34; 1 Cor. 2:16] [v][ch. 34:10]
24 [w]Luke 1:46; [Ps. 92:5; Rev. 15:3] [x][ch. 33:27; Ps. 104:33]
26 [y][ch. 37:5; 1 Cor. 13:12] [z]Ps. 90:2; 102:27
27 [a]Gen. 2:6 (Heb.) [b]Ps. 147:8
28 [c]Prov. 3:20; [Deut. 33:28]
29 [d][ch. 26:9] [e]Ps. 18:11; 105:39
31 [f]ch. 37:13 [g]Ps. 104:27, 28; 136:25; 145:15; 147:9; Acts 14:17
32 [h]Hab. 3:4

36:16–17 Elihu refers to the change in Job's circumstances with a wordplay on the descriptions of when his **table was full of fatness** (v. 16; i.e., prosperity) and how he is now **full of the judgment on the wicked** (v. 17; i.e., calamity and distress). Just as Elihu has already referred to affliction with the imagery of captivity (see vv. 8, 13), he suggests quite plainly that Job should see his own suffering as God seizing him in **judgment** and **justice** (v. 17).

36:18 Elihu has already alluded to the possibility of a **ransom** (see 33:24). Here he makes it explicit: Job should consider the **greatness** of the loss of his family, his reputation, and all that belonged to his household as the means by which the Lord is arresting his attention and turning him from sin.

36:22–37:13 Having described how God speaks through affliction (36:5–21), Elihu focuses now on the majestic and unsearchable ways of God (vv. 22–33) and the way in which his majesty is partially revealed in his governing of the power and purposes of storms (37:1–13). The speech is structured by the calls to the hearer/reader to see (**Behold**, 36:22, 26, 30) and hear (**Keep listening**, 37:2) what Elihu is describing—further implying that Job is simply not attending to the places where God is actually speaking.

36:30 he scatters his lightning. The lightning of the storm represents God's glory in it (cf. Ps. 104:2–3). His glory **covers** (lights up) even the depths of the **sea**.

36:31 he judges peoples. Judging and nourishing are often parallel aspects of God's provision. The clouds bear God's throne, from which he governs and feeds his people.

36:32 covers his hands. "Hands" may be a way of describing the great arches or vaulted chamber of heaven, filled with God's light.

37:2–5 Elihu makes repeated reference to God's **voice** in connection with both the audible (**thunder**) and visible (**lightning**) manifestations of a storm, through which God communicates something of his majesty.

3 Under the whole heaven he lets it go,
and his [i]lightning to the [j]corners of the earth.
4 After it [k]his voice roars;
[l]he thunders with his majestic voice,
and he does not restrain the lightnings[1] when his voice is heard.
5 God thunders wondrously with his voice;
he does [m]great things that we cannot [n]comprehend.
6 For to [o]the snow he says, 'Fall on the earth,'
likewise to the downpour, his mighty downpour.
7 He [p]seals up the hand of every man,
that all men whom he made may [q]know it.
8 Then the beasts go into their [r]lairs,
and remain in their [s]dens.
9 From [t]its chamber [u]comes the whirlwind,
and [v]cold from the scattering winds.
10 By the breath of God [w]ice is given,
and [x]the broad waters are frozen fast.
11 He loads the thick cloud with moisture;
the clouds scatter his lightning.
12 They [y]turn around and around by his [z]guidance,
[z]to accomplish all that he commands them
on the face of [a]the habitable world.
13 Whether for [b]correction or for his [c]land
or for [d]love, he causes it to happen.

14 "Hear this, O Job;
stop and [e]consider the wondrous works of God.
15 Do you know how God lays his command upon them
and causes the lightning of his cloud to shine?
16 Do you know the balancings[2] of the clouds,
the wondrous works of him who is [f]perfect in knowledge,
17 you whose garments are hot
when the earth is still because of the south wind?
18 Can you, like him, [g]spread out the skies,
hard as a cast metal [h]mirror?
19 Teach us what we shall say to him;
we cannot draw up our case because of [i]darkness.
20 Shall it be told him that I would speak?
Did a man ever wish that he would be swallowed up?
21 "And now no one looks on the light
when it is bright in the skies,
when the wind has passed and cleared them.
22 Out of the north comes golden splendor;
God is clothed with [j]awesome majesty.
23 The Almighty—we [k]cannot find him;
he is [l]great in power;
[m]justice and abundant righteousness he will not [n]violate.

[1] Hebrew *them* [2] Or *hoverings*

Chapter 37
3 [i]ch. 36:30, 32 [j]ch. 38:13; [Isa. 11:12; Ezek. 7:2]
4 [k]ch. 40:9; Ps. 68:33; See Ps. 29:3-9 [l]Ps. 18:13
5 [m]See ch. 5:9 [n]ch. 36:26
6 [o]Ps. 147:16, 17
7 [p]Dan. 12:9; [ch. 14:17] [q]Ps. 109:27
8 [r]ch. 38:40 [s]Ps. 104:22
9 [t]ch. 9:9 [u]Isa. 21:1; [ch. 1:19] [v]Ps. 147:17
10 [w]ch. 38:29, 30; Ps. 147:17 [x][ch. 36:16]
12 [y]Gen. 3:24 [z]Ps. 148:8 [a][Prov. 8:31]
13 [b]Ex. 9:18, 23; 1 Sam. 12:18, 19; Ezra 10:9; [ch. 36:31; 38:22, 23] [c]ch. 38:26, 27 [d]1 Kgs. 18:45
14 [e][Ps. 111:2]
16 [f]ch. 36:4; [1 Sam. 2:3]
18 [g]Isa. 42:5; 44:24; [Gen. 1:6] [h][Ex. 38:8]
19 [i]Isa. 60:2; [Eph. 4:18]
22 [j][Ps. 104:1]
23 [k]1 Tim. 6:16 [l]ch. 36:5 [m]Ps. 99:4 [n]Lam. 3:33

37:7 He seals up the hand of every man. This probably refers to the way severe weather causes people to take shelter (as the animals do, v. 8) and thus prevents them from working.

37:13 God's providential purposes may relate to people (**correction** or **love**), or may be **for his land** (see also 38:25–27).

37:14–20 Elihu focuses on God's majesty and calls on Job to listen (**Hear this, O Job**) and apply the weight of this description to his complaint before God, just as he had called Job to do in relation to affliction (see 36:16–21).

37:16 Elihu refers to God as one who is **perfect in knowledge**, a description he first applied to himself in offering this speech on God's behalf (see 36:4).

37:21–23 Elihu likens the **light** that comes after a storm has **cleared** (v. 21) to the God who is **clothed with awesome majesty** (v. 22), who cannot

24 Therefore men [o]fear him;
he does not regard any who are [p]wise in their own conceit."[1]

The Lord Answers Job

38 Then the Lord [q]answered Job out of the whirlwind and said:

2 "Who is this that [r]darkens counsel by words [s]without knowledge?
3 [t]Dress for action[2] like a man;
I will question you, and you make it known to me.

4 "Where were you when I [u]laid the foundation of the earth?
Tell me, if you have understanding.
5 Who determined its measurements—surely you know!
Or who stretched the line upon it?
6 On what were its bases sunk,
or who laid its cornerstone,
7 when the morning stars [v]sang together
and all [w]the sons of God [x]shouted for joy?

8 "Or who [y]shut in the sea with doors
when it burst out from the womb,
9 when I made clouds its garment
and [z]thick darkness its swaddling band,
10 and prescribed [a]limits for it
and set bars and doors,
11 and said, 'Thus far shall you come, and no farther,
and here shall your [b]proud waves be stayed'?

12 "Have you [c]commanded the morning since your days began,
and caused the dawn to know its place,

[1] Hebrew *in heart* [2] Hebrew *Gird up your loins*

24[o]Ps. 130:4; [Matt. 10:28] [p][Isa. 5:21; Matt. 11:25; 1 Cor. 1:26]

Chapter 38

1[q]ch. 40:6; [ch. 13:22]
2[r]ch. 42:3 [s]See ch. 35:16
3[t]1 Kgs. 18:46
4[u]Ps. 104:5; [Prov. 30:4; Isa. 40:12-14]; See Prov. 8:24-29
7[v][Ps. 19:1-4] [w]See ch. 1:6 [x][Luke 2:13, 14]
8[y]Gen. 1:9; Ps. 33:7; 104:8, 9; Jer. 5:22
9[z]ch. 22:13
10[a][ver. 33 (Heb.)]
11[b][Ps. 65:7; 89:9; 93:4]
12[c]Ps. 65:8; 74:16

simply be found, who is extremely powerful, and who does not **violate** what is right (v. 23).

37:24 Elihu presents the options of responding to God's majesty in two stark categories: either people are wise and exhibit **fear** of God, or they are **wise in their own** heart (see ESV footnote).

38:1–42:6 *Challenge: The Lord Answers Job.* The Lord responds in two speeches, each followed by a brief response from Job. In the first, the Lord asks Job whether he knows how creation and its creatures are governed (38:1–40:2). Job, now made conscious of his ignorance, responds by pledging silence (40:3–5). In his second speech, the Lord asks Job particularly about power in relation to himself and other creatures he has made (40:6–41:34). Job, directly aware of God as never before, responds by humbly submitting to God's sovereignty and penitently despising himself for his earlier wild words (42:1–6). While Job had rightly defended himself against his friends' accusations of sin and had defined his circumstances as being governed by God, he had drawn conclusions about what his affliction meant that did not account sufficiently for what was hidden in the knowledge and purposes of God.

38:1–40:2 *The First Challenge: Understanding the Universe.* After addressing Job and calling him to prepare himself (38:1–3), the Lord asks whether he knows how creation was established (38:4–11) and if he has the knowledge or ability to govern it (38:12–38) or to shape the lives of its wonderful variety of creatures (38:39–40:2).

38:1 the Lord answered Job out of the whirlwind. The heading of the speech is brief but important for what it signifies in the context of the book as a whole. The three friends and Elihu had all assumed in one way or another that Job's circumstances and/or his response to them revealed a repudiation of the God whom he claimed to serve faithfully. They warned that if he did not repent and accept his affliction as corrective, he could only expect further judgment. However, the heading suggests that God reveals himself to Job in a display of both majestic power and relational presence: "the Lord" (Hb. *YHWH*), the name most often used to signify God's covenant character and promises (see Ex. 3:14–15), was used in the prologue where God describes Job's relationship to him (see Job 1:8; 2:3); the fact that the Lord "answered Job" contrasts with what the friends and Elihu indicated he should expect (see 35:9–13). Although Elihu had already described the display of God's power and purposes in elements of weather (see 36:22–37:13), it is a covenantal gesture when the Lord reveals his power and his presence as he speaks to Job "out of the whirlwind." While he does not come simply to justify Job, the Lord's presence shows that his reproof comes in the context of steadfast love toward Job and not as judgment for what the friends assumed was Job's repudiation of the path of righteousness.

38:2 Elihu had accused Job of being someone whose words were generally "without knowledge" (34:35; 35:16) or insight (34:35) and represented rebellion in addition to his sin (34:37). The Lord does not reprove Job so extensively when he indicates that he **darkens counsel by words without knowledge**. There appears to be a play on the notion of darkness and something being hidden (see Job's reference to the image in 42:3). Job had drawn conclusions about the nature of God's rule from what was revealed on earth in his and others' circumstances. However, he did not account fully for what is hidden from him, and thus his words cast a shadow on the wisdom and righteousness of God's rule. In his speech, God will question Job in order to remind him that, even in what is revealed of God's powerful and majestic governance of the natural world and its inhabitants, much is still hidden. And if this is true for creation and its creatures, how much more is it true in relation to the wisdom and purpose of the Creator?

38:4–11 Job had begun by lamenting his birth and the time of his life (ch. 3). Using the same language of birth, God now asks Job about the birth of the universe. Can Job explain how the origin of the cosmos could or should have been different?

38:7 sons of God. This is the same expression found in the prologue (see 1:6 and note). It refers to the members of the heavenly court surrounding God's throne.

38:12–38 The Lord questions Job about whether he has either the knowledge or the ability to govern elements of creation that he experiences regularly. In

13 that it might take hold of [d]the skirts of the earth,
and the wicked be [e]shaken out of it?
14 It is changed like clay under the seal,
and its features stand out like a garment.
15 From the wicked their [f]light is withheld,
and [g]their uplifted arm is broken.

16 "Have you [h]entered into the springs of the sea,
or walked in the recesses of the deep?
17 Have [i]the gates of death been revealed to you,
or have you seen the gates of [j]deep darkness?
18 Have you comprehended the expanse of the earth?
Declare, if you know all this.

19 "Where is the way to the dwelling of light,
and where is the place of darkness,
20 that you may take it to its territory
and that you may discern [k]the paths to its home?
21 You know, for [l]you were born then,
and the number of your days is great!

22 "Have you entered [m]the storehouses of the snow,
or have you seen [m]the storehouses of the hail,
23 which I have reserved [n]for the time of trouble,
[n]for the day of battle and war?
24 What is the way to the place where the light is distributed,
or where the east wind is scattered upon the earth?

25 "Who has cleft a channel for the torrents of rain
and [o]a way for the thunderbolt,
26 to bring rain on [p]a land where no man is,
on [q]the desert in which there is no man,
27 to satisfy the waste and desolate land,
and to make the ground sprout with [r]grass?

28 "Has [s]the rain a father,
or who has begotten the drops of dew?
29 From whose womb did [t]the ice come forth,
and who has given birth to [t]the frost of heaven?
30 The waters become hard like stone,
and the face of the deep is [u]frozen.

31 "Can you bind the chains of [v]the Pleiades
or loose the cords of [v]Orion?
32 Can you lead forth the Mazzaroth[1] in their season,
or can you guide [v]the Bear with its children?
33 Do you know [w]the ordinances of the heavens?
Can you establish their rule on the earth?

34 "Can you lift up your voice to the clouds,
that [x]a flood of waters may cover you?

13[d]ch. 37:3 [e][Neh. 5:13]
15[f]ch. 18:5; [Matt. 6:23]; See ch. 24:13-17 [g]Ps. 10:15; 37:17; Ezek. 30:21, 22
16[h]Ps. 77:19
17[i]Ps. 9:13; 107:18; [Isa. 38:10; Matt. 16:18] [j]See ch. 3:5
20[k]ch. 24:13
21[l][ch. 15:7]
22[m][Ps. 135:7]
23[n]Josh. 10:11; Isa. 28:17; 30:30; Ezek. 13:11, 13; 38:22; Rev. 16:21; [ch. 37:13]
25[o]ch. 28:26
26[p][ch. 37:13] [q]Ps. 107:35
27[r]Gen. 1:11; 2 Sam. 23:4
28[s]Ps. 147:8; Jer. 14:22
29[t]Ps. 147:16, 17
30[u][ch. 37:10]
31[v]ch. 9:9; Amos 5:8
32[v][See ver. 31 above]
33[w]Jer. 31:35
34[x]ch. 22:11

[1] Probably the name of a constellation

light of the obvious answer, the Lord also reminds Job that he cannot see fully what the Lord is doing with respect to justice and judgment (see vv. 13, 15, 17, 22–23).

38:13–15 The repeated reference to the **wicked** (vv. 13, 15) indicates that the situations Job was lamenting on earth (e.g., 24:1–12) are not exhaustive of the Lord's counsel in relation to them (see also 38:22–23).

38:14 features stand out like a garment. The coming of the dawn (see v. 12) is compared to the dyeing of a garment.

38:22–23 The reference to **storehouses** (v. 22) that are reserved for **the time of trouble** (v. 23) is another reminder to Job that the Lord's governance of earth's inhabitants is not limited to what is revealed on earth (see vv. 13–15).

38:32 the Mazzaroth. This is a transliteration of a Hebrew word, otherwise unknown. In the context, it must refer to one of the constellations. **the Bear**. This is also a constellation, as indicated by the reference to it along with Orion and Pleiades in 9:9 (see 38:31).

35 Can you send forth lightnings, that they may go
and say to you, 'Here we are'?
36 Who has [y]put wisdom in [z]the inward parts[1]
or given understanding to the mind?[2]
37 Who can number the clouds by wisdom?
Or who can tilt the waterskins of the heavens,
38 when the dust runs into a mass
and [a]the clods stick fast together?
39 "Can you hunt the prey for the lion,
or [b]satisfy the appetite of the young lions,
40 when they crouch in their [c]dens
or lie in wait [d]in their thicket?
41 Who provides for [e]the raven its prey,
when its young ones cry to God for help,
and wander about for lack of food?

39

1 "Do you know when [f]the mountain goats give birth?
Do you observe [g]the calving of the does?
2 Can you number the months that they fulfill,
and do you know the time when they give birth,
3 when they [h]crouch, bring forth their offspring,
and are delivered of their young?
4 Their young ones become strong; they grow up in the open;
they go out and [i]do not return to them.
5 "Who has let the wild donkey go free?
Who has [j]loosed the bonds of the swift donkey,
6 to whom I have given [k]the arid plain for his home
and [l]the salt land for his dwelling place?
7 He scorns the tumult of the city;
he hears not the shouts of the driver.
8 He ranges the mountains as his pasture,
and he searches after every green thing.
9 "Is [m]the wild ox willing to serve you?
Will he spend the night at your [n]manger?
10 Can you bind [m]him in the furrow with ropes,
or will he harrow the valleys after you?
11 Will you depend on him because his strength is great,
and will you leave to him your labor?
12 Do you have faith in him that he will return your grain
and gather it to your threshing floor?
13 "The wings of the ostrich wave proudly,
but are they the pinions and plumage of love?[3]
14 For she leaves her eggs to the earth
and lets them be warmed on the ground,
15 forgetting that a foot may crush them
and that the wild beast may trample them.

[1] Or *in the ibis* [2] Or *rooster* [3] The meaning of the Hebrew is uncertain

36 [y]See ch. 32:8 [z]Ps. 51:6
38 [a]ch. 21:33
39 [b][Ps. 104:21]
40 [c]ch. 37:8 [d]Ps. 17:12
41 [e]Ps. 147:9; Luke 12:24; [Matt. 6:26]

Chapter 39

1 [f]1 Sam. 24:2; Ps. 104:18 [g]Ps. 29:9
3 [h]1 Sam. 4:19
4 [i][Gen. 8:12]
5 [j][ch. 12:18; Ps. 116:16]
6 [k]ch. 24:5; Jer. 2:24 [l]Ps. 107:34; Jer. 17:6; [Deut. 29:23]
9 [m]Num. 23:22 [n]Prov. 14:4; Isa. 1:3
10 [m][See ver. 9 above]

38:36 The translation of this line is difficult because the Hebrew terms are rare. If they are translated as "ibis" and "rooster" (see ESV footnote), the line has a sense that fits well in the context of the section to come (38:39–40:2). The combination of **wisdom** and **understanding** may make it more likely that these terms refer to **inward parts** or **mind**, as that which governs a person's actions and appropriates wisdom from the Lord.

38:39–39:30 The Lord now turns from describing his governance of creation to governance of specific creatures. The speech finishes with a request for Job to answer (40:1–2).

39:9 Hunting the **wild ox** was a sport of royalty. Shalmaneser III of Assyria had it portrayed among the items of tribute on his famous monument, the Black Obelisk.

39:15 foot may crush them. The ostrich lays her eggs in a shallow nest on the ground and sometimes scatters some of them, or deliberately destroys them if the nest is discovered.

16 She [o]deals cruelly with her young, as if they were not hers;
though her [p]labor be in vain, yet she has no fear,
17 because God has made her forget wisdom
and [q]given her no share in understanding.
18 When she rouses herself to flee,[1]
she laughs at the horse and his rider.

19 "Do you give the horse his might?
Do you clothe his neck with a mane?
20 Do you make him leap like the locust?
His majestic [r]snorting is terrifying.
21 He paws[2] in the valley and exults in his strength;
he [s]goes out to meet the weapons.
22 He laughs at fear and is not dismayed;
he does not turn back from the sword.
23 Upon him rattle the quiver,
the flashing spear, and the javelin.
24 With fierceness and rage he swallows the ground;
he cannot stand still at [t]the sound of the trumpet.
25 When the trumpet sounds, he says 'Aha!'
He smells the battle from afar,
the thunder of the captains, and the shouting.

26 "Is it by your understanding that the hawk soars
and spreads his wings toward the south?
27 Is it at your command that the eagle mounts up
and makes his [u]nest on high?
28 On the rock he dwells and makes his home,
on [v]the rocky crag and stronghold.
29 From there he spies out the prey;
his eyes behold it from far away.
30 His young ones suck up blood,
and [w]where the slain are, there is he."

40 And the LORD [x]said to Job:

2 "Shall a faultfinder [y]contend with the Almighty?
He who argues with God, let him answer it."

Job Promises Silence

3 Then Job answered the LORD and said:

4 "Behold, I am [z]of small account; what shall I answer you?
[a]I lay my hand on my mouth.
5 I have spoken [b]once, and I will not answer;
[b]twice, but I will proceed no further."

The LORD Challenges Job

6 Then the LORD [c]answered Job out of the whirlwind and said:

7 [d]"Dress for action[3] like a man;
[e]I will question you, and you make it known to me.

[1] The meaning of the Hebrew is uncertain [2] Hebrew *They paw* [3] Hebrew *Gird up your loins*

16 [o][Lam. 4:3] [p]Isa. 49:4; 65:23
17 [q][ch. 35:11]
20 [r]Jer. 8:16
21 [s][Jer. 8:6]
24 [t]Jer. 4:19; Amos 3:6
27 [u][Num. 24:21; Jer. 49:16; Obad. 4; Hab. 2:9]
28 [v]1 Sam. 14:5
30 [w]Matt. 24:28; Luke 17:37

Chapter 40

1 [x]ch. 38:1
2 [y]See ch. 33:13
4 [z][ch. 42:6; Ezra 9:6] [a]ch. 21:5; 29:9; Judg. 18:19
5 [b]ch. 33:14; Ps. 62:11
6 [c]ch. 38:1
7 [d]ch. 38:3 [e]ch. 38:3; 42:4

39:18 rouses herself to flee. The ostrich makes sport of the fearless warhorse. As it flees, the ostrich reaches a height of over 8 feet (2.4 m), strides of over 15 feet in length (4.6 m), and speeds of more than 40 miles (64 km) an hour.

40:1–2 The Lord refers to Job as a **faultfinder** and asks him to answer; but the questions help Job to recognize what is beyond the reach of any mortal's knowledge or power.

40:3–5 *Job's Response: Silence.* In the face of the Lord's questions, Job puts his hand over his mouth (v. 4), just as princes had done in his own presence (see 29:9), and pledges silence (40:5).

40:6–41:34 *The Second Challenge: Understanding Justice and Power.* At the hands of his three friends, Job knew what it felt like to have what was hidden about him (e.g., the state of his heart before God) questioned and judged by those who had drawn wrong conclusions from what was

8 Will you even put me in the wrong?
Will you condemn me that [f]you may be in the right?
9 Have you [g]an arm like God,
and can you thunder with [h]a voice like his?
10 "Adorn yourself with majesty and dignity;
[i]clothe yourself with glory and splendor.
11 Pour out the overflowings of your anger,
and look on everyone who is [j]proud and abase him.
12 Look on everyone who is proud and bring him low
and [k]tread down the wicked [l]where they stand.
13 [m]Hide them all in [n]the dust together;
bind their faces in the world below.[1]
14 Then will I also acknowledge to you
that your own [o]right hand can save you.

15 "Behold, Behemoth,[2]
which I made as I made you;
he eats [p]grass like an ox.
16 Behold, his strength in his loins,
and his power in the muscles of his belly.
17 He makes his tail stiff like a cedar;
the sinews of his thighs are knit together.
18 His bones are tubes of bronze,
his limbs like bars of iron.
19 "He is [q]the first of [r]the works[3] of God;
let him who made him bring near his sword!
20 For the mountains yield food for him
where all the wild beasts play.
21 Under the lotus plants he lies,
in the shelter of [s]the reeds and in the marsh.
22 For his shade the lotus trees cover him;
the willows of the brook surround him.
23 Behold, if the river is turbulent he is not frightened;
he is confident though Jordan rushes against his mouth.
24 Can one take him by his eyes,[4]
or pierce his nose with a snare?

41[5]

1 "Can you draw out [u]Leviathan[6] with a fishhook
or press down his tongue with a cord?
2 Can you put [v]a rope in his nose
or pierce his jaw with [v]a hook?

8 [f]See ch. 32:2
9 [g]Ps. 89:13; Isa. 63:12 [h]See ch. 37:4
10 [i][Ps. 93:1; 104:1]
11 [j][Dan. 4:37]; See Isa. 2:11-17
12 [k]Isa. 63:3 [l][ch. 36:20]
13 [m]Isa. 2:10 [n]ch. 21:26
14 [o]Ps. 98:1; Isa. 59:16; 63:5
15 [p]Num. 22:4
19 [q][Prov. 8:22] [r]ch. 26:14
21 [s]Ps. 68:30

Chapter 41

1 [u]ch. 3:8; Ps. 74:14; 104:26; Isa. 27:1
2 [v][2 Kgs. 19:28; Isa. 37:29]

[1] Hebrew *in the hidden place* [2] A large animal, exact identity unknown [3] Hebrew *ways* [4] Or *in his sight* [5] Ch 40:25 in Hebrew [6] A large sea animal, exact identity unknown

visible in his circumstances. The Lord now questions Job for overextending his judgment of what his suffering meant about the Lord's just governance of the world (40:6–9). In his faithfulness, Job had embodied aspects of the Lord's just and right character (see 29:11–17). However, the Lord makes the point that, in speaking about justice on earth, Job is referring to something much more extensive than he could comprehend or accomplish (40:10–14). The Lord illustrates this point further by describing two beasts of creation: Behemoth (40:15–24) and Leviathan (ch. 41). If Job is unable to subdue these powerful beasts who are themselves a part of creation, how much less should he presume to be able to maintain his own right toward the Lord (see 41:9–11).

40:6–14 The Lord addresses Job (v. 7) and questions him particularly about how Job sought to defend his integrity in such a way that he seemed to imply that it was God who was acting out of accord with his own character (v. 8). In doing so, Job has spoken beyond his knowledge or power to act justly (vv. 9–14).

40:13 Hide them . . . in the dust is a euphemism for "bury." **Faces** is metonymy for the whole person. **bind**. Death is an imprisonment; the image is that of faces pushed into the grave.

40:15–24 The Lord describes the power of Behemoth.

40:15 Behemoth usually refers to cattle, but in at least one other reference it most likely signifies a hippopotamus (see ESV footnote). It is almost universally so interpreted in this passage, taking the description of vv. 16–18 as poetical extravagance. Some, however, suppose that the description requires some kind of mythical beast to be in view, as a parallel to Leviathan (41:1); the first option is simpler.

40:17 tail stiff like a cedar. "Tail" is a common euphemism for phallus. It is to be so interpreted in this verse, considering the description of the anatomy of

4[w]Ex. 21:6; Deut. 15:17
11[x]Rom. 11:35; [ch. 35:7] [y]See Ps. 24:1
17[z]ver. 23
18[a]ch. 3:9
21[b]2 Sam. 22:13; [Ps. 18:8]
23[c]ver. 17

3 Will he make many pleas to you?
Will he speak to you soft words?
4 Will he make a covenant with you
to take him for [w]your servant forever?
5 Will you play with him as with a bird,
or will you put him on a leash for your girls?
6 Will traders bargain over him?
Will they divide him up among the merchants?
7 Can you fill his skin with harpoons
or his head with fishing spears?
8 Lay your hands on him;
remember the battle—you will not do it again!
9[1] Behold, the hope of a man is false;
he is laid low even at the sight of him.
10 No one is so fierce that he dares to stir him up.
Who then is he who can stand before me?
11 [x]Who has first given to me, that I should repay him?
[y]Whatever is under the whole heaven is mine.

12 "I will not keep silence concerning his limbs,
or his mighty strength, or his goodly frame.
13 Who can strip off his outer garment?
Who would come near him with a bridle?
14 Who can open the doors of his face?
Around his teeth is terror.
15 His back is made of[2] rows of shields,
shut up closely as with a seal.
16 One is so near to another
that no air can come between them.
17 They are [z]joined one to another;
they clasp each other and cannot be separated.
18 His sneezings flash forth light,
and his eyes are like [a]the eyelids of the dawn.
19 Out of his mouth go flaming torches;
sparks of fire leap forth.
20 Out of his nostrils comes forth smoke,
as from a boiling pot and burning rushes.
21 His breath [b]kindles coals,
and a flame comes forth from his mouth.
22 In his neck abides strength,
and terror dances before him.
23 The folds of his flesh [c]stick together,
firmly cast on him and immovable.
24 His heart is hard as a stone,
hard as the lower millstone.

[1] Ch 41:1 in Hebrew [2] Or *His pride is in his*

the animal. Potency is often associated with procreative power. In the medieval period, Behemoth was conceived as a symbol of sensuality and sin. **sinews of his thighs**. The word for "sinews" is otherwise unknown. Some ancient versions (see Targum, Latin) took it to mean "testicle," in keeping with the interpretation of the first line.

41:1–34 The Lord describes the power of Leviathan by focusing on the inability of man to subdue him, then applies such power analogously to himself (vv. 9–11).

41:1 Leviathan. The animal described in this section may be the crocodile (see ESV footnote). Interpreters sometimes suggest it is a mythical creature representing forces overcome by God's power in creation (see 3:8 and note). However, the focus of this section is on the fact that, whatever powerful creature is being referred to, it is a part of God's creation and is governed by his power (see note on Ps. 74:14).

41:9–11 If it is futile for people to presume that they could lay their hands on Leviathan, who is a part of God's creation (vv. 9, 11), then how much more should Job be cautious about his presumption in wanting to bring his case and **stand before** God.

41:24 His heart. "Heart" is metonymy for "chest" (see Ex. 28:29).

25 When he raises himself up the mighty[1] are afraid;
at the crashing they are beside themselves.
26 Though the sword reaches him, it does not avail,
nor the spear, the dart, or the javelin.
27 He counts iron as straw,
and bronze as rotten wood.
28 The arrow cannot make him flee;
for him sling stones are turned to stubble.
29 Clubs are counted as stubble;
he laughs at the rattle of javelins.
30 His underparts are like sharp [d]potsherds;
he spreads himself like [e]a threshing sledge on the mire.
31 He makes the deep boil like a pot;
he makes the sea like a pot of ointment.
32 Behind him he leaves a shining wake;
one would think the deep to be white-haired.
33 [f]On earth there is not his like,
a creature without fear.
34 He sees everything that is high;
he is king over all the [g]sons of pride."

Job's Confession and Repentance

42 Then Job answered the LORD and said:

2 "I know that you can [h]do all things,
and that no purpose of yours can be thwarted.
3 [i]'Who is this that hides counsel without knowledge?'
Therefore I have uttered what I did not understand,
things [j]too wonderful for me, which I did not know.
4 'Hear, and I will speak;
[k]I will question you, and you make it known to me.'
5 I had heard of you by the hearing of the ear,
but now my eye sees you;
6 therefore I despise myself,
and repent[2] in [l]dust and ashes."

The LORD Rebukes Job's Friends

7 After the LORD had spoken these words to Job, the LORD said to Eliphaz [m]the Temanite: "My anger burns against you and against your two friends, for you have not spoken of me what is right, as my servant Job has. 8 Now therefore take [n]seven bulls and seven rams

[1] *Or gods* [2] *Or and am comforted*

30 [d]ch. 2:8 [e]Isa. 28:27; 41:15
33 [f]ch. 19:25
34 [g]ch. 28:8

Chapter 42
2 [h]Gen. 18:14; Matt. 19:26
3 [i]ch. 38:2 [j]Ps. 40:5; 131:1; 139:6
4 [k]ch. 38:3; 40:7
6 [l][ch. 30:19; Gen. 18:27]; See ch. 2:8
7 [m]ch. 2:11; 1 Chr. 1:45
8 [n]Num. 23:1; 1 Chr. 15:26

42:1–6 *Job's Response: Submission.* In response to the Lord's reproof, Job confesses that the Lord's power and purposes will not fail (v. 2) and that he spoke of things beyond his knowledge (v. 3). In the presence of the Lord who is speaking and appearing to him, Job repents of what in the dialogue he was wildly blurting out (vv. 4–6).

42:3–4 In the first part of each of these verses, Job is quoting the Lord's questions (see 38:2–3; also 40:7) before responding to them.

42:6 The Lord has already embodied his mercy to Job in the way he graciously reproved and questioned Job for his good. **I despise myself**. That is, "I recognize the ignorance behind my own words." God's mercy is pictured further in the humble posture of Job, who in **dust and ashes** finally enjoys the comfort of relational peace that had been withheld from him by his friends: **repent** translates a form from the same root used of the friends' intention to "comfort" Job in 2:11 (see ESV footnote). The translation of the ESV footnote ("I despise myself and *am comforted* in dust and ashes") finds support in the way it corresponds to Job's search for comfort that runs through the book (see Introduction: Literary Features), and is consistent with God's declaration that what Job has spoken of him is right (42:7).

42:7–17 *Epilogue: The Vindication, Intercession, and Restoration of Job.* The final section of the book brings to light on earth what the prologue had described to be true before God: Job's suffering was not a consequence of sin (see 1:1–2:13). The narrative of this section describes two aspects of the conclusion to the dialogue: the Lord charges Eliphaz and the other friends with speaking wrong words about him and calls upon them to offer sacrifices to him and seek intercession from Job (42:7–9), and the Lord restores Job's fortunes (vv. 10–17).

42:7–9 *The Lord Rebukes the Three Friends.* In God's presence Job finds the arbiter for whom he had longed, as the Lord assigns a sacrifice to the three friends and requires them to seek Job's intercession. Notably, Elihu is absent from this final scene. Neither do Job's wife and Satan—so prominent in the prologue—feature in the close of the book.

42:7 My anger burns against you. The Lord's anger is directed against Eliphaz the Temanite and the other two friends (Bildad the Shuhite, and Zophar the Naamathite; see 2:11). This contrasts with Elihu who had presumed to speak, though harshly, on God's behalf (36:2), and whose anger

8 [o]ch. 1:5 [p]Gen. 20:7; 1 Sam. 12:23; James 5:16; 1 John 5:16
9 [q]ch. 2:11
10 [r]See Ps. 14:7 [s]Isa. 40:2; 61:7
11 [t]ch. 19:13 [u]ch. 2:11 [v]Gen. 33:19; Josh. 24:32 [w]Gen. 24:22
12 [x]ch. 8:7 [y][ver. 10; ch. 1:3]
13 [z]ch. 1:2
15 [a]See Num. 27:1-8
16 [b]Gen. 50:23; [Ps. 128:6; Isa. 53:10]
17 [c]See ch. 5:26

and go to my servant Job and [o]offer up a burnt offering for yourselves. And my servant
Job shall [p]pray for you, for I will accept his prayer not to deal with you according to your
folly. For you have not spoken of me what is right, as my servant Job has." **9** [q]So Eliphaz
the Temanite and Bildad the Shuhite and Zophar the Naamathite went and did what the
LORD had told them, and the LORD accepted Job's prayer.

The LORD Restores Job's Fortunes

10 And the LORD [r]restored the fortunes of Job, when he had prayed for his friends. And
the LORD gave Job [s]twice as much as he had before. **11** Then came to him all his [t]brothers
and sisters and all who had [t]known him before, and ate bread with him in his house. And
they [u]showed him sympathy and comforted him for all the evil[1] that the LORD had brought
upon him. And each of them gave him [v]a piece of money[2] and [w]a ring of gold.

12 And the LORD blessed [x]the latter days of Job more than his beginning. And he had
[y]14,000 sheep, 6,000 camels, 1,000 yoke of oxen, and 1,000 female donkeys. **13** He had also
[z]seven sons and three daughters. **14** And he called the name of the first daughter Jemimah,
and the name of the second Keziah, and the name of the third Keren-happuch. **15** And in all
the land there were no women so beautiful as Job's daughters. And their father gave them
an inheritance [a]among their brothers. **16** And after this Job lived 140 years, and [b]saw his
sons, and his sons' sons, four generations. **17** And Job died, an old man, and [c]full of days.

[1] Or *disaster* [2] Hebrew *a qesitah*; a unit of money of unknown value

had burned against Job as well as his friends (see 32:2–3). **spoken of me what is right, as my servant Job has**. Job's words certainly expressed deep anguish and frustration; but God does not count these words sinful. This is probably because Job never lost his earnest desire to appear before God, and his words are testimony to that.

42:8 for I will accept his prayer not to deal with you according to your folly. What is revealed to the friends is tragically ironic for them: they had been so sure they were defending wisdom against Job's "folly," only to find out they were totally mistaken. This conclusion is also a picture of God's mercy and Job's faithfulness: Job has the chance to intercede on behalf of the people who had brought him further suffering rather than the comfort he needed and should have received from them. By interceding for his friends, Job images the character of the Lord (e.g., slow to anger, abounding in steadfast love and mercy) and embodies the very mercy he himself had received. By doing so, he also continues the intercessory role he had faithfully performed for his family (see 1:5).

42:10–17 *The Lord Restores Job.* It is of utmost significance to note that Job's restoration occurs only at this point, when he has capitulated to God and has been reconciled with his friends—still in his broken and bereaved state. Precisely at this point, community is reestablished (vv. 10–11) and Job himself restored (vv. 12–15). As the restoration proceeds, his previous possessions of livestock are doubled (v. 12; cf. 1:3, and see note on 42:16), and a further 10 children born to him (v. 13; cf. 1:2).

42:11 After he was restored, Job's siblings and other friends came to him and **showed him sympathy and comforted him**, which restored a loss that Job had earlier lamented (cf. 19:13–19). This was the original intention of the three friends (see 2:11), but Job ends up receiving comfort primarily through his matured relationship with the Lord (see 42:6) and also through being vindicated by the Lord before those from whom he previously, and rightly, received respect (see Introduction: Literary Features).

42:14 Jemimah . . . Keziah . . . Keren-happuch. The name of the first daughter means "dove"; the second, a kind of perfume; and the third, a type of eye shadow. Their beauty indicates a special status.

42:16 Job **lived 140 years**—double the normal span of life (cf. Ps. 90:10). This is in keeping with the restoration of all Job's fortunes (Job 42:10).

INTRODUCTION TO THE PSALMS

Title

The book of Psalms, or Psalter, has supplied to believers some of their best-loved Bible passages. It is a collection of 150 poems that express a wide variety of emotions, including: love and adoration toward God, sorrow over sin, dependence on God in desperate circumstances, the battle of fear and trust, walking with God even when the way seems dark, thankfulness for God's care, devotion to the word of God, and confidence in the eventual triumph of God's purposes for the world.

The English title comes from the Greek word *psalmos*, which translates Hebrew *mizmor*, "song," found in many of the Psalm titles and simply translated as "psalm" (e.g., Psalm 3). This Greek name for the book was established by the time of the NT (Luke 20:42; Acts 1:20). The Hebrew name for the book is *Tehillim*, "Praises," pointing to the characteristic use of these songs as praises offered to God in public worship.

Theme

The Hebrew label for the psalms, "Praises," may have originally reflected the idea, readily found today, that adoration and thanks to God are the primary acts of worship; but it would be better to learn from the title of the entire Psalter that the whole range of the psalms—from adoration and thanks to the needy cry for help (even the desolate moan of Psalm 88)—praises God when offered to him in the gathered worship of his people.

Authorship, Occasion, and Date

Many of the psalms have titles (e.g., see Psalms 3 and 4). These titles can include liturgical directions, historical notes, and—possibly—the identity of the author. The Hebrew word translated "of" (as in "of David") can mean, according to its context, "belonging to," "authored by," or "about" (see note on Psalm 72); the same word can also be translated "to" (as in "to the choirmaster"). In the expression "a Psalm of David" (Psalm 3), the most natural sense is that it is "of" David because David wrote it; this is reflected in NT citations (e.g., Mark 12:36; Acts 2:25; Rom. 4:6; 11:9). Based on this, the simple "of David" (e.g., Psalm 11) is most readily taken in the same way.

Interpreting the titles this way yields David as the most common author of the Psalms: he appears in 73 titles, and the NT adds two more (Acts 4:25 for Psalm 2; and Heb. 4:7 for Psalm 95). Other authors include the Sons of Korah (11 psalms), Asaph (12 psalms), Solomon (possibly two psalms), and Moses (one). Other psalms do not identify the author at all.

Davidic authorship corresponds well with biblical testimony. David was "skillful in playing the lyre" (1 Sam. 16:16–23) and an accomplished songwriter (2 Sam. 1:17–27; 22:1–23:7); his reputation as "the sweet psalmist of Israel" (2 Sam. 23:1) is highly credible, as is the way 1 Chronicles presents him as taking an active role in developing Israel's worship (e.g., 1 Chron. 16:4–7, 37–42; 23:2–6; 25:1–7). The Sons of Korah served in the sanctuary (1 Chron. 9:19), and some of them along with Asaph were "in charge of the service of song in the house of the LORD" (1 Chron. 6:31). (It is also conceivable that these last two names represent the headwaters of choirs or guilds that bear their names.) Solomon is known for his achievements in "wisdom," but he also wrote "songs" (1 Kings 4:32), which could include two psalms (Psalm 127, and possibly Psalm 72). Moses provided songs for the whole assembled people (Ex. 15:1–18; Deut. 31:30–32:44; cf. 33:1–29).

By the end of the nineteenth century, many scholars had concluded that the titles in Psalms had little or no validity; some of their strongest arguments involved the presence of words and phrases in the psalms that look more at home in later Hebrew or even Aramaic than in standard Biblical Hebrew; this would imply that the psalms as they exist today come from the first few centuries B.C. But the discovery of more ancient Near Eastern writings since that time has made it possible to give a fuller history of the Hebrew language and a fuller appreciation of ancient literary conventions, and it is now harder to sustain these arguments for late dating. Many scholars will now allow that quite a few of the psalms come from before the Babylonian exile. Coupled with the apparent antiquity of the authorship inscriptions, this provides a good reason for taking these inscriptions at face value. The NT authors accept David as author of the psalms attributed to him (e.g., Mark 12:36; Acts 1:16; 2:25; Rom. 4:6; 11:9), and sometimes the characters in a story make David's authorship a key part of their case (e.g., Luke 20:42; Acts 2:29, 34; 13:36–39). (For the question of what use to make of the authorship, esp. of David, see The Psalms as Scripture.)

Fourteen of the Davidic psalms add further information in their titles, connecting the psalm to a specific incident in David's life (see chart below). It is often said that they are later additions to the psalms, since they narrate events in the third person (while the psalm is in the first person). Some wonder as well whether such polished productions (e.g., Psalm 34) could have arisen from the circumstances described in the title. In reply, there is no reason why an author cannot narrate about himself in the third person (e.g., Isa. 20:2; Jer. 20:1–2; 21:1–3; 26:1–24; Hos. 1:2–6; etc.); further, the titles do not imply that David composed the psalm at the time of the event, only that the event led to the psalm. The fact that two of the titles cannot be correlated with anything in 1–2 Samuel argues against the idea that a later editor added these titles after carefully examining biblical texts. Finally, this historical information often lends help to both interpreting the psalm and discerning how it should be applied. Therefore the notes that follow employ this information.

A few of the psalms seem originally to have been written for a particular occasion, and the individual expositions will discuss that possibility (e.g., Psalms 24; 68; 118). Perhaps they came to be used in specific festivals in order to commemorate the original events. Some scholars have suggested that the liturgical calendar found in Leviticus is a late invention, and that the early period of Israel (when some of the psalms were first written) had annual festivals analogous to those found in other cultures; hence they tried to associate particular psalms with places in these hypothetical festivals. The evidence for such a construction is poor, and many today try to connect various psalms with the biblical festivals. One difficulty with this is that there is so little information in the OT itself about how many aspects of the worship were conducted. In addition to the festivals, Leviticus 23:3 sets the weekly Sabbath as a day of "holy convocation." It is unclear what kind of meeting is expected in the villages week by week, but it seems to be some kind of worship. Therefore, while it seems true that some psalms are intended for particular festivals or celebrations (e.g., Psalm 65 as a harvest thanksgiving), it also is clear that many psalms are suitable year round, and could be used as needed; indeed, Psalm 92 is a thanksgiving for the weekly Sabbath worship.

Psalm	Incident	References
3	David flees from and battles Absalom	2 Samuel 15–17
7	The words of Cush, a Benjaminite (persecution by Saul?)	Unknown
18	David delivered from enemies and from Saul	2 Samuel 22
30	Dedication of the temple	Nothing in David's lifetime; cf. 1 Kings 8:63
34	David delivered from danger by feigning madness in the presence of King Achish of Gath	1 Sam. 21:12–22:1
51	Nathan confronts David about his adultery with Bathsheba	2 Samuel 11–12
52	Doeg the Edomite tells Saul that David went to the house of Ahimelech	1 Sam. 22:9–19
54	The Ziphites tell Saul that David is hiding among them	1 Sam. 23:19
56	The Philistines seize David in Gath	1 Sam. 21:10–11
57	David flees from Saul into a cave	1 Sam. 22:1 or 24:3
59	Saul sends men to watch David's house in order to kill him	1 Sam. 19:11
60	David's victory over Transjordan	2 Sam. 8:1–14
63	David in the desert of Judah	2 Samuel 15–17?; 1 Sam. 23:14–15?
142	David flees from Saul into a cave	Same as Psalm 57

The individual psalms come from diverse periods of Israel's history: from the time of Moses (15th or 13th century B.C.), to that of David and Solomon (10th century), down to exilic and postexilic times (e.g., Psalm 137). A number of factors clearly indicate that the book of Psalms in its present form is the product of a process of collecting (and possibly of editing) from a variety of sources; such factors include:

- The division into five books and the affinity groupings, e.g., Psalms 1–2; 113–118 (the Egyptian Hallel; see notes on Psalms 113–118); Psalms 120–134 (the Songs of Ascents); and the final Hallelujah of Psalms 146–150 (see discussion of Structure);
- the existence of the almost identical Psalms 14 and 53;
- the notice in 72:20 about the end of David's prayers (while there are still plenty of Davidic psalms to follow).

There is no way to tell what kind of editing the collectors might have done as they incorporated a composition into the developing Psalter; recognized scribal practices include minor things like updating spelling and grammar, and clarifying place names. If the regard for an author's inspiration was as high as it should have been (1 Chron. 25:1–5 describes some of the psalmists as "prophesying" and as "seers," which means they convey God's own words), then it is unlikely that the editors went much beyond the recognized scribal practices. It is likely that many of the psalms began as intensely personal poems, which were then adapted for congregational use (e.g., see note on Psalm 51), possibly even by the original author. It is also likely that some psalms were composed by stitching together preexisting material (e.g., Psalm 108); but, for the faithful, it is the final form that is canonical, and that is the focus of these notes.

It appears that at every stage of this editorial process, the Psalter served as the songbook of the worshiping people of God.

Key Themes

The Psalter is fundamentally the hymnbook of the *people of God* at worship. The Psalms take the basic themes of OT theology and turn them into song. Thus, themes common throughout the OT (see pp. 29–31) reappear in the Psalms and include the following:

1. *Monotheism.* The one true God, Maker of heaven and earth and ruler of all things, will vindicate his own goodness and justice, in his own time. Every human being must know and love this God, whose spotless moral purity, magnificent power and wisdom, steadfast faithfulness, and unceasing love are breathtakingly beautiful.

2. *Creation and fall.* Though God made man with dignity and purpose, all people since the fall are beset with sins and weaknesses that only God's grace can heal.

3. *Election and covenant.* The one true God chose a people for himself and bound himself to them by his covenant. This covenant expressed God's intention to save the people, and through them to bring light to the rest of the world.

4. *Covenant membership.* In his covenant, God offers his grace to his people: the forgiveness of their sins, the shaping of their lives in this world to reflect his own glory, and a part to play in bringing light to the Gentiles. Each member of God's people is responsible to lay hold of this grace from the heart: to believe the promises, to grow in obeying the commands, and to keep on doing so all their lives long. Those who lay hold in this way are the faithful, as distinct from the unfaithful among God's people; they enjoy the full benefits of God's love, and they find boundless delight in knowing God. Each of the faithful is a member of a people, a corporate entity; the members have a mutual participation in the life of the whole people. Therefore the spiritual and moral well-being of the whole affects the well-being of each of the members, and each member contributes to the others by his own spiritual and moral life. Thus each one shares the joys and sorrows of the others, and of the whole. The faithful will suffer in this life, often at the hands of the unfaithful, and sometimes from those outside God's people. The right response to this suffering is not personal revenge but believing prayer, confident that God will make all things right in his own time.

5. *Eschatology.* The story of God's people is headed toward a glorious future, in which all kinds of people will come to know the Lord and join his people. It is part of the dignity of God's people that, in God's mysterious wisdom, their personal faithfulness contributes to the story getting to its goal. The Messiah, the ultimate heir of David, will lead his people in the great task of bringing light to the Gentiles.

History of Salvation Summary

Throughout history God has been fashioning a people for himself who will love and obey him, and who will express and nourish their corporate life in gathered worship. The Psalms served as a vehicle for the prayers and praises of God's people in Israel, and Christians today, who have been grafted into the olive tree of God's ancient people (Rom. 11:17, 24), can join their voices together with these ancient people in their worship. There are indeed adjustments to be made, now that Jesus has died and risen (see The Psalms as Scripture), and yet Gentile believers in Jesus may rejoice with the people of God of all ages. (For an explanation of the "History of Salvation," see the Overview of the Bible, pp. 23–26. See also History of Salvation in the Old Testament: Preparing the Way for Christ, pp. 2635–2661.)

Musical Terms

There are several Hebrew words and phrases in the Psalms, such as "Selah" (e.g., 3:2), "The Sheminith" (Psalm 6 title), "Shiggaion" (Psalm 7 title), whose exact meaning is uncertain—which is why the translators have simply transliterated them, as any attempt to translate would be misleading. The ESV footnotes indicate that these are probably terms for musical or liturgical direction. (Cf. how Psalms 4 and 5 refer to musical instruments in their titles.) In some cases these may be things like names of tunes or chant styles (see note on "Do not destroy" in Psalm 57 title).

Curses in the Psalms

Many psalms call on God for help as the faithful are threatened with harm from enemies (often called "the wicked"—frequently the unfaithful who persecute the godly, and sometimes Gentile oppressors). In a number of places, the requested help is that God would punish these enemies. Christians, with the teaching and example of Jesus (in passages like Matt. 5:38–48; Luke 23:34; 1 Pet. 2:19–23; cf. Acts 7:6), may wonder what to make of such curses: How can it possibly be right for God's people to pray in this way? Many have supposed that this is an area in which the ethics of the NT improve upon and supersede the OT. Others suggest that these only apply to the church's warfare with its ultimate enemy, Satan, and his demons. Neither of these is fully satisfying, both because the NT authors portray themselves as heirs of OT ethics (cf. Matt. 22:34–40) and because the NT has some curses of its own (e.g., 1 Cor. 16:22; Gal. 1:8–9; Rev. 6:9–10), even finding instruction in some of the Psalms' curses (e.g., Acts 1:20 and Rom. 11:9–10, using Psalms 69 and 109). Each of the psalm passages must be taken on its own, and the notes address these questions (e.g., see notes on 5:10; 35:4–8; 58:6–9; 59:11–17; 69:22–28; 109:6–20; and the note on Psalm 137, which contains the most striking curse of all). At the same time, some general principles will help in understanding these passages.

First, one must be clear that the people being cursed are not enemies over trivial matters; they are people who hate the faithful precisely for their faith; they mock God and use ruthless and deceitful means to suppress the godly (cf. 5:4–6, 9–10; 10:15; 42:3; 94:2–7).

Second, it is worth remembering that these curses are in poetic form and can employ extravagant and vigorous expressions. (The exact fulfillment is left to God.)

Third, these curses are expressions of moral indignation, not of personal vengeance. For someone who knows God, it is unbearably wrong that those who persecute the faithful and turn people away from God should get away with it, and even seem to prosper. Zion is the city of God, the focus of his affection (cf. Psalms 48; 122); it is unthinkable that God could tolerate cruel men taking delight in destroying it. These psalms are prayers for God to vindicate himself, displaying his righteousness for all the world to see (cf. 10:17–18). Further, these are prayers that God will do what he said he will do: 35:5 looks back to 1:4, and even 137:9 has Isaiah 13:16 as its backdrop. Most of these prayers assume that the persecutors will not repent; however, in one place (Ps. 83:17), the prayer actually looks to the punishment as leading to their conversion.

Fourth, the OT ethical system forbids personal revenge (e.g., Lev. 19:17–18; Prov. 24:17; 25:21–22), a prohibition that the NT inherits (cf. Rom. 12:19–21).

Thus, when the NT writers employ these curses or formulate their own (as above), they are following the OT guidelines. Any prayer for the Lord to hasten his coming must mean disaster for the impenitent (2 Thess. 1:5–10). Yet Christians must keep as their deepest desire, even for those who mean harm to the church, that others would come to trust in Christ and love his people (cf. Luke 23:34; Rom. 9:1–3; 10:1; 1 Tim. 2:4; 2 Pet. 3:9). Hence, when they pray for God to protect his people against their persecutors, they should be explicit about asking God to lead such people to repentance. With these things in mind, then, it is still possible that the faithful today might sing or read aloud even these sections of the Psalms, if it takes place in a service of worship, under wise leadership, for the good of the whole people of God.

The Psalms as Scripture

The OT certainly presents the Psalms as part of God's inspired Word: 1 Chronicles 25:1–6 says that a number of sanctuary personnel "prophesied," and that one was a "seer" (a synonym for "prophet"). Some of these men appear as authors of canonical psalms. It is important to clarify just how the psalms are to function for the people of God.

Their primary function has already been mentioned: the Psalter is the songbook of the people of God in their gathered worship. These songs cover a wide range of experiences and emotions, and give God's people the words to express these emotions and to bring these experiences before God. At the same time, the psalms do not simply *express* emotions: when sung in faith, they actually *shape* the emotions of the godly. The emotions are therefore not a problem to be solved but are part of the raw material of now-fallen humanity that can be shaped to good and noble ends. The psalms, as songs, act deeply on the emotions, for the good of God's people. It is not "natural" to trust God in hardship, and yet the Psalms provide a way of doing just that, and enable the singers to trust better as a result of singing them. A person staring at the night sky might not know quite what to do with the mixed fear and wonder he finds in himself, and singing Psalm 8 will enrich his ability to respond.

The Psalms also provide guidance in the approach to worship: at times they offer content that is difficult to digest, calling on God's people to use their minds as well as their hearts and voices. They show profound respect for God as well as uninhibited delight in him. They enable the whole congregation to take upon themselves, to own, the troubles and victories of the individual members, so that everyone can "rejoice with those who rejoice and weep with those who weep" (Rom. 12:15). They enable God's people more fully to enjoy being under his care, and to want more keenly to be pure and holy, seeing purity and holiness as part of God's fatherly gift rather than as a burden.

David is the author of about half the Psalms. His role as king over Israel was more than that of a ruler, and more than that of an inspired author. The king was to represent and even embody the people, and the well-being of the whole people was tied to the faithfulness of the king (see notes on the royal psalms, e.g., Psalms 2; 89; 132). As a representative, the king was to aim to be the ideal Israelite. David, then, writes as a representative, and the readers must discern whether the emphasis of the psalm is more on his role as *ruler*—which he does not share with "ordinary" Israelites—or more on his role as *ideal Israelite*, in which he is an example for all. Most of the historical occasions in the psalm titles allow the reader to appreciate the way in which exemplary faith meets concrete situations, and then to apply that faith to features of his or her own situation that are analogous to those in the psalm.

These notes reflect the conviction that Christians are the heirs of the ancient people of God. Much has changed: the final heir of David has arrived and taken his throne (Rom. 1:4), and the people of God are no longer defined as a particular nation. The sacrifice of Jesus has radically altered the way that Christians look at the Levitical system. And yet Paul can include Gentile Christians as heirs of Abraham (Rom. 4:11–12), and ask Gentile Christians to think of the OT people as their "fathers" (1 Cor. 10:1). Therefore a large portion of these functions of the Psalms already mentioned still apply to Christians. The notes include suggestions as to how Christians might employ the psalms, making the necessary changes for application to their own lives.

Christians have generally used the Psalms in their worship (cf. Eph. 5:19; Col. 3:16), even though they have not agreed on whether they may use *only* canonical psalms. That topic goes far beyond this discussion; it will be enough to say that all Christians would profit from a more deliberate effort to use the Psalms in their worship.

Literary Features

As already mentioned, the book of Psalms is an anthology of individual poems. It is important to remember that these are poems to be sung, and thus are to be read differently than, say, a doctrinal or ethical treatise. Because the content of these songs is expressed in a poetic idiom, readers need to be ready to interpret such staples of poetry as image, metaphor, simile, personification, hyperbole, and apostrophe (see chart, p. 940). All of these factors contribute to the rhetoric of a psalm—the way it enables the singers to own the psalm's view of the world, and how it shapes their emotional structure so that they can "lean into" the world in a godly manner.

Guiding principles for reading the psalms include the following: The individual psalms should first be read as self-contained compositions. Sometimes it is helpful to see them as part of an ongoing sequence (e.g., Psalms 111–112). Further, within a particular psalm, the author does not always spell out his flow of

Term	Explanation	Example
Image	A word or phrase that names a concrete action or thing; by extension, a character, setting, or event in a story is an image—a concrete embodiment of human experience or an idea.	the way (or path); the congregation (or assembly); nature (or harvest) (Psalm 1)
Metaphor	An implied comparison that does not use the formula *like* or *as*.	"The LORD is my shepherd" (Ps. 23:1).
Simile	A figure of speech in which a writer compares two things using the formula *like* or *as*.	"He is like a tree planted by streams of water" (Ps. 1:3).
Personification	A figure of speech in which human attributes are given to something nonhuman, such as animals, objects, or abstract qualities.	Light and truth are personified as guides in Psalm 43:3.
Hyperbole	A figure of speech in which a writer consciously exaggerates for the sake of effect; usually that effect is emotional, and thus, loosely put, hyperbole usually expresses emotional truth rather than literal truth.	"My tears have been my food day and night" (Ps. 42:3).
Apostrophe	A figure of speech in which the writer addresses someone absent as though present and capable of responding. By slight extension, an apostrophe might be an address to something nonhuman as though it were human and capable of responding, even if the speaker is in the presence of the object.	The poet in Psalm 148:3 might well be looking up at the sun, moon, or stars as he commands them to praise God.

thought; one must use a disciplined imagination to follow the connections. Finally, readers must begin with the premise that poets present their material in images rather than abstractions, and that they prefer the figurative or nonliteral to the literal.

All of the Psalms are written in the verse form of parallelism, on which see Introduction to the Poetic and Wisdom Literature, pp. 865–868.

Scholars have tended to identify psalms according to their types (praise, lament, etc.). Unfortunately, scholars vary in their list of types, and it is easy to multiply categories to account for the particularities of each psalm—and soon one can end up with 150 categories! Nevertheless, used reasonably, this approach can shed light on the different purposes of the various psalms. The basic categories include:

- *Laments*, whose primary function is to lay a troubled situation before the Lord, asking him for help. There are community laments, dealing with trouble faced by the people of God as a whole (e.g., Psalm 12), and individual laments, where the troubles face a particular member of the people (e.g., Psalm 13). This category is the largest by far, including as much as a third of the whole Psalter.
- *Hymns of praise*, whose primary goal is to call and enable God's people to admire God's great attributes and deeds. These can focus, e.g., on a particular set of attributes (e.g., on God's benevolence in Psalm 145), on God's universal kingship over his creation (e.g., Psalm 93), or on God's works of creation (e.g., Psalm 8).
- *Hymns of thanksgiving*, which thank God for his answer to a petition; sometimes the petition can be identified as one of the lament psalms. Like laments, there are community (e.g., Psalm 9) and individual (e.g., Psalm 30) thanksgiving psalms.
- *Hymns celebrating God's law*, which speak of the wonders of the Torah (the Law of Moses) and help worshipers to aspire to obey it more fully (e.g., Psalm 119).
- *Wisdom psalms*, which take themes from the Wisdom Books (Job, Proverbs, Ecclesiastes, Song of Solomon) and make them the topic of song (e.g., Psalms 1; 37).
- *Songs of confidence*, which enable worshipers to deepen their trust in God through all manner of difficult circumstances (e.g., Psalm 23).
- *Royal psalms*, which are concerned with the Davidic monarchy as the vehicle of blessing for the people of God. Some of these are prayers (e.g., Psalm 20), some are thanksgivings (e.g., Psalm 21). All relate to the Messiah, the ultimate heir of David, either by setting a pattern (Psalms 20–21) or by portraying the king's reign in such a way that only the Messiah can completely fulfill it (e.g., Psalms 2; 72), or by focusing primarily on the future aspect (e.g., Psalm 110).
- *Historical psalms*, which take a lesson from the history of God's dealings with his people; these are generally corporate in their focus (e.g., Psalm 78).
- *Prophetic hymns*, which echo themes found in the Prophets, especially calling the people to covenant faithfulness (e.g., Psalm 81).

There are other elements in the psalms, such as penitence (see Psalms 6; 25; 32; 38; 51; 130; 143), claims of innocence (e.g., Psalm 26), yearning for God (e.g., Psalm 27), curses or imprecations (see Curses in the Psalms,

p. 938). There are psalms that seem to have been written for specific liturgical occasions (e.g., Psalm 24 and possibly Psalms 68 and 118). There are groups of psalms, such as the Egyptian Hallel (Psalms 113–118) and Songs of Ascents (Psalms 120–134); see notes on the individual psalms. Further, a psalm may fit mostly in one category, but that does not mean that elements of another category cannot also appear (cf. the note on Psalm 34, a thanksgiving psalm with a wisdom section; and the note on Psalm 56, which combines lament and thanksgiving).

Structure

The most basic structure of the Psalter is the easiest to see: it is a collection of 150 separate songs. It is possible that Psalms 42–43 are really two parts of one combined song, and Psalms 9–10 are companions (though not part of the same psalm; see note on Psalm 9).

The standard Hebrew text divides the Psalms into five "books," perhaps in imitation of the five books of the Pentateuch. The psalm that ends each book finishes with a doxology (see note on Ps. 41:13), and Psalm 150 as a whole is the conclusion both of Book 5 and of the entire Psalter.

Book 1	Psalms 1–41	Psalms 1–2 have no titles that attribute authorship (but see Acts 4:25 for Psalm 2); they provide an introduction to the Psalms as a whole. The remainder of Book 1 is made up almost entirely of psalms of David: only Psalms 10 (but see note on Psalm 9) and 33 lack a Davidic superscription. Prayers issuing from a situation of distress dominate, punctuated by statements of confidence in the God who alone can save (e.g., 9; 11; 16; 18), striking the note that concludes the book (40–41). Reflections on ethics and worship with integrity are found in Psalms 1; 14–15; 19; 24; and 26.
Book 2	Psalms 42–72	From the Davidic voice of Book 1, Book 2 introduces the first Korah collection (42–49, although 43 lacks a superscription), with a single Asaph psalm at Psalm 50. A further Davidic collection is found in Psalms 51–65 and 68–69, including the bulk of the "historical" superscriptions (51–52; 54; 56–57; 59–60; 63). Once again, lament and distress dominate the content of these prayers, which now also include a communal voice (e.g., Psalm 44; cf. Psalms 67; 68). The lone psalm attributed to Solomon concludes Book 2 with the Psalms' pinnacle of royal theology (72; cf. 45).
Book 3	Psalms 73–89	The tone darkens further in Book 3. The opening Psalm 73 starkly questions the justice of God before seeing light in God's presence; that light has almost escaped the psalmist in Psalm 88, the bleakest of all psalms. Book 2 ended with the high point of royal aspirations; Book 3 concludes in Psalm 89 with these expectations badly threatened. Sharp rays of hope occasionally pierce the darkness (e.g., Psalms 75; 85; 87). The brief third book contains most of the psalms of Asaph (Psalms 73–83), as well as another set of Korah psalms (Psalms 84–85; 87–88).
Book 4	Psalms 90–106	Psalm 90 opens the fourth book of the psalms. It may be seen as the first response to the problems raised by the third book (Psalms 73–89). Psalm 90, attributed to Moses, reminds the worshiper that God was active on Israel's behalf long before David. This theme is taken up in Psalms 103–106, which summarize God's dealings with his people before any kings reigned. In between there is a group of psalms (93–100) characterized by the refrain "The LORD reigns." This truth refutes the doubts of Psalm 89.
Book 5	Psalms 107–150	The structure of Book 5 reflects the closing petition of Book 4 in 106:47. It declares that God does answer prayer (Psalm 107) and concludes with five Hallelujah psalms (146–150). In between there are several psalms affirming the validity of the promises to David (Psalms 110; 132; 144), two collections of Davidic psalms (108–110; 138–145); the longest psalm, celebrating the value of the law (Psalm 119); and 15 psalms of ascent for use by pilgrims to Jerusalem (Psalms 120–134).

There are other evidences of editorial arrangement: e.g., Psalms 1–2 form the doorway into the whole Psalter; Psalms 111–112 illuminate each other; and some "affinity groupings" of psalms celebrating God's universal kingship (Psalms 93; 95–99), historical psalms (e.g., Psalms 104–107; see note on Psalm 107), the Egyptian Hallel (Psalms 113–118), the Songs of Ascents (Psalms 120–134), and the final Hallelujah Psalms (Psalms 146–150). There appear to be other factors that have led to psalms being grouped together, as the notes observe.

However, the question of whether there is an overarching scheme that governs all 150 psalms remains a recurring topic in scholarly discussion. It is entirely possible that those who compiled the Psalter arranged the individual psalms to address the concerns of their age. The difficulty is that many structural schemes have been proposed but none has won universal agreement, nor does any of them seem fully persuasive (therefore no overall outline of the book has been included here). But the absence of an overall structural scheme is no surprise when dealing with a songbook, which is what the Psalter is.

THE PSALMS

BOOK ONE

The Way of the Righteous and the Wicked

1 1 Blessed is the man[1]
who [a]walks not in [b]the counsel of the wicked,
nor stands in [c]the way of sinners,
nor [d]sits in [e]the seat of [f]scoffers;
2 but his [g]delight is in the law[2] of the LORD,
and on his [h]law he meditates day and night.

3 He is like [i]a tree
planted by [j]streams of water
that yields its fruit in its season,
and its [k]leaf does not wither.
[l]In all that he does, he prospers.
4 The wicked are not so,
but are like [m]chaff that the wind drives away.

5 Therefore the wicked [n]will not stand in the judgment,
nor sinners in [o]the congregation of the righteous;

[1] The singular Hebrew word for *man* (*ish*) is used here to portray a representative example of a godly person; see Preface [2] Or *instruction*

Psalm 1
1[a]Prov. 4:14, 15 [b]Job 21:16 [c]Prov. 1:10 [d]Ps. 26:4; Jer. 15:17 [e][Ps. 107:32] [f]Prov. 1:22; 3:34; 19:29; 21:24; 29:8; [Isa. 28:14]
2[g]Ps. 112:1; 119:35, 47, 92 [h]Ps. 119:1, 97; Josh. 1:8
3[i]Jer. 17:8; Ezek. 19:10; [Num. 24:6; Job 29:19] [j]Ps. 46:4 [k]Ezek. 47:12; [Isa. 34:4] [l]Gen. 39:3, 23; [Ps. 128:2; Isa. 3:10]
4[m]See Job 21:18
5[n]Ps. 5:5; 76:7; Nah. 1:6; Luke 21:36; Eph. 6:13 [o][Ezek. 13:9]

Psalm 1. The first psalm serves as the gateway into the entire book of Psalms, stressing that those who would worship God genuinely must embrace his Law (or Torah), i.e., his covenant instruction. This psalm takes topics found in wisdom literature such as Proverbs and makes them the subject of song; the purpose is that those who sing the psalm will own its values—namely, they will want more and more to be people who love the Torah, who believe it, who see themselves as the heirs and stewards of its story of redemption and hope, and who seek to carry out its moral requirements. They can delight in the idea of being among the "righteous," feeling that nothing can compare with such blessedness. By its sustained contrast, the psalm reminds readers that in the end there are really only two ways to live.

1:1–2 *Contrasting Sources of Values.* The truly happy person guides his life by God's instruction rather than by the advice of those who reject that instruction.

1:1 Blessed. The truly happy person is happy because God showers him with favor. Jesus uses the Greek equivalent in Matt. 5:3–11; cf. also James 1:12. The Latin translation, *beatus*, is the source of the word *beatitude*. **the man**. A specific, godly individual (Hb. *ha'ish*, "the man") is held up as an example for others to imitate. Such teaching by use of a concrete example is common in OT wisdom literature. **wicked . . . sinners . . . scoffers**. These are people, even within Israel, who refuse to live by the covenant; the godly person refuses to follow the moral orientation of such people's lifestyle. Some have seen an increasing level of sinfulness in the terms "wicked-sinners-scoffers," together with an increasing loyalty in the metaphors "walk-stand-sit"; however, it is likely that the terms "wicked" and "sinner" here are equivalent, while a "scoffer" is certainly more committed to evil (see note on Prov. 19:25–20:1).

1:2 the law of the LORD. As the ESV footnote indicates, this could be taken as God's *instruction* (Hb. *Torah*, which often designates the Law of Moses), particularly as he speaks in his covenant. For this reason no one should ever think that such a person receives his blessedness by deserving it, since the covenant is founded on God's grace. **Meditates** describes an active pondering, perhaps even muttering to oneself in pursuit of insight. Some suppose **day and night** speaks of the work of professional scholars who spend all their time pondering the words of the law, but in view of the similar instruction in Josh. 1:8, readers should see this as setting the ideal of facing every situation, be it ever so mundane, with a view to pleasing the Lord by knowing and following his Word.

1:3–4 *Contrasting Fruitfulness.* Here are two similes, based on agriculture in ancient Palestine, describing the effects of the two kinds of people.

1:3 The first image is that of a **tree** in a dry climate, which nevertheless thrives because of its constant supply of **water**. A tree bears fruit, not for itself, but for others; thus, when the faithful **prospers**, it is not for himself, nor is the prospering even necessarily material, but he succeeds in bringing benefit to others. See Jer. 17:8 for the same image.

1:4 wicked. See v. 1. **chaff**. This is the husks and straw removed by threshing, and it is lighter than the edible kernels; when a farmer tosses threshed wheat into the air, **the wind drives away** the chaff. Those who reject God's covenant are like chaff in that they bring no benefit to anyone (cf. 35:5).

1:5–6 *Contrasting Outcomes of Their Lives.* These two verses lead readers to reflect on where these two kinds of life are headed, showing that God will make the contrast last forever.

1:5 Therefore indicates that these verses are the conclusion of the psalm. **judgment**. This could be any particular judgment that falls on **the wicked** in this life, but it is more likely the final judgment, which allows some to enter the **congregation of the righteous**, while excluding others (Eccles. 12:14).

6[p]Ps. 31:7; 37:18; 144:3; Nah. 1:7; [John 10:14; 2 Tim. 2:19] [q]Ps. 37:5
Psalm 2
1[r]Cited Acts 4:25, 26 [s][Ps. 46:6]
2[t]Ps. 18:50; 20:6; 45:7; 89:20
3[u]Jer. 5:5
4[v]Ps. 11:4; 29:10; [Isa. 40:22] [w]Ps. 37:13; 59:8; Job 22:19; Prov. 1:26
5[x]Rev. 6:16, 17
6[y]Prov. 8:23 [z]2 Sam. 5:7; Ps. 110:2 [a]Ps. 3:4; 15:1; 43:3; 99:9
7[b]Rom. 1:4; Cited Acts 13:33; Heb. 1:5; 5:5
8[c][Ps. 72:8; 89:27; Dan. 7:14]
9[d]Ps. 89:23; Job 34:24 [e]Rev. 2:27; 12:5; 19:15 [f]Isa. 30:14; Jer. 19:11

6 for the LORD [p]knows [q]the way of the righteous,
but the way of the wicked will perish.

The Reign of the LORD's Anointed

2

1 [r]Why do [s]the nations rage[1]
and the peoples plot in vain?
2 The kings of the earth set themselves,
and the rulers take counsel together,
against the LORD and against his [t]Anointed, saying,
3 "Let us [u]burst their bonds apart
and cast away their cords from us."

4 He who [v]sits in the heavens [w]laughs;
the Lord holds them in derision.
5 Then he will speak to them in his [x]wrath,
and terrify them in his fury, saying,
6 "As for me, I have [y]set my King
on [z]Zion, my [a]holy hill."

7 I will tell of the decree:
The LORD said to me, [b]"You are my Son;
today I have begotten you.
8 Ask of me, and I will make the nations your heritage,
and [c]the ends of the earth your possession.
9 You shall [d]break[2] them with [e]a rod of iron
and dash them in pieces like [f]a potter's vessel."

10 Now therefore, O kings, be wise;
be warned, O rulers of the earth.

[1] Or *nations noisily assemble* [2] Revocalization yields (compare Septuagint) *You shall rule*

1:6 Knows must be something stronger than simply "knows about," since God knows about the wicked and their deepest secrets (cf. 94:8–11). Some have argued that the word means "cares for," but it is better to take this as "knows with affection and approval, i.e., prefers" (cf. Gen. 18:19; Amos 3:2). **will perish**. That is, end in destruction.

Psalm 2. When the people of God sing Psalm 2, they remind themselves of how God made David and his descendants to be kings in order to enable them to fulfill the very purpose for which Abraham was called (to bring blessing to all nations, Gen. 12:1–3). Thus it can be called a *royal psalm*. The pious Israelite realizes that his hope of blessing is now irrevocably tied to the house of David (cf. 2 Sam. 7:12–16), and so he prays that God will keep the king pure. At a time when the Gentile kingdoms that are part of the Davidic empire seek to throw off Israelite rule, this psalm recalls the promises made to the Davidic king at his coronation and notes that the Gentiles will find lasting joy only as subjects of this king. With its prospect of a worldwide rule for the house of David, the psalm also looks to the future, when the Davidic Messiah will indeed accomplish this; in fact, the scope of such an accomplishment calls for a ruler who is more than a mere man.

2:1–3 *The Gentile Kings in Revolt.* In vv. 1–2 several kings of Gentile peoples who are vassals of the Davidic king propose a revolt to throw off Israelite rule; in v. 3 they speak their goal.

2:2 Anointed. Samuel anointed both Saul (1 Sam. 10:1) and David (1 Sam. 16:13), setting them apart as king, whose task was to rule Israel and to embody covenant faithfulness. The word *Messiah* comes from transliterating the Hebrew word for "Anointed," and the word *Christ* comes from translating "Anointed" into Greek. For the Gentiles to rebel against the heir of David is to rebel against the Lord who installed him; it is also to cut themselves off from their only hope of knowing the one true God. In Acts 4:25–26, the early Christians saw the persecution they faced as the same kind of foolish rebellion.

2:4–6 *Heaven's Perspective on the Revolt.* Since the Lord is not dismayed, neither do his people need to be. In fact, God laughs at the rebels and declares his firm purpose to establish the throne of David as he has promised.

2:7–9 *The Davidic King Speaks.* The king recalls what God had said at his coronation. Lying behind this is the promise that the line of David will be sure forever before the Lord (2 Sam. 7:16) and that the obedience of the peoples will come to the ruler from the tribe of Judah (Gen. 49:10), together with the very purpose for choosing Abraham and his offspring.

2:7 decree. That is, the divine oracle spoken when the king took his throne. **The LORD said**. Although many suppose that this psalm is for the crowning of a king, the past tense indicates that the king recalls the oracle at a later time of trouble. **You are my Son**. In 2 Sam. 7:14, God says that he will take the heir of David as a "son." The people as a whole are called the "son of God" (see Ex. 4:22–23; Ps. 80:15; Hos. 11:1), and the king is called the "son of God" because he represents and embodies the people (see also Ps. 89:27). Hebrews 1:5 brings Ps. 2:7 together with 2 Sam. 7:14: this shows that the argument of that book assumes that Jesus is the messianic heir of David (the Son of God), into whom God has also folded the priestly office. In Acts 13:33 (a speech of Paul) and Rom. 1:4, Paul portrays the resurrection of Jesus as his coronation, his entry into his Davidic rule.

2:8 nations. That is, the Gentiles, including those in revolt (v. 1). The primary messianic picture of the OT is of the heir of David who will lead his people in bringing the light to the nations, by making them his subjects; this is how the nations of the earth will find blessing for themselves in him (see Gen. 22:18; see also Ps. 72:8–11, 17); thus Paul looks forward to the obedience of faith among all the nations (Rom. 1:5).

2:9 break (Hb. *tero'em*). As the ESV footnote says, the Septuagint (used in Rev. 2:27; 12:5; 19:15) renders this as "rule"; this comes from using the same Hebrew consonants with different vowels (*tir'em*).

2:10–12 *Advice to the Gentile Kings.* The kings must understand that the ruler whom they reject is not just another human ruler but is God's own appointed king for the sake of the whole world. Therefore they serve their best interest by submitting to David's heir.

2:10 kings . . . rulers of the earth. See v. 2.

11 [g]Serve the LORD with [h]fear,
and [i]rejoice with [h]trembling.
12 [j]Kiss [k]the Son,
lest he be angry, and you perish in the way,
for his [l]wrath is quickly kindled.
[m]Blessed are all who take refuge in him.

Save Me, O My God

3

A PSALM OF DAVID, [n]WHEN HE FLED FROM ABSALOM HIS SON.

1 O LORD, [o]how many are my foes!
Many are [p]rising against me;
2 many are saying of my soul,
[q]there is no salvation for him in God. *Selah*[1]

3 But you, O LORD, are [r]a shield [s]about me,
my glory, and [t]the lifter of my head.
4 I [u]cried aloud to the LORD,
and he [v]answered me from his [w]holy hill. *Selah*

5 I [x]lay down and slept;
I woke again, for the LORD sustained me.
6 I [y]will not be afraid of many thousands of people
who have [z]set themselves against me all around.

7 [a]Arise, O LORD!
Save me, O my God!
For you [b]strike all my enemies on the cheek;
you [c]break the teeth of the wicked.

8 [d]Salvation belongs to the LORD;
your blessing be on your people! *Selah*

[1] The meaning of the Hebrew word *Selah*, used frequently in the Psalms, is uncertain. It may be a musical or liturgical direction

11 [g]Heb. 12:28 [h]Phil. 2:12 [i]Phil. 4:4
12 [j]1 Sam. 10:1; 1 Kgs. 19:18; [John 5:23] [k]Prov. 31:2 [l]ver. 5 [m]Ps. 34:8; 84:12; Prov. 16:20; Jer. 17:7; [Ps. 146:5; Isa. 30:18]

Psalm 3

[n]See 2 Sam. 15:14-17
1 [o]2 Sam. 15:12 [p]2 Sam. 18:31, 32
2 [q]Ps. 71:11; [2 Sam. 16:8]
3 [r]Ps. 28:7; 84:9; 119:114; Gen. 15:1 [s]Job 1:10 [t]Ps. 27:5, 6; [Job 10:15]
4 [u]Ps. 77:1; 142:1 [v]Ps. 34:4; 60:5; 108:6; [Ps. 6:8; 34:6] [w]See Ps. 2:6
5 [x]Ps. 4:8; [Lev. 26:6; Job 11:18, 19; Prov. 3:24]
6 [y][Ps. 23:4; 27:3] [z]Isa. 22:7; [1 Kgs. 20:12]
7 [a]Ps. 7:6; 9:19; 10:12; Num. 10:35 [b]See Job 16:10 [c]Ps. 58:6; Job 29:17
8 [d]Ps. 37:39; 62:7; Isa. 43:11; 45:21; Jer. 3:23; Hos. 13:4; Jonah 2:9; Rev. 7:10; 19:1

2:12 Kiss the Son. "Son" (*bar*) is Aramaic in form, leading some to offer other translations (such as "purely"), or even to suggest large-scale repairs to the Hebrew text (e.g., to make it say "his feet"). But the Aramaic-sounding term is well-suited to a Gentile audience (the kings in revolt). The Son is the heir of David (v. 7). The kiss denotes religious homage, and the Davidic king deserves it (v. 2). It is possible that the **he** and **him** of this verse refer to the Lord (from v. 11), though it is more natural to find a reference to the Son, who acts in God's name. He is therefore the one in whom the faithful **take refuge**.

Psalm 3. This is the first psalm with a title. The title names David as the author and ties the psalm to the occasion of Absalom's rebellion (2 Samuel 15–16), although this need not mean that David actually composed it then. As explained in the Introduction: Authorship, Occasion, and Date, David as author is the representative of God's people. Readers must discern whether the emphasis is on his role as the ruler of God's people, in which case the congregation joins in offering his prayer, or else on David as the ideal member of the people of God, with the song being well-adapted for the use of Israelites in their various kinds of distress. The second option seems more likely, and thus the psalm can be considered an individual lament. The purpose, then, of the information in the title is to add concreteness: here is how David models genuine faith in his dire straits, and readers can learn to do the same in theirs.

3:1–2 *What He Sees.* The opening of the psalm lays out the desperate situation, with its repetition of **many**. The description here ties in well with 2 Sam. 15:12–13 ("many") and 16:8 ("no salvation for him").

3:2 Salvation here, as generally in the OT, refers to both physical and spiritual deliverance from danger. The fact that they are saying this of his **soul** indicates that the enemies are taunting him: his sins are so bad, they imply, that God cannot save him.

3:3–6 *What He Believes.* The singer calls to mind the variety of ways in which God has cared for him in the past, and how he was able in faith to sleep peacefully in the face of danger. These past experiences build his confidence for the present, enabling him to walk by faith and not by sight.

3:7–8 *What He Prays For.* The singer calls on the Lord to save him now as he has in the past. "Save" (v. 7) and "salvation" (v. 8) look back to the taunt in v. 2: this rescue is the Lord's to give or withhold as he sees fit, and not under the control of the enemies. The prayer does not replace work; instead it is what makes the work effective.

3:7 Arise. Cf. Num. 10:35; a request for God to show his favor by scattering the enemies. **For you strike . . . you break**. The singer is emboldened to ask God for help because God has regularly protected him from enemies, by shaming them and rendering them powerless.

3:8 Salvation belongs to the LORD. By looking back to v. 2, the singer remembers that it is the decision of the Lord, and not of the enemies, that makes the difference (for the same exclamation, cf. Jonah 2:9; Rev. 7:10; 19:1). **your blessing be on your people**. A merciful word indeed, wishing well even for the people who oppose him; but the blessing will require their defeat.

Psalm 4. This psalm expresses quiet trust amid troubling circumstances, combining the categories of individual lament and confidence. Many take this as a companion to Psalm 3, because 4:8 seems to echo 3:5. If there is a connection, the past tense of 3:5 sets it in the morning, while

Psalm 4

[e]Ps. 61, title; Hab. 3:19
1 [f]Isa. 54:17; Jer. 23:6 [g]See Job 36:16
2 [h][Ps. 5:6]
3 [i][Ex. 11:7] [j][Ps. 50:5]
4 [k]Cited Eph. 4:26 [l]Ps. 77:6 [m]See Ps. 42:8
5 [n]Ps. 51:19; Deut. 33:19 [o]Ps. 37:3; 62:8
6 [p]Num. 6:26 [q]Ps. 89:15; [Ps. 31:16; 67:1; 80:3, 7, 19; 119:135]
7 [r][Isa. 9:3; 16:10; Jer. 48:38]
8 [s]See Ps. 3:5 [t]Ps. 16:9; Lev. 25:18, 19; 26:5; Deut. 33:28

Psalm 5

1 [u][Ps. 39:3]
2 [v]Ps. 84:3 [w]Ps. 65:2
3 [x]Ps. 88:13; 119:147; 130:6 [y][Hab. 2:1]

Answer Me When I Call

4

To the [e]choirmaster: with [e]stringed instruments. A Psalm of David.

1 Answer me when I call, O God of my [f]righteousness!
You have [g]given me relief when I was in distress.
Be gracious to me and hear my prayer!

2 O men,[1] how long shall my honor be turned into shame?
How long will you love vain words and seek after [h]lies? *Selah*
3 But know that the Lord has [i]set apart [j]the godly for himself;
the Lord hears when I call to him.

4 [k]Be angry,[2] and do not sin;
[l]ponder in your own hearts [m]on your beds, and be silent. *Selah*
5 Offer [n]right sacrifices,
and put your [o]trust in the Lord.

6 There are many who say, "Who will show us some good?
[p]Lift up [q]the light of your face upon us, O Lord!"
7 You have put [r]more joy in my heart
than they have when their grain and wine abound.

8 In peace I will both [s]lie down and sleep;
for you alone, O Lord, make me [t]dwell in safety.

Lead Me in Your Righteousness

5

To the choirmaster: for the flutes. A Psalm of David.

1 Give ear to my words, O Lord;
consider my [u]groaning.
2 Give attention to the sound of my cry,
my [v]King and my God,
for [w]to you do I pray.
3 O Lord, in [x]the morning you hear my voice;
in the morning I prepare a sacrifice for you[3] and [y]watch.

[1] Or *O men of rank* [2] Or *Be agitated* [3] Or *I direct my prayer to you*

the future tense of 4:8 sets it in the evening; any further connection is speculative.

4:1 *Confident Prayer.* The recollection of past experience (**You have given me relief**) between two urgent requests is similar to the rhetoric of 3:7: past experience emboldens the faithful to confident prayer.

4:2–3 *Words to the Faithless.* The singer turns from his prayer to address those who slander the pious; such people should know that the Lord has set his favor upon the faithful and will listen to their prayers.

4:3 set apart. The same Hebrew word is rendered "set apart" in Ex. 8:22, and "make a distinction" in Ex. 9:4; 11:7; 33:16; the idea is that God sets his special attention and affection on a person or a people in order to distinguish them. **the godly**. The Hebrew word (*hasid*) is the adjective form of "steadfast love" (Hb. *hesed*). This term, variously rendered "godly," "saint," "faithful one," and "holy one" in the Psalms, refers to those who have genuinely laid hold of God's steadfast love; here it is singular, to stress that each faithful member of the people may have this confidence.

4:4–5 *Words to the Godly.* The singer tells the godly not to give in to the anger that would lead them to take revenge; instead they must remain steadfast in their worship and trust.

4:4 Be angry, and do not sin. This should perhaps be taken as a conditional sentence: "If you feel anger at those who slander you (which you may well do), nevertheless do not sin by seeking revenge against them." The way to prevent sin is to **ponder** and **be silent**: that is, reflect on how the Lord has shown himself trustworthy. This does not discourage the faithful from using legal recourse when necessary; instead it speaks against personal revenge that circumvents the law and consumes the lives of the vengeful. Cf. Eph. 4:26.

4:6–8 *Words to the Lord.* The singer finishes by offering a plea to the Lord. Each godly person is to see himself giving the plaintive cry of v. 6, and is to find the answer in remembering all that the Lord has done for him (vv. 7–8).

4:7 Joy in the OT is not focused on materialistic prosperity in itself; cf. 37:16; 73:28; Prov. 15:16; 16:8.

Psalm 5. This is another individual lament, and the first instance of a psalm with prayers for the personal downfall of the enemies. As indicated in Introduction: Literary Features, such Psalms have in view a situation where one is faced with bloodthirsty and deceitful persecutors. David is the attributed author, but there is no information on whether a particular experience of his was the occasion for the psalm.

5:1–3 *Asking for God's Attention.* As is common in the laments, the psalm opens by calling out to God. The tone is one of urgency and expectation.

5:2 my King and my God. Some psalms that speak of the Lord as "king" have in mind his rule over all his creation. Others, such as this one, refer to him as king over his people. The Davidic kingship, when it functioned properly, did not usurp either kind of divine kingship, though a faithless king could lead to God punishing the people (cf. 1 Sam. 8:7; 12:12–15).

5:3 I prepare a sacrifice for you is difficult in the Hebrew, which could also be rendered as in the ESV footnote, "I direct my prayer to you." The mention of the **morning** here, and the Lord's house in v. 7, favors "sacrifice";

4 For you are not a God who delights in wickedness;
evil may not dwell with you.
5 The [z]boastful shall not [a]stand before your eyes;
you [b]hate all evildoers.
6 You destroy those who speak [c]lies;
the LORD abhors [d]the bloodthirsty and deceitful man.
7 But I, through the abundance of your steadfast love,
will enter your house.
I will [e]bow down [f]toward your [g]holy temple
in the fear of you.
8 [h]Lead me, O LORD, in your righteousness
because of my enemies;
[i]make your way straight before me.
9 For there is no truth in their mouth;
their inmost self is [j]destruction;
[k]their throat is [l]an open grave;
they [m]flatter with their tongue.
10 [n]Make them bear their guilt, O God;
let them [o]fall by their own counsels;
because of the abundance of their transgressions cast them out,
for they have rebelled against you.

11 But let all who [p]take refuge in you [q]rejoice;
let them ever sing for joy,
and spread your protection over them,
that those who love your name may [r]exult in you.
12 For you [s]bless the righteous, O LORD;
you [t]cover him with favor as with [u]a shield.

O LORD, Deliver My Life

6 TO THE CHOIRMASTER: WITH STRINGED INSTRUMENTS;
ACCORDING TO [v]THE SHEMINITH.[1] A PSALM OF DAVID.

1 O LORD, [w]rebuke me not in your anger,
nor [x]discipline me in your wrath.

[1] Probably a musical or liturgical term

5[z]Ps. 73:3; 75:4; [Hab. 1:13] [a]See Ps. 1:5 [b]Ps. 11:5
6[c][Ps. 4:2]; Rev. 21:8; 22:15 [d]Ps. 55:23
7[e]Ps. 132:7 [f]1 Kgs. 8:29, 30 [g]Ps. 11:4; 79:1
8[h][Ps. 23:3; 25:4, 5] [i][Ezra 8:21]
9[j]Ps. 52:2 [k]Cited Rom. 3:13 [l]Jer. 5:16 [m]Ps. 12:2; Prov. 2:16; 7:5
10[n][Isa. 24:6] [o][2 Sam. 15:31; 17:14, 23]
11[p]Ps. 2:12 [q]Ps. 33:21 [r][Ps. 9:2; 1 Sam. 2:1]
12[s]Ps. 115:13 [t][Ps. 103:4] [u][Ps. 35:2]

Psalm 6

[v]1 Chr. 15:21
1[w]Ps. 38:1 [x][Ps. 94:12; 118:18; Prov. 3:11, 12; Jer. 30:11; 46:28]; See Heb. 12:3-11

the idea here is that the prayer comes in the context of a faithful worshiper who receives assurance and expresses personal consecration by way of these ordinances; it is small wonder that such a person will **watch**, looking around and ahead in expectant faith.

5:4–6 *The God Who Loves Justice.* The singer praises God for loving what is right. The argument of the psalm is that the success of these persecutors would contradict the biblical view of God's commitment to righteousness. The terms describing evil and evildoers are status words; that is, they describe people who reject God's kingship, as well as denoting the behavior that stems from such rejection (as vv. 7–8 will make clear).

5:4 dwell with you. For this theme, cf. 15:1; 61:4; Isa. 33:14.

5:7–8 *Confidence of the Pious.* The genuinely godly recognize that they come before God only through "the abundance of your steadfast love" (v. 7); and thus they pray that God will **lead** them to walk in the **way** that is morally **straight** (v. 8). There is nothing self-righteous about the confidence and prayers here.

5:7 abundance of your steadfast love. The phrase comes from Ex. 34:6, the basic confession of OT faith, describing the Lord's benevolence.

5:9–10 *Prayer against the Evildoers.* After a further description of the deceitful means and destructive schemes of these people (v. 9) comes a prayer that God would thwart the schemes and judge the schemers. It is actually a mercy to potential "evildoers" that this occurs in a hymn sung in public worship: it warns them of what awaits any who pursue such evil.

5:9 Paul uses this verse in Rom. 3:13 as part of his argument that both Jews and Gentiles are under the power of sin.

5:10 These prayers describe the judgment that must eventually fall on those members of God's people who harden themselves to persecute the godly, because to harm the godly is to attack God. The request, then, is for God to vindicate his commitment to his people, here in this life for all to see. Prayers of this sort generally carry the unstated assumption that the evildoers will not repent and seek forgiveness.

5:11–12 *Confidence for All the Godly.* The psalm closes by expressing the assurance enjoyed by the faithful. The song prays that the truly faithful, in contrast to the evildoers, will always rejoice in the Lord and be assured of his care and protection.

Psalm 6. This is an individual lament, also from David. It is especially suited to one whose hard circumstances have led him to see his sins and to repent of them. For this reason Psalm 6 is often included in the "Penitential Psalms" (cf. Psalms 32; 38 [and note]; 51; 130; 143).

6:1–5 *Plea for Mercy.* These verses arise from some life-threatening situation; a sickness would fit the description, as would a number of other desperate crises. The song interprets the situation as coming from God's displeasure at some particular sins. This does not mean that all desperate situations are

2 Be gracious to me, O LORD, for I am languishing;
[y]heal me, O LORD, [z]for my bones are troubled.
3 My [a]soul also is greatly troubled.
But you, O LORD—[b]how long?

4 Turn, O LORD, deliver my life;
save me for the sake of your steadfast love.
5 For in [c]death there is no remembrance of you;
in Sheol who will give you praise?

6 I am [d]weary with my [e]moaning;
every night I flood my bed with tears;
I drench my couch with my weeping.
7 My [f]eye wastes away because of grief;
it grows weak because of all my foes.

8 [g]Depart from me, all you [h]workers of evil,
for the LORD [i]has heard the sound of my weeping.
9 The LORD has heard my [j]plea;
the LORD accepts my prayer.
10 All my enemies shall be ashamed and greatly troubled;
they shall [k]turn back and be put to shame in a moment.

In You Do I Take Refuge

7

A [l]SHIGGAION[1] OF DAVID, WHICH HE SANG TO THE LORD CONCERNING THE WORDS OF CUSH, A BENJAMINITE.

1 O LORD my God, in you do I [m]take refuge;
[n]save me from all my pursuers and deliver me,
2 lest like [o]a lion they tear my soul apart,
rending it in pieces, with [p]none to deliver.

3 O LORD my God, [q]if I have done this,
if there is [r]wrong in my hands,
4 if I have repaid [s]my friend[2] with evil
or [t]plundered my enemy without cause,
5 let the enemy pursue my soul and overtake it,
and let him [u]trample my life to the ground
and lay my glory in the dust. *Selah*

2 [y]Ps. 30:2; 41:4; 103:3 [z]See Ps. 31:10
3 [a][John 12:27] [b]Ps. 90:13
5 [c]Ps. 30:9; 88:10-12; 115:17; Isa. 38:18
6 [d]Ps. 69:3 [e]Ps. 38:9
7 [f]Ps. 31:9; 88:9; [Ps. 38:10; Job 17:7; Lam. 2:11; 5:17]
8 [g]Ps. 119:115; 139:19; Matt. 7:23; 25:41; Luke 13:27 [h]Ps. 94:4 [i][Ps. 3:4]
9 [j]Ps. 55:1; 1 Kgs. 8:38
10 [k]Ps. 40:14; 56:9

Psalm 7

[l]Hab. 3:1
1 [m]See Ps. 11:1 [n]Ps. 31:15
2 [o]See Job 10:16 [p]Ps. 50:22
3 [q][2 Sam. 16:7, 8] [r]1 Sam. 24:11; 26:18; [Ps. 59:3]
4 [s]Ps. 55:20 [t]1 Sam. 24:7; 26:9
5 [u]Dan. 8:7; [Ps. 89:39]

[1] Probably a musical or liturgical term [2] Hebrew *the one at peace with me*

evidence of God's displeasure, only that some may be; the psalm provides a vehicle for singing to God properly *in such cases*.

6:4 for the sake of your steadfast love. Those who are penitent appeal to God's love and mercy, and not to their own well-doing.

6:5 Sheol is a proper name in Hebrew; sometimes it serves as a poetic name for the grave, to which all go (e.g., 141:7), and other times it names the dim destination to which the wicked go but not the faithful (e.g., 49:14–15). If it refers to the grave here, the idea is that the dead do not have the privilege of recounting God's praise in public worship. The verse expresses the fear that the psalmist's sins, if not forgiven, would separate him from God's presence.

6:6–7 *Weariness and Weeping.* Now the psalmist describes the effects of realizing that his circumstances stem from his sins; he moans and cries and loses sleep from sorrow over his sins.

6:8–10 *The Lord Has Heard.* Those who are truly sorry for their sins can be assured that God hears their cries for mercy and will not give them over to the schemes of their enemies.

6:8 Depart from me, all you workers of evil. This seems to be spoken to those who would take advantage of the singer's distress, slandering him and perhaps even trying to hasten his death. But if **the LORD has heard**, then these enemies are "all bark and no bite." Jesus uses these words in Luke 13:27, likening any Jews of his day who resist his message to the enemies in this psalm; they will discover in the end that Jesus really does have God's favor.

6:9 The particular **plea** and **prayer** is that of vv. 1–5; the Lord, in hearing it, forgives.

6:10 There is a reversal here: the singer's bones and soul were troubled (vv. 2–3), but now the **enemies** will be **greatly troubled**.

Psalm 7. This is another individual lament from David. The title refers to an otherwise unknown incident in his life when a man of Benjamin (the tribe of Saul) slandered David. The psalm provides a vehicle by which those unfairly criticized and persecuted may call to God for help.

7:1–2 *Cry for Safety.* In the face of desperate circumstances, the first words express trust (**my God**, **refuge**), leading to the specific request.

7:3–5 *Claim of Innocence.* These verses make it clear that this psalm is for those cases in which the danger stems from the malice of the persecutors, and not from the wrongdoing of the person in trouble. There is an implicit warning to those who commit the evils listed here—that they may not use this psalm to ask for God's help in *their* troubles.

6 [v]Arise, O LORD, in your anger;
[w]lift yourself up against the fury of my enemies;
[x]awake for me; you have appointed a judgment.
7 Let the assembly of the peoples be gathered about you;
over it return on high.

8 The LORD [y]judges the peoples;
[z]judge me, O LORD, according to my righteousness
and according to the integrity that is in me.
9 Oh, let the evil of the wicked come to an end,
and may you establish the righteous—
you who [a]test [b]the minds and hearts,[1]
O righteous God!
10 My shield is [c]with God,
who saves [d]the upright in heart.
11 God is [e]a righteous judge,
and a God who feels [f]indignation every day.

12 If a man[2] does not repent, God[3] will [g]whet his sword;
he has [h]bent and [i]readied his bow;
13 he has prepared for him his deadly weapons,
making his [j]arrows [k]fiery shafts.
14 Behold, the wicked man [l]conceives evil
and is [l]pregnant with mischief
and gives birth to lies.
15 He makes [m]a pit, digging it out,
and falls into the hole that he has made.
16 His [n]mischief returns upon his own head,
and on his own skull his violence descends.

17 I will give to the LORD the thanks due to his righteousness,
and I will [o]sing praise to the name of the LORD, the Most High.

How Majestic Is Your Name

8

TO THE CHOIRMASTER: ACCORDING TO THE [p]GITTITH.[4] A PSALM OF DAVID.
1 O LORD, our Lord,
how majestic is your [q]name in all the earth!

[1] Hebrew *the hearts and kidneys* [2] Hebrew *he* [3] Hebrew *he* [4] Probably a musical or liturgical term

6 [v]See Ps. 3:7 [w]Ps. 94:2; Isa. 33:10 [x]Ps. 35:23; 44:23; 59:4; Job 8:6
8 [y]See Ps. 58:11 [z]Ps. 26:1; 35:24; 43:1; [Ps. 18:20]
9 [a]Ps. 11:5; Job 23:10; [Ps. 139:1; 1 Sam. 16:7; 1 Chr. 28:9] [b]Ps. 26:2; Jer. 11:20; 17:10; 20:12; Rev. 2:23
10 [c][Ps. 62:8] [d]2 Chr. 29:34
11 [e][Job 8:3] [f]Nah. 1:2, 6
12 [g]Deut. 32:41 [h]Ps. 11:2; 37:14 [i]Ps. 21:12
13 [j]See Ps. 18:14 [k][Eph. 6:16]
14 [l]Job 15:35; Isa. 59:4; [Isa. 33:11; James 1:15]
15 [m]Ps. 9:15; 57:6; 119:85; Prov. 26:27; 28:10; Eccles. 10:8
16 [n][Ps. 94:23; 141:10; Judg. 9:24; 1 Kgs. 2:32; Esth. 7:10; 9:25; Prov. 5:22]
17 [o]Ps. 9:2

Psalm 8

[p]Ps. 81, title; 84, title
1 [q]Ps. 148:13; Isa. 12:4; [Ex. 34:5]

7:6–11 *Call to God to Arise as Judge.* The singers see their requests as part of the larger picture: God is a **righteous judge** (v. 11), to whom all the **peoples** of mankind, and not just Israel, are accountable (vv. 7, 8); thus his **anger** (v. 6) and **indignation** (v. 11) are directed against those who threaten his faithful ones (the **righteous**, v. 9; and the **upright in heart**, v. 10). In the Psalms, judging is more often than not a saving action, God intervening on behalf of the innocent and oppressed. (In English the word "judge" tends to focus more on condemning than on rescuing.) The particular deliverance, then, is part of God's larger project of putting the whole world back to its right order (v. 9).

7:12–16 *Evil Returns upon the Evildoers.* God's anger toward the persecutors shows itself by turning their own schemes against them.

7:12 If a man does not repent. There is a way out for the persecutors: namely, they can seek the Lord. This phrase warns the wicked and invites them to repentance; it also helps the faithful to prefer and wish that their oppressors would turn to God rather than suffer punishment.

7:17 *Closing Confidence.* For the faithful, the Lord's **righteousness** and his status as **the Most High** (expounded in vv. 6–11) lead to giving thanks and singing praise, because God's purpose of justice will prevail.

Psalm 8. This is a hymn of praise, enabling the Lord's people to celebrate their privileged place in the created order, which speaks of the glorious Creator. Genesis 1–2 lies behind the words here, especially in presenting mankind as the pinnacle of the creation week, as the rulers over the animal world, and as the object of God's special attention. At the same time, the mention of "foes," "enemy," and "avenger" (Ps. 8:2), as well as the covenantal name "LORD" (vv. 1, 9), show that readers cannot ignore Genesis 3 and God's plan for fallen mankind. Although the psalm is covenantal, and thus specifically for Israelite voices to sing, it nevertheless speaks of "man" in general terms, including all humanity. Israel's calling was to be the firstfruits of restored humanity; thus the Israelite worshiper could embrace his dignity and seek to live worthily of it. This points the way to understanding how Heb. 2:6–8 uses Ps. 8:4–6: Jesus, as Davidic king, is the ideal Israelite, and thus the ideal human being, in this case by being crowned with glory and honor after his suffering on behalf of mankind.

8:1–2 *God's Majestic Name.* The opening words (v. 1) set the theme of the psalm, which v. 9 then repeats. The majesty of God's name (his revealed character) is seen in the dignity he gives to mankind.

8:1 The covenant **name** (**LORD**) was given specifically to Israel, but it is **majestic . . . in all the earth**, even if not all people acknowledge it.

You have set your [r]glory above the heavens.
2 [s]Out of the mouth of babies and infants,
you have established [t]strength because of your foes,
to still [u]the enemy and the avenger.

3 When I [v]look at your heavens, the work of your [w]fingers,
the moon and the stars, [x]which you have set in place,
4 [y]what is man that you are [z]mindful of him,
and [a]the son of man that you [b]care for him?

5 Yet you have made him a little lower than [c]the heavenly beings[1]
and crowned him with [d]glory and honor.
6 You have given him [e]dominion over the works of your hands;
[f]you have put all things under his feet,
7 all sheep and oxen,
and also the beasts of the field,
8 the birds of the heavens, and the fish of the sea,
whatever passes along the paths of the seas.

9 O LORD, our Lord,
how majestic is your name in all the earth!

I Will Recount Your Wonderful Deeds

9[2] TO THE CHOIRMASTER: ACCORDING TO MUTH-LABBEN.[3] A PSALM OF DAVID.

1 I will give thanks to the LORD with my whole heart;
I will recount all of your [g]wonderful deeds.
2 I will be glad and [h]exult in you;
I will [i]sing praise to your name, [j]O Most High.

3 When my enemies turn back,
they stumble and perish before[4] your presence.

[1] Or *than God*; Septuagint *than the angels* [2] Psalms 9 and 10 together follow an acrostic pattern, each stanza beginning with the successive letters of the Hebrew alphabet. In the Septuagint they form one psalm [3] Probably a musical or liturgical term [4] Or *because of*

1 [r]Ps. 113:4
2 [s]Cited Matt. 21:16; [Matt. 11:25; 1 Cor. 1:27] [t]Jer. 16:19 [u]Ps. 44:16
3 [v][Ps. 111:2] [w]Ex. 8:19; 31:18 [x]Gen. 1:16
4 [y]Cited Heb. 2:6-8; [Ps. 144:3; Job 7:17; 25:6] [z][Gen. 8:1] [a]Ps. 80:17 [b]Ps. 65:9; Gen. 21:1; 50:24
5 [c][Gen. 1:26] [d]Ps. 21:5
6 [e]Gen. 1:26, 28 [f]Cited 1 Cor. 15:27; [Matt. 28:18]

Psalm 9

1 [g]Ps. 26:7; 40:5; 96:3; 105:5
2 [h]Ps. 5:11 [i]Ps. 7:17 [j]See Ps. 83:18

8:2 Perhaps the **babies** and **infants** are the people of Israel, seen as weak in comparison with the mighty unbelieving Gentiles, the **foes**, the **enemy**, the **avenger**. It is through these insignificant mouths that God reveals his majesty. The Greek translation of the Septuagint (see Matt. 21:16) rightly interprets **strength** as "strength attributed to God in song," or "praise."

8:3–8 *Man's Place in the Created Order.* This section falls into two parts: first, the psalmist beholds the countless stars and the bright moon, and marvels at God's interest in mankind (vv. 3–4); second, he marvels at the dominion God has given to mankind (vv. 5–8).

8:3–4 It is astonishing that the God who is great enough to have made the heavens can take notice of mere man; but he goes beyond taking notice: he is **mindful of** man, he cares **for him**. God's greatness does not mean remoteness but rather an eye for detail, no matter how small.

8:5 the heavenly beings. The Hebrew could mean "the gods," that is, the angels in the heavenly court, or it could mean God himself. The ESV text takes the first option, agreeing with the Greek of the Septuagint (quoted in Heb. 2:7). **Crowned him with glory and honor** describes mankind as God's kingly representative.

8:6 This echoes Gen. 1:26. **put all things under his feet**. Paul combines this with the explicitly messianic Ps. 110:1 (1 Cor. 15:25–27; cf. Eph. 1:22), reflecting an approach similar to that of Hebrews (Heb. 2:6–9).

8:9 *God's Majestic Name.* Serving as an envelope, the closing lines repeat v. 1 and link it with 7:17 and 9:2.

Psalm 9. As the ESV footnote indicates, Psalms 9–10 together follow a basically acrostic pattern, with Psalm 10 beginning where Psalm 9 leaves off. The acrostic is not perfect, however: several letters of the alphabet are missing or are out of order. Further, Psalm 10 lacks a title, which is unusual for this section of the Psalter. Both psalms refer to God's interest in "the oppressed" (9:9; 10:18), both mention "times of trouble" (9:9; 10:1), both call on God to "arise" (9:19; 10:12), and both are sure that God will not "forget the afflicted" (9:12; 10:12). Thus it is not surprising that the Greek and Latin versions have these combined as a single psalm. On the other hand, there are enough differences to justify finding two songs here: the tone of Psalm 9 is predominantly praise and thanks, while that of Psalm 10 is largely lament. Further, whereas in Psalm 9 the enemies are clearly Gentiles (vv. 5–8, 15–16, 19–20), in Psalm 10 they may be faithless Israelites (see esp. 10:4, 13), with the "nations" being mentioned (10:16) to show that the faithless are imitating the wicked Canaanites. Thus these two psalms are probably best taken as companions placed together in light of their similarities. Psalm 9 praises God for the success of the Davidic king in defending Israel from its Gentile foes. The "I" in this psalm is either David as the representative of the people, or each member of Israel, who celebrates the blessings that come to him by way of the whole nation's success.

9:1–2 *The Worshiper's Intent to Give Thanks.* The psalm opens with the singer's desire to thank God for his **wonderful deeds**.

9:1 with my whole heart. The biblical ideal is for the whole inner self to be engaged in loving and praising God (cf. Deut. 6:5), whether in private or in public (as here).

9:3–6 *The Enemies Have Fallen.* The psalm begins to recount the particular wonderful deeds in view, envisioning a successful campaign to protect God's people and their king from some evil scheme of Gentile powers; the victory is decisive (vv. 5–6). When an Israelite sings of his **just cause** (v. 4), he should think beyond the simple right to live unmolested by foreigners, to the very

4 For you have [k]maintained my just cause;
you have [l]sat on the throne, giving righteous judgment.

5 You have [m]rebuked the nations; you have made the wicked perish;
you have [n]blotted out their name forever and ever.
6 The enemy came to an end in everlasting ruins;
their cities you rooted out;
the very memory of them has perished.

7 But the LORD sits enthroned forever;
he has established his throne for justice,
8 and he [o]judges the world with righteousness;
he [p]judges the peoples with uprightness.
9 The LORD is [q]a stronghold for [r]the oppressed,
a stronghold in [s]times of trouble.
10 And those who [t]know your name put their trust in you,
for you, O LORD, have not forsaken those who seek you.

11 Sing praises to the LORD, who [u]sits enthroned in Zion!
Tell among the peoples his [v]deeds!
12 For he who [w]avenges blood is mindful of them;
he [x]does not forget the cry of the afflicted.

13 [y]Be gracious to me, O LORD!
See my affliction from those who hate me,
O you who lift me up from [z]the gates of death,
14 that I may recount all your praises,
that in the gates of [a]the daughter of Zion
I may [b]rejoice in your salvation.

15 The nations have sunk in [c]the pit that they made;
in [d]the net that they hid, their own foot has been caught.
16 The LORD has made himself [e]known; he has executed judgment;
the wicked are snared in the work of their own hands. *Higgaion.*[1] *Selah*

17 The wicked shall [f]return to Sheol,
all the nations that [g]forget God.

18 For the needy shall not always be forgotten,
and [h]the hope of the poor shall not perish forever.

[1] Probably a musical or liturgical term

4[k]Ps. 140:12 [l]Ps. 29:10
5[m]Ps. 68:30 [n]Deut. 9:14; 29:20; [Prov. 10:7]
8[o]Ps. 58:11; 96:13; 98:9 [p]Ps. 96:10
9[q]2 Sam. 22:3; [Prov. 18:10] [r]Ps. 10:18; 74:21 [s]Ps. 10:1
10[t]Ps. 91:14
11[u]Ps. 76:2 [v]Ps. 77:12; [Ps. 107:22]
12[w]Gen. 9:5; [Ps. 10:13]; See 1 Kgs. 21:17-19 [x]ver. 18; Ps. 10:12; [Ps. 12:5]
13[y]Ps. 4:1 [z]See Job 38:17
14[a]2 Kgs. 19:21; Isa. 37:22 [b]Ps. 13:5; 20:5; 21:1; 35:9; 1 Sam. 2:1
15[c]See Ps. 7:15 [d]See Job 18:8
16[e]Ex. 7:5; 14:4
17[f][Gen. 3:19] [g]Ps. 50:22; Job 8:13; Isa. 51:13
18[h][Prov. 23:18; 24:14]

purpose of the call of Israel, namely, to be a light to the Gentiles through living faithfully in the covenant (cf. v. 11).

9:7–10 *The Lord's Just Rule Is His People's Security.* The singer celebrates the security of God's righteous rule. To speak of God's throne (v. 7) is to remember his awesome might; to speak of justice, righteousness, and uprightness (vv. 7–8) is to remember the good and holy ends for which God wields his might, namely, to protect those who know his name (v. 10) and to achieve his purpose of bringing light to the benighted world.

9:7 The terms **sits** and **throne** continue the idea of v. 4, as does the concern with **justice** and righteousness (v. 8).

9:8 That Israel's God **judges the world** and all its **peoples** would be a bold claim if he was not the same God who made heaven and earth and all that is in them. In this particular case the judging is punitive, but this need not be true in every case and at all times (cf. Isa. 2:4).

9:9 God's judgment involves vindicating the **oppressed**, the people of Israel seen as weak and needy. This psalm grew out of an occasion in which the Gentile rulers sought to oppress them.

9:10 To **know** God's **name**, to put **trust in** him, and to **seek** him are all ideals of OT piety, of which the people of Israel often fell short. Here the people are viewed in terms of their ideal.

9:11–12 *A Call for God's Faithful to Sing His Praises.* The singer urges the people of God to make his praises known to the world.

9:11 Tell among the peoples his deeds. See 105:1 and Isa. 12:4 (cf. 1 Chron. 16:8) for a similar expression; and Ps. 18:49 and 96:3 for the idea. God called Abram and Israel for the sake of the whole world, and one function of passages like these is to cultivate in Israel a yearning for the time when the Gentiles would receive the blessing; Paul cites a number of texts to this effect in Rom. 15:8–12 in order that the Roman Christians might see that such a time has now come.

9:12 Mindful of them, namely, of the oppressed people of Israel (v. 9), whose **blood** God **avenges** when the Gentiles would spill it unjustly.

9:13–14 *A Prayer for Relief.* In these verses the song moves to a prayer for deliverance from affliction. The previous threat (vv. 3–6) makes it clear that others are yet to come, while the decisive victory has displayed God's commitment to protect and preserve his people. The result of God's answer to the prayer will be further praise in worship (v. 14; cf. vv. 1–2).

9:15–18 *God Protects the Needy by Defeating the Wicked.* The song again celebrates how God defends the poor by defeating their oppressors. Here the **wicked** (vv. 16, 17) are expressly those Gentiles who oppose God's purposes (vv. 15, 17), while the **needy** and **poor** are the people of Israel under threat (v. 18).

19[i]See Ps. 3:7 [j][Ps. 10:18]
20[j][See ver. 19 above]

Psalm 10

1[k]Ps. 22:1, 11, 19; 35:22; 38:21 [l]Ps. 13:1 [m]Ps. 9:9
2[n][Ps. 7:15, 16]
3[o]Ps. 94:4; [Isa. 3:9] [p]ver. 13 [q]Job 1:5, 11
4[q][See ver. 3 above] [r]Ps. 14:1; 53:1
5[s][Isa. 26:11] [t]Ps. 12:5
6[u]ver. 11, 13 [v][Rev. 18:7]
7[w]Cited Rom. 3:14 [x]Ps. 36:3 [y]Ps. 55:11; 72:14 [z]Job 20:12; [Ps. 140:3; Song 4:11] [a]Ps. 7:14 [b]Ps. 5:5; 6:8
8[c]Ps. 17:12; 64:4; [Hab. 3:14]
9[d]Ps. 17:12 [e]Job 38:40 [f]Ps. 59:3; Mic. 7:2 [g]Ps. 9:15
11[h][Ps. 73:11]; Job 22:13 [i]Ps. 94:7; Ezek. 8:12; 9:9; [Zeph. 1:12]
12[j]See Ps. 3:7 [k]Mic. 5:9 [l]Ps. 9:12, 18

19 [i]Arise, O LORD! Let not [j]man prevail;
let the nations be judged before you!
20 Put them in fear, O LORD!
Let the nations know that they are but [j]men! *Selah*

10

Why Do You Hide Yourself?

1 Why, O LORD, do you stand [k]far away?
Why [l]do you hide yourself in [m]times of trouble?
2 In arrogance the wicked hotly pursue the poor;
let them [n]be caught in the schemes that they have devised.
3 For the wicked [o]boasts of the desires of his soul,
and the one greedy for gain [p]curses[1] and [q]renounces the LORD.
4 In the pride of his face[2] the wicked does not [q]seek him;[3]
all his thoughts are, [r]"There is no God."
5 His ways prosper at all times;
your judgments are on high, [s]out of his sight;
as for all his foes, he [t]puffs at them.
6 He [u]says in his heart, "I shall not be moved;
throughout all generations I [v]shall not meet adversity."
7 [w]His mouth is filled with cursing and [x]deceit and [y]oppression;
[z]under his tongue are [a]mischief and [b]iniquity.
8 He sits in ambush in the villages;
in [c]hiding places he murders the innocent.
His eyes stealthily watch for the helpless;
9 he lurks in ambush like [d]a lion in his [e]thicket;
he [f]lurks that he may seize the poor;
he seizes the poor when he draws him into his [g]net.
10 The helpless are crushed, sink down,
and fall by his might.
11 He says in his heart, "God has forgotten,
he has [h]hidden his face, he [i]will never see it."

12 [j]Arise, O LORD; O God, [k]lift up your hand;
[l]forget not the afflicted.

[1] *Or and he blesses the one greedy for gain* [2] *Or of his anger* [3] *Or the wicked says, "He will not call to account"*

9:17 Sheol. See note on 6:5.

9:18 forgotten. As in v. 12, and in contrast to those who forget God in v. 17.

9:19–20 *Prayer for God to Judge the Nations.* By referring to these Gentiles as **man** (v. 19) and **men** (v. 20), the song contrasts their schemes with the just and good plan of God himself.

Psalm 10. Cf. note on Psalm 9. Psalm 10 is a lament, designed for cases in which "the wicked hotly pursue the poor" (v. 2). These wicked could be faithless, wealthy Israelites (vv. 4, 13), and the poor are the defenseless pious. While it was the task of the Davidic king to ensure justice (by force if necessary), it was the task of the general public to pray, and thus to use a psalm like this.

10:1–11 *Why Do You Let the Wicked Get Away with It?* Beginning with a blunt question to the Lord, the song details the ways in which the wicked make the helpless poor suffer, while they themselves prosper. These wicked are boastful and greedy; they renounce the Lord (v. 3) and feel secure from divine judgment (vv. 4–6, 11). They look for opportunities to destroy the innocent in order to advance their own interests (vv. 8–10). The question of why God "stands far away" (v. 1) does not stem from doubting God but from believing that he is reliable and just. It is this faith that leads to perplexity over how God can tolerate such conditions among his people.

10:1 hide yourself. That is, ignoring cries for help (cf. 55:1; Prov. 28:27; Isa. 1:15; 58:7).

10:3 curses. Literally, "blesses," used euphemistically for cursing God (as in Job 1:5). **renounces the LORD**. Cf. Ps. 10:13. See also Num. 14:11 and Isa. 1:4, where God's own people faithlessly "despise" him (same Hb. word).

10:6 I shall not be moved. See 15:5 and 55:22 (where it is the assurance of the godly); cf. 30:6 (the false confidence of the complacent). It is galling to the pious when the impious feel safe in their impiety.

10:7 Paul uses the Greek (LXX) wording of this verse in Rom. 3:14 as part of his proof that "all, both Jews and Greeks, are under sin" (Rom. 3:9); this text supports his case about the Jews.

10:11 God has forgotten. In the mouth of the wicked, this would attribute a weak memory to God, or perhaps indifference to human suffering. Either way it is blasphemy, and the faithful mention it to God in order to stir him to action that would prove the wicked to be in the wrong (see vv. 12–14).

10:12–15 *A Prayer for God to Protect the Helpless.* In view of the dreadful situation, the song asks God to defend the defenseless and afflicted. These verses repeat many words from the first section (such as "mischief," vv. 7, 14; "forget," vv. 11, 12; "see," vv. 11, 14; "renounce," vv. 3, 13; "helpless," vv. 8, 10, 14; and "wicked," vv. 2–4, 13, 15) in order to show that God's action is a direct answer to the injustice described.

13 Why does the wicked [m]renounce God
and say in his heart, "You will not [n]call to account"?
14 But you do see, for you [o]note mischief and vexation,
that you may take it into your hands;
to you the helpless [p]commits himself;
you have been [q]the helper of the fatherless.
15 [r]Break the arm of the wicked and evildoer;
[s]call his wickedness to account till you find none.

16 [t]The LORD is king forever and ever;
the [u]nations perish from his land.
17 O LORD, you hear the desire of the afflicted;
you will [v]strengthen their heart; you will incline your ear
18 to [w]do justice to the fatherless and [x]the oppressed,
so that [y]man who is of the earth may strike terror no more.

The LORD Is in His Holy Temple

11

TO THE CHOIRMASTER. OF DAVID.

1 In the LORD I take refuge;
how can you say to my soul,
[z]"Flee like a bird to your mountain,
2 for behold, the wicked [a]bend the bow;
[b]they have fitted their arrow to the string
to shoot in the dark at the upright in heart;
3 if [c]the foundations are destroyed,
what can the righteous do?"[1]

4 [d]The LORD is in his holy temple;
the LORD's [e]throne is in heaven;
his eyes see, his eyelids [f]test the children of man.
5 The LORD [g]tests the righteous,
but [h]his soul hates the wicked and the one who loves violence.

[1] *Or for the foundations will be destroyed; what has the righteous done?*

13[m]ver. 3 [n]Ps. 9:12
14[o]Ps. 33:13 [p]2 Tim. 1:12; 1 Pet. 4:19 [q]Ps. 68:5; 146:9; Hos. 14:3
15[r]See Ps. 37:17 [s][Ps. 37:36; Isa. 41:12]
16[t]Ps. 29:10; Ex. 15:18; Jer. 10:10; Lam. 5:19; Dan. 4:34; 6:26; 1 Tim. 1:17; Rev. 11:15 [u]Deut. 8:20
17[v]1 Chr. 29:18
18[w]Ps. 82:3; [Isa. 1:17; 11:4] [x]Ps. 9:9; 74:21 [y]Ps. 9:19, 20; 17:14

Psalm 11
1[z][1 Sam. 23:14, 19; 24:2; 26:19, 20]
2[a]Ps. 7:12; 64:4; [Jer. 9:3] [b]Ps. 21:12; 58:7; See Ps. 7:10
3[c]Ps. 82:5; Ezek. 30:4
4[d]Ps. 18:6; Mic. 1:2; Hab. 2:20 [e]Ps. 2:4; Isa. 66:1; Matt. 5:34; 23:22; Acts 7:49 [f]See Job 23:10
5[g]Gen. 22:1; James 1:12 [h]Ps. 5:5

10:14 the fatherless. The OT law is full of warnings about oppressing such people (see Ex. 22:22; Deut. 10:18); the true Israelite will care for them.

10:15 Break the arm. That is, make them powerless, so that they can no longer torment the godly. **call his wickedness to account**. That is, do precisely what the wicked deny you will do (v. 13). **till you find none**. That is, until there is no more wickedness to account for.

10:16–18 *Confidence in God's Justice and Power.* The psalm concludes with confidence that God will powerfully bring justice to the oppressed.

10:16 The LORD is king forever and ever. Cf. the very similar Ex. 15:18, where God's reign is for the sake of his people, to promote their peace and purity. Just as he removes unbelieving **nations** from **his land**, he can be trusted to purge unbelieving Israelites from it as well.

10:17 Contrary to appearances (as in v. 1), God does in fact attend to these cries for justice.

10:18 man who is of the earth. Similar to 9:19–20.

Psalm 11. This psalm expresses the confidence that the faithful may have, even in a time of severe crisis—and crisis seems to be its proper setting (vv. 1–3). This may or may not be tied to a particular event in David's life, but that really does not matter, as the psalm is adaptable to a variety of desperate situations, showing how to face them in faith.

11:1–3 *The Crisis Described.* The psalm first recounts the crisis. The **wicked** threaten to kill the **upright** (v. 2), and their obvious response is to **flee like a bird** (v. 1).

11:1 how can you say? The words do not require that someone has actually made the suggestion; the idea is that this would be the natural reaction.

11:3 the foundations. These would be either the people who ensure that Israel is managed justly (cf. "the pillars" of Isa. 19:10) or the principles of justice upon which Israel was founded. When these **are destroyed**, giving the unfaithful in Israel free rein, **what can the righteous do**—what security does he have?

11:4–7 *The Righteous Lord Gives Us Confidence.* The second part of the song reveals the answer to the psalmist's question. Thus the song looks beyond the immediate danger to the God who so rules all things as to vindicate his righteousness and his love for the righteous (that is, for those who keep his covenant).

11:4 his holy temple. This is more likely God's heavenly palace (his **throne is in heaven**) than his earthly temple, although one must not press the distinction too far: in the OT, the earthly sanctuary is the doorway into the heavenly (as in Isa. 6:1), and thus, in worship, God's people join the heavenly choir.

11:5 Just as God carefully assesses the inner condition of all mankind (11:4; cf. 7:9; 17:3), he especially assesses (**tests**) the **righteous**; thus the faithful should see their danger as an opportunity to prove that their faith is genuine. In contrast, the Lord **hates the wicked**—i.e., those among God's people who would exploit and harm others, and thereby foil the very purpose of the covenant, arouse God's anger, and render themselves liable to severe judgment (v. 6).

11:6 fire and sulfur. As upon Sodom and Gomorrah (Gen. 19:24). **portion of their cup**. That is, what God has assigned for them, whether in this life or

6 Let him rain coals on the wicked;
[i]fire and sulfur and a scorching wind shall be [j]the portion of their cup.
7 For the LORD is righteous;
he [k]loves righteous deeds;
[l]the upright shall behold his face.

The Faithful Have Vanished

12

TO THE CHOIRMASTER: ACCORDING TO THE SHEMINITH.[1] A PSALM OF DAVID.

1 Save, O LORD, for [m]the godly one is gone;
for the faithful have vanished from among the children of man.
2 Everyone [n]utters lies to his neighbor;
with [o]flattering lips and [p]a double heart they speak.

3 May the LORD cut off all [o]flattering lips,
the tongue that makes [q]great boasts,
4 those who say, "With our tongue we will prevail,
our lips are with us; who is master over us?"

5 "Because [r]the poor are plundered, because the needy groan,
[s]I will now arise," says the LORD;
"I will place him in the [t]safety for which he longs."
6 [u]The words of the LORD are pure words,
like silver refined in a furnace on the ground,
purified seven times.

7 You, O LORD, will keep them;
you will guard us[2] from this generation forever.
8 On every side the wicked prowl,
as vileness is exalted among the children of man.

How Long, O LORD?

13

TO THE CHOIRMASTER. A PSALM OF DAVID.

1 [v]How long, O LORD? Will you [w]forget me forever?
How long will you [x]hide your face from me?

[1] Probably a musical or liturgical term [2] Or *guard him*

6 [i]Gen. 19:24; Job 18:15; Ezek. 38:22 [j]Ps. 75:8; [Job 21:20]
7 [k]See Ps. 33:5 [l][Ps. 17:15; 140:13; 1 John 3:2; Rev. 22:4]

Psalm 12

1 [m]Isa. 57:1; Mic. 7:2
2 [n]Ps. 41:6; 144:8 [o]Ps. 5:9; Jer. 9:8; Rom. 16:18 [p]1 Chr. 12:33; James 1:8
3 [o][See ver. 2 above] [q]Dan. 7:8; Rev. 13:5; [Ps. 17:10]
5 [r]Ps. 9:12 [s]Isa. 33:10; [Ps. 82:8] [t]See Ps. 55:18
6 [u]Ps. 18:30; 119:140; Prov. 30:5; [Ps. 19:8]

Psalm 13

1 [v]Ps. 79:5; 89:46; [Rev. 6:10] [w]Ps. 10:12; 44:24; 74:19, 23; Lam. 5:20 [x]See Job 13:24

the next (Jer. 13:25; cf. Ps. 16:5 for the pious). The judgment may be visible in history, or it may be ultimate: that is God's business.

Psalm 12. This is a community lament, suited to occasions when the people of God are dominated by liars in positions of authority. It is not clear whether these liars are unfaithful Israelites or Gentile oppressors; the psalm works for either situation.

12:1–2 *The Liars Prevail.* As usual in laments, the psalm describes the situation: the particular kinds of **lies** are **flattering lips** and insincere speech (**a double heart**), both of which manipulate others for the sake of gain (v. 2). In such an environment the **godly** and the **faithful** become so rare that it seems as if they have disappeared (v. 1), either because they have been suppressed or because they have been seduced into lying themselves.

12:3–4 *May the Lord Cut Off the Liars.* The psalm moves on to prayer. The mention of **flattering lips** takes up a term from v. 2, showing the flow of thought. Note how the **lips** and **tongue** of v. 3 appear in reverse order in v. 4.

12:3 cut off. By removing them from his people, as in Lev. 20:3.

12:5–6 *The Reliable Promises of God Are Refreshing.* In such a climate of insincerity (cf. vv. 3–4), God's promises give hope.

12:5 The **poor** and **needy** are familiar groups whom the true Israelites will not oppress but care for (as in Deut. 15:11; 24:14); to oppress them arouses God to action (as in Ps. 9:18).

12:6 To say that God's **words** are **pure**, **refined**, and **purified** is to insist that they have no "dross" of lies, flattery, or insincerity: God means what he says; his words are completely pure. This general truth gives bite to his specific promise of v. 7 (cf. Prov. 30:5).

12:7–8 *God Will Guard His Faithful.* The psalm closes with assurance: God will protect his faithful followers.

12:7 It seems best to take **them** as the poor and needy (v. 5) and the godly (v. 1). Their disappearance (v. 1) was not absolute (see note on vv. 1–2).

12:8 This final verse returns to describe the prevailing conditions (cf. vv. 1–2); though this is a somber note on which to close, it keeps the faithful mindful of their constant dependence on God to guard them. The psalm has also shown that this trust is well placed.

Psalm 13. This is an individual lament for circumstances where the worshiper is on the verge of despair, his powers of endurance spent.

13:1–2 *How Long?* The psalm begins with the question, "How long?" (repeated four times). The question is not asking for information but expressing the feeling of being unable to endure any longer. The questions move from God's apparent indifference (v. 1) to the singer's circumstances of anguish.

13:1 For God to **forget** and to **hide** his **face** from someone is to deliberately abandon that person, to withhold his loving care; it is not a description of God's own mental state. If psalms were theological treatises, they would affirm that God will not forget his people (cf. 9:12) and that the abandonment described here is only apparent. But a song, whose goal is to describe feelings, does not need the same level of precision and detachment as a treatise.

2 How long must I take [y]counsel in my soul
and have sorrow in my heart all the day?
How long shall my enemy be exalted over me?

3 [z]Consider and answer me, O LORD my God;
[a]light up my eyes, lest [b]I sleep the sleep of death,
4 [c]lest my enemy say, "I have prevailed over him,"
lest my foes rejoice because I am [d]shaken.

5 But I have [e]trusted in your steadfast love;
my heart shall [f]rejoice in your salvation.
6 I will sing to the LORD,
because he has dealt bountifully with me.

The Fool Says, There Is No God

14

TO THE CHOIRMASTER. OF DAVID.

1 [g]The [h]fool says in his heart, [i]"There is no God."
They are [j]corrupt, they do abominable deeds,
[k]there is none who does good.
2 The LORD [l]looks down from heaven on the children of man,
to see if there are any who understand,[1]
who [m]seek after God.

3 They have all turned aside; together they have become [n]corrupt;
there is none who does good,
not even one.

4 Have they no [o]knowledge, all the evildoers
who [p]eat up my people as they eat bread
and [q]do not call upon the LORD?

5 There they are in great terror,
for God is with [r]the generation of the righteous.
6 You would shame the plans of the poor,
but[2] the LORD is his [s]refuge.

[1] Or *that act wisely* [2] Or *for*

2 [y][Ps. 77:6]
3 [z]Ps. 5:1; 119:153 [a]Ps. 19:8; Ezra 9:8; Prov. 29:13; Eph. 1:18; [1 Sam. 14:27] [b][Jer. 51:39]
4 [c]Deut. 32:27 [d]See Ps. 10:6
5 [e]See Ps. 11:1 [f]See Ps. 9:14

Psalm 14

1 [g]For ver. 1-7, see Ps. 53:1-6 [h]Ps. 74:18, 22; Job 2:10 [i]Ps. 10:4 [j]Gen. 6:5, 11, 12 [k]Cited Rom. 3:10-12
2 [l]Ps. 102:19; [Ps. 11:4] [m]2 Chr. 15:2; 19:3
3 [n]Job 15:16
4 [o]Ps. 82:5; [Isa. 1:3; Jer. 4:22] [p]Prov. 30:14; Jer. 10:25; Hos. 7:7; [Ps. 27:2; Amos 8:4; Mic. 3:3] [q]Ps. 79:6; Jer. 10:25; Hos. 7:7; [Isa. 64:7]
5 [r]Ps. 24:6; 73:15
6 [s]Ps. 46:1; 61:3; 62:7, 8; 91:2; 142:5

13:2 The **enemy** is typically one who hates. Often in the Psalter, the hatred leads the enemy to want to do violence to the singer; in other places, as here, it leads the enemy to gloat over the singer's misfortunes. Since the Psalms presuppose that their singers are faithful to the covenant, readers may safely assume that the enemy hates the singer's faithfulness.

13:3–4 *Prayer for Help.* The singer calls upon God to intervene.

13:3 For God to **consider and answer** would be for him to relieve the singer's circumstances. Some take the request, **light up my eyes, lest I sleep the sleep of death**, to imply that the psalm originated during a severe illness; but while the words could apply to such a case, they are general enough to apply to a wider variety of situations.

13:5–6 *Reaffirming His Trust in the Lord.* Confidence in the **steadfast love** of God (v. 5), as revealed in the covenant (Ex. 34:6), leads to a trusting expectation of salvation (Ps. 13:5) and God's bountiful dealing.

13:5 salvation. See note on 3:2.

Psalm 14. This is a community lament in which the people of God mourn the fact that humans in general do not seek after God and thus they treat God's people cruelly. It is almost identical to Psalm 53, which was probably an alternate version of the hymn prior to both of them being collected into the Psalter.

14:1–4 *The Godless Devour God's People.* These godless would be Gentiles ("the children of man," v. 2, as opposed to "my people," v. 4) who have not been given the light and "do not call upon the LORD" (v. 4). Some, however, suppose that v. 3 narrows the focus to those in Israel who have "turned aside," but the words themselves do not require this.

14:1 fool. There are three Hebrew words for *fool*, and all speak of moral orientation rather than intellectual ability. The term here denotes someone who stubbornly rejects wisdom; the word lies behind the name Nabal (see 1 Sam. 25:25). As in Ps. 10:4, **there is no God** expresses not philosophical atheism but the idea that God, if he exists, takes no interest in human affairs and will not call people to account for their deeds. The result of this denial is that **they are corrupt** and **do abominable deeds**, and thus **none** of them **does good**.

14:3 The word **all** in this verse refers to the Gentiles described in v. 2, and v. 4 reveals that they oppose God's people. Paul adapts the Greek of the Septuagint of vv. 1–3 in Rom. 3:10–12 as part of his argument that "all, both Jews and Greeks, are under sin" (Rom. 3:9).

14:4 The person speaking here may be God, or it may simply be the pious Israelite; either could talk about "my people." To **eat up my people** is to consume their wealth and freedom, and possibly even their lives (cf. Mic. 3:1–3, where it is Israelite rulers who do this). **call upon the LORD**. That is, to rely on the God of the covenant for life and well-being (see Ps. 18:3, 6; 118:5).

14:5–6 *The Lord Is the Refuge for the Poor.* In the face of such threats (v. 4) the faithful must remember that God is their refuge and that he will protect them and defeat the evildoers.

14:7 *Prayer for Community Salvation.* In light of both the situation and the assurance, the singing community prays that God would rescue them and promote their well-being; their prayer concludes with firm hope (**when,**

7 Oh, that salvation for Israel would come out of Zion!
When the LORD [t]restores the fortunes of his people,
let Jacob rejoice, let Israel be glad.

Who Shall Dwell on Your Holy Hill?

15

A PSALM OF DAVID.

1 O LORD, [u]who shall sojourn in your [v]tent?
Who shall dwell on your [w]holy hill?

2 He who [x]walks blamelessly and [y]does what is right
and [z]speaks truth in his heart;
3 who [a]does not slander with his tongue
and does no evil to his neighbor,
nor [b]takes up a reproach against his friend;
4 [c]in whose eyes a vile person is despised,
but who honors those who fear the LORD;
who [d]swears to his own hurt and does not change;
5 who [e]does not put out his money at interest
and [f]does not take a bribe against the innocent.
He who does these things shall never be [g]moved.

You Will Not Abandon My Soul

16

A [h]MIKTAM[1] OF DAVID.

1 Preserve me, O God, for in you I [i]take refuge.
2 I say to the LORD, "You are my Lord;
[j]I have no good apart from you."

3 As for [k]the saints in the land, they are the excellent ones,
in whom is all my delight.[2]

7 [t]Ps. 85:1; 126:1; Job 42:10; Jer. 30:18; Ezek. 16:53; 39:25; Hos. 6:11; Joel 3:1

Psalm 15

1 [u]For ver. 1-5, see Ps. 24:3-5; Isa. 33:14-16 [v]Ps. 61:4 [w]See Ps. 2:6
2 [x]Prov. 28:18 [y]Ps. 106:3; [Matt. 6:1] [z]Zech. 8:16; Eph. 4:25; [John 1:47; Col. 3:9]
3 [a]Lev. 19:16; [Ps. 34:13] [b]Ex. 23:1
4 [c][Esth. 3:2] [d][Judg. 11:35]
5 [e]Ex. 22:25; Lev. 25:36; Deut. 23:19; Ezek. 18:8; 22:12 [f]Ex. 23:8; Deut. 16:19 [g]See Ps. 10:6

Psalm 16

[h][Ps. 56, title; 57, title; 60, title]
1 [i]See Ps. 11:1
2 [j][Ps. 73:25]
3 [k][Ex. 19:6; Deut. 7:6; 1 Pet. 2:9]

[1] Probably a musical or liturgical term [2] Or *To the saints in the land, the excellent in whom is all my delight, I say:*

not *if*). **out of Zion**. Because the Lord dwells in a special way in Zion, namely, in his sanctuary.

Psalm 15. This is a hymn celebrating the ideal worshiper of the Lord. Some call it an entrance liturgy, prescribing questions and answers by which the priests examine would-be worshipers for their qualifications for entering holy space. This is unlikely, however, since the qualities described in this hymn are matters of the heart, and thus no priest could know whether or not they were present. Similar passages appear in 24:3–6 and Isa. 33:14–16. The singing congregation does not claim to have achieved these character qualities; instead, in describing them the members yearn to have them more and more.

15:1 *Question: Who Shall Dwell with God?* The **tent** (cf. 27:4–6) and **holy hill** speak of the sanctuary where God is especially present with his people; to **sojourn** or **dwell** there is to be a divinely welcomed guest in God's house (cf. 61:4; 65:4), the end for which humans were made.

15:2–5b *Answer: He Who Walks Blamelessly.* The terms **walks blamelessly** and **does what is right** (v. 2) are general, and the rest of the answer spells out some specific examples. One striking feature of these specifics is that they are matters of character and go beyond what the laws of the Pentateuch require. Another interesting feature is the social orientation of these specifics: i.e., they are aimed at promoting the well-being of other members of God's people—by speaking honestly (v. 2), by protecting their welfare and reputation (v. 3), by promoting their holiness (v. 4), and by seeking justice above personal gain (vv. 4c–5b).

15:4 vile person. This is the member of God's people who rejects covenant life (cf. Jer. 6:30, "rejected"). Such a person **is despised** because he brings disgrace on the God whose people they are. **Those who fear the LORD** are those who embrace the covenant, and the ideal person **honors** them. He **does not change** when he **swears to his own hurt**, i.e., he keeps his promises and does not seek to get out of them, even if that ends up being costly to him—because when he swears he has taken God as his witness.

15:5 put out his money at interest. When the Pentateuch laws regulate loans, they are generally envisioning private loans to a neighbor (say, when his crops fail and he needs help buying seed for planting) rather than commercial transactions. In such cases Israelites are forbidden to charge interest to their fellow Israelites (see Deut. 23:19–20, "your brother"); they may charge interest to a foreigner. The psalm does not mention "his brother," which seems to suggest that the ideal person deals generously and fairly with all people; he goes beyond what the law requires. To **take a bribe against the innocent** is an outrage against the justice that should characterize God's people (Deut. 16:19; 27:25); it also scorns the very character of God (Deut. 10:17).

15:5c *Assurance: Such a Person Shall Never Be Moved.* The person who has embraced the covenant promises may be confident that God will ensure his stability (21:7; 55:22).

Psalm 16. When the faithful sing Psalm 16, they entrust themselves to the Lord and foster their confidence and contentment in his care. The psalm uses imagery from Israel's allocation of the land (vv. 5–6) to express contentment in this life, and goes on to look forward to everlasting life in God's presence (vv. 9–11).

16:1–2 *The Lord Is My Refuge.* The Lord is the only one on whom the psalmist relies for well-being (**no good apart from you**, v. 2).

16:3–4 *My Preferred Company: The Godly.* There is a contrast between "the saints," **in whom is all my delight** (v. 3), and **those who run after another god** (v. 4; idolaters, among whom would be unfaithful Israelites), whose practices the faithful will shun.

16:3 the saints. That is, the holy ones. All Israel is holy in the sense of

4 The sorrows of those who run after[1] another god shall multiply;
their drink offerings of blood I will not pour out
or [l]take their names on my lips.

5 The LORD is [m]my chosen portion and my [n]cup;
you hold my [o]lot.
6 [p]The lines have fallen for me in pleasant places;
indeed, I have a beautiful inheritance.

7 I bless the LORD who [q]gives me counsel;
in [r]the night also my [s]heart instructs me.[2]
8 [t]I have [u]set the LORD always before me;
because he is at my [v]right hand, I shall not be [w]shaken.

9 Therefore my heart is glad, and my [x]whole being[3] rejoices;
my flesh also dwells secure.
10 For you will not abandon my soul to [y]Sheol,
[z]or let your [a]holy one see [b]corruption.[4]

11 You make known to me [c]the path of life;
in your presence there is [d]fullness of joy;
at your right hand are [e]pleasures forevermore.

In the Shadow of Your Wings

17 A [f]PRAYER OF DAVID.

1 Hear a just cause, O LORD; [g]attend to my cry!
Give ear to my prayer from lips free of deceit!
2 From your presence [h]let my vindication come!
Let your eyes behold the right!

[1] *Or who acquire* [2] Hebrew *my kidneys instruct me* [3] Hebrew *my glory* [4] *Or see the pit*

4 [l]Ex. 23:13; Josh. 23:7
5 [m]Ps. 73:26; 119:57; 142:5; Num. 18:20; Lam. 3:24; [Deut. 32:9; Jer. 10:16; 51:19] [n]Ps. 23:5; 116:13 [o]Ps. 125:3
6 [p]Mic. 2:5
7 [q]See 1 Sam. 23:9-12; 2 Sam. 5:18, 19 [r]Ps. 17:3; See Ps. 42:8 [s]Ps. 7:9
8 [t]Cited Acts 2:25-28 [u]Ps. 119:30 [v]Ps. 109:31; 110:5; 121:5 [w]Ps. 10:6; 15:5
9 [x]Ps. 30:12; 57:8; 108:1; Gen. 49:6
10 [y]See Job 21:13 [z]Cited Acts 13:35 [a]Ps. 89:18; [Mark 1:24] [b]Ps. 49:9; 103:4
11 [c]Matt. 7:14 [d][Ps. 21:6] [e]Ps. 36:8

Psalm 17
[f][Ps. 86, title; 142, title]
1 [g]Ps. 142:6; [Ps. 61:1; Jer. 7:16]
2 [h][Ps. 26:1]

being consecrated to the God who is himself holy; this does not guarantee, however, that every member of Israel will actually live out his holy status, and thus the command to "be holy" (Lev. 20:7–8). Here, the saints are those who have actually embraced their privilege; these are the ones whom the faithful singers should esteem, and whose company they should prefer.

16:4 The psalmist utterly refuses to participate in idolatrous practices (probably carried out by unfaithful Israelites). **Their names** probably refers to the names of the false gods being worshiped rather than the names of the idolaters.

16:5–6 *Contentment with My Chosen Portion.* The psalm now describes the psalmist's satisfaction with the Lord and his provision. The terms **portion**, **lot**, **lines**, and **inheritance** evoke the allocation of the land into family plots (perhaps with an allusion to the Lord as the Levites' portion and inheritance; Num. 18:20); the song promotes contentment with the arrangements of one's life, seeing them as providentially ordered.

16:7–8 *Delight in God's Constant Presence.* God's presence, in which the psalmist delights, is seen in the moral instruction he receives (v. 7), and it results in his assurance of stability (v. 8). The psalmist's **heart instructs** him during the **night** (v. 7), a result of deliberate reflection (cf. 1:2); likewise to **set the LORD always before me** expresses intention.

16:8 Shaken. Cf. "moved," 15:5.

16:9–11 *Hope of Everlasting Joy.* As in 49:15 and 73:24–26, here there is a clear affirmation that the human yearning to be near to God and to know the pleasure of his welcome forever, beyond the death of the body, finds its answer in the covenant. Peter cites 16:8–11 in his Pentecost speech (Acts 2:25–28), applying the verses to the resurrection of Jesus; Paul used Ps. 16:10 in his similar speech (Acts 13:35). If the apostles meant that David's words were a straight prediction of the death and resurrection of Jesus, it is difficult to know what function the psalm could have played in ancient Israel: the congregation would have scratched their heads in puzzlement every time they sang it. This puzzlement goes away if the psalm is seen as cultivating the hope of everlasting glory for the faithful, with the resurrection of Jesus (the **holy one** par excellence) as the first step in bringing this hope to fruition (cf. Rom. 8:23; 1 Cor. 15:23).

16:9 my whole being. The Greek in the Septuagint (cited in Acts 2:26) renders this as "my tongue."

16:10 Sheol. See note on 6:5. Here it is likely the abode of the wicked. Likewise, **corruption** probably describes the experience of being far from God forever. These are not likely terms for the grave, since everyone singing these words would know that his body would one day die and rot.

16:11 path of life. A master metaphor of the Bible: the covenant provides a "path" by which one walks to life in all its fullness (Prov. 5:6; 6:23; 10:17; 12:28; 15:24; Matt. 7:14); this is what the Lord makes **known to** his followers. To enjoy God's **presence**, or his face, is the fruition of the covenant (cf. Ex. 33:14–15; Num. 6:24–26). The word **pleasures** is related to "pleasant places" (Ps. 16:6); the pleasure that he has begun in this life will continue into its fullness in the world to come.

Psalm 17. This is an individual lament, especially geared toward cases in which the person suffering considers himself unjustly accused of wrong (thus resembling Psalm 7) by a worldly enemy. The psalm is a prayer for vindication, ending by expressing confidence in the true portion of the faithful (thus resembling Psalm 16).

3[j]See Job 23:10 [j]Job 31:14 [k]Ps. 16:7; [Job 33:15] [l]Judg. 7:4; Zech. 13:9; 1 Pet. 1:7; [Ps. 139:1; Mal. 3:2, 3]
5[m]Job 23:11; [Ps. 44:18]
6[n]Ps. 86:6, 7; 116:1, 2 [o]See Ps. 31:2
7[p]Ps. 31:21 [q]Ps. 44:5; 59:1; 139:21
8[r]Deut. 32:10; Zech. 2:8 [s]Ps. 36:7; 57:1; 63:7; 91:4; [Matt. 23:37; Luke 13:34]; See Ruth 2:12
9[t][1 Sam. 23:26]
10[u][Ps. 119:70] [v]Ps. 31:18; 1 Sam. 2:3
11[w][Ps. 89:51] [x]Ps. 62:4
12[y][Ps. 10:8, 9]
14[z][Ps. 10:18; Luke 16:8; 20:34] [a]Matt. 6:2, 5, 16; Luke 16:25 [b][Job 21:11]
15[c]Job 33:26; 1 John 3:2; [Ps. 11:7] [d]Isa. 26:19; Dan. 12:2 [e][Ps. 16:11]

3 You have [i]tried my heart, you have [j]visited me by [k]night,
you have [l]tested me, and you will find nothing;
I have purposed that my mouth will not transgress.
4 With regard to the works of man, by the word of your lips
I have avoided the ways of the violent.
5 My steps have [m]held fast to your paths;
my feet have not slipped.

6 I [n]call upon you, for you will answer me, O God;
[o]incline your ear to me; hear my words.
7 [p]Wondrously show[1] your steadfast love,
O Savior of those who seek refuge
from [q]their adversaries at your right hand.

8 Keep me as [r]the apple of your eye;
hide me in [s]the shadow of your wings,
9 from the wicked who do me violence,
my deadly enemies who [t]surround me.

10 [u]They close their hearts to pity;
with their mouths they [v]speak arrogantly.
11 They have now surrounded our [w]steps;
they set their eyes to [x]cast us to the ground.
12 He is like a lion eager to tear,
as a young lion [y]lurking in ambush.

13 Arise, O LORD! Confront him, subdue him!
Deliver my soul from the wicked by your sword,
14 from men by your hand, O LORD,
from [z]men of the world whose [a]portion is in this life.[2]
You fill their womb with treasure;[3]
they are satisfied with [b]children,
and they leave their abundance to their infants.

15 As for me, I shall [c]behold your face in righteousness;
when I [d]awake, I shall be [e]satisfied with your likeness.

[1] Or *Distinguish me by* [2] Or *from men whose portion in life is of the world* [3] Or *As for your treasured ones, you fill their womb*

17:1–2 *Request for Vindication.* The words suggest someone under attack or accusation, asking God to bring the singer's innocence to light.

17:3–5 *Claim of Innocence.* These verses amplify the assertion of innocence (the claim begins in v. 1, "lips free of deceit"). The singer has opened himself to the Lord's examination (**tried**, **visited**, **tested**), and he recounts his efforts to stay pure (**purposed**, **avoided**, **steps have held fast**, **feet have not slipped**). For the proper use of such claims, see note on 7:3–5.

17:6–9 *Request for Protection.* The song makes a general request for an answer to the prayer (v. 6) and then specifies the request, namely, for protection from violent adversaries (vv. 7–9).

17:8 apple of your eye. For this colorful biblical term for the pupil, see Deut. 32:10 and Prov. 7:2. **Shadow of your wings** always refers to a place of safety (see Ps. 36:7; 57:1; 63:7).

17:10–12 *The Pitiless Enemies.* No appeal to the attackers' **pity** or remorse is possible, since they **close their hearts** to such feelings, preferring instead to **speak arrogantly** (v. 10). They eagerly watch for the opportunity to trip up the innocent singer and then to destroy him (vv. 11–12).

17:13–14 *May God Defeat Them!* In such an environment of threat and faith, the proper recourse is prayer for the enemy's defeat. Though their repentance may be preferred, that avenue seems closed (v. 10), and thus deliverance for the pious requires defeat for the attacker. The specific kind of defeat is left up to God.

17:14 As indicated by the ESV footnotes, the Hebrew presents some challenges; the text describes these attackers as people whose only reward is in this life (their **treasure** and their **children**); they leave all their wealth behind when they die. This contrasts with the expectation that the pious have in v. 15.

17:15 *Confidence for Everlasting Satisfaction.* The psalm finishes in triumph, anticipating eternal fellowship in God's presence. **behold your face**. Cf. 11:7 and Rev. 22:4. **When I awake** is generally taken as implying "from the sleep of death"; thus the beholding and the satisfaction of this verse refer to the everlasting bliss that the godly look for (one may even go as far as seeing the general resurrection here).

The Lord Is My Rock and My Fortress

18

To the choirmaster. A Psalm of David, [f]the servant of the Lord, [g]who addressed the words of this [h]song to the Lord on the day when the Lord rescued him from the hand of all his enemies, and from the hand of Saul. He said:

1 I love you, O Lord, my strength.
2 The Lord is my [i]rock and my [j]fortress and my deliverer,
my God, my [i]rock, in [k]whom I take refuge,
my [l]shield, and [m]the horn of my salvation, my [n]stronghold.
3 I call upon the Lord, who is [o]worthy to be praised,
and I am saved from my enemies.

4 [p]The cords of death encompassed me;
[q]the torrents of destruction assailed me;[1]
5 [p]the cords of Sheol entangled me;
the snares of death confronted me.

6 [r]In my distress I called upon the Lord;
to my God I cried for help.
From his [s]temple he heard my voice,
and my cry to him reached his ears.

7 Then the earth [t]reeled and rocked;
the foundations also of the mountains trembled
and quaked, because he was angry.
8 Smoke went up from his nostrils,[2]
and devouring [u]fire from his mouth;
glowing coals flamed forth from him.
9 He [v]bowed the heavens and [w]came down;
[x]thick darkness was under his feet.
10 He rode on a cherub and flew;
he came swiftly on [z]the wings of the wind.
11 He made darkness his covering, his [a]canopy around him,
thick clouds [b]dark with water.
12 Out of the brightness before him
[c]hailstones and coals of fire broke through his clouds.

13 The Lord also [d]thundered in the heavens,
and the Most High uttered his [e]voice,
hailstones and coals of fire.
14 And he sent out his [f]arrows and scattered them;
he flashed forth lightnings and [g]routed them.
15 Then [h]the channels of the sea were seen,
and the foundations of the world were laid bare

[1] Or *terrified me* [2] Or *in his wrath*

Psalm 18
[f]Ps. 36, title; 89:3, 20; [2 Sam. 3:18; 7:5] [g]See 2 Sam. 22 [h]Ex. 15:1; Deut. 31:30
2 [i]ver. 31, 46; Ps. 19:14; 31:3 [j]Ps. 91:2; 144:2 [k][Heb. 2:13] [l]ver. 30; Gen. 15:1 [m]Ps. 112:9; Luke 1:69 [n]See Ps. 9:9
3 [o]Ps. 48:1; 96:4; 113:3; 145:3
4 [p]Ps. 116:3; [Ps. 119:61] [q]See Ps. 32:6
5 [p][See ver. 4 above]
6 [r]Ps. 66:14; 102:2; 120:1; [Jonah 2:2] [s]See Ps. 11:4
7 [t][Judg. 5:4; Acts 4:31; 16:26]
8 [u]See Ps. 21:9
9 [v]Ps. 144:5 [w]Isa. 64:1 [x]See Ex. 20:21
10 [z]Ps. 104:3
11 [a]Job 36:29; [Ps. 97:2] [b][Ps. 29:3]
12 [c][Ps. 148:8; Josh. 10:11]
13 [d]1 Sam. 2:10; 7:10; See Job 37:4 [e]Isa. 30:30; See Ps. 29:3-9
14 [f]Ps. 7:13; 64:7; 77:17; 144:6; Deut. 32:23, 42; Hab. 3:11 [g]Ex. 14:24; Josh. 10:10
15 [h]Ps. 42:1; Joel 1:20 (Heb.); [Job 36:30]

Psalm 18. This is a royal psalm, i.e., it celebrates the way that God has shown his love to his people by giving them the Davidic monarchy and by preserving David through many dangers (see the title and v. 50). The text of the psalm is almost identical to 2 Samuel 22. The two songs differ, however, in their context: Second Samuel 22 is David's personal expression of gratitude to the Lord, while Psalm 18 is the adaptation of that song for the whole people to sing, because their well-being is now tied to the offspring of David (2 Sam. 7:4–17). When God's people sang this, then, they were to give thanks for the Davidic line and to pray that its heirs would be faithful to the Lord and would be valiant military leaders, so that Israel might carry out its God-given purpose of bringing light to the Gentiles.

18:1–3 *The Lord Is My Strength.* The opening verses summarize the theme of the psalm, namely, that David has found the Lord to be a reliable defender against his enemies.

18:4–6 *In My Distress I Prayed.* These verses amplify v. 3, as David describes a particular danger that threatened to kill him.

18:6 his temple. Likely his heavenly palace (cf. 11:4).

18:7–19 *The Lord's Marvelous Rescue.* This vivid picture allows readers to imagine God in his heavenly fortress suddenly taking notice of David's need and hastening to bring aid. The images shift quickly: v. 8 speaks of God responding to David's danger as if he were an angry dragon, while vv. 10–15 picture his coming as if it were by way of a raging thunderstorm. David portrays his rescue (vv. 16–19) as if his enemies were swirling waters about to drown him, from which God plucked him and set him on a **broad place**, ground that is high and dry (v. 19).

at your [i]rebuke, O LORD,
at the blast of [j]the breath of your nostrils.

16 He [k]sent from on high, he took me;
he [l]drew me out of [m]many waters.
17 He rescued me from my strong enemy
and from those who hated me,
for they were [n]too mighty for me.
18 They confronted me in the day of my calamity,
but the LORD was my support.
19 He brought me out into [o]a broad place;
he rescued me, because he [p]delighted in me.

20 The LORD dealt with me [q]according to my righteousness;
according to [r]the cleanness of my hands he rewarded me.
21 For I have [s]kept the ways of the LORD,
and have not wickedly departed from my God.
22 For [t]all his rules[1] were before me,
and his statutes I did not put away from me.
23 I was [u]blameless before him,
and I kept myself from my guilt.
24 So the LORD has rewarded me according to my righteousness,
according to the cleanness of my hands in his sight.

25 With [v]the merciful you show yourself merciful;
with the blameless man you show yourself blameless;
26 with the purified you show yourself pure;
and with [w]the crooked you make yourself seem tortuous.
27 For you save [x]a humble people,
but [y]the haughty eyes you bring down.
28 For it is you who light my [z]lamp;
the LORD my God lightens my darkness.
29 For by you I can run against a troop,
and by my God I can [a]leap over [b]a wall.
30 This God—his way is [c]perfect;[2]
the word of the LORD [d]proves true;
he is [e]a shield for all those who [f]take refuge in him.

31 For [g]who is God, but the LORD?
And who is [h]a rock, except our God?—
32 the God who [i]equipped me with strength
and made my way [j]blameless.
33 He made my feet like the feet of a [k]deer
and set me secure on [l]the heights.
34 He [m]trains my hands for war,
so that my arms can bend a bow of bronze.

15 [i]Ps. 106:9; Nah. 1:4 [j][Ex. 15:8]
16 [k][Ps. 144:7] [l][Ex. 2:10] [m]See Ps. 32:6; Job 22:11
17 [n]Ps. 142:6
19 [o]Ps. 31:8; 118:5; [ver. 36] [p]Ps. 22:8; 2 Sam. 15:26
20 [q]Ps. 7:8; 1 Sam. 24:19; 26:23; 1 Kgs. 8:32 [r]See Job 22:30
21 [s][Gen. 18:19; Prov. 8:32]
22 [t]Ps. 119:30, 102
23 [u]Gen. 17:1; [1 Kgs. 14:8]
25 [v]Matt. 5:7
26 [w]Ps. 81:12; Lev. 26:23, 24; Prov. 3:34; Acts 7:42; Rom. 1:28
27 [x][Ex. 3:7] [y]See Ps. 101:5
28 [z]Ps. 132:17; 1 Kgs. 11:36; 15:4; 2 Kgs. 8:19; [2 Sam. 21:17]; See Job 18:5, 6
29 [a][Isa. 35:6] [b]See 2 Sam. 5:6-9
30 [c]Deut. 32:4; Dan. 4:37; Matt. 5:48; [Rev. 15:3] [d]See Ps. 12:6 [e]ver. 2 [f]Ps. 17:7
31 [g][Ps. 86:8] [h]See ver. 2
32 [i]1 Sam. 2:4; Isa. 45:5 [j]Ps. 101:2, 6; 119:1; Job 22:3
33 [k]Hab. 3:19 [l]Deut. 32:13; Isa. 58:14
34 [m]Ps. 144:1

[1] Or *just decrees* [2] Or *blameless*

18:20–30 *David's Claim of Faithfulness.* In these verses David claims that he has faithfully **kept the ways of the LORD** (v. 21), and thus God has **rewarded** him (vv. 20, 24). This could be taken as absurdly self-righteous if it were not for two obvious facts: first, this song comes from 2 Samuel, which is plain about David's sins; and second, the ways, **rules**, and **statutes** of the Lord (Ps. 18:22) include provisions for receiving forgiveness of sins. Thus the claim of v. 21, **I . . . have not wickedly departed from my God**, clarifies it all by saying that he has held fast to the life of faith.

18:30 his way is perfect. The ESV footnote ("blameless") indicates that following the Lord's blameless way (cf. v. 21) is what enables a man to become blameless (vv. 23, 25).

18:31–45 *The Lord Has Given Me Victory.* David's rescue (vv. 16–19) came by way of his military prowess, which was itself God's gift. In the books of Samuel those enemies included both Israelites and Gentiles, and both are in view here, especially in v. 43: **the people**, namely, Israel (see also v. 41, **they cried to the LORD**), and **the nations**, **people whom I had not known** (cf. vv. 44–45, **foreigners**).

35 You have given me the shield of your salvation,
and your right hand [n]supported me,
and your [o]gentleness made me great.
36 You [p]gave a wide place for my steps under me,
and my feet did not slip.
37 I pursued my enemies and overtook them,
and did not turn back till they were consumed.
38 I thrust them through, so that they were not able to rise;
they fell under my feet.
39 For you equipped me with strength for the battle;
you made those who rise against me sink under me.
40 You made my enemies [q]turn their backs to me,[1]
and those who hated me I destroyed.
41 [r]They cried for help, but there was none to save;
they cried to the LORD, but he did not answer them.
42 I beat them fine as [s]dust before the wind;
I cast them out like [t]the mire of the streets.

43 You delivered me from [u]strife with the people;
you made me [v]the head of the nations;
[w]people whom I had not known served me.
44 As soon as they heard of me they obeyed me;
[x]foreigners [y]came cringing to me.
45 [x]Foreigners lost heart
and [z]came trembling out of their fortresses.

46 The LORD lives, and blessed be my rock,
and exalted be the God of my salvation—
47 the God who gave me vengeance
and [a]subdued peoples under me,
48 who delivered me from my enemies;
yes, you [b]exalted me above those who rose against me;
you rescued me from [c]the man of violence.

49 [d]For this I will praise you, O LORD, among the nations,
and [e]sing to your name.
50 Great [f]salvation he brings to his king,
and shows steadfast love to his [g]anointed,
to [h]David and his offspring forever.

The Law of the LORD Is Perfect

19

TO THE CHOIRMASTER. A PSALM OF DAVID.

1 [i]The heavens declare the glory of God,
and the sky above[2] proclaims his handiwork.

[1] Or *You gave me my enemies' necks* [2] Hebrew *the expanse*; compare Genesis 1:6–8

35 [n]Ps. 20:2 [o][Isa. 63:9]
36 [p]Ps. 31:8; Prov. 4:12; [ver. 19]
40 [q]Ex. 23:27; [Ps. 21:12]
41 [r]See Job 27:9
42 [s]2 Kgs. 13:7 [t]Isa. 10:6; Mic. 7:10; Zech. 10:5
43 [u][2 Sam. 3:1; 19:9, 43; 20:1] [v][Ps. 2:8]; See 2 Sam. 8:1-14 [w]Isa. 55:5; [Ps. 22:27]
44 [x]Ps. 144:7 [y]Ps. 66:3; 81:15; Deut. 33:29
45 [x][See ver. 44 above] [z]Mic. 7:17
47 [a]Ps. 47:3; 144:2; [Isa. 45:1]
48 [b]Ps. 59:1 [c]Ps. 140:1
49 [d]Cited Rom. 15:9 [e]Ps. 66:4
50 [f]Ps. 144:10 [g]See Ps. 2:2 [h][Ps. 89:29; 2 Sam. 7:12, 13, 29]

Psalm 19
1 [i]Ps. 50:6; [Rom. 1:19, 20]

18:46–50 *God Is Faithful to His Anointed King.* This section stresses that David's place of prominence has come from the Lord and is therefore not the product of his own greed and lust for power. Indeed, the expectation that he **will praise** the Lord **among the nations** (v. 49) returns readers to the call of Abram, in whom the nations were to find blessing (Gen. 12:1–3).

18:49 Paul employs this verse in Rom. 15:9 as a part of his proof that it was always God's plan that the Gentiles should receive the light, especially through the Davidic line (of which Jesus is the ultimate heir).

18:50 salvation. See note on 3:2. The psalm puts the victories and escapes into perspective, as part of God's commitment to his people and the whole world. **Steadfast love to . . . David and his offspring forever** echoes 2 Sam. 7:12–16.

Psalm 19. In singing this psalm, God's people celebrate his law, the Torah, as his supreme revelation of himself. The psalm recounts the way the creation speaks of its Maker (vv. 1–6), and then the way in which the Mosaic law addresses the soul (vv. 7–11), followed by the humble response that this calls for (vv. 12–14). As Moses does in Genesis 1–2, the psalm identifies the transcendent Creator ("God," v. 1) with the covenant God of Israel ("the LORD," vv. 7–9).

19:1–6 *The Eloquent Heavens.* These verses describe how features of the sky bear witness to their Maker; in so doing, the song directs attention to divine speech that goes out to all humanity. The ode to the sun (vv. 4c–6) follows from the opening, giving a very specific way in which the voice of the heavens

2 Day to day pours out speech,
and night to night reveals knowledge.
3 There is no speech, nor are there words,
whose voice is not heard.
4 [j]Their [k]voice[1] goes out through all the earth,
and their words to the end of the world.
In them he has set a tent for [l]the sun,
5 [m]which comes out like [n]a bridegroom leaving his chamber,
and, like a strong man, runs its course with joy.
6 Its rising is from the end of the heavens,
and its circuit to the end of them,
and there is nothing hidden from its heat.

7 [o]The law of the LORD is perfect,[2]
[p]reviving the soul;
[q]the testimony of the LORD is [r]sure,
[s]making wise [t]the simple;
8 [u]the precepts of the LORD are right,
rejoicing the heart;
the commandment of the LORD is [v]pure,
[w]enlightening the eyes;
9 the fear of the LORD is clean,
enduring forever;
the rules[3] of the LORD are [x]true,
and righteous altogether.
10 More to be desired are they than [y]gold,
even much [z]fine gold;
[a]sweeter also than honey
and drippings of [b]the honeycomb.
11 Moreover, by them is your servant warned;
[c]in keeping them there is great reward.

12 [d]Who can discern his errors?
[e]Declare me innocent from [f]hidden faults.
13 [g]Keep back your servant also from [h]presumptuous sins;
let them not have [i]dominion over me!

[1] Or *Their measuring line* [2] Or *blameless* [3] Or *just decrees*

4 [j]Cited Rom. 10:18 [k][Isa. 28:10] [l][Eccles. 1:5]
5 [m][Judg. 5:31] [n]Joel 2:16
7 [o]Rom. 7:12 [p]Ps. 23:3; [2 Tim. 3:16] [q]Ex. 25:16; See Ps. 78:5 [r]Ps. 111:7 [s][Matt. 11:25; 1 Cor. 1:27; 2 Tim. 3:15] [t]Ps. 119:130; Prov. 1:4
8 [u]Ps. 103:18; 111:7; 119:4, 27 [v][Ps. 12:6] [w]See Ps. 13:3
9 [x]Ps. 119:142, 151, 160
10 [y]Ps. 119:72, 127; Prov. 8:10 [z]Job 28:17; Prov. 8:19 [a]Ps. 119:103 [b]Prov. 16:24
11 [c][Prov. 29:18]
12 [d]Ps. 40:12; [1 Cor. 4:4] [e][Lev. 4:2; Num. 15:27] [f]Ps. 90:8; See Job 34:32
13 [g]Gen. 20:6; 1 Sam. 25:33, 34, 39 [h][Num. 15:30] [i]Ps. 119:133; Rom. 6:12, 14

is revealed to all mankind; the thought of its scorching heat leads to the next section, the searching and pure law of the Lord.

19:1 The heavens and **the sky above** (see ESV footnote) recall Genesis 1. **The glory of God**, i.e., his power, wisdom, and worthiness of honor and worship.

19:3 The **speech** here is that mentioned in v. 2a; its **voice is not heard**, i.e., all people receive it (although not all attend to it).

19:4 Paul uses these words in Rom. 10:18–19 (see note) to show that all the world has received some kind of message.

19:7–11 *The Perfect Torah.* These verses describe some characteristics and effects of God's revelation to Moses. The terms **law**, **testimony**, **precepts**, **commandment**, and **rules** all come from the Pentateuch and are ways of referring to the Mosaic covenant. The whole section builds up to the delight expressed in vv. 10–11.

19:7 On **law**, see note on 1:2. **perfect**. See note on 19:13. **reviving the soul**. That is, giving refreshment (see Prov. 25:13, "refreshes the soul"; Ps. 23:3 uses a similar expression). **Sure**, or trustworthy. **simple**. See Introduction to Proverbs: Character Types in Proverbs.

19:8 pure. Unmixed with evil (cf. 24:4). **enlightening the eyes**. For the eyes to have light or to be bright is for the person to be alert and active (cf. 1 Sam. 14:27; Ezra 9:8; Ps. 13:3; 38:10; Prov. 29:13).

19:9 The fear of the LORD often means revering God, but here it is the revealed way by which one properly reveres God, i.e., the precepts of the covenant (similarly 34:11). **true**. A reliable transcript of God's will.

19:10 The fundamental attitude here is one of delight: God's instructions are more desirable than the best riches (cf. 119:127; Prov. 8:19) and more pleasurable than the finest tastes (cf. Prov. 24:13–14).

19:11 reward. The proper outcome, in this case assurance and character growth (see notes on vv. 12 and 13).

19:12–14 *The Humble Response.* Although some may use the law of God as a means of self-promotion, that is not what this psalm instills. Instead it leads the singers to reflect on their own moral failures, known and unknown; to rely on God's forgiveness; and to seek protection from sin's domination.

19:12 The word **hidden** shows the flow of thought in the psalm: just as the sun's heat searches every nook and cranny so that "there is nothing hidden from its heat" (v. 6), so too the law searches all the hiding places of the soul; the honest faithful can only ask God to **declare** them **innocent**. This prayer includes a request for forgiveness even from "hidden" sins which one does not remember, or which were committed in ignorance.

19:13 Presumptuous sins are sins committed in arrogant disregard of divine commands (Deut. 17:12). These, when repeated, come to **have dominion**, and thus to enslave. Instead the desire is to become **blameless** (which is what the law is; see ESV footnote on Ps. 19:7; see also note on 18:30). The

Then I shall be blameless,
and innocent of great transgression.

14 Let the words of my mouth and the meditation of my heart
be acceptable in your sight,
O LORD, my [j]rock and my [k]redeemer.

Trust in the Name of the LORD Our God

20

TO THE CHOIRMASTER. A PSALM OF DAVID.

1 May the LORD [l]answer you in the day of trouble!
May [m]the name of the God of Jacob [n]protect you!
2 May he send you help from [o]the sanctuary
and give you support from [p]Zion!
3 May he [q]remember all your offerings
and regard with favor your burnt sacrifices! *Selah*

4 May he [r]grant you your heart's desire
and fulfill all your plans!
5 May we shout for joy over [s]your salvation,
and in the name of our God set up our [t]banners!
May the LORD fulfill all your petitions!

6 Now I know that the LORD saves his anointed;
he will answer him from his holy heaven
with [u]the saving might of his right hand.
7 Some trust in [v]chariots and some in [w]horses,
[x]but we trust in the name of the LORD our God.
8 They collapse and fall,
but we rise and stand upright.

9 O LORD, save [y]the king!
May he answer us when we call.

The King Rejoices in the LORD's Strength

21

TO THE CHOIRMASTER. A PSALM OF DAVID.

1 O LORD, in your [z]strength the king rejoices,
and in your [a]salvation how greatly he exults!
2 You have [b]given him his heart's desire
and have not withheld the request of his lips. *Selah*
3 For you [c]meet him with rich blessings;
you set [d]a crown of [e]fine gold upon his head.
4 He asked life of you; you [f]gave it to him,
[g]length of days forever and ever.

14 [j]See Ps. 18:2 [k]See Job 19:25

Psalm 20

1 [l][Gen. 35:3] [m]Prov. 18:10 [n]Ps. 59:1; 69:29
2 [o]Ps. 73:17; 2 Chr. 20:8 [p]Ps. 128:5
3 [q][Acts 10:4]
4 [r]Ps. 21:2
5 [s]Ps. 9:14 [t]Ps. 60:4; Song 6:4, 10
6 [u][Ps. 28:8]
7 [v]Isa. 31:1; 36:9 [w]Prov. 21:31 [x][1 Sam. 17:45; 2 Chr. 32:8]
9 [y]Ps. 48:2

Psalm 21

1 [z]Ps. 8:2; 28:7, 8 [a]Ps. 9:14
2 [b]Ps. 20:4, 5
3 [c]Ps. 59:10 [d][2 Sam. 12:30; 1 Chr. 20:2] [e]Ps. 19:10
4 [f]Ps. 61:6; [2 Sam. 7:19] [g]Ps. 91:16; [1 Kgs. 1:31; Neh. 2:3]

term **innocent** points back to 19:12; there the singer asked to be *declared* innocent, while here he desires innocence in his own practice as well.

19:14 Be acceptable comes from the language of sacrifice (as in Lev. 22:20); thus the request is that this song be a suitable act of worship before God, like a sacrifice.

Psalms 20–21. These two psalms form a pair of royal psalms. Psalm 20 is a prayer that God will give success to the Davidic king, particularly in battle. Psalm 21 gives thanks to God for answering the request of Psalm 20.

20:1–5 *Prayer for the King's Success.* In these verses the congregation addresses the Davidic king ("you") with a prayer that God will answer his prayers, protect him from enemies, send him help, and support him. To call all of this "salvation" (v. 5) is to recognize that it comes from God as a gift and that it must further the ends for which God called his people to begin with. In other words, it is not a blank check for greed and land-grabbing.

20:2 The sanctuary in **Zion** is the place where God especially makes himself present among his people.

20:3 The **offerings** and **burnt sacrifices** were the means by which the worshiper received assurance of God's love and devoted himself to God.

20:6–8 *Sound Confidence in the Lord Alone.* Now the worshipers shift from speaking *to* the king to speaking *about* the king. They place their confidence in God alone as the one who **saves his anointed**, and thus the **chariots** and **horses** that they must use are not the final cause of success, only the means that God may be pleased to prosper (as they hope for themselves) or thwart (as they hope for the enemy).

20:9 *God Save the King!* The terms **save** and "salvation" are repeated in this psalm (vv. 5, 6, 9); see notes on vv. 1–5 (and cf. note on 3:2).

Psalm 21. See note on Psalms 20–21.

21:1–7 *Thanksgiving.* These verses are addressed to the Lord (**you**) about the king (**he**), celebrating the military success prayed for in Psalm 20. It is clear from such terms as **salvation** (21:1, 5), **your presence** (v. 6), and **trusts**

5[h]Ps. 8:5 [i]Ps. 45:3; 96:6
6[j]Ps. 45:7; See Ps. 16:11
7[k]Ps. 10:6; 16:8
8[l][Isa. 10:10]
9[m]Mal. 4:1; [Ps. 83:14] [n]Ps. 2:5 [o]Ps. 18:8; 50:3; 97:3; Isa. 26:11; [Job 20:26; Dan. 7:10; Hab. 3:5]
10[p]Ps. 34:16; 1 Kgs. 13:34 [q]Ps. 37:28; 109:13; Job 18:16, 17, 19; Isa. 14:20
11[r]Ps. 2:1; 10:2
12[s]Ps. 18:40 [t]Ps. 7:12; 11:2

Psalm 22
1[u]Cited Matt. 27:46; Mark 15:34 [v]ver. 11 [w]Ps. 32:3; 38:8; Job 3:24; Isa. 59:11; [Heb. 5:7]
2[x]Ps. 88:1
3[y]Lev. 19:2 [z][Ps. 80:1; 99:1] [a][Ps. 9:11, 14; 65:1; 102:21; 147:12]

5 His [h]glory is great through your salvation;
[i]splendor and majesty you bestow on him.
6 For you make him most blessed forever;[1]
you make him glad with the [j]joy of your presence.
7 For the king trusts in the LORD,
and through the steadfast love of the Most High he shall not be [k]moved.

8 Your hand will [l]find out all your enemies;
your right hand will find out those who hate you.
9 You will make them as [m]a blazing oven
when you appear.
The LORD will swallow them up in his [n]wrath,
and [o]fire will consume them.
10 You [p]will destroy their [q]descendants from the earth,
and their offspring from among the children of man.
11 Though they plan evil against you,
though they [r]devise mischief, they will not succeed.
12 For you will put them [s]to flight;
you will [t]aim at their faces with your bows.

13 Be exalted, O LORD, in your strength!
We will sing and praise your power.

Why Have You Forsaken Me?

22

TO THE CHOIRMASTER: ACCORDING TO THE DOE OF THE DAWN. A PSALM OF DAVID.

1 [u]My God, my God, why have you forsaken me?
Why are you so [v]far from saving me, from the words of my [w]groaning?
2 O my God, I cry by [x]day, but you do not answer,
and by night, but I find no rest.

3 Yet you are [y]holy,
[z]enthroned on [a]the praises[2] of Israel.

[1] Or *make him a source of blessing forever* [2] Or *dwelling in the praises*

(v. 7) that the psalm assumes a pious and faithful king and is not intended to offer endorsement to sinful plans.

21:7 not be moved. Cf. 10:6 and 15:5.

21:8–12 *Confidence for the Future.* The person addressed (**you**) may still be God, as above, but it seems better to take it as the king, who will continue his military exploits on behalf of the people. As above, it is necessary to see that these **enemies** are **those who hate** the king (who is the Lord's anointed, 20:6) and **plan evil against** him (21:11). When the king lives by the Davidic ideal, God takes hostility against the king as hostility against his own purposes and thus as against himself; thus the godly king is the tool of God's **wrath** (v. 9).

21:10 This probably assumes that the **descendants** and **offspring** of these hostile Gentiles carry on the hostility of their parents.

21:13 *Be Exalted!* As in 18:46, the Lord is **exalted** when he shows his power in making the faithful king successful.

Psalm 22. This psalm has the appearance of an especially anguished individual lament, where the suffering comes from the attacks of unscrupulous people and is intensified by the mockery of those who should feel sympathy; this person, nevertheless, looks forward to vindication and joyful worship with the rest of God's people. However, in view of its prominent place in the crucifixion story, Christian readers have found in it a description of the sufferings of Jesus. Many Christians have taken it as a straight prediction of Jesus' sufferings, as if the primary function of the psalm was to foretell the work of the Savior; others have read it as a lament in its OT context, with a "fuller meaning" revealed by Jesus' use of it. It is better to see the psalm as providing a lament for the innocent sufferer, and then to see how all the Gospels use this to portray Jesus as the innocent sufferer par excellence. Consider how Matthew 27 uses the psalm. Matthew 27:35 echoes Ps. 22:18 (dividing the garments by lot); Matt. 27:39 echoes Ps. 22:7 (wagging heads); Matt. 27:43 echoes Ps. 22:8 (the derisive challenge for God to rescue him); and Matt. 27:46 cites Ps. 22:1 (Jesus crying out). See chart, p. 964. Matthew presents Jesus as a thoroughly good and faithful person who is brutally and unjustly executed, and mocked by those who should have supported him. But this portrayal of Jesus in light of Psalm 22 allows Christ's followers as well to expect some kind of vindication, as vv. 22–31 describe; and they are not disappointed as they read the resurrection account. Hebrews 2:12 cites Ps. 22:22, from the vindication section, to show that Jesus shares the humanity of his followers, since he calls them "brothers." To make this argument, the author of Hebrews must also see Jesus as the ideal human being, which means he is using the psalm much as the Gospels do.

22:1–2 *Why Have You Forsaken Me?* This anguished question expresses just what a person in the circumstances described in the psalm feels: distress at receiving no relief to his pain or answer to his prayers (v. 2).

22:3–5 *Yet the Lord Has Been Our Trust.* The singer knows himself to be a member of God's own people, who is therefore the object of God's special attention. God is especially present in Israel's worship (v. 3), and has rescued **our fathers** when they called for help (vv. 4–5).

4 In you our fathers trusted;
they trusted, and you delivered them.
5 To you they [b]cried and were rescued;
in you they [c]trusted and were not put to shame.

6 But I am [d]a worm and not a man,
[e]scorned by mankind and [f]despised by the people.
7 All who see me [g]mock me;
they make mouths at me; they [h]wag their heads;
8 [i]"He trusts in the LORD; let him [j]deliver him;
let him rescue him, for he [k]delights in him!"

9 Yet you are he who [l]took me from the womb;
you made me trust you at my mother's breasts.
10 On you was I cast from my birth,
and from [m]my mother's womb you have been my God.
11 Be not [n]far from me,
for trouble is near,
and there is [o]none to help.

12 Many bulls encompass me;
[p]strong bulls of [q]Bashan surround me;
13 they [r]open wide their mouths at me,
like a ravening and roaring lion.

14 I am [s]poured out like water,
and all my bones are [t]out of joint;
my [u]heart is like [v]wax;
it is melted within my breast;
15 my strength is [w]dried up like a potsherd,
and my [x]tongue sticks to my jaws;
you lay me in the dust of death.

16 For [y]dogs encompass me;
a company of evildoers [z]encircles me;
they have [a]pierced my hands and feet[1]—
17 I can count all my bones—

5[b]See Judg. 3:9 [c]Ps. 25:2; 31:1; 71:1; Isa. 49:23; Rom. 9:33
6[d]Job 25:6; Isa. 41:14 [e]Ps. 69:19; 109:25 [f]Isa. 49:7; 53:3
7[g]See Matt. 27:39-43; Mark 15:29-32; Luke 23:35, 36 [h]Ps. 109:25; [Ps. 44:14; 2 Kgs. 19:21; Isa. 37:22; Lam. 2:15]
8[i][Ps. 37:5; Prov. 16:3] [j]Ps. 91:14 [k]Ps. 18:19; Matt. 3:17; Mark 1:11; Luke 3:22
9[l]Ps. 71:6
10[m]Isa. 46:3; 49:1; Gal. 1:15
11[n]See ver. 1; Ps. 10:1 [o]Ps. 107:12; 2 Kgs. 14:26; Isa. 63:5
12[p][Ps. 68:30 (Heb.)] [q]Amos 4:1
13[r]Ps. 35:21; Job 16:10; Lam. 2:16; 3:46
14[s][Lam. 2:11] [t][Dan. 5:6] [u][Job 23:16; Nah. 2:10]; See Josh. 2:11 [v]See Ps. 68:2
15[w]Prov. 17:22 [x][John 19:28; See Job 29:10]
16[y][Phil. 3:2; Rev. 22:15] [z]Ps. 88:17 [a]Matt. 27:35; Mark 15:24; Luke 23:33; 24:40; John 19:23, 37; 20:25; [Zech. 12:10]

[1] Some Hebrew manuscripts, Septuagint, Vulgate, Syriac; most Hebrew manuscripts *like a lion* [they are at] *my hands and feet*

22:6–8 *Yet I Am Derided.* In contrast to the history of vv. 3–5, the singer describes the mockery he encounters from his fellow members of **the people** (v. 6). They even deride his faith (v. 8), perhaps implying that they consider him a hypocrite.

22:9–11 *But the Lord Has Cared for Me All My Life.* The singer again recalls the past, as in vv. 3–5, but this time it is more personal. In effect he tells God, "Not only did you show yourself faithful to our ancestors in Israel, you have been faithful to me from the very beginning of my existence." In this light he can pray confidently, **be not far from me** (v. 11).

22:12–18 *I Am Surrounded by Enemies.* The song returns to describing the situation: enemies who are bent on evil like **bulls** (v. 12), a **lion** (v. 13), and

The Use of Psalm 22 in Matthew 27

Ps. 22:18	They divide my garments among them, and for my clothing they cast lots.	And when they had crucified him, they *divided his garments among them by casting lots.*	Matt. 27:35
Ps. 22:7	All who see me mock me; they make mouths at me; they wag their heads.	And those who passed by derided him, *wagging their heads.*	Matt. 27:39
Ps. 22:8	"He trusts in the LORD; let him deliver him; let him rescue him, for he delights in him!"	*He trusts in God; let God deliver him now,* if he desires him. For he said, "I am the Son of God."	Matt. 27:43
Ps. 22:1	My God, my God, why have you forsaken me? Why are you so far from saving me, from the words of my groaning?	And about the ninth hour Jesus cried out with a loud voice, saying, "Eli, Eli, lema sabachthani?" that is, *"My God, my God, why have you forsaken me?"*	Matt. 27:46

they [b]stare and gloat over me;
18 [c]they divide my garments among them,
and for my clothing they cast lots.

19 But you, O LORD, [n]do not be far off!
O you my help, [d]come quickly to my aid!
20 Deliver my soul from the sword,
my precious life from the power of [e]the dog!
21 Save me from [f]the mouth of the lion!
You have rescued[1] me from the horns of [g]the wild oxen!

22 [h]I will tell of your name to my [i]brothers;
in the midst of the congregation I will praise you:
23 You who [j]fear the LORD, praise him!
All you offspring of Jacob, [k]glorify him,
and stand in awe of him, all you offspring of Israel!
24 For he has not despised or abhorred
the affliction of [l]the afflicted,
and he has not [m]hidden his face from him,
but has heard, when he [n]cried to him.

25 From you comes my praise in the great [o]congregation;
my [p]vows I will [q]perform before those who fear him.
26 [r]The afflicted[2] shall [s]eat and be satisfied;
those who seek him shall praise the LORD!
May your hearts [t]live forever!

27 All [u]the ends of the earth shall remember
and turn to the LORD,
and all [v]the families of the nations
shall worship before you.
28 For [w]kingship belongs to the LORD,
and he rules over the nations.

29 All [x]the prosperous of the earth eat and worship;
before him shall [y]bow all who go down to the dust,
even the one who could not [z]keep himself alive.
30 Posterity shall serve him;
it shall be told of the Lord to the coming [a]generation;
31 they shall [b]come and proclaim his righteousness to a people yet
[c]unborn,
that he has done it.

[1] Hebrew *answered* [2] Or *The meek*

17[b]Luke 23:35
18[c]Cited John 19:24; [Matt. 27:35; Luke 23:34]
19[n][See ver. 11 above] [d]Ps. 38:22
20[e][Phil. 3:2; Rev. 22:15]
21[f]2 Tim. 4:17 [g]See Num. 23:22
22[h]Cited Heb. 2:12; [Ps. 102:21; John 17:6] [i]Matt. 28:10; John 20:17; Rom. 8:29
23[j]Ps. 135:20 [k]Ps. 50:15, 23
24[l][Isa. 53:4, 7] [m]Ps. 10:1; 13:1; See Job 13:24 [n]Heb. 5:7
25[o]Ps. 35:18; 40:9, 10; 111:1 [p]Lev. 7:16 [q]Ps. 66:13; Jonah 2:9; See Ps. 50:14
26[r]Ps. 69:32 [s]Isa. 25:6; 65:13 [t]John 6:51
27[u]Ps. 2:8; 67:7 [v]Ps. 96:7
28[w]Obad. 21; [Ps. 47:8; Zech. 14:9]
29[x][Ps. 45:12] [y]Ps. 72:9; [Phil. 2:10] [z]Ezek. 18:27
30[a]Ps. 48:13; 71:18
31[b]Ps. 86:9; [Isa. 60:3] [c]Ps. 78:6; 102:18

dogs (v. 16) leave the singer without energy (v. 14) or strength (v. 15). Peter borrows the image of a "roaring lion" (v. 13) for the devil (1 Pet. 5:8), the evil enemy behind all evil enemies of the faithful.

22:17 I can count all my bones, that is, "My flesh is so wasted away that my bones poke through my skin." **They stare**, that is, the enemies (see v. 18).

22:18 This verse is quoted in John 19:24 (cf. Matt. 27:35; Mark 15:24; Luke 23:34); see note on Psalm 22.

22:19–21 *Save Me as You Have Done Before!* Picking up from v. 11 (v. 19, **do not be far off** and **help**), the singer lays out his request. In recalling God's past answers to his prayers, he asks for relief in his present distress. Note how **dog**, **lion**, and **wild oxen** (vv. 20–21) reverse the order of the threats in vv. 12–18.

22:22–31 *Praise Will Result: From Me, From Israel, From All Nations.* The song closes with confidence that when God answers the prayer, the singer will be vindicated and will again be able to join with God's people in worship. The song helps readers to see the outcome of this personal trial in its relation to the whole of God's people: the vindicated singer looks forward to telling forth God's praise among the assembled congregation (vv. 22, 25), and thus all the **offspring of Israel** will take encouragement and join in giving thanks (vv. 23–24, 26). Indeed, the praising company will extend to the whole world (v. 27, **all the families of the nations**, echoing Gen. 12:3; 22:18; etc.); that is, the singer's personal story of trouble and vindication is part of the larger story of God's redemptive work in the world.

The Lord Is My Shepherd

23

A PSALM OF DAVID.

1 The LORD is my [d]shepherd; I shall not [e]want.
2 He makes me lie down in green [f]pastures.
He leads me beside still waters.[1]
3 He [g]restores my soul.
He [h]leads me in [i]paths of righteousness[2]
for his [j]name's sake.

4 Even though I [k]walk through the valley of [l]the shadow of death,[3]
I will [m]fear no evil,
for [n]you are with me;
your [o]rod and your staff,
they comfort me.

5 You [p]prepare a table before me
in [q]the presence of my enemies;
you [r]anoint my head with oil;
my [s]cup overflows.
6 Surely[4] goodness and mercy[5] shall follow me
all the days of my life,
and I shall [t]dwell[6] in the house of the LORD
[u]forever.[7]

The King of Glory

24

A PSALM OF DAVID.

1 [v]The earth is the LORD's and the fullness thereof,[8]
the world and those who dwell therein,

[1] Hebrew *beside waters of rest* [2] Or *in right paths* [3] Or *the valley of deep darkness* [4] Or *Only* [5] Or *steadfast love* [6] Or *shall return to dwell* [7] Hebrew *for length of days* [8] Or *and all that fills it*

Psalm 23

1 [d]Ps. 78:52; 80:1; Isa. 40:11; Jer. 31:10; Ezek. 34:11, 12, 23; John 10:11; Heb. 13:20; 1 Pet. 2:25; 5:4 [e]Ps. 34:9, 10; [Matt. 6:33]
2 [f]Ezek. 34:14; John 10:9
3 [g]Ps. 19:7 [h]Ps. 5:8; 31:3; 139:10, 24; 143:10; Isa. 40:11; 49:10 [i]Prov. 4:11; 8:20 [j]Ps. 25:11; 31:3; 79:9; 109:21; Ezek. 20:9, 14
4 [k]Ps. 138:7 [l]See Job 3:5 [m]Ps. 3:6; 27:1, 3; 118:6 [n]Ex. 3:12; Isa. 43:2 [o]Mic. 7:14
5 [p]Ps. 78:19; [Prov. 9:2; John 6:51]; See 2 Sam. 17:27-29 [q][Ps. 31:19] [r]Ps. 45:7; 133:2; Luke 7:46; [Ps. 92:10] [s]Ps. 16:5
6 [t]Ps. 27:4 [u]Ps. 21:4

Psalm 24

1 [v]Ps. 50:12; 89:11; Ex. 9:29; 19:5; Deut. 10:14; Job 41:11; Cited 1 Cor. 10:26

Psalm 23. This hymn is usually classified as a psalm of confidence in the Lord's care. It uses two images: the Lord as Shepherd who cares for the sheep (vv. 1–4), and the Lord as Host who cares for his guest (vv. 5–6). These images would be familiar from everyday experience (for David's own, cf. 1 Sam. 17:34); but they also evoke other ideas common in the ancient Near East (including the OT), with the deity as shepherd of his people and the deity as host of the meal. In worship, the faithful celebrate God's greatness and majesty; and when they sing this psalm, they see his majesty in the way he personally attends to each of his covenant lambs. He is the shepherd for Israel as a whole; and in being such, he is the shepherd for each faithful Israelite as well.

23:1–4 *The Lord as Shepherd.* Just as a shepherd cares for his sheep, so the Lord cares for his people, providing for their needs, guiding them, and protecting them.

23:1 shepherd. The deity-as-shepherd motif is common in the Bible (e.g., Gen. 48:15; 49:24; Ps. 28:9; 80:1; 95:7; 100:3; Rev. 7:17; cf. Ps. 49:14). The Lord is the Shepherd of the people as a whole, as well as individual members; and in this psalm the particular member is in view. **want.** That is, to lack what one needs.

23:2 Green pastures and **still waters** are peaceful places for rest and feeding.

23:3 The restoration, refreshment, or revival of the **soul** (or life) indicates the returning of life or vitality (cf. 19:7; Ruth 4:15; Prov. 25:13; Lam. 1:19). The **paths** in which God **leads** his faithful are the basic moral direction of their lives, toward **righteousness** (seen here as a blessing, not a burden). **for his name's sake.** That is, in order to preserve his reputation for being true to his revealed character (cf. 1 Kings 8:41; Ps. 25:11; 31:3).

23:4 The shadow of death may be the shadow that death casts, or it may be, as the ESV footnote has it, "deep darkness." Perhaps the idea is that in a **valley** in the desert (or wadi) in Judah one can encounter deep shadows, and cannot know for sure who (bandits) or what (animals, flash floods) lurks in them; even in such periods of suspense and danger, the faithful find assurance that God is with them, and thus they need not **fear**.

23:5–6 *The Lord as Host.* Some have argued that the image of shepherd and sheep is still present here; but the mention of a **table**, of putting **oil** on the **head**, the **cup**, and the Lord's "house," all show that the psalm now describes the faithful person as God's guest at a meal ("prepare a table"). The **enemies** are powerless to prevent the enjoyment of God's generous hospitality (perhaps they are there as captives at a victory celebration). **Goodness and mercy** (ESV footnote, "steadfast love") are the assurance for the faithful that God has showered his grace upon them. For a non-Levite to **dwell in the house of the LORD** is to have ready access to the sanctuary for worship (cf. 27:4). As the ESV footnote explains, **forever** is literally, "for length of days"; this may simply be another way of saying **all the days of my life**, but is more likely to be meant as "for days without end" (cf. 21:4; 93:5, "forevermore").

Psalm 24. This psalm seems fitted for some liturgical occasion, perhaps one that celebrates the way that David brought the ark of the Lord into Jerusalem (2 Samuel 6); this would explain the interest in God's presence in Ps. 24:3–6, and the address to the gates in vv. 7–10. The psalm asserts the astounding idea that the God who created and owns everything is the very same God into whose presence the faithful worshiper enters because of the covenant with Israel. Such is the privilege of being Israel, and such too defines their mission, namely, to bring God's fame to all his creation, and especially to all mankind.

24:1–2 *The Lord Is Creator and Owner of All.* The Lord, the covenant God of Israel, is the one who **founded** the world (cf. Gen. 1:1–2:3, where he is called God, the transcendent Creator). The focus here is on the **earth** as the dry land, where human beings **dwell**, as distinguished from the waters (cf. Gen.

2[w]Ps. 104:5; Job 38:6; Prov. 8:29 [x]Ps. 136:6; Gen. 1:9
3[y]For ver. 3-5, see Ps. 15:1-5 [z]Ps. 2:6
4[a][Deut. 10:12; Isa. 33:15, 16; Mic. 6:8] [b]See Job 22:30 [c]Ps. 73:1; Matt. 5:8 [d][Ezek. 18:6] [e]Ps. 31:6; 119:37
5[f][Gen. 22:17, 18] [g]Isa. 46:13; 56:1 [h]Ps. 27:9; 38:22; 51:14; 88:1
6[i]Ps. 14:5 [j]Ps. 27:8; 105:4
7[k][Ps. 118:19, 20; Isa. 26:2] [l][1 Cor. 2:8]
8[m][Ex. 15:3]
10[n]Mal. 1:14

Psalm 25

1[o]Ps. 86:4; 143:8; Lam. 3:41; [Ps. 24:4]
2[p]See Ps. 11:1 [q]ver. 20; Ps. 31:1, 17; 71:1 [r][Ps. 13:4]

2 for he has [w]founded it upon [x]the seas
and established it upon the rivers.

3 [y]Who shall ascend the hill of the LORD?
And who shall stand in his [z]holy place?
4 [a]He who has [b]clean hands and [c]a pure heart,
who does not [d]lift up his soul to [e]what is false
and does not swear deceitfully.
5 He will receive [f]blessing from the LORD
and [g]righteousness from [h]the God of his salvation.
6 Such is [i]the generation of those who seek him,
who [j]seek the face of the God of Jacob.[1] *Selah*

7 [k]Lift up your heads, O gates!
And be lifted up, O ancient doors,
that [l]the King of glory may come in.
8 Who is this King of glory?
The LORD, strong and mighty,
the LORD, [m]mighty in battle!
9 Lift up your heads, O gates!
And lift them up, O ancient doors,
that the King of glory may come in.
10 Who is this King of glory?
[n]The LORD of hosts,
he is the King of glory! *Selah*

Teach Me Your Paths

25[2]

OF DAVID.

1 To you, O LORD, I [o]lift up my soul.
2 O my God, in you I [p]trust;
[q]let me not be put to shame;
[r]let not my enemies exult over me.

[1] Septuagint, Syriac, and two Hebrew manuscripts; Masoretic Text *Jacob, who seek your face* [2] This psalm is an acrostic poem, each verse beginning with the successive letters of the Hebrew alphabet

1:9–10). Paul quotes Ps. 24:1 in 1 Cor. 10:26 to explain that since God owns everything, foods are included, and thus may be enjoyed without qualms.

24:3–6 *Who Receives Blessing from Him?* This section reminds the worshipers of a recurring theme in the OT: although every Israelite may attend worship at the sanctuary (**the hill of the LORD, his holy place**), not everyone will really **receive blessing** (v. 5) or will genuinely enjoy the status of **righteousness** (v. 5). God expects his people to embrace their privileges from their hearts, and to show that in their behavior (vv. 4, 6). This theme appears elsewhere in the Psalms (e.g., Ps. 15:1–5; 51:16–19) as well as in Proverbs (e.g., Prov. 15:8) and the Prophets (e.g., Isa. 1:11–17). The Hebrew for **clean** (Ps. 24:4) can also be translated "innocent"; clean **hands** are those that have acted innocently toward others (Gen. 20:5; Ps. 26:6; 73:13). Likewise the **pure heart** is the one cleansed of all unworthy motives toward other people. (The LXX [Gk.] for "pure heart" lies behind the sixth beatitude, Matt. 5:8.) Thus true piety is shown both in hunger for God (Ps. 24:6) and in fair and generous dealing with one another (v. 4). **to what is false**. I.e., to idols.

24:7–10 *Lift Up Your Heads, O Gates!* Readers may imagine this as the call and response before the gates of Jerusalem: in v. 7 the procession bearing the ark announces God's presence in the ark, seeking entry into his sanctuary; **Who is this King of glory?** (v. 8a) is the reply, asking for further identification. The procession then says who the Lord is (**The LORD, strong and mighty, the LORD, mighty in battle!**), and then repeats the request for entry (v. 9). Again the doorkeepers reply, asking for identification (v. 10a), and again the procession identifies the Lord (v. 10b).

Psalm 25. This is a lament in which individual members of the worshiping assembly ask God for help in their various troubles. While it expresses faith in God's kindness toward the faithful, it does not end in the confident way of most laments (vv. 16–22). The psalm also includes penitential elements, where the worshipers confess their sins and pray for forgiveness (vv. 6–7, 11, 18). As the notes will show, there are echoes of Pentateuch promises here, showing that the godly in Israel were to view the Sinai covenant as a gracious one. As the ESV footnote explains, this psalm is acrostic, each verse beginning with a successive letter of the Hebrew alphabet. This is the first psalm that is a consistent acrostic (cf. note on Psalm 9). Like other acrostics attributed to David (Psalms 9–10; 25; 34; 37; 145), this does not perfectly follow the acrostic pattern: the verse beginning with *w* is missing (it should be between 25:5–6); v. 18 begins with the letter *r* (as does v. 19), while *q* is expected; and v. 22 begins with *p*, as does v. 16. The acrostic pattern makes it harder for the poem to have a clear flow of thought, but the notes will show that the poet nevertheless provided one.

25:1–3 *Expression of Trust.* The psalm opens by expressing confidence in the Lord; the request of v. 2 is reaffirmed as assurance in v. 3.

25:1 lift up my soul. This Hebrew expression appears in Deut. 24:15; Prov. 19:18; Jer. 22:27; 44:14; and Hos. 4:8, where it is translated with terms such as "long," "desire," "set the heart on," "be greedy," "count on"; thus it is an idiom for "I direct my desire" (cf. Ps. 24:4; 86:4; 143:8).

25:2–3 To **be put to shame** (vv. 2, 3, 20) is to be publicly shown to have relied on a false basis for hope. The worshipers, who side with the genuinely faithful (**I trust . . . wait for you**), expect that their hope in the Lord has a worthy basis, while those who seek to harm them (**enemies . . . wantonly treacherous**, i.e., the unfaithful) have founded their hopes on lies.

3 Indeed, [s]none who wait for you shall be put to shame;
they shall be ashamed who are [t]wantonly [u]treacherous.

4 [v]Make me to know your ways, O LORD;
teach me your paths.
5 Lead me in your [w]truth and teach me,
for you are the God of my salvation;
for you I wait all the day long.
6 Remember your [x]mercy, O LORD, and your steadfast love,
[y]for they have been from of old.
7 Remember not [z]the sins of my youth or my transgressions;
according to your [a]steadfast love remember me,
for the sake of your goodness, O LORD!

8 [b]Good and upright is the LORD;
therefore he [c]instructs sinners in the way.
9 He leads the humble in what is right,
and teaches the humble his way.
10 All the paths of the LORD are [d]steadfast love and faithfulness,
for those who keep his covenant and his testimonies.

11 For your [e]name's sake, O LORD,
pardon my guilt, for it is [f]great.
12 Who is the man who fears the LORD?
Him [c]will he instruct in the way that he should choose.
13 His soul shall [g]abide in well-being,
and his [h]offspring [i]shall inherit the land.
14 [j]The friendship[1] of the LORD is for those who fear him,
and he makes known to them his covenant.
15 My [k]eyes are ever toward the LORD,
for he will [l]pluck my feet out of the net.

16 [m]Turn to me and be gracious to me,
for I am lonely and afflicted.
17 The troubles of my heart are enlarged;
bring me out of my distresses.
18 [n]Consider my affliction and my trouble,
and forgive all my sins.

19 Consider how many are my foes,
and with what violent hatred they hate me.

[1] Or *The secret counsel*

3 [s]Isa. 49:23; [Rom. 5:5; Phil. 1:20] [t][Ps. 59:3, 4] [u][Jer. 3:20]
4 [v]Ps. 27:11; 86:11; 143:8, 10; Ex. 33:13; [Ps. 5:8; 119:35]
5 [w]Ps. 26:3; 86:11
6 [x]Ps. 51:1; [Ps. 103:17; Isa. 63:15] [y][Gen. 8:1; 9:15; 19:29]
7 [z]Job 13:26; 20:11; Jer. 3:25 [a]Ps. 51:1
8 [b]Ps. 100:5 [c]Ps. 32:8
10 [d][John 1:17]
11 [e]See Ps. 23:3 [f][Rom. 5:20]
12 [c][See ver. 8 above]
13 [g][Prov. 1:33; 19:23] [h]Ps. 112:2 [i]See Ps. 37:9
14 [j][Amos 3:7; See Job 29:4]
15 [k]Ps. 123:1, 2; 141:8; [2 Chr. 20:12] [l]Ps. 31:4
16 [m]Ps. 69:16; 86:16; 119:132
18 [n][Job 10:15]

25:4–5 *Desire for Guidance.* Those who trust in the Lord seek his guidance, i.e., they want to learn what manner of life (**ways, paths**) pleases him and how his commands apply to their specific circumstances. God's guidance in the Bible is almost always concerned with the moral virtues he wants in his faithful people (cf. vv. 8–10, 12); in light of these virtues they make their choices in the various circumstances of life. **I wait.** Cf. v. 3.

25:6–7 *Desire for Forgiveness.* For God's covenant people to make progress in virtue, they must rely on God's grace and kindness, and not on their own virtue (which comes from God's guidance anyway). The terms **mercy, steadfast love, sins,** and **transgressions** evoke Ex. 34:6–7, which tells Israel of God's gracious disposition to them (cf. Ps. 25:10, "faithfulness"). For God to **remember** something is for him to attend to it in order to act (cf. 8:4; 9:12; 20:3); the faithful ask God to attend to them in mercy rather than according to their sins (cf. 79:8).

25:8–11 *Praise for the Lord's Goodness and Mercy.* This section picks up the ideas of God's goodness, steadfast love, and faithfulness from vv. 6–7, and his guidance from vv. 4–5. It celebrates the character of God, by which he forgives his people and guides them in moral growth. The OT expects that the people will **keep his covenant**, i.e., lay hold of the forgiveness and guidance that it graciously offers.

25:12–15 *Confidence in the Lord's Friendship.* The faithful have a close and intimate relationship with God. Verse 12 focuses on the particular person (**the man**, taken as an example for all the pious regardless of sex or age) who **fears the LORD**; such a person will know God's guidance, blessing, and **friendship** (v. 14; i.e., welcome into his intimate company; cf. 55:14; Prov. 3:32). The **well-being** of Ps. 25:13 is the expression of God's goodness (vv. 7, 8).

25:16–21 *Request for Forgiveness and Protection.* The psalm gathers all these confident thoughts and turns them into prayer for the particular circumstances of trouble, asking for deliverance from the **affliction**, **trouble**, and **foes** that threaten (vv. 17–19), on the basis of forgiven **sins** (v. 18b). The virtues of **integrity** and **uprightness** (v. 21), which are recognized as gifts (cf. God's uprightness, v. 8), are God's means of protection (cf. Prov. 2:11–12).

20 Oh, guard my soul, and deliver me!
[o]Let me not be put to shame, for I take refuge in you.
21 May integrity and uprightness preserve me,
for I wait for you.

22 [p]Redeem Israel, O God,
out of all his troubles.

I Will Bless the Lord

26

Of David.

1 [q]Vindicate me, O Lord,
for I have [r]walked in my integrity,
and I have [s]trusted in the Lord without wavering.
2 [t]Prove me, O Lord, and try me;
test my heart and [u]my mind.[1]
3 For your [v]steadfast love is before my eyes,
and I [w]walk in your [v]faithfulness.

4 I do not [x]sit with men of [y]falsehood,
nor do I consort with hypocrites.
5 I [z]hate the assembly of evildoers,
and I will not sit with the wicked.

6 I [a]wash my hands in innocence
and go around your altar, O Lord,
7 proclaiming thanksgiving aloud,
and telling all your [b]wondrous deeds.

8 O Lord, I [c]love the habitation of your house
and the place where your glory dwells.
9 [d]Do not sweep my soul away with sinners,
nor my life with bloodthirsty men,
10 in whose hands are evil devices,
and whose right hands are full of [e]bribes.

11 But as for me, I shall walk in my integrity;
redeem me, and be gracious to me.

[1] Hebrew *test my kidneys and my heart*

20[o]See ver. 2
22[p]Ps. 34:22; 71:23; 130:8; Lam. 3:58; [2 Sam. 4:9]

Psalm 26
1[q]See Ps. 7:8 [r]ver. 11 [s]See Ps. 11:1
2[t]See Ps. 7:9; 17:3; 139:23 [u]Ps. 7:9
3[v][Ps. 25:10] [w]2 Kgs. 20:3; [Ps. 86:11]
4[x]See Ps. 1:1 [y]Job 11:11
5[z]Ps. 31:6; 139:21, 22
6[a]Ps. 73:13; [Ex. 30:19, 20; Deut. 21:6]
7[b]See Ps. 9:1
8[c][Ps. 27:4]
9[d][Ps. 28:3]
10[e]Ex. 23:8; Deut. 16:19

25:22 *Prayer for the Whole People.* **Redeem** generally conveys the idea of rescue and protection, especially when its object is **Israel** (e.g., 44:26; 111:9; 130:7–8) or a faithful worshiper (e.g., 34:22; 55:18; 71:23). In some places (though not here) it carries the idea of exchanging a substitute or ransom (e.g., Ex. 13:13; Lev. 27:29).

Psalm 26. A variety of settings for Psalm 26 have been suggested, such as a prayer for public exoneration offered by someone seriously or falsely accused of wrongdoing; or perhaps part of an entrance liturgy by which pilgrims came into the sanctuary. There is scant evidence for any of these, though the latter is helpful because it links the theme with that of Psalms 15 and 24. That is, the psalm mirrors for those who attend worship what the ideal covenant participant should actually look like. Some have taken the claims of innocence here as a kind of self-righteous boasting, but this is a mistake. First, the mention of God's steadfast love and faithfulness (26:3), a clear echo of Ex. 34:6, shows that divine grace is the foundation for holy living; similarly, the references to worship in God's house (Ps. 26:6–8) indicate that the covenantal means of grace, with their focus on atonement and forgiveness, are in view; and third, singing this psalm serves to enable worshipers more and more to like and embrace the ideal of faithful covenant membership—but it does not make achieving that ideal a precondition for true worship.

26:1–3 *Prayer for Vindication.* For God to **vindicate** the worshiper is for God to distinguish between the faithful and the impious; perhaps there is the additional nuance of showing the distinction publicly (cf. 35:24; 43:1). The faithful are those who take the covenant to heart, and who as a general pattern of life **have walked in** their **integrity** and **have trusted in the Lord without wavering**. They also keep God's **steadfast love . . . before** their **eyes** and **walk in** God's **faithfulness**—i.e., they live by the grace revealed in Ex. 34:6.

26:4–8 *Claim of Innocence.* Here the psalm describes some of the features of the faithful covenant participant: he refuses to join with the unfaithful (**hypocrites**, **evildoers**, **wicked**) in their crooked schemes, because he renounces their values (cf. 1:1); and he aims to take part in public worship with moral **innocence** and with delight (**love**, 26:8). (On the **glory** as God's special presence in the sanctuary, see Ex. 40:34–35.)

26:9–10 *Separate from the Bloodthirsty.* These verses amplify the prayer for vindication in v. 1, namely, the desire to be treated differently from the unfaithful.

26:11–12 *Confidence and Commitment.* The person who owns this ideal, who determines to **walk in** his **integrity**, may be sure of God's continuing care. On **redeem**, see note on 25:22.

12 My foot stands on [f]level ground;
in [g]the great assembly I will bless the LORD.

The LORD Is My Light and My Salvation

27

OF DAVID.

1 The LORD is my [h]light and my [i]salvation;
[j]whom shall I fear?
The LORD is the stronghold[1] of my life;
of whom shall I be afraid?

2 When evildoers assail me
to [k]eat up my flesh,
my adversaries and foes,
it is they who stumble and fall.

3 [l]Though an army encamp against me,
my heart shall not fear;
though war arise against me,
yet[2] I will be confident.

4 [m]One thing have I asked of the LORD,
that will I seek after:
that I may [n]dwell in the house of the LORD
all the days of my life,
to gaze upon [o]the beauty of the LORD
and to inquire[3] in his temple.

5 For he will [p]hide me in his shelter
in the day of trouble;
he will conceal me under the cover of his tent;
he will [q]lift me high upon a rock.

6 And now my [r]head shall be lifted up
above my enemies all around me,
and I will offer in his tent
sacrifices with shouts of [s]joy;
[t]I will sing and make melody to the LORD.

7 [u]Hear, O LORD, when I cry aloud;
be gracious to me and answer me!

8 You have said, [v]"Seek[4] my face."

[1] Or *refuge* [2] Or *in this* [3] Or *meditate* [4] The command (*seek*) is addressed to more than one person

12 [f]See Ps. 27:11 [g]Ps. 22:25

Psalm 27

1 [h]Isa. 60:20; Mic. 7:8; [Ps. 84:11] [i]Ps. 118:14; Ex. 15:2; Isa. 12:2; 62:11 [j]See Ps. 23:4
2 [k]Ps. 14:4
3 [l]Ps. 3:6
4 [m][Ps. 26:8; 84:1, 2] [n]Ps. 23:6; 65:4; [Luke 2:37] [o]Ps. 90:17
5 [p]Ps. 31:20; [Ps. 91:1; Job 5:21; Isa. 4:6] [q]Ps. 40:2
6 [r]Ps. 3:3 [s][Num. 10:10] [t]Eph. 5:19; Col. 3:16
7 [u]Ps. 30:10
8 [v]Ps. 24:6; 105:4

Psalm 27. In singing Psalm 27, God's people have a way of not simply expressing confidence in him but of cultivating that confidence for the widest range of challenging life situations. The psalm uses several synonyms for "enemies" (vv. 2, 6, 11, 12), giving it the concrete setting of a faithful person beset by those who would destroy him with bloodthirsty and deceitful means; one who can trust God in those circumstances can trust him in other situations as well.

27:1–3 *Whom Shall I Fear?* The terms **fear** (vv. 1, 3) and **be afraid** (v. 1) contrast with **be confident** (v. 3): the faithful must learn to base their confidence on God's ever-present protection (**light, salvation, stronghold**, v. 1); this will be a confidence that grows through experiences of deliverance (as v. 2 recounts).

27:2 to eat up my flesh. The picture here is probably of **evildoers** as wild animals who would "devour" the faithful (cf. 14:4 and Mic. 3:3 for similar expressions; see Ps. 7:2; 10:9; 17:12; 22:13, 21 for the comparison).

27:4–6 *Shelter in His Sanctuary.* "House of the LORD," "temple," "tent," and "sacrifices" show that these verses focus on public worship; they view unhindered access to God's presence in worship as the best of all gifts. This is the place of true delight and true safety.

27:4 David, the author of this psalm, could have called the tabernacle a "house" (Josh. 6:24; 1 Sam. 1:7; 3:15) and a **temple** (1 Sam. 1:9; 3:3). On **dwell in the house of the LORD**, see Ps. 23:6. God's **beauty** is what the faithful yearn to **gaze upon** (i.e., to behold with admiration and affection) as they seek him in worship.

27:7–12 *Prayer for Continued Favor.* These verses turn to address the Lord directly, making it clear that the deliverance asked for is for the purpose of continuing to seek God.

27:8 As the ESV footnote points out, God addresses his words, **Seek my face**, to more than one person; the singer responds by acting personally on the invitation. The connection between this and v. 4 ("seek") indicates that the seeking is done in the sanctuary.

9 [w]Ps. 69:17; 102:2; 143:7 [x]See Ps. 24:5
10 [y][Isa. 49:15; 63:16] [z][Isa. 40:11]
11 [a]See Ps. 25:4 [b][Ps. 5:8]
12 [c]Ps. 41:2 [d]Ps. 35:11; [1 Kgs. 21:13; Matt. 26:59, 60; Mark 14:55, 56] [e]Acts 9:1
13 [f]Ex. 33:19 [g]Ps. 52:5; 116:9; 142:5; Job 28:13
14 [h]Ps. 37:34; 62:5; Prov. 20:22 [i]Ps. 31:24; Deut. 31:7; Josh. 1:6, 9, 18

Psalm 28

1 [j]See Ps. 18:2 [k]Ps. 35:22; 39:12; 83:1; 109:1 [l]Ps. 88:4; 143:7
2 [m]Ps. 140:6 [n]Ps. 134:2; 141:2; Lam. 2:19; 1 Tim. 2:8; [Ps. 119:48] [o]Ps. 5:7; 138:2; [1 Kgs. 8:29]
3 [p][Ps. 26:9; Ezek. 32:20] [q]Jer. 9:8; [Ps. 5:9; 12:2; 55:21; 62:4]

My heart says to you,
"Your face, LORD, do I seek."[1]
9 [w]Hide not your face from me.
Turn not your servant away in anger,
O you who have been my help.
Cast me not off; forsake me not,
[x]O God of my salvation!
10 For [y]my father and my mother have forsaken me,
but the LORD will [z]take me in.

11 [a]Teach me your way, O LORD,
and lead me on [b]a level path
because of my enemies.
12 [c]Give me not up to the will of my adversaries;
for [d]false witnesses have risen against me,
and they [e]breathe out violence.

13 I believe[2] that I shall look upon [f]the goodness of the LORD
in [g]the land of the living!
14 [h]Wait for the LORD;
[i]be strong, and let your heart take courage;
wait for the LORD!

The LORD Is My Strength and My Shield

28 OF DAVID.

1 To you, O LORD, I call;
[j]my rock, be not deaf to me,
lest, if you [k]be silent to me,
I become like those who [l]go down to the pit.
2 [m]Hear the voice of my pleas for mercy,
when I cry to you for help,
when I [n]lift up my hands
[o]toward your most holy sanctuary.[3]

3 Do not [p]drag me off with the wicked,
with the workers of evil,
[q]who speak peace with their neighbors
while evil is in their hearts.

[1] The meaning of the Hebrew verse is uncertain [2] Other Hebrew manuscripts *Oh! Had I not believed* [3] Hebrew *your innermost sanctuary*

27:11 Teach . . . lead. On guidance in the psalms, see note on 25:4–5.

27:13–14 *Wait for the Lord.* The singing worshiper addresses each of the other worshipers, with the admonition to live in continued confidence, returning to the trust expressed in vv. 1–3.

27:13 As the ESV footnote explains, other Hebrew manuscripts start the verse with an extra word; either way, the import is that the singer has believed. **Look upon** is similar to "gaze upon" (v. 4) and carries the same nuance of admiration and affection. The **goodness of the LORD** is probably his gracious character (Ex. 33:19; 34:6–7), thus these verses carry the expectation that the prayer of Ps. 27:4–6, for ready access to worship, will be answered. On the **land of the living** as this life's arena, cf. Isa. 38:11; 53:8; Jer. 11:19.

27:14 To **wait for the LORD** is to look to him with dependence and trust, not passivity; this is what enables one to **be strong** and courageous (cf. Deut. 31:6).

Psalm 28. This is a lament, a cry for help amid the threat posed by evildoers. It is not clear whether the threat is to the individual or to the whole community; if the speaker is a representative figure like King David, he could be speaking both for himself and for the community. It is probably best to see the hostility as a threat to the whole community (vv. 8–9), which each of the faithful is personally involved in (the references to "I," "me," and "my" throughout).

28:1–2 *Hear Me When I Call!* This model prayer brings its requests before God with urgency. The situation is desperate; to be **like those who go down to the pit** is probably more than simply to die, but to be like those who suffer divine judgment (cf. 30:3, 9; 88:4; 143:7; Isa. 14:19; Ezek. 26:20); the godly do not want to be treated in the same way as the wicked (cf. Ps. 28:3).

28:2 most holy sanctuary. This is the "innermost sanctuary" (see ESV footnote), the place mentioned in 1 Kings 6:16.

28:3–5 *Do Not Drag Me Off with the Wicked.* The psalms generally recognize that God will indeed hold the wicked (i.e., those who defy the Lord) accountable for their deeds. The pious wish to see God's justice vindicated, when those who defy his rule receive their due, and they do not want to suffer when the judgment falls (cf. 2 Thess. 1:9–10). The **wicked** here are not simply people who commit sins (even the faithful do that, cf. Ps. 32:6), but those who oppose God and his people with deceit and treachery (**evil is in their hearts**). Note the contrast between **their work** (i.e., of the wicked) and **the work of their hands** (28:4), and God's **works** and **the work of his hands** (v. 5).

4 [r]Give to them according to their work
and according to the evil of their deeds;
give to them according to the work of their hands;
[s]render them their due reward.
5 Because they [t]do not regard the works of the LORD
or the work of his hands,
he will tear them down and build them up no more.

6 Blessed be the LORD!
For he has [u]heard the voice of my pleas for mercy.
7 The LORD is my strength and [v]my shield;
in him my heart [w]trusts, and I am helped;
my heart exults,
and with my [x]song I give thanks to him.

8 The LORD is the strength of his people;[1]
he is [y]the saving refuge of his anointed.
9 Oh, save your people and bless [z]your heritage!
[a]Be their shepherd and [b]carry them forever.

Ascribe to the LORD Glory

29

A PSALM OF DAVID.

1 Ascribe to the LORD, O heavenly beings,[2]
[c]ascribe to the LORD glory and strength.
2 Ascribe to the LORD the glory due his name;
worship the LORD in [d]the splendor of holiness.[3]

3 The voice of the LORD is over [e]the waters;
the God of glory [f]thunders,
the LORD, over many waters.
4 The voice of the LORD is [g]powerful;
the voice of the LORD is full of majesty.

5 The voice of the LORD breaks the cedars;
the LORD breaks [h]the cedars of Lebanon.
6 He makes Lebanon to [i]skip like a calf,
and [j]Sirion like a young [k]wild ox.

7 The voice of the LORD flashes forth flames of fire.
8 The voice of the LORD shakes the wilderness;
the LORD shakes the wilderness of [l]Kadesh.

4 [r]Jer. 50:15, 29; Rev. 18:6; [2 Tim. 4:14] [s][Ps. 137:8]
5 [t]Isa. 5:12; [Job 34:27]
6 [u]ver. 2
7 [v]See Ps. 3:3 [w]See Ps. 11:1 [x]Ps. 69:30
8 [y]Ps. 140:7; [Ps. 20:6]
9 [z]Deut. 9:29; 32:9 [a]Ps. 78:71, 72 [b]Isa. 40:11; 46:3; 63:9

Psalm 29

1 [c]Ps. 96:7, 8; 1 Chr. 16:28, 29; [Ps. 68:34]
2 [d]Ps. 110:3; 1 Chr. 16:29; [Ex. 28:2]
3 [e][Ps. 18:11] [f]Job 37:4, 5
4 [g]Ps. 68:33
5 [h]Ps. 104:16; Judg. 9:15
6 [i]Ps. 114:4, 6 [j]Deut. 3:9 [k]Num. 23:22
8 [l]Num. 13:26

[1] Some Hebrew manuscripts, Septuagint, Syriac; most Hebrew manuscripts *is their strength* [2] Hebrew *sons of God, or sons of might* [3] Or *in holy attire*

28:6–9 *The Lord Has Heard Me.* The psalm ends with confidence that God will protect his **people** and his **anointed** (i.e., the Davidic king, who represents and embodies the whole people, cf. 2:8). This leads to prayer for God to **save** them and to **bless** his **heritage** (cf. Deut. 4:20; 9:26, 29; 32:9). On God as **shepherd**, see note on Ps. 23:1.

Psalm 29. This is a hymn of praise to God for his awesome power, where a thunderstorm serves as a visible emblem of God's majestic voice. It was once common to think that this psalm was based on a Canaanite or Phoenician original, but the evidence for this is poor. It seems reasonable, however, to suppose that the setting of the psalm in a thunderstorm deliberately sets Yahweh over Baal, the storm-god widely worshiped in Syria-Palestine. Biblical authors do not present the phenomena of nature in themselves as problems; they are God's creation, serve his purposes, and demonstrate his power, wisdom, glory, faithfulness, and even love.

29:1–2 *Call to Ascribe Glory to the Lord.* The psalm begins by urging the **heavenly beings** or angels (cf. ESV footnote, lit., "sons of God"; cf. 89:6) to **ascribe to the LORD glory and strength**, i.e., to acknowledge that these are true of God, and that he deserves admiration for them. **in the splendor of holiness**. As the ESV footnote explains, the Hebrew expression can be taken in more than one way; but the ESV text is more likely implying "for the splendor of God's holiness" (cf. 96:9; 1 Chron. 16:29).

29:3–9 *The Voice of the Lord in a Thunderstorm.* In these verses there are six descriptions of the **voice of the LORD**, of which the thunderstorm is an emblem. The reader should imagine a magnificent storm coming eastward from the Mediterranean, making landfall to the north in the mountains of **Lebanon**, and heading south to sweep through Israel, from **Sirion** (i.e., Mount Hermon, Deut. 3:9) in the northern end to **Kadesh** at the southern end. The faithful, worshiping in the **temple** in Jerusalem, see the awesome power of the storm and from it know that the **voice of the LORD** is even more **powerful**, and even more **full of majesty**; hence their responsive cry, **Glory!**

9[m][Job 39:1-3]
10[n][Gen. 6:17] [o]Ps. 10:16
11[p]Ps. 68:35; [Isa. 40:29] [q]Phil. 4:7

Psalm 30
[r]2 Sam. 5:11; 1 Chr. 22:1
1[s]Ps. 107:32 [t]Ps. 25:2; 35:19, 24; [Ps. 13:4]
2[u]Ps. 88:13 [v]See Ps. 6:2
3[w]See Ps. 16:10 [x]Ps. 28:1
4[y]Ps. 50:5 [z]Ps. 97:12; [1 Chr. 16:4]
5[a][Ps. 103:9; Job 33:26; Isa. 26:20; 54:7, 8] [b]Ps. 63:3 [c][2 Cor. 4:17, 18] [d]Ps. 126:5 (Heb.)
6[e][Job 29:18; Prov. 1:32] [f]Ps. 10:6
7[g][2 Sam. 5:9] [h]Ps. 104:29; [Deut. 31:17] [i][2 Sam. 24:10]
8[j]Ps. 142:1

9 The voice of the LORD makes [m]the deer give birth[1]
and strips the forests bare,
and in his temple all cry, "Glory!"

10 The LORD sits enthroned over [n]the flood;
the LORD sits enthroned [o]as king forever.
11 May the LORD give [p]strength to his people!
May the LORD bless[2] his people with [q]peace!

Joy Comes with the Morning

30

A PSALM OF DAVID. A SONG AT THE DEDICATION OF [r]THE TEMPLE.

1 I will [s]extol you, O LORD, for you have drawn me up
and have not let my foes [t]rejoice over me.
2 O LORD my God, I [u]cried to you for help,
and you have [v]healed me.
3 O LORD, you have brought up my soul from [w]Sheol;
you restored me to life from among those who [x]go down to the pit.[3]

4 Sing praises to the LORD, O you [y]his saints,
and [z]give thanks to his holy name.[4]
5 [a]For his anger is but for a moment,
and [b]his favor is for a lifetime.[5]
[c]Weeping may tarry for the night,
but [d]joy comes with the morning.

6 As for me, I said in my [e]prosperity,
"I shall never be [f]moved."
7 By your favor, O LORD,
you made my [g]mountain stand strong;
you [h]hid your face;
I was [i]dismayed.

8 To you, O LORD, I cry,
and [j]to the Lord I plead for mercy:
9 "What profit is there in my death,[6]
if I go down to the pit?[7]

[1] Revocalization yields *makes the oaks to shake* [2] Or *The LORD will give . . . The LORD will bless* [3] Or *to life, that I should not go down to the pit* [4] Hebrew *to the memorial of his holiness* (see Exodus 3:15) [5] Or *and in his favor is life* [6] Hebrew *in my blood* [7] Or *to corruption*

29:10–11 *The Lord Enthroned.* The temple (v. 9) is the place where God **sits enthroned** (9:11; 22:3; 1 Sam. 4:4; 2 Sam. 6:2) as **king forever**, especially over his people; worship is coming into his majestic presence. The word for **flood** here (Hb. *mabbul*) is used elsewhere only of Noah's flood (Gen. 6:17); this shows that God's power (unlike that of the storm) makes distinctions between the faithful and the unfaithful; hence the prayer that God will **give strength** (cf. Ps. 29:1) **to his people** and **bless his people with peace**—which requires that they be true to him always.

Psalm 30. According to the title, David composed Psalm 30 for the dedication of the temple (an event that took place after David died, 1 Kings 8:63). The temple does not figure much in the psalm itself, except for the address to fellow worshipers in Ps. 30:4. The theme of the whole psalm is one of personal thanksgiving for God's repeated care and deliverance over the course of a life; the title makes the concrete situation of David's experience the background, and the worshipers can liken their own experiences to his.

30:1–3 *Reasons Why I Will Extol.* The opening phrase, **I will extol you**, is followed by three experiences that lead the singer to extol God: deliverance from the attacks of the **foes**, answered prayer in desperate circumstances, and rescue from impending death. The mention of **Sheol** and **the pit** in v. 3 probably indicates that the threatened death would have been death under divine judgment (cf. 28:1).

30:4–5 *Joy Comes with the Morning.* After stating his own intention to extol the Lord, the singer turns to his fellow worshipers and urges them to join him, to **sing praises** and **give thanks**. Though there is indeed **weeping** in the lives of the faithful (sometimes because their misdeeds have incurred God's **anger**, and sometimes just because of suffering that comes from living in a fallen world), it comes to an end. **Morning** stands for the time when God gives relief (cf. 90:14); it might not arrive until the last day (cf. 49:14), but it will surely come.

30:6–7 *You Alone Are My Security.* It is easy, in times of **prosperity**, for God's people to trust in themselves for continued well-being; but they must always remember that it is God who makes one's **mountain stand strong** (a figure for unshakable security), and if he should remove his care, the faithful are undone.

30:8–10 *My Cry to the Lord.* After recording one thing he had said (v. 6), David moves on to another recollection: he had been in desperate circumstances and prayed for continued life. It is clear from v. 9 that the mere prolonging of earthly days is not the goal of these deliverances, precious as that is: the faithful live to **praise** God, to **tell of** his **faithfulness**. The books of Samuel recount many instances of just this in the life of David; the psalm expects the worshipers to reflect on the events of their own lives, and to renew their own intention to live well.

Will [k]the dust praise you?
Will it tell of your faithfulness?
10 [l]Hear, O LORD, and be merciful to me!
O LORD, be my helper!"

11 You have turned for me my mourning into [m]dancing;
you have loosed my sackcloth
and clothed me with gladness,
12 that my [n]glory may sing your praise and not be silent.
O LORD my God, I will give thanks to you forever!

Into Your Hand I Commit My Spirit

31

TO THE CHOIRMASTER. A PSALM OF DAVID.

1 [o]In you, O LORD, do I [p]take refuge;
[q]let me never be put to shame;
in your [r]righteousness deliver me!
2 Incline your ear to me;
rescue me speedily!
Be [s]a rock of [t]refuge for me,
a strong fortress to save me!

3 For you are my rock and my fortress;
and for your [u]name's sake you lead me and guide me;
4 you [v]take me out of [w]the net they have hidden for me,
for you are my [x]refuge.
5 [y]Into your hand I commit my spirit;
you have redeemed me, O LORD, [z]faithful God.

6 I [a]hate[1] those who pay [b]regard to worthless [c]idols,
but I trust in the LORD.
7 I will rejoice and be glad in your steadfast love,
because you have seen my affliction;
you have [d]known the distress of my soul,
8 and you have not [e]delivered me into the hand of the enemy;
you have set my feet in [f]a broad place.

9 Be gracious to me, O LORD, for I am [g]in distress;
[h]my eye is wasted from grief;
my soul and my body also.
10 For my life is spent with sorrow,
and my years with sighing;

[1] Masoretic Text; one Hebrew manuscript, Septuagint, Syriac, Jerome *You hate*

9 [k]See Ps. 6:5
10 [l]Ps. 27:7
11 [m]Ex. 15:20; 2 Sam. 6:14; Jer. 31:4, 13; [Ps. 149:3; 150:4; Lam. 5:15]
12 [n]See Ps. 16:9

Psalm 31

1 [o]For ver. 1-3, see Ps. 71:1-3 [p]See Ps. 11:1 [q]ver. 17 [r]Ps. 143:1
2 [s]See Ps. 18:2 [t][Ps. 91:2]
3 [u]See Ps. 23:3
4 [v]Ps. 25:15 [w]See Job 18:8 [x]Ps. 43:2
5 [y]Cited Luke 23:46; [Acts 7:59] [z]Deut. 32:4
6 [a]Ps. 26:5 [b]Jonah 2:8 [c]Deut. 32:21; Jer. 8:19; 14:22
7 [d]See Ps. 1:6
8 [e][Deut. 32:30] [f]See Job 36:16
9 [g]Ps. 66:14 [h]See Ps. 6:7

30:11–12 *I Will Give Thanks Forever.* The experiences in which sorrow has turned to joy lead the psalmist, and all who worship with him, to expect to **sing** God's **praise** and **give** him **thanks** (cf. v. 4) forever. **My glory** is a poetical term in the Psalms for one's whole being (cf. 16:9; 108:1).

Psalm 31. This is a lament that seeks help from God for a faithful person worn out with trouble and beset by enemies who want to do him harm (vv. 4, 8, 11, 13, 15, 18, 20). It is not hard to connect many of the particulars with the life of David, the author; but the wording is general enough for all kinds of people to find themselves in this prayer.

31:1–2 *Hear My Prayer.* The opening words, **I take refuge**, exhibit dependence and trust (cf. 5:11; 16:1; 25:20); this is the kind of person who may seek God's help. On **be put to shame**, see note on 25:2–3. God's **righteousness** here is his faithfulness to his promises; it is grounds for assurance, not for fear. The images of **rock** and **fortress**, using several different words, are common ways of describing God. Psalm 71:1–3 is very similar.

31:3–8 *You Have Always Kept Me Safe in the Past.* The psalm recounts previous experiences of calling for help in time of trouble. God has shown himself a reliable deliverer; thus the singer expects always to **rejoice and be glad** (v. 7).

31:5 Into your hand I commit my spirit. Jesus uses these words on the cross (Luke 23:46); he dies as the innocent sufferer, trusting in God for vindication (cf. note on Psalm 22). On **redeemed**, see note on 25:22.

31:6 I hate. A strong term, stressing the decisive way in which the faithful reject all sympathy with the wicked. It is possible for God to "hate" those who oppose him (5:5; 11:5), and at the same time to be "good" (or kind) to all (145:9); therefore, it must be desirable for the faithful to do the same.

31:9–13 *I Am in Distress Again.* After looking back over the past, the song turns to the present, a situation of **distress**. There is **grief**, **sorrow**, and **sighing** (vv. 9–10) because of the **adversaries** (v. 11) who **plot to take my life** (v. 13).

31:10 because of my iniquity. This interprets the distress as God's chastise-

my strength fails because of my iniquity,
  and [i]my bones waste away.

11 Because of all my adversaries I have become [j]a reproach,
  especially to my [k]neighbors,
and an object of dread to my acquaintances;
  those who see me in the street [l]flee from me.
12 I have been [m]forgotten like one who is dead;
  I have become like [n]a broken vessel.
13 For I [o]hear the whispering of many—
  terror on every side!—
[p]as they scheme together against me,
  as they plot to take my life.

14 But I [q]trust in you, O LORD;
  I say, "You are my God."
15 My [r]times are in your hand;
  [s]rescue me from the hand of my enemies and from my persecutors!
16 [t]Make your face shine on your servant;
  save me in your steadfast love!
17 O LORD, [u]let me not be put to shame,
  for I call upon you;
let the wicked be put to shame;
  let them go [v]silently to Sheol.
18 Let the lying lips be mute,
  which [w]speak [x]insolently against the righteous
  in pride and contempt.

19 Oh, how abundant is your goodness,
  which you have stored up for those who fear you
and worked for those who take refuge in you,
  [y]in the sight of the children of mankind!
20 In [z]the cover of your presence you hide them
  from the plots of men;
you [a]store them in your shelter
  from the strife of tongues.

21 Blessed be the LORD,
  for he has wondrously [b]shown his steadfast love to me
  when I was in [c]a besieged city.
22 I had said in my [d]alarm,[1]
  "I am [e]cut off from [f]your sight."
But you heard the voice of my pleas for mercy
  when I cried to you for help.
23 Love the LORD, all you his [g]saints!
  The LORD preserves the faithful
  but abundantly [h]repays the one who acts in pride.
24 [i]Be strong, and let your heart take courage,
  all you who wait for the LORD!

10 [i]Ps. 6:2; 32:3; 38:3; 102:3
11 [j][Ps. 41:7, 8; Isa. 53:3] [k]See Job 19:13, 14 [l][Matt. 26:56; Mark 14:50]
12 [m]Ps. 88:5; Eccles. 9:5 [n]Isa. 30:14
13 [o]Jer. 20:10 [p][Matt. 27:1]; See 2 Sam. 17:1-4
14 [q]ver. 1, 6
15 [r]1 Chr. 29:30; Job 24:1 [s]Ps. 7:1
16 [t]See Ps. 4:6
17 [u]ver. 1 [v]1 Sam. 2:9; [Ps. 94:17; 115:17]
18 [w][Jude 15] [x]Ps. 17:10
19 [y]Ps. 23:5
20 [z]See Ps. 32:7 [a]See Ps. 27:5
21 [b]Ps. 17:7 [c][1 Sam. 23:7]
22 [d]Ps. 116:11; [2 Sam. 15:14] [e]Isa. 38:11, 12; Lam. 3:54 [f]Jonah 2:4
23 [g]Ps. 30:4 [h]Deut. 32:41
24 [i]See Ps. 27:14

[1] Or *in my haste*

ment; but if it is that, then the purposes of God (and not of the evildoers) will prevail.

31:14–18 *My Times Are in Your Hand.* This section expresses **trust** in the Lord amid the present distress. This trust is built not only on the experiences recounted in vv. 3–8 but also on the promises of the covenant: e.g., for **make your face shine** (v. 16), cf. Num. 6:25. On **Sheol** (Ps. 31:17), see note on 6:5. As usual in the Psalms, people are designated by their stance toward God: the **righteous** (31:18) are those who trust in God, believe his word, and seek to please him; the **wicked** (v. 17), who are commonly everyone else besides the "righteous," are here those who seek to destroy the faithful.

31:19–24 *Confidence that the Lord Will Again Keep Me Safe.* The psalm closes with assurance: the God who has made promises and who has kept them in the past will continue to do so. On v. 24, cf. 27:14.

Blessed Are the Forgiven

32

A Maskil[1] of David.

1 [j]Blessed is the one whose [k]transgression is forgiven,
whose sin is covered.
2 Blessed is the man against whom the LORD [l]counts no iniquity,
and in whose spirit [m]there is no deceit.

3 For when I kept silent, my [n]bones wasted away
through my [o]groaning all day long.
4 For day and night your [p]hand was heavy upon me;
my strength was dried up[2] as by the heat of summer. *Selah*

5 I [q]acknowledged my sin to you,
and I did not cover my iniquity;
I said, "I [r]will confess my transgressions to the LORD,"
and you forgave the iniquity of my sin. *Selah*

6 Therefore let everyone who is [s]godly
offer prayer to you at a time when you [t]may be found;
surely in the rush of [u]great waters,
they shall not reach him.
7 You are a [v]hiding place for me;
you preserve me from [w]trouble;
you surround me with [x]shouts of deliverance. *Selah*

8 I will [y]instruct you and teach you in the way you should go;
I will [z]counsel you with my eye upon you.
9 [a]Be not like a horse or a mule, without understanding,
which must be curbed with [b]bit and bridle,
or it will not stay near you.

10 [c]Many are the sorrows of the wicked,
but steadfast love surrounds the one who [d]trusts in the LORD.
11 [e]Be glad in the LORD, and rejoice, O righteous,
and [f]shout for joy, all you [g]upright in heart!

[1] Probably a musical or liturgical term [2] Hebrew *my vitality was changed*

Psalm 32
1 [j]Cited Rom. 4:7, 8; [Ps. 85:2] [k][Ex. 34:7; John 1:29]
2 [l][2 Cor. 5:19] [m]John 1:47
3 [n]See Ps. 31:10 [o]See Ps. 22:1
4 [p]1 Sam. 5:6, 11; [Ps. 38:2]
5 [q]Ps. 51:3 [r]Ps. 38:18; Job 33:27; Prov. 28:13; [Luke 15:18, 21; 1 John 1:9]
6 [s]Ps. 30:4 [t]See Ps. 69:13 [u][Ps. 18:4, 16; 42:7; 69:1; 144:7]; See Job 22:11
7 [v]Ps. 91:1; 119:114; [Ps. 27:5; 31:20] [w]Ps. 9:9 [x][Ps. 18, title]; See Ex. 15:1-18; Judg. 5:1-31
8 [y]Ps. 25:8, 12 [z]Ps. 73:24
9 [a]Prov. 26:3; [Job 35:11] [b]James 3:3
10 [c][Prov. 13:21; Rom. 2:9] [d]Ps. 34:8; 84:12; Prov. 16:20; Jer. 17:7
11 [e]Ps. 64:10; 68:3; 97:12; [Ps. 33:1] [f]Deut. 32:43 [g]See Ps. 7:10

Psalm 32. This is usually classified as a thanksgiving hymn, in which the worshipers give thanks to God for the joy of having their sins forgiven. Because of v. 3 ("when I kept silent"), it has been common to connect this psalm with Psalm 51; but as there is no clear indication of this from either the title of the psalm or its body, it is better to take this psalm as geared more generally to the experience of confession and forgiveness. Psalm 32 can be classified as a "penitential psalm" (cf. Psalms 6; 38 [and note]; 51; 130; 143).

32:1–5 *The Doctrine: Only the Forgiven Are Truly Happy.* Verses 1–2 state the theme, answering the question, "Who is truly happy (or blessed)?" Then vv. 3–5 recount a personal experience that supports this theme. The terms "transgression," "forgiven," "sin," and "iniquity" all echo Ex. 34:6–7, the fundamental expression of God's kindness and mercy toward those who receive his covenant. No one needs to compel God to show mercy; rather, the faithful confess their sins because they believe he *is* merciful. Note how several words here appear in a mirror pattern, which binds all five verses together: "forgiven . . . covered [Ps. 32:1] . . . cover . . . forgave [v. 5]." There is a contrast in the kind of covering: when God "covers" sin, he graciously blots it out (cf. 85:2); when man "covers" his sin, he is sinfully hiding it (cf. Prov. 28:13).

32:1–2 On **blessed**, see note on 1:1. Paul uses 32:1–2a in Rom. 4:7–8 to show that "not counting sin" (which he treats as another way of counting righteousness) has always been done "apart from works." **Deceit** refers to deceiving man or God about one's own sins. To mention the **spirit** reinforces in the worshipers that they must combine the right words with the right intentions.

32:3–5 For. These verses support the theme that only the forgiven are truly happy. They recount a time **when I kept silent**, i.e., when the singer refused to confess his sins in order to have God forgive them. The lost vitality of vv. 3–4 is really a mercy; it is God's **hand . . . heavy upon** his faithful, to help them come to the point of confessing. Having come to that point, the singer **acknowledged** his sin, and God **forgave the iniquity of** his **sin**; this brings the psalm back to v. 1, with the implication that the singer has now learned more fully the blessedness of being forgiven.

32:6–11 *Application: Confess Our Sins Freely.* The opening word of this section, **therefore**, shows that it is drawing a lesson for **everyone who is godly**, namely, to **offer prayer** (of confession) **. . . at a time when** God **may be found**; i.e., do not be foolish and wait indefinitely (cf. v. 9). The godly are not expected to be sinless; rather, they are those who believe God's promises and confess their sins (similarly the **righteous**, v. 11). Verses 6–7 are addressed to God, whom the faithful find to be a **hiding place**; vv. 8–11 are addressed to fellow worshipers, urging them to accept this instruction about ready confession and to **be glad** in the Lord, who shows such goodness to his people.

33

The Steadfast Love of the Lord

1 [h]Shout for joy in the LORD, O you righteous!
[i]Praise befits the upright.
2 Give thanks to the LORD with the [j]lyre;
make melody to him with [j]the harp of [k]ten strings!
3 Sing to him [l]a new song;
play skillfully on the strings, with loud shouts.

4 For the word of the LORD is upright,
and all his work is done in [m]faithfulness.
5 He [n]loves righteousness and justice;
[o]the earth is full of the steadfast love of the LORD.

6 By [p]the word of the LORD the heavens were made,
and by [q]the breath of his mouth all [r]their host.
7 He gathers the waters of the sea as [s]a heap;
he [t]puts the deeps in storehouses.

8 Let all the earth fear the LORD;
let all the inhabitants of the world stand in awe of him!
9 For [u]he spoke, and it came to be;
he commanded, and it stood firm.

10 The LORD [v]brings the counsel of the nations to nothing;
he frustrates the plans of the peoples.
11 [w]The counsel of the LORD stands forever,
the plans of his heart to all generations.
12 [x]Blessed is the nation whose God is the LORD,
the people whom he has [y]chosen as his heritage!

13 The LORD [z]looks down from heaven;
he sees all the children of man;
14 from [a]where he sits enthroned he [b]looks out
on all the inhabitants of the earth,
15 he who fashions the hearts of them all
and observes all their deeds.
16 [c]The king is not saved by his great army;
a warrior is not delivered by his great strength.
17 [d]The war horse is a false hope for salvation,
and by its great might it cannot rescue.

Psalm 33
1[h][Ps. 32:11] [i]Ps. 147:1
2[j]Ps. 71:22 [k]Ps. 144:9
3[l]Ps. 40:3; 96:1; Isa. 42:10
4[m]Ps. 119:75
5[n]Ps. 11:7; 36:5, 6; 45:7; 89:14 [o]Ps. 119:64
6[p]Gen. 1:6, 7; Heb. 11:3; 2 Pet. 3:5; [John 1:3] [q][Job 26:13; Isa. 11:4] [r]Gen. 2:1
7[s]Ps. 78:13; Ex. 15:8; Josh. 3:13, 16 [t]See Job 38:8
9[u]Ps. 148:5, 6; Gen. 1:3; [Ps. 147:15, 18]
10[v]Isa. 19:3; Luke 1:51; [2 Sam. 15:34; 17:14; Neh. 4:15; Job 5:12; Isa. 8:10]
11[w]Prov. 19:21; Isa. 46:10
12[x]Ps. 144:15; Deut. 33:29 [y]Ps. 65:4; Deut. 7:6; [Ex. 19:5]
13[z]Job 28:24; See Ps. 11:4
14[a]1 Kgs. 8:39, 43, 49 [b][Prov. 15:3; Jer. 32:19]
16[c][Ps. 44:6]
17[d]Ps. 20:7; 147:10; Prov. 21:31; Hos. 1:7

Psalm 33. This is a hymn of praise to the God who made all things, who rules all things for his own purposes, and who has chosen a people to be his own for the sake of the whole world. The texts in Genesis that convey these notions underlie the psalm's ideas. The thought flows from the call to praise God, to several reasons for praise, to a closing filled with glad and peaceful hope.

33:1–3 *Call to Sing Praise.* The opening words of the psalm, **shout for joy** and **righteous**, echo 32:11, which may be why this psalm is placed here. Here, the righteous and the **upright** are the people of God, who have received his covenant and his steadfast love. The stringed instruments named here accompany this exuberant song of praise. **New song** (cf. 40:3; 96:1; 98:1; 144:9; 149:1; Isa. 42:10; Rev. 5:9; 14:3) need not imply a freshly composed song; instead it may mean singing this song as a response to a fresh experience of God's grace.

33:4–9 *Reason 1: God's Word Is Upright.* The first reason for this kind of praise is God's **word** (vv. 4, 6, 9): it is **upright**, expressing the very best of motives on God's part (vv. 4–5), and it is spoken by the same God who made everything (vv. 6–9). Verses 6–9 echo the creation account (Gen. 1:1–2:3), where each time God **spoke**, what he **commanded** produced its effect. The Septuagint Greek of Ps. 33:6, with the **word** (Gk. *logos*) as the means of creation, probably lies behind John 1:3; the Word came to be seen as a personal agent, whom John identifies as Christ himself (cf. John 1:14). Since the Lord is the Creator of everything, **all the earth** and **all the inhabitants of the world**, and not just Israel, should **fear** him (Ps. 33:8–9).

33:10–12 *Reason 2: God's Will Prevails.* The God who made the world also rules it according to his own purposes. In the creation account God's purposes always prevail; so it is after the creation: there is no power able to oppose God successfully, because all these powers derive their being and power from God. In view of such majesty, v. 12 stands out: God deserves the love of all mankind, and rules them, and yet there is one particular **people whom he has chosen as his heritage**, namely, Israel (see note on 28:6–9). It is clear from the call of Abram (Gen. 12:1–3) that Israel was called to be God's means by which the whole world would come to know him.

33:13–19 *Reason 3: God's Gaze Discerns All.* The Lord **sits enthroned** high over the earth, but that does not make him distant; rather, he is so great that he **observes all** the **deeds** of mankind. Further, his **eye . . . is on those who fear him**, to care for them as a people (v. 18) and as individuals (v. 19).

18 Behold, [e]the eye of the LORD is on those who fear him,
[f]on those who hope in his steadfast love,
19 that he may [g]deliver their soul from death
and keep them alive in [h]famine.

20 Our soul [i]waits for the LORD;
he is our [j]help and [k]our shield.
21 For our heart is [l]glad in him,
because we [m]trust in his holy name.
22 Let your steadfast love, O LORD, be upon us,
even as we hope in you.

Taste and See That the LORD Is Good

34

OF DAVID, WHEN HE [n]CHANGED HIS BEHAVIOR BEFORE [o]ABIMELECH, SO THAT HE DROVE HIM OUT, AND HE WENT AWAY.[1]

1 I will bless the LORD [p]at all times;
his praise shall continually be in my mouth.
2 My soul [q]makes its boast in the LORD;
let the humble hear and [r]be glad.
3 Oh, [s]magnify the LORD with me,
and let us exalt his name together!

4 I [t]sought the LORD, and he answered me
and delivered me from all my fears.
5 Those who look to him are [u]radiant,
and their faces shall never be ashamed.
6 [v]This poor man cried, and the LORD heard him
and [w]saved him out of all his troubles.
7 [x]The angel of the LORD [y]encamps
around those who fear him, and delivers them.

8 Oh, [z]taste and see that [a]the LORD is good!
[b]Blessed is the man who takes refuge in him!
9 Oh, fear the LORD, you his saints,
for those who fear him have no lack!

[1] This psalm is an acrostic poem, each verse beginning with the successive letters of the Hebrew alphabet

18 [e]Ps. 34:15; Job 36:7; 1 Pet. 3:12 [f]Ps. 147:11
19 [g][Acts 12:11] [h]Ps. 37:19; Job 5:20
20 [i]Ps. 62:1, 5; 130:6; Isa. 8:17 [j]Ps. 115:9-11 [k]See Ps. 3:3
21 [l]Zech. 10:7; See Ps. 9:14 [m]See Ps. 11:1

Psalm 34

[n]1 Sam. 21:13 [o][1 Sam. 21:10, 11, 12, 14]
1 [p][Eph. 5:20; 1 Thess. 5:18]
2 [q]Ps. 44:8; 1 Sam. 2:1; Jer. 9:24 [r]Ps. 119:74
3 [s]Ps. 35:27; 40:16; 69:30; 70:4; Luke 1:46
4 [t]2 Chr. 15:2; [Matt. 7:7]
5 [u]Isa. 60:5; [Ps. 4:6]
6 [v]ver. 15, 17 [w]ver. 17, 19; 2 Sam. 22:1
7 [x]Dan. 6:22; Heb. 1:14 [y][Gen. 32:1, 2; 2 Kgs. 6:17]
8 [z]Heb. 6:5; 1 Pet. 2:3 [a]Ps. 100:5 [b]See Ps. 2:12

33:20–22 *Therefore We Hope in God.* Each member of the faithful who sings this, and takes to heart the greatness and wonder of God, is enabled more and more to rest his soul on the Lord, confident that God's plans will succeed in the earth.

Psalm 34. This psalm is an expression of thanksgiving for God's protection and care for those who trust in him. There is also a "wisdom" section embedded in the thanksgiving (vv. 11–14); it is appropriate, because it is the "wise" (i.e., those who live out their trust in God) who have occasion to give such thanks. As the ESV footnote explains, the psalm follows an acrostic pattern (see note on Psalm 25). Like other Davidic acrostics, Psalm 34 is imperfect: the *w*-verse is missing (between vv. 5–6), and the last verse begins with *p* (cf. 25:22). The title connects the psalm to 1 Sam. 21:10–15, where David is delivered from danger by feigning madness in the presence of King Achish of Gath (1 Sam. 21:13, "he changed his behavior"). Probably the name "Abimelech" in the psalm is a title or alternate name for the king of Gath. This was a narrow escape, and David does not take credit for it; nor does he deny the importance of the faithful using their wits in desperate situations.

34:1–3 *Join Me in Blessing the Lord.* After announcing his intention to **bless the LORD at all times**, the singer invites all the **humble** to join him in song. Behind this lies the idea that the ideal praise to God is his assembled people joining their voices in thanking him. The idea behind "bless" is to speak a good word about someone: when God blesses someone (e.g., 29:11), he speaks a good word over that person for his well-being; when a human blesses God (e.g., 26:12), he speaks a good word about God's kindness and generosity (cf. Eph. 1:3). To **magnify the LORD** is to tell how great he is (cf. Luke 1:46).

34:4–7 *He Answered My Prayers.* The psalmist now moves to specific instances of God's kindness: he **sought the LORD** for help and he **cried** in his distress, and God rescued him from the things he feared. **ashamed** (v. 5). That is, disappointed at not finding what was hoped for.

34:8–14 *Therefore Fear the Lord with Me.* Now that the song has mentioned the humble (v. 2) and those who fear the Lord (v. 7), it moves on to encourage all who sing it to **fear the LORD** (v. 9), i.e., to revere him; and it seeks to teach them what it means to fear him (vv. 11–14). The verb **taste** (v. 8), which in the OT is commonly used in the literal sense, is a metaphor for personal experience; the NT uses the metaphor widely (e.g., John 8:52; Heb. 2:9; 6:4). The **saints** (Ps. 34:9), or holy ones, are those whom God has consecrated to himself, namely, his people. They should live holy lives in response to his kindness (Lev. 20:7–8). Observe how the holy life is distinguished by dealing well with others (Ps. 34:13–14). First Peter uses texts from this section: 1 Pet. 2:3, "you have tasted that the Lord is good," where "the Lord" is Jesus; 1 Pet. 3:10–12 uses Ps. 34:12–16 to summarize the ideal behavior and lifestyle for Christians.

10 [c]The young lions suffer want and hunger;
but those who [d]seek the LORD lack no good thing.

11 [e]Come, O children, listen to me;
[f]I will teach you the fear of the LORD.
12 [g]What man is there who desires life
and loves many days, that he may [h]see good?
13 [i]Keep your tongue from evil
and your lips from [j]speaking deceit.
14 [k]Turn away from evil and do good;
seek peace and [l]pursue it.

15 [m]The eyes of the LORD are toward the righteous
[n]and his ears toward their cry.
16 [o]The face of the LORD is against those who do evil,
to [p]cut off the memory of them from the earth.
17 [n]When the righteous cry for help, the LORD hears
and delivers them out of all their troubles.
18 The LORD is near to [q]the brokenhearted
and saves [r]the crushed in spirit.

19 [s]Many are the afflictions of the righteous,
[t]but the LORD delivers him out of them all.
20 He keeps all his bones;
[u]not one of them is broken.
21 [v]Affliction will slay the wicked,
and those who hate the righteous will be condemned.
22 The LORD [w]redeems the life of his servants;
none of those who take refuge in him will be [x]condemned.

Great Is the LORD

35

OF DAVID.

1 Contend, O LORD, with those who [y]contend with me;
[z]fight against those who fight against me!
2 Take hold of [a]shield and buckler
and rise for my help!
3 Draw the spear and javelin[1]
against my pursuers!
Say to my soul,
"I am your salvation!"

4 [b]Let them be [c]put to shame and dishonor
who seek after my life!

10[c]Job 4:10, 11 [d][Ps. 84:11]
11[e]Ps. 66:16 [f][Ps. 32:8]
12[g]Cited 1 Pet. 3:10-12 [h]Eccles. 3:13; 6:6
13[i]Ps. 15:3; 39:1; 141:3; Prov. 13:3; 21:23; James 1:26; 3:2; 1 Pet. 2:1, 22 [j]John 1:47; Rev. 14:5
14[k]Ps. 37:27; Isa. 1:16, 17; [Job 28:28] [l]Rom. 14:19; Heb. 12:14; [Rom. 12:18]
15[m]See Ps. 33:18 [n]ver. 6, 8; Ps. 145:18; [John 9:31]
16[o]Jer. 44:11; Amos 9:4 [p]See Ps. 21:10
17[n][See ver. 15 above]
18[q]Ps. 51:17; 147:3; Isa. 61:1 [r]Isa. 57:15; 66:2; See Luke 15:17-24
19[s]2 Tim. 3:11, 12 [t]ver. 6, 17, 22; [Acts 12:11]
20[u]John 19:36
21[v]Ps. 94:23; Prov. 24:16; [Ps. 7:15, 16]
22[w]See Ps. 25:22 [x][Rom. 8:33, 34]

Psalm 35

1[y]Isa. 49:25 [z][Ex. 14:25; Isa. 42:13]
2[a]Ps. 91:4; [Ps. 5:12]
4[b]For ver. 4-8, see Ps. 69:22-28; 109:6-15 [c]ver. 26; Ps. 40:14; 70:2; 71:13; 83:17

[1] *Or and close the way*

34:15–22 *The Lord Cares for Those Who Trust Him.* The final section speaks generally about how the Lord cares for his faithful ones—i.e., it does not recount specific instances as vv. 4–7 do. There is also a stress here on the difference between the way God treats the faithful and the wicked. The Hebrew expressions **brokenhearted** and **crushed in spirit** (v. 18) refer to the pride and stubbornness in one's heart being humbled (cf. 51:17; 69:20; 147:3). The psalm is clear that both the **righteous** and the **wicked** will have **afflictions** (see the repetition in 34:19, 21); the difference is in the outcomes (**none . . . condemned**, v. 22; and **condemned**, v. 21). It is possible that John 19:36 has combined Ps. 34:20 (**he keeps all his bones; not one of them is broken**) with Ex. 12:46 to emphasize that Jesus was not only the Passover Lamb but also a righteous sufferer whom God would vindicate. On **redeems**, see note on Ps. 25:22.

Psalm 35. This psalm shows how the faithful should pray when they know that malicious people are seeking to harm them. The prayer recounts the evil schemes of the persecutors and asks God to fight on behalf of his faithful one.

35:1–3 *Cry for Help against Pursuers.* In the imagery of combat, the psalm opens by asking God to take up the cause of the singer.

35:4–8 *Let Them Be Ashamed.* The faithful pray that the schemes of the pursuers would fail, and that the pursuers themselves would suffer disappointment and humiliation, and finally destruction. There are many reasons that such a prayer is proper for God's people to pray. First of all, it is realistic; God's protection of the faithful means that he must thwart the schemes of those who would harm them. Second, it is just, since the pursuers **devise evil** (v. 4), and **without cause they hid their net for me** (v. 7). (Observe the repetition of "without cause," in vv. 7, 19.) Third, it takes God at his word (cf. v. 5 with 1:4). Finally, from all of this it is plain that the prayer is not a vindictive response to personal injury but an appeal based on faith.

Let them be [d]turned back and disappointed
who devise evil against me!
5 Let them be like [e]chaff before the wind,
with the angel of the LORD driving them away!
6 Let their way be dark and [f]slippery,
with the angel of the LORD pursuing them!
7 For [g]without cause [h]they hid their net for me;
without cause they dug [i]a pit for my life.[1]
8 Let [j]destruction come upon him [k]when he does not know it!
And let the net that he hid ensnare him;
let him fall into it—to his destruction!

9 Then my soul will rejoice in the LORD,
[l]exulting in his salvation.
10 All my [m]bones shall say,
"O LORD, [n]who is like you,
delivering the poor
from him who is too strong for him,
the poor and needy from him who robs him?"

11 [o]Malicious[2] witnesses rise up;
they ask me of things that I do not know.
12 [p]They repay me evil for good;
my soul is bereft.[3]
13 But I, [q]when they were sick—
I [r]wore sackcloth;
I [s]afflicted myself with fasting;
I prayed [t]with head bowed[4] on my chest.
14 I went about as though I grieved for my friend or my brother;
as one who laments his mother,
I [u]bowed down in mourning.

15 But at my stumbling they rejoiced and gathered;
they gathered together against me;
[v]wretches whom I did not know
tore at me without ceasing;
16 like profane mockers at a feast,[5]
they [w]gnash at me with their teeth.

17 How long, O Lord, will you [x]look on?
Rescue me from their destruction,
[y]my precious life from the lions!
18 I will thank you in [z]the great congregation;
in the mighty throng I will praise you.

19 [a]Let not those rejoice over me
who are [b]wrongfully my foes,
and let not those [c]wink the eye
who [d]hate me [e]without cause.

4 [d]Ps. 129:5
5 [e]See Job 21:18
6 [f]Ps. 73:18; Jer. 23:12
7 [g]See Ps. 69:4 [h]See Job 18:8 [i]See Ps. 7:15
8 [j][1 Thess. 5:3] [k]Isa. 47:11
9 [l]Luke 1:47; See Ps. 9:14
10 [m]Ps. 51:8 [n]Ps. 71:19; 86:8; 89:6, 8; 113:5; Ex. 15:11
11 [o]See Ps. 27:12
12 [p]Ps. 38:20; 109:4; Jer. 18:20; [John 10:32]
13 [q][Job 30:25] [r]Ps. 69:11; [1 Kgs. 20:31] [s]Ps. 69:10; Num. 29:7 [t][Matt. 10:13]; Luke 10:6
14 [u]See Ps. 38:6
15 [v]Job 30:1, 8, 12
16 [w]Ps. 37:12; Job 16:9; Lam. 2:16
17 [x]Hab. 1:13 [y]Ps. 22:20
18 [z]Ps. 22:25
19 [a]ver. 24; See Ps. 13:4 [b]Ps. 38:19; 69:4; 119:78, 86 [c]Prov. 6:13; 10:10 [d]Ps. 69:4; Cited John 15:25 [e]ver. 7

[1] The word *pit* is transposed from the preceding line; Hebrew *For without cause they hid the pit of their net for me; without cause they dug for my life* [2] Or *Violent* [3] Hebrew *it is bereavement to my soul* [4] Or *my prayer shall turn back* [5] The meaning of the Hebrew phrase is uncertain

35:9–10 *Then I Shall Rejoice.* The song looks forward to joy and gratitude when its request is answered.

35:11–16 *They Repay Me Evil for Good.* The song returns to say more about the schemes of the pursuers: they **rise** as **malicious witnesses** (v. 11), and **they repay me evil for good**, especially in gloating over the misfortunes of those who have shown them kindness (vv. 12–16).

35:17–18 *How Long Will It Take?* The request is urgent, and waiting is hard.

35:19–21 *They Are Gloating Deceivers.* The song again tells more about the pursuers; they scheme (**wink the eye**), particularly against the hardworking pious (**those who are quiet in the land**). In John 15:25 Jesus uses Ps. 35:19, **hate me without cause** (cf. also 69:4), to portray himself as the quintessential innocent sufferer and to imply that his followers may expect the same treatment.

21[f] See Ps. 22:13 [g] ver. 25; Ps. 40:15; 70:3
22[h] [Ex. 3:7] [i] Ps. 28:1 [j] See Ps. 10:1
23[k] Ps. 44:23; 59:4; 80:2 [l] Ps. 7:6
24[m] Ps. 7:8 [n] ver. 19
25[o] ver. 21 [p] 2 Sam. 17:16; Lam. 2:16
26[q] See ver. 4 [r] See Job 8:22 [s] See Job 19:5
27[t] Ps. 40:16; 70:4 [u] Ps. 34:3 [v] Ps. 149:4
28[w] Ps. 51:14; 71:8, 15, 24

Psalm 36
[x] See Ps. 18, title
1[y] Cited Rom. 3:18
2[z] Deut. 29:19; [Ps. 10:3; 49:18]
3[a] [Ps. 12:2] [b] [Jer. 4:22]
4[c] Mic. 2:1; [Prov. 4:16] [d] Ps. 10:7 [e] Isa. 65:2 [f] [Ps. 97:10]

20 For they do not speak peace,
but against those who are quiet in the land
they devise words of deceit.
21 They [f] open wide their mouths against me;
they say, [g] "Aha, Aha!
Our eyes have seen it!"
22 [h] You have seen, O LORD; [i] be not silent!
O Lord, [j] be not far from me!
23 Awake and [k] rouse yourself for [l] my vindication,
for my cause, my God and my Lord!
24 [m] Vindicate me, O LORD, my God,
according to your righteousness,
and [n] let them not rejoice over me!
25 Let them not say in their hearts,
[o] "Aha, our heart's desire!"
Let them not say, [p] "We have swallowed him up."

26 Let them be [q] put to shame and disappointed altogether
who rejoice at my calamity!
Let them be [r] clothed with shame and dishonor
who [s] magnify themselves against me!

27 Let those who delight in my righteousness
shout for joy and be glad
[t] and say evermore,
[u] "Great is the LORD,
who [v] delights in the welfare of his servant!"
28 Then my [w] tongue shall tell of your righteousness
and of your praise all the day long.

How Precious Is Your Steadfast Love

36

TO THE CHOIRMASTER. OF DAVID, THE [x] SERVANT OF THE LORD.

1 Transgression speaks to the wicked
deep in his heart;[1]
[y] there is no fear of God
before his eyes.
2 [z] For he flatters himself in his own eyes
that his iniquity cannot be found out and hated.
3 The words of his mouth are [a] trouble and deceit;
[b] he has ceased to act wisely and do good.
4 He [c] plots [d] trouble while on his bed;
he sets himself in [e] a way that is not good;
[f] he does not reject evil.

[1] Some Hebrew manuscripts, Syriac, Jerome (compare Septuagint); most Hebrew manuscripts *in my heart*

35:22–26 *Vindicate Me!* Now the song returns to pray for vindication and deliverance. Verses 22–23 use vivid imagery, asking God to **be not silent** (as if he were complacent toward evil) and **awake and rouse yourself** (as if he were asleep); this shows how urgent the singer feels the situation to be. On **vindicate** (v. 24), see note on 26:1–3. God's **righteousness**, as often in the OT, is here his faithfulness in keeping his promises (also 35:28). Verse 26 is very similar to v. 4.

35:27–28 *Then I and Those Who Love Me Shall Rejoice.* The singer again looks forward to rejoicing, but this time not only his own but also that of all the faithful (**those who delight in my righteousness**). The high point is the prospect of telling all the faithful of God's faithfulness (v. 28; cf. vv. 9–10, 18).

Psalm 36. This is a lament that reflects on the wicked who oppose the faithful, and on the steadfast love of the Lord; it concludes with a prayer that God in his steadfast love will protect his people from the attacks of the wicked.

36:1–4 *The Wicked Act without Fear of God.* This stanza describes the **wicked** person, who has **no fear of God before his eyes** and who pursues evil courses, as one who particularly schemes to bring trouble to others (esp. to the godly). "Wicked" here, as generally in the Psalms, does not describe faithful people who have moral flaws; it describes those given over to doing evil (even if they are nominally within the covenant people), as these verses make clear. Paul uses v. 1b in Rom. 3:18 as part of his charge that both Jews and Gentiles are under sin.

5 Your steadfast love, O LORD, extends to the heavens,
your faithfulness to the clouds.
6 [g]Your righteousness is like the mountains of God;
[h]your judgments are like the great deep;
man and beast you [i]save, O LORD.
7 [j]How precious is your steadfast love, O God!
The children of mankind take refuge [k]in the shadow of your wings.
8 They feast on [l]the abundance of your house,
and you give them drink from [m]the river of [n]your delights.
9 For with you is [o]the fountain of life;
[p]in your light do we see light.
10 Oh, continue your steadfast love to those who [q]know you,
and your righteousness to [r]the upright of heart!
11 Let not the foot of arrogance come upon me,
nor the hand of the wicked drive me away.
12 There [s]the evildoers lie fallen;
they are thrust down, [t]unable to rise.

He Will Not Forsake His Saints

37[1]

OF DAVID.

1 [u]Fret not yourself because of evildoers;
be not [v]envious of wrongdoers!
2 For they will soon [w]fade like [x]the grass
and wither [y]like the green herb.
3 [z]Trust in the LORD, and do good;
[a]dwell in the land and befriend faithfulness.[2]
4 [b]Delight yourself in the LORD,
and he will [c]give you the desires of your heart.

6 [g][Ps. 71:19] [h]Ps. 92:5; Rom. 11:33 [i]Ps. 104:14, 15; 145:9, 15, 16; Neh. 9:6
7 [j][Ps. 31:19] [k]See Ruth 2:12
8 [l]Ps. 23:5; 27:4; 65:4; Isa. 25:6; See Jer. 31:12-14 [m]Ps. 46:4; Rev. 22:1 [n]Ps. 16:11
9 [o]Jer. 2:13; John 4:10, 14; 5:26 [p]John 1:9; Acts 26:18; 1 Pet. 2:9
10 [q]Jer. 22:16; Gal. 4:9; [Ps. 79:6] [r]See Ps. 7:10
12 [s]Ps. 94:4 [t]See Ps. 1:5

Psalm 37

1 [u]ver. 7, 8; Prov. 24:19 [v]Ps. 73:3; Prov. 3:31; 23:17; 24:1, 19
2 [w]Job 14:2; See Job 27:13-23 [x]Ps. 90:5, 6 [y]Ps. 129:6
3 [z]Ps. 62:8; 115:9-11; Prov. 3:5; Isa. 26:4 [a]Lev. 26:5; Prov. 2:21
4 [b]Job 22:26; Isa. 58:14; [Phil. 3:1; 4:4] [c]Matt. 6:33

[1] This psalm is an acrostic poem, each stanza beginning with the successive letters of the Hebrew alphabet [2] Or *and feed on faithfulness*, or *and find safe pasture*

36:5–9 *God's Precious Steadfast Love.* This stanza has two descriptions of God's **steadfast love**: it **extends to the heavens**, so that God can save **man and beast**; and it is **precious** to those who know it from the **children of mankind**. The pairing of **steadfast love** and **faithfulness** evokes Ex. 34:6, describing God's benevolence; this helps readers to see that the other terms, **righteousness** and **judgments**, also express God's enduring commitment to act kindly toward his creatures and to **save** them. In view of this, people can **take refuge** under his **wings** and find themselves welcome guests at his table. Although the psalm is a hymn for Israel, it looks beyond Israel to the rest of mankind (Ps. 36:6, 7); Israel's calling was to live in their land in a way that displayed the true image of God, with a view toward bringing its blessing to the whole world.

36:9 The **fountain of life** is a source for all that refreshes and sustains life; cf. Prov. 10:11; 13:14; 14:27; 16:22. To **see light** is an idiom for "experience life" (e.g., Job 33:28; Ps. 49:19; in Isa. 9:2 it is light that shines into darkness), and this depends on God's **light** that illuminates the world for his people.

36:10–12 *Show Your Steadfast Love by Protecting Us from the Wicked.* The final stanza is a prayer in response to the reflections of the first two stanzas. It follows the topics in reverse order: God's **steadfast love** (v. 10), and the **wicked** (v. 11). It is an appeal to God's reliable love for his faithful ones (**those who know you**, i.e., **the upright of heart**, v. 10), in the face of the scheming of those who would harm them.

Psalm 37. This can be called a wisdom psalm because it is a hymn that reflects on themes normally dealt with in the Wisdom Literature. In particular, it addresses the problem caused when godless people prosper; it helps the faithful to see that it really is better to stay loyal to the Lord—a loyalty expressed in contentment, honest dealing, generosity, and just speech. The Lord will make the distinction between the two groups clear in his own time, and the faithful must wait patiently. This psalm has many parallel texts in Proverbs. As the ESV footnote explains, it follows an acrostic pattern, although it is slightly different from that of Psalms 25 and 34; here each grouping of (usually) two verses begins with the next successive letter of the Hebrew alphabet. True to form for Davidic acrostics, this one is imperfect: the *s* grouping includes Ps. 37:27–29, and there is no *'ayin* grouping after it (v. 30 begins with *p*).

37:1–11 *Do Not Be Envious of Evildoers.* The opening stanza sets forth the overall theme: "fret not yourself because of evildoers" (esp. when it seems that they are prospering), "trust in the LORD, and do good." The reason not to fret is the assurance that justice will come in the end: the evildoers "will soon fade like the grass" (v. 2) and "shall be cut off" (v. 9), while the faithful—those who "wait for the LORD"—"shall inherit the land" (v. 9; i.e., they will remain after the Lord purges the wicked from the land; cf. Prov. 2:21–22). Those who "befriend faithfulness" (Ps. 37:3) will "delight" themselves "in the LORD" (v. 4), "commit" their "way" to him (v. 5), "be still before" him (v. 7), and "wait patiently for him" (v. 7); thus they will be able to "refrain from anger" (v. 8; i.e., from the resentment they would naturally feel toward the godless who prosper).

37:1 This verse is almost identical to Prov. 24:19; cf. also Prov. 23:17–18.

37:4 the desires of your heart. Some take "the desires" as referring to the *feeling* of desire, i.e., "God will shape your heart so that it desires the right things"; but the sense is rather, "he will give you what your heart desires." It is safe to say this to those who embrace the advice of this psalm, because as they **delight** themselves **in the LORD**, their hearts will desire the right things (cf. vv. 16, 31).

5 [d]Commit your way to the LORD;
[z]trust in him, and he will act.
6 [e]He will bring forth your righteousness as the light,
and your justice as [f]the noonday.

7 [g]Be still before the LORD and wait patiently for him;
[h]fret not yourself over the one who [i]prospers in his way,
over the man who carries out evil devices!

8 [j]Refrain from anger, and forsake wrath!
[h]Fret not yourself; it tends only to evil.
9 [k]For the evildoers shall be cut off,
but those who wait for the LORD shall [l]inherit the land.

10 In [m]just a little while, the wicked will be no more;
though you look carefully at [n]his place, he will not be there.
11 But [o]the meek shall inherit the land
and delight themselves in [p]abundant peace.

12 The wicked [q]plots against the righteous
and [r]gnashes his teeth at him,
13 but the Lord [s]laughs at the wicked,
for he sees that his [t]day is coming.

14 The wicked draw the sword and [u]bend their bows
to bring down the poor and needy,
to slay those whose [v]way is upright;
15 their sword shall enter their own heart,
and their [w]bows shall be broken.

16 [x]Better is the little that the righteous has
than the abundance of many wicked.
17 For [y]the arms of the wicked shall be broken,
but the LORD [z]upholds the righteous.

18 The LORD [a]knows the days of the blameless,
and their [b]heritage will remain forever;
19 they are not put to shame in evil times;
in [c]the days of famine they have abundance.

20 But the wicked will perish;
the enemies of the LORD are like [d]the glory of the pastures;
they vanish—like [e]smoke they vanish away.

21 The wicked borrows but does not pay back,
but the righteous [f]is generous and gives;

5 [d]Ps. 22:8; 55:22; Prov. 16:3; 1 Pet. 5:7 [z][See ver. 3 above]
6 [e]Isa. 58:8, 10; Mic. 7:9 [f]Job 11:17
7 [g][Ps. 62:1; Isa. 30:15; Lam. 3:26] [h]ver. 1 [i]Jer. 12:1
8 [j][Eph. 4:26] [h][See ver. 7 above]
9 [k]ver. 2, 22 [l]Ps. 25:13; Prov. 2:21; Isa. 57:13; 60:21
10 [m]Job 24:24 [n]Job 7:10
11 [o]Cited Matt. 5:5 [p]Ps. 119:165; [Isa. 32:17]
12 [q]Ps. 31:13 [r]See Ps. 35:16
13 [s]See Ps. 2:4 [t]See Job 18:20
14 [u]Ps. 7:12 [v]See Ps. 7:10
15 [w]See 1 Sam. 2:4
16 [x]Prov. 15:16; 16:8; [1 Tim. 6:6]
17 [y]Ps. 10:15; Job 38:15; Ezek. 30:21, 22 [z]ver. 24
18 [a]See Ps. 1:6 [b]ver. 9
19 [c]Ps. 33:19; Job 5:20
20 [d][Matt. 6:30; James 1:11] [e]Ps. 68:2; 102:3; Hos. 13:3
21 [f]ver. 26

37:9 The contrast between the two outcomes, those who **shall be cut off** and those who **shall inherit the land**, recurs throughout the psalm: vv. 11, 22, 28–29, 34. "Cut off" generally refers to divine judgment, which removes a person from the people of God (e.g., Gen. 17:14; Lev. 7:20); in this psalm, it looks forward to the "future of the wicked" (Ps. 37:38), which likely refers to his afterlife (since it contrasts with one's "hope" in Prov. 23:18; 24:14). Wisdom Literature recognizes that God may wait until the afterlife to fully display his distinction between the faithful and the godless (cf. notes on Psalms 49 and 73).

37:11 Jesus uses the first half of this verse in the third beatitude (Matt. 5:5). The benefits Jesus describes there are all revealed at the last day, and it is legitimate to see Ps. 37:11 referring to this in its original context. First, the psalm is concerned with ultimate outcomes, not simply the benefits of this present world; second, OT Wisdom Literature as a whole addresses the same concern (cf. note on v. 9).

37:12–20 *The Lord Thwarts the Schemes of the Wicked.* The **wicked** person may hatch all manner of schemes **against the righteous** person (v. 12), but God will see to it that they come to nothing and that **the wicked will perish**, unfulfilled (v. 20). The faithful who take this to heart can live in contentment, even with **little** (v. 16; cf. Prov. 15:16; 16:8), confident that **the LORD knows the days of the blameless** (Ps. 37:18) and thus can provide for them even **in the days of famine** (v. 19). Biblical wisdom does not have a simplistic "just trust God and you will be well off" mentality; it speaks to the very challenging life situations that God's people often face.

37:21–31 *Therefore Commit Yourself to Doing Good.* The person who is content is free to do good, e.g., to give generously to those in need. Without such contentment one might be greedy and envious, or else be fearful over one's own poverty. He is also free to **do good** (v. 27), because he will not resort to unjust means of acquiring wealth. He knows that **the steps of** such **a man are established by the LORD** (v. 23), and thus even **though he fall** (probably, "suffer material hardship"), he can recover, **for the LORD upholds his hand** (v. 24). A person like this, with **the law of his God . . . in his heart** (v. 31), is one whose words are worth listening to: he **utters wisdom** (v. 30). Verse 25 does not deny that there may be temporary setbacks for the **righteous** or his **children**; the focus is on the

22 for those blessed by the LORD[1] shall [g]inherit the land,
but those cursed by him [h]shall be cut off.
23 The [i]steps of a man are [j]established by the LORD,
when he delights in his way;
24 [k]though he fall, he shall not be cast headlong,
for the LORD [l]upholds his hand.
25 I have been young, and now am old,
yet I have not seen the righteous forsaken
or his children [m]begging for bread.
26 He is ever [n]lending generously,
and his children become a blessing.
27 [o]Turn away from evil and do good;
so shall you [p]dwell forever.
28 For the LORD [q]loves justice;
he will not forsake his [r]saints.
They are preserved forever,
but the children of the wicked shall be [s]cut off.
29 The righteous shall inherit the land
and [p]dwell upon it forever.
30 The mouth of the righteous utters wisdom,
and his tongue speaks justice.
31 [t]The law of his God is in his heart;
his [u]steps do not slip.
32 The wicked [v]watches for the righteous
and seeks to put him to death.
33 The LORD will not [w]abandon him to his power
or let him [x]be condemned when he is brought to trial.
34 [y]Wait for the LORD and keep his way,
and he will exalt you to inherit the land;
you will look on [z]when the wicked are cut off.
35 [a]I have seen a wicked, ruthless man,
spreading himself like [b]a green laurel tree.[2]
36 But he passed away,[3] and behold, [c]he was no more;
though I sought him, he could not be found.
37 Mark the blameless and behold the upright,
for there is a future for the man of [d]peace.
38 But [e]transgressors shall be altogether destroyed;
the future of the wicked [f]shall be cut off.
39 [g]The salvation of the righteous is from the LORD;
he is their stronghold in [h]the time of trouble.
40 The LORD helps them and [i]delivers them;
[j]he delivers them from the wicked and saves them,
because they [k]take refuge in him.

22 [g]See ver. 9 [h]ver. 2
23 [i]Ps. 25:12; 1 Sam. 2:9 [j]Ps. 40:2; 119:5
24 [k]Prov. 24:16; Mic. 7:8; 2 Cor. 4:9 [l]ver. 17
25 [m][Ps. 109:10; Job 15:23]
26 [n]Ps. 112:5, 9; Deut. 15:8, 10; Matt. 5:42; Luke 6:35
27 [o]See Ps. 34:14 [p][Ps. 102:28]
28 [q]See Ps. 11:7 [r]See Ps. 16:10 [s]ver. 2, 9; Ps. 21:10; Prov. 2:22; Isa. 14:20
29 [p][See ver. 27 above]
31 [t]Ps. 40:8; 119:11; Deut. 6:6; Isa. 51:7; Jer. 31:33; [Rom. 7:22] [u][Ps. 73:2]
32 [v]Ps. 10:8
33 [w][2 Pet. 2:9] [x]Ps. 109:31
34 [y]ver. 9; See Ps. 27:14 [z]Ps. 52:5, 6; 91:8
35 [a]See Job 5:3 [b][Ps. 52:8]
36 [c]ver. 10; Job 20:5
37 [d]ver. 11; Ps. 119:165; Isa. 57:2
38 [e][Ps. 52:5; 104:35; Prov. 2:22] [f]Ps. 73:17; Job 18:17
39 [g]See Ps. 3:8 [h]Ps. 9:9
40 [i][Isa. 31:5; Acts 12:11] [j][1 Chr. 5:20; Dan. 3:17, 28; 6:23] [k]See Ps. 11:1

[1] Hebrew *by him* [2] The identity of this tree is uncertain [3] Or *But one passed by*

ultimate outcomes (cf. the mention of being **young** and then **old**, presenting a long-run perspective). Further, the observation took place within Israel, which was under God's special care; as the people of God have spread over the world, there is more opportunity for them to suffer under the evil of those who oppose them.

37:32–40 *The Lord Protects the Righteous from the Plots of the Wicked.* A common theme in the Psalms is that the faithful are always under threat from the devices of the wicked, but that they may trust the Lord to preserve them. In this final section the assurance comes from the fact that **the LORD will not abandon** the faithful to the **power** of the **wicked** (vv. 32–33), but will ensure that both the righteous and the wicked receive their proper reward in due time (probably in the world to come, vv. 37–38; cf. note on v. 9).

Psalm 38
[l]Ps. 70, title; [1 Chr. 16:4]
1 [m]Ps. 6:1
2 [n]Job 6:4 [o]See Ps. 32:4
3 [p]Isa. 1:6 [q]See Ps. 31:10
4 [r]Ps. 40:12; Ezra 9:6
6 [s]Ps. 35:14; 42:5, 6, 11; 43:5 [t]Isa. 21:3 [u][Job 30:28]
7 [p][See ver. 3 above]
8 [v]See Ps. 22:1
9 [w]Ps. 6:6
10 [x]See Ps. 6:7
11 [y]Ps. 88:18; See Job 19:13-20 [z][Luke 10:31, 32] [a]Ps. 39:10; Isa. 53:4, 8 [b][Matt. 27:55; Mark 15:40; Luke 23:49]
12 [c][Matt. 22:15]; Mark 12:13; Luke 20:20; See 2 Sam. 17:1-3 [d][2 Sam. 16:7, 8] [e]Ps. 35:20
13 [f]Ps. 39:2, 9; Isa. 53:7; 1 Pet. 2:23
14 [g][Job 23:4]
15 [h]Ps. 39:7; [2 Sam. 16:12]
16 [i][Ps. 13:4] [j]See Job 19:5 [k]Ps. 94:18

Do Not Forsake Me, O Lord

38

A Psalm of David, [l]for the memorial offering.

1 O Lord, [m]rebuke me not in your anger,
nor discipline me in your wrath!
2 For your [n]arrows have sunk into me,
and your hand [o]has come down on me.

3 There is [p]no soundness in my flesh
because of your indignation;
there is no health in my [q]bones
because of my sin.
4 For my [r]iniquities have gone over my head;
like a heavy burden, they are too heavy for me.

5 My wounds stink and fester
because of my foolishness,
6 I am [s]utterly bowed down and [t]prostrate;
all the day I [u]go about mourning.
7 For my sides are filled with burning,
and there is [p]no soundness in my flesh.
8 I am feeble and crushed;
I [v]groan because of the tumult of my heart.

9 O Lord, all my longing is before you;
my [w]sighing is not hidden from you.
10 My heart throbs; my strength fails me,
and [x]the light of my eyes—it also has gone from me.
11 My [y]friends and companions [z]stand aloof from my [a]plague,
and my nearest kin [b]stand far off.

12 Those who seek my life [c]lay their snares;
those who seek my hurt [d]speak of ruin
and meditate [e]treachery all day long.

13 But I am like a deaf man; I do not hear,
like [f]a mute man who does not open his mouth.
14 I have become like a man who does not hear,
and in whose mouth are no [g]rebukes.

15 But for [h]you, O Lord, do I wait;
it is you, O Lord my God, who will answer.
16 For I said, "Only [i]let them not rejoice over me,
who [j]boast against me when my [k]foot slips!"

Psalm 38. This is a lament that lays a person's troubles before God, when that person realizes that these troubles result from his own sin. The psalm describes anguish of body and mind, desertion by friends, and how the singer's folly has made him vulnerable to enemies ready to pounce. Because the psalm acknowledges that the singer's sins lie behind these troubles, it is often called a "penitential" psalm (along with Psalms 6; 32; 51; 130; 143). Of course, not all troubles result from one's own sins; but this psalm is geared to those that do. The title associates the psalm with the "memorial offering" (cf. Lev. 2:2), the portion of the grain offering that the priest burns on the altar; its purpose was probably to "remind" God that the worshiper had consecrated these gifts of God's own abundant providence.

38:1–8 *The Tumult of My Heart.* The singer describes the anguish of his body and mind, acknowledging that he deserves it because of his sin (**anger**, **wrath**, v. 1; **because of**, vv. 3, 5, 8), and that these troubles come from God (**your arrows**, v. 2). The physical and emotional distress is complete.

38:9–14 *I Am a Lonely Victim.* The description of anguish intensifies as the singer tells of his loneliness. He knows himself to be open to God's inspection (v. 9), and yet his **friends and companions stand aloof** (v. 11), thus compounding the helplessness with loneliness (vv. 10–11). Further, his own humbled condition, together with the aloofness of his friends, leaves him vulnerable to **those who seek** his **life** (vv. 12–14). The psalms frequently describe the faithful as being in danger from unscrupulous and unfaithful people, who will seize any opportunity to exploit or even destroy them (by legal accusations if possible, or by illegal means if necessary); the present weakness offers them just such an opportunity.

38:15–22 *You Alone Are My Hope.* In such a hopeless situation, the faithful must look to God alone, and here he implores God to come to his aid. He

17 For I am [l]ready to fall,
and my pain is ever before me.
18 I [m]confess my iniquity;
I am [n]sorry for my sin.
19 But my foes are vigorous, they are mighty,
and many are those who hate me [o]wrongfully.
20 Those who [p]render me evil for good
[q]accuse me because I [r]follow after good.
21 Do not forsake me, O LORD!
O my God, be not [s]far from me!
22 [t]Make haste to help me,
O Lord, my [u]salvation!

What Is the Measure of My Days?

39

TO THE CHOIRMASTER: TO [v]JEDUTHUN. A PSALM OF DAVID.

1 I said, "I will [w]guard my ways,
that I [x]may not sin with my tongue;
I will [y]guard my mouth with a muzzle,
so long as the wicked are in my presence."
2 I was [z]mute and silent;
I held my peace to no avail,
and my distress grew worse.
3 My [a]heart became hot within me.
As I mused, the fire burned;
then I spoke with my tongue:
4 "O LORD, [b]make me know my end
and what is the measure of my days;
let me know how fleeting I am!
5 Behold, you have made my days a few handbreadths,
and [c]my lifetime is as nothing before you.
Surely [d]all mankind stands as a mere breath! *Selah*
6 Surely a man [e]goes about as a shadow!
Surely for nothing[1] they are in turmoil;
man [f]heaps up wealth and does not know who will gather!
7 "And now, O Lord, for what do I wait?
[g]My hope is in you.
8 Deliver me from all my transgressions.
[h]Do not make me the scorn of the fool!
9 [i]I am mute; I do not open my mouth,
[j]for it is you who have done it.
10 [k]Remove your stroke from me;
I am spent by the hostility of your hand.

[1] Hebrew *Surely as a breath*

17[l]Ps. 35:15; Jer. 20:10
18[m]See Ps. 32:5 [n][2 Cor. 7:9, 10]
19[o]Ps. 35:19
20[p]See Ps. 35:12 [q]Ps. 109:4 [r][3 John 11]
21[s]See Ps. 10:1
22[t]See Ps. 40:13 [u]See Ps. 27:1
Psalm 39
[v]Ps. 62, title; 77, title; 1 Chr. 16:41; 25:1
1[w]1 Kgs. 2:4; 2 Kgs. 10:31 [x]Job 2:10 [y]See Ps. 34:13
2[z]ver. 9; Job 40:4, 5; See Ps. 38:13
3[a]Jer. 20:9; Luke 24:32; [Job 32:18, 19]
4[b]Ps. 90:12
5[c]Ps. 89:47; 90:4 [d]ver. 11; [Job 14:2]
6[e][1 Cor. 7:31; James 4:14] [f]Ps. 49:10; Job 27:16, 17; Luke 12:20; [Eccles. 2:18, 21, 26; Jer. 17:11]
7[g]Ps. 38:15
8[h]See Ps. 44:13
9[i]ver. 2 [j]2 Sam. 16:10; Job 2:10
10[k]Job 9:34; 13:21

shows true faith in confessing the iniquity for which he is being disciplined (v. 18) and in calling the Lord his **salvation** (v. 22).

Psalm 39. This psalm allows those who are suffering to express their bewilderment to God. The circumstances of the suffering are left vague, although there is acknowledgment of sin (vv. 8, 11); the focus is on how suffering is a reminder of how fleeting a human life is.

39:1–3 *My Silent Musing.* The singer describes his experience of watching carefully over what he says in the presence of the wicked; after a while he could no longer contain himself. He is probably concerned with what he might say aloud in his suffering, perhaps blaming God. But the faithful know they need to say something, and worship is the way to do it.

39:4–6 *My Fleeting Life.* The singer prays to **know** his **end**, and **how fleeting** he is, i.e., the brevity of human life. To really know this would protect him from wasting his life in **turmoil** that results when one **heaps up wealth**; there truly is a wiser way to live.

39:7–13 *Request for Forgiveness and Relief.* Being sure that the circumstances come from God, the singer declares his **hope** in God, asks God to **deliver** him **from all** his **transgressions**, and furthermore to take away the **discipline**. The act of making such a request is a frank admission that he has sinned and deserves God's **rebukes for sin**; it also takes to heart the lesson prayed for in vv. 4–6 (cf. v. 11b with v. 5b). **Sojourner** stresses his temporary residence in this life (cf. 1 Chron. 29:15). **Look away** (Ps. 39:13; cf. Job 7:19; 14:6) here does not mean that he wants God to cease caring for him; rather, he asks God to turn away his angry gaze (cf. Ps. 39:10).

11 When you discipline a man
with [l]rebukes for sin,
you [m]consume like a [n]moth what is dear to him;
[o]surely all mankind is a mere breath! *Selah*

12 [p]"Hear my prayer, O LORD,
and give ear to my cry;
hold not your peace at my tears!
For I am [q]a sojourner with you,
[q]a guest, like all my fathers.
13 [r]Look away from me, that I may smile again,
[s]before I depart and [t]am no more!"

My Help and My Deliverer

40

TO THE CHOIRMASTER. A PSALM OF DAVID.

1 I [u]waited patiently for the LORD;
he inclined to me and [v]heard my cry.
2 He drew me up from [w]the pit of destruction,
out of [x]the miry bog,
and [y]set my feet upon a rock,
[z]making my steps secure.
3 He put [a]a new song in my mouth,
a song of praise to our God.
Many will [b]see and fear,
and put their trust in the LORD.

4 Blessed is the man who [c]makes
the LORD his trust,
who does not turn to the proud,
to those who [d]go astray after a lie!
5 You have multiplied, O LORD my God,
your [e]wondrous deeds and your [f]thoughts toward us;
none can compare with you!
I will proclaim and tell of them,
yet they are [g]more than can be told.

6 [h]In sacrifice and offering you have not delighted,
but you have given me an open [i]ear.[1]
Burnt offering and sin offering
you have not required.
7 Then I said, "Behold, I have come;
in the scroll of the book it is written [j]of me:
8 [k]I delight to do your will, O my God;
your law is [l]within my heart."

9 I have told the glad news of deliverance[2]
in [m]the great congregation;

[1] Hebrew *ears you have dug for me* [2] Hebrew *righteousness*; also verse 10

11 [l]Ps. 80:16 [m]Ps. 49:14 [n]Job 13:28; Isa. 50:9 [o]See ver. 5
12 [p]Ps. 102:1 [q]Ps. 119:19; Lev. 25:23; 1 Chr. 29:15; Heb. 11:13; 1 Pet. 2:11; [Gen. 47:9]
13 [r]Job 7:19 [s]Job 10:21 [t]Job 7:8; 14:10-12; 20:9

Psalm 40

1 [u]Ps. 27:14; 37:7 [v]Ps. 39:12
2 [w][Jer. 38:6] [x]Ps. 69:2, 14 [y]Ps. 27:5 [z]Ps. 37:23
3 [a]See Ps. 33:3 [b]Ps. 52:6; 64:8, 9; Deut. 13:11
4 [c]See Ps. 2:12 [d]Ps. 101:3; 125:5; Lev. 19:4; Deut. 29:18; Job 23:11; Hos. 3:1
5 [e]Ps. 9:1; Ex. 15:11 [f]Ps. 92:5; 139:17; Isa. 55:8 [g]Ps. 71:15; 139:18
6 [h]Ps. 51:16; 1 Sam. 15:22; Cited Heb. 10:5-7; See Prov. 21:3 [i]See Job 33:16
7 [j]Luke 24:44
8 [k]Ps. 119:16, 24, 35, 92; [John 4:34] [l]See Ps. 37:31
9 [m]See Ps. 22:25

Psalm 40. This psalm combines two parts: first, it gives thanks for the many past mercies the singer has received from God, and then it presents a fresh instance of need for God's help. Both parts recognize that an individual's experiences of God's mercy can lead to others rejoicing in God (vv. 3, 9–10, 16).

40:1–10 *Many Past Mercies to Be Thankful For.* The singer reflects on previous situations of need in which he called on God for help, and **he inclined to me and heard my cry** (v. 1). These situations have reinforced the lesson, **blessed is the man who makes the LORD his trust, who does not turn to the proud** (so as to depend on them and to become like them, v. 4). The song also shapes its singers to share their experiences with the faithful in worship (vv. 3, 9–10): one's reception of God's help is not complete until he gives public thanks. These deliverances express God's **steadfast love** and **faithfulness** (v. 10; cf. Ex. 34:6).

40:6–8 These verses are part of the OT corrective to any who think that the sacrificial system worked automatically, apart from expressing faith, repentance, and obedience (cf. 50:8–15; 51:16–19; Prov. 14:9; Isa. 1:11–17). This is probably why Heb. 10:5–7 uses these verses (from the LXX), because its audience was tempted to abandon their specifically Jewish Christianity and revert to "ordinary" Judaism, with its sacrifices, thinking they would still be pleasing to God. They must see the sacrifices as a means of furthering God's larger purposes, not as producing effects on their own. **An open ear** (Ps. 40:6) is one ready to listen to and obey God's words.

behold, I have not [n]restrained my lips,
[o]as you know, O LORD.
10 I have not hidden your deliverance within my heart;
I have spoken of your faithfulness and your salvation;
I have not concealed your steadfast love and your faithfulness
from the great congregation.

11 As for you, O LORD, you will not restrain
your mercy from me;
your [p]steadfast love and your faithfulness will
ever preserve me!
12 For evils have [q]encompassed me
beyond number;
my [r]iniquities have overtaken me,
and I cannot [s]see;
they are [t]more than the hairs of my head;
my heart [u]fails me.

13 [v]Be pleased, O LORD, to [w]deliver me!
O LORD, [x]make haste to help me!
14 [y]Let those be put to shame and disappointed altogether
who seek to snatch away my life;
let those be [z]turned back and brought to dishonor
who delight in my hurt!
15 Let those be appalled because of their shame
who [a]say to me, "Aha, Aha!"

16 But may all who seek you
rejoice and be glad in you;
may those who love your salvation
[b]say continually, "Great is the LORD!"
17 As for me, I am [c]poor and needy,
but [d]the Lord takes thought for me.
You are my help and my deliverer;
do not delay, O my God!

O LORD, Be Gracious to Me

41

TO THE CHOIRMASTER. A PSALM OF DAVID.

1 [e]Blessed is the one who considers the poor![1]
[f]In the day of trouble the LORD delivers him;
2 the LORD protects him and keeps him alive;
he is called blessed in the land;
you [g]do not give him up to the will of his enemies.
3 The LORD sustains him on his sickbed;
in his illness you restore him to full health.[2]

4 As for me, I said, "O LORD, [h]be gracious to me;
[i]heal me,[3] for I have sinned against you!"

[1] Or *weak* [2] Hebrew *you turn all his bed* [3] Hebrew *my soul*

9 [n]Ps. 119:13; [Acts 20:20, 27] [o]Josh. 22:22
11 [p]Ps. 57:3; 61:7; Prov. 20:28; See Ps. 36:5
12 [q]Ps. 116:3 [r]Ps. 38:4 [s][Ps. 38:10] [t]Ps. 69:4 [u]Ps. 73:26
13 [v]For ver. 13-17, see Ps. 70:1-5 [w]Ps. 22:20 [x]Ps. 22:19; 38:22; 71:12; 141:1
14 [y]Ps. 35:4, 26; 71:13 [z]Ps. 6:10
15 [a]Ps. 35:21, 25; 70:3
16 [b]Ps. 35:27
17 [c]Ps. 86:1; 109:22 [d][1 Pet. 5:7]

Psalm 41
1 [e]Prov. 14:21 [f]Ps. 37:19
2 [g]Ps. 27:12
4 [h]Ps. 4:1 [i]Ps. 6:2; 147:3; 2 Chr. 30:20

40:11–17 *I Am Again in Need.* Verse 11 continues the allusion to Ex. 34:6 from Ps. 40:10, saying that the previous experiences provide assurance that, in the current distress (**evils . . . beyond number** and **my iniquities**, v. 12), God will likewise **make haste to help** the singer (v. 13). As is often the case in the Psalms, the distress comes at the hands of people eager to hurt and to gloat over the faithful (vv. 14–15). To pray for deliverance from the schemes of such people (i.e., to ask that they be **put to shame, disappointed, turned back**, and **brought to dishonor**, v. 14) should not be considered vindictive. In contrast, the faithful (**all who seek** the Lord) will **rejoice and be glad** (v. 16) when the singer tells the "glad news" in the "great congregation" (v. 9).

Psalm 41. This is a lament in which a person who fulfills his responsibilities to the poor, and yet is suffering severely, prays for God's help and vindication. The psalm describes a serious illness but can be applied more generally if the illness is taken as simply one example of severe suffering.

41:1–3 *The Lord Sustains Those Who Are Kind to the Poor.* The opening section expresses true covenantal faith: the person **who considers the poor** is kind to them because they are fellow members of God's own people (usually "the poor" in the OT refers specifically to the poor in Israel); presumably his

5 My enemies say of me in malice,
"When will he die, and his name perish?"
6 And when one comes to see me, [j]he utters empty words,
while his heart gathers iniquity;
when he goes out, he tells it abroad.
7 All who hate me whisper together about me;
they imagine the worst for me.[1]

8 They say, "A deadly thing is poured out[2] on him;
he will not rise again from where he lies."
9 Even my [k]close friend in whom I trusted,
who [l]ate my bread, has lifted his heel against me.
10 But you, O LORD, be gracious to me,
and raise me up, that I may repay them!

11 By this I know that [m]you delight in me:
my enemy will not shout in triumph over me.
12 But [n]you have upheld me because of [o]my integrity,
and [p]set me in your presence [q]forever.

13 [r]Blessed be the LORD, the God of Israel,
from everlasting to everlasting!
Amen and Amen.

BOOK TWO

Why Are You Cast Down, O My Soul?

42

TO THE CHOIRMASTER. A MASKIL[3] OF [s]THE SONS OF KORAH.
1 [t]As a deer pants for flowing streams,
so pants my soul for you, O God.
2 [u]My soul thirsts for God,
for [v]the living God.
When shall I come and [w]appear before God?[4]
3 [x]My tears have been my food
day and night,

[1] *Or they devise evil against me* [2] *Or has fastened* [3] Probably a musical or liturgical term [4] Revocalization yields *and see the face of God*

6 [j]Ps. 12:2; 144:8
9 [k]Ps. 55:12, 13, 20; Job 19:13, 14, 19; Jer. 9:4; 20:10; Mic. 7:5; [2 Sam. 15:12] [l]Cited John 13:18
11 [m][2 Sam. 15:25, 26]
12 [n]Ps. 63:8 [o]Ps. 26:1 [p]Job 36:7 [q]Ps. 23:6
13 [r]Luke 1:68; [Ps. 72:18, 19; 89:52; 106:48; 150:6]

Psalm 42

[s]1 Chr. 6:33, 37
1 [t][Joel 1:20]
2 [u]Ps. 63:1; John 7:37; [Isa. 41:17; 55:1]; See Ps. 84:2 [v]Ps. 84:2; Josh. 3:10; Dan. 6:26 [w]Ps. 84:7; [Ex. 23:17]
3 [x]Ps. 80:5; 102:9

kindness includes both financial help and energetic protection of them from exploitation. These "poor" are "weak" (ESV footnote) in influence, and therefore this person's kindness is also generous, extended in the knowledge that they cannot pay it back. God honors the person who shows such kindness in true covenant faith; he **delivers him**, **protects him**, and more specifically, **sustains him on his sickbed**.

41:4–10 *My Enemies Hope for My Death.* From the statement of faith the singer turns to his present situation of serious illness, compounded with the malice of those impatient for his death.

41:9 One expects enemies to be treacherous, but here the pain of betrayal comes from his **close friend**, who had received only kindness and who has now **lifted his heel against** the singer. In John 13:18 Jesus applies this to Judas, who has received only kindness (including footwashing) from Jesus; this enables the reader both to see the pain Jesus underwent for the sake of his own, and the callous treachery of Judas.

41:11–12 *But I Am Sure You Will Uphold Me.* The singer returns to the faith of vv. 1–3; given that faith, he can be confident that God will continue to honor his **integrity** (specifically, his dedicated kindness to the poor, v. 1).

41:13 *Doxology Concluding Book 1.* Each of the five books of the Psalter ends with a doxology (see also 72:18–19; 89:52; 106:48; 150:6); three do not seem to be part of their psalms (41:13; 72:18–19; 89:52). Psalm 150 as a whole concludes both Book 5 and the Psalter.

Psalms 42–43. While each of these psalms can be taken separately, Psalms 42–43 go well together as a song with three stanzas: they share a refrain (42:5, 11; 43:5); 43:2 is almost the same as 42:9; and they both express the longing to return to God's presence in the sanctuary (42:2; 43:3–4). In these psalms the singer laments his circumstances (connected with enemies who despise God and oppress his faithful servants), which keep him from attending worship at the central sanctuary. Singing this in corporate worship would especially foster a sense of yearning and expectation in the faithful, so that they would learn to attend worship looking for God's presence, to mourn any circumstances that prevent them from attendance, and to count their attendance at worship as a great gift from God (certainly not a burdensome duty!). Other psalms that express yearning for God include Psalms 63 and 84.

42:1–5 *My Soul Pants for God.* The song begins with a poignant expression of longing for God himself, using the image of thirst: **As a deer pants for flowing streams**. For the pious, the answer to this longing comes in public worship; this is clear from the phrase **appear before God** (i.e., at the sanctuary; cf. Ex. 23:17), and from Ps. 42:4, which recollects the former participation in sanctuary worship. The singer represents himself as separated from this worship and subject to taunts from those who despise his faith. The singer closes the stanza by encouraging himself that God will return him to worship. (Observe that the first words of v. 6, "and my God," belong with the refrain.)

[y]while they say to me all the day long,
"Where is your God?"
4 These things I remember,
as I [z]pour out my soul:
[a]how I would go [b]with the throng
and lead them in procession to the house of God
with glad shouts and songs of praise,
[c]a multitude keeping festival.

5 [d]Why are you cast down, O my soul,
and why are you [e]in turmoil within me?
[f]Hope in God; for I shall again praise him,
my salvation[1] 6 and my God.

My soul is cast down within me;
therefore I [g]remember you
[h]from the land of Jordan and of [i]Hermon,
from Mount Mizar.
7 Deep calls to deep
at the roar of your waterfalls;
[j]all your breakers and your [k]waves
have gone over me.
8 By day the LORD [l]commands his steadfast love,
and at [m]night his song is with me,
a prayer to the God of my life.
9 I say to God, [n]my rock:
"Why have you forgotten me?
[o]Why do I go mourning
because of the oppression of the enemy?"
10 As with a deadly wound in my bones,
my adversaries taunt me,
[p]while they say to me all the day long,
"Where is your God?"

11 [q]Why are you cast down, O my soul,
and why are you in turmoil within me?
Hope in God; for I shall again praise him,
my salvation and my God.

Send Out Your Light and Your Truth

43

1 [r]Vindicate me, O God, and [s]defend my cause
against an ungodly people,
from [t]the deceitful and unjust man
deliver me!
2 For you are [u]the God in whom I take refuge;
why have you [v]rejected me?

[1] Hebrew *the salvation of my face*; also verse 11 and 43:5

3 [y]ver. 10; Ps. 79:10; 115:2; Joel 2:17; Mic. 7:10
4 [z]Ps. 62:8; 1 Sam. 1:15; Job 30:16; Lam. 2:19 [a][Isa. 30:29] [b]Ps. 55:14 [c][2 Sam. 6:15]
5 [d]ver. 11; Ps. 43:5; [Matt. 26:38; John 12:27] [e]Ps. 77:3 [f]Lam. 3:24
6 [g]Jonah 2:7 [h]2 Sam. 17:22, 24 [i]Deut. 3:9
7 [j]Jonah 2:3 [k]Ps. 88:7; See Ps. 32:6
8 [l]Ps. 44:4; 68:28; 71:3; 133:3 [m]Job 35:10; [Ps. 4:4; 16:7; 63:6; 77:6; 119:55, 62, 148; 149:5]
9 [n]See Ps. 18:2; 2 Sam. 22:2 [o]Ps. 38:6; 43:2
10 [p]See ver. 3
11 [q]See ver. 5

Psalm 43

1 [r]Ps. 7:8; 26:1 [s]See 1 Sam. 24:15 [t]Ps. 5:6
2 [u]Ps. 31:4 [v]See Ps. 44:9

42:6–11 *Has God Forgotten Me?* The second stanza sharpens the description of the singer's situation. He is in **the land of Jordan and of Hermon**, and near the otherwise unknown **Mount Mizar**; this would probably locate him north of the Sea of Galilee (at the source of the Jordan River)—but at any rate he is far from Jerusalem, where the sanctuary is. He knows that God is not literally absent (v. 6), but he also feels that the sanctuary is where he meets God most fully; hence his separation has left his soul **cast down within** him (v. 6), because he wonders **why** God has **forgotten** him (v. 9). This stanza ends, like the first, with self-encouragement.

42:7 This verse uses two images of unruly water, perhaps to contrast with the "flowing streams" of v. 1: the first portrays two waterfalls plunging into a valley, calling to one another with a **roar**, while the second portrays the raging sea, in which one might drown (Jonah 2:3).

43:1–5 *Vindicate Me So That I Can Come Back to the Temple.* In the third stanza of Psalms 42–43, the singer focuses on the **ungodly people** and the **deceitful and unjust man** who torment him with their taunts (42:3), asking God to **vindicate** him against them (43:1; see note on 26:1–3). He personifies God's **light** and **truth** as if they were guides sent to **lead** him back to the sanctuary at God's **holy hill** (43:3). The stanza closes, like the others, with encouragement.

2[w]Ps. 42:9
3[x]Ps. 40:11; 57:3 [y]See Ps. 2:6; 46:4 [z]Ps. 84:1
5[a]See Ps. 42:5 [b]Ps. 42:5, 11

Psalm 44

[c]Ps. 42, title
1[d]Ps. 78:3; Ex. 10:2; 12:26, 27; 13:8, 14, 15; Judg. 6:13; See Deut. 6:20-23 [e]See Ps. 77:5
2[f]Ps. 78:55; 80:8; Josh. 3:10 [g]Ex. 15:17; 2 Sam. 7:10 [h]Ps. 80:9-11; [Jer. 17:8]
3[i]Josh. 24:12; Hos. 1:7 [j]See Ps. 4:6 [k]Deut. 4:37; 7:7, 8; 10:15
4[l]Ps. 74:12 [m]See Ps. 42:8
5[n][Deut. 33:17; Dan. 8:4] [o]Ps. 60:12
6[p][Ps. 33:16; 1 Sam. 17:47]
7[q]See Ps. 35:4
8[r]See Ps. 34:2
9[s]ver. 23; Ps. 43:2; 60:1, 10; 74:1; 108:11; See Ps. 89:38-45 [t][Judg. 4:14; 2 Sam. 5:24]

Why do I [w]go about mourning
because of the oppression of the enemy?
3 [x]Send out your light and your truth;
let them lead me;
let them bring me to your [y]holy hill
and to your [z]dwelling!
4 Then I will go to the altar of God,
to God my exceeding joy,
and I will praise you with the lyre,
O God, my God.

5 [a]Why are you cast down, O my soul,
and why are you in turmoil within me?
[b]Hope in God; for I shall again praise him,
my salvation and my God.

Come to Our Help

44

TO THE CHOIRMASTER. [c]A MASKIL[1] OF THE SONS OF KORAH.

1 O God, we have heard with our ears,
[d]our fathers have told us,
what deeds you performed in their days,
[e]in the days of old:
2 you with your own hand [f]drove out the nations,
but [g]them you planted;
you afflicted the peoples,
but [h]them you set free;
3 for not [i]by their own sword did they win the land,
nor did their own arm save them,
but your right hand and your arm,
and [j]the light of your face,
[k]for you delighted in them.

4 [l]You are my King, O God;
[m]ordain salvation for Jacob!
5 Through you we [n]push down our foes;
through your name we [o]tread down those who rise up against us.
6 For not in [p]my bow do I trust,
nor can my sword save me.
7 But you have saved us from our foes
and have [q]put to shame those who hate us.
8 [r]In God we have boasted continually,
and we will give thanks to your name forever. *Selah*
9 But you have [s]rejected us and disgraced us
and [t]have not gone out with our armies.

[1] Probably a musical or liturgical term

Psalm 44. This is a hymn for when the people of God as a whole have suffered some great calamity at the hands of their enemies and are seeking God's help. The calamity is particularly painful, since God has chosen his people, given them a special place, and favored them over their enemies in the past. The corporate focus is not impersonal, however; each member of the congregation identifies with the whole people, using the singular "I" (vv. 4, 6, 15). When the worshiping congregation sings this, they do more than simply present the request to God; they remind themselves of their privileged standing with God, of the obligation to faith and holiness that is laid upon them, and of God's unfailing loyalty to his purpose for his people. Similar psalms include Psalms 74; 77; 79; 80; and 83. In some cases, the cause for the calamity is mysterious (as here); in others, it is acknowledged as due to the people's unfaithfulness (e.g., 79:8).

44:1–8 *We Have Heard What You Did for Us in the Past.* The song opens by recounting the ways God has favored his people over the Gentiles in the past: he **drove out the nations** from Canaan and **planted** his own people there (v. 2); and after that he **saved** them **from** their **foes** (v. 7). The people recognize that God's special provision, not their own abilities, was responsible for their well-being (vv. 3, 6), and that they should boast in God and **give thanks to** his **name forever** (v. 8).

44:9–16 *But Now You Have Rejected Us.* In light of this past (vv. 1–8), the current situation is unintelligible. God has apparently **rejected** and **disgraced**

10 You have made us [u]turn back from the foe,
and those who hate us have gotten spoil.
11 You have made us like [v]sheep for slaughter
and have [w]scattered us among the nations.
12 [x]You have sold your people for a trifle,
demanding no high price for them.
13 You have made us [y]the taunt of our neighbors,
the derision and [z]scorn of those around us.
14 You have made us [a]a byword among the nations,
[b]a laughingstock[1] among the peoples.
15 All day long my disgrace is before me,
and [c]shame has covered my face
16 at the sound of the taunter and reviler,
at the sight of [d]the enemy and the avenger.

17 [e]All this has come upon us,
though we have not forgotten you,
and we have not been false to your covenant.
18 Our heart has not turned back,
nor have our [f]steps [g]departed from your way;
19 yet you have [h]broken us in the place of [i]jackals
and covered us with [j]the shadow of death.
20 If we had forgotten the name of our God
or [k]spread out our hands to [l]a foreign god,
21 [m]would not God discover this?
[n]For he knows the secrets of the heart.
22 Yet [o]for your sake we are killed all the day long;
we are regarded as sheep to be slaughtered.

23 [p]Awake! Why are you sleeping, O Lord?
Rouse yourself! [q]Do not reject us forever!
24 Why [r]do you hide your face?
Why do you forget our affliction and oppression?
25 For our [s]soul is bowed down to the dust;
our belly clings to the ground.
26 Rise up; [t]come to our help!
[u]Redeem us for the sake of your steadfast love!

[1] Hebrew *a shaking of the head*

10[u]Lev. 26:17; Deut. 28:25; Josh. 7:8, 12
11[v][ver. 22] [w]Ps. 106:27; Lev. 26:33; Deut. 4:27; 28:64; Isa. 52:3; Ezek. 20:23; [John 7:35; 1 Pet. 1:1]
12[x][Deut. 32:30; Judg. 2:14; 3:8; Jer. 15:13]
13[y]Ps. 39:8; 79:4; 89:41; 119:22; [Neh. 2:17] [z][Ps. 80:6]
14[a]Jer. 24:9; See Job 17:6 [b]See Job 16:4
15[c]2 Chr. 32:21
16[d]Ps. 8:2
17[e]Dan. 9:13
18[f]Ps. 37:31 [g]Ps. 119:51, 157; Job 23:11
19[h]Ps. 51:8 [i]See Job 30:29 [j]See Job 3:5
20[k]Ps. 68:31; Job 11:13 [l]See Ps. 81:9
21[m]Ps. 139:1; Jer. 17:10 [n][John 2:25; Heb. 4:13]
22[o]ver. 11; Cited Rom. 8:36
23[p]See Ps. 35:23 [q]ver. 9
24[r]See Job 13:24
25[s]Ps. 119:25
26[t]Ps. 63:7 [u]See Ps. 25:22

his people (v. 9), no longer giving them success against their foes; he has given them over to be slaughtered and allowed the unbelieving nations to **taunt** them (v. 13).

44:17–22 *But We Have Not Forsaken You.* The pain of the situation is especially sharp because the community cannot discover what unfaithfulness of theirs could have brought on the calamity. They claim not to have **forgotten** God, or to have been **false to** his **covenant** (v. 17); they acknowledge that if they had done so, God would know it and would be right to discipline them. The community is not claiming absolute sinlessness. The OT recognizes that the pious commit sins, even grievous ones, and it makes provision for them without calling such people "wicked" (cf. 32:6). But it tends to reserve terms like "unfaithfulness" or "wickedness" for the actual turning of the heart's fundamental loyalty away from God, as in idolatry (44:20) or in persecution of the godly.

44:19 The **place of jackals** would be a place of ruins (cf. Isa. 34:13; Jer. 9:11).

44:22 This verse describes God's people suffering death at the hands of those who oppose God; in Rom. 8:36, Paul uses this verse to remind believers that God's people have always had to face such situations, yet they must not conclude that they are thereby separated from the love of Christ.

44:23–26 *Therefore Come Now to Help Us.* To remember God's history with his people emboldens the community to pray for his aid in the present. The language of vv. 23–24 uses bold imagery, as if God were asleep (cf. 35:23) or forgetful; even though the faithful know that this is imagery, they also have canonical warrant for boldly appealing to God to keep his word. The last word is a request for God to **redeem** (see note on 25:22), **for the sake of** his **steadfast love**—a request that God is sure to honor.

Psalm 45. This is a hymn celebrating a royal wedding; as the title says, it is a "love song." It is impossible to be sure for which king in David's line the song was first composed, but it does not matter; after 2 Sam. 7:11–16, the line of David was the appointed channel through which God would bless his people and carry out his mission

Psalm 45
[v]Ps. 42, title
1 [w][Ezra 7:6]
2 [x][Isa. 33:17] [y][Luke 4:22]; See Isa. 61:1-3
3 [z]Ex. 32:27 [a][Isa. 49:2; Heb. 4:12; Rev. 1:16; 19:15] [b][Ps. 24:8; Isa. 9:6] [c]Ps. 21:5; 96:6, 7
4 [d][Rev. 16:2] [e]See Ps. 65:5
6 [f]Ps. 93:2; 110:2; Cited Heb. 1:8, 9 [g][Ps. 67:4; 96:10]
7 [h]See Ps. 11:7 [i]Isa. 61:1 [j]Ps. 2:2; 1 Kgs. 1:39; [Acts 10:38] [k][Ps. 21:6] [l][1 Kgs. 3:13]
8 [m]John 19:39; [Matt. 2:11] [n]Ps. 150:4
9 [o][1 Kgs. 2:19; Neh. 2:6] [p]See Job 28:16
11 [q]Isa. 54:5 [r]Ps. 95:6
12 [s][Job 11:19] [t]Ps. 96:8 [u]Ps. 22:29; 68:29; 72:10; Isa. 49:7

Your Throne, O God, Is Forever

45

TO THE CHOIRMASTER: ACCORDING TO LILIES. A MASKIL[1]
OF [v]THE SONS OF KORAH; A LOVE SONG.

1 My heart overflows with a pleasing theme;
I address my verses to the king;
my tongue is like the pen of [w]a ready scribe.

2 You are [x]the most handsome of the sons of men;
[y]grace is poured upon your lips;
therefore God has blessed you forever.
3 [z]Gird your [a]sword on your thigh, O [b]mighty one,
in [c]your splendor and majesty!

4 In your majesty [d]ride out victoriously
for the cause of truth and meekness and righteousness;
let your right hand teach you [e]awesome deeds!
5 Your arrows are sharp
in the heart of the king's enemies;
the peoples fall under you.

6 [f]Your throne, O God, is forever and ever.
The [g]scepter of your kingdom is a scepter of uprightness;
7 [h]you have loved righteousness and hated wickedness.
Therefore [i]God, your God, has [j]anointed you
with the oil of [k]gladness [l]beyond your companions;
8 your robes are all fragrant with [m]myrrh and aloes and cassia.
From ivory palaces [n]stringed instruments make you glad;
9 daughters of kings are among your ladies of honor;
[o]at your right hand stands the queen in [p]gold of Ophir.

10 Hear, O daughter, and consider, and incline your ear:
forget your people and your father's house,
11 and the king will desire your beauty.
Since he is your [q]lord, [r]bow to him.
12 The people[2] of Tyre will [s]seek your favor with [t]gifts,
[u]the richest of the people.[3]

[1] Probably a musical or liturgical term [2] Hebrew *daughter* [3] Or *The daughter of Tyre is here with gifts, the richest of people seek your favor*

to the whole world. The psalm has sometimes been taken as directly messianic, because Heb. 1:8–9 cites Ps. 45:6–7, applying the verses to Christ. The notes below will make clear how the book of Hebrews uses these verses.

45:1 *A Song for a King.* Whether these words are to be sung by the congregation or by a choir, they are addressed **to the king**. As a psalm, used in Jerusalem, this would refer to a king in David's line. A **ready scribe** was probably one who wrote quickly and neatly.

45:2–9 *You Are a King of Beauty, Majesty, and Justice.* These words speak to the king, praising him for his appearance and gracious speech (v. 2), military power (v. 3), and commitment to promoting justice for his subjects (vv. 4–7a). These words focus the attention of a young king on the ideals he should hold for his reign and character. These are what lead to God's blessing for his people's king, and to the king's own respected position in the world (vv. 7b–9).

45:6–7 Your throne, O God. Many have supposed that these words must address the Davidic king, either as foretelling Christ or as a type that Christ would eventually fulfill. Although the OT does foretell a divine Messiah (e.g., Isa. 9:6), this kind of interpretation does not easily fit this context. It seems better to think that the song speaks to God about his throne ("your throne, O God"), namely, the one that the heir of David occupies, and then goes on to describe the divine ideals for a king's reign (**scepter of uprightness**). Hebrews 1:8–9 cites these verses in Greek from the Septuagint as part of the author's argument that the "Son" is superior to the angels. Hebrews 1 applies the term "Son" to Jesus, probably in his role as the heir of David. Thus Heb. 1:5 puts Ps. 2:7 with 2 Sam. 7:14, where "Son of God" is a title for the Davidic king (see note on Ps. 2:7). This also accounts for the use of the messianic 110:1 in Heb. 1:3, 13. (Hebrews does go on, like the rest of the NT, to apply to Jesus an OT passage about Yahweh; see note on Ps. 102:25–27.)

45:10–12 *O Bride, Honor This King.* Now the song turns to the bride (**O daughter**); her loyalty now is to her husband (**the king**), no longer to her **father's house**. The reference to her **people** need not mean that she is from a foreign people; the word can simply mean the people of her hometown (e.g., 1 Sam. 9:12–13). In her new position, she will receive honor from the king's subjects.

13 All glorious is [v]the princess in her chamber, with robes interwoven with
gold.
14 [w]In many-colored robes [x]she is led to the king,
with her virgin companions following behind her.
15 With joy and gladness they are led along
as they enter the palace of the king.

16 In place of your fathers shall be your sons;
you will make them [y]princes in all the earth.
17 [z]I will cause your name to be remembered in all generations;
therefore nations will praise you forever and ever.

God Is Our Fortress

46

TO THE CHOIRMASTER. OF [a]THE SONS OF KORAH.
ACCORDING TO [b]ALAMOTH.[1] A SONG.

1 God is our [c]refuge and strength,
a very [d]present[2] help in [e]trouble.
2 Therefore we will not fear [f]though the earth gives way,
though the mountains be moved into [g]the heart of the sea,
3 though [h]its waters roar and foam,
though the mountains tremble at its swelling. *Selah*

4 There is [i]a river whose streams make glad [j]the city of God,
the holy [k]habitation of the Most High.
5 [l]God is in the midst of her; she shall not be moved;
God will help her when morning dawns.
6 [m]The nations rage, the kingdoms totter;
he [n]utters his voice, the earth [o]melts.
7 [p]The LORD of hosts is with us;
the God of Jacob is our fortress. *Selah*

8 [q]Come, behold the works of the LORD,
how he has brought desolations on the earth.
9 [r]He makes wars cease to the end of the earth;
he [s]breaks the bow and shatters the spear;
[t]he burns the chariots with fire.
10 [u]"Be still, and know that I am God.
[v]I will be exalted among the nations,
I will be exalted in the earth!"
11 [p]The LORD of hosts is with us;
the God of Jacob is our fortress. *Selah*

[1] Probably a musical or liturgical term [2] Or *well proved*

13[v][Rev. 19:7, 8]
14[w][Judg. 5:30; Ezek. 16:18; 26:16] [x][Song 1:4]
16[y]1 Pet. 2:9; Rev. 1:6; 5:10; 20:6
17[z][Mal. 1:11]

Psalm 46

[a]Ps. 42, title [b]1 Chr. 15:20
1[c]See Ps. 14:6 [d]Ps. 145:18; Deut. 4:7 [e]Ps. 9:9
2[f][Ps. 18:7] [g]Ezek. 27:26
3[h][Ps. 93:3, 4; Jer. 5:22]
4[i]Ps. 36:8; 65:9; [Isa. 8:6; 33:21; Rev. 22:1, 2] [j]Ps. 48:1; 87:3; [Isa. 60:14] [k]Ps. 43:3; 84:1
5[l]Lev. 26:12; Deut. 23:14; Isa. 12:6; Ezek. 43:7, 9; Hos. 11:9; Joel 2:27; Zeph. 3:15; Zech. 2:5, 10, 11; 8:3
6[m]Ps. 2:1 [n]Ps. 18:13; 68:33; 76:8; Jer. 25:30; Joel 2:11; 3:16; Amos 1:2 [o]Ex. 15:15; Josh. 2:9, 24; Amos 9:5
7[p]ver. 11; 2 Chr. 13:12; 20:17; [Num. 14:9]
8[q]Ps. 66:5
9[r]Isa. 2:4; Mic. 4:3 [s]Ps. 76:3; 1 Sam. 2:4 [t]Ezek. 39:9
10[u][Ex. 14:13] [v]Isa. 2:11, 17; 33:10
11[p][See ver. 7 above]

45:13–15 *The Bride's Procession.* Now the song describes the splendid attire of the bride (**the princess**) as she leaves **her chamber** and **is led to the king**, accompanied by a procession of **virgin companions**.

45:16–17 *O King, Your Line Will Continue in Your Sons.* The song turns back to the king and speaks of his enduring line. The marriage of a Davidic king is not a private matter; it is crucial for the fulfilling of God's promises, not simply to Israel but to the **nations**.

Psalm 46. The psalm is a hymn celebrating Zion as the special city, to which God has pledged himself and through which he will bless the world. Other psalms like this include Psalms 48; 76; 87; and 122. The psalm has two stanzas, marked by a refrain (46:7, 11).

46:1–7 *A Mighty Fortress Is Our God.* The people of God are secure, even in times of tumult and upheaval, because God is their **refuge and strength** (v. 1). God is present in his city (an emblem of his people as a whole) to protect it in all circumstances. Verses 2–3 use earthquakes, landslides, and the raging sea as images of raging **nations** and tottering **kingdoms** (v. 6). There is also a contrast: **though the mountains be moved** (v. 2), Zion **shall not be moved** (v. 5). The reason is that God has chosen Zion to be his **holy habitation**, i.e., the place of his sanctuary, where his people meet him in worship (v. 4). **a river**. In contrast to the roaring seas (vv. 2–3), the **streams** of this river (perhaps an image of the grace found in worshiping the true God; cf. Ezek. 47:1–12) **make glad the city of God**.

46:8–11 *God Will Be Exalted Among All Nations.* God's goal for his choosing of Zion is that out of it the word might go forth to the peoples of the whole world, bringing them all to live in godly peace with one another (Isa. 2:1–5). This will be the means by which he **makes wars cease** (Ps. 46:9). Since the address in v. 10, **be still, and know**, is plural, readers should imagine God speaking these words to the **nations**, among whom he will eventually **be exalted**. This is the meaning of the **LORD of hosts** being **with** his people (v. 11; cf. Matt. 28:20): he will indeed see to it that the mission of Gen. 12:1–3 is accomplished.

God Is King over All the Earth

47

To the choirmaster. A Psalm of [w]the Sons of Korah.

1 [x]Clap your hands, all peoples!
[y]Shout to God with loud songs of joy!
2 For the LORD, the Most High, [z]is to be feared,
[a]a great king over all the earth.
3 He [b]subdued peoples under us,
and nations under our feet.
4 He chose our [c]heritage for us,
[d]the pride of Jacob whom he loves. *Selah*

5 God [e]has gone up with a shout,
the LORD with the sound of a trumpet.
6 Sing praises to God, sing praises!
Sing praises to our King, sing praises!
7 For God is [f]the King of all the earth;
sing praises [g]with a psalm![1]

8 God [h]reigns over the nations;
God sits on his holy throne.
9 [i]The princes of the peoples gather
as the people of the God of Abraham.
For [j]the shields of the earth belong to God;
he is highly exalted!

Zion, the City of Our God

48

A Song. A Psalm of [k]the Sons of Korah.

1 [l]Great is the LORD and greatly to be praised
in [m]the city of our God!
His [n]holy mountain, 2 [o]beautiful in elevation,
is [p]the joy of all the earth,
Mount Zion, in the far north,
[q]the city of the great King.
3 Within her citadels God
has made himself known as a fortress.

4 For behold, [r]the kings assembled;
they came on together.

[1] Hebrew *maskil*

Psalm 47
[w]Ps. 42, title
1 [x]2 Kgs. 11:12; Isa. 55:12; Nah. 3:19 [y]Ps. 95:1; [1 Sam. 10:24]
2 [z]Ps. 66:3, 5; 68:35; Deut. 7:21 [a]Mal. 1:14
3 [b]See Ps. 18:47
4 [c]Ps. 2:8; [1 Pet. 1:4] [d]Amos 6:8; 8:7; Nah. 2:2
5 [e]2 Sam. 6:15; [Ps. 68:18]
7 [f]Zech. 14:9 [g]1 Cor. 14:15
8 [h]Ps. 22:28; 1 Chr. 16:31
9 [i][Ps. 72:11; Isa. 49:7, 23] [j]Ps. 89:18

Psalm 48
[k]Ps. 42, title; 46, title
1 [l]Ps. 96:4; 145:3 [m]See Ps. 46:4 [n]Ps. 2:6; 87:1; Zech. 8:3; [Isa. 2:3; Mic. 4:1]
2 [o]See Ps. 50:2 [p]Lam. 2:15; [Ezek. 20:6] [q]Matt. 5:35
4 [r]See 2 Sam. 10:6-19

Psalm 47. This psalm celebrates God's kingship, i.e., his rule over all the earth (see note on 5:2). The promises to Abraham (47:9), that all peoples will be blessed in him (Gen. 12:3), are founded on the fact that there is only one true God, to whom all mankind owes love and loyalty. Other psalms like this are Psalms 93; 96–99.

47:1–4 *The Lord Is to Be Feared by All.* The Lord **loves** Israel and gave them their **heritage**; but this is in order that **all peoples** might come to fear and love him. Thus God's subduing of the Canaanites is not his final word for the Gentiles. To **clap** the **hands** is here an expression of exultation (cf. Nah. 3:19).

47:5–7 *Sing Praises to Our King.* This probably looks back to the ark going to reside in Jerusalem; 2 Sam. 6:15 tells of how the ark was made to go **up with a shout** (cf. Psalm 24). The Lord is Israel's acknowledged king and the rightful **King of all the earth**, to whom all ought to **sing praises**.

47:8–9 *God Reigns over All Nations.* God's **throne** is his sanctuary in Jerusalem, from which he will extend his rule **over the nations**; the psalm looks forward to the time when the Gentile **princes of the peoples gather** for worship **as the people of the God of Abraham**, i.e., the people to whom the blessing of Abraham has finally come.

Psalm 48. Like Psalm 46, Psalm 48 is a hymn celebrating Zion as God's special city, which he defends for the sake of the world. It commemorates some great event, in which Gentile powers had besieged Jerusalem but came away dismayed; it recognizes that though material fortresses may have their place, it is crucial that God himself be the defense of his people.

48:1–3 *The Lord, the King, Resides in Zion.* The mention of **his holy mountain** (v. 1) and the temple (v. 9) shows that God resides in his sacred city through the sanctuary, in which his people come most fully into his presence. **In the far north** (v. 2) is apparently an idiom for where God has his throne (cf. Isa. 14:13), and thus the physical location of **Mount Zion** is not itself the focus here. It is **the joy of all the earth**, not yet in fact but in God's own plan (cf. Ps. 48:10). Jesus gets a name for Jerusalem, **the city of the great King**, from v. 2 (cf. Matt. 5:35); the sacredness of the city to God is why one should not take oaths by it.

48:4–8 *The Kings of the Earth Thwarted from Attacking Her.* These verses recount an event in which Gentile **kings assembled** to assault Jerusalem but were foiled by the magnificence that God gave the city, together with an

5 As soon as they saw it, they were astounded;
they were in panic; they took to flight.
6 [s]Trembling took hold of them there,
anguish [t]as of a woman in labor.
7 By [u]the east wind you [v]shattered
the ships of [w]Tarshish.
8 As we have heard, so have we seen
in the city of the LORD of hosts,
in [m]the city of our God,
which God will [x]establish forever. *Selah*

9 We have thought on your [y]steadfast love, O God,
in the midst of your temple.
10 As your [z]name, O God,
so your praise reaches to [a]the ends of the earth.
Your right hand is filled with righteousness.
11 Let Mount [b]Zion be glad!
Let [b]the daughters of Judah rejoice
because of your judgments!

12 Walk about Zion, go around her,
number her towers,
13 consider well her [c]ramparts,
go through her citadels,
[d]that you may tell the next generation
14 that this is God,
our God forever and ever.
He will [e]guide us forever.[1]

Why Should I Fear in Times of Trouble?

49

TO THE CHOIRMASTER. A PSALM OF [f]THE SONS OF KORAH.
1 [g]Hear this, all peoples!
Give ear, all inhabitants of the world,
2 [h]both low and high,
rich and poor together!
3 My mouth shall speak [i]wisdom;
the meditation of my heart shall be understanding.

[1] Septuagint; another reading is (compare Jerome, Syriac) *He will guide us beyond death*

6[s][Ex. 15:15] [t]Isa. 13:8; Hos. 13:13
7[u]Jer. 18:17 [v]1 Kgs. 22:48; Ezek. 27:26 [w]1 Kgs. 10:22
8[m][See ver. 1 above] [x]Ps. 87:5; Isa. 2:2; Mic. 4:1
9[y]Ps. 26:3; 40:10
10[z]Ps. 113:3; [Ex. 34:5, 6; Deut. 28:58; Mal. 1:11, 14] [a]See Ps. 22:27
11[b]Ps. 97:8
13[c]Ps. 122:7 [d][Ps. 78:4-6]
14[e]Ps. 23:3, 4

Psalm 49
[f]Ps. 42, title
1[g]Ps. 78:1; Isa. 1:2; Mic. 1:2
2[h]Ps. 62:9
3[i]Prov. 1:20; 9:1

east wind that destroyed their fleet. The lesson is that **God will establish** his city **forever**.

48:7 Ships of Tarshish were capable of long voyages in the Mediterranean, Tarshish probably being at the western end of the sea, in modern Spain.

48:9–11 *The Lord's Presence Brings Joy to His People.* The people assembled for worship reflect on how God has displayed his **steadfast love**, not simply in personal deliverance and forgiveness but in preserving them as his people, whom he called so that his **praise** might reach **to the ends of the earth**, i.e., so that the Gentiles would come to know him. Such reflections on God's judgments, which display his **righteousness** (i.e., covenant faithfulness), should lead the **daughters** (i.e., towns and villages) **of Judah** to **rejoice**.

48:12–14 *Zion Endures to Tell the Next Generation.* The singing congregation addresses one another, inviting them to review the strength of Zion; as vv. 1–3 made clear, this is not purely the city's material defenses. The worshipers know that the people of God are secure, and are commissioned to **tell the next generation** of their security and their mission (v. 13).

Psalm 49. This is a wisdom psalm, i.e., a hymn that reflects on topics typically covered in the Bible's Wisdom Literature. In particular, it addresses the perplexity that the pious often feel when they encounter trouble, while unfaithful people seem to get along so well. Is not God expected to show his favor for the pious in how he treats them? The answer is that God will distinguish between the faithful and the unfaithful in what happens to them when they die. The psalm follows a very simple argument: it calls everyone to pay attention (vv. 1–4); then it reminds the singers that everyone has a common outcome, namely, all will die (vv. 5–12); and it finishes by stressing the contrasting destinations for the faithful and the unfaithful (vv. 13–20). Verses 12 and 20 are very similar, the key difference being in the words translated "remain" and "understanding," which sound almost the same in Hebrew (*yalin* and *yabin*). The element of understanding makes the difference, as the notes will show. Those who sing this will want to continue living faithfully, and will be strengthened against the temptation either to despair or to give up and join the unfaithful. Other psalms that address the same topic include Psalms 37 and 73.

49:1–4 *Call to Pay Attention.* This section indicates that the message is for **all** sorts of **peoples, low and high**, throughout the world. The terms **wisdom** and **understanding** are used in the Wisdom Books for genuine spiritual perception, the ability to approach life from God's perspective; they are features

4 I will incline my ear to [j]a proverb;
I will solve my [k]riddle to the music of the lyre.

5 [l]Why should I fear in [m]times of trouble,
when the iniquity of those who cheat me surrounds me,
6 those who [n]trust in their wealth
and boast of the abundance of their riches?
7 Truly no man [o]can ransom another,
or [p]give to God [q]the price of his life,
8 for [r]the ransom of their life is costly
and can never suffice,
9 that he should live on forever
and [s]never see the pit.

10 For he sees [t]that even the wise die;
[u]the fool and the stupid alike must perish
and [v]leave their wealth to others.
11 Their [w]graves are their homes forever,[1]
their dwelling places [x]to all generations,
though they [y]called lands by their own names.
12 Man in his pomp [z]will not remain;
[a]he is like the beasts that perish.

13 This is the path of those who have [b]foolish confidence;
yet after them people approve of their boasts.[2] *Selah*
14 Like sheep they are appointed for Sheol;
death shall be their shepherd,
and the upright [c]shall rule over them in the morning.
[d]Their form shall be consumed [e]in Sheol, with no place to dwell.
15 But God will [f]ransom my soul from the power of Sheol,
for he will [g]receive me. *Selah*

16 Be not afraid when a man becomes rich,
when the glory of his house increases.
17 [h]For when he dies he will [i]carry nothing away;
his glory will not go down after him.
18 For though, while he lives, he counts himself [j]blessed
—and though you get praise when you do well for yourself—
19 his soul will [k]go to the generation of his fathers,
who will never again [l]see light.
20 [m]Man in his pomp yet without understanding is like the beasts that perish.

4 [j][Ps. 78:2; Matt. 13:35] [k]Num. 12:8; Prov. 1:6
5 [l][Ps. 37:1] [m]Ps. 94:13
6 [n]Ps. 52:7; Prov. 11:28; Mark 10:24, 25; [Job 31:24]
7 [o][Matt. 25:9] [p][Matt. 16:26] [q]See Job 33:24
8 [r]Job 36:18, 19
9 [s]Ps. 16:10; [Ps. 89:48]
10 [t]Eccles. 2:16 [u]Ps. 73:22; 92:6; 94:8; Prov. 30:2 [v]See Ps. 39:6
11 [w]Ps. 5:9; 64:6 [x]Ps. 10:6 [y][Gen. 4:17]
12 [z]ver. 20; [Ps. 39:5; 82:7] [a]ver. 20; Eccles. 3:19
13 [b][Luke 12:20]
14 [c][Dan. 7:22; Mal. 4:3; Luke 22:30; 1 Cor. 6:2; Rev. 2:26; 20:4] [d]Ps. 39:11 [e]Job 24:19, 20
15 [f]Hos. 13:14; [Dan. 12:2] [g]Ps. 16:11; 17:15; 73:24; [Gen. 5:24]
17 [h][Job 27:19] [i]1 Tim. 6:7
18 [j]Ps. 10:3; 36:2; Deut. 29:19; Luke 12:19
19 [k]Gen. 15:15 [l]Ps. 56:13; Job 33:30
20 [m]ver. 12

[1] Septuagint, Syriac, Targum; Hebrew *Their inward thought was that their homes were forever* [2] Or *and of those after them who approve of their boasts*

marking those who have true faith. The song will expound a **proverb** and **solve** a **riddle**, i.e., the puzzle presented in vv. 5–6.

49:5–12 *Common Outcome: We All Die.* After presenting the puzzle, the song reminds all its singers that every single person has the same end (death). From vv. 5–6 the puzzle is clear: the pious (the **I** in this psalm) face **times of trouble** (v. 5), finding themselves surrounded by **the iniquity of those who cheat me** (v. 5), which is the same group as **those who trust in their wealth** (v. 6). It is likely that in this psalm the pious and the unfaithful are alike members of the covenant people of God; not all of the people lay hold of the blessings of the covenant. The point about all dying is made in two ways: in vv. 7–9, no one can bribe death, either to **ransom another** or to **give to God the price of his** own **life** (v. 7); in vv. 10–12, all kinds of people die, whether one is **wise** (embracing God's covenant) or a **fool** (stupidly rejecting God's covenant). Thus even the wealthy must die, and their **wealth** cannot prevent it.

49:13–20 *Contrasting Destinations: We Go to God, Not Sheol.* There are two groups of people here, **they** (the unfaithful, **those who have foolish confidence**) and "**I**" (the faithful, who sing this); and God treats them differently when they die. The unfaithful are **like sheep . . . appointed for Sheol**, while **God will ransom** the faithful person's **soul from the power of Sheol** (vv. 14–15). Since the impious go to Sheol, and the pious do not, here it represents the grim place of destruction for the wicked, and not simply the grave (see note on 6:5). A genuine grasp of this will enable a person to resist being **afraid when a man becomes rich** (49:16)—the fear that might lead the faithful to despair of God's justice and goodness, or to give up piety in order to join the wicked and to **get praise when** they **do well for** themselves (v. 18).

49:15 Quite often in the Bible, "soul" describes the life principle that animates the body, or the person's inner self, and can simply be another way of saying "the self." At other times, however, it can describe that inner self as something that survives the death of the body, as it does here, where **my soul** is parallel to **me**, the self that after death will not go to Sheol. In the larger picture of the Bible, the separation of body and soul is unnatural, a product of sin (Gen. 3:19), and will be healed with their reunion at the resurrection (Dan. 12:2–3; cf. 2 Cor. 5:1–4).

God Himself Is Judge

50

A Psalm of [n]Asaph.

1 [o]The Mighty One, God the Lord,
speaks and summons the earth
[p]from the rising of the sun to its setting.
2 Out of Zion, [q]the perfection of beauty,
[r]God shines forth.

3 Our God comes; he [s]does not keep silence;[1]
before him is a devouring [t]fire,
around him a mighty tempest.
4 [u]He calls to the heavens above
and to the earth, that he may judge his people:
5 "Gather to me my faithful ones,
who made [v]a covenant with me by sacrifice!"
6 [w]The heavens declare his righteousness,
for [x]God himself is judge! *Selah*

7 [y]"Hear, O my people, and I will speak;
O Israel, I will testify against you.
[z]I am God, your God.
8 Not for your sacrifices [a]do I rebuke you;
your burnt offerings are continually before me.
9 I will not accept a bull from your house
or goats from your folds.
10 For every beast of the forest is mine,
the cattle on a thousand hills.
11 [b]I know all the birds of the hills,
and all that moves in the field is mine.

12 "If I were hungry, I would not tell you,
[c]for the world and its fullness are mine.
13 Do I eat the flesh of bulls
or drink the blood of goats?
14 [d]Offer to God a sacrifice of thanksgiving,[2]
and [e]perform your vows to the Most High,
15 and [f]call upon me in the day of trouble;
I will [g]deliver you, and you shall [h]glorify me."

[1] *Or May our God come, and not keep silence* [2] *Or Make thanksgiving your sacrifice to God*

Psalm 50
[n]1 Chr. 6:39; 15:17; 16:5, 7; 25:2; 2 Chr. 29:30
1[o]Josh. 22:22 [p]Ps. 113:3
2[q][Lam. 2:15]; See Ps. 48:2 [r]Ps. 80:1; 94:1; Deut. 33:2
3[s][Ex. 19:16] [t]Ps. 21:9; 97:3; Lev. 10:2; Num. 16:35; Dan. 7:10
4[u]Deut. 4:26; 31:28; 32:1; Isa. 1:2; Mic. 6:1, 2
5[v]Ex. 24:7, 8; See Gen. 15:9-18
6[w]Ps. 89:5; 97:6; [Rev. 16:5, 7; 19:2] [x]Ps. 58:11; 75:7
7[y]Ps. 81:8; [Ps. 49:1] [z]Ex. 20:2
8[a]See Ps. 40:6
11[b][Matt. 10:29]
12[c]See Ps. 24:1
14[d]ver. 23; Ps. 27:6; 69:30; 107:22; Heb. 13:15; [Hos. 14:2; Rom. 12:1] [e]Ps. 22:25; 61:8; 65:1; 76:11; 116:14, 18; Num. 30:2; Deut. 23:21; Job 22:27; Eccles. 5:4, 5
15[f]Ps. 81:7; Zech. 13:9; [Ps. 107:6] [g]Ps. 91:15 [h]ver. 23; Ps. 22:23

Psalm 50. It is probably best to describe this psalm as an "oracular hymn," i.e., with it the worshipers sing God's pronouncement about how they should live as part of his covenant people. The God who speaks and summons the earth (v. 1) especially plans to judge his own people (v. 4), particularly to warn any of them who presume on the privileges of the sacrificial system, thinking that it is a way to buy God off, apart from a living relationship with him.

50:1–6 *God Summons the Earth to Assemble before Him.* **The Lord**, the God of Israel, is **the Mighty One**, who made and rules heaven and earth; when he **speaks and summons the earth**, he has the right to expect all mankind to pay attention; he especially expects it from Israel, whose very calling was to be the first installment of renewed mankind. When the song goes on to say that **God shines forth** from **Zion**, it focuses the reader's attention on God's particular people, Israel, and their privileged position (cf. Ex. 19:4–6): they are his **faithful ones, who made a covenant with** him **by sacrifice** (Ps. 50:5; cf. Ex. 24:8). Great privilege brings with it great responsibility, and thus God will **judge his people** (Ps. 50:4)—i.e., exercise his righteous rule over them, not necessarily punish them.

50:7–15 *He Speaks to His People: Worship Him from the Heart.* God's act of judgment is an oracle, explaining what it really means to be his people. He speaks to their use of **sacrifices** (v. 8); in the light of vv. 10–13, as well as v. 16, he is addressing people tempted to think that God somehow needs the sacrifices, and that they can be used almost as a bribe to satisfy him. God's reply (an obvious one for those who think clearly about the creation account) is that he owns the entire created order and does not depend on it in any way. The oracle then turns to the right use of sacrifices (cf. note on 40:6–8), focusing on the **sacrifice of thanksgiving** and **vows** (50:14). These were both kinds of peace offerings (Lev. 7:11–12, 16), which was the only kind of sacrifice in which the worshiper ate some of the sacrificial animal; its primary function was to eat a meal, in company with the sacrificer's family and the needy, with God as the host. (First Corinthians 10:16–18 shows that this is the basic meaning of the Christian Lord's Supper.) Membership in God's people is about being welcome in his presence (Ps. 50:14), depending on him (v. 15), and dealing justly with others (vv. 19–20, 23); thus it engages the heart.

17[i][Rom. 2:21, 22] [j]1 Kgs. 14:9; Neh. 9:26
18[k]Rom. 1:32 [l][1 Tim. 5:22]
19[m][Ps. 52:2]
21[n]Eccles. 8:11; Isa. 57:11 [o]Ps. 90:8; 2 Kgs. 19:4 [p]Job 13:18; 23:4
22[q]See Ps. 9:17 [r]Ps. 7:2
23[s]ver. 14, 15 [t][Gal. 6:16] [u]Ps. 91:16

Psalm 51
[v]2 Sam. 12:1
1[w]See Ps. 4:1 [x]See Ps. 106:45 [y]ver. 9; Isa. 43:25; 44:22; Acts 3:19; Col. 2:14
2[z]ver. 7; Isa. 1:16; Jer. 4:14; Mal. 3:3; Acts 22:16 [a]Heb. 9:14; 1 John 1:7, 9; [Lev. 13:6]
3[b]Ps. 32:5; [Prov. 28:13]

16 But to the wicked God says:
"What right have you to recite my statutes
or take my covenant on your lips?
17 [i]For you hate discipline,
[j]and you cast my words behind you.
18 If you see a thief, [k]you are pleased with him,
[l]and you keep company with adulterers.

19 "You give your mouth free rein for evil,
[m]and your tongue frames deceit.
20 You sit and speak against your brother;
you slander your own mother's son.
21 These things you have done, and I [n]have been silent;
you thought that I[1] was one like yourself.
But now I [o]rebuke you and [p]lay the charge before you.

22 "Mark this, then, you who [q]forget God,
lest I tear you apart, and there be [r]none to deliver!
23 The one who [s]offers thanksgiving as his sacrifice glorifies me;
to one who [t]orders his way rightly
I will show the [u]salvation of God!"

Create in Me a Clean Heart, O God

51

TO THE CHOIRMASTER. A PSALM OF DAVID, WHEN [v]NATHAN THE PROPHET WENT TO HIM, AFTER HE HAD GONE IN TO BATHSHEBA.

1 [w]Have mercy on me,[2] O God,
according to your steadfast love;
according to your [x]abundant mercy
[y]blot out my transgressions.
2 [z]Wash me thoroughly from my iniquity,
and [a]cleanse me from my sin!
3 [b]For I know my transgressions,
and my sin is ever before me.

[1] *Or that the I AM* [2] *Or Be gracious to me*

50:16–22 *He Speaks to the "Wicked": He Rebukes Them.* It is clear that the **wicked** here are members of the covenant people who despise the privileges of the covenant: in v. 16 they **take** his **covenant on** their **lips**, but they lack the right to do so; in v. 17 they **hate** the fatherly **discipline** that God gives his children (Prov. 3:11–12); and in Ps. 50:22 they **forget God** (implying that they knew something of him to begin with). The covenant should have knit them together with all of God's people in the great project of showing forth true humanity for the sake of the world, but instead they prefer the **thief** and **adulterers**, and use their tongues for destructive purposes (vv. 18–20). They misinterpreted God's silence; they thought he was as greedy as they are; but God in his mercy now issues his **rebuke** (v. 21) and invites them to change their ways.

50:21 The ESV footnote explains that it is possible to translate, **you thought that** [the] **I** [AM] **was one like yourself**; cf. Ex. 3:14. This sharpens the rebuke, as God's name is especially connected with his promises of faithfulness and kindness to his people (Ex. 3:12; 6:6–8), and the wicked are abusing this.

50:23 *He Sums It Up: Worship Him with the Heart.* The final thought sums up the psalm, with its interest in what membership in God's favored people should mean: joyfully to delight in God's presence (**thanksgiving as his sacrifice**), and a just and kind life in fellowship with God's people (**orders his way rightly**).

Psalm 51. This is probably the best known of the "Penitential Psalms" (Psalms 6; 25; 32; 38; 51; 130; 143). According to the title, David composed this psalm as a result of Nathan the prophet convicting him of his sins, both in his committing adultery with Bathsheba and in his arranging for the murder of Bathsheba's husband, Uriah the Hittite (2 Sam. 12:1–14). At the same time, this is more than David's personal prayer: its instructional elements (e.g., Ps. 51:16–19) show that, though the situation that led to the psalm was intensely personal, the psalm in its current form is well-suited to be a hymn by which the members of the worshiping congregation confess their own sins. As is the case with Psalms 25 and 32, the psalm enables its singers to appeal to God's own gracious character as the grounds for their cry for forgiveness, echoing Ex. 34:6–7 (see note on Ps. 51:1–2). The psalm also reinforces the view, found in the Levitical system itself, that the sacrifices bestow their benefits only on those who use them in humble and penitent faith.

51:1–2 *Have Mercy on Me.* The psalm opens with an appeal to God for forgiveness. The terms **mercy** and **steadfast love**, as well as **transgressions**, **iniquity**, and **sin**, all evoke God's proclamation of his own name (Ex. 34:6–7), with its focus on his grace and kindness. The plea for mercy here is a humble one, based entirely on God's mercy, frankly recognizing that the worshiper does not deserve it. The terms **wash** (cf. Ex. 19:10) and **cleanse** (cf. Num. 19:19) come from the ceremonial system, where they refer to rites that allow a person to come safely into God's presence. Here the psalm focuses on the inner condition that the ceremony points to.

51:3–5 *I Own Up to My Sin.* The next section builds on the humility expressed in the opening section, freely acknowledging that the sin is the worshiper's own and that God is free from all blame. Indeed, God would be fully justified in refusing the request for mercy and bringing judgment instead.

4 [c]Against you, you only, have I sinned
and done what is evil [d]in your sight,
[e]so that you may be justified in your words
and blameless in your judgment.
5 Behold, [f]I was brought forth in iniquity,
and in sin did my mother conceive me.
6 Behold, you delight in truth in [g]the inward being,
and you teach me wisdom in the secret heart.

7 Purge me [h]with hyssop, and I shall be clean;
[z]wash me, and I shall be [i]whiter than snow.
8 Let me hear joy and gladness;
[j]let the bones [k]that you have broken rejoice.
9 [l]Hide your face from my sins,
and [y]blot out all my iniquities.
10 [m]Create in me a [n]clean heart, O God,
and [o]renew a right[1] spirit within me.
11 [p]Cast me not away from your presence,
and take not [q]your Holy Spirit from me.
12 Restore to me the joy of your salvation,
and uphold me with a willing spirit.

13 Then I will teach transgressors your ways,
and sinners will [r]return to you.
14 Deliver me from [s]bloodguiltiness, O God,
O [t]God of my salvation,
and [u]my tongue will sing aloud of your [v]righteousness.

[1] Or *steadfast*

4 [c]Gen. 20:6; 39:9; 2 Sam. 12:13; [1 Cor. 8:12] [d]Luke 15:18, 21 [e]Cited Rom. 3:4
5 [f]Rom. 5:12, 19; Eph. 2:3; See Job 14:4; 15:14
6 [g]Job 38:36
7 [h]Ex. 12:22; Lev. 14:4; Num. 19:18; Heb. 9:19 [z][See ver. 2 above] [i]Isa. 1:18
8 [j]Ps. 35:10 [k]Ps. 44:19; Isa. 38:13
9 [l]Jer. 16:17 [y][See ver. 1 above]
10 [m]1 Sam. 10:9; Jer. 24:7; Ezek. 11:19; 36:26; Eph. 4:23, 24 [n]Ps. 24:4; Matt. 5:8; Acts 15:9 [o]Lam. 5:21
11 [p]Ps. 102:10; 2 Kgs. 13:23; 17:20; 24:20; Jer. 7:15 [q]Rom. 8:9; Eph. 4:30
13 [r][Luke 22:32]
14 [s]2 Sam. 11:17; 12:9 [t]Ps. 24:5 [u]Ps. 35:28; 71:8, 15, 24 [v][1 John 1:9]

51:4 Against you, you only, have I sinned. Of course, in doing wrong he has hurt others; the point here is that God is the ultimate judge for all sin (thus harming others is given not less weight but more). Cf. David's response to Nathan, 2 Sam. 12:13. **so that you may be justified in your words and blameless in your judgment**. The psalmist acknowledges his guilt before God "so that" God's justice in all he does will be clear. In Rom. 3:4 Paul cites this part of the verse from the Septuagint in support of his argument that God is just and is entitled to judge.

51:5 I was brought forth (that is, from the womb) **in iniquity**. David thinks of himself as a sinful person from the time of his birth. **in sin did my mother conceive me**. The idea is not that the act of conception was itself sinful, but (as the parallel first line shows) that each worshiper learns to trace his sinful tendencies to the very beginning of his existence—not only from birth but even from before that, to conception. (This certainly attributes moral accountability, the most important aspect of "personhood," to the developing baby in the womb. This is why many see this passage as implying that an unborn child should be thought of as a human person from the point of conception in his mother's womb.) See The Beginning of Life and Abortion, pp. 2537–2539.

51:6–13 *I Seek Restoration and Renewal.* The proper posture of the penitent is to crave a fresh sense of God's presence (vv. 8–9, 11), a deeper purification of the moral life (vv. 6, 10, 12), and a credible witness to the unfaithful (v. 13). The focus is on the inmost self, from which obedient actions flow: **inward being, secret heart** (v. 6); **clean heart, right spirit** (v. 10). The goal of this confession is not self-abasement but a renewal of the **joy and gladness** (v. 8) that the faithful have in God's presence.

51:7 hyssop. A plant with hairy leaves and branches; bunches of the branches are good for sprinkling. For its use in a cleansing ceremony, cf. Lev. 14:6; Num. 19:6. As with Ps. 51:2 (see note on vv. 1–2), the psalm highlights the inner condition to which the ceremonies point.

51:8 bones. The feeling of God's displeasure, and of his favor, penetrates into the whole person; cf. 32:3.

51:9 Usually when God is said to **hide** his **face from** someone, it means that he will no longer look upon that person with favor (cf. 13:1; 22:24; 27:9; 88:14; 102:2; 143:7; Deut. 31:17; 32:20; Isa. 8:17; 54:8; 59:2; 64:7). Here the singer asks God no longer to look upon his **sins**. To **blot out** (cf. Ps. 51:1) is to remove completely from the record book; cf. Ex. 32:32.

51:11 take not your Holy Spirit from me. Some have taken this to imply that the Holy Spirit can be taken from someone, at least in the OT; others have suggested that the Holy Spirit is viewed here in his role of empowering David for his kingly duties, and that this is a prayer that God not take the kingship and the divine anointing for kingship from David as he did from Saul (see note on 1 Sam. 16:14; cf. 1 Sam. 16:13). To evaluate these views, one should observe that the OT rarely discusses the Holy Spirit's role in cleansing the inner life (besides here, Ezek. 36:27 is the main OT text on the subject), and certainly does not enter into technical questions of the Spirit's permanent indwelling. Further, the fact that this is a psalm for the whole congregation argues against the idea that this is David's personal prayer about his kingship. The whole tenor of this psalm is that, if strict justice were God's only consideration, he would have the right to bring dire judgment on those who sin (which includes all of his own people), and that the only possible appeal is to his mercy. The function of the psalm, as a song sung by the entire congregation, is to shape their hearts so that they feel this at the deepest level, lest they ever presume upon God's grace.

51:13 As usual in the Psalms, the **transgressors** and **sinners** are members of the covenant people who do not faithfully embrace the provisions of God's covenant; the faithful call them to embrace God's grace, from the perspective of those who themselves deserve to be cast out.

51:14–17 *Then I Will Worship Truly.* The terms in this section, such as **sing aloud** (v. 14), **declare** (v. 15), and **sacrifice** (vv. 16–17), all point to activities of public worship. The person who has used this psalm to confess his sins and to receive God's assurance of pardon is the one who can genuinely worship the gracious God of the covenant.

51:14 bloodguiltiness. Probably a reference to the slaying of Uriah (cf. 2 Sam. 12:9). The faithful may not have committed this particular sin, but should instead take heart: if God can forgive David this evil, he can certainly forgive all else!

16[w]See Ps. 40:6
17[x]See Ps. 34:18
18[y][Ps. 69:35; 122:6] [z]Ps. 147:2
19[a]Ps. 4:5; [Mal. 3:3] [b]Deut. 33:10

Psalm 52
[c]1 Sam. 22:9
2[d]Ps. 50:19 [e][Ps. 57:4] [f]Ps. 101:7
3[g][Jer. 9:4, 5]
5[h]Prov. 2:22 [i]See Ps. 27:13
6[j]See Ps. 40:3 [k]See Ps. 2:4
7[l]See Ps. 49:6
8[m]Jer. 11:16; [Ps. 1:3; 37:35; 92:12, 13; 128:3; 144:12; Hos. 14:6]

15 O Lord, open my lips,
and my mouth will declare your praise.
16 [w]For you will not delight in sacrifice, or I would give it;
you will not be pleased with a burnt offering.
17 The sacrifices of God are [x]a broken spirit;
a broken and contrite heart, O God, you will not despise.

18 [y]Do good to Zion in your good pleasure;
[z]build up the walls of Jerusalem;
19 then will you delight in [a]right sacrifices,
in burnt offerings and [b]whole burnt offerings;
then bulls will be offered on your altar.

The Steadfast Love of God Endures

52

To the choirmaster. A Maskil[1] of David, when [c]Doeg, the Edomite, came and told Saul, "David has come to the house of Ahimelech."

1 Why do you boast of evil, O mighty man?
The steadfast love of God endures all the day.
2 Your [d]tongue plots destruction,
like [e]a sharp razor, you [f]worker of deceit.
3 You love evil more than good,
and [g]lying more than speaking what is right. *Selah*
4 You love all words that devour,
O deceitful tongue.

5 But God will break you down forever;
he will snatch and [h]tear you from your tent;
he will uproot you from [i]the land of the living. *Selah*
6 The righteous shall [j]see and fear,
and shall [k]laugh at him, saying,
7 "See the man who would not make
God his refuge,
but [l]trusted in the abundance of his riches
and sought refuge in his own destruction!"[2]

8 But I am like [m]a green olive tree
in the house of God.

[1] Probably a musical or liturgical term [2] Or *in his work of destruction*

51:16–17 These verses seem to make **sacrifice** and **burnt offering** relatively unimportant for the faithful, even replacing them with the inner disposition (**a broken and contrite heart**). However, since v. 19 goes on to speak of offering physical sacrifices, it is better to take these verses as implying that the animal sacrifices look to the worshiper offering himself to God (cf. notes on vv. 1–2 and v. 7) as "a living sacrifice" (Rom. 12:1), and without this they forfeit significance.

51:18–19 *Do Good to Zion.* The psalm closes by enabling worshipers to see the relationship between their own spiritual health and the well-being of the whole body of God's people (**Zion**). That is, each member is linked to all the others in a web of relationships, and together they share in the life of God as it pulses through the whole body. Thus each member contributes to (or else detracts from) the health of the whole. The ideal Israel is a community of forgiven penitents, faithfully embracing God's covenant and worshiping him according to the rites he appointed; this is the community that can bring light to the whole world.

Psalm 52. This psalm enables the faithful to develop confidence in God's care and protection, particularly when surrounded by ruthless enemies. The title sets the psalm during David's flight from Saul (1 Sam. 21:1–7), which led to the slaughter at Nob of the priests who had helped David (1 Sam. 22:9–19). Doeg's report put the priests' hospitality to David in the worst light (see note on 1 Sam. 22:10); when none of Saul's Israelite men would strike the priests down, Doeg willingly did so. He is thus an example of the enemies that the faithful might face.

52:1–4 *The Gloating Evildoer.* This section has the speech of the enemy in view, as can be seen from **boast** (v. 1), **tongue** (vv. 2, 4), **lying** (v. 3), and **words** (v. 4). But the speech of this enemy is not only false in itself, it is using falsehood to plot the **destruction** of the faithful. The most important answer to such evil is the confidence that **the steadfast love of God endures all the day** (v. 1; cf. v. 8).

52:5–7 *But God Will Deal with You in the Sight of All.* The faithful person (**righteous**, v. 6) who will trust in God (unlike the enemy, v. 7) is confident that he is always safe. On the other hand, the enemy is clearly presented as an enemy of both God's covenant and his faithful people (v. 7)—and this is the reason he plots such evil; it is only a matter of time until this enemy falls into disaster at God's own hands.

52:8–9 *I Am Safe in Your Keeping, O God.* This section develops more fully the confidence that v. 1 hinted at. In contrast to the wicked who are "uprooted" (v. 5), the faithful (**the godly**, v. 9) will be **a green olive tree** (an image of vitality and fruitfulness, cf. Jer. 11:16; Hos. 14:6; cf. Ps. 92:12–14 for a palm tree in God's courts). For the **house of God** as an image of God's hospitality, cf. 23:6; 27:4. In contrast to the enemy who trusts in the abundance of his riches (52:7), the faithful **trust in the steadfast love of**

I trust in the steadfast love of God
forever and ever.
9 I will thank you forever,
because you have done it.
I will wait for your name, [n]for it is good,
in the presence of the [o]godly.

There Is None Who Does Good

53 TO THE CHOIRMASTER: ACCORDING TO [p]MAHALATH. A MASKIL[1] OF DAVID.

1 [q]The fool says in his heart, "There is no God."
They are corrupt, doing abominable iniquity;
there is none who does good.

2 God looks down from heaven
on the children of man
to see if there are any who understand,[2]
who seek after God.

3 They have all fallen away;
together they have become corrupt;
there is none who does good,
not even one.

4 Have those who work evil no knowledge,
who eat up my people as they eat bread,
and do not call upon God?

5 There they are, in great terror,
[r]where there is no terror!
For God [s]scatters the bones of him who encamps against you;
you put them to shame, for God has rejected them.

6 Oh, that salvation for Israel would come out of Zion!
When God restores the fortunes of his people,
let Jacob rejoice, let Israel be glad.

The Lord Upholds My Life

54 TO THE CHOIRMASTER: WITH [t]STRINGED INSTRUMENTS. A MASKIL[3] OF DAVID, [u]WHEN THE ZIPHITES WENT AND TOLD SAUL, "IS NOT DAVID HIDING AMONG US?"

1 O God, save me by your [v]name,
and vindicate me by your might.

[1] Probably musical or liturgical terms [2] Or *who act wisely* [3] Probably a musical or liturgical term

9[n]Ps. 54:6 [o]See Ps. 50:5
Psalm 53
[p]Ps. 88, title
1[q]For ver. 1-6, see Ps. 14:1-7
5[r][Lev. 26:17, 36; Prov. 28:1] [s]Ps. 89:10; 141:7; Jer. 8:1, 2; Ezek. 6:5
Psalm 54
[t]Ps. 4, title [u]1 Sam. 23:19; 26:1
1[v]Ps. 5:11; 52:9

God forever and ever (52:8). The prospect that God will bring judgment upon the enemies enables the faithful to **wait for** God's **name**, i.e., for God to vindicate his name by protecting those who trust in him. Thus they need not be consumed with thoughts of vengeance.

Psalm 53. This psalm is almost identical to Psalm 14, and the two psalms were probably alternate versions of the same hymn before they were included in the Psalter. The two hymns serve the same function, namely, to mourn the fact that mankind does not seek after God and thus treats God's people cruelly. (See notes on Psalm 14 for exposition.) The chief difference between the two psalms is that 53:5 is as long as 14:5–6 together (and thus 53:6 = 14:7). In 53:5 the psalmist describes in greater detail the terror that will befall the wicked instead of emphasizing God's care for the poor (14:5–6). Also, Psalm 53 uses "God" throughout to refer to the deity, while Psalm 14 uses "the LORD" in several of these places.

Psalm 54. This is an individual lament, asking (as many laments do) for God's help against those who threaten the lives of the faithful. The title connects the song to the events of 1 Sam. 23:19, where the Ziphites, among whom David was hiding, informed Saul of where David was, promising to hand David over to him. The psalm directs its singers to God's protection and is therefore well-suited for the pious to use when they are under threat of deadly persecution; for those who do not face such persecution, this psalm is appropriate to sing on behalf of their brethren in danger.

54:1–3 *O God, Save Me from the Ruthless.* The psalm opens by describing the circumstances: **ruthless men**, who have no respect for God (**they do not set God before themselves**) **seek my life** (v. 3). In such a case the proper appeal is to God's **name** (vv. 1, 6; God's name can be an image for his personal presence, cf. Lev. 19:12; Deut. 6:13; or else as the sum of his revealed character; cf. Ex. 34:6). There is also an appeal to God's **might** (which is always greater than any might of the enemies).

2 [w]See Ps. 55:1
3 [x]Ps. 86:14 [y]Ps. 18:44; 144:7; Isa. 25:5 [z][1 Sam. 23:15]
4 [a]Ps. 118:7
5 [b][Ps. 89:49] [c]Ps. 143:12
6 [d]Ps. 52:9
7 [e]Ps. 59:10; 92:11; 112:8; 118:7

Psalm 55
[f]Ps. 4, title
1 [g]Ps. 54:2; 61:1; 86:6
2 [h]ver. 17; Ps. 64:1 [i][Isa. 38:14; 59:11]
3 [j][2 Sam. 16:7, 8]
4 [k]Ps. 116:3
5 [l]Job 21:6; Isa. 21:4; Ezek. 7:18 [m]Ps. 78:53
7 [n][Jer. 9:2]

2 O God, [w]hear my prayer;
give ear to the words of my mouth.

3 [x]For [y]strangers[1] have risen against me;
ruthless men [z]seek my life;
they do not set God before themselves. *Selah*

4 Behold, [a]God is my helper;
the Lord is the upholder of my life.
5 He will return the evil to my enemies;
in your [b]faithfulness [c]put an end to them.

6 With a freewill offering I will sacrifice to you;
I will give thanks to your name, O LORD, [d]for it is good.
7 For he has delivered me from every trouble,
and my eye has [e]looked in triumph on my enemies.

Cast Your Burden on the LORD

55

TO THE CHOIRMASTER: WITH [f]STRINGED INSTRUMENTS. A MASKIL[2] OF DAVID.

1 [g]Give ear to my prayer, O God,
and hide not yourself from my plea for mercy!
2 Attend to me, and answer me;
I am restless [h]in my complaint and I [i]moan,
3 because of the noise of the enemy,
because of the oppression of the wicked.
For they [j]drop trouble upon me,
and in anger they bear a grudge against me.

4 My heart is in anguish within me;
[k]the terrors of death have fallen upon me.
5 Fear and trembling come upon me,
and [l]horror [m]overwhelms me.
6 And I say, "Oh, that I had wings like a dove!
I would fly away and be at rest;
7 [n]yes, I would wander far away;
I would lodge in the wilderness; *Selah*

[1] Some Hebrew manuscripts and Targum *insolent men* (compare Psalm 86:14) [2] Probably a musical or liturgical term

54:3 The term **strangers** can refer to people from outside Israel (e.g., "foreigners," Isa. 1:7; Obad. 11). In context the Ziphites, who belong to Judah, are acting like Gentiles in opposing God's faithful. As the ESV footnote explains, some Hebrew manuscripts read "insolent men" (Hb. זדים, *zdym*, in place of זרים, *zrym*, a change of only one letter to another with similar appearance), which is the term found in the very similar Ps. 86:14. This word is also well-suited to the situation, where Israelites are acting unfaithfully (cf. 119:21, 51, 69, 78, 85, 122; the same word is rendered "arrogant" in Prov. 21:24; Mal. 3:15; 4:1).

54:4–5 *God Is My Helper.* The prayer directed to God in vv. 1–3 is a wise one, because God has promised to be the **helper** and **upholder of . . . life** for each of his faithful. Thus each believer can trust that God **will return the evil to my enemies** (i.e., the evil they intend to carry out, cf. 5:10; 7:15), and thus can leave the timing of that to God (it may or may not be in the particular worshiper's lifetime).

54:6–7 *I Will Bring a Freewill Offering.* The worshiper looks forward to continued enjoyment of God's presence and favor. The **freewill offering** is a kind of peace offering (Lev. 7:16), which means that its purpose is to celebrate God's goodness with a meal in his presence. The schemes of the ruthless cannot keep the faithful away from God forever.

Psalm 55. Like many other individual laments, this psalm prays for God's help against dangerous enemies who hate the faithful. There is a unique twist here, though: the danger comes from betrayal by a close friend (vv. 13–14, 20–21) who had seemed a fellow pilgrim on the path of life. Some deny that David could be the author of this psalm, because there is no clear instance of such betrayal in the recorded life of David. But that misses the point: the psalms are hymns, not merely autobiography. David has provided this psalm for God's people to sing under this kind of duress. In addition, David was betrayed by his son Absalom (2 Sam. 15:1–12; 16:15–23) and by his counselor Ahithophel (2 Sam. 15:12; 16:15–23).

55:1–3 *Hear My Prayer.* The prayer is earnest (**plea for mercy**, **restless in my complaint**), and its occasion is **the noise of the enemy** and **the oppression of the wicked**, namely, **they drop trouble upon me** (i.e., as if they were dropping stones) because **they bear a grudge against me**. As usual in the psalms, these are not simply people who dislike the singer; they are enemies of true piety, who will even take violent measures to ruin the godly and stamp out true faith (vv. 3, 9–11, 21, 23).

55:4–8 *I Am Desperate.* This section describes more fully the earnestness of the singer: **in anguish**, **terrors of death**, **fear**, **trembling**, and **horror**. If he could **fly** (the **dove** is probably a symbol of both innocence and

8 I would hurry to find a shelter
from [o]the raging wind and tempest."

9 Destroy, O Lord, [p]divide their tongues;
for I see [q]violence and strife in the city.
10 Day and night they go around it
on its walls,
and [r]iniquity and trouble are within it;
11 ruin is in its midst;
[s]oppression and fraud
do not depart from its marketplace.

12 For it is not an enemy who taunts me—
then I could bear it;
it is not an adversary who [t]deals insolently with me—
then I could hide from him.
13 [u]But it is you, a man, my equal,
my companion, my familiar friend.
14 We used to take sweet counsel together;
within God's house we walked in [v]the throng.
15 Let death steal over them;
let them go down to Sheol [w]alive;
for evil is in their dwelling place and in their heart.

16 But I call to God,
and the LORD will save me.
17 [x]Evening and [y]morning and at [z]noon
I [a]utter my complaint and moan,
and he hears my voice.
18 He redeems my soul in safety
from the battle that I wage,
for [b]many are arrayed against me.
19 God will give ear and humble them,
he who is [c]enthroned from of old, *Selah*
because they do not [d]change
and do not fear God.

20 My companion[1] [e]stretched out his hand against his friends;
he violated his covenant.
21 His [f]speech was [g]smooth as butter,
yet war was in his heart;
his words were softer than oil,
yet they were [h]drawn swords.

[1] Hebrew *He*

8 [o]Ps. 83:15
9 [p][Gen. 11:9] [q]Jer. 6:7
10 [r]Ps. 5:9
11 [s][Ps. 10:7]
12 [t]Job 19:5
13 [u][2 Sam. 15:12; 16:23]; See Ps. 41:9
14 [v]Ps. 42:4
15 [w]Num. 16:30, 33; Prov. 1:12; [Ps. 124:3]
17 [x]Ps. 141:2; Acts 3:1; 10:3, 30 [y]Ps. 5:3; 88:13; 92:2 [z]Acts 10:9; [Dan. 6:10] [a]ver. 2
18 [b][Ps. 56:2]
19 [c]Deut. 33:27 [d]Job 10:17; See Job 21:7-15
20 [e]Acts 12:1
21 [f]See Ps. 28:3 [g]Prov. 5:3, 4 [h]See Ps. 57:4

swiftness), he would take refuge **in the wilderness** (away from the **raging** in the city).

55:9–11 *Destroy Those Who Bring Such Ruin.* In such a situation the singer prays for deliverance, which ordinarily means the thwarting of the wicked schemes of the enemies. It cannot be compassionate to remain indifferent to the suffering that these enemies bring to the innocent (**violence, strife, iniquity and trouble, ruin, oppression and fraud**). In such hymns, the singer would prefer that the enemies repent of their evil; but here the singer seems to expect that they will not (cf. v. 19). For more on such prayers, see notes on 5:10 and 35:4–8.

55:9 divide their tongues. "Divide" (Hb. *palag*) probably evokes the name Peleg, "in [whose] days the earth was divided" (Gen. 10:25), which in turn is probably a reference to the Tower of Babel (Gen. 11:1–9, where God confused the language of the human schemers). The prayer is thus for the enemies to be prevented from working together to carry out their evil.

55:12–15 *I Am Betrayed by My Own Friend!* Now the pain sharpens: it is not a nameless **enemy** or **adversary** who is seeking to harm the pious singer, but **my companion, my familiar friend**. Cf. 41:9.

55:15 Let death. See note on vv. 9–11. **Sheol**. See note on 6:5.

55:16–19 *I Call to God and Trust He Will Hear Me.* This section is similar to vv. 1–3, except it is talking about praying, with God in the third person (**he**, v. 17) and not second person (e.g., yourself, v. 1). The psalmist describes both desperation (v. 17) and confidence (vv. 18–19).

55:18 redeems. See note on 25:22.

55:20–21 *My Treacherous Friend.* This section returns to describing a painful betrayal. This is not simply a friend who has let another down; he has planned destruction of those who had trusted him, all the while disguising his evil intent. **covenant**. He had sealed his friendship with a solemn obligation; see 1 Sam. 18:3.

22 [i]Cast your burden on the LORD,
and he will sustain you;
[j]he will never permit
the righteous to be moved.

23 But you, O God, [k]will cast them down
into [l]the pit of destruction;
men of [m]blood and treachery
shall not [n]live out half their days.
But I will [o]trust in you.

In God I Trust

56

TO THE CHOIRMASTER: ACCORDING TO THE DOVE ON FAR-OFF TEREBINTHS. A [p]MIKTAM[1] OF DAVID, WHEN THE [q]PHILISTINES SEIZED HIM IN GATH.

1 [r]Be gracious to me, O God, for man [s]tramples on me;
all day long an attacker oppresses me;
2 my enemies trample on me all day long,
for many attack me proudly.
3 When I am afraid,
I [t]put my trust in you.
4 In God, whose word I praise,
in God I trust; [u]I shall not be afraid.
What can flesh do to me?

5 All day long they injure my cause;[2]
all their thoughts are against me for evil.
6 They [v]stir up strife, they [w]lurk;
they [x]watch my steps,
as they have waited for my life.
7 For their crime will they escape?
[y]In wrath [z]cast down the peoples, O God!

8 You have kept count of my tossings;[3]
[a]put my tears in your bottle.
[b]Are they not in your book?
9 Then my enemies will turn back
[c]in the day when I call.
This I know, that[4] [d]God is for me.
10 In God, whose word I praise,
in the LORD, whose word I praise,
11 in God I trust; [u]I shall not be afraid.
What can man do to me?

[1] Probably a musical or liturgical term [2] Or *they twist my words* [3] Or *wanderings* [4] Or *because*

22[i]See Ps. 37:5 [j]Ps. 10:6
23[k]ver. 15; Ps. 56:7; 59:11 [l]Ps. 69:15; 94:13 [m]Ps. 5:6 [n]Prov. 10:27; See Job 15:32 [o]See Ps. 11:1

Psalm 56
[p]Ps. 16, title; 57, title [q][1 Sam. 21:10, 11; 22:1]
1[r]Ps. 57:1; See Ps. 4:1 [s]Ps. 57:3
3[t]See Ps. 11:1
4[u]Ps. 27:1; 118:6; Isa. 51:12; Heb. 13:6
6[v]Ps. 59:3; 140:2; Isa. 54:15 [w]Ps. 10:8 [x]Ps. 71:10
7[y]Ps. 7:6; 59:5 [z]See Ps. 55:23
8[a][Ps. 39:12; 2 Kgs. 20:5] [b][Mal. 3:16]
9[c]Ps. 102:2 [d]Ps. 118:6; [Rom. 8:31]
11[u][See ver. 4 above]

55:22–23 *Cast Your Burden on the LORD*. The singer addresses each of his fellow singers (**your**, v. 22), and then God (**you, O God**, v. 23). The reason the faithful can **cast** their **burden on the LORD** is that he can be trusted to bring judgment upon the evildoers. The psalms do not say *when* God will **cast them down**; the faithful will wait for God's own good timing.

55:22 Cast your burden. The Septuagint renders this "cast your anxieties," and 1 Pet. 5:7 urges Christians to a similar faith in the face of persecution. **moved**. See note on Ps. 10:6.

Psalm 56. Many take this to be an individual lament, but it could also be a psalm of (anticipated) thanksgiving: the description of troubles and prayer is taken up into gratitude that God has heard and will act (as he has acted in the past). The specific troubles arise from people who aim to hurt the pious singer, as is common with lament psalms. The title links the psalm with the events of 1 Sam. 21:10–15 (similar to Psalm 34).

56:1–4 *Man Tramples on Me.* The singer describes his circumstances and sets his mind on the right response. The situation can be seen in the repetition of **trample** and **attack** (vv. 1, 2); the response is seen in the repetition of **trust** (vv. 3, 4). This enables those who sing the psalm to set their own hearts on the right response: when they are **afraid**, this is the antidote.

56:5–7 *They Have Waited for My Life.* The psalm goes on to give more detail on the enemies' schemes. It is clear, as is usually true with the psalms, that the enemies are not simply personal opponents of the singer but opponents of all that is good. In David's experience, they would be the Philistines who thought he should be put to death (cf. **peoples**, v. 7; i.e., Gentiles).

56:8–11 *God Is for Me.* These verses fill out the picture of trust: God keeps account of the **tears** of his faithful ones; he does not ignore their concerns. He is **for** those who trust in him. Verses 10–11 repeat v. 4 with slight variations. The pious singer expects that his **enemies will turn back**, because God is trustworthy.

12 I must perform my [e]vows to you, O God;
I will [e]render thank offerings to you.
13 [f]For you have delivered my soul from death,
yes, my feet from falling,
[g]that I may walk before God
[h]in the light of life.

Let Your Glory Be over All the Earth

57

TO THE CHOIRMASTER: ACCORDING TO [i]DO NOT DESTROY. A [j]MIKTAM[1] OF DAVID, WHEN HE FLED FROM SAUL, IN [k]THE CAVE.

1 [l]Be merciful to me, O God, be merciful to me,
for in you my soul [m]takes refuge;
in [n]the shadow of your wings I will take refuge,
[o]till the storms of destruction pass by.
2 I cry out to God Most High,
to God who [p]fulfills his purpose for me.
3 [q]He will send from heaven and save me;
he will put to shame [r]him who tramples on me. *Selah*
[s]God will send out [t]his steadfast love and his faithfulness!

4 My soul is in the midst of [u]lions;
I lie down amid fiery beasts—
the children of man, whose [v]teeth are spears and arrows,
whose [w]tongues are sharp swords.

5 [x]Be exalted, O God, above the heavens!
Let your glory be over all the earth!

6 They set [y]a net for my steps;
my soul was [z]bowed down.
They [a]dug a pit in my way,
but they have fallen into it themselves. *Selah*
7 [b]My heart is [c]steadfast, O God,
my heart is steadfast!
I will sing and make melody!
8 [d]Awake, [e]my glory![2]

[1] Probably a musical or liturgical term [2] Or *my whole being*

12[e]See Ps. 50:14
13[f]Ps. 49:15; 116:8 [g]Ps. 116:9 [h][Ps. 49:19]

Psalm 57
[i][Ps. 58, title; 59, title; 75, title] [j]Ps. 16, title; 56, title [k]1 Sam. 22:1; 24:1-3; [Ps. 142, title]
1[l]Ps. 56:1; See Ps. 4:1 [m]Ps. 91:4 [n]See Ps. 17:8 [o]Isa. 26:20
2[p]Ps. 138:8
3[q]Ps. 144:5, 7; [Ps. 18:16] [r]See Ps. 56:1 [s]Ps. 43:3 [t]See Ps. 36:5; 40:11
4[u]Ps. 58:6 [v]Prov. 30:14 [w]Ps. 55:21; 59:7; 64:3; Prov. 12:18; [Ps. 52:2; Jer. 9:8]
5[x]Ps. 108:5; [Ps. 113:4]
6[y]See Job 18:8 [z]Ps. 145:14; 146:8 [a]See Ps. 7:15
7[b]For ver. 7-11, see Ps. 108:1-5 [c]Ps. 112:7
8[d]Judg. 5:12 [e]See Ps. 16:9

56:12–13 *You Have Delivered My Soul from Death.* The singer expresses his confidence that, if "God is for him" (v. 9), it is as good as done: God has **delivered** his **soul from death**. The **vows** and **thank offerings** are varieties of the peace offerings that celebrate God's answer to prayer (cf. 54:6; Lev. 7:15–16).

56:13 Walk before God in the light of life probably describes enjoying God's presence in "life," i.e., in true faithfulness; cf. 89:15 (walking in the light of God's face) and Isa. 2:5 (walking in God's light).

Psalm 57. This is another individual lament, based on an event in David's life (probably 1 Sam. 22:1, but possibly 1 Sam. 24:3; Psalm 142 is likewise from one of these passages). Like Psalms 34; 52; 54; 56; 59; 63; and 142, Psalm 57 arose from Saul's persecution of David. The psalm has two sections, each ended by the refrain (vv. 5, 11), and each mentioning God's "steadfast love and faithfulness" (vv. 3, 10, drawing on Ex. 34:6). In the first section (Ps. 57:1–5), the dominant strain is cheerful confidence amid danger, while in the second (vv. 6–11), the accent is on the expectation of victory, and thus of God's vindication. The faithful who sing this hymn can identify with David's confidence in the presence of serious dangers, and can look through those dangers to seek God's honor. Psalm 108:1–5, also by David, uses 57:7–11. "Do not destroy" in the title (Psalms 57–59; 75) may be some kind of tune or chant pattern, perhaps influenced by the phrase in Deut. 9:26 and 1 Sam. 26:9.

57:1–5 *Confident Request for Mercy.* The circumstances are dire (**storms of destruction**, v. 1; **tramples on me**, v. 3; **lions** and **fiery beasts**, v. 4), and yet the faithful person will **cry out to God** in confidence that he hears and that he **fulfills his purpose** for his children (v. 2).

57:1 Be merciful is a humble request for God to show kindness and grant relief, recognizing that God cannot be compelled to do this (cf. 30:10; 51:1; 123:3); the word can also be rendered "be gracious" (e.g., 4:1; 6:2; 56:1).

57:3 save. See note on 3:2. **His steadfast love and his faithfulness** (see also 57:10) alludes to Ex. 34:6.

57:5 Since God is already "high" or **exalted** (cf. 113:4; 138:6), this is a prayer that people would acknowledge his greatness. For his **glory** to **be over all the earth** is for people to honor God for his splendor and high position.

57:6–11 *Confident Expectation of Victory.* This section mentions the danger (**net** and **pit**, v. 6), only to exult in its reversal (**they have fallen into it themselves**, v. 6). The singer moves on to urge himself to praise, and to look forward to bringing testimony of God's goodness beyond the present people of Israel to the whole world (**peoples** and **nations**, v. 9; cf. Gen. 12:1–3; Ex. 19:5–6).

57:8 my glory. A term for the whole person, probably focusing on its most noble faculties (cf. 30:12; Gen. 49:6; and ESV footnotes on Ps. 16:9; 108:1); here the singer's "glory" gives the right response to God's "glory" (57:5, 11).

8[f]1 Chr. 15:16
10[g]See Ps. 36:5
11[x][See ver. 5 above]

Psalm 58
[h]See Ps. 57, title [i]See Ps. 16, title
2[j][Ps. 94:20]
3[k]Ps. 51:5; Isa. 48:8
4[l]Ps. 140:3; [Deut. 32:33]
5[m]Jer. 8:17
6[n]Ps. 3:7; Job 4:10; 29:17
7[o]Ps. 112:10; Josh. 7:5 [p]Ps. 64:3
8[o][See ver. 7 above] [q]See Job 3:16
9[r]Ps. 118:12; Eccles. 7:6 [s][Job 27:21; See Prov. 10:25]
10[t]Deut. 32:43; See Job 22:19 [u]Ps. 68:23

Awake, [f]O harp and lyre!
I will awake the dawn!
9 I will give thanks to you, O Lord, among the peoples;
I will sing praises to you among the nations.
10 For your [g]steadfast love is great to the heavens,
your faithfulness to the clouds.

11 [x]Be exalted, O God, above the heavens!
Let your glory be over all the earth!

God Who Judges the Earth

58 TO THE CHOIRMASTER: ACCORDING TO [h]DO NOT DESTROY. A [i]MIKTAM[1] OF DAVID.

1 Do you indeed decree what is right, you gods?[2]
Do you judge the children of man uprightly?
2 No, in your hearts you devise wrongs;
your hands [j]deal out violence on earth.

3 The wicked are [k]estranged from the womb;
they go astray from birth, speaking lies.
4 [l]They have venom like the venom of a serpent,
like the deaf adder that stops its ear,
5 so that it [m]does not hear the voice of charmers
or of the cunning enchanter.

6 O God, [n]break the teeth in their mouths;
tear out the fangs of the young lions, O LORD!
7 Let them [o]vanish like water that runs away;
when he [p]aims his arrows, let them be blunted.
8 Let them be like the snail [o]that dissolves into slime,
like [q]the stillborn child who never sees the sun.
9 Sooner than your pots can feel the heat of [r]thorns,
whether green or ablaze, may he [s]sweep them away![3]

10 [t]The righteous will rejoice when he sees the vengeance;
he will [u]bathe his feet in the blood of the wicked.

[1] Probably a musical or liturgical term [2] Or *you mighty lords* (by revocalization; Hebrew *in silence*) [3] The meaning of the Hebrew verse is uncertain

Psalm 58. God's people should sing this song when they are confronted with injustice among their own rulers (it is thus a community lament). In the time of David, of course, the focus was on those who ruled Israel, a theocracy (which was thus, at least in name, supposed to be governed by the principles of the Pentateuch); and yet Christians may pray this way since the rulers of God's people, indeed all people, everywhere and at all times, ought to embody the highest human ideals of justice (see notes on Prov. 31:1–9). Singing this in worship helps the faithful to pray more earnestly for godly leadership, and forms in the leaders of the community a true moral compass for their own leadership. It also celebrates the prospect that—one day, sooner or later—God will vindicate his justice in the world, and those who trust him will rejoice exceedingly.

58:1–2 *The Challenge to the Tyrants.* The song opens by addressing the tyrants directly: v. 1 asks questions about whether there is justice in their rule, and v. 2 answers the questions with a clear **No**. In context, the **wrongs** and **violence** are the kind a ruler too often condones—especially the exploitation of the weaker members of society.

58:1 you gods. As the ESV footnote explains, this translation is obtained by a change in vowels from the received Hebrew text (which may have been mistakenly altered through a copyist's error). The received vowels (Hb. *'elem*) yield "in silence," which does not make much sense, while a slight adjustment of the vowels yields "gods" or "mighty lords" (Hb. *'elim*), which can refer to human rulers who wield their might by God's appointment (cf. Ex. 15:15, "leaders"; Job 41:25, "mighty"; Ezek. 17:13; 32:21, "chiefs"; possibly also Ps. 82:6, see note). This fits well as a word for those who should **decree what is right** and **judge the children of man uprightly**.

58:3–5 *The Charge against the Tyrants.* Now the song describes these unjust rulers, calling them **wicked**; this term, when applied to an Israelite, denotes someone who does not honor God, i.e., does not fear him. They are Israelites who do not embrace the covenantal grace from their hearts; and thus, rather than devote themselves to serving the well-being of the community, they instead use their position to squeeze the life out of their fellow Israelites (employing **lies**, v. 3, as well as "violence," v. 2). In so doing they destroy the community, every bit as much as the **venom** of a dangerous **serpent** (such as the **deaf adder**; perhaps a kind of cobra, if the reference to the **charmers** in v. 5 is any indication) destroys the one it bites.

58:6–9 *The Curse upon the Tyrants.* The congregation prays that such rulers may fail in their vicious purposes. The **teeth in their mouths** (v. 6) looks back to the serpents' teeth of v. 4, as well as to the **fangs of the young lions** in v. 6. The verse is a prayer that these evildoers may no longer have their present power to do harm. Verses 7–9 continue this prayer, that they should **vanish** (v. 7) and dissolve (v. 8), that God will **sweep them away** as with a whirlwind (v. 9). As is generally the case with such prayers (see note on 5:10), this prayer assumes that the wicked will not repent and seek justice (which would be better by far).

58:10–11 *The Celebration When God Judges the Tyrants.* The faithful remember who their God is: the Creator who loves to see his creation functioning properly (which is why he loves justice). Believers (the **righteous**) may suffer here and now, but they can know that one day God will vindicate

11 Mankind will say, "Surely there is [v]a reward for the righteous;
surely there is a God who [w]judges on earth."

Deliver Me from My Enemies

59

TO THE CHOIRMASTER: ACCORDING TO [x]DO NOT DESTROY. A [y]MIKTAM[1] OF DAVID, [z]WHEN SAUL SENT MEN TO WATCH HIS HOUSE IN ORDER TO KILL HIM.

1 [a]Deliver me from my enemies, O my God;
[b]protect me from those who [c]rise up against me;
2 deliver me from [d]those who work evil,
and save me from [e]bloodthirsty men.

3 For behold, they [f]lie in wait for my life;
fierce men [g]stir up strife against me.
[h]For no transgression or sin of mine, O LORD,
4 for no fault of mine, they run and make ready.
[i]Awake, come to meet me, and see!
5 You, [j]LORD God of hosts, are God of Israel.
Rouse yourself to punish all the nations;
spare none of those who treacherously plot evil. *Selah*

6 Each evening they [k]come back,
howling like dogs
and prowling about the city.
7 There they are, [l]bellowing with their mouths
with [m]swords in their lips—
for [n]"Who," they think,[2] "will hear us?"

8 But you, O LORD, [o]laugh at them;
you hold all the nations in derision.
9 O my Strength, I will watch for you,
for you, O God, are [p]my fortress.
10 [q]My God in his steadfast love[3] [r]will meet me;
God will let me [s]look in triumph on my enemies.

11 Kill them not, lest my people forget;
make them totter[4] by your power and [t]bring them down,
O Lord, our [u]shield!

[1] Probably a musical or liturgical term [2] Hebrew lacks *they think* [3] Or *The God who shows me steadfast love* [4] Or *wander*

11 [v]Isa. 3:10 [w]Ps. 67:4; 94:2; Gen. 18:25; Job 19:29; Eccles. 12:14

Psalm 59

[x]Ps. 57, title [y]Ps. 16, title [z][1 Sam. 19:11]
1 [a]Ps. 143:9; [Ps. 18:48] [b]See Ps. 20:1 [c]See Ps. 17:7
2 [d]Ps. 94:4 [e]Ps. 5:6
3 [f]Ps. 10:9 [g]See Ps. 56:6 [h]1 Sam. 24:11; [Ps. 7:3; 69:4]
4 [i]See Ps. 35:23
5 [j]Ps. 80:4; 84:8
6 [k][Ps. 22:16]
7 [l]Prov. 15:2, 28; [Ps. 94:4] [m]See Ps. 57:4 [n]See Job 22:13
8 [o]See Ps. 2:4
9 [p]ver. 16, 17; See Ps. 9:9
10 [q]ver. 17 [r]Ps. 21:3 [s]See Ps. 54:7
11 [t]See Ps. 55:23 [u]See Ps. 3:3

his justice in the world. The **reward for the righteous** is the enjoyment of God and of a renewed community and world that God promises they will receive (cf. Gal. 6:9).

Psalm 59. This is another individual lament, seeking God's protection from enemies who threaten the pious person's life. The title connects the psalm to 1 Sam. 19:11, where David escaped from Saul's men through a window. The psalm is geared for the particular case in which the enmity is "for no fault of mine" (v. 4). The song has two sections (vv. 1–10, 11–17). Verses 6–7 (description of howling dogs) correspond to vv. 14–15; and vv. 9–10 ("O my strength . . . steadfast love") correspond to v. 17. The first section is a cry for help in the face of fierce and bloodthirsty enemies, and the second section voices confidence that God will protect the singer and make an example of the persecutors.

59:1–10 *Deliver Me from My Enemies, O God.* The enemies are described as **those who work evil** and **bloodthirsty men** who **lie in wait for my life** (vv. 2–3). They are **fierce men**, they **stir up strife against me**—and **for no fault of mine** (v. 4). That is, this psalm is for situations in which the pious may profess innocence; they face hostility even though they have done no injury to the enemies. The enemies are **howling like dogs**, **prowling about the city** (v. 6) like a pack of scavengers. (Although dogs were apparently used in Israel as watchdogs [Isa. 56:10] and as herd dogs [Job 30:1], in a city the dogs roamed as semi-wild packs, feeding on carrion, trash, and anything they could kill [cf. Ps. 22:16]. Thus they posed a danger to any human who might venture out alone in the **evening**.) But the faithful should not despair at such threats: God is greater than the enemies and is well able to thwart their schemes (59:8–10).

59:5 When used in the plural, as here, **nations** (cf. v. 8) usually refers to Gentiles. The title, however, sets the psalm in a situation in which the enemies are Israelites. Perhaps the simplest way to interpret this term, then, is to see the psalm as describing these Israelites who sought to kill David as acting like Gentiles (cf. note on 54:3).

59:11–17 *Stop Them, that They May Know that You Rule.* The basic request in this section is that God will bring judgment on these people in such a way that all people, both in Israel (**my people**, v. 11) and elsewhere (**to the ends of the earth**, v. 13), **may know that** a just, loving, and mighty **God rules over Jacob** and protects his faithful. The "curse" is that the enemies would fail in their purpose, **trapped in their pride**; this is not angry vengefulness (which would be out of place in the Psalms) but a cry for God to teach people a lesson. The song closes with confidence that the worshiper will survive these threats in order to **sing aloud of your steadfast love**, i.e., with the congregation of the faithful. (**In the morning**, v. 16, corresponds to **each evening**, v. 14.)

12[v]See Prov. 12:13
13[w][Ps. 7:9] [x]Ps. 83:18 [y]Ps. 22:27
14[z][Ps. 22:16]
15[a]Ps. 109:10; Job 15:23
16[b]ver. 9 [c]2 Sam. 22:3 [d]Ps. 18:6
17[b][See ver. 16 above] [e]ver. 10

Psalm 60

[f]Ps. 80, title [g]See Ps. 16, title [h]Deut. 31:19 [i][2 Sam. 8:3, 13, 14; 10:16; 1 Chr. 18:3, 12]
1[j]ver. 10; See Ps. 44:9 [k][2 Sam. 5:20] [l]See Ps. 80:3
2[m][2 Chr. 7:14]
3[n]Ps. 71:20 [o]Job 21:20 [p]Isa. 51:17, 22
4[q]Isa. 5:26; 11:12; 13:2; [Ps. 20:5] [r]Prov. 22:21
5[s]For ver. 5-12, see Ps. 108:6-13 [t]Deut. 33:12; Jer. 11:15
6[u]Ps. 89:35; Amos 4:2 [v][Josh. 1:6] [w]Gen. 12:6; 33:18; Josh. 17:7 [x]Gen. 33:17; Josh. 13:27

12 For [v]the sin of their mouths, the words of their lips,
let them be trapped in their pride.
For the cursing and lies that they utter,
13 [w]consume them in wrath;
consume them till they are no more,
that they may [x]know that God rules over Jacob
to [y]the ends of the earth. *Selah*

14 [z]Each evening they come back,
howling like dogs
and prowling about the city.
15 They [a]wander about for food
and growl if they do not get their fill.

16 But I will sing of your strength;
I will sing aloud of your steadfast love in the morning.
For you have been to me [b]a fortress
and [c]a refuge in [d]the day of my distress.
17 O my Strength, I will sing praises to you,
for you, O God, [b]are my fortress,
[e]the God who shows me steadfast love.

He Will Tread Down Our Foes

60

TO THE CHOIRMASTER: ACCORDING TO [f]SHUSHAN EDUTH. A [g]MIKTAM[1] OF DAVID; [h]FOR INSTRUCTION; WHEN HE [i]STROVE WITH ARAM-NAHARAIM AND WITH ARAM-ZOBAH, AND WHEN JOAB ON HIS RETURN STRUCK DOWN TWELVE THOUSAND OF EDOM IN THE VALLEY OF SALT.

1 O God, [j]you have rejected us, [k]broken our defenses;
you have been angry; [l]oh, restore us.
2 You have made the land to quake; you have torn it open;
[m]repair its breaches, for it totters.
3 [n]You have made your people see hard things;
[o]you have given us [p]wine to drink that made us stagger.

4 You have set up [q]a banner for those who fear you,
that they may flee to it [r]from the bow.[2] *Selah*
5 [s]That your [t]beloved ones may be delivered,
give salvation by your right hand and answer us!

6 God has spoken [u]in his holiness:[3]
"With exultation [v]I will divide up [w]Shechem
and portion out the Vale of [x]Succoth.

[1] Probably musical or liturgical terms [2] Or *that it may be displayed because of truth* [3] Or *sanctuary*

Psalm 60. This is a lament for the whole community, at a time when Israel's continued life in the land is under threat from Gentile neighbors. The title says it is "for instruction"; perhaps this means that it is to instruct the people how to pray when their troops must fight. The original setting is Israel, which by God's appointment dwelt in the land and was to be the source of blessing to the rest of the world (which often came, at least in Israel's better days, by making the other nations their subjects). Christians, who are not limited to one theocratic nation, recognize that God's process of conquering the Gentiles is through the witness of faithful believers (cf. Matt. 28:18–20); but they may still use this psalm to pray for God's blessing on this endeavor. The title seems to link the psalm with the events of 2 Sam. 8:1–14; but 2 Sam. 8:13 reports the number of Edomites killed as 18,000 instead of the "twelve thousand" here. If these are the same events, then probably the different numbers represent different ways of computing the casualties (e.g., 12,000 could be the number in an earlier report, while 18,000 could be the adjusted tally, after some time had passed). The campaign resulted in a great victory for David and brought several Gentile kingdoms under David's rule. This psalm, with its air of lament, would thus represent the prayers of the people before the campaign had been completed. Verses 5–12 of Psalm 60 are taken up again in Ps. 108:6–13.

60:1–5 *O God, You Have Rejected Us.* The song opens by laying out the heart of the matter: the community counts itself as if God has **rejected** them, i.e., treated them as if they were not his own people. In this psalm, **us** refers to the people of God as a whole, who are to view themselves as God's treasured possession, called for his own purposes (**your people**, v. 3; **that they may flee**, v. 4; **your beloved ones**, v. 5). That is why the complaint is so touching, and why they may confidently pray for restoration and repair. The **salvation** that they pray for (v. 5) is specifically success in their military endeavors, with a view toward Israel fulfilling its calling in the world.

60:6–8 *God Has Spoken: "These Lands Are Mine!"* These verses seem to recall an oracle (**God has spoken**) that gives God's plan for Israel's place in the world. The places mentioned in vv. 6–7 (**Shechem**, **Succoth**, **Gilead**, **Manasseh**, **Ephraim**, and **Judah**) are all parts of the land that God promised

7 [y]Gilead is mine; Manasseh is mine;
[z]Ephraim is [a]my helmet;
Judah is my [b]scepter.
8 [c]Moab is my washbasin;
upon Edom I [d]cast my shoe;
over [e]Philistia I shout in triumph."[1]

9 Who will bring me to the fortified city?
[f]Who will lead me to Edom?
10 Have you not [g]rejected us, O God?
You [h]do not go forth, O God, with our armies.
11 Oh, grant us help against the foe,
for [i]vain is the salvation of man!
12 With God we shall [j]do valiantly;
it is he who will [k]tread down our foes.

Lead Me to the Rock

61

To the choirmaster: with [l]stringed instruments. Of David.

1 Hear my cry, O God,
[m]listen to my prayer;
2 from the end of the earth I call to you
when my heart is [n]faint.
Lead me to [o]the rock
that is higher than I,
3 for you have been [p]my refuge,
a strong [q]tower against the enemy.

4 Let me [r]dwell in your tent forever!
Let me take refuge under [s]the shelter of your wings! *Selah*
5 For you, O God, have heard my vows;
you have given me the heritage of those who fear your name.
6 [t]Prolong [u]the life of the king;
may his years endure to all generations!
7 May he be enthroned forever before God;
appoint [v]steadfast love and faithfulness to watch over him!
8 So will I ever sing praises to your name,
as I [w]perform my vows day after day.

[1] Revocalization (compare Psalm 108:10); Masoretic Text *over me, O Philistia, shout in triumph*

7 [y]Josh. 13:31 [z]Deut. 33:17 [a]Ps. 140:7 [b]Gen. 49:10
8 [c][2 Sam. 8:2] [d][Matt. 3:11] [e][2 Sam. 8:1]
9 [f][2 Sam. 8:14]
10 [g]ver. 1 [h]See Ps. 44:9
11 [i][Ps. 146:3]
12 [j]Ps. 108:13; 118:15, 16; Num. 24:18 [k]Ps. 44:5; Isa. 63:3

Psalm 61
[l]Ps. 4, title
1 [m]Ps. 55:1, 2
2 [n]Ps. 77:3 [o][Ps. 18:2]
3 [p]See Ps. 14:6 [q]Prov. 18:10
4 [r]See Ps. 15:1; 27:4 [s]See Ps. 17:8
6 [t]See Ps. 21:4 [u]Ps. 63:11
7 [v]See Ps. 40:11
8 [w]See Ps. 50:14

to Israel; the places in v. 8 (**Moab**, **Edom**, **Philistia**) are neighboring lands, which also belong to the Lord (cf. Ex. 19:5). Israel exists to bring blessing to the Gentiles; in the time of David this normally happened as these nations came under Israelite sovereignty (cf. note on Psalm 2). Thus the military campaign is put in the context of Israel's mission; mere territorial expansion, as such, was not a part of Israel's calling.

60:9–12 *Grant Us Help, for Vain Is the Salvation of Man!* To come to **Edom** is the culmination of the military campaign of the title. If it is to do God's work, the army of Israel must seek God's **help**. To rely merely on their human capacities would not only be fruitless (**vain is the salvation of man**), it would mean they were rejecting God's calling.

Psalm 61. This is an individual lament of sorts: it serves as a general request for God's help in times of trouble for particular members of God's people. At the same time it is certainly not individualistic: in praying for the (Davidic) king, vv. 6–7 tie royal well-being to the well-being of the whole people; and v. 8 looks forward to acts of public worship as the proper result of the help for which the psalm prays.

61:1–3 *Hear My Prayer, for You Have Been My Refuge.* As the congregation sings this, they imagine themselves in all manner of places (**the end of the earth**) and circumstances (**when my heart is faint**) in which they feel needy and exposed; in such cases they should lift their **cry** to God, who is a reliable **refuge** and **strong tower**. **The rock that is higher than I** is an image of safety (cf. 27:5). For "rock" and "refuge" together, cf. 18:2.

61:4–5 *Let Me Dwell in Your Tent, for You Have Heard My Vows.* To **dwell in** God's **tent** is to be a welcome guest in God's presence in worship (cf. 15:1; 23:6; 27:4). In this context the **vows** are promises of special peace offerings, which the worshiper will celebrate in due course (see note on 56:12–13). For **shelter of your wings**, see note on 17:8.

61:6–7 *Prolong the Life of the King.* If God will **prolong the life of the king**, and **appoint steadfast love and faithfulness to watch over him** (cf. Prov. 20:28), then the community of God's people may rest secure in God's blessing. Such a king would be faithful to God and committed to the well-being of the people (contrast the unjust rulers of Psalm 58).

61:8 *I Will Always Sing Praises to You.* In the biblical worldview, one finds the fullness of God's presence in public worship, and the right response to

Psalm 62
[x]See Ps. 39, title
1 [y]See Ps. 33:20 [z][Ps. 37:7]
2 [a]Ps. 18:2 [b]See Ps. 9:9 [c]See Ps. 10:6
3 [d][Isa. 30:13]
4 [e]Job 13:11 [f]See Ps. 28:3
5 [y][See ver. 1 above]
6 [a][See ver. 2 above]
7 [g]See Ps. 3:8 [h]See Ps. 14:6
8 [i]See Ps. 37:3 [j]See Ps. 42:4 [h][See ver. 7 above]
9 [k]Ps. 39:5; [Isa. 40:17] [l][Ps. 116:11]
10 [m]See Prov. 1:10-19 [n]Luke 12:15; See Ps. 49:6
11 [o]Job 33:14; 40:5

My Soul Waits for God Alone

62

To the choirmaster: according to [x]Jeduthun. A Psalm of David.

1 For God alone [y]my soul [z]waits in silence;
from him comes my salvation.
2 [a]He alone is my rock and my salvation,
my [b]fortress; [c]I shall not be greatly shaken.

3 How long will all of you attack a man
to batter him,
like [d]a leaning wall, a tottering fence?
4 They only plan to thrust him down from his [e]high position.
They take pleasure in falsehood.
[f]They bless with their mouths,
but inwardly they curse. *Selah*

5 For God alone, O [y]my soul, wait in silence,
for my hope is from him.
6 [a]He only is my rock and my salvation,
my fortress; I shall not be shaken.
7 On God rests my [g]salvation and my glory;
my mighty rock, [h]my refuge is God.

8 [i]Trust in him at all times, O people;
[j]pour out your heart before him;
God is [h]a refuge for us. *Selah*

9 [k]Those of low estate are but a breath;
those of high estate [l]are a delusion;
in the balances they go up;
[k]they are together lighter than a breath.
10 Put no trust in extortion;
[m]set no vain hopes on robbery;
[n]if riches increase, set not your heart on them.

11 [o]Once God has spoken;
[o]twice have I heard this:

God's goodness is to **sing praises** and **perform** one's **vows** in the company of God's people.

Psalm 62. God's people sing this psalm to foster confidence in his care, especially as they are faced with people who use power and wealth to oppress them. The strong temptation in such a case is either to despair or else to seek security in power and wealth rather than in God. The simplest way to follow the flow of thought in the psalm is to observe how the addressees shift: from a description of "my soul" and God (vv. 1–2), to speaking directly to and about the attackers (vv. 3–4), then back to "my soul" and God (vv. 5–7), on to exhorting the whole of the worshiping congregation (vv. 8–10), and finally back to a description of God's trustworthiness (vv. 11–12).

62:1–2 *My Soul Waits for God Alone.* On its surface, this section is descriptive of **my soul** as relying on God alone **in silence**, and of God, who is a **rock** and **fortress**. **God alone. . . . He alone** lays stress on God as the only reliable hope, though it does not exclude all human activity: the psalm makes a contrast between God's **salvation** (which is received through faith and faithfulness) and the kind that comes through unjust means (cf. v. 10, "put no trust in extortion"). The description of a trusting soul is there to set an ideal for God's people: each one should aspire to this kind of quiet faith. On **salvation**, see note on 3:2. On **shaken** (62:2), see note on 16:8.

62:3–4 *To the Attackers: We Know What You Want.* The next section speaks to those who **attack a man**, particularly using lies and injustice. As indicated in the note on 13:1–2, the expression **how long** is not asking for information but is expressing the sense that the behavior has gone on far too long already. The purpose of singing this is to remind the godly that such attacks have **only** (Hb. *'ak*, cf. 63:1–2) one **plan**, and only one **pleasure**. There is thus only one safe recourse: trust in God (preparing for the next section).

62:5–7 *O My Soul, Wait for God Alone.* The first two verses here are quite close to vv. 1–2; the main difference is that the descriptive "waits in silence" (which sets an ideal) is now explicitly an imperative, **wait in silence**. Verse 7 develops the thought of God's reliability from v. 6.

62:8–10 *To the Faithful: Evil Men Are but a Breath.* From addressing his own soul in vv. 5–7, the singer turns to address the whole congregation (**O people**) with whom he is singing this hymn. He urges them all to trust in God and to find in him a **refuge** (v. 8), as he had described (v. 7). They express their trust by prayer (**pour out your heart**, v. 8, describes earnest prayer; cf. 1 Sam. 1:15; Ps. 42:4; Lam. 2:19) and by refusing to have any part in the methods of the attackers (**put no trust in extortion**, Ps. 62:10). Humans cannot outweigh God (they are **together lighter than a breath**, v. 9); so any human effort that does not arise from true faith will fail to achieve lasting good.

62:11–12 *God's Word Is Certain.* To say **once . . . twice** is to indicate that the idea is sure, namely, that to God belong both **power** (by which he can carry out his will; contrast v. 9) and **steadfast love** (in which he has pledged himself to the faithful, and for which they may safely trust him). God **will render to a man according to his work**; i.e., a person's "work" shows whether his faith is real or counterfeit (the attackers are probably Israelites), and God will sort out who is who. This is therefore a ground of confidence for the believer and a warning to the unfaithful.

that [p]power belongs to God,
12 and that to you, O Lord, [q]belongs steadfast love.
For you will [r]render to a man
according to his work.

My Soul Thirsts for You

63

A PSALM OF DAVID, [s]WHEN HE WAS IN THE WILDERNESS OF JUDAH.

1 O God, you are my God; [t]earnestly I seek you;
[u]my soul thirsts for you;
my flesh faints for you,
as in [v]a dry and weary land where there is no water.
2 So I have looked upon you in the sanctuary,
beholding [w]your power and glory.
3 Because your [x]steadfast love is better than life,
my lips will praise you.
4 So I will bless you [y]as long as I live;
in your [z]name I will [a]lift up my hands.

5 My soul will be [b]satisfied as with fat and rich food,
and my mouth will praise you with joyful lips,
6 when I remember you [c]upon my bed,
and meditate on you in [c]the watches of the night;
7 for you have been my help,
and in [d]the shadow of your wings I will sing for joy.
8 My soul [e]clings to you;
your right hand [f]upholds me.

9 But those who seek to destroy my life
[g]shall go down into [h]the depths of the earth;

11[p]Rev. 19:1; [Ps. 59:9, 17]
12[q]Ps. 86:5, 15; 103:8; Dan. 9:9 [r]See Job 34:11

Psalm 63

[s][2 Sam. 16:14; 17:2, 29]
1[t]Ps. 78:34; Isa. 26:9 [u]See Ps. 84:2 [v]Ps. 143:6; Isa. 32:2
2[w]Ps. 78:61; [Ps. 27:4]
3[x][Ps. 69:16]
4[y]Ps. 104:33; 146:2 [z]Ps. 20:1, 5 [a]See Ps. 28:2
5[b]See Ps. 36:8
6[c]See Ps. 42:8
7[d]See Ps. 17:8
8[e][Num. 14:24] [f]See Ps. 41:12
9[g]Ps. 9:17; 55:15 [h]Ezek. 26:20; 31:14; Eph. 4:9

62:12 render to a man according to his work. The Greek translation of this phrase is almost identical to the Greek of Prov. 24:12 (the Hb. is different, but conveys the same idea), and Paul uses it in Rom. 2:6. If Paul is speaking specifically to a Jew who passes judgment in Rom. 2:1 (which seems likely), then he is reminding such a person that mere Jewishness does not guarantee eternal life; one must embrace the covenant and prove the genuineness of one's faith by one's deeds (i.e., along the lines of the original intent of both Ps. 62:12 and Prov. 24:12). If, however, Paul is speaking to moralizers without respect to their place in the covenant, then he is using Ps. 62:12 as an instance of the more general principle of God's just judgment. The idea that the final judgment will use believers' deeds to vindicate the reality of their faith appears in Matt. 12:33–37; 16:27; John 5:28–29; James 1:12; Rev. 20:13; and possibly (though debatably) in Rom. 2:13; 2 Cor. 5:10; and Gal. 6:7–8.

Psalm 63. This psalm opens as if it were a lament, seeking God in a time of trouble; and yet the overall flow of the song is one of confident expectation. Hence it is best to see the psalm as enabling each of God's people to develop confidence during their times of trouble. In particular, the psalm inculcates the confidence that the worshiper will indeed be able to return to the sanctuary to worship God. Biblically, the highest privilege a mortal can enjoy is to be a welcome member of the worshiping congregation; and the psalm, in instilling such confidence, also enables its singers to treasure this worship as the gift that it is. The several references to "my soul" (vv. 1, 5, 8) point to the intensely personal devotion to God that infuses the whole song. The title links the psalm to David's days as a refugee, but it is not immediately clear whether the reference is to fleeing from Saul (1 Sam. 23:14–15; 24:1) or from Absalom (2 Sam. 15:23, 28). The latter may seem more likely, since the author calls himself a king (Ps. 63:11); cf. also 2 Sam. 16:14 for the term "weary" found in Ps. 63:1. On the other hand, the land through which David fled is not normally counted as part of the wilderness of Judah, and David could have thought of himself as a king even when he was fleeing Saul, since Samuel had already anointed him.

63:1–2 *Remembering Past Worship.* The song opens with passionate expressions of longing for God: **earnestly I seek, my soul thirsts, my flesh faints**. (No doubt the arid conditions of the wilderness of Judah provided the image of a **dry and weary land where there is no water**.) Clearly the singer misses God; but in particular, he misses his experience of God in public worship: the **sanctuary** is the place of corporate worship, and God's **glory** is his special presence with his people, which is given and enjoyed in the sanctuary (see note on 26:4–8). People are said to see (or look upon or behold) this glory (e.g., Ex. 16:7; 33:18; Num. 14:10; Deut. 5:24).

63:3–4 *Confidence for Future Worship.* The past tense recollection of v. 2 becomes a future expectation: **my lips will praise you, I will bless you, I will lift up my hands**. This activity of praising, blessing, and lifting up hands (cf. 28:2; 134:2) takes place in the sanctuary. Lifting up hands is a sign of directing one's prayers and praise toward God, and helps the worshiper to focus his thoughts on God. The ground of this expectation is 63:3: **because your steadfast love is better than life**.

63:5–8 *My Soul Clings to You.* The delight in God is not limited to the sanctuary, of course; the memory of God's presence and promises mediated in public worship, and of God's help in times past, produces joy and praise; even **in the watches of the night** (time normally devoted to sleep) people deal with sleeplessness by meditating on God.

63:7 shadow of your wings. See note on 17:8.

63:8 clings. Or "holds fast" (Hb. *dabaq*); cf. Deut. 4:4; 10:20; 11:22; 30:20; 1 Cor. 6:16–17 (see ESV footnote).

63:9–11 *Those Who Seek My Life Will Fail, but I Will Rejoice.* Now the song explains where the troubles came from: **those who seek to destroy my life**. In David's experience (as in the title), these were Israelites who rebelled against God's choice of David as king. In order to apply this psalm, the ordinary believer should observe the analogy: these are people hostile to God's purposes, especially hostile to the house of David (and Christians follow David's heir, Jesus). The confidence is that these people will fail in their

10 they shall be given over to the power of the sword;
they shall be a portion for jackals.
11 But [i]the king shall rejoice in God;
all who [j]swear by him shall exult,
[k]for the mouths of [l]liars will be stopped.

Hide Me from the Wicked

64

TO THE CHOIRMASTER. A PSALM OF DAVID.

1 Hear my voice, O God, in my [m]complaint;
preserve my life from dread of the enemy.
2 Hide me from [n]the secret plots of the wicked,
from the throng of evildoers,
3 who [o]whet their tongues like swords,
who [p]aim bitter words like arrows,
4 shooting from [q]ambush at the blameless,
shooting at him suddenly and [r]without fear.
5 They [s]hold fast to their evil purpose;
they talk of [t]laying snares secretly,
thinking, [u]"Who can see them?"
6 They search out injustice,
saying, "We have accomplished a diligent search."
For [v]the inward mind and heart of a man are deep.
7 [w]But God shoots his arrow at them;
they are wounded suddenly.
8 They are brought to ruin, with their own [x]tongues turned against them;
all who [y]see them will [z]wag their heads.
9 Then all mankind [y]fears;
they [a]tell what God has brought about
and ponder what he has done.

10 Let [b]the righteous one rejoice in the LORD
and [c]take refuge in him!
Let all [d]the upright in heart exult!

11 [i]Ps. 61:6 [j]Deut. 6:13; Isa. 45:23; 65:16 [k]Ps. 107:42; Job 5:16; [Rom. 3:19] [l][Ps. 38:12; 41:5-8]

Psalm 64

1 [m]Ps. 55:2
2 [n][Ps. 55:14]
3 [o]See Ps. 57:4 [p]See Ps. 11:2
4 [q][Ps. 10:8] [r]Ps. 55:19
5 [s]Jer. 23:14; Ezek. 13:22 [t]See Ps. 140:5 [u]See Job 22:13
6 [v]Ps. 49:11
7 [w]Ps. 7:12, 13; [Ps. 58:7]
8 [x]See Prov. 12:13; 18:7 [y]See Ps. 40:3 [z]Jer. 18:16; 48:27; See Ps. 22:7
9 [y][See ver. 8 above] [a]Jer. 50:28; 51:10
10 [b]See Ps. 32:11; Job 22:19 [c]See Ps. 11:1 [d]See Ps. 7:10

goal of destroying God's faithful. (If the setting is Absalom's revolt, then the **power of the sword** was fulfilled literally [2 Sam. 18:6–8]; again, ordinary believers should use analogy to apply this.) **The king** (i.e., David), and those who adhere to him, will not fall prey to these enemies but **shall rejoice in God**, because when **the mouths of liars** are **stopped**, God's love and faithfulness are clearly on display.

63:10 portion for jackals. Because jackals often scavenge, this image is a grim description of dead bodies, lying unburied after a battle.

63:11 swear by him. This could be "swear by the king," or it could be "swear by God." The second is more likely (cf. Deut. 6:13; 10:20, where swearing by the Lord's name displays loyalty to God). Thus the psalmist (King David) invites all the covenantally pious to join him in his confidence.

Psalm 64. This psalm shares many themes with Psalm 63, namely, confidence in God's victory over those who bring troubles on the righteous. However, since the psalm begins with a request, it is best to see it as an individual lament. The psalm has two parts: a request for help against deadly schemes (vv. 1–6), and confident expectation that God will fight on behalf of his faithful (vv. 7–10). The psalm presents God's purpose for his victory as instruction for mankind (v. 9) and the bringing of joy to the godly (v. 10).

64:1–6 *Hide Me from the Secret Plans of the Wicked.* This psalm lays out the danger to the devoted believer with three requests (**hear my voice, preserve my life, hide me**) and an extensive description of the enemies and their malevolent schemes. As usual in these psalms of lament, the **enemy** is made up of **wicked** people (v. 2) who have an **evil purpose** (v. 5) to carry out **injustice** (v. 6) against the faithful (**the blameless**, v. 4). The particular strategy is to use **bitter words** (vv. 3–4), which form **snares** secretly (v. 5); these terms are vague enough to range from lies that sow discord or despair to slander that destroys reputations. (This breadth of possibilities is probably intentional, allowing the psalm to be relevant to a variety of situations.)

64:7–10 *God Makes an Example of the Wicked.* Those who would shoot their bitter words like arrows aimed at the innocent (vv. 3–4) will find that **God shoots his arrow at them** (v. 7). This is keeping the imagery of the first section; it refers to God bringing them down as they deserve, with **their own tongues turned against them**, which is also a phrase vague enough to cover a wide range of possibilities (because the focus is more on confidence in their failure, whatever their schemes may have been). By their lies, the evildoers **are brought to ruin** (of an unnamed sort). Whatever their ruin may be, its effect brings a benefit: **all who see them will wag their heads** (v. 8), an expression of astonishment (perhaps even of compassion), cf. Jer. 18:16 and 48:27; **all mankind fears** (Ps. 64:9), and they **ponder what** God **has done**, taking instruction from God's vindication (cf. 58:11). In view of this, **let the righteous** (i.e., the faithful covenant member) **rejoice in the LORD** (64:10).

O God of Our Salvation

65

To the choirmaster. A Psalm of David. A Song.

1 Praise [e]is due to you,[1] O God, in Zion,
and to you shall [f]vows be performed.
2 O you who [g]hear prayer,
to you [h]shall all flesh come.
3 When [i]iniquities prevail against me,
you [j]atone for our transgressions.
4 [k]Blessed is the one you choose and bring near,
to [l]dwell in your courts!
We shall be [m]satisfied with the goodness of your house,
the holiness of your temple!

5 By [n]awesome deeds you answer us with righteousness,
O God of our salvation,
the hope of all [o]the ends of the earth
and of the farthest seas;
6 the one who by his strength established the mountains,
being [p]girded with might;
7 who [q]stills the roaring of the seas,
the roaring of their waves,
[r]the tumult of the peoples,
8 so that those who dwell at the ends of the earth are in awe at your signs.
You make the going out of the morning and the evening to shout for joy.

9 You visit the earth and [s]water it;[2]
you greatly enrich it;
[t]the river of God is full of water;
[u]you provide their grain,
for so you have prepared it.
10 You water its furrows abundantly,
settling its ridges,
softening it with [v]showers,
and blessing its growth.
11 You crown the year with your bounty;
your wagon tracks [w]overflow with abundance.
12 [x]The pastures of the wilderness overflow,
the hills [y]gird themselves with joy,

[1] *Or Praise waits for you in silence* [2] *Or and make it overflow*

Psalm 65
1 [e]Ps. 62:1 [f]See Ps. 50:14
2 [g]2 Kgs. 19:20 [h]See Ps. 86:9
3 [i]See Ps. 38:4 [j]Ps. 79:9; Isa. 6:7; See Ps. 51:2
4 [k][Ps. 33:12] [l]Ps. 84:4; See Ps. 27:4 [m]See Ps. 16:11
5 [n]Ps. 45:4; 106:22; Deut. 10:21; 2 Sam. 7:23; [Rev. 15:3] [o]See Ps. 22:27
6 [p]Ps. 93:1
7 [q]Ps. 89:9; 93:3, 4; 107:29; Matt. 8:26; [Jer. 5:22] [r]Ps. 74:23; Isa. 17:12, 13
9 [s]Ps. 68:9; 72:6; Lev. 26:4; See Job 5:10 [t][Ps. 46:4] [u][Ps. 147:14]
10 [v]Deut. 32:2
11 [w]Job 36:28
12 [x]Joel 2:22; [Job 38:26, 27] [y]Isa. 55:12

Psalm 65. This is a thanksgiving; the specific occasion is a fruitful harvest (vv. 9–13). Perhaps this good harvest has come after a drought, which was seen as a sign of divine displeasure (see vv. 3, 9–10; cf. Deut. 28:23–24); or perhaps the psalm is celebrating the Feast of Weeks (Pentecost). The harvest is set in the context of God's faithfulness to his covenant promises (Ps. 65:1–8). The Sinai covenant ties together God's grace, the believing response of the people, and the fruitfulness of the land. Singing this song should develop a deep spirit of gratitude in the hearts of the worshipers.

65:1–4 *Praise for God in Zion.* **Zion** is the name of the city that David captured and made his capital (2 Sam. 5:7), and which became the site of the tabernacle, and later of the temple. These verses describe acts of public worship at the central sanctuary: **praise**, **vows**, **prayer**, **shall all flesh come**, **atone**, **courts**, **house**, **temple**. The passage celebrates the unlimited kindness and mercy of God to his people: God atones for his people's transgressions through the sacrifices, which is what allows them to draw near in worship, **to dwell in** his courts (see note on Ps. 23:5–6). The **holiness of** God's temple is to such people a matter of delight, and not of terror.

65:5–8 *You Have Shown Us Awesome Deeds.* This section recounts some of the **awesome deeds** God has done for his people; the special focus is the work of creation (which is suited to the occasion: the Creator is the one who has blessed the harvest). The point that the OT often makes is that the Creator of heaven and earth and of all mankind is **the hope of all the ends of the earth**, i.e., the one true God whom all mankind should worship as their only hope. The marvel is that this universal Creator has chosen a particular people to receive his blessing and care (which itself should bring benefit to the rest of mankind: "to you all flesh shall come" in due course, v. 2).

65:9–13 *You Have Made the Land Produce Abundantly.* This section enables God's people to delight in his bountiful supply for his land by enabling them to imagine what the ground itself would feel under God's blessing: the abundance of **water** in an arid land, **softening it with showers** so that the farmers can work it and the plants can grow; the fields clothing themselves with grass, grazing animals, and grain; and the overflowing **wagon tracks**. These images convey the thought of a land producing abundantly for man and beast. In the personification, the very **pastures**, **hills**, **meadows**, and **valleys . . . shout and sing together for joy**. The faithful people can see their song as joining the celebration of the fruitful land.

13 [z]the meadows clothe themselves with flocks,
the valleys deck themselves with grain,
they [a]shout and sing together for joy.

How Awesome Are Your Deeds

66

To the choirmaster. A Song. A Psalm.

1 [b]Shout for joy to God, all the earth;
2 sing the glory of his name;
[c]give to him glorious praise!
3 Say to God, [d]"How awesome are your deeds!
So great is your power that your enemies [e]come cringing to you.
4 [f]All the earth worships you
and sings praises to you;
they sing praises to your name." *Selah*

5 [g]Come and see what God has done:
[d]he is awesome in his deeds toward the children of man.
6 He [h]turned the sea into dry land;
they [i]passed through the river on foot.
There did we rejoice in him,
7 who rules by his might forever,
whose [j]eyes keep watch on the nations—
let not the rebellious exalt themselves. *Selah*

8 Bless our God, O peoples;
let the sound of his praise be heard,
9 who has kept our soul among the living
and [k]has not let our feet slip.
10 For you, O God, have [l]tested us;
you have tried us as silver is tried.
11 You brought us into [m]the net;
you laid a crushing burden on our backs;
12 you let men [n]ride over our heads;
we went through fire and through [o]water;
yet you have brought us out to a place of abundance.

13 I will come into your house with burnt offerings;
I will [p]perform my vows to you,

13[z]Isa. 30:23 [a]Ps. 98:8; [Isa. 44:23]
Psalm 66
1[b]Ps. 81:1; 95:1; 98:4; 100:1
2[c][Josh. 7:19; Isa. 42:12]
3[d]See Ps. 65:5 [e]See Ps. 18:44
4[f]See Ps. 22:27
5[g]ver. 16; Ps. 46:8 [d][See ver. 3 above]
6[h][Ex. 14:21] [i]Ps. 74:15; See Josh. 3:14-17
7[j]See Ps. 11:4
9[k]See Ps. 121:3
10[l]See Job 23:10
11[m]Lam. 1:13; Ezek. 12:13
12[n]Isa. 51:23 [o]Isa. 43:2
13[p]See Ps. 50:14

Psalm 66. This is a thanksgiving for God's answer to the prayer of a particular member of God's people. Perhaps it was especially suited to the occasion on which a worshiper brought various sacrifices to express his thanks and consecration (cf. vv. 13–15). The marvel of this psalm is the way in which the first half (vv. 1–12)—with its references to "us" (i.e., to the people of God as a whole) and to "all the earth," and its recounting of God's "awesome deeds" for Israel (v. 6 describes the exodus and the crossing of the Jordan)—sets God's deeds for the particular person into the context of his commitment to the people as a whole (indeed, to mankind as a whole, for whose sake the people exist). The biblical worldview does not require a choice between "corporate" and "particular": rather, the particular person experiences God's love as a member of his people. Psalms 66–67 represent a break in the pattern of Davidic authorship that began in Psalm 51; Psalms 68–70 resume the pattern. At the same time, there are connections between Psalms 65 and 66, such as the mention of vows and sacrifices (65:1–4; 66:13–15).

66:1–4 *Let All the Earth Worship God!* The psalm opens with a universal call (**Shout for joy to God, all the earth**), and this section closes by declaring how **all the earth worships** the true God (v. 4). The biblical story line has the one true God creating all that there is; every human can genuinely express his or her humanness only by loving and worshiping this one God. Even now the nonhuman creation honors its Creator (cf. 19:1–6), and the OT nurtures the hope that one day all mankind will do so as well (e.g., 117:1, cited in Rom. 15:11 as part of Paul's rationale for his efforts among the Gentiles).

66:5–7 *Come and See How God Brought Israel out of Egypt!* From all the earth the focus narrows down to one people, Israel, as the reference to the exodus (**turned the sea into dry land**) and the crossing of the Jordan River (**passed through the river on foot**) in v. 6 makes plain. At the same time, Israel exists for the very purpose of bringing God's light to the world (Ex. 19:5–6); hence what God has done for Israel he has done for all peoples—**he is awesome in his deeds** (a reference to what he does for Israel) **toward the children of man** (i.e., for all mankind, not just Israel).

66:8–12 *Let All Peoples Bless the God Who Has Preserved Us!* The song moves on to the ways in which God has preserved Israel (**us**) through all manner of trials, without dwelling on whether those trials were brought on by Israel's own unfaithfulness (as in Judges) or by God's mysterious purposes (as in Ps. 44:17–22). Strikingly, God has brought Israel through all these, **to a place of abundance**, and the call goes out to the Gentiles, **Bless our God, O peoples**! God has chosen his people to be the vehicle by which light comes to the whole world, and thus the preserving of Israel is crucial to all mankind. Gentile Christians can see themselves as part of the fruition of all that God has done for Israel.

66:13–15 *I Will Come to His House with Offerings.* Here is where the focus shifts from Israel as a whole to the particular worshiper (**I**). A person in Israel (including sojourners), in a time of need, could make a vow to the Lord, which he could fulfill with **burnt offerings** or vow offerings (**perform my vows**); cf. Lev. 22:18 and Num. 15:3. As Ps. 50:7–15 makes clear, under no circum-

14 that which my lips uttered
and my mouth promised [q]when I was in trouble.
15 I will offer to you burnt offerings of fattened animals,
with the smoke of the sacrifice of rams;
I will make an offering of bulls and goats. *Selah*

16 [r]Come and hear, all you who fear God,
and I will tell what he has done for my soul.
17 I cried to him with my mouth,
and high praise was on[1] my tongue.[2]
18 If I had [s]cherished iniquity in my heart,
[t]the Lord would not have listened.
19 But truly [u]God has listened;
he has attended to the voice of my prayer.

20 Blessed be God,
because he has not rejected my prayer
or removed his steadfast love from me!

Make Your Face Shine upon Us

67 TO THE CHOIRMASTER: WITH [v]STRINGED INSTRUMENTS. A PSALM. A SONG.
1 May God [w]be gracious to us and bless us
and make his face to [x]shine upon us, *Selah*
2 that [y]your way may be known on earth,
your [z]saving power among all nations.
3 [a]Let the peoples praise you, O God;
let all the peoples praise you!

4 Let the nations be glad and sing for joy,
for you [b]judge the peoples with equity
and guide the nations upon earth. *Selah*
5 [a]Let the peoples praise you, O God;
let all the peoples praise you!

[1] Hebrew *under* [2] Or *and he was exalted with my tongue*

14[q]See Ps. 18:6
16[r]ver. 5; Ps. 34:11
18[s]Job 36:21 [t][Prov. 28:9; Isa. 59:2; John 9:31; James 4:3; See Job 27:9]
19[u]Ps. 116:1, 2
Psalm 67
[v]Ps. 4, title
1[w]Num. 6:25 [x]See Ps. 4:6
2[y][Acts 18:25] [z]Ps. 98:3; Luke 2:30; Titus 2:11
3[a]See Ps. 22:27
4[b]See Ps. 58:11
5[a][See ver. 3 above]

stances should these ever be treated as bribes for God; they are responses of personal consecration (a function of the burnt offering) and gratitude (a function of the vow offering, a kind of peace offering) to God for his freely given kindness. The psalm presents them as a joyful occasion.

66:16–20 *Let Me Tell You How God Has Heard My Prayer.* The reason for this thanksgiving is that God **has attended to the voice of my prayer** (v. 19). The OT insists that each member of the people must own the covenant for himself; thus each one would have some report of **what** God **has done for** his **soul** (and not just for the people as a whole). The wording here is quite general, allowing the song to be used in a wide variety of situations. The one requirement is that the worshiper has not **cherished** (lit., "looked forward to," "aimed for") **iniquity in** his **heart** (v. 18). The term "iniquity" here (Hb. *'awen*) refers to what is vile and abhorrent to God. To "cherish iniquity" is to aim at it; in context it refers to praying for God's help in order to be able to commit some form of sin—a practice the truly pious reject. Therefore it would be a misinterpretation to read this as implying that absolute sinlessness is a condition for answered prayer; rather, it reminds the faithful to pray for God's help in order to give him thanks and to serve him better (cf. James 4:3).

Psalm 67. This psalm, like Psalm 65, seems to be a thanksgiving for a fruitful harvest. Unlike Psalm 65, it is not really a thanksgiving hymn; it is rather a prayer that God will bless his people Israel so that the rest of the world may come to know the true God. Verses 3 and 5 of Psalm 67 are the same, marking the ends of their stanzas; they summarize the desire of this psalm, "Let all the peoples praise you!" Singing this helps Israel to keep its own calling in view: their blessing is not simply for themselves but for the Gentiles too (cf. Gen. 12:2–3). Each Israelite is a player in a grand story that stretches far beyond the boundaries of his own life, or even of his own land.

67:1–3 *May God Bless Us, So that All Nations May Know Him.* Verse 1 adapts the priestly blessing (Num. 6:24–26: **may God be gracious**, **bless**, **make his face to shine**), and Ps. 67:2 follows it with a purpose clause: the goal for which the congregation prays for God's blessing is **that** God's **way may be known on earth**—specifically, that his **saving power** might be known **among all nations**. God called Abram both to bless him and his descendants and to make them a vehicle of blessing to the Gentiles (Gen. 12:2–3). These words turn that calling into a song.

67:4–5 *May All Nations Be Glad in His Rule.* In addition to their knowing God's saving power, the psalmist prays that **the nations be glad and sing for joy** because he rules over (**you judge**) them **with equity**. This could be a prayer that these Gentiles come to appreciate the author of that general and kind providence they have experienced, and then to worship him (cf. Acts 14:17); but, since the term "judge" seems to indicate a more direct rule than simply oversight (cf. also the term **guide**, or "lead"; see Ps. 73:24; 77:20), it is more likely that this is praying for the day when God's acknowledged rule is extended to include the Gentiles (cf. Isa. 2:4; 11:3–4, both using the same word, "judge," applied to the Gentiles). (In the OT, the first duty of the judge was to protect the innocent; he was a kind of savior.) The OT very decidedly looks to a future era in which the Gentiles receive God's light, and this song fosters this hope in each ordinary believer. (See also the note on Ps. 67:6–7, "the ends of the earth.") The Christian

6 The earth has [c]yielded its increase;
God, our God, shall bless us.
7 God shall bless us;
let [d]all the ends of the earth fear him!

God Shall Scatter His Enemies

68

TO THE CHOIRMASTER. A PSALM OF DAVID. A SONG.

1 [e]God shall arise, his enemies shall be [f]scattered;
and those who hate him shall flee before him!
2 As [g]smoke is driven away, so you shall drive them away;
[h]as wax melts before fire,
so the wicked shall perish before God!
3 But [i]the righteous shall be glad;
they shall exult before God;
they shall be jubilant with joy!

4 Sing to God, [j]sing praises to his name;
[k]lift up a song to him who [l]rides through [m]the deserts;
his name is [n]the LORD;
exult before him!
5 [o]Father of the fatherless and [p]protector of widows
is God in his holy habitation.
6 God [q]settles the solitary in a home;
he [r]leads out the prisoners to prosperity,
but [s]the rebellious dwell in [t]a parched land.

7 O God, when you [u]went out before your people,
[v]when you marched through [w]the wilderness, *Selah*
8 [x]the earth quaked, the heavens poured down rain,
before God, the One of Sinai,
before God, the God of Israel.
9 [y]Rain in abundance, O God, you shed abroad;
you restored your inheritance as it languished;
10 your flock[1] found a dwelling in it;
in your goodness, O God, you [z]provided for the needy.

[1] Or *your congregation*

6[c]Ps. 85:12; Lev. 26:4; Ezek. 34:27; [Hos. 2:22]
7[d]See Ps. 22:27

Psalm 68

1[e]Num. 10:35; Isa. 33:3 [f][Ps. 89:10; 92:9]
2[g]See Ps. 37:20 [h]Ps. 22:14; 97:5; Mic. 1:4
3[i]See Ps. 32:11
4[j]Ps. 66:4 [k][Isa. 62:10] [l]ver. 33; [Ps. 18:10] [m]Isa. 40:3 [n]Ps. 89:8
5[o]See Ps. 10:14 [p]Deut. 10:18
6[q]Ps. 113:9; 1 Sam. 2:5 [r]Ps. 69:33; 107:10, 14; 146:7; Acts 12:7; 16:26 [s]ver. 18 [t][Ps. 107:33, 40]
7[u]Ex. 13:21; Judg. 4:14; Hab. 3:13; Zech. 14:3 [v]Judg. 5:4 [w]Ps. 78:40
8[x]Ex. 19:18; Judg. 5:4
9[y]See Ps. 65:9, 10
10[z]Ps. 65:9; 78:20

message includes the announcement that this era has arrived, due to Jesus' resurrection, which installs him on the throne of David (Rom. 1:1–5).

67:6–7 *God Will Bless Us, So that All Nations May Fear Him.* The final stanza repeats the idea of blessing from the first, and indicates one particular kind of blessing for which the people should give thanks: **the earth has yielded its increase**. To **fear** God means to hold him and his word in reverence, a disposition of true faith (e.g., 5:7; 15:4; 25:12). For **the ends of the earth** turning to the Lord (esp. in the messianic age), cf. 2:8; 22:27; 72:8 (Zech. 9:10); Isa. 45:22; 52:10; Jer. 16:19.

Psalm 68. This is a hymn by which God's people celebrate his continued care and protection for Israel, remembering how God led them through the wilderness into their inheritance, and daily bears his people up (v. 19). The celebration does not stop with Israel, however: it recognizes that defeating Gentile kingdoms "who delight in war" is for the sake of all the Gentiles coming to worship the true God. It is possible that David composed this psalm to commemorate the moving of the ark into the tabernacle (2 Sam. 6:12–15): Ps. 68:1 echoes Num. 10:35 (Moses' words when the ark set out); Ps. 68:16 mentions the mountain of God's abode; vv. 24–25 describe God's procession; and vv. 17, 35 speak of the sanctuary. In any event the overall theme of the psalm is God's residence in Zion and his care for his people.

68:1–3 *Gladness When God Arises.* Verse 1 adapts the words of Num. 10:35 ("Arise, O LORD, and let your enemies be scattered, and let those who hate you flee before you"), thus recalling the movement of the ark in the wilderness; from the perspective of the psalm, the ark was headed to its destination on Zion. For the ark to take up residence in Zion is for God to be among his people where they now live (cf. Ps. 68:17, "Sinai is now in the sanctuary"; the ark is a portable Sinai, where God made himself present with his people). This brings the happy promise that the **wicked** (those who reject God's covenant) **shall perish before God**, while the **righteous** (those who embrace the covenant) **shall be glad**, because God is carrying out his purpose of reversing the effects of sin in the world.

68:4–6 *Exhortation to Sing to God.* The faithful are to **sing to God** because he has shown himself kind, especially to helpless people (**fatherless**, or "orphans"; **widows**, cf. 146:9; Deut. 10:18; James 1:27; **solitary**; **prisoners**). The **rebellious** (i.e., those against God's gracious covenant), however, he exiles to a **parched land**: they may not dwell among his people.

68:7–10 *God's March from Sinai.* These verses recall the way God led his people **through the wilderness** (v. 7), from **Sinai** to his **inheritance** (i.e., Canaan, now the land of Israel), where God's **flock** (i.e., his people) **found a dwelling**. Not only did God give Israel a place to live, he made it fruitful: **Rain in abundance, O God, you shed abroad**. Verse 8 echoes Judg. 5:4–5, which also describes God's progress to the land with his people.

11 The Lord gives [a]the word;
[b]the women who announce the news are a great host:
12 [c]"The kings of the armies—they flee, they flee!"
The women at home [d]divide the spoil—
13 though you men lie among [e]the sheepfolds—
the wings of a dove covered with silver,
its pinions with shimmering gold.
14 When the Almighty scatters kings there,
let snow fall on [f]Zalmon.
15 O mountain of God, mountain of Bashan;
O many-peaked[1] mountain, mountain of Bashan!
16 Why do you look with hatred, O many-peaked mountain,
at the mount that God [g]desired for his abode,
yes, where the LORD will dwell forever?
17 [h]The chariots of God are twice ten thousand,
thousands upon thousands;
the Lord is among them; Sinai is now in the sanctuary.
18 [i]You ascended on high,
[j]leading a host of captives in your train
and [k]receiving gifts among men,
even among [l]the rebellious, [m]that the LORD God may dwell there.

19 Blessed be the Lord,
who daily [n]bears us up;
God is our salvation. *Selah*
20 Our God is a God of salvation,
[o]and to GOD, the Lord, belong deliverances from death.
21 [p]But God will strike the heads of his enemies,
the hairy crown of him who walks in his guilty ways.
22 The Lord said,
"I will bring them back [q]from Bashan,
[r]I will bring them back from the depths of the sea,
23 that you may [s]strike your feet in their blood,
that [t]the tongues of your dogs may have their portion from the foe."

24 Your procession is[2] seen, O God,
the procession of my God, my King, into the sanctuary—

11[a][Ps. 33:9] [b][Ex. 15:20; 1 Sam. 18:6]
12[c]Ps. 110:5; [Num. 31:8; Josh. 10:16; Judg. 5:19]; See Josh. 12:7-24 [d]Judg. 5:30
13[e][Gen. 49:14; Judg. 5:16]
14[f]Judg. 9:48
16[g]Ps. 132:13, 14; [Ps. 78:54; 87:1, 2; Deut. 12:5]
17[h]2 Kgs. 6:17; Hab. 3:8
18[i]Ps. 7:7; 47:5; Cited Eph. 4:8; [Acts 1:9] [j]Judg. 5:12 [k][Acts 2:4, 33] [l][Rom. 5:8; 1 Tim. 1:13] [m]Ps. 78:60; Ex. 29:45; Rev. 21:3; [John 14:23]
19[n][Isa. 46:4]
20[o]Deut. 32:39; Eccles. 7:18; Rev. 1:18
21[p]Ps. 110:6; Hab. 3:13
22[q]Num. 21:33 [r]See Amos 9:2-4
23[s]Ps. 58:10 [t][1 Kgs. 21:19; 22:38]

[1] Or *hunch-backed;* also verse 16 [2] Or *has been*

68:11–14 *Victory over Gentile Kings.* This section describes what happens **when the Almighty scatters** Gentile **kings** on behalf of his people. Even when the able-bodied of Israel were not all faithful to fight in the wars (v. 13, some **men** would even **lie among the sheepfolds** instead of endure the hardships of battle; cf. Judg. 5:16), the Lord brought about great victories—so that **the women at home divide the spoil** that their men have brought. **The women who announce the news** are probably groups like those in Ex. 15:20–21 and 1 Sam. 18:6–7, who declare from village to village the exciting news of the victory of Israel's army. **The wings of a dove covered with silver, its pinions with shimmering gold** is a fanciful image of enjoying wealth and beauty under God's care.

68:14 Zalmon. Judges 9:48 mentions a mountain with this name, but it is not certain that this is the intended reference. It is likely a mountain in any case, in view of the **snow**.

68:15–18 *The Mountain of God's Abode.* The ark's destination is the "sanctuary" on Mount Zion, the **mountain of God**. The previous section ended by referring to a mountain, and now this section compares God's mountain to the larger **mountain of Bashan** (to the north). Observe how the Lord dwells in the place where his ark does; God is especially present by way of his ark (cf. Josh. 3:11, ESV footnote). **Sinai is now in the sanctuary.** The ark is a portable Sinai, conveying God's presence to his people.

68:18 Ephesians 4:8–11 uses this verse to describe how the exalted Christ (who **ascended** after he descended in the incarnation) distributed gifts to his people, i.e., assigned to each of the members different ways of serving the body. That Paul can apply this to Christ shows that he considered Jesus divine. The quotation in Eph. 4:8 does not quite match the Septuagint (which follows the Hb.); Paul says that "he gave gifts to men" rather than **receiving gifts among men**. The difference is only superficial, however: the verb "receive" (Hb. *laqakh*) can have the idea of "receive in order to give," or "to fetch" (e.g., Gen. 18:4–5, where it is "bring"). Further, after a conquest, the spoils were distributed among the leader's men. Thus the psalm focuses on the conqueror who acquired the spoils from the defeated, while Paul's adaptation of the truth of the psalm focuses on how that conqueror distributed the spoils to his own.

68:19–23 *God Protects His People from His (and Their) Enemies.* This section celebrates how God **daily bears us** (Israel) **up** and is **salvation** for his people (cf. 14:7; see note on 20:1–5). The particular kind of salvation here is protection from enemies, which means military victories over them (**strike the heads, strike your feet in their blood**).

68:23 the tongues of your dogs. As they scavenge among the corpses and lick up the blood (cf. 1 Kings 21:19; 22:38).

68:24–27 *The Procession.* These verses describe a **procession** of Israelites, which consists of **singers**, followed by **virgins playing tambourines**, with

25[u]Ps. 47:5; 1 Chr. 13:8; 15:16 [v]See Ps. 33:3 [w]Ex. 15:20; Judg. 11:34
26[x]Ps. 22:25; 26:12 [y]Deut. 33:28; Isa. 48:1; [Isa. 51:1]
27[z][1 Sam. 9:21] [a][Judg. 5:18]
28[b]See Ps. 42:8
29[c]Ps. 45:12; 76:11; 1 Kgs. 10:10, 25; 2 Chr. 32:23; Isa. 18:7
30[d]Job 40:21; Isa. 19:6; Ezek. 29:3, 4; [Ezek. 32:2] [e]Ps. 22:12 [f][2 Sam. 8:2, 6]
31[g]Isa. 19:19, 21 [h]Ps. 87:4; Isa. 45:14; Zeph. 3:10 [i]Ps. 44:20
32[j]Ps. 102:22
33[k]Ps. 18:10; 104:3; Deut. 33:26 [l]Deut. 10:14; 1 Kgs. 8:27 [m]Ps. 29:4; See Ps. 46:6
34[n]Ps. 29:1 [o]Ps. 150:1 [p]Ps. 36:5; 57:10; 108:4
35[q][Ps. 65:5]; See Ps. 47:2 [r][Ps. 110:2] [s]Isa. 40:29; See Ps. 29:11

Psalm 69
[t]Ps. 45, title
1[u]ver. 14, 15; See Ps. 32:6; 130:1; Job 22:11

25 [u]the singers in front, [v]the musicians last,
between them [w]virgins playing tambourines:
26 [x]"Bless God in the great congregation,
the LORD, O you[1] who are of [y]Israel's fountain!"
27 There is [z]Benjamin, the least of them, in the lead,
the princes of Judah in their throng,
the princes of [a]Zebulun, the princes of Naphtali.

28 [b]Summon your power, O God,[2]
the power, O God, by which you have worked for us.
29 Because of your temple at Jerusalem
kings shall [c]bear gifts to you.
30 Rebuke [d]the beasts that dwell among the reeds,
the herd of [e]bulls with the calves of the peoples.
[f]Trample underfoot those who lust after tribute;
scatter the peoples who delight in war.[3]
31 Nobles shall come from [g]Egypt;
[h]Cush shall hasten to [i]stretch out her hands to God.

32 [j]O kingdoms of the earth, sing to God;
sing praises to the Lord, *Selah*
33 to him [k]who rides in [l]the heavens, the ancient heavens;
behold, he [m]sends out his voice, his mighty voice.
34 [n]Ascribe power to God,
whose majesty is over Israel,
and whose [o]power is in [p]the skies.
35 [q]Awesome is God from his[4] [r]sanctuary;
the God of Israel—he is the one who gives [s]power and strength to his people.
Blessed be God!

Save Me, O God

69

TO THE CHOIRMASTER: ACCORDING TO [t]LILIES. OF DAVID.
1 Save me, O God!
For [u]the waters have come up to my neck.[5]

[1] The Hebrew for *you* is plural here [2] By revocalization (compare Septuagint); Hebrew *Your God has summoned your power* [3] The meaning of the Hebrew verse is uncertain [4] Septuagint; Hebrew *your* [5] Or *waters threaten my life*

the musicians last, as they enter **into the sanctuary** in a worship setting. Included in the procession are **princes** from the various tribes (**Benjamin**, **Judah**, **Zebulun**, and **Naphtali** probably represent the whole of Israel). Verse 26 is apparently a summary of their song. The mention of these tribes indicates that the psalm dates from before the kingdom was divided, when Benjamin and Judah became the southern kingdom, while Zebulun and Naphtali became part of the northern kingdom.

68:28–31 *The Gentiles Will Come to the True God.* The defeat of the Gentile enemies (here described as fierce wild animals, an image of **those who lust after tribute** and **who delight in war**, v. 30) is a good thing, both because their designs are greedy and bloody, and because as a result they and others will come to worship the true God (vv. 29, 31). **kings shall bear gifts to you**. These are Gentile kings; cf. Isa. 60:7; Hag. 2:7; Zech. 6:15. For the expectation that people from **Egypt** and **Cush** (Nubia, the region south of Egypt, called "Ethiopia" by ancient writers) will come to know God, cf. Isa. 45:14. God's presence in his **temple at Jerusalem** (Ps. 68:29) will draw Gentiles to the light (cf. 1 Kings 8:41–43). The oracle of Isa. 2:1–5 foretells the Gentiles coming to worship at God's temple "in the last days"; the NT explains that this is taking place in the time after Christ's resurrection (see notes on Ps. 67:4–5; Isa. 2:1–5).

68:32–35 *Closing Call to Praise.* After all the recollections in the psalm, the call goes out to all the Gentile **kingdoms of the earth**, urging them to **sing to God** now (why wait for the messianic era?). Their praise should **ascribe power to God** and recognize that his **majesty is over Israel**. That is, they should recognize Israel's unique role as God's own people, among whom God has set his **sanctuary** and to whom he **gives power and strength**. As Israelites sing this, they should be overwhelmed with gratitude at the astonishing privilege of being God's vehicle of blessing to the world. Today, believers from all nations can sing this with gratitude that God was faithful to his promises to bring the light to the world; they too can share in grateful awe at their privilege of being God's vehicle for bringing the world further blessing.

Psalm 69. This is an individual lament, geared especially to a situation in which a faithful Israelite is suffering for wrongs he has done (v. 5) but also finds attackers piling on, taking advantage of his suffering and making it worse (v. 26). The NT cites several passages from this psalm, applying them to the life of Christ. Some have argued that NT use shows that the right way to read the psalm is as David's personal prayer, which believers sing in order to identify with him. A better approach comes from remembering that David was the representative for the people of God, and in that role he wrote this as a prayer that is well-suited to each of God's people in analogous situations, providing the ideal response to such trials (see note on Psalm 3, where the issues are similar); the notes will show how this sheds light on the NT writers' portrait of Jesus.

69:1–4 *I Am in Deep Trouble from Treacherous Enemies.* The singer lays the situation before God, first with colorful imagery (like drowning, or quicksand, vv. 1–2; cf. vv. 14–15), then with his own sad state (v. 3), and finally, with the actual case: **those who hate me without cause**. Since the psalm will

2 I sink in deep [v]mire,
where there is no foothold;
I have come into deep waters,
and the flood [w]sweeps over me.
3 [x]I am weary with my crying out;
[y]my throat is parched.
[z]My eyes grow dim
with [a]waiting for my God.

4 [b]More in number than the hairs of my head
are [c]those who hate me [d]without cause;
mighty are those who would destroy me,
[e]those who attack me with lies.
What I did not steal
must I now restore?
5 O God, you know my folly;
the wrongs I have done are not hidden from you.

6 Let not those who hope in you [f]be put to shame through me,
O Lord GOD of hosts;
let not those who seek you be brought to dishonor through me,
O God of Israel.
7 For it is [g]for your sake that I have borne reproach,
that dishonor has covered my face.
8 I have become [h]a stranger to my brothers,
an alien to my mother's sons.

9 For [i]zeal for your house has consumed me,
and [j]the reproaches of those who reproach you have fallen on me.
10 When I wept and humbled[1] my soul with fasting,
it became my reproach.
11 When I made [k]sackcloth my clothing,
I became [l]a byword to them.
12 I am the talk of those who [m]sit in the gate,
and the drunkards make [n]songs about me.

[1] Hebrew lacks *and humbled*

2 [v]ver. 14; Ps. 40:2 [w]Ps. 124:4
3 [x]Ps. 6:6 [y][Ps. 22:15] [z]Ps. 119:82, 123; Deut. 28:32; Isa. 38:14 [a]See Ps. 31:24
4 [b]Ps. 40:12 [c]Cited John 15:25 [d][Ps. 35:7; 59:3, 4; 109:3; 119:161] [e]Ps. 35:19; 38:19
6 [f]See Ps. 25:2
7 [g]Jer. 15:15; [Ps. 44:22]
8 [h][Ps. 31:11; 38:11; Job 19:13; John 1:11]
9 [i]Cited John 2:17; [Ps. 119:139]; See Ps. 132:1-5 [j]Cited Rom. 15:3; [Ps. 89:41, 50]
11 [k]See Ps. 35:13 [l]See Job 17:6
12 [m][Gen. 19:1; Esth. 2:19] [n]See Job 30:9

go on to acknowledge that the singer is not perfect, this cannot be a claim of total innocence; rather, it is a claim that the singer has not done harm to the particular people who **attack** him **with lies**.

69:4 hate me without cause. In John 15:25 Jesus uses these words to describe himself, and to lead his followers to expect the same. In John's presentation of Jesus, he is the perfect embodiment of a faithful Israelite, who may expect the impious to hate him.

69:5–8 *Let Not My Folly Bring Shame on Those Who Love You.* The singer admits that he is not perfect, which God knows full well (**the wrongs I have done are not hidden from you**); he agrees that his wrongs could put others of the faithful (**those who hope in you**) to shame (i.e., could subject them to scorn), and prays that this will not happen. In singing this the pious acknowledge that they do commit sins, and that these sins can cause trouble for themselves and for others, and even damage the reputation of God and his faithful people. Such acknowledgment should help them to be more honest about their weaknesses, and more careful about their deeds.

69:9–12 / *Bear Your Reproach.* The idea of **reproach**, introduced in v. 7, dominates this section. Here the song is speaking of the current condition: the **reproaches** that fall on the singer are not really the proper response of other godly people to his wrongs; they are instead the weapons of **those who reproach** God, scorning God himself, his covenant, and his faithful people. They even turn the signs of devout mourning and repentance (**fasting**, **sackcloth**) into an occasion to mock and humiliate the pious person. (Even though the singer is a penitent, he is still **consumed** with **zeal for** God's **house**, i.e., is loyal to the covenant and its ordinances.)

69:9 zeal for your house has consumed me. In John 2:17, Jesus' disciples remember this text after Jesus has driven the livestock merchants and money-changers out of the temple. Jesus embodies the ideal pious member of God's people, which is the calling of the Davidic king (though unlike all the heirs of David before him, Jesus does not have "folly" and "wrongs" [Ps. 69:5] to repent of; cf. John 8:46). **The reproaches of those who reproach you have fallen on me**. In Rom. 15:3, Paul applies this text to Jesus, because he saw Jesus as the ideal covenant member who was willing to suffer reproach for the sake of God's truth. In this he is an example to the Roman Christians, for whom the issue of the weak and the strong probably included elements of shame in Roman society: Romans are known to have looked down upon those with Jewish scruples about food (the weak). The faithful Christian should be willing to suffer the scorn that some people might heap on him if he has close fellowship with the socially "unworthy"; nothing, not even social reproach, should be allowed to prevent these Christians from worshiping together.

69:13–18 *My Prayer Is Directed to You.* The next section of the psalm expresses the singer's reliance on God: **my prayer is to you, answer me, hide not your face, draw near**. His case is desperate, and he urgently

13 [o]Ps. 109:4 [p]Isa. 49:8; 2 Cor. 6:2; [Ps. 32:6]
14 [q]ver. 2 [r]Ps. 144:7 [s]ver. 1, 2
15 [t]Ps. 55:23 [u]Num. 16:33
16 [v]Ps. 63:3; 109:21 [w]Ps. 106:45 [x]See Ps. 25:16
17 [y]See Ps. 27:9 [z]See Ps. 18:6 [a]Ps. 102:2; 143:7
19 [b]ver. 10, 11; [Heb. 12:2]; See Ps. 22:6
20 [b][See ver. 19 above] [c][Matt. 26:37] [d]Ps. 142:4; [Isa. 63:5] [e]Jer. 15:5 [f]Job 16:2
21 [g]Deut. 29:18; Matt. 27:34 [h]Matt. 27:48; Luke 23:36; John 19:29; [Mark 15:23]
22 [i]Cited Rom. 11:9, 10; See Ps. 35:4-8; 109:6-15 [j]Ps. 23:5 [k][1 Thess. 5:3]
23 [l]Isa. 6:10; [Matt. 13:14] [m]Dan. 5:6; Nah. 2:10

13 But as for me, my [o]prayer is to you, O LORD.
At [p]an acceptable time, O God,
in the abundance of your steadfast love answer me in your saving faithfulness.
14 Deliver me
from sinking in [q]the mire;
[r]let me be delivered from my enemies
and from [s]the deep waters.
15 Let not the flood sweep over me,
or the deep swallow me up,
or [t]the pit close [u]its mouth over me.

16 Answer me, O LORD, for your [v]steadfast love is good;
according to your abundant [w]mercy, [x]turn to me.
17 [y]Hide not your face from your servant;
[z]for I am in distress; [a]make haste to answer me.
18 Draw near to my soul, redeem me;
ransom me because of my enemies!

19 You know my [b]reproach,
and my shame and my dishonor;
my foes are all known to you.
20 [b]Reproaches have broken my heart,
so that I am in [c]despair.
I [d]looked for [e]pity, but there was none,
and for [f]comforters, but I found none.
21 They gave me [g]poison for food,
and for my thirst they gave me [h]sour wine to drink.

22 [i]Let their own [j]table before them become a snare;
[k]and when they are at peace, let it become a trap.[1]
23 [l]Let their eyes be darkened, so that they cannot see,
[m]and make their loins tremble continually.
24 Pour out your indignation upon them,
and let your burning anger overtake them.

[1] Hebrew; a slight revocalization yields (compare Septuagint, Syriac, Jerome) *a snare, and retribution and a trap*

needs God's help. The prayer appeals to what God has revealed about himself: **the abundance of your steadfast love** and **faithfulness** (v. 13) and **steadfast love** and **mercy** (v. 16) echo Ex. 34:6, God's revelation of his character ("merciful and gracious, . . . abounding in steadfast love and faithfulness"). It is clear in this case that for God to **answer** (Ps. 69:16–17) means for him to do something to relieve the situation ("no" does not qualify as an answer here!). Regarding "hide not your face," see note on 51:9. **redeem.** See note on 25:22.

69:19–21 *You Know My Reproach and Shame.* Here the psalm describes the sense of **shame**, **dishonor**, **despair**, and abandonment the singer must feel; and though these are emotions of the heart and not necessarily visible to man, nevertheless he can say to God, "**you know**," for God searches all hearts at all times.

69:21 for my thirst they gave me sour wine to drink. Sour wine would have been very unpleasant to someone suffering from severe thirst. John 19:28–29 uses these words in connection with one of Jesus' last words on the cross (cf. also Matt. 27:34, 48; Mark 15:23, 36; Luke 23:36). The sour wine would have been the cheap beverage that the soldiers used to satisfy their thirst; but Jesus felt God-forsaken (Mark 15:34), and the thirst to which he was testifying must have been far more severe and deep-seated than anything this drink was meant for. When Jesus received it, he briefly prolonged his life (and his agony), and perhaps moistened his lips enough finally to cry out, "It is finished!" (John 19:30). In Luke 23:34, Jesus prays, "Father, forgive them, for they know not what they do." Since Luke alluded to this psalm (as above), he might well have intended a contrast: the psalm will go on to call down curses on the enemies, while Jesus did not, but instead prayed for mercy. Nevertheless, the judgment requested by the curses is only delayed, and will be set loose when Christ returns as Judge of all. (This does not exhaust the Christian view of these curses, since other NT texts use them; see notes on Ps. 69:22–23 and 69:25.)

69:22–28 *May They Suffer the Punishment They Deserve.* The next section asks God to vindicate his faithful one by bringing on the enemies the troubles they deserve (and that they would bring on the faithful if they could). The description in vv. 22–25 uses imagery to convey the idea of a life devastated and sad in various ways: in home life (v. 22), in personal health (v. 23), and in its posterity (vv. 24–25). It is clear from v. 26 that these people are grievous sinners; they are Israelites who do not embrace the covenant and who can wield influence to harm the faithful. As with these curses in general, the unstated assumption is that they will not repent, which of course would be preferable (see notes on 5:10; 35:4–8).

69:22–23 In Rom. 11:9–10, Paul cites this curse to explain why his fellow Jews who reject the message of Christ have been hardened. Nevertheless, in the rest of Romans 11, he also explains why the curse is not irrevocable: it is a "partial hardening," which will be relieved if and when they repent (Rom. 11:23–25).

25 [n]May their camp be a desolation;
let no one dwell in their tents.
26 For they [o]persecute him whom [p]you have struck down,
and they recount the pain of [q]those you have wounded.
27 [r]Add to them punishment upon punishment;
may they have no acquittal from you.[1]
28 Let them be [s]blotted out of the book of the living;
let them not be [t]enrolled among the righteous.

29 But I am afflicted and in pain;
let your salvation, O God, [u]set me on high!

30 I will [v]praise the name of God with a song;
I will [w]magnify him with [x]thanksgiving.
31 This will [y]please the LORD more than an ox
or a bull [z]with horns and hoofs.
32 When [a]the humble see it they will be glad;
you who seek God, [a]let your hearts revive.
33 For the LORD hears the needy
and [b]does not despise his own people who are prisoners.

34 Let [c]heaven and earth praise him,
the seas and everything that moves in them.
35 For [d]God will save Zion
and build up the cities of Judah,
and people shall dwell there and possess it;
36 [e]the offspring of his servants shall inherit it,
and those who love his name shall dwell in it.

O LORD, Do Not Delay

70

TO THE CHOIRMASTER. OF DAVID, [f]FOR THE MEMORIAL OFFERING.
1 [g]Make haste, O God, to deliver me!
O LORD, make haste to help me!
2 Let them be put to shame and confusion
who seek my life!
Let them be turned back and brought to dishonor
who delight in my hurt!
3 Let them turn back because of their shame
who say, "Aha, Aha!"

[1] Hebrew *may they not come into your righteousness*

25[n]Cited Acts 1:20; [Matt. 23:38; Luke 13:35]
26[o][Zech. 1:15] [p]Isa. 53:4 [q][Job 19:21]
27[r]Neh. 4:5
28[s]Ex. 32:32; Rev. 3:5; [Phil. 4:3] [t][Ezek. 13:9; Luke 10:20; Heb. 12:23]
29[u]Ps. 20:1
30[v]Ps. 28:7 [w]See Ps. 34:3 [x]See Ps. 50:14, 23
31[y]Ps. 50:13 [z]Lev. 11:3
32[a]Ps. 22:26; 34:2
33[b][Ps. 68:6]
34[c]Ps. 96:11; 98:7; Isa. 44:23; 49:13; See Ps. 148:1-12
35[d]See Ps. 51:18; [Isa. 44:26]
36[e]Ps. 102:28; Isa. 65:9; [Ps. 37:29]

Psalm 70
[f]Ps. 38, title; [1 Chr. 16:4]
1[g]For ver. 1-5, see Ps. 40:13-17

69:25 In Acts 1:20, this text is applied to Judas, who had taken part in destroying Jesus, the perfect embodiment of this psalm. If it is part of Peter's speech, then he is combining it with Ps. 109:8 to show why the disciples should give up on Judas and replace him with another.

69:27–28 no acquittal . . . blotted out . . . not be enrolled. These prospects go beyond temporal punishments to include an eternal one. Again, the assumption is that the people in question will not repent. These words could prove to be a mercy to the evildoers, should any of them be present at worship when the congregation sings them, and they heed the warning.

69:29–33 *Deliver Me for the Sake of the Humble.* The argument of this section is that if God's **salvation** should **set** the pious singer **on high**, he will **magnify** God with public **thanksgiving**, presumably in a worship service (cf. the mention of potential sacrifice in v. 31; see note on 66:13–15). This will enable the **humble** (another term for the genuinely faithful) to **see it** and **be glad**; they will know that **the LORD hears the needy** who seek him in faith.

69:34–36 *Let Everything Praise the God Who Dwells in Zion.* The psalm moves on to sing of all creation praising God, and of God's enduring commitment to populate **Zion** with the faithful **offspring of his** (faithful) **servants**. Behind this section lies the recognition that God intends the whole world to be able to praise him, and he intends for Zion to flourish as the paradigm of true piety. This cannot happen when the kind of evildoers described in this psalm have a free rein to oppress the faithful and to corrupt the corporate life of God's people.

Psalm 70. This short psalm is an individual lament, an urgent prayer for rescue from gloating enemies. The whole psalm is very close to 40:14–16. The title specifies the psalm as "for the memorial offering" (cf. note on Psalm 38).

70:1–3 *Deliver Me from Those Who Seek My Life.* The first stanza sounds the note of desperation and danger. The threat comes from those **who seek my life, who delight in my hurt**, and **who say, "Aha, Aha!"** These are people who are eager to hurt and gloat over the faithful. The enemies could be powerful Israelites, unfaithful to the covenant and therefore hostile to true piety, or they could be foreigners who seek to impose other gods upon God's people. The song prays urgently that God would **make haste . . . to deliver** and **help me**; the specific kind of help is the thwarting of the enemies' schemes, i.e., that they would **be put to shame and confusion**, and that they would **be turned back and brought to dishonor**.

4 May all who seek you
rejoice and be glad in you!
May those who love your salvation
say evermore, "God is great!"
5 But I am poor and needy;
[h]hasten to me, O God!
You are my help and my deliverer;
O LORD, do not delay!

Forsake Me Not When My Strength Is Spent

71

1 [i]In you, O LORD, do I take refuge;
let me never be put to shame!
2 In your righteousness deliver me and rescue me;
incline your ear to me, and save me!
3 Be to me a rock of [j]refuge,
to which I may continually come;
you have [k]given the command to save me,
for you are my [l]rock and my fortress.

4 [m]Rescue me, O my God, from the hand of the wicked,
from the grasp of the unjust and cruel man.
5 For you, O Lord, are my [n]hope,
my trust, O LORD, from my youth.
6 Upon you I have leaned [o]from before my birth;
you are he who [p]took me from my mother's womb.
My praise is continually of you.

7 I have been as [q]a portent to many,
but you are my strong refuge.
8 My [r]mouth is filled with your praise,
and with your glory all the day.
9 [s]Do not cast me off in the time of old age;
forsake me not when my strength is spent.
10 For my enemies speak concerning me;
those who [t]watch for my life [u]consult together
11 and say, "God has forsaken him;
pursue and seize him,
for there is none to deliver him."

5 [h]Ps. 141:1

Psalm 71

1 [i]For ver. 1-3, see Ps. 31:1-3
3 [j][Ps. 90:1; 91:9; Deut. 33:27] [k]See Ps. 42:8 [l]See Ps. 18:2
4 [m]Ps. 140:1, 4
5 [n]Jer. 14:8; 17:13; 50:7; 1 Tim. 1:1
6 [o]See Ps. 22:10 [p]Ps. 22:9
7 [q]Isa. 8:18; [1 Cor. 4:9]
8 [r]ver. 24
9 [s]ver. 18
10 [t]Ps. 56:6 [u]Ps. 83:5; [Ps. 41:7, 8]

70:4–5 *May Those Who Seek You Rejoice at My Deliverance.* This stanza echoes the first stanza in several ways. First, **who seek you** (v. 4) contrasts with "who seek my life" (v. 2): clearly these are two contrasting groups of people. Then **hasten** (v. 5) echoes "make haste" (v. 1), while **help** and **deliverer** (v. 5) look back to "deliver" and "help" (v. 1), in reverse order (the Hb. uses two synonyms for deliver). In this stanza each person in the singing congregation identifies himself with the faithful in Israel (i.e., those who seek God and love his salvation) and prays that the whole company of the faithful might **rejoice . . . in** God when they see the rescue of the person in trouble. The person in trouble is **poor and needy**, and thus socially powerless; therefore his deliverance will be striking evidence that God keeps his promises.

Psalm 71. This is another individual lament, suited to a faithful person in danger from enemies who would cause hurt by taking advantage of any weakness or distress (vv. 9–11). These enemies could be foreign, and they could be Israelite; the wording is general enough to apply to either. There is no title for the psalm; it would appear that its author composed it using material from earlier psalms (esp. Davidic ones), albeit with variations (e.g., 71:1–3 echoes 31:1–3; the cross-references give other examples). The exposition here discerns the stanza structure of the psalm by following the vocatives, "O God" or "O LORD."

71:1–3 *Be My Refuge Always.* The song opens with a sturdy profession of faith, taking assurance from God's covenant promises: God's **righteousness** is his faithfulness to keep his promises, and this is the ground of hope (cf. vv. 15, 16, 19, 24).

71:4–11 *Rescue Me from the Wicked Who Want to Hurt Me.* The next section identifies the specific occasion for the prayer: the **wicked**, namely, **unjust and cruel** men who look for any opening to do harm to the faithful (vv. 4, 10–11). As usual in the Psalms, the term "wicked" refers to those who oppose true faith in God. The singer professes not to be in this category, but among the faithful **from my youth**, and prays that God will not **cast** him **off in the time of old age**. This is to remind Israel that the benefits of the covenant are not automatic but are for those who are faithful to its provisions. Hence the congregation will come to love piety, and each will yearn to have his **mouth . . . filled with** God's **praise**.

71:5–6 from my youth . . . from before my birth . . . from my mother's womb. The Israelites singing this came into the world as members of Abraham's family, the recipients of God's promises. These believers learn here to trace God's work in their lives back to the very beginning of their personal existence, before they were even born. Indeed, they even consider the faith that they articulate now to have begun then, before they could speak it. Cf. 22:9–10; 139:13–16; Luke 1:41–44.

12 O God, be not [v]far from me;
O my God, [w]make haste to help me!
13 May my accusers be [x]put to shame and consumed;
[y]with scorn and disgrace may they be covered
who [z]seek my hurt.
14 But I will [a]hope continually
and will [b]praise you yet more and more.
15 My [c]mouth will tell of your righteous acts,
of your deeds of salvation all the day,
for [d]their number is past my knowledge.
16 With the mighty deeds of the Lord GOD I will come;
I will remind them of your righteousness, yours alone.

17 O God, from my youth you have taught me,
and I still proclaim your wondrous deeds.
18 So even to [e]old age and gray hairs,
O God, [f]do not forsake me,
until I proclaim your might to another generation,
your power to all those to come.
19 Your [g]righteousness, O God,
reaches the high heavens.
You who have done [h]great things,
O God, [i]who is like you?
20 You who have [j]made me see many troubles and calamities
will [k]revive me again;
from the depths of the earth
you will bring me up again.
21 You will increase my greatness
and comfort me again.

22 I will also praise you with [l]the harp
for your faithfulness, O my God;
I will sing praises to you with the lyre,
O [m]Holy One of Israel.
23 My lips will shout for joy,
when I sing praises to you;
my soul also, which you have [n]redeemed.
24 And my [o]tongue will talk of your righteous help all the day long,
for they have been [p]put to shame and disappointed
who sought to do me hurt.

12[v]See Ps. 10:1 [w]Ps. 70:5; See Ps. 40:13
13[x]ver. 24; See Ps. 35:4, 26 [y]Ps. 109:29 [z]ver. 24; Esth. 9:2; [Ps. 70:2]
14[a]ver. 5 [b]ver. 22
15[c]ver. 8, 24 [d]See Ps. 40:5
18[e]Isa. 46:4 [f]ver. 9
19[g]Ps. 36:5 [h]Ps. 126:2; 1 Sam. 12:24; Luke 1:49 [i]Ps. 35:10
20[j]Ps. 60:3 [k]Ps. 80:18; 85:6; 119:25; 138:7; 143:11; Hos. 6:2
22[l]Ps. 33:2 [m]Ps. 78:41; 89:18; 2 Kgs. 19:22; Isa. 60:9
23[n]Ps. 34:22
24[o][ver. 8, 15]; See Ps. 35:28 [p][ver. 13]

71:12–16 *Do Not Be Far from Me.* The next appeal to God is **be not far from me** and **make haste to help me**. Under threat from such people as are described as **accusers** and those **who seek my hurt** (v. 13; see also vv. 4, 10–11), the pious singer looks to God for help. He promises to **hope continually**, leaving to God the timing of the answer to these prayers. He also looks forward to sharing his story of God's **righteous acts** with his fellow worshipers: **praise, tell,** and **remind them** (i.e., "remind my fellow believers") describe activities among the congregation. **Come** is "come to worship."

71:17–21 *Care for Me from Youth through Old Age.* This stanza returns to the topic of the second stanza: since **from my youth you have taught me** (i.e., to trust in you, cf. vv. 5–6), **so even to old age and gray hairs . . . do not forsake me** (cf. v. 9). The song goes on to foster an ideal for a pious person's life, asking God to make it long enough so that the singer might **proclaim your might to another generation, your power to all those to come**; the life of faith is meant to be passed on to one's descendants. The book of Psalms readily confesses that the believer's life is full of **many troubles and calamities** and acknowledges that these are under God's control (**you who have made me see**); and since God governs these troubles, he can also relieve them (hence the confidence of vv. 20–21).

71:22–24 *I Will Praise You for Your Deliverance.* The psalm closes by bringing to conclusion the previous parts of the psalm, especially the confidence (vv. 20–21), and the anticipation of giving testimony in worship (vv. 14–16). Not only does the singer look forward to joyful songs in worship, he expects to **talk of** God's **righteous help all the day long** (i.e., even outside of the gathered congregation).

71:22 Holy One of Israel. This is the common name for God in Isaiah (25 times), and is rare outside of that book, appearing only in 2 Kings 19:22 (= Isa. 37:23); Ps. 71:22; 78:41; 89:18; Jer. 50:29; 51:5. See Introduction to Isaiah: Date.

Psalm 72
[q]Ps. 127, title
1[r][1 Chr. 22:12]
2[s]Isa. 9:7; 11:2-4; 32:1; See Ps. 122:5
3[t][Ps. 85:10; Isa. 32:17; 52:7]
5[u]ver. 7, 17; Ps. 89:36, 37; Jer. 31:35, 36; [Jer. 33:20, 25] [v]Ps. 89:4; [Luke 1:33]
6[w]2 Sam. 23:4; Hos. 6:3 [x]Amos 7:1 [y]Deut. 32:2; [Ps. 65:10; Job 5:10]
7[z]See Ps. 92:12 [a]Isa. 2:4; [Eph. 2:14]
8[b]Ex. 23:31; 1 Kgs. 4:21, 24; Zech. 9:10; [Ps. 80:11; 89:25] [c]See Ps. 2:8
9[d]Ps. 22:29 [e]Isa. 49:23; Mic. 7:17
10[f]1 Kgs. 10:22 [g]Isa. 42:10, 12; 51:5; 60:9 [h]See Ps. 68:29; 1 Sam. 10:27 [i]See 1 Kgs. 10:1 [j]Gen. 10:7; Isa. 43:3; 45:14
11[k]Isa. 49:7, 23
12[l]See Job 29:12-17

72

Give the King Your Justice

OF [q]SOLOMON.

1 Give the king your [r]justice, O God,
and your righteousness to the royal son!
2 May he [s]judge your people with righteousness,
and your poor with justice!
3 Let the mountains bear [t]prosperity for the people,
and the hills, in righteousness!
4 May he defend the cause of the poor of the people,
give deliverance to the children of the needy,
and crush the oppressor!

5 May they fear you[1] while [u]the sun endures,
and as long as the moon, [v]throughout all generations!
6 May he be like [w]rain that falls on [x]the mown grass,
like [y]showers that water the earth!
7 In his days may [z]the righteous flourish,
and [a]peace abound, till the moon be no more!

8 May he have dominion from [b]sea to sea,
and from [b]the River[2] to the [c]ends of the earth!
9 May desert tribes [d]bow down before him,
and his enemies [e]lick the dust!
10 May the kings of [f]Tarshish and of [g]the coastlands
render him [h]tribute;
may the kings of [i]Sheba and [j]Seba
bring gifts!
11 May all kings [k]fall down before him,
all nations serve him!

12 For he delivers [l]the needy when he calls,
the poor and him who has no helper.

[1] Septuagint *He shall endure* [2] That is, the Euphrates

Psalm 72. The last psalm of Book 2 (see note on 41:13) is a royal psalm, praying that the heirs of David's line (beginning with Solomon) might have success in the task that God has assigned the king (namely, ruling God's people well, protecting the poor and needy, and bringing blessing to all nations of the earth). Like Psalm 2, this song looks forward to a worldwide rule that embraces in full what the Messiah will accomplish: the OT anticipates the ultimate heir of David, who will take the throne and bring the light of God to all nations (cf. Isa. 2:1–5; 11:1–10), and the NT is careful to explain that Jesus, by virtue of his resurrection, has begun to fulfill this task through the Christian mission (cf. Matt. 28:18–20; Rom. 1:1–6). Therefore Christian hymns based on this psalm, such as "Jesus Shall Reign" and "Hail to the Lord's Anointed," have used the song according to its proper meaning. (This also explains why Christian witness, when it is true to the messianic picture of the Bible, goes beyond basic gospel proclamation and also fosters social justice and the moral transformation of whole societies.) The title, "of Solomon," can mean that Solomon was the author (just as "of David" normally means that David wrote the psalm). On the other hand, it could mean that someone (perhaps David) spoke these words of (i.e., about) Solomon, setting out the goal for his reign (and for the reigns of his heirs). The reference in Ps. 72:20 to the prayers of David may favor this view, although David did not author all the songs of Book 2 (cf. Psalms 42–50; 66–67; 71), and thus this reference is not decisive.

72:1–4 *Let the King Judge Your People Justly.* The ideal for the Davidic king is that he promote the well-being of the whole people of God by embodying true piety and by governing in such a way that justice prevails at all times (usually this means protecting the weaker members from the oppressive schemes of the stronger ones). Under such conditions, godliness should thrive among all the people, and thus they would experience the covenant blessings (Lev. 26:3–13; Deut. 28:1–14), where the land looks like a renewed Eden and the Gentiles are drawn to worship the true God. The psalm begins, then, with a prayer for the character and rule of the Davidic king, knowing that the people depend upon God to give him **righteousness** and **justice** by which to rule (**judge**).

72:5–7 *May People Fear You Because of His Reign.* The next section prays for a blessed reign **while the sun endures** and **till the moon be no more** (i.e., always). This extension of time suggests that this psalm ultimately refers to the Messiah. **May they fear you**. "They" may be God's people (vv. 1–4), or people in general (vv. 8–11); in either case, the heir of David serves as God's representative to the people, and is to be "feared," i.e., honored and obeyed. Of course this should help David's heirs to love being honorable, the kind of person who is an unmitigated blessing and refreshment to God's people (just like **rain** and **showers** were in ancient Israel).

72:8–11 *May All the Kings of the Earth Serve Him.* The blessing is to go beyond the borders of Israel: by submitting to the Davidic king, the Gentile kings bring themselves and their peoples under God's own rule (see note on 2:10–12). Verses 8–10 of Psalm 72 give examples of places in the world as the ancient Israelites knew it, as parts of the world standing for the whole world. **From sea to sea** is as far as the land extends (cf. Amos 8:12). **The River** is the Euphrates (see ESV footnote). **Desert tribes . . . Sheba and Seba** refer to inhabitants of the Arabian peninsula and the Horn of Africa.

72:8 This verse is almost identical to the second part of Zech. 9:10, which is messianic.

72:12–14 *He Brings Justice and Relief to the Poor and Needy.* Proverbs 31:1–9 portrays the ideal human ruler, and the biblical desire is that the Davidic king embody that ideal. These verses lay stress on the **needy**, the **poor**, and **the weak** (cf. Ps. 72:2–4): these are the people most easily

13 He has pity on the weak and the needy,
and saves the lives of the needy.
14 From oppression and violence he redeems their life,
and [m]precious is their blood in his sight.

15 Long may he live;
may [n]gold of Sheba be given to him!
May prayer be made [o]for him continually,
and blessings invoked for him all the day!
16 May there be abundance of grain in the land;
on the tops of the mountains may it wave;
may its fruit be like Lebanon;
and may people [p]blossom in the cities
like the [q]grass of the field!
17 [r]May his name endure forever,
his fame continue as long as the sun!
[s]May people be blessed in him,
[t]all nations call him blessed!

18 [u]Blessed be the LORD, the God of Israel,
who alone does [v]wondrous things.
19 Blessed be his [w]glorious name forever;
may [x]the whole earth be filled with his glory!
[y]Amen and Amen!

20 [z]The prayers of [a]David, the son of Jesse, are ended.

BOOK THREE

God Is My Strength and Portion Forever

73 A PSALM OF [b]ASAPH.
1 Truly God is good to [c]Israel,
to those who are [d]pure in heart.
2 But as for me, my feet had almost stumbled,
my steps had nearly slipped.
3 [e]For I was [f]envious of the arrogant
when I saw the [g]prosperity of the wicked.

4 For they have no pangs until death;
their bodies are fat and sleek.

14 [m]Ps. 116:15; 2 Kgs. 1:13
15 [n]1 Kgs. 10:10 [o]Deut. 9:20
16 [p]Ps. 92:7 [q]Job 5:25
17 [r]Ps. 104:31; [Ps. 89:36] [s]Gen. 12:3; 18:18; 22:18; 26:4 [t]Luke 1:48
18 [u]See Ps. 41:13 [v]Ps. 77:14; 86:10; 136:4; Ex. 15:11; See Job 5:9
19 [w]Neh. 9:5 [x]Num. 14:21 [y]Ps. 41:13
20 [z]Ps. 17, title; 55:1; 86, title [a]2 Sam. 23:1

Psalm 73
[b]See Ps. 50, title
1 [c]John 1:47 [d]See Ps. 24:4
3 [e]See Job 21:7 [f]Ps. 37:1; Prov. 23:17 [g][Ps. 37:7; 92:7; Jer. 12:1]

subjected to **oppression and violence** on the part of powerful nobles or regional lords. **redeems**. That is, rescues so that they may live faithfully for God. **precious is their blood in his sight**. Such a king will not allow the powerful to shed that blood.

72:15–17 *May All Peoples Be Blessed in Him.* With such a king, Israel would see its crops and people flourish, and the rest of the world would indeed come to know the true God. **Long may he live**, and **may his name endure forever**, indeed!

72:17 be blessed in him, all nations. The wording of this closely follows Gen. 22:18, "in your offspring shall all the nations of the earth be blessed," speaking of a particular offspring (the Messiah; cf. note on Gen. 22:15–18).

72:18–20 *Blessed Be the LORD (Doxology Concluding Book 2).* This does not seem to be part of the psalm itself (see note on 41:13), and yet the prayer **may the whole earth be filled with his glory** is appropriate to the theme. "To be filled with God's glory" is to be a holy site of worship, where God makes his presence known (cf. Ex. 40:34–35; 1 Kings 8:10–11), and this prayer is that the whole earth be such a sanctuary (cf. note on Isa. 6:3). **The prayers of David . . . are ended**. This could refer to the psalm itself, but more likely refers to a stage in the collection of the Psalter (since there are Davidic psalms yet to come in Books 3–5).

Psalm 73. This is a wisdom psalm, helping those who sing it to rest content even when unbelievers seem to get along without a care in the world, so that the faithful are tempted to join them. Their help comes from taking to heart where the different life paths of the faithful and the unbelievers are headed: each one is going toward either nearness to God or separation from him, a nearness or separation that will apply both now and in the afterlife. Psalm 73 is thus a companion to Psalm 49. The singer remembers that he discerned these different destinations while he was in the sanctuary of God, namely, at public worship (which points the congregation to what they should look for as they worship).

73:1–3 *The Theme: I Envied the Wicked.* The motto in v. 1 makes it clear that the whole psalm is a meditation on the problem that **God is good to Israel** (and esp. to those in Israel **who are pure in heart**, i.e., for those who love God wholeheartedly; cf. Deut. 6:5), while there seem to be **arrogant** (or "boastful," Ps. 5:5; 75:4) people who enjoy **prosperity**. The latter despise the covenant and are proud of their disdain for the faithful (cf. 73:11). The motto is true, but must be properly understood; a person holding a simplistic understanding of that motto would become **envious**, and might even conclude that the whole basis of godliness is a lie.

5[h][Isa. 53:4]
6[i][Judg. 8:26] [j][Ps. 109:18]
7[k]See Job 15:27
8[l][2 Pet. 2:18; Jude 16]
10[m][Job 15:16]
11[n]See Job 22:13
12[o][ver. 3]
13[p][ver. 1]; See Job 34:9 [q]See Ps. 26:6
14[h][See ver. 5 above] [r]Rev. 3:19 [s][Ps. 101:8]
15[t][Ps. 14:5]
16[u]Eccles. 8:17
17[v]Ps. 20:2 [w]Ps. 37:38
18[x]Ps. 35:6
19[y][Num. 16:21] [z]See Job 18:11
20[a]See Job 20:8 [b]Ps. 78:65

5 They are not in trouble as others are;
they are not [h]stricken like the rest of mankind.
6 Therefore pride is [i]their necklace;
violence covers them as [j]a garment.
7 Their [k]eyes swell out through fatness;
their hearts overflow with follies.
8 They scoff and [l]speak with malice;
loftily they threaten oppression.
9 They set their mouths against the heavens,
and their tongue struts through the earth.
10 Therefore his people turn back to them,
and find [m]no fault in them.[1]
11 And they say, [n]"How can God know?
Is there knowledge in the Most High?"
12 Behold, these are the wicked;
always at ease, they [o]increase in riches.
13 All in vain have I [p]kept my heart clean
and [q]washed my hands in innocence.
14 For all the day long I have been [h]stricken
and [r]rebuked [s]every morning.
15 If I had said, "I will speak thus,"
I would have betrayed [t]the generation of your children.

16 But when I thought how to understand this,
it seemed to me [u]a wearisome task,
17 until I went into [v]the sanctuary of God;
then I discerned their [w]end.

18 Truly you set them in [x]slippery places;
you make them fall to ruin.
19 How they are destroyed [y]in a moment,
swept away utterly by [z]terrors!
20 Like [a]a dream when one awakes,
O Lord, when [b]you rouse yourself, you despise them as phantoms.
21 When my soul was embittered,
when I was pricked in heart,

[1] Probable reading; Hebrew *the waters of a full cup are drained by them*

73:4–12 *They Are Free from the Troubles We All Face.* This section describes the apparently carefree lives of the arrogant wicked of v. 3 in a sort of vivid character sketch. They have no **pangs**, **their bodies are fat and sleek** (like well-fed animals). In v. 7, **their eyes swell out through** the **fatness** of their faces (a sign of prosperity; Job 15:27); yet on the inside, **their hearts overflow with follies**. The height of their arrogance comes to expression in Ps. 73:11, when they say, **How can God know? Is there knowledge in the Most High?** They are virtually defying God to prove that he knows their evil and intends to do anything about it. Verse 12 serves as a nice summary of the whole section.

73:13–15 *My Bitter Feelings.* The singer unveils his inner turmoil: feeling that it has been worthless to practice faithfulness (**all in vain have I kept my heart clean**). The faithful are **stricken**, **all the day long**, in contrast to the arrogant, who "are not stricken like the rest of mankind" (v. 5). At the same time, being pious, the singer recognizes that to put his bitter feelings into words **would have betrayed the generation of your children**, i.e., would undermine others' faith.

73:16–17 *I Found the Answer in the Sanctuary.* To walk around with such an inner conflict is deeply painful, made worse by how **wearisome** it is **to understand this**: it seems impossible. But when the singer goes **into the sanctuary of God**, the holy place where God's people gather for worship, the light is finally allowed to break through. The key is to contemplate the **end** (the outcome) of the lives of the arrogant and the faithful.

73:18–20 *You Will Destroy Them.* Here is "their end" (v. 17): God has **set** the arrogant **in slippery places**, so that **they are destroyed in a moment**. This may imply that they will die suddenly and unexpectedly, which certainly does happen; more likely it speaks of the effect of death (see v. 20: **you despise them as phantoms**). "Phantom" (Hb. *tselem*) is often rendered "image"; the idea is that what is left over after they die is a "mere image" of the wicked person's personality—such a person does not have the prospect of a glad afterlife that the godly have.

73:21–28 *You Keep Me Near You, and That Is What I Need.* The final section begins by noting what the singer was like when he harbored his bitter thoughts: **I was like a beast toward you**. And yet God still had his firm hold on his faithful servant: **I am continually with you; you hold my right hand** (which is why he brought the singer into the sanctuary, v. 17). Verse 24 sums up the confidence: during the singer's earthly life, **you guide me with your counsel** (i.e., with instruction from God's Word), **and afterward** (i.e., after the singer dies) **you will receive me to glory** (the heavenly honor that awaits the faithful). Thus the godly can be satisfied, because they are **near God**, and thus they have him as **the strength of** their **heart and** their **portion forever**, while the arrogant are now **far from** God and will remain far from him forever.

22 I was [c]brutish and ignorant;
I was like [d]a beast toward you.

23 Nevertheless, I am continually with you;
you [e]hold my right hand.
24 You [f]guide me with your counsel,
and afterward you will [g]receive me to glory.
25 [h]Whom have I in heaven but you?
And there is nothing on earth that I desire besides you.
26 [i]My flesh and my heart may fail,
but God is [j]the strength[1] of my heart and my [k]portion [l]forever.

27 For behold, those who are [m]far from you shall perish;
you put an end to everyone who is [n]unfaithful to you.
28 But for me it is good to [o]be near God;
I have made the Lord GOD my [p]refuge,
that I may [q]tell of all your works.

Arise, O God, Defend Your Cause

74

A MASKIL[2] OF [r]ASAPH.

1 O God, why do you [s]cast us off forever?
Why does your anger [t]smoke against [u]the sheep of your pasture?
2 [v]Remember your congregation, which you have [w]purchased of old,
which you have [x]redeemed to be [y]the tribe of your heritage!
Remember Mount Zion, [z]where you have dwelt.
3 Direct your steps to [a]the perpetual ruins;
the enemy has destroyed everything in the sanctuary!

4 Your foes have [b]roared in the midst of your meeting place;
[c]they set up their [d]own signs for [e]signs.
5 They were like those who swing [f]axes
in a forest of trees.[3]
6 And all its [g]carved wood
they broke down with hatchets and hammers.
7 They [h]set your sanctuary on fire;
they [i]profaned [j]the dwelling place of your name,
bringing it down to the ground.
8 They [k]said to themselves, "We will utterly subdue them";
they burned all the meeting places of God in the land.

9 We do not see our [l]signs;
[m]there is no longer any prophet,
and there is none among us who knows how long.

[1] Hebrew *rock* [2] Probably a musical or liturgical term [3] The meaning of the Hebrew is uncertain

22[c]See Ps. 49:10 [d]Job 18:3; [Job 11:12]
23[e]Ps. 63:8; [Ps. 41:12]
24[f]Ps. 32:8 [g]See Ps. 49:15
25[h]Ps. 16:2; [Phil. 3:8]
26[i]Ps. 40:12; See Ps. 84:2 [j]Ps. 18:2 [k]See Ps. 16:5 [l][Dan. 12:3]
27[m]Ps. 119:155 [n]Ps. 106:39; Ex. 34:15; Num. 15:39; James 4:4
28[o]James 4:8; [Heb. 10:22] [p]See Ps. 14:6 [q]See Ps. 118:17

Psalm 74

[r]See Ps. 50, title
1[s]See Ps. 44:9 [t]Deut. 29:20; [Ps. 18:8] [u]Ps. 79:13; 100:3; Jer. 23:1; Ezek. 34:31; [Ps. 95:7]
2[v]ver. 18, 22 [w]Ex. 15:16; Deut. 32:6; [Ps. 78:54] [x]Ps. 77:15; Isa. 63:9 [y]Isa. 63:17; Jer. 10:16; 51:19 [z]Ps. 9:11
3[a][Isa. 61:4]
4[b]Lam. 2:6, 7 [c][Matt. 24:15] [d]Num. 2:2 [e][ver. 9]
5[f][Jer. 46:22]
6[g][1 Kgs. 6:18, 29, 32, 35]
7[h]2 Kgs. 25:9; [Ps. 79:1] [i]Ps. 89:39; [Lam. 2:2] [j][Ps. 26:8]
8[k]Ps. 83:4
9[l][ver. 4] [m][1 Sam. 3:1; Lam. 2:9; Ezek. 7:26; Amos 8:11]

73:24 receive. Cf. 49:15, using the same term for the same idea.

73:25 besides you. That is, "if set beside you, in comparison (and potential competition) with you."

Psalm 74. This psalm is a cry of anguish over a disaster that has befallen God's people; the temple has been laid to ruin (quite possibly the Babylonian destruction of Jerusalem). Thus this is a community lament, resembling Psalm 79 in tone. In distinction from Psalm 79, however, the guilt of the covenant people does not come into view in this psalm (of course, that does not deny that the disaster is a judgment on their unfaithfulness). Some community laments deal with situations for which the guilt of the people is not the explanation (e.g., Psalm 44; possibly Psalm 77). Psalm 74, like Psalm 77, recounts God's mighty deeds in the past, especially the exodus; here that recounting serves as a ground for the prayer: do not let the Gentiles scorn the God who has done such things.

74:1–3 *O God, Why Do You Cast Us Off?* God has **cast . . . off** his people (**us**, i.e., **the sheep of your pasture**). For God's people as a whole as his sheep, cf. 77:20; 79:13; 95:7; 100:3. The terms **purchased** and **redeemed** are taken from Ex. 15:13, 16; Israel is God's people, for whom he has done great deeds in the past, marking them out as his own. This makes the current disaster—where **the enemy has destroyed everything in the sanctuary**, laying it to **perpetual ruins**—all the more painful.

74:4–8 *They Have Destroyed the Sanctuary.* The next section details how the Gentiles devastated the sanctuary: they chopped up the wood and set fire to the building. The song calls it **your meeting place** (the place that God appointed to meet with his people) and **your sanctuary** (the holy place, **the dwelling place of your name**). Given the importance that God himself had placed on the temple, and the promises he had made to be present with his people, it is horrific that these Gentiles have **profaned** it (i.e., destroyed something holy).

74:9–11 *And You Seem Silent!* It is therefore puzzling that God gives no **signs**, that he has raised up no **prophet** to guide his people in such dire

10[n] ver. 18, 22; Ps. 79:12; 89:51
11[o] Lam. 2:3
12[p] Ps. 44:4
13[q] Ex. 14:21 [r] Isa. 51:9 [s] Isa. 27:1
14[t] See Job 41:1
15[u] Ps. 78:15; 105:41; Ex. 17:5, 6; Num. 20:11; Isa. 48:21 [v] Josh. 2:10; 4:23; Isa. 51:10; [Ps. 66:6]; See Ex. 14:21-25; Josh. 3:13-17
16[w] Ps. 104:19; See Gen. 1:14-16
17[x] Deut. 32:8; [Acts 17:26] [y] Gen. 8:22
18[z] ver. 2, 22; Ps. 89:50; Rev. 16:19; 18:5 [a] Ps. 39:8; Deut. 32:6
19[b] Song 2:14 [c] [Ps. 68:10]
20[d] Ps. 106:45; Gen. 17:7, 8; Lev. 26:44, 45; Jer. 33:21 [e] [Ps. 10:8]
21[f] Ps. 9:9; 10:18 [g] [Ps. 6:10] [h] Ps. 86:1
22[i] [1 Sam. 24:15] [j] ver. 2, 18
23[k] See Ps. 65:7
Psalm 75
[l] See Ps. 57, title [m] See Ps. 50, title
1[n] Ps. 145:18

10 How long, O God, [n]is the foe to scoff?
Is the enemy to revile your name forever?
11 Why [o]do you hold back your hand, your right hand?
Take it from the fold of your garment[1] and destroy them!

12 Yet [p]God my King is from of old,
working salvation in the midst of the earth.
13 You [q]divided the sea by your might;
you [r]broke the heads of [s]the sea monsters[2] on the waters.
14 You crushed the heads of [t]Leviathan;
you gave him as food for the creatures of the wilderness.
15 You [u]split open springs and brooks;
you [v]dried up ever-flowing streams.
16 Yours is the day, yours also the night;
you have established [w]the heavenly lights and the sun.
17 You have [x]fixed all the boundaries of the earth;
you have made [y]summer and winter.

18 [z]Remember this, O LORD, how the enemy scoffs,
and [a]a foolish people reviles your name.
19 Do not deliver the soul of your [b]dove to the wild beasts;
[c]do not forget the life of your poor forever.

20 Have regard for [d]the covenant,
for [e]the dark places of the land are full of the habitations of violence.
21 Let not [f]the downtrodden [g]turn back in shame;
let [h]the poor and needy praise your name.

22 Arise, O God, [i]defend your cause;
[j]remember how the foolish scoff at you all the day!
23 Do not forget the clamor of your foes,
[k]the uproar of those who rise against you, which goes up continually!

God Will Judge with Equity

75

TO THE CHOIRMASTER: ACCORDING TO [l]DO NOT DESTROY. [m]A PSALM OF ASAPH. A SONG.

1 We give thanks to you, O God;
we give thanks, for your name is [n]near.
We[3] recount your wondrous deeds.

[1] Hebrew *from your bosom* [2] Or *the great sea creatures* [3] Hebrew *They*

distress or to tell them **how long** it will last. It is even more puzzling why God allows the enemy to continue to **scoff** and to **revile** God's **name**: how can he not strike them down?

74:12–17 *But You Have Done Wonders in the Past.* The next section recalls God's mighty deeds from the past, in which he has worked **salvation** (see note on 18:50), including the exodus from Egypt and the journey through the wilderness (74:12–15), and God's creation and governance of the whole world (vv. 16–17). The OT is constantly reminding its readers that the God who chose Israel to be his people is in fact the very same God who made everything there is. This is the wonder of being Israel; the point of mentioning it here is to show how wrong it is for the Gentiles to disdain this God.

74:14 The name **Leviathan** appears five times in the OT; in Canaanite myths it is the name of a dangerous, dragon-like monster (cf. Job 3:8). The biblical authors are confident that the Lord triumphs over all powers, including the most feared (cf. Isa. 27:1); here, this monster is used as a figure for Egypt. Elsewhere the name is used for fearsome creatures, over which God has control (Job 41:1, probably a crocodile; Ps. 104:26, probably a whale).

74:18–23 *Have Regard for the Covenant and Deliver Us!* The psalm goes on to plead with God, "**remember this**," as if God could forget (though it feels like he has done so). It is unthinkable for God to **deliver the soul of** his **dove** (a clean bird, i.e., Israel) **to the wild beasts** (i.e., foreign powers), to be torn and devoured. There is no appeal to the people's merit; rather, the appeal is **have regard for the covenant** (God's promises to the patriarchs) and **defend your cause** (God chose the people of Israel for his purposes, to bring light to the Gentiles; how will the Gentiles receive the light if they are so busy mocking?).

Psalm 75. This is a hymn of praise, thanking God for the wondrous deeds he has done for Israel, and celebrating the fact that he is the judge of all the earth and will, in his own time, put down the wicked and lift up the faithful. There is no indication of a specific occasion for which someone wrote this psalm or the congregation sang it, but this is not surprising; its lesson of faith (God's sovereign rule that this psalm celebrates is often invisible) is needful at all times.

75:1 *O God, We Recount Your Wondrous Deeds.* The subject (**we**) is Israel: they are the ones to whom God's **name is near**, they are the people on whose account God has done his **wondrous deeds**. (In the Psalms, deeds that are "wondrous," "mighty," "awesome," etc., are the great acts God

2 "At [o]the set time that I appoint
I will judge [p]with equity.
3 When the earth [q]totters, and all its inhabitants,
it is I who keep steady its [r]pillars. *Selah*
4 I say to the boastful, 'Do not boast,'
and to the wicked, [s]'Do not lift up your horn;
5 do not lift up your horn on high,
or speak with haughty neck.'"

6 For not from the east or from the west
and not from the wilderness comes [t]lifting up,
7 but it is [u]God who executes judgment,
[v]putting down one and lifting up another.
8 [w]For in the hand of the LORD there is [x]a cup
with foaming wine, [y]well mixed,
and he pours out from it,
and all the wicked of the earth
shall [z]drain it down to the dregs.

9 But I will declare it forever;
I will sing praises to the God of Jacob.
10 [a]All the horns of the wicked I will cut off,
[b]but the horns of the righteous shall be lifted up.

Who Can Stand Before You?

76

TO THE CHOIRMASTER: WITH [c]STRINGED INSTRUMENTS. A PSALM OF [d]ASAPH. A SONG.

1 In Judah God is [e]known;
his name is great in Israel.
2 His [f]abode has been established in [g]Salem,
his [h]dwelling place in Zion.
3 There he [i]broke the flashing arrows,
the shield, the sword, and the weapons of war. *Selah*

2 [o]Dan. 8:19; Hab. 2:3; See Ps. 102:13 [p]Ps. 17:2
3 [q]Isa. 24:19 [r]1 Sam. 2:8
4 [s]ver. 10; Zech. 1:21
6 [t]See Ps. 3:3
7 [u]See Ps. 50:6 [v]1 Sam. 2:7; Dan. 2:21
8 [w]See Job 21:20 [x]Ps. 11:6 [y]Prov. 23:30 [z]Ps. 73:10
10 [a]Jer. 48:25 [b]ver. 4; Ps. 89:17; 112:9; 1 Sam. 2:1

Psalm 76

[c]Ps. 4, title [d]See Ps. 50, title
1 [e]Ps. 48:3
2 [f]Ps. 27:5; Lam. 2:6 [g]Gen. 14:18 [h]Ps. 9:11; 74:2
3 [i]Ps. 46:9; [Ezek. 39:9]

has done to guide and guard his people so that they can flourish in true piety; e.g., the plagues of Egypt, the crossing of the Jordan River, defeating enemies.)

75:2–5 *God Declares that He Will Judge the Earth with Equity.* In this section, God speaks, promising that he will work his perfect judgment over the earth. This judgment will be **with equity**, preserving the stability of God's creation order (**pillars**). Specifically, he will rebuke the **boastful** and the **wicked** (names for people who do not know God, and who are preeminent for their unbelief). The psalm does not make clear whether this **set time** is the time of the final judgment for all the earth, or any time in which God chooses to make his justice visible. The words fit both senses.

75:4 lift up your horn. The horn is a symbol of power (cf. 1 Kings 22:11; Zech. 1:18–21), and thus to lift it up (or "exalt" it) is to make a public assertion of power. God warns the ungodly not to lift up their horn, and promises that he will lift up the horn of the faithful. The term "lift up" recurs throughout the psalm (Ps. 75:4–6, 10). To "cut off" the horns (v. 10) is to render powerless and to humiliate.

75:6–8 *It Is God Who Lifts Up and Puts Down.* This section takes up the idea of **lifting up** from vv. 4–5, and makes it clear that ultimately it is God who **executes judgment, putting down one and lifting up another**. The "lifting up" here is the display of authority; those whom God "puts down" are the boastful wicked (v. 4), and the time is his act of judgment (whenever that might be, and however it relates to the final judgment; cf. note on vv. 2–5). The congregation that sings this is taking the stance of faith; certainly there are many times when God's faithful people must simply await his timing and not give in to despair.

75:9–10 *I Will Always Sing God's Praises.* Each member of the congregation pledges himself to the life of faith that this psalm fosters. It is possible that **I** in v. 10 is speaking in the name of Israel, the agent of God's judgment; but in view of vv. 2–8 it seems that God is the speaker.

Psalm 76. This is a hymn celebrating Zion as the place God has chosen to dwell, and the capital of the people he has chosen to bless and protect; it is a companion to Psalms 46; 48; 87; 122. The psalm is suited to an occasion in which God has delivered Zion from invaders. The congregation that sings this will marvel at the privilege of going to Zion and worshiping there, and will thank God for it.

76:1–2 *God Has Made His Abode in Zion.* The Maker of heaven and earth, to whom all mankind belongs, has chosen one people, **Judah** (which represents all **Israel**), and one particular spot called **Salem** (an old name for Jerusalem, Gen. 14:18) or **Zion**, to be **his dwelling place**. The OT is clear that this does not confine God in any way (1 Kings 8:27–30; Isa. 66:1–2); rather, it is the means by which his people have access to his presence.

76:3–9 *None Can Stand before You When You Rise to Judge.* The past-tense verbs show that this psalm is particularly geared to celebrating an occasion in which God has protected Zion from Gentile invaders: **he broke the flashing arrows, the stouthearted** (Gentile warriors) **were stripped of their spoil, rider and horse lay stunned**. Verses 6–9 trace the victory to God's **rebuke**, his **judgment**, and his plan **to save all the humble of the earth** (the faithful among his people). This could refer to the deliverance from Sennacherib (2 Kings 19:35), but the words are general enough for other occasions, and there is no reason to tie this psalm to that event over any other (cf. also Ps. 46:9).

4 Glorious are you, more majestic
[j]than the mountains full of [k]prey.
5 [l]The stouthearted were stripped of their spoil;
[m]they sank into sleep;
all the men of war
were unable to use their hands.
6 At your rebuke, O God of Jacob,
both [n]rider and horse lay stunned.

7 [o]But you, you are to be feared!
Who can [p]stand before you
when once your anger is roused?
8 From the heavens you uttered judgment;
[q]the earth feared and was still,
9 when God [r]arose to establish judgment,
to save all the humble of the earth. *Selah*

10 Surely [s]the wrath of man shall praise you;
the remnant[1] of wrath you will put on like a belt.
11 [t]Make your vows to the LORD your God and perform them;
let all around him [u]bring gifts
to him who [v]is to be feared,
12 who [w]cuts off the spirit of princes,
who [x]is to be feared by the kings of the earth.

In the Day of Trouble I Seek the Lord

77

TO THE CHOIRMASTER: ACCORDING TO [y]JEDUTHUN. A PSALM OF [z]ASAPH.

1 I [a]cry aloud to God,
aloud to God, and he will hear me.
2 [b]In the day of my trouble I seek the Lord;
in [c]the night my [d]hand is stretched out without wearying;
my soul [e]refuses to be comforted.
3 When I remember God, I [f]moan;
when I meditate, my spirit faints. *Selah*

[1] Or *extremity*

4[j][Isa. 14:25; Ezek. 39:4] [k]Nah. 2:13
5[l]Isa. 46:12 [m]Ps. 13:3; 2 Kgs. 19:35; Jer. 51:39; Nah. 3:18
6[n]Ex. 15:1, 21
7[o]Ps. 47:2 [p]Ps. 130:3
8[q]2 Chr. 20:29, 30; [Hab. 2:20]
9[r][Ps. 9:7, 8]
10[s][Ex. 9:16]
11[t]See Ps. 50:14 [u]See Ps. 68:29 [v]Ps. 89:7; Gen. 31:42, 53; Isa. 8:13
12[w][Isa. 18:5] [x]See Ps. 47:2

Psalm 77

[y]Ps. 39, title [z]Ps. 50, title
1[a]See Ps. 3:4
2[b]Ps. 86:7; [Ps. 20:1; 50:15; Isa. 26:16] [c]Ps. 63:6; Isa. 26:9 [d][Ps. 143:6] [e]Gen. 37:35
3[f]Ps. 42:5, 11; 43:5

76:10–12 *Let All the People Praise the Lord.* Since God gets praise even out of the schemes of unjust men, it is only right that his favored ones worship and love him. **The wrath of man shall praise you**, i.e., the way that God thwarts their wrathful schemes leads people to acknowledge God's rule. The phrase **the remnant of wrath you will put on like a belt** is obscure; by virtue of the parallelism, it probably means that God takes the last futile efforts of human wrath and wears it like an ornamental belt, extracting every last bit of honor from it. (Another possibility sees the "remnant of wrath" as the survivors of wrath, whom God attaches to his belt; but this makes less of a parallel with the first line.) **vows . . . perform**. See note on 56:12–13. The expression **to be feared**, referring to God, is two-edged: God's people fear him in reverential love, while the Gentile **kings** fear him because he **cuts off the spirit of princes** (although the OT hope is that the Gentiles will one day come to fear him in the first way).

Psalm 77. This is a community lament, suitable to a time when the people of God are in a low condition. The description of the low condition is general enough that the psalm cannot be tied to any specific occasion. The psalm acknowledges that the reason for the trouble may be some fault in the people: to refer to God's "anger" (v. 9) raises the question of whether his people's unfaithfulness provoked it; hence this is like Psalms 74; 79; and 80 in their recognition of this factor. (Psalm 44, on the other hand, is a community lament suited to an occasion in which the community's unfaithfulness is not the cause of its trouble.) That this is a community lament is clear from the nature of the appeal in 77:10–20: "the years of the right hand of the Most High" (v. 10) refer to ancient times in which God "redeemed your people" (v. 15) and "led" them "like a flock" (v. 20). Thus the emphasis is on the condition of God's people as a body; but this corporate focus is certainly not impersonal. Each person singing this owns his or her membership in the people, and acknowledges that his or her well-being is bound up with the well-being of the whole: "*I* cry aloud to God" (v. 1), "the day of *my* trouble" (v. 2), "*I* am so troubled" (v. 4). The Bible presents the individual as a member of the community and encourages each member to seek the good of the whole. The repeated key words here are "remember" and "meditate" (vv. 3, 6, 11–12), both of which appear in each of the main sections. The psalm moves from remembering and meditating on God (as the one who has made promises to his people), to remembering and meditating on how things once were better, to remembering and meditating on God's mighty deeds of old that build confidence for his people's future.

77:1–3 *Opening Statement: I Cry Aloud to God.* This section describes earnest prayer coming from a troubled heart: the statements **I cry aloud to God** (v. 1), **I moan**, and **my spirit faints** (v. 3) convey deep feeling, and **my hand is stretched out** (to God) is a common posture of prayer (cf. 44:20; 88:9; 143:6; Job 11:13; 1 Tim. 2:8). Here, however, it is not limited to prayer in public worship: it preoccupies his private moments as well (Ps. 77:2, **in the night**; cf. v. 4).

4 You hold my eyelids open;
I am so [g]troubled that I cannot speak.
5 I consider [h]the days of old,
the years long ago.
6 I said,[1] "Let me remember my [i]song in the night;
let me [j]meditate in my heart."
Then my spirit made a diligent search:
7 "Will the Lord [k]spurn forever,
and never again [l]be favorable?
8 Has his steadfast love forever ceased?
Are his [m]promises at an end for all time?
9 [n]Has God forgotten to be gracious?
[o]Has he in anger shut up his compassion?" *Selah*

10 Then I said, "I will appeal to this,
to the years of the [p]right hand of the Most High."[2]

11 I will remember the deeds of the LORD;
yes, I will [q]remember your wonders of old.
12 I will ponder all your [r]work,
and meditate on your [s]mighty deeds.
13 Your way, O God, is [t]holy.
[u]What god is great like our God?
14 You are the God who [v]works wonders;
you have [w]made known your might among the peoples.
15 You [x]with your arm redeemed your people,
the children of Jacob and Joseph. *Selah*

16 When [y]the waters saw you, O God,
when the waters saw you, they were afraid;
indeed, the deep trembled.
17 The clouds poured out water;
the skies [z]gave forth thunder;
your [a]arrows flashed on every side.

[1] Hebrew lacks *I said* [2] Or *This is my grief: that the right hand of the Most High has changed*

4[g][Gen. 41:8]
5[h]ver. 10, 11; Ps. 44:1; 143:5; Deut. 32:7; Isa. 51:9
6[i]See Ps. 42:8 [j]Ps. 4:4
7[k]See Ps. 44:9 [l]Ps. 85:1
8[m][Rom. 9:6]
9[n][Isa. 49:15] [o][Hab. 3:2]
10[p][Ps. 118:15]
11[q]ver. 5; Ps. 105:5
12[r]Ps. 90:16 [s]Ps. 9:11
13[t]Ps. 73:17 [u]See Ps. 35:10
14[v]See Ps. 72:18 [w]Ps. 106:8
15[x][Ps. 74:2; Ex. 6:6; Deut. 9:29]
16[y]Ps. 114:3; Ex. 14:21; Josh. 3:15, 16; Hab. 3:10
17[z][Ps. 68:33] [a]See Ps. 18:14

77:4–9 *Specific Complaint: Has God Forgotten to Be Gracious?* Now the psalm describes what gives so much unrest to the singer: during the night, when he cannot sleep (vv. 4–6), he ponders the question of whether God will **spurn** his people **forever** (vv. 7–9).

77:5 The **days of old** and the **years long ago** refer to earlier times, when it seemed that the condition of the people of God was better—this provokes the question, did God use up his favor? The answer is in vv. 10–11, repeating parts of these expressions: the "years of the right hand of the Most High" and the "wonders of old."

77:6 my song in the night. Since the word for "song" (Hb. *neginah*) occurs often in the sense of "stringed instruments" used in public worship (titles of Psalms 4; 6; 55; 61; 67; 76; Hab. 3:19; cf. Isa. 38:20), it is reasonable to suppose that these songs are worship songs, celebrating God's mighty deeds for his people, which the faithful Israelite might sing in private for edification or comfort.

77:7–9 It does not offend God when his troubled people raise these questions with an interest in the explanation. Indeed, just putting the questions invites the answer, since they touch on the points of Ex. 34:6, which describes the enduring benevolence of God toward his people: if God abounds in **steadfast love**, then it cannot cease, nor can his **promises** be **at an end**; if God is **gracious**, he cannot forget to continue that grace, nor can he **shut up his compassion**. The key matter is the last line: **has he** done this **in anger**? God's anger is a response to unfaithfulness on the part of his people, and will only remain if they remain impenitent. Hence this calls the people to examine themselves and to lay hold of the covenant afresh.

77:10–20 *The Appeal: What God Has Done in the Past for His People.* This psalm directs attention to what God has done for his people in the past, especially in the exodus and in the wilderness, as grounds for confidence that God will not abandon his purpose for his people: the spiritual condition of any particular generation will not derail that purpose, though it may indeed prevent members of that generation from receiving saving benefits from God, and from participating constructively in the outworking of that purpose in the world. This is why the **appeal** is not to the people, but **to the years of the right hand of the Most High**. God's "right hand" is the expression of his power for the sake of his people (e.g., Ex. 15:6, 12). God's **deeds**, **wonders**, **work**, and **mighty deeds** (Ps. 77:11–12) are likewise great things he has done to save and preserve his people. The colorful recollection of the exodus (vv. 16–19) comes to a soft landing with the simple statement that God **led** his **people like a flock** through the wilderness, **by the hand of Moses and Aaron** (v. 20). The singing congregation is left to draw the conclusion for themselves: the God who has done these great things certainly has the power to do them again if need be; and all the records of these events (the Pentateuch) speak clearly of God's unwavering commitment to bring blessing to Abraham's children, and through them to the world. So this song helps God's people to refresh their hope and renew their commitment to be a holy people, an attractive advertisement of the true God to the rest of the world.

77:14–15 God **made known** his **might among the peoples** (Ex. 15:14–16), and yet he **redeemed** just one **people** (Ex. 15:13), **the children of Jacob and Joseph**. On "redeem," see note on Isa. 41:14.

18[b]Ps. 104:7 [c]Ps. 97:4 [d]See Ps. 18:7
19[e]Hab. 3:15 [f]See Ps. 36:6
20[g]Ps. 78:52, 53; 80:1; Ex. 13:21; 14:19; Isa. 63:11, 12

Psalm 78
[h]Ps. 50, title
1[i][Isa. 51:4]; See Ps. 49:1; 50:7
2[j]Cited Matt. 13:35; See Ps. 49:4 [k][Num. 21:27]
3[l]See Ps. 44:1
4[m]Job 15:18 [n][Ex. 12:26, 27; 13:8, 14; Deut. 11:19; Josh. 4:6, 7; Joel 1:3] [o]ver. 11, 32
5[p]Ps. 19:7; [Ps. 81:5] [q]Ps. 147:19
6[r]ver. 4; Ps. 102:18

18 [b]The crash of your thunder was in the whirlwind;
[c]your lightnings lighted up the world;
the earth [d]trembled and shook.
19 Your [e]way was through the sea,
your path through the great waters;
yet your footprints [f]were unseen.[1]
20 You [g]led your people like a flock
by the hand of Moses and Aaron.

Tell the Coming Generation

78

A MASKIL[2] OF [h]ASAPH.

1 [i]Give ear, O my people, to my teaching;
incline your ears to the words of my mouth!
2 [j]I will open my mouth [k]in a parable;
I will utter dark sayings from of old,
3 things that we have heard and known,
that our [l]fathers have told us.
4 We will not [m]hide them from their children,
but [n]tell to the coming generation
the glorious deeds of the LORD, and his might,
and [o]the wonders that he has done.

5 He established [p]a testimony in [q]Jacob
and appointed a law in [q]Israel,
which he commanded our fathers
to teach to their children,
6 that [r]the next generation might know them,
the children yet unborn,
and arise and tell them to their children,
7 so that they should set their hope in God

[1] Hebrew *unknown* [2] Probably a musical or liturgical term

77:20 flock. For the image of God's people as sheep, and God as their Shepherd, see notes on 23:1; 74:1–3.

Psalm 78. This is a "historical psalm" (cf. Psalms 105; 106) recounting events from Israel's past that show how God persevered with his people, even when they disbelieved—while at the same time he cleansed his people by purging them of the unbelievers along the way. The psalm has selected events primarily from the Pentateuch, Joshua, Judges, and Samuel, ending with the reign of David. The psalm is clear about its purpose: to recount these events in song so that future generations of God's people might take the lessons to heart, particularly that they not be unbelieving and rebellious like the generations described here. The emphasis is on the people as a whole and the members' obligation to embrace the covenant faithfully in each generation. Terms for "remember" and "forget" run through the psalm (Ps. 78:7, 11, 35, 42; cf. v. 39, where God remembers): the psalmist hopes that those who sing this will never again forget. The psalm opens with its purpose statement (vv. 1–8), followed by several episodes of sin and unbelief, each new section beginning with "they sinned" or "they rebelled" (vv. 17, 32, 40, 56), followed by a final section on God's gift of David as the pinnacle expression of his enduring commitment (vv. 65–72). Christians will of course see the final section, on David, as important: Jesus is David's heir, who now occupies his throne. At the same time, they should not overlook God's patient preservation of his people, the descendants of Abraham—the people into which God has engrafted Gentile Christians. Christians may properly see themselves as the beneficiaries of God's patience: without it, there would be no people for them to be part of! And God will continue his purposes for his people until the very end.

78:1–8 *I Must Recount the Past Deeds So that Our Children Do Not Forget.* The song begins by calling for attention and explaining what it aims to do: **tell . . . the glorious deeds of the LORD . . . that the next generation might know them, . . . and that they should not be like their fathers, a stubborn and rebellious generation**. The **parable** and **dark sayings** (v. 2) are not secret teachings; they are **things that we have heard and known** (v. 3), which must be passed on to **the coming generation** (v. 4). The OT describes the people of God as those whom God has chosen to receive his particular revelation (**testimony** and **law**, v. 5), with the responsibility **to teach to their children**, "that the next generation might know them" (vv. 5–6; cf. Gen. 17:7; 18:19; Deut. 6:6–9). The process does not bring its benefits in any "automatic" way: each of the members must take the provisions of the covenant as his own, embrace God's grace, **set their hope in God**, and **keep his commandments**. Sadly, far too many Israelites, and too many generations, received the covenant as an external arrangement but did not embrace it from their hearts; thus they were "stubborn and rebellious," their **heart was not steadfast**, and their **spirit was not faithful to God** (these phrases describe a condition of unbelief or apostasy, not simply the sins that even genuine believers commit). But if each generation will take to heart the lessons of this psalm, they need not repeat these episodes of unbelief.

78:2 Parables and **dark sayings** (or "riddles," cf. 49:4) are the tools of wisdom teachers, and require imagination to unlock their meaning. Here the stories of Israelite history are the vehicle of this wisdom teaching. Jesus uses 78:2 to describe his own practice of telling parables (Matt. 13:35): he may simply find this text a convenient summary of what a wisdom teacher does, in order to challenge his audiences to apply themselves to his wisdom; but he may also be suggesting that at least some of his parables are like this psalm in drawing lessons from Israel's history (e.g., Matt. 21:33–44).

and not forget [s]the works of God,
but [t]keep his commandments;
8 and that they should not be [u]like their fathers,
[v]a stubborn and rebellious generation,
a generation [w]whose heart was not steadfast,
whose spirit was not faithful to God.

9 The Ephraimites, armed with[1] the bow,
[x]turned back on the day of battle.
10 They [y]did not keep God's covenant,
but refused to walk according to his law.
11 They [z]forgot his works
and [a]the wonders that he had shown them.
12 In the sight of their fathers [b]he performed wonders
in the land of Egypt, in [c]the fields of Zoan.
13 He [d]divided the sea and let them pass through it,
and made the waters [e]stand like a heap.
14 [f]In the daytime he led them with a cloud,
and all the night with a fiery light.
15 He [g]split rocks in the wilderness
and gave them drink abundantly as from the deep.
16 He made streams come out of [h]the rock
and caused waters to flow down like rivers.

17 Yet they sinned still more against him,
[i]rebelling against the Most High in the desert.
18 They [j]tested God in their heart
by demanding the food they craved.
19 They spoke against God, saying,
[k]"Can God [l]spread a table in the wilderness?
20 [m]He struck the rock so that water gushed out
and streams overflowed.
Can he also give bread
or provide meat for his people?"

21 Therefore, when the LORD heard, he was full of wrath;
[n]a fire was kindled against Jacob;
his anger rose against Israel,
22 because they [o]did not believe in God
and did not trust his saving power.
23 Yet he commanded the skies above
and [p]opened the doors of heaven,
24 and he [q]rained down on them manna to eat
and gave them [r]the grain of heaven.

[1] Hebrew *armed and shooting*

7 [s]Ps. 77:12 [t]Ps. 105:45
8 [u]2 Kgs. 17:14; 2 Chr. 30:7; Ezek. 20:18 [v]Ex. 32:9; 33:3; Deut. 9:7, 24; 31:27; Jer. 5:23 [w]ver. 37; Job 11:13
9 [x]ver. 57
10 [y][2 Kgs. 17:15]
11 [z]See Ps. 106:13 [a]ver. 4
12 [b]ver. 43; See Ex. 7-12; Ps. 72:18 [c]ver. 43; Num. 13:22; Isa. 19:11, 13; Ezek. 30:14
13 [d]Ps. 136:13; Ex. 14:21 [e]Ex. 15:8
14 [f]See Ps. 105:39
15 [g]ver. 20; Ps. 105:41; 114:8; Ex. 17:6; Isa. 48:21
16 [h]Num. 20:8, 10, 11
17 [i]ver. 40, 56; Deut. 9:22; Isa. 63:10
18 [j]ver. 41, 56; Ps. 95:9; 106:14; Deut. 6:16; 1 Cor. 10:9
19 [k][Ex. 16:3; Num. 11:4; 20:3; 21:5] [l]See Ps. 23:5
20 [m]ver. 15, 16
21 [n]Num. 11:1
22 [o]ver. 8, 32, 37
23 [p]Gen. 7:11; [Mal. 3:10]
24 [q]Ex. 16:4 [r]Ps. 105:40; [John 6:31]

78:9–16 *God's People Forgot His Great Deeds of the Exodus.* The first historical section recounts an otherwise unknown incident in which **the Ephraimites . . . turned back on the day of battle**; presumably this was a battle in which Israel was defending itself, and in which all Israel was expected to participate, each tribe serving the others because of their bond as God's people. Their failure, then, was not simply a failure in patriotism but also in brotherhood and faith; **they did not keep God's covenant**, and the reason is that **they forgot** God's **works**—this is not a simple mental lapse but a deliberate turning away from the implications of these great deeds, which marked them out as the body of God's chosen people, under obligation both to God and to each other. Verses 12–16 mention some of these deeds, such as the exodus from Egypt (vv. 12–13) and God's care for the people in the wilderness (vv. 14–16). Israel in every generation should have learned from these works of God, but often they did not.

78:12 Zoan is a city in Egypt (Num. 13:22), not far from where the Israelites lived. It is paired with **Egypt** again in Ps. 78:43, as a place where God's **wonders** upon the Egyptians would have been visible to the Israelites (cf. also Isa. 19:13).

78:17–31 *Yet They Sinned Still More in the Wilderness.* The next section advances the people's worthiness of blame with **yet they sinned still more against** God (in spite of the deeds they had seen, vv. 12–16). The verses that follow stress the people's disbelief of God's continued ability or commitment to care for them, as they demanded food, and God provided manna (vv. 21–25; cf. Ex. 16:1–21) and quail, for which they suffered a plague (Ps. 78: 26–31; cf. Num. 11:31–34, which corresponds to the description better than Ex. 16:13 does). These acts of provision preserved the covenant people, though God cut off the disbelieving along the way (Ps. 78:22, **did not believe**; v. 31, **anger of God** at their disbelief).

25 Man ate of the bread of [s]the angels;
he sent them food [t]in abundance.
26 He [u]caused the east wind to blow in the heavens,
and by his power he led out the south wind;
27 he rained meat on them like [v]dust,
winged birds like [w]the sand of the seas;
28 he [x]let them fall in the midst of their camp,
all around their dwellings.
29 And they [y]ate and were well filled,
for he gave them what they [z]craved.
30 But before they had satisfied their craving,
[a]while the food was still in their mouths,
31 the anger of God rose against them,
and he killed [b]the strongest of them
and laid low [c]the young men of Israel.

32 In spite of all this, they [d]still sinned;
[e]despite his wonders, they did not believe.
33 So he made [f]their days [g]vanish like[1] a breath,[2]
and their years in terror.
34 When he killed them, they [h]sought him;
they repented and sought God earnestly.
35 They remembered that God was their [i]rock,
the Most High God their [j]redeemer.
36 But they [k]flattered him with their mouths;
they [l]lied to him with their tongues.
37 Their [m]heart was not [n]steadfast toward him;
they were not faithful to his covenant.
38 Yet he, being [o]compassionate,
[p]atoned for their iniquity
and did not destroy them;
he restrained his anger often
and did not stir up all his wrath.
39 He [q]remembered that they were but [r]flesh,
[s]a wind that passes and comes not again.
40 How often they [t]rebelled against him in the wilderness
and [u]grieved him in [v]the desert!
41 They [w]tested God again and again
and provoked [x]the Holy One of Israel.
42 They [y]did not remember his power[3]
or the day when he redeemed them from the foe,
43 [z]when he performed his [a]signs in Egypt
and his [b]marvels in [c]the fields of Zoan.

[1] Hebrew *in* [2] Or *vapor* [3] Hebrew *hand*

25 [s]Ps. 103:20 [t][ver. 29]
26 [u]Num. 11:31
27 [v][Gen. 13:16] [w][Gen. 22:17]
28 [x]Ex. 16:13; Num. 11:31
29 [y]Num. 11:19, 20 [z]Num. 11:4, 34
30 [a]Num. 11:33; [Job 20:23]
31 [b]Isa. 10:16 [c]ver. 63
32 [d]See Num. 14; 16; 17 [e]ver. 22; Num. 14:11
33 [f]Num. 14:29, 35; 26:64, 65 [g]Ps. 39:5
34 [h]Hos. 5:15
35 [i]Deut. 32:4, 15, 31 [j]Ex. 15:13; See Ps. 74:2
36 [k]Isa. 29:13; Ezek. 33:31 [l]Isa. 57:11
37 [m]ver. 8 [n]Ps. 51:10
38 [o]Ex. 34:6 [p]Num. 14:20
39 [q][Ps. 103:14; Job 10:9] [r]Gen. 6:3 [s]Job 7:7
40 [t]ver. 17, 56; Ps. 107:11 [u][Eph. 4:30] [v]Ps. 106:14
41 [w]See ver. 18 [x]See Ps. 71:22
42 [y]Judg. 8:34
43 [z]For ver. 43-51, see Ps. 105:27-36 [a]Ex. 7:3; [Ps. 106:22]; Acts 7:36 [b]Ex. 4:21; 11:9, 10 [c]See ver. 12

78:32–39 *In Spite of All They Saw, They Still Sinned.* The mighty works of God described in vv. 9–31 should have been enough, but they were not: **In spite of all this, they still sinned, they did not believe**. This section focuses on the judgments with which the Lord disciplined his people, again and again seeking to lead them to repentance. **When he killed them, they sought him; they repented and sought God earnestly**, yet their repentance was not deep and sincere (v. 36, they only **flattered** and **lied** in their professions of faith), so it did not last: **their heart was not steadfast toward him; they were not faithful to his covenant** (v. 37; cf. v. 8). However, God did not do what one might expect, namely, wipe them out and start over: even though he could have purged them of unbelieving members, he **did not destroy them**, he **did not stir up all his wrath**. All this was because he is **compassionate**, and therefore he **atoned for their iniquity** (v. 38, which means that he accepted the sacrifices that they offered and conveyed his blessing of forgiveness).

78:40–55 *How Often They Rebelled, Forgetting the Exodus and Conquest.* The next section goes back to the exodus, describing all the plagues God brought against the Egyptian oppressors (vv. 42–53), with a brief summary of the conquest of the Promised Land (vv. 54–55). And yet, **how often they rebelled**, **grieved**, **tested**, and **provoked**! The reason: **they did not remember his power or the day when he redeemed them from the foe** (cf. 77:15). The story is one of constant disbelief in the face of unimaginable grace, and even more grace being granted in the face of disbelief!

78:40 grieved. Cf. Isa. 63:10, where God's people "rebelled and grieved his Holy Spirit"; cf. also Eph. 4:30.

44 He [d]turned their rivers to blood,
so that they could not drink of their streams.
45 He sent among them swarms of [e]flies, which devoured them,
and [f]frogs, which destroyed them.
46 He gave their crops to [g]the destroying locust
and the fruit of their labor to the locust.
47 He destroyed their vines with [h]hail
and their sycamores with frost.
48 He gave over their [i]cattle to the hail
and their flocks to thunderbolts.
49 He let loose on them his burning anger,
wrath, indignation, and distress,
a company of [j]destroying angels.
50 He made a path for his anger;
he did not spare them from death,
but gave their lives over to the plague.
51 He struck down every [k]firstborn in Egypt,
the firstfruits of their strength in the tents of [l]Ham.
52 Then he led out his people [m]like sheep
and guided them in the wilderness like a flock.
53 [n]He led them in safety, so that they [o]were not afraid,
but [p]the sea overwhelmed their enemies.
54 And he brought them to his [q]holy land,
[r]to the mountain which his right hand had [s]won.
55 He [t]drove out nations before them;
he [u]apportioned them for a possession
and settled the tribes of Israel in their tents.

56 Yet they [v]tested and [w]rebelled against the Most High God
and did not keep his testimonies,
57 but turned away and acted treacherously like their fathers;
they twisted like [x]a deceitful bow.
58 For they [y]provoked him to anger with their [z]high places;
they [a]moved him to jealousy with their [b]idols.
59 When God heard, he was full of [c]wrath,
and he utterly rejected Israel.
60 He [d]forsook his dwelling at [e]Shiloh,
the tent where he dwelt among mankind,
61 and delivered his [f]power to captivity,
his [g]glory to the hand of the foe.
62 He [h]gave his people over to the sword
and [i]vented his wrath on his heritage.
63 [j]Fire devoured their young men,
and their young women had no [k]marriage song.
64 Their [l]priests fell by the sword,
and their [m]widows made no lamentation.
65 Then the Lord [n]awoke as from sleep,
like a strong man shouting because of wine.

44 [d]See Ex. 7:17-24
45 [e]See Ex. 8:21-24 [f]See Ex. 8:2-14
46 [g]See Ex. 10:12-15
47 [h]See Ex. 9:23-25
48 [i]See Ex. 9:19-21
49 [j]Ex. 12:13, 23; [2 Sam. 24:16]
51 [k]Ex. 12:29; [Ps. 105:36; 135:8; 136:10] [l]Ps. 105:23, 27; 106:22
52 [m]See Ps. 77:20
53 [n][Ex. 14:19, 20] [o][Ex. 14:13] [p]Ex. 14:27, 28; 15:10
54 [q]Ex. 15:17 [r]Isa. 11:9; 57:13; [Ps. 68:16] [s]Ps. 74:2
55 [t]See Ps. 44:2 [u]Josh. 23:4; [Ps. 135:12; 136:21, 22; Acts 13:19]
56 [v]ver. 18; Judg. 2:11, 12 [w]ver. 40
57 [x]Hos. 7:16; [ver. 9]
58 [y]Deut. 31:29 [z]Lev. 26:30; Deut. 12:2; 1 Kgs. 11:7; 12:31; Ezek. 20:28 [a]Num. 25:11; Deut. 32:16, 21; Judg. 2:12 [b]Deut. 7:5, 25; 12:3
59 [c]ver. 62; Ps. 106:40; Deut. 3:26
60 [d]1 Sam. 4:11; Jer. 7:12, 14; 26:6 [e]Josh. 18:1
61 [f]Ps. 132:8; [Ps. 63:2; 96:6] [g][1 Sam. 4:21]
62 [h][1 Sam. 4:10] [i]ver. 59
63 [j][Ps. 79:5; 89:46] [k][Jer. 7:34]
64 [l]1 Sam. 4:11 [m]Job 27:15
65 [n]Ps. 73:20; See Ps. 35:23

78:56–64 *They Tested and Rebelled against God in the Promised Land.* Now that Israel has come to the Promised Land (vv. 54–55), this section describes the time of the judges, leading up to the captivity of the ark and the death of Eli and his sons (vv. 60–64; cf. 1 Samuel 4). Just as before, **they tested and rebelled against the Most High**, and **provoked him to anger**. The cycles of apostasy followed by repentance, followed by more apostasy, so familiar from the book of Judges, are in view (Ps. 78:56–58). The sons of the high priest Eli, who ministered in God's **tent** at **Shiloh**, brought the ark (in which the **glory** dwelt) to battle as a good-luck charm against the Philistines; but the Philistines won and took the ark into **captivity**. It would appear that the victorious Philistines went on to devastate the site of Shiloh as well (cf. Jer. 7:12–15).

78:59 utterly rejected. In context, God's "rejection" means that he cut off many of the Israelites for their unbelief; he nevertheless retains his interest in the people (as vv. 65–72 will make plain).

78:65–72 *Finally God Answered by Choosing the Line of David.* The final

66[o][Ps. 40:14]
67[p]Ps. 80:1; 81:5
68[q]Ps. 87:2
69[r]See 1 Kgs. 6
70[s]1 Sam. 16:12, 13
71[t]2 Sam. 7:8 [u]2 Sam. 5:2; [Ps. 28:9] [v]1 Sam. 10:1
72[w]Ps. 101:2; 1 Kgs. 9:4 [x][Ps. 77:20]
Psalm 79
[y]Ps. 50, title
1[z]Lam. 1:10 [a]Ex. 15:17; See Ps. 74:2 [b][Ps. 74:7] [c]Jer. 26:18; Mic. 3:12; [2 Kgs. 25:9, 10]; 2 Chr. 36:19
2[d]Deut. 28:26; Jer. 7:33; 16:4; 19:7; 34:20 [e]See Ps. 50:5 [f]Ps. 74:19
3[g]Jer. 14:16; [2 Kgs. 9:10]
4[h]Dan. 9:16; See Ps. 44:13

66 And he [o]put his adversaries to rout;
he put them to everlasting shame.
67 He rejected the tent of [p]Joseph;
he did not choose the tribe of Ephraim,
68 but he chose the tribe of Judah,
Mount Zion, which he [q]loves.
69 He [r]built his sanctuary like the high heavens,
like the earth, which he has founded forever.
70 He [s]chose David his servant
and took him from the sheepfolds;
71 from [t]following the nursing ewes he brought him
to [u]shepherd Jacob his people,
Israel his [v]inheritance.
72 With [w]upright heart he shepherded them
and [x]guided them with his skillful hand.

How Long, O Lord?

79

A Psalm of [y]Asaph.

1 O God, [z]the nations have come into your [a]inheritance;
they have defiled your [b]holy temple;
they have [c]laid Jerusalem in ruins.
2 They have given [d]the bodies of your servants
to the birds of the heavens for food,
the flesh of your [e]faithful to [f]the beasts of the earth.
3 They have poured out their blood like water
all around Jerusalem,
and there was [g]no one to bury them.
4 We have become [h]a taunt to our neighbors,
[h]mocked and derided by those around us.

section celebrates how God graciously answered this recurring pattern by raising up David to be king of Israel. **the Lord awoke as from sleep**. This is a bold image, conveying what the believer can feel like when he has not so far seen how God is active. God stirs himself from apparent inactivity to take action on behalf of his suffering people, even when, as here, they are suffering for their own unbelief (cf. 35:23; 44:23; 59:5). The action that God took was to install a king, selecting a man from the **tribe of Judah** rather than from the **tribe of Ephraim** (which, as a descendant of **Joseph**, might have seemed a more likely candidate); cf. Gen. 49:10, which foretold exactly this. God also chose **Mount Zion** (Jerusalem) to be not only the capital but the location of **his sanctuary**. David was taken **from the sheepfolds**. Like Moses (Ex. 3:1), he learned how to shepherd with literal sheep. (For the image of God's people as sheep, see notes on Ps. 23:1; 74:1–3.) **to shepherd**. The king is ideally a shepherd of his people (cf. 2 Sam. 5:2), caring for them, protecting them, and leading them in faithfulness to the covenant. David at his best did his work **with upright heart** and **skillful hand**, though he had his own moral failures; many kings in his line were much less upright and skillful. The term "shepherd" came to be used of leaders in Israel (priests, nobles, and judges), and the prophet Ezekiel spoke out about the greedy shepherds in his day (Ezekiel 34). He looked forward to the time after the exile when God would raise up "his servant David" (i.e., the Messiah) who would be the "shepherd" of his people (Ezek. 34:23–24). When Jesus called himself the "good shepherd" (John 10:11, 14), he claimed to be the long-awaited heir of David, who would guide his people perfectly.

78:70 David his servant. The Lord's "servant" is someone he appoints for a special purpose on behalf of his people (cf. 89:20; 132:10; 144:10). In the book of Isaiah, the servant of the Lord is never called an heir of David; but the fact that David can be called this helps support the messianic interpretation of that figure in Isaiah (see note on Isa. 42:1–9).

Psalm 79. This is a community lament, which was occasioned by a great disaster that fell upon Jerusalem (most likely the Babylonian destruction), and has many similarities to Psalm 74. It recounts the violence and impiety of the Gentile conquerors and asks God how long he intends to put up with such things. Running through the psalm is a recognition that, just as by reason of the covenant, Israel expects God to treat them differently than he treats the other nations, so too Israel should live faithfully to that covenant. The disaster came because Israel did not embrace the covenant in true faith; the psalm confesses that, asks for forgiveness, and pledges renewed faithfulness.

79:1–4 *The Nations Have Defiled Your Holy Temple and Slain Your People.* The first section chillingly describes the destruction that the **nations** (probably Babylon and its allies) have wrought on God's **inheritance** (i.e., the land where his own people dwell). **They have defiled your holy temple**, treating something holy as unclean, which is an atrocity against God (and invites a severe penalty from God, Lev. 20:3); **they have laid Jerusalem** (God's favored city and the home of David's dynasty, cf. Ps. 78:68) **in ruins**; and they have wantonly slaughtered God's own people (and left their bodies unburied, for wild animals to eat). **We have become a taunt to our neighbors**. This would hurt anyway, but the people singing this are God's people, and the neighbors are Gentiles; God's people were supposed to be an advertisement to the Gentiles of how great and good a God Yahweh is.

79:1 The land is called God's **inheritance** (or "heritage") because Israel is his inheritance and he gave the land to them as their inheritance (cf. Deut. 4:20–21; Ps. 28:9; 74:2).

5 [i]How long, O LORD? Will you be angry [j]forever?
Will your [k]jealousy [l]burn like fire?
6 [m]Pour out your anger on the nations
that [n]do not know you,
and on the kingdoms
that [o]do not call upon your name!
7 For they have devoured Jacob
and laid waste his habitation.

8 [p]Do not remember against us [q]our former iniquities;[1]
let your compassion come speedily to meet us,
for we are [r]brought very low.
9 [s]Help us, O God of our salvation,
for the glory of your name;
deliver us, and [t]atone for our sins,
for your [u]name's sake!
10 [v]Why should the nations say,
"Where is their God?"
Let [w]the avenging of the outpoured blood of your servants
be known among the nations before our eyes!

11 Let [x]the groans of the prisoners come before you;
according to your great power, preserve those [y]doomed to die!
12 Return [z]sevenfold into the [a]lap of our neighbors
the [b]taunts with which they have taunted you, O Lord!
13 But we your people, the [c]sheep of your pasture,
will [d]give thanks to you forever;
from generation to generation we will recount your praise.

Restore Us, O God

80

TO THE CHOIRMASTER: ACCORDING TO [e]LILIES.
A TESTIMONY. OF [f]ASAPH, A PSALM.

1 Give ear, O Shepherd of Israel,
you who lead [g]Joseph like [h]a flock.

[1] *Or the iniquities of former generations*

5 [i][Ps. 74:10; 80:4] [j][Ps. 74:1; 85:5]; See Ps. 13:1 [k]Ps. 78:58 [l]Ps. 78:21; 89:46
6 [m]Cited Jer. 10:25; [Zeph. 3:8] [n]2 Thess. 1:8 [o]See Ps. 14:4
8 [p]Isa. 64:9 [q]Jer. 11:10 [r]Ps. 116:6; 142:6
9 [s]2 Chr. 14:11 [t]See Ps. 65:3 [u]Jer. 14:7, 21; See Ps. 23:3
10 [v]See Ps. 42:3 [w]See Ps. 94:1
11 [x]Ps. 102:20 [y][1 Sam. 20:31]
12 [z]Gen. 4:15, 24; Lev. 26:21, 28; Prov. 6:31 [a]Isa. 65:6, 7; Jer. 32:18 [b]See Ps. 74:10
13 [c]See Ps. 74:1 [d]Isa. 43:21

Psalm 80

[e]Ps. 60, title [f]Ps. 50, title
1 [g]Ps. 78:67; 81:5 [h][Ps. 95:7]; See Ps. 77:20

79:5–7 *How Long, O LORD, Will You Let This Go On?* This section guides God's people in what they should feel at such a time. The right question is not, "How long will you let us suffer like this?" After all, they suffer because God is **angry** with their unfaithfulness. Rather, the question is, "How long will you allow the **nations**, who **do not know you**, to get away with what they have done?" Even though **Jacob** (i.e., Israel) has been unfaithful, the Israelites still belong to the Lord.

79:5 jealousy. God's jealousy is an analogy, based on the "marriage" relationship between God and his people (cf. "hold fast" in Gen. 2:24; Deut. 10:20). Unlike human jealousy, which can be irrational (cf. Num. 5:14), God's is a passionate commitment to receiving exclusive loyalty from his people—a commitment for their good. Cf. Ex. 34:14 and Ps. 78:58, where false worship provokes it. When this psalm acknowledges that God is jealous, it is admitting that the people have been unfaithful (cf. 79:8–9).

79:8–10 *Forgive Us, Help Us, and Let the Nations Know about It!* This section now faces the basic problem: God's people have been untrue to him and must seek his forgiveness. The psalm weaves two themes together: the first is the understandable desire for relief (**we are brought very low; deliver us**), and the second is the desire, born of true faith, for God's honor in the world (**for the glory of your name, for your name's sake, why should the nations say**?). This psalm takes these two as connected: God's reputation is tied to his people's well-being, and their well-being cannot be separated from their faithfulness. Like the Assyrians before them, the Babylonians were but the "rod of [God's] anger," sent to discipline his people; but they went about their work too eagerly and boastfully—and thus made themselves liable to God's judgment (cf. Isa. 10:5–19). Therefore the psalm prays for this to **be known among the nations before our eyes**: if everyone sees it, then everyone can learn its lessons (just as this disgrace has taught a lesson to God's people). The forgiveness and help requested are for the people as a whole, that they be allowed to continue under God's special care. (For more on this kind of forgiveness, cf. notes on Num. 14:13–19; 14:36–38.)

79:9 atone for our sins. Usually it takes a sacrifice to effect "atonement"; but here, the temple is no more (v. 1), so this is likely a metaphorical use of the word, meaning "forgiveness." This helps to show that the OT does not suppose that somehow God's hands are tied and he can only effect forgiveness through the sacrifices; the companion idea, that the sacrifices do not work "automatically," without respect to the worshiper's faith, is also crucial to the OT.

79:11–13 *Preserve Us, Return Their Taunts, and We Will Praise You.* Verses 8–10 prayed for forgiveness; here, the effect of that forgiveness will be that God will **preserve those** of his people who are **doomed to die**. Perhaps the reference to **prisoners** means that they are literally to be executed, but it is more likely that the people praying this see themselves under a sentence of "death," i.e., abandonment by God. The **taunts** of the **neighbors** against God's people (v. 4) are taken to be against God himself; v. 12 asks that God would give the destroyers what they deserve for daring to taunt God. Verse 13 looks forward to the granting of forgiveness, and pledges that **we your people . . . will give thanks to you forever**—this is what he made them for, and to sing this psalm sincerely is to accept this as a call to a genuine embrace of the covenant.

79:12 Sevenfold seems to be an idiom for "completely" (cf. Gen. 4:15; Ps. 12:6; Prov. 6:31).

1[i]Ps. 99:1; Ex. 25:22; 1 Sam. 4:4; 2 Sam. 6:2 [j]See Ps. 50:2
2[k]See Num. 2:18-24 [l]See Ps. 35:23 [m][Ps. 118:14, 21]
3[n]ver. 19; Ps. 60:1; 85:4; Lam. 5:21 [o]Num. 6:25; See Ps. 4:6
4[p]See Ps. 59:5 [q][Ps. 74:10; 79:5]
5[r]Ps. 42:3; 102:9; [1 Kgs. 22:27; Isa. 30:20]
6[s]See Ps. 44:13
7[n][See ver. 3 above]
8[t]Isa. 5:1; 27:2; Jer. 2:21; 12:10; Ezek. 17:6; Matt. 21:33; Mark 12:1; Luke 20:9 [u]See Ps. 44:2
9[v][Josh. 24:12]
11[w]See Ps. 72:8
12[x]Ps. 89:40; Isa. 5:5
13[y][Jer. 5:6]

You who are [i]enthroned upon the cherubim, [j]shine forth.
2 Before [k]Ephraim and Benjamin and Manasseh,
[l]stir up your might
and [m]come to save us!

3 [n]Restore us,[1] O God;
[o]let your face shine, that we may be saved!

4 O [p]LORD God of hosts,
[q]how long will you be angry with your people's prayers?
5 You have fed them with [r]the bread of tears
and given them tears to drink in full measure.
6 [s]You make us an object of contention for our [s]neighbors,
and our enemies laugh among themselves.

7 [n]Restore us, O God of hosts;
let your face shine, that we may be saved!

8 You brought [t]a vine out of Egypt;
you [u]drove out the nations and planted it.
9 You [v]cleared the ground for it;
it took deep root and filled the land.
10 The mountains were covered with its shade,
the mighty cedars with its branches.
11 It sent out its branches to [w]the sea
and its shoots to [w]the River.[2]
12 Why then have you [x]broken down its walls,
so that all who pass along the way pluck its fruit?
13 [y]The boar from the forest ravages it,
and all that move in the field feed on it.

[1] Or *Turn us again*; also verses 7, 19 [2] That is, the Euphrates

Psalm 80. This is a community lament geared to a situation in which the people (or at least a part of them) have received hard treatment from the Gentiles; it poignantly asks God to "restore us, let your face shine that we may be saved!" The specific tribes mentioned are Joseph (with his sons Ephraim and Manasseh) and Benjamin (vv. 1–2), namely, the two sons of Jacob's wife Rachel. Some have taken this to indicate that the psalm came from the northern kingdom, but Benjamin remained with Judah at the breakup of the kingdom (1 Kings 12:21). Further, when Ps. 80:1 speaks of the Lord as "enthroned upon the cherubim," it is describing his place at the ark, in the Jerusalem temple. Thus it is more likely that these tribes are mentioned as a part of the whole people, and the whole congregation owns the distress of the part (Rom. 12:15 exercised on a corporate level). A notable feature of the psalm is its refrain, "Restore us, O [LORD] God [of hosts]; let your face shine, that we may be saved!" (Ps. 80:3; cf. vv. 7, 19). As the ESV footnote explains, "restore us" could be rendered "turn us again," and this shows how "turn again, O God of hosts" (v. 14) is a variation of these words. In this light, vv. 14–15 form a long version of the refrain, explaining more fully what it would mean for God to restore his people and let his face shine.

80:1–3 *Stir Up Your Might to Save Us.* The psalm opens by setting out the basic request: a portion of the people need God to **stir up** his **might and come to save** them. (The second stanza spells out the specifics of the situation.)

80:1 Shepherd . . . flock. See notes on 23:1; 74:1–3. **enthroned upon the cherubim**. Cf. 1 Sam. 4:4; 2 Sam. 6:2 (1 Chron. 13:6); 2 Kings 19:15 (Isa. 37:16); Ps. 99:1. (Cherubim is the plural of cherub.) These are the golden representations of two cherubim at either end of the mercy seat on top of the ark (Ex. 25:17–22; cf. illustration, p. 184). God is especially present through the ark, for the sake of his worshiping people (Ps. 22:3).

80:2 save. See notes on 20:1–5 and 20:9.

80:3 See note on Psalm 80 for the refrain. **Let your face shine** recalls the words of Aaron's blessing for the people (Num. 6:25).

80:4–7 *How Long Will You Be Angry with Us?* Now the psalm takes up the reason for the cry of distress, namely, God is **angry with** his **people's prayers** (which implies that they have been unfaithful, cf. 74:1) and thus has brought sorrows upon them, especially that they have become **an object of contention for** their Gentile **neighbors** (cf. 79:4). As the next stanza will make clear, this is because these Gentiles have ravaged the land and people of Israel. Underlying this is the idea that faithful Israel ought to be the envy of the Gentiles, drawing them to the light by moral purity, social justice, and political stability (as in Psalm 79). Thus the current situation is a reversal of how things should be.

80:8–15 *We Are Your Vine, Which They Have Ruined.* This is the longest stanza, with its image of God's people as a **vine** for which God has cared and provided. The branches of this vine were to give **shade** to the **mighty cedars** (much taller trees, esp. associated with Lebanon), and were to extend **to the sea** (either the Red Sea or the Mediterranean) and **to the** Euphrates **River**, the ideal borders of the Promised Land (cf. Ex. 23:31), which always included Gentile nations. The branches and shoots are therefore an image of the benefits that come to all who are under the rule of this people. It is God who has **broken down** the **walls** that had protected the "vine" from **all who pass** by and from the **boar from the forest**, i.e., had removed from his people his own protection against marauding and empire-building Gentiles. In such a case, **why**? is a question that invites the singers to ponder: if God has shown such care for his vine, would he lightly allow such violence against it? Verse 4 of Psalm 80 has already admitted that the people's unfaithfulness is the likely reason. Verse 14 appeals to God to **look down from heaven** and **have regard for this vine** again, i.e., to restore it to its proper role in the world.

80:8 vine. On this image for Israel (and thus for John 15:1), see notes on Jer. 2:21 and Ezek. 15:1–8. See also Isa. 5:1–7.

14 Turn again, O God of hosts!
[z]Look down from heaven, and see;
have regard for this vine,
15 the stock that your right hand planted,
and for the son whom you made strong for yourself.
16 They have [a]burned it with fire; they have [a]cut it down;
may they perish at [b]the rebuke of your face!
17 But [c]let your hand be on the man of your right hand,
the son of man whom you have made strong for yourself!
18 Then we shall not turn back from you;
[d]give us life, and we will call upon your name!

19 [e]Restore us, O LORD God of hosts!
Let your face shine, that we may be saved!

Oh, That My People Would Listen to Me

81

TO THE CHOIRMASTER: ACCORDING TO [f]THE GITTITH.[1] OF [g]ASAPH.

1 [h]Sing aloud to God our strength;
[i]shout for joy to the God of Jacob!
2 Raise a song; sound [j]the tambourine,
[k]the sweet lyre with [k]the harp.
3 Blow the trumpet at [l]the new moon,
at the full moon, on our feast day.

4 For it is a statute for Israel,
a rule[2] of the God of Jacob.
5 He made it [m]a decree in [n]Joseph
when he [o]went out over[3] the land of Egypt.
[p]I hear a language [q]I had not known:
6 "I [r]relieved your[4] shoulder of [s]the burden;
your hands were freed from the basket.

[1] Probably a musical or liturgical term [2] Or *just decree* [3] Or *against* [4] Hebrew *his*; also next line

14[z][Isa. 63:15]
16[a]Isa. 33:12 [b]Ps. 76:6; [Ps. 39:11]
17[c]Ps. 89:21
18[d]See Ps. 71:20
19[e]ver. 3, 7

Psalm 81
[f]Ps. 8, title; 84, title [g]Ps. 50, title
1[h][Deut. 32:43] [i]See Ps. 66:1
2[j]Ex. 15:20 [k]Ps. 71:22
3[l]Lev. 23:24; Num. 10:10; 29:1
5[m]Ps. 122:4; [Ps. 78:5] [n]Ps. 77:15; 78:67; 80:1 [o]Ex. 11:4 [p]Ps. 114:1 [q][Deut. 28:49; Jer. 5:15]
6[r]Isa. 9:4; 10:27 [s]Ex. 1:11

80:14–15 This is a variation in the refrain pattern of the psalm; see note on Psalm 80.

80:15 the son. Israel as a whole is God's "son" (cf. Ex. 4:22–23; Hos. 11:1).

80:16–19 *Make Us Faithful!* The final stanza continues the vine imagery from the previous section, describing the monstrous deeds of these Gentile marauders: **they have burned it** (i.e., the vine) **with fire; they have cut it down.** For such an outrage against God's own plant, **may they perish at the rebuke of your face!** The terms in v. 17, **the man of your right hand** and **the son of man**, probably refer to the people of Israel, for several reasons. First, "the man of your right hand" is probably a play on the name Benjamin (v. 2), which means "son of the right hand" (see Gen. 35:18, ESV footnote). Here Israel is at God's right hand, called to carry out his purpose in the world. Second, the words "son whom you made strong for yourself" were applied to Israel in Ps. 80:15; the additional "of man" emphasizes Israel's frailty and dependence on God. (One reason NT writers call Jesus God's Son, and the Son of Man, is to show that he embodies all that Israel was called to be, which makes him the ideal heir of David.) Israel as a whole pledges itself to God: if he will **let** his **hand be on** Israel (i.e., put forth his power on their behalf, esp. in protecting them from the ravaging Gentiles), then Israel will **not turn back** (again) **from** God and **will call upon** his **name**, i.e., will exercise true faithfulness.

Psalm 81. It is not easy to put this psalm in a category; it actually resembles the oracles of the OT prophets; perhaps it is therefore best to think of it as a prophetic hymn. Prediction is not the primary function of the OT prophets, any more than it is of this psalm: rather, their goal is to challenge God's people to covenant faithfulness, speaking to them of covenant blessings or punishments that will come, depending on their response. This psalm reviews the basic history of the covenant (using the Pentateuch), charges Israel with unfaithfulness, and urges them to embrace the covenant—then God would subdue Israel's enemies. Verse 2 refers to the trumpet at the new moon and at the full moon. This may well indicate that the psalm was suited to the Feasts of Trumpets (the first day of the seventh month, the new moon) and Booths (the 15th day of the same month, when the moon was full), with the solemnity of the Day of Atonement in between them (Lev. 23:23–36). Certainly the overall theme of the psalm fits this setting.

81:1–3 *Sing Aloud to God.* The call to worship is a jubilant one; the people should **shout for joy** as well as play the various musical instruments, **tambourine**, **lyre**, **harp**, and **trumpet**. The **new moon** and **full moon** are the beginning and middle of months in ancient Israel; as the note on Psalm 81 suggests, this may show that the psalm was intended for the **feast day** of Trumpets (Lev. 23:23–25) and then Booths (Lev. 23:33–36), the beginning and middle of the seventh month. The rest of the psalm is quite somber in tone, and the exuberance of these verses reminds worshipers that even hearing some hard words from the Lord is a privilege, worthy of song and celebration.

81:4–7 *God's Work to Care for Israel in the Past.* The second section recounts the way in which **the God of Jacob** worked on behalf of his people to deliver them from slavery in **Egypt**, where their **shoulder** bore a **burden** and their **hands** carried **the basket** in which they hauled bricks and clay (cf. Ex. 6:6). Israel **called** and God **delivered** (cf. Ex. 2:23–25), bringing them through the desert. The psalm probably mentions **Meribah** (Ex. 17:7, where the people **tested** the Lord) because it is on the journey to Sinai and because it is also an example of the way Israel kept putting God to the test with their lack of trust.

7 In distress you [t]called, and I delivered you;
I [u]answered you in the secret place of thunder;
I [v]tested you at the waters of Meribah. *Selah*
8 [w]Hear, O my people, while I admonish you!
O Israel, if you would but listen to me!
9 There shall be no [x]strange god among you;
you shall not bow down to a [y]foreign god.
10 [z]I am the LORD your God,
who brought you up out of the land of Egypt.
[a]Open your mouth wide, and I will fill it.

11 "But my people did not listen to my voice;
Israel [b]would not submit to me.
12 So I [c]gave them over to their [d]stubborn hearts,
to follow their own [e]counsels.
13 [f]Oh, that my people would listen to me,
that Israel would [g]walk in my ways!
14 I would soon subdue their enemies
and [h]turn my hand against their foes.
15 Those who hate the LORD would [i]cringe toward him,
and their fate would last forever.
16 But he would feed you[1] with [j]the finest of the wheat,
and with [k]honey from the rock I would satisfy you."

Rescue the Weak and Needy

82

A PSALM OF [l]ASAPH.

1 [m]God [n]has taken his place in the divine council;
in the midst of [p]the gods he [q]holds judgment:

7[t]Ps. 50:15; [Ex. 2:23; 14:10] [u]Ex. 19:19; See Ps. 18:11-14 [v]Ex. 17:7; Num. 20:13
8[w]See Ps. 50:7
9[x]Ps. 44:20; Isa. 43:12; [Ex. 20:3] [y]Deut. 32:12
10[z]Ex. 20:2 [a][Ps. 37:3, 4]
11[b]Ex. 32:1; Deut. 32:15, 18; Prov. 1:25, 30
12[c]Job 8:4; [Acts 7:42; 14:16; Rom. 1:24, 26] [d][Deut. 29:19] [e]Ps. 106:43; Jer. 7:24; Mic. 6:16
13[f]Deut. 5:29; 32:29; Isa. 48:18 [g]Deut. 5:33
14[h]Amos 1:8
15[i]Ps. 18:44
16[j]Ps. 147:14; Deut. 32:14 [k]Deut. 32:13; [Job 29:6; Ezek. 16:19]

Psalm 82

[l]See Ps. 50, title
1[m][2 Chr. 19:5, 6; Eccles. 5:8] [n]Isa. 3:13 [p][1 Sam. 28:13] [q]See Ps. 58:11

[1] That is, Israel; Hebrew *him*

81:8–10 *God Calls His People to Worship Only Him.* This section follows closely on the previous one, especially evoking the covenant-making at Sinai. **I am the LORD your God, who brought you up out of the land of Egypt** (v. 10) is very close to the preface to the Ten Commandments (Ex. 20:2), and the basic admonition, **there shall be no strange god among you; you shall not bow down to a foreign god** (Ps. 81:9), is an effective summary of the first two commandments (Ex. 20:3–6). The Lord wants his people to **listen to** him (Ps. 81:8): to receive the covenant as an expression of his grace, believe in him, and live as he directs. (**Open your mouth wide, and I will fill it** is an indication of God's boundless generosity toward those he has rescued.) The expression **if you would** (v. 8) indicates that it is God's desire; the song moves to "my people did not listen" (v. 11), and back again to, "Oh, that my people would listen" (v. 13).

81:11–16 *If Only His People Would Listen to Him.* The final section starts from the sad fact that God's **people did not listen to** his **voice** (v. 11), which led to sad consequences (v. 12). But God has not given up, and he addresses his people afresh with the opportunity to **listen**, to embrace the covenant and thus to **walk in** God's good **ways** (v. 13). The consequences of this genuine covenant participation would be victory over **their enemies** (v. 14), while **those who hate the LORD** (the same Gentile enemies) **would cringe toward** God in submission (which would be to their benefit, cf. 2:10–12). The land of Israel would also then enjoy fruitfulness, yielding the **finest of the wheat** (Deut. 32:14) and **honey from the rock** (apparently an image of abundant wild honey, Deut. 32:13).

Psalm 82. Some call this a community lament since it addresses God directly with a request on behalf of the whole people (v. 8). Others call it a prophetical hymn (like Psalm 81), interpreting its address to the "gods" (82:6) as directed to unjust human rulers, whom God will judge. Both of these classifications have merit, which shows that one must use the psalm categories only as a rule of thumb, because the Psalms do not always fit neatly in only one category. Singing this psalm should enable the faithful, many of whom were socially weak and lowly in Israel (as often was the case with the early Christians as well; cf. 1 Cor. 1:26–28), to take courage in the face of unjust rule, so that they do not yield to the ever-present temptation to cooperate with the injustices of their wicked rulers. Even the most powerful rulers must die and face God's final judgment. The song should also help those who hold social and political power to use that power in service to others, especially to protect those who are easiest to exploit. The people of God are called to aspire to be an ideal society, with their justice visible to all peoples, that all nations might come to know the true God (Deut. 4:5–8); Christians are called to the same aspiration for their own present society. They must also testify about God's justice to their wider culture, since, as Prov. 31:1–9 shows (see note there), this kind of justice is applicable to all mankind; this is what properly functioning human nature looks like everywhere.

82:1–4 *The Task of the "Gods."* The first section gives the job description of human rulers (the **gods**), especially those who rule God's covenant people: they are to **give justice to the weak and the fatherless**, and **rescue the weak and the needy . . . from the hand of the wicked** (vv. 3–4). Far too often, however, they **judge unjustly and show partiality to the wicked** (i.e., people who take the lead in opposing God's purpose and oppressing others). The words of the psalm do not specify whether the rulers are Israelites, or Gentiles ruling Israel as a subject state (as in the Babylonian or Persian Empires). Both the ideal Davidic king in Psalm 72 and the ideal Gentile ruler in Prov. 31:1–9 are called to protect the powerless from those who would oppress them. Certainly the people of God should aim to embody this most clearly.

82:1 in the divine council; in the midst of the gods. Many would take these terms in vv. 1 and 6 as describing the assembly of angelic beings who surround God's throne as a divine court (cf. 1 Kings 22:19; Job 1:6; 2:1). This finds support in the way that the title "sons of the Most High" matches the label "sons of God" in Job; cf. also the "heavenly beings" (or "gods") in Ps. 8:5 (see note there). On the other hand, these "gods" are said to "judge" among men (82:2–4) and to die like men (v. 7); **God** is to judge the earth and to

2 "How long will you judge unjustly
and [r]show partiality to [s]the wicked? *Selah*
3 [t]Give justice to [u]the weak and the fatherless;
[v]maintain the right of the afflicted and the destitute.
4 [w]Rescue the weak and the needy;
[x]deliver them from the hand of the wicked."

5 [y]They have neither knowledge nor understanding,
[z]they walk about in darkness;
[a]all the foundations of the earth are [b]shaken.

6 [c]I said, "You are gods,
sons of the Most High, all of you;
7 nevertheless, like men [d]you shall die,
and fall like any prince."[1]

8 [e]Arise, O God, judge the earth;
for you shall [f]inherit all the nations!

O God, Do Not Keep Silence

83

A SONG. A PSALM OF [g]ASAPH.

1 O God, do not keep silence;
[h]do not hold your peace or be still, O God!
2 For behold, your enemies [i]make an uproar;
those who hate you have [j]raised their heads.
3 They lay [k]crafty plans against your people;
they consult together against your [l]treasured ones.
4 They say, "Come, [m]let us wipe them out as a nation;
let the name of Israel be remembered no more!"
5 For they conspire with one accord;
against you they make a covenant—

2 [r]Deut. 1:17 [s]Prov. 18:5
3 [t]Ps. 10:18 [u]Ps. 41:1 [v]Jer. 22:3
4 [w]Job 29:12 [x]Prov. 24:11
5 [y][Mic. 3:1]; See Ps. 14:4 [z]Prov. 2:13 [a]See Ps. 11:3 [b]Ps. 10:6
6 [c]ver. 1; Cited John 10:34
7 [d]Ps. 49:12; Job 21:32; Ezek. 31:14; See Ezek. 28:2-10
8 [e]See Ps. 12:5 [f]Ps. 2:8; [Rev. 11:15]

Psalm 83

[g]See Ps. 50, title
1 [h]See Ps. 28:1
2 [i][Ps. 2:1] [j]Judg. 8:28
3 [k][Neh. 4:8] [l]See Ps. 27:5; 31:20
4 [m]Jer. 48:2; [Ps. 74:8; Esth. 3:6]

[1] *Or fall as one man, O princes*

inherit the nations (where mankind lives, v. 8). This makes it better to see these as human rulers, who hold their authority as representatives of the true God (and therefore deserve respect; cf. 58:1; Rom. 13:1–7; 1 Pet. 2:13–17). Of course this does not require ultimate loyalty that overrides faithfulness to God, or that silences testimony about God's justice, as this very psalm makes clear. Jesus seems to have read the psalm in this way, since in John 10:34–35 he cites Ps. 82:6, describing the "gods" as those to whom the word of God came, which means they were human. See also note on v. 6.

82:5–7 *The "Gods" Who Fail in Their Task.* The next section describes God's verdict on those rulers who refuse to carry out their divinely given assignment. In saying that **they have neither knowledge nor understanding** (v. 5), the psalm is speaking of the moral perception necessary for promoting justice (cf. 1 Kings 3:9). When such people rule, the **foundations of the earth** (the moral principles that God instilled in the creation order) **are shaken** (cf. note on Ps. 11:3). There is only one true God **Most High**, however; as for these unjust "gods," **like** (other) **men** they **shall die, and fall like any prince**. The Lord will have the last word, vindicating his justice.

82:6 You are gods. John 10:34–35 tells how Jesus cited this text in a debate (see note on Ps. 82:1) to deflect criticism for calling himself the Son of God. Since the title "Son of God" is sometimes a designation of David's heir (see note on 2:7), Jesus is probably inviting his audience to reflect more deeply on its implications. **sons of the Most High**. If these are Gentile rulers, they serve the purposes of God, who is the highest of all powers. This may suggest that Israelite rulers are especially in view, since Deut. 14:1 calls God's people his "sons" (i.e., the whole people is God's "son," cf. Ps. 80:15; and the members are each "sons"). In this latter case, the injustice is even more reprehensible since it defies the gracious covenant of God.

82:8 *Prayer that the True God Would Judge the Earth.* The psalm closes with prayer that God will **judge the earth**. Since "judging" is the activity of rulers in this psalm (vv. 2–3), and since when God judges he rebukes the unjust rulers (v. 1), this prayer is for God to rebuke the present unjust rulers and raise up good ones. **you shall inherit all the nations**. The grounds of the request is that all nations belong to God already; perhaps this also alludes to 2:8, where the messianic king will have the nations as his heritage (or inheritance). The OT looks forward to a Messiah who will bring all nations under his sway, shedding God's light into their hearts and yielding a world dominated by true justice (cf. Isa. 2:1–5; 11:1–10; 42:4).

Psalm 83. This is a community lament, geared to a situation in which God's people are threatened by Gentile enemies (vv. 6–8) who aim to destroy them. The psalm prays that God will make such enemies fail miserably, being put to shame and perishing—so that they might come to know the Lord. It is possible (see note on vv. 9–18) that the psalm assumes that Israel must defend themselves, and the prayer is for military victory. Christians would use this psalm not against "national enemies" (Christians transcend national boundaries) but in cases where their persecutors would destroy them and all traces of their faith. They use this prayer rightly when they ask God to thwart these plans in such a way that even the persecutors might come to seek God's name.

83:1–8 *O God, Your Enemies Conspire against Israel.* The first section describes the Gentile coalition and their evil, **crafty plans: let us wipe them out as a nation; let the name of Israel be remembered no more!** The Gentiles, as to character, are **your** (i.e., God's) **enemies** and **those who hate you** (v. 2); then they are specific peoples from around Israel (vv. 6–7), with **Asshur** (probably Assyria, far off to the east, but possibly the tribe mentioned in Num. 24:22, 24, from the northern Sinai) joining them. The psalm is not limited to threats from these peoples alone, of course; prayer in this specific case is a guide to prayer in other cases like it. In such danger,

6 [n]Ps. 137:7; See 2 Chr. 20:10 [o]See Gen. 25:12-16 [p]2 Chr. 20:10 [q]1 Chr. 5:10
7 [r]Josh. 13:5 [p][See ver. 6 above] [s]1 Sam. 15:2 [t]1 Sam. 4:1; [Amos 1:6] [u]Ezek. 27:3; [Amos 1:9]
8 [v]2 Kgs. 15:19 [w]Deut. 2:9, 19
9 [x]Num. 31:7; See Isa. 9:4 [y]Judg. 4:15, 24 [z]Judg. 4:7; 5:21
10 [a]Josh. 17:11; 1 Sam. 28:7 [b]See Job 20:7
11 [c]Judg. 7:25; 8:3 [d]See Judg. 8:5-21
12 [e][2 Chr. 20:11]
13 [f]Isa. 17:13 [g]Job 13:25; 21:18; [Ps. 1:4]
14 [h][Isa. 9:18]; See Isa. 10:16-19 [i]Deut. 32:22
15 [j]Job 9:17
16 [k][Ps. 35:4, 26; Job 10:15]
17 [l]Ps. 35:4
18 [m]Ps. 59:13 [n]Ex. 6:3 [o]Ps. 9:2; 18:13; 97:9

Psalm 84

[p]Ps. 8, title; 81, title [q]Ps. 42, title
1 [r][Ps. 27:4] [s]Ps. 43:3; 132:5

6 the tents of [n]Edom and [o]the Ishmaelites,
[p]Moab and [q]the Hagrites,
7 [r]Gebal and [p]Ammon and [s]Amalek,
[t]Philistia with the inhabitants of [u]Tyre;
8 [v]Asshur also has joined them;
they are the strong arm of [w]the children of Lot. *Selah*

9 Do to them as you did to [x]Midian,
as to [y]Sisera and Jabin at [z]the river Kishon,
10 who were destroyed at [a]En-dor,
who became [b]dung for the ground.
11 Make their nobles like [c]Oreb and Zeeb,
all their princes like [d]Zebah and Zalmunna,
12 who said, [e]"Let us take possession for ourselves
of the pastures of God."

13 O my God, make them like [f]whirling dust,[1]
like [g]chaff before the wind.
14 As [h]fire consumes the forest,
as the flame [i]sets the mountains ablaze,
15 so may you pursue them [j]with your tempest
and terrify them with your hurricane!
16 [k]Fill their faces with shame,
that they may seek your name, O LORD.
17 Let them be [l]put to shame and dismayed forever;
let them perish in disgrace,
18 that they may [m]know that you alone,
[n]whose name is the LORD,
are [o]the Most High over all the earth.

84

My Soul Longs for the Courts of the LORD

TO THE CHOIRMASTER: ACCORDING TO [p]THE GITTITH.[2] A PSALM OF [q]THE SONS OF KORAH.

1 How [r]lovely is your [s]dwelling place,
O LORD of hosts!

[1] Or *like a tumbleweed* [2] Probably a musical or liturgical term

the people urge God, **do not keep silence** (i.e., do not suspend or disguise your power and commitment to your people).

83:9–18 *Defeat Them, that They Might Know that You Rule.* The basic request in this section is fairly simple: that these enemies would utterly fail in their scheme. This request begins with historical examples from Judges: **Midian, Oreb, Zeeb, Zebah and Zalmunna** (vv. 9, 11) all come from the story of Gideon (Judg. 7:1–8:28), while **Sisera and Jabin** come from the story of Deborah and Barak (Judges 4). These were deadly enemies, and from a merely human perspective their forces were superior to Israel's. Yet with God's help they were soundly defeated, which probably explains why the psalm uses them as examples. Verses 13–15 of Psalm 83 are colorful depictions of these enemies being thwarted and defeated. Verses 16–18 make explicit an element that is often only implicit in psalms asking for such victories: the goal in asking for their defeat is **that they may seek your name** (their conversion to the true God), or at least **that they may know that you alone . . . are the Most High over all the earth** (this may be conversion, or it may simply be the recognition that the God of Israel is the highest power there is, a recognition that may fall short of true conversion). The ultimate reason for Israel's existence is to serve God's purpose of restoring true worship and authentic human life among all mankind; therefore it is really for the good of these hostile Gentiles that they fail in their plan to "wipe out Israel" (v. 4). The genuine dependence on God expressed in this prayer is thus both devotion to God and goodwill to all mankind.

Psalm 84. This is a psalm celebrating pilgrimage to Jerusalem in order to worship at the temple. It is very much like the hymns in praise of Zion as God's special place (e.g., Psalm 122), although this one especially focuses on the delight of going to worship there. The purpose of singing this psalm is to cultivate that delight, to open the eyes and hearts of God's people to the staggering privilege of being a welcome guest in God's own house, and to write deep into their souls the conviction that wickedness offers no reward that can even remotely compare to the joy and pleasure of God's house. The psalm most likely comes from a time when the sanctuary was located in Zion (84:7), and when a king ruled and protected the pilgrims (v. 9): he is called the anointed, and is probably from David's line (though even Saul was called "the LORD's anointed," 1 Sam. 24:6; however, Saul was a poor protector of the sanctuary and its personnel, 1 Sam. 22:6–19). The psalm has three parts, in each of which people are pronounced "blessed" (Ps. 84:4, 5, 12).

84:1–4 *Blessed Are Those Who Dwell in God's Courts.* The song opens by describing God's house, the central sanctuary in Jerusalem. It is **lovely** and delightful, because it is the Lord's **dwelling place**; this is why the pious **soul longs, yes, faints for the courts of the LORD**: this is where the worshiper actually meets **the living God**—no wonder his **heart and flesh sing for joy**. (Israelite worship was not "quiet" or "restrained": how could it be, if these beliefs are true?) The marvel is that God's house is a welcoming place;

2 My soul [t]longs, yes, [u]faints
for the courts of the LORD;
my heart and flesh sing for joy
to [v]the living God.

3 Even the sparrow finds a home,
and the swallow a nest for herself,
where she may lay her young,
at your altars, O LORD of hosts,
[w]my King and my God.
4 [x]Blessed are those who dwell in your house,
ever [y]singing your praise! *Selah*
5 Blessed are those whose strength is in you,
[z]in whose heart are the highways to Zion.[1]
6 As they go through the Valley of Baca
they make it a place of springs;
[a]the early rain also covers it with [b]pools.
7 They go [c]from strength to strength;
each one [d]appears before God in Zion.

8 O [e]LORD God of hosts, hear my prayer;
give ear, O God of Jacob! *Selah*
9 [f]Behold our [g]shield, O God;
look on the face of your anointed!

10 For a day [h]in your courts is better
than a thousand elsewhere.
I would rather be [i]a doorkeeper in the house of my God
than dwell in the tents of wickedness.
11 For the LORD God is [j]a sun and [g]shield;
the LORD bestows favor and honor.
[k]No good thing does he withhold
from those who [l]walk uprightly.
12 O LORD of hosts,
[m]blessed is the one who trusts in you!

Revive Us Again

85 To the choirmaster. A Psalm of [n]the Sons of Korah.

1 LORD, you were [o]favorable to your land;
you [p]restored the fortunes of Jacob.

[1] Hebrew lacks *to Zion*

2 [t][Ps. 42:1, 2; 63:1] [u][Ps. 73:26; 119:81; 143:6; Job 19:27] [v]See Ps. 42:2
3 [w]Ps. 5:2
4 [x]See Ps. 65:4 [y]Ps. 42:5, 11; 43:5
5 [z][Ps. 122:1]
6 [a]Joel 2:23 [b]Ezek. 34:26
7 [c]Prov. 4:18; Isa. 40:31; [John 1:16; 2 Cor. 3:18] [d]See Ps. 42:2
8 [e]See Ps. 59:5
9 [f]Ps. 80:14 [g]See Ps. 3:3
10 [h]ver. 2 [i]1 Chr. 26:19
11 [j]Isa. 60:19, 20; See Ps. 27:1; Mal. 4:2; Rev. 21:23 [g][See ver. 9 above] [k]Ps. 85:12; [Ps. 34:9, 10; Matt. 6:33; 7:11] [l]Ps. 15:2; Prov. 2:7
12 [m]See Ps. 2:12

Psalm 85
[n]Ps. 42, title
1 [o]Ps. 77:7 [p]Ps. 14:7

if **even the sparrow finds a home** there, and the **swallow** too, then the humble and faithful Israelite need not fear that God will turn him away. **those who dwell in your house**. These are people with constant access to the sanctuary (see note on 23:5–6); they are **ever singing** God's **praise** because they can attend the services so readily. Such people are **blessed**, truly happy (see note on 1:1).

84:5–9 *Blessed Are Those Who Journey to Zion.* The next section describes those who make the journey to Zion to worship at such a sanctuary; they are **blessed**. Their **strength is in** God, to sustain them on the way; the **highways** are in their hearts, which probably means that they actually want to go (pilgrimage was obligatory [Deut. 16:16], but should never become mechanical or burdensome). The location of the **Valley of Baca** is unknown; it seems to have been a dry place, but the faithful pilgrims **make it a place of springs** (which probably means that they delight in this valley as much as if it were well-watered, being so happy to be on the way). These pilgrims **go from strength to strength** (i.e., they keep on finding new levels of strength for the journey), until **each one appears before God in Zion** (cf. Deut. 16:16). Prayer for the king (the **shield** and **anointed**) closes the section; not only does he protect the pilgrims, but he is called to represent Israel before God, to model faithfulness for the whole people, and thus to keep the whole people securely serving God.

84:10–12 *Blessed Are Those Who Trust in the LORD.* The final section describes the person **who trusts in** the Lord: he sincerely prefers one **day in** God's **courts** to a **thousand** anywhere else; and he prefers even the lowest task of service in the **house of my God** to any gain he might have if he were to **dwell in the tents of wickedness** (i.e., to fashion his life in opposition to the covenant, perhaps along the familiar lines of the Gentiles). This is the person who finds God to be a **sun and shield** (he gives the light of life, and protection), upon whom **the LORD bestows favor and honor** (such a person will not trust in these or turn them into a source of pride). **Those who walk uprightly** are those whose faith is genuine, which leads to a life that aims at doing God's will; **no good thing does** God **withhold from** them, because they are living in his light. The chief good thing, in this psalm, is to be welcomed in the temple. The faithful can enjoy other

2 [q]Ps. 32:1
3 [r]Ps. 78:38; 106:23; Ex. 32:12; Deut. 13:17; Jonah 3:9
4 [s]See Ps. 80:3
5 [t][Ps. 79:5]
6 [u]Ps. 71:20 [v]Ps. 90:14; 149:2
8 [w][Hab. 2:1] [x]Zech. 9:10; [Hag. 2:9] [y]See Ps. 50:5 [z][2 Pet. 2:21] [a][Ps. 49:13]
9 [b]Isa. 46:13 [c]Zech. 2:5; [John 1:14]
10 [d]Ps. 89:14; See Ps. 40:11 [e][Isa. 45:8]; See Ps. 72:3
12 [f]Ps. 84:11; [James 1:17] [g]See Ps. 67:6
13 [h]Ps. 89:14; Isa. 58:8

2 You [q]forgave the iniquity of your people;
you [q]covered all their sin. *Selah*
3 You withdrew all your wrath;
you [r]turned from your hot anger.

4 [s]Restore us again, O God of our salvation,
and put away your indignation toward us!
5 [t]Will you be angry with us forever?
Will you prolong your anger to all generations?
6 Will you not [u]revive us again,
that your people may [v]rejoice in you?
7 Show us your steadfast love, O LORD,
and grant us your salvation.

8 [w]Let me hear what God the LORD will speak,
for he will [x]speak peace to his people, to his [y]saints;
but let them not [z]turn back to [a]folly.
9 Surely his [b]salvation is near to those who fear him,
that [c]glory may dwell in our land.

10 [d]Steadfast love and faithfulness meet;
[e]righteousness and peace kiss each other.
11 Faithfulness springs up from the ground,
and righteousness looks down from the sky.
12 Yes, [f]the LORD will give what is good,
and our land [g]will yield its increase.
13 [h]Righteousness will go before him
and make his footsteps a way.

things only insofar as they express the life of the upright. Such people are **blessed** indeed!

Psalm 85. This is a community lament, at a time when God has shown his displeasure over his people's unfaithfulness, perhaps by withholding fruitfulness from the land (vv. 1, 12). The people singing this are seeking forgiveness for the whole people ("us"), asking God to show the steadfast love and faithfulness he proclaimed in Ex. 34:6; and because God is righteous (Ps. 85:10–11, 13)—that is, reliable about his promises—the psalm closes with confidence. Exodus 34:6–7 provides the background to this psalm, particularly in the terms "steadfast love and faithfulness" (Ps. 85:10; cf. vv. 7, 11) and "forgave iniquity" (v. 2). The Lord explained his "name" to Moses by emphasizing his benevolence, which is where the people's hope lies. Many churches use the psalm at Christmastime, the supreme occasion when God was favorable to his land and spoke peace to his saints.

85:1–3 *Lord, Once You Showed Us Favor and Forgave Us.* The verbs in this section are all past tense, looking back to what God has done for the people before: he was **favorable to** the **land**, i.e., he made it produce abundant crops to sustain his people; he **restored the fortunes of Jacob** after he had disciplined his people for their unfaithfulness; he **forgave** their **iniquity**, **covered all their sin**, **withdrew all** his **wrath**, and **turned from** his **hot anger**. As mentioned in the note on Psalm 85, "forgave iniquity" evokes Ex. 34:7; cf. also Ps. 32:1 for "covered sin." The expression "turned from his hot anger" (cf. Ex. 32:12, part of the same context as Ex. 34:6; cf. also Josh. 7:26) implies that God forgave his people after they repented of serious unfaithfulness and apostasy. God has done this in the past for his people, because he is boundlessly kind.

85:4–7 *Restore and Forgive Us Again.* The next section appeals to the benevolence God has claimed and shown, asking him to **restore us again**, i.e., **put away your indignation toward us**. For God to **be angry with us forever** would be contrary to this revealed character; therefore the people pray, **show us your steadfast love** (proclaimed in Ex. 34:6), **and grant us your salvation**. The specific "salvation" (see note on Ps. 3:2) is for God to turn away his anger, to forgive his people corporately (see notes on Num. 14:13–19; 14:20–35), and to **revive** them, i.e., to renew their genuine hold on the covenant and make the land fruitful.

85:8–9 *I Will Listen to Hear His Word of Peace.* Now the members of the congregation declare their patience in watching for God to act on their prayer. The song has shifted from the plural "we" to the singular "I": **let me hear**. Each member is thus making this pledge. There is confidence that God **will speak peace to his people**, i.e., he will agree to the reconciliation they have asked for in vv. 4–7. At the same time, the psalmist prays, **let them not turn back to folly**; i.e., the people who are appealing to God's benevolence should make sure that their repentance is genuine, and that they really do aim for faithfulness and really intend not to repeat the folly (moral stupidity) that provoked God's anger. The word **saints** (Hb. *khasid*) reinforces this, since it refers to members of the covenant people who take the covenant to heart and walk in obedience before God. Therefore the force of this is, "to his people, *especially* to his saints." Likewise God's **salvation** (which they had requested in v. 7) **is near to those who fear him**, i.e., again, to those who lay hold of the promises of God's covenant by genuine faith and obedience. The people should never presume upon God's gracious response to their prayers, as if it comes "automatically." Thus, as the Israelites wait for God to speak, they can evaluate their own sincerity.

85:9 glory may dwell in our land. The "glory" is God's special presence with his people (see note on 63:1–2); cf. Ex. 24:16 for the same expression. From the verb "dwell" (Hb. *shakan*) is derived a noun, "dwelling, that which dwells" (Hb. *shekinah*), which is why the glory that dwells with God's people in the sanctuary is called the "Shekinah." This dwelling of the glory is a gift to God's people, whose aim is to foster true piety. (Cf. John 1:14.)

85:10–13 *The Lord Will Give What Is Good.* The psalm closes with the confident expectation that God will hear their prayer and give what they ask. **Steadfast love and faithfulness meet**, i.e., in God they are in harmony.

Great Is Your Steadfast Love

86

[i]A PRAYER OF DAVID.

1 [j]Incline your ear, O LORD, and answer me,
for I am [k]poor and needy.
2 Preserve my life, for I am [l]godly;
save your servant, who [m]trusts in you—you are my God.
3 [n]Be gracious to me, O Lord,
for to you do I cry all the day.
4 Gladden the soul of your servant,
for [o]to you, O Lord, do I lift up my soul.
5 For you, O Lord, are good and [p]forgiving,
[q]abounding in steadfast love to all who call upon you.
6 [r]Give ear, O LORD, to my prayer;
listen to my plea for grace.
7 In [s]the day of my trouble I call upon you,
[t]for you answer me.
8 There is [u]none like you among the gods, O Lord,
[v]nor are there any works like yours.
9 [w]All the nations you have made shall come
and worship before you, O Lord,
and shall glorify your name.
10 For [x]you are great and [y]do wondrous things;
[z]you alone are God.
11 [a]Teach me your way, O LORD,
that I may [b]walk in your truth;
[c]unite my heart to fear your name.
12 I give thanks to you, O Lord my God, with my whole heart,
and I will glorify your name forever.
13 [d]For great is your steadfast love toward me;
you have [e]delivered my soul from the depths of Sheol.
14 O God, insolent men have [f]risen up against me;
a band of ruthless men seeks my life,
and they do not set you before them.

Psalm 86
[i][Ps. 72:20]
1[j]See Ps. 31:2 [k]Ps. 40:17
2[l]See Ps. 50:5 [m]See Ps. 11:1
3[n]ver. 16; Ps. 56:1; 57:1; See Ps. 4:1
4[o]See Ps. 25:1
5[p]Ps. 130:4 [q]ver. 15; Ps. 103:8; 145:8, 9; Ex. 34:6; Joel 2:13
6[r]Ps. 55:1, 2
7[s]See Ps. 77:2 [t]Ps. 17:6
8[u][Ps. 89:6; Ex. 15:11] [v]Deut. 3:24
9[w]Ps. 66:4; [Ps. 22:31; 65:2; Isa. 66:23; Zech. 14:18; Rev. 15:4]
10[x]Ps. 77:13 [y]See Ps. 72:18 [z]Deut. 6:4; Isa. 37:16; 44:6, 8; 1 Cor. 8:4, 6
11[a]See Ps. 25:4 [b]Ps. 26:3 [c][Jer. 32:39]
13[d][ver. 5] [e]Ps. 30:3; [Ps. 88:6; Ezek. 26:20]
14[f]Ps. 54:3

God's **righteousness** here is his character of reliably keeping his promises (esp. to his people), and therefore it guarantees the **peace** (cf. v. 8); they **kiss each other** like the affectionate greeting of relatives (e.g., Gen. 29:13; 45:15). Verse 11 of Psalm 85 keeps the image of greeting, with its picture of **faithfulness** springing up and **righteousness** looking down. Because God has this character, they can be sure that he will honor his promises; therefore **the LORD will give what is good**, namely, **our land will yield its increase** of abundant crops. Such confidence is based on God's own **righteousness** (v. 13): the God of Israel keeps his promises to his people, and forgives and renews them when they seek him.

Psalm 86. This is an individual lament, geared (as many of these laments are) to a situation in which "a band of insolent men seek my life" (v. 14). The psalm confesses that the Lord is "good and forgiving" (v. 5), acknowledging that the singer's own sins may have contributed to his enemies' plans. The psalmist explicitly grounds his request in Ex. 34:6, a fundamental confessional statement of the OT (Ps. 86:15; cf. vv. 5, 13); he also prays for a "united" heart to live faithfully to God (v. 11). The middle of the psalm strikingly professes faith in one God, to whom all nations shall come (vv. 8–10)—another vital OT theme. This is the only psalm of David in Book 3 of the Psalms; the last one encountered was Psalm 70, and the next one will be Psalm 101.

86:1–7 *Save Your Servant, Who Trusts in You.* The beginning of the psalm is a general call for help (**preserve my life, save your servant**), without specifying the nature of the **trouble**—that will come in the third section (vv. 14–17). The person praying offers reasons that God should answer, as indicated by the clauses introduced by **for** in vv. 2–5: first is the genuineness of his faith (v. 2, **I am godly . . . who trusts in you**); second is the earnestness with which he prays, relying on the Lord, not other gods (vv. 3–4, **to you do I cry all the day . . . to you, O Lord, do I lift up my soul**); and third is the crucial confession of God's benevolent character, as revealed in the Pentateuch (v. 5, **you, O Lord, are good and forgiving, abounding in steadfast love to all who call upon you**). Thus everyone who sings this prayer from the heart may be assured of God's attention.

86:8–13 *Praise to the Faithful and Majestic God.* In the second section, the singer offers up praise to the magnificent God he has petitioned for help and forgiveness. The praise comes in two parts; first, he praises the Lord, who alone is God (vv. 8–10); second, he praises the Lord who has shown his covenant kindness (**steadfast love**, v. 13). In between is a prayer for his own moral growth (v. 11).

86:8–10 These verses move from **there is none like you** who is worthy of worship **among the gods** (i.e., the angels and other heavenly beings), to **you alone are God**. This is why **all the nations you have made shall come and worship before you**: all human beings (Gen. 12:3)

15[g]ver. 5; Ps. 111:4; 112:4; Num. 14:18; Neh. 9:17; Jonah 4:2; See Ps. 62:12
16[h]See Ps. 25:16 [i]See Ps. 116:16
17[j][Judg. 6:17] [k]Neh. 5:19; 13:31

Psalm 87
[l]Ps. 42, title
1[m]See Ps. 48:1 [n]Isa. 28:16
2[o]Ps. 78:67, 68
3[p][Isa. 60:1]; See Isa. 54:1-3 [q]Ps. 46:4
4[r]Ps. 36:10; [John 10:14] [s]See Job 9:13; See Isa. 19:22-25 [t]See Ps. 68:31
5[u]Ps. 48:8
6[v]See Ps. 69:28
7[w]Ps. 68:25 [x]2 Sam. 6:14 [y]Ps. 36:9; Isa. 12:3; Rev. 21:6

15 But you, O Lord, are a God [g]merciful and gracious,
slow to anger and abounding in steadfast love and faithfulness.
16 [h]Turn to me and be gracious to me;
give your strength to [i]your servant,
and save [i]the son of your maidservant.
17 [j]Show me a sign of your [k]favor,
that those who hate me may see and be put to shame
because you, LORD, have helped me and comforted me.

Glorious Things of You Are Spoken

87

A PSALM OF [l]THE SONS OF KORAH. A SONG.

1 On [m]the holy mount [n]stands the city he founded;
2 the LORD [o]loves the gates of Zion
more than all the dwelling places of Jacob.
3 [p]Glorious things of you are spoken,
O [q]city of God. *Selah*

4 Among those who [r]know me I mention [s]Rahab and Babylon;
behold, Philistia and Tyre, with [t]Cush[1]—
"This one was born there," they say.
5 And of Zion it shall be said,
"This one and that one were born in her";
for the Most High himself will [u]establish her.
6 The LORD records as he [v]registers the peoples,
"This one was born there." *Selah*

7 [w]Singers and [x]dancers alike say,
"All my [y]springs are in you."

[1] Probably *Nubia*

were made to know and love the one true God. God called Abraham so that his family would be the vehicle of bringing this knowledge to the rest of mankind; the OT looks forward to an era in which this will actually happen, and the NT authors claim that this era has begun with the resurrection of Jesus. The words of Ps. 86:9 are incorporated into a song in Rev. 15:4.

86:11 Teach me your way. Cf. 25:8, 12; 27:11; 32:8 (and note on 25:4–5). The Bible regularly pictures the moral course of one's life as a "way" or path, and one's conduct as a "walk" or journey. A faithful person seeks instruction in the ways that please God in order to learn how better to **walk in** God's **truth**. **Unite my heart**, i.e., make it "one" (cf. Jer. 32:39), undivided in its loyalty (so that all of it can give thanks, Ps. 86:12).

86:13 Sheol. See note on 6:5.

86:14–17 *Save Me from the Insolent.* The third section of the psalm explains the source of the trouble: **insolent men** and **a band of ruthless men**. These people **do not set you before them** (i.e., they have no respect for God), therefore it is not surprising that they seek the **life** of the faithful (cf. note on vv. 1–7 for the "I" singing this psalm). But the faithful need not despair, since they have no grounds for worry that God will abandon them to enemies because of their sins: God is **merciful and gracious**, and therefore his faithful ones can trust him to forgive and to guard (cf. note on 32:6–11). Therefore the singer is bold and finishes by repeating his request. **that those who hate me may see and be put to shame**. When the enemies realize that the true God actually cares for the pious, they will also realize that they have relied on a false basis of hope; this may actually lead to their conversion. This lament does not, unlike most others, end with a certainty of being heard, but that certainty has been implicit throughout.

Psalm 87. This is a psalm celebrating Zion as the chosen city of God; it looks forward to people of all nations—even nations that have been enemies to Israel—becoming citizens of this city (carrying forward the ideas of 86:9). This brief song provided themes for the Christian hymn, "Glorious things of thee are spoken, Zion, city of our God" (see 87:3).

87:1–3 *The Lord Loves Zion.* The opening section describes Zion, the capital of God's people, as the **city** God **founded**, the city whose **gates** the Lord **loves**, the **city of God**. Its location **on the holy mount** shows why it is so **glorious**: it is the place of the temple, where God's people meet him.

87:4–6 *Zion, the Mother City of All Manner of People.* The second section is startling: one expects a reference to **those who know me**, but the list is composed of Gentile nations: **Rahab** (a nickname for Egypt, cf. Isa. 30:7), **Babylon**, **Philistia**, **Tyre** (a Phoenician city, culturally Canaanite), and **Cush** (Nubia, the region south of Egypt)—all of which had been, at one time or another, enemies of God's people and the city of Jerusalem. And yet, **the Most High himself will establish** Zion, in order to allow **the peoples** to be treated as **born in her**. When the people of God sing this, they are keeping themselves focused on their God-given purpose, to be a light for the Gentiles; cf. note on Ps. 86:8–10. Paul can call the full citizenship of Gentile Christians in the people of God a "mystery," because it was not made known in the OT in the same way it has been revealed to the apostles (Eph. 3:4–6), but this passage certainly points that way, anticipating what is to come.

87:7 *All Alike Delight in Zion.* The **singers and dancers**, who assist in the worship that takes place at the sanctuary in Zion, have this as their song: **all my springs are in you** (i.e., in Zion). This probably is an image of the life and refreshment that will pour forth from Zion in this future era (Ezek. 47:1–12; cf. Ps. 46:4).

I Cry Out Day and Night Before You

88

A SONG. A PSALM OF [z]THE SONS OF KORAH. TO THE CHOIRMASTER: ACCORDING TO [a]MAHALATH LEANNOTH. A MASKIL[1] OF [b]HEMAN THE EZRAHITE.

1 O LORD, [c]God of my salvation;
I [d]cry out day and night before you.
2 Let my prayer come before you;
[e]incline your ear to my cry!
3 For my soul is full of troubles,
and [f]my life draws near to [g]Sheol.
4 I am counted among those who [h]go down to the pit;
I am a man who has no strength,
5 like one set loose among the dead,
like the slain that lie in the grave,
like those whom [i]you remember no more,
for they are [j]cut off from your hand.
6 You have put me in [k]the depths of the pit,
in the [l]regions dark and [m]deep.
7 Your wrath [n]lies heavy upon me,
and you overwhelm me with [o]all your waves. *Selah*

8 You have caused [p]my companions to shun me;
you have made me [q]a horror[2] to them.
I am [r]shut in so that I cannot escape;
9 [s]my eye grows dim through sorrow.
Every day I call upon you, O LORD;
I [t]spread out my hands to you.
10 Do you work wonders for the dead?
[u]Do the departed rise up to praise you? *Selah*
11 Is your steadfast love declared in the grave,
or your faithfulness in Abaddon?

[1] Probably musical or liturgical terms [2] Or *an abomination*

Psalm 88
[z]Ps. 42, title [a]Ps. 53, title [b]1 Kgs. 4:31; 1 Chr. 2:6
1 [c]See Ps. 24:5 [d]Ps. 22:2; Luke 18:7
2 [e]See Ps. 31:2
3 [f][Ps. 107:18] [g]See Ps. 16:10
4 [h]See Ps. 28:1
5 [i][Ps. 31:12] [j]Isa. 53:8
6 [k][Ps. 63:9] [l]ver. 12, 18; Ps. 143:3; Lam. 3:6 [m]Ps. 69:15
7 [n][Ps. 32:4] [o]Ps. 42:7
8 [p]ver. 18; Ps. 142:4; See Job 19:13 [q]Job 30:10 [r]Jer. 32:2
9 [s][Ps. 6:7] [t]See Job 11:13
10 [u][Ps. 6:5]

Psalm 88. This is an individual lament, suited for a person who is so overwhelmed with troubles that even his friends shun him, and who wrestles with the dread that comes from suspecting that the Lord has shunned him as well. The psalm does not specify the troubles, only that they feel like expressions of God's relentless wrath; this allows the psalm to be used by the faithful for a wide variety of hardships. Most laments let in a ray of sunshine, usually closing on a confident note; Psalm 88 is distinct from all the rest in that there is no explicit statement of confidence. There is an implicit confidence, however, in vv. 6 and 14: the song confesses that it is God who has brought these troubles, implying that relief is also in God's hand. Further, there is insistent appeal to God (v. 1, "day and night"; v. 9, "every day"; v. 13, "in the morning"): the psalm instills a tough faith in its singers by reminding them to keep turning to God (the "God of my salvation," v. 1), even during these times when it seems that there is no answer being given. (The experiences of Job provide a good example of this kind of suffering. Sickness, bereavement, and persecution can easily lead to such distress.) Since Psalm 88 is in the canonical Psalms, the faith of this psalm cannot be separated from the faith expressed in the rest of the book, and it helps its singers to see that faith can be real, even when it cannot arrive at strong hope after prayer. Those without such problems may pray this psalm on behalf of those suffering.

88:1–2 *I Cry to You, O Lord.* The song opens by declaring its purpose: **Let my prayer come before you**. The psalm is therefore a petition; it belongs to a circumstance that is earnest (**day and night**, i.e., there is nothing easy-going here!) and urgent (**I cry out**, **my cry**; i.e., a great feeling of distress lies behind it).

88:3–9 *My Soul Is Full of Troubles.* The next section describes the trouble in general terms, focusing more on the feelings (**my soul is full of troubles**) than on the external circumstances. **my life draws near to Sheol**. Sheol may be a poetical name for the grave (see note on 6:5), but since the psalm says **your wrath lies heavy upon me** (cf. 88:5, **like those whom you remember no more**), it more likely refers to the place where the wicked go. The idea of vv. 3–7 is, "it feels like I am dying, and worse than that, dying under your wrath, with no hope either now or ever." The psalm allows the singer to lay out these despairing feelings; it does not claim that such feelings correspond to reality. Indeed, anyone genuinely singing this *to the Lord*, however miserable he may feel, can be assured that he is still expressing true faith. And yet these despairing feelings produce genuine pain, whether or not they correspond to reality: and the fact that **you have caused my companions** (who ought to have stood by me) **to shun me** (v. 8) only makes it harder to bear. The pain keeps building: he feels **shut in**, his **eye grows dim through sorrow**. And yet, tough faith will not let go: **every day I call upon you, O LORD; I spread out my hands to you**. The members of the singing congregation are learning here to keep coming to the Lord, even when they feel this way.

88:10–12 *Do the Dead Praise You?* The mention of dying under God's wrath (vv. 3–7) leads to the question: **Do you work wonders for the dead?** The purpose of this question is not to deny that the OT has a hope for the afterlife (see Psalms 49; 73; cf. note on Ezek. 37:12–13) but rather to allow worshipers who feel the pain of Ps. 88:3–9 to continue expressing their fears. If one were to die under God's wrath, then he could not anticipate any experience of God's wonders, or any chance to praise him, in **Abaddon** (the place of destruction). The person who sings this in the worshiping congregation obviously does not want to perish in this way (an important component of faith), cut off from God's **steadfast love** and **faithfulness** (v. 11).

12 Are your [v]wonders known in [w]the darkness,
or your righteousness in the land of [x]forgetfulness?

13 But I, O LORD, cry [y]to you;
[z]in the morning my prayer comes before you.
14 O LORD, why [a]do you cast my soul away?
Why [b]do you hide your face from me?
15 Afflicted and close to death from my youth up,
I suffer your terrors; I am helpless.[1]
16 Your wrath has swept over me;
your [c]dreadful assaults destroy me.
17 They [d]surround me like a flood [e]all day long;
they [f]close in on me together.
18 You have caused [g]my beloved and my friend to shun me;
my companions have become darkness.[2]

I Will Sing of the Steadfast Love of the LORD

89

A MASKIL[3] OF [h]ETHAN THE EZRAHITE.

1 [i]I will sing of [j]the steadfast love of the LORD, forever;
with my mouth I will make known your [k]faithfulness to all generations.
2 For I said, [j]"Steadfast love will be built up forever;
in the heavens [l]you will establish your [k]faithfulness."
3 You have said, "I have made [m]a covenant with my [n]chosen one;
I have [o]sworn to David my servant:
4 'I will establish your [p]offspring forever,
and build your [q]throne for all generations.'" *Selah*

5 Let [r]the heavens praise your [s]wonders, O LORD,
your faithfulness in the assembly of [t]the holy ones!

[1] The meaning of the Hebrew word is uncertain [2] Or *darkness has become my only companion* [3] Probably a musical or liturgical term

12[v]Ps. 89:5 [w]ver. 6; Job 10:21 [x][Eccles. 9:5]
13[y]Ps. 30:2 [z]See Ps. 5:3
14[a]See Ps. 44:9 [b]See Job 13:24
16[c]Job 6:4; 9:34
17[d]See Ps. 118:10-12 [e]Ps. 86:3 [f]Ps. 18:4; 22:16; [Ps. 118:10]
18[g]See Job 19:13, 14

Psalm 89

[h]1 Kgs. 4:31; 1 Chr. 2:6
1[i]Ps. 101:1 [j]ver. 14, 24, 28, 33, 49; [Isa. 55:3] [k]ver. 5, 8, 24, 33, 49; Ps. 88:11; 119:90
2[j][See ver. 1 above] [l]See Ps. 36:5 [k][See ver. 1 above]
3[m]ver. 28, 34, 39 [n]ver. 19; 1 Kgs. 8:16; Isa. 42:1 [o]ver. 35, 49; Ps. 132:11; See 2 Sam. 7:8-16; 1 Chr. 17:7-14; Jer. 33:17-21
4[p]ver. 29, 36; John 12:34 [q]ver. 29, 36; [Isa. 9:7; Luke 1:32, 33]
5[r]Ps. 19:1; 50:6; 97:6; See Rev. 7:10-12 [s]Ps. 88:12 [t]ver. 7; Job 5:1; 15:15; [Job 1:6]

88:13–18 *I Continue to Pray but Feel No Reply.* And so the prayer goes on; this section recapitulates the previous themes. Earnest and urgent prayer continues (v. 13), the feeling of abandonment by God continues (vv. 14, 16–17), and the fear of death under God's wrath continues (v. 15). The psalm ends (v. 18) with an echo of v. 8: **my beloved and my friend** will continue to **shun me**, and **my companions** (as in v. 8, the people from whom the psalmist might have expected help and sympathy) **have become darkness** (and not the light that is needed). This somber word, "darkness," is the last word in the psalm; and yet, as the preceding notes argue, even this does not mean that the ultimate outcome will be totally bleak. The faithful know that there is no alternative but to keep seeking the Lord in prayer.

Psalm 89. This is a community lament, but with a distinctive flavor: it celebrates the Davidic kingship as a special gift of God's love to his people, and mourns the distress into which the people have fallen, interpreting that distress as God's wrath against his anointed (i.e., the king in the line of David). For the people to sing this faithfully is for them to choose as their own the way that God has chosen to administer his people, accepting that the covenant with David (2 Sam. 7:8–16) defines the heir of David as the divinely appointed representative for God's people, whose task is to lead them in faithfulness. Owning this arrangement, they pray earnestly for God to bless his people through blessing the Davidic king with wisdom, goodness, and might. This psalm is for those who acknowledge the house of David as their legitimate ruler, i.e., for the united kingdom under David and Solomon, and for Judah after the division. (The prophets also instructed the people of the northern kingdom that their hope lay with David's house, cf. Hos. 3:5; Amos 9:11.) Crises during this period, including the exile to Babylon, would have been suitable occasions to sing this psalm. Christians sing this too, recognizing that, in Jesus, God has kept his promises to David, forcefully displaying his steadfast love and faithfulness. Under no circumstances will God ever "reject" (Ps. 89:38) Jesus; and even though God may be displeased with his people, and chastise them, he will not allow their mission to fail. As this psalm reassured God's people of old, so it reassures Christians that God's steadfast love and faithfulness are a solid foundation for the promise to David, even when it *feels like* God has abandoned that promise.

89:1–4 *The Covenant with David Expresses God's Steadfast Love and Faithfulness.* The theme of this opening section is straightforward: in raising up David and his line to be kings for his people, God has displayed his **steadfast love** and his **faithfulness**. These words, which evoke Ex. 34:6 (a fundamental aspect of God's character is his enduring love for his people), appear throughout the psalm (Ps. 89:1, 2, 14, 24, 28 [see ESV footnote], 33, 49). Verses 3–4 refer to the events of 2 Sam. 7:8–16: God's promise to David to **establish** his **offspring forever**. Because the promise is rooted in God's enduring love for his people, and is a **covenant** and an oath, i.e., a sworn purpose (Ps. 89:3), the term "forever" (v. 4) should receive its full weight. This sets up the "problem" that occasioned the psalm, namely, the humiliation that has come to the people ruled by David's heir (vv. 38–45); it also provides the confidence by which God's people can offer this prayer: they are asking God to be true to his own word.

89:5–18 *God Is above All Other Powers, and Has Shown Favor to Israel.* This section is praise to God, who is the Maker and Ruler of both the material creation and the angels (vv. 5–16). The marvel for Israel is that this God has pledged himself especially to them (vv. 15–17) and to their king (v. 18). This special privilege of Israel is a point frequently made in the OT (e.g., Ex. 19:5; Deut. 10:14–15).

89:5–7 holy ones. These are the angels (Job 15:15; Dan. 4:13; 8:13; Mark 8:38; Acts 10:22; Rev. 14:10), pictured as an **assembly** (Ps. 89:5) and **council** (v. 7), surrounding God and doing his will (cf. 1 Kings 22:19; Job 1:6; 2:1; Ps. 103:20–21). They are also called **heavenly beings** (ESV footnote, "sons

6 For [u]who in the skies can be compared to the LORD?
[u]Who among the heavenly beings[1] is like the LORD,
7 a God greatly [v]to be feared in the council of [t]the holy ones,
and awesome above all [w]who are around him?
8 O LORD God of hosts,
[x]who is mighty as you are, O [y]LORD,
with your faithfulness all around you?
9 You rule the raging of the sea;
when its waves rise, you [z]still them.
10 You [a]crushed [b]Rahab like a carcass;
you [c]scattered your enemies with your mighty arm.
11 [d]The heavens are yours; the earth also is yours;
[e]the world and all that is in it, you have [f]founded them.
12 [g]The north and the south, you have created them;
[h]Tabor and [i]Hermon [j]joyously praise your name.
13 You have a mighty arm;
strong is your hand, high your right hand.
14 [k]Righteousness and justice are the foundation of your throne;
[l]steadfast love and faithfulness go before you.
15 Blessed are the people who know [m]the festal shout,
who walk, O LORD, in [n]the light of your face,
16 who exult in your [o]name all the day
and in your righteousness are [p]exalted.
17 For you are [q]the glory of their strength;
by your favor our [r]horn is exalted.
18 For our [s]shield belongs to the LORD,
our king to [t]the Holy One of Israel.

19 [u]Of old you spoke in a vision to your godly one,[2] and said:
"I have [v]granted help to one who is [w]mighty;
I have exalted one [x]chosen from the people.
20 [y]I have found David, my servant;
with my holy oil I have [z]anointed him,
21 so that my [a]hand shall be established with him;
my arm also shall strengthen him.

6 [u]ver. 8; [Ps. 86:8]
7 [v]See Ps. 47:2 [t][See ver. 5 above] [w][Ps. 103:20, 21]
8 [x][1 Sam. 2:2]; See Ps. 35:10 [y]See Ps. 68:4
9 [z]Ps. 65:7; Job 38:11
10 [a][Ex. 14:30] [b]See Job 9:13 [c]See Ps. 53:5
11 [d]Gen. 1:1; 1 Chr. 29:11 [e]See Ps. 24:1 [f]See Ps. 104:5
12 [g]Job 26:7 [h]Jer. 46:18 [i]Deut. 3:9 [j]Ps. 98:8
14 [k]Ps. 97:2 [l]ver. 2; [Ps. 85:13]
15 [m]See Ps. 66:1 [n]See Ps. 4:6
16 [o][Ps. 20:5, 7] [p][Job 36:7]
17 [q][Ps. 78:61] [r]ver. 24; See Ps. 75:10
18 [s]Ps. 47:9 [t]See Ps. 71:22
19 [u][ver. 3, 4] [v][Ps. 21:5] [w]2 Sam. 17:10 [x]See ver. 3
20 [y]Cited Acts 13:22 [z]1 Sam. 16:13
21 [a]Ps. 80:17

[1] Hebrew *the sons of God, or the sons of might* [2] Some Hebrew manuscripts *godly ones*

of God"). The Lord is exalted above these most exalted of all creatures, and is worthy of their praise.

89:8–10 God is more **mighty** than any other being: he governs even the **raging of the sea** (unmanageable chaos to an Israelite) and the powers that dwell in it (**Rahab** could be a name for Egypt, seen as a great world power [cf. 87:4], but most take it to be a mythological beast that personifies the forces of chaos [cf. Job 9:13; 26:12; Isa. 51:9]).

89:11–12 Cf. 24:1–2. Because God is the Creator, the whole world belongs to him; and his creation will **joyously praise** his **name** (103:22). **Tabor** and **Hermon** are notable mountains in the land, Tabor in the Jezreel Valley and Hermon at the northern end. The most impressive features of the landscape acknowledge the greatness of their Creator.

89:13–14 These verses describe some of God's attributes, stressing his faithful commitment to his people. The pairing of God's **hand** and his **right hand** can refer to his power, as in Isa. 48:13, but here it is specifically his power for the sake of his own people (cf. Ps. 74:11; 138:7). Likewise God's **righteousness**, **justice**, **steadfast love**, and **faithfulness** all point to his reliability, his keeping of his promises, and his patient and enduring care even for people who are unworthy.

89:15–18 It is no wonder that the song moves on to glory in the privileges of being God's **people**, to whom God has given revelation (the **festal shout** is uttered in worship [cf. 27:6; 33:3]; they also have **the light of** God's **face** to guide their **walk**, i.e., lifestyle, and have received his **name**, i.e., the unveiling of his character [cf. Ex. 34:6–7]). God has also given them a special place in his plan for the world (they are **exalted**, and God pledges his **strength** on their behalf). The **shield** here is the **king**, whose task is to protect the people by representing them before God, embodying covenant faithfulness (cf. Ps. 84:9). Although the "shields" of all nations belong to God, Israel's king enjoys a distinctive role, just as Israel enjoys a distinctive role for the sake of the world. **Holy One of Israel**. See note on 71:22.

89:19–37 *God Promised an Enduring Dynasty to David.* The mention of the king's role in Israel (v. 18) leads to the story of how the line of David came into the kingship, and what promises God made to that line. The psalm draws on the story of David's anointing (1 Sam. 16:1–13) and God's oath to David (2 Sam. 7:4–17).

89:19 Your godly one most likely refers to Nathan, who received God's instructions by night in a **vision** (cf. 2 Sam. 7:17). If the Hebrew manuscripts that have the plural "godly ones" (see ESV footnote) are correct, then it refers to both Nathan and Samuel (cf. 1 Sam. 16:1–3; prophets typically received God's speech in dreams and visions [1 Sam. 3:1; cf. Num. 12:6]). On God's choice of David, cf. 1 Sam. 13:14 and 15:28.

89:20 servant. See note on 78:70. **anointed**. See 1 Sam. 16:13, and note on Ps. 2:2.

89:21 For God's **hand** and **arm**, see v. 13.

22[b][2 Sam. 7:10]
23[c][2 Sam. 7:9]; See Ps. 2:9
24[d]ver. 1 [e]ver. 17
25[f]See Ps. 72:8
26[g][2 Sam. 7:14] [h][Ps. 18:2]
27[i]Ex. 4:22; [Rom. 8:29; Col. 1:15, 18; Heb. 1:5] [j]Num. 24:7; [Rev. 19:16]
28[k]See ver. 3
29[l]See ver. 4 [m]See Job 14:12
30[n]2 Sam. 7:14; 1 Kgs. 2:4
32[o]See Job 9:34
34[k][See ver. 28 above]
35[p]See Ps. 60:6 [q][Heb. 6:18]
36[l][See ver. 29 above] [r]See ver. 4 [s]See Ps. 72:5
37[s][See ver. 36 above] [t]See Job 16:19
38[u]See Ps. 44:9 [v]ver. 20, 51
39[w]Lam. 2:7 [x]See ver. 3 [y]See Ps. 74:7 [z]Job 19:9

22 The enemy shall not outwit him;
[b]the wicked shall not humble him.
23 I will [c]crush his foes before him
and strike down those who hate him.
24 My [d]faithfulness and my [d]steadfast love shall be with him,
and in my name shall his [e]horn be exalted.
25 I will set his hand on [f]the sea
and his right hand on [f]the rivers.
26 He shall cry to me, 'You are my [g]Father,
my God, and [h]the Rock of my salvation.'
27 And I will make him the [i]firstborn,
[j]the highest of the kings of the earth.
28 My steadfast love I will keep for him forever,
and my [k]covenant will stand firm[1] for him.
29 I will establish his [l]offspring forever
and his [l]throne as [m]the days of the heavens.
30 [n]If his children forsake my law
and do not walk according to my rules,[2]
31 if they violate my statutes
and do not keep my commandments,
32 then I will punish their transgression with [o]the rod
and their iniquity with stripes,
33 but I will not remove from him my steadfast love
or be false to my faithfulness.
34 I will not violate my [k]covenant
or alter the word that went forth from my lips.
35 Once for all I have sworn [p]by my holiness;
I will not [q]lie to David.
36 His [l]offspring shall endure forever,
[r]his [l]throne as long as [s]the sun before me.
37 Like [s]the moon it shall be established forever,
[t]a faithful witness in the skies." *Selah*

38 But now you have [u]cast off and rejected;
you are full of wrath against your [v]anointed.
39 You have [w]renounced [x]the covenant with your servant;
you have [y]defiled his [z]crown in the dust.

[1] *Or will remain faithful* [2] *Or my just decrees*

89:22–23 On God's commitment to grant success to David and his heirs, see note on 21:8–12.

89:24–25 steadfast love. Cf. v. 33; 2 Sam. 7:15. **horn be exalted**. Cf. Ps. 89:17, where it is the people's "horn": the people's horn is exalted in connection with David's horn being exalted. (On the image, see note on 75:4.) The heirs of David represent and embody the people. For **hand** and **right hand**, cf. 89:13, where it is God's hand. The king also serves the people as God's representative.

89:26–28 Father . . . firstborn. Cf. 2 Sam. 7:14. Just as Israel is God's "firstborn" (Ex. 4:22), so the king is the firstborn as the people's embodiment (see note on Ps. 2:7). The NT calls Jesus the "firstborn," portraying him as the exalted heir of David who represents his people (Rom. 8:29; Col. 1:15, 18; Heb. 1:6; Rev. 1:5); he is the one who fulfills the prospect of being **the highest of the kings of the earth** (Rev. 1:5; 19:16; cf. Matt. 28:18–19; he is bringing the Gentiles to acknowledge this).

89:28–37 Cf. 2 Sam. 7:12–16. David's dynasty will not fail, but will indeed achieve its purpose (see note on Ps. 89:26–28). This does not mean that the particular occupants of the throne will be successful regardless of their faithfulness, nor does it imply that the dynasty can never go into obscurity (as it did during the exile). The lineage did survive, though its heir Zerubbabel was only a "governor" (Hag. 1:1); even so, God kept his promise (Hag. 2:23; see Matt. 1:12–16; Luke 3:23–27).

89:36–37 sun . . . moon. Cf. 72:5, 17.

89:38–45 *But Now You Have Renounced Your Promises to David.* With all this glorious background, the psalm moves to its current situation: it *looks* and *feels* as if God has forsaken his promises to the house of David (and thus to his people). This section takes up words from the preceding parts of the psalm in order to stress the feeling of reversal: God's **anointed** (v. 38) was his special choice (v. 20), but now God is **full of wrath against** him; the **covenant** (v. 39) that should have meant security (v. 34), God has **renounced**; the king's "right hand" (v. 42) should govern even the rivers (v. 25), but now God has **exalted the right hand of his foes**; David's **throne** (v. 44) was to endure as long as the sun (vv. 29, 36), but now God has **cast it to the ground**. Rather than the reigning heir of David being "the highest of the kings of the earth" (v. 27), now all the Gentiles triumph over him and his people (vv. 40–43). Although this description sounds bleak, the psalm is not hopeless. In recognizing that the current situation seems to express God's "wrath against the anointed" (v. 38), it looks back to vv. 30–32: this current hardship may be God's chastisement upon the king for unfaithfulness, and thus be a call to repentance.

40 You have [a]breached all his walls;
you have laid his strongholds in ruins.
41 [a]All who pass by plunder him;
he has become [b]the scorn of his neighbors.
42 You have exalted the right hand of his foes;
you have made all his enemies rejoice.
43 You have also turned back the edge of his sword,
and you have not made him stand in battle.
44 You have made his splendor to cease
and cast his throne to the ground.
45 You have cut short [c]the days of his youth;
you have [d]covered him with shame. *Selah*

46 [e]How long, O LORD? Will you hide yourself forever?
How long will your wrath [f]burn like fire?
47 [g]Remember [h]how short my [i]time is!
For what vanity you have created all the children of man!
48 [j]What man can live and never [k]see death?
Who can deliver his soul from the power of [l]Sheol? *Selah*

49 Lord, where is your [m]steadfast love of old,
which by your [m]faithfulness you swore to David?
50 [n]Remember, O Lord, how your servants are mocked,
and how I bear in my [o]heart the insults[1] of all the many nations,
51 with which your enemies mock, O LORD,
with which they mock [p]the footsteps of your [q]anointed.

52 [r]Blessed be the LORD forever!
Amen and Amen.

BOOK FOUR

From Everlasting to Everlasting

90

A [s]PRAYER OF MOSES, THE [t]MAN OF GOD.

1 Lord, you have been our [u]dwelling place[2]
in all generations.

[1] Hebrew lacks *the insults* [2] Some Hebrew manuscripts (compare Septuagint) *our refuge*

40[a]See Ps. 80:12
41[a][See ver. 40 above] [b][ver. 50]; See Ps. 44:13; 69:9, 19
45[c]Ps. 102:23 [d]Ps. 71:13; 109:29
46[e]See Ps. 13:1 [f]Ps. 78:63; 79:5
47[g]Job 7:7; 10:9 [h][Job 14:1] [i]Ps. 39:5
48[j][Ps. 49:9] [k][Luke 2:26; Heb. 11:5] [l]See Ps. 16:10
49[m][ver. 1, 2]
50[n][ver. 41]; See Ps. 74:18, 22 [o]Ps. 79:12
51[p][Ps. 17:11; 56:6] [q]ver. 20, 38
52[r]See Ps. 41:13

Psalm 90
[s]Ps. 17, title; 55:1 [t]Deut. 33:1; Josh. 14:6; Ezra 3:2
1[u]See Ps. 71:3

89:46–51 *O Lord, Show Your Steadfast Love by Restoring David's Throne.* There is great comfort in the promise of an enduring Davidic house, and thus the present low estate of God's people is not the end of their story; yet the faithful pray that even now God may see fit to relieve the hardship. Each generation of the faithful knows that its time is short (vv. 47–48) and yearns to see some foretaste of God's ultimate vindication of his promises to his people. It *feels* wrong for God's people, whose king is eventually to rule all the kings of the earth (v. 27), to be subject to the **insults of all the many nations** (v. 50), so that the Gentiles **mock the footsteps of** God's **anointed** (v. 51). The appeal is to God's **steadfast love** and **faithfulness** (v. 49, see note on vv. 1–4) expressed in his oath to David (v. 24), and not to any claims of merit.

89:52 *Doxology Concluding Book 3.* See note on 41:13.

Psalm 90. This community lament has some unspecified disaster (vv. 13, 15) as its background, and asks God to have pity on his people and bless them. The title, which ascribes the psalm to Moses, invites the singing congregation to picture Israel around the time of Deuteronomy, as they were about to cross the Jordan River and enter the Promised Land. Their parents had followed Moses out of Egypt, through the parted Red Sea—and yet they rebelled, so that God swore that they would not enter the land (Num. 14:20–36). For the Israelites to accomplish their mission and for God to establish the work of their hands (Ps. 90:17) would require that the people embrace the covenant and live in faith toward God. Those who sing this should see themselves as the heirs of that generation, seeking like them the blessing of God so that they can carry out their mission. This psalm stresses time and how it passes, as can be seen from the various time words throughout: "days" (vv. 4, 9, 12, 14, 15); "years" (vv. 4, 9–10, 15); cf. the description of God as eternal and unchanging, "in all generations" (v. 1); "from everlasting to everlasting" (v. 2). The awareness of how short human life is (v. 10) leads to earnest prayer for God's help, without which his people can accomplish nothing of lasting value (vv. 16–17). This psalm is the basis of the familiar hymn, "O God, Our Help in Ages Past." The title points to this lament as a prayer by "Moses, the man of God." Cf. Deut. 33:1; Josh. 14:6. Generally, the OT uses the expression "man of God" for a prophet, e.g., 1 Sam. 2:27; 9:6; 1 Kings 12:22; 13:1; 17:18; 2 Kings 4:7. Moses was, of course, a prophet par excellence.

90:1–2 *The Lord Is Eternal.* The Lord is the **dwelling place**, i.e., the home and refuge, for his people **in all generations** because he himself is eternal. He has been God since **before** the creation. That God is the Creator is assumed, and that the Lord has always been God indicates that he always will be, i.e., that he will not change.

2 [v]Before the [w]mountains were brought forth,
or ever you had formed the earth and the world,
[x]from everlasting to everlasting you are God.

3 You return man to dust
and say, [y]"Return, [z]O children of man!"[1]
4 For [a]a thousand years in your sight
are but as [b]yesterday when it is past,
or as [c]a watch in the night.

5 You [d]sweep them away as with a flood; they are like [e]a dream,
like [f]grass that is renewed in the morning:
6 in [i]the morning it flourishes and is renewed;
in the evening it [j]fades and [k]withers.

7 For we are brought to an end by your anger;
by your wrath we are dismayed.
8 You have [l]set our iniquities before you,
our [m]secret sins in the light of your presence.

9 For all our days pass away under your wrath;
we bring our years to an end like a sigh.
10 The years of our life are seventy,
or even by reason of strength eighty;
yet their span[2] is but toil and trouble;
they are soon gone, and we fly away.
11 Who considers the power of your anger,
and your wrath according to the fear of you?

12 [n]So teach us to number our days
that we may get a heart of wisdom.
13 [o]Return, O LORD! [p]How long?
Have [q]pity on your servants!
14 Satisfy us in the [s]morning with your steadfast love,
that we may [t]rejoice and be glad all our days.
15 Make us glad for as many days as you have [u]afflicted us,
and for as many years as we have seen evil.
16 Let your [v]work be shown to your servants,
and your glorious power to their children.

2 [v]Prov. 8:25 [w][Deut. 33:15; Job 15:7] [x]See Job 36:26
3 [y]Gen. 3:19 [z]Eccles. 12:7
4 [a]2 Pet. 3:8 [b][Ps. 39:5] [c]Ex. 14:24; Judg. 7:19
5 [d]Ps. 58:9 [e]See Job 20:8 [f]Ps. 37:2; 103:15; 2 Kgs. 19:26; Isa. 40:6-8; 1 Pet. 1:24
6 [i]See Job 4:20 [j]Job 14:2; [Ps. 92:7] [k]James 1:11
8 [l]Jer. 16:17; Heb. 4:13 [m]Ps. 19:12
12 [n]Ps. 39:4
13 [o]Ps. 6:4 [p]See Ps. 74:9, 10 [q]Ps. 106:45; 135:14; Ex. 32:12; Deut. 32:36; Judg. 2:18; Jonah 3:10; See Gen. 6:6
14 [s]See Ps. 46:5 [t]See Ps. 85:6
15 [u][Deut. 8:2]
16 [v]Ps. 77:12; 92:4; 95:9; Deut. 32:4; Hab. 3:2

[1] *Or of Adam* [2] *Or pride*

90:3–6 *But Man's Life Is Fleeting.* In contrast to God's eternity, human life—even the longest imaginable (**a thousand years**, v. 4)—is insignificantly brief (as expressed in the images of **a watch in the night**, **a flood**, **a dream**, and **grass**). Cf. 103:15–18; Job 14:1–2; Isa. 40:6–8; James 1:11. The psalm evokes God's sentence in Eden on the sin of Adam and Eve (Ps. 90:3), which means that the fleeting life span is due to the entry of sin into the world (i.e., it is not an inherent part of being human).

90:3 return man to dust. Even though the word "dust" here (Hb. *dakka'*) is not the same as that in Gen. 3:19 (Hb. *'apar*, the ordinary word), the coupling of "return" with a word for loose soil makes the reference to Genesis clear.

90:7–11 *We Are Brought to an End by Your Wrath.* The people of God reflect on the unfaithfulness of past generations (in which they harbored **iniquities** and **secret sins**, v. 8), which resulted in God's **anger** and **wrath** (vv. 7, 9, 11). The whole body of God's people suffers from the presence and influence of its unfaithful members, and God's judgments that purge them from his people are hard even for the faithful to endure. Hence the whole people experience **toil and trouble** during their brief span of life.

90:10 seventy . . . eighty. This gives an "ordinary" life span; many live fewer years (due to violence, accident, and disease), and a few live longer (e.g., Joseph, Gen. 50:26; Moses, Deut. 34:7; Joshua, Josh. 24:29). In any case, it is much briefer than a thousand years (Ps. 90:4), let alone God's eternity.

90:11 your wrath according to the fear of you. God's wrath toward his unfaithful people is in accordance with the "fear" (reverence, faith, and humble, holiness-seeking love) that they ought to have toward him (cf. note on Prov. 1:7).

90:12–17 *Teach Us Wisdom and Establish Our Work.* These considerations lead to eager prayer for God to guide his people in faithful living (v. 12), to draw near to them and make them glad (vv. 13–15), and to bless their endeavors (vv. 16–17).

90:12 teach us to number our days. In view of the theme of the psalm, this refers especially to the ability to make the most of one's days, since they are so few. The **heart of wisdom** would enable the faithful to live by the right priorities (cf. the "fear" of God, v. 11).

90:13–15 Return, i.e., come back to us, turn from your anger (cf. Ex. 32:12). **in the morning**. Probably a metaphor, where the current situation is the night and the singers look eagerly for the light of morning (cf. Ps. 30:5; 46:5; 59:16; 130:6; 143:8), the time when God will make his **steadfast love** clear to his people. Then they will be able to **rejoice and be glad all** their **days**.

90:16–17 Let your work be shown, i.e., display your love toward your people in great deeds of power that enable them to flourish. **to their children**. God made his covenant with Abraham and with his offspring (who must themselves embrace the covenant), and the OT faithful seek the continuation of the people through their own pious children (cf. 78:3–8; 103:17; 145:4). **favor**. Or "beauty" (see ESV footnote; Hb. *no'am*, cf. 27:4). God's own beauty

17 Let the [x]favor[1] of the Lord our God be upon us,
and establish [y]the work of our hands upon us;
yes, establish the work of our hands!

My Refuge and My Fortress

91

1 He who dwells in [a]the shelter of the Most High
will abide in [b]the shadow of the Almighty.
2 I will say[2] to the LORD, "My [c]refuge and my [d]fortress,
my God, in whom I [e]trust."
3 For he will deliver you from [f]the snare of the fowler
and from the deadly pestilence.
4 He will [g]cover you with his pinions,
and under his [h]wings you will [i]find refuge;
his [j]faithfulness is [k]a shield and buckler.
5 [l]You will not fear [m]the terror of the night,
nor the arrow that flies by day,
6 nor the pestilence that stalks in darkness,
nor the destruction that wastes at noonday.

7 A thousand may fall at your side,
ten thousand at your right hand,
but it will not come near you.
8 You will only look with your eyes
and [n]see the recompense of the wicked.

9 Because you have made the LORD your [o]dwelling place—
the Most High, who is my [c]refuge[3]—
10 [p]no evil shall be allowed to befall you,
[q]no plague come near your tent.

11 [r]For he will command his [s]angels concerning you
to [t]guard you in all your ways.

[1] Or *beauty* [2] Septuagint *He will say* [3] Or *For you, O LORD, are my refuge! You have made the Most High your dwelling place*

17 [x]Ps. 27:4 [y][Ps. 128:2]; [Isa. 26:12]

Psalm 91

1 [a]See Ps. 32:7 [b]Ps. 121:5; [Isa. 25:4; 32:2]
2 [c]ver. 9; See Ps. 14:6 [d]See Ps. 18:2 [e]See Ps. 11:1
3 [f]Ps. 124:7; 140:5; 141:9; Prov. 6:5
4 [g][1 Kgs. 8:7] [h]See Ps. 17:8 [i]Ps. 57:1 [j]See Ps. 36:5 [k]See Ps. 35:2
5 [l]Prov. 3:23; Isa. 43:1; See Job 5:19-23 [m]Song 3:8
8 [n]See Ps. 37:34
9 [o]See Ps. 71:3 [c][See ver. 2 above]
10 [p][ver. 5]; See Prov. 12:21 [q]Ps. 38:11
11 [r]Cited Matt. 4:6; Luke 4:10, 11 [s]See Ps. 34:7 [t]Ex. 23:20

is on display through his faithful servants. **The work of our hands** is the work that God's people do in pursuit of their calling (Deut. 14:29; 16:15; 24:19).

Psalm 91. This tender and intimate psalm describes the confidence that the believer may have through all manner of dangers and challenges. The psalm speaks about the faithful person as "he" (vv. 1, 14–16), addresses him directly as "you" (singular; vv. 3–13), and gives him words to say as "I" (v. 2). Some have suggested that all of these are Israel speaking as a whole, but the situations in view in the psalm (e.g., pestilence, vv. 3, 6; terrors by night and arrows, v. 5; one's fellows falling, v. 7) are those primarily faced by particular persons. Of course, Israel as a whole finds refuge in God and is covered by his divine wings, but the nation's members see this in their individual lives as well.

91:1–2 *God Is My Refuge.* The opening section sets out the basic theme of the whole psalm: the Lord is a secure defense for those who take refuge in him. Several terms for security appear: **shelter** (that hides one from danger), **shadow** (e.g., of the wings, v. 4; cf. 17:8; 36:7; 57:1; 63:7), **refuge** (a place of security), and **fortress** (protecting one from attack). The titles of God support this idea: **Most High** (Hb. *'elyon*, high above every other power) and **Almighty** (Hb. *Shadday*; see note on Gen. 17:1–2). The term **my God, in whom I trust** displays the utter reliance that is the ideal of biblical faith. The purpose of this psalm is to instill greater faith in God's people, and the first section helps the singers to feel that God is trustworthy.

91:3–8 *He Will Protect You from Danger.* **you**. These verses personally address each one who sings this, listing the benefits that come to those who trust in the Lord. The **snare of the fowler** (v. 3) seems to be a metaphor for the schemes of those who hate the pious (cf. 119:110; 140:1–5). **Pestilence** (91:3, 6) and **destruction** are diseases that God sends on his enemies or his unfaithful people (cf. Ex. 5:3; 9:15; Lev. 26:25; Deut. 32:24, "plagues"). The **terror** and **arrow**, together with **a thousand may fall**, envision God's people under attack. If the psalm were describing every situation of danger, it would clearly be untrue: faithful people have fallen prey to these and other perils. It is better to allow Ps. 91:8 to guide the interpretation, pointing to cases in which these events (plague, battle) are sent as God's **recompense** on the **wicked** (whether Gentile or Israelite); in such cases, the faithful can be sure of God's protection.

91:4 pinions . . . wings. For the image of God as a protecting bird, cf. Ex. 19:4; Deut. 32:11; see also note on Ps. 91:1–2 ("shadow").

91:9–13 *His Angels Will Watch over You.* This section continues the description of safety, adding the involvement of God's **angels** to watch over those who make **the Most High** their **refuge** (cf. vv. 1–2). The mention of a **plague** (v. 10) is reminiscent of the plagues that fell on Egypt (cf. Gen. 12:17; Ex. 11:1), again clarifying that this is describing the safety of the faithful in a time of God's judgment.

91:11–12 In Matt. 4:6 (cf. Luke 4:10–11), the devil quotes these verses in a ploy to get Jesus to seek a demonstration of the angels' care for all the Jews to see (throwing himself down from the pinnacle of the temple), which would no doubt win Jesus a great following among the people. Jesus denounces the idea as testing God; it is certainly a willful misuse of the psalm passage, which does not encourage the faithful to put themselves in unnecessary danger.

12[u]Prov. 3:23; [Ps. 37:24]
13[v][Dan. 6:23] [w][Acts 28:5] [x]See Ps. 74:13 [y]Luke 10:19; [Mark 16:18]
14[z]Deut. 7:7; 10:15 [a]Ps. 9:10
15[b]Job 12:4; See Ps. 50:15 [c]1 Sam. 2:30; John 12:26
16[d]Ps. 21:4; Deut. 6:2; 1 Kgs. 3:14; Prov. 3:2, 16 [e]Ps. 50:23; [Ps. 118:14, 21]
Psalm 92
1[f]Ps. 147:1; [Ps. 71:22] [g][Gen. 14:19, 20]
2[h]See Ps. 36:5 [i][Ps. 119:147, 148]
3[j]See Ps. 33:2
4[k]See Ps. 90:16 [l]Ps. 8:6
5[m]Ps. 111:2; Rev. 15:3 [n]Ps. 40:5; 139:17 [o][Rom. 11:33]; See Ps. 36:6
7[p]See Job 21:7 [q]Ps. 94:4; 125:5
8[r]Ps. 93:4
9[s]See Ps. 68:1

12 On their hands they will bear you up,
lest you [u]strike your foot against a stone.
13 You will tread on [v]the lion and the [w]adder;
the young lion and [x]the serpent you will [y]trample underfoot.

14 "Because he [z]holds fast to me in love, I will deliver him;
I will protect him, because he [a]knows my name.
15 When he [b]calls to me, I will answer him;
I will be with him in trouble;
I will rescue him and [c]honor him.
16 With [d]long life I will satisfy him
and [e]show him my salvation."

How Great Are Your Works

92

A PSALM. A SONG FOR THE SABBATH.

1 [f]It is good to give thanks to the LORD,
to sing praises to your name, [g]O Most High;
2 to declare your [h]steadfast love in [i]the morning,
and your [h]faithfulness by [i]night,
3 to the music of [j]the lute and [j]the harp,
to the melody of [j]the lyre.
4 For you, O LORD, have made me glad by your [k]work;
at [l]the works of your hands I sing for joy.

5 How [m]great are your works, O LORD!
Your [n]thoughts are very [o]deep!
6 The stupid man cannot know;
the fool cannot understand this:
7 that though [p]the wicked sprout like grass
and all [q]evildoers flourish,
they are doomed to destruction forever;
8 but you, O LORD, are [r]on high forever.
9 For behold, your enemies, O LORD,
for behold, your enemies shall perish;
all evildoers shall be [s]scattered.

91:13 The lion and the adder are probably images for people bent on harming the faithful (cf. 58:3–6; Deut. 32:33), or perhaps the demonic agents that inspire the harm.

91:14–16 *"Because He Loves Me, I Will Deliver Him."* The psalm closes by laying out what the ideal of trust looks like (**holds fast to me in love, knows my name,** and **calls to** God in times of trouble) and repeating God's pledge to care for his faithful ones (**deliver, protect, answer, be with him in trouble, rescue, honor**). Such a person will have **long life** (Hb. *'orek yamim*, "length of days," probably implying eternal life; cf. note on 23:5–6) and will enjoy God's **salvation** (see note on 3:2).

Psalm 92. This is a hymn of thanks and praise to God, specifically celebrating the blessing of the Sabbath institution in Israel. The Sabbath was a day of rest and a day for gathered worship (Lev. 23:3), and worship is the focus of the psalm. Besides the title ("A song for the Sabbath"), features that display this specific focus include the references to morning and evening worship (Ps. 92:2), to the musical instruments used in worship (v. 3), and to the temple (v. 13).

92:1–5 *Weekly Sabbath Worship Is Good.* One of the most basic features of worship on the Sabbath day is celebrating God's greatness in presiding over his creation and his goodness toward his faithful. The words **give thanks, sing praises, declare,** and **sing for joy** all describe the significance of the songs sung in gathered worship, along with musical accompaniment (**lute, harp, lyre**). The songs honor God for what he has revealed about himself, recalling Ex. 34:5–7, where God explained his **name** (Ps. 92:1), especially his benevolence toward his people (he is abounding in **steadfast love** and **faithfulness**). God's **work** and **works** are the great deeds he has done in creating the world and in caring for his people.

92:6–11 *Contrasts: The Godless Will Perish, but I Will Only See Them Perish.* The next section draws a contrast between the members of the people who are unfaithful to the covenant (called **stupid, fool, wicked,** God's **enemies,** and **evildoers,** vv. 6–9) and those who hold fast to God in love and trust (the "I" singing the psalm; cf. **my** and **me** in vv. 10–11). The unfaithful are unable to grasp that no matter how they might **flourish** (v. 7) for the moment, God's will alone prevails in the end; God will bring judgment upon those who despise him (esp. those among his people). God, who is **on high forever,** openly displays those who are faithful to him, "exalting" (v. 10; "making high") their **horn** (a symbol of power and strength derived from the image of the horns of an animal; cf. note on 75:4). The terms **my eyes have seen** and **my ears have heard** indicate that the destruction of the wicked, who seemed so prosperous and dangerous (92:7), vindicates the way the faithful kept their loyalty to God in the face of the seductive temptation to give in to the unfaithful.

92:9 The three lines of this verse build up to a peak, each adding something to the previous line (cf. 93:3). **perish . . . scattered.** Like "destruction" (92:7), these terms describe the judgment on the wicked as if it is a defeat in battle. Judgment extends, when necessary, into the afterlife (see note on 49:13–20). A Ugaritic text from the second millennium B.C. has a structure very similar to 92:9, although it praises Baal (rather than Yahweh): "Now your enemies, O Baal; now your enemies you will smite; now you will vanquish your foes." The biblical poets used the literary forms of their culture but always were clear that it was Yahweh who deserved their praise.

10 But you have exalted my [t]horn like that of [u]the wild ox;
you have [v]poured over me[1] fresh oil.
11 My [w]eyes have seen the downfall of my enemies;
my ears have heard the doom of my evil assailants.

12 [x]The righteous flourish like the palm tree
and grow like a cedar in Lebanon.
13 They are planted in the house of the LORD;
they flourish in [y]the courts of our God.
14 They still bear fruit in old age;
they are ever full of sap and green,
15 [z]to declare that the LORD is upright;
he is my [a]rock, and there is [b]no unrighteousness in him.

93

The LORD Reigns

1 [c]The LORD reigns; he is [d]robed in majesty;
the LORD is [e]robed; he has [f]put on strength as his belt.
[g]Yes, the world is established; [h]it shall never be moved.
2 [i]Your throne is established from of old;
[j]you are from everlasting.

3 [k]The floods have lifted up, O LORD,
the floods have lifted up their voice;
the floods lift up their roaring.
4 Mightier than the thunders of many waters,
mightier than the waves of the sea,
[l]the LORD [m]on high is mighty!

5 Your [n]decrees are very trustworthy;
[o]holiness befits your house,
O LORD, forevermore.

[1] Compare Syriac; the meaning of the Hebrew is uncertain

10 [t]See Ps. 75:10; 1 Sam. 2:1 [u]Num. 23:22 [v]See Ps. 23:5
11 [w]See Ps. 37:34; 54:7
12 [x]Ps. 1:3; 52:8; 72:7; Prov. 11:28; [Num. 24:6; Isa. 61:3]; See Hos. 14:5-8
13 [y]Ps. 100:4; 116:19; 135:2
15 [z][Ps. 58:11] [a]See Ps. 18:2 [b]See Job 34:10

Psalm 93

1 [c]Ps. 96:10; See 1 Chr. 16:31 [d]Ps. 104:1 [e]Isa. 51:9 [f]Ps. 65:6 [g]Ps. 96:10; [Ps. 46:5] [h]See Ps. 125:1
2 [i][Ps. 45:6] [j]Ps. 90:2
3 [k][Ps. 98:7, 8; Hab. 3:10]
4 [l]See Ps. 65:6, 7 [m]Ps. 92:8
5 [n][Ps. 89:28, 37] [o]See Ps. 29:2

92:10 exalted my horn. See note on 75:4. **The wild ox** is the aurochs, which is the ancestor of domestic cattle but is now extinct. The animal was known for its strength, and its horns were effective for goring (cf. 22:21; Deut. 33:17). Because the Greek translators used "one-horned" (Gk. *monokerōs*) to translate (incorrectly) the Hebrew term here, older English versions translated the word "unicorn" (the Latin Vulgate used a word signifying either rhinoceros or unicorn).

92:12–15 *The Everlasting Sabbath.* Cf. Heb. 4:9. This section describes the permanent security enjoyed by the faithful. They **flourish like the palm tree** (Ps. 92:12; the date palm, long-lived and stately, cf. v. 14), and they **flourish in the courts of our God**, which indicates enduring residence in God's presence (cf. 23:6) as opposed to the temporary "flourishing" of the evildoers (92:7), who "are doomed to destruction." In these courts, the faithful will **declare** (cf. v. 2) with enjoyment God's perfect faithfulness and righteousness. For the imagery of a tree, cf. 1:3. This passage, with its aura of permanent vitality, enables the faithful to look forward to an eternity in God's presence, singing his praise (see note on 23:5–6).

Psalm 93. Psalms 29; 93; and 95–99 are hymns of praise for divine kingship, namely, God's kingly rule over creation. The idea of God as universal king is of course rooted in the creation account; the specific words first appear in Ex. 15:18. When the OT speaks of the kingship of God, it can mean his kingship over all creation, or it can mean God's acknowledged kingship over his people (1 Sam. 8:7; 12:12–15); the NT expression "kingdom of God" focuses on the way God ministers to and governs his people through the heir of David. In each case, it is important to discern which of these is primarily in view. The psalms of divine kingship especially celebrate God's kingship over his creation. Even though it is important to distinguish these ideas, one should not separate them: it is Israel's great privilege that the God who rules over them is the universal Creator and Lord, who one day will rule all nations. Psalm 93 ends with this experience of wonder. The conviction that God reigns is the ultimate antidote to doubt and despair (cf. 89:38–51).

93:1–2 *The Lord Reigns, and Thus the World and God's Throne Are Stable.* The Lord **reigns** as king; because his **throne is established** (v. 2) and secure, therefore **the world is established** (v. 1), a stable and reliable place to live. The security of God's throne is here traced to his awesome and majestic power (he is **robed, he has put on strength as his belt**) and his eternity (he is **from everlasting**).

93:1 the world . . . shall never be moved. At one time this passage (cf. 96:10; 104:5) was taken to support the picture of the universe in which the earth is stationary and everything revolves around it. However, the verse does not imply this, for the term translated "moved" simply implies some kind of instability, and "never be moved" points to God-given security. (The psalmist is not concerned with the kind of motion that physics studies.) Cf. 46:5; 125:1; note on 10:6. The expression probably means that the world's ongoing order (and the moral principles that underlie that order) are faithful and sure, guaranteed by God's own faithfulness.

93:3–4 *The Lord Is Mightier than the Raging Sea.* To an Israelite, the raging sea (also called **floods** and **many waters**) was the most vivid emblem of uncontrollable chaos. This section insists that the divine king is **mightier** than even that. Both of these verses use "building parallelism," a kind of parallelism in which each successive line adds to or clarifies the line before it (cf. 92:9).

93:5 *God's Decrees Are Trustworthy.* God's **decrees are very trustworthy** and **holiness befits** his **house**, because the moral order of the universe reflects God's own character and is therefore stable and reliable. The laws given to Israel are based on this stable moral order, because Israel's calling is to be God's renewed humanity after the fall of Adam and Eve, and thus it is a fixed point that only those who constantly pursue holiness will constantly enjoy God.

Psalm 94

1[p]Deut. 32:35, 41, 43; Isa. 35:4; Jer. 51:56; Nah. 1:2; Rom. 12:19 [q]See Ps. 50:2
2[r]See Ps. 7:6 [s]See Ps. 58:11 [t]Luke 1:51
3[u]Rev. 6:10; See Ps. 74:10 [v][Job 20:5]
4[w]Ps. 31:18; 1 Sam. 2:3; [Jude 15] [x]Ps. 92:7, 9; 125:5
5[y][Prov. 22:22; Isa. 3:15]
6[z][Isa. 10:2]
7[a]See Job 22:13
8[b]See Ps. 49:10
9[c][Ex. 4:11; Prov. 20:12]
10[d][Job 12:23] [e]See Job 35:11
11[f]Cited 1 Cor. 3:20 [g][Ps. 30:5, 11]

94

The Lord Will Not Forsake His People

1 O Lord, God of [p]vengeance,
O God of vengeance, [q]shine forth!
2 [r]Rise up, O [s]judge of the earth;
repay to the [t]proud what they deserve!
3 O Lord, [u]how long shall the wicked,
how long shall [v]the wicked exult?
4 They pour out their [w]arrogant words;
all [x]the evildoers boast.
5 They [y]crush your people, O Lord,
and afflict your heritage.
6 They kill [z]the widow and the sojourner,
and murder [z]the fatherless;
7 [a]and they say, "The Lord does not see;
the God of Jacob does not perceive."

8 [b]Understand, O dullest of the people!
Fools, when will you be wise?
9 [c]He who planted the ear, does he not hear?
He who formed the eye, does he not see?
10 He who [d]disciplines the nations, does he not rebuke?
He who [e]teaches man knowledge—
11 [f]the Lord—knows the thoughts of man,
that they are [g]but a breath.[1]

[1] Septuagint *they are futile*

Psalm 94. This is a community lament, for a time when the wicked not only exult (v. 3) but also oppress the faithful (many of whom are socially weak, vv. 5–6), doing so with no fear of God. The song asks God to take action to protect the faithful. At the same time, it strengthens the pious to endure this oppression without losing heart or going over to join the wicked; it does this by recounting God's exhaustive knowledge of all that people think, do, and say (vv. 8–11); by remembering God's steadfast love for his own (v. 18); and by rejoicing in God's righteous commitment to bring justice by caring for the weak and putting down the wicked. Thus the godly can view their current circumstances as God's discipline (v. 12), even while they pray for deliverance (v. 16). The "wicked" in this psalm are members of God's people (v. 8) who in their hearts do not believe in the God of the covenant (v. 7). They seem to have political power, or at least influence with the ruling authorities (cf. v. 20, "wicked rulers"), which enables them to crush the faithful. Though such wicked persons are in one sense "members" of the covenant people, they are distinguished from God's true "people" or "heritage" (vv. 5, 14) and will suffer the full force of God's judgment. It puzzles scholars why this psalm is placed here, interrupting the sequence of divine kingship psalms (Psalms 93; 95–99). Perhaps the simplest explanation is that God's powerful kingship guarantees his final victory over all who oppose him, even if they are members of his own people (who ought to have acknowledged his rule!). It is always worth being on God's side.

94:1–3 *O Lord, Pay the Proud as They Deserve.* The psalm opens by addressing the Lord as **God of vengeance**, asking him to **repay to the proud what they deserve**. As the song develops, it will be clear who these "proud" are and why it is right to pray that God will "pay them back."

94:1 The notion of **vengeance** here is founded on God's justice: he brings his righteous judgment on those who oppose him and harm his people (cf. Deut. 32:35, 41, 43; Ps. 18:47). It is forbidden for individuals to take personal vengeance (Lev. 19:18; cf. Rom. 12:19), but one function of the civil government is to ensure just vengeance against wrongdoers (Ex. 21:20; cf. Rom. 13:4)—a function not being carried out in the context of this psalm. God will carry out vengeance against those who despise him (2 Thess. 1:8), and the faithful will rejoice because God's justice has been vindicated (Ps. 58:10; 79:10; Rev. 6:10). There is no double standard: God will judge the unfaithful among his own people as well as the Gentiles (cf. Ps. 99:8).

94:2–3 The people called **proud** here are not simply those among the faithful who commit the sin of pride; rather, in their unbelief they exalt themselves against God, defying him to punish them (v. 7), and they use their power to exploit the weak (vv. 5–6, 21). God's people feel that it is wrong for anyone to do that, and it is hideous for members of his own people to **exult**, i.e., to be jubilant over this, their apparent triumph. The right response is to pray to the **judge of the earth**.

94:4–7 *They Are Arrogant Oppressors.* The next section lists the activities of these **evildoers**: they **pour out their arrogant words** and **boast** (the quoted words of v. 7 provide a sample of their speech), they **crush** God's **people**, and they **kill** the helpless (such as the **widow**, **sojourner**, and **fatherless**), in direct defiance of God's attitude (cf. Deut. 10:18; 14:29; 24:17, 19; 27:19).

94:7 This denial that God takes notice of such misdeeds is the height of arrogance and folly, flowing from an unbelieving heart (cf. 10:11; 59:7; 64:5; 73:11; Isa. 29:15; Ezek. 8:12; 9:9).

94:8–11 *The Lord Knows the Plans of All Mankind.* This section is the reply to v. 7: the God **who planted the ear**, **who formed the eye**, **who disciplines the nations**, and **who teaches man knowledge**, is himself fully aware of everything that goes on, even the **thoughts of man**. Although these words speak directly to those who arrogantly defy God, they are not the only ones to receive this wisdom: the faithful sing the song and remember it, and do not lose heart.

94:8 As in the Wisdom Literature generally, the terms **dullest** (Hb. *bo'ar*, related to *ba'ar*, "stupid," cf. 49:10; 92:6; Prov. 12:1) and **fools** refer to people who resist the offer of grace found in God's covenant. (Observe that these are members **of the people**, i.e., of Israel.) To **understand** or to **be wise** means to grasp the fundamental truths about God, man, and the covenant.

94:11 In 1 Cor. 3:20, Paul adapts the Greek Septuagint of this verse to remind his readers not to set human wisdom against God's wisdom. (**Breath** commonly conveys "futility" [the LXX rendering], e.g., Ps. 62:9.)

12 [h]Blessed is the man whom you [i]discipline, O LORD,
and whom you teach out of your law,
13 to give him [j]rest from [k]days of trouble,
until [l]a pit is dug for the wicked.
14 [m]For the LORD will not forsake his [n]people;
he will not abandon his [n]heritage;
15 for [o]justice will return to the righteous,
and all the upright in heart will [p]follow it.

16 [q]Who rises up for me against the wicked?
Who stands up for me against evildoers?
17 [r]If the LORD had not been my help,
my soul would soon have lived in the land of [s]silence.
18 When I thought, [t]"My foot slips,"
your steadfast love, O LORD, [u]held me up.
19 When the cares of my heart are many,
your consolations cheer my soul.
20 Can [w]wicked rulers be allied with you,
those who frame injustice by [x]statute?
21 They [y]band together against the life of the righteous
and condemn [z]the innocent to death.[1]
22 But the LORD has become my [a]stronghold,
and my God [b]the rock of my [c]refuge.
23 He will bring back on them [d]their iniquity
and [e]wipe them out for their wickedness;
the LORD our God will wipe them out.

Let Us Sing Songs of Praise

95

1 Oh come, let us sing to the LORD;
let us [f]make a joyful noise to [g]the rock of our salvation!
2 Let us [h]come into his presence with thanksgiving;
let us [f]make a joyful noise to him with songs of praise!

[1] Hebrew *condemn innocent blood*

12[h]Prov. 3:11, 12; Heb. 12:5, 6; See Job 5:17 [i]Deut. 8:5; 1 Cor. 11:32
13[j]Job 34:29 [k]Ps. 49:5 [l]Ps. 55:23
14[m]1 Sam. 12:22; Rom. 11:2 [n]Deut. 32:9
15[o][Isa. 42:3] [p]1 Sam. 12:14; 1 Kgs. 14:8
16[q]See Ps. 12:5
17[r]Ps. 124:1, 2 [s]See Ps. 31:17
18[t]Ps. 38:16; [Ps. 73:2] [u][Ps. 20:2]
20[w][Amos 6:3] [x]Ps. 50:16; 58:2; Isa. 10:1
21[y]Matt. 27:1 [z]Matt. 27:4
22[a]See Ps. 9:9 [b]See Ps. 18:2 [c]See Ps. 14:6
23[d]See Ps. 7:16; 34:21; [Prov. 2:22] [e][Ps. 92:9]

Psalm 95

1[f]See Ps. 66:1 [g]Ps. 89:26; [Ps. 94:22]
2[h]Mic. 6:6 [f][See ver. 1 above]

94:12–15 *The Lord Cares for the Righteous.* This section explains how the faithful, who receive instruction from God's word and live by it (**the man whom you discipline, O LORD, and whom you teach out of your law**) are **blessed**. They can be sure that punishment (**a pit**, v. 13) will surely overtake the **wicked**, while **the LORD will not forsake his people** (v. 14) but will bring them **justice** (v. 15).

94:14 It is striking that even though the wicked in this psalm are members of "the people" (v. 8), they are nevertheless distinct from God's **people** and **heritage**; this implies that the faithful are God's people in the truest sense, while the faithless among them are not. For God's people as his heritage or inheritance, cf. 28:9; 33:12; 74:2; 78:62, 71; Deut. 4:20; 9:26; 32:9.

94:16–23 *The Lord Will Rise Up on Behalf of His Beloved.* The song finishes with confidence: the Lord will keep his faithful ones firm in their faith (v. 18), will protect them (v. 22), and will bring the unfaithful into the judgment they deserve (v. 23).

94:16 Who rises up for me? The speaker is the person singing (the same as "my," "I," and "me" referred to in vv. 17–19, 22); the answer is, "God does."

94:19 The specific **cares** are those expressed in the psalm, e.g., v. 3. The **consolations** are the assurances that God knows (vv. 9–11), that he has shown his support already (vv. 17–18), and that he will surely judge (v. 23).

94:20–21 wicked rulers. The ungodly here have power, and they use it to **frame injustice** and to **condemn the innocent to death** (which God hates; Ex. 23:7). Cf. Ps. 94:5–6. This verse denies that such rulers could possibly be **allied with** God, under his favor.

94:22 stronghold, rock. Cf. 9:9; 18:2; 59:16–17; 62:2, 6; 144:2.

94:23 bring back on them. It is common to expect the **iniquity** of the unfaithful to recoil upon their own heads; cf. 7:15; 57:6; Prov. 26:27.

Psalm 95. This psalm summons those singing it to learn the lesson from the rebellion of a previous generation and to commit themselves to faithfully heeding God's "voice." This psalm can be called a prophetic hymn (cf. Psalm 81 [which also remembers Meribah] and Psalm 82), as it echoes themes found in the OT Prophets; or it can be called a historical psalm (cf. Psalm 78, esp. vv. 7–8), as it draws a lesson from the history of Israel. (There is a fine line between the two categories.) The combination of Meribah and Massah shows that the psalm draws its lesson from the Israelites' grumbling against Moses because they had no water (Ex. 17:1–7). At the same time, this event did not lead to God's decisive oath found in the psalm. That oath comes in Num. 14:21–35, after the people had listened to the report of the 10 faithless spies and refused to enter the land to take it. The Lord swore ("as I live," Num. 14:21, 28) that not one of those who grumbled in disbelief "shall come into the land" (Num. 14:29–30); the 40 days of spying would yield 40 years of wandering (Num. 14:34). That is, those who refuse in unbelief to obey God's voice (Num. 14:11) would be removed from the people, and there would be a delay in the people carrying out their calling to occupy the land. The psalm takes the incident at Meribah and Massah as an early installment of this persistent unbelief, which culminated in refusal to enter the land. The psalm has two parts: the first a celebration of God's kingship and the privilege that his people enjoy as they worship him (Ps. 95:1–7a), and the second a warning not to repeat the rebellion of their ancestors (vv. 7b–11). The first section explains why the psalm appears with Psalms 93–99, and also serves to highlight the folly of any kind of rebellion in the face of such an astounding privilege. Hebrews 3:7–11 uses Ps. 95:7b–11, placing its audience in an analogous situation to the Israelites in the wilderness: for these Jews to abandon

3 [i]Ps. 93:4; 135:5 [j]Ps. 86:8; 96:4; 97:9; 2 Chr. 2:5
5 [k]Gen. 1:9, 10; Jonah 1:9
6 [l]2 Chr. 6:13; Dan. 6:10 [m]Ps. 100:3; 149:2; Deut. 32:6, 15, 18
7 [n]Ps. 48:14 [o]See Ps. 74:1 [p]Cited Heb. 3:7-11, 15; 4:7 [q]Num. 14:22
8 [r]Ex. 9:34; 1 Sam. 6:6; 2 Chr. 36:13; Prov. 28:14 [s]Ex. 17:7; Num. 20:13 [t]Ex. 17:7; Deut. 6:16
9 [u]1 Cor. 10:9; [Ps. 78:18, 41, 56] [v]See Ps. 90:16; [Num. 14:22]
10 [w]Acts 7:36; 13:18; Heb. 3:17; [Deut. 9:7] [x][Ps. 81:13]
11 [y]Num. 14:23, 28, 30; Deut. 1:35; Cited Heb. 3:11; 4:3, 5 [z]Deut. 12:9

Psalm 96

1 [a]For ver. 1-13, see 1 Chr. 16:23-33 [b]Ps. 98:1; See Ps. 33:3
2 [c][Isa. 52:7; 60:6]

3 For the LORD is [i]a great God,
and a great King [j]above all gods.
4 In his hand are the depths of the earth;
the heights of the mountains are his also.
5 The sea is his, for [k]he made it,
and his hands formed [k]the dry land.

6 Oh come, let us worship and bow down;
let us [l]kneel before the LORD, our [m]Maker!
7 For he is our [n]God,
and we are the people of his [o]pasture,
and the sheep of his hand.
[p]Today, if you [q]hear his voice,
8 [r]do not harden your hearts, as at [s]Meribah,
as on the day at [t]Massah in the wilderness,
9 when your fathers put me to the [u]test
and put me to the proof, though they had seen my [v]work.
10 [w]For forty years I loathed that generation
and said, "They are a people who go astray in their heart,
and they have not known [x]my ways."
11 Therefore I [y]swore in my wrath,
"They shall not enter [z]my rest."

96

Worship in the Splendor of Holiness

1 [a]Oh sing to the LORD [b]a new song;
sing to the LORD, all the earth!
2 Sing to the LORD, bless his name;
[c]tell of his salvation from day to day.

their explicit faith in Jesus in order to return to the safety of "ordinary" Judaism would be like the rebellion of Israel in the wilderness, a mark of unbelief. As in the psalm, Hebrews makes every day a "today" that calls for renewed faithfulness.

95:1–7a *The Lord Is King.* The members of the congregation singing these verses invite one another to the great privilege of worshiping **the LORD**, the **great God**, the **great King above all gods**. On the kind of kingship attributed to God here, see note on Psalm 93. God is King over creation: it **is his, he made it**, and he rules over it all (it is **in his hand**, i.e., under his authority). The marvel of being Israel is that such a majestic King has pledged himself to his people, making them the **sheep of his hand** (cf. note on 74:1–3). It is no surprise, then, that worship offered to him would be both exuberant (**sing, make a joyful noise**, **thanksgiving**, **songs of praise**) with astonished wonder, and humble (**bow down**, **kneel**) before such majesty. The whole person, body and soul, must offer this worship.

95:7b–11 *We His People Must Heed His Voice.* Since worship includes the priests reading and expounding the Scriptures, the worshipers will **hear his voice** (v. 7b), and in the rest of the psalm the congregation reminds itself that they must take it to heart, believing and obeying their great King. A previous generation of Israel had instead **put** God **to the test** by their unbelief. This section focuses on the inner self, the heart (v. 8, **do not harden your hearts**; and v. 10, **go astray in their heart**), where one lays hold of or rejects the grace of the covenant. As explained in the note on Psalm 95, the psalm uses Ex. 17:1–7 together with Num. 14:21–35 to make its point. God will preserve the corporate entity, the "people," in order to achieve his purposes in the world; but he wants the members of the people to be joined to him in true faith. If they rebel, they must be removed.

95:7b–8 Today, if you hear his voice, do not. Some scholars prefer to take the word "if" in the sense, "if only": "Today, if only you would hear his voice! Do not . . ." This, however, loses the connection between "today" (the day on which and of which the congregation sings) and **the day at Massah**. **harden your hearts**. The biblical writers use "heart" for the central core of the person's thoughts, feelings, and choices (cf. Prov. 4:23). To "harden the heart" is to make it dull and unresponsive to God, and thus to strengthen it in disbelief.

95:11 They shall not enter my rest. In the wilderness context, the "rest" is specifically the place of rest, i.e., the land (cf. Deut. 12:9; finally secured with David's reign, cf. 2 Sam. 7:1, 11); but, since the singing congregation is already in the land, it follows that the psalm is using "rest" as an image of enjoying God's presence forever (much as Heb. 4:1, 11 does).

Psalm 96. This is a hymn celebrating how God's kingship over all creation (see note on Psalm 93) means that all kinds of people should love and worship him. The psalm has three sections, each beginning with a command ("sing," 96:1; "ascribe," v. 7; "say," v. 10), and each mentioning the Gentiles ("all the earth," "the nations," and "the peoples" in vv. 1–6; "families of the peoples" and "all the earth" in vv. 7–9; and "the nations," "the peoples," and "the world" in vv. 10–13). God called Israel to be a vehicle of blessing for all mankind, bringing them knowledge of the true God for whom all human beings yearn, and this psalm keeps this mission prominent in the Israelites' view of the world and their role in it. Verses 8–9 even call the Gentiles to join Israel in their worship in God's courts. The psalm looks forward to a time when the Lord will come and judge all peoples with equity, without specifying how this will take place. The term "judge" is probably not limited to sifting between the righteous and the unrighteous; the wider sense of "execute justice, rule justly" fits the context better (cf. Isa. 2:4; 11:3–4). Thus the psalm is more focused on a time in which Gentiles acknowledge the true God, and the benefits that will bring to all the earth, than it is on the final judgment. Christians sing this, knowing that God has ushered in this long-awaited epoch with the resurrection of Jesus (see note on Isa. 11:3–4). This psalm appears in 1 Chron. 16:23–33, indicating that the people sang an adaptation (or perhaps an early edition) of it when David brought the ark to Jerusalem.

96:1–6 *Sing to the Lord All the Earth, for He Is Great!* The psalm begins by calling the inhabitants of **all the earth** to **sing to the LORD**. The activities (**sing to the LORD, bless his name, tell of his salvation**; cf. **praised** and **feared**) all describe the privilege of Israelite worship **in** God's **sanctuary**; here the Gentiles are invited to join in (see also vv. 8–9).

96:1 new song. See note on 33:1–3.

3 Declare his glory among the nations,
his marvelous works among all the peoples!
4 For [d]great is the LORD, and [e]greatly to be praised;
he is to be feared above [f]all gods.
5 For all the gods of the peoples are worthless idols,
but the LORD [g]made the heavens.
6 Splendor and majesty are before him;
[h]strength and beauty are in his sanctuary.

7 Ascribe to the LORD, O [i]families of the peoples,
[j]ascribe to the LORD glory and strength!
8 Ascribe to the LORD [k]the glory due his name;
bring [l]an offering, and [m]come into his courts!
9 Worship the LORD in [n]the splendor of holiness;[1]
[o]tremble before him, all the earth!

10 Say among the nations, [p]"The LORD reigns!
Yes, the world is established; it shall never be moved;
he will [q]judge the peoples with equity."

11 Let [r]the heavens be glad, and let [s]the earth rejoice;
let [t]the sea roar, and all that fills it;
12 let [u]the field exult, and everything in it!
Then shall all [v]the trees of the forest sing for joy
13 before the LORD, for he comes,
for he comes [w]to judge the earth.
He will judge the world in righteousness,
and the peoples in his faithfulness.

4[d]See Ps. 48:1 [e]Ps. 18:3 [f]See Ps. 95:3
5[g]Ps. 115:15; Isa. 42:5; 44:24; Jer. 10:12
6[h][Ps. 78:61]
7[i]Ps. 22:27 [j]See Ps. 29:1
8[k]Ps. 29:2 [l][Ps. 45:12]; See Ps. 68:29; 72:10 [m]Ps. 100:4
9[n]See Ps. 29:2 [o]Ps. 114:7
10[p]See Ps. 93:1 [q]ver. 13; See Ps. 9:8; 58:11
11[r]See Ps. 69:34 [s]Ps. 97:1 [t]Ps. 98:7
12[u][Isa. 35:1] [v][Isa. 55:12]
13[w]See Isa. 11:1-9

Psalm 97

1[x]See Ps. 93:1 [y]Ps. 96:11 [z]See Ps. 72:10
2[a]Ex. 19:9; Deut. 4:11; 5:22; 1 Kgs. 8:12; See Ps. 18:11 [b]Ps. 89:14

The LORD Reigns

97

1 [x]The LORD reigns, [y]let the earth rejoice;
let the many [z]coastlands be glad!
2 [a]Clouds and thick darkness are all around him;
[b]righteousness and justice are the foundation of his throne.

[1] Or *in holy attire*

96:4–5 These verses explain to the Gentiles that there is only one God truly worthy of worship. He is **to be feared above all gods** (because he **made the heavens**, while they are powerless, indeed unreal). The words **gods** (Hb. *'elohim*) and **worthless idols** (Hb. *'elilim*) sound alike, providing a play on words; in English this would be close to "these mighty beings are mighty useless!"

96:6 Splendor and majesty describe royal magnificence (21:5; 45:3), which is suited to the theme of divine kingship (cf. 104:1; 111:3; 145:3; Job 40:10). These, along with **strength and beauty**, are attributes of God, into whose presence people come **in his sanctuary**.

96:7–9 *All Nations, Ascribe Glory to the Lord!* These verses develop the thought of v. 7, inviting the Gentiles to worship **into his courts**, i.e., in the temple precincts. The OT describes the future era, when the Gentiles receive the light, by picturing them coming to the Jerusalem temple (Isa. 2:2–3; even the lesser temple after the exile, Hag. 2:7–9). The Gentiles are to **bring an offering** and to **worship the LORD in the splendor of holiness** (i.e., the splendid presence of the all-holy one). Their uncleanness (cf. Isa. 52:1) can be cured by conversion, and then they too will be welcome in God's house.

96:7–8 Ascribe . . . ascribe. . . . Ascribe. These three lines are very similar to 29:1–2, except that there the heavenly beings are called to worship, while here it is the **families of the peoples** (i.e., Gentiles). **Strength** looks back to the same word in 96:6, and **glory** (Hb. *kabod*) is a synonym of "beauty" (Hb. *tip'eret*). Verse 6 listed God's attributes, and the Gentiles are called to "ascribe" (or acknowledge) these attributes. The **glory due his name** is the respect and honor God's character deserves.

96:10–13 *Let All Nations Know that the Lord Will Judge in Righteousness.* The Gentiles addressed throughout this psalm (cf. vv. 1, 7) are to spread the news among all their fellow Gentiles (**among the nations**, v. 10; cf. v. 3), namely, that **the LORD reigns!** The universal rule of the one true God (who is above all other gods, who are worthless anyway, vv. 4–5) is good news to those who will acknowledge his kingship. These verses describe a time when God **will judge** (i.e., rule justly; see note on Psalm 96) **the peoples with equity** (v. 10; cf. v. 13). When all kinds of people gladly receive God's rule, worshiping him according to his gracious character, the rest of the creation (**the heavens**, **the earth**, **the sea**, and **the field** with all their inhabitants, and **the trees of the forest**) will all celebrate (**be glad**, **rejoice**, **roar**, **exult**, and **sing for joy**). The creation suffers from the curse upon mankind, and from God's discipline of wayward human beings, and from the evil that people do; but when they genuinely come under the rule of the true God, the blessings will spread throughout the world. Cf. note on Rom. 8:20–21.

96:10 the world . . . shall never be moved. See note on 93:1. The world is founded on secure moral principles, the unchanging character of God (cf. **equity**; and "righteousness" and "faithfulness," 96:13).

Psalm 97. This is a hymn celebrating God's kingship over all his creation (see note on Psalm 93), particularly focusing on how God's universal rule assures the faithful of his final victory over evil and idolatry. This victory

3 [c]Fire goes before him
and burns up his adversaries all around.
4 His [d]lightnings light up the world;
the earth sees and [e]trembles.
5 The mountains [f]melt like [g]wax before the LORD,
before [h]the Lord of all the earth.

6 [i]The heavens proclaim his righteousness,
and all [j]the peoples see his glory.
7 All worshipers of images are [k]put to shame,
who make their boast in [l]worthless idols;
[m]worship him, all you gods!

8 Zion hears and [n]is glad,
and the daughters of Judah rejoice,
because of your judgments, O LORD.
9 For you, O LORD, are [o]most high over all the earth;
you are exalted far above [p]all gods.

10 O you who love the LORD, [q]hate evil!
He [r]preserves the lives of his [s]saints;
he [t]delivers them from the hand of the wicked.
11 [u]Light [v]is sown[1] for the righteous,
and joy for the upright in heart.
12 [w]Rejoice in the LORD, O you righteous,
and [x]give thanks to his holy name!

[1] Most Hebrew manuscripts; one Hebrew manuscript, Septuagint, Syriac, Jerome *Light dawns*

3[c]See Ps. 21:9; 50:3
4[d]Ps. 77:18 [e][Ps. 96:9]
5[f]Nah. 1:5; [Judg. 5:5] [g]See Ps. 68:2 [h]Josh. 3:11
6[i]See Ps. 50:6 [j]Isa. 40:5; 66:18; [Ps. 96:3]
7[k]Isa. 42:17; 44:9 [l]Ps. 96:5 [m]Heb. 1:6
8[n]Ps. 48:11
9[o]See Ps. 83:18 [p]See Ps. 95:3
10[q]Prov. 8:13; Amos 5:15; Rom. 12:9; See Ps. 34:14 [r]Ps. 31:23; 37:28; 121:4; 145:20; Prov. 2:8 [s]See Ps. 30:4 [t]Dan. 3:28; 6:27; Acts 12:11
11[u]Ps. 112:4; 118:27; Prov. 4:18 [v][Prov. 11:18; Hos. 10:12; James 3:18]
12[w]See Ps. 32:11 [x]See Ps. 30:4

involves God's protection of his faithful ones from evildoers (97:10), the vindication of Zion as God's chosen place for revealing himself (vv. 8–9), and the Gentiles ultimately coming to know the true God (vv. 6–7). Such assurance does not come from observing the course of events in the world, as God's universal kingship is often invisible; it is an affirmation of biblical faith that produces profound joy in those who embrace it (vv. 11–12). The psalm has a number of echoes of the Pentateuch, especially Exodus: e.g., Ps. 97:1 ("the LORD reigns") and Ex. 15:18; Ps. 97:2–5 and Ex. 19:9, 16, 18 (God's appearance at Sinai); Ps. 97:6 and Ex. 16:7 ("see his glory") and Num. 14:21 (all the earth shall be filled with the Lord's glory); and Ps. 97:9 and Ex. 15:11 (the Lord far above all other gods). The reference to Zion hearing and being glad in Ps. 97:8 indicates that the psalm arose from some great deliverance of the city, although the particular deliverance in view is not clear.

97:1–5 *The Glorious Presence of the Lord.* In words that echo the appearance of God's glory on Sinai (Ex. 19:16–18; cf. Deut. 4:11; 5:22), the psalm describes the magnificence of God's presence. The **clouds and thick darkness** (Ps. 97:2) convey the mystery of God's unapproachable majesty, while **righteousness and justice** as **the foundation of his throne** show that the mysterious majesty is not that of an arbitrary despot but of one who can be trusted. The expressions **burns up his adversaries all around** (v. 3), **the earth sees and trembles** (v. 4), and **melt like wax** (v. 5; cf. 68:2; Mic. 1:4) direct the singers' attention to how the universal kingship of God means that he is completely able to clear away all opposition. Although the psalms can certainly describe God's coming judgment on those who disbelieve him (whether in Israel or among the nations), that is not the focus here: this psalm looks forward to the Gentiles coming to know the magnificent Creator and Ruler of all; and thus, **let the earth** (and its inhabitants) **rejoice** (Ps. 97:1).

97:1 many coastlands. The biblical authors commonly used the nations around the Mediterranean Sea as representatives of all nations everywhere (cf. Isa. 42:4).

97:6–9 *He Is High above All Gods, Therefore Worship Him Alone.* These verses concern the false worship found among the nations who are **worshipers of images** (v. 7), comparing the false gods to the Lord, who is **most high over all the earth** and **exalted far above all gods** (v. 9). The purpose here is not to gloat but to look forward to the time when **all the peoples see his glory**: the OT anticipates this era (cf. Num. 14:21) and connects it to the reign of the Davidic Messiah (cf. Isa. 11:1–10). There is a general declaration to all mankind (Ps. 97:6, **the heavens proclaim his righteousness**), and one day the specific message of redemption will come to the nations as well (the "glory"; cf. note on 63:1–2, see also Isa. 40:5). **Zion hears and is glad** (Ps. 97:8), because God's **judgments** (his historical acts that protect his people) provide the assurance that the purpose for which Israel was called will in fact be carried out.

97:7 worship him, all you gods! The Septuagint translators rendered this phrase into Greek as "worship him, all you his angels," and this may be the OT text quoted in Heb. 1:6. The author of Hebrews, like other NT authors, is willing to apply OT texts about the Lord (Yahweh) to Jesus (cf. Heb. 1:10–12, using Ps. 102:25–27); these authors were not saying that the OT texts were directly messianic, but they were certainly recognizing that if Jesus was in fact the God of Israel in human flesh (cf. John 1:14), then these texts apply to him.

97:10–12 *Hate Evil and Rejoice in the Lord.* This assurance for the big story of the whole world enables all of the faithful (those **who love the LORD**) to live their little stories in faith (i.e., to **hate evil** and to reject all its attractions). If God's righteous purpose will prevail in his world, this means that individual godly people (**his saints**, v. 10) will know his care and protection in their own lives. God fills their lives with **light** and **joy** (v. 11), and when they realize this, they willingly **rejoice in the LORD** and **give thanks to his holy name** (v. 12). The stanza has several terms for the same group of people, whose faith is genuine: those "who love the Lord" (v. 10); God's "saints" (v. 10); the "righteous" (vv. 11, 12); and the "upright in heart" (v. 11).

97:11 Light is sown. The image would be that God's "light" (i.e., guidance for a life that is good and healthy, cf. 118:27; 119:130) and **joy** are scattered along their path like seed, ready to sprout. The image of "sowing" is

Make a Joyful Noise to the Lord

98

A Psalm.

1 Oh sing to the Lord [y]a new song,
for he has done [z]marvelous things!
His [a]right hand and his holy arm
have worked salvation for him.
2 The Lord has [b]made known his salvation;
he has [c]revealed his righteousness in [d]the sight of the nations.
3 He has [e]remembered his [f]steadfast love and faithfulness
to the house of Israel.
All [g]the ends of the earth have seen
[h]the salvation of our God.

4 [i]Make a joyful noise to the Lord, all the earth;
[j]break forth into joyous song and sing praises!
5 Sing praises to the Lord with the lyre,
with the lyre and the [k]sound of melody!
6 With [l]trumpets and the sound of [m]the horn
[i]make a joyful noise before the King, the Lord!

7 [n]Let the sea roar, and [o]all that fills it;
[o]the world and those who dwell in it!
8 Let the rivers [p]clap their hands;
let [q]the hills sing for joy together
9 before the Lord, for he comes
to [r]judge the earth.
He will judge the world with righteousness,
and the peoples with equity.

Psalm 98

1 [y]See Ps. 33:3 [z][Ps. 96:3]; Ps. 72:18 [a][Ex. 15:6; Luke 1:51]; See Job 40:14
2 [b]Isa. 49:6; 52:10; Luke 2:30, 31; [Isa. 59:16; 63:5] [c]Isa. 62:2; Rom. 3:25, 26 [d]Ps. 96:2, 3
3 [e]Luke 1:54, 72 [f]See Ps. 36:5 [g]Ps. 22:27 [h]ver. 2
4 [i]See Ps. 66:1 [j]Isa. 44:23
5 [k]Isa. 51:3
6 [l]Num. 10:10; 1 Chr. 15:24 [m]2 Chr. 15:14 [i][See ver. 4 above]
7 [n]Ps. 96:11 [o]Ps. 24:1
8 [p]Isa. 55:12; [Ps. 93:3] [q]Ps. 89:12
9 [r]Ps. 96:13; See Ps. 58:11

unusual, and some have preferred the reading of one Hebrew manuscript and some ancient versions (see ESV footnote) that gives "light dawns," as found in 112:4 (the difference is slight: *z–r–kh*, "dawns"; in place of *z–r–'*, "sown"). However, in the second line "joy" is also "sown" or "dawns," and the ESV text makes more sense of this.

Psalm 98. This hymn celebrates God's universal kingship (v. 6) by referring to the "marvelous things" and "salvation" that God has worked in the sight of the Gentiles, on behalf of his people. The flow of thought is straightforward: God has worked salvation (rescue from evil) for Israel, which all the ends of the earth have seen (vv. 1–3); all people in the earth should join Israel's celebration, because God is their rightful king, too (vv. 4–6); the material creation should join all mankind in jubilant praise of the one true God, as they look forward to his rule (vv. 7–9). There are many overlaps with Psalm 96, as in the opening invitation (98:1; cf. 96:1); the interest in the Gentiles (98:4; cf. 96:7); the rejoicing of the material world (98:7–8; cf. 96:11–12); and the Lord as universal "judge" (98:9; cf. 96:13). This psalm lies behind Isaac Watts's famous hymn "Joy to the World." The psalm and the hymn have come to be associated with Christmas; like Psalm 96, this is not inappropriate, provided it is clear that the coming of Jesus as the Davidic king who will bring light to the Gentiles is what establishes the connection.

98:1–3 *Sing, for God Has Worked Salvation for His People.* This section calls on God's people to sing aloud together in celebration of God's faithfulness to his promises. The term **salvation** appears in each verse of this section; it describes the great deeds of God for the sake of his people as a whole, providing protection from their enemies and the conditions in which piety can flourish (as did the deliverance from Egypt, Ex. 14:13, 30; 15:2). Several other terms are used for the same deeds: **marvelous things** (Ps. 98:1; deeds that display God's supernatural control over events); **his righteousness** (v. 2; God's faithfulness in keeping his promises); God **has remembered his steadfast love and faithfulness** (v. 3; see note on 25:6–7; cf. Ex. 2:24; 34:6). God has done these great deeds **to the house of Israel** (Ps. 98:3), but the benefit is not limited to them: **all the ends of the earth have seen the salvation of our God** (i.e., the "salvation" he has worked for Israel, as described in vv. 1–2). The next stanza will invite the rest of the nations to join in the song.

98:1 new song. See 96:1 and note on 33:1–3.

98:3 all the ends of the earth. Cf. Isa. 52:10.

98:4–6 *Let All the Earth Sing Loudly and Joyfully.* The previous section ended with "all the ends of the earth"; this section addresses **all the earth**, i.e., all the people who dwell in all the earth. These varied peoples are all invited to join the **joyous song** offered to the one true God. What God has done for Israel (vv. 1–3) is for the sake of bringing the light to the whole world.

98:7–9 *Let all Nature Join in the Song.* This section extends the invitation from the human inhabitants of the world (**the world and those who dwell in it**) to include even the **sea** and **all that fills it**, the **rivers**, and the **hills**. The entire creation, human and otherwise, can rejoice at the prospect of God's just rule (as in 96:13, the sense of **judge** is "administer justice through a just rule"; see note on Psalm 96). Human beings were made to submit to God's rule and to govern the creation in wisdom and love; when they acknowledge God's kingship, they and the rest of the creation will flourish.

98:9 the peoples. As with Psalm 96, this is realized under the kingly rule of the Messiah (see note on Psalm 96).

Psalm 99. This is another hymn celebrating God's kingship over all his creation (see Psalm 93), this time focusing on his exalted holiness (99:3, 5, 9) and the wonder that he has made a way for his people to come

Psalm 99
1[s]Ps. 93:1; See 1 Chr. 16:31 [t][Ps. 96:9] [u]See Ps. 80:1 [v][Isa. 24:19, 20]
2[w][Isa. 24:23] [x]Ps. 113:4; [Ps. 92:8; 93:4]
3[y][Ps. 111:9; Deut. 28:58] [z]Josh. 24:19; Isa. 6:3; Rev. 15:4
4[a][ver. 1] [b]Ps. 11:7; Isa. 61:8; [Job 36:5-7]
5[c]Ps. 107:32; 118:28; Ex. 15:2; Isa. 25:1 [d]Ps. 132:7; 1 Chr. 28:2 [e]Isa. 60:13; Lam. 2:1; Ezek. 43:7 [z][See ver. 3 above]
6[f][Jer. 15:1] [g]See Ex. 24:6-8; 40:22-27; Lev. 8:1-30 [h]1 Sam. 7:9; 12:18; See Ps. 105:1 [i]Ps. 106:23; Ex. 14:15; 17:11, 12; 32:30; Num. 12:13; 16:48; Deut. 9:18
7[j]Ex. 33:9; Num. 12:5 [k][Ps. 105:28]
8[l]Num. 14:20 [m]Ex. 32:35; Num. 20:12; Deut. 9:20; [Jer. 46:28]
9[n]See Ps. 2:6

99

The Lord Our God Is Holy

1 [s]The Lord reigns; [t]let the peoples tremble!
He [u]sits enthroned upon the cherubim; [v]let the earth quake!
2 The Lord is [w]great in Zion;
he is [x]exalted over all the peoples.
3 Let them praise your [y]great and awesome name!
[z]Holy is he!
4 [a]The King in his might [b]loves justice.[1]
You have established equity;
you have executed justice
and righteousness in Jacob.
5 [c]Exalt the Lord our God;
[d]worship at his [e]footstool!
[z]Holy is he!

6 [f]Moses and Aaron were among his [g]priests,
Samuel also was among those who [h]called upon his name.
They [i]called to the Lord, and he answered them.
7 In [j]the pillar of the cloud he spoke to them;
they [k]kept his testimonies
and the statute that he gave them.

8 O Lord our God, you answered them;
you were [l]a forgiving God to them,
but [m]an avenger of their wrongdoings.
9 Exalt the Lord our God,
and worship at his [n]holy mountain;
for the Lord our God is holy!

[1] Or *The might of the King loves justice*

into his presence without danger. Although the emphasis falls specifically on God's covenant people, Israel, the element of universal hope for the Gentiles is also present: vv. 2–3 express the wish that "all the peoples" might praise the great and awesome name of the Lord.

99:1–5 *The Lord Is a Holy and Majestic King.* The first section stresses the stunning majesty of God's kingship (v. 1, he **reigns** and is **enthroned upon the cherubim**; v. 2, he is **great** and is **exalted over all the peoples**; vv. 3, 5, he is **holy**). It also emphasizes the proper human response to him (v. 1, **let the peoples tremble**; v. 3, **let them**—i.e., the peoples, v. 2—**praise your great and awesome name**; v. 5, people should **exalt the Lord** and **worship**). Verses 3 and 5 repeat the phrase, **holy is he**: the Lord is spotlessly pure and righteous, and separate above his creation. This universal God has made himself known in **Zion** (v. 2) and has established his just and gracious rule in **Jacob** (v. 4): here among his chosen people, Israel, the perfect kingship of God is supposed to be on display. The place of worship (the sanctuary) is God's **footstool** (cf. 132:7; 1 Chron. 28:2), in keeping with the royal image, where God the universal king is the acknowledged king over his people.

99:1 enthroned upon the cherubim. See note on 80:1. **let the peoples tremble**. This may be simply the humble response to God's majesty; but, in view of the interest in Zion (99:2) and Jacob (v. 4), i.e., in God's people Israel, it probably also stresses that the Gentiles should fear to harm God's own people (cf. Ex. 15:14; Deut. 2:25) and should instead join them in worship (Ps. 99:3; cf. 96:7–9).

99:4 loves justice. The **might** that this king wields is directed entirely to good and pure ends. In the true God there is absolute might combined with absolute right, and this endears him to his faithful worshipers. (On the idea of God's just rule, see note on Psalm 96.)

99:5 Exalt (see also v. 9). The Lord is "exalted," i.e., high in majesty, and people are to "exalt" him, i.e., to honor God for his high majesty.

99:6–9 *The Holy God Has Provided for His People to Worship Him.* The first section described the exalted holiness of the one true God and hinted at the privilege of the chosen people. This section explores more of the wonder of what it means to be God's people, whom he actually welcomes into his presence. In mentioning **Moses**, **Aaron**, and **Samuel** (v. 6), the psalm reminds its singers of how these men were God's gifts to lead his people. Here they further serve as examples of those who **called to the Lord, and he answered them** (see also v. 8), and who **kept his testimonies** and his **statute**. Those of God's faithful who heed the call to **worship at his holy mountain** (v. 9) can be sure that God has preserved his people through such servants as these and has called each of his people to a similar life of faith and obedience.

99:8 forgiving God. God describes himself this way in Ex. 34:7, and his people, even the best of **them** (i.e., Moses, Aaron, and Samuel of Ps. 99:6), rely on this, and not their own moral excellence, as their confidence. **avenger of their wrongdoings**. Although this could be taken to mean that God avenges the wrong done to them (Deut. 32:43), it is better to see it as affirming that God "avenges" the wrong committed by his people, chastising them in order to help them on to greater holiness. The God described here forgives his people, not because he is indifferent to their moral condition but so that they can have the joy of ever-deepening moral excellence.

99:9 Exalt. See note on v. 5. **holy mountain**. This can be the mountain on which Jerusalem sits (e.g., 87:1), or more specifically, the mountain where the temple is located (e.g., 15:1). Observe how this verse echoes 99:5.

His Steadfast Love Endures Forever

100

A PSALM FOR [o]GIVING THANKS.

1 [p]Make a joyful noise to the LORD, all the earth!
2 [q]Serve the LORD with gladness!
[r]Come into his presence with singing!

3 Know that [s]the LORD, he is God!
It is he who [t]made us, and [u]we are his;[1]
we are his [v]people, and [w]the sheep of his pasture.

4 [x]Enter his gates with thanksgiving,
and his [y]courts with praise!
Give thanks to him; [z]bless his name!

5 [a]For the LORD is good;
his steadfast love endures forever,
and his [b]faithfulness to all generations.

I Will Walk with Integrity

101

A PSALM OF DAVID.

1 I will sing of [c]steadfast love and justice;
to you, O LORD, I will make music.
2 I will [d]ponder the way [e]that is blameless.
Oh when will you [f]come to me?

[1] *Or and not we ourselves*

Psalm 100
[o][Ps. 50:14]
1 [p]See Ps. 66:1
2 [q][Ps. 2:11] [r][Ps. 95:2]
3 [s]1 Kgs. 18:39 [t]See Ps. 95:6; Job 10:3, 8 [u]Isa. 43:1 [v]Ezek. 34:30 [w]See Ps. 74:1
4 [x][Ps. 66:13] [y]Ps. 96:8 [z]Ps. 96:2
5 [a]Ps. 25:8; 106:1; 119:68; 2 Chr. 5:13; Ezra 3:11; Jer. 33:11; Nah. 1:7 [b]See Ps. 36:5

Psalm 101
1 [c][Ex. 34:7]
2 [d][Ps. 4:4] [e]Ps. 119:1; Prov. 11:20; [Matt. 5:48] [f][Ex. 20:24; John 14:23]

Psalm 100. This hymn, though not explicitly a psalm celebrating God's kingship, brings the collection of kingship hymns to a close with its exuberant call to come before the Lord in worship. Like the divine kingship psalms, this hymn invites "all the earth" (i.e., all the Gentiles) to join the song of praise. The title declares that this psalm is "for giving thanks." That is certainly fitting, as the worshipers thank the universal Creator for the privilege of being "the sheep of his pasture." The term "giving thanks" (Hb. *todah*) can also be the name for the thanksgiving offering, one kind of peace offering (Lev. 7:12–15). Since the peace offering is a meal enjoyed in God's presence, this too is fitting for the psalm; but there is no reason to be so specific. Further, Ps. 100:4 uses the word in its ordinary sense (in parallel with "praise"). There are several phrases shared between this psalm and Psalm 95, as the notes will point out.

100:1 joyful noise. Cf. 95:1–2. Also rendered, "shout for joy" (66:1). **all the earth.** The Lord is the Creator of all people, not just Israel; and Israel exists to bring light to the entire earth.

100:2 gladness . . . singing. Awareness of the goodness of God (v. 5) and of the great privilege of worshiping him produces joy in those who know they are welcome in his presence.

100:3 he who made us. This could be a reference to God's work as Creator of all; but, in view of what follows in the verse, it seems to be more specifically, "made us [Israel] to be his people." **and we are his.** Earlier English translations read "not" in place of "his" (see ESV footnote, "and not we ourselves"); the Hebrew for both sounds almost identical ("his," Hb. *lo*; "not," Hb. *lo'*), but "his" is the better reading. **his people, and the sheep of his pasture.** For the image of God's people as his sheep and the Lord as their shepherd, see note on 74:1–3. See also 95:7.

100:4 gates . . . courts. Parts of the temple complex.

100:5 good. Full of generosity (cf. 23:6; 25:7–8). **steadfast love . . . faithfulness.** These terms evoke Ex. 34:6; the foundation of joy for God's people is his enduring character of gracious love, of keeping his promises. **to all generations.** Exodus 34:7 says that God keeps his steadfast love "for thousands," which, in view of Deut. 7:9, is probably "generations in their thousands." The worshipers delight to think of the people of God being preserved forever, and of the prospect of their own descendants being members of that people (cf. Gen. 17:7; Ps. 103:17–18); this, too, is the measure of God's enduring love.

Psalm 101. This is a royal psalm, a song about the place that the Davidic monarchy has in God's plan for his people. This psalm sets out, for David and his heirs, the ideal kind of ruler that they should aim to be. The people who sing this will find their desires for their king shaped by it, and will receive guidance for their prayers for the ruling king. The psalm's "I" is the Davidic king, in whom the people are included (cf. 2 Sam. 20:1; 1 Kings 12:16), and therefore along with whom they sing. The king's task is his devotion to achieving covenant faithfulness, both in his personal life and in the social life of Israel. As God's people, Israel is called to display the true humanness which is godliness in active operation. The Davidic king should set the pattern for covenant faithfulness, and each Israelite should have the same aims in his own daily life. In the context of Book 4 (Psalms 90–106), this psalm is already understood to be looking forward to a new David (cf. Psalm 72). So even before Jesus, the psalm must have been understood to describe the Messiah's reign and his requirements. Christians sing this, rejoicing that they have in Jesus the perfect embodiment of the Davidic ideal; this can lead them to reflect on what kind of people they should aim to be, with such a king. They further can embrace its ideal of leadership in church and state, and seek to honor such leaders when they appear. This is the first psalm attributed to David since Psalm 86; the only other Davidic psalm in Book 4 is Psalm 103.

101:1–4 *The King Will Aim to Be Blameless.* The song opens by declaring the king's firm commitment to live out covenant faithfulness: he will **ponder the way that is blameless** (cf. 18:32; 119:1; Prov. 11:20; 13:6) in order to **walk** in that way (cf. Ps. 101:6, which echoes v. 2 here); he wants to display **integrity of heart within** his own **house** (i.e., in his private life); when it comes to whose advice and help he will seek in ruling, he will also reject **those who fall away** and those who have **a perverse heart** (i.e., those who are openly unfaithful). The policies and plans of a Davidic king should be focused on serving the people, especially in promoting the conditions in which piety can flourish; unfaithful advisers do not share these goals.

2 [g]1 Kgs. 9:4 [h]Ps. 78:72
3 [i]Deut. 15:9 [j]See Ps. 40:4
4 [k]Prov. 11:20; 17:20 [l][1 Cor. 5:11]
5 [m]Ps. 15:3 [n]ver. 8 [o]Ps. 18:27; 131:1; Prov. 6:17; 21:4; 30:13 [p]Prov. 16:5
6 [q]Ps. 119:1; Prov. 11:20; [Matt. 5:48]
7 [r]Ps. 52:2 [s]Ps. 102:28
8 [t][Ps. 73:14] [u]Ps. 75:10 [v]Ps. 94:4 [w]Ps. 48:1, 8; [Isa. 52:1]

Psalm 102
[x]Ps. 61:2 [y]Ps. 142:2
1 [z]Ps. 39:12 [a]Ps. 18:6; Ex. 2:23; 1 Sam. 9:16
2 [b]See Ps. 27:9 [c]See Ps. 18:6 [d]See Ps. 31:2 [e]See Ps. 69:17 [f]Ps. 56:9

I will [g]walk with [h]integrity of heart
within my house;
3 I will not set before my eyes
anything [i]that is worthless.
I hate the work of those who [j]fall away;
it shall not cling to me.
4 [k]A perverse heart shall be far from me;
I will [l]know nothing of evil.

5 Whoever slanders his neighbor [m]secretly
I will [n]destroy.
Whoever has a [o]haughty look and an [p]arrogant heart
I will not endure.

6 I will look with favor on the faithful in the land,
that they may dwell with me;
he who walks in [q]the way that is blameless
shall minister to me.

7 No one who [r]practices deceit
shall dwell in my house;
no one who utters lies
shall [s]continue before my eyes.

8 [t]Morning by morning I will destroy
all the wicked in the land,
[u]cutting off all [v]the evildoers
from [w]the city of the LORD.

Do Not Hide Your Face from Me

102

A PRAYER OF ONE AFFLICTED, WHEN HE IS [x]FAINT AND [y]POURS OUT HIS COMPLAINT BEFORE THE LORD.

1 [z]Hear my prayer, O LORD;
let my cry [a]come to you!
2 [b]Do not hide your face from me
in [c]the day of my distress!
[d]Incline your ear to me;
[e]answer me speedily [f]in the day when I call!

101:5–8 *The King Will Destroy the Wicked and Favor the Faithful.* The king should promote faithfulness among the people, and this includes protecting the weaker members from those who would do them harm. The king can carry this out in a judicial way against those who break specific laws: when someone **slanders his neighbor secretly** (cf. Lev. 19:16; this is an attack on the neighbor's life), the king can **destroy** the wrongdoer (Ps. 101:5; cf. also v. 8) by pronouncing sentence against him. There are situations in which the king does not have legal punishment to give, as when someone shows disdain for the covenant and for its people (e.g., **a haughty look and an arrogant heart**; **practices deceit**); and yet the faithful king will **not endure** such people (v. 5; i.e., he will not pretend that such people are pleasing, cf. Isa. 1:13), nor will they **dwell in** his **house** (Ps. 101:7; i.e., he will not count them as intimate friends). At the same time, the ideal king will **look with favor on the faithful in the land** (v. 6): they **may dwell with** him (contrast v. 7), and he will rely on them to **minister to** him (see note on v. 6). Under this kind of leadership, the **city of the LORD** can be a happy and holy place, a blessing to the world.

101:6 The word for **minister** (Hb. *sh-r-t*) means "serve" or "assist"; e.g., Joshua "ministered to" or "assisted" Moses (Ex. 24:13; 33:11). This is the likely sense here (cf. Prov. 29:12, where "his officials" are "those ministering to him"). The word also refers to the work of a priest, who ministers to the Lord (e.g., Deut. 10:8; 17:12), but this does not fit the present context.

Psalm 102. The title, "a prayer of one afflicted," makes it clear that this is an "individual lament." At the same time, it is certainly not individualistic: the "I" who sings this, whose troubles are so poignantly described here in all their inexplicability (vv. 1–11, 23–24), sees himself as a member of a community, "Zion" (vv. 12–22); his own well-being is ultimately bound up with the promised well-being of God's people. The psalm also contrasts the shortness of human life (e.g., v. 3, "my days pass away"; v. 11, "I wither away"; vv. 23–24) with God's enduring life (vv. 12, 25–28). Probably the repeated "my days" (vv. 3, 11, 23, 24) are intended to put "your [God's] years" (vv. 24, 27) into relief. As mentioned, the psalm is suited for one whose troubles seem to be unexplained (like Job's): even God's "indignation and anger" (v. 10) does not appear to be directed toward any specific sin. Nevertheless, singing this prayer equips the eye of faith to see God's ultimate purposes for the whole people of God and to look forward to participation in that blessedness (vv. 13, 21–22, 28).

102:1–2 *O Lord, Hear Me When I Call!* The psalm opens by sounding a note of bold urgency: the **cry** is desperate, and the singer wants God to respond **speedily**. He fears that God may (continue to) **hide** his **face from me** (see note on 13:1; cf. 22:24; 27:9; 30:7; 44:24; 69:17; 88:14; 143:7). The faithful can present their troubles to God with confidence.

3 For my days [g]pass away like smoke,
and my [h]bones burn like a furnace.
4 My heart is [i]struck down like grass and [j]has withered;
I [k]forget to eat my bread.
5 Because of my loud groaning
my [l]bones cling to my flesh.
6 I am like [m]a desert owl of the wilderness,
like an owl[1] of the waste places;
7 I [n]lie awake;
I am like a lonely sparrow on the housetop.
8 All the day my enemies taunt me;
those who [o]deride me [p]use my name for a curse.
9 For I eat ashes like bread
and [q]mingle tears with my drink,
10 because of your indignation and anger;
for you have [r]taken me up and [s]thrown me down.
11 My days are like [t]an evening shadow;
I [j]wither away like grass.

12 But you, O LORD, are [u]enthroned forever;
you [v]are remembered throughout all generations.
13 You will [w]arise and have [x]pity on Zion;
it is the time to favor her;
[y]the appointed time has come.
14 For your servants hold her [z]stones dear
and have pity on her dust.
15 Nations will [a]fear the name of the LORD,
and all [b]the kings of the earth will fear your glory.
16 For the LORD [c]builds up Zion;
he [d]appears in his glory;
17 he [e]regards the prayer of the destitute
and does not despise their prayer.

18 Let this be [f]recorded for [g]a generation to come,
so that [h]a people yet to be created may praise the LORD:

[1] The precise identity of these birds is uncertain

3[g][James 4:14]; See Ps. 37:20 [h]Job 30:30; Lam. 1:13; See Ps. 31:10
4[i]Ps. 121:6 [j]Ps. 37:2; Isa. 40:7; [James 1:10, 11] [k][1 Sam. 1:7; 2 Sam. 12:17; 1 Kgs. 21:4; Job 33:20]
5[l]See Job 19:20
6[m]Isa. 34:11; Zeph. 2:14; [Job 30:29]
7[n]Ps. 77:4
8[o][Acts 26:11] [p]Isa. 65:15; Jer. 29:22
9[q]See Ps. 42:3
10[r]Ezek. 3:12, 14 [s]Ps. 51:11
11[t]Ps. 109:23; 144:4; Job 8:9 [j][See ver. 4 above]
12[u]ver. 26; See Ps. 9:7 [v]Ps. 135:13; Ex. 3:15
13[w]Ps. 68:1 [x]Isa. 60:10; Zech. 1:12 [y]Ps. 75:2; Jer. 29:10; Dan. 9:2; [Isa. 40:2]
14[z]Neh. 4:2; [Lam. 4:1]
15[a]1 Kgs. 8:43; Isa. 59:19 [b]Ps. 138:4; Isa. 60:3
16[c]Ps. 147:2 [d]Isa. 60:1, 2
17[e]Neh. 1:6, 11
18[f][Deut. 31:19; Rom. 15:4; 1 Cor. 10:1] [g]Ps. 48:13; See Ps. 78:4, 6 [h]See Ps. 22:31; [Isa. 43:21]

102:3–11 *I Am in Distress as My Enemies Taunt Me.* These verses go on to describe what the singer feels like amid his distress. The psalm leaves out the specifics of the external troubles in order to focus on the singer's sense of discouragement: **bones burn**, **heart is struck down**, **forget to eat my bread**, **loud groaning**, **my bones cling to my flesh**—these all are vivid images of what it feels like to be consumed by sorrow and tempted to despair, which has such withering effects on one's body. There is a terrible sense of being alone (the solitary birds of vv. 6–7), which makes the taunts of the **enemies** pierce all the more deeply. The situation is one of mourning (expressed by **ashes** and **tears**), because it makes one think that these circumstances must be due to God's **indignation and anger**; and yet there is no suggestion in the psalm that there are specific sins to be confessed and forsaken. A person feeling such things inevitably senses his own mortality: his **days pass away like smoke** (v. 3; i.e., quickly) and **are like an evening shadow** (v. 11; i.e., soon gone).

102:6 desert owl . . . owl. As the ESV footnote explains, exact identification of these birds is not possible. Fortunately, the point is still clear: the stress is on their solitary life in desolate places (**the wilderness**, **the waste places**).

102:12–17 *O Lord, You Will Have Pity on Zion.* The previous section begins and ends with a sense of how short the life of a sufferer seems (vv. 3, 11); this section looks from that to the enduring life and reign of God (**enthroned forever**, **remembered throughout all generations**), which secures the ultimate success of his saving purposes in the world (v. 15). The connection between the afflicted individual and God having **pity on Zion** (v. 13) is not immediately obvious: probably v. 17 (God **regards the prayer of the destitute**) indicates that God's ultimate good for Zion (its role in bringing to pass that the **nations will fear the name of the LORD**, v. 15) includes ultimate good for each of the faithful members of God's people. Because God **does not despise their prayer** (cf. the same word in the title, and in v. 1), they can be assured that their momentary grieving is part of a larger scheme, and their endurance in faith contributes to it.

102:12 remembered throughout all generations. The phrase is borrowed from Ex. 3:15, describing God's "name," Yahweh.

102:15 For the OT expectation that one day Gentile **nations** and **kings** will come to know the true God by way of Israel (or its Messiah), see also 72:11; Isa. 52:1; 60:3; 62:2.

102:18–22 *Let Them Always Remember This in Zion.* This section further develops the previous section's reflections on Zion's future. The days of Zion's glory lie in the future, in the time of **a generation to come** (v. 18), who will need this record of God's promises and faithfulness to his people of all eras. In particular, the psalm allows the singers to see their present troubles, along with God's help, as a contribution to the praises to be offered in the future. The time will come when God's people will reflect on how God **looked down . . . to hear** (a past event to them, though still future to the singers!) and lift their voices to **declare in Zion the name of the LORD**; apparently the Gentiles will also celebrate (cf. v. 15).

19[i] See Ps. 11:4
20[j] Ps. 79:11 [k] Ps. 79:11
21[l] See Ps. 22:22
22[m] [Isa. 45:14]; See Ps. 22:27
23[n] Ps. 89:45
24[o] [Isa. 38:10] [p] Ps. 90:2; Job 36:26; Hab. 1:12
25[q] Gen. 1:1; 2:1; Cited Heb. 1:10 [r] See Ps. 96:5
26[s] Isa. 34:4; 51:6; Matt. 24:35; 2 Pet. 3:7, 10, 12; Rev. 20:11; 21:1; Cited Heb. 1:11, 12 [t] ver. 12
27[u] Isa. 41:4; 48:12; Mal. 3:6; [Heb. 13:8; James 1:17]
28[v] See Ps. 69:36 [w] Ps. 37:29 [x] Ps. 112:2
Psalm 103
1[y] ver. 22; Ps. 104:1

19 that he [i]looked down from his holy height;
from heaven the LORD looked at the earth,
20 to hear [j]the groans of the prisoners,
to set free [k]those who were doomed to die,
21 that they may [l]declare in Zion the name of the LORD,
and in Jerusalem his praise,
22 when [m]peoples gather together,
and kingdoms, to worship the LORD.

23 He has broken my strength in midcourse;
he [n]has shortened my days.
24 "O my God," [o]I say, "take me not away
in the midst of my days—
[p]you whose years endure
throughout all generations!"

25 [q]Of old you laid the foundation of the earth,
and [r]the heavens are the work of your hands.
26 [s]They will perish, but [t]you will remain;
they will all wear out like a garment.
You will change them like a robe, and they will pass away,
27 but [u]you are the same, and your years have no end.
28 [v]The children of your servants [w]shall dwell secure;
[x]their offspring shall be established before you.

Bless the LORD, O My Soul

103

OF DAVID.

1 [y]Bless the LORD, O my soul,
and all that is within me,
bless his holy name!

102:23–24 *O Lord, Do Not Shorten My Life!* As already mentioned, the person who feels what vv. 3–11 describe is keenly aware of his own mortality; it seems like the troubles will shorten his life even further. Probably, in view of the long-range expectations for Zion's future (vv. 12–22), the prayer is that the God **whose years endure throughout all generations** would preserve the life of his faithful ones so that they may see something of this wonderful future.

102:25–28 *The Lord Is Eternal, and His Faithfulness Outlasts the World.* The psalm finishes with words addressed to God, meditating on God's everlasting being and purpose. The average person experiences the physical world as a long-established operation (cf. the English saying, "as old as the hills"); and yet God is older still. **Of old** God **laid the foundation of the earth**; he was there before the world was created (cf. 90:1–2). And though the earth and heavens **will perish** and **will all wear out like a garment**, God **will remain**. In fact, the years will not change him; **you are the same**. This means that his purposes will not change either, and, even if it takes (what seems to us) a long time to bring those purposes about, he will never grow weary or give up. Thus the psalm closes with confidence that goes well beyond the individual worshipers' lifetime, expecting God to keep his promises to many faithful generations descended from today's faithful (102:28).

102:25–27 Hebrews 1:10–12 cites these verses from the Greek Septuagint, which is very close to the Hebrew. Because the book of Hebrews applies the words to Jesus, some interpreters think of this passage as "messianic." But it is better to observe that the text is not explicitly messianic; rather, NT authors call Jesus "Lord" (Gk. *Kyrios*, the LXX rendering of Yahweh) and apply to him several OT texts about Yahweh (e.g., Phil. 2:10–11, using Isa. 45:23; 1 Pet. 2:3, using Ps. 34:8; 1 Pet. 3:15, using Isa. 8:13); further, Christ's involvement in creation supports this pattern (e.g., John 1:1; Col. 1:16; Heb. 1:2). (See note on Ps. 97:7.) The author of Hebrews uses the expression **the same** again for Jesus (Heb. 13:8).

102:28 children . . . offspring. Cf. notes on 100:5 and 103:17–18. The Lord, who is everlasting, can ensure that the descendants of his **servants** will **dwell secure**, i.e., will enjoy God's love and Zion's future.

Psalm 103. This is a hymn of praise, celebrating the abundant goodness and love of the Lord for his people. It is the first of four psalms reflecting on God's dealings with his people from creation to exile. Psalm 103 introduces the sequence by recalling that Israel's survival in the time of Moses was due to God's steadfast love. It begins with each individual singer exhorting his or her own soul to bless the Lord, and then goes on to list the benefits that the soul should be careful not to forget. The crowning benefit is God's enduring love to the descendants of the faithful, which leads the worshipers to exhort all the angelic hosts and all the material creation to join in blessing the Lord. These benefits come to the individual ("you" in vv. 3–5 refers to "my soul," i.e., to me) but are not individualistic: he or she is a member of the community (vv. 6–14, thinking of the people of God), and he or she contributes to the progress of that community (vv. 17–18). As the notes will show, the psalm takes the Pentateuch story for granted, with evocations of Gen. 2:7; 17:7; Exodus 32–34. Christians enter into the joy of this psalm as they celebrate how the biblical story that has developed since that time has displayed even more of God's goodness and kindness. Psalm 104, though not by David, is probably placed next to this one because it too begins and ends with "Bless the LORD, O my soul." Psalm 145 is the other example of a Davidic psalm that is a sustained celebration of God's goodness and benevolence.

103:1–2 *Bless the Lord, O My Soul, and Do Not Forget His Benefits.* Each member of the worshiping congregation urges himself to **bless the LORD**, i.e., to speak well of him for his abundant generosity. Thus **forget not all his benefits** is a crucial step in blessing the Lord, and the body of the psalm lists these benefits in order to bring each singer to an admiring gratitude.

2 [y]Bless the LORD, O my soul,
and [z]forget not all his benefits,
3 who [a]forgives all your iniquity,
who [b]heals all your diseases,
4 who [c]redeems your life from the pit,
who [d]crowns you with steadfast love and mercy,
5 who [e]satisfies you with good
so that your youth is renewed like [f]the eagle's.

6 The LORD works [g]righteousness
and justice for all who are oppressed.
7 He made known his [h]ways to Moses,
his [i]acts to the people of Israel.
8 The LORD is [j]merciful and gracious,
slow to anger and abounding in steadfast love.
9 [k]He will not always chide,
nor will he [l]keep his anger forever.
10 He does not deal with us [m]according to our sins,
nor repay us according to our iniquities.
11 For [n]as high as the heavens are above the earth,
so great is his [o]steadfast love toward [p]those who fear him;
12 as far as the east is from the west,
so far does he [q]remove our transgressions from us.
13 As [r]a father shows compassion to his children,
so the LORD shows compassion [p]to those who fear him.
14 For he knows our frame;[1]
he [s]remembers that we are dust.

15 As for man, his days are like [t]grass;
he flourishes like [u]a flower of the field;
16 for [v]the wind passes over it, and [w]it is gone,
and [x]its place knows it no more.

[1] *Or knows how we are formed*

2 [y][See ver. 1 above] [z]Deut. 6:12; 8:11
3 [a]Ex. 34:7; Isa. 33:24; Matt. 9:2; Mark 2:5; [Luke 7:47] [b]Ps. 107:20; 147:3; Ex. 15:26; [Matt. 8:17]
4 [c]See Ps. 56:13 [d][Ps. 5:12]
5 [e]Ps. 107:9 [f]Isa. 40:31
6 [g]Ps. 146:7
7 [h]Ex. 33:13; [Ps. 25:4] [i][Ps. 78:11; Ex. 34:10]
8 [j]See Ps. 86:15
9 [k]Isa. 57:16 [l]Ps. 30:5; Jer. 3:5, 12; Mic. 7:18
10 [m]Ezra 9:13
11 [n]See Ps. 36:5 [o]Ps. 117:2 [p]ver. 13, 17; Luke 1:50
12 [q][Isa. 38:17; 43:25; Mic. 7:19]
13 [r]Mal. 3:17 [p][See ver. 11 above]
14 [s]Ps. 78:39
15 [t]Ps. 90:5 [u]See Job 14:2
16 [v]Isa. 40:7 [w]Ps. 37:36 [x]See Job 7:10

103:3–19 *The Benefits.* The benefits all express God's steadfast love (vv. 4, 8, 11, 17) and mercy, as God explains his own name in Ex. 34:6–7. These include the personal and communal experience of God's forgiveness and constant care.

103:3 Heals often refers to curing someone from a physical sickness, but it can also be used as a metaphor for restoring the moral and spiritual life (e.g., Isa. 6:10; 53:5; Jer. 3:22; Hos. 14:4). Since it is in parallel with **forgives**, the metaphorical use may be intended here. Thus **iniquity** is like **diseases**, which weaken and corrupt; it is God's mercy that takes them away. These sentiments reflect David's own experience of God's forgiveness (cf. 2 Samuel 12; Psalm 51).

103:4–5 These verses speak of God's constant care and provision. **redeems**. See note on Isa. 1:24–28; see also note on Ps. 25:22. **steadfast love and mercy**. See note on 103:8–13. **like the eagle's**. The eagle is an emblem of strength, vitality, and youthful endurance (cf. Isa. 40:31).

103:6–14 The list of benefits shifts to a survey of how God has dealt with his people as a whole, in spite of their many provocations. The key is v. 8. The terms "us," "our," and "we" refer to the people; the verses focus especially on "those who fear" the Lord (vv. 11, 13), i.e., on those who take the covenant to heart (see note on vv. 17–18).

103:6 Righteousness and **justice** are the blessings of protection from those who might exploit or harm (cf. 33:5; 97:2; Deut. 16:18; Isa. 5:7). The Lord extends these blessings to all who are **oppressed**, but especially to his own people (cf. Ps. 146:7).

103:7 his ways. God's character as it governs his deeds (Ex. 33:13). **his acts**. These reveal his enduring commitment to his people, i.e., they express God's "ways." "Acts" can also be rendered "deeds" (see Ps. 9:11; 66:5; 77:12; Isa. 12:4).

103:8–13 Verse 8 is based on Ex. 34:6, where God proclaims his own name (the OT's fundamental confession of God's character); Ps. 103:9–13 expounds this further. The terms **sins**, **iniquities** (v. 10), and **transgressions** (v. 12) are names for what God forgives in Ex. 34:7a. Likewise **steadfast love** (Ps. 103:11) and **shows compassion** (v. 13; the word is related to **merciful** in v. 8) reveal that this is an application of Ex. 34:6–7.

103:9 nor will he keep his anger forever. Cf. 30:5 and Mic. 7:18.

103:11–13 These are three comparisons for the kindness of God toward his people, to show its abundance (v. 11; cf. 36:5), decisiveness (103:12), and enduring quality (v. 13).

103:13 God is a **father** to his people as a whole (Ex. 4:22–23), and to the particular faithful members (Prov. 3:12). Of course many human fathers fail to embody this idea; this image assumes that biblically informed people have an intuition of what fathers ideally should be like. But it also serves as a goal for faithful fathers: they will seek more and more to be the kind of father who **shows compassion to his children**.

103:14 he knows our frame. As the ESV footnote explains, this could also be "he knows how we are formed," which, together with **we are dust** looks back to Gen. 2:7. The Lord **remembers** the finiteness of the human perspective ("dust" is not eternal or omniscient), and he is patient with his people.

103:15–18 The song reaches its crescendo here: amid the shortness of human life (vv. 15–16), God's steadfast love for his faithful is everlasting (v. 17a), bestowing on them the privilege of nurturing those who will be his people in coming generations (vv. 17b–18). For the image of **grass** and **flower** for the transience of life, cf. 90:5 and Isa. 40:7; for other reflections on the shortness of life, cf. Ps. 102:3, 11. **the wind passes over it, and it is gone**. The wind dries out the plants in a dry climate.

17[y]Ps. 25:6 [p][See ver. 11 above] [z]Ex. 20:5, 6
18[a]Deut. 7:9 [b]Ps. 19:8
19[c]Ps. 11:4; 93:2 [d]Ps. 47:2; Dan. 4:17
20[e]Ps. 148:2; [Luke 2:13] [f]Ps. 78:25 [g]Matt. 6:10
21[h]Gen. 32:2; Josh. 5:14; 1 Kgs. 22:19 [i]Ps. 104:4; Dan. 7:10; Heb. 1:14
22[j]Ps. 145:10 [k]ver. 1, 2

Psalm 104

1[l]Ps. 103:1, 2, 22 [m]See 2 Sam. 7:22 [n]Ps. 93:1; Job 40:10; [Job 37:22]
2[o]See Job 9:8 [p]Isa. 40:22

17 But [y]the steadfast love of the LORD is from everlasting to everlasting on [p]those who fear him,
and his righteousness to [z]children's children,
18 to those who [a]keep his covenant
and [b]remember to do his commandments.
19 The LORD has [c]established his throne in the heavens,
and his [d]kingdom rules over all.

20 Bless the LORD, O you [e]his angels,
you [f]mighty ones who [g]do his word,
obeying the voice of his word!
21 Bless the LORD, all his [h]hosts,
his [i]ministers, who do his will!
22 [j]Bless the LORD, all his works,
in all places of his dominion.
[k]Bless the LORD, O my soul!

O LORD My God, You Are Very Great

104

1 [l]Bless the LORD, O my soul!
O LORD my God, you are [m]very great!
[n]You are clothed with splendor and majesty,
2 covering yourself with light as with a garment,
[o]stretching out the heavens [p]like a tent.

103:17–18 the steadfast love of the LORD is from everlasting to everlasting. Cf. 25:6; 100:5. **Those who fear him** (103:11, 13) are the same as **those who keep his covenant and remember to do his commandments**; they are the faithful, who believe the promises and obey the commands (Ex. 19:5; Deut. 7:9; cf. John 14:15, 21; 15:10; Rev. 1:3; 3:8). The covenant of circumcision, which Abraham's descendants were to "keep," included the promise that the Lord would be God to both the offspring and their parents. This psalm goes beyond that, however: the faithful expect that God sets his saving love on their **children's children**. This is the crowning privilege that God gives to his faithful: though their lives are short and appear almost insignificant, they may still contribute to the future well-being of the people of God by their godly and prayerful parenting and grandparenting. Cf. also Ps. 100:5; 102:28; in Ex. 34:7a God keeps steadfast love for thousands (i.e., thousands of generations; cf. Deut. 7:9) of the faithful (Ex. 20:6).

103:19 His throne . . . his kingdom refers to God's universal rule over all creation (see note on Psalm 93). The marvel of being God's people is that the one whose kingdom **rules over all** offers the privilege of gratefully embracing his rule.

103:20–22 *Let All Creation Join in Blessing the Lord.* After listing all these benefits, the psalm returns to urging various creatures to **bless the LORD**, echoing vv. 1–2. The addressees go beyond the individual "soul" to include the **angels** and **mighty ones** (vv. 20–21) and even the material creation (**all his works, in all places of his dominion**; cf. v. 19). The overflow of goodness and steadfast love that God's works reveal compels his people to call on the angels and all of nature (cf. 19:1) to join in their celebration. The song closes with the singer returning to urge his own **soul** to **bless the LORD**, with a deeper appreciation of how much praise and admiration he owes.

103:21 who do his will. Jesus echoes this in Matt. 6:10, teaching his followers to pray that God's "will be done" with the same ready obedience shown by the angels ("in heaven").

Psalm 104. The phrase "Bless the LORD, O my soul," which opens and closes the psalm, shows that the psalm is about reasons for speaking well about God. This hymn of praise celebrates the way the created order reveals God's glory by providing so abundantly for all living things. Although it does not use many specific words from Gen. 1:1–2:3, it is generally agreed that the creation account's ideas lie behind the psalm. Some have even suggested that the psalm is structured around the six workdays of God (see chart, p. 1070). This structure, however, should not be pressed, since the land animals and man (Ps. 104:21–24) here precede the sea creatures (vv. 25–26), while the Genesis account has them in the opposite order. Even more, this is not a straight retelling of the Genesis account as an event: rather, it celebrates the way in which the creation order still continues in human experience. The psalm acknowledges the existence of human sin, but in only one verse (Ps. 104:35, "sinners" and "wicked"). This psalm shapes the worshipers' hearts in two ways. First, it leads them to delight in the world that God made, recognizing it as a gift. Second, it enables them to see that "sinners" and "the wicked" (i.e., those who dwell in their sin and refuse God's grace) defile God's world; the faithful will not want to be identified with such people. Genesis 1:1–2:3 uses the term "God" for the deity, stressing his role as the transcendent Creator. Psalm 104 primarily uses "the LORD," the personal name of the deity, following the biblical claim that the covenant God of Israel is the same being as the majestic Creator (see note on Gen. 2:4). This psalm joins Psalm 8 as a reflection on God's continuing commitment to, and care for, his creation (cf. also 136:5–9). This psalm is often said to be connected to the Great Hymn to Aten, which is generally attributed to the Egyptian Pharaoh Akhenaten, who ruled 1352–1336 B.C. This Pharaoh attempted a drastic revision of Egyptian religion, aiming to focus worship on only one god, Aten, represented by the disk of the sun. Egyptologists continue to debate whether he was a true monotheist (believing that there is only one God) or a henotheist (worshiping one god while allowing for others). The hymn celebrates the works of this deity, including his provision of water and food for man and beast; it distinguishes between creatures active during daylight and those active at night (even mentioning the lions). There are certainly similarities between this Egyptian hymn and Psalm 104, but there is no evidence that the psalm *derives from* the Egyptian hymn. As the notes will show, the psalm reflects the covenantal and creational perspective of the Pentateuch. If there is any connection to the Egyptian hymn (and it is questionable whether most Israelites would have known of it), it is that this psalm renders the right kind of praise to the universal Creator.

104:1–4 *The Lord Is Clothed with Splendor and Majesty.* The first section of the psalm sets the tone by expounding the cry, **O LORD my God, you are very great!** The various images all express the magnificence of the God who made the world and continues to rule it.

104:1–2 splendor and majesty. See note on 96:6. **stretching out the heavens like a tent**. See note on Isa. 40:22.

3 He [q]lays the beams of his [r]chambers on the waters;
he makes [s]the clouds his chariot;
he rides on [t]the wings of the wind;
4 he [u]makes his messengers winds,
his [v]ministers [w]a flaming fire.
5 He [x]set the earth on its foundations,
so that it should never be moved.
6 You [y]covered it with the deep as with a garment;
the waters stood above the mountains.
7 At [z]your rebuke they fled;
at [a]the sound of your thunder they [b]took to flight.
8 The mountains rose, the valleys sank down
to the place that you [c]appointed for them.
9 You set [d]a boundary that they may not pass,
so that they [e]might not again cover the earth.

10 You make springs gush forth in the valleys;
they flow between the hills;
11 they [f]give drink to every beast of the field;
the wild donkeys quench their thirst.
12 Beside them the birds of the heavens dwell;
they sing among the branches.
13 [g]From your lofty abode you [h]water the mountains;
the earth is satisfied with the fruit of your work.

14 You cause [i]the grass to grow for the livestock
and [j]plants for man to cultivate,
that he may bring forth [k]food from the earth
15 and [l]wine to gladden the heart of man,
[m]oil to make his face shine
and bread to [n]strengthen man's heart.

3 [q]Amos 9:6 [r]ver. 13 [s]Isa. 19:1 [t]Ps. 18:10; 2 Sam. 22:11
4 [u]Cited Heb. 1:7; [Ps. 148:8] [v]Ps. 103:21 [w][2 Kgs. 1:10; 2:11]
5 [x]Ps. 24:2; 89:11; 136:6; See Job 38:4
6 [y]Gen. 7:19
7 [z]Ps. 18:15; [Ps. 106:9; Gen. 1:9; 8:1, 5; Matt. 8:26] [a]Ps. 77:18 [b]Ps. 48:5
8 [c][Job 38:8, 10, 11]
9 [d]See Job 26:10 [e]See Gen. 9:11-16
11 [f][ver. 13]
13 [g]ver. 3 [h][Ps. 65:9; 147:8; Deut. 11:11; Job 5:10; Jer. 10:13; 14:22]
14 [i]Ps. 147:8, 9 [j]Gen. 1:11, 29, 30; 3:18; 9:3 [k]Job 28:5; [Ps. 136:25; 147:9]
15 [l]Judg. 9:13; Eccles. 10:19; [Prov. 31:6, 7] [m][Ps. 23:5; Judg. 9:9] [n][Gen. 18:5]

104:4 makes his messengers winds. Hebrews 1:7 quotes this verse from the Greek Septuagint, with the term "messengers" (Hb. *mal'akim*) translated as "angels" (Gk. *angeloi*); it reinforces the argument that Jesus is superior to the angels by showing that Jesus receives higher honor than the angels.

104:5–9 *The Lord Set Bounds for the Land and the Sea.* This section stresses the reliability of the world God made, based on the third day of creation (where the land and the water become separate); the dry land is a safe and suitable place for its inhabitants. The telling in Gen. 1:9–10 is very sparse and broad-stroke, while here the narration is more imaginative. Some have supposed that these verses are referring to the flood story, but the setting of the whole psalm is God's continuing care for his creation, rather than his judgment.

104:5 never be moved. This describes the stability of the earth (see note on 93:1), in this case the secure allocation of water and dry land to their proper places.

Creation day	Psalm 104 verses
Day 1	2a: light
Day 2	2b–4: the "expanse" divides the waters
Day 3	5–13: land and water distinct 14–18: vegetation and trees
Day 4	19–24: light-bearers as time-keepers
Day 5	25–26: sea creatures
Day 6	21–24: land animals and man 27–30: food for all creatures

104:7 At your rebuke. Mark may have had this text in mind when he wrote that Jesus "rebuked the wind" and commanded the sea (Mark 4:39), implying that Jesus wielded the same authority as the Lord God (cf. Mark 2:7).

104:10–13 *The Lord Provides Water for the Creatures on Land.* This section moves from the boundary between water and land, to the way God abundantly supplies the water that the land animals depend on. The term **beast of the field** (v. 11) refers to wild animals (see notes on Gen. 1:24–25; 2:20); the **wild donkeys** are onagers, a species of donkey that does not seem ever to have been domesticated. This suggests that these **valleys**, **hills** (Ps. 104:10), and **mountains** (v. 13) are uninhabited by man. Although God made the world an ideal place for human beings to live, his creation is filled with more creatures than simply the ones useful to man; and this helps the pious to admire God's bountiful care.

104:14–18 *The Lord Provides Food and Homes for the Land Creatures.* The thought of water naturally leads to the growth of vegetation (the second part of the third day of creation; Gen. 1:11–12): **grass**, **plants**, grapes (yielding **wine**), olives (yielding **oil**), grains (yielding **bread**), and **trees** of various kinds. While Ps. 104:14–15 stresses life on a farm (with **livestock** and **food from the earth**), vv. 16–18 join vv. 10–13 in focusing on the wild environment (e.g., where the **wild goats**, or ibexes, live). God's care extends to the unclean animals, such as the **stork** (Lev. 11:19; Deut. 14:18) and the **rock badgers** (or hyraxes, Lev. 11:5; Deut. 14:7; see note on Prov. 30:24–28). God cares for all kinds of animals, even for those that he has specifically forbidden the Israelites to eat.

104:15 The **bread** here serves human need; and the uses of **wine** and **oil** described here go beyond what is purely necessary to include what adds enjoyment.

16 The trees of the LORD are watered abundantly,
[o]the cedars of Lebanon [p]that he planted.
17 In them the birds build their nests;
the stork has her home in the fir trees.
18 The high mountains are for [q]the wild goats;
the rocks are a refuge for [r]the rock badgers.

19 He made the moon to mark the [s]seasons;[1]
the sun knows its time for setting.
20 [t]You make darkness, and it is night,
when all the beasts of the forest creep about.
21 [u]The young lions roar for their prey,
seeking their food from God.
22 When the sun rises, they steal away
and lie down in their [v]dens.
23 [w]Man goes out to his work
and to his labor until the evening.

24 O LORD, how manifold are your works!
In [x]wisdom have you made them all;
the earth is full of your creatures.
25 Here is the sea, great and wide,
[y]which teems with creatures innumerable,
living things both small and great.
26 There go the ships,
and [z]Leviathan, which you formed to [a]play in it.[2]

27 These [b]all look to you,
to [c]give them their food in due season.
28 When you give it to them, they gather it up;
when you [d]open your hand, they are filled with good things.
29 When you [e]hide your face, they are [f]dismayed;
when you [g]take away their breath, they die
and [h]return to their dust.
30 When you [i]send forth your Spirit,[3] they are created,
and you [j]renew the face of the ground.

[1] *Or the appointed times* (compare Genesis 1:14) [2] *Or you formed to play with* [3] *Or breath*

16[o]See Judg. 9:15 [p][Num. 24:6]
18[q]See Job 39:1 [r]Lev. 11:5; Prov. 30:26
19[s]Gen. 1:14; Lev. 23:4
20[t]Isa. 45:7
21[u]Job 38:39
22[v]Job 37:8
23[w][Gen. 3:19]
24[x]Prov. 3:19
25[y]Ps. 69:34
26[z]See Job 41:1 [a][Job 40:20]
27[b]Ps. 145:15 [c][ver. 14]; See Job 36:31
28[d]Ps. 145:16
29[e]Ps. 30:7; [Deut. 31:17] [f]Job 23:15 [g]See Job 34:14 [h]See Job 10:9
30[i]See Job 33:4 [j][Rev. 21:5]

104:19–24 *The Lord Governs the Rhythm of Day and Night.* These verses take up the fourth creation day, when God appointed the celestial lights to mark off time for mankind; the lights still do what God appointed them to do. The **moon** will **mark the seasons** (i.e., the "appointed times" of the liturgical calendar, see note on Gen. 1:14–19) with its phases, but it also joins the **sun** in marking off day and night. During the night, many wild animals are active: **all the beasts of the forest creep about**, and **the young lions roar for their prey**. At daybreak, they **steal away** for shelter, while **man goes out to his work**. These verses help the Israelites to see the rhythm of their life, by which they work during the day and rest at night, as inherent in the creation order (cf. note on Gen. 1:3–5) and also in the larger context of the other animals' activities. Hard work is not an evil distortion of the original creation; man was given work to do in the garden of Eden (Gen. 2:15). The curse did not introduce work; it infected work with pain (Gen. 3:17–18). Verse 24 of Psalm 104 brings to a close this section (about the **creatures** that live on the **earth**, i.e., on land), with its exclamation of wonder and delight: **how manifold are your works!**

104:21 Predators, such as **young lions**, go after **their prey, seeking their food from God**. This activity is admired, and even seen as part of the proper working of the world, so long as these beasts do not threaten stock animals (cf. 1 Sam. 17:34–35; Isa. 31:4; Amos 3:12) or man (Judg. 14:5; 2 Kings 17:25).

104:25–26 *The Lord Delights in the Sea Creatures, Too.* After celebrating God's care for the land animals, the song moves on to the open **sea . . . which teems with creatures innumerable** (corresponding to the fifth creation day, Gen. 1:20–23). (The **ships** that men sail for merchant activities do not defile the creation order.) **Leviathan** (see note on Ps. 74:14) here is probably a poetic name for a whale, and is therefore one of the "great sea creatures" (Gen. 1:21). Although the word can be used for an enemy of God, this psalm joins the creation account in portraying the various creatures as subject to the Lord, not opposing him. The admiration continues, as the song says that God **formed** Leviathan **to play in** the sea (or, if the alternate rendering in the ESV footnote is followed, he formed it to be his partner in play); throughout this psalm, delight takes the singing congregation far beyond mere utility!

104:27–30 *All Creatures Everywhere Depend on the Lord's Provision.* Each living thing on the land and sea (**these all**) depends on God to supply their **food in due season** and their very **breath**, in order to continue their lives; they also depend on God to **renew the face of the ground**, i.e., to give success to their reproduction. In keeping with this entire psalm, the God on whom all depend is generous (**they are filled with good things**), someone safe on whom to rely.

104:29 return to their dust. An allusion to Gen. 3:19.

31 May the glory of the LORD [k]endure forever;
may the LORD [l]rejoice in his works,
32 who looks on the earth and it [m]trembles,
who [n]touches the mountains and they smoke!
33 I will sing to the LORD [o]as long as I live;
I will sing praise to my God while I have being.
34 May my [p]meditation be pleasing to him,
for I rejoice in the LORD.
35 Let [q]sinners be consumed from the earth,
and let the wicked be no more!
[r]Bless the LORD, O my soul!
[s]Praise the LORD!

Tell of All His Wonderful Works

105 1 [t]Oh give thanks to the LORD; [u]call upon his name;
[v]make known his deeds among the peoples!
2 Sing to him, sing praises to him;
[w]tell of all his wondrous works!
3 Glory in his holy name;
let the hearts of those who seek the LORD rejoice!
4 Seek the LORD and his [x]strength;
[y]seek his presence continually!
5 Remember the [z]wondrous works that he has done,
his miracles, and [a]the judgments he uttered,
6 O offspring of [b]Abraham, his servant,
children of Jacob, his [c]chosen ones!

7 He is the LORD our God;
his [d]judgments are in all the earth.
8 He [e]remembers his covenant forever,
the word that he commanded, for [f]a thousand generations,

31 [k]Ps. 72:17 [l][Gen. 1:31; Prov. 8:31]
32 [m][Hab. 3:10] [n]Ps. 144:5; Ex. 19:18; [Amos 9:5]
33 [o]See Ps. 63:4
34 [p]Job 15:4
35 [q]See Ps. 37:38 [r]See ver. 1 [s]Ps. 105:45; 106:48; 113:9; 150:6

Psalm 105

1 [t]Ps. 106:1; 1 Chr. 16:34; Isa. 12:4; For ver. 1-15, see 1 Chr. 16:8-22 [u]Ps. 99:6; 116:13, 17; [Gen. 4:26] [v]Ps. 145:4, 5, 11, 12
2 [w]Ps. 77:12
4 [x]See Ps. 78:61 [y][Ps. 27:8]
5 [z]Ps. 77:11; See Ps. 72:18 [a]Ex. 6:6; 7:4
6 [b]ver. 42 [c]ver. 43; Ps. 106:5; [Ps. 135:4]
7 [d]Isa. 26:9
8 [e]ver. 42; Ps. 106:45; 111:5; Luke 1:72 [f]Deut. 7:9

104:31–35 *May I Ever Rejoice in the Lord's Works Like He Does.* The key to the final section is the repeated "rejoice": **may the LORD rejoice in his works** (v. 31; i.e., the works he does in caring for his creation), and **I rejoice in the LORD** (v. 34; i.e., who shows such abundant generosity in his works). This **meditation** on God's bounty will **be pleasing to him** if the singing congregation can learn from it to admire and trust the Creator and Ruler of all, and to **sing praise to** him from the heart. Verse 35 is the only mention of human sin in the entire psalm, though the curse on sin is alluded to in v. 29. **Sinners** and the **wicked** are, as generally in the psalms, those who reject God's gracious rule and dwell in their rebellion. Such a moral condition of hardness against God is a blemish on God's good world; the prayer that they be **consumed from the earth** will be answered in God's good time. The purpose of this prayer in this context is not to foster hatred of human sinners but instead hatred of all sorts of sin that so stains and defiles God's good creation. The faithful will not want to be identified with such people, and will want their own lives to be more and more in tune with the goodness of God.

104:35 Praise the LORD! (Hb. *hallelu-yah*). The Greek Septuagint makes this phrase a part of Psalm 105, matching the last phrase of 105:45. This would result in Psalms 103–106 each having a literary envelope, with the closing phrase echoing the opening. However, there is no evidence for this in the Hebrew manuscripts.

Psalm 105. This is a hymn celebrating God's faithful dealings with his people, particularly reflecting on episodes from the Pentateuch in which the people interacted with powerful foreigners who might have harmed them: Abimelech (Genesis 20), Potiphar (Genesis 39–41), and Pharaoh (Exodus, esp. chs. 7–14). The tone of Psalm 105 is one of gratitude (vv. 1–6): each member of the singing congregation should recognize that he is an heir and beneficiary of all these great deeds that God has done, so that each one will embrace his calling to live as a member of God's holy people (vv. 43–45). It is the only psalm to recall explicitly the promises to the patriarchs. Psalm 105 is a "historical psalm," like Psalms 78 and 106. Psalm 106 takes up events that follow those of Psalm 105, stressing God's patience with his people when they disbelieved and rebelled. The theme of the people's disbelief is absent from Psalm 105. Verses 28–36 recount eight of the 10 plagues sent upon the Egyptians, leaving out the fifth and sixth (Ex. 9:1–12). The psalm mentions the ninth plague first (Ps. 105:28), and has the third and fourth in reverse order (v. 31). There is no doubt that the psalm depends on Exodus; the difference between the two tellings is due to the different purposes behind the tellings. Exodus gives the fuller narrative, while Psalm 105 focuses on features that display God's faithfulness. Verses 1–15 also appear in 1 Chron. 16:8–22, followed by a version of Psalm 96, giving the song for moving the ark to Jerusalem.

105:1–6 *Call to Give Thanks to the Lord.* The opening section invites the congregation to celebrate what the Lord has done, setting a tone of gladness with terms such as **give thanks**, **sing**, **sing praises**, **tell**, **glory**, and **rejoice**. The foundation of gratitude is remembering **the wondrous works that** the Lord **has done**, particularly those on behalf of his people, the **offspring of Abraham** (cf. Gen. 15:5, 13, 18; 17:7).

105:1 call upon his name. An expression for seeking the Lord in public worship (cf. Gen. 4:26; 12:8). **make known his deeds among the peoples**. Cf. Ps. 9:11; Isa. 12:4.

105:6 servant . . . chosen. See vv. 26, 42–43.

105:7–11 *The Lord Makes and Keeps His Covenant.* The next section describes in general what the Lord has done: he has displayed his **judgments . . . in all the earth**, and he **remembers his covenant forever**. The rest of the psalm will give specific examples to back up this claim.

105:8 remembers his covenant forever. For this expression, see 106:45; 111:5; Gen. 9:15; Ex. 2:24; 6:5; Lev. 26:42, 45; Jer. 14:21; Ezek. 16:60. For

9 [g]the covenant that he made with Abraham,
his [h]sworn promise to Isaac,
10 which he confirmed to [i]Jacob as a statute,
to Israel as an everlasting covenant,
11 saying, [j]"To you I will give the land of Canaan
as [k]your portion for an inheritance."

12 When they were [l]few in number,
of little account, and [m]sojourners in it,
13 wandering from nation to nation,
from one kingdom to another people,
14 he [n]allowed no one to oppress them;
he [o]rebuked kings on their account,
15 saying, [p]"Touch not my anointed ones,
do my prophets no harm!"

16 When he [q]summoned a famine on the land
and [r]broke all supply[1] of bread,
17 he had [s]sent a man ahead of them,
Joseph, who was [t]sold as a slave.
18 His [u]feet were hurt with fetters;
his neck was put in a collar of iron;
19 until [v]what he had said came to pass,
the word of the LORD [w]tested him.
20 [x]The king sent and [y]released him;
the ruler of the peoples set him free;
21 he [z]made him lord of his house
and ruler of all his possessions,
22 to bind[2] his princes at his pleasure
and to teach his elders wisdom.

23 Then [a]Israel came to Egypt;
Jacob [b]sojourned in [c]the land of Ham.
24 And the LORD [d]made his people very fruitful
and made them stronger than their foes.
25 He [e]turned their hearts to hate his people,
to [f]deal craftily with his servants.

26 He [g]sent Moses, his servant,
and Aaron, [h]whom he had chosen.

[1] Hebrew *staff* [2] Septuagint, Syriac, Jerome *instruct*

9[g]Gen. 17:2; See Gen. 22:15-18 [h]Gen. 26:3
10[i]Gen. 28:13, 14; 35:11, 12
11[j]Gen. 13:15; 15:18 [k]Ps. 78:55
12[l]Gen. 34:30; Deut. 7:7; 26:5 [m]Heb. 11:9
14[n][Gen. 35:5] [o]Gen. 12:17; 20:3
15[p]Gen. 20:6, 7; [Gen. 26:11]
16[q]Gen. 41:54; [2 Kgs. 8:1; Hag. 1:11] [r]Lev. 26:26; Isa. 3:1; Ezek. 4:16; [Ps. 104:15]
17[s]Gen. 45:5; 50:20 [t]Gen. 37:28, 36; Acts 7:9
18[u][Gen. 39:20]
19[v]Gen. 40:20, 21; 41:53, 54 [w][Judg. 7:4]
20[x]Gen. 41:14 [y]Ps. 146:7
21[z]Gen. 41:40
23[a]Gen. 46:6; Acts 7:15 [b]Acts 13:17 [c]Ps. 106:22; [Ps. 78:51]
24[d]Ex. 1:7; Deut. 26:5
25[e][Ex. 9:12; Rom. 11:8]; See Ex. 1:8-14 [f]Ex. 1:10; Acts 7:19
26[g]Ex. 3:10; 4:12 [h]Num. 16:5; 17:5

God remembering, see note on Ps. 25:6–7. **a thousand generations**. See Ex. 34:7 and Deut. 7:9; cf. note on Ps. 100:5.

105:10 everlasting covenant. Here this refers to the promise that Israel will possess the land and remain as God's people (see Gen. 17:7, 19).

105:12–15 *He Watched over His People While They Wandered in Canaan.* The first specific example comes from Genesis 20, where Abraham sojourned in Gerar. **Prophets** (Ps. 105:15) recalls Gen. 20:7, "for [Abraham] is a prophet." When the king of Gerar took Sarah to be his wife, he placed in jeopardy God's promise to raise up a son for Abraham from Sarah, but God ensured the integrity of the promise.

105:12 Sojourners are resident aliens, who do not have citizenship rights (cf. Gen. 23:4).

105:15 anointed ones. This (with the companion 1 Chron. 16:22) is the only place in the OT that uses the plural of "anointed one," applying it here to the family of Abraham (perhaps treating the descendants as included in the ancestor). God calls Abraham and his offspring his "anointed ones" because he specially selected them to be his people. **prophets**. In Gen. 20:7, Abraham as a prophet is both under God's special care and a worthy intercessor on behalf of others.

105:16–23 *He Brought Israel to Egypt to Sojourn.* The next example is the account of Joseph (Genesis 39–41): Joseph went from being a slave in Potiphar's house (Ps. 105:17) to prison (v. 18; cf. Gen. 39:20), where he interpreted dreams (Ps. 105:19; cf. Gen. 41:13). He then became next in command to Pharaoh (Ps. 105:20–22; cf. Gen. 41:40). Following Joseph's words in Gen. 50:20, the psalm interprets the way Joseph was sold into slavery (the psalm does not need to add, "by his own brothers") and rose to power in Egypt as an expression of God's faithful care for his people.

105:16–17 famine. Gen. 41:57; 42:5. The psalm sees Joseph's troubles with the eye of faith, saying that God **had sent** Joseph (cf. Gen. 45:5), i.e., before the famine, God had already planned it.

105:23 came to Egypt. Gen. 46:5–7. **sojourned**. See note on Ps. 105:12.

105:24–38 *He Brought Them out of Egypt by the Hand of Moses.* The next section recounts events from the book of Exodus, focusing on how God used Moses to lead the people out of Egypt, in keeping with his promises (cf. Gen. 15:13–16). On the eight plagues described here (Ps. 105:28–36), see the note on Psalm 105.

105:24–25 made his people very fruitful. Cf. Ex. 1:7–11.

105:26 servant . . . chosen. See v. 6.

27 [i]They performed his signs among them
and miracles in [c]the land of Ham.
28 He [j]sent darkness, and made the land dark;
they [k]did not rebel[1] against his words.
29 He turned their waters into blood
and [l]caused their fish to die.
30 Their land swarmed with frogs,
even in [m]the chambers of their kings.
31 He spoke, and there came [n]swarms of flies,
[o]and gnats throughout their country.
32 He gave them hail for rain,
and fiery [p]lightning bolts through their land.
33 He struck down their vines and fig trees,
and [q]shattered the trees of their country.
34 He spoke, and the [r]locusts came,
young locusts without number,
35 which devoured all the vegetation in their land
and ate up the fruit of their ground.
36 He [s]struck down all the firstborn in their land,
[s] the firstfruits of all their strength.

37 Then he brought out Israel with [t]silver and gold,
and there was none among his tribes who stumbled.
38 [u]Egypt was glad when they departed,
for [v]dread of them had fallen upon it.

39 He [w]spread a cloud for a covering,
and fire to give light by night.
40 [x]They asked, and he [y]brought quail,
and gave them [z]bread from heaven in abundance.
41 He opened the rock, and [a]water gushed out;
it flowed through [b]the desert like a river.
42 For he [c]remembered his holy promise,
and [d]Abraham, his servant.

43 So he brought his people out with joy,
his [d]chosen ones with [e]singing.
44 And he [f]gave them the lands of the nations,
and they took possession of the fruit of the peoples' toil,

[1] Septuagint, Syriac omit *not*

27[i]For ver. 27-36, see Ps. 78:43-51 [c][See ver. 23 above]
28[j]Ex. 10:21-23 [k]Ps. 99:7
29[l]Ex. 7:21
30[m]Ex. 8:3
31[n]Ex. 8:21 [o]Ex. 8:16
32[p]Ex. 9:23
33[q]Ex. 9:25
34[r]See Ex. 10:12-15
36[s]See Ps. 78:51
37[t]Ex. 12:35, 36
38[u]Ex. 12:23 [v]Ex. 15:16
39[w][Job 36:20; Isa. 4:5]; See Ex. 13:21
40[x]Ps. 78:18, 27 [y]Ex. 16:13 [z]Ps. 78:24, 25; [John 6:31]
41[a]See Ps. 78:15 [b]See Ps. 63:1
42[c]ver. 8, 9; Ex. 2:24 [d][Gen. 15:14]; See ver. 6
43[d][See ver. 42 above] [e][Isa. 35:10]; See Ex. 15:1-21
44[f]Josh. 24:13; [Ps. 78:55]

105:27 The combination **signs** and **miracles** can also be rendered "signs and wonders" (cf. Ex. 7:3); these are the mighty deeds Moses and Aaron did before Pharaoh to demonstrate that God had sent them.

105:28 darkness. The ninth plague (Ex. 10:21–23). Perhaps the psalm puts it first because it seems to have overcome the resistance of most Egyptians (Ex. 11:3), though not yet of Pharaoh; that is, the Egyptian populace **did not rebel against** God's **words** any further.

105:29 waters into blood. The first plague (Ex. 7:20–21).

105:30 frogs. The second plague (Ex. 8:1–6).

105:31 flies. The fourth plague (Ex. 8:20–24). **gnats**. The third plague (Ex. 8:16–17).

105:32–33 hail, fiery lightning bolts. The seventh plague (Ex. 9:22–26).

105:34–35 locusts. The eighth plague (Ex. 10:12–15).

105:36 the firstborn. The tenth and climactic plague (Ex. 12:29–30). Cf. also Ps. 78:51. For the "firstborn" as the **firstfruits of all their strength**, see Gen. 49:3 and Deut. 21:17.

105:37 silver and gold. The plundering of the Egyptians (Ex. 12:35–36).

105:38 Egypt was glad. Ex. 12:33. **dread of them**. Ex. 15:17.

105:39–41 ***He Cared for His People in the Desert.*** The next section continues with a few more examples from Exodus that support the claim of Ps. 105:7–11.

105:39 cloud. Ex. 13:21–22.

105:40 quail. Ex. 16:1–13. **bread from heaven**. Manna (Ex. 16:4).

105:41 opened the rock. Ex. 17:6; cf. Ps. 78:15.

105:42–45 ***He Gave Them Canaan as He Had Promised.*** The final section rushes ahead from the events of Exodus to the time of Joshua, recalling that God **remembered his holy promise** to establish his people in the land, in order **that they might keep his statutes and observe his laws**, living faithfully under God's care (cf. 2 Kings 17:37) and deeply grateful to their faithful God.

105:42–43 servant . . . chosen ones. See vv. 6, 26.

45[g]Deut. 4:1, 40 [h]Ps. 78:7 [i]See Ps. 104:35

Psalm 106

1[i][See Ps. 105:45 above] [j]See Ps. 105:1 [k]See Ps. 100:5 [l]See 1 Chr. 16:34, 41
3[m][Ps. 15:2]
4[n][Ps. 119:132]
5[o]Ps. 105:6, 43
6[p]1 Kgs. 8:47; Ezra 9:6; Neh. 1:6, 7; 9:16; Jer. 3:25; 14:20; Dan. 9:5 [q]Ps. 79:8; Lev. 26:40

45 that they might [g]keep his statutes
and [h]observe his laws.
[i]Praise the LORD!

Give Thanks to the LORD, for He Is Good

106

1 [i]Praise the LORD!
[j]Oh give thanks to the LORD, [k]for he is good,
[l]for his steadfast love endures forever!
2 Who can utter the mighty deeds of the LORD,
or declare all his praise?
3 Blessed are they who observe justice,
who [m]do righteousness at all times!

4 [n]Remember me, O LORD, when you show favor to your people;
help me when you save them,[1]
5 that I may look upon the prosperity of your [o]chosen ones,
that I may rejoice in the gladness of your nation,
that I may glory with your inheritance.

6 [p]Both we and [q]our fathers have sinned;
we have committed iniquity; we have done wickedness.
7 Our fathers, when they were in Egypt,
did not consider your wondrous works;

[1] *Or Remember me, O LORD, with the favor you show to your people; help me with your salvation*

105:45 Praise the LORD! See note on 104:35.

Psalm 106. This historical psalm (see notes on Psalms 78 and 105) recites a series of events from Israel's history to illustrate God's steadfast love in the face of Israel's rebellion and unfaithfulness. The events are selected from Israel's time following Moses in the wilderness (Exodus and Numbers) and from the time when Israel repeatedly indulged in rebellion against the Lord after the death of Joshua (Judges). All of the episodes are instances of the whole people being unfaithful, and of God's continuing commitment to maintain this people and to foster among them the conditions in which piety can flourish. The focus is therefore on corporate unfaithfulness and forgiveness. The psalm begins by calling on the people to give thanks and praise to God (Ps. 106:1–3); and it ends in a prayer that the God who has shown such forbearance will once again deliver his people, apparently this time from exile (v. 47). In view of where the psalm ends up, it is best to call it a community lament. The specific occasion for this psalm is some kind of exile, in which the people must be gathered "from among the nations" (v. 47). The obvious candidate for this is the Babylonian exile. One difficulty with this conclusion is that there is no mention of the dynasty of David, so caution is appropriate. In any case, the psalm is suited for a variety of recurring situations in which the people of God (including some Christians even today) are in a crisis that results from their persistent unfaithfulness. A version of vv. 47–48 appears in 1 Chron. 16:35–36 as part of the song for bringing the ark to Jerusalem. Assuming that Chronicles records something like the actual song on the occasion, then probably the psalmist adapted the words of that song for his purposes (see notes on Psalms 96; 105).

106:1–3 *Praise to the Lord for His Mighty Deeds.* The psalm begins in a way reminiscent of Psalm 105, calling the people to **give thanks** and to reflect on his **mighty deeds**. Verse 3 of Psalm 106, with its description of covenant faithfulness for the members of Israel (**observe justice** and **do righteousness at all times**; cf. 1 John 2:29; 3:7; Rev. 22:11), reminds the singing congregation that they must authentically take hold of God's grace—an authenticity that is absent in most of the events described in this psalm.

106:1 Give thanks to the LORD . . . endures forever. See 107:1; 118:1, 29; and 136:1 for the same words; and cf. 100:5.

106:4–5 *Request to Share in the Future of God's People.* A crucial principle of biblical faith is that the story of God's people is going somewhere; in the OT, primarily to the time when God so blesses his people with godliness that the Gentiles are drawn into the light. This section looks to that future (**when you show favor to your people**); true piety wants to participate in the **gladness of** God's **nation**, and recognizes that for this, along with personal forgiveness, covenant authenticity is required (v. 3).

106:6–46 *Illustrating God's Faithfulness and the People's Unfaithfulness.* The body of the psalm is a list of incidents in which **both we and our fathers have sinned**. This list begins at the shore of the Red Sea (vv. 7–12); this is the only case listed in which the result of God's response to the unfaithfulness was that the people "believed his words." The list then moves to Kibroth-hattaavah (vv. 13–15), then to the revolt of Dathan and Abiram (vv. 16–18), then to the golden calf (vv. 19–23), then to the rebellion due to the spies' bad report (vv. 24–27), then to the sin with the Baal of Peor (vv. 28–31), then to Meribah (vv. 32–33), then to the wearying cycle of unfaithfulness followed by deliverance followed by more unfaithfulness that Judges records (Ps. 106:34–46). Each of these events can be tied to a passage in the Pentateuch and Judges; the psalm is probably based directly on the way that the narrative books describe the events. However, even though the overall movement, from the Red Sea to the time of the judges, is sequential, the incidents in between do not strictly follow the chronology of the Pentateuch. Perhaps the simplest explanation for this (see also note on Psalm 105) is that this poem does not depend as much on sequence as narrative tends to depend.

106:6 Both we and our fathers have sinned. This verse is the theme and focus of the whole list of incidents. The sins, **iniquity**, and **wickedness** described here are the kind that reveal that the people of Israel have unfaithful hearts. It is entirely possible that the penitent generation singing this psalm has not **committed** the kinds of unfaithfulness that brought about their exile (v. 47); and yet the psalm presents the current generation as having been present in their representatives, their ancestors, and thus incorporates the current generation in their ancestors' sin (see note on Deut. 1:20–21; cf. similar prayers of confession—Ezra 9:6–15; Neh. 1:5–11; Dan. 9:4–19—all expressing multigenerational solidarity in wrongdoing). The words "we have sinned" derive from Solomon's prayer (1 Kings 8:47).

106:7–12 The first incident is from the shore of the Red Sea (Ex. 14:10–31), when the people of Israel who had followed Moses saw the pursuing army of Egypt. To say that they **did not consider** God's **wondrous works** and that they **rebelled** is to indicate that their reaction was more than justifiable fear of the Egyptians; it was evidence of unbelieving hearts. Nevertheless the Lord **saved them for his name's sake**, i.e., **that he might make known his mighty power** (both to Israel, Ex. 6:7; and to the nations, Ex. 14:18). The terms **saved** and **redeemed** (Ps. 106:10) come from Exodus (Ex. 14:30;

they [r]did not remember the abundance of your steadfast love,
but [s]rebelled by the sea, at the Red Sea.
8 Yet he saved them [t]for his name's sake,
[u]that he might make known his mighty power.
9 He [v]rebuked the Red Sea, and it [w]became dry,
and he [x]led them through the deep as through a desert.
10 So he [y]saved them from the hand of the foe
and [z]redeemed them from the power of the enemy.
11 And [a]the waters covered their adversaries;
not one of them was left.
12 Then [b]they believed his words;
they [c]sang his praise.

13 But they soon [d]forgot his works;
they did not wait for [e]his counsel.
14 But they had [f]a wanton craving in the wilderness,
and [g]put God to the test in the desert;
15 he [h]gave them what they asked,
but sent [i]a wasting disease among them.

16 When men in the camp [j]were jealous of Moses
and Aaron, [k]the holy one of the LORD,
17 [l]the earth opened and swallowed up Dathan,
and covered the company of Abiram.
18 [m]Fire also broke out in their company;
the flame burned up the wicked.

19 They [n]made a calf in Horeb
and worshiped a metal image.
20 They [o]exchanged the glory of God[1]
for the image of an ox that eats grass.
21 They [p]forgot God, their Savior,
who had done great things in Egypt,
22 wondrous works in [q]the land of Ham,
and awesome deeds by the Red Sea.
23 Therefore [r]he said he would destroy them—
had not Moses, his [s]chosen one,
[t]stood in the breach before him,
to turn away his wrath from destroying them.

24 Then they [u]despised [v]the pleasant land,
having [w]no faith in his promise.

[1] Hebrew *exchanged their glory*

7 [r][ver. 13, 21] [s]Ex. 14:11, 12
8 [t]Ezek. 20:9, 14 [u]Ex. 9:16
9 [v][Ps. 18:15; 104:7] [w]Ex. 14:21; [Isa. 50:2; 51:10] [x]Isa. 63:13
10 [y]Ex. 14:30 [z]Ps. 107:2
11 [a]Ex. 14:28; 15:5
12 [b]Ex. 14:31 [c]See Ex. 15:1-21
13 [d]Ps. 78:11; [Ex. 15:24; 16:2; 17:2] [e][Ps. 107:11]
14 [f]Num. 11:4; 1 Cor. 10:6; [Ps. 78:18] [g]Ex. 17:2; 1 Cor. 10:9
15 [h]Ps. 78:29 [i]Isa. 10:16
16 [j]See Num. 16:1-3 [k]Deut. 33:2; Zech. 14:5; Jude 14
17 [l]Num. 16:31, 32; Deut. 11:6
18 [m]Num. 16:35
19 [n]Ex. 32:4; Deut. 9:8; Acts 7:41
20 [o]Jer. 2:11; [Rom. 1:23]
21 [p]ver. 7, 13; Ps. 78:11; Deut. 32:18
22 [q]Ps. 105:23, 27; [Ps. 78:51]
23 [r]Ex. 32:10; Deut. 9:14; Ezek. 20:8 [s]Ps. 105:6 [t]Ezek. 22:30
24 [u]Num. 14:31 [v]Zech. 7:14 [w]Deut. 1:32; 9:23

15:13) and speak of the great deeds God has done to rescue his people as a whole and to bring about the conditions in which their piety may flourish. The result was that **they believed his words** (cf. Ex. 14:31) and **sang his praise** (cf. Ex. 15:1).

106:13–15 Sadly, the people of Israel **soon forgot** God's **works**, i.e., descended back into unfaithfulness (cf. v. 7), such that they **put God to the test in the desert** (a hideous sin; cf. Num. 14:22). The specific incident in view is not the very next event in Exodus; the term **wanton craving** points to Num. 11:4, 31–35, at Kibroth-hattaavah (Hb. for "the Graves of Craving"). The **wasting disease** here is called a "very great plague" (Num. 11:33), and it killed many Israelites, indicating God's disapproval of the unbelief behind the asking.

106:16–18 The next event is the rebellion led by **Dathan** and **Abiram** (Num. 16:1–40), who apparently enlisted the Levite Korah as their chief spokesman. Korah spoke against **Moses and Aaron**, and the specific question he raised was over whether Aaron was **holy** in a way distinct from the holiness of the whole congregation. Because these people were **jealous**, they rebelled against God's appointed spokesman, Moses. Such a situation is intolerable among the leaders of God's people, and God brought a dramatic judgment upon them: **the earth opened and swallowed up** the tents of the conspirators, and **fire also broke out** and slew those who had dared to violate the priestly requirements (Num. 14:31–35). Neither the psalm nor Numbers gives any hope that people came to believe as a result.

106:19–23 The psalm moves on to the **calf in Horeb**, the **metal image**, the "golden calf" (Ex. 32:1–14). The reason why they committed this horror was, at bottom, unfaithfulness: **they forgot God, their Savior, who had done great things in Egypt** (cf. Ps. 106:7, 13). Moses **stood in the breach before** God (an image taken from risking one's own life to close up a gap broken in a wall; cf. Neh. 6:1; Ezek. 13:5; 22:30), **to turn away** God's **wrath from destroying** the Israelites, i.e., by earnestly interceding for them, reminding God of his promises and his reputation (Ex. 32:11–14).

106:20 exchanged the glory of God. In Rom. 1:23, Paul uses this expression to describe Gentile idolatry: people "exchanged the glory of the immortal God for images resembling mortal man and birds and animals and reptiles" (cf. Jer. 2:11). It is even more senseless when Israel does it.

106:24–27 The sad list now moves to what happened when the 12 spies

25[x]Num. 14:2; Deut. 1:27
26[y]Ex. 6:8; Num. 14:30; Deut. 32:40; Ezek. 20:6, 15, 23; [Ps. 95:11]
27[z]See Ps. 44:11
28[a]Num. 25:3; Hos. 9:10 [b]Isa. 8:19
30[c]Num. 25:7, 8
31[d][Gen. 15:6]; See Num. 25:10-13
32[e]See Num. 20:2-13; Deut. 1:37
33[f]Ps. 107:11; [Ps. 78:40; Isa. 63:10] [g]Num. 20:10
34[h]See Judg. 1:21, 27-36 [i]Deut. 7:2, 16; Judg. 2:2
35[j]Judg. 3:5, 6; [Ezra 9:2]
36[k]Ex. 23:33; Deut. 7:16; Judg. 2:3
37[l]2 Kgs. 16:3; Isa. 57:5; Ezek. 16:20; 20:26 [m]Deut. 32:17; [1 Cor. 10:20]
38[n]Isa. 24:5
39[o]Ezek. 20:18, 30, 31 [p]See Ps. 73:27

25 They [x]murmured in their tents,
and did not obey the voice of the LORD.
26 Therefore he [y]raised his hand and swore to them
that he would make them fall in the wilderness,
27 and would make their offspring fall among the nations,
[z]scattering them among the lands.

28 Then they [a]yoked themselves to the [a]Baal of Peor,
and ate sacrifices offered to [b]the dead;
29 they provoked the LORD to anger with their deeds,
and a plague broke out among them.
30 Then [c]Phinehas stood up and intervened,
and the plague was stayed.
31 And that was [d]counted to him as righteousness
from generation to generation forever.

32 They [e]angered him at the waters of Meribah,
and it went ill with Moses on their account,
33 for they [f]made his spirit bitter,[1]
and he [g]spoke rashly with his lips.

34 They did not [h]destroy the peoples,
[i]as the LORD commanded them,
35 but they [j]mixed with the nations
and learned to do as they did.
36 They served their idols,
which became [k]a snare to them.
37 They [l]sacrificed their sons
and their daughters to [m]the demons;
38 they poured out innocent blood,
the blood of their sons and daughters,
whom they sacrificed to the idols of Canaan,
and the land was [n]polluted with blood.
39 Thus they [o]became unclean by their acts,
and [p]played the whore in their deeds.

[1] *Or they rebelled against God's Spirit*

returned from their mission to scout out the land that God had promised (Num. 13:32–14:38): 10 of them gave a "bad report," which led Israel to give in to fear. As a result, **they despised the pleasant land, having no faith in his promise**: they refused God's command to enter the land to conquer it. The psalm follows the Mosaic account in attributing the basic problem to unfaithfulness (cf. Num. 14:11). This is a major turning point in the Pentateuch: a generation must now **fall in the wilderness** (cf. Num. 14:32; cf. Ps. 95:11), Israel must wander for another 38 years, and the children must take on the task of conquering. This section closes with an ominous foreshadowing of the singers' current situation: just as God made the Israelites fall in the wilderness, so he **would make their offspring fall among the nations, scattering them among the lands** (cf. Ps. 106:47).

106:28–31 Next is the time when the Israelites **yoked themselves to the Baal of Peor** (Num. 25:1–15). Participation in **sacrifices offered to the dead** (i.e., to the lifeless gods of the Moabites, see Num. 14:2) led to other kinds of immorality as well, which would have corrupted the people of God and ruined their ability to carry out their calling in the world (Num. 25:1, 6). It took the prompt and drastic action of **Phinehas** to stay the **plague** that **broke out among** the Israelites as a result of God's anger (see note on Num. 25:7–8). This deed was **counted to** Phinehas **as righteousness**, i.e., God considered it a deed of covenant faithfulness (rather than as giving legal status; see note on Deut. 6:25), and it led to his family having the priesthood **from generation to generation forever** (Num. 25:13–14).

106:32–33 At the waters of Meribah the people complained about lack of water and accused Moses of bringing them out of Egypt, apparently forgetting that Moses had acted throughout as God's spokesman (Num. 20:2–13; see note there). Their unbelief led Moses to speak **rashly** (i.e., to become careless about acting by faith) and thus to lose his right to enter the Promised Land. This is the last event from the Pentateuch in this list.

106:34–46 This description is unlike the previous episodes in that it refers not to a specific event but to the recurring pattern found in Judg. 2:11–3:6, in which the people of Israel **did not destroy the peoples** in Canaan (disobeying what **the LORD commanded them**): instead **they mixed with the nations** (esp. by intermarriage, Judg. 3:6; cf. Ezra 9:2) **and learned to do as they did** (Ps. 106:34–35). This led to the unspeakable practice of child sacrifice (vv. 36–39). This is in itself a hideous moral outrage, and it attacks the very heart of God's covenant with his people (Gen. 17:7; cf. Ps. 103:17–18), and what it means to be human (Gen. 1:28). Hence **the anger of the LORD was kindled against his people**, and **he gave them into the hand of the nations** (Ps. 106:40–41; cf. Judg. 2:14). The stunning thing about the period of the judges is the side-by-side themes: **many times he delivered them** while yet **they were rebellious in their purposes** (Ps. 106:43). **Nevertheless** God **looked upon their distress** (v. 44) and kept coming to their aid. The expressions **remembered his covenant** and **the abundance of his steadfast love** (v. 45, a reference to Ex. 34:6) look back to Ps. 106:7 and put the faithful Lord in stark contrast with the unfaithful people. In keeping with Solomon's prayer (1 Kings 8:50), God **caused** his repentant people **to be pitied by all those who held them captive** (Ps. 106:46), and he restored them.

40 Then [q]the anger of the LORD was kindled against [r]his people,
and he abhorred his [r]heritage;
41 he [s]gave them into the hand of the nations,
so that those who hated them ruled over them.
42 Their enemies [t]oppressed them,
and they were brought into subjection under their power.
43 [u]Many times he delivered them,
but they were rebellious in their [v]purposes
and were [w]brought low through their iniquity.
44 Nevertheless, he looked upon their distress,
when he [x]heard their cry.
45 For their sake he [y]remembered his covenant,
and [z]relented according to [a]the abundance of his steadfast love.
46 He caused them to be [b]pitied
by all those who held them captive.
47 [c]Save us, O LORD our God,
and [d]gather us from among the nations,
that we may give thanks to your holy name
and glory in your praise.
48 [e]Blessed be the LORD, the God of Israel,
from everlasting to everlasting!
[e] And let all the people say, "Amen!"
[f]Praise the LORD!

BOOK FIVE

Let the Redeemed of the LORD Say So

107 1 [g]Oh give thanks to the LORD, [h]for he is good,
for his steadfast love endures forever!
2 Let [i]the redeemed of the LORD say so,
whom he has [j]redeemed from trouble[1]

[1] *Or from the hand of the foe*

40 [q]Ps. 78:59, 62; Judg. 2:14 [r]See Ps. 28:9
41 [s]Neh. 9:27
42 [t]Judg. 4:3; 10:12
43 [u]Judg. 2:16 [v]See Ps. 81:12 [w]Lev. 26:39
44 [x]Judg. 3:9; 4:3; 6:7; 10:10
45 [y]Ps. 105:8; Lev. 26:42 [z]See Ps. 90:13 [a]ver. 7; Ps. 51:1; 69:16; Isa. 63:7; Lam. 3:32
46 [b]1 Kgs. 8:50; 2 Chr. 30:9; Ezra 9:9; Neh. 1:11; Jer. 42:12
47 [c]For ver. 47, 48, see 1 Chr. 16:35, 36 [d]See Ps. 107:3
48 [e]See Ps. 41:13 [f]See Ps. 104:35

Psalm 107
1 [g]See Ps. 105:1 [h]See Ps. 100:5
2 [i]Ps. 106:10 [j]Isa. 62:12; 63:4

106:47–48 *Concluding Prayer that God Will Save His People.* The previous sad recital clearly establishes that nothing is more certain than God's continuing commitment to his people as a body, so that when they come to their senses and repent they may appeal to God to **save** them and **gather** them **from among the nations** (cf. Deut. 30:3). He will do so when they share his goal for them, **that we may give thanks to your holy name and glory in your praise**.

106:48 This doxology closes Book 4 of the Psalms (see note on 41:13). Unlike those that close Books 1–3, this doxology belongs to its psalm, as the final words, **praise the LORD!** (Hb. *hallelu-yah*), echo the opening phrase of 106:1 and provide, so to speak, bookends or an envelope enclosing the psalm as a whole. In view of what this list of events establishes about God's faithfulness, **blessed be the LORD** indeed, and **all the people** may well—and should indeed—**say, "Amen!"**

Psalm 107. With this psalm the members of the community call one another to give thanks for God's enduring "steadfast love," which he has shown not only to the people as a whole but to the particular members as well. The distinctive feature of this psalm is its four accounts of people in distress ("some," vv. 4, 10, 17, 23), whom God rescued. Because the psalm concerns gratitude for Judah's return from exile (v. 3), it is likely that these four accounts describe the activities of members of the tribe of Judah in their exile. Some scholars think that these are four descriptions of the same group, but the activities of the groups are different enough to make it easier just to take these as four ways in which God's people have been scattered away from their Promised Land, to which God has now brought them back. Key repetitions in the psalm include: after the initial invitation to "give thanks to the Lord" (v. 1), the psalm describes how each of the four groups cried to the Lord in their trouble, and he delivered them (vv. 6, 13, 19, 28), and it calls on them to thank the Lord (vv. 8, 15, 21, 31). The theme of God's "steadfast love"—his enduring kindness toward his people and his willingness to forgive them even in the face of their rampant unfaithfulness—recurs throughout as the topic of thanks (vv. 1, 8, 15, 21, 31) and meditation (v. 43). With this focus on the restoration of the exiles, the psalm is at first glance more concerned with the thanks of the whole community than of any individual; at the same time, the persons who sing this have themselves received the benefits of the deliverance, so that the individual gives thanks as a member of the community. Even though this psalm begins a new book of the Psalter (see note on 106:48), there are clear connections with Psalms 105–106. For example, in 105:44 the Promised Land is the place God gave to his people that they might serve him there faithfully; 106:27 brings in the prospect of exile from the land for the people's unfaithfulness, and the prayer of 106:47, "gather us from among the nations," is presented as being answered in 107:3. More broadly, all three psalms reflect with praise and hope on aspects of sacred history.

107:1–3 *Let the Redeemed of the Lord Give Him Thanks.* The opening section states the purpose of the psalm (to call the congregation to **give thanks to the LORD**, v. 1) and the theme (**his steadfast love endures forever**). The specific occasion is that God has **redeemed** his people (i.e., rescued them from their **trouble**) and **gathered** them **in from the lands** (i.e., from exile, cf. 106:47; Deut. 30:3).

107:2 redeemed. See note on Isa. 1:24–28. In Ps. 106:10, God "redeemed"

3 and [k]gathered in from the lands,
from the east and from the west,
from the north and from the south.

4 Some [l]wandered in desert wastes,
finding no way [m]to a city to dwell in;
5 hungry and thirsty,
their soul [n]fainted within them.
6 Then they [o]cried to the LORD in their trouble,
and he delivered them from their distress.
7 He led them by [p]a straight way
till they reached [m]a city to dwell in.
8 [q]Let them thank the LORD for his steadfast love,
for his wondrous works to the children of man!
9 For he [r]satisfies the longing soul,
[s]and the hungry soul he fills with good things.

10 [t]Some sat in darkness and in [u]the shadow of death,
prisoners in [v]affliction and in irons,
11 for they [w]had rebelled against the words of God,
and [x]spurned the counsel of the Most High.
12 So he bowed their hearts down with hard labor;
they fell down, [y]with none to help.
13 [z]Then they cried to the LORD in their trouble,
and he delivered them from their distress.
14 He brought them out of [a]darkness and the shadow of death,
and [b]burst their bonds apart.
15 [c]Let them thank the LORD for his steadfast love,
for his wondrous works to the children of man!
16 For he [d]shatters the doors of bronze
and cuts in two the bars of iron.

17 Some were [e]fools through their sinful ways,
and because of their iniquities suffered affliction;
18 [f]they loathed any kind of food,
and they [g]drew near to [h]the gates of death.
19 [i]Then they cried to the LORD in their trouble,
and he delivered them from their distress.
20 He [j]sent out his word and [k]healed them,
and [l]delivered them from their destruction.
21 [m]Let them thank the LORD for his steadfast love,
for his wondrous works to the children of man!

3[k]Ps. 106:47; Deut. 30:3; Isa. 11:12; 43:5; 56:8; Jer. 29:14; 31:8, 10; Ezek. 20:34, 41; 39:27
4[l]ver. 40; [Deut. 32:10] [m]ver. 36
5[n]Ps. 77:3
6[o]ver. 13, 19, 28; Ps. 106:44
7[p]Ezra 8:21 [m][See ver. 4 above]
8[q]ver. 15, 21, 31
9[r][Ps. 34:10; 146:7] [s]Luke 1:53
10[t]Luke 1:79; [Isa. 42:7; 49:9; Mic. 7:8] [u]ver. 14; Job 10:21 [v][Job 36:8]
11[w]Ps. 106:7, 33, 43; See Ps. 78:40 [x]Prov. 1:30; 5:12; 15:5; [Deut. 31:20; Luke 7:30]
12[y]See Ps. 22:11
13[z]ver. 6, 19, 28
14[a]See ver. 10 [b][Ps. 2:3]
15[c]ver. 8, 21, 31
16[d]Isa. 45:2
17[e]Prov. 1:7; 14:9
18[f]Job 33:20 [g]Ps. 88:3; Job 33:22 [h]See Job 38:17
19[i]ver. 6, 13, 28
20[j]Ps. 147:15, 18; [Matt. 8:8] [k]Ps. 30:2, 3; 2 Kgs. 20:5; Job 33:29, 30 [l]Ps. 103:4
21[m]ver. 8, 15, 31

his people from their enemy, Egypt (cf. 74:2; 77:15); the return from exile is like a second exodus.

107:3 The mention of the four points of the compass (**east**, **west**, **north**, **south**) suggests the ways in which the people had been scattered; for a similar description of the return from exile, see Isa. 43:5–6.

107:4–9 *First Group: Those Who Wandered in Barren Places.* This is the first group of those who were banished from the land as a result of the exile: **some** of the exiles **wandered in desert wastes**, such as the Sinai Desert (cf. 106:14; Deut. 32:10). **finding no way to a city to dwell in**. Their proper home was the Promised Land, but God had sent them away. When **they cried to the LORD**, God **delivered them**, bringing them to a **city to dwell in** (Ps. 107:7, which answers v. 4). The proper response is for them to **thank the LORD for his steadfast love**. The Lord has done **wondrous works** for his people in the past (cf. 105:2, 5; 106:7, 22), and the restoration of Judah to Jerusalem after exile is a crowning achievement. Even as this applies to the whole community, God also **satisfies the longing soul**, i.e., the particular members of the restored community who recognize God's grace in their own lives.

107:10–16 *Second Group: Those Who Sat in Darkness.* The next group of exiles **sat in darkness and in the shadow of death**. The second line (**prisoners**) indicates that these people suffered as captives and forced laborers (v. 12, **hard labor**) because **they had rebelled against the words of God**. But even though they rejected God's covenant by their rebellion, God still heard them when **they cried to the LORD in their trouble**, and **brought them out of darkness and the shadow of death** (v. 14; cf. v. 10). They too should **thank the LORD for his steadfast love**.

107:17–22 *Third Group: Those Who Suffered for Their Own Folly.* **Some** of the exiles **were fools through their sinful ways**: their own folly (the stupidity that results from turning away from God) brought on their **affliction**, so that **they loathed any kind of food**. Nevertheless God heard and relieved them when **they cried to the LORD in their trouble**. In context, **healed them** is not simply the relief of bodily ailments (v. 18) but also their return to the Promised Land. These people should **thank the LORD**, specifically with **sacrifices of thanksgiving** (see note on 50:7–15; cf. 116:17), using **songs of joy** in their worship to **tell of** God's **deeds**.

22 And let them [n]offer sacrifices of thanksgiving,
and [o]tell of his deeds in [p]songs of joy!

23 Some [q]went down to the sea in ships,
doing business on the great waters;
24 they saw the deeds of the LORD,
his wondrous works in the deep.
25 For he [r]commanded and [s]raised the stormy wind,
which lifted up the waves of the sea.
26 They mounted up to heaven; they went down to the depths;
their courage [t]melted away in their evil plight;
27 they reeled and [u]staggered like drunken men
and [v]were at their wits' end.[1]
28 [w]Then they cried to the LORD in their trouble,
and he delivered them from their distress.
29 He [x]made the storm be still,
and the waves of the sea were hushed.
30 Then they were glad that the waters[2] were quiet,
and he brought them to their desired haven.
31 [y]Let them thank the LORD for his steadfast love,
for his wondrous works to the children of man!
32 Let them [z]extol him in [a]the congregation of the people,
and praise him in the assembly of the elders.

33 He [b]turns rivers into a desert,
springs of water into thirsty ground,
34 [c]a fruitful land into a salty waste,
because of the evil of its inhabitants.
35 He [d]turns a desert into pools of water,
[e]a parched land into springs of water.
36 And there he lets the hungry dwell,
and they establish [f]a city to live in;
37 they sow fields and plant vineyards
and get a fruitful yield.
38 [g]By his blessing they multiply greatly,
and he does not let their livestock diminish.

39 When they are diminished and brought low
through oppression, evil, and sorrow,
40 [h]he pours contempt on princes
and [i]makes them wander [j]in trackless wastes;
41 but [k]he raises up the needy out of affliction
and [l]makes their families like flocks.
42 [m]The upright see it and are glad,
and [n]all wickedness shuts its mouth.

[1] Hebrew *and all their wisdom was swallowed up* [2] Hebrew *they*

22 [n]See Ps. 50:14 [o]Ps. 9:11; See Ps. 118:17 [p]Ps. 105:43
23 [q]Isa. 42:10
25 [r]Ps. 105:31, 34 [s]Ps. 148:8; Jonah 1:4
26 [t]Ps. 119:28; See Ps. 22:14
27 [u]Isa. 24:20; 29:9; See Job 12:25 [v]Isa. 19:3
28 [w]ver. 6, 13, 19
29 [x]See Ps. 65:7
31 [y]ver. 8, 15, 21
32 [z]See Ps. 99:5 [a]Ps. 22:22, 25
33 [b]Isa. 50:2; [Isa. 42:15]
34 [c][Gen. 13:10; 14:3; Deut. 29:23]; See Gen. 19:24-28
35 [d]Ps. 114:8; Isa. 41:18; [Isa. 35:6, 7; 43:19, 20] [e]Job 38:26, 27
36 [f]ver. 4, 7
38 [g]Gen. 12:2; 17:20; Ex. 1:7
40 [h]Job 12:21 [i]Job 12:24 [j][Deut. 32:10]
41 [k]Ps. 113:7, 8; 1 Sam. 2:8 [l]Job 21:11
42 [m]See Job 22:19 [n]See Ps. 63:11

107:23–32 *Fourth Group: Those Who Went Down to the Sea in Ships.* The fourth group consists of sailors caught in a storm; if these are exiles, they are sailing in the service of a foreign king (Israelites rarely went to sea on their own). As the storm increased in its fury, threatening them with shipwreck and drowning, **they cried to the LORD in their trouble**, and God **made the storm be still**. These people should **thank the LORD for his steadfast love**; they have returned to the Promised Land, where they can **extol** God **in the congregation**.

107:33–42 *The Lord Vindicates Himself through Reversals.* This section moves on to reflect more generally about the reversals that God accomplishes in order to display his own righteousness. God may take a pleasant and prosperous land and turn it into a waste if **the evil of its inhabitants** calls for it (vv. 33–34), and he may reverse this judgment and make the land fruitful and pleasant again, in his mercy to the **hungry** (vv. 35–38). Verses 39–41 look at this from another angle: when people are **diminished and brought low**, God can humble their oppressors and raise up the **needy**. This psalm celebrates how God has fulfilled this pattern in restoring Judah after the exile. The **upright** (here, the faithful among God's people) **see it and are glad**, because God has vindicated his faithfulness to his people; **and all wickedness** (i.e., whatever repudiates God's covenant) **shuts its mouth** for the same reason.

43[o][Ps. 64:9; Jer. 9:12; Hos. 14:9]

Psalm 108

1[p]For ver. 1-5, see Ps. 57:7-11
4[q][Ps. 113:4]
6[r]For ver. 6-13, see Ps. 60:5-12
9[s][Ps. 60:8]

43 [o]Whoever is wise, let him attend to these things;
let them consider the steadfast love of the LORD.

With God We Shall Do Valiantly

108

A SONG. A PSALM OF DAVID.

1 [p]My heart is steadfast, O God!
I will sing and make melody with all my being![1]
2 Awake, O harp and lyre!
I will awake the dawn!
3 I will give thanks to you, O LORD, among the peoples;
I will sing praises to you among the nations.
4 For your steadfast love is great [q]above the heavens;
your faithfulness reaches to the clouds.

5 Be exalted, O God, above the heavens!
Let your glory be over all the earth!
6 [r]That your beloved ones may be delivered,
give salvation by your right hand and answer me!

7 God has promised in his holiness:[2]
"With exultation I will divide up Shechem
and portion out the Valley of Succoth.
8 Gilead is mine; Manasseh is mine;
Ephraim is my helmet,
Judah my scepter.
9 Moab is my washbasin;
upon Edom I cast my shoe;
[s]over Philistia I shout in triumph."

10 Who will bring me to the fortified city?
Who will lead me to Edom?
11 Have you not rejected us, O God?
You do not go out, O God, with our armies.
12 Oh grant us help against the foe,
for vain is the salvation of man!
13 With God we shall do valiantly;
it is he who will tread down our foes.

[1] Hebrew *with my glory* [2] Or *sanctuary*

107:43 *Let the Wise Attend to These Things.* The final verse closes by inviting **whoever is wise** (i.e., those who genuinely seek to be skillful in godly living; see Introduction to Proverbs: Character Types in Proverbs) to **attend to these things**, specifically, to the many ways in which God has displayed his **steadfast love**. Such a meditation will increase one's wisdom.

Psalm 108. It would appear that David composed this community lament using material from two other psalms, with small variations: vv. 1–5 are from 57:7–11 (an individual lament), and 108:6–13 are from 60:5–12 (a community lament). The result has its own flow of thought: in the midst of a dangerous situation, the members of the singing congregation express their confident hope of thanking God "among the peoples" (108:3), including the peoples who are the present threat. This confidence is based on God's own oracles about the land (vv. 7–9), and not on how things look from a purely human perspective (vv. 10–13). Psalms 108–110 are all attributed to David (as are Psalms 122; 124; 131; 133; 138–145). It is unclear why this group of Davidic psalms was put here; perhaps the terms "give thanks" and "the peoples" (108:3) establish a link with Psalms 105–107 (cf. 105:1; 106:1, 47; 107:1–3; cf. also 109:30).

108:1–4 *Confidently Expecting to Give Thanks.* Cf. 57:7–10. The opening section expresses confidence (**my heart is steadfast**) and anticipation (**I will sing and make melody . . . awake the dawn . . . give thanks . . . sing praises**). The dangerous situation for which Psalm 108 is suited does not appear until v. 6 hints at it. The basis for the confidence is God's own character, his **steadfast love** and **faithfulness** (Ex. 34:6). These words lead the singing congregation to feel their own confidence as they remember the promises that God has made to his people.

108:1 with all my being. Lit., "with my glory" (see ESV footnote); see note on 57:8.

108:5–6 *Prayer for God to be Exalted.* The next section is the general prayer, **be exalted**, with the more specific **that your beloved ones may be delivered**. Verse 5 comes from 57:5, 11 (see note on 57:5), and 108:6 comes from 60:5 (see note on 60:1–5).

108:7–9 *God Has Spoken: "These Lands Are Mine!"* As with 60:6–8 (see note there), these verses seem to recall an oracle (**God has promised**) that gives God's plan for Israel's place in the world.

108:10–13 *Grant Us Help, for Vain Is the Salvation of Man!* These verses come from 60:9–12 (see note there). Part of the background of Psalm 60 is a campaign that led to Edom; here, **Edom** is more generally a foe of God's people.

Help Me, O LORD My God

109

TO THE CHOIRMASTER. A PSALM OF DAVID.

1 [t]Be not silent, O [u]God of my praise!
2 For wicked and [v]deceitful mouths are opened against me,
speaking against me with lying tongues.
3 They encircle me with words of hate,
and attack me [w]without cause.
4 In return for my love they [x]accuse me,
but I [y]give myself to prayer.[1]
5 So they [z]reward me evil for good,
and hatred for my love.

6 [a]Appoint a wicked man [b]against him;
let an accuser stand [c]at his right hand.
7 When he is tried, let him come forth guilty;
let his [d]prayer be counted as sin!
8 May his [e]days be few;
may [f]another take his [g]office!
9 May his [h]children be fatherless
and his wife a widow!
10 May his children [i]wander about and beg,
[j]seeking food far from the ruins they inhabit!
11 May [k]the creditor seize all that he has;
may [k]strangers plunder the fruits of his toil!
12 Let there be none to [l]extend kindness to him,
nor any to [m]pity his fatherless children!

[1] Hebrew *but I am prayer*

Psalm 109
1[t]See Ps. 28:1 [u]Deut. 10:21; [Ps. 71:6; Jer. 17:14]
2[v]Ps. 52:4
3[w]See Ps. 69:4
4[x]Ps. 38:20 [y][Ps. 69:13]
5[z]See Ps. 35:12
6[a]For ver. 6-15, see Ps. 35:4-8; 69:22-28 [b][1 Chr. 21:1; Zech. 3:1] [c]Job 30:12
7[d]Prov. 28:9; [Prov. 15:8; 21:27]
8[e][Ps. 55:23] [f]Cited Acts 1:20 [g]Num. 4:16; [1 Chr. 24:3]
9[h]Ex. 22:24
10[i][Gen. 4:12]; See Ps. 59:15 [j][Ps. 37:25]
11[k][Deut. 28:43, 44]
12[l][Ps. 36:10] [m][Job 5:4]

Psalm 109. This is an individual lament, geared to a situation in which a faithful Israelite is suffering the attacks of vicious accusers who return evil to him for the good he has done to them (vv. 1–5). It contains an extensive prayer that his accusers (or their chief) would receive what they deserve (vv. 6–20), and finishes with a prayer that appeals to, and rests confidently on, God's "steadfast love" (vv. 21–31). An important repeated word is "accuse" (vv. 4, 6, 20, 29), indicating the invidious situation. The tone and content of this psalm are reminiscent of Psalm 69. A major difference is that the sufferer in Psalm 69 acknowledges that wrongs he has done have played a role in his troubles, while the sufferer in Psalm 109 professes innocence. This facilitates its application to Jesus and to Judas. Though readers may instinctively feel that Jesus would not have said such things about his betrayer and those who plotted against him, the Gospels do include his harsh condemnations of Judas (Matt. 26:24; Mark 14:21), Pilate, and the Jewish leaders (John 19:11). Jesus asked only for the soldiers to be forgiven, "for they know not what they do" (Luke 23:34). Nevertheless both contain curses on the enemies (see notes on Ps. 69:22–28), and both are appropriated by Christians (69:25 and 109:8 in Acts 1:20). In both psalms the "enemies" are influential Israelites who are unfaithful to the covenant. The same principle applies to David's authorship as with Psalm 69, namely, that this is a prayer well-suited to each of God's people in analogous situations.

109:1–5 *I Need Help against Those Who Accuse Me.* The opening section describes the situation: people **attack** the singer **without cause**; they **accuse** him **in return for** his **love**. The singer has shown the accusers **love** and **good**, which they repay with **evil** and **hatred**. The psalm offers the right response: **I give myself to prayer**, both prayers for his enemies in the past (cf. 35:13) and now in prayer for God's help in the present.

109:1 be not silent. I.e., "Let people not think that you are complacent toward evil" (cf. 28:1; 35:22; 39:12; 50:3; 83:1). **God of my praise**. I.e., "The God whom I praise" (109:30; cf. 71:8; 145:21; Deut. 10:21).

109:5 reward me evil for good (cf. 35:12; 38:20; Gen. 44:4; 1 Sam. 24:17; Prov. 17:13). Since Bible authors generally tell the faithful not to return evil for evil in their interpersonal dealings (Prov. 20:22; 24:29; cf. Rom. 12:21; 1 Thess. 5:15), it is clear that to return evil for good is heinous.

109:6–20 *May He Suffer What He Deserves.* This section asks God to vindicate his faithful one by bringing on the enemies the troubles that they deserve (and that they have been bringing on the faithful). This is clear from the way that **wicked man** and **accuser** (v. 6) echo vv. 2, 4: they have opened "wicked mouths" against the psalmist, they "accuse" him, so therefore let them suffer the same fate. Cf. v. 12 with v. 16; cf. also v. 17. Like the curse of 69:22–28 (see notes there), the description here uses imagery to depict a life that is devastated and sad (109:18–19) in its various aspects: a shortened life (v. 8), poverty for himself and his dependents (vv. 9–12), no posterity (v. 13), and no forgiveness (vv. 14–15), which goes beyond merely temporal punishments. As with Psalm 69, one must recall that the people cursed are grievous sinners, covenant members who are unfaithful to the covenant, who would use whatever means they can to oppress the faithful. Further, the unstated assumption is that they will not repent (see notes on 5:10; 35:4–8).

109:6 against him. Although vv. 2–5 speak of attackers (plural), vv. 6–19 speak of only one (singular: "he," "him," "his"), and v. 20 returns to the plural. Possibly the singular focuses on the chief attacker (cf. v. 8, an officeholder), or else it is to apply to each and every one of the group.

109:7 When he is tried. Because he now has an "accuser" (v. 6). **his prayer**. In contrast to the devotion of the faithful singer (v. 4).

109:8 may another take his office. That is, his "office of oversight" (cf. Num. 3:32; 1 Chron. 26:30; Ezek. 44:11), a responsible position among the people of God. In Acts 1:20 the disciples combine this verse with Ps. 69:25 (see note there) to explain why someone else should take Judas's "office of oversight" (Gk. *episkopē*; cf. 1 Tim. 3:1).

109:9–12 children . . . wife. The man's early death (v. 8) has its inevitable effect of impoverishing his dependents (contrast 37:25). See also Ex. 34:7 ("visiting the iniquity of the fathers on the children"); each member of the people is linked to others, and the unfaithfulness of one makes others suffer, especially those closest to him. Again, the assumption is that neither the man nor his family escapes the judgment through repentance.

13 [n]See Ps. 21:10 [o]Prov. 10:7
14 [p]Ex. 20:5 [q]Neh. 4:5; Jer. 18:23
15 [r][Ps. 90:8] [s]Ps. 34:16
16 [t]ver. 22; Ps. 40:17 [u]See Ps. 34:18
17 [v][Prov. 14:14; Ezek. 35:6]
18 [w][ver. 29; Ps. 73:6] [x][Num. 5:22]
20 [y]ver. 6, 29
21 [z][Jer. 14:7]; See Ps. 23:3 [a]Ps. 69:16; [Ps. 63:3]
22 [b]ver. 16
23 [c]See Ps. 102:11 [d]Ex. 10:19; [Neh. 5:13; Job 38:13]
24 [e]Ps. 35:13 [f][Job 16:8]
25 [g]Ps. 22:6; 69:19 [h]See Ps. 22:7
26 [i]Ps. 119:86
27 [j][Job 37:7]
28 [k][2 Sam. 16:12] [l][Isa. 65:14]
29 [m]ver. 18; See Job 8:22 [n]Ps. 71:13; [Ps. 35:26]
30 [o][Ps. 22:25]

13 May his [n]posterity be cut off;
may his [o]name be blotted out in the second generation!
14 May [p]the iniquity of his fathers be remembered before the LORD,
and let not the sin of his mother be [q]blotted out!
15 [r]Let them be before the LORD continually,
that he may [s]cut off the memory of them from the earth!

16 For he did not remember to show kindness,
but pursued [t]the poor and needy
and [u]the brokenhearted, to put them to death.
17 [v]He loved to curse; let curses come[1] upon him!
He did not delight in blessing; may it be far[2] from him!
18 He [w]clothed himself with cursing as his coat;
may it [x]soak[3] into his body like water,
like oil into his bones!
19 May it be like a garment that he wraps around him,
like a belt that he puts on every day!
20 May this be the reward of my [y]accusers from the LORD,
of those who speak evil against my life!

21 But you, O GOD my Lord,
deal on my behalf [z]for your name's sake;
because your [a]steadfast love is good, deliver me!
22 For I am [b]poor and needy,
and my heart is stricken within me.
23 I am gone like [c]a shadow at evening;
I am [d]shaken off like a locust.
24 My knees are weak [e]through fasting;
my [f]body has become gaunt, with no fat.
25 I am [g]an object of scorn to my accusers;
when they see me, they [h]wag their heads.

26 [i]Help me, O LORD my God!
Save me according to your steadfast love!
27 Let them [j]know that this is your hand;
you, O LORD, have done it!
28 [k]Let them curse, but you will bless!
They arise and are put to shame, but [l]your servant will be glad!
29 May my accusers be [m]clothed with dishonor;
may they [n]be wrapped in their own shame as in a cloak!

30 With my mouth I will give great thanks to the LORD;
I will [o]praise him in the midst of the throng.

[1] Revocalization; Masoretic Text *curses have come* [2] Revocalization; Masoretic Text *it is far* [3] Revocalization; Masoretic Text *it has soaked*

109:13 posterity be cut off. Part of the blessing of being Israel is the prospect of one's family line continuing (cf. Deut. 25:6), with one's descendants under God's perfect care (cf. Deut. 7:9; Ps. 103:17–18). The unfaithful may forfeit that blessing.

109:14–15 let not the sin . . . be blotted out. See note on 69:27–28.

109:16 did not remember to show kindness. This is the explanation for v. 12. Covenant faithfulness is most clearly seen in showing kindness to the most vulnerable (**the poor and needy and the brokenhearted**), especially those among one's fellow members of God's people; the cursed person has repudiated this, seeking to harm and exploit them instead.

109:17 For the theme of proportional reversal, cf. 7:15; 9:15; 57:6; Prov. 28:10.

109:20 my accusers. Now the psalm returns to the whole group of enemies (cf. vv. 4, 6, 20, 29).

109:21–29 *Deliver Me from Their Accusations.* The next section asks for God's protection from the attacks, and for the **accusers** to be disgraced (v. 29), i.e., to be rendered ineffective in their power to intimidate and harm. The appeal is to God's **steadfast love** (vv. 21, 26) and to the singer's own powerlessness (vv. 22–25). The ideal would be for the accusers to **know that this is** God's **hand**; this will **put** them **to shame** and might even lead to their repentance (cf. 83:17–18).

109:22 poor and needy. Cf. v. 16, where he is one of the persecuted; and v. 31, where he is nevertheless assured of God's care.

109:28 curse . . . bless. Cf. v. 17. On the safety of the faithful when the unfaithful curse, cf. Prov. 26:2.

109:30–31 *I Will Give Thanks to God Who Protects Me.* The psalm closes with hope, the singer confident that he will **give great thanks to the LORD** in public worship (so that all the faithful can join in the praise). He will be

31 For he stands [p]at the right hand of the needy one,
to save him from those who condemn his soul to death.

Sit at My Right Hand

110

A PSALM OF DAVID.

1 [q]The LORD says to my Lord:
[r]"Sit at my right hand,
[s]until I make your enemies your [t]footstool."

2 The LORD sends forth [u]from Zion
[v]your mighty scepter.
[w]Rule in the midst of your enemies!
3 [x]Your people will [y]offer themselves freely
on the day of your [z]power,[1]
in [a]holy garments;[2]
from the womb of the morning,
the dew of your youth will be yours.[3]
4 [b]The LORD has [c]sworn
and will [d]not change his mind,
[e]"You are [f]a priest [g]forever
after the order of [h]Melchizedek."

5 The Lord is at your [i]right hand;
he will [j]shatter kings on [k]the day of his wrath.

[1] Or *on the day you lead your forces* [2] Masoretic Text; some Hebrew manuscripts and Jerome *on the holy mountains* [3] The meaning of the Hebrew is uncertain

31[p]ver. 6; See Ps. 16:8

Psalm 110

1[q]Cited Matt. 22:44; Mark 12:36; Luke 20:42, 43; Acts 2:34, 35 [r]Cited Heb. 1:13; [Matt. 26:64; Eph. 1:20; Col. 3:1; Heb. 1:3; 8:1; 10:12; 12:2] [s]Heb. 10:13; [1 Cor. 15:25; Eph. 1:22; Heb. 2:8; 1 Pet. 3:22] [t][Ps. 8:6; 18:38; Josh. 10:24]
2[u][Ps. 68:35] [v]Jer. 48:17; Ezek. 19:14; [Ps. 45:6] [w]Ps. 72:8; [Dan. 7:13, 14]
3[x]Judg. 5:2; Neh. 11:2 [y][Ex. 35:29] [z][Isa. 13:3, 4] [a][Rev. 19:14]; See 1 Chr. 16:29
4[b]Cited Heb. 7:21 [c]Ps. 132:11; Heb. 6:17, 18 [d]Num. 23:19 [e]Cited Heb. 5:6; 7:17, 21; [Heb. 6:20] [f]Zech. 6:13 [g]Heb. 7:24, 28; [John 12:34] [h]Gen. 14:18
5[i]See Ps. 16:8 [j][Ps. 68:14] [k]Rom. 2:5; Rev. 6:17; [Ps. 2:5, 12]

found **in the midst of the throng** in worship, rather than fall prey to **those who condemn his soul to death**.

109:31 stands at the right hand of the needy. Contrast this with the unfaithful man (v. 6), for whom the psalm prays that someone else will "stand at his right hand"!

Psalm 110. This is a royal psalm, i.e., its theme deals with the role of the house of David in the life of God's people (see also Psalms 2; 18; 20–21; 45; 72; 101; 132; 144; and possibly 89). Like Psalms 2 and 72, this psalm goes well beyond the achievements of any merely human heir of David and thus looks forward to the Messiah; in fact, unlike those two psalms, it is almost entirely future in its orientation (see note on 110:4). When the people of God would sing this in faith, they would celebrate God's promises to David, yearn for the day in which the Gentiles receive the light (the coming accomplishment of the Messiah), and seek to be faithful to their calling until that great day. This psalm is one of the most cited OT texts in the NT, with quotations or allusions appearing in the Gospels, Acts, the Pauline epistles, Hebrews, and the Petrine epistles. Christians sing this psalm to celebrate that Jesus has taken his Davidic kingship by his resurrection (see note on Ps. 2:7), and that God is busy now subduing the Gentiles into the empire of Jesus.

110:1 *The LORD to My Lord.* The psalm opens with an oracle from God (**the LORD**/Yahweh) to the Davidic king (**my Lord**). **Sit at my right hand.** This is the position of honor (cf. 1 Kings 2:19; Ps. 45:9), occupied by the human king. The Davidic king "sat on the throne of the LORD" (1 Chron. 29:23). **make your enemies your footstool**. Cf. 1 Kings 5:3. God will subdue these enemies, making them subject to the authority of the Davidic king (cf. Ps. 2:8; 72:8–11, 17; Isa. 11:1–10). In Matt. 22:44 (Mark 12:36; Luke 20:42) Jesus draws attention to the fact that David (the psalm's author) calls the king "my Lord," which implies that the king (whom all agreed was the Messiah) was greater than David. The idea that the risen Lord Jesus is the reigning messianic king seated at "God's right hand" appears in Acts 2:32–35; 1 Cor. 15:25; Eph. 1:20; Col. 3:1; Heb. 1:3, 13; 8:1; 10:12; 12:2; 1 Pet. 3:22; cf. Matt. 26:64. In 1 Cor. 15:25 and Eph. 1:20 Paul combines this with Ps. 8:6 (see note there).

110:2–4 *The King Will Rule over God's People.* The next section looks to the Davidic king's effectual rule over God's people, even under threat from hostile forces: **rule in the midst of your enemies!** The people of God will **offer themselves freely on the day of your power**, i.e., on the day God exerts his power to take possession of the Gentiles (vv. 5–7).

110:3 in holy garments. In festive clothing, in honor of the great moment (cf. 2 Chron. 20:21). **from the womb of the morning, the dew of your youth will be yours**. As the ESV footnote observes, the meaning of the Hebrew is obscure. The "womb of the morning" is probably a poetic expression for the east, or for the dawn (which is when the dew appears). The "dew of your youth" may be a poetic term for refreshment, implying that the king has continual sources of fresh energy; or it might suggest willing soldiers as numerous as the dewdrops.

110:4 The LORD has sworn and will not change his mind. Once this takes effect, it cannot be revoked. **a priest forever after the order of Melchizedek**. Melchizedek was "king of Salem" (i.e., of Jerusalem) and a "priest of God Most High" (Gen. 14:18–20) who met Abraham after a battle, blessed him, and received a tenth of his spoil. The Davidic king is to be "after his order," i.e., like him, probably in the sense that he is both a king and a priest (these are two distinct offices in Israel), ruling in Jerusalem (cf. Zion, Ps. 110:2). The prophet Zechariah foresaw a merger of these two offices in the person of the Messiah, or "the Branch" (Zech. 6:9–14). Since the OT records this of no other king of David's line, this shows that the psalm is primarily about the final king, the Messiah. The author of Hebrews (Heb. 5:6), who cited Ps. 110:1 (see note) throughout his book, uses this verse to explain to his Jewish audience why Jesus, the now-reigning heir of David (cf. Heb. 1:3; 5:5), is also the ultimate priest; now that Jesus has arrived, Christian Jews may not legitimately return to "ordinary" Judaism in order to escape persecution, hoping that the old sacrifices will still "work," for they will not. There is a text from Qumran (11QMelchizedek) that also foresees Melchizedek as a heavenly judge and deliverer.

110:5–7 *The Warrior King Will Be Victorious over His Enemies.* The final section takes up a common messianic theme of the OT: the ultimate heir of David will be the triumphant conqueror of the Gentiles. The scene of victory in battle here may portray the final judgment, but is more likely the overcoming of all the Gentile leaders, so that the peoples themselves can serve their new king, the Messiah (cf. Isa. 11:4). **He will lift up his head** in victory, ready to enjoy his rule (cf. Ps. 27:6).

6[l]Isa. 2:4; Joel 3:12; Mic. 4:3 [m]See Ezek. 39:17-19; Rev. 19:17, 18 [n][Ps. 68:21]
7[o][Judg. 7:5, 6]
Psalm 111
1[p]See Ps. 104:35 [q]Ps. 138:1 [r][Ps. 149:1]
2[s]Ps. 92:5; Rev. 3:2; [Ps. 139:14] [t]Ps. 119:45, 94, 155; [Ps. 112:1; 143:5]
3[u]Ps. 145:5 [v]Ps. 112:3, 9
4[w][Ps. 78:4]
5[x]See Ps. 105:8
7[y]Ps. 93:5; [Ps. 19:7]
8[z]Isa. 40:8; Matt. 5:18 [a]Ps. 19:9; Rev. 15:3
9[b][Matt. 1:21]; Luke 1:68 [c][Ps. 133:3] [d]Ps. 99:3; Luke 1:49; [Ps. 8:1]

6 He will [l]execute judgment among the nations,
[m]filling them with corpses;
he will [n]shatter chiefs[1]
over the wide earth.
7 He will [o]drink from the brook by the way;
therefore he will lift up his head.

Great Are the LORD's Works

111[2]

1 [p]Praise the LORD!
I [q]will give thanks to the LORD with my whole heart,
in the company of [r]the upright, in the congregation.
2 Great are the [s]works of the LORD,
[t]studied by all who delight in them.
3 [u]Full of splendor and majesty is his work,
and his [v]righteousness endures forever.
4 He has [w]caused his wondrous works to be remembered;
the LORD is gracious and merciful.
5 He provides food for those who fear him;
he [x]remembers his covenant forever.
6 He has shown his people the power of his works,
in giving them the inheritance of the nations.
7 The works of his hands are faithful and just;
all his precepts are [y]trustworthy;
8 they are [z]established forever and ever,
to be performed with [a]faithfulness and uprightness.
9 He sent [b]redemption to his people;
he has [c]commanded his covenant forever.
[d]Holy and awesome is his name!

[1] Or *the head* [2] This psalm is an acrostic poem, each line beginning with the successive letters of the Hebrew alphabet

110:5 The Lord is at your right hand. The form of the word "Lord" (Hb. *'Adonay*) is reserved for the deity in the OT (see note on Gen. 18:3). Most of this section describes what "he" will do, and this most likely refers to the same person as "the Lord." But the image of the conquering king is a messianic image; and the messianic king is at God's right hand (Ps. 110:1). This implicitly attributes deity to the messianic Lord (cf. Isa. 9:6 and note).

Psalm 111. This is a hymn of praise, celebrating the great works that the Lord has done for his people in calling them to be his, in caring for them, and in protecting them. These great works express God's unstinting goodness toward his people. The purpose of singing the psalm is to remind the people of these deeds and to encourage them to embrace the privileges that God's call has bestowed, by a heartfelt "fear of the LORD" (v. 10). Psalm 111 focuses on the deeds God has done for his people as a body. The "covenant" (v. 5) established Israel as God's people, and the "works" sustain and protect Israel as a whole. The "redemption" described here (v. 9) is for the sake of calling and protecting the whole people and for fostering the conditions under which true piety may thrive (see note on Isa. 1:24–28). Psalms 111–112 go together. Both follow an acrostic pattern: after the initial "Praise the LORD" (Hb. *hallelu-yah*), the first word of each line begins with the successive letter of the Hebrew alphabet. For both psalms, the flow of thought is governed by the acrostic structure. Psalm 111:10 brings its praise to a close with a reference to the fear of the Lord—a "wisdom" idea, coupled with "understanding"—while Ps. 112:1 leads off its wisdom meditation with "the man who fears the LORD." This clear connection helps readers in interpretation: in Psalm 111 it is the Lord whose "righteousness endures forever" (v. 3) and who is "gracious and merciful" (v. 4, echoing Ex. 34:6), while in Psalm 112 it is the godly person whose "righteousness endures forever" (112:3) and who is "gracious and merciful" (112:4). The implication is that the person who fears the Lord and attends to his commandments has God's own moral traits reflected in his character. This is the goal of redemption, to renew the image of God in human beings. Psalm 111, in stressing God's mighty deeds of redemption for his people, focuses on the "big story" for the whole people; Psalm 112, in stressing "wisdom," encourages each member of God's people in a day-to-day walk, a "little story," that contributes to the big story of the whole people. Christians sing these psalms in the same way, with the mighty deeds including Jesus' resurrection and installation as the heir of David, and God's continuing care for his people.

111:1 give thanks. Cf. 105:1. Each member of the **congregation** participates in the task of giving thanks and praise.

111:2 works (cf. vv. 6, 7). These are God's deeds in creation (e.g., 8:3, 6; 104:24), and especially in redeeming his people (e.g., 145:9; Ex. 34:10; Deut. 3:24; 11:7; Dan. 9:14). **studied**. Carefully pondered.

111:3 splendor and majesty. See note on 96:6. **his righteousness endures forever**. Cf. 119:142; Isa. 51:8. God shows his righteousness, his uprightness and faithfulness to his promises, in his great deeds. See note on Ps. 112:3.

111:4 remembered. See note on 112:6–8. **gracious and merciful**. From Ex. 34:6. See note on Ps. 112:4.

111:5 those who fear him. See v. 10; 112:1. **remembers his covenant**. See notes on 25:6–7; 105:8. Just as God "remembers," so should his people remember (111:4).

111:6 This describes the taking of the Promised Land.

111:7–8 God's **precepts** (instructions; cf. 19:8; 119:4) given to his people express his love and faithfulness as much as do **the works of his hands** in redemptive history. Thus the precepts are **established forever**, in order for God's people to perform them **with faithfulness and uprightness**.

111:9 redemption. See note on Psalm 111.

10 [e]The fear of the LORD is the beginning of wisdom;
all those who practice it have [f]a good understanding.
His [g]praise endures forever!

The Righteous Will Never Be Moved

112[1]

1 [h]Praise the LORD!
[i]Blessed is the man who fears the LORD,
who [j]greatly delights in his commandments!
2 His [k]offspring will be mighty in the land;
[l]the generation of the upright will be blessed.
3 [m]Wealth and riches are in his house,
and his [n]righteousness endures forever.
4 Light dawns in the darkness [o]for the upright;
he is gracious, merciful, and [p]righteous.
5 It is well with the man who [q]deals generously and lends;
who conducts his affairs with justice.
6 For the righteous will [r]never be moved;
[s]he will be remembered forever.
7 He is not [t]afraid of bad news;
his [u]heart is firm, [v]trusting in the LORD.
8 His heart is steady; he will not be afraid,
until he looks in triumph on his adversaries.
9 He has [w]distributed freely; he has given to the poor;
his righteousness endures forever;
his [x]horn is exalted in honor.
10 The wicked man sees it and is angry;
he [y]gnashes his teeth and [z]melts away;
[a]the desire of the wicked will perish!

[1] This psalm is an acrostic poem, each line beginning with the successive letters of the Hebrew alphabet

10[e]Prov. 9:10; See Prov. 1:7 [f][Prov. 3:4; 13:15; John 7:17] [g][Ps. 44:8]

Psalm 112

1[h]See Ps. 104:35 [i]Ps. 128:1, 4; [Ps. 111:10; 115:13] [j]See Ps. 1:2
2[k][Ps. 25:13; 102:28; Prov. 11:21; 20:7] [l]Ps. 37:26
3[m]See Prov. 3:16 [n][Ps. 111:3]
4[o][Job 11:17]; See Ps. 97:11 [p][Matt. 1:19]
5[q]See Ps. 37:26
6[r]Ps. 55:22 [s][Prov. 10:7]
7[t]Prov. 1:33 [u]Ps. 57:7 [v]Ps. 11:1; 64:10
9[w]Cited 2 Cor. 9:9 [x]See Ps. 75:10
10[y][Matt. 8:12; Luke 13:28]; See Job 16:9 [z][Ps. 58:8] [a]See Job 8:13

111:10 The fear of the LORD is the beginning of wisdom. See note on Prov. 1:7. By mentioning this and **good understanding** (i.e., sound insight into God's moral order for the world), the psalm paves the way for Psalm 112, a "wisdom psalm."

Psalm 112. This wisdom psalm joins Psalms 1; 37; 49; 73; 127; and 128 (with 34:11–14) in making themes from the Wisdom Literature the topic of prayer, praise, and instruction in worship. Psalm 112 is also a companion to Psalm 111, as seen in the acrostic pattern they both follow and in the links between their wording (see note on Psalm 111). This psalm focuses on the moral character of the faithful, and on the benefits such people bring to themselves and to others.

112:1 Blessed. See note on 1:1. **man**. As with 1:1, the Hb. word is masculine, and the psalm uses a particular man as a pattern of godliness, inviting women and children to make the necessary adaptations to their own circumstances (see Introduction to Proverbs: Literary Features, on concreteness). **fears the LORD**. This links with Ps. 111:10 (see note there) and shows that the two psalms belong together. **greatly delights in his commandments**. This shows that the "fear" is not craven terror but reverent love (cf. 1:2).

112:2 offspring. See note on 109:13. The godly person brings blessing to others, particularly to his descendants.

112:3 Wealth and riches. See note on Prov. 10:4. **his righteousness endures forever**. In Ps. 111:3, this referred to God's righteousness, his moral uprightness and faithfulness to his promises. Now the same expression is used of the faithful: God's own character is visible in them (cf. 2 Pet. 1:4). The godly, with their character genuinely reflecting God's image, will dwell forever under God's love and watchful care.

112:4 Light dawns in the darkness for the upright. As in 97:11 (see note), the image of light is that of God's guidance; here that guidance makes the right path clear for those who pursue covenant faithfulness (see note on Prov. 4:18–19). **he is gracious, merciful, and righteous**. "The upright" is plural; now the verse speaks of each one of them. They show the character of the Lord himself (Ps. 111:4; see note on 112:3). Particular aspects of this character include generosity and fair dealing (vv. 5, 9).

112:5 deals generously and lends. See Prov. 14:21 (and note), 31; 19:17. **It is well with** such a **man** because he works for the good of God's whole community (cf. Prov. 11:25). Cf. also Ps. 112:9.

112:6–8 never be moved. See note on 15:5c; verses 7–8 of Psalm 112 describe his security. **be remembered**. By the people, just as they remember the Lord's own wondrous works (111:4), and perhaps by the Lord himself, who remembers his covenant **forever** (112:6). The righteous **is not afraid of bad news**, because he fears the Lord (112:1).

112:9 Paul quotes from this verse in 2 Cor. 9:9, encouraging the Corinthian Christians to give generously to the collection for poor Jewish Christians in Judea. The psalm shows why they should not fear (because God will **honor** and care for them); it also shows a lovely community orientation that provides a stark contrast to the ugly selfishness that Paul had to correct in 1 Corinthians. The NT "community" now transcends national and ethnic boundaries, including people of all kinds who believe in Jesus.

112:10 The **wicked man** is the person who despises the covenant; here he is probably an Israelite. The **desire** of such people will not bear fruit; instead it **will perish**, because the God who made and rules the world delights in those who fear him.

Who Is like the LORD Our God?

113

1 [b]Praise the LORD!
[c]Praise, O [d]servants of the LORD,
praise the name of the LORD!
2 [e]Blessed be the name of the LORD
from this time forth and forevermore!
3 [f]From the rising of the sun to its setting,
[g]the name of the LORD is [h]to be praised!
4 The LORD is [i]high above all nations,
and his [j]glory above the heavens!
5 [k]Who is like the LORD our God,
who is seated on high,
6 who [l]looks far down
on the heavens and the earth?
7 He [m]raises the poor from the dust
and lifts the needy from the ash heap,
8 to make them [n]sit with princes,
with the princes of his people.
9 He [o]gives the barren woman a home,
making her the joyous mother of children.
[b]Praise the LORD!

Tremble at the Presence of the Lord

114

1 When [p]Israel went out from Egypt,
the house of Jacob from [q]a people of strange language,
2 Judah became his [r]sanctuary,
Israel his dominion.
3 [s]The sea looked and fled;
[t]Jordan turned back.

Psalm 113
1 [b]See Ps. 104:35 [c]Ps. 135:1 [d]Ps. 34:22; 69:36; 102:28
2 [e]Ps. 115:18; See Job 1:21
3 [f]Ps. 50:1; Isa. 59:19; Mal. 1:11 [g]See Ps. 48:10 [h]See Ps. 18:3
4 [i]Ps. 99:2 [j]Ps. 8:1; 57:5, 11; 148:13
5 [k]See Ps. 35:10
6 [l]See Ps. 11:4; [Ps. 138:6]
7 [m][Ps. 136:23]; See Ps. 107:41
8 [n][Job 36:7]
9 [o]Ps. 68:6; 1 Sam. 2:5; [Ex. 1:21; Isa. 54:1] [b][See ver. 1 above]

Psalm 114
1 [p]Ex. 12:37 [q]Ps. 81:5; [Gen. 42:23]
2 [r]Ps. 78:68, 69; [Ex. 15:17; 25:8]
3 [s]See Ps. 77:16 [t]See Josh. 3:13-16

Psalm 113. This short hymn of praise celebrates the way in which the great and majestic God who rules over all takes notice of the lowly. Such a God is indeed worthy to be praised by all mankind. Verses 7–8 overlap with 1 Sam. 2:8, part of Hannah's Song. Perhaps the psalm borrowed the words, as the reference to a "barren woman" suggests. Psalms 113–118 have been called the "Egyptian Hallel" (Hb. *hallel* means "praise"; "Egyptian" because of the later connection with Passover), which came to be a regular part of the great festivals of the liturgical year (including Hanukkah, the Dedication, once it was instituted in the intertestamental period; cf. John 10:22). These psalms likely provided the hymn that Jesus and his disciples sang after their Passover meal (Matt. 26:30).

113:1–3 *The Lord Is to Be Praised through All the World.* The theme of the whole psalm is set by the words that open and close the psalm, **Praise the LORD!** (Hb. *hallelu-yah*). The **servants of the LORD** (esp. faithful Israelites; cf. 136:22, where the whole people is called God's "servant"), who have received his covenant, should lead the way in praise; but they live in confidence that one day their God will be praised **from the rising of the sun to its setting**, i.e., all over the world by all kinds of people, as he deserves.

113:4–9 *Though He Is on High, He Looks upon the Lowly.* This section develops the universal theme of the previous section in a surprising way: the God who deserves to be praised by all mankind **is seated on high** (ruling over the whole world), and yet he **looks far down** and **raises the poor from the dust**. The imagery of vv. 7–8 describes a position of extreme degradation and misery ("dust" and **ash heap**) being transformed to one of dignity and privilege (**sit with princes**). For an Israelite woman to be **barren** (i.e., unable to bear children) was a misery, too (cf. 1 Sam. 1:2–17), and this likewise provides an image of God's tender care for his loved ones. God's majesty never implies his remoteness from those who look to him; it implies instead his exhaustive attention to detail, and his inexhaustible ability to care for his faithful.

Psalm 114. This hymn of praise celebrates the special status of God's people in his plan: the Lord is the one whom all nature obeys, and even trembles before, and yet he has chosen little Israel to be his own, and he exerts his power on their behalf. The psalm mentions the exodus from Egypt, the covenant at Sinai that made Israel to be God's "dominion," the crossing of the Jordan River under Joshua's leadership, and God's provision for his people as they traveled through the wilderness. When the believing congregation sings this, they are better able to accept their current circumstances as under God's governance as well. The psalm uses exuberant personification, describing the Red Sea and Jordan River as if they fled from God, the mountains as skipping like lambs, and the earth as trembling at God's presence. The imagery conveys how powerful the Lord is: even the strongest natural forces would not dream of resisting him. However, the events of the psalm are not simply displays of raw power: God used his power for the sake of his people.

114:1–2 *Israel Became God's Holy Kingdom.* The opening section recalls the exodus (**when Israel went out from Egypt**) and its consequence: **Judah became** God's **sanctuary**, and **Israel** became God's **dominion**, i.e., Israel is the holy place where God rules. Judah probably represents all Israel here, which would make sense if, as most scholars think, this psalm comes from after the Babylonian exile (when Judah was all that was left of the ancient people). Describing Egypt as **a people of strange language** further supports this: Judah had recently dwelt among another people speaking an unfamiliar language (cf. Deut. 28:49; Jer. 5:15; Ezek. 3:5–6).

114:3–6 *The Red Sea and the Jordan River.* The next section recalls how God split the Red **sea** (Ex. 14:21–22), and later the **Jordan** River (Josh.

4 [u]The mountains skipped like rams,
the hills like lambs.
5 What [v]ails you, O sea, that you flee?
O Jordan, that you turn back?
6 O mountains, that you skip like rams?
O hills, like lambs?
7 [w]Tremble, O earth, at the presence of the Lord,
at the presence of the God of Jacob,
8 who turns [x]the rock into [y]a pool of water,
[z]the flint into a spring of water.

To Your Name Give Glory

115 1 [a]Not to us, O LORD, not to us, but to your name give glory,
[b]for the sake of your steadfast love and your faithfulness!
2 Why should the nations say,
[c]"Where is their God?"
3 [d]Our God is in the heavens;
[e]he does all that he pleases.
4 [f]Their idols are silver and gold,
[g]the work of human hands.
5 They have mouths, [h]but do not speak;
eyes, but do not see.
6 They have ears, but do not hear;
noses, but do not smell.
7 They have hands, but do not feel;
feet, but do not walk;
and they do not make a sound in their throat.
8 [i]Those who make them become like them;
so do all who trust in them.

4[u][Ps. 18:7; 29:6; Ex. 19:18]
5[v][Hab. 3:8]
7[w]Ps. 96:9
8[x]Num. 20:11; See Ps. 78:15 [y]See Ps. 107:35 [z]Deut. 8:15

Psalm 115
1[a][Isa. 48:11; Ezek. 36:22; Dan. 9:18, 19] [b]See Ps. 36:5
2[c][Ex. 32:12; Num. 14:13, 14]; See Ps. 42:3
3[d]See Ps. 11:4 [e]Ps. 135:6; Dan. 4:35
4[f]For ver. 4-8, see Ps. 135:15-18 [g]Deut. 4:28; 2 Kgs. 19:18; Isa. 37:19; Acts 19:26; See Isa. 44:10-20; Jer. 10:3-5
5[h][Isa. 46:7; Hab. 2:18]
8[i][Isa. 44:9]

3:15–17; cf. Josh. 4:21–24, where the two events are explicitly joined), for the sake of his people. The **mountains** may refer to God's arrival at Sinai (Ex. 19:18–20). The natural elements are personified, as if the sea, the river, and the mountains were all terrified of the Lord. This imagery is designed to show the absolute power that God has over his own creation.

114:7–8 *Tremble, O Earth, at God's Presence!* The third section continues to speak of God's power over his world. **Tremble, O earth**. As with 97:4, this directs the singers' attention to how God can sweep away all opposition. **turns the rock into a pool**. There are two events like this in the Pentateuch, Ex. 17:6 and Num. 20:8–13 (cf. Deut. 8:15), and both are probably in view. In both cases God showed his power over the elements in order to care for his people. God's people in each generation may sing this and take courage from his great power.

Psalm 115. This is a hymn urging God's people to trust and worship the Lord alone, by reminding them that he alone is worthy of their deepest loyalty. In the background lurks the temptation to turn to the gods worshiped in other nations, and the congregation must grasp how hopeless it is to serve such deities. Some scholars suppose that the Gentiles' taunt, "Where is their God?" (v. 2), and the description of useless idols (vv. 4–8) is evidence that the psalm arose after the exile, when Israel had close exposure to such taunts and temptations. And some have taken the expression, "you who fear the LORD" (vv. 11, 13), to address Gentiles who worship the Lord (cf. Acts 10:2; 13:16), which began to be a notable feature of Jewish life in the Greek period (i.e., after 330 B.C.). None of these arguments is decisive, however: as the comments show, the taunts and temptations existed at all periods, and the expression "fearing the Lord" readily applies to any of the faithful in Israel at any time. Nevertheless, if the psalm originated before the exile, it certainly took on a renewed relevance in the postexilic period; and the Gentiles attending the synagogue might see themselves included among those who fear the Lord, the true God. Indeed, Christians can sing this psalm for the same purpose of fortifying their loyalty to, and confidence in, the true God.

115:1–8 *Only One God Deserves Praise.* This section develops the idea that only the Lord deserves **glory** (i.e., honor): first, because of his **steadfast love** and **faithfulness** (cf. Ex. 34:6); and second, because he **is in the heavens** (in a position of rule over all, cf. Ps. 113:4–5), and in sovereign power **he does all that he pleases** (cf. 135:6; Isa. 46:10), unlike the gods that the Gentiles worship (Ps. 115:4–8).

115:2 Why should the nations say? The concern for the Lord's reputation among the nations occurs as early as Ex. 32:12 and Num. 14:13–14. When Israel remembers that its very calling includes making God's name known among the Gentiles (cf. Josh. 4:24; 1 Kings 8:41–43), they will see that more than their own self-esteem is at stake here: if the Gentiles think this way, they will not receive God's light.

115:3 The confession that God **does all that he pleases** is pertinent in reply to the Gentiles' taunt (v. 2), because in Dan. 4:35 and Jonah 1:14, Gentiles confess this once they realize that the Lord is the true God.

115:4–8 This satirical passage exposes the folly of worshiping **idols**, much like Isa. 44:9–20. This builds on Deut. 4:28 (cf. the regular denunciation of idols as **the work of human hands**, and therefore unworthy of human worship: Deut. 27:15; 31:29; 2 Kings 19:18; Isa. 2:8; Jer. 1:16; Mic. 5:13). Psalm 135:15–18 repeats most of these verses. If these gods are unworthy of Israel's worship, it is a tragedy that the Gentiles both **make them** and **become like them** (i.e., lifeless and useless); let Israel take warning!

9 O [j]Israel,[1] [k]trust in the LORD!
He is their [l]help and their shield.
10 O [j]house of Aaron, trust in the LORD!
He is their help and [m]their shield.
11 You [n]who fear the LORD, trust in the LORD!
He is their help and their shield.

12 The LORD has remembered us; he will bless us;
he will bless [o]the house of Israel;
he will bless [o]the house of Aaron;
13 he will [p]bless those who fear the LORD,
[q]both the small and the great.

14 May the LORD [r]give you increase,
you and your children!
15 May [s]you be blessed by the LORD,
[t]who made heaven and earth!

16 The heavens are the LORD's heavens,
but the earth he has given to the children of man.
17 [u]The dead do not praise the LORD,
nor do any who go down into [v]silence.
18 But [w]we will bless the LORD
from this time forth and forevermore.
[x]Praise the LORD!

116

I Love the LORD

1 I [y]love the LORD, because he has [z]heard
my voice and my pleas for mercy.
2 Because he [a]inclined his ear to me,
therefore I will call on him as long as I live.
3 [b]The snares of death encompassed me;
the pangs of Sheol laid hold on me;
I suffered distress and anguish.

[1] Masoretic Text; many Hebrew manuscripts, Septuagint, Syriac *O house of Israel*

9[j][Ps. 118:2-4; 135:19, 20] [k]Ps. 37:3; 62:8 [l]Ps. 33:20
10[j][See ver. 9 above] [m]See Ps. 3:3
11[n]Ps. 22:23; 103:11, 13, 17
12[o][Ps. 118:2-4; 135:19, 20]
13[p]See Ps. 112:1 [q]Jer. 16:6; 31:34
14[r]Deut. 1:11
15[s]See Ruth 2:20 [t]Ps. 121:2; 124:8; 134:3; 146:6; Acts 14:15; Rev. 14:7; [Gen. 1:1; 14:19; Jer. 10:11]
17[u]See Ps. 6:5 [v]See Ps. 31:17
18[w]Ps. 113:2 [x]See Ps. 104:35

Psalm 116

1[y]Ps. 18:1 [z]Ps. 66:19; 118:21
2[a][Ps. 31:2]
3[b]See Ps. 18:4

115:9–11 *Let God's People Trust Him as Their Help and Shield.* In response to the warning (v. 8), this section calls all the members of God's people (**Israel, house of Aaron, you who fear the LORD**; cf. 118:2–4) to **trust in the LORD**. The Lord alone is qualified to be **their help and their shield** (cf. 28:7; 33:20; Deut. 33:29).

115:10 The **house of Aaron** was the specific family within the tribe of Levi that supplied the priests (Ex. 28:1; Num. 16:8–11).

115:11 You who fear the LORD. By the time of the NT, Gentiles who adhered to the synagogue were called "God-fearers" (Acts 10:2; 13:16). Although the OT expected that Gentiles would come to "fear the LORD" (cf. 1 Kings 8:43), there is no evidence from either the OT or the Apocrypha (intertestamental books) that this term had taken on its specialized sense early enough for the psalm to use it. The term describes Israel as a community bound to the Lord by covenant, and perhaps especially designates those members with true piety. At the same time, the term is wide enough to include all who worship the Lord—even if they are neither from the house of Aaron nor from ethnic Israel—and once Gentiles in the Greco-Roman world began attending synagogue, they could see themselves addressed here.

115:12–15 *The Lord Blesses His Faithful People.* The next section expresses the confidence that God will indeed bless his people, and prays that he will continue to do so.

115:14–15 Verse 14 echoes Deut. 1:11 (anticipating that God's people will **increase** through their **children**), and Ps. 115:15 echoes Gen. 1:28, 31; God called Israel in order to give them the privileges that Adam forfeited.

115:16–18 *We Will Bless the Lord Forever.* The psalm closes by having the congregation sing of their renewed dedication to **bless the LORD** (in response to his blessing, vv. 12–15).

115:16 As v. 15 agrees, the Lord made heaven and earth; **the heavens** are where the Lord dwells (in the place of rule, see v. 3), while **the earth he has given to the children of man** (i.e., to mankind in general, for whom Israel is the first installment of their renewal in God's image).

115:17 The dead do not praise the LORD. See notes on 6:5 and 88:10–12.

Psalm 116. This is a hymn of personal thanksgiving for God's care. The specific circumstance is a deliverance from impending death (vv. 3, 8–9, 15); the words of the psalm may be generalized to other kinds of dramatic answers to prayer in a time of dire need. The psalm is notable for its assumption that one's thanks for this very personal deliverance are properly consummated in public worship. These words are an excellent form for God's people to use in giving public thanks after their own emergencies (e.g., some churches use the psalm in a service of thanksgiving after a woman has given birth).

116:1–4 *I Love the Lord, Who Has Heard My Prayer.* The psalm opens with a straightforward statement of its overall theme: **I love the LORD, because he has heard my voice and my pleas for mercy**. The people of Israel are urged to love the Lord in response to his covenant blessings (e.g., Deut. 6:5; 11:1); that love grows as the faithful experience God's work among the community and in their own lives. Likewise, the singer **called on the name of the LORD** in distress (Ps. 116:4), and now resolves to **call on him as long as I live** (v. 2).

116:3 The snares of death and **the pangs of Sheol** are probably the

4 Then [c]I called on the name of the LORD:
"O LORD, I pray, deliver my soul!"
5 [d]Gracious is the LORD, and [e]righteous;
our God is [f]merciful.
6 The LORD preserves [g]the simple;
when [h]I was brought low, he saved me.
7 Return, O my soul, to your [i]rest;
for the LORD has [j]dealt bountifully with you.

8 For [k]you have delivered my soul from death,
my eyes from tears,
my feet from stumbling;
9 I will walk before the LORD
[l]in the land of the living.

10 [m]I believed, [n]even when[1] I spoke:
"I am greatly afflicted";
11 [o]I said in my alarm,
[p]"All mankind are liars."

12 What shall I [q]render to the LORD
for all his benefits to me?
13 I will lift up [r]the cup of salvation
and [s]call on the name of the LORD,
14 I will [t]pay my vows to the LORD
in the presence of all his people.

15 [u]Precious in the sight of the LORD
is the death of his [v]saints.
16 O LORD, I am your [w]servant;
I am your servant, [x]the son of your maidservant.
You have [y]loosed my bonds.
17 I will [z]offer to you the sacrifice of thanksgiving
and [s]call on the name of the LORD.
18 I will [t]pay my vows to the LORD
in the presence of all his people,
19 in [a]the courts of the house of the LORD,
in your midst, O Jerusalem.
[b]Praise the LORD!

[1] Or *believed, indeed;* Septuagint *believed, therefore*

4 [c]Ps. 118:5; See Ps. 18:6
5 [d]See Ps. 86:15 [e]Ps. 7:9; 119:137; 145:17; Ezra 9:15; Neh. 9:8; Jer. 12:1; Dan. 9:7 [f]See Ps. 62:12
6 [g]See Ps. 19:7 [h]Ps. 79:8; 142:6
7 [i]Jer. 6:16; [Matt. 11:28] [j]See Ps. 13:6
8 [k]Ps. 49:15; 56:13; [Ps. 86:13]
9 [l]See Ps. 27:13
10 [m]Cited 2 Cor. 4:13 [n][Ps. 39:3]
11 [o]Ps. 31:22 [p][Ps. 62:9]
12 [q]2 Chr. 32:25
13 [r][Ps. 16:5] [s]See Ps. 99:6; 105:1
14 [t]See Ps. 50:14
15 [u]See Ps. 72:14 [v]See Ps. 50:5
16 [w]Ps. 119:125; 143:12; [Ps. 113:1] [x]Ps. 86:16 [y][Job 12:18]
17 [z]See Ps. 50:14 [s][See ver. 13 above]
18 [t][See ver. 14 above]
19 [a]See Ps. 92:13 [b]See Ps. 104:35

same thing; he was on the brink of dying (cf. vv. 8, 15). On Sheol as a poetic name for the grave, see note on 6:5.

116:4 called on the name of the LORD. This can be a general term for invoking a deity in prayer (e.g., 1 Kings 18:24), but more often refers to a prayer that is part of public worship (cf. Gen. 4:26; 12:8; Ps. 105:1), which is likely the case here in view of the same term in 116:13. Thus the request was made as part of a worship service.

116:5–7 *The Lord Deals Bountifully with His Own.* The answer to the urgent prayer leads to reflection on the character of God, namely, that he is **gracious, merciful** (cf. Ex. 34:6), and **righteous** (i.e., reliably faithful). The pious should know this already; and yet the experience being celebrated has made these notions all the more real to the believer.

116:8–11 *You Delivered My Soul from Death.* The song returns to the desperate situation from which the person has been delivered: **death, tears, stumbling**. These cover a wider variety of circumstances than simply the death of one's body, and may be the psalmist's invitation to the singers to apply the psalm more generally to experiences of need. The psalm also leads the thankful person to see how to make good use of the deliverance: **I will walk before the LORD** (i.e., in love, faith, and obedience toward him).

116:10 I believed, even when I spoke. In 2 Cor. 4:13, Paul uses the Greek Septuagint of this line, "I believe, and so I spoke." Paul is narrating the kinds of desperate trials from which God has rescued him, and thus it is fitting that he would borrow these words.

116:11 All mankind are liars. In Rom. 3:3 Paul borrows the Greek wording, "every (human) one is a liar," to emphasize God's truthfulness (which honors the context of the psalm, cf. Ps. 116:5).

116:12–19 *How Shall I Show My Thanks to Him?* The final section raises the question, **What shall I render to the LORD for all his benefits to me?** The answer is, with acts of public worship, as the following phrases show: **the cup of salvation** (perhaps a part of the sacrifice of thanksgiving, v. 14); **call on the name of the LORD** (see note on v. 4); **pay my vows** and **offer to you the sacrifice of thanksgiving** (see notes on 50:7–15; 56:12–13; 61:8; 66:13–15); **in the presence of all his people**; and **in the courts of the house of the LORD**. The personal deliverance is a benefit to the whole people, and the entire congregation shares in giving thanks (cf. Rom. 12:15).

Psalm 117
1[c]Cited Rom. 15:11
2[d]Ps. 103:11; [Ps. 116:5] [e][Ps. 100:5] [b][See Ps. 116:19 above]
Psalm 118
1[f]ver. 29; See Ps. 100:5
2[g][Ps. 115:9, 10, 11]
3[g][See ver. 2 above]
4[g][See ver. 2 above]
5[h][Jonah 2:1] [i][Ps. 116:4] [j]See Ps. 18:19
6[k]Ps. 56:9; Cited Heb. 13:6 [l]See Ps. 23:4; 56:4, 11
7[m]Ps. 54:4 [n]See Ps. 54:7
8[o][Ps. 40:4; 62:8] [p]Ps. 146:3
9[p][See ver. 8 above]
10[q][Ps. 88:17]

The LORD's Faithfulness Endures Forever

117

1 [c]Praise the LORD, all nations!
Extol him, all peoples!
2 For [d]great is his steadfast love toward us,
and [e]the faithfulness of the LORD endures forever.
[b]Praise the LORD!

His Steadfast Love Endures Forever

118

1 [f]Oh give thanks to the LORD, for he is good;
for his steadfast love endures forever!

2 [g]Let Israel say,
"His steadfast love endures forever."
3 [g]Let the house of Aaron say,
"His steadfast love endures forever."
4 [g]Let those who fear the LORD say,
"His steadfast love endures forever."

5 [h]Out of my distress I [i]called on the LORD;
the LORD answered me and set me [j]free.
6 [k]The LORD is on my side; [l]I will not fear.
What can man do to me?
7 [m]The LORD is on my side as my helper;
I shall [n]look in triumph on those who hate me.

8 [o]It is better to take refuge in the LORD
[p]than to trust in man.
9 It is better to take refuge in the LORD
[p]than to trust in princes.

10 [q]All nations surrounded me;
in the name of the LORD I cut them off!

Psalm 117. This short hymn invites **all nations** to **praise the LORD**. The Lord's **steadfast love** and **faithfulness** (Ex. 34:6) is pledged to Israel but is intended for all the world; hence the Gentiles addressed are included in the word **us**. The calling of Israel was for the sake of the whole world (Gen. 12:2–3; Ex. 19:5–6; 1 Kings 8:41–43), and the OT constantly nurtures the hope that a day will come when the Gentiles will gladly join in worshiping the one true God (see note on Psalm 96). When Israel sang this in faith, they would recall both their privileged position (cf. 147:19–20) and their reason for existence. Paul quotes 117:1 in Rom. 15:11 as part of his argument (Rom. 15:8–13) for Jewish and Gentile Christians welcoming one another and worshiping together (Rom. 15:5–7): the long-awaited time has arrived.

Psalm 118. This joyful song of thanksgiving closes the Egyptian Hallel (see note on Psalm 113). The psalm calls on all of God's people to praise the Lord for his steadfast love (118:1–4), and then moves to what seems to be a personal testimony of God's rescue from distress (vv. 5–18), and then to a liturgical occasion at the Lord's house, which involves the whole people again (vv. 19–29). The psalm describes a festive procession into Jerusalem after some great deliverance. The original occasion is hard to identify. It could be the rebuilding of the temple or the walls of Jerusalem. In later times it was sung at the Feast of Tabernacles as well as Passover. It was evidently recited by the crowds when Jesus entered Jerusalem on Palm Sunday (Matt. 21:9; Mark 11:9; Luke 19:38). And Jesus may imply that it will be sung again at his second coming (Matt. 23:39). It was the last psalm Jesus sang at the Last Supper with his disciples before they left for Gethsemane (Matt. 26:30), and vv. 25–26 of Psalm 118 are often still recalled in prayers at the Lord's Supper. The liturgical section inclines most scholars to think that the psalm was originally composed for some special ceremony, such as laying the foundation of the new temple (cf. v. 1 with Ezra 3:11), or the dedication of the new temple (Ezra 6:16–22). In any case, that connection would make the "I" giving the personal testimony of each member of the congregation, identifying himself with the trials of the whole people. God's many acts of deliverance show that his "steadfast love endures forever" and is not limited to one generation.

118:1–4 *Let Everyone Give Thanks to the Lord.* The opening section calls on the congregation to **give thanks to the LORD** (see note on 106:1), **for he is good** (see note on 100:5). Each group among the people (**Israel, the house of Aaron**, and **those who fear the LORD**; see note on 115:9–11) should recite this marvelous truth: God's **steadfast love endures forever**. (See Psalm 136 for a similar repetition of this phrase.)

118:5–7 *I Called, and He Answered.* The "personal testimony" part of the psalm (see note on Psalm 118) begins by recounting an instance in which **I called on the LORD** and **the LORD answered me and set me free**. God's answer shows that he **is on my side** and ensures that **I shall look in triumph on those who hate me** (who brought about the psalmist's distress).

118:6 Hebrews 13:6 urges its Jewish Christian readers to apply this verse to themselves, especially as they are tempted to fear what man can do to them (which is why they considered returning to "ordinary" Judaism; see note on Ps. 110:4).

118:8–9 *The Lord Is a Sure Refuge.* The experiences of God's help show that **it is better to take refuge in the LORD** (see note on 31:1–2; cf. 62:8) **than to trust in man**, particularly in **princes** (i.e., in merely human power, which the enemies of118:7 seem to trust in; cf. 146:3).

118:10–13 *The Gentiles Surrounded Me, and the Lord Delivered Me.* This section recounts a particular distress in a battle. **All nations surrounded me** (when they should have joined me in worship; cf. 117:1) and would have killed me, **but the LORD helped me**, and **in the name of the LORD** (i.e., acting as his representative) **I cut them off**.

11 They surrounded me, surrounded me on every side;
in the name of the LORD I cut them off!
12 [r]They surrounded me like bees;
they went out like [s]a fire among thorns;
in the name of the LORD I cut them off!
13 I was [t]pushed hard,[1] so that I was falling,
but the LORD helped me.

14 The LORD is my strength and my song;
[u]he has become my salvation.
15 Glad songs of salvation
are in the tents of the righteous:
[v]"The right hand of the LORD [w]does valiantly,
16 the right hand of the LORD exalts,
the right hand of the LORD [w]does valiantly!"

17 [x]I shall not die, but I shall live,
and [y]recount the deeds of the LORD.
18 The LORD has [z]disciplined me severely,
but he has not given me over to death.

19 [a]Open to me the gates of righteousness,
that I may enter through them
and give thanks to the LORD.
20 This is the gate of the LORD;
[b]the righteous shall enter through it.
21 I thank you that [c]you have answered me
[u]and have become my salvation.
22 [d]The stone that the builders rejected
has become the cornerstone.[2]
23 This is the LORD's doing;
it is marvelous in our eyes.
24 This is the day that the LORD has made;
let us rejoice and be glad in it.

25 Save us, we pray, O LORD!
O LORD, we pray, give us success!

26 [e]Blessed is he who comes in the name of the LORD!
We [f]bless you from the house of the LORD.

[1] Hebrew *You (that is, the enemy) pushed me hard* [2] Hebrew *the head of the corner*

12 [r]Deut. 1:44 [s][Ps. 58:9]
13 [t][Ps. 140:4]
14 [u]See Ps. 27:1
15 [v]Ex. 15:6; Luke 1:51 [w]Ps. 60:12
16 [w][See ver. 15 above]
17 [x][Hab. 1:12] [y]Ps. 73:28; 107:22; [Ps. 6:5]
18 [z][Jer. 30:11; 2 Cor. 6:9]
19 [a]Isa. 26:2; [Ps. 24:7, 9]
20 [b]Rev. 21:27; 22:14; [Isa. 35:8]
21 [c]Ps. 116:1 [u][See ver. 14 above]
22 [d]Cited Matt. 21:42; Mark 12:10, 11; Luke 20:17; [Isa. 28:16]; Acts 4:11; Eph. 2:20; 1 Pet. 2:4-7
26 [e]Matt. 21:9; 23:39; Mark 11:9; Luke 13:35; 19:38 [f]Ps. 129:8

118:14–16 *We Sing Glad Songs of Salvation.* The deliverance of vv. 10–13 leads to celebration in the camp of God's people. Verse 14 uses the victory song of Ex. 15:2 (cf. Isa. 12:2), and Ps. 118:15–16 describes what one can hear in the camp after the battle. **The right hand of the LORD**. Cf. Ex. 15:6.

118:17–18 *Though the Lord Disciplines Me, I Will Not Die.* The experience of deliverance, and the security that the faithful have in God, lead to the reflection, **I shall not die, but I shall live**. The next line also clarifies for each member of the congregation why God would extend life: that I might **recount the deeds of the LORD** (see note on 116:8–11). The situations of danger (118:5, 10–13) were not God's rejection of the singer but his severe discipline, aiming to bring the singer to see more clearly that in him the singer is secure.

118:19–27 *Let Me Enter the Gate of the Lord's House.* The next section seems to picture the singers in a liturgical procession, approaching the **gates** that lead into the temple courts (cf. **the house of the LORD**, v. 26; **the festal sacrifice** and **the altar**, v. 27).

118:19–21 The gates of righteousness are the gates of the temple, through which the worshipers **enter** (vv. 19, 20) in order to **give thanks to the LORD** (cf. vv. 1, 21, 28–29). **The righteous** refers to God's own people (because they have God's righteous laws; Deut. 4:8), especially the faithful, who keep those laws. **become my salvation**. See Ps. 118:14.

118:22–23 These verses use an image from ancient building practices (perhaps suggested by the newly built temple itself). The **cornerstone** is probably the large stone at the corner of the building's foundation, though some think it is the keystone or capstone of an arch (but the very similar expression in Isa. 28:16 makes the foundation interpretation more likely). The **builders** are the wise and knowledgeable, and they have **rejected** some particular **stone** as unsuited for this purpose. They were wrong in their judgment. The psalm is likening Israel (and perhaps particularly the person who had suffered) to such a stone; the imperial powers had thought little of Israel, but God had chosen his people to be the cornerstone of his great plan for the world. **This is the LORD's doing**, i.e., not a mere human accomplishment. The NT writers use this text (Matt. 21:42; Mark 12:10–11; Luke 20:17; Acts 4:11; 1 Pet. 2:7) to indicate that the powerful figures who rejected Jesus (esp. the Jewish leaders) were no wiser than the world powers that thought so little of Israel.

118:24 This is the day probably refers to the festival day that occasioned the psalm.

118:25 Save us, we pray. Cf. vv. 14–15, 21 (and see note on 3:2). This expression (Hb. *hoshi'ah na'*), when transliterated into Greek, becomes *hōsanna* (cf. Matt. 21:9, 15; Mark 11:9, 10; John 12:13).

118:26 Blessed is he who comes in the name of the LORD! The crowds

27 The LORD is God,
and he has made [g]his light to shine upon us.
Bind the festal sacrifice with cords,
up to [h]the horns of the altar!

28 You are my God, and I will give thanks to you;
you are my God; I will [i]extol you.
29 [j]Oh give thanks to the LORD, for he is good;
for his steadfast love endures forever!

Your Word Is a Lamp to My Feet

ALEPH

119[1] 1 Blessed are those whose [k]way is blameless,
who [l]walk in the law of the LORD!
2 Blessed are those who [m]keep his [n]testimonies,
who [o]seek him with their whole heart,
3 who also [p]do no wrong,
but walk in his ways!
4 You have commanded your [q]precepts
to be kept diligently.

[1] This psalm is an acrostic poem of twenty-two stanzas, following the letters of the Hebrew alphabet; within a stanza, each verse begins with the same Hebrew letter

27 [g]Ps. 18:28; 97:11; [Esth. 8:16; 1 Pet. 2:9] [h]See Ex. 27:2
28 [i]See Ps. 99:5
29 [j]ver. 1

Psalm 119

1 [k]Prov. 11:20; 13:6; [Ps. 101:2, 6] [l]Ps. 128:1; [Gen. 17:1]
2 [m][ver. 22] [n][Ps. 78:5] [o][ver. 10; 2 Chr. 15:2]
3 [p]1 John 3:9; 5:18
4 [q]Ps. 19:8

used these words in their shouts at Jesus' triumphal entry (Matt. 21:9; Mark 11:9; Luke 19:38; John 12:13), indicating that they thought it was a special occasion. Jesus used it in speaking to Jerusalem; because of her resistance to God, her "house" (probably the temple) was desolate, and she would have to greet Jesus with these words if she was to "see" him properly (Matt. 23:39; Luke 13:35).

118:27 made his light to shine upon us. Using the words of the Aaronic benediction (Num. 6:24–26); cf. Ps. 31:16; 67:1; 80:3, 7, 19.

118:28–29 *I Will Give You Thanks and Praise.* With these closing words the individual members of the congregation pledge themselves to the song in which they invited each other to join in v. 1.

Psalm 119. This psalm celebrates the gift of God's Torah, or covenant instruction, as the perfect guide for life. It thus belongs conceptually with Psalm 19 and overlaps with such wisdom psalms as Psalms 1 and 112. It is far more extensive, and far more elaborate, than they are; it is the longest psalm (and the longest chapter in the Bible, longer than many of the books) and the most carefully structured. By singing and praying its contents, one expresses heartfelt admiration to God, who has so lovingly bestowed this great gift upon his people, and fervent yearning for one's personal life to reflect the loveliness and goodness of the Torah. The psalm's structure observes a strict acrostic pattern (see ESV footnote at 119:1): there are 22 stanzas of eight verses each, following the 22 letters of the Hebrew alphabet in sequence. Within a stanza, the first word of each verse begins with the same letter, the letter to which the entire stanza corresponds. This pattern severely limits the author's liberty in sustaining his flow of thought, but this does not hinder the psalm from accomplishing its goal, which is to enable God's people to admire his Word so strongly that they will work and pray hard to have it shape their character and conduct. The cumulative impact of the psalm is huge.

The psalm uses a number of terms for God's covenantal revelation: "law" (v. 1: Hb. *torah*, i.e., instruction); "testimonies" (v. 2: Hb. *'edot*, i.e., what God solemnly testifies to be his will); "precepts" (v. 4: Hb. *piqqudim*, i.e., what God has appointed to be done); "statutes" (v. 5: Hb. *khuqqim* and *khuqqot*, i.e., what the divine Lawgiver has laid down); "commandments" (v. 6: Hb. *mitswot*, i.e., what God has commanded); "rules" (v. 7: Hb. *mishpatim*, i.e., what the divine Judge has ruled to be right); "word" (v. 9: Hb. *'imrah* and *dabar*, i.e., what God has spoken). Except for "precepts" (which appears only in the Psalms), all of these words can be found in Deuteronomy (e.g., Deut. 4:8, 44–45; 6:1; 33:9), and denote God's Word, focusing on its role in moral instruction for his people. The person who will "keep" God's instructions (Ps. 119:2: Hb. *shamar* and *natsar*, i.e., attend to them carefully, watch over them, treasure them) will find that his "way" (v. 5: Hb. *derek* and *'orakh*, i.e., the moral quality and orientation of his life) will more and more reflect God's own character (cf. 18:30; 145:17). (See chart, p. 1094.) Only a few verses in this psalm lack an explicit mention of God's Word: 119:84, 90–91, 120, 122, 132, 149. The psalm calls these instructions "righteous" (vv. 7, 75, 123, 138, 144, 160, 172), "true" and "sure" (vv. 86, 138, 142, 151, 160), and worthy of trust, hope, and faith (vv. 42, 43, 66). All of these are attributes of God himself, and it is no surprise that God's words would partake of his character. Indeed, the law expresses God's own "steadfast love" (v. 124; cf. vv. 41, 64, 76, 88, 149) and "faithfulness" (vv. 89–91). This psalm reflects the view that the Lord, who abounds in steadfast love and faithfulness and who therefore freely and fully forgives his people when they confess their sins (Ex. 34:6–7), loves his people without limit, and therefore also guides the faithful in the way of life that is genuinely good and beautiful (cf. Ps. 119:124). The psalm speaks the language of one ravished with moral beauty, to which there is only one fitting response—to try to reproduce this beauty, as much as possible, in one's daily life. There is no pretense of perfection here (cf. v. 5), only yearning, and trust (vv. 41, 176), and dependence on God (v. 125). To say that these commands are "true" (v. 160) is to confess that, with all their elements geared to a particular culture and phase of redemptive history, the principles that underlie them are founded on the very nature of things, and of God. This is why Christians can sing these words with the same yearning, trust, and dependence. The psalm does not tell who its author was, nor when it was written. Many scholars think it comes from after the Babylonian exile, but this cannot be proven. The psalmist identifies with the faithful among God's people, when they face trials (vv. 50, 67, 71, 75, 107, 153), and when they suffer contempt and ill treatment for their faithfulness, even from members of God's people who reject his grace (vv. 22–23, 39, 42, 51, 61, 69, 78, 84–86, 95, 121, 122, 134, 150, 157, 161). Even when many of God's own people forsake him (vv. 21, 53, 139), there will be those who want to pursue faithfulness. This fits, e.g., the time before Ezra and Nehemiah carried out their reforms, but it fits many other times as well. The words of this psalm can enable Christians to embrace its aspiration, both when they sing it and when they use those words as prayers for illumination as they attend to God's word in public and in private.

119:1 Blessed. See note on 1:1. **blameless**. See note on 15:2–5b.

119:2 seek. Cf. vv. 10, 45, 94, 155. **with their whole heart**. Cf. v. 10 and Deut. 4:29.

5 Oh that my ways may [r]be steadfast
in keeping your statutes!
6 [s]Then I shall not be put to shame,
having my eyes fixed on all your commandments.
7 I will praise you with an upright heart,
when I learn [t]your righteous rules.[1]
8 I will keep your statutes;
[u]do not utterly forsake me!

BETH

9 How can [v]a young man keep his way pure?
By guarding it according to your word.
10 [w]With my whole heart I seek you;
let me not [x]wander from your commandments!
11 I have [y]stored up your word in my heart,
that I might not sin against you.
12 Blessed are you, O LORD;
[z]teach me your statutes!
13 With my lips I [a]declare
all the rules[2] of your mouth.
14 In the way of your testimonies I [b]delight
as much as in all [c]riches.
15 I will [d]meditate on your precepts
and fix my eyes on your [e]ways.
16 I will [f]delight in your statutes;
I will not forget your word.

GIMEL

17 [g]Deal bountifully with your servant,
[h]that I may live and keep your word.
18 Open my eyes, that I may behold
wondrous things out of your law.
19 I am [i]a sojourner on the earth;
[j]hide not your commandments from me!
20 My soul is consumed with [k]longing
for your rules[3] at all times.
21 You rebuke [l]the insolent, [m]accursed ones,
who [n]wander from your commandments.

[1] *Or your just and righteous decrees; also verses 62, 106, 160, 164* [2] *Or all the just decrees* [3] *Or your just decrees; also verses 30, 39, 43, 52, 75, 102, 108, 137, 156, 175*

5[r]Ps. 37:23; [Prov. 16:9; Jer. 10:23]
6[s]ver. 80; [1 John 2:28]
7[t]ver. 62, 106; Ex. 24:3
8[u]Ps. 38:21; 71:9, 18
9[v][Ps. 25:7]
10[w][2 Chr. 15:2] [x][ver. 21, 118]
11[y]Luke 2:19, 51; See Ps. 37:31
12[z]ver. 26, 64, 68, 108, 124, 135, 171; See Ps. 25:4
13[a]Ps. 40:9; [Deut. 6:7]
14[b]ver. 111, 162 [c]See Prov. 3:13-15; 8:10, 11, 18, 19
15[d]ver. 23, 78, 97 [e]Ps. 25:4
16[f]ver. 24, 47, 70, 77, 92, 143, 174
17[g]See Ps. 13:6 [h]ver. 144
19[i]See Ps. 39:12 [j][Isa. 6:9, 10]
20[k]ver. 40, 131, 174; [Ps. 42:1, 2]
21[l]See ver. 51 [m]Deut. 27:26 [n][ver. 10]

Terms in Psalm 119 for God's Covenant Revelation

English	Hebrew	Meaning
law	*torah*	instruction
testimonies	*'edot*	what God solemnly testifies to be his will
precepts	*piqqudim*	what God has appointed to be done
statutes	*khuqqim; khuqqot*	what the divine Lawgiver has laid down
commandments	*mitswot*	what God has commanded
rules	*mishpatim*	what the divine Judge has ruled to be right
word	*'imrah; dabar*	what God has spoken

119:5 The goal of the whole psalm is that each member of the congregation would share in this eager yearning.

119:9 young man. Cf. 34:11 and Prov. 2:1.

119:11 stored up your word in my heart. By careful memorization and pondering (see note on 1:2); cf. 119:97.

119:18 Open my eyes. Give me insight beyond my abilities. **wondrous things**. Probably the wondrous works recorded there and what they reveal of God himself (cf. v. 27; Ex. 3:20; Josh. 3:5; Ps. 78:32; 145:5).

119:19 sojourner. See note on 39:7–13.

119:21 insolent, accursed ones. In the psalm, these are Israelites who reject the covenant, **who wander from your commandments**. See vv. 51, 69, 78, 85, 122; 86:14.

119:23 princes. In this psalm, these are rulers among God's people, who might use their power to suppress the faithful. Cf. vv. 84, 86–87, 121–122, 134, 150, 157, 161.

119:27 Make me understand. See note on v. 18; cf. v. 34.

22 Take away from me [o]scorn and contempt,
[p]for I have kept your testimonies.
23 Even though [q]princes sit plotting against me,
your servant will [r]meditate on your statutes.
24 Your testimonies are my [s]delight;
they are my [t]counselors.

Daleth

25 [u]My soul clings to the dust;
[v]give me life [w]according to your word!
26 When [x]I told of my ways, you answered me;
[y]teach me your statutes!
27 [z]Make me understand the way of your precepts,
and I will [a]meditate on your wondrous works.
28 [b]My soul melts away for sorrow;
strengthen me according to your word!
29 Put false ways far from me
and graciously [c]teach me your law!
30 I have chosen the way of faithfulness;
I [d]set your rules before me.
31 I cling to your testimonies, O Lord;
[e]let me not be put to shame!
32 I will run in the way of your commandments
when you [f]enlarge my heart![1]

He

33 [g]Teach me, O Lord, the way of your statutes;
and I will keep it [h]to the end.[2]
34 [i]Give me understanding, that I may keep your law
and observe it with my whole heart.
35 [j]Lead me in the path of your commandments,
for I [k]delight in it.
36 [l]Incline my heart to your testimonies,
and not to [m]selfish gain!
37 [n]Turn my eyes from looking at worthless things;
and [o]give me life in your ways.
38 [p]Confirm to your servant your promise,
[q]that you may be feared.
39 Turn away the [r]reproach that I dread,
for your rules are good.
40 Behold, I [s]long for your precepts;
[t]in your righteousness give me life!

Waw

41 Let your [u]steadfast love come to me, O Lord,
your salvation [v]according to your promise;
42 then [w]shall I have an answer for him [r]who taunts me,
for I trust in your word.
43 And take not the word of truth utterly out of my mouth,
for my [x]hope is in your rules.

[1] Or *for you set my heart free* [2] Or *keep it as my reward*

22 [o]See Ps. 44:13 [p][ver. 2]
23 [q]ver. 161; [Dan. 6:4] [r]ver. 15, 27, 28
24 [s][Rom. 7:22]; See ver. 16 [t][ver. 104]
25 [u]Ps. 44:25 [v]ver. 37, 40, 88, 107, 149, 154, 156, 159; See Ps. 71:20 [w]ver. 65
26 [x][Ps. 37:5] [y]ver. 12
27 [z]ver. 18, 34, 73, 125, 144, 169; [Job 32:8] [a]ver. 15, 23, 78
28 [b]See Ps. 22:14
29 [c][ver. 27]
30 [d][Ps. 16:8]
31 [e]ver. 116
32 [f]1 Kgs. 4:29; Isa. 60:5; 2 Cor. 6:11, 13
33 [g]ver. 12, 26 [h]ver. 112; [Matt. 10:22; Heb. 3:6; Rev. 2:26]
34 [i]ver. 27; Prov. 2:6; James 1:5
35 [j]See Ps. 25:4, 5 [k]ver. 16; See Ps. 1:2
36 [l]ver. 112; 1 Kgs. 8:58; [Ps. 141:4] [m][Luke 12:15; 1 Tim. 6:10; Heb. 13:5]
37 [n][Prov. 23:5; Isa. 33:15] [o]ver. 25
38 [p]2 Sam. 7:25 [q][Ps. 25:10; 112:1; 128:1; 130:4]
39 [r]ver. 22
40 [s]ver. 20 [t][ver. 149, 156]
41 [u]ver. 77; [Ps. 106:4] [v]ver. 58, 65, 76, 116, 170
42 [w]Prov. 27:11 [r][See ver. 39 above]
43 [x]ver. 49, 74, 81, 114, 147; [Ps. 31:24]

119:32 enlarge my heart. Or "make my heart broad"; cf. 1 Kings 4:29, where "breadth of heart or mind" is an expanded ability to perceive God's truth.

119:36 Incline my heart. As in v. 5, the singer knows that God must supply the deepest motivation; cf. v. 112; also 141:4; 1 Kings 8:58; Prov. 2:2.

119:39 reproach. The scorn that comes from the unfaithful (cf. vv. 22, 42, 51).

119:41 steadfast love. A recurring theme of the psalm (vv. 64, 76, 88, 124, 149, 159). It is the genuine experience of God's grace and mercy that impels the faithful to seek his moral guidance (see notes on 25:6–7; 25:8–11). **salvation**. See note on 3:2.

119:42 for I trust in your word. Cf. 115:9, "trust in the Lord."

119:43 my hope is in your rules. Cf. vv. 49, 74, 81, 114, 147. For

44 I will keep your law continually,
forever and ever,
45 and I shall walk [y]in a wide place,
for I have [z]sought your precepts.
46 I will also speak of your testimonies [a]before kings
and shall not be put to shame,
47 for I [b]find my delight in your commandments,
which I love.
48 I will [c]lift up my hands toward your commandments, which I love,
and I will [d]meditate on your statutes.

Zayin

49 Remember [e]your word to your servant,
in which you have made me [f]hope.
50 This is [g]my comfort in my affliction,
that your promise [h]gives me life.
51 [i]The insolent utterly deride me,
but I do not [j]turn away from your law.
52 When I think of your rules from of old,
I take comfort, O LORD.
53 [k]Hot indignation seizes me because of the wicked,
who forsake your law.
54 Your statutes have been my songs
in the house of my [l]sojourning.
55 I [m]remember your name in the night, O LORD,
and keep your law.
56 This blessing has fallen to me,
that [n]I have kept your precepts.

Heth

57 [o]The LORD is my portion;
I promise to keep your words.
58 I [p]entreat your favor with all my heart;
be gracious to me [q]according to your promise.
59 When I [r]think on my ways,
I turn my feet to your testimonies;
60 I hasten and do not delay
to keep your commandments.
61 Though [s]the cords of the wicked ensnare me,
I do not [t]forget your law.
62 At [u]midnight I rise to praise you,
because of your [v]righteous rules.
63 [w]I am a companion of all who fear you,
of those who keep your precepts.
64 [x]The earth, O LORD, is full of your steadfast love;
[y]teach me your statutes!

45 [y]Prov. 4:12 [z]ver. 94, 155
46 [a][Matt. 10:18; Acts 26:1, 2]
47 [b]ver. 16
48 [c]See Ps. 28:2 [d]ver. 13
49 [e]ver. 41, 42, 43 [f]ver. 43
50 [g][Rom. 15:4] [h]ver. 25; See Ps. 71:20
51 [i]ver. 69, 78, 85, 122; Jer. 20:7; [Ps. 42:3; 123:4] [j]ver. 157; Ps. 44:18; Job 23:11
53 [k][Neh. 13:25]
54 [l]See Ps. 39:12
55 [m]See Ps. 42:8
56 [n]ver. 22, 69, 100
57 [o]See Ps. 16:5
58 [p]Ps. 45:12 [q]ver. 41
59 [r][Luke 15:17]
61 [s]ver. 110 [t]ver. 83
62 [u][Acts 16:25] [v]ver. 7
63 [w][Ps. 101:6]
64 [x]Ps. 33:5 [y]ver. 12

hoping in God, cf. 33:22; 131:3; 147:11; for hoping in God and in his word, cf. 130:5, 7.

119:46 before kings. Like Daniel and his friends, or Ezra and Nehemiah.

119:48 lift up my hands. Cf. 28:2; 88:9, where this is to the Lord.

119:50 affliction. Cf. vv. 67, 71, 75, 92, 107, 153.

119:53 Hot indignation. Mixed with sorrow (v. 136), because these who **forsake** are Israelites, bound to love and obey the Lord. Contrast v. 87.

119:54 house of my sojourning. Cf. v. 19.

119:57 my portion. See note on 16:5–6.

119:59–60 When I think on my ways. The believer considers his own character and conduct, in order to bring them into greater conformity to God's **commandments**.

119:61 the cords of the wicked ensnare me. Cf. v. 110.

119:62 At midnight. Cf. v. 55.

119:63 companion of all who fear you. Among the pious there should be a bond of love and loyalty. Cf. vv. 74, 79.

Teth

65 You have dealt well with your servant,
O Lord, [z]according to your word.
66 Teach me [a]good judgment and knowledge,
for I believe in your commandments.
67 [b]Before I was afflicted I went astray,
but now I keep your word.
68 [c]You are good and do good;
[d]teach me your statutes.
69 [e]The insolent [f]smear me with lies,
but with my whole heart I [g]keep your precepts;
70 their heart is unfeeling [h]like fat,
but I [i]delight in your law.
71 It is [j]good for me that I was afflicted,
that I might learn your statutes.
72 [k]The law of your mouth is better to me
than thousands of gold and silver pieces.

Yodh

73 [l]Your hands have made and fashioned me;
[m]give me understanding that I may learn your commandments.
74 Those who fear you shall see me and [n]rejoice,
because I have [o]hoped in your word.
75 I know, O Lord, that your rules are [p]righteous,
and that in [q]faithfulness you have afflicted me.
76 Let your steadfast love comfort me
according to your promise to your servant.
77 Let your [r]mercy come to me, that I may live;
for your law is my [s]delight.
78 Let [t]the insolent be put to [u]shame,
because they have [v]wronged me with falsehood;
as for me, I will [w]meditate on your precepts.
79 Let those who fear you [x]turn to me,
that they may know your testimonies.
80 May my heart be [y]blameless in your statutes,
[z]that I may not be put to shame!

Kaph

81 My soul [a]longs for your salvation;
I [b]hope in your word.
82 My [c]eyes long for your promise;
I ask, [d]"When will you comfort me?"
83 For I have [e]become like a [f]wineskin in the smoke,
yet I have not forgotten your statutes.
84 [g]How long must your servant endure?[1]
[h]When will you judge those who persecute me?
85 [i]The insolent have [j]dug pitfalls for me;
they do not live according to your law.
86 All your commandments are [k]sure;
they persecute me [l]with falsehood; [m]help me!

65 [z][ver. 41]
66 [a]Phil. 1:9; [James 1:5]
67 [b]ver. 71, 75; Jer. 31:18, 19; See Heb. 12:5-11
68 [c]Ps. 106:1 [d]ver. 12
69 [e]ver. 51 [f]Job 13:4; [Ps. 109:2] [g]ver. 56
70 [h]Isa. 6:10; See Ps. 17:10 [i]ver. 16
71 [j][ver. 67]
72 [k]ver. 127; Ps. 19:10; Prov. 8:10
73 [l]Job 10:8; See Ps. 95:6; Job 31:15 [m]ver. 27
74 [n]Ps. 34:2; 35:27; 107:42 [o]ver. 43; Ps. 130:5
75 [p]ver. 138 [q]Ps. 33:4; See ver. 67
77 [r]ver. 41 [s]ver. 24, 47, 174
78 [t]See ver. 51 [u]Ps. 25:3 [v]ver. 86 [w]ver. 15, 23
79 [x][Jer. 15:19]
80 [y]ver. 1 [z]ver. 6
81 [a]See Ps. 84:2 [b]ver. 74, 114
82 [c]See Ps. 69:3 [d][Ps. 101:2]
83 [e][Job 30:30] [f][Matt. 9:17; Mark 2:22]
84 [g][Ps. 39:4] [h]Rev. 6:10; [Zech. 1:12]
85 [i]ver. 51 [j]See Ps. 7:15
86 [k]ver. 138 [l]ver. 78; Ps. 35:19 [m]Ps. 109:26

[1] Hebrew *How many are the days of your servant?*

119:76–77 steadfast love . . . mercy. Cf. Ex. 34:6.

119:80 blameless. See v. 1.

119:81 salvation. See v. 41.

119:83 like a wineskin in the smoke. An unused wineskin, hanging in the rafters, becomes shriveled by the smoke; this is an image of one's vitality "drying up."

87 They have almost made an end of me on earth,
but I have not forsaken your precepts.
88 In your steadfast love [n]give me life,
that I may keep the testimonies of your mouth.

LAMEDH

89 Forever, O LORD, your [o]word
is firmly fixed in the heavens.
90 Your [p]faithfulness endures to all generations;
you have [q]established the earth, and it [r]stands fast.
91 By your [s]appointment they stand this day,
for all things are your servants.
92 If your law had not been my [t]delight,
I would have perished in my affliction.
93 I will never forget your precepts,
for by them you have [u]given me life.
94 I am yours; save me,
[v]for I have sought your precepts.
95 The wicked lie in wait to destroy me,
but I consider your testimonies.
96 I have seen a limit to all perfection,
but your commandment is exceedingly [w]broad.

MEM

97 Oh how [x]I love your law!
It is my [y]meditation all the day.
98 Your commandment makes me [z]wiser than my enemies,
for it is ever with me.
99 I have more understanding than all my teachers,
for [a]your testimonies are my meditation.
100 I understand more than [b]the aged,[1]
for I [c]keep your precepts.
101 I [d]hold back my feet from every evil way,
in order to keep your word.
102 I do not turn aside from your rules,
for you have taught me.
103 How [e]sweet are your words to my taste,
sweeter than honey to my mouth!
104 Through your precepts I get understanding;
therefore [f]I hate every false way.

NUN

105 [g]Your word is a lamp to my feet
and a light to my path.
106 I have [h]sworn an oath and confirmed it,
to keep your [i]righteous rules.
107 I am severely [j]afflicted;
[k]give me life, O LORD, according to your word!

[1] *Or the elders*

88[n]ver. 25; See Ps. 71:20
89[o]ver. 152; [Matt. 24:35; 1 Pet. 1:25]; [Jer. 31:35-37]
90[p]See Ps. 36:5 [q][Ps. 148:6] [r]Eccles. 1:4
91[s]Jer. 33:25
92[t]ver. 77
93[u]ver. 25; See Ps. 71:20
94[v]ver. 45
96[w][Ps. 18:19]
97[x]ver. 113, 163, 165; [Ps. 1:2] [y]ver. 15
98[z][Deut. 4:6]
99[a][2 Tim. 3:15]
100[b]See Job 32:7-9 [c]ver. 56, 69
101[d]Prov. 1:15
103[e]Ps. 19:10
104[f]ver. 128
105[g]Prov. 6:23
106[h]Neh. 10:29 [i]ver. 7
107[j][ver. 25, 50] [k]ver. 88; See Ps. 71:20

119:89–91 These verses stress how God's word expresses his **faithfulness,** and its terms are therefore **firmly fixed**.

119:94 save me. Cf. vv. 41, 81, 94, 117, 123, 146, 155, 166, 174.

119:96 The Lord's **broad** commandment has no **limit to** its **perfection,** because it partakes of God's own limitless perfection.

119:98–100 wiser . . . more understanding . . . understand more. Because, in the setting of the psalm, neither **my enemies** nor **my teachers** nor **the aged** attend carefully to God's word.

119:104 understanding. See note on Prov. 3:5. **hate.** Cf. Ps. 119:128, 163.

119:105 lamp . . . light. See note on 112:4. The common style of lamp in ancient Israel was a small bowl with a pinched lip which was used to support a wick.

119:106 sworn an oath. Perhaps like that of Neh. 10:29.

108[l][Hos. 14:2] [m]ver. 12
109[n]See Judg. 12:3 [o]ver. 83
110[p]See Ps. 91:3 [q]ver. 10
111[r]Deut. 33:4 [s]ver. 14, 162
112[t]ver. 36 [u]See ver. 33
113[v][1 Kgs. 18:21; James 1:8; 4:8] [w]ver. 97
114[x]See Ps. 32:7 [y]See Ps. 3:3 [z]ver. 74
115[a]See Ps. 6:8 [b][ver. 22]
116[c]ver. 41 [d]ver. 31; See Ps. 25:2 [e]Ps. 146:5
117[f][Ps. 20:2]
118[g]Lam. 1:15 [h]ver. 10, 21, 110
119[i]Isa. 1:25; [Ezek. 22:18; Mal. 3:2, 3] [j]ver. 97
120[k][Job 4:14; Hab. 3:16]
122[l]See Job 17:3 [m]ver. 51
123[n]ver. 82
124[o]ver. 12
125[p]See Ps. 116:16 [q]ver. 27
127[r]ver. 72; Ps. 19:10
128[s]ver. 104

108 Accept [l]my freewill offerings of praise, O LORD,
and [m]teach me your rules.
109 I hold my life [n]in my hand continually,
but I do not [o]forget your law.
110 The wicked have laid [p]a snare for me,
but [q]I do not stray from your precepts.
111 Your testimonies are [r]my heritage forever,
for they are [s]the joy of my heart.
112 I [t]incline my heart to perform your statutes
forever, [u]to the end.[1]

SAMEKH

113 I hate [v]the double-minded,
but I love [w]your law.
114 You are my [x]hiding place and my [y]shield;
I [z]hope in your word.
115 [a]Depart from me, you evildoers,
that I may [b]keep the commandments of my God.
116 Uphold me [c]according to your promise, that I may live,
and let me not be [d]put to shame in my [e]hope!
117 [f]Hold me up, that I may be safe
and have regard for your statutes continually!
118 You [g]spurn all who [h]go astray from your statutes,
for their cunning is in vain.
119 All the wicked of the earth you discard like [i]dross,
therefore [j]I love your testimonies.
120 My flesh [k]trembles for fear of you,
and I am afraid of your judgments.

AYIN

121 I have done what is just and right;
do not leave me to my oppressors.
122 Give your servant [l]a pledge of good;
let not [m]the insolent oppress me.
123 My [n]eyes long for your salvation
and for the fulfillment of your righteous promise.
124 Deal with your servant according to your steadfast love,
and [o]teach me your statutes.
125 I am your [p]servant; [q]give me understanding,
that I may know your testimonies!
126 It is time for the LORD to act,
for your law has been broken.
127 Therefore I [r]love your commandments
above gold, above fine gold.
128 Therefore I consider all your precepts to be right;
I hate every [s]false way.

[1] Or *statutes; the reward is eternal*

119:108 freewill offerings. See notes on 54:6–7; 56:12–13; 66:13–15. The piety of this psalm is intensely personal, and the liturgical ordinances of the covenant are part of it.

119:111 my heritage. Cf. v. 57.

119:113 double-minded. Cf. 1 Kings 18:21; these are people who should be devoted to the Lord but who allow their loyalties to be divided. The strong terms **hate** and **love** refer not so much to irrational emotions as to deliberate rejection and adherence. Cf. Ps. 119:158; see also v. 118, where this reflects God's own attitude.

119:126 time for the LORD to act. When God's **law has been broken** by his own people and they seem to get away with it, it seems that God is inactive; this is a prayer that he would vindicate his own justice for the sake of his faithful.

Pe

129 Your testimonies are [t]wonderful;
therefore my soul [u]keeps them.
130 The unfolding of your words gives light;
it imparts [v]understanding to the simple.
131 I [w]open my mouth and [x]pant,
because I [y]long for your commandments.
132 [z]Turn to me and be gracious to me,
as is your way with those who love your name.
133 [a]Keep steady my steps according to your promise,
and let no iniquity [b]get dominion over me.
134 [c]Redeem me from man's oppression,
that I may keep your precepts.
135 [d]Make your face shine upon your servant,
and [e]teach me your statutes.
136 My eyes [f]shed streams of tears,
because people [g]do not keep your law.

Tsadhe

137 [h]Righteous are you, O Lord,
and right are your rules.
138 You have appointed your testimonies in [i]righteousness
and in all [j]faithfulness.
139 My [k]zeal consumes me,
because my foes forget your words.
140 Your promise is well [l]tried,
and your servant [m]loves it.
141 I am small and despised,
yet I do not [n]forget your precepts.
142 Your righteousness is righteous forever,
and your law is [o]true.
143 Trouble and anguish have found me out,
but your commandments are my [p]delight.
144 Your testimonies are righteous forever;
[q]give me understanding that I may [r]live.

Qoph

145 With my [s]whole heart I cry; answer me, O Lord!
I will [t]keep your statutes.
146 I call to you; save me,
that I may observe your testimonies.
147 I rise before [u]dawn and cry for help;
I [v]hope in your words.
148 My eyes are awake before [w]the watches of the night,
that I may meditate on your promise.
149 Hear my voice according to your steadfast love;
O Lord, [x]according to your justice [y]give me life.

129 [t]ver. 18, 27 [u]ver. 22
130 [v]See Ps. 19:7
131 [w]Ps. 81:10; Job 29:23 [x]Ps. 42:1 [y]ver. 20
132 [z]See Ps. 25:16
133 [a][Ps. 17:5] [b]Ps. 19:13
134 [c][Luke 1:74]
135 [d]See Ps. 4:6 [e]ver. 12
136 [f]Jer. 9:1, 18; 14:17; Lam. 3:48; [Ezek. 9:4; Phil. 3:18] [g]ver. 158
137 [h]See Ps. 116:5
138 [i]ver. 75, 172; See Ps. 19:7-9 [j]ver. 86
139 [k]See Ps. 69:9
140 [l]See Ps. 12:6 [m]ver. 97
141 [n]ver. 83
142 [o]ver. 151, 160; John 17:17; [Ps. 19:2]
143 [p]ver. 24
144 [q]ver. 27 [r]ver. 17
145 [s]ver. 2, 10 [t]ver. 22, 33
147 [u]See Ps. 5:3 [v]ver. 74
148 [w]See Ps. 42:8
149 [x]ver. 156; [ver. 40] [y]ver. 25; See Ps. 71:20

119:129 wonderful. Far beyond merely human in their origin and excellence (cf. 139:6).

119:130 The unfolding of your words. As they are pondered, explained, and understood. **gives light**. See note on v. 105. **the simple**. Cf. 19:7; see Introduction to Proverbs: Character Types in Proverbs; Prov. 19:25 and note.

119:134 Redeem. Cf. v. 154; see note on 25:22.

119:135 Make your face shine. Cf. Num. 6:25.

119:136 Cf. vv. 53, 126. The **streams of tears** are probably for sorrow and pity toward the unfaithful; this qualifies vv. 113, 158.

119:140 Your promise is well tried. Cf. 12:6; 18:30; Prov. 30:5.

119:141 I am small and despised, in contrast to the powerful oppressors (cf. v. 23). Nevertheless he refuses to succumb to the temptation to give in to such people.

119:142 your law is true. Cf. vv. 151, 160; John 17:17.

119:145 whole heart. See v. 2.

119:147–148 rise before dawn . . . awake before the watches of the night. Cf. v. 62.

150 They draw near who persecute me with evil purpose;
they are far from your law.
151 But [z]you are near, O LORD,
and all your commandments are [a]true.
152 Long have I known from your testimonies
that you have [b]founded them forever.

Resh

153 Look on my [c]affliction and deliver me,
for [d]I do not forget your law.
154 [e]Plead my cause and redeem me;
[f]give me life according to your promise!
155 [g]Salvation is far from the wicked,
[h]for they do not seek your statutes.
156 [i]Great is your mercy, O LORD;
[f]give me life according to your rules.
157 [j]Many are my persecutors and my adversaries,
but I do not [k]swerve from your testimonies.
158 I look at [l]the faithless with [m]disgust,
because they do not keep your commands.
159 Consider how I [n]love your precepts!
[f]Give me life according to your steadfast love.
160 [o]The sum of your word is [p]truth,
and every one of your [q]righteous rules endures forever.

Sin and Shin

161 [r]Princes persecute me [s]without cause,
but my heart [t]stands in awe of your words.
162 I [t]rejoice at your word
like one who [u]finds great spoil.
163 I hate and abhor falsehood,
but I love [v]your law.
164 Seven times a day I praise you
for your [q]righteous rules.
165 Great [w]peace have those who love your law;
[x]nothing can make them stumble.
166 I [y]hope for your salvation, O LORD,
and I do your commandments.
167 My soul keeps your testimonies;
I [v]love them exceedingly.
168 I keep your precepts and testimonies,
[z]for all my ways are before you.

Taw

169 Let my [a]cry come before you, O LORD;
[b]give me understanding [c]according to your word!
170 Let my plea come before you;
[d]deliver me according to your word.

151 [z]See Ps. 145:18 [a]See ver. 142
152 [b]ver. 89, 160; [Matt. 5:18]
153 [c]Job 36:15 [d]ver. 83
154 [e]Ps. 35:1 [f]ver. 25
155 [g]Job 5:4 [h][ver. 150]
156 [i]2 Sam. 24:14 [f][See ver. 154 above]
157 [j]Ps. 3:1, 2 [k]See ver. 51
158 [l][Jer. 3:20] [m]Ps. 139:21; [ver. 136]
159 [n]ver. 97 [f][See ver. 154 above]
160 [o]Ps. 139:17 [p][ver. 142, 172] [q]ver. 7
161 [r]ver. 23; [1 Sam. 24:11; 26:18] [s]See Ps. 69:4 [t][Ps. 2:11]
162 [t][See ver. 161 above] [u]1 Sam. 30:16; Isa. 9:3; [Matt. 13:44]
163 [v]ver. 97
164 [q][See ver. 160 above]
165 [w]Ps. 37:11, 37; [Prov. 3:2] [x]Prov. 3:23; 1 John 2:10; [Matt. 13:41]
166 [y]ver. 174; Gen. 49:18
167 [v][See ver. 163 above]
168 [z]Ps. 139:3; Prov. 5:21
169 [a][ver. 145] [b]See ver. 34 [c]ver. 65
170 [d]ver. 41

119:152 founded them forever. Cf. vv. 89–91.

119:155 For they do not seek implies that the cause is not God's stinginess but their refusal.

119:164 Seven times a day. The number is probably a figure for "many times," as seven is often used that way (e.g., Gen. 4:15). Cf. Paul's "pray without ceasing" (1 Thess. 5:17).

119:165 stumble. Using the image of one's life as "walking" (cf. vv. 1, 3), this expresses a failure to walk well; see v. 133 for a similar idea, and see vv. 105 and 130 for the reason why **those who love your law** have **great peace** and confidence.

119:167 My soul keeps your testimonies. The love for God's words goes right down to the deepest core of the singer's being; cf. v. 175.

119:168 all my ways are before you. God is well aware of every detail of one's life, and this is good motivation to keep a clear conscience (Eccles. 12:14; Matt. 12:36; Acts 24:15–16).

119:169–170 The **cry** and **plea** are both for **understanding** and for God to **deliver** him.

171 My lips will [e]pour forth praise,
for you [f]teach me your statutes.
172 My tongue will sing of your word,
for [g]all your commandments are right.
173 Let your hand be ready to help me,
for I have [h]chosen your precepts.
174 I [i]long for your salvation, O LORD,
and your law is my [j]delight.
175 Let my soul live and praise you,
and let your rules help me.
176 I have [k]gone astray like a lost sheep; seek your servant,
for I do not [l]forget your commandments.

Deliver Me, O LORD

120 A SONG OF [m]ASCENTS.
1 In my distress I called to the LORD,
and he answered me.
2 Deliver me, O LORD,
from lying lips,
from a deceitful tongue.

3 What shall be given to you,
[n]and what more shall be done to you,
you deceitful tongue?
4 [o]A warrior's [p]sharp arrows,
with glowing [q]coals of the broom tree!

5 Woe to me, that I sojourn in [r]Meshech,
that I dwell among [s]the tents of [t]Kedar!

171 [e]Ps. 145:7 [f]ver. 12
172 [g][ver. 160]
173 [h]Josh. 24:22; [Prov. 1:29]
174 [i]ver. 20 [j]ver. 24
176 [k]Isa. 53:6; 1 Pet. 2:25; [Matt. 18:12; Luke 15:4] [l]ver. 83

Psalm 120
[m]Ex. 34:24; 1 Kgs. 12:27; Isa. 30:29
3 [n][1 Sam. 3:17]
4 [o]Ps. 127:4; Jer. 50:9 [p]Ps. 45:5 [q]Ps. 140:10; Prov. 25:22
5 [r]Gen. 10:2; Ezek. 27:13; 38:2, 3; 39:1 [s]Song 1:5 [t]Gen. 25:13; Isa. 60:7; Jer. 49:28; Ezek. 27:21

119:171–172 The **lips** and **tongue** declare God's **praise** in song (in private, and in public worship).

119:176 I have gone astray like a lost sheep. The proper stance for praying this psalm is the humility and penitence of one who rests his life on God's grace and forgiveness, his steadfast love (see note on v. 41), and who asks God to **seek** him. One who has drunk deeply of this grace will not easily **forget** God's **commandments**.

Psalm 120. Psalm 120 is the first of the "Songs of Ascents" (Psalms 120–134). This diverse group includes individual and corporate laments, songs of confidence, thanksgiving hymns, a song celebrating Zion, wisdom psalms, a royal psalm, and a psalm for a liturgical occasion. Some traditional Jewish interpreters have suggested that these were songs sung on the "steps" (as the same word can mean, e.g., Ex. 20:26), either in parts of the temple or up from a spring in Jerusalem; others have taken them as geared toward returning to Jerusalem from exile (cf. Ezra 1:3). Neither of these makes good sense of David's authorship of Psalms 122; 124; 131; and 134. It is probably enough to take them simply as suited to the "ascent" to Jerusalem for worship (122:4; cf. 1 Kings 12:28; Zech. 14:16), even if they were not originally composed for that purpose.

Psalm 120 is an individual lament, sung by someone living away from Israel (v. 5); his distress concerns the way that deceitful people are stirring up war, while the psalmist prefers peace. It is possible that the psalm originated during the exile, when God told his dispersed people to seek the "welfare" (or "peace," Hb. *shalom*) of the city to which they were sent (Jer. 29:7). Because the Gentile lands of Meshech and Kedar are so far apart, some have suggested that "I" in this psalm is the people personified, but this is unnecessary (see note on Ps. 120:5). Worship in Jerusalem, both for the singer and for the Gentiles, is the remedy for this violence (cf. Isa. 2:3–4).

120:1–2 *I Called to the Lord, and He Answered Me.* The psalm opens by remembering: there have been times of **distress** in the past, and each time **I called to the LORD, he answered me** with rescue. This now provides encouragement to pray, and v. 2 explains the specific cause of distress: people with **lying lips** and a **deceitful tongue**.

120:1 called . . . answered. This word-pair expresses the prayer situation well: the believer calls out and expects God to answer; cf. 3:4; 4:1; 17:6; 20:9; 27:7; 86:7; 91:15; 99:6; 102:2; 118:5; 119:145; 138:3; Isa. 58:9; 65:24; Jer. 33:3; Zech. 13:9.

120:3–4 *The Liar Deserves the Warrior's Sharp Arrows.* The psalm now addresses the person who is causing the trouble, the one with the **deceitful tongue**. Such a person only courts God's judgment (of which the **sharp arrows** and **glowing coals** are emblems: 7:12–13; 11:6; 140:10).

120:4 The wood of the **broom tree** can be used to make excellent charcoal, which becomes a hot fire and retains its heat for a long time.

120:5–7 *Woe to Me that I Dwell among the Warlike.* The psalmist then reflects on the larger situation, i.e., that the people among whom he dwells are Gentiles, who do not have the advantage of the influence of God's word: this is why they **hate peace**. The ideal Israelite exile is **for peace**, seeking it for the city in which he is exiled (Hb. *shalom*; in Jer. 29:7 this is "welfare," see ESV footnote on Jer. 29:11). As a Song of Ascents, this psalm invites the people to suppose that Jerusalem's influence is the ultimate answer to this readiness for war (cf. Isa. 2:2–5).

120:5 sojourn. To live as a resident alien, not as a native-born citizen. **Meshech** was a people on the southeastern edge of the Black Sea (see note on Ezek. 27:13), while **Kedar** was a people dwelling in the Arabian desert (see note on Song 1:5). Since it is unlikely that one person would live in two places so far apart, some have suggested that the psalm's speaker, **I**, is a personification of Israel. This is possible, but it is probably simpler to see these two names as summarizing the Gentile world into which God's people have been dispersed.

7[u][Ps. 109:4]
Psalm 121
[m][See Ps. 120, title]
1[v]See Ps. 123:1 [w]Ps. 87:1; 133:3; Jer. 3:23; [Ps. 48:1]
2[x]Ps. 124:8; [Ps. 20:2] [y]See Ps. 115:15
3[z]Ps. 66:9; Prov. 3:23, 26; [1 Sam. 2:9] [a]Ps. 41:2; 127:1; [Isa. 27:3]; See Ps. 97:10
5[b]Ps. 91:1 [c]See Ps. 16:8
6[d]Isa. 49:10; Rev. 7:16 [e]2 Kgs. 4:19; Jonah 4:8
7[a][See ver. 3 above]
8[f]Deut. 28:6; 31:2; [Num. 27:17; 1 Sam. 29:6; 1 Kgs. 3:7; Acts 1:21]
Psalm 122
[m][See Ps. 120, title]
1[g]Isa. 2:3; Mic. 4:2; Zech. 8:21
3[h]Ps. 147:2 [i]Neh. 4:6

6 Too long have I had my dwelling
among those who hate peace.
7 [u]I am for peace,
but when I speak, they are for war!

My Help Comes from the Lord

121

A Song of [m]Ascents.
1 I [v]lift up my eyes to [w]the hills.
From where does my help come?
2 [x]My help comes from the Lord,
who [y]made heaven and earth.

3 He will not [z]let your foot be moved;
he who [a]keeps you will not slumber.
4 Behold, he who keeps Israel
will neither slumber nor sleep.

5 The Lord is your keeper;
the Lord is your [b]shade on your [c]right hand.
6 [d]The sun shall not [e]strike you by day,
nor the moon by night.

7 The Lord will [a]keep you from all evil;
he will [a]keep your life.
8 The Lord will keep
your [f]going out and your coming in
from this time forth and forevermore.

Let Us Go to the House of the Lord

122

A Song of [m]Ascents. Of David.
1 I was glad when they said to me,
[g]"Let us go to the house of the Lord!"
2 Our feet have been standing
within your gates, O Jerusalem!

3 Jerusalem—[h]built as a city
that is [i]bound firmly together,

Psalm 121. This psalm seems to be intended to instill confidence in those making the pilgrimage to Jerusalem to worship (see note on Psalm 120 for the Songs of Ascents). The successful journey becomes a parable for the whole of one's life, in which the faithful can be confident of God's tireless care.

121:1–2 *Where Does My Help Come From?* The person on pilgrimage to Jerusalem will **lift up** his **eyes to the hills** (possibly as a place to be feared, or else to the hills around Jerusalem, cf. 125:2), and wonders, **From where does my help come?** The reply shows that the question, which originally applied to "help to finish the journey," can be generalized to cover all of the believer's life. The **help comes from the Lord, who made heaven and earth**, and therefore no other power can hinder it.

121:2 who made heaven and earth. Biblical authors cite this idea, based on Gen. 2:4 and Ex. 20:11, to stress that the God of Israel has universal and unbounded power: cf. 2 Kings 19:15 (= Isa. 37:16); 2 Chron. 1:12; Ps. 115:15; 124:8; 134:3; 146:6; Jer. 32:17.

121:3–8 *The Lord Will Keep You at All Times.* These verses are dominated by the word "keep" (Hb. *shamar*, to keep, guard, watch over, attend to carefully): the Lord who **keeps Israel** (the corporate entity) also **keeps you** (the particular member). This means that **he will not let your foot be moved** (i.e., slip as you walk, cf. 38:16; 66:9), nor will he let you suffer from the dangers of **day** and **night**. When 121:7 speaks of **all evil**, and v. 8 of **your going out and your coming in** (cf. Deut. 28:6), they are probably taking the safe journey to Jerusalem as a parable for all of one's life: **the Lord is your keeper** at all times; he **will neither slumber nor sleep**. Not only is God all-powerful (Ps. 121:2), he is ever-watchful (v. 4). This is the confidence the faithful are to enjoy.

Psalm 122. This psalm celebrates Zion as God's chosen city (cf. Psalms 46; 48; 76; 87), and specifically the privilege of going there on a pilgrimage (cf. Psalm 84). Not only is "the house of the Lord" there, but so are "the thrones of the house of David." Christians who sing this recognize that in their gathered worship they are carrying out the task of the temple, and their Davidic king (Jesus) is present with them (1 Pet. 2:4–5; cf. Eph. 2:19–22).

122:1–2 *Joyful Arrival in Jerusalem.* The song begins by remembering (**they said** is past tense) the invitation to go to Jerusalem for worship (**the house of the Lord**), from the perspective of having arrived (**our feet have been standing**). The anticipation (**I was glad**) is now to be fulfilled.

122:3–5 *The Beauty of Jerusalem.* The singer, as it were, looks around Jerusalem: **bound firmly together** probably goes from the physical coziness of the city to the sense of unity the pilgrim expects to find there ("bound," Hb. *khubberah*, is related to "companion," Hb. *khaber*, 119:63). If this sense of unity is not always there in reality, it ought to be. This idealization also appears in the reference to the **house of David**, whose first goal should be the carrying out of **judgment** (i.e., ruling justly for the people).

4 to which the tribes [j]go up,
the tribes of the LORD,
as was [k]decreed for[1] Israel,
to give thanks to the name of the LORD.
5 There [l]thrones for judgment were set,
the thrones of the house of David.

6 [m]Pray for the peace of Jerusalem!
"May they be secure who love you!
7 Peace be within your [n]walls
and security within your [n]towers!"
8 For my brothers and companions' sake
I will say, [o]"Peace be within you!"
9 For the sake of the house of the LORD our God,
I will [p]seek your good.

Our Eyes Look to the LORD Our God

123

A SONG OF [m]ASCENTS.
1 To you I [q]lift up my eyes,
O you who are [r]enthroned in the heavens!
2 Behold, as the eyes of servants
look to the hand of their master,
as the eyes of a maidservant
to the hand of her mistress,
so our eyes look to the LORD our God,
till he has mercy upon us.

3 [s]Have mercy upon us, O LORD, have mercy upon us,
for we have had more than enough of [t]contempt.
4 Our soul has had more than enough
of [u]the scorn of [v]those who are at ease,
of the contempt of [w]the proud.

Our Help Is in the Name of the LORD

124

A SONG OF [m]ASCENTS. OF DAVID.
1 [x]If it had not been the LORD who was on our side—
[y]let Israel now say—

[1] *Or as a testimony for*

4 [j]Deut. 16:16 [k]Ps. 78:5
5 [l]Deut. 17:8; 2 Sam. 15:2; 1 Kgs. 3:16; 7:7; 2 Chr. 19:8
6 [m][Ps. 51:18; Jer. 29:7]
7 [n]Ps. 48:13
8 [o][1 Sam. 25:6; Ps. 85:8]
9 [p]Neh. 2:10; Esth. 10:3

Psalm 123

[m][See Ps. 120, title]
1 [q]Ps. 121:1; [Ps. 141:8]; See Ps. 25:15 [r]See Ps. 2:4
3 [s]Ps. 4:1 [t][Neh. 4:4]
4 [u][Neh. 2:19] [v]Isa. 32:9, 11; Amos 6:1 [w]See Ps. 119:51

Psalm 124

[m][See Ps. 120, title]
1 [x]Ps. 94:17 [y]Ps. 129:1

122:4 decreed. This interprets the Jerusalem temple as fulfilling the requirements of Deuteronomy about the place that God would choose (e.g., Deut. 12:5; 14:23; 16:16).

122:6–9 *Pray for the Peace of Jerusalem.* In light of what Jerusalem should be, the psalm ends by urging God's people to seek the conditions that will make that a reality: **the peace of Jerusalem** will ensure its stability and accessibility, in order that God's people might be able always to journey to the **house of the LORD**.

Psalm 123. This is a community lament, as the references to "we" and "us" show. As a Song of Ascents (see note on Psalm 120), it envisions a situation in which the faithful pilgrims feel themselves to be the objects of scorn and contempt—whether from the unfaithful in Israel or from unbelieving Gentiles among whom they must pass, the psalm does not say (the words are general enough to include both). The psalm goes beyond simply asking for a safe journey; it seeks relief from the scorn (a visible sign of God's mercy, which might even benefit those showing scorn). Christians should have no difficulty in praying the same way.

123:1–2 *Our Eyes Look to You, O Lord.* The first section describes the way God's faithful look trustingly toward God (for help, as **till he has mercy upon us** makes clear; and see vv. 3–4). The image of **servants** looking to a **master** and a **maidservant** to a **mistress** has suggested to some the idea of waiting for orders. But the context shows that the image is that of waiting patiently and trustingly for God to act; the psalm is concerned with gaining God's help.

123:3–4 *Have Mercy on Us at Last, O Lord.* The wait for mercy (v. 2) becomes a prayer, **have mercy upon us**. The specific mercy is relief from those who show **contempt** and **scorn** toward the faithful pilgrims. **Those who are at ease** can refer to unfaithful Israelites who do not trouble themselves with piety, preferring to enjoy luxury instead (e.g., Isa. 32:9; Amos 6:1), or it can apply to Gentiles indifferent to the true God (Zech. 1:15). Likewise the **proud** are arrogant in their unbelief (see Ps. 94:2). At many times during the history of God's people, they are under threat from those who hold power.

Psalm 124. This is a thanksgiving hymn for the community, particularly for an occasion in which God's people have been under threat but have been delivered. It is conceivable that David wrote this psalm in response to some deliverance such as those in 2 Sam. 5:17–25, but the words are quite general, applicable in a wide variety of settings; God's people have known many occasions on which this psalm provides just the right hymn. The implication of the psalm being now a Song of Ascents (see note on Psalm 120) seems to be that the faithful would sing it in connection with their pilgrimage to Jerusalem; the deliverance of the whole people allows them to continue journeying there (see note on 122:6–9).

3 [z]See Ps. 56:1
4 [a]See Ps. 32:6; Job 22:11 [b]Ps. 69:2; Isa. 8:8 [c]Ps. 69:1
7 [d]See Ps. 91:3
8 [e]Ps. 121:2

Psalm 125
[m][See Ps. 120, title]
1 [f]Ps. 25:2, 3 [g]Ps. 93:1; 104:5; [Prov. 10:30]
2 [h][2 Kgs. 6:17; Zech. 2:5]
3 [i]Isa. 14:5 [j]Isa. 30:30 [k]See Ps. 16:5 [l]Gen. 3:22; Ex. 22:8
4 [m]Ps. 119:68 [n]See Ps. 7:10

2 if it had not been the LORD who was on our side
when people rose up against us,
3 then they would have [z]swallowed us up alive,
when their anger was kindled against us;
4 then [a]the flood would have [b]swept us away,
the torrent would have gone [c]over us;
5 then over us would have gone
the raging waters.

6 Blessed be the LORD,
who has not given us
as prey to their teeth!
7 We have escaped like a bird
from [d]the snare of the fowlers;
the snare is broken,
and we have escaped!

8 [e]Our help is in the name of the LORD,
who made heaven and earth.

The LORD Surrounds His People

125

A SONG OF [m]ASCENTS.
1 Those who [f]trust in the LORD are like Mount Zion,
which [g]cannot be moved, but abides forever.
2 As the mountains surround Jerusalem,
so [h]the LORD surrounds his people,
from this time forth and forevermore.
3 For [i]the scepter of wickedness shall not [j]rest
on [k]the land allotted to the righteous,
lest the righteous [l]stretch out
their hands to do wrong.
4 [m]Do good, O LORD, to those who are good,
and to those who are [n]upright in their hearts!

124:1–5 *Had the Lord Not Helped Us.* The first section describes a situation in which **people** (apparently Gentiles) **rose up against us** (i.e., against Israel); these **would have swallowed us up alive** (v. 3) or **swept us away** like a **flood** (v. 4). And they would have succeeded **if it had not been the LORD who was on our side** to rescue us (cf. 94:17).

124:6–7 *We Have Had a Narrow Escape.* The second section stresses that the outcome could have been different, indeed it should have been: **we have escaped like a bird from the snare of the fowlers**, i.e., surprisingly. Therefore the psalm gives credit where it belongs: **Blessed be the LORD**!

124:8 *Our Help.* The psalm closes with its basic point, namely, that **our help is in the name of the LORD** (i.e., his personal presence, cf. Deut. 12:11), **who made heaven and earth** (see note on Ps. 121:2). Biblical authors certainly affirm the importance of human diligence; but such diligence makes no lasting difference unless it is a tool in the Lord's hand (cf. 127:1). David was a wily and sturdy warrior, and he had valiant fighters in his service (2 Sam. 23:8–39), as was proper; at the same time, it was the Lord who worked each great victory through them (2 Sam. 23:12).

Psalm 125. This psalm instills confidence in the Lord's people, that remaining loyal to him really is worth it. The leading image is of Zion as a city surrounded by sheltering mountains. It is possible that some of Zion's citizens might go over to evil, but the Lord will see to it that he publicly vindicates his faithful ones. This is like Psalm 122, in that it stresses the ideal of what the city should be (and the faithful will do their part to make it live up to the ideal).

125:1–2 *The Security of Zion.* The psalm begins by describing the secure position of **those who trust in the LORD**: they are **like Mount Zion, which cannot be moved** (see 10:6 and note; 46:5). **the mountains surround Jerusalem.** The hills on which Jerusalem sits are a little lower than the hills around it, so that one can picture the surrounding hills as a wall. This serves as an image of the Lord's protection, as he **surrounds his people** like a high wall encircling the city.

125:3 *Righteous Rule over Zion.* The middle of the psalm stresses that the Lord intends to protect his city, not simply from enemies without (v. 2) but from enemies within: the **scepter of wickedness** is kingly power held by Israelites who do not serve God and his people (the **righteous**). The disastrous effects of such rule show up frequently in OT history, where the bulk of the people do in fact **stretch out their hands to do wrong** (in defiance of the very purpose for which God chose them). Therefore no one could suppose that in affirming that this godless regime **shall not rest on the land**, the psalmist was ignoring the obvious; rather, he was both instilling the ideal toward which the Israelites should always press, and indicating that God will not allow the unrighteous to rule over his people forever. Christians rejoice that God raised Jesus to the throne of David in keeping with this principle, and pray that leaders in their churches (and in their nations) would model themselves after Jesus.

125:4–5 *May the Lord Vindicate His Truth!* The final section looks forward to the Lord vindicating his own character: he really does reward the faithful (**those who are good** and **those who are upright in their hearts**), and he really does purge the unfaithful (**those who turn aside to their crooked ways**) from his people (he **will lead** them **away with evildoers**). **Peace** will certainly **be upon Israel** when God so visibly vindicates the truthfulness of his words and when his people take it to heart.

5 But those who [o]turn aside to their [p]crooked ways
the LORD will lead away with [q]evildoers!
[r]Peace be upon Israel!

Restore Our Fortunes, O LORD

126

A SONG OF [m]ASCENTS.

1 When the LORD [s]restored the fortunes of Zion,
we were like those who [t]dream.
2 Then our [u]mouth was filled with laughter,
and our tongue with shouts of joy;
then they said among the nations,
[v]"The LORD has done great things for them."
3 The LORD has done great things for us;
we are glad.

4 Restore our fortunes, O LORD,
like streams in the Negeb!
5 [w]Those who sow in tears
shall reap with shouts of joy!
6 He who goes out weeping,
bearing the seed for sowing,
shall come home with shouts of joy,
bringing his sheaves with him.

Unless the LORD Builds the House

127

A SONG OF [m]ASCENTS. OF SOLOMON.

1 Unless the LORD builds the house,
those who build it labor in vain.
Unless the LORD [x]watches over the city,
the watchman stays awake in vain.
2 It is in vain that you rise up early
and go late to rest,

5 [o]See Ps. 40:4 [p]Prov. 2:15 [q]Ps. 92:7, 9; 94:4 [r]Ps. 128:6; Gal. 6:16

Psalm 126

[m][See Ps. 120, title]
1 [s]See Ps. 14:7 [t][Acts 12:9]
2 [u]Job 8:21 [v]See Ps. 71:19
5 [w][Ezra 6:22; Neh. 12:43; Jer. 31:9; Gal. 6:9]; See Hag. 2:3-9

Psalm 127

[m][See Ps. 120, title]
1 [x]See Ps. 121:4

Psalm 126. This is a community lament that recalls a previous time of God's mercy on his people (v. 1) and asks for a fresh show of that mercy (v. 4). The psalm does not specify which particular mercy or crisis is in view (see note on v. 1), and it is well-suited to a wide variety of comparable situations. In such crises, God's people may take encouragement from past events of mercy and pray for more of it. Repeated words that tie together the two halves of the psalm are "restore the fortunes" (vv. 1, 4) and "shouts of joy" (vv. 2, 5, 6). The psalm also reminds God's people that their well-being impacts the nations around them (v. 2).

126:1–3 *Recalling the Past Restoration of Zion.* The psalm opens by remembering some event in the past in which God **restored the fortunes of Zion** (see note on v. 1). This great mercy, which they could hardly believe (**like those who dream**) filled the people with gladness (v. 2); it also impressed **the nations** with God's care for his people, and the people themselves took up the Gentiles' cry: **the LORD has done great things for us**.

126:1 restored the fortunes. Some scholars think that this is specifically "returned from exile" (cf. Deut. 30:3), but the expression is more general than that (Job 42:10; cf. Ps. 14:7; 85:1; Lam. 2:14); vv. 5–6 of Psalm 126 refer to the more general type of restoration.

126:2 they said among the nations. Israel was called to be God's living testimony among the nations that he is the one true God, Maker of heaven and earth. Sometimes this testimony would be through God's purifying judgments (Deut. 29:24–28); ideally it would be through Israel's faithfulness and verbal witness (Ps. 96:10). God's great deeds for his people also provide testimony (e.g., Josh. 4:24; Ezek. 36:23).

126:4–6 *Prayer for a Renewed Restoration.* The words of v. 1 here become a prayer: **Restore our fortunes, O LORD**, i.e., "show us mercy now as you have done in the past." The images that follow (**streams in the Negeb**; **seed for sowing**) seem to illustrate the kind of renewal asked for, namely, a good year for crops. Since Israel's life in the land was to show forth a new Eden for all the world to see, such agricultural fruitfulness would necessarily be tied to active faithfulness on the part of the people (cf. Deut. 30:9–10).

126:4 The **Negeb** is the arid southern region of Judah; for its dry gullies to run as **streams** would turn the land green with plants.

Psalm 127. The basic theme of this wisdom psalm is that without the Lord's blessing, all human toil is worthless. This is explicit in vv. 1–2; and implicit in vv. 3–5, where the pious are to see their children as the Lord's gift. Psalms 127–128 are wisdom poems in the Songs of Ascents. Wisdom themes are suited to worshipful pilgrims, because in the OT, faithfulness in everyday life (the emphasis of wisdom) and vitality in worship go together (see note on Psalm 111). Christians need the same reminders. This psalm, along with Psalm 72, is attributed to Solomon. God gave Solomon great wisdom (1 Kings 4:29–34), though Solomon himself did not always abide by it (1 Kings 11:1–8).

127:1–2 *All Effort Is in Vain without the Lord.* A little reflection on v. 1 makes the point clear: of course **those who build** a house must **labor** on it, and certainly the **watchman** of a **city** must stay **awake**. At the same time they must carry out their efforts in faith, trusting God to make the work beneficial. Similarly, a farmer must be diligent (v. 2; cf. 128:2), but he must practice his diligence in faith—in this case by receiving the **sleep** that God wants to give **to his beloved**. These verses share their theme with the wisdom in Proverbs, which promotes diligence but clarifies that diligence is neither greed nor restless anxiety (see notes on Prov. 10:22; 23:4–5). The Sabbath commandment (Ex. 20:8–11) is a gift to enable God's people to live by faith, requiring them not to work all the time, as they trust him for their future well-being.

eating the bread of anxious [y]toil;
for he gives to his [z]beloved [a]sleep.

3 Behold, [b]children are a heritage from the LORD,
[c]the fruit of the womb a reward.
4 Like arrows in the hand of [d]a warrior
are the children[1] of one's youth.
5 Blessed is the man
who fills his quiver with them!
He shall not be put to shame
when he speaks with his enemies [e]in the gate.[2]

Blessed Is Everyone Who Fears the LORD

128

A SONG OF [m]ASCENTS.
1 [f]Blessed is everyone who fears the LORD,
who [g]walks in his ways!
2 You [h]shall eat the fruit of the labor of your hands;
you shall be blessed, and it shall be well with you.

3 Your wife will be like [i]a fruitful vine
within your house;
your children will be like [j]olive shoots
around your table.
4 Behold, thus shall the man be blessed
who fears the LORD.

5 [k]The LORD bless you [l]from Zion!
May you see [m]the prosperity of Jerusalem
all the days of your life!
6 May you see your [n]children's children!
[o]Peace be upon Israel!

They Have Afflicted Me from My Youth

129

A SONG OF [m]ASCENTS.
1 "Greatly[3] have they [p]afflicted me [q]from my youth"—
[r]let Israel now say—

[1] Or *sons* [2] Or *They shall not be put to shame when they speak with their enemies in the gate* [3] Or *Often*; also verse 2

2[y]Gen. 3:17, 19 [z]Ps. 60:5 [a][Mark 4:26, 27]
3[b][Gen. 33:5] [c]Deut. 28:4; [Ps. 132:11]
4[d]Ps. 120:4
5[e]See Job 5:4

Psalm 128
[m][See Ps. 120, title]
1[f]See Ps. 112:1 [g]Ps. 119:1; [Prov. 8:32]
2[h]Isa. 3:10; [Ps. 109:11]
3[i]Ezek. 19:10; [Gen. 49:22] [j]See Ps. 52:8
5[k]Ps. 134:3 [l]Ps. 20:2; 135:21 [m][Ps. 122:9]
6[n]Prov. 17:6; See Job 42:16 [o]Ps. 125:5

Psalm 129
[m][See Ps. 120, title]
1[p][Ex. 1:14; Judg. 3:8, 14; 4:3; 6:2; 10:8] [q]Isa. 47:12; Jer. 2:2; 22:21; Hos. 2:15 [r]Ps. 124:1

127:3–5 *The Blessedness of Children.* Like the first section, this does not eliminate human activity: **children are a heritage from the LORD**, and therefore his gift, and yet husband and wife must do something in bringing the children into the world and in raising them to be faithful members of God's people. Here the stress falls on **the children of one's youth**, now grown up and standing with their father **when he speaks with his enemies in the gate** (i.e., the place where justice was administered, see note on Ruth 4:1–2). It will be hard for the enemies (who are assumed to be unfaithful) to intimidate such a man.

127:5 Blessed. See note on 1:1.

Psalm 128. This wisdom psalm expands some of the topics in Psalm 127. Psalm 127 ended with the "blessed . . . man" (127:5), and Psalm 128 gives a further description of this man's blessedness: in the context of ancient Israel, it consisted of a productive farm, and a faithful wife and children around the table together (see note on Prov. 10:4). The ending of the psalm shows that neither wisdom nor blessedness are individualistic; both relate to the larger reality of the well-being of God's people.

128:1–4 *The Godly Enjoy Blessedness in Their Homes.* The opening section gives an attractive picture of how the faithful person (**who fears the LORD**, i.e., **who walks in his ways**; cf. 112:1; Deut. 8:6) sees blessedness (or true happiness) in his home: he is able to work his farm and to **eat the fruit of the labor of** his **hands** (a covenant blessing, cf. Deut. 28:1–6 and contrast Deut. 28:33); he has a wife who is **like a fruitful vine** (i.e., a bringer of joy like wine, and the mother of children; cf. Ps. 127:3), and children **like olive shoots around** the **table** (i.e., full of energy and promise). Nothing suggests that such happiness is "automatic"; the rest of the Wisdom Literature fills out how those who fear the Lord work diligently, love their spouses well, and faithfully train their children in godliness. The focus of this psalm is the aura of divine blessing that surrounds such a family.

128:5–6 *May the Lord Allow You to See Such Happiness.* This section prays that each member of God's people might know such a condition of blessedness—a condition that will benefit the whole of God's people (**Jerusalem**). **May you see your children's children**. This includes living to be old enough to see one's grandchildren and the delight they give (Prov. 17:6); within the people of God it includes the prospect of a faithful family line (Ps. 103:17). With such faithfulness and blessedness, **peace** would indeed **be upon Israel**.

Psalm 129. It is reasonable to call this song a psalm of confidence for the community, as it reflects on what God's people have endured and how God has sustained them. It could also be called a community thanksgiving, which celebrates God's sustaining presence, or a community lament, asking that God continue to sustain his people against those who would harm them. As a Song of Ascents, it is well-suited to remind the pilgrims never to take their privileges for granted.

129:1–4 *Those Who Hate Israel Have Not Prevailed.* The opening section has God's people as a whole (the **me** here) speaking, recalling that Israel

2 "Greatly have they [p]afflicted me [q]from my youth,
[s]yet they have not prevailed against me.
3 [t]The plowers plowed [u]upon my back;
they made long their furrows."
4 The LORD is righteous;
he has cut [v]the cords of the wicked.
5 May all who hate Zion
be [w]put to shame and turned backward!
6 Let them be like [x]the grass on the housetops,
which [y]withers before it grows up,
7 with which the reaper does not fill his hand
nor the binder of sheaves his arms,
8 nor do those who pass by say,
[a]"The blessing of the LORD be upon you!
We [b]bless you in the name of the LORD!"

My Soul Waits for the Lord

130

A SONG OF [m]ASCENTS.

1 Out of [c]the depths I cry to you, O LORD!
2 O Lord, hear my voice!
[d]Let your ears be attentive
to [e]the voice of my pleas for mercy!

3 If you, O LORD, should [f]mark iniquities,
O Lord, who could [g]stand?
4 But with you there is [h]forgiveness,
[i]that you may be feared.

5 I [j]wait for the LORD, [k]my soul waits,
and [l]in his word I hope;
6 my soul [m]waits for the Lord
more than [n]watchmen for [o]the morning,
more than watchmen for the morning.

7 O Israel, [p]hope in the LORD!
For [q]with the LORD there is steadfast love,
and with him is plentiful redemption.
8 And he will [r]redeem Israel
from all his iniquities.

2 [p][See ver. 1 above] [q][See ver. 1 above] [s][2 Cor. 4:8-10]
3 [t]Mic. 3:12 [u][Isa. 50:6; 51:23]
4 [v]Ps. 2:3
5 [w]See Ps. 35:4
6 [x]2 Kgs. 19:26; Isa. 37:27 [y]Ps. 37:2; Job 8:12
8 [a]Ruth 2:4 [b]Ps. 118:26

Psalm 130

[m][See Ps. 120, title]
1 [c]Ps. 69:2, 14; Lam. 3:55; Jonah 2:2
2 [d]Ps. 86:6; 2 Chr. 6:40 [e]Ps. 140:6
3 [f][Ps. 90:8]; See Job 10:14 [g]Ps. 76:7; Amos 2:15; Nah. 1:6; Mal. 3:2; Eph. 6:13; Rev. 6:17; [Ps. 143:2]
4 [h]ver. 7; Isa. 55:7; Dan. 9:9; See Ps. 86:5, 15 [i]1 Kgs. 8:39, 40; Jer. 33:8, 9; [Rom. 2:4]
5 [j]Ps. 40:1; Isa. 8:17; 26:8 [k]See Ps. 33:20 [l]Ps. 119:74, 81
6 [m][Ps. 123:2] [n][Ps. 63:6; 119:147] [o]See Ps. 5:3
7 [p]Ps. 131:3 [q]ver. 4
8 [r]Ps. 111:9; Luke 1:68; Titus 2:14; [Matt. 1:21]; See Ps. 25:22

has long (**from my youth**) endured people who have **afflicted** them, and yet **they have not prevailed against** Israel. They have done terrible things (**plowed upon my back**), but because **the LORD is righteous** (i.e., true to his promises), **he has cut the cords** (which bound Israel to be subjects) **of the wicked** (in this case, those who hate God's people).

129:5–8 *May Those Who Hate Zion Never Prevail.* The second section prays that **all** such enemies (**who hate Zion**) should always fail in their purposes (**be put to shame and turned backward**; see note on 25:2–3). The image of 129:6–8 is that of withered grass, which brings no blessing to others. (On why this is not vindictive, see notes on 35:4–8; 40:11–17; 70:1–3.)

Psalm 130. This is an individual lament, expressing penitence and trust in God's mercy. (Other psalms with prominent penitential themes are Psalms 6; 25; 32; 38; 51; 143.) The penitential element is geared toward helping worshipers to see themselves as forgiven people, whose only right to enter God's presence lies in his mercy.

130:1–2 *O Lord, Hear My Cry for Mercy!* The psalm climbs from **out of the depths** of misery over sin, to confession of it (vv. 3–4), to hope (vv. 5–6) and assurance (vv. 7–8). The tone is urgent, and the topic is **my pleas for mercy**.

130:3–4 *With You There Is Forgiveness.* The song acknowledges that if God **should mark iniquities** (as if he kept them in a record book), no one, not even the faithful who are singing this, **could stand**. And yet **with** the Lord **there is forgiveness**: this is what God promises his people who come to him in faith (cf. 86:5; 103:3; Neh. 9:17; Dan. 9:9), and this is why he **may be feared** (i.e., worshiped and served in loving reverence).

130:5–8 *I Earnestly Wait for the Lord to Hear Me.* The pious person now sings, **I wait for the LORD**, and **in his word I hope**, probably specifically for the word of forgiveness connected with the sacrifices to be offered (e.g., Lev. 4:21). This waiting proceeds to assurance, as each singer invites everyone else to **hope in the LORD**, with whom **there is steadfast love** and **plentiful redemption**. The Lord is the one who **will redeem Israel from all his iniquities**, i.e., deliver them from the penalties their iniquities deserve (on "redeem," see note on Ps. 25:22). The ideal Israel is a people where every single member readily acknowledges his or her dependence on God's mercy and grace.

I Have Calmed and Quieted My Soul

131

A SONG OF [m]ASCENTS. OF DAVID.

1 O LORD, my heart is not [s]lifted up;
my eyes are not [t]raised too high;
I do not [u]occupy myself with things
too great and [v]too marvelous for me.
2 But I have calmed and quieted my soul,
like a weaned [w]child with its mother;
like a weaned child is my soul within me.

3 [x]O Israel, hope in the LORD
from this time forth and forevermore.

The LORD Has Chosen Zion

132

A SONG OF [m]ASCENTS.

1 Remember, O LORD, in David's favor,
all [y]the hardships he endured,
2 how he swore to the LORD
and [z]vowed to [a]the Mighty One of Jacob,
3 "I will not enter my house
or get into my bed,
4 I will not [b]give sleep to my eyes
or slumber to my eyelids,
5 until I [c]find a place for the LORD,
a dwelling place for [a]the Mighty One of Jacob."

6 Behold, we heard of it in [d]Ephrathah;
we found it in [e]the fields of Jaar.
7 "Let us go to his dwelling place;
let us [f]worship at his [g]footstool!"

8 [h]Arise, O LORD, and go to your [i]resting place,
you and the ark of your [j]might.
9 Let your [k]priests be [l]clothed with righteousness,
and let your [m]saints shout for joy.

Psalm 131
[m][See Ps. 120, title]
1[s][Ps. 138:6; Isa. 57:15] [t]See Ps. 101:5 [u][Jer. 45:5; Rom. 12:16] [v]See Job 42:3
2[w][Matt. 18:3; 1 Cor. 14:20]
3[x]Ps. 130:7

Psalm 132
[m][See Ps. 120, title]
1[y]1 Chr. 22:14
2[z]Ps. 50:14 [a]ver. 5; Gen. 49:24; Isa. 49:26; 60:16
4[b]Prov. 6:4
5[c]1 Chr. 22:7; Acts 7:46 [a][See ver. 2 above]
6[d]1 Sam. 17:12; [Gen. 35:19] [e][1 Sam. 7:1]
7[f]Ps. 5:7 [g]See Ps. 99:5
8[h]Ps. 68:1; 2 Chr. 6:41, 42 [i]ver. 14 [j]Ps. 78:61
9[k]ver. 16 [l]See Job 29:14 [m][Ps. 149:5]

Psalm 131. This psalm of confidence in the Lord models the ideal frame of soul before God, a "calmed and quieted soul."

131:1–2 *I Have Quieted My Soul.* The opening section describes the humility that befits the faithful person: his **heart is not lifted up** and his **eyes are not raised too high** (expressions for arrogance and pride); nor does he **occupy** himself **with things too great and too marvelous for** him (i.e., with matters beyond human powers to comprehend; cf. Deut. 29:29). This person has **calmed and quieted** his **soul, like a weaned child with its mother**: just as a weaned child is content simply having his mother's presence, so the faithful worshiper is content with God's presence, even when there are many things he would like God to explain (such as how one's own little story relates to the big story; see note on Psalm 111).

131:1 When the **heart** is **lifted up** the person is proud; cf. the same expression translated "the heart is proud" in 2 Chron. 32:26 and Ezek. 28:2. Similarly, when the **eyes** are **raised too high**, they are "haughty eyes" (Ps. 18:27; Prov. 6:17; 21:4).

131:3 *O Israel, Hope in the Lord!* With such a disposition of trust and contentment, Israel may **hope in the LORD** at all times.

Psalm 132. The theme of this royal psalm is God's covenant with the house of David (2 Sam. 7:4–16) to establish the dynasty for the good of the people and, eventually, of the world. Most of the psalm expresses confidence in these promises; the requests are for God to carry out his purpose (Ps. 132:1, 8–9). As a Song of Ascents, this psalm recalls how the dynasty of David is to ensure the stability of the realm, especially of Jerusalem (cf. the Davidic Psalm 122). In the era in which the Psalter was edited, the inclusion of this psalm in the collection shows the editors' faith that in due course God will renew the Davidic line (132:11–12).

132:1–5 *Remember David's Service to the Ark.* The psalm opens with a request that God will **remember** (see note on 25:6–7) all that David did to prepare the temple, **a dwelling place for the Mighty One of Jacob** (cf. 2 Sam. 7:2; 1 Chron. 22:2–19). Perhaps the other sufferings of David to retain his rule are included in the **hardships**. The prayer expresses the feeling that such sacrifice and hard work ought not go to waste.

132:6–7 *We Are Going There to Worship.* The pilgrims come from various villages in Judah (**Ephrathah**, the district whose best-known villages were Bethlehem and **Jaar**; or Kiriath-jearim, where the ark had once lodged, 1 Sam. 7:2) to **worship at his footstool** (cf. 1 Chron. 28:2; Ps. 99:5).

132:8–10 *Continue Blessing the People and Its Leaders.* Adapting the words of Solomon's prayer, the worshipers pray that God will be present in his chosen **resting place**. Envisioning the scene in Jerusalem, the worshipers pray that Israel will be true to its calling, i.e., that the **priests** (who lead worship and teach the Scriptures at the sanctuary) would **be clothed with righteousness** (i.e., would be genuinely godly men; cf. Mal. 2:6–7), that the **saints** (the people, esp. the pious ones) would **shout for joy** (celebrating what God has done; cf. Ps. 126:2), and that God would **not turn away the face of** his **anointed one** (i.e., would continue showing favor to David's heirs, so that Israel would remain a secure home for piety).

10 For the sake of your servant David,
[n]do not turn away the face of [o]your anointed one.
11 [p]The LORD swore to David a sure oath
[q]from which he will not turn back:
[r]"One of the sons of your body[1]
I will set on your throne.
12 If your sons keep my covenant
and my testimonies that I shall teach them,
their sons also forever
shall [s]sit on your throne."
13 For the LORD has [t]chosen Zion;
he has [u]desired it for his dwelling place:
14 "This is my [v]resting place forever;
here I will [w]dwell, for I have desired it.
15 I will abundantly [x]bless her provisions;
I will [y]satisfy her poor with bread.
16 Her [z]priests I will clothe with salvation,
and her [z]saints will shout for joy.
17 There I will make [a]a horn to sprout for David;
I have prepared [b]a lamp for [c]my anointed.
18 His enemies I will [d]clothe with shame,
but on him his crown will shine."

When Brothers Dwell in Unity

133

A SONG OF [m]ASCENTS. OF DAVID.

1 Behold, how good and pleasant it is
when [e]brothers dwell in unity![2]
2 It is like the precious [f]oil on [g]the head,
running down on the beard,
on the beard of Aaron,
running down on [h]the collar of his robes!
3 It is like [i]the dew of [j]Hermon,
which falls on [k]the mountains of Zion!
For there the LORD [l]has commanded the blessing,
life forevermore.

[1] Hebrew *of your fruit of the womb* [2] Or *dwell together*

10 [n][2 Kgs. 18:24] [o]ver. 17; [1 Kgs. 1:39]
11 [p]Ps. 89:3, 34 [q]Ps. 110:4 [r]2 Sam. 7:12; 2 Chr. 6:16; Luke 1:32; Acts 2:30
12 [s]1 Kgs. 8:25; [Job 36:7]
13 [t]Ps. 78:68; [Ps. 135:21] [u]See Ps. 68:16
14 [v]ver. 8 [w]Matt. 23:21
15 [x]Ps. 147:14 [y]Ruth 1:6
16 [z]ver. 9
17 [a]Ezek. 29:21; [Luke 1:69] [b]1 Kgs. 11:36; 15:4; 2 Kgs. 8:19; 2 Chr. 21:7 [c]ver. 10
18 [d]See Job 8:22

Psalm 133
[m][See Ps. 120, title]
1 [e][Gen. 13:8; Heb. 13:1]
2 [f]Ex. 30:25, 30 [g]Ex. 29:7; Lev. 8:12 [h]Ex. 28:33; 39:24; [Ex. 28:32; 39:23; Job 30:18]
3 [i]Prov. 19:12; Mic. 5:7 [j]Deut. 3:9; 4:48 [k]See Ps. 48:1 [l]Lev. 25:21; Deut. 28:8; See Ps. 42:8

132:10 anointed one. See note on 2:2.

132:11–18 *The Lord's Promise to David and Zion.* The final section of the psalm is about half the total length; it reviews the **sure oath** that God **swore to David**. This promise is God's answer to the prayer of vv. 8–10. God promised to preserve the dynasty, and expects the individual heirs of David to be faithful to the **covenant**. The psalm does not mention that some of these may fail in their faithfulness and the people suffer for it; but with 2 Sam. 7:14–15 and 1 Kings 2:2–4 in the background (see note on Ps. 89:28–37), no one could miss that. With the Lord present in **Zion**, which he **has chosen**, the people will be happy and secure. Singing these words enables the worshipers to delight in their privileges, and not to take them lightly.

132:16–17 These verses closely echo the prayer of vv. 9–10.

132:18 Sung in exilic times, when the Psalter was compiled, this is a declaration of faith that God would again fulfill his promises and raise up a new David.

Psalm 133. This wisdom psalm celebrates the beauty of brothers in Israel dwelling together with two colorful similes that describe the blessedness of Israel being true to its calling ("when brothers dwell in unity").

133:1 brothers dwell in unity. The expression appears in Gen. 13:6; 36:7, where a particular region could not support "brothers" (relatives) and their families dwelling close together. If this is the background for the psalm, then Ps. 133:1 describes a situation in which the land is fruitful enough for brothers to live nearby (perhaps a family inheritance, cf. Deut. 25:5). Since this is a Song of Ascents, the "brothers dwelling in unity" would be the fellow Israelite pilgrims gathered in Jerusalem, abiding in peace with one another. The ideal Israel is a community of true brotherhood, where the members practice mutual concern for one another; if this were achieved, it would indeed be **good and pleasant**. This should be the goal of church life (John 17:20–23).

133:2 The first simile is the ordination **oil** on the **head** of **Aaron** and his descendants (cf. Ex. 30:22–33). This oil made the priests "holy," consecrated to God's purpose. The image means that when Israel is true to its ideal, it is displaying genuine consecration and carrying out its calling in the world.

133:3 Hermon is a high, snowcapped mountain at the northern end of the land (see note on Deut. 3:8–10); it is not clear exactly how its **dew . . . falls on the mountains of Zion**: perhaps the clouds above Hermon are pictured as dropping their moisture on Jerusalem, or perhaps "the dew of Hermon" is an idiom for "a heavy fall of dew." In any case, the dew is crucial for the vegetation during the dry season (Gen. 27:28; Deut. 33:28; 2 Sam. 1:21; 1 Kings 17:1; Prov. 3:20; 19:12; Hos. 14:5; Hag. 1:10; Zech. 8:12), and the image conveys the thought of a fruitful land. This too was part of the covenantal ideal (cf. Deut. 28:1–14).

Psalm 134
[m][See Ps. 120, title]
1 [m]Ps. 135:1 [n]Deut. 10:8; 18:7; 1 Chr. 23:30; 2 Chr. 29:11; 35:5 [o]1 Chr. 9:33; [Lev. 8:35]
2 [p]See Ps. 28:2 [q]Ps. 63:2
3 [r]Num. 6:24 [s]Ps. 128:5 [t]See Ps. 115:15

Psalm 135
1 [u]See Ps. 104:35 [v]See Ps. 113:1
2 [n][See Ps. 134:1 above] [w]Ps. 92:13
3 [x]See Ps. 100:5 [y]Ps. 147:1; [Ps. 52:9]
4 [z]Deut. 7:6, 7; 10:15; See Ps. 105:6 [a]Ex. 19:5
5 [b]Ps. 95:3
6 [c]Ps. 115:3
7 [d]Jer. 10:13; 51:16 [e][Job 28:25, 26; 38:25; Zech. 10:1] [f]Job 38:22
8 [g]See Ps. 78:51

Come, Bless the Lord

134

A Song of [m]Ascents.

1 Come, bless the Lord, all you [m]servants of the Lord,
who [n]stand [o]by night in the house of the Lord!
2 [p]Lift up your hands to [q]the holy place
and bless the Lord!

3 May the Lord [r]bless you [s]from Zion,
he who [t]made heaven and earth!

Your Name, O Lord, Endures Forever

135

1 [u]Praise the Lord!
Praise the name of the Lord,
give praise, O [v]servants of the Lord,
2 who [n]stand in the house of the Lord,
in [w]the courts of the house of our God!
3 Praise the Lord, for [x]the Lord is good;
sing to his name, [y]for it is pleasant![1]
4 For the Lord has [z]chosen Jacob for himself,
Israel as his [a]own possession.

5 For I know that [b]the Lord is great,
and that our Lord is above all gods.
6 [c]Whatever the Lord pleases, he does,
in heaven and on earth,
in the seas and all deeps.
7 [d]He it is who makes the clouds rise at the end of the earth,
who [e]makes lightnings for the rain
and brings forth the wind from his [f]storehouses.

8 He it was who [g]struck down the firstborn of Egypt,
both of man and of beast;

[1] *Or for he is beautiful*

Psalm 134. This final Song of Ascents is geared toward a liturgical occasion, perhaps the opening or closing of a festival (depending on the identity of the "servants of the Lord," v. 1). By the reading argued for here, this would suit well the close of a worship service.

134:1–2 *Call to the Temple Helpers to Bless the Lord.* The psalm opens by calling a group described as the **servants of the Lord** to **bless the Lord**. The title "servants of the Lord" could refer to Israelites in general (as it seems to in 135:1); but since they are said to **stand by night in the house of the Lord**, it seems better to take these words as addressed to Levitical personnel, whether priests (1 Kings 8:10–11) or attendants from the non-priestly Levitical families (1 Chron. 9:33). The worshiping congregation calls on them to **lift up** their **hands to the holy place and bless the Lord** (cf. Ps. 28:2).

134:3 *Blessing upon Each Worshiper.* The priests then address the worshipers and pronounce on each one of them ("you" is singular), **May the Lord bless you** (cf. Num. 6:24) **from Zion** (i.e., "from the place where you have been worshiping").

Psalm 135. This hymn calls God's people to praise him for his majestic power that he has displayed in his deeds on behalf of Israel. Each generation that sings this would strengthen their faith in and loyalty to the Lord, and deepen their gratitude toward him for their privileges. A side effect should also be an increasing compassion for the Gentiles, who suffer from worshiping lifeless idols. Many phrases in this psalm closely resemble phrases found elsewhere in the OT, as the cross-references show. This could mean that the author of the psalm used those other texts as his sources; it could also mean that this psalm and some of those other texts used phrases and ideas from a common stock. The psalm names no author, nor does it state whether the "house of the Lord" (v. 2) is the first or second temple. The psalm serves the needs of God's people at all times, in order to renew their faith and gratitude.

135:1–4 *Praise the Lord Who Has Chosen Israel.* The psalm begins by calling the worshiping community to **praise the Lord** (Hb. *hallelu-yah*). The term **servants of the Lord** could be the Levitical attendants (as in 134:1) but is more likely the faithful (cf. 19:11, 13; 27:9; 113:1; etc.) gathered for worship in the **house of the Lord** (the temple). On the Lord's **name** (135:1, 3), see note on v. 1. The reason for the praise is given at the end: **for the Lord has chosen Jacob for himself** (v. 4). This is a call to humility, gratitude, and faithfulness on the part of the worshipers (Deut. 7:6–11 expounds this idea).

135:1 In the Psalms, **the name of the Lord** is often the object of religious affections, such as praise, love, trust, and hope (e.g., 5:11; 7:17; 8:1, 9; 18:49; 33:21; 92:1; 96:2; 102:15; and many other places). The way that Deuteronomy speaks of God's "name" dwelling in the sanctuary helps here (e.g., Deut. 12:5, 11; cf. Ps. 74:7): the Lord's "name" there is a way of talking about his personal presence (i.e., the "name" as such, Yahweh, is not the issue), and particularly as he makes himself known through his covenant (cf. 20:1, 7).

135:5–7 *Praise Him Because He Is Great.* The psalm moves to another reason to praise the Lord, namely, that he **is great** and **is above all gods** (cf. 95:3). This means that **whatever the Lord pleases, he does** (cf. 115:3 and note), and there is no power that can stop him. He controls the weather (135:7); the implication is that the gods worshiped by the nations do not, and therefore God's people should neither fear nor honor them (which they were often tempted to do).

135:8–12 *The Lord Delivered His People from Egypt and Brought Them to Canaan.* The Lord has displayed his great power and his enduring love in the history of Israel; these verses mention the exodus from Egypt (vv. 8–9) and

9 who in your midst, O Egypt,
sent [h]signs and wonders
against Pharaoh and all his servants;
10 [i]who struck down many nations
and killed mighty kings,
11 [j]Sihon, king of the Amorites,
and [k]Og, king of Bashan,
and [l]all the kingdoms of Canaan,
12 and [m]gave their land as a heritage,
a heritage to his people Israel.

13 [n]Your name, O LORD, endures forever,
[o]your renown,[1] O LORD, throughout all ages.
14 [p]For the LORD will vindicate his people
and [q]have compassion on his servants.

15 [r]The idols of the nations are silver and gold,
the work of human hands.
16 They have mouths, but do not speak;
they have eyes, but do not see;
17 they have ears, but do not hear,
nor is there any breath in their mouths.
18 Those who make them become like them,
so do all who trust in them.

19 [s]O house of Israel, bless the LORD!
O house of Aaron, bless the LORD!
20 O house of Levi, bless the LORD!
You who fear the LORD, bless the LORD!
21 Blessed be the LORD [t]from Zion,
he who [u]dwells in Jerusalem!
[v]Praise the LORD!

His Steadfast Love Endures Forever

136 1 [w]Give thanks to the LORD, for he is good,
[x]for his steadfast love endures forever.
2 Give thanks to [y]the God of gods,
for his steadfast love endures forever.

[1] Or *remembrance*

9 [h]Deut. 6:22
10 [i]For ver. 10-12, see Ps. 136:17-22
11 [j]Deut. 29:7; See Num. 21:21-26 [k]See Num. 21:33-35 [l]See Josh. 12:7-24
12 [m]Deut. 29:8; See Ps. 78:55
13 [n]Ex. 3:15 [o]Ps. 102:12
14 [p]Deut. 32:36 [q]See Ps. 90:13
15 [r]For ver. 15-18, see Ps. 115:4-8
19 [s]See Ps. 115:9
21 [t]Ps. 128:5 [u]Ps. 132:13, 14 [v]ver. 1

Psalm 136

1 [w]Ps. 106:1; 107:1; 118:1 [x]See 1 Chr. 16:41
2 [y]Deut. 10:17

the conquest of the Promised Land (vv. 10–12; see 136:17–22). The defeat of **Sihon** and **Og** (Num. 21:21–35) was the first taste of victory for the new generation of Israel, and it strengthened their faith (cf. Deut. 2:26–3:11; 29:7; 31:4; Josh. 2:10; Neh. 9:22). Israel is under the special care of the Creator-Redeemer who exercises his power for their sake—what a privilege!

135:13–14 *The Lord's Name Will Endure Forever.* Verse 13 (see note) evokes Ex. 3:15, which is part of God's explanation for his "name": it signifies his continuing faithfulness to his people (see note on Ex. 3:14), and therefore ensures that he **will vindicate his people and have compassion on his servants** (i.e., rescue them from trouble and oppression, even when it is their own fault, cf. Deut. 32:36), as his deeds have already shown him doing (Ps. 135:8–12).

135:13 As the ESV footnote shows, the word **renown** could also be rendered "remembrance"; the psalm is alluding to Ex. 3:15, "This is my name forever, and thus I am to be remembered throughout all generations."

135:15–18 *The Idols of the Nations Are Worthless.* The next section adapts the words of 115:4–8 (see note there) to contrast the God who has chosen and cared for Israel, doing what he pleases (see note on 135:5–7) with the lifeless and useless gods that the Gentiles worship.

135:19–21 *Let Everyone in Israel Bless the Lord!* The only fitting response to such a great and lively God is for the various members of the worshiping company (the **house of Israel**, the **house of Aaron**, the **house of Levi**, and those **who fear the LORD**) to **bless the LORD** (cf. 115:9–11 and note; 118:2–4). The psalm closes as it began, **Praise the LORD!** (Hb. *hallelu-yah*).

135:19 Bless the LORD. See note on 103:1–2.

135:21 Blessed be. The passive form of "bless," v. 19. The mention of **Zion** and **Jerusalem** is a reminder that this is where the whole people gathered to worship in the OT era; it is where God made his "name" dwell (see note on v. 1).

Psalm 136. This hymn calls on the worshiping congregation to give thanks to the Lord, who has shown his steadfast love throughout the history of God's people: from creating the world, to bringing Israel out of Egypt and leading them through the wilderness, to giving them victory over those who opposed them as they took the Promised Land. The psalm includes more recent acts of God's deliverance and care (vv. 23–25), interpreting them as the continuation of God's enduring commitment to his people. Each verse in this psalm has the same refrain, "for his steadfast love endures forever"; one cannot miss the theme. Perhaps the psalm was to be sung responsively, with a priest leading with the first line of each verse, and a Levitical choir or the whole congregation replying with the refrain (cf. 2 Chron. 7:3, 6; Ezra 3:11).

3[y][See ver. 2 above]
4[z]See Ps. 72:18
5[a]Prov. 3:19; Jer. 10:12; 51:15 [b]See Gen. 1:1
6[c]Isa. 42:5; 44:24 [d]Ps. 24:2
7[e]Gen. 1:16
10[f]See Ps. 78:51
11[g]Ex. 12:51; 13:3
12[h]Deut. 4:34
13[i]See Ps. 78:13
14[j]Ex. 14:21, 22
15[k]Ex. 14:27; [Ps. 78:53]
16[l]Ex. 15:22; Deut. 8:15; See Ps. 77:20
17[m]For ver. 17-22, see Ps. 135:10-12

3 Give thanks to [y]the Lord of lords,
for his steadfast love endures forever;

4 to him who alone [z]does great wonders,
for his steadfast love endures forever;
5 to him who [a]by understanding [b]made the heavens,
for his steadfast love endures forever;
6 to him who [c]spread out the earth [d]above the waters,
for his steadfast love endures forever;
7 to him who [e]made the great lights,
for his steadfast love endures forever;
8 the sun to rule over the day,
for his steadfast love endures forever;
9 the moon and stars to rule over the night,
for his steadfast love endures forever;

10 to him who [f]struck down the firstborn of Egypt,
for his steadfast love endures forever;
11 and [g]brought Israel out from among them,
for his steadfast love endures forever;
12 with [h]a strong hand and an outstretched arm,
for his steadfast love endures forever;
13 to him who [i]divided the Red Sea in two,
for his steadfast love endures forever;
14 [j]and made Israel pass through the midst of it,
for his steadfast love endures forever;
15 but [k]overthrew[1] Pharaoh and his host in the Red Sea,
for his steadfast love endures forever;
16 to him who [l]led his people through the wilderness,
for his steadfast love endures forever;

17 to him [m]who struck down great kings,
for his steadfast love endures forever;
18 and killed mighty kings,
for his steadfast love endures forever;
19 Sihon, king of the Amorites,
for his steadfast love endures forever;
20 and Og, king of Bashan,
for his steadfast love endures forever;
21 and gave their land as a heritage,
for his steadfast love endures forever;

[1] Hebrew *shook off*

136:1–3 *Give Thanks to the One True God.* The song opens with its main thrust, to call God's people to **give thanks** to him: **he is good**, he is **the God of gods**, and he is **the Lord of lords**. As the psalm develops, it will be clear that this affirmation of the Lord's supremacy never makes him remote; instead, it shows why his **steadfast love**, which **endures forever**, is effective for his people.

136:1 Cf. 106:1; 107:1; 118:1, 29; 2 Chron. 5:13; Jer. 33:11. For **good** and **steadfast love**, see note on Ps. 100:5.

136:2–3 The titles **God of gods** and **Lord of lords** come from Deut. 10:17.

136:4–9 *Give Thanks to God for His Great Wonders in Creation.* In terms based mostly on Genesis 1, the next section celebrates the "wonders" that the Lord did in making the world. The OT is often at pains to remind God's people that the God who has redeemed them is also the very God who created the world. Sometimes that reminder is given to reassure the people of God's power; and sometimes (as here) that reminder is given so that the people will see their own lives in relation to God's continuing commitment to his creation.

136:4 wonders. Also translated "marvels," this word is usually applied to works of "redemption," i.e., to God's deeds of rescuing his people and protecting and caring for them (e.g., 9:1; 78:11; 98:1; Ex. 3:20; 34:10). Here it is applied specifically to creation, showing that God's creating work is wonderful, too.

136:10–16 *Give Thanks to God for Deliverance from Egypt.* The next section recounts, in terms based mostly on Exodus and Deuteronomy, how the Lord **brought Israel out from among** the Egyptians **with a strong hand and an outstretched arm**, and **led his people through the wilderness**. Echoing the Pentateuch (Ex. 15:13), these are clear deeds of **his steadfast love**.

136:17–22 *Give Thanks to God for Giving a Land to His People.* The next section recounts how God **struck down great kings** and **gave their land** to Israel **as a heritage**. The specific event here is the defeat of **Sihon** and **Og** (see note on 135:8–12).

22 a heritage to Israel his [n]servant,
for his steadfast love endures forever.

23 It is he who [o]remembered us in our low estate,
for his steadfast love endures forever;
24 and [p]rescued us from our foes,
for his steadfast love endures forever;
25 he who [q]gives food to all flesh,
for his steadfast love endures forever.

26 Give thanks to [r]the God of heaven,
for his steadfast love endures forever.

How Shall We Sing the LORD's Song?

137 1 By the waters of Babylon,
there we sat down and wept,
when we remembered Zion.
2 On the willows[1] there
we hung up our lyres.
3 For there our captors
required of us songs,
and our tormentors, mirth, saying,
"Sing us one of the songs of Zion!"

4 [s]How shall we sing the LORD's song
in a foreign land?
5 If I forget you, O Jerusalem,
[t]let my right hand forget its skill!
6 Let my [u]tongue stick to the roof of my mouth,
if I do not remember you,

[1] *Or poplars*

22[n]Ps. 105:6, 26
23[o]Gen. 8:1; [Deut. 32:36]
24[p]Ps. 107:2
25[q]Ps. 104:27; See Job 36:31
26[r]Ezra 5:12; Neh. 1:4; Dan. 2:18

Psalm 137

4[s][Neh. 2:3]
5[t][Ps. 76:5]
6[u]Job 29:10; Ezek. 3:26

136:22 Israel his servant. The people as a whole can be God's "servant" (cf. 1 Chron. 16:13; Isa. 41:8), and the individual members are "servants" (cf. Lev. 25:55).

136:23–26 *God Continues to Care for His People and for His Creation.* Now the song turns to an apparently more recent event, when the Lord **remembered us** (cf. 25:6–7 and note; 98:3; 106:45) **in our low estate,** and **rescued us from our foes**. Many think this is the return from exile, but even though that event would certainly qualify for this description, there is no easy way to date this psalm; thus there are many fresh instances of God's care for his people that put his **steadfast love** on display. The universal reference, **food to all flesh** (i.e., not just to Israel; cf. 104:27; 145:15), returns to the theme of the Lord as the universal Creator (136:4–9), whom it is Israel's privilege to serve.

136:26 *Give Thanks to the God of Heaven.* With the words **give thanks to the God of heaven**, the psalm returns to where it began (vv. 1–3). The title "God of heaven" is found in all periods of Israel's history (Gen. 24:7; Ezra 1:2; Neh. 1:4; Jonah 1:9).

Psalm 137. This community lament remembers the Babylonian captivity, and provides words by which the returned exiles can express their loyalty to Jerusalem and pray that God would pay out his just punishment on those who gloat over its destruction. This psalm is notable for the ferocity of its final wish (v. 9). This is a vivid application of the principle of *talion*, the principle that punishment should match the crime (Gen. 9:6; Ex. 21:23–24). It is a prayer that the Babylonians, who had smashed Israelite infants, should be punished appropriately. Three additional comments may be made. First, even though Babylon was the Lord's tool for disciplining his people, they apparently went about their work with cruel glee (cf. Isa. 47:6; cf. the Assyrians, Isa. 10:5–7). Second, the vile practice of destroying the infants of a conquered people is well-attested in the ancient world (e.g., 2 Kings 8:12; Hos. 10:14; 13:16; Nah. 3:10; Homer's *Iliad* 22.63), and was therefore foretold of the fall of Babylon (Isa. 13:16). Further, the Babylonians had apparently done this to the Judeans (as the connection with Ps. 137:8 suggests), and the prophets led the people to await God's justice (Isa. 47:1–9; Jer. 51:24). In this light, the psalm is not endorsing the action in itself but is instead seeing the conquerors of Babylon as carrying out God's just sentence (even unwittingly). Neither Israelites nor Christians are permitted to indulge personal hatred and vengeance (cf. Lev. 19:17–18; Matt. 5:44); generally speaking, the repentance of those who hate God's people is preferred (see note on Ps. 83:9–18), and yet, failing that, any prayer for God's justice (and for Christ's return) will involve punishment for those who have oppressed his people (cf. Rev. 6:9–10).

137:1–3 *Our Sadness as Captives in Babylon.* The opening section recalls the captivity **by the waters of Babylon** (the Euphrates River, several streams and canals), where the Babylonian captors had **required of us songs**. The **songs of Zion** would be sacred songs (such as the psalms), and apparently the **captors** wanted the Judeans to sing them for entertainment (and perhaps gloating) rather than for worship.

137:1 sat down and wept. The past tense distances the singers from these events, which favors the conclusion that the psalm comes from after the exile.

137:2 willows. Or "poplars" (cf. ESV footnote). In either case this kind of tree grows beside flowing water.

137:4–6 *May We Never Forget Jerusalem.* To a pious Judean, the request of v. 3 would be like asking him to **forget . . . Jerusalem**, which would be an act of treachery against God, his covenant, and his people. His prayer is that if he should consent to such treachery, the very **right hand** that would play the lyre would instead **forget its skill**, and the **tongue** that might

7 [v]Isa. 34:5, 6; Lam. 4:21, 22; Ezek. 35:2; [Amos 1:11, 12]; See Jer. 49:7-22; Ezek. 25:12-14; Obad. 8-14 [w]See Job 18:20 [x]Hab. 3:13; Zeph. 2:14
8 [y]Isa. 21:9; 47:1-15; Jer. 25:12; 50:1-46; 51:1-64; See Isa. 13:1-22 [z]Jer. 51:24, 56; [Ps. 28:4]
9 [a]2 Kgs. 8:12; Isa. 13:16; Hos. 10:14; Nah. 3:10

Psalm 138

1 [b]Ps. 111:1 [c]Ps. 95:3; 96:5
2 [d]Ps. 28:2; 1 Kgs. 8:29 [e]Ps. 5:7
4 [f]See Ps. 102:15
5 [g]Ps. 103:7
6 [h][Ps. 131:1; Prov. 3:34; Luke 1:48; James 4:6]; See Ps. 113:5, 6
7 [i][Ps. 23:4] [j]See Ps. 71:20 [k][1 Sam. 24:6; Job 1:12] [l]Ps. 60:5

if I do not set Jerusalem
above my highest joy!

7 Remember, O LORD, against the [v]Edomites
[w]the day of Jerusalem,
how they said, [x]"Lay it bare, lay it bare,
down to its foundations!"
8 O daughter of Babylon, [y]doomed to be destroyed,
blessed shall he be who [z]repays you
with what you have done to us!
9 Blessed shall he be who takes your little ones
and [a]dashes them against the rock!

Give Thanks to the LORD

138

OF DAVID.

1 [b]I give you thanks, O LORD, with my whole heart;
before [c]the gods I sing your praise;
2 I bow down [d]toward your [e]holy temple
and give thanks to your name for your steadfast love and your faithfulness,
for you have exalted above all things
your name and your word.[1]
3 On the day I called, you answered me;
my strength of soul you increased.[2]

4 [f]All the kings of the earth shall give you thanks, O LORD,
for they have heard the words of your mouth,
5 and they shall sing of [g]the ways of the LORD,
for great is the glory of the LORD.
6 [h]For though the LORD is high, he regards the lowly,
but the haughty he knows from afar.

7 [i]Though I walk in the midst of trouble,
you [j]preserve my life;
you [k]stretch out your hand against the wrath of my enemies,
and your [l]right hand delivers me.

[1] *Or you have exalted your word above all your name* [2] Hebrew *you made me bold in my soul with strength*

sing would instead **stick to the roof of my mouth** (cf. Job 29:10; Lam. 4:4; Ezek. 3:26).

137:7–9 *May the Lord Repay Those Who Destroyed Jerusalem.* The recollection of these hurtful taunts leads to a prayer that God will **remember** (see note on 25:6–7) the deeds of his people's enemies; he selects the **Edomites** (a conventional representative of all those who hate God's people, as in Obadiah) as well as the **daughter of Babylon** (the personified city). The Edomites took great delight in destroying Jerusalem utterly (cf. Obad. 11–14), while the Babylonians had carried out excessive violence against the helpless in Jerusalem. (On Ps. 137:9, see note on Psalm 137.)

Psalm 138. This psalm provides a way of offering thanks to God for signs of his constant care. The mention of the "holy temple" (v. 2) has led some to connect the psalm specifically to a thank-offering, which is reasonable (cf. Jer. 33:11). Psalms 138–145 are the final collection of psalms attributed to David.

138:1–3 *I Will Give God Thanks for Answering My Prayer.* The opening section explains the theme: **I give you thanks** because **on the day I called, you answered me.**

138:1 before the gods. This may well refer to the angels, as the Greek Septuagint took it (see 8:5 and note; 29:1). Others suppose these are human rulers (see note on 82:1), while still others think these are false deities. Since the setting is worship in the temple (138:2), the first option is most likely (cf. 1 Cor. 11:10).

138:2 give thanks to your name. See note on 135:1. **you have exalted above all things your name and your word**. As the ESV footnote indicates, the Hebrew is difficult; the ESV text is more likely than the footnote, though: the particular experience for which the psalm gives thanks shows that God has "exalted" his "name" (to which the singer gives thanks) and his "word" (i.e., his word of promise to care for his servants).

138:4–6 *The Lord Is High, and Looks on the Lowly.* The very personal experience of God's help is now put in perspective: the God to whom the singer had prayed is the universal Lord (he **is high**), to whom all the Gentiles will one day come in worship (**all the kings of the earth shall give you thanks**; cf. 102:15; Isa. 52:15); and yet **he regards the lowly** person (such as the one giving thanks in this psalm).

138:7–8 *The Lord Preserves Me through All Troubles.* The psalm closes by telling of God's constant care for each of his faithful. It is not easy for even the most faithful believer to be mindful of this care at all times, and singing this will help the members of the congregation be more aware of the ways in which God preserves and protects them.

8 The LORD will [m]fulfill his purpose for me;
[n]your steadfast love, O LORD, endures forever.
Do not forsake [o]the work of your hands.

Search Me, O God, and Know My Heart

139

TO THE CHOIRMASTER. A PSALM OF DAVID.

1 O LORD, you have [p]searched me and known me!
2 You [q]know when I sit down and when I rise up;
you [r]discern my thoughts from afar.
3 You search out my path and my lying down
and are acquainted with all my ways.
4 Even before a word is on my tongue,
behold, O LORD, [s]you know it altogether.
5 You [t]hem me in, behind and before,
and [u]lay your hand upon me.
6 [v]Such knowledge is [w]too wonderful for me;
it is high; I cannot attain it.

7 [x]Where shall I go from your Spirit?
Or where [y]shall I flee from your presence?
8 [z]If I ascend to heaven, you are there!
[a]If I make my bed in Sheol, you are there!
9 If I take the wings of the morning
and dwell in the uttermost parts of the sea,
10 even there your hand shall [b]lead me,
and your right hand shall hold me.
11 If I say, [c]"Surely the darkness shall cover me,
and the light about me be night,"
12 [d]even the darkness is not dark to you;
the night is bright as the day,
for darkness is as light with you.

13 For you [e]formed my inward parts;
you [f]knitted me together in my mother's womb.
14 I praise you, for I am fearfully and wonderfully made.[1]

[1] Or *for I am fearfully set apart*

8 [m]Ps. 57:2; [Phil. 1:6] [n]Ps. 136:1; See 1 Chr. 16:41 [o]See Ps. 100:3

Psalm 139

1 [p]Jer. 12:3; See Ps. 7:9; 17:3; 44:21
2 [q]2 Kgs. 19:27; Lam. 3:63 [r][Job 14:16; 31:4; Matt. 9:4; John 2:24, 25]
4 [s]Heb. 4:13
5 [t]Job 19:8 [u]Job 9:33
6 [v]Rom. 11:33 [w]Job 42:3
7 [x][Jer. 23:24] [y]Jonah 1:3
8 [z][Amos 9:2] [a][Job 26:6]
10 [b]ver. 24; Ps. 23:3
11 [c][Job 22:14]
12 [d]Job 34:22; [Dan. 2:22]
13 [e]Deut. 32:6 [f][Job 10:11]

138:8 fulfill his purpose for me. As God has begun to care for me, so he will finish the job all my life long (cf. 57:2).

Psalm 139. In this hymn the closing request ("search me, O God, and know my heart") echoes the opening statement ("you have searched me and known me"). The key word of the psalm is "know": God knows (vv. 1, 2, 4, 6, 23), and the faithful soul knows (v. 14). These features highlight the Psalm's theme: God's intimate knowledge of his people (a theme that vv. 1–6 begins). Then vv. 7–12 declare that there is no place one can go to get away from that knowledge, and vv. 13–16 illustrate the point by describing life in a very dark place (the mother's womb). Verses 17–18 exclaim how delightful this "knowledge of God's knowledge" is; vv. 19–22 affirm the singer's loyalty to the Lord; and vv. 23–24 invite God to continue examining the singer's inner life, in order to purge it from all that hinders him from walking in "the way everlasting."

139:1–6 *The Lord Knows All There Is to Know about Me.* Verse 1 states the theme of the whole psalm (**you have searched me and known me**), and vv. 2–6 develop that further as a general assertion: God knows all of my activities, all of my words, even my inmost thoughts. The response (v. 6) is, **such knowledge is too wonderful for me**, i.e., beyond my ability to comprehend (see note on "too marvelous," 131:1–2).

139:5 lay your hand upon me. A gentle gesture (cf. Gen. 48:14, 17), giving reassurance.

139:7–12 *There Is No Place I Can Be Hidden from Your View.* The next section makes it clear that there is no way the singer can escape such knowledge: there is nowhere in the universe that God will not be present to **lead** and **hold** the believer (vv. 7–10), and nowhere too **dark** for God to see him (vv. 11–12). Some have supposed that the impulse to **flee** (v. 7) comes from a guilty conscience, or from a desire for independence, but this is unlikely: these verses take delight in the fact that God will "lead" him, an entirely positive benefit (cf. v. 24; 23:3; 73:24; 143:10), and "hold" him (cf. 73:23). There is no place where he is beyond God's care (see 139:5).

139:8–9 These verses use two pairs of opposites: **heaven** and **Sheol**; **the wings of the morning** (i.e., the farthest east, where the sun rises) and **the uttermost parts of the sea** (i.e., the far end of the Mediterranean, to the west of Israel). This rhetorical device, using two polar opposites, indicates that everything in between is included.

139:13–16 *You Even Saw and Loved Me before I Was Born.* These verses illustrate the point of vv. 11–12 (the section begins with **for**, showing the connection to the previous) by describing a particular "dark place" where the Lord saw and cared for the singer, namely, his **mother's womb**. God was active as the **unformed substance** (embryo) grew and developed; indeed he is the one who **formed my inward parts** and **knitted me together**. God **saw** him, and even had **written** in his **book**, **every one of . . . the days that were formed for me**. The worshiper realizes that, even before his mother knew she was pregnant, the Lord was already showing his care for him. His personal life began in the womb (see note on 51:5), and God had already laid out its course.

139:14 I am fearfully and wonderfully made. If the ESV text is followed,

14[g]See Ps. 72:18
15[h][Job 10:8-10; Eccles. 11:5] [i]Ps. 63:9
16[j]Ps. 56:8
17[k]Ps. 92:5
18[l]Ps. 40:5 [m]Gen. 22:17
19[n]Isa. 11:4; [Ps. 9:17] [o]Ps. 5:6 [p]See Ps. 6:8
20[q][Jude 15] [r]Ex. 20:7
21[s]See Ps. 26:5 [t]Ps. 119:158 [u]Ps. 59:1
23[v]Ps. 26:2
24[w]ver. 10 [x][Jer. 6:16; 18:15]

Psalm 140

1[y]Ps. 71:4; 119:153, 170 [z]Ps. 18:48; Prov. 3:31
2[a]See Ps. 56:6

[g]Wonderful are your works;
my soul knows it very well.
15 [h]My frame was not hidden from you,
when I was being made in secret,
intricately woven in [i]the depths of the earth.
16 Your eyes saw my unformed substance;
in your [j]book were written, every one of them,
the days that were formed for me,
when as yet there was none of them.

17 How precious to me are your [k]thoughts, O God!
How vast is the sum of them!
18 [l]If I would count them, they are more than [m]the sand.
I awake, and I am still with you.

19 Oh that you would [n]slay the wicked, O God!
O [o]men of blood, [p]depart from me!
20 They [q]speak against you with malicious intent;
your enemies [r]take your name in vain.[1]
21 [s]Do I not hate those who hate you, O LORD?
And do I not [t]loathe those who [u]rise up against you?
22 I hate them with complete hatred;
I count them my enemies.

23 Search me, O God, and know my heart!
[v]Try me and know my thoughts![2]
24 And see if there be any grievous way in me,
and [w]lead me in [x]the way everlasting![3]

Deliver Me, O LORD, from Evil Men

140

TO THE CHOIRMASTER. A PSALM OF DAVID.

1 [y]Deliver me, O LORD, from evil men;
preserve me from [z]violent men,
2 who plan evil things in their heart
and [a]stir up wars continually.

[1] Hebrew lacks *your name* [2] Or *cares* [3] Or *in the ancient way* (compare Jeremiah 6:16)

the statement helps the worshiper to marvel over the mysterious process of a developing baby. The word translated "wonderfully made" (Hb. *nipleti*) has a slightly unusual spelling (the expected spelling is *niple'ti*), which favors the ESV footnote: "I am fearfully set apart." This takes the word to be the term for God setting his people apart (Ex. 8:22; Ps. 4:3) or making a distinction between them and those who are not his people (Ex. 9:4; 11:7; 33:16). The faithful person singing this, who in the OT would be the child of faithful parents, can affirm that God set his special love upon him from the earliest stages of his personal life (cf. Ps. 22:9–10; 71:5–6).

139:15 in the depths of the earth. As a parallel to **in secret**, this would be a poetic expression for the darkness and secrecy of the womb.

139:17–18 *How Precious Are Your Thoughts to Me!* These verses provide the right response to the **vast** extent of God's **thoughts** (cf. v. 6). Verse 18 seems to picture the hopelessness of trying to **count** God's thoughts: the number is so large that one would fall asleep; and even so, God will not abandon his faithful (**I awake, and I am still with you**).

139:19–22 *Please Slay the Wicked!* Sadly, not everyone delights in God and in his knowledge and presence: the **wicked** person, who joins with **men of blood** (i.e., who ruthlessly shed blood), who **speak against** God **with malicious intent**, is someone who actively opposes God and his gracious purpose (see note on 1:1). When God displays his justice in the earth, if these people will not repent, he will indeed **slay** them; until then, the faithful do not want to be identified with them (**depart from me**); cf. note on 104:31–35. This loyalty to God goes so far as to own God's attitudes (5:5; 11:7; see notes on 31:6 and 119:113; cf. 26:5; 101:3).

139:23–24 *Search Me, O God!* In view of these reflections, the members of the congregation invite God to continue his work of "searching" and "knowing" their hearts. This will expose any **grievous way** (i.e., aspects of character that lead to grief) and will **lead** the faithful **in the way everlasting** (i.e., the way that God loves; cf. 1:6).

Psalm 140. This individual lament serves the needs of people under threat from ungodly people who intend serious harm (cf. Psalms 5; 35; 54; 56; 59; 69; 70; 71; 109). The psalm does not clarify whether these ungodly people are Israelites, but this is the most likely identification in a psalm of David. This psalm, in praying for protection (140:1–5) and expressing trust (vv. 6–8), also prays for the defeat of these enemies (vv. 9–11) and looks forward to God's display of his justice (vv. 12–13).

140:1–5 *Deliver Me from the Plots of the Wicked!* The basic request is clear from the verbs **deliver** (v. 1), **preserve** (vv. 1, 4), and **guard** (v. 4). The threat is from **evil men**, who are further defined as **violent men** and **the arrogant**, who **plan evil things**. These enemies prefer wickedness to godliness, and they pose a serious danger to the faithful.

140:1 For the connection of "evil" (or "wickedness") with "violence," cf. 11:5; Prov. 4:17; 10:6, 11.

3 They make [b]their tongue sharp as [c]a serpent's,
and [d]under their lips is the [e]venom of asps. *Selah*

4 Guard me, O LORD, from the hands of the wicked;
preserve me from [z]violent men,
who have planned to trip up my feet.
5 The arrogant have [f]hidden a trap for me,
and with cords they have spread [g]a net;[1]
beside the way they have set [h]snares for me. *Selah*

6 [i]I say to the LORD, You are my God;
give ear to [j]the voice of my pleas for mercy, O LORD!
7 O LORD, my Lord, [k]the strength of my salvation,
you have covered my head in the day of battle.
8 [l]Grant not, O LORD, the desires of the wicked;
do not further their[2] evil plot, or [m]they will be exalted! *Selah*

9 As for the head of those who surround me,
let [n]the mischief of their lips overwhelm them!
10 Let [o]burning coals fall upon them!
Let them be cast into fire,
into miry pits, no more to rise!
11 Let not the slanderer be established in the land;
let evil hunt down the violent man speedily!

12 I know that the LORD will [p]maintain the cause of the afflicted,
and [q]will execute justice for the needy.
13 Surely [r]the righteous shall give thanks to your name;
[s]the upright shall dwell in your presence.

Give Ear to My Voice

141

A PSALM OF DAVID.

1 O LORD, I call upon you; [t]hasten to me!
Give ear to my voice when I call to you!
2 Let [u]my prayer be counted as incense before you,
and [v]the lifting up of my hands as [w]the evening sacrifice!

3 [x]Set a guard, O LORD, over my mouth;
[y]keep watch over the door of my lips!

3[b][Ps. 52:2] [c]Ps. 58:4 [d]Ps. 10:7 [e]Cited Rom. 3:13
4[z][See ver. 1 above]
5[f]Ps. 35:7; 141:9; 142:3; Jer. 18:22 [g]Job 18:8-10 [h]Ps. 64:5
6[i]Ps. 142:5 [j]Ps. 28:2; 31:22; 130:2
7[k]Ps. 28:8
8[l][Ps. 35:25] [m]Isa. 14:21
9[n][Prov. 12:13; 18:7]; See Ps. 7:16
10[o][Ps. 11:6; 18:13]
12[p]Ps. 9:4 [q]1 Kgs. 8:45, 49, 59
13[r][Ps. 64:10] [s][Ps. 11:7]

Psalm 141

1[t]Ps. 40:13; 70:5
2[u]Luke 1:10; Rev. 5:8; 8:3, 4 [v]See Ps. 28:2 [w]See Ex. 29:41
3[x]Ps. 34:13 [y]Mic. 7:5

[1] *Or they have spread cords as a net* [2] Hebrew *his*

140:3 under their lips is the venom of asps. In Rom. 3:13 Paul uses this phrase as part of his argument that Jews and Greeks are alike "under sin."

140:6–8 *O LORD, My Strength, Hear Me!* The right response to such danger is to reaffirm trust in God, and to ask him for help. Specifically, the singer asks God not to allow **the wicked** to have their **desires**.

140:6 You are my God. The Lord is the covenant God of Israel, but with these words the faithful worshiper affirms that he has personally laid hold of God's love.

140:7 salvation. See note on 3:2.

140:9–11 *Let Their Schemes Recoil on Them!* These verses pray that the evil schemes would recoil on the heads of those who plot them (cf. note on 94:23). On the nature of these "curses," see notes on 5:10; 35:4–8; 109:6–20. The success of such people would defile the **land**.

140:12–13 *I Am Confident that the Lord Will Protect Me.* The psalm closes, as many laments do, by expressing confidence in the Lord (he **will maintain the cause of the afflicted, and will execute justice**; cf. note on vv. 9–11) and by guiding the faithful in what they can expect (**give thanks to your name** and **dwell in your presence**).

Psalm 141. This is an individual lament, geared to a situation much like that of Psalm 140. The particular contribution of this psalm is its earnest prayer for God to protect the faithful person against all insincerity and compromise amid such dangers.

141:1–2 *O Lord, Hear My Prayer.* The singer earnestly asks God to **give ear to my voice when I call to you!** The **prayer** that he offers, which is sung in corporate worship, is likened to sacrificial acts that are also performed in worship: the **incense** (Ex. 30:8; Luke 1:10; cf. the image in Rev. 5:8) and the **evening sacrifice** (Ex. 29:41). On **the lifting up of my hands** in worship, cf. Ps. 28:2; 63:4; 119:48; 134:2.

141:3–5 *Keep Me from Taking Part in Their Evil.* The singer may be inclined to avoid danger by joining the **men who work iniquity**, and this section asks God to help him avoid all such temptation. The request of v. 3, **set a guard, O LORD, over my mouth**, is probably to be taken in that light: it is a prayer that God would protect the faithful from playing along with schemers in speech who betray the Lord and his godly ones. While the faithful person will accept correction from others of the faithful, his **prayer is continually against** the **evil deeds** of the schemers. This prayer reveals great insight into how a person in these circumstances would actually feel.

4 [z]Do not let my heart incline to any evil,
to busy myself with wicked deeds
in company with men who [a]work iniquity,
and [b]let me not eat of their delicacies!

5 [c]Let a righteous man strike me—it is a kindness;
let him rebuke me—it is oil for my head;
let my head not refuse it.
Yet [d]my prayer is continually against their evil deeds.
6 When their judges are [e]thrown over the cliff,[1]
then they shall hear my words, for they are pleasant.
7 As when one plows and breaks up the earth,
so shall our bones [f]be scattered at the mouth of Sheol.[2]

8 But [g]my eyes are toward you, O GOD, my Lord;
[h]in you I seek refuge; leave me not defenseless![3]
9 Keep me from [i]the trap that they have laid for me
and from the snares of evildoers!
10 Let the wicked [j]fall into their own nets,
while I pass by safely.

You Are My Refuge

142

A MASKIL[4] OF DAVID, WHEN HE WAS IN [k]THE CAVE. A PRAYER.

1 With my voice I [l]cry out to the LORD;
with my voice I [m]plead for mercy to the LORD.
2 I [n]pour out my complaint before him;
I tell my trouble before him.

3 When my spirit [o]faints within me,
you know my way!
In the path where I walk
they have [p]hidden a trap for me.
4 [q]Look to the [r]right and see:
[s]there is none who takes notice of me;
[t]no refuge remains to me;
no one cares for my soul.

5 I cry to you, O LORD;
I say, "You are my [u]refuge,
my [v]portion in [w]the land of the living."

4 [z]Ps. 119:36 [a]ver. 9; Ps. 94:4 [b]Prov. 23:6
5 [c][Prov. 9:8; 19:25; 25:12; 27:6; Eccles. 7:5] [d][Ps. 109:4]
6 [e]2 Chr. 25:12; [Luke 4:29]
7 [f]Ps. 53:5; [Ezek. 37:1]
8 [g]Ps. 25:15 [h]See Ps. 11:1
9 [i]See Ps. 140:5
10 [j][Ps. 7:15]

Psalm 142
[k]Ps. 57, title
1 [l]Ps. 3:4 [m]Ps. 30:8
2 [n][Isa. 26:16]; See Ps. 102, title
3 [o]See Ps. 77:3 [p]Ps. 140:5
4 [q]Ps. 69:20 [r]Ps. 16:8 [s][Ps. 31:11] [t]Job 11:20; Jer. 25:35
5 [u]See Ps. 14:6 [v]Ps. 16:5 [w]Ps. 27:13

[1] Or *When their judges fall into the hands of the Rock* [2] The meaning of the Hebrew in verses 6, 7 is uncertain [3] Hebrew *refuge; do not pour out my life!*
[4] Probably a musical or liturgical term

141:5 strike me . . . rebuke me. Cf. Prov. 27:5–6.

141:6–7 *Judgment Shall Overtake Them at Last.* As the ESV footnote explains, the Hebrew of these verses presents some difficulties. The ESV text is a reasonable rendering; the main point is that eventually God will bring his judgment upon the **judges** (apparently the leaders among the ungodly schemers); then the faithful person will be vindicated, and the unfaithful might even learn wisdom (**they shall hear my words, for they are pleasant**).

141:8–10 *I Trust You to Keep Me Safe.* In the meanwhile, the faithful keep the **eyes** of their hearts looking **toward** God in trust. Verses 9–10 reveal that the **evildoers** (introduced in v. 4) are laying schemes to harm the faithful (**trap**, **snares**, and **nets**). The prayer that God would **keep me** from falling prey to their schemes becomes a prayer that the **wicked** would "fall into their own nets" (cf. 140:9–11 and note).

Psalm 142. This individual lament, with its title that refers to David being "in the cave," is a companion to Psalm 57 (see note on Psalm 57). It is also similar to Psalms 140–141, the faithful person praying for protection from persecutors. Unlike the previous two psalms, this one has no prayers for the enemies' downfall (and thus is like Psalm 143).

142:1–2 *I Pour out My Complaint before the Lord.* The words here express earnest prayer in the face of imminent danger: **cry out**, **plead for mercy**, **pour out my complaint**, and **tell my trouble**. Each of these acts is directed toward the Lord, upon whom the worshiper depends.

142:3–4 *I Have None to Trust but You.* These verses express what people often feel in the kind of situation for which this psalm is geared: out of energy (**my spirit faints within me**; see note on 143:4), beset by dangers and confused (**they have hidden a trap for me**), and painfully alone (**none who takes notice of me, no one cares for my soul**). There is the reminder, **you know my way** (cf. 1:6), which the next section will develop.

142:5–7 *Deliver Me from My Persecutors.* The final section ties the whole psalm together. In v. 5, **cry to you** echoes v. 1, while **you are my refuge** echoes v. 4 ("no refuge," using a synonym); and **I am brought very low** (v. 6) summarizes vv. 3–4. This section enables the faithful to pray with boldness and with confidence in the Lord's unflagging care. The person praying recognizes how he should respond when he sees the answer (**that I may give thanks to your name**) and expects all the **righteous** to rejoice with him (as often is the case in the psalms, personal experiences of blessing profit the whole people; cf. notes on 109:30–31 and 116:12–19).

6 [x]Attend to my cry,
for [y]I am brought very low!
Deliver me from my persecutors,
[z]for they are too strong for me!
7 [a]Bring me out of prison,
that I may give thanks to your name!
The righteous will surround me,
for you will [b]deal bountifully with me.

My Soul Thirsts for You

143

A PSALM OF DAVID.

1 Hear my prayer, O LORD;
[c]give ear to my pleas for mercy!
In your [d]faithfulness answer me, in your [d]righteousness!
2 [e]Enter not into judgment with your servant,
for no one living is righteous [f]before you.

3 For the enemy has pursued my soul;
[g]he has crushed my life to the ground;
[h]he has made me sit in darkness like those long dead.
4 Therefore my spirit [i]faints within me;
my heart within me is appalled.

5 [j]I remember the days of old;
[k]I meditate on all that you have done;
I ponder the work of your hands.
6 [l]I stretch out my hands to you;
[m]my soul thirsts for you like [n]a parched land. *Selah*

7 [o]Answer me quickly, O LORD!
[p]My spirit fails!
[q]Hide not your face from me,
[r]lest I be like those who go down to the pit.
8 [s]Let me hear in the morning of your steadfast love,
for in you I [t]trust.
[u]Make me know the way I should go,
[v]for to you I lift up my soul.

9 [w]Deliver me from my enemies, O LORD!
I have fled to you for refuge.[1]

[1] One Hebrew manuscript, Septuagint; most Hebrew manuscripts *To you I have covered*

6 [x]Ps. 17:1 [y]Ps. 79:8 [z]Ps. 18:17
7 [a]Isa. 42:7; [Ps. 143:11] [b]Ps. 13:6

Psalm 143
1 [c]Ps. 140:6 [d]1 John 1:9; [Ps. 31:1]
2 [e][Job 14:3] [f]Ps. 130:3; 1 Kgs. 8:46; Job 9:2; 15:14; 25:4; Eccles. 7:20; Rom. 3:23; 1 Cor. 4:4
3 [g]See Ps. 88:3-6 [h]Lam. 3:6
4 [i]See Ps. 77:3
5 [j]Ps. 77:5, 11 [k]Ps. 77:12; 111:2
6 [l]See Job 11:13 [m]Ps. 42:2 [n][Ps. 63:1]
7 [o]Ps. 69:17; 102:2 [p][Ps. 84:2] [q]Ps. 27:9 [r]Ps. 28:1; 88:4
8 [s][Ps. 90:14] [t]Ps. 11:1; 25:2 [u]Ps. 25:4 [v]Ps. 25:1
9 [w]Ps. 59:1; 142:6

Psalm 143. This individual lament is suited to a situation in which the person's troubles make him aware of his own sins (v. 2); it is thus classified as a "penitential psalm" (see note on Psalm 130), of which its nearest kin are Psalms 6 and 38.

143:1–2 *Hear Me, and Do Not Put Me on Trial.* The opening cry for help asks God to **give ear to my pleas for mercy**; the person praying here is aware of his own sins that would warrant God forsaking him. Hence v. 2 prays, **enter not into judgment with your servant, for no one living** (and thus the person praying) **is righteous before you**. The term "righteous" is commonly used in the Psalms to describe either the people of God in general (e.g., 125:3) or especially the faithful within the people (e.g., 140:13). Here, however, the idea seems to be "qualified to stand in God's presence" (cf. Rom. 4:9–11), and not even the faithful are that in themselves (cf. note on Ps. 32:6–11). Therefore the "mercy" that the singer prays for is not only relief from the immediate situation but God's merciful acceptance of him.

143:3–4 *I Am Faint because the Enemy Pursues Me.* The next section describes how the enemy's pursuit has drained him of all vigor (cf. 142:3–4).

143:4 my spirit faints. When the "spirit" or "soul" is said to "faint," the person is at the end of his strength and ability to strive: 77:3; 107:5; 142:3; Isa. 57:16; Jonah 2:7.

143:5–6 *I Reach Out to You in Trust.* Being at the end of his strength need not mean that he gives up; instead, if he can **remember the days of old** (i.e., the great deeds God has done for his people as a whole and for so many needy individuals in the past), he can have fresh courage to **stretch out** his **hands to** God. The weary **soul thirsts for** God as its source of energy.

143:7–8 *Answer Me Quickly!* The situation is still dire, and the person praying is still desperate; therefore he asks, **answer me quickly**. He wants to **hear in the morning of** God's **steadfast love**—whatever time of day he prays, he looks for reassurance soon! The specific relief may take longer, but the reminder of God's steadfast love enables him to endure (cf. v. 12). He also prays for moral guidance: **make me know the way I should go** (see 25:4–5 and note; Ex. 18:20). The expression **lift up my soul** is one of deep dependence and allegiance (cf. Ps. 24:4; 25:1); the same expression in Deut. 24:15 is rendered "he counts on it."

143:9–12 *Deliver Me, and Teach Me to Do Your Will.* The prayer closes by repeating the request for deliverance (vv. 9, 11) and for guidance (v. 10; cf. v. 8), expressing trust in a number of ways: **I have fled to you for refuge** (v. 9), **you are my God** (v. 10; see note on 140:6), and the expectation

10[x][Ps. 119:12] [y]Neh. 9:20 [z]See Ps. 23:3 [a]Isa. 26:10; [Ps. 27:11]
11[b]Ps. 23:3; 25:11 [c]See Ps. 71:20 [d]Ps. 142:7
12[e]Ps. 54:5 [f]See Ps. 116:16
Psalm 144
1[g]See Ps. 18:2, 31, 46 [h]Ps. 18:34
2[i][Ps. 59:10, 17; Jonah 2:8] [j]Ps. 18:2; 91:2 [k]Ps. 18:2; 59:9 [l]Ps. 7:10; 18:2 [m]Ps. 18:47
3[n]See Ps. 8:4 [o]See Ps. 31:7
4[p]Ps. 39:5 [q]Ps. 102:11; 109:23 [r]Job 8:9
5[s]Ps. 18:9; [Isa. 64:1] [t]See Ps. 104:32
6[u]See Ps. 18:14
7[v]Ps. 18:16 [w]Ps. 69:14 [x]Ps. 18:44, 45
8[y]Ps. 12:2; 41:6 [z][Ps. 106:26; Gen. 14:22; Deut. 32:40; Isa. 62:8]
9[a]Ps. 33:2, 3

10 [x]Teach me to do your will,
for you are my God!
[y]Let your good Spirit [z]lead me
on [a]level ground!

11 [b]For your name's sake, O LORD, [c]preserve my life!
In your righteousness [d]bring my soul out of trouble!
12 And in your steadfast love you will [e]cut off my enemies,
and you will destroy all the adversaries of my soul,
for I am your [f]servant.

My Rock and My Fortress

144 OF DAVID.
1 Blessed be the LORD, my [g]rock,
[h]who trains my hands for war,
and my fingers for battle;
2 he is my [i]steadfast love and my [j]fortress,
my [k]stronghold and my deliverer,
my [l]shield and he in whom I take refuge,
who [m]subdues peoples[1] under me.

3 O LORD, [n]what is man that you [o]regard him,
or the son of man that you think of him?
4 [p]Man is like a breath;
his days are like [q]a passing [r]shadow.

5 [s]Bow your heavens, O LORD, and come down!
[t]Touch the mountains so that they smoke!
6 [u]Flash forth the lightning and scatter them;
[u] send out your arrows and rout them!
7 [v]Stretch out your hand from on high;
[w]rescue me and deliver me from the many waters,
from the hand [x]of foreigners,
8 whose mouths speak [y]lies
and whose right hand is [z]a right hand of falsehood.

9 I will sing [a]a new song to you, O God;
upon [a]a ten-stringed harp I will play to you,

[1] Many Hebrew manuscripts, Dead Sea Scroll, Jerome, Syriac, Aquila; most Hebrew manuscripts *subdues my people*

based on God's **steadfast love** (143:12). The appeal in v. 11, **for your name's sake,** means "for the sake of your good reputation," particularly God's reputation for faithfulness to his promises (see how **righteousness** is in parallel): the singer wants everyone else to know that those who have fled to God for refuge have a sure protection in him.

Psalm 144. This royal psalm asks for God to give victory to the reigning heir of David, which will lead to a condition of blessing for his people. The "I" in vv. 1–11 is the Davidic king, and "our" in vv. 12–14 is the whole people. God's promise to the house of David (2 Sam. 7:4–17) has tied the well-being of the whole people to the faithfulness of the reigning heir of David (see notes on Psalms 18; 89; 132). When God's faithful people sing this, they are praying for the success of this arrangement, so that the people might flourish under God's blessing. Christians, who recognize Jesus as the final heir of David, pray that God will protect his people from persecutors, will further the expansion of the people, and will prosper the faithful in their daily lives.

144:1–2 *The Lord Prospers the King in His Warfare.* With echoes of Psalm 18, this psalm begins by reviewing how God has equipped the king to fight for the sake of the people (**trains my hands for war, and my fingers for battle**). As the leader of God's people (like Psalms 20–21), the singer has found the Lord to be his **stronghold** and **deliverer**, who in his blessing **subdues peoples under me**.

144:2 my steadfast love. That is, "my hope of steadfast love"; cf. Jonah 2:8, where "their hope of steadfast love" is lit., "their steadfast love." **Peoples** (Hb. *'ammim*) could be "my people" (Hb. *'ammi*; see ESV footnote). Though this latter reading has more textual support, the many parallels with Psalm 18 (cf. 18:47) support the reading of the ESV text.

144:3–4 *How Can You Take Notice of Mankind?* The king does not take God's help for granted. He knows that if God should **regard him**, it is a condescension (cf. 8:4): he, and the people he serves, are **like a breath** (cf. 39:5); their lives quickly pass by.

144:5–8 *Come Down and Rescue Me from the Foreigners!* After the review of God's faithfulness and condescension, the psalm moves on to request: **rescue me and deliver me . . . from the hand of foreigners**. These words suggest that the psalm is especially suited to a time when the king must again lead the people in war, when Gentiles would conquer and oppress them. It was not true of all Gentiles that their **mouths speak lies**, and those who lead God's people in worship must be careful to guard against mere nationalism.

144:9–11 *Rescue Me, That I May Sing Your Praises.* The song looks to the future: once God has given the deliverance of vv. 5–8, the king (**David his servant**) will lead the people in public thanks (on the **new song** and the

10 who gives victory to kings,
who [b]rescues David his servant from the cruel sword.
11 Rescue me and deliver me
from the hand [x]of foreigners,
whose mouths speak [y]lies
and whose right hand is a right hand of falsehood.
12 May our sons in their youth
be like [c]plants full grown,
our daughters like [d]corner pillars
cut for the structure of a palace;
13 [e]may our granaries be full,
[f]providing all kinds of produce;
may our sheep bring forth thousands
and ten thousands in our fields;
14 may our cattle be heavy with young,
suffering no mishap or failure in bearing;[1]
may there be no [g]cry of distress in our streets!
15 [h]Blessed are the people to whom such blessings fall!
[i]Blessed are the people whose God is the LORD!

Great Is the LORD

145[2] A SONG OF PRAISE. OF DAVID.
1 [j]I will extol you, my God and [k]King,
and bless your name forever and ever.
2 Every day I will bless you
[l]and praise your name forever and ever.
3 [m]Great is the LORD, and greatly to be praised,
and his [n]greatness is unsearchable.
4 [o]One generation shall commend your works to another,
and shall declare your mighty acts.

[1] Hebrew *with no breaking in or going out* [2] This psalm is an acrostic poem, each verse beginning with the successive letters of the Hebrew alphabet

10 [b]Ps. 18:50
11 [x][See ver. 7 above] [y][See ver. 8 above]
12 [c][Ps. 128:3] [d][Zech. 9:15]
13 [e][Joel 2:24] [f][Isa. 30:23]
14 [g][Isa. 24:11; Jer. 14:2; 46:12]
15 [h]Deut. 33:29 [i]Ps. 33:12; 146:5

Psalm 145
1 [j]Ps. 99:5, 9 [k]Ps. 98:6
2 [l][Ps. 146:2]
3 [m]Ps. 48:1 [n]Job 5:9; [Isa. 40:28]
4 [o]Isa. 38:19

ten-stringed harp, see note on 33:1–3). Verse 11 of Psalm 144 repeats the request of vv. 7b–8.

144:10 The word rendered **victory** can also be translated "salvation" (as at 20:5): the requested victory furthers God's purpose for his people, and thus the king is not allowed to pursue selfish ends with the people's wars (see note on 20:1–5).

144:12–15 *May Your People Know Your Blessing.* The closing section shows the purpose of the fight, namely, to protect God's people so that they can flourish under God's blessing. The people (**our**) ask for healthy children and productive farms (cf. Deut. 28:1–14). They recognize that **such blessings** are a pure privilege and God's generous gift. Israel is **the people whose God is the LORD**, who are to bring blessedness to the rest of the world (cf. Ps. 33:12).

144:14 no mishap or failure in bearing. This is a good resolution of the obscure Hebrew (see ESV footnote), in light of Deut. 28:4, 11. Another possibility is that "breaking in" refers to being conquered, and "going out" to exile.

Psalm 145. This is the last of the psalms of David, and it introduces the hymns of praise that finish the Psalms. This hymn (or "song of praise," see title) specifically praises the Lord for his goodness and generosity toward his creatures, especially to his people (both corporate and individual). One remarkable feature of this psalm is the way it uses so many different words for "praising": "extol" (v. 1: to tell how great God is); "bless" (vv. 1, 2, 10, 21: to speak well of God for his generosity); "praise" (vv. 2, 3, 21: to glorify God for his magnificent qualities); "commend" (v. 4: to speak highly of God); cf. "declare" (synonyms in vv. 4, 6), "meditate" (v. 5), "speak" (v. 6), "pour forth" (v. 7), "sing aloud" (v. 7), and "give thanks" (v. 10). The author has exploited all the vocabulary he can muster to describe this great activity, praising God for his greatness and goodness. Further, there are repeated terms for the enduring nature of this praise: "forever and ever" (vv. 1, 2, 21); the "generations" (vv. 4, 13); and "everlasting" (v. 13). As the ESV footnote explains, this psalm follows an acrostic pattern (see Psalms 9–10; 25; 34; 37 for the other Davidic acrostics). Like the other acrostics from David, this one (at least in most Hb. manuscripts) is "imperfect," in this case lacking the *n*-verse (between 145:13–14). The ESV includes the "missing" verse (v. 13b), but in square brackets due to its uncertainty (see ESV footnote there). The Septuagint and Dead Sea Scroll evidence may witness to an earlier text, but they may just as easily witness to an early editor "helpfully" adding what he thought was a missing verse; the evidence is finely balanced. The sentiment of v. 13b, of course, is fully in line with the psalm and with the Bible as a whole.

145:1–3 *O God, I Will Ever Bless Your Name.* The psalm opens by stating its theme of joy and celebration. Each member of the congregation pledges himself to this (**I will**).

145:1 my God and King. For the different nuances of God's kingship, see note on Psalm 93. Here it is God's acknowledged kingship over his people, which the members of the congregation personally grasp—he is "*my* king," not just "*our* king." **forever and ever**. Repeated in 145:2, 21.

145:3 his greatness is unsearchable. That is, past the capacity of the human mind to fully describe or comprehend. It will take many worshipers, and a long duration (forever and ever, vv. 1, 2, 21), even to begin to do justice to what the Lord deserves.

145:4–7 *Each Generation Shall Tell Your Praise to the Next.* This section focuses the praise on God's great deeds that have protected his people and fostered the conditions in which they can flourish in true piety (his **works, mighty acts, wondrous works**, and **awesome deeds**). These actions

5[p]ver. 12
6[q][Ps. 78:4]
7[r]Isa. 63:7
8[s]See Ps. 86:5, 15
9[t]See Ps. 100:5
10[u][Ps. 19:1; 103:22] [v][Ps. 132:9, 16]
12[w]Ps. 105:1 [x]ver. 4; Ps. 150:2; Deut. 3:24 [y]ver. 5
13[z]See Ps. 10:16
14[a][Ps. 37:17, 24] [b]Ps. 146:8
15[c]Ps. 104:27
16[d]Ps. 104:28 [e][Ps. 104:21; 147:8]
17[f]See Ps. 116:5 [g]Ps. 18:25; Jer. 3:12
18[h][Ps. 34:18; 119:151; Deut. 4:7] [i]John 4:23, 24
19[j]Prov. 10:24; [John 9:31] [k]Ps. 31:22
20[l]See Ps. 97:10

5 On [p]the glorious splendor of your majesty,
and on your wondrous works, I will meditate.
6 They shall speak of [q]the might of your awesome deeds,
and I will declare your greatness.
7 They shall pour forth the fame of your [r]abundant goodness
and shall sing aloud of your righteousness.

8 The LORD is [s]gracious and merciful,
slow to anger and abounding in steadfast love.
9 The LORD is [t]good to all,
and his mercy is over all that he has made.

10 [u]All your works shall give thanks to you, O LORD,
and all your [v]saints shall bless you!
11 They shall speak of the glory of your kingdom
and tell of your power,
12 to [w]make known to the children of man your[1] [x]mighty deeds,
and [y]the glorious splendor of your kingdom.
13 [z]Your kingdom is an everlasting kingdom,
and your dominion endures throughout all generations.

[The LORD is faithful in all his words
and kind in all his works.][2]
14 The LORD [a]upholds all who are falling
and [b]raises up all who are bowed down.
15 The eyes of all [c]look to you,
and you give them their food in due season.
16 You [d]open your hand;
you [e]satisfy the desire of every living thing.
17 The LORD is [f]righteous in all his ways
and [g]kind in all his works.
18 The LORD is [h]near to all who call on him,
to all who call on him [i]in truth.
19 He [j]fulfills the desire of those who fear him;
he also [k]hears their cry and saves them.
20 The LORD [l]preserves all who love him,
but all the wicked he will destroy.

[1] Hebrew *his*; also next line [2] These two lines are supplied by one Hebrew manuscript, Septuagint, Syriac (compare Dead Sea Scroll)

express God's **abundant goodness** (see note on 100:5) and his **righteousness** (his faithfulness to keep his promises; see note on 31:1–2).

145:4 One generation shall commend your works to another. This is the biblical pattern for households (cf. Gen. 18:19; Deut. 6:1–9; Ps. 78:4), and the Passover makes this a ritual (Ex. 12:26–27; 13:8).

145:8–9 *Theme: God's Goodness.* These two verses fill out the idea of God's "goodness" and "righteousness" (v. 7).

145:8 This verse is based on Ex. 34:6. **slow to anger**. Showing wrath is not God's preferred option; he gives humans time to repent.

145:9 good to all. God's covenanted grace came to Israel in a special way, but it was never meant to be for them alone; Israel was to be the vehicle by which God's goodness and mercy became evident in **all that he has made**.

145:10–13a *God's Kingdom Is Everlasting.* This section celebrates the wonder of being part of God's **kingdom** (vv. 11, 12, 13). This refers to God's acknowledged kingship (see note on v. 1), as seen from the mention of the **saints** (the faithful among his people, as in 37:28) and his **mighty deeds**, which God has done to further his purposes for his people (see note on 145:4–7). God's people are to see his kingship as a gift of his goodness, not a burden.

145:13a an everlasting kingdom. These words are similar to Nebuchadnezzar's confession (Dan. 4:34), although Nebuchadnezzar is there granting God's universal rule. In Dan. 7:14, 27 the reference is to God's kingship over his people administered through the Davidic Messiah.

145:13b–20 *God Provides Generously for His Creatures.* Building on vv. 8–9, these verses develop the notion of God's kindness to all his creatures (vv. 15–17), which is especially received by his chosen people (vv. 18–20), particularly those **who call on him in truth** (the same people who **fear him** and **love him**).

145:13b See note on Psalm 145. **Faithful** (Hb. *ne'eman*) supplies the "missing" *n*-segment; for the idea, cf. Deut. 7:9; Ps. 93:5; Isa. 49:7. The second line is the same as the second line of Ps. 145:17. **Kind** (Hb. *hasid*) means that he shows "kindness" (Hb. *hesed*, also rendered "steadfast love").

145:14 In view of vv. 18–20, **all who are falling** (and **who are bowed down**) would apply to the faithful (cf. 37:24).

145:15–17 God's enduring kindness and provision for all his creatures is the theme of Psalm 104; cf. 147:8–9.

145:20 The English brings out the mirror pattern of the Hebrew: *verb* (**preserves**), then *object* (**all who love him**); *object* (**all the wicked**), then *verb* (**he will destroy**). The verbs and objects are the opposites of each other; and the two verbs even sound alike ("preserves," Hb. *shomer*; "destroy," Hb.

21 My mouth will speak the praise of the LORD,
and [m]let all flesh bless his holy name forever and ever.

Put Not Your Trust in Princes

146

1 [n]Praise the LORD!
Praise the LORD, O my soul!
2 I will praise the LORD [o]as long as I live;
[p]I will sing praises to my God while I have my being.

3 [q]Put not your trust in princes,
[r]in a son of man, in whom there is [s]no salvation.
4 When [t]his breath departs, he returns to the earth;
on that very day his plans perish.

5 [u]Blessed is he whose help is the God of Jacob,
whose [v]hope is in the LORD his God,
6 [w]who made heaven and earth,
the sea, and all that is in them,
[x]who keeps faith forever;
7 [y]who executes justice for the oppressed,
[z]who gives food to the hungry.

[a]The LORD sets the prisoners free;
8 [b]the LORD opens the eyes of the blind.
[c]The LORD lifts up those who are bowed down;
[d]the LORD loves the righteous.
9 [e]The LORD watches over the sojourners;
[f]he upholds the widow and the fatherless,
but [g]the way of the wicked he brings to ruin.

10 [h]The LORD will reign forever,
your God, O Zion, to all generations.
[n]Praise the LORD!

He Heals the Brokenhearted

147

1 [i]Praise the LORD!
For [j]it is good to sing praises to our God;
for [k]it is pleasant,[1] and [l]a song of praise is fitting.

[1] Or *for he is beautiful*

21 [m][Ps. 150:6]

Psalm 146

1 [n]See Ps. 135:1
2 [o]Ps. 63:4; [Ps. 145:2] [p]Ps. 104:33
3 [q]Ps. 118:9 [r]Ps. 118:8; [Isa. 2:22; Jer. 17:5] [s]Ps. 60:11; 108:12
4 [t]Ps. 104:29; [Eccles. 12:7]; See Job 10:9; 34:14, 15
5 [u][Ps. 144:15] [v]Ps. 119:116; See Ps. 2:12
6 [w]See Ps. 115:15 [x][Ps. 100:5; 117:2]
7 [y]Ps. 103:6 [z]Ps. 107:9; 145:15 [a]Ps. 105:20; Isa. 61:1; [Ps. 68:6]
8 [b]Matt. 9:30; John 9:7 [c]Ps. 145:14; [Ps. 147:6] [d]Ps. 11:7
9 [e][Ex. 22:21] [f]Deut. 10:18; [Ex. 22:22]; See Ps. 10:14 [g][Ps. 147:6]
10 [h]See Ps. 10:16 [n][See ver. 1 above]

Psalm 147

1 [i]See Ps. 135:1 [j]Ps. 92:1 [k]Ps. 135:3 [l]Ps. 33:1

hishmid). True faith is the key to the full enjoyment of the goodness of God celebrated in this psalm.

145:21 *Let All Flesh Bless His Name Forever.* With several echoes of the opening section (**praise**, cf. vv. 2–3; **bless his holy name**, cf. v. 1; **forever and ever**, vv. 1–2), the psalm closes with the only fitting response to such a meditation on God's goodness: to look forward to praising God forever and ever (and the faithful soul looks for this in all its fullness), and to wish that every creature might join in this glad song.

Psalm 146. The first and last phrase of this psalm (and Psalms 147–150), "Praise the LORD" (Hb. *hallelu-yah*), makes it plain that this hymn calls God's people to praise him. The theme is that the Lord's reign makes him a sure hope for God's suffering people.

146:1–2 *I Will Always Praise the Lord.* The opening verses set the tone for the whole psalm: the whole congregation receives the invitation, **Praise the LORD**, and then each member applies it to himself (**Praise the LORD, O my soul**). Joining in this song, **as long as I live**, is the best occupation for a human being.

146:3–4 *Do Not Trust in Mere Princes.* This section acts as a foil for the section that follows: in contrast to the Lord, the true God, it is vain to put one's **trust in princes**, who are mere mortals. Governments and armies have their proper place, but their merely human power is not ultimately decisive in the world that God rules (see note on 118:8–9; cf. 20:7; 147:10).

146:3 no salvation. See note on 20:1–5.

146:5–9 *Blessed Is He Whose Trust Is in the Real God.* Yahweh, **the God of Jacob**, is the very one **who made heaven and earth, the sea, and all that is in them** (words from Ex. 20:11, reflecting Genesis 1). His power is unlimited; and he has the character that **keeps faith forever**. Verses 7–9 of Psalm 146 list groups of weak people (**oppressed, hungry, prisoners, the blind, bowed down, sojourners, widow, fatherless**), probably God's own faithful (cf. **the righteous**, v. 8, in contrast to "the wicked," v. 9), for whom God shows his power and faithfulness in providing the relief they need. When God's people sing these words in faith, they will own these qualities as virtues toward which they too will strive. **the way of the wicked he brings to ruin**. Though such people seem to thrive for the time being, and even to hold power over the faithful, God will not allow that to continue (cf. 1:6).

146:10 *Praise the Lord Forever!* Because **the LORD will reign forever** (Ex. 15:18; Ps. 29:10), God's faithful should **praise** him now (in hopes of everlasting praise; cf. 145:21 and note).

Psalm 147. Like Psalm 146, this hymn of praise begins and ends with "Praise the LORD!" Here the praise is focused on gratitude for some great work of "building up Jerusalem" (or rebuilding it after the exile), and for the Creator who sustains his creation, especially his chosen people as

2 The LORD [m]builds up Jerusalem;
he [n]gathers the outcasts of Israel.
3 He heals [o]the brokenhearted
and [p]binds up their wounds.
4 He [q]determines the number of the stars;
he [r]gives to all of them their names.
5 [s]Great is our Lord, and [t]abundant in power;
[u]his understanding is beyond measure.
6 The LORD [v]lifts up the humble;[1]
he casts the wicked to the ground.

7 [w]Sing to the LORD with thanksgiving;
make melody to our God on [x]the lyre!
8 He covers the heavens with clouds;
he prepares [y]rain for the earth;
he makes [z]grass grow on the hills.
9 He [a]gives to the beasts their food,
and to [b]the young ravens that cry.
10 His delight is not in [c]the strength of the horse,
nor his pleasure in the legs of a man,
11 but the LORD [d]takes pleasure in those who fear him,
in those who [e]hope in his steadfast love.

12 Praise the LORD, O Jerusalem!
Praise your God, O Zion!
13 For he strengthens [f]the bars of your gates;
he blesses your children within you.
14 He [g]makes peace in your borders;
he [h]fills you with the [i]finest of the wheat.
15 He [j]sends out his command to the earth;
his word runs swiftly.
16 He gives [k]snow like wool;
he scatters [l]frost like ashes.
17 He hurls down his crystals of [m]ice like crumbs;
who can stand before his [n]cold?
18 He [o]sends out his word, and melts them;
he makes his wind blow and the waters flow.

2 [m]Ps. 51:18; 102:16 [n]Deut. 30:3; Isa. 11:12; 27:13; 56:8; Ezek. 39:28
3 [o]Ps. 34:18 [p]Ezek. 34:16
4 [q][Gen. 15:5] [r]Isa. 40:26
5 [s]Ps. 48:1 [t]Nah. 1:3 [u]Isa. 40:28; [Job 5:9]
6 [v][Ps. 146:8, 9]
7 [w]Ex. 15:21; [Ps. 95:1, 2] [x]See 1 Chr. 15:16
8 [y]See Job 5:10 [z]Ps. 104:14; Job 38:27
9 [a]Ps. 104:27, 28 [b]See Job 38:41
10 [c]Ps. 33:17
11 [d]Ps. 149:4 [e]Ps. 33:18
13 [f]Neh. 7:3
14 [g]Ex. 34:24; Prov. 16:7; Isa. 60:17, 18 [h]Ps. 132:15 [i]Ps. 81:16; Deut. 32:14
15 [j][Ps. 148:8]
16 [k]Job 37:6 [l][Job 38:29]
17 [m]Job 37:10 [n]Job 37:9
18 [o]ver. 15; [Job 37:12]; See Ps. 33:9; 107:20

[1] Or *afflicted*

they depend on him. The psalm alternates between universality (God rules over and cares for all) and particularity (he has set his own people apart and cares for them). Each new section begins with an imperative: "praise" (147:1), "sing" (v. 7), and "praise" (v. 12).

147:1–6 *Praise the Lord Who Sustains the Humble.* It is a good and fitting thing to sing in praise of the God who rules the universe, who **determines the number of the stars**, and who at the same time **builds up Jerusalem**, **gathers the outcasts of Israel** (perhaps after the exile, see note on v. 2), **heals the brokenhearted**, **lifts up the humble**, and **casts the wicked to the ground**. In this psalm, the "brokenhearted" and "humble" are members of his own people who look to him in faith. The God whose **understanding is beyond measure** is well able to carry out his great plan for Jerusalem. His greatness never implies remoteness from his faithful, nor does it mean indifference to the unfaithful ("the wicked," v. 6; cf. 146:9).

147:2 The terms **builds up** and **outcasts** (cf. Deut. 30:4; Neh. 1:9) may well suggest that the rebuilding of Jerusalem by the returned exiles is in view.

147:4–5 Isaiah 40:25–29 uses the same idea to encourage the faithful never to lose heart: God has the wisdom and the power to carry through his purposes, with such care that "not one is missing."

147:7–11 *Praise the Lord Who Provides for Those Who Fear Him.* The next section moves from God's universal provision (**rain**, so that all animals have **food**) to his special care for his faithful. The godly are secure, not because they have superior **strength** (whether by the warrior's **horse** or **legs**), but because they **fear** God and **hope in his steadfast love** (pledged in his covenant), and the Lord **takes pleasure in** them. See note on 146:3–4.

147:10 strength of the horse. Though it is easy to think of the horse here as an animal used for pulling loads, the image is most likely that of a war horse (cf. 20:7; Job 39:19); likewise, **the legs of a man** are swift for battle (cf. Ps. 18:33; Amos 2:14–15).

147:12–20 *Praise the Lord Who Favors Jerusalem.* Jerusalem, standing for all of God's people, should **praise the LORD**, who alone provides security and prosperity (vv. 13–14) for her people. The Lord governs all the processes of nature (the **snow**, **frost**, and **ice**, when melted, produce flowing **waters**), and he is well able to supply **peace** and the **finest of the wheat** to his people; and above all that, he has distinguished his people out of all peoples (**he has not dealt thus with any other nation**) with **his word** and **his statutes and rules**. These are terms for God's covenantal revelation to his people (see note on Psalm 119), and are grounds for his faithful ones to **praise the LORD**.

19 He declares his word to Jacob,
his [p]statutes and rules[1] to Israel.
20 He [q]has not dealt thus with any other nation;
they do not know his rules.[2]
[r]Praise the LORD!

Praise the Name of the LORD

148

1 [r]Praise the LORD!
Praise the LORD [s]from the heavens;
praise him [t]in the heights!
2 Praise him, all his angels;
praise him, all his [u]hosts!

3 Praise him, sun and moon,
praise him, all you shining stars!
4 Praise him, you [v]highest heavens,
and you [w]waters above the heavens!

5 [x]Let them praise the name of the LORD!
For [y]he commanded and they were created.
6 And he [z]established them forever and ever;
he gave [a]a decree, and it shall not [b]pass away.[3]

7 Praise the LORD [c]from the earth,
you [d]great sea creatures and all deeps,
8 [e]fire and hail, [f]snow and mist,
[g]stormy wind [h]fulfilling his word!

9 [i]Mountains and all hills,
[j]fruit trees and all [k]cedars!
10 [l]Beasts and all livestock,
creeping things and [m]flying birds!

11 Kings of the earth and [n]all peoples,
princes and all rulers of the earth!
12 Young men and maidens together,
old men and children!

13 [o]Let them praise the name of the LORD,
for [p]his name alone is exalted;
[q]his majesty is above earth and heaven.

[1] *Or and just decrees* [2] *Or his just decrees* [3] *Or it shall not be transgressed*

19[p]Mal. 4:4; [Ps. 78:5]; See Deut. 33:2-4
20[q]Deut. 4:7; See Deut. 4:32-34 [r]See Ps. 135:1

Psalm 148

1[r][See Ps. 147:20 above] [s][ver. 7]; See Ps. 69:34 [t]Matt. 21:9
2[u]See Ps. 103:20, 21
4[v]Ps. 68:33; Deut. 10:14; Neh. 9:6; See 1 Kgs. 8:27 [w]Gen. 1:7
5[x]ver. 13 [y]See Ps. 33:6, 9
6[z]Ps. 119:90, 91 [a][Job 28:26; Jer. 31:35, 36; 33:25] [b][Ps. 104:9; Esth. 1:19; Job 14:5]
7[c][ver. 1] [d][Gen. 1:21]; See Ps. 74:13
8[e]Ps. 18:12; 105:32 [f]Ps. 147:16 [g]Ps. 107:25 [h]Ps. 103:20; See Ps. 147:15-18
9[i]Isa. 44:23; 49:13; 55:12 [j]Gen. 1:11 [k]Ps. 104:16
10[l]Gen. 1:24 [m]Gen. 1:20, 21
11[n][Rev. 7:9]
13[o]ver. 5 [p]Ps. 8:1 [q]See Ps. 113:4

Psalm 148. This hymn of praise (see note on Psalm 146) calls on all of God's creatures to join in praising him: from the heavenly hosts, to the heavenly bodies, to the inhabitants of sea and land, to all mankind. The concluding note, regarding God's special people Israel, may refer to some particular event such as the return from exile, or it may be a more general reference to the protection God has given his people; in either case, God's favor for Israel is put into the larger context of his plan to bring light to all mankind through Israel.

148:1–6 *Praise to the Lord from the Heavens.* The **heavens** and everything found in them—whether **angels** or light-bearers (**sun, moon, stars**; Gen. 1:14–19), or **waters above the heavens** (Gen. 1:7)—should **praise the LORD**, who **commanded** with the result that **they were created** (see note on Ps. 33:4–9). By his **decree** they are **established**, standing firm and reliable.

148:7–12 *Praise to the Lord from the Earth and Seas.* Next the psalm invites the creatures under the heavens to **praise the LORD**: the **great sea creatures** (Gen. 1:21) **and all** ocean **deeps**, along with wet weather (**fire**, or lightning, **hail**, **snow**, **mist**, and **stormy wind**; cf. Ps. 147:15–18), then the features of the land (**mountains and all hills**, which are well-known in Palestine), trees (taking **fruit trees**, Gen. 1:11, **and all cedars** as representatives), and then the animals (**beasts and all livestock, creeping things and flying birds**, Gen. 1:20–25). All these creatures should give their praise according to their natures (cf. Ps. 103:22), for this is what they were made for; likewise all of mankind, of **all peoples** and of all age groups, should praise him according to their natures, for this is what they were made for.

148:13–14 *Let All Peoples Praise the Lord Who Has Exalted His People.* A recurring theme in the Psalms is the fact that all mankind should praise the Lord, the one true God, whose **name alone is exalted**; and God has bestowed unimaginable privilege upon Israel in calling them to be **near to him**, in making promises to them, and in fashioning them to be a fit vehicle by which to bring knowledge of God to the rest of the world. Therefore the special deeds God has done to bring **praise for all his saints** will ultimately enable all the world to answer the invitation of v. 13: **Let them praise the name of the LORD.**

14 He has [r]raised up a horn for his people,
[s]praise for all his saints,
for the people of Israel who are [t]near to him.
[u]Praise the LORD!

Sing to the LORD a New Song

149

1 [u]Praise the LORD!
Sing to the LORD [v]a new song,
his praise in [w]the assembly of the godly!
2 Let Israel [x]be glad in [y]his Maker;
let the children of Zion rejoice in their [z]King!
3 Let them praise his name with [a]dancing,
making melody to him with [b]tambourine and [c]lyre!
4 For the LORD [d]takes pleasure in his people;
he [e]adorns the humble with salvation.
5 Let the godly exult in glory;
let them [f]sing for joy on their [g]beds.
6 Let [h]the high praises of God be in their throats
and [i]two-edged swords in their hands,
7 to execute vengeance on the nations
and punishments on the peoples,
8 to bind their kings with [j]chains
and their nobles with fetters of iron,
9 to execute on them the judgment [k]written!
[l]This is honor for all his godly ones.
[u]Praise the LORD!

Let Everything Praise the LORD

150

1 [u]Praise the LORD!
Praise God in his [m]sanctuary;
praise him in [n]his mighty heavens![1]
2 Praise him for his [o]mighty deeds;
praise him according to his excellent [p]greatness!

[1] Hebrew *expanse* (compare Genesis 1:6–8)

14[r]See 1 Sam. 2:1 [s][Deut. 10:21; Jer. 17:14] [t]Deut. 4:7; Eph. 2:17 [u]See Ps. 135:1

Psalm 149

1[u][See Ps. 148:14 above] [v]See Ps. 33:3 [w]Ps. 89:5, 7
2[x]Ps. 85:6 [y]See Ps. 95:6; Job 35:10 [z]1 Sam. 12:12; Zech. 9:9
3[a]Ps. 150:4; [Ps. 30:11] [b]Ps. 150:4; Ex. 15:20 [c]Ps. 150:3
4[d]Ps. 35:27; 147:11 [e][Isa. 61:3]
5[f]See Job 35:10 [g]Ps. 4:4; 63:6; [Hos. 7:14]
6[h][Ps. 66:17] [i]Heb. 4:12; Rev. 1:16; 2:12; [Prov. 5:4]
8[j][Job 36:8]
9[k]Isa. 65:6; [Job 13:26] [l][Ps. 148:14] [u][See Ps. 148:14 above]

Psalm 150

1[u][See Ps. 148:14 above] [m][Ps. 11:4; 134:2] [n][Ps. 68:34]
2[o]Ps. 145:12 [p]Deut. 3:24

148:14 raised up a horn. For the expression, see note on 75:4. See also 89:24; 92:10; 112:9; 1 Sam. 2:1, 10.

Psalm 149. This hymn of praise (see note on Psalm 146) calls on God's people to praise the Lord for their special privileges. In particular, if Psalm 148 recalls the benefits that the whole world will one day receive through God's work on behalf of the faithful in Israel, Psalm 149 ends by calling to mind the expectation that the faithful will one day be God's agents of judgment through the world (cf. 1 Cor. 6:2–3; Jude 14–15; Rev. 19:14).

149:1–4 *Let the Godly Sing to Their Maker Who Delights in Them.* The members of the worshiping congregation (**the assembly of the godly**) call one another to **praise the LORD**, and to **sing to** him **a new song** (see note on 33:1–3). The tone is one of jubilant, even exuberant, gladness: **be glad**, **rejoice**, **dancing**, **making melody**. God's people can call him their **Maker** and their **King**, and know that he **takes pleasure in his people**. This idea would be unbearably arrogant had not the Lord himself declared it (147:11; cf. Ex. 19:5); the psalm also clarifies that the full benefit (**salvation**, see note on Ps. 3:2) comes to the **humble** (those who receive it properly, without presumption).

149:1 the godly. See note on 4:3.

149:5–9 *Let the Godly Exult in the Honor of Sharing in God's Rule.* This section begins like the first, with a call to the **godly** to **exult** and **sing for joy** (even **on their beds**, when they ought to be sleeping; contrast 4:4; 6:6; 77:4). Psalm 149:6 takes a startling turn, with the **high praises of God . . . in their throats** (cf. 66:17) and **two-edged swords in their hands** (an unexpected element in corporate worship!). Psalm 149:7–9 explains that the faithful will do God's work of bringing **vengeance on the nations** (assuming that they refuse the invitation to "praise the name of the LORD," 148:13); such is the **honor** that God shares with **all his godly ones**.

Psalm 150. This hymn closes the Psalter with its call for "everything that has breath" to praise the Lord with every kind of jubilant accompaniment. This psalm may have been intended for some particular liturgical use (say, the opening of a joyful service of celebration), but it now also serves as the final doxology of the whole book (see note on 41:13). The list of musical instruments in 150:3–5, with its mixture of wind, strings, percussion, and rhythmic dance, gives the impression of loud song and ceaseless motion—the worshiper's whole body offering praise to God.

150:1–2 *Praise God in the Sanctuary.* The members of the congregation invite one another to **praise God in his sanctuary**, where they are gathered to worship; the call to **praise him in his mighty heavens** may be addressed to the angels and heavenly lights, inviting them to join in (cf. 148:1–4). The reasons given in 150:2—**his mighty deeds** for his people (see note on 145:10–13a) and the **excellent greatness** of his character—indicate that,

3 Praise him with [q]trumpet sound;
praise him with [r]lute and [r]harp!
4 Praise him with [s]tambourine and [s]dance;
praise him with [t]strings and [u]pipe!
5 Praise him with sounding [v]cymbals;
praise him with loud clashing cymbals!
6 Let [w]everything that has breath praise the LORD!
[x]Praise the LORD!

3 [q]Ps. 98:6 [r]Ps. 33:2; 71:22
4 [s]Ps. 149:3 [t]Ps. 45:8; [Isa. 38:20] [u]Job 21:12
5 [v]2 Sam. 6:5; 1 Chr. 15:16, 19, 28; 25:1, 6
6 [w][Ps. 145:21] [x]ver. 1

with this topic of praise, the voices of human worshipers alone are too feeble; let the heavenly host help!

150:3–6 *Praise Him with Music and Dance.* Not only is the topic too great for merely human voices to do it justice; it also deserves the full expression of human energy and devotion, with instruments as varied as **trumpet**, **lute**, **harp**, **strings**, **pipe**, and various **cymbals**. The **tambourine** is commonly coupled with the **dance** (149:3; Ex. 15:20; 1 Sam. 18:6; Jer. 31:4) in a joyful procession. This builds to the final wish, **let everything that has breath** (all Israel, all mankind, all animals; cf. Ps. 148:10–11) **praise the LORD**: here is where they are most fully alive. Cf. Rev. 5:13–14. Hallelujah!

INTRODUCTION TO PROVERBS

Author and Date

Proverbs itself mentions Solomon (reigned c. 971–931 B.C.) as author or collector of its contents (1:1; 10:1), including the proverbs copied by Hezekiah's men (25:1). There are also two batches of sayings from a group called "the wise" (22:17–24:22; 24:23–34), and "oracles" from Agur (30:1–33) and Lemuel (31:1–9). But no author is named for the song in praise of the excellent wife that ends the book (31:10–31).

Solomon's interest in proverbs is corroborated by 1 Kings 4:29–34: "Solomon's wisdom surpassed the wisdom of all the people of the east and all the wisdom of Egypt. . . . He also spoke 3,000 proverbs, and his songs were 1,005." However, the proverbs mentioned in Kings are not necessarily identical to those of the book of Proverbs. First Kings speaks of Solomon composing proverbs about trees, beasts, birds, reptiles, and fish (1 Kings 4:33), but there are few such sayings in the Solomonic parts of Proverbs. Even so, there is nothing in the Bible to contradict the idea that Solomon was responsible for the portions of this book attributed to him. It is possible that he sponsored those who collected material from other sources (the wise, Agur, and Lemuel), but no one can be sure. At any rate the book does not claim that Solomon put it into its final form, since Hezekiah (see Prov. 25:1) reigned c. 715–686 B.C., long after Solomon's time. (For a discussion of the identities of Agur and Lemuel, see notes on 30:1–33 and 31:1–9.)

Today, many scholars assert that most of Proverbs was written much later than the time of Solomon, and many interpreters ascribe most of the contents of the book and certainly its final form to the postexilic period (i.e., after 539 B.C., when the Hebrews were in contact with the Persians and then the Greeks). There is little clear evidence to support such skepticism, however. The Hebrew of Proverbs is not demonstrably of a late variety, and there are no bits of historical evidence within the text that speak against an origin in the tenth century B.C. for the Solomonic portions of Proverbs. To the contrary, there are three principal arguments for dating this material to the reign of Solomon, apart from the claim of 1:1.

First, wisdom texts very similar to Proverbs predate the book of Proverbs by as much as a millennium. In addition to proverb texts from early Mesopotamia, a wide array of wisdom literature from Egypt has numerous and striking parallels to Proverbs. Some important ones are: *The Instruction of Vizier Ptah-hotep* (written in the 5th or 6th Egyptian Dynasty, c. 2500–2190 B.C.); *The Instruction for Merikare* (10th Dynasty, c. 2106–2010 B.C.); and *The Instruction of Amenemope* (probably written c. 1250 B.C.). The existence of these and other wisdom texts shows that the practice of composing discourses on wisdom and collecting wise sayings was already ancient by the time of Solomon. The notion that interest in such material could not have evolved until late in Israelite history conflicts with the evidence.

The second argument is based in the nature of the Solomonic kingdom as described in the Bible. It is referred to as a golden age of peace, prosperity, and international prestige for Israel. As a rule, it is in such times that a flowering of literature occurs. For example, of the above Egyptian texts, *Ptah-hotep* is from the powerful Old Kingdom period, and *Amenemope* is from the New Kingdom period. *Merikare* is an exception, coming from the weaker First Intermediate Period of Egypt, but it is rooted in the wisdom of the Old Kingdom. Similarly, the giants of Greek dramatic literature (Aeschylus, Sophocles, Euripides, and Aristophanes) emerged in the fifth century B.C., during the time of the Athenian Empire, and it was also at that time that Socrates propelled Western philosophy forward. The greatest works of Latin literature, and in particular the *Aeneid* of Virgil, were written in the golden age of Augustus. Based on these analogies, it is much more likely that the bulk of Proverbs comes from the golden age of Solomon than from the much more humble age of Hezekiah, to say nothing of the postexilic period, when Jerusalem was a cultural backwater.

Third, the Jewish wisdom literature known to be from the postexilic period, especially *Sirach* (also called *Ecclesiasticus*; c. 180 B.C.) and the pseudepigraphal *Wisdom of Solomon* (1st century B.C.), is noteworthy for being quite unlike Proverbs, clearly displaying the concerns of Hellenistic Judaism. *Sirach* seeks for a pious ideal based in following the already completed Hebrew Scriptures, and mentions particular figures in biblical and postbiblical history. The *Wisdom of Solomon* is concerned with matters of immortality, eschatology, and philosophy in a different way from Proverbs. There is a Lady Wisdom in the *Wisdom of Solomon* but, although clearly derived from Proverbs 8, this Lady Wisdom is described as an "emanation of the glory of the Almighty" and the "radiance of eternal light" (*Wisd. Sol.* 7:25–26), i.e., using terms unlike any used for Lady Wisdom in Proverbs 8 and thus reflecting a later era. Proverbs itself shows no indication of the postexilic age, either of the Persian or the Hellenistic period.

In summary, there is nothing that speaks against and much that speaks in favor of dating the materials in Proverbs to the Solomonic era. This does not mean that Solomon personally composed every proverb in the book, and the text does not say that he did. Further, the present form of the book is from a later time than the age of Solomon, but probably no later than Hezekiah.

Theme

Proverbs states its theme right at the book's beginning (1:1–7): its goal is to describe and instill "wisdom" in God's people, a wisdom that is founded in the "fear of the LORD" and that works out covenant life in the practical details of everyday situations and relationships.

Purpose, Occasion, and Background

Proverbs is the prime example of "Wisdom Literature" in the OT, the other books being Job, Ecclesiastes, and the Song of Solomon, together with the wisdom psalms (e.g., Psalm 112). In the NT, James is usually counted as a wisdom book, and parts of Jesus' teaching belong in this category as well. (See Introduction to the Poetic and Wisdom Literature, pp. 865–868.)

It is sometimes said that the Wisdom Literature is separate from the rest of the OT, lacking an interest in God's choice of Israel and his overarching purpose for the nations, the law, the temple and priesthood, and sacred history. Wisdom Literature, it is said, is more about living in the creation than it is about God's work of redemption. This is a false opposition for several reasons.

First, the OT presents God's redemption as restoring the damaged creature, man, to his proper functioning (as set out in the creation narrative of Genesis). This covenant given through Moses does not specify all of God's rules; its purpose is to set out the constitution of the theocracy, to give general moral guidance, and to provide a system by which God's people can know his forgiveness. Some principles like those in Proverbs can be discerned by wise observation of God's world, and not all of the worthy observers come from Israel (see note on Prov. 31:1–9). Second, the wisdom psalms take wisdom themes and make them a part of Israel's hymnody (and thus of its public worship). Third, Proverbs bases its instruction on the fear of the LORD (1:7, using the special covenantal name of God), implying that its audience is the covenant people (cf. Deut. 6:2, 24; 10:12). Fourth, as the notes will show, Proverbs has plenty of connections to the law: e.g., cf. Proverbs 11:1 to Deuteronomy 25:13–16; and see Proverbs 29:18 for a positive assessment of both prophetic vision and the Law of Moses.

Nevertheless, Proverbs is not at all the same as the Law or the Prophets. The difference is one of emphasis rather than basic orientation. The Law and the Prophets lay their stress on the covenant people as a whole, called to show the world what restored humanity can be; Proverbs focuses on what such restoration should look like in day-to-day behavior and in personal character.

A key term in Proverbs is of course "wisdom." The word (Hb. *khokmah*) can have the nuance of "skill" (as it does in Ex. 28:3), particularly the skill of choosing the right course of action for the desired result. In the covenantal framework of Proverbs, it denotes "skill in the art of godly living."

The opening of the book also discloses its intended audience (Prov. 1:4–5): the simple, the youth, the wise, and the one who understands. (See Character Types in Proverbs.) Questions about the book's purpose have focused on the identity of "the youth" (1:4): is this any Israelite boy or girl, or is it specifically young men on the verge of adulthood, or is it young men who will serve the royal court?

The last option gets most of its support from the wisdom literature found in other lands of the ancient Near East, particularly Egypt and Mesopotamia, which seems to be oriented to preparing diligent and honest men to serve the royal bureaucracy. Since Proverbs has points of contact with this larger wisdom tradition, and since the "words of the wise" (22:17–24:34) show an even closer connection to Egyptian wisdom (see note on 22:17–24:22), it can seem reasonable to attribute to Proverbs a similar function to wisdom in these other lands.

Such an attribution, however, runs into the simple fact that the collection of Proverbs, taken as a whole, repels the idea of a selective, elite audience, stressing instead the home and life in the village and farm. For example, the instructions are father (and sometimes mother, see 1:8) to son (for the inclusion of daughters, see Literary Features), and the situations envisioned are staples of ordinary life (marriage, raising children, discreet speech, diligence in harvest, concern for the poor neighbor, etc.). Indeed, when Lady Wisdom offers her benefits, she calls out to everyone (8:4–5), particularly to every member of the covenant people.

Considering these aspects, and the list of addressees in 1:4–5, it is easy to see that the book is addressed to all the people of Israel (and through them to all mankind). The situations faced by the youth receive much attention, probably because they supply concrete examples from which others can generalize. Additionally, the "wise" who pay attention will also benefit (1:5), so the audience is not limited to the youth. The best way to put this in light of the rest of the ancient Near East is to say that Proverbs represents the "democratization" of wisdom, the offer of it to all people.

The nature of Proverbs shows why Christians, who do not live in the theocracy established by the Mosaic covenant, should still find in this book wisdom for their lives. God gave the Mosaic covenant to his people out of his grace, in order to restore human life to its proper functioning within the specific context of the Israelite theocracy. In the same way the Christian message is God's gracious way of restoring human life for all kinds of people, fulfilling the promises made to the patriarchs. Both situations express the same grace of God, and both have the goal of restoring the image of God in man. Further, many of the proverbs make use of wise observations of God's world—which is the same world in which Christians live today. For all the "local" features found in the book (e.g., a society based on agriculture; Palestinian climate; Mosaic institutions), its wisdom is universally applicable. Therefore it is no surprise that NT authors readily make use of its individual proverbs (e.g., Rom. 12:20, using Prov. 25:21–22; Heb. 12:5–6, using Prov. 3:11–12) and its broader themes (e.g., James as a wisdom book), setting the pattern for Christians of all ages.

Key Themes

Proverbs covers a wide array of topics from daily life: diligence and laziness (6:6–11); friendship (3:27–28; 18:24); speech (10:19–21); marriage (18:22; 19:14); child rearing (22:6); domestic peace (15:17; 17:1); work (11:1); getting along and good manners (23:1–2; 25:16–17; 26:17–19; 27:14); eternity (14:32; 23:17–18); and much more. In each of these areas it offers wisdom for realizing the life of the covenant in the details; it shows that "godliness is of value in every way, as it holds promise for the present life and also for the life to come" (1 Tim. 4:8). It demonstrates clearly that:

1. God's will is intensely practical, applying to every aspect of his people's lives. A proper relation to God involves, first, trying hard to understand his truth, and then embracing and obeying what one understands.
2. A life lived by God's will is a happy life (3:21–26).
3. A life lived by God's will is a useful life (3:27–28; 12:18, 25).
4. A life lived by God's will does not just happen; one must seek after it, study, pursue it, and discipline oneself.
5. Such a life is available to those who go after it (9:1–6).

History of Salvation Summary

The history of salvation generally deals with the overarching story of God's work in calling, preserving, and shaping a people for himself, through whom he will bring blessing to the whole world. It also takes up the unfolding of God's revelation, especially the developing idea of who the Messiah will be and what he will do. At first glance, Proverbs has little to do with this, focused as it is on the daily life of particular members of God's people. However, it has much in every way to offer. First, the people in Proverbs are God's covenant people, and the kings are Davidic. Second, concern for the well-being of the people as a whole is never absent from the book (e.g., 11:14; 14:34; 29:2, 18).

The connection of Proverbs to salvation history can be seen more fully from noticing how Psalms 111–112 work together: Psalm 111, a hymn of praise, celebrates the great works of the Lord that further his redemptive purpose for his people, while Psalm 112 is a wisdom psalm, looking very much like Proverbs set to music. The two psalms have much in common (see notes there), which invites the reader to connect them. The wisdom described in Psalm 112 and in Proverbs guides the particular Israelite in his priorities and choices, and enables him to contribute to the whole body of God's people. It is what leads the covenant members toward the ideal of likeness to God and properly functioning humanity, so that their lives carry something of a taste of Eden—and this is what the Gentiles need to see in them. (For an explanation of the "History of Salvation," see the Overview of the Bible, pp. 23–26. See also History of Salvation in the Old Testament: Preparing the Way for Christ, pp. 2635–2661.)

Character Types in Proverbs

To read Proverbs well, one must have a good grasp of who the character types are and what function they serve in the book.

The most obvious characters in the book are the wise, the fool, and the simple. Proverbs urges its readers to be wise, that is, to embrace God's covenant and to learn the skill of living out the covenant in everyday situations (cf. 2:2). The *wise* person has done that (cf. 10:1); usually Proverbs focuses on the one who has made good progress in that skill, whose example is worth following (cf. 9:8b).

The *fool* is the person steadily opposed to God's covenant (cf. 1:7b). The setting of Proverbs assumes there can be fools even among God's people. There are three Hebrew terms translated "fool" (*kesil, 'ewil, nabal*), with little difference among them. This kind of person resists even the offer of forgiveness found in the covenant (14:9; 15:8). These people are dangerous in their influence (13:20; 17:12) and cause grief to their parents (10:1); but they are not beyond hope (8:5).

The *simple* is the person who is not firmly committed, either to wisdom or to folly; he is easily misled (cf. 14:15). His trouble is that he does not apply himself to the discipline needed to gain and grow in wisdom.

Proverbs also uses other terms, both positive (e.g., righteous, upright, diligent, understanding, prudent) and negative (e.g., wicked, lazy, lacking sense). These do not designate different groups of people from the wise and the fools; rather, the terms are commonly "co-referential," i.e., they apply to the same people looked at from different angles. The *righteous* is the one who has embraced the covenant, seen from the perspective of his faithfulness to God's will; the *wise* is the same person, seen from the perspective of his skill in living out God's will; the *prudent* is the same individual seen as one who carefully plans out his obedience. Likewise, the *wicked* is the one who rejects God's covenant, seen from the angle of his opposition to God; the *fool* is this same person, seen from the angle of the stupid course of life he has chosen.

The co-referential use of these terms helps the reader to discern the many-sided fruits of godliness and ungodliness.

Also, these characters usually serve as idealized portraits: that is, they denote people exemplary for their virtue and wisdom or especially despicable for their evil. The literary name for this is "caricature": portraits of people with features exaggerated for easy identification. The positive figures serve as ideals for the faithful, to guide their conduct and character formation. The negative figures are exaggerated portraits of those who do not embrace the covenant, so the faithful can recognize these traits in themselves and flee them.

Beyond the co-referential negative terms, there are some gradations: the *scoffer* is worse than a fool (21:24), and the person *wise in his own eyes* is almost beyond hope (cf. 26:12). The difference is one of hardness in unteachability (the great sin in Proverbs). The *simple* is not as far gone as the fool. All of these are what the OT calls "uncircumcised" in heart, and what Christian theology calls "unregenerate."

Personified Wisdom and Christ

Proverbs commends pursuing "wisdom," portraying it as a virtue. In four poems in chapters 1–9, wisdom is also personified as a noble lady whom one should pursue: 1:20–33; 3:13–20; 8:1–36; 9:1–18 (contrasted with Lady Folly). The poem of chapter 8 seems to go beyond personification to describing a personality, which has led to discussions of whether Christians should relate this description to Christ.

In the first few Christian centuries it was widely accepted that Christ was the incarnation of Wisdom in chapter 8. The Septuagint translation of 8:22 was read to mean, "the LORD created me" (see ESV footnote; the Gk. might not be that specific), and thus the Arians (who denied the deity of Christ) found here a proof that the Logos (the "Word" of John 1:1) was a creature, and not God. But Athanasius, defending the deity of Christ, took the text to refer to Christ's incarnation, and not to his preexistence. The ESV renders the Hebrew verb *qanah* as "possessed," which is a more accurate translation. The verse means that wisdom is the character of God by which he created (cf. 3:19), and therefore should not be taken as his creature; this is the wisdom he gives to those who will learn from Proverbs. In this light, neither side of those who based their discussion on the Septuagint had the correct understanding of the original Hebrew text.

It would appear, however, that Proverbs 8 played a role in the way NT authors described Christ. Paul's "*before* all things" (Col. 1:17) seems to draw on Proverbs 8:23–26, with its repeated "before." Wisdom in Proverbs 8 seems to be a personality—indeed, it seems to be what rationality would be if it were a person—by which God made the world. This is like Psalm 33:6, "By the word of the LORD the heavens were made." The NT authors further expand this idea in texts such as John 1:1–3; Colossians 1:16–17; and Hebrews 1:3, 10–12, all of which insist that Jesus Christ is the incarnation of that divine person through whom God made the world.

Literary Features

The book of Proverbs is what the title implies—a collection or anthology of individual proverbs. In addition to being teachers and authority figures, the wise men of ancient cultures were literary craftsmen—careful observers of the human condition and masters of a particular kind of discourse (the proverb).

The first nine chapters of the book are wisdom poems that extend over several verses, urging the reader to pursue wisdom. The proverbs proper—the concise, memorable statement of two or three lines—begin in 10:1.

A proverb works by making a *comparison*, and leaving it to the reader to work out how the proverb applies to different situations, following current cultural conventions. In English, "You can lead a horse to water but you cannot make him drink" is regularly applied to human relationships rather than ranching, and the competent reader knows this.

One question in reading Proverbs concerns *context*, namely, *is* there any? The Purpose, Occasion, and Background section has already argued that the covenant provides the theological context (hence God's grace and Israel's life in the land are always assumed); likewise, one can easily recognize subsistence agriculture (living from one crop to the next) as the basic cultural context (hence wealth and poverty are understood in that setting). There is also literary context: chapters 1–9 provide the ideals and motivation for pursuing wisdom, giving the right frame of mind in which to read the one-sentence proverbs. Additionally, chapters 1–9 are composed of coherent paragraphs in which the individual verses have their meaning. But do paragraphs occur in chapters 10–31 (besides the acrostic poem, 31:10–31)? It appears that in many cases they do, and so in reading the individual one-sentence proverbs, one must take account of their possible location in a paragraph context. The notes aim to apply this principle.

A feature of wisdom literature is its *concreteness*: i.e., the principle is often given in terms of a specific circumstance or a specific person, rather than in terms of a generalization about people (plural). The false balance, contrasted with the just weight (11:1), is a particular instance of the difference between swindling and honesty in one's work ethic and commercial dealings. A father speaks to his son, recalling his own boyhood (4:1–4), as a specific parent speaking to a particular child (rather than to one's children or to children in general). The idea is not to exclude, say, fathers speaking to daughters (or mothers speaking to sons and daughters); rather, by reflecting on a specific instance the wise reader will perceive the application to his or her own situation (making the appropriate adaptations).

In some cases individual proverbs seem to supply *contradictions*; the best example is 26:4–5, admonishing not to answer a fool, and then to answer a fool. These are only contradictory if it is forgotten that they are proverbs, and not laws: the successive verses apply in different situations (see note on 25:28–26:12). Most languages have the same phenomenon: English has "Many hands make light work" and "Too many cooks spoil the broth." At first sight these seem contradictory, but wisdom includes competence in matching the proverb to the right situation.

Proverbs of necessity focus on *consequences*, and this raises the question of whether they are "promises." Proverbs by nature deal with general truths, and are not meant to cover every conceivable situation. Consider the English proverb, "Short cuts make long delays"; the very form of the proverb forbids adding qualifiers, whether of frequency (often, usually, four times out of five) or of conditions (except in cases where . . .); these would lessen the memorability of the sentence. The competent reader knows that the force of the proverb is not statistical, but behavioral—in the case of the English proverb cited, to urge due caution. In biblical proverbs, the consequences generally make God's basic attitude clear, and thus commend or discourage behavior.

Proverbs often seem to be mere observations about life, but their deeper meanings will reveal themselves if the following grid is applied: (1) What *virtue* does this proverb commend? (2) What *vice* does it hold up for disapproval? (3) What *value* does it affirm?

Outline

I. Title, Goal, and Motto (1:1–7)

II. A Father's Invitation to Wisdom (1:8–9:18)

A. First paternal appeal: do not join those greedy for unjust gain (1:8–19)
B. First wisdom appeal (1:20–33)
C. Second paternal appeal: get wisdom (2:1–22)
D. Third paternal appeal: fear the Lord (3:1–12)
E. A hymn to wisdom (3:13–20)
F. Fourth paternal appeal: walk securely in wisdom (3:21–35)
G. Fifth paternal appeal: wisdom is a tradition worth maintaining (4:1–9)
H. Sixth paternal appeal: the two ways (4:10–19)
I. Seventh paternal appeal: maintain a heart of wisdom (4:20–27)
J. Eighth paternal appeal: sexuality (5:1–23)
K. Warnings relating to securing debt, sloth, and sowing discord (6:1–19)
L. Ninth paternal appeal: adultery leads to ruin (6:20–35)
M. Tenth paternal appeal: keep away from temptations to adultery (7:1–27)
N. Second wisdom appeal (8:1–36)
O. Lady Wisdom and Lady Folly (9:1–18)

III. Proverbs of Solomon (10:1–22:16)

IV. The Thirty Sayings of "the Wise" (22:17–24:22)

V. Further Sayings of "the Wise" (24:23–34)

VI. Hezekiah's Collection of Solomonic Proverbs (25:1–29:27)

VII. The Sayings of Agur (30:1–33)

VIII. The Sayings of King Lemuel (31:1–9)

IX. An Alphabet of Womanly Excellence (31:10–31)

PROVERBS

Chapter 1
1[a]ch. 10:1; 25:1; 1 Kgs. 4:32; Eccles. 12:9
3[b]ch. 2:9
4[c]ch. 8:5; 14:15, 18 [d]ch. 2:11; 3:21
5[e]ch. 9:9
6[f]ch. 22:17 [g]Judg. 14:12; Ps. 78:2
7[h]ch. 9:10; [ch. 15:33]; See Job 28:28
8[i]ch. 6:20; [Ps. 34:11; Eph. 6:1, 2]

The Beginning of Knowledge

1 [a]The proverbs of Solomon, son of David, king of Israel:

2 To know wisdom and instruction,
to understand words of insight,
3 to receive instruction in wise dealing,
in [b]righteousness, justice, and equity;
4 to give prudence to [c]the simple,
knowledge and [d]discretion to the youth—
5 Let the wise hear and [e]increase in learning,
and the one who understands obtain guidance,
6 to understand a proverb and a saying,
[f]the words of the wise and their [g]riddles.

7 [h]The fear of the LORD is the beginning of knowledge;
fools despise wisdom and instruction.

The Enticement of Sinners

8 [i]Hear, my son, your father's instruction,
and forsake not your mother's teaching,

1:1–7 *Title, Goal, and Motto.* Although perhaps originally written as the prologue to the first major division of Proverbs (1:1–9:18), these verses now effectively introduce the reader to the entire book in its final shape. After the title (1:1), there is an introduction that describes the goal of the whole book (vv. 2–6) and the motto that underlies every instruction in the book (v. 7). As discussed in the Introduction (Purpose, Occasion, and Background), this enables one to read the book properly.

1:1 For the origin of Proverbs in the reign of **Solomon**, see Introduction: Author and Date.

1:2–6 These verses give the purpose and benefit of the book: it instills wisdom in the reader. The wisdom offered here is practical (**instruction in wise dealing**), intellectual (**increase in learning**), moral (**righteousness, justice, and equity**), and probing (**to understand a proverb and . . . riddles**). It is for all people, be they naive and ignorant (**the simple . . . the youth**) or already experienced (**Let the wise hear**).

1:5 Let the wise hear and increase in learning. The great virtue that this book seeks to instill is *teachability*, the willingness to grow in wisdom no matter how far along a person already is.

1:7 The fear of the LORD is the beginning of knowledge. This is the core maxim of the book: the quest for wisdom begins with the fear of the Lord (cf. 9:10 and Ps. 111:10, "The fear of the LORD is the beginning of wisdom"). "Knowledge" and "wisdom" are closely tied together in Proverbs: "knowledge" tends to focus on correct understanding of the world and oneself as creatures of the magnificent and loving God, while "wisdom" is the acquired skill of applying that knowledge rightly, or "skill in the art of godly living" (see Introduction: Purpose, Occasion, and Background). On the fear of the Lord, see notes on Acts 5:5; 9:31; Rom. 3:18; Phil. 2:12–13; 1 Pet. 1:17; 1 John 4:18. The reason that the fear of the Lord is the beginning of both knowledge and wisdom is that the moral life begins with reverence and humility before the Maker and Redeemer. The idea of a quest for knowledge sets biblical wisdom in the broad context of the ancient Near Eastern quest for truth, and this verse also validates such a quest as legitimate and good. Thus it affirms a kind of "creational revelation," the idea that one can find moral and theological truth through observing the world. At the same time, it distinguishes the biblical pursuit of knowledge and wisdom from those of the surrounding cultures, for it asserts that submission to the Lord is foundational to the attainment of real understanding (cf. Ps. 111:10; Prov. 9:10). By using the covenant name "the LORD" in preference to the more generic "God," this verse makes the point that truth is found through Israel's God. (For fearing the Lord in Proverbs as the right response to his covenant, see 1:29; 2:5; 3:7; 8:13; 10:27; 14:2, 26–27; 15:16, 33; 16:6; 19:23; 22:4; 23:17; 24:21; 31:30; see note on Ps. 19:9.) In addition, the verse asserts that **fools despise wisdom and instruction**, thus setting up the alternative between the two ways of wisdom and folly. This contrast dominates the entire book, as the way of wisdom, righteousness, and the fear of the Lord is set against the way of folly, evil, and scoffing.

1:8–9:18 *A Father's Invitation to Wisdom.* This section describes the two paths implied in 1:7: the wise (grounded in the fear of the Lord) and the foolish (despising such wisdom and instruction). The appeals consist of: (1) a father (and mother in 1:8; 6:20) exhorting a son to seek wisdom (e.g., 2:1–22) and warning him against the ruin that comes from folly (e.g., 6:1–19); (2) Wisdom (personified as a woman) calling on all who will listen to seek her (1:20–33; 8:1–36); and (3) a final contrast of the two paths represented by Lady Wisdom and Lady Folly (9:1–18). The purpose of the section is to instruct the young and simple to embrace wisdom and to instill in them the desire to discern and persevere in the path of wisdom.

9 for they are [j]a graceful garland for your head
and [k]pendants for your neck.
10 My son, if sinners [l]entice you,
do not consent.
11 If they say, "Come with us, [m]let us lie in wait for blood;
[n]let us ambush the innocent without reason;
12 like Sheol let us [o]swallow them alive,
and whole, like [p]those who go down to the pit;
13 we shall find all precious goods,
we shall fill our houses with plunder;
14 throw in your lot among us;
we will all have one purse"—
15 my son, [q]do not walk in the way with them;
[r]hold back your foot from their paths,
16 for [s]their feet run to evil,
and they make haste to shed blood.
17 [t]For in vain is a net spread
in the sight of any bird,
18 but these men [u]lie in wait for their own blood;
they [u]set an ambush for their own lives.
19 [v]Such are the ways of everyone who is [w]greedy for unjust gain;
[x]it takes away the life of its possessors.

The Call of Wisdom

20 [y]Wisdom cries aloud in the street,
in the markets she raises her voice;
21 at the head of the noisy streets she cries out;
at [z]the entrance of the city gates she speaks:
22 "How long, O [a]simple ones, will you love being simple?
How long will [b]scoffers delight in their scoffing
and fools [c]hate knowledge?
23 If you turn at my reproof,[1]
behold, I will [d]pour out my spirit to you;
I will make my words known to you.

[1] Or *Will you turn away at my reproof?*

9 [j]ch. 4:9; [ch. 3:22] [k][Gen. 41:42; Dan. 5:29]
10 [l]ch. 16:29
11 [m]ver. 18; ch. 12:6; Jer. 5:26 [n]ver. 18; Ps. 10:8; 64:5
12 [o]Ps. 124:3; [Num. 16:32, 33] [p]Ps. 28:1
15 [q]ch. 4:14; 24:1; Ps. 1:1 [r][Ps. 119:101]
16 [s]ch. 6:18; Isa. 59:7; [Rom. 3:15]
17 [t][Job 40:24]
18 [u]ver. 11
19 [v][Job 8:13] [w]ch. 15:27 [x][1 Tim. 6:10]
20 [y]ch. 8:1; 9:3; [John 7:37]
21 [z]ch. 8:3
22 [a]See ver. 4 [b]See Ps. 1:1 [c]ver. 29; ch. 5:12; [Job 21:14]
23 [d]Joel 2:28; Acts 2:17

1:8–19 *First Paternal Appeal: Do Not Join Those Greedy for Unjust Gain.* The appeal opens, like most of the paternal addresses, with a personal address and an encouragement to heed the instruction as a prized and beneficial possession (vv. 8–9). This first appeal is a warning against those who might seek aid in unjust gain and consists of two parts: the hypothetical invitations of those who seek to "ambush the innocent" (vv. 11–14), bordered by warnings to reject such pleas (vv. 10, 15) and the grounds for doing so (vv. 16–19). The purpose of the warning is to instill the wisdom to recognize that while such plots offer companionship and immediate gain, they lead down a path that ends in destruction.

1:8 my son. On the address to a particular son, see the discussion of "concreteness" in Introduction: Literary Features. **your father's instruction . . . your mother's teaching**. Coming directly after the prologue (vv. 1–7), this verse begins the first section by indicating that the training in wisdom referred to in Proverbs includes instruction in the home by father and mother (see also 6:20; 23:22; 31:26; cf. Ex. 20:12).

1:13 The temptation for **precious goods** and **plunder** is one of the ways in which "the love of money is a root of all kinds of evils" (1 Tim. 6:10).

1:17–19 These verses conclude the first appeal by contrasting the sensible actions of a **bird** with the foolish actions of those who seek unjust gain. A bird that sees a fowler spreading a **net** will flee the danger to its life rather than take the bait. However, those who seek to trap the innocent do not recognize that though they may gain the desired prize (goods and plunder, v. 13) they foolishly overlook the full consequences of their actions: in setting the trap, they ultimately **set an ambush for their own lives** (v. 18). Unlike the sensible flying away of the bird, they take plunder, further forming their character on their way to ultimate peril. Their own words highlight their blindness. In v. 12 the sinners refer to capturing the innocent in ambush by saying, "like Sheol let us swallow them alive, and whole, like those who go down to the pit," comparing their actions to the physical effects of death. However, when v. 19 speaks of the result of **the ways of everyone who is greedy for unjust gain** (see note on v. 13)—that **it takes away the life of its possessors**—it is not saying simply that their actions will bring about their own death (though they may). Rather it says that such actions lead to the ultimate end of the way of the wicked, an even more profound loss of "life," with all that that involves (see also 22:22–23).

1:20–33 *First Wisdom Appeal.* Wisdom is personified here as a woman and is pictured appealing to simple ones, scoffers, and fools to heed her words. (Other personifications appear in chs. 8–9.) Since wisdom in Proverbs is set out in the prologue as a quality rooted in the fear of the Lord (1:1–7), it should not be surprising that in its personification, Wisdom speaks in a way that evokes the words of the Lord (e.g., "I will pour out my spirit to you; I will make my words known to you," v. 23). The appeal consists of a description of Wisdom's pursuit and plea (vv. 20–23), a warning about the consequences of refusing to heed her call (vv. 24–31), and the grounds for listening to her (vv. 32–33).

24 [e]Because I have called and [f]you refused to listen,
have [g]stretched out my hand and no one has heeded,
25 because you have [h]ignored all my counsel
and [i]would have none of my reproof,
26 I also [j]will laugh at your calamity;
I will mock when [k]terror strikes you,
27 when terror strikes you like [l]a storm
and your calamity comes like a whirlwind,
when distress and anguish come upon you.
28 [m]Then they will call upon me, but I will not answer;
they will seek me diligently but will not find me.
29 Because they [c]hated knowledge
and [n]did not choose the fear of the LORD,
30 [h]would have none of my counsel
and [i]despised all my reproof,
31 therefore they shall eat [o]the fruit of their way,
and have [p]their fill of their own devices.
32 For the simple are killed by [q]their turning away,
and [r]the complacency of fools destroys them;
33 but [s]whoever listens to me will dwell secure
and will be [t]at ease, without dread of disaster."

The Value of Wisdom

2
1 [u]My son, [v]if you receive my words
and treasure up my commandments with you,
2 making your ear attentive to wisdom
and inclining your heart to understanding;
3 yes, if you call out for insight
and raise your voice [w]for understanding,
4 if you seek it like [x]silver
and search for it as for [y]hidden treasures,
5 then [z]you will understand the fear of the LORD
and find the knowledge of God.
6 For [a]the LORD gives wisdom;
from his mouth come knowledge and understanding;
7 he stores up sound wisdom for the upright;
he is [b]a shield to those who [c]walk in integrity,

24[e]Isa. 65:12; 66:4; Jer. 7:13 [f]Zech. 7:11 [g]Rom. 10:21
25[h]See Ps. 107:11 [i][Ps. 81:11; Luke 7:30]
26[j]See Ps. 2:4 [k]ch. 10:24; Jer. 48:43; 49:5
27[l][Zeph. 1:15]
28[m]See 1 Sam. 8:18; Job 27:9
29[c][See ver. 22 above] [n][Job 21:14]
30[h][See ver. 25 above] [i][See ver. 25 above]
31[o]Jer. 6:19 [p]ch. 14:14; Isa. 3:11; [Job 4:8]
32[q]Jer. 2:19 [r][Ps. 73:18, 19]
33[s][Ps. 25:12, 13] [t]Ps. 112:7, 8

Chapter 2

1[u]See ch. 1:8 [v][ch. 4:1, 10, 20; 7:1]
3[w]ch. 4:1, 5, 7
4[x]ch. 3:14 [y]Job 3:21; [Matt. 13:44]
5[z][Ps. 25:14; John 7:17; 14:21]
6[a]Job 32:8
7[b]ch. 30:5; See Ps. 3:3 [c]Ps. 84:11

1:28 Wisdom declares that when calamity falls upon the scoffers, **they will call upon me, but I will not answer**. Although the language is similar to texts such as 1 Sam. 8:18, actual prayer is probably not in view here. Lady Wisdom here is not God but simply a personification (on whether the personification in Prov. 8:22–31 is different, see Introduction: Personified Wisdom and Christ). The meaning is that fools and scoffers, when disaster overtakes them, will frantically seek the wisdom to get out of trouble. But it will be too late for them.

1:29 The content of vv. 24–25 is repeated in vv. 28 and 30 as the foolish refusal to listen to instruction is reflected back to the wayward one in his distress. The effect of this repetition is to highlight the additional comment of v. 29, which warns that the foolish refusal to heed Wisdom's call manifests hatred of **knowledge** and rejection of **the fear of the LORD** (see v. 7).

1:31 therefore they shall eat the fruit of their way. Proverbs refers to the way of wisdom and the way of foolishness as sharing this reality: each works according to its nature. A person's actions both manifest the state of the heart and also shape it further in the way a person will walk. The direction of each path indicates the end to which it is headed. Those who refuse to listen to Wisdom's reproof walk in a way that will ultimately produce for their own consumption the very fruit they offered to others: the fruit of calamity, terror, and destruction. For a similar description of the paths and their ends, see Jer. 6:16–19.

2:1–22 *Second Paternal Appeal: Get Wisdom.* The appeal consists of one long sentence intricately structured in both its grammar (it is a conditional sentence: If . . . , then . . .) and its vocabulary (it contains repeated words as well as sets of words that refer in different ways to the same thing). The function of this structure is to aid in communicating the message of the appeal: setting one's heart on wisdom (vv. 1–4) is possible because the Lord gives it, and he does so for the purpose of protecting the path of those who fear him (vv. 5–8, 9–20), a path that leads ultimately to the blessed end of the righteous (vv. 21–22).

2:1–4 The protasis (the if-clause of the conditional) is set out in these verses and calls upon the listener or reader to **seek** wisdom diligently. Where Wisdom is pictured calling out in the streets in 1:20–21, these verses indicate that wisdom is something to be sought after (**if you call out for insight and raise your voice for understanding**, 2:3).

2:5–8 The first result of heeding wisdom is that one **will understand the fear of the LORD** (v. 5). This knowledge is possible only because the Lord gives it to the **upright** (vv. 6, 7). Thus, while wisdom is to be sought diligently and cultivated in practice, it is not something merited by the actions of an individual. (On wisdom's foundation in God's gracious covenant, see Introduction: Purpose, Occasion, and Background.) Verse 8 states that the purpose of the gift of wisdom is to protect the paths of the saints.

8 guarding the paths of justice
and [d]watching over the way of his [e]saints.
9 [f]Then you will understand [g]righteousness and justice
and equity, every good path;
10 for wisdom will come into your heart,
and knowledge will be pleasant to your soul;
11 [h]discretion will [i]watch over you,
understanding will guard you,
12 delivering you from the way of evil,
from men of perverted speech,
13 who forsake the paths of uprightness
to [j]walk in the ways of darkness,
14 who [k]rejoice in doing evil
and [l]delight in the perverseness of evil,
15 men whose [m]paths are crooked,
[n]and who are [o]devious in their ways.

16 So [p]you will be delivered from the forbidden[1] woman,
from [q]the adulteress[2] with [r]her smooth words,
17 who forsakes [s]the companion of her youth
and forgets [t]the covenant of her God;
18 [u]for her house sinks down to death,
and her paths to the departed;[3]
19 none who go to her come back,
nor do they regain the paths of life.

20 So you will walk in the way of the good
and keep to the paths of the righteous.
21 For the upright [v]will inhabit the land,
and those with integrity will remain in it,
22 but the wicked will be [w]cut off from the land,
and the treacherous will be [x]rooted out of it.

Trust in the Lord with All Your Heart

3
1 [y]My son, do not forget my teaching,
[z]but let your heart keep my commandments,
2 for [a]length of days and years of life
and [b]peace they will add to you.

[1] Hebrew *strange* [2] Hebrew *foreign woman* [3] Hebrew *to the Rephaim*

8 [d]1 Sam. 2:9; Ps. 66:9; 97:10 [e]See Ps. 30:4
9 [f][ver. 5] [g]ch. 1:3
11 [h]ch. 1:4 [i]ch. 6:22
13 [j]Ps. 82:5; [John 3:19, 20]
14 [k]Jer. 11:15; [ch. 10:23] [l][Ps. 50:18; Rom. 1:32]
15 [m]Ps. 125:5; [ch. 21:8] [n]ch. 14:2 [o]ch. 3:32
16 [p]ch. 7:5 [q]ch. 6:24; 23:27 [r]ch. 6:24; Ps. 5:9
17 [s]Jer. 3:4; [Ps. 55:13] [t][Mal. 2:14, 15]
18 [u]ch. 7:27
21 [v]ch. 10:30
22 [w]See Ps. 37:38 [x]ch. 15:25; Deut. 28:63; Ps. 52:5

Chapter 3

1 [y]See ch. 1:8 [z]Deut. 8:1; 30:16, 20
2 [a]ver. 16; ch. 4:10; 9:11; 10:27; See Ps. 91:16 [b]ch. 1:33; Ps. 119:165

2:9–11 The second result of heeding wisdom is that one gains an understanding of **righteousness and justice and equity** (v. 9) because wisdom takes root in the heart and acts to protect the person who embraces it (vv. 10, 11). There is a reversing sequence between v. 8 and v. 11 (v. 8, "guarding," "watching"; v. 11, **watch, guard**) that links the then-clause in vv. 5–8 with the then-clause in vv. 9–11 and indicates that the means by which the Lord will be "watching over the way of his saints" (v. 8) is through the wisdom and **understanding** he will give them (v. 11).

2:12–20 Following the description of the wisdom that the Lord grants (vv. 9–11), this section gives three statements of its purpose: it delivers from the deception of those on the evil path (vv. 12–15), it delivers from being flattered into unfaithfulness (vv. 16–19), and it directs one instead to walk in the way that is both true and good (v. 20).

2:12–15 Those who **walk** the wicked path are described as **men of perverted speech** (v. 12) who **rejoice** in what is ultimately harmful (v. 14) and thus deceive themselves while seeking to entrap others (see 1:10–19).

2:16–19 Like those who walk the crooked path in the preceding description (vv. 12–15), a woman who seeks to entice a man to adultery both practices deception (she flatters with **smooth words**, v. 16) and is herself deceived (for her **house sinks down to death**, v. 18).

2:16–17 The ESV footnote indicates that **forbidden woman** is lit., "strange woman" and **adulteress** is lit., "foreign woman." "Strange" is likely used here in the sense of "forbidden" or "unauthorized" (cf. the use of the same word in a different context in Lev. 10:1) since the description that follows in Prov. 2:17 refers to someone who has forsaken another relationship. Likewise, "foreign" is probably used not in the sense of being a member of another nation but rather of being a member of another household. The parallel description of forgetting **the covenant of her God** along with forsaking **the companion of her youth** indicates that the covenant being referred to here is her marriage vow (see Gen. 2:24; Mal. 2:14).

2:21–22 As vv. 18–19 refer to the paths of death and life to indicate where these paths ultimately lead, **the upright will inhabit the land** also looks not simply to the possibility of long life on earth but to the inheritance to which the path is headed (and this is contrasted with the **wicked** being **cut off from the land**). For a similar reference to the "land" used in the context of wisdom language referring to the way of the wicked and the righteous, see note on Ps. 37:11.

3:1–12 *Third Paternal Appeal: Fear the Lord.* The address to "my son" brackets these verses (vv. 1, 11), which consist of six sets of instruction. Each section includes a call to act in wisdom and the grounds for doing so (vv. 1–2, 3–4, 5–6, 7–8, 9–10, 11–12). As a whole, the appeal calls for living in light of the fear of the Lord in all respects: cultivation of faithfulness and humility (vv. 1, 3, 5–6a, 7), gratitude that treats the products of one's labors as a gift (v. 9),

3[c][Ps. 85:10] [d][ch. 20:28; Isa. 59:14] [e][ch. 1:9; 6:21; 7:3] [f]ch. 7:3; [Jer. 17:1; 2 Cor. 3:3]
4[g][1 Sam. 2:26; Luke 2:52; Rom. 14:18] [h]See Ps. 111:10
5[i]Ps. 37:3, 5 [j][Jer. 9:23]
6[k]1 Chr. 28:9 [l][Ps. 73:24]
7[m][Rom. 12:16]; See ch. 12:15 [n]Job 1:1; 28:28
8[o][ch. 4:22] [p]See Job 21:24
9[q]Ex. 23:19; 34:26; Deut. 26:2
10[r]Deut. 28:8
11[s]Cited Heb. 12:5, 6; See Job 5:17
12[t]Deut. 8:5; [1 Cor. 11:32]
13[u]ch. 8:34, 35
14[v]See Job 28:15-19 [w]ch. 8:10, 19; 16:16; Ps. 19:10
15[x]Job 28:18 [y]ch. 8:11
16[z]ver. 2 [a]ch. 8:18; 22:4

3 Let not [c]steadfast love and [d]faithfulness forsake you;
[e]bind them around your neck;
[f]write them on the tablet of your heart.
4 So you will [g]find favor and [h]good success[1]
in the sight of God and man.

5 [i]Trust in the LORD with all your heart,
and [j]do not lean on your own understanding.
6 In all your ways [k]acknowledge him,
and he [l]will make straight your paths.
7 [m]Be not wise in your own eyes;
[n]fear the LORD, and turn away from evil.
8 It will be [o]healing to your flesh[2]
and [p]refreshment[3] to your bones.

9 Honor the LORD with your wealth
and with [q]the firstfruits of all your produce;
10 then your [r]barns will be filled with plenty,
and your vats will be bursting with wine.

11 [s]My son, do not despise the LORD's discipline
or be weary of his reproof,
12 for the LORD reproves him whom he loves,
as [t]a father the son in whom he delights.

Blessed Is the One Who Finds Wisdom

13 [u]Blessed is the one who finds wisdom,
and the one who gets understanding,
14 [v]for the gain from her is better than gain from silver
and her profit better than [w]gold.
15 She is more precious than [x]jewels,
and [y]nothing you desire can compare with her.
16 [z]Long life is in her right hand;
in her left hand are [a]riches and honor.

[1] Or *repute* [2] Hebrew *navel* [3] Or *medicine*

and willingness to submit to reproof (v. 11). Obeying this instruction brings favor and success before God and man (vv. 2, 4, 6b, 8, 10) so that one lives in light of the Lord's delight (v. 12).

3:3 steadfast love and faithfulness. These terms are used together in the Lord's self-declaration to Moses of his character in covenantal relationship (Ex. 34:6, "abounding in steadfast love and faithfulness"). In light of the appeals to trust (Prov. 3:5), fear (v. 7), and honor (v. 9) the Lord, the call here to **bind them around your neck** and **write them on the tablet of your heart** is best understood as encouragement to live faithfully to the covenant (see also 14:22; 16:6; 20:28) by heeding faithful parental instruction (cf. Ps. 25:10).

3:5–8 Subordinating one's own **understanding** to the Lord is in keeping with the major thesis of Proverbs, that the fear of the Lord is the beginning of knowledge (1:7).

3:5 Trust in the LORD is necessary for fulfilling any of the wise ways of life taught in Proverbs; trusting the Lord is closely connected to "fearing" him (cf. 1:7; 2:5; 9:10; 15:33; 19:23; etc.). **With all your heart** indicates that trust goes beyond intellectual assent to a deep reliance on the Lord, a settled confidence in his care and his faithfulness to his Word. **Do not lean on your own understanding** further explains trusting in the Lord. One's "understanding" in Proverbs is his perception of the right course of action. The wise will govern themselves by what the Lord himself declares, and will not set their own finite and often-mistaken understanding against his.

3:6 To **make straight** a person's **paths** means to make the course of the person's life one that continually progresses toward a goal. In Proverbs, the emphasis is on the moral quality of one's life path (here, its moral "straightness").

3:9–10 Honor the LORD. This requires giving proper weight to **your wealth** by using it only for righteous, just, and equitable purposes ("in all your ways acknowledge him," v. 6), which begins with offering the **firstfruits** of everything to the Lord (see Deut. 18:1–5). To give the firstfruits is to imply that the whole belongs to God, indeed the whole worshiper. The prosperity described in Prov. 3:10 is the blessing of the covenant (Deut. 28:1–14), a kind of restored Eden. **Your barns will be filled with plenty** is a generalization concerning the effect of honoring the Lord with all that one has and is. It is not, however, more than a generalization (as Job's comforters held), for to view this as a mechanical formula dishonors God and his inscrutable sovereign purposes.

3:11–12 A father who reflects on these words will take pains to mold his own parenting (esp. **discipline**) according to the pattern set by **the LORD's** parenting. Hebrews 12:5–6 cites these verses, commending endurance to harried believers.

3:13–20 *A Hymn to Wisdom.* In extolling their benefits, this section makes it clear in the repeated reference to **wisdom** and **understanding** (vv. 13, 19) that they are both given and governed by **the LORD** (vv. 19, 20). Following the encouragement to humbly trust the Lord's instruction and discipline (vv. 1–12), this section describes the benefits of wisdom as **more precious** than anything that could be gained on earth (vv. 14, 15), as the way of true **peace** and **life** (vv. 16–18a), and thus as the means by which those who cling to her are **blessed** (vv. 13, 18) by the Lord. Just as wisdom is the means by which the Lord **founded** and **established** creation (v. 19), so it is also the means by which the one who **finds** it will be sustained (vv. 13–18) and established (vv. 21–35).

17 Her [b]ways are ways of pleasantness,
and all her paths are peace.
18 She is [c]a tree of life to those who [d]lay hold of her;
those who hold her fast are called blessed.

19 [e]The LORD by wisdom founded the earth;
by understanding [e]he established the heavens;
20 by his knowledge [f]the deeps broke open,
and [g]the clouds drop down the dew.

21 My son, [h]do not lose sight of these—
keep sound wisdom and discretion,
22 and they will be [i]life for your soul
and [j]adornment for your neck.
23 [k]Then you will walk on your way securely,
[l]and your foot will not stumble.
24 [m]If you lie down, you will not be afraid;
when you lie down, [n]your sleep will be sweet.
25 [o]Do not be afraid of sudden terror
or of [p]the ruin[1] of the wicked, when it comes,
26 for the LORD will be your confidence
and will [q]keep your foot from being caught.
27 [r]Do not withhold good from those to whom it is due,[2]
when it is in your power to do it.
28 [s]Do not say to your neighbor, "Go, and come again,
tomorrow I will give it"—when you have it with you.
29 [t]Do not plan evil against your neighbor,
who [u]dwells trustingly beside you.
30 [v]Do not contend with a man for no reason,
when he has done you no harm.
31 [w]Do not envy [x]a man of violence
and do not choose any of his ways,
32 for [y]the devious person is an abomination to the LORD,
but the upright are [z]in his confidence.
33 [a]The LORD's curse is on the house of the wicked,
but he [b]blesses the dwelling of the righteous.
34 Toward the [c]scorners he [d]is scornful,
[e]but to the humble he gives favor.[3]
35 The wise will inherit honor,
but fools get[4] disgrace.

[1] Hebrew *storm* [2] Hebrew *Do not withhold good from its owners* [3] Or *grace* [4] The meaning of the Hebrew word is uncertain

17 [b][Matt. 11:29, 30]
18 [c]ch. 11:30; 13:12; 15:4; Gen. 2:9; 3:22; Rev. 2:7; 22:2 [d]ch. 4:13
19 [e]ch. 8:27; Ps. 104:5, 24; 136:5
20 [f]Gen. 7:11; [Job 38:8] [g]Job 36:28
21 [h]ch. 4:21
22 [i]See ch. 4:22 [j][ch. 1:9]
23 [k]ch. 10:9; [ch. 28:18; Ps. 91:11] [l]ch. 4:12; Ps. 91:12
24 [m][ch. 6:22; Ps. 3:5; 4:8]; See Job 11:19 [n]Jer. 31:26
25 [o][1 Pet. 3:14]; See Ps. 91:5 [p][Job 5:21]
26 [q]See 1 Sam. 2:9
27 [r]Gal. 6:10
28 [s][Lev. 19:13; Deut. 24:15]
29 [t]ch. 6:14; 12:20; 14:22 [u][Judg. 18:7, 27]
30 [v][Rom. 12:18]
31 [w]See Ps. 37:1 [x]Ps. 18:48; 140:1
32 [y]ch. 2:15 [z]See Job 29:4
33 [a]Ps. 37:22; Zech. 5:4; Mal. 2:2; See Lev. 26:14-39 [b][Job 8:6]
34 [c]See Ps. 1:1 [d][James 4:6; 1 Pet. 5:5; See Ps. 138:6] [e][James 4:6; 1 Pet. 5:5]; See Ps. 138:6

3:17 peace. See note on John 14:27.

3:18 The **tree of life** first appears in Genesis (Gen. 2:9; 3:22, 24) and is referred to as if it had the effect of confirming a person in his moral state (see esp. Gen. 3:22). Through obedience, Adam and Eve would have had continued access to the tree and would have been confirmed in an unblemished state, but upon disobedience they were mercifully removed from the garden to keep from being confirmed in a state of guilt. This helps explain the image in Proverbs: the things that are called a "tree of life" are pictured as means by which the righteous continue on and are further confirmed in the way that is blessed in the end (cf. Prov. 11:30; 13:12; 15:4). The tree appears again in Revelation with a similar function of confirming in holiness those who conquer (see Rev. 2:7; 22:2, 14, 19).

3:19–20 For an extended description of **wisdom** as the means by which **the LORD** worked in creation, see the speech of personified Wisdom in 8:4–36. The essential point is that God has built the principles of wisdom into the structure of the world itself; wisdom is the ordering principle by which everything functions and does not devolve into chaos. Thus, when one lives without integrity, one violates the very rules whereby everything is held together. One cannot do this and thrive. This idea is developed at length in 8:22–31.

3:21–35 *Fourth Paternal Appeal: Walk Securely in Wisdom.* This appeal encourages the one who "finds wisdom" (vv. 13–20) to guard it and walk in its ways, knowing that the Lord sustains and secures the path of the righteous (vv. 21–26). At the center of this section is a series of commands (vv. 27–31) prohibiting actions that would contravene Lev. 19:9–18 (i.e., "love your neighbor as yourself") because such behavior treats others in a manner detestable to **the LORD** (Prov. 3:32). The appeal ends with the reminder that those who walk in wisdom will **inherit honor** (cf. v. 16) because it is the Lord who **blesses** the one who walks in humility (vv. 33–35).

3:25–26 These verses encourage those who seek to walk in wisdom not to live in fear of the **ruin** that will come upon the **wicked** (cf. 1:26–27) but to trust that the **LORD** will keep them safe through the just and equitable lifestyle he requires of the righteous.

3:34 James 4:6 and 1 Pet. 5:5 cite this verse from the Septuagint, encouraging humility.

A Father's Wise Instruction

4

1 [f]Hear, O sons, a father's instruction,
and be attentive, that you may [g]gain[1] insight,
2 for I give you good [h]precepts;
do not forsake my teaching.
3 When I was a son with my father,
[i]tender, [j]the only one in the sight of my mother,
4 he [k]taught me and said to me,
[l]"Let your heart hold fast my words;
[m]keep my commandments, and live.
5 [n]Get wisdom; get [g]insight;
do not forget, and do not turn away from the words of my mouth.
6 Do not forsake her, and she will keep you;
[o]love her, and she will guard you.
7 [p]The beginning of wisdom is this: Get wisdom,
and whatever you get, get [g]insight.
8 Prize her highly, and she will exalt you;
she will [q]honor you [r]if you embrace her.
9 She will place on your head [s]a graceful garland;
she will bestow on you a beautiful crown."

10 [f]Hear, [t]my son, and accept my words,
that [u]the years of your life may be many.
11 I have [v]taught you the way of wisdom;
I have led you in the paths of uprightness.
12 When you walk, [w]your step will not be hampered,
and [x]if you run, you will not stumble.
13 [y]Keep hold of instruction; do not let go;
guard her, for she is your [z]life.
14 [a]Do not enter the path of the wicked,
and do not walk in the way of the evil.
15 Avoid it; do not go on it;
turn away from it and pass on.
16 For they [b]cannot sleep unless they have done wrong;
they are robbed of sleep unless they have made someone stumble.
17 For they eat the bread of wickedness
[c]and drink the wine of violence.
18 But [d]the path of the righteous is like [e]the light of dawn,
which shines [f]brighter and brighter until [g]full day.

[1] Hebrew *know*

Chapter 4
1 [f]ch. 1:8; [ch. 5:7; 7:24; 8:33; Ps. 34:11] [g]ch. 2:2
2 [h]Job 11:4
3 [i]See 1 Chr. 22:5 [j]Zech. 12:10
4 [k]1 Chr. 28:9; [Eph. 6:4] [l][ch. 3:1] [m]ch. 7:2; Lev. 18:5; Isa. 55:3
5 [n]ch. 2:2 [g][See ver. 1 above]
6 [o][2 Thess. 2:10]
7 [p][ch. 1:7] [g][See ver. 1 above]
8 [q]1 Sam. 2:30 [r][Song 2:6]
9 [s]ch. 1:9
10 [f][See ver. 1 above] [t]ch. 2:1 [u]See ch. 3:2
11 [v]See 1 Sam. 12:23
12 [w][Job 18:7; Ps. 18:36; 119:45] [x]ch. 3:23
13 [y]ch. 3:18 [z]ver. 22; [John 1:4; 1 John 5:12]
14 [a]ch. 1:15; Ps. 1:1
16 [b][Ps. 36:4]
17 [c][Amos 2:8]
18 [d]Job 11:17; 22:28; Isa. 60:3; 62:1, 2; Dan. 12:3 [e]2 Sam. 23:4; See Ps. 97:11 [f][Ps. 84:7] [g][1 John 3:2]

4:1–9 *Fifth Paternal Appeal: Wisdom Is a Tradition Worth Maintaining.* In this appeal the father cites the appeal that his own father made to him. The effect is threefold. First, the father shows he can identify with his sons. He, too, was once young and under the tutelage of a father. Second, the father implies that wisdom did not begin with him but goes back through many generations. It is not a novelty, but is enduring. Third, he suggests that godliness and prudence are part of their family heritage, and he wants his sons to maintain the legacy. The text is structured in two parts: the opening encouragement (vv. 1–2) and the citation of the boy's grandfather (vv. 3–9).

4:1 sons. Usually Proverbs addresses the reader as "my son," but the plural is used here and in 5:7 and 7:24.

4:7 Although at first glance the statement that the **beginning of wisdom** is to **get wisdom** appears redundant, it represents a central theme in the book of Proverbs. Notice the words of Wisdom personified in 8:17: "those who seek me diligently find me." The nature of wisdom's benefits is such that the reader is encouraged to search for it and guard it continually—both because it is an invaluable treasure (cf. 2:4; 3:13–15; 4:20–23), and also because humans are so prone to spiritual laziness and moral laxity. However, as is true for many themes in Proverbs, this statement is complementary to and informed by the overall framework of Proverbs that wisdom is grounded in the fear of the Lord (cf. 1:1–7; 9:10) and ultimately is given by him (2:6–8).

4:10–19 *Sixth Paternal Appeal: The Two Ways.* This text lays out one of the core teachings of Proverbs: the doctrine of the two ways. It asserts that there lies before everyone a choice between entering the way of wisdom and the way of folly. Which path is taken will determine the outcome of one's life. This appeal has an opening encouragement (v. 10), an exhortation to take the right way (vv. 11–13), a warning against taking the wrong way (vv. 14–17), and a summarizing review of the two ways (vv. 18–19).

4:12 The image of stumbling is thematic for vv. 10–19: hold on to the way of wisdom and **you will not stumble** (v. 12) and instead will avoid the path of the wicked. Their resolve to make others stumble (v. 16) is reflected in their own stumbling (v. 19).

4:14–17 These verses warn against turning to the way of the **wicked** (vv. 14–15) by describing how it creates an insatiable and destructive hunger (v. 16). That hunger is perpetuated by what the path offers those who walk along it: the **bread of wickedness** and the **wine of violence**, v. 17.

4:18–19 The path of the righteous is the way of wisdom (v. 11). **dawn . . . full day**. The image here is of ever-increasing brightness, from first light until

19 [h]The way of the wicked is like deep [i]darkness;
they do not know over what they [j]stumble.

20 [k]My son, be attentive to my words;
incline your ear to my sayings.

21 [l]Let them not escape from your sight;
[m]keep them within your heart.

22 For they are [n]life to those who find them,
and healing to all their[1] flesh.

23 Keep your heart with all vigilance,
for [o]from it flow [p]the springs of life.

24 Put away from you [q]crooked speech,
and put [r]devious talk far from you.

25 [s]Let your eyes look directly forward,
and your gaze be straight before you.

26 [t]Ponder[2] the path of your feet;
[u]then all your ways will be sure.

27 [v]Do not swerve to the right or to the left;
turn your foot away from evil.

Warning Against Adultery

5

1 [w]My son, be attentive to my wisdom;
[x]incline your ear to my understanding,

2 that you may keep [y]discretion,
and your lips may [z]guard knowledge.

3 For the lips of [a]a forbidden[3] woman drip honey,
and her speech[4] is [b]smoother than oil,

4 but in the end she is [c]bitter as [d]wormwood,
[e]sharp as [f]a two-edged sword.

5 Her feet [g]go down to death;
her steps follow the path to[5] Sheol;

[1] Hebrew *his* [2] Or *Make level* [3] Hebrew *strange;* also verse 20 [4] Hebrew *palate* [5] Hebrew *lay hold of*

19 [h]1 Sam. 2:9; Isa. 59:9, 10; Jer. 23:12; John 12:35; [Job 18:5] [i][Matt. 6:23] [j][John 11:10; 1 John 2:10]
20 [k]ver. 10
21 [l]ch. 3:21 [m][ch. 2:1]
22 [n]ver. 13; ch. 8:35; 21:21; Deut. 32:47; [1 Tim. 4:8]
23 [o][Matt. 12:35] [p][Ps. 16:11]
24 [q]ch. 6:12 [r]ch. 2:15
25 [s][Heb. 12:2]
26 [t]ch. 5:6, 21; [Heb. 12:13] [u][Ps. 119:5]
27 [v]Deut. 5:32; 28:14; Josh. 1:7; 1 Kgs. 15:5

Chapter 5

1 [w]ch. 4:20; [ch. 2:1, 2] [x]ch. 22:17
2 [y]ch. 1:4 [z]Mal. 2:7
3 [a]See ch. 2:16 [b]Ps. 55:21
4 [c][Eccles. 7:26] [d]Deut. 29:18; Jer. 9:15; Lam. 3:15, 19; Rev. 8:11 [e]Ps. 57:4; [Ps. 55:21] [f]See Ps. 149:6
5 [g]See ch. 7:27

noon. The path of a person refers to the moral orientation of his or her life (v. 14; cf. 2:8, 13, 15, 20; 3:6; Ps. 25:4). It is this that **shines brighter and brighter**, i.e., keeps increasing in the way in which it displays God's light (cf. Ps. 19:8; 119:105, 130; Prov. 6:23). This contrasts with **the way of the wicked** (4:19), which is the way of "evil" (v. 14). The person whose life is oriented toward evil will stumble through life in **deep darkness**.

4:20–27 *Seventh Paternal Appeal: Maintain a Heart of Wisdom.* This appeal consists primarily of imperatives that encourage the son to attend to wise instruction and guard wisdom's presence in his heart (vv. 20–21, 23a) by turning from evil in speech and actions (vv. 24–26a, 27). That is because wisdom brings health (v. 22) and continues to sustain (v. 23b) and secure (v. 26b) the path of the one who does this.

4:20–23 The commands in vv. 20–21 all encourage internalizing wisdom. **Heart** in Proverbs regularly refers to the center of one's inner life and orientation to God, from which a person does all thinking, feeling, and choosing. Taking words of wisdom into the heart is vital (**they are life**, v. 22), and wisdom's presence in the heart is worth guarding because out of the heart flow all the thoughts and words and choices of a person's life (**from it flow the springs of life**, v. 23; cf. Mark 7:21–23; Luke 6:45).

4:24 As Proverbs makes clear throughout, **crooked speech** points one in the path of the wicked. Crooked speech includes not only dishonest speech but also any good and honest communication (e.g., rebuke) without the proper content, context, or purpose. Guarding the heart in wisdom includes guarding against any speech that contains elements contrary to what the Lord loves (note the numerous references to the misuse of speech as detestable to the Lord in 6:12–19).

4:25 The idea that the **eyes** should **look directly forward** suggests resolution about remaining in the right way. Metaphorically, it suggests that when a person turns his eyes away from the path, he is apt to stumble.

4:26–27 Vital to keeping the heart formed in wisdom is the need to recognize and stay on the path that will shape it further in the way of righteousness. **Do not swerve to the right or to the left** (see Deut. 5:32; Josh. 1:7) refers to both attending to where **the path of your feet** (Prov. 4:26) is going and seeking to stay on the right path by turning **your foot away from evil** (v. 27; cf. 3:7; 16:6, 17).

5:1–23 *Eighth Paternal Appeal: Sexuality.* After the introductory words in vv. 1–2, the entire appeal concerns matters of sexual morality. First, the immoral woman is introduced: she is alluring but deadly (vv. 3–6). An exhortation to stay far from such promiscuous women follows (vv. 7–14). The text then gives a brief but powerful presentation of the essentials of biblical teaching on sexual ethics. It asserts that sexual pleasure is good but that it must be confined to marriage (vv. 15–20). The passage concludes with a brief account of the woes that befall the immoral man (vv. 21–23). This illustrates the principle of "concreteness" (see Introduction: Literary Features). Of course other sexual dangers exist (such as a woman being tempted by an immoral man, temptations to homosexual conduct, incest, or sexual abuse of children), and the wise person applies this counsel by making the appropriate adaptations.

5:2–3 One of the purposes of attending to wisdom is that the son's **lips may guard knowledge** (v. 2), that is, his lips should not let anything go out from them that is inconsistent with true knowledge and wisdom. Such "guarded" speech has the best interest of both the speaker and the hearer in view (cf. Mal. 2:7, referring to the proper function of the priest). In contrast, **the lips of a forbidden woman** are flattering (they **drip honey**, Prov. 5:3)

6[h]ver. 21; ch. 4:26
7[i]See ch. 4:1
10[j]Ps. 127:2
11[k]Ezek. 24:23
12[l]ch. 1:22, 29; See ch. 12:1 [m]ch. 1:25; See Ps. 107:11
14[n][Ps. 94:17]
15[o]ver. 18; [ch. 9:17; Song 4:12, 15; Jer. 2:13]
16[p]See Ps. 68:26 [q][Jer. 9:21; Zech. 8:5]
17[r][ch. 14:10]
18[o][See ver. 15 above] [s]Deut. 24:5 [t]Mal. 2:14
19[u]Song 2:9, 17; 8:14 [v][Jer. 31:14]
20[w]See ch. 2:16
21[x]Ps. 119:168 [y]Hos. 7:2; Heb. 4:13; See Job 14:16; Ps. 11:4 [z]ver. 6

6 she [h]does not ponder the path of life;
her ways wander, and she does not know it.

7 And [i]now, O sons, listen to me,
and do not depart from the words of my mouth.
8 Keep your way far from her,
and do not go near the door of her house,
9 lest you give your honor to others
and your years to the merciless,
10 lest strangers take their fill of your strength,
and your [j]labors go to the house of a foreigner,
11 and at the end of your life you [k]groan,
when your flesh and body are consumed,
12 and you say, [l]"How I hated discipline,
and my heart [m]despised reproof!
13 I did not listen to the voice of my teachers
or incline my ear to my instructors.
14 [n]I am at the brink of utter ruin
in the assembled congregation."

15 Drink [o]water from your own cistern,
flowing water from your own well.
16 Should your [p]springs be scattered abroad,
streams of water [q]in the streets?
17 [r]Let them be for yourself alone,
and not for strangers with you.
18 Let your [o]fountain be blessed,
and [s]rejoice in [t]the wife of your youth,
19 a lovely [u]deer, a graceful doe.
Let her breasts [v]fill you at all times with delight;
be intoxicated[1] always in her love.
20 Why should you be intoxicated, my son, with [w]a forbidden woman
and embrace the bosom of [w]an adulteress?[2]
21 For [x]a man's ways are [y]before the eyes of the LORD,
and he [z]ponders[3] all his paths.

[1] Hebrew *be led astray*; also verse 20 [2] Hebrew *a foreign woman* [3] Or *makes level*

and her words are persuasive (**her speech is smoother than oil**), but her own end proves her words to be hollow and destructive (vv. 4–6).

5:7–8 These elements of instruction are repeated in one way or another throughout the book: recognize the right path and seek to stay on it. Taking in words of wisdom is itself a part of the path (**do not depart from the words of my mouth**, v. 7; cf. 4:20–21), as is the good sense to keep one's feet on the path by avoiding evil (**keep your way far from her**, 5:8; cf. 4:26–27).

5:9–14 Verses 9 and 10 begin the description of consequences (**lest**) for failing to heed the instruction of vv. 7 and 8. Following the lures of the forbidden woman (see note on 2:16–17) results in having what is meant for enjoyment (**honor** and **years**, 5:9; **strength** and **labors**, v. 10) being given over to others, and also produces regret over the wasting of body and soul (vv. 11–13) and shame within the corporate body (v. 14). Although the terms in vv. 9–10 (**others**, **merciless**, **strangers**, and **foreigner**) could refer to the husband and family of the woman with whom adultery would be committed (cf. 6:34–35), they need not be understood as referring exclusively to them. Proverbs often describes the foolish path as one that squanders the very good it deceptively offers (see 1:10–19).

5:15–18 The wife is pictured as the source of water in these images of "cistern," "well," "springs," "streams," and "fountain," which is clear both in the repeated phrase **from your own cistern/well** (v. 15) and the conjunction of "your fountain" and **the wife of your youth** (v. 18). The force of v. 16 is thus to call the hearer to imagine how he would feel if his wife were to commit adultery (**Should your springs be scattered abroad, streams of water in the streets?**) and to follow the principle of doing unto others what you would have done to you (see Matt. 7:12; Luke 6:31), i.e., be faithful to her as he wishes her to be faithful to him.

5:18–19 Proverbs calls unabashedly for seeking fulfillment in the sexual intimacy of marriage (**Let her breasts fill you at all times with delight . . . be intoxicated**) as the relational context where these desires are rightly fostered for the enjoyment (**rejoice in the wife of your youth**) and good (**Let your fountain be blessed**) of both husband and wife. (Regarding "be intoxicated," see ESV footnote: Hb. "be led astray"—i.e., in the sense of being "swept away" with delight in one's wife.)

5:21–23 **For a man's ways are before the eyes of the LORD** (v. 21) provides the grounds for the instruction of the chapter and acts as a reminder of the promises of God's blessing if one stays on the good path (cf. the vocabulary with 4:26). It also provides warning if one's path is heading toward an end consistent with its nature. Being **led astray** (5:23; the same Hb. word as "intoxicated," vv. 19–20, see ESV footnote; thus there is ironic contrast of the two kinds of being "led astray"—one into delight and the other into destruction) by the forbidden woman can result in being **held fast in . . . sin** (v. 22) and thus in a life that lays hold (cf. ESV footnote on v. 5) of the path leading to death.

22 The [a]iniquities of the wicked [b]ensnare him,
and he is held fast in the cords of his sin.
23 [c]He dies for lack of discipline,
and because of his great folly he is [d]led astray.

Practical Warnings

6 1 My son, if you have put up [e]security for your neighbor,
have [e]given your pledge for a stranger,
2 if you are [f]snared in the words of your mouth,
caught in the words of your mouth,
3 then do this, my son, and save yourself,
for you have come into the hand of your neighbor:
go, hasten,[1] and [g]plead urgently with your neighbor.
4 [h]Give your eyes no sleep
and your eyelids no slumber;
5 save yourself like a gazelle from the hand of the hunter,[2]
[i]like a bird from the hand of the fowler.

6 [j]Go to [k]the ant, O [l]sluggard;
consider her ways, and [m]be wise.
7 [n]Without having any chief,
[o]officer, or ruler,
8 she prepares her bread [p]in summer
and [q]gathers her food in harvest.
9 [r]How long will you lie there, [l]O sluggard?
When will you arise from your sleep?
10 [s]A little sleep, a little slumber,
[t]a little [s]folding of the hands to rest,
11 [u]and poverty will come upon you like a robber,
and want like an armed man.

12 [v]A worthless person, a wicked man,
goes about with [w]crooked speech,

[1] Or *humble yourself* [2] Hebrew lacks *of the hunter*

22[a]See Ps. 7:15, 16 [b]ch. 6:2
23[c]See Job 4:21 [d][Job 12:24]

Chapter 6

1[e]See Job 17:3
2[f][ch. 5:22]
3[g][Luke 11:8; 18:5]
4[h]ch. 20:13; Ps. 132:4
5[i]See Ps. 91:3
6[j][Job 12:7] [k]ch. 30:25 [l]ch. 10:26 [m]ch. 23:19; 27:11
7[n][ch. 30:27] [o]Ex. 5:6, 15
8[p][ch. 10:5] [q][ch. 10:5]
9[r][Jonah 1:6] [l][See ver. 6 above]
10[s]ch. 24:33 [t]Eccles. 4:5
11[u]ch. 24:34
12[v]ch. 16:27 [w]ch. 4:24

6:1–19 *Warnings Relating to Securing Debt, Sloth, and Sowing Discord.* This section gives instruction in wise dealing (see 1:3) that takes into account both the nature of a situation and the sort of person involved. The instruction, which refers to types of people with increasing responsibility for their plight, includes: a warning against putting up security because it can lead to harm (6:1–5), an exhortation of the sluggard to follow the example of the ant lest he come to ruin (vv. 6–11), and a description of the sort of characteristics that the Lord hates (vv. 12–19).

6:1–5 These proverbs describe putting up **security** (v. 1) for someone else's debt (i.e., promising to pay his debt if he defaults) as a trap in which one's life is endangered. The son is to be tireless in trying to get out of the position in which his labor, wealth, or goods could be squandered because someone else who is ultimately responsible for satisfying the debt has defaulted. The warning is intended to instill prudence in such situations. Therefore it does not imply that putting up security for someone is morally wrong in every possible situation, but rather that it is generally unwise. Wisdom recognizes that in nearly all cases putting up security is ultimately not good for either party involved (cf. 11:15; 17:18; 20:16; 22:26; 27:13).

6:2 The image of being trapped by one's own words uses verbs typical of capturing animals (**snared**, **caught**), which foreshadows the images of v. 5 and highlights the danger: one who puts up security is trapped because he is at the mercy of a debtor who no longer has any stake in satisfying the debt.

6:3–5 The main point of the appeal begins in v. 3: **save yourself** from the whim of the one in debt and **plead urgently** with him. The point of such pleading is made clear by the comparison to game caught in a trap: focus all your energy and seek to get out of such a situation and thus **save yourself** (v. 5) from ruin.

6:6–11 The sluggard is addressed twice in these proverbs (vv. 6, 9) and instructed to observe the careful labor of the ant (vv. 6–8) so that he may gain wisdom and heed the warning about the result of his sloth (vv. 9–11). The ruinous end that awaits the sluggard is described with some of the same images in 24:30–34, and the ant is called wise in laboring for its provision in 30:24.

6:7 The fact that the ant has no **chief, officer, or ruler** shows that it has initiative, which the sluggard lacks.

6:10 A little sleep, a little slumber. The sluggard may rationalize his late rising and his too-frequent naps as "just a little," but they destroy his productivity.

6:11 The similes used to describe the end of the sluggard are tragic. The **poverty** and **want** that his idleness has created are likened to external forces that will bring about his destitution (a **robber** and an **armed man**).

6:12–19 A person who seeks to cause strife among others is heading for an end of irreparable damage. These verses use repeated vocabulary to highlight the characteristics of such a person in two representative descriptions: characteristics of a worthless person (vv. 12–15), and things hateful to the Lord (vv. 16–19). These descriptions give a unified warning that it is the Lord himself (v. 16) who brings about the final end of the worthless person (v. 15).

6:12–14 The designation **a worthless person, a wicked man** indicates that he lacks "worth" in the sense of any desire to act in accord with righteousness, for that is what God values (cf. Deut. 13:13; 15:9). The four following phrases, each beginning with a participle in Hebrew (**signals, points, goes, winks**), describe the person more fully as one desiring to cause conflict, exploit situations, and gain personal advantage in all that he does. Not only his mouth (**crooked speech**) but also his **eyes**, **feet**, and **finger** are used to communicate deceptively. The final participle (**devises**) indicates that the external character of a worthless person's communication stems from a **per-**

13[x]ch. 10:10; Ps. 35:19
14[y]See ch. 2:12 [z][Mic. 2:1]; See ch. 3:29 [a][ch. 16:28]
15[b]Isa. 30:13, 14; Jer. 19:11 [c]ch. 29:1; 2 Chr. 36:16
16[d]See Job 5:19
17[e][ch. 8:13; 16:5; 21:4]; See Ps. 101:5 [f]ch. 12:22; 17:7; Ps. 31:18; 120:2 [g]Deut. 19:10; Isa. 1:15; 59:3, 7
18[h]Gen. 6:5 [i]See ch. 1:16
19[j]See Ps. 27:12 [k]ch. 12:17; 14:5, 25; 19:5, 9 [a][See ver. 14 above]
20[l]See ch. 1:8
21[m]See ch. 3:3 [n][Job 31:36]
22[o]See ch. 3:23, 24 [p]ch. 2:11
23[q]Ps. 119:105; [Ps. 13:3] [r][ch. 10:17]
24[s]See ch. 2:16
25[t][Matt. 5:28] [u][2 Kgs. 9:30]
26[v][ch. 29:3] [w]ch. 28:21; 1 Sam. 2:36 [x]Ezek. 13:18
27[y]Job 31:12 [z]Ps. 79:12

13 [x]winks with his eyes, signals[1] with his feet,
points with his finger,
14 with [y]perverted heart [z]devises evil,
continually [a]sowing discord;
15 therefore calamity will come upon him suddenly;
[b]in a moment he will be broken [c]beyond healing.

16 There are [d]six things that the LORD hates,
[d]seven that are an abomination to him:
17 [e]haughty eyes, [f]a lying tongue,
and [g]hands that shed innocent blood,
18 [h]a heart that devises wicked plans,
[i]feet that make haste to run to evil,
19 [j]a false witness who [k]breathes out lies,
and one who [a]sows discord among brothers.

Warnings Against Adultery

20 [l]My son, keep your father's commandment,
[l]and forsake not your mother's teaching.
21 [m]Bind them on your heart always;
[n]tie them around your neck.
22 [o]When you walk, they[2] will lead you;
[o]when you lie down, they will [p]watch over you;
and when you awake, they will talk with you.
23 For the commandment is [q]a lamp and the teaching a light,
and the [r]reproofs of discipline are the way of life,
24 to preserve you from the evil woman,[3]
from the smooth tongue of [s]the adulteress.[4]
25 [t]Do not desire her beauty in your heart,
and do not let her capture you with her [u]eyelashes;
26 for [v]the price of a prostitute is only [w]a loaf of bread,[5]
but a married woman[6] [x]hunts down a precious life.
27 Can a man carry [y]fire next to his [z]chest
and his clothes not be burned?

[1] Hebrew *scrapes* [2] Hebrew *it*; three times in this verse [3] Revocalization (compare Septuagint) yields *from the wife of a neighbor* [4] Hebrew *the foreign woman* [5] Or (compare Septuagint, Syriac, Vulgate) *for a prostitute leaves a man with nothing but a loaf of bread* [6] Hebrew *a man's wife*

verted heart that seeks to plant seeds of distrust and suspicion among others (**continually sowing discord**).

6:15 therefore. The primary justification for the conclusion of this verse is the content of v. 16: the Lord hates and thus also knows and judges these things. The unity of vv. 12–19 around these two central verses is indicated by the way vv. 12–14 and 17–19 are knit together in vocabulary and theme (see note on vv. 17–19).

6:16 six things . . . seven. This numeric literary device presents a representative rather than exhaustive list (cf. 30:15–16, 18–19, 21–31) that seeks to draw particular attention to the final item as the focus of God's hatred. It is easy to agree that God hates the first six items; it is also easy to overlook the seventh (v. 19b), and thus the author pulls the reader up short.

6:17–19 The repeated vocabulary from vv. 12–14 indicates that the things listed here are embodied in the character of the worthless person: **eyes, tongue, hands, feet**, and mouth (**breathes**) used for wrong purposes (see vv. 12–13), a **heart that devises wicked plans** (see v. 14a), and the same evil intent of **one who sows discord among brothers** (see v. 14b).

6:20–35 *Ninth Paternal Appeal: Adultery Leads to Ruin.* This is the second of three paternal appeals that focus on sexual ethics (cf. 5:1–23; 7:1–23). Wisdom here helps the son see past the immediate temptation to the consequences, namely, spiritual ruin in the midst of social and financial disgrace (and possibly even death). The fuller description of disaster here evokes and intensifies the description in 5:7–14. The emphasis on sexual sin may be due to the fact that it is an obvious representative of various kinds of sins; probably it is such a good representative because a person in the throes of sexual temptation easily ignores the consequences, and the results are so destructive. Wisdom, then, is the means by which God protects his faithful from such disaster (see note on 2:9–11).

6:20 your mother's teaching. In the appeals of chs. 1–9, usually only the father is mentioned. The mother as teacher appears here and in 1:8 (see note on 1:8). The young man's mother represents respect for the institutions of family and marriage.

6:24–26 the adulteress. The specific situation here is another man's wife who would willingly commit adultery with the son being addressed. Such a case would present sexual temptation in its most powerful form. There are other kinds of temptation, of course, and the wise reader will apply this example by making the appropriate adaptations (see Introduction: Literary Features; also note on 5:1–23).

6:25 Do not desire her beauty in your heart. See Matt. 5:28.

6:26 The Hebrew of this verse is very difficult, and translations vary, but the ESV rendering is most likely correct. The meaning is that a prostitute may be quite cheap—as cheap as a **loaf of bread**—but that having an affair with a **married woman** is fatal.

6:27–31 The father applies two analogies to make his point that succumbing to this temptation leads to disaster. First, he says that one cannot engage in outrageously foolish behavior and not suffer for it (vv. 27–29). Embracing a **neighbor's wife** is taking **fire** to one's **chest**. Second, using an argument from lesser to greater, he reasons that if someone who **steals** under a sense

28 Or can one [a]walk on hot coals
and his feet not be scorched?
29 So is he who goes in to his neighbor's wife;
none who touches her [b]will go unpunished.
30 People do not despise a thief if he steals
to [c]satisfy his appetite when he is hungry,
31 but [d]if he is caught, he will pay [e]sevenfold;
he will give all the goods of his house.
32 He who commits adultery lacks sense;
he who does it destroys himself.
33 He will get wounds and dishonor,
and his disgrace will not be wiped away.
34 For [f]jealousy makes a man furious,
and he will not spare when [g]he takes revenge.
35 He will accept no compensation;
he will refuse though you multiply gifts.

Warning Against the Adulteress

7
1 [h]My son, keep my words
and [h]treasure up my commandments with you;
2 [i]keep my commandments and live;
keep my teaching as [j]the apple of your eye;
3 [k]bind them on your fingers;
[k]write them on the tablet of your heart.
4 Say to wisdom, "You are my sister,"
and call insight your intimate friend,
5 to keep you from [l]the forbidden[1] woman,
from [l]the adulteress[2] with her smooth words.

6 For at [m]the window of my house
I have looked out through my lattice,
7 and I have seen among [n]the simple,
I have perceived among the youths,
a young man [o]lacking sense,
8 passing along the street [p]near her corner,
taking the road to her house
9 in [q]the twilight, in the evening,
at [r]the time of night and darkness.

10 And behold, the woman meets him,
[s]dressed as a prostitute, wily of heart.[3]

[1] Hebrew *strange* [2] Hebrew *the foreign woman* [3] Hebrew *guarded in heart*

28[a]Isa. 43:2
29[b]ch. 16:5
30[c]Job 38:39
31[d][Ex. 22:4] [e]See Ps. 79:12
34[f]ch. 27:4; Song 8:6 [g][Lev. 20:10]

Chapter 7
1[h]See ch. 2:1
2[i]See ch. 4:4 [j]Deut. 32:10
3[k]See ch. 3:3
5[l]See ch. 2:16
6[m]Judg. 5:28
7[n]See ch. 1:4 [o]See ch. 6:32
8[p]ver. 12
9[q]Job 24:15 [r]ch. 20:20
10[s][Gen. 38:14]

of compulsion has to pay a severe penalty, how much greater penalty will a man suffer for committing a more disgraceful and altogether unnecessary offense.

6:29 none . . . will go unpunished. The obvious question is, "By whom?" In Proverbs, the term "go unpunished" (Hb. *naqah*) usually implies that God does the punishing (11:21; 16:5; 17:5; 19:5, 9; 28:20).

6:35 He will accept no compensation. The offended husband will not be satisfied until **you** (singular, bringing the passage back to the son being addressed, vv. 20–25) have paid the full penalty.

7:1–27 *Tenth Paternal Appeal: Keep Away from Temptations to Adultery.* The appeal begins with the plea for the son to take the father's wise instruction to heart in order to keep himself away from the adulteress (vv. 1–5). The main section is a narrative about a man who willingly allows himself to be entrapped by the adulteress (vv. 6–23). The final verses appeal to the sons (plural, v. 24) to learn the point of the narrative: wisdom includes keeping off paths that one knows will lead to temptation, paths on which many have walked naively to their own ruin (vv. 24–26). This is the third paternal warning about adultery (see 5:1–23; 6:20–35).

7:4 Sister in ancient texts sometimes refers to one's wife as a dear companion, as in Song 5:1. Thus, the idea may be that one should bind himself to Wisdom and not the adulteress.

7:6–9 The father begins an account, based on something he has observed through his own **window**. The man is **simple** (see Introduction: Character Types in Proverbs) and **young**. As 6:20–35 expands on the consequences of adultery described in 5:9–14, this appeal plays out the way in which the reckless stumble into adultery by putting themselves in the wrong place (**passing . . . near her corner, taking the road to her house**) at the wrong time (**twilight, evening, time of night and darkness**) in contrast to the clear instruction of 5:8 to "keep your way from her, and do not go near the door of her house."

11 [t]ch. 9:13 [u][Hos. 4:16] [v]1 Tim. 5:13; [Titus 2:5]
12 [w]ver. 8 [x]ch. 23:28
13 [y]ch. 21:29
14 [z]Lev. 7:11 [a]See Ps. 50:14
16 [b]ch. 31:22 [c][Isa. 19:9]
17 [d]Ps. 45:8 [e]Ex. 30:23
19 [f]Matt. 20:11
21 [g]ch. 5:3; 6:24; See Ps. 12:2
23 [h]Eccles. 9:12
24 [i]See ch. 4:1
26 [j][Neh. 13:26]; See Judg. 16:1-5
27 [k][ch. 2:18; 5:5; 9:18]

11 She is [t]loud and [u]wayward;
[v]her feet do not stay at home;
12 now in the street, now in the market,
and [w]at every corner she [x]lies in wait.
13 She seizes him and kisses him,
and with [y]bold face she says to him,
14 "I had to [z]offer sacrifices,[1]
and today I have [a]paid my vows;
15 so now I have come out to meet you,
to seek you eagerly, and I have found you.
16 I have spread my couch with [b]coverings,
colored linens from [c]Egyptian linen;
17 I have perfumed my bed with [d]myrrh,
aloes, and [e]cinnamon.
18 Come, let us take our fill of love till morning;
let us delight ourselves with love.
19 For [f]my husband is not at home;
he has gone on a long journey;
20 he took a bag of money with him;
at full moon he will come home."

21 With much seductive speech she persuades him;
with [g]her smooth talk she compels him.
22 All at once he follows her,
as an ox goes to the slaughter,
or as a stag is caught fast[2]
23 till an arrow pierces its liver;
as [h]a bird rushes into a snare;
he does not know that it will cost him his life.

24 And [i]now, O sons, listen to me,
and be attentive to the words of my mouth.
25 Let not your heart turn aside to her ways;
do not stray into her paths,
26 for many a victim has she laid low,
and all her slain are [j]a mighty throng.
27 Her house is [k]the way to Sheol,
going down to the chambers of death.

[1] Hebrew *peace offerings* [2] Probable reading (compare Septuagint, Vulgate, Syriac); Hebrew *as an anklet for the discipline of a fool*

7:11–12 The woman is described in terms somewhat like Wisdom, who cried aloud in the streets and markets (see 1:20–21), but the implication is that her actions (**loud, wayward, in the street, in the market**) embody a deceptive heart and are those of the woman Folly (see 9:13–18).

7:13–20 The woman uses whatever she can as part of her appeal. She puts the young man off his guard: Israelite culture apparently discouraged the romantic kiss in public (see note on Song 8:1), and this **bold face** (Prov. 7:13) would set the man back; she flatters him into thinking he is someone special (**to meet you, to seek you eagerly**, v. 15); she promises sensual delights (vv. 16–18) and security from discovery (her **husband** will not be back anytime soon, vv. 19–20). The **sacrifices** (v. 14) are probably "peace offerings" (see ESV footnote). The implication is that she has a supply of meat at home (a luxury item; cf. 17:1). This is a stark example of a disconnect between her religious practice (the peace offering was intended to foster communion with God) and the path of her life—a disconnect that the prophets so often condemn (see note on Isa. 1:10–20).

7:22–23 Once again the foolish path is described as a trap (**slaughter**, **caught fast**, **snare**) that ends in destruction (cf. 1:17–19; 5:22; 6:2, 5).

7:24–25 The father now expands his audience to include all his **sons**. The narrative of the fool and the trap are meant to instill in the sons the good sense to keep far from such **ways** or **paths**. Such caution, stemming from the father's commandments being written on the heart (v. 4), is the means by which wisdom will keep them from the forbidden woman or the adulteress (v. 5).

7:26–27 The image of **many a victim . . . a mighty throng** having fallen to her advances, as if she were a warrior, is given as further grounds for staying away, and warns the sons against the foolish pride of presuming they would be different. Although the woman invites the fool to her bed (v. 17) in her home (v. 19) for immediate pleasure, the nature of the path to her **house** will entangle him in a way that, in the end, leads to the **chambers of death**. In mentioning **Sheol**, the text is indicating that the consequences go beyond this life (cf. 23:13–14): life and death in Proverbs commonly correspond to a right relationship to God and estrangement from him, continuing beyond the grave (cf. 12:28).

The Blessings of Wisdom

8

1 Does not [l]wisdom call?
Does not [m]understanding raise her voice?
2 On [n]the heights beside the way,
at the crossroads she takes her stand;
3 beside [o]the gates in front of [p]the town,
at the entrance of the portals she cries aloud:
4 "To you, O [q]men, I call,
and my cry is to [q]the children of man.
5 O [r]simple ones, learn [s]prudence;
O [t]fools, learn sense.
6 Hear, for I will speak [u]noble things,
and from my lips will come [v]what is right,
7 for my [w]mouth will utter truth;
wickedness is an abomination to my lips.
8 All the words of my mouth are righteous;
there is nothing [x]twisted or crooked in them.
9 They are all [y]straight to him who understands,
and right to those who find knowledge.
10 [z]Take my instruction instead of silver,
and knowledge rather than choice gold,
11 [a]for wisdom is better than jewels,
and [b]all that you may desire cannot compare with her.

12 "I, wisdom, dwell with prudence,
and I find knowledge and [c]discretion.
13 [d]The fear of the LORD is [e]hatred of evil.
[f]Pride and arrogance and the way of evil
and [g]perverted speech I hate.
14 I have [h]counsel and [i]sound wisdom;
I have insight; [j]I have strength.
15 By me [k]kings reign,
and rulers decree what is just;
16 by me princes rule,
and nobles, all who govern justly.[1]
17 [l]I love those who love me,
and [m]those who seek me diligently find me.

[1] Most Hebrew manuscripts; many Hebrew manuscripts, Septuagint *govern the earth*

Chapter 8
1 [l]See ch. 1:20 [m]Job 28:12
2 [n]ch. 9:3, 14
3 [o]ch. 1:21 [p]Job 29:7
4 [q][Ps. 49:1, 2]
5 [r]See ch. 1:4 [s]ver. 12 [t][ch. 1:22]
6 [u][ch. 22:20] [v]ch. 23:16
7 [w]Ps. 37:30
8 [x]Deut. 32:5
9 [y][ch. 14:6; 1 Cor. 2:10]
10 [z]ver. 19; ch. 3:14; Ps. 119:72, 127
11 [a][ch. 16:16]; See Job 28:12-19 [b]ch. 3:15
12 [c]ch. 1:4
13 [d][ch. 16:6] [e]See Ps. 97:10 [f][ch. 6:17; 16:5] [g]ch. 2:12; 4:24
14 [h]Isa. 11:2; [Isa. 9:6] [i][ch. 2:7] [j]Eccles. 7:19; [Ps. 89:19]
15 [k][Dan. 2:21; Rom. 13:1; Rev. 19:16]
17 [l]Ps. 91:14; John 14:21; [1 Sam. 2:30] [m]James 1:5; [ch. 1:28]

8:1–36 *Second Wisdom Appeal.* This section begins with a personification of wisdom as a woman calling out in the streets (vv. 1–3), followed by the very words of her appeal (vv. 4–36). Her discourse consists of five main sections: an address (vv. 4–5), a call to listen to her instruction and the grounds for doing so (vv. 6–11), a description of her righteous character and purposes (vv. 12–21), a description of her divine origin and use (vv. 22–31), and a concluding appeal that again addresses the "sons" and thus evokes all the preceding paternal appeals as integral to her instruction (vv. 32–36). As in 1:20–33, Wisdom is personified as a great lady, which helps illustrate the central message of Proverbs: the origin, existence, and purpose of true wisdom are properly framed in relationship with the covenant Lord, who is also the Maker of heaven and earth. As a result, the realm of wisdom encompasses every aspect of life in every corner of creation.

8:5 simple . . . fools. For these terms see Introduction: Character Types in Proverbs. Though they have not embraced the covenant, they are still invited to do so.

8:6–9 Wisdom describes the righteous character of her speech (**noble things**, **right**, **righteous**, **nothing twisted or crooked**) in contrast to the speech of the forbidden woman (cf. 2:16; 5:3; 6:24; 7:5) and of those who use their words for wicked purposes (e.g., the one who sows discord among others, 6:12, 19). In proclaiming the upright character of her speech, Wisdom also indicates that the ability to recognize it as such requires a heart that has embraced wisdom (8:9, **They are all straight to him who understands**).

8:13 One of the main purposes of the **fear of the LORD** in Proverbs is to align a person's heart with what the Lord loves. Describing what wisdom hates (and therefore what the Lord hates) calls a person to examine his or her heart, to guard it from such things, to walk in accord with what the Lord loves, and to seek wisdom for all relationships and interactions (cf. the similar function of 6:12–19). Whether a person's heart and path are aligned with wisdom is a recurring theme of this chapter (see 8:17, 21, 36).

8:14–16 What wisdom offers to the simple is the same **insight** used by **kings** and **rulers** when they **govern** nations **justly**.

8:17 I love those who love me reinforces the calls to seek wisdom (e.g., 2:1–4; 4:5, 7), for she will show favor and then grant multiplied benefits. **Those who seek me diligently find me** reinforces the promise that the Lord will give wisdom (e.g., 2:5–11; James 1:5) and its benefits (see Prov. 8:18–21, 35).

18[n] ch. 3:16 [o] Ps. 112:3; [Matt. 6:33; Luke 16:11; Eph. 3:8]
19[p] ch. 3:14 [q] ver. 10 [r] ch. 10:20
22[s] See Job 28:25-28 [t] Gen. 14:19, 22; [Ps. 104:24; 136:5] [u] Ps. 93:2
23[v] Ps. 2:6 [w] [John 17:5]
24[x] ver. 27, 28; ch. 3:20; Gen. 1:2 [y] Job 15:7; Ps. 51:5
25[z] Job 38:6 (Heb.) [a] Ps. 90:2
27[b] ch. 3:19 [c] Job 26:10
28[d] Gen. 1:6
29[e] Gen. 1:9, 10 [f] See Job 26:10 [g] See Ps. 104:5
30[h] Zech. 13:7; [John 1:1, 2] [i] Ps. 16:3; [Matt. 3:17]
31[j] [Gen. 1:31; Ps. 104:31] [k] Isa. 45:18
32[l] ch. 5:7; 7:24; [1 John 3:1] [m] Ps. 119:1, 2; 128:1, 2; [Luke 11:28]
33[n] See ch. 4:1
34[o] [ch. 3:13]
35[p] ch. 3:18; See ch. 4:22 [q] John 1:4; 17:3 [r] ch. 12:2; 18:22
36[s] [ch. 15:32; 20:2; 29:24] [t] ch. 12:1 [u] ch. 21:6

18 [n] Riches and honor are with me,
[o] enduring wealth and [o] righteousness.
19 My fruit is [p] better than [q] gold, even fine gold,
and my yield than [r] choice silver.
20 I walk in the way of righteousness,
in the paths of justice,
21 granting an inheritance to those who love me,
and filling their treasuries.

22 [s] "The LORD [t] possessed[1] me at the beginning of his work,[2]
the first of his acts [u] of old.
23 Ages ago I was [v] set up,
at the first, [w] before the beginning of the earth.
24 When there were no [x] depths I was [y] brought forth,
when there were no springs abounding with water.
25 Before the mountains [z] had been shaped,
[a] before the hills, I was brought forth,
26 before he had made the earth with its fields,
or the first of the dust of the world.
27 When he [b] established the heavens, I was there;
when he drew [c] a circle on the face of the deep,
28 when he [d] made firm the skies above,
when he established[3] the fountains of the deep,
29 when he [e] assigned to the sea its [f] limit,
so that the waters might not transgress his command,
when he marked out [g] the foundations of the earth,
30 then [h] I was beside him, like a master workman,
and I was daily his[4] [i] delight,
rejoicing before him always,
31 [j] rejoicing in his [k] inhabited world
and delighting in the children of man.

32 "And now, [l] O sons, listen to me:
[m] blessed are those who keep my ways.
33 [n] Hear instruction and be wise,
and do not neglect it.
34 [o] Blessed is the one who listens to me,
watching daily at my gates,
waiting beside my doors.
35 For [p] whoever finds me [q] finds life
and [r] obtains favor from the LORD,
36 but he who fails to find me [s] injures himself;
all who [t] hate me [u] love death."

[1] Or *fathered*; Septuagint *created* [2] Hebrew *way* [3] The meaning of the Hebrew is uncertain [4] Or *daily filled with*

8:18–21 Riches and honor come with wisdom (this often happens when a society is functioning justly), but also something even greater: an unspecified kind of **enduring wealth and righteousness** (v. 18), a **fruit** that is **better than gold** and **silver** (v. 19), and an abundant **inheritance** (v. 21). While this description would include any material blessings that come to those who seek wisdom, these things cannot compare to the greater value of what is promised here: life and favor from the Lord (see v. 35).

8:22–31 the first of his acts of old (v. 22). The same wisdom that makes this invitation is the wisdom that was present with God when he created the world and established it as a coherent system, for Wisdom (personified) says, **I was daily his delight** (v. 30; cf. also 3:19–20). The wisdom that enters the lives of the faithful actually enables them to participate in the rationality at the heart of things. This is why the impious are called "foolish" or even "stupid" (12:1); they are self-haters (cf. 8:36). On the question of whether the personification of Wisdom here goes beyond personification and describes an actual person, see Introduction: Personified Wisdom and Christ.

8:32–36 By using the address **O sons**, this section not only concludes Wisdom's appeal in vv. 1–31, but also draws together all of the paternal appeals as sharing her overall purpose: to extol the benefits of wisdom for faithful covenant living. The reasons given for heeding Wisdom's call also extend to those given in the preceding appeals: you will be **blessed** (see 3:13, 18), find **life** (see 2:21), and obtain **favor from the LORD** (see 3:4, 32–33). The final statement that **all who hate me love death** presents previous warnings (see 1:19, 32; 2:22; 3:33a; 5:22–23) in stark terms: those who practice what wisdom hates (see 8:13) show by their affections that they are on the way that leads not to life and favor (v. 35) but to injury and death.

The Way of Wisdom

9

1 [v]Wisdom has built her house;
she has hewn her [w]seven [x]pillars.
2 She has [y]slaughtered her beasts; she has [z]mixed her wine;
she has also [a]set her table.
3 She has [b]sent out her young women to [c]call
from [d]the highest places in the town,
4 [e]"Whoever is simple, let him turn in here!"
[f]To him who lacks sense she says,
5 "Come, [g]eat of my bread
and [h]drink of [z]the wine I have mixed.
6 Leave [i]your simple ways,[1] and [j]live,
[k]and walk in the way of insight."
7 Whoever corrects a scoffer gets himself abuse,
and he who reproves a wicked man incurs injury.
8 [l]Do not reprove a scoffer, or he will hate you;
[m]reprove a wise man, and he will love you.
9 Give instruction[2] to a wise man, and he will be [n]still wiser;
teach a righteous man, and he will [o]increase in learning.
10 [p]The fear of the LORD is the beginning of wisdom,
and [q]the knowledge of the Holy One is insight.
11 For by me [r]your days will be multiplied,
and years will be added to your life.
12 [s]If you are wise, you are wise for yourself;
if you scoff, you alone will bear it.

The Way of Folly

13 [t]The woman Folly is [u]loud;
she is seductive[3] and [v]knows nothing.
14 She sits at the door of her house;
she takes a seat on [w]the highest places of the town,
15 calling to those who pass by,
who are [x]going straight on their way,

[1] Or *Leave the company of the simple* [2] Hebrew lacks *instruction* [3] Or *full of simpleness*

Chapter 9
1 [v][Matt. 16:18; 1 Pet. 2:5]; See Eph. 2:20-22 [w][Rev. 1:4] [x][1 Tim. 3:15]
2 [y][Matt. 22:4] [z]ch. 23:30; Song 8:2 [a]Ps. 23:5; [Luke 14:17]
3 [b][Ps. 68:11; Matt. 22:3; 23:34] [c]ch. 8:1, 2 [d]ver. 14; ch. 8:2; [Matt. 10:27]
4 [e]ver. 16; [Matt. 11:25; 1 Cor. 1:26] [f]ch. 6:32
5 [g][Song 5:1; Isa. 55:1; John 6:27] [h][John 7:37] [z][See ver. 2 above]
6 [i]See ch. 1:4 [j][ver. 11] [k][ch. 23:19]
8 [l][Matt. 7:6] [m]See Ps. 141:5
9 [n][Matt. 13:12] [o]ch. 1:5
10 [p]See ch. 1:7 [q]ch. 30:3
11 [r][ch. 10:27]; See ch. 3:2
12 [s][Job 22:2, 3; 1 Cor. 3:8; Gal. 6:5]
13 [t]For ver. 13-18, see ch. 7:7-27 [u]ch. 7:11 [v]ch. 5:6
14 [w]ver. 3
15 [x][ver. 6]

9:1–18 *Lady Wisdom and Lady Folly.* The final poem of the first major section of the book (1:8–9:18) contains contrasting personifications of wisdom (9:1–12) and of folly (vv. 13–18). Each consists of a description of the women (Wisdom, vv. 1–3; Folly, vv. 13–15), a call to the simple (Wisdom, v. 4; Folly, v. 16), an invitation to eat (Wisdom, v. 5; Folly, v. 17), and a statement about where each invitation will lead (Wisdom, vv. 11–12; Folly, v. 18). The purpose of the similarity is to highlight the differences, which present Lady Wisdom as clearly desirable in all respects. The description of Lady Wisdom is given more space (12 out of 18 verses), contains a summary of her teaching (vv. 6–10), and has her narrating the consequences of her way (vv. 11–12). The description of Lady Folly, by contrast, while emphasizing the emptiness of her character (v. 13), lacks any of her crooked instruction (i.e., nothing follows the address and appeal in vv. 16–17), and has her end narrated *about* her rather than *by* her (v. 18). In the flow of the book, this concluding chapter acts as a bookend with the introduction (cf. 1:7 and 9:10) to unify the entire section in its call to recognize, internalize, and walk in the way of wisdom.

9:1–3, 13–14, 17 The description of Wisdom's **house** (she **built** it and hewed **seven pillars**) and her preparations (**slaughtered her beasts, mixed her wine, set her table**, and **sent out her young women**) is a picture of the prudence, strength, riches, and honor that she described as hers (see 8:12–21). In contrast, the description of Folly is a picture of one who lacks sense (**she . . . knows nothing**), strength and honor (**she sits at the door**), and riches (she offers **stolen water** and **bread**).

9:1 Some have likened Wisdom's **house** to a temple; this is unnecessary, since the overall image is of a noble lady inviting people to a great feast. Clearly, Wisdom does not compete with the Lord's own temple (cf. v. 10)! The **seven pillars** have also provoked many guesses. It is simplest, however, to take them as indicating that the house is of good size, and to consider that seven is often symbolic of perfection.

9:4–6 let him (who is simple) **turn in here**. Cf. the invitation in 8:5. **Leave your simple ways**. Wisdom calls the simple to her feast so that they may become wise. Folly calls the simple to come and not only remain simple but also to be further formed in the way of foolishness.

9:7–9 These verses present three statements about what happens if one **corrects a scoffer** or the **wicked** (vv. 7a, 7b, 8a) plus three contrasting statements about reproving a **wise man** (vv. 8b, 9a, 9b). The point is twofold: if a person desires to be wise, he must examine how his heart responds to wise reproof or correction (see v. 12); and in order to be wise with others, he must have the prudence to observe other people's actions. It is clear that the "wise" or "righteous" person does not rest content with his attainment, nor is he presented as morally "perfect." He becomes **still wiser**, and **will increase in learning**, through correction.

9:10 The fear of the LORD. Together with 1:7 (see note), this verse stands as the grounding and thematic statement for all of the appeals to wisdom throughout 1:1–9:18.

9:12 The contrast of this verse (**wise** or **scoff**) picks up that of vv. 7–9 and further emphasizes the responsibility of the individual to respond to Wisdom's call and to recognize her benefits.

9:13–14 The woman Folly . . . sits at the door. For the contrasts with Wisdom see note on vv. 1–3, 13–14, 17.

16 [y]"Whoever is simple, let him turn in here!"
And to him who lacks sense she says,
17 [z]"Stolen water is sweet,
and [a]bread eaten in secret is pleasant."
18 But he does not know [b]that the dead[1] are there,
that her guests are in the depths of Sheol.

The Proverbs of Solomon

10 [c]The proverbs of Solomon.

[d]A wise son makes a glad father,
[e]but a foolish son is a sorrow to his mother.
2 [f]Treasures gained by wickedness do not profit,
[g]but righteousness delivers from death.
3 [h]The LORD does not let the righteous go hungry,
[i]but he thwarts the craving of the wicked.
4 A slack hand [j]causes poverty,
[k]but the hand of the diligent makes rich.
5 He who [l]gathers in summer is a prudent son,
but he who sleeps in harvest is [m]a son who brings shame.
6 Blessings are on the head of the righteous,
but [n]the mouth of the wicked conceals violence.
7 [o]The memory of the righteous is a blessing,
but [p]the name of the wicked will rot.
8 [q]The wise of heart will receive commandments,
but a babbling fool will come to ruin.
9 [r]Whoever walks in integrity walks securely,
but he who makes his ways crooked [s]will be found out.

[1] Hebrew *Rephaim*

16 [y]ver. 4
17 [z][ch. 5:15] [a][ch. 20:17; 30:20]
18 [b]See ch. 7:27

Chapter 10

1 [c]See ch. 1:1 [d]See ch. 29:3 [e]ch. 17:25; 29:15
2 [f][ch. 21:6; Ezek. 7:19; Luke 12:19, 20] [g]ch. 11:4, 6
3 [h]Ps. 34:9, 10; 37:25; [Matt. 6:33] [i][Ps. 112:10; James 4:3]
4 [j][ch. 6:11; 12:24; 13:4] [k]ch. 21:5
5 [l][ch. 6:8] [m]ch. 17:2; 19:26
6 [n]ver. 32
7 [o]Ps. 112:6 [p][Ps. 9:5]
8 [q][Matt. 7:24, 25]
9 [r]ch. 3:23; 28:18; Ps. 23:4; Isa. 33:15, 16 [s][Matt. 10:26; 1 Tim. 5:25]

9:18 The first major section of Proverbs (1:8–9:18) closes with a description of where the foolish way will end: although the one who heeds Folly's call **does not know** it, her way ends in death (cf. 7:27; 8:36). **He** refers to anyone who turns aside and follows the woman Folly (see 9:13). The force of the contrast with the end of the way of wisdom throughout this section makes the point clear that this refers not simply to physical death but to the spiritual reality bound up with where that path is headed.

10:1–22:16 *Proverbs of Solomon.* Here begins what may be called the "proverbs proper," individual maxims or aphorisms, after the longer wisdom poems of chs. 1–9. Often, however, individual proverbs are grouped together into small collections which, taken together, give the reader a more complete understanding of a given topic (see Introduction: Literary Features).

10:1–5 The purpose of these proverbs is to encourage the pursuit of one's labors in righteousness, which excludes acquiring gain by unjust means (v. 2a) or squandering it by sloth (vv. 4–5). At the center of these verses is the reason: **The LORD does not let the righteous go hungry**. It is the Lord who provides (v. 3), and through righteousness he delivers not only from hunger but also from **death** (v. 2b). The encouragement of the whole section to walk in righteousness is framed by the appeal to be a son who is **wise** (v. 1a) or **prudent** (v. 5a) rather than **foolish** (v. 1b) or shameful (v. 5b). To see vv. 1–5 as a paragraph should prevent taking any of its verses out of context (see note on v. 4).

10:1 This verse opens 10:1–22:16 by echoing the previous chapters' appeals of a **father** and **mother** (1:8) to be a **wise son**. Thus it stands as a signpost to the reader that the instruction of 1:1–9:18 is essential for a proper understanding and appropriation of the proverbs that follow.

10:4 makes rich. Cf. v. 22a. The **diligent** is another name applied to the "wise" and the "righteous" (vv. 1, 3; see Introduction: Character Types in Proverbs). The paragraph context (cf. v. 3) indicates that the diligence the Lord instills in the righteous is his means to provide for their material needs. The contrasts of vv. 6–32 further indicate that the diligence referred to is grounded in "the fear of the LORD" (v. 27a) and has more than simply physical needs in view (vv. 16–17). In a culture like ancient Israel, based on subsistence agriculture, "wealth" means good crops, a well-fed family, and a stable farm to pass on to one's children, rather than the luxurious wealth a modern reader may think of. Further, Proverbs has a clear set of priorities in which wisdom is far better than wealth, and righteousness with few possessions is better than wealth without knowing the Lord and without walking in righteousness (3:13–15; 8:19; 15:16–17; 16:8, 16; 17:1).

10:6–32 Although set in clusters, vv. 6–32 as a whole act to contrast the **righteous** and the **wicked** in order to illustrate that "righteousness" (v. 2) is the path for a wise son. The phrase "the mouth of the wicked" opens (vv. 6, 11) and closes (v. 32) the section, which also includes other terms for the same idea (e.g., "lips" in vv. 13a, 18a, 21a, 32a; "babbling fool" is lit., "foolish of lips," vv. 8b, 10b). The recurring terms relating to the mouth (lips, tongue, etc.) are connected to their relation to both hunger (or desire) and speech: what people desire and how they attain it are both indicators of the path they walk.

10:6–11 Neither the **blessings . . . on the head of the righteous** nor the **violence** that is hidden by the **mouth of the wicked** are necessarily obvious to an observer who sees only external facts (v. 6). However, the one who is **wise of heart** (v. 8a) . . . **walks securely** (v. 9a), whereas the **fool** (vv. 8b, 10) who **makes his ways crooked** (v. 9b) will **come to ruin** (vv. 8b, 10b). Thus, the **mouth of the righteous** manifests what is good for the speaker and for others (it **is a fountain of life**, v. 11a), whereas the **mouth of the wicked conceals** what is harmful both for others and finally for the fool himself (**violence**, v. 11b).

10 Whoever [t]winks the eye causes trouble,
and a babbling fool will come to ruin.
11 [u]The mouth of the righteous is [v]a fountain of life,
but the mouth of the wicked [n]conceals violence.
12 Hatred stirs up strife,
but [w]love covers all offenses.
13 On the lips of him who has understanding, wisdom is found,
but [x]a rod is for the back of him who [y]lacks sense.
14 The wise [z]lay up knowledge,
but [a]the mouth of a fool brings ruin near.
15 [b]A rich man's wealth is his strong city;
the poverty of the poor is their ruin.
16 The wage of the righteous leads [c]to life,
the gain of the wicked to sin.
17 Whoever heeds instruction is on [d]the path to life,
but he who rejects reproof leads others astray.
18 The one who conceals hatred has lying lips,
and whoever utters slander is a fool.
19 [e]When words are many, transgression is not lacking,
[f]but whoever restrains his lips is prudent.
20 The tongue of the righteous is [g]choice silver;
the heart of the wicked is of little worth.
21 The lips of the righteous feed many,
but fools die for [h]lack of sense.
22 [i]The blessing of the LORD makes rich,
and he adds no sorrow with it.[1]
23 Doing wrong is [j]like a joke to a fool,
but [k]wisdom is pleasure to a man of understanding.
24 [l]What the wicked dreads [m]will come upon him,
but [n]the desire of the righteous will be granted.

[1] *Or and toil adds nothing to it*

10[t]ch. 6:13
11[u]Ps. 37:30 [v]ch. 13:14; Ps. 36:9 [n][See ver. 6 above]
12[w]1 Pet. 4:8; [James 5:20]
13[x]ch. 19:29; 26:3 [y]See ch. 6:32
14[z][ver. 8; ch. 12:23] [a]ch. 18:7
15[b]ch. 18:11; [Ps. 52:7; Mark 10:24, 25]
16[c]ch. 11:19; 19:23
17[d][ch. 6:23]
19[e][Matt. 12:36, 37] [f]ch. 17:27; [James 3:2]
20[g]ch. 8:19; 16:16
21[h][Hos. 4:6]
22[i][Gen. 24:35; 26:12; Deut. 8:18]
23[j]ch. 2:14; 15:21 [k][ch. 8:30]
24[l]Isa. 66:4; Heb. 10:27; [Job 15:21] [m]Job 3:25 [n]Ps. 145:19; Matt. 5:6; 1 John 5:14, 15

10:10 Whoever winks the eye probably describes a person giving a concealed signal that he is lying.

10:12–18 These verses constitute a paragraph, with both vv. 12 and 18 mentioning **hatred** and both using the word **covers/conceals** (Hb. *kasah*); the individual verses relate to this overall theme. At the center of the section is a statement about **wealth** and **poverty** (v. 15) that requires careful attention. Though wealth can represent strength, and poverty can lead to ruin, the verses that precede and follow v. 15 (vv. 12–14 and 16–18) reinforce the call to recognize that what people pursue and how they pursue it are more important than what they possess (see 28:6, 20). Deception conceals a hatred (10:18a) that causes contention among others (v. 12a) and **ruin** for the person who deals in it (vv. 14b, 16b). Seeking wisdom (vv. 13a, 14a, 17a) through obedience, by contrast, fosters a love that can make peace with others (v. 12b); such a path leads to life (vv. 16a, 17a).

10:12 Where the wicked are described as concealing violence (vv. 6b, 11b) or **hatred** (vv. 12a, 18a) and thus deceiving others for their own sinful purposes, the one who is wise seeks the good of others even when he or she is the offended party: **love covers** (the same Hb. verb, *kasah*, is translated as "conceal" in vv. 6b, 11b, 18a) **all offenses**. Cf. the similar instruction in Matt. 5:44; James 5:20; 1 Pet. 4:8.

10:15 The point of this proverb is to invite reflection on the benefit of **wealth** vs. the ruinous effect of **poverty**. Whereas wealth can be like a **strong city**, providing safety, resources, and protection against misfortune, poverty leads only to ruin and thus should not be embraced out of laziness or romanticism. Although there are benefits from wealth, it is a mistake (as shown elsewhere in Proverbs) to place one's trust in wealth rather than in "the name of the LORD" (18:10–11), for "treasures gained by wickedness do not profit" (10:2).

10:16 A **wage** earned by the **righteous** brings positive benefits, because it **leads to life**, but when the wicked **gain** wealth, they use it in sinful ways, so their gain leads **to sin**.

10:19–21 These three proverbs contrast the prudent and productive character of righteous speech with the revealed emptiness of what is concealed in foolish speech (see v. 18).

10:20 The value of **righteous** speech reveals that it is wise to seek further the well from which it flows, whereas the speech of the **wicked** shows that such a pursuit is vain because the **heart** of such a person is of **little worth**.

10:21 The lips of the righteous feed many. The actions of the righteous produce that which is good not only for himself but also for others. "Lips" can relate both to speech and to hunger; if the proverb plays on this double reference, then the feeding here may refer to material provision (what one eats), but probably also signifies speech that leads others in the way of life (cf. the contrast in v. 17).

10:22 This verse stands at the center of vv. 12–32 as an important qualification, relating to both the source and the nature of one's wealth. If it is the **blessing of the LORD** that **makes rich** (see also v. 4), then how one seeks wealth (e.g., vv. 4b, 15a) is necessarily governed by a commitment to act righteously, and always to manifest a hope that rests not in material things but in the Lord who provides (see vv. 23–30). **he adds no sorrow with it**. When the Lord gives material blessing, he does not give it grudgingly or with condemnation but freely and with joy.

10:23–25 The contrasting patterns of speech described in vv. 19–21 show the state of the heart. The heart of the **righteous** finds **pleasure** in **wisdom** and can hope that such a path leads to being **established forever**. The heart of the **wicked** treats **doing wrong** as a trivial matter yet **dreads** the inevitable end to which such a path leads.

25 [o]When the tempest passes, the wicked is no more,
but [p]the righteous is established forever.
26 Like vinegar to the teeth and smoke to the eyes,
so is the sluggard to those who send him.
27 [q]The fear of the LORD prolongs life,
[r]but the years of the wicked will be short.
28 [s]The hope of the righteous brings joy,
[t]but the expectation of the wicked will perish.
29 [u]The way of the LORD is a stronghold to the blameless,
but destruction to evildoers.
30 [v]The righteous will never be removed,
but [w]the wicked will not dwell in the land.
31 [x]The mouth of the righteous brings forth wisdom,
but the perverse tongue will be cut off.
32 The lips of the righteous [y]know what is acceptable,
but the mouth of the wicked, [z]what is perverse.

11

1 [a]A false balance is an abomination to the LORD,
[b]but a just weight is his delight.
2 [c]When pride comes, then comes disgrace,
but with [d]the humble is wisdom.
3 [e]The integrity of the upright guides them,
[f]but the crookedness of the treacherous destroys them.
4 [g]Riches do not profit in the day of wrath,
[h]but righteousness delivers from death.
5 The righteousness of the blameless [i]keeps his way straight,
but the wicked falls by his own wickedness.
6 [h]The righteousness of the upright delivers them,
but the treacherous [j]are taken captive by their lust.
7 When the wicked dies, his [k]hope will perish,
and [l]the expectation of wealth[1] perishes too.

[1] Or *of his strength*, or *of iniquity*

25[o][Job 21:18; Ps. 58:9]; See Matt. 7:26, 27 [p]ch. 12:3; Ps. 15:5; [Matt. 7:24, 25]
27[q]See ch. 3:2 [r]See Job 15:32, 33
28[s][Luke 21:28] [t]See Job 8:13
29[u][Ps. 25:12; Matt. 22:16; Acts 9:2]
30[v]ver. 25; Ps. 37:22, 29; 125:1 [w]ch. 2:21, 22
31[x]Ps. 37:30
32[y][Eccles. 10:12] [z]ch. 2:12

Chapter 11

1[a]ch. 16:11; 20:10, 23; See Lev. 19:35, 36 [b][ch. 12:22]
2[c]ch. 16:18; 18:12; 29:23; [Dan. 4:30, 31] [d]Mic. 6:8
3[e]ch. 13:6 [f]ch. 19:3
4[g]Zeph. 1:18; See ch. 10:2 [h][Gen. 7:1]
5[i]ch. 3:6
6[h][See ver. 4 above] [j]See Ps. 7:15, 16
7[k]ch. 10:28 [l]See Job 8:13, 14

10:26 Vinegar and **smoke** are major irritants to the **teeth** and **eyes**. In the same way, shiftless people are irritating because they can never be relied upon.

10:27–30 The hope of the righteous and **the expectation of the wicked** are set in repeated contrast in these verses. The effect of the comparison is to emphasize **the LORD** as the one who secures the end of the righteous as well as the one who brings the path of the wicked to futility.

10:27 The fear of the LORD prolongs life (cf. 9:11; Ps. 61:6) as a general rule, because of the Lord's blessing (cf. Deut. 5:16). **The years of the wicked will be short** (likewise a general rule) whether because the Lord brings about premature death as a judgment or because sinful patterns often destroy both physical health and peace of mind.

10:30 The declarations **will never be removed** and **will not dwell** indicate that the **land** here refers not to the geography of the original recipients, but to the promised end of the righteous path (cf. note on 2:21–22).

10:31–32 The repetition of the **mouth of the righteous** (see v. 11a) and the **mouth of the wicked** (see vv. 6b, 11b) frames vv. 6–32 and concludes the chapter by drawing the contrast into focus. The **perverse tongue** manifests the state of the person's heart (see the related contrast of v. 20), and the fact that it **will be cut off** indicates that what the wicked have concealed (violence, vv. 6b, 11b; hatred, v. 18a) in their speech has ruined them from the inside out. The mouth/**lips of the righteous** manifest a heart that **brings forth wisdom**, which is a blessing to themselves and others (cf. vv. 11a, 21a).

11:1–8 These proverbs focus on matters of financial and personal security.

11:1–4 The **riches** of the wicked that will not save them (v. 4) and the **false balance** whereby a wicked man increases his income (v. 1) are contrasted with the just weight (v. 1) and righteousness (v. 4). Similarly, the **pride** (v. 2) and **crookedness** (v. 3) that lead people to ruin are contrasted with the **humble** attitude (v. 2) and **integrity** (v. 3) that guides people through the troubles of life. Thus these verses form a unit, with vv. 1 and 4 answering each other as vv. 2 and 3 parallel each other, indicating that compromising just standards is not worth the immediate gain it may offer.

11:1 A **false balance** refers to deception by altering the standard of either the scale or the weight used to measure the quantity of an item being bought or sold. The Pentateuch instructs against such practice as out of accord with what the Lord desires (see Lev. 19:35–36; cf. Deut. 25:13–16, which also calls it **an abomination to the LORD**), and the prophets condemn it as an intolerable injustice among the Lord's people (see Ezek. 45:9–12; Amos 8:5; Mic. 6:11). Compare also the further statements in Proverbs on this subject: 16:11; 20:10, 23.

11:5–6 These two verses parallel each other (**The righteousness of the blameless/upright**) and emphasize a common theme of the section: the faithfulness of the righteous guides (vv. 3a, 5a) and **delivers them** (see vv. 4b, 6a, 8a, 9b) from the fate of the wicked. The repeated phrases in vv. 1 and 20 help make explicit that the Lord is the one who brings about the deliverance of those in whom he delights, as well as the fall of those who are an abomination to him.

11:7–8 The **expectation** and **hope** represented in wealth (with the likely implication that it is unjustly accumulated) will be in vain **when the wicked dies**. Proverbs contrasts this with the hope of the **righteous** (see 10:28) to warn against being fooled by the apparent security in dishonest gain and to assure those who fear the Lord that their hope, manifested in seeking the path of wisdom, will not be in vain (see 23:18; 24:14).

8 [m]The righteous is delivered from trouble,
and the wicked walks into it instead.
9 With his mouth the godless man would destroy his neighbor,
but by knowledge the righteous are delivered.
10 [n]When it goes well with the righteous, the city rejoices,
and when the wicked perish there are shouts of gladness.
11 By the blessing of the upright a city is exalted,
but [o]by the mouth of the wicked [p]it is overthrown.
12 Whoever [q]belittles his neighbor lacks sense,
but a man of understanding remains silent.
13 Whoever [r]goes about slandering reveals secrets,
but he who is trustworthy in spirit keeps a thing covered.
14 Where there is [s]no guidance, a people falls,
[s]but in an abundance of counselors there is safety.
15 [t]Whoever puts up security for a stranger will surely suffer harm,
but he who hates striking hands in pledge is secure.
16 [u]A gracious woman gets honor,
and [v]violent men get riches.
17 [w]A man who is kind benefits himself,
but a cruel man hurts himself.
18 The wicked earns deceptive wages,
but one who [x]sows righteousness gets a sure reward.
19 Whoever is steadfast in righteousness [y]will live,
but [z]he who pursues evil will die.
20 Those of [a]crooked heart are [b]an abomination to the LORD,
but those of [c]blameless ways are [d]his delight.
21 [e]Be assured, [f]an evil person will not go unpunished,
but [g]the offspring of the righteous will be delivered.
22 Like [h]a gold ring in a pig's snout
is a beautiful woman without discretion.
23 The desire of the righteous ends only in good;
[i]the expectation of the wicked in wrath.

8[m]ver. 6; [ch. 21:18] **10**[n][ch. 28:12; Esth. 8:15] **11**[o]Ps. 10:7 [p][ch. 14:1; 29:8] **12**[q]ch. 14:21; [Matt. 7:1] **13**[r]ch. 20:19; Lev. 19:16 **14**[s]ch. 15:22; 20:18; 24:6 **15**[t][ch. 6:1; Job 17:3] **16**[u][ch. 31:30] [v][Luke 11:21] **17**[w][Matt. 5:7]; See Matt. 25:34-40 **18**[x]Hos. 10:12; Gal. 6:8, 9; [James 3:18] **19**[y]ch. 10:16; 19:23 [z][Rom. 6:23; Gal. 6:8] **20**[a][ch. 17:20] [b]ch. 12:22; 16:5 [c]ch. 13:6; Ps. 119:1 [d]1 Chr. 29:17 **21**[e]ch. 16:5 [f]ch. 12:7; [Ps. 37:2, 9]; See Isa. 28:15-18 [g]See Ps. 112:2 **22**[h][Gen. 24:47; Isa. 3:21; Ezek. 16:12] **23**[i]Rom. 2:8, 9

11:9–12 These verses are framed by reference to imprudent speech relating to others: the **godless man** slanders **his neighbor** (v. 9), and one who **belittles his neighbor lacks sense** (v. 12). Verses 10–11 parallel each other and broaden the focus beyond the individual to a **city**. The city benefits or suffers respectively from the presence of the righteous or the wicked, and the attitude of the city toward each type of character is appropriate. In contrast to the typical modern city, the city described in these verses is a small community where people know each other well and where all would suffer from the person who slanders his neighbors.

11:9 by knowledge the righteous are delivered. Some understand "knowledge" as specifically knowledge of the true facts regarding the situation in which the **godless man** seeks to **destroy his neighbor** with slander, and this is possible. Yet in Proverbs, "knowledge" is more commonly knowledge of God and of his will, so the saying may well be making the point that, even when slandered, the (idealized) righteous person knows how to conduct himself uprightly.

11:12 A man of understanding remains silent rather than spreading harmful information that he might know about **his neighbor** because of living so close to him.

11:13 This is an afterword to vv. 9–12. The person who slanders cannot be trusted with private matters. In contrast, one who is **trustworthy in spirit** knows when to keep things in confidence. One should be prudent regarding the people with whom one chooses to share confidential matters.

11:14 The role of **counselors** is to aid a person in making wise decisions (cf. 15:22; 24:6). While this is particularly important for those who lead **a people**, Proverbs also stresses its broader application to people's decision making in all sorts of situations—cf. 11:5 and the contrasting description of how the wicked **falls** "by his own wickedness."

11:15 To put up **security** is equivalent to cosigning a loan (see note on 6:1–5), and to do so on behalf of a **stranger** is ill-advised. **Striking hands** most likely refers to some kind of gesture used to seal such a deal, analogous to a handshake.

11:16–21 There are three pairs of proverbs here (vv. 16–17, 18–19, 20–21), all relating to a common theme. The **gracious woman** (v. 16) and the **man who is kind** (v. 17) contrast with **violent men** (v. 16) and the **cruel man** (v. 17). By itself, v. 16 might suggest that there is wisdom in pursuing violence, since one can get rich by that means. But in the larger context of vv. 16–21, it is clear that their wealth brings the violent no happiness, and that it comes at a high price. The idea of striving to gain something governs vv. 18–19. Verse 18 speaks of laboring (**earns** and **sows**), whether it be for **deceptive wages** for the evil or for a **sure reward** for the good. Verse 19, similarly, speaks of pursuing **righteousness** or **evil** and of the results that follow. Verses 20 and 21 both concern divine judgment, with punishment for the evil and deliverance for the good.

11:20–21 The shared structure and vocabulary of vv. 1 and 20 draw attention to the character and actions that are either an **abomination** or a **delight** to **the LORD**. The implication is that it is the Lord himself who makes the consequences of v. 21 **assured** (and this implies that the consequences of vv. 3–9 and 18–19 are also brought about by the Lord).

11:22 The attractiveness of a **gold ring** would be nullified by its strange presence in the snout of a pig. This image turns typical notions of value on their head: the attractiveness of a **beautiful woman** is insignificant if there is a lack of **discretion** in her character (see 31:30).

11:23–31 The ultimate destinies of the **wicked** and the **righteous** (e.g., vv. 23 and 31) are reflected in their actions (v. 27) and are prefigured in the response of those affected by such actions (v. 26). The particular actions in

24 [j]One gives [k]freely, yet grows all the richer;
another withholds what he should give, and only suffers want.
25 [l]Whoever brings blessing [m]will be enriched,
and [n]one who waters will himself be watered.
26 [o]The people curse him who holds back grain,
but [p]a blessing is on the head of him who [q]sells it.
27 Whoever diligently seeks good seeks favor,[1]
but evil comes to [r]him who searches for it.
28 Whoever [s]trusts in his riches will fall,
but the righteous will [t]flourish like a green leaf.
29 Whoever [u]troubles his own household will [v]inherit the wind,
and the fool will be servant to the wise of heart.
30 The fruit of the righteous is [w]a tree of life,
and whoever [x]captures souls is wise.
31 If [y]the righteous is repaid on earth,
how much more the wicked and the sinner!

12

1 Whoever loves discipline loves knowledge,
but he who [z]hates reproof is [a]stupid.
2 A good man [b]obtains favor from the LORD,
but a man of evil devices he condemns.
3 No one is established by wickedness,
but the root of [c]the righteous will never be moved.
4 [d]An excellent wife is [e]the crown of her husband,
but she who [f]brings shame is like [g]rottenness in his bones.
5 [h]The thoughts of the righteous are just;
the counsels of the wicked are deceitful.
6 The words of the wicked [i]lie in wait for blood,
but [j]the mouth of the upright delivers them.
7 [k]The wicked are [l]overthrown and are no more,
[m]but the house of the righteous will stand.
8 A man is commended according to his good sense,
but one of twisted mind is [n]despised.
9 Better to be lowly and have a servant
than to play the great man and lack bread.

24 [j]ch. 13:7 [k]Ps. 37:21; 112:9; [ch. 19:17]
25 [l]See 2 Cor. 9:6-11 [m]ch. 13:4; 28:25 [n][Matt. 7:2]
26 [o]ch. 24:24 [p][Job 29:13] [q][Gen. 42:6]
27 [r]See Ps. 7:16
28 [s]See Ps. 49:6 [t]Jer. 17:8; See Ps. 92:12
29 [u]ch. 15:27 [v][Eccles. 5:16]
30 [w]See ch. 3:18 [x]Dan. 12:3; James 5:20; See 1 Cor. 9:19-22
31 [y][Jer. 25:29; 1 Pet. 4:18]

Chapter 12

1 [z]ch. 5:12; 15:10 [a]Ps. 49:10
2 [b]ch. 8:35
3 [c]See ch. 10:25
4 [d]See ch. 31:10 [e]Song 3:11 [f]ch. 10:5 [g]ch. 14:30
5 [h][Matt. 12:35]
6 [i]See ch. 1:11 [j]ch. 14:3
7 [k]See ch. 11:21 [l]Job 34:25 [m][ch. 10:25, 30]
8 [n][1 Sam. 20:30]

[1] Or *acceptance*

focus are the way a person relates to provisions and people (vv. 24–26, 28). The benefit of the generous life of the righteous for themselves and for others is represented throughout the section in several agricultural images: **waters/watered** (v. 25), **flourish like a green leaf** (v. 28), **fruit** (v. 30), and **tree of life** (v. 30). These images represent a fuller illustration of the statement in v. 18b: "one who sows righteousness gets a sure reward."

11:24 Because there is a God who blesses generosity and withholds blessing from the greedy, this paradoxical proverb makes perfect sense (cf. note on 3:9–10).

11:30 The Hebrew phrase translated **whoever captures souls** is used elsewhere in places where the sense is "to take life" or "to kill" (e.g., 1 Sam. 24:11; 1 Kings 19:10, 14; Jonah 4:3). However, this proverb appears to be purposely playing off the usual sense of the phrase to focus on the effect of **the fruit of the righteous**. The life of the righteous leads not only to blessing for themselves but also provides fruit that "captures souls" in the sense of leading people out of the path that ends in death. For similar declarations, cf. Dan. 12:3, equating "those who are wise" to "those who turn many to righteousness"; see also James 5:20, where the one "who brings back a sinner from his wandering" will "save his soul from death."

11:31 First Peter 4:18 cites this verse from the Septuagint. **repaid on earth**. Though the earthly consequences of a righteous or wicked life may not appear immediately, over the course of a person's earthly life such consequences will appear. Like other proverbs (see Introduction: Literary Features), this statement is a general truth about human behavior, though there may at times be exceptions, such as when evil governments oppress the righteous and reward evildoers (as Proverbs recognizes, cf. 13:23), or when some of God's righteous people (e.g., Job) endure suffering. Yet even in these cases, the Lord vindicates his faithful (although that may await the final judgment).

12:1–4 This section begins by encouraging the reader to be one who **loves discipline** and not one who **hates reproof** or moral correction (v. 1); such an attitude produces a life that **will never be moved** (v. 3).

12:4 crown. A woman of good character helps her husband live faithfully and brings him visible public honor. **excellent wife**. Cf. ch. 31.

12:5–7 These three proverbs are united by the word pairs **righteous/wicked** (v. 5), **wicked/upright** (v. 6), and **wicked/righteous** (v. 7). The proverbs progress from righteous counsel vs. wicked counsel (v. 5), to treachery vs. deliverance (v. 6), and finally to the destruction of the wicked vs. the stability of the righteous (v. 7).

12:8 A person gains the respect of others through speaking or acting with wisdom.

12:9–11 These are sayings about ordinary workers that illustrate either the "good sense" or the "twisted mind" of v. 8. **Lack bread** (end of v. 9) is paralleled by **lacks sense** (end of v. 11), and both verses speak of the importance of prudent labor in order to provide enough to eat. The point of the whole is that the **righteous** person cares even for his animals (v. 10a) and provides for his household by a sensible perspective on life (v. 9a) and sensible labors (v. 11a). By contrast, **he who follows worthless pursuits** (v. 11; such as get-rich-quick schemes, gambling, or lotteries, in a modern context) lacks

10 [o]Whoever is righteous has regard for the life of his beast,
but the mercy of the wicked is cruel.
11 [p]Whoever works his land [q]will have plenty of bread,
[r]but he who follows [s]worthless pursuits lacks sense.
12 Whoever is wicked covets [t]the spoil of evildoers,
but the root of the righteous bears fruit.
13 An evil man is ensnared [u]by the transgression of his lips,
[v]but the righteous escapes from trouble.
14 From the fruit of his mouth [w]a man is satisfied with good,
[x]and the work of a man's hand comes back to him.
15 [y]The way of a fool is right in his own eyes,
but a wise man listens to advice.
16 [z]The vexation of a fool is known at once,
but the prudent ignores an insult.
17 [a]Whoever speaks[1] the truth gives honest evidence,
but [b]a false witness utters deceit.
18 [c]There is one whose rash words are like sword thrusts,
but the tongue of the wise brings [d]healing.
19 Truthful lips endure forever,
but [e]a lying tongue is but for a moment.
20 Deceit is in the heart of [f]those who devise evil,
but those who plan peace have joy.
21 [g]No ill befalls the righteous,
but the wicked are filled with trouble.
22 [h]Lying lips are [i]an abomination to the LORD,
[j]but those who act faithfully are his delight.
23 [k]A prudent man conceals knowledge,
[k]but the heart of fools proclaims folly.
24 [l]The hand of the diligent will rule,
while the slothful will be [m]put to forced labor.
25 [n]Anxiety in a man's heart weighs him down,
but a good word makes him glad.
26 One who is righteous is a guide to his neighbor,[2]
but the way of the wicked leads them astray.
27 [o]Whoever is slothful will not roast his game,
but the diligent man will get precious wealth.[3]
28 [p]In the path of righteousness is life,
and in its pathway there is no death.

[1] Hebrew *breathes out* [2] Or *The righteous chooses his friends carefully* [3] Or *but diligence is precious wealth*

10[o][Deut. 25:4]
11[p]ch. 28:19 [q]ch. 20:13 [r]ch. 28:19 [s]Judg. 9:4
12[t][Ps. 10:9]
13[u]ch. 18:7; [Ps. 64:8; Matt. 12:37] [v]ch. 21:23
14[w]ch. 13:2; 14:14; 18:20 [x]ch. 19:17; Isa. 3:10, 11; [Judg. 9:16, 56]
15[y]ch. 3:7; 16:2; 21:2; 26:12; [ch. 14:12; 16:25]
16[z][ch. 14:33; 29:11]
17[a]ch. 14:5 [b]See ch. 6:19
18[c]See Ps. 57:4 [d]See ch. 4:22
19[e]ch. 19:9; [Ps. 52:4, 5]
20[f]ch. 3:29
21[g]Ps. 91:10; [1 Pet. 3:13; 2 Pet. 2:9]
22[h][Rev. 22:15]; See ch. 6:17 [i]ch. 11:20 [j][ch. 11:1]
23[k][ch. 13:16; 15:2]
24[l][ch. 10:4; 13:4] [m][Gen. 49:15; 1 Kgs. 9:21]
25[n]ch. 15:13; [ch. 17:22]
27[o][ver. 24]
28[p]See ch. 10:2

sense and, by contrast with the first half of the verse, will probably live in poverty as well (cf. 28:19).

12:12–14 The contrast between sensible labors and worthless pursuits (vv. 9–11) leads to the images of what each path produces. Where one who **covets** illegitimate **spoil** (v. 12a) will be trapped by his own **transgression** (v. 13a), the labor of the **righteous** takes **root, bears fruit** (vv. 12b, 14a), and leads in a path that ultimately **escapes from trouble** (v. 13b). The fact that **the work of a man's hand comes back to him** (v. 14b) is thus either a blessing or a curse, depending on the character of the person and the nature of the work (cf. 14:14).

12:15 In Proverbs, one who is **right** (or wise) **in his own eyes** sees no need to seek instruction or counsel from others and is thus also unwilling to listen to reproof. Proverbs strongly warns against this (see 3:5–7), because no one is immune to self-deception (see 16:2; 21:2), which can lead to the nearly hopeless state of having a hard heart (see 26:12).

12:16–23 The fool's perspective of being "right in his own eyes" (v. 15) is illustrated here in his speech, which is contrasted with that of the wise. The section is framed by reference to the actions of the **prudent** and the **fool** (vv. 16, 23). The fool quickly spills forth the **vexation** (v. 16) in his **heart** (v. 23), where the prudent **ignores** the intended effect of an **insult** (v. 16) because his heart **conceals** (v. 23; "ignores" and "conceals" translate the same Hb. verb) **knowledge** of the bad effects of such speech (v. 18); so he shrugs the insult off. The section reinforces the teaching of Proverbs that a person's speech comes out from the **heart** (vv. 17, 20) and that **the LORD** is the one who knows both and finds them accordingly either an **abomination** or a **delight** (vv. 21–22).

12:18 Some people's normal speech pattern is constantly to accuse, belittle, manipulate, mock, insult, or condemn, and their **rash words** hurt other people and feel **like sword thrusts**. This is opposite of the way of wisdom taught in Proverbs, for **the tongue of the wise brings healing** (cf. Eph. 4:29).

12:22 For other references to what is either **an abomination to the LORD** or **his delight**, see 11:1, 20; 15:8 ("acceptable to him" translates the same Hb. word as "his delight").

12:24–28 Adding to the contrast of the previous section regarding prudent and foolish speech, these verses contrast the related actions of one who is **diligent** (vv. 24a, 27b) and one who is **slothful** (vv. 24b, 27a).

13

1 A wise son hears his father's instruction,
but [q]a scoffer does not listen to rebuke.
2 From the fruit of his mouth a man [r]eats what is good,
but the desire of the treacherous [s]is for violence.
3 [t]Whoever guards his mouth preserves his life;
[u]he who opens wide his lips [v]comes to ruin.
4 [w]The soul of the sluggard craves and gets nothing,
while the soul of the diligent [x]is richly supplied.
5 The righteous hates falsehood,
but the wicked brings shame[1] and disgrace.
6 [y]Righteousness guards him whose [z]way is blameless,
but sin overthrows the wicked.
7 [a]One pretends to be rich, yet has nothing;
[b]another pretends to be poor, yet has great wealth.
8 The ransom of a man's life is his wealth,
but a poor man [c]hears no threat.
9 [d]The light of the righteous rejoices,
but [e]the lamp of the wicked will be put out.
10 [f]By insolence comes nothing but strife,
but with those who take advice is wisdom.
11 [g]Wealth gained hastily[2] will dwindle,
but whoever gathers little by little will increase it.
12 Hope deferred makes the heart sick,
[h]but a desire fulfilled is [i]a tree of life.
13 Whoever [j]despises [k]the word brings destruction on himself,
but he who reveres the commandment will be [l]rewarded.
14 The teaching of the wise is [m]a fountain of life,
that one may [n]turn away from the snares of death.
15 [o]Good sense wins [p]favor,
but the way of the treacherous is their ruin.[3]
16 [q]In everything the prudent acts with knowledge,
[r]but a fool flaunts his folly.
17 A wicked messenger falls into trouble,
but [s]a faithful envoy brings healing.
18 Poverty and disgrace come to him who [t]ignores instruction,
[u]but whoever [v]heeds reproof is honored.
19 [w]A desire fulfilled is sweet to the soul,
but to turn away from evil is an abomination to fools.
20 Whoever walks with the wise becomes wise,
but the companion of fools will suffer harm.

[1] Or *stench* [2] Or *by fraud* [3] Probable reading (compare Septuagint, Syriac, Vulgate); Hebrew *is rugged, or is an enduring rut*

Chapter 13
1 [q]ch. 1:22; See Ps. 1:1
2 [r]ch. 12:14 [s][ch. 1:31; 26:6]
3 [t]ch. 21:23; [ch. 12:13; 18:21; James 3:2] [u]ch. 20:19 [v]ch. 18:7
4 [w]See ch. 6:9-11 [x]ch. 11:25
6 [y]ch. 11:3, 5, 6 [z]ch. 11:20
7 [a]ch. 11:24; [Luke 12:21; Rev. 3:17] [b][Luke 12:33; 2 Cor. 6:10; James 2:5]
8 [c][ver. 1]
9 [d][Job 29:3] [e]See Job 18:5
10 [f][ch. 28:25]
11 [g][ch. 10:2; 20:21; 21:6; 28:20, 22]
12 [h][ver. 19] [i]See ch. 3:18
13 [j][ch. 19:16; Num. 15:31; 2 Chr. 36:16] [k]ch. 16:20; Deut. 30:14 [l][ver. 21]
14 [m]See ch. 10:11 [n]ch. 14:27; [Ps. 18:5; 2 Tim. 2:26]
15 [o][Luke 2:52]; See Ps. 111:10 [p]ch. 3:4; 22:1
16 [q][ch. 12:23; 15:2] [r][ch. 18:2; Eccles. 10:3]
17 [s]ch. 25:13; [ch. 14:5]
18 [t][ch. 15:5, 31, 32] [u][ch. 15:5] [v][ch. 15:31]
19 [w][ver. 12]

13:1–6 Headed by the call to be a **wise son** (cf. 10:1), these proverbs also utilize a play on words (cf. 10:6–32) relating to both speech (**hears/listen**, 13:1; **mouth**, vv. 2–3; **lips**, v. 3; **falsehood**, v. 5) and eating/desire (**eats**, v. 2; **desire**, v. 2; **craves** and **richly supplied**, v. 4) in order to assure those who seek to guard their mouth (v. 3) through **righteousness** (v. 6) that such a path has mutually reinforcing benefits in both heart and actions. The purpose of the section is integrated further by the repeated Hebrew *nepesh*, translated as "desire" (v. 2), **life** (v. 3), and **soul** (twice in v. 4): guarding the mouth protects the heart from being further confirmed in **violence** (v. 2; see 10:11) or **sin** (13:6), which **overthrows** (v. 6) a person and leads to **ruin** (v. 3).

13:7–8 Things are not always as they seem. In particular, one may have money but live in fear because of the threats one faces (v. 8). Verse 8 also looks back to v. 1: **hears no threat** translates the same Hebrew words as "does not listen to rebuke" in v. 1. The poor man has little at risk, so threats of robbery or extortion do not concern him (as they would the rich), but the poor man might also tend to brush off warnings and rebukes. The message is that life is sometimes paradoxical. The scoffer will not shut his mouth but will soon have nothing to put into it (vv. 1–4); the man known to be rich is impoverished by paying off those who are constantly threatening him (vv. 7–8).

13:9 The images of **light** and **lamp** refer to a person's joy, energy, and visible success in life, all of which cause the **righteous** to rejoice, but for the **wicked** this **will be put out**. This may also imply the actual end of life and the lack of a future for the wicked (cf. 24:20).

13:10 The contrast of **insolence** and **wisdom** is similar to the warning against being "right in his own eyes" rather than lining up with **those who take advice** (see 12:15).

13:11 Wealth gained hastily will dwindle. The person who receives sudden wealth has not worked for it enough to understand its value and has not gained sufficient skill in managing it (cf. 28:20). By contrast, Proverbs prefers diligent, patient, careful labor that will **increase** wealth over time.

13:20 Regular companions inevitably influence each other, for good or for ill.

21 [x]Disaster[1] pursues sinners,
[y]but the righteous are rewarded with good.
22 [z]A good man leaves an inheritance to his children's children,
but [a]the sinner's wealth is laid up for the righteous.
23 The fallow ground of the poor would yield much food,
but it is swept away through [b]injustice.
24 [c]Whoever spares the rod hates his son,
but he who loves him is diligent to discipline him.[2]
25 [d]The righteous has enough to satisfy his appetite,
but the belly of the wicked suffers want.

14

1 [e]The wisest of women [f]builds her house,
but folly with her own hands [g]tears it down.
2 Whoever [h]walks in uprightness fears the LORD,
but he who is [i]devious in his ways despises him.
3 By the mouth of a fool comes [j]a rod for his back,[3]
[k]but the lips of the wise will preserve them.
4 Where there are no oxen, the manger is clean,
but abundant crops come by the strength of the ox.
5 [l]A faithful witness does not lie,
but [m]a false witness breathes out lies.
6 [n]A scoffer seeks wisdom [o]in vain,
but [p]knowledge is easy for a man of understanding.
7 Leave the presence of a fool,
for there you do not meet words of knowledge.
8 The wisdom of the prudent is to discern his way,
but the folly of fools is deceiving.
9 [q]Fools mock at the guilt offering,
but the upright enjoy acceptance.[4]
10 The heart knows its own [r]bitterness,
and no stranger shares its joy.

[1] Or *Evil* [2] Or *who loves him disciplines him early* [3] Or *In the mouth of a fool is a rod of pride* [4] Hebrew *but among the upright is acceptance*

21[x][Ps. 11:6; 32:10] [y][ver. 13; Luke 6:38]
22[z][Ezra 9:12; Ps. 37:25] [a]ch. 28:8; See Job 27:16, 17
23[b][ch. 16:8]
24[c][ch. 19:18; 22:15; 23:13, 14; 29:15, 17]
25[d]See ch. 10:3

Chapter 14
1[e][ch. 9:1; 24:3] [f]Deut. 25:9; Ruth 4:11 [g][ch. 11:11]
2[h]ch. 19:1; 28:6 [i]ch. 2:15
3[j][Jer. 18:18] [k]ch. 12:6
5[l][Ex. 23:1] [m]See ch. 6:19
6[n][ch. 24:7] [o][Ps. 25:9; 1 Pet. 5:5] [p][ch. 8:9; 15:14; 17:24]
9[q][ch. 10:23]
10[r][1 Sam. 1:10]; See Job 3:20

13:22–25 Walking with the wise (see vv. 20–21) includes prudence to care for children (1) by providing a material **inheritance** that extends even to grandchildren (on inheritance in Israel, see Num. 27:5–11; Deut. 21:15–17), and (2) by providing moral **discipline** (Prov. 13:24). In thus seeking to provide, parents ought also to pursue justice (v. 23), exhibiting their faith that the **righteous** will have **enough to satisfy** (v. 25; cf. v. 21).

13:23 The causes of poverty are complex: it can be caused by injustice and oppression (as here; cf. 22:16; 28:3, 15); by sloth (6:9–11; 28:19); by God's punishment on wickedness (10:2–3; 13:25); or by his mysterious providence (e.g., 22:2).

13:24 Physical **discipline** is a common theme in Proverbs (see e.g., 10:13; 17:10; 22:15; 23:13–24; 29:15). It is viewed as an important part of the correction and training of a child, to teach him to avoid wrong behavior, to embrace what is right, and to build godly character. Equally important, physical discipline is an expression of love for a child, while the one who **spares the rod hates his son**. Taking into account all of the teaching of Proverbs, physical discipline of a child must never be severe and must always be exercised in love. Cf. Heb. 12:5–11.

14:1–3 The benefits of the sensible labor of the **wisest of women** (v. 1a) and the prudent speech of the **wise** (v. 3b) are contrasted with the way in which the acts of **folly** (v. 1b) and the words of the **fool** (v. 3a) ultimately result in self-harm. **with her own hands tears it down**. Sinful people sometimes become highly irrational and foolishly destroy the fruit of many years of work.

14:4 If the **strength of the ox** is the means for plowing the ground to produce **abundant crops**, then keeping **oxen** in a stable is a necessary part of the overall labor, even though it involves the unpleasant work of cleaning the stable. An empty stable may be **clean** (thus not requiring any unpleasant work), but it won't produce any abundance.

14:5–7 These verses refer to character manifested, in part, through speech: the **faithful** vs. **false witness** (v. 5), the **scoffer** (v. 6), the lack of **words of knowledge** from a **fool** (v. 7), and the implication that such words can be found with a **man of understanding** (v. 6). The verses appear to be prescriptive (walk the path of the faithful witness) as well as descriptive (look out for those who manifest lying, scoffing, or foolishness). The Lord desires that his people be faithful witnesses; cf. the Ten Commandments (Ex. 20:16; Deut. 5:20) and the further instruction of the law (cf. Ex. 23:1–4; Deut. 19:15–21).

14:8–15 This section is framed by verses that contrast the approach of the **prudent** (vv. 8a, 15b) with that of **fools** (v. 8b) and the **simple** (v. 15a). It is prudent to recognize that appearances can be deceptive (a person's exterior vs. the state of the **heart**, vv. 10 and 13; the solidity of the **house** vs. the **tent**, v. 11; and **a way that seems right**, v. 12) and that whatever the appearance, the path of one's life has consequences consistent with how it is walked.

14:8 The approach of **fools** to their path is **deceiving** because they believe it to be **wisdom** (and it appears so to the simple, v. 15) when actually it is void of what is required for wisdom (they mock legitimate sacrifices to the Lord, v. 9); their path is thus **folly**.

14:9 The reference to the **guilt offering** (see Lev. 5:14–6:7) indicates that the **acceptance** enjoyed by the **upright** likely means that the Lord accepts his sacrifice because it is given in sincerity (cf. Lev. 1:3–4). The Hebrew *ratson* ("acceptance") is also used in Proverbs to refer to what is a "delight" to the Lord (see Prov. 11:1, 20; 12:22) or to one finding "favor" with him (see 8:35; 12:2; 18:22).

11[s][ch. 3:33; 15:25; Job 8:15; 21:28]
12[t]ch. 16:25; See ch. 12:15 [u][ch. 5:5; Rom. 6:21]; See ch. 7:27
13[v][Eccles. 2:2; Luke 6:25] [w]ch. 10:1
14[x][ch. 1:31; Matt. 6:2, 5] [y]ch. 12:14; Isa. 3:10
15[z]See ch. 1:4
16[a][ch. 22:3; 27:12] [b][ch. 3:7]; See Job 28:28; Ps. 34:14
17[c][ver. 29]
19[d][Gen. 42:6; 1 Sam. 2:36]
20[e]ch. 19:7 [f]ch. 19:4
21[g]ch. 11:12 [h]Ps. 41:1
22[i]See ch. 3:29 [j]ch. 3:3
23[k][ch. 11:24; 21:5; 22:16]
25[l]ver. 5
26[m][ch. 1:33] [n][Ps. 73:15] [o]See Ps. 14:6
27[p]See ch. 10:11 [q]See ch. 13:14
28[r][1 Kgs. 4:20]

11 [s]The house of the wicked will be destroyed,
but the tent of the upright will flourish.
12 [t]There is a way that seems right to a man,
but [u]its end is the way to death.[1]
13 Even in laughter the heart may ache,
and [v]the end of joy may be [w]grief.
14 The backslider in heart will be [x]filled with the fruit of his ways,
and [y]a good man will be filled with the fruit of his ways.
15 [z]The simple believes everything,
but the prudent gives thought to his steps.
16 [a]One who is wise is cautious[2] and [b]turns away from evil,
but a fool is reckless and careless.
17 A man of [c]quick temper acts foolishly,
and a man of evil devices is hated.
18 The simple inherit folly,
but the prudent are crowned with knowledge.
19 [d]The evil bow down before the good,
the wicked at the gates of the righteous.
20 [e]The poor is disliked even by his neighbor,
[f]but the rich has many friends.
21 Whoever [g]despises his neighbor is a sinner,
but [h]blessed is he who is generous to the poor.
22 Do they not go astray who [i]devise evil?
Those who devise good meet[3] [j]steadfast love and faithfulness.
23 In all toil there is profit,
but mere talk [k]tends only to poverty.
24 The crown of the wise is their wealth,
but the folly of fools brings folly.
25 A truthful witness saves lives,
but one who [l]breathes out lies is deceitful.
26 In the fear of the LORD one has [m]strong confidence,
and [n]his children will have [o]a refuge.
27 The fear of the LORD is [p]a fountain of life,
that one may [q]turn away from the snares of death.
28 In [r]a multitude of people is the glory of a king,
but without people a prince is ruined.

[1] Hebrew *ways of death* [2] Or *fears* [the LORD] [3] Or *show*

14:16–17 The **wise** gives thought to his path and **turns away from evil** (cf. ESV footnote on **cautious** with the use of this phrase in 3:7; 16:6). In contrast, the **fool** is **reckless** on his path (14:16b), a quality of heart that is aggravated further by a **quick temper** and results in his being **hated** (v. 17) for its ruinous effects.

14:18–24 The effects of inheriting **folly** (v. 18a) or being **crowned with knowledge** (v. 18b) are borne out in the fruit of each: a further **crown** for the **wise** (v. 24a) and further **folly** for **fools** (v. 24b). The verses in between show that the promised state of affairs in vv. 19 and 22 is an encouragement to walk in the way of the **good** and **righteous** and not to devalue the **poor** or a **neighbor** according to their material means (vv. 20, 21).

14:20 The poor is disliked is an observation on how the world works, not an endorsement of such an attitude (cf. v. 21; and note on 10:15).

14:21 Proverbs commends being **generous to the poor**, particularly those among God's people (see v. 31; 19:17; 21:13; 22:9; 28:27; 31:20; cf. Deut. 15:7–11).

14:23 This is a rebuke against people who are always talking and planning but never accomplishing anything.

14:24 The circularity of the phrase **the folly of fools brings folly** appropriately captures the self-perpetuating nature of the foolish path. Cf. v. 8; 15:2, 14; 16:22; 26:11. The **wise** are free to enjoy their **wealth** (and it is safe for them to do so, as they will not be led astray by greed). A **crown** can be anything that gives visible, public honor (see note on 12:4).

14:25 A person called to be a **witness** (esp. in legal matters; cf. 12:17; 19:28) must be **truthful** (or faithful, see 14:5); the person who **lies** perverts justice—something that the Lord hates (6:19).

14:26–27 The **fear of the LORD** brings with it the **confidence** of lasting security (v. 26) and molds a person's character to follow the right path (v. 27). Note that "the teaching of the wise" is also called **a fountain of life** in an otherwise identical proverb (13:14), indicating that such teaching fosters the fear of the Lord (cf. also 10:11).

14:28–35 Verses 28 and 35, both of which concern a **king**, form a frame for this paragraph. Verses 29–34 contain various proverbs on the life and heart of an individual. A person must rule his **heart** with **wisdom** (vv. 29–30, 33), understand that all are under a higher sovereign (v. 31), and have confidence that the wicked, however powerful they are, will be cast down (v. 32). A **nation** perishes if its people lack **righteousness** (v. 34). Ultimately, many of the same rules that govern one person's life also govern a nation.

29 Whoever is [s]slow to anger has great understanding,
but he who has a hasty temper exalts folly.
30 A tranquil[1] heart gives [t]life to the flesh,
but [u]envy[2] makes [v]the bones rot.
31 Whoever oppresses a poor man [w]insults his [x]Maker,
[y]but he who is generous to the needy honors him.
32 [z]The wicked is overthrown through his evildoing,
but [a]the righteous finds refuge in his death.
33 Wisdom [b]rests in the heart of a man of understanding,
but it makes itself known even in the midst of fools.[3]
34 Righteousness exalts a nation,
but sin is a reproach to any people.
35 A servant who deals wisely has [c]the king's favor,
but his wrath falls on one who acts shamefully.

15

1 [d]A soft answer turns away wrath,
but [e]a harsh word stirs up anger.
2 The tongue of the wise commends knowledge,
but [f]the mouths of fools pour out folly.
3 [g]The eyes of the LORD are in every place,
keeping watch on the evil and the good.
4 [h]A gentle[4] tongue is [i]a tree of life,
but [j]perverseness in it breaks the spirit.
5 [k]A fool [l]despises his father's instruction,
but [m]whoever heeds reproof is prudent.
6 In the house of the righteous there is much treasure,
but trouble befalls the income of the wicked.
7 [n]The lips of the wise spread knowledge;
[n] not so the hearts of fools.[5]
8 [o]The sacrifice of the wicked is an abomination to the LORD,
but [p]the prayer of the upright is acceptable to him.
9 The way of the wicked is an abomination to the LORD,
but he loves him [q]who pursues righteousness.
10 There is [r]severe discipline for him who forsakes the way;
[s]whoever hates reproof will die.

[1] *Or healing* [2] *Or jealousy* [3] *Or Wisdom rests quietly in the heart of a man of understanding, but makes itself known in the midst of fools* [4] *Or healing* [5] *Or the hearts of fools are not steadfast*

29[s]ch. 16:32; 19:11; [ver. 17; Eccles. 7:9; James 1:19]
30[t]See ch. 4:22 [u][Ps. 112:10] [v]ch. 12:4
31[w]ch. 17:5; [Matt. 25:40, 45] [x]ch. 22:2; See Job 35:10 [y]ch. 28:8
32[z]ch. 24:16 [a]Gen. 49:18; Ps. 16:11; 17:15; 23:4; 2 Cor. 1:9; 5:8; 2 Tim. 4:18; [Num. 23:10]; See Job 19:25-27
33[b]Eccles. 7:9; ch. 12:16; 29:11
35[c][ch. 16:13; 22:11]; See Matt. 24:45-47

Chapter 15

1[d][ch. 25:15]; See Judg. 8:1-3 [e]See 1 Sam. 25:10-13; 1 Kgs. 12:13-16
2[f][ver. 28; ch. 12:23; 13:16; 18:2]
3[g]See Job 31:4
4[h][ch. 12:18] [i]See ch. 3:18 [j]ch. 11:3
5[k][ch. 10:1] [l][Ps. 107:11] [m][ch. 13:18]
7[n][Matt. 12:34, 35]
8[o]ch. 21:27; Eccles. 5:1; Isa. 1:11, 15 [p][ver. 29]
9[q]ch. 21:21; 1 Tim. 6:11; [ch. 11:19]
10[r][Isa. 1:5] [s]See ch. 12:1

14:29 The person who is **slow to anger** (cf. 15:18; 16:32; 19:11; James 1:19–20) reflects the Lord's character (see Ex. 34:6).

14:32 The one who is **righteous** lives in the fear of the Lord and thus **finds refuge in his death** because the Lord rewards him (see Ps. 49:15).

14:33 Wisdom resides in the **heart** of the wise, but **even in the midst of fools** it **makes itself known** by manifesting the effects of folly (cf. the picture of Wisdom calling out in the street to the simple, and the effects of rejecting her reproof, 1:20–33).

14:34 Righteousness exalts a nation. Morally righteous behavior has far-reaching effects—especially in the administration of justice and the compassionate care of people. Both the moral behavior and the well-being of the people are exalted.

15:1–17 This is a series of proverbs dealing primarily with the use of the tongue, submission to instruction, and God's governance of the world.

15:1–2, 4 Harsh word (v. 1) is lit., "word of pain," that is, a word that is hurtful. Words wisely chosen promote calm interactions rather than provoking **anger** (v. 1), they instruct by example (v. 2), and they encourage rather than discourage (v. 4).

15:3 The **eyes of the LORD** is a major theme in Proverbs: the Lord knows the actions and hearts of all, so he is neither pleased with nor fooled by one who offers sacrifices while continuing in the way of wickedness (cf. vv. 8–9, 11, 26, 29).

15:4 A gentle tongue . . . perverseness. A gentle, rightly spoken word will often bring life and healing, but gentle speech can also be used to mask perverse intent—crushing the spirit, damaging morale, and causing injury.

15:5 The description of a **fool** who **despises his father's instruction** is complemented by that of v. 20 and the foolish man who "despises his mother." In Proverbs, the nature of one's response to wise parental instruction is representative of and formative in the paths of wisdom or folly, respectively (cf. 1:8; 4:1; 6:20; 13:1). Note also the related references in this chapter to how a person responds to **reproof** (15:5, 10, 12, 31, 32).

15:6 Much treasure is the expected outcome for the **righteous** who walk in the paths of honesty, diligence, hard work, and the fear of the Lord, which is the path of wisdom described in Proverbs (but see the word of caution in v. 16). However, the **wicked** will earn **income** only to find **trouble** with it.

15:7 Similar to v. 2, this verse encourages people to be careful in what they say and to whom they listen (cf. 14:7).

15:8–9 The **sacrifice of the wicked** (v. 8a) is hollow, while the **prayer of the upright** (v. 8b)—i.e., his public worship (cf. Psalm 86 title; Isa. 56:7), as a part of a life that **pursues righteousness** (Prov. 15:9b)—is pleasing to the Lord (cf. also vv. 26, 29; 21:3, 27; 28:9).

15:10–12 These verses concern divine judgment and submission to correction. Both the apostate (v. 10a) and the obstinate (v. 10b) face judgment. Verse 12,

11 Sheol and Abaddon lie open before the LORD;
how much more [t]the hearts of the children of man!
12 [u]A scoffer [v]does not like to be reproved;
he will not go to the wise.
13 [w]A glad heart makes a cheerful face,
but by [x]sorrow of heart the spirit is [y]crushed.
14 [z]The heart of him who has understanding seeks knowledge,
but the mouths of fools feed on folly.
15 All the days of the afflicted are evil,
but [a]the cheerful of heart has a continual feast.
16 [b]Better is a little with the fear of the LORD
than great treasure and trouble with it.
17 [c]Better is a dinner of herbs where love is
than [d]a fattened ox and hatred with it.
18 [e]A hot-tempered man [f]stirs up strife,
but he who is [g]slow to anger quiets contention.
19 The way of [h]a sluggard is like a hedge of [i]thorns,
but the path of the upright is [j]a level highway.
20 [k]A wise son makes a glad father,
but a foolish man despises his mother.
21 [l]Folly is a joy to him who lacks sense,
but a man of understanding [m]walks straight ahead.
22 [n]Without counsel plans fail,
but with many advisers they succeed.
23 To make an apt answer is a joy to a man,
and [o]a word in season, how good it is!
24 The path of life leads upward [p]for the prudent,
that he may turn away from Sheol beneath.
25 The LORD tears down the house of [q]the proud
but [r]maintains [s]the widow's boundaries.
26 [t]The thoughts of the wicked are an abomination to the LORD,
but [u]gracious words are pure.
27 Whoever is [v]greedy for unjust gain [w]troubles his own household,
but he who hates [x]bribes will live.

11 [t]2 Chr. 6:30; Ps. 44:21; John 2:24; See 1 Sam. 16:7
12 [u]See Ps. 1:1 [v]Amos 5:10
13 [w][ver. 15; ch. 17:22] [x]See ch. 12:25 [y]ch. 18:14
14 [z]ch. 14:6; 19:24
15 [a]ver. 13
16 [b]ch. 16:8; Ps. 37:16; [1 Tim. 6:6]
17 [c]ch. 17:1 [d][Matt. 22:4; Luke 15:23]
18 [e]ch. 29:22; [ch. 16:28; 26:21] [f]ch. 28:25 [g]See ch. 14:29
19 [h]ch. 19:24; 22:13 [i]ch. 22:5 [j]Jer. 18:15
20 [k]See ch. 29:3
21 [l]ch. 10:23 [m][Eph. 5:15]
22 [n]ch. 11:14; [ch. 20:18]
23 [o]ch. 25:11; [Isa. 50:4]
24 [p]Col. 3:1, 2; [ch. 2:18, 19; Phil. 3:20]
25 [q][ch. 29:23] [r][ch. 23:10] [s][Ps. 68:5; 146:9]
26 [t]ch. 6:16, 18 [u]ch. 16:24
27 [v]ch. 1:19; [Isa. 5:8; Jer. 17:11] [w]ch. 11:29; [Josh. 7:25] [x]ch. 17:23

like v. 10b, concerns reproof and the fact that some people will not accept it. Verse 11, similar to v. 3, reminds the reader that God judges all.

15:13–15 These proverbs focus on the **heart**. A **cheerful face** indicates a positive attitude toward life; this comes about when the inner self is healthy (v. 13a). Such a person has inner joy all the time (v. 15b). But circumstances, whether internal (v. 13b) or external (v. 15a), can rob a person of tranquility. The key to gaining a joyful heart is in v. 14: seek **knowledge**.

15:16–17 These verses help establish a proper value system for forming the kind of heart described in vv. 13–15. One who "seeks knowledge" (v. 14) recognizes that contentment is found not primarily in external circumstances but in a life governed by the **fear of the LORD** (v. 16a). To gain wealth through **trouble** (v. 16b) or attended by **hatred** (v. 17b) is to "feed on folly" (v. 14b), which afflicts the heart and crushes the spirit.

15:18–33 This is another extended section of proverbs that, like vv. 1–17, begins with a proverb on avoiding provocative, argumentative language (cf. v. 1 and v. 18) and ends with a reference to "the fear of the LORD" (cf. vv. 16–33). The sections also share references to the folly of despising parental instruction (vv. 5, 20) and reproof (vv. 10, 12, 31–32) on the grounds that it is the Lord who knows and judges in these matters (vv. 3, 8–9, 25–26, 29).

15:19–24 This section is framed by references to the **path of the upright** (v. 19b) and the **path of life** (v. 24a), which are contrasted with the **way of a sluggard** (v. 19a) and the end of such a path (v. 24b). Verses 20–23 illustrate the wisdom of heeding instruction (vv. 20a, 21b, 23) and counsel (v. 22b); despising such things (vv. 20b, 22a) is like rejoicing in what is actually **folly** (v. 21a).

15:19 Because of his past actions and resultant lack of God's blessing, the life of the **sluggard** has become **like a hedge of thorns**, which can be traversed only with great pain and effort.

15:20 On the fool who **despises his mother**, see the complementary proverb of v. 5.

15:21 The Hebrew noun translated as **joy** is repeated in v. 23 referring to an "apt answer" and is related to the verb "makes glad" in v. 20. The interrelated vocabulary helps make the point that the "wise son" (v. 20a) finds joy in a fitting response (to tense situations, instruction, and the need of others for a good word) rather than in **folly** (despising wise instruction and ignoring counsel).

15:23 An **apt answer** or good **word** likely applies as much to a fitting response to receiving instruction as it does to giving counsel to another.

15:25–33 These proverbs are framed by a contrast: **the LORD** opposes the **proud** (v. 25a), but is near those who act in **humility** born out of the **fear of the LORD** (v. 33; cf. v. 25a). Verses 24–32 expand on this by illustrating the pride of the **wicked** as represented in their: **thoughts** (v. 26a), greed for **unjust gain** (v. 27a), harmful speech (v. 28b), and refusal to listen to **reproof** (v. 32a). These are the opposite of the way of the **righteous** represented in: **gracious words** (vv. 26b, 28a), maintaining justice (v. 27b), and heeding **instruction** (vv. 31, 32b). At the center of this section is the further reminder that the Lord is **far from the wicked**, but **hears the prayer of the righteous** (v. 29).

28 The heart of the righteous [y]ponders how to answer,
but [z]the mouth of the wicked pours out evil things.
29 The LORD is [a]far from the wicked,
but he [b]hears the prayer of the righteous.
30 [c]The light of the eyes rejoices the heart,
and [d]good news refreshes[1] the bones.
31 [e]The ear that listens to [f]life-giving reproof
will dwell among the wise.
32 Whoever [g]ignores instruction [h]despises himself,
but he who listens to reproof [i]gains intelligence.
33 [j]The fear of the LORD is instruction in wisdom,
and [k]humility comes before honor.

16

1 The plans of the heart belong to man,
but [l]the answer of the tongue is from the LORD.
2 [m]All the ways of a man are pure in his own eyes,
but the LORD [n]weighs the spirit.
3 [o]Commit your work to the LORD,
and your plans will be established.
4 [p]The LORD has made everything for its purpose,
even [q]the wicked for the day of trouble.
5 Everyone who is arrogant in heart is [r]an abomination to the LORD;
[s]be assured, he will not go unpunished.
6 By [t]steadfast love and faithfulness iniquity is atoned for,
and by [u]the fear of the LORD one [v]turns away from evil.
7 When a man's ways please the LORD,
[w]he makes even his enemies to be at peace with him.
8 [x]Better is a little with righteousness
than great revenues with injustice.
9 [y]The heart of man plans his way,
but [z]the LORD establishes his steps.
10 [a]An oracle is on the lips of a king;
his mouth does not sin in judgment.
11 [b]A just balance and scales are the LORD's;
all the weights in the bag are his work.
12 It is an abomination to kings to do evil,
for [c]the throne is established by righteousness.
13 [d]Righteous lips are the delight of a king,
and he loves him who speaks what is right.
14 [e]A king's wrath is a messenger of death,
and a wise man will [f]appease it.
15 [g]In the light of a king's face there is life,
and his [d]favor is like [h]the clouds that bring the spring rain.

[1] Hebrew *makes fat*

28 [y]Ps. 37:30 [z][1 Pet. 3:15]; See ver. 2
29 [a][Ps. 18:41; 34:16] [b]Ps. 145:18, 19; [ver. 8]
30 [c]Ps. 38:10 [d][ch. 25:25]
31 [e]ver. 5; ch. 20:12; 25:12 [f][ch. 6:23]
32 [g][ch. 8:33] [h]See ch. 8:36 [i][ch. 19:8]
33 [j]See ch. 1:7 [k]ch. 18:12

Chapter 16

1 [l][Matt. 10:19, 20]
2 [m]ch. 21:2; [ch. 12:15]; See ch. 30:12 [n]ch. 24:12; See 1 Sam. 16:7
3 [o]See Ps. 37:5
4 [p]Rom. 11:36 [q]Job 21:30; [Ex. 9:16]
5 [r]ch. 6:16, 17; 8:13; Luke 16:15 [s]ch. 11:21; [ch. 28:20]
6 [t]Dan. 4:27 [u]ch. 14:16 [v]ver. 17; Job 28:28
7 [w][Gen. 26:28; 2 Chr. 17:10]
8 [x]See ch. 15:16
9 [y][ver. 1; ch. 19:21] [z]ch. 20:24; [Ps. 37:23; Jer. 10:23]
10 [a][1 Kgs. 3:28]
11 [b]See ch. 11:1
12 [c]ch. 25:5; [ch. 20:28; 29:14; Isa. 16:5]
13 [d][ch. 14:35; 22:11]
14 [e]ch. 19:12; 20:2 [f][ch. 25:15]
15 [g][Job 29:24] [d][See ver. 13 above] [h][Ps. 72:6]; See Job 29:23

16:1–9 The comparison between the **plans** of a man's **heart** (vv. 1a, 9a) and the sovereign direction of **the LORD** (vv. 1b, 9b) unifies this section. Verses 2–8 focus on the importance of the heart-action connection.

16:6 This proverb portrays the sacrificial system, by which **iniquity is atoned for**, as an expression of God's **steadfast love and faithfulness** (cf. Ex. 34:6; Prov. 3:3; 14:22; 20:28). The right response is **the fear of the LORD**, by which **one turns away from** doing **evil** (a common "wisdom" phrase: 3:7; 13:19; 14:16; 16:17; Job 1:1, 8; 2:3; 28:28; Ps. 34:14; 37:27). The Bible consistently presents moral effort as the right response to God's grace.

16:10–33 The remaining sections of ch. 16 further illustrate the themes of vv. 1–9 on the benefits of wisdom for the well-being of the heart (vv. 16–19, 20–24, 25–33) in light of the sovereign governance of the Lord (vv. 10–15, 33).

16:10–15 These verses concern the **king**, who is mentioned explicitly in all but v. 11. Verses 10 and 12 appear to represent the king as flawlessly wise, especially since he is descended from David. These proverbs represent the ideal and imply that people should have respect for their highest officials. Verses 13–15 indicate that people should be careful around kings simply because absolute rulers—as all kings were in biblical times—have great power. Verse 11 seems out of place but is actually very important: ultimately, justice (as symbolized by the scales, representing commercial transactions in general) is maintained by God—it is above the power of the king.

16:16–19 The "better" sayings of vv. 16 and 19 seek to instill the value of

16[i]ch. 8:10, 11, 19 [j]See ch. 3:14 [k]ch. 10:20
17[l]ver. 6
18[m]See ch. 11:2
19[n]ch. 29:23; Isa. 57:15 [o]See Ex. 15:9
20[p]ch. 19:8 [q]See Ps. 2:12
21[r]ver. 23
22[s]See ch. 10:11
23[t][Ps. 37:30; Matt. 12:34]
24[u]ch. 15:26 [v]Ps. 19:10 [w]See ch. 4:22
26[x][Eccles. 6:7]
27[y][ch. 6:12, 14, 19] [z]James 3:6
28[a]See ch. 15:18 [b][ch. 18:8; 26:20, 22] [c]ch. 17:9
29[d]ch. 1:10
30[e]See ch. 2:12 [f][ch. 6:13]
31[g]ch. 20:29 [h]ch. 17:6 [i]See ch. 3:1, 2
32[j]ch. 14:29; [ch. 19:11; 25:28]
33[k][Acts 1:26] [l]ch. 29:26

16 [i]How much better to get wisdom than [j]gold!
To get understanding is to be chosen rather than [k]silver.
17 The highway of the upright [l]turns aside from evil;
whoever guards his way preserves his life.
18 [m]Pride goes before destruction,
and a haughty spirit before a fall.
19 [n]It is better to be of a lowly spirit with the poor
than to [o]divide the spoil with the proud.
20 Whoever gives thought to the word[1] [p]will discover good,
and blessed is he [q]who trusts in the LORD.
21 The wise of heart is called discerning,
and sweetness of speech [r]increases persuasiveness.
22 Good sense is [s]a fountain of life to him who has it,
but the instruction of fools is folly.
23 [t]The heart of the wise makes his speech judicious
and adds persuasiveness to his lips.
24 [u]Gracious words are like [v]a honeycomb,
sweetness to the soul and [w]health to the body.
25 There is a way that seems right to a man,
but its end is the way to death.[2]
26 A worker's appetite works for him;
his [x]mouth urges him on.
27 [y]A worthless man plots evil,
and his speech[3] is like [z]a scorching fire.
28 [a]A dishonest man spreads strife,
and [b]a whisperer [c]separates close friends.
29 A man of violence [d]entices his neighbor
and leads him in a way that is not good.
30 Whoever winks his eyes plans[4] [e]dishonest things;
he who [f]purses his lips brings evil to pass.
31 [g]Gray hair is [h]a crown of glory;
it [i]is gained in a righteous life.
32 [j]Whoever is slow to anger is better than the mighty,
and he who rules his spirit than he who takes a city.
33 [k]The lot is cast into the lap,
but its every decision is [l]from the LORD.

[1] *Or to a matter* [2] Hebrew *ways of death* [3] Hebrew *what is on his lips* [4] Hebrew *to plan*

wisdom over wealth (v. 16) and of humility **with the poor** over **spoil with the proud** (v. 19). The middle verses offer guidance on how to continue in the way of the wise (tread the **highway of the upright**, v. 17) and humble (do not foster a **haughty spirit**, v. 18). For similar statements of what it is wise to value, cf. 15:16–17; 16:8; 19:1, 22; 28:6.

16:20–24 These verses commend the speech characteristic of the **wise of heart** (vv. 21a, 23a): the wise consider their words carefully (vv. 20a, 23a) so that their words are both persuasive (vv. 21b, 23b) and good for **body** and **soul** (v. 24); they exhibit faithfulness to God (v. 20b) and are considered **discerning** by others (v. 21a). Such wisdom is a **fountain of life**, and foolish speech is empty of any such benefits (v. 22).

16:23–24 Persuasiveness is a skill that can be learned and improved. This is one aspect of the wisdom taught in Proverbs (cf. v. 21).

16:25–32 a way that seems right . . . but. People often have the wrong idea about what is good and what is bad. Hunger seems a bad thing, but it forces people to work and keeps them from idleness (v. 26). Verses 27–30 likewise describe types of evil that seem clever to those who practice them but which are actually vile and destructive. This includes general troublemaking (v. 27), spreading discord (v. 28), drawing others to join in crime (v. 29), and conspiring with others to commit crime (v. 30). **Gray hair** seems to be a mark of infirmity but actually is a **crown of glory** (v. 31; cf. 20:29). Finally, a mighty warrior seems to be the strongest man of all, but in reality a man who can control himself is stronger than a conqueror (16:32).

16:32 Contrary to the many who would say it is good to vent one's anger, Proverbs advocates being **slow to anger**. Only a **mighty** person, likened to the person who is strong enough to take a city, is capable of controlling his anger (**rules his spirit**). (On the harmful effects of anger, see 14:29; 15:1, 18; 19:11; 22:24; 27:4; 29:22; 30:33; see also Gal. 5:20; Eph. 4:31; Col. 3:8.)

16:33 "Casting lots" involves the random selection or distribution of objects in order to make a choice uncontrolled and unbiased by the participants. In Israel it was typically performed "before the Lord" (see Josh. 18:8) in order to receive his direction. **from the LORD**. Not only the careful plans of the heart (Prov. 16:1, 9) but also the apparently random practice of casting lots falls under God's providential governance. On the question of whether Christians should make decisions in this way, see note on Acts 1:26.

17

1 [m]Better is a dry morsel with quiet
than a house full of feasting[1] with strife.
2 A servant who deals wisely will rule over [n]a son who acts shamefully
and [o]will share the inheritance as one of the brothers.
3 [p]The crucible is for silver, and the furnace is for gold,
[q]and the LORD tests hearts.
4 An evildoer listens to wicked lips,
and a liar gives ear to a mischievous tongue.
5 Whoever mocks the poor [r]insults his Maker;
he who is [s]glad at calamity will not go [t]unpunished.
6 [u]Grandchildren are [v]the crown of the aged,
and the glory of children is their fathers.
7 Fine speech is not [w]becoming to a fool;
still less is [x]false speech to a prince.
8 [y]A bribe is like a magic stone in the eyes of the one who gives it;
wherever he turns he prospers.
9 Whoever [z]covers an offense seeks love,
but he who repeats a matter [a]separates close friends.
10 A rebuke goes deeper into a man of understanding
than a hundred blows into a fool.
11 An evil man seeks only rebellion,
and [b]a cruel messenger will be sent against him.
12 Let a man meet [c]a she-bear robbed of her cubs
[d]rather than a fool in his folly.
13 If anyone [e]returns evil for good,
[f]evil will not depart from his house.
14 The beginning of strife is like letting out water,
so [g]quit before the quarrel breaks out.
15 He who [h]justifies the wicked and he who [i]condemns the righteous
are both alike an abomination to the LORD.
16 Why should a fool have money in his hand [j]to buy wisdom
when he has no sense?
17 [k]A friend loves at all times,
and a brother is born for adversity.

[1] Hebrew *sacrifices*

Chapter 17
1[m]ch. 15:17
2[n]ver. 21, 25; ch. 10:5; 19:26 [o][2 Sam. 16:4]
3[p]ch. 27:21 [q]1 Chr. 29:17; Ps. 26:2; Jer. 17:10; Mal. 3:3
5[r]ch. 14:31; [Matt. 25:40, 45] [s]Job 31:29; Obad. 12; [ch. 24:17] [t]ch. 16:5
6[u]Ps. 128:6; [Ps. 127:3, 4] [v]ch. 16:31
7[w][ch. 19:10; 26:1] [x]ch. 6:17
8[y]ver. 23; ch. 18:16; 19:6; 21:14; [Ex. 23:8; Isa. 1:23; Amos 5:12]
9[z]ch. 10:12 [a]ch. 16:28
11[b][1 Kgs. 2:29]
12[c]2 Sam. 17:8; Hos. 13:8 [d][ch. 27:3]
13[e]Ps. 35:12; 109:4, 5; [ch. 20:22; Matt. 5:39] [f][2 Sam. 12:10]
14[g]ch. 20:3; 25:8
15[h]ch. 24:24; Ex. 23:7; Isa. 5:23 [i]Job 34:17; Ps. 94:21; [ver. 26; ch. 18:5]
16[j][ch. 23:23]
17[k]ch. 18:24; 27:10; [Ruth 1:16; Job 6:14]

17:1 Like 15:17, this proverb asserts that a poor but loving home is better than a home filled with **feasting** and **strife**. As the ESV footnote indicates, "feasting" is lit., "sacrifices," specifically peace offerings; such offerings would provide for a meal including meat—a luxury in ancient times.

17:2 Through diligence one can overcome disadvantages of birth; through being undisciplined one can lose advantages of birth.

17:3 Crucible and **furnace** suggest that **the LORD tests hearts** by adversity.

17:4 This proverb concerns both the one who spreads and the one who **listens to** malicious gossip.

17:5 mocks the poor. Such mocking can involve saying that those who suffer deserve it (e.g., the attitude of Job's friends) or simply being callous or indifferent to their plight.

17:6 Families depend on one another for their identity and joy. Both young and old should cherish their intergenerational relationships.

17:7 False speech is especially disconcerting when coming from a **prince**, whose job it is to promote justice.

17:8 A bribe is like a magic stone . . . prospers. This proverb observes but does not condone a fact of life (cf. note on 14:20). The wise person will ponder this reality and face it as a temptation.

17:9–19 These verses include two collections of proverbs (vv. 9–13 and vv. 14–19) that revolve around interpersonal conflict.

17:9–13 This section begins by contrasting wise and foolish responses to situations where a person is either the offended (v. 9) or offending (v. 10) party. The remaining verses warn against the calamitous effects of pursuing the foolish path; a situation of mortal danger (e.g., a **she-bear** protecting **her cubs**) is more desirable than the possibly ruinous effect of meeting a **fool in his folly** (v. 12).

17:14–19 Verse 14 advises the reader to avoid, resolve, or walk away from conflict before things get out of hand and true calamity ensues. In v. 19, to make the **door high** symbolizes the pride of the owner and is a picture of the arrogance and pride of the one who "seeks destruction." These two verses form a frame for vv. 15–18, each of which more or less describes the wisdom and shape of a right relationship.

17:14 like letting out water. Once a dam has been breached, there is no holding back the water—an apt image for the rapid and damaging escalation of a quarrel.

17:15 Though wisdom calls for the careful avoidance of strife, this does not excuse the one who **justifies the wicked** (calls a guilty person innocent) or who **condemns the righteous** (calls an innocent person guilty). Both of these actions are an **abomination to the LORD**.

17:16 This proverb either (1) expresses the irony of thinking that **wisdom** is a commodity that can be bought with **money**, or (2) suggests that a fool, because he **has no sense**, would refuse to buy wisdom even if he could.

18 One who lacks sense gives a pledge
and puts up security in the presence of his neighbor.
19 Whoever loves transgression loves strife;
he who [l]makes his door high seeks destruction.
20 [m]A man of crooked heart does not discover good,
and one with a dishonest tongue falls into calamity.
21 He who [n]sires a fool gets himself sorrow,
and the father of a fool has no joy.
22 [o]A joyful heart is good medicine,
but a crushed spirit [p]dries up the bones.
23 The wicked accepts [q]a bribe in secret[1]
to [r]pervert the ways of justice.
24 [s]The discerning sets his face toward wisdom,
but the eyes of a fool are on the ends of the earth.
25 [n]A foolish son is a grief to his father
[t]and bitterness to [u]her who bore him.
26 [v]To impose a fine on a righteous man is not good,
nor to strike the noble for their uprightness.
27 Whoever [w]restrains his words has knowledge,
and he who has a cool spirit is a man of understanding.
28 Even a fool [x]who keeps silent is considered wise;
when he closes his lips, he is deemed intelligent.

18

1 Whoever [y]isolates himself seeks his own desire;
he breaks out against all sound judgment.
2 A fool takes no pleasure in understanding,
but only [z]in expressing his opinion.
3 When wickedness comes, contempt comes also,
and with dishonor comes disgrace.
4 The words of a man's mouth are [a]deep waters;
the fountain of wisdom is a bubbling brook.
5 It is not good to [b]be partial to[2] the wicked
or to [c]deprive the righteous of justice.
6 A fool's lips walk into a fight,
and his mouth invites [d]a beating.

19 [l][ch. 11:2; 29:23]
20 [m][ch. 11:20]
21 [n]ch. 10:1; 19:13
22 [o]See ch. 15:13 [p]Ps. 22:15; [ch. 12:25]
23 [q]See ver. 8 [r][Mic. 3:11; 7:3]
24 [s][ch. 14:6; 15:14; Eccles. 2:14]; See Deut. 30:11-14
25 [n][See ver. 21 above] [t]ch. 10:1 [u]ch. 23:25
26 [v][ver. 15]
27 [w]ch. 10:19; [James 1:19]
28 [x]Job 13:5

Chapter 18

1 [y][Jude 19]
2 [z]ch. 13:16; [Eccles. 10:3]
4 [a]ch. 20:5
5 [b]ch. 24:23; 28:21; Lev. 19:15; Deut. 1:17; Ps. 82:2 [c]See ch. 17:15
6 [d]See ch. 19:29

[1] Hebrew *a bribe from the bosom* [2] Hebrew *to lift the face of*

17:18 There are wise limits to what it means to be a friend (cf. v. 17), e.g., when one is asked to put up a **pledge** or **security** for a loan for another person's debt (see note on 6:1–5). Such an action is labeled here as the sheer stupidity of a person who altogether **lacks sense**.

17:19 Transgression and **strife** go hand-in-hand (cf. v. 14). Transgression is in the heart of the person who **loves** strife, i.e., who is unwilling to "quit before the quarrel breaks out" (cf. v. 14). Such a person is characterized by pride and arrogance (**makes his door high**; see note on vv. 14–19); though he seeks the ruin of others, in reality he is seeking his own **destruction**, which God will bring about in due course (cf. Ps. 55:23; 2 Pet. 3:7).

17:20–26 These two sets of proverbs (vv. 20–22 and vv. 23–26) for the most part describe things that bring grief.

17:20–22 Three things will bring sorrow to the heart: a **crooked** and **dishonest** life (v. 20), a foolish son (v. 21), and too much discouragement (v. 22).

17:23–26 Verses 23 and 26 speak of perversions of justice. Verse 24 speaks of the fool who wastes his life chasing unattainable goals (**the ends of the earth**), and v. 25 speaks of the fool who gives distress to his parents. Folly and injustice have this in common, that they both fill life with grief and vexation.

17:25 The picture of a **foolish son** grieving the mother **who bore him** expands on the similar statement in v. 21 (cf. also 15:5, 20; 23:22–25). Such images should encourage both children and parents to seek the benefits of wisdom.

17:26 To impose a fine on a righteous man is not good. Governments should not punish innocent people (cf. 1 Pet. 2:14). In Israel, of all places, this should never happen!

17:27–18:4 This section is framed by two proverbs on the careful, restrained use of words (17:27; 18:4). Between these, 17:28 asserts that a fool would do well to keep his mouth shut, while 18:2 asserts that this is the one thing a fool cannot do. Also, 18:1 asserts that some people are irrational in their determination to be antisocial; this is answered by 18:3, which declares that wicked behavior brings people into contempt. Together, these six proverbs call for people to be careful with their words in the public arena lest they risk exclusion and humiliation.

18:1 Whoever isolates himself translates a Hebrew word that refers to someone who is either reclusive or divisive. Either way, antisocial tendencies seem to be implied.

18:5–8 These verses all concern the misuse of words and the consequences thereof. Verses 6 and 7 obviously parallel each other. Of itself, v. 5 is a simple condemnation of injustice in the courts; but in this context, and especially against v. 8, the implication is that the legal system will malfunction in a setting dominated by innuendo, gossip, and lying. Verse 8 explains why gossip is so deadly: people love to hear it and to share it.

7 [e]A fool's mouth is his ruin,
and his lips are a snare to his soul.
8 [f]The words of a whisperer are like delicious morsels;
they go down into [g]the inner parts of the body.
9 Whoever is slack in his work
is a [h]brother to him who destroys.
10 [i]The name of the LORD is [j]a strong tower;
the righteous man runs into it and [k]is safe.
11 [l]A rich man's wealth is his strong city,
and like a high wall in his imagination.
12 [m]Before destruction a man's heart is haughty,
but [n]humility comes before honor.
13 If one gives an answer [o]before he hears,
it is his folly and shame.
14 A man's spirit will endure sickness,
but [p]a crushed spirit who can bear?
15 An intelligent heart acquires knowledge,
and the ear of the wise seeks knowledge.
16 A man's [q]gift makes room for him
and brings him before the great.
17 The one who states his case first seems right,
until the other comes and examines him.
18 [r]The lot puts an end to quarrels
and decides between powerful contenders.
19 A brother offended is more unyielding than a strong city,
and quarreling is like the bars of a castle.
20 [s]From the fruit of a man's mouth his stomach is satisfied;
he is satisfied by the yield of his lips.
21 [t]Death and life are in the power of the tongue,
and those who love it will eat its fruits.
22 He who finds [u]a wife finds [v]a good thing
and [w]obtains favor [x]from the LORD.
23 The poor use entreaties,
but [y]the rich answer roughly.

7 [e]ch. 10:14; 12:13; 13:3; Ps. 64:8; 140:9; Eccles. 10:12
8 [f]ch. 26:22; [ch. 16:28] [g]ch. 20:27
9 [h][ch. 28:24]
10 [i]See Ex. 34:5-7 [j]Ps. 61:3; [Ps. 18:2]; See 2 Sam. 22:3 [k][Ps. 20:1]
11 [l]See ch. 10:15
12 [m]See ch. 11:2 [n]ch. 15:33
13 [o][John 7:51]
14 [p]ch. 15:13
16 [q][Gen. 32:20; 1 Sam. 25:27]; See ch. 17:8
18 [r][ch. 16:33]
20 [s]See ch. 12:14
21 [t]Matt. 12:36, 37; [ch. 4:23; 12:13]
22 [u]ch. 12:4; 19:14; See ch. 31:10-31 [v][Gen. 2:18] [w]ch. 8:35 [x]ch. 19:14
23 [y][James 2:3, 6]

18:9–12 Verses 10 and 11 describe two types of security (**the LORD** and riches), while vv. 9 and 12 describe two things that bring about one's destruction (laziness and pride). Taken together, these proverbs imply that riches can give a false sense of security that leads to laziness, pride, and a downfall, but that humility and the fear of God exalt people.

18:13 This proverb relates to every area of life, not just a courtroom setting.

18:14 A person's **spirit**, if it is hopeful and good, can endure **sickness** and adversity, but if the spirit is despondent, even when there is nothing overtly wrong, then life itself becomes difficult to **bear**.

18:15–19 These proverbs could be applied to many settings in life, though here they seem to be particularly focused on a courtroom setting. In hearing a case, one should seek with one's **heart** (Hb. *leb*, "reason, emotions, and will") to acquire **knowledge**, and likewise with one's **ear** to listen carefully to what is being said, for this is the way that **the wise** (person) **seeks knowledge**. One reason for this is the danger of bribery (condemned in 15:27)—that is, because of the **gift** that **makes room for him**, providing access to the **great**. Thus the warning of 18:17 not to be easily swayed by the person who **states his case first**; rather, the wise person **examines** the evidence in a careful, probing manner (cf. v. 13). Still, in some cases it is impossible to reach a verdict, because the matter is hidden and there is not enough evidence to make a well-informed judgment. In such cases (v. 18), it is better to settle **quarrels** by means of casting a **lot** ("before the Lord"), thus leaving the outcome in the Lord's hands, rather than allowing **powerful contenders** to do violence to each other. Even so, whether by means of a lot or judicial determination, the reconciliation of one brother to another (i.e., reconciliation of close friends) is difficult to achieve. **A brother offended** can be **more unyielding than a strong city**—for the resolution of **quarreling** meets with resistance **like the bars of a castle**.

18:18 On whether Christians should cast lots, see note on Acts 1:26.

18:20–21 Since the **tongue** can produce either **death** or **life**, the wise person will guard his or her speech (cf. 12:13–14; 13:2–3).

18:22–20:4 A number of proverbs in this section of the book are so similar to each other that they appear to serve as markers, setting boundaries for separate proverb collections. Proverbs 18:22 and 19:14 both assert that a good wife is from the Lord; while 19:15, 24, and 20:4 concern laziness. Proverbs 19:11–12 deals first with patience and then with the king's anger, and 20:2–3 deals first with the king's anger and then with patience. Between these markers, 18:23–19:10 concerns misfortune, while 19:16–23 can be described as an inventory of the essential elements of a good life. Over against 19:16–23, the proverbs in 19:25–20:1 present the antithesis of the good life, the life of the mocker.

18:22 This verse refers to both the human action (**finds**) and the divine governance (**from the LORD**) of a marital relationship, while the pronouncement **good** agrees with the Lord's assessment that it was "not good" for Adam to be alone (Gen. 2:18).

18:23–19:4 These proverbs observe misfortune from various angles. The **poor** are reduced to begging and taking abuse (18:23), but a few friends stick by a man even in his worst times (18:24). The great majority of one's companions, however, only stay close by so long as one's fortunes are good; in bad times, they disappear (19:4). Poverty with **integrity** is better than immorality (19:1), but hunger, such as is produced by poverty, can lead to thoughtless, hasty

24 A man of many companions may come to ruin,
but [z]there is a friend who sticks closer than a brother.

19

1 [a]Better is a poor person who [b]walks in his integrity
than one who is crooked in speech and is a fool.
2 Desire[1] without knowledge is not good,
and whoever [c]makes haste with his feet misses his way.
3 When a man's folly [d]brings his way to ruin,
his heart [e]rages against the LORD.
4 [f]Wealth brings many new friends,
[f]but a poor man is deserted by his friend.
5 [g]A false witness will not go unpunished,
and he who [h]breathes out lies will not escape.
6 Many seek the favor of a generous man,[2]
and everyone is a friend to a man who gives [i]gifts.
7 [j]All a poor man's brothers hate him;
[k]how much more do his friends go far from him!
He pursues them with words, but does not have them.[3]
8 [l]Whoever gets sense loves his own soul;
he who keeps understanding will [m]discover good.
9 [g]A false witness will not go unpunished,
and he who [h]breathes out lies will perish.
10 [n]It is not fitting for a fool to live in luxury,
much less for [o]a slave to rule over princes.
11 [p]Good sense makes one slow to anger,
and it is his glory to overlook an offense.
12 A king's wrath is like [q]the growling of a lion,
but his [r]favor is like [s]dew on the grass.
13 [t]A foolish son is ruin to his father,
and [u]a wife's quarreling is [v]a continual dripping of rain.
14 [w]House and wealth are inherited from fathers,
but a prudent wife is [x]from the LORD.
15 [y]Slothfulness casts into [z]a deep sleep,
and [a]an idle person will suffer hunger.
16 Whoever [b]keeps the commandment keeps his life;
he who despises his ways will die.

[1] Or *A soul* [2] Or *of a noble* [3] The meaning of the Hebrew sentence is uncertain

24[z]See ch. 17:17
Chapter 19
1[a]ch. 28:6 [b]ch. 14:2; 20:7; Ps. 26:1, 11
2[c][ch. 21:5; 28:20; 29:20]
3[d][ch. 11:3] [e][Ps. 37:7; Isa. 8:21; Rev. 16:11]
4[f]ch. 14:20
5[g][ch. 12:19; 21:28]; See Deut. 19:16-19 [h]See ch. 6:19
6[i]See ch. 17:8
7[j][ver. 4] [k][Ps. 38:11]
8[l][ch. 15:32] [m]ch. 16:20
9[g][See ver. 5 above] [h][See ver. 5 above]
10[n][ch. 17:7; 26:1] [o]ch. 30:22; Eccles. 10:6, 7
11[p]See ch. 14:29
12[q]ch. 20:2; [ch. 16:14, 15; 28:15] [r]ch. 14:35 [s]Ps. 133:3; Hos. 14:5; Mic. 5:7
13[t]ch. 10:1; 17:21 [u]See ch. 21:9 [v]ch. 27:15
14[w][2 Cor. 12:14] [x]ch. 18:22
15[y]See ch. 6:9-11 [z]Job 4:13 [a][ch. 10:4; 20:4, 13; 23:21]
16[b][ch. 13:13; Luke 10:28]

acts of folly (see 19:2 and note). People often blame God for their misfortune when they should be blaming themselves (19:3).

18:24 a friend . . . closer than a brother. Cf. 17:17 and 27:10.

19:2 Whoever makes haste with his feet could refer to a person hurrying to sin (in contrast with the one walking in integrity in v. 1), but more likely it refers to an impulsive person who unwisely acts before thinking or planning the right way. He has a "desire" to get somewhere but he does not have sufficient **knowledge** to reach his goal.

19:5–9 Verses 5 and 9 are virtually identical and frame this section. Of itself, v. 5 is a general proverb on the importance of honest testimony (for further implications of and warnings against being a **false witness**, see 6:19; 12:17; 14:5). In this context, dominated by the idea of poverty and misfortune, "false witness" could relate either to those who exploit the poor in the courts or to poor people who will perjure themselves for a little money. Verses 6–7 of ch. 19 return to the idea mentioned in v. 4, that the prosperous seem to have many friends but the poor man has no friends at all. Verse 8 picks up on the teaching of vv. 1–2, that even in misfortune one must seek wisdom.

19:10 Not fitting . . . for a slave to rule over princes does not mean it is always wrong for a slave to rise to power; otherwise, Joseph's ascent in the Egyptian government would be an example of moral disorder in the world. Rather, it suggests that fortune and misfortune are not always fair: sometimes a **fool** becomes wealthy without doing anything to merit that wealth, and sometimes a slave rises to power without an ability to rule well.

19:11 In many cultures, any sign of disrespect to a man is a challenge to his honor, and he can regain it only by fighting whoever insults him. Here, patience and overlooking slights bring honor to a man.

19:12 The growling of a lion is frightening and precedes an act of violence; **dew** is gentle and gives life. The proverb does not say that a king's anger (or **favor**) is always right, but that it is powerful.

19:13–14 Verse 13 gives balance to v. 14 in the recognition that family life can be painful and some wives are a great burden to their husbands. (Of course, some husbands are a great burden to their wives; see Introduction: Literary Features, regarding "concreteness"; and see note on 21:9.) The **continual dripping** brings to mind a leaking roof. This is not a minor irritation but a source of structural damage that can make a house uninhabitable. The point is that such a woman ruins her house (see 14:1). Verse 14 of ch. 19 implies not only that **a prudent wife is** a gift **from the LORD** (see Introduction: Character Types in Proverbs), but also that she manages the household so well that she increases its assets. **inherited from fathers**. **House and wealth** come in the ordinary course of things, in contrast to the prudent wife, who is a sign of special favor.

19:15 Slothfulness casts into a deep sleep. The lazy person is always too tired to work. Then his laziness becomes more and more severe until he is in dire poverty.

19:16–23 These verses lay out some essential features of a good life, which can be summarized as shown in the chart on p. 1168. This list moves from

17 [c]Whoever is generous to the poor lends to the LORD,
and he [d]will repay him for his [e]deed.
18 [f]Discipline your son, for there is hope;
do not set your heart on [g]putting him to death.
19 A man of great wrath will pay the penalty,
for if you deliver him, you will only have to do it again.
20 Listen to advice and accept instruction,
that you may gain wisdom in [h]the future.
21 [i]Many are the plans in the mind of a man,
but [j]it is the purpose of the LORD [k]that will stand.
22 What is desired in a man is steadfast love,
and a poor man is better than a liar.
23 The fear of the LORD [l]leads to life,
and whoever has it rests [m]satisfied;
he will [n]not be visited by harm.
24 [o]The sluggard buries his hand in [p]the dish
and will not even bring it back to his mouth.
25 [q]Strike [r]a scoffer, and the simple will [s]learn prudence;
[t]reprove a man of understanding, and he will gain knowledge.
26 He who does violence to his father and chases away his mother
is [u]a son who brings shame and reproach.
27 Cease to hear instruction, my son,
[v]and you will stray from the words of knowledge.
28 A worthless witness mocks at justice,
and the mouth of the wicked [w]devours iniquity.
29 Condemnation is ready for [r]scoffers,
and [x]beating for the backs of fools.

20

1 [y]Wine is a mocker, [z]strong drink a brawler,
and whoever [a]is led astray by it is not wise.[1]
2 The terror of a king is like [b]the growling of a lion;
whoever provokes him to anger [c]forfeits his life.
3 It is an honor for a man to [d]keep aloof from strife,
but every fool will be quarreling.
4 [e]The sluggard does not plow in the autumn;
[f]he will seek at harvest and have nothing.

[1] Or *will not become wise*

17 [c][ch. 22:9; 28:27; Eccles. 11:1; Matt. 10:42; Heb. 6:10]; See Deut. 15:7-10; Matt. 25:40; 2 Cor. 9:6-8 [d][Luke 6:38] [e]See ch. 12:14
18 [f]See ch. 13:24 [g][ch. 23:13]; See Deut. 21:18-21
20 [h]Ps. 37:37
21 [i]Ps. 33:10, 11 [j]Job 23:13; Isa. 14:26, 27 [k]Isa. 46:10
23 [l]ch. 10:16; 11:19; [Isa. 38:5; Mark 10:30] [m][Ps. 25:13] [n][Lev. 26:6]
24 [o]ch. 26:15; [ch. 15:19; 20:4] [p][Matt. 26:23; Mark 14:20]
25 [q]ch. 21:11 [r]See Ps. 1:1 [s]See Deut. 13:6-11 [t][ch. 9:8]
26 [u]ch. 10:5; 17:2
27 [v][2 Pet. 2:21]
28 [w]Job 15:16; [ch. 18:8; Job 34:7]
29 [r][See ver. 25 above] [x]ch. 10:13; 18:6; 26:3

Chapter 20
1 [y][Gen. 9:21]; See ch. 23:29-32 [z]ch. 31:4 [a]Isa. 28:7; [Hos. 4:11]
2 [b]See ch. 19:12 [c]Num. 16:38; Hab. 2:10; See ch. 8:36
3 [d][ch. 17:14]
4 [e][ch. 19:24] [f]ch. 19:15; [ch. 6:11]

basic principles of wisdom to the significance of love and then finally to fearing God as the supreme principle of life.

19:24 In a humorous caricature (echoing v. 15), the **sluggard** here is so foolish and so lazy that he will not even feed himself. Laziness is irrational and leads to poverty and hunger.

19:25–20:1 In contrast to the features of a good life described in 19:16–23 is the description in these verses of the **scoffer** or mocker. This person is a complete reprobate and the quintessential fool. Of such a person it can be said: (1) the only hope for correcting his stubborn attitude lies in beatings, which may or may not have the desired effect (19:25); (2) he has no respect for parents (19:26); (3) he will not listen to sound teaching (19:27); (4) he rejects all notions of right and wrong (19:28); and (5) again, he gets beaten for his behavior (19:29). Finally, **wine** is called a **mocker** and **strong drink a brawler** in 20:1. That is, excessive drinking leads to picking fights and an abandonment of principles of right and wrong. It is implied that drunkenness is common among scoffers.

Some Essential Features of a Good Life (Proverbs 19)

listen to instruction	vv. 16, 20
be kind to the poor	v. 17
be involved in your children's lives and discipline them	v. 18
avoid friendships with those who lack self-control	v. 19
acknowledge the rule of God	v. 21
understand that love and integrity are what bring real happiness	v. 22
fear the Lord	v. 23

19:25 The **simple** learn by seeing a beating, but the wise take instruction from a simple word of reproof. Notably, although the simple can **learn prudence**, no such teachable spirit is attributed to the **scoffer**.

20:2 The first line of this proverb is almost identical to 19:12a, but whereas 19:12b speaks of the king's favor, 20:2b continues to speak only of his anger (see also note on 15:10–12). The text does not say that a king's anger is always justified, only that it is lethal. Therefore, one should take care.

20:3 Of itself, this is another exhortation to patience (cf. 19:11). Its position after 20:2 may suggest that a king also should learn patience.

20:4 In Israel, the grain **harvest** began after Passover (around April), and the

5[g]ch. 18:4
6[h][ch. 25:14; Matt. 6:2; Luke 18:11] [i][Ps. 12:1]
7[j]See ch. 19:1 [k][1 Kgs. 15:4; Ps. 37:26; 112:2; Jer. 33:20, 21]
8[l][ch. 16:10] [m][ver. 26; ch. 25:5; Ps. 101:5]
9[n]See 1 Kgs. 8:46
10[o]ver. 23; See ch. 11:1
11[p][Matt. 7:16]
12[q]ch. 15:31; 25:12 [r]Ex. 4:11; Ps. 94:9
13[s][ch. 6:4; 19:15; 31:15; Rom. 12:11] [t][ver. 4] [u]ch. 12:11
15[v]Job 28:18 [w][ch. 3:14, 15]
16[x]ch. 27:13; [ch. 6:1; 22:26] [y]See Job 22:6
17[z][ch. 9:17] [a][Lam. 3:16]
18[b][ch. 11:14; 15:22] [c]ch. 24:6 [d]Luke 14:31
19[e]ch. 11:13 [f]ch. 13:3; [Rom. 16:18]
20[g]ch. 30:11, 17; See Ex. 21:17 [h]See 2 Sam. 21:17; Job 18:5

5 The purpose in a man's heart is like [g]deep water,
but a man of understanding will draw it out.
6 Many a man [h]proclaims his own steadfast love,
but [i]a faithful man who can find?
7 The righteous who [j]walks in his integrity—
[k]blessed are his children after him!
8 [l]A king who sits on the throne of judgment
[m]winnows all evil with his eyes.
9 [n]Who can say, "I have made my heart pure;
I am clean from my sin"?
10 [o]Unequal[1] weights and unequal measures
are both alike an abomination to the LORD.
11 Even a child [p]makes himself known by his acts,
by whether his conduct is pure and upright.[2]
12 [q]The hearing ear and the seeing eye,
[r]the LORD has made them both.
13 [s]Love not sleep, lest you [t]come to poverty;
open your eyes, and you will have [u]plenty of bread.
14 "Bad, bad," says the buyer,
but when he goes away, then he boasts.
15 There is gold and abundance of [v]costly stones,
[w]but the lips of knowledge are a precious jewel.
16 [x]Take a man's garment when he has put up security for a stranger,
and [y]hold it in pledge when he puts up security for foreigners.[3]
17 [z]Bread gained by deceit is sweet to a man,
but afterward his mouth will be full of [a]gravel.
18 [b]Plans are established by counsel;
by [c]wise guidance [d]wage war.
19 Whoever [e]goes about slandering reveals secrets;
therefore do not associate with [f]a simple babbler.[4]
20 [g]If one curses his father or his mother,
[h]his lamp will be put out in utter darkness.

[1] Or *Two kinds of*; also verse 23 [2] Or *Even a child can dissemble in his actions, though his conduct seems pure and upright* [3] Or *for an adulteress* (compare 27:13)
[4] Hebrew *with one who is simple in his lips*

sowing of this crop (in a field that had just been plowed) was done **in the autumn**, after the Feast of Tabernacles (around November).

20:5–21:8 The proverbs of this section primarily give teachings about judgment and, to a lesser extent, money. The section is framed by 20:5–7 and 21:8; 20:5 asserts that one must be discerning to understand what another person is really up to, and 20:6 observes that people's pretenses of virtue are often false and asks how to find true goodness. Verse 7a of chapter 20 answers the question of 20:6. While it looks like an empty truism, 20:7a really means that people's behavior is a good indicator of what they are. The blessing of 20:7b serves as a transition line to the catalog of proverbs that follows. It begins with the word "blessed," a word that often introduces wisdom poems (e.g., Ps. 1:1; 112:1). At the end, Prov. 21:8 repeats the basic rule of discernment found in 20:7a: **crooked** people do evil, and **upright** people do good.

20:8–12 This catalog of proverbs looks at judgment from various angles. The purpose of a **king**, representing human government, is to curb evil through acts of judgment (v. 8). Awareness of one's own guilt should make one forbearing in judging others (v. 9). Scales (economic tools that are also symbols of judgment) should be fair, balanced, and impartial (v. 10; see 11:1). The first principle of discernment, that people's actions show what they are, is simple and obvious; it applies even to evaluating children (20:11). As God made both **eye** and **ear**, he better than anyone knows how to assess a person or situation, and his judgment will be final and decisive (v. 12). Sometimes these proverbs balance one another. God's people do need to be forbearing, but that does not mean being unwilling to discern good and evil in others.

20:8 winnows all evil. That is, he sorts and separates it out, and then removes it.

20:13–17 These proverbs all relate to wealth: laziness leads to **poverty** (v. 13); people will set a value on something as it suits them (v. 14); wisdom is better than wealth (v. 15); one should not trust a man who gets involved in foolish debts (v. 16); and the pleasures of dishonest gain are brief (v. 17).

20:14 "Bad, bad." The buyer says the item he desires is worth very little, in order to drive the price down. But after he buys it, the item belongs to him, so his words change: now he **boasts** of its value. The proverb says this happens, without commending such activity. Wisdom requires weighing the words of other people.

20:18–19 One should not make major decisions without seeking the **counsel** of others. On the other hand, one should be careful about who is brought into one's private deliberations. The example of making **war** particularly points to the need to find advisers who can keep a matter private.

20:20–21 The person who despises parental authority will not live long (v. 20; see Ex. 20:12; 21:17). **An inheritance gained hastily in the beginning**. Too much wealth given too soon will be used foolishly and **will not be blessed** later in life (cf. note on Prov. 13:11). In Israel, land was given to sons as an inheritance for the continued welfare of the family (cf. 13:22).

21 [i]An inheritance gained hastily in the beginning
will not be blessed in the end.
22 Do not say, [j]"I will repay evil";
[k]wait for the LORD, and he will deliver you.
23 [l]Unequal weights are an abomination to the LORD,
and [m]false scales are not good.
24 A man's [n]steps are from the LORD;
how then can man understand his way?
25 It is a snare to say rashly, "It is holy,"
and to reflect only [o]after making vows.
26 A wise king [p]winnows the wicked
and drives [q]the wheel over them.
27 [r]The spirit[1] of man is the lamp of the LORD,
[s]searching all [t]his innermost parts.
28 [u]Steadfast love and faithfulness preserve the king,
and by steadfast love his [v]throne is upheld.
29 The glory of young men is their strength,
but [w]the splendor of old men is their gray hair.
30 [x]Blows that wound cleanse away evil;
strokes make clean [t]the innermost parts.

21 1 The king's heart is a stream of water in the hand of the LORD;
he [y]turns it wherever he will.
2 [z]Every way of a man is right in his own eyes,
but the LORD [a]weighs the heart.
3 [b]To do righteousness and justice
is more acceptable to the LORD than sacrifice.
4 [c]Haughty eyes and a proud heart,
[d]the lamp[2] of the wicked, are sin.
5 The plans of [e]the diligent lead surely to abundance,
but everyone who is [f]hasty comes [g]only to poverty.
6 [h]The getting of treasures by a lying tongue
is a [i]fleeting [j]vapor and a [k]snare of death.[3]
7 The violence of the wicked will [l]sweep them away,
because they refuse to do what is just.
8 The way of the guilty [m]is crooked,
but the conduct of the pure is upright.
9 It is [n]better to live in a corner of the housetop
than in a house shared with a quarrelsome wife.

[1] Hebrew *breath* [2] Or *the plowing* [3] Some Hebrew manuscripts, Septuagint, Latin; most Hebrew manuscripts *vapor for those who seek death*

21 [i]See ch. 13:11
22 [j]ch. 24:29; [ch. 17:13; Matt. 5:39; Rom. 12:17, 19; 1 Thess. 5:15; 1 Pet. 3:9] [k]Ps. 27:14
23 [l]ver. 10 [m]See ch. 11:1
24 [n]See ch. 16:9
25 [o][Eccles. 5:4, 5]
26 [p][Matt. 3:12] [q]Isa. 28:27
27 [r][1 Cor. 2:11] [s][Zeph. 1:12] [t]ch. 18:8
28 [u]ch. 3:3 [v]See ch. 16:12
29 [w]ch. 16:31
30 [x][Isa. 53:5] [t][See ver. 27 above]

Chapter 21

1 [y][Ezra 6:22]
2 [z]ch. 16:2; [ch. 12:15] [a]ch. 24:12; [Luke 16:15; 1 Cor. 4:4]; See 1 Sam. 16:7
3 [b]See ch. 15:8; 1 Sam. 15:22
4 [c]See ch. 6:17; Ps. 101:5 [d]1 Kgs. 11:36
5 [e]ch. 10:4 [f][ch. 19:2] [g][ch. 11:24; 14:23; 22:16]
6 [h]ch. 20:21; See ch. 10:2 [i][ch. 13:11] [j]Job 13:25 [k][ch. 8:36]
7 [l][Jer. 30:23]
8 [m][ch. 2:15]
9 [n]ch. 25:24; [ver. 19; ch. 19:13; 27:15]

20:22–25 These four proverbs teach that God, not people (20:22), is the judge and avenger, and that he detests all willful distortions of human judgment, as represented by biased **scales** (v. 23). Verse 24 emphasizes the mystery of divine sovereignty (see Ps. 37:23; Jer. 10:23). A person makes his own decisions and is responsible for them, but paradoxically God directs the **steps** of each. This paradox demonstrates the limitations of human discernment; if a person does not fully comprehend the pattern of his own life, how can he be competent to judge others? Proverbs 20:25 warns against falling under divine judgment by making ill-conceived **vows** (see Eccles. 5:4–5).

20:26–27 For the health of his kingdom, a **wise king** must root out evildoers. **Drives the wheel over them** is not meant literally but is an agricultural image using the picture of a heavy cart being drawn over the grain to separate the wheat from the chaff. **winnows**. See note on v. 8. The king can only look on the exterior; God, by contrast, sees the **innermost parts** (cf. 1 Sam. 16:7). God's judgment is thus more fair and more effective.

20:28 This verse balances what is said in v. 26. Although a king must separate out and punish evildoers, the real security of his throne is in **steadfast love and faithfulness**. This may refer to the king's character, but more likely it refers to *God's* steadfast love and faithfulness, which was the foundation of the Davidic dynasty (1 Kings 3:6; 8:23; Ps. 89:28). This is the idea in view when steadfast love and faithfulness are said to **preserve** or watch over someone (Ps. 40:11; 61:7). This is a striking truth, given that one expects a king's security to be in his army.

20:29 Gray hair (cf. 16:31) is a concrete example of a general truth: many of the physical evidences of old age have a dignity and splendor of their own, often representing experience, maturity, wisdom, and holiness (see the discussion of "concreteness" in Introduction: Literary Features).

21:1–4 Like 20:22–25, this section has three proverbs on divine judgment followed by a fourth proverb that is related but does not explicitly mention the Lord. God is a much higher judge than the king, whom he controls (cf. 21:1; on the "king" in Proverbs, see also 16:10–15; 20:8, 28; 24:21–22; 29:14; the Solomonic origin of these passages shows that the king is specifically the Davidic king). People are not vindicated by their own consciences but by God's judgment (21:2), which cannot be averted simply with sacrifices and religious rites (v. 3; cf. 1 Sam. 15:22). The thing most likely to bring divine judgment on one's head is pride (Prov. 21:4).

21:1 The **stream of water** describes water flowing through a channel or an irrigation ditch, which a skillful farmer can turn to flow wherever he wishes.

11[o]ch. 19:25; See Ps. 1:1
12[p]Ps. 37:35, 36
13[q][James 2:13]; See Matt. 18:30-34
14[r][ch. 17:8; 18:16]
15[s][ch. 10:29]
16[t][Ps. 49:14]
18[u][ch. 11:8] [v]Isa. 43:3
19[w][ver. 9]
20[x][Ps. 112:3] [y][Job 20:15, 18]
21[z]ch. 15:9; Matt. 5:6; [ch. 3:3] [a]ch. 3:16; 1 Kgs. 3:11; Matt. 6:33; See ch. 4:22
22[b][ch. 24:5; Eccles. 7:19]; See 2 Sam. 5:6-9; Eccles. 9:14-18
23[c]See ch. 13:3 [d]ch. 22:5 [e]ch. 12:13
24[f]ch. 1:22; See Ps. 1:1
25[g][ch. 13:4]
26[h]See Ps. 37:26

10 The soul of the wicked desires evil;
his neighbor finds no mercy in his eyes.
11 When [o]a scoffer is punished, the simple becomes wise;
when a wise man is instructed, he gains knowledge.
12 The Righteous One [p]observes the house of the wicked;
he throws the wicked down to ruin.
13 [q]Whoever closes his ear to the cry of the poor
will himself call out and not be answered.
14 [r]A gift in secret averts anger,
and a concealed bribe,[1] strong wrath.
15 When justice is done, it is a joy to the righteous
[s]but terror to evildoers.
16 One who wanders from the way of good sense
[t]will rest in the assembly of the dead.
17 Whoever loves pleasure will be a poor man;
he who loves wine and oil will not be rich.
18 [u]The wicked is a [v]ransom for the righteous,
and the traitor for the upright.
19 It is [w]better to live in a desert land
than with a quarrelsome and fretful woman.
20 [x]Precious treasure and oil are in a wise man's dwelling,
but a foolish man [y]devours it.
21 Whoever [z]pursues righteousness and kindness
will find [a]life, righteousness, and honor.
22 [b]A wise man scales the city of the mighty
and brings down the stronghold in which they trust.
23 [c]Whoever keeps his mouth and his tongue
[d]keeps himself out of [e]trouble.
24 [f]"Scoffer" is the name of the arrogant, haughty man
who acts with arrogant pride.
25 The desire of [g]the sluggard kills him,
for his hands refuse to labor.
26 All day long he craves and craves,
but the righteous [h]gives and does not hold back.

[1] Hebrew *a bribe in the bosom*

21:9–19 Verses 9 and 19, on the **quarrelsome wife**, frame this unit on the rewards for the wise and the troubles of the wicked.

21:9 The wise husband will reflect on what aspects of his behavior have led his **wife** to become **quarrelsome** (cf. 19:13; 21:19; 25:24).

21:10–13 Just as the **wicked** offers no **mercy** to his **neighbor** (v. 10), so his own pleas for help will **not be answered** (v. 13) because God both knows and judges the wicked (v. 12). Though it may take an example of the wicked being **punished** for the **simple** to learn, those who are **wise** take instruction to heart (v. 11; cf. 19:25).

21:14 A **bribe** achieves its temporary end of avoiding punishment at the expense of true justice (cf. 17:8, 23). In the broader context of 21:10–18, it is clear that, though a bribe may appease the immediate situation, no one can evade justice forever.

21:15–18 When **justice** is practiced, it is a **joy** for those who have walked in its ways and a **terror** to those who have perverted them (v. 15). Verses 16–18 describe the reality of the terror for the wicked: they have turned from the path that leads to life (v. 16), loved mere **pleasure** and luxury to their own impoverishment (v. 17), and are themselves a **ransom**—an image that likely reflects the merciless manner in which they treated others (v. 18; cf. vv. 10, 13).

21:17 This proverb does not imply that **pleasure** or **wine** or **oil** are wrong in themselves, but when they are enjoyed apart from thanksgiving to God, or enjoyed more than following in God's paths, they will destroy a person's life.

21:19 The life of a desert outcast is better than the life of marriage to a **quarrelsome** woman (see note on v. 9).

21:20–22:1 This unit is held together by an *inclusio* (literary "bookends") consisting of three verses at 21:20–22 and three verses at 21:30–22:1. In 21:20, wealth is achieved by wisdom and lost by folly, but 21:21 speaks of pursuing **righteousness and kindness**; 22:1 teaches that one should choose a **good name** (emblematic of being a righteous and kind person) over wealth. Thus, 22:1 answers 21:20–21; wisdom can enable a person to achieve prosperity, but one should always pursue a good name through righteousness and kindness over riches. Verse 22 of ch. 21, which speaks of the importance of wisdom in a military action—besieging a city—is answered by 21:30–31, which assert that **no wisdom . . . can avail against the Lord** (21:30) and that however carefully one may plan a military action, victory is in the hands of **the Lord** (21:31). The whole unit teaches that success comes by wisdom, but that no amount of intelligence can stand against the Lord's sovereign will, and that in the end a good and kind heart is better than great wealth and power.

21:23–24 The man who **keeps his mouth and his tongue** (of v. 23) is the opposite of the **scoffer** (of v. 24).

21:25–26 Laziness leads to constant greed and craving, whereas the diligence of the righteous allows them to be generous (see note on 10:4).

27 [i]The sacrifice of the wicked is an abomination;
how much more [j]when he brings it with evil intent.
28 [k]A false witness will perish,
but the word of a man who hears will endure.
29 A wicked man puts on a bold face,
but the upright [l]gives thought to[1] his ways.
30 [m]No wisdom, no understanding, no counsel
can avail against the LORD.
31 [n]The horse is made ready for the day of battle,
but [o]the victory belongs to the LORD.

22

1 [p]A good name is to be chosen rather than great riches,
and favor is better than silver or gold.
2 [q]The rich and the poor meet together;
the LORD is [r]the maker of them all.
3 [s]The prudent sees danger and hides himself,
but the simple go on and suffer for it.
4 The reward for humility and fear of the LORD
is [t]riches and honor and life.[2]
5 [u]Thorns and snares are in the way of the crooked;
whoever [v]guards his soul will keep far from them.
6 [w]Train up a child in the way he should go;
even when he is old he will not depart from it.
7 [x]The rich rules over the poor,
and the borrower is the slave of the lender.
8 Whoever [y]sows injustice will reap calamity,
and [z]the rod of his fury will fail.
9 [a]Whoever has a bountiful[3] eye will be blessed,
for he [b]shares his bread with the poor.
10 [c]Drive out a scoffer, [d]and strife will go out,
and [e]quarreling and abuse will cease.
11 He who [f]loves purity of heart,
and whose [g]speech is gracious, [h]will have the king as his friend.
12 The eyes of the LORD keep watch over knowledge,
but he [i]overthrows the words of the traitor.
13 [j]The sluggard says, "There is a lion outside!
I shall be killed in the streets!"

[1] *Or establishes* [2] *Or The reward for humility is the fear of the LORD, riches and honor and life* [3] Hebrew *good*

27[i]Isa. 66:3; See ch. 15:8 [j][ch. 24:9]
28[k]ch. 19:5, 9
29[l]Ps. 119:5
30[m]Isa. 8:9, 10; 1 Cor. 3:19, 20; [ch. 19:21]
31[n][Ps. 20:7; 33:17; Isa. 31:1] [o]Jer. 3:23

Chapter 22

1[p][Eccles. 7:1]
2[q][ch. 29:13] [r]ch. 14:31; Job 31:15
3[s]ch. 27:12; [ch. 14:16]
4[t][ch. 21:20, 21]
5[u]ch. 15:19 [v]ch. 21:23; [1 John 5:18]
6[w]Eph. 6:4; 2 Tim. 3:15
7[x]James 2:6
8[y]Job 4:8; [Hos. 10:13] [z][Isa. 14:6; 30:31]
9[a][ch. 19:17; 2 Cor. 9:6] [b][ch. 19:17; Luke 14:13, 14]
10[c][Gen. 21:9, 10] [d][ch. 26:20] [e]ch. 26:20
11[f][ch. 16:13; Ps. 101:6] [g][Eccles. 10:12] [h][ch. 14:35]
12[i]ch. 21:12; [ch. 11:3]
13[j]ch. 26:13

21:27 The sacrifice of the wicked that God abhors is a kind of lie, a false pretense of piety (cf. 15:8–9).

21:28 The contrast of a **false witness** with one who **hears** indicates that a person who testifies falsely has chosen not to listen carefully to either the matter at hand or the requirements that a witness act justly. Both the person and the perjury of such a witness will ultimately **perish,** because it is the Lord who clearly sees and judges these things (vv. 2, 12) and causes the **word** of the faithful witness to **endure** (cf. 12:19; 19:5, 9).

21:29 A **bold face** is a futile attempt to cover up or compensate for a path that is **wicked,** but the **upright** does not need a cover-up because he is wise in attending honestly to **his ways.**

21:30–22:1 These form the final three verses of the *inclusio* described in the note on 21:20–22:1.

22:2–16 This text is bounded by a frame consisting of vv. 2–6 at the beginning and vv. 15–16 at the end. Verses 2–5 are a tightly bound unit dealing with aspects of wealth, poverty, and the way to ruin (see note on vv. 2–5), while v. 6 asserts that one should train one's children. At the end of this collection, v. 15 teaches that parents should discipline their children, and v. 16 discusses the rich, the poor, and the road to ruin.

22:2–5 These four verses are bound together by a parallel structure:

A: **the LORD** is the maker of **rich** and **poor** (v. 2)
B: the **prudent** are cautious but the **simple** are not (v. 3)
A′: **fear of the LORD** leads to **riches and honor** (v. 4)
B′: the **crooked** wander off into **thorns** but the wise man **guards his soul** (v. 5)

22:6 Train up a child. This proverb, founded on the covenant with Abraham (cf. Gen. 18:19), encourages parents to "train" (i.e., to "dedicate" or "initiate"; this is the sense of the word in Deut. 20:5; cf. Ezra 6:16) their children **in the way** (i.e., the right moral orientation) by pointing to the kinds of conduct that please or displease the Lord, and to the normal outcome of each kind of conduct (on the matter of consequences, see Introduction: Literary Features). The training will include love and instruction as well as "the rod of discipline" (Prov. 22:15).

22:7–9 The **rich . . . lender** who rules the **poor . . . borrower** (v. 7) is in contrast to the **bountiful** person who **shares** with the **poor** (v. 9). Between these two, v. 8 describes the powerful man who will come to ruin.

22:10–11 The **scoffer,** who will be driven out, is contrasted with the person of pure **heart** and gracious **speech,** who will be welcomed by the **king.**

22:12 God's **eyes . . . watch over knowledge** in the sense that he is the guarantor that the teachings of wisdom will be vindicated.

22:13 This proverb shows how far a **sluggard** will go to avoid work. But

14[k]See ch. 2:16 [l]ch. 23:27] [m]Eccles. 7:26
15[n]See ch. 13:24
16[o]ch. 28:22
17[p]ch. 5:1 [q]ch. 1:6; 24:23 [r][ch. 23:12]
20[s]ch. 8:6
21[t][Luke 1:3, 4]
22[u][Ex. 23:6; Zech. 7:10; Mal. 3:5] [v]See Job 5:4 [w]Job 31:21
23[x]ch. 23:11; 1 Sam. 25:39; Ps. 12:5; 35:10; 68:5; 140:12; Jer. 51:36
26[y]See Job 17:3
27[z][ch. 20:16; Ex. 22:26]
28[a]ch. 23:10; Deut. 19:14; 27:17; Job 24:2; Hos. 5:10
29[b]1 Kgs. 10:8; See Gen. 41:46

14 The mouth of [k]forbidden[1] women is [l]a deep pit;
[m]he with whom the LORD is angry will fall into it.
15 Folly is bound up in the heart of a child,
but [n]the rod of discipline drives it far from him.
16 Whoever oppresses the poor to increase his own wealth,
or gives to the rich, [o]will only come to poverty.

Words of the Wise

17 [p]Incline your ear, and hear [q]the words of the wise,
[r]and apply your heart to my knowledge,
18 for it will be pleasant if you keep them within you,
if all of them are ready on your lips.
19 That your trust may be in the LORD,
I have made them known to you today, even to you.
20 Have I not written for you [s]thirty sayings
of counsel and knowledge,
21 to [t]make you know what is right and true,
that you may give a true answer to those who sent you?

22 [u]Do not rob the poor, because he is poor,
or [v]crush the afflicted at [w]the gate,
23 for [x]the LORD will plead their cause
and rob of life those who rob them.
24 Make no friendship with a man given to anger,
nor go with a wrathful man,
25 lest you learn his ways
and entangle yourself in a snare.
26 Be not one of those who [y]give pledges,
who put up security for debts.
27 If you have nothing with which to pay,
why should [z]your bed be taken from under you?
28 Do not move the ancient [a]landmark
that your fathers have set.
29 Do you see a man skillful in his work?
He will [b]stand before kings;
he will not stand before obscure men.

[1] Hebrew *strange*

what will actually devour him is not the imaginary **lion** of his excuses but the reality of poverty.

22:14 The **forbidden** woman is a **deep pit**—something from which a man cannot escape by himself. She ruins him financially, and probably in other ways as well, relating to health, strength, relationships, and above all the man's relationship to God. She is thus a means God uses to punish the wicked.

22:15–16 These verses form the end of the frame described in the note on vv. 2–16. On the **rod of discipline**, see notes on v. 6 and 23:13–14.

22:15 Folly is bound up in the heart of a child. Children will learn to do wrong on their own; parents are needed to train them to act rightly.

22:17–24:22 *The Thirty Sayings of "the Wise."* This section easily divides into 30 discrete teachings, as indicated in 22:20, and these reflect an awareness of the Egyptian wisdom text, *The Instruction of Amenemope*, dated to about 1250 B.C. Clearly 22:17–24:22 did not slavishly copy *Amenemope*, but there are many affinities in content. The most significant difference between the two is the devotion to the Lord exhibited in Proverbs. The identity of "the wise" (22:17) is unknown; perhaps they are the scholars who assembled these proverbs (possibly under Solomon's sponsorship).

22:17–21 Like the prologue in 1:1–7, this text asserts that it can impart wisdom to the reader, give him practical skills for dealing with people, and encourage the fear of the Lord.

22:22–23 *Saying One.* One should never **rob the poor, because he is poor** (and therefore has little power to defend himself) or **crush the afflicted at the gate**. The gate was the place of legal transactions; i.e., one should not use the courts to deprive the poor of their property. Teachings that reflect concern for the well-being of the poor are common in the ancient Near East, but biblical wisdom is distinctive for its assertion that the Lord is the champion of the poor. The Lord cares particularly for the poor among his people, and will punish those who hurt them.

22:24–25 *Saying Two.* **lest you learn his ways**. A bad attitude toward life and people is contagious and deadly; therefore the wise will choose their friends carefully.

22:26–27 *Saying Three.* **why should your bed be taken from under you?** Cf. Deut. 24:10–13, which specifies that a poor man's cloak, the "bed" on which he slept, was not to be held in pledge overnight.

22:28 *Saying Four.* The **landmark** was the boundary stone (Deut. 19:14; 27:17), and to move it was to steal a man's real property as well as his ancestral heritage.

22:29 *Saying Five.* People of great skill, whatever their craft may be, win the respect even of **kings**. The implied exhortation is that one should never be careless about the quality of one's **work**.

23

1 When you sit down to eat with a ruler,
observe carefully what[1] is before you,
2 and put a knife to your throat
if you are given to appetite.
3 [c]Do not desire his delicacies,
for they are deceptive food.
4 [d]Do not toil to acquire wealth;
[e]be discerning enough to desist.
5 When your eyes light on it, it is gone,
[f]for suddenly it sprouts wings,
flying like an eagle toward heaven.
6 [g]Do not eat the bread of a man who is [h]stingy;[2]
[i]do not desire his delicacies,
7 for he is like one who is inwardly calculating.[3]
"Eat and drink!" he says to you,
but his [j]heart is not with you.
8 You will vomit up the morsels that you have eaten,
and waste your pleasant words.
9 Do not speak in the hearing of a fool,
for he will despise the good sense of your words.
10 [k]Do not move an ancient landmark
or enter the fields of the fatherless,
11 for their [l]Redeemer is strong;
he will [m]plead their cause against you.
12 Apply your heart to instruction
and your ear to words of knowledge.
13 Do not withhold [n]discipline from a child;
[o]if you strike him with a rod, he will not die.
14 If you strike him with the rod,
you will [p]save his soul from Sheol.
15 [q]My son, if your heart is wise,
my heart too will be glad.
16 My [r]inmost being[4] will exult
when your lips speak [s]what is right.
17 Let not your heart [t]envy sinners,
but continue in [u]the fear of the LORD all the day.

[1] *Or who* [2] Hebrew *whose eye is evil* [3] *Or for as he calculates in his soul, so is he* [4] Hebrew *My kidneys*

Chapter 23
3 [c]ver. 6
4 [d]ch. 15:27; 28:20; Matt. 6:19; 1 Tim. 6:9, 10; Heb. 13:5 [e][ch. 3:5, 7; 26:12; Isa. 5:21; Rom. 12:16]
5 [f]ch. 27:24
6 [g][Ps. 141:4] [h]ch. 28:22; Deut. 15:9 [i]ver. 3
7 [j][Ps. 12:2]
10 [k]See ch. 22:28
11 [l][Ex. 6:6]; See Job 19:25 [m]See ch. 22:23
13 [n]See ch. 13:24 [o][ch. 19:18]
14 [p][1 Cor. 5:5]
15 [q]ver. 24, 25; See ch. 29:3
16 [r]Ps. 7:9; 73:21 [s][ch. 8:6]
17 [t]See Ps. 37:1 [u][ch. 28:14]

23:1–3 *Saying Six.* The warning here is that the rich host may be using the luxuries he can provide to entrap his less-wealthy guests so that they feel obliged to do his bidding. His hospitality is **deceptive**.

23:4–5 *Saying Seven.* The workaholic is exhorted to **be discerning enough to desist** in his pursuit of wealth. **suddenly it sprouts wings**. Wealth is fleeting; there should come a point where a person decides he has enough, and he will devote some of his time and effort to valuable activities that bring no financial reward. See also note on 8:18–21.

23:6–8 *Saying Eight* is similar to the warning of vv. 1–3, but here the host is **a man who is stingy**. **You will vomit up the morsels that you have eaten** probably signifies eventual revulsion and regret on the part of the guest when he realizes what a fool he has been.

23:9 *Saying Nine.* The problem is not the fool's lack of intelligence but his obstinacy.

23:10–11 *Saying Ten* reaffirms the warning of 22:28, but the reference to orphans suggests that the victims may be too weak to defend themselves. In this case, the movement of the boundary stone is not something surreptitiously done but is an open seizure of another family's land, perhaps through the courts. **Their Redeemer** is the Lord himself (cf. Gen. 48:16; Ps. 19:14; 119:154), perhaps portrayed here as the near kin (Lev. 25:25–26).

23:12 *Saying Eleven.* The command suggests that one should doggedly pursue wisdom. It cannot be acquired without determination.

23:13–14 *Saying Twelve* clearly affirms the place of corporal punishment in child rearing. At the same time, the father's overriding desire is to teach the child, rather than to vent his anger. The connection of the two verses shows that **he will not die** and **you will save his soul from Sheol** are parallel ideas. On the use of the proper name "Sheol," see note on Ps. 6:5. Since Proverbs generally contrasts "life" and "death" as a right relationship with God vs. estrangement from him (which lasts beyond one's bodily death; see note on Prov. 7:26–27), Sheol here is the place where the ungodly go (cf. Ps. 49:14). The point is that the discipline has character training as its goal, not simply behavior; and this training equips the child to persevere in the way of life (cf. Prov. 22:15), which is the godly parents' chief aim (cf. 23:15–18, 22–25).

23:15–16 *Saying Thirteen* develops the teaching of vv. 13–14. The father speaking here is motivated to teach by love, and his joy is in seeing his son succeed in life.

23:17–18 *Saying Fourteen.* Instead of envying those who disregard God's way, one should make pleasing the Lord one's top priority (v. 17), because such a path embodies the true **hope** that there is a **future** for the godly (cf. 24:14, 20; Ps. 37:9–11, 34, 37–38). Although Proverbs does not refer explicitly to the nature of this "future" (cf. Prov. 10:2; 11:4; 14:32), its encour-

18 [v]ch. 24:14, 20 [w]Ps. 9:18
19 [x]ch. 6:6 [y][ch. 9:6]
20 [z][ver. 29, 30; Isa. 5:11, 22; Matt. 24:49; Luke 21:34; Rom. 13:13; Eph. 5:18] [a]ch. 28:7
21 [b][ch. 6:10, 11]
22 [c]See ch. 1:8 [d][ch. 30:17]
23 [e][ch. 4:5, 7; 18:15; Matt. 13:44]
24 [f]ver. 15; See ch. 29:3
25 [f][See ver. 24 above] [g]ch. 17:25
27 [h][ch. 22:14] [i]See ch. 2:16 [j]Ps. 55:23
28 [k]ch. 7:12; [Eccles. 7:26]
29 [l][ver. 20, 21] [m][ver. 35] [n]Gen. 49:12
30 [o]Isa. 5:11 [p]ch. 9:2, 5; Ps. 75:8; Isa. 5:22; 65:11
32 [q]Job 20:16
33 [r]See ch. 2:12
35 [s]Jer. 5:3; [ver. 29]

18 Surely [v]there is a future,
and your [w]hope will not be cut off.
19 Hear, my son, and [x]be wise,
and [y]direct your heart in the way.
20 Be not among [z]drunkards[1]
or among [a]gluttonous eaters of meat,
21 for the drunkard and the glutton will come to poverty,
and [b]slumber will clothe them with rags.

22 [c]Listen to your father who gave you life,
[d]and do not despise your mother when she is old.
23 [e]Buy truth, and do not sell it;
buy wisdom, instruction, and understanding.
24 [f]The father of the righteous will greatly rejoice;
he who fathers a wise son will be glad in him.
25 [f]Let your father and mother be glad;
let [g]her who bore you rejoice.

26 My son, give me your heart,
and let your eyes observe[2] my ways.
27 For a prostitute is [h]a deep pit;
[i]an adulteress[3] is a narrow [j]well.
28 [k]She lies in wait like a robber
and increases the traitors among mankind.

29 [l]Who has woe? Who has sorrow?
Who has strife? Who has complaining?
Who has [m]wounds without cause?
Who has [n]redness of eyes?
30 Those who [o]tarry long over wine;
those who go to try [p]mixed wine.
31 Do not look at wine when it is red,
when it sparkles in the cup
and goes down smoothly.
32 In the end it [q]bites like a serpent
and stings like an adder.
33 Your eyes will see strange things,
and your heart utter [r]perverse things.
34 You will be like one who lies down in the midst of the sea,
like one who lies on the top of a mast.[4]
35 "They [s]struck me," you will say,[5] "but I was not hurt;
they beat me, but I did not feel it.

[1] Hebrew *those who drink too much wine* [2] Or *delight in* [3] Hebrew *a foreign woman* [4] Or *of the rigging* [5] Hebrew lacks *you will say*

agement to walk **in the fear of the LORD** presents the benefits of wisdom as fixing and guarding not only the present path but also the eternal destiny to which the path leads.

23:19–21 *Saying Fifteen.* **Slumber** (v. 21) here describes the results of intoxication or gluttony. Eating and drinking to excess will impoverish people.

23:22–25 *Saying Sixteen.* Acquiring wisdom is a duty in that it is the best way one can fulfill the command to honor one's parents.

23:26–28 *Saying Seventeen.* The **prostitute** is compared to a **deep pit** or **well** (in that she entraps a young man and he cannot escape; cf. note on 22:14) and to a **robber** (in that she will cost him dearly). Prostitution is used as a striking example of those "personal sins" that, far from affecting the sinner alone, corrupt and bankrupt society and so ruin communities. The preface, **give me your heart**, guides parents in their nurturing task: their target must ever be the deepest core of the child's inner life. **Observe my ways** further guides parents. They must aim to embody the virtues they commend.

23:29–35 *Saying Eighteen.* This exposition on the folly of drunkenness opens with a poignant question and answer (vv. 29–30); commands those who would listen to heed a warning (vv. 31–32); and, in order to communicate the tragic consequences of overindulgence in **wine**, presents a painfully comedic image of the drunkard deluded about his self-harm (vv. 33–35). The final two lines are as clear a picture as any in Proverbs of "a fool who repeats his folly" (see 26:11). **Your eyes will see strange things** (23:33). A drunken person does not "see" clearly, i.e., he cannot perceive the cause-and-effect connections of events. **like one who lies on the top of a mast** (v. 34). This is a notoriously unstable place to stay: the comparison is either to the staggering gait of the drunk person, or to the nausea he will feel (as uncontrollable as seasickness).

When shall I awake?
I [t]must have another drink."

24

1 Be not [u]envious of evil men,
nor desire to be [v]with them,
2 for their hearts [w]devise violence,
and their lips [x]talk of trouble.

3 By [y]wisdom a house is built,
and by understanding it is established;
4 by knowledge the rooms are filled
with all [z]precious and pleasant riches.
5 [a]A wise man is full of strength,
and a man of knowledge enhances his might,
6 for by [b]wise guidance you can wage your war,
and in [c]abundance of counselors there is victory.
7 Wisdom is [d]too high for a fool;
in [e]the gate he does not open his mouth.

8 Whoever [f]plans to do evil
will be called a schemer.
9 [g]The devising[1] of folly is sin,
and [h]the scoffer is an abomination to mankind.

10 If you [i]faint in the day of adversity,
your strength is small.
11 [j]Rescue those who are being taken away to death;
hold back those who are stumbling to the slaughter.
12 If you say, "Behold, we did not know this,"
[k]does not he who [l]weighs the heart perceive it?
Does not he who [m]keeps watch over your soul know it,
and will he not repay man [n]according to his work?

13 My son, [o]eat honey, for it is good,
and [p]the drippings of the honeycomb are sweet to your taste.
14 Know that wisdom is such to your soul;
if you find it, there will be [q]a future,
and your hope will not be cut off.

[1] Or *scheming*

35 [t]Isa. 56:12

Chapter 24

1 [u]ver. 19; See Ps. 37:1 [v]See ch. 1:15
2 [w][Isa. 59:13] [x]Ps. 10:7
3 [y][ch. 14:1]
4 [z][ch. 23:23; Luke 16:11]
5 [a][ch. 21:22]
6 [b]ch. 20:18 [c]See ch. 11:14
7 [d][ch. 14:6] [e]See Job 5:4
8 [f]Rom. 1:30
9 [g][ch. 21:27] [h]See Ps. 1:1
10 [i][Heb. 12:3]
11 [j]Ps. 82:4; [Isa. 58:6, 7]
12 [k][Eccles. 5:8] [l]ch. 16:2; See 1 Sam. 16:7 [m][Ps. 91:11] [n]See Job 34:11
13 [o][Ps. 19:10; 119:103; Song 5:1; Isa. 7:15] [p]Song 4:11
14 [q]See ch. 23:18

24:1–2 *Saying Nineteen.* The young man's peers can be the greatest threat to his moral life (cf. 23:17).

24:3–4 *Saying Twenty.* The images of wisdom's benefits (a **house . . . built, established**, and **filled**) include material provision in addition to a blessed family life. However, the means by which they are received (**by wisdom, understanding**, and **knowledge**) are presented in Proverbs as stemming from the fear of the Lord. Thus the nature of and posture toward **riches** is always to be governed by the priority of pursuing wisdom.

24:5–6 *Saying Twenty-one.* The source of true strength is found in wisdom; by implication, strength and might apart from wisdom will be ineffective. **Wise guidance** obtained in consultation with an **abundance of counselors** is the key to **victory** whether in war or in any circumstance that requires might and power. Wisdom carefully acquired and applied is the means of success in all of life.

24:7 *Saying Twenty-two.* Other proverbs indicate that the **fool** can never stop talking (e.g., 10:19; 13:3). The point here is that he is at a loss when a situation calls for serious analysis.

24:8–9 *Saying Twenty-three.* Those who plan **to do evil** (v. 8) quickly get a reputation for it.

24:10 *Saying Twenty-four.* Although framed as an observation, this is actually an exhortation for the reader to show himself strong and courageous in times of **adversity**.

24:11–12 *Saying Twenty-five.* This further expands on the call of v. 10 to act with strength of character amid difficulty. Although the circumstances of those **taken away to death** and **stumbling to the slaughter** are not specified, the themes of Proverbs make it likely that the images refer to those suffering under the injustice of the wicked (see 1:11–13) and possibly to those walking a path that leads to death (cf. 7:25–27). Proverbs calls the righteous to integrity of character that protects justice, proclaims the benefits of wisdom, and warns against living as if such things are unknown or do not matter (24:12). Claiming ignorance of a widely known evil is no excuse for not rescuing the victims of slaughter, for God knows the true condition of the **heart**. The one who embraces wisdom can never be content with merely seeking the well-being of himself or of his family; he will also seek justice as widely as he can. That God will **repay man according to his work** (cf. Job 34:11; Ps. 62:12; Matt. 16:27; Rom. 2:6; 2 Tim. 4:14; Rev. 18:6) implies that a person's deeds reveal the true state of his heart, whether he walks on the path of life or of death.

24:13–14 *Saying Twenty-six.* Just as **honey** is **sweet** to the taste and good for the body, so **wisdom** is pleasant to the **soul** that feeds on it, fostering a secure **hope** (cf. v. 20; see notes on 23:17–18; Ps. 37:9).

15[r]Ps. 10:9, 10
16[s]See Ps. 37:24 [t]See Job 5:19 [u]ch. 14:32
17[v]Ps. 35:15, 19; [Mic. 7:8]; See ch. 17:5
19[w][Jer. 12:1]; See Ps. 37:1 [x]ver. 1
20[q][See ver. 14 above] [y]ch. 13:9; See Job 18:5
21[z]1 Pet. 2:17; [Rom. 13:7]
23[a]ch. 1:6; 22:17 [b]See ch. 18:5
24[c]See ch. 17:15 [d]ch. 11:26
27[e][Luke 14:28]
28[f][ch. 25:18]
29[g]See ch. 20:22

15 [r]Lie not in wait as a wicked man against the dwelling of the righteous;
do no violence to his home;
16 [s]for the righteous falls [t]seven times and rises again,
but [u]the wicked stumble in times of calamity.

17 [v]Do not rejoice when your enemy falls,
and let not your heart be glad when he stumbles,
18 lest the LORD see it and be displeased,
and turn away his anger from him.

19 [w]Fret not yourself because of evildoers,
and be not [x]envious of the wicked,
20 for the evil man has no [q]future;
[y]the lamp of the wicked will be put out.

21 My son, [z]fear the LORD and the king,
and do not join with those who do otherwise,
22 for disaster will arise suddenly from them,
and who knows the ruin that will come from them both?

More Sayings of the Wise

23 These also are sayings of [a]the wise.

[b]Partiality in judging is not good.
24 Whoever [c]says to the wicked, "You are in the right,"
[d]will be cursed by peoples, abhorred by nations,
25 but those who rebuke the wicked will have delight,
and a good blessing will come upon them.
26 Whoever gives an honest answer
kisses the lips.

27 [e]Prepare your work outside;
get everything ready for yourself in the field,
and after that build your house.

28 [f]Be not a witness against your neighbor without cause,
and do not deceive with your lips.
29 Do not say, [g]"I will do to him as he has done to me;
I will pay the man back for what he has done."

24:15–16 *Saying Twenty-seven.* This warns against joining with the **wicked** in injustice because it forms a person's character in a way that will not be beneficial in **calamity**. The **righteous** is able to rise repeatedly because both his person and his path are sustained by the Lord (cf. 2:6–8; 15:29).

24:17–18 *Saying Twenty-eight.* If vv. 15–16 are aimed at the wicked, who commit crimes against the righteous, this saying is directed against the righteous, who might be tempted to gloat over the downfall of the wicked (cf. 17:5b). **Do not rejoice** reflects the heart of God, who has no pleasure in the death of the wicked (see note on Ezek. 33:11).

24:19–20 *Saying Twenty-nine*. This saying, building on vv. 13–18, once again reassures the reader that the **wicked** have **no future**. In short, the righteous must beware of two attitudes: gloating celebration when the wicked fall (v. 17), and a despairing fear that they never will fall (v. 19). The words of v. 19 are very close to those of Ps. 37:1; the wisdom psalm is in truth a hymnic reflection on this topic.

24:21–22 *Saying Thirty.* Both God and the (Davidic) **king** appear in Proverbs as agents of wrath (cf. 14:35; 16:10–15; 19:12; 20:2). The young man should respect authority, both human and divine.

24:23–34 *Further Sayings of "the Wise."* (See note on 22:17–24:22.) These sayings are grouped in a parallel fashion, as follows:

A: justice in court (vv. 23–26)
B: economy lesson for the home (v. 27)
A′: justice in court (vv. 28–29)
B′: economy lesson for the home (vv. 30–34)

24:23–25 Partiality in judging is not good. Courts must render honest verdicts, convicting the guilty and acquitting the innocent. People may be prejudiced for or against a person because he or she is rich and famous or of a certain race, but partiality of any kind is to be rejected.

24:26 The Hebrew phrase translated **kisses the lips** is found only here in the OT. It is either an act of homage (e.g., those who have not kissed Baal, 1 Kings 19:18) or an act of affection (e.g., Esau kissed Jacob upon their meeting, Gen. 33:4). Either sense fits the verse well in that an **honest answer** treats the other person involved with both respect and affection (note the appeals to honest speech in the surrounding text, Prov. 24:23–25, 28–29). (The sexually oriented kiss, though known in Israel—cf. Prov. 7:13; Song 8:1—is not relevant here.)

24:27 Proverbs encourages sensible preparation before building a **house**, so that one may attend well to the life lived in it.

24:28–29 Commitment to giving an honest answer (v. 26) includes refraining from paying back a **neighbor**, through false testimony or deception, for past acts of injustice (cf. Lev. 19:15–18; Matt. 5:43–48).

30 [h]I passed by the field of a sluggard,
by the vineyard of a man [i]lacking sense,
31 and behold, it was all overgrown with thorns;
the ground was covered with nettles,
and its stone [j]wall was broken down.
32 Then I saw and [k]considered it;
I looked and received instruction.
33 [l]A little sleep, a little slumber,
a little folding of the hands to rest,
34 and poverty will come upon you like a robber,
and want like an armed man.

More Proverbs of Solomon

25 These also are [m]proverbs of Solomon which the men of Hezekiah king of Judah copied.

2 It is the glory of God to [n]conceal things,
but the glory of kings is to [o]search things out.
3 As the heavens for height, and the earth for depth,
so the heart of kings is [p]unsearchable.
4 Take away [q]the dross from the silver,
and [r]the smith has material for a vessel;
5 take away [s]the wicked from the presence of the king,
and his [t]throne will be established in righteousness.
6 Do not put yourself forward in the king's presence
or stand in the place of the great,
7 for [u]it is better to be told, "Come up here,"
than to be put lower in the presence of a noble.

What your eyes have seen
8 [w]do not hastily bring into court,
for[1] what will you do in the end,
when your neighbor puts you to shame?
9 [x]Argue your case with your neighbor himself,
and do not reveal another's secret,
10 lest he who hears you bring shame upon you,
and your ill repute have no end.

11 [y]A word fitly spoken
is like apples of gold in a setting of silver.

30 [h][Job 5:3] [i]See ch. 6:32
31 [j]Isa. 5:5
32 [k][ch. 22:17]
33 [l]For ver. 33, 34, see ch. 6:10, 11

Chapter 25

1 [m]See ch. 1:1
2 [n][Deut. 29:29; Rom. 11:33] [o]Job 29:16
3 [p][Ps. 145:3]
4 [q][Ezek. 22:18; 2 Tim. 2:20, 21] [r][Mal. 3:2, 3]
5 [s][ch. 20:8] [t]See ch. 16:12
7 [u]See Luke 14:8-11
8 [w]Matt. 5:25; Luke 12:58; [ch. 17:14]
9 [x]Matt. 18:15
11 [y]ch. 15:23; [Isa. 50:4]

[1] Hebrew *or else*

24:30–34 These verses illustrate how proverbs are supposed to function: upon walking by a **field** and **vineyard** that has fallen into ruin through laziness (vv. 30–31), the observer takes it to heart and rightly recognizes (v. 32) that the wise instruction he has heard about the **sluggard** applies to the situation at hand (vv. 33–34 are identical to 6:10–11). Both the observer and the reader are encouraged to believe that sustained and steadfast labor is a part of the path of wisdom.

25:1–29:27 *Hezekiah's Collection of Solomonic Proverbs.* The present form of the book of Proverbs came into existence, at earliest, in the reign of Hezekiah (reigned 715–686 B.C.; see Introduction: Author and Date). Hezekiah is credited with reviving Judah's religious traditions (2 Kings 18:3–7). A new, expanded edition of Solomonic proverbs was apparently part of that revival.

25:2–3 The **glory of kings** (v. 2) is set here as subordinate to and derived from the **glory of God** because the king's searching is a function of his role under the overall governance of God, who keeps some things hidden (see Deut. 29:29). Proverbs 25:3 further describes the king from the perspective of his subjects and asserts by implication (reference to the **heavens** and the **earth**) that though his **heart** is hidden to those under him, it remains subject to the Creator (cf. 21:1–2). The references to Solomon and Hezekiah (25:1) indicate that, as usual in Proverbs, the kingship assumed is Davidic (14:28, 35; 16:10–15; 19:12; 20:2, 8, 26, 28; 21:1; 22:11, 29; 25:2–7b; 29:4, 14). **to search things out**. According to Proverbs, the ideal king will both govern through the use of his wisdom and investigate and understand the world and its people.

25:4–5 take away the wicked from the presence of the king. The close advisers of a ruler must be chosen with careful attention to their moral character (cf. 13:20). Following the picture of governance by the king under God in 25:2–3, here is wise counsel for those living and serving in that realm: every individual is called to search his or her own heart and seek to practice and pursue **righteousness** for the sake of the kingdom and the good of its people. Though this may particularly apply to those serving in the court of the king, the breadth of the imagery in vv. 2–3 and the nature of the instruction that follows (vv. 6–15) indicate that any attempt to act in accord with this passage, no matter how small it may seem, honors God and king (see 24:21).

25:6–7b These verses encourage proper humility; honor is better bestowed than wrongly presumed in the presence of the king (cf. Luke 14:7–11).

25:7c–10 The last line of v. 7 is understood by some ancient versions

12[z][Gen. 24:22] [a]ch. 15:31; 20:12
13[b]ch. 13:17
14[c]Jude 12 [d]ch. 20:6
15[e]ch. 15:1; 16:14; [Eccles. 10:4]
16[f][Judg. 14:8; 1 Sam. 14:25] [g][ver. 27]
18[h][ch. 24:28] [i]ch. 12:18; See Ps. 57:4
20[j][Rom. 12:15]
21[k]Cited Rom. 12:20; [2 Kgs. 6:22; 2 Chr. 28:15]; See Ex. 23:4, 5
22[l]Ps. 140:10
24[m]ch. 21:9
25[n][Ps. 42:2] [o]ch. 15:30
26[p][Ezek. 32:2; 34:18, 19]

12 Like [z]a gold ring or an ornament of gold
is a wise reprover to [a]a listening ear.
13 Like the cold of snow in the time of harvest
is [b]a faithful messenger to those who send him;
he refreshes the soul of his masters.
14 Like [c]clouds and wind without rain
is a man who [d]boasts of a gift he does not give.

15 With [e]patience a ruler may be persuaded,
and a soft tongue will break a bone.
16 If you have [f]found honey, eat [g]only enough for you,
lest you have your fill of it and vomit it.
17 Let your foot be seldom in your neighbor's house,
lest he have his fill of you and hate you.
18 A man who [h]bears false witness against his neighbor
is like a war club, or [i]a sword, or a sharp arrow.
19 Trusting in a treacherous man in time of trouble
is like a bad tooth or a foot that slips.
20 Whoever [j]sings songs to a heavy heart
is like one who takes off a garment on a cold day,
and like vinegar on soda.
21 [k]If your enemy is hungry, give him bread to eat,
and if he is thirsty, give him water to drink,
22 for you will heap [l]burning coals on his head,
and the LORD will reward you.
23 The north wind brings forth rain,
and a backbiting tongue, angry looks.
24 [m]It is better to live in a corner of the housetop
than in a house shared with a quarrelsome wife.
25 Like cold water to [n]a thirsty soul,
so is [o]good news from a far country.
26 Like [p]a muddied spring or a polluted fountain
is a righteous man who gives way before the wicked.

(Septuagint, Vulgate) and most modern versions as opening vv. 8–10. This section encourages working out conflict with a **neighbor** in the context of personal relationship (v. 9a) rather than imprudently rushing either to present a case in **court** (v. 8) or to perpetuate a grievance by reporting it to others (vv. 9b–10). Similar principles are operative in the instruction that Jesus gives in Matt. 18:15–20 (see notes there; and note on Matt. 5:25–26).

25:11–12 The **apples** refer to a decorative motif in jewelry, similar to the more familiar "pomegranate" pattern (Ex. 39:24–25; 1 Kings 7:18). The image represents godly speech (**a word fitly spoken**, i.e., suited to its occasion). **A wise reprover to a listening ear** (cf. Prov. 9:8b–9) is like **gold** jewelry; that is, stunningly beautiful and valuable (possibly because of its rarity).

25:13 The **time of harvest** for the various crops runs from June through September, and the heat can be withering. At such a time, the **cold of snow**—however it was brought—would refresh the workers (a literal snowfall is probably not in view, as that could be a catastrophe; cf. 26:1).

25:14 In an agrarian context, skies that promise but never produce **rain** would be a familiar image to illustrate a person who brags that he will give a **gift**, most likely to incur some sort of favor, but who has no intention to fulfill his promise.

25:15 a soft tongue will break a bone. Diplomacy with superiors means using tact even while trying to persuade.

25:16–17 Verse 16 is at first glance a warning against gluttony (and perhaps, by extension, an encouragement to take care in enjoying all pleasant things). But in context it is a metaphor leading into v. 17: one's presence, even though it may be pleasant, may become too much of a good thing.

25:18–20 In this collection, three types of men—the liar, the untrustworthy, and the insensitive—are each described with a pair of appropriate metaphors.

25:20 Putting **vinegar** (which is acidic) on **soda** (which is alkaline) does no good, destroying the distinctive properties of both.

25:21–22 Although interpreters differ about the meaning of the metaphor of heaping **burning coals on** the enemy's **head**, it is likely an image for leading him to repentance or shame, suggesting that he will feel inward burning pangs of guilt for his wrongdoing. In any case, the message is clearly to repay evil with good (see Rom. 12:17–21). The image of "burning coals" does not imply something that harms the enemy, because it further explains the **bread** and **drink** in Prov. 25:21, which do him good, and also because Proverbs forbids taking personal vengeance (see 20:22). Finally, **the LORD will reward you** (25:22) implies a good result from these "burning coals," which is most consistent with leading the person to repentance.

25:23 The **north wind** is not the usual source of **rain** in Palestine, but when it is, it brings unexpected and damaging rain. So a **backbiting tongue** brings sudden anger and damage.

25:24 quarrelsome wife. See note on 21:9.

25:25–26 These two proverbs are joined by **water** metaphors relating to the proximity and expectation of the source. **Good news** that comes from a **far country** is unexpected and revitalizing (v. 25). However, a **righteous man** who yields to injustice or to evil pollutes his way (v. 26)—a way that people close to him had likely come to trust as a "fountain of life" (cf. 10:11; 13:14; 14:27).

27 It is [q]not good to eat much honey,
nor is it glorious to [r]seek one's own glory.[1]
28 A man [s]without self-control
is like [t]a city broken into and left without walls.

26

1 Like snow in summer or [u]rain in harvest,
so [v]honor is [w]not fitting for a fool.
2 Like [x]a sparrow in its flitting, like a swallow in its flying,
[y]a curse that is causeless does not alight.
3 [z]A whip for the horse, a bridle for the donkey,
and [a]a rod for the back of fools.
4 [b]Answer not a fool according to his folly,
lest you be like him yourself.
5 [c]Answer a fool according to his folly,
lest he be [d]wise in his own eyes.
6 Whoever sends a message by the hand of a fool
cuts off his own feet and [e]drinks violence.
7 Like a lame man's legs, which hang useless,
is a proverb in the mouth of fools.
8 Like one who binds the stone in the sling
is [f]one who gives honor to a fool.
9 Like [g]a thorn that goes up into the hand of a drunkard
is a proverb in the mouth of fools.
10 Like an archer who wounds everyone
is one who hires a passing fool or drunkard.[2]
11 Like [h]a dog that returns to his vomit
is [i]a fool who repeats his folly.
12 Do you see a man who is [j]wise in his own eyes?
[k]There is more hope for a fool than for him.
13 [l]The sluggard says, "There is a lion in the road!
There is a lion in the streets!"
14 As a door turns on its hinges,
so does a sluggard on his bed.
15 [m]The sluggard buries his hand in the dish;
it wears him out to bring it back to his mouth.
16 The sluggard is [j]wiser in his own eyes
[n]than seven men who can answer sensibly.

27[q][ver. 16] [r][ch. 27:2]
28[s][ch. 16:32] [t][2 Chr. 32:5; 36:19; Neh. 1:3]

Chapter 26

1[u][1 Sam. 12:17] [v][ver. 8] [w]ch. 17:7; 19:10
2[x]ch. 27:8; Ps. 84:3 [y][Num. 23:8; Deut. 23:5; 2 Sam. 16:12]
3[z][Ps. 32:9] [a]See ch. 19:29
4[b][2 Sam. 16:11; 2 Kgs. 18:36; Luke 23:9]
5[c]See Matt. 16:1-4; 21:24-27 [d]ch. 28:11; [Rom. 12:16]
6[e][ch. 13:2; Job 15:16]
8[f][ver. 1]
9[g][ch. 23:35]
11[h]Cited 2 Pet. 2:22 [i][Ex. 8:15]
12[j]ch. 28:11; [Rom. 12:16] [k]ch. 29:20
13[l]ch. 22:13
15[m]ch. 19:24
16[j][See ver. 12 above] [n][ver. 25; ch. 6:16]; See Job 5:19

[1] The meaning of the Hebrew line is uncertain [2] Or *hires a fool or passersby*

25:27 The solution adopted by the ESV for the difficult second line has fairly wide support. The point is that to **seek one's own glory** can make people sick (see v. 16).

25:28–26:12 All of these proverbs focus on the **fool**, who is mentioned explicitly in every verse except 25:28 and 26:2.

25:28 Self-control relates to the passions (such as anger or love), the appetites (for food, sex, etc.), and the will (as illustrated by impulsive decisions). The lack of self-control is a mark of a fool. He is like **a city . . . left without walls**, that is, with no means of defense against enemies.

26:2 A curse that is causeless is a wish for harm to come to a righteous person, or a word of condemnation wrongly spoken against him. But it **does not alight** because God (who is sovereign over all) gives no heed to it but rather protects the righteous person.

26:4–5 These verses are especially striking in that they appear to contradict each other. To **answer a fool according to his folly** (v. 5) is to keep replying to his remarks in order to show up their folly. Verse 4 gives the general policy (**answer not a fool**), because you will end up **like him yourself** as he responds to your reply with further folly: the interchange will have no end. Verse 5 gives the exception (answer a fool), because sometimes he or others may think to their own harm that he cannot be answered (cf. v. 12).

26:8 One who fastens into a **sling** a **stone** that is meant to be flung out of the sling shows that he has neither the knowledge nor the skill to use it, and is in danger of hurting himself. Likewise, one who bestows **honor** on a **fool** shows a failure to understand the purpose of giving such recognition and stands to suffer harm when the fool proves unworthy of the honor and thus damages the reputation of the one who wrongly honored him.

26:9 A proverb in the mouth of fools is **like a thorn** in the **hand** of the **drunkard** because when a fool uses a proverb, he is insensitive to the fact that it applies principally to himself.

26:11 The first line supplies a vivid image for 2 Pet. 2:22.

26:12 After 11 verses describing the terrible state of the **fool**, this verse becomes a forceful punch line: even more hopeless than the situation of the fool is the situation of the stubbornly unteachable person, who is **wise in his own eyes** (see v. 5). The reference to a better **hope** for the fool indicates just how dire the situation is, since the fool is described as one who already considers his way to be "right in his own eyes" (12:15). Yet there are degrees of folly, and some of the more thoughtless type of fools can sometimes be reclaimed.

26:13–16 These proverbs focus on the **sluggard**. Verses 13–15 present him as comically ludicrous in his laziness, and v. 16 gives this portrait a twist by observing that the sluggard considers himself the paradigm of wisdom. His fear of the **lion** (v. 13) uses a remote possibility of danger as an excuse for not working.

18[o][Isa. 50:11]
20[p]ch. 16:28 [q]ch. 22:10
21[r]See ch. 15:18
22[s]ch. 18:8 [p][See ver. 20 above]
23[t][Matt. 23:27; Luke 11:39] [u]See ch. 25:4
25[v]See Ps. 28:3 [w][ver. 16]
27[x][ch. 28:10]; See Ps. 7:15

Chapter 27

1[y]Luke 12:19, 20; James 4:13, 14
2[z]2 Cor. 10:12, 18; [ch. 25:27; 2 Cor. 12:11]
3[a][ch. 12:16; 17:12]
4[b]ch. 6:34
5[c][ch. 28:23]
6[d]Ps. 141:5
7[e][ch. 25:16]

17 Whoever meddles in a quarrel not his own
is like one who takes a passing dog by the ears.
18 Like a madman who throws [o]firebrands, arrows, and death
19 is the man who deceives his neighbor
and says, "I am only joking!"
20 For lack of wood the fire goes out,
and where there is no [p]whisperer, [q]quarreling ceases.
21 As charcoal to hot embers and wood to fire,
so is [r]a quarrelsome man for kindling strife.
22 [s]The words of [p]a whisperer are like delicious morsels;
they go down into the inner parts of the body.
23 [t]Like the [u]glaze[1] covering an earthen vessel
are fervent lips with an evil heart.
24 Whoever hates disguises himself with his lips
and harbors deceit in his heart;
25 [v]when he speaks graciously, believe him not,
for there are [w]seven abominations in his heart;
26 though his hatred be covered with deception,
his wickedness will be exposed in the assembly.
27 [x]Whoever digs a pit will fall into it,
and a stone will come back on him who starts it rolling.
28 A lying tongue hates its victims,
and a flattering mouth works ruin.

27

1 Do not boast about tomorrow,
[y]for you do not know what a day may bring.
2 Let [z]another praise you, and not your own mouth;
a stranger, and not your own lips.
3 A stone is heavy, and sand is weighty,
but [a]a fool's provocation is heavier than both.
4 Wrath is cruel, anger is overwhelming,
but who can stand before [b]jealousy?
5 [c]Better is open rebuke
than hidden love.
6 Faithful are [d]the wounds of a friend;
profuse are the kisses of an enemy.
7 One who is full loathes [e]honey,
but to one who is hungry everything bitter is sweet.

[1] By revocalization; Hebrew *silver of dross*

26:17–22 These proverbs describe a person who uses his **words** carelessly. Examples include interfering in other people's arguments (v. 17), deceiving people as a joke without concern for the consequences (vv. 18–19), and gossiping, especially where gossip provokes conflict (vv. 20–21). Verse 22 directly warns the reader that gossip is seductive, and the proverb serves as a bridge to the next section (vv. 23–28), on the liar.

26:17 Someone who stands behind a **passing dog** and grabs it **by the ears** is temporarily safe from harm, but he is actually trapped because when he lets go, the angry dog will attack him.

26:23–28 These verses concern the liar. He artfully conceals his lies, and one should take care not to be fooled by him (vv. 23–25). But eventually his lies will be exposed and he will be entrapped in his own web of deceit (vv. 26–28). The Hebrew of v. 23a presents a challenge: the Masoretic text, as in the ESV footnote ("silver of dross"), suggests that the dross from refining silver was actually used to make a glaze for ceramics; the ESV text is based on a related Ugaritic word for the **glaze** on a pot. In either case, just as cheap pottery can be made to look beautiful, so **fervent** speech can disguise an **evil heart**.

26:27 Whoever digs a pit probably refers to the hostile enemy described in vv. 24–26. He is preparing a hidden trap for someone, but he is the one who will be harmed.

27:1–2 These proverbs both concern boasting (**boast** in v. 1 and **praise** in v. 2 are different forms of the same Hb. root, *h-l-l*). In v. 1, a person should not boast of his prospects; in v. 2, he should not boast of himself.

27:3–4 Both proverbs have the same pattern (two items mentioned for comparison's sake, followed by a single item that is worse than both of them). In v. 3, the two compared items are physical (**stone** and **sand**), and in v. 4 they are psychological (**wrath** and **anger**). Together, the proverbs suggest that a fool is more unbearable than any kind of physical or psychological malaise. The **provocation** a fool gives (v. 3) could be from a variety of behaviors associated with this character type (laziness, verbosity, a tendency to promote discord, etc.). **Jealousy** (v. 4), unlike ordinary anger, will not yield to reason.

27:5–6 Open rebuke affords a person the chance to reflect on the course of the path he or she is walking, where **hidden love** perceives but fails to communicate the possibility of such a need (v. 5). The **wounds of a friend** are meant to cut to the heart for the good of the person, whereas the **kisses of an enemy** are devised to appease the heart in order to hide the hurt that has or is to come (v. 6). Cf. 28:23.

27:7–10 These four proverbs each teach an element of wisdom that can stand on its own, but they have additional application when taken together. Verse 7 deals with **honey**, a pleasant treat, and v. 9 deals with **oil** and

8 Like [f]a bird that strays from its nest
is a man who strays from his home.
9 [g]Oil and perfume make the heart glad,
and the sweetness of a friend comes from his earnest counsel.[1]
10 Do not forsake your friend and [h]your father's friend,
and do not go to your brother's house in the day of your calamity.
[i]Better is a neighbor who is near
than a brother who is far away.
11 [j]Be wise, [k]my son, and [l]make my heart glad,
that I may [m]answer him who reproaches me.
12 [n]The prudent sees danger and hides himself,
but [o]the simple go on and suffer for it.
13 [p]Take a man's garment when he has put up security for a stranger,
and hold it in pledge when he puts up security for an adulteress.[2]
14 Whoever blesses his neighbor with a loud voice,
rising early in the morning,
will be counted as cursing.
15 [q]A continual dripping on a rainy day
and a quarrelsome wife are alike;
16 to restrain her is to restrain the wind
or to grasp[3] oil in one's right hand.
17 Iron sharpens iron,
and one man sharpens another.[4]
18 [r]Whoever tends a fig tree will eat its fruit,
and he who [s]guards his master will be honored.
19 As in water face reflects face,
so the heart of man reflects the man.
20 [t]Sheol and Abaddon are [u]never satisfied,
and [v]never satisfied are the eyes of man.

[1] *Or and so does the sweetness of a friend that comes from his earnest counsel* [2] Hebrew *a foreign woman;* a slight emendation yields (compare Vulgate; see also 20:16) *foreigners* [3] Hebrew *to meet with* [4] Hebrew *sharpens the face of another*

8 [f]ch. 26:2
9 [g][Ps. 23:5]
10 [h]See 1 Kgs. 12:6-8; 2 Chr. 10:6-8 [i]See ch. 17:17
11 [j]ch. 6:6 [k]ch. 10:1; 23:15, 24 [l]See ch. 29:3 [m]Ps. 119:42; [Ps. 127:5]
12 [n]ch. 22:3 [o]See ch. 1:4
13 [p]See ch. 20:16
15 [q]ch. 19:13
18 [r]Song 8:12; 1 Cor. 3:8; 9:7; 2 Tim. 2:6 [s][Matt. 25:21]
20 [t]ch. 15:11; See Job 26:6 [u]ch. 30:15, 16; Hab. 2:5; [ch. 1:12] [v]Eccles. 1:8; 4:8

perfume, luxuries that here represent a banquet (an ancient host provided perfumed oils for his guests at a banquet). Also, v. 7 says that something **bitter** is **sweet** to a **hungry** man, while v. 9 speaks of the **sweetness** of **earnest counsel**. Together, vv. 7 and 9 suggest that it is good to have friends for the occasional party, but it is better yet to have a friend willing and able to give good advice. Verse 8 speaks of someone who wanders far from **his home** (his immediate family) and leaves it unprotected, while v. 10 concerns someone in need whose **brother** (his immediate family) is **far away**. Together, they teach that there are benefits in remaining close to family, but a person should not hesitate to turn to a true friend when in need.

27:11–28:1 This section opens (27:11) with a paternal appeal similar to those in chs. 1–9 and then has an *inclusio* (literary "bookends") made up of 27:12 (the simple plunge heedlessly into danger) and 28:1 (the wicked flee when there is no danger). Between these two are various pieces of advice for the young man on prudence and integrity. The point of the whole section (27:12–28:1) is this: the one who has both prudence and integrity will neither stumble into trouble nor live in fear of retribution.

27:12–14 It takes wisdom to distinguish between rightful courage and foolish walking into **danger**. One should not cosign a loan for a **stranger** or an immoral woman (a repeat of 20:16). **loud voice . . . early in the morning**. Friendliness can seem obnoxious to a neighbor. Even in being sociable, one should be tactful.

27:15–16 In light of v. 12, these proverbs encourage a man to be careful, for a **quarrelsome** character would likely be evident before marriage. A husband should also examine the way *his* behavior affects his **wife**, since marriage is a mutually formative relationship. The fact that the husband tries but fails to **restrain** his wife pictures the consequences of a marriage working against itself, rather than each person working with and for the other (cf. the contrasting description of 31:11–12, 23, 28, 31).

27:17 Another is, as the ESV footnote reads, "the face of another." Since the word "face" (Hb. *panim*) can refer to the edge of an axe or sword (Eccles. 10:10; possibly Ezek. 21:16), the image is that interaction with a good man (both as he encourages and corrects) hones one's skill in handling challenges. **Man** translates Hebrew *'ish*, a word that specifically refers to a male human being. But such concrete examples in Proverbs invite broader application (see Introduction: Literary Features; cf. also notes on Prov. 31:10–31; 31:26; 31:28–29; 31:30; 31:31).

27:18 Faithful servants will eventually eat the **fruit** that comes through their labors.

27:19–22 Just as **water** reflects a person's actual appearance, so the **heart** reflects a person's true nature (v. 19). Looking at a reflection in water is an experience common to all people, but who is able to see into the heart? Proverbs indicates that while a person may conceal or reveal his heart through speech and actions, it lies open and transparent only before God (see 21:2). The comparisons of 27:20–22 draw attention to the state of the person's heart: dissatisfaction and greed that always want more (v. 20), the fostering of either humility or pride in response to receiving **praise** (v. 21), and folly that is so deeply rooted in a **fool** that it is unaffected even if he is ground to a pulp (v. 22). This focus on the heart as known and weighed by God is also evoked by the images of v. 20a (**Sheol** and **Abaddon**) and v. 21a (**crucible** and **furnace**), particularly since, in the one place where each of these phrases is found elsewhere in Proverbs (15:11a and 17:3a, respectively), it is followed by a second line that refers to the heart as either open before (15:11b) or tested by (17:3b) the Lord.

21 [w]The crucible is for silver, and the furnace is for gold,
and a man is tested by his praise.
22 [x]Crush a fool in a mortar with a pestle
along with crushed grain,
yet his folly will not depart from him.
23 [y]Know well the condition of your flocks,
and [y]give attention to your herds,
24 for [z]riches do not last forever;
and does a crown endure to all generations?
25 [a]When the grass is gone and the new growth appears
and the vegetation of the mountains is gathered,
26 [b]the lambs will provide your clothing,
and the goats the price of a field.
27 [b]There will be enough goats' milk for your food,
for the food of your household
and maintenance for your girls.

28

1 [c]The wicked flee when no one pursues,
but [d]the righteous are bold as a lion.
2 When a land transgresses, [e]it has many rulers,
but with a man of understanding and knowledge,
its stability will long continue.
3 [f]A poor man who oppresses the poor
is a beating rain that leaves no food.
4 Those who forsake the law [g]praise the wicked,
but those who keep the law [h]strive against them.
5 Evil men [i]do not understand justice,
but those who seek the LORD [j]understand it completely.
6 [k]Better is a poor man who [l]walks in his integrity
than a rich man who is [l]crooked in his ways.
7 The one who keeps the law is a son with understanding,
but [m]a companion of gluttons shames his father.
8 Whoever multiplies his wealth [n]by interest and profit[1]
[o]gathers it for him who is [p]generous to the poor.
9 If one turns away his ear from hearing the law,
even his [q]prayer is an abomination.

[1] That is, profit that comes from charging interest to the poor

21[w]ch. 17:3
22[x][ch. 23:35; Isa. 1:5; Jer. 5:3]
23[y][John 10:3, 14; Acts 20:28; 1 Pet. 5:2, 4]
24[z]ch. 23:5
25[a]Ps. 37:2; 90:5, 6
26[b][1 Tim. 6:8]
27[b][See ver. 26 above]

Chapter 28

1[c]Lev. 26:17; Ps. 53:5 [d]Lev. 26:8; 1 Sam. 17:32
2[e][1 Kgs. 15:27]; See 1 Kgs. 16:8-28; 2 Kgs. 15:8-15
3[f][Matt. 18:28]
4[g]Ps. 10:3; Rom. 1:32 [h][1 Kgs. 18:18, 21; Neh. 13:11, 15; Matt. 3:7; 14:4; Eph. 5:11]
5[i]Ps. 92:6; [John 12:39, 40] [j]Ps. 119:100; [John 7:17; 1 Cor. 2:15; James 1:5; 1 John 2:20, 27]
6[k]ch. 19:1 [l]ver. 18
7[m][ch. 23:20; 29:3]
8[n]Ex. 22:25; Lev. 25:36 [o]See Job 27:17 [p]ch. 14:31
9[q][Ps. 109:7]; See ch. 15:8

27:23–27 Though a person may think his wealth will **last forever** (v. 24), it will not. Therefore even those who have **flocks** and **herds** (v. 23) should keep careful account of them in order to be wise stewards.

28:2–12 For the most part, the meanings of these proverbs, taken individually, are self-evident. Taken as a group, however, they indicate that righteous individuals are an essential component of a just society. That is, one will not have good social order where many individuals, and especially those with power, are unjust. The structure of the text suggests its unity. Verse 2, which says that a society thrives when people have understanding but that it has many rulers when it is evil, brackets the entire section when connected with v. 12, which says that people celebrate the success of the righteous but hide when the wicked come to power. So these verses form an *inclusio*. Also, two catchwords link vv. 2 and 12. In v. 2, rulers are "many" (Hb. *rab*), but in v. 12, glory is "great" (Hb. *rab*); v. 2 speaks of a wise "man" (Hb. *'adam*), but v. 12 speaks of "people" (Hb. *'adam*) hiding. Between these two verses there are many other parallels among the proverbs. Verses 3 and 8 both concern how one treats the "poor," whether with oppression (v. 3) or with kindness (v. 8). Verses 4, 7, and 9 teach that one's attitude toward the "law" (Hb. *torah*) is the fundamental determiner of whether one will be good or evil. Verses 5 and 10 speak about knowing right from wrong (v. 5) and about leading others in the right or wrong path (v. 10). Also, the word evil (Hb. *ra'*) links v. 5 to v. 10. Finally, v. 6 says that a poor man can be morally superior to a "rich man," and v. 11 says that a poor man can see through the pretension of a "rich man." Taken together, this section shows that, for the society as a whole to be well off, each member must practice integrity, and that is especially true for its rulers. The three proverbs on the law (vv. 4, 7, 9) indicate that a healthy fear of the Lord, as reflected in people's respect for the Torah, is the only thing that will enable people to maintain integrity.

28:2 The **many rulers** may refer to the increasing number of officials in the bureaucracy, or to rapid changes of ruling dynasty (as in the northern kingdom of Israel), or to the breakup of central government with local lords dominating. Any of these can follow from the lack of moral integrity in the people, and especially in those charged with leading the **land**.

28:5 In Proverbs, **evil men** are people committed to opposing God's will. They **do not understand justice** and what it requires in a government or a society. **Those who seek the LORD**, in contrast, should have the most accurate grasp of justice.

28:9 The **law** is *torah* (Hb.), God's covenantal instruction, especially the books of Moses. On **prayer** as specifically prayer offered in public worship, see note on 15:8–9.

10 Whoever misleads the upright into an evil way
[r]will fall into his own pit,
but the blameless [s]will have a goodly inheritance.
11 A rich man is wise in his [t]own eyes,
but a poor man who has understanding [u]will find him out.
12 When [v]the righteous triumph, there is great glory,
but when [w]the wicked rise, people hide themselves.
13 Whoever [x]conceals his transgressions will not prosper,
but he who [y]confesses and forsakes them will obtain mercy.
14 Blessed is the one who [z]fears the LORD always,
but whoever [a]hardens his heart will fall into calamity.
15 Like [b]a roaring lion or [c]a charging bear
is [d]a wicked ruler over a poor people.
16 A ruler who [e]lacks understanding is a cruel oppressor,
but he who hates unjust gain will prolong his days.
17 If one is burdened with [f]the blood of another,
he will be a fugitive until death;[1]
let no one help him.
18 [g]Whoever [h]walks in integrity will be delivered,
but he who is crooked in his ways will suddenly fall.
19 [i]Whoever works his land will have plenty of bread,
but he who follows worthless pursuits will have plenty of poverty.
20 A faithful man will abound with blessings,
but whoever hastens to be rich [j]will not go unpunished.
21 To show [k]partiality is not good,
but for [l]a piece of bread a man will do wrong.
22 A [m]stingy man[2] [n]hastens after wealth
and does not know that [o]poverty will come upon him.
23 Whoever [p]rebukes a man will afterward find more favor
than [q]he who flatters with his tongue.
24 Whoever robs his father or his mother
and says, "That is no transgression,"
is [r]a companion to a man who destroys.
25 A greedy man [s]stirs up strife,
but the one who trusts in the LORD will [t]be enriched.
26 Whoever [u]trusts in his own mind is a fool,
but he who walks in wisdom will be delivered.
27 Whoever [v]gives to the poor will not want,
but he who [w]hides his eyes will get many a curse.
28 When [x]the wicked rise, [y]people hide themselves,
but when they perish, the righteous increase.

10 [r]See Ps. 7:15 [s][Matt. 6:33]
11 [t]ch. 26:5, 16 [u]Job 13:9
12 [v]ch. 11:10 [w]ver. 28; [ch. 29:2; Eccles. 10:5, 6]
13 [x][Job 31:33; Ps. 32:3]; See 1 John 1:8-10 [y]Ps. 32:5; 1 John 1:9
14 [z]ch. 23:17; Isa. 66:2; Phil. 2:12 [a]See Ps. 95:8
15 [b]ch. 19:12; 1 Pet. 5:8 [c][2 Kgs. 2:24] [d][Ex. 1:14, 16, 22; Matt. 2:16]
16 [e]See ch. 6:32
17 [f][Gen. 9:6]
18 [g][ch. 3:23; 10:9] [h]ver. 6
19 [i]ch. 12:11
20 [j]ch. 16:5
21 [k]See ch. 18:5 [l]Ezek. 13:19
22 [m]See ch. 23:6 [n][ver. 20] [o]ch. 22:16
23 [p]ch. 27:5, 6 [q]ch. 29:5
24 [r][ch. 18:9]
25 [s]See ch. 15:18 [t]ch. 11:25; 13:4
26 [u][1 Cor. 3:18]
27 [v][ch. 11:24]; See ch. 19:17 [w][ch. 29:7]
28 [x]See ver. 12 [y]Job 24:4

[1] Hebrew *until the pit* [2] Hebrew *A man whose eye is evil*

28:13–14 Although the words **the LORD** (v. 14) are not stated explicitly in Hebrew, they are appropriate to the sense of the verse, in view of the piety described in v. 13. To fear the Lord (see note on 1:7) involves confessing and forsaking one's sins, rather than concealing them and hardening one's heart. Such a person receives mercy and is therefore truly happy.

28:15–16 A **wicked ruler** is pictured as a powerful, destructive wild animal who feeds off of **poor people** rather than protecting and providing for them (v. 15). Such a ruler is a **cruel oppressor** who lacks the wisdom obligated by his position to hate **unjust gain**.

28:17–18 These proverbs concern being delivered from trouble: v. 17 teaches that no one should assist a murderer who is a **fugitive** fleeing from justice, and v. 18 teaches that people of **integrity** will get the help they need. For v. 17, cf. Gen. 9:6.

28:19–27 These proverbs all concern the desire to secure prosperity and favor for oneself. They speak of having **plenty of bread** (v. 19), of having **blessings** (v. 20), of doing **wrong** for a **piece of bread** (v. 21), of **wealth** and **poverty** (v. 22), of finding **favor** (v. 23), of someone who **robs** father and mother (v. 24), of the **greedy man** in contrast to the one who will **be enriched** (v. 25), of those who **will be delivered** (v. 26), and of those who do **not want** because they give **to the poor** (v. 27). Along the way, these verses condemn get-rich-quick schemes (vv. 19, 20; cf. 13:11), hastening after wealth (28:20, 22), accepting bribes (v. 21), seeking to get ahead by flattery (v. 23), wrongfully taking a parent's money (v. 24), causing turmoil through greed (v. 25), and lacking charity (v. 27). The best way to prosperity and security is through hard work (v. 19), integrity and honesty (vv. 20, 21, 23, 24), trusting in God and in the principles that wisdom teaches (vv. 25, 26), and paradoxically, through generosity (v. 27). The greed that produces strife in v. 25 has a particular application to the robbery of parents in v. 24: when a person tries to snatch up all of his parents' estate for himself, it inevitably produces strife in the family.

28:28–29:2 Like 21:20–22:1 and 28:2–12, this short passage has an *inclusio*

Chapter 29
1[z][1 Sam. 2:25]; See ch. 1:24-27 [a][Isa. 30:14; Jer. 19:11] [b]ch. 6:15
2[c]ch. 11:10; 28:12, 28; [Esth. 8:15] [d][Esth. 3:15]
3[e][ch. 10:1; 15:20; 27:11; 28:7] [f][ch. 5:9, 10; 6:26] [g]Luke 15:13, 30
4[h][ver. 14; 2 Chr. 9:8]
5[i]ch. 28:23 [j][Ps. 9:15]
6[k][Eccles. 9:12] [l][Ex. 15:1, 21; Ps. 35:27]
7[m]Job 29:16; Ps. 41:1 [n][ch. 28:27]
8[o][ch. 11:11]
9[p][Eccles. 4:6]
10[q][Gen. 4:5, 8; 1 John 3:12]
13[r][ch. 22:2] [s]Ps. 13:3; See Job 25:3
14[t][Ps. 72:4] [u][ver. 4]; See ch. 16:12
15[v]See ver. 17 [w]ch. 10:1; 17:25
16[x]Ps. 37:34, 36; 58:10; 91:8; 92:11
17[y]See ch. 13:24

29

1 [z]He who is often reproved, yet stiffens his neck,
will suddenly be [a]broken [b]beyond healing.
2 When [c]the righteous increase, the people rejoice,
but when [d]the wicked rule, the people groan.
3 He who [e]loves wisdom makes his father glad,
but [f]a companion of prostitutes [g]squanders his wealth.
4 By justice a king [h]builds up the land,
but he who exacts gifts[1] tears it down.
5 [i]A man who flatters his neighbor
spreads [j]a net for his feet.
6 An evil man is [k]ensnared in his transgression,
but a righteous man [l]sings and rejoices.
7 A righteous man [m]knows the rights of the poor;
a wicked man does not [n]understand such knowledge.
8 [o]Scoffers set a city aflame,
but the wise turn away wrath.
9 If a wise man has an argument with a fool,
the fool only rages and laughs, and there is [p]no quiet.
10 Bloodthirsty men [q]hate one who is blameless
and seek the life of the upright.[2]
11 A fool gives full vent to his spirit,
but a wise man quietly holds it back.
12 If a ruler listens to falsehood,
all his officials will be wicked.
13 The poor man and the oppressor [r]meet together;
the LORD [s]gives light to the eyes of both.
14 If a king [t]faithfully judges the poor,
his throne will [u]be established forever.
15 [v]The rod and reproof give wisdom,
but a child left to himself [w]brings shame to his mother.
16 When the wicked increase, transgression increases,
but [x]the righteous will look upon their downfall.
17 [y]Discipline your son, and he will give you rest;
he will give delight to your heart.

[1] *Or who taxes heavily* [2] *Or but the upright seek his soul*

(literary "bookends") on how a society thrives or suffers when, respectively, success comes to the righteous or to the wicked (28:28 and 29:2). Also, 28:28 ends with **the righteous increase** and 29:2 begins with **when the righteous increase**, indicating that the latter verse complements the former. Only one proverb (29:1) is between these two; it obviously means that people who obstinately refuse to turn from evil and folly will be ruined. Why is it placed here? It may serve to reassure the reader that eventually the wicked will fall. Or, the man who is **often reproved, yet stiffens his neck** may stand for Israelite society as a whole; the whole population can be warned to repent and can suffer for not doing so.

29:3–4 Verse 3 describes how a son may squander his inheritance, and v. 4 describes how a king can squander the kingdom that he inherited. The ruler **who exacts gifts** fosters a system of bribes and corruption, and so destroys his nation. (The alternative meaning in the ESV footnote, "who taxes heavily," has a similar sense; in either case the ruler demands large amounts of money, putting his own interests ahead of the good of the nation, with ruinous results.)

29:5–6 The metaphor of the **net** and of ensnaring someone binds these two proverbs together. Each proverb is clear by itself; together they suggest that the man who seeks to ensnare others eventually ensnares himself (cf. 1:17–19).

29:7 A wicked man does not understand such knowledge because he is not truly concerned for the poor, but for himself, and any professions of concern for the poor probably have ulterior motives (see 28:5).

29:8–11 These four proverbs describe the rage, havoc, and violence that accompany evil and folly. Such men **set a city aflame** (v. 8), are abusive and rude in a dispute (v. 9), **hate** people of integrity (v. 10), and give **full vent** to every passion they feel (v. 11). The ESV footnote for v. 10b, "but the upright seek his soul," means that the upright are concerned to vindicate the hated blameless man.

29:12–14 A king's administration will fall apart if he gives heed to corrupt counselors (v. 12), but it will thrive if he is just to even the weakest in his kingdom (v. 14). The Davidic king should be the protector of his people and the paradigm of integrity. Between these two verses, v. 13 asserts that all men are equal before God and thus implies that God will judge even the king without any favoritism. To give **light to the eyes** (v. 13) means to give life (cf. 22:2).

29:15–18 Verses 15 and 17 both insist that parents should teach their children, and vv. 16 and 18 both describe a society in upheaval. The chaos of a child out of control is comparable to the chaos of a people who have abandoned integrity and revelation. Verse 18 is notable in that it speaks of both **prophetic vision** and the **law**. The teachings of wisdom are not opposed to either the prophets or the Torah. As Proverbs endorses the fear of the Lord (1:7), so also it endorses divine revelation in the Scriptures.

18 Where [z]there is no prophetic vision the people [a]cast off restraint,[1]
but blessed is he who [b]keeps the law.
19 By mere words a servant is not disciplined,
for though he understands, he will not respond.
20 Do you see a man who is hasty in his words?
[c]There is more hope for a fool than for him.
21 Whoever pampers his servant from childhood
will in the end find him his heir.[2]
22 [d]A man of wrath stirs up strife,
and one given to anger causes much transgression.
23 [e]One's pride will bring him low,
[f]but he who is lowly in spirit will obtain honor.
24 The partner of a thief [g]hates his own life;
[h]he hears the curse, but discloses nothing.
25 [i]The fear of man lays a snare,
but whoever trusts in the LORD is safe.
26 Many [j]seek the face of a ruler,
but it is from the LORD that a man [k]gets justice.
27 [l]An unjust man is an abomination to the righteous,
but one whose way is straight is an abomination to the wicked.

The Words of Agur

30 The words of Agur son of Jakeh. The oracle.[3]

The man declares, I am weary, O God;
I am weary, O God, and worn out.[4]
2 Surely I am too [m]stupid to be a man.
I have not the understanding of a man.
3 I have not learned wisdom,
nor have I knowledge of [n]the Holy One.
4 Who has [o]ascended to heaven and come down?
Who has [p]gathered the wind in his fists?

18[z]1 Sam. 3:1; [2 Chr. 15:3; Ps. 74:9; Amos 8:11, 12] [a]Ex. 32:25 [b]Luke 11:28; John 13:17; James 1:25
20[c]ch. 26:12
22[d]See ch. 15:18
23[e]ch. 17:19; 2 Sam. 22:28; Matt. 23:12; James 4:6; See ch. 11:2 [f]ch. 15:33; 18:12
24[g]See ch. 8:36 [h]See Lev. 5:1
25[i]Luke 12:4; [Gen. 12:12, 13; 20:2, 11; 26:7; John 12:42, 43]
26[j]ch. 19:6 [k]Isa. 49:4; 1 Cor. 4:4, 5
27[l][2 Cor. 6:14]

Chapter 30

2[m]See Ps. 49:10
3[n]ch. 9:10
4[o]John 3:13 [p][Isa. 40:12]; See Job 38:4-11; Ps. 104:3-6

[1] Or *the people are discouraged* [2] The meaning of the Hebrew word rendered *his heir* is uncertain [3] Or *Jakeh, the man of Massa* [4] Revocalization; Hebrew *The man declares to Ithiel, to Ithiel and Ucal*

29:19–22 Verses 19 and 21 both advise maintaining discipline with those under authority, not through **mere words**, but also through negative and positive incentives of various kinds.

29:23 Paradoxically, **pride** brings humiliation while humility brings **honor**.

29:24 Companions of criminals cannot avoid getting mixed up in their crimes. The **curse** such a person hears is the call to testify in a criminal proceeding (see Lev. 5:1). But he dare not testify against his criminal friends, and so he brings the force of the curse on his own head.

29:25–26 One who acts primarily out of a **fear of man** shows that he does not trust **the LORD** to preserve and protect him (v. 25). Similarly, one who seeks only the **face** of the king for **justice** (v. 26) manifests a lack of belief that it is ultimately God who works to bring it about (cf. 24:21a, where the order reflects the priority).

29:27 The Hezekiah collection ends with a simple antithesis: righteousness and evil are detestable to one another. No one can serve both, and no one can be the companion of both righteous and evil people. Those who are faithful to God should not be surprised when they are hated by the **wicked** without any reason (cf. John 15:18–20, 25; 1 John 3:12–13).

30:1–33 *The Sayings of Agur.* The identity of Agur, son of Jakeh, is unknown (the name occurs nowhere else in the Bible). One traditional Jewish interpretation argued that Agur is a nickname for Solomon, though the argument is based on fanciful interpretations of the names Agur and Jakeh. Some suggest he was a court counselor to Solomon, which is possible, but evidence for this is lacking. Another interpretation claims that the word translated as **oracle** (Hb. *massa'*) actually should be rendered as the proper name "Massa," giving for v. 1, **Agur son of Jakeh**, "the man of Massa" (see ESV footnote). If so, then it might refer to a tribe in northwest Arabia (the name appears in some Akkadian sources), and Agur could have been a Gentile. One motivation for this interpretation is the view that an "oracle" is unsuited to Proverbs, since it is common in the Prophets; but the word **declares** (v. 1) is also common in the Prophets (see also note on 29:15–18). When all factors are considered, the ESV gives the best rendering of the Hebrew.

30:1 The ESV translation, **I am weary, O God; I am weary, O God, and worn out**, is achieved by means of a widely accepted pair of minor emendations to a difficult Hebrew text, slightly revising the division of two words and adjusting two vowels (on the assumption that a small copyist's error led to the current Hb. text). The ESV footnote renders the Masoretic text, which would suggest that Agur is addressing his words to Ithiel and Ucal (his sons?).

30:2–6 I am too stupid to be a man. Wisdom texts often begin with a kind of advertisement in which the teacher proclaims that he is wise and therefore that his words ought to be heeded. Here, Agur does just the opposite: he confesses that he is not learned in wisdom (vv. 2–3). Agur then asks a series of rhetorical questions meant to indicate the limitations on human perception and achievement (v. 4). Like the questions of God in Job 38–39, these questions point to things that only God can do; silent reverence is the only proper human response.

30:4 The rhetorical question, **What is his name, and what is his son's name?** is remarkable since the obvious answer is that God is the only one who moves between heaven and earth and who controls the wind and the waters. What, then, does the text mean by asking about his son? The Christian

Who has [q]wrapped up the waters in a garment?
Who has established all [r]the ends of the earth?
[s]What is his name, and what is his son's name?
Surely you know!

5 [t]Every word of God proves true;
he is [u]a shield to those who take refuge in him.
6 [v]Do not add to his words,
lest he rebuke you and you be found a liar.

7 Two things I ask of you;
deny them not to me [w]before I die:
8 Remove far from me falsehood and lying;
give me neither poverty nor riches;
feed me with the food that is [x]needful for me,
9 lest I be [y]full and [z]deny you
and say, [a]"Who is the LORD?"
or lest I be poor and steal
[b]and profane the name of my God.

10 [c]Do not slander a servant to his master,
[d]lest he curse you, and you be held guilty.

11 There are those[1] who [e]curse their fathers
and do not bless their mothers.
12 There are those who are [f]clean in their own eyes
but are not washed of their filth.
13 There are those—how [g]lofty are their eyes,
how high their eyelids lift!
14 There are those whose teeth are [h]swords,
whose [i]fangs are knives,
to [j]devour the poor from off the earth,
the needy from among mankind.

15 The leech has two daughters:
Give and Give.[2]
[k]Three things are never satisfied;
[k]four never say, "Enough":

4 [q]Job 26:8 [r]Ps. 22:27 [s][Rev. 19:12]
5 [t]Ps. 12:6; 18:30 [u]See Ps. 3:3
6 [v]Deut. 4:2; 12:32; [Rev. 22:18]
7 [w]Gen. 45:28
8 [x]Job 23:12; Matt. 6:11; Luke 11:3
9 [y]Deut. 8:12; 31:20; 32:15; Neh. 9:25; [ver. 22] [z]Josh. 24:27 [a]Ex. 5:2 [b][Job 21:14, 15]; See Ex. 20:7
10 [c][Ps. 15:3; 101:5] [d]Eccles. 7:21
11 [e]ch. 20:20; [ver. 17]; See Ex. 21:17
12 [f]ch. 16:2; [Luke 18:11; Rev. 3:17]
13 [g]See Ps. 101:5
14 [h]See Ps. 57:4 [i]Job 29:17 [j]See Ps. 14:4
15 [k]ver. 18, 21, 29; [ch. 6:16]

[1] Hebrew *There is a generation;* also verses 12, 13, 14 [2] Or *"Give, give," they cry*

reader naturally thinks of the Son of God, but the purpose of the words here is simply to say that no mere human being (whether father or son) has done these things, and that God is "the Holy One" (v. 3) whose ways are high and exalted, infinitely greater than "the understanding of man" (v. 2).

30:5–6 Every word of God proves true (cf. 2 Sam. 22:31; Ps. 18:30). "Proves true" can also mean "refined" (cf. Ps. 12:6) or "well tried" (Ps. 119:140); the implication is that God's words are a proven foundation for one's life. The proverb's emphasis on every "word" (Hb. *'imrah*) underscores the truthfulness, trustworthiness, and reliability of the Bible, not just in its overall message but also of every detail. This verse supplies support for the doctrine of the "plenary" (full, complete) inspiration of Scripture, extending even to "every word." Thus Prov. 30:6 warns against adding to God's **words**. The whole of vv. 2–6 thus teaches that human wisdom is limited, that the wisest people recognize their ignorance, that truth resides in the word of God, and that no one should think he is able to enhance the wisdom that God has given.

30:7–9 This is the only prayer in Proverbs. Agur asks for **two things**. It seems most likely that the first request is **remove far from me falsehood and lying** and that the second is **give me neither poverty nor riches; feed me with the food that is needful for me** (cf. the petition for "daily bread," Matt. 6:11). The first request probably implies both that he does not want to become a liar and that he does not want to have people lie to him and deceive him. The second request reflects the caution that Proverbs instills in the wise about trusting in wealth.

30:10 This proverb warns against someone speaking lies (**slander**) specifically against a **servant** to the servant's **master**, which could damage the servant's position and livelihood. But in such a case the slanderer is warned against committing such an injustice because the servant is likely to utter a **curse** against the slanderer (that is, he would express a wish that judgment would fall on the slanderer). The fact that the slanderer would then be found **guilty** indicates that God hears and judges rightly.

30:11–14 Here are four types of loathsome people: those who show no respect to parents (v. 11; cf. 20:20), those who are atrociously immoral but who refuse to admit it (30:12), those who are arrogant (v. 13), and those who plunder the **poor** (v. 14). All four proverbs begin with the same Hebrew word (*dor*, usually "generation"), which is translated as, **There are those**.

30:15–16 This text contains two sayings involving numbers (v. 15a and vv. 15b–16). Both concern insatiable things, and together they give the number sequence 2, 3, 4. The first (v. 15a) indicates that the **leech** has **two daughters** named **Give**. The saying probably alludes to the two suckers on a leech's body, and it may have been a common byword used to describe a selfish or demanding person. A frustrated mother may have said this when her children were clamoring for something. It is easy to see in what sense the four things of vv. 15b–16 are insatiable, but it is harder to guess at the point

16 [l]Sheol, [m]the barren womb,
the land never satisfied with water,
and the fire that never says, "Enough."
17 The eye that [n]mocks a father
and [o]scorns to obey a mother
will [p]be picked out by [q]the ravens of the valley
and eaten by the vultures.
18 [k]Three things are [r]too wonderful for me;
[k] four I do not understand:
19 the way of an eagle in the sky,
the way of a serpent on a rock,
the way of a ship on the high seas,
and the way of a man with a virgin.
20 This is the way of an adulteress:
she eats and wipes her mouth
and says, "I have done no wrong."
21 Under [k]three things [s]the earth trembles;
under [k]four it cannot bear up:
22 [t]a slave when he becomes king,
and a fool when he is [u]filled with food;
23 [v]an unloved woman when she [w]gets a husband,
and a maidservant when she displaces her mistress.
24 [k]Four things on earth are small,
but they are exceedingly wise:
25 [x]the ants are a people not strong,
yet they provide their food in the summer;
26 [y]the rock badgers are a people not mighty,
yet they make their homes in the cliffs;
27 the locusts have no [z]king,
yet all of them march in [a]rank;
28 the lizard you can take in your hands,
yet it is in kings' palaces.
29 [b]Three things are stately in their tread;
[b] four are stately in their stride:
30 the lion, which is mightiest among beasts
and [c]does not turn back before any;

16[l]See ch. 27:20 [m][Gen. 30:1]
17[n][ver. 11; Gen. 9:22] [o][ch. 23:22] [p][Num. 16:14] [q][Jer. 16:4]
18[k][See ver. 15 above] [r]See Job 42:3
21[k][See ver. 15 above] [s]Joel 2:10; Amos 8:8
22[t]ch. 19:10 [u][ver. 9]
23[v]Deut. 21:15 [w][Isa. 54:1; 62:4]
24[k][See ver. 15 above]
25[x]ch. 6:6-8
26[y]Lev. 11:5; Ps. 104:18
27[z][ch. 6:7] [a][Joel 2:7, 8, 25]
29[b]ver. 15, 18, 21; [ch. 6:16]
30[c][Job 39:22]

of the list. It may be that this was simply a byword used of any situation or task that has no end, and that it is here simply to say that life is full of such situations and tasks; in that case, Eccles. 1:3–7 is comparable.

30:17 This is actually a curse rather than a simple proverb. Agur obviously regards respect for parents as supremely important (see v. 11).

30:18–20 The numerical saying of vv. 18–19 is a riddle. What do these four things have in common, and why is the teacher amazed by them? Verse 20 is a clue to the meaning of the riddle; it is linked to v. 19 by the catchword **way** (Hb. *derek*). The **adulteress . . . eats and wipes her mouth**, and says she has **done no wrong**. Taking the words literally, what she says is true; eating is no sin. But eating here is symbolic of her life of adultery—wiping the mouth after eating suggests cleansing herself after illicit sex. She is of the opinion that after she has washed up, nothing remains of the sexual encounter and there are no moral ramifications to her behavior. In v. 19, the **eagle**, the **serpent**, and the **ship** leave no trail behind them (the serpent is on a large rock and not on sand, and the ship is a slow-moving sailboat). The relationship of a **man** and a **virgin**, if it is chaste, likewise leaves no observable change in either of them. An alternative interpretation of what the items in v. 19 have in common is that they all make apparently effortless, almost instinctive, progress toward a goal. These things happen, but the speaker finds them amazing and does not **understand** quite how they happen.

30:21–23 The four persons described here are insufferable because they have been granted things they have no capacity to enjoy or handle wisely. A modern example would be a person who is promoted above his level of competence.

30:24–28 These creatures are weak and **small** but give important lessons. The lesson of the **ants** is in making provision for the future; the lesson of the **rock badgers** (the hyrax, an unclean herbivore, Lev. 11:5, that lives in crevices in the **cliffs**) is in taking care to have a place of refuge; the lesson of the **locusts** is cooperation; and the lesson of the **lizard** (unknown species, perhaps a kind of gecko) is that even the humblest creature can attain to the highest circles of society.

30:29–31 The **king** is the main point here; the animals serve as comparisons. The lesson is that a king's majesty is not in himself (in contrast to the animals) but in his subjects (see 14:28). **Strutting rooster** (30:31) is the best guess on the meaning of the obscure Hebrew (see ESV footnote).

31[d][Job 40:16]
32[e]Mic. 7:16; See Job 21:5
Chapter 31
2[f]Isa. 49:15 [g][1 Sam. 1:27]
3[h][ch. 5:9] [i][ch. 7:26; Deut. 17:17; 1 Kgs. 11:1; Neh. 13:26]
4[j]Eccles. 10:17; [1 Kgs. 16:9; 20:16] [k][Hos. 4:11] [l]ch. 20:1
5[m][Isa. 5:22, 23]
6[n]Job 29:13 [o]Job 3:20
7[p][Ps. 104:15]
8[q]Job 29:12, 15, 16; [Isa. 1:17]
9[r]Lev. 19:15; Deut. 1:16 [s]Jer. 22:16; [Isa. 1:17] [t]ver. 20; Ps. 40:17; 86:1
10[u]ch. 12:4; Ruth 3:11; [ch. 18:22; 19:14] [v]Job 28:18

31 the [d]strutting rooster,[1] the he-goat,
and a king whose army is with him.[2]
32 If you have been foolish, exalting yourself,
or if you have been devising evil,
[e]put your hand on your mouth.
33 For pressing milk produces curds,
pressing the nose produces blood,
and pressing anger produces strife.

The Words of King Lemuel

31 The words of King Lemuel. An oracle that his mother taught him:

2 What are you doing, my son?[3] What are you doing, [f]son of my womb?
What are you doing, [g]son of my vows?
3 Do [h]not give your strength to women,
your ways to those [i]who destroy kings.
4 [j]It is not for kings, O Lemuel,
it is not for kings [k]to drink wine,
or for rulers to take [l]strong drink,
5 lest they drink and forget what has been decreed
and [m]pervert the rights of all the afflicted.
6 Give strong drink to the one who [n]is perishing,
and wine to [o]those in bitter distress;[4]
7 [p]let them drink and forget their poverty
and remember their misery no more.
8 [q]Open your mouth for the mute,
for the rights of all who are destitute.[5]
9 Open your mouth, [r]judge righteously,
[s]defend the rights of [t]the poor and needy.

The Woman Who Fears the LORD

10[6] [u]An excellent wife who can find?
She is far more precious than [v]jewels.

[1] *Or the magpie, or the greyhound;* Hebrew *girt-of-loins* [2] *Or against whom there is no rising up* [3] Hebrew *What, my son?* [4] Hebrew *those bitter in soul*
[5] Hebrew *are sons of passing away* [6] Verses 10–31 are an acrostic poem, each verse beginning with the successive letters of the Hebrew alphabet

30:32–33 Those given to obnoxious and conniving behavior would do well to become quiet and still, or they will soon be embroiled in conflict.

31:1–9 *The Sayings of King Lemuel.* The word translated **oracle** in v. 1 is the same as the word for "oracle" in 30:1; and, as in 30:1, some have preferred to see it as the name for a place called Massa. The ESV has followed the Masoretic text here; see note on 30:1–33 for more. No one knows who **Lemuel** was, or where he was **king**. Most suppose that he was not an Israelite (which is consistent with the fact that the words for **son** in 31:2 and **kings** in v. 3b have Aramaic spellings, and with the absence of the special name Yahweh, the covenant God of Israel, from any of the sayings). The purpose of vv. 2–9 is to instruct in what the ideal human king ought to look like: he is judicious personally (vv. 3–4) so that he may attend well to protect others through justice (vv. 5, 9) and compassion (vv. 6–8). This description runs contrary to ordinary experience, now as in Bible times, where power is often pursued and used to the gain of the individual rather than for the sake of those being led. If Lemuel was in fact a ruler from outside Israel, then the call of these verses underscores the teaching of Proverbs that all rulers are called upon to rule justly and are judged accordingly (cf. the comments of Lady Wisdom in 8:14–16).

31:3 That this proverb refers to mistresses (or a harem) rather than to monogamous marriage is obvious from the plural **women** rather than "a woman." Having mistresses is a waste of a man's **strength** (perhaps meaning his wealth, but, in the present context of a king, more likely his energy and vigor for ruling well).

31:4–5 The calling of **kings** is to serve the well-being of their subjects, especially in protecting the **rights of all the afflicted**. They must never allow their judgment to be clouded by **wine** or **strong drink**.

31:6–7 The **strong drink** would help **those in bitter distress** to **forget their poverty**. This is often taken to mean that the king should provide strong drink to those who are **perishing** or in **misery** for medicinal purposes, that is, to relieve their pain. But it could also mean that the king should invite these people to a banquet where they can have some innocent merriment and forget their troubles for a while.

31:10–31 *An Alphabet of Womanly Excellence.* As the ESV footnote to v. 10 explains, this wisdom poem is an acrostic, in which each verse begins with the successive letter of the Hebrew alphabet. The poem begins and ends with mention of the woman's "excellence" (vv. 10, 29–31). The probable intention of putting this together with the acrostic pattern is to show that this woman's character runs the whole range of excellence. The woman is married (as expected in that culture), and she is devoted to the well-being of her household (vv. 11–13, 15, 17, 19, 21–22, 25, 27), to which she contributes by her participation in outside economic concerns (vv. 14, 16, 18, 24). At the same time she makes her home the center of ministry by giving generously to the poor (v. 20) and by instructing her children and household workers in true kindness (v. 26; neighbors may be included in this audience). So her husband and

11 The heart of her husband trusts in her,
and he will have no lack of gain.
12 She does him good, and not harm,
all the days of her life.
13 She [w]seeks wool and flax,
and works with willing hands.
14 She is like the ships of the merchant;
she brings her food from afar.
15 She [x]rises while it is yet night
and [y]provides food for her household
and portions for her maidens.
16 She considers a field and buys it;
with the fruit of her hands she plants a vineyard.
17 She [z]dresses herself[1] with strength
and makes her arms strong.
18 She perceives that her merchandise is profitable.
Her lamp does not go out at night.
19 She puts her hands to the distaff,
and her hands hold the spindle.
20 She [a]opens her hand to [b]the poor
and reaches out her hands to [b]the needy.
21 She is not afraid of snow for her household,
for all her household are clothed in [c]scarlet.[2]
22 She makes [d]bed coverings for herself;
her clothing is [e]fine linen and [f]purple.
23 Her husband is known in [g]the gates
when he sits among the elders of the land.
24 She makes [h]linen garments and sells them;
she delivers sashes to the merchant.

[1] Hebrew *She girds her loins* [2] Or *in double thickness*

13 [w][ver. 21, 22, 24]
15 [x][ch. 20:13] [y]Luke 12:42; [Ps. 111:5]
17 [z][ver. 25]
20 [a][Rom. 12:13; Eph. 4:28] [b][ver. 9]
21 [c]2 Sam. 1:24
22 [d]ch. 7:16 [e]Gen. 41:42; Rev. 19:8, 14 [f]Judg. 8:26
23 [g]See Ruth 4:1, 2
24 [h]Judg. 14:12; Isa. 3:23

children enjoy their lot and honor her for her industry (vv. 11–12, 23, 28–29). This lofty portrait of excellence sets such a high standard that it can be depressing to godly women today until its purpose is understood. First, the woman embodies in all areas of life the full character of wisdom commended throughout this book. This shows that even though the concrete situations up to now have generally envisioned a cast of males, the teaching of the entire book is intended for all of God's people (see the discussion of "concreteness" in Introduction: Literary Features). Second, as with other character types, this profile is an *ideal*: a particular example of full-scale virtue and wisdom toward which the faithful are willing to be molded (see Introduction: Character Types in Proverbs). It is not expected that any one woman will look exactly like this in every respect.

31:10 An excellent wife who can find? reminds the reader that a good wife is from the Lord (see 12:4; 18:22; 19:14).

31:12 does him good. The diligence of the good wife (vv. 13–19) is not for herself alone but also for her husband and household.

31:13 seeks wool and flax. She is skilled in working with textiles to provide for the clothing needs of her household.

31:14 Trading **ships** is a poetic analogy; she does not literally sail the seas. She goes out of her way to secure fine **food** for her family.

31:15 By providing for **her household** and **her maidens** before the day begins, the "excellent wife" (v. 10) multiplies the effectiveness of her work, because her planning enables everyone else in her household to be productive throughout the day. She does not lie in bed and wait for servants to attend to her.

31:16 She is not confined to the home but is engaged in business. This verse demonstrates remarkable financial independence for a woman in the ancient world: she herself **considers a field** (indicating wise judgment) **and buys it** (indicating control of a substantial amount of money).

31:18 Profitable indicates that she is able to realize economic gain from the diligence of her labor, which she uses to purchase a field (v. 16) and provide for her household (v. 15). **Her lamp does not go out at night**. See v. 15, "She rises while it is yet night"; if the verses are taken to a literal extreme, they would imply that she never sleeps at all! But surely that is not true, nor is it intended (see Ps. 127:2). Rather, this is an idealized picture of a woman who is diligent to complete her work both in the morning and in the evening.

31:19 A **distaff** is a staff with a fork at the end that holds flax or wool that has yet to be spun, from which thread is drawn when a person is spinning thread or yarn on a spinning wheel. A **spindle** is a rod with tapered ends on which thread is wound once it has been spun by hand. The point of this and several other verses is the remarkable range of manual, commercial, administrative, and interpersonal skills at which this woman demonstrates excellence.

31:20 Active concern for the **poor** is a cardinal virtue of all wisdom literature.

31:21 Her careful preparation of necessary clothing in advance means that she is **not afraid** of sudden changes in weather, for they will not catch her unprepared.

31:22 Fine linen and purple indicates clothing of beauty and considerable expense, appropriate visual indications of the excellence of her work and character.

31:23 Gates were the center of civic and economic life in an Israelite city, where the leading men gathered. The wife's excellent work and noble character have contributed significantly to her husband's success and reputation **when he sits among the elders of the land**.

31:24 Making **linen garments** and **sashes**, which she sells to the **merchant**, indicates skill in creating clothing of beauty and value. Such activity

25[i] [ver. 17]
29[j] Song 6:9 [k] [ver. 10]
30[l] [ch. 11:16]

25 [i] Strength and dignity are her clothing,
and she laughs at the time to come.
26 She opens her mouth with wisdom,
and the teaching of kindness is on her tongue.
27 She looks well to the ways of her household
and does not eat the bread of idleness.
28 Her children rise up and call her blessed;
her husband also, and he praises her:
29 "Many [j] women have done [k] excellently,
but you surpass them all."
30 [l] Charm is deceitful, and beauty is vain,
but a woman who fears the LORD is to be praised.
31 Give her of the fruit of her hands,
and let her works praise her in the gates.

exemplifies a high degree of entrepreneurial skill and responsibility in making financial decisions and undertaking commercial activity (cf. note on v. 16).

31:25 Strength and dignity are so much a part of her character and conduct that they seem to be almost like **her clothing**. **She laughs** at the future, in contrast with being worried or fearful about it.

31:26 Although Proverbs has often used men as concrete examples of wisdom, the proverbs apply equally well to women, and the **wisdom** that God teaches in Proverbs can be well understood by both men and women (cf. note on 1:8).

31:27 She looks well to the ways of her household focuses on this woman's diligence in caring for her home and her children and servants. Her rejection of **idleness** embodies one of the chief virtues of Proverbs.

31:28–29 In a loving family, the members recognize the value of each other. Here the **children** and **husband** offer their praise. Verse 29 gives the words of the husband, or perhaps of both husband and children. **Excellently** recalls "excellent" in v. 10.

31:30 The mention of a **woman who fears the LORD** at the end of this long list of excellent qualities brings back the theme of the book of Proverbs stated in 1:7 (see note). It reminds readers that this woman excels in her fear of the Lord, and therefore that she is a model of the character traits and wisdom taught throughout the book's 31 chapters. The appearance of this woman's fear of the Lord at the end of this list is also a reminder that this quality is more important than even great skill and talent, and is foundational to the wise and right use of all activities and skills. A godly woman may well have outward **charm** and **beauty**, but these are of secondary importance to her godliness.

31:31 Although it is the husband, and not the excellent wife, who sits among the elders (v. 23), the wife's works are known and appreciated **in the gates**, and therefore throughout the town. **Give her of the fruit of her hands** means that she should be given some personal reward for her excellent work. **let her works praise her**. The excellent character and work of such a woman calls for public honor.

INTRODUCTION TO

ECCLESIASTES

Author, Title, and Date

The traditional English title comes from the book's heading in the Latin Vulgate translation (*Liber Ecclesiastes*) and is an anglicized version of the Greek and Latin renderings of the speaker's designation in Ecclesiastes 1:1 (Gk. *ekklēsiastēs*; Hb. *Qoheleth*). The Hebrew word is related to the term for "assembly" (Hb. *qahal*) and may be a title for someone who addresses an assembly (hence it is often translated "Preacher"). It could also refer to someone who possesses some other leadership role within an assembly. Scholars have debated whether *Qoheleth* is best understood as a personal name or a title, though the latter seems more likely in view of 12:8, where the definite article ("the") precedes the word.

Strictly speaking, then, the book is anonymous, given that no personal name is attached to it. Nevertheless, traditional Jewish and Christian scholarship has often ascribed authorship to Solomon (10th century B.C.), since the book describes the Preacher as the "son of David, king in Jerusalem" (1:1) and as someone who was surpassingly wise (1:16) and had a very prosperous reign (2:1–9; cf. 1 Kings 3–4). However, such arguments for Solomonic authorship have been called into question on several grounds: (1) The phrase "son of David" could refer to any legitimate Davidic descendant, as it does in Matthew 1:20 with reference to Joseph and frequently throughout the NT with reference to Jesus Christ. (2) The distinctive nature of the Hebrew language used in the book is widely believed to be indicative of a date much later than the 10th century B.C. (though some scholars explain the linguistic evidence in terms of other factors, such as a later modernizing of the language, the influence of foreign languages such as Phoenician or Aramaic, or the possibility of a regional dialect). (3) The Preacher's remarks imply a historical setting that seems in tension with the Solomonic era, such as the fact that many have preceded him as king in Jerusalem (e.g., Eccles. 1:16; 2:7, 9—though these may include non-Israelite kings), that injustice and oppression are openly practiced (3:16–17; 4:1–3; 8:10–11), and that he has observed firsthand the foolishness of kings (4:13–16; 10:5–6) and their abuse of royal power (8:2–9).

On the other hand, other proposals also have difficulties, for it is difficult to find any later "king in Jerusalem" (1:1) who is a better candidate than Solomon for being able to claim that he had "acquired great wisdom, surpassing all who were over Jerusalem before me" (1:16), or that he had great possessions, "more than any who had been before me in Jerusalem" (2:7). In light of the book's anonymity and the difficulty in using linguistic evidence to establish its date of composition, it is best simply to recognize that some interpreters have concluded the author was Solomon, while others think it was some other writer later than Solomon. Regardless, the book claims that its wisdom ultimately comes from the "one Shepherd" (12:11), i.e., from God (Gen. 48:15; Ps. 23:1; 28:9; 80:1).

Theme and Interpretation of Ecclesiastes

The theme of Ecclesiastes is the necessity of fearing God in a fallen, and therefore frequently confusing and frustrating, world. The unique character of the book, however, has led to its being interpreted in widely diverse ways: as a statement of pessimism, optimism, religious and philosophical skepticism (either the Preacher's own or a skepticism assumed for the purpose of demonstrating the futility of an irreligious point of view), faithful belief, heterodoxy, and orthodoxy, to name only a few. Such contradictory understandings of the book are made possible by several of its distinctive features: (1) The book's refrain "vanity of vanities" is open to very different interpretations (see Key Themes), and one's understanding of this important thematic statement will significantly influence one's interpretation of the book as a whole. (2) The attempt to identify any consistent message in the book encounters difficulty because of a number of alleged contradictions within it (e.g., wisdom "preserves life" in 7:12 but fails to do so in 2:16; death is preferable to life's misery in 4:2 but life is superior to death in 9:4–6). (3) The Preacher makes a number of statements which, on the surface, appear highly unorthodox (e.g., 7:16) and at odds with other biblical statements (compare, e.g., 2:16 with Prov. 3:18, or Eccles. 11:9 with Num. 15:39). While the book's epilogue (Eccles. 12:9–12) affirms the Preacher's wisdom, a number of scholars have asserted that these closing verses misrepresent his teaching and his purpose in writing, and therefore conclude that they are to be viewed as a misguided later addition that was intended to make the heterodoxy of the book more palatable to the original readers.

According to the basic interpretative approach adopted here, the Preacher is not to be viewed as some kind of skeptical iconoclast but rather as a teacher of orthodoxy, whose musings on God and human existence present a consistent message that is to be viewed as standing within the broad stream of the biblical wisdom tradition. The epilogue faithfully distills the weightiest themes of the book (see Key Themes, along with the note on 12:13–14). In several instances the book affirms themes from elsewhere in the Wisdom Literature (compare 5:2 with Prov. 10:19; Eccles. 5:15 with Job 1:21; Eccles. 7:1 with Prov. 22:1; Eccles. 8:12 with Prov. 1:7; Eccles. 10:3 with Prov. 13:16), most notably the importance of "the fear of the LORD" (see notes on Eccles. 3:14; 5:7; 12:13–14), thus indicating its basic agreement with the larger biblical message.

At the same time, however, the Preacher is distinctly original and creative in his thought and manner of expression and is not merely restating what other sages have taught. As a genuine wisdom teacher, he has a gift for penetrating observation and for stating things in a profound and challenging manner that spur the listener on to deeper thought and reflection. Many of the difficulties or paradoxes in the book can be reasonably explained in terms of: (1) his provocative style; (2) the general method of wisdom teaching, which can state apparently contradictory principles (e.g., Prov. 26:4–5) and leave it to the listener to work out which principle applies in a particular situation; and (3) the fact that, rather than focusing primarily on stating general truths that are applicable to most situations (as is the tendency with the teaching of the book of Proverbs), the Preacher devotes much of his attention to examining unique individual situations (e.g., Eccles. 4:7–8; 5:13–14; 9:13–16), which can represent deviations from what one might normally expect (e.g., 4:13–16; 9:11). Thus, while he does not deny the validity of the general depiction of reality found in the Wisdom Literature, the Preacher is also keenly aware of the complexities of life in a fallen world, which result in many individual exceptions to the "rules" of biblical wisdom.

One can see the Preacher's most distinctive contribution from the way he uses the term "find out" (see note on 3:11). Every human being wants to find out and understand all the ways of God in the world, but he cannot, because he is not God. And yet the faithful do not despair but cling to God, who deserves their trust; they can leave it to him to make sense of it all, while they seek to learn what it means to "fear God and keep his commandments," even when they cannot see what God is doing. This is true wisdom.

Purpose, Occasion, and Background

Like the rest of the Bible's Wisdom Literature, Ecclesiastes is concerned with imparting wisdom and knowledge to the people of God (12:9–11) and teaching them to fear the Lord. The speaker's designation indicates that he is addressing an assembly of some kind (see Author, Title, and Date), though his counsel in 5:1–7 would seem to suggest a setting outside of the temple. The socioeconomic diversity of his audience is indicated by his remarks directed toward royal counselors (e.g., 8:1–9) as well as common farmers (e.g., 11:6).

Key Themes

1. *The tragic reality of the fall.* The Preacher is painfully aware that the creation has been "subjected to futility" and is "groaning . . . in the pains of childbirth" (Rom. 8:20, 22), and his more troubled musings are to be viewed as the cry of the heart of one who likewise is "groaning inwardly" as he eagerly awaits the resurrection age (see Rom. 8:23). It is especially noteworthy that when Paul refers to the creation being "subjected to futility," the Greek word he uses (*mataiotēs*) is the one utilized 38 times in the LXX version of Ecclesiastes to render the word "vanity" (Hb. *hebel*), indicating that this book might well have formed the background to Paul's thought in Romans 8:18ff. The emphasis on the fall and its disastrous effects is closely related to the book's other key themes described below.

2. *The "vanity" of life.* The book begins and ends with the exclamation, "Vanity of vanities! All is vanity" (Eccles. 1:2; 12:8). While "vanity" is obviously a key word throughout the book (its 38 occurrences account

for more than half of its total usage in the OT), it is notoriously difficult to translate. Literally the word means "vapor" (see ESV footnote on 1:2) and conjures up a picture of something fleeting, ephemeral, and elusive, with different nuances to be ascertained from each context. When applied to human undertakings or the pleasures and joys of earthly life, it indicates that "the present form of this world is passing away" (1 Cor. 7:31); applied to the darker realities of living in a fallen world (e.g., death), it expresses frustration, anger, or sorrow; applied to the Preacher's search for understanding of all things, it indicates something that remained incomprehensible or inscrutable to him (e.g., Eccles. 1:14–15). This last-mentioned usage is particularly significant, as the book presents itself as primarily a quest to "figure out" all of life (see esp. 1:12–18).

3. *Sin and death.* Human beings forfeited the righteousness they originally possessed before God (7:29), and thus all people are sinners (7:20). The opening chapters of Genesis make it clear that death was a result of the fall (Gen. 2:16–17; 3:19), and the Preacher is only too aware of this dreadful reality that affects everyone (e.g., Eccles. 2:14–17; 3:18–21; 6:6).

4. *The joy and the frustration of work.* God gave Adam work to accomplish prior to the fall (Gen. 2:15), but part of the punishment of his sin was that it would become painful toil (Gen. 3:17–19). Both realities are borne out in the Preacher's experience, as he finds his work to be both satisfying (Eccles. 2:10, 24; 3:22; 5:18–20; 9:9–10) as well as aggravating (2:18–23; 4:4ff.).

5. *The grateful enjoyment of God's good gifts.* The Preacher spends a great deal of time commenting on the twisted realities of a fallen world, but this does not blind him to the beauty of the world God created (3:11) or cause him to despise God's good gifts of human relationships, food, drink, and satisfying labor (2:24–26; 3:12–13; 5:18–20; 7:14; 8:15; 9:7, 9). These are to be received humbly and enjoyed fully as blessings from God.

6. *The fear of God.* The fact that "all is vanity" should drive people to take refuge in God, whose work endures forever (3:14) and who is a "rock" for those who take shelter in him (e.g., Ps. 18:2; 62:8; 94:22). In other words, it summons people to "fear" or "revere" God (see notes on Eccles. 3:14; 5:7; 12:13–14; cf. also 7:18 and 8:12–13).

History of Salvation Summary

The history of salvation is the grand overarching story of the Bible; embracing it gives coherence to all of life. It calls each of God's people to own the story, and it dignifies each one with a role in the further outworking of the story. Nevertheless it is impossible for any human being to fully grasp how his or her decisions will contribute to God's grand scheme; and Ecclesiastes helps people to see that they do not have to understand this. Each of the faithful, by "fearing God and keeping his commandments" (12:13), participates in ways that he cannot "find out," trusting that God will take care of the big plan. Despite the fact that the Preacher is a great king and a teacher of true wisdom, he ultimately surpasses Solomon and others (1:16; 2:7, 9). From a Christian theological perspective, reading the biblical story line as a whole, one can see analogies between the Preacher and Jesus Christ who is the "Son of David" (Matt. 1:1), king (Matt. 2:2; Acts 17:7; Rev. 17:14; 19:16), "wisdom from God" (1 Cor. 1:24, 30), and "one Shepherd" (Ezek. 34:23; 37:24; John 10:11, 16), in whose ministry "something greater than Solomon" has arrived (Luke 11:31). (For an explanation of the "History of Salvation," see the Overview of the Bible, pp. 23–26. See also History of Salvation in the Old Testament: Preparing the Way for Christ, pp. 2635–2661.)

Literary Features

Although Ecclesiastes is wisdom literature, it does not read like a typical collection of proverbs. The proverbs are molded into clusters, and furthermore there is a unifying plot line that organizes the units together. The units fall into the three categories of recollections, reflections, and mood pieces. All of these are expressed by a narrator who in effect tells the story of his quest to find satisfaction in life. This quest is reconstructed from the vantage point of someone whose quest ended satisfactorily. The transitions between units often keep the quest in view: "so I turned to consider," "again I saw," "then I saw," etc. As the quest unfolds, one is continuously aware of the discrepancy between the narrator's present outlook and his futile search undertaken in the past. In effect, the speaker recalls the labyrinth of dead ends that he pursued, recreating his restless past with full vividness but not representing it as his mature outlook. Along with the narrative thread, the observational format of much of the material gives the book a meditative cast.

This mini-anthology is strongly unified by recurrent words and motifs. The phrase "under the sun" or its equivalent occurs more than 30 times. The Hebrew words translated "vanity" (*hebel*; see Key Themes, point 2) and "find" (*matsa'*; see Theme and Interpretation of Ecclesiastes) appear throughout the book and suggest the fleetingness of any human being's grasp of the full meaning of events. To keep the reader rooted in the real world, the author repeatedly uses the imagery of eating, drinking, toil, sleep, death, and the cycles of nature.

The proverb is the basic building block of the book. While all wisdom literature tends to make use of the resources of poetry, including the verse form of parallelism, the book of Ecclesiastes flaunts its poetic medium much more than ordinary wisdom literature does. The author is a master of image, metaphor, and simile. The book is partly observational and descriptive in format; one should approach such passages in a meditative way, reflecting on experience of the phenomena that the author describes. The book is also very affective, so the reader needs to be receptive of the moods that it seeks to instill.

Outline

I. Introduction and Theme (1:1–3)

II. First Catalog of "Vanities" (1:4–2:26)
- A. The "vanity" of the natural world (1:4–11)
- B. The "vanity" of wisdom and knowledge (1:12–18)
- C. The "vanity" of pleasures, possessions, and accomplishments (2:1–11)
- D. More on the "vanity" of wisdom (2:12–17)
- E. The "vanity" of labor (2:18–26)

III. Poem: A Time for Everything (3:1–8)

IV. Fear God, the Sovereign One (3:9–15)

V. Second Catalog of "Vanities" (3:16–4:16)
- A. The "vanity" of mortal life (3:16–4:3)
- B. More on the "vanity" of labor (4:4–12)
- C. More on the "vanity" of wisdom (4:13–16)

VI. Fear God, the Holy and Righteous One (5:1–7)

VII. Life "Under the Sun" (5:8–7:24)
- A. Injustice (5:8–9)
- B. Greed vs. contentment (5:10–6:9)
- C. Wisdom for living "under the sun" (6:10–7:24)

VIII. The Heart of the Problem: Sin (7:25–29)

IX. More on Life "Under the Sun" (8:1–12:7)
- A. Wisdom in dealing with foolish authorities (8:1–9)
- B. The importance of fearing God (8:10–13)
- C. The limits of human knowledge (8:14–17)
- D. The unpredictability of life and certainty of death (9:1–6)
- E. Finding enjoyment as circumstances allow (9:7–10)
- F. More on the unpredictability of life (9:11–12)
- G. The paths of wisdom and foolishness (9:13–11:6)
  1. The power of wisdom (9:13–18)
  2. Proverbs concerning wisdom and foolishness (10:1–20)
  3. Wise practices in light of the unpredictability of life (11:1–6)
- H. Aging and the "vanity" of mortal life (11:7–12:7)

X. Final Conclusion and Epilogue (12:8–14)

ECCLESIASTES

Chapter 1
1 [a]ver. 12; ch. 7:27; 12:8-10 [b]ver. 12
2 [c]ch. 12:8 [a][See ver. 1 above] [d][Rom. 8:20]
3 [e]ver. 14; Ps. 144:4; See Job 7:16; Ps. 39:5 [f]ch. 2:11, 22; 3:9; 5:16
4 [g]Ps. 104:5; 119:90
5 [h][Ps. 19:4-6]
6 [i][ch. 11:5; John 3:8]
7 [j]Ps. 104:8, 9
8 [k]ch. 4:8; Prov. 27:20
9 [l]ch. 3:15; 6:10; [ch. 2:12]
10 [m]ch. 3:15

All Is Vanity

1 The words of [a]the Preacher,[1] the son of David, [b]king in Jerusalem.

2 [c]Vanity[2] of vanities, says [a]the Preacher,
[c]vanity of vanities! [d]All is vanity.
3 [e]What [f]does man gain by all the toil
at which he toils under the sun?
4 A generation goes, and a generation comes,
but [g]the earth remains forever.
5 [h]The sun rises, and the sun goes down,
and hastens[3] to the place where it rises.
6 [i]The wind blows to the south
and goes around to the north;
around and around goes the wind,
and on its circuits the wind returns.
7 All [j]streams run to the sea,
but the sea is not full;
to the place where the streams flow,
there they flow again.
8 All things are full of weariness;
a man cannot utter it;
[k]the eye is not satisfied with seeing,
nor the ear filled with hearing.
9 [l]What has been is what will be,
and what has been done is what will be done,
and there is nothing new under the sun.
10 Is there a thing of which it is said,
"See, this is new"?
It has been [m]already
in the ages before us.

[1] Or *Convener*, or *Collector*; Hebrew *Qoheleth* (so throughout Ecclesiastes) [2] The Hebrew term *hebel*, translated *vanity* or *vain*, refers concretely to a "mist," "vapor," or "mere breath," and metaphorically to something that is fleeting or elusive (with different nuances depending on the context). It appears five times in this verse and in 29 other verses in Ecclesiastes [3] Or *and returns panting*

1:1–3 *Introduction and Theme.* The speaker introduces himself and his theme.

1:1 the Preacher, the son of David, king in Jerusalem. See Introduction: Author, Title, and Date.

1:2 vanity of vanities! All is vanity. This extremely important thematic word (Hb. *hebel*, lit., "vapor," taken figuratively as "vanity"; see ESV footnote) occurs frequently throughout the book; at this early point, however, the Preacher leaves it unexplained. It is only as the book progresses that its meaning becomes clear (for further discussion of its meaning, see Introduction: Key Themes).

1:3 What does man gain? This repeated question (3:9; 5:15; cf. 2:11; 6:11; 10:11) is born out of the Preacher's realization that "all is vanity" (1:2): if life frequently makes no sense and pleasures and achievements are "fleeting," is there any significance to human existence? The phrase **under the sun** does not indicate a "secular" point of view, as is often claimed (the Preacher's frequent references to God exclude such an interpretation) but rather refers to the world and to mankind in their current fallen state, much like NT expressions such as "this age" or "this present age."

1:4–2:26 *First Catalog of "Vanities."* The Preacher proceeds to give specific examples to prove his thesis that all is "vanity."

1:4–11 *The "Vanity" of the Natural World.* The endless repetition of natural seasons and cycles never produces anything "new" (v. 9) and thus appears to be without direction or purpose.

11 There is no [n]remembrance of former things,[1]
nor will there be any remembrance
of later things[2] yet to be
among those who come after.

The Vanity of Wisdom

12 I [o]the Preacher have been king over Israel in Jerusalem. 13 And I [p]applied my heart[3] to
seek and to search out by wisdom all that is done under heaven. It is an unhappy [q]business
that God has given to the children of man to be busy with. 14 I have seen everything that is
done under the sun, and behold, all is [r]vanity[4] and a striving after wind.[5]

15 [s]What is crooked cannot be made straight,
and what is lacking cannot be counted.

16 I said in my heart, "I have acquired great [t]wisdom, surpassing all who were over
Jerusalem before me, and my heart has had great experience of wisdom and knowledge."
17 And I [u]applied my heart to know wisdom and to know [v]madness and folly. I perceived
that this also is but [r]a striving after wind.

18 For [w]in much wisdom is much vexation,
and he who increases knowledge increases sorrow.

The Vanity of Self-Indulgence

2 I [x]said in my heart, "Come now, I will test you with pleasure; enjoy yourself." But behold,
this also was vanity.[6] 2 I [y]said of laughter, "It is mad," and of pleasure, "What use is it?"
3 I [z]searched with my heart how to cheer my body with wine—my heart still guiding me
with wisdom—and how to lay hold on [a]folly, till I might see what was good for the children of man to do under heaven during the few days of their life. 4 I made great works. I
[b]built houses and planted [c]vineyards for myself. 5 I made myself [d]gardens and parks, and
planted in them all kinds of fruit trees. 6 I made myself pools from which to water the forest of growing trees. 7 I bought male and female slaves, and had [e]slaves who were born in
my house. I had also great possessions of [f]herds and flocks, more than any who had been
before me in Jerusalem. 8 I also gathered for myself silver and [g]gold and the treasure of
[h]kings and [i]provinces. I got [j]singers, both men and women, and many [k]concubines,[7] the
delight of the sons of man.

[1] Or *former people* [2] Or *later people* [3] The Hebrew term denotes the center of one's inner life, including mind, will, and emotions [4] The Hebrew term *hebel* can refer to a "vapor" or "mere breath" (see note on 1:2) [5] Or *a feeding on wind*; compare Hosea 12:1 (also in Ecclesiastes 1:17; 2:11, 17, 26; 4:4, 6, 16; 6:9) [6] The Hebrew term *hebel* can refer to a "vapor" or "mere breath"; also verses 11, 15, 17, 19, 21, 23, 26 (see note on 1:2) [7] The meaning of the Hebrew word is uncertain

11 [n]ch. 2:16; See ch. 9:5
12 [o]ver. 1
13 [p]ver. 17; [1 Kgs. 4:33] [q]ch. 2:23, 26; 3:10; [Gen. 3:19]
14 [r]ver. 2; ch. 2:11, 17, 26; 4:4; 6:9
15 [s]See ch. 7:13
16 [t]ch. 2:9; [1 Kgs. 3:12, 13; 4:30; 10:7, 23]
17 [u]ver. 13; [ch. 2:3, 12; 7:23, 25] [v]ch. 9:3 [r][See ver. 14 above]
18 [w][ch. 12:12]

Chapter 2

1 [x]Luke 12:19
2 [y][Prov. 14:13]
3 [z][ch. 1:17] [a]ch. 7:25
4 [b]See 1 Kgs. 7:1-12 [c]Song 8:11
5 [d]Song 4:16; 5:1
7 [e]Gen. 14:14; 15:3 [f][1 Kgs. 4:23]
8 [g]1 Kgs. 9:28; 10:10, 14, 21 [h][1 Kgs. 4:21; 10:15] [i]1 Kgs. 20:14; Ezek. 19:8 [j]2 Sam. 19:35; 2 Chr. 35:25 [k]1 Kgs. 11:3

1:11 There is no remembrance of former things, nor . . . of later things. Or, if the reading in the footnote is accepted, "There is no remembrance of former people . . . nor . . . of later people" (see Lev. 26:45; Deut. 19:14; Eccles. 4:16). As the generations come and go (1:4), there are very few people who make any significant impact on the course of world history; the majority of the human race lives and dies in obscurity. The seemingly never-ending march of human generations thus appears to be as purposeless as the repetitive cycles of the natural world.

1:12–18 *The "Vanity" of Wisdom and Knowledge.* The Preacher states his basic quest (namely, to understand all of reality) and summarizes its results.

1:12 I the Preacher have been king over Israel. See Introduction: Author, Title, and Date.

1:13 The Preacher perceives that in this world **God has given** an **unhappy business**, i.e., a troubling or burdensome task, **to the children of man**. The same Hebrew phrase occurs in 4:8 and 5:14 ("bad venture"), where it refers to the burdens and trials experienced by those who live **under heaven** (this phrase is interchangeable with the expression "under the sun"; cf. 1:14). For some inscrutable reason, God ordains that mankind should endure painful experiences in this present fallen order.

1:14 The Preacher examined everything **under the sun**, just as he set out to do (v. 13). However, he is unable to comprehend it all and draws the conclusion that everything is **vanity** (see note on v. 2) **and a striving after wind**. This latter expression is almost always directly linked with the word for "vanity" (see 2:11, 17, 26; 4:4; 6:9).

1:15 Crooked is to be understood in the sense of "inscrutable," rather than in an ethical sense of "wicked" or "corrupt." There will always be aspects of life in a fallen world that remain mysterious because God has chosen not to reveal the answers to all of mankind's questions.

1:16 surpassing all who were over Jerusalem before me. If anyone possessed the wisdom to comprehend the meaning of life, it was the Preacher.

1:17 As part of his quest **to know wisdom**, the Preacher also seeks to comprehend **madness and folly** (see also 2:3, 12; 7:25). It is not that he seriously considers these to be viable alternatives to the path of wisdom (cf. 2:13–14; 9:3; 10:1, 13). Rather, his intent is to come to a better understanding of wisdom by simultaneously examining wisdom's opposite (foolishness); cf. the Lord's knowledge of "good and evil" (Gen. 3:22; see also Gen. 2:9, 17).

1:18 Wisdom is a mixed blessing: to gain **wisdom** and understanding is to gain a clearer view into the tragedies of life in a world marred by sin.

2:1–11 *The "Vanity" of Pleasures, Possessions, and Accomplishments.* The Preacher turns to examine the significance of less "intellectual" pursuits.

2:1–2 The Hebrew word for **pleasure** used here (*simkhah*) can mean either "joy" or "mirth," and the reference to **laughter** in v. 2 indicates that the latter is what the Preacher has in mind (cf. 7:4, where *mirth* renders the related Hb. noun *simkhah*). A lighthearted approach to life is foolish, in view of the tragic realities of a fallen world.

2:3 my heart still guiding me with wisdom. The Preacher did not indulge

9 [l]1 Chr. 29:25; See ch. 1:16
10 [m][Prov. 8:31] [n]ch. 3:22; 5:18; 9:9
11 [o]See ch. 1:14 [p]See ch. 1:3
12 [q]ch. 7:25 [r]See ch. 1:17 [s]ch. 1:9, 10
14 [t][Prov. 17:24] [u]ch. 3:19; 9:2, 3; Ps. 49:10
15 [v][ver. 16; ch. 6:8]
16 [w]ch. 1:11; See ch. 9:5 [x]See ver. 14
17 [o][See ver. 11 above]
18 [y]ch. 1:3 [z]Ps. 39:6; 49:10
20 [a]ch. 7:25 [b]ch. 1:3
22 [c]See ch. 1:3
23 [d]Job 5:7; 14:1 [e]See ch. 1:13
24 [f]ch. 3:12, 13, 22; 5:18; 8:15; [1 Tim. 6:17] [g][ch. 9:7; Luke 12:19; 1 Cor. 15:32] [h][ch. 3:13; 5:19]
26 [i]Job 32:8 [e][See ver. 7 above] [j][Job 27:16, 17; Prov. 13:22] [k]See ch. 1:14

9 So I became great and [l]surpassed all who were before me in Jerusalem. Also my [l]wis-
dom remained with me. 10 And whatever my eyes desired I did not keep from them. I kept
my heart from no pleasure, for my heart [m]found pleasure in all my toil, and this was my
[n]reward for all my toil. 11 Then I considered all that my hands had done and the toil I had
expended in doing it, and behold, all was [o]vanity and a striving after wind, and there was
nothing [p]to be gained under the sun.

The Vanity of Living Wisely

12 [q]So I turned to consider [r]wisdom and madness and folly. For what can the man do who
comes after the king? Only [s]what has already been done. 13 Then I saw that there is more
gain in wisdom than in folly, as there is more gain in light than in darkness. 14 [t]The wise
person has his eyes in his head, but the fool walks in darkness. And yet I perceived that
the [u]same event happens to all of them. 15 Then I said in my heart, [v]"What happens to the
fool will happen to me also. Why then have I been so very wise?" And I said in my heart
that this also is vanity. 16 For of the wise as of the fool there is [w]no enduring remembrance,
seeing that in the days to come all will have been long forgotten. [x]How the wise dies just
like the fool! 17 So I hated life, because what is done under the sun was grievous to me, for
[o]all is vanity and a striving after wind.

The Vanity of Toil

18 I hated [y]all my toil in which I toil under the sun, seeing that I must [z]leave it to the man
who will come after me, 19 and who knows whether he will be wise or a fool? Yet he will
be master of all for which I toiled and used my wisdom under the sun. This also is vanity.
20 So I [a]turned about and gave my heart up to despair [b]over all the toil of my labors under
the sun, 21 because sometimes a person who has toiled with wisdom and knowledge and
skill must leave everything to be enjoyed by someone who did not toil for it. This also is
vanity and a great evil. 22 What has a man from [c]all the toil and striving of heart with which
he toils beneath the sun? 23 For [d]all his days are full of sorrow, and his [e]work is a vexation.
Even in the night his heart does not rest. This also is vanity.

24 [f]There is nothing better for a person than that he should [g]eat and drink and find
enjoyment[1] in his toil. This also, I saw, is [h]from the hand of God, 25 for apart from him[2]
who can eat or who can have enjoyment? 26 For to the one who pleases him [i]God has given
wisdom and knowledge and joy, but to the sinner he has given [e]the business of gathering
and collecting, [j]only to give to one who pleases God. [k]This also is vanity and a striving
after wind.

[1] *Or and make his soul see good* [2] Some Hebrew manuscripts, Septuagint, Syriac; most Hebrew manuscripts *apart from me*

himself so excessively with wine that he lost his ability to think with genuine discernment. On his attempt **to lay hold on folly**, see the note on 1:17.

2:10–11 The Preacher comes to the unpleasant realization (v. 11) that his work resulted in no permanent gain **under the sun**; nevertheless, he did receive a **reward** in return for his work (v. 10), namely, the **pleasure** which the work itself gave him.

2:12–17 *More on the "Vanity" of Wisdom.* Although he knows wisdom is better than folly, the Preacher still finds "vanity" in his practice of it.

2:12 The Preacher's reign as king surpassed all others (1:16; 2:7, 9), and thus anyone **who comes after the king** will at best only be able to copy **what has already been done**. Having determined that even his own impressive reign was "vanity" (vv. 1–11), he turns again to examine the value of wisdom (cf. 1:12–18). On **madness and folly**, see the note on 1:17.

2:13 there is more gain in wisdom than in folly. Despite the fact that wisdom is a mixed blessing (1:18) with distressing limitations (e.g., 2:14–16), it is incomparably superior to a life of foolishness.

2:14–16 Wisdom, though infinitely better than folly, does not grant immortality to those who possess it: **the same event** (i.e., death, cf. v. 16) **happens** to both the wise and the foolish (cf. 3:19; 9:2–3, 11). To make matters still worse, even the wise are typically forgotten after their death and receive **no enduring remembrance** by others.

2:17 The limitations of wisdom mentioned in vv. 14–16 lead the Preacher to say that he **hated life**. The fact that he elsewhere states that life is superior to death (9:4–5) and commends its enjoyment (e.g., 3:12–13; 9:9) indicates that this statement is not to be interpreted as a capitulation to utter despair. Rather, his use of "hate" in this instance is to be understood as the common rhetorical technique of stating a relative contrast in absolute terms (see the use of "hate" in Gen. 29:30–31; Deut. 21:15; Luke 14:26). The Preacher "hates" life in the sense that he finds it deeply disappointing in certain key respects; life has lost much of its sweetness for him.

2:18–26 *The "Vanity" of Labor.* Considering the fruits of all his toil also leads the Preacher to declare it "vanity."

2:18–20 I hated all my toil. See the note on v. 17 concerning the Preacher's use of "hate." While at times he found pleasure in his toil (vv. 10, 24), his enjoyment is severely diminished by the knowledge that he must eventually hand over his life's work to someone else, **and who knows whether he will be wise or a fool?** As the **master of all** that the Preacher has acquired and achieved, his successor has the potential to squander everything. This painful realization causes the Preacher to **despair** that his life's work will, in the grand scheme of things, amount to anything significant (cf. 1:3; 2:11).

2:24–26 If one has no certainty of making a lasting impact on the world through the results of one's work (vv. 11, 18–23), the best that one can hope for is to **find enjoyment** in **toil** and in God's simple gifts of food and **drink**. Such enjoyment is to be viewed as a gift **from the hand of God**, granted **to the one who pleases him**, rather than to the **sinner**.

A Time for Everything

3 For everything there is a season, and [l]a time for every matter under heaven:

2 a time to be born, and a time to [m]die;
a time to plant, and a time to pluck up what is planted;
3 a time to kill, and a time to heal;
a time to break down, and a time to build up;
4 a time to [n]weep, and a time to laugh;
a time to mourn, and a time to [o]dance;
5 a time to [p]cast away stones, and a time to [q]gather stones together;
a time to embrace, and a time to [r]refrain from embracing;
6 a time to seek, and a time to [s]lose;
a time to keep, and a time to [t]cast away;
7 a time to [u]tear, and a time to sew;
a time to [v]keep silence, and a time to speak;
8 a time to love, and a time to [w]hate;
a time for war, and a time for peace.

The God-Given Task

9 What [x]gain has the worker from his toil? 10 I have seen [y]the business that [z]God has given
to the children of man to be busy with. 11 He has [a]made everything beautiful in its time.
Also, he has put eternity into man's heart, yet so that he cannot [b]find out what God has
done from the beginning to the end. 12 I perceived that there is [c]nothing better for them
than to be joyful and to [d]do good as long as they live; 13 also [e]that everyone should eat and
drink and take pleasure in all his toil—this is [f]God's gift to man.
14 I perceived that whatever God does endures forever; [g]nothing can be added to it, nor
anything taken from it. God has done it, so that people fear before him. 15 That which is,
[h]already has been; that which is to be, already has been; and God [i]seeks what has been
driven away.[1]

From Dust to Dust

16 Moreover, [j]I saw under the sun that in the place of justice, even [k]there was wickedness, and in the place of righteousness, even there was wickedness. 17 I said in my heart,
[l]God will judge the righteous and the wicked, for there is [m]a time for every matter and
for every work. 18 I said in my heart with regard to the children of man that God is testing

[1] Hebrew *what has been pursued*

Chapter 3
1 [l]ver. 17; ch. 8:6
2 [m]Heb. 9:27
4 [n][Rom. 12:15] [o][2 Sam. 6:14]; See Ex. 15:20
5 [p][2 Kgs. 3:25] [q][Isa. 5:2] [r][Joel 2:16]
6 [s][Matt. 10:39] [t][Prov. 11:24]
7 [u]See Gen. 37:29 [v]Amos 5:13
8 [w][Luke 14:26]
9 [x]See ch. 1:3
10 [y]See ch. 1:13 [z]See Gen. 3:17-19
11 [a][Gen. 1:31] [b]ch. 8:17; [Job 5:9; Rom. 11:33]
12 [c][ver. 22] [d]Ps. 34:14; 37:3
13 [e]See ch. 2:24 [f][ch. 2:24; 5:19]
14 [g][James 1:17]
15 [h][ch. 1:9] [i][ch. 12:14]
16 [j]ch. 4:1 [k]ch. 5:8; [ch. 4:1]
17 [l]Matt. 16:27; 2 Cor. 5:10; See Rom. 2:6-11; 2 Thess. 1:6-10 [m]ver. 1; ch. 8:6

3:1–8 *Poem: A Time for Everything.* There is an appropriate occasion for every human event or activity; life is endlessly complex. Several of the items mentioned in this poem have already been examined by the Preacher (e.g., compare v. 2 "a time to die" with 2:14–17; 3:2 "a time to plant" and v. 3 "a time to build up" with 2:4–5).

3:6 a time to lose. To give up looking for a lost item.

3:8 a time to hate. While love for one's neighbor is the norm for biblical ethics (Lev. 19:18; Gal. 5:14; James 2:8), there is also a righteous anger that is legitimate under the appropriate circumstances (see Ps. 15:4; 26:5; 31:6; 139:21–22).

3:9–15 *Fear God, the Sovereign One.* The "vanity" of life causes the Preacher to reflect on what is permanent and lasting, namely, God and his sovereign ordering of human affairs.

3:11 Despite the repetitiveness of the natural world (1:4–11), the Preacher can see that God **has made everything beautiful in its time**. The problem is that God has also placed **eternity** (that is, a sense that life continues beyond this present existence) **into man's heart, yet so that he cannot find out what God has done from the beginning to the end**. The word "find," or "find out" (Hb. *matsa'*) has the sense of "figure out, comprehend by study" in this verse and other places in the book (7:14, 24, 26, 27, 28, 29; 8:17). The Preacher thus realizes that both his desire to understand all of life, as well as the limitations on his ability to do so, have been ordained by God.

3:12–13 Rather than becoming embittered by what God has *not* granted human beings (namely, the ability to comprehend all of reality), one should enjoy the gifts that God *has* given.

3:14 The short-lived "vanities" of this world reveal all the more clearly the enduring work of **God**, to which **nothing can be added**. The absolute sovereignty of God and his purposes is meant to bring human beings to a sense of humble reverence and awe of him: **God has done it, so that people fear before him** (cf. 5:7; 12:13; also note on Acts 9:31). See Introduction: Key Themes.

3:16–4:16 *Second Catalog of "Vanities."* The Preacher returns to examining more of life's "vanities" (cf. 1:4–2:26).

3:16–4:3 *The "Vanity" of Mortal Life.* The fact that people die is a further aspect of "vanity."

3:16–17 The effects of the fall extend to human relationships (cf. Genesis 4), and thus in a fallen world one suffers outright injustice and **wickedness** at the hand of other human beings. What makes this sad reality tolerable is

18 [n]Ps. 49:12, 20; 73:22
19 [o]See ch. 2:14
20 [p]ch. 12:7; Gen. 3:19
21 [q][ch. 12:7]
22 [r]See ch. 2:24 [s]See ch. 2:10 [t]ch. 2:19; 6:12; 8:7; 10:14

Chapter 4

1 [u]ch. 9:11 [v]ch. 3:16 [w]ch. 5:8; Job 35:9 [x]Lam. 1:2
2 [y]See Job 3:11-26
3 [z]ch. 6:3
4 [a]See ch. 1:14
5 [b]Prov. 6:10; 24:33 [c][Isa. 9:20]
6 [d]See Prov. 15:16 [e]ch. 6:5
7 [u][See ver. 1 above]
8 [f]ch. 1:8; [Prov. 27:20; 1 John 2:16] [g]ch. 2:18; Ps. 39:6 [h]See ch. 1:13
11 [i]See 1 Kgs. 1:1-4
13 [j][ch. 9:15, 16] [k][Prov. 12:15]
14 [l]See Gen. 41:14, 41-43
16 [m]See ch. 1:14

them that they may see that they themselves are but [n]beasts. 19 [o]For what happens to the
children of man and what happens to the beasts is the same; as one dies, so dies the other.
They all have the same breath, and man has no advantage over the beasts, for all is vanity.[1]
20 All go to one place. All are from [p]the dust, and to dust all return. 21 Who knows whether
[q]the spirit of man goes upward and the spirit of the beast goes down into the earth? 22 So
I saw that there is [r]nothing better than that a man should rejoice in his work, for [s]that is
his lot. Who can bring him to see [t]what will be after him?

Evil Under the Sun

4 [u]Again I [v]saw all [w]the oppressions that are done under the sun. And behold, the tears of
the oppressed, and they had [x]no one to comfort them! On the side of their oppressors
there was power, and there was no one to comfort them. 2 And I [y]thought the dead who
are already dead more fortunate than the living who are still alive. 3 But [z]better than both
is he who has not yet been and has not seen the evil deeds that are done under the sun.
4 Then I saw that all toil and all skill in work come from a man's envy of his neighbor.
This also is [a]vanity[2] and a striving after wind.
5 The fool [b]folds his hands and [c]eats his own flesh.
6 [d]Better is a handful of [e]quietness than two hands full of toil and a striving after wind.
7 [u]Again, I saw vanity under the sun: 8 one person who has no other, either son or brother,
yet there is no end to all his toil, and his [f]eyes are never satisfied with riches, so that he
never asks, [g]"For whom am I toiling and depriving myself of pleasure?" This also is vanity
and an unhappy [h]business.
9 Two are better than one, because they have a good reward for their toil. 10 For if they fall,
one will lift up his fellow. But woe to him who is alone when he falls and has not another
to lift him up! 11 Again, if two lie together, they keep warm, [i]but how can one keep warm
alone? 12 And though a man might prevail against one who is alone, two will withstand
him—a threefold cord is not quickly broken.
13 Better was [j]a poor and wise youth than an old and foolish king who no longer knew
how [k]to take advice. 14 For he went [l]from prison to the throne, though in his own kingdom
he had been born poor. 15 I saw all the living who move about under the sun, along with
that[3] youth who was to stand in the king's[4] place. 16 There was no end of all the people,
all of whom he led. Yet those who come later will not rejoice in him. Surely this also is
[m]vanity and a striving after wind.

[1] The Hebrew term *hebel* can refer to a "vapor" or "mere breath" (see note on 1:2) [2] The Hebrew term *hebel* can refer to a "vapor" or "mere breath"; also verses 7, 8, 16 (see note on 1:2) [3] Hebrew *the second* [4] Hebrew *his*

the certainty that **God will judge the righteous and the wicked**, i.e., ultimately justice will be done.

3:18–19 The children of man . . . are but beasts in the sense that both human beings and animals die (vv. 19–21). In terms of mortality, then, **man has no advantage over the beasts**.

3:21 Who knows whether the spirit of man goes upward. For the Preacher, the human spirit is a mysterious entity: while he affirms that the spirit returns to God when a person dies (12:7), he does not know how it comes to reside in the human body in the first place (11:5). In this verse the verb "know" has either the sense of "to comprehend, to understand completely" (as in, e.g., 1:17; 7:25; 8:16) or else "to perceive, to observe" (as in 2:14; 3:12, 14).

4:2–3 Some people's circumstances are so tragic that they even welcome death. The Preacher, however, considers those who have not yet lived or died to be even more fortunate than those who die in such misery, thus indicating that he would still consider death to be an "enemy" (1 Cor. 15:26), despite its ability to provide relief from earthly suffering.

4:4–12 *More on the "Vanity" of Labor.* This continues and develops the theme of 2:18–26.

4:4–6 The Preacher observes that much of what is achieved by skillful human labor stems **from a man's envy of his neighbor**. The term translated "envy" (Hb. *qin'ah*) can have either negative or positive moral connotations, depending on the context (much like English "jealousy" and "zeal"). Here the Preacher focuses on the **vanity** that comes to those who make such **striving** their ultimate good, rather than a desire to serve the Lord (cf. Col. 3:24). If a man **folds his hands**—i.e., refuses to work—he only ruins himself. Finally, the Preacher adds a word of caution against excessive striving: instead of **two hands full of toil** and **striving after wind** (something fleeting; see Eccles. 4:8), one should learn to be content with less (one single **handful of quietness**).

4:7–11 The Preacher makes a sharp contrast in these verses. On the one hand there is **one person** who continues in endless **toil**, yet who is **never satisfied** even though he acquires great **riches** for himself (he **has no other**). This, the Preacher says, is **vanity and an unhappy business**. On the other hand the Preacher affirms how much better **two are . . . than one**. Thus the wise person will work side by side with another, enjoying **a good reward** and finding help in times of need.

4:9 Two . . . have a good reward for their toil. The wise person will pursue cooperative ventures rather than give in to jealous striving to be first (contrast vv. 8, 10, 11), a striving that isolates him from others.

4:12 A **threefold cord** stands for the great value of "plurality" (more than one or even two) as opposed to being alone (vv. 7–11).

4:13–16 *More on the "Vanity" of Wisdom.* The Preacher relates an instance he observed of how the results of wisdom can be fleeting. In contrast to **an old and foolish king**, there once was **a poor and wise youth** (v. 13) who managed to rise above his humble beginnings and ascend **to the throne** (v. 14) and an influential reign (vv. 15–16a). Yet later generations would not **rejoice in him** (v. 16b); his success and popularity, even though gained by true wisdom, did not last.

Fear God

5 [1] [n]Guard your steps when you go to [o]the house of God. To draw near to listen is better
than to [p]offer the sacrifice of fools, for they do not know that they are doing evil. 2 [2] Be
not rash with your mouth, nor let your heart be hasty to utter a word before God, for God
is in heaven and you are on earth. Therefore [q]let your words be few. 3 For a dream comes
with much business, and a fool's voice with [r]many words.
4 When [s]you vow a vow to God, [t]do not delay paying it, for he has no pleasure in fools.
[u]Pay what you vow. 5 [v]It is better that you should not vow than that you should vow and
not pay. 6 Let not your mouth lead you[3] into sin, and do not say before [w]the messenger[4]
that it was [x]a mistake. Why should God be angry at your voice and destroy the work of
your hands? 7 For when dreams increase and words grow many, there is vanity;[5] but[6] [y]God
is the one you must fear.

The Vanity of Wealth and Honor

8 [z]If you see in a province the oppression of the poor and the violation of justice and
righteousness, [a]do not be amazed at the matter, [b]for the high official is watched by a higher,
and there are yet higher ones over them. 9 But this is gain for a land in every way: a king
committed to cultivated fields.[7]
10 He who loves money will not be satisfied with money, nor he who loves wealth
with his income; this also is vanity. 11 When goods increase, they increase who eat them,
and what advantage has their owner but to see them with his eyes? 12 Sweet is the sleep
of a laborer, whether he eats little or much, but the full stomach of the rich will not let
him sleep.
13 [c]There is a grievous evil that I have seen under the sun: riches were kept by their
owner to his hurt, 14 and those riches were lost in a bad venture. And he is father of a son,
but he has nothing in his hand. 15 [d]As he came from his mother's womb he shall go again,
naked as he came, and shall take nothing for his toil that he may carry away in his hand.
16 This also is a grievous evil: just as he came, so shall he go, and what [e]gain is there to him
who [f]toils for the wind? 17 Moreover, all his days he [g]eats in darkness in much vexation
and sickness and anger.
18 Behold, what I have seen to be [h]good and fitting is to eat and drink and find enjoyment[8] in all the toil with which one toils under the sun the few days of his life that God
has given him, for this is his [i]lot. 19 Everyone also to whom [j]God has given [k]wealth and
possessions [l]and power to enjoy them, and to accept his lot and rejoice in his toil—this is
[m]the gift of God. 20 For he will not much remember the days of his life because God keeps
him occupied with joy in his heart.

Chapter 5
1 [n][Ex. 3:5; Isa. 1:12] [o][Gen. 28:17] [p]Prov. 15:8; See 1 Sam. 15:22
2 [q][Matt. 6:7]
3 [r]Prov. 10:19; [Job 11:2]
4 [s]Num. 30:2 [t]Deut. 23:21; Ps. 50:14; 76:11 [u][Ps. 66:13, 14]
5 [v][Prov. 20:25; Acts 5:4]
6 [w][1 Cor. 11:10] [x]ch. 10:5; Num. 15:25, 26
7 [y]ch. 12:13
8 [z]ch. 3:16; 4:1 [a][1 Pet. 4:12] [b][Ps. 12:5; 58:11; 82:1]
13 [c]ch. 6:1
15 [d]See Job 1:21
16 [e]See ch. 1:3 [f][Prov. 11:29]
17 [g][Ps. 127:2]
18 [h]See ch. 2:24 [i]See ch. 2:10
19 [j]ch. 6:2; [ch. 2:24] [k]2 Chr. 1:11 [l][ch. 6:2] [m]See ch. 3:13

[1] Ch 4:17 in Hebrew [2] Ch 5:1 in Hebrew [3] Hebrew *your flesh* [4] Or *angel* [5] The Hebrew term *hebel* can refer to a "vapor" or "mere breath"; also verse 10 (see note on 1:2) [6] Or *For when dreams and vanities increase, words also grow many; but* [7] The meaning of the Hebrew verse is uncertain [8] Or *and see good*

5:1–7 *Fear God, the Holy and Righteous One.* The previous exhortation to "fear God" was motivated by God's sovereignty (3:9–15); in this section, it is motivated by his holy and righteous character.

5:4 When you vow a vow to God. The Preacher wishes to keep people from uttering rash or meaningless words during the worship of God (vv. 1–2), and in particular he has in mind the careless taking of a religious **vow** as an act of piety (cf. Deut. 23:21–23). By taking a vow, a worshiper would promise to perform a specific act (such as making a sacrifice) if God would respond favorably to a particular petition (Gen. 28:20–22; Judg. 11:30–31; 1 Sam. 1:11). Since making a sacrifice was costly, however, people often looked for some excuse to avoid following through with it (e.g., Eccles. 5:6).

5:7 God is the one you must fear. Cf. 3:14; 12:13; and see Introduction: Key Themes.

5:8–7:24 *Life "Under the Sun."* Having demonstrated that all things are "vanity" and that the proper human response is, first and foremost, to "fear God," the Preacher makes further observations on the hardships of life in a fallen world and provides practical counsel for dealing with them.

5:8–9 *Injustice.* In a world like this, it is no surprise to find officials violating justice. **the high official is watched**. The political maneuvering of sinful ruling officials results in suffering for the powerless.

5:10–6:9 *Greed vs. Contentment.* The Preacher observes the destructive nature of greed and concludes that contentment is a key characteristic of the godly life in this world (cf. Phil. 4:11; 1 Tim. 6:6, 8; Heb. 13:5).

5:13–14 Riches were kept . . . to his hurt, i.e., the owner endured hardship and sacrifice in order to acquire his wealth but was never able to enjoy it, as it was **lost in a bad venture**, so that he neither enjoyed his riches nor did anything worthwhile with them. To make matters worse, he had a family to provide for.

5:17 This continues the story begun in v. 13. The man's selfish, fearful greed resulted in a truly wretched life.

5:20 he will not much remember . . . his life. This does not indicate an unreflective attitude toward life but simply means that the one to whom God grants contentment will not allow the darker realities of human existence to overshadow divinely bestowed blessings.

Chapter 6
1[n]ch. 5:13
2[o]ch. 5:19 [p][1 Kgs. 3:13] [q]Ps. 17:14; 73:7; See Job 21:7-13 [r][ch. 5:19; Luke 12:20]
3[s]Gen. 47:8, 9 [t][ver. 6] [u]Isa. 14:20; Jer. 8:2; 22:19; [2 Kgs. 9:35] [v]ch. 4:3; Job 3:16
5[w]ch. 7:11; 11:7 [x]ch. 4:6
7[y][Prov. 16:26]
8[z][ch. 2:15]
9[a]ch. 11:9 [b]See ch. 1:14
10[c]ch. 1:10; 3:15 [d]Job 9:32; Isa. 45:9; [1 Cor. 10:22]
12[e][ch. 7:15; 9:9] [f]ch. 8:13; See Job 14:2 [g][ch. 2:18; 3:22]

Chapter 7
1[h]Prov. 22:1; [Song 1:3] [i]ch. 4:2
2[j][Ps. 90:12]
3[k][2 Cor. 7:10]
5[l]Prov. 13:18; 15:31, 32; [Ps. 141:5]
6[m][Joel 2:5] [n][Ps. 58:9; 118:12]
7[o][ch. 4:1] [p]Deut. 16:19; See Prov. 17:8
8[q]See Prov. 14:29

6 [n]There is an evil that I have seen under the sun, and it lies heavy on mankind: 2 a man
[o]to whom [p]God gives wealth, possessions, and honor, so that he [q]lacks nothing of all
that he desires, yet God [r]does not give him power to enjoy them, but a stranger enjoys
them. This is vanity;[1] it is a grievous evil. 3 If a man fathers a hundred children and lives
many years, so that [s]the days of his years are many, but his soul is not satisfied with life's
[t]good things, and he also has no [u]burial, I say that [v]a stillborn child is better off than
he. 4 For it comes in vanity and goes in darkness, and in darkness its name is covered.
5 Moreover, it has not [w]seen the sun or known anything, yet it finds [x]rest rather than he.
6 Even though he should live a thousand years twice over, yet enjoy[2] no good—do not all
go to the one place?

7 [y]All the toil of man is for his mouth, yet his appetite is not satisfied.[3] 8 For what advantage has the wise man [z]over the fool? And what does the poor man have who knows how
to conduct himself before the living? 9 Better [a]is the sight of the eyes than the wandering
of the appetite: this also is [b]vanity and a striving after wind.

10 Whatever has come to be has [c]already been named, and it is known what man is, and
that he is not able to [d]dispute with one stronger than he. 11 The more words, the more
vanity, and what is the advantage to man? 12 For who knows what is good for man while
he lives the few days of his [e]vain[4] life, which he passes like [f]a shadow? For who can tell
man what will be [g]after him under the sun?

The Contrast of Wisdom and Folly

7 1 [h]A good name is better than precious ointment,
and [i]the day of death than the day of birth.
2 It is better to go to the house of mourning
than to go to the house of feasting,
for this is the end of all mankind,
and the living will [j]lay it to heart.
3 Sorrow is better than laughter,
[k]for by sadness of face the heart is made glad.
4 The heart of the wise is in the house of mourning,
but the heart of fools is in the house of mirth.
5 It is [l]better for a man to hear the rebuke of the wise
than to hear the song of fools.
6 [m]For as the crackling of [n]thorns under a pot,
so is the laughter of the fools;
this also is vanity.[5]
7 Surely [o]oppression drives the wise into madness,
and [p]a bribe corrupts the heart.
8 Better is the end of a thing than its beginning,
and [q]the patient in spirit is better than the proud in spirit.

[1] The Hebrew term *hebel* can refer to a "vapor" or "mere breath"; also verses 4, 9, 11 (see note on 1:2) [2] Or *see* [3] Hebrew *filled* [4] The Hebrew term *hebel* can refer to a "vapor" or "mere breath" (see note on 1:2) [5] The Hebrew term *hebel* can refer to a "vapor" or "mere breath" (see note on 1:2)

6:3–6 In the OT era, long life and numerous children were considered some of the highest of all earthly blessings (e.g., Gen. 15:15; Psalm 127), but a discontented heart will be unsatisfied even with these in excessive measure. Even **a stillborn child**—who does not have the prolonged conscious experience of suffering—**is better off** than such a discontented individual. Since all go to **one place** (i.e., the grave: Eccles. 3:20; 9:10), one is well advised to learn contentment in this life.

6:10–7:24 *Wisdom for Living "Under the Sun."* In the face of "vanity," it is still possible to know and do what is good.

6:10–11 God is the one who has already **named** all things. To "name" something is to exercise authority over it (Gen. 2:19–20). The Preacher thus confesses that God rules over all things, and he points out that it would be foolish for mankind **to dispute** with God's sovereign ordering of the world; to do so would only produce **more words** and **more vanity**.

6:12 For who knows what is good for man? The proverbs that follow (7:1–24) are clustered around the thematic words "good" or "better" (7:1, 2, 3, 5, 8, 10, 11, 14, 18, 20), and they attempt to provide at least a partial answer to this question. From one perspective, even the greatest wisdom teachers cannot give infallible advice based upon an absolutely certain knowledge of **what will be**; nevertheless, the sanctified counsel of the wise is a useful source of guidance for ordinary living.

7:1 A **precious ointment** was a costly luxury in ancient Israel (see Est. 2:12; Ps. 45:8; Amos 6:6; Matt. 26:7). The verses which follow (esp. Eccles. 7:2, 4) indicate that **the day of death** refers not to one's own passing but rather to that of another. Bereavement, while painful, is a more effective prod to growth in spiritual wisdom and maturity than the elation one feels over a newborn child.

7:6 The **crackling of thorns under a pot** refers to the meaningless roar of a fire.

7:7 In this instance, **oppression** refers to "extortion" or "blackmail" (see Lev. 6:4).

9 [r]Be not quick in your spirit to become angry,
[s]for anger lodges in the heart[1] of fools.
10 Say not, "Why were the former days better than these?"
For it is not from wisdom that you ask this.
11 Wisdom is good with an inheritance,
an advantage to those who [t]see the sun.
12 For the protection of wisdom is like [u]the protection of money,
and the advantage of knowledge is that [v]wisdom preserves the life of
him who has it.
13 Consider [w]the work of God:
[x]who can make straight what he has made crooked?

14 [y]In the day of prosperity be joyful, and in the day of adversity consider: God has made the
one as well as the other, [z]so that man may not find out anything that will be after him.
15 In my [a]vain[2] life I have seen everything. There is [b]a righteous man who perishes in his
righteousness, and there is a wicked man who [c]prolongs his life in his evildoing. 16 Be not
overly righteous, and do not [d]make yourself too wise. Why should you destroy yourself?
17 Be not overly wicked, neither be a fool. [e]Why should you die before your time? 18 It is
good that you should take hold of [f]this, and from [g]that [h]withhold not your hand, for the
one who fears God shall come out from both of them.
19 [i]Wisdom gives strength to the wise man more than ten rulers who are in a city.
20 Surely [j]there is not a righteous man on earth who does good and never sins.
21 Do not take to heart all the things that people say, lest you hear [k]your servant cursing
you. 22 Your heart knows that [l]many times you yourself have cursed others.
23 All this I have tested by wisdom. [m]I said, "I will be wise," but it was far from me. 24 That
which has been is far off, and [n]deep, very deep; [o]who can find it out?
25 [p]I turned my heart to know and to search out and to seek wisdom and the scheme of
things, and to know the wickedness of folly and the foolishness that is madness. 26 And I
find something more [q]bitter than death: [r]the woman whose heart is [s]snares and nets, and
whose hands are fetters. He who pleases God escapes her, but [t]the sinner is taken by her.
27 Behold, this is what I found, says [u]the Preacher, while adding one thing to another to find
the scheme of things— 28 which my soul has sought repeatedly, but I have not found. [v]One
man among a thousand I found, but [w]a woman among all these I have not found. 29 See, this
alone I found, that [x]God made man upright, but [y]they have sought out many schemes.

[1] Hebrew *in the bosom* [2] The Hebrew term *hebel* can refer to a "vapor" or "mere breath" (see note on 1:2)

9 [r][Prov. 14:17; 16:32; James 1:19] [s][Eph. 4:26]
11 [t]ch. 6:5; 11:7
12 [u][ch. 10:19] [v]Prov. 3:18
13 [w][ch. 3:11] [x][ch. 1:15; Job 12:14; Isa. 14:27]
14 [y][ch. 3:4, 22; Deut. 28:47] [z][ch. 3:22; 6:12]
15 [a]ch. 6:12; 9:9 [b]See ch. 8:14 [c]ch. 8:12, 13
16 [d][Rom. 12:3]
17 [e][Prov. 10:27]; See Job 22:16
18 [f][ver. 17] [g][ver. 16] [h]ch. 11:6
19 [i]ch. 9:16, 18; Prov. 21:22; 24:5
20 [j]See 1 Kgs. 8:46
21 [k]Prov. 30:10
22 [l][Gal. 6:1]
23 [m][Rom. 1:22]
24 [n][Rom. 11:33] [o]Job 28:12, 20; [1 Tim. 6:16]
25 [p]See ch. 1:17
26 [q]Prov. 5:4 [r]See Prov. 2:16 [s]Prov. 12:12; [Prov. 23:28] [t]Prov. 22:14
27 [u]See ch. 1:1
28 [v]Job 33:23; [ver. 20] [w][1 Kgs. 11:3]
29 [x][Gen. 1:27] [y][Gen. 3:6, 7]

7:11–12 A fool squanders his birthright (cf. Luke 15:11–32), but **wisdom is good with an inheritance** and enables one to make good use of it. Wisdom is similar to money in that both offer the possessor some real **protection** against the misfortunes of life. A point in favor of **wisdom**, however, is that it **preserves the life of him who has it**. As a general rule, living wisely receives God's blessing, including long life, even if it cannot provide eternal life.

7:13 crooked. See note on 1:15.

7:15 a righteous man . . . a wicked man . . . in his evildoing. In the OT, the terms "righteous" and "righteousness" do not refer exclusively to ethical or moral behavior but can also refer to being "right" or "just" in one's cause (e.g., in a legal case; see Deut. 25:1), which appears to be the sense that the Preacher has in mind here. He has observed instances in which a person who was technically in the right still lost his case, while someone who was actually in the wrong won the dispute (cf. Eccles. 8:14).

7:16 Be not overly righteous. The Preacher is not advocating moral laxity (cf. 8:12–13). Bearing in mind that he is using the term "righteous" in the sense of being "right in one's cause" (see note on 7:15), his counsel is a warning against the obsession of always being proved right in an argument or dispute. To insist on this is ultimately self-destructive: people who have to win every argument will eventually alienate everyone around them. See 1 Cor. 6:7 for Paul's advice on this.

7:17–18 Be not overly wicked, neither be a fool. By the same token (cf. note on v. 16), a willingness to suffer wrong, if not tempered with the wisdom to know when to insist on the justice of one's cause, can also lead to self-destruction. One must strike the proper balance between the two principles (v. 18).

7:25–29 *The Heart of the Problem: Sin.* The Preacher has already made numerous references to human sinfulness (3:16–17; 4:1; 5:8; 7:7, 20); this short section provides insight as to how this sorry condition came about in the first place.

7:25 to know the wickedness of folly. See note on 1:17.

7:27 this is what I found . . . the scheme of things. The verb "to find" is a key word in this section (vv. 26, 27, 28, 29) and has the meaning of "find out, figure out, comprehend" (see note on 3:11). As stated earlier (1:13), the Preacher is on a quest to understand all of reality.

7:28–29 One man . . . I found, but a woman . . . I have not found. The term "found" here means "figured out, comprehended by study" (see notes on 3:11 and 7:27). The Preacher is admitting that he is unable to "figure out" (see note on v. 27) the vast majority of people he encounters, whether male or female; even his successes in understanding his own sex are extremely unimpressive (only "one man among a thousand"). The one firm conclusion he is able to draw is **that God made man upright, but they have sought out many schemes**, i.e., they were not content to remain in their state of uprightness but instead rebelled against God (cf. Genesis 3).

Chapter 8
1[z]Prov. 4:8, 9; [Acts 6:15] [a]Prov. 21:29; [Deut. 28:50]
2[b]Ex. 22:11; 2 Sam. 21:7; 1 Kgs. 2:43; [2 Chr. 36:13; Ezek. 17:18]
3[c][ch. 10:4]
4[d]Dan. 4:35; See Job 9:12
6[e]ch. 3:1, 17
7[f][Prov. 24:22] [g]ch. 3:22; 6:12; 9:12; 10:14
8[h][Job 14:5] [i][ch. 3:19; 9:11] [j]See Deut. 20:5-8
9[k][ch. 1:13]
10[l][Neh. 11:1; Matt. 24:15] [m][ch. 9:5; Prov. 10:7]
11[n][Ps. 10:6; 50:21; Isa. 26:10; Rom. 2:4, 5; 2 Pet. 3:9] [o][Esth. 7:5; Acts 5:3]
12[p]ch. 7:15; Isa. 65:20 [q][Deut. 12:25; Isa. 3:10] [r][Ps. 37:11, 18, 19; Prov. 1:33; Matt. 25:34]
13[s]Isa. 3:11 [t]ch. 6:12; See Job 14:2
14[u]ch. 7:15; [Ps. 73:3]; See ch. 2:14 [v][Job 21:7; Ps. 17:9, 10; 73:12; Jer. 12:1]

Keep the King's Command

8

1 Who is like the wise?
  And who knows the interpretation of a thing?
[z]A man's wisdom makes his face shine,
  and [a]the hardness of his face is changed.

2 I say:[1] Keep the king's command, because of [b]God's oath to him.[2] **3** Be not hasty to [c]go
from his presence. Do not take your stand in an evil cause, for he does whatever he pleases.
4 For the word of the king is supreme, and [d]who may say to him, "What are you doing?"
5 Whoever keeps a command will know no evil thing, and the wise heart will know the
proper time and the just way. **6** For there is a time and a way [e]for everything, although
man's trouble[3] lies heavy on him. **7** For he [f]does not know what is to be, for [g]who can tell
him how it will be? **8** No man has power to [h]retain the spirit, [i]or power over the day of
death. There is no [j]discharge from war, nor will wickedness deliver those who are given
to it. **9** [k]All this I observed while applying my heart to all that is done under the sun, when
man had power over man to his hurt.

Those Who Fear God Will Do Well

10 Then I saw the wicked buried. They used to go in and out of [l]the holy place and were
[m]praised[4] in the city where they had done such things. This also is vanity.[5] **11** Because [n]the
sentence against an evil deed is not executed speedily, [o]the heart of the children of man
is fully set to do evil. **12** Though a sinner does evil a hundred times and [p]prolongs his life,
yet I know that [q]it will be well with [r]those who fear God, because they fear before him.
13 But it will [s]not be well with the wicked, neither will he prolong his days like [t]a shadow,
because he does not fear before God.

Man Cannot Know God's Ways

14 There is a vanity that takes place on earth, that there are righteous people [u]to whom it
happens according to the deeds of the wicked, and there are wicked people [v]to whom it happens according to the deeds of the righteous. I said that this also is vanity. **15** And I commend

[1] Hebrew lacks *say* [2] Or *because of your oath to God* [3] Or *evil* [4] Some Hebrew manuscripts, Septuagint, Vulgate; most Hebrew manuscripts *forgotten*
[5] The Hebrew term *hebel* can refer to a "vapor" or "mere breath"; also twice in verse 14 (see note on 1:2)

8:1–12:7 *More on Life "Under the Sun."* The Preacher continues his observations on life in a fallen world, and gives appropriate counsel for living wisely.

8:1–9 *Wisdom in Dealing with Foolish Authorities.* Kings are sinners like the rest of mankind (7:20, 29) and they abuse their authority (8:9). The nearly unlimited power they possessed in the ancient world meant that those who had to deal directly with them required exceptional wisdom.

8:1 Who is like . . . and who knows . . . ? The questions are rhetorical, not in the sense of denying that such wise men exist but in indicating that true wisdom is a rare commodity (Job 28:12, 20; Prov. 2:1–4). For the one who possesses such **wisdom**, however, it **makes his face shine**—it is as evident to others as if it were "written all over his face," just as a fool's stupidity is obvious to others (Eccles. 10:3).

8:2 Keep the king's command. Lit., "keep the mouth of the king"; the verb "keep" in this instance indicates not so much "obeying" as "protecting, guarding, keeping watch over" (cf. Prov. 21:23; Mic. 7:5). The Preacher is reminding the king's counselor that he is obligated to help restrain the king from making foolish decisions on account of his "oath to God" (ESV footnote), i.e., his taking an oath of service to the king in God's name (cf. Ex. 22:11; 2 Sam. 21:7; 1 Kings 2:43).

8:3 In a fallen world, there are foolish kings who issue imprudent commands, but that does not mean that a counselor is free to disassociate himself completely from his master. At the same time, however, he ought not to exercise such unthinking obedience to the king that he becomes implicated **in an evil cause**.

8:4–6 Given the nearly absolute authority of monarchs in the ancient world, it would take a great deal of courage for someone to question the wisdom of the king's decision, i.e., to **say to him, "What are you doing?"** The wise counselor, however, will find **the proper time and the just way** for doing so.

8:7–8 It is a risky proposition to offer correction to the king, and one cannot be absolutely certain ahead of time how it will be received (cf. Prov. 13:1). But, lest the counselor be intimidated into silent submission, he should remember that **no man**—not even the king—**has power to retain the spirit, or power over the day of death**, and that wickedness will surely be judged.

8:10–13 *The Importance of Fearing God.* See Introduction: Key Themes. The Preacher has already pointed out that people do not always get what they deserve in this life (3:16; 4:1; 5:8), and here he notes that the wicked—who do not fear God—apparently do not get punished for their sins but instead live long lives (8:12) and receive the treatment due to the righteous, such as an honorable burial (v. 11). While God undoubtedly has a reason for allowing this to happen, he has not revealed it to mankind; hence it is an inexplicable **vanity** (v. 10). One ought not to conclude from this, however, that it makes no difference whether or not one fears God: the Preacher insists that **it will be well with those who fear God** and that **it will not be well with the wicked**. The Preacher trusts divine revelation to be more reliable than his own empirical observation and knows that, ultimately, justice will be done (vv. 12–13; see also 3:17).

8:14–17 *The Limits of Human Knowledge.* The puzzling situation described in vv. 10–13 leads the Preacher to draw a larger conclusion regarding the limits of human understanding.

8:14–15 Not only is it an inexplicable **vanity** that the wicked appear to escape judgment and receive blessings (vv. 10–13), there is also no satisfying explanation for the fact that the righteous receive the treatment due to the wicked. Since this mystery cannot be completely solved, one should not become so obsessed with attempting to unravel it that he neglects to enjoy God's gifts.

joy, for man [w]has nothing better under the sun but to [x]eat and drink and be joyful, for
this will go with him in his toil through the days of his life that God has given him under
the sun.
16 When I applied my heart to know wisdom, and to see [y]the business that is done on
earth, how neither [z]day nor night do one's eyes see sleep, 17 then I saw all the work of God,
that [a]man cannot find out the work that is done under the sun. However much man may
toil in seeking, he will not find it out. Even though a wise man claims to know, [b]he cannot find it out.

Death Comes to All

9 But all this I laid to heart, examining it all, [c]how the righteous and the wise and their
deeds are [d]in the hand of God. Whether it is love or hate, man does not know; both are
before him. 2 [e]It is the same for all, since [f]the same event happens to the righteous and the
wicked, to the good and the evil,[1] to the clean and the unclean, to him who sacrifices and
him who does not sacrifice. As the good one is, so is the sinner, and he who [g]swears is as he
who shuns an oath. 3 This is an evil in all that is done under the sun, that [e]the same event
happens to all. Also, the hearts of the children of man are full of evil, and [h]madness is in
their hearts while they live, and after that they go to the dead. 4 But he who is joined with
all the living has hope, for a living dog is better than a dead lion. 5 For the living know that
they will die, but [i]the dead know nothing, and they have no more reward, for [j]the memory
of them is forgotten. 6 Their love and their hate and their envy have already perished, and
forever they have no more share in all that is done under the sun.

Enjoy Life with the One You Love

7 Go, [k]eat your bread with joy, and drink your wine with a merry heart, for God has
already approved what you do.
8 [l]Let your garments be always white. Let not [m]oil be lacking on your head.
9 Enjoy life with the wife whom you love, all the days of your [n]vain[2] life that he has given
you under the sun, because that is your [o]portion in life and in your toil at which you toil
under the sun. 10 Whatever your hand finds to do, [p]do it with your might,[3] [q]for there is no
work or thought or knowledge or wisdom in Sheol, to which you are going.

Wisdom Better than Folly

11 [r]Again I saw that under the sun [s]the race is not to the swift, nor [t]the battle to the strong,
nor bread to the wise, nor riches to the intelligent, nor favor to those with knowledge, but
time and [u]chance [v]happen to them all. 12 For man [w]does not know his time. Like fish that
are taken in an evil net, and [x]like birds that are caught in a snare, so the children of man
are [y]snared at an evil time, when it suddenly falls upon them.
13 I have also seen this example of wisdom under the sun, and it seemed great to me.
14 There was a little city with few men in it, and a great king came against it and besieged
it, building great siegeworks against it. 15 But there was found in it [z]a poor, wise man, and
he by his [a]wisdom delivered the city. Yet no one remembered that poor man. 16 But I say

15 [w]See ch. 2:24 [x]1 Kgs. 4:20
16 [y]ch. 1:13; 3:10 [z][Ps. 127:2]
17 [a][Prov. 25:2]; See ch. 3:11 [b][Ps. 73:16]

Chapter 9

1 [c][ch. 8:14] [d]Deut. 33:3
2 [e]Job 9:22 [f]See ch. 2:14 [g]Zech. 5:3; [Mal. 3:5]
3 [e][See ver. 2 above] [h]ch. 1:17
5 [i]Job 14:21 [j]ch. 1:11; 8:10; Ps. 31:12; 88:5, 12; Isa. 26:14
7 [k]See ch. 2:24
8 [l][Rev. 3:4] [m]Ps. 23:5
9 [n]ch. 6:12; 7:15 [o]See ch. 2:10
10 [p]Rom. 12:11; Col. 3:23 [q][ver. 5]
11 [r]ch. 4:1, 7 [s]Amos 2:14, 15; [Rom. 9:16] [t][2 Chr. 20:15; Jer. 9:23] [u][1 Kgs. 22:34] [v]See ch. 2:14
12 [w][ch. 8:7] [x]Prov. 7:23 [y][Prov. 29:6; Ezek. 12:13; Hos. 7:12; Luke 21:34, 35; 1 Thess. 5:3]
15 [z][ch. 4:13] [a]ver. 18; [2 Sam. 20:22]

[1] Septuagint, Syriac, Vulgate; Hebrew lacks *and the evil* [2] The Hebrew term *hebel* can refer to a "vapor" or "mere breath" (see note on 1:2) [3] Or *finds to do with your might, do it*

8:17 man cannot find out the work that is done under the sun. True wisdom includes the humility to admit that man cannot fully "figure out" (see note on 3:11) all of reality in a fallen world.

9:1–6 *The Unpredictability of Life and Certainty of Death.* No one knows whether a person's life in this world will be pleasant or difficult, regardless of whether the person is righteous or wicked. Nevertheless, in spite of this apparent "randomness," one can be assured that the godly person is **in the hand of God** (v. 1). However, one unpleasant reality is certain for everyone: death (v. 3; cf. 2:14–17). No matter how difficult or humble a person's circumstances may be, they are to be preferred to dying, because **a living dog is better than a dead lion.** (Here the "dog" is seen as an unclean scavenger, while the "lion" is a powerful predator.)

9:7–10 *Find Enjoyment as Circumstances Allow.* Life is superior to death (vv. 4–6), but there is no predicting whether one's life in this world will be hard or easy (vv. 1–3). Therefore, one is advised to enjoy life when circumstances are conducive for it. When godly people do so, they will acknowledge that it is due to God's "approval" or "favor" (v. 7; cf. 2:24–26; 3:13; 5:19–20).

9:11–12 *More on the Unpredictability of Life.* While not denying God's sovereign ordering of human affairs (e.g., 3:1–15; 7:14), the Preacher admits that from a finite, fallible human perspective, many things that occur in the world have the appearance of being the result of pure **chance** (cf. 9:1–6).

9:13–11:6 *The Paths of Wisdom and Foolishness.* The following section is somewhat loosely organized, but two contrasting key themes that appear throughout are "wisdom" (9:13, 15–18; 10:1–2, 10, 12) and "folly" (9:17; 10:1–3, 6, 12–15).

9:13–18 *The Power of Wisdom.* Wisdom can achieve much good and is therefore worth pursuing, and yet its benefits can be undone by evil.

9:13–16 The Preacher has observed an instance of wisdom's ability to snatch a remarkable victory from the jaws of defeat. Even when such wisdom is forgotten or **despised** by others, it is still to be prized over earthly **might**.

16[b]See ch. 7:19 [c][Mark 6:2, 3]
17[d]ch. 4:6
18[e]ver. 16 [f][Josh. 7:1]
Chapter 10
1[g]Ex. 30:25
2[h][ch. 2:14]
3[i][Prov. 13:16; 18:2]
4[j][ch. 8:3] [k][1 Sam. 25:24, 32, 33]; See Prov. 25:15
5[l]ch. 5:6
6[m][Esth. 3:1; Prov. 28:12; 29:2]
7[n]Prov. 19:10; [Prov. 30:22] [o][Esth. 6:8]
8[p]See Ps. 7:15 [q]Amos 5:19
9[r][1 Chr. 22:2] [s][Deut. 19:5]
11[t][Jer. 8:17]
12[u]Prov. 10:32; 22:11; [Luke 4:22] [v]See Prov. 18:7
14[w]See Prov. 15:2 [x]See ch. 3:22
15[y][Isa. 35:8]
16[z]Isa. 3:4, 12; [2 Chr. 13:7]
17[a][Prov. 31:4; Isa. 5:11]

that [b]wisdom is better than might, though [c]the poor man's wisdom is despised and his words are not heard.

17 The words of the wise heard in [d]quiet are better than the shouting of a ruler among
fools. 18 [e]Wisdom is better than weapons of war, but [f]one sinner destroys much good.

10

1 Dead flies make [g]the perfumer's ointment give off a stench;
so a little folly outweighs wisdom and honor.
2 [h]A wise man's heart inclines him to the right,
but a fool's heart to the left.
3 Even when the fool walks on the road, he lacks sense,
and he [i]says to everyone that he is a fool.
4 If the anger of the ruler rises against you, [j]do not leave your place,
[k]for calmness[1] will lay great offenses to rest.

5 There is an evil that I have seen under the sun, as it were [l]an error proceeding from
the ruler: 6 [m]folly is set in many high places, and the rich sit in a low place. 7 [n]I have seen
slaves [o]on horses, and princes walking on the ground like slaves.

8 He who [p]digs a pit will fall into it,
and [q]a serpent will bite him who breaks through a wall.
9 [r]He who quarries stones is hurt by them,
and he who [s]splits logs is endangered by them.
10 If the iron is blunt, and one does not sharpen the edge,
he must use more strength,
but wisdom helps one to succeed.[2]
11 If the serpent bites before it is [t]charmed,
there is no advantage to the charmer.

12 The words of a wise man's mouth [u]win him favor,[3]
but [v]the lips of a fool consume him.
13 The beginning of the words of his mouth is foolishness,
and the end of his talk is evil madness.
14 [w]A fool multiplies words,
though no man knows what is to be,
and who can tell him [x]what will be after him?
15 The toil of a fool wearies him,
for he does not know [y]the way to the city.
16 [z]Woe to you, O land, when your king is a child,
and your princes feast in the morning!
17 Happy are you, O land, when your king is the son of the nobility,
and your princes feast at the proper time,
for strength, and not for [a]drunkenness!

[1] Hebrew *healing* [2] Or *wisdom is an advantage for success* [3] Or *are gracious*

9:17–18 The Preacher balances his praise of wisdom's power and effectiveness (vv. 13–16) by observing that, just as one wise man can successfully overcome the worst odds, so also **one sinner destroys much good**.

10:1–20 *Proverbs Concerning Wisdom and Foolishness.* Observations and advice on everyday life.

10:2 right . . . left. The "right hand" is often associated with strength and blessing in the OT (e.g., Ex. 15:6, 12; Ps. 16:11; 17:7; Isa. 41:10, etc.), and the Preacher is either referring to the "left hand" with a correspondingly negative connotation (Gen. 48:14; Judg. 3:15) or else is simply stating that wisdom and foolishness invariably reveal themselves in one's behavior (cf. Eccles. 10:3; see also the note on 8:1).

10:6–7 The Preacher has observed **folly**, i.e., a foolish person, placed in a position of authority where **rich** people and **princes** belong. He is aware that the poor can also possess wisdom (4:13–14; 9:15–16) and that those from the wealthy ruling classes are not immune to corruption (5:8–12; 10:16–17; cf. Luke 6:24; James 2:6; 5:1). Nevertheless, the Bible often associates wealth with prudent, godly living (Prov. 10:4) and poverty with foolishness (Prov. 6:11; 13:18); moreover, the wealth of the nobleman affords him greater opportunity to pursue learning and wisdom. Thus, the Preacher is surprised by the situation described here.

10:8, 12 The various calamities described in vv. 8–11 are all accidental in nature, indicating that the one **who digs a pit** is not necessarily doing so with malicious intent (contrast Ps. 7:15; 57:6; Prov. 26:27; 28:10). The point is simply that fools destroy themselves by their own foolishness.

10:14 The fact that **no man knows what is to be** does not prevent a **fool** from multiplying **words** about it, i.e., making many groundless predictions.

10:15 A fool's **toil** in the fields is more tiring than others' because he is ignorant of important fundamental truths that would make his work easier, such as how to get back **to the city**.

18 Through sloth the roof sinks in,
and through indolence the house leaks.
19 Bread is made for laughter,
and [b]wine gladdens life,
and [c]money answers everything.
20 Even in your thoughts, [d]do not curse the king,
nor in your [e]bedroom curse the rich,
for a bird of the air will carry your voice,
or some winged creature tell the matter.

Cast Your Bread upon the Waters

11 1 [f]Cast your bread upon the waters,
[g]for you will find it after many days.
2 [h]Give a portion to [i]seven, or even to eight,
[j]for you know not what disaster may happen on earth.
3 If the clouds are full of rain,
they empty themselves on the earth,
and if a tree falls to the south or to the north,
in the place where the tree falls, there it will lie.
4 He who observes the wind will not sow,
and he who regards the clouds will not reap.

5 As you do not know the way [k]the spirit comes to [l]the bones in the womb[1] of a woman
with child, so you do not know the work of God who makes everything.
6 In the morning sow your seed, and at evening [m]withhold not your hand, for you do
not know which will prosper, this or that, or whether both alike will be good.
7 Light is sweet, and it is pleasant for the eyes to [n]see the sun.
8 So if a person lives many years, let him rejoice in them all; but let him remember [o]that
the days of darkness will be many. All that comes is [p]vanity.[2]
9 [q]Rejoice, O young man, in your youth, and let your heart cheer you in the days of your
youth. [r]Walk in the ways of your heart and [s]the sight of your eyes. But know that for all
these things [t]God will bring you into judgment.
10 Remove vexation from your heart, and [u]put away pain[3] from your body, for youth
and the dawn of life are vanity.

Remember Your Creator in Your Youth

12 Remember also your Creator in [v]the days of your youth, before [w]the evil days come
and the years draw near of which [x]you will say, "I have no pleasure in them"; 2 before
[y]the sun and the light and the moon and the stars are darkened and the clouds return after

[1] Some Hebrew manuscripts, Targum; most Hebrew manuscripts *As you do not know the way of the wind, or how the bones grow in the womb* [2] The Hebrew term *hebel* can refer to a "vapor" or "mere breath"; also verse 10 (see note on 1:2) [3] Or *evil*

19 [b]See Ps. 104:15 [c][ch. 7:12]
20 [d]Ex. 22:28 [e]See 2 Kgs. 6:12; Luke 12:3

Chapter 11

1 [f][Isa. 32:20] [g][Deut. 15:10; Prov. 19:17; Matt. 10:42; Luke 14:14; 2 Cor. 9:8; Gal. 6:9, 10; Heb. 6:10]
2 [h][Ps. 112:9; Matt. 5:42; Luke 6:30; 1 Tim. 6:18, 19] [i]Mic. 5:5; See Job 5:19; Prov. 6:16 [j][Luke 16:9; Eph. 5:16]
5 [k][ch. 1:6; John 3:8] [l]See Ps. 139:13-16
6 [m]ch. 7:18
7 [n]ch. 6:5; 7:11
8 [o][ch. 12:1, 2] [p]ch. 2:23; See ch. 1:2
9 [q][ch. 2:10; 9:7] [r][Num. 15:39; Job 31:7] [s]ch. 6:9 [t]See ch. 12:14
10 [u]2 Cor. 7:1; 2 Tim. 2:22

Chapter 12

1 [v][Lam. 3:27] [w][ch. 11:8] [x][2 Sam. 19:35]
2 [y][Job 3:9; Isa. 5:30; Ezek. 32:7, 8]

10:19 Bread . . . wine . . . money. The Preacher comments favorably here on each of these, but he concludes by saying that money **answers everything**: i.e., money is freely exchangeable and has the ability to exert a powerful influence over the course of affairs to produce the result one desires. Money, however, can never satisfy (cf. 5:10).

11:1–6 *Wise Practices in Light of the Unpredictability of Life.* Since life in a fallen world is largely unpredictable (vv. 2, 6; see also 9:1, 11; 10:14), this section gives wise counsel in such a world.

11:1 To **cast . . . bread upon the waters** is a metaphor without any contemporary parallels, so interpreters are uncertain about its meaning. Three suggestions are most common: (1) It refers to maritime commerce. (2) It refers to taking steps to spread out one's financial resources in multiple directions. (3) In older Jewish and Christian interpretation, it was taken to refer to giving to the poor, in which case finding it again represents others being kind in return.

11:2 Rather than speculating about such uncertainties (see note on vv. 1–6), it is financially more prudent to explore multiple avenues for making one's living and investing one's resources (vv. 2, 6), which could involve giving a "portion" or "compensation" to several different areas (**seven, or even to eight**), because such diversification gives protection against unforeseen **disaster** in one or two of the areas.

11:4 Too much time spent trying to "read the skies" will only distract one from the task at hand, and those who always wait for the "perfect" time to begin a project **will not sow** and **will not reap**.

11:5 the way the spirit comes to the bones in the womb. See note on 3:21. There is variation in the Hebrew manuscripts at this point (see ESV footnote).

11:7–12:7 *Aging and the "Vanity" of Mortal Life.* Being confronted with others' mortality causes one to grow in spiritual wisdom (e.g., 7:1–4); in this section, the Preacher urges his readers to embrace wisdom in view of their own mortality.

11:7–8 Light . . . darkness refers to the contrast between life and death.

11:9 Proper enjoyment of life is possible only within the moral boundaries established by God, who will evaluate all human deeds according to his righteous **judgment** (cf. 12:13–14).

11:10 Remove vexation . . . put away pain. Whatever woes or ailments one has, one should not dwell on them excessively.

12:1 In this context, **evil days** refers not to the consequences of wicked

the rain, 3 in the day when the keepers of the house tremble, and the strong men are bent,
and the grinders cease because they are few, and [z]those who look through the windows
are dimmed, 4 and [a]the doors on the street are shut—when [b]the sound of the grinding is
low, and one rises up at the sound of a bird, and all [c]the daughters of song are brought
low— 5 they are afraid also of what is high, and [d]terrors are in the way; the almond tree
blossoms, the grasshopper drags itself along,[1] and desire fails, because man is going to
his [e]eternal [f]home, and the [g]mourners go about the streets— 6 before the silver cord is
snapped, or [h]the golden bowl is broken, or the pitcher is [i]shattered at the fountain, or the
wheel broken at the cistern, 7 and [j]the dust returns to the earth as it was, and [k]the spirit
returns to God [l]who gave it. 8 [m]Vanity[2] of vanities, says [n]the Preacher; all is vanity.

Fear God and Keep His Commandments

9 Besides being wise, [n]the Preacher also taught the people knowledge, weighing and
studying and arranging [o]many proverbs with great care. 10 [n]The Preacher sought to find
words of delight, and uprightly he wrote words of truth.
11 [p]The words of the wise are like goads, and like [q]nails firmly fixed are the collected
sayings; they are [r]given by [s]one Shepherd. 12 My son, beware of anything beyond these. Of
making [u]many books there is no end, and [v]much study is a weariness of the flesh.
13 The end of the matter; all has been heard. [w]Fear God and keep his commandments,
for this is the whole duty of man.[3] 14 For [x]God will bring every deed into judgment, with[4]
every secret thing, whether good or evil.

[1] Or *is a burden* [2] The Hebrew term *hebel* can refer to a "vapor" or "mere breath" (three times in this verse); see note on 1:2 [3] Or *the duty of all mankind* [4] Or *into the judgment on*

3 [z][Gen. 27:1; 48:10; 1 Sam. 3:2]
4 [a][Ps. 141:3] [b][Jer. 25:10; Rev. 18:22] [c][ch. 2:8]
5 [d][Prov. 26:13] [e][Ps. 143:3] [f][Job 17:13; 30:23; Isa. 14:18] [g][2 Chr. 35:25; Jer. 9:17; Matt. 9:23]
6 [h][Zech. 4:2, 3] [i][Isa. 30:14]
7 [j]Ps. 90:3; 103:14; See ch. 3:20; Job 34:15 [k][ch. 3:21] [l][Job 34:14; Isa. 57:16; Zech. 12:1]; See Gen. 2:7
8 [m]ch. 1:2 [n]See ch. 1:1
9 [n][See ver. 8 above] [o]See Prov. 1:1
10 [n][See ver. 8 above]
11 [p]Prov. 22:17 [q]Ezra 9:8; Isa. 22:23 [r]Prov. 1:6; 2:6 [s]Ps. 80:1; Ezek. 34:23; John 10:11, 16
12 [u][1 Kgs. 4:32, 33] [v][ch. 1:18]
13 [w]ch. 5:7; Deut. 6:2; 10:12
14 [x]ch. 11:9; Job 19:29; Matt. 12:36; Acts 17:31; Rom. 2:16; 14:10, 12; 1 Cor. 4:5; [ch. 3:15, 17; Gen. 18:25; Ps. 58:11]

living but rather to the unpleasantness of physical deterioration in old age (see vv. 2–7).

12:2–7 This section contains a metaphorical description of the aging process and death. In many instances the specific metaphor is clear (e.g., in v. 3 the **grinders** refer to teeth), though some are more difficult to interpret. The common link between most of the images used in v. 6 (**bowl . . . pitcher . . . wheel broken at the cistern**) appears to be that they are water receptacles: since water is a symbol of life (2 Sam. 14:14; John 4:14; Rev. 21:6; 22:1, 17), the destruction of these various items indicates the moment when mortal life ceases **and the spirit returns to God who gave it** (see note on Eccles. 3:21).

12:8–14 *Final Conclusion and Epilogue.* The Preacher restates his claim that all is "vanity" (v. 8; cf. 1:2). The epilogue affirms the wisdom of the Preacher by pointing out the care which he took in writing (12:9–10), summons the reader to pay careful attention to the words of the wise (vv. 11–12), and summarizes the overall message of the book (vv. 13–14).

12:11 The words of the wise are like goads, i.e., they help guide one along the proper path. (A "goad" is a long, pointed stick used for prodding and guiding oxen while plowing.) Moreover, the words of the wise provide moral and intellectual stability **like nails firmly fixed**. Ultimately, such wisdom is **given by one Shepherd**, God (see Introduction: Author, Title, and Date).

12:13–14 The Preacher has already pointed out the need to **fear God** (see the notes on 3:14 and 5:7) and to **keep his commandments** (cf. 5:4–6; 7:17–18). The **whole duty of man** thus involves genuine faith in God, as well as works, which are the inevitable result of true faith (cf. James 2:14, 17, 26). **God will bring every deed into judgment** (cf. Eccles. 11:9), thus the importance of obeying his commands.

INTRODUCTION TO

THE SONG OF SOLOMON

Author and Date

The questions of who wrote the Song of Solomon, when it was written, how to read it properly, and what it means as part of Scripture are intertwined, and have occasioned many disagreements.

Jews and Christians have traditionally taken 1:1 ("The Song of Songs, which is Solomon's") to mean that Solomon, the son and successor to David, wrote the entire Song of Solomon, pointing to 1 Kings 4:32 ("his songs were 1,005") for evidence of Solomon's authorial work. However, there are several reasons to hesitate on that matter. First, Song of Solomon 1:1 is grammatically ambiguous: it need not mean that Solomon wrote the Song of Solomon, only that it was written in his honor. Second, what is known of Solomon himself from 1 Kings raises problems with the suggestion that Solomon was the author. For example, 1 Kings 2 gives a concise summary of how Solomon's kingdom was established (cf. 1 Kings 2:46), which is followed immediately by the statement in 1 Kings 3:1 that "Solomon made a marriage alliance with Pharaoh king of Egypt." Pharaoh's daughter, however, could not have been the country girl (a Shulammite) who is the heroine of the Song of Solomon (though some hold that Solomon might have married the Shulammite before he married Pharaoh's daughter). Likewise, Solomon's full harem (1 Kings 11:1–8) makes him a very bad example of married love for Israel (though some have replied that the Song of Solomon reflects Solomon's wisdom that came from his chastened perspective as he reflected on his own life). Third, the book mentions Solomon (Song 1:5; 3:7, 9, 11; 8:11–12), but generally as a distant, even idealized figure.

If it is not entirely certain that Solomon wrote the book, one can still argue that the book was written during Solomon's reign (971–931 B.C.). The book mentions him and seems to assume his glorious reign as a known fact. At the same time, the heroine is a young Shulammite woman (6:13); most take this to mean that she comes from the village of Shunem (Josh. 19:18; 2 Kings 4:8), which is in the tribal inheritance of Issachar. Furthermore, the town of Tirzah is mentioned along with Jerusalem in comparisons of beauty (Song 6:4). The towns of Shunem and Tirzah were located in what became the northern kingdom. These features make it likely that the book comes from the time before Israel was divided into the northern and southern kingdoms, which took place just after Solomon's death (931 B.C.).

Thus, the book was probably written sometime between c. 960 B.C. (when Solomon's reign was well established) and 931, perhaps under Solomon's oversight.

Theme, Title, and Interpretation

The Song of Solomon, or Song of Songs (1:1), contains beautiful and sensuous poetry expressing romantic love between a young man (a shepherd, 1:7) and a young woman (a shepherdess, 1:8) in ancient Israel. On this point there is general agreement; but agreement ends once the discussion moves to *how* the Song of Solomon works to convey its theme. The Song of Solomon has in fact been subject to a broader range of interpretation probably than any other book in the Bible. Thus the Song of Solomon was first understood by early Jewish interpreters as an allegory of God's love for Israel; and then, through many centuries of Christian interpretation, as primarily an allegory of Christ's love for the church, or as Christ's love for the soul. In contrast to this, most Christian interpreters since the nineteenth century have understood the Song of Solomon as a beautifully crafted love poem describing either: (1) the relationship between King Solomon and his Shulammite bride, or (2) the relationship between a simple shepherd and the Shulammite shepherdess, or (3) a three-character relationship involving Solomon, a shepherd boy, and the Shulammite shepherdess. Still many others, since the beginning of the twentieth century, have understood the Song of Solomon as simply a collection of sensuous love poems on a common theme, rather than the unfolding of a single poetic love story. Given this wide range of interpretative diversity, it has seemed best in these notes to focus mainly on a single cohesive interpretation of the Song of Solomon, while at the same time acknowledging that other interpretations are also commonly held among Bible-believing Christian interpreters (see Alternative Interpretations).

Reading the Song of Solomon. These notes recognize that one needs a strategy for reading this book, and to follow one reading means that one does not follow others. The issue is especially acute in the Song of Solomon: the book reads very differently under the different reading strategies that scholars have offered, and there is no clear consensus among them as to which is the right one. The approach taken in these notes, then, is to show why one particular strategy commends itself, and to mention briefly some other common strategies.

One may organize the interpretative disagreements among the scholars around the questions of coherence, characters, and consummation.

Coherence: Is there a single plot line from beginning to end? Traditional interpretations have said yes, the plot describes the love between the shepherd and his betrothed. Starting in the twentieth century, however, it became common for some scholars to deny that there is a coherent story, understanding the Song of Solomon as a collection of love songs. By this scheme, the title of the book means that it is a song composed of multiple songs. The commentary here, however, will argue that there is indeed coherence: first, because one can follow the story of a romantic love from the initial longing right through to the marital enjoyment; and second, because the characters have consistent patterns in how they speak to and about one another. Hence, it is better to see the title "Song of Songs" (Song 1:1) as describing this as the best of songs (just as "King of kings and Lord of lords" refers to the best king and lord), rather than as a collection.

Characters: How many are there, and who are they? In the Song of Solomon there are four main characters: a young woman (*SHE* in the ESV headings); the shepherd boy whom she loves (*HE*); King Solomon; and a chorus-like group (*OTHERS*). (As the ESV footnote at 1:2 indicates, it is generally possible to identify the speakers and addressees based on the gender [masculine or feminine] and number [singular or plural] of the Hebrew words.) Traditional interpretations have seen Solomon and the shepherd boy as the same person, but in light of 1 Kings 3:1 and the way that the rest of 1 Kings portrays Solomon, this assumption seems to raise significant difficulties (see Author and Date).

Consummation: When does the couple engage in sexual relations? Traditional readings have seen the couple's love leading to marriage, and only after that to sexual relations, in accord with biblical standards. Thus traditional readings have understood the wedding procession and wedding day (cf. Song 3:11) to be described in 3:6 through 4:16a, with the sexual consummation of the marriage being reflected in 4:16b and 5:1. However, some studies now suggest that the Song of Solomon is simply a collection of love songs that do not address the question of marriage, and that sexual relations are implied at a number of places in the Song of Solomon. In contrast to the collection interpretation, the understanding represented in the following notes views all of 3:1–6:3 as a dream in anticipation of the marriage and its consummation. Therefore, on this understanding, 5:2–8 is part of the dream ("I slept, but my heart was awake," 5:2), and chapter 7 is an eager anticipation of the enjoyment the couple will have once they are married (in ch. 8). In any case, the fact that the Song of Solomon is in the canon of Scripture, and the fact that it harmonizes with Proverbs 5:15–19 in commending sexual delight within marriage, lends further support to the conclusion that the consummation occurs only after the couple is married. The reading adopted in these notes, then, is that the actual marital consummation is reflected in Song of Solomon 8:5. This is supported by the consistent refrain urging restraint—i.e., not to "stir up or *awaken* love until it pleases" (cf. 2:7; 3:5; 8:4). Thus, immediately following the last occurrence of the refrain (see 8:4), in 8:5 the woman declares, "Under the apple tree I *awakened* you"—which is the only place where she is said to have (sexually) awakened her lover.

Purpose, Occasion, and Background

As has been indicated, it is preferable to read the Song of Solomon as a single literary whole (rather than a collection of love poems) telling the story of two betrothed Israelites who look forward to their marriage and the pleasure of their union.

It is common to group the Song of Solomon with the Wisdom Literature of the Bible (see Introduction to the Poetic and Wisdom Literature, pp. 865–868), and this finds support in the connection with Solomon (see Author and Date) and in the parallels with Proverbs 5:15–19 (see Theme, Title, and Interpretation). Like other Wisdom Literature, the Song of Solomon assumes that the covenant God of Israel ("the LORD,"

Song 8:6) is the one true God, Maker of heaven and earth. The purpose of the redemptive covenants is to restore fallen, damaged creatures (mankind) to the proper functioning of their humanity. Therefore obedience to the Lord's commands is the right way to enjoy the world God made, and it also displays to the rest of the world how refreshingly attractive it is to know the true God. The picture of the two lovers in the Song of Solomon is an ideal one, as are the character portraits in Proverbs: the picture provides the pattern into which God wishes to shape his faithful people, which is also the pattern toward which they will freely give themselves to be shaped. Indeed, one function of wisdom literature is to make that pattern attractive, as the Song of Solomon does in full measure.

Key Themes

1. God's covenant, which commands sexual purity, provides just the right framework (marriage) within which his people may properly enjoy the gift of sexual intimacy (cf. Gen. 2:23–24). Thus God's people honor him and commend him to the world when they demonstrate with their lives that obedience in such matters brings genuine delight.

2. Marriage is a gift of God, and is to be founded on loyalty and commitment (see Gen. 2:24, "hold fast"), which allows delight to flourish. As such, it is a fitting image for God's relationship with his people, in both the OT and the NT.

History of Salvation Summary

The fall of mankind damaged every aspect of human lives, and God's work of redemption aims to restore every aspect to its proper functioning. God's goal is that romantic love, with all its potential pain and degradation, should be an arena of enjoyment for his redeemed people. (For an explanation of the "History of Salvation," see the Overview of the Bible, pp. 23–26. See also History of Salvation in the Old Testament: Preparing the Way for Christ, pp. 2635–2661.)

Literary Features and Structure

The best label that can be assigned to the book is *love poetry*, in which the lovers are shepherd and shepherdess and the setting is a flowery and fruitful rural landscape (of which a vineyard is the prime example). If a love poem celebrates the occasion of a specific wedding, it is called an *epithalamion*, and that is what takes place here.

The Song of Solomon is most remembered for its extravagant comparisons—for example, the woman is compared to a horse in Pharaoh's court (1:9), and her hair to a flock of goats (4:1). The conventions within which the ancient poet wrote yield these ground rules for interpreting the comparisons: (1) the primary correspondence is not visual, and often there is no visual correspondence at all; (2) the comparisons are figurative rather than literal; (3) what the beloved has in common with what he or she is compared to is a certain *quality*—usually the quality of excellence, or of being the best of its kind; and (4) the carryover is the *value* of the two things that are compared (in 1:9, e.g., the woman is like a mare among Pharaoh's chariots in being the best that it is possible to be).

The author has presented the Song of Solomon as a series of exchanges, mostly between the shepherdess and the shepherd, with the chorus-like "others" sprinkled in. These others usually pick up items from the lovers' speeches and urge the two forward in love. There is also a refrain, "I adjure you, O daughters of Jerusalem, . . . that you not stir up or awaken love until it pleases" (2:7; 3:5; 8:4; variation in 5:8), spoken by the shepherdess, which is understood as her urging the other women not to push this love too fast, in order to let it reach its consummation at the right time (the marriage bed, which seems to begin in 8:5).

According to the reading followed here, the middle section of the book (3:1–6:3) describes the shepherdess's dream, anticipating the consummation of their love. This is suggested by 3:1 ("On my bed by night I sought him whom my soul loves") and 5:2 ("I slept, but my heart was awake"). The content is what one expects in such a dream: sexual longings, fears of loss, nightmarish scenes (5:7), and an imaginative transformation of the beloved into a Solomon figure (3:6–11). The dream expresses the eager erotic desires that the young man and woman have for each other; within the context of biblical morality, this longing is a part of God's good gift, looking forward to the consummation of their love.

The lovers speak in different ways, reflecting the difference between how a man and a woman experience being in love. The man's speech focuses entirely on the woman: he does not address anyone else in the Song of Solomon; he frequently addresses the woman directly, praising her admirable qualities; and though he does occasionally speak about himself (e.g., 5:1; 7:8; 8:13), readers learn only how fully his thoughts about the woman have taken over his imagination.

The woman is not nearly as exclusive in her speech, addressing "the daughters of Jerusalem" as well as the man. Of course, that does not make her distant: when she speaks to others, it is often about her beloved (e.g., 2:8–9), his admirable qualities (5:10–16), and her desire for him (2:5; 5:2–8). She describes what her beloved means to her (1:13–14), and her desire to be with him and give herself to him (7:12–13). She finds pleasure in the way her beloved desires her (7:10). The Song of Solomon portrays the young woman with sympathy and subtlety; she is perhaps the most clearly drawn female character in the Bible.

Alternative Interpretations

As noted above, perhaps no book in the biblical canon has had a greater diversity of interpretative strategies. In the interest of completeness, it will be helpful to describe briefly the following four diverse approaches that other interpreters have commonly taken.

1. *Allegorical interpretation.* The sensuous descriptions in this book have provided motivation to read the Song of Solomon as an allegory, namely, as an extended picture of the love between Israel's God and his people, and then between Christ and his bride (either the church or the individual soul). This approach, in fact, dominated exposition of the book until the nineteenth century. The limitation of such an approach, however, is that it runs the risk of diminishing the wisdom character of the Song of Solomon and its endorsement of God's good work of creation as evidenced in marital love. But even though virtually all scholarly interpreters today see the book primarily as a celebration of love and the gift of sexual intimacy, some would add that the Song of Solomon—by showing the pure and passionate love of the man and the woman in the story—can also enable believers to appreciate more deeply the intensity of the spiritual love-relationship between God and his people (as, e.g., this is further reflected in the picture of marriage depicted by Paul in Eph. 5:22–33).

2. *Anthology interpretation.* This interpretation views the Song of Solomon as a collection or anthology of interrelated love poems or lyrics, arranged around a common theme of intimate love between a man and a woman—in celebration of love's longing, ecstasy, joy, beauty, and exclusivity. This understanding, adopted by many interpreters beginning in the twentieth century, rejects the idea (advocated here) that the book contains a narrative plot. For criticisms of this approach, see Theme, Title, and Interpretation.

3. *The Shepherd Hypothesis.* In the nineteenth century the "Shepherd Hypothesis" became popular, whereby the young woman and the shepherd boy are two simple country folk in love, and King Solomon seeks to win the woman's consent to become part of his harem. The woman resists all his flattery and returns home to marry the shepherd. A number of evangelical interpreters now advocate this interpretation. Although this approach might be edifying, and could account for the problem of fitting the song with Solomon's known shortcomings, its weakness is that it does not supply any way for the reader to know when the shepherd speaks and when Solomon does. In fact, the speech patterns of the main characters (e.g., the descriptive titles they use for each other, the grammar by which they speak, and what they talk about) favor the conclusion that there are only two lovers, the woman and the shepherd. Another weakness of the Shepherd Hypothesis is that it seems unlikely that Solomon the king would be treated as an interloper in a work that is dedicated to Solomon himself. According to the interpretative strategy adopted in the notes below, Solomon is understood not as an intruder but as a somewhat distant figure, whom the woman brings into her dreams as her idealization of the young man she loves.

The following outline shows how advocates for the Shepherd Hypothesis might understand the structure of the book:

I. Title: The Best of Songs (1:1)
II. Solomon Meets the Shulammite in His Palace (1:2–2:7)
III. The Beloved Visits and the Shulammite Searches for Him in the Night (2:8–3:5)
IV. Solomon Displays His Wealth and Sings of His Love (3:6–5:1)
V. The Shulammite Yearns for the Beloved (5:2–6:3)
VI. The King Fails in His Pursuit of the Shulammite (6:4–8:14)

4. *The Solomon-Shulammite interpretation.* Another common interpretation also views the Song of Solomon as a unified love poem with a two-character plot, the two primary characters being King Solomon and the unnamed young Shulammite woman. Following this line of interpretation, chapters 1–2 lead up to the wedding; 3:1–5 is a dream; 3:6–11 recounts the wedding procession; chapter 4 praises the bride's beauty; and the consummation of the marriage is reflected in 4:16–5:1, possibly followed by another dream in

5:2–8. The rest of the book is understood, then, as recounting first a period of separation and marital difficulty (5:2–6:3); which is then resolved, resulting in the reaffirmation of their love for each other (6:4–8:4); followed by a brief concluding section of reflections and affirmations (8:5–14). Following this understanding, the structure of the book may be outlined as follows:

I. Title: The Best of Songs (1:1)
II. The Lovers Yearn for Each Other (1:2–3:5)
III. The Wedding (3:6–5:1)
IV. Temporary Separation and Reunion (5:2–6:3)
V. Delight in Each Other (6:4–8:4)
VI. Final Affirmations of Love (8:5–14)

Although 1 Kings 3:1 seems to indicate that Solomon married Pharaoh's daughter immediately after he established his kingdom (see 1 Kings 2:46), some advocates of the Solomon-Shulammite interpretation suggest that the Song of Solomon is a poetic retelling of the courtship and early days of Solomon's first marriage—after which, of course, Solomon abandoned the monogamous standard of Scripture, with grave consequences. In light of the way in which the rest of 1 Kings portrays Solomon, however, the assumption of an earlier marriage to the Shulammite seems to raise significant difficulties.

Outline

The following outline corresponds to the arguments presented in the introduction above and provides the structure for the interpretative strategy followed in the notes below:

I. Title: The Best of Songs (1:1)

II. The Lovers Yearn for Each Other (1:2–2:17)

III. The Shepherdess Dreams (3:1–6:3)

IV. The Lovers Yearn for Each Other Again (6:4–8:4)

V. The Lovers Join in Marriage (8:5–14)

The Song of Solomon

1 The Song of [a]Songs, which is Solomon's.

She Confesses Her Love

SHE[1]

2 Let him kiss me with the kisses of his mouth!
For your [b]love is better than wine;
3 your [c]anointing oils are fragrant;
your [d]name is oil poured out;
therefore virgins love you.
4 [e]Draw me after you; [f]let us run.
[g]The king has brought me into his chambers.

OTHERS

We will [h]exult and rejoice in you;
we will extol [b]your love more than wine;
rightly do they love you.

SHE

5 I am very dark, but [i]lovely,
O [j]daughters of Jerusalem,
like [k]the tents of [l]Kedar,
like the curtains of Solomon.
6 Do not gaze at me because I am dark,
because the sun has looked upon me.

[1] The translators have added speaker identifications based on the gender and number of the Hebrew words

Chapter 1
1 [a]1 Kgs. 4:32
2 [b]ch. 4:10
3 [c][Luke 7:46; John 12:3] [d]Eccles. 7:1
4 [e][Hos. 11:4; John 6:44; 12:32] [f]Ps. 119:32; See Phil. 3:12-14 [g]Ps. 45:14, 15; [ch. 2:4; John 14:2; Eph. 2:6] [h]Ps. 9:2; 45:15 [b][See ver. 2 above]
5 [i]ch. 2:14; 4:3; 6:4 [j]ch. 2:7; 3:5, 10, 11; 5:8, 16; 8:4; Luke 23:28 [k]Ps. 120:5 [l]Isa. 60:7

1:1 *Title: The Best of Songs.* "Song" refers to a joyful piece of literature with musical accompaniment. Laments, or mournful tunes, were separately identifiable in Hebrew literature. The name **Song of Songs** could either mean that it is a song composed of several songs (an anthology), or that it is the very best of songs (a superlative piece). On why the latter is preferable, see the paragraph on "Coherence" in Introduction: Theme, Title, and Interpretation.

1:2–2:17 *The Lovers Yearn for Each Other.* The two main characters, apparently betrothed, are introduced as they sing of their desire for each other. Throughout the Song of Solomon, the speakers and addressees are inferred from the gender and number of the Hebrew words.

1:2 him . . . your. The movement from the third to second person may seem odd to modern readers, but such a switch of pronouns is recognized as a poetical device in Hebrew. **Wine** is an obvious analogy for love—both cause exuberance and lightheadedness.

1:3 Name . . . oil is a wordplay (Hb. *shem . . . shemen*). "Name" refers to his reputation, which is as alluring as spilled perfume. **Anointing oils** were applied on special occasions. They were made from crushed aromatic blossoms or resins mixed with oil and reduced to an ointment by boiling.

1:4a The king is probably a term of endearment, indicating the woman's high regard for her lover rather than referring to his actual position. (However, many who follow the Shepherd Hypothesis read this as referring to Solomon; see Introduction: Alternative Interpretations.)

1:4b This is the first speech of the "others," who function like a chorus. They join the shepherdess in her praise for the shepherd (**you** is masculine) by picking up her words from v. 2. **They** probably refers back to the "virgins" of v. 3, who are presumably the same as the "daughters of Jerusalem" (v. 5).

1:5 dark, but lovely. The shepherd girl has spent her life working in the sun (in the vineyard, v. 6; caring for the flock, v. 8) and is not dainty like some refined young women. **daughters of Jerusalem**. See note on v. 4b; cf. 2:7; 3:5, 10; 5:8, 16; 8:4. Only the shepherdess addresses them. **tents of Kedar**. The black goat-hair tents of the nomadic descendants of Ishmael who lived in the east (cf. Gen. 25:13; Jer. 49:28–29). Between the eighth and fourth centuries B.C. they were the most powerful northern Arabian Bedouin tribe. **Curtains of Solomon** were no doubt luxuriously splendid (2 Chron. 3:14). The effect of these two parallel lines is to create a picture of the woman that engenders awe.

1:6 My own vineyard refers in a poetic image to the woman's physical appearance that has been marred by the sun as she has tended her family's vineyard.

My [m]mother's sons were angry with me;
they made me [n]keeper of [o]the vineyards,
but [p]my own vineyard I have not kept!
7 Tell me, you [q]whom my soul loves,
where you [r]pasture your flock,
where you make it [s]lie down at noon;
for why should I be like one who veils herself
beside the flocks of your [t]companions?

They Delight in Each Other

HE

8 If you do not know,
O [u]most beautiful among women,
follow in the tracks of the flock,
and pasture your young goats
beside the shepherds' tents.

9 I compare you, [v]my love,
to [w]a mare among Pharaoh's chariots.
10 [x]Your cheeks are lovely with ornaments,
your neck with strings of jewels.

OTHERS

11 We will make for you[1] ornaments of gold,
studded with silver.

SHE

12 While [y]the king was on his couch,
my [z]nard gave forth its fragrance.
13 My beloved is to me a sachet of [a]myrrh
that lies between my breasts.
14 My beloved is to me a cluster of [b]henna blossoms
in the vineyards of [c]Engedi.

HE

15 [d]Behold, [e]you are beautiful, [f]my love;
behold, you are beautiful;
your [g]eyes are doves.

SHE

16 Behold, you are beautiful, [h]my beloved, truly [i]delightful.
Our couch is green;
17 the beams of our house are [j]cedar;
our rafters are [j]pine.

2

1 I am a rose[2] of Sharon,
[k]a lily of the valleys.

[1] The Hebrew for *you* is feminine singular [2] Probably a bulb, such as a crocus, asphodel, or narcissus

6[m][Ps. 69:8] [n]Job 27:18; Prov. 27:18 [o]ch. 8:11, 12 [p][1 Cor. 9:27]
7[q]See ch. 3:1-4 [r]ch. 2:16; 6:3; [Ps. 23:1-3; Ezek. 34:14, 15] [s][Isa. 13:20; Jer. 33:12] [t]ch. 8:13
8[u]ch. 5:9; 6:1
9[v]See ver. 15 [w][2 Chr. 1:16, 17]
10[x][ch. 5:13]; See Ezek. 16:11-14
12[y][ver. 4] [z]ch. 4:13, 14; [Mark 14:3; John 12:3]
13[a]Ps. 45:8; [John 19:39]
14[b]ch. 4:13 [c]1 Sam. 23:29
15[d]ch. 4:1 [e][Ezek. 16:13] [f]ver. 9; ch. 2:2, 10, 13; 4:1, 7; 5:2; 6:4 [g]ch. 4:1; 5:12
16[h]ch. 2:3 [i][2 Sam. 1:23, 26]
17[j]Isa. 37:24; 60:13; Ezek. 31:8

Chapter 2

1[k]Hos. 14:5; [ch. 5:13]

1:7 Noon is the time to rest, providing an opportunity to meet. **whom my soul loves.** An all-encompassing love that meets all of her desires (not simply sexual; cf. 1 Sam. 20:17). The woman refers to her lover as a shepherd.

1:8 This is the man's first appearance. Here he offers a playful answer to the woman's question of where to find him. She cares for a **flock**, as he does (v. 7).

1:9 A mare among Pharaoh's chariots would be the best of its kind—noble and well-furnished with ornaments—captivating and exciting those around her.

1:10–11 ornaments. Within the Song of Solomon, the use of jewelry to heighten beauty is seen as natural and good (cf. 4:9). In 1:11, the chorus speaks to the woman (**you** is feminine), picking up from her comment in v. 10.

1:12 On the title **king**, see note on v. 4a. **Nard** was a **fragrance** extracted from a plant (cf. 4:13–14). For the erotic effect of a "fragrance," cf. 7:13.

1:13 My beloved is the woman's most common term of endearment for the man (31 times). **sachet of myrrh.** A pouch of aromatic resin that comes from various trees and shrubs.

1:14 White **henna blossoms** (which produced a red pigment) smell like roses. **Engedi** is an oasis of abundant water on the dry and desolate western bank of the Dead Sea—a location with obvious appeal.

1:16–17 The **couch, house,** and **rafters** are all likened to a lush woodland location and may indicate that the pair are outdoors.

2:1 Sharon is a coastal plain on the western side of Israel, north of present-day Tel-Aviv (Isa. 35:2). As the ESV footnote indicates, the **rose** of Sharon is

HE

2 As a lily among brambles,
so is [l]my love among the young women.

SHE

3 As an apple tree among the trees of the forest,
so is my [m]beloved among the young men.
With great delight I sat [n]in his shadow,
and his [o]fruit was sweet to my taste.
4 He [p]brought me to the banqueting house,[1]
and his [q]banner over me was love.
5 Sustain me with [r]raisins;
refresh me with apples,
[s]for I am sick with love.
6 His [t]left hand is under my head,
and his right hand [u]embraces me!
7 I [v]adjure you,[2] O [w]daughters of Jerusalem,
by [x]the gazelles or the does of the field,
that you not stir up or awaken love
until it pleases.

She Adores Her Beloved

8 The voice of my beloved!
Behold, he comes,
leaping [y]over the mountains,
bounding over the hills.
9 My beloved is like [z]a gazelle
or a young stag.
Behold, there he stands
behind our wall,
gazing through the windows,
looking through the lattice.
10 My beloved speaks and says to me:
[a]"Arise, my love, my beautiful one,
and come away,
11 for behold, the winter is past;
[b]the rain is over and gone.

[1] Hebrew *the house of wine* [2] That is, I put you on oath; so throughout the Song

2 [l]See ch. 1:15
3 [m]ch. 1:16 [n]Isa. 25:4; 32:2 [o][Rev. 22:2]
4 [p]ch. 1:4 [q][Ps. 20:5]
5 [r]2 Sam. 6:19; 1 Chr. 16:3; Hos. 3:1 [s]ch. 5:8
6 [t]ch. 8:3; [Deut. 33:27] [u][Prov. 4:8]
7 [v]ch. 3:5; 5:8, 9; 8:4 [w]See ch. 1:5 [x]See ver. 9
8 [y][Isa. 52:7]
9 [z]ch. 4:5; 7:3; 8:14; 2 Sam. 2:18; 1 Chr. 12:8; [Ps. 18:33; Hab. 3:19]
10 [a]ver. 13
11 [b][Joel 2:23]

"probably a bulb, such as a crocus, asphodel, or narcissus"—similar to the **lily** of the next line.

2:2 The man responds by elevating the woman's beauty well beyond her self-description, comparing her to others whom he refers to as **brambles** (prickly, thorny shrubs, or bushes).

2:3 Apple tree refers to a sweet fruit tree, providing pleasant shade and refreshing food; in this way, it is quite distinct from the other **trees of the forest**. Observe how the woman responds to his comparison from v. 2.

2:4 banqueting house (ESV footnote, "house of wine"). This is the only occurrence of this phrase in the OT (although there are similar expressions in Est. 7:8; Eccles. 7:2; Jer. 16:8). The exact location of this house is not critical. Rather, it is a place where wine is drunk and thus a place of love (see note on Song 1:2). This Hebrew term for **banner** is used elsewhere in the OT only in Numbers (Num. 2:2), where it is a standard flown at camps and carried into battle. Its use here would thus seem to indicate a public display of the lovers' identity, namely, that they belong to and are committed to each other.

2:5 For the refreshing and celebratory effects of **raisins**, see 2 Sam. 6:19. **sick with love**. See note on Song 5:8.

2:6 embraces. Sometimes this term refers to sexual activity (Prov. 5:20), but it can also describe the embrace of affection (e.g., Gen. 29:13; 33:4). Here it is not necessarily sexual, although the context would indicate great intimacy. These lines are repeated almost verbatim in Song 8:3.

2:7 This verse serves as a refrain (cf. 3:5; 8:4; a variation in 5:8). Love is demanding, and in giving of oneself, fatigue is inevitable. As appealing as love is, it should not be forced or rushed, hence the adjuration of the woman to the **daughters** in this verse. It is clear that the couple is already in love, but they must allow their love to proceed at its proper pace, which includes waiting until the right time to consummate it (in marriage, cf. 8:4; see also Introduction: Literary Features). Perhaps due to their shyness, **gazelles** were often associated with love in the ancient Near East (cf. 3:5).

2:8–17 These verses draw out the lovers' desire to be together in the face of various obstacles, with the woman quoting her lover in vv. 10–17. This yearning continues as the topic of the woman's dream in 3:1–5.

2:8 Mountains and **hills** are probably literary images for obstacles to their love (as in v. 15) that the man overcomes.

2:9 Our wall could refer to the wall of her mother's house (cf. 3:4; 8:2).

2:10 Arise, my love, my beautiful one, and come away is repeated at the end of v. 13, forming a literary envelope enclosing vv. 11–13.

2:11–13 Springtime is at hand, and with it come fresh, fragrant fruit and flowers, along with the cooing of the **turtledove**—stimulating all of the lovers' senses. Springtime is often celebrated as a time for lovers.

12 [c][2 Sam. 23:4] [d][Jer. 8:7]
13 [e][Matt. 24:32] [f]ch. 7:12 [g]ver. 10
14 [h]ch. 5:2; 6:9; [ch. 1:15] [i]Jer. 48:28; 49:16; Obad. 3 [j]ch. 8:13 [k]ch. 1:5; 4:3
15 [l][Ezek. 13:4] [f][See ver. 13 above]
16 [m]ch. 6:3; 7:10 [n]ch. 4:5; 6:3
17 [o]ch. 4:6; [Gen. 3:8] [p]Jer. 6:4 [q]See ver. 9

Chapter 3

1 [r]Isa. 26:9 [s]ch. 1:7 [t]ch. 5:6; [John 7:34]
2 [u]Jer. 5:1 [s][See ver. 1 above]
3 [v]ch. 5:7
4 [s][See ver. 1 above]

12 [c]The flowers appear on the earth,
the time of singing[1] has come,
and the voice of [d]the turtledove
is heard in our land.
13 [e]The fig tree ripens its figs,
and [f]the vines are in blossom;
they give forth fragrance.
[g]Arise, my love, my beautiful one,
and come away.
14 O my [h]dove, in the [i]clefts of the rock,
in the crannies of the cliff,
let me see your face,
let me [j]hear your voice,
for your voice is sweet,
and your face is [k]lovely.
15 Catch [l]the foxes[2] for us,
the little foxes
that spoil the vineyards,
[f]for our vineyards are in blossom."

16 [m]My beloved is mine, and I am his;
he [n]grazes[3] among the lilies.
17 Until [o]the day breathes
and [p]the shadows flee,
turn, my beloved, be like [q]a gazelle
or a young stag on cleft mountains.[4]

Her Dream

3

1 On my bed [r]by night
I sought [s]him whom my soul loves;
[t]I sought him, but found him not.
2 I will rise now and go about the city,
in [u]the streets and in the squares;
I will seek [s]him whom my soul loves.
I sought him, but found him not.
3 [v]The watchmen found me
as they went about in the city.
"Have you seen him whom my soul loves?"
4 Scarcely had I passed them
when I found [s]him whom my soul loves.

[1] *Or pruning* [2] *Or jackals* [3] *Or he pastures his flock* [4] *Or mountains of Bether*

2:14 my dove. Doves were associated with love, so this endearment used by the man identifies the woman with love; in her, he experiences love. The words occur in mirror form, **face . . . voice . . . voice . . . face**.

2:15–16 Foxes are pests that wreak havoc in vineyards (e.g., they will eat the grapes). Although the vineyard has been associated with the appearance of the woman (1:6), here it is described as **our vineyards** and thus refers to their relationship. The foxes represent some hindrances that are threatening to spoil their relationship.

2:17 Presumably the woman desires for her **beloved** to **turn** toward her rather than away from her.

3:1–6:3 *The Shepherdess Dreams.* Here the woman reports her dream, which comes from her eagerly anticipating the consummation of their love. That this is a dream is suggested by 3:1 ("On my bed by night I sought him whom my soul loves") and 5:2 ("I slept, but my heart was awake"). On this interpretation, the dream includes erotic longings, fears of losing her beloved, nightmarish scenes (5:7), and an imaginative transformation of the beloved into a Solomon-like figure (3:6–11).

3:1–5 The woman longs for her lover, searches for him persistently, eventually finds him, and takes him to an intimate place. This could simply be poetical imagination (to heighten her sense of longing for her lover), but it is more likely a dream (see note on v. 4).

3:1 Soul often refers to the whole person, encompassing the woman's desires, thoughts, feelings, etc.

3:4 chamber of her who conceived me. Her mother's bedroom presents a secure and intimate place for the two lovers. The woman has a similar desire to bring her lover to this place in 8:2, where she makes it clear that she will not do so until the right time; hence, it is best to read her search in 3:1–4 as not describing an actual event but rather as part of her dream. There are

I [w]held him, and would not let him go
until I had [x]brought him into my mother's house,
and into the chamber of [y]her who conceived me.
5 [z]I adjure you, [a]O daughters of Jerusalem,
[b]by the gazelles or the does of the field,
that you not stir up or awaken love
until it pleases.

He Arrives for the Wedding

6 [c]What is that coming up from the wilderness
like [d]columns of smoke,
perfumed with [e]myrrh and frankincense,
with all the fragrant powders of a merchant?
7 Behold, it is the litter[1] of Solomon!
Around it are [f]sixty [g]mighty men,
some of the mighty men of Israel,
8 all of them wearing swords
and expert in war,
each with his [h]sword at his thigh,
against [i]terror by night.
9 King Solomon made himself a carriage[2]
from the wood of Lebanon.
10 He made its posts of silver,
its back of gold, its seat of purple;
its interior was inlaid with love
by [j]the daughters of Jerusalem.
11 Go out, O [k]daughters of Zion,
and look upon King Solomon,
with the crown with which his mother crowned him
on [l]the day of his wedding,
on the day of the gladness of his heart.

He Admires Her Beauty

HE

4 1 Behold, [m]you are beautiful, my love,
behold, you are beautiful!
[n]Your eyes are doves
[o]behind your veil.

[1] That is, the couch on which servants carry a king [2] Or *sedan chair*

4 [w][Job 27:6] [x]ch. 8:2 [y][Hos. 2:5]
5 [z]See ch. 2:7 [a]See ch. 1:5 [b]See ch. 2:9
6 [c]ch. 8:5; [ch. 6:10; Isa. 60:8] [d]Ex. 13:21; Joel 2:30 [e]ch. 4:6, 14; Matt. 2:11; John 19:39
7 [f]ch. 6:8 [g]2 Sam. 23:8; 1 Chr. 11:10
8 [h]Ps. 45:3 [i]Ps. 91:5
10 [j]See ch. 1:5
11 [k]Isa. 3:16, 17; 4:4 [l][Isa. 62:5]

Chapter 4

1 [m]See ch. 1:15 [n]ch. 1:15; 5:12 [o]ch. 6:7

parallels between this passage and 5:2–8, which also seems to be placed within the context of a dream.

3:5 As in 2:7, the woman adjures the daughters not to force the progress of her love, presumably to avoid these consuming desires.

3:6–11 Apart from the context, it is difficult to know whether this is describing an actual event or whether it is the woman's own imagination (highlighting the great wealth and power of her lover, and consequently her own worth). Since, however, this fits in between vv. 1–5 and 5:2–8, the latter option is preferable (see also note on 3:6). On the use of Solomon (mentioned three times in this section), see Introduction: Theme, Title, and Interpretation; and Literary Features.

3:6 What is that? Although seen from a distance, the object in question has an aroma, suggesting that the impact of the image created by the poet is more important than the historical referents. The word translated "what" is actually feminine in Hebrew (i.e., "who"), and so one expects a woman to be the subject in question. If this is so, then there could be an element of the woman desiring to be this person. The answer given in v. 7 is that it is a "litter" (a portable couch; hence the English translation "what" in v. 6), suggesting that the question is simply posed in an evocative manner. **coming up from the wilderness**. Probably from the plains toward Jerusalem; the city itself is elevated on a hill. **frankincense**. Similar to **myrrh** (see note on 1:13).

3:7 litter. As the ESV footnote indicates, this is "the couch on which servants carry the king"; similar to a portable bed. **Sixty mighty men** (well-trained soldiers, v. 8) indicates the great wealth and power of the owner of the couch. By contrast, David had only 30 such men (cf. 2 Sam. 23:13).

3:9 Carriage probably refers to the litter in v. 7. Lebanese **wood** was of the highest quality available, hence its use in the temple (cf. 1 Kings 5:6).

3:10 Purple cloth was made using a pigment from the murex shellfish; it was even rarer than silver and gold.

3:11 Since the preceding verse mentions "the daughters of Jerusalem," and since "Zion" is a synonym for Jerusalem, the **daughters of Zion** probably refers to the same group (cf. note on 1:5).

4:1–7 The first part of v. 1 is repeated in v. 7, creating a literary envelope for a section that describes the woman's physical beauty, starting at the eyes and working systematically downward. Although the metaphors are vivid, they are

1 [p]ch. 6:5; [ch. 7:5] [q]Mic. 7:14
2 [r]ch. 6:6
3 [s][Josh. 2:18] [t]ch. 1:5; 2:14 [u]ch. 6:7 [o][See ver. 1 above]
4 [v][ch. 7:4] [w]Neh. 3:19 [x][Ezek. 27:10, 11] [y][2 Sam. 1:21]
5 [z]ch. 7:3; [ch. 8:10; Prov. 5:19] [a]See ch. 2:9 [b]ch. 2:16; 6:3
6 [c]ch. 2:17 [d]ver. 14; [ch. 3:6]
7 [e]See ch. 1:15 [f]ch. 5:2; [Eph. 5:27]
8 [g][Ps. 45:10, 11] [h]ch. 7:4; See 1 Kgs. 4:33 [i][Isa. 62:5] [j]Deut. 3:9; 1 Chr. 5:23 [k]Ps. 89:12
9 [l]ch. 5:1, 2 [m][Judg. 8:26]
10 [l][See ver. 9 above] [n]ch. 1:2, 4 [o][ch. 1:3]

[p]Your hair is like a flock of goats
leaping down [q]the slopes of Gilead.
2 Your [r]teeth are like a flock of shorn ewes
that have come up from the washing,
all of which bear twins,
and not one among them has lost its young.
3 Your lips are like [s]a scarlet thread,
and your mouth is [t]lovely.
Your [u]cheeks are like halves of a pomegranate
[o]behind your veil.
4 Your [v]neck is like the tower of David,
built in [w]rows of stone;[1]
on it [x]hang a thousand shields,
all of [y]them shields of warriors.
5 Your [z]two breasts are like two [a]fawns,
twins of a gazelle,
that [b]graze among the lilies.
6 [c]Until the day breathes
and the shadows flee,
I will go away to the mountain of [d]myrrh
and the hill of [d]frankincense.
7 [e]You are altogether beautiful, my love;
there is no [f]flaw in you.
8 [g]Come with me from [h]Lebanon, my [i]bride;
come with me from [h]Lebanon.
Depart[2] from the peak of Amana,
from the peak of [j]Senir and [k]Hermon,
from the dens of lions,
from the mountains of leopards.

9 You have captivated my heart, my [l]sister, my bride;
you have captivated my heart with one glance of your eyes,
with one [m]jewel of your necklace.
10 How beautiful is your love, my [l]sister, my bride!
How much [n]better is your love than wine,
and [o]the fragrance of your oils than any spice!

[1] The meaning of the Hebrew word is uncertain [2] Or *Look*

somewhat obscure to those who do not share the author's culture, and one must be careful not to press them too far. Nevertheless, they should still cause an emotional response in the reader.

4:1 Gilead is the area surrounding the Jabbok River, which flows into the lower half of the Jordan River from the east.

4:2 twins . . . not one . . . has lost its young. All her teeth are present (a not-so-common occurrence in the ancient world) and attractively matched within her mouth.

4:3 Pomegranate is a fruit with an orange-red leathery skin and deep pink succulent fleshy sacks with a subtle taste that is refreshing in the heat of summer. The metaphor is picking up on the beautiful color of either the skin or the flesh of this fruit.

4:4 The **Tower of David** is unmentioned outside of the Song of Solomon and little is known about it. The association with David, however, heightens the sense of dignity already implicit in the image of a tower. Dignity, rather than the physical attributes of the tower, probably provides the point of comparison.

4:5 Fawns (young deer) refers to the youthful appearance of her **two breasts**. **Gazelle** probably refers to her appealingly sleek form.

4:6 This verse starts with a phrase similar to that of 2:17, indicating the man's desire to spend time with the woman. The reference to a **mountain** and a **hill** could continue the theme of the previous verse and refer to the woman's breasts or, alternatively, to the woman as a whole. The point is that being with her is like inhaling an intoxicating fragrance.

4:7 In the man's eyes, this woman is without physical fault or **flaw** and is **altogether beautiful**.

4:8 Hermon (for which **Senir** is a synonym) is a peak in a range that starts in the extreme north of Israel near Dan and extends northward into **Lebanon** (and includes other peaks, such as **Amana**). These all represent the thought that the man is calling the woman from desolate places that have perils (cf. the references to **lions** and **leopards**). The term **my bride** (six times in 4:8–5:1 and nowhere else in the Song of Solomon) would seem appropriate only after the wedding; this probably indicates that this scene (4:1–5:1) also takes place in the woman's dream, as she looks forward to what the wedding day will bring.

4:9 The **heart** was considered the center of one's inner life, the place of thinking, feeling, and choosing (cf. Prov. 4:23). **Sister** was a common term of endearment between couples in the ancient Near East. **glance of your eyes**. See note on Song 6:5.

4:10 wine. See note on 1:2.

11 Your [p]lips drip nectar, my bride;
[q]honey and milk are under your tongue;
the fragrance of your garments is [r]like the fragrance of [h]Lebanon.
12 A garden locked is my [l]sister, my bride,
a spring locked, [s]a fountain [t]sealed.
13 Your shoots are [u]an orchard of pomegranates
with all [v]choicest fruits,
[w]henna with [x]nard,
14 nard and saffron, [y]calamus and [y]cinnamon,
with all trees of [z]frankincense,
[a]myrrh and [b]aloes,
with all [y]choice spices—
15 a garden fountain, a well of [c]living water,
and flowing streams from [h]Lebanon.

16 Awake, O north wind,
and come, O south wind!
Blow upon my [d]garden,
let its spices flow.

Together in the Garden of Love

SHE

[e]Let my beloved come to his [f]garden,
and eat its [v]choicest fruits.

HE

5

1 I [g]came to my garden, my [h]sister, my bride,
I gathered my [i]myrrh with my spice,
I ate my [j]honeycomb with my honey,
I [k]drank my wine with my milk.

OTHERS

Eat, [l]friends, drink,
and be drunk with love!

She Searches for Her Beloved

SHE

2 I slept, but my heart was awake.
A sound! My beloved is [m]knocking.

11[p][Prov. 5:3] [q]Prov. 24:13 [r]Hos. 14:6; [Gen. 27:27] [h][See ver. 8 above]
12[l][See ver. 9 above] [s][Gen. 29:3; Dan. 6:17] [t][Prov. 5:15]
13[u]Eccles. 2:5 [v]ch. 7:13 [w]ch. 1:14 [x]See ch. 1:12
14[y]Ex. 30:23 [z]ver. 6 [a]See ch. 3:6 [b]John 19:39
15[c]Jer. 2:13; [John 4:10; 7:38] [h][See ver. 8 above]
16[d][ch. 5:1; 6:2] [e][ch. 6:2] [f]ch. 6:2 [v][See ver. 13 above]

Chapter 5

1[g][ch. 4:16; 6:2] [h]ch. 4:9, 10, 12 [i]ver. 5, 13; ch. 4:14 [j]ch. 4:11 [k][Prov. 9:5] [l][John 15:14, 15]
2[m][Rev. 3:20]

4:11 Whereas the woman's lips and mouth were previously described in terms of beauty (v. 3), here her **lips** and **tongue** are described in terms of taste (**nectar**, **honey**, and **milk**, the latter two often being paired together in the Bible, as in the description of the Promised Land in Ex. 3:8). This heightens the sensuality of the man's continued description of his beautiful bride-to-be.

4:12 A **garden** (more like modern parks than flowerbeds) is not only a welcoming place for lovers but is regularly associated with a woman's sexuality in the ancient Near East. A **spring** or **fountain** reflects a similar concept (cf. Prov. 5:15–19). Notice that her garden and spring are **locked**, indicating that she reserves herself for her lover alone.

4:13 Her garden contains **choicest fruits** and spices in great array and abundance. See notes on 1:12 (**nard**) and 1:14 (**henna**).

4:14 **Saffron** is a kind of crocus with a purple flower, while **calamus** is a cane. Both can be used to produce a sweet-scented oil. **Cinnamon** is akin to the present-day aromatic bark, although its use was not limited to cooking (cf. Prov. 7:17, which also identifies **aloes** as a fragrant wood). On **frankincense** and **myrrh**, see notes on Song 1:13 and 3:6.

4:15 The garden-fountain metaphor is extended to indicate the refreshing quality of the woman's sexuality. In Hebrew, **living water** refers to fresh running water, the best kind available (e.g., Lev. 14:5; Jer. 2:13; cf. John 4:10; 7:38), as opposed to ground water or water stored in a cistern.

4:16 Awake, O north wind, and come, O south wind. The reference to the winds may reflect the man's desire for the woman to offer an invitation to him. This is granted in the second half of the verse.

5:1 I came to my garden. The man responds predictably and partakes of all that he described in 4:16, to the joyful acclaim of the chorus (who echo themes from 4:16–5:1). According to the reading strategy advocated in the Introduction, 4:16–5:1 represents the continuation of the dream sequence (see 5:2: "I slept, but my heart was awake"), with the sexual consummation of the marriage yet to come in 8:5 ("Under the apple tree I awakened you"). Many who follow the Shepherd Hypothesis, however, read 4:16–5:1 as referring to a visit (real or imagined) of the shepherd boy, for whom the girl really longs (see Introduction: Alternative Interpretations). Other approaches take this passage as describing the sexual consummation of the marriage of the two young people. Those who follow this approach base their interpretation in part on the fact that the consummation of the marriage would then fall in the structural center of the book, as an indication of the centrality of marriage in the literary structure of the book, but also as an indication of the centrality of marriage in the creation of man and woman.

5:2–6:3 It is not immediately clear whether the woman has been awoken by the knocking at the door or whether the knocking is in the dream. Her response to the chorus in 6:2 would indicate that the former is unlikely and that the significance of this section (5:2–6:3) is that it is a dream caused by

“Open to me, my [n]sister, my [o]love,
my [p]dove, my [q]perfect one,
for my head is wet with dew,
my [r]locks with the drops of the night.”
3 [s]I had put off my garment;
how could I put it on?
I had [t]bathed my feet;
how could I soil them?
4 My beloved put his hand to the latch,
and my heart was thrilled within me.
5 I arose to open to my beloved,
and my hands dripped with myrrh,
my fingers with [u]liquid myrrh,
on the handles of the bolt.
6 I opened to my beloved,
but my beloved had turned and gone.
My soul failed me when he [v]spoke.
[w]I sought him, but found him not;
[x]I called him, but he gave no answer.
7 [y]The watchmen found me
as they went about in the city;
they beat me, they bruised me,
they took away my veil,
those watchmen of the walls.
8 I [z]adjure you, O [a]daughters of Jerusalem,
if you find my beloved,
that you tell him
[b]I am sick with love.

OTHERS

9 What is your beloved more than another beloved,
O [c]most beautiful among women?
What is your beloved more than another beloved,
that you thus [z]adjure us?

She Praises Her Beloved

SHE

10 My beloved is radiant and [d]ruddy,
[e]distinguished among ten thousand.
11 His head is the finest gold;
[f]his locks are wavy,
black as a raven.

2[n]ch. 4:9, 10, 12 [o]See ch. 1:15 [p]See ch. 2:14 [q]ch. 6:9; [ch. 4:7] [r]ver. 11
3[s][Luke 11:7] [t]See Gen. 18:4
5[u]ver. 13
6[v][ver. 2] [w]ch. 3:1 [x][Prov. 1:28]
7[y]ch. 3:3
8[z]See ch. 2:7 [a]See ch. 1:5 [b]ch. 2:5
9[c]ch. 1:8; 6:1 [z][See ver. 8 above]
10[d][1 Sam. 16:12] [e][Ps. 45:2]
11[f]ver. 2

the way the lovers’ desires do not always synchronize—they are separated when they desire to be together.

5:2 The man’s request is clear: he wants to enter the house to be with the woman (note his urgency or even pushiness in his use of the imperative **open**, and the barrage of endearing names that follows).

5:3 Her initial response of petty objections could be a tease, or just a reluctance that comes from weariness, but it is more likely the kind of befuddlement that one encounters in a dream, leading to the confusing episode in vv. 4–7.

5:4–7 After warming to the man’s approach, but delaying to open the door to him, the woman soon realizes he has gone and she goes in pursuit of him, at which point the **watchmen** find her and, unlike in 3:3, they **beat** her, leaving her **bruised** (5:7). If this were an actual event, it would be unclear why the watchmen did this. If it is part of a dream, though, it would simply be a nightmarish episode, perhaps reflecting the woman’s fear of public hostility toward the couple or toward her pursuit of him: it underscores the painfulness of their separation.

5:8 In 2:5 the man was present when the woman uttered the words: **sick with love**. Now he is absent, suggesting that she is referring to her desire to be with him, and to the way that she, as a woman, can feel overwhelming physical weakness at the thought of her beloved, sometimes described as making the knees go weak as water. **I adjure you, O daughters of Jerusalem**. The wording of this verse is a variation of the refrain (also found in 2:7; 3:5; 8:4).

5:9–16 The chorus then asks how her lover compares to other men, and she responds.

5:9 The chorus is picking up the word **beloved** from v. 8; this, together with the echoed word **adjure**, indicates that the singers in the chorus are the “daughters of Jerusalem” addressed in v. 8.

5:10 Radiant and ruddy refers to an appealing complexion (cf. 1 Sam. 16:12).

12 His [g]eyes are like doves
beside streams of water,
bathed in milk,
sitting beside a full pool.[1]
13 His [i]cheeks are like [j]beds of spices,
mounds of sweet-smelling herbs.
His lips are [k]lilies,
dripping [u]liquid myrrh.
14 His arms are rods of gold,
set with [l]jewels.
His body is polished ivory,[2]
bedecked with [m]sapphires.[3]
15 His legs are alabaster columns,
set on bases of gold.
His appearance is like [o]Lebanon,
choice as the cedars.
16 His [p]mouth[4] is most sweet,
and he is altogether desirable.
This is my beloved and this is my friend,
O [a]daughters of Jerusalem.

OTHERS

6 1 Where has your beloved gone,
O [c]most beautiful among women?
Where has your beloved turned,
that we may seek him with you?

Together in the Garden of Love

SHE

2 My beloved has gone down to his [q]garden
to [r]the beds of spices,
to [s]graze[5] in the gardens
and to gather [t]lilies.
3 [u]I am my beloved's and my beloved is mine;
he grazes among the lilies.

They Delight in Each Other

HE

4 You are beautiful as [v]Tirzah, [w]my love,
[x]lovely as [y]Jerusalem,
[z]awesome as an army with banners.

[1] The meaning of the Hebrew is uncertain [2] The meaning of the Hebrew word is uncertain [3] Hebrew *lapis lazuli* [4] Hebrew *palate* [5] Or *to pasture his flock*; also verse 3

12 [g]ch. 1:15; 4:1
13 [i][ch. 1:10] [j]ch. 6:2 [k][ch. 2:1] [u][See ver. 5 above]
14 [l]Ex. 28:20; 39:13; Ezek. 1:16 [m]Ex. 24:10; Ezek. 1:26; 10:1
15 [o]See 1 Kgs. 4:33
16 [p][ch. 7:9] [a][See ver. 8 above]

Chapter 6

1 [c][See ch. 5:9 above]
2 [q]ch. 4:16; 5:1 [r]ch. 5:13 [s]ch. 1:7 [t][ch. 2:1]
3 [u]ch. 2:16; 7:10
4 [v]See 1 Kgs. 14:17 [w]See ch. 1:15 [x]ch. 1:5 [y]Ps. 48:2; 50:2; Lam. 2:15; [Rev. 21:2] [z]ver. 10

5:13 The description of his cheeks as **beds of spices** would apply more appropriately to a beard than to skin. Given that men in ancient Israel almost always had beards, this seems the likely meaning. As with many other metaphors in the Song of Solomon, the referent has an aromatic quality (spices and **sweet-smelling herbs**). On **myrrh**, see note on 1:13.

5:14–16 The continued description of the man refers to precious materials that are often used in statues and in the temple (**gold, jewels, ivory, alabaster**, and **cedars** from Lebanon). The man is thus clearly the object of great praise in this section; the woman considers him to be **altogether desirable**.

6:1 In 5:6 the woman lamented that her beloved "had turned and gone"; now the chorus asks her: **where has your beloved gone**, and **where has** he **turned**.

6:2 The woman's response may seem odd, given that she has enlisted the help of the group to find her lover, but see the comments at the start of the section (5:2–6:3). **garden**. See 4:12. The garden is **his**, for she has committed herself to him.

6:3 The lovers gladly declare that they have given themselves to each other (**I am my beloved's and my beloved is mine**).

6:4–8:4 *The Lovers Yearn for Each Other Again.* The dream is over, as the song turns from the absent beloved to the couple exchanging their praise for each other.

6:4 Tirzah (lit., "pleasing") was the capital of the northern kingdom for a short time (920–880 B.C.), while **Jerusalem** was the long-standing capital of the southern kingdom and an established icon of beauty (Psalms 48; 50). The hostility between the two kingdoms, represented by their capital cities, makes it unlikely that the Song of Solomon dates from the time of

5[a]ch. 4:1
6[b]ch. 4:2
7[c]ch. 4:3
8[d][ch. 3:7] [e][1 Kgs. 11:3] [f]Ps. 45:9, 14
9[g]See ch. 2:14 [h]ch. 5:2 [i]Prov. 17:25 [j][Gen. 30:13] [e][See ver. 8 above]
10[k]See ch. 3:6 [l]ver. 4
11[m][Job 8:11, 12] [n]ch. 7:12
12[o][Ps. 35:8; Prov. 5:6] [p][2 Kgs. 2:12; 13:14]
13[q][1 Kgs. 1:3; 2 Kgs. 4:12] [r][Judg. 21:21] [s]Gen. 32:2; 2 Sam. 17:24

Chapter 7

1[t]Ps. 45:13 [u]Prov. 25:12 [v][Prov. 8:30]

5 Turn away your eyes from me,
for they overwhelm me—
[a]Your hair is like a flock of goats
leaping down the slopes of Gilead.
6 [b]Your teeth are like a flock of ewes
that have come up from the washing;
all of them bear twins;
not one among them has lost its young.
7 [c]Your cheeks are like halves of a pomegranate
behind your veil.
8 There are [d]sixty [e]queens and eighty [e]concubines,
and [f]virgins without number.
9 My [g]dove, my [h]perfect one, is the only one,
the only one of her mother,
pure to [i]her who bore her.
[j]The young women saw her and called her blessed;
[e]the queens and [e]concubines also, and they praised her.

10 [k]"Who is this who looks down like the dawn,
beautiful as the moon, bright as the sun,
[l]awesome as an army with banners?"

SHE

11 I went down to the nut orchard
to look at [m]the blossoms of the valley,
[n]to see whether the vines had budded,
whether the pomegranates were in bloom.
12 [o]Before I was aware, my desire set me
among [p]the chariots of my kinsman, a prince.[1]

OTHERS

13[2] Return, return, O [q]Shulammite,
return, return, that we may look upon you.

HE

Why should you look upon [q]the Shulammite,
as upon [r]a dance before [s]two armies?[3]

7

1 How beautiful are your feet in sandals,
O [t]noble daughter!
Your rounded thighs are like [u]jewels,
the work of [v]a master hand.
2 Your navel is a rounded bowl
that never lacks mixed wine.

[1] Or *chariots of Ammi-Nadib* [2] Ch 7:1 in Hebrew [3] Or *dance of Mahanaim*

the divided kingdom (see Introduction: Author and Date). **awesome as an army with banners**. Not only is she beautiful, she inspires the most profound respect.

6:5 The woman's glances **overwhelm** the man (cf. 4:9, where they captivate his heart). On **Gilead**, see note on 4:1.

6:7 pomegranate. See note on 4:3.

6:8–9 Queens and **concubines** were positions within a royal harem, the latter being secondary in status to the former. There would usually be only one queen in an ancient Near Eastern harem (although within the harems of the kings of Israel and Judah, queens are never mentioned). **Virgins** refers to a group of women that were present in the court, but also in society at large. Notice how the numbers increase from **sixty** to **eighty** to **without number**, symbolizing that the woman of the Song of Solomon is without comparison among women, even royal women—all of whom praise her.

6:10 Dawn, **moon**, and **sun** all reflect the woman's radiant beauty.

6:13 The chorus picks up on the idea of "looking" (v. 11). As she had gone down to the orchard to look, so they want her to **return**, that they might **look upon** her. In the question **why should you look**, "you" is masculine plural (perhaps addressed to other men, or to society at large). **Shulammite** may be the feminine form of "Solomon," but here it more likely refers to the woman's origin; in a poem, however, it could easily evoke the idea of a suitable partner to the young man who is at times referred to and idealized as Solomon. The nature of the **dance before two armies** is unknown, but the repetition of "look upon" may suggest that if the woman did such a dance it would compromise her honor—and thus the beloved intervenes.

7:1–9a This description of the woman's beauty echoes that of 4:1–7 (cf. her description of the man in 5:10–16). They take erotic delight in each other's physical appearance.

Your belly is a heap of wheat,
encircled with [w]lilies.
3 [x]Your two breasts are like two fawns,
twins of a gazelle.
4 Your [y]neck is like an ivory tower.
Your [z]eyes are pools in [a]Heshbon,
by the gate of Bath-rabbim.
Your nose is like a tower of [b]Lebanon,
which looks toward [c]Damascus.
5 Your head crowns you like [e]Carmel,
and your [f]flowing locks are like purple;
a king is held captive in the tresses.

6 [g]How beautiful and [h]pleasant you are,
O loved one, with all your delights![1]
7 Your stature is like a palm tree,
and your breasts are like its clusters.
8 I say I will climb the palm tree
and lay hold of its fruit.
Oh may your breasts be like [i]clusters of the vine,
and the scent of your breath like apples,
9 and your [j]mouth[2] like the best wine.

SHE

It goes down smoothly for my beloved,
gliding over lips and teeth.[3]

10 [k]I am my beloved's,
[l]and his desire is for me.

She Gives Her Love

11 [m]Come, my beloved,
let us go out into the fields
and lodge in the villages;[4]
12 let us go out early to the vineyards
[n]and see whether the vines have budded,
whether [o]the grape blossoms have opened
and the pomegranates are in bloom.
There I will give you my love.
13 [p]The mandrakes give forth fragrance,
and beside our doors are all choice fruits,
[q]new as well as old,
which I have laid up for you, O my beloved.

[1]Or *among delights* [2]Hebrew *palate* [3]Septuagint, Syriac, Vulgate; Hebrew *causing the lips of sleepers to speak* [4]Or *among the henna plants*

2 [w]ch. 2:1
3 [x]ch. 4:5
4 [y][ch. 4:4] [z][ch. 5:12] [a]Num. 21:26 [b]ch. 4:8; See 1 Kgs. 4:33 [c]1 Kgs. 11:24; 2 Kgs. 5:12
5 [e]See Josh. 19:26 [f][ch. 4:1]
6 [g][ch. 1:15, 16] [h]2 Sam. 1:23, 26
8 [i][ch. 1:14; Mic. 7:1]
9 [j][ch. 5:16]
10 [k]ch. 2:16; 6:3 [l][Ps. 45:11]
11 [m][ch. 2:10; 4:8]
12 [n]ch. 6:11 [o]ch. 2:13, 15
13 [p]Gen. 30:14; ch. 4:13 [q][Matt. 13:52]

7:3 See note on 4:5.

7:4 As in 4:4, the woman's **neck** is likened to a **tower**. Since it is made of precious **ivory**, the dignity and beauty of her neck (rather than any physical aspect of it) is once again the reason for the simile. Similarly, the man praises the grandeur of her **nose** by comparing it to an elevated **tower of Lebanon** overlooking the important Syrian city of **Damascus**.

7:5 Mount **Carmel** is west of the Sea of Galilee near the Mediterranean coast. **Purple** is associated with royalty, as the related dye was expensive (see note on 3:10). As in the previous verse, these images portray the woman's dignity—no wonder she can hold a king captive!

7:7 It was not uncommon for a person with elegance to be compared to a **palm tree**. In the Bible, women with the name Tamar (lit., palm tree) are sensually alluring (cf. Genesis 38; 2 Samuel 13).

7:10 The first line of this verse echoes that of 6:3. The word **desire** in the second line appears elsewhere in the Bible only in Gen. 3:16 and 4:7; the context tells the reader what kind of desire it is, and here (unlike in Genesis) it is sexual. The thought of the man desiring her gives the shepherdess pleasure.

7:12 For the significance of a rural setting (and specifically **vineyards**), see Introduction: Literary Features.

7:13 It is possible that **mandrakes** (Hb. *duda'im*, which sounds like **my beloved**, *dodi*) were seen as an aphrodisiac (cf. Gen. 30:14–16). They appear to seduce as they **give forth fragrance** (as with the nard in Song 1:12). **New as well as old** is probably an idiom meaning "all," or perhaps it refers to a progression in love, from the already familiar ("old") to the "new" delights that they anticipate.

8:1 This verse seems to indicate that in Israelite culture, romantic kisses were to be reserved for private contexts, while the kiss of family affection was deemed appropriate in the open—hence the wish that he were a **brother**. (The wayward woman of Prov. 7:13 is thus seen to be shameless; probably Jacob's kiss for Rachel was a familial kiss [cf. Gen. 29:11–12].) The Hebrew for **I would kiss you** sounds like "I would give you . . . to drink" (Song 8:2).

8

Longing for Her Beloved

1 Oh that you were like a brother to me
who nursed at my mother's breasts!
If I found you outside, I would kiss you,
and none would despise me.
2 I would lead you and [r]bring you
into the house of my mother—
she who used to teach me.
I would give you [s]spiced wine to drink,
the juice of my pomegranate.
3 [t]His left hand is under my head,
and his right hand embraces me!
4 I [u]adjure you, O [v]daughters of Jerusalem,
[w]that you not stir up or awaken love
until it pleases.

5 [x]Who is that coming up from the wilderness,
leaning on her beloved?

Under the apple tree I awakened you.
There your mother was in labor with you;
there she who bore you was in labor.

6 Set me as a seal upon your heart,
as [y]a seal upon your arm,
for [z]love is strong as death,
[a]jealousy[1] is fierce as the grave.[2]
Its flashes are flashes of fire,
the very [b]flame of the LORD.
7 Many waters cannot quench love,
neither can floods drown it.
If a man offered for love
all the wealth of his [c]house,
he[3] would be utterly despised.

Final Advice

OTHERS

8 We have a little sister,
and she [d]has no breasts.

Chapter 8
2 [r]ch. 3:4 [s][Prov. 9:2, 5]
3 [t]ch. 2:6, 7
4 [u]See ch. 2:7 [v]See ch. 1:5 [w][ch. 2:7]
5 [x]See ch. 3:6
6 [y]Isa. 49:16; Jer. 22:24; Hag. 2:23 [z][Rom. 8:35] [a][Ex. 34:14]; Deut. 4:24 [b][Job 1:16]
7 [c]Prov. 6:35
8 [d][Ezek. 16:7]

[1] Or *ardor* [2] Hebrew *as Sheol* [3] Or *it*

8:2 house of my mother. See 3:4. **Wine** is linked to love and romance in the Song of Solomon (see 1:2; 2:4).

8:4 Here at the end of the period of longing and waiting is the final instance of the refrain urging the **daughters of Jerusalem** not to **stir up or awaken love** until the appropriate time (cf. 2:7; 3:5); it is now time to move on to the marriage (cf. 8:5, where the consummation is indicated by her finally "awakening" him).

8:5–14 *The Lovers Join in Marriage.* The Song of Solomon closes with a new stage in the relationship: the pair have gone from their yearning to be joined together, to actually being wed and consummating their union. The tension of the previous chapters—the anxious waiting, the concern for propriety—gives way to relaxed enjoyment.

8:5 It is possible that the two halves of this verse are spoken by different parties, since the first half is about the woman, and the second half has the woman speaking to her beloved (**you** is masculine singular). It is simpler, however, to suppose that the woman speaks both halves, and that in the first half she is quoting someone. The Hebrew term for **leaning** occurs only here in the OT, but its use in post-biblical Hebrew points to an intimate connection and thus implies that the pair are now wed. In 2:3 the **apple tree** was a place of love; here it is the place of childbirth (which is what erotic love ideally leads to). On **I awakened you**, cf. note on 8:4.

8:6 A **seal** could be a stamp or a cylinder (the latter being less common), and could be attached to a person by a band (and thereby hang from the neck or arm) or worn as a ring. It was pressed into clay to create an image or an inscription that assigned ownership of an object. **Love**, like **death**, is relentlessly persistent, always accomplishing its goal. Here **jealousy** (which parallels "love" in the preceding line) is a resolute devotion rather than a selfish ambition; only such devotion can rightly describe the relationship with God and with one's spouse. **flame of the LORD**. This is the only mention of the divine name in the entire Song of Solomon, but it is fitting in a book of covenant wisdom. This statement indicates that both love and a jealousy to protect marriage are given by God.

8:7 The image of **many waters** that **cannot quench love** picks up the image of love as a fire in v. 6; the **floods** that are unable to **drown** it (or "overwhelm"; cf. Isa. 43:2) are another image.

8:8–9 The chorus speaks, here anticipating the woman's speech in vv. 10–12. **The day when she is spoken for** is the day when the **little sister** will marry (cf. 1 Sam. 25:39). A **wall** carries the idea of resistance and probably refers to a chaste woman. The **door** which can be closed or open is an image for either cooperating with the wall (i.e., by propriety), or defying it (i.e., by promiscuity).

What shall we do for our sister
on the day when she is spoken for?
9 If she is a wall,
we will build on her a battlement of silver,
but if she is a door,
we will enclose her with [e]boards of cedar.

SHE

10 [f]I was a wall,
and my [g]breasts were like towers;
then I was in his eyes
as one who finds[1] peace.

11 Solomon had [h]a vineyard at Baal-hamon;
he [i]let out the vineyard to [j]keepers;
each one was to bring for its fruit [k]a thousand pieces of silver.
12 My vineyard, my very own, is before me;
you, O Solomon, may have the thousand,
and [l]the keepers of the fruit two hundred.

HE

13 [m]O you who dwell in the gardens,
with [n]companions listening for your voice;
[o]let me hear it.

SHE

14 [p]Make haste, my beloved,
and be [q]like a gazelle
or a young stag
on [r]the mountains of spices.

[1] Or *brings out*

9[e][1 Kgs. 6:15]
10[f][ch. 4:12, 13] [g][ch. 4:5; 7:3]
11[h]Eccles. 2:4 [i][Matt. 21:33] [j]ch. 1:6 [k][Isa. 7:23]
12[l]See Prov. 27:18
13[m][ch. 5:1] [n]ch. 1:7 [o]ch. 2:14
14[p][Rev. 22:17, 20] [q]See ch. 2:9 [r][ch. 4:6]

8:11–12 This is the second reference in the book to **Solomon** himself, outside of the title (see Introduction: Author and Date). Notice that he continues to be a distant figure, as in 3:6–11, as the reading strategy adopted in these notes suggests. As in 3:6–11, he is described as wealthy; here he has vineyards earning **a thousand pieces of silver** each (cf. Isa. 7:23). The woman's **vineyard** (Song 8:12) probably refers to her sexuality (cf. garden; see note on 4:12). It is hers alone, given to the one whom she chooses and not used for her gain, and thus is in contrast with Solomon's vineyard (8:11).

8:14 For **gazelle** and **young stag**, cf. 2:7, 17. **Mountains of spices** refers to the woman (cf. 4:6). The Song of Solomon closes with the man and woman delighting themselves with their enjoyment of each other.

Introduction to the Prophetic Books

Introduction

Mesopotamian texts indicate that long before Israel entered Canaan, other countries had prophets. These texts from Israel's neighbors indicate that their prophets claimed to intercede for people to the gods, speak for the gods, criticize the people's moral and ethical deficiencies on behalf of the gods, predict future events through special knowledge given by the gods, and denounce enemies by the power of the gods. Though the Bible asserts belief in one God, not many gods, it basically portrays Israel's prophets fulfilling the same tasks. This is not surprising if the idea of a "prophet" was of a person who spoke for a god to the people.

The OT includes three basic terms for the concept of "prophet," two of which have a similar connotation. First, on a few occasions the OT uses the terms *hozeh* or *ro'eh*. The former means "visionary," while the latter means "seer." These words imply that prophets were people who could "envision" or "see" things others could not. They could "see" or "envision" details about the present as well as what God wanted in the future. For example, Saul expected the "seer" Samuel to know where some lost donkeys had gone (1 Sam. 9:1–10). Samuel could indeed "see" where the donkeys had gone, but he could also "see" that God had chosen Saul to rule Israel (1 Sam. 9:15–17). Saul expected to pay the "seer" something for his trouble. Such expectations and the greed of some individuals calling themselves prophets eventually led people to think that all seers were after money (see Amos 7:12).

Second, the OT most commonly uses the word *nabi'* for "prophet." The origins of this word are uncertain; perhaps it comes from a root that means "to announce," which could imply that a prophet was one who announced or declared vital information. In any event the prophet serves as a spokesman: in Exodus 7:1 Moses will be like God to Pharaoh, while Aaron will be his prophet (i.e., his spokesman). Indeed, Israelite prophets claimed to declare the words of Yahweh, the God of Israel, while in other lands the prophets claimed to speak the words of other gods. Since so many prophets were active and were declaring conflicting messages, people had to determine who actually spoke for God and who was a false prophet.

The prophets addressed both future and present issues, with present issues often being the overwhelming concern of their messages. They did announce future events, such as the Messiah's coming and the final day of judgment, but typically they declared how God's people should live in light of their covenant with God (see below).

The Prophets in Israel's History

The Bible indicates that prophets who served the one true living God existed well before the careers of the writing prophets. Abraham (as early as 2000 B.C.), Moses (as early as 1450), Samuel (c. 1050–1010), Nathan (c. 1010–970), Elijah and Elisha (c. 860–850), and Huldah (627) are but a few of the persons whom Genesis–Psalms calls prophets.

Through Moses, God revealed his standards for prophets. According to Deuteronomy 13:1–11, Israel's prophets must never teach the people to serve any other god but Yahweh. Even if a prophet can perform signs and wonders, the people must not follow him if he advocates serving other gods. In Deuteronomy 18:9–22 Moses adds that other nations will have prophets who tell the future and communicate with spirits (Deut. 18:9–14); in contrast, God will put his own words in his prophets' mouths (Deut. 18:18). Further, a prophet can show that he has God's authorization by speaking the truth about future events (Deut. 18:21–22). Israel must wait for the perfect prophet whom God will send (see Acts 3:22–23). As they wait, they must obey prophets who proclaim faithfulness to God's covenant with Israel and whose predictions come true every time. Any prophet failing to meet these standards does not speak for God.

It is important to recognize that the prophets were not the regular teachers of God's word—that was the priests' calling (Deut. 33:10). Rather, God raised up prophets for particular times in the OT story (which is why their "calls" were so important, as in Isaiah 6).

The first Prophetic Books originated in the eighth century B.C. These books came about during the decline of the kingdoms of Israel and Judah and the rise of Assyria as a world power. Eventually Assyria destroyed Israel in 722 B.C., leaving only Judah as a remnant of David's kingdom. Hosea, Amos, and Jonah all ministered at mid-century (760–745 B.C.). Hosea and Amos decried social injustice fueled by covenantal disobedience and warned the covenant people and the nations of a future "day of the Lord," a day of judgment for their sins. Jonah reluctantly preached to Nineveh, the capital of Assyria, before Assyria became a dominant, oppressing nation. Isaiah, the greatest prophet of this era, shared his predecessors' concerns for sin and judgment and wrote some of the Bible's richest promises of a future Savior and his kingdom. Isaiah's book contains decades of writing (c. 745–690 B.C.). Micah ministered near the end of the century (overlapping with Isaiah), rebuking Judah for personal and societal sins and (like Isaiah) predicting God's victory over Assyria during the Sennacherib crisis of 701 B.C. (see 2 Kings 18–19). Micah promised that a leader born in Bethlehem would defeat God's enemies (Mic. 5:1–5; see Matt. 2:1–12).

Seventh-century B.C. prophets wrote against the background of the continuing power and ultimate demise of Assyria, which by 612 B.C. had lost its place as the world's greatest power to Babylon. These prophets pressed God's claims on the chosen people, especially the standards of the Mosaic covenant. Zephaniah (c. 640–609 B.C.) denounced Judah's worship of other gods, warned of judgment, and promised renewal beyond judgment. Nahum

(c. 660–630 B.C.) announced the end of Assyria's tyranny, and Habakkuk (c. 640–609) explored the ways of God in the days leading up to Babylon's capturing of Judah. Of course, Jeremiah also worked during this century and well into the next. He declared God's word of repentance to Judah for at least 40 years (627–587 B.C.; Jer. 1:1–3), decades that spanned from the period when Judah still had time to change its ways and avoid punishment, to the destruction of Jerusalem by Babylon in 587 and the subsequent exiling of the people. He repeatedly preached repentance, yet his most famous words are the promise of a future new covenant with the house of Israel (Jer. 31:31–34; see Heb. 8:8–12).

Sixth-century B.C. prophets lived under the shadow of exile. A few of them also lived during the shifting of world domination from Babylon to Persia, which occurred in 538 B.C. Daniel was taken to Babylon in 605 B.C. He worked there until at least 536 B.C. Ezekiel joined the exiles in Babylon in 597 B.C., where he wrote accounts of visions he received during 593–571. Both of these exiles envisioned perilous times and future days of glory for God's people. Obadiah witnessed the terrors of Babylon's invasion of Judah in 587 B.C. Haggai and Zechariah were among the people allowed to return to Jerusalem from Persia in 520–516 B.C. They participated in the rebuilding of the temple and looked forward to future glory for God's people under the Messiah's leadership.

Malachi served during the fifth century B.C. A contemporary of Ezra and Nehemiah (c. 460–425 B.C.), he experienced the problems associated with rebuilding Jerusalem and restoring faithful worship and covenantal obedience. Malachi identified flaws in the returned exiles' commitment to God, such as insincere worship, the failure of the priests to teach God's Word, and marital infidelity (Mal. 1:6–2:16). He also predicted the coming of a new Elijah and the Messiah (Mal. 4:5–6). The book of Joel probably comes from this period as well, as it makes no mention of a king in Judah. Joel calls the people to repentance at a time of national calamity (a locust plague).

Prophetic Books

Little is known about the Prophetic Books' composition and preservation, though some helpful information may be gleaned from the biblical text. For example, Isaiah had disciples who were able to preserve his words (Isa. 8:16), and Jeremiah's disciple Baruch was a scribe who wrote down some of the prophet's messages (Jer. 36:1–32). Many prophets were probably able to write their own words (Isa. 8:1–2; Jer. 1:4–19) since literacy was fairly widespread.

The prophets' words were originally copied on papyrus or leather scrolls that were passed on to future generations by persons who valued them (Jer. 36:1–4). Several such books existed at one time, for the author of 1–2 Chronicles reports sources composed by or about prophets (1 Chron. 29:29; 2 Chron. 9:29; 26:22). By Jeremiah's time the prophecy of Micah had been handed down and was considered authoritative (Jer. 26:18, quoting Mic. 3:12). According to the apocryphal book *Sirach*, by the second century B.C. (at the very latest) all the Prophetic Books were considered authoritative Scripture (see *Sir.* 48:22; 49:6, 8, 12; cf. *1 Macc.* 2:60).

Many types of literature appear in the Prophetic Books. There are narratives detailing what the prophets did and the circumstances in which they received and delivered their messages. There are also sermons, extended poems, dialogues between God and prophets, and visionary experiences. All of these forms reveal the great themes noted in the next section, and these themes provide the books' plot (or story line) and major characters.

Unifying Themes in the Prophetic Books

The Prophetic Books include most of the OT's greatest themes, preserving in written form for future generations the reasons Israel's history happened as it did. Though the authors wrote in different times and under different circumstances, their messages are in theological harmony with one another and with other types of biblical books. Several interrelated ideas unify the prophetic message, making it possible for readers to find their bearings in some difficult literature. It is often helpful to decide which of the following themes the biblical author is stressing when one becomes puzzled by the content of the books.

First, *the prophets assert that God has spoken through them*. They clearly considered themselves God's messengers and heralds, for they repeatedly preface their messages with the phrase, "Thus says Yahweh." In this way the prophets are claiming that their books are the written word of God. Peter explains that the prophets "were carried along by the Holy Spirit" (2 Pet. 1:21). Just as God used Moses to write and preach so that Israel could know God's will in his era, so God used the prophets in their generations. The prophets declared God's instructions in two basic ways: word and symbol. Usually the prophets presented God's word orally (e.g., Jer. 7:1–8:3) or in written form (e.g., Jer. 36:1–32) to varying types and sizes of audiences. Occasionally they performed symbolic acts that demonstrated God's purposes. For example, Isaiah went naked and barefoot for three years to teach God's people their future if they continued to seek help from other nations rather than from God (Isa. 20:1–6). Perhaps the saddest case of symbolic prophecy was Hosea's marriage to unfaithful Gomer, which portrayed God's relationship with unfaithful Israel (Hosea 1–3).

Second, *the prophets affirm that God chose Israel for covenant relationship*. The Pentateuch (the first five books of the OT) teaches that God chose Abraham and his family to bless all nations (Gen. 12:1–9), that he revealed salvation by grace to Abraham (Gen. 15:6), and that he assigned Moses to write a record of this revelation (Ex. 24:4). Furthermore, through Moses in Exodus–Deuteronomy he revealed the lifestyle that reflects that relationship. With these truths in mind, the prophets addressed Israel as a people with special responsibilities based on this special relationship (Jeremiah 2–6; Hosea 1–3; Amos 2:6–3:8; etc.). Through the prophets God revealed the success and failure of Israel's attempts or lack of attempts to fulfill their confession of faith in God and their God-given role as a kingdom of priests charged with serving the nations (see Ex. 19:5–6).

Third, sadly, *the prophets most often report that the majority of Israel has sinned against their God and his standards for their relationship*. They have failed to trust God (Isa. 7:1–14). Thus, they have broken the Ten Commandments (cf. Ex. 20:1–17 and Jer. 7:1–15; Hos. 4:2). They have worshiped other gods (Ezek. 8:1–18). They have mistreated one another and failed to preserve justice among God's people (Isa. 1:21–31). They have refused to repent (Amos 4:6–11). Of course, in these times there was always a faithful minority, called the "remnant" (see Isa. 4:3; 10:20–22; etc.), as the prophets' ministries themselves demonstrate (see Hebrews 11).

Fourth, *the prophets warn that judgment will eradicate sin.* This judgment is often called the "day of the LORD" (Isa. 2:12–22; Joel 2:1–11; Zeph. 1:7–18; etc.; see note on Amos 5:18–20). This is a day in history, as when Jerusalem was destroyed by Babylon (Jer. 42:18), but it is also a day to come, when God will judge all the world's inhabitants (Isa. 24:1–23). The prophets recorded these warnings in writing so readers can do what the prophets' original audience usually failed to do—turn from sin to God.

Fifth, *the prophets promise that renewal lies beyond the day of punishment that has occurred already in history and beyond the coming day that will bring history as we know it to a close.* The coming of the Savior lies beyond the destruction of Israel and other such events. He will rule Israel and the nations, and he will bring peace and righteousness to the world (Isa. 9:2–7; 11:1–16). This Savior must suffer, die, and rise from the dead (Isa. 52:13–53:12). He will be "like a son of man," and "the Ancient of Days" (God himself) will give him all the kingdoms of the world (Dan. 7:9–14). He will be the catalyst for a new covenant with Israel that will include all those, Jew or Gentile, whom God's Spirit fills and changes (Jer. 31:31–40; Ezek. 34:25–31; 36:22–32). This new people will serve him faithfully. Eventually he will cleanse the world of sin and recreate the earth (Isa. 65:17–25; 66:18–24; Zeph. 3:8–20). The creation now spoiled by sin will be whole again.

Scholarly Issues and the Prophetic Books

The past two centuries have seen many debates concerning the Prophetic Books. These discussions include many facets but may be summarized in the following categories: unity, authenticity, and relationship to the NT.

For centuries most scholars basically accepted that the Prophetic Books were written by the persons whose names were mentioned at the beginning of the books (Isa. 1:1; Jer. 1:1–3; etc.). They did so because they held traditional beliefs about the inspiration and authority of the Bible (see Ps. 19:1–14; 2 Tim. 3:14–17; 2 Pet. 1:21) yet also because the books are as well attested by other ancient sources, and as coherent in content and style, as any surviving ancient books.

Beginning in the late 1700s, however, several scholars began to argue that differences within individual books indicate that they were not composed of the words of the persons that the books name as the source of the material. For example, they noted that the book of Isaiah stresses judgment and renewal, mentions Assyria and Babylon as conquerors of Israel, and describes exile and return from exile. Therefore, they posited at least two authors, one who lived in the eighth century B.C. and one who lived in the sixth century, with perhaps a third in the fifth century. They soon made similar arguments about other prophetic books. As they continued to find other differences, they suggested still more authors. By the early 1900s such scholars wrote freely about the "authentic" passages (written or spoken by the persons the Bible names as authors) and the "inauthentic" passages (written by later editors of the books).

Many of these critical scholars also concluded that the OT prophets did not predict future events in the manner the NT claims. Rather, in their view the prophets wrote about events of their own day, but NT writers applied these texts to Jesus, the church, and other subjects. Thus, the unity of the OT and the NT, which Jesus and Paul are portrayed as affirming (Matt. 5:17–20; John 5:45–46; 10:35; 2 Tim. 3:14–17), simply does not exist. Church tradition may treat the Bible as a unity, but, they argued, historical research does not confirm that belief.

Evangelical scholars responded to these trends in several ways. First, they reaffirmed their belief in the inspiration and authority of the Bible and in the Holy Spirit's ability to provide information on the future to the prophets. Second, they observed that the OT and NT writers—the closest witnesses to the time of the books' writing and the most ancient teachers of that word—never name any writers of a biblical book other than the ones listed in the OT. Third, they offered treatments of the books that explained how the passages in question could come from the time period the books mention. Fourth, they described how the NT writers used the OT books in a contextual, not arbitrary, manner.

Recently evangelical scholars have been joined by less traditional experts in their critique of many of these assertions by critical scholars. These experts believe that differences in emphasis in a book do not necessarily mean different authors, since an author may stress many diverging themes that eventually constitute a unified composition. For instance, in order for a Greek comedy to end happily, there must be some negative reality overcome. For a Greek tragedy to end sadly, there must be some joy lost. Similarly, the prophetic message included punishment on the way to renewal and sin that marred the nation's once-positive relationship with God. The presence of different concepts helps comprise the whole; it does not necessitate multiple authors.

Despite this emerging agreement on the unified content of the Prophetic Books, evangelical scholars and their counterparts still often disagree on how the books came together. Many evangelical scholars continue to hold to the unity of the books as the words of the prophets that the books themselves identify, while their dialogue partners believe that the unity came about through the careful work of editors over a long period of time. What remains at stake in these discussions is the truthfulness of the text's claims to originate from a particular person in a particular era, addressing items specific to that era as well as items in the future. It is the special calling of the particular prophet that gives his writing canonical authority for God's people (Deut. 18:18–19).

Pronouns in the Prophets

As prepositions are to the letters of Paul, so pronouns are to the oracles of the prophets: crucial for meaning, but often puzzling. Hebrew prophets delivered messages on God's behalf, so identifying who is being addressed, and who is being spoken about, is central to understanding their preaching. Naturally, use of pronouns ("I," "we," "you," "she," etc.) can frustrate modern readers when their *antecedent* (the actual person or entity being referred to) either is missing or could have more than one possible candidate. Although pronoun confusion arises most naturally in the Prophets, it also crops up in the prayers of the Psalms. Sometimes modern biblical translations smooth out such difficulties for the reader by specifying the referent or adjusting the pronouns. The ESV approach, in general, prefers to represent the pronouns in English as equivalent to those appearing in the Hebrew, and not to make decisions for the reader about their referents.

In prophetic literature, confusing pronoun references occur especially in the following cases: (1) unmarked interjections; (2) unsignaled transitions in oracles or other passages; (3) differences in ancient and modern conventions for pronouns; and (4) obscurity in a passage beyond simply its pronouns. Also, (5) an author might be addressing the people as a whole (personified as a single "you"). The following are examples for each scenario.

(1) Who is "he" in Zechariah 10:11? The Lord speaks as "I" on either side of this verse; ancient versions and commentators often read "they" here, to link back to the last word of Zechariah 10:10. However, the context suggests that the action of Zechariah 10:10 belongs to the Lord, and in Zechariah 10:12b, the Lord's own voice seems to refer to himself in the third person ("his name"). Here the prophet's voice and the Lord's seem fused, and in spite of changing between "I" and "he/him," the reference is consistently to God.

(2) Who is "us" in Isaiah 41:22? The first-person plural reference continues in Isaiah 41:23, and then reappears in Isaiah 41:26, but never with an explicit referent. Here, help comes from the wider context. The setting is the divine courtroom ("set forth your case," Isa. 41:21), and this is introduced at Isaiah 41:1 ("let *us* draw near for judgment"), so "us" in Isaiah 41:22 remains the members of the divine court who are hearing the case against the idols of Isaiah 41:7.

(3) Who is "her" in Micah 7:10? The answer partly depends on who is "me" in Micah 7:8. "My enemy" in Micah 7:8, 10 is grammatically feminine (Hb. *'oyabti*), and so is the antecedent for "her" in Micah 7:10. It is likely, then, that the first-person voice is also feminine (cf. Mic. 6:9; 7:11)—Jerusalem personified. In biblical convention, cities are referred to as feminine and nations as masculine—unlike modern English usage in which cities are normally neuter ("it") and nations are feminine.

(4) A genuine difficulty is the "they" (fem.) reference of Ezekiel 30:17, represented in the ESV by "women" but with a textual note, "Or *the cities*; Hebrew *they*." The translation adopted in the text takes its cue from "young men" in Ezekiel 30:17a and "daughters" of Ezekiel 30:18b. "Cities" remains possible (see example 3), as "On" and "Pi-beseth" are the closest immediate antecedents in context.

(5) The prophets can personify God's people, viewed corporately, as if a single person. In Isaiah 41:8–10, "you" (masculine singular) refers to "Jacob," the whole people portrayed as God's "servant" (to accomplish his purposes for the world). It is to the people viewed corporately that God promises, "I will strengthen you, I will help you, I will uphold you" (Isa. 41:10). Similarly, in Isaiah 49:15–16, God addresses "you" (this time feminine singular), a personification of Zion (Isa. 49:14), representing the whole people (see also Isa. 54:1–17).

Awareness of these possibilities should assist the reader in untangling some of the pronoun references that might initially seem difficult to understand. ◂

Activity of the Writing Prophets during the Reigns of the Kings of Israel and Judah

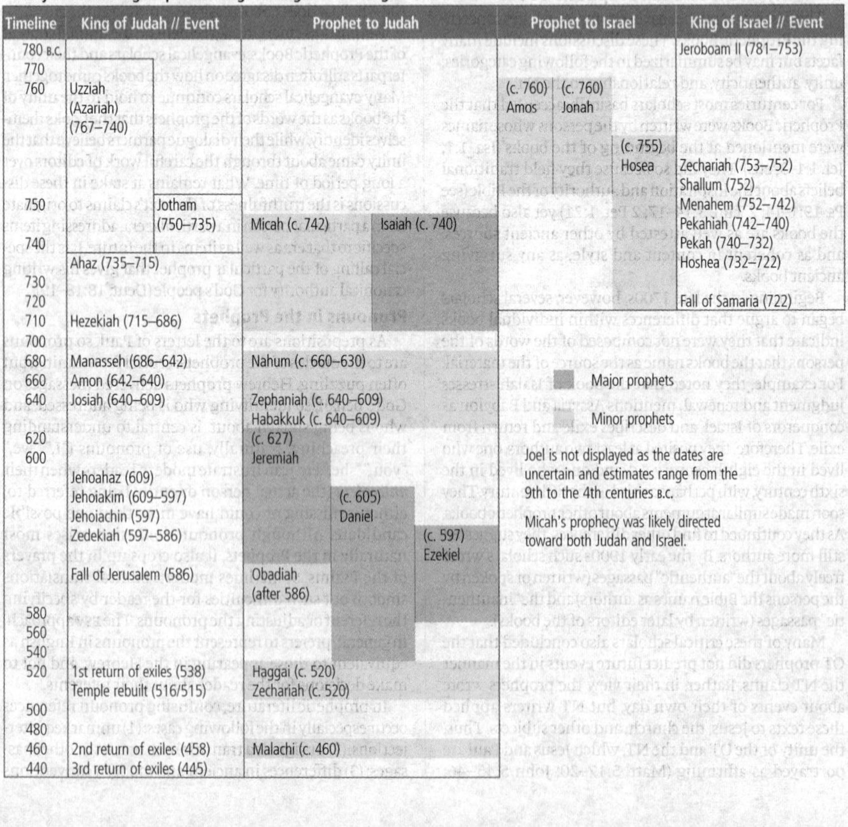

Timeline
King of Judah // Event
Prophet to Judah
Prophet to Israel
King of Israel // Event
780 B.C.
770
760
750
740
730
720
710
700
680
660
640
620
600
580
560
540
520
500
480
460
440
Uzziah (Azariah) (767–740)
Jotham (750–735)
Ahaz (735–715)
Hezekiah (715–686)
Manasseh (686–642)
Amon (642–640)
Josiah (640–609)
Jehoahaz (609)
Jehoiakim (609–597)
Jehoiachin (597)
Zedekiah (597–586)
Fall of Jerusalem (586)
1st return of exiles (538)
Temple rebuilt (516/515)
2nd return of exiles (458)
3rd return of exiles (445)
Micah (c. 742)
Isaiah (c. 740)
Nahum (c. 660–630)
Zephaniah (c. 640–609)
Habakkuk (c. 640–609)
(c. 627) Jeremiah
(c. 605) Daniel
(c. 597) Ezekiel
Obadiah (after 586)
Haggai (c. 520)
Zechariah (c. 520)
Malachi (c. 460)
(c. 760) Amos
(c. 760) Jonah
(c. 755) Hosea
Jeroboam II (781–753)
Zechariah (753–752)
Shallum (752)
Menahem (752–742)
Pekahiah (742–740)
Pekah (740–732)
Hoshea (732–722)
Fall of Samaria (722)
Major prophets
Minor prophets
Joel is not displayed as the dates are uncertain and estimates range from the 9th to the 4th centuries B.C.
Micah's prophecy was likely directed toward both Judah and Israel.

INTRODUCTION TO

ISAIAH

Author and Title

The opening words of the book explain that this is "the vision of Isaiah the son of Amoz" (1:1). Unlike Jeremiah, who discloses aspects of his inner personal life (e.g., Jer. 20:7–12), Isaiah says little about himself. Isaiah 6 records his call to prophesy, openly revealing his innermost thoughts on that occasion. Chapters 7–8; 20; and 37–39 offer glimpses into his public ministry. The parallel accounts in 2 Kings 19–20 add a little. The NT bears witness to his prophetic foresight (John 12:37–41) and boldness (Rom. 10:20). Beyond this, the Bible's sole interest is in Isaiah's message, which is summed up in the meaning of his name: "Yahweh is salvation."

Isaiah's father was Amoz (Isa. 1:1), but the Bible says nothing more of him. Jewish tradition claims that Amoz was a brother of Amaziah, king of Judah, putting Isaiah into the royal family. It is clear that Isaiah was a married man and a father (7:3; 8:3, 18). He appears to have been a resident of Jerusalem (7:3). Hebrews 11:37 ("they were sawn in two"; see note there) may allude to the tradition of Isaiah's death under persecution by Manasseh, king of Judah (687–642 B.C.; cf. *Lives of the Prophets* 1.1; *Martyrdom of Isaiah* 5.1–14).

Isaiah's record of the reign of King Uzziah (2 Chron. 26:22) is not to be identified with the biblical book of Isaiah.

The title presents the book as "the *vision* of Isaiah the son of Amoz" (Isa. 1:1). Israel's prophets were indeed seers (2 Kings 6:15–17; 17:13; Isa. 29:10; 30:10). Isaiah himself "saw the Lord" (6:1), but his visionary insights were made shareable by being put into a written message: "The *word* that Isaiah the son of Amoz saw" (2:1). Isaiah's book is a vision in that it reveals, through symbols and reasoned thought, a God-centered way of seeing and living. It offers everyone the true alternative to the false appearances of this world.

Date

Isaiah prophesied "in the days of Uzziah, Jotham, Ahaz, and Hezekiah, kings of Judah" (1:1). His call to ministry came "in the year that King Uzziah died" (6:1), around 740 B.C., and he lived long enough to record the death of Sennacherib (37:38), datable to 681. A few of the oracles can be dated, as the notes will show: e.g., chapter 7 comes from about 735 B.C.; chapters 36–38 come from the time of the Assyrian invasion, 701. Most of the material, however, can be dated only in very general terms because the book offers no such information.

Some scholars theorize that more than one author was responsible for this book. These scholars spread the authorship of the book through multiple hands writing over the course of around 200 years. This theory proposes that, though chapters 1–39 are largely the work of Isaiah, chapters 40–66 are the work of an anonymous prophet living during the Babylonian exile, over a century after Isaiah. Many propose further that chapters 56–66 were composed by yet another, still later, anonymous prophet. This would yield First Isaiah (chs. 1–39), from the late eighth century B.C.; Second Isaiah (chs. 40–55), from the middle of the sixth century; and Third Isaiah (chs. 56–66), from sometime in the fifth century. There are three primary reasons offered for not attributing chapters 40–66 to Isaiah the son of Amoz: (1) Chapters 40–66 assume the exilic period as their background. (2) Chapters 40–66 have differences in style from chapters 1–39. (3) The detailed predictions in the latter section of the book would have been meaningful to the exilic and postexilic community of Judah, but (according to this view) would not have been relevant to the people of Isaiah's own time.

These reasons for dividing the book suffer from severe shortcomings, and it is better to take the heading (1:1) as indicating that the entire book comes from Isaiah, the son of Amoz.

1. There is unified testimony from the ancient world for single authorship. (1) The NT refers to passages throughout the book as the work of Isaiah (see Matt. 3:3; 4:14–16; 8:17; 12:17–21; 13:14–15; 15:7–9; Mark 7:6–7; Luke 3:4–6; 4:17–19; John 1:23; 12:37–41; Acts 8:27–35; 28:25–27; Rom. 9:27–29; 10:16, 20–21; 15:12). The NT acknowledges no other author or authors. The testimony of John in John 12:41 is especially instructive: "Isaiah said these things because he saw his glory and spoke of him." "These things," which is plural, refers to the two previous quotations in John 12:38 (using Isa. 53:1, from the so-called "Second Isaiah") and John 12:40 (using Isa. 6:10, from so-called "First Isaiah"), but John refers to the one person, Isaiah, who both "saw his glory" and "spoke of him." (2) The intertestamental book of *Sirach* (48:24–25) and the first-century Jewish historian Josephus (*Jewish Antiquities* 11.5–6) attest Isaiah's authorship of the whole book. (3) A Hebrew manuscript of Isaiah in the Dead Sea Scrolls bears witness to the seamless unity of the book as the work of Isaiah. (4) It is hard to imagine how prophets could have issued such oracles as those of Isaiah 40–66, which were of such importance in the history of Judah, and yet fade into obscurity. (5) Later OT authors seem to cite prophecies from chapters 40–66, which they could not have done if the book were broken up as described (e.g., see note on 60:7, used in Ezra 7:27).

2. There are many distinctive features of Isaiah's style that run through all three parts. For example, Isaiah's characteristic title for the Lord is "the Holy One of Israel," which appears 25 times in the whole book (12 times in Isaiah 1–39; 11 times in chs. 40–55; and twice in chs. 56–66). It appears only six times outside of Isaiah: twice in Jeremiah, three times in the Psalms, and in 2 Kings 19:22 (cf. Isa. 37:33). The phrase "high and lifted up" is a feature of Isaiah, appearing in 2:12–14; 6:1; 52:13; 57:15 (i.e., in each of the three sections; see note on 6:1). The notes will show other aspects of coherent thought and expression in Isaiah. Any differences of style can be explained by the different topics of the chapters and by different stages in Isaiah's life (e.g., Isaiah may have written chapters 40–66 after the Assyrian invasion of 701 B.C.).

3. The predictive material in chapters 40–66 is highly relevant both to the exilic audience and to Isaiah's own day. Certainly it demonstrates the Lord's rule over history; these chapters appeal to it for that purpose (e.g., 41:21–29), and Josephus (*Jewish Antiquities* 11.5–7) records a story of the impression the specific prediction of Cyrus (Isa. 44:28) made on the Persian monarch when he learned of it (a prediction made about 150 years in advance). The biblical worldview, which begins with the majestic Creator, can readily accept this. Further, chapters 40–66 often mention pagan religion, but specifically Babylonian material is rare (46:1); most address Canaanite idolatry, which Judah mixed in with their worship of Yahweh (e.g., 57:5; 66:3, 17; cf. 40:19; 41:7, 29; 42:17; 45:16–20; 46:6; 48:5; and the extended satire on idolatry, 44:9–20)—and this was no longer a problem in Judah after the fall of Jerusalem.

However, the primary significance of this predictive material resides in a wider context. The whole book portrays God's plan for Judah as a story that is headed somewhere, namely, toward the coming of the final heir of David who will bring light to the Gentiles. Israel was created for this very purpose, and it will require that God's people be purified of those members whose lives destroy that mission (see note on 1:24–28). This prospect of a glorious future enlists all believing readers to dedicate themselves to living faithfully and to embrace the dignity of playing a part in its development (cf. 2:5).

At the heart of Isaiah's message is God's purpose of grace for sinners. If that ultimate miracle is accepted—and one cannot be a Christian without accepting it—then a lesser miracle is no barrier. Indeed, the prophet making predictions of future events is not a problem; it is, as Isaiah intended it to be, encouraging evidence of God's sovereign salvation intercepting a sinful world.

Theme

The central theme of the book is God himself, who does all things for his own sake (48:11). Isaiah defines everything else by its relation to God, whether it is rightly adjusted to him as the gloriously central figure in all of reality (45:22–25). God is the Holy One of Israel (1:4), the One who is high and lifted up but who also dwells down among the "contrite and lowly" (57:15), the Sovereign over the whole world (13:1–27:13) whose wrath is fierce (9:12, 17, 21; 10:4) but whose cleansing touch atones for sin (6:7), whose salvation flows in endless supply (12:3), whose gospel is "good news of happiness" (52:7), who is moving history toward the blessing of his people (43:3–7) and the exclusive worship due him (2:2–4). He is the only Savior (43:10–13), and the whole world will know it (49:26). To rest in the promises of this God is his people's only strength (30:15); to delight themselves in his word is their refreshing feast (55:1–2); to serve his cause is their worthy devotion (ch. 62); but to rebel against him is endless death (66:24).

A microcosm of the book's message appears in 1:2–2:5. The Lord announces his basic charge against the people: they have received so much privilege from God and ought to be grateful children, but "they have despised the Holy One of Israel" (1:2–4). He describes the purpose of the various judgments they face, namely, to bring them to repentance, or at least to preserve a remnant who *will* repent (1:5–9). Judah is very diligent to observe the divinely appointed sacrifices, but the people's hearts are far from God, as their unwillingness to protect their own weakest members exhibits (1:10–20). The Lord called his people to be the embodiment of faithfulness in this world, and yet they are now filled with rampant unfaithfulness at every level (personal, religious, and social); but God intends to purge Zion of its sinful members and set her up as a beacon of light for the whole world. In view of this glorious future, Isaiah's contemporaries should commit themselves afresh to walking "in the light of the LORD" (1:21–2:5).

Purpose, Occasion, and Background

Isaiah announces God's surprising plan of grace and glory for his rebellious people and, indeed, for the world. God had promised Abraham that through his descendants the world would be blessed (Gen. 12:1–3). God had promised David that his throne would lead the world into salvation (2 Sam. 7:12–16; Ps. 89:19–37). But by Isaiah's time, the descendants of Abraham and many members of the dynasty of David no longer trusted the promises of God, aligning themselves instead with the promises—and the fears—of this false world. Judah's unbelief in God during the pivotal events of Isaiah's lifetime redirected their future away from blessing and toward judgment. At this historic turning point, Judah moved from independence under God's power to subservience under pagan powers.

What, then, of God's ancient promises? Is the gracious purpose of God defeated by Judah's sin? Isaiah answers that question. After the prefatory chapters 1–5, his answer unfolds in chapters 6–27, and the rest of the book develops the serious but hopeful message of these chapters. Isaiah's answer is that, although God must purify his people through judgment, he has an overruling purpose of grace, beginning with Isaiah himself (ch. 6), spreading to Judah (7:1–9:7) and Israel (9:8–11:16), and resulting in endless joy (12:1–6). Even the nations of the world are taken into account (13:1–27:13). The purpose of Isaiah, then, is to declare the good news that God will glorify himself through the renewed and increased glory of his people, which will attract the nations. The book of Isaiah is a vision of hope for sinners through the coming Messiah, promising for the "ransomed" people of God a new world where sin and sorrow will be forever forgotten (35:10; 51:11).

Isaiah's book envisions three historical settings (see chart): (1) chapters 1–39 are set against the background of Isaiah's own times in the late eighth century B.C.; (2) chapters 40–55 assume the Jewish exiles in Babylon in the sixth century as their audience; and (3) chapters 56–66 take the returned exiles and subsequent generations of God's people as their backdrop. It would be a mistake, however, to suppose that the chapters have relevance only to their assumed audiences: the long-range prophecies of chapters 40–66, as already indicated, challenge all the people of Judah in Isaiah's time to accept their role in a story that is headed to a glorious future and to live faithfully in that light (cf. 2:5, on the heels of 2:1–4). Further, the entire book, as canonical Scripture, addresses all the people of God until Christ returns.

First, in his own times, Isaiah prophesied "in the days of Uzziah, Jotham, Ahaz, and Hezekiah, kings of Judah" (1:1). Called by God "in the year that King Uzziah died" (6:1), his long ministry began in 740 B.C. The external threat of Isaiah's day was the militant Assyrian Empire rising to power in the east. The question forced upon Judah by this threat was one of trust: in what will God's people trust for salvation—in human strategies of self-rescue, or in prophetic promises of divine grace?

This question of what and whom to trust intensified on two occasions. The first occurred c. 735 B.C., during the reign of King Ahaz. Under pressure from Assyria, the northern kingdom of Israel formed a pact of

Simplified Overview of Isaiah

	Isaiah 1–39	Isaiah 40–55	Isaiah 56–66
Date and Setting	The eighth century B.C. (700s); the Assyrian threat	Prophecies about the sixth century B.C. (500s); the Babylonian exile	Prophecies about all times and occasions until the end
Audience	God's rebellious people craving worldly security	God's defeated people under worldly domination	All who hold fast to God's covenant
Actions	God purifies a remnant of his apostate people through judgment	God consoles his discouraged people in exile	God prepares all of his true people for his promised salvation
Message	"In returning and rest you shall be saved; . . . But you were unwilling" (30:15)	"the glory of the LORD shall be revealed" (40:5)	"Keep justice, and do righteousness" (56:1)

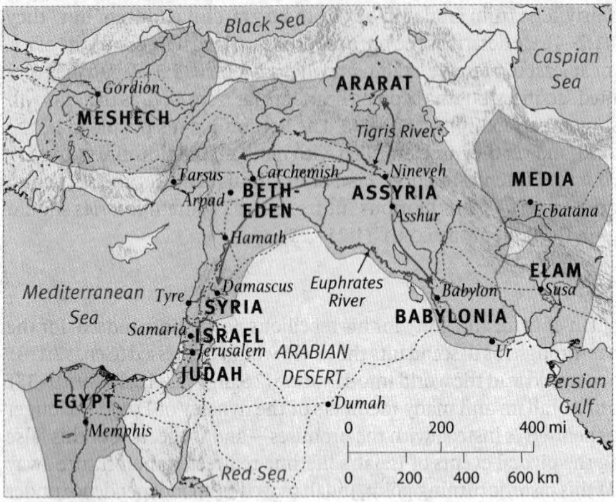

The Near East at the Time of Isaiah
c. 740 B.C.
The prophecies of Isaiah are set against the backdrop of a rising Assyrian Empire. This resurgent ancient nation posed a great threat to Israel and Judah, and it would eventually engulf nearly the entire Near East from Ur to Ararat to Egypt.

mutual defense with Syria, and together these two kingdoms aimed to force Judah into alignment with them (ch. 7). But God could be trusted to stand by his commitment to defend the Davidic throne. Accordingly, Isaiah assured Ahaz of God's saving purpose. But Ahaz refused God, preferring the power of Assyria, and negotiated for pagan protection (2 Kings 16:5–9). Thus Ahaz surrendered the sovereignty of the Davidic throne to a nation hostile to the kingdom of God, and achieved nothing in return. The coalition arrayed against Judah failed—Syria fell in 732 B.C. and Israel in 722, as God had said they would (Isa. 7:16; 8:4).

The second crisis occurred in 701 B.C., during the reign of Hezekiah. This time Assyria was the threat. As before, the temptation was to negotiate an alliance of defense with human powers, in this case with Egypt (30:1–7; 31:1–3; 36:6). Judah chose the false refuge of human promises rather than to rest on the Lord's "sure foundation" (28:14–22). Assyria then set out to punish Judah for its pact with Egypt. Hezekiah tried to buy peace from the Assyrians (2 Kings 18:13–16), but they turned on him (Isa. 33:1). Under extreme pressure, Hezekiah finally put his trust in the Lord and found him to be powerfully faithful (chs. 36–37).

The eventual downfall of Judah was foreseen in Hezekiah's unguarded openness to Babylonian influence (ch. 39). Isaiah discerned in Hezekiah's enthusiasm for Babylon a future of captivity there for God's people.

Second, Isaiah was enabled by God to address the Jewish captives far away in Babylon in the sixth century B.C. He announces a promise that God is coming with a world-changing display of his glory (40:5). To prepare for his coming, the exiles must return to the Promised Land (48:20). They must not be demoralized by the impressive but empty culture of idolatry in which they live (41:21–24), nor should they resent God's use of a pagan conqueror, Cyrus the Great, as their liberator from Babylon (44:24–28). They must look by faith for a greater liberator still to come, the messianic "servant of the Lord" (see note on 42:1–9). He will bring justice to the nations (42:1–4) and save his people from their ultimate captivity, the guilt of sin (52:13–53:12). Since the faith of God's people had already proven weak, God pledges that he alone will accomplish this, for his own glory (48:9–11).

Third, Isaiah addressed the returned exiles and subsequent generations of God's people with messages of challenge and hope, to keep their faith and obedience steady until God fulfills all his promises. Isaiah makes clear the spiritual and universal nature of God's true people (56:3–8; 66:18–23). He sees the final triumph of One who is "mighty to save" (63:1). His prophetic eye looks beyond the fraudulence of this world, all the way forward to the eternal finality of God's renewed people in a renewed cosmos (65:17; 66:22). "Therefore let us be grateful for receiving a kingdom that cannot be shaken" (Heb. 12:28).

Key Themes

With God himself as the center of Isaiah's vision, multiple supportive themes are entailed:

1. God is offended by religious ritual, however impressive, if it conceals an empty heart and a careless life (1:10–17; 58:1–12; 66:1–4).

2. God's true people will become a multinational community of worship and peace forever (2:2–4; 19:19–25;

25:6–9; 56:3–8; 66:18–23), and the predominant culture of a new world (14:1–2; 41:8–16; 43:3–7; 45:14–17; 49:19–26; 60:1–22).

3. God opposes all manifestations of human pride (2:10–17; 10:33–34; 13:11; 16:6; 23:9; 28:1–4).

4. The foolish idols that man creates are destined for destruction (2:20–21; 19:1; 31:6–7; 44:9–20; 46:1–7).

5. Though God's judgment will reduce his people to a remnant, his final purpose is the joyful triumph of his grace (1:9; 6:1–12:6; 35:1–10; 40:1–2; 49:13–16; 51:3; 54:7–8; 55:12–13).

6. God is able to judge people by rendering them deaf and blind to his saving word (6:9–10; 28:11–13; 29:9–14; 42:18–25).

7. The only hope of the world is bound up in one man—the promised Davidic king (4:2; 7:14; 9:2–7; 11:1–10), the servant of the Lord (42:1–9; 49:1–13; 50:4–9; 52:13–53:12), the anointed preacher of the gospel (61:1–3), and the lone victor over all evil (63:1–6).

8. God is actively using creation and history, and even the wrongs of man, for his own glory (10:5–19; 13:1–27:13; 36:1–39:8; 40:12–26; 44:24–45:13).

9. With a great and holy God ruling all things, man's duty is a repentant trust in him alone (7:9; 10:20; 12:2; 26:3–4; 28:12, 16; 30:15–18; 31:1; 32:17–18; 36:1–37:38; 40:31; 42:17; 50:10; 55:1–7; 57:13, 15; 66:2).

10. God's people, feeling abandoned by God (40:27; 49:14; 51:12–13), foolishly put their trust in worldly powers (7:1–8:22; 28:14–22; 30:1–17; 31:1–3; 39:1–8).

11. God will uphold his own cause with a world-transforming display of his glory (4:2–6; 11:10; 35:1–2; 40:3–5; 52:10; 59:19; 60:1–3; 66:18).

12. God uses predictive prophecy to prove that his hand is guiding human history (41:1–4, 21–29; 44:6–8; 44:24–45:13; 46:8–11; 48:3–11).

13. God's past faithfulness and the certainty of his final victory motivate his people toward prayer and practical obedience now (56:1–2; 62:1–64:12).

14. The wrath of God is to be feared above all else (5:25; 9:12, 17, 19, 21; 10:4–6; 13:9, 13; 30:27; 34:2; 59:18; 63:1–6; 66:15–16, 24).

History of Salvation Summary

Isaiah shares with the rest of the OT a high view of the mission of Israel. God called Abraham and his family to be the vehicle by which he would bring to the whole world the blessing of knowing the true God (Gen. 12:1–3). The great tragedy of Israel was their repeated faithlessness, which hid the light from the Gentiles. God will not be thwarted, however, and in order to bless the Gentiles he will purify his people (Isa. 1:24–28) and from them raise up the heir of David.

Though Isaiah denounces hypocrisy, greed, and idolatry as offenses against God, he also foresees the Savior of offenders, the Lord Jesus Christ, who is God-with-us (7:14), the child destined to rule forever (9:6–7), the hope of the Davidic throne (11:1), the glory of the Lord (40:5), the suffering servant of the Lord (42:1–9; 49:1–6; 50:4–9; 52:13–53:12), the anointed preacher of the gospel (61:1–3), the bloodied victor over all evil (63:1–6), and more. Isaiah is mentioned by name in the NT over 20 times and is quoted there extensively, for the message he preached is the very gospel of Jesus and the apostles.

Isaiah's message makes an impact on every reader in one of two ways. Either this book will harden the reader's pride against God (6:9–10; 28:13; 29:11–12) or it will become to the contrite reader a feast of refreshment in God (55:1–3; 57:15; 66:2). Through Isaiah's vision the eyes of faith see their iniquity laid on Another (53:6), they see a new Jerusalem of eternal gladness (65:17–18), they see all humanity giving God the worship that is his due forever (66:22–23), and that prophetic vision keeps their hope alive. As with the rest of the OT, these things were written "that through endurance and through the encouragement of the Scriptures we might have hope" (Rom. 15:4). (For an explanation of the "History of Salvation," see the Overview of the Bible, pp. 23–26. See also History of Salvation in the Old Testament: Preparing the Way for Christ, pp. 2635–2661.)

Literary Features

The overall genre of the book is prophecy. Although biblical prophets primarily *tell forth* God's message in their contemporary situation, and less frequently *foretell* the future, the last third of Isaiah is an exception in being mainly predictive of the future. It is important to clarify two literary features of the foretelling: first, having been received in visions, it has many figurative elements; and second, its purpose is not simply to tell the future but to express the author's sense of Israel's place in God's overarching redemptive plan for the world.

A book this large, and lacking a narrative line, must be viewed as an anthology or collection of individual compositions. It is often futile to look for a smooth flow from one unit to the next. The book swings back and forth between oracles of judgment and oracles of salvation. The general movement of the book is from an emphasis on evil and judgment to rapturous visions of a coming redemption, a movement from bad news to good news. But this is only a general pattern that should not lead readers to distort the smaller swings, between evil/judgment and redemption/restoration, which persist to the very last verses of the book.

The opening movement of the book is more of a warning against sin than a blueprint for the future. As Isaiah looks at his world, he *depicts* its evil, *denounces* that evil, and *predicts God's imminent judgment* against that evil. All three of these ingredients are typically couched in the form of the oracle of judgment, a divine indictment of present evil. Additionally, biblical prophets intermingle and end their books with visions of God's restored favor to his people; these visions are expressed in the form of the oracle of redemption (also called the oracle of salvation) and oracle of blessing.

The oracles of judgment need to be approached as examples of satire: they have an object of attack, a vehicle in which the attack is embodied, a stated or implied norm by which the criticism is conducted, and a prevailing tone of either ridicule or disgust. Because much of the book of Isaiah envisions things that either have not yet happened or do not literally happen (given the symbolic form in which they are portrayed), the genre of visionary writing is continuously operative in the book of Isaiah (the author *envisions* something that does not literally exist and/or that has not yet happened). A preponderance of the book is cast into the form of poetry, with the result that readers need to apply all that they know about staples of poetry, such as imagery, metaphor, simile, apostrophe, and hyperbole.

Many of the visions of redemption in the last third of Isaiah are lyric in form and effect. Apocalyptic writing appears prominently in chapters 24–27. Because the agents who interact with God are often nations rather than individuals, and because the forces of nature are also sometimes actors, the label "cosmic drama" is a helpful concept. Finally, in this book that encompasses such a diversity of material, there is even a full-fledged hero story involving King Hezekiah and the prophet Isaiah (chs. 36–39).

Outline

I. Introduction: "Ah, Sinful Nation!" (1:1–5:30)
   A. Judah's sins confronted (1:1–31)
   B. Judah's hope, guilt, hope (2:1–4:6)
      1. Hope (2:1–5)
      2. Guilt (2:6–4:1)
      3. Hope (4:2–6)
   C. Judah's sins condemned (5:1–30)

II. God Redefines the Future of His People: "Your Guilt Is Taken Away" (6:1–12:6)
   A. Grace—through judgment—for Isaiah (6:1–13)
   B. Grace—through judgment—for Judah (7:1–9:7)
   C. Grace—through judgment—for Israel (9:8–11:16)
   D. The enjoyment of God's grace (12:1–6)

III. God's Judgment and Grace for the World: "We Have a Strong City" (13:1–27:13)
   A. First series of oracles: the here and now (13:1–20:6)
      1. Babylon (13:1–14:27)
      2. Philistia (14:28–32)
      3. Moab (15:1–16:14)
      4. The Syria-Israel alliance (17:1–18:7)
      5. Egypt (19:1–20:6)
   B. Second series of oracles: the deeper truth (21:1–23:18)
      1. Babylon (21:1–10)
      2. Edom (21:11–12)
      3. Arabia (21:13–17)

4. Jerusalem (22:1–25)
5. Tyre (23:1–18)

C. Third series of oracles: the final end (24:1–27:13)
1. The wasted city (24:1–20)
2. The Lord will punish (24:21–23)
3. He will swallow up death forever (25:1–12)
4. He will ordain peace (26:1–21)
5. The whole world will be fruitful (27:1–13)

IV. God's Sovereign Word Spoken into the World: "Ah!" (28:1–35:10)

A. Six laments, with assurances (28:1–33:24)
1. The proud crown of Ephraim (28:1–29)
2. The city where David encamped (29:1–14)
3. Those who turn things upside down (29:15–24)
4. Stubborn children with their own plans (30:1–33)
5. Those who go down to Egypt for help (31:1–32:20)
6. The destroyer who has not been destroyed (33:1–24)

B. Two final outcomes: judgment or salvation (34:1–35:10)

V. Historical Transition: "In Whom Do You Now Trust?" (36:1–39:8)

A. Practical trust in God vindicated (36:1–37:38)
B. Human inconstancy sent into exile (38:1–39:8)

VI. Comfort for God's Exiles: "The Glory of the Lord Shall Be Revealed" (40:1–55:13)

A. The God of glory: his coming, exclusivity, power (40:1–31)
B. The one true God moving history for his people (41:1–20)
C. False hopes, the Lord's servant, a new song (41:21–42:17)
D. God reclaims his people for his glory (42:18–43:21)
E. God revives his people for his glory (43:22–44:23)
F. God predicts his use of Cyrus (44:24–45:25)
G. The gods and pride of Babylon doomed (46:1–47:15)
H. God will free his people from Babylon for his own sake (48:1–22)
I. The Lord's servant displayed, his people assured (49:1–50:3)
J. The Lord's servant taught, his people attentive (50:4–51:8)
K. Encouragements to a responsive faith (51:9–52:12)
L. The Lord's servant: the exalted sin-bearer (52:13–53:12)
M. Compassion for God's people, offered to all (54:1–55:13)

VII. How to Prepare for the Coming Glory: "Hold Fast My Covenant" (56:1–66:24)

A. The true people of God redefined (56:1–8)
B. The false people of God exposed (56:9–57:13)
C. The true people of God invited (57:14–21)
D. The path to blessing: ritual vs. responsibility (58:1–59:13)
E. Present failure, eternal covenant, future glory (59:14–60:22)
F. The anointed Preacher renewing the world (61:1–62:12)
G. The coming Victor; his past faithfulness (63:1–14)
H. Praying for the power of God (63:15–64:12)
I. The eagerness of God for his people's eternal joy (65:1–25)
J. True worship now and forever (66:1–24)

ISAIAH

1 The [a]vision of Isaiah the son of Amoz, which he saw concerning Judah and Jerusalem
[b]in the days of [c]Uzziah, [d]Jotham, [e]Ahaz, and [f]Hezekiah, kings of Judah.

The Wickedness of Judah

2 [g]Hear, O heavens, and give ear, O [h]earth;
for the LORD has spoken:
"Children[1] [i]have I reared and brought up,
but they have rebelled against me.
3 The ox [j]knows its owner,
and the donkey its master's crib,
but Israel does [j]not know,
my people do not understand."

4 Ah, sinful nation,
a people laden with iniquity,
[k]offspring of evildoers,
children who deal corruptly!
They have forsaken the LORD,
they have [l]despised [m]the Holy One of Israel,
they are utterly [n]estranged.

5 Why will you still be [o]struck down?
Why will you [p]continue to rebel?
The whole head is sick,
and the whole heart faint.

[1] Or *Sons*; also verse 4

Chapter 1

1 [a]ch. 6:1 [b]Hos. 1:1; Mic. 1:1 [c][2 Kgs. 15:1, 7]; See 2 Chr. 26 [d]See 2 Kgs. 15:32-38; 2 Chr. 27 [e]ch. 7:1, 3, 10, 12; 14:28; See 2 Kgs. 16; 2 Chr. 28 [f]See ch. 37:2–39:8; 2 Kgs. 18-20; 2 Chr. 29–32
2 [g]Deut. 32:1; [Deut. 4:26] [h]Mic. 1:2; 6:2 [i][Deut. 32:6, 10, 15]
3 [j][Jer. 8:7]
4 [k][Matt. 3:7] [l]ch. 5:24 [m]See ch. 31:1 [n]Ezek. 14:5
5 [o]Jer. 5:3; [ch. 9:13] [p]ch. 31:6

1:1–5:30 *Introduction: "Ah, Sinful Nation!"* The prophet rebukes the people of God in order for them to place themselves under the judgment of God's word. Isaiah includes promises of miraculous grace beyond the remedial judgments. On 1:2–2:5 as a microcosm of the book's message, see Introduction: Theme.

1:1–31 *Judah's Sins Confronted.* Isaiah explains why God's people (Judah) are in crisis. They do not comprehend that they have forsaken God, hollowed out their worship, and corrupted their society.

1:1 The superscription for the entire book. **vision**. A message from God (1 Sam. 3:1; Ezek. 7:26), given in symbolic form. **Isaiah the son of Amoz**. See Introduction: Author and Title. **Uzziah, Jotham, Ahaz, and Hezekiah**. See Introduction: Date, and chart to the left.

Kings of Judah in the Time of Isaiah

Isaiah prophesied "in the days of Uzziah, Jotham, Ahaz, and Hezekiah, kings of Judah" (1:1).

Kings of Judah	Years of Reign
Uzziah (Azariah)	767–740 B.C.
Jotham	750–735
Ahaz	735–715
Hezekiah	715–686

1:2–9 Isaiah indicts Judah's mindless revolt against God.

1:2 heavens . . . earth. Isaiah calls on the entire cosmos as a faithful witness to God's word (Deut. 30:19; 31:28; Ps. 50:4). **Children . . . they**. These emphatic words accent the contrast between God's grace and his people's ingratitude. Thus Isaiah summarizes Israel's history up to his time. Israel as a whole is God's "son" (Ex. 4:22–23), and individual Israelites are also "sons" (see ESV footnote; Deut. 14:1); this privilege should have led to gratitude, but it did not. **rebelled**. See Isa. 66:24.

1:4 Ah is a cry of pain and indignation. **sinful**. Isaiah's complex vocabulary uses a number of evocative Hebrew words for sin (translated here as **iniquity** and **corruptly**) that reveal to the people their true character. **the Holy One of Israel**. As described above (see Introduction: Date), this is Isaiah's characteristic title for God, occurring 25 times in the book (and rarely anywhere else in the OT); it reflects a central theme in Isaiah's thought. Perhaps it originated in the seraphic cry, "Holy, holy, holy" (6:3). When Isaiah saw God high and lifted up in infinite holiness, it defined his knowledge of God as the Holy One who is righteous (5:16), incomparable (40:25), redemptive (47:4), and lofty (57:15), and who has given himself to Israel. To despise the Holy One is to scorn, in practical ways, all that God is. **they are utterly estranged**. Their backwardness is beyond self-remedy.

6[q]Ps. 38:3 [r][Jer. 8:22]
7[s]ch. 5:5; 6:11, 12; Deut. 28:51, 52
8[t]ch. 10:32; 37:22; Zech. 2:10; 9:9 [u]Job 27:18
9[v]Lam. 3:22 [w]ch. 10:21, 22; Cited Rom. 9:29 [x]ch. 13:19; Gen. 19:24, 25
10[y]Ezek. 16:46, 48, 49, 55; [ch. 3:9; Rev. 11:8] [z][Deut. 32:32]
11[a]Prov. 15:8; Jer. 6:20; Mal. 1:10; [ch. 66:3]; See 1 Sam. 15:22
12[b]Ex. 23:17; 34:23
13[c]Num. 28:11; 1 Chr. 23:31 [d]Ex. 12:16; Lev. 23:36 [e][Jer. 7:9, 10] [f]See Joel 2:15-17
14[c][See ver. 13 above]
15[g]1 Kgs. 8:22

6 [q]From the sole of the foot even to the head,
there is no soundness in it,
but bruises and sores
and raw wounds;
they are [r]not pressed out or bound up
or softened with oil.

7 [s]Your country lies desolate;
your cities are burned with fire;
in your very presence
foreigners devour your land;
it is desolate, as overthrown by foreigners.
8 And [t]the daughter of Zion is left
like a [u]booth in a vineyard,
like a lodge in a cucumber field,
like a besieged city.

9 [v]If the LORD of hosts
had not left us [w]a few survivors,
we should have been like [x]Sodom,
and become like [x]Gomorrah.

10 Hear the word of the LORD,
you rulers of [y, z]Sodom!
Give ear to the teaching[1] of our God,
you people of [z]Gomorrah!
11 [a]"What to me is the multitude of your sacrifices?
says the LORD;
I have had enough of burnt offerings of rams
and the fat of well-fed beasts;
I do not delight in the blood of bulls,
or of lambs, or of goats.

12 "When you come to [b]appear before me,
who has required of you
this trampling of my courts?
13 Bring no more vain offerings;
incense is an abomination to me.
[c]New moon and Sabbath and the [d]calling of convocations—
I cannot endure [e]iniquity and [f]solemn assembly.
14 Your [c]new moons and your appointed feasts
my soul hates;
they have become a burden to me;
I am weary of bearing them.
15 When you [g]spread out your hands,
I will hide my eyes from you;

[1] Or *law*

1:5 Why? Not even painful experience makes an impact. Their minds are closed.

1:7–8 This imagery merged into reality in the foreign invasions during Isaiah's lifetime. **the daughter of Zion**. The city of Jerusalem (37:22).

1:9 Only the power of **the LORD of hosts** has preserved God's people (1 Kings 19:18). See Rom. 9:29, where Paul quotes this verse to teach God's gracious purpose to preserve a remnant that is truly his people. There is nothing within their own nature to keep God's people from the worst of paganism and its appropriate judgment (see Gen. 13:13; 18:16–19:28; 2 Pet. 2:6; Jude 7; Rev. 11:8).

1:10–20 These verses highlight the hypocrisy of the people's worship. Isaiah, like other prophets who comment on sacrificial practices, recognizes that God appointed the system of worship and authorized the central sanctuary. But these ordinances were always intended to foster true piety among God's people, which would move them to humble purity of heart and energetic promotion of others' well-being. Isaiah denounces the way his contemporaries have divorced the ordinances from their proper purpose. It seems that they treated their worship as a way of manipulating God; they also mixed in elements from Canaanite religions (v. 29). See note on Amos 4:4–5.

1:10–17 God rejects his people's worship, however lavish, because they use it as a pious evasion of the self-denying demands of helping the weak (cf. James 1:27). Even lifting their hands in prayer avails nothing, for **your hands are full of blood** (Isa. 1:15; see 59:3).

[h]even though you make many prayers,
I will not listen;
[i]your hands are full of blood.
16 [j]Wash yourselves; make yourselves clean;
remove the evil of your deeds from before my eyes;
[k]cease to do evil,
17 learn to do good;
[l]seek justice,
correct oppression;
[m]bring justice to the fatherless,
plead the widow's cause.
18 "Come now, [n]let us reason[1] together, says the LORD:
though your sins are like scarlet,
they shall be as [o]white as snow;
though they are red like crimson,
they shall become like wool.
19 [p]If you are willing and obedient,
you shall eat the good of the land;
20 but if you refuse and rebel,
you shall be eaten by the sword;
[q]for the mouth of the LORD has spoken."

The Unfaithful City

21 How the faithful city
[r]has become a whore,[2]
[s]she who was full of justice!
Righteousness lodged in her,
but now murderers.
22 [t]Your silver has become dross,
your best wine mixed with water.
23 Your princes are rebels
and companions of thieves.
Everyone [u]loves a bribe
and runs after gifts.
[v]They do not bring justice to the fatherless,
and the widow's cause does not come to them.

24 Therefore the [w]Lord declares,
the LORD of hosts,
the [x]Mighty One of Israel:
"Ah, I will get relief from my enemies
[y]and avenge myself on my foes.

[1] Or *dispute* [2] Or *become unchaste*

15 [h]Prov. 1:28; Mic. 3:4 [i]ch. 59:3
16 [j][Jer. 2:22] [k][1 Pet. 3:11]
17 [l]Jer. 22:3 [m][ver. 23; James 1:27]
18 [n]Mic. 6:2; [ch. 43:26] [o]Ps. 51:7; [Rev. 7:14]
19 [p]Deut. 30:15, 16
20 [q]ver. 2; ch. 24:3; 40:5; 58:14; Mic. 4:4; [Num. 23:19]
21 [r]Jer. 2:20; [Ex. 34:15] [s][Jer. 31:23]
22 [t][Jer. 6:30; Ezek. 22:18]
23 [u]Mic. 7:3; [Ex. 23:8] [v]Jer. 5:28; Zech. 7:10; [ver. 17]
24 [w]ch. 3:1; 10:33 [x]Ps. 132:2 [y][Deut. 32:41]

1:17 seek justice, correct oppression. Doing **good** in God's sight includes seeking the just functioning of society (note, by contrast, v. 23).

1:18–20 let us reason together. Rather than continue in their incomprehension, the people are urged to consider thoughtfully their actual position before God. **though your sins are like scarlet . . . red like crimson**. Their hands, red with blood (v. 15), can be cleansed (Ps. 51:7). But they must make a deliberate choice (Isa. 1:19–20).

1:21–23 Isaiah chronicles their social abuses.

1:21 a whore. Their covenant with God was comparable to a marriage (54:5). To depart from faithfulness to him is a more shocking sin than the people realize.

1:24–28 the Lord . . . the LORD of hosts, the Mighty One of Israel. In contrast to the worthless leaders of v. 23, Israel's God is a formidable Judge. Startlingly, he calls his own people his **enemies**! But the judgment here is not the end of the story; its purpose is to **smelt away** the **dross**, i.e., to remove the unbelieving members of the people (called **rebels and sinners, those who forsake the LORD**). **Afterward**, what remains will be a chastened people of God, **those . . . who repent** (i.e., who embrace their covenant privileges from the heart). **redeemed**. This word (Hb. *padah*) and its synonym (*ga'al*; see note on 41:14) generally convey the idea of rescue and protection, either for the whole people (1:27; 35:10; cf. 50:2; 51:11), or for a particular person (cf. 29:22). In some places either word carries the idea of exchanging a substitute or ransom (e.g., Ex. 13:13), but that is not relevant here. The prophet looks forward to a cleansed people after the historical judgment of the exile, restored to its mission (Isa. 2:1–5).

1:29 the oaks . . . the gardens. Suggesting pagan, and probably Canaanite, rites of worship (57:5; 65:3; 66:17) mixed into the life of God's own people.

1:31 Self-salvation, though it seems to make the people strong for a time,

25[z]Ps. 81:14; Amos 1:8; [ch. 5:25] [a][Ezek. 22:20; Mal. 3:3]
26[b]Jer. 33:7, 11 [c][Zech. 8:3]
27[d]Jer. 22:3, 4
28[e]Job 31:3; Ps. 1:6
29[f]Hos. 4:19 [g]ch. 57:5; Hos. 4:13 [h]ch. 65:3; 66:17
30[i][Jer. 17:8]
31[j]Judg. 16:9 [k]ch. 66:24

Chapter 2

2[l]For ver. 2-4, see Mic. 4:1-3 [m]ch. 14:13; 25:6 [n][ch. 56:7]
3[o]See Zech. 8:20-23

25 [z]I will turn my hand against you
and will smelt away your [a]dross as with lye
and remove all your alloy.
26 And I will restore your judges [b]as at the first,
and your counselors as at the beginning.
Afterward [c]you shall be called the city of righteousness,
the faithful city."

27 [d]Zion shall be redeemed by justice,
and those in her who repent, by righteousness.
28 [e]But rebels and sinners shall be broken together,
and those who forsake the LORD shall be consumed.
29 [f]For they[1] shall be ashamed of [g]the oaks
that you desired;
and you shall blush for [h]the gardens
that you have chosen.
30 For you shall be [i]like an oak
whose leaf withers,
and like a garden without water.
31 And the strong shall become [j]tinder,
and his work a spark,
and both of them shall burn together,
with [k]none to quench them.

The Mountain of the LORD

2 The word that Isaiah the son of Amoz saw concerning Judah and Jerusalem.

2 [l]It shall come to pass in the latter days
that [m]the mountain of the house of the LORD
shall be established as the highest of the mountains,
and shall be lifted up above the hills;
and [n]all the nations shall flow to it,
3 and [o]many peoples shall come, and say:
"Come, let us go up to the mountain of the LORD,
to the house of the God of Jacob,
that he may teach us his ways
and that we may walk in his paths."

[1] Some Hebrew manuscripts *you*

carries with it its own self-destruction. Apart from repentance (v. 27), the people and their syncretistic oaks and gardens (v. 29) will burn, **with none to quench them**.

2:1–4:6 *Judah's Hope, Guilt, Hope.* Within the reassuring context of glorious divine promises (2:2–4; 4:2–6), the prophet identifies the sinful human obstacles standing in the way of the promised hope (2:6–4:1).

2:1–5 *Hope.* Isaiah reveals the triumph of God's purpose for his people, when the nations will hurry to learn his ways as the only way. The fulfillment of this prophecy is foreseeable in the progress of Christian missions (see Luke 24:46–48).

2:1 This superscription marks the beginning of a new section. After the introductory, confrontational ch. 1, this section begins and ends with hope (2:2–4; 4:2–6), also taking into account the sinful human obstacles standing in the way of that hope (2:6–4:1). This vision expands the hope of 1:25–28.

2:2–4 Nearly the same wording appears in Mic. 4:1–3. It is possible that one borrowed from the other, or both used a common source; in any event the two were contemporaries and shared the same expectation for God's purpose.

2:2 The latter days is an expression for the future beyond the horizon (e.g., Num. 24:14; Deut. 4:30; Dan. 2:28), which sometimes refers specifically to the time of the Messiah (Hos. 3:5). It is not immediately clear here whether Isaiah is so specific, but the way Isa. 11:4 echoes 2:4 shows that the oracle speaks of the messianic era. NT authors use the various Greek translations of the expression (generally rendered "in the last days") in the belief that, since Jesus inaugurated his messianic kingship by his resurrection, the latter days have arrived in a decisive way, while at the same time the last days await their complete realization and final fulfillment at the end of the age (Acts 2:17; 2 Tim. 3:1; Heb. 1:2; James 5:3; 2 Pet. 3:3; and probably 1 Pet. 1:20; 1 John 2:18). Isaiah's future orientation in this section is also marked by his sevenfold use of "in that day" (Isa. 2:11, 17, 20; 3:7, 18; 4:1, 2) and "the LORD of hosts has a day" (2:12), including both the near and distant future. To the prophetic eye, the crises of the present are to be measured by the ultimate crisis of judgment and salvation toward which God is moving history (see Joel 2:28–3:21; Zeph. 1:7–2:3). **the mountain of the house of the LORD**. The Temple Mount in Jerusalem, though unimpressive from the lofty gaze of human religion, was God's choice (Ps. 68:15–16) and the true hope of the world (Ps. 48:1–2). **the highest of the mountains**. The gods of antiquity supposedly lived on mountains. The exaltation of the Lord's temple as the peak of world religion will be attractive to the nations. "Highest" here probably means "most exalted in honor," not actually physically highest. **all the nations shall flow to it**. By a miraculous magnetism, a river of humanity will flow uphill to worship the one true God (see John 12:32).

2:3 out of Zion. Out of Zion alone; the Gentiles will abandon all other religions for the true God.

For [p]out of Zion shall go the law,[1]
and the word of the LORD from Jerusalem.
4 He shall judge between the nations,
and shall decide disputes for many peoples;
[q]and they shall beat their swords into plowshares,
and their spears into pruning hooks;
[r]nation shall not lift up sword against nation,
neither shall they learn war anymore.

5 O house of Jacob,
come, let us walk
in [s]the light of the LORD.

The Day of the LORD

6 For you have rejected your people,
the house of Jacob,
because they are full of things [t]from the east
and [u]of fortune-tellers [v]like the Philistines,
and they [w]strike hands with the children of foreigners.
7 Their land is [x]filled with silver and gold,
and there is no end to their treasures;
their land is [y]filled with horses,
and there is no end to their chariots.
8 Their land is [z]filled with idols;
they bow down to [a]the work of their hands,
to what their own fingers have made.
9 So man [b]is humbled,
and each one [b]is brought low—
do not forgive them!
10 [c]Enter into the rock
and hide in the dust
[d]from before the terror of the LORD,
and from the splendor of his majesty.
11 [e]The haughty looks of man shall be brought low,
and the lofty pride of men shall be humbled,
and the LORD alone will be exalted in that day.

3[p][Luke 24:47; John 4:22]
4[q][Joel 3:10] [r]ch. 9:7; Ps. 72:3, 7; Hos. 2:18; Zech. 9:10
5[s]ch. 60:1, 2; [Eph. 5:8]
6[t][2 Kgs. 16:10, 11] [u]Mic. 5:12 [v]2 Kgs. 1:2 [w][2 Kgs. 16:7, 8]
7[x]ch. 39:2; [ch. 22:8, 11; Deut. 17:17] [y]ch. 30:16; [Deut. 17:16; Mic. 5:10]
8[z]ver. 18, 20; ch. 10:10, 11; Jer. 2:28 [a]See ch. 44:9-17
9[b]ch. 5:15
10[c]ver. 19, 21; [Rev. 6:15, 16] [d]Cited 2 Thess. 1:9
11[e]ver. 17; Ps. 18:27; [Mic. 2:3; 2 Cor. 10:5]

[1] *Or teaching*

2:4 nation shall not lift up sword against nation, neither shall they learn war anymore. Tiny Judah has been threatened by war for most of its existence. Now Isaiah predicts that, far from bringing oppression, the triumph of biblical faith will bring a peace the world has never known, when all nations **shall beat their swords into plowshares**. The description of the Messiah's reign in 11:1–10 echoes many of these themes; and 11:4 takes up the words **judge** and **decide disputes**, attributing the activity to the Messiah, in order to show that God will exercise this rule through his Messiah. Some Christian interpreters take this to describe the effect on the nations as their citizens and leaders submit to the rule of Christ; others understand this to point forward to an earthly reign of Christ in the millennium (see note on Rev. 20:1–6); still others see it as a prediction of Christ's reign in the new heavens and new earth. In any case, people of all ages have taken these words to express their longings for freedom from war, when the nations seek to follow the "ways" of "the God of Jacob" (Isa. 2:3) and when no mere human authority but the Lord Jesus himself shall judge **between the nations**.

2:5 Isaiah calls the people of God to live now in the **light** of the promised future. His exhortation applies the nations' future rallying cry in v. 3 to the people of God in the present. Judah is part of God's unfolding story, starting with Abraham's call, and the individuals within Judah must embrace their role in that story by faithfully keeping the covenant.

2:6–4:1 *Guilt.* In tragic contrast with the glory of the latter days (2:1–5; 4:2–6), God rejects Judah in Isaiah's time for their greed, idolatries, pride, and oppression (see Matt. 5:13).

2:6–22 Isaiah surveys the immensity of the present barriers to that happy future, but he is impressed by the Lord alone (vv. 10–11, 17, 19, 21).

2:6–8 For. The urgency of v. 5 is explained. **full . . . filled . . . no end**. Rather than the world coming to Zion to learn God's ways (vv. 2–4), the people of God in Isaiah's day are influenced by the ways of the world—to the point of saturation.

2:9 do not forgive them! Isaiah has given up on his generation. The mystery of forgiveness—for sin cannot be ignored—is revealed in ch. 53.

2:10, 19, 21 from before the terror of the LORD, and from the splendor of his majesty. Sennacherib, king of Assyria, boasted in terms of "the terror-inspiring splendor of my lordship" in his writings. Isaiah counters all human bravado with the prophetic vision of God as the only one who is truly terrifying: **when he rises to terrify the earth** (vv. 19, 21). The Lord is the Creator of all mankind, and therefore has an interest in all mankind (not just Israel).

2:11 the LORD alone will be exalted. Isaiah sees "the haughty looks/haughtiness of man" as central to what is wrong with the world and the exclusive exaltation of the Lord as the only remedy (cf. v. 17).

12[f][Job 40:11, 12; Mal. 4:1]
13[g]ch. 14:8; See Judg. 9:15 [h]Ezek. 27:6; Zech. 11:2
14[i][ch. 30:25]
16[j]ch. 60:9; 1 Kgs. 10:22
17[k]Ps. 18:27; [Mic. 2:3; 2 Cor. 10:5]
18[l]ver. 8
19[m]ver. 10; Hos. 10:8; Luke 23:30; Rev. 6:16 [n][Ps. 76:8, 9; Hab. 3:6]
20[o]ch. 30:22; 31:7 [p]Lev. 11:19; Deut. 14:18
21[m][See ver. 19 above] [n][See ver. 19 above]
22[q]Ps. 146:3 [r]Job 27:3; [James 4:14]

Chapter 3

1[s]ch. 1:24 [t]Lev. 26:26; Ezek. 4:16
2[u]2 Kgs. 24:14; Ezek. 17:13, 14

12 [f]For the LORD of hosts has a day
against all that is proud and lofty,
against all that is lifted up—and it shall be brought low;
13 against all the [g]cedars of Lebanon,
lofty and lifted up;
and against all the [h]oaks of Bashan;
14 against all [i]the lofty mountains,
and against all the uplifted hills;
15 against every high tower,
and against every fortified wall;
16 against all [j]the ships of Tarshish,
and against all the beautiful craft.
17 [k]And the haughtiness of man shall be humbled,
and the lofty pride of men shall be brought low,
and the LORD alone will be exalted in that day.
18 [l]And the idols shall utterly pass away.
19 [m]And people shall enter the caves of the rocks
and the holes of the ground,[1]
from before the terror of the LORD,
and from the splendor of his majesty,
[n]when he rises to terrify the earth.

20 In that day [o]mankind will cast away
their idols of silver and their idols of gold,
which they made for themselves to worship,
to the moles and to the [p]bats,
21 [m]to enter the caverns of the rocks
and the clefts of the cliffs,
from before the terror of the LORD,
and from the splendor of his majesty,
[n]when he rises to terrify the earth.
22 [q]Stop regarding man
[r]in whose nostrils is breath,
for of what account is he?

Judgment on Judah and Jerusalem

3 1 For behold, the [s]Lord GOD of hosts
is taking away from Jerusalem and from Judah
support and supply,[2]
all [t]support of bread,
and all support of water;
2 [u]the mighty man and the soldier,
the judge and the prophet,
the diviner and the elder,

[1] Hebrew *dust* [2] Hebrew *staff*

2:12–16 against all . . . against every. Ten times Isaiah asserts God's settled opposition to all human pride.

2:17 the LORD alone will be exalted. See note on v. 11.

2:20–21 their idols of silver and their idols of gold . . . to the moles and to the bats (i.e., into the ruins and caves in which they live). The precious but fraudulent ideals of the present world will be seen for the contemptible things they are and acted upon accordingly. True conversion does not quibble over the loss (cf. Phil. 3:8).

2:22 Stop regarding man. Matching the exhortation in v. 5, Isaiah urges a realistic assessment of the weakness of human power and pride.

3:1–4:6 The false and sinful glories of men and women, which are—and deserve to be—vulnerable, are replaced by the glory of the Lord, "a refuge and a shelter from the storm and rain" (4:6; cf. Ex. 13:21).

3:1–15 Bracketed by "the Lord GOD of hosts" (vv. 1, 15), this section announces God's intention to deprive Jerusalem and Judah of human leadership in their time of crisis.

3:1 For. The prophet explains why man is not to be regarded (2:22). **taking away**. See "take away" in 3:18. God takes away whatever keeps his people from him, but only in order that they might enjoy his glory (4:2–6). The words **support** and **supply** sound alike in Hebrew, and the combination suggests severe deprivation, i.e., **all support of bread, and all support of water**.

3:2–5 God judges his people by removing the leaders who were considered indispensable and replacing them with irresponsible **boys** and **infants**.

3 the captain of fifty
and the man of rank,
the counselor and the skillful magician
and the expert in charms.
4 [v]And I will make boys their princes,
and infants[1] shall rule over them.
5 [w]And the people will oppress one another,
every one his fellow
and every one his neighbor;
the youth will be insolent to the elder,
and the despised to the honorable.
6 For [x]a man will take hold of his brother
in the house of his father, saying:
"You have a cloak;
you shall be our leader,
and this heap of ruins
shall be under your rule";
7 in that day he will speak out, saying:
"I will not be a [y]healer;[2]
in my house there is neither bread nor cloak;
you shall not make me
leader of the people."
8 For Jerusalem has stumbled,
and Judah has fallen,
because their [z]speech and their deeds are against the LORD,
[a]defying his glorious presence.[3]
9 For the look on their faces bears witness against them;
they proclaim their sin [b]like Sodom;
they do not hide it.
Woe to them!
[c]For they have brought evil on themselves.
10 [d]Tell the righteous that it shall be well with them,
[e]for they shall eat the fruit of their deeds.
11 [f]Woe to the wicked! It shall be ill with him,
for what his hands have dealt out shall be done to him.
12 My people—[g]infants are their oppressors,
and women rule over them.
O my people, [h]your guides mislead you
and they have swallowed up[4] the course of your paths.
13 The LORD [i]has taken his place to contend;
he stands to judge peoples.
14 The LORD will enter into judgment
with the [j]elders and princes of his people:
"It is you who [k]have devoured[5] the vineyard,
[l]the spoil of the poor is in your houses.

4[v]ver. 12; Eccles. 10:16
5[w]See Mic. 7:3-6
6[x]ch. 4:1
7[y][ch. 1:6]
8[z]See Ps. 73:9-11 [a]ch. 65:3
9[b]Gen. 13:13; 18:20; Ezek. 16:46, 48, 49 [c][Rom. 6:23]
10[d]Eccles. 8:12; See Deut. 28:1-14 [e]Ps. 128:2
11[f]Eccles. 8:13; See Deut. 28:15-68
12[g]ver. 4 [h]See ch. 28:14-22
13[i]Ps. 7:6; Hos. 4:1
14[j]Mic. 3:1 [k]Ps. 14:4 [l]Amos 3:10

[1] Or *caprice* [2] Hebrew *binder of wounds* [3] Hebrew *the eyes of his glory* [4] Or *they have confused* [5] Or *grazed over;* compare Exodus 22:5

3:6 You have a cloak. The mere appearance of qualified leadership is seized upon by the leaderless people.

3:7 I will not be a healer, i.e., "I cannot fix your problems." Exposing human inadequacy discredits self-confidence.

3:8 For . . . because. The explanation for the nation's social collapse lies in their hostility toward God. **defying his glorious presence**. They obstinately disregard God's presence in their midst (Ex. 40:38; 1 Kings 8:10–11), though his nearness is the hope they ought to cherish (Isa. 4:5). On "glory" as the Lord's special presence, see note on 6:3.

3:10–11 The **righteous** may suffer and the **wicked** may prosper, but only in the short run.

3:12–15 My people . . . his people. The Lord demands an accounting from all who oppress his people, whether native-born or Gentile.

3:16–17 Because . . . therefore. The arrogant self-display of Jerusalem's women will be judged by humiliating exposure.

15 What do you mean by [m]crushing my people,
by grinding the face of the poor?"
declares the Lord GOD of hosts.

16 The LORD said:
[n]Because [o]the daughters of Zion are haughty
and walk with outstretched necks,
glancing wantonly with their eyes,
mincing along as they go,
[p]tinkling with their feet,
17 therefore the Lord [q]will strike with a scab
the heads of [o]the daughters of Zion,
and the LORD will lay bare their secret parts.

18 In that day the Lord will take away [r]the finery of the anklets, the [s]headbands, and the
[t]crescents; 19 the pendants, the bracelets, and the scarves; 20 the [u]headdresses, the armlets,
the sashes, the perfume boxes, and the amulets; 21 the signet rings and [v]nose rings; 22 the
[w]festal robes, the mantles, the cloaks, and the handbags; 23 the mirrors, the linen garments,
the turbans, and the veils.

24 Instead of [x]perfume there will be rottenness;
and instead of a [y]belt, a rope;
and instead of [z]well-set hair, [a]baldness;
and instead of a rich robe, a [b]skirt of sackcloth;
and [c]branding instead of beauty.
25 Your men shall fall by the sword
and your mighty men in battle.
26 And [d]her gates shall lament and mourn;
empty, she shall [e]sit on the ground.

4 [f]And seven women [g]shall take hold of [f]one man in that day, saying, "We will eat our
own bread and wear our own clothes, only let us be called by your name; [h]take away
our reproach."

The Branch of the LORD Glorified

2 In that day [i]the branch of the LORD shall be beautiful and glorious, and [j]the fruit of the
land shall be the pride and honor of the survivors of Israel. 3 [k]And he who is left in Zion
and remains in Jerusalem will be called [l]holy, everyone who has [m]been recorded for life
in Jerusalem, 4 when [n]the Lord shall have washed away the filth of [o]the daughters of Zion
and cleansed the bloodstains of Jerusalem from its midst by a spirit of judgment and by
[p]a spirit of burning.[1] 5 Then the LORD will create over the whole site of Mount Zion and
over her assemblies [q]a cloud by day, and smoke and the shining of a flaming fire by night;

[1] Or *purging*

15 [m][Ps. 94:5]
16 [n]See ch. 32:9-11 [o]ch. 4:4; Song 3:11 [p]ver. 18
17 [q][Deut. 28:60] [o][See ver. 16 above]
18 [r]ver. 16 [s][1 Pet. 3:3] [t]Judg. 8:21, 26
20 [u]Ex. 39:28; Ezek. 24:17
21 [v]Gen. 24:47; Ezek. 16:12
22 [w][Luke 15:22]
24 [x][Esth. 2:12] [y]Prov. 31:24 [z]1 Pet. 3:3 [a]ch. 15:2; 22:12; Ezek. 27:31; Amos 8:10; Mic. 1:16 [b]ch. 15:3; Gen. 37:34; Lam. 2:10 [c]Lev. 19:28
26 [d]Jer. 14:2; Lam. 1:4 [e]Job 2:13; Lam. 2:10

Chapter 4

1 [f][ch. 13:12] [g]ch. 3:6 [h]See Gen. 30:23
2 [i]Jer. 23:5; 33:15; Zech. 3:8; 6:12 [j][ch. 27:6]
3 [k]ch. 6:13; 10:20 [l]Obad. 17 [m]Ex. 32:32; Luke 10:20; Heb. 12:23; [Ps. 69:28]
4 [n]Ezek. 36:25 [o]ch. 3:16 [p]ch. 33:14; Mal. 3:2; Matt. 3:11; Luke 3:17
5 [q]Ex. 13:21

3:18–23 This inventory of extravagant female wardrobes matches the list of hoped-for male leaders in vv. 2–3. The Lord will take away both.

3:24 Instead of. Five times Isaiah asserts that God will replace the women's self-indulgence with the tragedies of exile and abuse.

3:25–4:1 Isaiah summarizes by predicting the defeat of the men (3:25), the emptying of Jerusalem (personified as an abandoned woman; 3:26), and the plight of the women begging for a man's protection (4:1; see 3:6).

4:2–6 *Hope*. Further developing the bright hope of 2:2–4, Isaiah reveals the worthy leadership and enduring beauty that God intends to provide for his people.

4:2 The branch of the LORD is the Messiah (see Jer. 23:5; 33:15; Zech. 3:8; 6:12; and, using different words, Isa. 11:1). He springs from the Lord, and his rule spreads over the world. His beginnings are unimpressive (53:2), but his triumph will be **beautiful and glorious. The fruit of the land** may also refer to the Messiah, with an emphasis on his human roots.

4:2–3 survivors . . . he who is left . . . and remains . . . recorded for life. The remnant preserved by God (see 1:9).

4:3–4 holy . . . when the Lord shall have washed away the filth . . . and cleansed the bloodstains. A permanent remedy will have been applied to God's people, so that never again would such language as "take away" (3:1, 18) be necessary.

4:5 Then the LORD will create. More than reversing the deprivation of 3:1–4:1. **a cloud by day, and smoke and the shining of a flaming fire by night**. Recalling Israel's early days, God's presence will be wonderfully manifest, this time not in wilderness wanderings but **over the whole site of Mount Zion and over her assemblies** (cf. Ex. 13:21–22; 40:34–38; Num. 9:15–23). **over all the glory there will be a canopy**. Perhaps, as in Joel 2:16, a wedding canopy; cf. Isa. 54:4–8; Rev. 21:9–11, 22–27. On the "glory," see note on Isa. 6:3.

for over all the glory there will be [r]a canopy. 6 [s]There will be a [t]booth for shade by day from the heat, and [u]for a refuge and a shelter from the storm and rain.

The Vineyard of the LORD Destroyed

5 1 Let me sing for my beloved
my love song concerning his vineyard:
My beloved had [v]a vineyard
on a very fertile hill.
2 He dug it and cleared it of stones,
and planted it with [w]choice vines;
he built a watchtower in the midst of it,
and hewed out a wine vat in it;
and [x]he looked for it to yield grapes,
but it yielded wild grapes.

3 And now, O inhabitants of Jerusalem
and men of Judah,
judge between me and my vineyard.
4 [y]What more was there to do for my vineyard,
that I have not done in it?
[x]When I looked for it to yield grapes,
why did it yield wild grapes?

5 And now I will tell you
what I will do to my vineyard.
I will remove [z]its hedge,
and it shall be devoured;[1]
[a]I will break down its wall,
and it shall be trampled down.
6 I will make it a waste;
it shall not be pruned or hoed,
and [b]briers and thorns shall grow up;
[c]I will also command the clouds
that they rain no rain upon it.

7 [d]For the vineyard of the LORD of hosts
is the house of Israel,
and the men of Judah
are his pleasant planting;
and he looked for justice,
but behold, bloodshed;[2]
for righteousness,
but behold, an outcry![3]

Woe to the Wicked

8 Woe to those who [e]join house to house,
who add field to field,

[1] Or *grazed over*; compare Exodus 22:5 [2] The Hebrew words for *justice* and *bloodshed* sound alike [3] The Hebrew words for *righteous* and *outcry* sound alike

5 [r][Rev. 7:15]
6 [s]ch. 25:4 [t]See Ps. 27:5 [u]ch. 25:4

Chapter 5

1 [v]Ps. 80:8; Matt. 21:33; Mark 12:1; Luke 20:9; [Hos. 9:10]
2 [w]Jer. 2:21 [x][Matt. 21:19; Mark 11:13; Luke 13:6]
4 [y][Mic. 6:3, 4] [x][See ver. 2 above]
5 [z][Jer. 5:10] [a]Ps. 80:12; [Prov. 24:31]
6 [b]See ch. 7:23-25 [c][1 Kgs. 17:1; Jer. 14:1, 22]
7 [d][ch. 3:14]; See Ps. 80:8-11
8 [e]Mic. 2:2

4:6 God's people will be forever protected from all distress.

5:1–30 ***Judah's Sins Condemned.*** Isaiah's introductory diagnosis of Judah's spiritual decline (chs. 1–5) now concludes with an unsparing assertion of his generation's apostasy and its consequences. The chapter is divided into the song of the vineyard (5:1–7) and the "wild grapes" that the vineyard produced (vv. 8–30).

5:1 Let me sing for my beloved my love song. To Isaiah, God is both the Holy One and his beloved. **Vineyard** is explained in v. 7 as a reference to Israel and Judah (cf. Jer. 12:10 and possibly Matt. 21:33; see also Ex. 15:17, where God plants them; and for Israel as a vine, Ps. 80:8–16; Jer. 2:21; Hos. 10:1; John 15:1).

5:2 God made every provision for his people to be a blessing to the world, as he had promised (cf. Gen. 12:1–3). **wild grapes**. Another possible translation is "stinking" or "sour" grapes, conveying the bad taste of wild grapes in contrast to the sweetness of the cultivated kind.

5:4 What more . . . ? leaves no room for excuses.

5:5–6 These verses use imagery to describe foreign invasion and national destruction.

5:7 God's high expectations of his people were fair. **he looked for justice, but behold, bloodshed; for righteousness, but behold, an outcry!** As the ESV footnotes on "bloodshed" and "outcry" explain, Isaiah uses wordplay here; he aims to show that sin does not simply fail to reach a standard; it distorts good into evil.

5:8–30 This section translates the metaphorical "wild grapes" of vv. 2 and

9 [f] ch. 6:12
10 [g] [Lev. 26:26; Hag. 1:6; 2:16] [h] Ezek. 45:11
11 [i] ver. 22; [Prov. 23:29, 30; Eccles. 10:16, 17]
12 [j] Amos 6:5, 6 [k] ch. 26:11
13 [l] ch. 1:3; Hos. 4:6 [m] [Lam. 4:2, 7, 8]
14 [n] Hab. 2:5 [o] Ps. 141:7 [p] [ver. 12; Job 1:18, 19]
15 [q] ch. 2:9
16 [r] ch. 2:11, 17
17 [s] Mic. 2:12 [t] [Judg. 6:3]
18 [u] Prov. 5:22
19 [v] [Ezek. 12:22; 2 Pet. 3:4]
20 [w] [Amos 5:7]

until there is no more room,
and you are made to dwell alone
in the midst of the land.
9 The LORD of hosts has sworn in my hearing:
[f] "Surely many houses shall be desolate,
large and beautiful houses, without inhabitant.
10 [g] For ten acres[1] of vineyard shall yield but one bath,
and a [h] homer of seed shall yield but an ephah."[2]

11 Woe to those who [i] rise early in the morning,
that they may run after strong drink,
who tarry late into the evening
as wine inflames them!
12 [j] They have lyre and harp,
tambourine and flute and wine at their feasts,
[k] but they do not regard the deeds of the LORD,
or see the work of his hands.
13 Therefore my people go into exile
[l] for lack of knowledge;[3]
their [m] honored men go hungry,[4]
and their multitude is parched with thirst.
14 Therefore Sheol has [n] enlarged its appetite
and opened [o] its mouth beyond measure,
and the nobility of Jerusalem[5] and her multitude will go down,
her revelers and he who [p] exults in her.
15 [q] Man is humbled, and each one is brought low,
and the eyes of the haughty[6] are brought low.
16 [r] But the LORD of hosts is exalted[7] in justice,
and the Holy God shows himself holy in righteousness.
17 Then shall the lambs graze [s] as in their pasture,
and [t] nomads shall eat among the ruins of the rich.

18 Woe to those who draw iniquity with [u] cords of falsehood,
who draw sin as with cart ropes,
19 who say: [v] "Let him be quick,
let him speed his work
that we may see it;
let the counsel of the Holy One of Israel draw near,
and let it come, that we may know it!"
20 Woe to [w] those who call evil good
and good evil,

[1] Hebrew *ten yoke*, the area ten yoke of oxen can plow in a day [2] A *bath* was about 6 gallons or 22 liters; a *homer* was about 6 bushels or 220 liters; an *ephah* was about 3/5 bushel or 22 liters [3] Or *without their knowledge* [4] Or *die of hunger* [5] Hebrew *her nobility* [6] Hebrew *high* [7] Hebrew *high*

4 into literal realities. Six "woes" lament the bitter fruits of Israel's character (vv. 8, 11, 18, 20, 21, 22), and four "therefores" anticipate the harvest of inescapable consequences (vv. 13, 14, 24, 25).

5:8–10 Leviticus 25 taught Israel to return purchased lands in the Year of Jubilee. "The land is mine," God said (Lev. 25:23), and he parceled it out to families as their permanent inheritance from him (Num. 26:55; 33:54; 1 Kings 21:1–3). Restoring property to the original owner ensured a fresh start for whomever had fallen on hard times. Therefore, **those who join house to house, who add field to field, until there is no more room** do business without regard for God's instructions for his land (see note on Amos 3:15). By accumulating more and more land, the powerful are driving the weaker members off the land that God allotted to them, and all for greed. But God sees to it that these landowners who force others out do not receive the profits they expect (cf. Isa. 5:10).

5:11–12 wine inflames them. The ungodly in Judah are marked by a visceral refusal to think.

5:13–14 The drunkenness of vv. 11–12 is answered here with **thirst**. The greed of vv. 8–10 is answered with the **appetite** of **Sheol** swallowing up the dead (see Ps. 88:3–6; 141:7; Prov. 9:18; Isa. 14:15; 38:18).

5:16 What sets Judah's God apart is his exalted moral character. He is not merely a provider who is useful to humans; he is **holy** in himself, and he proves it by enforcing his moral order.

5:17 This suggests the devastation of Jerusalem, as sheep **graze** and scavengers **eat** where the mighty once strolled.

5:18–23 Isaiah issues four laments over the cynicism of God's people. **Those who draw iniquity with cords of falsehood** (v. 18) eagerly pull sin their way, denying its heavy cost and daring God to punish them (v. 19). Cf. 2 Pet. 3:3–4.

5:20 those who call evil good and good evil. Evildoers can be so blinded in their moral judgment that their evaluations of good and evil are

[x]who put darkness for light
and light for darkness,
who put bitter for sweet
and sweet for bitter!
21 Woe to those who are [y]wise in their own eyes,
and shrewd in their own sight!
22 Woe to those who are [z]heroes at drinking wine,
and valiant men in mixing strong drink,
23 who [a]acquit the guilty for a bribe,
and deprive the innocent of his right!

24 Therefore, [b]as the tongue of fire devours the stubble,
and as dry grass sinks down in the flame,
so [c]their root will be [d]as rottenness,
and their blossom go up like dust;
for they have [e]rejected the law of the LORD of hosts,
and have [f]despised the word of the Holy One of Israel.
25 Therefore [g]the anger of the LORD was kindled against his people,
and he stretched out his hand against them and struck them,
and [h]the mountains quaked;
and their corpses were [i]as refuse
in the midst of the streets.
[j]For all this his anger has not turned away,
and his hand is stretched out still.

26 He will [k]raise a signal for nations far away,
and [l]whistle for them [m]from the ends of the earth;
and behold, quickly, speedily they come!
27 [n]None is weary, none stumbles,
none slumbers or sleeps,
not a waistband is loose,
not a sandal strap broken;
28 [o]their arrows are sharp,
all their bows bent,
their horses' hoofs seem like flint,
and their wheels [p]like the whirlwind.
29 Their roaring is like a lion,
like young lions they roar;
they growl and [q]seize their prey;
they carry it off, and none can rescue.
30 They will growl over it on that day,
like the growling of the sea.
And if one looks to the land,
behold, [r]darkness and distress;
and the light is darkened by its clouds.

20 [x][Job 17:12; Matt. 6:22, 23; Luke 11:34, 35]
21 [y]Prov. 3:7; Rom. 12:16
22 [z]ver. 11
23 [a]Ex. 23:8; Prov. 17:15
24 [b]ch. 47:14; Joel 2:5; [Ex. 15:7] [c]Job 18:16 [d]Hos. 5:12 [e]ch. 30:9 [f]ch. 1:4
25 [g]2 Kgs. 22:13, 17 [h]Jer. 4:24; [Ps. 97:5; Hab. 3:6] [i][2 Kgs. 9:37; Jer. 36:30] [j]ch. 9:12, 17, 21; 10:4
26 [k]ch. 11:12; 13:2; 18:3 [l]ch. 7:18; Zech. 10:8 [m]ch. 10:3; Deut. 28:49
27 [n]See ch. 10:28-31
28 [o]Ps. 7:12, 13 [p]ch. 21:1
29 [q]See 2 Kgs. 18:13-16
30 [r]ch. 8:22

the exact opposite of God's true perspective (cf. Matt. 12:24; John 8:44; 2 Thess. 2:11).

5:24–30 Two more outcomes, each marked by **therefore**, doom Isaiah's generation.

5:24 they have rejected . . . and have despised. God delighted in his people ("his pleasant planting," v. 7), but they have rejected and despised him (cf. 53:3).

5:26 Nations, including Assyria, are summoned by the sovereign God with a mere whistle. **Quickly, speedily they come**, to serve his purpose by humbling the arrogant taunt of v. 19.

5:27–30 With frightening realism Isaiah describes the approach of invading military forces—a far cry from the nations approaching Zion to learn the ways of God and cease from war (2:2–4).

5:30 darkness and distress . . . light is darkened. Having rejected the light of the Lord that was offered to them (2:5), Judah and Jerusalem find that the light they chose turns to darkness. Because they have refused God's grace (5:4), his wrath engulfs them. The rest of the book reveals that God's purpose of grace is still greater than his disciplinary wrath.

6:1–12:6 *God Redefines the Future of His People: "Your Guilt Is Taken Away."* God's grace will preserve a remnant of his people to enjoy forever

Isaiah's Vision of the Lord

6 In the year that [s]King Uzziah died I [t]saw the Lord sitting upon a throne, high and
lifted up; and the train[1] of his robe filled the temple. 2 Above him stood the seraphim.
Each had [u]six wings: with two he covered his face, and with two he covered his feet, and
with two he flew. 3 And one called to another and said:

> [u]"Holy, holy, holy is the LORD of hosts;
> [v]the whole earth is full of his glory!"[2]

4 And [w]the foundations of the thresholds shook at the voice of him who called, and [x]the
house was filled with smoke. 5 And I said: "Woe is me! [y]For I am lost; [z]for I am a man of
unclean lips, and I dwell in the midst of a people of unclean lips; for my eyes have seen
the [a]King, the LORD of hosts!"
6 Then one of the seraphim flew to me, having in his hand a burning coal that he had
taken with tongs from the altar. 7 And he [b]touched my mouth and said: "Behold, this has
touched your lips; your guilt is taken away, and your sin atoned for."

Isaiah's Commission from the Lord

8 And I heard the voice of the Lord saying, "Whom shall I send, and who will go for [c]us?"
Then I said, "Here I am! Send me." 9 And he said, "Go, and say to this people:

> [d]"'Keep on hearing,[3] but do not understand;
> keep on seeing,[4] but do not perceive.'

[1] *Or hem* [2] *Or may his glory fill the whole earth* [3] *Or Hear indeed* [4] *Or see indeed*

Chapter 6
1 [s]ch. 1:1; 2 Chr. 26:16-21 [t][John 12:41]
2 [u]Rev. 4:8
3 [u][See ver. 2 above] [v]Ps. 72:19
4 [w]Amos 9:1 [x]1 Kgs. 8:10, 11; Rev. 15:8; [Ex. 19:18]
5 [y][Judg. 13:22] [z][Luke 5:8] [a]ch. 33:17; Jer. 10:10; [1 Sam. 12:12]
7 [b]Jer. 1:9; Dan. 10:16
8 [c]See Gen. 1:26
9 [d]Cited Matt. 13:14, 15; Acts 28:26, 27; [Mark 4:12; Luke 8:10; Rom. 11:8]

his messianic kingdom and to fulfill the purpose for which he called them. That grace spreads from Isaiah (6:1–13) to the southern kingdom of Judah (7:1–9:7) to the northern kingdom of Israel (9:8–11:16), bringing God's people to the "wells of salvation" (12:1–6).

6:1–13 *Grace—through Judgment—for Isaiah.* God's grace leads Isaiah from "Woe is me!" (v. 5) to "Here I am!" (v. 8). This vision seems to recount Isaiah's commission as a prophet. His book conveys the lasting impression of this vision of God in his infinite holiness.

6:1 In the year. Around 740 B.C. **King Uzziah died**, marking the end of a lengthy era of national prosperity (see 2 Chronicles 26). Uzziah had contracted leprosy for flouting God's holiness, and his son Jotham had been his co-regent for about 10 years (2 Chron. 26:16–21). **I saw the Lord sitting upon a throne**. The undying King holds court above. The words **high and lifted up** appear elsewhere in Isaiah (Isa. 52:13; 57:15) and seem to be part of his distinctive style (see Introduction: Date). John 12:38–41 brings two of these together, implying that John saw the servant of Isa. 52:13–53:12 as not only messianic, but divine. The temple in Jerusalem modeled the **temple** in heaven (cf. Heb. 9:24; Rev. 4:1–4).

6:2 the seraphim. Fiery angelic beings (the Hb. word *serapim* means "flames"). **Six wings** suggest remarkable powers. The references to **face** and **feet**, with their capacity for speech in vv. 3 and 7, and "his hand" in v. 6, imply composite creatures, such as are represented in ancient Near Eastern art. **he covered**. Even a perfect, superhuman creature humbles himself before the all-holy God.

6:3 Holy, holy, holy. The threefold repetition intensifies the superlative (cf. Rev. 4:8). Holiness implies absolute moral purity and separateness above the creation (see note on Isa. 1:4). **his glory**. This is a technical term for God's manifest presence with his covenant people. It was seen in the cloud in the wilderness (Ex. 16:7, 10); it moved in to "fill" the tabernacle (Ex. 40:34–35) and then the temple (1 Kings 8:11), where the worshipers could "see" it (Ex. 29:43; Ps. 26:8; 63:2). Several passages look forward to the day when the Lord's glory would fill the earth, i.e., the whole world will become a sanctuary (Num. 14:21; Ps. 72:19; Hab. 2:14; cf. Isa. 11:9); and the ESV footnote suggests that the seraphic cry shares this anticipation. Other texts in Isaiah also look forward to the revealing of the Lord's glory to the world (11:10; 35:2; 40:5; 58:8; 59:19; 60:1–2; 66:18). John 1:14 asserts that this glory was present in Jesus.

6:4–5 The revelation of the Holy One is disturbing (see Ex. 19:16–18). **Woe is me!** For the first time in the book, Isaiah speaks, and his word is a prophetic woe against himself. He confesses his **unclean** (i.e., not permitted in God's presence) **lips**, unlike the seraphic choir, whose worship is pure. **I dwell in the midst**. Isaiah's generation is unfit for God, and Isaiah himself is no better. **my eyes have seen the King**. The holiness of the King is such that the very sight of him seems as though it would be fatal to a sinner (cf. Gen. 32:30; Ex. 33:20; Isa. 33:14).

6:6–7 this has touched your lips. The remedy of grace is personally applied. God's holiness and glory now redemptively enter Isaiah's experience. **atoned for**. Through the sacrifice on the **altar**, according to the Levitical ordinances (e.g., Lev. 1:4). Through his seraph (the singular form of *seraphim*, plural; see note on Isa. 6:2), God declares the remedy for Isaiah's sin to be sufficient and instantly effective. Now Isaiah is qualified to proclaim the only hope of the world—the overruling grace of God.

6:8 Whom shall I send, and who will go for us? See 1 Kings 22:19–20; Jer. 23:18, 22. **Here I am! Send me**. Isaiah's experience of grace has dealt with his problem, confessed in Isa. 6:5. "Us" is like "us" in Gen. 1:26 ("let us make man"): God could be addressing himself (in a way compatible with the Christian doctrine of the Trinity), or he could be addressing his heavenly court (less likely, since only God is doing the sending here). See notes on Gen. 1:26; 1:27.

6:9–10 God decrees that the prophet's ministry will have a hardening effect on his own generation, whose character was laid bare in chs. 1–5. The NT quotes this text to explain why some reject the good news of the gospel (cf. Matt. 13:14–15 par.; John 12:39–40; Acts 28:25–27). The openness of faith is a gift of grace, but the unresponsive hearer finds that the message only hardens him to God's gracious purposes (cf. Isa. 29:9–10; 42:18–25; 65:1–7; Luke 2:34; John 9:39; Acts 7:54; Rom. 11:7–10, 25; 2 Cor. 2:15–16; 1 Pet. 2:8).

Datable Events in the Book of Isaiah

Uzziah's death; Isaiah's call	ch. 6	740 B.C.
Days of Ahaz	ch. 7	c. 735
Assyrian invasion	chs. 36–38	701
Sennacherib's death	37:38	681
Babylonians will destroy Jerusalem	39:6–8	586
Israel will return from Babylonian exile	chs. 40–48	538

10 [e]Make the heart of this people [f]dull,[1]
and their ears heavy,
and blind their eyes;
[g]lest they see with their eyes,
and hear with their ears,
and understand with their hearts,
and turn and be healed."
11 Then I said, [h]"How long, O Lord?"
And he said:
"Until [i]cities lie waste
without inhabitant,
and houses without people,
and the land is a desolate waste,
12 and the LORD removes people far away,
and the forsaken places are many in the midst of the land.
13 [j]And though a tenth remain in it,
it will be burned[2] again,
like a terebinth or an oak,
whose stump [k]remains
when it is felled."
[l]The holy seed[3] is its stump.

10 [e]Cited John 12:40 [f]Ps. 119:70 [g][Jer. 5:21]
11 [h]Ps. 79:5; 89:46 [i][ch. 1:7; 27:10]
13 [j][ch. 10:22] [k][Job 14:7] [l]Ezra 9:2

Isaiah Sent to King Ahaz

7 In the days of [m]Ahaz the son of Jotham, son of Uzziah, king of Judah, [n]Rezin the king
of Syria and [n]Pekah the son of Remaliah the king of Israel came up to Jerusalem to
wage war against it, but could not yet mount an attack against it. 2 When the house of
David was told, [o]"Syria is in league with[4] [p]Ephraim," the heart of Ahaz[5] and the heart of
his people shook as the trees of the forest shake before the wind.
3 And the LORD said to Isaiah, "Go out to meet Ahaz, you and [q]Shear-jashub[6] your son,
at the end of [r]the conduit of the upper pool on the highway to the Washer's Field. 4 And
say to him, [s]'Be careful, [t]be quiet, do not fear, and do not let your heart be faint because
of these two [u]smoldering stumps of firebrands, at the fierce anger of Rezin and Syria
and [v]the son of Remaliah. 5 Because Syria, with Ephraim and [v]the son of Remaliah, has
devised evil against you, saying, 6 "Let us go up against Judah and terrify it, and let us
conquer it[7] for ourselves, and set up the son of Tabeel as king in the midst of it," 7 thus
says the Lord GOD:

Chapter 7

1 [m]ch. 1:1 [n]2 Kgs. 15:37; 16:5
2 [o][ch. 8:12] [p]ch. 9:9
3 [q][ch. 8:3, 18] [r]ch. 36:2; 2 Kgs. 18:17
4 [s][ch. 8:12] [t][Ex. 14:13] [u][Amos 4:11; Zech. 3:2] [v]ver. 1
5 [v][See ver. 4 above]

[1] Hebrew *fat* [2] Or *purged* [3] Or *offspring* [4] Hebrew *Syria has rested upon* [5] Hebrew *his heart* [6] *Shear-jashub* means *A remnant shall return* [7] Hebrew *let us split it open*

6:11–13 God's discipline will leave only a remnant of his people—**the holy seed**—like a single **stump** left after a forest has been **burned** over. The remaining believers are set apart for God by the same grace that saved Isaiah. They are the heirs of God's promises to Abraham, and thus the only hope for the whole world (see 10:20–23; 11:1–10).

7:1–9:7 *Grace—through Judgment—for Judah.* Though King Ahaz brings Assyrian oppression upon his nation, God promises a miraculous child who will rule forever from the throne of David. In the face of human failure, the "zeal of the LORD of hosts" alone will accomplish this (9:7).

7:1 In the days of Ahaz is c. 735 B.C., when Ahaz has just begun his reign. **Rezin the king of Syria and Pekah the son of Remaliah the king of Israel**. Syria and the northern kingdom of Israel ("Ephraim," v. 2) join forces against Assyria with the intention of forcing the southern kingdom of Judah into their alliance, perhaps trying to take advantage of Ahaz's inexperience (see map, p. 1253). Isaiah informs the reader that Ahaz has nothing to fear (v. 4).

7:2 the house of David. In God's covenant with David his forefather, Ahaz has clear warrant for confidence in God's protective care (cf. 2 Sam. 7:8–17; Ps. 89:3–4, 19–34). **the heart of Ahaz and the heart of his people shook**. The weakness of national character is revealed.

7:3 Shear-jashub means "a remnant shall return" and suggests both judgment (God's people will be reduced to a remnant) and grace (that remnant *will* return; cf. 10:20–22). See 8:18 for the symbolic significance of Isaiah's family.

7:4 Defiance in the face of evil is called for by the faithfulness of God.

7:6 the son of Tabeel. The puppet ruler meant to replace Ahaz, son of David. The promises of God were given only to the royal line of David (cf. 2 Sam. 7:12–16), and Tabeel is apparently not from this line.

7:7–9 Human threats are to be dismissed and divine promises firmly trusted, for **the Lord GOD** vetoes human intentions. **within sixty-five years**. The northern kingdom fell to Assyria in 722 B.C. By around 670 B.C. the ethnic identity of the former kingdom would have been decisively transformed, due to the importation of foreign settlers (cf. 2 Kings 17:24; Ezra 4:1–2, 10). **If you are not firm in faith, you will not be firm at all**. The southern kingdom still has an opportunity to hold fast to God, but their faith must be firm. The wordplay on firmness ("not firm . . . not be firm") connects unbelief with instability. Unbelief in God destabilizes everything for Ahaz, not just his religious life.

7[W]ch. 8:10
8[X]Gen. 14:15
9[Y]ver. 1 [Z][2 Chr. 20:20]

[W]"'It shall not stand,
and it shall not come to pass.
8 For the head of Syria is [X]Damascus,
and the head of Damascus is Rezin.
And within sixty-five years
Ephraim will be shattered from being a people.
9 And the head of Ephraim is Samaria,
and the head of Samaria is [Y]the son of Remaliah.
[Z]If you[1] are not firm in faith,
you will not be firm at all.'"

[1] The Hebrew for *you* is plural in verses 9, 13, 14

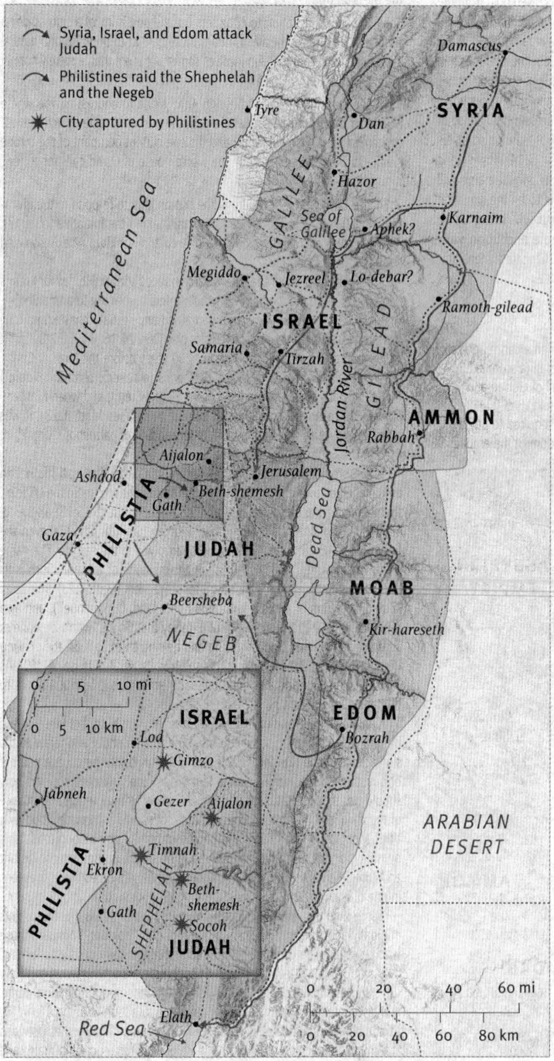

Syria and Israel Attack Judah
c. 740–732 B.C.
As the Assyrian Empire expanded westward, Syria and Israel sought to compel Judah and the other nearby states to form an anti-Assyrian alliance. Judah refused, leading Syria, Israel, and perhaps Edom and Philistia to attack Judah (2 Kings 15:29–37; 2 Chron. 28:1–19). Isaiah assured Ahaz that he needed only trust in God, who would call upon Assyria to deal with Syria and Israel.

The Sign of Immanuel

10 Again the LORD spoke to Ahaz, 11 "Ask [a]a sign of the LORD your[1] God; let it be deep
as Sheol or high as heaven." 12 But Ahaz said, "I will not ask, and I will not put the LORD
to the test." 13 And he[2] said, "Hear then, O house of David! Is it too little for you to weary
men, that you [b]weary my God also? 14 Therefore the [c]Lord himself will give you a sign.
[d]Behold, the [e]virgin shall conceive and bear a son, and shall call his name [f]Immanuel.[3]
15 He shall eat [g]curds and honey when he knows how to refuse the evil and choose the

[1] The Hebrew for *you* and *your* is singular in verses 11, 16, 17 [2] That is, Isaiah [3] *Immanuel* means *God is with us*

11 [a]See 2 Kgs. 19:29
13 [b]ch. 43:24
14 [c]ch. 37:30; 38:7, 8 [d]ch. 9:6; Cited Matt. 1:23; [Luke 1:31, 34] [e]Gen. 24:43 (Heb.); Ex. 2:8 (Heb.); Ps. 68:25 (Heb.); Prov. 30:19 (Heb.) [f]ch. 8:8, 10
15 [g]ver. 22

7:10–17 The basic issue in ch. 7 is that Ahaz and the Lord (speaking through Isaiah) have completely different views concerning the threat from the coalition of Syria and Ephraim. Though Ahaz is the heir of David's throne, he has put his firm faith (v. 9) in the king of Assyria and he has given gold from the temple to the Assyrians, to induce them to attack Syria (2 Kings 16:1–9). Thus Ahaz placed his hope for salvation in human power rather than in the Lord. But Isaiah calls for Ahaz and all of Jerusalem to put their firm faith in a far more reliable ally: "the Lord himself" (Isa. 7:14). Thus the Lord invites Ahaz to request a sign to strengthen his faith (v. 11), but Ahaz hypocritically refuses to do so (v. 12; cf. Deut. 6:16). Isaiah then addresses the "house of David," accusing the royal house of wearying God, but Isaiah also offers them ("you" plural) a **sign** from the Lord himself (Isa. 7:14). This sign is the famous announcement of a **son** born to a **virgin**, whose name will be **Immanuel** (see notes following). This child's life is to be the sign that confirms the truth of the divine word, which **the LORD will bring upon you** ("you" singular; i.e., Ahaz) **and upon your people and upon your father's house** (i.e., the house of David; cf. v. 13). Christian interpretation of this passage requires doing justice to the meaning of Isaiah's words both (1) as they were first addressed to Ahaz, and then (2) as these same prophetic words are used later by Matthew with respect to the birth of Jesus the Messiah (Matt. 1:21–23).

Assyria Captures Northern Israel

c. 733 B.C.

Suffering attacks on all sides due to his refusal to join an alliance against Assyria, King Ahaz of Judah called upon Tiglath-pileser III (also called Pul) of Assyria for help. The Assyrians captured Syria and all of Galilee and Gilead from Israel (2 Kings 15:29). As Isaiah had foretold (Isa. 7:17), however, Ahaz's petition came at a price, for he was required to pay a large tribute to Assyria and make Judah a vassal kingdom of the empire.

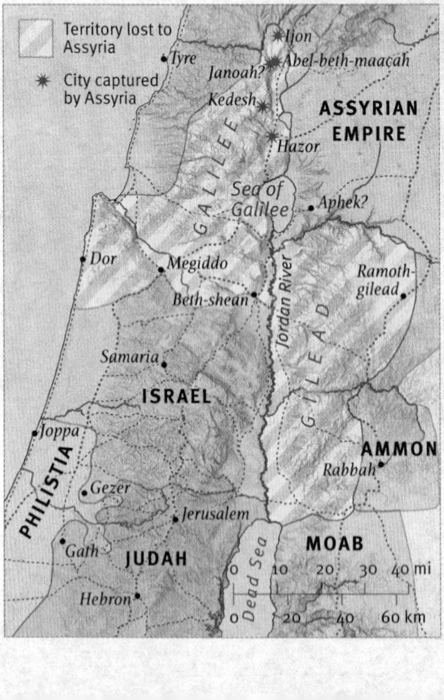

7:11 The Lord's invitation to Ahaz sets out the possibility of a sign as **deep as Sheol or high as heaven**, clearly inviting Ahaz to think beyond natural signs, indicating that the sign involves something more than a merely normal birth. See note on vv. 10–17.

7:13 The transition from addressing Ahaz alone to addressing the whole **house of David** provides a parallel with the previous oracle, which likewise concerned both the royal family and the one current occupant of the throne (vv. 2–3). The failure shared by the whole house of David calls for a new, future hope—the sign of v. 14.

7:14 the Lord himself. Failure of the human king to respond to the invitation (v. 12) results in the divine King again taking the initiative (cf. v. 17). Similarly, two such signs would be offered to Hezekiah, Ahaz's son and successor (see 37:30; 38:7).

Although some claim that the word translated **virgin** (Hb. *'almah*) refers generally to a "young woman," it actually refers specifically to a "maiden"—that is, to a young woman who is unmarried and sexually chaste, and thus has virginity as one of her characteristics (see Gen. 24:16, 43; Ex. 2:8, "girl"). Thus when the Septuagint translators, 200 years before the birth of Christ, rendered *'almah* here with Greek *parthenos* (a specific term for "virgin") they rightly perceived the meaning of the Hebrew term; and when Matthew applied this prophecy to the virgin birth of Christ (see Matt. 1:23), it was in accord with this well-established understanding of *parthenos* ("virgin") as used in the Septuagint and in other Greek writers.

Isaiah prophesies further that it is "the virgin" who shall **call his name** Immanuel. Bestowing a child's name often falls to the mother in the OT (e.g., the naming of the patriarchs in Gen. 29:31–30:24; but cf. 35:18; also Judg. 13:24; 1 Sam. 1:20), although other women (cf. Ruth 4:17) or even the father (Gen. 16:15; Judg. 8:31) could be involved in the naming. The name itself, **Immanuel**, "God is with us," is the message of the sign. Such is its importance that Matthew translates it for his readers (Matt. 1:23). Immanuel is used as a form of address in Isa. 8:8 ("your land, O Immanuel"), and as a sentence in 8:10 ("for God is with us"). To say that God is "with" someone or a people means that God is guiding and helping them to fulfill their calling (Gen. 21:22; Ex. 3:12; Deut. 2:7; Josh. 1:5; Ps. 46:7, 11; Isa. 41:10). As such, it would provide a pointed message either to the fearful Ahaz or to the failing royal house.

Christian interpretation follows Matthew in applying this verse to the birth of Jesus. However, some aspects of Isaiah's prophecy also relate to the significance of the sign for Isaiah's own day. This being the case, a number of questions are raised: To whose family does the virgin belong, and how should her marital status be understood? What is the precise significance of the child's name? Is it a personal name, or should it be understood as a title? Most importantly, does the fulfillment of this sign belong to Isaiah's own day, or does it rather point (even in his day) to a much more distant and complete fulfillment? Christians have typically answered these questions in one of two ways.

Some hold that the sign has a *single fulfillment*—that is, the sign points originally and solely to the birth of Jesus as the "ultimate" Messiah. Those who hold this view emphasize the understanding of *'almah* only as "virgin," thus precluding any "near term" fulfillment before the birth of Jesus; this view understands "Immanuel" as a title (as in 8:8) rather than a personal name. It is also noted that the variation in reference to a "son" (Hb. *ben*) in 7:14, as compared to a "boy" (Hb. *na'ar*) in v. 16, further distinguishes between the child of miraculous birth and a more generic reference to a male child

16[h][ch. 8:4] [i]ch. 6:12
17[j]ch. 8:7; [2 Chr. 28:20] [k]1 Kgs. 12:16
18[l]ch. 5:26
19[m]ch. 2:19; Jer. 13:4; 16:16
20[n]ch. 24:1; See 2 Kgs. 18:13-16 [o]Ezek. 5:1 [p][ch. 10:5, 15] [q]ch. 8:7; 11:15
21[r][ch. 5:17]
22[s]ver. 15
23[t]ch. 5:6
24[u][Judg. 5:11]
25[v]ch. 32:13, 14 [t][See ver. 23 above]

Chapter 8

1[w]ch. 30:8
2[x][ch. 43:10] [y]2 Kgs. 16:10, 11, 15, 16

good. 16 [h]For before the boy knows how to refuse the evil and choose the good, the land
whose two kings you dread will be [i]deserted. 17 [j]The LORD will bring upon you and upon
your people and upon your father's house such days as have not come since the day that
[k]Ephraim departed from Judah—the king of Assyria."

18 In that day the LORD will [l]whistle for the fly that is at the end of the streams of Egypt, and
for the bee that is in the land of Assyria. 19 And they will all come and settle in the steep ravines,
and [m]in the clefts of the rocks, and on all the thornbushes, and on all the pastures.[1]

20 In that day [n]the Lord will [o]shave with a razor that is [p]hired beyond [q]the River—
with the king of Assyria—the head and the hair of the feet, and it will sweep away the
beard also.

21 [r]In that day a man will keep alive a young cow and two sheep, 22 and because of the
abundance of milk that they give, he will eat curds, for everyone who is left in the land
will eat [s]curds and honey.

23 In that day every place where there used to be a thousand vines, worth a thousand
shekels[2] of silver, will become [t]briers and thorns. 24 [u]With bow and arrows a man will
come there, for all the land will be briers and thorns. 25 [v]And as for all the hills that used
to be hoed with a hoe, you will not come there for fear [t]of briers and thorns, but they will
become a place where cattle are let loose and where sheep tread.

The Coming Assyrian Invasion

8 Then the LORD said to me, "Take a large tablet [w]and write on it in common characters,[3]
'Belonging to Maher-shalal-hash-baz.'[4] 2 And [x]I will get reliable witnesses, [y]Uriah the
priest and Zechariah the son of Jeberechiah, to attest for me."

3 And I went to the prophetess, and she conceived and bore a son. Then the LORD said

[1] Or *watering holes, or brambles* [2] A *shekel* was about 2/5 ounce or 11 grams [3] Hebrew *with a man's stylus* [4] *Maher-shalal-hash-baz* means *The spoil speeds, the prey hastens*

unrelated to the divine promise. This has the effect of separating the reference to Isaiah's day (vv. 16–17) from the fulfillment of the announced miraculous son to be born at a future time (v. 14). According to this interpretation, then, the prediction of the virgin birth in v. 14 is a straightforward prediction of an event cast well into the future, and Matthew's application of this prophecy to Jesus (Matt. 1:20–23) provides the divinely inspired testimony to there being a single fulfillment of Isaiah's prophecy. By this interpretation, the sign is directed to the "house of David," to affirm God's intention of preserving David's dynasty (in keeping with the promises of 2 Sam. 7:12–16), in order to bring Israel's mission to its glorious fulfillment (Isa. 9:6–7; 11:1–10). God will use any means to do this, even miraculous ones: this is a rebuke to the faithless and secular outlook of Ahaz.

Those who see in this sign a more immediate application to Ahaz and his times usually argue that the prophecy has a *double fulfillment*—that is, both an immediate fulfillment in Isaiah's day and a long-term fulfillment in the birth of the Messiah. Those who hold this view argue that it is natural for the name "Immanuel" to be understood in terms of double fulfillment, since two other "sons" perform similar symbolic roles in the context (cf. 7:3; 8:3–4). They argue further that the prophet's own interpretation of the sign in 7:16–17 applies it directly to Ahaz's own day. It should be observed that this understanding of the text in no way diminishes Matthew's affirmation of the supernatural conception and virgin birth of Jesus (cf. also Luke 1:34–35). Even if the prophecy does include an immediate application to the time of Ahaz, however, the prophecy cannot have been fulfilled completely by the birth of someone like Maher-shalal-hash-baz (Isa. 8:1, 3) or by Hezekiah, as some have suggested, since 9:6 prophesies the birth of a son whose name will be "Wonderful Counselor, Mighty God, Everlasting Father, Prince of Peace"—a statement that could apply only to the Davidic Messiah. On this understanding, then, the prophecy of 7:14 foretells the birth of Immanuel, which was fulfilled partially in Isaiah's time but fully and finally in the person of Jesus Christ.

Faithful interpreters can be found on either side of this debate. One should not, therefore, lose sight of those truths on which all agree: the prophet speaks authoritatively for God; Ahaz and his house stand under judgment; the prophetic sign directly meets the failures of Ahaz's day; fulfillment of the prophecy comes about through direct divine intervention in human history; and the sign finds its final fulfillment in the virgin birth of Jesus the Messiah, who is literally "God with us."

7:15–17 These verses indicate that the Syro-Ephraimite threat will soon pass; it will not last longer than the time it takes for the **boy** (possibly in the sense of "any boy") to reach an age when he can **refuse the evil and choose the good**. In fact, Syria did fall to Assyria in 732 B.C. and Israel fell in 722. But the agent of deliverance—**the king of Assyria**—was a worse disaster for Judah. Ahaz forsook "the King, the LORD of hosts" (6:5) for a dreaded earthly king. He foolishly hired the military support of Assyria (2 Kings 16:5–9), for in his spiritual blindness he could not discern between his true ally and his true enemy. Ahaz's unbelief doomed the Davidic dynasty to loss of sovereignty under foreign domination. Now God must restore the throne of David and save the world.

7:18–25 Isaiah sets forth the devastating national consequences of foreign invasion, marked fourfold by the phrase, **in that day** (vv. 18, 20, 21, 23), referring back to "such days" in v. 17.

7:18–19 At the Lord's command, the Promised Land is infested with swarms of enemy troops.

7:20 In a culture of honor and shame, forced shaving was a mark of humiliation (cf. 2 Sam. 10:4–5). Isaiah foresees his nation scraped down to bare essentials, to their disgrace, by the very **razor** they **hired** to save them from humiliation. But the sovereign **Lord** fulfills his purpose.

7:21 The population of God's people is so diminished that it takes only a few animals to produce more than enough food for the remnant.

8:1–22 Isaiah reflects on the events of ch. 7, shifting from the third person ("And the LORD said to Isaiah," 7:3) to the first person ("Then the LORD said to me," 8:1).

8:1–2 Through Isaiah's son, God provides an openly attested witness to his promise of deliverance from the Syro-Ephraimite coalition. **Maher-shalal-hash-baz**. See ESV footnote, the relevance of which is explained in v. 4. The striking similarities between 7:14–17 and 8:1–4 suggest that, in addition to the Lord's promise of ultimate deliverance in ch. 7, he provides a rapidly approaching, short-term assurance in ch. 8, encouraging confidence in his long-term faithfulness.

8:2 Uriah worked closely with King Ahaz (cf. 2 Kings 16:10–16), while **Zechariah** was probably Ahaz's father-in-law (cf. 2 Kings 18:2; 2 Chron. 29:1).

8:3 Isaiah's wife, **the prophetess**, bears the "sign-child," **Maher-shalal-hash-baz** (cf. v. 18).

to me, [z]"Call his name Maher-shalal-hash-baz; 4 [a]for before the boy knows how to cry 'My
father' or 'My mother,' the [a]wealth of [b]Damascus and the spoil of [b]Samaria will be carried
away before the king of Assyria."
5 The LORD spoke to me again: 6 "Because this people has refused the waters of [c]Shiloah
that flow gently, and rejoice over [d]Rezin and the son of Remaliah, 7 therefore, behold, the
Lord is bringing up against them [e]the waters of [f]the River, mighty and many, the king
of Assyria and all his glory. And it [g]will rise over all its channels and go over all its banks,
8 and it will sweep on into Judah, it will overflow and pass on, [h]reaching even to the neck,
and its [i]outspread wings will fill the breadth of your land, [j]O Immanuel."

9 Be broken,[1] you peoples, and [k]be shattered;[2]
give ear, all you far countries;
strap on your armor and be shattered;
strap on your armor and be shattered.
10 Take counsel together, but it will come to nothing;
speak a word, [l]but it will not stand,
for God [m]is with us.[3]

Fear God, Wait for the LORD

11 For the LORD spoke thus to me with his strong hand upon me, and [n]warned me not
to walk in the way of this people, saying: 12 "Do not call [o]conspiracy all that this people
calls conspiracy, and [p]do not fear what they fear, nor be in dread. 13 But the LORD of hosts,
[q]him you shall honor as holy. Let him be your fear, and let him be your dread. 14 And he
will become a [r]sanctuary and [s]a stone of offense and a rock of stumbling to both houses
of Israel, a trap and a snare to the inhabitants of Jerusalem. 15 And many [t]shall stumble
on it. They shall fall and be broken; they shall be snared and taken."
16 Bind up [u]the testimony; [v]seal the teaching[4] among my disciples. 17 I will [w]wait for the
LORD, who is [x]hiding his face from the house of Jacob, and I will hope in him. 18 [y]Behold,
I and [z]the children whom the LORD has given me are signs and portents in Israel from
the LORD of hosts, who dwells on Mount Zion. 19 And when they say to you, "Inquire
of the [a]mediums and the necromancers who chirp and mutter," should not a people
inquire of their God? Should they inquire of [b]the dead on behalf of the living? 20 [c]To
the teaching and to the testimony! If they will not speak according to this word, it is
because they have no [d]dawn. 21 They will pass through the land,[5] greatly distressed and
hungry. And when they are hungry, they will be enraged and will speak contemptuously
against[6] their king and their God, and turn their faces upward. 22 [e]And they will look
to the earth, but behold, distress and darkness, the gloom of anguish. And they will be
thrust into [f]thick darkness.

[1] Or *Be evil* [2] Or *dismayed* [3] The Hebrew for *God is with us* is *Immanuel* [4] Or *law;* also verse 20 [5] Hebrew *it* [6] Or *speak contemptuously by*

3 [z][Hos. 1:4]
4 [a][ch. 7:16] [b]See ch. 7:8, 9
6 [c][Neh. 3:15; John 9:7, 11] [d]See ch. 7:1, 4
7 [e][ch. 17:12, 13] [f]See ch. 7:20 [g][Jer. 46:8]
8 [h]ch. 30:28 [i][ch. 36:1] [j]ch. 7:14
9 [k][Dan. 2:34, 35]
10 [l]ch. 7:7 [m][ver. 8; Rom. 8:31]
11 [n][Ezek. 2:8]
12 [o][ch. 7:2] [p]Cited 1 Pet. 3:14, 15
13 [q]See Num. 20:12
14 [r]Ezek. 11:16 [s]Cited Rom. 9:33; 1 Pet. 2:8; [ch. 28:16]
15 [t][ch. 28:13; Matt. 21:44; Luke 20:18]
16 [u]ver. 1, 2 [v]Dan. 12:4
17 [w]Ps. 27:14; 33:20; Hab. 2:3 [x]ch. 1:15; 54:8; Deut. 31:17
18 [y]Cited Heb. 2:13 [z][ch. 7:3]
19 [a]ch. 19:3; 2 Kgs. 21:6; 23:24; 2 Chr. 33:6; See Lev. 19:31 [b][Ps. 106:28]; See 1 Sam. 28:11-14
20 [c][Luke 16:29] [d][ch. 60:1]
22 [e]ch. 5:30 [f]Nah. 1:8

8:5–8 Judah celebrates their escape from Syria and Israel as their own achievement, despite the witness of Maher-shalal-hash-baz, only to find that their ally, Assyria, is really their oppressor.

8:6–7 The waters of Shiloah that flow gently is probably referring to the water system that preceded Hezekiah's construction of the conduit that brought water into the pool of Siloam (cf. 22:9; 2 Kings 20:20; Luke 13:4; John 9:7), used here as an image of God's faithful care, available to his people. **Rezin and the son of Remaliah**. See Isa. 7:1. **the waters of the** (Euphrates) **River**. In contrast to 8:6, v. 7 describes a swollen "river" of Assyrian military power flowing over Syria and Ephraim and flooding south into Judah, who will survive only by standing on tiptoe to keep her head above the tide (chs. 36–37). The way of faith in God seems inadequate to Judah, but the worldly alternative she prefers nearly drowns her in human oppression.

8:8 your land, O Immanuel. Immanuel's land (cf. 7:14) will be almost completely overrun (**even to the neck**) by the Assyrians (chs. 36–37).

8:9–10 In view of Immanuel's future triumph, Isaiah announces that the enemies of God who gather against his people will be shattered (cf. Gen. 3:15). At all times, in all conditions, even prior to the first coming of Christ, **God is with us** (Hb. "Immanuel"; see note on Isa. 7:14).

8:11–15 God deeply impressed upon Isaiah a surprising message. The holy God, who is the sanctuary for frightened human beings, is also the snare for those who do not fear him. Judah and Jerusalem wring their hands over surface-level crises (7:2, 6, 16), with little awareness of the grandeur of God. By disregarding God, they find him to be an obstacle they cannot evade. First Peter 3:15 uses language from Isa. 8:13 to identify Isaiah's **the LORD of hosts** (v. 13) with Jesus Christ.

8:16–22 The difference between the remnant (vv. 16–18) and the hardened nation (vv. 19–22) becomes clear. God marks his own as loyal disciples who preserve the **testimony** of his Word (v. 16). Isaiah speaks for them with the voice of patient trust in God during hard times (v. 17). He offers himself and his **children** as a prophetic presence in their nation, bearing witness to the enduring significance of Zion (v. 18; cf. Heb. 2:13). The prophet urges his followers not to be drawn into occult gibberish when their faithful God speaks clearly in his Word (Isa. 8:19–20). Enshrouded in spiritual darkness and sent into exile, unbelieving Judah rages at God (vv. 21–22).

For to Us a Child Is Born

9 [1] But there will be no [g]gloom for her who was in anguish. In the former time he
[h]brought into contempt the land of [i]Zebulun and the land of Naphtali, but in the
latter time he [j]has made glorious the way of the sea, the land beyond the Jordan, Galilee
of the nations.[2]

2 [3] [i]The people [k]who walked in darkness
have seen a great light;
those who dwelt in a land of [l]deep darkness,
on them has light shone.
3 [m]You have multiplied the nation;
you have increased its joy;
they rejoice before you
as with [n]joy at the harvest,
as they [o]are glad [p]when they divide the spoil.
4 [q]For the yoke of his burden,
[r]and the staff for his shoulder,
the rod of his oppressor,
you have broken as [s]on the day of Midian.
5 [t]For every boot of the tramping warrior in battle tumult
and every garment rolled in blood
will be burned as fuel for the fire.
6 [u]For to us a child is born,
to us [v]a son is given;
[w]and the government shall be [x]upon[4] his shoulder,
and his name shall be called[5]
Wonderful [y]Counselor, [z]Mighty God,
[a]Everlasting [b]Father, Prince of [c]Peace.
7 Of the increase of his government and of peace
[d]there will be no end,
on the throne of David and over his kingdom,
to establish it and to uphold it

[1] Ch 8:23 in Hebrew [2] Or *of the Gentiles* [3] Ch 9:1 in Hebrew [4] Or *is upon* [5] Or *is called*

Chapter 9
1 [g][ch. 8:22] [h][2 Kgs. 15:29; 2 Chr. 16:4] [i]Cited Matt. 4:15, 16 [j]ch. 26:15
2 [i][See ver. 1 above] [k][Luke 1:79; Eph. 5:8, 14] [l]See Job 3:5
3 [m]ch. 26:15 [n]Ps. 4:7; [John 4:36] [o]Ps. 119:162; [1 Sam. 30:16] [p][Judg. 5:30]
4 [q]ch. 10:27; 14:25; Nah. 1:13; [Matt. 11:29] [r]ch. 10:5, 24; 14:5 [s]ch. 10:26; Ps. 83:9; See Judg. 7:19-25; 8:10-21
5 [t]Ezek. 39:9
6 [u]Luke 2:11; [John 3:16] [v]ch. 7:14 [w][Matt. 28:18; 1 Cor. 15:25] [x]ch. 22:22 [y][ch. 28:29] [z]ch. 10:21; Deut. 10:17; Neh. 9:32; Jer. 32:18; [Ps. 45:3] [a]Ps. 72:17 [b]ch. 63:16; [John 14:18] [c]Ps. 72:7; [Eph. 2:14]; See ch. 11:6-9
7 [d]Ps. 89:4; Luke 1:32, 33

9:1–7 The spiritual gloom of 8:22 is dispelled forever by the light of the Messiah, Jesus Christ.

9:1 Her who was in anguish refers to Israel as the people of God under his discipline. **In the former time**. Isaiah's vision projects his thought out of the tragic present as if it were already past. **Brought into contempt**, i.e., humiliated with national defeat. **the land of Zebulun**. The northern regions of the Promised Land—first to come under attack by foreign invaders who approached by means of the Fertile Crescent (2 Kings 15:29)—are the first to see a glorious new era. **Galilee of the nations**. The Messiah launched his worldwide mission from Galilee (Matt. 4:12–16). **in the latter time he has made glorious**. A past-tense verb, because the prophetic eye sees the future in a vision. The people of God finally play the glorious role prophesied in Isa. 2:3 through the triumph of their Messiah.

9:2 The people who walked in darkness. Such people as those who refused the appeal of 2:5 (cf. also 5:30; 8:22; John 3:19–20). **on them has light shone**. Not subjective wishful thinking but an objective, surprising joy breaking upon sinners through the grace of Christ (cf. Isa. 42:6; 49:6; John 1:5; 2 Cor. 4:6).

9:3 You have multiplied the nation. No longer are the faithful a small remnant (cf. 26:15; 49:20–21; 54:1–5; 66:7–14). **the harvest . . . the spoil**. The joys of both peaceful abundance and military victory, i.e., fullness of joy (cf. 29:19; 35:10; 61:7).

9:4–7 Isaiah explains the overflowing joy of v. 3, introduced by a threefold **For**.

9:4 Like a freedom fighter, God breaks all human oppression **as on the day of Midian**. Cf. Judges 6–7, where Gideon achieves an improbable victory over Midian by the power of God.

9:5 every boot . . . will be burned as fuel for the fire. See Ps. 46:9; Isa. 2:4.

9:6 to us. A gift of divine grace to sinners. **a child . . . a son**. This is the invincible figure striding across the world stage, taking gracious command, according to vv. 4–5 (cf. Ps. 2:7–9; Luke 1:32). Isaiah presents the events as if it were the time of the child's arrival, with an expectation of what he will achieve (Isa. 9:7). **Wonderful Counselor**. A "counselor" is one who is able to make wise plans (cf. 11:2). He is a ruler whose wisdom is beyond merely human capabilities, unlike intelligent but foolish Ahaz (cf. 28:29). **Mighty God**. A title of the Lord himself (10:20–21; Deut. 10:17; Neh. 9:32; Jer. 32:18). **Everlasting Father**. A "father" here is a benevolent protector (cf. Isa. 22:21; Job 29:16), which is the task of the ideal king and is also the way God himself cares for his people (cf. Isa. 63:16; 64:8; Ps. 103:13). (That is, this is not using the Trinitarian title "Father" for the Messiah; rather, it is portraying him as a king.) **Prince of Peace**. He is the ruler whose reign will bring about peace because the nations will rely on his just decisions in their disputes (cf. Isa. 2:4; 11:6–9; 42:4; 49:7; 52:15). This kind of king contrasts with even the best of the Davidic line that Judah has experienced so far, because these titles show that this king will be divine. Thus this cannot refer to, say, Hezekiah (whose father Ahaz was king at the time), who for all his piety was nevertheless flawed (cf. 39:5–8) and only human.

9:7 God called Abraham to be the channel of blessing to the whole world (Gen. 12:1–3), and this was the purpose of Israel's life in their land (Ex. 19:5–6). Isaiah focuses the messianic hope on an heir of David who would extend his rule from Israel to include all the Gentiles, and thus finally to bring to them the blessing of knowing the true God (Gen. 49:10; 2 Sam. 7:8–16). **Of the increase . . . no end**. The empire of grace will forever expand, and

[e]with justice and with righteousness
from this time forth and forevermore.
[f]The zeal of the LORD of hosts will do this.

Judgment on Arrogance and Oppression

8 The Lord has sent a word against Jacob,
and it will fall on Israel;
9 and all the people will know,
[g]Ephraim and the inhabitants of Samaria,
who say in pride and in arrogance of heart:
10 "The bricks have fallen,
but we will build with dressed stones;
the sycamores have been cut down,
but we will put cedars in their place."
11 But the LORD raises the adversaries of Rezin against him,
and stirs up his enemies.
12 [h]The Syrians on the east and [i]the Philistines on the west
devour Israel with open mouth.
[j]For all this his anger has not turned away,
and his hand is stretched out still.

13 The people [k]did not turn to him who struck them,
nor inquire of the LORD of hosts.
14 So the LORD cut off from Israel [l]head and tail,
palm branch and reed in one day—
15 [m]the elder and honored man is the head,
and [n]the prophet who teaches lies is the tail;
16 for those who guide this people have been leading them astray,
and those who are guided by them are swallowed up.
17 Therefore the Lord does not [o]rejoice over their young men,
and has no compassion on their fatherless and widows;
for everyone is [p]godless and an evildoer,
and every mouth speaks [q]folly.[1]
[j]For all this his anger has not turned away,
and his hand is stretched out still.

18 For wickedness burns like [r]a fire;
it consumes briers and thorns;
it kindles the thickets of the forest,
and they roll upward in a column of smoke.
19 Through the wrath of the LORD of hosts
the land is scorched,

[1] Or *speaks disgraceful things*

7 [e]Jer. 23:5 [f]ch. 37:32; 2 Kgs. 19:31; [Zech. 1:14]
9 [g]ch. 7:2, 5, 8, 9, 17
12 [h][2 Kgs. 16:6] [i][2 Chr. 28:18] [j]ver. 17, 21; ch. 5:25; 10:4
13 [k][ch. 1:5; Hos. 7:10]
14 [l]ch. 19:15; Deut. 28:13
15 [m]ch. 3:2, 3 [n][ch. 28:7; Mic. 3:5]
17 [o]Ps. 147:10, 11 [p]ch. 10:6 [q]Gen. 34:7 [j][See ver. 12 above]
18 [r]Ps. 83:14; [James 3:5]

every moment will be better than the last. **the throne of David**. Cf. Luke 1:32. **with justice and with righteousness**. Unlike apostate Ahaz (cf. Jer. 33:15–16). **zeal**. The final victory is a miracle, accomplished with a passionate intensity of which only **the LORD of hosts** is capable (cf. Isa. 42:13; 59:15–19; 63:15).

9:8–11:16 *Grace—through Judgment—for Israel.* God reveals his gracious intentions toward Israel, the northern kingdom. Though his wrath works against them in the Assyrian invasion, God promises to punish Assyria for its arrogance and give his purified people a home in the messianic kingdom.

9:8–10:4 The section is marked by four assertions of God's unrelenting **anger** (9:12, 17, 21; 10:4).

9:8–12 Pride is the source of all the nation's disasters.

9:8–9 Jacob . . . Israel . . . Ephraim . . . Samaria. The northern kingdom rebelled against the throne of David and against the worship of the Lord (cf. 1 Kings 12:16–33).

9:10 Isaiah quotes the people's superficial response to national calamities. In their self-confident blindness to God, their need of repentance does not occur to them.

9:11 adversaries of Rezin. The Assyrians.

9:12 his anger. Not an impersonal process of cause and effect but God's own **hand** at work against evil. His love is intrinsic to his nature (1 John 4:16), but his anger can be provoked (Deut. 4:25). Far from arbitrary, as Isaiah shows, God's anger is principled, and therefore the more to be feared (Deut. 29:22–28; cf. Ex. 34:6–7; Isa. 13:9; 42:24–25; 48:9; 63:3–6; 66:15–16; Nah. 1:2–3; Rom. 2:5, 8). **stretched out still**. Human pride cannot wear God down and force him to compromise.

9:13–17 Impenitent leaders degrade the nation.

19[s]ch. 24:6 [t][Mic. 7:2]
20[u]ch. 8:21 [v]ch. 49:26; See Deut. 28:53-57
21[w][ch. 11:13]; See 2 Chr. 28:6-9 [x]See ver. 12
Chapter 10
1[y][Ps. 94:20] [z]Jer. 8:8
2[a]ch. 5:23
3[b]Jer. 5:29; Hos. 9:7; [Luke 19:44] [c]ch. 5:26
4[d]See ch. 9:12
5[e]ver. 24; ch. 9:4; [Mic. 5:1; 6:9]
6[f]ch. 9:17 [g]See 2 Kgs. 18:14-16 [h]ch. 5:5
7[i][Mic. 4:12]
8[j][2 Kgs. 18:24]
9[k]2 Kgs. 19:12, 13 [l][Gen. 10:10; Amos 6:2] [m]2 Chr. 35:20; Jer. 46:2 [n]ch. 11:11; Amos 6:2; Zech. 9:2 [o]2 Kgs. 18:34 [p][2 Kgs. 16:9; 17:6] [q]ch. 7:9
10[r][2 Kgs. 19:17, 18]

and [s]the people are like fuel for the fire;
[t]no one spares another.
20 [u]They slice meat on the right, but are still hungry,
and they devour on the left, but are not satisfied;
[v]each devours the flesh of his own arm,
21 Manasseh devours Ephraim, and Ephraim devours Manasseh;
together they are [w]against Judah.
[x]For all this his anger has not turned away,
and his hand is stretched out still.

10

1 Woe to those who [y]decree iniquitous decrees,
and the writers who [z]keep writing oppression,
2 to turn aside the needy from justice
and [a]to rob the poor of my people of their right,
that widows may be their spoil,
and that they may make the fatherless their prey!
3 What will you do on [b]the day of punishment,
in the ruin that will come [c]from afar?
To whom will you flee for help,
and where will you leave your wealth?
4 Nothing remains but to crouch among the prisoners
or fall among the slain.
[d]For all this his anger has not turned away,
and his hand is stretched out still.

Judgment on Arrogant Assyria

5 Ah, Assyria, [e]the rod of my anger;
the staff in their hands is my fury!
6 Against a [f]godless nation I send him,
and against the people of my wrath I command him,
to take [g]spoil and seize plunder,
and to [h]tread them down like the mire of the streets.
7 But he [i]does not so intend,
and his heart does not so think;
but it is in his heart to destroy,
and to cut off nations not a few;
8 for he says:
[j]"Are not my commanders all kings?
9 [k]Is not [l]Calno like [m]Carchemish?
Is not [n]Hamath like [o]Arpad?
[p]Is not [q]Samaria like Damascus?
10 As my hand has reached to [r]the kingdoms of the idols,
whose carved images were greater than those of Jerusalem and Samaria,

9:14 in one day. Judgment comes suddenly, perhaps referring to 722 B.C., when the northern kingdom fell.

9:17 their fatherless and widows. The moral decline is so pervasive that not even the weak are spared.

9:18–21 Self-seeking becomes self-destruction.

10:1–4 Corrupt **wealth** buys helplessness.

10:3 ruin that will come from afar. The Assyrian invasion.

10:4 fall among the slain. In his writings, the Assyrian king Shalmaneser III boasted of stacking the corpses of his defeated enemies and heaping up piles of their skulls (cf. Nah. 3:3). To give up in the face of such an enemy is profound despair.

10:5–15 God rules over the unwitting, arrogant Assyrians (cf. 14:24–27; Prov. 16:4).

10:6 a godless nation. Apostate Israel (9:17).

10:7 But he does not so intend. God uses human evil for his own just purpose, but he does not need humans to intend their cooperation. Events unfold through human intentions but also, more deeply, through the divine intention (cf. Luke 22:22; Acts 2:22–23; 4:27–28).

10:8–9 Are not my commanders all kings? The Assyrian is confident his army can prevail. **Is not Calno like Carchemish?** In each pair of cities listed, the first is geographically nearer to God's people than the second. The speaker is saying that, since he has conquered the latter, more distant of each pair of cities, surely he can conquer the former as well. His logic is clear, but blindly arrogant.

10:10–11 The Assyrian sees no end to his potential, for he cannot see the God of Jerusalem. Cf. the similar boasting by a later Assyrian, 36:13–20; 37:8–13.

11 shall I not do to Jerusalem and [s]her idols
[t]as I have done to Samaria and her images?"

12 [u]When the Lord has finished all his work on Mount Zion and on Jerusalem, [v]he[1] will
punish the speech of the arrogant heart of the king of Assyria and the boastful look in
his eyes. 13 [w]For he says:

"By the strength of my hand I have done it,
and by my wisdom, for I have understanding;
I remove the boundaries of peoples,
and plunder their treasures;
like a bull I bring down those who sit on thrones.
14 My hand has found like a nest
the wealth of the peoples;
and as one gathers eggs that have been forsaken,
so I have gathered all the earth;
and there was none that moved a wing
or opened the mouth or chirped."
15 Shall [x]the axe boast over him who hews with it,
or the saw magnify itself against him who wields it?
As if a rod should wield him who lifts it,
or as if a staff should lift him who is not wood!
16 Therefore the Lord GOD of hosts
will send wasting sickness among his [y]stout warriors,
and under his glory [z]a burning will be kindled,
like the burning of fire.
17 [a]The light of Israel will become a fire,
and [b]his Holy One a flame,
and [c]it will burn and devour
his thorns and briers [d]in one day.
18 The glory of [e]his forest and of his [f]fruitful land
the LORD will destroy, both soul and body,
and it will be as when a sick man wastes away.
19 The remnant of the trees of his forest will be so few
that a child can write them down.

The Remnant of Israel Will Return

20 [g]In that day [h]the remnant of Israel and the survivors of the house of Jacob will no more
[i]lean on him who struck them, but [j]will lean on the LORD, the Holy One of Israel, in truth.
21 A remnant will return, the remnant of Jacob, [k]to the mighty God. 22 [l]For though your
people Israel be as the sand of the sea, [m]only a remnant of them will return. [n]Destruction
is decreed, overflowing with righteousness. 23 For the Lord GOD of hosts will make a full
end, as decreed, in the midst of all the earth.
24 Therefore thus says the Lord GOD of hosts: "O my people, [o]who dwell in Zion, [p]be not
afraid of the Assyrians when they strike with the rod and lift up their staff against you

[1] Hebrew *I*

11 [s]ch. 2:8 [t]2 Kgs. 18:34
12 [u][ch. 29:4, 5; 30:18; 2 Kgs. 19:31] [v]See 2 Kgs. 19:35-37
13 [w]ch. 37:23-25; 2 Kgs. 19:22-24
15 [x][ver. 5; ch. 29:16; 45:9; Rom. 9:17]
16 [y]Ps. 78:31 [z][ch. 30:33]
17 [a][Obad. 18] [b]ch. 37:23 [c]ch. 27:4; [ch. 9:18; Nah. 1:10] [d][ch. 9:14; 2 Kgs. 19:35]
18 [e]ver. 33; [ch. 2:13] [f][Ps. 107:33-34]
20 [g]ver. 27; ch. 2:11 [h]ch. 4:2 [i][2 Kgs. 16:7; 2 Chr. 28:20, 21] [j]2 Kgs. 19:14
21 [k]ch. 9:6
22 [l]Cited Rom. 9:27, 28 [m][ch. 6:13] [n]ch. 28:22
24 [o][ch. 31:5] [p]2 Kgs. 19:6

10:12 Assyrian evil is used by God—**When the Lord has finished all his work**—but is still held accountable by God, down to the very thoughts of the Assyrian king's **heart** and the **look in his eyes**. God **will punish** Assyria, which fell in 612 B.C.

10:13–14 These verses further explain "the arrogant heart" (v. 12) of Assyria.

10:15 axe . . . saw . . . rod . . . staff. Assyria is a mere tool in the hand of God.

10:16–34 God moves history to preserve his remnant people. Isaiah marks this section with **the Lord GOD of hosts** (vv. 16, 23, 24, 33).

10:16–19 The mighty Assyrian army is reduced to near nothing.

10:19 the trees of his forest. The soldiers of the Assyrian army.

10:20–23 The remnant of Israel returns to God.

10:20 him who struck them. At one level, the blow to Israel was human. At a deeper level, it was divine (9:13).

10:21 A remnant will return. See note on 7:3.

10:22 See Gen. 22:17; 32:12. Paul quotes this verse, using the Septuagint (Rom. 9:27–28), to illustrate that the **remnant** idea comes from the OT. **Destruction . . . overflowing with righteousness**. God's acts of judgment are entirely just and fair.

10:24–26 Fearful Zion is made confident in God's promises.

10:26 as when he struck Midian at the rock of Oreb . . . as he did in Egypt. See Ex. 14:15–31 and Judg. 7:19–25. Israel was victorious only by the power of God.

as [q]the Egyptians did. 25 For [r]in a very little while my fury will come to an end, and my
anger will be directed to their destruction. 26 And [s]the LORD of hosts will wield against
them a whip, as when he struck [t]Midian [u]at the rock of Oreb. And his staff will be over
the sea, and he will lift it [v]as he did in Egypt. 27 And in that day [w]his burden will depart
from your shoulder, and [x]his yoke from your neck; and the yoke will be broken because
of the fat."[1]

28 He has come to Aiath;
he has passed through [y]Migron;
at Michmash he stores [z]his baggage;
29 they have crossed over [a]the pass;
at [b]Geba they lodge for the night;
[c]Ramah trembles;
[d]Gibeah of Saul has fled.
30 Cry aloud, O daughter of [e]Gallim!
Give attention, O Laishah!
O poor [f]Anathoth!
31 Madmenah is in flight;
the inhabitants of Gebim flee for safety.
32 This very day he will halt at [g]Nob;
he will shake his fist
at the mount of [h]the daughter of Zion,
the hill of Jerusalem.

33 Behold, the Lord GOD of hosts
[i]will lop [j]the boughs with terrifying power;

[1] The meaning of the Hebrew is uncertain

24 [q]Ex. 2:23
25 [r][ch. 17:14]
26 [s]2 Kgs. 19:35 [t]ch. 9:4 [u]Judg. 7:25; [ch. 9:4] [v][Ex. 14:30]
27 [w]2 Kgs. 18:14 [x][ch. 9:4; Nah. 1:13]
28 [y]1 Sam. 14:2 [z]Judg. 18:21; 1 Sam. 17:22; Acts 21:15; [ch. 46:1]
29 [a]1 Sam. 13:23 [b]1 Sam. 13:16 [c]1 Sam. 7:17 [d]1 Sam. 11:4
30 [e]1 Sam. 25:44 [f]Jer. 1:1
32 [g]1 Sam. 21:1; 22:19 [h]ch. 1:8; 37:22
33 [i][Nah. 1:12] [j]ver. 18

10:27–34 Proud Assyrian aggression is humbled by God.

10:27 the yoke will be broken because of the fat. Rather than being subdued under the yoke of Assyria, Israel will break the yoke by the fatness of its neck, just like a healthy ox.

10:28–32 Isaiah envisions the terrifying approach of the Assyrian army from one village to another toward Jerusalem (see map below). But the invader is stopped at the last moment and can only **shake his fist** at the holy city. **the daughter of Zion.** See note on 1:7–8.

10:33–34 an axe. The Assyrian "axe" of v. 15 is itself cut down for its arrogance (cf. chs. 36–37).

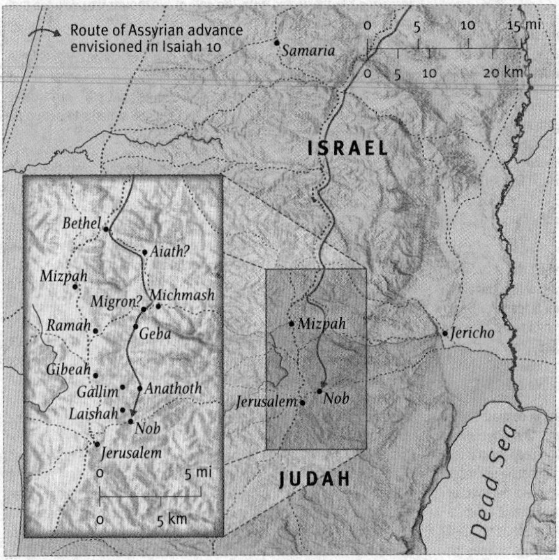

Assyria Advances toward Jerusalem
Isaiah prophesied that although Assyria would pose a great threat to God's people, God would stop them from fully carrying out their destruction. Isaiah 10:28–34 may recount how the prophet envisioned the Assyrian army advancing closer and closer to Jerusalem until they are finally stopped at Nob, just outside the city.

the great in height will be hewn down,
and the lofty will be brought low.
34 He will cut down [j]the thickets of the forest with an axe,
and [k]Lebanon will fall by the Majestic One.

The Righteous Reign of the Branch

11 1 There shall come forth a shoot from the stump of [l]Jesse,
and a branch from his roots shall bear fruit.
2 And [m]the Spirit of the LORD shall rest upon him,
the Spirit of wisdom and understanding,
the Spirit of counsel and might,
the Spirit of knowledge and the fear of the LORD.
3 And his delight shall be in the fear of the LORD.
[n]He shall not judge by [o]what his eyes see,
or decide disputes by [o]what his ears hear,
4 but [p]with righteousness he shall judge the poor,
and decide with equity for the meek of the earth;
and he shall [q]strike the earth with the rod of his mouth,
and [r]with the breath of his lips [s]he shall kill the wicked.
5 Righteousness shall be the belt of his waist,
and [t]faithfulness the belt of his loins.

6 [u]The wolf shall dwell with the lamb,
and the leopard shall lie down with the young goat,
and the calf and the lion and the fattened calf together;
and a little child shall lead them.
7 The cow and the bear shall graze;
their young shall lie down together;
and the lion shall eat straw like the ox.
8 The nursing child shall play over the hole of the cobra,
and the weaned child shall put his hand on the adder's den.
9 [u]They shall not hurt or destroy
in all [v]my holy mountain;

34[j][See ver. 33 above] [k][Ezek. 31:3; Amos 2:9]

Chapter 11

1[l]ver. 10; Acts 13:23
2[m]ch. 61:1; Matt. 3:16; Mark 1:10; Luke 3:22
3[n][John 7:24] [o][Eccles. 1:8]
4[p]Ps. 72:2, 4 [q]Ps. 2:9; [Mal. 4:6] [r]Job 4:9; 2 Thess. 2:8 [s]Ps. 139:19
5[t][Eph. 6:14]
6[u]ch. 65:25; [Hos. 2:18]
9[u][See ver. 6 above] [v]Ps. 78:54

11:1–16 The Messiah will transform the world.

11:1–10 These verses describe the paradise of the Messiah's triumph. Verse 10 rounds off this section with its reference to **Jesse**, echoing v. 1. The reference to Jesse's family indicates that this continues the theme of 7:10–14 and 9:1–7 about the coming heir of David (the Messiah).

11:1 a shoot from the stump. After portraying the destruction of arrogant human evil as the felling of a vast forest (10:33–34), Isaiah presents the Messiah as a shoot or twig growing from a stump remaining after God's judgment (cf. 4:2; 6:13; 53:2). **Jesse**. The father of David (cf. 1 Sam. 16:1–13; 2 Sam. 20:1). A greater David is prophesied (cf. Ezek. 34:23–24; Hos. 3:5). **bear fruit**. Unlike the human failure before him, especially King Ahaz, this son of Jesse bears the fruit of a new world.

11:2 the Spirit of the LORD. David was empowered by the Holy Spirit (1 Sam. 16:13), but the Messiah is more richly endowed with a threefold fullness of the Spirit: **wisdom and understanding** for leadership (Deut. 1:13; 1 Kings 3:9; cf. Isa. 10:13); **counsel and might** to carry out his wise plans (36:5; cf. Job 12:13; observe the connection to Isa. 9:6, "counselor" and "mighty"); **knowledge and the fear of the LORD** for holiness (Ps. 14:4; Prov. 2:5). For Jesus' fulfillment of this prophetic word, cf. Matt. 3:16–17.

11:3–4 his delight shall be in the fear of the LORD. In contrast to the way in which all other human beings live in rebellion against God, the coming Messiah will be the ideal in his human faithfulness, finding deep joy in living before God in reverence (see note on Prov. 1:7), and in promoting reverence among those he rules. Unlike human leaders, the Messiah is not deceived by appearances. The words **judge** and **decide disputes** echo Isa. 2:4, where the Lord will do this; this oracle shows that the breathtaking effects of 2:2–4 will come about through the Messiah's rule over the nations. He defends the weak and kills the wicked **with the rod of his mouth**, i.e., with the truth of his word (cf. 49:2; Rev. 1:16; 19:15).

11:5 The Messiah is not clothed with the trappings of human ego but is truly qualified to rule the world. Paul gets many of the parts of "the armor of God" (Eph. 6:11–17) from Isaiah; here he gets "the belt of truth" [or **faithfulness**]. (See also Isa. 52:7; 59:17.) To "put on" the armor is to put on the Messiah himself.

11:6–9 Isaiah uses the imagery of his time to make one point: **the earth shall be full of the knowledge of the LORD**. The One whom Israel rejected as unhelpful renews the world (cf. 35:9; 65:17–25; Ezek. 34:25–31). In Isaiah's time, Judah was to the nations, such as Assyria, as prey to fierce predators. Messiah's benevolent rule would change all that. **The wolf shall dwell with the lamb** (cf. **leopard . . . lion . . . bear**). In the context of once-predatory imperial powers coming under the Messiah's sway, and thus learning to be peaceable (cf. the connection between Isa. 11:3–4 and 2:4), some interpreters understand these fierce animals as images for these larger nations (such as Assyria, the looming threat of chs. 7–11); cf. Jer. 5:6 (with note) for the same image (with lion, wolf, and leopard together). Understood this way, Isa. 11:9 speaks of the future messianic age when the predatory nations will no longer **hurt or destroy** God's people, who will dwell in peace and safety in his **holy mountain**. Other interpreters, however, understand this as a reference to a future time when God will bring about a transformation of the earth, extending even to the animal kingdom, when the curse of Gen. 3:17–18 will be removed (cf. Rom. 8:19–22), that is, a future time when the present working order of the natural world will be changed, removing the carnivorous nature of the wolf, leopard, lion, and bear. Some interpreters think this will occur in a future millennial period (see note on Rev. 20:1–6), while others think it will occur in the new heavens and new earth.

9[w]Hab. 2:14
10[x]Cited Rom. 15:12 [y]ver. 1 [z]ch. 49:22; [Ex. 17:15]
11[a]ch. 10:20 [b]ch. 27:13; Mic. 7:12; Zech. 10:10 [c]Jer. 44:1, 15; Ezek. 29:14; 30:14 [d]See Gen. 10:6-12 [e]Gen. 10:22; 14:1, 9; Jer. 25:25; See Jer. 49:34-39 [f]Gen. 11:2 [g]See ch. 10:9 [h]Esth. 10:1
12[z][See ver. 10 above] [i]ch. 56:8; [Zech. 10:6]
13[j]Ezek. 37:16, 17; [ch. 9:21; Zech. 11:14]
14[k][2 Sam. 8:1; 2 Kgs. 18:8] [l]Judg. 6:3; See Jer. 49:28 [m]Ps. 60:8 [n][2 Sam. 8:14] [o][2 Sam. 8:2] [p]See 2 Sam. 12:26-31
15[q][Zech. 10:11] [r]See ch. 7:20
16[s]ch. 19:23; [ch. 35:8] [t]Ex. 14:29
Chapter 12
1[u]ch. 11:11 [v][ch. 10:4]

[w]for the earth shall be full of the knowledge of the LORD
as the waters cover the sea.

10 In that day [x]the root of [y]Jesse, who shall stand as [z]a signal for the peoples—of him
shall the nations inquire, and his resting place shall be glorious.
11 [a]In that day the Lord will extend his hand yet a second time to recover the remnant
that remains of his people, [b]from Assyria, [b]from Egypt, from [c]Pathros, from [d]Cush,[1] from
[e]Elam, from [f]Shinar, from [g]Hamath, and from [h]the coastlands of the sea.

12 He will raise [z]a signal for the nations
and will assemble [i]the banished of Israel,
and gather the dispersed of Judah
from the four corners of the earth.
13 [j]The jealousy of Ephraim shall depart,
and those who harass Judah shall be cut off;
Ephraim shall not be jealous of Judah,
and Judah shall not harass Ephraim.
14 [k]But they shall swoop down on the shoulder of the Philistines in the west,
and together they shall plunder [l]the people of the east.
They shall put out their hand [m]against [n]Edom and [o]Moab,
and [p]the Ammonites shall obey them.
15 And the LORD will utterly destroy[2]
[q]the tongue of the Sea of Egypt,
and will wave his hand over [r]the River
with his scorching breath,[3]
and strike it into seven channels,
and he will lead people across in sandals.
16 And there will be [s]a highway from Assyria
for the remnant that remains of his people,
[t]as there was for Israel
when they came up from the land of Egypt.

The LORD Is My Strength and My Song

12

1 You[4] will say [u]"in that day:
"I will give thanks to you, O LORD,
for though you were angry with me,
[v]your anger turned away,
that you might comfort me.

[1] Probably *Nubia* [2] Hebrew *devote to destruction* [3] Or *wind* [4] The Hebrew for *you* is singular in verse 1

11:10 Paul quotes this verse in Rom. 15:12 to describe his ambition to reach the Gentiles with the gospel: he sees himself as living in the messianic time the OT expected, in which the Gentiles would come to know the true God, and thus his own ministry involved spreading Messiah's rule among the Gentiles. **a signal for the peoples**. See Isa. 11:12; 49:22; 62:10. **glorious**. Lit., "glory," i.e., the place where God's presence is conveyed (see note on 6:3).

11:11–16 The gathering of the Messiah's people. This section is marked by **his hand** (vv. 11, 15) and by **the remnant that remains of his people** (vv. 11, 16). God's power gathers in all his people, and no earthly power can prevent their final homecoming.

11:11 yet a second time. The first deliverance was the exodus from Egypt (v. 16). **from Assyria . . . the coastlands of the sea**. From all over the known world—a greater exodus by far.

11:13–14 Rather than compete with one another, God's people unite to oppose evil. **their hand**. God's hand of power through them. The victory of Christ and the victory of his people are one victory. Isaiah is not predicting a new imperialism but is using the imagery of royal conquest for the spreading of the Messiah's reign of peace (cf. 9:6; 12:3–6), as the NT authors saw (e.g., Acts 15:12–17).

11:15 the LORD will . . . Isaiah uses evocative imagery here to convey the idea that no barrier anywhere can withstand God's purpose to restore his people. **the tongue of the Sea of Egypt**. I.e., the bay or gulf of the Red Sea. See Josh. 15:2, 5, where "bay" translates the Hebrew word for "tongue" (Hb. *lashon*). **the River**. The Euphrates (cf. Isa. 7:20; 8:7). **his scorching breath**. See Ex. 14:21–22. **seven channels**. As if the great Euphrates were miraculously reduced to easily passable brooks.

11:16 Mighty **Assyria** becomes an avenue for God's people into their salvation (cf. 35:8–10; 57:14; 62:10).

12:1–6 *The Enjoyment of God's Grace.* Isaiah concludes chs. 6–12 by foreseeing the day when God's people will praise him for the abundant joys of his salvation.

12:1 As the ESV footnote explains, in v. 1 **you** is singular, perhaps referring to the people of God as a whole (see v. 3). **In that day** links ch. 12 with ch. 11. **you were angry**. See 5:25; 9:12, 17, 19, 21; 10:4, 5, 6, 25. **your**

2 “Behold, God is my salvation;
I will trust, and will not be afraid;
for [w]“the LORD GOD[1] is my strength and my song,
and he has become my salvation.”

3 [x]With joy you[2] will draw water from the wells of salvation. 4 [y]And you will say in
that day:

[z]“Give thanks to the LORD,
call upon his name,
[a]make known his deeds among the peoples,
proclaim [b]that his name is exalted.

5 [c]“Sing praises to the LORD, for he has done gloriously;
let this be made known[3] in all the earth.
6 Shout, and sing for joy, O inhabitant of Zion,
for great [d]in your[4] midst is [e]the Holy One of Israel.”

The Judgment of Babylon

13 The oracle concerning [f]Babylon which [g]Isaiah the son of Amoz saw.

2 On a bare hill [h]raise a signal;
cry aloud to them;

[1] Hebrew *for Yah, the LORD* [2] The Hebrew for *you* is plural in verses 3, 4 [3] *Or this is made known* [4] The Hebrew for *your* in verse 6 is singular, referring to the *inhabitant of Zion*

2 [w]Ex. 15:2; Ps. 118:14
3 [x][John 4:13, 14; 7:37, 38]
4 [y]ch. 11:11 [z]Ps. 105:1 [a][Ps. 145:4-6] [b]Ps. 148:13
5 [c]Ex. 15:1; Ps. 98:1
6 [d]Ps. 46:5; Hos. 11:9 [e]ch. 5:24; 41:14, 16

Chapter 13

1 [f]ver. 19; ch. 14:4; 21:9; 47:1; See Jer. 51, 52 [g]ch. 1:1
2 [h]ch. 5:26

anger turned away. Only God can turn away the anger of God (cf. 6:6–7; 53:4–6). **that you might comfort me**. See 40:1; 66:13.

12:2 God is my salvation. See 45:17; 51:6; 59:16; 63:5. A supernatural salvation, such as King Ahaz did not believe in (cf. 7:2, 4, 9; 8:12; 10:24). Isaiah echoes Ex. 15:2–18. **the LORD GOD**. The ESV footnote explains the unusual name for God behind the English spelling. The Lord himself and the Lord alone is enough for strength, song, and salvation.

12:3 As the ESV footnote explains, **you** is plural here, perhaps referring to all of the members of God's people. **With joy**. See 29:19; 35:10; 51:3, 11; 55:12; 61:3, 7; 65:18–19; John 15:11; 16:24; 17:13. **draw water from**

Oracles against the Nations in the Prophets

	Isaiah	Jeremiah	Ezekiel	Joel	Amos	Obadiah	Jonah	Nahum	Zephaniah	Zechariah*
Ammon		49:1–6	25:1–7		1:13–15					
Arabia	21:13–17									
Assyria (Nineveh)	10:5–19; 14:24–27						(Nineveh)	(Nineveh)		
Babylon	13:1–14:23; 21:1–10; 46:1–47:15	50:1–51:64								2:9–12?
Damascus	17:1–6?	49:23–27			1:3–5					9:1
Edom	21:11–12	49:7–22	25:12–14		1:11–12	1–14?				
Egypt	18:1–20:6	46:2–26	29:1–32:32							
Elam		49:34–39								
Ethiopia									2:12–15	
Gaza					1:6–8					9:5
Kedar and Hazor		49:28–33								
Lebanon										11:1–3?
Moab	15:1–16:14	48:1–47	25:8–11		2:1–3				2:8–11	
Philistia	14:28–32	47:1–7	25:15–17	3:4–8					2:5–7	9:6
Tyre *Sidon*	23:1–18		26:1–28:19; *28:20–23*	3:4–8	1:9–10					9:2–3

**Additional cities/states are denounced in 9:1–8: Hadrach, Aram (v. 1); Ashkelon, Ekron (v. 5); Ashdod (v. 6)*

wave the hand for [i]them to enter
the gates of the nobles.
3 I myself have commanded my consecrated ones,
and have summoned my mighty men to execute my anger,
my proudly exulting ones.[1]

4 The sound [j]of a tumult is on the mountains
as of a great multitude!
The sound of an uproar of kingdoms,
of nations gathering together!
[k]The LORD of hosts is mustering
a host for battle.
5 [l]They come from a distant land,
from the end of the heavens,
the LORD and the weapons of his indignation,
to destroy the whole land.[2]
6 [m]Wail, for [n]the day of the LORD is near;
as destruction from the Almighty[3] it will come!
7 Therefore all hands will be feeble,
and every human heart [o]will melt.
8 They will be dismayed:
[p]pangs and agony will seize them;
[q]they will be in anguish like a woman in labor.
They will look aghast at one another;
their faces will be aflame.
9 Behold, [n]the day of the LORD comes,
cruel, with wrath and fierce anger,
to make the land a desolation
and [r]to destroy its sinners from it.
10 [s]For the stars of the heavens and their constellations
will not give their light;
[t]the sun will be dark at its rising,
and the moon will not shed its light.

2 [i][ch. 41:25]
4 [j][ch. 22:5] [k][Josh. 5:13, 14]
5 [l][ch. 46:11]
6 [m]ch. 14:31; 15:2, 3, 8; 16:7; Jer. 51:8; Ezek. 30:2 [n]ch. 2:12; Joel 1:15; Zeph. 1:7
7 [o]See Josh. 2:11
8 [p][Nah. 2:10] [q]ch. 26:17; Jer. 4:31; 6:24; Mic. 4:9, 10; John 16:21
9 [n][See ver. 6 above] [r][Ps. 104:35]
10 [s][ch. 34:4] [t]Ezek. 32:7; Joel 2:31; 3:15; Matt. 24:29; Mark 13:24; Luke 21:25

[1] Or *those who exult in my majesty* [2] Or *earth*; also verse 9 [3] The Hebrew words for *destruction* and *almighty* sound alike

the wells of salvation. Endless supplies of salvation, richly enjoyed (cf. Ps. 36:8; 63:1; 65:9; 107:35; 143:6; Isa. 8:6; 32:2; 35:6–7; 44:3; 55:1; Jer. 2:13; John 4:13–14; 7:37–39; Rev. 7:17; 21:6; 22:17).

12:4 God's salvation flows out to **the peoples** through the witness of his people. The message is **his name**, i.e., who he has revealed himself to be (cf. Ex. 3:13–15; 34:5–8).

12:6 inhabitant of Zion. The remnant people of God is personified (cf. 37:22). **in your midst**. God intends to dwell among his people (cf. Ex. 25:8; 40:34; Isa. 57:15; Zech. 2:10–11; Rev. 21:3). **the Holy One of Israel**. Isaiah concludes this section with his characteristic title for God. Because of God's gracious intervention, the sinner's greatest dread (Isa. 6:3–5) becomes his ultimate joy.

13:1–27:13 *God's Judgment and Grace for the World: "We Have a Strong City."* Isaiah reveals the sovereign ways of God with the nations, for he is no local, tribal deity but the Judge and Savior ruling over all the world. His purpose is moving human history forward for the benefit of his people.

13:1–20:6 *First Series of Oracles: The Here and Now.* The prophet helps Judah to see the nations of the day as entirely subject to the sovereign rule of God. Five oracles reveal God ruling over Babylon and Assyria (13:1–14:27), Philistia (14:28–32), Moab (15:1–16:14), Damascus/Israel (17:1–18:7), and Egypt (19:1–20:6). The OT prophets have numerous oracles about other nations (see chart, p. 1264). These display the basic biblical conviction that as universal Creator, the God of Israel is not limited to Israel but holds all nations accountable for their deeds (cf. 13:11; Rom. 3:29–30).

13:1–14:27 *Babylon.* The first oracle opens as the day of the Lord looms over the world (ch. 13).

13:1 oracle. A prophetic message (cf. 2:1). Isaiah sees in the prestigious culture of **Babylon** the proud evil that sets the whole world against God (13:11, 19; cf. Gen. 11:1–9; Isa. 14:26; Dan. 4:30; Rev. 14:8; 17:5; 18:2–3).

13:2 raise a signal. God arouses human action against Babylon.

13:3 my consecrated ones. The enemies of Babylon do not consecrate themselves to God; he consecrates them to his own purpose (cf. 10:5–15; 45:1).

13:4 The LORD of hosts. The commander-in-chief of all human armies.

13:5–6 As the ESV footnote explains, **the whole land** can also be translated "the whole earth" (likewise v. 9). **the day of the LORD**. Cf. 2:12; for this expression, see note on Amos 5:18–20.

13:9 land. See note on vv. 5–6.

13:10 For the stars of the heavens and their constellations will not give their light. See Matt. 24:29; Rev. 6:12; 8:12. The Lord does not limit his rule to his people alone, nor even to the earth. He rules over all (cf. Ps. 103:19).

11 I will punish [u]the world for its evil,
and the wicked for their iniquity;
I will [v]put an end to the pomp of the arrogant,
[w]and lay low the pompous pride of the ruthless.
12 I will make [x]people more rare than fine gold,
and mankind than the [y]gold of Ophir.
13 Therefore [z]I will make the heavens tremble,
and the earth will be shaken out of its place,
at the wrath of the LORD of hosts
in the day of his fierce anger.
14 And like a hunted gazelle,
or like sheep with none to gather them,
[a]each will turn to his own people,
and each will flee to his own land.
15 Whoever is found will be thrust through,
and whoever is caught will fall by the sword.
16 [b]Their infants will be dashed in pieces
before their eyes;
their houses will be plundered
and their wives ravished.

17 Behold, [c]I am stirring up the Medes against them,
who have no regard for silver
and do not delight in gold.
18 [d]Their bows will slaughter[1] the young men;
they will have no mercy on the fruit of the womb;
their eyes will not pity children.
19 And Babylon, [e]the glory of kingdoms,
the splendor and pomp of the Chaldeans,
will be [f]like Sodom and Gomorrah
when God overthrew them.
20 [g]It will never be inhabited
or lived in for all generations;
no [h]Arab will pitch his tent there;
no [i]shepherds will make their flocks lie down there.
21 But [j]wild animals will lie down there,
and their houses will be full of howling creatures;
there [k]ostriches[2] will dwell,
and there wild goats will dance.
22 Hyenas[3] will cry in its towers,
and [l]jackals in [m]the pleasant palaces;
its time is close at hand
and its days will not be prolonged.

The Restoration of Jacob

14 [n]For the LORD will have compassion on Jacob and will again choose Israel, and
[o]will set them in their own land, and [p]sojourners will join them and will attach
themselves to the house of Jacob. 2 And [q]the peoples will take them and bring them to

[1] Hebrew *dash in pieces* [2] Or *owls* [3] Or *foxes*

11 [u]ch. 24:21 [v][ch. 24:4] [w][ch. 2:11, 17]
12 [x]ch. 24:6 [y]1 Kgs. 10:11; Job 28:16
13 [z]Hag. 2:6
14 [a]Jer. 50:16; 51:9; [1 Kgs. 22:36]
16 [b]Ps. 137:9; Nah. 3:10
17 [c]ch. 21:2; Jer. 51:11, 28; Dan. 5:28, 31
18 [d]Jer. 50:14, 29; 51:3
19 [e][ch. 47:5] [f]ch. 1:9; Gen. 19:24; Jer. 50:40; Amos 4:11
20 [g]Jer. 51:37, 43 [h]Jer. 3:2 [i]Jer. 33:12
21 [j][ch. 34:13, 14] [k]ch. 34:13; Jer. 50:39
22 [l]ch. 35:7; Jer. 51:37 [m][ch. 25:2; Amos 3:15]

Chapter 14

1 [n]Ps. 102:13; Zech. 1:17 [o]2 Chr. 36:22, 23 [p]Zech. 8:22, 23; See Eph. 2:12-14
2 [q]ch. 49:22; 60:9; 66:20

13:12 This refers to the thorough destruction of "the arrogant" and "the ruthless" of v. 11.

13:14–15 Though worldwide, God's judgment reaches individuals (cf. Deut. 29:18–20).

13:17 The Medes conquered Babylon in 539 B.C. (cf. Jer. 51:11; Dan. 5:30–31). **no regard for silver**. These attackers cannot be bribed to withdraw.

13:19 The final end is made visible in the judgments of history.

13:20–22 It will never be inhabited. See note on Jer. 50:39–40. Animals live there because people do not. This eerie scene contrasts with the "splendor and pomp" of Isa. 13:19 and the messianic paradise of 11:6–8 (cf. similar imagery in 34:11–15; Jer. 50:39; 51:37; Zeph. 2:14–15; Rev. 18:2).

14:1–2 God reverses the roles of all oppressors with his persecuted people. God reestablishing the glory of his people, for his own glory, is an important element in Isaiah's message (e.g., ch. 62).

14:1 For the LORD will have compassion. Judgment (ch. 13) clears the

their place, and the house of Israel will possess them in the LORD's land [r]as male and
female slaves.[1] [s]They will take captive those who were their captors, [t]and rule over those
who oppressed them.

Israel's Remnant Taunts Babylon

3 When the LORD has given you rest from your pain and turmoil and the hard service with
which you were made to serve, 4 you will take up this [u]taunt against the king of Babylon:

"How the oppressor has ceased,
[v]the insolent fury[2] ceased!
5 The LORD has broken the [w]staff of the wicked,
the [w]scepter of rulers,
6 [x]that struck the peoples in wrath
with unceasing blows,
that ruled the nations in anger
with unrelenting persecution.
7 The whole earth is at rest and quiet;
[y]they break forth into singing.
8 [z, a]The cypresses rejoice at you,
[b]the cedars of Lebanon, saying,
'Since you were laid low,
no woodcutter comes up against us.'
9 Sheol beneath is stirred up
to meet you when you come;
it rouses the shades to greet you,
all who were leaders of the earth;
it raises from their thrones
all who were kings of the nations.
10 [c]All of them will answer
and say to you:
'You too have become as weak as we!
You have become like us!'
11 Your pomp is brought down to Sheol,
the sound of your harps;
maggots are laid as a bed beneath you,
and worms are your covers.
12 "How [d]you are fallen from heaven,
O Day Star, [e]son of Dawn!
How you are cut down to the ground,
you who laid the nations low!
13 You said in your heart,
[f]'I will ascend to heaven;

2 [r]ch. 61:5 [s][Joel 3:8] [t]ch. 60:14
4 [u]Mic. 2:4; Hab. 2:6 [v][Jer. 51:13; Rev. 18:16]
5 [w][ch. 9:4]
6 [x][Jer. 50:23]
7 [y]ch. 44:23; 49:13; 54:1; 55:12
8 [z][Ezek. 31:16] [a][ch. 37:24] [b]See ch. 2:13
10 [c][Jer. 51:48]
12 [d][ch. 24:21; 34:3] [e][Job 38:7]
13 [f]Jer. 51:53; Amos 9:2; [Matt. 11:23; Luke 10:15]

[1] Or *servants* [2] Dead Sea Scroll (compare Septuagint, Syriac, Vulgate); the meaning of the word in the Masoretic Text is uncertain

way for God's compassion. **will again choose Israel**. God restores them to his purpose of grace. **sojourners**. Gentiles who live among the people of Israel; see Ex. 23:9; Deut. 10:19. God's people multiply as outsiders join them (cf. Isa. 2:2–4; 56:3–8).

14:2 the house of Israel . . . the LORD's land. God's people become the predominant culture of the world (cf. 45:14; 49:22–23; 60:1–16; 61:5–7). **slaves**. The oppression of God's people by foreign nations will be reversed. This is probably not a reference to literal slavery but is a poetic symbol of Gentiles being welcomed (at some time in the future) among God's people and gladly taking places of service in God's kingdom. Some interpreters hold that the future fulfillment of this prophecy will take place in a millennial kingdom, where Christ's servants reign with him over the nations (cf. Luke 19:17; Rev. 20:4, 6).

14:3–21 God's people have the last laugh on their archenemy (cf. Revelation 18–19).

14:4 the king of Babylon. The royal figure, personifying Babylonian arrogance, is dismissed with the taunts of his victims, not immortalized in the praises of his admirers.

14:12–15 fallen from heaven, O Day Star, son of Dawn! Using rich poetic imagery, the king of Babylon is addressed with sarcastic irony. From the great heights of his pride, arrogance, and rebellion against God, his downfall brings him to the depths of **Sheol**. **the mount of assembly in the far reaches of the north**. In Canaanite mythology, the gods sat in assembly on a northern mountain (cf. Ps. 48:1–2). **like the Most High**. See Gen. 3:5; 11:4. Some have seen here a poetic allusion in which the fallen king of Babylon is likened to a fallen Satan. At the minimum, the extravagant pretensions of the king of Babylon are graphically and poetically portrayed, from the heights of God-defying arrogance ("I will make myself like the Most High") to the depths of destruction in **the far reaches of the pit**. (See also note on Ezek. 28:11–19.)

above the stars of God
[g]I will set my throne on high;
I will sit on the mount of assembly
in the far reaches of the north;[1]
14 I will ascend above the heights of the clouds;
I will make myself like the Most High.'
15 [h]But you are brought down to Sheol,
to the far reaches of the pit.
16 Those who see you will stare at you
and ponder over you:
'Is this [i]the man who made the earth tremble,
who shook kingdoms,
17 who made the world like a desert
and overthrew its cities,
[j]who did not let his prisoners go home?'
18 All the kings of the nations lie in glory,
each in his own tomb;[2]
19 but you are cast out, away from your grave,
like a loathed branch,
[k]clothed with the slain, those pierced by the sword,
who go down to the stones of the pit,
like a dead body trampled underfoot.
20 You will not be joined with them in burial,
because you have destroyed your land,
you have slain your people.

"May [l]the offspring of evildoers
nevermore be named!
21 Prepare slaughter for his sons
[m]because of the guilt of their fathers,
lest they rise and possess the earth,
and fill the face of the world with cities."

22 "I will rise up against them," declares the LORD of hosts, "and will cut off from Babylon
name and [n]remnant, [o]descendants and posterity," declares the LORD. 23 "And I will make
it a possession of the [p]hedgehog,[3] and pools of water, and I will sweep it with the broom
of destruction," declares the LORD of hosts.

An Oracle Concerning Assyria

24 The LORD of hosts has sworn:
[q]"As I have planned,
so shall it be,
and as I have purposed,
so shall it stand,
25 that [r]I will break the Assyrian in my land,
and on my mountains trample him underfoot;
and [s]his yoke shall depart from them,
and [s]his burden from their shoulder."

13 [g]Dan. 5:22, 23; [2 Thess. 2:4]
15 [h]Ezek. 32:23; Matt. 11:23; Luke 10:15
16 [i][Jer. 50:23]
17 [j][Jer. 50:33]
19 [k][Ezek. 32:20]
20 [l]Job 18:19; Ps. 21:10; 109:13
21 [m][Ex. 20:5; Matt. 23:35]
22 [n][Jer. 51:50, 62] [o]Job 18:19; [Gen. 21:23]
23 [p]ch. 34:11; Zeph. 2:14
24 [q][Prov. 19:21]
25 [r]ch. 37:36 [s]ch. 9:4; 10:27

[1] *Or in the remote parts of Zaphon* [2] Hebrew *house* [3] *Possibly porcupine, or owl*

14:21 Babylon's proud royal line will end forever, while Isaiah expects David's royal line to last forever and to bless all mankind (9:6–7; cf. Psalm 45; 72).

14:22–23 With three declarations of divine resolve—**declares the LORD**—the true Ruler of history vows to **sweep** the dynasty of Babylon away into oblivion, preserving no **remnant**.

14:24–27 The oracle concludes by applying its principles to the manifestation of Babylonian evil threatening in Isaiah's time, namely, Assyria. God's plan and purpose has the last say in his world; not even the great might of Assyria can prevent him from carrying out his plan.

14:25–26 As the Lord will eventually punish the world for its Babylonian evil (13:11), so, on a smaller scale and sooner, he will **break the Assyrian in**

26 This is the purpose that is purposed
concerning the whole earth,
and this is [t]the hand that is stretched out
over all the nations.
27 [u]For the LORD of hosts has purposed,
and who will annul it?
[t]His hand is stretched out,
and who will turn it back?

An Oracle Concerning Philistia

28 In the year that [v]King Ahaz died came this [w]oracle:

29 Rejoice not, [x]O Philistia, all of you,
that [y]the rod that struck you is broken,
for from the serpent's root will come forth an adder,
and its fruit will be a [z]flying fiery serpent.
30 And the firstborn of [a]the poor will graze,
and [a]the needy lie down in safety;
but I will kill your root with famine,
and your remnant it will slay.
31 [b]Wail, O [c]gate; cry out, O city;
melt in fear, [x]O Philistia, all of you!
[d]For smoke comes out of the north,
and there is no straggler in his ranks.

32 What will one answer the messengers of the nation?
[e]"The LORD has founded Zion,
and in her the afflicted of his people find refuge."

An Oracle Concerning Moab

15 An [w]oracle concerning [f]Moab.

Because [g]Ar of Moab is laid waste in a night,
Moab is undone;
because [h]Kir of Moab is laid waste in a night,
Moab is undone.
2 He has gone up to the temple,[1] and to [i]Dibon,
to the high places[2] to weep;
over [j]Nebo and over [j]Medeba
Moab [k]wails.
On every head is [l]baldness;
every beard is shorn;
3 in the streets they wear sackcloth;
on the housetops and in the squares
everyone wails and melts in tears.

[1] Hebrew *the house* [2] Or *temple, even Dibon to the high places*

26 [t][Deut. 4:34]
27 [u]2 Chr. 20:6; Job 9:12; Ps. 33:11; Prov. 21:30; Dan. 4:31, 33, 35 [t][See ver. 26 above]
28 [v]2 Kgs. 16:20 [w]See ch. 13:1
29 [x]Ex. 15:14; [Ps. 60:8; 87:4; 108:9] [y][ch. 10:24] [z]ch. 30:6; Num. 21:6; [Jer. 46:22]
30 [a][ch. 29:19; Zeph. 3:12]
31 [b]ch. 13:6 [c]ch. 24:12 [x][See ver. 29 above] [d][ch. 20:1]
32 [e]Ps. 87:1, 5; 102:16; 132:13; [ch. 28:16]

Chapter 15

1 [w][See ch. 14:28 above] [f]See Jer. 48; Ezek. 25:8-11; Amos 2:1-3; Zeph. 2:8, 9 [g]Num. 21:15, 28 [h][ch. 16:7, 11]
2 [i]Num. 21:30 [j]Deut. 34:1 [k]ch. 13:6 [l]See ch. 3:24

my land (see chs. 36–37). This interim fulfillment of his word encourages faith in the ultimate fulfillment of all that he says **concerning the whole earth**. Moreover, "in my land" implies that the only true safety is found among God's people, whatever their lot at any given time.

14:28–32 *Philistia.* The second oracle of 13:1–20:6 concerns Philistia.

14:28 the year that King Ahaz died. Around 715 B.C.

14:29 God warns Philistia not to gloat that **the rod that struck you is broken**, referring either to the Davidic dynasty, which Ahaz had reduced to puppet status under Assyria, or to the Assyrian Empire, which itself had suffered a setback. The interpretation of the **serpent's root . . . adder . . . flying fiery serpent** depends on the identification of "the rod." In any case, the future of Philistia is nothing to rejoice over.

14:30–32 God decrees **safety** for his own but **fear** for Philistia, without a **remnant**. Assyrian invasion **comes out of the north**. The only **refuge** is in **Zion**, the city of God, weakened though it is, because here alone God maintains his purpose of grace.

15:1–16:14 *Moab.* The third oracle concerns Moab. Jeremiah 48 parallels and expands this passage.

15:1–9 Moab is devastated by a sudden attack on its villages. Even God mourns for them (vv. 5–9; cf. Ezek. 33:11). For the location of these villages, see map, p. 1272.

15:2–3 On every head is baldness . . . sackcloth. An expression of mourning (cf. 22:12; Jer. 48:37–39; Lam. 2:10).

4 [m]Heshbon and [m]Elealeh cry out;
their voice is heard as far as [n]Jahaz;
therefore the armed men of Moab cry aloud;
his soul trembles.
5 My heart cries out for Moab;
her fugitives flee to Zoar,
to [n]Eglath-shelishiyah.
For at the [o]ascent of Luhith
they go up weeping;
on the road to [o]Horonaim
they raise a cry of destruction;
6 the waters of [p]Nimrim
are a desolation;
the grass is withered, the vegetation fails,
the greenery is no more.
7 [q]Therefore the abundance they have gained
and what they have laid up
they carry away
over the Brook of the Willows.
8 For a cry has gone
around the land of Moab;
her wailing reaches to Eglaim;
her wailing reaches to Beer-elim.
9 For the waters of [r]Dibon[1] are full of blood;
for I will bring upon Dibon even more,
[s]a lion for those of Moab who escape,
for the remnant of the land.

16

1 [t]Send the lamb to the ruler of the land,
from [u]Sela, by way of the desert,
to the mount of the daughter of Zion.
2 Like fleeing birds,
like a scattered nest,
so are the daughters of Moab
at [v]the fords of the Arnon.
3 "Give counsel;
grant justice;
[w]make your shade like night
at the height of noon;
shelter the outcasts;
do not reveal the fugitive;
4 let [x]the outcasts of Moab
sojourn among you;
be a shelter to them[2]
from the destroyer.
When the oppressor is no more,
and destruction has ceased,
and he who tramples underfoot has vanished from the land,
5 [y]then a throne will be established in steadfast love,
and on it will sit in faithfulness
in the tent of David

4[m]Num. 32:37 [n]Jer. 48:34
5[n][See ver. 4 above] [o]Jer. 48:5
6[p][Num. 32:36]
7[q]Jer. 48:36
9[r][ver. 2] [s][2 Kgs. 17:25; Jer. 50:17]

Chapter 16
1[t]2 Kgs. 3:4 [u]ch. 42:11; 2 Kgs. 14:7
2[v]Judg. 11:18
3[w][1 Kgs. 18:4]
4[x]1 Sam. 22:3
5[y]ch. 32:1, 2; Dan. 7:14, 27; Mic. 4:7; Luke 1:33

[1] Dead Sea Scroll, Vulgate (compare Syriac); Masoretic Text *Dimon*; twice in this verse [2] Some Hebrew manuscripts, Septuagint, Syriac; Masoretic Text *let my outcasts sojourn among you; as for Moab, be a shelter to them*

15:9 lion. The remnant of Moabites who escape the oncoming human invaders are met by a lion sent by God.

16:1–5 Fugitive **Moab** begs **Zion** for asylum. Moab had historical ties with the people of God (Gen. 19:30–37; Ruth 1:1–4; 4:13–17; 1 Sam. 22:3–4), but Moab's interest in Zion is not spiritual.

16:1 the lamb. A token of tribute (cf. 2 Kings 3:4).

6 [z]Jer. 48:29; Zeph. 2:10 [a]Judg. 3:14; 2 Kgs. 13:20; [2 Chr. 20:1]
7 [b]ch. 15:3 [c]2 Sam. 6:19; [ver. 9] [d]2 Kgs. 3:25; [ch. 15:1]
8 [e]Jer. 48:32
9 [f][ch. 15:5] [e][See ver. 8 above] [g][ver. 7]
10 [h]Jer. 48:33 [i][ch. 9:3] [j][Judg. 9:27] [k]ch. 63:3; Jer. 25:30 [l]ch. 5:2
11 [m]ch. 15:5; Jer. 48:36
12 [n][1 Kgs. 18:29] [o]ch. 15:2; [Num. 22:41; 23:14, 28]
13 [p]See Amos 2:1-3
14 [q]ch. 21:16 [r][ch. 10:22]

Chapter 17

1 [s]See ch. 13:1 [t]ch. 7:8; Zech. 9:1; See Jer. 49:23-27; Amos 1:3-5
2 [u]Deut. 2:36; Josh. 13:25

one who judges and seeks justice
and is swift to do righteousness."

6 [z]We have heard of the pride of Moab—
how proud he is!—
[a]of his arrogance, his pride, and his insolence;
in his idle boasting he is not right.
7 Therefore let Moab wail for Moab,
[b]let everyone wail.
Mourn, utterly stricken,
for the [c]raisin cakes of [d]Kir-hareseth.

8 For the fields of Heshbon languish,
and [e]the vine of Sibmah;
the lords of the nations
have struck down its branches,
which reached to Jazer
and strayed to the desert;
its shoots spread abroad
and passed over the sea.
9 Therefore [f]I weep with [e]the weeping of Jazer
for the vine of Sibmah;
I drench you with my tears,
O Heshbon and Elealeh;
for over [g]your summer fruit and your harvest
the shout has ceased.
10 [h]And joy and gladness are taken away from [i]the fruitful field,
and in the vineyards no [j]songs are sung,
no cheers are raised;
no [k]treader treads out wine [l]in the presses;
I have put an end to the shouting.
11 Therefore [m]my inner parts moan like a lyre for Moab,
and my inmost self for Kir-hareseth.

12 And when Moab presents himself, when [n]he wearies himself on [o]the high place, when
he comes to his sanctuary to pray, he will not prevail.
13 This is the word that the LORD spoke concerning Moab [p]in the past. 14 But now the
LORD has spoken, saying, "In three years, [q]like the years of a hired worker, the glory of
Moab will be brought into contempt, in spite of all his great multitude, and those who
remain will be [r]very few and feeble."

An Oracle Concerning Damascus

17 An [s]oracle concerning [t]Damascus.

Behold, Damascus will cease to be a city
and will become a heap of ruins.
2 The cities of [u]Aroer are deserted;
they will be for flocks,

16:4–5 When the oppressor is no more . . . then a throne will be established. God's reply to Moab's plea for safety from Assyrian oppression is the messianic throne of David, full of divine integrity but also demanding submission (cf. 9:7; 11:4–5, 10; 55:3).

16:6–12 Moab's **pride** is their doom, portrayed as a vineyard cut down. God is moved to compassion by their sufferings (vv. 9, 11), though he is the one who ends their happiness (v. 10). Verse 12 echoes 15:1–2, emphasizing the futility of misplaced religious trust in the face of disaster. **Therefore** (16:7, 9, 11). Three consequences flow from Moab's proud rejection of the Davidic throne (cf. Jer. 48:42).

16:13–14 As a token of ultimate fulfillment, God declares a more immediate fulfillment of his word. **In three years**, Moab's pride will be broken, presumably under Assyrian invasion around 715 B.C.

17:1–18:7 *The Syria-Israel Alliance.* The fourth oracle concerns the Damascus/Israel alliance of Isaiah's time (cf. 7:1–16; 8:1–4).

17:1 Damascus will cease to be a city. It was destroyed by Assyria in 732 B.C., after a terribly destructive siege.

17:1–3 The words **behold** (v. 1) and **declares the LORD of hosts** (v. 3) solemnize the decree.

which will lie down, and [v]none will make them afraid.
3 The fortress will disappear from [w]Ephraim,
and the kingdom from [w]Damascus;
and the remnant of Syria will be
like [x]the glory of the children of Israel,
declares the LORD of hosts.

4 And in that day [x]the glory of Jacob will be brought low,
and [y]the fat of his flesh will grow lean.
5 And it shall be [z]as when the reaper gathers standing grain
and his arm harvests the ears,
and as when one gleans the ears of grain
in [a]the Valley of Rephaim.
6 [b]Gleanings will be left in it,
as when an olive tree is beaten—
two or three berries
in the top of the highest bough,
four or five
on the branches of a fruit tree,
declares the LORD God of Israel.

2[v]Mic. 4:4
3[w]ch. 7:16; 8:4 [x][1 Sam. 4:21]
4[x][See ver. 3 above] [y]ch. 10:16
5[z][ch. 24:1] [a]See 2 Sam. 5:18
6[b]ch. 24:13

Isaiah Prophesies against Moab

c. 718 B.C.

Over a hundred years before Isaiah's time, the nation of Moab, distantly related to the Israelites (Genesis 19), had expanded their territory northward across the Arnon River into area formerly belonging to Israel. This may have led to the pride for which Isaiah condemned them. He foretold of the doom that awaited them in three years (Isa. 16:14), perhaps carried out by the Assyrians during their invasion of the nation.

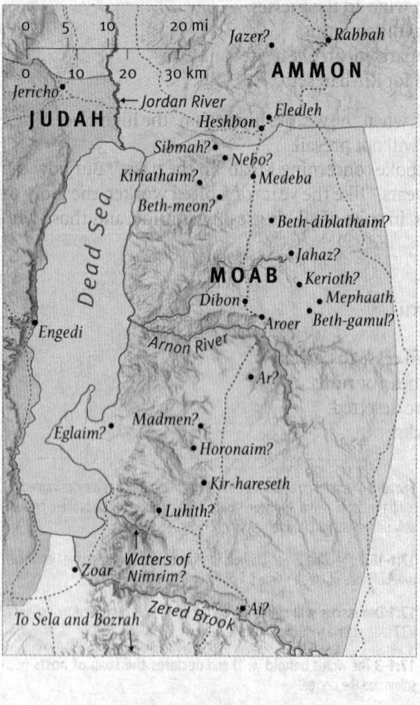

17:2 None will make them afraid, not because of peace but because **the cities . . . are deserted**.

17:3 like the glory of the children of Israel. See vv. 4–6.

17:4–11 A threefold use of **in that day** unites these verses. Israel's fraudulent glory brings them **low** (vv. 4–6), a remnant returns to God (vv. 7–8), and human power is discredited (v. 9). Verses 10–11 explain Israel's fall as a spiritual, not a political, miscalculation.

17:5–6 Stripped nearly clean after reaping and then gleaning, only the topmost fruit on a tree would be left. Even so, **the LORD God of Israel** will preserve, through judgment, a remnant of his people.

17:7–8 The faith that marks the remnant fixes its devoted attention on their **Maker** for all that he is and rejects all rivals of their own making. **Asherim**. Canaanite fertility idols (cf. Deut. 16:21; 2 Chron. 34:3–7; Isa. 27:9).

17:9 The Canaanites had deserted their **cities** centuries before because at that time Israel trusted in the power of God (cf. the book of Joshua), but Israel foolishly came to trust in the same human power that they themselves had defeated.

17:10 the vine-branch of a stranger. Perhaps a metaphor for Israel's alliance with foreign Damascus.

17:12–18:7 The prophetic horizon broadens to include the whole world, for the God-forgetting folly made obvious in the Syro-Ephraimite alliance (17:10–11) is universal.

17:12–14 Ah draws attention to the nations—mighty, restless, and destructive, but scattered by the mere rebuke of the sovereign God (cf. chs. 36–37).

18:1–7 Another **Ah** urges the world to acknowledge the Lord of hosts in Zion.

18:1 land of whirring wings. Perhaps buzzing insects, suggesting an exotic location. "Cush," also known as Nubia or Ethiopia (though not the same as modern Ethiopia), designates a region of northeast Africa along the Nile, which corresponds to present-day southern Egypt and northern Sudan, and is located northwest of present-day Ethiopia (cf. 11:11; Ezek. 29:10). Therefore **beyond the rivers of Cush** likely refers to a region near modern Ethiopia (see also note on Isa. 18:2).

18:2 Go. Isaiah overhears the world's response to emergency—securing its position, or trying to, through political alliance with formidable human power.

18:3 Isaiah calls the whole **world** to redirect its attention to the unmistakable signs of God's activity in history.

18:4–6 Working as silently as **heat** or **dew**, God frustrates human attempts at securing the world without him. He watches until the moment is right, and then acts. This is the truth underlying the appearance of human might in history.

7[c]In that day man will look to his Maker, and his eyes will look on the Holy One of Israel.
8 [d]He will not look to the altars, the work of his hands, and he will not look on what his
own fingers have made, either the [e]Asherim or the altars of incense.
9 [f]In that day their strong cities will be like the deserted places of the wooded heights
and the hilltops, which they deserted because of the children of Israel, and there will be
desolation.

10 For [g]you have forgotten the God of your salvation
and have not remembered the [h]Rock of your refuge;
therefore, though you plant pleasant plants
and sow the vine-branch of a stranger,
11 though you make them grow[1] on the day that you plant them,
and make them blossom in the morning that you sow,
yet the harvest will flee away[2]
in a day of grief and incurable pain.

12 Ah, [i]the thunder of many peoples;
they thunder like the thundering of the sea!
Ah, the roar of nations;
they roar like the roaring of mighty waters!
13 [j]The nations roar like the roaring of many waters,
[k]but he will rebuke them, and they will flee far away,
chased [l]like chaff on the mountains before the wind
and [m]whirling dust before the storm.
14 [n]At evening time, behold, terror!
Before morning, they are no more!
This is the portion of those who loot us,
and the lot of those who plunder us.

An Oracle Concerning Cush

18 1 Ah, land of [o]whirring wings
that is beyond the rivers of [p]Cush,[3]
2 which [q]sends ambassadors by the sea,
in vessels of papyrus on the waters!
Go, you swift messengers,
to a nation [r]tall and smooth,
to a people feared near and far,
a nation [s]mighty and conquering,
whose land the rivers divide.

3 All you inhabitants of the world,
you who dwell on the earth,
when [t]a signal is raised on the mountains, look!
When a trumpet is blown, hear!
4 For thus the LORD said to me:
"I will quietly look [u]from my dwelling
like clear heat in sunshine,
like a cloud of dew in the heat of harvest."
5 [v]For before the harvest, when the blossom is over,
and the flower becomes a ripening grape,
he cuts off the shoots with pruning hooks,
and the spreading branches he lops off and clears away.
6 [v]They shall all of them be left
to the birds of prey of the mountains
and to the beasts of the earth.

7[c][Hos. 8:14]
8[d]ch. 27:9; Mic. 5:13, 14 [e]Ex. 34:13; See Deut. 16:21
9[f][ch. 27:10]
10[g]Ps. 106:21 [h]ch. 26:4; [Deut. 32:4, 18, 31]
12[i]See ch. 22:5-7
13[j][ch. 33:3] [k]Ps. 9:5; [Joel 3:2] [l]See Ps. 1:4 [m]Ps. 83:13
14[n][Ps. 30:5]

Chapter 18

1[o][ch. 8:8; 17:12] [p]2 Kgs. 19:9
2[q]ch. 30:4 [r]ver. 7 [s][2 Sam. 8:2]
3[t]See ch. 5:26
4[u]Ps. 11:4
5[v][Ezek. 31:3, 12, 13]
6[v][See ver. 5 above]

[1] *Or though you carefully fence them* [2] *Or will be a heap* [3] *Probably Nubia*

And the birds of prey will summer on them,
and all the beasts of the earth will winter on them.

7 [w]At that time tribute will be brought to the LORD of hosts
from a people [x]tall and smooth,
from a people feared near and far,
a nation mighty and conquering,
whose land the rivers divide,
to [y]Mount Zion, the place of the [z]name of the LORD of hosts.

An Oracle Concerning Egypt

19 An [a]oracle concerning [b]Egypt.

Behold, the LORD [c]is riding on a swift cloud
and comes to Egypt;
and [d]the idols of Egypt will tremble at his presence,
and the heart of the Egyptians will [e]melt within them.
2 And I will stir up Egyptians against Egyptians,
[f]and they will fight, each against another
and each against his neighbor,
city against city, kingdom against kingdom;
3 and the spirit of the Egyptians within them will be emptied out,
and I will confound[1] their [g]counsel;
and they will inquire of the idols and the sorcerers,
and [h]the mediums and the necromancers;
4 and I will give over the Egyptians
into the hand of [i]a hard master,
and a fierce king will rule over them,
declares the Lord GOD of hosts.

5 And the waters of the sea will be dried up,
and the river will be dry and parched,
6 and its canals will become foul,
and the branches of Egypt's Nile will diminish and dry up,
reeds and rushes will rot away.
7 There will be bare places by the Nile,
on the brink of the Nile,
and all that is sown by the Nile will be parched,
will be driven away, and will be no more.
8 The [j]fishermen will mourn and lament,
all who cast a hook in the Nile;
and they will languish
who spread nets on the water.

[1] Or *I will swallow up*

7 [w]Ps. 68:31 [x]ver. 2 [y][ch. 25:10] [z]2 Sam. 7:13

Chapter 19

1 [a]See ch. 13:1 [b][Joel 3:19]; See Jer. 46:13–26; Ezek. 29:1–31:2; 31:18–32:32 [c]Ps. 18:10, 11; 104:3; [Matt. 26:64; Rev. 1:7] [d]Ex. 12:12; [1 Sam. 5:3; Jer. 43:12; 50:2] [e]ch. 13:7; See Josh. 2:11
2 [f][Judg. 7:22]
3 [g]ver. 11 [h]ch. 8:19
4 [i]ch. 20:4; Jer. 46:26; Ezek. 29:19
8 [j][Num. 11:5]

18:7 At that time. That is, when God consummates history with the victory of his own kingdom (either, as some would hold, at the time of the future millennial kingdom [see note on Rev. 20:1–6], or, as others would hold, when God establishes the new heavens and new earth [see Rev. 21:1]). **tribute will be brought to the LORD of hosts**. Gentile nations will worship God and give of their wealth to honor him (cf. Isa. 2:2; Rev. 21:24). The twofold mention of **the LORD of hosts** signals that God's purpose of grace for the nations will triumph by his power alone (cf. Ps. 68:28–35; 87:1–7; Isa. 2:2–4; 11:10; Acts 11:18; Rev. 7:9–10).

19:1–20:6 *Egypt*. The fifth oracle concerns Egypt. Judah turned to Egypt for deliverance from Assyria. But the God whom Judah overlooks has the power both to judge and to save Egypt.

19:1–15 God reveals his purpose against Egypt.

19:1–4 Egypt disintegrates from the inside (vv. 1–3) and is oppressed from the outside (v. 4).

19:1 the LORD is riding on a swift cloud. God approaches Egypt with power above human powers (cf. Deut. 33:26; Ps. 18:10–15; 68:33–34; 104:3–4). (Ugaritic literature employs the same descriptive title for the god Baal: "Seven years Baal will fail, eight years the rider of the clouds, no dew, no rain." Why would Isaiah ascribe a characteristic of Baal to Yahweh? It is an implicit criticism of Baalism: Baal does not ride on the clouds in the heavens; Yahweh does!) **the idols . . . the heart**. See Ezek. 14:3.

19:4 a hard master. Egypt suffered under tyrants from various nations in the following centuries.

19:5–10 Egypt's primary natural resource and economic base was the **Nile**.

9 [k][Ezek. 27:7]
10 [l][Gal. 2:9] [m]Jer. 46:21
11 [n]ch. 30:4; Num. 13:22; Ps. 78:43
12 [o]1 Kgs. 4:30; Acts 7:22
13 [n][See ver. 11 above] [p]Jer. 2:16; 44:1; 46:14, 19; Ezek. 30:13, 16 [q][Zech. 10:4]
14 [r][1 Kgs. 22:22] [s][ch. 24:20; 29:9]
15 [t]ch. 9:14
16 [u]Jer. 50:37; 51:30; Nah. 3:13 [v]ch. 10:32
18 [w]ver. 21 [x][ch. 30:17; 2 Kgs. 7:13] [y][Zeph. 3:9]
19 [z][2 Kgs. 5:17] [a][Gen. 28:18]
20 [a][See ver. 19 above] [b][Obad. 21]
21 [c][ver. 25] [d]Zech. 14:16-18; [ch. 2:2]
22 [e]Jer. 46:25, 26

9 The workers in [k]combed flax will be in despair,
and the weavers of white cotton.
10 Those who are the [l]pillars of the land will be crushed,
and all who [m]work for pay will be grieved.

11 The princes of [n]Zoan are utterly foolish;
the wisest counselors of Pharaoh give stupid counsel.
How can you say to Pharaoh,
"I am a son of the wise,
a son of ancient kings"?
12 Where then are your [o]wise men?
Let them tell you
that they might know what the LORD of hosts has purposed against
Egypt.
13 The princes of [n]Zoan have become fools,
and the princes of [p]Memphis are deluded;
those who are the [q]cornerstones of her tribes
have made Egypt stagger.
14 The LORD has mingled within her [r]a spirit of confusion,
and they will make Egypt stagger in all its deeds,
[s]as a drunken man staggers in his vomit.
15 And there will be nothing for Egypt
that [t]head or tail, palm branch or reed, may do.

Egypt, Assyria, Israel Blessed

16 In that day the Egyptians will be [u]like women, and [v]tremble with fear before the hand
that the LORD of hosts shakes over them. 17 And the land of Judah will become a terror to
the Egyptians. Everyone to whom it is mentioned will fear because of the purpose that
the LORD of hosts has purposed against them.
18 [w]In that day there will be [x]five cities in the land of Egypt that [y]speak the language
of Canaan and swear allegiance to the LORD of hosts. One of these will be called the City
of Destruction.[1]
19 In that day there will be an [z]altar to the LORD in the midst of the land of Egypt, and
a [a]pillar to the LORD at its border. 20 [a]It will be a sign and a witness to the LORD of hosts in
the land of Egypt. When they cry to the LORD because of oppressors, [b]he will send them a
savior and defender, and deliver them. 21 [c]And the LORD will make himself known to the
Egyptians, and the Egyptians will know the LORD in that day [d]and worship with sacrifice
and offering, and they will make vows to the LORD and perform them. 22 [e]And the LORD
will strike Egypt, striking and healing, and they will return to the LORD, and he will listen
to their pleas for mercy and heal them.

[1] Dead Sea Scroll and some other manuscripts *City of the Sun*

19:11–15 Egypt was famous for its wisdom (cf. 1 Kings 4:30).

19:12 your wise men. Human expertise, however brilliant, fails before the overruling purpose of God.

19:13 Zoan and **Memphis** were the most prominent cities along the Nile River in northeastern **Egypt**.

19:15 head or tail. Cf. 9:14–15.

19:16–25 The Lord will eventually restore Egypt, and the nations. This section is marked by a sixfold use of **in that day**, placing its fulfillment in an undated but inevitable future.

19:16–17 God's powerful hand reverses the roles of fearful Judah and mighty Egypt.

19:16 the Egyptians will be like women, and tremble with fear. In the face of the Lord's powerful opposition, the Egyptian soldiers would lose all courage for battle (portrayed as a manly virtue).

19:18 Isaiah envisions a Godward movement spreading from **five cities** in Egypt to that entire nation (v. 19) to the entire world (v. 23). **speak the language of Canaan**. Egyptians, who were prejudiced against Hebrews (Gen. 43:32), will adopt their language, melding with God's people as one (cf. Gen. 11:1–9). **the City of Destruction**. See ESV footnote, giving a strongly attested textual variant, "City of the Sun," which would refer to Heliopolis, the center of the worship of Ra, the Egyptian sun-god. A culture of idolatry will swear allegiance to the Lord.

19:19–22 Egypt experiences God's saving intervention, just as Israel did during the period of the judges.

19:20 a savior and defender. See Judg. 3:9; 1 Sam. 12:11; Neh. 9:27; Isa. 43:11.

19:21 Cf. Ex. 7:5. Rather than acting like Pharaoh, whose hardened heart refused to allow God's people to worship (Ex. 3:18–19), Egypt too will **worship**.

19:22 striking and healing. Striking in vv. 1–15, healing in vv. 16–25.

23 [f]In that day there will be a highway from Egypt to Assyria, and Assyria will come into
Egypt, and Egypt into Assyria, [g]and the Egyptians will worship with the Assyrians.
24 In that day Israel will be the third with Egypt and Assyria, [h]a blessing in the midst of
the earth, 25 whom the LORD of hosts has blessed, saying, "Blessed be Egypt [i]my people,
and Assyria [j]the work of my hands, and [k]Israel my inheritance."

A Sign Against Egypt and Cush

20 In the year that [l]the commander in chief, who was sent by Sargon the king of Assyria,
came to [m]Ashdod and fought against it and captured it— 2 at that time the LORD
spoke by Isaiah the son of Amoz, saying, "Go, and loose the sackcloth from your waist and
take off your sandals from your feet," and he did so, walking [n]naked and barefoot.
3 Then the LORD said, "As my servant Isaiah has walked naked and barefoot for three
years [o]as a sign and a portent against Egypt and Cush,[1] 4 so shall the [p]king of Assyria lead
away the Egyptian captives and the Cushite exiles, both the young and the old, naked
and barefoot, with buttocks uncovered, the nakedness of Egypt. 5 [q]Then they shall be
dismayed and ashamed because of Cush their hope and of Egypt their boast. 6 And the
inhabitants of [r]this coastland will say in that day, 'Behold, this is what has happened to
those in whom we hoped and [s]to whom we fled for help to be delivered from the king of
Assyria! And we, how shall we escape?'"

Fallen, Fallen Is Babylon

21 The [t]oracle concerning the wilderness of [u]the sea.

[v]As whirlwinds in the Negeb sweep on,
it comes from the wilderness,
from a terrible land.
2 A stern vision is told to me;
[w]the traitor betrays,
and the destroyer destroys.
Go up, O [x]Elam;
lay siege, O [y]Media;
all the [z]sighing she has caused
I bring to an end.

[1] Probably *Nubia*

23 [f]ch. 11:16 [g][ver. 18, 21; Zeph. 3:9]
24 [h][Gen. 12:2, 3]
25 [i][Hos. 2:23] [j]ch. 29:23 [k]Deut. 32:9

Chapter 20

1 [l]2 Kgs. 18:17 [m]1 Sam. 5:1
2 [n]Mic. 1:8, 11; [1 Sam. 19:24]
3 [o][ch. 8:18]
4 [p]ch. 19:4
5 [q]ch. 30:3, 5; [ch. 37:9]
6 [r]Jer. 47:7; [ch. 14:29, 31] [s][ch. 37:6]

Chapter 21

1 [t]See ch. 13:1 [u]Jer. 51:36, 42 [v]Jer. 51:1
2 [w]ch. 24:16; 33:1 [x]See ch. 11:11 [y]See ch. 13:17 [z]Ezek. 9:4

19:23 the Egyptians will worship with the Assyrians. A remarkable change in two of Israel's worst enemies: they too will worship the one true God. The whole world—represented by **Egypt** and **Assyria**, at either end of Isaiah's historical landscape—unites in worship.

19:24–25 God's overflowing **blessing** unites the entire world as his own (cf. Gen. 12:1–3; Gal. 3:7–9, 26–29; Eph. 2:11–22; 3:6; Col. 3:11; Rev. 7:9–10).

20:1–6 The Lord will soon expose the futility of man-centered hopes. An interim fulfillment encourages confidence in God's longer-term promises.

20:1 In the year. 711 B.C. **the commander in chief**. See 2 Kings 18:17, where "the Tartan" translates the same Hebrew word (Hb. *tartan*). **Sargon** (II) was **king of Assyria**, 722–705 B.C. **Ashdod**. A Philistine city (cf. 1 Sam. 5:1). The Assyrian defeat of this city was relevant to "Egypt and Cush" (Isa. 20:3) because Ashdod had relied on promises of Egyptian support against Assyrian attack, but Egypt reneged. How then can Egypt—no match for Assyria—be trusted (cf. 30:1–5; 31:1–3)? (This Ashdod campaign of 712/711 B.C. is documented in the Assyrian Annals of Sargon II from Khorsabad. The Annals confirm that Sargon II sent a military commander to capture Ashdod while he remained in his capital city. Excavations at Ashdod have uncovered fragments of an inscribed pillar of Sargon II, and it is a duplicate of a victory pillar found at Khorsabad. In addition, remains of skeletons of 3,000 persons have been found that probably died in Sargon's conquest of the city.)

20:2 naked and barefoot. Like a prisoner of war (cf. 2 Chron. 28:14–15). The prophets at times acted out their messages with dramatic and even bizarre behavior (cf. 1 Kings 18; Jeremiah 13; 19; 27–28; 43; Ezek. 3:22–5:17; 12:1–20; 24:15–27).

20:3 a sign and a portent. See 8:18. The **three years** need not imply that Isaiah did this continually; he may have done it intermittently as an acted out prophecy (see notes on Ezek. 4:4–6; 4:10).

20:4 the nakedness of Egypt. The sight of such captives revealed Egypt's spiritual plight.

20:5–6 they . . . the inhabitants of this coastland. The various peoples depending on Egypt for aid against Assyria. **And we, how shall we escape?** Isaiah asks his people to arrive at the obvious conclusion: there is no deliverance for them except in God.

21:1–23:18 *Second Series of Oracles: The Deeper Truth.* Isaiah again shows God ruling over the nations of the day, but now he reveals the inner character of these cultures. Five oracles reveal God's ruling over and holding accountable the wilderness by the sea (21:1–10), Dumah (21:11–12), Arabia (21:13–17), the valley of vision (22:1–25), and Tyre (23:1–18).

21:1–10 *Babylon.* The message of the first oracle is that human treachery leaves God's people with no earthly hope.

21:1 the wilderness of the sea. The oracle concerns Babylon (v. 9), but the cryptic title suggests a place both deserted (wilderness) and flooded (sea), thus doubly hopeless (cf. Jer. 51:42–43). Babylon represents the condition of the whole world. **it comes**. The ominous approach of a dreaded message.

21:2 traitor . . . destroyer. Isaiah is shown the vileness of human political backstabbing. **Elam . . . Media**. It is unclear from the text whether these nations are allied with or against Babylon, though Isaiah foretold the role of the Medes in Babylon's fall (13:17). **I bring to an end**. A human promise of relief through conquest, which Isaiah warned his generation not to trust.

3[a]See ch. 13:8
4[b][Deut. 28:67]
5[c]Jer. 51:39, 57 [d]2 Sam. 1:21
8[e]Hab. 2:1
9[f][Hab. 2:2] [g]Jer. 51:8; Cited Rev. 14:8; 18:2 [h]ch. 46:1
10[i]Jer. 51:33; Amos 1:3; [Mic. 4:13]
11[j]See ch. 13:1 [k]Gen. 25:14; 1 Chr. 1:30 [l]Deut. 2:8; Ezek. 35:2
12[m][Job 36:20; Amos 5:8]

3 Therefore my loins are filled with anguish;
[a]pangs have seized me,
like the pangs of a woman in labor;
I am bowed down so that I cannot hear;
I am dismayed so that I cannot see.
4 My heart staggers; horror has appalled me;
[b]the twilight I longed for
has been turned for me into trembling.
5 [c]They prepare the table,
they spread the rugs,[1]
they eat, they drink.
Arise, O princes;
[d]oil the shield!
6 For thus the Lord said to me:
"Go, set a watchman;
let him announce what he sees.
7 When he sees riders, horsemen in pairs,
riders on donkeys, riders on camels,
let him listen diligently,
very diligently."
8 Then he who saw cried out:[2]
[e]"Upon a watchtower I stand, O Lord,
continually by day,
and at my post I am stationed
whole nights.
9 And behold, here come riders,
horsemen in pairs!"
[f]And he answered,
[g]"Fallen, fallen is Babylon;
[h]and all the carved images of her gods
he has shattered to the ground."
10 O [i]my threshed and winnowed one,
what I have heard from the LORD of hosts,
the God of Israel, I announce to you.

11 The [j]oracle concerning [k]Dumah.

One is calling to me from [l]Seir,
"Watchman, what time of the night?
Watchman, what time of the night?"
12 The watchman says:
"Morning comes, and also [m]the night.

[1] Or *they set the watchman* [2] Dead Sea Scroll, Syriac; Masoretic Text *Then a lion cried out*, or *Then he cried out like a lion*

21:3–4 Isaiah is shocked by the nightmarish vision. **the twilight I longed for . . . trembling**. The prophet longed to see God intervene in the world, but he trembles when he sees the reality.

21:5 Others in Judah celebrate the promise of human power and worldly alliance.

21:6–9 God establishes Isaiah's self-understanding as a **watchman**, keeping constantly alert and faithfully reporting whatever he sees.

21:7, 9 riders. Mounted warriors. The prophet sees in his vision the downfall of Babylon, the type of worldly power opposed to God.

21:9 Fallen, fallen is Babylon. The repeated cry emphasizes Babylon's final and total destruction (cf. Rev. 14:8; 18:2). **Her gods** represent the worldview giving Babylon her legitimacy. Thus, the world's most cherished beliefs are **shattered**.

21:10 my threshed and winnowed one. Probably Judah, oppressed by Assyria and unrelieved by Babylon. This text reminds the reader of the primary task of the prophet: to **announce to** God's people **what** he has **heard from the LORD of hosts, the God of Israel**.

21:11–12 *Edom.* The second oracle of the second series (21:1–23:18) depicts prolonged darkness enveloping a frightened world.

21:11 The designation of Isaiah's **oracle concerning Dumah** (Hb. *dumah*, "silence," "stillness," or "the underworld," i.e., the land of silence; cf. Ps. 94:17; 115:17) most likely represents a wordplay for the land of Edom by which he calls attention both to the land of similarly sounding "Edom" and also to the "silence" or "stillness" of death that the oracle predicts. The mention of **Seir** confirms Edom as the explicit object of this oracle (cf. Gen. 32:3; 36:9). **Watchman, what time of the night?** An Edomite pleads with the prophet to announce how much longer his nation must endure the darkness of its troubled history. The repetition of his question conveys his desperation.

21:12 The prophet's answer is vague: **morning** is sure to come, with more **night** as well. But Edom is urged to keep inquiring.

If you will inquire, [n]inquire;
come back again."

13 The [o]oracle concerning [p]Arabia.

In the thickets in [p]Arabia you will lodge,
O [q]caravans of [p]Dedanites.
14 To the thirsty bring water;
meet the fugitive with bread,
O inhabitants of the land of [r]Tema.
15 For they have fled from the swords,
from the drawn sword,
from the bent bow,
and from the press of battle.

16 For thus the Lord said to me, "Within a year, [s]according to the years of a hired worker,
all the glory of [t]Kedar will come to an end. 17 And the remainder of the archers of the mighty
men of the sons of [t]Kedar will be few, [u]for the LORD, the God of Israel, has spoken."

An Oracle Concerning Jerusalem

22 The [v]oracle concerning [w]the valley of vision.

What do you mean that you have gone up,
all of you, to the housetops,
2 you who are full of shoutings,
tumultuous city, [x]exultant town?
Your slain are [y]not slain with the sword
or dead in battle.
3 [z]All your leaders have fled together;
without the bow they were captured.
All of you who were found were captured,
though they had fled far away.
4 Therefore I said:
"Look away from me;
[a]let me weep bitter tears;
do not labor to comfort me
concerning the destruction of the daughter of my people."
5 [b]For the Lord GOD of hosts has [c]a day
of tumult and [d]trampling and [e]confusion
in [w]the valley of vision,

12 [n][Ps. 37:36]
13 [o]See ch. 13:1 [p]Gen. 25:3; Jer. 25:23, 24 [q][Gen. 37:25]
14 [r]Job 6:19
16 [s]See ch. 16:14 [t]ch. 60:7; Gen. 25:13; Ps. 120:5, 6; Song 1:5; Jer. 2:10; 49:28; Ezek. 27:21
17 [t][See ver. 16 above] [u]ch. 1:20

Chapter 22

1 [v]See ch. 13:1 [w]ver. 5; Jer. 21:13; [Joel 3:12, 14]
2 [x]ch. 32:13 [y]Lam. 4:9
3 [z][ch. 1:10]
4 [a]Jer. 9:1; Mic. 1:8
5 [b]ch. 2:12-17 [c][ch. 37:3] [d]ch. 10:6; 18:2 [e]Mic. 7:4 [w][See ver. 1 above]

21:13–17 *Arabia.* The third oracle shows human ferocity scattering fugitives in a darkening world.

21:13 in Arabia. Isaiah plays on words with the title **concerning Arabia**, which sounds like "at evening." The sun is setting on the security of Arabian remoteness (cf. Jer. 49:28–32, esp. v. 31). **you will lodge**. I.e., you will pass the night. **O caravans of Dedanites**. Arabian merchants (cf. Ezek. 27:15, 20). They are driven off their caravan routes to spend the night **in the thickets**, i.e., off the beaten path.

21:14–15 Even in so remote a location as the hinterland of Arabia, exhausted fugitives of war appear, begging for Arabian hospitality as war's relentless destruction rolls on.

21:16–17 These verses depict an interim fulfillment, as in 16:13–14. The prestige of Arabia will soon be humbled and her warriors reduced to a remnant. Isaiah creates an "any moment now" sense of doom, without stating how the prophecy will be fulfilled, for his interest is the deeper meaning and urgency of events. **For**. The ultimate reason for Arabia's decline is not human militarism but the word of the God of Israel.

22:1–25 *Jerusalem.* The fourth oracle shows the light of the world growing dark.

22:1–14 The people of Jerusalem are marked by mindless escapism and frantic self-salvation.

22:1–4 Isaiah foresees the destruction of Jerusalem. He contrasts the unreasoning joviality of the people with his own sorrow.

22:1 valley of vision. Jerusalem (vv. 9–10). The irony is twofold: Mount Zion has become a valley, and the spiritual vision to be expected there has become a blind and reckless drive for present pleasure without regard for God (vv. 11, 13).

22:3 All your leaders have fled. See 2 Kings 25:4.

22:5 For. The reason for Jerusalem's fall is the will of **the Lord GOD of hosts**. The raucous partying of vv. 1–2 is replaced by the **tumult and trampling and confusion** of warfare (cf. Deut. 28:20).

22:6 Elam and **Kir** refer to foreign invaders, though the historical situation being alluded to is debated. Elam was east of the Tigris River, in modern Iran. The location of Kir is unknown (but see note on Amos 1:5). Isaiah may intend a less precise and more impressionistic view of the city's fall.

22:7 full of chariots. The fullness of jubilant shouting (v. 2) is replaced by a fullness of enemy chariots.

a battering down of walls
and a shouting to the mountains.
6 And [f]Elam bore the quiver
with chariots and horsemen,
and [g]Kir uncovered the shield.
7 Your choicest valleys were full of chariots,
and the horsemen took their stand at the gates.
8 He has taken away [h]the covering of Judah.

In that day you looked to [i]the weapons of the House of the Forest, 9 and you saw that
[j]the breaches of the city of David were many. [k]You collected the waters of the lower pool,
10 and you counted the houses of Jerusalem, and you broke down the houses to fortify the
wall. 11 [k]You made a reservoir between [l]the two walls for the water of [m]the old pool. But
[n]you did not look to him who did it, or see him who planned it long ago.

12 In that day [o]the Lord GOD of hosts
called for weeping and mourning,
for [p]baldness and [q]wearing sackcloth;
13 and behold, joy and gladness,
killing oxen and slaughtering sheep,
eating flesh and drinking wine.
[r]"Let us eat and drink,
for tomorrow we die."
14 The LORD of hosts [s]has revealed himself in my ears:
"Surely [t]this iniquity will not be atoned for you [u]until you die,"
says the Lord GOD of hosts.

15 Thus says the Lord GOD of hosts, "Come, go to this steward, to [v]Shebna, who is over
the household, and say to him: 16 What have you to do here, and whom have you here,
[w]that you have cut out here a tomb for yourself, you [x]who cut out a tomb on the height
and carve a dwelling for yourself in the rock? 17 Behold, the LORD will hurl you away
violently, O you strong man. [y]He will seize firm hold on you 18 and whirl you around and
around, and throw you like a ball into a wide land. There you shall die, and there shall be
[z]your glorious chariots, you shame of your master's house. 19 [a]I will thrust you from your
office, and you will be pulled down from your station. 20 In that day I will call my servant
[b]Eliakim the son of Hilkiah, 21 and [b]I will clothe him with your robe, and will bind your
sash on him, and will commit your authority to his hand. And he shall be [c]a father to the
inhabitants of Jerusalem and to the house of Judah. 22 And I will place [d]on his shoulder
[e]the key of the house of David. [f]He shall open, and none shall shut; and he shall shut, and
none shall open. 23 And I will fasten him [g]like a peg in a secure place, and he will become

6 [f]See ch. 11:11 [g]2 Kgs. 16:9
8 [h]ch. 30:1 [i]1 Kgs. 10:17
9 [j]ver. 5, 10; [2 Chr. 32:5] [k][Neh. 3:16]
11 [k][See ver. 9 above] [l][2 Kgs. 25:4] [m][ch. 7:3; 2 Kgs. 20:20; 2 Chr. 32:3, 4] [n][ch. 5:12]
12 [o][Joel 2:17] [p]See ch. 3:24 [q]See 2 Sam. 3:31
13 [r]ch. 56:12; Cited 1 Cor. 15:32
14 [s]ch. 5:9 [t][ch. 27:9; 1 Sam. 3:14] [u][ver. 13]
15 [v]ch. 36:3, 11, 22; 37:2; 2 Kgs. 18:18, 26, 37; 19:2
16 [w]2 Chr. 16:14 [x]Matt. 27:60
17 [y][Dan. 3:21]
18 [z][ch. 36:9]
19 [a][ver. 25]
20 [b]ch. 36:3; 37:2; 2 Kgs. 18:18, 26, 37; 19:2
21 [b][See ver. 20 above] [c]Gen. 45:8
22 [d]ch. 9:6 [e]Rev. 3:7 [f][Job 12:14]
23 [g][ch. 33:20; 54:2; Eccles. 12:11]

22:8b–11 These verses reveal the irony of attentive energies given to military readiness with thoughtless inattention to the sovereign God who controls the situation.

22:8b the House of the Forest. The armory in Jerusalem (cf. 1 Kings 7:2–5; 10:17).

22:9–11 You collected the waters . . . fortify the wall. In the face of Assyrian threat, the people (at Hezekiah's command; see 2 Chron. 32:30) diverted waters from the Gihon Spring outside the city walls to collection points within the city walls (2 Chron. 32:30). In order to prepare for possible attack, homes between the inner and outer wall were cleared for defensive purposes. Rubble from the clearing of these houses was used to repair and fortify existing walls. (See Jerusalem in the Time of Hezekiah, pp. 788–789.)

22:12–13 Isaiah contrasts what **the Lord GOD of hosts** called for with what his unrepentant people called down on themselves (v. 5). **joy and gladness**. In this case, a desperate counterfeit for true happiness (cf. 35:10). **Let us eat and drink**. The speech of God's people, who are heedless of him. Paul finds in this the perfect expression of an attitude that has no regard for deep and lasting realities (see 1 Cor. 15:32).

22:14 this iniquity. I.e., the sin of looking away from God to human self-rescue.

22:15–25 Isaiah addresses two officials in Jerusalem, **Shebna** (a worthless man) and **Eliakim** (a worthy man, but inadequate).

22:15–19 God dismisses self-seeking **Shebna** from high office.

22:15–16 this steward. Shebna is referred to scornfully, despite his position. **The household** is the royal palace (cf. 1 Kings 4:6a). **cut . . . for yourself**. See 2 Chron. 16:14. (The "Tomb of the Royal Steward," an elaborate tomb discovered outside Jerusalem in the village of Silwan, contains a Hebrew inscription at its entrance. This tomb probably belonged to **Shebna**.)

22:20–25 God promotes **Eliakim** to Shebna's office (cf. 36:3, 22; 37:2), but Eliakim cannot support the weight of Jerusalem's heavy problems (22:25).

22:20 my servant. See 20:3; 37:35; 41:8–9; 42:1.

22:22 the key. The authority of the steward to make binding decisions in the interests of the king (cf. Matt. 16:19; Rev. 3:7–8).

22:23–25 a peg. Set firmly in a wall and capable of bearing weight; and yet **in that day** (of God's judgment on Judah) even he (or his family line) **will give way**.

[h]a throne of honor to his father's house. 24 And they will hang on him the whole honor
of his father's house, the offspring and issue, every small vessel, from the cups to all the
flagons. 25 In that day, declares the LORD of hosts, [g]the peg that was fastened in a secure
place will give way, and it will be cut down and fall, and the load that was on it will be cut
off, for the LORD has spoken."

An Oracle Concerning Tyre and Sidon

23 The [i]oracle concerning [j]Tyre.

Wail, O [k]ships of Tarshish,
for Tyre is laid waste, [l]without house or harbor!
From [m]the land of Cyprus[1]
it is revealed to them.
2 Be still, O inhabitants of the coast;
the merchants of [n]Sidon, who cross the sea, have filled you.
3 And on many waters
your revenue was the grain of Shihor,
the harvest of the Nile;
you were [o]the merchant of the nations.
4 Be ashamed, O [n]Sidon, for the sea has spoken,
the stronghold of the sea, saying:
"I have neither labored nor given birth,
I have neither reared young men
nor brought up young women."
5 When the report comes to Egypt,
they will be in anguish[2] over the report about Tyre.
6 [p]Cross over to Tarshish;
wail, O inhabitants of the coast!
7 Is this your exultant city
[q]whose origin is from days of old,
whose feet carried her
to settle far away?
8 Who has purposed this
against Tyre, the bestower of crowns,
whose merchants were princes,
whose traders were the honored of the earth?
9 The LORD of hosts has purposed it,
[r]to defile the pompous pride of all glory,[3]
to dishonor all the honored of the earth.
10 Cross over your land like the Nile,
O daughter of Tarshish;
there is no restraint anymore.
11 [s]He has stretched out his hand over the sea;
he has shaken the kingdoms;

23[h][Rev. 3:21]
25[g][See ver. 23 above]

Chapter 23

1[i]See ch. 13:1 [j][Jer. 25:22; 27:2, 3]; See Ezek. 26:2–28:24; Joel 3:4-8; Amos 1:9, 10; Zech. 9:2-4 [k]ver. 14; 1 Kgs. 10:22; 22:48 [l]ch. 24:10 [m]Jer. 2:10; See Gen. 10:4
2[n]ver. 4, 12; Gen. 10:15; Josh. 19:28; Jer. 25:22; 27:3; Ezek. 27:8; 32:30; Joel 3:4; Zech. 9:2
3[o]See Ezek. 27:3-23
4[n][See ver. 2 above]
6[p]ver. 12
7[q][Gen. 10:15]
9[r][Ezek. 28:7]
11[s][Ex. 14:21]

[1] Hebrew *Kittim*; also verse 12 [2] Hebrew *they will have labor pains* [3] The Hebrew words for *glory* and *hosts* sound alike

23:1–18 *Tyre.* The fifth oracle concerns the judgment—and redemption—of Tyre, here characterized as the world's prostitute (vv. 15–17).

23:1–14 Tyre, a successful port on the Phoenician coast and "the merchant of the nations" (v. 3), is humbled by God (cf. Ezek. 28:1–10).

23:1 Word of Tyre's fall reaches her fleet off **Cyprus**. On **ships of Tarshish**, see 1 Kings 10:22 and Ps. 48:7.

23:2 Sidon. Another Phoenician city, sharing Tyre's doom (v. 12). See Joel 3:4.

23:3 Shihor. Perhaps a branch of the Nile in its delta region (cf. ESV footnote on 1 Chron. 13:5).

23:4 The **sea** laments the loss of Tyrian merchantmen as her children.

23:5–6 The news of Tyre spreads farther to **Egypt** and still farther to **Tarshish**.

23:7–9 The devastation of the city prompts the deeper question, Who could decree the downfall of so great a human power? **The LORD of hosts**. See 14:24–27. He will never make peace with human pride.

23:10 With Tyre's monopoly removed, **Tarshish** has an open market.

23:11 He has stretched out his hand over the sea in sovereign authority (cf. Ex. 14:16). Tyre and Sidon were part of what once was **Canaan** (cf. Josh. 5:1).

12[t]See ver. 2 [u]ver. 6 [v]ver. 1
13[w]ch. 47:1; 48:14
[x][2 Kgs. 25:1]
14[y]See ver. 1
15[z]Jer. 25:11, 22
17[a]Jer. 25:11, 22 [b]Rev. 17:1, 2

Chapter 24

1[c]ch. 13:9
2[d]Hos. 4:9; [Lam. 4:16]; See ch. 3:1-3 [e][Ezek. 7:12, 13] [f][Jer. 15:10]

the LORD has given command concerning Canaan
to destroy its strongholds.
12 And he said:
"You will no more exult,
O oppressed virgin daughter of [t]Sidon;
arise, [u]cross over to [v]Cyprus,
even there you will have no rest."

13 Behold the land of [w]the Chaldeans! This is the people that was not;[1] Assyria destined
it for wild beasts. They erected [x]their siege towers, they stripped her palaces bare, they
made her a ruin.

14 [y]Wail, O ships of Tarshish,
for your stronghold is laid waste.

15 In that day Tyre will be forgotten for [z]seventy years, like the days[2] of one king. At the
end of [z]seventy years, it will happen to Tyre as in the song of the prostitute:

16 "Take a harp;
go about the city,
O forgotten prostitute!
Make sweet melody;
sing many songs,
that you may be remembered."

17 At the end of [a]seventy years, the LORD will visit Tyre, and she will return to her wages
and [b]will prostitute herself with all the kingdoms of the world on the face of the earth.
18 Her merchandise and her wages will be holy to the LORD. It will not be stored or hoarded,
but her merchandise will supply abundant food and fine clothing for those who dwell
before the LORD.

Judgment on the Whole Earth

24

1 Behold, [c]the LORD will empty the earth[3] and make it desolate,
and he will twist its surface and scatter its inhabitants.
2 [d]And it shall be, as with the people, so with the priest;
as with the slave, so with his master;
as with the maid, so with her mistress;
[e]as with the buyer, so with the seller;
as with the lender, so with the borrower;
[f]as with the creditor, so with the debtor.

[1] Or *that has become nothing* [2] Or *lifetime* [3] Or *land*; also throughout this chapter

23:12 virgin daughter of Sidon. The city personified (cf. 37:22; 47:1).

23:13 The prophet directs Tyre's attention to Babylon in the **land of the Chaldeans**, ruined by the Assyrians (who ruled it as a puppet kingdom until a new Babylonian dynasty arose in 626 B.C.). If Babylon is vulnerable, so is Tyre.

23:15–18 The **prostitute** Tyre will soon be back in business, but v. 18 abruptly shows that it will ultimately be redeemed (like other nations, e.g., 19:23–25).

23:15–16 After a period of decline and recovery, Tyre charms her old customers back into trading with her. The **seventy years** are difficult to identify historically. Some take it as a symbolic expression for a "completed" period of diminished influence; some understand it as the same 70 years of Babylonian reign as represented in Jer. 25:11 (see note there); and some understand it as the period of Assyrian domination, from Sennacherib's campaign in 701 B.C. to the recovery of the strength of Tyre around 630. **prostitute**. Tyre lived by an anything-for-money ethic.

23:17–18 The inveterate whore, deeply bound to the corruption of wealth, in v. 18 is made **holy to the LORD** and devoted to his people. Deuteronomy 23:18 forbids the wages of a prostitute from being consecrated; the reversal here implies redemption. On hope for the nations, who will consecrate their wealth to God, cf. Isa. 60:10–11; Hag. 2:7–8; Rev. 21:24–27. On "holy to the LORD," see Ex. 28:36–38.

24:1–27:13 *Third Series of Oracles: The Final End.* The third and climactic vision of God ruling the nations in judgment and salvation. While chs. 13–20 and 21–23 address particular nations, chs. 24–27 foresee the whole world in crisis at the end of history, but with the people of God wonderfully secured in their own city (cf. 24:4; 25:8; 26:19; 27:6). These chapters are often called "apocalyptic," since they depict the final conflict and God's victory in vivid images.

24:1–20 *The Wasted City.* The Lord, ruling from Mount Zion, violently dismantles this present evil age and replaces it with the joy of worldwide worship.

24:1–6 The world order, in which human sin is exalted, is laid waste.

24:1 Behold, the LORD. The first impression conveyed by the vision is the active presence of God. **scatter**. The same word (Hb. *puts*) as "dispersed" in Gen. 11:4, 8, 9. Alluding to Babel, Isaiah foresees another, final judgment of human autonomy.

24:2 No position of social rank can serve as protection against the judgment of God (cf. Rev. 20:12).

3 [g]The earth shall be utterly empty and utterly plundered;
[h]for the LORD has spoken this word.

4 [i]The earth mourns and withers;
the world languishes and withers;
the highest people of the earth languish.
5 The earth lies [j]defiled
under its inhabitants;
for [k]they have transgressed the laws,
violated the statutes,
broken the everlasting covenant.
6 Therefore [l]a curse devours the earth,
and its inhabitants [m]suffer for their guilt;
therefore the inhabitants of the earth are scorched,
and few men are left.
7 [n]The wine mourns,
the vine languishes,
all the merry-hearted sigh.
8 [o]The mirth of the tambourines is stilled,
the noise of the jubilant has ceased,
the mirth of the lyre is stilled.
9 No more do they drink wine [p]with singing;
strong drink is bitter to those who drink it.
10 [q]The wasted city is broken down;
[r]every house is shut up so that none can enter.
11 [s]There is an outcry in the streets for lack of wine;
[t]all joy has grown dark;
the gladness of the earth is banished.
12 Desolation is left in the city;
the gates are battered into ruins.
13 For thus it shall be in the midst of the earth
among the nations,
[u]as when an olive tree is beaten,
as at the gleaning when the grape harvest is done.

14 They lift up their voices, they sing for joy;
over the majesty of the LORD they shout from the west.[1]
15 [v]Therefore in the east[2] give glory to the LORD;
in the coastlands of the sea, give glory to the name of the LORD, the God of Israel.
16 [w]From the ends of the earth we hear songs of praise,
of glory to [x]the Righteous One.

3 [g]ver. 1, 6 [h]See ch. 1:20
4 [i][ch. 16:8; Hos. 4:3]
5 [j]Num. 35:33 [k][ch. 2:6, 8]
6 [l]Zech. 5:3, 4 [m][Ps. 5:10]
7 [n][Joel 1:10, 12]
8 [o]Jer. 7:34; Hos. 2:11; [Amos 8:10]
9 [p][Amos 6:5, 6]
10 [q][ch. 34:11] [r]ch. 23:1
11 [s][ver. 7; Ps. 144:14; Joel 1:5] [t][Joel 1:12]
13 [u]ch. 17:6; [Mic. 7:1]
15 [v][ch. 45:6]
16 [w][ver. 14] [x][ch. 26:2; 60:21]

[1] Hebrew *from the sea* [2] Hebrew *in the realm of light*

24:4 The earth mourns and withers. See Hos. 4:3.

24:5 The earth lies defiled . . . for they have transgressed the laws. Human sin defiles the world in God's sight (cf. Num. 35:34). **violated the statutes**. Judgment comes as the world defies God's revealed will in order to construct an alternative social order. **the everlasting covenant**. Perhaps the covenant given through Noah (Gen. 9:16), which applies to all mankind; or the covenant with the house of David (2 Sam. 23:5; Isa. 55:3), through which all mankind is to be blessed. Other interpreters think this refers to the implicit covenant with all mankind contained in the "laws" and "statutes" of God that he imparts through human conscience (cf. Rom. 1:18–32; 2:12–15), although this option, unlike the first two, is not called an "everlasting covenant" in the OT.

24:6 Therefore . . . therefore. Isaiah explains the guilt of human sin and the justice of God's judgment.

24:7–13 The worldly lifestyle of escapist revelry falls silent.

24:10 The wasted city. The city is an important image in chs. 24–27 (cf. 24:12; 25:2; 26:1–2, 5; 27:10). Isaiah sees world culture as a city because it is a place both of concentrated population and of imagined safety. "Wasted" (Hb. *tohu*) is translated "without form" in Gen. 1:2. The world city of human civilization, though highly developed, rejects the will of God and thus wastes its own potential.

24:13 beaten . . . gleaning . . . harvest. These are metaphors for the "few men" of v. 6 left after judgment. This is a transitional verse into vv. 14–16.

24:14–16 The drunken binge of vv. 7–11 is replaced with the joyful worship of those redeemed from the world. They humbly admire the **majesty of the LORD**, giving glory to the covenant **LORD, the God of Israel. . . . the Righteous One** who alone rules in justice (cf. 12:1–6; 52:8–9; 65:14; Rev. 5:9–10; 15:2–4).

24:16 Woe is me! The prophet laments the present treachery of the world (cf. 6:5; 21:2–4).

16[y]ch. 21:2; 33:1
17[z]Jer. 48:43, 44; [Job 20:24; Amos 5:19]
18[z][See ver. 17 above] [a]See Gen. 7:11 [b]Ps. 18:7
20[c][ch. 19:14; 29:9] [d][ver. 5, 6]
21[e]Ps. 76:12; [ch. 10:12; 31:8]
22[f]Mic. 4:11, 12 [g]ch. 29:6
23[h]See ch. 13:10 [i]Ps. 99:1, 2; Mic. 4:7

Chapter 25

1[j]Ex. 15:2 [k][Ps. 107:32] [l][2 Kgs. 19:25]
2[m][ch. 17:1; Jer. 51:37]

But I say, "I waste away,
I waste away. Woe is me!
For [y]the traitors have betrayed,
with betrayal the traitors have betrayed."
17 [z]Terror and the pit and the snare[1]
are upon you, O inhabitant of the earth!
18 [z]He who flees at the sound of the terror
shall fall into the pit,
and he who climbs out of the pit
shall be caught in the snare.
For [a]the windows of heaven are opened,
and [b]the foundations of the earth tremble.
19 The earth is utterly broken,
the earth is split apart,
the earth is violently shaken.
20 The earth [c]staggers like a drunken man;
it sways like a hut;
[d]its transgression lies heavy upon it,
and it falls, and will not rise again.
21 On that day the LORD will punish
the host of heaven, in heaven,
and [e]the kings of the earth, on the earth.
22 [f]They will be gathered together
as prisoners in a pit;
they will be shut up in a prison,
and after many days [g]they will be punished.
23 [h]Then the moon will be confounded
and the sun ashamed,
for [i]the LORD of hosts reigns
on Mount Zion and in Jerusalem,
and his glory will be before his elders.

God Will Swallow Up Death Forever

25 1 O LORD, [j]you are my God;
[k]I will exalt you; I will praise your name,
for you have done wonderful things,
[l]plans formed of old, faithful and sure.
2 For you have made the city [m]a heap,
the fortified city a ruin;
the foreigners' palace is a city no more;
it will never be rebuilt.

[1] The Hebrew words for *terror, pit,* and *snare* sound alike

24:17–20 The judgment of the world is a deliberate and final act of God.

24:18 He who flees . . . shall fall . . . he who climbs . . . shall be caught. Not an accident but an act of God (cf. Amos 5:19). **the windows of heaven**. See Gen. 7:11. The pairing of "heaven" and **earth** indicates total disaster, as in Noah's flood.

24:21–23 *The Lord Will Punish.* The Lord rules in triumph over his enemies and in glory before his own people.

24:21 On that day. The focal point toward which God is leading history, foreseen seven times in chs. 24–27 (24:21; 25:9; 26:1; 27:1, 2, 12, 13). **the host of heaven . . . the kings of the earth**. All opposition to God everywhere, even angelic (i.e., demonic).

24:23 The **moon** and **sun** are outshone by the **glory** of **the LORD of hosts** reigning in triumph forever from his city, **Jerusalem** on **Mount Zion**. His **elders** lead his redeemed people, once unfaithful (3:14; 9:14–15), but now replaced by faithful ones (52:7; 60:19–20).

25:1–12 *He Will Swallow Up Death Forever.* The redeemed celebrate their liberation by God. The "elders" of 24:23 now sing.

25:1–5 Human tyranny is overthrown by God.

25:1 you are my God. Though worldwide in scope, redemption is personal. **Wonderful things** (Hb. *pele'*) refers especially to the remarkable acts of God, which bear the marks of his supernatural intervention in the natural world and human events (cf. 9:6). **plans formed of old**. Not a last-minute attempt but a long-assured victory (cf. 14:24–27).

25:2 the city. See note on 24:10. **the foreigners' palace**. Every bastion of foreign invasion and occupation disappears forever.

3 [n]Therefore strong peoples will glorify you;
cities of ruthless nations will fear you.
4 [o]For you have been a stronghold to the poor,
a stronghold to the needy in his distress,
[p]a shelter from the storm and a shade from the heat;
[q]for the breath of the ruthless is like a storm against a wall,
5 [r]like heat in a dry place.
You subdue the noise of the foreigners;
as heat by the shade of a cloud,
so the song of the ruthless is put down.

6 [s]On this mountain the LORD of hosts will make for all peoples
a feast of rich food, a feast of well-aged wine,
[t]of rich food full of marrow, of aged wine well refined.
7 And he will swallow up [s]on this mountain
the covering that is cast over all peoples,
[u]the veil that is spread over all nations.
8 [v]He will swallow up death forever;
and [w]the Lord GOD will wipe away tears from all faces,
and [x]the reproach of his people he will take away from all the earth,
[y]for the LORD has spoken.
9 It will be said on that day,
"Behold, this is our God; [z]we have waited for him, that he might save us.
This is the LORD; we have waited for him;
[a]let us be glad and rejoice in his salvation."
10 For the hand of the LORD will rest [s]on this mountain,
and [b]Moab shall be trampled down in his place,
as straw is trampled down in a dunghill.[1]
11 [c]And he will spread out his hands in the midst of it
as a swimmer spreads his hands out to swim,
but the LORD [d]will lay low his pompous pride together with the skill[2] of his hands.
12 And the high fortifications of his walls he will bring down,
lay low, and cast to the ground, to the dust.

[1] The Hebrew words for *dunghill* and for the Moabite town *Madmen* (Jeremiah 48:2) sound alike [2] Or *in spite of the skill*

3[n][ch. 18:7]
4[o]Nah. 1:7 [p]ch. 4:6 [q][2 Chr. 32:18]
5[r][ch. 32:2]
6[s]ch. 2:2, 3; 11:9; 24:23 [t][Ps. 63:5]
7[s][See ver. 6 above] [u][2 Cor. 3:15]
8[v]Cited 1 Cor. 15:54; [Hos. 13:14] [w]Rev. 7:17; [ch. 30:19] [x][ch. 37:4] [y]See ch. 1:20
9[z]ch. 26:8; [Gen. 49:18; Ps. 27:14] [a]Ps. 9:14
10[s][See ver. 6 above] [b]See ch. 15:1
11[c][ch. 16:12] [d][ch. 16:14]

25:3 Therefore. The destruction of human tyranny clears the way for the vindication of God. **glorify you**. See 45:23. The once **ruthless nations**, formerly united against God, come to **fear** him properly.

25:4–5 stronghold. The redeemed have in God something better than the "fortified city" of man (v. 2). Easily, silently—like **the shade of a cloud**—God defends his oppressed people until his final triumph. **The song of the ruthless** is their pompous boasting.

25:6–8 Human sorrow is relieved by God.

25:6 On this mountain. See 2:2–4; 4:5; 11:9; 24:23; 65:25; Heb. 12:22. **for all peoples**. The fivefold use of "all" in Isa. 25:6–8 suggests the fullness of God's salvation. The inclusiveness of "all peoples" is matched by the particularity of "this mountain." **a feast**. This is God's bountiful answer to the worldly partying silenced in 24:7–11 (cf. 55:1–2; Rev. 19:9).

25:7 the covering . . . the veil. The pall of death hanging over all human activity under the curse (cf. Gen. 3:17–19; Rev. 22:1–3). God will **swallow** it up and give back life (cf. Rev. 1:17–18).

25:8 He will swallow up death forever, defeating the swallowing power of death (cf. 5:14; 1 Cor. 15:54; Rev. 21:4). This is a promise that at some future time God's people will no longer be subject to death but will live forever. **the reproach of his people**. The appearance that they have been abandoned by God (cf. Deut. 28:37; Ps. 44:13–16; 69:9–12; 74:9–11, 22–23; 79:1–5; Isa. 43:28; 51:7; 54:4–8; Jer. 15:15; Ezek. 5:14–17; 36:6–7).

25:9–12 Human pride is humbled by God.

25:9 Behold. See 24:1. At last, the realization of the forward-looking faith that patiently **waited** for a renewed society and a renewed earth (cf. the expectation in 40:9–11). **this is our God**. An expression of wholehearted identification with him (cf. Ex. 29:45–46). **we have waited**. Salvation is worth the wait, and is even worth the reproach of Isa. 25:8. **Salvation** is **his** entirely, God's alone, from first to last (cf. Ex. 14:13; 15:2; Ps. 68:19–20; 98:2–3).

25:10 hand. A metaphor for God's powerful "salvation" in v. 9. **Moab** falls under God's foot and represents all nations and cultures lifted up against God, like Edom in 34:5–9 and 63:1. **dunghill**. The only alternative to the feast of 25:6.

25:11 He will spread out his hands to **swim** out of the muck of v. 10 by his own desperate methods of self-salvation. **his pompous pride**. See 16:6. Human pride is set in contrast to the glad patience of 25:9.

25:12 Observe the city imagery (cf. 24:10; 25:2).

Chapter 26
1[e][ch. 27:2] [f][ch. 60:18]
2[g]Ps. 118:19, 20
3[h][ch. 30:15]
5[i]ch. 25:12
6[j][ch. 25:4]
7[k]1 Sam. 2:9; Ps. 37:23
8[l]Ex. 3:15
9[m]ver. 16; [2 Chr. 33:12]
10[n]See Ps. 73:3-11
11[o][Mic. 5:9] [p][ch. 5:12]
[q]Ps. 21:9; [ch. 33:14]

You Keep Him in Perfect Peace

26 In that day [e]this song will be sung in the land of Judah:

"We have a strong city;
he sets up [f]salvation
as walls and bulwarks.
2 [g]Open the gates,
that the righteous nation that keeps faith may enter in.
3 [h]You keep him in perfect peace
whose mind is stayed on you,
because he trusts in you.
4 Trust in the LORD forever,
for the LORD GOD is an everlasting rock.
5 [i]For he has humbled
the inhabitants of the height,
the lofty city.
He lays it low, lays it low to the ground,
casts it to the dust.
6 The foot tramples it,
the feet of [j]the poor,
the steps of [j]the needy."

7 The path of the righteous is level;
[k]you make level the way of the righteous.
8 In the path of your judgments,
O LORD, we wait for you;
[l]your name and [l]remembrance
are the desire of our soul.
9 My soul yearns for you in the night;
my spirit within me earnestly seeks you.
[m]For when your judgments are in the earth,
the inhabitants of the world learn righteousness.
10 [n]If favor is shown to the wicked,
he does not learn righteousness;
in the land of uprightness he deals corruptly
and does not see the majesty of the LORD.
11 O LORD, [o]your hand is lifted up,
but [p]they do not see it.
Let them see your zeal for your people, and be ashamed.
Let [q]the fire for your adversaries consume them.

26:1–21 *He Will Ordain Peace.* God achieves for his people their final and complete victory. The time perspective in ch. 26 shifts between the past, present, and future.

26:1–6 A song of confidence.

26:1 a strong city. Contrast "the wasted city" in 24:10. **salvation as walls**. See Zech. 2:5.

26:2 Open the gates. Contrast "every house is shut up" in 24:10. Zion welcomes pilgrims and fears no threats. **the righteous nation**. A reference to many and various human beings, all keeping **faith** in the promises of God.

26:3 perfect peace. The peace described here is first the corporate peace of the city (v. 1) and the nation (v. 2) that comes from the "hand of the Lord" (25:10); but it is also the individual peace of the person whose **mind is stayed on** God. The source of such peace is the righteous, sovereign, saving God (25:9)—who "will swallow up death forever" and "will wipe away" every tear (25:8; cf. Rev. 21:4), and who alone is worthy of trust. (On the meaning of peace in the OT and NT, see note on John 14:27.)

26:4 Trust in the LORD. This is the practical challenge that the book of Isaiah lays down for God's people (cf. 7:9; 10:20; 12:2; 30:15; 31:1; 32:17; 36:15; 42:17; 50:10; 57:13). **the LORD GOD**. Hebrew *Yah YHWH*, an emphatic form of God's name. **everlasting rock**. The vindication of faith is secured by the solid dependability of God (cf. Deut. 32:4, 31; 1 Sam. 2:2; Ps. 18:2, 31; 61:2–3).

26:5 The lofty city of proud human self-sufficiency. **lays it low, lays it low**. Cf. the repeated "Fallen, fallen" in 21:9. **dust**. See 25:12.

26:6 the poor . . . the needy. Those despised by proud conquerors (10:2), but who trust in God (Zeph. 3:12).

26:7–9 A prayer of yearning.

26:7 God's promises lead along a **path** straight and true to fulfillment (cf. Prov. 3:6).

26:8–9 you . . . you . . . you. God himself is the wholehearted desire of his people. **the inhabitants of the world**. Desire for God inspires a longing that all would recognize him. These verses are transitional to vv. 10–11.

26:10–11 This cry for vindication is the centerpiece of ch. 26. **your hand is lifted up**. A gesture of opposition (cf. 2 Sam. 24:16; Isa. 9:12). In a world of spiritual blindness, God's people long for the truth to be seen. That truth is God's judgment on his enemies and his **zeal** for his own people, reversing the reproach of 25:8 and fulfilling the hopes of 24:14–16a, 23b; 25:1–12; 26:1–6.

12 O LORD, you will ordain [r]peace for us,
for you have indeed done for us all our works.
13 O LORD our God,
[s]other lords besides you have ruled over us,
[t]but your name alone we bring to remembrance.
14 They are dead, they will not live;
they are shades, they will not arise;
to that end you have visited them with destruction
and wiped out all remembrance of them.
15 [u]But you have increased the nation, O LORD,
you have increased the nation; you are glorified;
[v]you have enlarged all the borders of the land.

16 O LORD, [w]in distress they sought you;
they poured out a whispered prayer
when your discipline was upon them.
17 [x]Like a pregnant woman
who writhes and cries out in her pangs
when she is near to giving birth,
so were we because of you, O LORD;
18 [x]we were pregnant, we writhed,
but we have given birth to wind.
We have accomplished no deliverance in the earth,
and the inhabitants of the world have not fallen.
19 [y]Your dead shall live; their bodies shall rise.
You who dwell in the dust, awake and sing for joy!
For [z]your dew is a dew of light,
and the earth will give birth to the dead.

20 Come, my people, enter your chambers,
and shut your doors behind you;
hide yourselves [a]for a little while
until the fury has passed by.
21 [b]For behold, the LORD is coming out from his place
to punish the inhabitants of [c]the earth for their iniquity,
and the earth will disclose the blood shed on it,
and will no more cover its slain.

The Redemption of Israel

27 In that day the LORD with his hard and great and strong [d]sword will punish [e]Leviathan the fleeing serpent, [e]Leviathan the twisting serpent, and he will slay [f]the dragon that is in the sea.

12[r]ch. 9:7; Mic. 5:5
13[s][ch. 2:8; 2 Kgs. 16:3, 4] [t][ch. 2:20; Ps. 20:7]; See 2 Kgs. 18:4-6
15[u]ch. 9:3 [v][ch. 54:2, 3]
16[w]Hos. 5:15; See ch. 37:1-4
17[x]See ch. 13:8
18[x][See ver. 17 above]
19[y][Ezek. 37:12; Dan. 12:2; Hos. 13:14] [z][Hos. 14:5]
20[a]ch. 10:25
21[b]Mic. 1:3 [c][ch. 24:5]

Chapter 27

1[d][Jer. 47:6] [e]Ps. 74:14 [f]ch. 51:9; Ezek. 29:3

26:12–15 A confession of dependence.

26:12 The future is bright, because salvation belongs to God alone.

26:13–15 other lords. Human tyrants. **They are dead**. The redeemed will outlive all tyranny. **wiped out all remembrance**. Evil is not only defeated; it even fades from memory (cf. 35:10; 65:17). **increased . . . increased . . . enlarged**. God glorifies himself by reversing his suffering people's lot in life (cf. 9:3; 54:2).

26:16–18 An admission of failure. The nation's historic pattern of failure (**they**, v. 16) is owned by the present generation (**we**, vv. 17–18). Although Israel was to be God's agent of deliverance in the world (Gen. 12:1–3; Ex. 19:5–6), they failed, and the world went on as before.

26:19–21 The hope of glory is coming, but an interim caution is given.

26:19 In contrast with the finality of death in v. 14, v. 19 rejoices in a bodily resurrection of all God's people. The long-standing failure described in vv. 16–18 will be dramatically reversed by God's power alone. **your dew is a dew of light**. God's life-giving power falls on his deceased people.

26:20–21 shut your doors. Contrast "open the gates" in v. 2. Isaiah alludes to Gen. 7:16 and perhaps Ex. 12:21–23. **until the fury has passed by**. The remainder of history until the city of man is laid waste. **the earth will disclose the blood shed on it**. The unanswered persecutions of God's people will be avenged (cf. Gen. 4:10).

27:1–13 *The Whole World Will Be Fruitful.* God destroys evil and brings all his people home.

27:1 Leviathan. An ancient symbol of evil in all its monstrous horror, attested in Ugaritic myths that describe a powerful, dragon-like deity. The threefold designation—**the fleeing serpent**, **the twisting serpent**, and **the dragon that is in the sea**—is matched by the Lord's threefold description of the **hard and great and strong sword**. Although the image was supplied from an ancient myth, biblical revelation filled it with true meaning. Leviathan is but a created plaything of God (Ps. 104:26) and already is defeated (Ps. 74:12–14). See note on Ps. 74:14. Now Isaiah foresees God destroying it finally and forever (cf. Rev. 12:7–9).

2[g]ch. 5:7 [h][ch. 26:1]
4[i][ch. 10:17]
6[j]ch. 37:31; Hos. 14:5, 6
7[k]Hos. 6:1, 2 [l]See ch. 37:36-38 [m]ch. 37:18, 19
8[n][Jer. 10:24] [o][Jer. 18:17]
9[p][ch. 22:14] [q][2 Kgs. 18:4] [r]See Deut. 16:21
10[s]ch. 17:9; 32:14, 19; [Hos. 8:14; Mic. 5:11]
11[t]Deut. 32:28; See ch. 30:16-18
12[u]See Gen. 15:18
13[v]Lev. 25:9; [Matt. 24:31; Rev. 11:15] [w]ch. 11:11, 16; Mic. 7:12 [x][ch. 2:2]

2 In that day,
[g]"A pleasant vineyard,[1] [h]sing of it!
3 I, the LORD, am its keeper;
every moment I water it.
Lest anyone punish it,
I keep it night and day;
4 I have no wrath.
[i]Would that I had thorns and briers to battle!
I would march against them,
I would burn them up together.
5 Or let them lay hold of my protection,
let them make peace with me,
let them make peace with me."

6 [j]In days to come[2] Jacob shall take root,
Israel shall blossom and put forth shoots
and fill the whole world with fruit.

7 [k]Has he struck them [l]as he struck those who struck them?
Or have they been slain [m]as their slayers were slain?
8 [n]Measure by measure,[3] by exile you contended with them;
[o]he removed them with his fierce breath[4] in the day of the east wind.
9 Therefore by this [p]the guilt of Jacob will be atoned for,
and this will be the full fruit of the removal of his sin:[5]
[q]when he makes all the stones of the altars
like chalkstones crushed to pieces,
no [r]Asherim or incense altars will remain standing.
10 [s]For the fortified city is solitary,
a habitation deserted and forsaken, like the wilderness;
there the calf grazes;
there it lies down and strips its branches.
11 When its boughs are dry, they are broken;
women come and make a fire of them.
[t]For this is a people without discernment;
therefore he who made them will not have compassion on them;
he who formed them will show them no favor.

12 In that day [u]from the river Euphrates[6] to the Brook of Egypt the LORD will thresh
out the grain, and you will be gleaned one by one, O people of Israel. 13 And in that day [v]a
great trumpet will be blown, [w]and those who were lost in the land of Assyria and those
who were driven out to the land of Egypt [x]will come and worship the LORD on the holy
mountain at Jerusalem.

[1] Many Hebrew manuscripts *A vineyard of wine* [2] Hebrew *In those to come* [3] Or *By driving her away*; the meaning of the Hebrew word is uncertain [4] Or *wind* [5] Septuagint *and this is the blessing when I take away his sin* [6] Hebrew *from the River*

27:2–6 In that day the people will dwell in a fruitful vineyard (cf. 5:1–7).

27:2 pleasant vineyard. The city of God is also a vineyard.

27:3 every moment I water it. Contrast "I will also command . . . no rain" in 5:6.

27:4 Would that I had thorns and briers to battle! The vineyard is so clear of infestation that God wishes for some to appear to satisfy his passion to defend the vineyard's purity (cf. 5:6).

27:5 let them make peace with me. The repetition conveys God's desire (cf. 2 Pet. 3:9).

27:6 God's people become a worldwide garden of Eden (cf. 26:18). **Fill the whole world with fruit**, a different image from "fill the face of the world with cities" in 14:21.

27:7–11 The ways of God with his people and with his enemies.

27:7 Has God ever dealt with his people as harshly as he has dealt with their persecutors?

27:8 Measure by measure, by exile. God carefully measured his disciplines, even exile.

27:9 Therefore by this. Restraint has been God's pattern in the past; by the same loving restraint he will bring his people to idol-free purity before him.

27:10–11 The city of this world falls into desolation, fit only for animals and firewood, for the Creator **will show them no favor**.

27:12 from the river Euphrates to the Brook of Egypt. The boundaries of the Promised Land (cf. Gen. 15:18). **you will be gleaned one by one**. God will gather in his chosen people, with his hand on each individual. The agricultural metaphor matches the "vineyard" in Isa. 27:2–6.

27:13 a great trumpet. Matching the "great sword" of v. 1. The Year of Jubilee was announced with the blowing of the trumpet on the Day of Atonement to "proclaim liberty throughout the land" (Lev. 25:8–12). **Assyria . . . Egypt**. See Isa. 19:23–25. All of God's people will be gathered in, with not one lost. **the holy mountain**. See 2:2–4; 25:6–7; 65:17–25; 66:22–23; Rev. 21:9–11.

Judgment on Ephraim and Jerusalem

28

1 Ah, the proud crown of [y]the drunkards of Ephraim,
and the fading flower of its glorious beauty,
which is on the head of the rich valley of those overcome with wine!
2 Behold, the Lord has [z]one who is mighty and strong;
like a storm of hail, a destroying tempest,
like [a]a storm of mighty, overflowing waters,
he casts down to the earth with his hand.
3 [b]The proud crown of the drunkards of Ephraim
will be trodden underfoot;
4 [c]and the fading flower of its glorious beauty,
which is on the head of the rich valley,
will be like [d]a first-ripe fig before the summer:
when someone sees it, he swallows it
as soon as it is in his hand.

5 [e]In that day the LORD of hosts will be a crown of glory,[1]
and a diadem of beauty, to the remnant of his people,
6 and [f]a spirit of justice to him who sits in judgment,
and [g]strength to those who turn back the battle at the gate.

7 [h]These also reel with wine
and [i]stagger with strong drink;
the priest and [j]the prophet reel with strong drink,
they are swallowed by[2] wine,
they stagger with strong drink,
they reel in vision,
they stumble in giving judgment.
8 For all tables are full of filthy vomit,
with no space left.

9 [k]"To whom will he teach knowledge,
and to whom will he explain the message?
Those who are weaned from the milk,
those taken from the breast?
10 For it is precept upon precept, precept upon precept,
line upon line, line upon line,
here a little, there a little."

[1] The Hebrew words for *glory* and *hosts* sound alike [2] Or *confused by*

Chapter 28
1 [y][Hos. 7:5]
2 [z][ch. 8:7] [a]ver. 15, 18
3 [b]ver. 1
4 [c][Amos 8:1, 2] [d]Hos. 9:10; Mic. 7:1
5 [e]ch. 2:11
6 [f][1 Kgs. 3:28] [g][ch. 38:6]
7 [h][ch. 3:12] [i]Hos. 4:11 [j]ch. 9:15; 56:10, 12
9 [k]Jer. 6:10

28:1–35:10 *God's Sovereign Word Spoken into the World: "Ah!"* The Lord speaks into history (chs. 28–33), moving events toward final judgment and salvation (chs. 34–35). He is the powerful ally of his people, above all earthly powers. Therefore, to trust in him is a wise policy for real life in the here and now.

28:1–33:24 *Six Laments, with Assurances.* Isaiah warns his people—and Assyria—against the folly of self-trust, promising God's abundant blessings to those who trust him.

28:1–29 *The Proud Crown of Ephraim.* God's uncomprehending people do not relish his word but choose death.

28:1–6 The northern city of Samaria, with its complacent self-indulgence, will fall to Assyria.

28:1 Ah. Chapters 28–33 are marked by a sixfold exclamation of alarm (28:1; 29:1, 15; 30:1; 31:1; 33:1; cf. 5:8–30). "Ah" represents Hebrew *hoy*, an interjection signaling alarm or grief (LXX translates it as *ouai*, "woe"). **the proud crown of the drunkards of Ephraim.** Isaiah sees the proud city of Samaria, the crown of the northern kingdom, degraded by a degenerate lifestyle. **the fading flower.** The northern kingdom's days are nearly over. Israel fell to Assyria in 722 B.C.

28:2–4 one who is mighty and strong. Assyria. **like a storm of hail . . . like a first-ripe fig.** Isaiah contrasts the force of the invader with the ease of his conquest.

28:5–6 In that day the LORD of hosts will be a crown of glory . . . to the remnant. God preserves his true people who boast in him. **a spirit of justice . . . and strength.** Spiritual leaders are not "overcome with wine" (v. 1) but are filled with the Holy Spirit (cf. Eph. 5:18).

28:7–13 The southern kingdom shares the same drunken distaste for God's word.

28:7 These also. Judah in the south. **the priest and the prophet.** The leaders entrusted with God's word. **swallowed by wine.** The debauched leaders are consumed by what they consume.

28:8 filthy vomit. Though no doubt literal as well, the metaphorical "vomit" of cynicism pours out of Jerusalem's leaders, as in vv. 9–10.

28:9–10 The priests and prophets scoff at Isaiah's message as beneath their intelligence (cf. 1 Cor. 2:14).

11 [l]Cited 1 Cor. 14:21; See ch. 5:26-29
12 [m]ch. 30:15; [Matt. 11:28, 29]
13 [n]ch. 8:15
14 [o]ver. 22; ch. 29:20
15 [p]ver. 2, 18; [ch. 8:7, 8] [q][Rom. 1:25]
16 [r]Cited Rom. 9:33; 1 Pet. 2:6; [Ps. 118:22; Matt. 21:42; Acts 4:11] [s]ch. 14:32
17 [t][2 Kgs. 21:13]
18 [u]ver. 15
19 [v][ch. 50:4] [w][2 Chr. 32:18]
21 [x][2 Sam. 5:20; 1 Chr. 14:11] [y]See Josh. 10:10-14 [z]1 Chr. 14:16; See Josh. 9:3

11 [l]For by people of strange lips
and with a foreign tongue
the LORD will speak to this people,
12 to whom he has said,
[m]"This is rest;
give rest to the weary;
and this is repose";
yet they would not hear.
13 And the word of the LORD will be to them
precept upon precept, precept upon precept,
line upon line, line upon line,
here a little, there a little,
[n]that they may go, and fall backward,
and be broken, and snared, and taken.

A Cornerstone in Zion

14 Therefore hear the word of the LORD, you [o]scoffers,
who rule this people in Jerusalem!
15 Because you have said, "We have made a covenant with death,
and with Sheol we have an agreement,
when the [p]overwhelming whip passes through
it will not come to us,
for we have made [q]lies our refuge,
and in falsehood we have taken shelter";
16 therefore thus says the Lord GOD,
[r]"Behold, I am the one who has laid[1] as a foundation [s]in Zion,
a stone, a tested stone,
a precious cornerstone, of a sure foundation:
'Whoever believes will not be in haste.'
17 And I will make justice [t]the line,
and righteousness [t]the plumb line;
and hail will sweep away the refuge of lies,
and waters will overwhelm the shelter."
18 Then [u]your covenant with death will be annulled,
and your agreement with Sheol will not stand;
when the overwhelming scourge passes through,
you will be beaten down by it.
19 As often as it passes through it will take you;
[v]for morning by morning it will pass through,
by day and by night;
and it will be [w]sheer terror to understand the message.
20 For the bed is too short to stretch oneself on,
and the covering too narrow to wrap oneself in.
21 For the LORD will rise up [x]as on Mount Perazim;
[y]as in the Valley of [z]Gibeon he will be roused;

[1] Dead Sea Scroll *I am laying*

28:11–13 Now that God's people have rejected Isaiah's clear message of **rest** in God, God will speak to them by the **foreign tongue** of invaders (cf. Jer. 5:15). The same invitation saves some and hardens others (cf. Isa. 6:9–10; 8:11–15). (See further Paul's application of this passage to speaking in tongues; 1 Cor. 14:21–22.)

28:14–22 God rebukes the scoffing stupidity of Judah's leaders.

28:15 a covenant with death. Jerusalem's leaders rejoiced over their alliance with Egypt for protection from Assyria (cf. 30:1–5; 31:1–3), but Isaiah rephrases their glad report to reveal the truth of what they have done. **the overwhelming whip**. The Assyrian army.

28:16 God has established another **foundation** for the **Zion** of his remnant people. That **sure foundation**, embodied in Jesus Christ, is the good news that God saves as no one else can (Rom. 9:33; 1 Pet. 2:4–8 combines this with Isa. 8:14; cf. also Rom. 10:11). Isaiah heaps terms upon terms to emphasize that God's salvation is worth believing in. **not be in haste**. Unlike the nervous diplomats of Jerusalem, scurrying about to secure Egypt's guarantee of their salvation.

28:19 it will be sheer terror to understand the message. As the meaning of their repeated calamities dawns on the people, it intensifies their terror.

28:20 The **bed** of misplaced trust offers no rest, the blanket no comfort.

28:21 The Lord fought for Israel against the Philistines at **Mount Perazim** (2 Sam. 5:17–21) and against the Amorites in the **Valley of Gibeon** (Josh.

to do his deed—strange is his deed!
and to work his work—alien is his work!
22 Now therefore do not [a]scoff,
lest your bonds be made strong;
for I have heard [b]a decree of destruction
from the Lord GOD of hosts against the whole land.

23 Give ear, and hear my voice;
give attention, and hear my speech.
24 Does he who plows for sowing plow continually?
Does he continually open and harrow his ground?
25 [c]When he has leveled its surface,
does he not scatter dill, sow cumin,
and put in wheat in rows
and barley in its proper place,
and emmer[1] as the border?
26 [d]For he is rightly instructed;
his God teaches him.

27 Dill is not threshed with a threshing sledge,
nor is a cart wheel rolled over cumin,
but dill is beaten out with a stick,
and cumin with a rod.
28 Does one crush grain for bread?
No, he does not thresh it forever;[2]
when he drives his cart wheel over it
with his horses, he does not crush it.
29 This also comes from the LORD of hosts;
he is [e]wonderful in counsel
and excellent in wisdom.

The Siege of Jerusalem

29

1 Ah, Ariel, Ariel,
the city [f]where David encamped!
Add year to year;
let the feasts run their round.
2 Yet I will distress Ariel,
and there shall be moaning and lamentation,
and she shall be to me like an Ariel.[3]
3 [g]And I will encamp against you all around,
and will besiege you [h]with towers
and I will raise siegeworks against you.
4 [i]And you will be brought low; from the earth you shall speak,
and from the dust your speech will be bowed down;

22[a]ver. 14 [b]ch. 10:23
25[c][ch. 55:10, 11]
26[d][ch. 21:10]
29[e]Jer. 32:19; [ch. 9:6]

Chapter 29

1[f][2 Sam. 5:9]
3[g][2 Kgs. 25:1; Ezek. 4:2] [h][Ezek. 21:22; 26:8]
4[i][ch. 2:11, 12]

[1] A type of wheat [2] Or *Grain is crushed for bread; he will surely thresh it, but not forever* [3] *Ariel* could mean *lion of God*, or *hero* (2 Samuel 23:20), or *altar hearth* (Ezekiel 43:15–16)

10:1–11), but now he rises to do something **strange**—fighting against his own people (cf. Isa. 28:11).

28:22 Isaiah makes a final appeal to repent of scoffing and to hear the word of the Lord.

28:23–29 God's dealings with his people, though "strange" (v. 21), are wise. Like a farmer, God knows that the upheaval of plowing has its appointed season and purpose (vv. 23–26), and that the refining of harvested **grain** must take into account the desired outcome (vv. 27–28). Even so, God uses all the methods of perfect **wisdom** in working with his people (v. 29). He can be trusted in everything.

29:1–14 *The City Where David Encamped.* God will both punish and save Jerusalem, though Jerusalemites in their hypocrisy try to control him through false worship.

29:1–8 The divine Warrior conquers and preserves his people.

29:1 Ah. See note on 28:1. **Ariel, Ariel** (i.e., "Jerusalem, Jerusalem"). The address is repeated out of great sorrow and compassion. The exact meaning of the term "Ariel" is uncertain (Hb. *'Ari'el*). Of the options mentioned in the ESV footnote (29:2), "altar hearth" seems the best for this context. Jerusalem is the place where sacrifices are consumed by fire in order to assuage divine wrath against sin. However, if "Ariel" means "lion of God" or "hero," it is an ironic reminder of the city's former glory. **Add year to year** implies the futility of their repeated annual worship celebrations (cf. 1:11–15).

29:2 God **will distress Ariel** through the Assyrians, who are too incidental to be named. Jerusalem faces God. **she shall be to me like an Ariel.** Like a place where the wrath of God burns.

4[j]See ch. 8:19
5[k]ch. 17:13; Ps. 18:42 [l][ch. 17:14; 37:36; 2 Kgs. 19:35]
6[m][1 Kgs. 19:11, 12]
7[n][Zech. 12:9]; See Mic. 4:11-13 [o]ch. 17:14; [Job 20:8]
8[p][Ps. 73:20; 90:5]
9[r][ch. 19:14; 24:20]
10[s][ch. 6:10; Rom. 11:8]
11[t]ch. 8:16; Dan. 12:4
13[u]Cited Matt. 15:8, 9; Mark 7:6, 7; [Ezek. 33:31] [v][ch. 1:12; 58:2]
14[w]Hab. 1:5; See ch. 3:1-4 [x]Jer. 49:7; Cited 1 Cor. 1:19
15[y][ch. 30:1] [z]Ezek. 8:12

your voice shall come from the ground like [j]the voice of a ghost,
and from the dust your speech shall whisper.
5 But the multitude of your foreign foes shall be like [k]small dust,
and the multitude of the ruthless like passing chaff.
[l]And in an instant, suddenly,
6 [m]you will be visited by the LORD of hosts
with thunder and with earthquake and great noise,
with whirlwind and tempest, and the flame of a devouring fire.
7 And [n]the multitude of all the nations that fight against Ariel,
all that fight against her and her stronghold and distress her,
shall be [o]like a dream, a vision of the night.
8 [p]As when a hungry man dreams, and behold, he is eating
and awakes with his hunger not satisfied,
or as when a thirsty man dreams, and behold, he is drinking
and awakes faint, with his thirst not quenched,
so shall the multitude of all the nations be
that fight against Mount Zion.

9 Astonish yourselves[1] and be astonished;
blind yourselves and be blind!
Be drunk, but not with wine;
[r]stagger, but not with strong drink!
10 [s]For the LORD has poured out upon you
a spirit of deep sleep,
and has closed your eyes (the prophets),
and covered your heads (the seers).

11 And the vision of all this has become to you like the words of a book that is [t]sealed. When men give it to one who can read, saying, "Read this," he says, "I cannot, for it is sealed." 12 And when they give the book to one who cannot read, saying, "Read this," he says, "I cannot read."

13 And the Lord said:
"Because [u]this people [v]draw near with their mouth
and honor me with their lips,
while their hearts are far from me,
and their fear of me is a commandment taught by men,
14 therefore, behold, [w]I will again
do wonderful things with this people,
with wonder upon wonder;
and [x]the wisdom of their wise men shall perish,
and the discernment of their discerning men shall be hidden."

15 Ah, [y]you who hide deep from the LORD your counsel,
whose deeds are [z]in the dark,
and who say, "Who sees us? Who knows us?"

[1] Or *Linger awhile*

29:4 Their exultant festivals will be humbled to pathetic whispers.

29:5–8 See 37:36–38. **And in an instant, suddenly, you will be visited by the LORD of hosts**. The tedious unreality of their worship stands in ironic contrast with the active God whom they profess to worship. It is the nations who prove to be unreal when he dismisses them from usefulness (29:7–8). The mighty God who is able to besiege (vv. 1–4) and defend (vv. 5–8) his people is, to them, a religious bore. They need a radical awakening.

29:9–14 The divine Mystery blinds all who prefer not to see.

29:9–10 Astonish yourselves and be astonished. Isaiah gives up on his bewildered generation, seeing the judgment of God in their incomprehension of God (cf. Deut. 28:28–29; 29:2–4; Isa. 6:9–10; 30:9–10; 63:17; 64:7; Rom. 1:28; 11:7–8).

29:11–12 The nation is indifferent to the message revealed through Isaiah (cf. 28:13).

29:13–14 honor me with their lips. Outwardly proper worship offends God if it is a way of evading him at a deeper level (which is why Jesus quotes v. 13 in Matt. 15:8–9). But God will not be set aside. **wonderful things** (i.e., miraculous works). Even in the human cleverness that disregards him, God's overruling power is accomplishing his own purpose (cf. 1 Cor. 1:19).

29:15–24 *Those Who Turn Things Upside Down.* The divine Potter will reshape the world, as he promised.

29:15–16 Ah. See note on 28:1. Rather than demonstrate a forthright openness inspired by trust in God, the leaders of Judah are reduced to the secrecy of underhanded human politics. For them, the sovereign God might as well

16 [a]You turn things upside down!
Shall the potter be regarded as the clay,
that the thing made should say of its maker,
"He did not make me";
or the thing formed say of him who formed it,
"He has no understanding"?
17 Is it not yet a very little while
[b]until Lebanon shall be turned into a fruitful field,
and the fruitful field shall be regarded as a forest?
18 In that day [c]the deaf shall hear
[d]the words of a book,
and out of their gloom and darkness
[e]the eyes of the blind shall see.
19 [f]The meek shall obtain fresh joy in the LORD,
and the poor among mankind shall exult in the Holy One of Israel.
20 For the ruthless shall come to nothing
and [g]the scoffer cease,
and all who watch to do evil shall be cut off,
21 who by a word make a man out to be an offender,
and [h]lay a snare for him who reproves in the gate,
and with an empty plea [i]turn aside him who is in the right.

22 Therefore thus says the LORD, [j]who redeemed Abraham, concerning the house of Jacob:

"Jacob shall no more be ashamed,
no more shall his face grow pale.
23 For when he sees his children,
[k]the work of my hands, in his midst,
they will sanctify my name;
[l]they will sanctify the Holy One of Jacob
and will stand in awe of the God of Israel.
24 And those [m]who go astray in spirit will come to understanding,
and those who murmur will accept instruction."

Do Not Go Down to Egypt

30 1 "Ah, [n]stubborn children," declares the LORD,
[o]"who carry out a plan, but not mine,
and who make [p]an alliance,[1] but not of my Spirit,
that they may add sin to sin;
2 [q]who set out to go down to Egypt,
without asking for my direction,
to take refuge in the protection of Pharaoh
and to seek shelter in the shadow of Egypt!

[1] Hebrew *who weave a web*

16[a]See ch. 10:15
17[b][Ps. 107:33, 35]
18[c][ch. 32:3; 35:5; Matt. 11:5] [d]ver. 12 [e][ch. 35:5; Matt. 11:5]
19[f]ch. 61:1; [ch. 14:32; Zeph. 3:12; Matt. 5:3]
20[g]ch. 28:14, 22
21[h]Amos 5:10; [Ps. 127:5] [i]Amos 5:12
22[j][ch. 51:2]
23[k]ch. 19:25; 60:21; [Ps. 100:3] [l]ch. 8:13
24[m][ch. 28:7]

Chapter 30

1[n][ch. 1:2, 4] [o][ch. 29:15] [p]ch. 25:7
2[q]ch. 31:1; 36:6

not exist. For the **potter** and **clay** imagery (29:16), cf. 43:1; 45:9; 64:8; Rom. 9:20.

29:17–21 Despite human unbelief, God plans to transform the moral order of the world. The metaphors of v. 17 are explained in vv. 18–21. The gospel of Christ is God's means of accomplishing this transformation (cf. 61:1–3).

29:22–24 Despite their failures, God will keep his promises to the descendants of Abraham, who himself needed redemption (cf. Josh. 24:1–3, 14–15). Note that the empty worship of Isa. 29:13 will be replaced with the **awe** of v. 23, and the furtiveness of v. 15 will be replaced by the openness of v. 24 (which is the hope of every troubled church).

30:1–33 ***Stubborn Children with Their Own Plans.*** When his people are faithless, God remains faithful.

30:1–7 Judah trusts in Egypt, a worthless ally. Egypt had its own interest in keeping Judah as a buffer state for protection against Assyria.

30:1 Ah. See note on 28:1. **an alliance**. Judah, under threat from Assyria, negotiates a pact of defense with Egypt (cf. 36:6). But God had already promised to defend his people, while Egypt offers only death (cf. 28:14–15). **who carry out a plan, but not mine**. The Lord denounces all who make and carry out their own plans rather than submitting to and carrying out the plans that God has revealed to his people. The result of such lack of faith and disobedience is always "shame and disgrace" (30:5). To reject God's plan is to reject God himself and so to come under his judgment. **add sin to sin**. Once a practical trust in God is abandoned, one sin leads to another.

30:2 who set out to go down to Egypt. The envoys of Judah travel to Egypt to buy protection. Ironically, they return to their original oppressor, reversing their salvation (cf. Ex. 1:8–22).

3 [r]Therefore shall the protection of Pharaoh turn to your shame,
and the shelter in the shadow of Egypt to your humiliation.
4 For though his officials are at [s]Zoan
and [t]his envoys reach [u]Hanes,
5 everyone comes to shame
through [v]a people that cannot profit them,
that brings neither help nor profit,
but shame and disgrace."

6 An [w]oracle on [x]the beasts of [y]the Negeb.

Through a land of trouble and anguish,
from where come the lioness and the lion,
the adder and the [z]flying fiery serpent,
they carry their riches on the backs of donkeys,
and their treasures on the humps of camels,
to a people that cannot profit them.
7 Egypt's [a]help is worthless and empty;
therefore I have called her
[b]"Rahab who sits still."

A Rebellious People

8 And now, go, [c]write it before them on a tablet
and inscribe it in a book,
that it may be for the time to come
as a witness forever.[1]
9 [d]For they are a rebellious people,
lying children,
children unwilling to hear
the instruction of the LORD;
10 [e]who say to [f]the seers, "Do not see,"
and to the prophets, "Do not prophesy to us what is right;
speak to us [g]smooth things,
prophesy illusions,
11 leave the way, turn aside from the path,
let us hear no more about the Holy One of Israel."
12 Therefore thus says the Holy One of Israel,
"Because you despise this word
and trust in [h]oppression and perverseness
and rely on them,
13 therefore this iniquity shall be to you
[i]like a breach in a high wall, bulging out, and about to collapse,
whose breaking comes suddenly, in an instant;
14 and its breaking is [j]like that of a potter's vessel
that is smashed so ruthlessly

[1] Some Hebrew manuscripts, Syriac, Targum, Vulgate, and Greek versions; Masoretic Text *forever and ever*

3[r][ver. 7; ch. 20:5]
4[s]See ch. 19:11 [t][Ezek. 17:15] [u][Jer. 43:7]
5[v][ver. 7; Jer. 2:36]
6[w]See ch. 13:1 [x][ch. 51:9; Ps. 68:30] [y][Acts 8:26] [z][Deut. 8:15]
7[a]ch. 36:6 [b]ch. 51:9
8[c]Hab. 2:2
9[d]ver. 1
10[e]Amos 2:12; [Amos 7:12, 13] [f]See 1 Sam. 9:9 [g][1 Kgs. 22:13]; See Jer. 28:1-11; Ezek. 13:8-16
12[h][ch. 5:8, 20]
13[i]Ps. 62:3
14[j]Ps. 2:9

30:4 Zoan . . . Hanes. Cities of Egypt.

30:6–7 With ironic solemnity, Isaiah mocks the Judean embassy carrying payment to the court of Egypt. The danger and difficulty of the journey, the expense of the purchase, and its disappointing outcome reveal the stupidity of the plan. **Rahab who sits still**. For Rahab as a poetical name for Egypt, see Ps. 87:4; for another oracle against Egypt, see Ezek. 29:3. Like a monster inhabiting the Nile, Egypt appears formidable but, in fact, just sits there.

30:8–17 Judah prefers to trust in illusions, which God likens to an unsteady wall.

30:8 write it. God instructs Isaiah to record his message against Egyptian aid **for the time to come** (cf. 8:16). His ministry would benefit later generations.

30:9–12 Isaiah's generation feared Assyrian aggression. The prophet understands that the real threat to them is their unwillingness to hear God's saving word. **smooth things . . . illusions**. For the popularity of false prophets in Judah, see Jer. 6:13–14; 8:11; 14:13–14; 23:17; Ezek. 13:10–16; Mic. 2:6–11; 3:5, 11. The people prefer to hear false reassurances. More deeply, they are rejecting "the Holy One of Israel" himself. **Therefore thus says the Holy One of Israel**. The One they reject still speaks.

30:13–14 Therefore resumes "Therefore . . . because" in v. 12. **like a breach in a high wall**. Isaiah compares Egyptian protection with a wall under pressure, collapsible at any moment. **its breaking is like that of a potter's vessel**. Egypt's promises of aid will be smashed to bits. Appearances can be deceiving.

30:15–17 Isaiah articulates the heart of the matter. With the authority of

that among its fragments not a shard is found
with which to take fire from the hearth,
or to dip up water out of the cistern."

15 For thus said the Lord GOD, the Holy One of Israel,
"In [k]returning[1] and [l]rest you shall be saved;
in quietness and in trust shall be your strength."
But you were unwilling, **16** and you said,
"No! We will flee upon [m]horses";
therefore you shall flee away;
and, "We will ride upon swift steeds";
therefore your pursuers shall be swift.
17 [n]A thousand shall flee at the threat of one;
at the threat of five you shall flee,
till you are left
like a flagstaff on the top of a mountain,
like a signal on a hill.

The LORD Will Be Gracious

18 Therefore the LORD [o]waits to be gracious to you,
and therefore he [p]exalts himself to show mercy to you.
For the LORD is a God of justice;
[q]blessed are all those who wait for him.

19 For a people shall dwell [r]in Zion, in Jerusalem; you shall weep no more. He will surely
be gracious to you at the sound of your cry. As soon as he hears it, he answers you. **20** And
though the Lord give you the [s]bread of adversity and the [s]water of affliction, [t]yet your
Teacher will not hide himself anymore, but your eyes shall see your Teacher. **21** [u]And your
ears shall hear a word behind you, saying, "This is [v]the way, walk in it," when you turn to
the right or when you turn to the left. **22** Then you will defile your carved idols overlaid
with silver and your gold-plated metal images. [w]You will scatter them as unclean things.
You will say to them, "Be gone!"

23 [x]And he will give [y]rain for the seed with which you sow the ground, and bread, the
produce of the ground, which will be rich and plenteous. [z]In that day your livestock will
graze in large pastures, **24** and [a]the oxen and the donkeys that work the ground will eat
seasoned fodder, which has been winnowed with shovel and fork. **25** And [b]on every lofty
mountain and every high hill there will be brooks running with water, in the day of the
great slaughter, [c]when the towers fall. **26** [d]Moreover, the light of the moon will be as the
light of the sun, and the light of the sun will be sevenfold, as the light of seven days, in
the day when [e]the LORD binds up [f]the brokenness of his people, and heals the wounds
inflicted by his blow.

[1] Or *repentance*

15 [k]Hos. 14:1 [l][Ex. 14:14]
16 [m]ch. 31:1, 3; [Hos. 14:3]
17 [n][Lev. 26:8; Deut. 32:30]
18 [o][Hab. 2:3] [p]ch. 5:16 [q]Ps. 2:12; 34:8; Prov. 16:20; Jer. 17:7
19 [r][ch. 14:32]
20 [s]1 Kgs. 22:27; Ps. 127:2; [Ezek. 4:10, 11] [t][ch. 3:1, 2]
21 [u][Jer. 31:33, 34] [v]ch. 35:8; [Acts 9:2]
22 [w]ch. 2:20; 31:7; [Hos. 14:8]
23 [x][ch. 32:20; Ps. 144:13, 14] [y][Jer. 5:24] [z][Ps. 65:13]
24 [a]See Gen. 45:6
25 [b][ch. 33:21; Ps. 107:35; Joel 3:18] [c]ch. 32:19; [ch. 2:15]
26 [d]ch. 60:19, 20 [e][Hos. 6:1] [f][ch. 1:5, 6]

the Lord GOD, the Holy One of Israel, the secret to Judah's strength has been revealed: **In returning** (or repentance, see ESV footnote) **and rest . . . in quietness and in trust**. This is the true path to victory and peace, but their general disinclination to heed the word of God (v. 9) becomes clear in their rejection of this particular message (cf. 28:12). **We will flee upon horses**. Refusing God's salvation commits them to military action, which he will frustrate (cf. Lev. 26:7–8; Deut. 32:30; Josh. 23:10). **like a flagstaff**. See Isa. 1:7–8; 6:11–12.

30:18–26 God promises ultimate abundance, purified of idols.

30:18 Therefore the LORD waits to be gracious to you. Note the amazing logic of grace: God's people forsake him for a false salvation (vv. 1–17); therefore, he is gracious to them (v. 18). But he waits, for **the LORD is a God of justice**, i.e., he knows the perfect way to achieve his purpose, the perfect time to go into action, and the perfect disciplinary process that will awaken Judah.

30:20–21 your Teacher. Contrast v. 9. **This is the way, walk in it**. Contrast v. 11. Isaiah foresees the internalized law of the new covenant (cf. Jer. 31:31–34; Ezek. 36:25–27) and the internal guidance of the Holy Spirit (cf. Rom. 8:14; Gal. 5:16, 18, 25).

30:22 idols. Foreign entanglements are replaced by wholehearted loyalty to the Lord.

30:23–26 And he will . . . Isaiah portrays the anticipated new order that will establish the messianic kingdom (cf. Deut. 28:1–14). The details in this OT portrayal suggest the glorious reality and fullness of the blessing. Some would see this as a *poetic* description of the glorious new messianic order (something that will be so new and different that it can be described adequately only in poetic terms), though others would hold that this is a *literal* description of the new messianic order.

30:26 For **light** as an image, see 9:2; 60:19; John 8:12; Rev. 21:23; 22:5. **heals**. See Isa. 1:6; 53:5; 57:16–19; 61:1; Jer. 33:6; Rev. 22:2.

28[g]ch. 11:4; 2 Thess. 2:8 [h][ch. 8:8; Nah. 1:8] [i]ch. 37:29
29[j]1 Sam. 10:5; 1 Kgs. 1:40 [k]ch. 2:3 [l]ch. 26:4; 44:8; Deut. 32:18
30[m]Ps. 18:13 [n]ch. 29:6 [o]ch. 28:2; [Josh. 10:11]
31[p]ch. 9:4; [Mic. 6:9]
32[q]Ex. 15:1 [r]ch. 11:15; 19:16; [ch. 2:19]
33[s]2 Kgs. 23:10; Jer. 7:31 [t]Ezek. 24:9, 10 [u]Ps. 18:8; Ezek. 20:48

Chapter 31

1[v]ch. 30:2; 36:6 [w]Ps. 20:7; [ch. 30:16; 36:9] [x][ch. 22:11]
2[y][Ps. 94:8-10] [z][Num. 23:19] [a][ch. 22:14] [b]Ps. 94:4
3[c]Jer. 17:5

27 Behold, the name of the LORD comes from afar,
burning with his anger, and in thick rising smoke;[1]
his lips are full of fury,
and his tongue is like a devouring fire;
28 [g]his breath is [h]like an overflowing stream
that reaches up to the neck;
to sift the nations with the sieve of destruction,
and to place on the jaws of the peoples [i]a bridle that leads astray.

29 You shall have a song as in the night when a holy feast is kept, and gladness of heart,
[j]as when one sets out to the sound of the flute to go to [k]the mountain of the LORD, to
[l]the Rock of Israel. **30** And the LORD [m]will cause his majestic voice to be heard and the
descending blow of his arm to be seen, in furious anger [n]and a flame of devouring fire,
with a cloudburst [o]and storm and hailstones. **31** The Assyrians will be terror-stricken at the
voice of the LORD, [p]when he strikes with his rod. **32** And every stroke of the appointed staff
that the LORD lays on them [q]will be to the sound of tambourines and lyres. [r]Battling with
brandished arm, he will fight with them. **33** For [s]a burning place[2] has long been prepared;
indeed, for the king it is made ready, [t]its pyre made deep and wide, with fire and wood in
abundance; [u]the breath of the LORD, like a stream of sulfur, kindles it.

Woe to Those Who Go Down to Egypt

31

1 Woe to [v]those who go down to Egypt for help
and rely on horses,
who [w]trust in chariots because they are many
and in horsemen because they are very strong,
but [x]do not look to the Holy One of Israel
or consult the LORD!
2 And [y]yet he is wise and brings disaster;
[z]he does not call back his words,
but [a]will arise against the house of the evildoers
and against the helpers of [b]those who work iniquity.
3 The Egyptians are man, and not God,
and their horses [c]are flesh, and not spirit.
When the LORD stretches out his hand,
the helper will stumble, and he who is helped will fall,
and they will all perish together.

[1] Hebrew *in weight of uplifted clouds* [2] Or *For Topheth*

30:27–33 God promises immediate intervention, a glad victory.

30:27 The name of the LORD is matched by "the voice of the LORD" in v. 31 and "the breath of the LORD" in v. 33. With all that he is, God preserves his people. **From afar** is matched by "long" in v. 33. God may seem far away, but he is drawing near. Judgment may be long delayed, but it is coming. **burning**. See Ps. 18:6–15 and Hab. 3:2–15. Assyria and every earthly power are no match.

30:28–30 The wrath of God is greeted joyfully by his people, as he intervenes with an open display of his power on their behalf.

30:31 strikes with his rod. See 37:36–38.

30:32 he will fight. Not the worthless Egyptian army, but God himself. The role of his people is simply to celebrate with **tambourines and lyres** (cf. Ex. 15:19–21; 1 Sam. 18:6–7).

30:33 The victories of God within history foreshadow his final triumph. **a burning place**. Topheth (ESV footnote) was a location in the Hinnom Valley (2 Kings 23:10) where Judeans had burned their children in sacrifice; here it is a place where God's enemies are destroyed. **the king**. The Assyrian tyrant, and every other tyrant in history.

31:1–32:20 *Those Who Go Down to Egypt for Help.* God calls his people to stop trusting in man and return to him, promising them the Messiah and his Spirit.

31:1–5 The futility of Egypt is contrasted with the power of God.

31:1 Woe. See note on 28:1. **go down to Egypt for help**. See 28:15; 29:15; 30:1–7, 16. **horses . . . chariots . . . horsemen**. A military advantage desirable to Judah, but already defeated by God (cf. Ex. 14:5–28; 15:2, 4; Deut. 17:16; 1 Kings 10:28–29; Ps. 20:7; Isa. 2:7; 36:8–9). **many . . . very strong**. Judah is deceived by appearances (cf. Ps. 147:10–11).

31:2 he is wise and brings disaster. Judah's diplomats think they are wise in enlisting Egyptian aid to avert disaster, but God is wise enough to use their plans actually to bring disaster. **does not call back his words**. Unlike human leaders, God is so wise that he does not have to change course on the basis of new information.

31:3 Isaiah argues for the superiority of a spiritual ally (cf. 2 Chron. 32:8; Ps. 56:4; 146:3–4; Isa. 2:22; 40:28–30; Jer. 17:5–6). **stretches out his hand**. With minimal effort. The **helper** is Egypt; **he who is helped** is Judah.

4 For thus the LORD said to me,
[d]"As a lion or a young lion growls over his prey,
and when a band of shepherds is called out against him
he is not terrified by their shouting
or daunted at their noise,
[e]so the LORD of hosts will come down
to fight[1] on Mount Zion and on its hill.
5 [f]Like birds hovering, so the LORD of hosts
will protect Jerusalem;
he will protect and deliver it;
he will spare and rescue it."

6 [g]Turn to him from whom people[2] have [h]deeply revolted, O children of Israel. 7 For
in that day [i]everyone shall cast away his idols of silver and his idols of gold, which your
hands have sinfully made for you.

8 [j]"And the Assyrian shall fall by a sword, not of man;
and a sword, not of man, shall devour him;
and he shall flee from the sword,
and his young men shall be [k]put to forced labor.
9 [l]His rock shall pass away in terror,
and his officers desert the standard in panic,"
declares the LORD, whose [m]fire is in Zion,
and whose [n]furnace is in Jerusalem.

A King Will Reign in Righteousness

32 1 Behold, [o]a king will reign in righteousness,
and princes will rule in justice.
2 [p]Each will be like a hiding place from the wind,
a shelter from the storm,
[q]like streams of water in a dry place,
like the shade of a great rock in a weary land.
3 [r]Then the eyes of those who see will not be closed,
and the ears of those who hear will give attention.
4 The heart of the hasty will understand and know,
[s]and the tongue of the stammerers will hasten to speak distinctly.
5 [t]The fool will no more be called noble,
nor the scoundrel said to be honorable.
6 For [u]the fool speaks folly,
and his heart is busy with iniquity,
to practice ungodliness,
to utter error concerning the LORD,
[v]to leave the craving of the hungry unsatisfied,
and to deprive the thirsty of drink.

[1] The Hebrew words for *hosts* and *to fight* sound alike [2] Hebrew *they*

4 [d]Hos. 11:10; Amos 1:2; 3:8 [e][ch. 42:13]
5 [f]Deut. 32:11; [Ps. 91:4]
6 [g][ch. 30:15] [h]ch. 1:5
7 [i]ch. 2:20; 30:22
8 [j]ch. 37:36 [k][Gen. 49:15; Prov. 12:24]
9 [l]Deut. 32:31; See ch. 30:29 [m]ch. 30:33 [n]Ps. 21:9; Mal. 4:1

Chapter 32

1 [o]Ps. 72:1, 2, 4; Jer. 23:5; See ch. 11:1-4
2 [p]ch. 4:6; 25:4 [q]ch. 33:21
3 [r]See ch. 29:18
4 [s]ch. 35:6
5 [t][ch. 5:20]
6 [u]1 Sam. 24:13 [v][ch. 3:14, 15]

31:4–5 Judah's true Helper is like both an unperturbed **lion** straddling its defeated prey and a bird gently hovering over its nest. **Come down** matches "go down" in v. 1.

31:6–9 The victory of God should lead to the repentance of his people.

31:6–7 Turn to him. See 30:15. **deeply revolted**. Judah has to be told that their apostasy is serious. **idols**. See 2:20.

31:8 See 37:36–38. **a sword, not of man**. Judah does not need Egyptian defense.

31:9 His rock. Probably the king of Assyria, in contrast with the "Rock" of 30:29 and the king in 32:1. **fire**. See 6:6–7 and 33:14. When Assyria attacked Jerusalem, they walked into a furnace.

32:1–20 The messianic King rules his transformed people.

32:1 Behold, a king will reign. Isaiah foresees the triumph of the Messiah (cf. 7:14; 9:2–7; 11:1–10). **in righteousness**. Unlike the apostate leaders of Judah or the plundering king of Assyria. **princes**. See 1 Pet. 5:1–4 for the ideal leadership for God's people.

32:2 Each. The Messiah allows for no inept or corrupt leaders. God's people will be sheltered from every threat forever (cf. Jer. 3:15; 23:4).

32:3–4 Not only will a perfect king reign in righteousness, but his subjects will be perfected in responsiveness (cf. 29:24).

32:5–8 Social ideals are redefined so that prestige goes only to the truly noble.

32:5 The fool. The leaders of Judah were fools for setting God aside (cf. 7:10–12; 28:14; 29:14–16).

32:6 to leave the craving of the hungry unsatisfied. Isaiah denounces

7[w]Mic. 2:1, 2
9[x]See ch. 3:16–4:1 [y]Amos 6:1
11[y][See ver. 9 above] [z][ch. 47:2, 3] [a]See Gen. 37:34
12[b][ch. 24:7]
13[c]ch. 7:23; 34:13; Hos. 9:6 [d][ch. 24:11, 12]
14[e]Jer. 2:24
15[f][ch. 11:2; Joel 2:28] [g]ch. 35:1, 2; [ch. 29:17]
17[h]James 3:18; [ch. 1:27; Ps. 72:3; 119:165]
19[i]ch. 28:2, 17 [j]ch. 26:5

7 As for the scoundrel—[w]his devices are evil;
he plans wicked schemes
to ruin the poor with lying words,
even when the plea of the needy is right.
8 But he who is noble plans noble things,
and on noble things he stands.

Complacent Women Warned of Disaster

9 [x]Rise up, you women [y]who are at ease, hear my voice;
you complacent daughters, give ear to my speech.
10 In little more than a year
you will shudder, you complacent women;
for the grape harvest fails,
the fruit harvest will not come.
11 Tremble, you women [y]who are at ease,
shudder, you complacent ones;
[z]strip, and make yourselves bare,
[a]and tie sackcloth around your waist.
12 [b]Beat your breasts for the pleasant fields,
for the fruitful vine,
13 [c]for the soil of my people
growing up in thorns and briers,
[d]yes, for all the joyous houses
in the exultant city.
14 For the palace is forsaken,
the populous city deserted;
the hill and the watchtower
will become dens forever,
[e]a joy of wild donkeys,
a pasture of flocks;
15 until [f]the Spirit is poured upon us from on high,
and [g]the wilderness becomes a fruitful field,
and the fruitful field is deemed a forest.
16 Then justice will dwell in the wilderness,
and righteousness abide in the fruitful field.
17 [h]And the effect of righteousness will be peace,
and the result of righteousness, quietness and trust[1] forever.
18 My people will abide in a peaceful habitation,
in secure dwellings, and in quiet resting places.
19 [i]And it will hail when the forest falls down,
[j]and the city will be utterly laid low.

[1] Or *security*

leaders who disregard the proper needs of those in their charge (cf. Jer. 2:8; 10:21; 23:1).

32:8 Isaiah foresees a kingdom of true human nobility, by the grace of God. **he who is noble plans noble things**. Those who have the powerful position of "nobles" should aim at true nobility by planning ways to bring good to others and to advance the kingdom of God on the earth.

32:9 These verses make more pointed the general call to repentance in 31:6. The **women who are at ease** are the spiritually heedless women of Jerusalem (cf. 3:16–4:1).

32:10 The Assyrian invasion of 701 B.C. (see ch. 36) is **little more than a year** away, but the people are too careless to see it coming.

32:11–12 A call to serious repentance.

32:13 all the joyous houses in the exultant city. This is a false, escapist joy, which can be seen in 24:7–11 and is now active in Jerusalem.

32:15 until the Spirit is poured upon us from on high. Salvation is beyond all human capability. The One who is spirit (31:3) not only defends his people but also enriches them with new life: **the wilderness becomes a fruitful field**, reversing the disasters of 32:14 (cf. 44:3; 65:17–25; Joel 2:28–32).

32:17–18 quietness and trust forever. See 30:15. The word translated "complacent" in 32:9 (Hb. *batakh*) is from the same root as the word translated "trust" in v. 17 (Hb. *betakh*) and the word translated **"secure"** in v. 18 (Hb. *mibtakh*). In addition, the word translated "at ease" in v. 9 (Hb. *sha'anan*) is translated **"quiet"** in v. 18. The worldly counterfeit is replaced by the real.

32:19–20 Isaiah concludes the vision of messianic glory with two metaphors: the destruction of Assyria and the humbling of Jerusalem in the short term (v. 19), with the undisturbed peace of the Messiah's kingdom in the long term (v. 20). See 30:23–26.

32:19 it will hail when the forest falls down. The hail represents God's judgment on the nation of Assyria, the "forest" which God will fell (cf. 10:18, 33–34; 30:31). **The city . . . utterly laid low** in humiliation is Jerusalem (cf. 32:12–14), whose pride must be humbled before it can be restored to

20 [k]Happy are you who sow beside all waters,
who let the feet of the ox and the donkey range free.

O Lord, Be Gracious to Us

33

1 [l]Ah, you destroyer,
who yourself have not been destroyed,
you traitor,
whom none has betrayed!
When you have ceased to destroy,
you will be destroyed;
and when you have finished betraying,
they will betray you.

2 O LORD, be gracious to us; [m]we wait for you.
Be our arm every morning,
our salvation in the time of trouble.
3 [n]At the tumultuous noise peoples flee;
when you lift yourself up, nations are scattered,
4 and your spoil is gathered as the caterpillar gathers;
[o]as locusts leap, it is leapt upon.

5 [p]The LORD is exalted, for he dwells on high;
he will fill Zion with justice and righteousness,
6 [q]and he will be the stability of your times,
abundance of salvation, wisdom, and knowledge;
the fear of the LORD is Zion's[1] treasure.

7 Behold, their heroes cry in the streets;
[r]the envoys of peace weep bitterly.
8 [s]The highways lie waste;
the traveler ceases.
[t]Covenants are broken;
cities[2] are despised;
there is no regard for man.
9 [u]The land mourns and languishes;
Lebanon is confounded and withers away;
Sharon is like a desert,
and Bashan and Carmel shake off their leaves.

10 [v]"Now I will arise," says the LORD,
"now I will lift myself up;
now I will be exalted.
11 [w]You conceive chaff; you give birth to stubble;
your breath is [x]a fire that will consume you.

[1] Hebrew *his* [2] Masoretic Text; Dead Sea Scroll *witnesses*

20[k]Eccles. 11:1; [ch. 30:23]
Chapter 33
1[l]ch. 21:2; [ch. 17:14]
2[m]ch. 25:9; 26:8
3[n]ch. 17:13; [2 Kgs. 19:7]
4[o][Joel 2:4, 5]
5[p]ch. 2:17; 5:15, 16
6[q][ch. 39:8]
7[r][ch. 36:22; 2 Kgs. 18:37]
8[s][Judg. 5:6] [t][ver. 1]; See 2 Kgs. 18:14-17
9[u]ch. 24:4; [Nah. 1:4]
10[v]Ps. 12:5; 68:1; [ch. 10:26]
11[w][ch. 59:4; Ps. 7:14] [x]ch. 10:16, 17; [Ps. 80:16]

righteousness (vv. 16–17). Before Israel can become "a peaceful habitation, in secure dwellings" (v. 18), it too must undergo God's discipline for its sin.

33:1–24 ***The Destroyer Who Has Not Been Destroyed.*** Assyria, the enemy that has been destroying God's people with apparent impunity, will itself be destroyed, but God will visit his people with his saving presence.

33:1–6 The Lord defends his trusting people.

33:1 Ah. See note on 28:1. **destroyer . . . traitor**. Unscrupulous, successful Assyria.

33:2 This verse gives voice to the practical, daily trust in God that Isaiah is calling for.

33:3–4 when you. I.e., God. **your spoil**. I.e., the spoils of war, left after the defeat of the "destroyer" nations, gathered in by God's people who inherit his final victory (cf. Ex. 3:21–22; Isa. 9:3; 11:14; 33:23). Isaiah speaks to God (v. 3), then to God's people (v. 4).

33:5–6 stability. This confidence lies at the heart of Isaiah's message. **Zion's treasure**, unlike the treasures of the nations taken as spoil (v. 4), is an endless resource (cf. Ps. 31:19).

33:7–12 The Lord intervenes for his repentant people.

33:7–9 Covenants are broken. Judah paid Assyria to withdraw its army, but it still attacked, demanding total surrender (see ch. 36; hence, "you traitor" in 33:1).

33:7 Their heroes are Judah's soldiers; **the envoys** are their diplomats (cf. 36:22).

33:10 Now . . . now . . . now. God has waited, apparently inactive. Now that his people turn to his grace (v. 2), his kingdom comes.

33:11–12 God dooms Assyria's plan against Judah, repeating the prophecy of v. 1. For **fire** as an image of God protecting his people, see 9:19; 10:16–17; 26:11; 29:6; 31:9; 66:15–16.

12[x][See ver. 11 above] 14[y][Ps. 15:1; 24:3] [z]ch. 66:15; Heb. 12:29 15[a][Ps. 15:2; 24:4] [b]Ps. 119:37 16[c]ch. 30:23, 25 17[d]ch. 6:5; [Zech. 9:9] [e][ch. 54:2, 3] 18[f][Ps. 37:10] [g][2 Kgs. 18:14] [h][Ps. 48:12] 19[i][2 Kgs. 19:32, 33] [j]ch. 28:11; Deut. 28:49, 50 20[k]ch. 32:18 [l]ver. 6 21[m]Ps. 46:4, 5 [n][ch. 2:16; Ps. 48:7] 22[o][Judg. 2:16] [p]James 4:12 [q][1 Sam. 12:13]

12 And the peoples will be as if burned to lime,
[x]like thorns cut down, that are burned in the fire."

13 Hear, you who are far off, what I have done;
and you who are near, acknowledge my might.
14 The sinners in Zion are afraid;
trembling has seized the godless:
[y]"Who among us can dwell [z]with the consuming fire?
Who among us can dwell with everlasting burnings?"
15 [a]He who walks righteously and speaks uprightly,
who despises the gain of oppressions,
who shakes his hands, lest they hold a bribe,
who stops his ears from hearing of bloodshed
[b]and shuts his eyes from looking on evil,
16 he will dwell on the heights;
his place of defense will be the fortresses of rocks;
[c]his bread will be given him; his water will be sure.

17 [d]Your eyes will behold the king in his beauty;
[e]they will see a land that stretches afar.
18 [f]Your heart will muse on the terror:
"Where is he who counted, where is [g]he who weighed the tribute?
Where is [h]he who counted the towers?"
19 [i]You will see no more the insolent people,
the people [j]of an obscure speech that you cannot comprehend,
stammering in a tongue that you cannot understand.
20 Behold Zion, the city of our appointed feasts!
[k]Your eyes will see Jerusalem,
an untroubled habitation, an [l]immovable tent,
whose stakes will never be plucked up,
nor will any of its cords be broken.
21 But there the LORD in majesty will be for us
a place of [m]broad rivers and streams,
[n]where no galley with oars can go,
nor majestic ship can pass.
22 For the LORD is our [o]judge; the LORD is our [p]lawgiver;
the LORD is our [q]king; he will save us.

33:13–24 The Lord alone will secure his people forever.

33:13–14 You who are far off are the **godless**, and **you who are near** are **sinners in Zion**. All of God's people everywhere, called to share his holiness, are confronted by their own unholiness (cf. 6:1–7). See notes on 29:1 and 29:2.

33:15 See Ps. 15:1–5 and 24:3–6. Isaiah emphasizes the practical, transforming power of God's grace, because his generation's faith was diminished to the theoretical. But the kingdom is for transformed people. **who despises the gain of oppressions**. The righteous person who **walks righteously** refuses gain from oppression, even if such gain is obtained "legally" because the laws are skewed to protect the powerful and deprive the powerless of what is rightfully theirs. **who stops his ears from hearing of bloodshed and shuts his eyes from looking on evil**. The faithful person, who shares God's delights and grief, will refuse (1) to listen to plans to commit violence and (2) to look approvingly on any evildoing. While the godless person (Isa. 33:14) is captivated by graphic descriptions of violence and moral perversion, the righteous person is grieved and offended to read about or look at such things.

33:16 To **dwell on the heights** is to be near God (v. 5).

33:17 Your eyes will behold (i.e., you will enjoy the personal experience of) **the king in his beauty** (i.e., the Messiah wonderfully displayed). The Messiah-King is identified with the Lord in vv. 21–22. **A land that stretches afar** will provide freedom of movement, with no enemy pressing in.

33:18–19 The redeemed recall with wonder the victory of God. Isaiah describes the eternal joy of God's people in terms of the Assyrian threat in his own time. **people of an obscure speech**. See note on 28:11–13.

33:20 God's people are secured forever in their perfect home, reversing the distress of vv. 7–9 (cf. 4:5; 32:17–18).

33:21 broad rivers and streams. Abundant provision (cf. 41:18). **where no galley with oars can go**. No possible attack is by sea, matching the secure land in 33:17.

33:22 the LORD . . . the LORD . . . the LORD . . . he. The redeemed finally attribute all of their happiness to their all-sufficient Lord alone. Three different functions that are generally carried out by human governments are here attributed to the Lord: **judge** (for deciding proper interpretations and applications of laws), **lawgiver** (for making laws), and **king** (for enforcing the laws and defending the nation). This does not exclude human governments, but shows that government rightly fulfills its role only when it is carried out in submission to the will and purpose and laws of God. Isaiah looks forward to the future time when this will be fulfilled, when the messianic King will "reign in righteousness" (32:1).

23 Your cords hang loose;
they cannot hold the mast firm in its place
or keep the sail spread out.
[r]Then prey and spoil in abundance will be divided;
even [s]the lame will take the prey.
24 And no inhabitant will say, [t]"I am sick";
[u]the people who dwell there will be forgiven their iniquity.

Judgment on the Nations

34

1 Draw near, [v]O nations, to hear,
and give attention, O peoples!
Let the earth hear, and all that fills it;
the world, and all that comes from it.
2 For the LORD is enraged against all the nations,
and furious against all their host;
he has [w]devoted them to destruction,[1] has given them over for slaughter.
3 Their slain shall be cast out,
and [x]the stench of their corpses shall rise;
[y]the mountains shall flow with their blood.
4 [z]All the host of heaven shall rot away,
and the skies roll up like a scroll.
All their host shall fall,
as leaves fall from the vine,
like leaves falling from the fig tree.

5 For my sword has drunk its fill in the heavens;
behold, it descends for judgment upon [a]Edom,
upon the people [b]I have devoted to destruction.
6 The LORD has a sword; it is sated with blood;
it is gorged with fat,
with the blood of lambs and goats,
with the fat of the kidneys of rams.
[c]For the LORD has a sacrifice in Bozrah,
a great slaughter in the land of Edom.
7 [d]Wild oxen shall [e]fall with them,
and [f]young steers with [f]the mighty bulls.
Their land shall drink its fill of blood,
and their soil shall be gorged with fat.

8 [g]For the LORD has a day of vengeance,
a year of recompense for the cause of Zion.
9 [h]And the streams of Edom[2] shall be turned into pitch,
and her soil into sulfur;
her land shall become burning pitch.

[1] That is, set apart (devoted) as an offering to the Lord (for destruction); also verse 5 [2] Hebrew *her streams*

23[r][Gen. 49:27] [s][Ps. 68:12]
24[t][ch. 1:5, 6] [u]ch. 1:25, 26; Jer. 50:20

Chapter 34

1[v]Ps. 49:1; [Joel 3:1, 2]
2[w][Josh. 6:21]
3[x]Joel 2:20 [y][Ezek. 39:4]
4[z]Joel 2:31; 3:15; Matt. 24:29; Acts 2:20; Rev. 6:13, 14; [Ps. 102:26; Heb. 1:11]
5[a]See ch. 63:1-6; Jer. 49:7-22; Obad. 1-21; Mal. 1:2-4 [b][ver. 2]
6[c]ch. 63:1
7[d]Num. 23:22 [e]ch. 47:1 [f]Ps. 22:12
8[g]ch. 61:2; 63:4; Ps. 137:7
9[h]Deut. 29:23

33:23–24 God's people, in themselves, are like a drifting hulk of a ship. But **then**, even **the lame will take the prey**. God's sin-sick people will be **forgiven their iniquity** (cf. 53:4–6).

34:1–35:10 *Two Final Outcomes: Judgment or Salvation.* These chapters describe God's final judgment of the world (ch. 34) and vindication of his people (ch. 35), with their everlasting happiness.

34:1–17 God's word to all who oppose him: everlasting wrath is coming.

34:1 Draw near, O nations. Looking beyond the Assyrian crisis of Isaiah's time, God summons the whole world to judgment at the climax of history.

34:2 For the LORD is enraged. The Hebrew idiom could be translated, "The LORD has rage." Four times in ch. 34 Isaiah says, "The LORD has . . ." The Lord has rage (v. 2), a sword (v. 6), a sacrifice (v. 6), and a day of vengeance (v. 8) as his resources for judgment. **devoted them to destruction**. See Num. 21:2–3; Josh. 2:10; 1 Sam. 15:3; and note on Deut. 20:16–18. God's judgments within history foreshadow his final destruction of all evil.

34:4 All the host of heaven matches "all their host" in v. 2. The enemies of God in both heaven and earth are finally defeated (cf. Rev. 6:12–17).

34:5–7 Edom, the antithesis to God's people (Mal. 1:2–5), typifies "all the nations" (Isa. 34:2) under God's judgment (cf. 63:1; Ezekiel 35). **sacrifice . . . great slaughter**. The world becomes a bloody altar as God requires payment for sin (the only refuge for anyone is the sacrifice of Christ). **Bozrah**. The capital city of Edom (cf. Jer. 49:22).

34:8 vengeance . . . recompense. See Deut. 32:40–43; Ps. 94:1–2; Isa. 59:17–18; 2 Thess. 1:6–10; Rev. 22:12. God has scheduled a day of justice at the end of history. The wrong he will punish is opposition to the **cause of**

10[i]ch. 66:24 [j][Rev. 14:11; 18:18; 19:3] [k]Mal. 1:4
11[l]ch. 14:23; Zeph. 2:14; [Rev. 18:2] [m]2 Kgs. 21:13; Lam. 2:8; See Amos 7:7-9 [n][ch. 24:10]
13[o]See ch. 32:13 [p]ch. 13:22; Ps. 44:19; Mal. 1:3
14[q]See ch. 13:21
15[r]Deut. 14:13
17[s][Ps. 78:55]

Chapter 35

1[t]ch. 55:12, 13 [u][ch. 32:15]
2[v]Song 5:15 [w]Song 7:5 [x]ch. 33:9; Song 2:1 [y]ch. 40:5

10 Night and day [i]it shall not be quenched;
[j]its smoke shall go up forever.
[k]From generation to generation it shall lie waste;
none shall pass through it forever and ever.
11 [l]But the hawk and the porcupine[1] shall possess it,
the owl and the raven shall dwell in it.
[m]He shall stretch the line of [n]confusion[2] over it,
and the plumb line of emptiness.
12 Its nobles—there is no one there to call it a kingdom,
and all its princes shall be nothing.

13 [o]Thorns shall grow over its strongholds,
nettles and thistles in its fortresses.
It shall be the haunt of [p]jackals,
an abode for ostriches.[3]
14 [q]And wild animals shall meet with hyenas;
the wild goat shall cry to his fellow;
indeed, there the night bird[4] settles
and finds for herself a resting place.

15 There the owl nests and lays
and hatches and gathers her young in her shadow;
indeed, there [r]the hawks are gathered,
each one with her mate.
16 Seek and read from the book of the LORD:
Not one of these shall be missing;
none shall be without her mate.
For the mouth of the LORD has commanded,
and his Spirit has gathered them.
17 [s]He has cast the lot for them;
his hand has portioned it out to them with the line;
they shall possess it forever;
from generation to generation they shall dwell in it.

The Ransomed Shall Return

35 1 [t]The wilderness and the dry land shall be glad;
[u]the desert shall rejoice and blossom like the crocus;
2 it shall blossom abundantly
and rejoice with joy and singing.
[v]The glory of Lebanon shall be given to it,
the majesty of [w]Carmel and [x]Sharon.
[y]They shall see the glory of the LORD,
the majesty of our God.

[1] The identity of the animals rendered *hawk* and *porcupine* is uncertain [2] Hebrew *formlessness* [3] Or *owls* [4] Identity uncertain

Zion. Edom illustrated that opposition clearly (cf. Num. 20:14–21; Ps. 137:7; Ezek. 35:5–6; Obad. 10–14).

34:9–10 Isaiah portrays hell (cf. Rev. 14:9–11) by means of expanding on the vision of the destruction of Edom.

34:11–15 Edomite civilization reverts to a desolate wasteland, fit only for beasts and weeds (cf. 13:19–22; 14:22–23; Rev. 18:2).

34:11 Unclean creatures possess Edom (cf. Deut. 14:11–20). **confusion . . . emptiness**. These words (Hb. *tohu* and *bohu*) first appear in Gen. 1:2, describing the world before God ordered it and filled it with life. **stretch the line**. Isaiah implies that God will, with the precision of a plumb line, reduce the world's culture of rebellion to something subhuman.

34:13 Thorns . . . nettles and thistles. The curse intensified (cf. Gen. 3:17–18).

34:16 the book of the LORD. His decrees—in this case, as revealed by Isaiah (cf. Ps. 139:16; Jer. 49:20; Dan. 7:10; Rev. 5:1; 20:12). **none shall be without her mate**. God's decree will be carried out in detail, down to each hawk (Isa. 34:15) and its mate.

34:17 God hands Edom over to unclean creatures **forever**.

35:1–10 God's word to all who trust him is that everlasting joy is coming.

35:1–2 be glad . . . rejoice . . . rejoice with joy and singing. The tone of the chapter is established by these verbs and their echoes in v. 10. God's people once made their exodus through a desert (Ex. 15:22; Deut. 1:19), but their final homecoming is through glorious abundance exploding with joy, when the curse of Gen. 3:17–19 shall be reversed (cf. Rom. 8:20–21). **The glory of Lebanon . . . the majesty of Carmel and Sharon**. See Isa. 33:9. **They**. Identified in 35:9–10. **the glory of the LORD**. The reason for the transformation of the desert is that the Lord is coming (cf. 40:3–5). On "glory," see note on 6:3.

3 [z]Strengthen the weak hands,
and make firm the feeble knees.
4 Say to those who have an anxious heart,
"Be strong; fear not!
[a]Behold, your God
will come with vengeance,
with the recompense of God.
He will come and save you."

5 [b]Then the eyes of the blind shall be opened,
and the ears of the deaf unstopped;
6 [b]then shall the lame man leap like a deer,
and the tongue of the mute sing for joy.
[c]For waters break forth in the wilderness,
and streams in the desert;
7 [d]the burning sand shall become a pool,
and the thirsty ground springs of water;
in the haunt of [e]jackals, where they lie down,
the grass shall become reeds and rushes.

8 [f]And a highway shall be there,
and it shall be called the Way of Holiness;
[g]the unclean shall not pass over it.
It shall belong to those who walk on the way;
even if they are fools, they shall not go astray.[1]
9 No lion shall be there,
nor shall any ravenous beast come up on it;
they shall not be found there,
but the redeemed shall walk there.
10 [h]And the ransomed of the LORD shall return
and come to Zion with singing;
[i]everlasting joy shall be upon their heads;
they shall obtain gladness and joy,
and sorrow and sighing shall flee away.

Sennacherib Invades Judah

36 [j]In the fourteenth year of King Hezekiah, [k]Sennacherib king of Assyria came up
against all the fortified cities of Judah and took them. 2 [l]And the king of Assyria sent
the Rabshakeh[2] from [m]Lachish to King Hezekiah at Jerusalem, with a great army. And he
stood [n]by the conduit of the upper pool on the highway to the Washer's Field. 3 And there
came out to him [o]Eliakim the son of Hilkiah, who was over the household, and [o]Shebna
the secretary, and Joah the son of Asaph, the recorder.

[1] *Or if they are fools, they shall not wander in it* [2] *Rabshakeh* is the title of a high-ranking Assyrian military officer

3[z]Cited Heb. 12:12; [ch. 40:1]
4[a][ch. 40:10, 11]
5[b]ch. 32:3, 4
6[b][See ver. 5 above] [c][ver. 1; ch. 41:18; 43:19; 44:3, 4; John 7:38, 39]
7[d]ch. 48:20, 21; 49:10 [e]See ch. 13:22
8[f]ch. 40:3 [g]ch. 52:1
10[h]ch. 51:11 [i]ch. 65:19; [ch. 25:8; Rev. 7:17; 21:4]

Chapter 36

1[j]For ver. 1-22, see 2 Kgs. 18:13, 17-37 [k][2 Chr. 32:1]
2[l]2 Chr. 32:9 [m]Josh. 15:20, 39 [n]ch. 7:3
3[o]ch. 22:15, 20, 21

35:3–4 The hope of vv. 1–2 inspires strength and courage in God's weak, unsteady people. **Behold, your God will come**. Believing perseverance comes from God's commitment to his people ("your God") and the faithfulness of his promise ("will come").

35:5–7 Then . . . then. The prophet points to the promised future, inaugurated in the first coming of Jesus Christ (Luke 4:16–21; 7:18–23) and fully consummated at his second coming (Rev. 21:4; 22:1–5). Isaiah contrasts God's people, suffering now but destined for heightened powers of enjoyment in a new world, with the Edom of this age, with its present streams of privilege reverting to burning aridity, making Edom a haunt of jackals (cf. Isa. 34:9, 13). **the eyes of the blind shall be opened**. The salvation that God will provide includes both spiritual well-being and physical healing and wholeness, as was first demonstrated repeatedly in Jesus' own ministry and as will be fully realized in the resurrection bodies of God's people when Christ returns (see notes on 1 Cor. 15:20–55).

35:8–10 a highway. In an environment of joyful abundance, God's pilgrim people are led forward to Zion, singing their way into their eternal home (cf. 33:8; 34:10). **the Way of Holiness**. See 4:3–4; 6:6–7. **even if they are fools**. The highway is so clearly marked, even fools cannot miss it. **the redeemed . . . the ransomed**. These ancient words (Ex. 6:6) emphasize the gracious initiative of God as the only final explanation for the joy of his people. **They shall obtain** the **gladness and joy** that had always been out of reach. Isaiah 35:10 is quoted in 51:11.

36:1–39:8 *Historical Transition: "In Whom Do You Now Trust?"* These chapters form a narrative bridge between the mostly poetic chs. 1–35 and 40–66. Chapters 36–37 look back to chs. 28–35, proving through Hezekiah that faith in God is met by his blessing. Chapters 38–39 provide context for chs. 40–55, as Hezekiah's folly dooms his nation to Babylonian exile. Against the backdrop of divine faithfulness (chs. 36–37) and human inconstancy (chs. 38–39), God stands forth as the only hope of his people. Isaiah 36–39 is paralleled in 2 Kings 18:13–20:19 (see notes there).

4 [p][ch. 10:8]
6 [q]Ezek. 29:6, 7
7 [r]2 Kgs. 18:4; See Deut. 12:2-5
9 [s][ch. 10:8] [t][ch. 20:5; 30:3, 7; 31:1]
10 [u]ch. 10:5, 6
11 [v]Ezra 4:7; Dan. 2:4

4 And the Rabshakeh said to them, "Say to Hezekiah, 'Thus says the [p]great king, the
king of Assyria: On what do you rest this trust of yours? 5 Do you think that mere words
are strategy and power for war? In whom do you now trust, that you have rebelled against
me? 6 [q]Behold, you are trusting in Egypt, that broken reed of a staff, which will pierce the
hand of any man who leans on it. Such is Pharaoh king of Egypt to all who trust in him.
7 But if you say to me, "We trust in the LORD our God," is it not he [r]whose high places
and altars Hezekiah has removed, saying to Judah and to Jerusalem, "You shall worship
before this altar"? 8 Come now, make a wager with my master the king of Assyria: I will
give you two thousand horses, if you are able on your part to set riders on them. 9 How
then can you repulse [s]a single captain among the least of my master's servants, when [t]you
trust in Egypt for chariots and for horsemen? 10 Moreover, is it without the LORD that I
have come up against this land to destroy it? [u]The LORD said to me, Go up against this
land and destroy it.'"
11 Then Eliakim, Shebna, and Joah said to the Rabshakeh, "Please speak to your servants
[v]in Aramaic, for we understand it. Do not speak to us in the language of Judah within the
hearing of the people who are on the wall." 12 But the Rabshakeh said, "Has my master sent
me to speak these words to your master and to you, and not to the men sitting on the wall,
who are doomed with you to eat their own dung and drink their own urine?"
13 Then the Rabshakeh stood and called out in a loud voice in the language of Judah:

36:1–37:38 *Practical Trust in God Vindicated.* When God's people align themselves with his cause, trusting in his power alone, they find him faithful to keep his word.

36:1 In the fourteenth year. 701 B.C. Apparently, Hezekiah served as co-regent with his father Ahaz until 715 B.C., at which time he began to rule solely. **Sennacherib king of Assyria** reigned 705–681 B.C. See 8:5–8. **all the fortified cities of Judah**. Jerusalem is surrounded, with no hope of human rescue.

36:2 Rabshakeh is the title of a high-ranking Assyrian military officer (see ESV footnote). **the conduit of the upper pool**. See 7:3.

36:3 Eliakim, Shebna. See 22:15–25.

36:4 Thus says the great king. Speaking unwittingly as a false prophet, the Rabshakeh pronounces a royal decree, amplified in vv. 13–14, 16. It is answered by a higher royal decree in 37:6, 21–22, and 33. **On what do you rest this trust of yours?** The word "trust" appears seven times in the Hebrew text of this paragraph (36:4, 5, 6, 7, 9). At the heart of Isaiah's message is a call to God's people to trust his promises with an audacious faith amid the hard realities of life.

36:5 Mere words stand in contrast with "a great army" in v. 2.

36:6 you are trusting in Egypt. There is some truth in the Rabshakeh's speech, making its plausibility all the more cunning.

36:7 This reveals the uncomprehending Assyrian viewpoint and the key to their eventual doom. Because the Rabshakeh does not believe that the God of Israel is different from the gods of the pagan **high places and altars**, he misinterprets Hezekiah's reforms as offensive to the Lord (cf. 2 Kings 18:4; 2 Chron. 31:1).

36:8–9 The Rabshakeh patronizes Hezekiah as a tactic of psychological warfare.

36:10 I have come up against this land to destroy it. Hezekiah had paid Sennacherib heavy tribute (2 Kings 18:14–17), but the Assyrian attacked anyway. **The LORD said to me**. The Rabshakeh violates the third commandment ("You shall not take the name of the LORD your God in vain," Ex. 20:7) by putting his own words into the mouth of the Lord. There is some truth in what he says (Isa. 10:5–6), but not as intended by his arrogant self-confidence. He does not notice his own reliance here on "mere words" (36:5).

36:11 Aramaic was the language of international protocol. **The language of Judah** was Hebrew.

36:12 doomed with you to eat their own dung and drink their own urine. The starvation conditions under siege (cf. 2 Kings 6:25). The Rabshakeh may hope to terrorize the people listening so that they turn against Hezekiah and his advisers.

36:13–14 the great king, the king of Assyria. . . . Hezekiah. The Rabshakeh heaps honor on Sennacherib but does not recognize Hezekiah, the son of David, with any title (cf. 10:12).

Assyria Attacks Judah and Jerusalem

c. 701 B.C.

During the reign of Hezekiah of Judah, Sennacherib of Assyria came and attacked cities along the western edge of Judah, and he sent officials to besiege Jerusalem and convince Hezekiah to surrender. The Cushite king Tirhakah advanced from Egypt to support Hezekiah but apparently failed. The siege of Jerusalem was broken when the angel of the Lord killed 185,000 Assyrians in a single night (2 Kings 19:35). Sennacherib withdrew and returned to Nineveh in Assyria, where his own sons killed him.

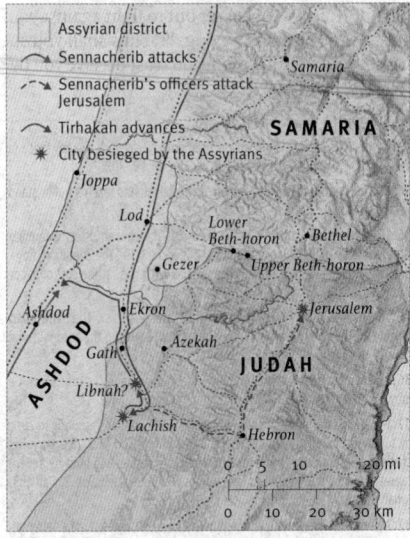

"Hear the words of the great king, the king of Assyria! 14 Thus says the king: [w]"Do not let
Hezekiah deceive you, for he will not be able to deliver you. 15 Do not let Hezekiah make
you trust in the LORD by saying, "The LORD will surely deliver us. This city will not be
given into the hand of the king of Assyria." 16 Do not listen to Hezekiah. For thus says the
king of Assyria: Make your peace with me[1] and come out to me. Then each one of you will
eat of his own vine, and each one of his own fig tree, and each one of you will drink the
water of his own cistern, 17 until [x]I come and take you away to a land like your own land,
a land of grain and wine, a land of bread and vineyards. 18 Beware lest Hezekiah mislead
you by saying, "The LORD will deliver us." Has any of the gods of the nations delivered
his land out of the hand of the king of Assyria? 19 [y]Where are the gods of [z]Hamath and
[z]Arpad? Where are the gods of Sepharvaim? [a]Have they delivered Samaria out of my hand?
20 [b]Who among all the gods of these lands have delivered their lands out of my hand, that
the LORD should deliver Jerusalem out of my hand?'"

21 But they were silent and answered him not a word, for the king's command was, "Do
not answer him." 22 [c]Then Eliakim the son of Hilkiah, who was over the household, and
Shebna the secretary, and Joah the son of Asaph, the recorder, came to Hezekiah with their
clothes torn, and told him the words of the Rabshakeh.

Hezekiah Seeks Isaiah's Help

37 [d]As soon as King Hezekiah heard it, he tore his clothes and covered himself with
sackcloth and went into the house of the LORD. 2 And he sent Eliakim, who was over
the household, and Shebna the secretary, and the senior priests, covered with sackcloth, to
the prophet [e]Isaiah the son of Amoz. 3 They said to him, "Thus says Hezekiah, 'This day
is a [f]day of distress, of rebuke, and of disgrace; [g]children have come to the point of birth,
and there is no strength to bring them forth. 4 [h]It may be that the LORD your God will
hear the words of the Rabshakeh, whom his master the king of Assyria has sent to mock
the living God, and will rebuke the words that the LORD your God has heard; therefore
lift up your prayer for [i]the remnant that is left.'"

5 When the servants of King Hezekiah came to Isaiah, 6 Isaiah said to them, "Say to your
master, 'Thus says the LORD: Do not be afraid because of the words that you have heard,
with which the young men of the king of Assyria have reviled me. 7 Behold, [j]I will put a
spirit in him, so that [k]he shall hear a rumor and return to his own land, and [l]I will make
him fall by the sword in his own land.'"

8 The Rabshakeh returned, and found the king of Assyria fighting against [m]Libnah, for
he had heard that the king had left [m]Lachish. 9 Now the king heard concerning Tirhakah
king of [n]Cush,[2] "He has set out to fight against you." And when he heard it, he sent messengers to Hezekiah, saying, 10 "Thus shall you speak to Hezekiah king of Judah: [o]'Do
not let your God in whom you trust deceive you by promising that Jerusalem will not be

[1] Hebrew *Make a blessing with me* [2] Probably Nubia

14 [w][ch. 37:10; 2 Chr. 32:6-8]
17 [x]2 Kgs. 18:11
19 [y]ch. 37:13 [z]Jer. 49:23 [a][2 Kgs. 17:6]
20 [b][2 Chr. 32:19]
22 [c]ver. 3; [ch. 33:7]

Chapter 37

1 [d]For ver. 1-38, see 2 Kgs. 19
2 [e]See ch. 1:1
3 [f][ch. 22:5] [g][ch. 13:8; Hos. 13:13]
4 [h][ver. 28, 29] [i]ch. 1:9
7 [j][ch. 19:14] [k]ver. 9 [l]ver. 38
8 [m]Josh. 10:31
9 [n]ch. 18:1, 2; 20:5
10 [o][ch. 36:14]

36:14 he will not be able to deliver you. "Deliver" is the key word in vv. 13–20, occurring seven times (vv. 14, 15, 18, 19, 20).

36:15 The LORD will surely deliver us. Hezekiah had taken a public stand of faith in God's promises.

36:16–17 his own vine . . . fig tree. The Rabshakeh offers a familiar Israelite blessing (cf. 1 Kings 4:25; Mic. 4:4; Zech. 3:10). The condition, however, is surrender to him: **Make your peace with me**, at the cost of peace with God.

36:18–20 See 10:7–11. **Who among all the gods . . . that the LORD should deliver.** The Assyrian takes a fatal step, equating the Lord with the gods of this world.

36:21 Do not answer him. Wisely, Hezekiah forbade his officials to be drawn into negotiations.

37:1–2 Unlike his faithless father Ahaz in ch. 7, Hezekiah responds to crisis by turning to God (37:1) and seeking a word from God (v. 2). **He tore his clothes and covered himself with sackcloth**, expressing humility, repentance, and dependence on God (see 1 Kings 21:27–29; Neh. 9:1–2; Dan. 9:3; Jonah 3:6–9; Matt. 11:21).

37:3 Hezekiah admits that, as the moment of crisis arrives, Judah's strength fails (cf. 66:7–9). There is no stopping the events now set in motion: the situation is desperate, and God's people have no capacity for response.

37:4 to mock the living God. Hezekiah understands what matters most—not the survival of his kingdom but the triumph of what his kingdom stands for: the glory of God. **the remnant that is left.** The city of Jerusalem (cf. 36:1).

37:6 reviled me. The sin that dooms Sennacherib is blasphemy against God.

37:7 Behold, I will put a spirit in him. The God whom Sennacherib reviles is in complete command of Sennacherib. His "great army" (36:2), too impressed with itself to respect "mere words" (36:5), will be dispersed by a **rumor**. Sennacherib will **fall by the sword**. See 37:38.

37:8–13 Drawn away from Jerusalem by news of an approaching Cushite force, the Assyrian king warns Hezekiah that he still intends to attack. **Libnah . . . Lachish.** See Josh. 10:29, 31; Isa. 36:2.

37:10 Do not let your God in whom you trust deceive you by promising. The Assyrian makes the issue clear as he intensifies his blasphemy. To him, what counts is not divine promise but human intimidation (cf. 36:5, 7, 15, 18).

12 [p]ch. 36:18, 19 [q]2 Kgs. 17:6 [r]Gen. 11:31, 32
13 [p][See ver. 12 above]
16 [s]Ex. 25:22; Ezek. 10:1 [t]Acts 4:24; [Jer. 10:11]
17 [u][2 Chr. 6:40] [v]2 Chr. 32:19
18 [w][ch. 10:13, 14]
22 [x][Mic. 4:13]; See ch. 1:8
23 [y]ch. 10:17
24 [z][ch. 8:7, 8] [a][ch. 14:8]

given into the hand of the king of Assyria. 11 Behold, you have heard what the kings of
Assyria have done to all lands, devoting them to destruction. And shall you be delivered?
12 [p]Have the gods of the nations delivered them, the nations that my fathers destroyed,
[q]Gozan, [r]Haran, Rezeph, and the people of Eden who were in Telassar? 13 [p]Where is the
king of Hamath, the king of Arpad, the king of the city of Sepharvaim, the king of Hena,
or the king of Ivvah?'"

Hezekiah's Prayer for Deliverance

14 Hezekiah received the letter from the hand of the messengers, and read it; and Hezekiah
went up to the house of the LORD, and spread it before the LORD. 15 And Hezekiah prayed
to the LORD: 16 "O LORD of hosts, God of Israel, [s]enthroned above the cherubim, you are
the God, you alone, of all the kingdoms of the earth; [t]you have made heaven and earth.
17 [u]Incline your ear, O LORD, and hear; open your eyes, O LORD, and see; and hear [v]all
the words of Sennacherib, which he has sent to mock the living God. 18 Truly, O LORD,
[w]the kings of Assyria have laid waste all the nations and their lands, 19 and have cast their
gods into the fire. For they were no gods, but the work of men's hands, wood and stone.
Therefore they were destroyed. 20 So now, O LORD our God, save us from his hand, that all
the kingdoms of the earth may know that you alone are the LORD."

Sennacherib's Fall

21 Then Isaiah the son of Amoz sent to Hezekiah, saying, "Thus says the LORD, the God
of Israel: Because you have prayed to me concerning Sennacherib king of Assyria, 22 this
is the word that the LORD has spoken concerning him:

"'She despises you, she scorns you—
[x]the virgin daughter of Zion;
she wags her head behind you—
the daughter of Jerusalem.

23 "'Whom have you mocked and reviled?
Against whom have you raised your voice
and lifted your eyes to the heights?
Against [y]the Holy One of Israel!
24 By your servants you have mocked the Lord,
and you have said, [z]With my many chariots
I have gone up the heights of the mountains,
to the far recesses of Lebanon,
[a]to cut down its tallest cedars,
its choicest cypresses,
to come to its remotest height,
its most fruitful forest.

37:14 Hezekiah says nothing to the messengers. His business is with God, for it is God's glory at stake.

37:16 Hezekiah does not put his own safety first, nor does he plead his own righteousness. He bases his prayer on the character of God. **enthroned above the cherubim**. See Ex. 25:10–22; Num. 7:89; 1 Sam. 4:4. The cherubim were composite creatures, symbolizing creation. The ark represented God's earthly throne. Hezekiah directs his thoughts to the King who is above all creation and yet decisively present in everything here below.

37:17 Hezekiah begs the God who is over all not to regard this slight upon his character as beneath his notice.

37:18–19 These verses show Hezekiah's realism. His faith is not a blind optimism but an overruling sense of God.

37:20 save us. Isaiah's life message was that the Lord alone saves (cf. 12:2–3; 25:9; 26:1; 30:15; 33:2, 6, 22; 35:4; 37:35; 43:3, 11; 45:15, 17, 21–22; 49:6, 25–26; 51:5–8; 52:7, 10; 56:1; 59:1, 16–17; 60:16, 18; 62:1, 11; 63:1, 5). Now Hezekiah gives voice to that faith, bringing the message of the book to a focal point. **that all the kingdoms of the earth may know**. The ultimate reason why God intervenes for his people is to make them living proof of his glory. **you alone are the LORD**. Hezekiah sees the exclusivity of God not as an embarrassing problem but as the message the world must know. A real salvation puts the unique reality of God on visible display in human experience.

37:21 Because you have prayed to me. Hezekiah expressed his dependence on God alone by praying and waiting for an answer before acting. Hezekiah's prayer actually affected the way God acted in history.

37:22 the word that the LORD has spoken. The final and decisive word in what has been a war of human words. **The virgin daughter of Zion** is Jerusalem, like a girl mocking her would-be but defeated rapist. Not only is Jerusalem untouched, she triumphs with a defiant joy, the weak over the strong.

37:23 Whom have you mocked and reviled? See vv. 4, 6. This question counters, "In whom do you now trust, that you have rebelled against me?" (36:5). **raised . . . lifted**. Rebellion and pride, belittling God. **the Holy One of Israel**. Sennacherib's fatal mistake is to lump the Holy One in with other gods and powers (cf. 36:18–20; 37:10–12). But the Holy One is unique, and to deny the truth of who he is defies reality (cf. 40:25).

37:24–25 Pride distorts perspective (cf. 10:5–19).

25 I dug wells
and drank waters,
to dry up with the sole of my foot
all [b]the streams [c]of Egypt.

26 [d]"'Have you not heard
that I determined it long ago?
I planned from days of old
what now I bring to pass,
that you should make fortified cities
crash into heaps of ruins,
27 while their inhabitants, shorn of strength,
are dismayed and confounded,
and have become like plants of the field
and like tender grass,
like grass on the housetops,
blighted[1] before it is grown.

28 "'I know your sitting down
and your going out and coming in,
and your raging against me.
29 [e]Because you have raged against me
and your complacency has come to my ears,
I will put my hook in your nose
and my bit in your mouth,
and [f]I will turn you back on the way
by which you came.'

30 "And this shall be the sign for you: this year you shall eat what grows of itself, and in
the second year what springs from that. Then in the third year sow and reap, and plant
vineyards, and eat their fruit. 31 And the surviving remnant of the house of Judah [g]shall again
take root downward and bear fruit upward. 32 [h]For out of Jerusalem shall go a remnant,
and out of Mount Zion a band of survivors. [i]The zeal of the LORD of hosts will do this.
33 "Therefore thus says the LORD concerning the king of Assyria: He shall not come into
this city or shoot an arrow there or come before it with a shield or [j]cast up a siege mound
against it. 34 By the way that he came, by the same he shall return, and he shall not come
into this city, declares the LORD. 35 [k]For I will defend this city to save it, for my own sake
and for [l]the sake of my servant David."
36 [m]And the angel of the LORD went out and struck down 185,000 in the camp of the
Assyrians. And when people arose early in the morning, behold, these were all dead bodies.
37 Then Sennacherib king of Assyria departed and returned home and lived at [n]Nineveh.
38 And as he was worshiping in the house of Nisroch his god, Adrammelech and Sharezer,
his sons, struck him down with the sword. And after they escaped into the land of [o]Ararat,
[p]Esarhaddon his son reigned in his place.

[1] Some Hebrew manuscripts and 2 Kings 19:26; most Hebrew manuscripts *like a field*

25 [b][ch. 19:6] [c][ch. 20:4]
26 [d][ch. 10:5, 15; 25:1, 2]
29 [e][ch. 10:12] [f]ver. 34
31 [g]ch. 27:6
32 [h][ch. 14:32] [i]See ch. 9:7
33 [j][Hab. 1:10; Luke 19:43]
35 [k]ch. 31:5; 38:6 [l][ch. 29:1]
36 [m]ch. 17:14; 30:31; 31:8; [ch. 10:33; 14:25; 29:5]
37 [n]Gen. 10:11; Jonah 1:2; 3:3; 4:11
38 [o]Gen. 8:4 [p]Ezra 4:2

37:26–29 Have you not heard. God holds Sennacherib responsible to acknowledge God (cf. Rom. 1:18–21). **I determined it long ago**. The ancient plan of God means that he is not responding to unfolding events, but that events reveal his own long-intended purpose (cf. Isa. 14:24–27; 25:1; 44:6–8). **I will put my hook in your nose**. The Assyrians handled their prisoners of war in this way (cf. Obad. 15).

37:30–32 the sign. God promises Hezekiah that he will faithfully preserve the land, feeding the people as they recover from the invasion, to show that his purpose, not chance, orchestrated the entire event. Moreover, the agricultural miracle will symbolize the spiritual miracle of a remnant preserved by grace.

37:33–35 God controls every **arrow** in the Assyrian arsenal. **He shall not come into this city**. The annals of Sennacherib boast, "I made [Hezekiah] a prisoner in Jerusalem, his royal residence, like a bird in a cage," leaving unstated his failure to enter the city (see notes on 2 Kings 18:13–19:37 and 18:13). God will defend his city for his own glory and out of covenant faithfulness to David, suggesting his larger kingdom purpose for history consummated in Jesus Christ (cf. 2 Sam. 7:12–13; Isa. 9:7; 11:1; 55:3–4; Rom. 1:1–5; Rev. 22:16).

37:36–38 God keeps his promise, vindicating Hezekiah's faith with a stunning demonstration of his power over his enemies (cf. 8:8–10; 10:33–34; 31:8). The narrative is brief and undramatic. The real drama took place in prayer (37:14–35). **the angel**. One against 185,000. **behold**. A visible, concrete historical event. **in the house of Nisroch his god**. Contrast v. 14. Hezekiah went to the house of the Lord and was saved. Sennacherib went to the house of his god and was assassinated (about 20 years later).

38:1–39:8 *Human Inconstancy Sent into Exile.* Man at his best, exposed now as self-centered and short-sighted, cannot be trusted. God himself is the only hope of his people.

Chapter 38
1[q]For ver. 1-8, see 2 Kgs. 20:1-6, 9-11 [r]2 Chr. 32:24 [s]See ch. 1:1
3[t]2 Kgs. 18:5, 6
5[u]2 Kgs. 18:2, 13
6[v]ch. 37:35
8[w][2 Kgs. 20:9, 10]
10[x][Ps. 102:24]
11[y]Ps. 27:13; [Ps. 88:5]
12[z][2 Cor. 5:1] [a]Job 7:6 [b][Heb. 1:12] [c]Job 6:9 [d][Job 4:20; Ps. 73:14]
13[e][Ps. 30:5] [f][Ps. 38:3]
14[g][Jer. 8:7] [h]ch. 59:11 [i]Ps. 69:3 [j]Ps. 119:122; [Ps. 86:17; Heb. 7:22]

Hezekiah's Sickness and Recovery

38 [q]In those days Hezekiah became [r]sick and was at the point of death. And [s]Isaiah
the prophet the son of Amoz came to him, and said to him, "Thus says the LORD:
Set your house in order, for you shall die, you shall not recover."[1] **2** Then Hezekiah turned
his face to the wall and prayed to the LORD, **3** and said, "Please, O LORD, remember how
[t]I have walked before you in faithfulness and with a whole heart, and have done what is
good in your sight." And Hezekiah wept bitterly.
4 Then the word of the LORD came to Isaiah: **5** "Go and say to Hezekiah, Thus says the
LORD, the God of David your father: I have heard your prayer; I have seen your tears.
Behold, I will add [u]fifteen years to your life.[2] **6** [v]I will deliver you and this city out of the
hand of the king of Assyria, and will defend this city.
7 "This shall be the sign to you from the LORD, that the LORD will do this thing that
he has promised: **8** [w]Behold, I will make the shadow cast by the declining sun on the dial
of Ahaz turn back ten steps." So the sun turned back on the dial the ten steps by which
it had declined.[3]

9 A writing of Hezekiah king of Judah, after he had been sick and had recovered from
his sickness:

10 I said, [x]In the middle[4] of my days
    I must depart;
I am consigned to the gates of Sheol
    for the rest of my years.
11 I said, I shall not see the LORD,
    the LORD [y]in the land of the living;
I shall look on man no more
    among the inhabitants of the world.
12 My dwelling is plucked up and removed from me
    [z]like a shepherd's tent;
[a]like a weaver [b]I have rolled up my life;
    [c]he cuts me off from the loom;
[d]from day to night you bring me to an end;
13 [e]I calmed myself[5] until morning;
like a lion [f]he breaks all my bones;
    from day to night you bring me to an end.
14 Like [g]a swallow or a crane I chirp;
    [h]I moan like a dove.
[i]My eyes are weary with looking upward.
    O Lord, I am oppressed; [j]be my pledge of safety!

[1] Or *live*; also verses 9, 21 [2] Hebrew *to your days* [3] The meaning of the Hebrew verse is uncertain [4] Or *In the quiet* [5] Or (with Targum) *I cried for help*

38:1 In those days. The events of chs. 38–39 take place near the time of the deliverance from Assyria in chs. 36–37. But "in those days" is intentionally vague. Isaiah 38:6 clarifies that Hezekiah's illness occurred prior to chs. 36–37. Isaiah locates the events of chs. 38–39 here in order to establish the context for chs. 40–55. **Hezekiah became sick**. Unlike the crisis of chs. 36–37, which was national in scope, this crisis is only personal. **at the point of death**. Hezekiah began his reign at 25 years of age and reigned for 29 years (2 Kings 18:2). With 15 years added to his life after this illness (Isa. 38:5), he would have been only 39 when this illness struck him ("In the middle of my days," v. 10). "**You shall not recover**" offers Hezekiah the opportunity to pray for a different outcome, as many prophecies do (cf. Jer. 18:1–11; Jonah 3:4).

38:3 Unlike Hezekiah's God-centered prayer in 37:15–20, now his thoughts withdraw into himself, perhaps even implying that he thinks God is being unfair to him. The **faithfulness**, wholeheartedness, and **good** that Hezekiah pleads were real (2 Kings 18:5–6) but not the whole story (2 Chron. 32:24–31). Moreover, his selfish thoughts in Isa. 39:8 reveal the state of his heart.

38:5 the God of David your father. God replaces Hezekiah's claims of merit with his own covenant faithfulness to David as the basis for his answer to the king's prayer.

38:6 God looks beyond Hezekiah's personal crisis to what matters more—the defense of the **city** of God.

38:7–8 God turns the clock back on Hezekiah's life, symbolized by this miracle. **the sun turned back on the dial**. See 7:11. Second Chronicles 32:31 implies that the sign was localized in Judah but known beyond. This appears to be a supernatural event, but the passage offers no explanation as to how it happened.

38:9–20 Hezekiah's psalm is clear about this truth: God alone has the power of life and death, and he prefers life. Therefore, Hezekiah's lack of spiritual awareness in ch. 39 is all the more inexcusable. The psalm divides into the anguish of death (38:10–15), the hope of deliverance (vv. 16–19), and a concluding confession of faith (v. 20).

38:10 To the gates of Sheol is matched in v. 20 by "at the house of the LORD." The crisis is death, and the resolution is endless worship. But Hezekiah's renewed sense of God-centered purpose in life will fade from view in ch. 39.

15 What shall I say? For he has spoken to me,
and he himself has done it.
[k]I walk slowly all my years
because of the bitterness of my soul.

16 [l]O Lord, by these things men live,
and in all these is the life of my spirit.
Oh restore me to health and make me live!
17 [m]Behold, it was for my welfare
that I had great bitterness;
[n]but in love you have delivered my life
from the pit of destruction,
[n] for you have cast all my sins
behind your back.
18 [o]For Sheol does not thank you;
death does not praise you;
those who go down to the pit do not hope
for your faithfulness.
19 The living, the living, he thanks you,
as I do this day;
[p]the father makes known to the children
your faithfulness.

20 The LORD will save me,
and we will play my music on stringed instruments
all the days of our lives,
[q]at the house of the LORD.

21 [r]Now Isaiah had said, "Let them take a cake of figs and apply it to the boil, that he
may recover." 22 Hezekiah also had said, "What is the sign that I shall go up to the house
of the LORD?"

Envoys from Babylon

39 [s]At that time Merodach-baladan the son of Baladan, king of Babylon, [t]sent envoys
with letters and a present to Hezekiah, for he heard that he had been sick and had
recovered. 2 And Hezekiah welcomed them gladly. And he showed them his treasure house,
[u]the silver, the gold, the spices, the precious oil, his whole armory, all that was found in
his storehouses. [v]There was nothing in his house or in all his realm that Hezekiah did not
show them. 3 Then Isaiah the prophet came to King Hezekiah, and said to him, "What
did these men say? And from where did they come to you?" Hezekiah said, "They have
come to me from a far country, from Babylon." 4 He said, "What have they seen in your
house?" Hezekiah answered, "They have seen all that is in my house. There is nothing in
my storehouses that I did not show them."

5 Then Isaiah said to Hezekiah, "Hear the word of the LORD of hosts: 6 [w]Behold, the days
are coming, when all that is in your house, and that which your fathers have stored up

15 [k]1 Kgs. 21:27
16 [l]Deut. 8:3
17 [m]Ps. 119:67, 75 [n][Ps. 103:12; Mic. 7:19]
18 [o]Ps. 88:10-12; 115:17; [Eccles. 9:10]
19 [p]Deut. 4:9; 6:7; Ps. 78:3, 4
20 [q]2 Kgs. 20:5
21 [r]2 Kgs. 20:7, 8

Chapter 39

1 [s]For ver. 1-8, see 2 Kgs. 20:12-19 [t][2 Chr. 32:31]
2 [u][2 Kgs. 18:15, 16] [v][2 Chr. 32:25]
6 [w]2 Kgs. 24:13; See 2 Kgs. 25:13-17

38:20 The LORD will save me. The statement implies the bias, as it were, of God's heart. Hezekiah's saving God should always be absolutely trusted and prized, which Hezekiah himself will fail to demonstrate in ch. 39.

38:21–22 That he may recover reverses "you shall not recover" in v. 1. In addition to the promise of v. 5, and in addition to the dramatic miracle of v. 8, Hezekiah also receives this medicinal application as a felt token of healing. But his faith wavers: **What is the sign that I shall go up to the house of the LORD?** His father Ahaz refused a sign because of closed-minded unbelief (7:12). Now the son asks for a sign beyond what was already given because of double-minded unbelief.

39:1 At that time connects these events with ch. 38. **Merodach-baladan** was the ruler of **Babylon**, subject to the Assyrian Empire. Upon the death of Sargon II (705 B.C.), he tried to establish independence from Assyria; that is the likely time of this embassy, aimed at splitting Assyrian attention. The Assyrians quickly squelched the rebellion. In the Bible, Babylon is more than an ancient culture; it represents everything in this world that is humanly impressive but opposed to God (cf. Gen. 11:1–9; Isa. 13:19; 1 Pet. 5:13; Rev. 14:8; 18:2–3).

39:2 Hezekiah welcomed them gladly. The man whose faith stood firm against Assyrian intimidation now melts in the face of Babylonian flattery. He is foolish not to look for ulterior motives and is unguarded in his openness to their visit. **he showed them his treasure house**. Perhaps Hezekiah wants to be counted on to play a role in Babylon's plan to topple Assyria from power. In any case, Hezekiah is losing his sense of God. He foolishly reveals the extent of his wealth, thus inviting plunder by Babylon.

39:3 Isaiah's questions reveal his alertness to the danger. **They have come to me from a far country**. Hezekiah is dazzled—by a doomed culture (cf. 13:1–14:27; 21:1–10; 24:1–27:13).

39:6 Isaiah foretells the deportation **to Babylon**, which is due to Judah's

7[x]Dan. 1:2, 3, 7
8[y][2 Chr. 32:26]

Chapter 40

1[z]ch. 51:12; [Luke 2:25]
2[a]Hos. 2:14 [b][2 Chr. 36:22; Jer. 25:12]
3[c]Cited Matt. 3:3; Mark 1:3; Luke 3:4; John 1:23 [d]Mal. 3:1; [ch. 57:14] [e]Ps. 68:4
4[f]Cited Luke 3:5; [ch. 49:11]
5[g][Luke 3:6] [h]ch. 1:20
6[i]Cited 1 Pet. 1:24, 25; [Job 14:2; Ps. 102:11; 103:15; James 1:10]

till this day, shall be carried to Babylon. Nothing shall be left, says the LORD. 7 [x]And some of your own sons, who will come from you, whom you will father, shall be taken away, and they shall be eunuchs in the palace of the king of Babylon." 8 Then Hezekiah said to Isaiah, "The word of the LORD that you have spoken is good." For he thought, [y]"There will be peace and security in my days."

Comfort for God's People

40

1 [z]Comfort, comfort my people, says your God.
2 [a]Speak tenderly to Jerusalem,
and cry to her
that [b]her warfare[1] is ended,
that her iniquity is pardoned,
that she has received from the LORD's hand
double for all her sins.

3 [c]A voice cries:[2]
[d]"In the wilderness prepare the way of the LORD;
[e]make straight in the desert a highway for our God.
4 [f]Every valley shall be lifted up,
and every mountain and hill be made low;
the uneven ground shall become level,
and the rough places a plain.
5 [g]And the glory of the LORD shall be revealed,
and all flesh shall see it together,
[h]for the mouth of the LORD has spoken."

The Word of God Stands Forever

6 A voice says, "Cry!"
And I said,[3] "What shall I cry?"
[i]All flesh is grass,
and all its beauty[4] is like the flower of the field.

[1] Or *hardship* [2] Or *A voice of one crying* [3] Revocalization based on Dead Sea Scroll, Septuagint, Vulgate; Masoretic Text *And someone says* [4] Or *all its constancy*

unfaithfulness (cf. 2 Kings 23:26–27, referring to the deeds of Hezekiah's own son). This prepares the way for Isaiah 40–66, which envisions Jerusalem in captivity in Babylon and ready to return.

39:8 There will be peace and security in my days. Irresponsibly, Hezekiah thinks only of himself (and he was one of the *good* kings of Judah!). Hezekiah is disappointing as a man and father; but even more so as the steward of David's dynasty. He is not allowed to act solely for himself: for his sons to serve as eunuchs (v. 7) threatens their ability to continue the family line. He failed to learn the lesson of 38:1 (see note), and thus failed to prepare his descendants to avoid the disaster.

40:1–55:13 *Comfort for God's Exiles: "The Glory of the Lord Shall Be Revealed."* The assumed addressees in these chapters are the exiles in Babylonian captivity; and yet this is a message for Isaiah's contemporaries (see Introduction: Date; and Purpose, Occasion, and Background). God comforts his exiled people by promising the world-transforming display of his glory. Isaiah's perspective moves forward from his own eighth-century setting to the Jews' sixth-century exile predicted in 39:5–7. Isaiah's tone changes from confrontation to assurance.

40:1–31 *The God of Glory: His Coming, Exclusivity, Power.* God provides a comforting promise of hope for the brokenhearted people of God. God is incomparably powerful over all things and promises strength for endurance to all who will wait for him.

40:1–11 A promise of glorious hope breaks upon the people of God.

40:1 Comfort, comfort. God commissions the voices of vv. 3 and 6 and the heralds of v. 9, repeating himself to emphasize his deep feeling. **my people . . . your God**. Though their unbelief has brought them low, God still identifies with his people.

40:2 Speak tenderly. God aims to win their hearts back. **to Jerusalem.** In Babylonian exile, they are far from Jerusalem, but God dignifies them with their true identity and assures them that he understands their sufferings.

40:3 A barren landscape, which God's people had become (64:10), is where he comes to them with refreshment (cf. 32:14–16; 35:1–10; 41:17–20; 43:19–21; 51:3). John the Baptist found here his own calling to his generation, implying the promises of these chapters had not yet fully come to pass (cf. Matt. 3:1–6 par.; John 1:23).

40:4 These are metaphors—based on the rough terrain as one approaches Jerusalem from the east—for personal repentance and social reformation, remaking the world as a place fit for the coming King.

40:5 glory. See 4:5; 6:3; 35:1–2; 60:1–3; 66:18–19; see note on 6:3. The glory is **revealed** (or seen) as God leads his people (cf. Ex. 16:7). **all flesh shall see it**. Not a private viewing for the remnant only, but out in front of the whole world (cf. Isa. 52:7–10). From this promise of God's presence flow all of God's gracious promises, and from this divine purpose flows the whole of history. **for the mouth of the LORD has spoken**. The fulfillment of this comforting promise depends not on favorable historical trends but only on the promise of God (cf. 55:10–11).

40:6–8 all its beauty (or "constancy," ESV footnote). Only God can be absolutely trusted, and his words will never prove false: **the word of our God will stand forever**. Contrast Hezekiah's weakness of character (39:1–8). Far from fading away, God's word of hope imparts life to weak people. First Peter 1:23–25 uses Isa. 40:6, 8 to illustrate that "the living and abiding word of God" is reliable, "imperishable . . . seed."

7 The grass withers, the flower fades
when the breath of the LORD blows on it;
surely the people are grass.
8 [j]The grass withers, the flower fades,
but the word of our God will stand forever.

The Greatness of God

9 Go on up to a high mountain,
O Zion, [k]herald of good news;[1]
lift up your voice with strength,
O Jerusalem, herald of good news;[2]
lift it up, fear not;
say to the cities of Judah,
"Behold your God!"
10 [l]Behold, the Lord GOD comes with might,
and his arm rules for him;
[m]behold, his reward is with him,
and his recompense before him.
11 [n]He will tend his flock like a shepherd;
[o]he will gather the lambs in his arms;
[p]he will carry them in his bosom,
and gently lead those that are with young.
12 [q]Who has measured the waters in the hollow of his hand
and marked off the heavens with a span,
enclosed the dust of the earth in a measure
and weighed the mountains in scales
and the hills in a balance?
13 [r]Who has measured[3] the Spirit of the LORD,
or what man shows him his counsel?
14 Whom did he consult,
and who made him understand?
[s]Who taught him the path of justice,
and taught him knowledge,
and showed him the way of understanding?
15 Behold, the nations are like a drop from a bucket,
and are accounted [t]as the dust on the scales;
behold, he takes up [u]the coastlands like fine dust.
16 Lebanon would not suffice for fuel,
nor are [v]its beasts enough for a burnt offering.
17 [w]All the nations are as nothing before him,
they are accounted by him as less than nothing and emptiness.
18 [x]To whom then will you liken God,
[y]or what likeness compare with him?
19 [y]An idol! A craftsman casts it,
and a goldsmith overlays it with gold
and casts for it silver chains.

[1] Or *O herald of good news to Zion* [2] Or *O herald of good news to Jerusalem* [3] Or *has directed*

8[j]Cited James 1:11
9[k]ch. 52:7
10[l]ch. 59:16, 17; [Luke 11:22] [m]ch. 62:11; [Rev. 22:12]
11[n]Ezek. 34:23; Zech. 11:7; [John 10:11; 21:15; Acts 20:28] [o][Matt. 18:12; Luke 15:5] [p][Num. 11:12]
12[q][Prov. 30:4]
13[r]Cited Rom. 11:34; [1 Cor. 2:16]
14[s]Job 21:22
15[t]ch. 29:5 [u]ch. 41:1
16[v][Ps. 50:10]
17[w]Ps. 62:9; Dan. 4:35; [ch. 41:12]
18[x]ver. 25; ch. 46:5; Acts 17:29 [y][Hos. 13:2]
19[y][See ver. 18 above]

40:9 high mountain. The reliability of God's promise calls for wholehearted public announcement (cf. 52:7). **fear not**. They are to proclaim the message by faith, whatever the conditions at the time (cf. 35:3–4). **cities of Judah**. The Jewish exiles will return to the Promised Land, for that is where the divine Messiah is to appear (cf. 48:20; Mic. 5:2).

40:10–11 The glorious Lord comes to his people as a conquering king, a generous benefactor, and a gentle **shepherd**.

40:12–26 God is able to keep his promise because no opposition can compare with the Creator of all things.

40:12–14 God alone established the creation. He is uniquely powerful and wise, so he is worthy of his people's trust (cf. Job 38–41; Rom. 11:34). **a span** (Hb. *zeret*). The distance between the ends of the thumb and the little finger when the hand is fully extended.

40:15–17 a drop from a bucket. The **nations** of mankind may seem insurmountable to Israel, but they are as **nothing** to God.

40:18–20 God alone is God. Isaiah looks with sarcasm at idol-manufacture. His simple description, without further comment, is mockery enough.

20 [z]ch. 46:6; Jer. 10:3-5; See ch. 44:9-15
21 [a]ver. 28; [Acts 14:17; Rom. 1:19, 20]
22 [b][Num. 13:33] [c]Job 9:8; Ps. 104:2
23 [d]Job 12:21; Ps. 107:40
24 [e]ch. 41:2; [Ps. 83:13]
25 [f]ver. 18
26 [g]Ps. 147:4
27 [h][ch. 49:14] [i][ch. 49:4]
28 [j][Ps. 121:4] [k]Ps. 147:5

20 [z]He who is too impoverished for an offering
chooses wood[1] that will not rot;
he seeks out a skillful craftsman
to set up an idol that will not move.

21 [a]Do you not know? Do you not hear?
Has it not been told you from the beginning?
Have you not understood from the foundations of the earth?
22 It is he who sits above the circle of the earth,
and its inhabitants are [b]like grasshoppers;
[c]who stretches out the heavens like a curtain,
and spreads them like a tent to dwell in;
23 [d]who brings princes to nothing,
and makes the rulers of the earth as emptiness.

24 Scarcely are they planted, scarcely sown,
scarcely has their stem taken root in the earth,
when he blows on them, and they wither,
[e]and the tempest carries them off like stubble.

25 [f]To whom then will you compare me,
that I should be like him? says the Holy One.
26 Lift up your eyes on high and see:
who created these?
[g]He who brings out their host by number,
calling them all by name,
by the greatness of his might,
and because he is strong in power
not one is missing.

27 Why do you say, O Jacob,
and speak, O Israel,
[h]"My way is hidden from the LORD,
[i]and my right is disregarded by my God"?
28 Have you not known? Have you not heard?
The LORD is [j]the everlasting God,
the Creator of the ends of the earth.
He does not faint or grow weary;
[k]his understanding is unsearchable.
29 He gives power to the faint,
and to him who has no might he increases strength.

[1] Or *He chooses valuable wood*

40:21–24 God rules effortlessly over world leaders.

40:22 the circle of the earth. Either the bowl-like sky over the earth (Job 22:14) or the outer horizon encircling the earth (Job 26:10). **stretches out the heavens like a curtain**. A number of passages (Job 9:8; Ps. 104:2; Isa. 42:5; 44:24; 45:12; 51:13; Jer. 10:12; 51:15; Zech. 12:1) use this image (with a verb that means to "pitch" or "stretch out" a tent, cf. Gen. 12:8; 26:25; 33:19; 35:21; Judg. 4:11) to stress that God alone fashioned the heavens and the earth, and prepared them as a place for habitation (**to dwell in**).

40:24 Scarcely. Human greatness briefly flourishes in one era of history, soon replaced by another brief display of human greatness. **He blows on them** with minimal effort. God controls the **tempest**, the chaotic processes of history.

40:25–26 Much of pagan religion, to which Isaiah's contemporaries had succumbed and with which the exiles were surrounded, worshiped astrological phenomena. In contrast to this, **the Holy One** of Israel is incomparable in his power (v. 12), wisdom (vv. 13–14), immensity (vv. 15–17), sovereignty (vv. 22–23), and authority (v. 25). Thus only Israel's God is worthy of worship, for he created, controls, and preserves what the pagans foolishly worship. **not one is missing**. God's creating the stars would have been awe-inspiring even in ancient Israel, where about 5,000 stars were visible at night. Astronomers now estimate, however, that there are more than 400 billion stars in the Milky Way galaxy, and that there are 125 billion galaxies in the universe. The total number of stars is estimated at $1x10^{22}$ or 10 billion trillions. Moreover, the God who created all of these, the Holy One of Israel, even calls **them all by name** and ensures that "not one is missing." Such a God will surely never forget even one of his people.

40:27–31 Faith in God's promise empowers his people for endurance.

40:27 Jacob . . . Israel. God is true to his covenant, despite his people's unbelief (cf. Gen. 35:9–15). **My way is hidden from the LORD**. While the despondent exiles could feel abandoned by God, it is the sovereign Creator (Isa. 40:21–26) who is the source of their strength (vv. 28–31). **my right**. The justice expected of God.

40:28–29 God never suffers setbacks, and he helps those who do.

30 Even youths shall faint and be weary,
and young men shall fall exhausted;
31 but [l]they who wait for the LORD shall renew their strength;
they shall mount up with wings [m]like eagles;
they shall run and not be weary;
they shall walk and not faint.

Fear Not, for I Am with You

41

1 [n]Listen to me in silence,[o]O coastlands;
let the peoples renew their strength;
let them approach, then let them speak;
let us together draw near for judgment.

2 [p]Who stirred up one from the east
whom victory meets at every [q]step?[1]
[r]He gives up nations before him,
so that he tramples kings underfoot;
he makes them like dust with his sword,
[s]like driven stubble with his bow.
3 He pursues them and passes on safely,
by paths his feet have not trod.
4 [t]Who has performed and done this,
calling the generations from the beginning?
[u]I, the LORD, the first,
and with the last; I am he.

5 [v]The coastlands have seen and are afraid;
the ends of the earth tremble;
they have drawn near and come.
6 Everyone helps his neighbor
and says to his brother, "Be strong!"
7 [w]The craftsman strengthens the goldsmith,
and he who smooths with the hammer him who strikes the anvil,
saying of the soldering, "It is good";
and they strengthen it with nails [x]so that it cannot be moved.

8 But you, Israel, [y]my servant,
Jacob, [z]whom I have chosen,
the offspring of Abraham, [a]my friend;
9 you whom I took from the ends of the earth,
and called [b]from its farthest corners,

[1] Or *whom righteousness calls to follow?*

31 [l]Ps. 103:5 [m][Ex. 19:4]

Chapter 41

1 [n][Hab. 2:20; Zech. 2:13] [o]See ch. 11:11
2 [p]ch. 46:11; [ch. 45:1] [q][Judg. 4:10] [r]2 Chr. 36:23 [s]ch. 40:24
4 [t][ver. 26] [u]ch. 43:10, 11; 44:6; 48:12; Rev. 1:8, 17; 22:13
5 [v]See ch. 11:11
7 [w]ch. 40:19 [x][ch. 40:20]
8 [y]ch. 44:1, 2 [z]Deut. 7:6; 10:15; 14:2; Ps. 135:4; [1 Pet. 2:9] [a]2 Chr. 20:7; James 2:23
9 [b]ch. 43:5, 6

40:30 Even youths. Human strength at its best inevitably fails. Only the promise of God can sustain human perseverance.

40:31 wait for the LORD. Savoring God's promise by faith until the time of fulfillment. **renew**. Find endless supplies of fresh strength.

41:1–20 *The One True God Moving History for His People.* God reassures his people that he alone is guiding all events in human history, for his glory and their benefit.

41:1–7 God argues for his sovereignty over history and the terrifying inadequacy of all idolatrous hopes.

41:1 let the peoples renew their strength. Let the unbelieving nations try to match the strength God gives his believing people (40:31). **let us together draw near for judgment**. God invites the nations to validate their own made-up explanations of history.

41:2 one from the east. Cyrus the Great, leader of the rising Persian Empire, soon to conquer Babylon (cf. 44:24–45:7). The Lord **gives up** (i.e., gives over) **nations before him** (that is, before Cyrus). **He** (the Lord) **makes them like dust with his sword** (that is, with Cyrus's sword). God is guiding "secular" events, even brutal events, by his own overruling redemptive purpose.

41:4 calling the generations from the beginning. The rise of Cyrus is not a unique event but is evidence of the one divine plan governing historical events from the beginning. On **the first** and **the last** in Isaiah, see also 44:6 and 48:12. These texts convey the idea that the Lord is the one and only God, the ruler of every last bit of history.

41:5–7 The nations respond to the upheavals of history by nervously constructing more gods to believe in. But how can created "creators" save?

41:8–20 God reassures his people that they have nothing to fear amid the turbulence he is stirring up in history.

41:8–9 God reminds his people of his active commitments to them. On **Israel** as the Lord's **servant**, see note on 42:1–9. Mention of God's having **chosen** Jacob and of Israel's status as the **offspring of Abraham** speaks clearly of God's promises (Gen. 17:7; 22:17) and therefore reminds them that they inhabit a story filled with God's purposes.

9[y][See ver. 8 above] [z][See ver. 8 above]
10[c]Ps. 48:10
11[d][ch. 45:24]
12[e]Ps. 37:10 [f]ch. 40:17
14[g][Ps. 22:6] [h]ch. 54:5; [Ps. 78:35]; See ch. 43:14
15[i]Mic. 4:13 [j][ch. 2:14]
16[k][Jer. 51:2] [l][ver. 2] [m]ch. 45:25
17[n][ch. 44:3]
18[o]ch. 35:6, 7 [p]Ps. 107:35

saying to you, "You are [y]my servant,
[z]I have chosen you and not cast you off";
10 fear not, for I am with you;
be not dismayed, for I am your God;
I will strengthen you, I will help you,
I will uphold you with [c]my righteous right hand.

11 [d]Behold, all who are incensed against you
shall be put to shame and confounded;
those who strive against you
shall be as nothing and shall perish.
12 [e]You shall seek those who contend with you,
but you shall not find them;
[f]those who war against you
shall be as nothing at all.
13 For I, the LORD your God,
hold your right hand;
it is I who say to you, "Fear not,
I am the one who helps you."

14 Fear not, you [g]worm Jacob,
you men of Israel!
I am the one who helps you, declares the LORD;
your [h]Redeemer is the Holy One of Israel.
15 [i]Behold, I make of you a threshing sledge,
new, sharp, and having teeth;
you shall thresh [j]the mountains and crush them,
and you shall make the hills like chaff;
16 [k]you shall winnow them, and [l]the wind shall carry them away,
and the tempest shall scatter them.
[m]And you shall rejoice in the LORD;
in the Holy One of Israel you shall glory.

17 [n]When the poor and needy seek water,
and there is none,
and their tongue is parched with thirst,
I the LORD will answer them;
I the God of Israel will not forsake them.
18 [o]I will open rivers on the bare heights,
and fountains in the midst of the valleys.
[p]I will make the wilderness a pool of water,
and the dry land springs of water.

41:10 You here is the people as a whole (called "Jacob" in v. 8). Unlike the terrified nations of v. 5, the people of God have in him reason to be fearless (cf. vv. 13–14). Unlike the gods of the nations, which must be strengthened and secured (v. 7), the God of Israel secures his people.

41:11–13 The fearful people of God, victimized by the cruel whims of human power, will be vindicated, for no human hostility can defeat God.

41:14–16 The weak people of God are made into a powerful force to remove even mountainous obstacles to his joyful purpose.

41:14 Worm (cf. 14:11; 66:24; Ex. 16:20; Deut. 28:39; Jonah 4:7) refers to various kinds of insect larvae and here is a symbol for weakness and insignificance (cf. Job 25:6; Ps. 22:6). **Redeemer**. There are two words for "redeem" in Isaiah (cf. note on Isa. 1:24–28), and both carry the idea of delivering and protecting. The term here (Hb. *ga'al*) is very common, especially in this part of Isaiah (35:9; 43:1, 14; 44:6, 22–24; 47:4; 48:17, 20; 49:7, 26; 51:10; 52:9; 54:5, 8; 59:20; 60:16; 62:12; 63:4, 9, 16); its use is based on its appearance in Ex. 6:6 and 15:13. The focus is on God's intent to rescue his people from their captivity and to foster the conditions under which their piety can flourish. Although in some places the word can imply the payment of a ransom, that is usually absent in Isaiah (although in Isa. 43:1–4, the prophet evokes this idea for rhetorical effect).

41:15–16 threshing sledge. A wooden platform studded underneath with sharp objects, dragged over harvested crops to rip open their husks. **The wind** and **the tempest** are the forces of history, created and guided by God for his own purpose.

41:17–20 The One stirring up the crises of history also pours out refreshment on his dry people for his own glory.

41:17 the poor and needy. The people of God, who refuse the false salvations of idolatry, look to God alone in faith. They are sustained as they make their way to Zion after release from exile. In vv. 8–9, God identifies his people from his perspective; here he describes them from their own perspective (cf. Ps. 37:14). **and there is none**. With every human resource exhausted, only God remains.

41:18–19 Abundant provision of both water and shade in a desolate environment.

19 [q]I will put in the wilderness the cedar,
the acacia, the myrtle, and the olive.
I will set in the desert [r]the cypress,
the plane and the pine together,
20 that they may see and know,
may consider and understand together,
that [s]the hand of the LORD has done this,
the Holy One of Israel has created it.

The Futility of Idols

21 Set forth your case, says the LORD;
bring your proofs, says the King of Jacob.
22 Let them bring them, and [t]tell us
what is to happen.
Tell us the former things, what they are,
that we may consider them,
that we may know their outcome;
or declare to us the things to come.
23 [t]Tell us what is to come hereafter,
that we may know that you are gods;
[u]do good, or do harm,
that we may be dismayed and terrified.[1]
24 Behold, [v]you are nothing,
and your work is less than nothing;
an abomination is he who chooses you.

25 [w]I stirred up one from the north, and he has come,
[x]from the rising of the sun, [y]and he shall call upon my name;
he shall trample on rulers as on mortar,
as the potter treads clay.
26 [z]Who declared it from the beginning, that we might know,
and beforehand, that we might say, "He is right"?
There was none who declared it, none who proclaimed,
none who heard your words.

[1] *Or that we may both be dismayed and see*

19[q]ch. 35:1, 2; 55:12, 13 [r]ch. 60:13
20[s]Job 12:9
22[t][ver. 26; ch. 44:7; 45:21; 46:10]
23[t][See ver. 22 above] [u][ch. 45:7]
24[v]ver. 29; [Ps. 115:8; 1 Cor. 8:4]
25[w]Jer. 50:3 [x]ver. 2 [y][Ps. 44:5]
26[z][ver. 22]

41:20 God acts in history, in both judgment and salvation, for his own glory. History is not only controlled by God; when understood rightly in light of God's word, history also displays the character of God, as everyone will ultimately acknowledge (cf. 45:22–23).

41:21–42:17 *False Hopes, the Lord's Servant, a New Song.* God challenges the false claims of human idols, he presents his servant as the only hope of the world, and he invites the whole human race to praise him for his salvation.

41:21–29 Set forth your case. God renews his challenge from v. 1, that the nations of the earth, with the help of their gods, demonstrate the truth of their beliefs. This is a recurring theme in this part of Isaiah: the Lord is superior to all other "gods," whether Canaanite (who tempted Isaiah's audience) or Mesopotamian (who confronted the exiles).

41:21 Your proofs are the nations' strongest arguments. The particular proofs concern which deities are successful at telling the future.

41:22 Let them bring them. I.e., let the nations bring their idols, which are motionless without human help! **Tell us**. "Us" refers to God and the people of Israel. **what is to happen**. A test case in this debate is the ability to prophesy future events. Canaanite and Mesopotamian religions claimed prophetic powers. Here and in the following chapters God claims that he alone can accurately predict the future, and this shows that he is the only true God (cf. 44:7–8; 45:21; 46:9–10). **the former things . . . the things to come**. A challenge to present the past and the future (42:9; 43:9, 18; 46:9; 48:3), providing a connected narrative of the overarching story of the world, a complete worldview, as offered in the Bible.

41:23 that we may know that you are gods. Sovereignty over history is required of deity. **do good, or do harm**. Do something, anything! **that we may be dismayed and terrified**. Human religion is intimidating but is empty, while the gospel is comforting (40:1) and comes with good and sufficient reasons for faith.

41:24 abomination. The debate that God calls for is no intellectual game. To prefer a false god is more than a mistake; it is perverse (cf. Lev. 18:30; Ps. 115:4–8; Rom. 1:18–32). **chooses**. To choose an idol is to forsake the choice of God (Isa. 41:8; cf. 1 John 5:21).

41:25–29 Having dismissed the false gods, the Lord predicts the rise of Cyrus as clear proof that he (the Lord) is God above all gods.

41:25 one from the north . . . from the rising of the sun. In v. 2 Cyrus is presented as "one from the east," and here as one from the north and the east. As head of the Medo-Persian Empire, he represents the north (Media) and the east (Persia). See Dan. 5:28; 8:3–4, 20. **he shall call upon my name**. Cyrus used diplomatic God-talk (Ezra 1:1–4), but he was not a believer (Isa. 45:4–5). Cyrus's policies, however, were part of God's strategy to reveal himself in history.

41:26 God points to the failure of idolatrous religions to foretell the rise of Cyrus. **that we might know . . . that we might say**. "We" refers to God and his people, as God speaks on their behalf and challenges the other nations; see notes on vv. 22 and 23. **your words**. Predictions from idolatrous oracles. See "your case" in v. 21.

27 [a]I was the first to say[1] to Zion, "Behold, here they are!"
and [b]I give to Jerusalem a herald of good news.
28 [c]But when I look, there is no one;
among these there is no counselor
who, when I ask, gives an answer.
29 [d]Behold, they are all a delusion;
their works are nothing;
their metal images are empty wind.

The LORD's Chosen Servant

42

1 [e]Behold [f]my servant, whom I uphold,
my chosen, [g]in whom my soul delights;
[h]I have put my Spirit upon him;
[i]he will bring forth justice to the nations.
2 He will not cry aloud or lift up his voice,
or make it heard in the street;
3 [j]a bruised reed he will not break,
and a faintly burning wick he will not quench;
[k]he will faithfully bring forth justice.
4 He will not grow faint or be discouraged[2]
till he has established justice in the earth;
and [l]the coastlands wait for his law.

5 Thus says God, the LORD,
who created the heavens [m]and stretched them out,
who spread out the earth and what comes from it,
[n]who gives breath to the people on it
and spirit to those who walk in it:
6 "I am the LORD; [o]I have called you[3] in righteousness;
I will take you by the hand and keep you;

27[a]ch. 51:12 [b]ch. 40:9; 52:7
28[c]See ver. 21-24
29[d][ver. 12]
Chapter 42
1[e]Cited Matt. 12:18-20 [f]ch. 41:8; 43:10; 52:13; 53:11; [ver. 19; Ezek. 34:24; Zech. 3:8; Acts 3:26; 4:27; Phil. 2:7] [g]Matt. 3:17 [h]ch. 11:2; 61:1 [i][ch. 2:4]
3[j][ch. 57:15] [k]Ps. 9:8
4[l]ch. 60:9; Gen. 10:5; [ch. 2:3; Matt. 12:21]
5[m]ch. 44:24; 45:12 [n]Acts 17:25
6[o]ch. 41:9

[1] Or *Formerly I said* [2] Or *bruised* [3] The Hebrew term for *you* is singular; four times in this verse

41:27 here they are. Presumably, Cyrus's conquests in v. 25b. **a herald of good news**. Isaiah, as a voice for the gospel.

41:29 they are all a delusion. I.e., all who look to the idols of their own making for guidance and stability. God thus concludes the debate.

42:1–9 This is the first of four Servant Songs, fulfilled in Jesus Christ (cf. 49:1–13; 50:4–9; 52:13–53:12). Isaiah sprinkles references to "the servant of the Lord" throughout chs. 40–55. Often it is a title for the people as a whole (41:8–9; 42:19; 43:10; 44:1–2, 21, 26; 45:4; 48:20), but at times the servant is a specific person within Israel who is distinct from the whole, with a calling to serve Israel and beyond (49:5–6; 50:10; see notes on 52:13; 53:11). The second Servant Song (49:1–13), which clarifies that the servant is distinct from Israel, also *calls* him Israel (49:3); this is best explained as identifying the servant as the representative and embodiment of the whole people. This last point shows why the traditional Christian reading, that the servant is a messianic figure, accurately captures Isaiah's intent. First, in the Davidic covenant, David's heirs represent and embody the people as a whole: Israel is God's "son" (Ex. 4:22–23), and the king becomes God's "son" on his coronation (2 Sam. 7:14; cf. Ps. 89:26–27). Therefore the servant follows the pattern of David's heirs. Second, the servant achieves the expansion of his rule throughout the Gentile world (Isa. 42:1–4; 52:13–15), which is the work of the Davidic Messiah in chs. 7–12. Third, later prophets describe an heir of David, and especially the Messiah, as the servant (Ezek. 34:23–24; 37:25; Hag. 2:23; Zech. 3:8; cf. Jer. 33:21–22, 26), which supports reading the servant in Isaiah as a messianic figure. In addition to his royal function, the servant also has a prophetic role (Isa. 49:1; 50:4, 10) and a priestly one (53:11; cf. Ps. 110:4, which folds a priestly role into Messiah's royal office). Isaiah's audience must know that God will restore the exiles and then fulfill the mission of Israel by means of the servant whom he will raise up at some unspecified time after the return from exile: this is where their story is headed.

42:1 Behold my servant. In contrast to the idols ("Behold, you," 41:24) and the idol-worshiping nations ("Behold, they," 41:29), God presents his servant as the only hope of the nations (cited in Matt. 12:18–21). **whom I uphold**. The servant's success is of God. **in whom my soul delights**. The servant is God's delight, in contrast with the "abomination" of Isa. 41:24 (cf. Matt. 3:17; Luke 9:35). **my Spirit**. The servant's power, in contrast with the "empty wind" of Isa. 41:29 (cf. 11:2; 61:1). The human race, by implication, is impressed with the wrong strategies, remedies, and powers. **justice**. The key word in 42:1–4. In the Bible, justice means fulfilling mutual obligations in a manner consistent with God's moral law. Biblical justice creates the perfect human society (cf. Deut. 10:18; Isa. 1:17; 16:5; 32:1–2; 61:8; Zech. 7:9). The messianic servant is the only hope for a truly just world. This Messiah will bring not only individual spiritual forgiveness and health (cf. Isa. 1:18) but also the establishment of perfect justice throughout all earthly governments.

42:2–3 In contrast with ruthless human conquerors, like Cyrus (41:2, 25), the Lord's quiet servant will not crush but will defend the weak (cf. 11:4; 40:11).

42:4 The servant is unweakened by the demands of his mission. **the coastlands**. Using the lands surrounding the Mediterranean Sea as the image, this designates the remotest peoples of the earth.

42:5 The Creator and Sustainer God is well able to keep the promises of vv. 1–4.

42:6–7 The servant is **a covenant for the people** (cf. 49:8), i.e., he represents the people in God's covenant. He will become **a light for the nations** (cf. 49:6), bringing the knowledge of God to them; this probably lies behind Jesus' saying in John 8:12. **to open the eyes . . . to bring out**. This is the purpose of God's grace for his people, using liberation from Babylonian exile as an image for spiritual liberation.

I will give you [p]as a covenant for the people,
[q]a light for the nations,
7 [r]to open the eyes that are blind,
to bring out the prisoners from the dungeon,
[s]from the prison those who sit in darkness.
8 I am the LORD; that is my name;
[t]my glory I give to no other,
nor my praise to carved idols.
9 Behold, the former things have come to pass,
[u]and new things I now declare;
before they spring forth
I tell you of them."

Sing to the LORD a New Song

10 [v]Sing to the LORD a new song,
his praise from the end of the earth,
[w]you who go down to the sea, and all that fills it,
[l]the coastlands and their inhabitants.
11 Let the desert and its cities lift up their voice,
the villages that [x]Kedar inhabits;
let the habitants of [y]Sela sing for joy,
let them shout from the top of the mountains.
12 Let them give glory to the LORD,
and declare his praise in [l]the coastlands.
13 [z]The LORD goes out like a mighty man,
like a man of war [a]he stirs up his zeal;
he cries out, [b]he shouts aloud,
he shows himself mighty against his foes.

14 For a long time I have held my peace;
I have kept still and restrained myself;
now I will cry out [c]like a woman in labor;
I will gasp and pant.
15 [d]I will lay waste mountains and hills,
and dry up all their vegetation;
I will turn the rivers into islands,[1]
and dry up the pools.

[1] Or *into coastlands*

6 [p]ch. 49:6, 8 [q]Luke 2:32
7 [r]ch. 35:5; 49:9; 61:1; Heb. 2:14, 15 [s]Luke 1:79
8 [t]ch. 48:11
9 [u][ch. 43:19]
10 [v]See Ps. 33:3 [w]Ps. 107:23 [l][See ver. 4 above]
11 [x]See ch. 21:16 [y]ch. 16:1
12 [l][See ver. 4 above]
13 [z]ch. 40:10 [a][ch. 9:7; 59:17] [b]Ps. 78:65
14 [c]See ch. 13:8
15 [d]ch. 50:2

42:8–9 Both the triumph of Cyrus (41:2–4, 25–29) and the greater triumph of the servant glorify the true Lord of history and discredit idolatrous claims of human mastery. The God who has promised the world-transforming display of his glory (40:5) directs all events as he pleases to that final end. **my glory I give to no other**. God must discredit all idols to receive his proper honor. He is not one of many; he is not superior among inferior gods; he is not even the best of all; he is the *only* God, and he will have his people know and rejoice in this truth. **new things I now declare**. God deliberately draws attention to the seemingly impossible predictions he is making, citing his previous prophecies as evidence of his credibility (cf. 41:22).

42:10–17 God calls all the nations to rejoice in his triumphant self-vindication.

42:10 a new song. See note on Ps. 33:1–3. This is unprecedented praise, such as has never been heard before, marking the greatness of the revelation of the servant in history (cf. Rev. 5:9; 14:3). The joy of his liberating approach stands in contrast with the dread felt among the nations at the rise of Cyrus (cf. Isa. 41:5–6).

42:11 Kedar. Nomads of the Arabian desert. **Sela**. Probably a Moabite town (cf. 16:1). Former enemies of God join in the widening scope of celebration (cf. Gal. 3:28; Col. 3:11).

42:12 declare his praise. The Septuagint translation of this phrase ("they will proclaim his excellencies") may lie behind the phrase "proclaim the excellencies" in 1 Pet. 2:9; it is the task of the converted Gentiles to praise God to even more Gentiles in order to bring them into the ranks of the people of God.

42:13 like a mighty man. As a soldier going into battle stirs up his emotions, God is committed to his victory from the depths of his being.

42:14 For a long time. To the Jewish exiles in Babylon, it would have seemed that God was delaying, but his passion for them was intensifying. **like a woman in labor**. As a woman cries out after finally going into labor, God, at the time he knows is best, will exert himself to bring his purpose to fulfillment (cf. Luke 12:50).

42:15 Cf. 41:18–19. In God's passion for his people and for his own glory (42:13–14), no obstacle in human society can stand in his way.

42:16 No human incapacity can defeat God's purpose of grace. His ways are so counterintuitive to human understanding that those he delivers might as well be **blind**, in **darkness** and on **rough** terrain, but God leads them through (cf. Ex. 13:21–22).

42:17 Every foolish object of trust leads to personal disgrace.

42:18–43:21 *God Reclaims His People for His Glory.* God promises to restore his confused people to clarity about himself as their only Savior.

16[e]ch. 35:5, 8 [f]ch. 40:4
17[g]ch. 1:29; 44:11; 45:16; Ps. 97:7
20[h]See Rom. 2:21-23 [i][Jer. 6:10]
22[j]ch. 14:17
25[k][ch. 47:11; Hos. 7:9] [l]ch. 57:1, 11

Chapter 43

1[m]ch. 44:2, 21, 24 [n]ch. 41:14 [o]ch. 45:3, 4; [Gen. 32:28]

16 [e]And I will lead the blind
in a way that they do not know,
in paths that they have not known
I will guide them.
I will turn the darkness before them into light,
[f]the rough places into level ground.
These are the things I do,
and I do not forsake them.
17 [g]They are turned back and utterly put to shame,
who trust in carved idols,
who say to metal images,
"You are our gods."

Israel's Failure to Hear and See

18 Hear, you deaf,
and look, you blind, that you may see!
19 Who is blind but my servant,
or deaf as my messenger whom I send?
Who is blind as my dedicated one,[1]
or blind as the servant of the LORD?
20 [h]He sees many things, but does not observe them;
[i]his ears are open, but he does not hear.
21 The LORD was pleased, for his righteousness' sake,
to magnify his law and make it glorious.
22 But this is a people plundered and looted;
they are all of them trapped in holes
[j]and hidden in prisons;
they have become plunder with none to rescue,
spoil with none to say, "Restore!"
23 Who among you will give ear to this,
will attend and listen for the time to come?
24 Who gave up Jacob to the looter,
and Israel to the plunderers?
Was it not the LORD, against whom we have sinned,
in whose ways they would not walk,
and whose law they would not obey?
25 So he poured on him the heat of his anger
and the might of battle;
it set him on fire all around, [k]but he did not understand;
it burned him up, [l]but he did not take it to heart.

Israel's Only Savior

43 1 But now thus says the LORD,
[m]he who created you, O Jacob,
he who formed you, O Israel:
[n]"Fear not, for I have redeemed you;
[o]I have called you by name, you are mine.

[1] *Or as the one at peace with me*

42:18–25 God's own people need deliverance as much as the nations do.

42:18–19 In vv. 1–4, the servant of the Lord is the Savior of the world, but now the servant needs salvation. According to v. 24, this servant is Jacob/Israel. What the nation failed to be, the servant is (see note on vv. 1–9). He alone qualifies as a covenant for the people of God and a light for the nations, to open many blind eyes (vv. 6–7). The designations **my servant, my messenger, my dedicated one**, and **the servant of the LORD** emphasize the spiritual privileges granted to Israel (cf. 41:8–10).

42:20–22 Exposure to the gospel makes no impact on blind Israel, though it is worthy of their trust (cf. 6:9–10). Rather than attracting the nations to God (2:2–5), Israel is **plundered** by the nations, beyond all self-remedy (cf. Deut. 28:25–34; 2 Kings 24:8–25:21).

42:23–25 The fall of Israel cannot be explained as a failure of God. He is powerful, but his power turned against them because they turned against his word. The real problem for God's people, therefore, is not their captivity in Babylon but their disobedience to God. That is what they do not understand (cf. 1:5–6).

43:1–7 God reassures his people that, for his own glory, he will ensure their wonderful restoration.

43:1 Fear not. Knowing what they deserve, the people should fear;

2 [p]When you pass through the waters, I will be with you;
and through the rivers, they shall not overwhelm you;
[p]when you walk through fire [q]you shall not be burned,
and the flame shall not consume you.
3 For [r]I am the LORD your God,
the Holy One of Israel, your Savior.
[s]I give Egypt as your ransom,
Cush and [t]Seba in exchange for you.
4 Because you are precious in my eyes,
and honored, and I love you,
I give men in return for you,
peoples in exchange for your life.
5 [u]Fear not, for I am with you;
[v]I will bring your offspring from the east,
and from the west I will gather you.
6 I will say to the north, Give up,
and to the south, Do not withhold;
bring [w]my sons from afar
and [w]my daughters from the end of the earth,
7 everyone who is called by my name,
whom I created for my glory,
whom I formed and made."
8 Bring out [x]the people who are blind, yet have eyes,
who are deaf, yet have ears!
9 [y]All the nations gather together,
and the peoples assemble.
Who among them can declare this,
and show us the former things?
Let them bring their witnesses to prove them right,
and let them hear and say, It is true.
10 [z]"You are my witnesses," declares the LORD,
"and [a]my servant whom I have chosen,
that you may know and believe me
and understand that I am he.
[b]Before me no god was formed,
nor shall there be any after me.
11 [c]I, I am the LORD,
and besides me there is no savior.
12 I declared and saved and proclaimed,
when there was no strange god among you;
and [z]you are my witnesses," declares the LORD, "and I am God.

2[p]Ps. 66:12 [q]ch. 42:25; [Dan. 3:25, 27]
3[r]See Ex. 20:2 [s][ch. 45:14; 52:3, 4] [t]Ps. 72:10
5[u]ch. 41:10, 13, 14; 44:2; Jer. 30:10, 11 [v]ch. 49:12; [ch. 60:8, 9; Ps. 107:3]
6[w][2 Cor. 6:18]
8[x]ch. 42:19
9[y]ch. 41:1, 21, 22
10[z]ver. 12; ch. 44:8 [a]ch. 42:1 [b]See ch. 41:4
11[c]ch. 45:21; Hos. 13:4
12[z][See ver. 10 above]

but hearing of their Redeemer's choice and promise, they should not fear. **redeemed**. See note on 41:14. **you are mine**. What defines them is not their guilty blindness (42:18–25) but the grace of the One who says, "You are mine" (cf. Ex. 6:7).

43:2 You designates the whole people (v. 1). Even when they are subject to the hardships of captivity and exile, God is still with his people (cf. 41:10).

43:3–4 God's people are secured by his resolve to be glorified through their salvation. **I give Egypt as your ransom . . . Cush and Seba**. Here Isaiah plays on the idea of a ransom price that is sometimes conveyed by "redeemed" (v. 1; see note on 41:14). God will move history for the sake of his people. "Egypt" alludes to the exodus. The more remote Cush and Seba may imply that God will go to any length and alter the history of any nation for his people's salvation. On "Cush," see note on 18:1. "Seba" was probably along the Red Sea, though it is uncertain whether it was on the African or Arabian side.

43:5–7 Wherever God's people may be scattered, he will bring them home (cf. Deut. 30:1–4). **whom I created for my glory**. God's people become living proof of his glory, which is his ultimate goal in salvation (cf. Eph. 1:3–6).

43:8–13 God's people exist in order to declare his exclusive deity.

43:8–9 Isaiah imagines a great gathering of Israel and the nations in which God challenges anyone to match his proven ability to achieve his purposes in history. **this**. Probably the rise of Cyrus the Great (cf. 41:2). **the former things**. Previous prophecies. **Let them bring their witnesses**. God is unafraid of a full and open presentation of the facts. Indeed, he commands it.

43:10–13 In this great trial, God's people are his **witnesses** to his exclusive reality as God (cf. Acts 1:8, where Jesus likewise declares his apostles his witnesses). God emphasizes repeatedly that he alone is God. Nineteen words in the Hebrew text of these verses are in a first-person singular form (I, me, my). Israel's exclusive loyalty to the Lord, and their witness to the nations, defines their identity.

13[d]ch. 41:4; Ps. 90:2; [John 8:58]
14[e][ver. 4] [f][ch. 47:1] [g]ch. 23:13
16[h]ch. 51:10; Ex. 14:21, 22; Ps. 77:19
17[i]See Ex. 14:4-9 [j][Ps. 76:5, 6] [k]ch. 1:31; [Ps. 118:12]
18[l][Jer. 16:14; 23:7]
19[m][ch. 42:9; 2 Cor. 5:17; Rev. 21:5] [n]ch. 35:8 [o]ch. 41:18; 48:21
20[p]See ch. 13:22 [q][ch. 49:10]
21[r]Ps. 79:13; [Ps. 22:3; 105:1; Luke 1:74, 75; 1 Pet. 2:9]
22[s]Mic. 6:3
23[t][Amos 5:25] [s][See ver. 22 above]

13 Also [d]henceforth I am he;
there is none who can deliver from my hand;
I work, and who can turn it back?"

14 Thus says the LORD,
your Redeemer, the Holy One of Israel:
[e]"For your sake I send to Babylon
and [f]bring them all down as fugitives,
[g]even the Chaldeans, in the ships in which they rejoice.
15 I am the LORD, your Holy One,
the Creator of Israel, your King."

16 Thus says the LORD,
[h]who makes a way in the sea,
a path in the mighty waters,
17 who [i]brings forth chariot and horse,
army and warrior;
they lie down, they cannot rise,
[j]they are extinguished, [k]quenched like a wick:
18 [l]"Remember not the former things,
nor consider the things of old.
19 [m]Behold, I am doing a new thing;
now it springs forth, do you not perceive it?
[n]I will make a way in the wilderness
[o]and rivers in the desert.
20 The wild beasts will honor me,
[p]the jackals and the ostriches,
[q]for I give water in the wilderness,
rivers in the desert,
to give drink to my chosen people,
21 the people whom I formed for myself
[r]that they might declare my praise.

22 "Yet you did not call upon me, O Jacob;
but [s]you have been weary of me, O Israel!
23 [t]You have not brought me your sheep for burnt offerings,
or honored me with your sacrifices.
I have not burdened you with offerings,
[s]or wearied you with frankincense.
24 You have not bought me sweet cane with money,
or satisfied me with the fat of your sacrifices.
But you have burdened me with your sins;
you have wearied me with your iniquities.

43:14–15 God promises that the Babylonian conquerors of the Jewish people will themselves be conquered and exiled. **Babylon** is mentioned explicitly here for the first time in chs. 40–55. **I am . . . your King**. The guarantor of God's promise is God himself.

43:16–21 God promises that his people will be released from exile through a new exodus.

43:16–17 Isaiah's language evokes the exodus through the Red Sea at the nation's birth (cf. Ex. 14:21–30). **makes . . . brings**. The present-tense verbs imply that the great exodus was representative of what God does and that it is therefore repeatable. **they lie down . . . like a wick**. God's enemies are absolutely defeated.

43:18–19 The original exodus did not exhaust God's power but provided a pattern of new exodus-like deliverances. The Jewish exiles should not live in the past but should look for God to bring them home from Babylon through another "exodus." **a way in the wilderness**. Where there is no clear path forward, God creates one. **rivers in the desert**. Where there is no natural relief or refreshment, God provides it.

43:20–21 These verses hint that a grander, more ultimate exodus still awaits God's people (cf. Rom. 8:20–21). God's ultimate goal is **that** his people **might declare** his **praise**.

43:22–44:23 *God Revives His People for His Glory.* God promises to pour his life-giving Spirit upon his weary people.

43:22–28 Far from declaring his praise, God's people have failed him. Therefore, he will save them **for** his **own sake** (v. 25).

43:22 you did not call upon me. Israel practiced their worship with the unspoken intention of evading God, not meeting God. **you have been weary of me**. Their attitude in worship implied that God is a demanding bore.

43:23–24 While in Babylonian exile, the Jewish people were unable to continue the Mosaic sacrificial system. God did not demand of them impossible observances, but they burdened him with their spiritual apathy.

25 “I, I am he
[u]who blots out [v]your transgressions for my own sake,
and I will not remember your sins.
26 Put me in remembrance; [w]let us argue together;
set forth your case, that you may be proved right.
27 [x]Your first father sinned,
and [y]your mediators transgressed against me.
28 Therefore [z]I will profane the princes of the sanctuary,
and [a]deliver Jacob to utter destruction
and Israel to reviling.

Israel the LORD’s Chosen

44

1 “But now hear, [b]O Jacob my servant,
Israel whom I have chosen!
2 Thus says the LORD who made you,
[c]who formed you from the womb and will help you:
[d]Fear not, O Jacob my servant,
[e]Jeshurun whom I have chosen.
3 [f]For I will pour water on the thirsty land,
and streams on the dry ground;
I will pour my Spirit upon your offspring,
and my blessing on your descendants.
4 They shall spring up among the grass
[g]like willows by flowing streams.
5 [h]This one will say, ‘I am the LORD’s,’
another will call on the name of Jacob,
and another will write on his hand, ‘The LORD’s,’
and name himself by the name of Israel.”

Besides Me There Is No God

6 Thus says the LORD, the King of Israel
and [i]his Redeemer, the LORD of hosts:
[j]“I am the first and I am the last;
besides me there is no god.
7 [k]Who is like me? Let him proclaim it.[1]
Let him declare and set it before me,
since I appointed an ancient people.
Let them declare what is to come, and what will happen.
8 Fear not, nor be afraid;
have I not told you from of old and declared it?
[l]And you are my witnesses!
[m]Is there a God besides me?
There is no [n]Rock; I know not any.”

[1] Or *Who like me can proclaim it?*

25 [u]ch. 44:22; [Ezek. 36:25, 26] [v][ch. 46:8]
26 [w]ch. 1:18
27 [x][Ezek. 16:3] [y][Jer. 5:31]
28 [z]Lam. 2:2 [a][Jer. 24:9; 29:22]

Chapter 44

1 [b]See ch. 41:8
2 [c]ver. 24; ch. 49:15; [Ps. 71:6; Jer. 1:5; Gal. 1:15] [d]See ch. 43:5 [e]Deut. 32:15
3 [f]Joel 2:28; John 7:38; Acts 2:18; See ch. 35:6
4 [g][Ps. 1:3]
5 [h][ch. 14:1]
6 [i]See ch. 43:14 [j]ch. 48:12; Rev. 1:8; See ch. 41:4
7 [k]ch. 41:26, 27
8 [l]ch. 43:10 [m]ch. 45:5; Deut. 4:35, 39; 32:39; 1 Sam. 2:2; Joel 2:27 [n]See ch. 30:29

43:25 I, I am he. God stands forth, boldly declaring the mystery of his grace. Why he forgives his people cannot be understood by human moral reasoning. **For my own sake** locates the reason for his grace deep within his own being and requires its glorious display before his creatures.

43:26–28 The people are invited to prove that they deserve God’s favor, in order that they may repent of all self-righteousness. Their record is a failure; their just reward is total judgment. **Your first father**. Abraham or Jacob. **your mediators**. Their religious leaders.

44:1–5 God reassures his people that his final purpose for them is blessing.

44:1–2 God reminds his people how fully he has committed himself to them. **Jeshurun** (probably meaning “upright one”) is a name for Israel (cf. Deut. 32:15; 33:5, 26).

44:3–4 The “utter destruction” of 43:28 reduces God’s people to **thirsty land** and **dry ground**, but under the outpouring of **my Spirit**, they thrive and multiply (cf. 32:15; 65:17–25; Joel 2:28–32; Luke 24:49). **your offspring . . . your descendants**. The blessing rolls on through the generations.

44:5 The imagery in v. 4 is explained as one enthusiastic conversion to the Lord after another. The Lord’s decisive grace (43:25) bears fruit in many new believers’ decisive faith (cf. Psalm 87). **The LORD’s . . . Israel**. Identification with the Lord entails identification with his people.

44:6–8 The Lord alone is God and therefore fully able to keep his promises.

44:8 you are my witnesses. God’s people exist to be living proof of his all-sufficiency (cf. note on 43:10–13). **Rock**. See Deut. 32:4, 15, 18, 30, 31; Isa. 8:14; 17:10.

The Folly of Idolatry

9 [o]All who fashion idols are nothing, and the things they delight in do not profit. Their
witnesses neither see nor know, that they may be put to shame. 10 [p]Who fashions a god or
casts an idol that is profitable for nothing? 11 [q]Behold, all his companions shall be put to
shame, and the craftsmen are only human. Let them all assemble, let them stand forth.
They shall be terrified; they shall be put to shame together.
12 [p]The ironsmith takes a cutting tool and works it over the coals. He fashions it with
hammers and works it with his strong arm. He becomes hungry, and his strength fails;
he drinks no water and is faint. 13 The carpenter stretches a line; he marks it out with a
pencil. He shapes it with planes and marks it with a compass. [r]He shapes it into the figure of a man, with the beauty of a man, to dwell in a house. 14 [s]He cuts down cedars, or
he chooses a cypress tree or an oak and lets it grow strong among the trees of the forest.
He plants a cedar and the rain nourishes it. 15 Then it becomes fuel for a man. He takes
a part of it and warms himself; he kindles a fire and bakes bread. Also he makes a god
and worships it; he makes it an idol and falls down before it. 16 Half of it he burns in the
fire. Over the half he eats meat; he roasts it and is satisfied. Also he warms himself and
says, "Aha, I am warm, I have seen the fire!" 17 And the rest of it he makes into a god, his
idol, and falls down to it and worships it. [t]He prays to it and says, "Deliver me, for you
are my god!"
18 They know not, nor do they discern, for he has shut their eyes, so that they cannot see,
and their hearts, so that they cannot understand. 19 No one considers, nor is there knowledge or discernment to say, "Half of it I burned in the fire; I also baked bread on its coals;
I roasted meat and have eaten. And shall I make the rest of it an [u]abomination? Shall I fall
down before a block of wood?" 20 [v]He feeds on [w]ashes; a deluded heart has led him astray,
and he cannot deliver himself or say, "Is there not [x]a lie in my right hand?"

The Lord Redeems Israel

21 Remember these things, O Jacob,
  and Israel, for you are [y]my servant;
I formed you; you are my servant;
  [z]O Israel, you will not be forgotten by me.
22 [a]I have blotted out your transgressions like a cloud
  and your sins like mist;
return to me, for I have redeemed you.

23 [b]Sing, O heavens, for the Lord has done it;
  shout, O [c]depths of the earth;
break forth into singing, O mountains,
  O forest, and every tree in it!

9 [o]ch. 41:24, 29
10 [p][ch. 40:19, 20; 41:6, 7; 46:6, 7; Hab. 2:18]; See Jer. 10:3-5
11 [q]ch. 45:16; Ps. 115:8; See ch. 42:17
12 [p][See ver. 10 above]
13 [r]See Ps. 115:5-7
14 [s][ch. 40:20]
17 [t][ch. 45:20]
19 [u]Deut. 27:15
20 [v]Hos. 12:1 [w][Job 13:12] [x]Ps. 144:8; [Rom. 1:25]
21 [y]ch. 42:19; See ch. 42:1 [z][ch. 49:15]
22 [a]ch. 43:25
23 [b]ch. 49:13; [ch. 55:12; Ps. 69:34; Jer. 51:48] [c]Ps. 63:9; [Hos. 2:21, 22]

44:9–20 The idols made by humans delude people into compulsive folly (cf. Acts 14:15; 17:24–25; Rom. 1:21–25; 1 Cor. 8:4–6; 1 Thess. 1:9; Rev. 21:8; 22:14–15).

44:9–11 All . . . all . . . all . . . together. A sweeping assertion, without a single exception. **do not profit . . . profitable for nothing**. Pagan culture, based on idolatry, brings no benefit to anyone; nor can it prevent God from keeping his promises. **Their witnesses** are the worshipers of idols, in contrast with "my witnesses" in v. 8. **put to shame . . . put to shame . . . put to shame**. The nothingness of idols dooms their worshipers to disgrace.

44:12–17 The embarrassing absurdity of man-made gods is obvious.

44:12 He fashions it. Contrast "he who formed you" in 43:1 and "I formed you" in 44:21. **his strong arm**. This is meant ironically, in view of 40:10–11, 26, 29–31. **his strength fails**. The human god-maker is himself limited.

44:13 the beauty of a man. The projection of human self-idealization (cf. Gen. 1:26–27). **a house**. I.e., a temple.

44:14 The false gods depend on human purpose for their existence. **the rain nourishes it**. The very materials of god-manufacture come from natural processes, sustained by a higher power.

44:15–17 the rest of it. The leftovers of ordinary human activity provide gods to whom people turn for deliverance. Isaiah is astonished.

44:18–20 As in v. 9, God judges idolatrous worship with subrational blindness. This explains why the stupidity described in vv. 12–17 is not obvious to those involved (cf. 6:9–10; 2 Cor. 4:4). **abomination**. Not a mere mistake (cf. Deut. 27:15).

44:21–23 God calls his people to clear awareness of his glorious grace.

44:21 Remember. God calls his people to focused thought, in contrast to the muddled delusions described in vv. 9–20 about **these things**, both the all-sufficiency of the God who makes true promises to his people and the emptiness of the false gods with their lies. **I formed you**. Contrast "all who fashion idols" in v. 9 and "he fashions it" in v. 12 (cf. 45:9, 11).

44:22 like a cloud . . . like mist. Before God's grace, sins fade away to nothing. **return to me, for I have redeemed you**. Repentance is motivated by grace (cf. Rom. 2:4).

44:23 The redemption of God's people will be the joy of the whole creation, because God's people will rule it wisely and well (cf. 35:1–2; 49:13; 55:12–13; Rom. 8:19–21). **forest . . . every tree**. See Isa. 44:14. The very creation, now misused for idolatrous purposes, will then sing to God.

For the LORD has redeemed Jacob,
[d]and will be glorified[1] in Israel.

24 Thus says the LORD, [e]your Redeemer,
[f]who formed you from the womb:
[g]"I am the LORD, who made all things,
[h]who alone stretched out the heavens,
who spread out the earth by myself,
25 who frustrates the signs of liars
and makes fools of diviners,
[i]who turns wise men back
and makes their knowledge foolish,
26 [j]who confirms the word of his servant
and fulfills the counsel of his messengers,
who says of Jerusalem, 'She shall be inhabited,'
[k]and of the cities of Judah, 'They shall be built,
and I will raise up their ruins';
27 [l]who says to the deep, 'Be dry;
I will dry up your rivers';
28 who says of [m]Cyrus, 'He is [n]my shepherd,
and he shall fulfill all my purpose';
saying of Jerusalem, 'She shall be built,'
[o]and of the temple, 'Your foundation shall be laid.'"

Cyrus, God's Instrument

45 1 Thus says the LORD to [p]his anointed, to Cyrus,
[q]whose right hand I have grasped,
to subdue nations before him
and [r]to loose the belts of kings,
to open doors before him
that gates may not be closed:
2 "I will go before you
and [s]level the exalted places,[2]
[t]I will break in pieces the doors of bronze
and cut through the bars of iron,
3 [u]I will give you the treasures of darkness
and the hoards in secret places,
that you may know that it is I, the LORD,
the God of Israel, [v]who call you by your name.
4 For the sake of my servant Jacob,
and Israel my chosen,

[1] Or *will display his beauty* [2] Masoretic Text; Dead Sea Scroll, Septuagint *level the mountains*

23[d]ch. 49:3; [ch. 55:5; 60:9]
24[e]See ch. 43:14 [f]See ver. 2 [g][ch. 42:5] [h]ch. 42:5; 45:12
25[i][ch. 19:3, 14]
26[j][2 Chr. 36:22] [k][Jer. 32:15, 44]
27[l]ch. 11:15; [ch. 51:10]
28[m]ch. 45:1 [n][2 Sam. 5:2; Ps. 78:72] [o]ch. 45:13; See 2 Chr. 36:22, 23; Ezra 1:1-3

Chapter 45

1[p][ch. 44:28] [q][ch. 41:13] [r]Job 12:21; [ver. 5; ch. 22:21]
2[s]ch. 40:4 [t]Ps. 107:16
3[u][Jer. 50:37; 51:13] [v]ch. 43:1

44:24–45:25 *God Predicts His Use of Cyrus.* God names Cyrus the Great as the one through whom he will restore postexilic Jerusalem.

44:24–28 God, sovereign over all things, promises his people a deliverer.

44:24 you. The people, i.e., Jacob (v. 21). **I am the LORD, who made all things**. God is not too great to care for his people; he is too great *not* to care for them. **alone . . . by myself**. The pagan gods, according to their legends, consulted together for wisdom.

44:25–26 frustrates . . . confirms. Even as God overrules human predictions of the future, he translates his own promises into realities. **his servant . . . his messengers**. Isaiah and other prophets. This short-term prophecy of the restoration of Judah, fulfilled within the experience of the Jewish exiles, verifies the credibility of longer-term prophecies.

44:27 I will dry up your rivers. Probably a reference to the miraculous crossing of the Red Sea at the exodus (cf. 11:15; 43:16–17; 51:10).

44:28 Cyrus is predicted by name, validating God's claim to be the One guiding history (see a similar prophetic naming in 1 Kings 13:1–3; 2 Kings 23:15–17). Josephus (*Jewish Antiquities* 11.5–7) records a story in which Cyrus, reading Isaiah's prophecy, was so impressed with the divine power to tell the future that he eagerly sought to fulfill what was written about him here. **my shepherd**. See 2 Sam. 5:2. After the failure of the kings of Judah, a pagan emperor plays the role of shepherd to God's people. **She shall be built**. The policy of Cyrus expresses the deeper purpose of God, revealed in Isa. 44:26, reversing 6:11 (cf. Ezra 1:1–5; 6:1–5; Isa. 45:13).

45:1–7 Through Cyrus God will demonstrate his own sovereignty over everything.

45:1 his anointed. This later became a specifically messianic title (Dan. 9:25–26), though it was not that in Isaiah. Here it denotes Cyrus as God's instrument for his purposes, a reminder that God rules all things.

45:2–3 The victories of Cyrus reveal God at work in history, accomplishing his own purpose. **that you may know that it is I**. Cyrus himself could and should have acknowledged God on the basis of these prophecies.

45:4 I call you by your name, I name you. The prediction of Cyrus by

4[v][See ver. 3 above] [w][ch. 62:2]
5[x]See ch. 44:8 [y][Job 12:21; ch. 22:21]
6[z][ch. 37:20; Mal. 1:11]
7[a][ch. 41:23; Amos 3:6]
8[b][Deut. 32:2] [c]Ps. 85:11; [Hos. 10:12]
9[d][Eccles. 6:10]; See ch. 10:15 [e]ch. 64:8; Cited Rom. 9:20
11[f]Ezek. 39:7 [g][ch. 41:23] [h][Jer. 31:9] [i]ch. 29:23; 64:8
12[j]Jer. 27:5 [k]ch. 42:5; 44:24 [l]Gen. 2:1
13[m]ch. 41:2 [n][ver. 2] [o]See ch. 44:28 [p]ch. 49:25; 51:14; 52:3
14[q][ch. 43:3] [r]ch. 14:2

[v]I call you by your name,
[w]I name you, though you do not know me.
5 [x]I am the LORD, and there is no other,
besides me there is no God;
[y]I equip you, though you do not know me,
6 [z]that people may know, from the rising of the sun
and from the west, that there is none besides me;
I am the LORD, and there is no other.
7 I form light and create darkness,
I make well-being and [a]create calamity,
I am the LORD, who does all these things.

8 [b]"Shower, O heavens, from above,
and [c]let the clouds rain down righteousness;
let the earth open, that salvation and righteousness may bear fruit;
let the earth cause them both to sprout;
I the LORD have created it.

9 [d]"Woe to him who strives with him who formed him,
a pot among earthen pots!
[e]Does the clay say to him who forms it, 'What are you making?'
or 'Your work has no handles'?
10 Woe to him who says to a father, 'What are you begetting?'
or to a woman, 'With what are you in labor?'"

11 Thus says [f]the LORD,
the Holy One of Israel, and the one who formed him:
[g]"Ask me of things to come;
will you command me [h]concerning my children and [i]the work of my hands?[1]
12 [j]I made the earth
and created man on it;
it was my hands [k]that stretched out the heavens,
and [l]I commanded all their host.
13 [m]I have stirred him up in righteousness,
[n]and I will make all his ways level;
[o]he shall build my city
[p]and set my exiles free,
not for price or reward,"
says the LORD of hosts.

The LORD, the Only Savior

14 Thus says the LORD:
[q]"The wealth of Egypt and the merchandise of Cush,
and the Sabeans, men of stature,
shall come over to you [r]and be yours;
they shall follow you;
they shall come over in chains and bow down to you.

[1] A slight emendation yields *will you question me about my children, or command me concerning the work of my hands?*

name (44:28; 45:1) is meant to awaken the faith of **my servant Jacob, and Israel my chosen**.

45:5–6 Predictive prophecy, fulfilled in history, proves that the Lord alone is God, and he wants the whole world to know it.

45:7 Beyond the case of Cyrus, the Lord's creative will and wise purposes stand behind everything. Therefore, his people should not be discouraged when the appearances of history seem contrary to his promises.

45:8 Far from a problem to cope with, God's sovereignty over all things, as affirmed in v. 7, is the only hope for the flowering of **salvation and righteousness** in this world.

45:9–13 Isaiah warns against challenging God's right to do his will in his own way.

45:9–10 Woe . . . Woe. Putting God under suspicious scrutiny is a serious offense. Created beings may not demand explanations from him (cf. Rom. 9:19–21).

45:11–13 The Lord asserts his right to be God. **I have stirred him up in righteousness**. Cyrus rose up in fulfillment of God's righteous purpose. **not for price or reward**. See Ezra 1:7–11; 6:3–5. With no financial incentive for Cyrus, his support of the rebuilding of the temple had to be of God.

45:14–19 God's plan goes beyond the return of his people to Jerusalem. His

They will plead with you, saying:
'Surely God is in you, and there is no other,
no god besides him.'"

15 [s]Truly, you are a God who hides himself,
O God of Israel, the Savior.
16 [t]All of them are put to shame and confounded;
the makers of idols go in confusion together.
17 But Israel is saved by the LORD
with everlasting salvation;
[u]you shall not be put to shame or confounded
to all eternity.

18 [v]For thus says the LORD,
who created the heavens
(he is God!),
who formed the earth and made it
(he established it;
he [w]did not create it empty,
[x]he formed it to be inhabited!):
"I am the LORD, and there is no other.
19 [y]I did not speak in secret,
in a land of darkness;
I did not say to the offspring of Jacob,
[z]'Seek me in vain.'[1]
I the LORD speak [a]the truth;
I declare what is right.

20 [b]"Assemble yourselves and come;
draw near together,
you survivors of the nations!
[c]They have no knowledge
who [d]carry about their wooden idols,
[e]and keep on praying to a god
that cannot save.
21 [f]Declare and present your case;
let them take counsel together!
Who told this long ago?
Who declared it of old?
Was it not I, the LORD?
And there is no other god besides me,
a righteous God [g]and a Savior;
there is none besides me.

22 "Turn to me and be saved,
[h]all the ends of the earth!
For I am God, and there is no other.

[1] Hebrew *in emptiness*

15[s]ch. 57:17
16[t]See ch. 42:17
17[u]ch. 54:4
18[v]ch. 42:5 [w][Gen. 1:2] [x][Ps. 115:16]
19[y]ch. 48:16; [Deut. 30:11] [z]Jer. 29:13, 14 [a]ver. 23
20[b][ch. 41:1] [c][ch. 44:18, 19; 48:5-7] [d]ch. 46:1, 7; Jer. 10:5 [e][ch. 44:17]
21[f][ch. 41:22, 26; 43:9] [g][ch. 43:11]
22[h]ch. 11:12; 43:5, 6

salvation will spread through them to all nations (cf. John 4:22; 10:16; Acts 1:8; Rom. 1:16; Gal. 3:28–29; Eph. 2:11–3:6; Col. 3:11; Rev. 7:9–10).

45:14 in chains. Isaiah uses the imagery of prisoners of war for Gentile conversions to Israel's faith—not forced on them but borne of personal conviction: **Surely God is in you**. If there is only one true God, then the only proper response is surrender. The new allegiance is to the Lord himself (v. 23), but faith in him entails humble identification with his people, too (cf. Ps. 68:29, 31; Isa. 2:2–4; Zech. 8:23). **there is no other**. See Isa. 45:6.

45:15 How God achieves his saving purpose, despite the appearances of history, excites wonder. God is not evasive, but he is counterintuitive.

45:17–18 The promise of everlasting salvation (v. 17) should be believed because the One making the promise is God (v. 18). **he formed it to be inhabited.** Cf. Gen. 1:2.

45:19 Unlike the idols, whose myths offer no light or hope, God can be taken at his word (cf. 40:8).

45:20–22 God invites all nations to renounce their idols and worship him alone.

45:21 Unbelieving opinion, however broad the consensus, cannot refute the evidence of predictive prophecy. **this**. Cyrus's conquest of Babylon and his release of the Jewish exiles (cf. 46:8–11).

45:22 be saved. Contrast "a god that cannot save" in v. 20. The idolatrous

23[i]See Gen. 22:16 [j]ver. 19 [k]Cited Rom. 14:11; [Phil. 2:10]
24[l][ch. 26:4; 44:8] [m][ch. 26:4; 44:8] [n][ch. 41:11]

Chapter 46

1[o]Jer. 50:2; 51:44; [ch. 21:9]
2[p][Jer. 48:7; Hos. 10:5, 6]
3[q][Deut. 1:31; 32:11]
4[r][Ps. 71:18]
5[s]See ch. 40:18
6[t]See ch. 44:10 [u]ch. 44:15
7[v]See ch. 45:20 [w]Ps. 115:7

23 [i]By myself I have sworn;
from my mouth has gone out in [j]righteousness
a word that shall not return:
[k]"To me every knee shall bow,
every tongue shall swear allegiance.'[1]
24 [l]"Only in the LORD, it shall be said of me,
are righteousness and [m]strength;
to him shall come and be ashamed
[n]all who were incensed against him.
25 In the LORD all the offspring of Israel
shall be justified and shall glory."

The Idols of Babylon and the One True God

46

1 [o]Bel bows down; Nebo stoops;
their idols are on beasts and livestock;
these things you carry are borne
as burdens on weary beasts.
2 They stoop; they bow down together;
they cannot save the burden,
but [p]themselves go into captivity.

3 "Listen to me, O house of Jacob,
all the remnant of the house of Israel,
[q]who have been borne by me from before your birth,
carried from the womb;
4 [r]even to your old age I am he,
and to gray hairs I will carry you.
I have made, and I will bear;
I will carry and will save.

5 [s]"To whom will you liken me and make me equal,
and compare me, that we may be alike?
6 [t]Those who lavish gold from the purse,
and weigh out silver in the scales,
hire a goldsmith, and he makes it into a god;
[u]then they fall down and worship!
7 [v]They lift it to their shoulders, they carry it,
they set it in its place, and it stands there;
[w]it cannot move from its place.
If one cries to it, it does not answer
or save him from his trouble.

[1] Septuagint *every tongue shall confess to God*

world is not scorned but invited. This invitation goes not only to Jewish people but to **all the ends of the earth**.

45:23–25 God's goal is a world without idols. Therefore, in the end, he will be either the Savior or the Judge of everyone. Paul cites v. 23 twice, from the Septuagint. In Rom. 14:11, the point is that God alone is the final judge. In Phil. 2:10–11, a hymn adapts the verse, applying it to Jesus (implying that Paul thought Jesus shared the position of Yahweh). **all the offspring of Israel**. All of God's people, Jew and Gentile alike (cf. Gal. 6:16).

46:1–47:15 *The Gods and Pride of Babylon Doomed.* The Lord will humiliate the idols of human self-worship and will demonstrate that he is the one true God.

46:1–7 The gods of Babylon fail their devotees, but the God of Israel saves his people.

46:1–2 Bel . . . Nebo. Isaiah aims his polemic at two of Babylon's chief gods. **these things you carry**. Images of these gods were carried in procession at the annual New Year's festival in Babylon. But rather than lead the way into the future, they **go into captivity** under historical forces beyond their control.

46:3–4 borne by me. While the idols must be carried, the God of Israel carries his people. **the remnant**. Those who survived the Babylonian captivity. **from before your birth . . . even to your old age**. There is never one moment when God fails his people. **I am he . . . I will carry and will save**. God emphasizes his personal commitments to his people.

46:5 To whom will you liken me? Biblical faith refuses to limit God to analogies within the creation. Though God teaches about himself with many analogies throughout the Bible, in the end no analogy, and no combination of analogies, can adequately describe his greatness.

46:6–7 Created gods are dependent on their creators. **they carry it**. If a god has to be carried, how can it unburden its worshipers? **it cannot move**. If a god cannot move, how can it intervene? **it does not answer or save**. Gold and silver are lavished on the god, to no benefit. Isaiah's contempt is obvious.

8 "Remember this and stand firm,
recall it to mind, [x]you transgressors,
9 remember the former things of old;
for I am God, and there is no other;
I am God, and there is none like me,
10 [y]declaring the end from the beginning
and from ancient times things not yet done,
saying, [z]'My counsel shall stand,
and I will accomplish all my purpose,'
11 [a]calling a bird of prey from the east,
the man of my counsel from a far country.
[b]I have spoken, and I will bring it to pass;
I have purposed, and I will do it.

12 "Listen to me, you stubborn of heart,
you who are far from righteousness:
13 [c]I bring near my righteousness; it is not far off,
and my salvation will not delay;
[d]I will put salvation in Zion,
for Israel my glory."

The Humiliation of Babylon

47 1 [e]Come down and sit in the dust,
O virgin [f]daughter of Babylon;
[g]sit on the ground without a throne,
O daughter of [h]the Chaldeans!
[i]For you shall no more be called
tender and delicate.
2 Take the millstones and [j]grind flour,
[k]put off your veil,
strip off your robe, uncover your legs,
pass through the rivers.
3 Your nakedness shall be uncovered,
and your disgrace shall be seen.
I will take vengeance,
and I will spare no one.
4 [l]Our Redeemer—the LORD of hosts is his name—
is the Holy One of Israel.

5 [m]Sit in silence, and go into darkness,
O daughter of [h]the Chaldeans;
for you shall no more be called
[n]the mistress of kingdoms.
6 [o]I was angry with my people;
I profaned my heritage;

8 [x][ch. 43:25]
10 [y]ch. 41:26 [z]ch. 44:26, 28; Ps. 33:11; Prov. 19:21; [Heb. 6:17]
11 [a]See ch. 41:2 [b]Num. 23:19
13 [c]ch. 51:5; [ch. 56:1; Ps. 85:9] [d]ch. 62:11; [Joel 2:32]
Chapter 47
1 [e][ch. 43:14] [f]Ps. 137:8 [g]ch. 3:26 [h]ch. 23:13; 48:14 [i][ver. 5; ch. 13:19]
2 [j]Judg. 16:21; [Matt. 24:41] [k][ch. 20:4]
4 [l]See ch. 43:14
5 [m][Jer. 8:14] [h][See ver. 1 above] [n][ver. 1]
6 [o][Zech. 1:15]

46:8–13 The only true God will succeed in his glorious purpose for his stubborn people.

46:8–11 stand firm. God calls his people to a bold trust in his sole deity and sovereign ways. **recall it to mind**. Mental focus on who God is must be renewed, for the idolatrous culture of the world erodes clarity. **transgressors**. The natural thoughts of the human mind resist the truth about God. **the former things of old**. The record of God's faithfulness in the past. **declaring . . . saying . . . calling**. God calls for a wholehearted trust in his unfailing word. **a bird of prey from the east**. Cyrus.

46:12–13 Even as the idols of the world are failing in their claims and God is succeeding in his promises, his people are still **stubborn of heart** to believe his word and accept his ways. **my righteousness . . . my salvation . . . my glory**. God does not need his people's faith to carry him forward. He will keep his promises to them for reasons springing from his own nature and purpose.

47:1–7 In contrast with Zion's salvation (46:13), Babylon is doomed to national disgrace.

47:1 The **virgin daughter of Babylon . . . tender and delicate** is Babylon itself, portrayed as a self-indulgent girl now subjected to the harsh realities of judgment. Babylon came to symbolize world culture in contempt of God (cf. Revelation 18).

47:2 God warns Babylon of the end of its luxurious selfishness and the beginning of slavery and exile.

47:4 The only safety in a world under judgment is the Lord himself, who acts for the sake of his people.

6[p][ch. 14:17; 51:23]
7[q][ver. 1]
8[q][See ver. 7 above] [r]Zeph. 2:15 [s][ch. 45:6, 18; Jer. 50:29] [t]Lam. 1:1; [Rev. 18:7]
9[u][ch. 51:19] [v][Jer. 50:31] [w][ver. 12, 13; Nah. 3:4]
10[x][ch. 45:6, 18; Jer. 50:29]
11[y][Ps. 35:8; Jer. 51:41]
12[z][ver. 9]
13[a][ch. 44:25; Dan. 2:2, 10]

I gave them into your hand;
[p]you showed them no mercy;
on the aged you made your yoke exceedingly heavy.
7 You said, "I shall be [q]mistress forever,"
so that you did not lay these things to heart
or remember their end.

8 Now therefore hear this, [q]you lover of pleasures,
[r]who sit securely,
who say in your heart,
[s]"I am, and there is no one besides me;
[t]I shall not sit as a widow
or know the loss of children":
9 [u]These two things shall come to you
in a moment, [v]in one day;
the loss of children and widowhood
shall come upon you in full measure,
[w]in spite of your many sorceries
and the great power of your enchantments.

10 You felt secure in your wickedness,
you said, "No one sees me";
your wisdom and your knowledge led you astray,
and you said in your heart,
[x]"I am, and there is no one besides me."
11 But evil shall come upon you,
which you will not know how to charm away;
disaster shall fall upon you,
for which you will not be able to atone;
[y]and ruin shall come upon you suddenly,
of which you know nothing.

12 [z]Stand fast in your enchantments
and your many sorceries,
with which you have labored from your youth;
perhaps you may be able to succeed;
perhaps you may inspire terror.
13 You are wearied with your many counsels;
let them stand forth and save you,
[a]those who divide the heavens,
who gaze at the stars,
who at the new moons make known
what shall come upon you.

47:5–7 Sit in silence. Babylon is left with nothing to say. God used the Babylonians to discipline his own people, as he said he would (cf. Deut. 28:49–50), but God still held Babylon accountable for their cruel abuses and unthinking arrogance (cf. Isa. 10:5–19).

47:8–11 Babylon's proud religion is exposed.

47:8 I am, and there is no one besides me. The self-deifying autonomy at the heart of Babylon blasphemes God (cf. 41:4; 44:6; 45:5–6, 18, 21–22; 46:9; Rev. 18:7). All nations, without exception, are accountable to God.

47:9 loss of children and widowhood. No future for Babylonian civilization. **your many sorceries . . . your enchantments**. See Ezek. 21:21; Babylon's religion claimed to guarantee favorable outcomes, but it proved powerless to avert the overwhelming disaster decreed by the God of Israel.

47:10 No one sees me. Defiant silencing of conscience. **your wisdom and your knowledge**. Intellectual pride distorts judgment. **I am**. See v. 8.

47:11 "You felt secure in your wickedness [Hb. *ra'ah*]" (v. 10) is answered by **but evil** (Hb. *ra'ah*) **shall come upon you**. This is the measure-for-measure "vengeance" of v. 3.

47:12–15 Babylon is left alone and helpless.

47:12 Stand fast . . . perhaps . . . perhaps. Isaiah mocks Babylon.

47:13 You are wearied. See 46:1. The idolatries of Babylon worked through the **many counsels** that their leaders turned to in national emergency. They leaned hard on their remedies, but nothing helped. **those who divide the heavens**. Astrology, a kind of false prophecy, was highly developed in Babylon (cf. Dan. 2:1–2).

14 Behold, [b]they are like stubble;
[c]the fire consumes them;
they cannot deliver themselves
from the power of the flame.
No coal for warming oneself is this,
no fire to sit before!
15 Such to you are those with whom you have labored,
who have done business with you from your youth;
they wander about, each in his own direction;
there is no one to save you.

Israel Refined for God's Glory

48 1 Hear this, O house of Jacob,
[d]who are called by the name of Israel,
and [e]who came from the waters of Judah,
[f]who swear by the name of the LORD
and confess the God of Israel,
but not in truth or right.
2 For they call themselves after the holy city,
[g]and stay themselves on the God of Israel;
the LORD of hosts is his name.

3 "The former things [h]I declared of old;
they went out from my mouth, and I announced them;
then suddenly I did them, and they came to pass.
4 Because I know that [i]you are obstinate,
and your neck is an iron sinew
and your forehead brass,
5 [h]I declared them to you from of old,
before they came to pass I announced them to you,
lest you should say, [j]'My idol did them,
my carved image and my metal image commanded them.'

6 "You have heard; now see all this;
and will you not declare it?
From this time forth [k]I announce to you new things,
hidden things that you have not known.
7 They are created now, not long ago;
before today you have never heard of them,
lest you should say, 'Behold, I knew them.'
8 You have never heard, you have never known,
from of old your ear has not been opened.
For I knew that you would surely deal treacherously,
and that [l]from before birth you were called a rebel.

9 [m]"For my name's sake I defer my anger,
for the sake of my praise I restrain it for you,

14 [b]ch. 41:2; Nah. 1:10; Mal. 4:1 [c]See ch. 10:17

Chapter 48

1 [d]ch. 43:1 [e]Ps. 68:26 [f]Jer. 7:9
2 [g][Mic. 3:11]
3 [h]ch. 41:26
4 [i][Ex. 32:9]
5 [h][See ver. 3 above] [j]See Jer. 44:15-17
6 [k]See ch. 43:19
8 [l]ch. 46:8
9 [m][Mal. 3:6]

47:14 Babylonian counselors burn like **stubble**, but the fire offers no benefit.

47:15 they wander about. When Babylon's partners in trade are most needed, they busy themselves elsewhere.

48:1–22 *God Will Free His People from Babylon for His Own Sake.* Despite Israel's stubborn unbelief, God pursues his purpose of redemption.

48:1–11 God puts up with his backward people for the sake of his own glory.

48:1 Hear. The imperative (repeated in vv. 12, 14, 16) calls Jacob to hear the word of God with the kind of hearing that makes an impact and produces action in response. They were **called by the name of Israel** (which is their identity and background) and are to **confess the God of Israel** (which is their profession of faith). **but not in truth or right**. Their faith is nominal, hypocritical, and imaginary.

48:2 The people of God do not grasp what it means that **the LORD of hosts is his name**. The central question of life is, "Who is God?" and even God's own people understand this only dimly.

48:3–5 God established a pattern of prophecies faithfully fulfilled, anticipating idolatrous thoughts rising from the hard hearts of his own people (as in Ezek. 3:7). God has prepared this defense for his own honor.

48:6–8 Now God intends to reveal surprising new prophecies. Unprecedented acts of God are on the horizon—unprecedented, lest his own people treat his deeds dismissively.

48:9–11 The deepest motive in the heart of God is his own **glory**, to the

10[n][1 Pet. 1:7] [o][Deut. 4:20; Ezek. 22:18, 20, 22]
11[p]ch. 43:25; Ezek. 20:9 [q]ch. 42:8
12[r]See ch. 41:4
13[s]ch. 51:13; [Ps. 102:25; Heb. 1:10] [t][ch. 40:26]
14[u][ch. 41:26] [v]ch. 46:10, 11 [w]ch. 23:13; 47:1
15[x]See ch. 45:1-3
16[y]ch. 45:19 [z]ch. 61:1
18[a]Ps. 81:13; Luke 19:42; [Deut. 32:29] [b]ch. 66:12
19[c]ch. 10:22; Gen. 22:17; Hos. 1:10
20[d]ch. 52:11; Jer. 50:8; 51:6, 45; Zech. 2:6, 7 [e]ch. 23:13; 47:1 [f][ch. 35:10; 52:9]

that I may not cut you off.
10 Behold, I have refined you, [n]but not as silver;
[o]I have tried[1] you in the furnace of affliction.
11 [p]For my own sake, for my own sake, I do it,
for how should my name[2] be profaned?
[q]My glory I will not give to another.

The Lord's Call to Israel

12 "Listen to me, O Jacob,
and Israel, whom I called!
I am he; [r]I am the first,
and I am the last.
13 My hand [s]laid the foundation of the earth,
and my right hand [s]spread out the heavens;
[t]when I call to them,
they stand forth together.

14 "Assemble, all of you, and listen!
[u]Who among them has declared these things?
The Lord loves him;
[v]he shall perform his purpose on Babylon,
and his arm shall be against [w]the Chaldeans.
15 [x]I, even I, have spoken and called him;
I have brought him, and he will prosper in his way.
16 [y]Draw near to me, hear this:
from the beginning I have not spoken in secret,
from the time it came to be I have been there."
And now [z]the Lord God has sent me, and his Spirit.

17 Thus says the Lord,
your Redeemer, the Holy One of Israel:
"I am the Lord your God,
who teaches you to profit,
who leads you in the way you should go.
18 [a]Oh that you had paid attention to my commandments!
[b]Then your peace would have been like a river,
and your righteousness like the waves of the sea;
19 [c]your offspring would have been like the sand,
and your descendants like its grains;
their name would never be cut off
or destroyed from before me."

20 [d]Go out from Babylon, flee from [e]Chaldea,
declare this [f]with a shout of joy, proclaim it,

[1] Or *I have chosen* [2] Hebrew lacks *my name*

exclusion of all other glories. He does not punish his unbelieving people as they deserve, for that would diminish the display of his glory in his persistent compassion (cf. Ps. 78:37–41; 103:8–14).

48:12–22 God will free his backward people from Babylon through Cyrus.

48:12–13 The God of the gospel is *the* commanding presence in the universe. Nothing disproves him; everything reveals his glory.

48:14–15 God reaffirms his plan to use Cyrus for his own redemptive purpose. **among them**. I.e., the idols. **The Lord loves him**. God is not reluctant to use Cyrus.

48:16 And now the Lord God has sent me, and his Spirit. This unidentified speaker appears more clearly in 49:1–6 as the servant of the Lord (cf. 42:1–13). Unlike Cyrus, the servant's power is not a human sword but the divine Spirit (cf. 11:2; 61:1). Many would see this as a reference to the three persons of the Trinity: the Father ("the Lord God"), the Son ("has sent me"), and the Holy Spirit ("his Spirit").

48:17–19 The cost of resisting God's word; the blessings of true listening. **who teaches you to profit**. Misplaced values are idols, which do not profit (cf. 44:9). **my commandments**. Even if God's prophecies of the future were difficult to believe, his practical commandments lay within range of human understanding. **peace . . . like a river**. Not seasonal but perpetual. **righteousness like the waves of the sea**. Covering sin again and again. **like the sand . . . like its grains**. See Gen. 15:5 and 22:17.

48:20–21 The Jewish exiles are called to take advantage of Cyrus's conquest of Babylon and return to the Promised Land. **They did not thirst**. The return of the exiles is a second exodus, marked again by God's miraculous provision. The Lord does not call his people out in order to abandon them but to provide for them lavishly (cf. Ex. 17:1–7; Ps. 105:41).

send it out to the end of the earth;
say, [g]"The LORD has redeemed his servant Jacob!"
21 [h]They did not thirst when he led them through the deserts;
[i]he made water flow for them from the rock;
he split the rock and the water gushed out.

22 [j]"There is no peace," says the LORD, "for the wicked."

The Servant of the LORD

49

1 Listen to me, [k]O coastlands,
and give attention, you peoples [l]from afar.
[m]The LORD called me from the womb,
from the body of my mother he named my name.
2 [n]He made my mouth like a sharp sword;
[o]in the shadow of his hand he hid me;
he made me a polished arrow;
in his quiver he hid me away.
3 And he said to me, "You are my servant,
Israel, [p]in whom I will be glorified."[1]
4 [q]But I said, "I have labored in vain;
I have spent my strength for nothing and vanity;
yet surely my right is with the LORD,
and my recompense with my God."

5 [r]And now the LORD says,
he [m]who formed me from the womb to be his servant,
to bring Jacob back to him;
and that Israel might be gathered to him—
for [s]I am honored in the eyes of the LORD,
and my God has become my strength—
6 he says:
"It is too light a thing that you should be my servant
to raise up the tribes of Jacob
and to bring back the preserved of Israel;
[t]I will make you [u]as a light for the nations,
that [v]my salvation may reach to the end of the earth."

7 Thus says the LORD,
[w]the Redeemer of Israel and his Holy One,

[1] Or *I will display my beauty*

20[g]ch. 44:23; [Ex. 19:4-6]
21[h][ch. 35:6; 44:3; Deut. 8:15] [i]ch. 43:19; Ex. 17:6; Num. 20:11
22[j]ch. 57:21

Chapter 49

1[k]See ch. 11:11 [l]ch. 33:13 [m]See ch. 44:2
2[n]ch. 11:4; Hos. 6:5; [Heb. 4:12; Rev. 1:16] [o]ch. 51:16
3[p]ch. 44:23
4[q][ch. 65:23]; See ch. 50:6-8; 53:10-12
5[r][ch. 50:4] [m][See ver. 1 above] [s][ch. 52:13]
6[t]Cited Acts 13:47 [u]ch. 42:6 [v][Ps. 98:3]
7[w]ch. 48:17

48:22 In contrast to the peace promised to God's people (26:13; 32:17; cf. 44:18), **there is no peace . . . for the wicked**. The comfort announced in 40:1 belongs only to those whose faith sends them on a pilgrimage into the promises of God (cf. 57:21).

49:1–50:3 ***The Lord's Servant Displayed, His People Assured.*** The trusting servant will save his despairing people with a salvation available for the whole world.

49:1–13 The servant of the Lord will restore Israel and save the nations. This is the second of four Servant Songs, describing the Messiah (see note on 42:1–9).

49:1 Listen to me. The servant of the Lord demands a worldwide hearing. **O coastlands . . . you peoples from afar**. Compared with "comfort, comfort my people" (40:1), the prophetic horizon is broadening to reveal more and more nations claimed by God's grace—an empire far greater than that of Cyrus. **He named my name** shows God's personal care for his servant (cf. 43:1; 45:3–4).

49:2 God alone prepared and equipped the servant. **my mouth like a sharp sword**. Unlike Cyrus, the servant conquers by the truth of his word (cf. 11:4; Rev. 1:16; 19:15, 21). The servant is a match for enemies both near and far ("sword," **arrow**).

49:3 my servant, Israel. Comparing vv. 5–6, this servant Israel restores the nation Israel. The servant is the true embodiment of what the nation failed to be, namely, the one **in whom I will be glorified**.

49:4 The servant confesses his sense of failure due to Israel's poor response (cf. v. 7; 53:1). **yet**. The servant does not turn from God in cynical unbelief; he accepts emotional suffering and frustrating toil with confidence that God will reward him.

49:5–6 It is too light a thing. It is too small a task to redeem only the **tribes of Jacob** (ethnic Israel). It is clear here that the servant, though he embodies Israel (v. 3), is nevertheless distinct from Israel, and has a calling to serve Israel and beyond. Far from failing, the servant is declared by God to be the only hope of the world. **a light for the nations**. See note on 42:6–7. **that my salvation may reach to the end of the earth**. A clear statement of salvation's worldwide scope, a theme that Acts develops by quoting this text (see Acts 1:8; 13:47).

49:7–13 The servant of the Lord triumphs worldwide.

49:7 Unlike the kings of this world, the servant of the Lord conquers by his sufferings (cf. 50:6; 52:14–15). **because of the LORD**. The triumph of the servant's mission is not due to any facile human idealism but to the purpose of God alone (cf. 9:7).

7[x]ver. 1; ch. 53:3; [ch. 50:6, 7] [y]ver. 23
8[z]Cited 2 Cor. 6:2 [a]Ps. 69:13 [b]ch. 42:6 [c]ch. 61:4
9[d]ch. 42:7 [e][ch. 41:18]
10[f]Cited Rev. 7:16 [g]Rev. 7:17; See ch. 40:11
11[h][ch. 40:4]
12[i]ch. 43:5, 6 [j][Ps. 107:3]
13[k]See ch. 44:23 [l]ch. 40:1
14[m][ch. 40:27; 54:6; 62:4]
15[n][ch. 43:1; Ps. 27:10]
16[o]Song 8:6; Rev. 13:16
17[p]See Zech. 1:18-21
18[q]ch. 60:4

[x]to one deeply despised, abhorred by the nation,
the servant of rulers:
[y]"Kings shall see and arise;
princes, and they shall prostrate themselves;
because of the LORD, who is faithful,
the Holy One of Israel, who has chosen you."

The Restoration of Israel

8 Thus says the LORD:
[z]"In a [a]time of favor I have answered you;
in a day of salvation I have helped you;
I will keep you [b]and give you
as a covenant to the people,
to establish the land,
[c]to apportion the desolate heritages,
9 [d]saying to the prisoners, 'Come out,'
to those who are in darkness, 'Appear.'
[e]They shall feed along the ways;
on all bare heights shall be their pasture;
10 [f]they shall not hunger or thirst,
neither scorching wind nor sun shall strike them,
for he who has pity on them [g]will lead them,
and by springs of water will guide them.
11 [h]And I will make all my mountains a road,
and my highways shall be raised up.
12 [i]Behold, these shall come from afar,
and behold, [j]these from the north and from the west,[1]
and these from the land of Syene."[2]

13 [k]Sing for joy, O heavens, and exult, O earth;
break forth, O mountains, into singing!
For the LORD [l]has comforted his people
and will have compassion on his afflicted.

14 But Zion said, [m]"The LORD has forsaken me;
my Lord has forgotten me."

15 [n]"Can a woman forget her nursing child,
that she should have no compassion on the son of her womb?
Even these may forget,
yet I will not forget you.
16 Behold, [o]I have engraved you on the palms of my hands;
your walls are continually before me.
17 Your builders make haste;[3]
[p]your destroyers and those who laid you waste go out from you.
18 [q]Lift up your eyes around and see;
they all gather, they come to you.

[1] Hebrew *from the sea* [2] Dead Sea Scroll; Masoretic Text *Sinim* [3] Dead Sea Scroll; Masoretic Text *Your children make haste*

49:8–12 The servant's faith is vindicated at the time of God's choosing. The **day of salvation** is now, as the gospel is being offered (as cited in 2 Cor. 6:2). **a covenant to the people**. See note on Isa. 42:6–7. Isaiah 49:8b–12 describes, with the "prisoners" imagery of 42:7, pilgrimage into the promises of God (cf. Rev. 7:9–17). **Syene**. I.e., Aswan in southern Egypt (cf. Ezek. 29:10; 30:6).

49:13 The servant's triumph inspires unprecedented joy (cf. 44:23; 55:12–13; Rom. 8:19–21).

49:14–26 Human despair is more than offset by divine grace.

49:14 The joy of v. 13 contrasts with the gloom of the Jewish exiles (cf. 40:27).

49:15–17 The Lord counters the despondency of his people. His attention to them is keener than a mother's to her child. **Behold, I have engraved you**. As if calling them to gaze upon his open hands. **your walls**. The rubble of Jerusalem, destroyed by the Babylonians (cf. Ps. 74:3; 102:14). But God intends to rebuild Zion (cf. Isa. 44:26, 28).

49:18 Isaiah sees the restoration of Zion as a mother welcoming her children and as a bride putting on her wedding gown. The prophet's vision extends to the worldwide growth of the people of God (cf. 54:1–3; Col. 1:3–6).

[r]As I live, declares the LORD,
[s]you shall put them all on as an ornament;
you shall bind them on as a bride does.

19 "Surely your waste and your desolate places
and your devastated land—
[t]surely now you will be too narrow for your inhabitants,
and those who swallowed you up will be far away.
20 [u]The children of your bereavement
will yet say in your ears:
[t]'The place is too narrow for me;
make room for me to dwell in.'
21 Then you will say in your heart:
'Who has borne me these?
[u]I was bereaved and barren,
exiled and put away,
but who has brought up these?
Behold, I was left alone;
from where have these come?'"

22 Thus says the Lord GOD:
"Behold, I will lift up my hand to the nations,
[v]and raise my signal to the peoples;
[w]and they shall bring your sons in their arms,[1]
and your daughters shall be carried on their shoulders.
23 [x]Kings shall be your foster fathers,
and their queens your nursing mothers.
[y]With their faces to the ground they shall bow down to you,
and [z]lick the dust of your feet.
Then you will know that I am the LORD;
[a]those who wait for me [b]shall not be put to shame."

24 Can the prey be taken from the mighty,
or the captives of a tyrant[2] be rescued?
25 For thus says the LORD:
[c]"Even the captives of the mighty shall be taken,
and the prey of the tyrant be rescued,
for I will contend with those who contend with you,
and I will save your children.
26 [d]I will make your oppressors eat their own flesh,
and they shall be drunk [e]with their own blood as with wine.
Then all flesh shall know
that [f]I am the LORD your Savior,
and your Redeemer, the Mighty One of Jacob."

Israel's Sin and the Servant's Obedience

50

1 Thus says the LORD:
"Where is [g]your mother's certificate of divorce,
with which [h]I sent her away?

[1] Hebrew *in their bosom* [2] Dead Sea Scroll, Syriac, Vulgate (see also verse 25); Masoretic Text *of a righteous man*

18 [r]Num. 14:21; See Ezek. 5:11 [s][Jer. 43:12]
19 [t][Zech. 10:10]
20 [u]ch. 54:1 [t][See ver. 19 above]
21 [u][See ver. 20 above]
22 [v]ch. 11:12 [w]ch. 14:2
23 [x]ch. 60:3, 16 [y]ch. 60:14 [z]Ps. 72:9; [Mic. 7:17] [a][ch. 40:31] [b]Ps. 25:3; Joel 2:27
25 [c][Matt. 12:29; Luke 11:21, 22]
26 [d][ch. 9:20; Zech. 11:9] [e][Rev. 14:20; 16:6] [f]ch. 43:3; See Ex. 20:2

Chapter 50

1 [g]Deut. 24:1 [h]Jer. 3:8; [Hos. 2:2]

49:19–21 God's restored people are astonished at the number to which they have miraculously grown. This promise contrasts with the doom of Babylon (47:8–9).

49:22–23 God moves history for the benefit of his people (cf. 45:14; 60:10–14). **I will lift up my hand . . . and raise my signal**. With ease, God's gesture causes the nations to do his will. **you will know**. The faith of God's people will finally be personal and rewarding. **Kings . . . queens**. Even those of highest status in other nations will serve God's people.

49:24–26 The people's skeptical question in v. 24 is answered by the Lord's strong assertion in vv. 25–26. **eat their own flesh . . . be drunk with their own blood** (as if under siege conditions). Defying God's purpose of grace is self-destructive (cf. Phil. 1:27–28). **Then all flesh shall know that I am the LORD**. This is God's ultimate purpose. This "recognition formula" ("all flesh shall know"), deriving from Ex. 6:7 and 14:18, occurs elsewhere in Isaiah (e.g., Isa. 7:20; 45:3, 6; 49:23; 60:16).

50:1–3 God challenges the despondency of his people.

50:1 The Jewish exiles feel abandoned (cf. 40:27; 49:14). But their hardships are not due to failure in God. They sinned their way into exile.

Or [i]which of my creditors is it
to whom I have sold you?
[j]Behold, for your iniquities you were sold,
and for your transgressions your mother was sent away.
2 [k]Why, when I came, was there no man;
why, when I called, was there no one to answer?
[l]Is my hand shortened, that it cannot redeem?
Or have I no power to deliver?
[m]Behold, by my rebuke [n]I dry up the sea,
[o]I make the rivers a desert;
[p]their fish stink for lack of water
and die of thirst.
3 [q]I clothe the heavens with blackness
and make sackcloth their covering."

4 The Lord God has given [r]me
the tongue of those who are taught,
that [s]I may know how to sustain with a word
[t]him who is weary.
Morning by morning he awakens;
he awakens my ear
to hear as those who are taught.
5 [u]The Lord God has opened my ear,
[v]and I was not rebellious;
I turned not backward.
6 [w]I gave my back to those who strike,
and my cheeks to those who pull out the beard;
I hid not my face
from disgrace and spitting.

7 But the Lord God helps me;
therefore I have not been disgraced;
[x]therefore I have set my face like a flint,
and I know that I shall not be put to shame.
8 [y]He who vindicates me is near.
Who will contend with me?
Let us stand up together.
Who is my adversary?
Let him come near to me.
9 [z]Behold, the Lord God helps me;
who will declare me guilty?
Behold, all of them will wear out like a garment;
the moth will eat them up.

10 Who among you fears the Lord
and obeys [a]the voice of his servant?

1 [i][2 Kgs. 4:1; Matt. 18:25] [j]ch. 59:2
2 [k][ch. 42:18-23] [l]ch. 59:1; Num. 11:23 [m]Ps. 104:7; 106:9; Nah. 1:4; [ch. 19:5, 6] [n][Ex. 14:21] [o]Josh. 3:16 [p][Ex. 7:18, 21]
3 [q]Jer. 14:22; Rev. 6:12
4 [r][Ex. 4:11] [s][ch. 40:1, 2] [t][Matt. 11:28]
5 [u]Ps. 40:6 [v][John 14:31; Phil. 2:8; Heb. 5:8; 10:7]
6 [w][ch. 53:5; Matt. 26:67; 27:26; Mark 15:19; Luke 22:63]
7 [x]Ezek. 3:8, 9
8 [y]Rom. 8:33, 34
9 [z]ch. 41:10
10 [a]ver. 4; ch. 49:2, 3

50:2–3 Why . . . was there no man? God's people snubbed the approach of his saving word. **I dry up the sea**. Cf. Ex. 7:21; 10:21–22; 15:8.

50:4–51:8 *The Lord's Servant Taught, His People Attentive.* The listening servant will sustain his listening people with a salvation that will last forever.

50:4–9 The servant of the Lord suffers in order to sustain others. This is the third of four Servant Songs, which anticipate the Messiah (see note on 42:1–9). This song focuses on the servant as a rejected prophet.

50:4 The Lord God. This title of the Sovereign Lord appears four times in this song (vv. 4, 5, 7, 9). The power of God takes the form of a servant. **the tongue of those who are taught**. The servant is a scholar, well schooled in the Word of God. **he awakens my ear**. Unlike the guilty silence of God's people (v. 2), the servant is responsive to God's Word (cf. 48:8).

50:6 those who strike. The gentle healer (42:3), patient worker (49:4), and wise comforter (50:4) is greeted with abusive opposition, and he accepts it. The description of the servant's rejection intensifies as the Servant Songs progress (49:7; 50:6; 52:14–53:9).

50:7 my face like a flint. The servant chose his sufferings willingly and he moves forward with resolute determination, confident in God's overruling help.

50:8–9 As 53:4–6 will make clear, the servant did not suffer because he was **guilty** but because others were guilty. For his innocence, God vindicated him (cf. 1 Tim. 3:16).

50:10–11 Isaiah defines the two responses to the servant of the Lord: (1) Fear the Lord by obeying the voice of his servant, trusting him even in the darkness

[b]Let him who walks in darkness
and has no light
trust in the name of the LORD
and rely on his God.
11 Behold, all you who kindle a fire,
who equip yourselves with burning torches!
Walk by the light of your fire,
and by the torches that you have kindled!
[c]This you have from my hand:
you shall lie down in torment.

The LORD's Comfort for Zion

51

1 [d]"Listen to me, you who pursue righteousness,
you who seek the LORD:
look to the rock from which you were hewn,
and to the quarry from which you were dug.
2 Look to Abraham your father
and to Sarah who bore you;
for [e]he was but one when I called him,
that I might bless him and multiply him.
3 For the LORD [f]comforts Zion;
he comforts all her waste places
and makes her wilderness like [g]Eden,
her desert like [h]the garden of the LORD;
[i]joy and gladness will be found in her,
thanksgiving and the voice of song.

4 [j]"Give attention to me, my people,
and give ear to me, my nation;
[k]for a law[1] will go out from me,
and I will set my justice for a light to the peoples.
5 [l]My righteousness draws near,
my salvation has gone out,
and my arms will judge the peoples;
[m]the coastlands hope for me,
and for my arm they wait.
6 [n]Lift up your eyes to the heavens,
and look at the earth beneath;
[o]for the heavens vanish like smoke,
the earth will wear out like a garment,
and they who dwell in it will die in like manner;[2]
[p]but my salvation will be forever,
and my righteousness will never be dismayed.

7 [q]"Listen to me, you who know righteousness,
the people [r]in whose heart is my law;
[s]fear not the reproach of man,
nor be dismayed at their revilings.
8 [t]For the moth will eat them up like a garment,
and the worm will eat them like wool;

[1] Or *for teaching*; also verse 7 [2] Or *will die like gnats*

10[b]ch. 42:16; [Mic. 7:8]
11[c][John 9:39]

Chapter 51

1[d]ver. 7
2[e]Ezek. 33:24
3[f]ch. 40:1; 52:9 [g]Gen. 2:8; Ezek. 28:13; 31:9; Joel 2:3 [h]Gen. 13:10 [i]ch. 35:10
4[j]Ps. 78:1 [k]ch. 2:3
5[l]ch. 46:13 [m]See ch. 11:11
6[n]ch. 40:26 [o]Ps. 102:26; [Matt. 24:25; 2 Pet. 3:10; Rev. 21:1] [p][Ps. 102:27, 28]
7[q]ver. 1 [r]Ps. 37:31 [s]ch. 41:14; Matt. 10:28
8[t]ch. 50:9

of this life. (2) Kindle the false light of one's own wisdom, but then **lie down in torment** forever (cf. Prov. 16:25).

51:1–8 These verses follow 50:10, giving three incentives for obeying the voice of the servant: vv. 1–3, 4–6, 7–8.

51:1–3 The first incentive (cf. note on vv. 1–8) is that, if God could make a great nation from one barren couple (**Abraham** and **Sarah**), then he can revive barren Zion as a joyful new Eden. This encouragement is intended not for all, but for **you who pursue righteousness, you who seek the LORD**.

51:4–6 The second incentive (cf. note on vv. 1–8) is that the truth of the Lord is going out to the nations with a saving power that will outlast the universe.

51:7–8 The third incentive (cf. note on vv. 1–8) is that, like the servant of the Lord, though believers are reviled, they will also be eternally vindicated (cf. John 16:33).

8[p][See ver. 6 above]
9[u]ver. 17; ch. 52:1 [v][Ps. 93:1] [w]ch. 40:10; 52:10; 53:1; Luke 1:51 [x]Ps. 44:1 [y]ch. 30:7 [z]ch. 27:1; Ps. 74:13, 14; Ezek. 29:3
10[a]ch. 43:16; Ex. 14:21; Ps. 106:9
11[b]See ch. 35:10
12[c]ch. 40:1; 66:13 [d]Ps. 118:6 [e]See ch. 40:6
13[f]ch. 40:22 [g]See ch. 48:13 [h]ch. 14:4
14[i]ch. 45:13 [j]Zech. 9:11
15[k]Jer. 31:35
16[l]ch. 59:21; [ch. 50:4] [m]ch. 49:2 [n]ch. 40:22 [o]See ch. 48:13
17[p]ver. 9; ch. 52:1

[p]but my righteousness will be forever,
and my salvation to all generations."

9 [u]Awake, awake, [v]put on strength,
O [w]arm of the LORD;
awake, [x]as in days of old,
the generations of long ago.
Was it not you who cut [y]Rahab in pieces,
who pierced [z]the dragon?
10 [a]Was it not you who dried up the sea,
the waters of the great deep,
who made the depths of the sea a way
for the redeemed to pass over?
11 [b]And the ransomed of the LORD shall return
and come to Zion with singing;
everlasting joy shall be upon their heads;
they shall obtain gladness and joy,
and sorrow and sighing shall flee away.

12 "I, I am he [c]who comforts you;
who are you that you are afraid of [d]man who dies,
of the son of man who is made [e]like grass,
13 and have forgotten the LORD, your Maker,
[f]who stretched out the heavens
and [g]laid the foundations of the earth,
and you fear continually all the day
because of the wrath of [h]the oppressor,
when he sets himself to destroy?
And where is the wrath of [h]the oppressor?
14 [i]He who is bowed down shall speedily be released;
he shall not die and go down [j]to the pit,
neither shall his bread be lacking.
15 I am the LORD your God,
[k]who stirs up the sea so that its waves roar—
the LORD of hosts is his name.
16 [l]And I have put my words in your mouth
[m]and covered you in the shadow of my hand,
[n]establishing[1] the heavens
and [o]laying the foundations of the earth,
and saying to Zion, 'You are my people.'"

17 [p]Wake yourself, wake yourself,
stand up, O Jerusalem,

[1] Or *planting*

51:9–52:12 *Encouragements to a Responsive Faith.* God's power for his people is always active, opening new ways forward through the gospel.

51:9–11 God's oppressed people pray for a new exodus into eternal joy.

51:9 Awake, awake. The discouraged people of God think of him as asleep. As in v. 17 and 52:1, the double imperative intensifies the urgency of the appeal. **as in days of old**. I.e., the days of the exodus. **Was it not you . . . ?** The helpless people wonder if God is as active as he once was. **Rahab** is Egypt (cf. 30:7). The ancient oppressor nation is perceived as a monster of mythic evil, slain by the power of God.

51:10 the sea. I.e., the Red Sea.

51:11 See the very similar 35:10.

51:12–16 God assures his people of his omnipotent salvation.

51:12–13 The Creator God rebukes the fears of his people. **I, I am he** answers the double "Awake, awake" of v. 9. Those who are **afraid of man who dies** have **forgotten the LORD**. Human opposition to God cannot last. **And where is the wrath of the oppressor?** Human wrath is nothing compared to divine wrath (cf. Matt. 10:28).

51:14 No bondage can keep God's people from their salvation (cf. Rom. 8:31–39).

51:15–16 I am the LORD your God . . . You are my people. God's covenant with his people defines both him and them. **I have put my words in your mouth**. This is the language by which God describes a prophet (cf. Deut. 18:18; Jer. 1:9). Here God speaks to his messianic servant, through whom he keeps his covenant.

51:17–23 God rouses his defeated people to renewed comforts.

51:17 Wake yourself, wake yourself. In v. 9, the people think God needs to be awakened to action; but in reality, they need to wake themselves. It was God, not their Babylonian captors, who force-fed Jerusalem the cup of wrath (cf. Ps. 75:8; Rev. 16:19). Now God invites his people to rise up from their stupor of despair.

[q]you who have drunk from the hand of the LORD
the cup of his wrath,
who have drunk to the dregs
the bowl, [r]the cup of staggering.
18 [s]There is none to guide her
among all the sons she has borne;
there is none to take her by the hand
among all the sons she has brought up.
19 [t]These two things have happened to you—
who will console you?—
devastation and destruction, famine and sword;
who will comfort you?[1]
20 [u]Your sons have fainted;
they lie at the head of every street
like an [v]antelope [w]in a net;
they are full of the wrath of the LORD,
the rebuke of your God.

21 [x]Therefore hear this, you who are afflicted,
who are drunk, but not with wine:
22 Thus says your Lord, the LORD,
your God [y]who pleads the cause of his people:
"Behold, I have taken from your hand [r]the cup of staggering;
the bowl of my wrath you shall drink no more;
23 [z]and I will put it into the hand of your tormentors,
[a]who have said to you,
'Bow down, that we may pass over';
and [b]you have made your back like the ground
and like the street for them to pass over."

The LORD's Coming Salvation

52

1 [c]Awake, awake,
put on your strength, O Zion;
[d]put on your beautiful garments,
O Jerusalem, [e]the holy city;
[f]for there shall no more come into you
the uncircumcised and the unclean.
2 [g]Shake yourself from the dust and arise;
be seated, O Jerusalem;
[h]loose the bonds from your neck,
O captive daughter of Zion.

3 For thus says the LORD: [i]"You were sold for nothing, and [j]you shall be redeemed without
money." 4 For thus says the Lord GOD: [k]"My people went down at the first into Egypt to
sojourn there, and the Assyrian oppressed them for nothing.[2] 5 Now therefore what have I
here," declares the LORD, "seeing that my people are taken away for nothing? Their rulers
wail," declares the LORD, "and [l]continually all the day my name is despised. 6 Therefore

[1] Dead Sea Scroll, Septuagint, Syriac, Vulgate; Masoretic Text *how shall I comfort you* [2] Or *the Assyrian has oppressed them of late*

17 [q]Job 21:20; Jer. 25:15; [Matt. 20:22; 26:39, 42; Mark 10:38; 14:36; Luke 22:42; John 18:11] [r]Ps. 60:3; Zech. 12:2
18 [s][Ps. 74:9; Jer. 5:31]
19 [t]ch. 47:9
20 [u]Lam. 2:11, 12 [v]Deut. 14:5 [w][Ps. 141:10]
21 [x]ch. 54:11
22 [y]Jer. 50:34; [ch. 49:25] [r][See ver. 17 above]
23 [z]Jer. 25:17, 26, 28 [a][ch. 47:6] [b][ch. 52:2]

Chapter 52
1 [c]ch. 51:17 [d][Ex. 28:2, 40]; See Zech. 3:1-4 [e]ch. 48:2; Neh. 11:1 [f]ch. 60:21; Joel 3:17; [ch. 35:8; Rev. 21:27]
2 [g][ch. 51:23] [h]ch. 51:14
3 [i]ch. 45:13; 50:1 [j][1 Pet. 1:18]
4 [k]Gen. 46:6
5 [l]Cited Rom. 2:24; [Ezek. 36:20, 23]

51:18–20 When God disciplines, no human help suffices. Jerusalem was left depopulated and defenseless.

51:21–23 The same divine power that humiliated Jerusalem turns the tables on her enemies.

52:1–10 God calls his royal people into a new era of blessing for themselves and the whole world.

52:1 Awake, awake. God turns the cry of his people (51:9) back on them. God has prepared a bright future, to be entered into by faith. **put on your strength.** I.e., live as what the one God says you are (cf. Eph. 4:22–24; Rev. 3:4–5). **there shall no more come into you.** Never again will foreign invaders violate the **holy city**, i.e., the people of God (cf. Rev. 21:22–27). Note the reversal of Isa. 47:1–2.

52:2 loose the bonds from your neck. Bondage is to be rejected.

52:3–6 The people of God will enter into their true identity, for it is all by his grace and for his glory.

52:3–4 You were sold for nothing. Judah was sold into Babylonian captivity, but not because of any lack in God. **you shall be redeemed without money.** See note on 43:3–4. **at the first.** The whole of Israel's history proves the faithfulness of God.

52:5–6 The defeat of God's people has brought shame upon his name, the

6[m][ch. 49:26]
7[n]Nah. 1:15; Cited Rom. 10:15 [o]ch. 40:9
8[p]See ch. 62:6 [q][ch. 33:17, 22; 1 Cor. 13:12; 1 John 3:2; Rev. 22:4]
9[r]Ps. 98:4 [s]ch. 58:12 [t]ch. 40:1; 51:3, 12
10[u]See ch. 51:9 [v]Ps. 98:3; [Luke 3:6]
11[w]ch. 48:20; Jer. 50:8; 51:6, 45; Zech. 2:6, 7; Cited 2 Cor. 6:17; [Rev. 18:4] [x]See Ezra 1:7-11
12[y][Ex. 12:11, 33, 39] [z]Mic. 2:13; [Ex. 14:19] [a][ch. 58:8]
13[b]See ch. 42:1
14[c][ch. 53:2, 3]

my people shall know my name. [m]Therefore in that day they shall know that it is I who speak; here I am."

7 [n]How beautiful upon the mountains
are the feet of him who brings good news,
who publishes peace, [o]who brings good news of happiness,
who publishes salvation,
who says to Zion, "Your God reigns."
8 The voice of [p]your watchmen—they lift up their voice;
together they sing for joy;
[q]for eye to eye they see
the return of the LORD to Zion.
9 [r]Break forth together into singing,
[s]you waste places of Jerusalem,
for [t]the LORD has comforted his people;
he has redeemed Jerusalem.
10 [u]The LORD has bared his holy arm
before the eyes of all the nations,
[v]and all the ends of the earth shall see
the salvation of our God.

11 [w]Depart, depart, go out from there;
touch no unclean thing;
go out from the midst of her; purify yourselves,
[x]you who bear the vessels of the LORD.
12 For you shall not [y]go out in haste,
and you shall not go in flight,
[z]for the LORD will go before you,
[a]and the God of Israel will be your rear guard.

He Was Pierced for Our Transgressions

13 Behold, [b]my servant shall act wisely;[1]
he shall be high and lifted up,
and shall be exalted.
14 As many were astonished at you—
[c]his appearance was so marred, beyond human semblance,
and his form beyond that of the children of mankind—

[1] Or *shall prosper*

most disastrous consequence (cf. Rom. 2:24). Therefore, he will vindicate himself with unmistakable clarity, for his own glory (cf. Ezek. 36:16–32).

52:7–10 God turns the wailing of his people and the despising of his name (as in v. 5) into rejoicing as the gospel of God's sovereign grace spreads over the world.

52:7 The "here I am" of v. 6 is experienced through the gospel. Isaiah prompts the people of God to welcome the approach of every gospel messenger (cf. Rom. 10:14–15). **the feet of him who brings good news**. As 2 Sam. 18:24–27 shows, this refers to someone who announces a great deed, usually a victory. (On how this verse relates to the "armor of God," see note on Isa. 11:5.) The longed-for message of **peace . . . good news of happiness . . . salvation** is summed up in one glad cry: **Your God reigns**—the victory of God over every oppression is now a reality (cf. Ps. 97:1; Acts 13:30–33; Rev. 19:6).

52:8–9 As the lone messenger approaches the city of God, the **watchmen** on the wall shout the good news that the King is returning.

52:10 The power of salvation spreads to the ends of the earth (cf. 49:6). **before the eyes of all the nations**. Restoring Jerusalem is a means to this great end.

52:11–12 Depart, depart. God calls his exiled people to leave Babylon as pilgrims, staking everything on his promises (cf. 2 Cor. 6:17). **touch no unclean thing**. I.e., do not bring any defilement with you as you return to rebuild the holy city. **you who bear the vessels of the LORD**. I.e., they are restoring these vessels to the temple service (cf. Ezra 1:1–11). **you shall not go out in haste**. Not as panicky fugitives but in confidence. **before you . . . your rear guard**. The Lord surrounds his Jerusalem-bound people as their escort (cf. Ex. 14:19–20; Ezra 8:21–23).

52:13–53:12 *The Lord's Servant: The Exalted Sin-bearer.* The fourth and final Servant Song, frequently quoted in the NT (e.g., Acts 8:30–35; 1 Pet. 2:22–25), describes the Messiah (see note on Isa. 42:1–9). Isaiah finally explains how the Holy One can bless sinful people: all the promises of God will come true for them because the suffering and triumphant servant removes their guilt before God by his sacrifice. To be clear on which parties are described, it helps to observe the pronouns: "I" in this passage is typically the Lord, "he" the servant, and "we" the servant's disciples, who themselves need the servant to bear their guilt (53:4–6), which is why the servant cannot be Israel or the pious within Israel.

52:13–15 The servant appeared repulsive but achieved redemption.

52:13 act wisely. Succeed at his task (cf. ESV footnote). **high and lifted up**. See note on 6:1. In John 12:38–41, John brings the vision of Isaiah 6 together with the fourth Servant Song and says that Isaiah saw Jesus' glory; this repeated phrase justifies John's reading.

52:14–15 As the servant was rejected by many (in his passion, Jesus was beaten into a shockingly inhuman mass of wounded flesh), **so** he will **sprinkle many nations** to make them clean (see the ministry of sprinkling in Ex. 29:21; Lev. 4:1–21; 14:7; 16:14–19; Heb. 9:13–14, 19–22; 10:19–22; 12:22–24;

15 so [d]shall he sprinkle[1] many nations;
[e]kings shall shut their mouths because of him;
[f]for that which has not been told them they see,
and that which they have not heard they understand.

53

1 [g]Who has believed what he has heard from us?[2]
And to whom has [h]the arm of the LORD been revealed?
2 For he grew up before him like a young plant,
[i]and like a root out of dry ground;
[j]he had no form or majesty that we should look at him,
and no beauty that we should desire him.
3 [k]He was despised and rejected[3] by men;
a man of sorrows,[4] and acquainted with[5] grief;[6]
and as one from whom men hide their faces[7]
he was despised, and [l]we esteemed him not.

4 [m]Surely he has borne our griefs
and carried our sorrows;
yet we esteemed him stricken,
[n]smitten by God, and afflicted.
5 [o]But he was pierced for our transgressions;
he was crushed for our iniquities;
upon him was the chastisement that brought us peace,
[p]and with his wounds we are healed.
6 [q]All we like sheep have gone astray;
we have turned—every one—to his own way;
[r]and the LORD has laid on him
the iniquity of us all.

7 He was oppressed, and he was afflicted,
[s]yet he opened not his mouth;
[t]like a [u]lamb that is led to the slaughter,
and like a sheep that before its shearers is silent,
so he opened not his mouth.
8 By oppression and judgment he was taken away;
and as for his generation, [v]who considered
that he was cut off out of the land of the living,
stricken for the transgression of my people?

15[d]Lev. 4:6, 17 [e]ch. 49:7, 23 [f]Cited Rom. 15:21; [Rom. 16:25]

Chapter 53

1[g]Cited John 12:38; Rom. 10:16 [h]See ch. 51:9
2[i]ch. 11:1 [j][ch. 52:14]
3[k]ch. 49:7; [Ps. 22:6; Mark 9:12] [l][John 1:10, 11]
4[m][Matt. 8:17] [n]Ps. 69:26
5[o][Rom. 4:25] [p]Cited 1 Pet. 2:24
6[q]Cited 1 Pet. 2:25; [Jer. 50:6, 17] [r]2 Cor. 5:21; [ver. 10; Col. 2:14]
7[s]Matt. 26:63; Mark 14:61; John 19:9; 1 Pet. 2:23 [t]Cited Acts 8:32 [u][Jer. 11:19]
8[v]ch. 57:1

[1] Or *startle* [2] Or *Who has believed what we have heard?* [3] Or *forsaken* [4] Or *pains*; also verse 4 [5] Or *and knowing* [6] Or *sickness*; also verse 4 [7] Or *as one who hides his face from us*

1 Pet. 1:2). **Kings** (representing the nations) **shall shut their mouths**, awed by his wretched humiliation and exalted glory (cf. Rom. 15:21). **that which has not been told them**. I.e., until revealed uniquely in the gospel.

53:1–3 The servant lived in rejection.

53:1 Us refers to the believing remnant of Israel (quoted in John 12:37–38; Rom. 10:16). **The arm of the LORD** is the power of God in action (cf. Isa. 40:10; 51:9; 62:8).

53:2 Unbelief in the servant was natural because he was an obscure, outwardly unimpressive person in a failed culture. "His generation" was blind (v. 8).

53:3 See 49:7; cf. John 1:10–11. Rejection of the servant reveals how misguided the human mind is. **a man of sorrows, and acquainted with grief**. Jesus experienced sorrow and grief of various sorts throughout his whole life. "Acquainted with" could also be rendered "knowing" (ESV footnote; see note on Isa. 53:11).

53:4–6 The servant bore the sins of other people; he was himself innocent. This paragraph is the heart of the passage.

53:4 Surely introduces the truth about the servant's sufferings. Acting as his people's substitute, with no support or understanding from them, the servant took upon himself the bitter consequences of their sin: **griefs, sorrows** (cf. Matt. 8:14–17). The sufferings of the servant would show the consequences that sin brings to fallen humanity, though he himself would not sin (Isa. 53:9). **smitten by God, and afflicted**. God would be the ultimate source of the sufferings of this faithful servant.

53:5 But contrasts with "our" incomprehension in v. 4b. The servant's anguish was "our" fault, not his own. **our transgressions, our iniquities**. His sufferings went to the root of all human woe (cf. Matt. 8:17; 1 Pet. 2:24). **pierced, crushed, chastisement, wounds**. Isaiah emphasizes how severely God punished the rejected servant for the sins of mankind.

53:6 All we . . . every one. The servant, who alone was sinless, was uniquely qualified to bear the sins of others, and all people contributed to his pain. **like sheep**. Stupid and helpless. **the LORD has laid on him the iniquity of us all**. See Lev. 16:21–22; 2 Cor. 5:21; 1 Pet. 2:25.

53:7–9 The servant dies in innocence.

53:7 like a lamb. I.e., innocent, submissive, not complaining (cf. John 1:29, 36; Acts 8:32–33; 1 Pet. 2:22–23).

53:8 By oppression and judgment. I.e., oppressive judgment. The servant was wrongly condemned. **who considered . . . ?** Those who condemned Jesus did not understand what they were doing (cf. Luke 23:34; Acts 3:14–18; 1 Cor. 2:8).

9[w]Matt. 27:57, 60 [x]Cited 1 Pet. 2:22; [Heb. 4:15; 1 John 3:5]
10[y][ver. 4] [z][ver. 6] [a][ch. 44:28]
11[b][1 John 2:1] [c]Acts 13:39; Rom. 5:18, 19 [d][ver. 5]
12[e]ch. 52:13; [Phil. 2:9] [f][Col. 2:15] [g]ver. 6, 8, 10

Chapter 54

1[h]Cited Gal. 4:27 [i]ch. 62:4 [j][1 Sam. 2:5]
2[k][ch. 49:19, 20]
3[l][ch. 11:14; Gen. 28:14]

9 And they made his grave with the wicked
[w]and with a rich man in his death,
although [x]he had done no violence,
and there was no deceit in his mouth.
10 Yet [y]it was the will of the LORD to crush him;
he has put him to grief;[1]
[z]when his soul makes[2] an offering for guilt,
he shall see his offspring; he shall prolong his days;
[a]the will of the LORD shall prosper in his hand.
11 Out of the anguish of his soul he shall see[3] and be satisfied;
by his knowledge shall [b]the righteous one, my servant,
[c]make many to be accounted righteous,
[d]and he shall bear their iniquities.
12 [e]Therefore I will divide him a portion with the many,[4]
[f]and he shall divide the spoil with the strong,[5]
because he poured out his soul to death
and was numbered with the transgressors;
[g]yet he bore the sin of many,
and makes intercession for the transgressors.

The Eternal Covenant of Peace

54

1 [h]"Sing, O barren one, who did not bear;
break forth into singing and cry aloud,
you who have not been in labor!
For the children of [i]the desolate one [j]will be more
than the children of her who is married," says the LORD.
2 [k]"Enlarge the place of your tent,
and let the curtains of your habitations be stretched out;
do not hold back; lengthen your cords
and strengthen your stakes.
3 [l]For you will spread abroad to the right and to the left,
and your offspring will possess the nations
and will people the desolate cities.

[1] Or *he has made him sick* [2] Or *when you make his soul* [3] Masoretic Text; Dead Sea Scroll *he shall see light* [4] Or *with the great* [5] Or *with the numerous*

53:9 they made his grave with the wicked and with a rich man. The numerous parallels between the description of the servant in this verse and the death of Jesus have led Christians through the ages to see this as fulfilled by the events surrounding Jesus' death. Although the servant was condemned as a criminal ("with the wicked"), he was buried in an expensive garden tomb belonging to a rich man. Likewise the servant is presented as someone who was completely innocent, both in deed (having **done no violence**) and in word (**there was no deceit in his mouth**). The servant is thus described as a person of total moral purity, the true substitute for sinners (cf. v. 7). See Matt. 27:57–60 for the fulfillment of this prophecy.

53:10–12 The servant was crushed but victorious.

53:10 the will of the LORD. There was a divine purpose for the oppression of the servant (cf. Luke 24:26; Acts 2:23; 4:27–28). **his soul**. He suffered not just in his body but in his deepest inner self. **an offering for guilt**. The servant's sacrificial death compensated for human sin by setting sinners free from their guilt before God (cf. Lev. 5:15–16). The Septuagint translates "offering for guilt" as "offering for sin," which explains why Paul could say that Christ's death "for our sins" was "in accordance with the Scriptures" (1 Cor. 15:3). **he shall see his offspring**. Those who strayed like sheep (Isa. 53:6) return as children. **he shall prolong his days**. Death is not the servant's end; he will receive everlasting life. Although resurrection is not explicit here, it is the natural inference (hence 1 Cor. 15:4 can speak of the resurrection as being "in accordance with the Scriptures"). **the will of the LORD shall prosper in his hand**. The servant becomes the executor of God's will and plan.

53:11 he shall see and be satisfied. The outcome of the servant's sufferings is not regret but the satisfaction of obvious accomplishment. **by his knowledge**. His experiential knowledge of grief (v. 3, see ESV footnote). **many**. His triumph, which does not secure the salvation of every individual without exception (universalism), spreads out beyond the remnant of Israel to "a great multitude that no one could number" (Rev. 7:9; cf. Rom. 5:15). **to be accounted righteous**. See Rom. 4:11–12.

53:12 Therefore. The sacrificial death of the servant explains his subsequent glory and the eternal blessings of those who believe in him. **a portion . . . the spoil**. The imagery is that of a conqueror sharing his victory with his allies. **numbered with the transgressors**. The servant is identified with rebels (cf. Luke 22:37). **makes intercession**. This is the servant's priestly work on behalf of those he represents, securing their acceptance before God.

54:1–55:13 *Compassion for God's People, Offered to All.* The everlasting love of God will heal all his people's sorrows, if they will enter in now on the terms of his glorious grace.

54:1–3 God commands his people to prepare joyfully for their future.

54:1 O barren one. The old covenant people of God, who failed to bless the world, were like a barren woman. Under the new covenant, God's people become the mother of a growing family (cf. Gal. 4:25–28).

54:2 The present task of God's people is to labor in expectancy. **Enlarge the place of your tent**, i.e., prepare for more people to be added to your family.

54:3 your offspring will possess the nations. See Gen. 22:17; 28:14; Ex. 34:24; Deut. 9:1; 11:23. God is not promising oppressive world domination but that, through his people, his righteous reign and the knowledge of him will spread throughout the world.

4 "Fear not, [m]for you will not be ashamed;
be not confounded, for you will not be disgraced;
for you will forget the shame of your youth,
and the reproach of your widowhood you will remember no more.
5 [n]For your Maker is your husband,
the LORD of hosts is his name;
[o]and the Holy One of Israel is your Redeemer,
[p]the God of the whole earth he is called.
6 [q]For the LORD has called you
like a wife deserted and grieved in spirit,
like a wife of youth when she is cast off,
says your God.
7 [r]For a brief moment I deserted you,
but with great compassion I will gather you.
8 [r]In overflowing anger for a moment
I hid my face from you,
[s]but with everlasting love I will have compassion on you,"
says the LORD, your Redeemer.

9 "This is like [t]the days of Noah[1] to me:
as I swore that the waters of Noah
should no more go over the earth,
so I have sworn that I will not be angry with you,
and will not rebuke you.
10 For the mountains may depart
and the hills be removed,
but my steadfast love shall not depart from you,
and [u]my covenant of peace shall not be removed,"
says the LORD, who has compassion on you.

11 [v]"O afflicted one, storm-tossed and not comforted,
behold, [w]I will set your stones in antimony,
[x]and lay your foundations with sapphires.[2]
12 I will make your pinnacles of agate,[3]
your gates of carbuncles,[4]
and all your wall of precious stones.
13 [y]All your children [z]shall be taught by the LORD,
[a]and great shall be the peace of your children.

[1] Some manuscripts *For this is as the waters of Noah* [2] Or *lapis lazuli* [3] Or *jasper, or ruby* [4] Or *crystal*

4 [m]ch. 45:17
5 [n]ch. 62:4, 5; [Hos. 2:7] [o]See ch. 43:14 [p]Zech. 14:9
6 [q]ver. 1; [ch. 49:14; 60:15; 62:4]
7 [r][ch. 26:20]
8 [r][See ver. 7 above] [s]ch. 55:3
9 [t]Gen. 8:21; 9:11
10 [u]Num. 25:12; Ezek. 34:25; 37:26; [Mal. 2:5]
11 [v]ch. 51:21 [w][ch. 60:10] [x][Rev. 21:19]
13 [y]Cited John 6:45 [z]Jer. 31:33, 34 [a][ch. 9:7; Ps. 119:165]

54:4–10 God commands his people to confidently expect his endless compassion.

54:4 the reproach of your widowhood. When God withdrew from his unfaithful people during the Babylonian exile, they were like a wife without a husband. God promises complete emotional restoration (cf. 40:1).

54:5 The certainty of the promise of v. 4 rests in the person of God, who would have to stop being God in order for his promises to fail. Isaiah heaps words upon words to convey the all-sufficiency of God for his weak people.

54:6 the LORD has called you like a wife. The future of God's people is not rejection or even cool relational distance, but the joy and passion of a marriage forever young (cf. Rev. 19:7, 9; 21:2, 9). **deserted and grieved**. God's discipline of his unfaithful people.

54:7–8 For a brief moment I deserted you. The Babylonian exile did not seem "brief" at the time (cf. Psalm 74), but it was momentary in comparison to God's everlasting love. **with great compassion**. Lavish displays of God's eternal love more than offset his momentary chastening.

54:9 like the days of Noah. God's wrath overwhelmed the Jewish exiles like Noah's flood, but like that ancient flood, his wrath also subsided. Now God renews his assurances of grace (cf. Gen. 8:20–9:17).

54:10 God's **love** for his people is not just a little greater than his wrath; it is massively greater and eternally unchanging. **my covenant of peace**. Cf. this term in Ezek. 34:25–31, describing a renewed covenant with God after the exile. When the language of these prophecies is compared to the accounts of the returnees (in Ezra–Nehemiah), it becomes clear that the physical return was only the first installment.

54:11–17 God assures his people of their glorious future.

54:11–12 Having endured much, the people of God will be restored like a ruined city rebuilt with the finest materials. **behold, I**. God alone glorifies his people.

54:13 taught by the LORD. Unlike the tragic record of ancient Israel, the future blessing of God's people is ensured because his grace will guarantee their allegiance to his word (cf. 50:4–5; Jer. 31:31–34; John 6:45). **peace**. The security and fullness that mankind has always desired but failed to achieve now stretch out into the future as the inheritance of God's children.

15[b][ch. 8:9, 10]
17[c]ch. 45:24, 25
Chapter 55
1[d]ch. 44:3; John 7:37; [Matt. 5:6] [e]Prov. 9:5
2[f][John 6:27]
3[g]Prov. 4:4 [h]ch. 61:8; Jer. 32:40; Ezek. 37:26; [ch. 54:8; 59:21] [i]Ps. 89:33-35; [Acts 13:34] [j]Jer. 30:9
4[k]Ps. 18:43 [l]Dan. 9:25; Mic. 5:2; Acts 5:31; Rev. 17:14; 19:16; [ch. 9:6, 7]
5[k][See ver. 4 above] [m]Zech. 8:22, 23 [n][ch. 44:23; Acts 3:13]
6[o]Ps. 32:6; Amos 5:4

14 In righteousness you shall be established;
you shall be far from oppression, for you shall not fear;
and from terror, for it shall not come near you.
15 [b]If anyone stirs up strife,
it is not from me;
whoever stirs up strife with you
shall fall because of you.
16 Behold, I have created the smith
who blows the fire of coals
and produces a weapon for its purpose.
I have also created the ravager to destroy;
17 no weapon that is fashioned against you shall succeed,
and you shall refute every tongue that rises against you in judgment.
This is the heritage of the servants of the LORD
[c]and their vindication[1] from me, declares the LORD."

The Compassion of the LORD

55

1 [d]"Come, everyone who thirsts,
come to the waters;
and he who has no money,
[e]come, buy and eat!
Come, buy wine and milk
without money and without price.
2 [f]Why do you spend your money for that which is not bread,
and your labor for that which does not satisfy?
Listen diligently to me, and eat what is good,
and delight yourselves in rich food.
3 Incline your ear, and come to me;
[g]hear, that your soul may live;
[h]and I will make with you an everlasting covenant,
[i]my steadfast, sure love for [j]David.
4 [k]Behold, I made him a witness to the peoples,
[l]a leader and commander for the peoples.
5 [k]Behold, you shall call a nation that you do not know,
and [m]a nation that did not know you shall run to you,
because of the LORD your God, and of the Holy One of Israel,
[n]for he has glorified you.
6 [o]"Seek the LORD while he may be found;
call upon him while he is near;

[1] Or *righteousness*

54:14 In righteousness . . . far from oppression. See 32:17–18.

54:15–17 The city of God is secure because (1) all the powers of evil are under God's control and (2) he will defend his people. **Behold, I**. God alone accomplishes the promised victory. **This is the heritage**. All the promises of ch. 54. **no weapon that is fashioned against you shall succeed**. God will protect his people and defeat every enemy, no matter how powerful.

55:1–13 God invites everyone to enter into his promised blessings.

55:1 Come, everyone who thirsts. The invitation is urgent in tone and universal in scope, addressing a deep spiritual longing to "seek the LORD while he may be found" (v. 6). Thirst is not a problem but an opportunity (cf. John 7:37–39). **come . . . come. . . . Come**. This is all one needs to do in order to find mercy in God.

55:2 Why do you spend your money? Isaiah exposes how costly but disappointing unbelief is. **Listen diligently to me** is how the banquet of the gospel of Christ is enjoyed (**and eat what is good**).

55:3 an everlasting covenant. This term appears in 61:8; Jer. 32:40; Ezek. 37:26, referring to the experience of the returned exiles. **steadfast, sure love for David**. The blessing is focused on the house of David, out of which the messianic servant will arise (cited from the Septuagint in Acts 13:34).

55:4 God established David (v. 3) as the authoritative world ruler—as a spokesman for God and as an ancestor of the Messiah (cf. Ps. 18:49–50).

55:5 You addresses the glorious son of David, the messianic servant, through whom God attracts the nations, bringing history to its appointed consummation (cf. Rom. 1:1–5). **a nation that you do not know**. I.e., people previously outside of God's covenant (cf. Eph. 2:11–12).

55:6–7 let him return to the LORD. Anyone may enter into the victory of God, but the time is short and the offer is conditioned upon repentance. The cost of enjoying God's feast of covenant love (vv. 1–3) is forsaking oneself, but the gain is abundant pardon.

55:6 Seek the LORD while he may be found. Since this is God's offer, he is free to withdraw it; therefore people should not be foolish and delay (cf. Ps. 32:6). The offer of salvation should never be despised or rejected, for the opportunity may end at any moment.

7 let the wicked forsake his way,
and the unrighteous man his thoughts;
let him return to the LORD, that he may have compassion on him,
and to our God, for he will abundantly pardon.
8 For my thoughts are not your thoughts,
neither are your ways my ways, declares the LORD.
9 [p]For as the heavens are higher than the earth,
so are my ways higher than your ways
and my thoughts than your thoughts.

10 [q]"For as the rain and the snow come down from heaven
and do not return there but water the earth,
making it bring forth and sprout,
[r]giving seed to the sower and bread to the eater,
11 so shall my word be that goes out from my mouth;
it shall not return to me empty,
but [s]it shall accomplish that which I purpose,
and shall succeed in the thing for which I sent it.

12 [t]"For you shall go out in joy
and be led forth in peace;
[u]the mountains and the hills before you
shall break forth into singing,
and all the trees of the field shall clap their hands.
13 [v]Instead of the thorn shall come up the cypress;
instead of the brier shall come up the myrtle;
and it shall make a name for the LORD,
an everlasting sign that shall not be cut off."

Salvation for Foreigners

56 1 Thus says the LORD:
"Keep justice, and do righteousness,
[w]for soon my salvation will come,
and my righteousness be revealed.
2 Blessed is the man who does this,
and the son of man who holds it fast,

9[p]Ps. 103:11
10[q][Ps. 148:8] [r][2 Cor. 9:10]
11[s]ch. 40:8
12[t]ch. 35:10; [ch. 48:20, 21; 52:12] [u]ch. 44:23; Ps. 98:8
13[v]ch. 35:1, 2; 41:19

Chapter 56

1[w]ch. 46:12, 13; 51:5, 6

55:7–9 let the wicked forsake his way . . . let him return. Thorough repentance is required, for God's **thoughts are not your thoughts**—that is, they are as high above man's thoughts as the **heavens** are above the **earth** and vastly superior to the expectations of human intuitions (cf. Ps. 145:3; 1 Cor. 2:9). **neither are your ways my ways.** In the immediate context, this is an appeal to people to exchange their sinful "thoughts" and "ways" (Isa. 55:7) for God's, which are **higher** (nobler and more magnificent). More broadly, theologians have recognized that God, the incomparable Creator, is far above his finite creatures and beyond their ability to describe him or comprehend him fully; though they may know him truly, such knowledge is always partial and imperfect. But because God is perfectly wise in all his thoughts and ways, his people can take great comfort amid hardship and when inevitably they are unable to understand the mysteries and tragedies of life.

55:10–11 As **the rain and the snow** cannot fail to nourish the earth, **so** God's **word** of promise cannot fail to bring his people into the richness and fullness of eternal life. Human good intentions fail, but God's promises succeed (cf. 40:6–8). The word of God not only *describes* a glorious future, it is God's appointed means to *create* that future (cf. Ezek. 37:1–14).

55:12–13 The prophet concludes both this chapter and all of chs. 40–55 with a vision of the triumph of God's grace, when the effects of sin and the fall (see Gen. 3:17; 6:11–13) are rectified and "the creation itself will be set free from its bondage to corruption and obtain the freedom of the glory of the children of God" (Rom. 8:21). **before you.** The redeemed, proceeding at last into their eternal joys, are the occasion for the creation to break forth into singing. **Instead of the thorn.** The image is of arid, unproductive land being transformed. **a name . . . an everlasting sign.** God will be forever glorified by the display of his triumphant grace.

56:1–66:24 *How to Prepare for the Coming Glory: "Hold Fast My Covenant."* Isaiah guides the people of God of all ages into the reviving power of the truths and promises of chs. 1–55, so that they may prepare for the salvation that will renew all things forever.

56:1–8 *The True People of God Redefined.* Outward disqualification for being included among God's people is offset by holding fast to his covenant love and lifestyle.

56:1 This verse serves as a summary of chs. 1–55. **Keep justice, and do righteousness** echoes the ideals of chs. 1–39; **soon my salvation will come, and my righteousness be revealed** sums up the promises of chs. 40–55 (cf. 1:21, 27; 5:7, 16; 9:7; 16:5; 28:17; 32:1, 16; 33:5; 45:8; 46:13; 51:5–8).

56:2 The **Sabbath** is a covenant sign that represents a lifestyle of devotion to the Lord, for it requires the practical reorganization of every week around him (cf. Ex. 31:12–17; Ezek. 20:18–20). True observance of the Sabbath entails not just refraining from work but also refraining **from doing any evil**. On the Sabbath command as it applies to Christian believers, see note on Rom. 14:5; also notes on Matt. 12:6–12; Mark 2:27–28; John 5:10; 5:17; 9:14; Gal. 4:10; Col. 2:17; Heb. 4:8–10.

2[x]ch. 58:13
3[y]ch. 14:1; [Deut. 23:7, 8] [z][Ezek. 17:24; 20:47]
4[x][See ver. 2 above]
5[a][1 Tim. 3:15; Rev. 3:12] [b][2 Sam. 18:18; John 1:12] [c][2 Tim. 2:19]
6[y][See ver. 3 above] [x][See ver. 2 above]
7[d]ch. 65:1; [ch. 19:24, 25] [e]ch. 2:2 [f][Rom. 15:16] [g]Cited Matt. 21:13; Mark 11:17; Luke 19:46
8[h]ch. 11:12 [i]John 10:16; Eph. 1:10; See Eph. 2:11-16
9[j]Jer. 12:9; Ezek. 34:8
10[k]ch. 62:6; Jer. 6:17 [l][Phil. 3:2]
11[m]Ezek. 34:2, 3

[x]who keeps the Sabbath, not profaning it,
and keeps his hand from doing any evil."
3 Let not [y]the foreigner who has joined himself to the LORD say,
"The LORD will surely separate me from his people";
and let not the eunuch say,
"Behold, I am [z]a dry tree."
4 For thus says the LORD:
"To the eunuchs [x]who keep my Sabbaths,
who choose the things that please me
and hold fast my covenant,
5 [a]I will give in my house and within my walls
a [b]monument and a name
better than sons and daughters;
[c]I will give them an everlasting name
that shall not be cut off.

6 "And [y]the foreigners who join themselves to the LORD,
to minister to him, to love the name of the LORD,
and to be his servants,
everyone [x]who keeps the Sabbath and does not profane it,
and holds fast my covenant—
7 [d]these I will bring to [e]my holy mountain,
and make them joyful in my house of prayer;
[f]their burnt offerings and their sacrifices
will be accepted on my altar;
for [g]my house shall be called a house of prayer
for all peoples."
8 The Lord GOD,
[h]who gathers the outcasts of Israel, declares,
[i]"I will gather yet others to him
besides those already gathered."

Israel's Irresponsible Leaders

9 [j]All you beasts of the field, come to devour—
all you beasts in the forest.
10 [k]His watchmen are blind;
they are all without knowledge;
they are all silent [l]dogs;
they cannot bark,
dreaming, lying down,
loving to slumber.
11 [m]The dogs have a mighty appetite;
they never have enough.

56:3–8 The true people of God, who will inherit all his promises, are universally inclusive of all who hold fast to his covenant, despite their outward, apparent disqualification.

56:3–5 The **foreigner**, approaching God's people, need not fear God's rejection if he **has joined himself to the LORD**. The **eunuch**, once he is gripped by the gospel, receives an eternal place with God (v. 5) that is better than producing physical descendants (although that is also good). The restrictions of Ex. 12:43, 45 and Deut. 23:1 no longer apply.

56:6 Covenant union with God defines the true people of God and their true worship. Contrast the futilities condemned in 1:11–15. **Sabbath**. See note on 56:2.

56:7 My holy mountain is the place of God's presence and his people's worship—**a house of prayer for all peoples**. See 1 Kings 8:41–43; Isa. 2:2–3; 25:6–8; Mark 11:17 (combining it with Jer. 7:11).

56:8 The Lord GOD, who gathers. He will gather in more than the Jewish exiles from Babylon (cf. 11:11–12). **Yet others** not only includes the foreigners and eunuchs of 56:3 but extends as far as the "everyone" of v. 6 and "all peoples" of v. 7 (cf. John 10:16).

56:9–57:13 *The False People of God Exposed.* Selfishly complacent leaders, morally lax people, and idol-worshiping hypocrites have no place in God's kingdom.

56:9–12 In contrast with "the outcasts of Israel" (v. 8) who possess an endless hope, the self-serving leaders of ancient Israel are warned of coming judgment.

56:9 The **beasts** are enemy nations (cf. Jer. 12:7–9).

56:10 Watchmen are prophets (cf. Ezek. 3:17; 33:1–9; Hab. 2:1), but they are asleep on their job. **Silent** watchdogs are useless.

56:11 Shepherds are rulers (see Jer. 25:34–35; Ezek. 34:1–10; cf. Isa. 40:10–11).

But [n]they are shepherds who have no understanding;
they have all turned to their own way,
[o]each to his own gain, one and all.
12 [p]"Come," they say, "let me get wine;
let us fill ourselves with strong drink;
[q]and tomorrow will be like this day,
great beyond measure."

Israel's Futile Idolatry

57
1 The righteous man perishes,
and no one lays it to heart;
[r]devout men are taken away,
while no one understands.
For the righteous man is taken away from calamity;
2 [s]he enters into peace;
they rest [t]in their beds
who walk in their uprightness.
3 But you, draw near,
sons of the sorceress,
[u]offspring of the adulterer and the loose woman.
4 Whom are you mocking?
Against whom [v]do you open your mouth wide
and stick out your tongue?
Are you not children of [w]transgression,
[x]the offspring of deceit,
5 you who burn with lust among [y]the oaks,[1]
under every green tree,
[z]who slaughter your children in the valleys,
under the clefts of the rocks?
6 Among the smooth stones of [a]the valley is your portion;
they, they, are your lot;
to them you have poured out a drink offering,
you have brought a grain offering.
Shall I relent for these things?
7 [b]On a high and lofty mountain
you have set your bed,
and there you went up to offer sacrifice.
8 Behind the door and the doorpost
you have set up your memorial;
for, deserting me, [c]you have uncovered your bed,
you have gone up to it,
[d]you have made it wide;
and you have made a covenant for yourself with them,
you have loved their bed,
you have looked on nakedness.[2]

11 [n][Jer. 23:1] [o]Jer. 6:13
12 [p][ch. 28:7] [q][ch. 22:13; Prov. 23:35; Luke 12:19; 1 Cor. 15:32]

Chapter 57
1 [r]Ps. 12:1
2 [s][Luke 2:29] [t]2 Chr. 16:14; Ezek. 32:25
3 [u][John 8:41, 42]
4 [v][Ps. 35:21] [w]ch. 46:8, 9 [x][ch. 1:4]
5 [y]ch. 1:29; 2 Kgs. 16:4 [z]Ezek. 16:20, 21
6 [a][2 Kgs. 23:10]
7 [b]1 Kgs. 14:23; Ezek. 16:16, 24
8 [c]Ezek. 16:25; [Hos. 1:2] [d][Ezek. 23:17]

[1] Or *among the terebinths* [2] Or *on a monument* (see 56:5); Hebrew *on a hand*

56:12 let me get wine. Cf. 5:11–12; 28:7–8.

57:1–13 Isaiah confronts apostasy, which he sees increasing among God's people.

57:1–2 The righteous man perishes. Isaiah sees a trend toward fewer righteous people, yet **no one lays it to heart**, i.e., the masses of people generally do not understand that this indicates a withdrawal of God's blessing. In such a troubled time, for the righteous, death is a mercy, for **he enters into peace** (cf. 2 Kings 22:20; Rev. 14:13).

57:3–10 Paganism has come in among God's unthinking people.

57:3 The Jewish people's physical descent from Abraham is meaningless, for the people's pagan morals reveal their true spiritual identity.

57:4–5 Contempt for God and for the righteous is linked with idol worship and human cruelty (cf. Jer. 2:20; 32:35).

57:6 The **smooth stones** are objects of pagan worship. **Shall I relent for these things?** This rhetorical question argues for the reasonableness of God's all-out opposition to idolatry (cf. 42:8).

57:7 you have set your bed. Idol worship is spiritual whoredom.

9 [e]Ezek. 16:26, 28, 29
10 [f]Jer. 2:25; 18:12
11 [g][ch. 51:12, 13] [h]Ps. 78:10, 36 [i]Ps. 50:21
13 [j]Jer. 11:12 [k]Ps. 37:9 [l]ch. 11:9; 56:7; 65:11, 25
14 [m]ch. 62:10; [ch. 40:3]
15 [n][Mic. 6:6] [o]Luke 1:49 [p]Ps. 113:6 [q]Ps. 34:18; 138:6 [r][ch. 42:3]
16 [s]Gen. 6:3; Ps. 103:9
17 [t]ch. 56:11; Jer. 6:13
18 [u]Jer. 3:22 [v]ch. 61:3
19 [w]ch. 50:4 [x]Heb. 13:15 [y][Eph. 2:17] [z]Acts 2:39 [u][See ver. 18 above]

9 You journeyed to the king with oil
and multiplied your perfumes;
[e]you sent your envoys far off,
and sent down even to Sheol.
10 You were wearied with the length of your way,
[f]but you did not say, "It is hopeless";
you found new life for your strength,
and so you were not faint.[1]
11 [g]Whom did you dread and fear,
[h]so that you lied,
and did not remember me,
did not lay it to heart?
[i]Have I not held my peace, even for a long time,
and you do not fear me?
12 I will declare your righteousness and your deeds,
but they will not profit you.
13 [j]When you cry out, let your collection of idols deliver you!
The wind will carry them all off,
a breath will take them away.
[k]But he who takes refuge in me shall possess the land
and shall inherit [l]my holy mountain.

Comfort for the Contrite

14 And it shall be said,
[m]"Build up, build up, prepare the way,
remove every obstruction from my people's way."
15 For thus says [n]the One who is high and lifted up,
who inhabits eternity, whose name is [o]Holy:
[p]"I dwell in the high and holy place,
and also [q]with him who is of a contrite and lowly spirit,
[r]to revive the spirit of the lowly,
and to revive the heart of the contrite.
16 [s]For I will not contend forever,
nor will I always be angry;
for the spirit would grow faint before me,
and the breath of life that I made.
17 Because of the iniquity of his [t]unjust gain I was angry,
I struck him; I hid my face and was angry,
but he went on backsliding in the way of his own heart.
18 I have seen his ways, [u]but I will heal him;
I will lead him [v]and restore comfort to him and his mourners,
19 [w]creating [x]the fruit of the lips.
[y]Peace, peace, [z]to the far and to the near," says the LORD,
[u]"and I will heal him.

[1] Hebrew *and so you were not sick*

57:8 uncovered your bed. Private sins reveal that the people are deserting the Lord and actively giving themselves to idolatry.

57:9–10 Idolatry also involved futile political alliances with foreign powers (cf. 30:1–17; 31:1–9). **even to Sheol**. The search for human alliances knew no bounds. Indeed, the people found it energizing.

57:11–13 The people do not fear God. They fear human threats and cling to false assurances (cf. Luke 12:4–5). **I will declare your righteousness**. See Isa. 58:1–5 and 64:6.

57:14–21 *The True People of God Invited.* God opens the way into his reviving presence for all the penitent.

57:14 The way back to God is clear. As far as he is concerned, there is no obstacle (cf. 62:10).

57:15 high and lifted up. See note on 6:1; cf. 52:13. God dwells in the **high and holy place** of his eternal transcendence, where no one else may go, and also dwells with **him who is of a contrite and lowly spirit**.

57:16–19 God knows how much discipline the human heart can take (cf. 1 Pet. 5:10). He heals those who mourn the low condition of his people (cf. Isa. 66:10). He even creates their spirit of repentance. **Peace, peace, to the far and to the near** includes both Jews and Gentiles (cf. Eph. 2:11–22).

20 [a]But the wicked are like the tossing sea;
for it cannot be quiet,
and its waters toss up mire and dirt.
21 [b]There is no peace," says my God, "for the wicked."

True and False Fasting

58

1 "Cry aloud; do not hold back;
[c]lift up your voice like a trumpet;
[d]declare to my people their transgression,
to the house of Jacob their sins.
2 [e]Yet they seek me daily
and delight to know my ways,
as if they were a nation that did righteousness
and did not forsake the judgment of their God;
they ask of me righteous judgments;
they delight to draw near to God.
3 [f]'Why have we fasted, and you see it not?
Why have we humbled ourselves, and you take no knowledge of it?'
Behold, in the day of your fast you seek your own pleasure,[1]
[g]and oppress all your workers.
4 Behold, you fast only to quarrel and to fight
and to hit with a wicked fist.
Fasting like yours this day
will not make your voice to be heard on high.
5 [h]Is such the fast that I choose,
[i]a day for a person to humble himself?
Is it to bow down his head like a reed,
and to spread sackcloth and ashes under him?
Will you call this a fast,
and a day acceptable to the LORD?

6 "Is not this the fast that I choose:
[j]to loose the bonds of wickedness,
to undo the straps [k]of the yoke,
to let the oppressed[2] go free,
and to break every yoke?
7 Is it not [l]to share your bread with the hungry
and bring the homeless poor into your house;
when you see the naked, to cover him,
[m]and not to hide yourself from your own flesh?
8 [n]Then shall your light break forth like the dawn,
[o]and your healing shall spring up speedily;

[1] *Or pursue your own business* [2] *Or bruised*

20[a]Jude 13
21[b]ch. 48:22

Chapter 58

1[c]Lev. 25:9; [Joel 2:1] [d]Mic. 3:8
2[e][ch. 1:11; 29:13; Zech. 7:5, 6]
3[f][Mal. 3:14] [g][ch. 60:17]; See Neh. 5:1-8
5[h]Zech. 7:5 [i]Lev. 16:29
6[j]See Neh. 5:10-12 [k]ver. 9
7[l]ver. 10; Ezek. 18:7; [Matt. 25:35] [m]Neh. 5:5
8[n][Job 11:17] [o]Jer. 30:17

57:20–21 like the tossing sea. The unsettled turbulence of wickedness brings its own punishment (see 48:22; Jude 12–13; cf. Isa. 32:17–18; 57:2).

58:1–59:13 ***The Path to Blessing: Ritual vs. Responsibility.*** God's true people experience his blessing in a personally godly and socially responsible way of life, owning up to their offenses.

58:1–14 Isaiah is commanded to confront the hypocrisy of God's people with boldness and to clarify the true path to God's blessing. See note on 1:10–20 regarding ritual vs. righteousness.

58:2 The people are not gripped by the practical implications of biblical faith (cf. 29:13). **Yet they seek me daily**. "Me" is emphatic in the Hebrew text, for ironic effect (cf. Luke 18:9–14).

58:3–4 The "delight" of v. 2 is false, for it is an emotional mechanism for pressuring God into compliance with human wishes. When God refuses to be used, the people are offended that their religion does not "work." Their unacknowledged attempt to gain advantage with God is exposed in their overbearing use of people: **oppress all your workers . . . hit with a wicked fist**. God called his people to show humanity in their social life, but they are failing to do this (cf. the recurring theme of Amos).

58:5 Isaiah uses sarcasm to dismiss false piety. What establishes true religion is not what is acceptable to man but what is **acceptable to the LORD** (cf. Ps. 51:17; Isa. 56:6–7).

58:6–7 God defines the true piety that he does bless, for it is true to his non-oppressive gospel (cf. 1:17; James 1:27). **Is not this . . . ? Is it not . . . ?** God dignifies his dishonest people with appeals to reasoned thought (cf. Isa. 1:18). **every yoke**. Every form of oppression (cf. Deut. 28:48; 1 Kings 12:4).

58:8–9a Then . . . Then. God promises to meet true fasting with true blessing. Unlike false gods, the Lord *responds* (cf. 64:5a). **your light**. See 9:1–7; Eph. 5:14. **your rear guard**. See Ex. 13:21; 14:19–20. **Here I am**. God humbly offers his availability (cf. Isa. 65:1; for men responding to God's call, cf. Gen. 22:1, 11; Ex. 3:4).

8[p]Ps. 85:13 [q][ch. 52:12]
9[r]ver. 6 [s]Prov. 6:13
10[t]ver. 7, 8 [n][See ver. 8 above]
11[u]Jer. 31:12
12[v]ch. 61:4; 65:21; [Ezra 6:14; Neh. 4:6]
13[w]ch. 56:2; See Neh. 13:15-21 [x]ver. 3
14[y]Deut. 32:13 [z]Jer. 50:19 [a]ch. 1:20
Chapter 59
1[b]ch. 50:2; Num. 11:23
2[c]Jer. 5:25
3[d]ch. 1:15

[p]your righteousness shall go before you;
[q]the glory of the LORD shall be your rear guard.
9 Then you shall call, and the LORD will answer;
you shall cry, and he will say, 'Here I am.'
If you take away [r]the yoke from your midst,
[s]the pointing of the finger, and speaking wickedness,
10 [t]if you pour yourself out for the hungry
and satisfy the desire of the afflicted,
[n]then shall your light rise in the darkness
and your gloom be as the noonday.
11 And the LORD will guide you continually
and satisfy your desire in scorched places
and make your bones strong;
and you shall be [u]like a watered garden,
like a spring of water,
whose waters do not fail.
12 [v]And your ancient ruins shall be rebuilt;
you shall raise up the foundations of many generations;
you shall be called the repairer of the breach,
the restorer of streets to dwell in.

13 [w]"If you turn back your foot from the Sabbath,
from doing your pleasure[1] on my holy day,
and call the Sabbath a delight
and the holy day of the LORD honorable;
if you honor it, not going your own ways,
or seeking [x]your own pleasure,[2] or talking idly;[3]
14 then you shall take delight in the LORD,
[y]and I will make you ride on the heights of the earth;[4]
[z]I will feed you with the heritage of Jacob your father,
[a]for the mouth of the LORD has spoken."

Evil and Oppression

59 1 Behold, [b]the LORD's hand is not shortened, that it cannot save,
or his ear dull, that it cannot hear;
2 [c]but your iniquities have made a separation
between you and your God,
and your sins have hidden his face from you
so that he does not hear.
3 [d]For your hands are defiled with blood
and your fingers with iniquity;
your lips have spoken lies;
your tongue mutters wickedness.

[1] Or *business* [2] Or *pursuing your own business* [3] Hebrew *or speaking a word* [4] Or *of the land*

58:9b–10a If . . . if. God again defines the conditions of the blessing in a manner consistent with his nature. **the pointing of the finger**. Either in false accusation, or in destructive gossip, or both. See Prov. 6:12–15.

58:10b–12 then. God reaffirms his readiness to bless his obedient people. **your bones**. The human person (cf. Ps. 6:2; 32:3; Prov. 15:30; Isa. 66:14; Jer. 23:9). **your ancient ruins**. The ruins of Jerusalem in the sixth century B.C. symbolized the deeper spiritual ruins of long-standing human failure (cf. Isa. 1:5–9; 44:26–28; 61:4).

58:13–14 If . . . if . . . then. For a third time in ch. 58, God clarifies the kind of religious practice that draws down his blessing. **the Sabbath**. See note on 56:2. **the heights of the earth**. Social prestige among the nations (cf. Deut. 26:16–19; 28:1; 33:29). **the heritage of Jacob**. The promises to the patriarchs.

59:1–13 Isaiah explains how God's people sink to a low condition.

59:1–8 Accusations of social evils.

59:1 God is unlimited in his capacity and readiness to help. This is another answer to the sullen question in 58:3a.

59:2 Iniquities and sins create a practical barrier between God and his people, typically resulting in God's discipline (see Heb. 12:5–11; cf. James 4:1–10). In this case, the extreme nature of their behavior may express total unbelief.

59:3–8 These sins, which keep God's presence away, are not religious but social. **your hands are defiled with blood**. See 1:15. **they conceive mischief and give birth to iniquity**. Sin comes naturally. **Their feet run to evil**, meaning they are eager for sin. Paul describes the entire sinful human race with Isaiah's language (Rom. 3:15–17), implying that

4 [e]No one enters suit justly;
no one goes to law honestly;
they rely on empty pleas, they speak lies,
[f]they conceive mischief and give birth to iniquity.
5 They hatch adders' eggs;
they weave the spider's web;
he who eats their eggs dies,
and from one that is crushed a viper is hatched.
6 [g]Their webs will not serve as clothing;
men will not cover themselves with what they make.
Their works are works of iniquity,
and deeds of violence are in their hands.
7 [h]Their feet run to evil,
and they are swift to shed innocent blood;
their thoughts are thoughts of iniquity;
desolation and destruction are in their highways.
8 The way of peace they do not know,
and there is no justice in their paths;
they have made their roads crooked;
[i]no one who treads on them knows peace.

9 Therefore justice is far from us,
and righteousness does not overtake us;
[j]we hope for light, and behold, darkness,
and for brightness, but we walk in gloom.
10 [k]We grope for the wall like the blind;
we grope like those who have no eyes;
we stumble at noon as in the twilight,
[l]among those in full vigor we are like dead men.
11 We all growl like bears;
[m]we moan and moan like doves;
[n]we hope for justice, but there is none;
for salvation, but it is far from us.
12 For our transgressions are multiplied before you,
and our sins testify against us;
for our transgressions are with us,
and we know our iniquities:
13 transgressing, and denying the LORD,
and turning back from following our God,
[o]speaking oppression and revolt,
conceiving and uttering from the heart lying words.

Judgment and Redemption

14 [p]Justice is turned back,
and righteousness stands far away;

4 [e][ver. 14] [f]Job 15:35; Ps. 7:14
6 [g]Job 8:14
7 [h]Prov. 1:16; Cited Rom. 3:15-17
8 [i]ch. 48:22; 57:21
9 [j][ver. 11; ch. 60:2]
10 [k]Deut. 28:29; Job 5:14; 12:25; See ch. 42:18-20 [l][1 Cor. 4:9, 10]
11 [m]ch. 38:14 [n][ver. 9; ch. 46:13; 56:1]
13 [o][ver. 3, 4]
14 [p][ch. 51:4, 5]

when God's people do not embrace his covenant, they can sin as badly as any others.

59:9–13 Sin and misery are confessed.

59:9 Therefore. Isaiah leads his people away from blaming God—their bitter spirit is implied in v. 1—to clear awareness of their own responsibility for their problems. Note the change to the first person ("us").

59:10 We grope for the wall . . . we stumble at noon. Metaphors for moral confusion.

59:11 We all growl like bears in sullen anguish.

59:12–13 For our transgressions. The people of God own up to their guilt as the cause of their miseries (cf. Ps. 51:3).

59:14–60:22 *Present Failure, Eternal Covenant, Future Glory.* God, the only Savior, through his covenant with the Redeemer, will glorify his people as the predominant culture of a new world, for his own glory.

59:14–20 Human sin is so radical that only God can redeem the guilty.

59:14–15a Guilty mankind has so rejected **justice, righteousness, truth**, and **uprightness** that godliness is persecuted. **truth has stumbled in the public squares**. The people no longer have any publicly acknowledged standard of truth. Falsehood is freely proclaimed and readily accepted. **He who departs from evil** (i.e., the evil that the people are doing) **makes himself a prey** (i.e., he is hunted like an animal).

59:15b–16 it displeased him . . . his own arm brought him salvation. God, who is offended by sin, is the only one able to accomplish salvation. **his righteousness upheld him**. His faithfulness to his covenant promises was expressed in what he did.

16[q][ch. 51:18; 63:5]
17[r]1 Thess. 5:8; See Eph. 6:13-17 [s][ch. 9:7]
18[t]ch. 63:4, 6 [u][ch. 41:1, 5]
19[v][Ps. 113:3] [w][ch. 30:27, 28]
20[x]Cited Rom. 11:26, 27; [ch. 40:9; Joel 2:32] [y]ch. 43:14
21[z]Jer. 31:31; Heb. 8:10; 10:16 [a]ch. 51:16; [Deut. 4:10]

Chapter 60

1[b][Eph. 5:14] [c]ch. 40:5; 58:8; Mal. 4:2
3[d]ch. 42:6; 49:6; Rev. 21:24

for truth has stumbled in the public squares,
 and uprightness cannot enter.
15 Truth is lacking,
 and he who departs from evil makes himself a prey.

The LORD saw it, and it displeased him[1]
 that there was no justice.
16 [q]He saw that there was no man,
 and wondered that there was no one to intercede;
then his own arm brought him salvation,
 and his righteousness upheld him.
17 [r]He put on righteousness as a breastplate,
 and a helmet of salvation on his head;
he put on garments of vengeance for clothing,
 and wrapped himself in [s]zeal as a cloak.
18 [t]According to their deeds, so will he repay,
 wrath to his adversaries, repayment to his enemies;
 [u]to the coastlands he will render repayment.
19 [v]So they shall fear the name of the LORD from the west,
 and his glory from the rising of the sun;
[w]for he will come like a rushing stream,[2]
 which the wind of the LORD drives.

20 [x]"And [y]a Redeemer will come to Zion,
 to those in Jacob who turn from transgression," declares the LORD.

21 "And as for me, [z]this is my covenant with them," says the LORD: "My Spirit that is upon you, [a]and my words that I have put in your mouth, shall not depart out of your mouth, or out of the mouth of your offspring, or out of the mouth of your children's offspring," says the LORD, "from this time forth and forevermore."

The Future Glory of Israel

60

1 [b]Arise, shine, for your light has come,
 and [c]the glory of the LORD has risen upon you.
2 For behold, darkness shall cover the earth,
 and thick darkness the peoples;
but the LORD will arise upon you,
 and his glory will be seen upon you.
3 [d]And nations shall come to your light,
 and kings to the brightness of your rising.

[1] Hebrew *and it was evil in his eyes* [2] Hebrew *a narrow river*

59:17 God displayed (**put on**) the powers of a fully equipped warrior. God not only forgives sin; he opposes it with all his might (cf. 42:13; 63:1–6). On the "armor of God" (Eph. 6:11–17) as the equipment of the Messiah, see note on Isa. 11:5.

59:18 According to . . . so. Perfect justice, measure-for-measure, in a final settlement. **to the coastlands**. There is no hiding place, however remote (cf. Amos 9:2–4).

59:19 To **fear the name of the LORD** is the right response to him (Deut. 28:58; Neh. 1:11; Ps. 61:5; 86:11; Mal. 4:2). This passage reflects the expectation that all kinds of people will know the Lord and fear his name (cf. 2 Chron. 6:33; Ps. 102:15; Mal. 1:11). **the west . . . the rising of the sun**. Opposite directions, suggesting the entire world (cf. Isa. 45:6; 52:10; Mal. 1:11). **a rushing stream . . . the wind**. The power of God, applied with double force.

59:20 a Redeemer. See note on 41:14. The Redeemer is the sole alternative to the wrath of God (see 59:18). Only the redemption of God saves from his wrath. In Rom. 11:26–27, Paul combines this verse (from the LXX) with Jer. 31:33 (and perhaps Isa. 27:9) to describe his hope for his ethnic kin.

59:21 And as for me. God declares his commitment to his people. **My covenant with them** is the messianic servant, the Redeemer of v. 20 (cf. 42:6; 49:8). **My Spirit that is upon you**, i.e., upon the Messiah (cf. 61:1). **my words**. All the words that God speaks to his people through his prophets (cf. Deut. 18:18). But the promise does not apply only to the prophets who first spoke God's words, for their **offspring** and their **children's offspring** shall also have these words and will speak them to others. This promise implies that God's people would preserve his words spoken by the prophets; this process ultimately resulted in the written words of the Bible.

60:1–22 Isaiah foresees the final glory of God's people, uniting all humanity in knowing the true God.

60:1–9 God will put his beauty upon his people, attracting the nations.

60:1 Arise, shine addresses Zion (cf. 59:20; 60:14). The bright future of God's people calls for cheerful expectancy now by faith. **your light has come**. Cf. 58:8. **the glory of the LORD**. Cf. 40:5. The false glories of mankind will finally fade away into the nothingness they really are.

60:2 God will make a clear public distinction between those who are his and those who are not his (cf. Ex. 8:22, 23; Rev. 21:10–11).

60:3 Isaiah predicts a reversal of the prestige presently given to unbelief and the shame heaped upon God's people (cf. 2:2–4; 11:10).

4 [e]Lift up your eyes all around, and see;
they all gather together, they come to you;
[f]your sons shall come from afar,
and your daughters shall be carried on the hip.
5 Then you shall see and [g]be radiant;
your heart shall thrill and exult,[1]
because the abundance of the sea shall be turned to you,
[h]the wealth of the nations shall come to you.
6 A multitude of camels shall cover you,
the young camels of [i]Midian and [j]Ephah;
all those from [k]Sheba shall come.
[l]They shall bring gold and frankincense,
and shall bring good news, the praises of the LORD.
7 All the flocks of [m]Kedar shall be gathered to you;
the rams of [n]Nebaioth shall minister to you;
[o]they shall come up with acceptance on my altar,
[p]and I will beautify my beautiful house.

8 Who are these that fly like a cloud,
and [q]like doves to their windows?
9 For [r]the coastlands shall hope for me,
[s]the ships of Tarshish first,
[t]to bring your children from afar,
their silver and gold with them,
for the name of the LORD your God,
and for the Holy One of Israel,
because [u]he has made you beautiful.
10 [v]Foreigners shall build up your walls,
and [v]their kings shall minister to you;
for in my wrath I struck you,
but in my favor I have had mercy on you.
11 [w]Your gates shall be open continually;
day and night they shall not be shut,
[w]that people may bring to you the wealth of the nations,
with their kings led in procession.

[1] Hebrew *your heart shall tremble and grow wide*

4 [e]ch. 49:18 [f]ver. 9; ch. 66:20
5 [g]Ps. 34:5 [h]ch. 61:6
6 [i]Judg. 6:5 [j]Gen. 25:4 [k]1 Kgs. 10:1; Ps. 72:10 [l][Matt. 2:11]
7 [m]See ch. 21:16 [n]Gen. 25:13; 28:9; 36:3 [o]ch. 56:7 [p]Hag. 2:7
8 [q]Hos. 11:11; [Gen. 8:9]
9 [r]ch. 51:5; See ch. 11:11 [s]See ch. 2:16 [t]Gal. 4:26 [u]ch. 44:23; 55:5
10 [v]ch. 45:1, 13; Zech. 6:15
11 [w][Rev. 21:25, 26]

60:4 Lift up your eyes. Isaiah calls believers to look expectantly for many converts to the Lord entering Zion as a growing family (cf. 43:5–7; 49:18; 54:1–8; 66:18–23).

60:5–7 A wonderful reordering of society, so that the people of God become the predominant culture of the world, honored by the nations. The victory of God includes the victory of his people and the blessing of the world, as God promised (cf. Gen. 12:1–3).

60:5 the wealth of the nations shall come to you. Cf. notes on 18:7; 60:6–7; 60:8–9.

60:6–7 Midian is one of Abraham's sons (by Keturah), and **Ephah** is Midian's son, and **Sheba** his nephew (Gen. 25:1–4). From Midian and Ephah descended an Arabian tribe that dwelt east of the Red Sea in what is today northwestern Saudi Arabia. "Those from Sheba" were a people and a kingdom in southern Arabia that corresponds to modern-day Yemen. Together with the place names pertaining to two sons of Ishmael (Gen. 25:13) named in Isa. 60:7—**Kedar** (approximately 240 miles or 386 km northeast of Midian, still in modern Saudi Arabia) and **Nebaioth** (associated with the Nabateans, whose kingdom was approximately 120 miles or 193 km north of Midian, in present-day Jordan)—the verses depict an abundance of wealth and goods flooding into Zion from Israel's near and far neighbors. **gold and frankincense**. This is the fulfillment of the promise given in v. 5. (See further the ultimate fulfillment, prefigured in Matt. 2:11, and the final fulfillment as seen in Rev. 21:24–26.)

60:7 Isaiah uses the language of his times to portray the exalted spiritual destiny of God's people. **they shall come up with acceptance on my altar**. See Rom. 15:16. **I will beautify my beautiful house**. Ezra 7:27 uses these words to describe the mission on which the Persian king sent him to Jerusalem, portraying that mission as part of the fulfillment of this passage.

60:8–9 These that fly like a cloud are rapidly approaching foreign ships—not an invading force but a merchant fleet bringing converts devoted to the Lord, for his glory. **the ships of Tarshish**. See 2:16 and 23:1. The nations see in the beauty of God's people the beauty of **the Holy One of Israel**. He glorifies his name by glorifying the people who bear his name.

60:10–14 God will fulfill his ancient promises to Abraham.

60:10 Instead of persecuting God's people, the nations will **build** them up. **your walls**. Zion, the city of God. See Neh. 2:7–8 for a short-term "down payment" on this promise, and Acts 15:12–16 for a longer-term, spiritual fulfillment. **I struck you**. God had used the hostile nations to discipline his own people (cf. Isa. 10:5–6). His disciplines are never final, only remedial, but his mercies are final and endless.

60:11 Your gates shall be open continually because there will be no more war or threat of war, or even the threat of plundering by thieves (cf. 2:4; 26:1–4; 33:20–22). Cf. the new Jerusalem, Rev. 21:25.

12 [x]For the nation and kingdom
that will not serve you shall perish;
those nations shall be utterly laid waste.
13 [y]The glory of Lebanon shall come to you,
the cypress, the plane, and [z]the pine,
to beautify the place of my sanctuary,
and I will make the place of my feet glorious.
14 [a]The sons of those who afflicted you
shall come bending low to you,
[b]and all who despised you
shall bow down at your feet;
[c]they shall call you the City of the LORD,
the Zion of the Holy One of Israel.

15 [d]Whereas you have been forsaken and hated,
with no one passing through,
[e]I will make you majestic forever,
a joy from age to age.
16 [f]You shall suck the milk of nations;
you shall nurse at the breast of kings;
and you shall know that [g]I, the LORD, am your Savior
and your Redeemer, [h]the Mighty One of Jacob.

17 Instead of bronze I will bring gold,
and instead of iron I will bring silver;
instead of wood, bronze,
instead of stones, iron.
I will make your overseers peace
[i]and your taskmasters righteousness.
18 [j]Violence shall no more be heard in your land,
devastation or destruction within your borders;
[k]you shall call your walls Salvation,
and your gates Praise.

19 [l]The sun shall be no more
your light by day,
nor for brightness shall the moon
give you light;[1]
but the LORD will be your everlasting light,
and your God will be your glory.[2]
20 Your sun shall no more go down,
nor your moon withdraw itself;
for the LORD will be your everlasting light,
and [m]your days of mourning shall be ended.
21 [n]Your people shall all be righteous;
[o]they shall possess the land forever,
[p]the branch of my planting, the work of my hands,
that I might be glorified.[3]

12[x][Zech. 14:17-19]
13[y]ch. 35:2 [z]ch. 41:19
14[a][ch. 14:1, 2; Zech. 8:23] [b]ch. 49:23; [Rev. 3:9] [c][ch. 1:26; 62:2]
15[d]ch. 54:6; 62:4 [e]Ps. 47:4; [ch. 65:18]
16[f][ch. 49:23; 66:11, 12] [g]ch. 43:3; 49:26; [ch. 47:4] [h]Gen. 49:24; Ps. 132:2
17[i][ch. 58:3]
18[j]ch. 11:9 [k]ch. 26:1
19[l]Zech. 14:6, 7; Rev. 21:23; 22:5; [ch. 24:23; 30:26]
20[m]ch. 35:10; 65:19; Rev. 21:4
21[n]ch. 52:1; Jer. 31:34 [o]Ps. 37:9; See Ezek. 37:25 [p]ch. 61:3

[1] Masoretic Text; Dead Sea Scroll, Septuagint, Targum add *by night* [2] *Or your beauty* [3] *Or that I might display my beauty*

60:12 The attitude of the **nations** toward God's people reveals their true attitude toward God (cf. Gen. 12:3). Serving God entails serving his people.

60:13 The glory of the nations will beautify, not profane, the worship of God. **the place of my feet**. I.e., the temple as his footstool on earth (cf. Ps. 99:5; 132:7; Ezek. 43:7).

60:15–22 God will reverse the present failures and sorrows of his people through the open display of his own presence forever.

60:16 The powerful people of this world will no longer trample on God's people but will care for them. This poetic imagery pictures the people of God as infants and pictures other nations—even leaders of nations—as caring for them. **you shall know**. God will move his people from their cynical unbelief (cf. 40:27; 49:14) to a wondering acknowledgment of him.

60:17 Instead of bronze . . . gold. See 1 Kings 10:21, 27.

60:18 Salvation and **Praise** portray dominant traits of Zion. Contrast 5:7.

60:19 the LORD will be your everlasting light. Cf. the new Jerusalem, Rev. 21:23.

60:21–22 The people of Zion will be **righteous**, not sinful; secure, not imperiled; fruitful, not disappointing; and influential, not ignored. **in its time I will**

22 [q]The least one shall become a clan,
and the smallest one a mighty nation;
[r]I am the LORD;
in its time I will hasten it.

The Year of the LORD's Favor

61

1 [s]The Spirit of the Lord GOD is upon me,
because the LORD has [t]anointed me
to bring good news to the poor;[1]
he has sent me to bind up the brokenhearted,
to proclaim liberty to the captives,
and [u]the opening of the prison to those who are bound;[2]
2 [v]to proclaim the year of the LORD's favor,
[w]and the day of vengeance of our God;
to comfort all who mourn;
3 to grant to those who mourn in Zion—
[x]to give them a beautiful headdress instead of ashes,
[y]the oil of gladness instead of mourning,
the garment of praise instead of a faint spirit;
[z]that they may be called oaks of righteousness,
the planting of the LORD, [a]that he may be glorified.[3]
4 [b]They shall build up the ancient ruins;
they shall raise up the former devastations;
they shall repair the ruined cities,
the devastations of many generations.
5 [c]Strangers shall stand and tend your flocks;
foreigners shall be your plowmen and vinedressers;
6 [d]but you shall be called the priests of the LORD;
they shall speak of you as the ministers of our God;
[e]you shall eat the wealth of the nations,
and in their glory you shall boast.
7 [f]Instead of your shame there shall be a double portion;
instead of dishonor they shall rejoice in their lot;
therefore in their land they shall possess a double portion;
they shall have everlasting joy.
8 [g]For I the LORD love justice;
I hate robbery and wrong;[4]
[h]I will faithfully give them their recompense,
[i]and I will make an everlasting covenant with them.

[1] *Or afflicted* [2] *Or the opening* [of the eyes] *to those who are blind;* Septuagint *and recovery of sight to the blind* [3] *Or that he may display his beauty*
[4] *Or robbery with a burnt offering*

22 [q][Matt. 13:31] [r]Hab. 2:3
Chapter 61
1 [s]ch. 11:2; 42:1; 48:16; Cited Luke 4:18, 19 [t]Ps. 45:7 [u]ch. 45:13; Ps. 146:7
2 [v][Lev. 25:10] [w]ch. 34:8
3 [x]ver. 10; [ch. 28:5] [y]Ps. 45:7; Heb. 1:9 [z][ch. 60:21] [a]John 15:8
4 [b]Amos 9:14; See ch. 58:12
5 [c]ch. 14:2; [ch. 60:10]
6 [d]Ex. 19:6; 1 Pet. 2:9; [Joel 1:9] [e]ch. 60:5, 11, 16
7 [f]ch. 40:2; [ch. 54:7, 8; Zech. 9:12]
8 [g]Ps. 11:7; [ch. 59:15] [h]ch. 40:10; 49:4 [i]See ch. 55:3

hasten it. The fulfillment of these promises does not await favorable historical conditions but depends directly on the act of God.

61:1–62:12 *The Anointed Preacher Renewing the World.* The Messiah will preach into existence his new, liberated people, who will pray into existence his new, redeemed world.

61:1–3 The Spirit of the Lord GOD is upon me. This looks back to 48:16, and thus the speaker is the messianic servant, who creates a new people by his Spirit-empowered preaching (cf. 11:2; 59:21). Isaiah explains the goal of Messiah's anointing with seven purpose clauses. **the poor**. See 11:4; 29:19; Matt. 5:3. **to proclaim liberty**. See Lev. 25:10. **the opening of the prison**. The return from Babylonian exile, but more than that: spiritual freedom from the oppression of sin and Satan. **the year of the LORD's favor**. A new era of blessing (cf. Isa. 34:8; 63:4; 2 Cor. 6:2). Quoting this text in Nazareth (Luke 4:18–19), Jesus did not include **and the day of vengeance of our God** because the display of his wrath awaits Christ's second coming (cf. Isa. 5:25–29; 63:1–6; Acts 17:31; Rev. 6:15–17). **oaks of righteousness**. Grand, fruitful, lasting, and strong (cf. Ps. 1:3).

61:4 They shall build up the ancient ruins. The poor become, through the Messiah, creative restorers of the sad situations that man has had to live with for so long (cf. 54:3; 58:12). Every human ideal falls into ruins in this world of death, but the new culture of life in the city of God will thrive forever.

61:5–7 Regarding the blessings of the Gentiles coming to God's people, see notes on 60:6–7 and references there; Rom. 15:27. **the priests of the LORD**. At long last, Israel will fulfill its role among the nations (Ex. 19:5–6; 1 Pet. 2:9). **your shame**. The failure of God's old covenant people (cf. Isa. 54:4). **they shall rejoice**. Isaiah shifts from one grammatical person to another (from "your" to "they"), in order to change his focus (cf. 1:29; 5:8; 52:14). **a double portion** (61:7). Inheriting twice what was expected.

61:8 The promises of God are guaranteed by the character of God (cf. 41:13; 42:6–8; 43:3, 15; 44:6, 24–28; 46:8–11; 48:17; 49:26; 51:12–16; 60:16). **an everlasting covenant**. See note on 54:10.

61:10–11 The speaker is either the Messiah, the prophet Isaiah, or Zion herself. With **the Lord GOD** echoing "The Spirit of the Lord GOD is upon me" in v. 1, it is likely that the Messiah is speaking here. **as a bridegroom . . .**

10[j]Hab. 3:18 [k][ch. 59:17; Zech. 3:4] [l]ver. 3 [m]ch. 49:18; Rev. 21:2
11[n][ch. 60:18; 62:7]

Chapter 62

1[o]ver. 6, 7 [p][Prov. 4:18]
2[q]ch. 60:3; Ps. 98:2 [r]ch. 60:14; [Rev. 2:17; 3:12]
3[s]Zech. 9:16; [ch. 54:11, 12]
4[t]Hos. 1:10; 1 Pet. 2:10; See ch. 54:6 [u]ch. 49:14; 54:1, 7; 60:15 [r][See ver. 2 above] [v]Mal. 3:12
5[w][ch. 51:18] [x]ch. 65:19
6[y]ch. 52:8; 56:10

9 Their offspring shall be known among the nations,
and their descendants in the midst of the peoples;
all who see them shall acknowledge them,
that they are an offspring the LORD has blessed.

10 [j]I will greatly rejoice in the LORD;
my soul shall exult in my God,
[k]for he has clothed me with the garments of salvation;
he has covered me with the robe of righteousness,
as a bridegroom decks himself [l]like a priest with a beautiful headdress,
[m]and as a bride adorns herself with her jewels.
11 For as the earth brings forth its sprouts,
and as a garden causes what is sown in it to sprout up,
so the Lord GOD will cause [n]righteousness and praise
to sprout up before all the nations.

Zion's Coming Salvation

62

1 [o]For Zion's sake I will not keep silent,
and for Jerusalem's sake I will not be quiet,
[p]until her righteousness goes forth as brightness,
and her salvation as a burning torch.
2 [q]The nations shall see your righteousness,
and all the kings your glory,
[r]and you shall be called by a new name
that the mouth of the LORD will give.
3 You shall be [s]a crown of beauty in the hand of the LORD,
and a royal diadem in the hand of your God.
4 [t]You shall no more be termed [u]Forsaken,[1]
and your land shall no more be termed Desolate,[2]
[r]but you shall be called [v]My Delight Is in Her,[3]
and your land Married;[4]
for the LORD delights in you,
and your land shall be married.
5 For as a young man marries a young woman,
so [w]shall your sons marry you,
and as the bridegroom rejoices over the bride,
so [x]shall your God rejoice over you.

6 On your walls, O Jerusalem,
I have set [y]watchmen;

[1] Hebrew *Azubah* [2] Hebrew *Shemamah* [3] Hebrew *Hephzibah* [4] Hebrew *Beulah*

as a bride. The Messiah will lead his people into the romance of eternal salvation (cf. Eph. 5:25–27; Rev. 21:2, 9). **As the earth . . . as a garden** suggests a bountiful harvest.

62:1–5 The desolation of God's people will be replaced with delight.

62:1 For Zion's sake. That is, for the sake of the redeemed people of God who dwell in Zion (another name for Jerusalem), the city of God. This emphasis on God's acting for the sake of his people lies at the heart of Isaiah's ministry: God will glorify himself in the renewed and increased glory of his people, and that future is worth living for now (cf. 1:26; 2:2–3; 4:2–6; 9:1–3; 10:20–21; 11:11–16; 14:1–2; 25:1–9; 26:1–21; 29:22–24; 30:19–26; 32:1–4, 15–18; 33:5–6, 17–24; 35:1–10; 40:1–5, 27–31; 41:8–20; 42:6–7; 43:1–7, 16–21; 44:1–5, 21–28; 45:14–17, 24–25; 49:5–6, 8–26; 51:1–3, 11; 52:1–10; 54:1–17; 55:12–13; 57:15–19; 59:20; 60:1–22; 61:1–9; 62:1–12; 65:8–10, 17–25; 66:10–14, 18–23). **I will not keep silent**. The speaker is either the prophet Isaiah, the Lord, or the Messiah. Since the prophetic intercessors of 62:6 "shall never be silent," it is likely that Isaiah is speaking here. The promises of God compel him to pray.

62:2 Your and **you** are feminine singular, addressing Zion. **a new name that the mouth of the LORD will give**. He alone defines the destiny of his people, explained in vv. 4, 12 (cf. 1:26; 56:5; 60:14, 18).

62:4 Reversing the situation of 60:15; cf. 6:12; 49:14.

62:5 Your sons are the loyal inhabitants of Zion (here, the eternal city of God; cf. Psalm 87). **shall . . . marry**. A poetic image indicating that the inhabitants of Jerusalem will love and cherish their city: the inhabitants of Zion will forever be committed to and delight in their eternal dwelling place, for the Lord's people are there, and the Lord himself is there. Isaiah's poetic imagery leaves an overwhelming impression of joy, delight, righteousness, beauty, safety, and peace. **so shall your God rejoice over you**. Boldly drawing on a familiar human image of inexpressible joy and delight, God says his delight in his people will be like that of a bridegroom's delight in his bride. Isaiah explains that in God's great plan of salvation, he not only forgives his people, protects them, heals them, provides for them, restores them to their home, reconciles them to each other, transforms them so they are righteous, honors them, exalts them above all nations, and makes them a blessing to all nations, as he called them to be—but more than all these things, he actually *delights* in his people.

62:6–7 I have set. The speaker is either the Messiah or the Lord. The **watchmen** were prophetic guardians, like sentries on a city wall, praying

all the day and all the night
  they shall never be silent.
You who put the LORD in remembrance,
  take no rest,
7 and give him no rest
  until he establishes Jerusalem
  and makes it [z]a praise in the earth.
8 The LORD has sworn [a]by his right hand
  and by his mighty arm:
"I will not again give [b]your grain
  to be food for your enemies,
[c]and foreigners shall not drink your wine
  for which you have labored;
9 but [d]those who garner it shall eat it
  and praise the LORD,
and [d]those who gather it shall drink it
  in the courts of my sanctuary."[1]

10 Go through, go through the gates;
  [e]prepare the way for the people;
[f]build up, build up the highway;
  clear it of stones;
  [g]lift up a signal over the peoples.
11 Behold, the LORD has proclaimed
  to the end of the earth:
[h]Say to the daughter of Zion,
  [i]"Behold, your salvation comes;
behold, his reward is with him,
  and his recompense before him."
12 [j]And they shall be called The Holy People,
  The Redeemed of the LORD;
[k]and you shall be called Sought Out,
  A City Not Forsaken.

The LORD's Day of Vengeance

63

1 Who is this who comes from [l]Edom,
  in crimsoned garments from [l]Bozrah,
he who is splendid in his apparel,
  [m]marching in the greatness of his strength?
"It is I, speaking in righteousness,
  mighty to save."

[1] *Or in my holy courts*

7[z]ch. 60:18; [ch. 61:11; Zeph. 3:20]
8[a][Heb. 6:13] [b]Deut. 28:33; Jer. 5:17 [c][ch. 65:21, 22]
9[d][Deut. 12:12; 14:23, 26]
10[e]ch. 40:3 [f]ch. 57:14 [g]ch. 11:10; 49:22
11[h]Zech. 9:9; [Matt. 21:5; John 12:15] [i]ch. 40:10
12[j]ch. 61:6 [k]ver. 4; [ch. 61:4]

Chapter 63
1[l]ch. 34:6 [m][Ps. 68:7]

and watching for the fulfillment of God's promises (cf. 2 Sam. 18:24; Isa. 56:10; Ezek. 3:17). **they shall never be silent**. Cf. note on Isa. 62:1. **take no rest**. Do not cease to cry out to him; see Ps. 132:1–5. **give him no rest**. Continue to pray to him, call out to him. See Gen. 32:24–28. **Jerusalem** (Isa. 62:7) is here the new city of God, the place where his people dwell in safety and in righteousness forever (cf. Rev. 21:2, 10).

62:8–9 not again. God disciplined his ancient people according to the curses of the old covenant (cf. Lev. 26:14–39; Deut. 28:15–68; Judg. 6:1–6), but here he swears, with great solemnity, to display his glory through his merciful restoration to satisfy his people.

62:10–12 God invites and commands everyone to enter into the salvation of Zion.

62:10 The people . . . the peoples refers to God's old covenant people Israel plus all others willing to join them (cf. 56:8; 57:19; John 10:16). **clear it of stones**. Make an easy way of access into Zion.

62:11 the end of the earth . . . the daughter of Zion. God extends to the nations the opportunity to become part of Zion (cf. 11:9; 19:23–25; 56:3–8).

62:12 they. The people and peoples of v. 10. **You** is feminine singular in the Hebrew text, referring to Zion. Logically, the two merge into one.

63:1–14 *The Coming Victor, His Past Faithfulness.* God comforts his people with a vision of his victory over all evil in the future and of his loving goodness in the past.

63:1–6 The Messiah comes in final vengeance.

63:1 Speaking as a watchman on the wall, Isaiah marvels at the Messiah marching toward Zion as a victorious warrior (cf. 52:8; 62:6). **Edom**, the unbelieving nation southeast of Jerusalem, typifies the world in its contempt for the promises of God (cf. Gen. 25:29–34; 27:41; Isa. 34:1–7; Ezekiel 35; Mal. 1:2–4). **Bozrah**. The capital city of Edom (cf. Isa. 34:6). **speaking in**

2[n]Rev. 19:13 [o][Lam. 1:15; Rev. 14:20; 19:15]
3[p][Joel 3:13] [q][ch. 59:16]
4[r]ch. 34:8
5[s][ch. 59:16]
6[t]ch. 49:26
7[u]Ps. 145:7
9[v]Judg. 10:16 [w]Deut. 7:7, 8; [Ezek. 16:5, 6] [x]See Deut. 32:10-12
10[y]Ex. 15:24; Num. 14:11; Ps. 78:17, 56; 95:9; Ezek. 20:8 [z]Ps. 78:40; Acts 7:51; [Eph. 4:30]
11[a]See Ps. 77:11-20 [b]See Ex. 14:19-22

2 Why is your [n]apparel red,
and your garments like his [o]who treads in the winepress?

3 [p]"I have trodden the winepress alone,
[q]and from the peoples no one was with me;
I trod them in my anger
and trampled them in my wrath;
their lifeblood[1] spattered on my garments,
and stained all my apparel.
4 [r]For the day of vengeance was in my heart,
and my year of redemption[2] had come.
5 I looked, but [s]there was no one to help;
I was appalled, but there was no one to uphold;
so my own arm brought me salvation,
and my wrath upheld me.
6 I trampled down the peoples in my anger;
[t]I made them drunk in my wrath,
and I poured out their lifeblood on the earth."

The Lord's Mercy Remembered

7 I will recount the steadfast love of the LORD,
the praises of the LORD,
according to all that the LORD has granted us,
[u]and the great goodness to the house of Israel
that he has granted them according to his compassion,
according to the abundance of his steadfast love.
8 For he said, "Surely they are my people,
children who will not deal falsely."
And he became their Savior.
9 [v]In all their affliction he was afflicted,[3]
and the angel of his presence saved them;
[w]in his love and in his pity he redeemed them;
[x]he lifted them up and carried them all the days of old.

10 [y]But they rebelled
[z]and grieved his Holy Spirit;
therefore he turned to be their enemy,
and himself fought against them.
11 Then he remembered [a]the days of old,
of Moses and his people.[4]
[b]Where is he who brought them up out of the sea
with the shepherds of his flock?

[1] Or *their juice*; also verse 6 [2] Or *the year of my redeemed* [3] Or *he did not afflict* [4] Or *Then his people remembered the days of old, of Moses*

righteousness. His claim to be **mighty to save** has integrity and truth. No Edom exists that can defeat him (cf. Rev. 17:14).

63:3 I have trodden the winepress. Trampling of grapes is an image of judgment. God's final judgment on human sin is a harvest of justice (cf. Joel 3:13; Rev. 14:18–20; 19:13, 15). **alone . . . no one**. The Messiah alone wins the victory for his people (cf. Isa. 59:15b–18).

63:4 the day of vengeance was in my heart. See note on 61:1–3. **my year of redemption**. See note on 41:14.

63:7–14 The present challenge to faith: "Where is he?"

63:7 I will recount. The same verb (Hb. *zakar*) is in "You who put the LORD in remembrance" (62:6). These are the reflections of one who brings things to remembrance, recalling God's history of mercies toward Israel. **the steadfast love of the LORD . . . his steadfast love**. God was always true to his old covenant people; cf. Ex. 34:6.

63:8 God gave himself to Israel as her **Savior**, but she betrayed him (cf. 1:2–4). Isaiah is not saying that God miscalculated, but that his people did not respond as they should have.

63:9 In all their affliction he was afflicted. God was sorrowful over the suffering of his people (even though it was their own sin that brought it on). See Ex. 2:23–25 and Judg. 10:16. **the angel of his presence**. An unparalleled expression, suggesting how God wonderfully drew near to his people (cf. Ex. 23:20–23; 33:14–15; Num. 20:16). **he redeemed them**. The word "he" is emphatic, for God acted directly and personally.

63:10–11 his Holy Spirit. . . . his Holy Spirit. Again Isaiah emphasizes God's generous self-giving to Israel. **grieved**. This attributes some personal characteristics to the Holy Spirit and is one of the hints the OT gives of the distinct, personal existence of the Holy Spirit within the being of God. **But they rebelled**. See Psalm 78; Isa. 1:2; 66:24; Acts 7:51. The Savior of Isa. 63:8 thus became **their enemy**. See 1:19–20 and 43:27–28. In Eph. 4:30 Paul warns against grieving the Holy Spirit.

Where is he who put in the midst of them
his Holy Spirit,
12 who caused his glorious arm
to go at the right hand of Moses,
[c]who divided the waters before them
[d]to make for himself an everlasting name,
13 who led them through the depths?
Like a horse in the desert,
they did not stumble.
14 Like livestock that go down into the valley,
[e]the Spirit of the LORD gave them rest.
So you led your people,
[d]to make for yourself a glorious name.

Prayer for Mercy

15 [f]Look down from heaven and see,
[g]from your holy and beautiful[1] habitation.
Where are [h]your zeal and your might?
The stirring of your inner parts and your compassion
are held back from me.
16 For [i]you are our Father,
though Abraham does not know us,
and Israel does not acknowledge us;
you, O LORD, are our Father,
[j]our Redeemer from of old is your name.
17 O LORD, why do you make us wander from your ways
and [k]harden our heart, so that we fear you not?
[l]Return for the sake of your servants,
the tribes of your heritage.
18 [m]Your holy people held possession for a little while;[2]
[n]our adversaries have trampled down your sanctuary.
19 [o]We have become like those over whom you have never ruled,
like those who are not called by your name.

64

1 [p]Oh that you would rend the heavens and come down,
[q]that the mountains might quake at your presence—
2[3] as when fire kindles brushwood
and the fire causes water to boil—
[r]to make your name known to your adversaries,
and that the nations might tremble at your presence!
3 [s]When you did awesome things that we did not look for,
you came down, the mountains quaked at your presence.
4 [t]From of old no one has heard
or perceived by the ear,

12[c]Ex. 14:21; Josh. 3:16 [d]2 Sam. 7:23; Neh. 9:10
14[e][Num. 10:33] [d][See ver. 12 above]
15[f]Deut. 26:15 [g]Ps. 33:14 [h]ch. 59:17; [Zech. 1:14]
16[i]ch. 64:8; Deut. 32:6 [j]ch. 43:14
17[k]ch. 6:10; [John 12:40] [l]Ps. 90:13
18[m][Deut. 4:25, 26] [n]ch. 64:11
19[o][Jer. 14:8]

Chapter 64

1[p][2 Sam. 22:10; Ps. 18:9; 144:5] [q]Judg. 5:5; Mic. 1:4
2[r][Josh. 2:9, 10]
3[s][Ex. 14:13; 15:11]
4[t][Ps. 31:19]

[1] *Or holy and glorious* [2] *Or They have dispossessed your holy people for a little while* [3] Ch 64:1 in Hebrew

63:12–14 his glorious arm . . . a glorious name. God displayed his beauty in the history of Israel. Isaiah has hope for the future, not because present appearances favor it but because God *must* be glorified (cf. Eph. 1:6, 12, 14).

63:15–64:12 *Praying for the Power of God.* Isaiah is moved to instruct God's people on how to pray for demonstrations of God's saving power.

63:15–16 Isaiah claims God's love for his people. **your holy and beautiful habitation**. See 6:1 and 64:11. **are held back**. See 64:12, where "restrain yourself" translates the same Hebrew verb. Isaiah is concerned that God is withholding himself from his people (cf. 42:14). **Abraham does not know us**. The people have drifted from their ancestral faith (cf. Gen. 15:6; 22:12; 26:5).

63:17 why do you make us wander? God did not force his people to sin but, in discipline, gave them over to the power of their sins (cf. Ex. 4:21; Deut. 32:4; Job 34:10; Isa. 6:3, 10; Rom. 1:24, 26). **Return**. Human repentance requires divine initiative (cf. Ps. 80:14–15; 90:13).

63:18 Your holy people held possession for a little while. The glory days of God's old covenant people, happily settled in the Promised Land, were all too brief (cf. Deut. 4:25–26).

64:1 Oh that you would rend the heavens and come down. Isaiah sees the heavens as a vast curtain, concealing God, and begs God to rip them apart and step down into this world with his felt presence (cf. 40:22).

64:3 Awesome things alludes to the history recalled in 63:7–14 (cf. Ex. 15:11; 19:16–20; 34:10; Deut. 10:21; 2 Sam. 7:23; Ps. 66:3–5; 106:21–22).

64:4 a God besides you. Essential to Isaiah's message is the uniqueness of Israel's God (cf. 43:11; 44:6; 45:5–6, 18, 21–22; 46:9; 47:8, 10). **who acts**. Unlike the idols, the God of Israel intervenes (cf. Ps. 135:5–18; Isa.

4[u][1 Cor. 2:9]
6[v]See ch. 59:12-15 [w]Ps. 90:5, 6
7[x]ch. 43:22; Hos. 7:7
8[y]ch. 63:16 [z]ch. 45:9; Rom. 9:20, 21 [a]ch. 29:23; 45:11
9[b][ch. 57:16; Ps. 74:1, 2] [c]Ps. 79:8
10[d]Neh. 1:3; 2:3
11[e]Hag. 1:9; 2:3; [2 Kgs. 25:9; 2 Chr. 36:19; Ps. 74:7]
12[f]ch. 42:14; [Zech. 1:12]

Chapter 65

1[g]Cited Rom. 10:20; [Eph. 2:12, 13] [h][ch. 2:2, 3; 18:7; 19:19, 25; Zech. 14:16]
2[i]Rom. 10:21

[u]no eye has seen a God besides you,
who acts for those who wait for him.
5 You meet him who joyfully works righteousness,
those who remember you in your ways.
Behold, you were angry, and we sinned;
in our sins we have been a long time, and shall we be saved?[1]
6 [v]We have all become like one who is unclean,
and all our righteous deeds are like a polluted garment.
[w]We all fade like a leaf,
and our iniquities, like the wind, take us away.
7 [x]There is no one who calls upon your name,
who rouses himself to take hold of you;
for you have hidden your face from us,
and have made us melt in[2] the hand of our iniquities.

8 [y]But now, O LORD, you are our Father;
[z]we are the clay, and you are our potter;
[a]we are all the work of your hand.
9 [b]Be not so terribly angry, O LORD,
[c]and remember not iniquity forever.
Behold, please look, we are all your people.
10 [d]Your holy cities have become a wilderness;
Zion has become a wilderness,
Jerusalem a desolation.
11 [e]Our holy and beautiful[3] house,
where our fathers praised you,
has been burned by fire,
and all our pleasant places have become ruins.
12 [f]Will you restrain yourself at these things, O LORD?
Will you keep silent, and afflict us so terribly?

Judgment and Salvation

65 1 [g]I was ready to be sought by [h]those who did not ask for me;
I was ready to be found by those who did not seek me.
I said, "Here I am, here I am,"
to a nation that was not called by[4] my name.
2 [i]I spread out my hands all the day
to a rebellious people,
who walk in a way that is not good,
following their own devices;

[1] Or *in your ways is continuance, that we might be saved* [2] Masoretic Text; Septuagint, Syriac, Targum *have delivered us into* [3] Or *holy and glorious* [4] Or *that did not call upon*

31:1–9; 37:14–38). He never fails to meet those with true faith. **who wait**. See note on 40:31.

64:5a him who joyfully works righteousness. See Deut. 28:47–48.

64:5b–7 With four similes, Isaiah laments the long-standing patterns of sin among God's people. **like one who is unclean**. A leper, infected and infectious (cf. Lev. 13:45–46; Isa. 6:5). **like a polluted garment**. Even their righteousness is disgusting to God (cf. 57:12; Ezek. 36:17). **like a leaf**. Decayed, brittle, lifeless (cf. Isa. 1:30; 40:6–8). **like the wind**. The overwhelming power of sin (cf. Ps. 1:4; Isa. 17:13; 40:24). **for you have hidden your face**. Cf. 8:17. When God's "face" shines upon his people, they live in his favor (Num. 6:25–26); when he hides it due to their unfaithfulness, they suffer.

64:8–9 you are our Father. Isaiah is not blaming God for Israel's condition; he puts his hope in God as the sovereign Father (cf. Ps. 103:13–14; Isa. 45:9–10). **Be not so terribly angry**. See Ps. 79:8; Isa. 54:7–8; 57:16–19. **remember not iniquity forever**. See 43:25; 53:4–6; Jer. 31:34. **we are all your people**. God chose them, and thus his fame in the world could suffer loss through them (cf. Ex. 32:11–14; Ezek. 36:20–23).

64:10–12 Jerusalem was **a desolation** as a result of the Babylonian invasion (cf. 6:11–12; Jer. 25:8–11). **Our holy and beautiful house**. The temple was lovely with the holy presence of God, as it matched God's "holy and beautiful habitation" (Isa. 63:15; cf. note on 60:7). **yourself . . . us**. God's own glory and his people's desire for restored happiness in him will surely move him to act.

65:1–25 *The Eagerness of God for His People's Eternal Joy.* Though the people of God have unfaithful sinners mixed among them now, he is eager to bring his true people into their glorious eternal home.

65:1–12 The eagerness of God is snubbed by Jews, welcomed by Gentiles.

65:1–2 These verses anticipate the drama of the book of Acts and the spread of the gospel to the Gentiles, as seen especially in Acts 28:17–28 (cf. Rom. 10:20–21). **Here I am**. God takes the initiative to reveal himself to the nations through the gospel (cf. Isa. 11:10; 56:3–8). **I spread out my hands all the day**. God patiently pleads with obstinate Israel (cf. John 1:11). **following their own devices** (or thoughts). See Isa. 55:8–9.

3 a people who provoke me
to my face continually,
[j]sacrificing in gardens
and making offerings on bricks;
4 who sit in tombs,
and spend the night in secret places;
[k]who eat pig's flesh,
and broth of tainted meat is in their vessels;
5 who say, "Keep to yourself,
do not come near me, for I am too holy for you."
[l]These are a smoke in my nostrils,
a fire that burns all the day.
6 Behold, [m]it is written before me:
[n]"I will not keep silent, but I will repay;
[o]I will indeed repay into their lap
7 both your iniquities [p]and your fathers' iniquities together,
says the LORD;
[q]because they made offerings on the mountains
[q] and insulted me on the hills,
I will measure into their lap
payment for their former deeds."[1]

8 Thus says the LORD:
[r]"As the new wine is found in the cluster,
and they say, 'Do not destroy it,
for there is a blessing in it,'
so I will do for my servants' sake,
[s]and not destroy them all.
9 [t]I will bring forth offspring from Jacob,
and from Judah possessors of my mountains;
my chosen shall possess it,
and my servants shall dwell there.
10 [u]Sharon shall become a pasture for flocks,
and [v]the Valley of Achor a place for herds to lie down,
for my people [w]who have sought me.
11 But [x]you who forsake the LORD,
who forget [y]my holy mountain,
who [z]set a table for Fortune
and [z]fill cups of mixed wine for Destiny,
12 I will destine you to the sword,
and all of you shall bow down to the slaughter,
[a]because, when I called, you did not answer;
when I spoke, you did not listen,
[b]but you did what was evil in my eyes
and chose what I did not delight in."

[1] Or *I will first measure their payment into their lap*

3[j]ch. 1:29; 66:17; [ch. 57:3-6]
4[k]ch. 66:17
5[l]ch. 1:31; 9:18
6[m][Jer. 2:22; 17:1] [n]Ps. 50:3 [o]Ps. 79:12; [Jer. 16:18]
7[p]Ex. 20:5; [Matt. 23:35] [q][Ezek. 20:27, 28]
8[r][ch. 17:6] [s][ch. 2:21]
9[t][ch. 27:6; 37:31]
10[u]ch. 33:9; 35:2 [v]Hos. 2:15; [Josh. 7:26] [w][ch. 51:1]
11[x][Josh. 24:20] [y]ver. 25; Joel 3:17 [z]Ezek. 23:41; [1 Cor. 10:21]
12[a]ch. 66:4; Prov. 1:24; Jer. 7:13 [b]ch. 66:4

65:3–4 who sit in tombs (v. 4). God laments over religious practices that offend him; apparently they mix Canaanite elements into Israelite religious life (cf. 1:29; 8:19; 66:17).

65:5 I am too holy for you. What they are claiming is actually false, a self-defined, unclean "holiness" that distorts true worship and improperly elevates some people over others (cf. Luke 18:9–14).

65:6–7 I will not keep silent answers the question of 64:12. **I will repay**. God vows a reckoning with Israel for their historic accumulation of sins (cf. 6:9–13; 10:22–23).

65:8–10 Though his judgments will destroy, God will also bless his old covenant people by preserving a remnant (cf. 1:9; 10:20–23; Matt. 13:24–30; Rom. 9:27–29; 11:1–5). **the cluster**. See Isa. 5:1–7. **Sharon shall become a pasture** (cf. 33:9). Sharon is the plain of rich pastureland beginning about 32 miles (51 km) northwest of Jerusalem and stretching along the Mediterranean coast from Joppa to Carmel. The **Valley of Achor** (see Josh. 7:22–26; Hos. 2:15) is a range of hills running through the plain of Jericho about 16 miles (26 km) northeast of Jerusalem. Their respective locations on the western and eastern borders of Israel signify God's restorative blessing covering the whole of the land.

65:11–12 Those Israelites who **forsake** their God for false gods will perish (cf. 57:3–13). **set a table for Fortune and fill cups of mixed wine for Destiny**. These are pagan rituals invoking good luck.

13 Therefore thus says the Lord GOD:
“Behold, [c]my servants shall eat,
but you shall be hungry;
behold, my servants shall drink,
but you shall be thirsty;
behold, my servants shall rejoice,
but you shall be put to shame;
14 behold, [d]my servants shall sing for gladness of heart,
but you shall cry out for pain of heart
and shall wail for breaking of spirit.
15 You shall leave your name to [e]my chosen [f]for a curse,
and the Lord GOD will put you to death,
but his servants [g]he will call by another name.
16 So that he who [h]blesses himself in the land
shall bless himself by [h]the God of truth,
and he who takes an oath in the land
shall swear by [i]the God of truth;
[j]because the former troubles are forgotten
and are hidden from my eyes.

New Heavens and a New Earth

17 “For behold, [k]I create new heavens
and a new earth,
and the former things shall not be remembered
or come into mind.
18 But be glad and rejoice forever
in that which I create;
for behold, [l]I create Jerusalem to be a joy,
and her people to be a gladness.
19 [m]I will rejoice in Jerusalem
and be glad in my people;
[n]no more shall be heard in it the sound of weeping
and the cry of distress.
20 No more shall there be in it
an infant who lives but a few days,
or an old man who does not fill out his days,
for [o]the young man shall die a hundred years old,
and [p]the sinner a hundred years old shall be accursed.
21 [q]They shall build houses and inhabit them;
they shall plant vineyards and eat their fruit.
22 [q]They shall not build and another inhabit;
they shall not plant and another eat;

13[c]ch. 55:1; Ps. 22:26
14[d][Ps. 5:11]
15[e]ver. 9 [f][Deut. 28:37; Jer. 29:22; Zech. 8:13] [g]ch. 62:2
16[h]Jer. 4:2 [i][Deut. 32:4] [j][ch. 43:18, 19]
17[k]ch. 66:22; 2 Pet. 3:13; Rev. 21:1
18[l][Jer. 31:7]
19[m]ch. 62:5; 66:10 [n]ch. 35:10; Rev. 21:4
20[o][Prov. 3:2] [p]Eccles. 8:12
21[q]Ezek. 28:26; [Deut. 28:30]
22[q][See ver. 21 above]

65:13–25 The Lord describes the joys of his true people in their eternal home.

65:13 my servants. Both Jews and Gentiles. God excluded disloyal Jews and included responsive Gentiles (cf. Matt. 3:7–10; 8:10–13).

65:15 You shall leave your name to my chosen for a curse. They will be remembered as objects of judgment. See Jer. 29:22–23. **his servants he will call by another name**. That is, a name of blessing. See Gen. 17:5; 32:28; Isa. 62:2, 4, 12.

65:16 the God of truth. He will keep his every promise, as his servants invoke his blessings.

65:17–25 Isaiah uses images from his age to paint a magnificent poetic picture to describe the joys of the world to come. Christians differ over whether to read this as (1) an idealized description of restored Jerusalem (leading into eternal joys), (2) an intermediate “millennial” state, or (3) the eternal state itself. Certainly the expression **new heavens and a new earth** would seem to suggest the eternal state (because of Rev. 21:1). On the other hand, the mention of people dying, even at an advanced age, as well as the presence of the **sinner** (Isa. 65:20), seem to suggest this is not the eternal state. To argue for a millennial state (which is not explicit here), one would have to understand the millennial state to include both death and unbelief among unbelievers during the millennial period. However, the mention of the animals (v. 25) evokes 11:6–9, which is part of an oracle describing the messianic era (see note on 11:10). Hence (and in view of the larger context of chs. 40–66) some interpreters read these verses as describing an idealized future for Jerusalem—not simply as a restored city but as the center of the world, in which all manner of people know and delight in God and live at peace with each other (as 2:2–4; 9:6–7; 11:1–10). Under such circumstances, human community and piety flourish. At the same time, the description goes far beyond anything that the world has ever seen, inviting the believing reader to yearn for more and to play his or her role as the story unfolds to its glorious end (cf. 2:5).

65:22 like the days of a tree. A picture of longevity and durability (some trees live 2,000 years), as compared (in 40:7–8) to grass, which withers and

[r]for like the days of a tree shall the days of my people be,
and my chosen shall long enjoy[1] the work of their hands.
23 [s]They shall not labor in vain
[t]or bear children for calamity,[2]
for [u]they shall be the offspring of the blessed of the LORD,
and their descendants with them.
24 [v]Before they call I will answer;
[w]while they are yet speaking I will hear.
25 [x]The wolf and the lamb shall graze together;
the lion shall eat straw like the ox,
and [y]dust shall be the serpent's food.
[z]They shall not hurt or destroy
in all my holy mountain,"
says the LORD.

The Humble and Contrite in Spirit

66
1 [a]Thus says the LORD:
[b]"Heaven is my throne,
and the earth is my footstool;
what is the house that you would build for me,
and what is the place of my rest?
2 [c]All these things my hand has made,
and so all these things came to be,
declares the LORD.
[d]But this is the one to whom I will look:
he who is humble and contrite in spirit
and trembles at my word.
3 [e]"He who slaughters an ox is like one who kills a man;
he who sacrifices a lamb, like one who breaks a dog's neck;
he who presents a grain offering, like one who offers [f]pig's blood;
he who makes a memorial offering of frankincense, like one who
blesses an idol.
[g]These have chosen their own ways,
and their soul delights in their abominations;
4 [h]I also will choose harsh treatment for them
and bring [i]their fears upon them,
[j]because when I called, no one answered,
when I spoke, they did not listen;
[k]but they did what was evil in my eyes
and chose that in which I did not delight."
5 Hear the word of the LORD,
you who tremble at his word:

22[r]See Ps. 92:12-14
23[s]ch. 49:4 [t][Deut. 28:41] [u]ch. 61:9; See Ps. 115:12-15
24[v][Ps. 32:5] [w][Dan. 9:21]
25[x]ch. 11:6, 7 [y]Gen. 3:14; Mic. 7:17 [z]ch. 11:9

Chapter 66

1[a]Cited Acts 7:49, 50; [1 Kgs. 8:27; Acts 17:24] [b][Matt. 5:34, 35]
2[c][1 Chr. 29:14] [d]ch. 57:15; Ps. 34:18
3[e]ch. 1:11 [f]See ch. 65:4 [g]Jer. 7:24
4[h][ch. 30:16] [i][ch. 51:12] [j]See ch. 65:12 [k][Jer. 7:31]

[1] Hebrew *shall wear out* [2] Or *for sudden terror*

fades. The picture also recalls the example of the righteous person who is "like a tree planted by streams of water that yields its fruit" (Ps. 1:3).

65:25 dust shall be the serpent's food. An allusion to Gen. 3:14; God's redemptive purpose (Gen. 3:15) has succeeded, and he has subdued the serpent in judgment as he promised.

66:1–24 *True Worship Now and Forever.* Though the worship of God is violated now, in the future falsehood will be judged, true worship will spread, and God will be honored forever.

66:1–6 The city of God is cleansed of religious hypocrisy.

66:1 The Creator cannot be walled in—not even by his own temple in Jerusalem (cf. 1 Kings 8:27; Jer. 7:8–15; John 2:19; Acts 7:44–50). The OT is constantly at pains to remind God's people that he is greater than the institutions he has authorized, and he will not be manipulated by their use.

66:2 I will look with favor (cf. Ps. 80:14; 84:9; Isa. 63:15). **he who is humble and contrite**. See Ps. 51:17; Isa. 57:15; Luke 18:9–14. **Trembles at my word** suggests pious reverence for God's word and eagerness to obey it (cf. Ezra 9:4; 10:3).

66:3–4 Even Levitical worship—without a trembling heart (see note on v. 2)—is abhorrent to God (cf. 1:10–17; Jer. 7:21–23) and is as bad as outright sin (**kills a man**) and idolatry (**breaks a dog's neck, offers pig's blood, blesses an idol**). **their fears**. Aiming at the illusion of control, false faith proves helpless before everything it hopes to avoid (see Isa. 48:18; 65:11–12). **they did not listen**. True faith is essentially an openhearted listening to the word of God and wholeheartedly believing it (cf. Deut. 6:4; Ps. 95:7–8; Isa. 55:3).

66:5–6 Your brothers who hate you. These are people who profess biblical faith but lack a trembling heart, who scorn the humble and contrite

5[l]ch. 5:19
6[m]ch. 63:4; 65:6
7[n]See ch. 13:8
8[n][See ver. 7 above]
10[o]ch. 65:19
12[p][ch. 48:18] [q]ch. 60:16
13[r]ch. 51:12; [ch. 35:10]
14[s]ch. 58:11

"Your brothers who hate you
and cast you out for my name's sake
have said, [l]'Let the LORD be glorified,
that we may see your joy';
but it is they who shall be put to shame.

6 "The sound of an uproar from the city!
A sound from the temple!
The sound of the LORD,
[m]rendering recompense to his enemies!

Rejoice with Jerusalem

7 [n]"Before she was in labor
she gave birth;
before her pain came upon her
she delivered a son.
8 Who has heard such a thing?
Who has seen such things?
Shall a land be born in one day?
Shall a nation be brought forth in one moment?
For [n]as soon as Zion was in labor
she brought forth her children.
9 Shall I bring to the point of birth and not cause to bring forth?"
says the LORD;
"shall I, who cause to bring forth, shut the womb?"
says your God.

10 [o]"Rejoice with Jerusalem, and be glad for her,
all you who love her;
rejoice with her in joy,
all you who mourn over her;
11 that you may nurse and be satisfied
from her consoling breast;
that you may drink deeply with delight
from her glorious abundance."[1]

12 For thus says the LORD:
[p]"Behold, I will extend peace to her like a river,
and the glory of the nations like an overflowing stream;
and [q]you shall nurse, you shall be carried upon her hip,
and bounced upon her knees.
13 As one whom his mother comforts,
so [r]I will comfort you;
you shall be comforted in Jerusalem.
14 You shall see, and your heart shall rejoice;
[s]your bones shall flourish like the grass;

[1] *Or breast*

(cf. 28:9–10; Rev. 2:9). **Let the LORD be glorified, that we may see your joy**. This is the cynical contempt of the self-righteous, excluding the humble (cf. Ps. 22:6–8; Luke 6:22; John 16:2). **A sound from the temple!** The Lord's answer to such people is **recompense**, because he counts them his **enemies**.

66:7–14 The people of God are set apart by miraculous blessing.

66:7–9 Mother Zion gives **birth**, effortlessly and instantly, to a new nation (cf. 49:19–21; 54:1–3). The questions of 66:9 answer fears that God might not prove faithful to perform all his promises to his helpless people.

66:10–14 The certainty of future blessing calls for joy in the present. **her consoling breast. . . . you shall be comforted in Jerusalem**. The poetic image is of a nursing baby who finds complete comfort, joy, nourishment, and satisfaction in the arms of its mother. Notably the same Hebrew word for **comfort** found in 40:1 ("Comfort, comfort my people, says your God") is repeated three times here in a similar word form in 66:13, underscoring the fact that the comfort proclaimed by the Lord in ch. 40 is the same comfort that the Lord will surely provide. **like a river**. See 48:18. **like the grass**. See 58:11.

66:12 the glory of the nations. See note on 60:5–7.

and [t]the hand of the LORD shall be known to his servants,
  and he shall show his indignation against his enemies.

Final Judgment and Glory of the LORD

15 "For behold, [u]the LORD will come in fire,
  and [v]his chariots like the whirlwind,
to render his anger in fury,
  and his rebuke with flames of fire.
16 For [w]by fire [x]will the LORD enter into judgment,
  and by his sword, with all flesh;
  and those slain by the LORD shall be many.

17 [y]"Those who sanctify and purify themselves to go into the gardens, following one in
the midst, [z]eating pig's flesh and the abomination and mice, shall come to an end together,
declares the LORD.

18 "For I know[1] their works and their thoughts, and the time is coming[2] [a]to gather all
nations and tongues. And they shall come and shall see my glory,
19 and I will set a sign
among them. And from them [b]I will send survivors to the nations, to [c]Tarshish, [d]Pul,
and [d]Lud, who draw the bow, to [e]Tubal and [e]Javan, [f]to the coastlands far away, [g]that have
not heard my fame or seen my glory. And they shall declare my glory among the nations.
20 [h]And they shall bring all your brothers from all the nations [i]as an offering to the LORD,
on horses and in chariots and in litters and on mules and on dromedaries, to my holy
mountain Jerusalem, says the LORD, just as the Israelites bring their grain offering in a
clean vessel to the house of the LORD.
21 [j]And some of them also I will take for priests and
for Levites, says the LORD.

22 "For as [k]the new heavens and the new earth
  that I make
shall remain before me, says the LORD,
  so [l]shall your offspring and your name remain.
23 [m]From new moon to new moon,
  and from Sabbath to Sabbath,
all flesh shall come to worship before me,
declares the LORD.

24 "And they shall go out and look on the dead bodies of the men who have rebelled
against me. For [n]their worm shall not die, [o]their fire shall not be quenched, and they shall
be an abhorrence to all flesh."

[1] Septuagint, Syriac; Hebrew lacks *know* [2] Hebrew *and it is coming*

14 [t][Ezra 8:22, 31]
15 [u]ch. 33:14; Mal. 3:1, 2; [2 Thess. 1:7, 8] [v]Ps. 68:17
16 [w]Ps. 97:3 [x]Joel 3:2
17 [y]ch. 65:3, 5 [z]See ch. 65:4
18 [a]ch. 2:2; Zech. 14:16
19 [b]ch. 45:20 [c]1 Kgs. 10:22 [d]Jer. 46:9; Ezek. 27:10 [e]Gen. 10:2; Ezek. 27:13 [f]Gen. 10:5 [g][Rom. 15:20, 21]
20 [h]See ch. 14:2; 49:22 [i][Rom. 15:16]
21 [j]ch. 61:6; Ex. 19:6; [1 Pet. 2:9; Rev. 1:6]
22 [k]See ch. 65:17 [l]ch. 53:10; [Ps. 89:29]
23 [m][Ps. 86:9; Zech. 14:16]
24 [n]Mark 9:48 [o][Rev. 21:8]

66:15–17 The enemies of God are destined for fiery judgment.

66:15 The holy wrath of God **will come in fire** (cf. 10:16–18; 29:5–6; 30:27, 30; 33:14). **like the whirlwind**. A storm of divine judgment will swoop down on the earth (cf. 19:1; 29:6; 30:30).

66:16 all flesh. Specifically, "his enemies" (v. 14).

66:17 Those who sanctify and purify themselves. See note on 66:3–4; cf. 57:3–13; 65:2–7, 11–12. **following one in the midst**. See Ezek. 8:7–11.

66:18–24 God's glory is declared worldwide, and man's rebellion is punished forever.

66:18 and the time is coming to gather all nations and tongues. See 2:2–4; 40:5; 45:23; Rev. 7:9–10.

66:19 a sign. See 7:14; 11:10, 12; 55:12–13. **I will send survivors**, i.e., the remnant of Israelite believers who survive the judgments of God (cf. Joel 2:28–32; Acts 2:1–12). **Tarshish** (probably in modern Spain), **Pul** (mentioned only here; perhaps another spelling of Put, which was Libya), **Lud** (ancient Lydia, in modern Turkey), **Tubal** (in modern Turkey), and **Javan** (Greece) exemplify the remote places of earth (cf. Matt. 28:18–20). On these place names see notes on Ezek. 27:10; 27:12–25; 27:13.

66:20 all your brothers from all the nations. Contrast "your brothers who hate you" in v. 5 (cf. John 11:52; Gal. 3:28–29; Col. 3:11). **an offering to the LORD . . . in a clean vessel**. See Rom. 15:15–16.

66:21 some of them also I will take for priests and for Levites. This speaks of Gentiles, perhaps as those who will carry out the calling of Israel (see note on 61:5–7), or else (in view of the mention of Levites) as those who will provide worship leadership within the people of God.

66:22–23 See 65:17. The cosmos, which bore witness to Israel's sins in 1:2–3, is renewed as the environment for the endless worship of the new people of God, who represent **all flesh**. God will keep his every promise to the praise of his glorious grace.

66:24 Isaiah uses the image of Jerusalem's city dump, just outside the city wall in the Hinnom Valley (cf. Jer. 7:30–34). **They shall go out and look**, not to gloat, but to agree with the victory of God in his judgment of the wicked and to know the peaceful assurance that God has judged wickedness forever. **rebelled**. See Isa. 1:2. **their worm . . . their fire**. A terrifying picture of unending judgment (see 50:11; Mark 9:43–48; Rev. 14:11). **They shall be an abhorrence**, though in this life they are often successful. The gospel is good news to the contrite but bad news to the rebellious.

INTRODUCTION TO

JEREMIAH

Author and Title

Determining the authorship of the book of Jeremiah is complicated by several factors: the variety of types of literature found in the book, the differences between the Hebrew and Greek versions of the book, and the difficult lives Jeremiah and his scribe Baruch lived. However, these complications described below do not make it impossible for the contents of the book to be Jeremiah's words, as the Bible says they are (1:1).

The variety of literary types in Jeremiah. The book of Jeremiah contains various types of literature. It includes autobiography (1:4–19), long poetic discourses (2:1–6:30), reports of oral sermons (7:1–8:3; 26:1–9), reports of sermons delivered in written form (36:1–8), historical narratives (37:1–43:13), messages to individuals (45:1–5), and messages denouncing foreign nations (46:1–51:64). Since this diverse material is not presented in chronological order, the book requires readers to know the outline of Judah's history and theology and to be able to move backward and forward in time. The book reports that Baruch wrote down some of Jeremiah's messages (36:1–4, 32). Therefore, it is quite possible that he wrote down the various types of "words of Jeremiah" (1:1) at Jeremiah's dictation.

The Hebrew and Greek versions of Jeremiah. The Greek version (Septuagint) of Jeremiah differs from the Hebrew version. It is shorter, in part, because it does not include all the section introductions (e.g., 2:1–2a; 7:1–2a; 16:1), all the repetition of material (e.g., 6:22–24 and 50:41–43), or all the instances of the phrase "says the LORD." Thus, the Greek version is shorter due to the lack of redundant material, not because vital doctrinal passages like 31:31–34 are absent. It also has a different structure: in the Greek version the messages against the nations appear after 25:13, and the nations are addressed in a different order.

Scholars offer two basic solutions to these differences. Some commentators believe that a later editor expanded the Hebrew underlying the Greek version to yield the present Hebrew text of Jeremiah. Others propose that a later editor trimmed the Hebrew version of material that seemed to be unnecessary and placed the messages to the nations at the point in the book when Jeremiah addressed the envoys of the nations in Jerusalem; that trimmed-down version later served as the basis for the Greek translation. A decision between the two options involves many theological, literary, and historical factors, but the second option is more compelling. Though editors differ in their approaches, it is unclear why an editor would add material that has already occurred in a book and remove messages from a clear context and place them at the end of a book. The Hebrew version is surely the more difficult to read in chronological and contextual order, which makes it more likely that someone tried to simplify it for later readers.

If this description is accurate, the Hebrew version of the book may be shaped as it is because Baruch and Jeremiah wrote it piecemeal in the midst of their turbulent lives. They preserved each part, and Baruch collected the pieces in an order intended to stress God's covenantal relationship with Israel in the midst of trying times. There is repetition because the whole of the parts was preserved. Thus, this book reads more like what political prisoners and refugees write than what persons writing in settled places and times produce. Of course, the book itself presents Jeremiah and Baruch as the former sort of writers.

Jeremiah's difficult life. Jeremiah was born and raised in Anathoth, a small town a few miles northeast of Jerusalem (1:1; see map, p. 1365). He was called to be a prophet c. 627 B.C. and served for over 40 years (1:2–3). At the time of his call he was a youth (1:6), still financially dependent on his parents, so he could have been born c. 645 B.C., though no certain date can be established. He became a priest and lived in an area allotted to the tribe of Benjamin (1:1), so he was possibly a descendant of Abiathar, high priest during David's reign.

Solomon removed Abiathar from service because of his support of Adonijah (1 Kings 2:13–26). Thus, Jeremiah was from a small town, served a small tribe, and perhaps came from a deposed priestly lineage. He lived close enough to Jerusalem to understand its people, their worship, and their daily activities. He was far enough removed from Jerusalem that he was not afraid to criticize what he saw happening there.

Jeremiah had a difficult life. His messages of repentance delivered at the temple were not well received (7:1–8:3; 26:1–11). His hometown plotted against him (11:18–23), and he endured much persecution in the pursuit of his ministry (20:1–6; 37:11–38:13; 43:1–7). At God's command he never married (16:1–4). A faithful preacher, he apparently had only two converts: Baruch, his scribe (32:12; 36:1–4; 45:1–5), and Ebed-melech, an Ethiopian eunuch who served the king (38:7–13; 39:15–18). These are the only two mentioned in the entire book who respond favorably to Jeremiah's preaching. Though the book does not reveal the time or place of Jeremiah's death, he presumably died in Egypt, where he had been taken by his countrymen against his will after the fall of Jerusalem (43:1–7).

Many authors have called Jeremiah the "weeping prophet." While he does occasionally weep for Israel's condition (8:18–9:3; 13:15–17), and this depth of concern speaks well of him, this emphasis on his weeping may mislead readers regarding his toughness. Jeremiah was a determined, dedicated, longsuffering, and visionary follower of God. His courage and stamina serve as examples to even the most faithful of all God's embattled servants. The apostle Paul certainly viewed his own ministry as being like Jeremiah's (see 2 Corinthians 3). Thus, Jeremiah's weeping hardly summarizes his character. He could perhaps more accurately be called "the persevering prophet."

Part of his perseverance was in the composition of the book that bears his name. It was not easy to remain invested in the production of what is now called the book of Jeremiah, for there were various reasons he could have given up the process. That Jeremiah and Baruch remained committed to composing the book is a testament to their faith, as well as to the power of the Holy Spirit (2 Pet. 1:21).

Date

It is impossible to know exactly when the book of Jeremiah reached its final form. Jeremiah certainly died within a decade or two of the last events recorded in the book, and the same is likely true of Baruch. Thus, the book was probably composed by 550 B.C.

Theme

Jeremiah exhibits many great themes that stress God's judgment on covenant infidelity and worldwide sin, as well as God's determination to restore an international people for himself through the establishing of a new covenant.

Purpose, Occasion, and Background

There is no way to determine with any level of accuracy the first readers of the book of Jeremiah in its present state or the specific occasion that led to its being read by that audience. Most likely it was read by persons awaiting the end of Judah's exile and the return of God's people to the land.

Its purpose is clearer: Jeremiah and Baruch wished to leave behind a record of the tumultuous times in which they lived, God's message for those times, and God's message for the future of Israel and the nations.

Jeremiah lived during troubled times. He became a prophet during Josiah's reign (640–609 B.C.). Josiah was the last faithful king in Judah's history (2 Kings 22:1–23:27). His death (2 Kings 23:28–30) marked the beginning of the last years of the nation of Judah. Political, social, financial, moral, and spiritual decay led to the country's demise within two short decades. Other prophets, such as Nahum, Habakkuk, and Zephaniah, also ministered to Judah during this time.

During Josiah's era the world political scene shifted greatly. Assyria had been the dominant world power since the reign of its mightiest king, Tiglath-pileser III (745–727 B.C.), though Babylon, Egypt, and other nations had regularly challenged Assyria. In 612 B.C. the Babylonians conquered Nineveh, the Assyrian capital, an event described in the book of Nahum. Assyria rallied with the aid of Egypt, but Babylon completed its triumph over its ancient foe in 609 B.C., the same year Josiah was killed fighting Egypt.

Immediately after Josiah's death Egypt dominated Judah's political landscape because Babylon could not yet consolidate all the territory that had been under Assyrian servitude. Unsatisfied to leave Jehoahaz on the throne, the Egyptians replaced him with Jehoiakim in 609 B.C. (2 Kings 23:31–35). Babylon marched south by 605 B.C., however, and Jehoiakim stayed in power only by shifting his allegiance from Egypt to Babylon. That year Babylon took its first group of exiles from Judah. Daniel and his friends were among

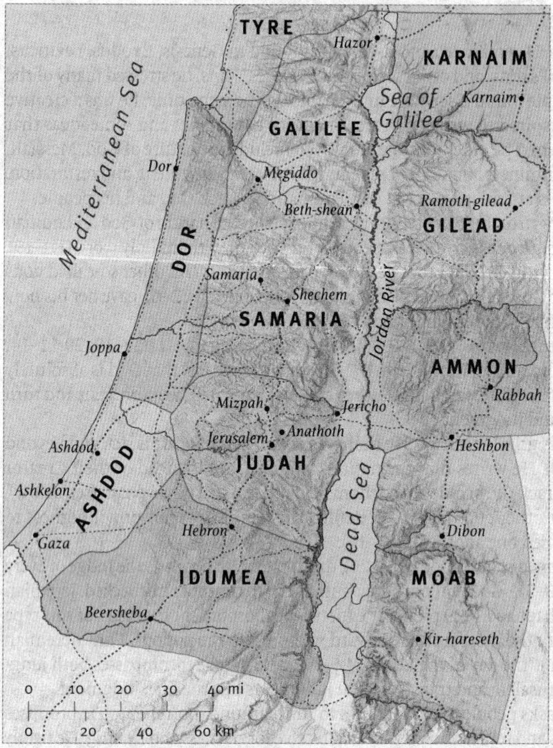

Israel and Judah at the Time of Jeremiah
c. 597 B.C.
The book of Jeremiah is set during the politically tumultuous times following the fall of the Assyrians and the rise of the Babylonians. Jeremiah witnessed multiple deportations of Judeans to Babylon and the destruction of Jerusalem and the temple. Though the precise boundaries of Judea and the surrounding regions during this period are difficult to ascertain, they likely resembled those that previously existed under Assyrian rule, with the exception that Edom (Idumea) had now migrated to the area formerly belonging to southern Judah.

the persons removed (Dan. 1:1–7). Jehoiakim rebelled against Babylon, but died in 598 B.C. before he could suffer the consequences of his actions (2 Kings 24:1–7). His successor, Jehoiachin, who reigned for only three months in 598–597 B.C., was left to feel the Babylonians' wrath. Babylon's King Nebuchadnezzar led his army to Jerusalem, deposed Jehoiachin, and placed Zedekiah on the throne (2 Kings 24:8–17). Babylon again took captives (2 Kings 24:16). Ezekiel was part of this group of exiles (Ezek. 1:1–3).

Zedekiah's reign (597–586 B.C.) was marked by decline, intrigue, indecision, and ultimately defeat. Judah aligned itself with nations committed to throwing off the Babylonian yoke (Jer. 27:1–15) while paying lip service to Nebuchadnezzar. Such a policy could not succeed for long. Eventually Zedekiah's rebellion became pronounced (2 Kings 24:20). In response, Nebuchadnezzar invaded Judah, laid siege to Jerusalem, and sacked the city (Jer. 39:1–10). He then appointed Gedaliah, a Judean, to be governor of Judah (40:5).

Gedaliah tried to work with the remaining inhabitants of the land, and the economy was good for those who still lived in the land during the early days after the Babylonian army left (40:7–12). But there were plots on Gedaliah's life (40:13–16). Ishmael succeeded in killing the governor. He also murdered several pilgrims coming to Jerusalem to worship and took several hostages (41:1–10). Though the hostages were rescued, the people feared what Babylon would do in retaliation for Gedaliah's murder (41:11–16).

The leaders advised everyone associated with the Gedaliah episode to flee to Egypt (41:17–18). Before doing so, however, they decided to ask Jeremiah to seek God's will on the matter (42:1–6). Despite his unequivocal urging that they should remain in the land (42:7–22), the people rejected Jeremiah's word, left for Egypt, and forced Jeremiah and Baruch to accompany them, as if they were some sort of magic charm against God's wrath (43:1–7). Once in Egypt, Jeremiah fulfilled his calling to be a prophet to the nations (1:5) by preaching against Judah's sins, Egypt's sins, and those of other countries, including Babylon (chs. 46–51). He most likely did not live to see the devastation he mentions in chapters 46–51, but he certainly would not have been surprised at how world events unfolded, given what he experienced in his lifetime.

Key Themes

Jeremiah was a biblical theologian. He embraced and used truths found in Genesis, Exodus, Leviticus, Numbers, Deuteronomy, Hosea, the Psalms, and other scriptural passages. Thus, he stressed many of the great themes about God and his people found elsewhere in the Bible. At the same time, he was a creative theologian whom the Holy Spirit inspired to write fresh treatments of old themes and some ideas that were new when Jeremiah penned them. The older ideas he employed include the nature of God, Messiah, God's covenant with Israel, human sinfulness and need of repentance, threat of judgment, and restoration. His chief unique contribution was his articulation of the new covenant between God and his people.

God and humanity. Jeremiah includes virtually every biblical teaching about the nature of God and human beings. He presents God as the sovereign one who calls and equips his servant with his holy word (1:1–19). Jeremiah claims that God alone is a living God and that he alone made the world. All other so-called gods are mere idols (10:1–16). This Creator God called Israel to a special relationship (chs. 2–6), gave her his holy word, and promised to bless her temple with his name and presence (7:1–8:3).

God rules the present and the future (1:4–16; 29:1–10), protects his chosen ones (1:17–19; 29:11–14; 39:15–18; 45:1–5), and saves those who turn to him (12:14–17). Jeremiah proclaims that God is absolutely trustworthy; he keeps his promises. Therefore, Jeremiah assures readers that when people repent and turn to God, his grace triumphs over sin and judgment.

Jeremiah's view of human beings is grimly realistic. He claims that the human heart is sick and beyond curing by anyone but God (17:9–10). He writes that the nations worship idols instead of their Creator (10:1–16). Worse yet, he notes how Israel, the people with whom God made a special covenant (see below), sinned against him. They went after other gods (chs. 2–6), defiled the temple by their unwillingness to repent (7:1–8:3; 26:1–11), and oppressed one another (34:8–16).

Since Israel and the nations have sinned against God (25:1–26), the Creator also becomes the Judge of every nation on the earth he created (chs. 46–51). God will not allow human sin to continue unchecked. Jeremiah warns that punishment is coming. Chapters 21–29 probably contain the most urgent messages of this type for Judah, and chapters 46–51 present the most straightforward warnings to the nations. Thus, Jeremiah contributes to the OT's teaching about "the day of the LORD" (4:5–12), a term that encompasses both judgments in history such as the fall of Jerusalem and transhistorical judgments like the final judgment.

Given this situation, the prophet asks people over 100 times to "turn around" or "repent." He promises that when people turn from their sins and return to God they will receive forgiveness and healing. He firmly believes that God will renew a repenting people, and he mourns the lack of repentance in his day (8:18–22). God comforts him with the knowledge that repentance and renewal would eventually come (33:14–26).

Old covenant, Messiah, and new covenant. Like the other true prophets in the Bible, Jeremiah believed that God had made a covenant with Israel. Though no brief definition can do justice to the concept, the covenant between God and Israel in biblical context was a binding relational agreement between God and Israel, based on deeds done by God and promises made by God, which Israel accepted by faith in God, for the purpose of living for God as his unique people in the world.

This covenant was rooted in God's promises to Abraham, Isaac, and Jacob (Genesis 12–50). It was based on God's redemption of Israel from slavery in Egypt (Ex. 1:1–20:2). It included standards of living (Exodus 20–24) that the people who were called to be "a kingdom of priests and a holy nation" (Ex. 19:6) should uphold as they trusted God and lived for him. It included faith-based sacrifices (Leviticus 1–16) and prayers (Psalm 32; 51; etc.) to deal with the people's sins. It included clear accountability for this kingdom of priests in the form of benefits (blessings) and consequences (curses) (Deuteronomy 27–28).

As time passed, God's covenant with Israel incorporated God's promise to David of an eternal kingdom (2 Samuel 7; 1 Chronicles 17). From this promise came the concept of a Messiah, which literally means "anointed one." Jeremiah does not mention the Messiah as often as Isaiah, but the concept is not missing altogether. Jeremiah conceives of a time when God will "gather the remnant" of Israel and raise up "for David a righteous Branch" who will reign over the faithful ones (Jer. 23:3–5). When he comes, this King will be "our righteousness" (23:6). In this way God's eternal covenant with David will be kept fully at a time in the future that Jeremiah leaves unspecified (32:14–25).

God established this covenant with all Israel, irrespective of faith in God on the part of many individuals. However, the only persons that God was pleased with and redeemed spiritually were persons like Jeremiah who placed their faith in God, which was demonstrated by obedience to his word (Hebrews 11). Such persons are part of the remnant that the Messiah will gather (Jer. 23:3–5). Sadly, as chapters 2–6 indicate, the nation of Israel had a long history of covenant breaking. Collectively they were not a faithful covenant partner, though Abraham, Moses, David, Isaiah, Jeremiah, and others proved that covenant faithfulness was possible through God's grace.

God used Jeremiah to deliver the good news that in future days God would "make a new covenant with the house of Israel and the house of Judah" (31:31). This covenant would be different in one chief respect: the new covenant partners will not break the covenant, as most of the old partners did even though God was unwaveringly faithful (31:32). Instead, the new covenant partners will have the word of God so ingrained in their hearts through God's power that they will know and follow God all their lives (31:33–34).

Thus, all the new covenant partners will be believers who are forgiven and empowered by God; he will "remember their sin no more" (31:34). Hebrews 8:8–12 quotes Jeremiah 31:31–34 as evidence that the new covenant has come through the life, death, and resurrection of Jesus. The coming of Jesus the Messiah fulfills God's promises to Abraham, Moses, David, and the prophets of a new faithful people of God in continuity with the old people of God.

History of Salvation Summary

Jeremiah was called to speak to the people of Jerusalem during a revival under King Josiah and continued to speak to them during that city's final fall to the Babylonians. His task was to hammer home the message that Jerusalem's fall was not due to any lack on God's part but was due entirely to Judah's unfaithfulness toward God, specifically by listening to false prophets rather than true ones (with Deut. 18:15–22 in the background). Even this horrifying disaster, however, was not the end: Jeremiah foretold a return from exile, an everlasting covenant, and a new covenant in which God's people would at last embrace the covenant in their hearts. Israel and Judah would be reunited and finally fulfill their calling to bring light to the world. (For an explanation of the "History of Salvation," see Overview of the Bible, pp. 23–26. See also History of Salvation in the Old Testament: Preparing the Way for Christ, pp. 2635–2661.)

Literary Features

Jeremiah is an anthology or collection of writings drawn from an entire lifetime of prophetic ministry. The narrative sections scattered throughout the book are loosely structured around the main events of Jeremiah's life in ministry, which themselves were shaped by Judah's decline, fall, and exile in Babylon. But most of the material in the book is prophetic, much of it in the form of poetry. This material does not always follow a historical sequence; the logic of its arrangement is sometimes topical rather than chronological.

It may be helpful to think of the book of Jeremiah as a notebook or scrapbook of things written by the prophet about his ministry. Jeremiah includes enough "news clippings" to piece together the story of his life, but just as important are the prophetic poems he wrote to address the spiritual needs of his generation and to express the emotions of his own suffering soul. The list of subgenres shows how diverse the anthology is: call narrative, covenant lawsuit, jeremiad (a long recitation of mournful complaints), doom poem, satire, sermon, oracle of judgment, oracle of salvation, memoir, lament or complaint, soliloquy, prophetic object lesson, predictive prophecy, messianic prophecy, epistle, prayer, royal audience, rescue narrative, murder story, and judgment narrative.

The two main unifying elements in the book are the person of Jeremiah himself and the city that he loved, Jerusalem. Reading the book of Jeremiah, one watches the prophet in action, following the broad contours of his biography in the years leading up to and following the cataclysmic fall of Jerusalem (to trace the prophet's story line, see esp. chs. 1, 4, 7, 11–13, 18–20, 24–29, 32, 34–43). At the same time, one sees through windows into the prophet's soul and witnesses the grief that he suffered in watching the people he loved persist in sin and finally fall under the judgment of God. The many minor characters in the book—especially the rebellious kings, lying prophets, and unruly priests who constantly oppose the prophet's ministry, as well as the handful of his faithful supporters—are all seen in relationship to Jeremiah. Viewed as a story, the book of Jeremiah has a unifying plot conflict: will God's people listen to God's warnings and repent of their sin, or will they reject the message of God's prophet and be destroyed? The city of Jerusalem also has a strong unifying presence in the book.

Outline

I. Introduction (1:1–19)
   - A. Jeremiah's historical setting (1:1–3)
   - B. Jeremiah's call and message (1:4–16)
   - C. God's promised protection of Jeremiah (1:17–19)

II. Israel's Covenantal Adultery (2:1–6:30)
  A. Israel has been a faithless spouse (2:1–3:5)
  B. Israel can and should repent (3:6–4:4)
  C. Disaster is coming (4:5–31)
  D. Judah's unwillingness to repent and its consequences (5:1–31)
  E. God has rejected his people (6:1–30)

III. False Religion and an Idolatrous People (7:1–10:25)
  A. Judah's improper reliance on the temple (7:1–8:3)
  B. Judah rejects God's Torah (8:4–17)
  C. Judah lives deceitfully (8:18–9:9)
  D. Judah grieves Jeremiah (9:10–26)
  E. Judah engages in idolatry (10:1–16)
  F. Judah will go into exile (10:17–25)

IV. Jeremiah's Struggles with God and Judah (11:1–20:18)
  A. Jeremiah surprised by opposition (11:1–12:17)
  B. Jeremiah feels betrayed by God (13:1–15:21)
  C. Jeremiah renewed by God (16:1–17:18)
  D. Jeremiah burdened by constant opposition (17:19–18:23)
  E. Jeremiah endures suffering and questions his calling (19:1–20:18)

V. Jeremiah's Confrontations (21:1–29:32)
  A. Jeremiah opposes Judah's kings (21:1–23:8)
  B. Jeremiah confronts false prophets (23:9–40)
  C. Jeremiah opposes Judah's people (24:1–25:38)
  D. Jeremiah opposes false belief (26:1–29:32)

VI. Restoration for Judah and Israel (30:1–33:26)
  A. God will restore the nation (30:1–24)
  B. God will make a new covenant with Israel (31:1–40)
  C. God will bring Israel back to the Promised Land (32:1–44)
  D. God will honor the Davidic covenant (33:1–26)

VII. God Judges Judah (34:1–45:5)
  A. God's faithfulness and Judah's infidelity (34:1–35:19)
  B. Judah rejects God's word (36:1–32)
  C. Jerusalem's last days (37:1–39:18)
  D. Judah's futile rebellion against Babylon (40:1–41:18)
  E. Judah's futile rebellion against God (42:1–45:5)

VIII. God's Judgment on the Nations (46:1–51:64)
  A. God will judge Egypt (46:1–28)
  B. God will judge Philistia (47:1–7)
  C. God will judge Moab (48:1–47)
  D. God will judge many nations (49:1–39)
  E. God will judge Babylon (50:1–51:64)

IX. Conclusion: The Fall of Jerusalem (52:1–34)
  A. Jerusalem's fall and Zedekiah's blinding (52:1–11)
  B. The destruction of the temple (52:12–23)
  C. The exiling of the people (52:24–30)
  D. The continuation of the Davidic lineage (52:31–34)

JEREMIAH

Chapter 1

1[a]Ezek. 1:3 [b]ch. 29:27; 32:7; Josh. 21:18
2[c]See 2 Kgs. 22; 23:1-30 [d]ch. 25:3; 36:2
3[e]ch. 25:1; 36:1; See 2 Kgs. 23:34–24:6 [f]ch. 39:2 [g]See 2 Kgs. 24:17–25:7 [h]See 2 Kgs. 25:8-11
5[i]See Isa. 44:2 [j][John 10:36] [k][Isa. 49:6]; See ch. 25:15-29; ch. 46–51

1 The words of Jeremiah, the son of Hilkiah, one [a]of the priests who were in [b]Anathoth
in the land of Benjamin, 2 to whom the word of the LORD came in the days of [c]Josiah
the son of Amon, king of Judah, in [d]the thirteenth year of his reign. 3 It came also in the
days of [e]Jehoiakim the son of Josiah, king of Judah, and [f]until the end of the eleventh year
of [g]Zedekiah, the son of Josiah, king of Judah, [h]until the captivity of Jerusalem in the fifth
month.

The Call of Jeremiah

4 Now the word of the LORD came to me, saying,

5 [i]"Before I formed you in the womb I knew you,
and before you were born [j]I consecrated you;
I appointed you a prophet [k]to the nations."

1:1–19 *Introduction.* These verses introduce the book's historical background (vv. 1–3), Jeremiah's call and message (vv. 4–16), and the Lord's promised protection of Jeremiah (vv. 17–19). Thus, this section introduces the book's major settings, themes, and characters.

1:1–3 *Jeremiah's Historical Setting.* Jeremiah lived in difficult times. He ministered from c. 627 B.C., or from the reign of Judah's last good king (Josiah), to sometime after the fall of Jerusalem at the hands of the Babylonians in 587. Despite his efforts, Jeremiah's preaching did not stop the nation's slide into exile.

1:1 words of Jeremiah. These are the prophet's words, yet they are also the inspired word of God (v. 4; see 2 Pet. 1:21). **one of the priests**. This indicates that Jeremiah knew the written word of God and was charged with teaching it to the people (Hos. 4:1–3; Mal. 2:1–9). **Anathoth** (Jer. 11:21–23; 32:6–9) was 2–4 miles (3.2–6.4 km) northeast of Jerusalem, so Jeremiah grew up in the shadow of the capital city and its temple. Anathoth was one of the four towns in Benjamin allotted to the priests (Josh. 21:17–18). Jeremiah was from the lineage of Abiathar, the priest deposed by Solomon in favor of Zadok (1 Kings 2:26–27, 35) in accordance with Yahweh's denunciation of Eli's family (1 Sam. 2:27–36). (For the name Yahweh, see notes on Ex. 3:14; 3:15.) Thus, Jeremiah was not an insider in temple politics. He was therefore in an unfavorable position to criticize the temple leadership. **land of Benjamin**. Benjamin and Judah were the two tribes that stayed with David's lineage when the kingdom divided at Solomon's death (1 Kings 11:35–12:24).

1:2 to whom the word of the LORD came. Again the text highlights that what follows comes from God. Jeremiah is God's messenger. Hezekiah and **Josiah** were the only two kings whom the author of 1–2 Kings considered fully faithful to God (2 Kings 18:1–20:18; 22:1–23:30). Josiah ruled c. 640–609 B.C. and led a reform of religion that began c. 622 (2 Kings 22:8–23:27). He was killed in an ill-advised battle with Pharaoh Neco (2 Kings 23:28–30). The **thirteenth year** was c. 627 B.C. Thus, Jeremiah was called to prophesy about five years prior to the beginning of Josiah's reform. It is not clear what role, if any, Jeremiah had in the reform movement.

1:3 Jehoiakim serves as the book's villain. He ruled c. 609–598 B.C., and he hated Jeremiah's preaching (36:1–26). He favored Egypt over Babylon, which led Babylon to invade Judah and take a number of captives c. 605 B.C. (Daniel and his friends were some of the exiles taken to Babylon at that time; Dan. 1:1–2.) Jehoiakim then switched allegiance to Babylon, only to change back to Egypt, which led to a second deportation of Judeans in 597 B.C. (Ezekiel went to Babylon at this time.) **Zedekiah** was the last king of Judah (c. 597–586 B.C.). He was an inconsistent man who sought Jeremiah's counsel but was unwilling to take his advice (Jer. 21:1–10; 38:14–28). His opposition to Babylon eventually led the Babylonians to conquer Jerusalem **in the fifth month**, or July/August (cf. 39:1–10), of 587 or 586 B.C. This **captivity** lasted until c. 538–535 B.C., when Cyrus, the Persian conqueror of Babylon, allowed the Jews to return to their homeland (Ezra 1). Jeremiah prophesied that the exile would last 70 years, and it did (counting from 605 B.C.; see note on Jer. 25:11).

1:4–16 *Jeremiah's Call and Message.* Jeremiah's calling (vv. 4–8) and message (vv. 9–16) were as difficult as his times, for the people were in no mood to hear God's word. Nevertheless, God directed him to preach and write about Judah's sin and its consequences.

1:4 to me. Verses 4–19 are an autobiographical account.

1:5 God is completely sovereign. He knows all things even before they happen, so he **knew** Jeremiah even before he was formed in his mother's **womb**. God's plan for Jeremiah was that he be **consecrated**, or "set apart," for preaching God's word. Jeremiah's ministry is to be a prophet **to the nations**, not just to Israel (25:1–14; 46:1–51:64).

The Date of Jeremiah's Call

Date	Event
628/627 B.C.	Josiah's cleansing of the temple (12th year of Josiah's reign)
627	Jeremiah's call (13th year of Josiah's reign)
626	Babylon's rebellion and independence (14th year of Josiah's reign)

6 Then I said, "Ah, Lord GOD! Behold, [l]I do not know how to speak, [m]for I am only a youth."
7 But the LORD said to me,

"Do not say, 'I am only a youth';
for to all to whom I send you, you shall go,
and [n]whatever I command you, you shall speak.
8 [o]Do not be afraid of them,
[p]for I am with you to deliver you,
declares the LORD."

9 [q]Then the LORD put out his hand and [r]touched my mouth. And the LORD said to me,

"Behold, I have put [s]my words in your mouth.
10 See, I have set you this day [k]over nations and over kingdoms,
[t]to pluck up and to break down,
to destroy and to overthrow,
to build and to plant."

11 And the word of the LORD came to me, saying, [u]"Jeremiah, what do you see?" And I
said, "I see an almond[1] branch." 12 Then the LORD said to me, "You have seen well, for I am
watching over my word to perform it."
13 The word of the LORD came to me a second time, saying, "What do you see?" And I said,
"I see [v]a boiling pot, facing away [w]from the north." 14 Then the LORD said to me, [w]"Out of
the north disaster[2] shall be let loose upon all the inhabitants of the land. 15 For behold, [x]I
am calling all the tribes of the kingdoms of the north, declares the LORD, [y]and they shall
come, and every one shall set his throne at the entrance of the gates of Jerusalem, against
all its walls all around and against all the cities of Judah. 16 And [z]I will declare my judgments against them, for all their evil [a]in forsaking me. [b]They have made offerings to other
gods and [c]worshiped the works of their own hands. 17 But you, [d]dress yourself for work;[3]
arise, and [e]say to them everything that I command you. [f]Do not be dismayed by them, lest
I dismay you before them. 18 And I, behold, I make you this day [g]a fortified city, [h]an iron

[1] *Almond* sounds like the Hebrew for *watching* (compare verse 12) [2] The Hebrew word can mean *evil, harm,* or *disaster,* depending on the context; so throughout Jeremiah [3] Hebrew *gird up your loins*

6 [l][Ex. 4:10] [m][1 Kgs. 3:7]
7 [n]ver. 17; Ezek. 2:7
8 [o]Ezek. 2:6; 3:9 [p]ch. 15:20; See Ex. 3:12
9 [q][Ezek. 2:9] [r][Isa. 6:7] [s]ch. 5:14
10 [k][See ver. 5 above] [t]ch. 18:7; 31:28; 45:4; [2 Cor. 10:4, 5]
11 [u][Amos 7:8]
13 [v]Ezek. 24:3; [Ezek. 22:21] [w]ch. 4:6; 6:1; 10:22
14 [w][See ver. 13 above]
15 [x][ch. 25:9] [y][ch. 39:3; 43:10]
16 [z]ch. 4:12 [a]ch. 19:4; 22:9 [b]ch. 7:9; 44:3 [c]ch. 25:6, 7; Isa. 2:8; Acts 7:41
17 [d][1 Kgs. 18:46; 1 Pet. 1:13] [e]ver. 7 [f]ver. 8; Ezek. 3:9
18 [g][Isa. 50:7] [h]Rev. 3:12

1:6 Jeremiah speaks humbly; he does not simply make excuses. He is in fact a **youth** (Hb. *na'ar*), which means that he remains dependent on parental support. He has not yet reached adulthood, though his exact age is impossible to determine.

1:7 God reassures Jeremiah by telling him he is God's ambassador. Jeremiah will **go** where God sends and say what God commands. He belongs to God; he has no other master, and there is no one else he should seek to please.

1:8 Jeremiah can fear either God (Prov. 1:7) or men. He need not fear men, for God will **deliver** him, though the mention of deliverance means Jeremiah will face trouble. **I am with you**. See note on Jer. 30:11.

1:9–10 God's touching of Jeremiah's **mouth** sets it apart for God's use (Isa. 6:4–7). That God puts his words in Jeremiah's mouth once again underscores the words' divine source (cf. Deut. 18:18). Jeremiah claims no credit for what follows. This word has power **over nations and over kingdoms**. The sovereign word of the sovereign God governs history. Jeremiah's message is threefold: (1) he must **pluck up** and **break down**, which refers to preaching against sin; (2) he must **destroy** and **overthrow**, which relates to messages concerning judgment; and (3) he must **build** and **plant**, which means he must preach about hope and renewal. One or more of these three word pairs occur again in Jer. 18:7–11; 31:28; and 45:4. Jeremiah will preach a full-orbed message over the 40 years of his ministry.

1:11–12 what do you see? This question is also used to introduce a vision in Amos 7:8; 8:2; Zech. 4:2; 5:2. Jeremiah's response and God's rejoinder produce a play on words (see ESV footnote for Jer. 1:11). Jeremiah says he sees an **almond** (Hb. *shaqed*) **branch**, and God states, **You have seen well, for I am watching over** (Hb. *shoqed*) **my word to perform it**. Since the almond tree was the first tree to bud in the spring, it was said to "watch for spring." Thus, God is watching over his word for the first opportunity to carry out his threats and promises. Jeremiah can expect that when he speaks God's words, the words will come true.

1:13–14 God asks Jeremiah a **second time** what he sees. This time Jeremiah sees a **boiling pot, facing away from the north**. This vision means that God's word, which he watches over to perform (v. 12), is that judgment will come from the north. Eventually Babylon fulfills this threat. **disaster**. As the ESV footnote for v. 14 explains, the same word (Hb. *ra'*) can be translated either "evil" or "disaster, harm," according to the context. Jeremiah loves to exploit these two possible meanings, as he does in vv. 14 and 16, with the implication turn from your "evil" or God will send "disaster" (cf. 4:4, 6; 11:8, 11, 17; 18:8–11; 23:11–12; 25:5, 7; 26:3; 32:32, 42; 35:15, 17; 36:3; 44:2–3, 22–23; see note on Jonah 1:2).

1:15 Invaders from the **north** will conquer Jerusalem and set up thrones for their leaders in the city **gates**, where judicial decisions are made. This threat comes true in 39:1–10.

1:16 Though human agents will sit in the gate (v. 15), God says it will be his **judgments against them, for all their evil in forsaking** him. The term "forsaking" indicates that they have abandoned their covenant God for other gods (2:1–8), which they demonstrate by making **offerings to other gods** and bowing down to the **works of their own hands**. Their sin amounts to harm or evil committed against God.

1:17–19 *God's Promised Protection of Jeremiah.* Persecution will be part of Jeremiah's life. He will face opposition from the entire nation, but God will deliver him, thereby ensuring that his ministry will be completed.

1:17 God gives Jeremiah four directives. He must **dress . . . for work**, which literally means (see ESV footnote) "gird up your loins" or "tie up your robe so your legs are free for work." He must **arise** and thus be ready for his work. He must **say** only what God commands him to say (v. 7). He must **not be dismayed by them** (his foes) as he works, or God will give him over to their terrors.

1:18 Jeremiah should not fear, because God makes him **a fortified city, an iron pillar, and bronze walls** that can withstand every possible assault

18[j]ch. 15:20; [ch. 6:27]
19[j][See ver. 18 above] [j]ver. 8; [Acts 18:9, 10]
Chapter 2
2[k]ch. 3:4 [l]Ezek. 16:8, 43, 60; [Rev. 2:4] [m]Deut. 2:7 [n]Deut. 8:2, 3
3[o]Ex. 28:36; [Ex. 19:5, 6] [p]James 1:18; [Ex. 4:22] [q]ch. 12:14; Ezek. 25:12, 13; [Gen. 12:3]
5[r]ver. 31; Isa. 5:4; Mic. 6:3 [s]2 Kgs. 17:15 [t]ch. 10:15; 14:22; 16:19
6[u][Isa. 63:11-13; Hos. 13:4, 5] [v]Deut. 8:15; 32:10
7[w]See Deut. 8:7-10 [x]Ps. 106:38; [Lev. 18:24, 25]

pillar, and [i]bronze walls, against the whole land, against the kings of Judah, its officials, its priests, and the people of the land. 19 [j]They will fight against you, but they shall not prevail against you, for [j]I am with you, declares the LORD, to deliver you."

Israel Forsakes the LORD

2 The word of the LORD came to me, saying, 2 "Go and proclaim in the hearing of Jerusalem, Thus says the LORD,

"I remember the devotion of [k]your youth,
your love [l]as a bride,
[m]how you followed me in the wilderness,
[n]in a land not sown.
3 [o]Israel was holy to the LORD,
[p]the firstfruits of his harvest.
[q]All who ate of it incurred guilt;
disaster came upon them,
declares the LORD."

4 Hear the word of the LORD, O house of Jacob, and all the clans of the house of Israel.
5 Thus says the LORD:

[r]"What wrong did your fathers find in me
that they went far from me,
[s]and went after [t]worthlessness, and became worthless?
6 They did not say, [u]'Where is the LORD
who brought us up from the land of Egypt,
who led us [v]in the wilderness,
in a land of deserts and pits,
in a land of drought and deep darkness,
in a land that none passes through,
where no man dwells?'
7 [w]And I brought you into a plentiful land
to enjoy its fruits and its good things.
But when you came in, [x]you defiled my land
and made my heritage an abomination.
8 The priests did not say, 'Where is the LORD?'

from the different segments of the population. He is invincible as long as he does God's work. God's sovereignty is his comfort. **the kings of Judah, its officials, its priests, and the people of the land**. These groups provide the book's major and minor characters.

1:19 but they shall not prevail against you. God promises to protect and sustain Jeremiah through persecution. God's presence (**for I am with you**) makes him like a fortified city (v. 18), able to endure what will follow, and the calling, word, and presence of God keep him safe.

2:1–6:30 *Israel's Covenantal Adultery.* These five related messages were probably delivered during Josiah's reign (3:6). Jeremiah declares that God's chosen people commit spiritual adultery by loving idols more than the living God. Thus, they have broken their covenant vows and made themselves ripe for judgment. The prophet asserts that Israel is a faithless spouse (2:1–3:5); Israel can and should repent (3:6–4:4); disaster is coming (4:5–31); there are consequences for Judah's unwillingness to repent (ch. 5); and God has rejected his people (ch. 6).

2:1–3:5 *Israel Has Been a Faithless Spouse.* Building on a theme found in his predecessor Hosea's prophecy, Jeremiah conveys God's contention that Israel has committed spiritual adultery (2:1–19) and yet tries to act as if she has been faithful to him (2:20–3:5).

2:1–2 God's **word** is aimed at **Jerusalem**, the heart of the nation. God recalls Israel's past **devotion** (Hb. *hesed,* the term used in covenantal passages to indicate loyalty, faithfulness, and commitment). While **in the wilderness** Israel had the **love** of a **bride** for her husband (Hos. 2:14–15).

2:3 Israel was holy to the LORD, set apart for his purposes, just as Jeremiah was set apart for the Lord's purposes in his role as a prophet (1:5). Israel was the **firstfruits of his** (God's) **harvest**, his chosen and blessed people. He protected Israel, for **all who ate of it** (i.e., of Israel as the holy firstfruits) faced **disaster**, such as befell Egypt at the Red Sea (Ex. 14:1–15:21). Now disaster awaits Israel (Jer. 1:14); a great reversal has occurred.

2:4 God's message is for **all the clans of the house of Israel**, for all the people with whom God made the Abrahamic, Mosaic, and Davidic covenants. Here, it is specifically Judah (and any remnants of the northern tribes who had taken refuge there).

2:5 Israel has been faithless to God though God was faithful to Israel. The Israelites found fault where there was no fault (31:32). They sought out lifeless, and therefore "worthless," idols (Isa. 44:9–20; Jer. 8:19; 10:1–25; 14:22; 16:19; 51:17–18) and as a result **became worthless** covenant partners.

2:6 The Israelites did not seek the Lord, the one whose sovereign power brought them **up from the land of Egypt**, the one who led them through a **land of deserts, pits, drought, darkness**, and desolation. They quickly forgot who had saved and sustained them.

2:7 God gave his people Canaan, a **plentiful land** full of **fruits** and . . . **good things**. God delivered them from Egypt, bringing them through the desert and into the Promised Land. Yet once there they **defiled** God's **land** by embracing Canaanite gods (Judg. 2:11–15).

2:8 Three groups (**priests, shepherds**, and **prophets**) bear heavy responsibility

[y]Those who handle the law did not know me;
[z]the shepherds[1] transgressed against me;
[a]the prophets prophesied by Baal
and went after [b]things that do not profit.

9 "Therefore [c]I still contend with you,
declares the LORD,
and [d]with your children's children I will contend.
10 For cross to the coasts of [e]Cyprus and see,
or send to [f]Kedar and examine with care;
see if there has been such a thing.
11 [g]Has a nation changed its gods,
[h]even though they are no gods?
But my people [i]have changed their glory
for [b]that which does not profit.
12 Be appalled, [j]O heavens, at this;
be shocked, be utterly desolate,
declares the LORD,
13 for my people have committed two evils:
[k]they have forsaken [l]me,
the fountain of [m]living waters,
and hewed out cisterns for themselves,
broken cisterns that can hold no water.

14 [n]"Is Israel a slave? Is he a homeborn servant?
Why then has he become a prey?
15 [o]The lions have roared against him;
they have roared loudly.
They have made his land a waste;
his cities are in ruins, [p]without inhabitant.
16 Moreover, the men of [q]Memphis and [r]Tahpanhes
[s]have shaved[2] the crown of your head.
17 [t]Have you not brought this upon yourself
by forsaking the LORD your God,
when [u]he led you in the way?
18 [v]And now what do you gain by going to Egypt

[1] Or *rulers* [2] Hebrew *grazed*

8 [y]ch. 18:18; [Mal. 2:7; Rom. 2:20] [z][ch. 5:5] [a]ch. 23:13; [ch. 5:31] [b][Hab. 2:18]
9 [c]ver. 35; Ezek. 17:20; 20:35, 36 [d]Ex. 20:5, 6
10 [e]See Gen. 10:4 [f]See Isa. 21:16
11 [g][Mic. 4:5]; See ch. 18:13-15 [h]ch. 16:20; Isa. 37:19; Gal. 4:8 [i]Ps. 106:20 [b][See ver. 8 above]
12 [j]Isa. 1:2
13 [k]ch. 17:13 [l]Ps. 36:9 [m]John 4:10
14 [n][Ex. 4:22]
15 [o]ch. 4:7; Isa. 5:29 [p]ch. 9:11; 46:19
16 [q]ch. 44:1; 46:14; Ezek. 30:16 [r]ch. 43:7-9 [s][Deut. 33:20]
17 [t]ch. 4:18 [u]ver. 6
18 [v]ver. 36; Isa. 30:1, 2; 31:1

for this unfaithfulness. The priests **handle the law** but **did not know** God. Their lack of saving, knowledgeable faith meant they could not teach the people the knowledge of God (Hos. 4:1–3). The shepherds, the nation's rulers (see note on Jer. 3:15), rebelled against God's rule. The prophets **prophesied by Baal** rather than by the Spirit of God, a clear contrast to the task of a true prophet (1:17–19). Baal was a Canaanite storm god. Considered the source of fertility, he was thought to make the earth and women bear fruit. Such power was important in an agricultural economy. Worship practices included sexual activities for men and women at sacred shrines. Thus, people could worship money, sex, and power and be considered righteous for doing so. In the ninth century B.C., Baalism was promoted by Jezebel and Ahab (of the northern kingdom) but opposed by Elijah (1 Kings 16:29–18:46).

2:9 Given this situation, God will **contend** with Israel. This word introduces a common lawsuit metaphor (25:31; Hos. 4:1–4).

2:10–11 The charge is that God's people have done worse than idolaters. Most nations are loyal to their lifeless deities, but Israel has forsaken **their glory** (i.e., Yahweh and the covenants) **for that which does not profit**. Their act is as unnatural as it is ungrateful.

2:12–13 The **heavens**, called as witnesses in the lawsuit (see note on v. 9), are appalled by Israel's twin evils of abandoning the **fountain of living waters** for **broken cisterns that can hold no water**. Palestine has three sources of water: the best is fresh running water, such as flows from a spring or stream, which is called "living water" (Hb. *mayim khayyim*; cf. Lev. 14:5, ESV footnote; Gen. 26:19; Song 4:15; John 4:10–11; 7:38; Rev. 7:17); next comes ground water, such as might collect in a well; and last is runoff water collected in a cistern (a pit hewn into the limestone and plastered to prevent seepage; see note on Jer. 38:6; it also collects silt and mosquito larvae). Thus, in Jeremiah's image, not only have the Israelites traded the best of water supplies for the worst, but their cistern is broken, with all its water leaked out and nothing but sludge remaining. Their covenant infidelity is not just ungrateful and unnatural; it is also foolish. It leaves them without help in the coming difficult days.

2:14 Is Israel a slave? This rhetorical question expects a negative answer. Israel is God's bride (v. 2), not a slave or **homeborn servant**. Yet she has become **prey**, or the "plunder" of war (Num. 14:3). How did Israel go from being the one God protected (Jer. 2:3) to the one God let enemies capture?

2:15 The **lions** are nations like Egypt, Assyria, and Babylon that have made Israel's cities lie **in ruins, without inhabitant** (vv. 18, 36).

2:16 Prior to the exiles of 605, 597, and 586 B.C., Egypt took parts of Judah's land and received many refugees. Egypt seemed like Judah's ally against Babylon (43:7–9), but actually took advantage of Judah.

2:17 The only answer to the question in v. 14 is that Israel has brought all of this on itself by turning from God's protection and has therefore left itself defenseless. See Lev. 26:14–33 and Deut. 28:15–63.

2:18–19 Resorting to allies like **Egypt** and **Assyria** cannot save Judah now.

18 [w]Isa. 23:3 [x][Hos. 7:11] [y]Gen. 31:21; Isa. 7:20; 8:7
19 [z]Isa. 3:9; Hos. 5:5 [a]ch. 3:22; 5:6; 14:7 [b]ch. 4:18 [c]ver. 13, 17
20 [d]ch. 5:5; 30:8 [e]ver. 31 [f]ch. 3:2; 17:2 [g]ch. 3:1; Isa. 1:21
21 [h]Ex. 15:17; Ps. 44:2; 80:8; Isa. 5:2 [i]Isa. 5:4; [Deut. 32:32]
22 [j][ch. 17:1]
23 [k]ver. 35 [l]ch. 7:31, 32; 19:2, 6
24 [m]ch. 14:6
25 [n]Deut. 29:5 [o]Ex. 17:6 [p]ch. 3:13; Deut. 32:16

to drink the waters of [w]the Nile?
[x]Or what do you gain by going to Assyria
to drink the waters of [y]the Euphrates?[1]
19 [z]Your evil will chastise you,
and [a]your apostasy will reprove you.
Know and see that it is evil and [b]bitter
for [c]you to forsake the LORD your God;
the fear of me is not in you,
declares the Lord GOD of hosts.

20 "For long ago I [d]broke your yoke
and burst your bonds;
but you said, [e]'I will not serve.'
Yes, [f]on every high hill
and under every green tree
you bowed down [g]like a whore.
21 [h]Yet I planted you a choice vine,
wholly of pure seed.
[i]How then have you turned degenerate
and become a wild vine?
22 Though you wash yourself with lye
and use much soap,
[j]the stain of your guilt is still before me,
declares the Lord GOD.
23 [k]How can you say, 'I am not unclean,
I have not gone after the Baals'?
Look at your way [l]in the valley;
know what you have done—
a restless young camel running here and there,
24 [m]a wild donkey used to the wilderness,
in her heat sniffing the wind!
Who can restrain her lust?
None who seek her need weary themselves;
in her month they will find her.
25 Keep [n]your feet from going unshod
and [o]your throat from thirst.
But you said, 'It is hopeless,
[p]for I have loved foreigners,
and after them I will go.'

26 "As a thief is shamed when caught,
so the house of Israel shall be shamed;

[1] Hebrew *the River*

In fact, doing so amounts to **apostasy** and **evil**. The Judeans do not **fear** God in the sense of respecting and trusting him and their covenant with him.

2:20 At the time of the exodus God broke Israel's **bonds**. He set the Israelites free, yet they refused to **serve** him. Indeed, **under every green tree**, the places where local idols were worshiped, the people **bowed down like a whore**. This stark language is meant to stir shame, though it pales in comparison to imagery found in Ezekiel 16, 20, and 23. Israel committed spiritual whoredom (see note on Jer. 3:1; cf. Hos. 2:1–13).

2:21 God **planted** Israel in the Promised Land (Ex. 15:17) out of **pure seed**. Yet Israel has become a **wild vine** that bears only putrid fruit. For the image of Israel as a vine and vineyard, see notes on Isa. 5:1 and Ezek. 15:1–8. The Septuagint of this verse reads, "Yet I planted you a fruitful vine, all true." This probably is the background for Jesus' words in John 15:1, "the true vine": he claims to embody the genuine people of God, unlike the Israelites of Isaiah's day.

2:22 Apparently the people tried to cover their sins through ritual cleansing using **lye** and **much soap** (cf. Ps. 51:2, 7; Isa. 1:15–20). A cleansing that is merely ritual does not remove **guilt**. Only repentance and God's forgiveness can do that.

2:23–24 Israel has become **unclean**, or unfit to appear before God, by serving Baal. All sorts of pagan observances occurred **in the valley** (7:31–32; 2 Kings 23:10; 2 Chron. 28:3). The Israelites have acted like a **wild donkey . . . in her heat sniffing the wind** and going where the scent leads her. They run to Baal, Egypt, and Assyria.

2:25 God gave Israel sandals (Deut. 29:5) and water (Ex. 17:6) in the desert. Her "Husband" thus supported her, but she **loved foreigners** and was determined to keep her lovers. Her decision defied logic.

2:26–27 All the culprits mentioned in 1:17–19 and 2:8 will be **shamed** like a captured **thief**. They **turned their back to** God, pretending to worship him (v. 22) while pursuing deities made from a **tree** or a **stone** (v. 27). Thus, they think they can receive God's deliverance whenever they need it.

[q]they, their kings, their officials,
their priests, and their prophets,
27 who say to a tree, 'You are my father,'
and to a stone, 'You gave me birth.'
For they have turned their back to me,
and not their face.
But [r]in the time of their trouble they say,
'Arise and save us!'
28 But [s]where are your gods
that you made for yourself?
Let them arise, [t]if they can save you,
in your time of trouble;
for [u]as many as your cities
are your gods, O Judah.

29 "Why do you contend with me?
You have all transgressed against me,
declares the LORD.
30 In vain have I [v]struck your children;
they took no correction;
[w]your own sword devoured your prophets
like a ravening lion.
31 And you, O generation, behold the word of the LORD.
Have I been a wilderness to Israel,
or a land of thick darkness?
Why then do my people say, 'We are free,
we will come no more to you'?
32 [x]Can a virgin forget her ornaments,
or a bride her attire?
Yet [y]my people have forgotten me
days without number.

33 "How well you direct your course
to seek love!
So that even to wicked women
you have taught your ways.
34 Also on your skirts is found
[z]the lifeblood of the guiltless poor;
you did not find them [a]breaking in.
Yet in spite of all these things
35 you say, 'I am innocent;
surely his anger has turned from me.'
[b]Behold, I will bring you to judgment
for [c]saying, 'I have not sinned.'
36 [d]How much you go about,

26 [q]ch. 13:13; 32:32; [ch. 8:1]
27 [r]Judg. 10:9, 10; Isa. 26:16
28 [s]Deut. 32:37, 38 [t]Isa. 45:20 [u]ch. 11:13
30 [v]ch. 5:3; Isa. 1:5; 9:13 [w]Neh. 9:26; 1 Thess. 2:15
32 [x]Isa. 3:20; 61:10 [y]ch. 3:21; 18:15; Deut. 32:18; Ps. 106:21; Isa. 17:10; Hos. 8:14
34 [z]ch. 19:4; 2 Kgs. 21:16; 24:4; Ps. 106:38 [a]Ex. 22:2
35 [b]Ps. 143:2 [c]Prov. 28:13; 1 John 1:8, 10
36 [d][ch. 31:22]

2:28–29 God is not fooled or moved. **Let them arise**. God challenges the Israelites to have their helpless, inanimate gods save them. After all, they worship as many **gods** as they have **cities**! In their prayers they **contend** (or bring suit) against God, when he has reason to contend with them (v. 9). They have **transgressed** (or broken faith with) their bridal covenant with God (v. 2). They have no case against God.

2:30 Though God **struck** the Israelites in order to bring them back to himself (Lev. 26:14–24; Amos 4:6–13), **they took no correction**. Instead, their **sword devoured . . . prophets**. They killed the very messengers of God sent to warn and help them (2 Kings 17:13–14; 21:16; Neh. 9:26; Jer. 26:20–23).

2:31–32 God's question basically means, "Have I failed to keep my **word** to bless you and thus have been like a **wilderness** and a **land of thick darkness**?" If not, then Israel is not **free** to forsake him. To do so is like a **bride** forgetting her jewelry and wedding dress on her wedding day. No bride forgets such things, yet Israel, God's bride (v. 2), has **forgotten** him repeatedly.

2:33 Israel's treachery is so complete and so well planned that **wicked women** learn from her.

2:34 Covenant infidelity always leads to ethical infidelity. God has **found the lifeblood of the guiltless poor** on Israel's **skirts** (Amos 4:1–5). Israel has harmed the poor though they did not break into her home (Ex. 22:2). She has brought false charges for her own gain.

2:35 Israel claims she is **innocent**, which only adds to her guilt. God will bring her **to judgment** for committing spiritual perjury.

2:36–37 Israel changes her political course of action (v. 18) very easily, but whoever she chooses (whether **Egypt** or **Assyria**) will bring her **shame**. Placing one's **hands** on one's **head** was a sign of grief brought on by

36[e]Isa. 30:3
37[f]2 Sam. 13:19

Chapter 3

1[g]See Deut. 24:1-4 [h]ver. 9; Ps. 106:38 [i]ch. 2:20
2[j]ver. 21, 23; ch. 4:11; 7:29; Num. 23:3 [k]Ezek. 16:25 [h][See ver. 1 above]
3[l]ch. 9:12; 14:22; Deut. 28:24 [m][ch. 6:15]; See Ezek. 3:7, 8
4[n][Luke 15:18]
5[o]Ps. 103:9
6[p]ch. 1:2 [q]See ch. 2:20 [i][See ver. 1 above]
7[r][Ezek. 16:46; 23:4]

changing your way!
You shall be [e]put to shame by Egypt
as you were put to shame by Assyria.
37 From it too you will come away
with [f]your hands on your head,
for the LORD has rejected those in whom you trust,
and you will not prosper by them.

3

1 [g]"If[1] a man divorces his wife
and she goes from him
and becomes another man's wife,
will he return to her?
[h]Would not that land be greatly polluted?
[i]You have played the whore with many lovers;
and would you return to me?
declares the LORD.
2 Lift up your eyes to [j]the bare heights, and see!
Where have you not been ravished?
[k]By the waysides you have sat awaiting lovers
like an Arab in the wilderness.
[h]You have polluted the land
with your vile whoredom.
3 [l]Therefore the showers have been withheld,
and the spring rain has not come;
yet you have [m]the forehead of a whore;
you refuse to be ashamed.
4 Have you not just now [n]called to me,
'My father, you are the friend of my youth—
5 [o]will he be angry forever,
will he be indignant to the end?'
Behold, you have spoken,
but you have done all the evil that you could."

Faithless Israel Called to Repentance

6 The LORD said to me in the days of [p]King Josiah: "Have you seen what she did, that
faithless one, Israel, [q]how she went up on every high hill and under every green tree, and
there [i]played the whore? 7 And I thought, 'After she has done all this she will return to
me,' but she did not return, and her treacherous [r]sister Judah saw it. 8 She saw that for all

[1] Septuagint, Syriac; Hebrew *Saying, "If*

sexual shame. Tamar did so when Amnon raped her (2 Sam. 13:19). But Israel is actually guilty of *seeking* sexual shame. Her shame will be apparent when Assyria and Egypt fail to defeat Babylon. Israel has trusted allies whom God has **rejected**. She will chase her lovers, lose her virtue, and forfeit her land.

3:1 Jeremiah may have Deut. 24:1–4 in mind, which answers the first question (**will he return to her?**) negatively and the second question (**Would not that land be greatly polluted?**) positively. With the words **played the whore** (cf. Jer. 2:20; 13:27), Jeremiah uses the image of Judah as God's promiscuously unfaithful wife; the image begins in the Pentateuch (Ex. 34:15; Deut. 31:16) and is widespread in the Prophets (Isa. 1:21; Ezekiel 16; 23; Hosea 1–3). Israel tries to alternate between God and idols (Jer. 2:25, 27, 35–36), but God rejects this arrangement. She must commit herself exclusively to God.

3:2 The imagery moves to Israel sitting by **waysides . . . awaiting lovers**. Such idolatry pollutes the Promised Land (Lev. 18:25–28).

3:3 God says the **showers have been withheld** as a means of trying to get Israel to change (Deut. 28:24; Amos 4:7). The nation's sin resulted in economic loss. Yet Israel has the **forehead of a whore**, which refers either to her blatant obstinacy (cf. Isa. 48:4; Ezek. 3:7) or to a special headpiece worn by prostitutes. Either way this metaphor highlights Israel's refusal **to be ashamed**.

3:4–5 Israel acts as if God has been **angry** for no reason, or perhaps for too long. She calls out to God after being with other lovers/gods (2:26–29), but God cannot accept her duplicity.

3:6–4:4 *Israel Can and Should Repent.* God offers forgiveness to the people of the northern kingdom (Israel). Josiah tried to extend his reform to Israel from Judah (2 Kings 23:15–20; 2 Chron. 35:16–19), which may be the background of this passage. Despite her past unfaithfulness, God is willing to take his straying bride back. Judgment does not have to be the final word. Past sins can be forgiven (Jer. 3:6–14), so the future can be bright (vv. 15–18). God calls the people to repentance (vv. 19–25), which requires a new heart (4:1–4).

3:6 God speaks to Jeremiah **in the days of King Josiah** (after 627 B.C.; see 1:1–3; and Dates of Events in Jeremiah, p. 1376) concerning the faithlessness of **Israel**, the northern kingdom. Israel **played the whore** by worshiping idols everywhere possible (2:20).

3:7 Despite God's centuries-long patience, **she did not return** to God. The same word (Hb. *shub*) may be translated "return" or "repent," depending on the context. Israel's failure "to return" was a refusal "to repent." Sadly, **her treacherous sister Judah** learned to behave as she did.

3:8 Judah saw that God sent Israel **away with a decree of divorce**,

the adulteries of that faithless one, Israel, [s]I had sent her away with [t]a decree of divorce.
[u]Yet her treacherous sister Judah did not fear, but she too went [i]and played the whore.
9 Because she took her whoredom lightly, she polluted the land, committing adultery with
[v]stone and tree. 10 Yet for all this her treacherous sister Judah did not return to me [w]with
her whole heart, but in pretense, declares the LORD."

11 And the LORD said to me, [x]"Faithless Israel has shown herself more righteous than
treacherous Judah. 12 Go, and proclaim these words toward [y]the north, and say,

[z]"'Return, faithless Israel,
declares the LORD.
I will not look on you in anger,
for [a]I am merciful,
declares the LORD;
[b]I will not be angry forever.
13 [c]Only acknowledge your guilt,
that you rebelled against the LORD your God
and scattered your favors among foreigners under [d]every green tree,
and that you have not obeyed my voice,
declares the LORD.

8 [s]2 Kgs. 17:18; [Hos. 1:6, 9] [t][Matt. 19:7; Mark 10:4]; See Deut. 24:1-4 [u]Ezek. 23:11 [i][See ver. 1 above]
9 [v]ch. 2:27
10 [w]Hos. 7:14
11 [x]Ezek. 16:51, 52
12 [y]See ver. 18 [z]Prov. 28:13; See Deut. 30:1-10 [a]Ps. 86:5, 15 [b]Ps. 103:9
13 [c]Lev. 26:40 [d]ver. 6

Dates of Events in Jeremiah

Dates	Passage
Under Josiah (627–609 B.C.)	1:1–19
	3:6–6:30
Under Jehoahaz (609) and Jehoiakim (609–597)	7:1–34
	25:1–38
	26:1–24
	35:1–19
	36:1–32
	45:1–5
	46:1–28
	47:1–7
	48:1–47
Under Jehoiachin (597) and Zedekiah (597–586)	20:1–22:30
	24:1–10
	27:1–22
	28:1–17
	29:1–32
	30:1–31:40
	32:1–44
	33:1–26
	34:1–22
	37:1–21
	38:1–28
	39:1–18
	49:1–39
	50:1–51:64
	52:1–34
After the Fall of Jerusalem (586)	40:1–42:22
	43:1–44:30

which here refers to the exiling that began in 732 B.C. and accelerated in 722 with the fall of Samaria. Undaunted, Judah **went and played the whore** anyway.

3:9–10 Judah **did not return** (repent). Rather, she only acted as if she had (2:26–29; 3:4–5). None of her prayers and sacrifices were offered in genuine repentance and trust.

3:11 God declares **faithless Israel . . . more righteous than treacherous Judah**. At least Israel was honest about her faithlessness. Judah tried to hide her adultery.

3:12 God commissions Jeremiah to make an extraordinary offer of grace to the fallen, exiled northern tribes, now scattered in **the north**. They should repent, since he will not deal with them angrily, for he is **merciful** (see Hos. 3:5 for a similar hope for the north). The word translated "merciful" (Hb. *hasid*) is used of God only here and in Ps. 145:17, where it is translated "kind." The one who is *hasid* extends *hesed*, the Hebrew term for covenant kindness and faithfulness, to others (see note on Jer. 2:1–2).

3:13 Israel must **acknowledge** her **guilt** and rebellion in committing idolatry with the gods of the nations. Repentance will lead to acceptance and renewal (Deut. 30:1–10).

3:14 God asks the **faithless children** (lit., "the turning-away ones") to turn, or **return**, to him. He claims to be their **master**, or their "husband." The Hebrew word for "master" (or "husband") in this verse is *ba'al*, the verb from the same root as the name of the god Baal. Historically, Israel followed Baal as her master rather than following her true husband, Yahweh (Hos. 2:16–17). If she will return to this true Husband, he will take Israel **one from a city and two from a family . . . to Zion**. This minority, this "remnant" of ones and twos, will be the true people of God (Isa. 6:11–13; 10:20–23).

3:15 God will give this remnant (see note on v. 14) **shepherds after** his **own heart**, that is, leaders (like David) who are kings in whom God takes delight (1 Sam. 13:14). These shepherds will **feed** the people **with knowledge and understanding**, the very qualities they lacked when they turned away from God and followed false teachers and priests (Hos. 4:1–3). The shepherds are a recurring theme in Jeremiah (Jer. 2:8; 3:15; 10:21; 23:1–4; 50:6; cf. Ezekiel 34). The term can refer specifically to civil leaders, such as the king (2 Sam. 5:2), or to leaders more generally (civil and religious): all were charged with the responsibility of leading God's people to show forth his holiness in their personal and corporate lives. The people need faithful shepherds, and God will supply them after the exile.

3:16 God will multiply the remnant into larger numbers **in those days** (i.e., the days when he leads Israel to Zion). Israel's exiles long for the **ark of the covenant of the LORD** in the temple at Jerusalem, for they consider it God's symbolic throne (2 Kings 19:15). In the days of restoration it will not **come to mind** and **it shall not be made again**. Whatever happens to the ark, it will no longer be essential to godly worship.

14 [e]Return, O faithless children,
declares the LORD;
[f]for I am your master;
I will take you, one from a city and two from a family,
and I will bring you to Zion.

15"'And [g]I will give you shepherds after my own heart, [h]who will feed you with knowledge and understanding. **16** And when you have multiplied and been fruitful in the land,
in those days, declares the LORD, they shall no more say, "The ark of the covenant of the
LORD." It shall not come to mind or be remembered or missed; it shall not be made again.
17 At that time Jerusalem shall be called the throne of the LORD, [i]and all nations shall
gather to it, [j]to the presence of the LORD in Jerusalem, and they shall no more stubbornly
follow their own evil heart. **18** [k]In those days the house of Judah shall join the house of
Israel, and together they shall come from the land [l]of the north to [m]the land that I gave
your fathers for a heritage.

19 "'I said,
How I would set you among my sons,
and give you a pleasant land,
a heritage most beautiful of all nations.
And I thought you would [n]call me, My Father,
and would not turn from following me.
20 [o]Surely, as a treacherous wife leaves her husband,
so have you been treacherous to me, O house of Israel,
declares the LORD.'"

21 A voice on the [p]bare heights is heard,
[q]the weeping and pleading of Israel's sons
because they have perverted their way;
they have forgotten the LORD their God.
22 [r]"Return, O faithless sons;
[s]I will heal your faithlessness."
"Behold, we come to you,
for you are the LORD our God.
23 Truly [t]the hills are a delusion,
the orgies[1] on the mountains.
[u]Truly in the LORD our God
is the salvation of Israel.

24"But from our youth the shameful thing has devoured all for which our fathers labored,
their flocks and their herds, their sons and their daughters. **25** [v]Let us lie down in our shame,

[1] Hebrew *commotion*

14 [e]ver. 22; Hos. 14:1 [f]Isa. 54:5; 62:5; Hos. 2:19, 20; Mal. 2:11
15 [g]ch. 23:4; Ezek. 34:23; [John 10:11] [h]Acts 20:28
17 [i]Isa. 2:2, 3 [j]Isa. 60:9
18 [k]ch. 50:4; Isa. 11:13; Ezek. 37:21, 22; Hos. 1:11 [l]ver. 12; ch. 16:15; 23:8; 31:8 [m]Amos 9:15
19 [n][Isa. 63:16]
20 [o]ver. 7, 8; ch. 5:11
21 [p]See ver. 2 [q]ch. 31:9
22 [r]ver. 14 [s]ch. 30:17; Isa. 57:18; Hos. 6:1
23 [t]ver. 21; [Ps. 121:1, 2] [u]Ps. 3:8
25 [v]Ezra 9:6; Job 8:22

3:17 At that time Jerusalem shall be called the throne of the LORD, thereby replacing the ark in symbolic function. Then **all nations shall gather to it** (Jerusalem) (Isa. 2:1–5), and those who live there will be faithful to God (Isa. 4:2–6). This Jerusalem is ultimately the new Jerusalem where God's people will live with him forever in the total absence of sin (Isa. 65:17–25; Rev. 21:1–8).

3:18 In those days the house of Judah and **Israel** will be united again in service to God. They shall come to the land of promise from all the places where their sins have driven them (Isa. 11:10–16). Their renewal will be complete.

3:19–20 God reiterates that Israel's **treacherous**, adulterous ways have kept him from blessing her with **a pleasant land, a heritage most beautiful of all nations**, something he longed to give.

3:21 Suddenly, a sound of the **weeping and pleading of Israel's sons** arises from the **bare heights.** Israel's sons finally recognize **they have perverted their way** and **have forgotten the LORD their God**.

3:22 God counsels the Israelites to **return** (repent) so he can **heal** their **faithlessness**, their worship of other gods. Here forgiveness is compared to physical healing (30:17; 33:6; Hos. 6:1; 14:4). **Behold, we come to you.** Israel responds positively by confessing that the Lord is their God.

3:23 The Israelites also confess that the **hills** (the places of idol worship) and the **orgies** (the worship services for the idols) **are a delusion**, falsehood, and hollow nothingness. Only God **is the salvation of Israel**. They further confess sole loyalty to their covenant husband, as he asked in vv. 11–18.

3:24 The Israelites admit that their idols (the **shameful thing**) have cost them their homes, land, and freedom, just as Lev. 26:27–33 and Deut. 28:64–68 warned.

3:25 The Israelites complete their confession by saying they merit **shame** and **dishonor** (Ps. 51:4). God was just in punishing them. They and their **fathers** sinned from their **youth**, from the nation's earliest days, and **have not obeyed the voice of the LORD** (cf. Neh. 9:1–38; Dan. 9:1–19) by following his teaching.

and let our dishonor cover us. For [w]we have sinned against the LORD our God, we and our fathers, from our youth even to this day, and we have not obeyed the voice of the LORD our God."

4

1 "If you return, O Israel,
declares the LORD,
[x]to me you should return.
If you remove your detestable things from my presence,
[y]and do not waver,
2 [z]and if you swear, 'As the LORD lives,'
in truth, in justice, and in righteousness,
then [a]nations shall bless themselves in him,
[b]and in him shall they glory."

3 For thus says the LORD to the men of Judah and Jerusalem:

[c]"Break up your fallow ground,
and [d]sow not among thorns.
4 [e]Circumcise yourselves to the LORD;
remove the foreskin of your hearts,
O men of Judah and inhabitants of Jerusalem;
[f]lest my wrath go forth like fire,
and burn with none to quench it,
[g]because of the evil of your deeds."

Disaster from the North

5 Declare in Judah, and proclaim in Jerusalem, and say,

[h]"Blow the trumpet through the land;
cry aloud and say,
[i]'Assemble, and let us go
into the fortified cities!'
6 [j]Raise a standard toward Zion,
flee for safety, stay not,
for I bring disaster from [k]the north,
[l]and great destruction.
7 [m]A lion has gone up from his thicket,
a destroyer of nations has set out;
he has gone out from his place
to make your land a waste;
your cities will be ruins
[n]without inhabitant.

25 [w]Ezra 9:7; Ezek. 2:3

Chapter 4

1 [x]Joel 2:12 [y][1 Kgs. 14:15]
2 [z]Deut. 6:13 [a]Isa. 65:16 [b]1 Cor. 1:31; 2 Cor. 10:17
3 [c]Hos. 10:12 [d]Matt. 13:7, 22; Mark 4:7, 18; Luke 8:7, 14
4 [e]Deut. 10:16; [ch. 9:26; Rom. 2:28, 29] [f]ch. 21:12 [g]Deut. 28:20
5 [h][ch. 6:1; Hos. 5:8; Joel 2:1] [i]ch. 8:14
6 [j][ch. 50:2; 51:12, 27] [k]See ch. 1:13 [l][Isa. 1:28]
7 [m]ch. 2:15; 5:6; 49:19 [n]ch. 33:10; 34:22; 46:19; Isa. 5:9; 6:11

4:1 God stresses that true repentance includes removing **detestable things** (idols) **from** his **presence** (Gen. 35:1–4) and not wavering in this decision. Israel must not try to serve both God and idols as Judah is currently doing (Jer. 2:23–37).

4:2 True repentance includes swearing that **the LORD** alone **lives**, and doing so with a commitment to live **in truth** (or in faithfulness), **in justice, and in righteousness** with God and neighbor (Lev. 19:18; Deut. 6:4–9). Grace leads to changed living. Israel's full repentance will glorify God, leading the nations to **bless themselves in him**—thus fulfilling God's promise to Abraham concerning the nations (Gen. 12:3)—and to **glory** (or "exult" as in Ps. 63:11) **in him**. God called Jeremiah to be a prophet to the nations (Jer. 1:5–10), and here he fulfills that calling.

4:3 God addresses the **men of Judah and Jerusalem**. Like wise farmers, they must plow their **fallow ground, and sow not among thorns**. Serving other gods amounts to farming the wrong spiritual soil.

4:4 Changing the image, God tells the people of Judah to **circumcise** themselves **to the LORD** by removing the **foreskin of** their **hearts** (Deut. 10:16). The heart symbolizes the totality of one's will and emotions. Loving God with all one's heart is the essence of faith (Deut. 6:4–9; Mark 12:28–32). True circumcision is of the heart, not simply the flesh (Gen. 17:10–14), and makes the Israelites followers of God (Rom. 2:28–29 articulates this OT principle). The lack of a changed heart leads to disobedience, which leads to God's **wrath** burning like unquenchable **fire** (Isa. 1:31; Jer. 7:20; 17:27; 21:12; Amos 5:6).

4:5–31 *Disaster Is Coming.* Unless Judah and Jerusalem repent, disaster in the form of a devastating invasion will come from the north (1:13–16). A defeat so terrible will occur that it will seem as if God's act of creation has been reversed. The invasion will lead to lamenting (4:5–13), though it *should* lead to repentance (vv. 14–18). Thus, refusing to repent is foolish (vv. 19–31).

4:5–6 Judah and **Jerusalem** must prepare for war. The **trumpet** announces peril, so the people living in the unwalled and unprotected countryside should flee **into the fortified cities** for protection. The threat comes **from the north** (1:13–16).

4:7 lion. Many ancient nations likened themselves to lions, but here the text refers to Babylon, the chief **destroyer of nations** in Jeremiah's times. The land will be a **waste . . . without inhabitant**, so fleeing (as in vv. 5–6) will be fruitless.

8[o]ch. 6:26; Isa. 22:12; 32:11 [p]Num. 25:4; Ps. 78:49; See Isa. 13:9-13
9[q][Ps. 48:4, 5]
10[r]Ezek. 14:9; [1 Kgs. 22:22]
11[s]See ch. 3:2
12[t]ch. 1:16
13[u]Isa. 5:28 [v]2 Sam. 1:23; Lam. 4:19 [w]ch. 9:19
14[x]Ps. 51:2, 7; Isa. 1:16; James 4:8
15[y]ch. 8:16 [z]See Josh. 24:33
16[a]ch. 5:15
17[b]ch. 6:3; See 2 Kgs. 25:1-4
18[c]ch. 2:19
19[d]Isa. 16:11; Hab. 3:16; [ch. 9:1; Isa. 22:4]

8 For this [o]put on sackcloth,
lament and wail,
for [p]the fierce anger of the LORD
has not turned back from us."

9"In that day, declares the LORD, [q]courage shall fail both king and officials. The priests shall
be appalled and the prophets astounded." 10Then I said, "Ah, Lord GOD, [r]surely you have
utterly deceived this people and Jerusalem, saying, 'It shall be well with you,' whereas the
sword has reached their very life."

11At that time it will be said to this people and to Jerusalem, "A hot wind from [s]the bare
heights in the desert toward the daughter of my people, not to winnow or cleanse, 12a wind
too full for this comes for me. Now it is I who [t]speak in judgment upon them."

13 Behold, he comes up like clouds;
[u]his chariots like the whirlwind;
his horses are [v]swifter than eagles—
woe to us, [w]for we are ruined!
14 O Jerusalem, [x]wash your heart from evil,
that you may be saved.
How long shall your wicked thoughts
lodge within you?
15 For a voice [y]declares from Dan
and proclaims trouble from [z]Mount Ephraim.
16 Warn the nations that he is coming;
announce to Jerusalem,
"Besiegers come [a]from a distant land;
they shout against the cities of Judah.
17 Like keepers of a field [b]are they against her all around,
because she has rebelled against me,
declares the LORD.
18 Your ways and your deeds
have brought this upon you.
This is your doom, and [c]it is bitter;
it has reached your very heart."

Anguish over Judah's Desolation

19 [d]My anguish, my anguish! I writhe in pain!
Oh the walls of my heart!
My heart is beating wildly;
I cannot keep silent,
for I hear the sound of the trumpet,
the alarm of war.

4:8 Lamenting and wailing (both ancient funeral practices) are appropriate, for God will vent his **fierce anger** on the unjust and unloving people (v. 4).

4:9 In that day refers to the day of the Lord, the day God judges, whether in history or at the final judgment that ends history. (See note on Amos 5:18–20 and The Day of the Lord in the Prophets, p. 1668.) **King and officials . . . priests** lead the people astray (Jer. 2:8) and oppose Jeremiah (1:17–19), so they will be useless when judgment comes.

4:10 Jeremiah speaks out of his agony of soul. He claims that God has said all **shall be well** when in fact divine wrath is coming. Apparently he is quoting the false prophets at this point (6:14; 14:13; 23:16–17). He wonders why God has allowed these prophets to speak at all if they are so wrong. But elsewhere in Scripture, God sometimes sends deceiving spirits into the false prophets (see note on 1 Sam. 16:14). Though God himself never does evil, he sometimes sends evil agents to accomplish his purposes of judgment.

4:11–12 A scorching sirocco (**hot wind**) bringing sand and dust is compared to the effects of the enemy's army. Such a wind only destroys; it does not **winnow or cleanse** (cf. Ruth 3:2; Isa. 30:24; on the process of winnowing, see note on Ps. 1:4).

4:13 The army is described as coming up suddenly **like clouds** before a storm, riding as hard as a **whirlwind**, and moving as swiftly as **eagles**. Jeremiah realizes his people **are ruined** in the face of such a foe.

4:15–17 Watchmen from the territory of **Dan**, the northernmost part of the old Israel, warn that siege warfare is coming to **Jerusalem** and Judah's **cities** because of Judah's rebellion against God.

4:18 The defeat will be so **bitter** it will touch Israel's **heart**, the very place God has tried to touch with his love.

4:19 Jeremiah responds feelingly. He cries, **"My anguish, my anguish,"** literally, "My entrails, my entrails," referring to internal digestive organs. Trouble in the entrails was a metaphor for extreme physical distress (Job 30:27; Lam. 1:20; 2:11). His **heart** (the center of his affections, will, and emotions) also trembles at the **sound of the trumpet** (Jer. 4:5).

20 [e]Crash follows hard on crash;
the whole land is laid waste.
[f]Suddenly my tents are laid waste,
my curtains in a moment.
21 How long must I see the standard
and hear the sound of the trumpet?
22 "For [g]my people are foolish;
they know me not;
they are stupid children;
they have no understanding.
[h]They are 'wise'—in doing evil!
But how to do good they know not."

23 I looked on the earth, and behold, it was [i]without form and void;
[j]and to the heavens, and they had no light.
24 I looked on [k]the mountains, and behold, they were quaking,
and all the hills moved to and fro.
25 [l]I looked, and behold, there was no man,
and all the birds of the air had fled.
26 I looked, and behold, the [m]fruitful land was a desert,
and all its cities were laid in ruins
before the LORD, before [n]his fierce anger.

27 For thus says the LORD, "The whole land shall be a desolation; [o]yet I will not make
a full end.

28 [p]"For this the earth shall mourn,
[q]and the heavens above be dark;
for I have spoken; I have purposed;
[r]I have not relented, nor will I turn back."

29 At the noise of horseman and archer
every city takes to flight;
they enter thickets; they climb among rocks;
all the cities are forsaken,
and [s]no man dwells in them.
30 And you, O desolate one,
what do you mean that you dress in scarlet,
[t]that you adorn yourself with ornaments of gold,
[u]that you enlarge your eyes with paint?
In vain you beautify yourself.
[v]Your lovers despise you;
they seek your life.
31 For I heard [w]a cry as of a woman in labor,
anguish as of one giving birth to her first child,

20[e]Ezek. 7:26 [f]ch. 10:20; 49:29
22[g]Ps. 82:5; Isa. 1:3 [h]Ps. 36:3; Isa. 1:16, 17; Rom. 16:19
23[i]Gen. 1:2 [j]Isa. 5:30
24[k]Nah. 1:5
25[l][Zeph. 1:3]
26[m]Ps. 107:34 [n]See ver. 8
27[o]ch. 5:10, 18; 30:11; 46:28; Neh. 9:31; Ezek. 11:13
28[p]ch. 12:4; Hos. 4:3 [q]Isa. 50:3 [r][Num. 23:19]
29[s]See ver. 7
30[t][Isa. 61:10] [u][2 Kgs. 9:30] [v]Lam. 1:2, 19; Ezek. 23:22
31[w]ch. 6:24; See Isa. 13:8

4:21 Like many Bible characters, Jeremiah wonders **how long** (Ps. 79:5; 89:46; Isa. 6:11) he must **see** the battle **standard** and **hear** the battle **trumpet** (Jer. 4:5–6).

4:22 God responds by stating that his **people** lack saving knowledge and a proper **understanding** of his ways and words (3:15; Hos. 4:1–3). Their only wisdom is **in doing evil**. Thus, they are **foolish** and **stupid children**. This strong language seeks to shock the people into repentance and to inform Jeremiah that his sympathy may be misplaced.

4:23–25 Jeremiah portrays the coming judgment as a reversal of the creation process. The earth is once again **without form and void** (Gen. 1:2), the **heavens** have **no light** (Gen. 1:3), the **mountains** and **hills** quake (Gen. 1:9–11), and mankind (Gen. 1:26–31) and **birds** (Gen. 1:20–23) disappear.

4:26 The fruitfulness of the Promised Land will be reversed (cf. note on 4:5–31). The **fruitful land** (3:19) has become a **desert** in the wake of God's **fierce anger** (4:8).

4:27 Despite the seeming totality of the destruction, God **will not make a full end** of the **whole land** (or "whole earth"). The creation will endure because of God's mercy (Hos. 11:1–9) and eternal plan (Eph. 1:3–14; 2 Pet. 3:1–13).

4:28 Just as God once spoke and the world came into existence, so now he will speak and devastation will come to pass. He will not relent, or **turn back**, for he knows there will be no repentance.

4:30 Jerusalem will try to make herself beautiful to her **lovers** (her old allies) but the efforts will be **in vain**.

4:31 The daughter of Zion refers to Jerusalem and the temple area. Jerusalem will suffer like a **woman . . . giving birth to her first child** when she faces her **murderers** (Lam. 1:8–22).

31[x]Isa. 1:15; Lam. 1:17
Chapter 5
1[y][2 Chr. 16:9] [z]See Gen. 18:23-32 [a][ver. 7]
2[b][Titus 1:16] [c]ch. 7:9
3[d]See ch. 2:30 [e]Ezek. 3:8
4[f]ch. 8:7; Mic. 3:1
5[g]ch. 2:20; Ps. 2:3; 107:14
6[h]See ch. 4:7 [i]Hab. 1:8; Zeph. 3:3 [j]Hos. 13:7 [k]ch. 2:19
7[l][ver. 1] [m]Deut. 32:21; Josh. 23:7; 2 Chr. 13:9; Gal. 4:8 [n]Deut. 32:15 [o]ch. 9:2; 23:10 [p]Mic. 5:1

the cry of the daughter of Zion gasping for breath,
[x]stretching out her hands,
"Woe is me! I am fainting before murderers."

Jerusalem Refused to Repent

5
1 [y]Run to and fro through the streets of Jerusalem,
look and take note!
Search her squares to see
[z]if you can find a man,
one who does justice
and seeks truth,
[a]that I may pardon her.
2 [b]Though they say, "As the LORD lives,"
[c]yet they swear falsely.
3 O LORD, do not your eyes look for truth?
[d]You have struck them down,
but they felt no anguish;
you have consumed them,
but they refused to take correction.
[e]They have made their faces harder than rock;
they have refused to repent.

4 Then I said, "These are only the poor;
they have no sense;
[f]for they do not know the way of the LORD,
the justice of their God.
5 I will go to the great
and will speak to them,
for they know the way of the LORD,
the justice of their God."
[g]But they all alike had broken the yoke;
they had burst the bonds.

6 Therefore [h]a lion from the forest shall strike them down;
a [i]wolf from the desert shall devastate them.
[j]A leopard is watching their cities;
everyone who goes out of them shall be torn in pieces,
because their transgressions are many,
their [k]apostasies are great.

7 [l]"How can I pardon you?
Your children have forsaken me
[m]and have sworn by those who are no gods.
[n]When I fed them to the full,
[o]they committed adultery
[p]and trooped to the houses of whores.

5:1–31 *Judah's Unwillingness to Repent and Its Consequences.* Despite Jeremiah's messages, the people do not repent (vv. 1–9). Indeed they prefer false teaching to the truth (vv. 10–13), for they wish to continue their immoral, unjust ways. They will soon experience the full force of Babylon's invasion (vv. 14–31).

5:1 What Abraham discovered when pleading for Sodom (Gen. 18:23–32), Jeremiah discovers now: there is not a single just, faithful, and covenant-keeping person in Jerusalem for whose sake God would **pardon** the whole people.

5:2 At best the people pay lip service to God (cf. 2:26–29).

5:3 struck them down, but they felt no anguish. God's discipline has not led to repentance but to a hardened resolve to sin (cf. 2:14–19, 30; Amos 4:6–13).

5:4–5 Jeremiah believes that perhaps **only** the **poor** (the ones uneducated in the **way of the LORD**, who do not know the **justice** of God's discipline) reject God's ways. Sadly, however, he learns that the **great** (those who should know God's ways) have also **broken the yoke** of God's rule in their lives.

5:6 lion . . . wolf . . . leopard. Sudden judgment will come in various forms, when the Israelites do not expect it. Their enemies are like hungry, deadly animals watching for prey. Their **transgressions** (rebellions) and **apostasies** (lit., "turnings"; cf. 2:19; 3:22) are **great** (or "numerous").

5:7 God cannot find a reason to **pardon** (see v. 1), for the Israelites swear by "those who are no gods" and have **committed adultery and trooped to the houses of whores** though their divine Husband has met all their needs (2:1–8; Hos. 2:1–13). This imagery depicts spiritual adultery committed through physically taking part in pagan fertility rites in Baal worship (Jer. 2:8).

8 They were well-fed, lusty stallions,
[q]each neighing [r]for his neighbor's wife.
9 [s]Shall I not punish them for these things?
declares the LORD;
and shall I not avenge myself
on a nation such as this?
10 [t]"Go up through her vine rows and destroy,
[u]but make not a full end;
strip away her branches,
for they are not the LORD's.
11 [v]For the house of Israel and the house of Judah
have been utterly treacherous to me,
declares the LORD.
12 They have spoken falsely of the LORD
and have said, 'He will do nothing;
[w]no disaster will come upon us,
[x]nor shall we see sword or famine.
13 The prophets will become wind;
the word is not in them.
Thus shall it be done to them!'"

The LORD Proclaims Judgment

14 Therefore thus says the LORD, the God of hosts:
"Because you have spoken this word,
behold, [y]I am making my words in your mouth [z]a fire,
and this people wood, and the fire shall consume them.
15 [a]Behold, I am bringing against you
a nation from afar, O house of Israel,
declares the LORD.
It is an enduring nation;
it is an ancient nation,
a nation whose language you do not know,
[b]nor can you understand what they say.
16 [c]Their quiver is like [d]an open tomb;
they are all mighty warriors.
17 [e]They shall eat up your harvest and your food;
they shall eat up your sons and your daughters;
they shall eat up your flocks and your herds;
they shall eat up your vines and your fig trees;
your [f]fortified cities in which you trust
they shall beat down with the sword."

18 "But even in those days, declares the LORD, [u]I will not make a full end of you. 19 And
when your people say, [g]'Why has the LORD our God done all these things to us?' you shall

8 [q]ch. 13:27; 50:11 [r]Ezek. 22:11
9 [s]ver. 29; ch. 9:9; [Rom. 2:2]
10 [t][ch. 39:8] [u]See ch. 4:27
11 [v]ch. 3:20
12 [w][Gen. 3:4] [x][ch. 14:13; Isa. 28:15]
14 [y][ch. 1:9, 10] [z][Obad. 18; Zech. 12:6; Rev. 11:5]
15 [a]ch. 34:21, 22; Deut. 28:49; [ch. 1:15; Amos 6:14] [b]Isa. 33:19
16 [c]See Isa. 5:28 [d]Ps. 5:9
17 [e]Lev. 26:16; Deut. 28:31, 33, 51 [f][Hos. 8:14]
18 [u][See ver. 10 above]
19 [g]ch. 13:22; 16:10, 11; 22:8, 9; Deut. 29:24, 25; 1 Kgs. 9:8, 9

5:8 Religious infidelity leads to marital infidelity (see note on 2:34). The men have no more control than **lusty stallions**.

5:9 Two more rhetorical questions follow those in vv. 3 and 7. Punishment and retribution await the adulterers.

5:10–11 God will **strip . . . Israel** and **Judah** like one strips a vineyard of fruit. Nonetheless, God will not make a **full end** at this time (4:27; 5:18). He will preserve a remnant for a new covenant (31:31–34).

5:12–13 The people believe God **will do nothing** (Zeph. 1:12) because of what they hear from false **prophets**. The Hebrew for "wind" and "spirit" is the same (*ruakh*). True prophets have God's spirit (*ruakh*), but these prophets merely have **wind** (*ruakh*), for God's **word is not in them**.

5:14 God of hosts is a title often used of God when he judges (Isa. 3:1; 5:16). Jeremiah's true and rejected words become a **fire** that will **consume** the **people**, and God will use him to judge the nation (Jer. 1:9–10).

5:15 The destroyer, Babylon, was indeed **ancient** and famous, renowned for literature, religion, and determination to wage war.

5:16–17 Babylon will **eat up** everything and everyone in Judah as if it were a hungry animal (v. 6). Judah will be left without resources of any kind.

5:18–19 Israel's punishment will be for disciplinary purposes, to bring them to their senses (cf. Lev. 26:14–20) and to educate them.

19[h]Deut. 4:27, 28; 28:47, 48, 68
21[i]Deut. 32:6; Isa. 6:9 [j][Matt. 13:14]
22[k]ch. 10:7 [l]Job 26:10; 38:10, 11; Ps. 104:9 [m]ch. 51:55; [Ps. 46:3]
23[n]ch. 6:28
24[o]ch. 14:22; Deut. 11:14; Job 5:10; Ps. 147:8; Matt. 5:45 [p]Gen. 8:22
25[q]ch. 3:3
26[r][Prov. 1:11] [s]Ps. 10:9; [Ps. 124:7]
28[t]Deut. 32:15 [u][ch. 7:6; Isa. 1:23; Zech. 7:10]
29[v]See ver. 9
30[w]ch. 23:14; Hos. 6:10

say to them, 'As you have forsaken me and served foreign gods in your land, [h]so you shall serve foreigners in a land that is not yours.'"

20 Declare this in the house of Jacob;
proclaim it in Judah:
21 "Hear this, [i]O foolish and senseless people,
[j]who have eyes, but see not,
who have ears, but hear not.
22 [k]Do you not fear me? declares the LORD.
Do you not tremble before me?
I placed the sand [l]as the boundary for the sea,
a perpetual barrier that it cannot pass;
though the waves toss, they cannot prevail;
though [m]they roar, they cannot pass over it.
23 [n]But this people has a stubborn and rebellious heart;
they have turned aside and gone away.
24 They do not say in their hearts,
'Let us fear the LORD our God,
[o]who gives the rain in its season,
the autumn rain and the spring rain,
and keeps for us
[p]the weeks appointed for the harvest.'
25 [q]Your iniquities have turned these away,
and your sins have kept good from you.
26 For wicked men are found among my people;
[r]they lurk like fowlers lying in wait.[1]
[s]They set a trap;
they catch men.
27 Like a cage full of birds,
their houses are full of deceit;
therefore they have become great and rich;
28 [t]they have grown fat and sleek.
They know no bounds in deeds of evil;
[u]they judge not with justice
the cause of the fatherless, to make it prosper,
and they do not defend the rights of the needy.
29 [v]Shall I not punish them for these things?
declares the LORD,
and shall I not avenge myself
on a nation such as this?"
30 An appalling and [w]horrible thing
has happened in the land:

[1] The meaning of the Hebrew is uncertain

5:20 Jeremiah continues to address both Israel (**Jacob**) and **Judah** (cf. v. 11).

5:21 Jeremiah preaches to **foolish and senseless people** (Deut. 32:6). They refuse to **hear** the prophets or **see** what is happening around them. They harden their hearts (Ps. 95:7–8; Isa. 6:9; Matt. 13:10–17; Heb. 3:7–19).

5:22 Two more rhetorical questions (cf. vv. 3, 7, 9) reveal that Israel and Judah do not **fear** (respect, revere) or **tremble before** the Creator, who rules the **sea**.

5:23 Rather than a circumcised heart (4:4), the people have a **stubborn and rebellious heart** (5:3–5) that turns **away** from (2:4–5) God, not toward (3:11–14) him.

5:24 God provides **rain** for harvest for the faithful (Deut. 11:13–17). He is the Creator and deserves reverence (**fear**), but Israel has not feared him.

5:25 Your iniquities have turned these away refers to the rain in v. 24, which had not come. The Israelites' sin had led to a change in weather and a loss of crops, through God's judgment. **good**. The blessings that could have been theirs (see note on v. 24).

5:26–29 Wicked men grow **fat and sleek** through **deeds of evil**. The **fatherless** had no adult male in the family to protect and provide for them (see note on 7:6). The rulers did not protect their rights or the rights of the **needy** (cf. Isa. 1:16–23; Amos 2:6–7; 4:1–5). God must **punish** such oppression, just as he must punish constant spiritual and physical adultery (Jer. 5:9).

5:30–31 The **prophets** and **priests** conspire to lie and oppress, rather than to teach God's word and rule justly (1:16–19; 2:8; 5:13; 6:13; 14:14; 20:1–6). Rather than one correcting the other, they reinforce each other's sins. And rather than challenging both prophets and priests, the people also reinforce the sin: **my people love to have it so**. They crave such false

31 [x]the prophets prophesy falsely,
and the priests rule at their direction;
[y]my people love to have it so,
but what will you do when the end comes?

Impending Disaster for Jerusalem

6 1 Flee for safety, [z]O people of Benjamin,
from the midst of Jerusalem!
Blow the trumpet in [a]Tekoa,
and raise a signal on [b]Beth-haccherem,
for disaster looms [c]out of the north,
and great destruction.
2 The lovely and delicately bred I will destroy,
[d]the daughter of Zion.[1]
3 [e]Shepherds with their flocks shall come against her;
[f]they shall pitch their tents around her;
they shall pasture, each in his place.
4 [g]"Prepare war against her;
arise, and let us attack [h]at noon!
Woe to us, for the day declines,
for the shadows of evening lengthen!
5 Arise, and let us attack by night
and destroy her palaces!"
6 For thus says the LORD of hosts:
[i]"Cut down her trees;
[j]cast up a siege mound against Jerusalem.
This is the city that must be [k]punished;
there is nothing but oppression within her.
7 [l]As a well keeps its water fresh,
so she keeps fresh her evil;
[m]violence and destruction are heard within her;
sickness and wounds are ever before me.
8 Be warned, O Jerusalem,
[n]lest I turn from you in disgust,
lest I make you [o]a desolation,
an uninhabited land."
9 Thus says the LORD of hosts:
[p]"They shall glean thoroughly as a vine
the remnant of Israel;

[1] Or *I have likened the daughter of Zion to the loveliest pasture*

31 [x]ch. 6:13; 14:14, 18; 20:6; 23:21, 25; 27:10, 15; 29:9; Ezek. 13:6 [y][Mic. 2:11]

Chapter 6

1 [z][Judg. 1:21] [a]See 2 Sam. 14:2 [b]Neh. 3:14 [c]See ch. 1:14
2 [d]See 2 Kgs. 19:21
3 [e][ch. 23:1] [f]ch. 4:17
4 [g]ch. 22:7; Joel 3:9; [ch. 51:27] [h]ch. 15:8
6 [i][Deut. 20:20] [j]2 Kgs. 19:32; Isa. 37:33; Ezek. 26:8; Luke 19:43 [k]Luke 19:44
7 [l]Isa. 57:20 [m]Ps. 55:9; Ezek. 7:11, 23
8 [n]Ezek. 23:18; [Hos. 9:12] [o]See ch. 4:7
9 [p][Deut. 24:21]

teaching (cf. Mic. 2:6, 11; 2 Tim. 4:3–4; 2 Pet. 2:1–3), but it will destroy them **when the end comes** (2 Kings 17:7–23; Jer. 39:1–10).

6:1–30 *God Has Rejected His People.* Having rejected the Lord, the people now find that he has rejected them. Hundreds of years of disobedience will be addressed. Now Judah must prepare for invasion and defeat (vv. 1–8) since she has rejected God's word (vv. 9–15) and refused to walk in God's ways (vv. 16–26). Jeremiah's ministry will prove that Judah is like base metal, fit only for punishment (vv. 27–30).

6:1 Jeremiah's tribe (**Benjamin**) should **flee for safety** out of **Jerusalem**. **Disaster** comes from the **north**, yet also from **Tekoa**, about 9 miles (15 km) south of Jerusalem. **Beth-haccherem** is of uncertain location, but it probably lies southwest of Jerusalem. Thus, the city is nearly surrounded.

6:2–3 the daughter of Zion. See note on 4:31. Jerusalem takes its life from Mount Zion. If the ESV footnote on 6:2 is followed, it adds detail to the prediction of v. 3: Jerusalem is like a lovely pasture in which **shepherds** (kings) and **their flocks** (armies) will **pasture** (invade).

6:4–5 These armies are ready to **attack at noon** or even **by night**. A night attack was rare and done only when victory was certain or when surprise was necessary (see Judg. 7:19–23).

6:6 Judah's own **trees** were used to make battering rams and a **siege mound**, a ramp to the city walls. God gives the orders here, so he directly punishes the oppressive city.

6:7 Jerusalem should repent of **evil** (harmful acts; see 4:14), but she keeps her evil as **fresh** as **well** water. **violence and destruction**. Constant brutality against others. **sickness and wounds**. This results in both discipline from God (Lev. 26:23; Jer. 31:18) and violence in the land.

6:8 Without repentance from the people, God's own heart will be "out of joint" concerning Jerusalem (**I turn from you in disgust**, lit., "my soul be disjointed concerning you"; Gen. 32:25), and she will be emptied.

6:9 the remnant. Those who survive, not those who believe. **pass your hand again**. God orders (v. 6) the armies to make sure every grape (survivor) is picked (taken captive).

10 [q]Isa. 28:9; 53:1 [r][Ex. 6:12; Acts 7:51] [s]ch. 7:26 [t]ch. 20:8
11 [u]ch. 20:9 [v]ch. 9:21 [w][Lam. 2:21] [x]ch. 8:9
12 [y]For ver. 12-15, see ch. 8:10-12
13 [z][ch. 31:34; 44:12; Jonah 3:5] [a]Isa. 56:11 [b]ch. 14:18; 23:11; Mic. 3:11; See ch. 5:31
14 [c]ch. 4:10; 14:13; 23:17; Ezek. 13:10; Mic. 3:5; [John 14:27] [d]Isa. 48:22; 57:21; Ezek. 7:25
15 [e][ch. 3:3; 8:12] [f][ver. 6]
16 [g]ch. 18:15; [Isa. 8:20; Mal. 4:4; Luke 16:29] [h]Matt. 11:29; [Ps. 116:7]
17 [i]Isa. 56:10; [Isa. 21:11] [j]Isa. 58:1; [ch. 4:19] [k]ch. 44:16

like a grape gatherer pass your hand again
over its branches."
10 [q]To whom shall I speak and give warning,
that they may hear?
[r]Behold, their ears are uncircumcised,
[s]they cannot listen;
behold, [t]the word of the LORD is to them an object of scorn;
they take no pleasure in it.
11 Therefore I am full of the wrath of the LORD;
[u]I am weary of holding it in.
[v]"Pour it out upon the children in the street,
and upon the gatherings of young men, also;
[w]both husband and wife [x]shall be taken,
the elderly and the very aged.
12 [y]Their houses shall be turned over to others,
their fields and wives together,
for I will stretch out my hand
against the inhabitants of the land,"
declares the LORD.
13 [z]"For from the least to the greatest of them,
everyone [a]is greedy for unjust gain;
and from [b]prophet to priest,
everyone deals falsely.
14 They have healed the wound of my people lightly,
saying, [c]'Peace, peace,'
[d]when there is no peace.
15 [e]Were they ashamed when they committed abomination?
No, they were not at all ashamed;
they did not know how to blush.
Therefore they shall fall among those who fall;
[f]at the time that I punish them, they shall be overthrown,"
says the LORD.

16 Thus says the LORD:
"Stand by the roads, and look,
and ask for [g]the ancient paths,
where the good way is; and walk in it,
[h]and find rest for your souls.
But they said, 'We will not walk in it.'
17 [i]I set watchmen over you, saying,
'Pay attention to [j]the sound of the trumpet!'
But they said, [k]'We will not pay attention.'
18 Therefore hear, O nations,
and know, O congregation, what will happen to them.

6:10 To whom shall I speak? Every segment of society (1:15–19; 5:3–5) has rejected God's **warning**. Their hearts (4:4) and **ears are uncircumcised**, rendering them unwilling and incapable of obeying the **word of the LORD**. They made God's precious word an **object of scorn** (see note on 36:23–24), leading to God's wrath being poured out (6:11). In any age, those who scoff at God's word and **take no pleasure in it** can expect eventual judgment from God.

6:11 God orders (vv. 6, 9) Jeremiah to pour out words of **wrath**, not warning, as before, so that all ages experience judgment.

6:12 houses . . . fields . . . wives. Spoils of war taken by victors.

6:13–15 Greed always leads to seeking **unjust gain**. **prophet . . . priest**. These religious leaders are as greedy as the people, so they promise **peace** (not the punishment of war) because their audiences wish for such reassurances (cf. 5:30–31). They feel no shame over their **abomination** (i.e., spiritual perversion; Lev. 18:27; 20:13). They must **fall** when the city falls.

6:16 the ancient paths. The way of faithfulness revealed to Moses and the earlier prophets. **the good way**. The proper life of faith-driven obedience. **walk**. A metaphor for patterned living (cf. Ps. 1:1). **We will not walk** describes strong rebellion against revealed truth.

6:17 watchmen. Moses and the prophets (2 Kings 17:7–18). **trumpet**. Blown to warn cities of danger (Jer. 4:5, 19, 21; 6:1). Here it refers to God's word of warning.

6:18–19 The **nations**, **congregation**, and **earth** are all called to **hear** God's testimony against **this people** (Judah and Israel). The crime is rejecting God's **words** from true prophets and his **law** (Hb. *torah*) given through Moses.

19 Hear, O earth; behold, I am bringing disaster upon this people,
[l]the fruit of their devices,
because they have not paid attention to my words;
and as for my law, they have rejected it.
20 [m]What use to me is [n]frankincense that comes from [o]Sheba,
or sweet cane from a distant land?
[p]Your burnt offerings are not acceptable,
nor your sacrifices pleasing to me.
21 Therefore thus says the LORD:
[q]'Behold, I will lay before this people
stumbling blocks against which they shall stumble;
fathers and sons together,
neighbor and friend shall perish.'"

22 Thus says the LORD:
[r]"Behold, a people is coming [s]from the north country,
a great nation is stirring from [t]the farthest parts of the earth.
23 They lay hold on bow and javelin;
they are [u]cruel and have no mercy;
[v]the sound of them is like the roaring sea;
they ride on horses,
set in array as a man for battle,
against you, O daughter of Zion!"
24 We have heard the report of it;
[w]our hands fall helpless;
anguish has taken hold of us,
[x]pain as of a woman in labor.
25 Go not out into the field,
nor walk on the road,
for the enemy has a sword;
[y]terror is on every side.
26 O daughter of my people, [z]put on sackcloth,
and [a]roll in ashes;
[b]make mourning as for an only son,
most bitter lamentation,
for suddenly the destroyer
will come upon us.

27 "I have made you [c]a tester of metals among my people,
that you may know and [d]test their ways.
28 [e]They are all stubbornly rebellious,
[f]going about with slanders;
they are [g]bronze and iron;
all of them act corruptly.

19[l]Prov. 1:31
20[m]Isa. 1:11 [n]Isa. 43:23; 60:6 [o]See 1 Kgs. 10:1 [p]ch. 7:21, 22; 14:12; Ps. 40:6; Isa. 1:11; Amos 5:21
21[q]Ezek. 3:20
22[r]For ver. 22-24, see ch. 50:41-43 [s]See ch. 1:13 [t]ch. 25:32; 31:8
23[u]Isa. 13:9, 18 [v]Isa. 17:12
24[w]ch. 38:4; 49:24; Ezek. 21:7; See 2 Sam. 4:1; Ezek. 7:17 [x]See Isa. 13:8
25[y]Ps. 31:13; Lam. 2:22; [Job 18:11]
26[z]See ch. 4:8; Esth. 4:1 [a]ch. 25:34; Ezek. 27:30; [Lam. 3:16; Mic. 1:10] [b]Amos 8:10; Zech. 12:10
27[c][ch. 1:18] [d]ch. 9:7
28[e]ch. 5:23 [f]ch. 9:4; [Lev. 19:16] [g]Ezek. 22:18, 20

6:20 Ritual without faith-induced obedience is unacceptable to God (Isa. 1:10–19; Amos 5:21–24; Mic. 6:6–8). **frankincense**. A fragrant white gum resin used to make incense for the temple (Ex. 30:34–38). **Sheba**. A country in faraway southwest Arabia famous for spices (Ezek. 27:22). **sweet cane**. Imported from India to make holy oil (Ex. 30:23). **burnt offerings . . . sacrifices**. Regular animal offerings in the temple.

6:21 stumbling blocks. These were obstacles such as invasion and famine that God sends to hamper all levels of society.

6:22–23 great nation. Babylon. **the farthest parts of the earth**. Babylon's army had outposts all over the ancient world. This army has **no mercy**; its **horses** are so numerous that their thundering hoofs sound **like the roaring sea** (4:13, 29).

6:24 Panic over the invading army will lead to physical helplessness like that of a **woman in labor** (Isa. 13:8; Mic. 4:9–10).

6:25 Jerusalemites dare not leave the city for fear of capture (Lam. 4:18–19). **terror is on every side**. A common phrase in Jeremiah depicting the experience of invasion (Jer. 20:3, 10; 46:5; 49:29; Lam. 2:22).

6:26 daughter. Jerusalem as representative of the whole nation (cf. 4:31). **sackcloth . . . ashes**. The dress of mourning, representing the pain of life and the fact of death respectively. **as for an only son**. Reflects mourning for a unique and irreplaceable person (cf. Amos 8:10).

6:27–29 tester of metals. Jeremiah's task is to assess how much dross (i.e., impurity) remains in a people called to be pure. Their rebellion marks them as **bronze and iron** rather than as pure silver (for the image, see Ezek. 22:18–22; similarly, Ps. 119:119; Isa. 1:22, 25). The ancient refining process used heated lead to draw out ore from silver. Despite Jeremiah's words being like a **bellows** and like **lead** used to purify silver, all is **in vain**, for the dross (the **wicked**) remains in the metal (the land).

29 [g][See ver. 28 above] [h][Isa. 1:25]
30 [i]Isa. 1:22; Ezek. 22:19, 20

Chapter 7

2 [j]ch. 26:2
3 [k]ch. 18:11; 26:13
4 [l][ver. 8]
5 [m]ch. 22:3 [n]Deut. 24:14
6 [n][See ver. 5 above] [m][See ver. 5 above] [o]ch. 13:10; 25:6; Deut. 6:14
7 [p]Deut. 4:40 [q]ch. 3:18
9 [r]Hos. 4:1, 2 [s]ch. 5:2 [t]ch. 1:16 [o][See ver. 6 above]
10 [u]ch. 32:34; 34:15
11 [v]Isa. 56:7 [u][See ver. 10 above] [w]Cited Matt. 21:13; Mark 11:17; Luke 19:46; [Ezek. 7:22]
12 [x]Judg. 18:31; 1 Sam. 1:3 [y]Deut. 12:11 [z]ch. 26:6; Ps. 78:60; See 1 Sam. 4:3-12
13 [a]ver. 25; 2 Chr. 36:15 [b]Prov. 1:24; [ver. 27; Isa. 50:2; 65:12]
14 [c]Deut. 12:5; 1 Kgs. 9:7 [u][See ver. 10 above] [z][See ver. 12 above]
15 [c][See ver. 14 above] [d]2 Kgs. 17:6, 23 [e]Ps. 78:67; Hos. 4:17; 5:3, 9; 6:4; 12:1
16 [f]ch. 11:14; 14:11; [Ex. 32:10; Deut. 9:14; 1 John 5:16]

29 The [g]bellows blow fiercely;
the lead is consumed by the fire;
[h]in vain the refining goes on,
for the wicked are not removed.
30 [i]Rejected silver they are called,
for the LORD has rejected them.”

Evil in the Land

7 The word that came to Jeremiah from the LORD: **2** [j]“Stand in the gate of the LORD’s
house, and proclaim there this word, and say, Hear the word of the LORD, all you men
of Judah who enter these gates to worship the LORD. **3** Thus says the LORD of hosts, the
God of Israel: [k]Amend your ways and your deeds, and I will let you dwell in this place.
4 [l]Do not trust in these deceptive words: ‘This is the temple of the LORD, the temple of the
LORD, the temple of the LORD.’
5 “For if you truly [m]amend your ways and your deeds, if you truly [n]execute justice one
with another, **6** if you [n]do not oppress the sojourner, the fatherless, or the widow, [m]or shed
innocent blood in this place, [o]and if you do not go after other gods to your own harm, **7** [p]then
I will let you dwell in this place, [q]in the land that I gave of old to your fathers forever.
8 “Behold, you trust in deceptive words to no avail. **9** [r]Will you steal, murder, commit
adultery, [s]swear falsely, [t]make offerings to Baal, [o]and go after other gods that you have
not known, **10** and then come and stand before me in this house, [u]which is called by my
name, and say, ‘We are delivered!’—only to go on doing all these abominations? **11** [v]Has
this house, [u]which is called by my name, [w]become a den of robbers in your eyes? Behold,
I myself have seen it, declares the LORD. **12** Go now to [x]my place that was in Shiloh, [y]where
I made my name dwell at first, and [z]see what I did to it because of the evil of my people
Israel. **13** And now, because you have done all these things, declares the LORD, and [a]when
I spoke to you persistently you did not listen, and [b]when I called you, you did not answer,
14 therefore I will do to [c]the house [u]that is called by my name, and in which you trust, and
to the place that I gave to you and to your fathers, [z]as I did to Shiloh. **15** [c]And I will cast you
out of my sight, [d]as I cast out all your kinsmen, all the offspring of [e]Ephraim.
16 “As for you, [f]do not pray for this people, or lift up a cry or prayer for them, and do not

6:30 The nation is impure, **rejected silver**. God’s word through the prophets and the law has not purified the people, so God rejects them.

7:1–10:25 *False Religion and an Idolatrous People.* These chapters give evidence of the truth of God’s accusations in chs. 2–6. Judah takes comfort in the temple while breaking God’s commands (7:1–8:3), rejecting the Torah (covenantal instruction, 8:4–17), living deceitfully (8:18–9:9), grieving the prophet (9:10–26), and engaging in idolatry (10:1–16). Exile awaits this rebellious community (10:17–25).

7:1–8:3 *Judah’s Improper Reliance on the Temple.* The existence of a temple does not guarantee God’s approval. Repentance must occur, or the temple will become like the sanctuary at Shiloh. Currently the people trust in the temple (7:1–7), offer corrupt worship (7:8–11), and act in a way that will lead to the temple’s destruction (7:12–15). God will no longer heed intercessory prayer for Judah (7:16–20), for mere external observances do not impress him (7:21–26). Judgment will put an end to Judah’s sins (7:27–8:3).

7:1–2 Jeremiah takes God’s message to the temple-going public. This sermon is undated, but may have been during Jehoiakim’s reign (609–598 B.C.; see notes on 1:3; 26:1).

7:3 Though the Israelites come to worship (v. 2), they must **amend** (lit., “make good”) their patterns of life. Such change is necessary if they are to **dwell in this place**, the Promised Land.

7:4 deceptive words. Either taught by false prophets or derived from a misunderstanding of Scripture. **temple of the LORD**. Apparently the Israelites either believed the temple would never be destroyed or thought swearing by the temple kept them safe.

7:5 The true (not deceptive) word was that Israel should **amend** oppressive **deeds** by executing **justice** (right and fair decisions).

7:6 sojourner. A resident alien living in Judah. **fatherless**. Either through death, desertion, or irresponsible sexual acts. **widow**. Either through death or desertion. These three groups lack social protection and are thus afforded special care (Deut. 16:11, 14; 24:19–21). **shed innocent blood**. For gain or revenge (Jer. 2:34; 26:20–24). **your own harm**. Such actions bring disaster on their perpetrators.

7:7 let you dwell . . . in the land. Obedience (Deut. 4:4) and repentance (Deut. 30:1–10) are essential prerequisites for a long tenure in the Promised Land. Loss of the land is possible (Deut. 28:64–68).

7:9–10 Judah has broken the Ten Commandments (Ex. 20:1–17) and has not repented. **called by my name**. See 1 Kings 8:41–43; 2 Chron. 6:33. **delivered**. Forgiven because of the completed ritual. **go on doing**. The people feel justified in sinning, as they did before they came to “worship.”

7:11 den of robbers. Jesus combined this passage with Isa. 56:7 (see Matt. 21:13 par.) to highlight the temple’s defilement. Here God declares the false worshipers to be violent thieves preying on others (cf. Isa. 7:5–9).

7:12–14 Shiloh. This was the central sanctuary (about 19 miles [31 km] north of Jerusalem) prior to the monarchy (Judg. 21:19; 1 Sam. 1:3). **because of the evil of my people**. Constant sin caused God to shut down this old site. What happened to Shiloh will happen to Jerusalem. Apparently after the battle of 1 Sam. 4:2–11, the Philistines overran Shiloh itself (cf. Ps. 78:60–64). Judah’s **trust** in a physical site is misplaced.

7:15 cast you out. To foreign lands (Deut. 28:64–68). **Ephraim** is another name for Israel, the northern kingdom, and also the area where Shiloh was located.

7:16 do not pray . . . do not intercede. This is an unusual command for a dire situation. After many warnings, God has made the decision to punish, and he will **not hear** (respond to) further pleas from Jeremiah. This is a decisive turn; previously (e.g., Ex. 32:10–14), God would accept intercession.

intercede with me, for I will not hear you. 17 Do you not see what they are doing in the
cities of Judah and in the streets of Jerusalem? 18 The children gather wood, the fathers
kindle fire, [g]and the women knead dough, to [h]make cakes for [i]the queen of heaven. And
[j]they pour out drink offerings to other gods, [k]to provoke me to anger. 19 [l]Is it I whom they
provoke? declares the LORD. Is it not themselves, [m]to their own shame? 20 Therefore thus
says the Lord GOD: Behold, [n]my anger and my wrath will be poured out on this place,
upon man and beast, upon the trees of the field and the fruit of the ground; [o]it will burn
and not be quenched."

21 Thus says the LORD of hosts, the God of Israel: [p]"Add your burnt offerings to your
sacrifices, and eat the flesh. 22 For in the day that I brought them out of the land of Egypt, I
did not speak to your fathers or command them [q]concerning burnt offerings and sacrifices.
23 But this command I gave them: [r]'Obey my voice, and [s]I will be your God, and you shall
be my people. [t]And walk in all the way that I command you, [u]that it may be well with you.'
24 [v]But they did not obey or incline their ear, [w]but walked in their own counsels and [x]the
stubbornness of their evil hearts, and [y]went backward and not forward. 25 From the day
that your fathers came out of the land of Egypt to this day, [z]I have persistently sent all
my servants the prophets to them, day after day. 26 [v]Yet they did not listen to me or incline
their ear, [a]but stiffened their neck. [b]They did worse than their fathers.

27 [c]"So you shall speak all these words to them, but they will not listen to you. [d]You shall
call to them, but they will not answer you. 28 And you shall say to them, 'This is the nation
that did not obey the voice of the LORD their God, and did not accept discipline; [e]truth
has perished; it is cut off from their lips.

29 [f]"'Cut off your hair and cast it away;
raise a lamentation on [g]the bare heights,
for the LORD has rejected and forsaken
the generation of his wrath.'

The Valley of Slaughter

30 "For the sons of Judah have done evil in my sight, declares the LORD. They have set
[h]their detestable things in the house [i]that is called by my name, to [h]defile it. 31 And they
have built the high places of [j]Topheth, which is in [k]the Valley of the Son of Hinnom, [l]to
burn their sons and their daughters in the fire, [m]which I did not command, nor did it
come into my mind. 32 [n]Therefore, behold, the days are coming, declares the LORD, when
it will no more be called [j]Topheth, or [k]the Valley of the Son of Hinnom, but the Valley of
Slaughter; [o]for they will bury in Topheth, because there is no room elsewhere. 33 [p]And the

18 [g]Hos. 7:4 [h]ch. 44:17, 19 [i][2 Kgs. 23:13] [j]ch. 19:13 [k]ch. 11:17; Deut. 32:16, 21; 1 Kgs. 14:9; 16:2; 2 Chr. 34:25
19 [l][Job 35:6] [m]ch. 51:51
20 [n]ch. 42:18; 44:6; 2 Chr. 34:25; Lam. 4:11 [o]ch. 17:27
21 [p]See ch. 6:20
22 [q]Hos. 6:6
23 [r]ch. 11:4, 7; Ex. 15:26; Deut. 6:3 [s]Lev. 26:12 [t]Deut. 5:33 [u]ch. 42:6; Deut. 4:40
24 [v]Ps. 81:11 [w]Ps. 81:12 [x][ch. 3:17; Hos. 4:16] [y]ch. 2:19, 27; 8:5; 15:6; 32:33
25 [z]2 Chr. 36:15, 16
26 [v][See ver. 24 above] [a]2 Chr. 30:8 [b]ch. 16:12
27 [c]ch. 1:17 [d][ver. 13]
28 [e]ch. 9:3
29 [f][Job 1:20] [g]See ch. 3:2
30 [h]ch. 32:34; Ezek. 5:11; 7:20; [ch. 19:5; 2 Kgs. 21:4, 7] [i]See ver. 10
31 [j]2 Kgs. 23:10 [k][ch. 31:40; Josh. 18:16] [l]Ps. 106:38 [m]Deut. 17:3; [ver. 21, 22]
32 [n]ch. 19:6 [j][See ver. 31 above] [k][See ver. 31 above] [o]ch. 19:11; [Ezek. 6:5]
33 [p]ch. 12:9; 16:4; 19:7; 34:20; Deut. 28:26; Ps. 79:2

7:18 Whole families work together to worship the **queen of heaven**, an astral deity named Astarte, whom the Assyrians and Babylonians believed aided fertility. She was popular in Judah for many years (2 Kings 23:4–14; Zeph. 1:5). **drink offerings**. Fluids poured out to show devotion to God (Num. 28:7) or other gods.

7:19 their own shame. See 3:25; 17:18.

7:20 God's **anger** and **wrath** (42:18; 44:6) will spill over from the city into the countryside. His anger will **not be quenched** until it achieves its purpose (17:27).

7:21 Burnt offerings were to be consumed by fire, but parts of some **sacrifices** could be eaten. Useless sacrifices cause God to treat the people all alike—with judgment.

7:22–23 Acceptable sacrifices are based on a right relationship brought about by faith in the God who delivers (Ex. 19:3–8; 20:1–2). Only those who believe will **obey**; only those who **walk in all** God's ways because of their faith can be God's people.

7:24 The Israelites **did not obey** because of the **stubbornness of their evil hearts** (3:17; 5:23). Only a new heart can repair their relationship with God (3:10; 4:3–4, 14).

7:25–26 Starting with Moses (Deut. 34:10–12), God sent his **servants the prophets** to instruct, exhort, and warn Israel. With few exceptions (e.g., Josh. 24:31), each generation **did worse than their fathers**.

7:28 not accept discipline. This refers to the Israelites' refusal to accept previous hardships as evidence that they needed to repent (2:30). **Truth** (honesty, 5:1) has been amputated from their mouths (9:2–4).

7:29 Cut off your hair. A symbol of mourning (Job 1:20; Mic. 1:16), this may also refer to a Nazirite vow (Num. 6:2–8). If so, the phrase may underscore again the end of false worship. **raise a lamentation**. A funeral dirge. **bare heights**. Where the Judeans worshiped idols (Jer. 3:2, 21). **the generation of his wrath**. The generation that experienced loss of the Promised Land.

7:30 detestable things. Images of false gods (4:1).

7:31 high places of Topheth . . . Hinnom. See 2 Kings 23:10; Isa. 30:33; Jer. 19:6–14. Children were burned alive at these places as sacrifices to Molech and other gods, even though human sacrifice was banned in the law (Lev. 18:21; 20:2–5). God hated such a practice; hence he **did not command** it, **nor did it come into** his **mind**. (This last expression does not mean that God was unaware of it or that he did not know it was going to happen, but that he did not have the slightest thought of approving such a horrible practice.) Child sacrifice was known from Canaanite/Phoenician contexts. The offering of children, especially firstborn, to the gods was seen as a means of manipulating deities to grant fertility to the offerer. Archaeological excavations at Carthage, a Phoenician colony founded in the eighth century B.C., include the charred remains of thousands of child sacrifices.

7:32 When Babylon conquers Jerusalem, the dead bodies will be heaped so high that the valley will be renamed the **Valley of Slaughter** (19:1–9).

7:33 food for the birds. See Deut. 28:26. This punishment will occur

33 [q][Isa. 17:2]
34 [r]ch. 16:9; 25:10; Ps. 78:63; Isa. 24:7, 8; Rev. 18:22, 23; [Ezek. 26:13; Hos. 2:11] [s]ch. 27:17; 44:2, 6; Lev. 26:31, 33

Chapter 8

2 [t]Deut. 4:19; 2 Kgs. 21:3; 23:5; [Job 31:26-28; Ezek. 8:16] [u][Job 27:19] [v]ch. 9:22; 16:4; 25:33
3 [w][Job 3:21, 22; 7:15, 16; Rev. 9:6] [x]ch. 23:3, 8; 29:14, 18; 32:37; Dan. 9:7
4 [y][Rom. 11:11]
5 [z]See ch. 7:24 [a]See ch. 2:19 [b]ch. 9:6
6 [c][2 Pet. 3:9] [d]See Job 39:19-25
7 [e]Song 2:12 [f]Isa. 38:14 [g][ch. 5:4, 5; Isa. 1:3]
8 [h][Rom. 2:17, 18]
9 [i][1 Cor. 1:19, 20] [j]Job 5:13
10 [k]For ver. 10-12, see ch. 6:12-15

dead bodies of this people will be food for the birds of the air, and for the beasts of the
earth, [q]and none will frighten them away. 34 [r]And I will silence in the cities of Judah and
in the streets of Jerusalem the voice of mirth and the voice of gladness, the voice of the
bridegroom and the voice of the bride, [s]for the land shall become a waste.

8 "At that time, declares the LORD, the bones of the kings of Judah, the bones of its officials,
the bones of the priests, the bones of the prophets, and the bones of the inhabitants
of Jerusalem shall be brought out of their tombs. 2 And they shall be spread [t]before the
sun and the moon and all the host of heaven, which they have loved and served, which
they have gone after, and which they have sought and worshiped. [u]And they shall not be
gathered or buried. [v]They shall be as dung on the surface of the ground. 3 [w]Death shall be
preferred to life by all the remnant that remains of this evil family [x]in all the places where
I have driven them, declares the LORD of hosts.

Sin and Treachery

4 "You shall say to them, Thus says the LORD:
[y]When men fall, do they not rise again?
If one turns away, does he not return?
5 Why then has this people [z]turned away
in perpetual [a]backsliding?
[b]They hold fast to deceit;
they refuse to return.
6 [c]I have paid attention and listened,
but they have not spoken rightly;
no man relents of his evil,
saying, 'What have I done?'
Everyone turns to his own course,
[d]like a horse plunging headlong into battle.
7 Even the stork in the heavens
knows her times,
and [e]the turtledove, [f]swallow, and crane[1]
keep the time of their coming,
[g]but my people know not
the rules[2] of the LORD.
8 [h]"How can you say, 'We are wise,
and the law of the LORD is with us'?
But behold, the lying pen of the scribes
has made it into a lie.
9 [i]The wise men shall be put to shame;
they shall be dismayed [j]and taken;
behold, they have rejected the word of the LORD,
so what wisdom is in them?
10 [k]Therefore I will give their wives to others
and their fields to conquerors,

[1] The meaning of the Hebrew word is uncertain [2] Or *just decrees*

due to covenant disobedience. **Dead bodies** should be buried, not left to scavengers.

7:34 I will silence . . . the voice of the bridegroom. Normal joy will cease, so weddings will cease (16:9; 25:10). The **land shall become a waste**—another consequence of covenantal disobedience (Lev. 26:31, 33).

8:1–2 Removing **bones** from a grave was a great insult (2 Kings 23:16–18) and was often done by victorious invaders (Amos 2:1). Ironically, these bones will be placed in full view of the very parts of creation that Judah **worshiped** when venerating astral deities (Jer. 7:17–19).

8:3 Death shall be preferred to life. Cf. Deut. 28:64–68.

8:4–17 *Judah Rejects God's Torah.* The roots of Judah's sin are in bad hearts and rejection of God's word.

8:4–5 Normally people get up after they **fall** and **return** after they walk away. Judah has entered into **perpetual backsliding** through a refusal **to return** (repent).

8:6 paid attention. God has patiently waited and listened carefully for words of repentance, to no avail. **relents**. Regrets and thus changes.

8:8 The Judeans possess God's **law**, just as they possess the temple. But their **scribes**, the professional copiers and teachers of the Scriptures, have altered God's word to fit their own desires. Thus, they have **made it into a lie**.

8:9 These so-called **wise men** will **be put to shame** (2:26; 6:15) because of their changing of God's word. Rejecting God's **word** proves they are really unwise.

8:10 When **prophet** and **priest** deal **falsely** with God's word, the nation becomes **greedy for unjust gain**, and enemies take their **wives** and **fields**.

because from the least to the greatest
everyone [l]is greedy for unjust gain;
from prophet to priest,
everyone deals falsely.
11 They have healed [m]the wound of my people lightly,
saying, 'Peace, peace,'
when there is no peace.
12 Were they ashamed when they committed abomination?
No, [n]they were not at all ashamed;
they did not know how to blush.
[o]Therefore they shall fall among the fallen;
when I punish them, they shall be overthrown,
says the LORD.
13 When I would gather them, declares the LORD,
there are [q]no grapes on the vine,
[r]nor figs on the fig tree;
[s]even the leaves are withered,
and what I gave them has passed away from them."[1]
14 Why do we sit still?
[t]Gather together; [t]let us go into the fortified cities
and perish there,
for the LORD our God has doomed us to perish
and has [u]given us [v]poisoned water to drink,
because we have sinned against the LORD.
15 [w]We looked for peace, but no good came;
for a time of healing, but behold, terror.
16 [x]"The snorting of their horses is heard [y]from Dan;
at the sound of the neighing [z]of their stallions
[a]the whole land quakes.
They come [b]and devour the land and all that fills it,
the city and those who dwell in it.
17 For behold, I am sending among you [c]serpents,
adders [d]that cannot be charmed,
[e]and they shall bite you,"
declares the LORD.

Jeremiah Grieves for His People

18 My joy is gone; grief is upon me;[2]
[f]my heart is sick within me.
19 Behold, the cry of the daughter of my people

[1] The meaning of the Hebrew is uncertain [2] Compare Septuagint; the meaning of the Hebrew is uncertain

10 [l][Isa. 56:11]
11 [m]ver. 21
12 [n]See ch. 3:3 [o][Hos. 4:5]
13 [q]Isa. 5:1, 2; Joel 1:7 [r][Matt. 21:19; Luke 13:6] [s]Isa. 1:30
14 [t]ch. 4:5 [u]ch. 9:15; 23:15; Lam. 3:15, 19; Amos 6:12; [Rev. 8:11] [v]ch. 23:15; Deut. 29:18
15 [w]ch. 14:19; Job 30:26
16 [x]Job 39:20 [y]ch. 4:15 [z]Judg. 5:22 [a]ch. 49:21; 51:29; Ps. 60:2 [b]ch. 10:25; 47:2
17 [c][Lev. 26:22] [d]Ps. 58:4, 5; [Eccles. 10:11] [e]Num. 21:6
18 [f]Isa. 1:5; Lam. 1:13, 22; 5:17

8:11 Peace, peace. See 6:12–15. The wicked prophets and priests are like incompetent doctors who tell a patient he or she is healthy when in fact the patient is desperately sick (17:9). Contrast Isa. 57:18–21.

8:12 they committed abomination. Prophets and priests engaged in idolatry (6:12–15).

8:13 God finds no good "fruit" in Judah, so the people will be "picked" by Babylon (5:10, 17; 6:9).

8:14 The people give lip service to having **sinned against the LORD** when the Babylonian invasion drives them **into the fortified cities** (4:5). Ultimately, they claim **God has doomed** them **to perish** no matter what they do.

8:15 Israel **looked for peace**, but only the peace offered by false teachers (v. 11). Such **healing** brings only **terror**.

8:16–17 Babylon's **horses** are so numerous and powerful (4:13; 6:23) that the **whole land quakes**. Its soldiers are like **serpents** (Num. 21:6–9) that resist charming (Ps. 58:4–5).

8:18–9:9 *Judah Lives Deceitfully.* Jeremiah mourns over his people (8:18–22) because they are deceitful and thus self-appointed for judgment by Judah's righteous God (9:1–9).

8:18–22 In these verses, the people's complaint is followed by God's response and then by another complaint (vv. 19b–20), with Jeremiah's own distress over what Judah faces serving as literary bookends to the section (vv. 18, 21–22; cf. 4:19–21). In the interchange between Judah and God, the Judeans assert that God has deserted them, but God notes their ongoing veneration of idols; they reply that they **are not saved** (and readers must infer that this is because they are not faithful). Jeremiah is **wounded** because of his people's wounds, or sins (8:11). This prophet cares deeply for his hearers. Their **health** has **not been restored** (v. 22) because they have consulted the wrong physicians (vv. 11–12). They prefer false prophets to God's written and revealed word.

from [g]the length and breadth of the land:
"Is the LORD not in Zion?
[h]Is her King not in her?"
[i]"Why have they provoked me to anger with their carved images
and with their foreign idols?"
20 "The harvest is past, the summer is ended,
and we are not saved."
21 For the wound of [j]the daughter of my people is my heart wounded;
[k]I mourn, and dismay has taken hold on me.

22 Is there no [l]balm in Gilead?
Is there no physician there?
Why then has the health of the daughter of my people
not been restored?

9[1] 1 [m]Oh that my head were waters,
and my eyes a fountain of tears,
that I might weep day and night
for the slain of [j]the daughter of my people!
2[2] Oh that I had in the desert
a travelers' lodging place,
that I might leave my people
and go away from them!
For they are all [n]adulterers,
a company of [o]treacherous men.
3 [p]They bend their tongue like a bow;
falsehood and not truth has grown strong[3] in the land;
for they proceed from evil to evil,
[q]and they do not know me, declares the LORD.
4 [r]Let everyone beware of his neighbor,
and put no trust in any brother,
for every [s]brother is a deceiver,
and every neighbor [t]goes about as a slanderer.
5 Everyone deceives his neighbor,
and no one speaks the truth;
they have taught their tongue to speak lies;
they weary themselves committing iniquity.
6 Heaping oppression upon oppression, and deceit upon deceit,
[u]they refuse to know me, declares the LORD.
7 Therefore thus says the LORD of hosts:
"Behold, [v]I will refine them and [w]test them,
for what else can I do, [j]because of my people?
8 [x]Their tongue is a deadly arrow;
[y]it speaks deceitfully;

19 [g]Isa. 39:3 [h]Isa. 33:17 [i]Deut. 32:21
21 [j]ver. 11; ch. 14:17 [k]Job 30:30; Lam. 4:8; Joel 2:6; Nah. 2:10
22 [l]ch. 46:11; [Gen. 37:25]
Chapter 9
1 [m]See ch. 13:17 [j][See ch. 8:21 above]
2 [n]ch. 5:7, 8; 23:10; Hos. 7:4 [o]Isa. 21:2
3 [p][Ps. 64:3] [q][Judg. 2:10; Hos. 4:1]
4 [r]ch. 12:6; Ps. 41:9; Mic. 7:5 [s][Gen. 27:36] [t]ch. 6:28; [Lev. 19:16]
6 [u]ch. 8:5
7 [v]Isa. 1:25 [w]ch. 6:27 [j][See ch. 8:21 above]
8 [x][Ps. 57:4] [y][Ps. 12:2; 120:3]

[1] Ch 8:23 in Hebrew [2] Ch 9:1 in Hebrew [3] Septuagint; Hebrew *and not for truth they have grown strong*

9:1 Jeremiah is often called the "weeping prophet" based on this verse, but this nickname does not do justice to his preaching messages of repentance and judgment. He cares for Judah, but he does much more than **weep**.

9:2 Despite his compassion, Jeremiah understands **they are all adulterers** and **treacherous men**. They swear covenant fidelity and then sin against God and neighbor. He wishes to flee from them.

9:3 tongue like a bow. The Israelites use their tongues as weapons (vv. 5, 8). Their speech conveys their character. They **proceed** into ever greater victories in doing **evil**. **not know me**. They have no saving knowledge of God, which is a reproach for any of his people, who should in fact know him in this way (2:8; 4:22; 5:4; 8:7; 10:25; cf. Judg. 2:10; 1 Sam. 2:12; 3:7; Isa. 1:3; Hos. 4:1, 6; 5:4; John 1:10; 8:55; 14:17; 15:21; 16:3; 17:25; 1 John 2:3; 3:6; 4:8).

9:4–6 Everyone deceives his neighbor, and no one speaks the truth. Deceit and slander dominate the Israelites' speech, so no one should trust friend or neighbor. Again, they refuse to know God and his will (v. 3). When God's own people turn away from him, and thus from his standards of truth, their everyday speech is increasingly filled with **lies**.

9:7 refine . . . and test. See 6:27–30. The Israelites leave a just, patient God with little recourse but to punish. He will purge them of their sin.

9:8 The Israelites deceive their **neighbor** by speaking **peace** (8:11, 15) while plotting evil in their hearts.

with his mouth [z]each speaks peace to his neighbor,
but in his heart [a]he plans an ambush for him.
9 [b]Shall I not punish them for these things? declares the LORD,
and shall I not avenge myself
on a nation such as this?

10 "I will take up weeping and wailing for the mountains,
and a lamentation for [c]the pastures of the wilderness,
[d]because they are laid waste so that no one passes through,
and the lowing of cattle is not heard;
[e]both the birds of the air and the beasts
have fled and are gone.
11 [f]I will make Jerusalem a heap of ruins,
[g]a lair of jackals,
[h]and I will make the cities of Judah a desolation,
without inhabitant."

12 [i]Who is the man so wise that he can understand this? To whom has the mouth of the
LORD spoken, that he may declare it? Why is the land ruined [j]and laid waste like a wilderness, so that no one passes through? 13 And the LORD says: [k]"Because they have forsaken
my law that I set before them, and have not obeyed my voice or walked in accord with it,
14 but [l]have stubbornly followed their own hearts and have gone after the Baals, as their
fathers taught them. 15 Therefore thus says the LORD of hosts, the God of Israel: [m]Behold,
I will feed this people with bitter food, and give them [n]poisonous water to drink. 16 [o]I will
scatter them among the nations [p]whom neither they nor their fathers have known, and I
will [q]send the sword after them, until I have consumed them."

17 Thus says the LORD of hosts:
[r]"Consider, and call for the mourning women to come;
send for the skillful women to come;
18 let them make haste [s]and raise a wailing over us,
[t]that our eyes may run down with tears
and our eyelids flow with water.
19 For a sound of wailing is heard from Zion:
[u]'How we are ruined!
We are utterly shamed,
because we have left the land,
because they have cast down our dwellings.'"
20 Hear, O women, the word of the LORD,
and let your ear receive the word of his mouth;
teach to your daughters a lament,
and each to her neighbor a dirge.
21 For death has come up into our windows;
it has entered our palaces,
[v]cutting off the children from the streets

8 [z]Ps. 28:3 [a]Hos. 7:6
9 [b]ch. 5:9, 29
10 [c]ch. 12:4; Ps. 65:12 [d]ver. 12 [e]ch. 4:25
11 [f]Isa. 25:2 [g]ch. 10:22; 49:33; 51:37 [h]ch. 34:22; 44:6
12 [i]ch. 23:18; Ps. 107:43; Hos. 14:9 [j]ver. 10
13 [k][Ps. 89:30-32]
14 [l]See ch. 3:17
15 [m]Deut. 29:18; [Ps. 80:5] [n]See ch. 8:14
16 [o]Lev. 26:33; Deut. 28:64 [p]ch. 15:14 [q]ch. 14:12; [ch. 49:37; Ezek. 5:2, 12]
17 [r][2 Chr. 35:25]
18 [s]Amos 5:16; [Matt. 9:23; Mark 5:38] [t]ver. 1; ch. 14:17
19 [u]ch. 4:13
21 [v]ch. 6:11

9:9 Shall I not punish? See 5:9, 29.

9:10–26 *Judah Grieves Jeremiah.* Once again Jeremiah mourns Judah's future, which includes terrible devastation. This devastation will be thorough, yet just (vv. 10–22). Knowing God is all that will matter when judgment comes (vv. 23–26).

9:10–11 Ancient laments often included depictions of defeated cities becoming wastelands populated only by animals (10:22; 49:33; 51:37; Isa. 13:21–22; Lam. 5:18).

9:12 man so wise. See 4:22 and 8:8–9, where Judah's only "wisdom" is in doing evil. Here the wise man (i.e., with the proper kind of wisdom) is whoever understands why Judah will fall.

9:13–14 The wise man knows the people of Judah have forsaken God's law, followed **their own hearts**, and followed **their fathers** in worshiping Baal (cf. 2:23).

9:15 Bitter food . . . poisonous water refer to both bitter hearts that prefer disobedience (Deut. 29:18; Heb. 12:12–17) and bitter experiences related to defeat (Lam. 3:15, 19).

9:16 scatter them. See Deut. 28:64–68.

9:17–18 The **mourning women** are professional mourners able to chant funeral songs. They will join Jeremiah's wailing (vv. 1, 10–11).

9:19 Jerusalem also mourns, for she has lost houses and **land** (cf. 4:19–21).

9:20–22 The **women** teach others to mourn. **Death** enters homes like an assassin and cuts down **children** in the **streets** (cf. Lam. 2:21–22; 4:1–2). Unburied **bodies** lie everywhere. See note on Jer. 7:33.

and the young men from the squares.
22 Speak: "Thus declares the LORD,
[w]'The dead bodies of men shall fall
like dung upon the open field,
[x]like sheaves after the reaper,
and none shall gather them.'"

23 Thus says the LORD: [y]"Let not the wise man boast in his wisdom, let not the mighty
man boast in his might, let not the rich man boast in his riches, 24 but [z]let him who boasts
boast in this, that he understands and knows me, that I am the LORD who practices steadfast love, justice, and righteousness in the earth. [a]For in these things I delight, declares
the LORD."
25 "Behold, the days are coming, declares the LORD, when [b]I will punish all those who
are circumcised merely in the flesh— 26 [c]Egypt, Judah, Edom, the sons of Ammon, Moab,
and [d]all who dwell in the desert who cut the corners of their hair, for all these nations are
uncircumcised, and all the house of Israel are [e]uncircumcised in heart."

Idols and the Living God

10 Hear the word that the LORD speaks to you, O house of Israel. 2 Thus says the
LORD:

"Learn not the way of the nations,
nor be dismayed at the signs of the heavens
because the nations are dismayed at them,
3 [f]for the customs of the peoples are vanity.[1]
[g]A tree from the forest is cut down
and worked with an axe by the hands of a craftsman.
4 [h]They decorate it with silver and gold;
[i]they fasten it with hammer and nails
so that it cannot move.
5 Their idols[2] are like scarecrows in a cucumber field,
and [j]they cannot speak;
[k]they have to be carried,
for they cannot walk.
Do not be afraid of them,
[l]for they cannot do evil,
neither is it in them to do good."
6 [m]There is none like you, O LORD;
you are great, and your name is great in might.
7 [n]Who would not fear you, O King of the nations?
For this is your due;
for among all the wise ones of the nations
and in all their kingdoms
there is none like you.
8 [o]They are both [p]stupid and foolish;
the instruction of idols is but wood!

[1] Or *vapor*, or *mist* [2] Hebrew *They*

22 [w]See ch. 8:2 [x][Lev. 23:22; Job 5:26]
23 [y]Prov. 3:5; 21:30; Eccles. 9:11
24 [z][Ps. 34:2; 1 Cor. 1:31; 2 Cor. 10:17] [a][Mic. 6:8; 7:18]
25 [b][Isa. 24:21]
26 [c][ch. 25:19-21] [d]ch. 25:23; 49:32; [Lev. 19:27] [e]Lev. 26:41; Deut. 10:16; Ezek. 44:7; Rom. 2:28, 29; [ch. 4:4]

Chapter 10
3 [f]Isa. 44:9 [g]Isa. 40:20; 45:20
4 [h]Isa. 40:19 [i]Isa. 41:7
5 [j]Ps. 115:5; 135:16; Hab. 2:18, 19; 1 Cor. 12:2 [k]Ps. 115:7; Isa. 46:7 [l]Isa. 41:23
6 [m]ch. 49:19; Ex. 15:11; Ps. 86:8, 10
7 [n]ch. 5:22; Rev. 15:4
8 [o][Isa. 41:29; Hab. 2:18; Zech. 10:2] [p]ver. 21

9:23–24 The truly **wise man** (4:22; 8:8–9; 9:12–14) learns what God teaches; he knows why Judah will fall and is grieved and humbled by that knowledge; thus he will not **boast in his wisdom**. Knowing God means knowing his **steadfast love** (covenant faithfulness), **justice** (right judgment), and **righteousness** (right behavior, esp. in keeping his promises). See Ex. 34:6–7; Ps. 103:8; Joel 2:12–14; Jonah 3:9–4:2. Paul applied the admonition "**let him who boasts boast in** the Lord," based on this text, to the Corinthian Christians (1 Cor. 1:31; 2 Cor. 10:17).

9:25–26 In coming **days** God will punish all Jews and Gentiles who are **uncircumcised in heart** (cf. 4:3–4). Jeremiah shockingly likens unfaithful Judah to these Gentile peoples.

10:1–16 *Judah Engages in Idolatry.* Idolatry remains the chief sin that God will judge, for it cuts people off from their only true source of salvation and guidance. Judah must reject idols (vv. 1–5) since God alone is the Lord (vv. 6–10) and Creator (vv. 11–16).

10:2 Judah must not adopt the **way** (practices) **of the nations**, which includes connecting phenomena like eclipses and comets with idol worship (7:18; 8:2).

10:3–5 **Idols** are made by people, so they have no power to **speak** or act. Serving them makes no sense (Isa. 44:9–20).

10:8–9 Taking **instruction** from **idols** is foolish. **Tarshish** is symbolic of the

9 [q]Beaten silver is brought from [r]Tarshish,
and gold from [s]Uphaz.
[q]They are the work of the craftsman and of the hands of the goldsmith;
their clothing is violet and purple;
[t]they are all the work of skilled men.
10 [u]But the LORD is the true God;
[v]he is the living God and the everlasting King.
At his wrath the earth quakes,
and the nations cannot endure his indignation.

11 Thus shall you say to them: [w]"The gods who did not make the heavens and the earth
[x]shall perish from the earth and from under the heavens."[1]

12 [y]It is he who [z]made the earth by his power,
[z]who established the world by his wisdom,
and [a]by his understanding stretched out the heavens.
13 [b]When he utters his voice, there is a tumult of waters in the heavens,
[c]and he makes the mist rise from the ends of the earth.
[c]He makes lightning [d]for the rain,
[c]and he brings forth the wind [e]from his storehouses.
14 [f]Every man is stupid and without knowledge;
[g]every goldsmith is put to shame by his idols,
for his images are false,
[h]and there is no breath in them.
15 They are worthless, a work of delusion;
at the time of their punishment they shall perish.
16 Not like these is he who is [i]the portion of Jacob,
for he is the one who formed all things,
[j]and Israel is the tribe of his inheritance;
[k]the LORD of hosts is his name.

17 [l]Gather up your bundle from the ground,
O you who dwell under siege!
18 For thus says the LORD:
[m]"Behold, I am slinging out the inhabitants of the land
at this time,
[n]and I will bring distress on them,
that they may feel it."

19 Woe is me because of my hurt!
[o]My wound is grievous.
But I said, "Truly this is an affliction,
and I must bear it."
20 [p]My tent is destroyed,
and all my cords are broken;
my children have gone from me,
[q]and they are not;

[1] This verse is in Aramaic

9 [q]Isa. 40:19 [r]Gen. 10:4; See 1 Kgs. 10:22 [s]Dan. 10:5 [t]Ps. 115:4
10 [u]Deut. 32:4; Ps. 31:5 [v]Ps. 42:2
11 [w][Ps. 96:5] [x]ver. 15; Isa. 2:18; Zech. 13:2
12 [y]For ver. 12-16, see ch. 51:15-19 [z]Gen. 1:1, 6, 9; Ps. 104:5; Prov. 3:19 [a]Job 9:8
13 [b][Job 38:34; Ps. 104:6, 7] [c]Ps. 135:7 [d]ch. 14:22; Job 5:10 [e]Job 38:22
14 [f]ver. 8; Prov. 30:2; [Rom. 1:22] [g]See Isa. 42:17 [h]Ps. 135:17; Hab. 2:19
16 [i]Ps. 16:5 [j]Deut. 32:9 [k]ch. 31:35; 32:18; 50:34
17 [l][ch. 6:1; Ezek. 12:3]
18 [m]1 Sam. 25:29 [n]Deut. 28:20
19 [o]ch. 14:17; 30:12
20 [p]ch. 4:20; [Isa. 54:2] [q]ch. 31:15

ends of the earth. The location of **Uphaz** is unknown. Idols may be made of the finest materials by the finest **craftsman**, but they remain human creations.

10:11–13 All false gods **shall perish**. They were created by humans, but the living God **made** and **established the world** by **wisdom** and **understanding** (51:15–19). The false gods' "instruction" (10:8) makes people foolish, while God's instruction makes people wise.

10:14–16 People are foolish without God's wisdom (Prov. 1:1–7), especially when practicing idolatry. God, Israel's **portion** and **inheritance**, is the Creator, the one who provides wisdom (cf. Prov. 8:22–31).

10:17–25 *Judah Will Go into Exile.* God will remove sinful Judah from the Promised Land. Exile will be horrible and could have been avoided.

10:17 bundle. The refugees from the countryside had brought just a few possessions into the city that is now **under siege**.

10:18 slinging out. God will hurl the people from the **land** into the unprotected **distress** of captivity.

10:19–20 Jerusalem expresses her woes (Lam. 1:20–22; 2:20–22). Her **tent** (the city) **is destroyed** and her **children** (the inhabitants) are captured.

20[p]ch. 4:20; [Isa. 54:2]
21[r]ch. 23:1; Ezek. 34:2 [s]ver. 8 [t]Ezek. 34:5, 6
22[u]See ch. 1:13 [v]See ch. 9:11
23[w]Prov. 16:1; 20:24; Dan. 5:23
24[x]ch. 30:11; 46:28; Ps. 6:1; 38:1
25[y]Ps. 79:6, 7 [z]ch. 8:16; 30:16; Ps. 14:4

Chapter 11

2[a]ver. 6, 8; [2 Kgs. 23:3]
3[b]Deut. 27:26; Gal. 3:10
4[c]Deut. 4:20 [d]ch. 7:22, 23; Lev. 26:3, 12
5[e]Deut. 7:12, 13; Ps. 105:9, 10 [f]See Ex. 3:8
6[g][ch. 19:2] [h]ver. 2, 8; [2 Kgs. 23:3]
7[i]ch. 7:25; See 2 Chr. 36:15 [d][See ver. 4 above]
8[j]ch. 7:26; 32:23 [k]See ch. 3:17 [h][See ver. 6 above]
9[l]Ezek. 22:25; [Isa. 8:12; Hos. 6:9]

there is no one to spread my tent again
and [p]to set up my curtains.
21 [r]For the shepherds [s]are stupid
and do not inquire of the LORD;
therefore they have not prospered,
[t]and all their flock is scattered.

22 A voice, a rumor! Behold, it comes!—
[u]a great commotion out of the north country
to make [v]the cities of Judah a desolation,
[v]a lair of jackals.

23 [w]I know, O LORD, that the way of man is not in himself,
that it is not in man who walks to direct his steps.
24 [x]Correct me, O LORD, but in justice;
not in your anger, lest you bring me to nothing.
25 [y]Pour out your wrath on the nations that know you not,
and on the peoples that call not on your name,
[z]for they have devoured Jacob;
they have devoured him and consumed him,
and have laid waste his habitation.

The Broken Covenant

11 The word that came to Jeremiah from the LORD: 2 [a]"Hear the words of this covenant,
and speak to the men of Judah and the inhabitants of Jerusalem. 3 You shall say to
them, Thus says the LORD, the God of Israel: [b]Cursed be the man who does not hear the
words of this covenant 4 that I commanded your fathers when I brought them out of the
land of Egypt, [c]from the iron furnace, saying, [d]Listen to my voice, and do all that I command you. [d]So shall you be my people, and I will be your God, 5 [e]that I may confirm the
oath that I swore to your fathers, [f]to give them a land flowing with milk and honey, as at
this day." Then I answered, "So be it, LORD."
6 And the LORD said to me, [g]"Proclaim all these words in the cities of Judah and in the
streets of Jerusalem: [h]Hear the words of this covenant and do them. 7 For I solemnly warned
your fathers when I brought them up out of the land of Egypt, [i]warning them persistently,
even to this day, saying, [d]Obey my voice. 8 [j]Yet they did not obey or incline their ear, [k]but
everyone walked in the stubbornness of his evil heart. Therefore I brought upon them all
[h]the words of this covenant, which I commanded them to do, but they did not."
9 Again the LORD said to me, [l]"A conspiracy exists among the men of Judah and the

10:21 shepherds. Judah's leaders (see note on 3:15). **do not inquire**. They refuse to seek God's word (cf. 1 Kings 22:5–8; 2 Kings 1:16; Isa. 9:13). **their flock is scattered**. Judah's citizens are in exile (Deut. 28:64–68).

10:22 rumor . . . commotion. Word of the invasion has reached Judah. **the north country**. Babylon.

10:23–25 Jeremiah turns to God for wisdom (vv. 11–16), for he needs God **to direct his steps**. He knows God can **correct** a person, and only does so justly (Heb. 12:5–11). He asks that the idolatrous **nations** attacking Judah may soon receive divine correction.

11:1–20:18 *Jeremiah's Struggles with God and Judah.* As the nation faces invasion, Jeremiah struggles to serve God faithfully. In turn he is surprised by opposition (11:1–12:17), stunned over feeling betrayed by God (13:1–15:21), renewed by God (16:1–17:18), burdened by opposition (17:19–18:23), and prepared to continue serving (19:1–20:18).

11:1–12:17 *Jeremiah Surprised by Opposition.* This section highlights Israel's history of covenant breaking (11:1–17), a plot hatched against Jeremiah (11:18–23), his complaint about his enemies (12:1–4), God's challenging of Jeremiah's attitude (12:5–13), and God's promises for Judah's future (12:14–17).

11:2 this covenant. The Mosaic law.

11:3 Cursed refers to the consequences of Israel not keeping its promises to God (Lev. 26:14–39; Deut. 28:15–68). **hear**. Obey.

11:4 I brought them out. God alone deserves credit for the exodus (Ex. 20:1–2). **iron furnace**. Egypt forced Israel to make bricks (Ex. 5:1–21). **My people . . . your God** underscores the relational nature of the covenant. For similar language, see Deut. 4:20 and 1 Kings 8:51.

11:5 confirm the oath. Staying in the Promised Land depended on Israel's obedience and repentance (Deut. 28:15–68; 30:1–10). **Milk and honey** signifies the land's richness (cf. Ex. 3:8).

11:6 Jeremiah had an itinerant ministry, proclaiming Judah's need to **hear** and **do** what the covenant required.

11:7 God was **warning them persistently** through Moses (Num. 14:5–9), chastisement (Ex. 16:27–30), instruction, and liturgy (Leviticus 16). **to this day**. Through Jeremiah at the time of this book.

11:8 The invasion described in 10:17–25 occurred because of covenant infidelity (4:22).

11:9 conspiracy. Against Yahweh, to serve other gods (v. 10).

inhabitants of Jerusalem. 10 They have turned back to [m]the iniquities of their forefathers,
who refused to hear my words. [m]They have gone after other gods to serve them. [n]The
house of Israel and the house of Judah have broken my covenant that I made with their
fathers. 11 Therefore, thus says the LORD, Behold, I am bringing disaster upon them that
they cannot escape. [o]Though they cry to me, I will not listen to them. 12 Then the cities of
Judah and the inhabitants of Jerusalem [p]will go and cry to the gods to whom they make
offerings, [p]but they cannot save them in the time of their trouble. 13 [p]For your gods have
become as many as your cities, O Judah, and as many as the streets of Jerusalem are the
altars you have set up to shame, [q]altars to make offerings to Baal.

14 "Therefore [r]do not pray for this people, or lift up a cry or prayer on their behalf, [o]for
I will not listen when they call to me in the time of their trouble. 15 [s]What right has my
beloved in my house, [t]when she has done many vile deeds? Can even sacrificial flesh avert
your doom? [u]Can you then exult? 16 The LORD once called you [v]'a green olive tree, beautiful with good fruit.' But [w]with the roar of a great tempest he will set fire to it, and [x]its
branches will be consumed. 17 The LORD of hosts, [y]who planted you, has decreed disaster
against you, because of the evil that the house of Israel and the house of Judah have done,
[z]provoking me to anger by making offerings to Baal."

18 The LORD made it known to me and I knew;
then you showed me their deeds.
19 But I was [a]like a gentle lamb
led to the slaughter.
I did not know [b]it was against me
they devised schemes, saying,
"Let us destroy the tree with its fruit,
[c]let us cut him off from [d]the land of the living,
that his name be remembered no more."
20 But, O LORD of hosts, who judges righteously,
who [e]tests [f]the heart and the mind,
[g]let me see your vengeance upon them,
for to you have I committed my cause.

21 Therefore thus says the LORD concerning the men of [h]Anathoth, [i]who seek your life, and
say, [j]"Do not prophesy in the name of the LORD, or you will die by our hand"— 22 therefore
thus says the LORD of hosts: "Behold, I will punish them. The young men shall die by the
sword, their sons and their daughters shall die by famine, 23 and none of them shall be left.
For I will bring disaster upon the men of [k]Anathoth, [l]the year of their punishment."

Jeremiah's Complaint

12 1 [m]Righteous are you, O LORD,
when I complain to you;
yet I would plead my case before you.
[n]Why does the way of the wicked prosper?

10 [m][ch. 17:23; Ps. 78:8; 79:8; Ezek. 20:18] [n]Deut. 31:16, 20
11 [o]Prov. 1:28; Isa. 1:15; Ezek. 8:18; Mic. 3:4
12 [p]ch. 2:28; [Acts 17:16]
13 [p][See ver. 12 above] [q][Hos. 9:10]; See Judg. 6:25-32
14 [r]ch. 7:16; [Heb. 10:26; 1 John 5:16] [o][See ver. 11 above]
15 [s]Isa. 1:11, 12 [t][Ezek. 16:25] [u]Prov. 2:14
16 [v]Ps. 52:8; [Hos. 14:6] [w][Ps. 83:2] [x]Rom. 11:17, 20
17 [y]ch. 2:21; Isa. 5:2 [z]See ch. 7:18
19 [a]Isa. 53:7; [Rev. 5:6] [b]ch. 18:18; Lam. 3:60, 61 [c]Ps. 83:4; Isa. 53:8 [d]Ps. 27:13
20 [e]ch. 17:10; 20:12; Ps. 7:9; Rev. 2:23 [f]See 1 Sam. 16:7 [g]ch. 15:15; 17:18; 20:12; Lam. 3:64
21 [h]Josh. 21:18 [i][ch. 12:6; Matt. 13:57] [j]Isa. 30:10
23 [k]Josh. 21:18 [l]ch. 23:12

Chapter 12

1 [m]Ezra 9:15; Ps. 51:4; Lam. 1:18; Dan. 9:7 [n]Job 12:6; Ps. 37:1, 7; 92:7; Hab. 1:13; Mal. 3:15; See Job 21:7-15; Ps. 73:3-12

11:10 iniquities of their forefathers. Idolatry committed with the golden calf (Ex. 32:1–6), Baal (Judg. 2:11–15), and astral deities (Jer. 7:16–20; 8:2).

11:11–12 disaster. The nation's destruction by Babylon. **not listen to them**. God has decided to judge (v. 14; 14:11). **cry to the gods**. See 2:27–28; Lam. 1:19. The gods **cannot save** because they are not real (Jer. 10:1–16).

11:13 Superstitious polytheism fills Jerusalem. **Baal**. Canaanite fertility god whose worship rituals included sexual acts committed with sacred prostitutes.

11:14 do not pray. God will not heed Jeremiah's prayer for a delay in punishment (cf. 7:16; 14:11).

11:15 Israel's spiritual adultery leads God to expel her from his home. **sacrificial flesh**. Sacrifices offered with no intent to change (7:1–15; Isa. 1:10–20).

11:16 Green olive tree signifies fruitfulness and economic prosperity (Ps. 52:8). **great tempest**. The storm of invasion (cf. Ezek. 1:24). Paul used Jeremiah's image of God's people as an "olive tree" with the members as **branches** (Rom. 11:17–24).

11:17 On the wordplay with **disaster** and **evil**, see note on 1:13–14. **provoking me**. See 7:18.

11:18–20 God reveals a plot against Jeremiah, who commits his future to his deliverer.

11:21 Anathoth. Jeremiah's hometown (1:1). **Do not prophesy**. Even his old friends hate his message, for it exposes their sins. They prefer false prophets (5:12–13).

11:22–23 God will protect his word and his prophet. **sword . . . famine**. Babylon's sword and natural disaster will overwhelm **Anathoth**.

12:1 Righteous. God defines and acts out what is fair and correct. **complain**. Jeremiah laments his situation. His basic question is universal and naive. It assumes that sinful persons never harm God's servants, despite the warnings in 1:17–19.

1 [o][Isa. 21:2]
2 [p]Isa. 29:13
3 [q]ch. 15:15; Ps. 139:1 [r]Ps. 17:3 [s][2 Pet. 2:12] [t]James 5:5
4 [u]ver. 11; ch. 9:10; 23:10 [v]Ps. 107:34 [w]ch. 4:25; 7:20; 9:10; Hos. 4:3; [Rom. 8:22]
5 [x]ch. 49:19; 50:44; Zech. 11:3; [Josh. 3:15]
6 [y]ch. 9:4; [ch. 11:19, 21] [o][See ver. 1 above] [z]Prov. 26:25
7 [a]Isa. 19:25 [b]ch. 11:15
8 [a][See ver. 7 above]
9 [a][See ver. 7 above] [c]Isa. 46:11 [d]ch. 7:33; Isa. 56:9; [Ezek. 39:17; Rev. 19:17]
10 [e]Isa. 63:18
11 [u][See ver. 4 above] [f]Isa. 42:25

Why do all [o]who are treacherous thrive?
2 You plant them, and they take root;
they grow and produce fruit;
[p]you are near in their mouth
and far from their heart.
3 [q]But you, O LORD, know me;
[r]you see me, and test my heart toward you.
[s]Pull them out like sheep for the slaughter,
and set them apart for [t]the day of slaughter.
4 [u]How long will the land mourn
and the grass of every field wither?
[v]For the evil of those who dwell in it
[w]the beasts and the birds are swept away,
because they said, "He will not see our latter end."

The LORD Answers Jeremiah

5 "If you have raced with men on foot, and they have wearied you,
how will you compete with horses?
And if in a safe land you are so trusting,
what will you do in [x]the thicket of the Jordan?
6 For [y]even your brothers and the house of your father,
[o]even they have dealt treacherously with you;
they are in full cry after you;
[z]do not believe them,
though they speak friendly words to you."
7 "I have forsaken my house;
I have abandoned [a]my heritage;
I have given [b]the beloved of my soul
into the hands of her enemies.
8 [a]My heritage has become to me
like a lion in the forest;
she has lifted up her voice against me;
therefore I hate her.
9 Is [a]my heritage to me like [c]a hyena's lair?
Are the [c]birds of prey against her all around?
Go, [d]assemble all the wild beasts;
bring them to devour.
10 Many shepherds have destroyed my vineyard;
[e]they have trampled down my portion;
they have made my pleasant portion
a desolate wilderness.
11 They have made it a desolation;
desolate, [u]it mourns to me.
The whole land is made desolate,
[f]but no man lays it to heart.
12 Upon all the bare heights in the desert

12:2 You plant them. Jeremiah believes God has blessed hypocrites who feign belief in him (Ps. 73:1–3). **you are near in their mouth**. They speak of God often. **and far from their heart**. They do not know him or love him (cf. Isa. 29:13; Matt. 15:8).

12:3 In contrast, Jeremiah's **heart** is right with God. Thus, he wants God to **set** his enemies **apart for the day of slaughter**.

12:4 How long? A common question asked by those waiting for justice (Ps. 13:1; 35:17; 79:5; 80:4; Rev. 6:10). **He will not see**. Sinners often believe God will not judge (Zeph. 1:12; 2 Pet. 3:1–13).

12:5–6 God responds with a rebuke and a caution: Jeremiah must prepare for worse times, and he cannot trust even family and friends.

12:7 God has **forsaken** his people, the **beloved of** his **soul**, consigning them to judgment. His suffering exceeds Jeremiah's.

12:9 The hyena and **birds** represent Babylon, the enemy who stalks Judah.

12:10–11 shepherds have destroyed my vineyard. On God's people as his vineyard, see note on Isa. 5:1. Judah's leaders have misled God's people, resulting in oppression and judgment (Isa. 3:1–5; 5:1–13; Jer. 2:8; 4:9–10). **no man lays it to heart**. No leader pays attention and guides Judah to repent (Isa. 42:18–25).

12:12 sword of the LORD. Babylon is simply God's instrument for punishing Judah; he rules the earth.

destroyers have come,
for the sword of the LORD devours
from one end of the land to the other;
no flesh has peace.
13 [g]They have sown wheat and have reaped thorns;
[h]they have tired themselves out but profit nothing.
They shall be ashamed of their[1] harvests
[i]because of the fierce anger of the LORD."

14 Thus says the LORD concerning all [j]my evil neighbors [k]who touch the heritage that [l]I
have given my people Israel to inherit: "Behold, I will pluck them up from their land, and
I will pluck up the house of Judah from among them. 15 And after I have plucked them up,
I will again have compassion on them, [m]and I will bring them again each to his heritage
and each to his land. 16 And it shall come to pass, if they will diligently learn the ways of
my people, [n]to swear by my name, 'As the LORD lives,' even as they taught my people to
swear by Baal, [o]then they shall be built up in the midst of my people. 17 [p]But if any nation
will not listen, then I will utterly pluck it up and destroy it, declares the LORD."

The Ruined Loincloth

13 Thus says the LORD to me, "Go and buy a linen loincloth and [q]put it around your
waist, and do not dip it in water." 2 So I bought a loincloth according to the word
of the LORD, and put it around my waist. 3 And the word of the LORD came to me a second
time, 4 "Take the loincloth that you have bought, which is around your waist, and arise,
[r]go to the Euphrates and hide it there in [s]a cleft of the rock." 5 So I went and hid it by the
Euphrates, as the LORD commanded me. 6 And after many days the LORD said to me, "Arise,
go to the Euphrates, and take from there [q]the loincloth that I commanded you to hide
there." 7 Then I went to the Euphrates, and dug, and I took [q]the loincloth from the place
where I had hidden it. And behold, the loincloth was [t]spoiled; it was [u]good for nothing.
8 Then the word of the LORD came to me: 9 "Thus says the LORD: [v]Even so will I spoil
the pride of Judah and the great [w]pride of Jerusalem. 10 This evil people, who refuse to
hear my words, [x]who stubbornly follow their own heart and have gone after other gods
to serve them and worship them, shall be like this loincloth, which is [u]good for nothing.
11 For as the loincloth clings to the waist of a man, so I made the whole house of Israel
and the whole house of Judah cling to me, declares the LORD, [y]that they might be for me
a people, [z]a name, a praise, and a glory, but they would not listen.

The Jars Filled with Wine

12 "You shall speak to them this word: 'Thus says the LORD, the God of Israel, "Every jar
shall be filled with wine."' And they will say to you, 'Do we not indeed know that [a]every
jar will be filled with wine?' 13 Then you shall say to them, 'Thus says the LORD: [b]Behold,
I will fill with drunkenness all the inhabitants of this land: [c]the kings who sit on David's
throne, [d]the priests, the prophets, and all the inhabitants of Jerusalem. 14 And I will [e]dash

[1] Hebrew *your*

13 [g][Lev. 26:16; Deut. 28:38; Mic. 6:15; Hag. 1:6] [h]Isa. 55:2; Hab. 2:13 [i]ch. 4:8, 26; 25:37, 38; 30:24; 49:37; 51:45; Lam. 1:12; 4:11
14 [j][Ps. 137:7]; See Ezek. 25 [k]Zech. 2:8 [l]ch. 3:18
15 [m]ch. 48:47; 49:6
16 [n]ch. 4:2 [o]ch. 24:6; [1 Pet. 2:5]
17 [p][Isa. 60:12]

Chapter 13

1 [q]Ex. 28:39; Lev. 16:4; [Acts 21:11]
4 [r][ch. 51:59, 63] [s]Isa. 7:19
6 [q][See ver. 1 above]
7 [q][See ver. 1 above] [t]ch. 18:4 [u][Ezek. 15:4, 5]
9 [v][Ps. 137:1] [w]Lev. 26:19
10 [x][ch. 3:17; 16:11, 12] [u][See ver. 7 above]
11 [y][Ex. 19:5] [z]ch. 33:9; Isa. 55:13; Zeph. 3:20
12 [a]ch. 48:12
13 [b]Ezek. 23:33 [c]ch. 17:20; 19:3; 22:2 [d][ch. 18:18]
14 [e]Ps. 2:9; [ch. 19:10, 11]

12:13 Sown wheat . . . reaped thorns indicates either an invasion keeping farmers from harvesting or the result of Judah reaping what it has sown morally.

12:14 pluck up. God will take Judah from the **land** (1:10; 18:7; 31:28; 42:10) and take Judah's **evil neighbors** from their land as well.

12:15 compassion. Wrath is never God's final word to his covenant people (Deut. 30:1–10; Lam. 3:19–38; Hos. 11:1–9).

12:16–17 God also has compassion on the nations who **learn** his **ways**, **swear by** his **name**, and obey his word. He is the Creator of all nations (10:1–16), not just Israel's national deity.

13:1–15:21 *Jeremiah Feels Betrayed by God.* As he probes God's character, the prophet complains about God's integrity. Jeremiah preaches that Judah is a ruined and drunken nation (13:1–14) that ought to glorify God before it is too late (13:15–27). As a terrible drought grips the land, Jeremiah intercedes for the people (14:1–22). God refuses Jeremiah's intercession (15:1–9), which leads Jeremiah to complain again (15:10–18), which prompts God's rebuke (15:19–21).

13:1 This is the first of several symbolic acts Jeremiah performs to reveal God's will.

13:2–7 God orders Jeremiah to place an intimate garment in a rocky place. Of course, it gets ruined by the weather. The **Euphrates** River lies hundreds of miles from Anathoth. If the Euphrates is intended, the prophet may have experienced it in a vision. A slight change in spelling in the Hebrew text from the name *perat* yields "Parah," a place less than 3 miles (4.8 km) from Anathoth, and some interpreters think that is what was intended, with a later copyist's error resulting in the more common *perat* ("Euphrates").

13:8–11 The Judeans' prideful, idolatrous ways cling to them like an intimate garment. Like Jeremiah's garment, this **pride** will be ruined.

13:12–14 "Every jar shall be filled with wine." Most likely a reveler's play on words, meaning that every *person* ought to be filled with wine. Israel's leaders have acted with no more sense than drunkards. They are jars filled with wine that shall be smashed.

them one against another, fathers and sons together, declares the LORD. I will not pity or
spare or have compassion, that I should not destroy them.'"

Exile Threatened

15 Hear and give ear; be not proud,
for the LORD has spoken.
16 [f]Give glory to the LORD your God
[g]before he brings darkness,
before your feet stumble
on the twilight mountains,
and [g]while you look for light
he turns it into gloom
and makes it [h]deep darkness.
17 But if you will not listen,
[i]my soul will weep in secret for your pride;
my eyes will weep bitterly and run down with tears,
because the LORD's flock has been taken captive.

18 Say to [j]the king and [j]the queen mother:
"Take a lowly seat,
for [k]your beautiful crown
has come down from your head."
19 [l]The cities of the Negeb are shut up,
with none to open them;
all Judah is taken into exile,
wholly taken into exile.

20 "Lift up your eyes [m]and see
those who come from the north.
Where is the flock that was given you,
your beautiful flock?
21 What will you say when they set as head over you
those whom you yourself have taught to be friends to you?
[n]Will not pangs take hold of you
like those of a woman in labor?
22 And if you say in your heart,
[o]'Why have these things come upon me?'
it is for the greatness of your iniquity
that [p]your skirts are lifted up
and you suffer violence.
23 [q]Can the Ethiopian change his skin
or [q]the leopard his spots?
Then also you can do good
who are accustomed to do evil.
24 I will scatter you[1] [r]like chaff
driven by the wind from the desert.
25 [s]This is your lot,
the portion I have measured out to you, declares the LORD,

16 [f][Josh. 7:19] [g]Isa. 5:30; 8:22; Amos 5:8; 8:9; [John 11:10] [h]Isa. 60:2
17 [i]ch. 9:1, 18; 14:17; Lam. 1:2, 16; 2:18; 3:49
18 [j]ch. 22:26; 2 Kgs. 24:12 [k]Prov. 4:9; Isa. 28:5; 62:3; Lam. 5:16
19 [l][Josh. 6:1]
20 [m]ch. 1:13, 14; 6:22
21 [n]See Isa. 13:8
22 [o]See ch. 5:19 [p]ver. 26; Isa. 3:17; Lam. 1:8; Nah. 3:5; [Hos. 2:10]
23 [q][Matt. 19:26]
24 [r]Ps. 1:4; 83:13
25 [s]Job 20:29; Ps. 11:6

[1] Hebrew *them*

13:15–17 be not proud. Jeremiah implores Judah to repent. **darkness**. A common ancient Near Eastern metaphor for judgment. **my eyes will weep**. Jeremiah's grief emerges again (cf. 4:19–21; 9:1).

13:18 queen mother. Often noted as a significant person in the king's administration (2 Kings 24:8, 18). **come down**. The whole royal house will suffer.

13:19 Negeb. Lands south of Jerusalem. **shut up**. They are awaiting or experiencing the Babylonian siege. If these cities are threatened, Jerusalem has already fallen.

13:20–22 flock. Judah's people. **friends**. Babylon was once Judah's ally (Isa. 39:1–8). **Why**? Unaware, self-serving leaders somehow consider themselves innocent sufferers (cf. Jer. 5:19).

13:23 change his skin? This is a rhetorical question assuming a negative answer.

13:24 scatter you like chaff. A metaphor for the judgment of the wicked (Deut. 28:64–68; Ps. 1:4; 35:5).

13:25 trusted in lies. God holds his people responsible for believing falsehoods. They should have known better.

because [t]you have forgotten me
and trusted in lies.
26 [p]I myself will lift up your skirts over your face,
and your shame will be seen.
27 I have seen [u]your abominations,
your adulteries and [v]neighings, your lewd whorings,
[w]on the hills in the field.
Woe to you, O Jerusalem!
How long will it be [x]before you are made clean?"

Famine, Sword, and Pestilence

14 The word of the LORD that came to Jeremiah concerning [y]the drought:

2 [z]"Judah mourns,
and [a]her gates languish;
her people lament on the ground,
and [b]the cry of Jerusalem goes up.
3 Her nobles send their servants for water;
they come to the cisterns;
they find no water;
they return with their vessels empty;
they are [c]ashamed and confounded
and [d]cover their heads.
4 Because of the ground that is dismayed,
since there is [e]no rain on the land,
the farmers are ashamed;
they cover their heads.
5 Even [f]the doe in the field forsakes her newborn fawn
because there is no grass.
6 [g]The wild donkeys stand on the bare heights;
they pant for air like jackals;
their eyes fail
because there is no vegetation.

7 "Though our iniquities testify against us,
act, O LORD, [h]for your name's sake;
[i]for our backslidings are many;
[j]we have sinned against you.
8 [k]O you hope of Israel,
its savior in time of trouble,
why should you be like a stranger in the land,
like a traveler who turns aside to tarry for a night?
9 Why should you be like a man confused,
[l]like a mighty warrior who cannot save?
Yet [m]you, O LORD, are in the midst of us,
and [n]we are called by your name;
[o]do not leave us."

25 [t]ch. 2:32
26 [p][See ver. 22 above]
27 [u]ch. 6:15 [v]ch. 5:8 [w]See ch. 2:20 [x]Isa. 1:16; [Ezek. 24:13]

Chapter 14

1 [y]ch. 17:8
2 [z]Lam. 1:4 [a]Isa. 3:26; [Lam. 2:8] [b][1 Sam. 5:12]
3 [c]Ps. 40:14 [d][2 Sam. 15:30]
4 [e]ch. 3:3
5 [f]Job 39:1; Ps. 29:9
6 [g]ch. 2:24
7 [h]ver. 21; Ps. 25:11 [i]ch. 2:19 [j]ver. 20
8 [k]ch. 17:13; 50:7; Ps. 71:5
9 [l][Isa. 59:1] [m][Ex. 29:45] [n]Dan. 9:18; [Eph. 3:15] [o]Ps. 119:121

13:26–27 skirts . . . shame. Judah's spiritual adultery will be exposed (Lam. 1:9). **lewd whorings**. See Ezek. 16:1–58; 23:1–48. **Woe**. Coming judgment (Isa. 5:8–23).

14:1 drought. Judah experiences drought alongside Babylon's invasion (cf. Deut. 28:23–24).

14:2 Judah mourns and prays because of the situation (cf. Lam. 1:3–4; 2:8).

14:3–4 Not even prominent people (**nobles**) have sufficient **water**, and **farmers** are ruined.

14:7 Jeremiah intercedes, noting Judah's rebellion and apostasy (cf. Amos 7:1–9).

14:8–9 we are called by your name. God has been Israel's deliverer in the past, and Jeremiah wonders if he will help the nation for the sake of his reputation (Lam. 1:20–22; 2:20–22).

10 Thus says the LORD concerning this people:
"They have loved to wander thus;
they have not restrained their feet;
[p]therefore the LORD does not accept them;
[q]now he will remember their iniquity
and punish their sins."

11 The LORD said to me: [r]"Do not pray for the welfare of this people. 12 Though they fast,
I will not hear their cry, [s]and though they offer burnt offering and grain offering, I will not
accept them. But I will consume them [t]by the sword, by famine, and by pestilence."

Lying Prophets

13 Then I said: "Ah, Lord GOD, behold, the prophets [u]say to them, 'You shall not see the
sword, nor shall you have famine, but I will give you assured peace in this place.'" 14 And the
LORD said to me: "The [v]prophets are prophesying lies in my name. [w]I did not send them,
nor did I command them or speak to them. They are prophesying to you a lying vision,
[x]worthless divination, and [y]the deceit of their own minds. 15 Therefore thus says the LORD
concerning the prophets who prophesy in my name although [w]I did not send them, and
who say, [t]'Sword and famine shall not come upon this land': [z]By sword and famine those
prophets shall be consumed. 16 And the people to whom they prophesy shall be cast out in
the streets of Jerusalem, victims of famine and sword, [a]with none to bury them—them,
their wives, their sons, and their daughters. For I will pour out their evil upon them.

17 "You shall say to them this word:
[b]'Let my eyes run down with tears night and day,
and let them not cease,
for the virgin [c]daughter of my people is shattered with a great wound,
[d]with a very grievous blow.
18 [e]If I go out into the field,
behold, those pierced by the sword!
[e]And if I enter the city,
behold, the diseases of famine!
[f]For both prophet and priest ply their trade through the land
and have no knowledge.'"

19 [g]Have you utterly rejected Judah?
Does your soul loathe Zion?
Why have you struck us down
[h]so that there is no healing for us?
[i]We looked for peace, but no good came;
[i]for a time of healing, but behold, terror.
20 [j]We acknowledge our wickedness, O LORD,
and the iniquity of our fathers,
[j]for we have sinned against you.
21 Do not spurn us, [k]for your name's sake;
do not dishonor your glorious throne;
[l]remember and do not break your covenant with us.

10 [p]Hos. 8:13 [q]Hos. 9:9
11 [r]See ch. 7:16
12 [s]Prov. 1:28; Isa. 1:15; Ezek. 8:18; Mic. 3:4; See ch. 6:20 [t]ch. 16:4; 24:10; 32:24; Ezek. 14:21
13 [u][ch. 4:10; 6:14]
14 [v]See ch. 5:31 [w]ch. 23:21; 27:15; Deut. 18:20; [Matt. 7:15; Mark 13:22] [x]Ezek. 13:6; [ch. 27:9; 29:8] [y]ch. 23:26
15 [w][See ver. 14 above] [t][See ver. 12 above] [z][ch. 23:34]
16 [a]Ps. 79:3
17 [b]See ch. 13:17 [c]See ch. 8:21 [d]ch. 10:19; 30:12
18 [e]Ezek. 7:15 [f][ch. 5:31]
19 [g]Lam. 5:22 [h][ch. 15:18] [i]ch. 8:15
20 [j][Ps. 106:6; Dan. 9:5, 8]
21 [k]ver. 7 [l]Lev. 26:42; Ps. 106:45

14:10 God is able to save, but Israel's constant wandering from him must be addressed. For God remembering his people's **iniquity** and **sins**, see Hos. 7:2; 8:13; 9:9; and contrast Ps. 25:7; 79:8; Isa. 43:25; 64:9; Jer. 31:34.

14:11–12 Do not pray. A rare instance when God will not accept intercession (see note on 7:16). Religious observances (14:1–2) will not move him, for they are false (7:1–29). For **sword**, **famine**, and **pestilence**, see 15:2–3.

14:13–14 the prophets say. Jeremiah seems to argue that God allowed other prophets to tell Judah that all was well (4:9–10; 6:13–15). **prophesying lies in my name**. In no uncertain terms God denies sending these prophets. Their messages are from their minds, not God's.

14:15 sword and famine. Babylon and the drought. The false prophets deny the very fate that will come upon the nation.

14:16 none to bury. The people's bodies will lie unburied; they are like dung in the street (cf. 9:22). See note on 7:33.

14:17–18 Again Jeremiah mourns, for the people are **shattered with a great wound**. Bodies lie everywhere (cf. 9:20–22). This is because the leaders have taught people falsehoods about God: **For both prophet and priest . . . have no knowledge**.

14:19 Why have you struck us? Jeremiah questions God again, declaring that the people were misled. He wonders if God has cast them off (cf. Lam. 5:22).

14:20–22 Jeremiah expresses his faith on behalf of Judah, but the people do not share his convictions, as God knows. **remember**. See v. 10.

22 Are there any among [m]the false gods of the nations [n]that can bring rain?
Or can the heavens give showers?
Are you not he, O LORD our God?
We set our hope on you,
[o]for you do all these things.

The LORD Will Not Relent

15 Then the LORD said to me, [p]"Though [q]Moses [r]and Samuel [s]stood before me, yet
my heart would not turn toward this people. Send them out of my sight, and let
them go! 2 And when they ask you, 'Where shall we go?' you shall say to them, 'Thus says
the LORD:

[t]"'Those who are for pestilence, to pestilence,
and those who are for the sword, to the sword;
those who are for famine, to famine,
and those who are for captivity, to captivity.'

3 [u]I will appoint over them four kinds of destroyers, declares the LORD: the sword to kill,
the dogs to tear, and [v]the birds of the air [w]and the beasts of the earth to devour and destroy.
4 [x]And I will make them a horror to all the kingdoms of the earth because of what [y]Manasseh
the son of Hezekiah, king of Judah, did in Jerusalem.

5 [z]"Who will have pity on you, O Jerusalem,
[z]or who will grieve for you?
Who will turn aside
to ask about your welfare?
6 [a]You have rejected me, declares the LORD;
[b]you keep going backward,
so I have stretched out my hand against you and destroyed you—
[c]I am weary of relenting.
7 [d]I have winnowed them with [e]a winnowing fork
in the gates of the land;
I have bereaved them; I have destroyed my people;
[f]they did not turn from their ways.
8 I have made their widows more in number
than [g]the sand of the seas;
I have brought against the mothers of young men
a destroyer at noonday;
I have made anguish and terror
fall upon them suddenly.
9 [h]She who bore seven has grown feeble;
[i]she has fainted away;
[j]her sun went down while it was yet day;
she has been shamed and disgraced.
And the rest of them I will give to the sword
before their enemies,
declares the LORD."

22 [m]ch. 10:15; [Deut. 32:21] [n]Job 28:26; 38:26, 28; Zech. 10:1, 2 [o]Job 12:9; Isa. 66:2

Chapter 15

1 [p]Ps. 99:6; [Ezek. 14:14] [q][Ps. 106:23]; See Ex. 32:11-13 [r][1 Sam. 7:9; 8:6; 12:23; 15:11] [s]ch. 35:19; [ver. 19]
2 [t]ch. 14:12; 16:4; 21:9; 43:11; Ezek. 5:12; 6:11, 12; Zech. 11:9
3 [u]See Lev. 26:16-22 [v]Deut. 28:26 [w]Rev. 6:8
4 [x]ch. 24:9; 29:18; 34:17; Deut. 28:25 [y][2 Kgs. 21:2, 11, 16, 17; 23:26; 24:3, 4]
5 [z]Isa. 51:19; [Nah. 3:7]
6 [a]Deut. 32:15 [b]See ch. 7:24 [c][Hos. 13:14]
7 [d][ch. 51:2; Isa. 41:16; Matt. 3:12; Luke 3:17] [e]Isa. 30:24 [f]ch. 5:3; Isa. 9:13; Amos 4:6, 8-11
8 [g]Gen. 22:17; Ps. 139:18
9 [h]1 Sam. 2:5; [Lam. 1:1] [i]Job 11:20 [j]Amos 8:9

15:1 Moses and Samuel. Two great leaders and intercessors (Ex. 32:11–14; 1 Sam. 7:3–11).

15:2–3 Judah has four places to **go**: plague (**pestilence**), battle (**sword**), starvation (**famine**), and exile (**captivity**). Carnivorous animals will consume what the sword leaves (cf. 14:12; 21:7–9; 24:10).

15:4 make them a horror. A cautionary tale for all nations (Deut. 28:25). **Manasseh** ruled Judah c. 697–642 B.C. He committed idolatry, practiced child sacrifice, used fortune-tellers, and generally led Judah to hate God's word (2 Chron. 33:1–9). He repented late in life (2 Chron. 33:10–20).

15:5 Who? Judah has no allies, and God has left them.

15:6 relenting. God is **weary** of turning back punishment on account of intercession, repentance, or kindness.

15:7 winnowed. The process of separating chaff from wheat is a metaphor for judgment (51:2; Isa. 41:16; on the process of winnowing, see note on Ps. 1:4). The primary cause for punishment was that **they did not turn from their ways**.

15:8 noonday. An unexpected time for an attack, since it lacks possible surprise.

15:9 She who bore seven. A mother with the perfect number of sons losing all she has in a metaphor for Judah's reversal of fortunes.

10[k]ch. 20:14 [l]Ex. 22:25; Ps. 15:5; Isa. 24:2
12[m]See ch. 1:13
13[n]ch. 17:3 [o]Ps. 44:12
14[p]ch. 9:16; 16:13; 17:4; 22:28 [q]Deut. 32:22
15[r]ch. 12:3 [s][Judg. 16:28] [t]ch. 11:20; 20:12 [u]ch. 17:16 [v]Ps. 69:7
16[w]Ezek. 3:1, 3; Rev. 10:9, 10 [x]Ps. 119:111, 162 [y]ch. 14:9
17[z]Ps. 26:4 [a]Ps. 102:7; Lam. 3:28
18[b]ch. 30:15; Job 34:6 [c]Job 6:15; Isa. 58:11
19[d]ch. 3:14 [e][ver. 1]
20[f][ch. 1:18; 6:27] [g]ch. 1:19; 20:11 [h]See ch. 1:8

Jeremiah's Complaint

10 [k]Woe is me, my mother, that you bore me, a man of strife and contention to the whole
land! [l]I have not lent, nor have I borrowed, yet all of them curse me. **11** The LORD said,
"Have I not[1] set you free for their good? Have I not pleaded for you before the enemy
in the time of trouble and in the time of distress? **12** Can one break iron, iron [m]from the
north, and bronze?
13 [n]"Your wealth and your treasures I will give as [o]spoil, without price, for all your sins,
throughout all your territory. **14** I will make you serve your enemies [p]in a land that you do
not know, [q]for in my anger a fire is kindled that shall burn forever."

15 [r]O LORD, you know;
[s]remember me and visit me,
[s, t]and take vengeance for me on my persecutors.
In your forbearance take me not away;
[u]know that [v]for your sake I bear reproach.
16 Your words were found, [w]and I ate them,
and [x]your words became to me a joy
and the delight of my heart,
[y]for I am called by your name,
O LORD, God of hosts.
17 [z]I did not sit in the company of revelers,
nor did I rejoice;
[a]I sat alone, because your hand was upon me,
for you had filled me with indignation.
18 Why is my pain unceasing,
[b]my wound incurable,
refusing to be healed?
Will you be to me [c]like a deceitful brook,
like waters that fail?

19 Therefore thus says the LORD:
[d]"If you return, I will restore you,
and you shall [e]stand before me.
If you utter what is precious, and not what is worthless,
you shall be as my mouth.
They shall turn to you,
but you shall not turn to them.
20 [f]And I will make you to this people
a fortified wall of bronze;
they will fight against you,
[g]but they shall not prevail over you,
[h]for I am with you
to save you and deliver you,
declares the LORD.

[1] The meaning of the Hebrew is uncertain

15:10 Woe is me. Jeremiah faces a new crisis (see 11:18–12:6). He claims the people are against him as if he had **borrowed** or **lent** money.

15:11–12 The exact meaning of these verses is uncertain. It may be that Jeremiah wonders why he has suffered in this way, given his prayer for the people and God's promise to make him like **iron** (1:17–19).

15:13–14 Again God states that Judah's **sins** have brought her to the brink of financial ruin and exile.

15:15 you know. God has seen Jeremiah's suffering. **take me not away.** Jeremiah asks to be spared when death strikes.

15:16 Your words were found, and I ate them. As a true prophet, Jeremiah digested, delighted in, and spoke God's words in God's **name** for the people's good.

15:17 Jeremiah took no part in the nation's sin (Ps. 1:1). **sat alone.** He was isolated because of his commitment.

15:18 pain unceasing. There was no relief from persecution. **a deceitful brook.** Jeremiah accuses God of failing to protect him.

15:19 If you utter what is precious. God rebukes Jeremiah, urging repentance and faithful, truthful speech about himself. Jeremiah must side with God, not with the people.

15:20–21 God repeats his promise to protect (1:17–19). God will **deliver**

21 [g]I will deliver you out of the hand of the wicked,
and redeem you from the grasp of [i]the ruthless."

Famine, Sword, and Death

16 The word of the LORD came to me: 2"You shall not take a wife, nor shall you have
sons or daughters in this place. 3For thus says the LORD concerning the sons and
daughters who are born in this place, and concerning the mothers who bore them and the
fathers who fathered them in this land: 4[j]They shall die of deadly diseases. [k]They shall not
be lamented, nor shall they be buried. [l]They shall be as dung on the surface of the ground.
[m]They shall perish by the sword and by famine, [n]and their dead bodies shall be food for
the birds of the air and for the beasts of the earth.
5"For thus says the LORD: [o]Do not enter the house of mourning, or go to lament or
grieve for them, for I have taken away my peace from this people, my steadfast love and
mercy, declares the LORD. 6Both great and small shall die in this land. [k]They shall not be
buried, and no one shall lament for them or [p]cut himself [q]or make himself bald for them.
7No one shall [r]break bread for the mourner, to comfort him for the dead, nor shall anyone
give him the cup of consolation to drink for his father or his mother. 8You shall not go
into the house of feasting to sit with them, to eat and drink. 9For thus says the LORD of
hosts, the God of Israel: [s]Behold, I will silence in this place, before your eyes and in your
days, the voice of mirth and the voice of gladness, the voice of the bridegroom and the
voice of the bride.
10"And when you tell this people all these words, and they say to you, [t]'Why has the
LORD pronounced all this great evil against us? What is our iniquity? What is the sin that
we have committed against the LORD our God?' 11then you shall say to them: [u]'Because
your fathers have forsaken me, declares the LORD, and [v]have gone after other gods and
have served and worshiped them, and have forsaken me and have not kept my law, 12and
because [w]you have done worse than your fathers, for behold, [x]every one of you follows his
stubborn, evil will, refusing to listen to me. 13Therefore [y]I will hurl you out of this land
into [z]a land that neither you nor your fathers have known, [a]and there you shall serve other
gods day and night, for I will show you no favor.'

The LORD Will Restore Israel

14[b]"Therefore, behold, the days are coming, declares the LORD, when it shall no longer
be said, [c]'As the LORD lives who brought up the people of Israel out of the land of Egypt,'
15but [c]'As the LORD lives who brought up the people of Israel [d]out of the north country
and out of all the countries where he had driven them.' For [e]I will bring them back to their
own land that I gave to their fathers.
16"Behold, [f]I am sending for many fishers, declares the LORD, and they shall catch them.
And afterward I will send for many hunters, and they shall hunt them from every mountain
and every hill, and out [g]of the clefts of the rocks. 17For [h]my eyes are on all their ways. [i]They are
not hidden from me, [i]nor is their iniquity concealed from my eyes. 18But first [j]I will doubly

21[g][See ver. 20 above] [i]Isa. 13:11; 25:4, 5; 29:5

Chapter 16

4[j]See ch. 15:2 [k]ch. 22:18, 19; 25:33 [l]See ch. 8:2 [m]See ch. 14:12 [n]See ch. 7:33
5[o]See Ezek. 24:16-23
6[k][See ver. 4 above] [p]Lev. 19:28; Deut. 14:1 [q]Job 1:20; [Isa. 3:24]
7[r]Isa. 58:7; Ezek. 24:17; [Deut. 26:14; Hos. 9:4]
9[s]See ch. 7:34
10[t]See ch. 5:19
11[u]ch. 5:19; 22:9; [Deut. 29:25, 26; 2 Kgs. 22:17; 2 Chr. 34:25] [v]ch. 13:10
12[w]ch. 7:26 [x]See ch. 3:17
13[y]ch. 10:18; 22:26; Isa. 22:17, 18; See Deut. 4:26-28; 28:64, 65 [z]See ch. 15:14 [a]Deut. 28:36, 64
14[b]For ver. 14, 15, see ch. 23:7, 8 [c]ch. 4:2
15[c][See ver. 14 above] [d][Isa. 43:5, 6]; See ch. 3:18 [e]ch. 24:6; 30:3; 32:37
16[f][Ezek. 12:13; Amos 4:2; Hab. 1:15] [g]ch. 13:4
17[h]ch. 32:19; 2 Chr. 16:9; Job 34:21; Prov. 5:21 [i][Ps. 51:9; 90:8]
18[j]ch. 17:18; Isa. 40:2

Jeremiah, but the promise implies continued persecution. **with**. See note on 30:11.

16:1–17:18 *Jeremiah Renewed by God.* Jeremiah responds positively to God's rebuke and undertakes new ministry. He preaches about the terrible times awaiting Judah (16:1–18) and the depths of human sin (16:19–17:11). He prays for and receives restoration (17:12–18).

16:2 As a symbol to the nation, Jeremiah is instructed not to marry. Such living messages were intended to shock the people into repentance (cf. 13:1–14), although it is a mercy for Jeremiah (16:3–4).

16:3–4 With **sword**, **famine**, and **diseases** coming as part of judgment (15:2–3), it will be better for Jeremiah not to have a wife or children to care for and not to have to watch them suffer and die (cf. 1 Cor. 7:29–32).

16:5 God commands Jeremiah not to attend funerals or mourn the dead, again as a testimony that God has **taken away** his **peace**. **steadfast love**. God's protection is based on his covenant relationship with Israel.

16:6–8 All mourning rituals such as burial, lamenting, and feasting will cease, because **no one** will be left to do them (cf. 7:33).

16:9 voice of the bridegroom. Weddings will cease as society disintegrates (cf. 7:34; 25:10).

16:10–12 you have done worse. God's condemnation comes because of constant covenant breaking that exceeds that of previous generations.

16:13 hurl. Violently expel (10:18). **a land**. A place of exile (15:14). **serve other gods**. The ultimate punishment (Deut. 28:64). **no favor**. A reversal of Ex. 34:6–7.

16:14–15 God will restore **Israel** after exile. This renewal will be so astounding it will surpass the first exodus (32:37; Deut. 30:1–10).

16:16–17 fishers, hunters. These are either enemy soldiers who will catch all refugees (Ezek. 12:13; 29:4–5; Amos 4:2; 9:1–4; Hab. 1:14–17) or God's servants who will pluck people out of exile (cf. Matt. 4:19; Mark 1:17).

16:18 Prior to any renewal, Yahweh will punish the polluters of his **inheritance**, i.e., God's people and their land.

18[k][Isa. 65:4]; See Ezek. 43:7-9
19[l]2 Sam. 22:33; Ps. 28:7; 31:3, 4; Isa. 25:4 [m]ch. 17:17 [n][Isa. 9:2; 49:6, 22, 23] [o]See ch. 18:15
20[p][1 Cor. 8:4]; See ch. 2:11
21[q]See ch. 33:2
Chapter 17
1[r]Job 19:24 [s]Prov. 3:3; 7:3; [2 Cor. 3:3] [t]Ex. 27:2; Ps. 118:27
2[u][ch. 19:5] [v]Judg. 3:7; See Deut. 16:21 [w][Isa. 1:29]; See ch. 2:20
3[x]Ps. 48:1, 2; 87:1; Isa. 2:3 [y]ch. 15:13
4[z]See ch. 15:14 [a]See Deut. 32:22
5[b]2 Chr. 32:8; Ps. 146:3
6[c]ch. 48:6 [d]ch. 29:32; Job 20:17; Ps. 34:12 [e]Deut. 29:23; Job 39:6
7[f]Ps. 25:2; 34:8; 125:1; See Ps. 2:12 [g]Ps. 71:5
8[h]Ps. 1:3; [Ezek. 47:12]

repay their iniquity and their sin, because they have polluted my land with the carcasses of their detestable idols, and [k]have filled my inheritance with their abominations."

19 [l]O LORD, my strength and my stronghold,
[m]my refuge in the day of trouble,
[n]to you shall the nations come
from the ends of the earth and say:
"Our fathers have inherited nothing but lies,
[o]worthless things in which there is no profit.
20 Can man make for himself [p]gods?
Such are not gods!"

21 "Therefore, behold, I will make them know, this once I will make them know my power and my might, and they shall know that [q]my name is the LORD."

The Sin of Judah

17 "The sin of Judah is written with [r]a pen of iron; with a point of diamond it is engraved
on [s]the tablet of their heart, and on [t]the horns of their altars, 2 while [u]their children
remember their altars and their [v]Asherim, [w]beside every green tree and on the high hills,
3 [x]on the mountains in the open country. [y]Your wealth and all your treasures I will give
for spoil as the price of your high places for sin throughout all your territory. 4 You shall
loosen your hand from your heritage that I gave to you, [z]and I will make you serve your
enemies in a land that you do not know, [a]for in my anger a fire is kindled that shall burn
forever."

5 Thus says the LORD:
"Cursed is the man [b]who trusts in man
and makes flesh his strength,[1]
whose heart turns away from the LORD.
6 [c]He is like a shrub in the desert,
[d]and shall not see any good come.
He shall dwell in the parched places of the wilderness,
in [e]an uninhabited salt land.

7 [f]"Blessed is the man who trusts in the LORD,
[g]whose trust is the LORD.
8 [h]He is like a tree planted by water,
that sends out its roots by the stream,
and does not fear when heat comes,
for its leaves remain green,
and is not anxious in the year of drought,
for it does not cease to bear fruit."
9 The heart is deceitful above all things,
and desperately sick;

[1] Hebrew *arm*

16:19–20 Jeremiah's confession of faith indicates he has repented, as 15:19–21 ordered. **my strength**. The one who delivers him (Ex. 15:2–3). **my refuge**. His place of protection (cf. Jer. 12:1–4; 15:10–12). The **nations** will **come** to Yahweh, rejecting their idols (10:1–16) and confessing that he alone is God and thus able to save. This is the OT expectation and the purpose of Israel's calling (Gen. 12:1–3).

16:21 I will make them know. All that will befall Judah and the nations will be for a redemptive purpose.

17:1–3 pen of iron . . . point of diamond. These were tools for carving on stone, which is what **their heart** has become. **beside every green tree, on the high hills, on the mountains**. Serving idols in every conceivable location is the sin engraved on their hearts.

17:4 serve your enemies. See 15:14 and Deut. 28:64. **my anger**. God's justifiable wrath at Judah's constant, baseless covenant breaking.

17:5 Cursed. Beset with negative consequences (Deut. 28:15–68). **makes flesh his strength**. He turns from God to seek help **in man**.

17:6 like a shrub in the desert. He will be alone and without resources when disaster comes.

17:7 Blessed. Filled with God-defined benefits. **whose trust is the LORD**. Only trust in God motivates confident obedience in times of crisis.

17:8 tree planted by water. Settled with resources no matter what happens. A perfect contrast to the "shrub in the desert" (v. 6; cf. Ps. 1:3).

17:9 heart. A metaphor for the human will and emotions (cf. vv. 5–7). **deceitful**. Tortuous, uneven, and crooked like a bad road. **desperately sick**. Medically incurable (15:18; 30:12, 15; Job 34:6; Isa. 17:11; Mic. 1:9). **who can understand it?** A rhetorical question expecting a negative answer. However, this strongly negative assessment of the human heart is not intended as a description of the heart of a believer under the new covenant, where

who can understand it?
10 [i]"I the LORD search the heart
[j]and test the mind,[1]
[k]to give every man according to his ways,
according to the fruit of his deeds."
11 Like the [l]partridge that gathers a brood that she did not hatch,
so is [m]he who gets riches but not by justice;
[n]in the midst of his days they will leave him,
[o]and at his end he will be a fool.
12 A glorious throne set on high from the beginning
is the place of our sanctuary.
13 O LORD, [p]the hope of Israel,
[q]all who forsake you shall be put to shame;
those who turn away from you[2] [r]shall be written in the earth,
for [s]they have forsaken [t]the LORD, the fountain of living water.

Jeremiah Prays for Deliverance

14 [u]Heal me, O LORD, and I shall be healed;
save me, and I shall be saved,
for [v]you are my praise.
15 [w]Behold, they say to me,
"Where is the word of the LORD?
Let it come!"
16 I have not run away from being your shepherd,
nor have I desired the day of sickness.
[x]You know [x]what came out of my lips;
it was before your face.
17 Be not a terror to me;
[y]you are my refuge in the day of disaster.
18 [z]Let those be put to shame who persecute me,
but let me not be put to shame;
[z]let them be dismayed,
but let me not be dismayed;
[a]bring upon them the day of disaster;
destroy them with double destruction!

Keep the Sabbath Holy

19 Thus said the LORD to me: "Go and stand in the People's Gate, by which [b]the kings of
Judah enter and by which they go out, and in all the gates of Jerusalem, 20 and say: 'Hear the
word of the LORD, [b]you kings of Judah, and all Judah, and all the inhabitants of Jerusalem,
who enter by these gates. 21 Thus says the LORD: Take care for the sake of your lives, and

[1] Hebrew *kidneys* [2] Hebrew *me*

10 [i]1 Sam. 16:7; 1 Chr. 28:9; Ps. 139:23; Rom. 8:27 [j]See ch. 11:20 [k]ch. 32:19; Job 34:11; Ps. 62:12
11 [l][1 Sam. 26:20] [m]Ps. 39:6 [n][Ps. 55:23] [o][Luke 12:20]
13 [p]See ch. 14:8 [q]Josh. 24:20; Ps. 73:27; Isa. 1:28 [r][Luke 10:20] [s]ch. 1:16 [t]ch. 2:13; [John 4:10, 14]
14 [u]Ps. 6:2 [v]Deut. 10:21
15 [w]Isa. 5:19; 2 Pet. 3:4
16 [x]ch. 15:15; Ps. 40:9; 139:4
17 [y]ch. 16:19
18 [z]Ps. 35:4; 40:14 [a]ch. 11:20; Ps. 35:8
19 [b]See ch. 13:13
20 [b][See ver. 19 above]

God promises to write his law on people's hearts (Jer. 31:33; 32:40; cf. Ezek. 36:26; Rom. 5:5; 6:17; Heb. 10:22; 1 John 3:21).

17:10 heart and . . . mind. God understands (v. 9) the inner recesses of human motives, thinking, and decisions. **to give every man**. God is a just and merciful Judge.

17:11 Just as some birds claim offspring that are not their own, some people take others' rights and **riches**.

17:12–13 glorious throne. The temple (14:21; Ps. 80:1). **our sanctuary**. A place of security when the people trust Yahweh, but a place of thieves when they do not (Jer. 7:1–15). **hope of Israel**. The one who secures the future of those who trust in him (14:8; 50:7; 1 Cor. 13:13). **written in the earth**. Those who turn away from God shall die and go to the dust ingloriously (Ps. 69:28). **fountain of living water**. Source of spiritual sustenance (Jer. 17:5–8; cf. note on 2:12–13).

17:14 Jeremiah prays for his own healing and salvation. **my praise**. That which he most values and speaks of with most joy.

17:15–16 Despite scoffing hearers, Jeremiah preaches faithfully. **your shepherd**. One entrusted to feed, protect, and guide. **the day of sickness**. Judah's apostasy and its punishment. **out of my lips . . . before your face**. He spoke only what he had received from God (15:19–21).

17:17–18 For now Jeremiah stands with God, not the people. Thus he fulfills God's commands in 1:7–10, 17–19; 15:19–21.

17:19–18:23 ***Jeremiah Burdened by Constant Opposition.*** Jeremiah remains faithful to his calling, but Judah remains "faithful" in its opposition. After hearing Jeremiah preach against Sabbath breaking (17:19–27) and compare them to a spoiled pot (18:1–17), the people renew their opposition to him (18:18–23).

17:19–20 God sends Jeremiah to condemn **all Judah**. The **People's Gate** is not mentioned elsewhere in Scripture, but was obviously a prominent city entrance.

17:21–23 Take care for . . . your lives. This message has life-or-death consequences. The **Sabbath** is a day of ceasing from work, thus a time for

[c]do not bear a burden on the Sabbath day or bring it in by the gates of Jerusalem. 22 And
do not carry a burden out of your houses on the Sabbath [d]or do any work, but [e]keep the
Sabbath day holy, as I commanded your fathers. 23 Yet [f]they did not listen or incline their
ear, [g]but stiffened their neck, that they [h]might not hear and receive instruction.
24 "'But if you listen to me, declares the LORD, and [c]bring in no burden by the gates
of this city on the Sabbath day, but [e]keep the Sabbath day holy and do no work on it,
25 then [i]there shall enter by the gates of this city kings and princes who sit on the throne
of David, riding in chariots and on horses, they and their officials, the men of Judah
and the inhabitants of Jerusalem. And this city shall be inhabited forever. 26 And people
shall come from [j]the cities of Judah [k]and the places around Jerusalem, [j]from the land of
Benjamin, [k]from the Shephelah, from the hill country, [k]and from [l]the Negeb, bringing
[m]burnt offerings and sacrifices, grain offerings and frankincense, and [m]bringing thank
offerings to the house of the LORD. 27 But if you do not listen to me, to [e]keep the Sabbath
day holy, [c]and not to bear a burden and enter by the gates of Jerusalem on the Sabbath
day, then I will [n]kindle a fire in its gates, and it shall [o]devour the palaces of Jerusalem
and [p]shall not be quenched.'"

The Potter and the Clay

18 The word that came to Jeremiah from the LORD: 2 "Arise, and go down to [q]the potter's house, and there I will let you hear my words." 3 So I went down to [r]the potter's
house, and there he was working at his wheel. 4 And the vessel he was making of clay was
[s]spoiled in the potter's hand, and [t]he reworked it into another vessel, as it seemed good
to the potter to do.
5 Then the word of the LORD came to me: 6 "O house of Israel, [u]can I not do with you as
this potter has done? declares the LORD. [v]Behold, like the clay in the potter's hand, so are
you in my hand, O house of Israel. 7 If at any time I declare concerning a nation or a kingdom, that I will [w]pluck up and break down and destroy it, 8 and if that nation, concerning
which I have spoken, [x]turns from its evil, [y]I will relent of the disaster that I intended to
do to it. 9 And if at any time I declare concerning a nation or a kingdom that I will [w]build
and plant it, 10 and if it does evil in my sight, not listening to my voice, then I will relent
of the good that I had intended to do to it. 11 Now, therefore, say to the men of Judah and
the inhabitants of Jerusalem: 'Thus says the LORD, Behold, I am shaping disaster against
you and devising a plan against you. [z]Return, every one from his evil way, and [a]amend
your ways and your deeds.'
12 "But they say, [b]'That is in vain! We will follow our own plans, and will every one act
according to [c]the stubbornness of his evil heart.'

13 "Therefore thus says the LORD:
[d]Ask among the nations,
Who has heard the like of this?

21 [c][John 5:10]; See Neh. 13:15-19
22 [d]See Num. 15:32-36 [e]Ex. 23:12; 31:13; Isa. 56:2; 58:13; Ezek. 20:12, 20; See Ex. 20:8-11; Deut. 5:12-15
23 [f]ch. 7:24, 26; [ch. 11:10] [g][2 Chr. 30:8; Acts 7:51] [h]See ch. 5:3
24 [c][See ver. 21 above] [e][See ver. 22 above]
25 [i]ch. 22:4
26 [j]ch. 32:44; 33:13 [k]Zech. 7:7 [l]Gen. 13:1 [m]Lev. 7:12; 22:29; 2 Chr. 33:16; Ps. 107:22; 116:17
27 [e][See ver. 22 above] [c][See ver. 21 above] [n]ch. 21:14; 43:12; 49:27; 50:32; Lam. 4:11; Amos 1:14 [o]ch. 52:13; 2 Kgs. 25:9 [p]ch. 7:20

Chapter 18

2 [q]ch. 19:1; 1 Chr. 4:23; [Zech. 11:13]
3 [r]ch. 19:1; 1 Chr. 4:23; [Zech. 11:13]
4 [s]ch. 13:7 [t][Rom. 9:21]
6 [u]Isa. 45:9; See Rom. 9:20-24 [v]Job 10:9; Isa. 64:8
7 [w]ch. 1:10; 42:10
8 [x]Ezek. 18:21 [y]ch. 26:3, 13, 19; Judg. 2:18; Jonah 3:10
9 [w][See ver. 7 above]
11 [z]ch. 35:15; 2 Kgs. 17:13; Jonah 3:8 [a]ch. 7:3; 25:5; 35:15
12 [b]ch. 2:25 [c]See ch. 3:17
13 [d]ch. 2:10, 11

physical and spiritual renewal (Ex. 20:8–11) and a gift to mankind (Mark 2:23–28).

17:24–27 Restoration of **Sabbath** rest and worship will result in perpetual rule by David's lineage, perpetual habitation, and perpetual worship. Refusal to keep the Sabbath will result in **fire in its gates**, a metaphor for destruction (Amos 1:3–2:5).

18:1–2 God commands another symbolic act (cf. 13:1–14; 16:1–13).

18:3 A potter was a maker of household vessels. **wheel**. Two flat, circular stones mounted on a rod; the potter spun the stones while placing mud and water on them.

18:4 spoiled. It did not develop properly. **reworked**. The potter shaped and reshaped the wet clay to keep the developing vessel symmetrical. **as it seemed good to the potter**. Cf. Rom. 9:21.

18:6 can I not do with you? As its maker, God can reshape **Israel**.

18:7 Pluck up, **break down**, and **destroy** were judgment metaphors from agriculture, construction, and war. See 1:10; 31:28; 45:4. **If**. Many of the biblical prophecies are conditional; the human response of repentance or disbelief matters because the goal of prophecy, more than simply telling the future, is the moral formation of God's people. See note on Jonah 3:4.

18:8 turns. From sin to God. **relent of the disaster**. See notes on 8:6 and 15:6. For this expression, see 26:3, 13, 19; 42:10; Ex. 32:12; Joel 2:13; Jonah 3:10; 4:2. God has prophets preach judgment so that repentance results. Repentance then removes the necessity for judgment. On the wordplay with **evil** and disaster, see note on Jer. 1:13–14.

18:9 Build and plant are restoration metaphors from construction and agriculture. See 1:10; 42:10.

18:10 does evil. Turns from God to sin based on **not listening to** God's **voice** as found in the written covenant (Deut. 6:4–9). **relent of the good**. Remove the blessing the people could have received.

18:11 God is **shaping disaster** (vv. 7–8), so Judah must **amend** (lit., "make good"; 7:3, 5) its **ways** (patterns of living) and **deeds**.

18:12 vain. Hopeless (2:25; Isa. 57:10) as a plan. **follow our own plans** (see Jeremiah 42–43). What the people say in their hearts, if not aloud.

18:13 Who has heard? Judah's covenant breaking is unprecedented. See 2:10–11 for a similar question.

The virgin Israel
has done [e]a very horrible thing.
14 Does the snow of Lebanon leave
the crags of Sirion?[1]
Do the mountain waters run dry,[2]
the cold flowing streams?
15 [f]But my people have forgotten me;
they make offerings to [g]false gods;
they made them stumble in their ways,
[h]in the ancient roads,
and to walk into side roads,
[i]not the highway,
16 making their land [j]a horror,
a thing [j]to be hissed at forever.
[k]Everyone who passes by it is horrified
[l]and shakes his head.
17 [m]Like the east wind [n]I will scatter them
before the enemy.
[o]I will show them my back, not my face,
in the day of their calamity."

18 Then they said, [p]"Come, let us make plots against Jeremiah, [q]for the law shall not perish from the priest, nor counsel from the wise, nor the word from the prophet. [r]Come, let
us strike him with the tongue, and let us not pay attention to any of his words."

19 Hear me, O LORD,
and [s]listen to the voice of my adversaries.
20 [t]Should good be repaid with evil?
Yet [u]they have dug a pit for my life.
[v]Remember how I stood before you
to speak good for them,
to turn away your wrath from them.
21 Therefore [w]deliver up their children to famine;
give them over to the power of the sword;
let their wives become childless [x]and widowed.
May their men meet death by pestilence,
their youths be struck down by the sword in battle.
22 [y]May a cry be heard from their houses,
when you bring the plunderer suddenly upon them!
For [u]they have dug a pit to take me
[z]and laid snares for my feet.
23 Yet [a]you, O LORD, know
all their plotting to kill me.
[b]Forgive not their iniquity,

[1] Hebrew *of the field* [2] Hebrew *Are foreign waters plucked up*

13 [e]ch. 5:30
15 [f]ch. 2:13, 32; 17:13 [g]ch. 2:5; 10:15; 16:19 [h]ch. 6:16 [i][Isa. 57:14]
16 [j]ch. 19:8; 25:9, 11, 18; 49:13, 17; 50:13; 51:37; 2 Chr. 29:8 [k]ch. 50:13; Lam. 2:15 [l]Job 16:4; Ps. 22:7; Matt. 27:39
17 [m]Gen. 41:6, 23, 27; Ex. 10:13; Job 27:21; Ps. 48:7; Ezek. 27:26; Hos. 13:15; Jonah 4:8 [n]ch. 13:24 [o][ch. 2:27]
18 [p]ch. 11:19 [q][ch. 2:8; 5:13, 31; 6:13] [r]ch. 9:3, 8; Job 5:21; [Ps. 31:20]
19 [s]Ps. 35:1; Isa. 49:25
20 [t]Ps. 35:12 [u]Ps. 35:7; 57:6; 119:85 [v][Neh. 13:14]
21 [w]Ps. 109:10 [x]Ps. 109:9
22 [y][ch. 20:16] [u][See ver. 20 above] [z]Ps. 140:5
23 [a][Ps. 35:22] [b]Neh. 4:5

18:14–16 The Hebrew in v. 14 is nearly impossible to translate with certainty (cf. the two ESV footnotes). **Does the snow of Lebanon . . . Do the mountain waters . . . ?** Both questions expect a negative answer. In contrast, Judah has done the unnatural thing and deserted God. **ancient roads**. Judah's relationship and covenant with God. **side roads**. Serving idols. **making their land a horror**. The result of God's judgment (4:7). **Everyone who passes by**. Judah will be a cautionary tale for others (Lam. 2:15).

18:17 scatter them. See 9:16; Deut. 28:64–68. **show them my back**. Remove God's protecting presence. Judah has already turned its back on God (Jer. 2:27).

18:18 Judah **plots against Jeremiah**. **law . . . priest**. Priests were to teach Moses' writings accurately. **counsel from the wise**. Advisers were to apply the law and wisdom writings correctly. **word from the prophet**. Both already revealed and yet-to-be-revealed words. The people rejected the notion that Jeremiah could be right and all their leaders wrong (1:17–19; 2:8; 5:13, 31; 6:13).

18:19–20 my adversaries. Those plotting against Jeremiah. **good . . . repaid with evil**. He told Judah the truth and interceded for them, and yet they plotted against him.

18:21–22 famine . . . sword . . . pestilence. These are what God said Judah would experience (15:2).

18:23 Jeremiah now fully agrees with God's assessment of and plans for Judah.

nor blot out their sin from your sight.
Let them be overthrown before you;
deal with them in the time of your anger.

The Broken Flask

19 Thus says the LORD, "Go, buy [c]a potter's earthenware [d]flask, and take some of [e]the
elders of the people and some of [e]the elders of the priests, 2 and go out [f]to the Valley
of the Son of Hinnom at the entry of the Potsherd Gate, and proclaim there the words that
I tell you. 3 You shall say, [g]'Hear the word of the LORD, [h]O kings of Judah and inhabitants
of Jerusalem. Thus says the LORD of hosts, the God of Israel: Behold, I am bringing such
disaster upon this place that [i]the ears of everyone who hears of it will tingle. 4 [j]Because
the people have forsaken me and have profaned this place by making offerings in it to
other gods whom neither they nor their fathers nor the kings of Judah have known; [k]and
because they have filled this place with the blood of innocents, 5 [l]and have built the high
places of Baal [l]to burn their sons in the fire as burnt offerings to Baal, [m]which I did not
command or decree, nor did it come into my mind— 6 therefore, [n]behold, days are coming, declares the LORD, when this place shall no more be called Topheth, or [o]the Valley of
the Son of Hinnom, but the Valley of Slaughter. 7 And in this place [p]I will make void the
plans of Judah and Jerusalem, [q]and will cause their people to fall by the sword before their
enemies, and by the hand of those who seek their life. [r]I will give their dead bodies for food
to the birds of the air and to the beasts of the earth. 8 And I will make this city [s]a horror, [s]a
thing to be hissed at. Everyone who passes by it will be horrified and will hiss because of
all its wounds. 9 [t]And I will make them eat the flesh of their sons and their daughters, and
everyone shall eat the flesh of his neighbor [u]in the siege and in the distress, with which
their enemies and those who seek their life afflict them.'

10 "Then [v]you shall break [w]the flask in the sight of the men who go with you, 11 and shall
say to them, 'Thus says the LORD of hosts: So will I break this people and this city, [x]as one
breaks a potter's vessel, [y]so that it can never be mended. [z]Men shall bury in Topheth because
there will be no place else to bury. 12 Thus will I do to this place, declares the LORD, and to
its inhabitants, making this city [a]like Topheth. 13 The houses of Jerusalem and the houses
of the kings of Judah—[b]all the houses on whose [c]roofs offerings have been offered [d]to all
the host of heaven, and [e]drink offerings have been poured out to other gods—shall be
defiled [a]like the place of Topheth.'"

14 Then Jeremiah came from [f]Topheth, where the LORD had sent him to prophesy, [g]and
he stood in the court of the LORD's house and said to all the people: 15 "Thus says the LORD
of hosts, the God of Israel, behold, I am bringing upon this city and upon all its towns
all the disaster that I have pronounced against it, [h]because they have stiffened their neck,
[i]refusing to hear my words."

Chapter 19
1 [c]See ch. 18:2 [d]ver. 10 [e]2 Kgs. 19:2; 23:1; Ezek. 8:1
2 [f]See Josh. 15:8
3 [g]ch. 17:20 [h]See ch. 13:13 [i]1 Sam. 3:11; 2 Kgs. 21:12
4 [j]See ch. 1:16 [k]2 Kgs. 21:16; See ch. 2:34
5 [l]ch. 7:31; 32:35; Lev. 18:21 [m]ch. 7:31; 32:35; Deut. 17:3
6 [n]ch. 7:32 [o]ver. 2
7 [p][Isa. 19:3] [q][Lev. 26:17] [r]See ch. 7:33
8 [s]See ch. 18:16
9 [t]Lev. 26:29; Deut. 28:53; Isa. 9:20; Lam. 2:20; 4:10; Ezek. 5:10 [u]Deut. 28:53, 55, 57
10 [v][ch. 51:63, 64] [w]ver. 1
11 [x]Ps. 2:9; Isa. 30:14; Lam. 4:2 [y][Prov. 6:15] [z]ch. 7:32
12 [a][2 Kgs. 23:10]
13 [b]ch. 32:29; 44:18; 2 Kgs. 23:12; Zeph. 1:5 [c]2 Sam. 11:2 [d]Deut. 4:19; Acts 7:42 [e]ch. 7:18; 44:18 [a][See ver. 12 above]
14 [f]ver. 2, 3 [g]ch. 26:2; [2 Chr. 20:5]
15 [h]ch. 7:26; 2 Chr. 30:8 [i]ch. 25:3

19:1–20:18 *Jeremiah Endures Suffering and Questions His Calling.* Though Jeremiah prophesies God's word faithfully (ch. 19), he endures persecution (20:1–6), which makes him question God and his calling (20:7–18).

19:1 Go, buy. The third symbolic act (cf. 13:1–7; 16:1–9). **earthenware flask**. A general term for a container. **elders of the people**. Civic leaders. **elders of the priests**. Religious leaders.

19:2 Hinnom. Probably the valley south of the city, used as a dumping place (7:31). **Potsherd Gate**. Uncertain location but likely a dumping ground (for broken containers).

19:3 Ears . . . will tingle with shock and horror at an account of judgment (cf. 1 Sam. 3:11; 2 Kings 21:12).

19:4 blood of innocents. Likely child sacrifices made to Molech (7:31).

19:5–6 burn their sons . . . to Baal. Perhaps an innovation to the worship of the fertility deity (7:31–32).

19:7 the plans of Judah and Jerusalem. I.e., their proposed solution to the threat that Babylon poses (see 18:12). **bodies for food**. Leaving bodies unburied was considered unacceptable (2 Sam. 21:10–14).

19:9 eat the flesh. Because of the lack of food caused by the **siege**, the people of Judah will turn to cannibalism (Lev. 26:29; Deut. 28:53; 2 Kings 6:24–29; Lam. 2:20; 4:10).

19:10 break the flask. A symbolic act representing Jerusalem's defeat.

19:11 break this people and this city. Babylon will crush and destroy. **mended**. Lit., "healed," a favorite image of Jeremiah (3:22; 6:14; 8:11; 15:18; 17:14; 30:17; 33:6; 51:8–9; cf. Lam. 2:13). **bury in Topheth**. Probably a cemetery already full (Jer. 7:32). **no place else**. No unused ground.

19:12 like Topheth. An overcrowded cemetery. Proper burial is impossible there.

19:13 offerings . . . to all the host of heaven. Sacrifices made on rooftops to astral deities (cf. 7:16–20; 44:15–19; Zeph. 1:4–5). **defiled**. Unclean or unfit for divine service or human habitation.

19:15 this city. Jerusalem. **all its towns**. The villages that depend on Jerusalem for protection. **all the disaster that I have pronounced**. See 18:13–17; Lev. 26:14–39; Deut. 28:15–68. **stiffened their neck**. See Jer. 7:26. **refusing to hear**. Rejected the covenant (Deut. 6:4–9).

Jeremiah Persecuted by Pashhur

20 Now [j]Pashhur the priest, the son of [k]Immer, who was [l]chief officer in the house of
the LORD, heard Jeremiah prophesying these things. 2 Then [j]Pashhur beat Jeremiah
the prophet, and put him [m]in the stocks that were in the upper [n]Benjamin Gate of the house
of the LORD. 3 The next day, when [j]Pashhur released Jeremiah from the stocks, Jeremiah
said to him, "The LORD does not call your name [j]Pashhur, but Terror on Every Side. 4 For
thus says the LORD: Behold, I will make you [o]a terror to yourself and to all your friends.
They shall fall by the sword of their enemies while you look on. And I will give all Judah
into the hand of the king of Babylon. He shall carry them captive to Babylon, and shall
strike them down with the sword. 5 Moreover, [p]I will give all the wealth of the city, all its
gains, all its [q]prized belongings, and all the treasures of the kings of Judah into the hand
of their enemies, who shall plunder them and seize them and carry them to Babylon. 6 And
you, [r]Pashhur, and all who dwell in your house, shall go into captivity. To Babylon you
shall go, and there you shall die, and there you shall be buried, you and all your friends,
[s]to whom you have prophesied falsely."

7 O LORD, [t]you have deceived me,
  and I was deceived;
[u]you are stronger than I,
  and you have prevailed.
[v]I have become a laughingstock all the day;
  everyone mocks me.
8 For whenever I speak, I cry out,
  I shout, [w]"Violence and destruction!"
For [x]the word of the LORD has become for me
  [y]a reproach and [y]derision all day long.
9 If I say, "I will not mention him,
  or speak any more in his name,"
[z]there is in my heart as it were a burning fire
  shut up in my bones,
and [a]I am weary with holding it in,
  and I cannot.
10 [b]For I hear many whispering.
  [c]Terror is on every side!
"Denounce him! [d]Let us denounce him!"
  say all my [e]close friends,
[f]watching for [g]my fall.
"Perhaps he will be deceived;
  then [h]we can overcome him
  and take our revenge on him."
11 But [i]the LORD is with me as a dread warrior;

Chapter 20
1 [j]ch. 21:1; 38:1; 1 Chr. 9:12; [Ezra 2:38] [k]1 Chr. 24:14; Ezra 2:37 [l][ch. 29:26]
2 [j][See ver. 1 above] [m]ch. 29:26; Acts 16:24 [n]ch. 37:13
3 [j][See ver. 1 above]
4 [o]See ch. 6:25
5 [p][2 Kgs. 20:17]; See 2 Kgs. 24:12-16; 25:13-17 [q]Job 28:10; Ezek. 22:25
6 [r]ch. 21:1; 38:1; 1 Chr. 9:12; [Ezra 2:38] [s]See ch. 14:14
7 [t][Ezek. 14:9] [u][2 Pet. 1:21] [v]Ps. 119:51; Lam. 3:14
8 [w]ch. 6:7 [x]ch. 6:10 [y]Ps. 44:13; 79:4
9 [z]Job 32:18, 19; Ps. 39:3 [a]ch. 6:11
10 [b]Ps. 31:13 [c]See ch. 6:25 [d][ch. 36:16, 20] [e]Ps. 41:9; 55:13; [ch. 9:4; 38:22] [f][Ps. 56:6] [g]Ps. 35:15 [h]ch. 1:19; 5:22
11 [i]See ch. 1:8

20:1 Pashhur. A common name (21:1). **chief officer**. Head overseer of temple supplies and activities; probably also handled troublemakers (29:26).

20:2 Pashhur beat Jeremiah for preaching disaster (19:14–15; see 1:17–19; 7:1–8:3; Matt. 5:11–12). **stocks**. A restraining device causing Jeremiah to stoop.

20:3 not . . . Pashhur, but Terror on Every Side. Pashhur may mean "tear off," i.e., God has "torn off" pieces of Judah and given them to invaders; but now he will cause terror on every side of Jerusalem.

20:4 False teachers are the ultimate terror, for they lead others to believe lies, which will result in **Babylon** capturing **all Judah**.

20:5 I will give. God, not Babylon, is the ruler. **all the treasures**. In the palace and temple. **carry them to Babylon**. Treasure, people, and the **kings of Judah** will go to Babylon (Isa. 39:1–8).

20:6 go into captivity. In 605, 597, or 587 B.C. **all your friends**. Those who believed Pashhur when he **prophesied falsely** that Jeremiah had erred (vv. 1–2).

20:7–8 deceived me . . . stronger than I . . . laughingstock. Jeremiah expresses his displeasure over his circumstances, even accusing God of deceiving and overpowering him (cf. 12:1–4; 15:10–21; Jeremiah's complaints are not always pure). Perhaps he wonders why God, who has called him to be a prophet, has not protected him from the suffering and mockery he has endured (20:1–2, 10, 18). Soon his complaint moves to praise (vv. 9–13), but then returns to distressed realism over his calling (vv. 14–18).

20:9 God does not allow Jeremiah to cease preaching. **burning fire . . . in my bones**. When Jeremiah decides not to preach, he apparently feels intense (and possibly bodily) pain, as if the words are trying to burst forth. He cannot stop proclaiming God's words.

20:10 many whispering. Jeremiah's enemies turn his words (v. 3) against him, planning **terror** for him **on every side**. They were **watching for** his **fall**, hoping for an incorrect prediction (cf. Luke 20:20, 26).

20:11 the LORD is with me. See note on 30:11. **dread warrior**. God fights for his people (Ex. 15:1–18). **not overcome me**. See Jer. 1:17–19; 15:19–21.

11[i]See ch. 1:8 [j]ch. 17:18; 23:40 [k]ch. 23:40
12[l]See ch. 11:20
13[m][Ps. 35:9, 10; 109:30, 31]
14[n]ch. 15:10; Job 3:3
15[o][John 16:21]
16[p]Gen. 19:25; Isa. 13:19 [q]ch. 18:22
17[r][Job 3:10, 11]
18[s][Job 3:20] [t][Lam. 3:1, 2]

Chapter 21

1[u]See ch. 20:1 [v]ch. 29:25; 37:3; 2 Kgs. 25:18 [w]ch. 35:4; 2 Chr. 34:8
2[x][ch. 37:7] [y][2 Kgs. 25:1] [z]Ps. 105:2, 5

therefore my persecutors will stumble;
[i]they will not overcome me.
[j]They will be greatly shamed,
for they will not succeed.
Their [k]eternal dishonor
will never be forgotten.
12 O LORD of hosts, who tests the righteous,
[l]who sees the heart and the mind,[1]
let me see your vengeance upon them,
for to you have I committed my cause.

13 [m]Sing to the LORD;
praise the LORD!
For he has delivered the life of the needy
from the hand of evildoers.

14 [n]Cursed be the day
on which I was born!
The day when my mother bore me,
let it not be blessed!
15 Cursed be the man who brought the news to my father,
"A son is born to you,"
[o]making him very glad.
16 Let that man be like [p]the cities
that the LORD overthrew without pity;
[q]let him hear a cry in the morning
and an alarm at noon,
17 [r]because he did not kill me in the womb;
so my mother would have been my grave,
and her womb forever great.
18 [s]Why did I come out from the womb
[t]to see toil and sorrow,
and spend my days in shame?

Jerusalem Will Fall to Nebuchadnezzar

21 This is the word that came to Jeremiah from the LORD, when King Zedekiah sent to
him [u]Pashhur the son of Malchiah and [v]Zephaniah the priest, the son of [w]Maaseiah,
saying, 2 [x]"Inquire of the LORD for us, [y]for Nebuchadnezzar[2] king of Babylon is making
war against us. Perhaps the LORD will deal with us according to [z]all his wonderful deeds
and will make him withdraw from us."
3 Then Jeremiah said to them: "Thus you shall say to Zedekiah, 4 'Thus says the LORD,

[1] Hebrew *kidneys* [2] Hebrew *Nebuchadrezzar*, an alternate spelling of *Nebuchadnezzar* (king of Babylon) occurring frequently from Jeremiah 21–52; this latter spelling is used throughout Jeremiah for consistency

20:12 See 11:20, where Jeremiah also asks the **LORD of hosts** (i.e., of armies) to judge between the wicked (his persecutors) and himself. **Mind** in this case represents a term (plural of Hb. *kilyah*, lit., "kidneys"; see ESV footnote) that refers particularly to the inner emotions.

20:13–14 praise the LORD! . . . Cursed be the day! On the one hand, God merits praise for his protection; on the other hand, Jeremiah lives a hard life. See 15:10 and Job 3:3.

20:15 Cursed be the man who brought the news. A son's birth was considered a blessing from God, but Jeremiah believes his birth was the opposite.

20:16–17 Let that man be defeated like Judah's cities because he did not kill Jeremiah at birth.

20:18 Jeremiah's ministry causes him hard work, **sorrow**, and **shame**. He accepts his role, but has no illusions of fame, approval, or appreciation.

21:1–29:32 *Jeremiah's Confrontations*. Having solidified his relationship with God, Jeremiah confronts his foes and their beliefs. He opposes kings (21:1–23:8), false prophets (23:9–40), the people (24:1–25:38), and false belief (26:1–29:32).

21:1–23:8 *Jeremiah Opposes Judah's Kings*. Jeremiah declares that the kingdom will perish (ch. 21), David's house will be left desolate (22:1–12), wicked kings will merit blame (22:13–30), and a righteous king will come (23:1–8).

21:1–2 Zedekiah. The last king of Judah (597–586 B.C.). **Pashhur**. Most likely a different man than in 20:1–2. **Zephaniah**. Not the prophet. **Nebuchadnezzar**. The greatest king of Babylon (605–562 B.C.). **making war against us**. Most likely in 588 B.C. due to Zedekiah not paying tribute money. **wonderful deeds**. Such as the exodus or the deliverance of Jerusalem in 701 B.C. (Isa. 36:1–37:36).

21:3–6 God will bring the Babylonians into the **city** (v. 4), **fight** alongside them **against** Judah (v. 5), and give them complete victory (v. 6).

the God of Israel: [a]Behold, I will turn back the weapons of war that are in your hands
and with which you are fighting against the king of Babylon and against the Chaldeans
who are besieging you outside the walls. [b]And I will bring them together into the midst
of this city. 5 I myself will fight against you [c]with outstretched hand and strong arm, [d]in
anger and in fury and in great wrath. 6 And I will strike down the inhabitants of this city,
both man and beast. They shall die of a great pestilence. 7 Afterward, declares the LORD,
[e]I will give Zedekiah king of Judah and his servants and the people in this city who survive the pestilence, sword, and famine into the hand of Nebuchadnezzar king of Babylon
and into the hand of their enemies, into the hand of those who seek their lives. He shall
strike them down with the edge of the sword. [f]He shall not pity them or spare them or
have compassion.'

8 "And to this people you shall say: [g]'Thus says the LORD: Behold, [h]I set before you the
way of life and the way of death. 9 He who stays in this city shall die [i]by the sword, by
famine, and by pestilence, but he who goes out and [j]surrenders to the Chaldeans who are
besieging you shall live [k]and shall have his life as a prize of war. 10 For [l]I have set my face
against this city for harm and [m]not for good, declares the LORD: [n]it shall be given into the
hand of the king of Babylon, and he shall burn it with fire.'

Message to the House of David

11 "And to the house of the king of Judah say, 'Hear the word of the LORD, 12 O house of
David! Thus says the LORD:

[o]"'Execute justice [p]in the morning,
and deliver from the hand of the oppressor
him who has been robbed,
[q]lest my wrath go forth like fire,
and burn with none to quench it,
because of your evil deeds.'"

13 [r]"Behold, I am against you, O inhabitant of the valley,
O rock of the plain,
declares the LORD;
you who say, [s]'Who shall come down against us,
or who shall enter our habitations?'
14 [t]I will punish you according to [u]the fruit of your deeds,
declares the LORD;
[v]I will kindle a fire in her forest,
[v]and it shall devour all that is around her."

22 Thus says the LORD: "Go down to the house of the king of Judah and speak there
this word, 2 and say, [w]'Hear the word of the LORD, O king of Judah, who sits on the
throne of David, you, and your servants, and your people who enter these gates. 3 Thus says
the LORD: [x]Do justice and righteousness, and deliver from the hand of the oppressor him
who has been robbed. And [y]do no wrong or violence [z]to the resident alien, [x]the fatherless,
and the widow, nor [a]shed innocent blood in this place. 4 For if you will indeed obey this

4 [a][ch. 32:5; 37:10] [b][Isa. 13:4]
5 [c]ch. 27:5; 32:17, 21; Ex. 6:6; Deut. 4:34; Ezek. 20:33 [d]ch. 32:37; Deut. 29:28
7 [e]ch. 37:17; 39:5; 52:9 [f]Deut. 28:50; 2 Chr. 36:17; Ezek. 5:11
8 [g]Deut. 30:15, 19 [h]ch. 38:2
9 [i]See ch. 15:2 [j]ch. 37:13, 14 [k]ch. 39:18; 45:5
10 [l]ch. 44:11; Lev. 20:3, 5; Ps. 34:16; Ezek. 14:8; [Amos 9:4] [m][ch. 14:11] [n]ver. 7; ch. 34:2; 37:8, 10; 38:17, 18, 23; 39:8; 52:13; 2 Chr. 36:19
12 [o]ch. 22:3; Zech. 7:9; [ch. 22:16] [p]Ps. 101:8 [q]ch. 4:4
13 [r][ver. 10]; See Ezek. 13:8 [s][ch. 49:4]
14 [t]ch. 9:25 [u]Prov. 1:31; Isa. 3:10 [v]Ezek. 20:47

Chapter 22

2 [w]ch. 21:12
3 [x]ch. 7:5, 6; 21:12 [y]Lev. 19:33 [z][Ps. 82:3; Isa. 1:17] [a]ver. 17; [ch. 26:15]

21:7 Those who survive **pestilence, sword, and famine** (15:2–3) will be given to **their enemies**, who will kill them pitilessly.

21:8–9 Jerusalemites have two choices: surrender to Babylon and **live**, or fight Babylon and **die**.

21:12 house of David. Zedekiah and his officials. **Execute justice**. Based on God's written word (Deut. 17:14–20). **deliver from the hand**. Make certain the weak receive protection and vindication. These are the marks of a great king. **wrath . . . like fire**. See Amos 1:3–2:16.

21:13 inhabitant of the valley. The valleys around Mount Zion. **rock of the plain**. The high and relatively flat area of Upper Jerusalem. **Who shall come** shows misplaced confidence in Jerusalem's natural defenses.

21:14 fruit of your deeds. Well documented by this point in the book: idolatry, oppression, and covenant infidelity. **devour**. See Isa. 5:24 and Amos 1:3–2:16.

22:1–2 This message is for the **king** and **people** alike.

22:3 The king and those with him are not to use their power for personal advantage, but are to rule in **justice and righteousness**. "Justice" (Hb. *mishpat*) means making right decisions according to God's commands and case laws. "Righteousness" (Hb. *tsedaqah*) means what is correct according to God's norms and moral standards (cf. 4:2; 9:24). **deliver**. Rescue from harm. **resident alien**. A foreigner residing permanently in Judah. **fatherless**. Due either to death or abandonment; see notes on 5:26–29; 7:6. **widow**. By death or abandonment. These spell out the responsibilities of the ideal king over God's people (cf. 7:6; contrast 22:13, 15). The messianic King will carry this out (23:5; 33:15).

22:4 obey this word. To protect the weak (v. 3), which is a major role of kings. **then there shall enter**. David's descendants would continue to rule Judah. This shows that the prophecies of destruction are conditional; the exile was not inevitable.

4[b]ch. 17:25
5[c]ch. 49:13; 51:14; Gen. 22:16; Amos 6:8; [Heb. 6:13] [d]ch. 7:34; 25:11, 18; 44:6, 22; Isa. 64:10; Ezek. 5:14
6[e]ver. 20, 23 [f][ch. 6:8]
7[g]ch. 6:4 [h]2 Kgs. 19:23; Isa. 37:24
8[i]See ch. 5:19
9[j]Deut. 29:25, 26
10[k][2 Chr. 35:24, 25] [l]ver. 11
11[m][2 Kgs. 23:34; 2 Chr. 36:4; Ezek. 19:4]
12[m][See ver. 11 above]
13[n]Hab. 2:12; See Isa. 5:18-23 [o][Mic. 3:10] [p]Lev. 19:13; 25:39, 40; Deut. 24:14, 15; James 5:4
14[q]Ezek. 23:14
15[r][2 Kgs. 23:25] [s]Ps. 128:2; Eccles. 8:12; Isa. 3:10
16[t]Prov. 31:9; [Isa. 1:17] [s][See ver. 15 above]

word, [b]then there shall enter the gates of this house kings who sit on the throne of David,
riding in chariots and on horses, they and their servants and their people. **5** But if you will
not obey these words, I [c]swear by myself, declares the LORD, that [d]this house shall become
a desolation. **6** For thus says the LORD concerning the house of the king of Judah:

"'You are like Gilead to me,
  like the summit of [e]Lebanon,
yet surely I will make you a desert,
  [f]an uninhabited city.[1]
7 [g]I will prepare destroyers against you,
  each with his weapons,
[h]and they shall cut down your choicest cedars
  and cast them into the fire.

8 "'And many nations will pass by this city, and every man will say to his neighbor,
[i]"Why has the LORD dealt thus with this great city?" **9** [j]And they will answer, "Because
they have forsaken the covenant of the LORD their God and worshiped other gods and
served them."'"

10 [k]Weep not for him who is dead,
  nor grieve for him,
[l]but weep bitterly for him who goes away,
  for he shall return no more
  to see his native land.

Message to the Sons of Josiah

11 For thus says the LORD concerning Shallum the son of Josiah, king of Judah, who
reigned instead of Josiah his father, and [m]who went away from this place: "He shall return
here no more, **12** but [m]in the place where they have carried him captive, there shall he die,
and he shall never see this land again."

13 [n]"Woe to him who builds his house by [o]unrighteousness,
  and his upper rooms by injustice,
[p]who makes his neighbor serve him for nothing
  and does not give him his wages,
14 who says, 'I will build myself a great house
  with spacious upper rooms,'
who cuts out windows for it,
  paneling it with cedar
  and [q]painting it with vermilion.
15 Do you think you are a king
  because you compete in cedar?
Did not your father eat and drink
  and [r]do justice and righteousness?
  [s]Then it was well with him.
16 [t]He judged the cause of the poor and needy;
  [s]then it was well.

[1] Hebrew *cities*

22:5 this house. See v. 1. **a desolation**. A ruin (39:1–10; 52:1–23).

22:6 Like Gilead . . . like . . . Lebanon suggests lush forests. **a desert**. The house of David after Jerusalem's fall.

22:7 destroyers . . . shall cut down your choicest cedars. Like the temple (Ps. 74:4–8), David's lineage will be cut down (Ps. 89:38–45).

22:8–9 pass by. See 18:16; 19:8.

22:10 him who is dead. Killed in the siege, yet free from pain. **him who goes away**. Exiles who deserve pity because they will never return home.

22:11 Shallum. Jehoahaz, king after Josiah (640–609 B.C.) for three months in 609 (2 Kings 23:31–33). **He shall return here no more**. Jehoahaz will never be restored to power (cf. Jer. 22:10).

22:12 Shallum will **die** in Egypt (2 Kings 23:34), as will all who flee there rather than surrender to Babylon (Jer. 21:8–10).

22:13–14 Jehoiakim (609–598 B.C.) built a palace for himself while his people suffered. He required his subjects to work on the project without compensation. Contrast this with v. 3.

22:15 The real mark of a good king is establishing justice (v. 3), not building ornate palaces. **your father**. Either David or Josiah, both better kings than Jehoiakim.

22:16–17 Jehoiakim's oppressive ways mean he did not **know** God. Jehoiakim saw only opportunity for wealth, not the needs of the **poor**.

Is not this [u]to know me?
declares the LORD.
17 But you have eyes and heart
only for your dishonest gain,
[v]for shedding innocent blood,
and for practicing oppression and violence."

18 Therefore thus says the LORD concerning Jehoiakim the son of Josiah, king of Judah:

[w]"They shall not lament for him, saying,
[x]'Ah, my brother!' or 'Ah, sister!'
They shall not lament for him, saying,
[y]'Ah, lord!' or 'Ah, his majesty!'
19 With the burial of a donkey [z]he shall be buried,
dragged and dumped beyond the gates of Jerusalem."
20 "Go up to Lebanon, and cry out,
and lift up your voice in Bashan;
cry out from [a]Abarim,
for all [b]your lovers are destroyed.
21 I spoke to you in your prosperity,
but you said, 'I will not listen.'
[c]This has been your way from [d]your youth,
that you have not obeyed my voice.
22 [e]The wind shall shepherd all your shepherds,
and [b]your lovers shall go into captivity;
[f]then you will be ashamed and confounded
because of all your evil.
23 O inhabitant of [g]Lebanon,
nested among the cedars,
how you will be pitied when pangs come upon you,
[h]pain as of a woman in labor!"

24 [i]"As I live, declares the LORD, though Coniah the son of Jehoiakim, king of Judah,
were [j]the signet ring on my right hand, yet I would tear you off 25 and [k]give you [l]into the
hand of those who seek your life, into the hand of those of whom you are afraid, even into
the hand of Nebuchadnezzar king of Babylon and into the hand of the Chaldeans. 26 [m]I
will hurl you and [n]the mother who bore you into another country, where you were not
born, and there you shall die. 27 But to the land to which they will long to return, there
they shall not return."

28 Is this man [o]Coniah a despised, broken pot,
a [p]vessel no one cares for?
Why are he and his children hurled and cast
into a [q]land that they do not know?
29 [r]O land, land, land,
hear the word of the LORD!

16 [u][Judg. 2:10]
17 [v]ver. 3; [ch. 26:15]
18 [w]Ps. 78:64; See ch. 16:4-6 [x][1 Kgs. 13:30] [y][ch. 34:5]
19 [z]ch. 8:2; 36:30; [Isa. 14:19]
20 [a]Num. 27:12; Deut. 32:49 [b][ch. 3:1]
21 [c]ch. 3:25 [d]Ps. 129:1, 2
22 [e]ch. 23:1; [Ezek. 34:10] [b][See ver. 20 above] [f]ch. 3:25
23 [g]ver. 6 [h]ch. 6:24; See Isa. 13:8
24 [i]Isa. 49:18; See Ezek. 5:11 [j]1 Kgs. 21:8; Song 8:6; Hag. 2:23
25 [k]ch. 34:20 [l]ch. 39:17; [Deut. 1:17]
26 [m]2 Kgs. 24:15; 2 Chr. 36:10 [n][2 Kgs. 24:8]
28 [o]ver. 24 [p][ch. 48:38; Ps. 31:12; Hos. 8:8] [q]See ch. 15:14
29 [r]Isa. 1:2

22:18 Jehoiakim is so unjust, no one will mourn his death.

22:19 burial of a donkey. Rather than the elaborate rituals kings usually receive.

22:20 Lebanon. Mountains to the north. **Bashan**. Mountains northeast of Jerusalem. **Abarim**. Mountains southeast in Moab. **lovers**. Judah's allies, all **destroyed** by Babylon.

22:21 Israel tended to disobey God during times of prosperity (Deut. 8:11–20; Judg. 2:6–3:6).

22:22 The wind shall shepherd all your shepherds. Judah's leaders/shepherds (2:8; 10:21) will be driven and scattered to the winds. **lovers**. See 22:20. **all your evil**. In trusting allies, not God.

22:23 Lebanon. In the north and thus first to experience Babylon's fury. **pain as of a woman in labor**. Metaphor for severe pain prior to a very painful event (4:31; 6:24; 13:21).

22:24 Coniah. Another name for Jehoiachin, who ruled three months (598–597 B.C.); also called Jeconiah (24:1). Babylon deposed him and put Zedekiah (597–587 B.C.) in power. Jehoiachin was later treated well in exile (52:31–34; 2 Kings 24:8–9; 25:27–30). **signet ring**. Used to imprint a person's signature and thus represent a person's authority (Hag. 2:23).

22:26–27 Sent to Babylon in 597 B.C., Jehoiachin and his **mother** died in exile. Some Judeans may have hoped he would **return** and reign.

22:28 broken pot. Like the nation itself, punished by God. **cast into a land**. Exiled in Babylon.

22:29–30 Judah (the **land**) must understand that David's lineage will cease

30 Thus says the LORD:
"Write this man down as [s]childless,
a man who shall not succeed in his days,
[t]for none of his offspring shall succeed
[t] in sitting on the throne of David
and ruling again in Judah."

The Righteous Branch

23 [u]"Woe to the shepherds who destroy and scatter the sheep of my pasture!" declares
the LORD. 2 Therefore thus says the LORD, the God of Israel, concerning [u]the shepherds who care for my people: "You have scattered my flock and have driven them away, and
you have not attended to them. [v]Behold, I will attend to you for your evil deeds, declares
the LORD. 3 [w]Then I will gather the remnant of my flock [x]out of all the countries where I
have driven them, and I will bring them back to their fold, [y]and they shall be fruitful and
multiply. 4 [z]I will set shepherds over them who will care for them, and they shall fear no
more, nor be dismayed, neither shall any be missing, declares the LORD.
5 [a]"Behold, the days are coming, declares the LORD, when I will raise up for David a
righteous [b]Branch, and [c]he shall reign as king and deal wisely, and shall execute justice and
righteousness in the land. 6 In his days Judah will be saved, and [d]Israel will [e]dwell securely.
And this is the name by which he will be called: [f]'The LORD is our righteousness.'
7 [g]"Therefore, behold, the days are coming, declares the LORD, when they shall no longer
say, 'As the LORD lives who brought up the people of Israel out of the land of Egypt,' 8 but
'As the LORD lives who brought up and led the offspring of the house of Israel out of the
north country and out of all the countries where he[1] had driven them.' Then they shall
dwell in their own land."

Lying Prophets

9 Concerning the prophets:

[h]My heart is broken within me;
[i]all my bones shake;
I am like a drunken man,
like a man overcome by wine,
because of the LORD
and because of his holy words.
10 [j]For the land is full of adulterers;
[k]because of the curse [l]the land mourns,
and [m]the pastures of the wilderness are dried up.
[n]Their course is evil,
and their might is not right.

[1] Septuagint; Hebrew *I*

30 [s][1 Chr. 3:17; Matt. 1:12] [t]ch. 36:30

Chapter 23

1 [u]ch. 6:3; 10:21; 22:22; 25:34, 36; Isa. 56:11; Ezek. 34:2; Zech. 11:17; [John 10:12, 13]
2 [u][See ver. 1 above] [v]ver. 22; ch. 4:4
3 [w]ch. 29:14; 32:37; Deut. 30:3; Ezek. 20:34, 41; 37:21; [Ps. 107:3]; See Ezek. 34:11-16 [x][ch. 8:3] [y][Gen. 1:28]
4 [z]ch. 3:15
5 [a]For ver. 5, 6, see ch. 33:14-16 [b]Isa. 4:2; 11:1 [c]ch. 30:9; Isa. 32:1; Ezek. 37:24; Hos. 3:5; Zech. 9:9; Matt. 2:2; Luke 1:32; 19:38; John 1:49
6 [d]Deut. 33:28; [Zech. 14:11] [e]ch. 32:37 [f]Rom. 10:4; 1 Cor. 1:30
7 [g]For ver. 7, 8, see ch. 16:14, 15
9 [h]Ezek. 6:9 [i]Hab. 3:16
10 [j]ch. 5:7, 8; 9:2 [k]Ps. 10:7; 59:12; Hos. 4:2, 3 [l]ch. 4:28 [m]ch. 9:10; 12:4; Ps. 107:34 [n][ch. 22:17]

to rule Judah. **none of his offspring**. This raises a severe problem: Will God keep his promise of 2 Sam. 7:16? And how? See Jer. 23:5–6.

23:1–2 shepherds. See note on 3:15. Rather than bind up, heal, protect, and feed their **sheep**, Judah's leaders have destroyed and **scattered** them (2:8; 10:21; 22:22; Ezek. 34:2; Zech. 11:15–17). **attend to you**. Judge them because they have not judged God's people well.

23:3 gather. Bring back to Judah from exile. This process began in 538 B.C. (Ezra 1–2). For the expectation, see Jer. 29:14; 31:8, 10; 32:37; Ezek. 11:17; 20:41; 28:25; 34:13; 36:24; 37:21. **remnant**. Originally this meant simply "survivors," but it came to mean "faithful ones" (Isa. 4:2–6; 10:22–24; Jer. 6:9).

23:5 God will honor his covenant with **David** (2 Sam. 7:1–25). **a righteous Branch** (see notes on Zech. 3:8–9; 6:12) . . . **shall reign as king**. This Davidic king, metaphorically a "branch" from the tree of David, will embody all good kingly characteristics of insightful decision making, fairness, and correct dispensing of **justice** (cf. Isa. 11:1–10). Such predictions of a coming king, part of the larger complex of messianic expectations, were seen by the NT authors as fulfilled in Jesus (Matt. 2:2; Luke 1:32; 19:38; John 1:49).

23:6 Judah will be saved. For the whole people being "saved," see Ex. 14:30. God rescues his people from danger—including the danger to which their own sin has subjected them—and fosters for them the conditions in which faithful life can flourish. **dwell securely**. Free from victorious enemies. **The LORD is our righteousness**. A play on the new king's name, Zedekiah, which means "the LORD is my righteousness." Even though Zedekiah fails, a new king will come. Cf. Isaiah 40–66, which foretells the return from exile, which leads to the raising up of David's heir.

23:7–8 they shall no longer say. The people's return and the Messiah's subsequent reign will be so great as to overshadow the exodus itself (cf. 16:14–15).

23:9–40 *Jeremiah Confronts False Prophets.* Prophets were supposed to preach God's covenant and make accurate predictions (Deut. 13:1–11; 18:15–22).

23:9 God's words are **holy words**, accurate and special words, and their current import staggers Jeremiah.

23:10 full of adulterers. Spiritual adultery has led God to take disciplinary measures (cf. 5:7–8; 9:2), such as sending drought (14:1–12).

11 [o]"Both prophet and priest are ungodly;
even [p]in my house I have found their evil,
declares the LORD.
12 [q]Therefore their way shall be to them
like slippery paths [r]in the darkness,
into which they shall be driven and fall,
for I will bring disaster upon them
[s]in the year of their punishment,
declares the LORD.
13 In the prophets of [t]Samaria
[u]I saw an unsavory thing:
[v]they prophesied by Baal
[w]and led my people Israel astray.
14 But in the prophets of Jerusalem
I have seen a horrible thing:
[x]they commit adultery and walk in lies;
[y]they strengthen the hands of evildoers,
so that no one turns from his evil;
[z]all of them have become like Sodom to me,
[z]and its inhabitants like Gomorrah."
15 Therefore thus says the LORD of hosts concerning the prophets:
[a]"Behold, I will feed them with bitter food
[a]and give them [b]poisoned water to drink,
for from the prophets of Jerusalem
ungodliness has gone out into all the land."

16 Thus says the LORD of hosts: "Do not listen to the words of the prophets who prophesy
to you, [c]filling you with vain hopes. [d]They speak visions of their own minds, not from the
mouth of the LORD. 17 They say continually to those who despise the word of the LORD,
[e]'It shall be well with you'; and to everyone who [f]stubbornly follows his own heart, they
say, [g]'No disaster shall come upon you.'"

18 For [h]who among them has stood in the council of the LORD
to see and to hear his word,
or who has paid attention to his word and listened?
19 [i]Behold, the storm of the LORD!
Wrath has gone forth,
[j]a whirling tempest;
it will burst upon the head of the wicked.
20 [k]The anger of the LORD will not turn back
until he has executed and [k]accomplished
the intents of his heart.
[l]In the latter days you will understand it clearly.
21 [m]"I did not send the prophets,
yet they ran;
I did not speak to them,

11 [o][ver. 33, 34; Zeph. 3:4]; See ch. 6:13 [p]ch. 7:30; 32:34; Ezek. 8:16; 23:39
12 [q]Ps. 35:6; 73:18 [r]Prov. 4:19; [ch. 13:16] [s]ch. 11:23
13 [t]Isa. 7:9; Ezek. 16:46, 51, 53, 55; 23:4, 33 [u]Lam. 2:14 [v]ch. 2:8 [w]Isa. 9:16; Mic. 3:5
14 [x]ch. 29:23 [y]Ps. 64:5; Ezek. 13:22 [z]Isa. 1:9, 10; 13:19
15 [a]ch. 9:15; Prov. 5:4 [b]ch. 8:14
16 [c][Ps. 12:2] [d][ver. 21, 26; Num. 16:28]
17 [e][Zech. 10:2]; See ch. 6:14 [f]See ch. 3:17 [g]ch. 5:12; Mic. 3:11
18 [h]ver. 22; Isa. 40:14
19 [i]ch. 30:23 [j]ch. 25:32
20 [k]ch. 30:24; [Isa. 55:11] [l]ch. 30:24
21 [m]See ch. 14:14

23:11–12 Spiritual adultery begins with ungodly spiritual leaders. Such "guides" will find their own way to be **like slippery paths in the darkness**. The people need their spiritual leaders—specifically **prophet and priest**—to be exemplary for their faithfulness and piety (a recurring theme in Jeremiah; 2:8; 5:31; 6:13; 8:10; 14:18).

23:13–14 Israel's **prophets** turned to Baal worship (1 Kings 18:20–46; 2 Kings 17:7–18), which led to exile (2 Kings 17:19–23). Judah's prophets have been even worse. They lie, **commit adultery**, and lead Judah to be like **Sodom** and **Gomorrah** (cf. Isa. 1:10).

23:15 See 9:15. Judah's **ungodliness** begins with those who teach God's ways falsely (see Ex. 20:7).

23:16 vain hopes. Of peace and security (6:14). **visions of their own minds**. This is what the false prophets want to happen, not what God says will happen.

23:17 "It shall be well with you." These prophets are clearly not from God, for they affirm the wicked in their ways (cf. Rom. 1:32).

23:18 council of the LORD. Where God reveals his plans (cf. 1 Kings 22:19–23; Isa. 6:1–13; Amos 3:7–8). See Jer. 1:9–10 on the divine origin of Jeremiah's words.

23:19 storm of the LORD (cf. 30:23–24). The bursting forth of God's **wrath** on the **wicked** is like a tornado.

23:21–22 "I did not send the prophets." True prophets would have led the people to repent of their unfaithfulness.

22[n]ver. 18 [o]ch. 25:5; [Luke 1:17] [p]ver. 2
23[q][Ps. 94:7, 9; Amos 9:2, 3]; See Ps. 139:7-12
24[q][See ver. 23 above] [r]Isa. 66:1; Acts 7:49
25[s]See ch. 5:31 [t][Zech. 10:2]
26[u][ver. 16, 21; Num. 16:28]
27[t][See ver. 25 above] [v]Judg. 3:7; 8:33, 34
28[w][Num. 12:6] [x]ver. 25 [y][Luke 3:17]
29[y][See ver. 28 above] [z][Dan. 2:34, 45]
30[a]Ezek. 13:8; [ch. 14:15; Deut. 18:20]
32[b]ver. 13 [c]ver. 21; See ch. 14:14
33[d]See Ezek. 14:1-11 [f][Hos. 4:6]
34[d][See ver. 33 above]
36[g][Matt. 15:6] [h]Ps. 42:2
39[f][See ver. 33 above]
40[i]ch. 20:11

Chapter 24

1[j]2 Kgs. 24:12; 2 Chr. 36:10 [k]Matt. 1:11; [ch. 22:18, 24, 28] [l]ch. 29:2; 2 Kgs. 24:12, 14

yet they prophesied.
22 [n]But if they had stood in my council,
then they would have proclaimed my words to my people,
[o]and they would have turned them from their evil way,
and [p]from the evil of their deeds.

23 [q]"Am I a God at hand, declares the LORD, and not a God far away? 24 [q]Can a man
hide himself in secret places so that I cannot see him? declares the LORD. [r]Do I not fill
heaven and earth? declares the LORD. 25 I have heard what the prophets have said [s]who
prophesy lies in my name, saying, [t]'I have dreamed, I have dreamed!' 26 How long shall
there be lies in the heart of [u]the prophets who prophesy lies, and who prophesy the
deceit of their own heart, 27 who think to make my people forget my name [t]by their
dreams that they tell one another, even as their [v]fathers forgot my name for Baal? 28 [w]Let
the prophet who has a dream [x]tell the dream, but let him who has my word speak my
word faithfully. [y]What has straw in common with wheat? declares the LORD. 29 [y]Is not
my word like fire, declares the LORD, and [z]like a hammer that breaks the rock in pieces?
30 [a]Therefore, behold, I am against the prophets, declares the LORD, who steal my words
from one another. 31 Behold, I am against the prophets, declares the LORD, who use their
tongues and declare, 'declares the LORD.' 32 Behold, I am against those who prophesy lying
dreams, declares the LORD, and who tell them and [b]lead my people astray by their lies
and their recklessness, when [c]I did not send them or charge them. So they do not profit
this people at all, declares the LORD.

33 [d]"When one of this people, or a prophet or a priest asks you, 'What is the burden of
the LORD?' you shall say to them, 'You are the burden,[1] and [f]I will cast you off, declares the
LORD.' 34 And as for the prophet, priest, or one of the people who says, 'The burden of
the LORD,' [d]I will punish that man and his household. 35 Thus shall you say, every one to
his neighbor and every one to his brother, 'What has the LORD answered?' or 'What has
the LORD spoken?' 36 But 'the burden of the LORD' you shall mention no more, for the
burden is every man's own word, and [g]you pervert the words of [h]the living God, the LORD
of hosts, our God. 37 Thus you shall say to the prophet, 'What has the LORD answered you?'
or 'What has the LORD spoken?' 38 But if you say, 'The burden of the LORD,' thus says the
LORD, 'Because you have said these words, "The burden of the LORD," when I sent to you,
saying, "You shall not say, 'The burden of the LORD,'" 39 therefore, behold, I will surely lift
you up and [f]cast you away from my presence, you and the city that I gave to you and your
fathers. 40 [i]And I will bring upon you everlasting reproach and [i]perpetual shame, which
shall not be forgotten.'"

The Good Figs and the Bad Figs

24 [j]After Nebuchadnezzar king of Babylon had taken into exile from Jerusalem [k]Jeconiah
the son of Jehoiakim, king of Judah, together with [l]the officials of Judah, the craftsmen, and the metal workers, and had brought them to Babylon, the LORD showed me this

[1] Septuagint, Vulgate; Hebrew *What burden?*

23:23–25 God is always present (**at hand**), so he always sees sinful acts, including false prophecies.

23:26–27 How long? God's exasperation over ongoing sin (Num. 14:11–12). **forget my name by their dreams**. False prophecy's worst trait is leading people away from a relationship with God.

23:28 The false prophet's dreams and Jeremiah's faithful preaching are as different as **straw** and **wheat**.

23:29 like fire. God's **word**, in contrast to that of the false prophets, would burn the straw of falsehood (v. 28). **like a hammer**. God's word shatters the sinful heart.

23:30 steal my words from one another. Quoting each other's false interpretations of God's words and purposes.

23:31–32 God opposes those who falsely claim to speak his words with their **lying dreams** and reckless **lies** (reckless, because they harm others). Deuteronomy 18:20–22 denounces such people for their presumption.

23:33 There is a wordplay here, because the same word can mean **burden** or "oracle," according to the context (e.g., Prov. 30:1; Isa. 13:1; Nah. 1:1; Hab. 1:1; Mal. 1:1). **You are the burden**. The false prophets, hypocritically asking Jeremiah for an oracle, are burdens that God will **cast . . . off**.

23:34–35 No new word (**burden**) concerning Judah's situation will come. **the LORD answered**. God has already decided not to turn aside his wrath (v. 28).

23:36 Any new **word** on the situation is a perversion of God's **words**.

23:38–40 Prophets who dare to disobey God's command in vv. 34–36 will receive **perpetual shame** (cf. ch. 28), a threat fulfilled by the existence of the book of Jeremiah.

24:1–25:38 *Jeremiah Opposes Judah's People.* Jeremiah compares the people to figs (ch. 24), announces they will be exiled for 70 years (25:1–14), and says Judah will not be alone in experiencing God's wrath (25:15–38).

24:1 Nebuchadnezzar (see 21:1–2). **taken into exile**. In 597 B.C. **Jeconiah**. Also called "Jehoiachin" (52:31) and "Coniah" (22:24). **officials**.

vision: behold, [m]two baskets of figs placed before the temple of the LORD. 2 One basket had
very good figs, [n]like first-ripe figs, but the other basket had [o]very bad figs, so bad that they
could not be eaten. 3 And the LORD said to me, "What do you see, Jeremiah?" I said, "Figs,
the good figs very good, and the bad figs very bad, so bad that they cannot be eaten."
4 Then the word of the LORD came to me: 5 "Thus says the LORD, the God of Israel: Like
these good figs, so I will regard as good the exiles from Judah, [p]whom I have sent away
from this place to the land of the Chaldeans. 6 [q]I will set my eyes on them for good, and I
will bring them back to this land. [r]I will build them up, and not tear them down; [s]I will
plant them, and not pluck them up. 7 [t]I will give them a heart to know that I am the LORD,
[u]and they shall be my people [u]and I will be their God, [v]for they shall return to me with
their whole heart.
8 "But thus says the LORD: Like [w]the bad figs that are so bad they cannot be eaten, so will
I treat [x]Zedekiah the king of Judah, his officials, the remnant of Jerusalem who remain in
this land, and those who [y]dwell in the land of Egypt. 9 I will make them [z]a horror[1] to all the
kingdoms of the earth, to be [a]a reproach, [b]a byword, [a]a taunt, and [c]a curse in all the places
where I shall drive them. 10 And I will send [d]sword, famine, and pestilence upon them, until
they shall be utterly destroyed from the land that I gave to them and their fathers."

Seventy Years of Captivity

25 [e]The word that came to Jeremiah concerning all the people of Judah, in the
fourth year of Jehoiakim the son of Josiah, king of Judah (that was the first year of
Nebuchadnezzar king of Babylon), 2 which Jeremiah the prophet spoke to all the people of
Judah and all the inhabitants of Jerusalem: 3 "For twenty-three years, [f]from the thirteenth
year of Josiah the son of Amon, king of Judah, to this day, the word of the LORD has come to
me, and I have spoken [g]persistently to you, [h]but you have not listened. 4 [h]You have neither
listened nor inclined your ears to hear, although the LORD [g]persistently sent to you all his
servants the prophets, 5 saying, '[i]Turn now, every one of you, [j]from his evil way and evil
deeds, and [k]dwell upon the land that the LORD has given to you and your fathers from of
old and forever. 6 [l]Do not go after other gods to serve and worship them, [m]or provoke me

[1] Compare Septuagint; Hebrew *horror for evil*

1 [m]Amos 8:1, 2
2 [n][Isa. 28:4] [o]ch. 29:17
5 [p]ch. 29:20
6 [q][Amos 9:4] [r]ch. 12:15; 29:10 [s]ch. 31:28; 42:10; [ch. 1:10; Amos 9:15]
7 [t]ch. 32:39; Deut. 30:6; Ezek. 11:19; 36:26, 27 [u]See ch. 30:22; 31:33 [v]ch. 29:13; Joel 2:12, 13
8 [w]ver. 2; ch. 29:17 [x]ch. 21:1 [y]See ch. 43–44
9 [z]See ch. 15:4 [a]ch. 29:18; 49:13; Neh. 2:17; Isa. 43:28 [b]Deut. 28:37; 2 Chr. 7:20 [c]ch. 25:18; 26:6; 29:22; 2 Kgs. 22:19
10 [d]See ch. 14:12

Chapter 25

1 [e]ch. 1:3; 36:1; [2 Kgs. 24:1]
3 [f]ch. 1:2 [g]ch. 7:13; 11:7, 8; 26:5; 29:19; 32:33; 35:14; 2 Chr. 36:15 [h]See ch. 7:13
4 [h][See ver. 3 above] [g][See ver. 3 above]
5 [i]See ch. 18:11 [j]ch. 23:22 [k]ch. 7:7
6 [l]See ch. 7:6 [m][ch. 32:30]

Civil servants. **craftsmen, metal workers**. Persons useful to the conquerors. **vision**. See 1:11–16. For the image of **figs**, see 29:14.

24:3 The **good figs** are the exiles.

24:5 regard as good. See 29:10–14.

24:6 build . . . plant. God will restore the exiles (1:10; 12:2; 18:9).

24:7 I will give them a heart to know. Saving knowledge of God (cf. 4:4; 31:31–34; see note on 9:3) based on God's sovereign grace. **be my people**. Special covenantal relationship (31:31–34). They **shall return**

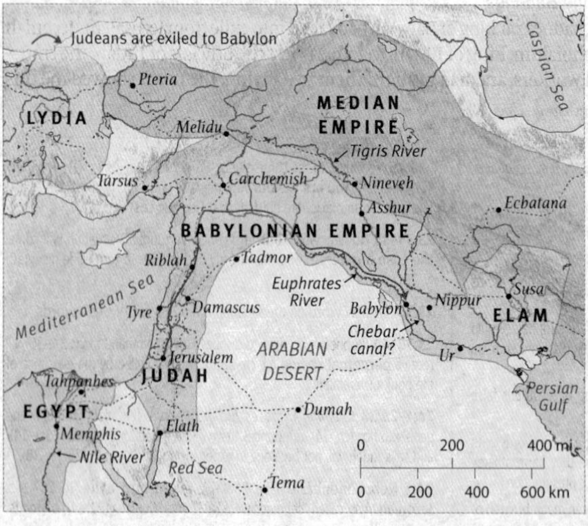

The Babylonian Empire
c. 597, 586, 582 B.C.
Jeremiah witnessed multiple deportations of many of his fellow Judeans to Babylon (see 52:28–30), which he and other prophets had foretold would happen if the people did not repent of their wickedness. Jeremiah specifically foretold that the exiles would remain in Babylon for 70 years, after which time the Lord would punish the Babylonians themselves for their wickedness (25:11–12).

to anger [m]with the work of your hands. Then I will do you no harm.' **7** [m]Yet you have not
listened to me, declares the LORD, [m]that you might provoke me to anger [m]with the work
of your hands to your own harm.
8 "Therefore thus says the LORD of hosts: Because you have not obeyed my words, **9** [n]behold,
I will send for all the tribes of the north, declares the LORD, and for Nebuchadnezzar the
king of Babylon, [o]my servant, and I will bring them against this land and its inhabitants,
and against all these surrounding nations. I will devote them to destruction, [p]and make
them a horror, a hissing, and an everlasting desolation. **10** Moreover, [q]I will banish from
them the voice of mirth and the voice of gladness, the voice of the bridegroom and the voice
of the bride, [r]the grinding of the millstones and [s]the light of the lamp. **11** [p]This whole land
shall become a ruin and a waste, and [t]these nations shall serve the king of Babylon [u]seventy
years. **12** Then after [u]seventy years are completed, [v]I will punish the king of Babylon and
that nation, [v]the land of the Chaldeans, for their iniquity, declares the LORD, [v]making the
land an everlasting waste. **13** I will bring upon that land all the words that I have uttered
against it, everything written [w]in this book, which Jeremiah prophesied against all the
nations. **14** [x]For many nations [x]and great kings shall make slaves even of them, [y]and I will
recompense them according to their deeds and the work of their hands."

The Cup of the LORD's Wrath

15 Thus the LORD, the God of Israel, said to me: [z]"Take from my hand this cup of the
wine of wrath, and make all the nations to whom I send you drink it. **16** They shall drink
and stagger and be crazed because of [a]the sword that I am sending among them."
17 So I took the cup from the LORD's hand, [b]and made all the nations to whom the LORD
sent me drink it: **18** [c]Jerusalem and the cities of Judah, its kings and officials, [d]to make
them a desolation and a waste, a hissing and a curse, as at this day; **19** [e]Pharaoh king of
Egypt, his servants, his officials, all his people, **20** and [f]all the mixed tribes among them;
all the kings of [g]the land of Uz and all the kings of [h]the land of the Philistines ([h]Ashkelon,
[h]Gaza, Ekron, and the remnant of [i]Ashdod); **21** [j]Edom, [k]Moab, and the sons of [l]Ammon;
22 all the kings of [m]Tyre, all the kings of [m]Sidon, and the kings of the coastland across [n]the
sea; **23** [o]Dedan, [p]Tema, [q]Buz, and all who cut [r]the corners of their hair; **24** all the [s]kings of
Arabia and all the kings of [f]the mixed tribes who dwell in the desert; **25** all the kings of
Zimri, all the kings of [t]Elam, and all the kings of [u]Media; **26** all the kings of [v]the north, far
and near, one after another, and all the kingdoms of the world that are on the face of the
earth. And after them the king of [w]Babylon[1] shall drink.
27 "Then you shall say to them, 'Thus says the LORD of hosts, the God of Israel: [x]Drink,

[1] Hebrew *Sheshach*, a code name for Babylon

6 [m][ch. 32:30]
7 [m][See ver. 6 above]
9 [n]ch. 1:15 [o]ch. 27:6; 43:10; [Isa. 44:28; 45:1]; See Ezek. 29:18-20 [p]See ch. 18:16
10 [q]See ch. 7:34 [r]Eccles. 12:4; Rev. 18:22 [s]Rev. 18:23
11 [p][See ver. 9 above] [t][ch. 28:14]; See ch. 27:3-6 [u]2 Chr. 36:21, 22; Ezra 1:1; Dan. 9:2; [Isa. 23:15]
12 [u][See ver. 11 above] [v]ch. 51:24, 26, 62; Isa. 13:19
13 [w]See ch. 46–51
14 [x]ch. 27:7; 50:9, 41; 51:27, 28 [y]ch. 50:29; 51:6, 24
15 [z]ch. 49:12; 51:7; Job 21:20; Ps. 60:3; 75:8; Isa. 51:17; Lam. 4:21; Rev. 14:10
16 [a][ch. 47:6]
17 [b][Isa. 51:22, 23]
18 [c][Zech. 12:2] [d]See ch. 18:16
19 [e]ch. 46:25
20 [f]ch. 50:37; [Ex. 12:38; Ezek. 30:5] [g]Job 1:1; Lam. 4:21 [h]ch. 47:1, 4, 5 [i][Isa. 20:1]
21 [j]ch. 9:26; See ch. 49:7-22 [k]See ch. 48 [l]See ch. 49:1-6
22 [m]ch. 47:4; Isa. 23:1, 2 [n][ch. 49:23]
23 [o]ch. 49:8; Isa. 21:13 [p]Job 6:19 [q][Job 32:2, 6] [r]See ch. 9:26
24 [s]2 Chr. 9:14 [f][See ver. 20 above]
25 [t]Isa. 11:11; See ch. 49:34-39 [u][2 Kgs. 17:6]
26 [v]ch. 50:9 [w]ch. 51:41
27 [x]Hab. 2:16

by repenting in their hearts (Deut. 30:1–10). Ezekiel 36:22–38 expresses a similar expectation.

24:8 The disgustingly **bad figs** are (1) the **king**, (2) the remaining people in Judah, and (3) the people who fled to **Egypt** to escape the invasion.

24:9 horror, reproach, byword, taunt, curse. See 15:4.

24:10 sword, famine, pestilence. See note on 15:2–3.

25:1 fourth year of Jehoiakim. 605 B.C. See Dates of Events in Jeremiah, p. 1376.

25:3–4 Judah has rejected Jeremiah and all those whom God **persistently sent** (7:13, 25; 11:7; 29:19; 32:33; 35:14–15; 44:4; 2 Kings 17:13–14).

25:5–6 Turn now. The consistent prophetic message was one of repentance from idolatry so that the people could have a right relationship with God.

25:7 provoke. Cf. 7:18–19.

25:8–9 tribes of the north. See 1:13–16; 3:12, 18; 4:6; 6:1; etc. **Nebuchadnezzar . . . my servant**. See 27:6; 43:10. Though earth's greatest king, he is God's vassal and instrument. Cyrus of Persia is also called God's "shepherd" and "anointed" (Isa. 44:28; 45:1). Nebuchadnezzar came to believe in God through Daniel's ministry (Dan. 4:1–2, 34–37). **devote them to destruction**. See note on Jer. 50:21. This is what God's people were to do to the Canaanites (Deut. 7:2); now it will be their fate instead.

25:10 Common joys will cease when judgment comes (cf. 7:34; 16:5–9).

25:11 seventy years. This is probably counted from the first exile in 605 B.C. to the first return, variously dated from 538 to 535 (2 Chron. 36:21; Ezra 1:1). However, 70 may be a rounded number, as it is elsewhere (Ps. 90:10; cf. Matt. 18:22).

25:12 Persia conquered **Babylon** in 539 B.C. God punishes sin wherever it exists.

25:13 This book may refer to the scroll mentioned in 36:1–4. The Septuagint places chs. 46–51 (in slightly different order) at this point.

25:14 many nations. Persia and its allies. **great kings**. Cyrus and his successors. **according to their deeds**. See v. 12.

25:15 cup of . . . wrath. See Isa. 51:17; Rev. 18:6.

25:16 drink and stagger. See 13:12–14.

25:17 made all the nations . . . drink it. Through a symbolic act in Jeremiah's role as prophet to the nations (1:5).

25:18 a hissing. See 18:16.

25:19 Egypt. Prior to 605 B.C., Egypt had dominated Judah, but Babylon's victory at Carchemish that year gave it power over Egypt and its vassals.

25:20–22 All of Judah's traditional regional foes opposed Babylon, to no avail (see 27:1–3).

25:23–26 Nations far distant from Judah will likewise bow to Babylon's might. Indeed, **all the kingdoms of the world** shall drink the cup of Babylon's wrath, but afterward the **king of Babylon shall drink** the cup of Persian wrath. All these cups come from God, who speaks through Jeremiah.

be drunk and vomit, fall and rise no more, because of [y]the sword that I am sending among
you.'
28 "And if they refuse to accept the cup from your hand to drink, then you shall say
to them, 'Thus says the LORD of hosts: [z]You must drink! 29 For behold, [a]I begin to work
disaster at the city that is called by my name, and shall you go unpunished? You shall not
go unpunished, [y]for I am summoning a sword against all the inhabitants of the earth,
declares the LORD of hosts.'
30 "You, therefore, shall prophesy against them all these words, and say to them:

[b]"'The LORD will roar from on high,
 and from his holy habitation utter his voice;
he will roar mightily against his fold,
 [c]and shout, like those who tread grapes,
 against all the inhabitants of the earth.
31 The clamor will resound to the ends of the earth,
 for [d]the LORD has an indictment against the nations;
[e]he is entering into judgment with all flesh,
 and the wicked he will put to the sword,
 declares the LORD.'

32 "Thus says the LORD of hosts:
Behold, disaster is going forth
 from nation to nation,
[f]and a great tempest is stirring
 [g]from the farthest parts of the earth!

33 [h]"And those pierced by the LORD on that day shall extend from one end of the earth
to the other. [i]They shall not be lamented, [j]or gathered, or buried; [j]they shall be dung on
the surface of the ground.

34 [k]"Wail, [l]you shepherds, and cry out,
 [m]and roll in ashes, you lords of the flock,
for the days of your slaughter and dispersion have come,
 and you shall fall like a choice vessel.
35 No refuge will remain [n]for the shepherds,
 nor escape for the lords of the flock.
36 A voice—the cry [n]of the shepherds,
 [o]and the wail of the lords of the flock!
For the LORD is laying waste their pasture,
37 [p]and the peaceful folds are devastated
 [q]because of the fierce anger of the LORD.
38 Like a lion [r]he has left his lair,
 for their land has become a waste
because of [s]the sword of the oppressor,
 [q]and because of his fierce anger."

27 [y]Ezek. 38:21; [ver. 16]
28 [z]ch. 49:12
29 [a]Prov. 11:31; Isa. 10:12; Amos 3:2; Obad. 16; [1 Pet. 4:17] [y][See ver. 27 above]
30 [b]Joel 3:16; Amos 1:2 [c][Judg. 9:27; Isa. 16:9]
31 [d]Hos. 4:1 [e]Isa. 66:16; [Joel 3:2]
32 [f]ch. 23:19; 30:23 [g]ch. 6:22
33 [h]Isa. 66:16 [i]See ch. 16:4 [j]See ch. 8:2
34 [k]ch. 4:8 [l]See ch. 23:1 [m]ch. 6:26
35 [n]See ch. 23:1
36 [n][See ver. 35 above] [o]ch. 4:8
37 [p][Isa. 32:18] [q]See ch. 12:13
38 [r][Job 38:40] [s]ch. 46:16; 50:16 [q][See ver. 37 above]

25:28–29 If judgment begins with Jerusalem (cf. 1 Pet. 4:17), then surely the other nations will not escape either.

25:30 will roar. Like a lion capturing prey (cf. Joel 3:16; Amos 1:2). Like **those who tread grapes**, they must shout to be heard over the noise of grapes being trodden.

25:31 God's voice will reach the **ends of the earth**, for his **indictment** of sin encompasses **all flesh**. His **sword** will touch all **wicked** persons (see v. 29).

25:32 great tempest. God's wrath will break out and punish like a sudden, destructive storm (23:19; 30:23–24).

25:33 shall not be lamented . . . or buried. The sword will slay so many that no one will be left to bury the dead (cf. 7:33; 14:16; 16:6).

25:34 shepherds. Leaders, either of the nations (vv. 19–26) or specifically of Judah, who have brought this disaster upon the people (cf. 2:8; 23:1). **roll in ashes**. A mourning ritual. **choice vessel**. See 22:28.

25:35–37 With no way to **escape**, the leaders can only **wail** for how their **folds**, their countries, are devastated **because of the fierce anger of the LORD**.

25:38 Like a lion. See 25:30. The **sword of the oppressor** (Babylon) is the result of God's **fierce anger**. This lion will devour his prey completely.

26:1–29:32 *Jeremiah Opposes False Belief.* Jeremiah speaks against believing that the temple's existence indicates God's approval of Judah (ch. 26), that Babylon will not conquer Judah (ch. 27), that Babylon's power would cease soon (ch. 28), and that the exile would end quickly (ch. 29).

26:1 The events of this chapter occur c. 609 B.C.

26:2 The setting is similar to 7:1ff., but may convey a second sermon.

26:3 God's reason for sending Jeremiah is to offer Judah one more chance to **turn from . . . evil** so that he may **relent** from punishing (see note on 1:13–14). This is generally the intent of prophetic preaching in Scripture (cf. 18:7–8).

Chapter 26
1[t]ch. 27:1 [u]2 Kgs. 23:36; 2 Chr. 36:5
2[v]ch. 19:14 [w][Ezek. 3:10] [x]Deut. 4:2; 12:32; [Acts 20:27]
3[y]ch. 36:3 [z]ver. 13, 19; See ch. 18:8
3[a]ch. 4:4
4[b]Lev. 26:14; Deut. 28:15
5[c]See ch. 25:3, 4
6[d]See ch. 7:12 [e]See ch. 24:9
7[f]ch. 23:33
8[f][See ver. 7 above]
9[d][See ver. 6 above] [g]See ch. 4:7
10[h]ch. 36:12 [i]ch. 36:10
11[f][See ver. 7 above] [j]ch. 38:4; [ver. 16]
13[k]See ch. 7:3 [l]Deut. 30:2 [z][See ver. 3 above]
14[m]Josh. 9:25
15[n][Matt. 27:24]
16[o]ver. 8 [p][ver. 11]
17[q][Acts 5:34] [r]See ch. 19:1
18[s]Mic. 3:12
19[t][2 Chr. 32:26] [u]Ex. 32:14; 2 Sam. 24:16; [1 Kgs. 13:6] [v][Acts 5:39]

Jeremiah Threatened with Death

26 [t]In the beginning of the reign of [u]Jehoiakim the son of Josiah, king of Judah, this
word came from the LORD: **2** "Thus says the LORD: [v]Stand in the court of the LORD's
house, and speak to all the cities of Judah that come to worship in the house of the LORD
[w]all the words that I command you to speak to them; [x]do not hold back a word. **3** [y]It may
be they will listen, and every one turn from his evil way, [z]that I may relent of the disaster
that I intend to do to them [a]because of their evil deeds. **4** You shall say to them, 'Thus says
the LORD: [b]If you will not listen to me, to walk in my law that I have set before you, **5** [c]and
to listen to the words of my servants the prophets whom I send to you [c]urgently, [c]though
you have not listened, **6** then I will make this house [d]like Shiloh, and I will make this city
[e]a curse for all the nations of the earth.'"

7 [f]The priests and the prophets and all the people heard Jeremiah speaking these words
in the house of the LORD. **8** And when Jeremiah had finished speaking all that the LORD had
commanded him to speak to all the people, then [f]the priests and the prophets and all the
people laid hold of him, saying, "You shall die! **9** Why have you prophesied in the name of
the LORD, saying, 'This house shall be [d]like Shiloh, and this city shall be desolate, [g]without
inhabitant'?" And all the people gathered around Jeremiah in the house of the LORD.

10 When [h]the officials of Judah heard these things, they came up from the king's house
to the house of the LORD and took their seat in the [i]entry of the New Gate of the house of
the LORD. **11** Then [f]the priests and the prophets said to the officials and to all the people,
[j]"This man deserves the sentence of death, because he has prophesied against this city, as
you have heard with your own ears."

12 Then Jeremiah spoke to all the officials and all the people, saying, "The LORD sent me
to prophesy against this house and this city all the words you have heard. **13** Now therefore
[k]mend your ways and your deeds, [l]and obey the voice of the LORD your God, [z]and the LORD
will relent of the disaster that he has pronounced against you. **14** [m]But as for me, behold, I am
in your hands. Do with me as seems good and right to you. **15** Only know for certain that if you
put me to death, [n]you will bring innocent blood upon yourselves and upon this city and its
inhabitants, for in truth the LORD sent me to you to speak all these words in your ears."

Jeremiah Spared from Death

16 [o]Then the officials and all the people said to the priests and the prophets, [p]"This man
does not deserve the sentence of death, for he has spoken to us in the name of the LORD
our God." **17** [q]And certain of [r]the elders of the land arose and spoke to all the assembled
people, saying, **18** "Micah of Moresheth prophesied in the days of Hezekiah king of Judah,
and said to all the people of Judah: 'Thus says the LORD of hosts,

[s]"'Zion shall be plowed as a field;
  Jerusalem shall become a heap of ruins,
  and the mountain of the house a wooded height.'

19 Did Hezekiah king of Judah and all Judah put him to death? [t]Did he not fear the LORD
and entreat the favor of the LORD, [u]and did not the LORD relent of the disaster that he had
pronounced against them? [v]But we are about to bring great disaster upon ourselves."

26:4–5 Sending the **prophets** was a gracious act on God's part. Failure to **listen** (obey) meant a rejection of that grace.

26:6 Shiloh. See note on 7:12–14. **a curse**. See 24:9 and 25:18.

26:7–8 priests . . . prophets . . . people. The ones who need God's word yet reject it (1:17–19). **You shall die!** A phrase traditionally used as a death sentence (cf. 1 Sam. 14:44; 1 Kings 2:37, 42).

26:9 Why have you prophesied? Jeremiah's audience considers a sermon against Jerusalem and the temple to be blasphemy. Jeremiah considers their deeds the real blasphemy (7:11–15).

26:10 officials. Judges, in this instance. **took their seat**. To judge the matter. **entry of the New Gate**. The place where judicial proceedings occurred (cf. Amos 5:10, 12, 15).

26:11 The priests and the prophets claim Jeremiah **has prophesied against this city**, or committed treason.

26:12 The LORD sent me. Jeremiah claims to speak only God's words (1:4–10) concerning the **city** and temple (**this house**).

26:13 mend your ways (lit., "make good"; 7:3; 18:11) **. . . and obey**. These are the true marks of repentance. **relent**. See 18:8, 10; 26:3.

26:14 good and right. The correct verdict in any judicial matter.

26:15 innocent blood. The condemning of just persons. Such unjust verdicts were common in Jeremiah's day (cf. 2:34; 7:6; 19:4; 22:17).

26:16 The **officials** (judges) and **people** (assembled community) oppose the religious leaders' wishes.

26:17 elders of the land. Most likely civic leaders from other cities.

26:18 Micah. The biblical prophet. **prophesied**. This verse quotes Mic. 3:12. **days of Hezekiah**. 715–687 B.C.

26:19 The elders note how **Hezekiah** and the people heeded Micah's words and repented, which led to God relenting of the disaster of Sennacherib's invasion of Judah in 701 B.C. (2 Kings 18–19). The elders counsel obedience to

20 There was another man who prophesied in the name of the LORD, Uriah the son of
Shemaiah from [w]Kiriath-jearim. He prophesied against this city and against this land in
words like those of Jeremiah. 21 And when [x]King Jehoiakim, with all his warriors and all
the officials, heard his words, the king sought to put him to death. But when Uriah heard
of it, he was afraid and fled and escaped to Egypt. 22 Then [x]King Jehoiakim sent to Egypt
certain men, [y]Elnathan the son of [z]Achbor and others with him, 23 and they took Uriah
from Egypt and brought him to King Jehoiakim, [a]who struck him down with the sword
and dumped his dead body into the burial place of the common people.
24 But the hand of [b]Ahikam the son of Shaphan was with Jeremiah so that he was not
given over to the people to be put to death.

The Yoke of Nebuchadnezzar

27 In the beginning of the reign of Zedekiah[1] the son of Josiah, king of Judah, this word
came to Jeremiah from the LORD. 2 Thus the LORD said to me: [c]"Make yourself straps
and [d]yoke-bars, and put them on your neck. 3 Send word[2] to the king of [e]Edom, the king
of [e]Moab, the king of the sons of [e]Ammon, the king of [e]Tyre, and the king of Sidon by the
hand of the envoys who have come to Jerusalem to Zedekiah king of Judah. 4 Give them this
charge for their masters: 'Thus says the LORD of hosts, the God of Israel: This is what you
shall say to your masters: 5 "It is I who [f]by my great power and my outstretched arm [g]have
made the earth, with the men and animals that are on the earth, [h]and I give it to whomever
it seems right to me. 6 [i]Now I have given all these lands into the hand of Nebuchadnezzar,
the king of Babylon, [j]my servant, [k]and I have given him also the beasts of the field to serve
him. 7 [l]All the nations shall serve him and [m]his son and [n]his grandson, [o]until the time of his
own land comes. [p]Then many nations and great kings shall make him their slave.
8 " ' "But if any nation or kingdom will not serve this Nebuchadnezzar king of Babylon,
[q]and put its neck under the yoke of the king of Babylon, I will punish that nation [r]with
the sword, with famine, and with pestilence, declares the LORD, until I have consumed
it by his hand. 9 So [s]do not listen to your [t]prophets, your diviners, your dreamers, your
[u]fortune-tellers, or your sorcerers, who are saying to you, 'You shall not serve the king of
Babylon.' 10 [v]For it is a lie that they are prophesying to you, with the result that you will
be removed far from your land, and I will drive you out, and you will perish. 11 [w]But any
nation that will bring its neck under the yoke of the king of Babylon and serve him, I will
leave on its own land, to work it and dwell there, declares the LORD." ' "
12 To [x]Zedekiah king of Judah I spoke in like manner: [w]"Bring your necks under the yoke
of the king of Babylon, and [y]serve him and his people and live. 13 [z]Why will you and your
people die [a]by the sword, by famine, and by pestilence, [b]as the LORD has spoken concerning any nation that will not serve the king of Babylon? 14 [c]Do not listen to the words of
the prophets who are saying to you, 'You shall not serve the king of Babylon,' [v]for it is a
lie that they are prophesying to you. 15 I have not sent them, declares the LORD, but [v]they
are prophesying falsely in my name, with the result that I will drive you out and you will
perish, you and the prophets who are prophesying to you."

[1] Or *Jehoiakim* [2] Hebrew *Send them*

20 [w]Josh. 9:17; 1 Sam. 6:21; 7:1, 2; 1 Chr. 13:5, 6
21 [x]ver. 1; ch. 27:1
22 [x][See ver. 21 above] [y]ch. 36:12, 25 [z]2 Kgs. 22:12, 14
23 [a][ch. 22:17; Neh. 9:26; Matt. 21:35; 23:37]
24 [b]2 Kgs. 22:12

Chapter 27

2 [c][1 Kgs. 22:11; Ezek. 7:23] [d]ch. 28:10, 12, 13; See Lev. 26:13
3 [e]ch. 25:21, 22
5 [f]See ch. 21:5 [g]Ps. 115:15; Isa. 45:12 [h]Ps. 115:16; Dan. 4:17, 25, 32
6 [i][Ezek. 30:21, 25] [j]See ch. 25:9 [k]ch. 28:14; Dan. 2:38
7 [l][Dan. 2:37, 38] [m]ch. 52:31 [n]Dan. 5:1, 30 [o]See ch. 25:12 [p]See ch. 25:14
8 [q]ver. 11, 12; [ch. 30:8] [r]See ch. 14:12
9 [s][ch. 14:14] [t][ch. 29:8] [u][Deut. 18:10; Isa. 2:6]
10 [v]See ch. 5:31
11 [w][ver. 2, 8]
12 [x]ch. 28:1; [ver. 1] [w][See ver. 11 above] [y]ver. 17; [ch. 38:17]
13 [z]Ezek. 18:31 [a]See ch. 14:12 [b]ver. 8
14 [c][ch. 14:14] [v][See ver. 10 above]
15 [v][See ver. 10 above]

Jeremiah's words. This shows that Micah's oracle was considered canonical by this time; it also shows that prophecy has a moral purpose, rather than simply telling the future (see note on Jer. 18:7; also Isa. 38:1–6).

26:20 Another prophet, **Uriah** (otherwise unknown), also **prophesied** in Jehoiakim's era in a manner similar to **Jeremiah**.

26:21–23 In contrast to the thoughtful response of Hezekiah (v. 19), **Jehoiakim** sought to kill **Uriah**, who had fled to **Egypt**. Jehoiakim had him brought back to Judah and executed.

26:24 Only by the intervention of **Ahikam** did **Jeremiah** escape Uriah's fate. The death of other faithful prophets underscores the unusual nature of God's promise of protection to Jeremiah (1:17–19). **Shaphan**. A scribe during Josiah's reform (2 Kings 22:3–14).

27:1 beginning of the reign of Zedekiah. 597 B.C.

27:2 Make yourself. Jeremiah was to engage in yet another symbolic act (cf. 13:1–11; 16:1–9; 19:1–15). **straps and yoke-bars**. Yokes were made of wooden bars affixed to the animal by leather thongs.

27:3–4 A group of **envoys** had **come to Jerusalem** to plot strategy for opposing Babylon. Jeremiah, God's envoy, gave a message for these envoys to take to their kings.

27:5 Jeremiah's message that Israel's God **made** and ruled the **earth** would likely have amused the envoys, all of whom served deities they considered Yahweh's equal.

27:6–7 Nebuchadnezzar . . . my servant. See 25:8–9. **make him their slave**. See 27:12, 14. Babylon's rule will not last forever.

27:8 Until the era of Nebuchadnezzar's grandsons, the nations must serve **Babylon** or face **sword**, **famine**, and **pestilence** (14:1–12; 15:1–2; 16:4; 18:21; 21:7–9; 24:10).

27:9–10 it is a lie. Any prophet or other teller of the future who disputes Jeremiah's word is a lying prophet like those described in 23:9–40.

27:11 God counsels all nations to **serve** Babylon. They should wear Babylon's **yoke** just as Jeremiah wears his symbolic yoke (v. 2).

16 Then I spoke to the priests and to all this people, saying, "Thus says the LORD: [c]Do
not listen to the words of your prophets who are prophesying to you, saying, [d]'Behold, the
vessels of the LORD's house will now shortly be brought back from Babylon,' [v]for it is a lie
that they are prophesying to you. 17 [c]Do not listen to them; [w]serve the king of Babylon and
live. Why should this city [e]become a desolation? 18 If they are prophets, and if the word of
the LORD is with them, then [f]let them intercede with the LORD of hosts, [g]that the vessels
that are left in the house of the LORD, in the house of the king of Judah, and in Jerusalem
may not go to Babylon. 19 [h]For thus says the LORD of hosts concerning the pillars, the sea,
the stands, and the rest of the vessels that are left in this city, 20 which Nebuchadnezzar
king of Babylon did not take away, [i]when he took into exile from Jerusalem to Babylon
Jeconiah the son of Jehoiakim, king of Judah, and all the nobles of Judah and Jerusalem—
21 thus says the LORD of hosts, the God of Israel, [h]concerning the vessels that are left in the
house of the LORD, in the house of the king of Judah, and in Jerusalem: 22 [j]They shall be
carried to Babylon [k]and remain there [l]until the day when I visit them, declares the LORD.
[m]Then I will bring them back [j]and restore them to this place."

Hananiah the False Prophet

28 In that same year, at the beginning of the reign of [n]Zedekiah king of Judah, in
the fifth month of the fourth year, Hananiah the son of [o]Azzur, the prophet from
[p]Gibeon, spoke to me in the house of the LORD, in the presence of the priests and all the
people, saying, 2 "Thus says the LORD of hosts, the God of Israel: [q]I have broken the yoke
of the king of Babylon. 3 [r]Within [s]two years I will bring back to this place all the vessels
of the LORD's house, which Nebuchadnezzar king of Babylon took away from this place
and carried to Babylon. 4 I will also bring back to this place [t]Jeconiah the son of Jehoiakim,
king of Judah, and all the exiles from Judah who went to Babylon, declares the LORD, [q]for
I will break the yoke of the king of Babylon."
5 Then the prophet Jeremiah spoke to Hananiah the prophet in the presence of the
priests and all the people who were standing in the house of the LORD, 6 and the prophet
Jeremiah said, [u]"Amen! May the LORD do so; may the LORD make the words that you have
prophesied come true, and bring back to this place from Babylon the vessels of the house
of the LORD, and all the exiles. 7 Yet hear now this word that I speak in your hearing and
in the hearing of all the people. 8 [v]The prophets who preceded you and me from ancient
times prophesied war, famine, and pestilence against many countries and great kingdoms.
9 [w]As for the prophet who prophesies peace, when the word of that prophet comes to pass,
then it will be known that the LORD has truly sent the prophet."
10 Then the prophet Hananiah took the [x]yoke-bars from the neck of Jeremiah the prophet
and broke them. 11 And Hananiah spoke in the presence of all the people, saying, [y]"Thus
says the LORD: [z]Even so will I break the yoke of Nebuchadnezzar king of Babylon from the
neck of [a]all the nations within two years." But Jeremiah the prophet went his way.
12 Sometime after the prophet [b]Hananiah had broken the yoke-bars from off the neck

16 [c][See ver. 14 above] [d]ch. 28:3; 2 Kgs. 24:13; 2 Chr. 36:7, 10, 18 [v][See ver. 10 above]
17 [c][See ver. 14 above] [w][See ver. 11 above] [e]See ch. 7:34
18 [f][Isa. 59:16] [g]Dan. 1:2
19 [h][2 Kgs. 25:13]
20 [i]2 Kgs. 24:14, 15; Matt. 1:11, 12; See ch. 24:1
21 [h][See ver. 19 above]
22 [j]ch. 52:17, 20, 21; 2 Kgs. 25:13; 2 Chr. 36:18 [k]ch. 32:5 [l]ch. 29:10; 2 Chr. 36:22; Ezra 1:1 [m]Ezra 1:7, 8; 5:14; 7:19

Chapter 28

1 [n]ch. 27:12 [o]Ezek. 11:1 [p]Josh. 9:3; 21:17
2 [q][ch. 27:2, 11, 12]
3 [r]ch. 27:16 [s]ver. 11
4 [t][ch. 22:10, 12, 26] [q][See ver. 2 above]
6 [u]1 Kgs. 1:36
8 [v][ch. 26:18]
9 [w]Deut. 18:22; See ch. 6:14
10 [x]ch. 27:2
11 [y][1 Kgs. 22:11] [z]ver. 2, 3 [a]ch. 27:7
12 [b]ver. 1, 10

27:12–15 Having delivered God's message to the other nations, Jeremiah now tells **Zedekiah** the same thing: serving **Babylon** is God's will.

27:16 vessels of the LORD's house. Some valuable articles were removed from the temple by Nebuchadnezzar in 605 B.C. (Dan. 1:1–2) and 597 (2 Kings 24:10–13). **shortly be brought back**. False prophets claimed that Babylon's oppression would soon end.

27:18 True **prophets** would pray that what remains in the temple not be taken away. Only serving **Babylon** can avert greater loss.

27:19 pillars. Located in the vestibule of the temple and overlaid with bronze (1 Kings 7:15–22). **sea**. A tank holding water to clean the area where sacrifices were made (1 Kings 7:23–26). **Stands** supported the sea and were overlaid with bronze (1 Kings 7:27–37). **vessels**. Bronze basins (1 Kings 7:38). See illustrations, pp. 604–605.

27:21–22 The articles noted in v. 19 will indeed go **to Babylon**, but will also return. The threat came true in 587 B.C., and the promise of their return came true in 538–535, when the Israelites returned to Jerusalem (Ezra 1:7, 8; 5:13–17).

28:1 same year. As in 27:16–22. **fourth year**. c. 594–593 B.C. **Gibeon**. A town 6 miles (9.7 km) northwest of Jerusalem. Thus, **Hananiah**, like Jeremiah, was a Benjaminite (1:1–3).

28:2–4 Thus says the LORD. Hananiah claimed divine authority for his false prophecy. **I have broken the yoke . . . Within two years**. Hananiah contradicts Jeremiah's prophecy concerning serving **Babylon** (27:8–11) and the temple's **vessels** (27:19–22). **bring back . . . Jeconiah . . . and all the exiles**. That is, Jeconiah (another name for Jehoiachin) and the others exiled in 597 B.C.—again a direct contradiction of Jeremiah's prophecy (22:24–27).

28:6 Amen! May the LORD do so. Jeremiah wishes that Hananiah's prophecy were true, for he has prayed for the people (11:14; 14:11) and preached for their benefit.

28:8–9 Jeremiah's point is that **peace** and security is the rarer of the two messages described here. Peace requires repentance (26:18–19), which has not occurred. **when the word . . . comes to pass**. Cf. Deut. 18:22.

28:10–11 False prophets could perform symbolic acts as easily as true ones. Hananiah's breaking of Jeremiah's **yoke-bars** (27:2) brought no response from **Jeremiah**.

28:12–15 Eventually God asserts that Hananiah's prophecy turns the

of Jeremiah the prophet, the word of the LORD came to Jeremiah: 13 "Go, tell Hananiah,
'Thus says the LORD: You have broken wooden bars, but you have made in their place
bars of iron. 14 For thus says the LORD of hosts, the God of Israel: I have put upon the neck
of all these nations [c]an iron yoke to serve Nebuchadnezzar king of Babylon, [d]and they
shall serve him, [e]for I have given to him even the beasts of the field.'" 15 And Jeremiah the
prophet said to the prophet Hananiah, "Listen, Hananiah, [f]the LORD has not sent you,
[g]and you have made this people trust in a lie. 16 Therefore thus says the LORD: 'Behold,
I will remove you from the face of the earth. This year you shall die, [h]because you have
uttered rebellion against the LORD.'"
17 In that same year, in the seventh month, the prophet Hananiah died.

Jeremiah's Letter to the Exiles

29 These are the words of the letter that Jeremiah the prophet sent from Jerusalem
to [i]the surviving elders of the exiles, and to [j]the priests, [j]the prophets, and [j]all the
people, whom Nebuchadnezzar had taken into exile from Jerusalem to Babylon. 2 This
was after [k]King Jeconiah and the queen mother, the eunuchs, the officials of Judah and
Jerusalem, the craftsmen, and the metal workers had departed from Jerusalem. 3 The letter
was sent by the hand of Elasah the son of [l]Shaphan and Gemariah the son of [m]Hilkiah,
whom Zedekiah king of Judah sent to Babylon to Nebuchadnezzar king of Babylon.
It said: 4 "Thus says the LORD of hosts, the God of Israel, to all the exiles whom I have
sent into exile from Jerusalem to Babylon: 5 [n]Build houses and live in them; plant gardens and eat their produce. 6 Take wives and have sons and daughters; take wives for
your sons, and give your daughters in marriage, that they may bear sons and daughters;
multiply there, and do not decrease. 7 But seek the welfare of the city where I have sent
you into exile, and [o]pray to the LORD on its behalf, for in its welfare you will find your
welfare. 8 For thus says the LORD of hosts, the God of Israel: [p]Do not let your prophets
and [q]your diviners who are among you deceive you, and do not listen to the dreams that
they dream,[1] 9 for [r]it is a lie that they are prophesying to you in my name; [s]I did not send
them, declares the LORD.
10 "For thus says the LORD: [t]When seventy years are completed for Babylon, [u]I will visit
you, [v]and I will fulfill to you my promise [v]and bring you back to this place. 11 [w]For I know
the plans I have for you, declares the LORD, plans for welfare[2] and not for evil, [x]to give
you a future and a hope. 12 [y]Then you will call upon me and come and pray to me, [y]and
I will hear you. 13 [z]You will seek me and find me, when you seek me [a]with all your heart.
14 I will be found by you, declares the LORD, [b]and I will restore your fortunes and [c]gather
you from all the nations and all the places [d]where I have driven you, declares the LORD,
and I will bring you back to the place from which I sent you into exile.

[1] Hebrew *your dreams, which you cause to dream* [2] Or *peace*

14 [c]Deut. 28:48 [d][ch. 25:11] [e]See ch. 27:6
15 [f]ch. 29:31; Deut. 18:20; [Ezek. 13:22, 23] [g]See ch. 5:31
16 [h]ch. 29:32; Deut. 13:5

Chapter 29

1 [i]Ezek. 8:1 [j][ch. 23:33]
2 [k]ch. 24:1; 2 Kgs. 24:12, 14
3 [l]2 Chr. 34:8 [m]1 Chr. 6:13
5 [n]ver. 28
7 [o][Ezra 6:10; 1 Tim. 2:1, 2]
8 [p][ch. 5:31; 6:14] [q]ch. 27:9, 15
9 [r]See ch. 5:31 [s]ver. 31
10 [t]See ch. 25:12 [u]ch. 27:22 [v]ch. 33:14; [ch. 24:6]
11 [w][Isa. 55:8, 9] [x]ch. 31:17
12 [y]ch. 33:3; Dan. 9:3
13 [z]2 Chr. 15:2; Ps. 32:6; 78:34; Prov. 8:17; Isa. 55:6; Hos. 3:5; See Lev. 26:39-42; Deut. 30:1-3 [a]ch. 24:7; Deut. 4:29
14 [b]ch. 30:3 [c]See ch. 23:3 [d]See ch. 8:3

yoke-bars of surrender into a yoke of devastation by leading people to ignore God's advice to surrender to **Nebuchadnezzar** (27:1–11).

28:16–17 Hananiah probably feared rebelling against Zedekiah, so he prophesied peace. However, he has rebelled **against the LORD**, so he dies two months after uttering his prophecy (vv. 1–4).

29:1 The purpose of this **letter** is to reassure these **exiles** that God has not abandoned them or forgotten his purpose for them. At the same time, since its contents would be widely known in Judah, it also reinforces Jeremiah's announcements of impending judgment on those left in Judah. **All the people** were **taken into exile** in 597 B.C. by **Nebuchadnezzar**.

29:2 queen mother. Nehushta (2 Kings 24:8). **eunuchs**. Royal servants and officials. See Jer. 24:1; and note on 2 Kings 9:32.

29:3 Elasah. Mentioned only here in Scripture. **Shaphan**. Perhaps an official under Josiah (2 Kings 22:3–13). **Gemariah**. Perhaps involved in reading Jeremiah's scroll in Jer. 36:10, 12, 25. **Hilkiah**. A common name (1:1), perhaps the chief priest for Josiah (2 Kings 22:4–23:4).

29:5–6 The exiles should plan for a long stay in Babylon. They will not return anytime soon, despite Hananiah's words (28:4).

29:7 The exiles should hope and work for Babylon's success, for they will share this success. **Welfare** is *shalom* (Hb.), which covers all aspects of peace and plenty (see note on John 14:27). The people of Israel were true to their calling when they brought blessing to the Gentiles (Gen. 12:2–3).

29:8–9 prophets and . . . diviners. False prophets went into exile and were deceiving the people by promising a return to the land (vv. 21–23).

29:10 God promises to **bring** the exiles home, but only after 70 years (see note on 25:11; also Ezra 1:1; Dan. 9:1–2).

29:11 God's **plans** for the exiles is **welfare** (Hb. *shalom*; see note on v. 7), not **evil**, or "calamity." Having sought Babylon's *shalom*, the exiles will receive God's *shalom* in the form of **a future and a hope** in their homeland.

29:12 Eventually, God will respond to his people's prayers for restoration.

29:13 You will seek me and find me. This amazing promise from the infinitely righteous, holy God to sinful people echoes a promise in Deut. 4:29 and remains true even to the present day (John 6:37). **all your heart**. See Jer. 4:4, 14; 11:20; 12:2; 17:9.

29:14 I will bring you back. After 70 years, Israel's penitent prayers and changed hearts will lead to God's restoration of the nation (Deut. 30:1–10).

15 “Because you have said, ‘The LORD has raised up prophets for us in Babylon,’ 16 thus
says the LORD concerning [e]the king who sits on the throne of David, and concerning all
the people who dwell in this city, your kinsmen who did not go out with you into exile:
17 ‘Thus says the LORD of hosts, behold, I am sending on them [f]sword, famine, and pestilence, and I will make them like [g]vile figs that are so rotten they cannot be eaten. 18 I will
pursue them with [f]sword, famine, and pestilence, [h]and will make them a horror to all the
kingdoms of the earth, [i]to be a curse, a terror, a hissing, and a reproach among all the nations
[d]where I have driven them, 19 because they did not pay attention to my words, declares
the LORD, [j]that I persistently sent to you by my servants the prophets, but you would not
listen, declares the LORD.’ 20 Hear the word of the LORD, all you exiles [k]whom I sent away
from Jerusalem to Babylon: 21 ‘Thus says the LORD of hosts, the God of Israel, concerning
Ahab the son of Kolaiah and Zedekiah the son of Maaseiah, [l]who are prophesying a lie to
you in my name: Behold, I will deliver them into the hand of Nebuchadnezzar king of
Babylon, and he shall strike them down before your eyes. 22 [m]Because of them [n]this curse
shall be used by all the exiles from Judah in Babylon: “The LORD make you like Zedekiah
and Ahab, [o]whom the king of Babylon roasted in the fire,” 23 because they have done an
outrageous thing in Israel, [p]they have committed adultery with their neighbors’ wives,
and [p]they have spoken in my name lying words that I did not command them. [q]I am the
one who knows, [q]and I am witness, declares the LORD.’”

Shemaiah’s False Prophecy

24 To [r]Shemaiah of Nehelam you shall say: 25 “Thus says the LORD of hosts, the God of
Israel: You have sent letters in your name to all the people who are in Jerusalem, and to
[s]Zephaniah the son of [t]Maaseiah the priest, and to all the priests, saying, 26 ‘The LORD has
made you priest instead of Jehoiada the priest, to have [u]charge in the house of the LORD
[v]over every madman who prophesies, to put him in [w]the stocks and neck irons. 27 Now
why have you not rebuked Jeremiah [x]of Anathoth who is prophesying to you? 28 For he
has sent to us in Babylon, saying, “Your exile will be long; [y]build houses and live in them,
and plant gardens and eat their produce.”’”

29 [s]Zephaniah the priest read this letter in the hearing of Jeremiah the prophet. 30 [z]Then
the word of the LORD came to Jeremiah: 31 “Send to all the exiles, saying, ‘Thus says the
LORD concerning [a]Shemaiah of Nehelam: Because [a]Shemaiah had prophesied to you [b]when
I did not send him, and has made you trust in a lie, 32 therefore thus says the LORD: Behold,
I will punish [a]Shemaiah of Nehelam and his descendants. He shall not have anyone living
among this people, [c]and he shall not see the good that I will do to my people, declares the
LORD, [d]for he has spoken rebellion against the LORD.’”

16 [e]See ch. 22:2
17 [f]See ch. 24:10 [g]ch. 24:8
18 [f][See ver. 17 above] [h]See ch. 15:4 [i]ch. 18:16; 42:18; See ch. 24:9 [d][See ver. 14 above]
19 [j]See ch. 25:4
20 [k]ch. 24:5
21 [l]ver. 9; See ch. 14:14
22 [m]See Isa. 65:15 [n]See ch. 24:9 [o][Dan. 3:6]
23 [p]ch. 23:14 [q]Mal. 3:5
24 [r]ver. 31, 32
25 [s]ch. 21:1; 2 Kgs. 25:18 [t]ch. 35:4
26 [u][ch. 20:1] [v][2 Kgs. 9:11; Acts 26:24] [w]ch. 20:2
27 [x]ch. 1:1; 32:7
28 [y]ver. 5
29 [s][See ver. 25 above]
30 [z]ver. 1, 20
31 [a]ver. 24 [b]ver. 9; See ch. 5:31
32 [a][See ver. 31 above] [c]See ch. 17:6 [d]ch. 28:16

29:15–17 prophets for us. See note on vv. 8–9. In contrast to the exiles, those who remain in Jerusalem will face **sword, famine, and pestilence** (5:12; 14:1–11; 15:1–4; 16:4; 21:1–10; 24:10). They are the **vile figs** first mentioned in ch. 24.

29:18 horror . . . hissing. See 15:4; 18:16; 19:8; 24:9; 25:9.

29:19 persistently sent. See note on 25:3–4.

29:20 God addresses the **exiles** again.

29:21–22 As vv. 8–9 indicate, false prophets addressed the exiles. **LORD of hosts** (“Yahweh of armies”) is often used in judgment passages to describe God (cf. 5:14). **Ahab the son of Kolaiah . . . Zedekiah the son of Maaseiah**. Neither is mentioned elsewhere in Scripture. **prophesying a lie**. See 27:10, 14, 16; 28:15; 29:9. The lie is not specified, but they probably promised a quick return from exile. **deliver them into the hand**. Have Ahab and Zedekiah arrested. **strike them down**. The penalty for their lies in contrast to God’s protection of Jeremiah (1:17–19). Their fate will be so terrible that they will become a **curse** used to condemn others.

29:23 outrageous thing. A technical term for extreme acts that contribute to the breakdown of society. It can refer to aberrant sexual acts (Deut. 22:21; Judg. 19:23–24; 20:6, 10; 2 Sam. 13:12) or to acts of defiance against God’s explicit orders (Josh. 7:10–15). **committed adultery**. See Jer. 23:13–15; 2 Tim. 3:1–6. **I am witness**. God has seen everything, even what the false prophets thought was done in secret (cf. Jer. 23:23–24).

29:24 Shemaiah is unmentioned elsewhere, and the location of **Nehelam** is unknown.

29:25 Shemaiah sent letters from Babylon to counter Jeremiah’s prior correspondence (vv. 4–23). **Zephaniah**. Not the prophet. See 21:1–2.

29:26 Shemaiah considered it Zephaniah’s duty to punish the **madman** (1 Sam. 21:14–15; 2 Kings 9:11; Hos. 9:7), a term that probably relates to a “babbler” pretending to be a prophet. Jeremiah was actually placed in stocks at least once (Jer. 20:2).

29:27–28 Shemaiah does not consider Jeremiah’s letter (vv. 4–23) either comforting or true. He believes prophets like Hananiah who prophesy a short **exile** (ch. 28). **Anathoth**. See 1:1–3.

29:29 Zephaniah never persecutes **Jeremiah** (21:1–2; 37:1–10; 38:24–28). Here he informs Jeremiah of Shemaiah’s demands.

29:31–32 Shemaiah is revealed as a false prophet who makes **people** trust in lies (28:15). **His descendants** (or “his offspring”) could mean near or distant descendants who presumably share his rebellion (see Ex. 20:5–6; Ezek. 18:1–4). **spoken rebellion**. By preaching what God has not said.

Restoration for Israel and Judah

30 The word that came to Jeremiah from the LORD: 2 “Thus says the LORD, the God of
Israel: [e]Write in a book all the words that I have spoken to you. 3 [f]For behold, days
are coming, declares the LORD, [g]when I will restore [h]the fortunes of my people, [i]Israel and
Judah, says the LORD, [j]and I will bring them back to the land that I gave to their fathers,
and they shall take possession of it.”
4 These are the words that the LORD spoke concerning [i]Israel and Judah:

5 “Thus says the LORD:
We have heard a cry of panic,
of terror, and no peace.
6 Ask now, and see,
can a man bear a child?
[k]Why then do I see every man
with his hands on his stomach [k]like a woman in labor?
[l]Why has every face turned pale?
7 Alas! [m]That day is so great
[n]there is none like it;
it is a time of distress for Jacob;
yet he shall be saved out of it.

8 “And it shall come to pass in that day, declares the LORD of hosts, that I will [o]break
his [p]yoke from off your neck, and I will [o]burst your bonds, [q]and foreigners shall no more
make a servant of him.[1] 9 But they shall serve the LORD their God and [r]David their king,
whom I will raise up for them.

10 [s]“Then fear not, [t]O Jacob my servant, declares the LORD,
nor be dismayed, O Israel;
for behold, [s]I will save you from far away,
[u]and your offspring from the land of their captivity.
[s]Jacob shall return and have quiet and ease,
and none shall make him afraid.
11 [v]For I am with you to save you,
declares the LORD;
[v]I will make a full end of all the nations
among whom I scattered you,
but of you I will not make a full end.

[1] *Or serve him*

Chapter 30
2 [e]ch. 36:2; Hab. 2:2
3 [f]Hab. 2:3 [g]ver. 18; ch. 29:14; 31:23; 32:44; 33:7, 11, 26; Job 42:10; Lam. 2:14 [h]Ezra 2:1 [i]Isa. 11:12, 13; Hos. 1:11 [j]ch. 12:15; Ezek. 20:42; See ch. 16:15; 23:3
4 [i][See ver. 3 above]
6 [k]See Isa. 13:8 [l]Nah. 2:10; [Joel 2:6]
7 [m]Joel 2:11; Zeph. 1:14 [n]Dan. 12:1
8 [o]ch. 2:20; Nah. 1:13 [p]See ch. 27:2 [q]Ezek. 34:27
9 [r]Isa. 55:3, 4; Ezek. 34:23; 37:24; Hos. 3:5; [Luke 1:69, 70; Acts 13:22, 23]; See ch. 23:5
10 [s]ch. 42:11; 46:27, 28; See Isa. 43:5 [t]Isa. 41:8 [u]See ch. 3:18
11 [v]ch. 46:28

30:1–33:26 *Restoration for Judah and Israel.* The book now turns to positive themes. At last Jeremiah may “build and plant” (1:10). He claims that God will restore the nation (ch. 30), make a new covenant with Israel (ch. 31), bring Israel back to the Promised Land (ch. 32), and honor the Davidic covenant (ch. 33).

30:1–24 *God Will Restore the Nation.* This chapter serves as an introduction to this section (chs. 30–33). Jeremiah emphasizes hope (30:1–11), healing (vv. 12–17), and rebuilding (vv. 18–24).

30:1 This message (chs. 30–31) is undated, unlike chs. 24–29.

30:2 Write in a book. See 25:13; 36:2. This would preserve the words for future generations. **all the words**. See 30:4ff.

30:3 days are coming. Seventy years in the future (25:12). **I will bring them back**. After the exiles seek God with all their heart (27:22; 29:10–14).

30:4 These promises of hope include the long-defeated **Israel**, not just **Judah**. The whole nation will be united again.

30:5–6 God announces a time of **terror**. Israel’s men (perhaps “soldiers”) writhe in pain and anguish **like a woman in labor**, due to the extreme situation (4:31; 6:24; 22:23).

30:7 That day. The day of the Lord, the day of judgment (Isa. 2:6–22; Amos 5:18–20; etc.; see also The Day of the Lord in the Prophets, p. 1668). **time of distress for Jacob**. Israel will suffer. **yet he shall be saved out of it**. The day of judgment will remove Israel’s foes.

30:8 yoke. See 2:20; 5:5; 27:8–12; 28:1–17. **burst your bonds**. See 2:20; 5:5. **foreigners**. Such as Egypt, Assyria, Babylon, and Persia. **servant**. As Israel was in pre-exodus days (Ex. 2:23–25; 5:10–23).

30:9 The people will respond to the deliverance by serving **God** and the Davidic king (23:1–8). For **David** as the name of the Davidic king (and ultimately the Messiah), see Ezek. 34:23–24; 37:24–25; Hos. 3:5. This service will be a complete reversal of their previous disobedience.

30:10 fear not. Because God will act on the nation’s behalf. **Jacob my servant**. See note on Isa. 42:1–9. **Jacob shall return**. The exile will end when the people return home.

30:11 I am with you to save you. For God to be “with” someone is for him to give his help for that person to carry out his calling (1:8, 19;

11[v]ch. 46:28 [w]See ch. 10:24
12[x]See ch. 15:18 [y]ch. 10:19; 14:17
13[z]ch. 46:11
14[a]Lam. 1:2; [ch. 4:30] [b]Job 13:24; 19:11; Isa. 63:10; Lam. 2:4 [c]Job 30:21; [ch. 6:23] [d]ch. 5:6
15[x][See ver. 12 above] [d][See ver. 14 above]
16[e][ver. 11; ch. 10:25; Isa. 41:11] [f][Ex. 23:22] [g][Isa. 33:1] [h]ch. 2:14
17[i]ch. 33:6 [j]ch. 8:22 [k]Ps. 6:2; Hos. 6:1 [l][Mic. 4:6, 7; Zeph. 3:19]
18[m][Amos 9:11]; See ver. 3 [n]Deut. 13:16
19[o]ch. 31:12, 13; 33:11; Isa. 35:10; 51:11 [p]Ezek. 36:10, 37; Zech. 10:8
20[q]Isa. 1:26
21[r][Gen. 49:10; Deut. 18:18] [s]Num. 16:5 [t]ch. 49:19; [Heb. 5:4]

[v]I will [w]discipline you in just measure,
and I will by no means leave you unpunished.

12 "For thus says the LORD:
[x]Your hurt is incurable,
[y]and your wound is grievous.
13 There is none to uphold your cause,
no medicine for your wound,
[z]no healing for you.
14 [a]All your lovers have forgotten you;
they care nothing for you;
for I have dealt you the blow of [b]an enemy,
the punishment [c]of a merciless foe,
because your guilt is great,
[d]because your sins are flagrant.
15 [x]Why do you cry out over your hurt?
[x]Your pain is incurable.
Because your guilt is great,
[d]because your sins are flagrant,
I have done these things to you.
16 [e]Therefore all who devour you shall be devoured,
and [f]all your foes, every one of them, shall go into captivity;
[g]those who plunder you shall be plundered,
[h]and all who prey on you I will make a prey.
17 [i]For I will restore [j]health to you,
and [k]your wounds I will heal,
declares the LORD,
because [l]they have called you an outcast:
'It is Zion, for whom no one cares!'

18 "Thus says the LORD:
Behold, [m]I will restore the fortunes of the tents of Jacob
and have compassion on his dwellings;
the city shall be rebuilt on [n]its mound,
and the palace shall stand where it used to be.
19 [o]Out of them shall come songs of thanksgiving,
and the voices of those who celebrate.
[p]I will multiply them, and they shall not be few;
I will make them honored, and they shall not be small.
20 [q]Their children shall be as they were of old,
and their congregation shall be established before me,
and I will punish all who oppress them.
21 [r]Their prince shall be one of themselves;
[r]their ruler shall come out from their midst;
[s]I will make him draw near, and he shall approach me,
[t]for who would dare of himself to approach me?
declares the LORD.

15:20; 20:11; 42:11; 46:28; see Gen. 39:2–3). **make a full end**. Completely destroy (Jer. 46:28).

30:14 lovers. Former allies and their gods (3:1–2; 4:30; 22:20–23; Lam. 1:2, 19). **the blow of an enemy**. God turned from fighting for Israel (Ex. 15:1–18) to fighting against Israel (Jer. 11:14–17; 15:1–9; 27:8). **guilt is great**. Israel sought other gods in violation of their covenant with God.

30:15 pain is incurable. Israel's defeat and resulting loss are terrible (see note on 17:9). **Because your guilt is great**. Covenant infidelity has caused devastation (6:1–15; 15:1–9).

30:18 Every possible level of society will be renewed, from clans living in **tents**, to city dwellers living in towns built on a **mound** of rubble, to royalty living in a restored **palace**.

30:19 Singing will replace sorrow, growth will replace decimation, and honor will replace shame.

30:20 congregation. The community gathered by God for instruction, worship, or judicial decision making (Ex. 12:3; 35:1; 1 Kings 8:5). **established before me**. Regain God's favor.

30:21 Israel's **ruler** will no longer be a foreigner, as during the exile, but will

22 [u]And you shall be my people,
and I will be your God."
23 [v]Behold [w]the storm of the LORD!
Wrath has gone forth,
a whirling tempest;
it will burst upon the head of the wicked.
24 [x]The fierce anger of the LORD will not turn back
until he has executed and accomplished
the intentions of his mind.
[y]In the latter days you will understand this.

The LORD Will Turn Mourning to Joy

31 [z]"At that time, declares the LORD, [a]I will be the God of all the clans of Israel, and
they shall be my people."

2 Thus says the LORD:
"The people who survived the sword
found grace in the wilderness;
[b]when Israel sought for rest,
3 the LORD appeared to him[1] from far away.
[c]I have loved you with an everlasting love;
therefore [d]I have continued [e]my faithfulness to you.
4 [f]Again I will build you, and you shall be built,
O virgin Israel!
[g]Again you shall adorn yourself with tambourines
and shall go forth in [h]the dance of the merrymakers.
5 [i]Again you shall plant vineyards
on the mountains of Samaria;
the planters shall plant
and shall enjoy the fruit.
6 For there shall be a day when watchmen will call
in [j]the hill country of Ephraim:
[k]'Arise, and let us go up to Zion,
to the LORD our God.'"
7 For thus says the LORD:
[l]"Sing aloud with gladness for Jacob,
and raise shouts for [m]the chief of the nations;
proclaim, give praise, and say,

[1] Septuagint; Hebrew *me*

22[u]ch. 24:7; 31:1; 32:38; See ch. 31:33; Lev. 26:12
23[v]ch. 23:19, 20 [w]ch. 25:32
24[x]See ch. 12:13 [y]Hos. 3:5

Chapter 31

1[z]ch. 30:24 [a][2 Cor. 6:18]; See ch. 30:22
2[b][ch. 30:10; Ps. 95:11; Isa. 63:14]
3[c]Deut. 7:8; 10:15; Mal. 1:2; Rom. 11:28 [d]Ps. 36:10 [e]Hos. 11:4
4[f]ver. 28; ch. 33:7 [g]Isa. 61:10 [h]ver. 13; Ex. 15:20; Judg. 11:34; 21:21; See 2 Sam. 6:14
5[i]Isa. 65:21; Amos 9:14
6[j]See Josh. 24:33 [k]Isa. 2:3; 27:13
7[l]Isa. 12:6; 65:18 [m]Amos 6:1

be **one of themselves**. He will be able, once again, to **draw near** to God as Israel's representative.

30:22 Jeremiah expects the privilege of the covenant (Ex. 29:45; Lev. 26:12; Deut. 27:9) to be renewed, especially after the exile (cf. Jer. 24:7; 31:1, 33; 32:38; Ezek. 11:20; 14:11; 36:28; 37:23, 27; Zech. 8:8).

30:23 storm of the LORD. A metaphor for the day of God's judgment (cf. 23:19–20; 25:32) that will fall **upon . . . the wicked**.

30:24 God's **intentions** include removing the wicked in Israel (v. 23), displacing Israel's enemies, and establishing Israel's king (v. 21). Israel will be God's people again, yet only **in the latter days**, that is, sometime in the unspecified future.

31:1–40 *God Will Make a New Covenant with Israel.* This chapter includes the most famous passage in Jeremiah, the promise of a new covenant (vv. 31–40). Leading up to that passage, God promises Israel that they will be his people (vv. 1–14), he will have mercy on weary Israel (vv. 15–26), and he will make Israel secure (vv. 27–30).

31:1 At that time. In the latter days (30:24), God will reunite **Israel** with Judah under his covenantal leadership. **my people**. See note on 30:22.

31:2 Israel's exile experience mirrors the exodus era. In both, those who escaped death **found grace** and **rest** in the desert. After exile, **Israel** will again follow God (2:1–3).

31:3 You is feminine singular, referring to the whole people (cf. v. 4). **everlasting love**. God's love was always based on grace (Deut. 7:6–11), and even the involvement of the majority in Israel's rejection of that love cannot cause this covenantal, relational love to cease (Hos. 1:10–11; 2:14–23; 11:1–9).

31:4 virgin Israel. The northern kingdom (vv. 5–6). **dance of the merrymakers**. Women who celebrated military victories (Ex. 15:20; Judg. 11:34; 1 Sam. 18:6) and participated in religious ceremonies (Lam. 1:4).

31:5–6 Samaria (both a city and region in Israel) and **Ephraim** (both a tribe and a representative name for Israel) will **plant** vineyards again. More importantly, they will **go up to Zion** to worship **the LORD** again (contrast 1 Kings 12:26–33).

31:7 The dancers in v. 4 will **raise shouts** of joy for Israel's restoration. **remnant of Israel**. A term that can denote survivors of a catastrophe (8:3), faithful ones in Judah and Israel (Isa. 4:2), and faithful ones in all nations (Isa. 11:11). The second option applies here. Some Israelites will serve God (cf. Hos. 3:5).

[n]"O LORD, save your people,
the remnant of Israel.'
8 Behold, I will bring them [o]from the north country
and [p]gather them from [q]the farthest parts of the earth,
among them [r]the blind and the lame,
the pregnant woman and she who is in labor, together;
a great company, they shall return here.
9 [s]With weeping they shall come,
[t]and with pleas for mercy I will lead them back,
I will make them [u]walk by brooks of water,
[v]in a straight path in which they shall not stumble,
for [w]I am a father to Israel,
and Ephraim is [x]my firstborn.

10 "Hear the word of the LORD, O nations,
and declare it in the coastlands far away;
say, 'He who scattered Israel will [p]gather him,
and will keep him [y]as a shepherd keeps his flock.'
11 [z]For the LORD has ransomed Jacob
and has redeemed him from [a]hands too strong for him.
12 They shall come and sing aloud on the height of Zion,
[b]and they shall be radiant [c]over the goodness of the LORD,
[d]over the grain, the wine, and the oil,
and over the young of the flock and the herd;
[e]their life shall be like a watered garden,
[f]and they shall languish no more.
13 [g]Then shall the young women rejoice in the dance,
and the young men and the old shall be merry.
[h]I will turn their mourning into joy;
I will comfort them, and give them gladness for sorrow.
14 [i]I will feast the soul of the priests with abundance,
and my people shall be satisfied with my goodness,
declares the LORD."

15 Thus says the LORD:
[j]"A voice is heard in [k]Ramah,
lamentation and bitter weeping.
[l]Rachel is weeping for her children;
she refuses to be comforted for her children,
[m]because they are no more."
16 Thus says the LORD:
"Keep your voice from weeping,
and your eyes from tears,

7 [n]Ps. 118:25
8 [o]See ch. 3:18 [p]See ch. 23:3 [q]See ch. 6:22 [r]Isa. 35:5, 6
9 [s]ch. 50:4; [Ezra 3:13; 10:1] [t]ch. 3:21; Zech. 12:10 [u]Isa. 35:6, 7; 49:10; [Ps. 23:2] [v]Isa. 35:8; 43:19; 49:11 [w]Rom. 8:15 [x][Ex. 4:22; Ps. 89:27]
10 [p][See ver. 8 above] [y]Isa. 40:11
11 [z]Isa. 43:1; 44:23; 48:20 [a][Isa. 49:24, 25]
12 [b]Isa. 2:2; Mic. 4:1 [c]Hos. 3:5 [d][Deut. 12:17] [e]Isa. 58:11 [f]Isa. 35:10
13 [g]See ver. 4 [h][John 16:20]
14 [i][ver. 25]
15 [j]Cited Matt. 2:18 [k]Josh. 18:25 [l][Gen. 35:19, 20; 48:7; 1 Sam. 10:2] [m]ch. 10:20

31:8 gather them from the farthest parts of the earth. Where Israel was driven over time after Samaria fell in 722 B.C. (2 Kings 17:18; Isa. 7:8). **the blind and the lame**. Physical infirmity will not keep the remnant from returning.

31:9 God will provide for all their needs as the exiles return. **father to Israel**. See Ex. 4:22–23; Hos. 11:1–9.

31:10 God, Israel's great **shepherd** (Isa. 40:11), will **gather** and **keep** (guard) his sheep.

31:11 Ransomed suggests financial payment for a debt (Hos. 13:14). **Redeemed** implies a family member acting on behalf of a relative to remove from trouble, pay a debt, or avenge a wrong (e.g., Ruth 4:1). See also Deut. 9:26; 13:5.

31:12 See Isa. 35:10; 51:10–11. The people shall flourish as they eat food and enjoy the prosperity that God provides.

31:13 When God restores Israel's lives he will also restore its **joy**. God will **comfort them**. See Isa. 40:1.

31:14 abundance. Literally "fatness," which probably refers to the portions of sacrificial meats set aside for the priests (Lev. 7:31–36).

31:15 Ramah. 5 miles (8 km) north of Jerusalem and on the route to exile (40:1). **Rachel**. Jacob's second, yet favorite, wife (Gen. 29:30), the mother of Joseph, who was father of Ephraim and Manasseh (Gen. 30:22–24; 41:50–52). Rachel was buried near Bethlehem (Gen. 35:19–20). The focus in Jeremiah is on the grief of the exile, as if it touched Rachel herself. Matthew 2:18 applies this verse to Herod killing the innocent children in an attempt to kill Jesus. Thus, by Jesus' time the phrase had become proverbial for the mistreatment of Jewish children.

31:16–17 God promises that Rachel's **children** will return from exile.

for there is a reward for your work,
declares the LORD,
and [n]they shall come back from the land of the enemy.
17 [o]There is hope for your future,
declares the LORD,
and your children shall come back to their own country.
18 I have heard [p]Ephraim grieving,
'You have disciplined me, and I was disciplined,
like an untrained calf;
[q]bring me back that I may be restored,
for you are the LORD my God.
19 For after [r]I had turned away, I relented,
and after I was instructed, [s]I struck my thigh;
[t]I was ashamed, and I was confounded,
because I bore the disgrace of my youth.'
20 [p]Is Ephraim my dear son?
[u]Is he my darling child?
For as often as I speak against him,
I do remember him still.
[v]Therefore my heart[1] yearns for him;
I will surely have mercy on him,
declares the LORD.
21 [w]"Set up road markers for yourself;
make yourself guideposts;
[x]consider well the highway,
[w] the road by which you went.
Return, O virgin Israel,
return to these your cities.
22 [y]How long will you waver,
[z]O faithless daughter?
For the LORD has created a new thing on the earth:
a woman encircles a man."

23 Thus says the LORD of hosts, the God of Israel: "Once more they shall use these words in the land of Judah and in its cities, [a]when I restore their fortunes:

[b]"'The LORD bless you, [c]O habitation of righteousness,
[d]O holy hill!'

24 [e]And Judah and all its cities shall dwell there together, and [e]the farmers and those who wander with their flocks. 25 For I will [f]satisfy the weary soul, and every languishing soul I will replenish."

26 At this I awoke and looked, and my sleep was pleasant to me.

[1] Hebrew *bowels*

16 [n]Ezra 1:5; Hos. 1:11
17 [o]ch. 29:11
18 [p][ver. 9] [q]Ps. 80:3; Lam. 5:21
19 [r]Deut. 30:2 [s]Ezek. 21:12 [t][ch. 3:25]
20 [p][See ver. 18 above] [u][Prov. 8:30] [v]Song 5:4; Isa. 16:11
21 [w][Isa. 57:14; 62:10] [x]ch. 50:4, 5
22 [y]ch. 2:18, 23, 36 [z]ch. 49:4
23 [a]See ch. 30:3 [b]Ps. 122:6, 7 [c]ch. 50:7; Isa. 1:26 [d]Zech. 8:3
24 [e]ch. 33:13
25 [f]Ps. 36:8; [ver. 14]

31:18 Ephraim recognizes God's discipline (cf. Lev. 26:14–26; Deut. 30:1–10) and pleads for restoration (Lam. 5:21–22).

31:19 Ephraim explains his path back to God. **struck my thigh**. A physical act of remorse (Ezek. 21:12). **disgrace of my youth**. Past shameful actions against God (Jer. 2:2–5; 3:24–25; etc.).

31:20 Despite all God has had to do to discipline **Ephraim**, he never stopped loving his **darling child**.

31:21 Israel should mark the way they **went** out (to exile), for they will **return** on the same road.

31:22 How long will you waver, i.e., how long will you wait to fulfill the prophecy of v. 6? **faithless daughter**. What Ephraim has been in the past. **a new thing**. A new beginning (Isa. 43:19; 48:7). **a woman encircles a man**. A proverbial phrase, the meaning of which may well be lost. Several interpretations have been proposed. (1) It most likely means "the weak will overcome the strong," so that Israel's return will be the weak (i.e., Israel, whose soldiers had become like women; Jer. 30:6) overcoming the strong (its captors) through God's power. (2) "Encircles" may mean "embraces, clings to" and speaks metaphorically of the relationship between Israel ("a woman") and God ("a man"). (3) Israel's soldiers may so decisively defeat the enemy that on their return they would be surrounded by women without fear of attack from outside. (4) Ancient commentators saw a prediction of the birth of Christ, since he was "encircled" by Mary's womb until he was born, but most modern interpreters conclude that this goes beyond the intent of the passage.

31:23–25 Jeremiah addresses **Judah**, who will soon join **Israel** in exile. God will **restore** Judah and its rejoicing, just as he will Israel's (vv. 2–7).

31:26 At this I awoke may indicate that vv. 3–25 were a vision.

27 [g]"Behold, the days are coming, declares the LORD, when [h]I will sow the house of Israel
and the house of Judah with [i]the seed of man and the seed of beast. 28 And it shall come to
pass that [j]as I have watched over them [k]to pluck up and break down, to overthrow, destroy,
and bring harm, [j]so I will watch over them [l]to build and to plant, declares the LORD. 29 In
those days they shall no longer say:

> [m]"'The fathers have eaten sour grapes,
> and the children's teeth are set on edge.'

30 [n]But everyone shall die for his own iniquity. Each man who eats sour grapes, his teeth
shall be set on edge.

The New Covenant

31 [o]"Behold, the days are coming, declares the LORD, when I will make [p]a new covenant
with the house of Israel and the house of Judah, 32 not like the covenant that I made with
their fathers on the day when [q]I took them by the hand to bring them out of the land of
Egypt, my covenant that they broke, [r]though I was their husband, declares the LORD. 33 [s]For
this is the covenant that I will make with the house of Israel after those days, declares the
LORD: [s]I will put my law within them, and I will write it [t]on their hearts. [u]And I will be
their God, and they shall be my people. 34 And no longer shall each one teach his neighbor
and each his brother, saying, 'Know the LORD,' [v]for they shall all know me, [w]from the least
of them to the greatest, declares the LORD. For [x]I will forgive their iniquity, and [y]I will
remember their sin no more."

> 35 Thus says the LORD,
> who [z]gives the sun for light by day
> and [a]the fixed order of the moon and the stars for light by night,
> who stirs up the sea so that its waves roar—
> [b]the LORD of hosts is his name:
> 36 [c]"If this fixed order departs
> from before me, declares the LORD,
> then shall the offspring of Israel cease
> from being a nation before me forever."
>
> 37 Thus says the LORD:
> "If the heavens above can be measured,
> and the foundations of the earth below can be explored,

27 [g]ch. 9:25 [h]Ezek. 36:11; Hos. 2:23; Zech. 10:9 [i][Ps. 22:30; Isa. 53:10]
28 [j]ch. 44:27; [ch. 32:42] [k][ver. 40]; See ch. 1:10 [l]See ch. 24:6
29 [m]Ezek. 18:2, 3; [Lam. 5:7]
30 [n]Ezek. 18:4
31 [o]ver. 31-34, cited Heb. 8:8-12 [p]Luke 22:20; 2 Cor. 3:6
32 [q][Deut. 1:31] [r]See ch. 3:14
33 [s]ch. 32:40; Ezek. 37:26; Cited Heb. 10:16 [t]Ps. 37:31; 2 Cor. 3:3 [u]Hos. 2:23; Zech. 8:8; 13:9; Rev. 21:7; See ch. 30:22
34 [v]Isa. 54:13 [w]See ch. 6:13 [x]ch. 33:8; 36:3; 50:20; Mic. 7:18; Acts 10:43; Rom. 11:27; Cited Heb. 10:17 [y]Isa. 43:25
35 [z]Gen. 1:16 [a]See ver. 36 [b]See ch. 10:16
36 [c][Ps. 148:6; Isa. 54:9, 10]; For ver. 36, 37, see ch. 33:20-26

31:27–40 These verses, describing the new covenant, can be divided into three subsections, each introduced with "Behold, the days are coming, declares the LORD" (vv. 27, 31, 38). The days that are coming will involve the return from exile and repopulation of Jerusalem (vv. 27, 38–40) but will also extend into the unspecified future. Here Jeremiah (see also 32:36–44; 50:5) expresses a theme similar to that of Isaiah 40–66 and Ezek. 11:14–21; 16:60–63; 34:25; 36:22–32; 37:26; namely, that the return from exile will also mean a renewal of the covenant for Judah, with the expectation that the nation will get it right this time. The experience of the postexilic community is seen as a down payment on the promises; the time when "they shall all know me" (Jer. 31:34) looks forward to the consummation of all things.

31:27 God will plant (cf. 1:10) **Israel** and **Judah** in the land again and **sow** people and animals everywhere.

31:28 At that time God will be as determined to **plant** and **build** as he was to tear down and **destroy** (cf. 1:10).

31:29–30 sour grapes . . . teeth are set on edge. This proverb was apparently common (cf. Lam. 5:7; Ezek. 18:2); the negation of the proverb (**they shall no longer say**) means that no one will suffer for the sins of others, for national rebellion against God will cease. The remnant will become the majority.

31:31–34 God will finally remedy the long-standing problem of his people, namely, that they are circumcised in body but so few are circumcised in heart (i.e., truly **know the LORD**). The benefits that God will provide—knowledge of the Lord and forgiveness—were all offered in the OT but all-too-rarely appropriated. Two major interpretative issues for the Christian reader are: (1) What does the author of Hebrews mean by connecting this prophecy concerning **the house of Israel and the house of Judah** (Jer. 31:31) with the Messiah (Heb. 8:8–12)? (2) Do the terms in Jer. 31:27, 31, 36–37 focus the prophecy on ethnic Israel or on a redefined Israel (the Jewish-Gentile church)? The second question is much like the one faced in interpreting "all Israel" in Rom. 11:26.

31:31 The **new covenant** will provide a fresh start for **Israel** and **Judah**, the recipients of both the old and now the new covenant (though many interpret the new covenant as beginning entirely with Jews but going on to include Gentiles; see note on vv. 31–34). This is the only OT passage to speak of a new covenant; for NT uses of the phrase, see Luke 22:20; 2 Cor. 3:6; Heb. 8:8–12.

31:32 This new **covenant** will be different in that it will not be broken, as Israel and Judah **broke** the first one despite God's faithfulness as a good **husband**.

31:33 Rather than writing the **law** on tablets and scrolls (see Ex. 34:1; Deut. 31:9–13) and asking the people to internalize it (Deut. 6:4–9), God will **write it on their hearts** from the start. He will be the God of this new covenant, just as he was for the old covenant partners who loved him. In Rom. 11:27, Paul takes the words "this will be my covenant with them" from this verse.

31:34 There will be no need for a faithful remnant within the covenant people to **teach** the unfaithful majority to know God, for **all** covenant partners will **know** him. This covenant will include only those who know him, and he **will remember their sin no more**.

31:35–36 God gives a **fixed order** to the natural creation, and it is just as impossible for the new covenant (vv. 31–34) to **cease** as it is for the natural order to cease.

31:37 The full extent of creation is unfathomable, and it is equally unfathomable that God would **cast off** the **Israel** of this new covenant.

[d]then I will cast off all the offspring of Israel
for all that they have done,
declares the LORD."

38 [e]"Behold, the days are coming, declares the LORD, when the city shall be rebuilt for the
LORD [f]from the Tower of Hananel to [g]the Corner Gate. 39 [h]And the measuring line shall go
out farther, straight to the hill Gareb, and shall then turn to Goah. 40 [i]The whole valley of
the dead bodies and the ashes, and all the fields as far as the [j]brook Kidron, to the corner
of [k]the Horse Gate toward the east, [l]shall be sacred to the LORD. [m]It shall not be plucked
up or overthrown anymore forever."

Jeremiah Buys a Field During the Siege

32 The word that came to Jeremiah from the LORD [n]in the tenth year of Zedekiah
king of Judah, [o]which was the eighteenth year of Nebuchadnezzar. 2 At that time
the army of the king of Babylon was besieging Jerusalem, and Jeremiah the prophet [p]was
shut up in [q]the court of the guard that was in the palace of the king of Judah. 3 For Zedekiah
king of Judah had imprisoned him, saying, "Why do you prophesy and say, 'Thus says the
LORD: [r]Behold, I am giving this city into the hand of the king of Babylon, and he shall
capture it; 4 [s]Zedekiah king of Judah shall not escape out of the hand of the Chaldeans,
[r]but shall surely be given into the hand of the king of Babylon, and shall speak with him
face to face and see him eye to eye. 5 And [t]he shall take Zedekiah to Babylon, and there he
shall remain until I visit him, declares the LORD. [u]Though you fight against the Chaldeans,
you shall not succeed'?"

6 Jeremiah said, "The word of the LORD came to me: 7 Behold, Hanamel the son of
Shallum your uncle will come to you and say, [v]'Buy my field that is at [w]Anathoth, [x]for
the right of redemption by purchase is yours.' 8 Then Hanamel my cousin came to me
in [q]the court of the guard, in accordance with the word of the LORD, and said to me,
'Buy my field that is at [w]Anathoth in the land of Benjamin, for the right of possession
and redemption is yours; buy it for yourself.' Then I knew that this was the word of
the LORD.

9 "And I bought the field at [w]Anathoth from Hanamel my cousin, and [y]weighed out the
money to him, seventeen shekels of silver. 10 [z]I signed the deed, [a]sealed it, [b]got witnesses,
and [y]weighed the money on scales. 11 Then I took the sealed deed of purchase, containing
the terms and conditions and the open copy. 12 And I gave the deed of purchase to [c]Baruch
the son of Neriah son of Mahseiah, in the presence of Hanamel my cousin, in the presence
of [d]the witnesses who signed the deed of purchase, and in the presence of all the Judeans
who were sitting in [q]the court of the guard. 13 I charged [c]Baruch in their presence, saying,
14 'Thus says the LORD of hosts, the God of Israel: Take these deeds, both this sealed deed
of purchase and this open deed, and put them in an earthenware vessel, that they may last

37 [d]Rom. 11:1
38 [e]ver. 27, 31 [f]Neh. 3:1; 12:39; Zech. 14:10 [g]2 Kgs. 14:13
39 [h]Ezek. 40:3; Zech. 1:16; 2:1, 2; [Rev. 11:1]
40 [i][ch. 7:31, 32] [j]See 2 Sam. 15:23 [k]2 Chr. 23:15 [l]Isa. 52:1; Joel 3:17 [m][ver. 28]

Chapter 32

1 [n][ch. 37:5, 11; 39:1, 2; 52:4; 2 Kgs. 25:2] [o][ch. 52:12; 2 Kgs. 25:8]
2 [p]Ps. 88:8 [q]ver. 8, 12; ch. 33:1; 37:21; 38:6, 13; 39:14; [Neh. 3:25]
3 [r]ver. 25, 36, 43; ch. 21:10; 34:2; 37:17; 38:3
4 [s]ch. 34:3 [r][See ver. 3 above]
5 [t]ch. 39:7; 52:11 [u][ch. 21:4; 33:5]
7 [v]ver. 25 [w]ch. 1:1; 29:27; Josh. 21:18 [x]Lev. 25:25; [Ruth 4:4]
8 [q][See ver. 2 above] [w][See ver. 7 above]
9 [w][See ver. 7 above] [y]Gen. 23:16; Zech. 11:12; [Matt. 26:15]
10 [z]ver. 44 [a]Esth. 3:12 [b]ver. 25 [y][See ver. 9 above]
12 [c]ch. 36:4, 8, 10, 14, 26, 32; 43:3, 6; 45:1-3 [d][Isa. 8:2] [q][See ver. 2 above]
13 [c][See ver. 12 above]

31:38–40 Jerusalem will soon be destroyed, yet God will eventually rebuild it. When it is totally sacred to the Lord (Zech. 14:20–21), it will **not be plucked up or overthrown anymore forever**. At that time it will be Zion, the new Jerusalem, the city where God lives with his people in the permanent absence of sin (Isa. 4:2–6; 25:6–12; 65:17–25).

32:1–44 *God Will Bring Israel Back to the Promised Land.* This chapter revolves around God's commanding of Jeremiah to purchase land in Judah even though exile from the land is imminent. This seemingly irrational command (vv. 1–15) leads to Jeremiah questioning God and receiving a firm response (vv. 16–35) and to God's pledge to bring the exiles home (vv. 36–44).

32:1 tenth year. c. 588–587 B.C.

32:2–5 Babylon was besieging Jerusalem. This siege lasted about a year (see 39:1; 52:4). **Jeremiah** was **imprisoned** by **Zedekiah** (37:11–21) for prophesying that Babylon would take the city (21:1–10; 34:1–5; 37:6–10).

32:6–7 Hanamel . . . will come to you. God revealed what would occur. **right of redemption**. See Lev. 25:25–32. When property was sold due to financial problems, a next of kin would buy it back so that it could stay in the family. The person who bought it back was called a "kinsman-redeemer" (cf. "redeemer," Ruth 4:1).

32:8 Hanamel . . . came to me. What God said would happen (v. 7) did in fact occur. **Anathoth . . . land of Benjamin**. See 1:1–3.

32:9 Because of God's word, Jeremiah buys the **field**, despite the impending Babylonian invasion. **seventeen shekels**. About seven ounces. The size and actual value of the field are unknown.

32:10 Signed (lit., "wrote") may indicate that Jeremiah dictated the deed (36:1–32). **sealed**. He pressed his signature stamp into wax that covered the document's folds or rolls. **Witnesses** probably signed the outside of the document.

32:11 sealed deed . . . open copy. Scribes wrote two copies of the transaction; they rolled up and sealed the first copy, leaving the second open for viewing.

32:12 Baruch was Jeremiah's disciple and scribe (36:4; 45:1–5). The name means "blessed."

32:13–14 Jeremiah had **Baruch** place the precious document in an **earthenware** storage **vessel** for safekeeping. Many of the Dead Sea Scrolls were stored in such jars.

15 [e]ver. 43
16 [f]See ver. 12
17 [g]Isa. 37:16 [h]See ch. 21:5 [i]ver. 27; See Gen. 18:14
18 [j]Ex. 20:6; 34:7; Deut. 5:9, 10 [k][Ps. 79:12; Isa. 65:6-7] [l]Isa. 9:6 [m]See ch. 10:16
19 [n]Isa. 28:29 [o][Ps. 66:3, 5] [p]See ch. 16:17 [q]See ch. 17:10
20 [r]Ps. 135:9 [s]2 Sam. 7:23; See Neh. 9:10
21 [t]Ex. 6:6; Deut. 4:34; 1 Chr. 17:21 [u]See ch. 21:5
22 [v]Deut. 26:15; See Ex. 3:8
23 [w]Neh. 9:26, 27; See ch. 11:8; Dan. 9:10-14
24 [x]ch. 33:4; See ch. 6:6 [y]ver. 36; See ch. 14:12 [z]See ver. 3
25 [a]ver. 7 [b]ver. 10 [z][See ver. 24 above]
27 [c]Num. 16:22 [d]See Gen. 18:14
28 [e]ver. 3
29 [f]See ch. 21:10 [g]See ch. 19:13 [h]See ch. 7:18
30 [i]ch. 3:25 [h][See ver. 29 above] [j]ch. 25:6, 7
31 [k]2 Kgs. 23:27; 24:3
32 [l]ch. 2:26

for a long time. 15 For thus says the LORD of hosts, the God of Israel: Houses and [e]fields
and vineyards shall again be bought in this land.'

Jeremiah Prays for Understanding

16 "After I had given the deed of purchase to [f]Baruch the son of Neriah, I prayed to the
LORD, saying: 17 'Ah, Lord GOD! It is [g]you who have made the heavens and the earth by
your great power and by [h]your outstretched arm! [i]Nothing is too hard for you. 18 [j]You
show steadfast love to thousands, [j]but you repay the guilt of fathers [k]to their children after
them, O great and [l]mighty God, whose name is the [m]LORD of hosts, 19 [n]great in counsel and
[o]mighty in deed, [p]whose eyes are open to all the ways of the children of man, [q]rewarding
each one according to his ways and according to the fruit of his deeds. 20 You have shown
[r]signs and wonders in the land of Egypt, and to this day in Israel and among all mankind,
[s]and have made a name for yourself, as at this day. 21 [t]You brought your people Israel out
of the land of Egypt with signs and wonders, with a strong hand and [u]outstretched arm,
[t]and with great terror. 22 And you gave them this land, [v]which you swore to their fathers
to give them, [v]a land flowing with milk and honey. 23 And they entered and took possession of it. [w]But they did not obey your voice or walk in your law. They did nothing of all
you commanded them to do. Therefore you have made all this disaster come upon them.
24 Behold, [x]the siege mounds have come up to the city to take it, and [y]because of sword and
famine and pestilence [z]the city is given into the hands of the Chaldeans who are fighting
against it. What you spoke has come to pass, and behold, you see it. 25 Yet you, O Lord GOD,
have said to me, [a]"Buy the field for money [b]and get witnesses"—though [z]the city is given
into the hands of the Chaldeans.'"

26 The word of the LORD came to Jeremiah: 27 "Behold, I am the LORD, [c]the God of all
flesh. [d]Is anything too hard for me? 28 Therefore, thus says the LORD: [e]Behold, I am giving this city into the hands of the Chaldeans and into the hand of Nebuchadnezzar king
of Babylon, and he shall capture it. 29 The Chaldeans who are fighting against this city
[f]shall come and set this city on fire and burn it, [g]with the houses on whose roofs offerings have been made to Baal [g]and drink offerings have been poured out to other gods,
[h]to provoke me to anger. 30 For the children of Israel and the children of Judah have done
nothing but evil in my sight [i]from their youth. The children of Israel have done nothing
but [h]provoke me to anger [j]by the work of their hands, declares the LORD. 31 This city has
aroused my anger and wrath, from the day it was built to this day, [k]so that I will remove it
from my sight 32 because of all the evil of the children of Israel and the children of Judah
that they did to provoke me to anger—[l]their kings and their officials, their priests and

32:15 Now the point of this symbolic act (cf. 13:1–14; 16:1–13; 18:1–11; 19:1–15; 27:1–28:17) is revealed: **God** will return the people to the **land**, and **fields** will be **bought** and sold **again**.

32:17 Jeremiah's prayer begins by confessing that God is the all-powerful Creator (**made the heavens**), for whom **nothing is too hard** (cf. Gen. 18:14). This supports the doctrine of God's omnipotence: God has infinite power and can do all that he wills to do. However, it does not mean that God can do anything, for he cannot act contrary to his own character (cf. 2 Tim. 2:13; Heb. 6:18).

32:18 steadfast love to thousands. Covenant love to countless generations. See Ex. 34:6–7; Joel 2:12–14; Jonah 4:2. **repay the guilt**. In many cases, both **fathers** and **children** have sinned in the same ways, so both suffer the consequences of their actions. See Ex. 20:5–6; Jer. 3:25; 7:26; 13:14; 14:20; 31:29. One of the most horrible aspects of sin, however, is that it often harms other people, especially those closest to the person committing the sin. **hosts**. Armies that God commands for purposes of judgment.

32:19 great in counsel. Wise and rich in revelation. **mighty in deed**. Able to act as well as think and talk. **eyes are open**. God sees **all the ways of the children of man**. **rewarding each one**. Giving justly to each according to his sense of justice (cf. 17:10; Ps. 62:12; Matt. 16:27; 2 Cor. 5:9–10; 1 Pet. 1:17).

32:20–23 God has revealed the characteristics noted in vv. 17–19 by his great acts, such as sending the plagues in **Egypt**, leading **Israel** in the exodus, giving Israel the Promised Land, and bearing with Israel until he sent Babylon to Jerusalem.

32:20 signs and wonders. Miracles (see notes on Mark 13:22; Acts 3:16; Rom. 15:19; 2 Cor. 12:12; 2 Thess. 2:9–10). **and to this day**. Such miraculous evidences of God's presence and care for his people were not limited to the generation of the exodus, for from the exodus until the time of Jeremiah, God had continued to work miracles among his people, for the glory of his **name**.

32:24 siege mounds. Ramps built near city walls so that battering rams could strike. **sword and famine and pestilence**. See 14:1–12; 15:1–4. **What you spoke has come to pass**. All of God's threats, beginning with 1:9–16, were fulfilled.

32:25 Given the inevitable Babylonian victory, Jeremiah wonders why God has directed him to **buy** land now.

32:26–27 God confirms Jeremiah's confession (v. 17); he is the Creator of **all flesh**, and nothing is **too hard** for him to accomplish.

32:28–29 Because God is all-powerful, he will give Jerusalem to **Babylon**, who will **burn it** and all its idols (21:1–10; 27:1–15; 29:1–32).

32:31–32 Even Jerusalem has **aroused** God's **anger and wrath**, for the entire populace has broken the covenant (cf. 1:17–19; 2:8, 26; 8:1–3; 13:13–14; 23:9–20).

their prophets, the men of Judah and the inhabitants of Jerusalem. **33** [m]They have turned
to me their back and not their face. And though I have taught them [n]persistently, they
have not listened [o]to receive instruction. **34** They set up [p]their abominations in the house
that is called by my name, to defile it. **35** They built the high places of Baal [q]in the Valley
of the Son of Hinnom, [r]to offer up their sons and daughters to Molech, [s]though I did not
command them, nor did it enter into my mind, that they should do [p]this abomination,
[t]to cause Judah to sin.

They Shall Be My People; I Will Be Their God

36 "Now therefore thus says the LORD, the God of Israel, concerning this city of which
you say, [u]'It is given into the hand of the king of Babylon by sword, by famine, and by
pestilence': **37** [v]Behold, I will gather them from all the countries [w]to which I drove them in
[x]my anger and my wrath and in great indignation. I will bring them back to this place, [y]and
I will make them dwell in safety. **38** [z]And they shall be my people, and I will be their God.
39 [a]I will give them one heart and one way, that they may fear me forever, [b]for their own
good and the good of their children after them. **40** [c]I will make with them an everlasting
covenant, that I will not turn away from doing good to them. [d]And I will put the fear of
me in their hearts, that they may not turn from me. **41** [e]I will rejoice in doing them good,
[f]and I will plant them in this land in faithfulness, with all my heart and all my soul.
42 "For thus says the LORD: [g]Just as I have brought all this great disaster upon this people,
so I will bring upon them all the good that I promise them. **43** [h]Fields shall be bought in
this land [i]of which you are saying, 'It is a desolation, without man or beast; [j]it is given into
the hand of the Chaldeans.' **44** Fields shall be bought for money, and [k]deeds shall be signed
and [k]sealed and [k]witnessed, [l]in the land of Benjamin, [l]in the places about Jerusalem, [l]and
in the cities of Judah, [l]in the cities of the hill country, [l]in the cities of the Shephelah, and
in the cities of the Negeb; for [m]I will restore their fortunes, declares the LORD."

The LORD Promises Peace

33 The word of the LORD came to Jeremiah a second time, while he was still [n]shut up
in the court of the guard: **2** "Thus says [o]the LORD who made the earth,[1] the LORD
who formed it to establish it—[p]the LORD is his name: **3** [q]Call to me and I will answer you,
[r]and will tell you great and hidden things that you have not known. **4** For thus says the
LORD, the God of Israel, concerning the houses of this city and the houses of the kings
of Judah that were torn down to make a defense against [s]the siege mounds and against

[1] Septuagint; Hebrew *it*

33 [m]ch. 2:27; [Ezek. 8:16]; See ch. 7:24 [n]See ch. 25:3 [o]See ch. 5:3
34 [p]See ch. 7:30; 23:11
35 [q]ch. 7:31; See Josh. 18:16 [r]Lev. 18:21 [s]ch. 7:31 [p][See ver. 34 above] [t][1 Kgs. 16:19]
36 [u]See ver. 3
37 [v]See ch. 23:3 [w]See ch. 8:3 [x]ch. 21:5; Deut. 29:28 [y]ch. 23:6; 33:16; Ezek. 34:25
38 [z]See ch. 30:22; 31:33
39 [a]Ezek. 11:19, 20 [b]Deut. 6:24
40 [c]ch. 50:5; Ps. 89:34; Isa. 55:3; Ezek. 16:60 [d]See ch. 31:33
41 [e][Deut. 28:63] [f]See ch. 24:6
42 [g][ch. 31:28]
43 [h]ver. 15 [i]ch. 33:10 [j]See ver. 3
44 [k]ver. 10 [l]See ch. 17:26 [m]See ch. 30:3

Chapter 33

1 [n]See ch. 32:2
2 [o][Isa. 37:26] [p][ch. 16:21; Ex. 6:3; Ps. 83:18; Amos 4:13]
3 [q]ch. 29:12; Ps. 91:15 [r]Isa. 48:6
4 [s]ch. 32:24

32:33 turned . . . their back. An act of defiance (cf. 7:24). **I have taught them**. Through Moses, David, Solomon, and the prophets (7:13, 25–26). **not listened to receive instruction**. The root of foolish behavior (Prov. 1:7).

32:34 abominations in the house. See 7:30; 23:11–12; 2 Kings 16:10–20; Ezek. 8:16–18.

32:35 high places . . . sons . . . daughters. See 7:31.

32:36 this city. See vv. 24, 28–29.

32:37 I will gather them. See 23:7–8; 29:10–14; 31:1–9. **dwell in safety**. God will protect the exiles from their enemies (31:38–40; 2 Sam. 7:10).

32:38 they shall be my people. See 24:7; 30:22; 31:33.

32:39 one heart. United together to serve God (2 Chron. 30:12; Ps. 86:11; Ezek. 11:19; cf. Deut. 6:4–9; Jer. 4:4). **one way**. One way of life that is based on reverence (**fear**) for God. **their own good**. Rather than to their own harm (25:7). **the good of their children**. Rather than teaching their children to follow in their wicked ways (7:31; 31:29–30).

32:40–41 everlasting covenant. See Isa. 55:3; 61:8; Ezek. 16:60; 37:26; cf. Jer. 31:31–40. God's covenant will not cease because he will do **good to them**, place **fear** of him **in their hearts**, and **plant them in this land**. God will make every provision for the keeping of the covenant. **I will rejoice in doing them good**. God keeps his promises, not grudgingly but with great delight.

32:42 God will be as thorough in doing **good** for his faithful ones as he was in punishing his unfaithful ones.

32:43 Jeremiah rightly preached the coming **desolation** of Judah, but this situation will not be permanent.

32:44 Just as Jeremiah has purchased land (vv. 1–15), so will others do the same in future times. God will restore Jeremiah's tribe (**Benjamin**), place of ministry (**Jerusalem**), and native towns (**cities of Judah**). Beyond these areas, places in the **hill country** northward, **Shephelah** (central Israel), and **Negeb** (southern Israel) will also be restored.

33:1–26 *God Will Honor the Davidic Covenant.* God always keeps his promises, and here he promises to direct the future (vv. 1–5), heal the land (vv. 6–13), and fulfill the Davidic covenant (vv. 14–26).

33:1 second time . . . in the court of the guard. See 32:1–2.

33:2 God the Creator (10:16; 32:17), who **formed** and established the **earth**, makes the promises that follow. His word was as powerful in Jeremiah's time as in Gen. 1:1–2:3. His promises cannot fail; they are as firm as the earth.

33:3 Call. See 29:12. **I will answer**. Because of his love and grace. **hidden things**. Future things that God will now reveal. **You** is singular, addressed specifically to Jeremiah, but this great promise also has wider application to all the people of God, particularly as they call out for understanding and he gives them understanding of his word and his purposes in their lives.

33:4 Cities under siege often tore down buildings, using the stones and wood to reinforce the city walls against battering rams that attackers carried up **siege mounds**.

5[t][ch. 32:5] [u]Ezek. 22:20 [v]Deut. 31:17, 18
6[w]ch. 30:17
7[x]See ch. 30:3 [y]See ch. 24:6 [z]Isa. 1:26
8[a]Ezek. 36:25; [Ps. 51:2, 7; Heb. 9:13, 14] [b]See ch. 31:34
9[c]See ch. 13:11 [d][Ps. 130:4; Isa. 60:5]
10[e]ch. 32:43
11[f]See ch. 7:34 [g]1 Chr. 16:34; Ps. 106:1; 107:1; Isa. 12:4 [h]ch. 30:19; Lev. 7:12; Ps. 107:22 [x][See ver. 7 above]
12[i][Ezek. 36:11] [j][ch. 31:24; 50:19; Isa. 65:10; Ezek. 34:14, 15] [k]Song 1:7
13[l]See ch. 17:26 [m][Lev. 27:32] [n][John 10:3]
14[o]For ver. 14-16, see ch. 23:5, 6 [p]ch. 29:10
15[q]ch. 23:5; [Isa. 4:2; 11:1]
16[r]ch. 23:6; 32:37 [s]ch. 23:6
17[t]2 Sam. 7:16; 1 Kgs. 2:4; Ps. 89:3, 4
18[u][Isa. 66:21]
20[v]For ver. 20-26, see ch. 31:36, 37 [w]ver. 25; [Isa. 54:9] [x]Gen. 8:22; Ps. 72:5
21[y]Ps. 89:34
22[z]Gen. 22:17

the sword: **5** They are coming in [t]to fight against the Chaldeans and to fill them[1] with the
dead bodies of men whom I shall strike down [u]in my anger and my wrath, [v]for I have hidden my face from this city because of all their evil. **6** [w]Behold, I will bring to it health and
healing, and I will heal them and reveal to them abundance of prosperity and security.
7 [x]I will restore the fortunes of Judah and the fortunes of Israel, [y]and rebuild them as they
were [z]at first. **8** [a]I will cleanse them from all the guilt of their sin against me, [b]and I will
forgive all the guilt of their sin and rebellion against me. **9** [c]And this city[2] shall be to me
a name of joy, a praise and a glory before all the nations of the earth who shall hear of all
the good that I do for them. They shall [d]fear and tremble because of all the good and all
the prosperity I provide for it.
10 "Thus says the LORD: In this place [e]of which you say, 'It is a waste without man or
beast,' in the cities of Judah and the streets of Jerusalem that are desolate, without man
or inhabitant or beast, there shall be heard again **11** [f]the voice of mirth and the voice of
gladness, the voice of the bridegroom and the voice of the bride, the voices of those who
sing, as they bring [g]thank offerings to the house of the LORD:

> [h]" 'Give thanks to the LORD of hosts,
> for the LORD is good,
> for his steadfast love endures forever!'

[x]For I will restore the fortunes of the land as at first, says the LORD.
12 "Thus says the LORD of hosts: [i]In this place that is waste, without man or beast, and
in all of its cities, there shall again be [j]habitations of shepherds [k]resting their flocks. **13** [l]In
the cities of the hill country, [l]in the cities of the Shephelah, [l]and in the cities of the Negeb,
in the land of Benjamin, [l]the places about Jerusalem, [l]and in the cities of Judah, [m]flocks
shall again pass under the hands [n]of the one who counts them, says the LORD.

The LORD's Eternal Covenant with David

14 [o]"Behold, the days are coming, declares the LORD, when [p]I will fulfill the promise I made
to the house of Israel and the house of Judah. **15** In those days and at that time I will cause a
righteous [q]Branch to spring up for David, and he shall execute justice and righteousness
in the land. **16** In those days Judah will be saved, [r]and Jerusalem will dwell securely. And
this is the name by which it will be called: [s]'The LORD is our righteousness.'
17 "For thus says the LORD: [t]David shall never lack a man to sit on the throne of the house
of Israel, **18** [u]and the Levitical priests shall never lack a man in my presence to offer burnt
offerings, to burn grain offerings, and to make sacrifices forever."
19 The word of the LORD came to Jeremiah: **20** [v]"Thus says the LORD: [w]If you can break
my covenant with the day and my covenant with the night, [x]so that day and night will
not come at their appointed time, **21** [y]then also my covenant with David my servant may
be broken, so that he shall not have a son to reign on his throne, and my covenant with
the Levitical priests my ministers. **22** As [z]the host of heaven cannot be numbered and [z]the

[1] That is, the torn-down houses [2] Hebrew *And it*

33:5 God reveals that all current efforts to repel Babylon will fail. Because of its evil deeds, God will fill Jerusalem with **dead bodies**. He has declared the future.

33:6–8 God promises **health and healing** for Jerusalem's "wounds"—its devastation, disgrace, and sin (30:16–17; see 33:7–8)—but first he will **cleanse them from all the guilt of their sin**.

33:9 Jerusalem was once a cautionary tale for other **nations** (cf. 15:4; 24:9; 29:18), but in the future it will be a testimony to God's goodness.

33:10–11 voice of gladness. Jeremiah correctly prophesied that joy would cease when **Jerusalem** was made desolate (7:34; 16:9; 25:10). But now he prophesies that joy will be restored, with worship being the most important joy (30:19; Ps. 107:22; 136:1–26).

33:12–13 See 32:14–15. Raising sheep was a major part of the ancient Near Eastern economy. The return of **shepherds** and **flocks** signifies renewed prosperity.

33:15 Branch. The Davidic messianic offspring (cf. Isa. 4:2; Zech. 3:8; 6:12). **execute justice and righteousness**. A key role God and his Messiah play (Isa. 9:7; 11:5; Jer. 23:5–6; cf. 22:3, 13, 15).

33:16 The Messiah's coming will mean salvation for **Judah** and **Jerusalem**. The city will be so changed that **it will be called: "The LORD is our righteousness,"** the name given to the Messiah in 23:6.

33:17 The Branch's coming will fulfill God's promise to **David** of an eternal kingdom (2 Sam. 7:16; 1 Chron. 17:11–12); see note on Jer. 22:29–30.

33:18 The Messiah's coming will also mean that the covenant with Levi (Mal. 2:1–9) will be kept. The Messiah will be both king (2 Sam. 7:16) and priest (Ps. 110:4).

33:19–21 See 31:35–37. Like the new covenant, God's **covenant with David** and Levi will endure forever. This does not contradict the NT teaching about a new covenant (31:31), for Christ fulfills the promise that one of David's descendants will always reign over the house of Israel.

33:22 Like Abraham's descendants, the **offspring of David** will be innumerable (Gen. 15:1–6), for believers in the Messiah will be innumerable. They will share the Messiah's inheritance (Rom. 8:17). They will also serve as God's

sands of the sea cannot be measured, so I will multiply the offspring of David my servant,
and the Levitical priests who minister to me."
23 The word of the LORD came to Jeremiah: 24 "Have you not observed that these people
are saying, 'The LORD has rejected the two clans that he chose'? Thus they have despised
my people so that they are no longer a nation in their sight. 25 Thus says the LORD: [a]If I
have not established my covenant with day and night and the fixed order of heaven and
earth, 26 then I will reject the offspring of Jacob and David my servant and will not choose
one of his offspring to rule over the offspring of Abraham, Isaac, and Jacob. [b]For I will
restore their fortunes and will have mercy on them."

Zedekiah to Die in Babylon

34 The word that came to Jeremiah from the LORD, when [c]Nebuchadnezzar king of
Babylon and all his army [d]and all the kingdoms of the earth under his dominion
and all the peoples were fighting against Jerusalem and all of its cities: 2 "Thus says the
LORD, the God of Israel: Go and speak to [e]Zedekiah king of Judah and say to him, 'Thus
says the LORD: [f]Behold, I am giving this city into the hand of the king of Babylon, and he
shall burn it with fire. 3 [g]You shall not escape from his hand but shall surely be captured
and delivered into his hand. [g]You shall see the king of Babylon eye to eye and speak with
him face to face. And you shall go to Babylon.' 4 Yet hear the word of the LORD, O Zedekiah
king of Judah! [h]Thus says the LORD concerning you: [h]'You shall not die by the sword. 5 You
shall die in peace. [i]And as spices were burned for your fathers, the former kings who were
before you, so people shall [j]burn spices for you [k]and lament for you, saying, "Alas, lord!"'
For I have spoken the word, declares the LORD."
6 Then Jeremiah the prophet spoke all these words to Zedekiah king of Judah, in
Jerusalem, 7 when the army of the king of Babylon was fighting against Jerusalem and
against all the cities of Judah that were left, [l]Lachish and [m]Azekah, [n]for these were the only
[o]fortified cities of Judah that remained.
8 The word that came to Jeremiah from the LORD, after King Zedekiah [p]had made a
covenant with all the people in Jerusalem [q]to make a proclamation of liberty to them,
9 [r]that everyone should set free his Hebrew slaves, male and female, [s]so that no one should
enslave a Jew, his brother. 10 And they obeyed, all the officials and all the people who had
entered into the covenant that everyone would set free his slave, male or female, so that
they would not be enslaved again. They obeyed and set them free. 11 But afterward they
turned around and took back the male and female slaves [r]they had set free, and brought
them into subjection as slaves. 12 The word of the LORD came to Jeremiah from the LORD:
13 "Thus says the LORD, the God of Israel: I myself made a covenant with your fathers when
[t]I brought them out of the land of Egypt, out of the house of slavery, saying, 14 [u]'At the end

25 [a]Ps. 74:16, 17; 104:19
26 [b]ver. 7, 11; See ch. 30:3

Chapter 34

1 [c]ch. 39:1; 52:4; 2 Kgs. 25:1 [d]ch. 1:15; [ch. 51:28]
2 [e]2 Kgs. 25:2 [f]See ch. 21:10
3 [g]See ch. 32:4
4 [h][ch. 38:17, 20; 39:4, 7]
5 [i]1 Sam. 31:12; 2 Chr. 21:19 [j]2 Chr. 16:14 [k][ch. 22:18]
7 [l]Josh. 10:3 [m]Josh. 10:10; 15:35 [n]2 Kgs. 18:13 [o]ch. 4:5
8 [p]ver. 15 [q]ver. 15, 17; Ex. 21:2; Lev. 25:10; [Isa. 61:1]
9 [r]See Lev. 25:39-46 [s][Neh. 5:8]
11 [r][See ver. 9 above]
13 [t]Ex. 20:2
14 [u]Ex. 21:2; Deut. 15:12

priests (Ex. 19:5–6; Isa. 66:21; 1 Pet. 2:5, 9). **my servant.** Like Moses (Num. 12:7), David was God's servant in that he was God's undershepherd for Israel, God's means of writing revelation, and God's close friend. The Messiah was to be the greatest servant (see note on Isa. 42:1–9).

33:24 these people. The nations who observe what has happened to Israel and Judah. These observers think God has **despised** and rejected the **two clans that he chose** (i.e., Israel and Judah).

33:25–26 Once again (cf. 31:35–37; 33:19–22) God asserts that Judah and Israel's renewal and permanent relationship with him are as secure as the natural **order**. God will keep his promises no matter what.

34:1–45:5 *God Judges Judah.* Having declared Judah and Israel's current sins (chs. 2–29) and future renewal (chs. 30–33), Jeremiah now depicts Judah's final days. He does so while declaring God's faithfulness and Judah's infidelity (chs. 34–35), Judah's rejection of God's word (ch. 36), Judah's last days before Jerusalem's destruction (chs. 37–39), Judah's futile rebellion against Babylon after the city's fall (chs. 40–41), and Judah's futile rebellion against God (chs. 42–45).

34:1–35:19 *God's Faithfulness and Judah's Infidelity.* While God remains faithful to his word (34:1–17), the people of Judah act unfaithfully toward one another (34:18–22) and God (ch. 35).

34:1 This message came when Babylon's invasion was in full force (c. 587 B.C.).

34:3–5 Zedekiah will lose the battle and his freedom. He will go to Babylon with many of his people (21:7). Second Kings 25:6–7 records the fulfillment: after Zedekiah meets the **king of Babylon eye to eye** (in Riblah), his sons are slain and his eyes are put out, and then he is led off **to Babylon**. Nonetheless, God will allow **Zedekiah** to **die in peace**, for he is David's descendant (cf. Jer. 52:11).

34:6–7 With only weeks remaining before Jerusalem's fall, **Jeremiah** spoke to **Zedekiah** again. **Lachish** is 27 miles (43 km) southwest of Jerusalem. **Azekah** is 11 miles (18 km) north of Lachish and 18 miles (29 km) southwest of Jerusalem; originally fortified under Rehoboam (2 Chron. 11:5), it was one of the last towns to fall to Nebuchadnezzar in 587 B.C. The Lachish Letters (21 letters from this era found by archaeologists) describe the circumstances of the city's demise. **the only fortified cities . . . that remained.** All other walled, armed cities with commanding views had been taken.

34:8–11 When Jerusalem feared that defeat was imminent, the people freed all **Hebrew slaves,** or bondservants, so they could fight. **but afterward.** When the threat eased, however, they rescinded the freedom.

34:13 covenant with your fathers. The Mosaic covenant, which was based on God freeing **Israel** from the **house of slavery** (see Ex. 20:2).

34:14 Israelites could become indentured servants of one another for a

of seven years each of you must set free the fellow Hebrew who has been sold to you and
has served you six years; [r]you must set him free from your service.' But [v]your fathers did
not listen to me or incline their ears to me. **15** You recently repented and did what was right
in my eyes [q]by proclaiming liberty, each to his neighbor, and [w]you made a covenant before
me in the [x]house that is called by my name, **16** but then you turned around [y]and profaned
my name when each of you took back his male and female slaves, [z]whom you had set free
according to their desire, and you brought them into subjection to be your slaves.
17 "Therefore, thus says the LORD: You have not obeyed me [q]by proclaiming liberty, every
one to his brother and to his neighbor; [a]behold, I proclaim to you liberty [b]to the sword, to
pestilence, and to famine, declares the LORD. [c]I will make you a horror to all the kingdoms
of the earth. **18** And the men who transgressed my covenant and did not keep the terms
of [w]the covenant that they made before me, I will make them like[1] [d]the calf that they cut
in two and passed between its parts— **19** the officials of Judah, the officials of Jerusalem,
[e]the eunuchs, the priests, and all the people of the land who passed between the parts of
the calf. **20** And I will give them into the hand of their enemies [f]and into the hand of those
who seek their lives. [g]Their dead bodies shall be food for the birds of the air and the beasts
of the earth. **21** And [h]Zedekiah king of Judah and his officials I will give into the hand of
their enemies and into the hand of those who seek their lives, into the hand of the army of
the king of Babylon [i]which has withdrawn from you. **22** Behold, [j]I will command, declares
the LORD, and will [k]bring them back to this city. [k]And they will fight against it and take it
and burn it with fire. [l]I will make the cities of Judah a desolation [m]without inhabitant."

The Obedience of the Rechabites

35 The word that came to Jeremiah from the LORD in the days of [n]Jehoiakim the son
of Josiah, king of Judah: **2** "Go to the house of the [o]Rechabites and speak with them
and bring them to the house of the LORD, into one of [p]the chambers; then offer them wine
to drink." **3** So I took Jaazaniah the son of Jeremiah, son of Habazziniah and his brothers
and all his sons and the whole house of the Rechabites. **4** I brought them to the house of
the LORD into [p]the chamber of the sons of Hanan the son of Igdaliah, [q]the man of God,
which was near [p]the chamber of the officials, above [p]the chamber of [r]Maaseiah the son of
Shallum, [s]keeper of the threshold. **5** Then I set before the Rechabites pitchers full of wine,
and cups, and I said to them, "Drink wine." **6** But they answered, "We will drink no wine, for
[t]Jonadab the son of Rechab, our father, commanded us, 'You shall not drink wine, neither
you nor your sons forever. **7** You shall not build a house; you shall not sow seed; you shall
not plant or have a vineyard; but you shall live in tents all your days, [u]that you may live
many days in the land where you sojourn.' **8** We have obeyed the voice of Jonadab the son of

[1] Hebrew lacks *them like*

14 [r][See ver. 9 above] [v]ch. 7:24, 26; 11:8; 17:23; 25:4; 35:15; 44:5
15 [q][See ver. 8 above] [w]ver. 8; [2 Kgs. 23:3] [x]See ch. 7:10
16 [y]Lev. 18:21; 19:12 [z]ver. 11
17 [q][See ver. 8 above] [a][Matt. 7:2; Gal. 6:7; James 2:13] [b]See ch. 14:12 [c]See ch. 15:4
18 [w][See ver. 15 above] [d][Gen. 15:10]
19 [e]ch. 29:2
20 [f]See ch. 22:25 [g]See ch. 7:33
21 [h][ver. 2, 4, 8] [i]ch. 37:5, 11
22 [j]Isa. 10:6 [k]ch. 37:8; 38:3 [l]ch. 9:11 [m]See ch. 4:7

Chapter 35

1 [n]ch. 25:1
2 [o]1 Chr. 2:55 [p]1 Kgs. 6:5, 6; 1 Chr. 9:26, 33
4 [p][See ver. 2 above] [q][Deut. 33:1] [r]ch. 21:1; 29:25; 37:3 [s]2 Kgs. 12:9; 25:18
6 [t]2 Kgs. 10:15, 23
7 [u][Ex. 20:12; Eph. 6:2, 3]

period of **six years**, but then were to be set **free** (Ex. 21:2; Deut. 15:12). Historically many in Israel rejected this teaching, finding ways to keep persons enslaved.

34:15 repented. Of not obeying God's word on indentured persons. **made a covenant**. Performed a solemn covenant ceremony in the temple, setting the servants free.

34:16 turned around. Repented of repenting. **profaned my name**. Invoked in the ceremony. **took back**. Enslaved again those set free according to God's word.

34:17 Because the servants have not been set free, God sets the nation "free" to be consumed by **sword**, **pestilence**, and **famine**. See 14:1–12; 15:1–4; 29:17–18; 32:24.

34:18–20 make them like the calf. Put the covenant breakers to death by the sword. **passed between its parts**. Covenant-ratification ceremonies (vv. 16–17) often included cutting a sacrifice in two and having the parties walk between the halves of the sacrifice (Gen. 15:7–17). Presumably the cutting of the sacrifice would warn the parties of the consequences of breaking the covenant. All the people of Judah and their leaders have broken the covenant and must suffer the consequences of their actions.

34:22 bring them back. Babylon had lifted its siege of Jerusalem for some unspecified reason, which probably motivated the revocation of the servants' freedom (v. 11). This time was only a reprieve before destruction.

35:1 days of Jehoiakim. King 609–598 B.C. See Dates of Events in Jeremiah, p. 1376. These events are not sequential to ch. 34, which took place in 587 B.C. (see note on 34:1).

35:2 Rechabites. Nomadic tribe that originated with the Kenites (Judg. 4:11; 1 Sam. 15:6; 1 Chron. 2:55) and was associated with Jehu's purge in 842 B.C. (2 Kings 10:15–17). The **chambers** of the **house of the LORD** were used for storage or for living quarters (cf. 1 Kings 6:5; Neh. 13:4–9). **offer them wine**. Normally associated with hospitality.

35:3–4 Jeremiah took the **Rechabites** to the living quarters of **Igdaliah**. **man of God**. Synonym for "prophet" (1 Sam. 2:27; 9:6; 1 Kings 12:22; 17:24). **officials**. Court officials. The temple and royal palace were adjacent to one another. **keeper of the threshold**. The priest who managed the temple entrances and the collecting of temple taxes (2 Kings 12:9; Jer. 52:24).

35:5–7 The **Rechabites** refuse the wine because their ancestor had bound them not to **drink wine** or **build** permanent homes (a voluntary commitment, perhaps something like a Nazirite vow; Num. 6:2–4).

35:8–11 The Rechabites have **obeyed the voice** of their ancestor. They came to **Jerusalem** only out of necessity when **Babylon** began its invasion.

Rechab, our father, in all that he commanded us, to drink no wine all our days, ourselves,
our wives, our sons, or our daughters, 9 and not to build houses to dwell in. We have no
vineyard or field or seed, 10 but we have lived in tents and have obeyed and done all that
Jonadab our father commanded us. 11 But [v]when Nebuchadnezzar king of Babylon came
up against the land, we said, 'Come, and let us go to Jerusalem for fear of [w]the army of the
Chaldeans and [w]the army of the Syrians.' [x]So we are living in Jerusalem."
12 Then the word of the LORD came to Jeremiah: 13 "Thus says the LORD of hosts, the
God of Israel: Go and say to the people of Judah and the inhabitants of Jerusalem, [y]Will
you not receive instruction and listen to my words? declares the LORD. 14 The command
that Jonadab the son of Rechab gave to his sons, to drink no wine, has been kept, and
they drink none to this day, for they have obeyed their father's command. I have spoken
to you [z]persistently, but you have not listened to me. 15 I have sent to you all my servants
the prophets, sending them [z]persistently, saying, [a]'Turn now every one of you from his
evil way, and amend your deeds, and [b]do not go after other gods to serve them, and then
you shall dwell in the land that I gave to you and your fathers.' [c]But you did not incline
your ear or listen to me. 16 The sons of Jonadab the son of Rechab have kept the command
that their father gave them, but this people has not obeyed me. 17 Therefore, thus says the
LORD, the God of hosts, the God of Israel: Behold, I am bringing upon Judah and all the
inhabitants of Jerusalem all the disaster that I have pronounced against them, [d]because
I have spoken to them and they have not listened, [d]I have called to them and they have
not answered."
18 But to the house of the Rechabites Jeremiah said, "Thus says the LORD of hosts, the God
of Israel: Because you have obeyed the command of Jonadab your father and kept all his
precepts and done all that he commanded you, 19 therefore thus says the LORD of hosts, the
God of Israel: Jonadab the son of Rechab shall never lack a man [e]to stand before me."

Jehoiakim Burns Jeremiah's Scroll

36 In the [f]fourth year of Jehoiakim the son of Josiah, king of Judah, this word came
to Jeremiah from the LORD: 2 "Take [g]a scroll and [h]write on it all the words that I
have spoken to you against Israel and [i]Judah [j]and all the nations, [k]from the day I spoke
to you, from the days of Josiah until today. 3 [l]It may be that the house of Judah will hear
all the disaster that I intend to do to them, [m]so that every one may turn from his evil way,
and [n]that I may forgive their iniquity and their sin."
4 Then Jeremiah called [o]Baruch the son of Neriah, and [o]Baruch wrote on [g]a scroll at the
dictation of Jeremiah all the words of the LORD that he had spoken to him. 5 And Jeremiah
ordered [o]Baruch, saying, [p]"I am banned from going to the house of the LORD, 6 so you are
to go, and [q]on a day of fasting in the hearing of all the people in the LORD's house you shall
read the words of the LORD from the scroll that you have written at my dictation. You shall
read them also in the hearing of all the men of Judah who come out of their cities. 7 [l]It may

11 [v]ch. 46:2; 2 Kgs. 24:1; [ver. 1] [w]2 Kgs. 24:2 [x][ver. 7]
13 [y]See ch. 5:3
14 [z]See ch. 25:3
15 [z][See ver. 14 above] [a]2 Kgs. 17:13; See ch. 18:11 [b]See ch. 7:6 [c]See ch. 34:14
17 [d][Isa. 50:2]
19 [e]See ch. 15:1

Chapter 36

1 [f]ch. 25:1; 45:1; [ver. 9]
2 [g]Ezra 6:2; Ps. 40:7; Ezek. 2:9; Zech. 5:1, 2 [h]ch. 30:2; [ch. 51:60] [i]ch. 25:2 [j]See ch. 25:15-26; 46–51 [k]ch. 1:2; 25:3
3 [l]ch. 26:3; Ezek. 12:3; Zeph. 2:3; [Amos 5:15] [m][ch. 18:8] [n]See ch. 31:34
4 [o]See ch. 32:12 [g][See ver. 2 above]
5 [o][See ver. 4 above] [p]ch. 32:2; 33:1; 39:15
6 [q][ver. 9]
7 [l][See ver. 3 above]

35:12–14 The Lord points out the stark contrast between the Rechabites, who have **kept** the command of **Jonadab**, and his people Israel, who have **not listened** to him.

35:15–16 God **sent** regular reminders of his covenant with Judah through the **prophets** (7:23–25; 11:6, 7; 25:3–4; 29:19; 32:33), to no avail, whereas the Rechabites needed be told only once to obey their ancestor.

35:17 all the disaster. See 34:22. **called to them**. Through Moses and the prophets (Luke 16:29–31). **not answered**. By believing, repenting, and obeying (Hos. 11:1–2).

35:18–19 The Lord tells the **Rechabites** that, **because** they have **obeyed** their own spiritual leader (vv. 8–10), they will **stand before** the God of Israel. "Stand before" is a synonym for serving God in his presence, often in the temple (cf. 7:10; 15:19).

36:1–32 *Judah Rejects God's Word.* Judah's rebellion against God's word receives further elaboration. God has mercifully revealed his word (vv. 1–19), yet Jehoiakim callously rejects it (vv. 20–26). Nonetheless, God's word stands when kingdoms fall (vv. 27–32).

36:1 fourth year. Probably in 605 B.C., prior to Babylon's forcing **Judah** to become its vassal (2 Kings 24:1) and also prior to Babylon taking captives from Judah (Dan. 1:1–4).

36:2 scroll. See 32:9–15. **all the words . . . from the days of Josiah until today**. From 627 to 605 B.C. (1:1–3).

36:3 God's merciful purpose in sending his written word was to lead **Judah** to repentance (35:12–15) so they could avoid the consequences of their covenant disobedience. On the wordplay with **disaster** and **evil**, see note on 1:13–14.

36:4 Baruch (see 32:12–16) was Jeremiah's friend and fellow servant of God (36:32; 45:1–5). Jeremiah dictated the words for the **scroll** to Baruch. A seal with the name "Berachyahu son of Neriyahu the scribe" has been found; this may be Jeremiah's Baruch.

36:5 banned from . . . the house of the LORD. For some unspecified reason, but perhaps for his preaching about the temple. See 7:1–8:3; 26:1–24.

36:6 you are to go. Evidence of Baruch's commitment to God and his word. **day of fasting**. Usually called in times of emergency (see Joel 2:15–17), perhaps on the occasion of the Babylonian invasion of 605 B.C. (Jer. 36:1). **read the words**. As Jeremiah's emissary, Baruch was to make a public proclamation of God's warning.

36:7 their plea for mercy. Prayers for deliverance from Babylon as part of Judah's day of fasting. **turn from his evil way** (cf. v. 3). It is vain to pray for deliverance unaccompanied by repentance (7:9–15).

7[m][See ver. 3 above]
9[r][ver. 1] [s]ver. 22 [t][2 Chr. 20:3]
10[u][ch. 35:2]
11[v]ch. 26:24; 40:5; 2 Chr. 34:8, 15, 18
12[w]ch. 26:10 [x]ver. 20; ch. 41:1; 2 Kgs. 25:25 [y]ver. 25 [z]ch. 26:22
14[a]ver. 26; ch. 37:3, 13; 38:1
16[b]ver. 20
18[c]ver. 32; [Rom. 16:22]
20[d]ver. 12
22[e]ver. 9; [John 10:22] [f]Amos 3:15
24[g][ver. 16] [h]See Josh. 7:6
25[i]ver. 12 [j][Isa. 59:16]
26[k][1 Kgs. 22:26; Zeph. 1:8] [l]ver. 14 [m]See ch. 45:1-3

be that their plea for mercy will come before the LORD, [m]and that every one will turn from
his evil way, for great is the anger and wrath that the LORD has pronounced against this
people." 8 And Baruch the son of Neriah did all that Jeremiah the prophet ordered him
about reading from the scroll the words of the LORD in the LORD's house.

9 [r]In the fifth year of Jehoiakim the son of Josiah, king of Judah, [s]in the ninth month, all
the people in Jerusalem and all the people who came from the cities of Judah to Jerusalem
[t]proclaimed a fast before the LORD. 10 Then, in the hearing of all the people, Baruch read the
words of Jeremiah from the scroll, in the house of the LORD, in [u]the chamber of Gemariah
the son of Shaphan the secretary, which was in the upper court, at the entry of the New
Gate of the LORD's house.

11 When Micaiah the son of Gemariah, son of [v]Shaphan, heard all the words of the LORD
from the scroll, 12 he went down to the king's house, into the secretary's chamber, and [w]all the
officials were sitting there: [x]Elishama the secretary, [y]Delaiah the son of Shemaiah, [y]Elnathan
[z]the son of Achbor, [y]Gemariah the son of [z]Shaphan, Zedekiah the son of Hananiah, and
all the officials. 13 And Micaiah told them all the words that he had heard, when Baruch
read the scroll in the hearing of the people. 14 Then all the officials sent Jehudi the son of
Nethaniah, son of [a]Shelemiah, son of Cushi, to say to Baruch, "Take in your hand the scroll
that you read in the hearing of the people, and come." So Baruch the son of Neriah took
the scroll in his hand and came to them. 15 And they said to him, "Sit down and read it."
So Baruch read it to them. 16 When they heard all the words, they turned one to another in
fear. And they said to Baruch, [b]"We must report all these words to the king." 17 Then they
asked Baruch, "Tell us, please, how did you write all these words? Was it at his dictation?"
18 Baruch answered them, "He dictated all these words to me, [c]while I wrote them with
ink on the scroll." 19 Then the officials said to Baruch, "Go and hide, you and Jeremiah, and
let no one know where you are."

20 So they went into the court to the king, having put the scroll in [d]the chamber of
Elishama the secretary, and they reported all the words to the king. 21 Then the king sent
Jehudi to get the scroll, and he took it from the chamber of Elishama the secretary. And
Jehudi read it to the king and all the officials who stood beside the king. 22 It was [e]the ninth
month, and the king was sitting in [f]the winter house, and there was a fire burning in the
fire pot before him. 23 As Jehudi read three or four columns, the king would cut them off
with a knife and throw them into the fire in the fire pot, until the entire scroll was consumed in the fire that was in the fire pot. 24 Yet [g]neither the king nor any of his servants
who heard all these words was afraid, [h]nor did they tear their garments. 25 Even when
[i]Elnathan and Delaiah and Gemariah [j]urged the king not to burn the scroll, he would not
listen to them. 26 And the king commanded Jerahmeel the [k]king's son and Seraiah the son
of Azriel and [l]Shelemiah the son of Abdeel to seize [m]Baruch the secretary and Jeremiah
the prophet, but the LORD hid them.

27 Now after the king had burned the scroll with the words that Baruch wrote at Jeremiah's
dictation, the word of the LORD came to Jeremiah: 28 "Take another scroll and write on it
all the former words that were in the first scroll, which Jehoiakim the king of Judah has

36:8–10 Baruch obeyed Jeremiah's orders. **fifth year . . . ninth month**. December 604 B.C. **a fast**. See v. 6. **chamber**. See 35:2–4. **upper court**. Above the courtyards where the people gathered. **New Gate**. Where the officials gathered to decide cases. See 26:10. In one of the four-room domestic buildings from the seventh–sixth centuries B.C. a cache of 50 bullae (round seals, often made of clay) for sealing documents was found. One of the bullae included the seal impression of Gemaryahu (a variant spelling of **Gemariah**), the **son of Shaphan**.

36:11 Micaiah the son of Gemariah. Gemariah was probably the brother of Ahikam, who defended Jeremiah in 26:24, and the uncle of Gedaliah, who guarded Jeremiah in 39:14.

36:12–13 For reasons not mentioned, Micaiah was anxious for the king's **officials** to know Jeremiah's words.

36:14–16 Upon hearing the words, the **officials** want Jehoiakim to hear them as well. **fear**. Probably due to their fear of God's judgment, but possibly due to the appearance of treason.

36:17–19 Once again (cf. 26:16–24) the officials show concern for preserving the lives of Jeremiah and Baruch.

36:22 ninth month. See v. 9. **winter house**. Rooms set aside in the inner house that retained heat (it was December; cf. vv. 8–10). See Amos 3:15. **fire pot**. Either a portable fire pan or a fixed hearth.

36:23–24 The **king** and **his servants** show no regard for God's word. To them the scroll is merely fuel for the **fire**. To **cut . . . off** God's words **with a knife** and burn them showed foolish, haughty disregard for a message from their omnipotent Creator and Judge.

36:25 Elnathan. See 26:22–23. **Gemariah**. See 29:3.

36:26 king's son. Since Jehoiakim was only about 30 years old at this time (v. 1; 2 Kings 23:36), the phrase probably means a favored or special servant of the king (Jer. 36:8). **the LORD hid them**. Probably using human agents, as in 26:24.

burned. 29 And concerning Jehoiakim king of Judah you shall say, 'Thus says the LORD, You
have burned this scroll, saying, [n]"Why have you written in it that the king of Babylon will
certainly come and destroy this land, and will cut off from it man and beast?" 30 Therefore
thus says the LORD concerning Jehoiakim king of Judah: [o]He shall have none [p]to sit on the
throne of David, [q]and his dead body shall be cast out to the heat by day and the frost by
night. 31 [r]And I will punish him and his offspring and his servants for their iniquity. I will
bring upon them and upon the inhabitants of Jerusalem and upon the people of Judah
all the disaster that I have pronounced against them, but they would not hear.'"
32 Then Jeremiah took another scroll and gave it to [s]Baruch the scribe, the son of Neriah,
who [t]wrote on it at the dictation of Jeremiah all the words of the scroll that Jehoiakim king
of Judah had burned in the fire. And many similar words were added to them.

Jeremiah Warns Zedekiah

37 [u]Zedekiah the son of Josiah, [v]whom Nebuchadnezzar king of Babylon made king
in the land of Judah, reigned instead of [w]Coniah the son of Jehoiakim. 2 [x]But neither
he nor his servants nor the people of the land listened to the words of the LORD that he
spoke through Jeremiah the prophet.
3 King Zedekiah sent [y]Jehucal the son of [z]Shelemiah, and [a]Zephaniah the priest, the son
of [b]Maaseiah, to Jeremiah the prophet, saying, "Please [c]pray for us to the LORD our God."
4 [d]Now Jeremiah was still going in and out among the people, [e]for he had not yet been put
in prison. 5 [f]The army of Pharaoh had come out of Egypt. And when [g]the Chaldeans who
were besieging Jerusalem heard news about them, [h]they withdrew from Jerusalem.
6 Then the word of the LORD came to Jeremiah the prophet: 7 "Thus says the LORD, God
of Israel: Thus shall you say to the king of Judah who [i]sent you to me to inquire of me,
'Behold, [j]Pharaoh's army that came to help you is about to [k]return to Egypt, to its own land.
8 And [l]the Chaldeans shall come back and fight against this city. [l]They shall capture it and
burn it with fire. 9 Thus says the LORD, Do not deceive yourselves, saying, "The Chaldeans
will surely go away from us," for they will not go away. 10 [m]For even if you should defeat the
whole army of Chaldeans who are fighting against you, and there remained of them only
wounded men, every man in his tent, they would rise up and [l]burn this city with fire.'"

Jeremiah Imprisoned

11 Now when [n]the Chaldean army had withdrawn from Jerusalem at the approach of
Pharaoh's army, 12 Jeremiah set out from Jerusalem to go to [o]the land of Benjamin [p]to receive
his portion there [q]among the people. 13 When he was at [r]the Benjamin Gate, a sentry there
named Irijah the son of [s]Shelemiah, son of Hananiah, seized Jeremiah the prophet, saying,
[t]"You are deserting to the Chaldeans." 14 And Jeremiah said, "It is a lie; I am not deserting
to the Chaldeans." But Irijah would not listen to him, and seized Jeremiah and brought
him to [u]the officials. 15 And the officials were enraged at Jeremiah, and they beat him [v]and
imprisoned him in the house of Jonathan the secretary, for it had been made a prison.

29 [n]See ch. 26:9
30 [o][ch. 22:30] [p][ch. 22:2, 4] [q][ch. 22:19]
31 [r][ch. 1:16]
32 [s]See ver. 4 [t]ver. 18

Chapter 37

1 [u]2 Kgs. 24:17; 2 Chr. 36:10 [v][Ezek. 17:13] [w]ch. 22:24
2 [x]See 2 Chr. 36:12-14
3 [y][ch. 38:1] [z]ver. 13; ch. 38:1 [a]See ch. 21:1 [b]See ch. 35:4 [c][ch. 21:2]
4 [d][Num. 27:17] [e][ch. 32:2; 33:1]
5 [f][Ezek. 17:15] [g]ch. 32:2 [h]ver. 11; ch. 34:21
7 [i][ch. 21:2] [j][Ezek. 29:2, 6] [k][ch. 46:17; 2 Kgs. 24:7; Lam. 4:17]
8 [l]ch. 34:22
10 [m][ch. 21:4] [l][See ver. 8 above]
11 [n]ver. 5
12 [o]ch. 1:1; 32:8 [p][ch. 32:9] [q]ver. 4; ch. 39:14
13 [r]ch. 38:7; Zech. 14:10 [s]ver. 3; ch. 38:1 [t][ch. 21:9; 38:19; 39:9; 52:15]
14 [u]ch. 36:12
15 [v][Heb. 11:36]

36:29 Jehoiakim **burned** the **scroll** because he did not believe Babylon's invasion would succeed (7:1–15; 26:9).

36:30 Because of his disregard for God's word, **Jehoiakim** will have no heir to succeed him and will not receive a respectable burial (22:18–19). This judgment is fulfilled in 37:1.

36:31 would not hear. Would not obey (cf. Deut. 6:4–9).

36:32 Jeremiah obeys God's command to make a second papyrus **scroll** (vv. 27–28). **many similar words**. Jeremiah expanded his messages, but the manner in which he did so is unstated.

37:1–39:18 *Jerusalem's Last Days.* At last Jerusalem falls (39:1–10). Prior to this event, Jeremiah warns Zedekiah of self-deception (37:1–10), Zedekiah imprisons Jeremiah (37:11–21), Ebed-melech frees Jeremiah (38:1–16), and Jeremiah counsels Zedekiah to surrender (38:17–18). After Jerusalem falls (39:1–10), God delivers Jeremiah and Ebed-melech (39:11–18).

37:1 Zedekiah. Reigned c. 597–586 B.C. **Coniah**. Another name for Jehoiachin, who reigned for only three months in 598–597 B.C. (2 Kings 24:8–9); also called Jeconiah (Jer. 24:1). He was removed in keeping with the prophecy found in 36:30.

37:2 A new regime did not mean a new attitude toward God's **words**.

37:3 pray for us. See 21:1–2.

37:4 not yet been put in prison. See 29:24–32 and 37:11–38:6.

37:5–9 Egypt marched against Babylon c. 588 B.C., drawing the Babylonians away from **Jerusalem**. But God's **word** for Zedekiah is that Babylon will **come back**. Believing anything else is self-deception.

37:10 God's word is that Babylon could defeat Judah with only **wounded men** for soldiers, for God has decided to give Jerusalem to Babylon.

37:11–12 when . . . had withdrawn. See 37:5. **land of Benjamin**. Jeremiah's home territory. See 1:1–3. The meaning of **receive his portion** is uncertain. It may relate to the field he had purchased (32:1–15).

37:13 The **Benjamin Gate** opened to the north toward the land of Benjamin. **sentry**. Literally, "master of the guard," thus an important officer. **Irijah**. Mentioned only here and in v. 14. **deserting to the Chaldeans**. A natural assumption, since Jeremiah had counseled surrender (21:9).

37:14 Despite Jeremiah's denials and his long track record of truth-telling, **Irijah** detained him and **brought him to the officials** (26:10–24).

37:15 enraged. At Jeremiah's teaching and denial (36:29). **beat him**. See

[16] [w]When Jeremiah had come to the dungeon cells and remained there many days, [17] King
Zedekiah sent for him and received him. The king questioned him [x]secretly in his house and
said, "Is there any word from the LORD?" Jeremiah said, "There is." Then he said, [y]"You shall
be delivered into the hand of the king of Babylon." [18] Jeremiah also said to King Zedekiah,
"What wrong have I done to you or your servants or this people, [v]that you have put me in
prison? [19] [z]Where are your prophets who prophesied to you, saying, 'The king of Babylon
will not come against you and against this land'? [20] Now hear, please, O my lord the king:
[a]let my humble plea come before you and [b]do not send me back to the house of Jonathan
the secretary, lest I die there." [21] So King Zedekiah gave orders, and they committed Jeremiah
to [c]the court of the guard. And a loaf of bread was given him daily from the bakers' street,
[d]until all the bread of the city was gone. So Jeremiah remained in [c]the court of the guard.

Jeremiah Cast into the Cistern

38 Now Shephatiah the son of Mattan, Gedaliah the son of Pashhur, [e]Jucal the son
of Shelemiah, and [f]Pashhur the son of Malchiah heard the words that Jeremiah
was saying to all the people, [2] "Thus says the LORD: [g]He who stays in this city shall die
by the sword, by famine, and by pestilence, [g]but he who goes out to the Chaldeans shall
live. He shall have his life as a prize of war, and live. [3] Thus says the LORD: [h]This city shall
surely be given into the hand of the army of the king of Babylon and be taken." [4] Then the
officials said to the king, [i]"Let this man be put to death, [j]for he is weakening the hands
of the soldiers who are left in this city, and the hands of all the people, by speaking such
words to them. For this man is not seeking [k]the welfare of this people, but their harm."
[5] King Zedekiah said, "Behold, he is in your hands, [l]for the king can do nothing against
you." [6] So they took Jeremiah [m]and cast him into the cistern of Malchiah, the king's son,
which was in [n]the court of the guard, letting Jeremiah down [o]by ropes. [p]And there was no
water in the cistern, but only mud, and [q]Jeremiah sank in the mud.

Jeremiah Rescued from the Cistern

[7] When [r]Ebed-melech [s]the Ethiopian, [t]a eunuch who was in the king's house, heard that
they had put Jeremiah into the cistern—the king was sitting [u]in the Benjamin Gate—
[8] [r]Ebed-melech went from the king's house and said to the king, [9] "My lord the king, these
men have done evil in all that they did to Jeremiah the prophet by casting him into the
cistern, and he will die there of [v]hunger, [w]for there is no bread left in the city." [10] Then the
king commanded [r]Ebed-melech the Ethiopian, "Take thirty men with you from here,
and lift Jeremiah the prophet out of the cistern before he dies." [11] So [r]Ebed-melech took
the men with him and went to the house of the king, to a wardrobe in the storehouse,
and took from there old rags and worn-out clothes, which he let down to Jeremiah in

16 [w]See ch. 38:6-14
17 [x]ch. 38:16 [y]See ch. 21:7
18 [v][See ver. 15 above]
19 [z][ch. 28:2, 11, 17]
20 [a][ch. 38:26] [b][ch. 38:28]
21 [c]See ch. 32:2 [d]ch. 38:9; 52:6; Ezek. 4:10, 16

Chapter 38

1 [e][ch. 37:3] [f]See ch. 20:1
2 [g]ch. 21:9; [ver. 17, 18]
3 [h]See ch. 32:3
4 [i]ch. 26:11 [j]See ch. 6:24 [k][ch. 33:9]
5 [l]See ver. 24-28
6 [m]ch. 37:16 [n]See ch. 32:2 [o]ver. 11, 13 [p][Gen. 37:24; Zech. 9:11] [q][Ps. 69:14]
7 [r]ch. 39:16 [s][Acts 8:27] [t]ch. 29:2; Isa. 56:3, 4 [u]See ch. 37:13
8 [r][See ver. 7 above]
9 [v]ch. 11:22; [ch. 14:16, 18; 19:9] [w][ch. 37:21]
10 [r][See ver. 7 above]
11 [r][See ver. 7 above]

20:1–2. **house of Jonathan**. See 37:16. Perhaps other prisons were full. Regardless, it proved a terrible place (v. 20).

37:16 dungeon cells. The phrase refers to either a cell in a cistern (see note on 38:6) or a vaulted room underground. Either option indicates a damp, unhealthy place.

37:17 Desperate for good news (21:1–2), **Zedekiah** sends for **Jeremiah**, only to learn that God's word remains one of judgment.

37:18–19 What wrong? Indeed Jeremiah had done no wrong, other than deliver an unpleasant truth when asked. **Where are your prophets**? Those who had told him lies (23:9–40; 28:1–17). Jeremiah's words have proven true, so why should he be punished?

37:20 humble plea. Jeremiah genuinely feared for his life, so he asked for a new prison.

37:21 court of the guard. Next to the palace (32:1–2). **loaf of bread**. A day's ration in time of war, siege, and famine (14:1–12). **until all the bread . . . was gone**. Eventually Jerusalem faced great privation, if not actual starvation.

38:1 Even after imprisonment, Jeremiah did not stop speaking God's truth. **Shephatiah . . . Gedaliah**. Not mentioned elsewhere. **Jucal**. Another name for Jehucal. See 37:3. **Pashhur**. See 21:1. All these courtiers were apparently pro-Egyptian in foreign policy matters.

38:2–3 This is a summary of Jeremiah's message concerning Jerusalem for all 10 years of Zedekiah's reign. See 27:1–15.

38:4 Unlike in 26:16–24, the **officials** think Jeremiah should die. They believe his words undermine the war effort. Ironically, though his advice is sound, they believe it will **harm** the **people**.

38:5 Forsaking his responsibility, Zedekiah gives Jeremiah to his opponents, but God has promised to protect his life (1:17–19).

38:6 Unlike in 37:20–21, Jeremiah cannot avoid imprisonment in a **cistern**. Cisterns were dug out of rock, had a small opening, and spread out at the bottom. Escape from such a place was virtually impossible, so perhaps only notorious prisoners were put there (cf. Gen. 37:20, with ESV footnote). **sank in the mud**. A slow, filthy way to die.

38:7 Ebed-melech. Means "servant of the king." **the Ethiopian**. A foreigner who most likely was forced to serve Judah's king. **eunuch**. Maybe, as in Gen. 37:36, a generic term for "officer." Ebed-melech may or may not have been a physical eunuch. **Benjamin Gate**. See Jer. 37:13.

38:8–9 Ebed-melech shows himself superior in character to the weak Zedekiah. He recognizes the injustice **Jeremiah** has suffered and his life-threatening circumstances (cf. 39:16–18).

38:11–13 Ebed-melech continues to prove resourceful on Jeremiah's behalf. Using **old rags and worn-out clothes** to cushion the **ropes**, he and his helpers liberate **Jeremiah**, once again fulfilling God's promise of protection

the cistern [x]by ropes. **12** Then [r]Ebed-melech the Ethiopian said to Jeremiah, "Put the rags
and clothes between your armpits and [x]the ropes." Jeremiah did so. **13** Then they drew
Jeremiah up with [x]ropes and lifted him out of the cistern. And Jeremiah remained in the
[n]court of the guard.

Jeremiah Warns Zedekiah Again

14 King Zedekiah sent for Jeremiah the prophet and received him at the third entrance
of the temple of the LORD. The king said to Jeremiah, "I will ask you a question; hide
nothing from me." **15** Jeremiah said to Zedekiah, "If I tell you, will you not surely put me
to death? And if I give you counsel, you will not listen to me." **16** Then King Zedekiah swore
[y]secretly to Jeremiah, [z]"As the LORD lives, [a]who made our souls, I will not put you to death
or deliver you into the hand of [b]these men who seek your life."

17 Then Jeremiah said to Zedekiah, "Thus says the LORD, the God of hosts, the God of
Israel: [c]If you will surrender to [d]the officials of the king of Babylon, [e]then your life shall
be spared, and this city shall not be burned with fire, and you and your house shall live.
18 But if you do not surrender to [d]the officials of the king of Babylon, [f]then this city shall
be given into the hand of the Chaldeans, [f]and they shall burn it with fire, and you shall
not escape from their hand." **19** King Zedekiah said to Jeremiah, "I am afraid of the Judeans
[g]who have deserted to the Chaldeans, lest I be handed over to them and they deal cruelly
with me." **20** Jeremiah said, "You shall not be given to them. Obey now the voice of the LORD
in what I say to you, [h]and it shall be well with you, and your life shall be spared. **21** But if
you refuse to [c]surrender, this is the vision which the LORD has shown to me: **22** Behold,
all the women left in the house of the king of Judah were being led out to the officials of
the king of Babylon and were saying,

[i]"'Your trusted friends have deceived you
  and prevailed against you;
now that your feet are sunk in the mud,
  they turn away from you.'

23 All your wives and [j]your sons shall be led out to the Chaldeans, and you yourself shall
not escape from their hand, but shall be seized by the king of Babylon, and this city shall
be burned with fire."

24 Then Zedekiah said to Jeremiah, "Let no one know of these words, and you shall not die.
25 If [k]the officials hear that I have spoken with you and come to you and say to you, 'Tell us
what you said to the king and what the king said to you; hide nothing from us and we will
not put you to death,' **26** then you shall say to them, [l]'I made a humble plea to the king that
he would not send me back to the house of Jonathan to die there.'" **27** Then all the officials
came to Jeremiah and asked him, and he answered them as the king had instructed him.
So they stopped speaking with him, for the conversation had not been overheard. **28** And
Jeremiah remained [m]in the court of the guard until the day that Jerusalem was taken.

The Fall of Jerusalem

39 [n]In the ninth year of Zedekiah king of Judah, in the tenth month, Nebuchadnezzar
king of Babylon and all his army came against Jerusalem and besieged it. **2** In
the eleventh year of Zedekiah, in the fourth month, on the ninth day of the month, a
breach was made in the city. **3** Then all [o]the officials of the king of Babylon came [p]and sat

11 [x]ver. 6
12 [r][See ver. 7 above] [x][See ver. 11 above]
13 [x][See ver. 11 above] [n][See ver. 6 above]
16 [y]ch. 37:17 [z]See Ruth 3:13 [a][Isa. 57:16] [b]See ver. 1-9
17 [c]ver. 2, 21; [ch. 27:12, 13; 2 Kgs. 24:12] [d]ch. 39:3 [e][ch. 34:4, 5]
18 [d][See ver. 17 above] [f]See ch. 21:10
19 [g]See ch. 37:13
20 [h]ch. 40:9
21 [c][See ver. 17 above]
22 [i]See ch. 20:10
23 [j]ch. 39:6; 41:10; 43:6
25 [k][ver. 5]
26 [l][ch. 37:20]
28 [m]See ch. 32:2

Chapter 39

1 [n]For ver. 1-10, see ch. 52:4-16; 2 Kgs. 25:1-12
3 [o]ch. 38:17, 18, 22 [p][ch. 1:15]

(cf. 1:17–19). They **drew Jeremiah up** out of the mud (cf. David's words of praise in Ps. 40:2).

38:14 third entrance. Unmentioned elsewhere. Perhaps the king's private entrance. **hide nothing**. As if **Jeremiah** has been doing so! See 37:17.

38:15 Jeremiah suspects that the king **will not listen** this time any more than he did previously. Jeremiah also dreads further punishment (cf. 32:1–2).

38:16 secretly. Zedekiah's promise had no public weight (37:17). **men who seek your life. Zedekiah** was well aware of the dangers **Jeremiah** faced (38:5).

38:17–18 Once again Jeremiah counsels **surrender** (21:1–10; 27:1–15; 32:1–5; 38:1–5).

38:19–20 Zedekiah feared displeasing people in Jerusalem (vv. 4–5) and feared being turned over to **Judeans** who had already surrendered to Babylon. But Jeremiah promises that obedience to God's word (27:1–15) will result in his survival.

38:21–22 Refusal to obey carries dire consequences. **women . . . being led out**. To exile. **trusted friends**. The king's counselors and lying prophets (37:19; 38:1–5). **feet are sunk in the mud**. Zedekiah's political fortunes were sinking even as Jeremiah had been sinking in the cistern (v. 6). **they turn away**. When disaster comes.

38:23 Without obedience to God's word, Zedekiah, his family, and Jerusalem will all suffer terrible fates.

3 [q] ver. 13; 2 Kgs. 18:17
4 [r] See Deut. 1:1
5 [s] Josh. 5:10 [t] See 2 Kgs. 23:33 [u] [Ezek. 17:15]
6 [v] ch. 52:10 [t] [See ver. 5 above]
7 [w] [ch. 32:4; Ezek. 12:13]
8 [x] See ch. 21:10 [y] Neh. 1:3; [Ps. 80:12; Isa. 5:5]
9 [z] ch. 40:1; 52:12; 2 Kgs. 25:8 [a] Gen. 37:36 [b] See ch. 37:13
10 [c] ch. 40:7; 2 Kgs. 25:12
12 [d] ch. 40:4
13 [e] [ver. 3]
14 [f] ch. 38:28; See ch. 32:2

in the middle gate: Nergal-sar-ezer of Samgar, Nebu-sar-sekim [q] the Rab-saris, Nergal-
sar-ezer the Rab-mag, with all the rest of the officers of the king of Babylon. 4 When
Zedekiah king of Judah and all the soldiers saw them, they fled, going out of the city
at night by way of the king's garden through the gate between the two walls; and they
went toward [r] the Arabah. 5 But the army of the Chaldeans pursued them and overtook
Zedekiah in [s] the plains of Jericho. And when they had taken him, they brought him
up to Nebuchadnezzar king of Babylon, at [t] Riblah, in the land of Hamath; [u] and he
passed sentence on him. 6 The king of Babylon [v] slaughtered the sons of Zedekiah at
[t] Riblah before his eyes, and the king of Babylon [v] slaughtered all the nobles of Judah.
7 [w] He put out the eyes of Zedekiah and bound him in chains to take him to Babylon.
8 [x] The Chaldeans burned the king's house and the house of the people, [y] and broke down
the walls of Jerusalem. 9 Then [z] Nebuzaradan, the [a] captain of the guard, carried into exile
to Babylon the rest of the people who were left in the city, [b] those who had deserted to
him, and the people who remained. 10 Nebuzaradan, the captain of the guard, [c] left in the
land of Judah some of the poor people who owned nothing, and gave them vineyards
and fields at the same time.

The LORD Delivers Jeremiah

11 Nebuchadnezzar king of Babylon gave command concerning Jeremiah through
Nebuzaradan, the captain of the guard, saying, 12 [d] "Take him, look after him well, and
do him no harm, but deal with him as he tells you." 13 So [e] Nebuzaradan the captain of
the guard, Nebushazban the Rab-saris, Nergal-sar-ezer the Rab-mag, [e] and all the chief
officers of the king of Babylon 14 sent and took Jeremiah from [f] the court of the guard. They

Babylon Attacks Judah

586 B.C.

The Babylonians had invaded Judah at least once before in 597 B.C., but in 586 Nebuchadnezzar completely destroyed the walls of Jerusalem and the temple as punishment for Zedekiah's rebellion. Zedekiah himself fled Jerusalem but was caught by the Babylonians near Jericho and sent to Riblah to face judgment.

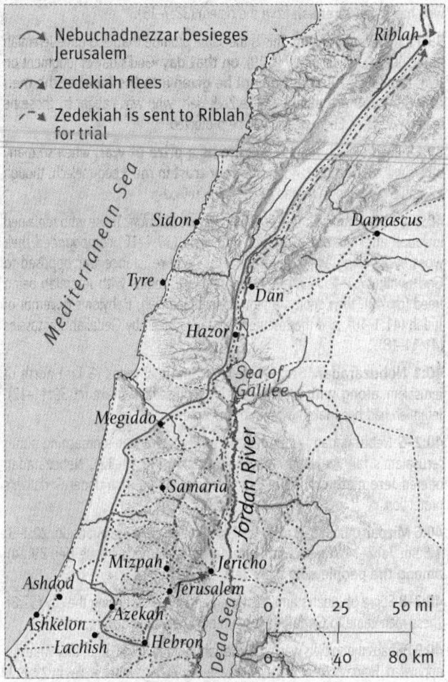

38:24 Let no one know. Jeremiah's future seems to lie in Zedekiah's hands, but God has promised him protection (1:17–19).

38:25–27 If the officials . . . say to you. Once again, Zedekiah has no control over the situation. **"I made a humble plea."** Cf. 37:20. **the conversation had not been overheard.** The king's secret was safe.

38:28 court of the guard. See 37:21. **the day that Jerusalem was taken.** Babylon renewed the siege, as Jeremiah had promised (see 37:6–10), and eventually triumphed.

39:1 ninth year . . . tenth month. Perhaps December 589/January 588 B.C. **Babylon . . . came against Jerusalem.** See map to the left.

39:2 eleventh year . . . fourth month. Perhaps June/July 587 B.C. The siege lasted over two years. **a breach.** Babylon broke through the defenses and walls in the middle of the **city**. See v. 3.

39:3 middle gate. Mentioned only here. Perhaps in the middle of the northern wall, since **Babylon** would likely have attacked from the north, the flattest terrain. The **officials . . . sat in the** gate, thus asserting judicial authority. **Nergal-sar-ezer.** Perhaps Neviglissar, who succeeded Nebuchadnezzar's son on Babylon's throne (c. 560–556 B.C.). **Rab-saris.** A chief attendant. **Rab-mag.** A court official.

39:4 Zedekiah now learns that Jeremiah was God's true prophet. **king's garden.** Most likely on the south side of Jerusalem. **Arabah.** A region extending from the Jordan River Valley to the area south of the Dead Sea.

39:5 In fleeing (v. 4), Zedekiah did not get far; the **plains of Jericho** were perhaps as few as 14 miles (23 km) east of Jerusalem. **Riblah.** In Syria, 65 miles (105 km) north of Damascus; **Nebuchadnezzar** ruled his armies and pronounced judgment on enemies here.

39:6–7 Nebuchadnezzar was harsher than what **Zedekiah** feared from his countrymen (38:19). He **slaughtered** Zedekiah's **sons** and **nobles**, blinded him, and took him **in chains** to **Babylon**.

39:8 As Jeremiah had predicted (21:1–10; 27:1–15; 32:1–5; 37:1–10), Babylon sacked, **burned**, and destroyed **Jerusalem**.

39:9–10 Babylon took the **people who were left in the city** and **those who had deserted** to **Babylon**. Not every Judean was taken, for the poorest people, **who owned nothing**, were given what remained in Judea.

39:11–12 Apparently **Nebuchadnezzar** had learned of **Jeremiah** from those who had surrendered (see 38:19). **do him no harm**. God was still protecting Jeremiah (cf. 1:19).

39:13–14 Nebuchadnezzar's officials (v. 3) released **Jeremiah** from prison,

entrusted him to [g]Gedaliah the son of [h]Ahikam, son of [i]Shaphan, that he should take him
home. So [j]he lived among the people.
15 The word of the LORD came to Jeremiah [k]while he was shut up in the court of the
guard: 16 "Go, and say to [l]Ebed-melech the Ethiopian, 'Thus says the LORD of hosts, the
God of Israel: [m]Behold, I will fulfill my words against this city for harm and [n]not for good,
and they shall be accomplished before you on that day. 17 But I will deliver you on that
day, declares the LORD, and you shall not be given into the hand of the men [o]of whom
you are afraid. 18 For I will surely save you, and you shall not fall by the sword, but you
shall have your [p]life as a prize of war, [q]because you have put your trust in me, declares
the LORD.'"

Jeremiah Remains in Judah

40 The word that came to Jeremiah from the LORD [r]after Nebuzaradan the captain
of the guard had let him go from [s]Ramah, when he took him [t]bound in chains
along with all the captives of Jerusalem and Judah who were being exiled to Babylon. 2 The
captain of the guard took Jeremiah and said to him, [u]"The LORD your God pronounced
this disaster against this place. 3 The LORD has brought it about, and has done as he said.
[v]Because you sinned against the LORD and did not obey his voice, this thing has come upon
you. 4 Now, behold, I release you today from [t]the chains on your hands. [w]If it seems good
to you to come with me to Babylon, come, and I will look after you well, [w]but if it seems
wrong to you to come with me to Babylon, do not come. [x]See, the whole land is before you;
go wherever you think it good and right to go. 5 If you remain,[1] then return to [y]Gedaliah
the son of Ahikam, son of Shaphan, [z]whom the king of Babylon appointed governor of
the cities of Judah, and dwell with him among the people. Or go wherever you think it

[1] Syriac; the meaning of the Hebrew phrase is uncertain

14 [g]ch. 43:6; See ch. 40:5-9, 11-16; 41:1-4, 6; 2 Kgs. 25:22-25 [h]2 Kgs. 22:12 [i]2 Kgs. 22:3 [j]ch. 37:12
15 [k]ch. 36:5; 38:13
16 [l]See ch. 38:7 [m]Dan. 9:12 [n]ch. 21:10; [ch. 14:11]
17 [o]ch. 22:25
18 [p]ch. 21:9; 45:5 [q]Ps. 25:2; 37:40

Chapter 40

1 [r][ch. 39:14] [s]Josh. 18:25 [t][Ps. 149:8]
2 [u][Deut. 29:24, 28]
3 [v]ch. 44:3, 23; Deut. 29:25; See Dan. 9:10-12
4 [t][See ver. 1 above] [w][ch. 39:12] [x][Gen. 20:15]
5 [y]See ch. 39:14 [z]ch. 41:2

The Fall of Jerusalem
586 B.C.
As punishment for Zedekiah's rebellion, Nebuchadnezzar attacked Jerusalem. After the Babylonians had made a breach in the wall at the middle gate, Zedekiah realized his fate was sealed if he stayed in the city, so he and his soldiers attempted to escape during the night through a gate between two walls at the southeast corner of the city. The Babylonians overtook him near Jericho, however, and he was sent to Riblah for judgment. Then Nebuchadnezzar destroyed the walls of Jerusalem and the temple and exiled many of the people to Babylon (see 52:1–34).

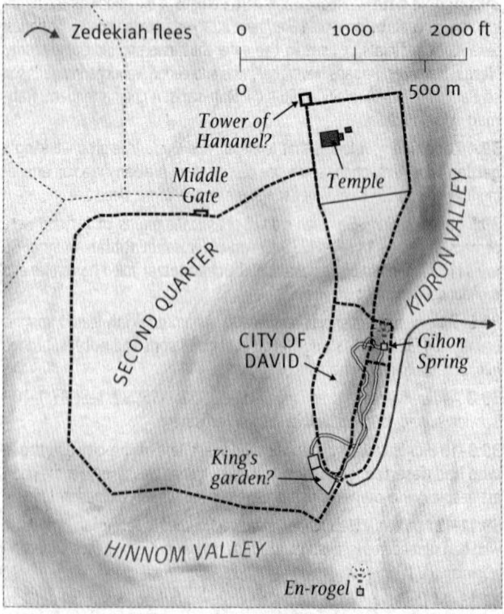

which probably branded him as a collaborator in some Judeans' minds. **Gedaliah**. A Judean who was named governor by Nebuchadnezzar. **take him home**. To the governor's house. **lived among the people**. Those described in v. 10.

39:15–16 Before Jerusalem fell, **God** sent a word concerning **Ebed-melech**, who had saved **Jeremiah** from the cistern (38:7–13).

39:17 I will deliver you. This is the same promise that God gave Jeremiah at the outset of his ministry (1:19). **on that day**. God's day of judgment on Jerusalem (39:1–10). **you shall not be given into the hand of the men of whom you are afraid**. Unlike Zedekiah, who was caught by those he feared (vv. 4–7), Ebed-melech will be protected.

39:18 Ebed-melech will have his **life as a prize of war**, when so many others will die. See 21:9; 45:5. **put your trust in me**. Ebed-melech, though a Gentile (an Ethiopian), had saving faith in God.

40:1–41:18 *Judah's Futile Rebellion against Babylon.* Those who remained in Judah after the destruction of Jerusalem (39:1–10) compounded their woes by rebelling against Babylon. This futile resistance was opposed to God's will (27:1–15; 29:1–32). This segment begins with Jeremiah being freed (ch. 40), then depicts a plot against Gedaliah, Babylon's governor of Judah (41:1–10), and the rescue of hostages taken by Gedaliah's assassins (41:11–18).

40:1 Nebuzaradan. See 39:11–14. **Ramah**. 5 miles (8 km) north of Jerusalem. **along with all the captives**. By some mistake (cf. 39:11–12), Jeremiah had been taken away with the exiles.

40:2–5 Nebuzaradan recognizes the truth of Jeremiah's preaching about Jerusalem's fall. As Nebuchadnezzar ordered (39:11–12), Nebuzaradan offered **Jeremiah** a choice of where to live and put him under Gedaliah's protection.

40:6 Mizpah. About 5–8 miles (8–13 km) north of Jerusalem (Judg. 20:1–3; 1 Sam. 7:12–14). **lived with him**. In the governor's house (Jer. 39:14). **among the people who were left**. See 39:10, 14.

40:7–8 Some of Judah's army scattered and hid after fleeing the city (52:8). These men came to **Gedaliah** to learn how he would govern.

40:9 Perhaps the soldiers wanted **Gedaliah** to lead a revolt. If so, they were disappointed. He gave them the same advice Jeremiah gave the exiles in 29:1–9.

6[y][See ver. 5 above] [a]ch. 41:6; Josh. 18:26 [b]ch. 37:12; 39:14 [c]ch. 39:10
7[d]For ver. 7-9, see 2 Kgs. 25:23, 24 [e]ver. 5 [f]ch. 39:10; 2 Kgs. 25:12
8[a][See ver. 6 above] [g]ver. 14, 15, 16; See ch. 41:1-3 [h]ver. 13, 15, 16; ch. 42:1, 8 [i]ch. 42:1
9[j]ch. 38:20
10[a][See ver. 6 above] [l][ver. 12]
11[m][Num. 22:1; 2 Sam. 8:2] [n]1 Sam. 11:1; 12:12 [o]Gen. 36:8
12[p][ch. 43:5] [q][ver. 10]
13[r]ver. 8, 15, 16; ch. 42:1, 8 [s]ch. 41:11; 42:1

right to go." So the captain of the guard gave him an allowance of food and a present, and
let him go. 6 Then Jeremiah went to [y]Gedaliah the son of Ahikam, at [a]Mizpah, and lived
with him [b]among the people [c]who were left in the land.

7 [d]When all the captains of the forces in the open country and their men heard that [e]the
king of Babylon had appointed Gedaliah the son of Ahikam governor in the land and
had committed to him men, women, and children, those of [f]the poorest of the land who
had not been taken into exile to Babylon, 8 they went to Gedaliah at [a]Mizpah—[g]Ishmael
the son of Nethaniah, [h]Johanan the son of Kareah, Seraiah the son of Tanhumeth, the
sons of Ephai the Netophathite, [i]Jezaniah the son of the Maacathite, they and their men.
9 Gedaliah the son of Ahikam, son of Shaphan, swore to them and their men, saying, "Do
not be afraid to serve the Chaldeans. Dwell in the land and serve the king of Babylon, [j]and
it shall be well with you. 10 As for me, I will dwell at [a]Mizpah, to represent you before the
Chaldeans who will come to us. But as for you, [l]gather wine and summer fruits and oil,
and store them in your vessels, and dwell in your cities that you have taken." 11 Likewise,
when all the Judeans who were in [m]Moab and among [n]the Ammonites and in [o]Edom
and in other lands heard that the king of Babylon had left a remnant in Judah and had
appointed Gedaliah the son of Ahikam, son of Shaphan, as governor over them, 12 [p]then
all the Judeans returned from all the places to which they had been driven and came to
the land of Judah, to Gedaliah at Mizpah. And they [q]gathered wine and summer fruits
in great abundance.

13 Now [r]Johanan the son of Kareah and [s]all the leaders of the forces in the open country

40:10 represent you. As a Judean trusted by Babylon. **gather . . . store . . . dwell**. These poorer people could now reap the harvest in their fellow citizens' absence. **cities that you have taken**. Those who remained had moved into the exiles' homes and towns.

40:11–12 Many **Judeans** fled to neighboring countries, but **returned** at this point and **gathered wine and summer fruits in great abundance**. All was going well for those who remained in Judea.

40:13–14 Apparently the former soldiers (vv. 7–9) appreciated **Gedaliah**, for they warned him of a plot against his **life** involving **Baalis the king of the Ammonites**, and **Ishmael**, one of the "captains of the forces in the open country" (vv. 7–8), but he did **not believe** the rumors. The Ammonites opposed Babylon (27:3) and would therefore oppose Gedaliah. The archaeological record confirms the existence of "Baalis, the king of the Ammonites" in the sixth century B.C. An Ammonite seal from this time reads, "Belonging to Baalis, king of the Ammonites." An inscription from Tel el-Umeiri in Jordan on a seal impression of a high-court official says, "Milqom servant of Baalis."

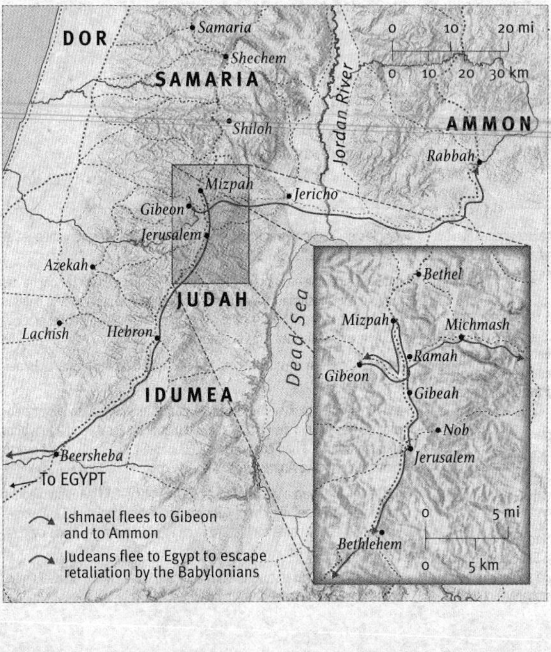

Gedaliah Is Assassinated

586 B.C.

After depopulating Judah of all but the poorest of its inhabitants, the Babylonians set up a new governor, Gedaliah, in Mizpah. Among Gedaliah's new officers was Ishmael, a member of the Judean royal family. King Baalis of the Ammonites incited Ishmael to assassinate Gedaliah at Mizpah, and then he slaughtered many pilgrims from Shechem, Shiloh, and Samaria and took captives to Gibeon. Another leader named Johanan, however, overtook Ishmael at Gibeon and freed the captives, but Ishmael escaped to Ammon. Fearing what the Babylonians might do in retaliation for Gedaliah's murder, many of the freed captives fled to Egypt.

came to Gedaliah at Mizpah 14 and said to him, "Do you know that Baalis the king of [t]the
Ammonites has sent Ishmael the son of Nethaniah to take your life?" But Gedaliah the
son of Ahikam would not believe them. 15 Then Johanan the son of Kareah spoke secretly
to Gedaliah at Mizpah, "Please let me go and strike down Ishmael the son of Nethaniah,
and no one will know it. Why should he take your life, so that all the Judeans who are
gathered about you would be scattered, [u]and the remnant of Judah would perish?" 16 But
Gedaliah the son of Ahikam said to Johanan the son of Kareah, "You shall not do this
thing, for you are speaking falsely of Ishmael."

Gedaliah Murdered

41 [v]In the seventh month, Ishmael the son of Nethaniah, son of Elishama, of the
royal family, one of the chief officers of the king, came with ten men to Gedaliah
the son of Ahikam, at [w]Mizpah. As they [x]ate bread together there at Mizpah, 2 [y]Ishmael
the son of Nethaniah and the ten men with him rose up and struck down Gedaliah the
son of Ahikam, son of Shaphan, with the sword, and killed him, [z]whom the king of
Babylon had appointed governor in the land. 3 Ishmael also struck down all the Judeans
who were with Gedaliah at [w]Mizpah, and the Chaldean soldiers who happened to be
there.

4 On the day after the murder of Gedaliah, before anyone knew of it, 5 eighty men arrived
from [a]Shechem and [b]Shiloh and [c]Samaria, with [d]their beards shaved and [e]their clothes
torn, and [d]their bodies gashed, [f]bringing grain offerings and incense to present at the
temple of the LORD. 6 And Ishmael the son of Nethaniah came out from [g]Mizpah to meet
them, weeping as he came. As he met them, he said to them, "Come in to Gedaliah the
son of Ahikam." 7 When they came into the city, Ishmael the son of Nethaniah and the
men with him slaughtered them and cast them into a cistern. 8 But there were ten men
among them who said to Ishmael, "Do not put us to death, for we have [h]stores of wheat,
barley, oil, and honey hidden in the fields." So he refrained and did not put them to death
with their companions.

9 Now the cistern into which Ishmael had thrown all the bodies of the men whom he
had struck down along with[1] Gedaliah was the large cistern that [i]King Asa had made for
defense against [i]Baasha king of Israel; Ishmael the son of Nethaniah filled it with the slain.
10 Then Ishmael took captive all the rest of the people who were in Mizpah, [j]the king's
daughters and all the people who were left at Mizpah, whom [k]Nebuzaradan, the captain
of the guard, had committed to Gedaliah the son of Ahikam. Ishmael the son of Nethaniah
took them captive and set out to cross over to [l]the Ammonites.

11 But when [m]Johanan the son of Kareah and [n]all the leaders of the forces with him heard
of all the evil that Ishmael the son of Nethaniah had done, 12 they took all their men and
went to fight against Ishmael the son of Nethaniah. They came upon him at [o]the great pool
that is in [p]Gibeon. 13 And when all the people who were with Ishmael saw Johanan the son of

[1] Hebrew *by the hand of*

14[t][ch. 41:10]
15[u][ch. 42:2]

Chapter 41

1[v]2 Kgs. 25:25 [w]See ch. 40:6, 8, 10 [x][Ps. 41:9]
2[y][2 Sam. 13:28, 29] [z]ch. 40:5
3[w][See ver. 1 above]
5[a]Josh. 17:7 [b]Josh. 18:1 [c]1 Kgs. 16:24; See ch. 23:13 [d][ch. 48:37; Deut. 14:1; Isa. 15:2] [e]ch. 36:24 [f][2 Kgs. 25:9]
6[g]ch. 40:6, 8, 10
8[h][Judg. 6:11]
9[i][1 Kgs. 15:22; 2 Chr. 16:6]
10[j]See ch. 38:23 [k][ch. 40:7] [l][ch. 40:14]
11[m]See ch. 40:8 [n]ch. 40:13
12[o][2 Sam. 2:13] [p]Josh. 9:3, 17

40:15–16 Once again **Johanan** warned **Gedaliah** of the plot against him by **Ishmael** (see note on vv. 13–14), this time recommending a preemptive strike. But the magnanimous (or naive) **Gedaliah** could not imagine that **Ishmael** would be guilty of treason.

41:1 seventh month. October, most likely 587 B.C., though perhaps as late as 582 (see 52:30). The Feast of Booths took place in this month, and the pilgrims mentioned in 41:4–5 may have come for that festival. **Ishmael**. See 40:13–16. **royal family**. Thus he may have harbored hopes of renewing David's lineage to power. **Mizpah**. See 40:6. **ate bread together**. Gedaliah offered hospitality to Ishmael and his **ten men**.

41:2 As Johanan had feared (40:13–16), **Ishmael** did plan to kill **Gedaliah**. Killing a host was considered a cowardly, heinous act. Killing the man Nebuchadnezzar **had appointed governor** was akin to committing suicide.

41:3 Ishmael killed **all the Judeans who were with Gedaliah**, thus carrying out a political massacre.

41:4–5 Others share Gedaliah's tragedy. **eighty men**. Probably pilgrims for the Feast of Booths. They were from three Israelite cities: **Shechem**, **Shiloh**, and **Samaria**. Some northerners came to Jerusalem to worship even after the nations were divided in 930 B.C. **beards shaved**. They probably mourned the temple's destruction. **grain offerings and incense**. Worship continued at the **temple** site after 587 B.C.

41:6–8 Under the guise of offering safe passage to Gedaliah (whom he has just killed; v. 2), **Ishmael** slaughters 70 of the pilgrims, apparently in order to leave no witnesses of his first crime. He spares 10 because they offer precious food. He throws the dead into a **cistern**.

41:9 This **cistern** was dug when **Asa** of Judah fought **Baasha** of **Israel**. See 1 Kings 15:16–22.

41:10 Ishmael took hostages. **king's daughters**. Some prominent **people** had been left in the land, perhaps to pacify the local populace. **whom Nebuzaradan . . . had committed**. Cf. 39:13–14. Ishmael then **set out to cross over to the Ammonites**, who also opposed Babylon (27:3).

41:11–12 Johanan and other former soldiers (40:7–8, 13–16) pursued the treasonous **Ishmael**. The city of **Gibeon** was about 3 miles (4.8 km) southwest of Mizpah. Ishmael took a circuitous route, perhaps to elude capture, but he did not get far.

41:13–15 Johanan rescued the hostages and killed two of Ishmael's men, but **Ishmael . . . escaped** to Ammon.

Kareah and [q]all the leaders of the forces with him, they rejoiced. 14 [r]So all the people whom
Ishmael had carried away captive from Mizpah turned around and came back, and went
to Johanan the son of Kareah. 15 But Ishmael the son of Nethaniah escaped from Johanan
with eight men, and went to [s]the Ammonites. 16 Then Johanan the son of Kareah and [q]all
the leaders of the forces with him took from Mizpah all the rest of the people whom he
had recovered from Ishmael the son of Nethaniah, after he had struck down Gedaliah
the son of Ahikam—soldiers, [t]women, children, and eunuchs, whom Johanan brought
back from [u]Gibeon. 17 And they went and stayed at Geruth [v]Chimham near [w]Bethlehem,
intending to go to Egypt 18 because of the Chaldeans. For they were afraid of them, because
Ishmael the son of Nethaniah had struck down Gedaliah the son of Ahikam, [x]whom the
king of Babylon had made governor over the land.

Warning Against Going to Egypt

42 Then [y]all the commanders of the forces, and [z]Johanan the son of Kareah and
Jezaniah the son of [a]Hoshaiah, and all the people [b]from the least to the greatest, came near 2 and said to Jeremiah the prophet, "Let [c]our plea for mercy come before
you, and [d]pray to the LORD your God for us, for all [e]this remnant—[f]because we are
left with but a few, as your eyes see us— 3 that [g]the LORD your God may show us the
way we should go, and the thing that we should do." 4 Jeremiah the prophet said to
them, "I have heard you. Behold, I will pray to the LORD your God according to your
request, and [h]whatever the LORD answers you I will tell you. [h]I will keep nothing back
from you." 5 Then they said to Jeremiah, [i]"May the LORD be a true and [j]faithful witness
against us [k]if we do not act according to all the word [l]with which the LORD your God
sends you to us. 6 Whether it is good or bad, we will obey the voice of the LORD our God
to whom we are sending you, [m]that it may be well with us when we obey the voice of
the LORD our God."

7 [n]At the end of ten days the word of the LORD came to Jeremiah. 8 Then he summoned
[z]Johanan the son of Kareah and [y]all the commanders of the forces who were with him,
and all the people [b]from the least to the greatest, 9 and said to them, "Thus says the LORD,
the God of Israel, [o]to whom you sent me to present your plea for mercy before him: 10 If
you will remain in this land, [p]then I will build you up and not pull you down; I will plant
you, and not pluck you up; [q]for I relent of the disaster that I did to you. 11 [r]Do not fear
the king of Babylon, [r]of whom you are afraid. [s]Do not fear him, declares the LORD, [s]for I
am with you, to save you and to deliver you from his hand. 12 [t]I will grant you mercy, that
he may have mercy on you and let you remain in your own land. 13 [u]But if you say, 'We
will not remain in this land,' disobeying the voice of the LORD your God 14 and saying,
'No, [v]we will go to the land of Egypt, where we shall not see war or [w]hear the sound of
the trumpet or [x]be hungry for bread, and we will dwell there,' 15 then hear the word of
the LORD, O remnant of Judah. Thus says the LORD of hosts, the God of Israel: [y]If you

13 [q]ch. 40:13
14 [r]ver. 10, 16
15 [s][ch. 40:14]
16 [q][See ver. 13 above] [t]ch. 40:7 [u]Josh. 9:3, 17
17 [v][2 Sam. 19:37, 38] [w][Matt. 2:1, 14]; See Gen. 35:19
18 [x]ver. 2; ch. 40:5

Chapter 42

1 [y]ch. 40:13; 41:11 [z]See ch. 40:8 [a]ch. 43:2 [b][ch. 6:13]
2 [c]See ch. 36:7 [d]ver. 20; [1 Sam. 7:8; 12:19] [e][ch. 40:15; Isa. 37:4] [f][Lev. 26:22]
3 [g][ch. 37:17; Ezra 8:21]
4 [h]1 Sam. 3:18; [Num. 22:18]
5 [i][Gen. 31:50] [j][Rev. 1:5; 3:14] [k]Judg. 11:10 [l]ver. 21
6 [m]ch. 7:23
7 [n][Ezek. 3:16]
8 [z][See ver. 1 above] [y][See ver. 1 above] [b][See ver. 1 above]
9 [o]ver. 2, 3
10 [p]See ch. 24:6 [q]ch. 18:8; Gen. 6:6; [Deut. 32:36]
11 [r][ch. 22:25; 41:18] [s]ch. 30:10, 11; [Rom. 8:31]
12 [t][Neh. 1:11]
13 [u]ch. 43:4; [ch. 44:16, 17]
14 [v][ch. 41:17] [w]ch. 4:19 [x][ch. 37:21]
15 [y]ch. 44:12; [ver. 19; Deut. 17:16]

41:16 soldiers, women, children, and eunuchs. Defines all the **people** mentioned in v. 10.

41:17–18 Geruth Chimham. Location unknown. **Bethlehem**. About 5 miles (8 km) southwest of Jerusalem, so Johanan and his soldiers had traveled 10–15 miles (16–24 km). **go to Egypt**. The nation farthest from Babylon-controlled territory. **because of the Chaldeans**. Johanan and his soldiers obviously feared retaliation for Gedaliah's murder despite their innocence in the matter.

42:1–45:5 *Judah's Futile Rebellion against God.* The only thing more futile than rebelling against Babylon was rebelling against God. The survivors now take this foolish step. They request a word from God (42:1–6), and Jeremiah delivers it (42:7–22). They reject the word (43:1–7), so God rejects them (43:8–13). Though God despises idolatry (44:1–14), the people love it (44:15–19). Thus, God pronounces a final word on the faithless people (44:20–30), yet offers hope to Jeremiah and Baruch (ch. 45).

42:1–4 Before Judah goes to Egypt, the leaders ask **Jeremiah** to seek God's will. They are desperate and decimated and claim to desire the **thing that** they **should do**. As in 21:1–10 and 37:16–21, Jeremiah promises to deliver God's word accurately.

42:5–6 The people promise in most emphatic terms that they will **obey** God's word no matter what it is.

42:7–9 Jeremiah waits for the word (cf. 28:11–12), and when it comes he summons the **people. At the end of ten days**. Though Jeremiah was a faithful and true prophet of God, he could not give prophecies whenever he wanted, but had to wait for the Lord to speak to him.

42:10 Jeremiah delivers a word of promise: God has ceased bringing **disaster**. If the people stay in Judah, God will **build** and **plant** them, which are metaphors for renewal (1:10; 24:6; 31:28).

42:11 Do not fear. The retaliation that Judah's leaders expect will not come. **with you, to save you and to deliver you**. God gives the people the same promise he gave Jeremiah at his call (1:19). Their lives will be as safe as Jeremiah's has been.

42:12 Nebuchadnezzar is God's servant (27:6), so he will **grant** these persons **mercy** if God commands him to do so.

42:13–17 Rejecting God's promise and fleeing to Egypt will result in **Judah** experiencing what they fear. Babylon will defeat **Egypt**; the exiles are safer in Judah.

42:18 God's **anger** and **wrath** were warned about (4:4; 7:20; 21:5), then poured out (39:1–10). **execration, horror, curse, taunt**. See 15:4; 18:16;

set your faces to enter Egypt [z]and go to live there, 16 then the sword [a]that you fear shall
overtake you there in the land of Egypt, and the famine of which you are afraid shall
follow close after you to Egypt, [b]and there you shall die. 17 All the men who set their faces
to go to Egypt to live there shall die by the sword, by famine, and by pestilence. They
shall have [c]no remnant or survivor from the disaster that I will bring upon them.
18 "For thus says the LORD of hosts, the God of Israel: [d]As my anger and my wrath were
poured out on the inhabitants of Jerusalem, so my wrath will be poured out on you when
you go to Egypt. [e]You shall become an execration, a horror, a curse, and a taunt. You shall
see this place no more. 19 The LORD has said to you, O remnant of Judah, [f]'Do not go to
Egypt.' [g]Know for a certainty that I have warned you this day 20 that you have gone astray
at the cost of your lives. [h]For you sent me to the LORD your God, saying, [h]'Pray for us to
the LORD our God, and [i]whatever the LORD our God says declare to us and we will do it.'
21 And I have this day declared it to you, but you have not obeyed the voice of the LORD
your God in anything [j]that he sent me to tell you. 22 [k]Now therefore know for a certainty
that you shall die by the sword, by famine, and by pestilence in the place where you desire
to go to live."

Jeremiah Taken to Egypt

43 When Jeremiah finished speaking to all the people all these words of the LORD
their God, with which the LORD their God had sent him to them, 2 Azariah the son
of [l]Hoshaiah and [m]Johanan the son of Kareah and [n]all the insolent men said to Jeremiah,
"You are telling a lie. The LORD our God did not send you to say, [o]'Do not go to Egypt to
live there,' 3 but [p]Baruch the son of Neriah [q]has set you against us, [r]to deliver us into the
hand of the Chaldeans, that they may kill us or take us into exile in Babylon." 4 So [m]Johanan
the son of Kareah and all [s]the commanders of the forces and all the people did not obey
the voice of the LORD, to remain in the land of Judah. 5 But Johanan the son of Kareah and
all the commanders of the forces took [t]all the remnant of Judah who had returned to live
in the land of Judah from all the nations to which they had been driven— 6 [u]the men, the
women, the children, [v]the princesses, and every person whom [w]Nebuzaradan the captain
of the guard had left with [x]Gedaliah the son of Ahikam, son of Shaphan; also Jeremiah the
prophet and Baruch the son of Neriah. 7 And they came into the land of Egypt, for they
did not obey the voice of the LORD. And they arrived at [y]Tahpanhes.
8 Then the word of the LORD came to Jeremiah in [y]Tahpanhes: 9 "Take in your hands large
stones and hide them in the mortar in the pavement that is at the entrance to Pharaoh's
palace in [y]Tahpanhes, in the sight of the men of Judah, 10 and say to them, 'Thus says the
LORD of hosts, the God of Israel: Behold, I will send and take Nebuchadnezzar the king
of Babylon, [z]my servant, [a]and I will set his throne above these stones that I have hidden,
and he will spread his royal canopy over them. 11 He shall come [b]and strike the land of
Egypt, [c]giving over to the pestilence those who are doomed to the pestilence, to captivity
those who are doomed to captivity, and to the sword those who are doomed to the sword.
12 [d]I shall kindle a fire [e]in the temples of the gods of Egypt, and he shall burn them [f]and
carry them away captive. [g]And he shall clean the land of Egypt [g]as a shepherd cleans his

15 [z]ch. 44:27; See ch. 44:1, 12-14
16 [a]Ezek. 11:8 [b]ver. 22; ch. 44:12
17 [c]Lam. 2:22
18 [d]See ch. 7:20 [e]See ch. 18:16
19 [f]ch. 43:2; [ver. 14-16] [g][Ezek. 2:5]
20 [h]ver. 2 [i]ver. 3
21 [j]ver. 5
22 [k]ver. 16, 17

Chapter 43

2 [l]ch. 42:1 [m]See ch. 40:8 [n]Ps. 86:14; Isa. 13:11; Mal. 4:1 [o]ch. 42:19
3 [p]See ch. 32:12 [q][ch. 38:22] [r][ch. 37:13]
4 [m][See ver. 2 above] [s]ch. 40:13
5 [t][ch. 40:11, 12]
6 [u]ch. 44:20 [v]See ch. 38:23 [w]ch. 39:10; 40:7 [x]See ch. 39:14
7 [y]ch. 2:16; 44:1; 46:14; [Isa. 30:4]
8 [y][See ver. 7 above]
9 [y][See ver. 7 above]
10 [z]See ch. 25:9 [a]ch. 1:15
11 [b]ch. 44:13; 46:13 [c]See ch. 15:2
12 [d]See ch. 17:27 [e]ch. 46:25; Ezek. 30:13; [Ex. 12:12; Isa. 19:1] [f][ch. 48:7] [g][Ps. 104:2; Isa. 49:18]

19:8; 24:9; 29:18; 34:17. If they flee to Egypt, they will become what the Jerusalemites had been: "bad figs" (ch. 24) ripe for punishment rather than people to whom God gives hope (ch. 29).

42:19–20 Jeremiah could hardly speak more plainly: to obey means life; to disobey means death.

42:21–22 Jeremiah senses that the decision has been made. His hearers **have not obeyed** before, and they will not obey now.

43:1 What **Jeremiah** delivered to the exiles were the **words of the LORD their God**.

43:2 Azariah. Not mentioned elsewhere in Jeremiah. **Johanan.** See 40:13–16; 41:11–18. **insolent men.** As their words to **Jeremiah** demonstrate. **a lie.** They accuse Jeremiah of false prophecy.

43:3 For unspecified reasons, the men accuse **Baruch** (32:12; 36:1–32), Jeremiah's friend and scribe, of scheming to deliver them to the **Chaldeans**. Apparently they consider Jeremiah and Baruch to be pro-Babylonian.

43:4–6 Johanan and company **did not obey the voice of the LORD.** Rather, they took to Egypt the captives they had rescued (41:11–18), along with **Jeremiah** and **Baruch** (43:6) as hostages. They even took some people **who had returned** from exile.

43:7 Tahpanhes. Located in the eastern delta of Egypt. See 2:16.

43:9–10 Jeremiah performs another symbolic act. Cf. 13:1–14; 16:1–13; 19:1–15; 27:1–28:17; 32:1–15. This time he places **large stones** near one of **Pharaoh's** palaces and promises that **God** will place Nebuchadnezzar's **throne** on **these stones**.

43:11 The people will face **pestilence**, **captivity**, and **sword**, all of which they experienced in Jerusalem (14:1–12; 15:1–9). Their nightmare will begin afresh because their disobedience to God's word continues.

43:12 kindle a fire. See 17:27. **the gods of Egypt.** See 10:11. **carry them away captive.** Other nations' gods were often carried away to the conqueror's home temple. **as a shepherd cleans his cloak of vermin.** Nebuchadnezzar will pick off Egypt's cities as easily as a shepherd picks small insects such as lice off his clothing.

13[h][Ex. 23:24] [e][See ver. 12 above]
Chapter 44
1[i]ch. 46:14; Ex. 14:2 [j]See ch. 43:7-9 [k]ver. 15; See Isa. 11:11
2[l]ver. 6
3[m]ver. 8; See ch. 7:18, 19 [n]See ch. 1:16 [o]ch. 19:4; Deut. 6:14
4[p]See 2 Chr. 36:15

cloak of vermin, and he shall go away from there in peace. 13 He shall break the [h]obelisks
of Heliopolis, which is in the land of Egypt, [e]and the temples of the gods of Egypt he
shall burn with fire.' "

Judgment for Idolatry

44 The word that came to Jeremiah concerning all the Judeans who lived in the land of
Egypt, at [i]Migdol, at [j]Tahpanhes, at Memphis, and in the land of [k]Pathros, 2 "Thus
says the LORD of hosts, the God of Israel: You have seen all the disaster that I brought upon
Jerusalem and upon all the cities of Judah. Behold, this day [l]they are a desolation, and no one
dwells in them, 3 because of the evil that they committed, [m]provoking me to anger, [n]in that
they went to make offerings [o]and serve other gods that they knew not, neither they, nor you,
nor your fathers. 4 [p]Yet I persistently sent to you all my servants the prophets, saying, 'Oh, do

43:13 obelisks of Heliopolis. Sacred pillars in the temples of Heliopolis, about 5 miles (8 km) northeast of Cairo. Jeremiah takes special pains to highlight the gods' impotence. See 10:1–16.

44:1 Migdol. Probably located near Tahpanhes in the eastern delta. **Tahpanhes**. See 43:7. **Memphis**. The major city of northern Egypt, about 13 miles (21 km) south of today's Cairo. **land of Pathros**. Southern Egypt. This diversity of locations underscores that the message that follows is for **all the Judeans . . . in the land of Egypt**. Clearly many Judean refugees had fled to Egypt.

44:2–3 God has brought **all the disaster** he threatened. **Jerusalem** has become a **desolation** (4:27; 6:8; 9:11; 10:22; 12:11; 22:5; 25:9; etc.). On the wordplay with "disaster" and **evil**, see note on 1:13–14.

44:4–5 This disaster has come because the people rejected God's **servants the prophets** and refused **to turn** from idolatry (7:25; 25:4; 26:5; 29:19; 35:15).

44:7 against yourselves. See 26:19. **infant and child**. These groups suffered greatly in the invasion and siege. See Lam. 2:19–20 and 4:10.

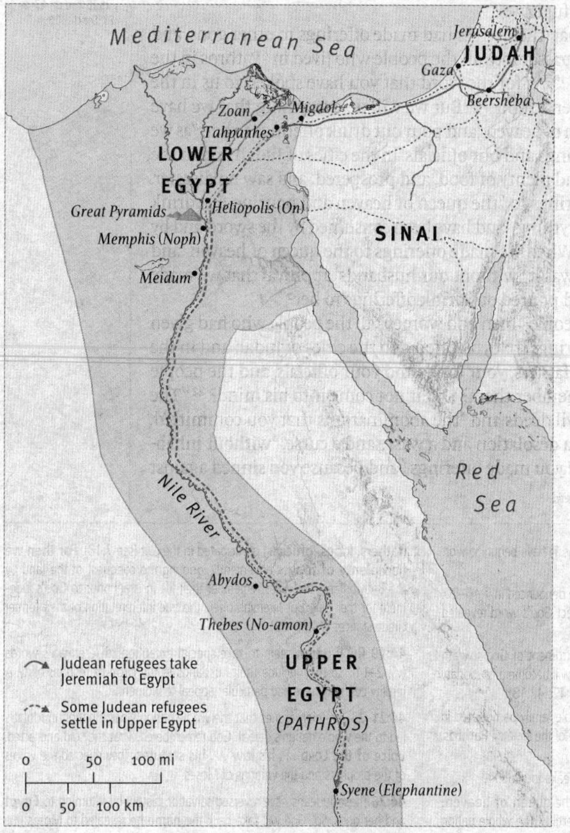

Jeremiah Prophesies against Egypt
c. 586 B.C.
Many of the leading families who had been freed from Ishmael chose to flee to Egypt to escape the Babylonians' wrath over Gedaliah's murder. Though Jeremiah himself warned against this course of action, he apparently was forced to accompany the refugees to Tahpanhes in Egypt, where he delivered a prophecy against Egypt and all the Judeans who had fled there. Archaeological evidence has corroborated the influx of significant populations of Judean refugees during this time as far south as Elephantine (near Syene), at the first cataract of the Nile River.

not do this abomination that I hate!' 5 [q]But they did not listen [q]or incline their ear, to turn
from their evil and make no offerings to other gods. 6 [r]Therefore my wrath and my anger
were poured out and kindled in the cities of Judah and in the streets of Jerusalem, [s]and they
became a waste and a desolation, as at this day. 7 And now thus says the LORD God of hosts,
the God of Israel: Why do you commit this great evil [t]against yourselves, to cut off from
you [u]man and woman, [u]infant and child, from the midst of Judah, leaving you no remnant?
8 [m]Why do you provoke me to anger with the works of your hands, [n]making offerings to
other gods in the land of Egypt where you have come to live, so that you may be cut off and
become [v]a curse and a taunt among all the nations of the earth? 9 Have you forgotten the
evil of your fathers, [w]the evil of the kings of Judah, [x]the evil of their[1] wives, your own evil,
[y]and the evil of your wives, which they committed in the land of Judah and in the streets
of Jerusalem? 10 They have not humbled themselves even to this day, [z]nor have they feared,
nor walked in my law and my statutes that I set before you and before your fathers.

11 "Therefore thus says the LORD of hosts, the God of Israel: [a]Behold, I will set my face
against you for harm, to cut off all Judah. 12 I will take the remnant of Judah who have [b]set
their faces to come to the land of Egypt to live, and they shall all be consumed. [c]In the land
of Egypt they shall fall; by the sword and by famine [c]they shall be consumed. [d]From the
least to the greatest, they shall die by the sword and by famine, [e]and they shall become an
oath, a horror, [v]a curse, and a taunt. 13 [f]I will punish those who dwell in the land of Egypt,
as I have punished Jerusalem, with the sword, with famine, and with pestilence, 14 [g]so that
none of the remnant of Judah who have come to live in the land of Egypt shall escape or
survive [h]or return to the land of Judah, to which they desire to return to dwell there. For
they shall not return, [i]except some fugitives."

15 Then all the men who knew that [j]their wives had made offerings to other gods, and
all the women who stood by, a great assembly, all the people who lived in [k]Pathros in the
land of Egypt, answered Jeremiah: 16 "As for the word that you have spoken to us in the
name of the LORD, [l]we will not listen to you. 17 [m]But we will do everything that we have
vowed, make offerings to [n]the queen of heaven [o]and pour out drink offerings to her, [p]as we
did, both we and our fathers, our kings and our officials, in the cities of Judah and in the
streets of Jerusalem. For then we had plenty of food, and prospered, and saw no disaster.
18 But since we left off making offerings to [n]the queen of heaven and pouring out drink
offerings to her, we have lacked everything [q]and have been consumed by the sword and by
famine." 19 And the women said,[2] "When we made offerings to the queen of heaven [r]and
poured out drink offerings to her, was it [s]without our husbands' approval that we made
cakes for her bearing her image and poured out drink offerings to her?"

20 Then Jeremiah said to all the people, [t]men and women, all the people who had given
him this answer: 21 [u]"As for the offerings that you offered in the cities of Judah and in the
streets of Jerusalem, you and your fathers, your kings and your officials, and the people
of the land, [v]did not the LORD remember them? Did it not come into his mind? 22 [w]The
LORD could no longer bear your evil deeds and [x]the abominations that you committed.
[y]Therefore your land has become [z]a desolation and a waste and a curse, [a]without inhabitant, as it is this day. 23 It is because you made offerings [b]and because you sinned against

[1] Hebrew *his* [2] Compare Syriac; Hebrew lacks *And the women said*

5 [q]See ch. 34:14
6 [r]See ch. 7:20 [s]See ch. 7:34; 9:11
7 [t]Hab. 2:10; [Num. 16:38; Prov. 20:2] [u][ch. 38:23; Lam. 2:11]
8 [m][See ver. 3 above] [n][See ver. 3 above] [v]ch. 42:18; See ch. 18:16
9 [w][ch. 15:4] [x]1 Kgs. 11:1, 8; 15:13; 2 Kgs. 11:1 [y]ver. 15, 25
10 [z][Prov. 28:14]
11 [a]See ch. 21:10
12 [b]ch. 42:15 [c]ch. 42:16 [d]See ch. 6:13 [e]See ch. 18:16 [v][See ver. 8 above]
13 [f]ch. 43:11
14 [g]ch. 42:17 [h][ch. 22:27] [i][ver. 28]
15 [j]ver. 9, 25 [k]See ver. 1
16 [l]ch. 6:16; 42:13
17 [m][Judg. 11:36] [n]ch. 7:18 [o]ch. 19:13 [p][1 Kgs. 11:33; 2 Kgs. 21:3]
18 [n][See ver. 17 above] [q][Lam. 3:22]
19 [r]ch. 7:18 [s][Num. 30:6, 7]
20 [t]ch. 43:6
21 [u]ver. 17; [Ezek. 8:10, 11] [v][Ezek. 21:24]
22 [w]ch. 5:9, 29 [x]Ezek. 8:6 [y]See ch. 7:34 [z]See ch. 18:16 [a]See ch. 4:7
23 [b]See ch. 40:3

44:8 Already the Judeans who have fled to **Egypt** (v. 1) have begun to worship the **gods** that their new nation serves.

44:9–10 The people commit the same acts Jeremiah denounced in 7:16–20. Despite all they have endured, they continue to reject God's word revealed through Moses (9:13–14; 26:4–6).

44:11–14 Babylon will complete its role as an instrument of God's wrath (27:1–15) against Judah's idolatrous **remnant**. They will become a cautionary tale to other peoples (15:4; 18:16; 24:9; 29:18; 34:17; 42:18).

44:15 all the men who knew. See 7:18. The whole family participated in the idolatry. **A great assembly** testifies to the scope of the idolatry. **Pathros**. Southern Egypt; see 44:1.

44:16 This assembly does not care that Jeremiah speaks for God.

44:17–18 These people will continue to worship the **queen of heaven**, which most likely refers to Ishtar, the goddess of fertility. The whole nation (**fathers**, **kings**, **officials**) participated in the cult (see 7:18). **For then we had plenty of food**. Conveniently ignoring the conquest of the land by the Babylonians, the exiles remember their life in Israel prior to God's judgment for their sins. But Jeremiah offers the true interpretation of their former circumstances (44:20–23).

44:19 The **women** seem to take special exception to Jeremiah's words (vv. 2–14), so they include their husbands in the circle of responsibility. A fertility cult may have had particular appeal to women.

44:21–23 Jeremiah argues that the whole nation's participation in idolatry led to the whole nation's defeat. God remembered what they did and acted. **voice of the LORD . . . his law . . . his statutes**. They rejected the voices of the prophets and the writings of Moses.

44:26 These Judeans have reversed salvation history by returning to **Egypt** and her gods. So, God will take back the **name** he revealed to Moses (Ex.

the LORD and did not obey the voice of the LORD or walk in his law and in his statutes and
in his testimonies [c]that this disaster has happened to you, as at this day."
24 Jeremiah said to all the people and all the women, "Hear the word of the LORD, [d]all
you of Judah who are in the land of Egypt. 25 Thus says the LORD of hosts, the God of
Israel: [e]You and your wives have declared with your mouths, and have fulfilled it with
your hands, saying, 'We will surely perform our vows that we have made, [f]to make offerings to the queen of heaven and to pour out drink offerings to her.' Then confirm your
vows and perform your vows! 26 Therefore hear the word of the LORD, [d]all you of Judah
who dwell in the land of Egypt: [g]Behold, I have sworn by my great name, says the LORD,
[h]that my name shall no more be invoked by the mouth of any man of Judah in all the land
of Egypt, [i]saying, 'As the Lord GOD lives.' 27 [j]Behold, I am watching over them for disaster
and not for good. [k]All the men of Judah who are in the land of Egypt shall be consumed
by the sword and by famine, until there is an end of them. 28 [l]And those who escape the
sword shall return from the land of Egypt to the land of Judah, [m]few in number; and all
the remnant of Judah, who came to the land of Egypt to live, [n]shall know whose word
will stand, mine or theirs. 29 This shall be the sign to you, declares the LORD, that I will
punish you in this place, in order that you may know that [o]my words will surely stand
against you for harm: 30 Thus says the LORD, Behold, I will give [p]Pharaoh Hophra king of
Egypt into the hand of his enemies [q]and into the hand of those who seek his life, as I gave
[r]Zedekiah king of Judah into the hand of Nebuchadnezzar king of Babylon, who was his
enemy and sought his life."

Message to Baruch

45 The word that Jeremiah the prophet spoke to [s]Baruch the son of Neriah, [t]when
he wrote these words in a book at the dictation of Jeremiah, [u]in the fourth year
of Jehoiakim the son of Josiah, king of Judah: 2 "Thus says the LORD, the God of Israel,
to you, O Baruch: 3 You said, [v]'Woe is me! For the LORD has added sorrow to my pain. [w]I
am weary with my groaning, [x]and I find no rest.' 4 Thus shall you say to him, Thus says
the LORD: [y]Behold, what I have built I am breaking down, and what I have planted I am
plucking up—that is, the whole land. 5 And [z]do you seek great things for yourself? Seek
them not, for behold, [a]I am bringing disaster upon all flesh, declares the LORD. But I will
give you [b]your life as a prize of war in all places to which you may go."

Judgment on Egypt

46 The word of the LORD that came to Jeremiah the prophet [c]concerning the
nations.
2 About Egypt. [d]Concerning the army of Pharaoh Neco, king of Egypt, which was by the

23 [c][Deut. 31:29]
24 [d]ver. 15; See ch. 43:5-7
25 [e]ver. 16 [f]ver. 17
26 [d][See ver. 24 above] [g]See ch. 22:5 [h][Ezek. 20:39] [i][ch. 4:2]
27 [j]ch. 31:28 [k]ch. 42:16
28 [l][ver. 14; Isa. 27:13] [m]Ezek. 6:8 [n]ver. 17, 25, 26
29 [o]Prov. 19:21
30 [p]ch. 46:17; See Ezek. 29:2-5; 30:21-24 [q]ch. 46:26 [r][ch. 39:5]

Chapter 45

1 [s]See ch. 32:12 [t]See ch. 36:4, 18 [u]ch. 36:1
3 [v][ch. 36:26] [w]Ps. 6:6 [x]Lam. 1:3; 5:5
4 [y]ch. 31:28; [Isa. 5:5]
5 [z][Ps. 131:1, 2; Rom. 12:16] [a][ch. 25:26, 29] [b]ch. 21:9; 39:18

Chapter 46

1 [c][ch. 1:5; 25:13]; See ch. 25:15-26
2 [d]2 Kgs. 23:29; 2 Chr. 35:20

3:14; 6:2–3) and the saving, covenantal presence his name symbolizes. No one can then swear by his (recalled) name and his presence.

44:27 watching over them. To keep God's words concerning the sending **disaster**. See 1:11–12. **sword . . . famine**. See 14:1–15:4 and 44:12–13.

44:28 The **remnant** of the remnant that fled to **Egypt** will be quite **few in number**, but some will return to **Judah**. When this happens they will see that just as they carry out their promises to the "queen of heaven" (vv. 24–25), so will God carry out his words of judgment.

44:29–30 God offers the people a sign: when Egypt's current king dies, they will know that God has spoken truly. **Hophra** ruled Egypt c. 589–570 B.C. He supported **Zedekiah** against Babylon (37:5), so he was probably a special favorite of the Judeans. **hand of his enemies**. Domestic enemies deposed Hophra in 570 B.C. and killed him three years later.

45:1 Baruch. See 32:12; 36:1–32; 43:3. **at the dictation of Jeremiah**. See 36:1–4, 32. **fourth year of Jehoiakim**. About 605 B.C. See 36:1 and Dates of Events in Jeremiah, p. 1376.

45:3 Baruch felt the effects of sharing Jeremiah's ministry and persecution (36:19; 43:3, 6). **the LORD has added**. Baruch felt God was unjust, and he viewed the great events of the day as difficulties for him.

45:4 God informs Baruch that he (God) has lost much more than Baruch has. God has lost all he had **built** and **planted**—Israel's people and **land**.

45:5 Apparently Baruch hoped for great personal success, not pain and suffering. **Seek them not**. Fame and ease are not available. **I am bringing disaster upon all flesh**. Not just Judah, but Egypt (44:29–30; 46:1–28) and many other nations (chs. 47–51). **give you your life**. A great promise in such times. See 1:17–19 and 39:15–18.

46:1–51:64 *God's Judgment on the Nations.* Jeremiah has already declared God's sovereignty over the nations (27:1–15). Here he describes God's coming judgment on Egypt (ch. 46), Philistia (ch. 47), Moab (ch. 48), Ammon (49:1–6), Edom (49:7–22), Damascus (49:23–33), the ends of the earth (49:34–39), and Babylon (chs. 50–51).

46:1–28 *God Will Judge Egypt.* This chapter declares God's displeasure with Egypt, Israel's old foe and recent ally. Jeremiah claims that God will put Egypt to shame (vv. 1–12) and judge Egypt's gods and kings (vv. 13–26), then notes that God is with Israel (vv. 27–28).

46:1 The Septuagint places chs. 46–51 (in slightly different order) after 25:13a. Jeremiah 46:1 serves as a superscription for chs. 46–51. The **word of the LORD . . . concerning the nations**. God is not the God of the Jews only, but is Lord of all the earth. In chs. 46–51 his words show that he holds all nations and all people accountable before him (see notes on Mark 6:18; Acts 17:31; Rom. 2:14–16).

46:2 At Carchemish, Babylon defeated **Egypt**, thus taking full control of the region. **fourth year of Jehoiakim**. 605 B.C. (25:1; 36:1; 45:1).

river Euphrates at Carchemish and which Nebuchadnezzar king of Babylon defeated in
[e]the fourth year of Jehoiakim the son of Josiah, king of Judah:

3 [f]"Prepare buckler and shield,
and advance for battle!
4 [g]Harness the horses;
mount, O horsemen!
Take your stations with your helmets,
[f]polish your spears,
put on your armor!
5 Why have I seen it?
They are dismayed
and have turned backward.
Their [h]warriors are beaten down
and have fled in haste;
[i]they look not back—
[j]terror on every side!
declares the LORD.
6 "The swift cannot flee away,
nor the warrior escape;
[d]in the north by the river Euphrates
[k]they have stumbled and fallen.

7 "Who is this, [l]rising like the Nile,
like rivers [m]whose waters surge?
8 Egypt rises like the Nile,
like rivers [m]whose waters surge.
He said, 'I will rise, I will cover the earth,
I will destroy cities and their inhabitants.'
9 [n]Advance, O horses,
and rage, O chariots!
Let the warriors go out:
men of Cush and [o]Put who handle the shield,
[p]men of Lud, skilled in handling the bow.
10 [q]That day is the day of the Lord GOD of hosts,
[r]a day of vengeance,
[s]to avenge himself on his foes.
[t]The sword shall devour and be sated
and drink its fill of their blood.
For the Lord GOD of hosts holds [u]a sacrifice
[v]in the north country [w]by the river Euphrates.
11 [x]Go up to Gilead, and take [x]balm,
O virgin daughter of Egypt!

2 [e]ch. 25:1; 36:1; 45:1
3 [f][ch. 51:11]
4 [g][Nah. 3:2] [f][See ver. 3 above]
5 [h][2 Sam. 1:19, 25] [i]ver. 21; ch. 47:3 [j]See ch. 6:25
6 [d][See ver. 2 above] [k][Dan. 11:19]
7 [l][ch. 47:2; Isa. 8:7, 8; Dan. 11:22] [m][Ezek. 32:2]
8 [m][See ver. 7 above]
9 [n]Nah. 3:2; [Judg. 5:22] [o]Ezek. 27:10 [p]Isa. 66:19
10 [q]Isa. 13:9; Joel 1:15 [r]ch. 50:15 [s]Isa. 1:24 [t][ver. 14; Isa. 34:5] [u][Isa. 34:6] [v]ver. 6 [w]ver. 2
11 [x][ch. 8:22]

Jehoiakim was placed in power by Egypt (2 Kings 23:34). When Babylon defeated Egypt, Jehoiakim switched sides, yet only after **Nebuchadnezzar** attacked Judah (2 Kings 24:1; Dan. 1:1).

46:3 The **buckler** was a small shield held in the left hand to protect the head; the **shield** refers to a large shield held in the right hand to protect the full body. The infantry used these implements.

46:4 The charioteers wore **helmets** and body **armor** and used **spears**.

46:5 Egypt's infantry and chariots flee in total disarray. **terror on every side**. A phrase used also to describe the invader from the north (6:25), as a name for Pashhur (20:3), and as a threat by Jeremiah's enemies (20:10). In this instance God brings the terror.

46:7–8 The **Nile** rises and falls throughout the year. Jeremiah compares Egypt's armies to flood **waters** bent on covering the **earth** (Isa. 8:7–8; Amos 8:8).

46:9 Egypt's infantry and chariots (vv. 3–4) **advance** against Babylon. **Cush**. Ethiopia, in the Nile region south of Egypt. **Put**. Perhaps on the north coast of Africa (Libya). **Lud**. Perhaps Lydia, in Asia Minor. Soldiers from these areas were probably mercenaries in Egypt's army.

46:10 day of the Lord. The day that **GOD** judges Egypt by sending Babylonian swords. See The Day of the Lord in the Prophets, p. 1668. **holds a sacrifice**. Egypt's army is the sacrifice (Isa. 34:1–7; Zeph. 1:7–9).

46:11 Gilead. On the eastern side of the Jordan River. **balm**. Soothing substance placed in wounds (8:22; Gen. 37:25). **Virgin daughter of Egypt** refers to the whole population of Egypt and recalls a similar term of endearment used of Israel (Jer. 31:4, 21; see note on 4:31). **many medicines**. A metaphor for strategy. **no healing**. A metaphor for aid from another country.

46:12 Egypt's **shame** has international proportions. Judah felt the shame of loss as well (2:36; 3:25; 23:40).

11[y][Ezek. 30:21]
12[z]ver. 6
13[a]ch. 43:10, 11; 44:30; [Isa. 19:4; Ezek. 29:10]
14[b]See ch. 44:1 [c][ver. 3, 4] [d][ver. 10]
16[f]Lev. 26:37 [g]ch. 50:16
17[h][Isa. 30:7]
18[i]See ch. 4:2 [j]ch. 48:15; 51:57; Isa. 47:4; 48:2 [k]Judg. 4:6 [l]1 Kgs. 18:42, 44
19[m][Ezek. 12:3] [n][ch. 48:18] [o]See ch. 44:1 [p]See ch. 4:7
20[q][Hos. 10:11] [r]ver. 6, 10, 24; See ch. 1:13
21[s]Amos 6:4; Mal. 4:2 [t]ch. 50:27
22[u][Isa. 29:4]

In vain you have used many medicines;
[y]there is no healing for you.
12 The nations have heard of your shame,
and the earth is full of your cry;
[z]for warrior has stumbled against warrior;
they have both fallen together."

13 The word that the LORD spoke to Jeremiah the prophet about the coming of
[a]Nebuchadnezzar king of Babylon to strike the land of Egypt:

14 "Declare in Egypt, and proclaim in [b]Migdol;
proclaim in [b]Memphis and [b]Tahpanhes;
say, [c]'Stand ready and be prepared,
for [d]the sword shall devour around you.'
15 Why are your mighty ones face down?
They do not stand[1]
because the LORD thrust them down.
16 He made many stumble, [f]and they fell,
and they said one to another,
'Arise, and let us go back to our own people
and to the land of our birth,
[g]because of the sword of the oppressor.'
17 Call the name of [h]Pharaoh, king of Egypt,
'Noisy one who lets the hour go by.'

18 [i]"As I live, declares the King,
[j]whose name is the LORD of hosts,
like [k]Tabor among the mountains
and like [l]Carmel by the sea, shall one come.
19 [m]Prepare yourselves baggage for exile,
O [n]inhabitants of Egypt!
For [o]Memphis shall become a waste,
a ruin, [p]without inhabitant.

20 "A beautiful [q]heifer is Egypt,
but a biting fly [r]from the north has come upon her.
21 Even her hired soldiers in her midst
are like [s]fattened calves;
yes, they have turned and fled together;
they did not stand,
for the day of their calamity has come upon them,
[t]the time of their punishment.

22 "She makes [u]a sound like a serpent gliding away;
for her enemies march in force

[1] Hebrew *He does not stand*

46:13 Nebuchadnezzar advanced against **Egypt** after the battle of Carchemish. He also campaigned there c. 570–567 B.C.

46:14 Migdol . . . Memphis . . . Tahpanhes. See 44:1. These were places Judeans had fled to, and God said Babylon would punish them (44:1–14).

46:15–16 God causes Egypt's defeat. Babylon remains God's instrument for punishing idolatry (27:1–15).

46:17 The Egyptian name of **Pharaoh** Hophra (44:30) was "Haabire" (Gk. *Apries*). The Hebrew for **lets . . . go by** (*he'ebir*) sounds like Haabire. The pun may refer to Egypt's poor response to Judah's hour of need in 587 B.C. (37:5–6).

46:18 the King. God rules the heavens and earth (Ps. 103:19). **hosts**. Armies. **Tabor**. Isolated mountain in the plain of Jezreel in northern Israel. **Carmel**. A famous mountain on the west coast of Israel near the Mediterranean Sea (1 Kings 18:19–40). Nebuchadnezzar shall tower over Egypt like these two **mountains**.

46:19 Memphis was the capital of **Egypt**. It will suffer Jerusalem's fate (4:7–8).

46:20 biting fly. Perhaps the gadfly, a metaphor for Babylon, who will come **from the north** and "sting" **Egypt** in battle.

46:21 Egypt's mercenary **soldiers** were **like fattened calves** ready for slaughter. The day of the Lord is the **day of their calamity**.

46:22–23 Like a snake exposed, Egypt hisses at Babylon and crawls into the **forest**. Babylon's soldiers **are more numerous than locusts**, so they simply **cut down** the whole forest (Isa. 10:34).

and come against her with axes
[v]like those who fell trees.
23 [v]They shall cut down her forest,
declares the LORD,
though it is impenetrable,
because [w]they are more numerous than locusts;
they are without number.
24 The daughter of Egypt shall be put to shame;
she shall be delivered into the hand of [r]a people from the north."

25 The LORD of hosts, the God of Israel, said: "Behold, I am bringing punishment upon
[x]Amon of [y]Thebes, and Pharaoh and Egypt [z]and her gods and her kings, upon Pharaoh
and those who trust in him. 26 [a]I will deliver them into the hand of those who seek their
life, into the hand of Nebuchadnezzar king of Babylon and his officers. [b]Afterward Egypt
shall be inhabited [c]as in the days of old, declares the LORD.

27 [d]"But fear not, O Jacob my servant,
nor be dismayed, O Israel,
for behold, I will save you from far away,
and your offspring from the land of their captivity.
Jacob shall return and have quiet and ease,
and none shall make him afraid.
28 [d]Fear not, O Jacob my servant,
declares the LORD,
for I am with you.
I will make a full end of all the nations
to which I have driven you,
but of you I will not make a full end.
[e]I will discipline you in just measure,
and I will by no means leave you unpunished."

Judgment on the Philistines

47 The word of the LORD that came to Jeremiah the prophet [f]concerning the Philistines, before Pharaoh struck down [g]Gaza.

2 "Thus says the LORD:
[h]Behold, waters are rising [i]out of the north,
[h]and shall become an overflowing torrent;
they shall overflow [j]the land and all that fills it,
the city and those who dwell in it.
Men shall cry out,
and every inhabitant of the land shall wail.
3 At the noise of the stamping of the hoofs of his stallions,
[l]at the rushing of his chariots, at the rumbling of their wheels,
the fathers [m]look not back to their children,
so feeble are their hands,
4 because of the day that is coming to destroy
all [f]the Philistines,
to cut off from [n]Tyre and Sidon
every helper that remains.

22 [v][Isa. 10:34; 14:8]
23 [v][See ver. 22 above] [w][Judg. 6:5; 7:12]
24 [r][See ver. 20 above]
25 [x][Nah. 3:8] [y]Ezek. 30:14, 15, 16 [z]See ch. 43:12
26 [a]ch. 44:30; Ezek. 30:4; 32:11 [b]Ezek. 29:13, 14; See Isa. 19:22-25 [c]Isa. 51:9
27 [d]See ch. 30:10, 11; Isa. 43:5
28 [d][See ver. 27 above] [e]ch. 10:24

Chapter 47

1 [f]ch. 25:20; Ezek. 25:15, 16; Zeph. 2:5 [g]Amos 1:6, 7; Zeph. 2:4
2 [h][ch. 46:7, 8; Isa. 8:7] [i]See ch. 1:13 [j][ch. 8:16]
3 [l]Nah. 3:2 [m]ch. 46:5
4 [f][See ver. 1 above] [n]Isa. 23:1, 2; Joel 3:4; See ch. 25:22

46:24 daughter of Egypt. See v. 11. **put to shame**. See v. 12. **people from the north**. Babylon. See v. 20.

46:25 Israel's **God** commands armies (**hosts**), and he sends these armies against **Egypt and her gods and her kings. Amon** was the chief god of **Thebes**, the capital of Upper (southern) Egypt. Babylon's conquest will include Egypt's southern regions.

46:26 Despite the devastation, **Egypt** will endure. God will leave Egypt with a remnant, perhaps one that will turn to him (Isa. 19:19–25).

46:27–28 fear not. See 30:10–11 and Isa. 41:8–10. This promise of renewal includes **Israel**, not just Judah.

47:1–7 *God Will Judge Philistia.* Philistia was one of Israel's most ancient foes (Josh. 13:2–3; Judg. 3:31; 13:1). This brief chapter asserts that God will destroy the Philistines (Jer. 47:1–4) at the hands of a foe from the north, for his sword cannot rest until then (vv. 5–7). Evidence of such a conflagration appears in the excavations of Ashkelon. Remains from the destruction of the

4[o]Amos 1:8 [p]Gen. 10:14; Amos 9:7
5[q][ch. 48:37; Isa. 3:24] [r]ch. 25:20; [Judg. 1:18] [s][ch. 48:37]
6[t]Deut. 32:41; See Ezek. 21:3-5
7[u][Ezek. 14:17] [v]ch. 25:20; [Judg. 1:18] [w]Mic. 6:9
Chapter 48
1[x]ch. 25:21; 2 Kgs. 24:2; See Isa. 15–16; Ezek. 25:8-11; Amos 2:1-3; Zeph. 2:8, 9 [y]ver. 22; Num. 32:3 [z]ver. 23; Num. 32:37; Josh. 13:19; Ezek. 25:9

For the LORD is destroying the Philistines,
[o]the remnant of the coastland of [p]Caphtor.
5 [q]Baldness has come upon Gaza;
[r]Ashkelon has perished.
O remnant of their valley,
[s]how long will you gash yourselves?
6 [t]Ah, sword of the LORD!
How long till you are quiet?
Put yourself into your scabbard;
rest and be still!
7 How can it[1] be quiet
[u]when the LORD has given it a charge?
Against [v]Ashkelon and against the seashore
[w]he has appointed it."

Judgment on Moab

48 [x]Concerning Moab.
Thus says the LORD of hosts, the God of Israel:
"Woe to [y]Nebo, for it is laid waste!
[z]Kiriathaim is put to shame, it is taken;

[1] Septuagint, Vulgate; Hebrew *you*

city by Nebuchadnezzar in 604 B.C. include a layer with much smashed pottery and a male skeleton with a crushed skull.

47:1 before Pharaoh struck down Gaza. It is uncertain when this event occurred. Nebuchadnezzar destroyed Ashkelon, one of Philistia's major cities (alongside Gaza, Ekron, Gath, and Ashdod), in 604 B.C. Philistia sent no envoy to the multinational meeting (27:3) held in Jerusalem early in Zedekiah's reign (597–586 B.C.), so Gaza's defeat may have come prior to that time.

47:2 Babylon comes against Gaza like flood **waters** that **overflow the land and all that fills it**. Isaiah 8:8 and 28:17 use similar imagery to describe Assyria's invasion of Judah.

47:3 The swiftness and **noise** of the approaching army will leave **fathers** helpless to aid their **children** (46:5).

47:4 because of the day. This day of loss is a day of God's judgment (46:10). **Tyre and Sidon**. These Phoenician cities were likely Gaza's allies. Coastal cities were often the last places to fall in land-dominated wars. **coastland of Caphtor**. The original home of the Philistines (Amos 9:7). Perhaps Crete and the Aegean islands. The Philistines were well settled in Palestine by the late thirteenth century B.C.

47:5 Baldness. This means either that Gaza's citizens shaved their heads as part of a mourning ritual (cf. Isa. 22:12; Amos 8:10) or that the land was shaved clean of inhabitants and cities. **Ashkelon has perished**. See Jer. 47:1. **gash yourselves**. Either as a sign of mourning (41:5) or when praying to one's gods (1 Kings 18:28).

47:6–7 God's punishing **sword** (12:12) will not rest until it completes its work **against Ashkelon** (47:1) and the **seashore**.

48:1–47 *God Will Judge Moab.* Israel's dealings with Moab date back even farther than its relationship with Philistia. Moab's origins in Abraham's era (c. 2000 B.C.) began with the tawdry episode of Lot and his daughters (Gen. 19:30–38). Moab opposed Israel in Moses' era (Numbers 22–25), served Israel in David's era (2 Sam. 8:2), and plotted with Judah against Babylon in Zedekiah's era (Jer. 27:3). Here Jeremiah claims God will judge Moab's arrogance and idolatry (48:1–10), make Moab ashamed of its god (vv. 11–20), silence Moab's boasts (vv. 21–44), and someday restore Moab (vv. 45–47).

48:1 The location of **Nebo** is uncertain; perhaps it was near Mount Nebo, 12 miles (19 km) east of the northernmost point of the Dead Sea. **Kiriathaim** was probably near Nebo. **fortress**. One or both of the cities were citadels that could house refugees from the countryside. When such places fell, defeat was total.

Jeremiah Prophesies against Moab

In a series of prophetic condemnations of nations surrounding Judah, Jeremiah foretold of the doom of Moab and its cities. Moab had often acted as an enemy of Judah, from the time God's people were preparing to enter the Promised Land (Numbers 22–24) to the time the Moabites formed a coalition with the Ammonites and the Meunites against Judah (2 Chron. 20:1–29). Along with the Ammonites, Moabites were also specifically forbidden from entering the assembly of the Lord (Deut. 23:3).

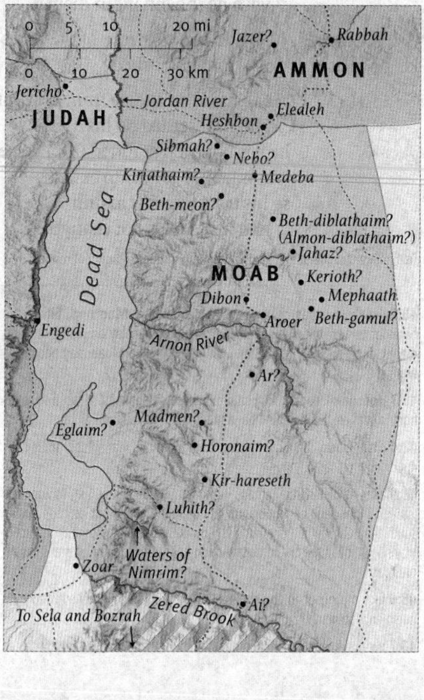

the fortress is put to shame [a]and broken down;
2 the renown of Moab is no more.
In [b]Heshbon they planned disaster against her:
'Come, let us cut her off [c]from being a nation!'
You also, O [d]Madmen, shall be brought to silence;
the sword shall pursue you.

3 "A voice! A cry from [e]Horonaim,
'Desolation and great destruction!'
4 Moab is destroyed;
her little ones have made a cry.
5 [e]For at the ascent of Luhith
they go up weeping;[1]
for [e]at the descent of Horonaim
they have heard the distressed cry[2] of destruction.
6 Flee! Save yourselves!
You will be like [f]a juniper in the desert!
7 For, [g]because you trusted in your works and your treasures,
you also shall be taken;
and [h]Chemosh [i]shall go into exile
with [j]his priests and his officials.
8 [k]The destroyer shall come upon every city,
and no city shall escape;
the valley shall perish,
and [l]the plain shall be destroyed,
as the LORD has spoken.
9 "Give wings to Moab,
for she would fly away;
her cities shall become a desolation,
with no inhabitant in them.

10 [m]"Cursed is he who does [n]the work of the LORD with slackness, and cursed is he who keeps back his sword from bloodshed.

11 "Moab has been at ease from his youth
and has [o]settled on his dregs;
he has not been emptied from vessel to vessel,
nor has he gone into exile;
so his taste remains in him,
and his scent is not changed.

[1] Hebrew *weeping goes up with weeping* [2] Septuagint (compare Isaiah 15:5) *heard the cry*

1 [a]ver. 20, 39
2 [b]ver. 34, 45; ch. 49:3; Num. 32:37; Isa. 15:4 [c][ch. 31:36] [d][Isa. 10:31]
3 [e]Isa. 15:5; [ver. 34]
5 [e][See ver. 3 above]
6 [f]ch. 17:6
7 [g]ch. 49:4 [h]Num. 21:29 [i][Isa. 46:2] [j]ch. 49:3
8 [k]ch. 6:26 [l]ver. 21; Josh. 13:9, 17, 21; [Deut. 3:10]
10 [m]Judg. 5:23; [1 Sam. 15:3, 9; 1 Kgs. 20:42] [n][1 Cor. 15:58]
11 [o]Zeph. 1:12

48:2 Heshbon was northeast of Mount Nebo. **Madmen**. Either the name of an unknown city or a play on words. If a play on words, it could mean "dung pit" (Isa. 25:10 and ESV footnote), so Moab may become a dung pit.

48:3 Horonaim. Location uncertain, perhaps in southwest Moab. If so, cities from north (vv. 1–2) to south have suffered in the invasion.

48:4 little ones. The most helpless of all victims of war (cf. Isa. 16:2; Lam. 4:4).

48:5 ascent of Luhith. Perhaps in southern Moab on the way to Zoar. See Isa. 15:5. **descent of Horonaim**. Location unknown, but perhaps farther south than Luhith. See Isa. 15:5. The contrast between ascent and descent may simply mean the **cry of destruction** has reached the heights and depths of Moab.

48:6 like a juniper in the desert. A short shrub that barely survived in its harsh environment (17:6).

48:7 works, treasures. Moab once raised vast numbers of sheep, boasted fierce warriors (2 Kings 3), and was likely proud of building a nation in a desert region. **Chemosh** was Moab's national deity. Human sacrifice was part of Moab's rituals for Chemosh (2 Kings 3:27). **shall go into exile**. Images of a defeated nation's gods were often taken to the temples of the victorious nation (1 Sam. 5:1–12; Isa. 46:1–2; Amos 5:25–27).

48:8 destroyer. Babylon. Nebuchadnezzar defeated Moab c. 582 B.C. Every **city** and region, **valley** or **plain** was devastated.

48:9 she would fly away. Moab's only escape route is the sky, so she has no hope of eluding Babylon. See Isa. 15:5–9 and 16:6–12 for similar imagery of a defeat **Moab** suffered at Assyria's hand c. 713–711 B.C.

48:10 Babylon will do its work as God's instrument of judgment (27:1–15) with urgency, not laziness.

48:11 Moab has survived many previous invasions (v. 9). Thus, Moab has become complacent and **settled on his dregs** (Zeph. 1:12), like wine allowed to age. Moab produced wine (Isa. 16:8–11), so the metaphor is apt.

13[p][Num. 21:29; Isa. 16:14] [q][Hos. 10:6] [r][1 Kgs. 12:29]
15[s]ver. 8, 18, 20; Isa. 15:1 [t]ch. 50:27 [u]See ch. 46:18
17[v][Isa. 15:4, 5; 16:7] [w][Isa. 9:4; 14:5]
18[x][Isa. 47:1] [y]Num. 21:30; Isa. 15:2
19[z][1 Sam. 4:13, 16; Nah. 2:1] [a]Deut. 2:36; Josh. 13:9
20[v][See ver. 17 above] [b]Isa. 16:2 [s][See ver. 15 above]
21[c]ver. 8; Num. 21:23 [d]Josh. 13:18
22[y][See ver. 18 above] [e]Num. 33:46; Isa. 15:2
23[f]See ver. 1 [g][Josh. 13:17; 1 Chr. 5:8]
24[h]Amos 2:2 [i]ch. 49:13, 22; Isa. 63:1
25[j][Ps. 75:10] [k][Ezek. 30:21]
26[l]ch. 25:27; 51:39; Isa. 19:14 [m]ver. 42 [n]ver. 39
27[o]Zeph. 2:8; [Ezek. 25:8] [p][ch. 2:26] [q]Ps. 64:8; Lam. 2:15; Matt. 27:39
28[r]ver. 9

12 "Therefore, behold, the days are coming, declares the LORD, when I shall send to him
pourers who will pour him, and empty his vessels and break his[1] jars in pieces. **13** Then
[p]Moab shall be ashamed of Chemosh, as [q]the house of Israel was ashamed of [r]Bethel,
their confidence.

14 "How do you say, 'We are heroes
and mighty men of war'?
15 The destroyer of [s]Moab and his cities has come up,
and the choicest of his young men have [t]gone down to slaughter,
declares [u]the King, [u]whose name is the LORD of hosts.
16 The calamity of Moab is near at hand,
and his affliction hastens swiftly.
17 [v]Grieve for him, all you who are around him,
and all who know his name;
say, [w]'How the mighty scepter is broken,
the glorious staff.'

18 [x]"Come down from your glory,
and sit on the parched ground,
O inhabitant of [y]Dibon!
For the destroyer of Moab has come up against you;
he has destroyed your strongholds.
19 [z]Stand by the way [z]and watch,
O inhabitant of [a]Aroer!
Ask him who flees and her who escapes;
say, 'What has happened?'
20 Moab is put to shame, for it is broken;
[v]wail and cry!
Tell it beside [b]the Arnon,
that [s]Moab is laid waste.

21 "Judgment has come upon [c]the tableland, upon Holon, and [d]Jahzah, and Mephaath,
22 and [y]Dibon, and [e]Nebo, and Beth-diblathaim, **23** and [f]Kiriathaim, and Beth-gamul, and
[g]Beth-meon, **24** and [h]Kerioth, and [i]Bozrah, and all the cities of the land of Moab, far and
near. **25** [j]The horn of Moab is cut off, and [k]his arm is broken, declares the LORD.
26 [l]"Make him drunk, [m]because he magnified himself against the LORD, so that Moab
shall [l]wallow in his vomit, [n]and he too shall be held in derision. **27** [o]Was not Israel a derision to you? [p]Was he found among thieves, that whenever you spoke of him [q]you wagged
your head?

28 [r]"Leave the cities, and dwell in the rock,
O inhabitants of Moab!

[1] Septuagint, Aquila; Hebrew *their*

48:12 pour him . . . break his jars. Babylon will empty Moab like one pours wine from a jar; it will smash Moab like one smashes and disposes of old jars (13:12–14; 19:1–15).

48:13 ashamed of Chemosh. Because this god cannot save (10:1–25; Isa. 15:2; 16:12). **ashamed of Bethel**. See Hos. 10:6. At Bethel, Jeroboam I established one of his chief high places in his syncretistic religion (1 Kings 12:25–33). Worship there was part of the reason God judged **Israel** (2 Kings 17:9).

48:15 See 46:18. The **LORD** is the **King** of all nations. Even Babylon must obey him (cf. 27:1–15).

48:16 near at hand. See v. 8. **Moab** had only a few years to change its ways.

48:17 all you who are around him. Neighboring nations that once plotted with Moab against Babylon (27:3). **scepter**. A symbol of royal power (cf. Gen. 49:10). **staff**. A symbol of the king's rule as shepherd of his people (cf. Ps. 23:4).

48:19 Aroer. About 3 miles (4.8 km) southeast of Dibon. Its citizens stand beside the road as Dibon's people flee from the north.

48:20 The fleeing ones explain that Moab **is broken** (v. 12). The **Arnon** is a river just south of Aroer.

48:21–24 All Moab's cities are lost in this **judgment** time. **the tableland**. The region north of the Arnon as far as Heshbon (v. 8). **Holon**. Location uncertain. **Jahzah**. Perhaps near **Dibon** (v. 18). **Mephaath**. Location uncertain. **Nebo**. See v. 1. **Beth-diblathaim**. Location uncertain. **Kiriathaim**. See v. 1. **Beth-gamul**. Perhaps 8 miles (13 km) east of Dibon. **Beth-meon**. 5 miles (8 km) southwest of Medeba. **Kerioth**. See Amos 2:2. **Bozrah**. Location uncertain.

48:25 horn . . . arm. Symbols of strength (Deut. 11:2; Ps. 18:2; 75:5).

48:26 drunk. By drinking the cup of God's wrath (25:15–26). **wallow in his vomit**. See 25:27.

48:27 derision. See Zeph. 2:8–11. **wagged your head**. See Lam. 2:15.

48:28 God counsels **Moab** to seek refuge in the mountains, as David once did (1 Sam. 24:1–3).

Be [s]like the dove that nests
in the sides of the mouth of a gorge.
29 [t]We have heard of the pride of Moab—
he is very proud—
of his loftiness, his pride, and his arrogance,
and the haughtiness of his heart.
30 I know his insolence, declares the LORD;
[u]his boasts are false,
his deeds are false.
31 [v]Therefore I wail for Moab;
I cry out for all Moab;
for the men of [w]Kir-hareseth I mourn.
32 More than for [x]Jazer I weep for you,
[y]O vine of [z]Sibmah!
[a]Your branches passed over the sea,
reached to the Sea of [x]Jazer;
on your summer fruits and your grapes
the destroyer has fallen.
33 [b]Gladness and joy have been taken away
from the fruitful land of Moab;
I have made the wine cease from the winepresses;
no one treads them with shouts of joy;
the shouting is not the shout of joy.

34 [c]"From the outcry at Heshbon even to Elealeh, as far as Jahaz they utter their voice,
from Zoar to [d]Horonaim and Eglath-shelishiyah. For the waters of Nimrim also have
become desolate. 35 And I will bring to an end in Moab, declares the LORD, him who offers
sacrifice in [e]the high place and makes offerings to his god. 36 Therefore my heart moans for
Moab like a flute, and my heart moans like a flute for the men of [f]Kir-hareseth. [g]Therefore
the riches they gained have perished.

37 [h]"For every head is shaved and every beard cut off. [i]On all the hands are gashes, and
[j]around the waist is sackcloth. 38 On all the housetops of Moab and in the squares there
is nothing but lamentation, for I have broken Moab like [k]a vessel for which no one cares,
declares the LORD. 39 How it is broken! How they wail! [l]How Moab has turned his back in
shame! So Moab [m]has become a derision and a horror to all that are around him."

40 For thus says the LORD:
"Behold, [n]one shall fly swiftly like an eagle
[o]and spread his wings against Moab;
41 [p]the cities shall be taken
and the strongholds seized.
[q]The heart of the warriors of Moab shall be in that day
like the heart of [r]a woman in her birth pains;

28 [s]Ps. 55:6, 7; Song 2:14
29 [t]Isa. 16:6
30 [u][ch. 50:36]
31 [v]Isa. 15:5; 16:7, 11 [w][2 Kgs. 3:25]
32 [x]Num. 21:32 [y]Isa. 16:8, 9 [z]Josh. 13:19 [a][Ps. 80:11]
33 [b]Isa. 16:10
34 [c]See Isa. 15:4-6 [d]ver. 3
35 [e][Isa. 15:2; 16:12; Ezek. 20:29]
36 [f]See ver. 31 [g]Isa. 15:7
37 [h]Isa. 15:2, 3 [i][ch. 47:5] [j]ch. 49:3; Lam. 2:10; See ch. 4:8
38 [k][ch. 22:28]
39 [l][ver. 6] [m]ver. 26
40 [n]ch. 49:22; [Deut. 28:49; Ezek. 17:3] [o][Isa. 8:8]
41 [p]ver. 24 [q][Isa. 13:7, 8] [r]See ch. 6:24

48:29–30 the pride of Moab. See Isa. 16:6.

48:31 This verse is close in content to Isa. 16:7, 11. God mourns over the necessity of judging **Moab**. **Kir-hareseth**. Probably 17 miles (27 km) south of the Arnon River and 10 miles (16 km) east of the Dead Sea.

48:32 Jazer. Probably 10 miles (16 km) north of Heshbon (Num. 21:32). **Sibmah**. Probably 3 miles (4.8 km) southwest of Heshbon. This area was covered with vineyards.

48:33 The **shout of joy** heard when new wine is made will be replaced by warriors' **shouts** (25:30–31). See Isa. 16:8–10.

48:34 Heshbon. See v. 2. **Elealeh**. Two miles (3.2 km) north of Heshbon. **Jahaz**. Located in southwest Moab. **Zoar**. At the south end of the Dead Sea (Gen. 14:2; 19:22). **Horonaim**. See Jer. 48:5. **Eglath-shelishiyah**. Location unknown. **waters of Nimrim**. Either 10 miles (16 km) from the southern end of the Dead Sea or 8 miles (13 km) from its northern end.

48:35 God's judgment **will bring** Moab's idolatry **to an end** (cf. Isa. 15:2, 5).

48:36 my heart moans. God himself mourns that Moab's people will lose the possessions they spent a lifetime collecting (Isa. 15:7; 16:11). Though God in his justice brings righteous judgment against sinners and takes delight in the purity and holiness of his judgment, he also feels sorrow at the destruction that the judgment brings upon human beings created in his image (cf. Ezek. 18:32; 33:11; Matt. 23:37; Luke 19:41).

48:37 Moab will take on every conceivable indication of mourning. See 16:6 and 47:5.

48:38 broken Moab like a vessel. See 19:11 and 48:11–12.

48:40 spread his wings against. Babylon will swoop down on Moab like a bird capturing prey (cf. 49:22; Lam. 4:19; Ezek. 17:3–8).

48:41 Moab will be as capable of stopping the invasion as a **woman** giving birth is able to stop **birth pains** (4:31; 6:24; Isa. 13:7–8).

42 Moab shall be [s]destroyed and be no longer a people,
because [t]he magnified himself against the LORD.
43 [u]Terror, pit, and snare
are before you, O inhabitant of Moab!
declares the LORD.
44 He who flees from the terror
shall fall into the pit,
and he who climbs out of the pit
shall be caught in the snare.
[v]For I will bring these things upon Moab,
the year of their punishment,
declares the LORD.

45 "In the shadow of Heshbon
fugitives stop without strength,
for fire came out from Heshbon,
flame from the house of Sihon;
it has destroyed [w]the forehead of Moab,
the crown of [w]the sons of tumult.
46 [x]Woe to you, O Moab!
The people of [y]Chemosh are undone,
for your sons have been taken captive,
and your daughters into captivity.
47 [z]Yet I will restore the fortunes of Moab
in the latter days, declares the LORD."
Thus far is the judgment on Moab.

Judgment on Ammon

49 [a]Concerning the Ammonites.
Thus says the LORD:

"Has Israel no sons?
Has he no heir?
Why then has [b]Milcom [c]dispossessed Gad,
and his people settled in its cities?
2 Therefore, behold, the days are coming,
declares the LORD,
when I will cause [d]the battle cry to be heard
against [e]Rabbah of the Ammonites;
it shall become a desolate [f]mound,
and its villages shall be burned with fire;
then Israel shall dispossess those who dispossessed him,
says the LORD.

42 [s][Isa. 7:8] [t]ver. 26
43 [u]Isa. 24:17, 18; Lam. 3:47
44 [v][ch. 11:23]
45 [w]Num. 24:17
46 [x]See ver. 1 [y]ver. 13
47 [z][ch. 46:27; 49:39]

Chapter 49

1 [a]ch. 25:21; [Ezek. 21:28; 25:2] [b][1 Kgs. 11:5, 33; 2 Kgs. 23:13] [c][Amos 1:13]
2 [d]ch. 4:19 [e]Ezek. 21:20; 25:5; Amos 1:14 [f]ch. 30:18

48:42 Moab . . . magnified itself **against the LORD** by failing to accept God's word concerning Babylon's role as a divine instrument of judgment. See 27:1–15.

48:43–44 Moab will be hunted down and captured like animals. See Isa. 24:17–18; Lam. 3:52–55; Amos 5:18–20.

48:45 Heshbon. See v. 2. **fugitives stop without strength**. These people have fled only as far as the northern regions of Moab. **fire came out from Heshbon**. The city has been torched. **house of Sihon**. See Num. 21:21. **forehead . . . crown**. Probably a reference to Moab's northern regions.

48:46 This verse echoes Num. 21:29, which celebrates Israel's victory over the Amorites and Moabites before Israel entered Canaan.

48:47 God makes the same promise of restoration to **Moab** as he did to Judah in 29:14. **The latter days** most likely refers to a time when Moabites will take refuge in the Messiah (cf. 49:6, 39; Isa. 16:3–5).

49:1–39 *God Will Judge Many Nations.* God will judge Ammon (vv. 1–6), Edom (vv. 7–22), Damascus (vv. 23–33), and the ends of the earth (vv. 34–39).

49:1 Ammonites. People living north of Moab. Their capital was Rabbah, present-day Amman. During Jehoiakim's reign they raided Judah (2 Kings 24:2), and they conspired with Judah and others against Babylon in Zedekiah's reign (Jer. 27:3). **Milcom**. Or Molech, Ammon's chief god (1 Kings 11:5, 7). Milcom means "their king." **dispossessed Gad**. In the aftermath of the Assyrian invasion of 734–732 B.C., Ammon occupied some territory belonging to the Israelite tribe Gad.

49:2 Like Jerusalem (38:18, 23), **Rabbah** (49:1) will be **burned** by invaders. **Israel shall dispossess**. Israel will retake the cities lost in 734–732 B.C. (v. 1).

3 “Wail, O [g]Heshbon, for Ai is laid waste!
Cry out, O daughters of [e]Rabbah!
[h]Put on sackcloth,
lament, and run to and fro among the hedges!
For [i]Milcom shall go into exile,
[j]with his priests and his officials.
4 Why do you boast of your valleys,[1]
[k]O faithless daughter,
[l]who trusted in her treasures, saying,
‘Who will come against me?’
5 Behold, [m]I will bring terror upon you,
declares the Lord GOD of hosts,
from all who are around you,
and you shall be driven out, every man straight before him,
with none to gather the fugitives.

6 “But [n]afterward I will restore the fortunes of the Ammonites, declares the LORD.”

Judgment on Edom

7 Concerning [o]Edom.
Thus says the LORD of hosts:

[p]“Is wisdom no more in [p]Teman?
[q]Has counsel perished from the prudent?
[q]Has their wisdom vanished?
8 [r]Flee, turn back, dwell in the depths,
O inhabitants of [s]Dedan!
For I will bring the calamity of Esau upon him,
[t]the time when I punish him.
9 [u]If grape gatherers came to you,
would they not leave [v]gleanings?
[u]If thieves came by night,
would they not destroy only enough for themselves?
10 [w]But I have stripped Esau bare;
[u]I have uncovered his hiding places,
and he is not able to conceal himself.
His children are destroyed, and his brothers,
and his neighbors; and [x]he is no more.
11 [y]Leave your fatherless children; I will keep them alive;
[y]and let your widows trust in me.”

12 For thus says the LORD: [z]“If those who did not deserve to drink the cup must drink
it, [a]will you go unpunished? You shall not go unpunished, but you must drink. 13 [b]For I

[1] Hebrew *boast of your valleys, your valley flows*

3 [g]ch. 48:2 [e][See ver. 2 above] [h]ch. 48:37; See ch. 4:8 [i][1 Kgs. 11:5, 33; 2 Kgs. 23:13] [j]ch. 48:7
4 [k]ch. 3:14 [l]ch. 48:7
5 [m][ch. 48:43]
6 [n][ver. 39; ch. 48:47]
7 [o]ch. 25:21; Isa. 34:5; Amos 1:11; Obad. 1; [Mal. 1:2]; See Ezek. 25:12-14 [p]ver. 20; Obad. 9 [q][Isa. 19:11, 12]
8 [r]ver. 30 [s]ch. 25:23; Gen. 25:3 [t]ch. 50:27, 31; [ch. 46:21; 50:27]
9 [u]Obad. 5, 6 [v][Judg. 8:2]
10 [w]Mal. 1:3 [u][See ver. 9 above] [x]ch. 31:15; Isa. 17:14
11 [y][Ps. 10:14, 18; 68:5]
12 [z]ch. 25:28; [Obad. 16] [a]ch. 25:29
13 [b]See ch. 22:5

49:3 Heshbon. See 48:2. **Ai**. Location unknown; not the Ai of Josh. 7:1–9. **Rabbah**. See Jer. 49:2. **Milcom shall go into exile**. See 48:7.

49:4 boast of your valleys. Perhaps a fertile part of the Jabbok River Valley. **trusted in her treasures**. See 48:7. Like Moab, Ammon believed that her wealth insulated her from trouble. Perhaps this wealth was used to pay tribute money.

49:5 I will bring terror. God is sovereign over all nations; he will send an invader. **every man straight before him**. The Ammonites will flee by the quickest route possible, and there will be **none to gather the fugitives**. Nebuchadnezzar defeated Ammon c. 582 B.C.

49:6 God will **restore** Ammon's **fortunes**, just as he will for Israel and Moab. See 29:14 and 48:47.

49:7–22 There is much overlap between this prophecy against Edom and the book of Obadiah.

49:7 Edom. Descendants of Esau (Gen. 36:1–19) who lived south of the Dead Sea toward the Gulf of Aqaba. Obadiah 10–14 indicates that Edom benefited from Jerusalem's fall. **wisdom . . . in Teman**. Teman was in northern Edom. Obadiah 8 indicates Edom was famous for its “wise men”; they will soon vanish.

49:8 Dedan. A site southeast of Edom. The warning is either for Dedanites living in Edom to return home or for Dedan to cease relations with Edom to avoid trouble with Edom's conqueror.

49:9–10 Unlike **grape gatherers** and **thieves**, who **leave** something behind, God has **stripped Esau bare** of protection and **hiding places**.

49:11–12 God may protect Edom's **fatherless children** and **widows**, but the nation as a whole will **drink** the **cup** of destruction (25:28–29; Lam. 4:21).

49:13 Bozrah. Capital of Edom, 25 miles (40 km) southeast of the Dead Sea. Moab also had a city by this name (48:24). Like Jerusalem (15:4; 24:9), Bozrah shall become a **horror** to other nations.

13[c]ver. 22; See ch. 48:24 [d]See ch. 24:9
14[e]See Obad. 1-4 [f][Isa. 13:4]
16[g][ch. 48:28]
17[h]Ezek. 35:3, 7, 9 [i][ch. 50:13]
18[j]See Isa. 13:19 [k][Deut. 29:23] [l]ver. 33
19[m]For ver. 19-21, see ch. 50:44-46 [n]See ch. 4:7 [o]See ch. 12:5 [p]See ch. 10:6 [q]Job 9:19 [r][ch. 30:21]
20[s]Ezek. 35:3, 7, 9 [t]See ver. 7 [u]ch. 50:45
21[v]ch. 8:16; 50:46; [Ezek. 26:15]
22[w]See ch. 48:40 [x]ver. 13 [y]ver. 24; See ch. 6:24
23[z]Isa. 17:1; Amos 1:3 [a]1 Kgs. 8:65; Zech. 9:2 [b]2 Kgs. 18:34 [c]Zech. 9:4
24[z][See ver. 23 above] [d][ch. 46:5] [y][See ver. 22 above]

have sworn by myself, declares the LORD, that [c]Bozrah shall become [d]a horror, a taunt, a waste, and a curse, and all her cities shall be perpetual wastes."

14 [e]I have heard a message from the LORD,
and an envoy has been sent among the nations:
[f]"Gather yourselves together and come against her,
and rise up for battle!
15 For behold, I will make you small among the nations,
despised among mankind.
16 The horror you inspire has deceived you,
and the pride of your heart,
you who live in the clefts of the rock,[1]
who hold the height of the hill.
Though you [g]make your nest as high as the eagle's,
I will bring you down from there,
declares the LORD.

17 [h]"Edom shall become a horror. [i]Everyone who passes by it will be horrified [i]and will
hiss because of all its disasters. 18 [j]As when Sodom and Gomorrah and their [k]neighboring
cities were overthrown, says the LORD, [l]no man shall dwell there, [l]no man shall sojourn
in her. 19 [m]Behold, [n]like a lion coming up from [o]the jungle of the Jordan against a perennial pasture, I will suddenly make him[2] run away from her. And I will appoint over her whomever I choose. [p]For who is like me? [q]Who will summon me? [r]What shepherd can
stand before me? 20 Therefore hear the plan that the LORD has made against [s]Edom and the purposes that he has formed against the inhabitants of [t]Teman: [u]Even the little ones of the flock shall be dragged away. Surely their fold shall be appalled at their fate. 21 At the
sound of their fall [v]the earth shall tremble; the sound of their cry shall be heard at the
Red Sea. 22 Behold, [w]one shall mount up and fly swiftly like an eagle and spread his wings against [x]Bozrah, and the heart of the warriors of Edom shall be in that day like the heart [y]of a woman in her birth pains."

Judgment on Damascus

23 Concerning [z]Damascus:

[a]"Hamath and [b]Arpad are confounded,
for they have heard bad news;
they melt in fear,
[c]they are troubled like the sea that cannot be quiet.
24 [z]Damascus has become feeble, [d]she turned to flee,
and panic seized her;
anguish and sorrows have taken hold of her,
as [y]of a woman in labor.

[1] Or *of Sela* [2] Septuagint, Syriac *them*

49:14 Once Edom sent envoys to Judah to plot against Babylon (27:3); now God sends an **envoy** to gather **nations** against Edom (Obad. 1).

49:15 small. See Obad. 2.

49:16 Edom was in mountainous terrain and her citadels were well fortified, so she felt safe. But no topography can protect Edom from the invaders that God sends.

49:17 a horror. See 15:4; 29:18; 49:13; Lam. 1:12; 2:15.

49:18 God utterly destroyed **Sodom and Gomorrah and their neighboring cities**, Admah and Zeboiim (Gen. 14:2; 19:23–29), and he will do the same to Edom.

49:19 the jungle of the Jordan. An area of the Jordan Valley where the Asiatic lion and other wild animals roamed (12:5). **perennial pasture**. Lush grazing ground for sheep. These sheep **run away** when the lion approaches. God will devour Edom's sheep (people) and **appoint** new shepherds (leaders) over them.

49:20 See 50:45. God's plans never fail, so Edom's whole **flock**—even its **little ones**—will **be dragged away**.

49:21 See 50:46. Edom's **cry** will **be heard** at the **Red Sea**, or as far as the Egyptian border.

49:22 The invader will be like an **eagle** swift to pursue prey. See 48:40. **Bozrah**. Probably the capital of Edom; see note on 49:13. **a woman in her birth pains**. See 4:31 and 48:41.

49:23 Damascus. See Isa. 17:1–6 and Amos 1:3–5. The chief Aramean city, home to kings Ben-hadad (1 Kings 20) and Hazael (2 Kings 8:7–15). Assyria dominated Damascus from 732 to 609 B.C., and Babylon did so after 605. **Hamath and Arpad**. Hamath was 115 miles (185 km) north of Damascus, and Arpad was 95 miles (153 km) north of Hamath. **heard bad news**. About Damascus and from a great distance.

49:24 Damascus's distress is so great she is too terrified **to flee**. She is like a **woman in labor**. See 4:31 and 48:41.

25 How is [e]the famous city not forsaken,
the city of my joy?
26 [f]Therefore her young men shall fall in her squares,
and all her soldiers shall be destroyed in that day,
declares the LORD of hosts.
27 And [g]I will kindle a fire in the wall of [z]Damascus,
and it shall devour the strongholds of [h]Ben-hadad."

Judgment on Kedar and Hazor

28 Concerning [i]Kedar and the kingdoms of Hazor that Nebuchadnezzar king of Babylon
struck down.

Thus says the LORD:
[j]"Rise up, advance against [i]Kedar!
Destroy [k]the people of the east!
29 [l]Their tents and their flocks shall be taken,
their [l]curtains and all their goods;
their camels shall be led away from them,
and men shall cry to them: [m]'Terror on every side!'
30 [n]Flee, wander far away, dwell in the depths,
O inhabitants of Hazor!
declares the LORD.
For Nebuchadnezzar king of Babylon
has made a plan against you
and formed a purpose against you.
31 [j]"Rise up, advance against a nation [o]at ease,
[p]that dwells securely,
declares the LORD,
[p]that has no gates or bars,
that dwells alone.
32 [q]Their camels shall become plunder,
their herds of livestock a spoil.
[r]I will scatter to every wind
[s]those who cut the corners of their hair,
and I will bring their calamity
from every side of them,
declares the LORD.
33 Hazor shall become [t]a haunt of jackals,
an everlasting waste;
[u]no man shall dwell there;
[u]no man shall sojourn in her."

Judgment on Elam

34 The word of the LORD that came to Jeremiah the prophet concerning [v]Elam, in the
beginning of the reign of [w]Zedekiah king of Judah.
35 Thus says the LORD of hosts: "Behold, I will break [x]the bow of [y]Elam, the mainstay
of their might. 36 And I will bring upon [y]Elam the four winds from the four quarters of

25 [e][ch. 33:9]
26 [f]ch. 50:30
27 [g]See ch. 17:27 [z][See ver. 23 above] [h]1 Kgs. 15:18; 20:1; 2 Kgs. 6:24; 8:7; 13:3
28 [i]Isa. 21:16; 60:7 [j]ver. 14, 31 [k]Isa. 11:14; Ezek. 25:4, 10; See Judg. 6:3
29 [l]Ps. 120:5; Song 1:5 [m]See ch. 6:25
30 [n]ver. 8
31 [j][See ver. 28 above] [o]Job 16:12 [p]Ezek. 38:8, 11
32 [q][Ezek. 38:12] [r]ver. 36 [s]See ch. 9:26
33 [t]See ch. 9:11 [u]ver. 18
34 [v]ch. 25:25; Gen. 14:1; Isa. 11:11; 21:2; Ezek. 32:24; Dan. 8:2 [w]2 Kgs. 24:17, 18
35 [x]Isa. 22:6 [y][See ver. 34 above]
36 [y][See ver. 34 above]

49:26 See 50:30. Damascus is left with no defenders.

49:27 See Amos 1:4–5, where similar phraseology is applied to **Damascus**.

49:28 Kedar. A significant Arab clan (2:10; Isa. 21:16–17). Kedar engaged in sheep breeding (Isa. 60:7) and traded with Phoenicia (Ezek. 27:21). **kingdoms of Hazor**. Probably a term designating several nomadic tribes in northern Arabia (Ps. 120:5; Isa. 42:11). **Nebuchadnezzar . . . struck down**. Babylonian records indicate that Nebuchadnezzar raided Arabia in 599 B.C., but another (unknown) event could be intended. **people of the east**. A general term for people living east of Judah, perhaps the Midianites and Amalekites (Judg. 6:2–3).

49:29 "Terror on every side!" See 6:25; 20:3, 10; 46:5.

49:30 plan . . . purpose. See v. 20. God devises plans that **Nebuchadnezzar** implements (27:1–15).

49:31–32 These tribes did not have walled, fortified cities, so they were as vulnerable as the sheep in v. 19.

49:33 Hazor. See v. 28. These metaphors for desolation occur in 9:11 to describe Jerusalem and in 10:22 to describe Judah's cities. See also Isa. 13:19–22.

49:34 Elam. East of Babylon in the lower Tigris River Valley. Conquered by Assyria in 640 B.C. **beginning of the reign of Zedekiah**. c. 597 B.C.

49:36–38 God will send invaders against **Elam** and destroy it. **set my throne**. Most likely the throne of Nebuchadnezzar (27:1–15). Babylonian

heaven. And I will scatter them to all those winds, and there shall be no nation to which
those driven out of [v]Elam shall not come. **37** I will [y]terrify [v]Elam before their enemies and
before those who seek their life. I will bring disaster upon them, [z]my fierce anger, declares
the LORD. [a]I will send the sword after them, until I have consumed them, **38** and I will set
my throne in [v]Elam and destroy their king and officials, declares the LORD.
39 "But in the latter days [b]I will restore the fortunes of [v]Elam, declares the LORD."

Judgment on Babylon

50 The word that the LORD spoke concerning [c]Babylon, concerning the land of the
Chaldeans, [d]by Jeremiah the prophet:

2 "Declare among the nations and proclaim,
set up a banner and proclaim,
conceal it not, and say:
[e]'Babylon is taken,
[f]Bel is put to shame,
Merodach is dismayed.
[e]Her images are put to shame,
her idols are dismayed.'

3 "For [g]out of the north a nation has come up against her, [h]which shall make her land a
desolation, and none shall dwell in it; [i]both man and beast shall flee away.

4 [j]"In those days and in that time, declares the LORD, [l]the people of Israel and the people
of Judah shall come together, [k]weeping as they come, and they [l]shall seek the LORD their
God. **5** [m]They shall ask the way to Zion, with faces turned toward it, [n]saying, 'Come, let us
join ourselves to the LORD in an [o]everlasting covenant that will never be forgotten.'

6 [p]"My people have been lost sheep. [q]Their shepherds have led them astray, turning
them away on the mountains. From mountain to hill they have gone. They have forgotten
their fold. **7** All who found them have devoured them, [r]and their enemies have said, 'We
are not guilty, for [s]they have sinned against the LORD, [t]their habitation of righteousness,
the LORD, [u]the hope of their fathers.'

8 [v]"Flee from the midst of Babylon, [v]and go out of the land of the Chaldeans, and be as
male goats before the flock. **9** For behold, I am stirring up and bringing against Babylon
[w]a gathering of great nations, from the north country. And they shall array themselves
against her. From there she shall be taken. Their arrows are like a skilled warrior who
does not return empty-handed. **10** [x]Chaldea shall be plundered; all who plunder her shall
be sated, declares the LORD.

36 [v][See ver. 34 above]
37 [y][ch. 1:17] [v][See ver. 34 above] [z]See ch. 12:13 [a]See ch. 9:16
38 [v][See ver. 34 above]
39 [b][ch. 48:47] [v][See ver. 34 above]

Chapter 50

1 [c]See Isa. 13:1–14:27; 21:1-10 [d][ch. 51:59, 60]
2 [e]Isa. 21:9 [f]See Isa. 46:1
3 [g]See ch. 1:14 [h]ver. 13, 23; ch. 51:29 [i]ch. 51:62; [Ps. 135:8]
4 [j]See ch. 3:18 [k]ch. 31:9, 18; Ezra 8:21; Ps. 126:6 [l]Hos. 3:5
5 [m][ch. 31:21] [n][Isa. 2:3] [o]See ch. 32:40
6 [p]ver. 17; Isa. 53:6; [Matt. 18:12; Luke 15:4] [q]Zech. 10:2; See Ezek. 34:1-6
7 [r][ch. 40:2, 3] [s][ver. 14] [t]ch. 31:23 [u]See ch. 14:8
8 [v]ch. 51:6, 45; See Isa. 48:20
9 [w]See ch. 25:14
10 [x][ch. 25:12]

records indicate Nebuchadnezzar may have campaigned against Elam in 596–595 B.C.

49:39 For the same promise to other nations, see 33:26; 49:6; and note on 48:47. These verses predict a future salvation for Gentiles.

50:1–51:64 *God Will Judge Babylon.* Babylon was the great world power during the second half of Jeremiah's ministry (609–587 B.C.). Jeremiah predicts that this great kingdom will fall, an event that occurred in 539 B.C. Jeremiah asserts that Babylon and its gods will be destroyed (50:1–10) because the people have sinned against God (50:11–16). He claims that God will gather and pardon Israel (50:17–20) but will make Babylon like Sodom and Gomorrah (50:21–40), for God's plans must be fulfilled (50:41–46). He promises that God has not forsaken Israel (51:1–10). God is the Creator (51:11–23) who will destroy Babylon for Israel's sake (51:24–64).

50:1–2 Babylon is taken. Persia conquered Babylon in 539 B.C. (Isa. 13:1–14:23; 21:9). **Bel** (corresponds to Hb. *Ba'al*) was the title ("Lord") of the chief god of Babylon, depicted as a storm god and source of life (Isa. 46:1). **Merodach** (Babylonian "Marduk") was the personal name of this god.

50:3 In Jeremiah, trouble always comes from the **north** (1:14). Like Judah's cities (4:27; 10:22; 25:18; etc.), Babylon shall become a **desolation** (Isa. 13:9).

50:4–5 When Babylon falls, **Israel** and **Judah** shall join together (3:6–18) to **seek the LORD their God** (31:9). **Zion** was both the mountain in Jerusalem and the eternal home of God and his people (31:6, 12; Isa. 4:2–6). **everlasting covenant**. The new covenant (Jer. 32:40; cf. 31:31–40).

50:6 shepherds. Judah's and Israel's religious, political, and social leaders have **led them astray**. See 2:8; 3:15; 6:3; 10:21; 12:10; 23:1–4. **From mountain to hill they have gone**. Probably for fertility cult worship (2:20).

50:7 Because their leaders have led them astray and then forsaken them, Israel and Judah have been plundered by their foes, all of whom God has sent (27:1–15). **their habitation of righteousness**. God is his people's only security (31:23) and only righteousness (23:6). **the hope of their fathers**. He is the covenant God of Abraham, Isaac, Jacob, David, and their offspring (33:26).

50:8 male goats before the flock. Just as male goats rushed out first when gates were opened, so Israel will be among the first to leave **Babylon**.

50:9 gathering of great nations. See 51:27–28; Isa. 13:1–5.

11 [y]"Though you rejoice, though you exult,
O plunderers of my heritage,
though you frolic like a heifer in the pasture,
and neigh like stallions,
12 your mother shall be utterly shamed,
and she who bore you shall be disgraced.
Behold, she shall be the last of the nations,
[z]a wilderness, a dry land, and a desert.
13 [a]Because of the wrath of the LORD she shall not be inhabited
but shall be an utter desolation;
[b]everyone who passes by Babylon shall be appalled,
[b]and hiss because of all her wounds.
14 [c]Set yourselves in array against Babylon all around,
[d]all you who bend the bow;
shoot at her, spare no arrows,
[e]for she has sinned against the LORD.
15 [f]Raise a shout against her all around;
she has surrendered;
her bulwarks have fallen;
[g]her walls are thrown down.
For [h]this is the vengeance of the LORD:
take vengeance on her;
[i]do to her as she has done.
16 Cut off from Babylon the sower,
and the one who handles the sickle in time of harvest;
[j]because of the sword of the oppressor,
[k]every one shall turn to his own people,
and every one shall flee to his own land.

17 [l]"Israel is a hunted sheep [m]driven away by lions. [n]First the king of Assyria [o]devoured
him, and now at last [p]Nebuchadnezzar king of Babylon [q]has gnawed his bones. 18 Therefore,
thus says the LORD of hosts, the God of Israel: Behold, [r]I am bringing punishment on the
king of Babylon and his land, [s]as I punished the king of Assyria. 19 [t]I will restore Israel to
his pasture, and [t]he shall feed on [u]Carmel and in [u]Bashan, and his desire shall be satisfied on the hills of Ephraim and in [u]Gilead. 20 In those days and in that time, declares the
LORD, [v]iniquity shall be sought in Israel, and there shall be none, and sin in Judah, and
none shall be found, for [w]I will pardon those whom I leave as a remnant.

21 "Go up against the land of Merathaim,[1]
and against the inhabitants of Pekod.[2]
Kill, [x]and devote them to destruction,[3]
declares the LORD,
and do all that I have commanded you.
22 [y]The noise of battle is in the land,

[1] *Merathaim* means *double rebellion* [2] *Pekod* means *punishment* [3] That is, set apart (devote) as an offering to the Lord (for destruction)

11 [y][Lam. 4:21]
12 [z]ch. 51:43
13 [a]ver. 39 [b]See ch. 18:16
14 [c]ver. 9; ch. 51:11; Isa. 21:2 [d]ver. 29; [ch. 51:3] [e][ver. 7]
15 [f][Josh. 6:16] [g]ch. 51:58 [h]ch. 46:10; 51:6, 11 [i]ver. 29; ch. 51:56
16 [j]ch. 46:16 [k][ch. 51:9]; See Isa. 13:14
17 [l]See ver. 6 [m]ch. 2:15; 4:7; Isa. 5:29 [n]2 Kgs. 17:6; 18:13 [o]ch. 51:34 [p]2 Kgs. 24:10, 14; See 2 Kgs. 25:1-11 [q][ch. 51:34]
18 [r]Isa. 10:12; 24:21; [Ps. 76:12] [s]Isa. 14:24, 25
19 [t]Ezek. 34:13, 14 [u]Mic. 7:14
20 [v][Isa. 40:2] [w]Isa. 33:24; See ch. 31:34
21 [x]ver. 26; [ch. 51:3]
22 [y]ch. 51:54

50:11–13 Babylon once rejoiced over its plundering of Judah, God's **heritage**, like a calf frolicking or a stallion snorting. Soon Babylon will be ashamed and become an **utter desolation** (cf. v. 2). **everyone who passes by**. Just as Judah became a cautionary tale for others, so **Babylon** will become one as well.

50:14–15 Just as Judah and Israel faced defeat because they **sinned against the LORD**, so the same will happen to **Babylon** for the same reason. Babylon's defeat is the **vengeance of the LORD** for all her oppressive ways.

50:16 Just as Babylon's army has ruined other lands, so its **land** will now be ruined by foreign forces.

50:17 a hunted sheep. See vv. 6–7. **Assyria devoured him**. In 734–732 B.C. (Isa. 7:1–9), 722 (2 Kings 17:1–6), and 701 (2 Kings 18:13–18; Isa. 36:1). **Nebuchadnezzar . . . has gnawed his bones**. In 605 B.C. (2 Kings 24:1; Dan. 1:1), 597 (2 Kings 24:1–7), and 587 (Jer. 39:1–10; 2 Kings 25:1–21).

50:18 Just as God used **Babylon** to punish **Assyria** (c. 612–609 B.C.), so God uses Persia to punish Babylon (539).

50:19 God's sheep (23:1–8) will feed in lush pastures. **Carmel**. See 46:18. **Bashan**. See 22:20. **Ephraim**. See 4:15. **Gilead**. See 46:11.

50:20 When God restores his people, no sin will be found in them, not because they have never sinned, but because he will **pardon** them (31:34) and completely purify their hearts (see note on 31:38–40; cf. Rev. 21:27).

50:21 Merathaim. Region where the Tigris and Euphrates rivers converge. **Pekod**. Region in eastern Babylonia. **devote them to destruction**. Set apart as the goods given to God as the spoils of holy war (cf. Josh. 7:10–26).

23 [z]Isa. 14:6 [a][Rev. 18:19, 21] [b]ver. 3, 13
24 [c][Ps. 141:9] [d][ch. 51:31; Dan. 5:30]
25 [e]Isa. 13:5
26 [f][Neh. 4:2]
27 [g][Ps. 22:12; Isa. 34:7, 8] [h]ch. 46:21
28 [i][ver. 8] [j]ch. 51:10; Ps. 64:9 [k][ch. 51:11; 52:13; Dan. 5:3, 23]
29 [l][ver. 14; Job 16:13] [m]ch. 25:14 [n]Isa. 47:10
30 [o]ch. 49:26
31 [n][See ver. 29 above] [p]ver. 27; ch. 49:8
32 [n][See ver. 29 above] [q]See ch. 17:27
33 [r][ver. 17] [s][Isa. 14:17]

and great destruction!
23 [z]How the hammer of the whole earth
is cut down and broken!
[a]How Babylon [b]has become
a horror among the nations!
24 [c]I set a snare for you and you were taken, O Babylon,
and [d]you did not know it;
you were found and caught,
because you opposed the LORD.
25 The LORD has opened his armory
and brought out [e]the weapons of his wrath,
for the Lord GOD of hosts has a work to do
in the land of the Chaldeans.
26 Come against her from every quarter;
open her granaries;
[f]pile her up like heaps of grain, and devote her to destruction;
let nothing be left of her.
27 Kill all [g]her bulls;
let them go down to the slaughter.
Woe to them, for their day has come,
[h]the time of their punishment.

28 "A voice! They [i]flee and escape from the land of Babylon, [j]to declare in Zion the vengeance of the LORD our God, vengeance for [k]his temple.

29 [l]"Summon archers against Babylon, all those who bend the bow. [l]Encamp around
her; let no one escape. [m]Repay her according to her deeds; do to her according to all that
she has done. For she has [n]proudly defied the LORD, the Holy One of Israel.
30 [o]Therefore
her young men shall fall in her squares, and all her soldiers shall be destroyed on that
day, declares the LORD.

31 "Behold, I am against you, O [n]proud one,
declares the Lord GOD of hosts,
[p]for your day has come,
the time when I will punish you.
32 [n]The proud one shall stumble and fall,
with none to raise him up,
[q]and I will kindle a fire in his cities,
and it will devour all that is around him.

33 "Thus says the LORD of hosts: [r]The people of Israel are oppressed, and the people of
Judah with them. All who took them captive have held them fast; [s]they refuse to let them

50:23 hammer of the whole earth. Babylon hammered all other nations into submission (27:6). **a horror**. See 15:4; 18:16; 19:8; 34:17; 48:39; 49:13, 16, 17.

50:24 God set a trap for and snared Babylon. He willed that it face defeat. **you did not know it**. The defeat completely surprised Babylon. **opposed the LORD**. In part, through prideful attributing of its success to its own prowess and its own gods (Isa. 10:5–19), but more significantly by not worshiping and serving the one true God.

50:25 The armies that defeat Babylon carry the **weapons of** God's **wrath** (v. 9; Isa. 13:1–5). **a work to do**. See Jer. 48:10.

50:26 Babylon's dead will be piled up **like heaps of grain** pouring out of **granaries**. **devote her to destruction**. See note on v. 21.

50:27 bulls. A technical term (Hb. *par*) for choice young bulls, probably referring to Babylon's soldiers (Isa. 34:6–7). **go down to the slaughter**. A metaphor for defeat in battle (Jer. 48:15).

50:28 Fugitives (most likely Israelites) will **declare** God's retribution for Babylon's destruction of Jerusalem's **temple**.

50:29 The scene is of siege warfare. **Archers** peppered the city walls with arrows to provide cover for the men building and using ramps and battering rams. **Encamp**. Invading armies camped outside the besieged city's walls. **let no one escape**. Fugitives from besieged cities were chased, captured, and killed (39:5–6; Lam. 4:19). **proudly defied the LORD**. See Jer. 50:24. **Holy One of Israel**. One of Isaiah's favorite names for God (Isa. 1:4; 5:19; 10:20; 12:6; 60:14).

50:30 See 49:26. **on that day**. God's day of judging Babylon (Isa. 13:1–6).

50:31 O proud one. As was true of Assyria (Isa. 10:5–34), Babylon's pride was the cause of its downfall.

50:32 none to raise him up. No ally will be able to deliver Babylon on the day of punishment. **kindle a fire**. See 21:14; Amos 1:4, 7, 10, 12, 14; 2:2, 5.

50:33 held them fast. Part of Babylon's sin against God is its oppression of Israelite and Judean captives. Once held, they were never released. Babylon has become like the pharaoh of the exodus (Ex. 5:2).

go. **34** [t]Their Redeemer is strong; [u]the LORD of hosts is his name. [v]He will surely plead their
cause, that he may give rest to the earth, but unrest to the inhabitants of Babylon.

35 "A sword against the Chaldeans, declares the LORD,
and against the inhabitants of Babylon,
and against [w]her officials and her [x]wise men!
36 A sword against the diviners,
that they may become fools!
A sword against her [y]warriors,
that they may be destroyed!
37 A sword against her horses and against her chariots,
and against all [z]the foreign troops in her midst,
that [a]they may become women!
[b]A sword against all her treasures,
that they may be plundered!
38 [c]A drought against her waters,
that they may be dried up!
[d]For it is a land of images,
and they are mad over idols.

39 [e]"Therefore wild beasts shall dwell with hyenas in Babylon, and ostriches shall dwell
in her. She shall never again have people, nor be inhabited for all generations. **40** [f]As when
God overthrew Sodom and Gomorrah and their neighboring cities, declares the LORD,
[g]so no man shall dwell there, and no son of man shall sojourn in her.

41 [h]"Behold, a people comes from the north;
a mighty nation and many kings
are stirring from the farthest parts of the earth.
42 They lay hold of bow and spear;
they are cruel and have no mercy.
The sound of them is like the roaring of the sea;
they ride on horses,
arrayed as a man for battle
against you, O daughter of Babylon!

43 "The king of Babylon heard the report of them,
and his hands fell helpless;
anguish seized him,
pain as of a woman in labor.

44 [i]"Behold, like a lion coming up from the thicket of the Jordan against a perennial pasture, I will suddenly make them run away from her, and I will appoint over her whomever
I choose. For who is like me? Who will summon me? What shepherd [j]can stand before me?
45 Therefore hear [k]the plan that the LORD has made against Babylon, [k]and the purposes that
he has formed against the land of the Chaldeans: [l]Surely the little ones of their flock shall be
dragged away; surely their fold shall be appalled at their fate. **46** [m]At the sound of the capture
of Babylon the earth shall tremble, and her cry shall be heard among the nations."

34 [t]See Isa. 43:14 [u]See ch. 10:16 [v]ch. 51:36; Isa. 51:22
35 [w]ch. 51:57; Dan. 5:30 [x]Dan. 4:6
36 [y]ch. 51:57
37 [z]See ch. 25:20 [a]ch. 51:30 [b][Isa. 45:3]
38 [c]Isa. 44:27; [ch. 51:36] [d]ver. 2; ch. 51:47, 52
39 [e]Isa. 13:21, 22
40 [f]Gen. 19:25; See Isa. 13:19 [g]ch. 51:43
41 [h]For ver. 41-43, see ch. 6:22-24
44 [i]For ver. 44-46, see ch. 49:19-21 [j]Job 41:10
45 [k]ch. 51:11, 12, 29; Isa. 14:24 [l]ch. 49:20
46 [m]See ch. 49:21

50:34 Redeemer. A kinsman who avenged, protected, secured release, and retained property for a relative (Lev. 25:23–34, 47–55). **plead their cause**. Act as Israel's advocate in a legal case. **rest to the earth**. From Babylon's oppressive ways. **unrest to . . . Babylon**. Lit., "shake" Babylon with war and destruction.

50:35–36 officials. Probably court functionaries. **wise men**. Persons who attempt to interpret dreams, omens, and other means of determining the future (Dan. 4:6–7). **diviners**. Individuals who read omens to discern the future, especially future battles and their results (Jer. 27:9; 29:8).

50:37 foreign troops. Mercenaries. **that they may become women!** That is, weak in terms of physical strength in combat. It was shameful for a nation to allow women to fight in war. See note on Nah. 3:12–13.

50:38 Babylon's **idols** will not be able to help when God dries up the nation's **waters**.

50:39–40 See Isa. 13:19–22. These verses present common metaphors of defeat and desolation. **She shall never again have people**. Ancient **Babylon** is still an uninhabited ruin today, though it is surrounded by the city of Al Hillah, Iraq (about 50 miles [81 km] south of Baghdad).

50:41–43 These verses are close in content to 6:22–24. What happened to Judah will happen to **Babylon**. Invasion will come **from the north**. See 50:3. **mighty nation and many kings**. See v. 3 and Isa. 13:1–5.

50:44–46 These verses are very close in content to 49:19–21. Thus, what happened to Edom will happen to **Babylon**.

Chapter 51
1 [n][ch. 4:11; Isa. 21:1]
2 [o][Matt. 3:12]; See ch. 15:7 [p][ch. 2:28]
3 [q][ch. 50:14, 29] [r][ch. 50:21]
4 [s]ch. 49:26
5 [t]See Isa. 54:5-7
6 [u]ver. 45; ch. 50:8 [v][Gen. 19:15] [w]ch. 50:15
7 [x][Ps. 75:8; Rev. 17:4] [y]Rev. 14:8 [z]See ch. 25:15, 16
8 [a]See Isa. 21:9 [b]Isa. 13:6; Rev. 18:9, 11, 19; [ch. 48:20] [c][ch. 46:11]
9 [d]ver. 6, 45; ch. 50:8 [e][ch. 50:16]; See Isa. 13:14 [f]Rev. 18:5
10 [g]Ps. 37:6; [ch. 23:6] [h]ch. 50:28

The Utter Destruction of Babylon

51

1 Thus says the LORD:
"Behold, I will stir up [n]the spirit of a destroyer
against Babylon,
against the inhabitants of Leb-kamai,[1]
2 and I will send to Babylon winnowers,
and [o]they shall winnow her,
and they shall empty her land,
when they come against her from every side
[p]on the day of trouble.
3 [q]Let not the archer bend his bow,
and let him not stand up in his armor.
Spare not her young men;
[r]devote to destruction[2] all her army.
4 They shall fall down slain in the land of the Chaldeans,
[s]and wounded in her streets.
5 [t]For Israel and Judah have not been forsaken
by their God, the LORD of hosts,
but the land of the Chaldeans[3] is full of guilt
against the Holy One of Israel.

6 [u]"Flee from the midst of Babylon;
let every one save his life!
[v]Be not cut off in her punishment,
[w]for this is the time of the LORD's vengeance,
the repayment he is rendering her.
7 Babylon was [x]a golden cup in the LORD's hand,
[y]making all the earth drunken;
[z]the nations drank of her wine;
therefore the nations went mad.
8 [a]Suddenly Babylon has fallen and been broken;
[b]wail for her!
[c]Take balm for her pain;
perhaps she may be healed.
9 We would have healed Babylon,
but she was not healed.
[d]Forsake her, and [e]let us go
each to his own country,
for [f]her judgment has reached up to heaven
and has been lifted up even to the skies.
10 [g]The LORD has brought about our vindication;
[h]come, let us declare in Zion
the work of the LORD our God.

[1] A code name for Chaldea [2] That is, set apart (devote) as an offering to the Lord (for destruction) [3] Hebrew *their land*

51:1 Leb-kamai (lit., "heart of my adversaries") is a code name for Chaldea (i.e., **Babylon**; see ESV footnote), and it may simply refer to Babylon as God's enemy because she opposed God (50:24).

51:2 Just as God winnowed Judah (15:7), so he will winnow **Babylon . . . on the day of trouble** (see 2:28; on the process of winnowing, see note on Ps. 1:4).

51:3 The meaning of this verse is uncertain. It refers either to the futility of Babylon resisting the invasion or the ease with which the invader will succeed.

51:4 in her streets. See 49:26 and 50:30.

51:5 Despite all the judgments that God has sent on **Judah** and **Israel**, he has **not . . . forsaken** them, for he will unite them (3:6–18) and give them a new covenant (31:31–40). **full of guilt**. See 50:24 and 51:1. **Holy One of Israel**. See note on 50:29.

51:6 Flee probably refers to Israelites who are counseled to avoid the coming devastation. **vengeance**. See 50:15, 28.

51:7 golden cup. A metaphor for Babylon's wealth (v. 13) and role as God's instrument of judgment (25:15–26). **making all the earth drunken**. A metaphor for the nations' helplessness before Babylon's invasions (25:27).

51:8 balm. See 8:22 and 46:11.

51:9 We. Perhaps Babylon's allies. **would have healed Babylon**. Would have come to her aid, but such attempts would be pointless because her sins have **reached up to heaven**, where God sees and judges.

51:10 our vindication. God has vindicated Judah and Israel by judging Babylon (v. 5). This action merits God's praise **in Zion**, his city.

11 [i]"Sharpen the arrows!
Take up the shields!

[j]The LORD has stirred up the spirit of the kings of [k]the Medes, because [l]his purpose concerning Babylon is to destroy it, [m]for that is the vengeance of the LORD, the vengeance
for [m]his temple.

12 [n]"Set up a standard against the walls of Babylon;
[o]make the watch strong;
set up watchmen;
prepare the ambushes;
[l]for the LORD has both planned and done
what he spoke concerning the inhabitants of Babylon.
13 [p]O you who dwell by many waters,
rich in treasures,
your end has come;
the thread of your life is cut.
14 [q]The LORD of hosts has sworn by himself:
Surely I will fill you with men, [r]as many as locusts,
[s]and they shall raise the shout of victory over you.

15 [t]"It is he who made the earth by his power,
who established the world by his wisdom,
and by his understanding stretched out the heavens.
16 When he utters his voice there is a tumult of waters in the heavens,
and he makes the mist rise from the ends of the earth.
He makes lightning for the rain,
and he brings forth the wind from his storehouses.
17 Every man is stupid and without knowledge;
every goldsmith is put to shame by his idols,
for his images are false,
and there is no breath in them.
18 They are worthless, a work of delusion;
at the time of their punishment they shall perish.
19 Not like these is he who is the portion of Jacob,
for he is the one who formed all things,
and Israel is the tribe of his inheritance;
the LORD of hosts is his name.

20 "You are my hammer and weapon of war:
with you I [u]break nations in pieces;
with you I destroy kingdoms;
21 with you I break in pieces the horse and his rider;
with you I break in pieces the chariot and the charioteer;
22 with you I break in pieces man and woman;
with you I break in pieces [v]the old man and the youth;
with you I break in pieces [v]the young man and the young woman;
23 with you I break in pieces the shepherd and his flock;
with you I break in pieces the farmer and his team;
with you I break in pieces [w]governors and commanders.

11 [i]ch. 46:4 [j]See Isa. 13:17 [k]2 Kgs. 17:6; Dan. 5:31 [l][ch. 50:45] [m]ch. 50:28
12 [n]ver. 27; ch. 50:2; [Isa. 13:2] [o][Isa. 21:5; Nah. 2:1] [l][See ver. 11 above]
13 [p]Rev. 17:1, 15; [ver. 36]
14 [q]See ch. 22:5 [r][Ps. 105:34; Joel 1:4; 2:25] [s]Isa. 16:9
15 [t]For ver. 15-19, see ch. 10:12-16
20 [u][Dan. 7:7, 19, 23]
22 [v]2 Chr. 36:17; [Isa. 13:16, 18]
23 [w]ver. 28, 57

51:11 Medes. See Isa. 13:17–18. The Medes were incorporated into the Persian Empire by Cyrus in 550 B.C. The Medes and Persians are connected as one kingdom in Dan. 5:28; 6:8, 12, 15. **vengeance for his temple**. See Jer. 50:28.

51:12 standard. Signal. See 4:6 and Isa. 13:2. **watchmen**. Persons charged with making certain **Babylon** has not grown wise to the invader's plan. **ambushes**. Intended to catch Babylon unaware as soldiers leave the city.

51:13 many waters. A metaphor for Babylon's fertility.

51:14 sworn by himself. The highest name and authority (22:5; 49:13; Gen. 22:16; Isa. 45:23; 62:8; Amos 4:2; 6:8; Heb. 6:13). **as many as locusts**. The invaders will swarm over Babylon (Joel 1:4; 2:25).

51:15–19 Stated also in 10:12–16. God alone created and rules the **earth**. **Israel** forgot this and was judged; Babylon ignored this and will be judged (Dan. 5:13–30).

51:20–23 In the past Babylon was God's **hammer**, or instrument of judgment (50:23), but now a new nation will play that role as Babylon becomes like the **nations** it defeated.

24 [x]"I will repay Babylon and all the inhabitants of Chaldea before your very eyes for all
the evil that they have done in Zion, declares the LORD.

25 "Behold, I am against you, O destroying mountain,
declares the LORD,
which destroys the whole earth;
I will stretch out my hand against you,
and roll you down from the crags,
[y]and make you a burnt mountain.
26 No [z]stone shall be taken from you for a corner
and no stone for a foundation,
but you shall be [a]a perpetual waste,
declares the LORD.

27 [b]"Set up a standard on the earth;
[c]blow the trumpet among the nations;
[d]prepare [e]the nations for war against her;
summon against her [f]the kingdoms,
[g]Ararat, Minni, and [h]Ashkenaz;
appoint a [i]marshal against her;
[j]bring up horses like bristling locusts.
28 [d]Prepare [e]the nations for war against her,
the kings of [k]the Medes, [l]with their governors [l]and deputies,
and every [m]land under their dominion.
29 [n]The land trembles and writhes in pain,
[o]for the LORD's purposes against Babylon stand,
to make the land of Babylon a desolation,
without inhabitant.
30 The warriors of Babylon have ceased fighting;
they remain in their strongholds;
their strength has failed;
[p]they have become women;
[q]her dwellings are on fire;
[r]her bars are broken.
31 One [s]runner runs to meet another,
and one messenger to meet another,
to tell the king of Babylon
that his city is taken on every side;
32 the fords have been [t]seized,
the marshes are burned with fire,
and the soldiers are in panic.
33 For thus says the LORD of hosts, the God of Israel:
[u]The daughter of Babylon is like [u]a threshing floor
at the time when it is trodden;
yet a little while
and [v]the time of her harvest will come."

24 [x]ch. 50:15, 29; [Ps. 137:8]
25 [y]Rev. 8:8; [Rev. 18:8, 9]
26 [z][Ps. 118:22; Isa. 28:16] [a]ver. 62; ch. 25:12
27 [b]See ver. 12 [c]See ch. 4:5 [d]See ch. 6:4 [e]See ch. 25:14 [f][ch. 50:41] [g]Gen. 8:4; 2 Kgs. 19:37 [h]Gen. 10:3; 1 Chr. 1:6 [i]Nah. 3:17 [j]See ver. 14
28 [d][See ver. 27 above] [e][See ver. 27 above] [k]See ver. 11 [l]ver. 23, 57 [m][ch. 34:1]
29 [n]See ch. 8:16 [o]ch. 50:45
30 [p]ch. 50:37; [Isa. 19:16] [q]Isa. 47:14 [r]Lam. 2:9; Nah. 3:13
31 [s][2 Chr. 30:6]
32 [t]ver. 41
33 [u]See Isa. 21:10 [v][Isa. 17:5; Joel 3:13; Rev. 14:15]

51:24 all the evil that they have done in Zion. See 50:28 and 51:11.

51:25 As in Dan. 2:35, 44–45, Babylon is compared to a great **mountain** that once destroyed others but will now be destroyed. A volcano may be the basis for the metaphor, but the exact meaning is uncertain.

51:26 Once destroyed, Babylon will never be rebuilt. No one will even begin the process by starting to set up a **corner** or lay a **foundation**.

51:27 Set up a standard. See v. 12. **Ararat**. Assyrian "Urartu," in eastern Turkey (see note on Gen. 8:2–4). **Minni**. Assyrian "Mannay," located in northwest Iran. **Ashkenaz**. Also known as the Scythians, located in the Caucasus region. These groups were all ruled by the Medes until the Persians defeated the Medes c. 550 B.C.

51:28 Medes. See v. 11. **land under their dominion**. See v. 27.

51:29 land trembles and writhes in pain. See 8:16. **desolation**. See 50:3, 13.

51:30 they have become women. See note on 50:37. **on fire**. See 50:32. **bars are broken**. See 49:31.

51:31–32 Several messengers tell Babylon's **king** the same news: the city is surrounded, the water escape routes cut off, and the places of hiding (**marshes**) have been torched. No wonder the **soldiers are in panic**.

51:33 Babylon has been prepared for judgment **like a threshing floor** awaiting harvest. Her **time** is coming soon.

34 “Nebuchadnezzar the king of Babylon [w]has devoured me;
he has crushed me;
he has made me an empty vessel;
[x]he has swallowed me like [y]a monster;
he has filled his stomach with my delicacies;
he has rinsed me out.[1]
35 The violence done to me and to my kinsmen be upon Babylon,”
let the inhabitant of Zion say.
“My blood be upon the inhabitants of Chaldea,”
let Jerusalem say.
36 Therefore thus says the LORD:
“Behold, [z]I will plead your cause
and take vengeance for you.
[a]I will dry up her sea
and [b]make her fountain dry,
37 and Babylon shall become [c]a heap of ruins,
[d]the haunt of jackals,
[e]a horror [e]and a hissing,
without inhabitant.

38 [f]“They shall roar together [g]like lions;
they shall growl like lions’ cubs.
39 [h]While they are inflamed [h]I will prepare them a feast
and [i]make them drunk, that they may become merry,
[i]then sleep a perpetual sleep
and not wake, declares the LORD.
40 I will bring them down like lambs to the slaughter,
like rams and male goats.

41 “How [j]Babylon[2] is taken,
[k]the praise of the whole earth [l]seized!
How Babylon has become
a horror among the nations!
42 [m]The sea has come up on Babylon;
she is covered with its tumultuous waves.
43 Her cities have become a horror,
[n]a land of drought and a desert,
[o]a land in which no one dwells,
and through which no son of man passes.
44 And I will punish [p]Bel in Babylon,
and [q]take out of his mouth [r]what he has swallowed.
[s]The nations shall no longer flow to him;
[t]the wall of Babylon has fallen.

45 “Go out of the midst of her, [u]my people!
Let every one save his life
from [v]the fierce anger of the LORD!

[1] Or *he has expelled me* [2] Hebrew *Sheshach*, a code name for Babylon

34 [w]ch. 50:17 [x]ver. 44 [y]Ps. 74:13
36 [z]ch. 50:34 [a]Isa. 44:27; [ch. 50:38] [b][ver. 13]
37 [c]Isa. 25:2 [d]Isa. 13:22 [e]See ch. 18:16
38 [f][Amos 3:4] [g]Nah. 2:11, 12
39 [h][Isa. 21:5] [i]ver. 57
41 [j]ch. 25:26 [k][Isa. 13:19] [l]ver. 32
42 [m][ver. 55; Isa. 8:7, 8]
43 [n]ch. 50:12 [o]ch. 50:40
44 [p]ch. 50:2; See Isa. 46:1 [q]ver. 34; [Ezra 1:7, 8] [r]ver. 34 [s][ch. 31:12; Isa. 2:2] [t]ver. 58
45 [u]See ver. 6 [v]See ch. 12:13

51:34–35 like a monster. Though **Nebuchadnezzar** was sent by God against **Jerusalem** (27:1–15), he was unnecessarily violent and brutal in how he treated the Jews (50:17–18; 51:11, 24).

51:36 plead your cause. See 50:33–34. **dry up her sea**. Cut off her fertility. See 51:13.

51:37 heap of ruins. See 50:23 and Isa. 13:17–22.

51:38–40 Babylon roars like a hungry lion. God gives it intoxication instead of food (25:15–29), and it will become food for other power-hungry nations. See 5:6 for the image.

51:41 praise of the whole earth. The most powerful, richest, and most glorious kingdom on earth (Isa. 13:19).

51:42 Babylon’s foes are compared to floodwaters that overwhelm the city.

51:43 In contrast to v. 42, Babylon is compared to a **desert** land too desolate for human travel.

51:44 Bel. See note on 50:1–2. **what he has swallowed**. Babylon believed that its god gave its victories, but he has no power to help in its time of need. **wall**. The tops of Babylon’s walls were wide enough for several chariots to travel side by side.

51:45 “Go out of the midst of her.” See 50:8 and 51:6.

46[w][Isa. 37:7] [x]Matt. 24:6, 7
47[y][ch. 50:2] [z][ch. 50:12]
48[a][Rev. 18:20]; See Isa. 44:23 [b]ch. 50:3
49[c][ver. 24]
50[d][ch. 44:28]
51[e]ch. 7:19; Ps. 44:15, 16 [f]Lam. 1:10
52[y][See ver. 47 above] [g]Job 24:12; Ezek. 26:15
53[h][ver. 25]; See Isa. 14:13 [i][ch. 49:16]
54[j]ch. 50:22
55[k][ver. 42]; See ch. 5:22
56[l]ch. 50:15; Isa. 59:18

46 Let not your heart faint, and be not fearful
[w]at the report heard in the land,
[x]when a report comes in one year
and afterward a report in another year,
and violence is in the land,
[x]and ruler is against ruler.
47 "Therefore, behold, the days are coming
when [y]I will punish the images of Babylon;
[z]her whole land shall be put to shame,
and all her slain shall fall in the midst of her.
48 [a]Then the heavens and the earth,
and all that is in them,
shall sing for joy over Babylon,
[b]for the destroyers shall come against them out of the north,
declares the LORD.
49 Babylon must fall for the slain of Israel,
[c]just as for Babylon have fallen the slain of all the earth.
50 [d]"You who have escaped from the sword,
go, do not stand still!
Remember the LORD from far away,
and let Jerusalem come into your mind:
51 [e]'We are put to shame, for we have heard reproach;
[e]dishonor has covered our face,
[f]for foreigners have come
into the holy places of the LORD's house.'
52 "Therefore, behold, the days are coming, declares the LORD,
when [y]I will execute judgment upon her images,
[g]and through all her land
the wounded shall groan.
53 Though Babylon should [h]mount up to heaven,
and though she should [i]fortify her strong height,
yet destroyers would come from me against her,
declares the LORD.
54 [j]"A voice! A cry from Babylon!
The noise of great destruction from the land of the Chaldeans!
55 For the LORD is laying Babylon waste
and stilling her mighty voice.
[k]Their waves roar like many waters;
the noise of their voice is raised,
56 for a destroyer has come upon her,
upon Babylon;
her warriors are taken;
their bows are broken in pieces,
[l]for the LORD is a God of recompense;

51:46 Israel's exiles should not worry about all the intrigue in Babylon. There will be **violence**, political unrest, and rulers vying for power.

51:47 images. See 50:2 and 51:44. **slain shall fall**. See 51:4.

51:48 All of creation will **sing for joy** when **Babylon**, the great destroyer, falls. Its **destroyers shall come . . . out of the north** (50:3, 9, 41).

51:49 Babylon made other nations drink the cup of God's wrath (25:15–25), and soon Babylon will drink the same cup (25:26).

51:50 Remember the LORD. Israel must recall and renew its covenant with God (2:2–3; 31:31–40). The Israelites should **let Jerusalem** enter their thoughts and draw them home.

51:51 foreigners have come into the holy places. Babylon destroyed the temple (52:12–13) and in doing so profaned God's dwelling place (Ps. 74:4–8; Lam. 1:10).

51:52 execute judgment upon her images. See 50:2 and 51:44, 47.

51:53 No amount of preparation or military buildup can save **Babylon** from destruction.

51:54 A voice. See 50:28.

51:55–56 her mighty voice. A metaphor for Babylon's power. **noise of their voice is raised**. The invader's power will become greater than Babylon's. **he will surely repay**. See 46:10; 50:15, 28; 51:6, 11, 36.

he will surely repay.
57 [m]I will make drunk her officials and her wise men,
[n]her governors, her commanders, and her warriors;
they shall sleep a perpetual sleep and not wake,
declares [o]the King, whose name is the LORD of hosts.

58 "Thus says the LORD of hosts:
The broad [p]wall of Babylon
shall be leveled to the ground,
[q]and her high gates
shall be burned with fire.
[r]The peoples labor for nothing,
and [s]the nations weary themselves only for fire."

59 The word that Jeremiah the prophet commanded Seraiah [t]the son of Neriah, son of
Mahseiah, when he went with Zedekiah king of Judah to Babylon, [u]in the fourth year
of his reign. Seraiah was the quartermaster. 60 [v]Jeremiah wrote in a book all the disaster
that should come upon Babylon, [w]all these words that are written concerning Babylon.
61 And Jeremiah said to Seraiah: "When you come to Babylon, see that you read all these
words, 62 and say, 'O LORD, you have said concerning this place that you will cut it off, so
[x]that nothing shall dwell in it, neither man nor beast, and it shall be [y]desolate forever.'
63 When you finish reading this book, [z, a]tie a stone to it [z]and cast it into the midst of the
Euphrates, 64 and say, [z]'Thus shall Babylon sink, to rise no more, because of the disaster
that I am bringing upon her, [b]and they shall become exhausted.'"

Thus far are the words of Jeremiah.

The Fall of Jerusalem Recounted

52 [c]Zedekiah was twenty-one years old when he became king, and he reigned eleven
years in Jerusalem. His mother's name was Hamutal the daughter of Jeremiah of
Libnah. 2 And he did what was evil in the sight of the LORD, [d]according to all that Jehoiakim
had done. 3 For because of the anger of the LORD it came to the point in Jerusalem and
Judah that he cast them out from his presence.

And Zedekiah rebelled against the king of Babylon. 4 [e]And in the ninth year of his reign,
in the tenth month, on the tenth day of the month, Nebuchadnezzar king of Babylon

57 [m]ver. 39 [n]ver. 23, 28 [o]See ch. 46:18
58 [p]ver. 44; ch. 50:15 [q][Isa. 45:2] [r]Hab. 2:13 [s]ver. 64
59 [t][ch. 32:12] [u][ch. 28:1]
60 [v][ch. 36:2] [w]See ver. 1-58; ch. 50:1-46
62 [x]ch. 50:3 [y]ver. 26
63 [z][ch. 19:10, 11] [a][Rev. 18:21]
64 [z][See ver. 63 above] [b]ver. 58

Chapter 52

1 [c]For ver. 1-27, see 2 Kgs. 24:18–25:21
2 [d]2 Kgs. 23:37; See ch. 22:13-17
4 [e]For ver. 4-16, see ch. 39:1-10

51:57 make drunk. See 25:15–29; 51:38–40. **the King**. God, not human monarchs like Nebuchadnezzar, rules the universe (46:18).

51:58 broad wall of Babylon. See v. 44. **high gates**. Babylon's walls and gates were for defensive purposes, but they could not protect her in the end (v. 53). **peoples labor for nothing**. Humans weary themselves to build great cities to make names for themselves, but God rules history and makes reputations (45:1–5; Hab. 2:12–14).

51:59 Seraiah the son of Neriah. Probably Baruch's brother (32:12). **went with Zedekiah**. Apparently Zedekiah was summoned to Babylon to explain his questionable behavior recounted in 27:1–15. **fourth year**. 594–593 B.C. **quartermaster**. Responsible for the king's travel arrangements.

51:60–62 Jeremiah wrote in a book all these words concerning **Babylon** (most likely 50:2–51:58). **read all these words**. Apparently **Seraiah** was sent to deliver this message, as Baruch was sent in 36:1–8.

Jeremiah 52	*Parallels in 2 Kings 24–25*	*Parallels in Jeremiah 39*
vv. 1–11	24:18–25:7	
vv. 4–11		vv. 1–7
vv. 12–27	25:8–21	
vv. 31–34	25:27–30	

51:63–64 Jeremiah's final symbolic act (cf. 13:1–14; 16:1–9; 19:1–15; etc.) fulfills his initial call to be a prophet to the nations (1:5). **Thus far are the words of Jeremiah** indicates the end of Jeremiah's words either for the whole book or for the scroll composed in 594–593 B.C.

52:1–34 *Conclusion: The Fall of Jerusalem.* The book ends by describing Jerusalem's fall and Zedekiah's blinding (vv. 1–11), the destruction of the temple (vv. 12–23), the exiling of the people (vv. 24–30), and the continuation of the Davidic lineage (vv. 31–34). There are parallels with Jeremiah 39 as well as 2 Kings 24–25 (see chart to the left).

52:1–11 *Jerusalem's Fall and Zedekiah's Blinding.* The content of these verses and 2 Kings 24:18–25:7 is nearly identical, and the content of Jer. 52:4–11 and 39:1–7 is also nearly identical. Thus, this section begins a summary of the results of Jeremiah's preaching (1:10).

52:1 Zedekiah ruled c. 597–586 B.C. Nebuchadnezzar placed him in power to replace Jehoiachin, Zedekiah's nephew (2 Kings 24:17). **Hamutal**. See 2 Kings 24:18. Not mentioned elsewhere. **Jeremiah of Libnah**. Otherwise unknown. Jeremiah the prophet, this Jeremiah, and one other person (Jer. 35:3) have the same name.

52:2 Both Zedekiah and **Jehoiakim** failed to heed God's warnings (21:1–10; 36:1–31).

52:3 cast them out from his presence. Sent the Judeans into exile, as God had warned (Lev. 26:27–39; Deut. 28:64–68). **Zedekiah rebelled** against the man who put him in power (2 Kings 24:17; Jer. 52:1).

10 [f]ver. 26, 27
11 [g][Ezek. 12:13]
12 [h]ch. 1:3 [i][2 Kgs. 25:8] [j][ver. 29] [k]ch. 40:10
15 [l]See ch. 37:13
17 [m]ch. 27:19; See 2 Chr. 4:12-15 [n]2 Chr. 4:2, 10 [o]See ch. 27:22
18 [p]2 Kgs. 25:14
19 [q]1 Kgs. 7:50; 2 Kgs. 25:15 [r]1 Kgs. 7:49 [s]Ex. 25:29; 37:16
20 [t]1 Kgs. 7:25, 44
21 [u]1 Kgs. 7:15
22 [v]1 Kgs. 7:16; [2 Kgs. 25:17]

came with all his army against Jerusalem, and laid siege to it. And they built siegeworks
all around it. **5** So the city was besieged till the eleventh year of King Zedekiah. **6** On the
ninth day of the fourth month the famine was so severe in the city that there was no food
for the people of the land. **7** Then a breach was made in the city, and all the men of war fled
and went out from the city by night by the way of a gate between the two walls, by the
king's garden, and the Chaldeans were around the city. And they went in the direction of
the Arabah. **8** But the army of the Chaldeans pursued the king and overtook Zedekiah in
the plains of Jericho, and all his army was scattered from him. **9** Then they captured the
king and brought him up to the king of Babylon at Riblah in the land of Hamath, and he
passed sentence on him. **10** The king of Babylon slaughtered the sons of Zedekiah before
his eyes, and also slaughtered all the officials of Judah at [f]Riblah. **11** [g]He put out the eyes
of Zedekiah, and bound him in chains, and the king of Babylon took him to Babylon, and
put him in prison [g]till the day of his death.

The Temple Burned

12 [h]In the fifth month, on [i]the tenth day of the month—that was [j]the nineteenth year
of King Nebuchadnezzar, king of Babylon—Nebuzaradan the captain of the bodyguard,
who [k]served the king of Babylon, entered Jerusalem. **13** And he burned the house of the
LORD, and the king's house and all the houses of Jerusalem; every great house he burned
down. **14** And all the army of the Chaldeans, who were with the captain of the guard, broke
down all the walls around Jerusalem. **15** And Nebuzaradan the captain of the guard carried
away captive some of the poorest of the people and the rest of the people who were left
in the city and [l]the deserters who had deserted to the king of Babylon, together with the
rest of the artisans. **16** But Nebuzaradan the captain of the guard left some of the poorest
of the land to be vinedressers and plowmen.

17 And the [m]pillars of bronze that were in the house of the LORD, and the stands and
the [n]bronze sea that were in the house of the LORD, the Chaldeans broke in pieces, and
[o]carried all the bronze to Babylon. **18** And they took away [p]the pots and the shovels and the
snuffers and the basins and the dishes for incense and all the vessels of bronze used in
the temple service; **19** [q]also the small bowls and the fire pans and the basins and the pots
and [r]the lampstands and [s]the dishes for incense [s]and the bowls for drink offerings. What
was of gold the captain of the guard took away as gold, and what was of silver, as silver.
20 As for the two pillars, the one sea, [t]the twelve bronze bulls that were under the sea,[1] and
the stands, which Solomon the king had made for the house of the LORD, the bronze of
all these things was beyond weight. **21** As for the pillars, the height of the one pillar was
eighteen cubits,[2] [u]its circumference was twelve cubits, and its thickness was four fingers,
and it was hollow. **22** On it was a capital of bronze. The height of the one capital was [v]five
cubits. A network and pomegranates, all of bronze, were around the capital. And the second
pillar had the same, with pomegranates. **23** There were ninety-six pomegranates on the
sides; all the pomegranates were a hundred upon the network all around.

[1] Hebrew lacks *the sea* [2] A *cubit* was about 18 inches or 45 centimeters

52:4–6 Nebuchadnezzar punished Zedekiah's rebellion by laying **siege** to **Jerusalem** (39:1–2). Because the siege lasted over a year and because of **famine** in the land (15:1–4), **the city** could hold out no longer.

52:7 breach. See 39:2–3.

52:8–9 The words **and all his army was scattered from him** do not appear in 39:5.

52:10–11 The words **and put him in prison till the day of his death** do not appear in 39:7.

52:12–23 *The Destruction of the Temple.* Though 39:8 has already described the city's burning in general terms, this passage focuses on the pillaging and burning of God's house.

52:12 fifth month. One month after the breach in the city walls (v. 6) **Nebuzaradan** (39:9–10), Nebuchadnezzar's representative, **entered Jerusalem** to complete its destruction.

52:13 See 39:8. Nebuzaradan set fire to the temple, the palace, and all large **houses**. These fires must have destroyed other parts of the city as well. The burning of the temple is not mentioned in 39:8.

52:14 The Chaldean **army . . . broke down all the walls**, thus leaving the city defenseless. Nehemiah began rebuilding the walls c. 445 B.C. (Neh. 2:11–3:32).

52:15–16 carried away captive. See 39:9–10.

52:17–23 See 2 Kings 25:13–17. For a description of these temple furnishings, see the notes on 1 Kings 7:13–47. Nebuzaradan took these ornaments before burning the temple (Jer. 52:13).

The People Exiled to Babylon

24 And the captain of the guard took [w]Seraiah the chief priest and [x]Zephaniah the second
priest and the three keepers of the threshold; 25 and from the city he took an officer who had
been in command of the men of war, and [y]seven men of the king's council, who were found
in the city; and the secretary of the commander of the army, who mustered the people of
the land; and sixty men of the people of the land, who were found in the midst of the city.
26 And Nebuzaradan the captain of the guard took them and brought them to the king of
Babylon at [z]Riblah. 27 And the king of Babylon struck them down and put them to death
at [z]Riblah in the land of Hamath. So Judah was taken into exile out of its land.
28 This is the number of the people whom Nebuchadnezzar carried away captive: [a]in
the seventh year, 3,023 Judeans; 29 [b]in the eighteenth year of Nebuchadnezzar he carried
away captive from Jerusalem 832 persons; 30 in the twenty-third year of Nebuchadnezzar,
Nebuzaradan the captain of the guard carried away captive of the Judeans 745 persons;
all the persons were 4,600.

Jehoiachin Released from Prison

31 [c]And in the thirty-seventh year of the exile of Jehoiachin king of Judah, in the twelfth
month, on the twenty-fifth day of the month, Evil-merodach king of Babylon, in the year
that he began to reign, graciously freed[1] [d]Jehoiachin king of Judah and brought him out
of prison. 32 And he spoke kindly to him and gave him a seat above the seats of [e]the kings
who were with him in Babylon. 33 So Jehoiachin put off his prison garments. And every
day of his life he dined regularly at the king's table, 34 and for his allowance, a regular
allowance was given him by the king, according to his daily needs, until the day of his
death, as long as he lived.

[1] *Hebrew king, lifted up the head of*

24 [w][1 Chr. 6:14, 15] [x][ch. 29:25]
25 [y][Esth. 1:14]
26 [z]ver. 9, 10
27 [z][See ver. 26 above]
28 [a][2 Kgs. 24:12, 14]
29 [b][ver. 12]
31 [c]For ver. 31-34, see 2 Kgs. 25:27-30 [d]ch. 37:1; See ch. 22:24-30
32 [e][ch. 27:3]

52:24–30 *The Exiling of the People.* Babylon removes Judah's chief religious, civic, and military leaders, leaving the nation without wise direction. The exile is not one event, but three or more deportations linked to political machinations.

52:24 Seraiah the chief priest. The grandson of Hilkiah, chief priest during Josiah's reign (1 Chron. 6:13–15). **Zephaniah the second priest**. Probably next in line to be high priest (Jer. 29:24–32). **three keepers of the threshold**. See 35:3–4. The temple's chief leaders were taken into exile.

52:25 Nebuzaradan also exiled several civic leaders. **officer . . . in command of the men of war**. A position perhaps akin to a minister of defense. **seven men of the king's council**. The king's personal advisers or cabinet. **secretary of the commander**. Probably responsible for military personnel. **sixty men of the people of the land**. Most likely leaders of various parts of Judah who took refuge in Jerusalem during the invasion.

52:26–27 Riblah in the land of Hamath. The same place where Nebuchadnezzar judged Zedekiah (39:5).

52:28–30 Nebuchadnezzar took captives from Judah in stages. Many people had fled to other lands (44:1, 8), and many were left in the land (ch. 40). The **seventh year** was c. 597 B.C., when Nebuchadnezzar replaced Jehoiachin with Zedekiah (2 Kings 24:17). **3,023**. This may count only males or leaders, since 2 Kings 24:11–16 gives a larger number. **eighteenth year**. c. 586 B.C. **twenty-third year**. c. 582 B.C. This deportation may have been in response to Gedaliah's assassination (Jeremiah 41) or some other revolt, but specific details are not known.

52:31–34 *The Continuation of the Davidic Lineage.* God's promises cannot fail, and God promised David a permanent kingdom (2 Sam. 7:16; 1 Chron. 17:14) from which the Messiah would come (Jer. 23:1–8; 33:14–22). These verses are virtually identical to 2 Kings 25:27–30.

52:31 the exile of Jehoiachin. See vv. 1, 29; 2 Kings 24:17. **Evil-merodach**. Nebuchadnezzar's successor, who reigned c. 562–560 B.C. Perhaps to show his benevolence, he treated Jehoiachin (who may have been the longest-imprisoned opposing king) with favor.

52:32–34 Whatever Evil-merodach's motives, **Jehoiachin** was treated well **as long as he lived**. The Davidic lineage, like the people, waited in exile for the 70 years to end (25:12; 29:1–14).

INTRODUCTION TO
LAMENTATIONS

Author and Title

In the Hebrew Bible, Lamentations is called *Ekah* ("How"), after the first word in the book. This word occurs in 1:1, 2:1, and 4:1 to emphasize how much Jerusalem has suffered.

The book does not identify its author, which should keep interpreters from unnecessarily contentious debates. Many scholars consider Jeremiah the author. They base this decision on (1) the statement in 2 Chronicles 35:25 that Jeremiah "uttered a lament for Josiah"; (2) the fact that Jeremiah was an eyewitness of Jerusalem's destruction; and (3) the similarities in theological emphasis and vocabulary between the books of Jeremiah and Lamentations. In addition, much Jewish tradition (such as the Septuagint, the Targum on Jeremiah, and the Babylonian Talmud, *Baba Bathra* 15a) attributes this book to Jeremiah. The problems with this view include: (1) Lamentations does not name Jeremiah as its author; (2) the book of Jeremiah details much of Jeremiah's post-587 B.C. activities but says nothing about his writing Lamentations; (3) there are differences in key vocabulary between Jeremiah and Lamentations; and (4) Lamentations provides material for worship in Jerusalem, whereas Jeremiah spent his last years in Egypt.

Others think Lamentations was written by several persons over several years. They argue that the intricately detailed poetry must be the product of an extended period of reflection. They consider the theological variety in the poems to be evidence of multiple authors. The problem with this view is that it does not take fully into account the commonalities between Jeremiah and Lamentations and the book's eyewitness quality.

Given these considerations, it is best to treat Lamentations as the book itself does. That means accepting it as (1) an anonymous work that agrees with the theology of books like Deuteronomy and Jeremiah (see Key Themes); (2) a literary masterpiece; and (3) a work that reflects eyewitness testimony. Though it is possible that Lamentations was penned by more than one poet (as were the Psalms), its unity of theme, movement, and poetic form is best accounted for by accepting a one-author hypothesis.

Date

Lamentations describes the results of Babylon's destruction of Jerusalem in 587 B.C. in vivid (though stylized) detail. The book has the flavor of personal experience and eyewitness testimony, particularly in the descriptions of death and starvation in 4:1–22. Though it is possible that a long time passed between the destruction and the book's composition, there is no compelling reason to accept this conclusion. Since temple worship had begun again by 520–516 B.C. (during the time of Haggai and Zechariah), it is likely that the mourning for the city and temple had reached its height before then. The date of the writing of Lamentations probably falls between 587 and 516 B.C., with a time earlier in the era being more likely.

Theme

The key passage in Lamentations is 3:19–24, where the speaker affirms that belief in God's mercy and faithfulness is the key to a restored relationship with God. This fact is true even for people who have merited and received God's judgment (1:18). Hope, not despair, is the final word in Lamentations.

This theme becomes clear as the book unfolds. Lamentations presents five intricately interconnected poems. Together they describe a movement from horrible loss and personal shame, to restored hope and prayer for renewal. This movement has both individual and community components, and is conveyed by the literary type, acrostic forms, meter, and basic movement of Lamentations. (See Literary Features.)

Purpose, Occasion, and Background

Lamentations was most likely written to be prayed or sung in worship services devoted to asking God's forgiveness and seeking restoration to a covenant relationship with God. Such observances began as early as the months after the temple's destruction in 587 B.C. (Jer. 41:4–5). They continued when the temple was rebuilt during Zechariah's time (c. 520 B.C.; see Zech. 7:3–5; 8:19). As time passed, Lamentations was read and sung as part of annual observances related to remembering the temple's destruction.

Key Themes

Lamentations is a neglected book. This is unfortunate because it presents key theological concepts composed creatively during an important era in Israel's history.

1. It offers compelling prayers that confess sin, express renewed hope, and declare total dependence on God's grace.
2. It is the only book in the Bible written by a person who endured one manifestation of the divine judgment the Bible consistently calls "the day of the LORD" (cf. Joel 2:1–2; Amos 5:18; Zeph. 1:14–16).
3. The book's authorship, setting, contents, and theology underline its value for understanding the nature of pain, sin, and redemption.
4. Lamentations agrees with the theology of Leviticus 26, Deuteronomy 27–30, Joshua–Kings, and Jeremiah in that it affirms that Jerusalem fell:
   a. because of the people's sins (Lam. 1:18);
   b. because they rejected God's word sent through the prophets (2:8, 14, 17);
   c. because their leaders led them astray (4:13). God warned (2:17), but the people did not heed the warning.
5. It affirms God's faithful, never-ceasing mercy (3:19–24; cf. Deut. 30:1–10). Therefore, readers can know that God is not finished with his people even when they sin greatly.
6. The book agrees with Psalms in that it affirms that prayers of confession and petition are the means for restoring a broken relationship with God. These poems also coincide with the Psalms in their honest expressions of pain and their dismay at what God has allowed to happen. By attributing what has occurred to God's will, the poems also share the Psalms' emphasis on God's sovereignty as King of creation (Ps. 103:19).
7. Lamentations agrees with the emphasis on "the day of the LORD" found in the prophetic books. This "day" is the day God comes to judge sin. It can occur in historical contexts like 587 B.C., or it can occur at the end of time and be the final "day of the LORD." Regardless, such "days" do occur, and people need to take seriously the warnings about such days in Lamentations and the rest of the Bible.

History of Salvation Summary

Isaiah had foretold God's future for Jerusalem: she would be the vehicle for bringing light to all the Gentiles (Isa. 2:1–5) in the Messianic era; but the unfaithful in her midst, who dominated her life and testimony, must be purged from her by disaster, while the faithful remain to build her up (Isa. 1:24–28). Lamentations is a book for the faithful, enabling them to mourn for Zion's disaster and to pray in hope for her renewal, and thus for the completion of God's saving purpose for the world. (For an explanation of the "History of Salvation," see the Overview of the Bible, pp. 23–26. See also History of Salvation in the Old Testament: Preparing the Way for Christ, pp. 2635–2661.)

Literary Features

As its title indicates, the book of Lamentations is a collection of laments, or melancholy dirges, for a ruined society. The poems in the book could also be termed elegies or funeral orations, in which the author expresses deep personal and communal grief for the dead and for all of the suffering that surrounds their loss. In terms of structure, the first four poems are acrostics. This structure, using the entire Hebrew alphabet, matches the poet's intent, which is to give full expression to the suffering of his people and the sorrows of his own soul—in effect, to offer a lament "from A to Z" (or *aleph* to *taw*). Perhaps the highly structured form of the acrostic is also an attempt to impose some sense of order on a tragic situation that is chaotic beyond what anyone can bear.

Lamentations is not an emotional outburst but a formal expression of grief in a high literary style. However, each lament moves rapidly from one topic to the next, revealing that the writer's soul is still in turmoil. Like most elegies, the lyrics in Lamentations deal with profound loss by recollecting past glories and cataloging what is now gone forever, lamenting the finality of the losses while at the same time seeking consolation in present sorrows and some hope for the future.

Literary type. Each chapter of Lamentations is a lament, many examples of which exist in the Psalms (e.g., Psalms 3, 13, 44, 77). Laments in the Psalms vary in format, but they regularly include a description of the problem, protests of innocence, a plea for help, a statement of faith, and a pledge of service when the situation changes. Except for "pleas of innocence," all these characteristics occur in Lamentations. The "confession of faith" and "pledge of service" are also less evident, perhaps because the book focuses on sinful persons returning to the Lord rather than faithful persons pouring out their hearts to God because of unjust suffering.

Acrostic forms. An acrostic poem uses the Hebrew alphabet as a key organizing principle. Several examples exist in the Bible; Psalm 119 is probably the best known. There is great variety in the acrostic form. Indeed, Lamentations utilizes four different types.

Some acrostic poems begin each succeeding line with the next letter of the alphabet. For example, chapter 1 consists of 22 one-verse sentences. Therefore 1:1 starts with a word that begins with *aleph*, 1:2 uses a word that begins with *beth*, and so forth through the 22 letters of the Hebrew alphabet.

Other acrostic poems open a segment with *aleph* and then begin each succeeding segment with the succeeding letter of the alphabet. Only the first word in a stanza exhibits the acrostic pattern. For example, chapters 1 and 2 feature 22 three-line verses, for a total of 66 lines. The first word in 1:1, 2:1, and 4:1 begins with an *aleph*; the first word in 1:2, 2:2, and 4:2 begins with *beth*; and so forth.

There are variations on that second type. For example, chapter 4 follows the same procedure as chapters 1 and 2, except that each segment is two lines long, for a total of 44 lines.

Still other acrostic poems have stanzas of three lines each that begin with the same letter of the alphabet. Thus, chapter 3 has 66 lines, like chapters 1 and 2. But each line in 3:1–3 begins with *aleph*; 3:4–6 has each line begin with *beth*; and so forth. The composition of acrostics requires great skill.

Meter. Lamentations often utilizes *qinah* meter, a type used in some passages that mourn the dead (e.g., Isaiah 14; Ezekiel 27). This rhythm is based on lines of two unequal parts. The first part normally consists of three words and the second part usually includes two words. This pattern creates three accents, then two, thereby creating a falling, rising, and falling cadence. In this way the poems seem to "limp," as if the reader is walking haltingly along behind a funeral procession.

Basic movement. The acrostic forms noted above convey the book's movement from Jerusalem's protest concerning what she has suffered (1:1–22) to her penitent turning to God again (5:1–22). Chapters 1–2 relate Jerusalem's horrible defeat at the hands of Babylon. People, property, opportunity, and hope have been lost. A narrator and a prophetic voice encourage Jerusalem to turn to God. Jerusalem prays, but almost solely in protest. These chapters are the least acrostic of all the poems, and they portray the least movement toward God.

Chapter 3 presents an individual who counsels Jerusalem to turn to God, just as he has done. His counsel includes statements of what he endured, and of the justice of what he endured, and of the way he came to trust in God's faithfulness (3:19–24). This "most acrostic" of the chapters exhibits the most faith in God.

Chapter 4 is much like chapters 1–2 in its speakers and tone. Jerusalem continues to question the justice of what she has endured, but she admits her sin and takes comfort in the fact that her pain will soon end. Thus, the two-line acrostic form conveys protest, but less protest than chapters 1–2.

Chapter 5 is a community lament that presents Jerusalem crying out to God and casting all her future on him. Chapter 5 is to the community what chapter 3 was for the individual, in that the whole community has come to accept what the individual in chapter 3 advised.

Outline

I. How Lonely Sits the City (1:1–22)

   A. Jerusalem's devastation (1:1–11)

   B. Jerusalem's call for help (1:12–22)

II. God Has Set Zion under a Cloud (2:1–22)

A. The effects of God's punishment (2:1–10)
B. The need to cry out to God (2:11–19)
C. Jerusalem asks God to see and act (2:20–22)

III. I Am the Man Who Has Seen Affliction (3:1–66)

A. Enduring suffering, experiencing faithfulness (3:1–24)
B. Responding to God's goodness and sovereignty (3:25–39)
C. Praying for renewal (3:40–47)
D. Maintaining confidence in God (3:48–66)

IV. How the Gold Has Grown Dim (4:1–22)

A. The suffering of Jerusalem's children (4:1–10)
B. God's punishing of Jerusalem's religious leaders (4:11–16)
C. The power of Jerusalem's enemies (4:17–20)
D. The end of Jerusalem's suffering (4:21–22)

V. Restore Us to Yourself, O Lord (5:1–22)

A. Opening petition (5:1)
B. The woes Jerusalem has faced (5:2–18)
C. A concluding prayer for restoration (5:19–22)

LAMENTATIONS

1

How Lonely Sits the City

1 [a]How lonely sits the city
that was full of people!
How like [b]a widow has she become,
she who was great among the nations!
She who was [c]a princess among the provinces
has become [d]a slave.

2 [e]She weeps bitterly in the night,
with tears on her cheeks;
[f]among all her lovers
she has [g]none to comfort her;
[h]all her friends have dealt treacherously with her;
they have become her enemies.

3 [i]Judah has gone into exile because of affliction
and hard servitude;
[j]she dwells now among the nations,
[k]but finds no resting place;
her pursuers have all overtaken her
in the midst of her distress.[1]

4 The roads to Zion mourn,
for none come to [l]the festival;
[m]all her gates are desolate;
her priests [n]groan;
her virgins have been afflicted,[2]
and she herself suffers bitterly.

5 [o]Her foes have become the head;
her [p]enemies prosper,
because [q]the LORD has afflicted her
[r]for the multitude of her transgressions;

[1] Or *in the narrow passes* [2] Septuagint, Old Latin *dragged away*

Chapter 1

1 [a][Jer. 7:34] [b][Jer. 15:8] [c][ch. 5:16; Ezra 4:20; Eccles. 2:8] [d]Isa. 31:8
2 [e]Ps. 6:6; Jer. 9:1; 13:17 [f]ver. 19; Jer. 22:22; 30:14 [g]ver. 9, 16, 17, 21; Eccles. 4:1 [h]See Ezek. 23:22-26
3 [i]Jer. 52:27 [j][ch. 2:9; Deut. 28:64, 65] [k]Jer. 45:3
4 [l]See ch. 2:6 [m]Jer. 14:2 [n]ver. 8, 11, 21, 22
5 [o][Deut. 28:13, 44; Jer. 13:21] [p]Jer. 12:1 [q]ver. 12; ch. 3:33 [r]Jer. 30:14, 15; Dan. 9:16

1:1–22 *How Lonely Sits the City.* Lamentations begins with a description of Jerusalem's devastation (vv. 1–11) and reports of her calls for help (vv. 12–22). Jerusalem speaks in vv. 9b, 11b–16, and 18–22. A narrator speaks in vv. 1–9a, 10–11a, and 17.

1:1–11 *Jerusalem's Devastation.* Jerusalem lies in waste from invasion and conquest. This section depicts her reversals (vv. 1–3), emptiness (vv. 4–6), uncleanness and guilt (vv. 7–9), and groaning (vv. 10–11).

1:1 How (Hb. *'ekah*). An exclamation often associated with funeral language for people or cities (cf. Isa. 1:21; Jer. 48:17). Note the contrasts: **full of people/lonely; great/widow; princess/slave.** Jerusalem's reversal of fortunes is total.

1:2 Jerusalem **weeps bitterly in the night** because of her losses (v. 1). **lovers . . . friends.** Her former allies (cf. vv. 9, 16, 17, 21; Jer. 22:20–22; 30:14; Ezek. 16:37–41; 23:22–29).

1:3 gone into exile. See Jer. 52:24–30. **because of affliction and hard servitude**. See Lam. 1:7, 9; 3:1, 19. Exiles were often forced to work unstintingly. Such labor evokes memories of Israel's Egyptian bondage (cf. Ex. 1:1–14; 2:23; 5:11; 6:6, 9). **dwells now among the nations . . . no resting place**. A reversal of God's own promises to Israel (e.g., Deut. 12:10). **pursuers have all overtaken her**. See Jer. 39:1–10 (cf. 52:1–11); 40:1–6.

1:4 Devastated Jerusalem lacks worshipers (cf. Jer. 41:4–5) to travel her **roads**, enter her **gates**, and attend any **festival**. The chief priests have been killed (Jer. 52:24–27), and the remaining **priests groan**. The **virgins** were women who participated in joyful processions (Ps. 68:24–25), rejoicings and dances (Jer. 31:4), and generally expressed joy. Now they suffer.

1:5 her enemies prosper. Babylon has conquered Jerusalem (Jer. 52:1–30) because of her **transgressions**, i.e., her willfully breaking God's law (cf. Lam. 1:5, 14, 22; Amos 1:3, 6, 9; etc.). Jerusalem's sins have affected **her children**, that is, her inhabitants.

[s]her children have gone away,
captives before the foe.

6 From the daughter of Zion
all her majesty has departed.
Her princes have become like deer
[t]that find no pasture;
they fled without strength
before the pursuer.

7 Jerusalem remembers
in the days of her affliction and wandering
[u]all the precious things
that were hers from [v]days of old.
When her people fell into the hand of the foe,
and there was none to help her,
her foes gloated over her;
they [w]mocked at her downfall.

8 [x]Jerusalem sinned grievously;
therefore she became filthy;
all who honored her despise her,
[y]for they have seen her nakedness;
she herself [z]groans
and turns her face away.

9 Her uncleanness was [a]in her skirts;
[b]she took no thought of her future;[1]
therefore her fall is terrible;
[c]she has no comforter.
"O LORD, behold my affliction,
for the enemy has [d]triumphed!"

10 The enemy has stretched out his hands
over all her [e]precious things;
for she has seen [f]the nations
enter her sanctuary,
those whom you [g]forbade
to enter your congregation.

11 All her people [z]groan
as [h]they search for bread;
they trade their [e]treasures for [i]food
to revive their strength.

5 [s]2 Chr. 36:17, 20; See Jer. 52:28-30
6 [t][Jer. 14:6]
7 [u]ver. 10, 11 [v]ch. 2:17; Jer. 46:26 [w]Obad. 12, 13; [Ps. 119:51]
8 [x][Zech. 13:1] [y][Ezek. 16:37] [z]ver. 4, 21, 22
9 [a][Jer. 13:22] [b][Deut. 32:29; Isa. 47:7] [c]ver. 2 [d]Jer. 48:26
10 [e]ver. 7 [f]Ps. 79:1; Jer. 51:51 [g][Deut. 23:3; Neh. 13:1]
11 [z][See ver. 8 above] [h]ch. 2:12; 4:4; [Jer. 38:9; 52:6] [e][See ver. 10 above] [i]ver. 19

[1] *Or end*

1:6 daughter of Zion. A metaphor for Jerusalem, which rested on Mount Zion like a child on a parent's shoulder (cf. note on 3:48). **her majesty has departed**. Most likely God's glory (Ps. 96:6; 145:5) and kingship (Ps. 104:1; 111:3; 145:5, 12). Judah's **princes** were famished with hunger when they **fled** and were captured (cf. 2 Kings 25:3–5; Jer. 52:6–11).

1:7 In exile the people recall the days of David, Solomon, and Josiah (**all the precious things**) in **days of old**. These precious things have been replaced with worthless things like the gloating and mocking of enemies.

1:8 Jerusalem sinned grievously. See v. 5. **filthy** (lit., "impurity"; cf. v. 17). This may refer to menstrual discharge (Lev. 12:2, 5) but could refer to a willing display of **her nakedness**. By becoming naked for her lovers (Lam. 1:2) she has become impure to her covenant husband (see Jer. 31:32).

1:9 Her uncleanness. The sins she committed (v. 8) were **in her skirts**, i.e., they clung to her. She **took no thought of her future** in the sense that she did not expect things to turn out as they had, despite God's warnings in Lev. 26:14–46, Deut. 28:15–68, and the Prophetic Books. **no comforter**. Neither God nor her allies (Lam. 1:2) comfort her. **O LORD, behold my affliction**. Jerusalem speaks for the first time, asking God to take note of what the **enemy** has done.

1:10 The narrator agrees that the **enemy** has succeeded; the enemy has taken **her precious things**, such as her children (v. 5). **the nations enter her sanctuary**. Babylon plundered the temple in 597 B.C. (Jer. 28:1–3) and burned it in 587 (Jer. 52:13). **those whom you forbade**. See Deut. 23:3–6.

1:11 they search for bread. Jerusalem's people sought bread during Babylon's siege (Jer. 37:21). Jerusalem asks God a second time (cf. Lam. 1:9) to **see** how the enemy treats her.

12[j]Job 21:29; Ps. 80:12 [k][Dan. 9:12] [l]ver. 5 [m]See Jer. 12:13
13[n]Ps. 102:3 [o]Ps. 9:15; Ezek. 12:13; 17:20 [p]ch. 3:11; See Jer. 8:18
14[q]Deut. 28:48
15[r][Isa. 63:2, 3]
16[s]See Jer. 13:17 [t]ver. 2, 21 [u][ver. 11]
17[v]Isa. 1:15; Jer. 4:31 [t][See ver. 16 above]

"Look, O LORD, and see,
for I am despised."

12 "Is it nothing to you, all [j]you who pass by?
[k]Look and see
if there is any sorrow like my sorrow,
which was brought upon me,
which [l]the LORD inflicted
on [m]the day of his fierce anger.

13 "From on high he [n]sent fire;
into my bones[1] he made it descend;
[o]he spread a net for my feet;
he turned me back;
[p]he has left me stunned,
faint all the day long.

14 "My transgressions were bound[2] into [q]a yoke;
by his hand they were fastened together;
they were set upon my neck;
he caused my strength to fail;
the Lord gave me into the hands
of those whom I cannot withstand.

15 "The Lord rejected
all my mighty men in my midst;
he summoned an assembly against me
to crush my young men;
[r]the Lord has trodden as in a winepress
the virgin daughter of Judah.

16 "For these things [s]I weep;
my eyes flow with tears;
for [t]a comforter is far from me,
one to [u]revive my spirit;
my children are desolate,
for the enemy has prevailed."

17 [v]Zion stretches out her hands,
but [t]there is none to comfort her;
the LORD has commanded against Jacob
that his neighbors should be his foes;
Jerusalem has become
a filthy thing among them.

[1] Septuagint; Hebrew *bones and* [2] The meaning of the Hebrew is uncertain

1:12–22 *Jerusalem's Call for Help.* Jerusalem expresses her acute sorrow (vv. 12–16), which is attested by the narrator (v. 17) and which leads to prayer for relief (vv. 18–22).

1:12 Jerusalem now speaks (vv. 12–16). She addresses those **who pass by**, perhaps because God has not answered. She wants them to **look and see**, just as she wanted God to see and act (vv. 9, 11). **day of his fierce anger**. Cf. Isa. 2:6–22; Jer. 12:3.

1:13 From on high he sent fire. Fire is a common metaphor for judgment (Amos 1:3–2:5). The phrase reminds readers of Sodom and Gomorrah (cf. Gen. 19:23–29; Lam. 4:6). **into my bones**. The very core of Jerusalem's being (Jer. 20:9). **spread a net**. As one does to trap an animal (cf. Ps. 35:7; 57:6; Prov. 29:5; Hos. 7:12).

1:14 A **yoke** represents power and authority (e.g., Jer. 27:8). God placed Jerusalem under the power of her own sins, which **caused** her **strength to fail**, resulting in God giving her **into the hands of** her foes (cf. Deut. 28:64–68; Jer. 52:1–30).

1:15 rejected. Or "spurned" (Ps. 119:118). **he summoned an assembly**. God brought an overwhelming fighting force against Jerusalem (Jer. 52:1–30). **trodden as in a winepress**. Cf. Isa. 63:1–6.

1:16 Jerusalem weeps after the devastation, just like Jeremiah wept (Jer. 13:17) when he predicted it. **comforter**. See Lam. 1:9. **enemy has prevailed**. See vv. 7–10.

1:17 The narrator verifies Jerusalem's claims of loneliness and lack of **comfort** (cf. vv. 9, 16), God's sovereignty in the situation (vv. 12–13), and Jerusalem's sinful past (vv. 5, 9, 14).

18 [w]"The LORD is in the right,
[x]for I have rebelled against his word;
but hear, all you peoples,
and see my suffering;
[y]my young women and my young men
have gone into captivity.

19 "I called to [z]my lovers,
but they deceived me;
my priests and elders
perished in the city,
while [a]they sought food
to revive their strength.

20 "Look, O LORD, for I am in distress;
[b]my stomach churns;
my heart is wrung within me,
because I have been very rebellious.
[c]In the street the sword bereaves;
in the house it is like death.

21 "They heard[1] [d]my groaning,
yet [e]there is no one to comfort me.
All my enemies have heard of my trouble;
[f]they are glad that you have done it.
You have brought[2] the day you announced;
[f]now let them be as I am.

22 [g]"Let all their evildoing come before you,
and deal with them
as [h]you have dealt with me
because of all my transgressions;
for [d]my groans are many,
and [i]my heart is faint."

The Lord Has Destroyed Without Pity

2 1 How the Lord in his anger
has set the daughter of Zion [j]under a cloud!
[k]He has cast down from heaven to earth

[1] Septuagint, Syriac *Hear* [2] Syriac *Bring*

18[w]See Jer. 12:1 [x]1 Sam. 12:14, 15 [y][Deut. 28:41]
19[z]See ver. 2 [a]ver. 11
20[b]ch. 2:11; Job 30:27; Isa. 16:11 [c]Deut. 32:25; Ezek. 7:15; See Jer. 15:2
21[d]ver. 4, 8, 11 [e]ver. 2, 16, 17 [f][ch. 4:21; Jer. 50:11]
22[g]Ps. 109:14, 15 [h]ver. 12; ch. 2:20 [d][See ver. 21 above] [i]See Jer. 8:18

Chapter 2

1[j][ch. 3:44] [k][Matt. 11:23]; See Isa. 14:15

1:18 Jerusalem confesses that God **is in the right** (cf. Ps. 51:4) for judging her rebellion. **but hear.** Nonetheless, she desires comfort from **all you peoples**.

1:19 I called to my lovers. Jerusalem asked her allies for help (cf. Jer. 27:1–15; 37:1–10), but to no avail. **they deceived me.** They promised help they could not or would not deliver. **priests and elders.** Religious and civic leaders who misled the people (cf. Jer. 2:8, 26). **perished . . . while they sought food.** A pitiable end, regardless of their spiritual condition.

1:20 Again Jerusalem asks God to **look** at her **distress** (cf. vv. 9, 11). Her **stomach churns**. Her "inward parts" (Isa. 16:11), i.e., the emotions, are in turmoil. **I have been very rebellious.** See Lam. 1:18. **the sword bereaves.** See Jer. 15:1–4.

1:21 no one to comfort me. See vv. 9, 16, 17. **the day you announced.** The day of judgment promised by Moses and the prophets (see vv. 12–13). **let them be as I am.** Jerusalem asked that God judge her foes, which Jer. 27:7 and 46:1–51:64 indicate will occur in due course.

2:1–22 *God Has Set Zion under a Cloud.* This chapter emphasizes the totality of God's judgment of Jerusalem. The verses unfold in three parts, each of which has a different main speaker. In vv. 1–10 the narrator describes the effects of God's punishment; in vv. 11–19 a prophetic voice like Jeremiah's grieves the city's losses and counsels her to cry out to God; and in vv. 20–22 Jerusalem again asks God to see what she has suffered and to act on her behalf.

2:1–10 *The Effects of God's Punishment.* The narrator stresses God's unrelenting attack (vv. 1–3); his treatment of Jerusalem like an enemy (vv. 4–5); and his devastation of Jerusalem's temple (vv. 6–7), defenses (vv. 8–9a), and leaders (vv. 9b–10).

2:1 How. See note on 1:1. **the Lord in his anger.** Over Judah's long-term, ingrained sin (1:9, 14, 18, 20, 22). **under a cloud.** A metaphor for the darkness of God's punishment (cf. 2 Sam. 22:12; Ps. 18:11; Jer. 13:16). **He has cast down.** See Lam. 1:12, 21–22. **From heaven to earth** describes Israel's fall from greatest favor (cf. Deut. 28:1–14) to terrible devastation (cf. Deut. 28:15–68). **he has not remembered.** In contrast to when he mercifully reached out to deliver his people (Ex. 2:23–25). **his footstool.** A metaphor for either the ark of the covenant or the temple in Ps. 99:5; 132:7; and 1 Chron. 28:2; here probably Jerusalem itself. **day of his anger.** See Lam. 1:12–13, 21.

the splendor of Israel;
he has not remembered [l]his footstool
in the day of his anger.

2 The Lord [m]has swallowed up [n]without mercy
all the habitations of Jacob;
in his wrath [o]he has broken down
the strongholds of the daughter of Judah;
he has brought [p]down to the ground [p]in dishonor
the kingdom [q]and its rulers.

3 He has cut down in [r]fierce anger
all [s]the might of Israel;
[t]he has withdrawn from them his right hand
in the face of the enemy;
[u]he has burned like a flaming fire in Jacob,
consuming all around.

4 [v]He has bent his bow like an enemy,
with his right hand set [w]like a foe;
and he has killed all who were delightful in our eyes
in the tent of the daughter of Zion;
he has poured out his fury like fire.

5 [w]The Lord has become like an enemy;
[x]he has swallowed up Israel;
[y]he has swallowed up all its palaces;
he has laid in ruins its strongholds,
and he has multiplied in the daughter of Judah
[z]mourning and lamentation.

6 He has laid waste his booth like a garden,
laid in ruins [a]his meeting place;
[a] the LORD has made Zion forget
festival and [b]Sabbath,
and in his fierce indignation has spurned king and priest.

7 [c]The Lord has scorned his altar,
[d]disowned his sanctuary;
[e]he has delivered into the hand of the enemy
the walls of her palaces;

1 [l]1 Chr. 28:2
2 [m]ver. 16; [Ps. 35:25; 56:2; Ezek. 36:3] [n]ver. 17, 21; ch. 3:43; [Ezek. 9:5, 10] [o]Ps. 89:40 [p]Ps. 74:7 [q]Isa. 43:28
3 [r]See Jer. 12:13 [s]1 Sam. 2:1 [t]Ps. 74:11 [u]Ps. 79:5; 89:46
4 [v]ch. 3:12 [w]See Jer. 30:14
5 [w][See ver. 4 above] [x]ver. 16; [Ps. 35:25; 56:2; Ezek. 36:3] [y][2 Kgs. 25:9] [z]Isa. 29:2
6 [a]ch. 1:4; Isa. 1:13; Zeph. 3:18 [b]Isa. 1:13
7 [c][Ps. 89:38] [d][Ezek. 24:21] [e]Deut. 32:30

2:2 without mercy. In contrast to his typical attitude toward Israel (cf. 2 Chron. 36:15; Joel 2:18). **brought down . . . in dishonor**. See Jer. 52:1–30.

2:3 God's **right hand**, which in times past shattered Pharaoh's army (Ex. 15:6, 12) was now **withdrawn . . . in the face of the enemy**.

2:4 bent his bow. In contrast to how he fought for Israel in the past, now God has fought against them. **right hand**. See note on v. 3. **like a foe**. God has sided with Babylon (cf. Jer. 27:6–11). **he has killed**. See Jer. 15:1–4; 52:1–11, 24–27.

2:6 laid waste his booth. Destroyed the temple, the place where his name and his presence dwell (1 Kings 9:1–9). **his meeting place**. The temple, where he communes with worshipers. **forget**. The memory of these celebrations is growing dim, for they occur no more. **festival**. The great national annual gathering before God (Deut. 16:1–17).

2:7 Disowned occurs only here and Ps. 89:39 ("renounced"), which notes that God has rejected the Davidic covenant. **Sanctuary** ("holy place") implies all the buildings and walls of the temple complex (cf. Ps. 74:2–3). **her palaces**. Perhaps those of the king, which were adjacent to the temple (cf. 1 Kings 7:1–12). **raised a clamor**. Israel's enemies rejoiced over their victory as if they were having a party (cf. Ps. 74:4–8).

Parallels between Jeremiah and Lamentations

Jeremiah	Lamentations
I will make this house like Shiloh (chs. 7, 26)	The Lord has scorned . . . his sanctuary (2:7)
Let my eyes run down with tears (14:17–22)	my eyes flow with rivers of tears (3:48–51)
can I not do with you as this potter has done? (18:6)	regarded as earthen pots, the work of a potter's hands! (4:2)
eat the flesh of their sons and their daughters (19:9)	Should women eat the fruit of their womb? (2:20)
vain hopes (23:16)	Your prophets have seen for you false and deceptive visions (2:14)

[f]they raised a clamor in the house of the LORD
as on the day of festival.

8 [g]The LORD determined to lay in ruins
[h]the wall of the daughter of Zion;
[i]he stretched out the measuring line;
he did not restrain his hand from destroying;
[j]he caused rampart and wall to lament;
[j] they languished together.

9 Her gates have sunk into the ground;
[k]he has ruined [k]and broken her bars;
[l]her king and princes are among the nations;
the law is no more,
and [m]her prophets find
no vision from the LORD.

10 The elders of the daughter of Zion
[n]sit on the ground [o]in silence;
[p]they have thrown dust on their heads
and [q]put on sackcloth;
the young women of Jerusalem
have bowed their heads to the ground.

11 [r]My eyes are spent with weeping;
[s]my stomach churns;
[t]my bile is poured out to the ground
[u]because of the destruction of the daughter of my people,
[v]because infants and babies [w]faint
in the streets of the city.

12 They cry to their mothers,
[x]"Where is bread and wine?"
[w]as they faint like a wounded man
in the streets of the city,
as their life is poured out
on their mothers' bosom.

13 What can I say for you, [y]to what compare you,
O daughter of Jerusalem?
[y]What can I liken to you, that I may comfort you,
O virgin daughter of Zion?
[z]For your ruin is vast as the sea;
who can heal you?

14 [a]Your prophets have seen for you
false and deceptive visions;

7 [f]Ps. 74:4
8 [g][Jer. 5:10] [h]ver. 18 [i]See 2 Kgs. 21:13 [j]Jer. 14:2
9 [k]Jer. 51:30; Nah. 3:13 [l][Hos. 3:4] [m]Ps. 74:9
10 [n]ch. 1:1; 3:28; Isa. 3:26 [o]Ezek. 3:15 [p]See Josh. 7:6 [q]Jer. 48:37; Ezek. 7:18; Amos 8:10; See Jer. 4:8
11 [r][ver. 18; ch. 5:17; Ps. 6:7] [s]See ch. 1:20 [t][Job 16:13] [u]ch. 3:48 [v][ch. 4:4; Jer. 44:7] [w]ver. 19; [Isa. 51:20]
12 [x]See ch. 1:11 [w][See ver. 11 above]
13 [y][ch. 1:12] [z]2 Sam. 5:20; [Ezek. 26:3]
14 [a]See Jer. 5:31

2:8 The LORD determined. God's plan (cf. Jer. 18:11; 29:20; 36:3; 50:45) was to overthrow the rebellious, impenitent people. **measuring line**. God marked off what would be destroyed and what would be spared (cf. Amos 7:7–9).

2:9 God caused loss of protection (**gates**, **bars**, walls [v. 7]), loss of leadership (**king and princes**), loss of written revelation (**the law**), and loss of specific revelatory direction (**her prophets find no vision**).

2:10 The people's civic leaders (elders, cf. 1:19) have no direction to give. The **young women** sang and danced joyously at ceremonies (1:4; cf. Ex. 15:20; Judg. 21:21; Ps. 68:25; Jer. 31:13); now they mourn.

2:11–19 *The Need to Cry Out to God.* An eyewitness who shares Jeremiah's theology notes the fate of Jerusalem's children (vv. 11–12), regrets her trust in false prophets (vv. 13–14) and status as a byword for ruin (vv. 15–16), and counsels her to cry out to the sovereign God for help (vv. 17–19).

2:11 stomach churns. See note on 1:20. **my bile**. Lit., "my liver," i.e., emotions. **daughter of my people**. A term of endearment for Jerusalem (cf. Jer. 8:19–22; 14:17; and note on Lam. 3:48). **infants and babies**. Jerusalem's most vulnerable inhabitants suffer because of their parents' failures (cf. 2:20; 4:10; Deut. 28:41, 50, 53–57; Jer. 10:20).

2:12 Children **cry** out **to their mothers** for food, only to die in their mothers' arms. Adult sins cause grief to children.

2:14 Judah's **prophets** were part of the problem (cf. Jer. 14:13–22; 23:9–40; 27:1–29:32; Ezek. 13:1–19; Hos. 4:5). **false and deceptive visions**. See Jer. 27:14–15; 37:18–19. **not exposed your iniquity**. Their sins were the ultimate source of their problems, but the prophets avoided this subject (cf. Jer. 5:30–31). **to restore your fortunes**. Repentance would have led to renewal, but the prophets offered only **false and misleading** sermons of peace (Jer. 6:14) and safety.

14[b][Isa. 58:1] [c]See Jer. 30:3 [d]See Jer. 5:31 [e][Jer. 23:33, 34]
15[f]See 2 Chr. 29:8 [g]Ps. 48:2; Ezek. 16:14
16[h]ch. 3:46; [Job 16:9, 10] [i]See ver. 2 [j][Ps. 35:21]
17[k]See Lev. 26:14-45; Deut. 28:15-68 [l]ch. 1:7; Jer. 46:26 [m]See ver. 2 [n]ver. 2, 21 [o][Ps. 38:16; 89:42] [p][ver. 3]
18[q]ver. 8 [r]See ver. 11 [s]Ps. 32:4; 42:3 [t]Ps. 77:2 [u]Ps. 17:8
19[v]Ps. 119:147, 148 [w]Ps. 62:8; [1 Sam. 7:6] [x][1 Tim. 2:8] [y]See ver. 11, 12
20[z]ch. 1:22 [a]ch. 4:10; See Jer. 19:9

[b]they have not exposed your iniquity
to [c]restore your fortunes,
[d]but have seen for you [e]oracles
that are false and misleading.

15 All who pass along the way
clap their hands at you;
[f]they hiss and wag their heads
at the daughter of Jerusalem:
"Is this the city that was called
[g]the perfection of beauty,
[g]the joy of all the earth?"

16 [h]All your enemies
rail against you;
they hiss, they gnash their teeth,
they cry: "We [i]have swallowed her!
Ah, this is the day we longed for;
now we have it; [j]we see it!"

17 The LORD has done what he purposed;
he has carried out [k]his word,
which he commanded [l]long ago;
[m]he has thrown down [n]without pity;
[o]he has made the enemy rejoice over you
and exalted the [p]might of your foes.

18 Their heart cried to the Lord.
O [q]wall of the daughter of Zion,
[r]let tears stream down like a torrent
[s]day and night!
[t]Give yourself no rest,
[u]your eyes no respite!

19 "Arise, [v]cry out in the night,
at the beginning of the night watches!
[w]Pour out your heart like water
before the presence of the Lord!
[x]Lift your hands to him
for the lives of your children,
[y]who faint for hunger
at the head of every street."

20 Look, O LORD, and see!
[z]With whom have you dealt thus?
[a]Should women eat the fruit of their womb,

2:15 Jerusalem's foes mock her downfall. They even quote a line from Ps. 48:2 (which celebrates Jerusalem as the **joy of all the earth**) to gloat over her current woeful condition.

2:16 Jerusalem's enemies claim they have **swallowed her**, which vv. 2, 5, and 8 assert God has done; they were merely God's instruments in this process (Jer. 27:1–15). **the day we longed for**. See Obad. 10–14.

2:17 what he purposed. See 1:18 and 2:8. God banished the people because of their sins (cf. Lev. 26:14–39; Deut. 28:64–68). God **carried out his word**, which he delivered through Moses and the prophets (2 Kings 17:7–23). **thrown down without pity**. Once judgment began, it proceeded without interruption. Jerusalem had so often rejected the mercy of forgiveness received through repentance that only punishment remained as an option. **he has . . . exalted . . . your foes**. Rather than defeating them on Judah's behalf.

2:18–19 Now Jerusalem (**daughter of Zion**) must cry out to God, just as the speaker (v. 11) has cried out for Jerusalem. She must turn to God for the sake of her children, who are fainting **for hunger** (see v. 12).

2:20–22 *Jerusalem Asks God to See and Act.* Jerusalem notes her people's suffering (v. 20), asserts God's lack of pity (v. 21), and remarks on the totality of the day of wrath (v. 22).

2:20 With whom have you dealt thus? Jerusalem was God's chosen city (1 Kings 9:1–9), yet God has judged her (Jer. 7:1–8:3). **eat the fruit of their womb**. Cannibalism of this type did occur in wartime (see 2 Kings 6:24–31). Moses had warned that such would happen when Israel broke her covenant with God (cf. Lev. 26:29; Deut. 28:52–57; Jer. 19:1–9; Ezek. 5:10). **priest and prophet**. Careless priests (Lev. 10:1–7; 1 Sam. 4:12–22) and false prophets (Jer. 28:1–17) repeatedly come to a bad end in Scripture.

the children of [b]their tender care?
Should [c]priest and prophet be killed
in the sanctuary of the Lord?

21 In the dust of the streets
[d]lie the young and the old;
[d]my young women and my young men
have fallen by the sword;
[e]you have killed them in the day of your anger,
slaughtering [f]without pity.

22 You summoned as if to [g]a festival day
[h]my terrors on every side,
[i]and on the day of the anger of the LORD
no one escaped or survived;
[j]those whom I held and raised
my enemy destroyed.

Great Is Your Faithfulness

3

1 [k]I am the man who has seen affliction
under the [l]rod of his wrath;
2 he has driven and brought me
[m]into darkness without any light;
3 surely against me he turns his hand
again and again the whole day long.

4 He has made my flesh and my skin waste away;
[n]he has broken my bones;
5 [o]he has besieged and enveloped me
with [p]bitterness and tribulation;
6 [q]he has made me dwell in darkness
like the dead of long ago.

7 [r]He has walled me about so that [s]I cannot escape;
he has made my chains heavy;
8 though [t]I call and cry for help,
he shuts out my prayer;
9 [r]he has blocked my ways with blocks of stones;
he has made my paths crooked.

10 [u]He is a bear lying in wait for me,
a lion in hiding;
11 [v]he turned aside my steps and [u]tore me to pieces;
[w]he has made me desolate;

20 [b]ver. 22 [c][ch. 4:13]
21 [d][2 Chr. 36:17] [e]ch. 3:43 [f]ver. 2, 17
22 [g][ver. 6] [h]See Jer. 6:25 [i][Jer. 42:17; 44:14] [j]ver. 20

Chapter 3
1 [k]Jer. 20:18 [l]Ps. 2:9
2 [m]Isa. 5:30
4 [n]Ps. 51:8; Isa. 38:13; Jer. 50:17
5 [o][Job 19:12] [p]ver. 19; Deut. 29:18
6 [q]Ps. 143:3
7 [r]Job 19:8 [s]Ps. 88:8
8 [t]Job 19:7; 30:20; Ps. 22:2
9 [r][See ver. 7 above]
10 [u]See Hos. 13:8
11 [v][Jer. 18:15] [u][See ver. 10 above] [w]ch. 1:13

2:22 a festival day. The old festivals (cf. 1:4, 15; 2:6, 7) have been replaced by a new "festival": **the day of the anger of the LORD**. The phrase **terrors on every side** is distinctly Jeremianic (Jer. 6:25; 20:3,10; 46:5; 49:29; cf. Ps. 31:13). **no one escaped**. With only a few exceptions, such as Jeremiah (see Jer. 39:11–14). Jerusalem's children (**those whom** she **held and raised**) perished in the battle.

3:1–66 *I Am the Man Who Has Seen Affliction.* Chapter 3 has one speaker, a man who has endured suffering and experienced God's faithfulness (vv. 1–24) and responded to God's sovereignty and goodness (vv. 25–39). He prays for renewal (vv. 40–47) and maintains confidence in God's concern for him and Israel (vv. 48–66).

3:1–24 *Enduring Suffering, Experiencing Faithfulness.* This section describes the speaker's loss (vv. 1–18) and regaining of hope (vv. 19–24).

3:1–2 I am the man. A new speaker, who has experienced God's wrath and desires to teach others what he has learned. **Darkness without any light** describes the severity of the day of the Lord (cf. Joel 2:1–2; Amos 5:18; Zeph. 1:14–16).

3:4–6 He has made my flesh and my skin waste away. Lit., "he has swallowed up my flesh and my skin." For "swallow" as a metaphor for judgment, see 2:2, 5, 8, 16. **he has broken**. For "breaking" as a metaphor for punishment, see 1:15 ("crush") and 2:9. Jerusalem was besieged by Babylon; the speaker in this chapter (see note on 3:1–2) was **besieged** by **bitterness and tribulation**. For **darkness**, see note on vv. 1–2. **like the dead of long ago**. Like persons put in a dark place and forgotten (cf. Ps. 74:18–20; 88:3–7; 143:3).

3:7–9 walled. God has imprisoned the speaker (Job 19:8; Hos. 2:6). Even if the speaker had escaped his prison, God made certain that his path to freedom was **blocked**.

3:10–11 Even if the speaker had taken the dangerous path to freedom, God was like a **bear** waiting to attack.

12[x]ch. 2:4 [y][Job 16:12]
13[z]Job 6:4; Ps. 38:2
14[a]See Jer. 20:7 [b]ver. 63; Job 30:9; Ps. 69:12
15[c][Isa. 51:17, 21] [d]Jer. 9:15
16[e][Prov. 20:17] [f]See Jer. 6:26
18[g][Ps. 9:18]
19[h][ch. 1:9, 11, 20] [d][See ver. 15 above] [i]ver. 5
20[j]Ps. 42:6; 44:25
21[k][Ps. 42:5, 11]
22[l][Mal. 3:6]
23[m]Job 7:18 [n]Ps. 36:5
24[o]Ps. 16:5; 73:26 [k][See ver. 21 above]
25[p]Ps. 130:6; [Isa. 30:18]
26[q]Ps. 130:5, 7; Mic. 7:7
27[r][Matt. 11:29] [s][Eccles. 12:1]

12 [x]he bent his bow [y]and set me
as a target for his arrow.

13 He drove into my kidneys
[z]the arrows of his quiver;
14 [a]I have become the laughingstock of all peoples,
[b]the object of their taunts all day long.
15 [c]He has filled me with bitterness;
he has sated me with [d]wormwood.

16 [e]He has made my teeth grind on gravel,
and [f]made me cower in ashes;
17 my soul is bereft of peace;
I have forgotten what happiness[1] is;
18 [g]so I say, "My endurance has perished;
so has my hope from the LORD."

19 [h]Remember my affliction and my wanderings,
[d]the wormwood and [i]the gall!
20 My soul continually remembers it
[j]and is bowed down within me.
21 But this I call to mind,
and [k]therefore I have hope:

22 [l]The steadfast love of the LORD never ceases;[2]
[l]his mercies never come to an end;
23 they are new [m]every morning;
[n]great is your faithfulness.
24 [o]"The LORD is my portion," says my soul,
[k]"therefore I will hope in him."

25 The LORD is good to those who [p]wait for him,
to the soul who seeks him.
26 [q]It is good that one should wait quietly
for the salvation of the LORD.
27 [r]It is good for a man that he bear
the yoke [s]in his youth.

[1] Hebrew *good* [2] Syriac, Targum; Hebrew *Because of the steadfast love of the LORD, we are not cut off*

3:12–13 God **bent his bow** (see 2:4) and made the speaker a **target**. Indeed, God succeeded in hitting the speaker with the **arrows of his quiver**.

3:14 Like Jerusalem (1:7), the speaker has endured shame and mocking.

3:15 bitterness. For his food; see v. 5. **wormwood**. For his drink. This plant has a bitter taste and is often used as a metaphor for hardship and sorrow (v. 19; Prov. 5:4; Amos 5:7; 6:12).

3:16 teeth grind on gravel. Akin to the English phrase "eating dirt."

3:17–18 Since God treats both Jerusalem (2:4–5) and the speaker (3:1–16) as enemies, he has lost **peace**, **happiness**, and **hope**. The true source of a believer's hope for the future is **from the LORD**.

3:19–20 A prayer for God to **remember** all that the man has suffered. God has not remembered Jerusalem, to protect her (cf. note on 2:1). **wormwood**. See 3:15. **gall**. Or, "bitterness," cf. vv. 5, 15. Remembering what he asks God to remember causes his **soul** to bow down.

3:21 This verse marks a change in the speaker's attitude. The contentment he remembers renews the **hope** lost in v. 18. In view of vv. 22–23, 32, he may be reflecting on Ex. 34:6–7, which these verses echo.

3:22 God's **steadfast love** (his "covenant mercy" or beneficial action on his people's behalf) **never ceases**, even in the face of Judah's unfaithfulness and the resulting "day of the LORD" (cf. Joel 2:1–2; Amos 5:18; Zeph. 1:14–16). **mercies**. Or "compassion." This type of mercy goes the second mile, replacing judgment with restoration. **never come to an end**. God is willing to begin anew with those who repent.

3:23 new every morning. Each day presents another opportunity to experience God's grace. **faithfulness**. God's covenantal fidelity and personal integrity remain intact no matter what happens.

3:24 my portion. As with the Levites (Num. 18:20), God is the speaker's only inheritance (see Ps. 73:26). **says my soul**. This is what the speaker remembers in Lam. 3:21. **I will hope in him**. God daily offers fresh opportunities for reconciliation (cf. v. 18).

3:25–39 *Responding to God's Goodness and Sovereignty.* The speaker emphasizes God's goodness (vv. 25–30), justice (vv. 31–36), and lordship (vv. 37–39).

3:25 The LORD is good. God's goodness, or gracious sovereignty, is the core of his character (Neh. 9:25; Ps. 34:8; 86:5; Hos. 3:5). **wait for him**. Not passive, listless sitting, but faithful serving until God acts (Ps. 37:1–11). **seeks him**. Desires to know him and to do his will (Ps. 34:10; Amos 5:4, 6, 14).

3:26 wait quietly. In a posture of prayer and expectation. **salvation**. In this instance, deliverance from peril, not salvation from sin.

3:27 He must **bear the yoke** of punishment for sin (v. 18; cf. 1:14). **In his youth** indicates that the suffering is temporary.

28 Let him [t]sit alone in silence
when it is laid on him;
29 [u]let him put his mouth in the dust—
there may yet be hope;
30 [v]let him give his cheek to the one who strikes,
and let him be filled with insults.

31 [w]For the Lord will not
cast off forever,
32 but, though he [x]cause grief, [y]he will have compassion
[z]according to the abundance of his steadfast love;
33 [a]for he does not afflict from his heart
or [b]grieve the children of men.

34 To crush underfoot
all [c]the prisoners of the earth,
35 [d]to deny a man justice
in the presence of the Most High,
36 to subvert a man in his lawsuit,
[d]the Lord does not approve.

37 [e]Who has spoken and it came to pass,
unless the Lord has commanded it?
38 [f]Is it not from the mouth of the Most High
that good and bad come?
39 [g]Why should a living man complain,
a man, about the punishment of his sins?

40 Let us test and examine our ways,
[h]and return to the LORD!
41 [i]Let us lift up our hearts and hands
to God in heaven:
42 [j]"We have transgressed and [k]rebelled,
and you have not forgiven.

43 "You have wrapped yourself with anger and pursued us,
[l]killing without pity;
44 [m]you have wrapped yourself with a cloud
so that no prayer can pass through.

28[t]ch. 1:1; 2:10; Isa. 3:26
29[u]Job 42:6
30[v]Isa. 50:6; Matt. 5:39
31[w]Ps. 103:9
32[x]ch. 1:5 [y]Ps. 103:8 [z]Ps. 106:45
33[a][Heb. 12:6, 10] [b][Heb. 12:11]
34[c][Ps. 107:10]
35[d][Hab. 1:13]
36[d][See ver. 35 above]
37[e][Ps. 33:9]
38[f]Isa. 45:7; Amos 3:6
39[g]Prov. 19:3
40[h]Joel 2:12, 13
41[i]Ps. 25:1; 119:48
42[j]See Dan. 9:5 [k]Ps. 78:17
43[l]ch. 2:2, 17, 21
44[m]ver. 8; [ch. 2:1]

3:28 sit alone in silence. See 1:1 and 2:10.

3:29 put his mouth in the dust. Assume a posture that expresses humility and dependence on God. **There may yet be hope** because of God's covenant fidelity (cf. v. 24).

3:30 give his cheek. Those who wait on and seek for God can accept humiliation as coming from God for a purpose.

3:31–33 not cast off forever. God's anger is only temporary (Ps. 103:9), for he sends judgment in order to effect restoration. **Though he cause grief**, in this instance, because of the people's covenant infidelity, **he will have compassion**. See Ex. 34:6–7; Lam. 3:22; Hos. 11:1–9. **steadfast love**. See Lam. 3:22. **does not afflict from his heart**. God's first instinct is not to punish. He does so only when his patience with sinners does not lead to their repentance.

3:34–36 The Lord does not approve (v. 36) of those who **crush** others **underfoot** (perhaps a reference to the Israelites who were crushed by Babylon), of those who **deny a man justice** (cf. Ex. 23:2, 6; Deut. 16:19; 24:17; 27:19; Ps. 94:1–7), or of those who **subvert a man in his lawsuit**, that is, who make the innocent party guilty.

3:37 spoken and it came to pass. Just as in creation (cf. Gen. 1:3; Ps. 33:9), God sovereignly speaks and commands in history and things happen, including Jerusalem's destruction (Lam. 1:5, 12–16; 2:1–10).

3:38 good and bad. As experienced by human beings (cf. Isa. 45:7; Amos 3:6). The God who sent judgment can also send renewal.

3:39 When people suffer for their sins, they suffer because of what they have done, not because God enjoys punishing them (cf. v. 33).

3:40–47 *Praying for Renewal.* With his hope renewed, the speaker exhorts others to join him in prayer for restoration.

3:41 The people should **lift up** their **hearts** (where repentance originates; cf. Deut. 4:30–31; 30:1–10; Jer. 4:3–4) and their **hands**, showing their total dependence on God. **God in heaven**. A reference to his sovereignty (cf. Lam. 3:37–39).

3:42 We have transgressed. See 1:5, 14, 22. **rebelled**. See 1:18, 20. **you have not forgiven**. God has not let their actions go unpunished.

3:43–44 God has **pursued** his people (see 1:3, 6; 4:19; 5:5), **killing** them (see 2:4, 21) **without pity** (see 2:2, 17, 22). His judgment has been thorough. He has **wrapped** himself in **anger** toward Jerusalem but has also **wrapped** himself in a **cloud**, having seemingly become unavailable to his own people.

45 [n]You have made us scum and garbage
among the peoples.

46 [o]"All our enemies
open their mouths against us;
47 [p]panic and pitfall have come upon us,
devastation and [q]destruction;
48 [r]my eyes flow with rivers of tears
because of the destruction of the daughter of my people.

49 [r]"My eyes will flow without ceasing,
without respite,
50 [s]until the LORD from heaven
looks down and sees;
51 my eyes cause me grief
at the fate of all the daughters of my city.

52 [t]"I have been hunted [u]like a bird
by those who were my enemies [v]without cause;
53 [w]they flung me alive into the pit
[x]and cast stones on me;
54 [y]water closed over my head;
I said, [z]'I am lost.'

55 [a]"I called on your name, O LORD,
from the depths of the pit;
56 [b]you heard my plea, 'Do not close
your ear to my cry for help!'
57 [c]You came near when I called on you;
you said, [d]'Do not fear!'

58 "You have [e]taken up my cause, [f]O Lord;
you have [e]redeemed my life.
59 You have seen the wrong done to me, [g]O LORD;
judge my cause.
60 You have seen all their vengeance,
all [h]their plots against me.

45[n][1 Cor. 4:13]
46[o]ch. 2:16, 17
47[p]Isa. 24:17; Jer. 48:43 [q]Isa. 51:19
48[r]ch. 1:16; See Jer. 13:17
49[r][See ver. 48 above]
50[s]Ps. 14:2; Isa. 63:15
52[t]ch. 4:18 [u]Ps. 11:1 [v]See Ps. 35:19
53[w]Jer. 37:16; 38:6, 9, 10 [x][Dan. 6:17]
54[y]Ps. 69:2 [z]Ps. 88:5; [Ezek. 37:11]
55[a]Ps. 130:1
56[b][Ps. 130:2]
57[c][James 4:8] [d]See Josh. 1:9
58[e]Ps. 119:154 [f][1 Sam. 24:15]
59[g]Ps. 35:22, 23
60[h]See Jer. 11:19

3:45 Jerusalem has become **garbage** in the eyes of other nations (cf. 1:7–8; 2:15–16; 3:14). She endures great shame.

3:47 panic. The natural human reaction to divine judgment (cf. Ex. 15:16; Isa. 19:16; 33:14; Jer. 49:5; Mic. 7:17). **pitfall**. A trap or pit dug for catching animals; thus, a metaphor for judgment (cf. Isa. 24:17; Jer. 48:43). **devastation and destruction**. See Lam. 2:11; 3:48; 4:10. Such are the effects of the "day of the LORD" (cf. Joel 2:1–2; Amos 5:18; Zeph. 1:14–16).

3:48–66 *Maintaining Confidence in God.* The speaker continues his efforts to lead the people back to God. He describes his grief over Jerusalem's predicament (vv. 48–51), declares what the enemy has done (vv. 52–54), confesses God's past help (vv. 55–58), and confidently asks God to punish Jerusalem's foes (vv. 59–66).

3:48 my eyes flow with . . . tears. Like Jerusalem (1:16; 2:11, 18), the speaker weeps for what has happened to the city. **the daughter of my people**. A term of endearment for Jerusalem (cf. 2:11). For similar imagery, see 1:6; 2:1, 4, 8, 10, 13, 18; 4:22 ("daughter of Zion"); 1:15; 2:2, 5 ("daughter of Judah"); 2:13, 15 ("daughter of Jerusalem"); and 3:51 ("daughters of my city").

3:49–50 Like Jeremiah (Jer. 14:17), the speaker mourns **without ceasing** for the people's situation so that God will answer **from heaven**.

3:51 my eyes cause me grief. What he has witnessed penetrates to the speaker's inner being. **the fate of all the daughters of my city**. Jerusalem's women were taken into captivity, and many were likely raped or abused in other ways (cf. Jer. 52:28–30; Amos 1:13–15).

3:52–54 hunted like a bird. See vv. 12–13. The speaker has suffered alongside the people. **enemies without cause**. Like Jeremiah, he endured some measure of persecution by those he tried to help. This may also refer to Judah suffering at the hands of nations like Edom (cf. 4:21; Obad. 10–14). **flung me alive into the pit**. To silence and punish him (cf. Jer. 37:11–16; 38:4–28). **cast stones on me**. As if to bury him alive. **water closed over my head**. An even worse fate than Jeremiah suffered (cf. Ps. 88:6–7; Jonah 2:3–5). **I am lost**. There seemed to be no hope (cf. Lam. 3:18).

3:55–57 In the **depths of the pit** (the extremity of his suffering), the speaker **called** upon the very one who had placed him there. **you heard my plea**. Cf. Ps. 30:2; 40:2–4; 103:4. God not only **came near**, offering his comforting and saving presence, but also gave reassuring and empowering words of courage (**Do not fear!**). Cf. Jer. 1:17–19.

3:58 taken up my cause. God has become the speaker's advocate against his attackers (v. 52). **redeemed my life**. God's advocacy resulted in deliverance (cf. Lev. 25:47–54; Ruth 4:1–12; Jer. 1:17–19; 39:11–40:6).

3:59–60 God has **seen the wrong done to** the speaker. Jerusalem prayed for this in 1:9, 11, 20. True relief cannot come until God judges in favor of the speaker and against his enemies for **all their plots** (cf. Jer. 11:18–12:6; 17:18; 18:23).

61 [i]"You have heard their taunts, O LORD,
all [h]their plots against me.
62 The lips and thoughts [j]of my assailants
are against me all the day long.
63 [k]Behold their sitting and their rising;
[l]I am the object of their taunts.

64 [m]"You will repay them,[1] O LORD,
[n]according to the work of their hands.
65 You will give them[2] dullness of heart;
your curse will be[3] on them.
66 You will pursue them[4] in anger and [o]destroy them
from under [p]your heavens, O LORD."[5]

The Holy Stones Lie Scattered

4

1 [q]How the gold has grown dim,
how the pure gold is changed!
The holy stones lie scattered
[r]at the head of every street.

2 The precious sons of Zion,
worth their weight in [s]fine gold,
how they are regarded as [t]earthen pots,
the work of a potter's hands!

3 Even jackals offer the breast;
they nurse their young,
but the daughter of my people has become cruel,
like the ostriches in the wilderness.

4 The tongue of the nursing infant [u]sticks
to the roof of its mouth for thirst;
[v]the children beg for food,
but no one gives to them.

5 Those who once feasted on delicacies
perish in the streets;
[w]those who were brought up in purple
embrace ash heaps.

6 [x]For the chastisement[6] of the daughter of my people has been greater
than the punishment[7] of Sodom,

61[i]ch. 5:1 [h][See ver. 60 above]
62[j]Ps. 18:39, 48
63[k][Ps. 139:2] [l]See ver. 14
64[m]See Jer. 11:20 [n]Ps. 28:4; [2 Tim. 4:14]
66[o][Deut. 25:19; Jer. 10:11] [p]Ps. 8:3

Chapter 4

1[q][Isa. 1:22; Jer. 6:30] [r]ch. 2:19
2[s]Ps. 19:10 [t]See Jer. 19:11
4[u]Ps. 22:15 [v][ch. 2:11]
5[w][2 Sam. 1:24]
6[x]Matt. 10:15; Luke 10:12

[1] Or *Repay them* [2] Or *Give them* [3] Or *place your curse* [4] Or *Pursue them* [5] Syriac (compare Septuagint, Vulgate); Hebrew *the heavens of the LORD* [6] Or *iniquity* [7] Or *sin*

3:61–63 taunts. See v. 30; Ps. 69:9; 79:4; Jer. 20:10–12. **all their plots**. See Lam. 3:60. **Behold**. Or "look closely" (cf. 1:11; 2:20; 5:1).

3:65 You will give them dullness of heart. God will give them hard hearts, unwilling to repent and avoid judgment (Isa. 6:8–10). **your curse**. The judgment that comes as the consequences of their actions (cf. Deut. 28:15–68), not some sort of magical incantation.

3:66 You will pursue . . . and destroy them. For "pursue," see 1:3, 6; 3:43; 4:19; 5:5. **in anger**. Or "wrath" (cf. 1:12; 2:1, 3, 6; 3:43). God will bring the same type of justice to Jerusalem's enemies that Jerusalem has experienced (cf. v. 64).

4:1–22 *How the Gold Has Grown Dim*. Chapter 4 returns to themes found in chs. 1–2 yet also announces the completion of Jerusalem's punishment. The chapter can be divided into four segments: the suffering of Jerusalem's children (vv. 1–10), God's punishing of Jerusalem's religious leaders (vv. 11–16), the power of Jerusalem's enemies (vv. 17–20), and the end of Jerusalem's suffering (vv. 21–22).

4:1–10 *The Suffering of Jerusalem's Children*. Jerusalem's children have been scattered (vv. 1–2) and starved (vv. 3–6), and their elders have hardly fared better.

4:1 How. See note on 1:1. **the gold has grown dim**. Perhaps because it has been covered with dirt or has been burned. **holy stones**. The people, according to 3:2. **at the head of every street**. Cf. 2:19; 4:5, 8, 14. Suffering occurs in every section of the ravaged city.

4:2 worth their weight in fine gold. In the eyes of their parents and countrymen. **earthen pots**. To be shattered.

4:3–4 Even wild animals feed their young, but Jerusalem's mothers cannot feed their children because of the severity of the siege, famine, and devastation (cf. Jer. 15:1–4). **like the ostriches in the wilderness**. Job 39:13–17 depicts these creatures abandoning their eggs.

4:5 Some of these children were raised in luxury, but now they live in abject poverty. **delicacies**. Foods normally reserved for royalty. **perish**. Probably due to starvation. **purple**. Expensive clothing colored by the best dyeing processes. **embrace ash heaps**. Scavenge among garbage dumps.

6[y]Gen. 19:25; 2 Pet. 2:6; Jude 7
8[z]ch. 5:10; Job 30:30; [Ps. 119:83]
10[a]See Jer. 19:9 [b][1 Kgs. 3:26; Isa. 49:15] [c][2 Kgs. 6:29] [d]Deut. 28:57
11[e]Ezek. 5:13 [f]See Jer. 17:27
12[g][Isa. 52:15; 53:1]
13[h][ch. 2:20]; See Jer. 5:31; 23:21
14[i][Isa. 59:10] [j][Num. 19:16]

[y]which was overthrown in a moment,
and no hands were wrung for her.[1]

7 Her princes were purer than snow,
whiter than milk;
their bodies were more ruddy than coral,
the beauty of their form[2] was like sapphire.[3]

8 [z]Now their face is blacker than soot;
they are not recognized in the streets;
their skin has shriveled on their bones;
it has become as dry as wood.

9 Happier were the victims of the sword
than the victims of hunger,
who wasted away, pierced
by lack of the fruits of the field.

10 [a]The hands of [b]compassionate women
[c]have boiled their own children;
[d]they became their food
during the destruction of the daughter of my people.

11 [e]The LORD gave full vent to his wrath;
he poured out his hot anger,
and [f]he kindled a fire in Zion
that consumed its foundations.

12 [g]The kings of the earth did not believe,
nor any of the inhabitants of the world,
that foe or enemy could enter
the gates of Jerusalem.

13 This was for [h]the sins of her prophets
and [h]the iniquities of her priests,
who shed in the midst of her
the blood of the righteous.

14 [i]They wandered, blind, through the streets;
they were so defiled with blood
[j]that no one was able to touch
their garments.

[1] The meaning of the Hebrew is uncertain [2] The meaning of the Hebrew is uncertain [3] Hebrew *lapis lazuli*

4:6 Jerusalem's sin has been greater than that of **Sodom**, due to her greater knowledge of God's will; therefore, her **punishment** has been greater than Sodom's. Sodom **was overthrown in a moment**, but Jerusalem has suffered over a long time.

4:7 purer than snow. Their skin was untouched by the sun; they were not common laborers. **more ruddy than coral**. Their bodies were perfectly formed and healthy. **beauty of their form**. Their faces were handsome.

4:8 blacker than soot. A compete reversal of v. 7.

4:9 Happier were the victims of the sword. Because they died quickly (cf. v. 6). **pierced by lack**. Rather than by a sword.

4:10 The most **compassionate women** in the land **boiled their own children**, due to gnawing hunger and as a consequence of covenant infidelity (cf. 2:20; Lev. 26:29; Deut. 28:52–57; 2 Kings 6:29). **during the destruction**. During Babylon's siege of Jerusalem (Jer. 37:21).

4:11–16 *God's Punishing of Jerusalem's Religious Leaders*. A more detached speaker addresses Jerusalem's punishment as part of the day of the Lord (vv. 11–12; cf. Joel 2:1–2; Amos 5:18; Zeph. 1:14–16) and describes the sins and suffering of Jerusalem's priests and prophets.

4:11 his wrath. See 1:12; 2:1, 3, 6, 21, 22; 3:43, 66. **gave full vent**. Poured it out until it achieved its purpose (2:11, 22). **he kindled a fire in Zion**. See 2:3, 4; Amos 1:3–2:5. **that consumed its foundations**. Babylon served as God's instrument in carrying out this task (Jer. 52:12–13).

4:12 did not believe. Jerusalem had stood despite invasions by Egypt (1 Kings 14:25–28), Israel (2 Kings 14:13–14), Assyria (2 Kings 18:1–19:35), and Babylon (2 Kings 24:10–17), so it must have surprised those who heard that it had fallen.

4:13 sins of her prophets. In failing to warn and rebuke the people (cf. Jer. 5:30–31; 23:9–40). **iniquities of her priests**. In failing to teach the people God's word and its ramifications for godly living (cf. Hos. 4:1–9; Mal. 2:1–9). **shed . . . the blood of the righteous**. Persecuted those who told the truth.

4:14 The **blood** of the righteous covers the prophets and priests' **garments**, thereby rendering them morally and ritually unclean.

15 "Away! [k]Unclean!" people cried at them.
"Away! Away! Do not touch!"
So they became fugitives and wanderers;
people said among the nations,
"They shall stay with us no longer."

16 [l]The LORD himself[1] has scattered them;
he will regard them no more;
[m]no honor was shown to the priests,
[n]no favor to the elders.

17 [o]Our eyes failed, ever watching
[o]vainly for help;
in our watching we watched
for [p]a nation which could not save.

18 [q]They dogged our steps
so that we could not walk in our streets;
[r]our end drew near; our days were numbered,
for our end had come.

19 Our pursuers were [s]swifter
than the eagles in the heavens;
they chased us on the mountains;
they lay in wait for us in the wilderness.

20 [t]The breath of our nostrils, [u]the LORD's anointed,
was captured [v]in their pits,
of whom we said, [w]"Under his shadow
we shall live among the nations."

21 [x]Rejoice and be glad, O daughter of Edom,
you who dwell in [y]the land of Uz;
but to you also [z]the cup shall pass;
you shall become drunk and strip yourself bare.

22 [a]The punishment of your iniquity, O daughter of Zion, is accomplished;
he will keep you in exile no longer;[2]
but [b]your iniquity, O daughter of Edom, he will punish;
he will uncover your sins.

[1] Hebrew *The face of the LORD* [2] Or *he will not exile you again*

15[k][Lev. 13:45]
16[l]ch. 2:17 [m][Isa. 24:2] [n]ch. 5:12
17[o]Ps. 119:82, 123; [Jer. 3:23] [p]Jer. 37:7, 8
18[q]ch. 3:52 [r]Ezek. 7:2, 3, 6; Amos 8:2
19[s]Jer. 4:13; [2 Sam. 1:23; Hab. 1:8]
20[t][Gen. 2:7] [u][ch. 2:9; 2 Kgs. 25:5, 6] [v][Ezek. 12:13; 17:20; 19:4, 8] [w][Judg. 9:15; Ezek. 31:6, 17]
21[x][ch. 1:21] [y]Job 1:1; Jer. 25:20 [z]See Jer. 25:15, 16
22[a][Isa. 40:2] [b]Obad. 10

4:15 These blood-soaked, blind, unclean religious leaders find no refuge **among the nations**. No one wants such undesirable **fugitives and wanderers**.

4:16 God **himself . . . scattered them**. See 1:4, 19; 4:13; 5:12. **no honor . . . no favor**. The priests and prophets lost the respect usually reserved for their persons and offices because of their sins (4:13).

4:17–20 *The Power of Jerusalem's Enemies.* Babylon cut off Jerusalem's allies (v. 17), prevented all attempts to escape (vv. 18–19), and captured David's heir (v. 20).

4:17 Jerusalem watched **vainly for help** during Babylon's siege. Most often they watched for help from Egypt (Jer. 37:1–10).

4:18 dogged our steps. Babylon tracked Jerusalem's every move to get free. **we could not walk in our streets**. No place felt safe, for the walls could be breached at any time. **our end had come**. The day of the Lord (cf. Joel 2:1–2; Amos 5:18; Zeph. 1:14–16) broke upon them at last.

4:19 Once the city was breached, Jerusalem's citizens fled, yet only into Babylon's clutches (Jer. 39:1–40:6). Babylon was relentless (Lam. 1:3, 6).

4:20 Jerusalem's king, **the LORD's anointed**, was the very **breath** of their **nostrils**, so much did they depend on him. They had lived **under** the **shadow** of his protection. Yet he **was captured**. See Jer. 39:1–10.

4:21–22 *The End of Jerusalem's Suffering.* Nations that rejoice over Jerusalem's day of punishment will experience God's wrath in due course (v. 21), but Jerusalem can take comfort that her punishment has concluded (v. 22).

4:21 Edom took great joy in Jerusalem's fall and profited from her destruction (Ps. 137:7; Jer. 49:7; Joel 3:19; Obad. 10–14), perhaps because of the ancient Israel/Edom conflict (Gen. 25:19–34; 36:2–8). **but to you also the cup shall pass**. See Jer. 49:7–22, especially v. 12. **drunk . . . bare**. Metaphors for confusion and shame.

4:22 accomplished. Their **punishment** has ceased, and the long, hard, slow recovery of life, worship, and society can begin. **keep you in exile no longer**. Jews began to return to the area by 538–535 B.C. (cf. Ezra 1:1–2:70; Jer. 29:10–14; Dan. 9:1–2). **but . . . Edom**. See Jer. 49:7–22 and Lam. 4:21.

Chapter 5
1[c]Ps. 89:50 [d]ch. 3:61
2[e]Ps. 79:1
5[f][Josh. 10:24]
6[g][Hos. 12:1]
7[h]Jer. 31:29; Ezek. 18:2
8[i][Prov. 30:21, 22]
9[j][Jer. 6:25]
10[k]See ch. 4:8 [l][Deut. 32:24]
12[m]See 2 Kgs. 25:19-21 [n]ch. 4:16
13[o][Judg. 16:21] [p][Josh. 9:27]
14[n][See ver. 12 above] [q][Isa. 24:8]
15[q][See ver. 14 above] [r][Amos 8:10]

5

Restore Us to Yourself, O Lord

1 [c]Remember, O LORD, what has befallen us;
look, and see [d]our disgrace!
2 [e]Our inheritance has been turned over to strangers,
our homes to foreigners.
3 We have become orphans, fatherless;
our mothers are like widows.
4 We must pay for the water we drink;
the wood we get must be bought.
5 [f]Our pursuers are at our necks;[1]
we are weary; we are given no rest.
6 We have given the hand to [g]Egypt, and to [g]Assyria,
to get bread enough.
7 Our fathers sinned, and are no more;
[h]and we bear their iniquities.
8 [i]Slaves rule over us;
there is none to deliver us from their hand.
9 [j]We get our bread at the peril of our lives,
because of the sword in the wilderness.
10 [k]Our skin is hot as an oven
with [l]the burning heat of famine.
11 Women are raped in Zion,
young women in the towns of Judah.
12 [m]Princes are hung up by their hands;
[n]no respect is shown to the elders.
13 Young men are compelled to [o]grind at the mill,
and boys stagger [p]under loads of wood.
14 [n]The old men have left the city gate,
the young men [q]their music.
15 [q]The joy of our hearts has ceased;
[r]our dancing has been turned to mourning.

[1] Symmachus *With a yoke on our necks*

5:1–22 *Restore Us to Yourself, O Lord.* This concluding chapter is the community's plea for restoration. It includes an opening petition (v. 1), a description of the woes the people have faced (vv. 2–18), and an urgent plea for restored relationship (vv. 19–22).

5:1 *Opening Petition.* This verse continues the book's emphasis on God "seeing" the people's plight (cf. 1:11, 20; 2:20; 3:63). **Remember, O LORD.** A common theme in the book (cf. 1:7; 2:1; 3:19, 20), "remember" evokes covenantal redemptive events like the exodus (Ex. 2:23–25), when God acted on Israel's behalf. **our disgrace.** Due to Jerusalem's exposed and humiliating posture (Ps. 74:4–8, 18; 89:50–51; Lam. 1:11, 12; 2:20).

5:2–18 *The Woes Jerusalem Has Faced.* These woes include economic impoverishment (vv. 2–10), social humiliation (vv. 11–14), and social and political disintegration (vv. 15–18).

5:2 Our inheritance. The Promised Land, which was the tangible evidence of Israel's relationship with God (Deut. 4:21, 38). **Foreigners** denotes aggressive, harsh opponents, not just non-Israelites.

5:3 orphans, fatherless. They have lost their fathers, presumably through war, exile, and starvation. **like widows.** They have no resources, whether their husbands are alive or dead.

5:4 must pay for the water. Not only do the people lack land (v. 2) and family (v. 3), they also lack the essentials for survival.

5:5 pursuers. Probably persons to whom they owe money, or the foreign taskmasters who rule over them. **are at our necks.** Desiring payment or more work. **given no rest.** They get no break from their labor. They are at their rulers' mercy.

5:6 In the past, the people reached out to allies like **Egypt** and **Assyria** for aid rather than trusting God. Some of them did so after Jerusalem fell (cf. Jer. 44:1). The gesture proved every time to be folly.

5:7 Past mistakes (v. 6) have led to terrible present realities. Though people are not condemned for others' sins (cf. Jer. 31:29–30; Ezek. 18:2), they can certainly suffer for what others have done. It is also possible to sin in a manner similar to one's ancestors (cf. Dan. 9:16).

5:8 Slaves (or "servants") **rule over us.** Either nations that once served Judah, or (more likely) servants of Babylon's kings.

5:9 Necessities are expensive near Jerusalem (v. 4), but leaving the area to get food is dangerous. **sword.** A metaphor for bandits (2 Kings 13:20–21) or famine (Deut. 28:22).

5:10 skin is hot as an oven. One of the many effects of slowly starving to death (cf. 4:7–8).

5:11 Women are not safe even after the city has fallen (cf. 1:4, 18). Lawlessness of the worst sort abounds.

5:12 Princes. Or "officials." **hung up by their hands.** Most likely for execution (cf. Gen. 40:19; Est. 2:23), perhaps by Babylon's servants to ward off rebellion. **elders.** See Lam. 1:19; 2:10; 4:16.

5:13 grind at the mill. A task usually performed by animals. **stagger under loads.** Forced to do arduous manual labor beyond their years, until they collapse.

5:14–15 old men. Civic leaders. **have left the city gate.** They no longer sit where decisions were made and business was conducted. **Music** was also offered at the city gates, but now such joyous occasions have ceased (Jer. 16:1–13).

16 [s]The crown has fallen from our head;
woe to us, for we have sinned!
17 For this [t]our heart has become sick,
for these things [u]our eyes have grown dim,
18 for Mount Zion which lies desolate;
[v]jackals prowl over it.
19 [w]But you, O LORD, reign forever;
your throne endures to all generations.
20 [x]Why do you forget us forever,
why do you forsake us for so many days?
21 [y]Restore us to yourself, O LORD, that we may be restored!
Renew our days as of old—
22 [z]unless you have utterly rejected us,
and you remain exceedingly angry with us.

16[s]Ps. 89:39; Jer. 13:18; [ch. 1:1]
17[t]Isa. 1:5 [u]See ch. 2:11
18[v][Isa. 34:13]
19[w]Ps. 9:7; 102:12; 145:13
20[x]Ps. 13:1
21[y]Jer. 31:18; [Ps. 80:3, 7, 19]
22[z]Jer. 14:19

5:16 The crown has fallen. Both the Davidic kingship (4:20) and Jerusalem itself were considered crowning glories (cf. Jer. 13:18). **we have sinned**. Punishment has followed transgression (cf. Lam. 1:5, 8, 14, 18, 22; 2:14; 3:42; 4:6, 13, 22).

5:17 our heart has become sick. Over the condition of the people and the city (cf. 1:13, 22). **our eyes have grown dim**. Perhaps with tears (cf. 1:2, 16; 2:18; 3:48).

5:18 desolate. Without people, kingship, palace, or temple (1:4, 16; 3:11; 4:5). **jackals**. Animals known to inhabit ruins (cf. Ezek. 13:4).

5:19–22 *A Concluding Prayer for Restoration.* The book closes with a plea for renewal. The people confess God's permanence and kingship (v. 19), decry their ongoing suffering (v. 20), ask for renewal (v. 21), and wonder when renewal will come, given God's justifiable anger (v. 22).

5:19 Unlike frail humanity, God reigns as king of the universe (Ps. 103:19) **forever** (Ps. 90:1–17; 102:12–13). Whatever forgiveness, renewal, and relief Jerusalem will receive must come from the one whose **throne endures to all generations** (Ps. 45:6–7; 93:1–2).

5:20 forever. See Ps. 74:1; 89:46. **for so many days**. A seemingly endless sequence of days (cf. Ps. 23:6; 93:5, where the same expression means "forever"). **Forget . . . forsake** indicate feelings of covenantal abandonment (Isa. 49:14–15).

5:21 Restore us. Restoration depends on a right relationship with God (Jer. 31:18), and only God can do the restoring. **as of old**. Before covenant infidelity had broken the relationship (Jeremiah 2–6; Lam. 1:7).

5:22 unless. Denotes God's ongoing delay in restoring his elect people and chosen city. **utterly rejected us**. Because of their sin (vv. 16, 20; Lev. 26:15–39; Jer. 6:19, 30). **remain exceedingly angry**. A situation that cannot remain permanent, given God's promises (cf. Lev. 26:44–45; Deut. 30:1–10; Isa. 57:14–21; Jeremiah 31–32; Hos. 11:1–9).

INTRODUCTION TO

EZEKIEL

Author and Title

Ezekiel is both the name of the sixth-century B.C. prophet and the title of the book that records his preaching. Ezekiel's name (Hb. *Yekhezqe'l*) means "God strengthens" or "May God strengthen," appropriate for a prophet called to proclaim a message of uncompromising judgment and later a message of a restoration for God's sake, not Israel's. Ezekiel lived out his prophetic career among the community of exiled Judeans in Babylon. He belonged to the priestly class and was married (see 24:15–24), but it is doubtful that he had any children.

If Ezekiel was thirty years old at the time of the inaugural vision (see note at 1:1), an intriguing connection can be made with the final vision of the book, which is dated to the twenty-fifth year of the exile (40:1), when Ezekiel would have been fifty. As Numbers 4 makes clear, the ages of thirty and fifty mark the span of the active service of the priests. As a member of the exilic community, Ezekiel would not have been able to participate in the ritual life of the Jerusalem temple, nor would he have undergone initiation into priestly service while living outside the land. But perhaps the timing of these visions coincided with what would have been Ezekiel's "working life" as a priest had he lived in Jerusalem prior to the exile.

The relationship between the Hebrew prophets and the books that bear their names is complex. For both Isaiah (see Isa. 8:16) and Jeremiah (e.g., Jeremiah 36) there is evidence of individuals or groups who preserved the prophet's words. Such is not the case with Ezekiel. No such disciples are named, and Ezekiel's autobiographical style suggests his close involvement with recording the written traditions that bear his name. At the same time, the very preservation of his scroll implies the existence of a support group, which may also have provided some editorial input.

Date

Ezekiel's oracles are more frequently dated than those of other OT prophets. The first date of the book takes the reader to the summer of 593 B.C., five years after the first group of exiles was deported to Babylon by Nebuchadnezzar. The latest-dated oracle comes 22 years after that summer, in April of 571 B.C. The book is arranged chronologically in three parts: chapters 1–24 and 33–48 form one sequence, while the foreign-nation oracles of chapters 25–32 have their own order (see Outline). Caution must be exercised in attempting to align Ezekiel's dates with those of the modern calendar, but the rough equivalents are as shown in the chart, Dates in Ezekiel.

Theme and Purpose

Ezekiel spoke to a community forced from its home, a people who had broken faith with their God. As the spokesman for the God of Israel, Ezekiel spoke oracles that vindicate the reputation of this holy God. This radically God-centered point of view finds its sharpest expression in 36:22–23 ("It is not for your sake, O house of Israel, that I am about to act, but for the sake of my holy name. . . . And I will vindicate the holiness of my great name. . . . And the nations will know that I am the LORD"). Thus the primary purpose of Ezekiel's message was to restore God's glory before the people who had spurned it in view of the watching nations. But Israel's own welfare was bound up with its God. So the prophet pleads: "Why will you die, O house of Israel? For I have no pleasure in the death of anyone, declares the Lord GOD; so turn, and live" (18:31–32).

Dates in Ezekiel

Reference	Year / month / day following exile of Jehoiachin	Modern equivalent*/year B.C.	Situation
1:2	5th year / 4th month / 5th day	July 593***	inaugural vision
8:1	6th year / 6th month / 5th day	September 592	first temple vision
20:1	7th year / 5th month / 10th day	August 591	elders come to inquire
24:1	9th year / 10th month / 10th day**	January 588 or 587	siege of Jerusalem begins
26:1	11th year / month (?) / 1st day	c. 587–586	oracle against Tyre, before Babylon besieged it
29:1	10th year / 10th month / 12th day	January 587	oracle against Egypt
29:17	27th year / 1st month / 1st day	April 571****	Egypt assigned to Babylon; after end of Babylon's siege of Tyre
30:20	11th year / 1st month / 7th day	April 587	oracle against Egypt
31:1	11th year / 3rd month / 1st day	June 587	oracle against Egypt
32:1	12th year / 12th month / 1st day	March 585	oracle against Egypt
32:17	12th year / 12th month / 15th day	April 585	oracle against Egypt
33:21	12th year / 10th month / 5th day	January 585	fugitive arrives in Babylon
40:1	25th year / 1st month (?) / 10th day (?)	April 573	second temple vision

**For simplicity, here and in the notes that follow, only the second month of the modern equivalent is given (cf. Months in the Hebrew Calendar, p. 34)*
***Unique dating formula in Hebrew; see notes ***earliest recorded oracle ****latest recorded oracle*

Ezekiel's message was unrelenting. Of all the books in the OT, only Psalms, Jeremiah, and Genesis are longer. Ezekiel's uncompromising message is matched by language that often seems hard and sometimes offensive. If there is no softening his language, at least it appears that the grandeur of Ezekiel's vision of God rendered much of the earthly reality he observed as sordid, and worse. The appropriate response, in Ezekiel's terms, is not simply revulsion but repentance and a longing for the restoration of God's glory.

Occasion and Background

Ezekiel prophesied during a time of great confusion. In 597 B.C. the Babylonians had exiled Judah's king Jehoiachin—only 18 years old, and on the throne for only three months—along with several thousand of its leading citizens (2 Kings 24:10–16). Ezekiel was among their number; he was probably about 25 years old. The political situation was complex: a Judean king was among the exiles (Jehoiachin), but the Babylonians had appointed a puppet king to the throne in Jerusalem (Jehoiachin's uncle, Zedekiah).

The pattern in the history of the exiled northern kingdom of Israel, and now again for the southern kingdom of Judah, was that prophets emerged in times of crisis to bring God's message to his people. The time of Judah's exile was therefore a period of intense prophetic activity. Jeremiah was an older contemporary of Ezekiel (and, like Ezekiel, from a priestly family). Ezekiel clearly knows Jeremiah's message and develops some of the older prophet's themes. However, it is not known whether they ever met, and it seems Jeremiah was not aware of Ezekiel, whose ministry did not begin until after Ezekiel had been in exile for five years.

Although Ezekiel's fellow exiles formed his main audience, it seems likely that his oracles would have been communicated to their compatriots back in Judah. Ezekiel probably lived out his days in exile. His second temple vision—in which a new constitution for renewed, ideal Israel was spelled out—came well into the long exile Jeremiah predicted (Jer. 25:8–14). If Ezekiel was 30 years old when his ministry began, this vision came when he was about 50.

Key Themes

1. As a priest, Ezekiel was deeply concerned with *the holiness of God,* and consequently with *the sin of his people,* that is, with any behavior that offended the holy God. These twin themes can hardly be separated, as attention to matters of purity can be found on nearly every page. Ezekiel's perception of the depth of Israel's sin shows graphically in his version of Israel's history (ch. 20). Even the oracles of restored Israel in chapters 40–48 include provision for dealing with the people's sin so they can survive in the presence of a holy God. This concern also accounts for the many echoes in Ezekiel's oracles of the priestly material in the

Pentateuch, particularly in the legislation of Leviticus and Numbers, as well as the resonances of Ezekiel's new temple (Ezekiel 40–42) with the Exodus tabernacle.

2. Israel was of course subject to its national God. However, Ezekiel's God is no tribal deity but rather is *supreme over all nations*. Therefore Nebuchadnezzar, king of mighty Babylon, was simply a tool in God's hand to accomplish God's purpose (e.g., 21:19–23; 30:25). God's absolute supremacy finds its most pronounced expression in the battle against Gog, the final enemy (chs. 38–39), where God alone crushes Gog's vast hostile forces.

3. The vigilance for holy living that the holy God demands places a claim both on *individuals* and on *the whole community*. Some see a significant milestone in biblical thought in Ezekiel's preaching on individual responsibility in chapter 18 (cf. Jer. 31:29–30). While this chapter certainly focuses on the individual in the modern sense, Ezekiel's clear expression of the requirements binding on communities should not thereby be ignored.

4. The very structure of the book declares *judgment* on those clinging to (false) hope, but true *hope* for those who accept judgment (37:11). Ezekiel's restoration message was heard both before and after the destruction of Jerusalem, but radically God-centered judgment is partnered with a hope ("salvation") that wholly depends on God's gifts of a new heart and spirit (36:22–32).

5. The *condemnation of Israel's "princes"* (e.g., ch. 19; Ezekiel is reluctant to use the title "king") finds its hopeful counterpart in the *promise of a future "prince"* who would rule with justice (34:23–24) and stand at the point of connection between God and people (46:1–18).

Style

Prophetic books often make use of formulaic statements, but such formulas have a frequency and consistency in Ezekiel not matched in other prophetic writings. Once recognized, these formulas can greatly help interpretation because they formally mark the introduction and conclusion of oracles. Introductory formulas include "the word of the LORD came to me" (50 times), or, at significant junctures, "the hand of the LORD" being upon Ezekiel (1:3; 3:14, 22; 8:1; 33:22; 37:1; 40:1). Conclusions are often marked with variations of the "recognition formula," e.g., "they shall know that I am the LORD" (more than 50 times), and the formula itself is an indication of the book's central purpose. Internally, oracles are frequently structured by the terms "because . . . therefore," identifying the motivation and the message of the oracle.

Some of the unusual aspects of Ezekiel's prophecies are inevitably some of the better known. This is true of his frequent recourse to street theater, and symbolic actions of a quite odd and striking kind (e.g., 4:1–5:17; 12:3–6; 24:16–18; 37:16–17). He also makes plentiful use of extended allegories (e.g., chs. 15–17; 19; 21; 23; etc.). Especially in the foreign-nation oracles, laments become vehicles for his message (e.g., 27:2; 28:11–12; 32:2).

Influence

This book stands at a turning point in the history of biblical prophecy. In part this has to do with Ezekiel's standing on the cusp between the predominant preexilic message, which called for repentance by threatening judgment, and postexilic prophecy, which regularly called for repentance by promising restoration. It has also to do with forms of prophetic experience. While the origins of apocalyptic literature are still debated, Ezekiel's visions must play a role in contributing to its development. In particular, the scenario in which a vision of heavenly realities is given in the company of a celestial guide-interpreter—so familiar from Zechariah and Daniel, as well as the NT book of Revelation—finds its headwaters in Ezekiel's prophecy.

Ezekiel inherited some of his themes from earlier prophets, but his handling of them contributes to their later shape in the NT. This seems particularly true of the imagery of the "good shepherd" (34:11–24) and "living water" (47:1–14; cf. Rev. 22:1–2). The book of Revelation draws inspiration from some of Ezekiel's most negative images—e.g., the "whoring" of Ezekiel 16 and 23, the enemy Gog of Magog (on the use of this in Rev. 20:8, see note on Ezek. 38:2)—but Ezekiel's vision of a new city also resonates there (Rev. 3:12; 21:1–22:5). There are few clear hints of resurrection in the OT, but one of them is found in the interpretation of Ezekiel's vision of the valley of dry bones (see Ezek. 37:12–13 and note). Whatever it might have meant to Ezekiel's audience, it makes an important contribution to the development of biblical thought.

History of Salvation Summary

Like other prophets called to explain the Babylonian exile, Ezekiel stressed that it was due to the people's faithlessness toward God, and therefore to their failure to live as God's renewed humanity. He also stressed

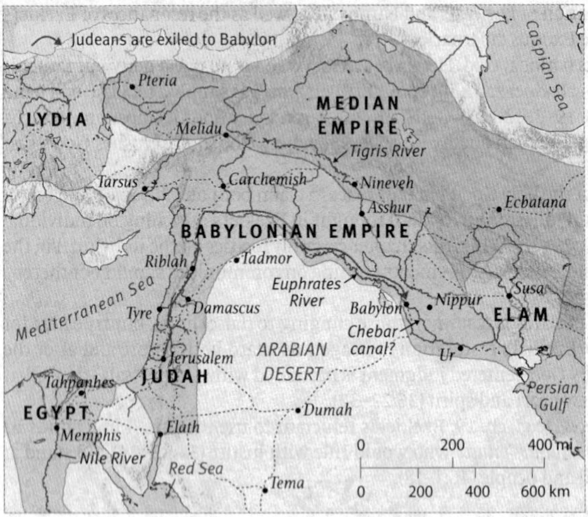

The Near East at the Time of Ezekiel
c. 593 B.C.
Ezekiel recorded his visions and prophecies while living in the vicinity of Babylon, where he had been exiled years earlier. By Ezekiel's time, the Babylonian Empire had engulfed virtually all of the area along the eastern coast of the Mediterranean Sea and would eventually subdue even the land of Egypt, where many other Judeans had fled.

that even this disaster was not the end of Israel's story. God would restore them morally and spiritually, and eventually use Israel to bring light to the Gentiles. Ezekiel adds a nuance to this prophetic refrain: Israel's calling was to show forth the holiness of God's name, but they had "profaned" that name (treated it as unholy); in restoring them, God would act to vindicate the holiness of his name before all nations, enabling them to know him. (For an explanation of the "History of Salvation," see the Overview of the Bible, pp. 23–26. See also History of Salvation in the Old Testament: Preparing the Way for Christ, pp. 2635–2661.)

Literary Features

The book of Ezekiel is one of the most complex books in the Bible because so many different genres converge in it. It is important to grasp right at the start that this book is an anthology of separate pieces of writing. There is no single overarching story line; the unity is that of a carefully arranged collection (see Outline). The general arrangement of the material is one that several other OT prophetic books also follow—a general movement from (1) oracles of judgment against the prophet's own nation of Judah (usually called Israel in the text), to (2) oracles of judgment against the surrounding pagan nations, to (3) oracles of future, eschatological blessing on those who believe in God.

Several observations are in order. First, much of the book consists of visionary writing, which transports readers to a world of the imagination where the rules of reality are obviously suspended in favor of highly unusual visions. To understand and relish the book of Ezekiel, readers often need to abandon expectations of realism. Second, Ezekiel employs a technique known as symbolic reality, which occurs when a writer consistently transports the reader to a world of visionary experience where the most important ingredients are symbols—symbols like a vine, a boiling pot, or a valley full of dry bones. Third, prophecy is itself a genre, made up of oracles (pronouncements from God through the agency of a prophet) that fall into two main categories—oracles of judgment and oracles of blessing. Oracles of judgment are ordinarily examples of satire, and in the prophetic satire of Ezekiel there are three motifs: (1) *description* of evil, (2) *denunciation* of this evil, and (3) *warnings and predictions* that God will judge the evil. Prophecy often merges with apocalyptic writing about epic, end-time struggles. These sections often portray events at the end of history. Finally, readers should not overlook the obvious—the prophet Ezekiel expresses himself in the form of poetry.

In addition to abandoning expectations of consistent realism, readers should give themselves to the sheer strangeness of what is presented. Ezekiel talks about real, historical events, but much of the time he does not portray these events in literal terms. Instead he prefers extravagant visions as his mode. Additionally, readers need to be ready for a kaleidoscope of details, always shifting and never in focus for very long. The best approach to the oracles of judgment is to analyze them according to the usual literary rules regarding satire.

Outline

Ezekiel is the most overtly and deliberately structured of the Major Prophets. The book as a whole is organized around the fulcrum of the destruction of Jerusalem in 586 B.C., with chapters 1–25 preceding its fall, and chapters 33–48 following. The foreign-nation oracles of chapters 26–32 also have a chronological ordering, as well as geographical and thematic organization (see notes for details). The book's major visions play a structuring role too. The inaugural vision of chapters 1–3 finds an explicit cross-reference in the middle of the first temple vision of chapters 8–11 (see 10:20–22). The "dry bones" vision of 37:1–14 is shorter than the others but plays a pivotal role in the movement toward restoration, seen in the culminating vision of chapters 40–48, which in turn makes a pronounced cross-reference back to the inaugural vision as well as the previous temple vision (43:1–5). These observations alone powerfully imply that in Ezekiel's book, both content and form contribute to the message.

I. Inaugural Vision (1:1–3:27)
  A. Setting (1:1–3)
  B. Inaugural vision (1:4–3:15)
    1. The throne of the Lord approaches (1:4–28)
    2. The prophet commissioned (2:1–3:11)
    3. The throne of the Lord withdraws (3:12–13)
    4. The vision concludes (3:14–15)
  C. The watchman (3:16–21) [cf. 33:1–9]
  D. Inaugural vision reprise (3:22–27)

II. Judgment on Jerusalem and Judah (4:1–24:27)
  A. God against Jerusalem (4:1–5:17)
    1. God against Jerusalem enacted (4:1–5:4)
    2. God against Jerusalem explained (5:5–17)
  B. Oracles against the "land" (6:1–7:27)
    1. Against the mountains of Israel (6:1–14)
    2. Against the land of Israel (7:1–27)
  C. Ezekiel's temple vision (8:1–11:25)
    1. Transportation and abominations (8:1–18)
    2. Slaughter in Jerusalem (9:1–11)
    3. The fire and the glory (10:1–22)
    4. Punishment for civic authorities (11:1–13)
    5. Promise of a new heart, spirit (11:14–21)
    6. The glory of the Lord departs (11:22–25)
  D. Anticipating exile (12:1–28)
    1. Exile predicted (12:1–20)
    2. Exile confirmed (12:21–28)
  E. False prophecy, true prophecy (13:1–14:11)
    1. False prophets (13:1–23)
    2. False inquirers (14:1–11)
  F. The consequences of infidelity (14:12–15:8)
    1. Noah, Daniel, Job (14:12–23)
    2. The useless vine (15:1–8)
  G. The faithless bride (16:1–63)
    1. Jerusalem, the foundling bride (16:1–43)
    2. Jerusalem and her sisters (16:44–58)
    3. The everlasting covenant (16:59–63)
  H. The parable of the eagles and the vine (17:1–24)
    1. The parable narrated (17:1–10)
    2. The parable explained (17:11–18)
    3. The parable interpreted (17:19–21)
    4. A new parable (17:22–24)
  I. Moral responsibility (18:1–32)

1. The one who sins dies (18:1–4)
2. Three case studies (18:5–18)
3. Two objections (18:19–29)
4. Conclusion: repent! (18:30–32)

J. Lament for the princes of Israel (19:1–14)
1. A lioness and her cubs (19:1–9)
2. A vine and its stem(s) (19:10–14)

K. Learning from history (20:1–44)
1. Looking to the past (20:1–31)
2. Unthinkable idolatry (20:32)
3. Looking to the future (20:33–44)

L. Fire and sword (20:45–21:32)
1. The parable of the fire (20:45–49)
2. The drawn sword (21:1–7)
3. The sharpened sword (21:8–17)
4. The sword of Nebuchadnezzar (21:18–29)
5. The sword sheathed and judged (21:30–32)

M. A city defiled (22:1–31)
1. The bloody city (22:1–16)
2. The city of dross (22:17–22)
3. Systemic failure (22:23–31)

N. Two sisters (23:1–49)
1. The sisters and politics (23:1–35)
2. The sisters and religion (23:36–49)

O. Two losses (24:1–27)
1. Jerusalem, the bloody pot (24:1–14)
2. No mourning for Ezekiel's wife (24:15–24)
3. Fugitive news (24:25–27)

III. Oracles against Foreign Nations (25:1–32:32)

A. Against Judah's neighbors (25:1–17)
1. Against Ammon (25:1–7)
2. Against Moab (25:8–11)
3. Against Edom (25:12–14)
4. Against Philistia (25:15–17)

B. Oracles against Tyre (26:1–28:19)
1. Against Tyre (26:1–21)
2. A lament against Tyre (27:1–36)
3. Against Tyre's king (28:1–19)

C. Oracle against Sidon (28:20–23)

D. Israel gathered in security (28:24–26)

E. Oracles against Egypt (29:1–32:32)
1. Against Pharaoh (29:1–16)
2. Nebuchadnezzar and Egypt (29:17–21)
3. Lament for Egypt (30:1–19)
4. The kings of Egypt and Babylon (30:20–26)
5. The fall of Pharaoh (31:1–18)
6. Lament over Pharaoh (32:1–16)
7. Egypt's descent to the pit (32:17–32)

IV. After the Fall of Jerusalem (33:1–39:29)

A. Reminders (33:1–20)
1. The watchman (reprise) (33:1–9) [cf. 3:16–21]
2. Moral responsibility (reprise) (33:10–20) [cf. 18:21–29]

B. The fall of Jerusalem (33:21–22)
C. Culpability (33:23–33)
  1. A word for the homelanders (33:23–29)
  2. A word for the exiles (33:30–33)
D. Shepherds and sheep (34:1–31)
  1. Wicked shepherds and the good shepherd (34:1–16)
  2. The flock: problems and prospects (34:17–31)
E. The mountains of Edom and Israel (35:1–36:15)
  1. Against Mount Seir (35:1–15)
  2. The mountains of Israel restored (36:1–15)
F. Restoration for the sake of God's name (36:16–38)
  1. State of impurity (36:16–21)
  2. Divine intervention: a new spirit (36:22–32)
  3. Land renewed (36:33–36)
  4. Populace increased (36:37–38)
G. The vision of dry bones (37:1–14)
H. The houses of Israel and Judah (37:15–28)
I. Gog of Magog (38:1–39:29)

V. Vision of Restoration (40:1–48:35)

A. Vision of the new temple (40:1–42:20)
  1. The vision begins (40:1–4)
  2. The outer court and its gates (40:5–27)
  3. The inner court, gates, and chambers (40:28–49)
  4. The temple interior (41:1–26)
  5. Chambers of the outer court (42:1–14)
  6. Exterior measurements (42:15–20)
B. The return of God's glory (43:1–5)
C. Regulations for renewed Israel (43:6–46:18)
  1. New people for new temple (43:6–12)
  2. The altar regulations (43:13–27)
  3. The prince's gate (44:1–3)
  4. Temple access and rules for priests (44:4–31)
  5. The temple districts (45:1–8)
  6. Legal measurements (45:9–12)
  7. Offerings and gatherings (45:13–46:15)
  8. Rules for inheritance of the prince (46:16–18)
D. The river flowing from the temple (46:19–47:12)
  1. The temple kitchens (46:19–24)
  2. The temple's river (47:1–12)
E. Dividing the land: allotment and access (47:13–48:35)
  1. The outer boundaries (47:13–23)
  2. Territories of the northern tribes (48:1–7)
  3. The central territories (48:8–22)
  4. Territories of the southern tribes (48:23–29)
  5. Access to the city (48:30–35)

EZEKIEL

Ezekiel in Babylon

1 [a]In the thirtieth year, in the fourth month, on the fifth day of the month, as I was among
the exiles by [b]the Chebar canal, [c]the heavens were opened, and I saw [d]visions of God.[1]
2 On the fifth day of the month (it was [e]the fifth year of [f]the exile of King Jehoiachin), 3 the
word of the LORD came to Ezekiel [g]the priest, the son of Buzi, in the land of the Chaldeans
by [b]the Chebar canal, and [h]the hand of the LORD was upon him there.

The Glory of the LORD

4 As I looked, behold, [i]a stormy wind came [j]out of the north, and a great cloud, with
[k]brightness around it, and fire flashing forth continually, and in the midst of the fire,
[l]as it were gleaming metal.[2] 5 And from the midst of it came the likeness of [m]four living
creatures. [n]And this was their appearance: they had a human likeness, 6 [o]but each had four
faces, and each of them had four wings. 7 Their legs were straight, and the soles of their feet
were like the sole of a calf's foot. And they sparkled [p]like burnished bronze. 8 Under their
wings [q]on their four sides [r]they had human hands. And the four had their faces and their
wings thus: 9 their wings touched one another. [s]Each one of them went straight forward,
[q]without turning as they went. 10 As for the likeness of their faces, [t]each had a human

[1] Or *from God* [2] Or *amber*; also verse 27

10 [t]ch. 10:14, 21

Chapter 1

1 [a][ver. 3; Num. 4:3] [b]ch. 3:15, 23; 10:15, 20, 22; 43:3 [c][Matt. 3:16; Mark 1:10; Luke 3:21; John 1:51; Acts 7:56; 10:11; Rev. 19:11] [d]ch. 8:3; 40:2; [ch. 11:24; Num. 12:6]
2 [e][ch. 8:1]; See ch. 20:1 [f]2 Kgs. 24:12, 15; [ch. 17:12; 19:8; 33:21; 40:1]
3 [g][ver. 1] [b][See ver. 1 above] [h]ch. 3:22; 8:1; 33:22; 37:1; 40:1; [1 Kgs. 18:46; 2 Kgs. 3:15]
4 [i]Jer. 23:19; 25:32; 30:23; [ch. 3:12] [j]See Jer. 1:14 [k]ver. 27 [l]ver. 27; ch. 8:2
5 [m]See Rev. 4:6-8 [n]ch. 10:14, 21
6 [o]ch. 10:21
7 [p]ch. 40:3; Rev. 1:15; 2:18
8 [q]ver. 17; ch. 10:11 [r]ch. 10:8, 21
9 [s]ch. 10:22 [q][See ver. 8 above]

1:1–3:27 *Inaugural Vision.* The opening sequence of Ezekiel is the most elaborate and complex of the prophetic call narratives in the OT, and also one of the most carefully structured. In a vision, Ezekiel witnesses the awesome approach of the glory of God (1:1–28). Ezekiel receives his prophetic commission through swallowing the scroll God offers (2:1–3:11), thus both fortifying him and training him in obedience. After the glory of God withdraws (3:12–15), Ezekiel's role is further refined by his appointment as a "watchman" (3:16–21). The sequence concludes with a further encounter with God's glory (3:22–27).

1:1–3 *Setting.* Unusually, Ezekiel opens with an autobiographical note (v. 1) and some accompanying explanation (vv. 2–3). These verses have echoes in 3:14–15; together they frame the book's opening vision.

1:1 What **the thirtieth year** signifies is obscure, as it does not follow the usual pattern for dates in Ezekiel. It may refer to the prophet's age. Reference to the **Chebar canal** locates the prophet near ancient Nippur (or, in modern terms, halfway between Baghdad and Basra) and thus not in the city of Babylon itself. **Visions of God** links this vision with 8:3 and 40:2; the other great vision in the book (37:1–14) does not use this language.

1:2 Probably the "thirtieth year" of v. 1 should be linked with the **fifth year of the exile of King Jehoiachin** (i.e., 593 B.C.). Jehoiachin's exile is the regular chronological marker for dates given throughout the book. Jehoiachin was only 18 at the time of exile in 597 B.C., and had then been king for only three months (see 2 Kings 24:8).

1:4–3:15 *Inaugural Vision.* The vision forms a unified whole, in spite of its being comprised of distinct episodes. It is symmetrically structured, having onion-like layers: the "frame" (1:1–3 and 3:14–15) is wrapped around the approach and departure of the cherub-throne (1:4–28 and 3:12–13), with the prophet's audience before the Lord contained in 2:1–3:11. That central section has its own internal "nesting."

1:4–28 *The Throne of the Lord Approaches.* The richness of detail in Ezekiel's account of this vision is both inspiring and perplexing. It recalls the traditions of the ark of the covenant (Ex. 25:10–22), especially within the context of Solomon's temple (1 Kings 8:6–8), and stands at the head of the later mystical *merkavah* (Hb. for "chariot") tradition within Judaism.

1:4 A **stormy wind** (Hb. *ruakh se'arah*) heralds the approach of the Lord, as in Job 38:1; 40:6. Likewise, the **north** is associated with the divine abode (see Ps. 48:2), and in Jeremiah it indicates the source of divine judgment (Jer. 1:13–15). The phrase **as it were** translates the Hebrew preposition *ke-*, "like," which is used 18 times in this description; half of those are in Ezek. 1:24–28. Clearly Ezekiel is groping for language to describe the vision.

1:5–14 The piling up of detail contrasts with the bland label of **living creatures**, only later identified as "cherubim" in 10:20. The first impression (1:6–9) is followed by closer detail (vv. 10–13). (A beautiful carved ivory that may depict one of these composite creatures has been found, dating to the 9th century B.C. It probably comes from the site of Arslan Tash in northern Syria. The figure combines all four features described in ch. 1: a human figure, wings of an eagle, forelegs of a lion, and hind legs of an ox.)

1:5 The many uses of the term **likeness** (Hb. *demut*, 10 times in ch. 1) emphasize the impressionistic nature of the vision's description.

1:9 The notice that **their wings touched** is reminiscent of the description of the cherubim in the Most Holy Place in Solomon's temple (1 Kings 6:27). The four-sided form of the creatures ensures that they can always do the impossible: go **straight forward**, in any direction, but **without turning** (cf. "went straight forward" [Ezek. 1:12] with "darted to and fro" [v. 14]).

1:10 The creatures had a predominantly human shape, but each had four different **faces**. This assemblage is unique, although complex combinations of supernatural beings are known throughout the ancient Near East. Many suggestions have been made to explain their symbolism. Certainly each creature is majestic in its realm, whether among the wild (**lion**; Prov. 30:30) and domestic (**ox**; Prov. 14:4) animals, or in the air (**eagle**; Prov. 23:5; cf. Obad. 4), with each of them noticed subsequently to the **human face** (cf. Gen.

face. The four had the face of a lion on the right side, the four had the face of an ox on the
left side, and the four had the face of an eagle. **11** Such were their faces. And their wings
were spread out above. Each creature had two wings, each of which touched the wing of
another, while [u]two covered their bodies. **12** [s]And each went straight forward. [v]Wherever
the spirit[1] would go, they went, without turning as they went. **13** As for the likeness of the
living creatures, their appearance was [w]like burning coals of fire, [w]like the appearance of
torches moving to and fro among the living creatures. [x]And the fire was bright, and out
of the fire went forth lightning. **14** And the living creatures [y]darted to and fro, [z]like the
appearance of a flash of lightning.

15 [a]Now as I looked at the living creatures, I saw a wheel on the earth beside the living
creatures, one for each of the four of them.[2] **16** [a]As for the appearance of the wheels and
their construction: their appearance was like [b]the gleaming of beryl. [c]And the four had the
same likeness, their appearance and construction being as it were a wheel within a wheel.
17 [d]When they went, they went [e]in any of their four directions[3] [f]without turning as they
went. **18** And their rims were tall and awesome, [g]and the rims of all four were full of eyes all
around. **19** [h]And when the living creatures went, the wheels went beside them; [i]and when
the living creatures rose from the earth, the wheels rose. **20** [j]Wherever the spirit wanted to
go, they went, and the wheels rose along with them, [j]for the spirit of the living creatures[4]
was in the wheels. **21** [h]When those went, these went; and when those stood, these stood;
[i]and when those rose from the earth, the wheels rose along with them, [j]for the spirit of
the living creatures was in the wheels.

22 Over the heads of the living creatures there was [k]the likeness of an expanse, shining
like awe-inspiring [l]crystal, spread out above their heads. **23** And under the expanse their
wings were [m]stretched out straight, one toward another. [n]And each creature had two
wings covering its body. **24** And when they went, I heard the sound of their wings [o]like
the sound of many waters, like [p]the sound of the [q]Almighty, a sound of tumult [r]like the
sound of an army. When they stood still, they let down their wings. **25** And there came
a voice from above [s]the expanse over their heads. When they stood still, they let down
their wings.

26 And above the expanse over their heads there was [t]the likeness of a throne, [t]in appearance [u]like sapphire;[5] and seated above the likeness of a throne was [v]a likeness with a human
appearance. **27** And [w]upward from what had the appearance of his waist I saw as it were
[x]gleaming metal, like the appearance of fire enclosed all around. And downward from
what had the appearance of his waist I saw as it were the appearance of fire, and [y]there
was brightness around him.[6] **28** Like the appearance of [z]the bow that is in the cloud on the
day of rain, so was the appearance of the brightness all around.

[1] Or *Spirit*; also twice in verse 20 and once in verse 21 [2] Hebrew *of their faces* [3] Hebrew *on their four sides* [4] Or *the spirit of life*; also verse 21 [5] Or *lapis lazuli* [6] Or *it*

11 [u]ver. 23; [Isa. 6:2]
12 [s][See ver. 9 above] [v]ch. 10:17
13 [w][Ps. 104:4] [x][Ps. 97:3, 4]
14 [y][Zech. 4:10] [z][Matt. 24:27; Luke 17:24]
15 [a]ch. 10:9; [Dan. 7:9]
16 [a][See ver. 15 above] [b][Dan. 10:6] [c]ch. 10:10
17 [d]ch. 10:11 [e]ver. 8 [f]ver. 9
18 [g]ch. 10:12; [Rev. 4:8]
19 [h]ch. 10:16 [i][ch. 10:19; 11:22]
20 [j]ch. 10:17
21 [h][See ver. 19 above] [i][See ver. 19 above] [j][See ver. 20 above]
22 [k][ver. 25, 26; ch. 10:1] [l][Rev. 4:6]
23 [m]ver. 7 [n]ver. 11
24 [o]ch. 43:2; [Rev. 1:15] [p]Ps. 29:3, 4; 68:33 [q]See Gen. 17:1 [r]Dan. 10:6; [Rev. 19:6]
25 [s][ver. 22]
26 [t]ch. 10:1; [1 Kgs. 22:19] [u]Ex. 24:10 [v]Dan. 8:15; [Rev. 1:13]
27 [w]ch. 8:2; [ver. 4] [x]See ver. 4 [y]ver. 4
28 [z]Gen. 9:13; [Rev. 4:3; 10:1]

1:26). This imagery is later echoed in the four (separate) creatures before the throne in Rev. 4:7.

1:11 The **two wings** of these creatures (also in v. 23) are similar to the three pairs of wings of the seraphim in Isaiah's throne vision (Isa. 6:2).

1:12 straight forward . . . without turning. See note on v. 9. Should this **spirit** (Hb. *ruakh*) be identified with that of v. 20? It is certainly different from the *ruakh* (Hb. for "wind") of v. 4. Given the closer identification of the spirit in v. 20, it seems likely that here the reference is to a "spirit" beyond the living creatures—in other words, the creatures' movements are responsive to the divine spirit (for "Spirit," see note on 3:12; and ESV footnote on 1:12).

1:14 darted to and fro. See note on v. 9.

1:15–21 The complex structure of their **wheels** is difficult to envisage, though something gyroscopic seems to be suggested.

1:16 Beryl (Hb. *tarshish*) is a crystalline mineral found in different colors. Here, it is likely to be the pale green to gold variety. The Septuagint does not use a consistent Greek equivalent.

1:18 The wheels' **eyes** should be understood metaphorically and as related to the "gleaming" beryl of v. 16 (perhaps protruding gemstones).

1:22–28 The climax of the vision: a form can be discerned **above** the wheels, above the creatures, above the expanse, on a throne. Wrapped in light, **the glory of the LORD** cannot be captured in human language.

1:22–23 Expanse appears four times in the immediate context (vv. 22–23, 25–26) and forms a strong link to Gen. 1:6–8, 14–20, where it is used nine times (out of a total of 17 times in the whole OT). There the expanse forms the dome of the sky; here it is borne on the wings of the creatures and forms a boundary *beyond* which comes the culmination of the vision.

1:24 For the first time in the vision, sound dominates sight, even though the preceding description includes a violent thunderstorm (v. 4). The sound of **many waters** will again accompany the approaching glory of God in 43:2.

1:25 While the sound of a **voice** is registered, report of speech is deferred until v. 28b.

1:28 The **bow . . . on the day of rain** could signal the covenant rainbow of Gen. 9:13–16. Given the ominous message that follows, the more likely symbolic reference is to the bow that is the Lord's weapon from the storm, which shoots arrows of lightning (see Ps. 7:12–13; Hab. 3:9). The **glory of the LORD** is his manifested presence with his people, visible in the wilderness (Ex. 16:7) and then accessible through the sanctuary (Ex. 40:34–35); in Ezekiel the term appears in Ezek. 1:28; 3:12, 23; 8:4; 9:3; 10:4, 18–19; 11:22–23; 43:2–5; 44:4. This glory will leave the temple (chs. 9–11) and then will return to the restored temple (43:2–5). See note on Isa. 6:3. **I fell on my face**.

Such was the appearance of the likeness of [a]the glory of the LORD. And when I saw it,
[b]I fell on my face, and I heard the voice of one speaking.

Ezekiel's Call

2 And he said to me, [c]"Son of man,[1] [d]stand on your feet, and I will speak with you." **2** And
as he spoke to me, [e]the Spirit entered into me and [f]set me on my feet, and I heard him
speaking to me. **3** And he said to me, "Son of man, I send you to the people of Israel, to
[g]nations of rebels, who have rebelled against me. [h]They and their fathers have transgressed
against me to this very day. **4** The descendants also are [i]impudent and stubborn: I send you
to them, and you shall say to them, 'Thus says the Lord GOD.' **5** And [j]whether they hear or
refuse to hear (for they are [g]a rebellious house) [k]they will know that a prophet has been
among them. **6** And you, son of man, [l]be not afraid of them, nor be afraid of their words,
[m]though briers and thorns are with you and you sit on [n]scorpions.[2] Be not afraid of their
words, nor be dismayed at their looks, for they are a rebellious house. **7** And you shall speak
my words to them, [j]whether they hear or refuse to hear, for they are a rebellious house.

8 "But you, son of man, hear what I say to you. [o]Be not rebellious like that rebellious
house; open your mouth and [p]eat what I give you." **9** And when I looked, behold, [q]a hand
was stretched out to me, and behold, [r]a scroll of a book was in it. **10** And he spread it before
me. And it had writing [s]on the front and on the back, and there were written on it words
of lamentation and mourning and woe.

3 And he said to me, [c]"Son of man, eat whatever you find here. [t]Eat this scroll, and go,
speak to the house of Israel." **2** So I opened my mouth, and he gave me this scroll to eat.
3 And he said to me, "Son of man, feed your belly with this scroll that I give you and fill
your stomach with it." [u]Then I ate it, and it was in my mouth [v]as sweet as honey.

4 And he said to me, [w]"Son of man, go to the house of Israel and speak with my words
to them. **5** For you are not sent to a people of foreign speech and a hard language, but to
the house of Israel— **6** not to many peoples of foreign speech and a hard language, whose
words you cannot understand. [x]Surely, if I sent you to such, they would listen to you. **7** [y]But
the house of Israel will not be willing to listen to you, for they are not willing to listen to
me: because all the house of Israel [z]have a hard forehead and a stubborn heart. **8** [a]Behold,
I have made your face as hard as their faces, and your forehead as hard as their foreheads.

[1] Or *Son of Adam*; so throughout Ezekiel [2] Or *on scorpion plants*

28 [a]ch. 3:23; 8:4; 9:3; 10:4, 18, 19; 11:22, 23; 43:4, 5; 44:4; [Ex. 24:16] [b]ch. 3:23; 43:3; 44:4; [Gen. 17:3, 17; Josh. 5:14; Dan. 8:17; Acts 9:4; Rev. 1:17]

Chapter 2

1 [c]ch. 3:1, 3, 4, 17, 25; 4:1, 16; 5:1 [d]Dan. 10:11
2 [e]ch. 3:24 [f]ch. 3:24; Dan. 8:18
3 [g][ver. 5, 6, 8; ch. 3:26; 24:3; 44:6] [h]ch. 20:16, 18, 21
4 [i][ch. 3:7]
5 [j]ch. 3:11; [ch. 3:27; 17:12] [g][See ver. 3 above] [k]ch. 33:33
6 [l]ch. 3:9; Jer. 1:8 [m][ch. 28:24; 2 Sam. 23:6; Mic. 7:4] [n][Deut. 8:15]
7 [j][See ver. 5 above]
8 [o][Isa. 50:5] [p]Rev. 10:9; [ch. 3:1, 3]
9 [q]ch. 8:3; Dan. 10:10; Rev. 10:2 [r]Jer. 36:2
10 [s]Rev. 5:1

Chapter 3

1 [c][See ch. 2:1 above] [t][ch. 2:8]
3 [u]Jer. 15:16; Rev. 10:9, 10 [v][Ps. 19:10; 119:103]
4 [w]See ch. 2:1
6 [x][Matt. 11:21, 23]
7 [y][John 15:20] [z][ch. 2:4]
8 [a]See Jer. 1:18

In the NT, John's vision of the risen Christ (Rev. 1:9–20, esp. v. 17) stirred a similar response.

2:1–3:11 *The Prophet Commissioned.* The vision of glory culminates in a call that is both sweet and severe. Two speeches bracket a test of obedience.

2:1 Ezekiel is never addressed by name, but 93 times as **son of man** (Hb. *ben-'adam*), out of a total of 99 times for the phrase in the OT; Daniel is the only other person so addressed in the OT (Dan. 8:17). The Hebrew idiom "son of x" indicates membership in a class. "Son of man" identifies Ezekiel as a creature before the supreme creator. This highlights the humanity and thus the proper humility and dignity of the servant before Israel's almighty, transcendent God.

2:2–4 The characterization of the people of Israel as **rebels** sounds a distinctive note throughout the commissioning vision. This deep-seated trait (**and their fathers**; cf. v. 4) will be emphasized again in Ezekiel's retrospective of Israel's history in ch. 20. Ezekiel is sent to speak on God's behalf (**you shall say to them**), but no content is given—yet.

2:5–7 The label **rebellious house**, used almost like a refrain in these verses, is unique to Ezekiel (see also 3:9, 26–27; 12:2–3, 9, 25; 24:3). This label joins 2:2–4 in pointing to a deeply ingrained bent to rebellion, while treating the Judean nation as a whole. On the parallel of vv. 6b–7 to 3:9b–11, see note on 3:9b–11.

2:8–3:3 The demand to **eat** the scroll immediately tests Ezekiel's obedience, a matter of contrast with the rebelliousness of his compatriots. The progression from command to compliance moves through three moments of speech and response (2:8–10; 3:1–2; 3:3).

2:8–10 The request to **open your mouth and eat** comes without any indication of what is to be given. The missing "content" of v. 4 is about to be provided, not as food but as the **scroll of a book**. This phrase (elsewhere found only in Ps. 40:8; Jer. 36:2, 4) emphasizes the scroll's physicality. When it is unrolled, the **writing** is visible front and back: the scroll is full, just as Ezekiel soon will be (Ezek. 3:3). Its **words** are all audible, though their precise content remains unspecified.

3:1–2 The command to **eat** is now combined with the commission to **go** and **speak**.

3:3 feed your belly. Does this third instruction imply hesitation on the prophet's part? Finally, having tasted, the prophet gets another surprise: the words of mourning are not bitter, as one would expect, but **sweet as honey**. Ezekiel has taken a first step in obedience to the Lord.

3:4–11 Following Ezekiel's obedient response, the emphasis shifts from prophet to people, though both remain in view.

3:4 The command to **go** and **speak** is repeated in v. 11, framing this second speech. While the first speech emphasized divine sending (2:3–4), here the focus is on the prophet's going.

3:5–7 Contrary to expectation, Ezekiel is cautioned that a cross-cultural mission would be easier than taking words of God to his own people. There is nothing inherently derogatory about **foreign speech and a hard language**, although the terms could be negatively applied to a foreign oppressor (cf. Isa. 33:19).

3:8–9a made your face as hard. This equipping forms the necessary step to the final charge.

3:9b–11 The conclusion to the second speech echoes and expands on that of the first (2:6b–7). Despite the striking resemblance of the English texts, the Hebrew is cast quite differently in the two passages. This could simply be stylistic variation. If the Hebrew constructions are intended to carry a nuance, then 2:6b–7 has the force of an immediate instruction ("don't be afraid [now]!") while 3:9b–11 has that of a blanket prohibition ("never fear!"). It could also

9[b][Isa. 50:7] [c]ch. 2:6
10[d]Jer. 26:2 [e][ver. 3]
11[f]ch. 33:2, 12, 17, 30 [g]ver. 27 [h]ch. 2:7
12[i]ch. 8:3; 11:1, 24; 43:5; [ch. 37:1] [j][ch. 1:24]
13[k]ch. 1:5, 15 [l][ch. 1:24]
14[m]ch. 8:3; 11:1, 24; 43:5; [ch. 37:1] [n]See ch. 1:3
15[o]See ch. 1:1 [p]Job 2:13; Ps. 137:1; Lam. 2:10 [q]ch. 4:17; Isa. 52:14; Jer. 14:9 [r][Gen. 50:10; 1 Sam. 31:13]
16[s][Jer. 42:7]
17[t]See ch. 2:1 [u]ch. 33:7; Isa. 52:8; 56:10; Jer. 6:17; [Heb. 13:17] [v]2 Chr. 19:10; [2 Kgs. 6:10]; See ver. 18-21; ch. 33:4-6
18[w]ch. 33:8 [x]Gen. 2:17 [v][See ver. 17 above] [y]ch. 18:18; Jer. 31:30; [John 8:21, 24] [z]ver. 20; ch. 33:6, 8; 34:10; [ch. 18:13; Acts 18:6; 20:26]
19[a]ch. 33:9 [b][1 Tim. 4:16] [c]ch. 14:14, 20
20[d]See ch. 18:24 [e]Jer. 6:21 [v][See ver. 17 above] [z][See ver. 18 above]
22[f]See ch. 1:3 [g]ch. 8:4; 37:1; Gen. 11:2 [h][Acts 9:6; 22:10]
23[i]See ch. 1:28 [j]See ch. 1:1
24[k]See ch. 2:2

9 Like [b]emery harder than flint have I made your forehead. [c]Fear them not, nor be dismayed
at their looks, for they are a rebellious house." 10 Moreover, he said to me, "Son of man, [d]all
my words that I shall speak to you receive [e]in your heart, and hear with your ears. 11 And
go to the exiles, [f]to your people, and speak to them and say to them, [g]'Thus says the Lord
GOD,' [h]whether they hear or refuse to hear."
12 [i]Then the Spirit[1] lifted me up, and I heard behind me the voice[2] of [j]a great earthquake:
"Blessed be the glory of the LORD from its place!" 13 It was the sound of the wings of [k]the
living creatures as they touched one another, and the sound of the wheels beside them,
and the sound of [l]a great earthquake. 14 [m]The Spirit lifted me up and took me away, and I
went in bitterness in the heat of my spirit, the [n]hand of the LORD being strong upon me.
15 [o]And I came to the exiles at Tel-abib, who were dwelling [o]by the Chebar canal, and I sat
where they were dwelling.[3] And [p]I sat there [q]overwhelmed among them [r]seven days.

A Watchman for Israel

16 [s]And at the end of seven days, the word of the LORD came to me: 17 [t]"Son of man, [u]I have
made you a watchman for the house of Israel. Whenever you hear a word from my mouth,
you shall [v]give them warning from me. 18 [w]If I say to the wicked, [x]'You shall surely die,' [v]and
you give him no warning, nor speak to warn the wicked from his wicked way, in order to
save his life, that wicked person [y]shall die for[4] his iniquity, [z]but his blood I will require at
your hand. 19 [a]But if you warn the wicked, and he does not turn from his wickedness, or
from his wicked way, he shall die for his iniquity, [b]but you [c]will have delivered your soul.
20 [d]Again, if a righteous person turns from his righteousness and commits injustice, [e]and
I lay a stumbling block before him, he shall die. [v]Because you have not warned him, he
shall die for his sin, [d]and his righteous deeds that he has done shall not be remembered,
[z]but his blood I will require at your hand. 21 But if you warn the righteous person not to
sin, and he does not sin, he shall surely live, because he took warning, and you will have
delivered your soul."
22 [f]And the hand of the LORD was upon me there. And he said to me, "Arise, go out into
[g]the valley,[5] and [h]there I will speak with you." 23 So I arose and went out into the valley, and
behold, [i]the glory of the LORD stood there, like the glory that I had seen [j]by the Chebar
canal, [i]and I fell on my face. 24 [k]But the Spirit entered into me and set me on my feet, and

[1] Or *the wind*; also verse 14 [2] Or *sound* [3] Or *Chebar, and to where they dwelt* [4] Or *in*; also verses 19, 20 [5] Or *plain*; also verse 23

carry the implication that Ezekiel, now that he has been divinely toughened, simply will not be afraid.

3:10 Embedded in this charge, God's words give one of the few descriptions of prophetic experience in the OT, involving both a psychological (**receive in your heart**) and an auditory (**hear with your ears**) element (cf. Job 32:18–20; Jer. 20:7–9).

3:12–13 *The Throne of the Lord Withdraws.* The departure of the glory of God is accompanied by the same sensory experiences as its approach (cf. 1:24).

3:12 the Spirit lifted me up. Simultaneous events are being described: Ezekiel is being taken away, but at the same time the throne of the Lord is departing. There is ambiguity in the Hebrew *ruakh*: "Spirit" implies the divine spirit (see notes on 1:4 and 1:12) but, given the stormy setting, "wind" (ESV footnote) or the Spirit manifested in the form of wind is also possible. However, there is a tacit "transportation" here (see 3:15), and the parallels in 8:3 and 37:1 point toward this certainly being the divine Spirit in action in some form.

3:13 In the audience with God, the **living creatures** have been momentarily forgotten, but their movement brings them dramatically into focus once more.

3:14–15 *The Vision Concludes.* In language echoing 1:1–3, Ezekiel's visionary encounter with the Spirit draws to an end. It is tempting to think of going **in bitterness in the heat of my spirit** simply as a state of agitation following this traumatic encounter, and the translation "in the heat" leaves open this possibility. But this idiom appears 30 times in the OT, and the ESV generally translates it "in wrath" or "in fury" or the like. Probably this nuance also applies here. Ezekiel has gained a divine perspective on his people's sin, and his anger reflects that shared viewpoint.

3:15 Although no "transportation" was narrated in the course of the vision that began by the **Chebar canal** (see note on 1:1), Ezekiel knows himself to have been elsewhere. The **seven days** of recovery echo the time of Job's recovery from tragedy before he finds his voice (Job 2:13). The term **Tel-abib** means "mound of the flood," but its precise location has not been determined. It was near the "Chebar canal," and therefore it should not be confused with modern Tel Aviv in Israel.

3:16–21 *The Watchman.* Ezekiel is assigned duty as an early warning system for Judah. This role is rehearsed and elaborated in 33:1–9, the passage introducing the second phase of Ezekiel's ministry.

3:17 The task of **watchman** is also found in Isaiah (Isa. 21:6–9), Hosea (Hos. 9:8), and Habakkuk (Hab. 2:1), but none provides a direct parallel to Ezekiel's commission (see 2 Sam. 18:24–27; 2 Kings 9:17–20). The insistence on speaking only the divine **word** persists from Ezek. 3:10.

3:18–19 Although the intent is clearly to **warn the wicked** and thus **save his life** (cf. 33:8), the more fundamental concern here remains the fidelity of the prophet to deliver warnings faithfully. Both scenarios result in the death of the wicked; but in the second, if the warning is issued, the prophet's life is saved (**delivered your soul**; see 3:21).

3:20–21 Even the **righteous** need warnings, for they remain susceptible to sin. Indeed, God's sovereignty includes taking responsibility for the fatal **stumbling block** of v. 20.

3:22–27 *Inaugural Vision Reprise.* This final piece of the complex vision sequence comes as something of an aftershock in the wake of the main event, with several direct parallels to the earlier vision.

3:22–23 Here the **valley** is the broad river valley of Mesopotamia, the same setting as the later vision of dry bones (37:1).

he spoke with me and said to me, "Go, shut yourself within your house. 25 And you, O
son of man, behold, [l]cords will be placed upon you, and you shall be bound with them,
so that you cannot go out among the people. 26 And I will make your tongue cling to the
roof of your mouth, so that [m]you shall be mute and unable to reprove them, [n]for they are
a rebellious house. 27 [o]But when I speak with you, I will open your mouth, and you shall
say to them, [p]'Thus says the Lord GOD.' [q]He who will hear, let him hear; and he who will
refuse to hear, let him refuse, for they are a rebellious house.

The Siege of Jerusalem Symbolized

4 "And you, [r]son of man, [s]take a brick and lay it before you, and engrave on it a city, even
Jerusalem. 2 [t]And put siegeworks against it, [u]and build a siege wall against it, [v]and cast
up a mound against it. Set camps also against it, [w]and plant battering rams against it all
around. 3 And you, take an iron griddle, and place it as an iron wall between you and the
city; [x]and set your face toward it, [y]and let it be in a state of siege, and press the siege against
it. This is [z]a sign for the house of Israel.

4 "Then lie on your left side, and place the punishment[1] of the house of Israel upon
it. For the number of the days that you lie on it, [a]you shall bear their punishment. 5 For
I assign to you a number of days, [b]390 days, [c]equal to the number of the years of their
punishment. [a]So long shall you bear [d]the punishment of the house of Israel. 6 And when
you have completed these, you shall lie down a second time, but on your right side, and
[e]bear [f]the punishment of the house of Judah. [g]Forty days I assign you, a day for each year.
7 [h]And you shall set your face toward the siege of Jerusalem, [i]with your arm bared, and
you shall prophesy against the city. 8 And behold, [j]I will place cords upon you, so that you
cannot turn from one side to the other, till you have completed [k]the days of your siege.

9 "And you, take wheat and barley, beans and lentils, millet and emmer,[2] and put them
into a single vessel and make your [l]bread from them. [m]During the number of days that

[1] Or *iniquity*; also verses 5, 6, 17 [2] A type of wheat

25 [l]ch. 4:8
26 [m][Isa. 8:16] [n][ch. 2:3]
27 [o][ch. 24:27; 29:21] [p]ver. 11 [q][Rev. 22:11]

Chapter 4

1 [r]See ch. 2:1 [s][ver. 3; Jer. 13:1, 2]
2 [t][2 Kgs. 25:1] [u]ch. 17:17; 21:22; 26:8 [v]Luke 19:43 [w]ch. 21:22; 26:9
3 [x]See ch. 21:2 [y][Isa. 29:3] [z]ch. 12:6, 11; 24:24, 27; [Isa. 8:18; 20:3]
4 [a]ch. 44:10, 12; [Lev. 16:22; Isa. 53:11, 12]
5 [b]ver. 9 [c][Num. 14:34] [a][See ver. 4 above] [d][ch. 23:4, 9, 10]
6 [e]ch. 44:10, 12; [Lev. 16:22; Isa. 53:11, 12] [f][ch. 23:11, 12] [g][Num. 14:34]
7 [h]See ch. 21:2 [i]Isa. 52:10
8 [j]ch. 3:25 [k][ver. 9; ch. 5:2]; See 2 Kgs. 25:1-3; Jer. 39:1, 2; 52:4-6
9 [l][1 Kgs. 22:27] [m]See ver. 8

3:25–27 Ezekiel has already ingested the message (vv. 1–3) and absorbed the divine perspective (v. 14). His identification with the prophetic message is pushed even further, with his actions and words under direct divine control. Ezekiel will be **mute** until Jerusalem's fall (see 33:22). Such constraint raises the problem: how will he warn if he cannot speak? The solution: oracles of God will be divinely enabled—**I will open your mouth**. The concluding words are familiar, echoing the terms of the divine commission in 2:4, 7.

4:1–24:27 *Judgment on Jerusalem and Judah.* In the roughly chronological ordering of Ezekiel's preaching, the oracles of chs. 4–24 precede the downfall of Jerusalem in 586 B.C. His message consistently points to approaching judgment; both the message and the messenger were vindicated by the fall of the city. Although the sequence appears to be chronological, there is also some grouping by theme and genre: chs. 4–7 include a high density of "symbolic actions"; chs. 8–11 comprise the second major vision sequence in the book, Ezekiel's first "temple vision"; chs. 15–23 are dominated by "parables" and extended metaphors. Almost the only relief from the relentless indictment of sin and announcement of judgment comes in 11:14–21, which anticipates the hopeful tone of the latter half of the book, but not without sounding the familiar warning.

4:1–5:17 *God against Jerusalem.* Commissioned, equipped, and positioned, Ezekiel now receives his first complex of oracles.

4:1–5:4 *God against Jerusalem Enacted.* Poetry is typically the vehicle for prophetic oracles—but not here. Ezekiel is called upon to perform "street theater": actions (rather than words) that convey a divine message. In most cases in Ezekiel, like this one, only the instructions are recorded, and not the report of the performance and its reception.

4:1–8 This complex of instructions is not dated. Although the "vision reprise" in the preceding section links it most naturally back to the beginning of the book, other terms (e.g., "cords" in 3:25; cf. 4:8) join it closely with this passage. If so, these symbolic actions would then belong to the same time frame as the prophet's commissioning (about 593 B.C.). In any case this passage ought to be dated before the events of 24:1 (roughly 587 B.C.), when the Babylonian siege of Jerusalem is reported to Ezekiel.

4:1–2 These verses describe a complete **siege** in miniature; **brick** was the common building material in Babylon, not Jerusalem. The fivefold repetition of **against it** strikes an insistent note.

4:3 The **iron griddle** (Hb. *makhabath barzel*) was part of the priestly equipment (see Lev. 2:5; 6:21; 7:9); domestic versions were probably not metal. The **sign** ensures that the siege, which could have been construed as God's passive neglect, be understood as deliberate hostility.

4:4–6 The instructions to **lie on your left side** and then again **lie down . . . on your right side** prescribe Ezekiel's disposition during the enacted siege (v. 7). The practicalities of what would amount to over 14 months in this posture are not spelled out (e.g., readers are not told for how many hours each day Ezekiel would lie down this way), but the implied identification of the prophet with his people remains strong.

4:4 Punishment (Hb. *'awon*, "punishment" or "iniquity," given as an alternative in ESV footnote; cf. vv. 5, 6, 17). The word may refer to either an offense or its penalty. Ezekiel's enactment points to "punishment," which is the most likely sense (see v. 12), although when combined with **bear**, *'awon* usually carries the nuance of "iniquity" (e.g., Lev. 10:17; Num. 18:1). The **number of the days**, stipulated in the following verses, corresponds to periods of exile. Both phrases strikingly parallel the pronouncement of the 40 years of wilderness wandering in Num. 14:33–34.

4:7 As the prophet takes God's role in the street drama, the **arm bared** (cf. Isa. 52:10) suggests the more common "outstretched arm" (e.g., Ex. 6:6; Deut. 4:34; Ezek. 20:33–34) with which the Lord acts on behalf of his people, but here it is wielded *against* Jerusalem. Ezekiel's muteness (3:26) gives way to speech with the instruction to **prophesy against the city**.

4:8 For **cords**, cf. 3:25.

4:9–17 Again, the actions commanded—in this case rationing of food and water—ensure that Ezekiel's symbolic identification with the besieged community is complete.

4:9 The combination of **wheat . . . emmer** (as the ESV footnote explains, emmer is a type of wheat; it is inferior to ordinary wheat) is not prohibited,

9[n]ver. 5
10[o]ch. 12:19; [Jer. 37:21] [p]ch. 45:12
11[o][See ver. 10 above]
12[q]See ch. 12:3
13[r]Hos. 9:3; [Dan. 1:8]
14[s]ch. 9:8; 11:13; 20:49 [t][Acts 10:14] [u]ch. 44:31; [Lev. 7:24] [v]Isa. 65:4; [Lev. 7:18]
16[w]See ch. 2:1 [x]ch. 5:16; 14:13; Lev. 26:26 [o][See ver. 10 above]
17[y]See ch. 3:15 [z]ch. 24:23; 33:10; Lev. 26:39

Chapter 5

1[a]See ch. 2:1 [b]Ps. 57:4; Isa. 49:2 [c][Isa. 7:20] [d][ch. 1:3; 44:20; Lev. 21:5]
2[e]See ver. 12 [f][ver. 5; ch. 4:1] [g]See ch. 4:8 [h][ver. 10] [i]ver. 12; ch. 12:14; [Jer. 9:16]
3[j][Jer. 40:6; 52:16]
4[k][Jer. 42:18; 44:14]
5[l][ver. 2; ch. 4:1] [m][ch. 38:12]
6[n]See ch. 16:47, 48 [m][See ver. 5 above]
7[o]Ps. 2:1; 46:6 [p]ch. 16:47 [q][ch. 11:12]
8[r]See ch. 13:8 [s]ch. 11:9; 16:41; 23:10 [t]ch. 22:16
9[u][2 Kgs. 21:12, 13; Lam. 1:12; Dan. 9:12]
10[v]See Jer. 19:9 [s][See ver. 8 above] [w]ch. 12:14; 17:21; 22:15; 36:19; Deut. 28:64; Jer. 9:16; 15:4; Zech. 2:6; [ver. 2; ch. 36:19]
11[x]See ch. 16:48 [y]ch. 8:3, 5, 6; 23:39; 2 Chr. 36:14; Jer. 7:30 [z]ch. 11:18

you lie on your side, [n]390 days, you shall eat it. **10** And your food that you eat shall be [o]by
weight, [p]twenty shekels[1] a day; from day to day[2] you shall eat it. **11** And water you shall
drink [o]by measure, the sixth part of a hin;[3] from day to day you shall drink. **12** And you
shall eat it as a barley cake, baking it [q]in their sight on human dung." **13** And the LORD
said, "Thus shall the people of Israel eat [r]their bread unclean, among the nations where
I will drive them." **14** Then I said, [s]"Ah, Lord GOD! Behold, I have never defiled myself.[4]
[t]From my youth up till now I have never eaten [u]what died of itself or was torn by beasts,
nor has [v]tainted meat come into my mouth." **15** Then he said to me, "See, I assign to you
cow's dung instead of human dung, on which you may prepare your bread." **16** Moreover,
he said to me, [w]"Son of man, behold, [x]I will break the supply[5] of bread in Jerusalem. They
shall eat bread [o]by weight and with anxiety, and they shall drink water [o]by measure and
in dismay. **17** I will do this that they may lack bread and water, and [y]look at one another in
dismay, and [z]rot away because of their punishment.

Jerusalem Will Be Destroyed

5 "And you, [a]O son of man, take a [b]sharp sword. Use it as [c]a barber's razor and [d]pass it
over your head and your beard. Then take balances for weighing and divide the hair.
2 [e]A third part you shall burn in the fire [f]in the midst of the city, [g]when the days of the siege
are completed. And a third part you shall take and strike with the sword all around the
city. [h]And a third part you shall scatter to the wind, and [i]I will unsheathe the sword after
them. **3** [j]And you shall take from these a small number and bind them in the skirts of your
robe. **4** [k]And of these again you shall take some and cast them into the midst of the fire and
burn them in the fire. From there a fire will come out into all the house of Israel.
5 "Thus says the Lord GOD: [l]This is Jerusalem. I have set her [m]in the center of the nations,
with countries all around her. **6** And she has rebelled against my rules by doing wickedness
[n]more than the nations, and against my statutes more than [m]the countries all around her;
for they have rejected my rules and have not walked in my statutes. **7** Therefore thus says the
Lord GOD: Because you are [o]more turbulent than the nations that are all around you, [p]and
have not walked in my statutes or obeyed my rules, [q]and have not[6] even acted according to
the rules of the nations that are all around you, **8** therefore thus says the Lord GOD: Behold,
I, even I, [r]am against you. [s]And I will execute judgments[7] in your midst [t]in the sight of the
nations. **9** And because of all your abominations I will do with you [u]what I have never yet
done, and the like of which I will never do again. **10** Therefore [v]fathers shall eat their sons
in your midst, and sons shall eat their fathers. [s]And I will execute judgments on you, [w]and
any of you who survive I will scatter to all the winds. **11** Therefore, [x]as I live, declares the
Lord GOD, surely, [y]because you have defiled my sanctuary [z]with all your detestable things

[1] A *shekel* was about 2/5 ounce or 11 grams [2] Or *at a set time daily*; also verse 11 [3] A *hin* was about 4 quarts or 3.5 liters [4] Hebrew *my soul* (or *throat*) *has never been made unclean* [5] Hebrew *staff* [6] Some Hebrew manuscripts and Syriac lack *not* [7] The same Hebrew expression can mean *obey rules*, or *execute judgments*, depending on the context

but it is not appealing. Desperation for food during a siege will drive one to eat even this—and worse.

4:10 The **twenty shekels** ration of bread amounts to just 8 ounces (0.23 kg). Since Ezekiel is acting out a symbolic message, it is not necessary to suppose that he ate or drank nothing else for 24 hours every day, but in any case his hardship was evident.

4:11 The sixth part of a hin is roughly equivalent to 1.4 pints (0.6 liters).

4:12–15 Ezekiel raises no objection until he is told to use **human dung** for fuel. Animal dung is a common fuel (v. 15; cf. 1 Kings 14:10), but Ezekiel, as a priest, regards food as holy (e.g., Lev. 21:6; 22:7–8) and excrement as defiling (Deut. 23:12–14).

4:16 Underlying the phrase **supply of bread** is the distinctive Hebrew "staff of bread" (*matteh-lekhem*; see ESV footnote), which probably refers to a method of storage. To **break** the staff (see 5:16; 14:13; also Lev. 26:26; Ps. 105:16) is synonymous with famine.

4:17 The context here reinforces the nuance of **punishment** for the Hebrew *'awon* (see note on v. 4).

5:1–4 razor. Although cleanliness from disease may underlie this action (Lev. 14:9), it is unlikely that that picture of purification is in mind here. Rather, the shaving of **head** and **beard** combines elements that are again both desecrating and shaming. Priests should not shave off their hair (Ezek. 44:20; see also Lev. 21:5), so this desecrates as the unclean food did in Ezekiel 4. Further, the shaming of the king of Assyria in Isa. 7:20 at God's own hands echoes Ezekiel's action here. Each of the three actions should be understood as proclaiming destruction, even for those who survive (**scatter to the wind**, Ezek. 5:2; **bind them**, v. 3). Even the remnant of vv. 3–4 faces a precarious and vulnerable future.

5:5–17 *God against Jerusalem Explained.* Naturally, these symbolic actions carry enigmatic elements, not the least of which is the motivation behind them. This oracular commentary on Ezekiel's street theater offers the rationale and alludes to each of the three phases of Jerusalem's destruction previously acted out. Since this passage is intended to be commentary, it is also in large part self-explanatory.

5:8–10 The hostility identified here with God's setting himself **against** Jerusalem points back to the actions in 4:1–2. **eat their sons**. This gruesome prospect arises not only out of the realities of siege warfare (see Lam. 4:10) but also from the **judgments** for breaking the covenant (Deut. 28:49–57).

5:11 Deuteronomy often steels the Israelites to inflict stern judgment—when issues of purity or loyalty are at stake—in terms of their "eye not pitying"

and with all your [a]abominations, [b]therefore I will withdraw.[1] [c]My eye will not spare, and I
will have no pity. **12** [d]A third part of you shall die of pestilence and be consumed with famine
in your midst; [d]a third part shall fall by the sword all around you; [d]and a third part I will
scatter to all the winds and will unsheathe the sword after them.
13 [e]"Thus shall my anger spend itself, and I will vent my fury upon them and satisfy
myself. And they shall know that [f]I am the LORD—that I have spoken in my jealousy—
[e]when I spend my fury upon them. **14** Moreover, I will make you [g]a desolation and [h]an object
of reproach among [i]the nations all around you and in the sight of all who pass by. **15** You
shall be[2] a reproach and a taunt, a warning [j]and a horror, to [i]the nations all around you,
[k]when I execute judgments on you in anger and fury, and [l]with furious rebukes—I am the
LORD; I have spoken— **16** when I send against you[3] [m]the deadly arrows of famine, arrows
for destruction, which I will send to destroy you, and when I bring more and more famine
upon [n]you and break your supply[4] of bread. **17** I will send famine and [o]wild beasts against
you, [p]and they will rob you of your children. Pestilence and [q]blood shall pass through you,
and I will bring the sword upon you. I am the LORD; I have spoken."

Judgment Against Idolatry

6 The word of the LORD came to me: **2** [r]"Son of man, [s]set your face toward [t]the mountains
of Israel, and [u]prophesy against them, **3** and say, [v]You mountains of Israel, hear the
word of the Lord GOD! Thus says the Lord GOD to [w]the mountains and [x]the hills, to [y]the
ravines and the valleys: Behold, I, even I, will bring a sword upon you, [z]and I will destroy
your high places. **4** [z]Your altars shall become desolate, and your [a]incense altars shall be
broken, and I will cast down your slain before your idols. **5** [z]And I will lay the dead bodies
of the people of Israel before their idols, [b]and I will scatter your bones around your altars.
6 Wherever you dwell, [c]the cities shall be waste and [d]the high places ruined, so that your
altars will be waste and ruined,[5] your idols broken and destroyed, your [a]incense altars cut
down, and your works wiped out. **7** And the slain shall fall in your midst, and you shall
know that I am the LORD.
8 [e]"Yet I will leave some of you alive. When you have among the nations [f]some who
escape the sword, and when you are scattered through the countries, **9** then those of you
who escape [g]will remember me among the nations where they are carried captive, how [h]I
have been broken over their whoring heart that has departed from me and over their eyes
[i]that go whoring after their idols. [g]And they will be loathsome in their own sight for the
evils that they have committed, for all their abominations. **10** And they shall know that I
am the LORD. [j]I have not said in vain that I would do this evil to them."
11 Thus says the Lord GOD: [k]"Clap your hands [l]and stamp your foot and say, Alas, because

[1] Some Hebrew manuscripts *I will cut you down* [2] Dead Sea Scroll, Septuagint, Syriac, Vulgate, Targum; Masoretic Text *And it shall be* [3] Hebrew *them*
[4] Hebrew *staff* [5] Or *and punished*

11 [a]ch. 7:20; 11:18, 21 [b]ch. 16:27 [c]ch. 7:4, 9; 8:18; 9:5, 10; [Jer. 21:7]
12 [d][ver. 2; ch. 6:11, 12; Jer. 15:2]
13 [e]ch. 6:12; 7:8; 20:8, 21; Lam. 4:11; [ch. 39:25] [f]ch. 36:5, 6; 38:19
14 [g]ch. 6:6; See Jer. 22:5 [h]ch. 22:4; Neh. 2:17; Ps. 79:4; Jer. 24:9 [i]ver. 5, 6
15 [j]ch. 14:8; Deut. 28:37 [i][See ver. 14 above] [k][ch. 14:21] [l]ch. 25:17
16 [m]Deut. 32:23, 24 [n]See ch. 4:16
17 [o]ch. 14:15; 33:27; 34:25; Deut. 32:24; [2 Kgs. 17:25] [p][ch. 36:12] [q]ch. 38:22

Chapter 6

2 [r]See ch. 2:1 [s]ch. 13:17; 20:46; 21:2; 25:2; 28:21; 29:2; 35:2; 38:2; [Luke 9:51] [t]ch. 19:9; 33:28; 34:13, 14; 35:12; 36:1, 4, 8; 37:22; 38:8; 39:2, 4, 17 [u]ch. 37:4, 9; 38:2
3 [v]ch. 36:1, 4 [w]ch. 36:4, 6 [x][ver. 13] [y][ch. 31:12; Isa. 57:5, 6] [z]Lev. 26:30
4 [z][See ver. 3 above] [a]See 2 Chr. 14:5
5 [z][See ver. 3 above] [b][2 Kgs. 23:14, 16]
6 [c]ch. 12:20; [Isa. 27:10] [d][ver. 3, 4] [a][See ver. 4 above]
8 [e]ch. 12:16; 14:22 [f]ch. 7:16
9 [g]ch. 16:61; 20:43; 36:31; Lev. 26:39, 40 [h][Jer. 23:9] [i]See Ex. 34:15
10 [j][Num. 23:19]
11 [k][ch. 21:14, 17] [l][ch. 25:6]

(e.g., Deut. 13:8; 19:13). The same Hebrew is used here for God's **eye** that **will not spare** (also six more times in Ezekiel).

5:12 The groupings of thirds point back to the symbolic action of the hair in vv. 1–4, as does the reference to scattering (cf. v. 10). With **pestilence**, **famine**, and **sword** (also v. 17; 6:11–12; 7:15; 12:16; and 14:21), Ezekiel employs one of Jeremiah's favorite groupings of three disasters (used 17 times), one of several examples of the younger prophet's use of language borrowed from his older contemporary.

5:16 The commentary now connects with the **famine**, alluding to the second symbolic action (4:9–17), including the distinctive **break your supply of bread** (see 4:16).

6:1–7:27 *Oracles against the "Land."* These two extended oracles share the feature of being addressed to "geography": the "mountains" (6:2) and "land" (Hb. *'adamah*; lit., "ground"; 7:2) of Israel, a feature also shared with 20:46; 21:2; 35:2; and 36:1, 6. Although in both cases the real audience is human (see 6:6), this form of address must have some significance beyond being simply symbolic. A deliberate connection of both "mountains" and "land" is found in ch. 36—one of the most theologically important chapters in the book, which forms a counterpart to chs. 6 and 7. Chapters 6 and 7 both describe coming punishment, but each addresses a different theme.

6:1–14 *Against the Mountains of Israel.* The address to the "mountains of Israel" (v. 2)—a phrase unique to Ezekiel in the OT—does more than strike a nostalgic note, although it does that as well. The hills were inherently linked to illicit worship (see 1 Kings 14:23; 2 Chron. 21:11; Jer. 3:6), and this is Ezekiel's focus. Variations of the "recognition formula" ("you shall know that I am the LORD," Ezek. 6:7; cf. vv. 10, 13, and 14) structure the chapter.

6:1–7 prophesy against them. Here the focus is on the death of idolaters.

6:2 set your face. Another favorite phrase of Ezekiel, expressing determination, reflects God's own orientation in Jer. 44:11 and that of the "servant" in Isa. 50:7. Luke used it of Jesus in Luke 9:51.

6:3 The treaty curses of Leviticus 26 lurk in the background. This is especially clear in the threat to **bring a sword upon you**, used five more times in Ezekiel (5:17; 11:8; 14:17; 29:8; and 33:2) and once in Lev. 26:25, but only in three other places in the entire OT. The **high places** (Hb. *bamot*) were not just the crests of hills. They were constructed cultic installations that could, therefore, be destroyed.

6:8–10 leave some of you alive. Complete annihilation is moderated with the promise of a remnant (cf. 5:3). The remorse of the survivors is matched by the striking description of the effect that idolatry had on God: **I have been broken** (6:9) uses the same term of God as was used in v. 6 ("idols broken"), and indicates God's deep sorrow at the people's sin.

6:11–13 The prophet's nonverbal actions here indicate the force with which

of all the evil abominations of the house of Israel, [m]for they shall fall by the sword, by
famine, and by pestilence. **12** [n]He who is far off shall die of pestilence, and he who is near
shall fall by the sword, and he who is left and is preserved shall die of famine. [o]Thus I will
spend my fury upon them. **13** And you shall know that I am the LORD, [p]when their slain lie
among their idols around their altars, [q]on every high hill, [r]on all the mountaintops, [s]under
every green tree, and under [t]every leafy oak, wherever [u]they offered pleasing aroma to all
their idols. **14** And [v]I will stretch out my hand against them and [w]make the land desolate
and waste, [x]in all their dwelling places, from the wilderness to [y]Riblah.[1] Then [z]they will
know that I am the LORD."

The Day of the Wrath of the LORD

7 The word of the LORD came to me: **2** "And you, [a]O son of man, thus says the Lord GOD to
the land of Israel: [b]An end! The end has come upon the four corners of the land.[2] **3** Now
[b]the end is upon you, and [c]I will send my anger upon you; [d]I will judge you according to
your ways, and I will punish you for all your abominations. **4** [e]And my eye will not spare
you, nor will I have pity, but [f]I will punish you for your ways, while your abominations
are in your midst. [g]Then you will know that I am the LORD.

5 "Thus says the Lord GOD: Disaster [h]after disaster![3] Behold, it comes. **6** [b]An end has come;
the end has come; it has awakened against you. Behold, it comes. **7** [i]Your doom[4] has come
to you, O inhabitant of the land. [j]The time has come; the day is near, a day of tumult, and
not [k]of joyful shouting on the mountains. **8** Now I will soon [l]pour out my wrath upon you,
and [m]spend my anger against you, [d]and judge you according to your ways, and I will punish you for all your abominations. **9** [e]And my eye will not spare, nor will I have pity. I will
punish you according to your ways, while your abominations are in your midst. [n]Then
you will know that I am the LORD, who strikes.

10 [o]"Behold, the day! Behold, it comes! [p]Your doom has come; [q]the rod has blossomed;
pride has budded. **11** [r]Violence has grown up into [q]a rod of wickedness. [s]None of them shall
remain, nor their abundance, nor their wealth; neither shall there be preeminence among
them.[5] **12** [j]The time has come; the day has arrived. Let not [t]the buyer rejoice, nor [t]the seller
mourn, [u]for wrath is upon all their multitude.[6] **13** For [v]the seller shall not return to what
he has sold, while they live. [w]For the vision concerns all their multitude; it shall not turn
back; and because of his iniquity, none can maintain his life.[7]

[1] Some Hebrew manuscripts; most Hebrew manuscripts *Diblah* [2] Or *earth* [3] Some Hebrew manuscripts (compare Syriac, Targum); most Hebrew manuscripts *Disaster! A unique disaster!* [4] The meaning of the Hebrew word is uncertain; also verse 10 [5] The meaning of this last Hebrew sentence is uncertain [6] Or *abundance*; also verses 13, 14 [7] The meaning of this last Hebrew sentence is uncertain

11 [m]See ch. 5:12
12 [n][ch. 7:15] [o]See ch. 5:13
13 [p][ver. 4, 5] [q][ch. 20:28] [r]Hos. 4:13 [s]Jer. 2:20 [t]Isa. 1:29 [u]ch. 16:19; 20:28; Gen. 8:21
14 [v]ch. 25:7, 13, 16; 35:3; Isa. 5:25 [w]ch. 33:28 [x][ver. 6] [y][Num. 34:11] [z]See ver. 7

Chapter 7

2 [a]See ch. 2:1 [b]Lam. 4:18; [Isa. 10:23]
3 [b][See ver. 2 above] [c]See ver. 8 [d]See ch. 18:30
4 [e]See ch. 5:11 [f]ch. 9:10; 11:21; 16:43; 22:31 [g]See ch. 6:7
5 [h][ch. 5:9]
6 [b][See ver. 2 above]
7 [i]ver. 10 [j]Zeph. 1:14, 15; [ch. 12:23] [k][Jer. 25:30]
8 [l]ch. 9:8; 14:19; 20:8, 13, 21, 33, 34; 22:22; 36:18 [m]See ch. 5:13 [d][See ver. 3 above]
9 [e][See ver. 4 above] [n][ch. 6:7]
10 [o][ver. 2] [p]ver. 7 [q][Isa. 10:5; 14:5]
11 [r][ver. 23] [q][See ver. 10 above] [s][ch. 17:13]
12 [j][See ver. 7 above] [t][Isa. 24:2; 1 Cor. 7:29, 30] [u]ver. 14
13 [v]Lev. 25:13, 14 [w]See ch. 9:8-10

the oracle is to be delivered. This catalog of illicit cultic locations occurs elsewhere in the OT and has its roots in Deut. 12:2.

6:14 The place name **Riblah**, a correction of the Masoretic text's "Diblah," is based on some Hebrew evidence (the mistake of *d* for *r* was very easy in both paleo-Hebrew as well as later square script). The area being described stretches from the Negeb to northern Syria.

7:1–27 *Against the Land of Israel.* The address to the "land [soil] of Israel" (v. 2) links this chapter to the previous one against the "mountains of Israel" (6:2). Two features of this chapter pull in different directions: the Hebrew is at points quite obscure and translation is difficult (see the "uncertain" readings in ESV footnotes); yet the imagery is striking and the overall sense plain. Although laid out as prose, many see Ezekiel's diction here inclining to poetry, as short staccato lines echo content. As in ch. 6, the "recognition formula" (7:4, 9, 27; cf. Introduction: Style) gives internal shape to the oracle, which falls into two main parts (vv. 1–9, 10–27). Together they form a "sermon" whose text is Amos 8. The resonance of language and overlap of themes and sequence between these chapters is impressive, and it seems likely that Ezekiel's oracle develops Amos's earlier prophecy.

7:1–9 The end has come (v. 2). This first section itself further divides in two, with introductory and concluding formulas framing vv. 1–4 and 5–9, with strong parallels between them: cf. vv. 2 and 5–6; 3 and 8; 4 and 9. Is this a first and second "edition," both of which were preserved? The "odd man out," v. 7, finds its echo in the second section at v. 12. These verses are mostly framed in the first person, as God announces the imminent outpouring of his wrath.

7:2 The address to the **land** (lit., "soil") **of Israel** uses a phrase unique to Ezekiel (found 17 times in the book, always referring to the people Israel). Similar to 6:2, it is evocative language on the lips of an exile. The announcement of **an end** (also 7:3, 6) picks up the language of Amos 8:2.

7:3 abominations (also vv. 4, 8, 9; plural of Hb. *to'ebah*). These are offenses repugnant to God that defile and that demand elimination. This is very frequent language in Ezekiel (mentioned 41 times), and is rooted more in Deuteronomy (e.g., Deut. 18:12) than Leviticus.

7:7 The **time** and **day** point forward to the second part of the chapter, and indicate a moment of reversal.

7:10–27 Behold, the day! (v. 10). The "day of the LORD" is a prominent theme in the Hebrew prophets, with origins in Amos 5:18–20 (see notes on Isa. 13:5–6; Amos 5:18–20). Ezekiel's development relates most closely to Amos 8:9–10. It was a time of great expectation but was turned to bitter anguish at the hands of God, who was wrongly assumed to be coming in blessing. Among the many motifs shared between Ezekiel 7 and Amos 8 are the "day" itself, violence and wealth, agricultural metaphors, foiled commerce, desecration of holy things, and withholding of divine direction. In contrast to the first-person oracle of Ezek. 7:1–9, the action of vv. 10–27 is mostly carried by third-person descriptions of the coming disaster.

7:12–13 The transactions described here connect with the laws of Lev. 25:26–27. There is no opportunity to redeem property because death will come first.

14 "They have blown the trumpet and made everything ready, but none goes to battle,
[x]for my wrath is upon all their multitude. 15 [y]The sword is without; pestilence and famine
are within. [z]He who is in the field dies by the sword, [z]and him who is in the city famine
and pestilence devour. 16 [a]And if any survivors escape, they will be on the mountains, like
[b]doves of the valleys, all of them moaning, each one over his iniquity. 17 [c]All hands are feeble,
and all knees turn to water. 18 [d]They put on sackcloth, and [e]horror covers them. Shame is
on all faces, and [f]baldness on all their heads. 19 They cast their silver into the streets, and
their gold is like an unclean thing. [g]Their silver and gold are not able to deliver them in
the day of the wrath of the LORD. They cannot satisfy their hunger or fill their stomachs
with it. [h]For it was [i]the stumbling block of their iniquity. 20 [j]His beautiful ornament they
used for pride, and [k]they made their abominable images and their detestable things of
it. Therefore [l]I make it an unclean thing to them. 21 And I will give it into the hands of
[m]foreigners for prey, [n]and to the wicked of the earth for spoil, and [l]they shall profane it.
22 I will turn my face from them, and [l]they shall profane my treasured[1] place. Robbers
shall enter [l]and profane it.

23 [o]"Forge a chain![2] [p]For the land is full of bloody crimes [q]and the city is full of violence.
24 I will bring [r]the worst of the nations to take possession of their houses. [s]I will put an
end to the pride of the strong, [t]and their holy places[3] shall be profaned. 25 [u]When anguish
comes, [v]they will seek peace, but there shall be none. 26 [w]Disaster comes upon disaster;
[x]rumor follows rumor. [y]They seek a vision from the prophet, while [z]the law[4] perishes
from the priest and [a]counsel from the elders. 27 The king mourns, the prince is wrapped
in despair, and the hands of the people of the land are paralyzed by terror. According to
their way [b]I will do to them, and according to their judgments I will judge them, [c]and
they shall know that I am the LORD."

Abominations in the Temple

8 [d]In the sixth year, in the sixth month, on the fifth day of the month, [e]as I sat in my
house, with [f]the elders of Judah sitting before me, [g]the hand of the Lord GOD fell
upon me there. 2 Then I looked, and behold, [h]a form that had the appearance of a man.[5]
[h]Below what appeared to be his waist was fire, and above his waist was something like
the appearance of brightness, like [i]gleaming metal.[6] 3 He [j]put out the form of a hand and
took me by a lock of my head, and the Spirit lifted me up [k]between earth and heaven and
[l]brought me in [m]visions of God to Jerusalem, [n]to the entrance of the gateway of the inner
court that faces north, [o]where was the seat of the [p]image of jealousy, [q]which provokes to
jealousy. 4 And behold, [r]the glory of the God of Israel was there, like the vision that I saw
[s]in the valley.

14 [x]ver. 12
15 [y][ch. 6:12; Lam. 1:20] [z]Jer. 14:18
16 [a]ch. 6:8 [b][Isa. 38:14]
17 [c]ch. 21:7; Isa. 13:7; Jer. 6:24
18 [d]Isa. 15:2, 3; Lam. 2:10 [e]Ps. 55:5 [f]See Isa. 3:24
19 [g]Prov. 11:4; Zeph. 1:18 [h][1 Tim. 6:10] [i]ch. 14:3, 4, 7; 44:12
20 [j][Isa. 64:11] [k][ch. 16:17]; See ch. 8:5-16 [l][ch. 9:7; 24:21; 25:3]
21 [m]See ch. 28:7 [n][ver. 24; ch. 23:46] [l][See ver. 20 above]
22 [l][See ver. 20 above]
23 [o][Jer. 27:2] [p]ch. 8:17; 9:9; 11:6; 22:3, 4; Jer. 6:7 [q][ver. 11]
24 [r][ver. 21; Hab. 1:6, 13] [s][ver. 11] [t]See ver. 20
25 [u][ver. 2] [v][Jer. 6:14; 8:15; 1 Thess. 5:3]
26 [w][Jer. 4:20] [x]See Job 1:16-19 [y][ch. 20:1, 3; Ps. 74:9] [z][Mal. 2:7] [a][1 Kgs. 12:6]
27 [b][ver. 4] [c]See ch. 6:7

Chapter 8

1 [d][ch. 1:2]; See ch. 20:1 [e][2 Kgs. 6:32] [f]ver. 11, 12; ch. 14:1; 20:1, 3 [g]See ch. 1:3
2 [h]ch. 1:27 [i]ch. 1:4, 27
3 [j][Dan. 5:5]; See ch. 2:9 [k][2 Cor. 12:2, 4] [l]ch. 11:1, 24; 40:2 [m]See ch. 1:1 [n]ver. 14 [o][ch. 5:11] [p][Deut. 4:16] [q]Deut. 32:16, 21
4 [r]See ch. 1:28 [s]See ch. 3:22

[1] Or *secret* [2] Probably refers to an instrument of captivity [3] By revocalization (compare Septuagint); Hebrew *and those who sanctify them* [4] Or *instruction*
[5] By revocalization (compare Septuagint); Hebrew *of fire* [6] Or *amber*

7:17 all knees turn to water. The Hebrew formulation suggests a loss of bladder control with the onset of panic (LXX, "all thighs will be defiled with moisture").

7:20 The **beautiful ornament** is an obscure reference, but imagery of the temple is probably in mind.

7:26 Loss of divine direction from the **prophet**, **priest**, and **elders** forges another link to Jeremiah, where the oblivious Judeans assume that such guidance will always be forthcoming (Jer. 18:18).

8:1–11:25 *Ezekiel's Temple Vision.* This is the second of Ezekiel's four dramatic visions, having overt connections with the opening vision (chs. 1–3). It also has strong links to the concluding vision (chs. 40–48), which offers a mirror image to this one. Ezekiel is shown a mounting series of vignettes of idolatrous worship in the temple (ch. 8), the citywide slaughter of idolaters (ch. 9), the destruction of Jerusalem by fire, and the gradual withdrawal of the presence of the Lord from the temple (ch. 10). The vision culminates in the contrast of judgment on wicked officials (11:1–13) with an oracle of hope (11:14–21) before God's glory departs completely (11:22–25). As a whole, the vision emphasizes God's rejection of this generation of Judeans and demonstrates the justice of God's stance.

8:1–18 *Transportation and Abominations.* Ezekiel is transported in his vision to the temple complex at the heart of Jerusalem (vv. 1–4). In a series of locations, including both the center and the periphery of the temple, various cultic practices, termed **abominations**, are revealed.

8:1–4 The vision begins with Ezekiel's "physical" transportation from his home in Babylon (v. 1) to the Jerusalem temple (v. 3), a detail without parallel in the canonical OT (but cf. *Bel and Dragon* 14:33–36). Otherwise the setting is reminiscent of the inaugural vision (Ezekiel 1–3).

8:1 The date formula places this vision in September 592 B.C., just over a year from the inaugural vision. No triggering event can be linked to this date with certainty, but the events leading up to the sinking of the anti-Babylonian scroll related in Jer. 51:59–64 may lurk in the background. Clearly there were "prophets" among the exiles fomenting rebellion (see Jer. 29:20–23). The **elders** (Ezek. 8:1) seek a word from Ezekiel.

8:2 The manifestation of God that Ezekiel sees on this occasion is like that of the inaugural vision in 1:27. In 8:4 this connection is made explicit.

8:3 When interpreting chs. 8–11 it must be borne in mind that what Ezekiel sees are dreamlike **visions of God**. This is spiritual, not "natural" reality. The inner **gateway** locates Ezekiel within the temple-palace complex, yet not at its center. (For the **image of jealousy**, see 8:5.)

8:4 glory. See note on 1:28.

5 Then he said to me, [t]"Son of man, lift up your eyes now toward the north." So I lifted
up my eyes toward the north, and behold, north of [u]the altar gate, in the entrance, was
this [p]image of jealousy. 6 And he said to me, "Son of man, [v]do you see what they are doing,
[w]the great abominations that the house of Israel are committing here, [x]to drive me far
from my sanctuary? But you will see still greater abominations."
7 And he brought me to the entrance of the court, and when I looked, behold, there was a
hole in the wall. 8 Then he said to me, "Son of man, [y]dig in the wall." So I dug in the wall, and
behold, there was an entrance. 9 And he said to me, "Go in, and see [z]the vile abominations
that they are committing here." 10 So I went in and saw. And there, [a]engraved on the wall
all around, was [b]every form of [c]creeping things and loathsome beasts, and all the idols of
the house of Israel. 11 And before them stood [d]seventy men of [e]the elders of the house of
Israel, with Jaazaniah the son of [f]Shaphan standing among them. Each had his censer in
his hand, and [g]the smoke of the cloud of incense went up. 12 Then he said to me, "Son of
man, have you seen what the elders of the house of Israel are doing [h]in the dark, each [i]in
his room of pictures? For they say, [j]'The LORD does not see us, the LORD has forsaken the
land.'" 13 He said also to me, [k]"You will see still greater abominations that they commit."
14 Then he brought me to [l]the entrance of the north gate of the house of the LORD, and
behold, there sat women weeping for Tammuz. 15 Then he said to me, "Have you seen this,
O [t]son of man? [k]You will see still greater abominations than these."
16 And he brought me into [m]the inner court of the house of the LORD. And behold, at
the entrance of the temple of the LORD, [n]between the [o]porch and [p]the altar, were about
twenty-five men, [q]with their backs to the temple of the LORD, and their faces toward the
east, worshiping [r]the sun toward the east. 17 Then he said to me, "Have you seen this, O
[s]son of man? Is it too light a thing for the house of Judah to commit [t]the abominations
that they commit here, that [u]they should fill the land with violence and [v]provoke me still
further to anger? Behold, they put the branch to their[1] nose. 18 Therefore [w]I will act in
wrath. [x]My eye will not spare, nor will I have pity. [y]And though they cry in my ears with
a loud voice, I will not hear them."

Idolaters Killed

9 Then he cried in my ears with a loud voice, saying, "Bring near the executioners of the
city, [z]each with his destroying weapon in his hand." 2 And behold, six men came from
the direction of [a]the upper gate, which faces north, each with his weapon for slaughter
in his hand, and with them was [b]a man clothed in linen, with a writing case at his waist.
And they went in and stood beside [c]the bronze altar.

[1] Or *my*

5 [t]See ch. 2:1 [u]See ver. 16 [p][See ver. 3 above]
6 [v][ch. 47:6] [w]See ch. 5:11 [x][ch. 10:18, 19]
8 [y][ch. 12:5]
9 [z]See ch. 5:11
10 [a]ch. 23:14 [b]See Ex. 20:4 [c]Lev. 11:20; Rom. 1:23
11 [d][Ex. 24:1; Num. 11:16] [e]See ver. 1 [f]2 Chr. 34:8 [g][ch. 6:13]
12 [h][ver. 7] [i][ver. 10] [j]ch. 9:9; Ps. 10:11; Isa. 29:15
13 [k]ver. 6
14 [l]ver. 3
15 [t][See ver. 5 above] [k][See ver. 13 above]
16 [m]ch. 10:3; 40:28; 43:5; 45:19; 46:1; 1 Kgs. 6:36 [n]Joel 2:17 [o]1 Kgs. 6:3 [p]ver. 5; ch. 40:47; Ex. 40:6, 29; [ch. 9:2] [q][Jer. 2:27; 32:33] [r]See Jer. 8:2
17 [s]See ch. 2:1 [t]See ch. 5:11 [u][ch. 7:11, 23] [v]Jer. 7:18, 19; [ch. 20:28]
18 [w]ch. 5:13 [x]See ch. 5:11 [y]Prov. 1:28; Isa. 1:15; Mic. 3:4

Chapter 9

1 [z][ch. 43:3]
2 [a]2 Kgs. 15:35; Jer. 20:2 [b]ch. 10:2, 6, 7; Dan. 10:5; 12:6, 7 [c][ch. 8:16]

8:5–6 The first of the four vignettes situates Ezekiel with his back to the altar, facing an **image of jealousy**, which remains unidentified. The vagueness is deliberate: focus remains on the provocation of divine outrage, not on the specifics of the image itself. It will get worse (**still greater abominations**; cf. vv. 13, 15). These sins are "greater" in the sense of being more hateful to God; this can be because of such factors as bringing him more dishonor, bringing greater harm to others, expressing more and more defiance to God's warnings or indifference to his love, being more boldly done in public, or being committed by those with greater responsibility.

8:7–13 This second scenario demonstrates the impossible possibilities of visions. To look inside the wall for a literal "room" that could hold 70 men is to miss the force of what Ezekiel is being shown: the interior of self-deceived (v. 12) idolaters.

8:10 The images **engraved** on the walls contravene not only the second commandment (Ex. 20:4) but also the list enumerated in Deut. 4:15–18.

8:11 The presence of **Jaazaniah the son of Shaphan** among the 70 elders may have been a shock. He was probably a member of the clan of Shaphan (2 Kings 22:8–10) which had proved so loyal to the cause of Yahweh in Jeremiah's ministry (e.g., Jer. 26:24). This identification is not certain, but would explain why Jaazaniah is singled out for mention here.

8:14–15 Moving farther north, Ezekiel sees **women weeping for Tammuz** (from the Sumerian name, Dumuzi). This ancient Mesopotamian cult celebrated the shepherd-king and god of vegetation, whose association with sacred marriage seems clear, while claims about his status as a dying and rising god remain controversial. (The term "sacred marriage" describes ancient practices of ritual prostitution intended to ensure agricultural fertility.) Mourning rites among women in his cult are well attested outside of the Bible.

8:16 The final vignette, also the briefest, states simply and starkly the climax of abominations. The **twenty-five men** are not further identified, but the location **between the porch and the altar** would normally be reserved for priests. At this sacred place they venerate the sun. Solar worship is prohibited in Deut. 4:19 (see also 2 Kings 23:11). The outrage of this action contrasts with what priests ought to do here (cf. Ps. 26:6–7; Joel 2:17).

8:17–18 The behavior described in vv. 1–16 must be punished by a holy God. The phrase **put the branch to their nose** remains obscure; it was probably a gesture of derision.

9:1–11 *Slaughter in Jerusalem.* A team of seven angels carries out the execution of the unfaithful in Jerusalem at God's command. Only one of them is assigned the job of protecting the faithful. The prophet's anguished intervention does not dissuade God from judgment. Cf. the Passover (Exodus 12): a mark protects the faithful from God's agents of death.

9:1–2 The first phrase of v. 1 ironically repeats the closing phrase of 8:18. Hebrew *pequddot*, here rendered **executioners**, also carries the sense of "governing officials." The angels of the seven cities of Revelation 1–3 may be an analogy. In Ezekiel 9, destruction is by **weapon**; in ch. 10 it is by fire.

3 Now [d]the glory of the God of Israel had gone up from the cherub on which it rested to
[e]the threshold of the house. And he called to [b]the man clothed in linen, who had the writing
case at his waist. 4 And the LORD said to him, "Pass through the city, through Jerusalem, and
[f]put a mark on the foreheads of the men who [g]sigh and groan over all the abominations
that are committed in it." 5 And to [h]the others he said in my hearing, "Pass through the
city after him, and strike. [i]Your eye shall not spare, and you shall show no pity. 6 [j]Kill old
men outright, young men and maidens, little children and women, but [k]touch no one on
whom is the mark. And [l]begin at my sanctuary." So they began with the elders who were
before the house. 7 Then he said to them, [m]"Defile the house, and fill the courts with the
slain. Go out." So they went out and struck in the city. 8 And while they were striking, and
I was left alone, [n]I fell upon my face, and cried, [o]"Ah, Lord GOD! [p]Will you destroy all the
remnant of Israel [q]in the outpouring of your wrath on Jerusalem?"

9 Then he said to me, [r]"The guilt of the house of Israel and Judah is exceedingly great.
[s]The land is full of blood, and the city full of injustice. For [t]they say, 'The LORD has forsaken
the land, and the LORD does not see.' 10 As for me, [u]my eye will not spare, nor will I have
pity; [v]I will bring their deeds upon their heads."

11 And behold, [w]the man clothed in linen, with the writing case at his waist, brought
back word, saying, "I have done as you commanded me."

The Glory of the LORD Leaves the Temple

10 Then I looked, and behold, [x]on the expanse that was over the heads of the cherubim there appeared above them something [y]like a sapphire,[1] in appearance like
a throne. 2 And he said to [z]the man clothed in linen, "Go in among [a]the whirling wheels
underneath the cherubim. Fill your hands with [b]burning coals from between the cherubim,
and [c]scatter them over the city."

And he went in [d]before my eyes. 3 Now the cherubim were standing [e]on the south side
of the house, when the man went in, and [f]a cloud filled [g]the inner court. 4 And [h]the glory
of the LORD [i]went up from the cherub to the threshold of the house, and the house [f]was
filled with the cloud, and the court was filled with [j]the brightness of the glory of the LORD.
5 And [k]the sound of the wings of the cherubim was heard as far as the outer court, [k]like
the voice of God Almighty when he speaks.

6 And when he commanded [l]the man clothed in linen, [m]"Take fire from between [n]the
whirling wheels, from between the cherubim," he went in and stood beside a wheel. 7 And
a cherub stretched out his hand from between the cherubim to the fire that was between
the cherubim, and took some of it and put it into the hands of the man clothed in linen,
who took it and went out. 8 The cherubim appeared to have [o]the form of a human hand
under their wings.

9 [p]And I looked, and behold, there were four wheels beside the cherubim, one beside each

[1] Or *lapis lazuli*

3 [d]See ch. 1:28 [e]ch. 10:4, 18; 46:2; 47:1 [b][See ver. 2 above]
4 [f]Rev. 3:12; 7:3; 9:4; 14:1; 22:4; [Ex. 12:7; Rev. 13:16, 17; 14:9; 20:4] [g][Ps. 119:53, 136, 158]
5 [h][ver. 2] [i]See ch. 5:11
6 [j][2 Chr. 36:17] [k][Rev. 9:4] [l]See Jer. 25:29
7 [m]ch. 7:21, 22
8 [n]ch. 11:13; [Num. 14:5] [o]See ch. 4:14 [p]ch. 11:13 [q]See ch. 7:8
9 [r]See 2 Chr. 36:14-16 [s]See ch. 7:23 [t]See ch. 8:12
10 [u]See ch. 5:11 [v]See ch. 7:4
11 [w]ch. 10:2, 6, 7; Dan. 10:5; 12:6, 7

Chapter 10

1 [x][ch. 1:22] [y]See ch. 1:26
2 [z]See ch. 9:2 [a]ver. 6, 13 [b]ch. 1:13 [c][Rev. 8:5] [d]ver. 19
3 [e][Luke 1:11] [f]See 1 Kgs. 8:10 [g]See ch. 8:16
4 [h]See ch. 1:28 [i]ver. 18, 19 [f][See ver. 3 above] [j][ch. 43:2]
5 [k]ch. 1:24
6 [l]See ch. 9:2 [m][ver. 2] [n]ver. 2
8 [o][ver. 21; ch. 1:8; 8:3]
9 [p][ch. 1:15]

9:3–7 Verse 3a is a parenthetic aside, foreshadowing the main focus of ch. 10. The seventh angel, in the role of scribe, puts **a mark on the foreheads** (9:4) of those faithful to the Lord. Preserving a remnant has been a feature of chs. 4–7. Here, the mark is the Hebrew *taw*, and in the script of Ezekiel's day would be an X. Ancient Christian interpretation saw in this symbol an anticipation of the cross. Verses 6–7 of ch. 9 indicate that the slaughter is to begin where Ezekiel's tour of ch. 8 ended. The command to **defile the house** (9:7) overcomes the reluctance to pollute the sanctuary with corpses (cf. 1 Kings 1:51; 2 Kings 11:15).

9:6 they began with the elders. Just as the leaders had led the people astray, so now judgment begins with them, from their place before God's **house** (the temple). This judgment is echoed in Peter's talk of a purifying judgment that will "begin at the household of God" (1 Pet. 4:17).

9:8–10 Ah, Lord GOD! Ezekiel's impassioned outburst pleads for the remnant, and prompts the question: was the preserving angel finding any faithful? See also 4:14; 11:13; 21:5. God reiterates the firm intention of his justice and pointedly responds to the delusion of divine ignorance voiced by the elders (cf. 8:12 and 9:9).

10:1–22 *The Fire and the Glory.* Two actions are interwoven here: the second (visionary) phase of city destruction (vv. 1–8), and the further withdrawal of the glory of God from the temple (vv. 9–22).

10:1–8 The **man clothed in linen** (v. 2), a "preserving angel" in ch. 9, here becomes an incendiary agent of destruction. The narrative remains elusive, as attention oscillates between the angel (10:2, 6–7) and the cherubim, who are both the "throne" for God's presence and the source of the **burning coals** that will ignite the city (vv. 1, 3–5, 8). On a natural level, sword and fire would coincide; in the vision, they are distinct phases.

10:4 glory. See note on 1:28.

10:9–22 Much of the description of the cherubim here overlaps with the account of the "living creatures" in ch. 1, and reference should be made to that passage for an explanation of the common features. Although the description itself already signals this equivalence, the visionary account makes it explicit in 10:15, 20–22. The assault of sight and sound on the senses seems overpowering, as it was in the inaugural vision. While description dominates this section, the action, confined to vv. 18–19, is crucial. At the **threshold** (v. 18) of the **east gate** (v. 19), the **glory of the God of Israel** is poised to depart from the midst of his sinful people slowly and in stages (perhaps symbolizing how he gives the people every opportunity to repent). The language is deliberate: "God of Israel" is used five times in this vision (8:4; 9:3; 10:19–20; 11:22),

cherub, and [q]the appearance of the wheels was [r]like sparkling [s]beryl. 10 And as for their
appearance, the four had the same likeness, as if a wheel were within a wheel. 11 [t]When
they went, they went in any of their four directions[1] [u]without turning as they went, [v]but
in whatever direction the front wheel[2] faced, the others followed without turning as they
went. 12 [w]And their whole body, their rims, and their spokes, their wings,[3] and the wheels
were full of eyes all around—the wheels that the four of them had. 13 As for the wheels,
they were called in my hearing [n]"the whirling wheels." 14 [x]And every one had four faces:
[y]the first face was the face of the cherub, and the second face was [z]a human face, and the
third the face of a lion, and the fourth the face of an eagle.
15 [a]And the cherubim mounted up. These were [b]the living creatures that I saw by [c]the
Chebar canal. 16 [d]And when the cherubim went, the wheels went beside them. And [d]when
the cherubim lifted up their wings to mount up from the earth, the wheels did not turn
from beside them. 17 [e]When they stood still, these stood still, and when they mounted up,
these mounted up with them, for the spirit of the living creatures[4] was in them.
18 [f]Then [g]the glory of the LORD went out from the threshold of the house, and stood
over the cherubim. 19 [h]And the cherubim lifted up their wings and mounted up from the
earth [i]before my eyes as they went out, with the wheels beside them. And they stood at
the entrance of the [j]east gate of the house of the LORD, and [k]the glory of the God of Israel
was over them.
20 [l]These were the living creatures that I saw [m]underneath the God of Israel by [n]the
Chebar canal; and I knew that they were cherubim. 21 [o]Each had four faces, and each four
wings, and underneath their wings [p]the likeness of human hands. 22 [q]And as for the likeness of their faces, they were the same faces whose appearance I had seen by the Chebar
canal. [r]Each one of them went straight forward.

Judgment on Wicked Counselors

11 [s]The Spirit lifted me up and brought me to [t]the east gate of the house of the LORD,
which faces east. And behold, at the entrance of the gateway there were [u]twenty-five
men. And I saw among them Jaazaniah [v]the son of Azzur, and [w]Pelatiah the son of Benaiah,
princes of the people. 2 And he said to me, [x]"Son of man, these are the men who devise
iniquity and who give wicked counsel in this city; 3 [y]who say, [z]'The time is not near[5] to
build houses. [a]This city is the cauldron, and we are the meat.' 4 Therefore prophesy against
them, prophesy, O son of man."
5 And [b]the Spirit of the LORD fell upon me, and he said to me, "Say, Thus says the LORD: So
you think, O house of Israel. [c]For I know the things that come into your mind. 6 [d]You have
multiplied your slain in this city and have filled its streets with the slain. 7 Therefore thus
says the Lord GOD: [e]Your slain whom you have laid in the midst of it, [a]they are the meat,
and [a]this city is the cauldron, but you shall be brought out of the midst of it. 8 [f]You have
feared the sword, and I will bring the sword upon you, declares the Lord GOD. 9 And I will
bring you out of the midst of it, and [g]give you into the hands of foreigners, and [h]execute
judgments upon you. 10 [i]You shall fall by the sword. I will judge you at the border of Israel,

[1] Hebrew *to their four sides* [2] Hebrew *the head* [3] Or *their whole body, their backs, their hands, and their wings* [4] Or *spirit of life* [5] Or *Is not the time near . . . ?*

9 [q]ch. 1:16 [r][ch. 1:4] [s][ch. 1:16; Dan. 10:6]
11 [t]ch. 1:17 [u]ch. 1:9 [v][ver. 22]
12 [w][ch. 1:18]
13 [n][See ver. 6 above]
14 [x][ch. 1:6] [y][ch. 1:10] [z][ch. 1:5, 10; 41:19]
15 [a]ver. 17, 19 [b]ch. 1:5 [c]See ch. 1:1
16 [d]ch. 1:19
17 [e]ch. 1:20
18 [f][ver. 4] [g]ch. 43:2; See ch. 1:28
19 [h]ch. 11:22 [i]ver. 2 [j]ch. 11:1 [k]ch. 43:2; See ch. 1:28
20 [l]ch. 1:5 [m]ch. 1:22, 26 [n]See ch. 1:1
21 [o][ch. 1:6] [p][ver. 8]
22 [q]ch. 1:10 [r][ver. 11]

Chapter 11

1 [s]ver. 24; See ch. 3:12 [t]ch. 10:19 [u]ch. 8:16 [v]Jer. 28:1 [w]ver. 13
2 [x]See ch. 2:1
3 [y][Jer. 29:28] [z][ch. 12:22, 27] [a]ch. 24:3, 6
5 [b]See ch. 2:2 [c]ch. 20:32; 38:10; [Isa. 29:15]
6 [d][ch. 7:23]
7 [e]ch. 24:7 [a][See ver. 3 above]
8 [f]Jer. 42:16
9 [g]ch. 7:21 [h]See ch. 5:8
10 [i]Jer. 39:6; See 2 Kgs. 25:18-21

and four of those with "glory of." Beyond these, this phrasing occurs in Ezekiel only at 43:2 and 44:2, when God's glory returns.

11:1–13 *Punishment for Civic Authorities.* The new introduction at v. 1 seems to interrupt the vision sequence at this point of tension, with God's glory poised at the threshold. Ezekiel sees 25 men—a different group from 8:16, and at a different location. And unlike the previous group, the problem here is not with worship but with politics, although the precise issue at stake remains elusive. The overall impression is that the thing they fear will come upon them (11:8; like the Tower of Babel in Gen. 11:1–9) and that they have brought divine judgment on themselves. This framework helps make sense of the details.

11:1 The named individuals are otherwise unknown; on **Pelatiah**, see v. 13. The Hebrew behind **princes of the people** (*sare ha'am*) need not refer to royalty, nor does it here; cf. the identical phrase translated "leaders of the people" at Neh. 11:1.

11:2–3 Unfortunately for interpretation, the **wicked counsel** announced in v. 2 and quoted in v. 3 is obscure. Verse 3a may be either a statement or a question. If the former, the **cauldron** and **meat** metaphor is negative ("we're cooked!"); but if the latter, the metaphor is positive ("we won't be burned!"). Since it is unlikely that being cooked is positive, the imagery is best understood to indicate fear, which led to mistrusting God. The metaphor is further developed in ch. 24.

11:6 Although the judgment that multiplies corpses is divine (9:7), it has been provoked by the people's guilt, and they remain responsible.

11:7–12 The focus here is on the distinction between the court officials and the people slain. The outcome here has clarity that the earlier part of the vision lacked: the departure of Zedekiah's court and its destruction at the hands of the Babylonians (see 2 Kings 25:4–7). Note the theological perspective of Ezek. 11:9 (**I will bring you out**), in contrast to the panicked flight of 2 Kings 25:4.

[j]and you shall know that I am the LORD. 11 [k]This city shall not be your cauldron, nor shall
you be the meat in the midst of it. I will judge you at the border of Israel, 12 and you shall
know that I am the LORD. For you have not walked in my statutes, nor obeyed my rules,
[l]but have acted according to the rules of the nations that are around you."
13 And it came to pass, while I was prophesying, [m]that [n]Pelatiah the son of Benaiah died.
[o]Then I fell down on my face and cried out with a loud voice and said, [o]"Ah, Lord GOD!
[p]Will you make a full end of the remnant of Israel?"

Israel's New Heart and Spirit

14 And the word of the LORD came to me: 15 [q]"Son of man, your brothers, even your
brothers, your kinsmen,[1] the whole house of Israel, all of them, are those of whom the
inhabitants of Jerusalem have said, [r]'Go far from the LORD; to us this land is given for
a possession.' 16 Therefore say, 'Thus says the Lord GOD: Though I removed them far off
among the nations, and though I scattered them among the countries, yet [s]I have been
a sanctuary to them for a while[2] in the countries where they have gone.' 17 Therefore say,
'Thus says the Lord GOD: [t]I will gather you from the peoples and assemble you out of the
countries where you have been scattered, [t]and I will give you the land of Israel.' 18 And
when they come there, [u]they will remove from it all its [v]detestable things and all its
abominations. 19 [w]And I will give them one heart, and [x]a new spirit I will put within them.
[y]I will remove the heart of stone from their flesh [z]and give them a heart of flesh, 20 [a]that
they may walk in my statutes and keep my rules and obey them. [b]And they shall be my
people, and I will be their God. 21 [c]But as for those whose heart goes after their detestable
things and their abominations, [d]I will[3] bring their deeds upon their own heads, declares
the Lord GOD."
22 [e]Then the cherubim lifted up their wings, with the wheels beside them, [e]and the
glory of the God of Israel was over them. 23 And the glory of the LORD went up from the
midst of the city and [f]stood on the mountain that is on the east side of the city. 24 [g]And
the Spirit lifted me up and brought me [h]in the vision by the Spirit of God [i]into Chaldea,
to the exiles. Then the vision that I had seen went up from me. 25 And I told the exiles all
the things that the LORD had shown me.

Judah's Captivity Symbolized

12 The word of the LORD came to me: 2 [j]"Son of man, you dwell in the midst of [k]a
rebellious house, [l]who have eyes to see, but see not, who have ears to hear, but
hear not, for they are [k]a rebellious house. 3 As for you, son of man, prepare for yourself
[m]an exile's baggage, and go into exile by day [n]in their sight. You shall go like an exile from

[1] Hebrew *the men of your redemption* [2] Or *in small measure* [3] Hebrew *To the heart of their detestable things and their abominations their heart goes; I will*

10 [j]See ch. 6:7
11 [k][ver. 3, 7]
12 [l][ch. 8:10, 14, 16]
13 [m][Acts 5:5] [n]ver. 1 [o]ch. 9:8 [p][ch. 20:17]
15 [q]See ch. 2:1 [r][1 Sam. 26:19]
16 [s][ch. 37:26, 28; Isa. 8:14; Rev. 21:22]
17 [t]ch. 20:41; 28:25; 34:13; 36:24; 37:21; [ch. 38:8; 39:27; Isa. 11:12]
18 [u]ch. 37:23 [v]ch. 5:11
19 [w]Jer. 32:39; [Acts 4:32] [x]ch. 36:26; [ch. 18:31; Ps. 51:10; Jer. 31:33] [y][Zech. 7:12] [z][2 Cor. 3:3]
20 [a]Ps. 105:45 [b]ch. 14:11; 36:28; Lev. 26:12; See Jer. 30:22; 31:33
21 [c]See ch. 9:4-6 [d]See ch. 7:4
22 [e]ch. 10:19
23 [f]Zech. 14:4; [ch. 43:2]
24 [g]ver. 1; See ch. 3:12 [h]See ch. 1:1 [i][ch. 1:3]

Chapter 12

2 [j]See ch. 2:1 [k]See ch. 2:3, 5 [l]Isa. 42:18; Matt. 13:13
3 [m]ver. 4, 7 [n]ch. 4:12; 21:6; 37:20; 43:11

11:13 The impact of the death of **Pelatiah the son of Benaiah** on Ezekiel is not immediately obvious. Perhaps it is due to Ezekiel's shock at seeing such an immediate judgment from God in fulfillment of his prophecies. Its significance may also lie in the symbolism of the name itself: "The LORD delivers," the son of "The LORD builds," has died.

11:14–21 *Promise of a New Heart, Spirit.* Ezekiel's outcry of v. 13 apparently prompts one of the most important statements of hope in the book, one closely connected to the famous "new heart" passage in 36:22–32. In 11:15 the voice of those left in Judah is heard baiting the exiles. The divine response of v. 16 both asserts God's own action in bringing about the exile (**I removed . . . I scattered**) and redefines the relationship between God and the remnant: the real **sanctuary** is not the temple but God himself. That new relationship is marked by a **new spirit** and a **heart of flesh** (v. 19) provided by God himself, which enables faithful living previously impossible with a **heart of stone**. There is a theological tension in Ezekiel between divine provision (here and 36:26–27) and human endeavor ("make yourselves a new heart and a new spirit," 18:31).

11:22–25 *The Glory of the Lord Departs.* The vision concludes on a tragic note: the departure of the God of Israel from his city denotes divine absence and thus death for the people. The **mountain . . . on the east** is the Mount of Olives. Both the action and location confirm that the emphasis falls on divine absence from Jerusalem rather than (by inference) presence with the exiles. God's absence persists until 43:1–5. The concluding report (11:25) links back to the setting of 8:1.

12:1–28 *Anticipating Exile.* The unfolding of events surrounding the collapse of Judah must always be borne in mind when reading Ezekiel. This is especially true for this chapter, as its predictions of exile come during a time when the exile has already begun. This only makes sense in the context of the uncertain decade between 597 B.C. (the deportation during the reign of Jehoiachin, during which Ezekiel was exiled) and 586 (the final fall of Jerusalem, during the reign of Zedekiah). It is the latter complex of events toward which these oracles point. Formulaic markers group them into two pairs: symbolic action is again a vehicle for the divine word in vv. 1–16 and 17–20; the passage of time prompted doubts about this further exile, and these are confronted in the pair of oracles in vv. 21–25 and 26–28.

12:1–20 *Exile Predicted.* Ezekiel, who was included in the first deportation to Babylon, predicts a further exile by means of symbolic actions, much like chs. 4–5.

12:1–16 Ironically, the issue of perception lies at the heart of this passage. Ezekiel's fellow exiles form the audience whose attitude, one must conclude, remained untouched by their own experience of exile and whose expectations were therefore deluded.

12:2 On Ezekiel's distinctive use of **rebellious house** (also vv. 9, 25), see note on 2:5–7. The unseeing **eyes** and unhearing **ears** emphasize the willfulness of the exiles' ignorance (cf. Isa. 6:9–10; Jer. 5:21).

12:3 In their sight is repeated seven times in vv. 3–7, further underlining

3 [n]ch. 4:12; 21:6; 37:20; 43:11 [o]See Jer. 36:3
4 [p][2 Kgs. 25:4; Jer. 39:4; 52:7]
5 [q][ch. 8:8]
6 [r]See ch. 4:3
7 [s]ch. 24:18; 37:7 [t][ver. 3]
9 [u]See ch. 2:1 [v]See ch. 2:3, 5 [w][ch. 17:12; 24:19; 37:18]
10 [x][ch. 21:25]; See 2 Chr. 36:11-13
11 [y][ver. 6] [z][ch. 24:24]
12 [a][2 Kgs. 25:4] [b][ver. 5] [c][ver. 6]
13 [d]ch. 17:20; 19:8; 32:3; [Hos. 7:12] [e][2 Kgs. 25:7; Jer. 32:4, 5; 52:11]
14 [f][2 Kgs. 25:5]; See ch. 5:10 [g]See ch. 5:2
15 [h]See ch. 6:7
16 [i]ch. 6:8, 9; 14:22 [j]See ch. 6:7
18 [k]See ch. 2:1 [l][ch. 4:10, 11]
19 [m]ch. 4:16 [n][ch. 32:15; Zech. 7:14] [o]ch. 7:11, 23
20 [p]ch. 6:6
22 [q][ch. 16:44; 18:2, 3] [r][ver. 27; ch. 11:3; 2 Pet. 3:4]
23 [s][ch. 7:7, 12]
24 [t]ch. 13:23 [u]ch. 13:6, 7
25 [v]Isa. 55:11 [w]Isa. 13:22 [x]See ch. 2:3, 5

your place to another place [n]in their sight. [o]Perhaps they will understand, though[1] they
are a rebellious house. **4** You shall bring out your baggage by day in their sight, as baggage
for exile, and you shall go out yourself [p]at evening in their sight, as those do who must
go into exile. **5** In their sight [q]dig through the wall, and bring your baggage out through
it. **6** In their sight you shall lift the baggage upon your shoulder and carry it out at dusk.
You shall cover your face that you may not see the land, for I have made you [r]a sign for
the house of Israel."

7 [s]And I did as I was commanded. [t]I brought out my baggage by day, as baggage for exile,
and in the evening I dug through the wall with my own hands. I brought out my baggage
at dusk, carrying it on my shoulder in their sight.

8 In the morning the word of the LORD came to me: **9** [u]"Son of man, has not the house
of Israel, [v]the rebellious house, said to you, [w]'What are you doing?' **10** Say to them, 'Thus
says the Lord GOD: This oracle concerns[2] [x]the prince in Jerusalem and all the house of
Israel who are in it.'[3] **11** Say, [y]'I am a sign for you: [z]as I have done, so shall it be done to them.
They shall go into exile, into captivity.' **12** [a]And the prince who is among them shall lift his
baggage upon his shoulder at dusk, and shall go out. [b]They shall dig through the wall to
bring him out through it. [c]He shall cover his face, that he may not see the land with his
eyes. **13** [d]And I will spread my net over him, and he shall be taken in my snare. And [e]I will
bring him to Babylon, the land of the Chaldeans, [e]yet he shall not see it, and he shall die
there. **14** [f]And I will scatter toward every wind all who are around him, his helpers and all
his troops, [g]and I will unsheathe the sword after them. **15** [h]And they shall know that I am
the LORD, when I disperse them among the nations and scatter them among the countries. **16** [i]But I will let a few of them escape from the sword, from famine and pestilence,
that they may declare all their abominations among the nations where they go, [j]and may
know that I am the LORD."

17 And the word of the LORD came to me: **18** [k]"Son of man, [l]eat your bread with quaking,
and drink water with trembling and with anxiety. **19** And say to the people of the land, Thus
says the Lord GOD concerning the inhabitants of Jerusalem in the land of Israel: [m]They
shall eat their bread with anxiety, [m]and drink water in dismay. In this way [n]her land will
be stripped of all it contains, [o]on account of the violence of all those who dwell in it. **20** [p]And
the inhabited cities shall be laid waste, and the land shall become a desolation; and you
shall know that I am the LORD."

21 And the word of the LORD came to me: **22** "Son of man, [q]what is this proverb that you[4]
have about the land of Israel, saying, [r]'The days grow long, and every vision comes to nothing'? **23** Tell them therefore, 'Thus says the Lord GOD: I will put an end to this proverb, and
they shall no more use it as a proverb in Israel.' But say to them, [s]The days are near, and
the fulfillment[5] of every vision. **24** [t]For there shall be no more any [u]false vision or flattering
divination within the house of Israel. **25** For I am the LORD; I will speak [v]the word that I
will speak, and it will be performed. [w]It will no longer be delayed, but in your days, [x]O
rebellious house, I will speak the word and perform it, declares the Lord GOD."

26 And the word of the LORD came to me: **27** "Son of man, behold, they of the house of

[1] Or *will see that* [2] Or *This burden is* [3] Hebrew *in the midst of them* [4] The Hebrew for *you* is plural [5] Hebrew *word*

the main point of the prophecy. The hope that **they will understand** (lit., that they will "see") also develops this theme.

12:8–15 The explanation of the symbolic actions has both a broad and a narrow application. Verse 10 targets the **prince in Jerusalem**—a reference to Zedekiah, whom Ezekiel resolutely refuses to refer to as "king"—while the rest of v. 10 and the plural references of v. 11 broaden the scope to the rest of the remaining Judeans. Verses 12–15 point in specific detail to the fate of Zedekiah narrated in 2 Kings 25, much as did the oracle of Ezek. 11:5–12. Still, this remains **a sign for you** (plural, 12:11), that is, for Ezekiel's fellow exiles.

12:13 he shall not see it. The fate of Zedekiah is clearly in view here: cf. 2 Kings 25:7; Jer. 52:11.

12:17–20 The demeanor of refugees is the focus of these verses. The symbolic action has some resonance with 4:9–17, but the emphasis here is psychological rather than ritual. The **people of the land** (12:19) refers to the commoners among Ezekiel's fellow exiles who are now, of course, landless.

12:21–28 *Exile Confirmed.* Apparently, the delay in fulfillment of the prophecy opened a window for counter-prophecies, which are here rebutted. This pair of oracles may be a longer and shorter version of the same prophecy given on different occasions, somewhat like 7:1–9. These verses provide an affirmation of the predictive element among the Hebrew prophets: their "forth-telling" is sometimes emphasized, but "foretelling" constituted a significant factor in their preaching.

12:21–25 The **proverb** that authorizes ignoring Ezekiel's warning, quoted in v. 22, is inverted in v. 23. It requires refutation, much as another proverb will in 18:2–3.

12:24 The introduction of the theme of false prophecy sets the stage for the next block of oracles.

12:26–28 Here, the tone is not so much the assumed failure of vision as its supposed interminable delay. But the God who gives the word will also bring it to pass, without fail.

Israel say, [y]'The vision that he sees is [z]for many days from now, and he prophesies of times
far off.' 28 Therefore say to them, Thus says the Lord GOD: [w]None of my words will be delayed
any longer, [v]but the word that I speak will be performed, declares the Lord GOD."

False Prophets Condemned

13 The word of the LORD came to me: 2 [a]"Son of man, prophesy against the prophets
of Israel, who are prophesying, and say to those [b]who prophesy from their own
hearts: 'Hear the word of the LORD!' 3 Thus says the Lord GOD, Woe to the foolish prophets
who follow their own spirit, and have seen nothing! 4 Your prophets have been like jackals
among ruins, O Israel. 5 [c]You have not gone up into the breaches, or built up a wall for
the house of Israel, that it might stand in battle in the day of the LORD. 6 [d]They have seen
false visions and lying divinations. They say, 'Declares the LORD,' [e]when the LORD has not
sent them, and yet they expect him to fulfill their word. 7 Have you not seen a false vision
and uttered a lying divination, [f]whenever you have said, 'Declares the LORD,' although I
have not spoken?"

8 Therefore thus says the Lord GOD: "Because you have uttered falsehood and seen lying
visions, therefore behold, [g]I am against you, declares the Lord GOD. 9 My hand will be
against the prophets who see false visions and who give lying divinations. They shall not
be in the council of my people, [h]nor be enrolled in the register of the house of Israel, [i]nor
shall they enter the land of Israel. [j]And you shall know that I am the Lord GOD. 10 Precisely
because they have misled my people, [k]saying, 'Peace,' when there is no peace, and because,
when the people build a wall, [l]these prophets smear it with whitewash,[1] 11 say to those
who smear it with whitewash that it shall fall! [m]There will be a deluge of rain, and you,
O great hailstones, will fall, and a stormy wind break out. 12 And when the wall falls, will
it not be said to you, 'Where is the coating with which you smeared it?' 13 Therefore thus
says the Lord GOD: [m]I will make a stormy wind break out in my wrath, [m]and there shall
be a deluge of rain in my anger, and great hailstones in wrath to make a full end. 14 And
I will break down the wall that you have smeared with whitewash, and bring it down to
the ground, so that its foundation will be laid bare. When it falls, you shall perish in the
midst of it, [n]and you shall know that I am the LORD. 15 Thus will I spend my wrath upon
the wall and upon those who have smeared it with whitewash, and I will say to you, The
wall is no more, nor those who smeared it, 16 the prophets of Israel who prophesied concerning Jerusalem [k]and saw visions of peace for her, when there was no peace, declares
the Lord GOD.

17 "And you, son of man, [o]set your face against [p]the daughters of your people, [q]who
prophesy out of their own hearts. Prophesy against them 18 and say, Thus says the Lord GOD:
Woe to the women [r]who sew magic bands upon all wrists, and [s]make veils for the heads
of persons of every stature, in [t]the hunt for souls! Will you hunt down souls belonging to

[1] Or *plaster*; also verses 11, 14, 15

27 [y][ver. 22; Amos 6:3] [z]ch. 38:8; Dan. 8:26; 10:14; [2 Pet. 3:4]
28 [w][See ver. 25 above] [v][See ver. 25 above]

Chapter 13

2 [a]See ch. 2:1 [b]ver. 17; Jer. 23:16, 26
5 [c]ch. 22:30; Ps. 106:23; [Ps. 80:12; Isa. 5:5; 58:12]
6 [d]ver. 23; ch. 12:24; 21:29; 22:28; Jer. 5:31 [e]See Jer. 14:14
7 [f]Jer. 23:21
8 [g]ch. 5:8; 21:3; 26:3; 28:22; 29:3; 30:22; 34:10; 35:3; 38:3; Jer. 21:13
9 [h][Ezra 2:59, 62; Neh. 7:5; Ps. 69:28; 87:6] [i]ch. 20:38 [j]See ch. 6:7
10 [k]ver. 16; Jer. 6:14; Mic. 3:5 [l]ch. 22:28
11 [m]ch. 38:22; Isa. 28:2, 17; [Isa. 30:13]
13 [m][See ver. 11 above]
14 [n]See ch. 6:7
16 [k][See ver. 10 above]
17 [o]See ch. 6:2 [p][Ex. 15:20; Judg. 4:4; 2 Kgs. 22:14] [q]ver. 2
18 [r]ver. 20 [s]ver. 21 [t]ver. 20

13:1–14:11 *False Prophecy, True Prophecy.* Chapters 13–14 express condemnation of speaking false prophecy and of ignoring true prophecy. The subject has already been broached in 12:24 in terms now repeated throughout ch. 13. The passage falls into two main sections: the condemnations against false speaking (ch. 13) and against false seeking (14:1–11).

13:1–23 *False Prophets.* Two groups come in for condemnation: male "prophets" who simply prophesy delusions (vv. 1–16), and women who are prophets by pretense (vv. 17–23). Each group is addressed twice, so that the broad architecture of ch. 12 is also seen here (two groups of two oracles). The masculine and feminine references tend to break down toward the end of the chapter. Although the text is difficult, it remains clear that the issue is not gender. The themes developed here appear in concentrated form in Mic. 3:5–7.

13:1–9 Introductory and concluding formulas as well as distinctive content bracket these verses from those that follow. The basic indictment—prophets speak their own delusions—is voiced in vv. 2–3 and developed throughout. The metaphors of vv. 4–5 are striking: like **jackals** (v. 4; cf. Jer. 9:11) they are no more than scavengers, when they ought to have been sentinels (Ezek. 13:5; cf. 22:30; Ps. 106:23). Hammering home the point, Ezek. 13:6, 7, and 9 each make explicit reference to **false visions** and **lying divinations**, the latter referring to the manipulation of some object to discern a divine message (v. 8 varies this pattern slightly). For this combination, cf. Jer. 14:14.

13:2 who prophesy from their own hearts. Cf. v. 17. "Hearts" (Hb. *leb*) could also be translated "minds" as in Jer. 14:14; 23:16.

13:9 The punishment is total exclusion. The **council** (Hb. *sod*) **of my people** provides an oblique contrast with the "council of the LORD" (Jer. 23:18, 22), where the prophet should stand.

13:10–16 A further connection with Jeremiah (Jer. 6:14; 8:11) brackets this second oracle: the false declaration of **peace** (also Ezek. 13:16). The false prophets' word of peace puts a delusive veneer on people's hopes.

13:17–21 Attention turns to women who give prophecies of their own devising. The term "prophetess," usually found with genuine agents of God (e.g., Miriam in Ex. 15:20; Deborah in Judg. 4:4; Huldah in 2 Kings 22:14), is avoided with reference to these impostors. Focus shifts resolutely onto magical practices that are very difficult to clarify any further. The striking language of **hunt for souls** (Ezek. 13:18, 20) identifies this generally as illicit spiritual manipulation. Such behavior is forbidden (e.g., in Lev. 19:26, 31; Deut. 18:10–14).

my people and keep your own souls alive? 19 You have profaned me among my people [u]for
handfuls of barley [v]and for pieces of bread, putting to death souls who should not die and
keeping alive souls who should not live, by your lying to my people, who listen to lies.
20 "Therefore thus says the Lord GOD: Behold, [w]I am against [x]your magic bands with
which you hunt the souls like birds, and I will tear them from your arms, and I will let
the souls whom you hunt go free, the souls like birds. 21 Your veils also I will tear off and
[y]deliver my people out of your hand, and they shall be no more in your hand as prey,
[z]and you shall know that I am the LORD. 22 [a]Because you have disheartened the righteous
falsely, although I have not grieved him, and [b]you have encouraged the wicked, that [c]he
should not turn from his evil way to save his life, 23 [d]therefore you shall no more see false
visions nor practice divination. I will deliver my people out of your hand. And you shall
know that I am the LORD."

Idolatrous Elders Condemned

14 Then certain of the [e]elders of Israel came to me [e]and sat before me. 2 And the word
of the LORD came to me: 3 [f]"Son of man, these men have taken their idols into their
hearts, and set [g]the stumbling block of their iniquity before their faces. [h]Should I indeed
let myself be consulted by them? 4 Therefore speak to them and say to them, Thus says the
Lord GOD: Any one of the house of Israel who takes his idols into his heart and sets the
stumbling block of his iniquity before his face, and yet comes to the prophet, [i]I the LORD
will answer him as he comes with the multitude of his idols, 5 [j]that I may lay hold of the
hearts of the house of Israel, [k]who are all estranged from me through their idols.
6 "Therefore say to the house of Israel, Thus says the Lord GOD: [l]Repent and turn away
from your idols, and turn away your faces from all your abominations. 7 For any one of the
house of Israel, or of the strangers who sojourn in Israel, [k]who separates himself from me,
taking his idols into his heart and putting the stumbling block of his iniquity before his
face, and yet comes to a prophet to consult me through him, [m]I the LORD will answer him
myself. 8 And [n]I will set my face against that man; I [o]will make him a sign and a byword [n]and
cut him off from the midst of my people, [p]and you shall know that I am the LORD. 9 And if
the prophet is deceived and speaks a word, [q]I, the LORD, have deceived that prophet, and
I will stretch out my hand against him and will destroy him from the midst of my people

19 [u][Mic. 3:5] [v][Prov. 28:21]
20 [w]See ver. 8 [x]ver. 18
21 [y][ch. 34:10] [z]See ch. 6:7
22 [a][Jer. 14:14]; See Jer. 28:15 [b]Jer. 23:14 [c]See ch. 18:21
23 [d]See ver. 6, 7, 9

Chapter 14

1 [e]See ch. 8:1
3 [f]See ch. 2:1 [g]ch. 7:19; 44:12 [h]ch. 20:3, 31; 2 Kgs. 3:13; [ch. 36:37]
4 [i][ver. 7]
5 [j][2 Thess. 2:11, 12] [k]Isa. 1:4
6 [l][ch. 18:30, 32]
7 [k][See ver. 5 above] [m][ver. 4]
8 [n]ch. 15:7; Lev. 17:10; Jer. 44:11 [o]ch. 5:15; Deut. 28:37 [p]See ch. 6:7
9 [q][1 Kgs. 22:23]

13:22–23 Those with spiritual power ought to strengthen the righteous and cast down the wicked; however, this has been inverted. The Hebrew of v. 22 is ambiguous in its reference, but the announcement of v. 23 (**you shall no more**) identifies the targets as the female false prophets of the preceding oracle. The conclusion (v. 23) forms a doublet with v. 21: God will deliver his people from this malicious power.

14:1–11 *False Inquirers.* That the theme of false prophecy continues is clear from vv. 9–11, although now the problem is viewed from the side of the recipients rather than the producers of false oracles. A second occasion of being approached by the **elders** (v. 1) in exile (cf. 8:1; 20:1) sets the context for this oracle against idolaters seeking a word from the Lord. Although the exilic setting is not required to explain the idolatry of these elders, the new cultural setting and dislocation could promote unthinking syncretism. This section turns on God's question in 14:3, which brings three successive responses. Verses 4–5 give an apparent "yes," but what it might mean to **lay hold of the hearts** (v. 5) is unpacked in the following verses. The second response comes in vv. 6–8: any divine answer to idolatrous inquirers will be tuned to their repentance (v. 6)—which, if not forthcoming, leads to their rejection by God (v. 8). The third response (vv. 9–11) joins inquirer and false prophet, as God asserts responsibility for deceptions that ensure punishment for both partners in delusion (cf. 1 Kings 22:13–28).

14:7 The **strangers** (Hb. *ger*) and native Israelites were to have one and the same code for life, according to priestly law (cf. Lev. 19:33–34; Num. 15:13–16).

14:9 I, the LORD, have deceived that prophet. One of the forms of God's judgment is allowing people to believe falsehood, or even (as in this verse) *leading* them to believe falsehood. Yet Scripture also consistently affirms the human decision to sin and human responsibility for that decision (note the idolatry [v. 7] that preceded this deception, and the just punishment from God [vv. 9–10]). Moreover, Scripture never says that God himself speaks falsehood (he cannot; Titus 1:2; Heb. 6:18), and it never excuses human beings for speaking or believing falsehood.

14:10 On **bear their punishment**, see note on 4:4.

14:12–15:8 *The Consequences of Infidelity.* Larger complexes of material are more difficult to discern, from this point through to the collection of oracles against foreign nations (chs. 25–32). The common thread in these verses is the certainty of divine judgment on Jerusalem.

14:12–23 *Noah, Daniel, Job.* Five clearly formed paragraphs make up this oracle: the first four detail four modes of divine judgment on Jerusalem: famine (vv. 12–14); beasts (vv. 15–16); sword (vv. 17–18); and pestilence (vv. 19–20). The final paragraph provides a summary and holds open the possibility of a remnant (vv. 21–23). For this oracle's holding up righteous heroes of the past, cf. Jer. 15:1. For its implied hope that a few righteous might suffice to save many wicked, cf. Gen. 18:22–33. The implicit assertion that each individual is held to account for his or her own life (the summary phrase of each paragraph here) was an implicit theme of Ezekiel from the start (see Ezek. 3:16–21) and will see its fullest treatment in ch. 18.

14:14, 20 Noah and **Job** are well-known righteous men of the past (see Gen. 6:9; Job 1:1). Noah saved only his family; the protection of Job's piety did not even extend that far. The identity of **Daniel** (cf. also Ezek. 28:3) has been disputed. Traditionally, he is identified with the hero of the book of Daniel, a contemporary of Ezekiel, who served in the court of Babylon and then of Persia. His reputation might have spread widely enough by this time for Ezekiel to expect his audience to recognize him (cf. Dan. 2:1, which is well before Ezekiel's call, although it is hard to say whether he was widely known outside the court, and Ezekiel was not in Babylon itself). Others suggest, however, that the Daniel mentioned here should be identified with an ancient sage of the Syrian region, known from the Ugaritic texts as a just and pious

Israel. 10 And they shall bear their punishment[1]—the punishment of the prophet and the
punishment of the inquirer shall be alike— 11 that the house of Israel may no more go
astray from me, nor [r]defile themselves anymore with all their transgressions, [s]but that
they may be my people and I may be their God, declares the Lord GOD."

Jerusalem Will Not Be Spared

12 And the word of the LORD came to me: 13 [t]"Son of man, when a land sins against me
[u]by acting faithlessly, and I stretch out my hand against it and [v]break its supply[2] of bread
and send famine upon it, and [w]cut off from it man and beast, 14 [x]even if these three men,
[y]Noah, [z]Daniel, and [a]Job, were in it, [b]they would deliver but their own lives by their righteousness, declares the Lord GOD.

15 [c]"If I cause wild beasts to pass through the land, and they ravage it, [d]and it be made
desolate, so that no one may pass through because of the beasts, 16 even if these three men
were in it, [e]as I live, declares the Lord GOD, they would deliver neither sons nor daughters.
They alone would be delivered, but [f]the land would be desolate.

17 "Or [g]if I bring a sword upon that land and say, Let a sword pass through the land, [h]and I
cut off from it man and beast, 18 [x]though these three men were in it, as I live, declares the Lord
GOD, they would deliver neither sons nor daughters, but they alone would be delivered.

19 "Or [i]if I send a pestilence into that land and pour out my wrath upon it with blood, to
cut off from it man and beast, 20 even if Noah, Daniel, and Job were in it, as I live, declares
the Lord GOD, they would deliver neither son nor daughter. They would deliver but their
own lives by their righteousness.

21 "For thus says the Lord GOD: How much more [j]when I send upon Jerusalem my four
disastrous acts of judgment, [k]sword, [l]famine, [m]wild beasts, and [n]pestilence, to cut off from
it man and beast! 22 But behold, [o]some survivors will be left in it, sons and daughters who
will be brought out; behold, when they come out to you, and [p]you see their ways and their
deeds, you will be consoled for the disaster that I have brought upon Jerusalem, for all
that I have brought upon it. 23 They will console you, when you see their ways and their
deeds, and you shall know that I have not done without cause all that I have done in it,
declares the Lord GOD."

Jerusalem, a Useless Vine

15 And the word of the LORD came to me: 2 [q]"Son of man, how does [r]the wood of the
vine surpass any wood, the vine branch that is among the trees of the forest? 3 Is
wood taken from it to make anything? Do people take [s]a peg from it to hang any vessel on
it? 4 [t]Behold, it is given to the fire for fuel. When the fire has consumed both ends of it, and
the middle of it is charred, is it useful for anything? 5 [u]Behold, when it was whole, it was
used for nothing. How much less, when the fire has consumed it and it is charred, can it
ever be used for anything! 6 Therefore thus says the Lord GOD: [v]Like the wood of the vine
among the trees of the forest, [t]which I have given to the fire for fuel, so have I given up
the inhabitants of Jerusalem. 7 [w]And I will set my face against them. Though [x]they escape
from the fire, the fire shall yet consume them, [y]and you will know that I am the LORD,
[w]when I set my face against them. 8 [z]And I will make the land desolate, because [a]they have
acted faithlessly, declares the Lord GOD."

[1] Or *iniquity*; three times in this verse [2] Hebrew *staff*

11 [r]ch. 37:23 [s]See ch. 11:20
13 [t]See ch. 2:1 [u]ch. 15:8; 17:20; 18:24; 20:27; 2 Chr. 36:14 [v]See ch. 4:16 [w]ver. 17, 19, 21
14 [x][Jer. 15:1] [y]See Gen. 6:9 [z]ch. 28:3; Dan. 9:23 [a]Job 1:1 [b]ch. 3:19
15 [c]See ch. 5:17 [d]ch. 6:6; 12:20
16 [e]See ch. 5:11 [f]ch. 6:14
17 [g]ch. 21:3, 4, 9; Lev. 26:25; [Jer. 47:6, 7] [h]ver. 13
18 [x][See ver. 14 above]
19 [i]ch. 38:22; [2 Sam. 24:15]
21 [j]ch. 5:17; Rev. 6:8; [ch. 33:27] [k]ver. 17 [l]ver. 13 [m]ver. 15 [n]ver. 19
22 [o]ch. 6:8; 12:16 [p]ver. 23; ch. 20:43; [ch. 16:54]

Chapter 15

2 [q]See ch. 2:1 [r]See ver. 6
3 [s][Isa. 22:23, 24]
4 [t][John 15:6]
5 [u][ver. 3]
6 [v][ch. 17:6; Ps. 80:8; Isa. 5:1]; See ch. 19:10-14 [t][See ver. 4 above]
7 [w]See ch. 14:8 [x][2 Kgs. 25:9] [y]See ch. 6:7
8 [z]ch. 6:14 [a]See ch. 14:13

ruler. This is suggested by the fact that the other two figures, Noah and Job, are from the distant past, and are not Israelite (contrast Jer. 15:1, using Moses and Samuel). Further, the book of Daniel consistently spells the name with the consonants *d-n-y-'-l* (with vowels, *Daniye'l*), in Ezekiel it is *d-n-'-l* (with vowels, *Dani'el*), which some students of Ezekiel suggest points to the Daniel in Ugaritic texts. On balance, however, there is no conclusive evidence indicating that the Daniel mentioned in Ezekiel is anyone other than the biblical prophet Daniel.

14:23 The expanded recognition formula (**you shall know**; cf. Introduction: Style) emphasizes the justice of God's actions.

15:1–8 *The Useless Vine.* This "parable of the vine" is very different from John 15! The metaphor of the vine for Israel is common in the OT (e.g., Ps. 80:8–16; Jer. 2:21; Hos. 10:1), which explains Jesus' claim in John 15:1 ("I am the true vine") to embody the people of God. (On Israel as a vineyard, cf. Isa. 5:1–7; Jer. 12:10; as an olive tree, cf. Jer. 11:16; Rom. 11:17–24.) The juxtaposition of vine and harlotry themes in Jer. 2:20–21 is exactly what one finds on a different scale in Ezekiel 15–16. Ezekiel himself further develops the vine metaphor in ch. 17 (cf. 19:10–14). Here, the point is simple: the wood of a vine is fit only for burning—and so it is with **the inhabitants of Jerusalem** (15:6). Such a pessimistic evaluation is not only consistent with Ezekiel's oracles up to this point, it also marks his evaluation of the whole of Israelite history in ch. 20.

15:2 how does the wood . . . surpass? The Hebrew is difficult to translate. The question may also be rendered, "Son of man, of any wood, what happens to the wood of a vine . . . ?"

The LORD's Faithless Bride

16 Again the word of the LORD came to me: 2 [b]"Son of man, [c]make known to Jerusalem
her abominations, 3 and say, Thus says the Lord GOD to Jerusalem: Your origin and
your birth are of the land of the Canaanites; your father was an [d]Amorite and your mother
a [e]Hittite. 4 And as for your birth, [f]on the day you were born your cord was not cut, nor
were you washed with water to cleanse you, nor rubbed with salt, nor wrapped in swaddling cloths. 5 No eye pitied you, to do any of these things to you out of compassion for
you, [g]but you were cast out on the open field, for you were abhorred, [f]on the day that you
were born.

6 "And when I passed by you and saw you wallowing [h]in your blood, I said to you [h]in
your blood, 'Live!' I said to you [h]in your blood, 'Live!' 7 [i]I made you flourish like a plant of
the field. And you grew up and became tall [j]and arrived at full adornment. Your breasts
were formed, and your hair had grown; yet [k]you were naked and bare.

8 "When I passed by you again and saw you, behold, you were at the age for love, and [l]I
spread the corner of my garment over you and covered your nakedness; I made my vow
to you [m]and entered into a covenant with you, declares the Lord GOD, [n]and you became
mine. 9 Then I bathed you with water and washed off your blood from you and [o]anointed
you with oil. 10 [p]I clothed you also with embroidered cloth and shod you with fine leather. I
wrapped you in fine linen and covered you with silk.[1] 11 [q]And I adorned you with ornaments
and [r]put bracelets on your wrists and a chain on your neck. 12 And I put a ring on your nose
and earrings in your ears and a beautiful crown on your head. 13 Thus you were adorned
with gold and silver, and your clothing was of fine linen and silk and embroidered cloth.
[s]You ate fine flour and honey and oil. [t]You grew exceedingly beautiful and advanced to
royalty. 14 And [u]your renown went forth among the nations because of your beauty, for it
was perfect through the splendor that I had bestowed on you, declares the Lord GOD.

15 [v]"But you trusted in your beauty [w]and played the whore[2] because of your renown

[1] *Or with rich fabric* [2] *Or were unfaithful*; also verses 16, 17, 26, 28

Chapter 16
2 [b]See ch. 2:1 [c]ch. 22:2
3 [d]ver. 45; Gen. 15:16; Deut. 7:1 [e]ver. 45; Deut. 7:1; Judg. 1:26
4 [f][Hos. 2:3]
5 [g][Deut. 32:10] [f][See ver. 4 above]
6 [h]ver. 22
7 [i][Ex. 1:7] [j][ver. 11, 13] [k]ver. 22, 39; ch. 23:29
8 [l]Ruth 3:9; [Jer. 2:2] [m][Ex. 24:7, 8] [n]See Ex. 19:5
9 [o]Ruth 3:3; [Ps. 23:5]
10 [p]ver. 13, 18; [ch. 26:16; 27:7, 16; Ex. 26:36]
11 [q][ch. 23:40] [r][ch. 23:42; Gen. 24:22, 30, 47]
13 [s]Deut. 32:13, 14 [t][ver. 15, 25; Ps. 48:2]
14 [u]Lam. 2:15; [ch. 23:10]
15 [v][ver. 13] [w]ch. 23:3, 8, 11, 12; Lev. 17:7; Isa. 1:21; 57:8; Jer. 2:20; 3:2, 6, 20; Hos. 1:2

16:1–63 *The Faithless Bride.* This is both the most infamous passage in the book and also its longest single oracle. The infamy rests not only on the brutal violence it depicts but also on Ezekiel's shocking use of sexual language. On a general level, the meaning of the passage is clear: the infidelity of Jerusalem has brought upon it the just punishment of God. However, at the level of detail it is very complex, and the boundary between the metaphorical and the literal is sometimes difficult to discern. Some interpreters have also voiced concerns about the legitimization that might be given by this metaphorical description of the violent attacks by the adulteress's husband (vv. 37–42). Yet it must be remembered that this is an extended metaphor portraying God's judgment on the nation, and it is by no means intended as a pattern for any human punishment of adultery. Structurally, the passage divides into two large sections, plus a conclusion: vv. 1–43 follow the story of the abandoned child who became a bride; vv. 44–58 broaden the "family" to include two "sisters," Samaria and Sodom; and vv. 59–63 conclude both parts.

16:1–43 *Jerusalem, the Foundling Bride.* This oracle is an extended metaphor, and so its details cannot simply be equated with certain aspects of literal history. It moves through three phases as God speaks through the prophet: (1) The story of the abandoned girl (v. 6) who becomes a queen (v. 13) is told in the first person through the actions of the king (by implication) who found her (vv. 1–14). (2) Verses 15–34 describe in the third person the sexual promiscuity of the "queen" despite her husband's generosity. (3) The first-person account resumes to announce the impending judgment on the faithless bride (vv. 35–43).

16:1–14 As in ch. 15, the oracle focuses on the city of Jerusalem, and not "Israel" per se. This accounts for the seemingly unusual account of origins given in 16:3 and is the reason why the "sisters" in the second half of the chapter are also both cities. The first stage of the oracle depicts Jerusalem's helpless and hopeless state—except for the intervention of the passerby (who is God).

16:2 The instruction to deliver the oracle comes in quasi-legal language: **make known** carries overtones of "arraign" (cf. 20:4; also Job 13:23). On **abominations**, see note on Ezek. 7:3.

16:3 land of the Canaanites. Jerusalem's recorded history predates its takeover by David (2 Sam. 5:6–10) by centuries. The parentage of **Amorite** and **Hittite** joins together two of the pagan peoples inhabiting Canaan in pre-Israelite times (cf. Ex. 3:8, and the close joining of these names in Neh. 9:8).

16:4–5 cast out. Exposure clearly implies an unwanted birth and certain death. Ezekiel also describes the usual practice for welcoming a newborn. The reason for rubbing with **salt** is not understood, although the custom persists in some traditional cultures, in the belief that it is beneficial.

16:6 Blood is an important motif throughout Ezekiel's book. Usually it refers to violence, but here to life (cf. Gen. 9:4) and the discharge of birthing.

16:7 The narrative quickly moves from infancy to puberty. Still **naked**, she is vulnerable and in need of resources.

16:8 Now at a marriageable **age**, she is taken as a wife; **spread . . . my garment** signals intent to marry (cf. Ruth 3:9), and the **covenant** signifies the formal commitment (Mal. 2:14). The bonds are formed before the cleansing of Ezek. 16:9.

16:9 The cleansing actions here mirror those of v. 4, though now of an adult; **blood** therefore is menstrual issue.

16:10–13 Only after the covenant has been entered are the beautifying gifts given. This culminates in status as **royalty** (v. 13).

16:14 The first-person verbs in the preceding verses find their summation here, as God asserts that Jerusalem's **renown** (Hb. *shem*, "name") and **beauty** were entirely of his making (**that I had bestowed**).

16:15–34 God's address switches now to focus on the actions of his bride in response to his life-giving gifts. The passage is marked by inversions, initially signaled by the phrasing **but you . . . beauty . . . renown** in v. 15, literally reversing the terms of v. 14. Throughout these verses, the gifts given in vv. 10–13, which enhanced and beautified, successively become the means of Jerusalem diminishing and debasing herself. She thus alienates herself from her husband. Structurally, vv. 15–22 present the initial indictment, vv. 23–29 develop the political aspects of the metaphor, and vv. 30–34 summarize the inversions of Jerusalem's behavior.

16:15 played the whore. This language in the OT (Hb. *zanah*) usually refers

[x]and lavished your whorings[1] on any passerby; your beauty[2] became his. 16 You took some
of your garments and made for yourself colorful shrines, and on them played the whore.
The like has never been, nor ever shall be.[3] 17 You also took [y]your beautiful jewels of my
gold and of my silver, which I had given you, and [z]made for yourself images of men, and
with them played the whore. 18 And you took your embroidered garments to cover them,
[a]and set my oil and my incense before them. 19 [b]Also my bread that I gave you—[s]I fed you
with fine flour and oil and honey—you set before them for [c]a pleasing aroma; and so it
was, declares the Lord GOD. 20 [d]And you took your sons and your daughters, whom you
had borne to me, and [e]these you sacrificed to them to be devoured. Were your whorings
so small a matter 21 that you slaughtered my children and delivered them up as an offering
by fire to them? 22 And in all your abominations and your whorings you did not remember
[f]the days of your youth, [g]when you were naked and bare, wallowing in your blood.

23 "And after all your wickedness (woe, woe to you! declares the Lord GOD), 24 you built
yourself [h]a vaulted chamber and made yourself a lofty place in every square. 25 At the head
of every street [i]you built your lofty place and made [j]your beauty an abomination, [k]offering
yourself[4] to any passerby and multiplying your whoring. 26 [w]You also played the whore
[l]with the Egyptians, your lustful neighbors, [m]multiplying your whoring, [n]to provoke me
to anger. 27 Behold, therefore, I stretched out my hand against you [o]and diminished your
allotted portion [p]and delivered you to the greed of your enemies, [q]the daughters of the
Philistines, who were ashamed of your lewd behavior. 28 [w]You played the whore also [r]with
the Assyrians, because you were not satisfied; yes, you played the whore with them, and
still you were not satisfied. 29 You multiplied your whoring also with the trading land [t]of
Chaldea, and even with this you were not satisfied.

30 "How sick is your heart,[5] declares the Lord GOD, because you did all these things, the
deeds of a brazen prostitute, 31 building your vaulted chamber at the head of every street,
and making your lofty place in every square. Yet you were not like a prostitute, [u]because
you scorned payment. 32 Adulterous wife, who receives strangers instead of her husband!
33 Men give gifts to all prostitutes, [v]but you gave your gifts to all your lovers, bribing them
to come to you from every side with your whorings. 34 So you were different from other
women in your whorings. No one solicited you to play the whore, and [v]you gave payment,
while no payment was given to you; therefore you were different.

35 "Therefore, O prostitute, hear the word of the LORD: 36 Thus says the Lord GOD, Because
your lust was poured out and your nakedness uncovered in your whorings with your lovers, and with all your abominable idols, [w]and because of the blood of your children that
you gave to them, 37 therefore, behold, [x]I will gather all your lovers with whom you took
pleasure, all those you loved and [y]all those you hated. [z]I will gather them against you from
every side [a]and will uncover your nakedness to them, that [b]they may see all your nakedness.
38 [c]And I will judge you [d]as women who commit adultery and [e]shed blood are judged, and

15 [x][ver. 25]
17 [y][ver. 11] [z][ch. 7:20; 23:14]
18 [a]ch. 23:41
19 [b][Hos. 2:8] [s][See ver. 13 above] [c]See ch. 6:13
20 [d][ver. 21, 36] [e]ch. 20:26, 31; 23:37
22 [f]ver. 43, 60 [g]ver. 6, 7
24 [h]ver. 39
25 [i]ver. 31; [Isa. 57:7; Jer. 2:20; 3:2] [j][ver. 14] [k][ver. 15]
26 [w][See ver. 15 above] [l]ch. 20:7, 8; 23:19-21 [m]ch. 23:14, 19 [n]Jer. 7:18, 19
27 [o][ch. 5:10, 11] [p][ver. 37] [q]ver. 57; [2 Sam. 1:20]
28 [w][See ver. 15 above] [r]ch. 23:12; Jer. 2:18, 36; See 2 Kgs. 16:7-18; 2 Chr. 28:16-21
29 [t]See ch. 23:14-16
31 [u][ver. 33, 34]
33 [v][ver. 41; Hos. 8:9]
34 [v][See ver. 33 above]
36 [w][ver. 20, 21, 38]
37 [x]Hos. 8:10 [y][ver. 27; ch. 23:28] [z]ch. 23:22 [a]ch. 23:10, 29; Hos. 2:10; Rev. 17:16; [ver. 39] [b]Lam. 1:8
38 [c]ch. 21:30 [d]ch. 23:45; Lev. 20:10; Deut. 22:22 [e]Gen. 9:6; [ch. 18:10; 23:37, 45]

[1] Or *unfaithfulness;* also verses 20, 22, 25, 26, 29, 33, 34, 36 [2] Hebrew *it* [3] The meaning of this Hebrew sentence is uncertain [4] Hebrew *spreading your legs*
[5] Revocalization yields *How I am filled with anger against you*

to wanton sexual immorality. When used metaphorically of one's relationship with God, it brings connotations of depraved worship.

16:20–22 took your sons and your daughters . . . these you sacrificed. Cf. the accusation against Manasseh in 2 Kings 21:6 (cf. Jer. 7:31).

16:22 did not remember the days of your youth. The failed memory refers both to infancy (v. 4) and puberty (vv. 7, 9). This theme reappears later in the chapter: vv. 43, 60 (cf. 23:19; Eccles. 12:1).

16:23–29 Jerusalem's "whorings" included multiple partners, each involving a turn away from God. The **Egyptians** (v. 26) had been involved in Judean politics (2 Kings 23:31–35) and proved a perennial temptation for illicit political alliance (cf. Isa. 31:1), as did the **Assyrians** (Ezek. 16:28) at this point in Judah's history (see Jer. 2:18).

16:30–34 The summary pointedly accuses Jerusalem of being uniquely (v. 34) promiscuous, drawing together the two preceding metaphors. The marriage metaphor relates to infidelity and adultery, offending against exclusive loyalty at the heart of the covenant relationship. The prostitution metaphor relates to the multiplicity of partners, secured by inverting the client relationship. Both metaphors, then, represent reversals, with the second intensifying the offense of the first.

16:35–43 An important question for interpretation turns on how far the metaphors are carried into the punishments announced, and where literal razing of Jerusalem shapes this language. The **because . . . therefore** terms in vv. 36–37 (Hb. *ya'an . . . laken*) and v. 43 (Hb. *ya'an . . . gam*) structure the grounds and outcome of the accusation in two unequally weighted parts (vv. 36–42, 43). Adultery, along with other illicit sexual relationships, was one of a number of capital crimes in Israel's law, and so the announcement of execution here is not surprising. Other aspects of the punishments listed do not fit Israelite law so simply. It is unclear how stripping the culprit (v. 37) relates to adultery law. It seems rather to be a case of "poetic justice," returning Jerusalem to the naked estate in which she was found (vv. 4, 7–8). Nor does entrusting punishment to the illicit partners (vv. 39b–42) or dismemberment (v. 40) appear in biblical law. Here Ezekiel crosses over into the language of city destruction, made explicit in the mention of **houses** in v. 41. In all this, the supreme element in view is the offense against God, who remains responsible for judgment (vv. 37–39a, 43).

bring upon you the blood of wrath and jealousy. **39** And I will give you into their hands, and
they shall throw down your [f]vaulted chamber and break down [g]your lofty places. [h]They
shall strip you of your clothes and take [i]your beautiful jewels and leave you [j]naked and
bare. **40** [k]They shall bring up a crowd against you, [l]and they shall stone you and cut you to
pieces with their swords. **41** [l]And they shall [m]burn your houses and [n]execute judgments
upon you in the sight of many women. [o]I will make you stop playing the whore, and [p]you
shall also give payment no more. **42** [q]So will I satisfy my wrath on you, and my jealousy
shall depart from you. I will be calm and will no more be angry. **43** Because you have not
remembered [r]the days of your youth, but have enraged me with all these things, therefore,
behold, [s]I have returned your deeds upon your head, declares the Lord GOD. Have you not
[t]committed lewdness in addition to all your abominations?

44 "Behold, everyone [u]who uses proverbs will use this proverb about you: 'Like mother,
like daughter.' **45** You are the daughter of your mother, who loathed her husband and her
children; and you are the sister of [v]your sisters, who loathed their husbands and their
children. [w]Your mother was a Hittite and [w]your father an Amorite. **46** And [x]your elder
sister is Samaria, who lived with her daughters to the north of you; and [y]your younger
sister, who lived to the south of you, is Sodom with her daughters. **47** [z]Not only did you
walk in their ways and do according to their abominations; within a very little time [a]you
were more corrupt than they in all your ways. **48** [b]As I live, declares the Lord GOD, your
sister [c]Sodom and her daughters have not done as you and your daughters have done.
49 Behold, this was the guilt of your sister Sodom: she and her daughters had pride, [d]excess
of food, and prosperous ease, but did not aid the poor and needy. **50** They were haughty
and [e]did an abomination before me. So [f]I removed them, when I saw it. **51** [g]Samaria has
not committed half your sins. You have committed more abominations than they, and
[h]have made your sisters appear righteous by all the abominations that you have committed. **52** [i]Bear your disgrace, you also, for you have intervened on behalf of your sisters.
Because of your sins in which you acted more abominably than they, they are more in the
right than you. So be ashamed, you also, and bear your disgrace, for you have made your
sisters appear righteous.

53 [j]"I will restore their fortunes, both the fortunes of Sodom and her daughters, and the
fortunes of Samaria and her daughters, and I will restore your own fortunes in their midst,
54 that you may bear your disgrace [k]and be ashamed of all that you have done, [l]becoming a
consolation to them. **55** As for your sisters, Sodom and her daughters shall return to their
former state, [j]and Samaria and her daughters shall return [m]to their former state, [j]and you
and your daughters shall return [m]to your former state. **56** Was not your sister Sodom a byword
in your mouth [n]in the day of your pride, **57** before your wickedness was uncovered? Now
you have become [o]an object of reproach for the daughters of Syria[1] and all those around
her, and for [p]the daughters of the Philistines, [q]those all around who despise you. **58** [r]You
bear the penalty of your lewdness and your abominations, declares the LORD.

The LORD's Everlasting Covenant

59 "For thus says the Lord GOD: I will deal with you as you have done, you [s]who have
despised the oath in breaking the covenant, **60** yet [t]I will remember my covenant with you

[1] Some manuscripts (compare Syriac) *of Edom*

39 [f]ver. 24 [g]ver. 25 [h]ch. 23:26; [Hos. 2:3] [i]ver. 11, 12 [j]ver. 7
40 [k]ch. 23:46 [l]ch. 23:47; [Josh. 7:24, 25]
41 [l][See ver. 40 above] [m]2 Kgs. 25:9; Jer. 39:8; 52:13 [n]See ch. 5:8 [o]ch. 23:27, 48 [p][ver. 33, 34]
42 [q]See ch. 5:13
43 [r]ver. 22, 60 [s]See ch. 7:4 [t]ch. 22:9
44 [u][ch. 12:22; 18:2, 3]
45 [v][ver. 46] [w]See ver. 3
46 [x]ver. 51, 53, 55; [ch. 23:4, 33] [y]ver. 48, 49, 53, 55; [Isa. 1:10]
47 [z]ch. 5:7 [a]ver. 48, 51, 52; ch. 5:6; [2 Kgs. 21:9; 2 Chr. 33:9; Jer. 2:10, 11]
48 [b]ch. 5:11; 14:16, 18, 20; 17:16, 19; 18:3; 20:3, 33; Isa. 49:18; Zeph. 2:9 [c]ver. 47; [Matt. 10:15; 11:24]
49 [d][Gen. 13:10]
50 [e]See Gen. 13:13 [f]See Gen. 19:24
51 [g]ver. 46, 47 [h]ver. 52; Jer. 3:11
52 [i]See ch. 32:24
53 [j][ch. 29:14; 39:25; Zeph. 2:7; 3:20]
54 [k]ver. 61 [l][ch. 14:22, 23]
55 [j][See ver. 53 above] [m]ch. 36:11
56 [n]See Isa. 2:6-11
57 [o]See 2 Kgs. 16:5-7; Isa. 7:1, 2 [p]ver. 27; [2 Chr. 28:18] [q]ch. 28:24, 26
58 [r][ch. 14:10; 23:35, 49]
59 [s][ch. 17:15, 16, 18, 19]
60 [t]See Lev. 26:42

16:44–58 *Jerusalem and Her Sisters.* The second major block in this chapter aligns Jerusalem's crimes with those of two more cities. Jerusalem suffers in comparison with both "sisters." The structure parallels that of the preceding section, with metaphorical reminiscence (vv. 44–48) giving way to analysis (vv. 49–52) before divinely imposed outcomes are announced (vv. 53–58).

16:44–48 A history much like that of v. 3 is sketched (v. 45), and the "proverb" of v. 44 (see note on 12:21–25) may account for bringing the Hittite **mother** to the foreground. The relationships are different and more laterally focused now, with no mention of the husband-wife metaphor of the first half of the chapter.

16:49–52 Jerusalem's crimes exceed those of her sisters, but these now fall into the category of social justice (v. 49), beyond that of idolatry.

16:49 Sodom . . . did not aid the poor and needy. There were other sins as well (as narrated in Gen. 19:4–9; cf. Jude 7), but this is the sin that God chooses to highlight through Ezekiel's prophecy at this point (along with Sodom's pride, Ezek. 16:50).

16:53–58 Unlike the "outcome" of vv. 35–43 (which detailed punishment), here judgment is presupposed and a future restoration envisaged. Neither here nor in the conclusion of vv. 59–63 does future hope exclude shame. Restoring each to **their former state** (v. 55) puts Jerusalem on the same level as her "sisters" who have been similarly graced.

16:59–63 *The Everlasting Covenant.* The final brief passage of ch. 16 explicitly refers back both to the sections on the abandoned child (vv. 8 and 59, 22 and 60) and the "sisters" (vv. 45 and 61), drawing them together in one conclusion. The malleability of the metaphors can be seen in the **sisters** being given as **daughters** in v. 61. The **everlasting covenant** (Hb. *berit 'olam*) of v. 60 finds parallels elsewhere in the OT, most significantly in 37:26 (cf. Isa.

[u]in the days of your youth, [v]and I will establish for you an everlasting covenant. 61 [w]Then
you will remember your ways [x]and be ashamed when you take [y]your sisters, both your
elder and your younger, and I give them to you [z]as daughters, but not on account of[1] the
covenant with you. 62 I will establish my covenant with you, [a]and you shall know that I
am the LORD, 63 that you may remember and be confounded, and [b]never open your mouth
again because of your shame, when I atone for you for all that you have done, declares
the Lord GOD."

Parable of Two Eagles and a Vine

17 The word of the LORD came to me: 2 [c]"Son of man, [d]propound a riddle, and speak
a parable to the house of Israel; 3 say, Thus says the Lord GOD: [e]A great eagle [f]with
great wings and long pinions, [f]rich in plumage of many colors, came [g]to Lebanon [h]and
took the top of the cedar. 4 He broke off the topmost of its young twigs and carried it to a
land of trade and set it in a city of merchants. 5 Then he took of the seed of the land [i]and
planted it in fertile soil.[2] He placed it beside abundant waters. [j]He set it like a willow twig,
6 and it sprouted and became a [k]low [l]spreading vine, and its branches turned toward him,
and its roots remained where it stood. So it became a vine and produced branches and
put out boughs.

7 [m]"And there was another great eagle with great wings and much plumage, [m]and behold,
this vine bent its roots toward him and shot forth its branches toward him from [n]the bed
where it was planted, that he might water it. 8 [i]It had been planted on good soil by abundant
waters, that it might produce branches and bear fruit and become a noble vine.

9 "Say, Thus says the Lord GOD: [m]Will it thrive? Will he not pull up its roots and cut off
its fruit, so that it withers, so that all its fresh sprouting leaves wither? It will not take a
strong arm or many people to pull it from its roots. 10 Behold, it is planted; will it thrive?
[o]Will it not utterly wither when the east wind strikes it—wither away on the bed where
it sprouted?"

11 Then the word of the LORD came to me: 12 "Say now to [p]the rebellious house, [q]Do
you not know what these things mean? Tell them, behold, [r]the king of Babylon came
to Jerusalem, and took her king and her princes and brought them to him to Babylon.
13 [s]And he took one of the royal offspring[3] [t]and made a covenant with him, [u]putting him
under oath ([v]the chief men of the land he had taken away), 14 that the kingdom might be
humble and not lift itself up, and keep his covenant that it might stand. 15 [w]But he rebelled
against him by sending his ambassadors [x]to Egypt, that they might give him horses and
a large army. [y]Will he thrive? Can one escape who does such things? Can he [z]break the
covenant and yet escape?

16 [a]"As I live, declares the Lord GOD, surely [b]in the place where the king dwells [c]who made

[1] *Or not apart from* [2] Hebrew *in a field of seed* [3] Hebrew *seed*

60 [u]ver. 8, 22, 43 [v]Jer. 32:40; 50:5
61 [w]See ch. 6:9 [x]ver. 54 [y][ver. 45, 46] [z][Isa. 54:1]
62 [a]See ch. 6:7
63 [b][Rom. 3:19]

Chapter 17

2 [c]See ch. 2:1 [d][ch. 20:49; 24:3]
3 [e]Jer. 48:40 [f]ver. 7 [g][Jer. 22:23] [h]ver. 22; ch. 31:3, 4, 10
5 [i]See Deut. 8:7-10 [j][Isa. 44:4]
6 [k][ver. 14] [l]ch. 15:6
7 [m][ver. 15] [n][ch. 31:4]
8 [i][See ver. 5 above]
9 [m][See ver. 7 above]
10 [o]ch. 19:12; [Hos. 13:15]
12 [p]See ch. 2:3-5 [q]See ch. 12:9-11 [r]2 Kgs. 24:11, 12
13 [s]2 Kgs. 24:17 [t]ver. 15, 16, 18; 2 Chr. 36:13 [u][ch. 21:23] [v]2 Kgs. 24:14, 15
15 [w][ver. 7; ch. 23:27; 2 Kgs. 24:20; 2 Chr. 36:13; Jer. 37:5-7] [x]Deut. 17:16; [Isa. 31:1, 3]; 36:6, 9 [y][ver. 9, 10] [z]ch. 16:59; [ver. 13]
16 [a]See ch. 16:48 [b][ch. 12:13] [c]ver. 13

61:8); also within the context of bringing back together the old kingdoms of north and south (cf. the hope expressed in Jer. 32:40).

17:1–24 *The Parable of the Eagles and the Vine.* The predominantly theological viewpoint of ch. 16 now gives way to a predominantly political one. It bears the hallmarks of a "fable," a story form in which flora and fauna take the lead roles in order to teach some lesson (e.g., Judg. 9:8–15). Here two eagles, a cedar, and a vine are the main protagonists, and the story turns on the fortunes of the vine (cf. Ezek. 19:10–14; Isa. 5:1–7). The whole is meant to illustrate the current and imminent state of Judah's political fortunes, and ultimately its future under God. The fable is narrated in Ezek. 17:1–12 and successively unpacked, first on the natural plane (vv. 11–18) and then in theological terms (vv. 19–21). Finally, the terms of the fable return to articulate an ideal future (vv. 22–24).

17:1–10 *The Parable Narrated.* Although the story is easily followed, it still puzzles the hearer. It proceeds in two phases. A **great eagle** (v. 3) transplants a twig from a cedar, then plants a seed, which becomes a flourishing vine. But then a second, lesser eagle (v. 7) attracts the vine's attention and draws it away from the first.

17:2 This oracle appears as a **riddle**, designed to provoke thought, and a **parable** (Hb. *mashal*, also translated "proverb"; see 12:22), which depends on some comparison.

17:3–5 The terms of the description are significant, as they indicate the relative status of the various characters. This is the greater eagle, taking a **topmost** twig as well as a **seed**.

17:7 The second **eagle** lacks the grandeur of the first, while still remaining "great."

17:8 The new orientation of the vine to the second eagle threatens its choice location and flourishing state.

17:9–10 The provocative questions clearly require a judgment on the part of the hearers and implicate them in that judgment—the function of all good parables.

17:11–18 *The Parable Explained.* The first phase of explanation identifies the characters of the fable (vv. 11–15) before spelling out the moral of the story (vv. 16–18). The first eagle is the **king of Babylon**, Nebuchadnezzar, who takes **her king**, i.e., Judah's king Jehoiachin (the "twig"), **to Babylon** (v. 12). The **royal offspring** (the "seed") is Zedekiah (v. 13), Jehoiachin's uncle and replacement to whom Ezekiel never refers as a "king." Zedekiah's failure was to break his **covenant** with Nebuchadnezzar (vv. 13–14) by turning to **Egypt** (v. 15), whose king was Hophra, the lesser eagle. Ultimately, hope in Egyptian aid will prove futile (v. 17; see Jer. 37:6–10). The breaking of this political covenant will bring disaster on Zedekiah and his people (Ezek. 17:18).

him king, whose oath he despised, and whose covenant with him he broke, in Babylon he
shall die. 17 [d]Pharaoh with his mighty army and great company will not help him in war,
[e]when mounds are cast up and siege walls built to cut off many lives. 18 He despised the
oath in breaking the covenant, and behold, he gave his hand and did all these things; he
shall not escape. 19 Therefore thus says the Lord GOD: As I live, surely it is my oath that he
despised, and my covenant that he broke. I will return it upon his head. 20 [f]I will spread
my net over him, and he shall be taken in my snare, and I will bring him to Babylon [g]and
enter into judgment with him there [h]for the treachery he has committed against me. 21 And
all the pick[1] of his troops shall fall by the sword, [i]and the survivors shall be scattered to
every wind, and you shall know that [j]I am the LORD; I have spoken."

22 Thus says the Lord GOD: [k]"I myself will take a sprig from the lofty top of the cedar
and will set it out. [l]I will break off from the topmost of its young twigs a tender one, and
[m]I myself will plant it on a high and lofty mountain. 23 [n]On the mountain height of Israel
will I plant it, that it may bear branches and produce fruit and become a noble cedar. [o]And
under it will dwell every kind of bird; in the shade of its branches birds of every sort will
nest. 24 And all the trees of the field shall know that I am the LORD; [p]I bring low the high
tree, and make high the low tree, dry up [q]the green tree, and make [q]the dry tree flourish.
[r]I am the LORD; I have spoken, and I will do it."

The Soul Who Sins Shall Die

18 The word of the LORD came to me: 2 "What do you[2] mean [s]by repeating this proverb
concerning the land of Israel, [t]'The fathers have eaten sour grapes, and the children's
teeth are set on edge'? 3 [u]As I live, declares the Lord GOD, [v]this proverb shall no more be
used by you in Israel. 4 Behold, all souls are mine; the soul of the father as well as the soul
of the son is mine: [w]the soul who sins shall die.

5 "If a man is righteous and does [x]what is just and right— 6 if he [y]does not eat upon the
mountains or [z]lift up his eyes to the idols of the house of Israel, [a]does not defile his neighbor's wife [b]or approach [c]a woman in her time of menstrual impurity, 7 [d]does not oppress
anyone, but [e]restores to the debtor his pledge, [f]commits no robbery, [g]gives his bread to
the hungry [g]and covers the naked with a garment, 8 [h]does not lend at interest [h]or take any
profit,[3] withholds his hand from injustice, [i]executes true justice between man and man,
9 [j]walks in my statutes, and keeps my rules by acting faithfully—he is righteous; [k]he shall
surely live, declares the Lord GOD.

10 "If he fathers a son who is violent, [l]a shedder of blood, who does any of these things
11 (though he himself did none of these things), [m]who even eats upon the mountains, [n]defiles
his neighbor's wife, 12 oppresses the poor and needy, [o]commits robbery, [o]does not restore
the pledge, [p]lifts up his eyes to the idols, [q]commits abomination, 13 [r]lends at interest, and

[1] Some Hebrew manuscripts, Syriac, Targum; most Hebrew manuscripts *all the fugitives* [2] The Hebrew for *you* is plural [3] That is, profit that comes from charging interest to the poor; also verses 13, 17 (compare Leviticus 25:36)

17 [d]ver. 15; See Jer. 37:5-8 [e]See ch. 4:2
20 [f]See ch. 12:13 [g][ch. 20:35; 38:22] [h]See ch. 14:13
21 [i]See ch. 5:10 [j]ch. 21:17, 32; 26:5, 14; 28:10; 30:12; 34:24; 39:5; [ver. 24]
22 [k]ver. 3 [l]ver. 4 [m][Ps. 2:6]
23 [n]ch. 20:40; 34:14 [o]ch. 31:6; Dan. 4:12; Matt. 13:32
24 [p][ch. 21:26, 27] [q]ch. 20:47; [Luke 23:31] [r]ch. 22:14; 24:14; 36:36; 37:14

Chapter 18

2 [s][ch. 12:22; 16:44] [t]Jer. 31:29
3 [u]See ch. 16:48 [v]Jer. 31:29, 30
4 [w]ver. 20
5 [x]ver. 19, 21, 27
6 [y]ver. 11, 15; ch. 22:9 [z]ch. 33:25 [a]ver. 11, 15; [ch. 22:11] [b]Lev. 18:19 [c]ch. 22:10
7 [d]ver. 12, 16; Ex. 22:21 [e]ver. 12; ch. 33:15; Ex. 22:26 [f]ver. 12, 16, 18 [g]ver. 16; Isa. 58:7; [Matt. 25:35, 36]
8 [h]ver. 13, 17; ch. 22:12; Ex. 22:25; Ps. 15:5 [i]Deut. 1:16; Zech. 8:16
9 [j]ver. 17 [k]ver. 17, 19, 21; ch. 20:11; Amos 5:4
10 [l]See ch. 16:38
11 [m]See ver. 6 [n]ver. 6; [Lev. 18:20]
12 [o]ver. 7 [p]ver. 6 [q]ch. 8:6, 17
13 [r]See ver. 8

17:19–21 *The Parable Interpreted.* The "natural," political explanation does not exhaust the meaning of the parable. Zedekiah's political covenant is now termed **my covenant** by God (v. 19). God takes full responsibility for the disaster to come (**return . . . spread . . . bring . . . enter**, all first-person verbs), now seen not as military defeat but as divine judgment.

17:22–24 *A New Parable.* God's action continues as the terms of the parable are used to sketch not a flawed present but an ideal messianic future. The eagles are absent. God chooses a new **sprig** from the **topmost** part of the cedar (v. 22) and plants it himself (v. 23). The terms asserting God's sovereignty in v. 24 resonate with 1 Sam. 2:1–10 and Luke 1:46–55.

18:1–32 *Moral Responsibility.* Chapter 18 is sometimes thought to present a novel understanding of Hebrew ethics, as the high politics of chs. 17 and 19 give way to the lot of ordinary people. Some view the notions of corporate responsibility (cf. Josh. 7:19–26) and accumulated guilt (cf. 2 Kings 23:26) as the primary context for Ezekiel's teaching and observe that, here in Ezekiel 18, he appears to depart from that context and focus on the moral responsibility of the individual. Of course, this reading sits well with modern individualism (which rightly stresses individual moral accountability) but it misses the primary communal focus of Ezekiel. Ezekiel's "you" addresses are consistently in the plural (note also "house of Israel" in vv. 25, 29). The primary focus of this chapter is not so much on legal individual culpability as on divine justice resting afresh on each generation in accord with what that generation deserves.

18:1–4 *The One Who Sins Dies.* **fathers have eaten sour grapes . . . children's teeth are set on edge**. Cf. Jer. 31:29. Once again a proverb (cf. Ezek. 12:22) is introduced as a vehicle for an oracle. The second-person plural forms (**What do you mean**?) address the whole community in exile. The exilic setting itself is significant; see note on 18:30–32.

18:5–18 *Three Case Studies.* Ezekiel exemplifies his teaching by means of three generations: a righteous father (vv. 5–9) and his wicked son (vv. 10–13), who in turn fathers a righteous son (vv. 14–18). Each paragraph follows the same format—the behavior and moral character is introduced, illustrated by a list of characteristic actions, and concluded by a statement regarding either life or death, as appropriate. There are obvious resonances with the Ten Commandments, but not so close as to suggest Ezekiel is citing them. Other such lists appear in Psalms 15 and 24; cf. also Job's declaration of innocence in Job 31.

takes profit; shall he then live? He shall not live. He has done all these abominations; he
shall surely die; [s]his blood shall be upon himself.
14 "Now suppose this man fathers a son who sees all the sins that his father has done;
he sees, and does not do likewise: 15 he does not eat upon the mountains or lift up his eyes
to the idols of the house of Israel, does not defile his neighbor's wife, 16 does not oppress
anyone, [t]exacts no pledge, [u]commits no robbery, [v]but gives his bread to the hungry [v]and
covers the naked with a garment, 17 withholds his hand from iniquity,[1] takes no interest or
profit, obeys my rules, [w]and walks in my statutes; he shall not die for his father's iniquity;
[x]he shall surely live. 18 As for his father, because he practiced extortion, robbed his brother,
and did what is not good among his people, [y]behold, he shall die for his iniquity.
19 "Yet you say, [z]'Why should not the son suffer for the iniquity of the father?' When the
son has done [a]what is just and right, and has been careful to observe all my statutes, [b]he shall
surely live. 20 [c]The soul who sins shall die. [d]The son shall not suffer for the iniquity of the
father, nor the father suffer for the iniquity of the son. [e]The righteousness of the righteous
shall be upon himself, [f]and the wickedness of the wicked shall be upon himself.
21 [g]"But if a wicked person turns away from all his sins that he has committed and keeps
all my statutes and does [h]what is just and right, [i]he shall surely live; he shall not die.
22 [j]None of the transgressions that he has committed shall be remembered against him;
for the righteousness that he has done he shall live. 23 [k]Have I any pleasure in the death of
the wicked, declares the Lord GOD, and not rather that he should turn from his way and
live? 24 [l]But when a righteous person turns away from his righteousness and does injustice
and does the same abominations that the wicked person does, shall he live? [m]None of the
righteous deeds that he has done shall be remembered; for [n]the treachery of which he is
guilty and the sin he has committed, for them he shall die.
25 [o]"Yet you say, 'The way of the Lord is not just.' Hear now, O house of Israel: Is my
way not just? Is it not your ways that are not just? 26 [l]When a righteous person turns away
from his righteousness and does injustice, he shall die for it; for the injustice that he has
done he shall die. 27 Again, [p]when a wicked person turns away from the wickedness he has
committed and does what is just and right, he shall save his life. 28 Because he considered
and turned away from all the transgressions that he had committed, he shall surely live;
he shall not die. 29 Yet the house of Israel says, 'The way of the Lord is not just.' O house of
Israel, are my ways not just? Is it not your ways that are not just?
30 "Therefore [q]I will judge you, O house of Israel, every one according to his ways, declares
the Lord GOD. [r]Repent and turn from all your transgressions, [s]lest iniquity be your ruin.[2]
31 [t]Cast away from you all the transgressions that you have committed, and [u]make yourselves a new heart and a new spirit! [v]Why will you die, O house of Israel? 32 [w]For I have no
pleasure in the death of anyone, declares the Lord GOD; [r]so turn, and live."

A Lament for the Princes of Israel

19 And you, [x]take up a lamentation for the princes of Israel, 2 and say:

What was your mother? [y]A lioness!
Among lions she crouched;

[1] Septuagint; Hebrew *from the poor* [2] Or *lest iniquity be your stumbling block*

13 [s]ch. 33:4; Lev. 20:9, 11; See ch. 3:18
16 [t][ver. 7, 12] [u]ver. 7 [v]See ver. 7
17 [w]ver. 9 [x]See ver. 9
18 [y]See ch. 3:18
19 [z]Ex. 20:5; [ver. 2] [a]ver. 5, 21, 27 [b]See ver. 9
20 [c]ver. 4 [d]See 2 Kgs. 14:6 [e]Isa. 3:10, 11 [f][Rom. 2:9]
21 [g]See ver. 27 [h]ver. 5, 19 [i]ver. 9
22 [j]ch. 33:16
23 [k]ver. 32; ch. 33:11; 1 Tim. 2:4, 6; 2 Pet. 3:9; [Titus 2:11]
24 [l]ch. 3:20; 33:12, 13, 18 [m][2 Pet. 2:20, 21] [n]See ch. 14:13
25 [o]ch. 33:17, 20
26 [l][See ver. 24 above]
27 [p]ver. 21; ch. 33:19; [ch. 13:22; 33:11, 12]
30 [q]ch. 7:3, 8; 33:20; 36:19; [ch. 39:24] [r][ch. 14:6; Hos. 14:1] [s][Isa. 3:8]
31 [t][ch. 20:7] [u]See ch. 11:19 [v]ch. 33:11
32 [w]See ver. 23 [r][See ver. 30 above]

Chapter 19

1 [x]ch. 26:17; 27:2, 32; 28:12; 32:2; Amos 5:1; [Jer. 7:29]
2 [y][Gen. 49:9]

18:19–29 *Two Objections.* The words **yet you say** (vv. 19, 25) introduce two objections from Ezekiel's exilic audience. Again, "you" is plural. Another edition of this teaching appears in 33:10–20.

18:19–24 Why should not the son suffer for the iniquity of the father? Ezekiel anticipates his audience clinging to their traditional understanding encapsulated in the now defunct proverb (vv. 1–2).

18:20–24 The soul who sins shall die. Verses 21–24 explain this teaching in what might seem a surprising way for Ezekiel. Verses 21–22 consider the wicked person who then repents and lives rightly before God. Verse 24 considers the opposite scenario. Sandwiched between these is the central declaration of God's "pleasure" (v. 23) in repentance, and a denial that he has **any pleasure in the death of the wicked** (see note on 33:11).

18:25–29 The way of the Lord is not just. The second objection, repeated in vv. 25 and 29, appears to be oriented to the immediately preceding teaching on repentance, rather than being a second objection to the main teaching of the chapter. "Just" (Hb. root *takan*, vv. 25, 29) has the sense of "weighed" or "measured," that is, in conformity to a standard (cf. 1 Sam. 2:3). The irony of this objection is rich, coming from people whose lives have not accorded with justice.

18:30–32 *Conclusion: Repent!* Repentance is not being urged on Jerusalem, for the preceding chapters affirm that its destruction is assured. Rather, the exiles are pressed to repent and take responsibility for their moral lives. Thus the appeal is to **make yourselves a new heart** and **spirit**, in contrast to 11:19 and 36:26, where these are the gift of God. The restatement of God's displeasure in anyone's death (18:32; cf. v. 23 and note on 33:11) is the basis for the final entreaty to **turn, and live**.

19:1–14 *Lament for the Princes of Israel.* Ezekiel presents two further political allegories, like that of ch. 17. Unfortunately the symbolism remains

3[z][ch. 22:25; 32:2; 2 Kgs. 23:30, 31] [a]ch. 22:25, 27
4[b]Lam. 4:20 [c][2 Kgs. 23:33, 34; Jer. 22:11, 12]
5[d]2 Kgs. 23:34, 36
8[e][2 Chr. 36:6] [f]See ch. 12:13 [b][See ver. 4 above]
9[e][See ver. 8 above] [g][Jer. 22:26, 27] [h]See ch. 6:2
10[i]See ch. 15:6 [j][Ps. 80:9] [k][Deut. 8:7]

in the midst of young lions
she reared her cubs.
3 And she brought up one of her cubs;
[z]he became a young lion,
[a]and he learned to catch prey;
he devoured men.
4 The nations heard about him;
[b]he was caught in their pit,
[c]and they brought him with hooks
to the land of Egypt.
5 When she saw that she waited in vain,
that her hope was lost,
[d]she took another of her cubs
and made him a young lion.
6 He prowled among the lions;
he became a young lion,
and he learned to catch prey;
he devoured men,
7 and seized[1] their widows.
He laid waste their cities,
and the land was appalled and all who were in it
at the sound of his roaring.
8 [e]Then the nations set against him
from provinces on every side;
[f]they spread their net over him;
[b]he was taken in their pit.
9 With hooks [e]they put him in a cage[2]
and [g]brought him to the king of Babylon;
they brought him into custody,
that his voice should no more be heard
on [h]the mountains of Israel.

10 Your mother was [i]like a vine in a vineyard[3]
planted by the water,
[j]fruitful and full of branches
[k]by reason of abundant water.
11 Its strong stems became
rulers' scepters;
it towered aloft
among the thick boughs;[4]
it was seen in its height
with the mass of its branches.

[1] Hebrew *knew* [2] Or *in a wooden collar* [3] Some Hebrew manuscripts; most Hebrew manuscripts *in your blood* [4] Or *the clouds*

unexplained here. In 19:1–9, a lioness produces two cubs who represent the fate of two Davidic princes, while in vv. 10–14 a vine produces branches, as well as a particular "stem" that appears to represent a single Davidic figure. The whole is presented as a **lamentation** (v. 1), a distinctive form of Hebrew poetry. Some see this lament as ironic, a pseudo-lament that infuses the literary form of the dirge with disparaging content. Others hear in these words genuine sadness, and the conclusion in v. 14b suggests this is the better reading. The political lesson is that even Davidic princes are not immune from the divine consequences of their actions.

19:1–9 *A Lioness and Her Cubs.* Both allegories refer to a **mother** (vv. 2, 10). One cannot be certain whether a literal queen mother is in view (then most likely Hamutal; 2 Kings 23:31; 24:18), or rather a symbolic reference to the nation of Judah (cf. Gen. 49:9 and "mother" of Babylon as nation, Jer. 50:12). Ezekiel 19:3–4 applies most closely to Jehoahaz, taken captive to Egypt by Pharaoh Neco (2 Kings 23:31–35). The second cub's identity in Ezek. 19:5–9 is much more problematic. Of possible candidates, Zedekiah remains plausible (see 2 Kings 25:6), but Jehoiachin is more likely (2 Kings 24:12). Both Jehoahaz and Jehoiachin reigned only three months, which is thought to be a problem for the negative assessment of the second "cub" (although cf. 2 Kings 24:8–9).

19:10–14 *A Vine and Its Stem(s).* For details, cf. the parable of the eagles and the vine in ch. 17. Whereas the lioness-and-cubs story fixed attention on the fate of individuals, the vine-and-**stems** (Hb. *mattot*, plural of *matteh*) passage makes more inclusive reference to the whole dynasty. Verses 12b and 14 of ch. 19 single out one particular **strong stem** (Hb. *matteh*), normally translated "staff," only here referring to a living branch. Wordplay undoubtedly motivated this choice. The reference seems to be to Zedekiah, the last reigning Davidic figure, whose attempts at power politics ended in disaster.

12 But the vine was plucked up in fury,
cast down to the ground;
[l]the east wind dried up its fruit;
they were stripped off and withered.
As for its strong stem,
fire consumed it.
13 [m]Now it is planted in the wilderness,
in a dry and thirsty land.
14 [n]And fire has gone out from the stem of its shoots,
has consumed its fruit,
[o]so that there remains in it no strong stem,
no scepter for ruling.

This is [p]a lamentation and has become a lamentation.

Israel's Continuing Rebellion

20 [q]In the seventh year, in the fifth month, on the tenth day of the month, certain of
[r]the elders of Israel came to inquire of the LORD, [s]and sat before me. 2 And the word
of the LORD came to me: 3 [t]"Son of man, speak to the elders of Israel, and say to them, Thus
says the Lord GOD, Is it to inquire of me that you come? [u]As I live, declares the Lord GOD, [v]I
will not be inquired of by you. 4 [w]Will you judge them, son of man, will you judge them? [x]Let
them know the abominations of their fathers, 5 and say to them, Thus says the Lord GOD: [y]On
the day when I chose Israel, [z]I swore[1] to the offspring of the house of Jacob, [a]making myself
known to them in the land of Egypt; [z]I swore to them, saying, I am the LORD your God. 6 On
that day I swore to them that [b]I would bring them out of the land of Egypt into a land that
I had searched out for them, a land [b]flowing with milk and honey, [c]the most glorious of all
lands. 7 And I said to them, [d]Cast away the detestable things [e]your eyes feast on, every one of
you, and do not defile yourselves with [f]the idols of Egypt; [g]I am the LORD your God. 8 [h]But
they rebelled against me and were not willing to listen to me. [i]None of them cast away the
detestable things their eyes feasted on, nor did they forsake the idols of Egypt.
"Then I said I would pour out my wrath upon them [j]and spend my anger against them
in the midst of the land of Egypt. 9 [k]But I acted [l]for the sake of my name, [m]that it should
not be profaned in the sight of the nations among whom they lived, [n]in whose sight I made

[1] Hebrew *I lifted my hand*; twice in this verse; also verses 6, 15, 23, 28, 42

12 [l]ch. 17:10; [Hos. 13:15]
13 [m][ch. 1:1; Hos. 2:3; See 2 Kgs. 24:12-16]
14 [n][2 Kgs. 24:20]; See ch. 17:15-19 [o][ver. 11, 12] [p]See ver. 1

Chapter 20

1 [q][ch. 1:2; 8:1; 24:1; 26:1; 29:1, 17; 30:20; 31:1; 32:1, 17; 33:21; 40:1] [r]See ch. 8:1 [s]ch. 14:1
3 [t]See ch. 2:1 [u]See ch. 16:48 [v]See ch. 14:3
4 [w]ch. 22:2; 23:36 [x]ch. 16:2; 22:2
5 [y]See Ex. 6:7 [z]ver. 15, 23, 28, 42; ch. 36:7; 47:14; [Gen. 14:22] [a][Ex. 3:8; 4:31; 6:2]
6 [b]ver. 15; See Ex. 3:8 [c]ver. 15; [Jer. 3:19; Zech. 7:14]
7 [d][ver. 8; ch. 18:31] [e][ver. 24] [f][ver. 18; Lev. 18:3] [g]ver. 19; See Ex. 20:2
8 [h]ver. 21 [i][ver. 7] [j]See ch. 5:13
9 [k]ver. 22, 44 [l]Ps. 106:8 [m][Isa. 48:11] [n]ver. 14

20:1–44 *Learning from History.* A deputation of elders is the occasion for an oracle. The end of this section is marked by a chapter division in the Hebrew Bible (20:45 is 21:1 in the MT), because the episode triggered by the visit is completed by 20:44. The sprawling oracle is comprised of two main phases: a review of Israel's history is the vehicle for the oracle in vv. 1–31, and one of the rare restoration passages in the first half of Ezekiel builds on it in vv. 33–44 (v. 32 seems to stand apart from this structure). Shared vocabulary and themes provide an overall unity for the section. Thus the pattern of the whole—diagnosis of behavior offensive to God, plus an appeal to look to a renewed future—is consistent with both chs. 17 and 18.

20:1–31 *Looking to the Past.* This recital of Israel's history by the inspired prophet is unique in the Bible, involving a very different interpretation of both the nature of the exodus experience and God's dealings with his people. Although some perceive tension between this presentation of the generations and that of ch. 18, still throughout ch. 20 each generation experiences God's wrath for its own actions, and divine forbearance is related solely to God's own reputation. Significantly, the narration focuses entirely on life outside the Promised Land—an important consideration for an audience of exiles. Absentees are also significant. There is no room for Moses or Joshua here, pointing to Ezekiel's "God-centeredness." Nor are any neighbors mentioned who tempted Israel to sin. Their rebellion was their own. Literary structure proves difficult. Varied analyses of the passage have been offered; none commands universal agreement. The complicating factor appears to be the repetition of phrases compounded by the cyclical nature of Ezekiel's story: divine actions are both initiating and responding, but a "response" also may prove to be an "initiative."

20:1–4 This is the third occasion on which elders seek an oracle (see also 8:1; 14:1). Their inquiry is to be denied. Justification for this "silence" comes in the form of historical recital. The narrative frame begun in 20:1–4 finds its conclusion in vv. 27–31.

20:1–3 The date formula locates this oracle in August 591 B.C. About a year has passed since the temple vision (see 8:1). The command to **speak** is renewed in 20:27.

20:5–26 Israel's story is told in five broad movements: the author describes the exodus generation first in Egypt (vv. 5–8), then in the exodus itself (vv. 9–13), and then in the wilderness (vv. 14–17). The story of the wilderness generation follows in two phases (vv. 18–21, 22–26). This outline is at best an approximation, as the narrative is fluid. Locating Israel's rebellion in Egypt itself marks out Ezekiel's interpretation of Israel's history from any other in the Bible. Likewise, although rebellion in the wilderness is known elsewhere (e.g., Psalm 106), there is nowhere the sort of "alluring" that Hosea describes (Hosea 2). In Ezekiel's view, there were no "good old days."

20:5–8 Although reference to **Jacob** (v. 5) makes clear there is a prehistory, Ezekiel's narrative begins in **Egypt**. The pattern, repeated with variations in the successive sections, sees divine initiative (vv. 5–6) that requires action on Israel's part (v. 7), then God being spurned (v. 8a), which in turn brings divine judgment (v. 8b).

20:5 I swore, lit., "I raised my hand"; cf. Ps. 106:26, where a more expansive translation is offered.

20:9–13 But I acted for the sake of my name (v. 9; cf. vv. 14, 22) strikes one of the insistent notes in Ezekiel, that God's reputation, not Israel's merit, is the basis for forbearance and grace. This phase includes the law-giving at

myself known to them in bringing them out of the land of Egypt. 10 [o]So I led them out of
the land of Egypt and brought them into the wilderness. 11 [p]I gave them my statutes and
made known to them my rules, [q]by which, if a person does them, he shall live. 12 Moreover,
I gave them [r]my Sabbaths, as a sign between me and them, [s]that they might know that
I am the LORD who sanctifies them. 13 [t]But the house of Israel rebelled against me in the
wilderness. [u]They did not walk in my statutes but rejected my rules, by which, if a person
does them, he shall live; [v]and my Sabbaths they greatly profaned.
[t]"Then I said I would pour out my wrath upon them in the wilderness, to make a full
end of them. 14 But I acted for the sake of my name, that it should not be profaned in the
sight of the nations, [w]in whose sight I had brought them out. 15 Moreover, [x]I swore to them
in the wilderness [y]that I would not bring them into the land that I had given them, a land
[z]flowing with milk and honey, [z]the most glorious of all lands, 16 because they rejected my
rules and did not walk in my statutes, and profaned my Sabbaths; [a]for their heart went
after their idols. 17 Nevertheless, [b]my eye spared them, and I did not destroy them or [c]make
a full end of them in the wilderness.
18 "And I said to [d]their children in the wilderness, Do not walk [e]in the statutes of your
fathers, nor keep their rules, [f]nor defile yourselves with their idols. 19 [g]I am the LORD your
God; [h]walk in my statutes, and be careful to obey my rules, 20 and [i]keep my Sabbaths holy
that [j]they may be a sign between me and you, that you may know that I am the LORD
your God. 21 [k]But the children [l]rebelled against me. [m]They did not walk in my statutes
and were not careful to obey my rules, by which, if a person does them, he shall live; they
profaned my Sabbaths.
[n]"Then I said I would pour out my wrath upon them and spend my anger against them
in the wilderness. 22 [o]But I withheld my hand [p]and acted for the sake of my name, [q]that it
should not be profaned in the sight of the nations, in whose sight I had brought them out.
23 [r]Moreover, [s]I swore to them in the wilderness [t]that I would scatter them among the nations
and disperse them through the countries, 24 because they had not obeyed my rules, but had
rejected my statutes and profaned my Sabbaths, [u]and their eyes were set on their fathers'
idols. 25 [v]Moreover, I gave them statutes that were not good and rules by which they could
not have life, 26 and I defiled them through [w]their very gifts [w]in their offering up all their
firstborn, that I might devastate them. I did it [x]that they might know that I am the LORD.
27 "Therefore, [y]son of man, speak to the house of Israel and say to them, Thus says the
Lord GOD: In this also your fathers blasphemed me, by [z]dealing treacherously with me.
28 For when I had brought them into the land that [a]I swore to give them, then wherever
they saw [b]any high hill or any leafy tree, there they offered their sacrifices and there they
presented [c]the provocation of their offering; there they sent up their pleasing aromas, and
there they poured out their drink offerings. 29 (I said to them, [d]What is the high place to
which you go? So its name is called Bamah[1] to this day.)
30 "Therefore say to the house of Israel, Thus says the Lord GOD: [e]Will you defile yourselves after the manner of your fathers and go [f]whoring after their detestable things?
31 When you present your gifts and [g]offer up your children in fire,[2] you defile yourselves
with all your idols to this day. And [h]shall I be inquired of by you, O house of Israel? [i]As I
live, declares the Lord GOD, I will not be inquired of by you.

[1] *Bamah* means *high place* [2] Hebrew *and make your children pass through the fire*

10 [o]Ex. 13:18, 20
11 [p]Deut. 4:8; [Neh. 9:13, 14; Ps. 147:19, 20] [q]Lev. 18:5; Rom. 10:5; Gal. 3:12; See ch. 18:9
12 [r][ver. 13, 16, 21, 24]; See Ex. 20:8-11; Deut. 5:12-15 [s]ch. 37:28; [Lev. 21:23]
13 [t]ver. 21 [u]ver. 21, 24 [v]ver. 21, 24; ch. 22:8; 23:38
14 [w]ver. 9
15 [x]See ver. 5 [y]Ps. 95:11; See Num. 14:28-30 [z]ver. 6; See Ex. 3:8
16 [a][ver. 24; Num. 15:39; Ps. 78:37]
17 [b]See ch. 5:11 [c][ch. 11:13]
18 [d]ver. 21; [ch. 2:3] [e]Josh. 24:14; 1 Pet. 1:18 [f][ver. 7]
19 [g]ver. 5; See Ex. 20:2 [h]Deut. 5:32, 33
20 [i]Jer. 17:22 [j]ver. 12; [Gen. 9:12; 17:11]
21 [k]Deut. 31:27 [l]ver. 8, 13 [m]ver. 13, 16 [n]ver. 8
22 [o]ver. 14 [p]ver. 9, 14, 44 [q]ver. 9
23 [r]ver. 15 [s]See ver. 5 [t]Deut. 28:64
24 [u][ver. 16]
25 [v]Ps. 81:12; Acts 7:42; Rom. 1:24, 28; 2 Thess. 2:11, 12; [ver. 39]
26 [w][ver. 31; ch. 16:20, 21] [x]See ch. 6:7
27 [y]See ch. 2:1 [z]See ch. 14:13
28 [a]See ver. 5 [b][ch. 6:13] [c][ch. 8:17]
29 [d][ver. 40]
30 [e][ver. 7] [f]Ps. 106:39
31 [g][ver. 26] [h]See ch. 14:3 [i]See ch. 16:48

Sinai (v. 10). Verse 11 (cf. vv. 13, 21) echoes Lev. 18:5 (see note there). The emphasis on **Sabbaths** (Ezek. 20:12) is another distinctive of this recital (see also vv. 13, 16, 20, 21, 24).

20:14–17 This phase shows some variations in wording, as the main formulas of this passage are missing, but the concepts remain. The parallels of vv. 6 and 15 envelop the story of the exodus generation.

20:18–21 Passing on to **their children** (v. 18), that is, the wilderness generation, gives another opportunity for faithful covenant living (vv. 19–20), which is again spurned (v. 21).

20:22–26 The final phase in the history includes a passage notoriously difficult to understand. Although the giving of laws in v. 11 held out the possibility of life, in v. 25 God asserts that he gave Israel **statutes that were not good and rules by which they could not have life**. The Mosaic laws were in fact good and were the means by which the people could enjoy God's presence and blessing among them. The laws that were "not good" refer rather to the infiltration of pagan customs of the surrounding nations, with which the people of Israel increasingly aligned their understanding of their own law. Verse 26, **offering up all their firstborn** (cf. v. 31), points this way. This phase is analogous to God giving up people to their own idolatrous desires and the consequences thereof (Num. 11:4–6, 31–35; Rom. 1:24, 26, 28; cf. Acts 7:42).

20:27–31 As Ezekiel turns from recitation to application, life on the land itself is in view for the first time. On worship on the high places (vv. 28–29), see note on 6:3. The appeal of 20:30 to be morally distinct from preceding generations resonates with 18:30–31, although the consistent rebellion is overtly the reason for God's refusing inquiry (20:31b). Still, the story of rebellion outside

32 [j]“What is in your mind shall never happen—the thought, [k]‘Let us be like the nations,
like the tribes of the countries, [l]and worship wood and stone.’

The LORD Will Restore Israel

33 [l]“As I live, declares the Lord GOD, [m]surely with a mighty hand and an outstretched
arm and [n]with wrath poured out I will be king over you. **34** [o]I will bring you out from the
peoples and gather you out of the countries where you are scattered, with a mighty hand
and an outstretched arm, and with wrath poured out. **35** [p]And I will bring you into the
wilderness of the peoples, [q]and there I will enter into judgment with you [r]face to face.
36 [s]As I entered into judgment with your fathers in the wilderness of the land of Egypt,
so I will enter into judgment with you, declares the Lord GOD. **37** I will make you [t]pass
under the rod, and I will bring you into the bond of the covenant. **38** [u]I will purge out the
rebels from among you, and those who transgress against me. [v]I will bring them out of
the land where they sojourn, [w]but they shall not enter the land of Israel. [x]Then you will
know that I am the LORD.

39 “As for you, O house of Israel, thus says the Lord GOD: [y]Go serve every one of you his
idols, now and hereafter, if you will not listen to me; [z]but my holy name you shall no more
profane with your gifts and your idols.

40 [a]“For on my holy mountain, the mountain height of Israel, declares the Lord GOD,
there [b]all the house of Israel, all of them, shall serve me in the land. [c]There I will accept
them, and there I will require your contributions and the choicest of your gifts, with all
your sacred offerings. **41** As a pleasing aroma I will accept you, when [d]I bring you out from
the peoples and gather you out of the countries where you have been scattered. And [e]I
will manifest my holiness among you in the sight of the nations. **42** [f]And you shall know
that I am the LORD, when I bring you into the land of Israel, the country that [g]I swore to
give to your fathers. **43** [h]And there you shall remember your ways and all your deeds with
which you have defiled yourselves, [h]and you shall loathe yourselves for all the evils that
you have committed. **44** And you shall know that I am the LORD, [i]when I deal with you for
my name’s sake, [j]not according to your evil ways, nor according to your corrupt deeds, O
house of Israel, declares the Lord GOD.”

45 [1] And the word of the LORD came to me: **46** [k]“Son of man, [l]set your face toward the southland;[2] [m]preach against the south, and prophesy against the forest land in the Negeb. **47** Say
to the forest of the Negeb, Hear the word of the LORD: Thus says the Lord GOD, Behold, [n]I
will kindle a fire in you, and it shall devour every [o]green tree in you and every [o]dry tree. The
blazing flame shall not be quenched, and [p]all faces from south to north shall be scorched
by it. **48** [q]All flesh shall see that I the LORD have kindled it; it shall not be quenched.” **49** Then
I said, [r]“Ah, Lord GOD! They are saying of me, [s]‘Is he not a maker of parables?’ ”

[1] Ch 21:1 in Hebrew [2] Or *toward Teman*

32 [j]See ch. 11:5 [k][Jer. 44:17] [l]Deut. 4:28; 2 Kgs. 19:18; Dan. 5:4, 23; Rev. 9:20
33 [l][See ver. 31 above] [m]See Jer. 21:5 [n][ver. 8]
34 [o][Jer. 31:8]
35 [p][ver. 10; Hos. 2:14] [q][ch. 17:20] [r][Deut. 5:4]
36 [s]See Num. 14:20-23, 28-30
37 [t]Lev. 27:32
38 [u]ch. 34:17, 20, 22; [Matt. 25:32, 33] [v][ver. 35] [w]ch. 13:9 [x]See ch. 6:7
39 [y][ver. 25, 26; Judg. 10:14] [z]ch. 39:7; 43:7; [Jer. 44:25, 26]
40 [a]ch. 17:23; [ch. 28:14; Isa. 56:7] [b]ch. 39:25 [c]ch. 43:27; Isa. 60:7; [Mal. 3:4; Rom. 12:1]
41 [d]ver. 34 [e]ch. 36:23; 39:27; [ch. 28:22; 38:16, 23; Num. 20:12; Isa. 8:13]
42 [f]See ch. 6:7 [g]See ver. 5
43 [h]See ch. 6:9
44 [i]ver. 9, 14, 22 [j][Ps. 103:10]
46 [k]See ch. 2:1 [l][ch. 21:2] [m]Amos 7:16; [Isa. 55:10, 11]
47 [n]Jer. 21:14 [o]ch. 17:24; [Luke 23:31] [p]ch. 21:4
48 [q]Isa. 40:5; [Isa. 30:33]
49 [r]See ch. 4:14 [s][ch. 17:2; 24:3]

the land holds within it multiple instances of divine forbearance. This grace contains the seed from which the next section grows.

20:32 *Unthinkable Idolatry.* This isolated verse acts as a pivot between the history of the preceding passage and the future orientation that follows. It is encouragement to heed the warning of Deut. 28:64.

20:33–44 *Looking to the Future.* The structure of two phases in the wilderness finds its mirror image in two phases of restoration: vv. 33–38 use exodus/wilderness motifs as the community is purified; vv. 39–44 focus on worship, in a reversal of ritual behavior in the land (vv. 27–31). Both movements here parallel the “bringing out” in the historical recital (vv. 5, 22 and 34, 41).

20:33–38 The history recited in vv. 5–26 is now compressed into a symbolic future for the exilic community, although with **wrath poured out** (vv. 33, 34) and **judgment** expressed (vv. 35, 36) it is not yet the idealized future of 11:14–20 or even 17:22–24.

20:39–44 With gathering complete, the worship life of the renewed community comes into focus. The contrast with the defiling practices of vv. 26 and 28 is complete. The lingering shame (v. 43) is consistent with the restoration picture in 16:54, 61. God’s own reputation is supremely the reason for the restoration of God’s people (20:44).

20:40 The **holy mountain** as the place of God’s renewed presence with his people is especially prominent in the latter chapters of Isaiah (e.g., Isa. 56:7; 66:20), and its **height** is celebrated in the psalms of Zion (cf. Ps. 48:1–3).

20:45–21:32 *Fire and Sword.* The chapter division in English versions can obscure the relationship of 20:45–49 to the following oracles. In the Hebrew text, 20:45 begins a new chapter. The abrupt change in subject, from fire to sword, reinforces this confusion. However, the conjunction of fire and sword appears in both literal (e.g., Judg. 1:8) and theological contexts (Isa. 66:16; Nah. 3:15). Seeming frustration at the symbolism of the “fire” oracle (Ezek. 20:45–49) prompts its unpacking in terms of the “sword” (21:1–32). Once the sword symbolism is introduced, it is developed in a cascading series of oracles linked by their common theme. Formulaic language (e.g., “the word of the LORD came to me,” and concluding formulas) help to demarcate distinct movements.

20:45–49 *The Parable of the Fire.* The command to **set your face**, distinctive in Ezekiel, and the orientation to **the southland** are both reminiscent of 6:2, which introduces another “sword of the LORD” passage. Here, however, all-consuming fire is the destroying agent, clearly announcing the totality of coming divine judgment (destroying both **green tree** and **dry tree**). But what of the addressees: the “southland” (Hb. *teman*), the **south** (*darom*), and the **forest of the Negeb** (*Negeb*)? This inclusive breadth of territory, rather than the fiery content itself, seems to prompt the outcry of 20:49, **Ah,**

Chapter 21
2[t]See ch. 2:1 [u][ch. 20:46] [v]See ch. 20:46
3[w]See ch. 13:8 [x]ver. 19, 30; [Deut. 32:41; Jer. 47:6] [y][ch. 20:47; Job 9:22]
5[z][ch. 20:48] [x][See ver. 3 above] [a][ver. 30]
6[b][ch. 6:11; 12:18] [c]See ch. 12:3
7[d][ch. 12:9] [e][ch. 7:5, 6] [f]See Josh. 2:11 [g]See ch. 7:17 [h]ch. 39:8
9[t][See ver. 2 above] [i]See ver. 3
10[j][ver. 15, 28] [k][James 5:5] [l][ch. 20:47]
11[m][ver. 19]
12[n][ver. 6] [o]Jer. 31:19
13[p][ver. 10]
14[q]See ch. 2:1 [r]ch. 22:13; Num. 24:10 [s][2 Kgs. 24:1, 10; 25:1]
15[t]ver. 10
17[r][See ver. 14 above] [u]See ch. 5:13 [v]See ch. 17:24

The LORD Has Drawn His Sword

21 [1]The word of the LORD came to me: **2** [t]“Son of man, [u]set your face toward Jerusalem
and [v]preach against the sanctuaries.[2] Prophesy against the land of Israel **3** and say
to the land of Israel, Thus says the LORD: [w]Behold, I am against you and will draw [x]my
sword from its sheath and [y]will cut off from you both righteous and wicked. **4** Because I
will cut off from you both righteous and wicked, therefore my sword shall be drawn from
its sheath against all flesh from south to north. **5** [z]And all flesh shall know that I am the
LORD. I have drawn [x]my sword from its sheath; [a]it shall not be sheathed again.
6 “As for you, son of man, [b]groan; with breaking heart and bitter grief, [c]groan before
their eyes. **7** [d]And when they say to you, ‘Why do you groan?’ you shall say, ‘Because of the
news [e]that it is coming. [f]Every heart will melt, and [g]all hands will be feeble; every spirit
will faint, and [g]all knees will be weak as water. [h]Behold, it is [e]coming, and it will be fulfilled,’ ” declares the Lord GOD.
8 And the word of the LORD came to me: **9** [t]“Son of man, prophesy and say, Thus says
the Lord, say:

> [i]“A sword, a sword is sharpened
> and also polished,
> **10** [j]sharpened for slaughter,
> [j]polished to flash like lightning!

(Or [k]shall we rejoice? You have despised the rod, my son, [l]with everything of wood.)[3] **11** So
the sword is given to be polished, that it may be grasped in the hand. It is sharpened and
polished [m]to be given into the hand of the slayer. **12** [n]Cry out and wail, son of man, for it
is against my people. It is against all the princes of Israel. They are delivered over to the
sword with my people. [o]Strike therefore upon your thigh. **13** For it will not be a testing—
what could it do if you despise [p]the rod?”[4] declares the Lord GOD.
14 “As for you, [q]son of man, prophesy. [r]Clap your hands and let the sword come down
twice, [s]yes, three times,[5] the sword for those to be slain. It is the sword for the great slaughter, which surrounds them, **15** that their hearts may melt, and many stumble.[6] At all their
gates I have given the glittering sword. Ah, it is made like lightning; [t]it is taken up[7] for
slaughter. **16** Cut sharply to the right; set yourself to the left, wherever your face is directed.
17 I also will [r]clap my hands, [u]and I will satisfy my fury; [v]I the LORD have spoken.”
18 The word of the LORD came to me again: **19** “As for you, son of man, mark two ways

[1] Ch 21:6 in Hebrew [2] Some Hebrew manuscripts, compare Septuagint, Syriac *against their sanctuary* [3] Probable reading; Hebrew *The rod of my son despises everything of wood* [4] Or *For it is a testing; and what if even the rod despises? It shall not be!* [5] Hebrew *its third* [6] Hebrew *many stumbling blocks* [7] The meaning of the Hebrew word rendered *taken up* is uncertain

Lord GOD! Once before, Ezekiel similarly cried out on his own behalf (4:14; cf. 9:8; 11:13). For **parables**, see note on 17:2.

21:1–7 *The Drawn Sword.* The opening words directly correspond with those of 20:46–47: **set your face**, **preach**, **prophesy**, and **say** all appear in the same order in those preceding verses. Now, however, the addressees are identified with clarity. The “southland” is **Jerusalem**, the “south” is now **sanctuaries**, the “forest land” is the **land of Israel** (in Ezekiel’s distinctive phrase; see note on 7:2). No doubt remains about the focus of the Lord’s judgment, while the destroying agent is translated into the metaphor of the drawn **sword** (21:3).

21:3–4 The **righteous and wicked** correspond to the “green” and “dry” trees of 20:47. Whereas elsewhere the fate of the righteous has been marked off from that of the wicked (e.g., 9:4–6), and the teaching of ch. 18 also points in a different direction, here God predicts a judgment that will come on the whole nation and will affect everyone, righteous and wicked alike. Sometimes the righteous suffer not as judgment for their own sin but simply as a trial that is part of life in a fallen world. One must allow here for God’s freedom to judge as he will. This is not the first or last time in Scripture that the righteous experience the heavy hand of God (e.g., Job; cf. James 5:11).

21:6–7 Intertextual connections suggest that these verses continue to address the destruction of both “righteous and wicked” (see note on vv. 3–4). The **groan** and **breaking heart** of v. 6 point back to 9:4, which identifies the righteous by this behavior and thus directly connects this passage to the one with which it is in greatest tension. Verse 7 of ch. 21 echoes 7:17 and the reaction to the coming day of the LORD. The closing phrase, **behold . . . it will be fulfilled**, echoes 7:5–6, 10. This passage, then, infers that all have at some level been defiled and provides a precedent within Ezekiel for the totality of judgment expressed in 21:3–4.

21:8–17 *The Sharpened Sword.* The Hebrew of these verses is notoriously difficult (thus the several ESV translation footnotes). Some phrases in translation are approximations at best. Even if the details are obscure, the gist is clear enough. Verses 8–13 focus on the nature of the sword itself, honed to razor sharpness; vv. 14–17 describe its lethal effect.

21:12 The **princes of Israel** may refer to the tragic events at Riblah (2 Kings 25:6–7). This prompts one of two gestures narrated here: **strike . . . your thigh** is an action associated with lament (see Jer. 31:19).

21:14, 17 As in 6:11, to **clap your hands** communicates agitation, perhaps in anticipation of the imminent judgment.

21:18–29 *The Sword of Nebuchadnezzar.* In v. 11 the sword was committed to the “hand of the slayer,” identified here as **the king of Babylon**. This sets a new trajectory for this “sword” oracle, as the campaign of Nebuchadnezzar is imagined (vv. 18–23), as well as its threat to Jerusalem (vv. 24–27) and its application to Ammon (vv. 28–29).

21:18–23 Ezekiel performs another symbolic action (see ch. 4), drawing (presumably on the ground) a map with a forked road, and supplying road signs. It is unknown how much of the rest of the action was actually performed or whether it was simply narrated. It depicts Nebuchadnezzar at his camp, probably somewhere in Syria, deciding whether to bear west toward

for [w]the sword of the king of Babylon to come. Both of them shall come from the same
land. And make [x]a signpost; make it [x]at the head of the way to a city. 20 Mark a way [y]for the
sword to come to Rabbah of the Ammonites and to Judah, into Jerusalem the fortified.
21 For the king of Babylon stands [z]at the parting of the way, at the head of the two ways,
to use divination. He shakes the arrows; he consults [a]the teraphim;[1] he looks at the liver.
22 Into his right hand comes the divination for Jerusalem, [b]to set battering rams, to open
the mouth with murder, to lift up the voice with shouting, to set battering rams against
the gates, [c]to cast up mounds, to build siege towers. 23 But to them it will seem like a false
divination. [d]They have sworn solemn oaths, but he brings their guilt to remembrance,
[e]that they may be taken.

24 "Therefore thus says the Lord GOD: Because you have made your guilt to be remembered, in that your transgressions are uncovered, so that in all your deeds your sins appear—
because you have come to remembrance, [f]you shall be taken in hand. 25 And you, O profane[2]
[g]wicked one, prince of Israel, [h]whose day has come, [i]the time of your final punishment,
26 thus says the Lord GOD: Remove the turban and take off the crown. Things shall not
remain as they are. [j]Exalt that which is low, and bring low that which is exalted. 27 A ruin,
ruin, ruin I will make it. [k]This also shall not be, [l]until he comes, the one to whom judgment belongs, and I will give it to him.

28 "And you, [m]son of man, prophesy, and say, Thus says the Lord GOD [n]concerning the
Ammonites and concerning their reproach; say, [o]A sword, a sword [p]is drawn for the slaughter. [o]It is polished to consume and to flash like lightning— 29 while [q]they see for you false
visions, while they divine lies for you—to place you on the necks of the profane wicked,
[r]whose day has come, the time of their final punishment. 30 [p]Return it to its sheath. In the
place where you were created, in the land of your origin, [s]I will judge you. 31 And [t]I will
pour out my indignation upon you; [u]I will blow upon you with the fire of my wrath, and
I will deliver you into the hands of [v]brutish men, skillful to destroy. 32 You shall be fuel for
the fire. Your blood shall be in the midst of the land. [w]You shall be no more remembered,
[x]for I the LORD have spoken."

Israel's Shedding of Blood

22 And the word of the LORD came to me, saying, 2 "And you, [y]son of man, [z]will you
judge, will you judge [a]the bloody city? [b]Then declare to her all her abominations.
3 You shall say, Thus says the Lord GOD: A city that sheds blood in her midst, so that [c]her
time may come, and that makes idols to defile herself! 4 You have become guilty [a]by the

[1] Or *household idols* [2] Or *slain*; also verse 29

19 [w]ver. 11 [x][ver. 21]
20 [y]See ch. 25:1-5; Jer. 49:1-6; Amos 1:13-15
21 [z][ver. 19] [a]See Gen. 31:19
22 [b]ch. 4:2; 26:9 [c]See ch. 4:2
23 [d][ch. 17:13] [e][ch. 17:20]
24 [f][ch. 17:20]
25 [g][ch. 17:19; 2 Chr. 36:13; Jer. 52:2] [h]ver. 29; ch. 22:3, 4 [i]ch. 35:5
26 [j][ch. 17:24; Luke 1:52]
27 [k][ver. 13] [l]Gen. 49:10; Zech. 6:12, 13; John 1:49; [Rev. 17:14]
28 [m]See ch. 2:1 [n]See ver. 20 [o][ver. 9, 10] [p][ver. 5]
29 [q]See ch. 13:6 [r]ver. 25
30 [p][See ver. 28 above] [s]ch. 16:38
31 [t]See ch. 7:8 [u]ch. 22:20, 21 [v]See Ps. 49:10
32 [w]ch. 25:10 [x]See ch. 17:24

Chapter 22

2 [y]See ch. 2:1 [z]See ch. 20:4 [a][ch. 16:38; 23:37; 24:6; 2 Kgs. 21:16]; See ch. 7:23 [b]ch. 16:2; 20:4
3 [c]ch. 21:25, 29
4 [a][See ver. 2 above]

Jerusalem or east toward **Rabbah** (21:20, modern Amman). He decides to attack Jerusalem (v. 22).

21:21 Three means of divination (manipulation of objects in search of a divine message) are described. **Shakes the arrows** may be akin to drawing lots; **consults the teraphim** may refer to small idol images (usually translated "household gods," e.g., Gen. 31:19; Hos. 3:4). **Liver** omens are well known throughout the ancient Near East. They involved examining the organ of a sacrificed animal.

21:24–27 With the sword committed to the Babylonian king, impending judgment is announced on Jerusalem. Although this section begins with plural references, it quickly focuses on an individual, the "wicked" **prince of Israel**, who must be Zedekiah.

21:26 Turban and **crown** are both insignias of office. The former is related to the priesthood (Ex. 28:4); the latter is clearly royal. It may be, however, that these are the same and the reference is simply to Zedekiah. This is often the way with Hebrew parallelism (cf. Prov. 4:9; Isa. 62:3).

21:28–29 The application of this prophecy to the **Ammonites** is in addition to the prophecy in 25:1–7, where the prophecy against Ammon stands first among the collection of oracles against foreign nations. The point here is that the visitation of the sword against Jerusalem does not preclude its coming to Ammon as well (21:20).

21:30–32 *The Sword Sheathed and Judged.* The instruction to **return** the sword **to its sheath** (v. 30) is the counterpart to the action begun in v. 3. With its work done, the "tool" is now itself subject to judgment. In this, Babylon is like Assyria in Isa. 10:5–19. The conclusion in Ezek. 21:31–32 points in two directions: **fire of my wrath** refers back to the parable of the fire that began this oracle complex (20:45–49), and it anticipates the conclusion to the oracle that follows (22:31); so too in 21:32, **fuel for the fire** points back to 20:45–49, while the reference to **blood** prepares the way for ch. 22.

22:1–31 *A City Defiled.* Again, introductory and concluding formulas mark out the bounds of three distinct but thematically related oracles. Each convicts Jerusalem of practicing vile impurities that God refuses to tolerate. The first, and longest, characterizes this behavior in detail (vv. 1–16); the second uses the metaphor of melting for ridding Jerusalem of its impurities (vv. 17–22); the third surveys the city's inhabitants; but none provides a reason for preventing its destruction (vv. 23–31).

22:1–16 *The Bloody City.* Issues of purity persist throughout the book, and come to the fore here. Although guilt is implicated, the issue is not primarily legal. The repetition of forms of the Hebrew *tame'* ("impure, unclean")—translated **defiled** in vv. 3–5 (also v. 11)—points rather to ethical or ritual impurity, as also does the distinctive conjunction of **blood** and **idols** in vv. 3–4 (only, it seems, in Ezekiel; cf. 16:36; 36:18). The catalog of abominations in 22:6–12 bears comparison with the similar lists of virtues and vices in 18:5–18. They are not identical, however, and it has been pointed out that some of the offenses listed here depend on powerful officials (22:6–7, 9, 12) and a functioning temple (v. 8). In other words, the addressees are members of pre-586-B.C. Jerusalem, in distinction to the audience of exiles in ch. 18. The list has strong parallels in Leviticus (see the cross-references).

4[c][See ver. 3 above] [d]See ch. 5:14
5[e][Isa. 1:21] [f]Isa. 22:2
6[g]ver. 27
7[h]Deut. 27:16; [Eph. 6:2]; See Ex. 20:12 [i]Ex. 22:21, 22
8[j][ver. 26] [k]See ch. 20:13
9[l]Lev. 19:16; [1 Sam. 22:9-19] [m]See ch. 18:6 [n]ch. 16:43
10[o]Lev. 18:7, 8; 20:11
11[p]Lev. 18:20; Jer. 5:8; [ch. 18:6] [q]Lev. 18:15; 20:12; [Amos 2:7] [r]Lev. 18:9; 20:17
12[s]Deut. 27:25 [t]See ch. 18:8 [u]ch. 23:35; See Jer. 2:32
13[v]ch. 21:14, 17 [w]ver. 27 [x]See ver. 2
14[y][ch. 21:7] [z]See ch. 17:24
15[a]See ch. 5:10 [b]ch. 24:11; [ver. 21, 22]
16[c][ver. 26; ch. 7:24] [d]ch. 5:8 [e]See ch. 6:7
18[f]See ch. 2:1 [g]Ps. 119:119; Isa. 1:22, 25 [h]Jer. 6:28 [i]Isa. 1:25
20[j]ch. 21:31; [Mal. 3:3] [k]Jer. 33:5
22[l]See ch. 7:8
24[m]See ver. 2-4 [n][ch. 34:26]; See 1 Kgs. 8:35, 36
25[o]See Jer. 11:9 [p]See ch. 19:3 [q]ver. 27
26[r][Mal. 2:8] [s]Zeph. 3:4 [t][ver. 8] [u]See Lev. 10:10 [v][Jer. 17:22, 24, 27] [w]See ch. 36:20
27[x]ver. 6; Mic. 3:1, 2; Zeph. 3:3; [Matt. 7:15] [y]ver. 25 [z][ver. 13]
28[a]ch. 13:10 [b]See ch. 13:6

blood that you have shed, and defiled by the idols that you have made, and you have brought
[c]your days near, the appointed time of[1] your years has come. [d]Therefore I have made you a
reproach to the nations, and a mockery to all the countries. **5** Those who are near and those
who are far from you will mock you; [e]your name is defiled; [f]you are full of tumult.
6 "Behold, [g]the princes of Israel in you, every one according to his power, have been bent
on shedding blood. **7** Father and mother [h]are treated with contempt in you; the sojourner
[i]suffers extortion in your midst; the fatherless and the widow [i]are wronged in you. **8** [j]You
have despised my holy things and [k]profaned my Sabbaths. **9** [l]There are men in you who
slander to shed blood, and people in you [m]who eat on the mountains; [n]they commit lewdness in your midst. **10** In you [o]men uncover their fathers' nakedness; in you they violate
women who are unclean in their menstrual impurity. **11** [p]One commits abomination with
his neighbor's wife; [q]another lewdly defiles his daughter-in-law; [r]another in you violates
his sister, his father's daughter. **12** In you [s]they take bribes to shed blood; [t]you take interest
and profit[2] and make gain of your neighbors by extortion; but [u]me you have forgotten,
declares the Lord GOD.
13 "Behold, [v]I strike my hand at [w]the dishonest gain that you have made, and at [x]the
blood that has been in your midst. **14** [y]Can your courage endure, or can your hands be
strong, in the days that I shall deal with you? [z]I the LORD have spoken, and I will do it.
15 [a]I will scatter you among the nations and disperse you through the countries, and [b]I will
consume your uncleanness out of you. **16** And [c]you shall be profaned by your own doing
[d]in the sight of the nations, [e]and you shall know that I am the LORD."
17 And the word of the LORD came to me: **18** [f]"Son of man, the house of Israel has become
[g]dross to me; all of them are [h]bronze and tin and iron and lead in the furnace; they are
[i]dross of silver. **19** Therefore thus says the Lord GOD: Because you have all become dross,
therefore, behold, I will gather you into the midst of Jerusalem. **20** As one gathers silver and
bronze and iron and lead and tin into a furnace, [j]to blow the fire on it in order to melt it,
so I will gather you [k]in my anger and in my wrath, and I will put you in and melt you. **21** I
will gather you and blow on you with the fire of my wrath, and you shall be melted in the
midst of it. **22** As silver is melted in a furnace, so you shall be melted in the midst of it, and
you shall know that I am the LORD; [l]I have poured out my wrath upon you."
23 And the word of the LORD came to me: **24** "Son of man, say to her, You are a land
that is [m]not cleansed [n]or rained upon in the day of indignation. **25** [o]The conspiracy of
her prophets in her midst is [p]like a roaring lion [q]tearing the prey; they have devoured
human lives; they have taken treasure and precious things; they have made many widows
in her midst. **26** [r]Her priests [s]have done violence to my law and [t]have profaned my holy
things. [u]They have made no distinction between the holy and the common, neither have
they taught the difference between the unclean and the clean, and [v]they have disregarded
my Sabbaths, [w]so that I am profaned among them. **27** [x]Her princes in her midst are like
wolves [y]tearing the prey, [z]shedding blood, destroying lives to get dishonest gain. **28** And
[a]her prophets have smeared whitewash for them, [b]seeing false visions and divining lies

[1] Some Hebrew manuscripts, Septuagint, Syriac, Vulgate, Targum; most Hebrew manuscripts *until* [2] That is, profit that comes from charging interest to the poor (compare Leviticus 25:36)

22:6–12 In you, that is, in Jerusalem, all the sins on this long list occur. Every area of life is defiled, for these sins violate God's laws for the protection of worship, parental authority, human life, marriage, property, and truth (in other words, all of the matters contained in the Ten Commandments; see Ex. 20:1–17).

22:9 The prohibition against **slander** is linked to **blood** in Lev. 19:16 (where the word translated "life" is Hb. *dam*, "blood"). To **eat on the mountains** (cf. Ezek. 18:6, 15) is to participate in forbidden sacrificial rites.

22:12 This verse provides a fitting summary to the list of ethical vices: **but me you have forgotten**. A holy God cannot tolerate such behavior.

22:17–22 *The City of Dross.* The metaphor of melting is found elsewhere in the OT: Jer. 6:29 makes similar use of it, while Isa. 48:10 provides a literal application. Here, however, the point is not to get purified silver but to be rid of the dross, i.e., Jerusalem's inhabitants (cf. Isa. 1:22, 25). Jerusalem is seen as a slag heap of useless dross.

22:23–31 *Systemic Failure.* Here, rather than surveying behaviors (as in vv. 6–12), Ezekiel surveys personnel. The issue is still impurity (**a land . . . not cleansed**, v. 24). This oracle almost serves as a commentary on 7:23–27 where prophet, priest, elders, and king mislead the city, although an even earlier "model" is found in Zeph. 3:3–4. The sum is a web of deceit, as these pillars of the community are seen as colluding.

22:25 The **conspiracy of her prophets** (Hb. *qesher nebi'im*) initiates this list. The lion metaphor was used of princes in 19:2–7.

22:26 The **priests** were meant to be guardians of moral discernment (cf. Lev. 10:10; Mal. 2:4–7).

22:27 princes (plural of Hb. *sar*). Not the same term as that used at 19:1, where the reference is to royal sons; here the wider nobility is intended, or perhaps simply officials in the royal service. **Wolves** are lesser predators than "lions" (see 22:25).

22:28 On false **prophets** being **smeared** with **whitewash**, cf. 13:10–16.

for them, saying, 'Thus says the Lord GOD,' when the LORD has not spoken. 29 The people
of the land [c]have practiced extortion and committed robbery. They have oppressed the
poor and needy, and [c]have extorted from the sojourner without justice. 30 [d]And I sought
for a man among them [e]who should build up the wall [e]and stand in the breach before
me for the land, that I should not destroy it, but I found none. 31 Therefore [f]I have poured
out my indignation upon them. I have consumed them with the fire of my wrath. I have
returned [g]their way upon their heads, declares the Lord GOD."

Oholah and Oholibah

23 The word of the LORD came to me: 2 [h]"Son of man, there were [i]two women, the
daughters of one mother. 3 [j]They played the whore in Egypt; [j]they played the whore
[k]in their youth; there their breasts were pressed and their virgin bosoms[1] handled. 4 Oholah
was the name of the elder and Oholibah the name of her sister. [l]They became mine, and
they [m]bore sons and daughters. As for their names, Oholah is [n]Samaria, and Oholibah is
Jerusalem.
5 "Oholah played the whore [o]while she was mine, and [p]she lusted after her lovers [q]the
Assyrians, warriors 6 clothed in purple, [r]governors and commanders, [s]all of them desirable young men, [t]horsemen riding on horses. 7 She bestowed her whoring upon them, the
choicest men of Assyria all of them, and she defiled herself with all the idols of everyone
after whom she lusted. 8 She did not give up her whoring [u]that she had begun in Egypt; for
in her youth men had lain with her and handled her virgin bosom and poured out their
whoring lust upon her. 9 Therefore [v]I delivered her into the hands of her lovers, into the
hands of the Assyrians, after whom she lusted. 10 [w]These uncovered her nakedness; [x]they
seized her sons and her daughters; and as for her, they killed her with the sword; and she
became [y]a byword among women, [z]when judgment had been executed on her.
11 [a]"Her sister Oholibah saw this, and she became [b]more corrupt than her sister[2] in her
lust and in her whoring, which was worse than that of her sister. 12 She lusted after the
Assyrians, governors and commanders, warriors clothed in full armor, horsemen riding on
horses, [s]all of them desirable young men. 13 And I saw that she was defiled; they both took
the same way. 14 But she carried her whoring further. She saw men [c]portrayed on the wall,
the [d]images of [e]the Chaldeans portrayed in vermilion, 15 wearing belts on their waists, with
flowing turbans on their heads, all of them having the appearance of officers, a likeness
of Babylonians whose native land was Chaldea. 16 When she saw them, she lusted after
them and [f]sent messengers to them [e]in Chaldea. 17 And the Babylonians came to her [g]into
the bed of love, and they defiled her with their whoring lust. And after she was defiled by
them, [h]she turned from them in disgust. 18 When she carried on her whoring so openly

[1] Hebrew *nipples*; also verses 8, 21 [2] Hebrew *than she*

29 [c][ver. 7]
30 [d]Isa. 59:16; Jer. 5:1 [e]See ch. 13:5
31 [f][ver. 21] [g]See ch. 7:4

Chapter 23
2 [h]See ch. 2:1 [i][ch. 16:45, 46]
3 [j]See ch. 16:15 [k][ch. 16:22]
4 [l]ch. 16:8 [m][ver. 37] [n][ch. 16:46]
5 [o]Num. 5:19, 20 [p][Hos. 2:5] [q]2 Kgs. 15:19; 17:3; Hos. 8:9
6 [r]ver. 23 [s]ver. 23 [t]ch. 38:15; [Isa. 5:28]
8 [u][ver. 3, 19]
9 [v][2 Kgs. 15:29]; See 2 Kgs. 17:4-6, 23; 18:9-11
10 [w]ver. 29; See ch. 16:37 [x]ver. 25 [y][ch. 16:14] [z]See ch. 5:8
11 [a]Jer. 3:8, 9 [b]Jer. 3:11; See ch. 16:47
12 [s][See ver. 6 above]
14 [c]ch. 8:10 [d][ch. 16:17] [e]ch. 16:29; [2 Kgs. 20:12, 13; 24:1]
16 [f][ver. 40; Isa. 57:9] [e][See ver. 14 above]
17 [g][ver. 41; Isa. 57:7, 8] [h]ver. 22, 28; [ch. 17:15]

22:30 There is no one to **stand in the breach** (cf. 13:5; Ps. 106:23) who might avert the destruction. Sometimes it takes only one courageous, righteous person to stop great evil, but there was no one.

23:1–49 *Two Sisters.* The allegory of the unfaithful sisters parallels ch. 16 (esp. 16:44–63) in employing this extended metaphor to portray the nature of God's relationship to Judah (and here, Israel) and its inevitable outcome in judgment (for common features, see the notes on ch. 16). Whereas ch. 16 focused primarily on religious fidelity and worship, with politics in the background, here those elements are reversed as political issues come to the fore. Also, ch. 16 is overtly framed on the basis of a marriage covenant, which here is implied rather than stated. Once again, Jeremiah's preaching provides background (cf. Jer. 3:6–10). The two sisters are again cities: **Oholah is Samaria, and Oholibah is Jerusalem** (Ezek. 23:4). Jerusalem's destruction is depicted as yet more just and certain in light of the judgment that befell her sister. The oracle falls into two main parts: vv. 1–35 tell the story and its outcome, with a condensed version found in vv. 36–49, which brings elements of social justice into the scenario.

23:1–35 *The Sisters and Politics.* In the first part of the oracle (vv. 1–21), the behavior of the sisters is individually described, with the younger sister (Jerusalem) not only exceeding her older sister's unfaithfulness quantitatively by involving more partners, but qualitatively, in that she "saw" (v. 11) what happened to Samaria yet it only deepened her own depravity. Judgment inevitably follows (vv. 22–31).

23:1–21 The sisters in this allegory are introduced (vv. 1–4), then the older sister's story, including her downfall, is told (vv. 5–10), which is another feature of this oracle that sets it apart from ch. 16. The younger sister's story follows, with greater development (23:11–21). The "partners" (Assyria, Babylonia, and Egypt) represent various political alliances sought by the respective capital cities.

23:3 Tracing depravity back to Egypt corresponds to the historical recital of 20:5–8.

23:4 The names **Oholah** ("her tent") and **Oholibah** ("my tent is in her") are given and quickly identified as Samaria and Jerusalem. The significance of the symbolism of these names has been largely lost, and the translations suggested here are approximate.

23:8 Samaria's **whoring** behavior began **in her youth** (i.e., **in Egypt**).

23:11 The notice that **Oholibah saw this** is the only hint Ezekiel gives that she ought to have learned the lessons of her older sister.

23:12 The **Assyrians** had dominated the period of Manasseh's rule (cf. 2 Chron. 33:11).

23:14–17 The empire of the **Babylonians** succeeded that of the Assyrians (v. 12).

and flaunted her nakedness, I turned in disgust from her, as I had turned in disgust from
her sister. 19 Yet she increased her whoring, [i]remembering the days of her youth, when she
played the whore in the land of Egypt 20 and lusted after her lovers there, whose members
were like those of donkeys, and whose issue was like that of horses. 21 Thus you longed
for the lewdness of your youth, when the Egyptians handled your bosom and pressed[1]
your young breasts."

22 Therefore, O Oholibah, thus says the Lord God: "Behold, I will stir up against you
your lovers [h]from whom you turned in disgust, [j]and I will bring them against you from
every side: 23 the Babylonians and all the Chaldeans, [k]Pekod and Shoa and Koa, and all
the Assyrians with them, [l]desirable young men, [l]governors and commanders all of them,
officers and men of renown, all of them riding on horses. 24 And they shall come against
you from the north[2] with chariots and wagons and a host of peoples. [m]They shall set themselves against you on every side with buckler, shield, and helmet; and [n]I will commit the
judgment to them, and [o]they shall judge you according to their judgments. 25 And I will
direct my jealousy against you, [p]that they may deal with you in fury. They shall cut off
your nose and your ears, and your survivors shall fall by the sword. [q]They shall seize your
sons and your daughters, and your survivors shall be devoured by fire. 26 [r]They shall also
strip you of your clothes and take away your beautiful jewels. 27 [s]Thus I will put an end
to your lewdness and [t]your whoring begun in the land of Egypt, so that you shall not lift
up your eyes to them or remember Egypt anymore.

28 "For thus says the Lord God: [u]Behold, I will deliver you into the hands of those whom
you hate, [v]into the hands of those from whom you turned in disgust, 29 and [w]they shall
deal with you in hatred and take away all the fruit of your labor [x]and leave you naked and
bare, and [y]the nakedness of your whoring shall be uncovered. Your lewdness and your
whoring 30 have brought this upon you, because [z]you played the whore with the nations
and defiled yourself with their idols. 31 You have gone the way of your sister; [a]therefore I
will give [b]her cup into your hand. 32 Thus says the Lord God:

"You shall drink your sister's cup
that is deep and large;
you shall be laughed at and held in derision,
for it contains much;
33 you will be filled with [c]drunkenness and sorrow.
[c]A cup of horror and desolation,
the cup of [d]your sister Samaria;
34 [e]you shall drink it and drain it out,
and gnaw its shards,
and tear your breasts;

for I have spoken, declares the Lord God. 35 Therefore thus says the Lord God: Because
[f]you have forgotten me and [g]cast me behind your back, you yourself [h]must bear the consequences of your lewdness and whoring."

36 The Lord said to me: [i]"Son of man, [j]will you judge Oholah and Oholibah? Declare to
them their abominations. 37 For [k]they have committed adultery, [l]and blood is on their hands.
With their idols they have committed adultery, and they have even [m]offered up[3] to them

[1] Vulgate, Syriac; Hebrew *bosom for the sake of* [2] Septuagint; the meaning of the Hebrew word is unknown [3] Or *have even made pass through the fire*

19 [i][ver. 3]; See ch. 16:15
22 [h][See ver. 17 above] [j]ch. 16:37
23 [k]Jer. 50:21 [l]ver. 6, 12
24 [m][2 Kgs. 19:32] [n][ch. 9:5, 6] [o]2 Kgs. 25:6
25 [p]ver. 29 [q]ver. 10
26 [r]ch. 16:39
27 [s]ver. 48; ch. 16:41 [t]ver. 3, 19
28 [u]ch. 16:37 [v]ver. 17, 22
29 [w]ver. 25 [x]ch. 16:7, 22, 39 [y]ver. 10; See ch. 16:37
30 [z]ch. 6:9; See Ex. 34:15
31 [a][ver. 9, 10] [b][Jer. 25:15]
33 [c]Isa. 51:17; Jer. 13:13; [Rev. 14:10] [d][ver. 4]
34 [e]Ps. 75:8
35 [f]ch. 22:12; See Jer. 2:32 [g]1 Kgs. 14:9 [h][ver. 49; ch. 14:10; 16:58]
36 [i]See ch. 2:1 [j][ch. 20:4; 22:2]
37 [k]See ch. 16:38 [l][ch. 22:2] [m]ch. 16:20, 21; [ch. 7:23]

23:19 Usually, "youthful memory" implies coming to one's senses (e.g., 16:22). Here, **remembering the days of her youth** inspires Oholibah to greater depths of depravity. **Egypt** again proves a temptation to Jerusalem; see notes on 16:23–29; 17:11–18.

23:22–31 As in ch. 16, the paramours become the punishers. Twice here the formula **thus says the Lord God** (23:22, 28) introduces announcements of judgment (vv. 22–27; 28–31). The longer first section details the political agents of destruction, leaving the second to provide a summary.

23:32–35 Two further **thus says** introductions frame the final outcomes. The mention of the **cup** in v. 31 triggers a different development here. The cup is well known in Jeremiah as an image of punishment (see Jer. 25:15–29; cf. Isa. 51:17–23), although here the metaphor of the sisters is not abandoned (Ezek. 23:33). Verse 35 concludes the entire oracle.

23:36–49 *The Sisters and Religion.* Having reached one stopping point, the oracle restarts, once again naming **Oholah and Oholibah** (v. 36; see note on v. 4). The familiar narrative pattern of accusation and analysis (vv. 36–45) leading to judgment (vv. 46–49) is again followed.

23:36–45 The actions listed in vv. 37–39 provide a more prosaic list of offenses than the consistently metaphorical language in the earlier part of the chapter. They echo other such lists seen previously, especially 22:6–12. The intensifying of interest in the worship life of the cities (for the most part, this list applies to both sisters) supplements the political infidelity identified in 23:5–21.

for food the children whom they had borne to me. 38 Moreover, this they have done to me:
[n]they have defiled my sanctuary on the same day and [o]profaned my Sabbaths. 39 For when
[p]they had slaughtered their children in sacrifice to their idols, on the same day [q]they came
into my sanctuary to profane it. And behold, [r]this is what they did in my house. 40 They even
sent for men to come from afar, [s]to whom a messenger was sent; and behold, they came.
For them you bathed yourself, [t]painted your eyes, [u]and adorned yourself with ornaments.
41 You sat on [v]a stately couch, with a table spread before it [w]on which you had placed my
incense and [x]my oil. 42 The [y]sound of a carefree multitude was with her; and with men of
the common sort, drunkards[1] were brought from the wilderness; and they put [z]bracelets
on the hands of the women, and [a]beautiful crowns on their heads.

43 "Then I said of her who was worn out by adultery, Now they will continue to use her
for a whore, even her![2] 44 For they have gone in to her, as men go in to a prostitute. Thus
they went in to Oholah and to Oholibah, lewd women! 45 But righteous men [b]shall pass
judgment on them with the sentence of adulteresses, and with the sentence of women
who shed blood, because they are adulteresses, and blood is on their hands."

46 For thus says the Lord GOD: [c]"Bring up a vast host against them, and make them [d]an
object of terror and [e]a plunder. 47 [f]And the host shall stone them and cut them down with
their swords. [g]They shall kill their sons and their daughters, and [h]burn up their houses.
48 [i]Thus will I put an end to lewdness in the land, that all women may take warning and
not commit lewdness as you have done. 49 And they shall return your lewdness upon you,
and [j]you shall bear the penalty for your sinful idolatry, and [k]you shall know that I am the
Lord GOD."

The Siege of Jerusalem

24 [l]In the ninth year, in the tenth month, on the tenth day of the month, the word of
the LORD came to me: 2 [m]"Son of man, write down the name of this day, this very
day. The king of Babylon has laid siege to Jerusalem this very day. 3 And [n]utter a parable
to [o]the rebellious house and say to them, Thus says the Lord GOD:

"Set on [p]the pot, set it on;
pour in water also;
4 put in it the pieces of meat,
all the good pieces, [q]the thigh and the shoulder;
fill it with choice bones.
5 Take the choicest one of the flock;
pile the logs[3] under it;
boil it well;
seethe also its bones in it.

6 "Therefore thus says the Lord GOD: [r]Woe to the bloody city, to [p]the pot whose corrosion is in it, and whose corrosion has not gone out of it! Take out of it piece after piece,
without making any choice.[4] 7 For the blood she has shed is in her midst; she put it on
[s]the bare rock; [t]she did not pour it out on the ground to cover it with dust. 8 To rouse
my wrath, to take vengeance, I have set on the bare rock the blood she has shed, that it

[1] Or *Sabeans* [2] The meaning of the Hebrew verse is uncertain [3] Compare verse 10; Hebrew *the bones* [4] Hebrew *no lot has fallen upon it*

38 [n]See ch. 5:11 [o]See ch. 20:13
39 [p]ver. 37; ch. 16:20, 21, 36 [q]ch. 44:7 [r][2 Kgs. 21:4]; See Jer. 23:11
40 [s][ver. 16] [t][2 Kgs. 9:30; Jer. 4:30] [u][ch. 16:11, 12]
41 [v][Esth. 1:6] [w]ch. 16:18; [Prov. 7:17] [x][Hos. 2:8]
42 [y][Isa. 22:2] [z][ch. 16:11] [a][ch. 16:12]
45 [b][ver. 24]; See ch. 16:38
46 [c]ch. 16:40 [d]Deut. 28:25 [e]ch. 7:21
47 [f]ch. 16:40, 41; [Josh. 7:24, 25] [g]ch. 24:21; See 2 Chr. 36:17 [h]2 Chr. 36:19
48 [i]ver. 27; [ch. 16:41]
49 [j][ver. 35] [k][See ch. 6:7]

Chapter 24

1 [l]See ch. 20:1
2 [m]See ch. 2:1
3 [n][ch. 17:2; 20:49] [o]See ch. 2:5 [p]ch. 11:3, 7, 11; 2 Kgs. 4:38
4 [q]See 1 Sam. 9:24
6 [r]ch. 22:2; [Nah. 3:1] [p][See ver. 3 above]
7 [s]ch. 26:4, 14 [t][Lev. 17:13; Deut. 12:16, 24]

23:46–49 Again, punishment is visited on the cities and the countryside surrounding them (**sons and . . . daughters**, v. 47; cf. vv. 4, 10, 25).

24:1–27 *Two Losses.* Although not explicitly linked, the two losses recounted here almost certainly belong together, and they come at a turning point in Ezekiel's prophetic career. The first loss (vv. 1–14) is that of the city of Jerusalem—with a Babylonian siege launched, it is the beginning of the end. The second loss, that of Ezekiel's own wife (vv. 15–24), triggers his most poignant symbolic action. Finally (vv. 25–27), the promise of the end is made, linking this chapter back to the prologue and forward to what lies beyond the destruction of Jerusalem.

24:1–14 *Jerusalem, the Bloody Pot.* This is the last of Ezekiel's "parables" (see 12:22). It uses imagery already found in the temple vision (see 11:2–3) but further developed and with greater clarity here. As the Babylonians lay siege to Jerusalem, it is likened to a boiling pot. A brief "song" in 24:3b–5 receives two explanations in vv. 6–14.

24:1–5 The oracle is precisely dated in v. 1. The notation here in Hebrew does not follow the pattern found for the dates in the rest of the book but corresponds exactly to that of 2 Kings 25:1 (see also Jer. 39:1; 52:4). It seems that here the date accords with the years of a king's reign rather than years of exile (Ezekiel's norm). It is thus equivalent to January 587 B.C. (or 588 if reckoned by years of exile). The content of the "parable" speaks for itself (in addition to Ezek. 11:2–3, cf. Mic. 3:3): anticipation builds as the fine stew cooks.

24:2 The king of Babylon has laid siege to Jerusalem this very day. Jerusalem was 880 miles (1,416 km) away, a journey of several weeks. God revealed it to Ezekiel at the same time it happened.

24:6–9 Some difficult Hebrew obscures the first phase of explanation. The

may not be covered. 9 Therefore thus says the Lord GOD: Woe to the bloody city! [u]I also
will make the pile great. 10 Heap on the logs, kindle the fire, boil the meat well, mix in
the spices,[1] and let the bones be burned up. 11 Then set it empty upon the coals, that it
may become hot, and its copper may burn, [v]that its uncleanness may be melted in it, its
corrosion consumed. 12 [w]She has wearied herself with toil;[2] its abundant corrosion does
not go out of it. Into the fire with its corrosion! 13 On account of your unclean lewdness,
because I would have cleansed you and you were not cleansed from your uncleanness,
[x]you shall not be cleansed anymore till [y]I have satisfied my fury upon you. 14 [z]I am the
LORD. I have spoken; it shall come to pass; I will do it. I will not go back; [a]I will not spare;
[b]I will not relent; [c]according to your ways and your deeds you will be judged, declares
the Lord GOD."

Ezekiel's Wife Dies

15 The word of the LORD came to me: 16 [d]"Son of man, behold, I am about to take the
delight of your eyes away from you at a stroke; yet you shall not mourn or weep, nor shall
your tears run down. 17 Sigh, but not aloud; make no mourning for the dead. [e]Bind on
your turban, and [f]put your shoes on your feet; do not cover your lips, [g]nor eat the bread
of men." 18 So I spoke to the people in the morning, and [h]at evening my wife died. And on
the next morning I did [i]as I was commanded.

19 And [j]the people said to me, "Will you not tell us what these things mean for us, that
you are acting thus?" 20 Then I said to them, "The word of the LORD came to me: 21 'Say
to the house of Israel, Thus says the Lord GOD: [k]Behold, I will profane my sanctuary, the
pride of your power, the delight of your eyes, and the yearning of your soul, and [l]your sons
and your daughters whom you left behind shall fall by the sword. 22 And [m]you shall do
as I have done; [m]you shall not cover your lips, [g]nor eat the bread of men. 23 [m]Your turbans
shall be on your heads and your shoes on your feet; you shall not mourn or weep, but [n]you
shall rot away in your iniquities and groan to one another. 24 Thus shall Ezekiel be to you
[o]a sign; [m]according to all that he has done you shall do. When this comes, then [p]you will
know that I am the Lord GOD.'

25 "As for you, [q]son of man, surely on the day when I take from them [r]their stronghold,
their joy and glory, the delight of their eyes and their soul's desire, and also their sons and
daughters, 26 [s]on that day a fugitive will come to you to report to you the news. 27 On that
day your mouth [t]will be opened to the fugitive, and you shall speak and be no longer mute.
[u]So you will be a sign to them, and [v]they will know that I am the LORD."

[1] Or *empty out the broth* [2] The meaning of the Hebrew is uncertain

9 [u]Isa. 30:33
11 [v]ch. 22:15
12 [w][Jer. 2:22]
13 [x]Isa. 22:14 [y]See ch. 5:13
14 [z]See ch. 17:24 [a]See ch. 5:11 [b][Num. 23:19; 1 Sam. 15:29] [c][ch. 20:43; 23:45]
16 [d]See ch. 2:1
17 [e]See Lev. 10:6 [f][2 Sam. 15:30; Isa. 20:2] [g]Hos. 9:4; See Jer. 16:5-7
18 [h][ver. 16] [i]ch. 12:7; 37:7
19 [j]See ch. 12:9
21 [k][Jer. 7:14]; See ch. 7:21 [l]ch. 23:47; See 2 Chr. 36:17
22 [m][ver. 17; ch. 12:11] [g][See ver. 17 above]
23 [m][See ver. 22 above] [n]See ch. 4:17
24 [o]ver. 27; See ch. 4:3 [m][See ver. 22 above] [p]See ch. 6:7
25 [q]See ch. 2:1 [r][ver. 21]
26 [s]See ch. 33:21, 22
27 [t]ch. 29:21; [ch. 3:26, 27] [u]ver. 24; See ch. 4:3 [v]See ch. 6:7

picture seems to be that of a corroded **pot** which has spoiled the broth. The reference to **blood** (vv. 7–9) is unexpected and takes the imagery in a different direction, reminiscent of 22:2–4.

24:10–14 The compounded nature of corruption and rot demands that both the pot and its contents be completely consumed (v. 11; see 22:15). The cleansing **fire** burns with such intensity that nothing will remain. The first-person forms of 24:14 are repetitive and insistent: this is God's work, and it is certain to come.

24:15–24 *No Mourning for Ezekiel's Wife.* No further reference is made to a date, but the placement of this account next to the oracle marking the siege of Jerusalem is significant. Ezekiel has performed other symbolic actions (4:1–5:17; 12:1–28; 21:19–20), but this must be the most painful. It elicits no protest (cf. 4:14; 20:49). Ezekiel has learned that there is nothing that God cannot ask of him. He is now about 35 years old, and he is told that his wife will die, and that he will not mourn. She dies; he complies. People are disturbed (24:19), but Ezekiel's action prefigures what awaits his countrymen in exile with him.

24:15–18 A bare glimpse is given of Ezekiel's inner life; there is little else like it in prophetic literature. One may wonder about the nature of marriages in ancient Judah, but Ezekiel's **wife** was **the delight of** his **eyes**. The list of mourning rites forbidden to him is easily understood, except for the reference to **bread of men** (v. 17), which must refer to bread provided to the bereaved (see Hos. 9:4). One can only imagine what this embodied oracle cost Ezekiel.

24:16 you shall not mourn or weep. This is a unique symbolic action commanded of Ezekiel alone, not intended as a pattern for believers generally to follow (cf. John 11:35; Acts 8:2).

24:19–24 Such apparent indifference to bereavement was unsettling, but Ezekiel's neighbors infer that this bizarre behavior is for their "benefit" (v. 19). The desecration of the temple would be devastating and numbing, breaking the people's spirit, and exile would ensue. Here too is a rare glimpse of the social devastation of exile, as the corresponding losses for Ezekiel's fellow exiles will be **your sons and your daughters whom you left behind** (v. 21). The recognition formula (v. 24; cf. Introduction: Style) concludes the oracle.

24:25–27 *Fugitive News.* **As for you, son of man**. The final verses of this oracle are for Ezekiel himself, and continue the language of bereavement found in the preceding verses. The prophecy foretells the destruction of Jerusalem and the arrival of a **fugitive** (v. 26) bearing the news. Much like Zechariah's renewed speech at the birth of John the Baptist (Luke 1:64), Ezekiel's speech will be regained at this event, and again Ezekiel **will be a sign to them**, as he has been at the death of his beloved. This brief passage forges connections that span the book. Ezekiel's muteness began with the report in Ezek. 3:26; it will be released with the arrival of the fugitive in 33:21, when the oracles about Jerusalem resume following the foreign-nation oracles (25:1–32:32).

Prophecy Against Ammon

25 The word of the LORD came to me: 2 [w]"Son of man, [x]set your face toward [y]the
Ammonites and prophesy against them. 3 Say to the Ammonites, Hear the word
of the Lord GOD: [z]Thus says the Lord GOD, Because you said, [a]'Aha!' over my [b]sanctuary
when it was profaned, and over the land of Israel when it was made desolate, and over
the house of Judah when they went into exile, 4 therefore behold, I am handing you over
to [c]the people of the East for a possession, and they shall set their encampments among
you and make their dwellings in your midst. They shall eat your fruit, and they shall drink
your milk. 5 I will make [d]Rabbah a [e]pasture for camels and Ammon[1] [e]a fold for flocks.
[v]Then you will know that I am the LORD. 6 For thus says the Lord GOD: Because [f]you have
clapped your hands [g]and stamped your feet and [h]rejoiced with all the [i]malice within your
soul against the land of Israel, 7 therefore, behold, [j]I have stretched out my hand against
you, and [k]will hand you over as plunder to the nations. And I will cut you off from the
peoples and will make you perish out of the countries; I will destroy you. Then you will
know that I am the LORD.

Prophecy Against Moab and Seir

8 "Thus says the Lord GOD: Because [l]Moab and [m]Seir[2] said, 'Behold, the [n]house of Judah
is like all the other nations,' 9 therefore [l]I will lay open the flank of Moab from the cities,
from its cities on its frontier, the glory of the country, [o]Beth-jeshimoth, [p]Baal-meon, and
[q]Kiriathaim. 10 I will give it [r]along with the Ammonites [s]to the people of the East as a possession, [t]that the Ammonites may be remembered no more among the nations, 11 [l]and I
will execute judgments upon Moab. [u]Then they will know that I am the LORD.

Prophecy Against Edom

12 "Thus says the Lord GOD: Because [v]Edom acted revengefully against the house of Judah
and has grievously offended [w]in taking vengeance on them, 13 therefore thus says the Lord

[1] Hebrew *and the Ammonites* [2] Septuagint lacks *and Seir*

Chapter 25
2 [w]See ch. 2:1 [x]See ch. 6:2 [y]ch. 21:20, 28; See Jer. 49:1-6
3 [z]ch. 2:4; 3:11, 27 [a]ch. 26:2; 36:2 [b]See ch. 7:22
4 [c]Judg. 6:3
5 [d]2 Sam. 11:1; 12:26; See ch. 21:20 [e][Zeph. 2:15] [v][See ch. 24:27 above]
6 [f]Ps. 98:8; Isa. 55:12 [g][ch. 6:11] [h][Zeph. 2:8, 10] [i]ver. 15; ch. 36:5
7 [j]See ch. 6:14 [k][ver. 4; ch. 7:21]
8 [l]See Isa. 15:1-9; Jer. 48:1-47 [m]See ver. 12 [n]See Jer. 25:17-26
9 [l][See ver. 8 above] [o]Josh. 12:3 [p]1 Chr. 5:8 [q]See Jer. 48:1
10 [r]ver. 2 [s]ver. 4 [t]ch. 21:32
11 [l][See ver. 8 above] [u]See ch. 6:7
12 [v]ver. 8; ch. 32:29; 35:2, 5; 2 Chr. 28:17; Ps. 137:7; Isa. 21:11; 34:5; Amos 1:11, 12; See Jer. 49:7-22; Obad. 1-21 [w]ver. 15

25:1–32:32 *Oracles against Foreign Nations.* Poised at this moment in the dramatic downfall of Jerusalem, Ezekiel's tirade ends and the focus shifts. The fate of the city is left hanging as a collection of oracles against foreign nations is presented. While not all the oracles in this collection are dated, most seem to fall within the period 587–585 B.C. (for the exception, see 29:17). Almost every Prophetic Book includes prophecies addressed to nations other than Israel and Judah (e.g., Isaiah 13–23; Jeremiah 46–51; Amos 1–2; Zephaniah 2). Their primary theological role is to show that all peoples are under the dominion and discipline of the King of kings. Israel is uniquely God's own, yet all nations are subject to the one true God (cf. Amos 3:2; 9:7). The fate of every nation, whether for judgment or for blessing, is in God's hands. Implied hope for Israel is thus a secondary message of the condemnatory foreign-nation oracles. Further, the reasons for judgment found in the foreign and domestic oracles tend to cohere within a given book. In Ezekiel, just as Judah and Jerusalem are punished for impurity and oppression, so too are the foreign nations. However, Ezekiel often simply announces God's opposition to these nations without offering an explicit rationale. The oracles are arranged in three large sections: first, Judah's nearest neighbors are condemned (Ezekiel 25), followed by the extended collections of oracles against Tyre (chs. 26–28) and Egypt (chs. 29–32). Two smaller oracles—one against Sidon, the other looking to Israel's regathering—are embedded at the halfway point (28:20–26). In all, seven nations stand condemned.

25:1–17 *Against Judah's Neighbors.* Apart from the old northern kingdom of Israel to the north, Judah had four immediate neighbors. Clockwise, they were Ammon on the northeast (vv. 1–7), Moab to the east across the Dead Sea (vv. 8–11), Edom to the south (vv. 12–14), and Philistia to the west (vv. 15–17). The oracles against these nations group into two pairs. Excluding Philistia, but including Tyre and Sidon (chs. 26–28), these nations had been part of a coalition with Judah against Babylon early in Zedekiah's reign (see Jer. 27:3). Each of these oracles has a similar structure, with formulaic address and conclusion, as well as similar content: condemnation for contemptuous cruelty of heart toward Judah.

25:1–7 *Against Ammon.* Ammon and Moab fell to the Babylonians much later than Judah. Clearly, talk of "coalition" did nothing to help Judah's cause when the Babylonians overran it. Ammon receives two oracles, and the pattern is followed in the succeeding indictments: the basis of judgment is stated (**because**, Hb. *ya'an*), the outcome announced (**therefore**, Hb. *laken*), and the recognition formula follows by way of conclusion. The Ammon oracle, then, falls into two sections, with vv. 1–5 being more detailed than vv. 6–7.

25:3 The leading reason for judgment against Ammon is the insult they gave to **my sanctuary**—God's own reputation is of primary concern. While **land** (Hb. *'adamah*; see note on 7:2) **of Israel** is a common phrase in Ezekiel, **house of Judah** is not; it is used outside this chapter only at 4:6 and 8:17. "House of Israel," by contrast, is used 83 times in Ezekiel, well over half of its occurrences in the entire OT.

25:4 The agents of divine justice are **the people of the East**, that is, desert nomads. This both accounts for the description that follows, and implies the ironic insult that the people unconquered by mighty Babylon will fall to nomads.

25:6 This second oracle is linked to the first (**for**, or "because," Hb. *ki*) as a further indictment.

25:8–11 *Against Moab.* For structure and general features, see note on vv. 1–7. Although the indictment is very brief, the insult to God behind the belittling of Judah (v. 8) can still be discerned.

25:8 and Seir. This phrase, lacking in the Septuagint (see ESV footnote), is surprising here and may be the result of a copyist's error. Seir is consistently identified with Edom in the OT, but nowhere else with Moab. It is not mentioned in the judgment of vv. 9–11.

25:9 These place names are known from sources outside the Bible. Although not leading cities themselves, they form a direct line pointing to Dibon and Aroer in the Moabite heartland.

GOD, [x]I will stretch out my hand against Edom and cut off from it man and beast. And
I will make it desolate; from [y]Teman even to [z]Dedan they shall fall by the sword. 14 And
I will lay my vengeance upon Edom [a]by the hand of my people Israel, and they shall do
in Edom according to my anger and according to my wrath, and [b]they shall know my
vengeance, declares the Lord GOD.

Prophecy Against Philistia

15 "Thus says the Lord GOD: Because [c]the Philistines [d]acted revengefully and took vengeance [e]with malice of soul to destroy in never-ending enmity, 16 therefore thus says the
Lord GOD, [x]Behold, I will stretch out my hand against the Philistines, and I will cut off
[f]the Cherethites and destroy the rest of the seacoast. 17 I will execute great vengeance on
them [g]with wrathful rebukes. [h]Then they will know that I am the LORD, when I lay my
vengeance upon them."

Prophecy Against Tyre

26 [i]In the eleventh year, on the first day of the month, the word of the LORD came to
me: 2 [j]"Son of man, because [k]Tyre said concerning Jerusalem, [l]'Aha, the gate of the
peoples is broken; it has swung open to me. I shall be replenished, now that she is laid
waste,' 3 therefore thus says the Lord GOD: [m]Behold, I am against you, O Tyre, and will

13 [x]See ch. 6:14 [y]1 Chr. 1:45; Amos 1:12 [z]ch. 27:15, 20; 38:13; Isa. 21:13
14 [a]Amos 9:12; Obad. 18 [b][ver. 17]
15 [c]Jer. 25:20; 47:1; Joel 3:4; Amos 1:6; Zeph. 2:4; See Isa. 14:29-31 [d]ver. 12 [e]ver. 6; ch. 36:5
16 [x][See ver. 13 above] [f]See 1 Sam. 30:14
17 [g]ch. 5:15 [h][ver. 14]

Chapter 26

1 [i]See ch. 20:1
2 [j]See ch. 2:1 [k]See Isa. 23:1-18 [l]ch. 25:3; 36:2
3 [m]See ch. 13:8

25:10 For **people of the East**, see note on v. 4.

25:12–14 *Against Edom.* The intense hatred felt for **Edom** by later Judeans is amply attested in the OT, e.g., Ps. 137:7; Jer. 49:7–22; Lam. 4:21–22. In the OT, Edom often serves as the chief representative of hostility to God and his people. The accusation of **taking vengeance** (Ezek. 25:12) coheres with this wider picture. The locations of the cities **Teman** and **Dedan** are not certain, but the suggestion that they represent the extremities of Edom (**from . . . to**) makes good sense. Assigning **my people Israel** (v. 14) to be the agent of God's wrath is not paralleled elsewhere in Ezekiel, but it does have the ring of poetic justice against this traditional foe.

25:15–17 *Against Philistia.* Philistia had already been subdued by Nebuchadnezzar before the campaigns against Judah. It was thus not in a position to be part of the conspiracy planned in Zedekiah's day (see note on vv. 1–17). This oracle is very much an echo of the preceding one. The Cherethites (v. 16) were coastal dwellers, identified with the **Philistines** also in Zeph. 2:5. Use of their name also provides a pun on their punishment: in the phrase **cut off the Cherethites**, the verb and the proper noun both have the same three consonants (*k-r-t*) in their root (Hb. *wehikrati 'et-Keretim*).

26:1–28:19 *Oracles against Tyre.* The Tyre oracles are neatly divided into three large segments by the concluding refrain at 26:21, 27:36, and 28:19. With further subdivisions, there are seven units in all. This lengthy collection, surpassed only by the Egypt oracles, immediately raises the question, why so much about Tyre? The answer seems to be that, of the states addressed by Ezekiel, only Tyre and Egypt had the power to withstand Babylon: Egypt's power was military, Tyre's was economic. This latter factor is especially prominent in Ezekiel's oracles. Some have claimed that the Tyre oracles, especially ch. 26, are examples of unfulfilled prophecy. Ezekiel announces the devastation of Tyre at the hands of Nebuchadnezzar (26:7–13). Tyre eventually capitulated but was not destroyed, as Ezekiel eventually knew (29:17–20). How is this so-called "failure" of the prophetic word to be explained? Some recent interpreters have preferred to identify Alexander the Great's victory over Tyre in 332 B.C. with Ezekiel's prophecy. This interpretation is unsatisfactory, however, because it does not do justice to the expectation that *Babylon* would destroy Tyre (cf. 26:7). Others appeal to God's sovereign freedom, claiming he is able not only to carry out a threat but also to relent, as with Nineveh in Jonah 3. However, there is no suggestion that Tyre repented as did Nineveh, and this approach renders the interpretation of prophecy quite arbitrary. A third strategy lays emphasis on the element of promise rather than prediction: no matter the actual outcome, the real intent was to subject Tyre to God's sovereignty by the prophetic word. However, this reading is unsatisfactory in that it seems to render insignificant the details of Ezekiel's language. A further possibility is to read Ezekiel 26 along the lines suggested in ch. 16, that is, that metaphorical language should not be confused with literal. Since much of this prophecy is metaphorical, one should not look for literal fulfillment. Finally, it is also clear that biblical prophecy is not necessarily exhausted in a single historical horizon (cf. Jeremiah's 70 years [Jer. 25:12; Dan. 9:2, 20–27]). So too here, Tyre's initial reduction in Ezekiel's day (see note on Ezek. 26:1–21) was but the firstfruits of the unfolding of God's judgment on Tyre. The exposition here seeks to steer carefully through these difficulties.

26:1–21 *Against Tyre.* The prophet announces the destruction of Tyre at the hands of the Babylonians in four oracles grouped into two pairs, each linked by the Hebrew *ki* (vv. 7, 19; "for," "because"; see 25:6): 26:1–6 and 7–14 look toward Tyre being razed; vv. 15–18 and 19–21 stand imaginatively on the other side of destruction, depicting reactions to Tyre's demise. To the claim that the prophecies in ch. 26 were never fulfilled, the best answer recognizes that the prophecy against Tyre in vv. 3–14 is a complex one. It combines elements that would be fulfilled in the attack of Nebuchadnezzar (he besieged Tyre for 13 years, from 585–572 B.C., an attack described in vv. 7–11), and in the subsequent attack and conquest by Alexander the Great in 332 (this provides a fulfillment for the complete destruction predicted in vv. 3–6 and vv. 12–14). OT prophecies often contain different elements that are fulfilled in the near future and in the more distant future. In addition, some parts of ch. 26 were not even fulfilled until a time later than Alexander (see note on v. 14).

26:1–6 Apart from the date formula (see note on v. 1), this unit bears striking similarity to those of ch. 25 and thus serves as a "hinge" between that sequence on Judah's nearest neighbors (see note on 25:1–32:32) and this larger complex of Tyrian oracles. Like those nations, Tyre had been involved with the coalition referred to in Jer. 27:3, and now is censured for its insult to and exploitation of Jerusalem (Ezek. 26:2).

26:1 The date formula lacks the month, and so cannot be fixed with precision. It falls within the span of 587/586 B.C. According to Josephus, Nebuchadnezzar's siege against Tyre was launched around 586/585 B.C. and lasted 13 years (*Jewish Antiquities* 10.228).

26:3 The agents of destruction here are **many nations**, described metaphorically as the crashing of the **sea** and **its waves**. The description that follows continues this figurative language. This was fulfilled partially by the siege of Nebuchadnezzar, and then more fully in the conquest by Alexander the Great in 332 B.C. (see note on 26:1–28:19). Both Nebuchadnezzar and Alexander the Great led the military forces from "many nations" whom they had conquered. Nebuchadnezzar's title "king of kings" (26:7) reflected this reality and echoes historical records of Assyrian royal language. Alexander the Great, in attacking Tyre, had the help of 80 ships from Persia and 120 from Cyprus, in addition to soldiers from other nations.

bring up [n]many nations against you, [o]as the sea brings up its waves. 4 They shall destroy
the walls of Tyre and break down her towers, and I will scrape her soil from her and [p]make
her a bare rock. 5 She [q]shall be in the midst of the sea a place for the spreading of nets,
[r]for I have spoken, declares the Lord GOD. And she shall become plunder for the nations,
6 and her daughters on the mainland shall be killed by the sword. [s]Then they will know
that I am the LORD.

7 "For thus says the Lord GOD: [t]Behold, I will bring against Tyre [u]from the north
Nebuchadnezzar[1] king of Babylon, [v]king of kings, with horses and chariots, and with
horsemen and a host of many soldiers. 8 He will kill with the sword [w]your daughters on
the mainland. [x]He will set up a siege wall against you and throw up a mound against
you, and raise [y]a roof of shields against you. 9 [z]He will direct the shock of his battering
rams against your walls, and with his axes he will break down your towers. 10 His horses
will be so many that their dust will cover you. Your walls will shake at the noise of the
horsemen and wagons and chariots, when he enters your gates as men enter a city that
has been breached. 11 With the hoofs of his horses he will trample all your streets. He will
kill your people with the sword, and your mighty pillars will fall to the ground. 12 They
will plunder [a]your riches and loot [a]your merchandise. They will break down your walls
and destroy your pleasant houses. Your stones and timber and [b]soil they will cast into the
midst of the waters. 13 [c]And I will stop the music of your songs, and [d]the sound of your
lyres shall be heard no more. 14 [p]I will make you a bare rock. [q]You shall be a place for the
spreading of nets. You shall never be rebuilt, [r]for I am the LORD; I have spoken, declares
the Lord GOD.

15 "Thus says the Lord GOD to Tyre: Will not [e]the coastlands shake at the sound of your
fall, [f]when the wounded groan, when slaughter is made in your midst? 16 Then all [g]the
princes of the sea will step down from their thrones and [h]remove their robes and strip off
their embroidered garments. They will clothe themselves with trembling; [i]they will sit
on the ground and [j]tremble every moment and [k]be appalled at you. 17 And they will [l]raise
a lamentation over you and say to you,

"'How you have perished,
you who were inhabited from the seas,
O city renowned,
[m]who was mighty on the sea;
she and her inhabitants [n]imposed their terror
on all her inhabitants!
18 Now the coastlands tremble
on the day of your fall,
and the coastlands that are on the sea
are dismayed at your passing.'

[1] Hebrew *Nebuchadrezzar*, so throughout Ezekiel

3 [n][ch. 32:3; Jer. 34:1] [o][Lam. 2:13]
4 [p]ch. 24:7
5 [q]ch. 47:10 [r]See ch. 17:24
6 [s]See ch. 6:7
7 [t][ch. 29:18] [u]See Jer. 1:14 [v]Ezra 7:12; Dan. 2:37; [Hos. 8:10]
8 [w]ver. 6 [x]See ch. 4:2 [y][2 Kgs. 19:32]
9 [z]ch. 4:2; 21:22
12 [a]See ch. 27:12-24 [b]ver. 4
13 [c][Isa. 24:8; Jer. 7:34; 16:9] [d][Isa. 5:12; 23:16]
14 [p][See ver. 4 above] [q][See ver. 5 above] [r][See ver. 5 above]
15 [e]ch. 27:35 [f]Jer. 51:52
16 [g][Isa. 23:8] [h][Jonah 3:6] [i]Isa. 3:26 [j]ch. 32:10 [k]ch. 27:35
17 [l]ch. 19:1; 27:2, 32; [Rev. 18:9] [m][Isa. 23:4] [n]See ch. 32:23

26:4–5 The location of Tyre **in the midst of the sea**, often seen in extrabiblical sources as a sign of its security, is now described with derision (see also v. 17). In the conquests of Alexander the Great, Tyre was indeed destroyed and made like a **bare rock**.

26:6 Her daughters on the mainland are the villages on the mainland that were opposite the island city of Tyre. They were destroyed by Nebuchadnezzar and again by Alexander.

26:7–14 This oracle develops its briefer partner (vv. 2–6), adding specificity and concreteness to the imagery as its message is reinforced. Some repeated vocabulary contributes to their coherence ("walls" and "towers," vv. 4 and 9; "bare rock," vv. 4 and 14; "a place for the spreading of nets," vv. 5 and 14).

26:7 Nebuchadnezzar (II) of Babylon reigned 605–562 B.C.

26:8–10 Ezekiel's oracle includes many of the traditional elements of siege warfare, at the same time conjuring up much of its claustrophobia. **daughters**. See note on v. 6.

26:12 That Tyre's wealth should be subject to **plunder** is not only inevitable in ancient warfare, it is also poetic justice, given its gloating (v. 2). However, by the time that Nebuchadnezzar conquered Tyre, much of value had been removed by sea, and apparently little wealth remained after 13 years of siege (see 29:18). Later, Alexander the Great conquered Tyre by building a 2,600-foot (800-m) causeway from the mainland out to the island fortress, thus fulfilling the prophecy of this verse, **your stones and timber and soil they will cast into the midst of the waters**. (These materials came from the destruction of the city's settlements on the mainland, 26:6, 8.)

26:14 You shall never be rebuilt. Tyre was rebuilt and reconquered several times after Alexander the Great, so the complete fulfillment of this prophecy did not come immediately. The modern city of Tyre is of modest size and is near the ancient site, though not identical to it. Archaeological photographs of the ancient site show ruins from ancient Tyre scattered over many acres of land. No city has been rebuilt over these ruins, however, in fulfillment of this prophecy.

26:15–18 Off the island itself, the vantage point is now that of the mainland cities (cf. vv. 6, 8) as their princes mourn the downfall of formerly majestic Tyre. The lament itself appears in vv. 17–18, an outpouring of fear-induced

19[o][ver. 3; ch. 27:34]
20[p][ch. 31:14, 16; 32:18, 24] [q]ch. 32:23, 27, 32; Ps. 27:13
21[r]ch. 27:36; 28:19 [s][Ps. 37:36]
Chapter 27
2[t]See ch. 2:1 [u]See ch. 19:1
3[v][Isa. 23:1] [w][Isa. 23:3] [x]ch. 28:12
4[y]ver. 25, 27

19 "For thus says the Lord GOD: When I make you a city laid waste, like the cities that are
not inhabited, [o]when I bring up the deep over you, and the great waters cover you, 20 then
[p]I will make you go down with those who go down to the pit, to the people of old, and I
will make you to dwell in the world below, among ruins from of old, [p]with those who go
down to the pit, so that you will not be inhabited; but I will set beauty [q]in the land of the
living. 21 I will bring you [r]to a dreadful end, and you shall be no more. [s]Though you be
sought for, you will never be found again, declares the Lord GOD."

A Lament for Tyre

27 The word of the LORD came to me: 2 "Now you, [t]son of man, [u]raise a lamentation
over Tyre, 3 and say to Tyre, who dwells at [v]the entrances to the sea, [w]merchant of
the peoples to many coastlands, thus says the Lord GOD:

"O Tyre, you have said,
'I am [x]perfect in beauty.'
4 Your borders are [y]in the heart of the seas;
your builders made perfect your beauty.

grief. Laments feature prominently in the Tyre and Egypt oracles (cf. 27:1–36; 28:11–19; 32:1–32).

26:19–21 The final oracle anticipates the closing of the entire foreign-nation oracle collection, which bemoans the arrival of the nations in the underworld place of the dead (32:17–32; cf. Job 3:13–19). The repeated phrase **those who go down to the pit** (twice, Ezek. 26:20; see 32:18) refers to the state of those whom death has separated from communion with God (cf. Isa. 38:13).

27:1–36 *A Lament against Tyre.* This remarkable passage, the second installment of the Tyre series, is both simple and complex. Its simplicity lies in the unfolding narrative line, set in the form of a lament. Its complexity is in the wealth of detail and technical artistry displayed throughout. Tyre is likened to a merchant ship, whose fortunes are traced from the shipyards (vv. 4–7) and crew (vv. 8–11) to its tragic loss at sea (vv. 26–27) and the outcry its loss provokes (vv. 28–32a)—all culminating in a lament-within-a-lament (vv. 32b–36). A lengthy aside in the middle of the chapter (vv. 12–25) offers a sort of commercial litany, as Tyre's many trading partners and their wares are dolefully itemized (see map below). A striking feature of the lament, lending to its somber tone, is the complete lack of invective; nor is God mentioned

Tyre's International Trade
c. 587 B.C.
During Ezekiel's time, the city of Tyre had grown very wealthy due to its strategic island location in the middle of the ancient Near East. Tyre served as a sort of international commodities exchange for the surrounding nations, and Ezekiel's extensive list of various nations who traded or collaborated with Tyre (shown here) gives a glimpse of the city's great influence. Merchants from as far away as Persia, southern Arabia (including Sheba, etc.), and perhaps even Spain (a possible location of Tarshish) traded their goods there.

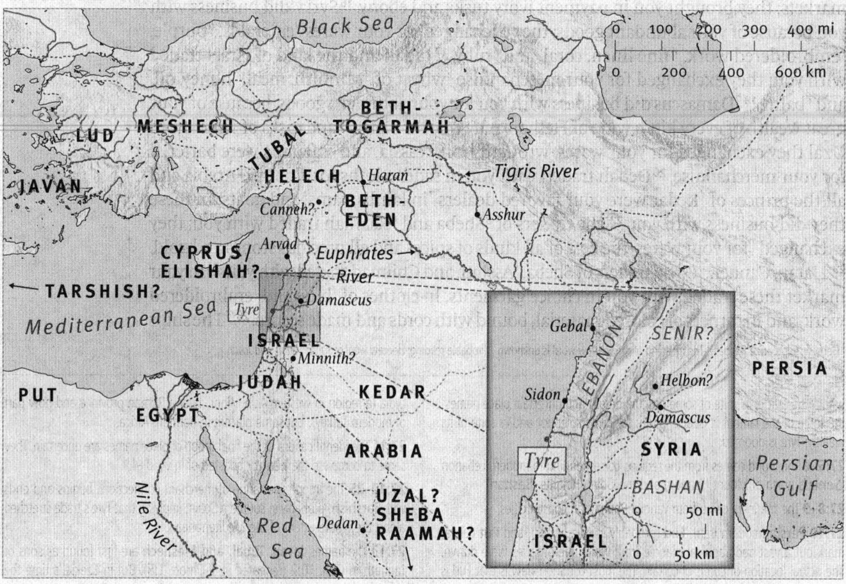

5 They made all your planks
  of fir trees from [z]Senir;
they took [a]a cedar from Lebanon
  to make a mast for you.
6 Of [b]oaks of Bashan
  they made your oars;
they made your deck of pines
  from [c]the coasts of Cyprus,
  inlaid with ivory.
7 [d]Of fine embroidered linen from Egypt
  was your sail,
  serving as your banner;
blue and purple from [c]the coasts of Elishah
  was your awning.
8 The inhabitants of Sidon and [e]Arvad
  were your rowers;
your skilled men, O Tyre, were in you;
  they were [f]your pilots.
9 The elders of [g]Gebal and her skilled men were in you,
  [h]caulking your seams;
all the ships of the sea with their mariners were in you
  to barter for your wares.

10 [i]“Persia and [j]Lud and [j]Put were in your army as your men of war. [k]They hung the
shield and helmet in you; they gave you splendor. 11 Men of [e]Arvad and Helech were on
your walls all around, and men of Gamad were in your towers. They hung their shields
on your walls all around; they made [x]perfect your beauty.
12 [l]“Tarshish did [m]business with you because of your great wealth of every kind; silver, iron, tin, and lead they exchanged for your [n]wares. 13 [o]Javan, [p]Tubal, and [p]Meshech
traded with you; they exchanged human beings and vessels of bronze for your merchandise. 14 From [q]Beth-togarmah they exchanged horses, war horses, and mules [r]for your
wares. 15 The men of [s]Dedan[1] traded with you. Many coastlands were your own special
markets; they brought you in payment ivory tusks and ebony. 16 Syria [t]did business with
you because of your abundant goods; they exchanged for your wares [u]emeralds, [u]purple,
[v]embroidered work, [w]fine linen, coral, and [x]ruby. 17 Judah and the land of Israel traded
with you; they exchanged for your merchandise [y]wheat of [z]Minnith, meal,[2] honey, oil,
and [a]balm. 18 [b]Damascus did business with you for your abundant goods, because of your
great wealth of every kind; wine of Helbon and [c]wool of Sahar 19 and casks of wine[3] from
Uzal they exchanged for your wares; wrought iron, [d]cassia, and [e]calamus were bartered
for your merchandise. 20 Dedan traded with you in saddlecloths for riding. 21 Arabia and
all the princes of [f]Kedar were your favored dealers [f]in lambs, rams, and goats; in these
they did business with you. 22 The traders of [g]Sheba and [g]Raamah traded with you; they
exchanged [h]for your wares [i]the best of all kinds of spices and all precious stones and gold.
23 [j]Haran, Canneh, [j]Eden, traders of Sheba, [k]Asshur, and Chilmad traded with you. 24 In your
market these traded with you in choice garments, in clothes of [l]blue and [l]embroidered
work, and in carpets of colored material, bound with cords and made secure. 25 [m]The ships

[1] Hebrew; Septuagint *Rhodes* [2] The meaning of the Hebrew word is unknown [3] Probable reading; Hebrew *wool of Sahar, Vedan, and Javan*

5 [z]Deut. 3:9 [a]Judg. 9:15
6 [b]See Isa. 2:13 [c]See Gen. 10:4
7 [d]See ch. 16:10 [c][See ver. 6 above]
8 [e]Gen. 10:18 [f]ver. 27, 29
9 [g]1 Kgs. 5:18; Ps. 83:7 [h]ver. 27
10 [i]ch. 38:5 [j]ch. 30:5; [Isa. 66:19; Jer. 46:9] [k][2 Sam. 8:7; Song 4:4]
11 [e][See ver. 8 above] [x][See ver. 3 above]
12 [l]ver. 25; ch. 38:13; See 1 Kgs. 10:22 [m]ver. 16, 18, 21 [n]ver. 14, 16, 19, 22
13 [o]Gen. 10:2 [p]ch. 32:26; 38:2; 39:1
14 [q]ch. 38:6; Gen. 10:3 [r]ver. 12
15 [s]Gen. 10:7; See ch. 25:13
16 [t]ver. 12 [u]ch. 28:13 [v]ver. 7 [w]1 Chr. 15:27; Job 28:18 [x]Isa. 54:12
17 [y]See 1 Kgs. 5:9, 11 [z]Judg. 11:33 [a]See Gen. 37:25
18 [b]Isa. 7:8; [ver. 16] [c]Rev. 1:14
19 [d]Ex. 30:24 [e][Ex. 30:23]
21 [f]Isa. 60:7
22 [g]ch. 38:13; Gen. 10:7 [h]ver. 12 [i]Ex. 30:23
23 [j]2 Kgs. 19:12 [k]Gen. 10:22
24 [l]ver. 7
25 [m]Ps. 48:7; Isa. 2:16; 23:14

within the oracle. In spite of some obscure details and uncertain place names, the force of the lament is clear enough: for all its splendor and in spite of its wealth, Tyre is doomed.

27:5–6 The wood comes from the regions corresponding to modern Lebanon (**Senir** is north of Mount Hermon) and the Golan Heights (**Bashan**).

27:8–9 The mariners came from various Phoenician coastal cities.

27:10 **Persia** (modern Iran), **Lud** (probably in Asia Minor), and **Put** (Libya) mark out a vast geographical triangle from which mercenaries were drawn. The actual location of Lud is uncertain. The most common view is that Lud is Lydia (a region in western Asia Minor, later a Roman province and now part of modern Turkey), but some place it in northern Africa.

27:11 The identifications of the final group of place names are uncertain. They serve to complete the **beauty** boasted of in vv. 3–4.

27:12–25 The impressive range of merchant connections begins and ends with **Tarshish**, probably in southern Spain, implying that Tyre's trade stretched along the whole extent of the Mediterranean.

27:13 The names **Javan, Tubal, and Meshech** are first found as sons of Japheth in Gen. 10:2 (repeated in 1 Chron. 1:5). But in Ezekiel's time the

25[n]See ver. 12 [o]ver. 4
26[p]See Jer. 18:17
27[q]ver. 8 [r]ver. 9 [s][ch. 26:18; 32:10]
28[t][ch. 45:2; 48:15, 17]
29[u][Rev. 18:17, 18]
30[u][See ver. 29 above] [v]Lam. 2:10; Rev. 18:19 [w]See Jer. 6:26
31[x]See Isa. 3:24
32[y]See ch. 19:1 [z][Rev. 18:18]
33[a][Rev. 18:15, 19]
34[b][ch. 26:19]
35[c]ch. 26:15, 16 [d][ch. 32:10]
36[e]Rev. 18:11 [f]See Jer. 18:16 [g]ch. 26:21; 28:19

of [n]Tarshish traveled for you with your merchandise. So you were filled and heavily laden [o]in the heart of the seas.

26 "Your rowers have brought you out
into the high seas.
[p]The east wind has wrecked you
in the heart of the seas.
27 Your riches, your wares, your merchandise,
your mariners and [q]your pilots,
[r]your caulkers, your dealers in merchandise,
and all your men of war who are in you,
with all your crew
that is in your midst,
sink into the heart of the seas
[s]on the day of your fall.
28 At the sound of the cry of your pilots
[t]the countryside shakes,
29 and down from their ships
[u]come all who handle the oar.
The mariners and all the pilots of the sea
stand on the land
30 [u]and shout aloud over you
and cry out bitterly.
[v]They cast dust on their heads
[w]and wallow in ashes;
31 they [x]make themselves bald for you
and put sackcloth on their waist,
and they weep over you in bitterness of soul,
with bitter mourning.
32 In their wailing they [y]raise a lamentation for you
and lament over you:
[z]'Who is like Tyre,
like one destroyed in the midst of the sea?
33 When your wares came from the seas,
[a]you satisfied many peoples;
with your abundant wealth and merchandise
[a]you enriched the kings of the earth.
34 Now [b]you are wrecked by the seas,
in the depths of the waters;
your merchandise and all your crew in your midst
have sunk with you.
35 [c]All the inhabitants of the coastlands
are appalled at you,
and [d]the hair of their kings bristles with horror;
their faces are convulsed.
36 [e]The merchants among the peoples [f]hiss at you;
[g]you have come to a dreadful end
and shall be no more forever.'"

names signified geographical regions, perhaps peopled by descendants of those men. The primary import of the names here is to signify the far-off places with which Tyre did business. More specifically, "Javan" (Hb. *Yawan*) was a collective OT name for Greece or the Greeks (the same Hb. term is translated "Greece" in Dan. 8:21; 10:20; 11:2; Zech. 9:13). "Tubal" refers to ancient Tabal, in what is now central Turkey (the province of Cappadocia in NT times). "Meshech" refers to a people known in Greek literature as the *Moschoi*, who settled in an area on the southeast edge of the Black Sea (the northeastern part of modern Turkey).

27:14 Beth-togarmah was located in the region of Carchemish and Harran.

27:32–36 The lament raised by the onlookers (vv. 28–29) offers a miniature version of the whole chapter: wealthy Tyre, who enriched the entire economy, has sunk, instilling fear in the watching nations.

Prophecy Against the Prince of Tyre

28 The word of the LORD came to me: 2 [h]"Son of man, say to [i]the prince of Tyre, Thus
says the Lord GOD:

[j]"Because your heart is proud,
and [k]you have said, 'I am a god,
I sit in the seat of the gods,
in the heart of the seas,'
yet [l]you are but a man, and no god,
[m]though you make your heart like the heart of a god—
3 [n]you are indeed wiser [o]than [p]Daniel;
no secret is hidden from you;
4 by your wisdom and your understanding
[q]you have made wealth for yourself,
and have gathered gold and silver
into your treasuries;
5 by your great wisdom in your trade
you have increased your wealth,
and [j]your heart has become proud in your wealth—
6 therefore thus says the Lord GOD:
[r]Because you make your heart
like the heart of a god,
7 therefore, behold, I will bring [s]foreigners upon you,
the most ruthless of the nations;
and they shall draw their swords against [t]the beauty of your wisdom
and defile [t]your splendor.
8 [u]They shall thrust you down into the pit,
[v]and you shall die the death of the slain
in the heart of the seas.
9 [w]Will you still say, 'I am a god,'
in the presence of those who kill you,
though [l]you are but a man, and no god,
in the hands of those who slay you?
10 [x]You shall die the death of the uncircumcised
by the hand of foreigners;
[y]for I have spoken, declares the Lord GOD."

A Lament over the King of Tyre

11 Moreover, the word of the LORD came to me: 12 [z]"Son of man, [a]raise a lamentation
over [b]the king of Tyre, and say to him, Thus says the Lord GOD:

Chapter 28
2 [h]See ch. 2:1 [i][ver. 12] [j][Rev. 18:7] [k][ver. 9] [l]Isa. 31:3 [m]ver. 6
3 [n][ver. 12; Zech. 9:2] [o]Dan. 1:17 [p]ch. 14:14
4 [q][Zech. 9:3]
5 [j][See ver. 2 above]
6 [r]ver. 2
7 [s]ver. 10; ch. 7:21; 30:12; 31:12 [t][ver. 17]
8 [u][ch. 32:18, 19] [v][ch. 32:20]
9 [w][ver. 2] [l][See ver. 2 above]
10 [x]ch. 31:18; 32:19, 21, 24, 25 [y]See ch. 17:24
12 [z]See ch. 2:1 [a]See ch. 19:1 [b][ver. 2]

28:1–19 *Against Tyre's King.* The final part of the Tyre oracles brings the movement of Tyre's hubris to a climax. While its pride was implied throughout ch. 26, and led to self-exaltation in ch. 27, here Tyre claims deity (28:2). Two distinct laments are presented: vv. 1–10 assail the pride of Tyre's king; vv. 11–19 present him as a primordial being fallen from grace. In neither case does a particular king seem to be in view; rather, Tyre is personified through its monarch. Tyre's wealth is constantly in view, as it has been throughout chs. 26–27, intrinsically bound up with its opposition to God.

28:1–10 Although cast in lament form, the structure of this oracle takes the familiar pattern of grounds of indictment (vv. 2b–6) and outcome (vv. 7–10) with a formulaic conclusion. Pride is at the center of the charge, reinforced by the repetition of the word "heart" (Hb. *leb* or *lebab*), used eight times in the span of vv. 2–8.

28:2 The king of Tyre is designated **prince** (Hb. *nagid*). It could simply be a stylistic variation for "king" (cf. Ps. 76:12, where it is a poetic parallel to "kings"). If it has further value beyond a simple designation for a national leader, this term could imply a divinely appointed, charismatic leader as it does in older Hebrew usage. If so, it further emphasizes the hubris of this figure.

28:3 On **Daniel**, see note on 14:14, 20.

28:4–5 Trade and commerce were the foundation of Tyre's wealth, but then that wealth led Tyre to become proud, which led to aspirations to deity.

28:6 The entire **because . . . therefore** structure (vv. 2, 7) is distilled in this single "hinge" verse.

28:7–8 Here the agents of divine punishment are unnamed **foreigners**, elsewhere identified with the Babylonians (26:7; 29:18; cf. 30:10–11). For descent to the **pit**, cf. 26:19–21.

28:11–19 The final anti-Tyre oracle adds a plethora of detail. As in ch. 27, there is no indictment (like in 28:1–10) but rather a narrative lament culminating in inevitable doom. The imagery is kaleidoscopic. Tyre is likened to a second Adam, clearly a created being (vv. 13, 15) and yet a "cherub" (v. 14). It is in the "garden of God" in v. 13, and on the "mountain of God" in vv. 14 and 16. Some would see v. 17 as a poetic allusion, wherein Ezekiel likens the downfall of the proud king of Tyre to the fall and curse on Satan in Gen. 3:1–15. At minimum, the extravagant pretensions of Tyre are graphically and poetically portrayed (cf. note on Ezek. 28:4–5), along with the utter devastation inflicted upon Tyre as a consequence (vv. 18–19).

12[c][ver. 3] [d]ch. 27:3
13[e]ch. 31:8, 9; See Isa. 51:3 [f][ch. 27:16] [g]Rev. 4:3; 21:19, 20 [i]ver. 15
14[j]Ex. 25:20; 1 Kgs. 8:7 [k][ch. 20:40]
15[l]ver. 13
16[m][ver. 5] [k][See ver. 14 above] [j][See ver. 14 above]
17[n]ver. 2, 5 [o][ver. 7]
18[p][ch. 30:8, 14, 16; Rev. 18:8] [q][ver. 17]
19[r]ch. 26:21; 27:36
21[s]See ch. 2:1 [t]See ch. 6:2 [u]See Isa. 23:2

"You were the signet of perfection,[1]
[c]full of wisdom and [d]perfect in beauty.
13 You were in [e]Eden, the garden of God;
[f]every precious stone was your covering,
[g]sardius, topaz, and diamond,
beryl, onyx, and jasper,
sapphire,[2] [f]emerald, and carbuncle;
and crafted in gold were your settings
and your engravings.[3]
[i]On the day that you were created
they were prepared.
14 You were an anointed [j]guardian cherub.
I placed you;[4] you were on [k]the holy mountain of God;
in the midst of the stones of fire you walked.
15 You were blameless in your ways
[l]from the day you were created,
till unrighteousness was found in you.
16 In the abundance of [m]your trade
you were filled with violence in your midst, and you sinned;
so I cast you as a profane thing from [k]the mountain of God,
and I destroyed you,[5] [j]O guardian cherub,
from the midst of the stones of fire.
17 [n]Your heart was proud because of [o]your beauty;
you corrupted your wisdom for the sake of your splendor.
I cast you to the ground;
I exposed you before kings,
to feast their eyes on you.
18 By the multitude of your iniquities,
in the unrighteousness of your trade
you profaned your sanctuaries;
so [p]I brought fire out from your midst;
it consumed you,
and I turned you to ashes on the earth
[q]in the sight of all who saw you.
19 All who know you among the peoples
are appalled at you;
[r]you have come to a dreadful end
and shall be no more forever."

Prophecy Against Sidon

20 The word of the LORD came to me: 21 [s]"Son of man, [t]set your face toward [u]Sidon, and
[t]prophesy against her 22 and say, Thus says the Lord GOD:

[1] The meaning of the Hebrew phrase is uncertain [2] Or *lapis lazuli* [3] The meaning of the Hebrew phrase is uncertain [4] The meaning of the Hebrew phrase is uncertain [5] Or *banished you*

28:13 Putting Tyre in **Eden, the garden of God,** forges a link with Genesis 2–3, but avoids connecting pagan Tyre with "the garden of Yahweh," as in Gen. 13:10 and Isa. 51:3. Some of the precious stones in this difficult list cannot be identified with confidence. It parallels similar lists in Exodus of the composition of the breastpiece of the priestly garments (see Ex. 28:17–20; 39:10–13).

28:14 As a **guardian cherub,** Tyre is like the cherubim guarding Eden (Gen. 3:24) rather than the "living creatures" seen in Ezekiel 1–3 and 8–11, who are throne-bearers.

28:15–16 Tyre was **blameless**, as was Job (Job 1:1; 12:4). But **trade**, coupled with **violence**, triggers the downfall of this previously admirable creature; see also Ezek. 28:18.

28:18 The priestly allusions are further developed as the **sanctuaries** are **profaned**.

28:20–23 *Oracle against Sidon.* Sidon is often mentioned alongside Tyre (e.g., Jer. 25:22; 47:4; Joel 3:4; Zech. 9:2), an association that survived into NT times (e.g., Matt. 11:21–22; Luke 10:13–14). This brief oracle is, on one hand, reminiscent of the collection in Ezekiel 25 (cf. 25:1–2 and 28:20–21) and continues the geographical sequence begun there. On the other hand, it contains no accusation against Sidon, but simply announces divine opposition to it.

28:22 Behold, I am against you will also be the opening formula in the Egypt oracles (29:3), forming a link to the following collection. Concern for

"Behold, [v]I am against you, O Sidon,
and [w]I will manifest my glory in your midst.
And [x]they shall know that I am the LORD
[y]when I execute judgments in her
and [z]manifest my holiness in her;
23 for I will send [a]pestilence into her,
and blood into her streets;
and the slain shall fall in her midst,
by the sword that is against her on every side.
Then they will know that I am the LORD.

24 "And for the house of Israel [b]there shall be no more a brier to prick or [c]a thorn to hurt them among all their neighbors [d]who have treated them with contempt. Then they will know that I am the Lord GOD.

Israel Gathered in Security

25 "Thus says the Lord GOD: [e]When I gather the house of Israel from the peoples among whom they are scattered, and [z]manifest my holiness in them in the sight of the nations, [f]then they shall dwell in their own land that I gave to my servant Jacob.
26 [g]And they shall dwell securely in it, and they shall build houses and plant vineyards. They shall dwell securely, [h]when I execute judgments upon all their neighbors [d]who have treated them with contempt. [x]Then they will know that I am the LORD their God."

Prophecy Against Egypt

29 [i]In the tenth year, in the tenth month, on the twelfth day of the month, the word of the LORD came to me:
2 [j]"Son of man, [k]set your face against [l]Pharaoh king of Egypt, [m]and prophesy against him and [n]against all Egypt;
3 speak, and say, Thus says the Lord GOD:

[o]"Behold, I am against you,
Pharaoh king of Egypt,
[p]the great dragon that lies
in the midst of his streams,

22 [v]See ch. 13:8 [w]ch. 39:13; [Ex. 14:4, 17, 18] [x]See ch. 6:7 [y]ver. 26 [z]See ch. 20:41
23 [a]ch. 38:22
24 [b]Num. 33:55; Josh. 23:13 [c][2 Cor. 12:7] [d]ch. 16:57
25 [e]See ch. 11:17 [z][See ver. 22 above] [f]ch. 36:28; 37:25
26 [g]Jer. 23:6; 32:37 [h]ver. 22 [d][See ver. 24 above] [x][See ver. 22 above]

Chapter 29

1 [i]See ch. 20:1
2 [j]See ch. 2:1 [k]See ch. 6:2 [l]ch. 32:2 [m]See ch. 6:2 [n]See Isa. 19:1
3 [o]See ch. 13:8 [p]ch. 32:2; Ps. 74:13, 14; Isa. 27:1; 51:9

God's **glory** and **holiness** picks up the underlying theme of ch. 25 (see note on 25:3).

28:23 This trio of **pestilence**, **blood**, and **sword** is characteristic of Ezekiel.

28:24–26 *Israel Gathered in Security.* Strategically, this hopeful note is struck precisely at the halfway point in the collection of foreign-nation oracles. Verses 24 and 26 make explicit what is sometimes implicit and often simply absent from foreign oracles: the subduing of God's enemies will result in the well-being of God's own people. Since "scattering" is one of the primary judgments on Israel (e.g., Lev. 26:33; Deut. 28:64), "gathering" (Ezek. 28:25) is one of God's distinctive saving responses (cf. Deut. 30:3), a theme to be repeated throughout the latter part of Ezekiel's book. The peaceful settlement in a bountiful land (Ezek. 28:26) anticipates the prophecy of the "covenant of peace" (34:25–30).

29:1–32:32 *Oracles against Egypt.* The seventh and last of the nations to be addressed, Egypt (like Tyre) receives seven oracles, clarified structurally by the date formula that heads all but one of them (30:1 is the exception). The Egypt oracles equal in bulk the rest of the collection in chs. 25–28. If the chief interest in Tyre was economic, the leading issue for Egypt is military power. As seen in chs. 17 and 19, Egypt was still closely bound up with Judean affairs at this time. The Egyptian king during the period covered by these oracles was Hophra (reigned 589–570 B.C.), named in the OT only in Jer. 44:30. His aspirations over this region were instrumental in fomenting Zedekiah's rebellion against Babylon. This accounts both for the belief that Judeans fleeing Babylonian reprisals would find safety in Egypt (Jeremiah 42–43) and Ezekiel's condemnation of Egypt's opposition to the Babylonians, who wielded the sword of the Lord's wrath.

29:1–16 *Against Pharaoh.* The two leading charges against Egypt come out clearly in this initial trio of oracles. Verses 1–6a portray the hubris of Egypt putting itself in the place of God, while vv. 6b–9a condemn it for its part in the destruction of Judah. The third section returns to the charge of hubris and subjects Egypt in a more extended way to the retributive hand of God. The date of these prophecies in v. 1, under which these oracles are gathered, equates to January 587 B.C., just after Babylon laid siege to Jerusalem, and after Hophra came to power in Egypt. In several prophecies, including this one, God shows Ezekiel what was happening hundreds of miles away (see note on 24:2).

29:1–6a Ezekiel delivered this oracle against **Pharaoh king of Egypt**, soon after Hophra ascended the throne (in 589 B.C.).

29:3 The confrontational formula, **Behold, I am against you**, also appears at 28:22, there addressed to Sidon, the last nation to be dealt with before Egypt (see also 26:3). The figure of the **dragon** takes Ezekiel's language to the boundary between the natural and supernatural realms. At one level, this is a symbolic name for the crocodile in the Nile (also 32:2), but at another level it represents a cosmic creature opposed to the rule of God and defeated by him (e.g., Ps. 74:13; Isa. 27:1; 51:9). The claim to be the maker of the Nile amounts to arrogation of divinity (cf. Tyre; Ezek. 28:2).

29:4–5 hooks in your jaws. The judgments against Pharaoh match the metaphorical framework of the accusation ("great dragon . . . in the midst of his streams"; v. 3).

29:6b–9a The second accusation is cast in the familiar **because . . . therefore** (Hb. *ya'an . . . laken*) form seen often in Ezekiel. A river-related metaphor is again used; this time, however, Egypt is the **staff of reed** (i.e., a useless staff made from a flimsy reed) that treacherously fails to give support. In all likelihood this metaphor relates to the events narrated in Jer. 37:5–11 and echoes the taunt hurled against Hezekiah's Jerusalem by the Assyrians (2 Kings 18:21).

29:9b–16 A brief **because** section (v. 9b) repeats the accusation against Egypt in v. 3 before a much longer and literal judgment speech (vv. 10–16).

3[q]ver. 9
4[r]ch. 19:9; 38:4; 2 Kgs. 19:28
5[s][ch. 32:4, 5] [t]Jer. 9:22 [u]See Jer. 8:2
6[v]See ch. 6:7 [w]2 Kgs. 18:21; Isa. 36:6
7[x][ch. 17:17; Isa. 20:5; 30:3, 5; Jer. 2:36; 37:5, 7]
8[y]See ch. 14:17
9[v][See ver. 6 above] [z]ver. 3; See ch. 13:8
10[z][See ver. 9 above] [a][ch. 30:12] [b]ch. 30:6
11[c]ch. 32:13; [ch. 35:7]
12[d]ch. 30:7 [e]ch. 30:23, 26; [Jer. 46:19]
13[f][Isa. 19:22, 23; Jer. 46:26]
14[g][ch. 39:25] [h]ch. 30:14; See Isa. 11:11
15[i][ch. 30:13]
16[j][Isa. 30:2, 3; 36:4, 6; Lam. 4:17] [k]ver. 6; See ch. 6:7
17[l]See ch. 20:1
18[m]See ch. 2:1 [n][ch. 26:7]
19[o]ch. 30:10, 24, 25; 32:11; Jer. 46:13

[q]that says, 'My Nile is my own;
I made it for myself.'
4 I will [r]put hooks in your jaws,
and make the fish of your streams stick to your scales;
and I will draw you up out of the midst of your streams,
with all the fish of your streams
that stick to your scales.
5 [s]And I will cast you out into the wilderness,
you and all the fish of your streams;
you shall fall [t]on the open field,
and [u]not be brought together or gathered.
To the beasts of the earth and to the birds of the heavens
[s]I give you as food.

6 Then all the inhabitants of Egypt [v]shall know that I am the LORD.
"Because you[1] have been [w]a staff of reed to the house of Israel, **7** [x]when they grasped you
with the hand, you broke and tore all their shoulders; and when they leaned on you, you
broke and made all their loins to shake.[2] **8** Therefore thus says the Lord GOD: [y]Behold, I
will bring a sword upon you, and will cut off from you man and beast, **9** and the land of
Egypt shall be a desolation and a waste. [v]Then they will know that I am the LORD.
[z]"Because you[3] said, 'The Nile is mine, and I made it,' **10** therefore, [z]behold, I am against
you and [a]against your streams, and [a]I will make the land of Egypt an utter waste and desolation, [b]from Migdol to Syene, as far as the border of Cush. **11** [c]No foot of man shall pass
through it, and no foot of beast shall pass through it; it shall be uninhabited forty years.
12 [d]And I will make the land of Egypt a desolation in the midst of desolated countries, and
her cities shall be a desolation forty years among cities that are laid waste. [e]I will scatter
the Egyptians among the nations, and disperse them through the countries.
13 "For thus says the Lord GOD: At the end of forty years [f]I will gather the Egyptians
from the peoples among whom they were scattered, **14** and [g]I will restore the fortunes of
Egypt and bring them back to [h]the land of Pathros, the land of their origin, and there
they shall be a lowly kingdom. **15** It shall be the most lowly of the kingdoms, [i]and never
again exalt itself above the nations. And I will make them so small that they will never
again rule over the nations. **16** And it shall never again be [j]the reliance of the house of
Israel, recalling their iniquity, when they turn to them for aid. [k]Then they will know that
I am the Lord GOD."
17 [l]In the twenty-seventh year, in the first month, on the first day of the month, the word
of the LORD came to me: **18** [m]"Son of man, [n]Nebuchadnezzar king of Babylon made his
army labor hard against Tyre. Every head was made bald, and every shoulder was rubbed
bare, yet neither he nor his army got anything from Tyre to pay for the labor that he had
performed against her. **19** Therefore thus says the Lord GOD: [o]Behold, I will give the land

[1] Hebrew *they* [2] Syriac (compare Psalm 69:23); Hebrew *to stand* [3] Hebrew *he*

The judgment has typical elements in vv. 10–12 that coincide with those leveled against Israel and Judah themselves. That Egypt should also be favored with restoration (vv. 13–16) is more surprising, but not unparalleled (see Jer. 46:26; cf. Jer. 48:47; 49:6, 39). Restored Egypt will, however, be cured of its hubris (Ezek. 29:14–15). Isaiah describes a future even farther off, with the Egyptians brought to knowing the true God (Isa. 19:18–25).

29:10–11 The **desolation** of Egypt, which lasts **forty years**, strikes at the assumption that the annual inundations of the Nile that supported Egypt guaranteed its perpetual well-being. The location of **Migdol** is unknown, but together with **Syene** (Aswan) it bounds Egypt north and south. **Cush** is the region roughly corresponding to modern Ethiopia. Most interpreters think this "forty years" does not refer to any specific period of time but is a symbolic number showing the parallel to the wandering of Israel in the wilderness for 40 years, or just symbolizing the completeness of God's judgment. Some interpreters have taken it to refer to the period when Egypt was under Babylonian rule from 568 to 525 B.C. (see note on v. 19).

29:14 Ancient Egyptian tradition located its national origins in the region of the Upper Nile where **Pathros** is located. The reference suggests that Ezekiel was well informed of Egyptian lore. Jewish mercenaries had been in the region for many years. Judean refugees fled there with Jeremiah (Jer. 44:15).

29:15 they will never again rule over the nations. Egypt never rebuilt the empire it once had.

29:17–21 *Nebuchadnezzar and Egypt.* This is the latest-dated oracle in the book, coming in April 571 B.C. Nebuchadnezzar's siege of Tyre had ended with Tyre intact, albeit subject to the Babylonians, who had little to show for 13 years of effort. (On this episode, see note on 26:1–28:19.) The concluding remark in 29:20 that **they worked for me** (i.e., Babylon was doing the Lord's work in besieging Tyre), emphasizes the point of view running through Ezekiel's foreign-nation oracles: opposition to Nebuchadnezzar's Babylon was opposition against the agents of God's wrath. Thus the **labor** they expended (v. 18) was to be rewarded with **wages** (v. 19) provided by God, but now coming from **Egypt** (v. 20).

29:19 I will give the land of Egypt to Nebuchadnezzar king of Babylon. This prophecy was given in 571 B.C. (see note on vv. 17–21), and Nebuchadnezzar conquered Egypt in 568 (this is described in detail

of Egypt to Nebuchadnezzar king of Babylon; [p]and he shall carry off its wealth[1] [q]and
despoil it and plunder it; and it shall be the wages for his army. 20 [r]I have given him the
land of Egypt as his payment for which he labored, because they worked for me, declares
the Lord GOD.

21 "On that day [s]I will cause a horn to spring up for the house of Israel, and [t]I will open
your lips among them. [u]Then they will know that I am the LORD."

A Lament for Egypt

30 The word of the LORD came to me: 2 [v]"Son of man, prophesy, and say, Thus says
the Lord GOD:

[w]"Wail, 'Alas for the day!'
3 [w]For the day is near,
[x]the day of the LORD is near;
it will be [y]a day of clouds,
a time of doom for[2] the nations.

[1] Or *multitude* [2] Hebrew lacks *doom for*

19 [p]ch. 30:4 [q]ch. 32:12
20 [r][Isa. 43:3]
21 [s]Ps. 132:17; [Luke 1:69] [t]ch. 24:27; 33:22; [ch. 16:63] [u]See ch. 6:7

Chapter 30

2 [v]See ch. 2:1 [w]See Isa. 13:6
3 [w][See ver. 2 above] [x]ch. 7:7, 12; Joel 1:15; 2:1; Zeph. 1:7 [y]ch. 34:12

in Jeremiah 43–44 and also recorded in Josephus, *Jewish Antiquities* 10.180–182). Egypt was subsequently subject to Persian rule (beginning in 525 B.C.), was conquered by Alexander the Great and made part of his empire in 332, and was conquered by the Romans and became part of the Roman Empire in 31.

29:21 The final note of promise appears to be for Ezekiel himself. The phrase **open your lips** does not relate to Ezekiel's muteness (which would have ended years earlier than the events foretold here; see 33:21–22). Rather, it affirms that, after all those years, Ezekiel's prophetic ministry was to be vindicated.

30:1–19 *Lament for Egypt.* The third of the seven anti-Egypt oracles is the only one undated, and it contains no written basis for dating. It is comprised of four relating prophecies, each introduced by **Thus says the Lord** (vv. 2, 6, 10, 13) and each echoing motifs and ideas seen elsewhere in Ezekiel's oracles. Together they announce the fall not only of Egypt but also of her allies, and again by the hand of Nebuchadnezzar (v. 10). Much like in the Tyre oracle in ch. 27, there is no specific charge brought against Egypt here; rather, God's judgment is simply pronounced. See map below.

30:2–5 The cry of **the day** (v. 2) and the announcement that **the day is near** (v. 3) point to the "day of the LORD" concept, developed in 7:10–27 (see notes there). The bare announcement of the day of the LORD finds its counterpart in the **time . . . for the nations**, explained almost at once as a time **of doom**. Ezekiel combines this motif with the "sword of the Lord" in a subtle way at 21:8–10, but here the connection is overt with the reference to the **sword** in 30:4.

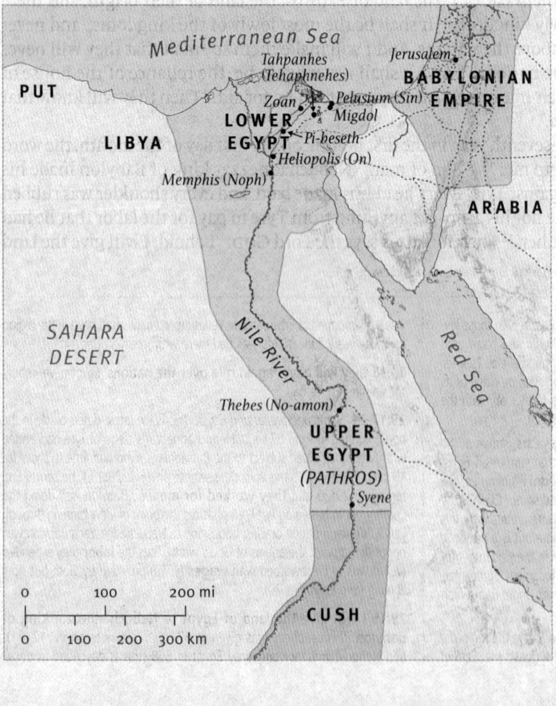

Ezekiel Prophesies against Egypt
c. 571 B.C.

Ezekiel prophesied that even the great nation of Egypt and its allies would fall to the Babylonians, who already occupied the land of Israel and Judah. The rule of the Babylonians would eventually extend as far as the borders of Cush, referred to elsewhere as Ethiopia. None of the great cities of Egypt would be spared Babylon's wrath.

4 [z]A sword shall come upon Egypt,
[a]and anguish shall be in [b]Cush,
when the slain fall in Egypt,
and [c]her wealth[1] is carried away,
and [d]her foundations are torn down.

5 [b]Cush, and [e]Put, and Lud, and [f]all Arabia, and Libya,[2] and the people of the land that is
in league,[3] shall fall with them by the sword.

6 "Thus says the LORD:
[g]Those who support Egypt shall fall,
and [h]her proud might shall come down;
[i]from Migdol to Syene
they shall fall within her by the sword,
declares the Lord GOD.
7 [j]And they shall be desolated in the midst of desolated countries,
and their cities shall be in the midst of cities that are laid waste.
8 [k]Then they will know that I am the LORD,
when [l]I have set fire to Egypt,
and [g]all her helpers are broken.

9 "On that day [m]messengers shall go out from me in ships to terrify the unsuspecting
[b]people of Cush, and [a]anguish shall come upon them on the day of Egypt's doom;[4] for,
behold, it comes!

10 "Thus says the Lord GOD:

[n]"I will put an end to the wealth of Egypt,
by the hand of Nebuchadnezzar king of Babylon.
11 He and his people with him, [o]the most ruthless of nations,
shall be brought in to destroy the land,
[z]and they shall draw their swords against Egypt
and fill the land with the slain.
12 And [p]I will [q]dry up the Nile
and will sell the land into the hand of [r]evildoers;
[s]I will bring desolation upon the land and everything in it,
by the hand of [t]foreigners;
[u]I am the LORD; I have spoken.

13 "Thus says the Lord GOD:

[v]"I will destroy the idols
and put an end to the images in [w]Memphis;
[x]there shall no longer be a prince from the land of Egypt;
so [y]I will put fear in the land of Egypt.
14 I will make [z]Pathros a desolation
and will set fire to [a]Zoan

4 [z]ch. 29:8 [a][Isa. 21:3] [b][Isa. 43:3] [c]ch. 29:19 [d][ver. 6]
5 [b][See ver. 4 above] [e]See ch. 27:10 [f]See Jer. 25:20
6 [g][ch. 32:21] [h]ver. 18; [ch. 33:28] [i]ch. 29:10
7 [j]ch. 29:12
8 [k]ch. 29:6; See ch. 6:7 [l][ch. 28:18] [g][See ver. 6 above]
9 [m][Isa. 18:1, 2] [b][See ver. 4 above] [a][See ver. 4 above]
10 [n]See ch. 29:19
11 [o]See ch. 28:7 [z][See ver. 4 above]
12 [p]Isa. 19:5, 6; [ch. 29:10] [q][ch. 29:3] [r][Isa. 19:4] [s][ch. 29:10] [t]See ch. 28:7 [u]See ch. 17:24
13 [v]See Jer. 43:12 [w]Isa. 19:13 [x][ch. 29:15; Zech. 10:11] [y][Isa. 19:16]
14 [z]ch. 29:14; See Isa. 11:11 [a]See Num. 13:22

[1] Or *multitude*; also verse 10 [2] With Septuagint; Hebrew *Cub* [3] Hebrew *and the sons of the land of the covenant* [4] Hebrew *the day of Egypt*

30:4–5 On **Cush**, see 29:10. **Put** refers to the same region as **Libya**; for it and **Lud**, see note on 27:10. The Hebrew underlying **Arabia** (*'Ereb*) literally means "mixed peoples." This geographical survey anticipates the central thrust of the next unit.

30:6–9 Here the allies of Egypt come into focus. They shall share the same fate as their master. On **Migdol to Syene**, see 29:10. The language of desolation also forges a link back to 29:8, 10.

30:10–12 The explicit identification of **Nebuchadnezzar** and the Babylonians as the agents of God's wrath links to 29:17–20, although it is likely that this unit comes from an earlier period. Likewise, the drying up of the **Nile** (30:12) links back to 29:9b–12.

30:13–19 The knowledge of Egypt demonstrated in 29:14 is seen in this unit's plethora of place names, often compared to Mic. 1:10–15. To each place is joined a facet of the judgment to fall upon it. This litany of divine actions amounts to a comprehensive rejection of Egyptian religion and politics. There is no clear geographical organization to the list, but where information is available, the judgments appear to be appropriate to the place. **Memphis** (Ezek. 30:13, 16) was the capital of Lower Egypt, south of the Nile delta. On **Pathros** (v. 14), see 29:14. **Zoan** (30:14), **Pelusium** (vv. 15–16), and **Tehaphnehes** (v. 18) were in the northeastern delta, with Pelusium being a strategic fortress at the border with the Sinai. **Thebes** (vv. 14–16) was capital of Upper Egypt, thus holding great symbolic value. **On** and **Pi-beseth** (v. 17) were in the southeastern delta, near the land of Goshen, the location of the sojourn of the people of Israel before the exodus (Gen. 45:10). Some of the judgments (Ezek. 30:18) provide allusions to the exodus plagues.

[b]and will execute judgments on [c]Thebes.
15 And I will pour out my wrath on Pelusium,
the stronghold of Egypt,
and cut off the multitude[1] of Thebes.
16 And I will set fire to Egypt;
Pelusium shall be in great agony;
Thebes shall be breached,
and [w]Memphis shall face enemies[2] by day.
17 The young men of On and of Pi-beseth shall fall by the sword,
and the women[3] shall go into captivity.
18 At [d]Tehaphnehes [e]the day shall be dark,
when I break there the yoke bars of Egypt,
and [f]her proud might shall come to an end in her;
she shall be covered by a cloud,
and her daughters shall go into captivity.
19 Thus [g]I will execute judgments on Egypt.
[h]Then they will know that I am the LORD."

Egypt Shall Fall to Babylon

20 [i]In the eleventh year, in the first month, on the seventh day of the month, the word of
the LORD came to me: 21 [j]"Son of man, [k]I have broken the arm of Pharaoh king of Egypt,
and behold, [l]it has not been bound up, to heal it by binding it with a bandage, so that
it may become strong to wield the sword. 22 Therefore thus says the Lord GOD: Behold,
I am against Pharaoh king of Egypt and [m]will break his arms, both the strong arm and
the one that was broken, and I will make the sword fall from his hand. 23 [n]I will scatter
the Egyptians among the nations and disperse them through the countries. 24 And [o]I will
strengthen the arms of the king of Babylon and put [p]my sword in his hand, but I will
break the arms of Pharaoh, and he will groan before him [q]like a man mortally wounded.
25 I will strengthen the arms of the king of Babylon, but the arms of Pharaoh shall fall.
[r]Then they shall know that I am the LORD, [s]when I put my sword into the hand of the
king of Babylon and he stretches it out against the land of Egypt. 26 And I will scatter the
Egyptians among the nations and disperse them throughout the countries. Then they
will know that I am the LORD."

Pharaoh to Be Slain

31 [t]In the eleventh year, in the third month, on the first day of the month, the word
of the LORD came to me: 2 [u]"Son of man, say to Pharaoh king of Egypt and to [v]his
multitude:

[w]"Whom are you like in your greatness?
3 Behold, [x]Assyria was a [y]cedar in [z]Lebanon,
with beautiful branches and [a]forest shade,

[1] Or *wealth* [2] Or *distress* [3] Or *the cities;* Hebrew *they*

14 [b]ver. 19 [c]Jer. 46:25
16 [w][See ver. 13 above]
18 [d]See Jer. 2:16 [e][Jer. 15:9; Amos 8:9] [f]ver. 6
19 [g]ver. 14 [h]See ch. 6:7
20 [i]See ch. 20:1
21 [j]See ch. 2:1 [k][Jer. 48:25] [l][Jer. 30:13; 46:11]
22 [m]See ver. 21
23 [n]ch. 29:12
24 [o]ver. 10 [p]See ch. 21:3 [q]Job 24:12
25 [r]See ch. 6:7 [s][ver. 8]

Chapter 31

1 [t]See ch. 20:1
2 [u]See ch. 2:1 [v][ch. 29:19; 30:4; 32:12, 16, 20, 31, 32] [w][ver. 18; ch. 32:19]
3 [x][Isa. 10:34]; See Dan. 4:10, 20-22 [y]See Judg. 9:15 [z][ver. 15, 16] [a][ch. 17:23]

30:17 The Hebrew text has only a feminine pronoun ("they"), and the ESV supplies the referent as **women**, anticipating the ending of v. 18; it could also be "cities," which is grammatically feminine (see ESV footnote).

30:20–26 *The Kings of Egypt and Babylon.* The dates return in this fourth Egypt oracle, locating this unit in April 587 B.C. This oracle contrasts the weakness of Hophra's forces with the might of Babylon. The direct confrontation between these kings has been announced in v. 10. The **sword** (vv. 21–22) will **fall** from the **hand** of Hophra, but Nebuchadnezzar wields the sword of the Lord (v. 24; cf. 29:11, 19). Again, the king of Babylon does God's work (29:20).

30:23 scatter . . . and disperse (see also v. 26). This language appeared in 29:12. The fear of dispersion is one of the most deep-seated in the OT (e.g., Gen. 11:4; cf. Ezek. 28:24–26).

31:1–18 *The Fall of Pharaoh.* Ezekiel's fifth oracle against Egypt dates to June 587 B.C., thus only a few weeks after the preceding unit. Here the prophet points to Assyria as an object lesson to Egypt. In its dying days, the once-mighty Assyrian Empire looked to Egypt for help against the mounting power of Babylon (c. 610 B.C.). Even together they could not withstand the Babylonian onslaught. That had been a mere 23 years earlier, well within living memory. In Isaiah's prophecies, given earlier still, Assyria—pride personified—was chopped down by the axe of the Lord (Isa. 10:5–19). This, the prophet says, is the fate awaiting Egypt. The motif of the "cosmic tree" that harbors the nations in its branches uses elements from ancient mythology, much as does the oracle of Tyre in the "garden of God" (see Ezek. 28:11–19).

31:2 The notice of **Pharaoh** and **his multitude** is repeated in v. 18b, but there as a statement rather than an address. Likewise, the rhetorical question in v. 2b is posed again and expanded in v. 18a. This provides an effective frame around the intervening verses.

31:3 Some find the reference to **Assyria** problematic, expecting rather immediate application to Egypt. However, the text is stable and clear, and there

3[b][Isa. 10:33]
4[c][ch. 17:7]
5[d][Dan. 4:11] [e]ch. 17:5; [Ps. 1:3]
6[f]ch. 17:23; Dan. 4:12, 21
7[g][ver. 2] [e][See ver. 5 above]
8[h][Amos 2:9] [i]ch. 28:13; [ver. 16, 18]
9[j]See Isa. 51:3
10[k][ver. 3] [l]Dan. 5:20; [Isa. 10:12]
12[m]See ch. 28:7 [n][ch. 32:5] [o][ch. 6:3] [p][Dan. 4:14]
13[q]ch. 32:4
14[r][ver. 5] [s][ver. 16, 18; ch. 26:20; 32:18, 24] [t]Ps. 63:9
15[u][ch. 32:18, 21; Isa. 14:9, 10]
16[v][ch. 26:15]

[b]and of towering height,
its top among the clouds.[1]
4 The waters nourished it;
the deep made it grow tall,
making [c]its rivers flow
around the place of its planting,
sending forth its streams
to all the trees of the field.
5 So [d]it towered high
above all the trees of the field;
its boughs grew large
and its branches long
from [e]abundant water in its shoots.
6 [f]All the birds of the heavens
made their nests in its boughs;
under its branches all the beasts of the field
gave birth to their young,
and under its shadow
lived all great nations.
7 It was [g]beautiful in its greatness,
in the length of its branches;
[e]for its roots went down
to abundant waters.
8 [h]The cedars [i]in the garden of God could not rival it,
nor the fir trees equal its boughs;
neither were the plane trees
like its branches;
no tree [i]in the garden of God
was its equal in beauty.
9 I made it beautiful
in the mass of its branches,
and all the trees of [j]Eden envied it,
that were in the garden of God.

10 "Therefore thus says the Lord GOD: Because [k]it[2] towered high and set its top among
the clouds, and [l]its heart was proud of its height, 11 I will give it into the hand of a mighty
one of the nations. He shall surely deal with it as its wickedness deserves. I have cast it out.
12 [m]Foreigners, [m]the most ruthless of nations, have cut it down and left it. [n]On the mountains and in all the valleys its branches have fallen, and its boughs have been broken in all
[o]the ravines of the land, and [p]all the peoples of the earth have gone away from its shadow
and left it. 13 [q]On its fallen trunk dwell all the birds of the heavens, and on its branches
are all the beasts of the field. 14 [r]All this is in order that no trees by the waters may grow
to towering height or set their tops among the clouds, and that no trees that drink water
may reach up to them in height. For they are all given over to death, [s]to the world [t]below,
among the children of man,[3] with those who go down to the pit.

15 "Thus says the Lord GOD: On the day [u]the cedar[4] went down to Sheol I caused mourning; I closed the deep over it, and restrained its rivers, and many waters were stopped. I
clothed Lebanon in gloom for it, and all the trees of the field fainted because of it. 16 [v]I

[1] Or *its top went through the thick boughs*; also verses 10, 14 [2] Syriac, Vulgate; Hebrew *you* [3] Or *of Adam* [4] Hebrew *it*

is no support from the ancient translations for suggested textual corrections (which are themselves not free from interpretative problems).

31:8–9 The **garden of God** is mentioned three times. As in 28:13 (see note), this garden is identified with **Eden** (also 31:16, 18). **I** (God) **made it beautiful**, leaving no room for self-exaltation (v. 9).

31:10–14 Pride precedes the fall, here brought about by the agency of a **mighty one of the nations** (v. 11), paralleled by the **most ruthless of nations** (v. 12), elsewhere a cryptic code for Babylon (28:7). Those who once prospered in Egypt's **shadow** now languish on its remains; no longer is it able to sustain life. The closing mention of **those who go down to the pit** (cf. 26:19–21) provides a bridge into the next paragraph.

31:15–17 While the judgment entailed in these verses echoes the content of those immediately preceding, the attention to **Sheol** (the place of the dead) prepares the way for the longer reflection on this theme in 32:17–32.

made the nations quake at the sound of its fall, [u]when I cast it down to Sheol with those
who go down to the pit. [w]And all the trees of Eden, the choice and best of Lebanon, all that
drink water, [x]were comforted in the world below. 17 They also went down to Sheol with
it, [y]to those who are slain by the sword; yes, [z]those who were its arm, [a]who lived under
its shadow among the nations.

18 [b]"Whom are you thus like in glory and in greatness [w]among the trees of Eden? [c]You
shall be brought down with [w]the trees of Eden to the world below. [d]You shall lie among
the uncircumcised, [y]with those who are slain by the sword.

[b]"This is Pharaoh and all his multitude, declares the Lord GOD."

A Lament over Pharaoh and Egypt

32 [e]In the twelfth year, in the twelfth month, on the first day of the month, the word
of the LORD came to me: 2 [f]"Son of man, [g]raise a lamentation over [h]Pharaoh king
of Egypt and say to him:

"You consider yourself [i]a lion of the nations,
  but you are like [j]a dragon [k]in the seas;
[l]you burst forth in your rivers,
  trouble the waters with your feet,
  and foul their rivers.
3 Thus says the Lord GOD:
  [m]I will throw my net over you
  with a host of [n]many peoples,
  and [o]they will haul you up in my dragnet.
4 And [p]I will cast you on the ground;
  on the open field I will fling you,
and will cause all the birds of the heavens to settle on you,
  and I will gorge the beasts of the whole earth with you.
5 I will strew your flesh [q]upon the mountains
  and fill the valleys with your carcass.[1]
6 I will drench the land even to the mountains
  with your flowing blood,
  and the ravines will be full of you.
7 [r]When I blot you out, [s]I will cover the heavens
  and make their stars dark;
I will cover the sun with a cloud,
  and the moon shall not give its light.
8 All the bright lights of heaven
  will I make dark over you,
  and [t]put darkness on your land,
    declares the Lord GOD.

9 "I will trouble the hearts of many peoples, when I bring your destruction among the
nations, into the countries that you have not known. 10 [u]I will make many peoples appalled
at you, and the hair of their kings shall bristle with horror because of you, when [v]I brandish

[1] Hebrew *your height*

16 [u][See ver. 15 above] [w]ver. 9; [Isa. 14:8] [x][ch. 32:31]
17 [y]ch. 32:20, 21; 35:8 [z][ch. 30:5, 6, 8] [a][ver. 6]
18 [b][ver. 2] [w][See ver. 16 above] [c][Matt. 11:23; Luke 10:15] [d]ch. 28:10; 32:19, 21, 24, 25, 28 [y][See ver. 17 above]

Chapter 32

1 [e]See ch. 20:1
2 [f]See ch. 2:1 [g]See ch. 19:1 [h]ch. 29:2 [i]ch. 19:3, 5, 6; 38:13 [j]ch. 29:3 [k][Isa. 18:2] [l][ver. 14; Jer. 46:8]
3 [m]See ch. 12:13 [n][ch. 26:3] [o][ch. 29:4]
4 [p][ch. 29:5]
5 [q][ch. 31:12]
7 [r][Isa. 14:12] [s][Isa. 13:10; Joel 2:31; Matt. 24:29; Mark 13:24, 25]
8 [t][Ex. 10:21; Isa. 5:30]
10 [u][ch. 27:35] [v][1 Chr. 21:16]

31:18 Pharaoh . . . multitude. See note on v. 2.

32:1–16 *Lament over Pharaoh.* Like the preceding oracle, this one is firmly bounded by a repeated element, the call to "lament" (vv. 2, 16)—although the poetic form itself is not strongly marked by this genre. The poem turns on the identification of Pharaoh as a "dragon" (v. 2), recalling 29:3 (see note). It is followed by two pronouncements of divine activity, one in 32:3–10, which develops the metaphorical world of the "dragon," and the second in vv. 11–15, which more briefly and literally applies divine judgment to Egypt.

32:1 The date formula corresponds to March 585 B.C., placing it some time after the fall of Jerusalem and its defining moment in Ezekiel at 33:21, breaking the book's chronological sequence in order to follow the thematic gathering of the foreign-nation oracles into a single collection.

32:2 Egypt may fancy itself a **lion**, a self-delusion like that in 29:3, but it is a **dragon**, the cosmic beast being associated with the Nile's crocodile (again, see 29:3). In the verses that follow, the cosmic and natural elements intermingle, although the metaphorical language predominates.

32:3–6 Slaying the monster affects the entire landscape. The gorging of the **birds** and **beasts** in v. 4 is a stage beyond settling on the remains of the "cosmic tree" in 31:13.

32:7–8 The "cosmic" scope of the language is obvious in these heavenly effects of the dragon's death. The **darkness on your land** again provides allusions to the exodus story (cf. 30:13–19; also Ex. 10:21–23).

32:9–10 The political dimension is introduced. The more literal language, along with the reference to **my sword**, provides a transition to the second unit.

10[w]ch. 26:16; [Deut. 28:66]
11[x][ch. 29:8, 19]; See Jer. 46:26
12[y]See ch. 31:2 [z]See ch. 28:7 [a]ch. 29:19
13[b]ch. 29:11
14[c][ver. 2]
15[d][ch. 12:19] [e][Ex. 7:5]; See ch. 6:7
16[f][ver. 2] [g]See ch. 31:2
17[h]See ch. 20:1
18[i]See ch. 2:1 [j][ver. 2] [g][See ver. 16 above] [k][ch. 26:20; 31:16] [l]See ch. 31:14
19[m][ch. 31:2, 18] [n]ver. 32; See ver. 28-30
20[o]ch. 31:17, 18 [p]See ch. 31:2
21[q]Isa. 14:9, 10 [r][ch. 30:6, 8] [s]ch. 28:10; 31:18 [o][See ver. 20 above]
22[t][ver. 24, 26, 29, 30] [u]ver. 25, 26
23[v]Isa. 14:15 [w]ver. 24, 25, 26, 27; [ch. 26:17] [x]Ps. 27:13
24[y]Isa. 11:11; See Jer. 49:34-39 [z][ver. 22] [a]ver. 20 [b]ver. 18; See ch. 31:14 [c]ver. 25, 30; ch. 16:52, 54; 36:7; 44:13; [ch. 34:29; 36:6; 39:26]
25[d][Isa. 30:33] [e][ver. 22]

my sword before them. [w]They shall tremble every moment, every one for his own life, on the day of your downfall.

11 "For thus says the Lord GOD: [x]The sword of the king of Babylon shall come upon
you. **12** I will cause [y]your multitude to fall by the swords of mighty ones, all of them [z]most
ruthless of nations.

[a]"They shall bring to ruin the pride of Egypt,
and all its multitude[1] shall perish.
13 I will destroy all its beasts
from beside many waters;
[b]and no foot of man shall trouble them anymore,
nor shall the hoofs of beasts trouble them.
14 Then [c]I will make their waters clear,
and cause their rivers to run like oil,
declares the Lord GOD.
15 When I make the land of Egypt desolate,
and when the land [d]is desolate of all that fills it,
when I strike down all who dwell in it,
then [e]they will know that I am the LORD.

16 [f]This is a lamentation that shall be chanted; the daughters of the nations shall chant it;
over Egypt, and over [g]all her multitude, shall they chant it, declares the Lord GOD."

17 [h]In the twelfth year, in the twelfth month,[2] on the fifteenth day of the month, the
word of the LORD came to me: **18** [i]"Son of man, [j]wail over [g]the multitude of Egypt, and
[k]send them down, her and the daughters of majestic nations, [l]to the world below, to those
who have gone down to the pit:

19 [m]'Whom do you surpass in beauty?
Go down and [n]be laid to rest with the uncircumcised.'

20 They shall fall amid those [o]who are slain by the sword. Egypt[3] is delivered to the sword;
drag her away, and [p]all her multitudes. **21** The mighty chiefs [q]shall speak of them, [r]with
their helpers, out of the midst of Sheol: 'They have come down, they lie still, [s]the uncircumcised, [o]slain by the sword.'

22 [t]"Assyria is there, and all her company, [u]its graves all around it, all of them slain, fallen
by the sword, **23** whose graves are set in [v]the uttermost parts of the pit; and her company
is all around her grave, all of them slain, fallen by the sword, [w]who spread terror [x]in the
land of the living.

24 [y]"Elam is [z]there, and all her multitude around her grave; all of them [a]slain, fallen by
the sword, who went down uncircumcised into [b]the world below, who spread their terror in the land of the living; and [c]they bear their shame [b]with those who go down to the
pit. **25** [d]They have made her a bed among the slain with all her multitude, [e]her graves all

[1] Or *wealth* [2] Hebrew lacks *in the twelfth month* [3] Hebrew *She*

32:11–13 Yet again the agent of God's punishment is identified as the **king of Babylon** (v. 11), once again bearing the **sword** of the Lord (v. 10). Here, the demise of Egypt provides an opportunity for nature to recover from its corrupting influence, with the "waters" and "rivers" of v. 14 pointing back to the initial picture drawn in v. 2.

32:16 The closing verse of the oracle also connects with v. 2, providing a literary envelope for the whole oracle.

32:17–32 *Egypt's Descent to the Pit.* The seventh and final oracle against Egypt—and the last of the entire foreign-nation oracle collection—returns to a theme introduced briefly in an oracle on the sinking of Tyre in 26:20, and already used against Egypt in 31:14, 16. In a grand finale, all the nations are gathered together in **the pit** (32:18), in **Sheol**, the place of the dead. Egypt joins them there, Pharaoh receiving cold comfort from the welcome he receives (v. 31). Ezekiel is instructed to **wail** (v. 18), not to "lament," so this dirge lacks the poetic structure of the lament genre. After a leading rhetorical question, which serves as a thematic superscription, Egypt's reception in Sheol is described in terms of the "welcoming party"—five nations already languishing there. In drawing the nations together in this place over which God alone has power, Ezekiel again demonstrates God's sovereignty, poised at this juncture of the book when Judah's own death seems assured.

32:17 This oracle occurs two weeks later than the previous one (**fifteenth day**; cf. "first day," v. 1).

32:19 The rhetorical question with its implied irony alludes to Tyre's proud claim in 27:3, but is framed in a way similar to the question posed to Egypt in 31:2b. The Egyptians practiced circumcision, thus their place with the **uncircumcised** would be cause for deep shame.

32:22–23 Assyria is the chief of the slain (cf. ch. 31), but in the **uttermost parts** of the pit. Ezekiel's Sheol knows gradations of shame, and Assyria's appears to be the deepest.

32:24–25 Elam, in modern terms bordering southern Iraq to the east, was not at this time a notable political power. Its inclusion may be to mark a remote eastern edge of the nations gathered.

around it, all of them uncircumcised, slain by the sword; for terror of them was spread in
the land of the living, and they bear their shame with those who go down to the pit; they
are placed among the slain.
26 [f]"Meshech-Tubal is [e]there, and all her multitude, [e]her graves all around it, all of them
uncircumcised, slain by the sword; for they spread their terror in the land of the living.
27 And [g]they do not lie with the mighty, the fallen from among the uncircumcised, who
went down to Sheol with their weapons of war, whose swords were laid under their heads,
and whose iniquities are upon their bones; for the terror of the mighty men was in the
land of the living. 28 But as for you, you shall be broken [h]and lie among the uncircumcised,
with those who are slain by the sword.
29 [i]"Edom is [j]there, her kings and all her princes, who for all their might are laid with
those who are killed by the sword; they lie with the uncircumcised, with those who go
down to the pit.
30 "The princes [k]of the north are there, all of them, and all the [l]Sidonians, who have gone
down in shame with the slain, [m]for all the terror that they caused by their might; they lie
uncircumcised with those who are slain by the sword, and [n]bear their shame with those
who go down to the pit.
31 "When Pharaoh sees them, he [o]will be comforted for [p]all his multitude, Pharaoh and
all his army, slain by the sword, declares the Lord GOD. 32 [q]For I spread terror [r]in the land
of the living; and he shall be laid to rest among [s]the uncircumcised, with those who are
slain by the sword, Pharaoh and all his multitude, declares the Lord GOD."

Ezekiel Is Israel's Watchman

33 The word of the LORD came to me: 2 [t]"Son of man, speak to [u]your people and say
to them, If [v]I bring the sword upon a land, and the people of the land take a man
from among them, and make him their [w]watchman, 3 and if he sees the sword coming
upon the land and [x]blows the trumpet and warns the people, 4 then if anyone who hears
the sound of the trumpet does not take warning, and the sword comes and takes him
away, [y]his blood shall be upon his own head. 5 [z]He heard the sound of the trumpet and
did not take warning; his blood shall be upon himself. But if he had taken warning, he
would have saved his life. 6 [a]But if the watchman sees the sword coming and does not
blow the trumpet, so that the people are not warned, and the sword comes and takes any
one of them, [a]that person is taken away in his iniquity, but his blood I will require at the
watchman's hand.
7 [b]"So you, [t]son of man, I have made a watchman for the house of Israel. [b]Whenever you
hear a word from my mouth, you shall give them warning from me. 8 [c]If I say to the wicked,
O wicked one, you shall surely die, [c]and you do not speak to warn the wicked to turn from
his way, [c]that wicked person shall die in his iniquity, but his blood I will require at your
hand. 9 [d]But if you warn the wicked to turn from his way, and he does not turn from his
way, [d]that person shall die in his iniquity, [e]but you will have delivered your soul.

26 [f]See ch. 27:13 [e][See ver. 25 above]
27 [g][Isa. 14:18, 19]
28 [h]ch. 28:10; 31:18
29 [i]See ch. 25:12-14 [j][ver. 22]
30 [k][ch. 38:6; 39:2] [l]ch. 28:21; See Isa. 23:2 [m]ver. 23 [n]See ver. 24
31 [o][ch. 31:16] [p]See ch. 31:2
32 [q][ver. 10] [r]ver. 23 [s]ver. 21, 27

Chapter 33

2 [t]See ch. 2:1 [u]ver. 12, 17, 30; ch. 3:11; 37:18 [v]See ch. 14:17 [w][Mic. 7:4]
3 [x][Amos 3:6]
4 [y]ch. 18:13; See ch. 3:18
5 [z][ch. 3:19]
6 [a][ch. 3:18]
7 [b]See ch. 3:17 [t][See ver. 2 above]
8 [c]ver. 6
9 [d][ver. 4] [e]ch. 3:19; [1 Tim. 4:16]

32:26–27 Not . . . with the mighty implies that residence in Sheol includes distinctions of shame and honor (cf. note on 32:22–23).

32:28 The focus of the mourning returns briefly to address Egypt directly.

32:29–30 Edom (v. 29; see 25:12–14) and the **Sidonians** (32:30; see 28:20–23) were Judah's near neighbors to the southeast and northwest respectively.

32:31–32 The oracle returns full circle (cf. vv. 18–21), affirming Pharaoh's destiny.

33:1–39:29 *After the Fall of Jerusalem.* Following the central collection of foreign-nation oracles, the focus returns to Judah (or "the house of Israel" in Ezekiel's preferred phrase). Before Jerusalem's fall, warning and doom dominated Ezekiel's message—although hints of hope were not absent. In the wake of Jerusalem's destruction (33:21–22), the balance is reversed. With false hopes shattered, Ezekiel's oracles now point to the true source and proper shape of life renewed. This reorientation is not an abrupt "about face" but rather a gradual turning that revisits the realities of life under judgment while building toward the solid promise of a renewed and permanent relationship of life with God.

33:1–20 *Reminders.* On the brink of hope, there is a brief pause to forge links back to chs. 1–24, and to remind Ezekiel and his audience of their mutual responsibilities: 33:1–9 again describes the role of the prophet in terms of the "watchman" seen also in 3:16–21; 33:10–20 offers a different edition of the teaching on individual responsibility seen in 18:21–29.

33:1–9 *The Watchman (Reprise).* See also 3:16–21. God, prophet, and people are inextricably bound together in these verses. The role of the **watchman** (33:2, 6, 7) dominates. He must act on what he **sees** (vv. 3, 6). Yet v. 2 frames the parable of vv. 2–6 about the **land** itself, and the whole oracle (vv. 2–9) is addressed **to your people**. They are responsible to attend to the watchman's warnings (vv. 4–5). The watchman must exercise vigilance to discern the actions of God (**If I bring the sword . . . and if he sees**, vv. 2–3), but God himself speaks the divine word to the prophet (v. 7). Verses 7–9 are almost identical to 3:17–19.

33:2 On God's own **sword**, cf. 21:3 and the context there.

10 [f]See ch. 2:1 [g]See ch. 4:17 [h][ch. 37:11; Isa. 49:14]
11 [i]See ch. 16:48 [j]See ch. 18:23 [k]ch. 18:31
12 [t][See ver. 2 above] [l]See ver. 2 [m][ver. 18]; See ch. 18:24 [n][2 Chr. 7:14]
13 [m][See ver. 12 above]
14 [o]ch. 3:18 [p][Gen. 2:17] [q]See ch. 18:27
15 [r]ch. 18:7 [s]Lev. 6:2, 4, 5; [Luke 19:8] [t]See ch. 20:11
16 [u]ch. 18:22
17 [l][See ver. 12 above] [v]ch. 18:25, 29
18 [w][ver. 12, 13; See ch. 18:26]
19 [x]ch. 18:27; [ver. 11, 12]
20 [y]See ch. 18:30
21 [z]See ch. 20:1 [a]ch. 40:1; See ch. 1:2 [b]ch. 24:26 [c]ch. 40:1; [ch. 26:2]; See 2 Kgs. 25:2-11
22 [d]ch. 24:26, 27 [e]See ch. 1:3
24 [f]See ch. 2:1 [g][ch. 36:4] [h]Isa. 51:2; [Acts 7:5] [i][Matt. 3:9; Luke 3:8]
25 [j][Gen. 9:4; Lev. 3:17] [k]ch. 18:6 [l]See ch. 22:3
26 [m][Gen. 27:40] [n]ch. 22:11
27 [o]See ch. 16:48 [p][ch. 36:4] [q][ch. 14:21]

Why Will You Die, Israel?

10 “And you, [f]son of man, say to the house of Israel, Thus have you said: ‘Surely our
transgressions and our sins are upon us, and [g]we rot away because of them. [h]How then can
we live?’ **11** Say to them, [i]As I live, declares the Lord GOD, [j]I have no pleasure in the death
of the wicked, but that the wicked turn from his way and live; [k]turn back, turn back from
your evil ways, [k]for why will you die, O house of Israel?
12 [t]“And you, son of man, say to [l]your people, [m]The righteousness of the righteous shall
not deliver him when he transgresses, [n]and as for the wickedness of the wicked, he shall
not fall by it when he turns from his wickedness, [m]and the righteous shall not be able to
live by his righteousness[1] when he sins. **13** Though I say to the righteous that he shall surely
live, yet [m]if he trusts in his righteousness and does injustice, none of his righteous deeds
shall be remembered, but in his injustice that he has done he shall die. **14** Again, [o]though I
say to the wicked, [p]‘You shall surely die,’ yet [q]if he turns from his sin and does what is just
and right, **15** if the wicked [r]restores the pledge, [s]gives back what he has taken by robbery,
and walks [t]in the statutes of life, not doing injustice, he shall surely live; he shall not die.
16 [u]None of the sins that he has committed shall be remembered against him. He has done
what is just and right; he shall surely live.
17 “Yet [l]your people say, [v]‘The way of the Lord is not just,’ when it is their own way that
is not just. **18** [w]When the righteous turns from his righteousness and does injustice, he
shall die for it. **19** And [x]when the wicked turns from his wickedness and does what is just
and right, he shall live by this. **20** Yet you say, ‘The way of the Lord is not just.’ O house of
Israel, [y]I will judge each of you according to his ways.”

Jerusalem Struck Down

21 In the [z]twelfth year [a]of our exile, in the tenth month, on the fifth day of the month,
[b]a fugitive from Jerusalem came to me and said, [c]“The city has been struck down.” **22** [d]Now
[e]the hand of the LORD had been upon me the evening before the fugitive came; and he
had opened my mouth by the time the man came to me in the morning, so my mouth
was opened, and I was no longer mute.
23 The word of the LORD came to me: **24** [f]“Son of man, the inhabitants of these [g]waste
places in the land of Israel keep saying, [h]‘Abraham was only one man, yet he got possession
of the land; but [i]we are many; the land is surely given us to possess.’ **25** Therefore say to them,
Thus says the Lord GOD: [j]You eat flesh with the blood and [k]lift up your eyes to your idols
and [l]shed blood; shall you then possess the land? **26** [m]You rely on the sword, [n]you commit
abominations, and [n]each of you defiles his neighbor’s wife; shall you then possess the land?
27 Say this to them, Thus says the Lord GOD: [o]As I live, surely those who are in [p]the waste
places shall fall by [q]the sword, and whoever is in the open field I will give to [q]the beasts

[1] Hebrew *by it*

33:10–20 *Moral Responsibility (Reprise).* As the reminders continue, the emphasis falls on the people. This passage parallels that of 18:19–29 (see the notes there), which concluded with a call to repentance (18:30–32). Here, no such call is issued. But the following oracle represents the most important juncture in the prophet’s ministry.

33:11 I have no pleasure in the death of the wicked. The Bible is clear that God will punish sin and vindicate his holiness and justice. At the same time, God feels sorrow over the punishment and death of creatures created in his image.

33:17 your people say, “The way of the Lord is not just.” When people do wrong, they are quick to complain about God rather than admitting their own sin.

33:21–22 *The Fall of Jerusalem.* This brief notice has an importance out of proportion to its size. It provides the hinge on which the main structure of the book turns. The readers, and Ezekiel, have had preparation for this precise moment: Ezekiel’s muteness was first encountered in 3:22–27, and a marker had been put down when the siege of Jerusalem began (24:1–2, 25–27). The date is now January 585 B.C., about five months after the fall of the city. The arrival of the **fugitive** confirms the word spoken at the beginning of the siege (24:25–27), affirms Ezekiel’s prophetic ministry, and establishes the work of God in bringing it about. It also gives weight to the words that follow.

33:23–33 *Culpability.* Although the movement toward restoration has begun, words from the LORD are castigating Judeans at home (vv. 23–29) and abroad (vv. 30–33) regarding ungodly living.

33:23–29 *A Word for the Homelanders.* Those left in Judah after its fall are addressed. The scenarios described (vv. 24–26) overlap with those listed in ch. 18. The connection is appropriate. Chapter 18 challenges the notion that ancestry ensures (or prohibits) blessing, and the claim confronted here, in part, is that “paternity” implies possession. Rather, the desolation of the land (33:27–29) is directly linked to the people’s own abominations.

33:24 The patriarchs (Abraham, Isaac, and Jacob) are rarely mentioned by the prophets. For this invocation of **Abraham**, cf. Isa. 41:8; 51:2. The Judeans’ “logic” of arguing from the **one** to the **many** here is deeply flawed. On possession of land at this time, see also Jer. 39:10.

33:25–26 On this catalog of crimes, cf. notes on 18:5–18. **You eat flesh with the blood**. The Hebrew is literally “you eat over the blood,” an idiom used also in Lev. 19:26. The reference is to illicit sacrifice. Ezekiel’s rhetorical questions (**shall you then possess the land?**) imply the terms of the covenant that the homelanders have seemingly forgotten.

to be devoured, and those who are in [r]strongholds and in caves shall die by [q]pestilence.
28 [s]And I will make the land a desolation and a waste, and [t]her proud might shall come
to an end, and [u]the mountains of Israel shall be so desolate that none will pass through.
29 [v]Then they will know that I am the LORD, when I have made the land a desolation and
a waste because of all their abominations that they have committed.
30 "As for you, [f]son of man, [w]your people who talk together about you by the walls and
at the doors of the houses, say to one another, each to his brother, 'Come, and hear what
the word is that comes from the LORD.' **31** [x]And they come to you as people come, and they
sit before you as my people, and they hear what you say but they will not do it; for [y]with
lustful talk in their mouths they act; their heart is set on their gain. **32** And behold, you
are to them like one who sings lustful songs with a beautiful voice and [z]plays[1] well on an
instrument, for [a]they hear what you say, but they will not do it. **33** [b]When this comes—and
come it will!—[c]then they will know that a prophet has been among them."

Prophecy Against the Shepherds of Israel

34 The word of the LORD came to me: **2** [d]"Son of man, prophesy against the shepherds
of Israel; prophesy, and say to them, even to the shepherds, Thus says the Lord GOD:
[e]Ah, shepherds of Israel [f]who have been feeding yourselves! [g]Should not shepherds feed
the sheep? **3** [h]You eat the fat, you clothe yourselves with the wool, [i]you slaughter the fat
ones, but you do not feed the sheep. **4** [j]The weak you have not strengthened, the sick you
have not healed, [h]the injured you have not bound up, [h]the strayed you have not brought
back, [k]the lost you have not sought, and with force and [l]harshness you have ruled them.
5 [m]So they were scattered, because there was no shepherd, and [n]they became food for all
the wild beasts. **6** My sheep were scattered; they wandered over all the mountains and on
every high hill. My sheep were scattered over all the face of the earth, [o]with none to search
or seek for them.
7 "Therefore, you shepherds, hear the word of the LORD: **8** [p]As I live, declares the Lord
GOD, surely because [q]my sheep have become a prey, and my sheep have become food for all
the wild beasts, since there was no shepherd, and because my shepherds have not searched
for my sheep, but the shepherds have fed themselves, and have not fed my sheep, **9** therefore, you shepherds, hear the word of the LORD: **10** Thus says the Lord GOD, [r]Behold, I am
against the shepherds, and [s]I will require my sheep at their hand and [t]put a stop to their
feeding the sheep. [u]No longer shall the shepherds feed themselves. [v]I will rescue my sheep
from their mouths, that they may not be food for them.

The Lord GOD Will Seek Them Out

11 "For thus says the Lord GOD: [w]Behold, I, I [x]myself will search for my sheep and will
seek them out. **12** As a shepherd seeks out his flock when he is among his sheep that have

[1] Hebrew *like the singing of lustful songs with a beautiful voice and one who plays*

27 [r][1 Sam. 23:29]
28 [s][ch. 35:3, 9; Jer. 44:2, 6, 22] [t][ch. 7:24; 30:6] [u]See ch. 6:2
29 [v]See ch. 6:7
30 [f][See ver. 24 above] [w]See ver. 2
31 [x]See ch. 8:1 [y]Ps. 78:36, 37; Isa. 29:13; Jer. 12:2; 1 John 3:18
32 [z][1 Sam. 16:17] [a][Matt. 7:26; Luke 6:49]
33 [b][ver. 29] [c]ch. 2:5

Chapter 34

2 [d]See ch. 2:1 [e]See Jer. 23:1 [f][ver. 8, 10; Jude 12] [g][2 Cor. 12:14]
3 [h]Zech. 11:16 [i]Zech. 11:4, 5; [Mic. 3:2, 3]
4 [j][ver. 16, 21] [h][See ver. 3 above] [k][Matt. 18:12; Luke 15:4] [l]Ex. 1:13, 14; [1 Pet. 5:3]
5 [m]1 Kgs. 22:17; Matt. 9:36 [n][Jer. 50:7, 17]
6 [o][ver. 11]
8 [p]See ch. 16:48 [q][ver. 22]
10 [r]See ch. 13:8 [s][Heb. 13:17]; See ch. 3:18 [t][Zech. 11:8] [u][ver. 2, 8] [v][ch. 13:21]
11 [w][Luke 19:10; John 10:11] [x][Mic. 4:6, 7]

33:30–33 *A Word for the Exiles.* If the "implied" audience for vv. 23–29 was the homelanders, the "real" audience listening in was Ezekiel's fellow exiles. Their enjoyment of the rebuke aimed at their land-hungry compatriots is cut short as Ezekiel turns to accuse *them* of also being marked by greed (v. 31). Compounding this, they treat prophetic words as mere entertainment (v. 32). No judgment is pronounced, but it is ominously implied (v. 33).

34:1–31 *Shepherds and Sheep.* The move toward restoration continues by way of further warning and indictment. Ezekiel develops the picture of the community and its leaders as flock and shepherds (used throughout Jeremiah). In Ezekiel, the metaphor is seen only in this chapter and in 37:24. The brief oracle in Jer. 23:1–4 focused only on the shepherds, and this is Ezekiel's starting point (Ezek. 34:1–16)—but here Ezekiel goes on to address the sheep (vv. 17–31).

34:1–16 *Wicked Shepherds and the Good Shepherd.* The passage moves from condemnation (vv. 1–10) to restoration (vv. 11–16). As in Jeremiah, the punishment of negligent shepherds (the leaders of the people) precedes the promise of a faithful shepherd, although the two prophets differ on details. The passage is emphatic that the role of the shepherd is to ensure the safety and well-being of the flock. This has been the distinctive failure of Judah's leaders.

34:1–10 Often in Ezekiel a concise accusation leads to a lengthy description of consequences and punishments. Here, the proportions are reversed. The situation is presented in vv. 1–6, it is summarized in vv. 7–8, and judgment is announced in vv. 9–10.

34:2 The metaphor of **shepherds** for the rulers of the community has ancient roots and was widespread in the ancient Near East (e.g., on Tammuz, 8:14–15). In the OT, David is the shepherd-king par excellence (2 Sam. 5:2; Ps. 78:70–72), but preeminently, it applies to God himself (e.g., Ps. 80:1). Jesus identifies himself as the "good shepherd" (John 10:11, 14). **feeding yourselves**. The failure here is not simply a matter of neglecting the sheep but of benefiting at the cost of the flock.

34:3–6 These verses pointedly describe how the shepherds misused their power by using it for their own gain rather than for the good of the people. Because of this covenant neglect (Lev. 26:33; Deut. 28:64) the **sheep** were **scattered**.

34:10 No punishment is identified except that this situation must stop, and divine intervention ensures that it does (see note on vv. 11–16).

34:11–16 God intervenes to reverse, step by step, the process described above. He successively undoes the damage inflicted by the failed shepherds (vv. 2–6, 8) by seeking the scattered (v. 12), gathering (v. 13) and feeding them (v. 14), and ensuring they live in security (v. 15). On the announcement of God himself as **shepherd** (v. 15), see v. 23. The summary in v. 16 portrays

been scattered, so will I seek out my sheep, and I will rescue them from all places where
they have been scattered on [y]a day of clouds and [z]thick darkness. **13** And I will bring them
out from the peoples [a]and gather them from the countries, and will bring them into their
own land. And I will feed them on [b]the mountains of Israel, by the ravines, and in all
the inhabited places of the country. **14** [c]I will feed them with good pasture, and on the
mountain heights of Israel shall be their grazing land. [d]There they shall lie down in good
grazing land, and on rich pasture they shall feed on the mountains of Israel. **15** [e]I myself
will be the shepherd of my sheep, [d]and I myself will make them lie down, declares the
Lord GOD. **16** [f]I will seek the lost, [g]and I will bring back the strayed, and I will bind up the
injured, and I will strengthen the weak, and [h]the fat and the strong I will destroy.[1] I will
feed them in justice.

17 "As for you, my flock, thus says the Lord GOD: [i]Behold, I judge between sheep and sheep,
between rams and [j]male goats. **18** Is it not enough for you to feed on the good pasture, that
you must tread down with your feet the rest of your pasture; and to drink of [k]clear water,
that you must muddy the rest of the water with your feet? **19** And must my sheep eat what
you have trodden with your feet, and drink what you have muddied with your feet?

20 "Therefore, thus says the Lord GOD to them: Behold, I, I myself will judge between
the fat sheep and the lean sheep. **21** Because you push with side and shoulder, and [l]thrust
at all the [m]weak with your horns, till you have scattered them abroad, **22** I will rescue[2] my
flock; [n]they shall no longer be a prey. And I will judge between sheep and sheep. **23** And [o]I
will set up over them one shepherd, [p]my servant David, and he shall feed them: he shall
feed them and be their shepherd. **24** And [q]I, the LORD, will be their God, and my servant
David shall be prince among them. [r]I am the LORD; I have spoken.

The LORD's Covenant of Peace

25 [s]"I will make with them a covenant of peace and [t]banish wild beasts from the land, [u]so
that they may dwell securely in the wilderness and sleep in the woods. **26** And I will make
them and the places all around my hill [v]a blessing, and [w]I will send down the showers
in their season; they shall be [x]showers of blessing. **27** [y]And the trees of the field shall yield
their fruit, and the earth shall yield its increase, [u]and they shall be secure in their land. And
[z]they shall know that I am the LORD, when [a]I break the bars of their yoke, and [a]deliver
them from the hand of those who enslaved them. **28** [n]They shall no more be a prey to the
nations, [t]nor shall the beasts of the land devour them. [u]They shall dwell securely, and none
shall make them afraid. **29** And I will provide for them [b]renowned plantations so that [c]they
shall no more be consumed with hunger in the land, and no longer [d]suffer the reproach
of the nations. **30** And they shall know that [q]I am the LORD their God with them, and that
they, the house of Israel, are my people, declares the Lord GOD. **31** And you are my sheep,
[e]human sheep of my pasture, and I am your God, declares the Lord GOD."

[1] Septuagint, Syriac, Vulgate *I will watch over* [2] Or *save*

12 [y]ch. 30:3 [z]Joel 2:2; Zeph. 1:15
13 [a]See ch. 11:17 [b]See ch. 6:2
14 [c]Ps. 23:2; [John 10:9] [d][Isa. 32:18; Jer. 33:12]
15 [e][ver. 23; Isa. 40:11] [d][See ver. 14 above]
16 [f][ver. 4] [g]Mic. 4:6 [h][ver. 20; Isa. 10:16; Amos 4:1]
17 [i]ver. 20, 22; [ch. 20:38; Matt. 25:32, 33] [j]Zech. 10:3
18 [k][ch. 32:14]
21 [l]Deut. 33:17; Dan. 8:4 [m][ver. 4]
22 [n][ver. 8]
23 [o]ch. 37:22, 24; Jer. 23:4, 5; Mic. 5:4; 7:14; [ver. 15; John 10:11, 16] [p]ch. 37:24, 25; [2 Sam. 5:2; Ps. 78:71, 72]
24 [q]See ch. 37:27; Ex. 29:45; Lev. 26:12 [r]See ch. 17:24
25 [s]ch. 37:26; See Isa. 54:10 [t]Lev. 26:6; Hos. 2:18; [Isa. 35:9]; See Isa. 11:6-9 [u]ch. 38:8, 14; 39:26
26 [v]Gen. 12:2; Isa. 19:24; Zech. 8:13 [w]Lev. 26:4; [ch. 22:24] [x]Mal. 3:10
27 [y]ch. 36:30; Lev. 26:4 [u][See ver. 25 above] [z]See ch. 6:7 [a]Jer. 30:8
28 [n][See ver. 22 above] [t][See ver. 25 above] [u][See ver. 25 above]
29 [b]Isa. 60:21; 61:3 [c]ch. 36:29 [d]See ch. 32:24
30 [q][See ver. 24 above]
31 [e]Ps. 74:1; 100:3; John 10:16

the judgment of the shepherds and the restoration of the flock as two aspects of a single work of God. In John 10:9, Jesus speaks of the sheep finding "pasture" (evoking Ezek. 34:14).

34:17–31 *The Flock: Problems and Prospects.* The remainder of the chapter is addressed to the flock in three stages: vv. 17–22 condemn victimization within the flock; vv. 23–24 return to the provision of a faithful shepherd; and vv. 25–31 attend to the implications of renewal for the natural world.

34:17–22 The structure is much like that of vv. 1–10. Behavior within the flock is described and condemned in vv. 17–19, and the consequent divine intervention is described (vv. 20–22), which includes a reiteration of the charges (v. 21). The "you" now addresses the flock rather than its shepherds.

34:17–19 The previous oracle concluded with a statement of "justice" (v. 16, Hb. *mishpat*); this pertains not only to the rulers but also to the people themselves. The selfish greed, which not only monopolizes but also squanders the resources of the community, is "judged" (v. 17, Hb. *shophet*, related to *mishpat*). Ezekiel's oracle anticipates Jesus' teaching in Matt. 25:31–46.

34:20–22 The description of the classes of **sheep** implies oppressive exploitation apart from failed leadership. The assertion of judgment that begins and ends this oracle distinguishes it from the next element in the chapter.

34:23–24 Ezekiel's announcement of a Davidic shepherd (v. 23; cf. 37:24) is similar to Jeremiah's (Jer. 23:5–6). The covenant formula in Ezek. 34:24 affirms the relationship of God and people. Because it is in such close proximity to v. 15, some commentators see a tension between those taking up the role of shepherd: is the shepherd divine (v. 15) or human (v. 23)? The dilemma may be solved by appeal to editorial layering, or in assuming a hierarchy of divine shepherd over human shepherd. A Christological reading finds here an anticipation of the divine-human nature of the Messiah. Such a reading explains John 10:11–18, where, in claiming to be the "good shepherd," Jesus claims to be both the Davidic Messiah (Ezek. 34:23) and the incarnate God of Israel (v. 15; cf. John 1:14). Ezekiel's uneasiness with any king except God is seen in designating David as **prince** (Hb. *nasi'*).

34:25–31 The **covenant of peace** announced in v. 25 extends the renewal of life from the human community to the natural world. These effects also come in tandem with the messianic age in Isa. 11:1–9. Covenant curses have been prominent until this point, but the covenant also entailed blessings (cf. Lev. 26:4–6; Deut. 28:8–14). **They shall be showers of blessing** refers not only to literal rain but also to abundant blessings from God. Ezekiel 34:31 returns explicitly to the pastoral metaphor to draw the threads of the chapter together.

Prophecy Against Mount Seir

35 The word of the LORD came to me: 2 [f]"Son of man, [g]set your face [h]against [i]Mount
Seir, and prophesy against it, 3 and say to it, Thus says the Lord GOD: [j]Behold, I am
against you, Mount Seir, and [k]I will stretch out my hand against you, [l]and I will make you
a desolation and a waste. 4 [m]I will lay your cities waste, and you shall become a desolation,
and you shall know that I am the LORD. 5 Because [n]you cherished perpetual enmity and
gave over the people of Israel to the power of the sword [o]at the time of their calamity, [p]at
the time of their final punishment, 6 therefore, [q]as I live, declares the Lord GOD, I will
prepare you for blood, and blood shall pursue you; [r]because you did not hate bloodshed,
therefore blood shall pursue you. 7 [l]I will make Mount Seir a waste [m]and a desolation, and
I will cut off from it [s]all who come and go. 8 And I will fill [t]its mountains with the slain.
On your hills and in your valleys and in all [t]your ravines [u]those slain with the sword shall
fall. 9 [l]I will make you a perpetual desolation, and [m]your cities shall not be inhabited. Then
[v]you will know that I am the LORD.
10 "Because you said, [w]'These two nations and these two countries shall be mine, and
[x]we will take possession of them'—although the [y]LORD was there— 11 therefore, [q]as I
live, declares the Lord GOD, I will deal with you [z]according to the anger and [z]envy that
you showed because of your hatred against them. And [a]I will make myself known among
them, when I judge you. 12 And you shall know that I am the LORD.
[b]"I have heard all the revilings that you uttered against the mountains of Israel, saying,
'They are laid desolate; [c]they are given us to devour.' 13 And [b]you magnified yourselves
against me [d]with your mouth, and multiplied your words against me; I heard it. 14 Thus
says the Lord GOD: [e]While the whole earth rejoices, I will make you desolate. 15 As you
[f]rejoiced over the inheritance of the house of Israel, because it was desolate, so I will deal
with you; you shall be desolate, [g]Mount Seir, and all Edom, all of it. Then [h]they will know
that I am the LORD.

Prophecy to the Mountains of Israel

36 "And you, [i]son of man, prophesy to [j]the mountains of Israel, and say, O mountains
of Israel, hear the word of the LORD. 2 Thus says the Lord GOD: Because [k]the enemy
said of you, [l]'Aha!' and, 'The ancient [m]heights have become our possession,' 3 therefore
prophesy, and say, Thus says the Lord GOD: Precisely because [n]they made you desolate and
crushed you from all sides, so that you became the possession of the rest of the nations, and

Chapter 35
2 [f]See ch. 2:1 [g]See ch. 6:2 [h]ch. 25:12; Isa. 21:11, 12; Amos 1:11; Mal. 1:4 [i]ch. 25:8; Gen. 32:3
3 [j]See ch. 13:8 [k]See ch. 6:14 [l][ch. 33:28]
4 [m][Isa. 17:9; 27:10]
5 [n][Ps. 137:7; Amos 1:11] [o]Obad. 13 [p]ch. 21:25
6 [q]See ch. 16:48 [r]See Gen. 9:6
7 [l][See ver. 3 above] [m][See ver. 4 above] [s]ch. 29:11
8 [t][ch. 31:12] [u]ch. 31:17, 18; 32:20, 21
9 [l][See ver. 3 above] [m][See ver. 4 above] [v]See ch. 6:7
10 [w][ch. 37:22] [x][ch. 36:2, 3, 5; Ps. 83:6, 12] [y]See ch. 48:35
11 [q][See ver. 6 above] [z][ver. 15; Matt. 7:2] [a][ver. 9]
12 [b][2 Kgs. 19:4, 28] [c][ver. 10]
13 [b][See ver. 12 above] [d][1 Sam. 2:3]
14 [e][Isa. 65:13, 14]
15 [f]ch. 36:5; Ps. 137:7 [g]ver. 2 [h]See ch. 6:7

Chapter 36
1 [i]See ch. 2:1 [j]See ch. 6:2
2 [k]ver. 5; ch. 35:10, 12 [l]ch. 25:3; 26:2 [m]Deut. 32:13
3 [n][ch. 6:3, 4]

35:1–36:15 *The Mountains of Edom and Israel.* In so highly structured a book as Ezekiel, it seems odd that an oracle against a foreign nation should appear outside the collection in chs. 25–32. However, that collection is itself highly structured, and it is clear that the prophecies against Mount Seir (Edom) in ch. 35 are a preface to the address to the mountains of Israel in 36:1–15, and these two passages are best regarded as a single unit in two parts.

35:1–15 *Against Mount Seir.* Mount Seir (v. 2) is identified with Edom (v. 15) much as Mount Zion is identified with Judah. An oracle against Edom appears in 25:12–14 (see note there), and its theme is echoed here. Edom's excesses against the stricken Judah (which inspired such animosity) are registered and judged. (Cf. also the book of Obadiah.) There is also considerable overlap of language with Ezekiel's earlier oracle against the "mountains of Israel" in Ezek. 6:1–7, 11–14. In this passage, the "recognition formula" (35:4, 9, 12a, 15; cf. Introduction: Style) punctuates a sequence of four related sayings. The key words "waste" and "desolation" recur throughout the passage, translating at least four Hebrew terms.

35:1–4 The first oracle is little more than a bare announcement of God's opposition to **Mount Seir** and his intention to destroy it. "Mount Seir" was not a single peak but rather the highland region southeast of the Dead Sea.

35:5–9 The familiar **because . . . therefore** structure of indictment sets out the key charges against Edom (v. 5) and details the judgment (vv. 6–9). Edom is treated here much as Israel was in ch. 6.

35:10–12a Edom's land-grab is condemned. **Two nations** refers to Israel and Judah as separate kingdoms (see 37:15–28). Punishment is presented as poetic justice: just as Edom treated Israel and Judah, so it will be treated in turn. The assertion in 35:10 that **the LORD was there** moderates the claims of those who portray Yahweh as having abandoned the land of promise (see 11:23) for the land of the exiles. This land remains the Lord's.

35:12b–15 The theme of derisive speech picks up one of the main issues from ch. 25. As there, so here the speech is more than simply taunting a vanquished people. God is himself the object of insult, and this is unacceptable. The sole mention of the name **Edom** comes in 35:15 (cf. note on vv. 1–15).

36:1–15 *The Mountains of Israel Restored.* The judgment of Mount Seir (ch. 35)—so reminiscent of God's prior judgment of the mountains of Israel (ch. 6)—contrasts with the announcement now of restoration in corresponding terms. The address here is fairly consistently to the "mountains of Israel" (36:1), and most of the second-person references ("you") are plural. A singular reference is occasionally made, however (e.g., to the "land [soil] of Israel," v. 6). Broadly, this oracle sets out an explanation for the wrath that befell the "mountains" (vv. 1–7), followed by the promise of their restoration (vv. 8–15). Within that simple division, the structure is complicated.

36:1–7 In vv. 1–7 there are a series of nested "because" and "therefore" statements whose relationships are difficult to disentangle, as apparent outcomes simply introduce further grounds. Three factors are intertwined: the encroachment of Israel's enemies, the desolation of the land, and the wrath of God. The enemies come to the fore in vv. 2 and 7, the situation of Israel is the focus of vv. 3–4 and 6, and God's wrath is the theme of v. 5.

36:2 The claim to the **ancient heights** points back to the intended dispossession of Israel's land, judged in ch. 35.

36:3 The enemy is seen to be legion: **they** came **from all sides**, without further identification (until v. 5). The derision (v. 4) inspired by the fall of Israel and Judah will be the closing concern of this oracle (vv. 13–15).

3[o][Lam. 2:15, 16]
4[p]ch. 6:3 [q][ch. 33:24, 27] [r][ch. 7:21]
5[s]Deut. 4:24 [t]ch. 35:15 [u][ver. 3; ch. 35:10] [v]ch. 35:15 [w]ch. 25:6
6[j][See ver. 1 above] [x][ver. 5] [y]See ch. 32:24
7[z]See ch. 20:5 [y][See ver. 6 above]
8[a]See ch. 17:23 [b]ch. 12:23; [Isa. 56:1]
9[c][ch. 5:8] [d][ver. 34]
10[e]ver. 37; ch. 37:26; Jer. 30:19 [f][ver. 33, 35]
11[g]Jer. 31:27; [Jer. 33:12] [h][Gen. 1:28] [i][ch. 16:55] [j][Job 42:12] [k]See ch. 6:7
12[l]Obad. 17 [m][ch. 5:17]
13[n][Num. 13:32]
15[y][See ver. 6 above]
17[o]See ch. 2:1 [p]See Lev. 18:25 [q]See Lev. 18:19
18[r]See ch. 7:8 [s]ch. 16:36; 22:3 [t]See ch. 5:11
19[u]See ch. 5:10 [v]See ch. 18:30
20[w]Isa. 52:5; [ch. 22:26; Rom. 2:24]
21[x][ch. 20:9; Isa. 43:25; 48:11]

[o]you became the talk and evil gossip of the people, 4 therefore, O mountains of Israel, hear
the word of the Lord GOD: Thus says the Lord GOD to [p]the mountains and the hills, the
ravines and the valleys, [q]the desolate wastes and the deserted cities, which have become [r]a
prey and derision to the rest of the nations all around, 5 therefore thus says the Lord GOD:
Surely I have spoken in [s]my hot jealousy against the rest of the nations and [t]against all
Edom, who [u]gave my land to themselves as a possession [v]with wholehearted joy and [w]utter
contempt, that they might make its pasturelands a prey. 6 Therefore prophesy concerning
the land of Israel, and say to [j]the mountains and hills, to the ravines and valleys, Thus says
the Lord GOD: [x]Behold, I have spoken in my jealous wrath, because you have suffered [y]the
reproach of the nations. 7 Therefore thus says the Lord GOD: [z]I swear that the nations that
are all around you [y]shall themselves suffer reproach.

8 "But you, O mountains of Israel, [a]shall shoot forth your branches and yield your fruit
to my people Israel, for [b]they will soon come home. 9 For [c]behold, I am for you, and I will
turn to you, and [d]you shall be tilled and sown. 10 And [e]I will multiply people on you, the
whole house of Israel, all of it. [f]The cities shall be inhabited and the waste places rebuilt.
11 And I will multiply on you [g]man and beast, and [h]they shall multiply and be fruitful.
And I will cause you to be inhabited as in [i]your former times, and [j]will do more good to
you than ever before. [k]Then you will know that I am the LORD. 12 I will let people walk on
you, even my people Israel. [l]And they shall possess you, and you shall be their inheritance,
and you shall no longer [m]bereave them of children. 13 Thus says the Lord GOD: Because
they say to you, [n]'You devour people, and you bereave your nation of children,' 14 therefore
you shall no longer devour people and no longer bereave your nation of children, declares
the Lord GOD. 15 And I will not let you hear anymore [y]the reproach of the nations, and
you shall no longer bear the disgrace of the peoples and no longer cause your nation to
stumble, declares the Lord GOD."

The LORD's Concern for His Holy Name

16 The word of the LORD came to me: 17 [o]"Son of man, when the house of Israel lived in
their own land, [p]they defiled it by their ways and their deeds. Their ways before me were
[q]like the uncleanness of a woman in her menstrual impurity. 18 So [r]I poured out my wrath
upon them [s]for the blood that they had shed in the land, for the idols [t]with which they
had defiled it. 19 [u]I scattered them among the nations, and they were dispersed through the
countries. [v]In accordance with their ways and their deeds I judged them. 20 But when they
came to the nations, wherever they came, [w]they profaned my holy name, in that people
said of them, 'These are the people of the LORD, and yet they had to go out of his land.'
21 But I had concern [x]for my holy name, which the house of Israel had profaned among
the nations to which they came.

36:5 That the judgment of **Edom** in ch. 35 was in part exemplary is seen here, as it takes its place within the welter of enemies that came against God's people.

36:8–15 But you signals a transition: although the address has been to the "mountains of Israel," now the focus is on Israel's promising future, rather than its bleak, enemy-ridden past. As in the "covenant of peace" (34:25–30), the prosperity of people is bound up with the bounty of the land. Verses 8–11 of ch. 36 present a series of blessings, reminiscent of the restoration of Job 42 as the new exceeds the old. The people themselves become the focus of Ezek. 36:12, reiterating right ownership (cf. v. 2).

36:13–14 The identity of the "mountains" with the "land" is seen here: the **you** of v. 13 is plural, but the **you** addressed in v. 14 is feminine singular, referring to the land (soil) of Israel (v. 6). The long history of unsettled relationship between people and land will no longer hold in God's restoration—a vision to sustain future hope.

36:15 The reproach that went beyond insulting people to dishonoring God is also consigned to the past.

36:16–38 *Restoration for the Sake of God's Name.* This key passage sets out in concentrated form Ezekiel's entire theology. It is one of the primary restoration passages, though it also contains an analysis of human failure that calls for divine judgment. It carries forward some ideas from the preceding "mountain" oracles, in particular the joint restoration of land and people, and the silencing of blasphemous taunts. Far overshadowing these, however, are the towering claims of the supremacy of a holy God. The impurity of God's people impelled him to scatter them (vv. 16–21). This in turn led to derision (v. 20), so in order to vindicate his reputation, God was moved to act on behalf of his people (vv. 22–32). The restoration of the land of Israel silences the nations, compelling them to recognize the true God (vv. 33–36), just as the flourishing of Israel confirms their recognition of their own God (vv. 37–38).

36:16–21 *State of Impurity.* With v. 15 ending on the note of reproach being lifted, this return to scrutinize Israel's failings initially jars. However, this account of Israel's impurity is the basis on which God's intervention to restore his people must be understood. The metaphor of **menstrual impurity** (v. 17; see Lev. 15:19–30) is likewise jarring, but Ezekiel uses it for at least two reasons: (1) it accords with his earlier portrayals of the abandoned child (Ezekiel 16) and the sisters (ch. 23), and (2) it emphasizes Israel's defiling the sacred. That is, the activity used as a metaphor for Israel's sin is not a criminal or moral failure so much as a willful disregard of the holiness of God. However, the judgment itself (36:18–19) resulted in God's holiness being yet further **profaned** (v. 20). So God looked now to his own interests (v. 21).

I Will Put My Spirit Within You

22 "Therefore say to the house of Israel, Thus says the Lord GOD: [y]It is not for your sake, O house of Israel, that I am about to act, but for the sake of my holy name, [w]which you have profaned among the nations to which you came. 23 [z]And I will vindicate the holiness of my great name, which has been profaned among the nations, and which you have profaned among them. [a]And the nations will know that I am the LORD, declares the Lord GOD, when through you I vindicate my holiness before their eyes. 24 [b]I will take you [c]from the nations and gather you from all the countries and [d]bring you into your own land. 25 [e]I will sprinkle clean water on you, and you shall be clean from [f]all your uncleannesses, and [g]from all your idols [h]I will cleanse you. 26 And I will give you [i]a new heart, and [i]a new spirit I will put within you. [i]And I will remove the heart of stone from your flesh and give you a heart of flesh. 27 [j]And I will put my Spirit within you, [i]and cause you to walk in my statutes and [k]be careful to obey my rules.[1] 28 [l]You shall dwell in the land that I gave to your fathers, and [m]you shall be my people, and I will be your God. 29 And [n]I will deliver you from all your uncleannesses. And [o]I will summon the grain and make it abundant and [p]lay no famine upon you. 30 [q]I will make the fruit of the tree and the increase of the field abundant, [o]that you may never again suffer the disgrace of famine among the nations. 31 Then [r]you will remember your evil ways, and your deeds that were not good, and you will loathe yourselves for your iniquities and your abominations. 32 [y]It is not for your sake that I will act, declares the Lord GOD; let that be known to you. Be ashamed and confounded for your ways, O house of Israel.

33 "Thus says the Lord GOD: On the day that [s]I cleanse you from all your iniquities, [t]I will cause the cities to be inhabited, and the waste places shall be rebuilt. 34 And the land that was desolate shall be tilled, instead of being the desolation that it was in the sight of all who passed by. 35 And they will say, 'This land that was desolate has become like [u]the garden of Eden, and the waste and desolate and ruined cities are now fortified and inhabited.' 36 Then [v]the nations that are left all around you shall know that I am the LORD;

[1] *Or my just decrees*

22 [y]ver. 32; [Deut. 9:5] [w][See ver. 20 above]
23 [z]See ch. 20:41 [a][ch. 30:19, 26; 38:23; 39:7, 21]; See ch. 6:7
24 [b]See ch. 11:17 [c]See Ps. 44:11 [d]ch. 37:12, 21
25 [e][Isa. 52:15; Heb. 10:22] [f]Isa. 4:4; [ver. 17] [g]ch. 37:23 [h]Jer. 33:8
26 [i]See ch. 11:19, 20
27 [j]ch. 37:14 [i][See ver. 26 above] [k]ch. 37:24
28 [l]ch. 28:25 [m]See ch. 11:20
29 [n]ch. 37:23; [Matt. 1:21] [o]Joel 2:19; [Zech. 9:17] [p]ch. 34:29
30 [q]ch. 34:27 [o][See ver. 29 above]
31 [r]See ch. 6:9
32 [y][See ver. 22 above]
33 [s][ver. 25] [t][ver. 9, 10]
35 [u]See Isa. 51:3
36 [v][Ps. 126:2]

36:22–32 *Divine Intervention: A New Spirit.* This theologically central passage is often compared to Jeremiah's "new covenant" text (Jer. 31:31–34; cf. 32:36–41). The overtones carried by Jeremiah's language resonate with political loyalty. Ezekiel's overtones, by contrast, have to do with ritual purity, as Ezek. 36:17–19 bears out. The structure of this passage reinforces its message. The outer verses relate the responses of God (vv. 22–23) and people (vv. 31–32). Nested within the next layer are the movements of return and purification brought about in renewal (vv. 24–25, 28–30). At the heart of the passage is the divine gift of the new heart and spirit, which enables right response (vv. 26–27). The physical return was only the beginning of the fulfillment for these prophecies.

36:22–23 It is not for your sake. The fundamental reason given for God's acting on Israel's behalf is not grace and mercy (though it is gracious and merciful) but to uphold the sanctity and greatness of God's reputation: **but for the sake of my holy name.** Although the "recognition formula" (**will know that I am the LORD**, v. 23; cf. Introduction: Style) is used repeatedly throughout the book of Ezekiel, here its significance is made plain. It is not just that Israel's God is "great" and "holy"; it is also imperative that God be given the recognition and respect, indeed the honor, that he is due. To **vindicate the holiness of** God's **great name** is also to "hallow his great name" (cf. Matt. 6:9) and is contrasted to "profaning his name" (i.e., treating it, and so him, as not holy).

36:24–25 The restoration of God's reputation first requires the external renovation of his people. God's actions are naturally sequential: gathering and return (v. 24) precede cleansing (v. 25). Purification with **clean water** echoes God's earlier cleansing of his people (16:4, 9) and once again relates to ritual cleansing in the Mosaic law (cf., e.g., Lev. 17:15–16; 22:6; Num. 19:19–21). The reference to cleansing by sprinkling "clean water on you" recalls the cleansing by sprinkling for touching a dead body (Num. 19:13, 20), perhaps suggesting that the **idols** of Ezek. 36:25 are comparable to dead things. Many interpreters see this picture of cleansing by water as the background to Jesus' words in John 3:5, "Unless one is born of water and the Spirit, he cannot enter the kingdom of God"; cf. the mention of "my Spirit" in Ezek. 36:27. Thus, Ezekiel's prophecy refers both to outward cleansing by a ceremony and to inward, spiritual cleansing.

36:26–27 God's initiative moves from external to internal with the gift of a **new heart** and **new spirit** (see 11:19; cf. 18:31). The outer purification will be no use without the inner disposition to live rightly before God (36:27). The connection of "water" (v. 25) and "Spirit" (v. 27) lies behind John 3:5. **I will put my Spirit within you** predicts an effective inward work of God in the "new covenant."

36:28–30 With God's people now graced with an inclination to keep faith with God, so too there will be an enduring habitation of the land (v. 28)—this time with no occasion for it to prove "treacherous" (cf. vv. 13–14). The conjunction of restoration of people and land is a continuing theme through this part of Ezekiel (see e.g., 34:25–31). The restoration of the people to the land is symbolic of, and probably implies the reality of, the return of the people to live in the presence of God, knowing once again his blessings on their lives (see 36:27).

36:31–32 you will loathe yourselves. The response of the renewed people is to see themselves as God sees them. **not for your sake.** The assertion of God acting for his own sake repeats and confirms the basis of God's action spelled out already in v. 22, thus bracketing this overtly theological account of renewal.

36:33–36 *Land Renewed.* As seen in vv. 28–30, the land enjoys the benefits of the people's cleansing (v. 33). The impact on the land is not simply on its fertility (vv. 34–35). The cityscape is renewed as well as the landscape (v. 33). The mention of **Eden** (v. 35) emphasizes the nature of this act as re-creation (see 28:13; cf. 37:1–14). One appointed function of Israel's experience in the land was to show the whole world a restored Edenic life, lived in God's presence and with his blessing.

36 [w][ch. 34:29] [x]See ch. 17:24
37 [y][ch. 14:3] [z]See ver. 10 [a][ch. 34:31]
38 [b][2 Chr. 35:7] [t][See ver. 33 above] [c]See ch. 6:7

Chapter 37

1 [d]See ch. 1:3 [e]See ch. 3:12
3 [f]See ch. 2:1 [g][1 Cor. 15:35] [h][Deut. 32:39; John 5:21]
4 [i][ch. 6:2] [j][John 5:28]
5 [k][Gen. 2:7]
6 [l][ver. 8] [m]See ch. 6:7
7 [n]ch. 12:7; 24:18 [o][1 Kgs. 19:11]
8 [p][ver. 5]
9 [i][See ver. 4 above] [f][See ver. 3 above] [q]Dan. 7:2; 11:4; Rev. 7:1
10 [n][See ver. 7 above] [r]Rev. 11:11
11 [f][See ver. 3 above] [s][ch. 33:10; Isa. 49:14] [t]Lam. 3:54
12 [i][See ver. 4 above] [u][Isa. 26:19; Hos. 13:14] [v]ver. 21, 25; ch. 36:24
13 [w]See ch. 6:7
14 [x]ch. 36:27 [y]See ch. 17:24

I have rebuilt the ruined places and [w]replanted that which was desolate. [x]I am the LORD;
I have spoken, and I will do it.
37 "Thus says the Lord GOD: This also [y]I will let the house of Israel ask me to do for
them: [z]to increase their people like [a]a flock. **38** Like the flock for sacrifices,[1] [b]like the flock
at Jerusalem during her appointed feasts, so [t]shall the waste cities be filled with flocks of
people. [c]Then they will know that I am the LORD."

The Valley of Dry Bones

37 [d]The hand of the LORD was upon me, and [e]he brought me out in the Spirit of the
LORD and set me down in the middle of the valley;[2] it was full of bones. **2** And he led
me around among them, and behold, there were very many on the surface of the valley,
and behold, they were very dry. **3** And he said to me, [f]"Son of man, [g]can these bones live?"
And [h]I answered, "O Lord GOD, you know." **4** Then he said to me, [i]"Prophesy over these
bones, and say to them, [j]O dry bones, hear the word of the LORD. **5** Thus says the Lord GOD
to these bones: Behold, I will cause [k]breath[3] to enter you, and you shall live. **6** [l]And I will
lay sinews upon you, and will cause flesh to come upon you, and [l]cover you with skin, and
put breath in you, and you shall live, [m]and you shall know that I am the LORD."
7 So I prophesied [n]as I was commanded. And as I prophesied, there was a sound, and
behold, [o]a rattling,[4] and the bones came together, bone to its bone. **8** And I looked, and
behold, there were sinews on them, and flesh had come upon them, and skin had covered
them. But [p]there was no breath in them. **9** Then he said to me, [i]"Prophesy to the breath;
prophesy, [f]son of man, and say to the breath, Thus says the Lord GOD: Come from [q]the
four winds, O breath, and breathe on these slain, that they may live." **10** So I prophesied
[n]as he commanded me, and [r]the breath came into them, and they lived and stood on their
feet, an exceedingly great army.
11 Then he said to me, [f]"Son of man, these bones are the whole house of Israel. Behold,
they say, 'Our bones are dried up, and [s]our hope is lost; [t]we are indeed cut off.' **12** Therefore
[i]prophesy, and say to them, Thus says the Lord GOD: Behold, [u]I will open your graves and
raise you from your graves, O my people. And [v]I will bring you into the land of Israel. **13** And
[w]you shall know that I am the LORD, when I open your graves, and raise you from your
graves, O my people. **14** And [x]I will put my Spirit within you, and you shall live, and I will
place you in your own land. Then you shall know that I am the LORD; [y]I have spoken, and
I will do it, declares the LORD."

[1] Hebrew *flock of holy things* [2] Or *plain*; also verse 2 [3] Or *spirit*; also verses 6, 9, 10 [4] Or *an earthquake* (compare 3:12, 13)

36:37–38 *Populace Increased.* The flourishing of the people in terms of a **flock** recalls the pastoral imagery of ch. 34 (see also 37:24). Applying the metaphor to a **flock for sacrifices** (36:38) may seem ironic, but the imagery suggests not impending death but festivals and great numbers, all set aside for God. **Then they will know**. The recognition formula (cf. Introduction: Style) is a fitting conclusion to a passage in which recognizing the true God is seen to be paramount.

37:1–14 *The Vision of Dry Bones.* This vision, Ezekiel's third in the book (see 1:1), is one of the most famous passages in Ezekiel. While it stands on its own as a powerful statement of God's power to re-create the community, the context is significant. The promised gift of new heart and spirit (36:26–27) left questions hanging (i.e., how can this be? and can it be true for us?). Chapter 37 addresses these questions. The vision itself is reported in vv. 1–10 with vivid power. The landscape is filled with bleached bones to which Ezekiel is commanded to prophesy. As he does, the bones are restored to life. The vision receives a double interpretation in vv. 11–14. The primary meaning relates directly to the exiles' despair (v. 11) and concludes the vision in v. 14. Verses 12–13 transpose the metaphor to a graveyard and contain one of the few hints of resurrection in the OT (see note).

37:1 The vast landscape of dry **bones** suggests the aftermath of battle, the ultimate outcome of the judgment of ch. 6.

37:3 The question **can these bones live?** anticipates the exiles' own self-perception (v. 11): total hopelessness. It also introduces one of the key words in the passage: the verb "to live" appears in vv. 3, 5, 6, 9, 10, and 14. Ezekiel's response leaves the outcome to God's sovereignty.

37:4–6 God commands Ezekiel to do what seems pointless (**prophesy over these bones**, v. 4), and includes the promise that he will perform the impossible (vv. 5–6)—bring them back to life. The key to "resuscitation" is stated in v. 5: **breath** is the Hb. *ruakh*, the same word used for "the Spirit" in v. 1, and which appears seven more times in the vision.

37:8 The first phase of prophesying results in the rebuilt bodies, which lack **breath**. So far this activity only yields corpses—but it is still a necessary first step.

37:9–10 The second phase of prophesying is addressed to the **breath** (or wind or spirit/Spirit; Hb. *ruakh*, which can take all three meanings). The coming of the wind/breath/spirit that gives life powerfully alludes to God's creative work in Gen. 2:7. God creates, and God re-creates.

37:12–13 I will open your graves and raise you from your graves, O my people. The vision of national revival is transposed into the metaphor of a cemetery, which seems to be related to the experience of exile (v. 12b). By using this language, Ezekiel also contributes to OT teaching on resurrection. Although clear statements of bodily life after death are not common in the OT, one of the clearest comes in Daniel (Dan. 12:2–3). In addition, there were hints in earlier texts that prepared the way. The influence of a number of these texts, including Isa. 26:19 and Hos. 6:1–2 and 13:14, is immediately apparent in the NT. Other passages include Job 19:25–27 and Ps. 17:15 (see note).

37:14 The fundamental lesson of the vision is repeated: when the **Spirit** is present, God's people are enabled to **live**. This is the only basis on which hope can be held out to the despairing community.

I Will Be Their God, They Shall Be My People

15 The word of the LORD came to me: 16 [z]“Son of man, [a]take a stick[1] and write on it, ‘For
[b]Judah, and [c]the people of Israel associated with him’; then take another stick and write
on it, ‘For [b]Joseph (the stick of [d]Ephraim) and all the house of Israel associated with him.’
17 And [e]join them one to another into one stick, that [f]they may become [g]one in your hand.
18 And when [h]your people say to you, [i]‘Will you not tell us what you mean by these?’ 19 say
to them, Thus says the Lord GOD: Behold, I am about to take [j]the stick of Joseph (that is
in the hand of Ephraim) and the tribes of Israel associated with him. And I will join with it
the [j]stick of Judah,[2] and [k]make them one stick, [g]that they may be one in my hand. 20 When
the sticks on which you write are in your hand [l]before their eyes, 21 then say to them, Thus
says the Lord GOD: Behold, [m]I will take the people of Israel from the nations among which
they have gone, and will gather them from all around, and [m]bring them to their own land.
22 And [n]I will make them one nation in the land, on [o]the mountains of Israel. And [p]one
king shall be king over them all, and they shall be no longer [q]two nations, and no longer
divided into two kingdoms. 23 [r]They shall not [s]defile themselves anymore [t]with their idols
and their detestable things, or with any of their transgressions. But [u]I will save them from
all the backslidings[3] in which they have sinned, and will cleanse them; and [v]they shall be
my people, and I will be their God.
24 “My servant [w]David [x]shall be king over them, and they shall all have [y]one shepherd.
[z]They shall walk in my rules and be careful to obey my statutes. 25 [a]They shall dwell
in the land that I gave to my servant Jacob, where your fathers lived. They and their
children and their children’s children shall dwell there [b]forever, and David my servant
shall be their prince [c]forever. 26 [d]I will make a covenant of peace with them. It shall be
[e]an everlasting covenant with them. And I will set them in their land[4] and [f]multiply
them, and will [g]set my sanctuary in their midst forevermore. 27 [h]My dwelling place shall
be with them, [v]and I will be their God, and they shall be my people. 28 Then [i]the nations
will know that [j]I am the LORD who sanctifies Israel, when [g]my sanctuary is in their
midst forevermore.”

Prophecy Against Gog

38 The word of the LORD came to me: 2 [k]“Son of man, [l]set your face toward [m]Gog, of
the land of [n]Magog, the [o]chief prince of [p]Meshech[5] and [p]Tubal, and [q]prophesy
against him 3 and say, Thus says the Lord GOD: Behold, [r]I am against you, O Gog, chief

16 [z]See ch. 2:1 [a][Num. 17:2] [b][Zech. 10:6] [c]2 Chr. 11:12, 13, 16; 15:9; 30:11, 18 [d]Gen. 48:13, 14, 19; [Hos. 5:3, 5]
17 [e][ver. 22, 24] [f][Isa. 11:13] [g][ch. 35:10]
18 [h]See ch. 33:2 [i]See ch. 12:9
19 [j][ver. 16] [k][ver. 17] [g][See ver. 17 above]
20 [l]See ch. 12:3
21 [m]ver. 25; ch. 36:24; See ch. 11:17
22 [n][ver. 17; Jer. 50:4] [o]See ch. 6:2 [p][ver. 24, 25; ch. 34:24] [q][ch. 35:10]
23 [r][ch. 36:25] [s]ch. 14:11 [t]ch. 36:25 [u]ch. 36:29 [v]ch. 34:24, 30; 2 Cor. 6:16; Rev. 21:3; See Ex. 29:45; Lev. 26:12
24 [w]See ch. 34:23 [x]See Jer. 23:5 [y][ver. 22] [z]ch. 36:27
25 [a]ch. 28:25 [b]Isa. 60:21; Joel 3:20; Amos 9:15 [c][John 12:34]
26 [d]ch. 34:25 [e]See Isa. 55:3 [f]See ch. 36:10 [g]ver. 28; ch. 43:7; See ch. 11:16
27 [h]Lev. 26:11; Rev. 21:3 [v][See ver. 23 above]
28 [i]See ch. 36:23 [j]See ch. 20:12 [g][See ver. 26 above]

Chapter 38

2 [k]See ch. 2:1 [l]See ch. 6:2 [m]ch. 39:1, 11; Rev. 20:8 [n]ch. 39:6; Gen. 10:2; Rev. 20:8 [o]ch. 39:1 [p]See ch. 27:13 [q][ver. 4, 9]
3 [r]See ch. 13:8

[1] Or *one piece of wood*; also verses 17, 19, 20 [2] Hebrew *And I will place them on it, the stick of Judah* [3] Many Hebrew manuscripts; other Hebrew manuscripts *dwellings* [4] Hebrew lacks *in their land* [5] Or *Magog, the prince of Rosh, Meshech*

37:15–28 *The Houses of Israel and Judah.* The re-creative activity of vv. 1–14 included homecoming (vv. 12, 14). Although homecoming remains a minor element in the “dry bones” vision, it provides a link to this oracle (vv. 21, 25–26)—a symbolic action as in chs. 4–5 but much simpler than those Ezekiel performed earlier in his ministry. The instructions for this bit of street theater are given in 37:16–17. The reunion of Israel and Judah is another theme that Ezekiel shared with Jeremiah (cf. Jer. 30:3; 50:4; esp. 33:14–16, which joins the same themes as this passage). This action prompts questions from the onlookers (Ezek. 37:18) and sets up two oracles: vv. 19–20 announce the reunification of old northern and southern kingdoms; vv. 21–23 give the renewed nation its moral and political shape. Verses 24–28 elucidate the second oracle. The closing verses, with their allusions to the temple, provide a bridge to chs. 40–48.

37:16 Joseph, as father of **Ephraim** (see Gen. 48:5, 8–20), here represents the northern kingdom of Israel. **Judah** represents the southern kingdom (cf. Ps. 78:67–68).

37:19 make them one stick. Although the hopes for a reunion were alive at this time, Israel’s deportation by the Assyrians was already 150 years in the past. It may be that the “dry bones” vision in vv. 1–14 allayed doubts as to the plausibility of this hope.

37:21–22 This renewed national unity requires a secure national home (v. 21). The reunion takes concrete political shape under the rule of **one king**, which is not Ezekiel’s usual title for the messianic figure (cf. “prince,” v. 25).

37:23 The life of this nation is consistently moral and pure. The people are enabled to live in this way by God (**I will save them**). The covenant formula appears here and in v. 27, one mirroring the other.

37:24–25 The assignment of David as shepherd-**king** recalls 34:23–24, there in terms of **prince** (v. 25), as well as several passages in Jeremiah (e.g., Jer. 23:5; 30:9). Divine enabling to live rightly (Ezek. 37:23) does not exclude moral vigilance on the part of the people but enforces it.

37:26 The **covenant of peace** (see 34:25) and **everlasting covenant** (see 16:60) appeared individually earlier in Ezekiel. Here they come together to provide the charter for the renewed nation. The joining of these covenants also combines political life and the natural world, as if people and land are in symbiotic unity.

37:27–28 My dwelling place shall be with them. The oracle’s conclusion emphasizes the centrality of God’s presence to the renewed people, the greatest of all blessings by far. The “dwelling place” (Hb. *mishkan*) recalls the wilderness tabernacle. The **sanctuary** (Hb. *miqdash*; see v. 26) points rather to the temple, in particular the renewed temple, which will occupy Ezekiel’s attention in ch. 44.

38:1–39:29 *Gog of Magog.* These initially obscure chapters, which form a single unit, deliver a powerful assertion of God’s sovereignty. The prophet addresses the mysterious Gog, ruler of the equally mysterious Magog (see note on 38:2). Gog commands his own army and a legion of allies (38:4–6). Ezekiel’s oracle pronounces judgment on him for attacking renewed Israel (38:1–3, 7–13). However, there is a power greater than Gog: the sovereign God of Israel reigns over Gog’s plans, which will be used to vindicate God’s

prince of Meshech[1] and Tubal. **4** [s]And I will turn you about and [t]put hooks into your jaws,
and I will bring you out, and [u]all your army, horses and horsemen, all of them clothed in
full armor, a great host, all of them with buckler and shield, wielding swords. **5** [v]Persia,
[w]Cush, and [v]Put are with them, all of them with shield and helmet; **6** [x]Gomer and all his
[y]hordes; [z]Beth-togarmah from [a]the uttermost parts of the north with all his hordes—
[u]many peoples are with you.

7 [b]"Be ready and keep ready, you and all your hosts that are assembled about you, and
be a guard for them. **8** [c]After many days you will be mustered. [d]In the latter years you will
go against [d]the land that is restored from war, the land whose people [e]were gathered
from many peoples upon [f]the mountains of Israel, which had been a continual waste. Its
people were brought out from the peoples and [g]now dwell securely, all of them. **9** You will
advance, coming on [h]like a storm. You will be [i]like a cloud covering the land, you and all
your [y]hordes, and many peoples with you.

10 "Thus says the Lord GOD: On that day, [j]thoughts will come into your mind, and
you will devise an evil scheme **11** and say, 'I will go up against [k]the land of unwalled
villages. I will fall upon [l]the quiet people who dwell securely, all of them dwelling
without walls, and having no bars or gates,' **12** to seize spoil and carry off plunder, to
turn your hand against [m]the waste places that are now inhabited, and [m]the people who
were gathered from the nations, who have acquired livestock and goods, [n]who dwell at
the center of the earth. **13** [o]Sheba and [p]Dedan and the merchants of Tarshish and all [q]its

[1] Or *Gog, prince of Rosh, Meshech*

4 [s]ch. 39:2 [t]See ch. 29:4 [u][ver. 15]
5 [v]ch. 27:10 [w]Gen. 10:8
6 [x]Gen. 10:2 [y]ver. 22 [z]Gen. 10:3; See ch. 27:14 [a]ch. 39:2; [ch. 32:30] [u][See ver. 4 above]
7 [b][Isa. 8:9, 10]
8 [c]Isa. 24:22 [d][ver. 16] [e]See ch. 11:17 [f]See ch. 6:2 [g]ch. 34:25, 27, 28
9 [h][Isa. 28:2] [i][Jer. 4:13] [y][See ver. 6 above]
10 [j]See ch. 11:5
11 [k][Zech. 2:4, 5] [l][Jer. 49:31]
12 [m][ver. 8] [n][ch. 5:5, 7, 14, 15]
13 [o]ch. 27:22 [p]ch. 25:13; 27:15 [q][ch. 32:2; Ps. 17:12]

holiness (38:14–16). Gog and his hordes attack, bringing peril to God's people and convulsions to the natural world. But they meet the wrath of God, who vindicates himself before the nations (38:17–23). God's judgment against this latter-day enemy results in Gog's complete destruction. His army falls (39:1–6), an event that galvanizes God's people as they see the greatness of their God (39:7–8). So great is the number of the dead, and so complete the victory, that Israel will use the weapons taken from Gog as fuel for seven years (39:9–10) and take seven months to cleanse the land of the dead (39:11–16). This "sacrifice" will yield a feast for predators (39:17–20). No question will remain about the reason for Israel's earlier exile: the all-powerful God withdrew from them because of their treachery, but this final victory displays God's supremacy (39:21–24) and marks the final restoration of his people (39:25–29). Sketched thus, the contours of Ezekiel's prophecy against Gog are clear, but obscurity remains at the level of detail. The structural signals that usually mark Ezekiel's oracles are of less help here, as the introductions and conclusions often do not coincide. Another problem for interpretation is the shifting viewpoint taken at different points in the oracle (somewhat like the parable of ch. 17). As the vantage point shifts from prophet to observer to an overtly theological outlook, so too the reader's perception of the narrative alters. The setting of this oracle in the context of restored Israel remains clear, and theological lessons emerge. The security Israel enjoys is not the result of a lack of threats but of an indissoluble bond between God and people. Nor is the presence of threat a sign of God's absence: the human, animal, and natural worlds are all under God's control.

38:2 Gog, of the land of Magog. These two names have been the focus of extensive investigation and speculation in both Jewish and Christian literature, but there is no consensus on their meaning. Some interpreters think "Gog" is a veiled reference to a historical figure, such as Gyges, a seventh-century B.C. king of Lydia in Asia Minor, in which case the prophecy would be about a future attacker similar to Gyges. Others have thought it was a prediction of Alexander the Great (356–323 B.C.). But elsewhere Ezekiel was willing to make firm identifications or use more obvious symbols, and a connection with Alexander would be anything but obvious. Therefore many interpreters understand this passage to be a prophecy concerning an attack against Israel in a more distant future. In rabbinic literature and the Targums, Gog and Magog are often seen as leaders of a great attack on Israel in a future messianic age. In particular, Magog is seen as representing the Scythian people (see Josephus, *Jewish Antiquities* 1.123), who ruled vast regions of Asia north of the Black Sea and the Caspian Sea (modern Russia, Ukraine, and Kazakhstan) and who also conquered peoples east and south of the Black Sea (modern Georgia, Armenia, and Turkey). In the NT, Gog and Magog are the names of the nations led by Satan to attack Jerusalem at the end of the "thousand years" (Rev. 20:8). Although the other geographical names in this passage can be identified (see notes on Ezek. 38:5; 38:6), "Gog" and "Magog" remain enigmatic, perhaps because the intention of the prophecy is simply to point to a yet-unknown future leader of a great attack against God's people, one whose identity will not be known until the prophecy is fulfilled. No time is specified in the prophecy either, except the vague "In the latter years" in v. 8 and "In the latter days" in v. 16. (As the ESV footnote indicates, an alternative translation of v. 2 is "Gog, prince of Rosh, Meshech, and Tubal," but no place named "Rosh" can be clearly identified either.) **Meshech** and **Tubal**, first named in Gen. 10:2, are in Asia Minor (see note on Ezek. 27:13).

38:4 I will bring you out. From the beginning, God's initiative in rousing Gog's hordes is apparent.

38:5 For **Persia** (modern Iran), cf. 27:10; **Cush** is in the region of Ethiopia (cf. 29:10); **Put** is identified with Libya (27:10; 30:4–5). Gog's allies are described in terms analogous to those of Tyre in 27:10. Together with 38:2, 6, this passage depicts enemies coming against Israel from all sides: Meshech, Tubal, Gomer, and Beth-togarmah from the north (vv. 2, 6), and here Persia, Cush, and Put from the south.

38:6 Gomer probably refers to the Cimmerians, who had lived north of the Black Sea (modern Ukraine and the southern part of Russia) but were expelled by the conquering Scythians and migrated to an area south of the Black Sea, in Anatolia (modern Turkey). For **Beth-togarmah**, see note on 27:14. **The uttermost parts of the north** seems to refer to enemies that will come from regions to the far north of Israel, without specifically identifying these enemies. This phrase (repeated in 38:15; 39:2) has led some interpreters to understand this as a prediction of a future attack against Israel by Russia (Russia is the country farthest north of Israel, and Moscow is directly north of Jerusalem). But others see it as a general prediction of invaders from the north (see note on 38:2). In other places in the OT, this phrase describes the place where God reigns (Ps. 48:2) or where God will set his throne (Isa. 14:13), which would suggest a more symbolic interpretation of this oracle.

38:8 Locating this episode in the **latter years** in the **land that is restored** casts this oracle into the future. See the "latter days" in v. 16 (cf. note on Isa. 2:2); thus, it is not necessarily the absolute end of time.

38:10–13 The clear insistence that Gog remains firmly under God's control and, in fact, acts at God's behest (vv. 4, 16), does not preclude Gog from forming plans to plunder the now-fertile land of restored Israel (**the quiet**

leaders[1] will say to you, 'Have you come to seize spoil? Have you assembled your hosts
to carry off plunder, to carry away silver and gold, to take away livestock and goods, to
seize great spoil?'
14 "Therefore, [r]son of man, prophesy, and say to [s]Gog, Thus says the Lord GOD: On
that day when my people Israel are [g]dwelling securely, [t]will you not know it? **15** You will
come from your place out of [u]the uttermost parts of the north, you and [v]many peoples
with you, [w]all of them riding on horses, a great host, a mighty army. **16** You will come up
against my people Israel, [i]like a cloud covering the land. [x]In the latter days I will bring you
against my land, that the nations may know me, when through you, O Gog, [y]I vindicate
my holiness before their eyes.
17 "Thus says the Lord GOD: Are you [z]he of whom I spoke in former days by my servants
the prophets of Israel, who in those days prophesied for years that I would bring you
against them? **18** But on that day, the day that Gog shall come against the land of Israel,
declares the Lord GOD, [a]my wrath will be roused in my anger. **19** For [b]in my jealousy and
in my blazing wrath I declare, On that day [c]there shall be a great earthquake in the land
of Israel. **20** [d]The fish of the sea and the birds of the heavens and the beasts of the field and
all creeping things that creep on the ground, and all the people who are on the face of
the earth, [e]shall quake at my presence. And [f]the mountains shall be thrown down, and
the cliffs shall fall, and every wall shall tumble to the ground. **21** [g]I will summon a sword
against Gog[2] on all my mountains, declares the Lord GOD. [h]Every man's sword will be
against his brother. **22** With pestilence and bloodshed [i]I will enter into judgment with
him, and [j]I will rain upon him and [k]his hordes and the many peoples who are with him
[l]torrential rains and hailstones, [m]fire and sulfur. **23** So I will show my greatness and my
[n]holiness and [o]make myself known in the eyes of many nations. Then [p]they will know
that I am the LORD.

39 "And you, [q]son of man, [r]prophesy against [s]Gog and say, Thus says the Lord GOD:
Behold, [t]I am against you, O Gog, [u]chief prince of [v]Meshech[3] and [v]Tubal. **2** [w]And I
will turn you about and drive you forward, and bring you up from [x]the uttermost parts
of the north, and lead you against the [y]mountains of Israel. **3** Then [z]I will strike your bow
from your left hand, and [z]will make your arrows drop out of your right hand. **4** [a]You shall
fall on [y]the mountains of Israel, you and all your [b]hordes and the peoples who are with you.
[c]I will give you to birds of prey of every sort and to the beasts of the field to be devoured.
5 You shall fall in the open field, for [d]I have spoken, declares the Lord GOD. **6** [e]I will send
fire on [f]Magog and on those [g]who dwell securely in [h]the coastlands, and [i]they shall know
that I am the LORD.
7 "And [j]my holy name I will make known in the midst of my people Israel, and [k]I will
not let my holy name be profaned anymore. And [l]the nations shall know that I am [m]the
LORD, the Holy One in Israel. **8** [n]Behold, it is coming and it will be brought about, declares
the Lord GOD. That is the day [o]of which I have spoken.
9 "Then those who dwell in the cities of Israel will go out and [p]make fires of the weapons
and burn them, shields and bucklers, bow and arrows, [q]clubs[4] and spears; and they will
make fires of them for seven years, **10** so that they will not need to take wood out of the

[1] Hebrew *young lions* [2] Hebrew *against him* [3] *Or Gog, prince of Rosh, Meshech* [4] *Or javelins*

14 [r]See ch. 2:1 [s]ver. 2, 3 [g][See ver. 8 above] [t][ver. 11]
15 [u]ver. 6; ch. 39:2 [v][ver. 6, 9, 22] [w]ch. 23:6
16 [i][See ver. 9 above] [x][ver. 8] [y]ver. 23; [ch. 39:13]; See ch. 20:41
17 [z][Jer. 6:22, 23]
18 [a][Ps. 18:8]
19 [b]See ch. 5:13 [c][Hag. 2:6, 7; Rev. 16:18]
20 [d][Hos. 4:3] [e][Ps. 114:7] [f]Jer. 4:24
21 [g]Jer. 25:29 [h][Judg. 7:22]
22 [i][ch. 17:20] [j]Ps. 11:6 [k]ver. 6, 9 [l]ch. 13:11, 13 [m]Ps. 11:6; [ch. 39:6; Rev. 20:9]
23 [n]See ver. 16 [o]ch. 36:23; 37:28 [p]See ch. 6:7

Chapter 39

1 [q]See ch. 2:1 [r]ch. 38:2, 3 [s]ch. 38:2 [t]ch. 38:3; See ch. 13:8 [u]ch. 38:2, 3 [v]ch. 38:2
2 [w]ch. 38:4 [x]ch. 38:6, 15; [ch. 32:30] [y]See ch. 6:2
3 [z][Ps. 76:3]
4 [a][ch. 38:21] [y][See ver. 2 above] [b]ch. 38:6, 9, 22 [c][ver. 17]
5 [d]See ch. 17:21
6 [e][ch. 28:18; 30:8, 14, 16; 38:22] [f]ch. 38:2 [g]ch. 38:8, 14 [h]ch. 27:3, 6, 7, 15 [i]See ch. 6:7
7 [j][ver. 22] [k]See ch. 20:39 [l]See ch. 36:23 [m]Isa. 45:11
8 [n]ch. 21:7 [o]ch. 38:17
9 [p][Ps. 46:9; Isa. 9:5] [q][1 Sam. 17:40]

people who dwell securely, v. 11) and being held responsible for those plans.

38:16 like a cloud. The vastness of Gog's hordes that come against Israel is a theme repeated throughout these chapters. Once again, God's sovereignty over Gog's actions is asserted (**I will bring you**), as Gog is a tool used to vindicate God's holiness. In this, Gog evokes Pharaoh in the exodus narratives (see Ex. 7:3–5; 14:4).

38:17 The Septuagint understands this sentence as an assertion rather than a question (though the Hb. is more naturally a question). Either way, it probably relates to the mysterious "foe from the north" tradition linked especially to Jeremiah (e.g., Jer. 4:6; 6:22).

38:19–20 Upheaval in nature, reflecting the cosmic outpouring of God's wrath, consequently affects God's own people. Such phenomena are also part of Jeremiah's vision of the future (cf. Jer. 4:23–26).

38:22–23 This battle is God's. So too the greatness belongs to him alone.

39:1–6 God's opposition to Gog is reiterated as the invasion of Israel proceeds, only for Gog's army to fall solely by the hand of God. On **Meshech** and **Tubal**, see note on 38:2. **uttermost parts**. See note on 38:6.

39:7–8 This brief passage asserting the devotion to the holy God by his own people is introduced at this point as the obvious peril implied in vv. 2–5 draws attention to the Israelites themselves. It also forges a link with 21:7, where the words of 39:8 were applied to Judah and Jerusalem. The fall of Gog's hordes is as certain as Jerusalem's own was.

39:9 The **seven years** of fuel provided by the abandoned weapons of the

field or cut down any out of the forests, for [p]they will make their fires of the weapons.
[r]They will seize the spoil of those who despoiled them, and plunder those who plundered
them, declares the Lord GOD.
11 "On that day I will give to [s]Gog a place for burial in Israel, the Valley of the Travelers,
east of the sea. It will block the travelers, for there Gog and all his multitude will be
buried. It will be called the Valley of [t]Hamon-gog.[1] 12 For [u]seven months the house of
Israel will be burying them, in order [v]to cleanse the land. 13 All the people of the land
will bury them, and it will bring them renown on the day that [w]I show my glory, declares
the Lord GOD. 14 They will set apart men to travel through the land regularly and bury
those travelers remaining on the face of the land, so as [v]to cleanse it. At[2] the end of [x]seven
months they will make their search. 15 And when these travel through the land and anyone sees a human bone, then he shall set up a sign by it, till the buriers have buried it
in the Valley of [y]Hamon-gog. 16 (Hamonah[3] is also the name of the city.) Thus shall they
cleanse the land.
17 "As for you, [z]son of man, thus says the Lord GOD: [a]Speak to [b]the birds of every sort
and to [b]all beasts of the field, 'Assemble and come, gather from all around to [c]the sacrificial
feast that I am preparing for you, a great sacrificial feast on the mountains of Israel, and
you shall eat flesh and drink blood. 18 [d]You shall eat the flesh of the mighty, and drink
the blood of the princes of the earth—of rams, of lambs, and of he-goats, of bulls, all
of them [e]fat beasts of Bashan. 19 And you shall eat fat till you are filled, and drink blood
till you are drunk, at the sacrificial feast that I am preparing for you. 20 And you shall be
filled at my table with horses and charioteers, with mighty men and all kinds of warriors,'
declares the Lord GOD.
21 "And [f]I will set my glory among the nations, and all the nations shall see [g]my judgment that I have executed, and [g]my hand that I have laid on them. 22 [h]The house of Israel
shall know that I am the LORD their God, from that day forward. 23 And [i]the nations shall
know that the house of Israel went into captivity for their iniquity, because they dealt so
treacherously with me that [j]I hid my face from them and [k]gave them into the hand of
their adversaries, and they all fell by the sword. 24 I dealt with them [l]according to their
uncleanness and their transgressions, and hid my face from them.

The LORD Will Restore Israel

25 "Therefore thus says the Lord GOD: Now [m]I will restore the fortunes of Jacob and have
mercy on [n]the whole house of Israel, and [o]I will be jealous for my holy name. 26 They shall
[p]forget their shame and all the treachery they have practiced against me, when [q]they dwell
securely in their land with [r]none to make them afraid, 27 [s]when I have brought them back
from the peoples and gathered them from their enemies' lands, [t]and through them have
vindicated my holiness in the sight of many nations. 28 [h]Then they shall know that I am
the LORD their God, because I sent them into exile among the nations and then assembled
them into their own land. I will leave none of them remaining among the nations anymore.
29 [u]And I will not hide my face anymore from them, when [v]I pour out my Spirit upon the
house of Israel, declares the Lord GOD."

[1] *Hamon-gog* means *the multitude of Gog* [2] Or *Until* [3] *Hamonah* means *multitude*

10 [p][See ver. 9 above] [r][Isa. 33:1]
11 [s]ch. 38:2 [t]ver. 15
12 [u][ver. 14] [v][Deut. 21:23]
13 [w]ch. 28:22
14 [v][See ver. 12 above] [x][ver. 12]
15 [y]ver. 11
17 [z]See ch. 2:1 [a][Rev. 19:17] [b]ver. 4; [Jer. 12:9] [c][Isa. 34:6; Zeph. 1:7]
18 [d][Rev. 19:18] [e][Ps. 22:12]
21 [f]ver. 7, 13; [ch. 28:22; 37:28; 38:23]; See ch. 36:23 [g][Ex. 7:4]
22 [h]ver. 28; Joel 2:27; See ch. 6:7
23 [i]See Deut. 29:24-28 [j]Deut. 31:17 [k][Lev. 26:25]
24 [l][See ch. 18:30]
25 [m]See Jer. 30:3 [n]ch. 20:40 [o][ch. 20:9]; See ch. 5:13
26 [p]See ch. 32:24 [q]ch. 34:25, 27, 28; 38:8 [r]ch. 34:28
27 [s]ch. 28:25; See ch. 11:17 [t]See ch. 20:41
28 [h][See ver. 22 above]
29 [u][ver. 23] [v][Joel 2:28]

enemy corresponds to the "seven months" of burial in v. 14. The number seven is also deliberately employed in the collection of oracles against foreign nations.

39:17–20 This grisly scene represents the wholesale inversion of what sacrifice intends, but God has inverted it. The slain of Gog's army are carrion for scavengers, a banquet celebrating condemnation. In John's vision of the end in Rev. 19:17–21, he sees an angel using this language and this imagery.

39:21–24 all the nations shall see my judgment. This absolute, unanswerable demonstration of God's power serves as vindication before the nations. It also puts Israel's exile into proper perspective. Their expulsion from their land was not because their God was incapable of preserving them. On the contrary, their treachery compelled God to hide his **face** (vv. 23, 24; cf. v. 29) from them, leaving them to the fate they deserved for their **iniquity** of turning against God (cf. Deut. 31:18).

39:25–29 The final element of the oracle attends now to Israel rather than to Gog. These brief verses echo many of the restoration passages in chs. 34–37, including the themes of renewal for the **whole house of Israel** (39:25), the turning away from previous **treachery** (v. 26), and the gathering and return of those once scattered (vv. 27–28).

39:29 God's promise (**I will not hide my face**) ensures that the abandonment reviewed in vv. 23–24 is consigned to the past (cf. Isa. 54:8). As in Ezek. 37:1–14, this final renewal coincides with the outpouring of **my Spirit**.

Vision of the New Temple

40 [w]In the twenty-fifth year [x]of our exile, at the beginning of the year, on the tenth
day of the month, [y]in the fourteenth year after the city was struck down, on that
very day, [z]the hand of the LORD was upon me, and he brought me to the city.[1] 2 In [a]visions
of God he brought me to the land of Israel, and set me down on [b]a very high mountain,
on which was a structure like a city to the south. 3 When he brought me there, behold,
there was [c]a man whose appearance was [d]like bronze, with [e]a linen cord and [f]a measuring
reed in his hand. And he was standing in the gateway. 4 And the man said to me, [g]"Son of
man, [h]look with your eyes, and [h]hear with your ears, and set your heart upon all that I
shall show you, for you were brought here in order that I might show it to you. [i]Declare
all that you see to the house of Israel."

The East Gate to the Outer Court

5 And behold, there was [j]a wall all around the outside of the temple area, and the length
of the measuring reed in the man's hand was six long cubits, [k]each being a cubit and a
handbreadth[2] in length. So he measured the thickness of the wall, one reed; and the height,
one reed. 6 Then he went into [l]the gateway facing east, [m]going up its steps, and measured
the threshold of the gate, one reed deep.[3] 7 And [n]the side rooms, one reed long and one reed
broad; and the space between the side rooms, five cubits; and the threshold of the gate by

[1] Hebrew *brought me there* [2] A cubit was about 18 inches or 45 centimeters; a *handbreadth* was about 3 inches or 7.5 centimeters [3] Hebrew *deep, and one threshold, one reed deep*

Chapter 40

1 [w]See ch. 20:1 [x]ch. 33:21; See ch. 1:2 [y][ch. 26:1, 2] [z]See ch. 1:3
2 [a]See ch. 1:1 [b][ch. 43:12; Rev. 21:10]
3 [c]ch. 43:6; 47:3; See ch. 9:2 [d]See ch. 1:7 [e][ch. 47:3] [f][Rev. 11:1]; See ch. 42:16-19
4 [g]See ch. 2:1 [h]ch. 44:5 [i]ch. 43:10
5 [j]ch. 42:20 [k][ch. 41:8; 43:13]
6 [l]See ch. 43:1 [m][ver. 22]
7 [n]ver. 29, 33, 36

40:1–48:35 *Vision of Restoration.* With the last date formula in the book appearing at 40:1, Ezekiel arrives at the beginning of the end. The post-destruction oracles of chs. 33–37 concluded with a promise of divine presence that anticipates the final words of the book (cf. 37:26–28; 48:35). The oracle against Gog in chs. 38–39 appeared to interrupt the movement toward realizing that presence. That interpretation, however, assumes a reading of the book that focuses on the human plane, which is not Ezekiel's perspective. The most important thing is not human hope but divine glory. The Gog oracle established God's absolute supremacy among the nations. The book's final vision accomplishes this same purpose, but within the community of God's own people. Understood this way, the details of Ezekiel's vision (which may strike the modern reader as mundane or obscure) take on their proper vitality and significance. The vision of chs. 40–48 is a direct counterpart to the pre-destruction vision in chs. 8–11, in which the abominations practiced in Jerusalem drove the holy God from his temple. In chs. 40–42, Ezekiel is again taken on a tour, this time of the new temple, which culminates with the return of the glory of God (43:1–5). The voice of the Lord now instructs Ezekiel in the regulations for Israel's renewed worship life (43:6–46:24). When the "tour" resumes, Ezekiel witnesses the river flowing from the temple, which brings life to the world (46:19–47:12). The book concludes with the division of the land among the tribes with the new city and new temple at its heart, with equal access for all (47:13–48:35).

With regard to the meaning of this passage as a whole: (1) Some interpreters understand this vision as a prophecy that will be fulfilled literally, with a rebuilt temple and Israel dwelling in the land according to its tribes—a future millennial kingdom on the earth (see notes on Rev. 20:1–6). Many who hold this position believe that literal animal sacrifices will be offered, but that in the future millennial kingdom they will function as reminders of the complete and sufficient death of Christ, a function different from what they had in the OT. (2) Other interpreters see this vision of a new temple and a renewal of the land of Israel as an extended, detailed metaphor predicting the presence of God among his people in the new covenant age (that is, his presence in the church). (3) Another view is that the vision predicts God's presence among his people in the new heavens and new earth (cf. Isa. 66:17; 2 Pet. 3:13; Rev. 21:1), not as physical details that will be literally fulfilled but as symbolic indications of the great blessings of that future age. In this interpretation, the details about worship and sacrifices are symbols of the centrality of worship of God: the temple represents the orderliness and beauty of God's heavenly dwelling place; the priests and their sacrifices represent the service and worship of all God's people; the division of the land represents the allocation of places to live for all God's people; and the river represents the outward flow of God's blessings to his people forever. (4) Finally, it is possible that there are both literal and symbolic elements in this vision, and that, as with the visions in Ezekiel 1, this vision describes future realities that cannot be fully expressed in terms of Ezekiel's present realities. Almost all interpreters agree that Ezekiel 40–48 is one of the most difficult passages in the entire Bible.

No matter which interpretation one adopts, certain primary emphases are quite clear. The whole vision may be understood as describing the actual presence of God within the temple of the new community: chs. 40–42 prepare for it; ch. 43 realizes it; chs. 44–46 provide the rules for it; ch. 47 describes its effects; and ch. 48 lays out access to it. The vision thus also presupposes threads and themes of earlier oracles: the supremacy of God; the requirements necessitated by his holiness; revitalization by the Spirit of God; honoring God by living in accord with his holiness; and ensuring the sanctity of the community by maintaining divine justice.

40:1–42:20 *Vision of the New Temple.* Fourteen years after the destruction of Jerusalem, Ezekiel is given a vision of a rebuilt temple, just as he had been given a temple vision 20 years earlier (8:1). (For a drawing of this temple plan, see pp. 1566–1567.) As on that occasion, a heavenly being leads him around the temple precincts. This time, however, the vision does not reveal the sin of Ezekiel's people but the splendor of his God. The temple itself appears to be geometrically idealized. It is a square structure, its areas nested, with the most sacred place being both the innermost and the uppermost, as each succeeding area is elevated from the preceding. It seems also to be symmetrical around the east-west axis, with the main entrance facing east. Ezekiel is led back to the outer court in ch. 42 where various chambers of the temple area are identified. Cf. illustration, p. 1567.

40:1–4 *The Vision Begins.* The date formula corresponds to April 573 B.C. About 12 years have passed since the last dated oracle (32:1). The phrase **visions of God** links this vision with 1:1 and 8:3. The ruined city is in the prophet's mind (40:1) as the vision of a new city comes to him (v. 2). His guide, with an **appearance** like **bronze**, is reminiscent of the guide of 8:2.

40:5–27 *The Outer Court and Its Gates.* The tour with accompanying measurements begins at the main east entrance. (A number of the Hb. technical architectural terms are of uncertain meaning, as the ESV footnotes illustrate.) The main units of measurement are given (v. 5): the **reed**, about 10 feet (3.1 m), which was equal to **six long cubits** of about 20 inches (50 cm). The outer wall is thus about 10 feet high and 10 feet thick (v. 5; 3.1 m high and 3.1 m thick). The main east gate with its chambers is described (vv. 6–16) in more detail than the other gates, which are built to the same plan. The

the vestibule of the gate at the inner end, one reed. **8** Then he measured the vestibule of the
gateway, on the inside, one reed. **9** Then he measured the vestibule of the gateway, eight
cubits; [o]and its jambs, two cubits; and the vestibule of the gate was at the inner end. **10** And
there were three side rooms on either side of the east gate. [p]The three were of the same
size, and the jambs on either side were of the same size. **11** Then he measured the width
of the opening of the gateway, ten cubits; and the length of the gateway, thirteen cubits.
12 There was a barrier before the side rooms, one cubit on either side. And the side rooms
were six cubits on either side. **13** Then he measured the gate from the ceiling of the one
side room to the ceiling of the other, a breadth of twenty-five cubits; the openings faced
each other. **14** He measured also [q]the vestibule, twenty cubits. And around the vestibule of
the gateway was the court.[1] **15** From the front of the gate at the entrance to the front of the
inner vestibule of the gate was fifty cubits. **16** And the gateway had [r]windows all around,
narrowing inwards toward the side rooms and toward their [s]jambs, and likewise the vestibule had windows all around inside, and on the jambs were [t]palm trees.

The Outer Court

17 Then he brought me into [u]the outer court. And behold, there were [v]chambers and a
[w]pavement, all around the court. [x]Thirty chambers faced the pavement. **18** And the pavement ran along the side of the gates, corresponding to the length of the gates. This was
the lower pavement. **19** Then he measured the distance from the inner front of the lower
gate to the outer front of the inner court,[2] a hundred cubits on the east side and on the
north side.[3]

The North Gate

20 As for [y]the gate that faced toward the north, belonging to [u]the outer court, he measured
its length and its breadth. **21** Its [n]side rooms, three on either side, and its jambs and its vestibule
were of the same size as those of [z]the first gate. Its length was [a]fifty cubits, and its breadth
[b]twenty-five cubits. **22** And [c]its windows, its vestibule, and [c]its palm trees were of the same
size as those of the gate that faced toward the east. And by seven steps [d]people would go up
to it, and find its vestibule before them. **23** And opposite the gate on the north, as on the east,
was a gate to [e]the inner court. And [f]he measured from gate to gate, a hundred cubits.

The South Gate

24 And he led me toward the south, and behold, there was a gate on the south. And [g]he
measured its jambs and its vestibule; they had the same size as the others. **25** Both it and
its vestibule [h]had windows all around, like the windows of the others. Its length was fifty
cubits, and its breadth twenty-five cubits. **26** And there were seven steps leading up to it,
and its vestibule was before them, and it had [i]palm trees on its jambs, one on either side.
27 And there was a gate on the south of [j]the inner court. And he measured from gate to
gate toward the south, a hundred cubits.

The Inner Court

28 Then he brought me to [j]the inner court through the south gate, and [k]he measured
the south gate. It was of the same size as the others. **29** Its [l]side rooms, its jambs, and its
vestibule were of the same size as the others, and both it and its vestibule [m]had windows
all around. [m]Its length was fifty cubits, and its breadth twenty-five cubits. **30** And there were
vestibules all around, twenty-five cubits long and five cubits broad. **31** Its vestibule faced
the outer court, and [i]palm trees were on its jambs, and [n]its stairway had eight steps.

32 Then he brought me to the inner court on the east side, and [o]he measured the gate. It
was of the same size as the others. **33** Its side rooms, its jambs, and its vestibule were of the

[1] Text uncertain; Hebrew *And he made the jambs sixty cubits, and to the jamb of the court was the gateway all around* [2] Hebrew *distance from before the low gate before the inner court to the outside* [3] Or *cubits. So far the eastern gate; now to the northern gate.*

9 [o]ch. 41:1
10 [p][ver. 7]
14 [q]ver. 9, 16
16 [r]ch. 41:16, 26; [1 Kgs. 6:4] [s]ver. 9, 14 [t]ch. 41:18
17 [u]ch. 42:1; [Rev. 11:2] [v]ver. 38, 44, 45, 46; ch. 41:10; See 2 Kgs. 23:11 [w][2 Chr. 7:3] [x]ch. 41:6; [ch. 45:5]
20 [y][ver. 6] [u][See ver. 17 above]
21 [n][See ver. 7 above] [z][ver. 6] [a][ver. 15] [b][ver. 13]
22 [c][ver. 16] [d][ver. 6]
23 [e]ver. 28; [ch. 8:3] [f]ver. 27
24 [g][ver. 21]
25 [h]ver. 22
26 [i][ver. 16]
27 [j]ver. 23; ch. 8:16
28 [j][See ver. 27 above] [k][ver. 24]
29 [l]See ver. 7 [m][ver. 25]
31 [i][See ver. 26 above] [n][ver. 22]
32 [o][ver. 21]

expanse of the main outer court is taken in (vv. 17–19) before inspection of first the north gate (vv. 20–23), then the south gate (vv. 24–27).

40:28–49 *The Inner Court, Gates, and Chambers.* Ezekiel's guide then leads him into the inner court by way of the south gate (v. 28), and the descriptions are more cursory since the design is repeated from the outer gates. The sequence now is south gate (vv. 28–31), east gate (vv. 32–34), and north gate (vv. 35–37). This area is reserved for priestly use, and the furnishings and implements for sacrificial rituals are described in vv. 38–43. The chambers for the use of ministering priests of two classes (see 44:9–31) are found in the north and south gates (40:44–47). They then approach the central structure of the inner court, the temple building itself (vv. 48–49). With 10 steps (v. 49; cf. vv. 22, 31), it has the tallest rise of any set of stairs.

EZEKIEL'S TEMPLE VISION

Ezekiel's final vision of an ideal temple (and city, and land; chs. 40–48) forms a counterpart to the vision of chs. 8–11. In each case he is taken on a tour of the structure, but whereas in the earlier vision he discovers abominations and perverted worship, in this final vision all is in readiness for the perpetual dwelling of the glory of the God of Israel. In chs. 8–10 most of the movement centers on the gate structures to the north and finally focuses on the main sacrificial altar, from which central point the slaughtering angels begin their work (9:6b). In this final vision Ezekiel's tour begins and ends at the East Gate, but passes by the same areas as those he saw in the earlier vision. With the "tour" completed, he is again outside the main East Gate as he senses the approach of the glory of God returning the same way as Ezekiel had seen him go.

Temple Plan

The labels below are arranged from the innermost, and most sacred, area and moving outward. It must be borne in mind that "temple" can have two quite distinct references: it can refer generally to the entire "temple" complex, including the outer gates and court; in its more "strict" reference the "temple" is the innermost structure itself, which has a single (eastern) entrance and contains the Most Holy Place.

	Reference	Explanation
A	41:4	The "Most Holy Place."
B	41:3	The inner room of the temple.
C	41:2	The entrance to the temple.
D	43:13–17	The imposing altar; although the number of stairs is not given, the entire altar structure is about 16 feet (4.9 m) tall, so many steps would have been required. This area of the inner court was accessible only by priests—not even the prince was permitted entry.
E	40:46	Chamber for Zadokite priests.
F	40:45	Chamber for "priests who have charge of the temple."
G	40:17–19	The outer court, with its 30 chambers in the outer wall (40:17).
H	46:21–24	The temple "kitchens," one in each corner of the outer court.
I	40:17	The 30 outer chambers.
J	46:2	The "prince's gate": from its threshold he worships on each Sabbath while the priests bring the offerings into the inner court.
K	43:1	The main east gate, through which "the glory of the God of Israel" returns to his temple (cf. 10:19; 11:22–23).

Temple Tour

	Reference	Explanation
1	40:6	The eastern (main) gate begins the tour; the E–W axis of the temple should be noted; if a line is drawn from the east gate to the Most Holy Place, there is a sequence of three elevations, as the space in the inner temple becomes increasingly constricted.
2	40:17	From this vantage point in the outer court, Ezekiel is shown the main features of this "plaza" area.
3	40:20	The northern-facing gate.
4	40:24	En route to the southern-facing gate, no details are given of the outer facade of the inner court; the architectural details of this area must remain speculative.
5	40:28	Ezekiel's entry to the inner court is by way of its south gate . . .
6	40:32	. . . then to the east gate (past the imposing altar, not yet described) . . .
7	40:35	. . . and on to the north gate, which includes areas for handling sacrificial animals.
8	40:48; 41:1	Ezekiel approaches the inner temple structure itself, first describing its entrance; he is then stationed outside the entrance while his guide first measures its interior, then the exterior.
9	42:1	They exit the inner court through its north gate to explore the northwestern quadrant of the outer court.
10	42:15	Ezekiel and his guide leave the temple from the east gate by which they first entered. From this vantage point, Ezekiel was able to watch the return of "the glory of the God of Israel" moments later (43:1–5).

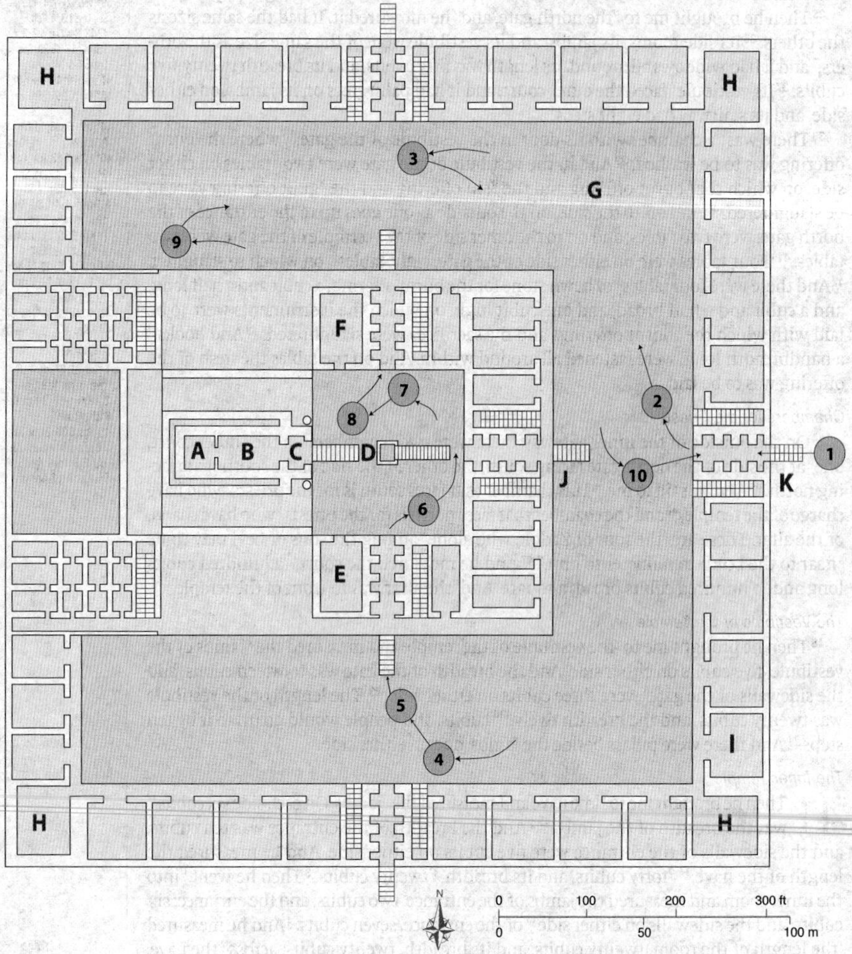

Letters in diagram represent locations within the temple complex; numbers indicate the stages in Ezekiel's temple tour (see charts on opposite page).

same size as the others, and both it and its vestibule had windows all around. Its length
was fifty cubits, and its breadth twenty-five cubits. 34 [p]Its vestibule faced the outer court,
and it had palm trees on its jambs, on either side, and its stairway had eight steps.
35 Then he brought me to [q]the north gate, and [r]he measured it. It had the same size as
the others. 36 Its side rooms, its jambs, and its vestibule were of the same size as the others,[1] and it had windows all around. Its length was fifty cubits, and its breadth twenty-five
cubits. 37 Its vestibule[2] faced the outer court, and it had palm trees on its jambs, on either
side, and its stairway had eight steps.
38 There was [s]a chamber with its door in the vestibule of the gate,[3] [t]where the burnt
offering was to be washed. 39 And in the vestibule of the gate were two [u]tables on either
side, on which the [v]burnt offering and the [w]sin offering and the [x]guilt offering were to
be slaughtered. 40 And off to the side, on the outside as one goes up to the entrance of the
north gate, were two tables; and off to the other side of the vestibule of the gate were two
tables. 41 [y]Four tables were on either side of the gate, eight tables, [z]on which to slaughter.
42 And there were four tables [a]of hewn stone for the burnt offering, a cubit and a half long,
and a cubit and a half broad, and one cubit high, on which the instruments were to be
laid with which the [v]burnt offerings and the sacrifices were slaughtered. 43 And hooks,[4]
a handbreadth long, were fastened all around within. And on the tables the flesh of the
offering was to be laid.

Chambers for the Priests

44 On the outside of the inner gateway there were two [b]chambers[5] in the [c]inner court,
one[6] at the side of the north gate facing south, the other at the side of the south[7] gate facing north. 45 And he said to me, "This chamber that faces south is for the priests [d]who have
charge of the temple, 46 and the chamber that faces north is for the priests [e]who have charge
of the altar. These are [f]the sons of Zadok, who alone[8] among the sons of Levi may come
[g]near to the LORD to minister to him." 47 And he measured the court, [h]a hundred cubits
long and [h]a hundred cubits broad, a square. And [i]the altar was in front of the temple.

The Vestibule of the Temple

48 Then he brought me to [j]the vestibule of the temple and measured the [k]jambs of the
vestibule, five cubits on either side. And the breadth of the gate was fourteen cubits, and
the sidewalls of the gate[9] were three cubits on either side. 49 [l]The length of the vestibule
was twenty cubits, and the breadth twelve[10] cubits, and people would go up to it by ten
steps.[11] And there were pillars beside the jambs, one on either side.

The Inner Temple

41 Then he brought me to [m]the nave and measured the [n]jambs. On each side six cubits[12]
was the breadth of the jambs.[13] 2 And the breadth of the entrance was ten cubits,
and the sidewalls of the entrance were five cubits on either side. And he measured the
length of the nave,[14] [o]forty cubits, and its breadth, [p]twenty cubits. 3 Then he went [q]into
the inner room and measured the jambs of the entrance, two cubits; and the entrance, six
cubits; and the sidewalls on either side[15] of the entrance, seven cubits. 4 And he measured
[r]the length of the room, twenty cubits, and its breadth, twenty cubits, across [s]the nave.
And he said to me, "This is [t]the Most Holy Place."
5 Then he measured the wall of the temple, six cubits thick, and the breadth of [u]the
side chambers, four cubits, [u]all around the temple. 6 And the side chambers were in three

[1] One manuscript (compare verses 29 and 33); most manuscripts lack *were of the same size as the others* [2] Septuagint, Vulgate (compare verses 26, 31, 34); Hebrew *jambs* [3] Hebrew *at the jambs, the gates* [4] Or *shelves* [5] Septuagint; Hebrew *were chambers for singers* [6] Hebrew lacks *one* [7] Septuagint; Hebrew *east* [8] Hebrew lacks *alone* [9] Septuagint; Hebrew lacks *was fourteen cubits, and the sidewalls of the gate* [10] Septuagint; Hebrew *eleven* [11] Septuagint; Hebrew *and by steps that would go up to it* [12] A *cubit* was about 18 inches or 45 centimeters [13] Compare Septuagint; Hebrew *tent* [14] Hebrew *its length* [15] Septuagint; Hebrew *and the breadth*

34 [p]ver. 31
35 [q]ch. 47:2 [r]ver. 32, 33
38 [s][ver. 17] [t][ch. 46:2; 2 Chr. 4:6]
39 [u][ver. 42] [v][ch. 46:2]; See Lev. 1:3, 4 [w]ch. 42:13; See Lev. 4:2, 3 [x]ch. 42:13; 46:20; See Lev. 5:1-6
41 [y][ver. 39, 40] [z][ver. 38]
42 [a][Ex. 20:25] [v][See ver. 39 above]
44 [b][ver. 17, 38] [c]1 Chr. 6:31, 32
45 [d]1 Chr. 9:23; [ch. 44:8, 14, 15, 16; 48:11]; See Lev. 8:35; Num. 1:53
46 [e][Num. 3:31]; See Num. 18:5 [f]ch. 43:19; 44:15; [1 Kgs. 2:35; 1 Chr. 24:3, 6] [g]ch. 42:13; 45:4
47 [h]See ch. 41:13-15 [i][ch. 43:13; Ex. 40:29; Matt. 23:35]
48 [j]ch. 41:25, 26 [k][ver. 9]
49 [l]1 Kgs. 6:3

Chapter 41

1 [m]ver. 21, 23; ch. 42:8 [n]ver. 3; ch. 40:9
2 [o]1 Kgs. 6:17 [p]1 Kgs. 6:2
3 [q]ch. 40:16
4 [r]1 Kgs. 6:20; 2 Chr. 3:8 [s]1 Kgs. 6:5 [t]ver. 21, 23; ch. 45:3; See 1 Kgs. 6:16
5 [u]1 Kgs. 6:5, 8; See ver. 6-9

41:1–26 *The Temple Interior.* The temple structure is now described in detail, including both floor plan and elevations. The **nave** (v. 1) is the main hall of the temple. Ezekiel is guided into its interior but does not follow his celestial guide into the **Most Holy Place** (v. 4). This might have been the climax of the tour, but it continues. Verses 5–11 describe the three-story structure built into the temple's walls. A building is located to the extreme west of the temple complex (v. 12), but no purpose is identified for it. The previous measurements are summarized in vv. 13–15a, while visual descriptions of the temple's decorations and layout are described in vv. 15b–26. The **cherubim**, carved on the walls in relief (vv. 18–20), are reminiscent of the cherubim woven into the fabric walls of the tabernacle (Ex. 26:1, 31). The **cherubim** and **palm trees** are combined in the decoration of Solomon's temple (1 Kings 6:29, 32).

stories, one over another, [v]thirty in each story. There were offsets[1] all around the wall of the
temple to serve as supports for the side chambers, [w]so that they should not be supported by
the wall of the temple. **7** And it became broader as it wound upward to the side chambers,
because the temple was enclosed upward all around the temple. Thus the temple had a
broad area upward, and [x]so one went up from the lowest story to the top story through
the middle story. **8** I saw also that the temple had a raised platform all around; the foundations of the side chambers measured a full reed of [y]six long cubits. **9** The thickness of the
outer wall of the side chambers was five cubits. [z]The free space between the side chambers
of the temple and the **10** [a]other chambers was a breadth of [b]twenty cubits all around the
temple on every side. **11** And the doors of the [c]side chambers opened on [d]the free space,
one door toward the north, and another door toward the south. And the breadth of the
free space was five cubits all around.

12 The building that was facing [e]the separate yard on the west side was seventy cubits broad,
and the wall of the building was five cubits thick all around, and its length ninety cubits.
13 Then he measured the temple, [f]a hundred cubits long; and the yard and the building
with its walls, a hundred cubits long; **14** also the breadth of the east front of the temple
and the yard, a hundred cubits.

15 Then he measured the length of [g]the building facing the yard that was at the back
and [h]its galleries[2] on either side, a hundred cubits.

The inside of the nave and the vestibules of the court, **16** [i]the thresholds and [j]the narrow windows and the galleries all around the three of them, opposite the threshold, were
paneled with wood all around, from the floor up to the windows (now the windows were
covered), **17** to the space above the door, even to the inner room, and on the outside. And
on all the walls all around, inside and outside, was a measured pattern.[3] **18** It was carved of
[k]cherubim and [l]palm trees, a palm tree between cherub and cherub. Every cherub had two
faces: **19** [m]a human face toward the palm tree on the one side, and the face of a young lion
toward the palm tree on the other side. They were carved on the whole temple all around.
20 From the floor to above the door, cherubim and palm trees were carved; similarly the
wall of the nave.

21 The doorposts of [n]the nave were squared, and in front of [o]the Holy Place was something
resembling **22** [p]an altar of wood, three cubits high, two cubits long, and two cubits broad.[4]
Its corners, its base,[5] and its walls were of wood. He said to me, "This is [q]the table that is
before the LORD." **23** The nave and the Holy Place had each [r]a double door. **24** The double
doors had two leaves apiece, [s]two swinging leaves for each door. **25** And on the doors of the
nave were carved cherubim and palm trees, [t]such as were carved on the walls. And there
was [u]a canopy[6] of wood in front of [v]the vestibule outside. **26** And there were [j]narrow windows and palm trees on either side, on the sidewalls of the vestibule, [w]the side chambers
of the temple, and the [u]canopies.

The Temple's Chambers

42 Then he led me out into [x]the outer court, [y]toward the north, and he brought me
to [x]the chambers that were opposite [z]the separate yard and opposite [a]the building
on the north. **2** The length of the building whose door faced north was [b]a hundred cubits,[7]
and [c]the breadth fifty cubits. **3** Facing [d]the twenty cubits that belonged to the inner court,
and facing [e]the pavement that belonged to the outer court, was [f]gallery[8] against gallery
in three stories. **4** And [g]before the chambers was a passage inward, ten cubits wide and [h]a
hundred cubits long,[9] and [g]their doors were on the north. **5** Now the upper chambers were
narrower, for the galleries took more away from them than from the lower and middle

6 [v]ch. 40:17 [w]1 Kgs. 6:6
7 [x]1 Kgs. 6:8
8 [y][ch. 40:5; 43:13]
9 [z][ver. 11]
10 [a]See ch. 40:17 [b]ch. 42:3
11 [c][ver. 5] [d][ver. 9]
12 [e]ch. 42:1, 10, 13; See ver. 13-15
13 [f]ch. 40:47
15 [g]ver. 12; ch. 42:1 [h]ch. 42:3, 5
16 [i]Isa. 6:4 [j]ver. 26; ch. 40:16, 25; [1 Kgs. 6:4]
18 [k]ver. 20, 25; 1 Kgs. 6:29, 32, 35; 7:36 [l]ch. 40:16, 22, 26, 31, 34, 37; 2 Chr. 3:5
19 [m][ch. 1:10; 10:14]
21 [n]ver. 1 [o]See ver. 4
22 [p]Rev. 11:1; See Ex. 30:1 [q]ch. 44:16; [ch. 23:41; Mal. 1:7, 12]
23 [r]See 1 Kgs. 6:31-33
24 [s][1 Kgs. 6:34]
25 [t]ver. 18, 20 [u]1 Kgs. 7:6 [v]ch. 40:48
26 [j][See ver. 16 above] [w]See ver. 5-9 [u][See ver. 25 above]

Chapter 42

1 [x]ch. 40:17 [y]ch. 40:20 [z]ver. 10, 13; ch. 41:12, 13 [a]ch. 41:12, 15
2 [b][ch. 41:13] [c][ver. 8]
3 [d]ch. 41:10 [e]ch. 40:17 [f][ver. 5; ch. 41:15, 16]
4 [g][ch. 46:19] [h][ver. 11]

[1] Septuagint, compare 1 Kings 6:6; the meaning of the Hebrew word is uncertain [2] The meaning of the Hebrew term is unknown; also verse 16 [3] Hebrew *were measurements* [4] Septuagint; Hebrew lacks *two cubits broad* [5] Septuagint; Hebrew *length* [6] The meaning of the Hebrew word is unknown; also verse 26 [7] A *cubit* was about 18 inches or 45 centimeters [8] The meaning of the Hebrew word is unknown; also verse 5 [9] Septuagint, Syriac; Hebrew *and a way of one cubit*

42:1–14 *Chambers of the Outer Court.* Ezekiel is led to the **outer court** and describes the construction of the **chambers** in the perimeter wall of the court's north area (vv. 1–9). Clearly the same arrangement is meant to be mirrored in vv. 10–12, although it appears that **south** is more likely the original reading in v. 10, following the Septuagint, rather than the Hebrew text's "east." The functions of these rooms are explained in vv. 13–14. They are to serve as sacristies, that is, rooms for the use of the priests to prepare for the exercise of their duties.

chambers of the building. 6 For they were in three stories, and they had no pillars like the
pillars of the courts. Thus the upper chambers were set back from the ground more than
the lower and the middle ones. 7 And [i]there was a wall outside parallel to the chambers,
toward the outer court, opposite the chambers, [j]fifty cubits long. 8 For the chambers on
the outer court were fifty cubits long, while those opposite [k]the nave[1] were [l]a hundred
cubits long. 9 Below these chambers was [m]an entrance on the east side, as one enters them
from the outer court.
10 In the thickness of [n]the wall of the court, on the south[2] also, opposite [o]the yard and
opposite [o]the building, there were [p]chambers 11 with [q]a passage in front of them. They
were similar to the chambers on the north, of the same length and breadth, with the
same exits[3] and arrangements and [q]doors, 12 as were the entrances of the chambers on
the south. There was an entrance at the beginning of the passage, the passage before [n]the
corresponding wall on the east as one enters them.[4]
13 Then he said to me, "The north chambers and the south chambers opposite [o]the yard
are the holy chambers, [r]where the priests who approach the LORD [s]shall eat the [t]most
holy offerings. There they shall put the most holy offerings—[t]the grain offering, [u]the sin
offering, and [u]the guilt offering—for the place is holy. 14 When the priests enter the Holy
Place, they shall not go out of it into the outer court [v]without laying there the garments
in which they minister, for these are holy. [v]They shall put on other garments before they
go near to that which is for the people."
15 Now when he had finished measuring the interior of the temple area, he led me out
by [w]the gate that faced east, and measured the temple area all around. 16 He measured the
east side with [x]the measuring reed, 500 cubits by the measuring reed all around. 17 He
measured the north side, 500 cubits by the measuring reed all around. 18 He measured
the south side, 500 cubits by the measuring reed. 19 Then he turned to the west side and
measured, 500 cubits by the measuring reed. 20 He measured it on the four sides. It had
[y]a wall around it, [z]500 cubits long and [z]500 cubits broad, [a]to make a separation between
the holy and the common.

The Glory of the LORD Fills the Temple

43 Then he led me to [b]the gate, the gate facing east. 2 And behold, [c]the glory of the
God of Israel was coming from the east. And [d]the sound of his coming was like the
sound of many waters, and [e]the earth shone with his glory. 3 And [f]the vision I saw was just
like the vision that I had seen [g]when he[5] came to destroy the city, and just like [h]the vision
that I had seen [i]by the Chebar canal. And [j]I fell on my face. 4 As [c]the glory of the LORD
[k]entered the temple by the gate facing east, 5 [l]the Spirit lifted me up and brought me into
[m]the inner court; and behold, [n]the glory of the LORD filled the temple.
6 [o]While the man was standing beside me, [p]I heard one speaking to me out of the temple,

[1] Or *temple* [2] Septuagint; Hebrew *east* [3] Hebrew *and all their exits* [4] The meaning of the Hebrew verse is uncertain [5] Some Hebrew manuscripts and Vulgate; most Hebrew manuscripts *when I*

7 [i][ver. 10, 12] [j][ver. 2]
8 [k]ch. 41:1, 21, 23 [l][ch. 41:13, 14]
9 [m]ch. 44:5; 46:19
10 [n][ver. 7] [o][ver. 1] [p]See ch. 40:17
11 [q][ver. 4]
12 [n][See ver. 10 above]
13 [o][See ver. 10 above] [r]ch. 40:46 [s]Lev. 6:16, 26; 10:13; 24:9 [t]Num. 18:9 [u]ch. 40:39
14 [v]ch. 44:19; Lev. 6:11
15 [w]See ch. 43:1
16 [x][ch. 40:3]
20 [y]ch. 40:5 [z][ch. 45:2; Rev. 21:16] [a][ch. 22:26; 43:12; 44:23; 48:15]

Chapter 43

1 [b]ver. 4; ch. 10:19; 11:1; 40:6; 42:15; 44:1
2 [c]ch. 10:18, 19; 11:23; [Rev. 21:11] [d]ch. 1:24; [Rev. 1:15] [e][ch. 10:4; Rev. 18:1]
3 [f]See ch. 1:28 [g][ch. 9:1, 2, 5] [h]See ch. 1:4-28 [i]See ch. 1:1 [j]See ch. 1:28
4 [c][See ver. 2 above] [k][ch. 44:2]
5 [l]See ch. 3:12 [m]See ch. 8:16 [n]ch. 10:4; 44:4; 1 Kgs. 8:10, 11; [Isa. 6:1]
6 [o]See ch. 40:3 [p][Ex. 25:22]

42:15–20 *Exterior Measurements.* Finally, Ezekiel and his guide return to the place where they began, the main east gate to the temple complex (v. 15; cf. 40:5–6). Starting there, and proceeding counterclockwise, the external dimensions are measured as **500 cubits** by **500 cubits** square (roughly 830 feet/253 m). The numbers of the internal dimensions, with fifties and hundreds featuring prominently, yield these ideal and perfect dimensions. The sacredness of the entire domain is emphasized by the closing comment, that the wall separates **the holy and the common**.

43:1–5 *The Return of God's Glory.* Clearly the return of God's glory to the temple is one of the most dramatic moments in the book. His return here is the restoration counterpart to the departure in 10:18–22 and 11:23. It also brings completion to the temple tour: all that was lacking from this sacred space was God. However, this moment also forms a new beginning. The arrival of God's glory in his temple inaugurates a new era in the relationship of God and people, and this becomes the focus of the remainder of the vision.

43:1 The action takes places at the **gate facing east**, the main temple entrance in the vision, and the equivalent to the gate of the old temple from which God had previously departed (10:19).

43:2 The approach of **the glory of the God of Israel** recalls the overwhelming sensory experience of Ezekiel's inaugural vision: the **sound of many waters** describes the roar of the approach (see 1:24); its brilliance caused **the earth** to shine **with his glory** (cf. 1:27–28).

43:3 Although there are implicit links to the two prior visions, here the connections are made explicit. The vision **when he came to destroy the city** refers to chs. 8–11. The vision **by the Chebar canal** is the inaugural vision of chs. 1–3. As in 1:28b, Ezekiel **fell on** his **face** (cf. 44:4) before the holiness and majesty of God.

43:5 the Spirit lifted me up. Ezekiel is transported (as in 8:3) to the inner court of the temple, where God's glory now resides.

43:6–46:18 *Regulations for Renewed Israel.* Although some aspects of Ezekiel's "tour" reappear from time to time, the emphasis now falls on the activities to take place in the temple, and the regulations for the officiants and leaders of the community. The main altar and its round of sacrifices is the first element put in place (43:13–27). The identification of the prince's gate in 44:1–3 introduces the regulations concerning access to the temple area and the rules governing priests (44:4–31). Chapter 45 brings together seemingly disparate interests, including the arrangements of the temple's hinterland (45:1–6), exhortations to justice (45:9–12), and regulations concerning

7 and he said to me, [q]"Son of man, this is [r]the place of my throne and [s]the place of the soles
of my feet, [t]where I will dwell in the midst of the people of Israel forever. And the house of
Israel shall no more [u]defile my holy name, neither they, nor their kings, by their whoring
and by the dead bodies[1] of their kings at their high places,[2] 8 by setting their threshold by
my threshold and their doorposts beside my doorposts, with [v]only a wall between me and
them. They have [w]defiled my holy name by their abominations that they have committed,
so I have consumed them in my anger. 9 Now let them put away their whoring and the
dead bodies of their kings far from me, [t]and I will dwell in their midst forever.
10 "As for you, [q]son of man, [x]describe to the house of Israel the temple, that they may be
ashamed of their iniquities; and they shall measure the plan. 11 And if they are ashamed of
all that they have done, [x]make known to them the design of the temple, its arrangement,
[y]its exits and its entrances, that is, its whole design; and make known to them as well all
its statutes and its whole design and all its laws, and write it down [z]in their sight, so that
they may observe all its laws and all its statutes and carry them out. 12 This is the law of the
temple: the whole territory on the top of [a]the mountain [b]all around shall be most holy.
Behold, this is the law of the temple.

The Altar

13 "These are the measurements of [c]the altar by cubits (the cubit being [d]a cubit and a
handbreadth):[3] its base shall be one cubit high[4] and one cubit broad, with a rim of one span[5]
around its edge. And this shall be the height of the altar: 14 from the base on the ground
to the lower ledge, two cubits, with a breadth of one cubit; and from the smaller ledge
to the larger ledge, four cubits, with a breadth of one cubit; 15 and the altar hearth, four
cubits; and from the altar hearth projecting upward, [e]four horns. 16 The altar hearth shall
be [f]square, twelve cubits long by twelve broad. 17 The ledge also shall be square, fourteen
cubits long by fourteen broad, with a rim around it half a cubit broad, and its base one
cubit all around. [g]The steps of the altar shall face east."
18 And he said to me, [h]"Son of man, thus says the Lord GOD: These are the ordinances
for the altar: On the day when it is erected for offering burnt offerings upon it and [i]for
throwing blood against it, 19 you shall give to [j]the Levitical priests [k]of the family of Zadok,
who draw near to me to minister to me, declares the Lord GOD, [l]a bull from the herd for
a sin offering. 20 And [m]you shall take some of its blood and put it on [e]the four horns of

[1] *Or the monuments*; also verse 9 [2] *Or at their deaths* [3] *A cubit* was about 18 inches or 45 centimeters; a *handbreadth* was about 3 inches or 7.5 centimeters
[4] *Or its gutter shall be one cubit deep* [5] *A span* was about 9 inches or 22 centimeters

7 [q]See ch. 2:1 [r][Ps. 99:1] [s][1 Chr. 28:2; Isa. 60:13] [t]See ch. 37:26, 28 [u][ver. 8]; See ch. 20:39
8 [v][ch. 42:20] [w][ver. 7]
9 [t][See ver. 7 above]
10 [q][See ver. 7 above] [x]ch. 40:4
11 [x][See ver. 10 above] [y][ch. 44:5] [z]See ch. 12:3
12 [a][ch. 40:2] [b]See ch. 42:15-20
13 [c][ch. 40:47; 47:1]; See Ex. 27:1-8 [d]ch. 40:5; [ch. 41:8]
15 [e]See Ex. 27:2
16 [f][ch. 40:47; Ex. 27:1]
17 [g][Ex. 20:26]
18 [h]See ch. 2:1 [i]See Lev. 1:5
19 [j]ch. 44:15; Deut. 17:9; 18:1; 24:8; 27:9 [k]See ch. 40:46 [l]ch. 45:18; Ex. 29:1, 10
20 [m]ch. 45:19; Ex. 29:12; Lev. 8:15 [e][See ver. 15 above]

offerings and sacrifices, Sabbaths, and festivals (45:13–46:15). Instructions concerning the "prince" are interspersed, but come to the fore at 45:7–8 and 46:16–18. There is no other body of legislation for the community like this outside the Pentateuch (thus its introduction by God as **the law of the temple**, 43:12b). It has the effect of placing Ezekiel in the role of a second Moses, meeting with God not at the mountain in Sinai (Ex. 19:1–5; 31:18, etc.) but on the mount of the new temple (Ezek. 43:12).

43:6–12 *New People for New Temple.* God's return sets everything right again, but there is no relenting from the rigorous demands his holiness places on his people. Verses 7–9 combine promise and warning—or, the promise is a warning—that the bond between God and people is indissoluble (**I will dwell . . . forever**, v. 7) but that he will not tolerate the challenge to his supremacy that their earlier behavior had brought (vv. 8–9). The serious point about the architecture of this temple (v. 10) is that no royal palace is adjoined to it, in contrast to Solomon's temple/palace complex (see 1 Kings 7:8) and the wayward royal cult it often harbored (cf. Isa. 42:8). As Ezek. 43:11–12 makes clear, these measurements and regulations are not merely interesting details but communicate something of the character of God.

43:6 The Hebrew indicates that **the man . . . standing beside me** is not the same as the **one speaking to me out of the temple**; that is, Ezekiel's heavenly guide remains by his side, so the voice is not his. It is the very voice of God, as the first-person speech of vv. 7–9 makes clear.

43:13–27 *The Altar Regulations.* Appropriately, given Ezekiel's priestly outlook, the starting point for the life of Israel before God is the altar. This was the location of the lowest point of Israel's sin in the previous temple vision (8:16). It again becomes the focal point for communion between God and people.

43:13–17 The altar's design is described, just as the temple architecture was before it (vv. 13–17; cf. vv. 10–11). The altar is square, like the temple itself, with a horned projection at each corner, as Israel's altars had long been (e.g., Ex. 29:12; Ps. 118:27). In spite of (or perhaps because of) the detail, it is surprisingly difficult to visualize the altar. In broad terms, it was layered, with each succeeding layer one cubit less on each side than the one below it. The base is one cubit tall, and the sum of the layers above it totals 10 cubits. The dimensions of the base are 16 cubits square, up to the hearth at the top of the altar, which is 12 cubits square. These dimensions make it slightly smaller than the altar of Solomon's temple in 2 Chron. 4:1. For the cubit measurements, see note on Ezek. 40:5–27.

43:18–27 This section describes the rituals of purification required for the altar before it is fit for regular use. Although the preceding verses have focused on the altar's design, its actual material required consecration for use in the sacred realm. This also explains why the ritual focuses on the application of the blood to the altar rather than on the sacrifice itself. The first day's sacrifice is described in detail in vv. 18–21 when a single **bull** is offered by the Zadokite priests. Less detail, but more sacrifice on day two (vv. 22–24) sets the pattern for the succeeding days until the seven days (vv. 25–26) of the consecration are complete. Once again a link is forged to Moses and the tabernacle, as a similar pattern is found in Ex. 29:36b–37. This sacred "isolation" of the altar addresses the abomination condemned in Ezek. 43:8.

43:18 The practice of **throwing blood against the altar** is well attested in the Pentateuch, especially those passages dealing with priests (e.g., Ex. 24:6; 29:20; and 11 more times in Leviticus alone).

the altar and on the four corners of the ledge and upon [n]the rim all around. [o]Thus you
shall purify the altar and make atonement for it. **21** You shall also take the bull of the sin
offering, and [p]it shall be burned in the appointed place belonging to the temple, outside
the sacred area. **22** And on the second day you shall offer a male goat without blemish for
a sin offering; and the altar shall be purified, as it was purified with the bull. **23** When you
have finished [o]purifying it, you shall offer a bull from the herd without blemish and [q]a
ram from the flock without blemish. **24** You shall present them before the LORD, and the
priests [r]shall sprinkle salt on them and offer them up as a burnt offering to the LORD.
25 [s]For seven days you shall provide daily a male goat for a sin offering; also, a bull from
the herd and a ram from the flock, without blemish, shall be provided. **26** Seven days shall
they make atonement for the altar and cleanse it, and so consecrate it.[1] **27** And when they
have completed these days, then [t]from the eighth day onward the priests shall offer on
the altar your burnt offerings and your [u]peace offerings, and [v]I will accept you, declares
the Lord GOD."

The Gate for the Prince

44 Then he brought me [w]back to the outer gate of the sanctuary, [x]which faces east. And
it was shut. **2** And the LORD said to me, "This gate shall remain shut; it shall not
be opened, and no one shall enter by it, for [y]the LORD, the God of Israel, has entered by it.
Therefore it shall remain shut. **3** Only [z]the prince may sit in it [a]to eat bread before the LORD.
He [b]shall enter by way of the vestibule of the gate, and shall go out by the same way."

4 Then he brought me by way of [c]the north gate to the front of the temple, and I looked,
and behold, [d]the glory of the LORD filled the temple of the LORD. And [e]I fell on my face.
5 And the LORD said to me, [f]"Son of man, mark well, [g]see with your eyes, [g]and hear with
your ears all that I shall tell you concerning [h]all the statutes of the temple of the LORD and
all its laws. And mark well [h]the entrance to the temple and all the exits from the sanctuary.
6 And say to [i]the rebellious house,[2] to the [j]house of Israel, Thus says the Lord GOD: O house
of Israel, [k]enough of all your abominations, **7** in [l]admitting foreigners, [m]uncircumcised
in heart and flesh, to be in my sanctuary, [n]profaning my temple, when you offer to me
my food, the fat and the blood. You[3] have broken my covenant, in addition to all your
abominations. **8** And [o]you have not kept charge of my holy things, but you have set others
to keep my charge for you in my sanctuary.

9 "Thus says the Lord GOD: [p]No foreigner, uncircumcised in heart and flesh, of all the
foreigners who are among the people of Israel, shall enter my sanctuary. **10** But [q]the Levites
who went far from me, going astray from me after their idols [r]when Israel went astray,
[s]shall bear their punishment.[4] **11** They shall be [t]ministers in my sanctuary, having oversight
[u]at the gates of the temple and ministering in the temple. They shall slaughter the burnt

[1] Hebrew *fill its hand* [2] Septuagint; Hebrew lacks *house* [3] Septuagint, Syriac, Vulgate; Hebrew *They* [4] Or *iniquity*; also verse 12

20 [n][ver. 13, 17] [o]Ex. 29:36; [ch. 45:18]
21 [p]Ex. 29:14
23 [o][See ver. 20 above] [q][Ex. 29:1]
24 [r]Lev. 2:13
25 [s]Ex. 29:35, 36; Lev. 8:33, 35
27 [t]Lev. 9:1 [u]See Lev. 3:1 [v]See ch. 20:40

Chapter 44
1 [w][ch. 43:5] [x]See ch. 43:1
2 [y][ch. 43:4]
3 [z]ch. 34:24; 37:25; 45:7; 46:2 [a][Gen. 31:54] [b]ch. 46:2, 12
4 [c]ch. 40:20 [d]See ch. 43:5 [e]See ch. 1:28
5 [f]See ch. 2:1 [g]ch. 40:4 [h][ch. 43:11]
6 [i]See ch. 2:3 [j]ch. 40:4 [k]ch. 45:9; [1 Pet. 4:3]
7 [l][ver. 9; Neh. 7:64, 65; Acts 21:28] [m][Jer. 9:26; Acts 7:51] [n]ch. 23:39
8 [o][ch. 22:26]
9 [p][ver. 7]
10 [q][ver. 15; ch. 48:11] [r]ch. 48:11 [s]See ch. 4:4
11 [t]ch. 46:24 [u][1 Chr. 26:1]

43:27 Only after the entire week of purification is the altar ready for the round of sacrificial offerings, which were provided to ensure continuing communion with God.

44:1–3 *The Prince's Gate.* The main east gate is significant on many levels (see note on 43:1–5). Ezekiel is taken back to the outer court to see the main east gate closed, no more to be used because **the LORD . . . has entered by it** (44:2). By implication, God is not going to need it again. Only one individual may use this divine entrance: **the prince** (v. 3; cf. 34:23–24; 37:24–25), mentioned in this vision for the first time. Significantly, even he does not use it merely for access but rather for sharing in a fellowship meal **before the LORD**.

44:4–31 *Temple Access and Rules for Priests.* The next phase of the vision begins with an echo of the previous phase. Returning to the inner court before the temple proper, Ezekiel is again overcome by the presence of God's glory and again receives a commission to report this vision to Israel (44:4–5; cf. 43:3–4, 10–11). Also as in the previous section, an indictment prefaces positive commands (44:6–8; cf. 43:7–9). Here the problem is that of allowing illegitimate access to the temple, and thus to God's presence, explicitly forbidden in 44:9. Resident aliens cannot play a role in the service of the temple. Proper access to sacred things is in the hands of the priests, and two classes are distinguished. Verses 10–14 specify the roles accorded to the Levitical priests; vv. 15–31 deal at greater length with the Zadokite priests.

44:4 The **way of the north gate** is the one designated for the use of "priests who have charge of the temple" (40:44–45) and is the gate most used by Ezekiel in this vision (e.g., 47:2; cf. 8:3, the starting point for the pre-destruction temple vision).

44:5–8 Access implies participation, and so the task of tending the gates is critical.

44:9 While resident aliens are forbidden a role in temple service, the qualifying phrase **uncircumcised in heart and flesh** (cf. v. 7) may suggest that aliens with the appropriate inner orientation announced in 36:26–27 could become members of the covenant community. Residence alone, however, was not enough to qualify.

44:10–14 The **Levites** are gatekeepers and temple attendants but are restricted from service at the altar. The vision maintains these as suitable roles for a class of priests who had previously failed in their sacred duties (v. 12). Priestly conflict and failure are as old as the priesthood itself (cf. Lev. 10:1–7; Numbers 16). Rivalry among priests continued into the period of the monarchy (e.g., 1 Kings 1:7–8). Ezekiel's vision places greater restrictions on Levites than is seen in the books of Chronicles (e.g., in the account of Josiah's Passover, 2 Chronicles 35; cf. also Deut. 18:1–8).

offering and the sacrifice for the people, and [v]they shall stand before the people, to minister
to them. 12 Because they ministered to them before their idols and became [w]a stumbling
block of iniquity to the house of Israel, therefore I have [x]sworn concerning them, declares
the Lord GOD, and they shall bear their punishment. 13 They [y]shall not come near to me,
to serve me as priest, nor come near any of my holy things and the things that are most
holy, but [z]they shall bear their shame and the abominations that they have committed.
14 Yet I will appoint them to keep [a]charge of the temple, [b]to do all its service and all that
is to be done in it.

Rules for Levitical Priests

15 "But [c]the Levitical priests, [c]the sons of Zadok, who kept [a]the charge of my sanctuary
[r]when the people of Israel went astray from me, shall come near to me [d]to minister to me.
And they shall stand before me to offer me [e]the fat and the blood, declares the Lord GOD.
16 They shall enter my sanctuary, and they shall approach [f]my table, to minister to me,
and they shall keep my charge. 17 When they enter the gates of the inner court, they shall
wear [g]linen garments. They shall have nothing of wool on them, while they minister at
the gates of the inner court, and within. 18 They shall have linen turbans on their heads,
and linen undergarments around their waists. They shall not bind themselves with anything that causes sweat. 19 And when they go out into the outer court to the people, they
shall put off the garments in which they have been ministering [h]and lay them in the holy
chambers. And [i]they shall put on other garments, [j]lest they transmit holiness to the people
with their garments. 20 [k]They shall not shave their heads or [l]let their locks grow long; they
shall surely trim the hair of their heads. 21 [m]No priest shall drink wine when he enters
the inner court. 22 [n]They shall not marry a widow or a divorced woman, but only virgins
of the offspring of the house of Israel, or a widow who is the widow of a priest. 23 [o]They
shall teach my people the difference between the holy and the common, and [o]show them
how to distinguish between the unclean and the clean. 24 [p]In a dispute, they shall act as
judges, and they shall judge it according to my judgments. They shall keep my laws and
my statutes in all my appointed feasts, and [q]they shall keep my Sabbaths holy. 25 [r]They
shall not defile themselves by going near to a dead person. However, for father or mother,
for son or daughter, for brother or unmarried sister they may defile themselves. 26 [s]After
he[1] has become clean, they shall count seven days for him. 27 And on the day that he goes
into the Holy Place, [t]into the inner court, to minister in the Holy Place, [u]he shall offer his
sin offering, declares the Lord GOD.

28 [v]"This shall be their inheritance: I am their inheritance: and [w]you shall give them
no possession in Israel; I am their possession. 29 [x]They shall eat the grain offering, the sin
offering, and the guilt offering, and [y]every devoted thing in Israel shall be theirs. 30 [z]And
the first of all the firstfruits of all kinds, and every offering of all kinds from all your offerings, shall belong to the priests. [a]You shall also give to the priests the first of your dough,
[b]that a blessing may rest on your house. 31 [c]The priests shall not eat of [d]anything, whether
bird or beast, that has died of itself or is torn by wild animals.

The Holy District

45 "When [e]you allot the land as an inheritance, [f]you shall set apart for the LORD a
portion of the land as a holy district, 25,000 cubits[2] long and 20,000[3] cubits broad.
It shall be holy throughout its whole extent. 2 [g]Of this a square plot of 500 by 500 cubits

[1] That is, a priest [2] A *cubit* was about 18 inches or 45 centimeters [3] Septuagint; Hebrew *ten*

11 [v]Num. 16:9
12 [w]ch. 7:19; 14:3, 4, 7; [Mal. 2:8] [x]Ps. 106:26
13 [y]Num. 18:3; 2 Kgs. 23:9 [z]See ch. 32:24
14 [a]See ch. 40:45 [b]1 Chr. 23:28, 32
15 [c]See ch. 43:19 [a][See ver. 14 above] [r][See ver. 10 above] [d][ver. 11; Deut. 10:8] [e][ver. 7]
16 [f]See ch. 41:22
17 [g]Ex. 28:39; 39:27
19 [h]ch. 42:14 [i]Lev. 6:11 [j][ch. 46:20; Ex. 29:37; 30:29; Lev. 6:27]
20 [k]Lev. 21:5; [ch. 5:1] [l][Num. 6:5]
21 [m]Lev. 10:9
22 [n]Lev. 21:7, 13, 14
23 [o][ch. 22:26]; See Lev. 10:10, 11
24 [p]Deut. 17:8, 9; [2 Chr. 19:8] [q][ch. 22:26]
25 [r]See Lev. 21:1-3
26 [s]Num. 19:11, 12
27 [t]ver. 17, 21 [u]ch. 40:39; 42:13; Lev. 4:2, 3
28 [v]See Num. 18:20 [w][ch. 45:4, 5]
29 [x]See Lev. 6:14-18, 25-29; 7:1-6 [y]Lev. 27:21, 28; Num. 18:14
30 [z]See Ex. 23:19 [a]See Num. 15:20 [b]Mal. 3:10
31 [c]Lev. 22:8; [Ex. 22:31]; See Lev. 7:24 [d]ch. 4:14

Chapter 45

1 [e][ch. 48:29]; See ch. 47:21, 22 [f]See ch. 48:8-10
2 [g]See ch. 42:16-20

44:15–31 The privilege of serving at the altar and in the sanctuary itself, that is, **before** the Lord (v. 15), falls to the Zadokite priests. Zadok was a priest of Aaron's line who came to prominence in David's time (2 Sam. 20:25) and remained faithful to David and then to Solomon in the power struggle over succession to David's throne (1 Kings 1:39). He and his successors are thus especially associated with the Jerusalem priests rather than the rural priests from among whom Jeremiah came. The regulations bearing on their activities have a close relationship with Pentateuchal legislation (esp. Leviticus 21 and Numbers 18; see ESV cross-references for parallels). These regulations were intended to maintain the Zadokite priests in a state of readiness for serving before the altar and in the sanctuary, in other words, to be holy. They include instructions concerning clothing and grooming (Ezek. 44:17–20), comportment (v. 21), and marriage (v. 22). They are to be teachers and arbitrators (vv. 23–24; cf. Lev. 10:8–11; Ezek. 22:26). When of necessity they defile themselves by tending to the dead, they must wait a period of seven days (cf. 43:26) before reentering sacred service. Like other priestly groups in antiquity, they do not hold landed property (44:28); their maintenance comes from their temple service itself and the offerings of those in the community who do have property (vv. 29–30). Finally, they are forbidden unclean meat, a restriction Ezekiel himself had long since taken to heart (see 4:14).

45:1–8 *The Temple Districts.* This definition of sacred space within the wider context of renewed Israel provides a summary anticipation of 48:8–22.

shall be for the sanctuary, with fifty cubits for [h]an open space around it. 3 And [i]from this
measured district you shall measure off a section 25,000 cubits long and 10,000 broad,
[j]in which shall be the sanctuary, [k]the Most Holy Place. 4 [l]It shall be the holy portion of the
land. It shall be for the priests, who minister in the sanctuary and approach the LORD to
minister to him, and it shall be a place for their houses and a holy place for the sanctuary.
5 [m]Another section, 25,000 cubits long and 10,000 cubits broad, shall be for the Levites
who minister at the temple, as their possession for cities to live in.[1]
6 "Alongside the portion set apart as the holy district [n]you shall assign for the property
of the city an area 5,000 cubits broad and 25,000 cubits long. [o]It shall belong to the whole
house of Israel.

The Portion for the Prince

7 [p]"And to [q]the prince shall belong the land on both sides of the holy district and the
property of the city, alongside the holy district and the property of the city, on the west
and on the east, corresponding in length to one of the tribal portions, and extending from
the western to the eastern boundary 8 of the land. It is to be his property in Israel. And [r]my
princes shall no more oppress my people, but [s]they shall let the house of Israel have the
land according to their tribes.
9 "Thus says the Lord GOD: [t]Enough, O princes of Israel! Put away violence and oppression, and execute justice and righteousness. Cease [u]your evictions of my people, declares
the Lord GOD.
10 [v]"You shall have just balances, a just ephah, and a just bath.[2] 11 The ephah and the
bath shall be [w]of the same measure, [x]the bath containing one tenth of a homer,[3] and the
ephah one tenth of a homer; the homer shall be the standard measure. 12 [y]The shekel
shall be twenty gerahs;[4] twenty shekels plus twenty-five shekels plus fifteen shekels shall
be your mina.[5]
13 [z]"This is the offering that you shall make: one sixth of an ephah from each homer of
wheat, and one sixth of an ephah from each homer of barley, 14 and as the fixed portion of
oil, measured in baths, one tenth of a bath from each cor[6] (the cor, like the homer, contains
[a]ten baths).[7] 15 And one sheep from every flock of two hundred, from the watering places of
Israel for grain offering, burnt offering, and peace offerings, [b]to make atonement for them,
declares the Lord GOD. 16 All the people of the land shall be obliged to give this offering to
the prince in Israel. 17 [c]It shall be the prince's duty to furnish the burnt offerings, grain offerings, and drink offerings, at the feasts, the new moons, and the Sabbaths, all the appointed
feasts of the house of Israel: he shall provide the sin offerings, grain offerings, burnt offerings, and peace offerings, to make atonement on behalf of the house of Israel.

[1] Septuagint; Hebrew *as their possession, twenty chambers* [2] An *ephah* was about 3/5 of a bushel or 22 liters; a *bath* was about 6 gallons or 22 liters [3] A *homer* was about 6 bushels or 220 liters [4] A *shekel* was about 2/5 ounce or 11 grams; a *gerah* was about 1/50 ounce or 0.6 gram [5] A *mina* was about 1 1/4 pounds or 0.6 kilogram [6] A *cor* was about 6 bushels or 220 liters [7] See Vulgate; Hebrew *(ten baths are a homer, for ten baths are a homer)*

2 [h][ch. 27:28; 48:15, 17]; See Lev. 25:34
3 [i][ver. 1] [j]ch. 48:10 [k]See ch. 41:4
4 [l][ch. 48:11, 12]
5 [m]ch. 48:13
6 [n]ch. 48:15 [o][ch. 48:18, 19]
7 [p]ch. 48:21 [q]See ch. 44:3
8 [r][ch. 22:27; 46:18] [s]ch. 47:13, 21; See ch. 48:1-7, 23-28
9 [t]ch. 44:6 [u][ch. 46:18]
10 [v]See Lev. 19:35, 36
11 [w][Deut. 25:14, 15] [x][Isa. 5:10]
12 [y]See Ex. 30:13
13 [z]ch. 44:30
14 [a]ver. 11
15 [b]See Lev. 1:4
17 [c][2 Chr. 30:24; 35:7]; See ch. 46:4-7

The two accounts offer the same layout of the temple district, although the later text provides more details. Ezekiel depicts three strips of **25,000 cubits** (about 7.7 miles/12 km) oriented from east to west as expected, given the temple's east-west axis. The central strip of **10,000 cubits** north to south (about 3 miles/4.8 km) contains the sanctuary (45:2) and is the region where the Zadokite **priests** live (vv. 3–4). The strip of equal size north of it is home for the **Levites** (v. 5). The southernmost strip, half as deep, is the district for **the whole house of Israel** (v. 6), which also contains the **city** itself. Included on either side to the east and west are the areas **5,000 cubits** wide (about 1.5 miles/2.4 km) but **25,000 cubits** deep allocated to the **prince** (vv. 7–8a), intended to satisfy the requirements of the royal domain (v. 8b; cf. 1 Kings 21). It is difficult to say why these details are included at this point. Perhaps it is sufficient to note that, in this vision, the "where" of location invariably precedes the "what" that is supposed to happen there. With the temple described and the duties of the priests detailed, the next "where" specifies the surrounding area from which the offerings and sacrifices will come. The districts extending from the temple describe this region.

45:9–12 *Legal Measurements.* The exhortation to the prince to be content with his holdings inspires a sharp reproof in v. 9, and a call to exercise **justice and righteousness**. It recalls the condemnation of 22:27. It is striking to find such a text in a restoration setting, and the context lends timelessness to the demand for justice: the future is now! The call for justice provides a transition to a listing of just weights and volumes, the measurements necessary for quantifying the offerings to follow (modern equivalents appear in the ESV footnotes).

45:10–11 At Tell Beit Mirsim, archaeologists uncovered a large storage jar with the Hebrew term "bath" inscribed on it. In Level III of Lachish (late 8th century B.C.), a storage jar had the words "royal bath" written on its neck. The bath is a liquid measure equaling about 5–6 gallons (19–23 liters).

45:13–46:15 *Offerings and Gatherings.* The contributions of people and prince to the sacred offerings are now described (45:13–17), along with the festivals and other gatherings at which these offerings are used—first the annual festivals (45:18–25), then those occurring more frequently throughout the year (46:1–15).

45:13–17 The set of levies on the community includes agricultural produce (vv. 13–14) and livestock (v. 15a), all of which goes toward the offerings given to God (v. 15b) by way of the prince (v. 16). Although the prince makes direct provision for the festivals and regular services (v. 17), the whole community is involved. The tax to be borne by the community is fairly small, at the rate of about 1/60 for cereals, 1/100 for oil, and 1/200 for sheep. It is noteworthy that provision for **sin offerings** (v. 17) persists into this restoration vision.

18[d][ch. 46:1, 3, 6] [e]Lev. 16:16; [ch. 43:20, 22, 23]
19[f]See ch. 43:20 [g][Ex. 12:7]
21[h]See Lev. 23:5
22[i][ver. 17]
23[j]Lev. 23:8 [k]Num. 28:15
24[l]ch. 46:5, 7 [m]See Lev. 2:1
25[n]See Lev. 23:34 [o]See ver. 22-24

Chapter 46

1[p]ch. 45:19 [q]See ch. 8:16 [r][ch. 45:18]
2[s]See ch. 44:3 [t][ch. 45:19] [u][ch. 40:38, 39] [v][ch. 9:3]
3[w]ver. 9
4[x]ch. 45:17 [y][Num. 28:9, 10]
5[z]ver. 14; ch. 45:24 [a][Deut. 16:17]
7[b]ver. 5
8[c][ver. 2]
9[d]ver. 3 [e][Deut. 16:16]; See Ex. 23:14-17

18 "Thus says the Lord GOD: In the first month, [d]on the first day of the month, you shall
take a bull from the herd without blemish, and [e]purify the sanctuary. 19 [f]The priest shall
take some of the blood of the sin offering and put it [g]on the doorposts of the temple, the
four corners of the ledge of the altar, and the posts of the gate of the inner court. 20 You
shall do the same on the seventh day of the month for anyone who has sinned through
error or ignorance; so you shall make atonement for the temple.
21 [h]"In the first month, on the fourteenth day of the month, you shall celebrate the Feast
of the Passover, and for seven days unleavened bread shall be eaten. 22 On that day the prince
[i]shall provide for himself and all the people of the land a young bull for a sin offering.
23 And on [j]the seven days of the festival he shall provide as a burnt offering to the LORD
seven young bulls and seven rams without blemish, on each of the seven days; and [k]a male
goat daily for a sin offering. 24 And [l]he shall provide as [m]a grain offering an ephah for each
bull, an ephah for each ram, and a hin[1] of oil to each ephah. 25 [n]In the seventh month, on
the fifteenth day of the month and for the seven days of the feast, [o]he shall make the same
provision for sin offerings, burnt offerings, and grain offerings, and for the oil.

The Prince and the Feasts

46 "Thus says the Lord GOD: [p]The gate of [q]the inner court that faces east shall be shut
on the six working days, but on the Sabbath day it shall be opened, and [r]on the day
of the new moon it shall be opened. 2 [s]The prince shall enter by the vestibule of the gate
from outside, and shall take his stand by [t]the post of the gate. [u]The priests shall offer his
burnt offering and his peace offerings, and he shall worship at [v]the threshold of the gate.
Then he shall go out, but the gate shall not be shut until evening. 3 [w]The people of the land
shall bow down at the entrance of that gate before the LORD on the Sabbaths and on the
new moons. 4 [x]The burnt offering that the prince offers to the LORD [y]on the Sabbath day
shall be six lambs without blemish and a ram without blemish. 5 And [z]the grain offering
with the ram shall be an ephah,[2] and the grain offering with the lambs shall be [a]as much
as he is able, together with a hin[3] of oil to each ephah. 6 On the day of the new moon he
shall offer a bull from the herd without blemish, and six lambs and a ram, which shall
be without blemish. 7 As a grain offering he shall provide an ephah with the bull and an
ephah with the ram, and with the lambs [b]as much as he is able, together with a hin of oil
to each ephah. 8 [c]When the prince enters, he shall enter by the vestibule of the gate, and
he shall go out by the same way.
9 [d]"When the people of the land [e]come before the LORD at the appointed feasts, he who
enters by the north gate to worship shall go out by the south gate, and he who enters by

[1] A *hin* was about 4 quarts or 3.5 liters [2] An *ephah* was about 3/5 bushel or 22 liters [3] A *hin* was about 4 quarts or 3.5 liters

45:18–25 There are several calendars of annual festivals in the Pentateuch (Ex. 23:14–17; 34:18–24; Lev. 23:4–44; Num. 28:16–29:39; Deut. 16:1–17), but Ezekiel's schedule matches none of them. It is not even clear if he has in mind the same basic trio of main festivals (Passover, Weeks/Pentecost, Day of Atonement/Tabernacles). The purification ritual assigned for the turn of the year in Ezek. 45:18–20 resembles the inauguration of the altar in 43:18–27, and it is not certain that this rite of purification is meant to be observed annually. However, it remains distinct from the inaugural altar cleansing, is assigned a place on the calendar, and deals with inevitable contamination (cf. Heb. 9:22), so probably it is to be an annual event. The Feasts of **Passover** (Ezek. 45:21–24) and Tabernacles (v. 25) follow. In both cases, dealing with **sin** (v. 25) is again integral to the feast. This represents a shift from the nature of Passover elsewhere in the OT, where it has the character rather of a memorial celebration (e.g., 2 Chron. 30:1–27 [Hezekiah]; 35:1–19 [Josiah]).

46:1–15 The instructions for the more frequent observance of the weekly **Sabbath** and monthly **new moon** are found in vv. 1–7, with v. 7 substantially repeated in v. 11. Regulations on access to the temple precinct and movement through it are given in vv. 8–10. The actions of the prince at the gate are further specified in v. 12. The most frequent repeating time period for sacrifice concludes the section with the prescriptions for **daily** offerings in vv. 13–15. Unlike for the annual festivals, instructions for these offerings make no explicit mention of dealing with sin. Activity at the gates recurs throughout these instructions, focusing on the **prince** in particular. These access points to the holy and the Holy One, in Ezekiel's thinking, are laden with significance for the communal life of sustained communion with God.

46:1–3 The whole community—**prince**, **priests** (v. 2), and **people** (v. 3)—are involved in the weekly and monthly observances, but the prince plays the pivotal role. The east **gate** of the **inner court** is the fulcrum for these exchanges between the most sacred and the outer court. The prince takes his place in the gateway but does not enter the inner court, which is exclusive to the priests. It remains open (v. 2), so that the people in the outer court have some visual contact with the inner sanctum (v. 3).

46:4–7 The **prince** provides the offerings (see 45:17) for the **Sabbath** (46:4–5) and **new moon** (vv. 6–7) celebrations.

46:8–10 The movements of **prince** and **people** are coordinated for festival gatherings. The prince's use of the east gate is limited to his station there; v. 8 prohibits its use as a thoroughfare. The regulation of crowd movement in v. 9 is clear, although no explanation is offered. It could simply be for practical crowd control. Little in Ezekiel's vision lacks deeper significance, however, and it is possible that this regulation also intends something more. One effect of the regulation is to ensure that the whole community makes use of the whole of the outer court, and thereby must pass the east gate to the inner court, which stands open to the presence of God's glory. By integration of the prince's movements with the rest of the people (v. 10), his special status is given its proper context: although he is the prince of the people, he belongs with them (cf. Deut. 17:14–20).

the south gate shall go out by the north gate: no one shall return by way of the gate by
which he entered, but each shall go out straight ahead. **10** When they enter, [f]the prince
shall enter with them, and when they go out, he shall go out.
11 "At the feasts and the appointed festivals, [z]the grain offering with a young bull shall
be an ephah, and with a ram an ephah, and with the lambs [b]as much as one is able to give,
together with a hin of oil to an ephah. **12** When the prince provides [g]a freewill offering,
either a burnt offering or peace offerings as a freewill offering to the LORD, [h]the gate facing
east shall be opened for him. And he shall offer his burnt offering or his peace offerings
[i]as he does on the Sabbath day. Then he shall go out, and after he has gone out the gate
shall be shut.
13 [j]"You shall provide a lamb a year old without blemish for a burnt offering to the
LORD daily; morning by morning you shall provide it. **14** And [k]you shall provide a grain
offering with it morning by morning, one sixth of an ephah, and one third of a hin of oil
to moisten the flour, as a grain offering to the LORD. This is a perpetual statute. **15** Thus
the lamb and the meal offering and the oil shall be provided, morning by morning, for
[l]a regular burnt offering.
16 "Thus says the Lord GOD: If the prince makes a gift to any of his sons as his inheritance,
it shall belong to his sons. It is their property by inheritance. **17** But if he makes a gift [m]out
of his inheritance to one of his servants, it shall be his to [n]the year of liberty. Then it shall
revert to the prince; surely it is his inheritance—it shall belong to his sons. **18** [o]The prince
shall not take any of the inheritance of the people, [p]thrusting them out of their property.
He shall give his sons their inheritance out of his own property, so that none of my people
shall be [q]scattered from his property."

Boiling Places for Offerings

19 Then he brought me through the entrance, which was [r]at the side of the gate, to the
north row of [s]the holy chambers for the priests, and behold, a place was there at the extreme
western end of them. **20** And he said to me, "This is the place where the priests [t]shall boil the
guilt offering and the sin offering, and where [u]they shall bake the grain offering, in order
not to bring them out into the outer court and so [v]transmit holiness to the people."
21 Then he brought me out to the outer court and led me around to the four corners of
the court. And behold, in each corner of the court there was another court— **22** in the four
corners of the court were small[1] courts, forty cubits[2] long and thirty broad; the four were of
the same size. **23** On the inside, around each of the four courts was a row of masonry, with
hearths made at the bottom of the rows all around. **24** Then he said to me, "These are the
kitchens where those who [w]minister at the temple [t]shall boil the sacrifices of the people."

Water Flowing from the Temple

47 Then he brought me back to [x]the door of the temple, and behold, [y]water was issuing
from below [z]the threshold of the temple toward the east (for the temple faced east).
The water was flowing down from below the south end of the threshold of the temple,

[1] Septuagint, Syriac, Vulgate; the meaning of the Hebrew word is uncertain [2] A *cubit* was about 18 inches or 45 centimeters

10 [f][Ps. 42:4]
11 [z][See ver. 5 above] [b][See ver. 7 above]
12 [g]Lev. 7:16; 22:23; Deut. 23:23 [h][ver. 1] [i][ver. 2]
13 [j]Ex. 29:38; Num. 28:3, 4
14 [k]ver. 5
15 [l]Num. 23:15, 17
17 [m][ch. 45:7] [n]See Lev. 25:10
18 [o][1 Sam. 8:14; 1 Kgs. 21:3, 7] [p][ch. 45:8] [q][ch. 34:4, 5]
19 [r][ver. 1] [s][ch. 42:4]
20 [t]2 Chr. 35:13 [u][Lev. 2:4] [v]See ch. 44:19
24 [w]ch. 44:11 [t][See ver. 20 above]

Chapter 47

1 [x][ch. 43:1, 2] [y]Ps. 46:4; Joel 3:18; [Zech. 14:8; Rev. 22:1] [z]See ch. 9:3

46:13–15 The daily offerings were to take place **morning by morning** (repeated three times). Again Ezekiel's vision differs from the practice seen in the Pentateuch, where sacrifices are prescribed for morning and evening (cf. Ex. 29:38–42; Num. 28:3–6).

46:16–18 *Rules for Inheritance of the Prince.* Encroachment by the prince on the land of the rest of the community has already been forbidden (45:7–9), and now the prince's territories are protected from slipping into other hands. These stipulations do not limit the prince's capacity for generosity—servants can still receive gifts (46:17)—but such property reverts to the prince in **the year of liberty** (v. 17, Hb. *shenat deror*). This recalls the Jubilee of Lev. 25:10, although Ezekiel does not indicate how frequent the "liberty" (Hb. *deror*) is to be; cf. Zedekiah's futile attempt to proclaim "liberty" in Jer. 34:8–22.

46:19–47:12 *The River Flowing from the Temple.* The style of the "temple tour" of chs. 40–42 returns briefly, as cooking sites (since offerings were, among other things, sacred communal meals) are identified (46:19–24), before the prophet catches sight of a river with its source at the heart of the temple itself (47:1–12).

46:19–24 *The Temple Kitchens.* First, an area in the inner courts is designated for the priests (vv. 19–20), thus protecting its sacred status. Then Ezekiel tours the four corners of the outer court, each equipped with a kitchen for the cooking of the wider community's sacrifices by the Levitical priests (vv. 21–24).

47:1–12 *The Temple's River.* The tour continues by bringing Ezekiel back into the inner court (the **door of the temple**, v. 1, is that of the sanctuary itself). There begins one of the most striking scenarios in the entire vision. A trickle of water miraculously issues from the south side of the threshold of the sanctuary and makes its way south of the altar (v. 1), out the east gate to the outer court, and then out of the main east gate (v. 2). The trickle becomes a powerful river as Ezekiel and his guide wade into the stream, the guide measuring as they go (vv. 3–5). Sitting at the river bank, the guide explains the life-giving properties of the river (vv. 6–12). This aspect of the vision coheres with 34:25–31 in affirming that renewal is not just moral and does not just come to people but affects the entire natural world. Here, however, the water brings life not just to the "world" but to that part of it least capable of sustain-

south of [a]the altar. 2 Then he brought me out by way of [b]the north gate and led me around
on the outside to [c]the outer gate that faces toward the east; and behold, the water was
trickling out on the south side.
3 Going on eastward with a measuring line in his hand, [d]the man measured a thousand
cubits,[1] and then led me through the water, and it was ankle-deep. 4 Again he measured a
thousand, and led me through the water, and it was knee-deep. Again he measured a thousand, and led me through the water, and it was waist-deep. 5 Again he measured a thousand,
and it was a river that I could not pass through, for the water had risen. It was deep enough
to swim in, a river that could not be passed through. 6 And he said to me, [e]"Son of man,
[f]have you seen this?"
Then he led me back to the bank of the river. 7 As I went back, I saw on the bank of the
river [g]very many trees on the one side and on the other. 8 And he said to me, "This water
flows toward the eastern region and goes down into [h]the Arabah, and enters the sea;[2]
when the water flows into [i]the sea, the water will become fresh.[3] 9 And wherever the river
goes,[4] every living creature that swarms will live, and there will be very many fish. For
this water goes there, that the waters of the sea[5] may become fresh; so everything will live
where the river goes. 10 Fishermen will stand beside the sea. From [j]Engedi to [k]Eneglaim
it will be a place for the spreading of nets. Its fish will be of very many kinds, like the fish
of [l]the Great Sea.[6] 11 But its swamps and marshes will not become fresh; they are to be left
for salt. 12 And on the banks, [m]on both sides of the river, there will grow [n]all kinds of trees
for food. [o]Their leaves will not wither, nor their fruit fail, [p]but they will bear fresh fruit
every month, because the water for them flows from the sanctuary. Their fruit will be for
food, and [p]their leaves for healing."

Division of the Land

13 Thus says the Lord GOD: "This is the boundary[7] by which [q]you shall divide the land
for inheritance among the twelve tribes of Israel. [r]Joseph shall have two portions. 14 And
you shall divide equally what [s]I swore [t]to give to your fathers. [u]This land shall fall to you
as your inheritance.
15 "This shall be the boundary of the land: On the north side, from [l]the Great Sea [v]by
way of Hethlon to Lebo-hamath, and on to [w]Zedad,[8] 16 [x]Berothah, Sibraim (which lies on
the border between [y]Damascus and [v]Hamath), as far as Hazer-hatticon, which is on the
border of Hauran. 17 So the boundary shall run from the sea to [z]Hazar-enan, which is on
the northern border of Damascus, with the border of Hamath to the north.[9] This shall
be the north side.[10]

1 [a]See ch. 43:13
2 [b]ch. 40:35 [c][ch. 40:6]
3 [d][ch. 40:3]
6 [e]See ch. 2:1 [f][ch. 8:6]
7 [g]ver. 12; [Rev. 22:2]
8 [h]See Deut. 1:1 [i]Deut. 3:17; 4:49; Josh. 3:16
10 [j]See 1 Sam. 23:29 [k]Isa. 15:8 [l]See Josh. 15:12
12 [m][ver. 7] [n][Gen. 2:9] [o]Ps. 1:3; [Jer. 17:8] [p][Rev. 22:2]
13 [q]ch. 45:8; See ch. 48:1-7, 23-28 [r][ch. 48:4, 5]; See Josh. 17:14-18
14 [s]See ch. 20:5 [t]See Gen. 12:7 [u][ch. 48:29]
15 [l][See ver. 10 above] [v]ch. 48:1 [w]Num. 34:8
16 [x]2 Sam. 8:8 [y]ch. 48:1; Isa. 7:8 [v][See ver. 15 above]
17 [z][ch. 48:1]

[1] A *cubit* was about 18 inches or 45 centimeters [2] That is, the Dead Sea [3] Hebrew *will be healed*; also verses 9, 11 [4] Septuagint, Syriac, Vulgate, Targum; Hebrew *the two rivers go* [5] Hebrew lacks *the waters of the sea* [6] That is, the Mediterranean Sea; also verses 15, 19, 20 [7] Probable reading; Hebrew *The valley of the boundary* [8] Septuagint; Hebrew *the entrance of Zedad, Hamath* [9] The meaning of the Hebrew is uncertain [10] Probable reading; Hebrew *and as for the north side*

ing life. The influence of this river is found in Zech. 14:8, but it extends into the NT as well, most pointedly in Rev. 22:1–2 near the climax of John's vision of the new heaven, earth, and city.

47:8 The **Arabah** generally refers to the Jordan (Rift) Valley, usually the part south of the Dead Sea, but here it probably refers in a more limited sense to the plains of Jericho (cf. 2 Kings 25:4–5), as the waters are en route to **the sea**, i.e., the Dead Sea.

47:10 Engedi and **Eneglaim** are both on the shores of the Dead Sea. Engedi is known (about the midpoint of the west side), but the location of Eneglaim remains uncertain.

47:11 The saltiness of the Dead Sea inhibits life, but provides **salt**. This essential element is preserved in spite of the overall revivification of the region.

47:13–48:35 *Dividing the Land: Allotment and Access.* The final element in the vision, and in the book, demarcates the territory for the whole of Israel (47:13–23), allots territories to the 12 tribes (48:1–7, 23–29), and allocates access to the new city (48:30–35). It includes a detailed version of the central area assigned to the sanctuary and city (48:8–22; cf. 45:1–8). These are clearly idealized boundaries, as strips are simply drawn east to west in equal chunks (see map, p. 1578). And yet the overall boundaries correspond to those of Num. 34:1–12 (cf. 1 Kings 8:65). Given the power of the river in Ezek. 47:1–12 to make things fruitful, it can be assumed that the whole of the land is envisaged as equally fertile.

47:13–23 *The Outer Boundaries.* The principles governing division of the land (vv. 13–14) introduce the description of Israel's borders (vv. 15–20). Verse 21 links with vv. 13–14, then makes provision for the settlement of resident aliens (vv. 22–23).

47:13 As seen in 37:16, **Joseph** is remembered among the patriarchs. His tribes (the **two portions**) are Ephraim and Manasseh.

47:15–20 The borders themselves are described beginning on the north, which happens to be the most difficult of the boundaries to describe. The starting point (**by way of Hethlon**, v. 15) is somewhere between modern-day Beirut and Lebanese Tripoli on the Mediterranean (**the Great Sea**) coast. The line circles north of Damascus (v. 16), and somewhere to the east of Damascus it turns south—many of the place names cannot be identified. The eastern border then follows the line of the **Jordan** to **Tamar**, a fort south of the Dead Sea (v. 18). From this point the southern border goes to the Mediterranean coast by way of **Meribah-kadesh**, emerging near modern Arish in Egypt (v. 19). The western **boundary** is naturally formed by the Mediterranean coast itself (v. 20).

18 "On the east side, the boundary shall run between Hauran and Damascus; along the
Jordan between [a]Gilead and the land of Israel; to [b]the eastern sea and as far as Tamar.[1]
This shall be the east side.
19 "On the south side, it shall run from [c]Tamar as far as [d]the waters of Meribah-kadesh,
from there along [e]the Brook of Egypt[2] to [f]the Great Sea. This shall be the south side.
20 "On the west side, the Great Sea shall be the boundary to a point [v]opposite Lebo-
hamath. This shall be the west side.
21 [g]"So you shall divide this land among you according to the tribes of Israel. 22 [h]You shall
allot it as an inheritance for yourselves and [i]for the sojourners who reside among you and
have had children among you. [j]They shall be to you as native-born children of Israel. With
you they shall be allotted an inheritance among the tribes of Israel. 23 In whatever tribe the
sojourner resides, there you shall assign him his inheritance, declares the Lord GOD.

48 "These are the names of the tribes: Beginning at the northern extreme, beside
[k]the way of Hethlon [l]to Lebo-hamath, as far as [m]Hazar-enan (which is on the
northern border of [n]Damascus over against Hamath), and[3] extending from the east side

[1] Compare Syriac; Hebrew *to the eastern sea you shall measure* [2] Hebrew lacks *of Egypt* [3] Probable reading; Hebrew *and they shall be his*

18 [a]Josh. 13:11 [b]Joel 2:20
19 [c]Gen. 14:7; 2 Chr. 20:2 [d]Num. 20:13 [e]Num. 34:5 [f]See Josh. 15:12
20 [v][See ver. 15 above]
21 [g]ver. 13
22 [h]ch. 45:1; 48:29 [i]Isa. 14:1; [Eph. 3:6] [j]Ex. 12:19, 48, 49; [Rom. 10:12; Gal. 3:28; Col. 3:11]

Chapter 48

1 [k]ch. 47:15 [l]ch. 47:20; See 1 Kgs. 8:65 [m][ch. 47:17] [n]ch. 47:16, 17, 18

47:21–23 Finally, provision is made for resident aliens, or **sojourners**, as permanent settlers among the people of Israel. The notion that they **shall be to you as native-born** recalls the qualification of legislation in Leviticus (e.g., Lev. 19:34) and Numbers (e.g., Num. 9:14).

48:1–7 *Territories of the Northern Tribes.* The equal distribution of this territory among the 12 tribes begins, as expected, in the north working south toward the central sacred district. Each tribe is allocated a strip running east-west (v. 1). There seems to be some rank order relating to proximity to the

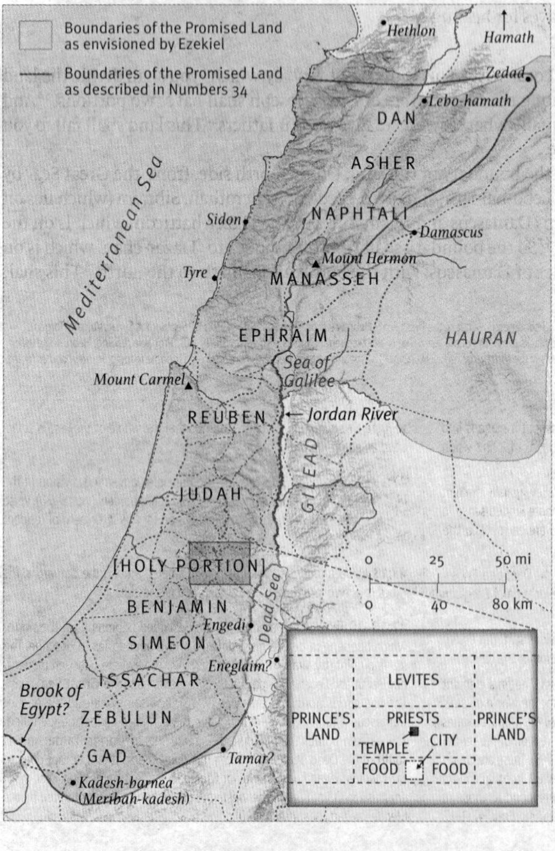

Ezekiel's Vision of Israel's New Boundaries
c. 571 B.C.

Ezekiel's final vision describes the boundaries of a restored Israel, including the allotment to each tribe and the temple. Rather than following the boundaries traditionally occupied by the Israelites, which included Gilead east of the Jordan River and excluded land north of Tyre, Ezekiel's new boundaries generally follow those described by Moses in Numbers 34. Ezekiel's vision also departs from the traditional allotment of the land among the 12 tribes and reassigns the land in horizontal bands from north to south.

to the west,[1] [o]Dan, one portion. 2 Adjoining the territory of Dan, from the east side to the
west, [o]Asher, one portion. 3 Adjoining the territory of Asher, from the east side to the west,
[o]Naphtali, one portion. 4 Adjoining the territory of Naphtali, from the east side to the west,
Manasseh, one portion. 5 Adjoining the territory of Manasseh, from the east side to the
west, Ephraim, one portion. 6 Adjoining the territory of Ephraim, from the east side to
the west, Reuben, one portion. 7 Adjoining the territory of Reuben, from the east side to
the west, Judah, one portion.
8 "Adjoining the territory of Judah, from the east side to the west, shall be [p]the portion
which you shall set apart, 25,000 cubits[2] in breadth, and in length equal to one of the
tribal portions, from the east side to the west, with [q]the sanctuary in the midst of it. 9 The
portion that you shall set apart for the LORD shall be 25,000 cubits in length, and 20,000[3]
in breadth. 10 [r]These shall be the allotments of the holy portion: the priests shall have an
allotment measuring 25,000 cubits on the northern side, 10,000 cubits in breadth on the
western side, 10,000 in breadth on the eastern side, and 25,000 in length on the southern
side, with the sanctuary of the LORD in the midst of it. 11 This shall be for [s]the consecrated
priests, [t]the sons of Zadok, who kept my charge, who did not go astray when the people
of Israel went astray, [u]as the Levites did. 12 And it shall belong to them as a special portion
from the holy portion of the land, a most holy place, adjoining the territory of the Levites.
13 [v]And alongside the territory of the priests, the Levites shall have an allotment 25,000
cubits in length and 10,000 in breadth. The whole length shall be 25,000 cubits and the
breadth 20,000.[4] 14 They [w]shall not sell or exchange any of it. They shall not alienate [x]this
choice portion of the land, for it is holy to the LORD.
15 [y]"The remainder, 5,000 cubits in breadth and 25,000 in length, shall be [z]for common
use for the city, for dwellings and for [a]open country. In the midst of it shall be the city,
16 and these shall be its measurements: [b]the north side 4,500 cubits, the south side 4,500,
the east side 4,500, and the west side 4,500. 17 And the city shall have open land: on the
north 250 cubits, on the south 250, on the east 250, and on the west 250. 18 The remainder
of the length alongside the holy portion shall be 10,000 cubits to the east, and 10,000
to the west, and it shall be alongside the holy portion. [c]Its produce shall be food for the
workers of the city. 19 And the workers of the city, from all the tribes of Israel, shall till it.
20 The whole portion that [d]you shall set apart shall be 25,000 cubits square, that is, the
holy portion together with the property of the city.
21 [e]"What remains on both sides of the holy portion and of the property of the city shall
belong to the prince. Extending from the 25,000 cubits of the holy portion to the east border,
and westward from the 25,000 cubits to the west border, parallel to the tribal portions, it
shall belong to the prince. [f]The holy portion with the sanctuary of the temple shall be in
its midst. 22 It shall be separate from the property of the Levites and the property of the
city, which are in the midst of that which belongs to the prince. The portion of the prince
shall lie between the territory of Judah and the territory of Benjamin.
23 "As for the rest of the tribes: from the east side to the west, Benjamin, one portion.
24 Adjoining the territory of Benjamin, from the east side to the west, Simeon, one portion. 25 Adjoining the territory of Simeon, from the east side to the west, Issachar, one
portion. 26 Adjoining the territory of Issachar, from the east side to the west, Zebulun,
one portion. 27 Adjoining the territory of Zebulun, from the east side to the west, Gad,
one portion. 28 And adjoining the territory of Gad to the south, the boundary shall run
[g]from Tamar to the waters of [g]Meribah-kadesh, from there along the Brook of Egypt[5] to

[1] Septuagint (compare verses 2–8); Hebrew *the east side the west* [2] A *cubit* was about 18 inches or 45 centimeters [3] Compare 45:1; Hebrew *ten* [4] Septuagint; Hebrew *10,000* [5] Hebrew lacks *of Egypt*

1 [o]Num. 2:25-31
2 [o][See ver. 1 above]
3 [o][See ver. 1 above]
8 [p]See ch. 45:1-6 [q]ver. 21
10 [r]ch. 45:4
11 [s]ch. 44:15 [t]See ch. 40:46 [u]ch. 44:10
13 [v]ch. 45:5
14 [w][Lev. 27:10, 28, 33] [x][ch. 44:30]
15 [y]ch. 45:6 [z]See ch. 42:20 [a][ch. 27:28; 45:2]
16 [b][ver. 20; Rev. 21:16]
18 [c][ch. 45:6]
20 [d][ch. 40:47]
21 [e]ch. 45:7 [f]ver. 8, 10
28 [g]ch. 47:19

temple area. **Judah** (v. 7), the leading tribe of the old southern kingdom, borders the temple area to the north, and next north of Judah is **Reuben** (v. 6), the firstborn of the patriarchs.

48:8–22 *The Central Territories.* Much of this material has already been seen in 45:1–8 (see notes there). The important addition is the location of the city and its surrounding region in the southernmost east-west strip adjoining the Levites' territory (48:15–19). At 4,500 cubits square, the **city** itself is about 1.4 miles (2.3 km) square. Work goes on in the city, although what kind is not stated; perhaps the work is to farm the adjacent land. See map, p. 1578. Verse 19 indicates the national character of the city, as its citizens come from each of the 12 tribes.

48:23–29 *Territories of the Southern Tribes.* The tribal distribution continues to the south of the city, beginning with **Benjamin** (v. 23; it had been to the immediate north of Judah in the old tribal land holdings), probably due to the proximity of the new city, since Jerusalem was in Benjaminite territory. The tribal territories seem to have some rank ordering. Judah

[h]the Great Sea.[1] **29** This is the land that [i]you shall allot as an inheritance among the tribes
of Israel, and these are their portions, declares the Lord GOD.

The Gates of the City

30 "These shall be [j]the exits of the city: On the north side, which is to be [k]4,500 cubits
by measure, **31** [l]three gates, the gate of [m]Reuben, the gate of [m]Judah, and the gate of [m]Levi,
the gates of the city being named after the tribes of Israel. **32** On the east side, which is
to be 4,500 cubits, three gates, the gate of Joseph, the gate of Benjamin, and the gate of
Dan. **33** On the south side, which is to be 4,500 cubits by measure, three gates, the gate of
Simeon, the gate of Issachar, and the gate of Zebulun. **34** On the west side, which is to be
4,500 cubits, three gates,[2] the gate of Gad, the gate of Asher, and the gate of Naphtali. **35** The
circumference of the city shall be 18,000 cubits. And [n]the name of the city from that time
on shall be, [o]The LORD Is There."

28 [h]ch. 47:10; See Josh. 15:12
29 [i]ch. 47:22
30 [j]Num. 34:4, 5, 8, 9, 12; Josh. 15:4, 7, 11 [k][ver. 16]
31 [l][Rev. 21:12, 13] [m]See Deut. 33:6-8
35 [n]Isa. 60:14; [Jer. 23:6; 33:16] [o]ch. 35:10; Jer. 3:17; Joel 3:21; [Zech. 2:10; Rev. 21:3]

[1] That is, the Mediterranean Sea [2] One Hebrew manuscript, Syriac (compare Septuagint); most Hebrew manuscripts *their gates three*

borders the central sacred area to the north, **Benjamin** to the south, both adjacent to the new Jerusalem. At the extreme north, Dan, Asher, and Naphtali are all sons of "concubines" (Asher of Zilpah, Dan and Naphtali of Bilhah), while at the extreme south, **Gad** is Bilhah's other son. The pattern of distribution, then, seems to combine aspects of political rank (Judah leading), territorial connections (Benjamin), birth order (Reuben and **Simeon** next "out" from Judah and Benjamin), the Joseph tribes (Ephraim to the south of Manasseh), and "birth mother," with the concubines' sons at the extremities.

48:30–35 *Access to the City.* Finally, the city gates are assigned to the 12 tribes—not now corresponding to the patriarchs of the territorial divisions but to the original 12 brothers, since the sons of **Levi** (the priests who have no property; see 44:28) require access to the city as well. Thus, Ephraim and Manasseh are here represented by **Joseph**. The round of the gates begins again in the north and proceeds clockwise. A rationale for the assignments is difficult to discern.

48:35 The city's new name is to be **The LORD Is There**, for its name indicates its true character. This name recalls the observation in the introduction to this vision complex: this vision, and by extension the book, is about the actualization of God's presence among his people (cf. Rev. 22:3).

INTRODUCTION TO DANIEL

Author and Title

The book of Daniel, named after and written by Daniel in the sixth century B.C., records the events of his life and the visions that he saw from the time of his exile in 605 (1:1) until the third year of King Cyrus (536; 10:1). Daniel, whose name means "God is my Judge," was a young man of noble blood who was exiled from Judah during the time of King Jehoiakim (609–597 B.C.) and lived thereafter at the Babylonian court. After the fall of the Babylonian Empire, he served the Medo-Persian Empire that succeeded it.

Date

Both Jewish and Christian (cf. Matt. 24:15) tradition have held that the author of this book is Daniel, a Jew who lived during the sixth-century B.C. Babylonian exile. Many of the chapters are dated and range from the first year of Nebuchadnezzar's reign (605 B.C.; Dan. 1:1) to Cyrus's third year (536; 10:1). But because of its detailed prophecies of events in the middle of the second century B.C. (see ch. 11) and alleged historical inconsistencies with what scholars know of sixth-century history (see note on 5:30–31), some scholars have argued that the book must be a second-century document, from the time when Antiochus IV Epiphanes (175–164 B.C.) was oppressing God's people. In that case, it would contain "prophecies after the fact," put into the mouth of a famous historical character rather than being written by Daniel himself. Thus, the visions that "Daniel" saw would attempt to interpret rather than predict history. It has also been argued that the book must be dated later than the sixth century due to its language, especially the presence of Persian and Greek loanwords.

However, the facts do not require a late date. In the first place, current knowledge of sixth-century B.C. history is far from complete, and there are plausible harmonizations that explain the alleged discrepancies.

Second, the Bible asserts clearly that the Lord announces ahead of time his plans through his prophets as a means of vindicating his sovereignty and encouraging his people (see Isa. 41:21–24; 44:6–7), and there is no reason in principle why such prophecies should not be detailed and precise. Some scholars, who allow in principle that God can foretell events, nevertheless suggest that such detailed foretelling is unparalleled in the rest of the canonical prophets, and that it cannot be reconciled with the usual purpose of prediction (namely, that the first audience should be faithful to the covenant). In reply, note that Jeremiah did give a specific amount of time for the exile (Jer. 25:11; cf. note on Dan. 9:2). Further, the high degree of specificity in Daniel's prophecies does serve its first audience as well as those to follow: this shows how carefully God has planned events and governs them for his perfect ends; therefore the faithful can recognize that none of their troubles take God by surprise, and none will derail his purpose of vindicating those who steadfastly love him. This is quite relevant to the people of God in Daniel's day, who are on the verge of horrendous devastations and persecutions (see notes on ch. 11); they must be assured that the story will continue to its appointed fulfillment, so that they do not lose heart.

Third, there were likely Greeks and Persians present at the Babylonian court as mercenaries and in other capacities, providing a ready explanation for the presence of loanwords.

Fourth, the book of Daniel was accepted as canonical by the community of Qumran (who produced the Dead Sea Scrolls). This is telling because this group emerged as a separate party in Judaism between 171 and 167 B.C., before the proposed late date. They would not have accepted the book if it had appeared after the split.

Fifth, some who favor a later date say that the author of Daniel represented Antiochus IV Epiphanes using the figure of Nebuchadnezzar. Literary studies, however, have shown that the book of Daniel puts Nebuchadnezzar in far too positive a light (e.g., he comes to acknowledge the true God) for him to be an effective image of the relentless persecutor Antiochus IV. Of course the book's lesson, about God's sovereignty over even the imperial forces, would have taken a heightened relevance in the days of Antiochus IV; but that is different from saying that the book was written *for* that particular occasion.

There are therefore no compelling reasons to deny that Daniel wrote this book.

Theme

The central theme of the book of Daniel is God's sovereignty over history and empires, setting up and removing kings as he pleases (2:21; 4:34–37). All of the kingdoms of this world will come to an end and will be replaced by the Lord's kingdom, which will never pass away (2:44; 7:27). Though trials and difficulties will continue for the saints up until the end, those who are faithful will be raised to glory, honor, and everlasting life in this final kingdom (12:1–3).

Purpose, Occasion, and Background

The book of Daniel is made up of two halves, each of which has its own genre. The first half (chs. 1–6) contains narratives from the lives of Daniel and his three friends, Shadrach, Meshach, and Abednego. These court stories exemplify faithful living in exile and provide models of how God's people should live as strangers and exiles in a world that is not their home (Heb. 13:14). They show Daniel and his friends serving their pagan masters loyally, as Jeremiah 29:5–7 had commanded, yet without compromising their greater loyalty to God. The second half of the book (Daniel 7–12) contains apocalyptic visions, which are designed to reassure God's people that in spite of their present persecution and suffering, God is in control and will ultimately be victorious. The Lord is aware of the suffering of his people and will bring their trials to an end on the day when he establishes his kingdom. The final victory belongs to the Ancient of Days and his representative, the Son of Man (ch. 7). When they triumph, the powers and authorities of this world will be defeated and judged, while the saints will be vindicated and rewarded (7:26–27).

The two parts of the book are linked by a variety of literary features: (1) the dates attached to the visions locate them during the same period of history as the narratives of chapters 1–6; (2) the book begins in Hebrew, switches into Aramaic from 2:4–7:28, and then returns to Hebrew for chapters 8–12; (3) the vision of the four beasts in chapter 7 mirrors in a number of ways Nebuchadnezzar's dream in chapter 2; and (4) the message of the visions of chapters 7–12 reinforces the message of the narratives in chapters 1–6: God's ultimate victory over the powers and authorities of this present evil age is sure, so the wise will be faithful to the Lord in the meantime, whatever pressures are brought to bear upon them.

Key Themes

1. It is possible to live a faithful life in exile, surrounded by pagan influences and propaganda, if one sets one's mind to serving the Lord wholeheartedly (ch. 1).
2. God can vindicate his faithful servants in front of pagan rulers by giving them unusual wisdom and insight into divine mysteries and by miraculously protecting them against the enmity of their pagan neighbors (chs. 2; 3; 6). Nevertheless, divine rescue from martyrdom cannot be assumed (3:16–18).
3. God humbles the proud and raises up the humble; even the hearts of the greatest kings are under his control (chs. 4; 5).
4. This world will be a place of torment and persecution for the saints until the end, getting worse and worse rather than better and better (chs. 2; 7). Yet the Lord will judge the kingdoms of this world and bring them to an end, replacing them with his own kingdom that will never end. This kingdom will be ruled by "one like a son of man" who comes "with the clouds," a figure who combines the distinctive traits of humanity and divinity (7:13).
5. God is sovereign over the course of history, even over those who rebel against him and seek to destroy his people (ch. 8).
6. The exile was not the end of Israel's history of rebellion and judgment. In the future, Israel would again transgress against the Lord, and Jerusalem would be handed over into the power of her enemies, who

The City of Babylon

The city of Babylon reached its zenith under Nebuchadrezzar II (Nebuchadnezzar of Scripture, who reigned 605–562 B.C.). He restored and enlarged it, making it the largest city seen in the world up to that time. The Euphrates River flowed through it, with the oldest quarter of the city lying on the east bank of the river. The city was surrounded by a city wall with fortified gates that were named after the various Babylonian deities. The Esagila Complex on the east bank of the Euphrates contained the Temple of Marduk with its associated seven-storied ziggurat Etemenanki.

From Esagila, the Processional Way (its walls lined with glazed bricks with representations of lions) led to the Ishtar Gate (which was decorated with glazed brick reliefs of dragons and young bulls). Beside the Ishtar Gate stood two immense fortified palaces. A bridge led over the Euphrates to the western part of the city. No evidence of the famed Hanging Gardens of Babylon has been found, but if anything like this was ever constructed here, it would have been during this time, at the height of the city's splendor. The city was captured by Cyrus the Persian in 539 B.C.

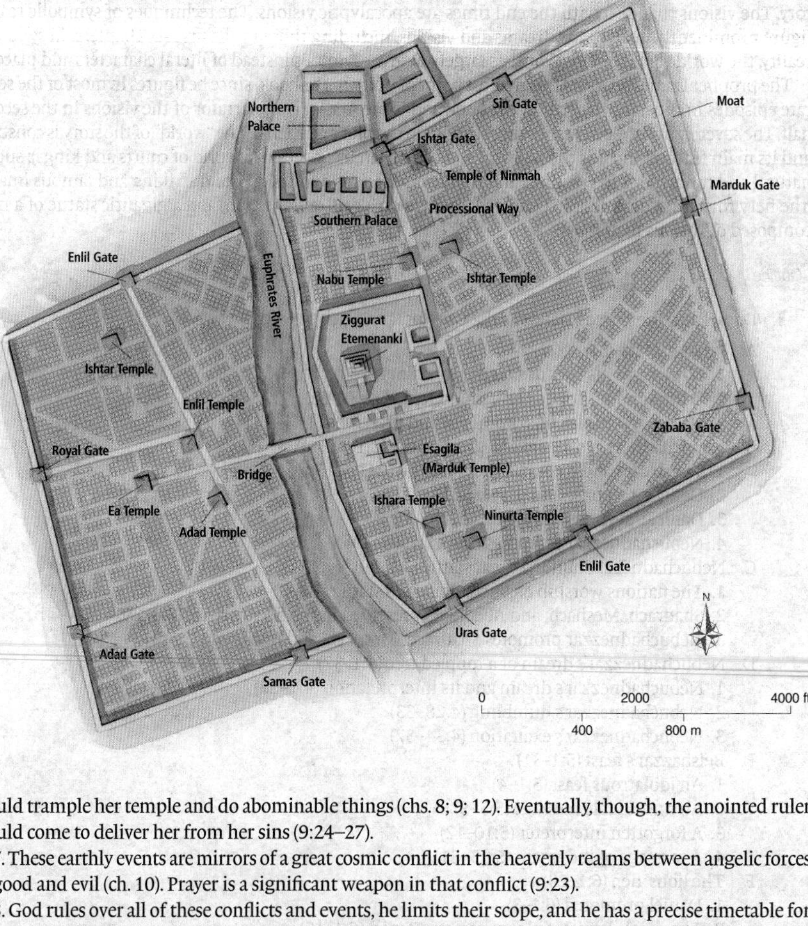

would trample her temple and do abominable things (chs. 8; 9; 12). Eventually, though, the anointed ruler would come to deliver her from her sins (9:24–27).

7. These earthly events are mirrors of a great cosmic conflict in the heavenly realms between angelic forces of good and evil (ch. 10). Prayer is a significant weapon in that conflict (9:23).

8. God rules over all of these conflicts and events, he limits their scope, and he has a precise timetable for the trials of the saints to be completed, when he will finally intervene to cleanse and deliver his people (ch. 12).

9. In the meantime, the saints must be patient and faithful amid a hostile world, looking to the Lord alone for deliverance (11:33–35).

History of Salvation Summary

The people of Judah could have interpreted their exile to Babylon as the end of their special relationship with God. But not only does the book of Daniel show them that it is possible to be faithful to God even away from the Promised Land, it also shows them that God has not abandoned his plan for the whole world: he controls all of history, even the most dire conflicts, to bring his Messiah's rule to all nations. (For an explanation of the "History of Salvation," see the Overview of the Bible, pp. 23–26. See also History of Salvation in the Old Testament: Preparing the Way for Christ, pp. 2635–2661.)

Literary Features

The book of Daniel is unique in the Bible in falling decisively into two distinct genres in its two halves. The first six chapters are hero stories comprised of six self-contained ordeals. The last six chapters are a series of visions that employ highly symbolic images to portray vast stretches of political and spiritual history. The visions that deal with the end times are apocalyptic visions. The techniques of symbolic reality figure prominently in all of the dreams and visions, including those in the first six chapters; in symbolic reality, the world that is entered consists largely of great symbols instead of literal characters and places.

The prophet Daniel provides the greatest point of unity in the book, since he figures in most of the separate episodes in the narrative half of the book and is the first-person narrator of the visions in the second half. The sovereignty of God is a unifying element in the plot and theme. The "world" of the story is constant, and its main features include the political and courtly arena of action (a world of courts and kings); supernatural and miraculous happenings and characters; dreams and visions; and striking and famous images (the fiery furnace; a disembodied hand that writes on a wall; a lions' den; and a gigantic statue of a man composed of various materials).

Outline

I. Daniel and the Three Friends at the Babylonian Court (1:1–6:28)
- A. Prologue (1:1–21)
  1. Daniel and his friends taken into exile (1:1–7)
  2. Daniel and his friends remain undefiled (1:8–16)
  3. Daniel and his friends promoted and preserved (1:17–21)
- B. Nebuchadnezzar's dream of a great statue (2:1–49)
  1. The dream and Nebuchadnezzar's threat (2:1–13)
  2. Daniel's response and prayer (2:14–24)
  3. Daniel interprets the dream (2:25–45)
  4. Nebuchadnezzar promotes Daniel (2:46–49)
- C. Nebuchadnezzar builds a great statue (3:1–30)
  1. The nations worship Nebuchadnezzar's statue (3:1–7)
  2. Shadrach, Meshach, and Abednego preserved in the fiery furnace (3:8–29)
  3. Nebuchadnezzar promotes Shadrach, Meshach, and Abednego (3:30)
- D. Nebuchadnezzar's dream of a toppled tree (4:1–37)
  1. Nebuchadnezzar's dream and its interpretation (4:1–27)
  2. Nebuchadnezzar's humbling (4:28–33)
  3. Nebuchadnezzar's exaltation (4:34–37)
- E. Belshazzar's feast (5:1–31)
  1. An idolatrous feast (5:1–4)
  2. An unreadable message (5:5–9)
  3. A forgotten interpreter (5:10–12)
  4. A message of judgment (5:13–31)
- F. The lions' den (6:1–28)
  1. Daniel promoted (6:1–3)
  2. The administrators plot to remove Daniel (6:4–15)
  3. Daniel preserved in the lions' den (6:16–24)
  4. Darius acknowledges the power of Daniel's God (6:25–27)
  5. Daniel preserved until the end of the exile (6:28)

II. The Visions of Daniel (7:1–12:13)
- A. The vision of four great beasts and the heavenly court (7:1–28)
  1. The four great beasts (7:1–8)

2. The Ancient of Days judges the beasts (7:9–12)
3. The coming of the Son of Man (7:13–14)
4. The interpretation of the vision (7:15–27)
5. Daniel's response (7:28)

B. The vision of the ram, the goat, and the little horn (8:1–27)
1. The vision of the ram and the goat (8:1–14)
2. The interpretation of the vision (8:15–26)
3. Daniel's response (8:27)

C. Daniel's prayer and its answer (9:1–27)
1. Daniel's prayer concerning the 70 years (9:1–19)
2. Gabriel's answer: 70 sevens before the promised redemption (9:20–27)

D. Daniel's vision of the final conflict (10:1–12:13)
1. A heavenly messenger brings news of heavenly conflict (10:1–11:1)
2. A detailed vision of future earthly conflicts among nations (11:2–45)
3. The promise of resurrection to glory or shame (12:1–4)
4. How long until the end? (12:5–13)

DANIEL

Daniel Taken to Babylon

1 In the third year of [a]the reign of Jehoiakim king of Judah, Nebuchadnezzar king of
Babylon came to Jerusalem and besieged it. 2 And the Lord gave Jehoiakim king of
Judah into his hand, with some of [b]the vessels of the house of God. And he brought them
to [c]the land of Shinar, to the house of his god, [d]and placed the vessels in the treasury of
his god. 3 Then the king commanded Ashpenaz, [e]his chief eunuch, to bring some of the
people of Israel, both of the royal family[1] and of [f]the nobility, 4 youths without [g]blemish,
of good appearance and [h]skillful in all wisdom, endowed with knowledge, understanding
learning, and competent to stand in the king's palace, and to [i]teach them the literature and
language of the [j]Chaldeans. 5 The king assigned them a daily portion of [k]the food that the
king ate, and of [l]the wine that he drank. They were to be educated for [m]three years, and
at the end of that time they were to [n]stand before the king. 6 Among these were [o]Daniel,
[p]Hananiah, [p]Mishael, and [p]Azariah of the tribe of Judah. 7 And [e]the chief of the eunuchs
[q]gave them names: [r]Daniel he called Belteshazzar, Hananiah he called Shadrach, Mishael
he called Meshach, and Azariah he called Abednego.

Daniel's Faithfulness

8 But Daniel [s]resolved that he would not [t]defile himself with [k]the king's food, or with
[l]the wine that he drank. Therefore he asked the chief of the eunuchs to allow him not to

[1] Hebrew *of the seed of the kingdom*

Chapter 1
1 [a]2 Kgs. 24:1, 2; 2 Chr. 36:6
2 [b]ch. 5:2; 2 Kgs. 24:13; 2 Chr. 36:7, 10; [Jer. 27:18] [c]Gen. 11:2; Zech. 5:11 [d]2 Chr. 36:7; Ezra 5:14
3 [e][2 Kgs. 20:18; Isa. 39:7] [f]Esth. 1:3
4 [g][Lev. 24:19, 20; 2 Sam. 14:25] [h][ver. 17; ch. 9:22] [i][Isa. 47:10] [j]ch. 2:2, 4, 5, 10; 3:8; 4:7; 5:7, 11
5 [k]ch. 11:26 [l]ver. 8, 16 [m][ver. 18] [n][ch. 2:2; 1 Kgs. 10:8]; See Gen. 41:46
6 [o]Ezek. 14:14, 20; Matt. 24:15 [p]ch. 2:17
7 [e][See ver. 3 above] [q][2 Kgs. 23:34; 24:17] [r]ch. 2:26; 4:8, 9, 18, 19; 5:12; 10:1
8 [s]2 Cor. 9:7 [t][Lev. 3:17; Ezek. 4:13; Hos. 9:3] [k][See ver. 5 above] [l][See ver. 5 above]

1:1–6:28 *Daniel and the Three Friends at the Babylonian Court.* The Hebrew exiles live faithfully to the Lord while serving in the court of Nebuchadnezzar and his successors, from 605 B.C. down to the fall of the Babylonian Empire (539) and into the early years of Persian rule; their service brings blessing to the Gentiles.

1:1–21 *Prologue.* Daniel describes how he and his three friends were taken into exile (vv. 1–7), remained undefiled (vv. 8–16), and were promoted and preserved (vv. 17–21).

1:1–7 *Daniel and His Friends Taken into Exile.* Here it is explained how the Hebrew youths came to be trainees for service in the Babylonian court.

1:1–2 In the third year of the reign of Jehoiakim (605 B.C.), **Nebuchadnezzar king of Babylon came to Jerusalem** and took Daniel and other promising young people to Babylon to be trained in Babylonian culture and literature. This deportation was the beginning of what came to be known as the Babylonian exile, which was the result of the Lord's judgment on his people. In Lev. 26:33, 39 the Lord threatened his people with exile if they were unfaithful to the terms of the covenant established at Mount Sinai (see also Deut. 4:27; 28:64). After a lengthy history of disobedience, this threat was carried out in several stages, culminating in the destruction of Jerusalem and the burning of the temple in 586 B.C. The final destruction and exile were foreshadowed by this earlier exile in which **vessels of the house of God** were taken into captivity along with some of his people. Daniel calls it the "third year of the reign of Jehoiakim," apparently using the Babylonian system for counting the length of a reign, while Jer. 25:1 calls it "the fourth year," using the Jewish system. (Reigns could be counted from the beginning of the new year preceding a king's ascension, or from the actual date of ascension, or from the beginning of the new year following his ascension; the third system was used in Babylon.)

1:3–4 Some of **the royal family** and **nobility** were also exiled. Like the temple vessels and sacrifices, they had to be **without blemish**. Their exile was a fulfillment of Isaiah's prophecy to King Hezekiah in 2 Kings 20 and Isaiah 39, a century earlier. Hezekiah had shown the representatives of Babylon around his treasuries, hoping to win a political partner against the Assyrians. This failure to trust in the Lord was met with a prophecy that the treasures he had shown the Babylonians and some of his own descendants would be carried off to Babylon.

1:5–7 Nebuchadnezzar sought to assimilate the exiles into Babylonian culture by obliterating their religious and cultural identity and creating dependence upon the royal court. For this reason, the exiles were given names linked with Babylonian deities in place of Israelite names linked with their God. **Daniel** ("God is my Judge"), **Hananiah** ("Yahweh is gracious"), **Mishael** ("Who is what God is?"), and **Azariah** ("Yahweh is a helper") became names that invoked the help of the Babylonian gods Marduk, Bel, and Nebo: **Belteshazzar** ("O Lady [wife of the god Bel], protect the king!"), **Shadrach** ("I am very fearful [of God]" or "command of Aku [the moon god]"), **Meshach** ("I am of little account" or "Who is like Aku?"), and **Abednego** ("servant of the shining one [Nebo]"). They were schooled in the language and mythological literature of the Babylonians, and their food was assigned from the king's table, reminding them constantly of the source of their daily bread.

1:8–16 *Daniel and His Friends Remain Undefiled.* Daniel and his three friends resisted the attempted assimilation. They retained their original names (see v. 11) and **resolved** not to **defile** themselves with **the king's food** and drink (v. 8). Many have thought that the four men's resolve came from their intent to eat only ceremonially clean food, not any "unclean" food as specified in Lev. 11:1–47 and Deut. 14:3–20—much as a group of Jewish priests later did in Rome, eating only figs and nuts (see Josephus, *Life of Josephus* 14; cf. Rom. 14:2). That may be part of the explanation, for the Babylonians would have eaten such things as pork, which was unclean for Jews. But **wine** (Dan. 1:8) would not have been prohibited by any law in Jewish Scripture, so that cannot be the entire explanation (unless the young men feared that

[t]defile himself. 9 [u]And God gave Daniel favor and compassion in the sight of the chief of
the eunuchs, 10 and the chief of the eunuchs said to Daniel, "I fear my lord the king, who
assigned your food and your drink; for why should he see that you were in worse condition than the youths who are of your own age? So you would endanger my head with the
king." 11 Then Daniel said to the steward whom the chief of the eunuchs had assigned
over Daniel, Hananiah, Mishael, and Azariah, 12 "Test your servants for [v]ten days; let us be
given vegetables to eat and water to drink. 13 Then let our appearance and the appearance
of the youths who eat [k]the king's food be observed by you, and deal with your servants
according to what you see." 14 So he listened to them in this matter, and tested them for ten
days. 15 At the end of ten days it was seen that they were better in appearance and fatter in
flesh than all the youths who ate [k]the king's food. 16 [w]So the steward took away their food
and the wine they were to drink, and gave them [x]vegetables.

17 As for these four youths, [y]God gave them learning and [z]skill in all literature and wisdom, and Daniel had [a]understanding in all visions and dreams. 18 At the end of [b]the time,
when the king had commanded that they should be brought in, the chief of the eunuchs
brought them in before Nebuchadnezzar. 19 And the king spoke with them, and among
all of them none was found like Daniel, Hananiah, Mishael, and Azariah. Therefore [c]they
stood before the king. 20 And in every matter of wisdom and understanding about which
the king inquired of them, he found them ten times better than all [d]the magicians and
[e]enchanters that were in all his kingdom. 21 And Daniel [f]was there until the first year of
[g]King Cyrus.

Nebuchadnezzar's Dream

2 In the second year of the reign of Nebuchadnezzar, Nebuchadnezzar had dreams;
[h]his spirit was troubled, and [i]his sleep left him. 2 Then the king commanded that [d]the
magicians, [e]the enchanters, the [j]sorcerers, and [k]the Chaldeans be summoned to tell the

8 [t][Lev. 3:17; Ezek. 4:13; Hos. 9:3]
9 [u][Gen. 39:21; Ps. 106:46; Prov. 16:7]
12 [v][Rev. 2:10]
13 [k][See ver. 5 above]
15 [k][See ver. 5 above]
16 [w]ver. 11 [x]ver. 12
17 [y][ch. 2:20, 23; Job 32:8; James 1:5] [z]ver. 4 [a]ch. 5:12; [ch. 9:23; 10:1, 11, 12]
18 [b][ver. 5]
19 [c]ch. 2:2
20 [d][ch. 2:27; Gen. 41:8, 24; Ex. 7:11, 22; 8:7, 18, 19; 9:11] [e]ch. 2:2, 10, 27; 4:7; 5:7, 11, 15
21 [f][ch. 6:28; 10:1] [g]See ch. 6:28

Chapter 2

1 [h][ch. 4:5; 5:9; Gen. 41:8] [i][ch. 6:18; Esth. 6:1]
2 [d][See ch. 1:20 above] [e][See ch. 1:20 above] [j]Deut. 18:10, 11; 2 Chr. 33:6; Isa. 47:9, 12 [k]See ch. 1:4

somehow the wine had been polluted through failure to grow the grapes according to the rule of Lev. 19:23–25; cf. Deut. 20:6). Another view is that they feared the meat and wine would have been first offered to Babylonian idols. Again, this may have provided part of the reason for their reluctance to partake of the Babylonian food, but the vegetables and grains would probably also have been offered to idols, so that does not seem to be the most persuasive explanation. A third view, that they were following a vegetarian diet for health reasons, is unhelpful, because no OT laws would have taught them that (modern) idea. A fourth view combines elements of the first two, and seems the best explanation: Daniel and his friends avoided the luxurious diet of the king's table as a way of protecting themselves from being ensnared by the temptations of the Babylonian culture. They used their distinctive diet as a way of retaining their distinctive identity as Jewish exiles and avoiding complete assimilation into Babylonian culture (which was the king's goal with these conquered subjects). With this restricted diet they continually reminded themselves, in this time of testing, that they were the people of God in a foreign land and that they were dependent for their food, indeed for their very lives, upon God, their Creator, not King Nebuchadnezzar. (It is possible that Daniel later came to accept some of the Babylonian food; see Dan. 10:3.) The Lord **gave Daniel favor** (1:9) with his captors, an answer to Solomon's prayer for the exiles (1 Kings 8:50), and the steward honored their request for a special diet. At the end of a trial period, Daniel and his friends looked fitter (**fatter in flesh**; Dan. 1:15) than those who had consumed a high-calorie diet. This confirmed that God's favor was upon them.

1:17–21 *Daniel and His Friends Promoted and Preserved.* God also gave to all four of them exceptional knowledge and understanding of the Babylonian **literature and wisdom**, and to Daniel the ability to discern **all visions and dreams** (v. 17). God's favor enabled them to answer all of Nebuchadnezzar's questions, so that he found them **ten times better than all** of his pagan advisers (v. 20). God placed them in a unique position where they could be a blessing to their captors and build up the society in which they found themselves (see Jer. 29:5–7), while at the same time enabling them to remain true to him amid extraordinary pressures.

1:21 until the first year of King Cyrus. That is, 539 B.C., when Cyrus conquered Babylon. God's faithfulness proved sufficient for Daniel throughout the 70 years of his exile. Babylonian kings came and went, and the Babylonians were replaced as the ruling world power by the Medo-Persian King Cyrus, yet God sustained his faithful servant (cf. 10:1).

2:1–49 *Nebuchadnezzar's Dream of a Great Statue.* Daniel's God shows himself superior by revealing to Daniel both the content and the interpretation of Nebuchadnezzar's dream.

2:1–13 *The Dream and Nebuchadnezzar's Threat.* Nebuchadnezzar expects his interpreters to also tell him the very content of his dream (perhaps to prove that they are genuinely qualified to interpret it).

2:1 In the ancient world, **dreams** were thought to be shadows of future events. A king's dreams had significance for the nation as a whole, and the interpretation was important so that the king might take steps to be ready for the events the dream anticipated, or even to counteract them. From the timing in **the second year of the reign of Nebuchadnezzar**, it is possible that the author implies that Daniel and his friends had not yet finished their three-year program (1:5). However, it may be better to use Babylonian conventions to count the years of a reign, such that the young men were taken and began their training in Nebuchadnezzar's accession year, and had their second and third years of training during what the Babylonians called the first and second years of Nebuchadnezzar's reign (see note on 1:1–2). In that case, "the second year of the reign of Nebuchadnezzar" would be 603–602 B.C.

2:2 Nebuchadnezzar had a staff of specialists in dream interpretation: **the magicians, the enchanters, the sorcerers, and the Chaldeans**. The name "Chaldeans" initially referred to a part of the Babylonian Empire, but it developed into a descriptive term for a special group, known for their expertise in magic lore and interpreting dreams.

Rulers During the Time of Daniel

Babylon	Nebuchadnezzar	605–562 B.C.
	Nabonidus	556–539
	Co-regent Belshazzar	550–539
Persia	Cyrus	539–530
	Darius I	522–486

king his dreams. So they came in and [l]stood before the king. 3 And the king said to them,
"I had a dream, and [h]my spirit is troubled to know the dream." 4 Then [k]the Chaldeans
said to the king in Aramaic,[1] [m]"O king, live forever! Tell your servants the dream, and we
will show the interpretation." 5 The king answered and said to [k]the Chaldeans, "The word
from me is firm: if you do not make known to me the dream and its interpretation, you
shall be [n]torn limb from limb, [n]and your [o]houses shall be laid in ruins. 6 But if you show
the dream and its interpretation, [p]you shall receive from me gifts and rewards and great
honor. [q]Therefore show me the dream and its interpretation." 7 They answered a second
time and said, "Let the king tell his servants the dream, and we will show its interpretation."
8 The king answered and said, "I know with certainty that you are trying to [r]gain time,
because you see that the word from me is firm— 9 if you do not make the dream known to
me, [s]there is but one sentence for you. You have agreed to speak lying and corrupt words
before me till [t]the times change. [u]Therefore tell me the dream, and I shall know that you
can show me its interpretation." 10 [v]The Chaldeans answered the king and said, "There is
not a man on earth who can meet the king's demand, for no great and powerful king has
asked such a thing of any magician or enchanter or [v]Chaldean. 11 The thing that the king
asks is difficult, and no one can show it to the king except [w]the gods, whose dwelling is
not with flesh."

12 Because of this the king was angry and [x]very furious, and [y]commanded that all [z]the
wise men of Babylon be destroyed. 13 So the decree went out, and the wise men were about
to be killed; and they sought [a]Daniel and his companions, to kill them. 14 Then Daniel
replied with prudence and discretion to [b]Arioch, the [c]captain of the king's guard, who
had gone out to kill the wise men of Babylon. 15 He declared[2] to Arioch, the king's captain,
"Why is the decree of the king [d]so urgent?" Then Arioch made the matter known to Daniel.
16 And Daniel went in and requested the king to appoint him a time, that he might show
the interpretation to the king.

God Reveals Nebuchadnezzar's Dream

17 Then Daniel went to his house and made the matter known to [e]Hananiah, [e]Mishael,
and [e]Azariah, his companions, 18 [f]and told them to seek mercy from the [g]God of heaven
concerning this mystery, so that Daniel and his companions might not [h]be destroyed with
the rest of the wise men of Babylon. 19 Then the mystery was revealed to Daniel in [i]a vision
of the night. Then Daniel [j]blessed the [g]God of heaven. 20 Daniel answered and said:

> [k]"Blessed be the name of God forever and ever,
> [l]to whom belong wisdom and might.
> 21 [m]He changes times and seasons;
> [n]he removes kings and sets up kings;

2 [l]See ch. 1:5
3 [h][See ver. 1 above]
4 [k][See ver. 2 above] [m]ch. 3:9; 5:10; 6:6, 21; See 1 Kgs. 1:31
5 [k][See ver. 2 above] [n]ch. 3:29 [o]Ezra 6:11; [2 Kgs. 10:27]
6 [p][ch. 5:7, 16] [q][ver. 7, 9]
8 [r]Eph. 5:16; Col. 4:5
9 [s]Esth. 4:11 [t][ver. 21; ch. 7:25] [u]ver. 6; [ver. 7]
10 [v]See ch. 1:4
11 [w][ch. 5:11, 14]
12 [x][ch. 3:19] [y][ver. 24] [z]ch. 4:6
13 [a]See ch. 1:4-7
14 [b]ver. 24, 25 [c][Gen. 37:36]
15 [d]ch. 3:22
17 [e]ch. 1:6
18 [f][Matt. 18:19] [g]ver. 19, 28, 37, 44; Rev. 11:13 [h][ver. 12, 24]
19 [i][Num. 12:6; Job 33:15, 16] [j]See Josh. 22:33 [g][See ver. 18 above]
20 [k]1 Chr. 29:10; Ps. 72:18; 113:2; 115:18; Luke 1:68 [l][Isa. 28:29]
21 [m][ver. 9; ch. 7:25] [n][ch. 4:17; 5:20; Job 12:18; Ps. 75:7; Rom. 13:1]

[1] The text from this point to the end of chapter 7 is in Aramaic [2] Aramaic *answered and said*; also verse 26

2:4 From this point until the end of ch. 7, the text switches from Hebrew into **Aramaic**, the court language of its Babylonian setting. Perhaps the change indicates that these chapters address matters of universal significance rather than those of more specifically Israelite concern.

Explicit References to Dates in Daniel

Babylon	Nebuchadnezzar's 1st year	605 B.C.	ch. 1
	Nebuchadnezzar's 2nd year	604	ch. 2
	Nebuchadnezzar's reign	605–562	chs. 3–4
	Belshazzar's 1st year	550	ch. 7
	Belshazzar's 3rd year	548	ch. 8
	Belshazzar's last year	539	ch. 5
Persia	Cyrus's 3rd year	536	chs. 10–12
	Darius's 1st year	522	ch. 9
	Darius's reign	522–486	ch. 6

2:5–6 Contrary to normal procedure, the king made the extraordinary demand that his interpreters recount the **dream** itself as well as **its interpretation**. If the interpreters succeeded, they would be given great **rewards**. If they failed, they would be executed and their **houses** would be destroyed.

2:11 These men consider the king's demand unreasonable because no human being could know another person's dream unless it was revealed by **the gods, whose dwelling is not with flesh**. Their own words reveal the power of Israel's God, who does exactly what they say is impossible. Israel's God is not only the high and holy God whose glory fills the heavens, but also the God who dwells with those of a humble and contrite spirit (Isa. 57:15).

2:12 Nebuchadnezzar's decree of death affected **all the wise men**, a wider group that would have also included Daniel and his friends.

2:14–24 *Daniel's Response and Prayer.* Daniel shows the right response: he leads his friends in praying to the true God for insight.

2:15–16 With remarkable faith, **Daniel** requested from **Arioch** an appointment with the **king** to reveal the dream and its **interpretation** even before God had revealed the dream to Daniel.

2:19 Unlike the gods of the Babylonian diviners, Daniel's God was able and willing to reveal such a **mystery** to his servants (see Isa. 44:7–8; Amos 3:7).

[o]he gives wisdom to the wise
[o]and knowledge to those who have understanding;
22 [p]he reveals deep and hidden things;
[p]he knows what is in the darkness,
[q]and the light dwells with him.
23 To you, O [r]God of my fathers,
[s]I give thanks and praise,
for [t]you have given me wisdom and might,
and have now made known to me what [u]we asked of you,
for you have made known to us the king's matter."

24 Therefore Daniel went in to [v]Arioch, whom the king had appointed to destroy the wise
men of Babylon. He went and said thus to him: "Do not destroy the wise men of Babylon;
bring me in before the king, and I will show the king the interpretation."
25 Then [v]Arioch brought in Daniel before the king [w]in haste and said thus to him: "I
have found [x]among the exiles from Judah a man who will make known to the king the
interpretation." 26 The king declared to Daniel, [y]whose name was Belteshazzar, [z]"Are you
able to make known to me the dream that I have seen and its interpretation?" 27 Daniel
answered the king and said, "No wise men, [a]enchanters, [a]magicians, or [b]astrologers can
show to the king the mystery that the king has asked, 28 but [c]there is a God in heaven
who reveals mysteries, and he has made known to King Nebuchadnezzar [d]what will be
in the latter days. Your dream and [e]the visions of your head as you lay in bed are these:
29 To you, O king, as you lay in bed came thoughts of what would be after this, [f]and he
who reveals mysteries made known to you what is to be. 30 But [g]as for me, this mystery
has been revealed to me, not because of any wisdom that I have more than all the living,
but in order that the interpretation may be made known to the king, and that [h]you may
know the thoughts of your mind.

Daniel Interprets the Dream

31 "You saw, O king, and behold, a great image. This image, mighty and of exceeding
brightness, stood before you, and its appearance was frightening. 32 [i]The head of this image
was of fine gold, [j]its chest and arms of silver, its middle and [j]thighs of bronze, 33 [k]its legs
of iron, its feet partly of iron and partly of clay. 34 As you looked, a stone was cut out [l]by
no human hand, and it struck the image on its feet of iron and clay, and [m]broke them in
pieces. 35 Then the iron, the clay, the bronze, the silver, and the gold, all together were
broken in pieces, and became [n]like the chaff of the summer threshing floors; and the wind
carried them away, so that [o]not a trace of them could be found. But the stone that struck
the image became [p]a great mountain [q]and filled the whole earth.
36 "This was the dream. Now we will tell the king its interpretation. 37 You, O king,
[r]the king of kings, to whom [s]the God of heaven [t]has given the kingdom, the power, and
the might, and the glory, 38 and into whose hand he has given, wherever they dwell, the
children of man, [u]the beasts of the field, and the birds of the heavens, making you rule
over them all—you are [v]the head of gold. 39 [w]Another kingdom inferior to you shall arise
after you, and yet a third kingdom [v]of bronze, [x]which shall rule over all the earth. 40 And

21 [o]See ch. 1:17
22 [p]Job 12:22; [Ps. 25:14; 139:12; Amos 4:13; Heb. 4:13] [q]1 Tim. 6:16; James 1:17; 1 John 1:5; [John 1:4, 5]
23 [r]Deut. 26:7; 1 Chr. 12:17; 29:18 [s][ch. 6:10] [t][ver. 20]; See ch. 1:17 [u][ver. 18]
24 [v]ver. 14, 15
25 [v][See ver. 24 above] [w]ch. 3:24 [x]ch. 5:13; Ezra 4:1; 6:16, 19, 20; 10:7, 16
26 [y]See ch. 1:7 [z][ch. 5:16]
27 [a]See ch. 1:20 [b]ch. 4:7; 5:7
28 [c]See ver. 22 [d]ch. 10:14; Hos. 3:5 [e]ch. 4:5; 7:15
29 [f]ver. 45
30 [g][Gen. 41:16; Acts 3:12] [h][Eccles. 3:18]
32 [i][ver. 38] [j][ver. 39]
33 [k][ver. 40]
34 [l][ch. 8:25; Job 34:20; Lam. 4:6; 2 Cor. 5:1] [m]ver. 35, 40, 44, 45; Isa. 8:9; [Matt. 21:44; Luke 20:18]
35 [n]Ps. 1:4 [o][Rev. 20:11] [p][Isa. 2:2] [q][Ps. 80:9]
37 [r]Ezra 7:12; Ezek. 26:7 [s]ver. 19 [t]ch. 5:18; [Ezra 1:2]; See ver. 21
38 [u]ch. 4:21; Jer. 27:6 [v][ver. 32]
39 [w][ver. 32; ch. 5:28, 31] [v][See ver. 38 above] [x][ch. 7:6]

2:23 Daniel gathered his companions to pray for the revelation of the mystery (vv. 17–18). When God answered his prayer, Daniel praised and thanked God for his **wisdom and might** before he went to see King Nebuchadnezzar.

2:25–45 *Daniel Interprets the Dream.* In successfully meeting the king's demands, Daniel makes sure that the God of heaven gets the credit.

2:25–28 Arioch was eager to claim the credit for finding an interpreter for the king's dream. **Daniel**, however, was careful to ascribe to God all of the credit for revealing the **mystery**. Daniel was able to interpret it not because of his own wisdom but only because **there is a God in heaven who reveals mysteries**. Daniel's statement contrasts God's ability with the inability of any pagan **wise men, enchanters, magicians, or astrologers** to know the "mysteries" of what the king dreamed and what it predicted.

2:30 God **made known** the **interpretation** of the dream so that Nebuchadnezzar would know this great God controlled future events, and so that he would be aware of what was coming.

2:37–38 According to Daniel's interpretation, the **head of gold** was Nebuchadnezzar. God gave him great dominion, **power**, and **glory**—reminiscent of that granted to Adam, with dominion over not only human beings but also the birds of the air and the beasts of the field. The nation had become a vast empire, and Nebuchadnezzar ruled ruthlessly. Babylon itself was an amazing achievement, with its hanging gardens (one of the famed Seven Wonders of the ancient world), many temples, and a bridge crossing the Euphrates River (see plan, p. 1583). Thus the head of gold is a fitting description.

2:39 After Nebuchadnezzar's time there would be two more kingdoms, each inferior to the previous one in glory and unity, though still strong and powerful (Medo-Persia [539–331 B.C.] and Greece [331–63]).

2:40 The **fourth kingdom** (i.e., the Roman Empire) would be **strong as iron**, yet also an unstable composite of different peoples who would not hold together (see v. 43).

[y]there shall be a fourth kingdom, strong as iron, because iron [z]breaks to pieces and shatters all things. And like iron that crushes, it shall [z]break and crush all these. **41** And as
you saw [a]the feet and toes, partly of potter's clay and partly of iron, it shall be a divided
kingdom, but some of the [y]firmness of iron shall be in it, just as you saw iron mixed with
the soft clay. **42** And as the toes of the feet were partly iron and partly clay, so the kingdom
shall be partly strong and partly brittle. **43** As you saw the iron mixed with soft clay, so
they will mix with one another in marriage,[1] but they will not hold together, just as iron
does not mix with clay. **44** And in the days of those kings [b]the God of heaven will set up [c]a
kingdom that shall never be destroyed, nor shall the kingdom be left to another people.
[d]It shall break in pieces all these kingdoms and bring them to an end, and [c]it shall stand
forever, **45** just as [e]you saw that [f]a stone was cut from a mountain by no human hand, and
that [d]it broke in pieces the iron, the bronze, the clay, the silver, and the gold. A [g]great
God has made known to the king what shall be after this. The dream is certain, and its
interpretation sure."

Daniel Is Promoted

46 Then King Nebuchadnezzar [h]fell upon his face and [i]paid homage to Daniel, and commanded that [j]an offering and [k]incense be offered up to him. **47** The king answered and
said to Daniel, "Truly, your [l]God is God of gods and [m]Lord of kings, and [n]a revealer of
mysteries, for you have been able to reveal this mystery." **48** Then the king gave Daniel high
honors and many great [o]gifts, and made him ruler over the whole [p]province of Babylon
and [q]chief prefect over all the wise men of Babylon. **49** Daniel made a request of the king,

[1] Aramaic *by the seed of men*

40 [y][ch. 7:7, 23] [z]See ver. 34
41 [a][ver. 33] [y][See ver. 40 above]
44 [b]ver. 19 [c]ch. 4:3, 34; 6:26; 7:14, 27; Mic. 4:7; [Matt. 3:2; Luke 1:33; John 18:36] [d][Isa. 60:12]; See ver. 34
45 [e][ver. 34] [f][Isa. 28:16] [d][See ver. 44 above] [g]ver. 28
46 [h][2 Sam. 14:22] [i][Matt. 8:2; Acts 10:25] [j][Acts 14:13] [k][Ezra 6:10]
47 [l]Deut. 10:17 [m][1 Tim. 6:15; Rev. 17:14; 19:16] [n]See ver. 22
48 [o][ver. 6] [p]ch. 3:1, 12, 30; [Esth. 1:1] [q]ch. 5:11; [ch. 4:9]

2:43–44 The Aramaic description of intermarriage as mixing "by the seed of men" (see ESV footnote) recalls the prohibition on sowing mixed seed in a field (Lev. 19:19). At that time, God will establish **a kingdom that shall never be destroyed**, his final kingdom, which will ultimately destroy all other **kingdoms**. Though it starts small, it will grow to fill the earth and, unlike the earthly kingdoms, it will endure forever (cf. "stone," "great mountain," Dan. 2:34–35). It is striking that God gave this dream to Nebuchadnezzar in the seventh century B.C. (about 602; see note on v. 1), for in this dream and in the subsequent visions linked to it in chs. 7 and 8, God predicts in accurate detail the future kingdoms that would arise to dominate world history in the sixth, fourth, and first centuries B.C. Traditional commentators through the history of the church have almost universally identified the four kingdoms as Babylon, Medo-Persia (established by Cyrus in 539 B.C.; specifically named in 8:20), Greece (under Alexander the Great, about 331; specifically named in 8:21), and Rome (the Roman Empire began its rule over Palestine in 63). Those scholars, however, who assume that Daniel's detailed visions cannot be predictive prophecies, but had to have been written after the events they claim to "predict," hold that Daniel was written not in the sixth century B.C. but in the second century, in the Maccabean period. Under this scheme the fourth kingdom cannot be the Roman Empire, which did not yet exist at that time. So they propose various other identifications for the kingdoms, such as (1) Babylon, (2) Media, (3) Persia, and (4) Greece; however, Media was never an independent world power after Babylon fell to Cyrus in 539 B.C. (it was also ruled by Cyrus). Another point being made in the dream is that each earthly kingdom has its own glory but also its own end: both have been assigned to it by God. The progression of world history is typically not upward to glory and unity but rather downward to dishonor and disunity. Thus the statue progresses from gold, to silver, to bronze, to iron, and from one head, to a chest and arms, to a belly and thighs, to feet and toes of composite iron and clay. (This list of metals shows a progressive decrease in the value and splendor of the materials but an increase in toughness and endurance. Some commentators understand this to indicate a general decline in the moral quality of the governments and an increase in the amount of time they lasted. See chart below. In contrast, God's kingdom grows from humble beginnings to ultimate, united glory as a single kingdom that fills the whole earth forever. The stone that will **break in pieces all these** other four kingdoms is most likely Christ (see Luke 20:18). He is the mystery of the ages, the one in whom God plans to unite all things in his glorious kingdom (Eph. 1:9–10).

2:46–49 *Nebuchadnezzar Promotes Daniel.* Nebuchadnezzar recognized and honored Daniel's God and promoted Daniel and his friends within the Babylonian court, giving them further opportunity to promote the peace and

The Traditional View of Daniel's Visions

	Babylonian Empire (625–539 B.C.)	**Medo-Persian Empire** (539–331 B.C.)	**Greek Empire** (331–63 B.C.)	**Roman Empire** (63 B.C.–A.D. 476)	**Future Events**
Vision of Statue (ch. 2)	head of gold (vv. 36–38)	chest and arms of silver (vv. 32, 39)	middle and thighs of bronze (vv. 32, 39)	legs of iron; feet of iron and clay (vv. 33, 40–43)	*messianic kingdom* stone (vv. 44–45)
Vision of Tree (ch. 4)	Nebuchadnezzar humbled (vv. 19–37)				
Vision of Four Beasts (ch. 7)	lion with wings of eagle (v. 4)	bear raised up on one side (v. 5)	leopard with four wings and four heads (v. 6)	terrifying beast with iron teeth (v. 7)	*Antichrist* little horn uttering great boasts (vv. 8–11)
Vision of Ram and Goat (ch. 8)		ram with two horns: one longer than the other (vv. 2–4)	male goat with one horn: it was broken and four horns came up (vv. 5–8); Antiochus IV (vv. 23–26)		

and he [r]appointed [s]Shadrach, Meshach, and Abednego over the affairs of [p]the province of
Babylon. But Daniel [t]remained at the king's court.

Nebuchadnezzar's Golden Image

3 King Nebuchadnezzar made an image of gold, whose height was sixty cubits[1] and
its breadth six cubits. He set it up on [u]the plain of Dura, in [v]the province of Babylon.
2 Then King Nebuchadnezzar sent to gather [w]the satraps, the prefects, and [x]the governors, the counselors, the treasurers, the justices, the magistrates, and all the officials of
the provinces to come to the dedication of the image that King Nebuchadnezzar had set
up. 3 Then [w]the satraps, the prefects, and the governors, the counselors, the treasurers, the
justices, the magistrates, and all the officials of the provinces gathered for the dedication
of the image that King Nebuchadnezzar had set up. And they stood before the image that
Nebuchadnezzar had set up. 4 And the herald [y]proclaimed aloud, "You are commanded, O
[z]peoples, nations, and languages, 5 that when you hear the [a]sound of the horn, pipe, lyre,
trigon, harp, bagpipe, and every kind of music, you [b]are to fall down and worship the
golden image that King Nebuchadnezzar has set up. 6 And whoever does not fall down
and worship shall immediately [c]be cast into a burning fiery furnace." 7 Therefore, as soon
as all the peoples heard the sound of the horn, pipe, lyre, trigon, harp, bagpipe, and every
kind of music, all [z]the peoples, nations, and languages fell down and worshiped the golden
image that King Nebuchadnezzar had set up.

The Fiery Furnace

8 Therefore at that time certain [d]Chaldeans [e]came forward and maliciously accused the
Jews. 9 They declared[2] to King Nebuchadnezzar, "O king, live forever! 10 You, O king, [f]have
made a decree, that every man who [g]hears the sound of the horn, pipe, lyre, trigon, harp,
bagpipe, and every kind of music, [g]shall fall down and worship the golden image. 11 And
whoever does not fall down and worship [c]shall be cast into a burning fiery furnace. 12 There
are certain Jews whom you have [h]appointed over the affairs of [v]the province of Babylon:
[i]Shadrach, Meshach, and Abednego. These men, O king, [j]pay no attention to you; they do
not serve your gods or worship the golden image that you have set up."
13 Then Nebuchadnezzar [k]in furious rage commanded that [i]Shadrach, Meshach, and
Abednego be brought. So they brought these men before the king. 14 Nebuchadnezzar
answered and said to them, "Is it true, O Shadrach, Meshach, and Abednego, that you do
not serve my gods or worship the golden image that I have set up? 15 Now if you are ready
when [l]you hear the sound of the horn, pipe, lyre, trigon, harp, bagpipe, and every kind of

[1] A *cubit* was about 18 inches or 45 centimeters [2] Aramaic *answered and said*; also verses 24, 26

49 [r]ch. 3:12 [s][ch. 1:7] [p][See ver. 48 above] [t]Esth. 2:19

Chapter 3

1 [u][Gen. 11:2] [v]ver. 12, 30; ch. 2:48, 49
2 [w]ver. 27; ch. 6:1, 2, 3, 4, 6, 7; [Ezra 8:36] [x]ch. 2:48
3 [w][See ver. 2 above]
4 [y]ch. 4:14; 5:7; [Rev. 18:2] [z]ver. 29; ch. 4:1; 5:19; 6:25; 7:14; [Rev. 5:9]
5 [a]ver. 7, 10, 15 [b][ch. 2:46]
6 [c][Jer. 29:22; Ezek. 23:25]
7 [z][See ver. 4 above]
8 [d]See ch. 1:4 [e]ch. 6:12
10 [f]ver. 29; ch. 4:6; 6:26 [g]ver. 5, 7, 15
11 [c][See ver. 6 above]
12 [h]ch. 2:49 [v][See ver. 1 above] [i][ch. 1:7] [j]ch. 6:13
13 [k]ch. 2:12 [i][See ver. 12 above]
15 [l]ver. 5, 7, 10

welfare of the city where the Lord had exiled them, as Jeremiah had counseled (cf. Jer. 29:5–7).

3:1–30 *Nebuchadnezzar Builds a Great Statue.* Nebuchadnezzar commands all peoples under his rule to worship his golden image, and, though his officials from other nations obey, Daniel's friends refuse out of loyalty to their God. When God delivers them from the fiery furnace, Nebuchadnezzar's respect for their God increases. A Babylonian document from the time of Nebuchadnezzar (605–562 B.C.) warns not to harm the statue that had been set up: "Beside my *statue* as king . . . I wrote an inscription mentioning my name, . . . I erected for posterity. May future kings respect the monument, remember the praise of the gods. . . . He who respects . . . my royal name, who does not abrogate my statutes and not change my decrees, his throne shall be secure, his life last long, his dynasty shall continue."

3:1–7 *The Nations Worship Nebuchadnezzar's Statue.* When Nebuchadnezzar has the statue built, representatives of the nations under his rule obey his command to worship it.

3:1 The **image of gold** reflects the enormous statue in Nebuchadnezzar's dream, except it is made entirely of gold, as if Nebuchadnezzar were asserting that there would be no other kingdoms after his. It was **sixty cubits** (90 feet/27 m) high and **six cubits** (9 feet/2.7 m) wide. Its location on a **plain** in **Babylon** recalls the location of the Tower of Babel (also on a plain, Gen. 11:2), as does its purpose to provide a unifying center for all the peoples of the earth.

3:2 satraps. A "satrap" was a governor of a "satrapy" (province); cf. Ezra 8:36.

3:3 This chapter repeatedly states that this was **the image that King Nebuchadnezzar had set up**. It is unclear whether the image represented Nebuchadnezzar or one of his gods. All of the leading officials from throughout his empire were **gathered** before the statue for its **dedication**, as a public statement that the unity of Nebuchadnezzar's empire was rooted in the common worship of the golden image.

3:5 The Aramaic names for the **lyre**, **harp**, and **bagpipe** may well be words loaned from Greek. Some conclude that the story must therefore have come from the time of Greek cultural dominance, namely, after Alexander the Great (d. 323 B.C.). But since there was Greek cultural influence in the Near East long before Alexander, this is not evidence of a late date for the book.

3:8–29 *Shadrach, Meshach, and Abednego Preserved in the Fiery Furnace.* Daniel's three friends, who serve Nebuchadnezzar as officials, refuse to obey the command to worship the statue, even under threat of a horrible death in a furnace. Sentenced to die, they are rescued, which amazes Nebuchadnezzar.

3:12 Certain "Chaldeans" (v. 8—that is, the magicians, enchanters, etc.; cf. 2:2, 4) observed the fact that **Shadrach, Meshach, and Abednego** had not joined in bowing to the statue. They charged the young men with ingratitude for the positions they held and impiety toward Nebuchadnezzar's gods. Daniel himself is curiously absent; perhaps he is away on a mission, or perhaps above the administrative rulers mentioned in 3:3 and thus immune from such displays of Nebuchadnezzar's pride, or perhaps the Chaldeans did not feel safe accusing Daniel.

music, to fall down and worship the image that I have made, well and good.[1] But if you
do not worship, [c]you shall immediately be cast into a burning fiery furnace. And [m]who is
the god who will deliver you out of my hands?"
16 [l]Shadrach, Meshach, and Abednego answered and said to the king, "O Nebuchadnezzar,
we have no need to answer you in this matter. 17 If this be so, [n]our God whom we serve is
able to deliver us from the burning fiery furnace, and he will deliver us out of your hand,
O king.[2] 18 But if not, be it known to you, O king, that we will not serve your gods or worship the golden image that you have set up."
19 Then Nebuchadnezzar was [o]filled with fury, and the expression of his face [p]was changed
against [l]Shadrach, Meshach, and Abednego. He ordered the furnace heated seven times
more than it was usually heated. 20 And he ordered some of the mighty men of his army [q]to
bind [l]Shadrach, Meshach, and Abednego, and to cast them into the burning fiery furnace.
21 Then these men were [q]bound in their cloaks, their tunics,[3] their hats, and their other
garments, and they were thrown into the burning fiery furnace. 22 Because the king's order
was [r]urgent and the furnace overheated, the flame of the fire killed those men who took
up [s]Shadrach, Meshach, and Abednego. 23 And these three men, Shadrach, Meshach, and
Abednego, fell [q]bound into the burning fiery furnace.
24 Then King Nebuchadnezzar was [t]astonished and rose up [u]in haste. He declared to
his [v]counselors, "Did we not cast three men [w]bound into the fire?" They answered and
said to the king, "True, O king." 25 He answered and said, "But I see four men unbound,
[x]walking in the midst of the fire, and they [y]are not hurt; and the appearance of the fourth
is like [z]a son of the gods."
26 Then Nebuchadnezzar came near to the door of the burning fiery furnace; he declared,
[s]"Shadrach, Meshach, and Abednego, servants of the [a]Most High God, come out, and come
here!" Then [s]Shadrach, Meshach, and Abednego came out from the fire. 27 And the [b]satraps,
the prefects, the governors, and [v]the king's counselors gathered together and saw that
[c]the fire had not had any power over the bodies of those men. The hair of their heads was
not singed, their [d]cloaks were not harmed, and no smell of fire had come upon them.
28 Nebuchadnezzar answered and said, "Blessed be the God of [s]Shadrach, Meshach, and
Abednego, who [e]has sent his angel and [f]delivered his servants, who [g]trusted in him, and
set aside[4] the king's command, and yielded up their bodies rather than [h]serve and worship any god except their own God. 29 Therefore [i]I make a decree: Any [j]people, nation, or
language that speaks anything against the God of [s]Shadrach, Meshach, and Abednego
[k]shall be torn limb from limb, and their houses laid in ruins, for there is no other god
who is able to rescue in this way." 30 Then the king promoted [s]Shadrach, Meshach, and
Abednego in [l]the province of Babylon.

[1] Aramaic lacks *well and good* [2] Or *If our God whom we serve is able to deliver us, he will deliver us from the burning fiery furnace and out of your hand, O king.*
[3] The meaning of the Aramaic words rendered *cloaks* and *tunics* is uncertain; also verse 27 [4] Aramaic *and changed*

15 [c][See ver. 6 above] [m][ch. 6:20; Ex. 5:2; 2 Kgs. 18:35]
16 [l][See ver. 12 above]
17 [n][ver. 15]
19 [o][ver. 13; Esth. 7:7] [p][ch. 2:49] [l][See ver. 12 above]
20 [q][ver. 24, 25] [l][See ver. 12 above]
21 [q][See ver. 20 above]
22 [r]ch. 2:15 [s][ch. 1:7]
23 [q][See ver. 20 above]
24 [t]ch. 4:19 [u]ch. 2:25 [v]ch. 4:36; 6:7 [w]ver. 20, 21, 23
25 [x][Isa. 43:2] [y][ch. 6:23] [z][ver. 28; Job 1:6]
26 [s][See ver. 22 above] [a]ch. 4:2; 5:18, 21
27 [b]ver. 2 [v][See ver. 24 above] [c][Heb. 11:34] [d]ver. 21
28 [s][See ver. 22 above] [e]ch. 6:22 [f][ver. 15, 17; Ps. 34:7] [g][Ps. 25:2] [h][Ex. 20:3]
29 [i]See ver. 10 [j]See ver. 4 [s][See ver. 22 above] [k]ch. 2:5
30 [s][See ver. 22 above] [l]ver. 1, 12; ch. 2:48, 49

3:18 But if not. There was no doubt in the three men's minds as to God's power to save them (see 2:20–23). Yet the way in which God would work out his plan for them in this situation was less clear. God's power is sometimes extended in dramatic ways to deliver his people, as when he parted the Red Sea for Israel on the way out of Egypt (Exodus 14); at other times, that same power is withheld, and his people are allowed to suffer. Either way, they would not bow down to Nebuchadnezzar's image.

3:19 In anger, Nebuchadnezzar ordered the furnace superheated: **seven times more than it was usually heated** is probably a figurative expression meaning "as hot as possible" (seven is a number signifying completion or perfection, cf. Prov. 24:16; 26:16).

3:22 Ironically, Nebuchadnezzar's order resulted in the death of his own soldiers, demonstrating the fact that the Lord is able to protect his servants better than Nebuchadnezzar can protect his.

3:23 After this verse the various Greek OT versions add *The Song of the Three Young Men*, which is an effort to elaborate the men's experience of deliverance in the furnace. (This addition to Daniel is also included in the Apocrypha: see article on The Apocrypha, pp. 2581–2583.)

3:24–25 Shadrach, Meshach, and Abednego were joined in the fire by a **fourth** individual, who had the appearance of a divine being **like a son of the gods**, who was either a Christophany (a physical appearance of Christ before his incarnation) or an angel (see v. 28). In either case, this is a physical demonstration of God's presence with believers in their distress, a graphic fulfillment of the Lord's promise in Isa. 43:2. The Lord promised his presence with his people, ensuring that their trials and difficulties would not utterly overwhelm them.

3:27 Shadrach, Meshach, and Abednego were completely untouched by the fire: their clothes were not **harmed** nor their hair **singed**, and they did not even **smell of fire**—a testimony to the comprehensiveness of the Lord's protection.

3:28 Nebuchadnezzar's question in v. 15 had been decisively answered, as he himself was forced to testify. Yet his heart was not yet changed: the God of whom he spoke was still **the God of Shadrach, Meshach, and Abednego**, or **their . . . God**, not his own.

3:30 *Nebuchadnezzar Promotes Shadrach, Meshach, and Abednego.* Nebuchadnezzar shows that he appreciates the integrity of these men.

4:1–37 *Nebuchadnezzar's Dream of a Toppled Tree.* Nebuchadnezzar has another dream, and Daniel again is the only one of his officials able to interpret it. This dream concerns Nebuchadnezzar's own need to acknowledge that

Chapter 4
1[m]See ch. 3:4 [n]ch. 6:25 [o]1 Pet. 1:2; 2 Pet. 1:2
2[p]ch. 6:27; [John 4:48] [q]ch. 3:26
3[p][See ver. 2 above] [r]See ch. 2:44
5[s]ch. 2:28; 7:15
6[t]See ch. 3:10 [u]ch. 2:12
7[v]See ch. 2:2 [w][ver. 18; ch. 2:27; 5:8, 15]
8[x]See ch. 1:7 [y]ver. 18; ch. 2:11; 5:11; Gen. 41:38; [Isa. 63:14]
9[z]ch. 5:11; [ch. 2:48] [y][See ver. 8 above] [a]ch. 2:18 [s][See ver. 5 above]
10[s][See ver. 5 above] [b][Ezek. 31:3]
11[c][Ps. 37:35]
12[d]Ezek. 31:7 [e]Ezek. 31:6
13[s][See ver. 5 above] [f]ver. 23 [g][Deut. 33:2; Zech. 14:5; Jude 14]
14[h]See ch. 3:4 [i]ver. 23; [Matt. 3:10; Luke 3:9] [j][Ezek. 31:12]
16[k][ver. 23, 25] [l][1 Chr. 29:30]
17[f][See ver. 13 above] [g][See ver. 13 above] [m]ver. 25, 32; ch. 5:21 [n]Jer. 27:5 [o]See 1 Sam. 2:8
18[p]See ch. 1:7 [q][ver. 7; ch. 5:8, 15; Gen. 41:8] [r]See ver. 8
19[p][See ver. 18 above] [s]ch. 3:24 [t]ch. 5:6 [u][1 Sam. 25:26; 2 Sam. 18:32]

Nebuchadnezzar Praises God

4 1[1] King Nebuchadnezzar to all [m]peoples, nations, and languages, [n]that dwell in all the
earth: [o]Peace be multiplied to you! 2 It has seemed good to me to show the [p]signs and
wonders that the [q]Most High God has done for me.

3 How great are [p]his signs,
how mighty his [p]wonders!
[r]His kingdom is an everlasting kingdom,
[r]and his dominion endures from generation to generation.

Nebuchadnezzar's Second Dream

4[2] I, Nebuchadnezzar, was at ease in my house and prospering in my palace. 5 I saw a
dream that made me afraid. As I lay in bed the fancies and [s]the visions of my head alarmed
me. 6 So [t]I made a decree that [u]all the wise men of Babylon should be brought before me,
that they might make known to me the interpretation of the dream. 7 Then [v]the magicians,
the enchanters, the Chaldeans, and the astrologers came in, and I told them the dream,
but [w]they could not make known to me its interpretation. 8 At last Daniel came in before
me—he who was named [x]Belteshazzar after the name of my god, and in whom is [y]the
spirit of the holy gods[3]—and I told him the dream, saying, 9 "O Belteshazzar, [z]chief of the
magicians, because I know that [y]the spirit of the holy gods is in you and that no [a]mystery
is too difficult for you, tell me [s]the visions of my dream that I saw and their interpretation.
10 [s]The visions of my head as I lay in bed were these: I saw, and [b]behold, a tree in the midst of
the earth, and its height was great. 11 [c]The tree grew and became strong, and its top reached
to heaven, and it was visible to the end of the whole earth. 12 [d]Its leaves were beautiful and
its fruit abundant, and in it was food for all. [e]The beasts of the field found shade under it,
and [e]the birds of the heavens lived in its branches, and all flesh was fed from it.
13 "I saw in [s]the visions of my head as I lay in bed, and behold, [f]a watcher, [g]a holy one,
came down from heaven. 14 He [h]proclaimed aloud and said thus: [i]'Chop down the tree
and [j]lop off its branches, [j]strip off its leaves and scatter its fruit. [j]Let the beasts flee from
under it and the birds from its branches. 15 But leave the stump of its roots in the earth,
bound with a band of iron and bronze, amid the tender grass of the field. Let him be wet
with the dew of heaven. Let his portion be with the beasts in the grass of the earth. 16 Let
his mind be changed from a man's, and let a beast's mind be given to him; [k]and let seven
periods of time [l]pass over him. 17 The sentence is by the decree of [f]the watchers, the decision
by the word of [g]the holy ones, to the end that the living may know that the Most High
[m]rules the kingdom of men [n]and gives it to whom he will and [o]sets over it the lowliest of
men.' 18 This dream I, King Nebuchadnezzar, saw. And you, O [p]Belteshazzar, tell me the
interpretation, because [q]all the wise men of my kingdom are not able to make known to
me the interpretation, but you are able, for [r]the spirit of the holy gods is in you."

Daniel Interprets the Second Dream

19 Then Daniel, whose name was [p]Belteshazzar, was [s]dismayed for a while, and [t]his
thoughts alarmed him. The king answered and said, "Belteshazzar, let not the dream
or the interpretation alarm you." Belteshazzar answered and said, "My lord, [u]may

[1] Ch 3:31 in Aramaic [2] Ch 4:1 in Aramaic [3] Or *Spirit of the holy God*; also verses 9, 18

the God of Israel is the one who rules the affairs of mankind, and through humiliation Nebuchadnezzar learns the lesson.

4:1–27 *Nebuchadnezzar's Dream and Its Interpretation.* Nebuchadnezzar tells his dream to his wise men, but they cannot interpret it. Finally he asks Daniel, who shows respect and kindness to the king by explaining that the dream threatens him with humiliation if he does not acknowledge that God is supreme.

4:1–3 The narrative begins at the end of the story, with the letter of praise to God that Nebuchadnezzar wrote after his recovery. The letter is addressed to **peoples, nations, and languages**, the same group summoned to bow down to the golden image (see 3:7). The "signs" and "wonders" the Lord has performed certainly include the fiery furnace, yet the key difference is that now Nebuchadnezzar speaks of **signs and wonders that the Most High God has done for me** (cf. note on 3:28). From being a persecutor of the faithful, Nebuchadnezzar has himself become a witness to the faith.

4:7 This time Nebuchadnezzar tells the wise men of Babylon the dream—perhaps Nebuchadnezzar was not worried about their honesty since he expected that Daniel could correct them if they tried to deceive him.

4:10–16 In this dream, Nebuchadnezzar saw an enormous **tree** whose **top** touched the heavens. While Nebuchadnezzar was looking on, however, **a watcher, a holy one** (an angel commissioned to carry out God's judgment on earth) **came down** and ordered that the tree be cut down. The tree was not utterly destroyed, however: its **stump** was to remain in the ground for **seven periods of time** (the text does not explain the length of time, but "seven" signifies completion and most ancient and modern scholars have argued it was "seven years"), bound in **iron and bronze**.

the dream be for those who hate you [u]and its interpretation for your enemies! **20** [v]The
tree you saw, which grew and became strong, so that its top reached to heaven, and it
was visible to the end of the whole earth, **21** [w]whose leaves were beautiful and its fruit
abundant, and in which was food for all, under which beasts of the field found shade,
and in whose branches the birds of the heavens lived— **22** [x]it is you, O king, who have
grown and become strong. [y]Your greatness has grown and reaches to heaven, [y]and your
dominion to the ends of the earth. **23** And because the king saw [z]a watcher, a holy one,
coming down from heaven and saying, [a]'Chop down the tree and destroy it, but leave
the stump of its roots in the earth, bound with a band of iron and bronze, in the tender grass of the field, and let him be wet with the dew of heaven, and let his portion
be with the beasts of the field, till [b]seven periods of time pass over him,' **24** this is the
interpretation, O king: It is a decree of the Most High, which has come upon my lord
the king, **25** [c]that you shall be driven from among men, and your dwelling shall be with
the beasts of the field. You shall be made [d]to eat grass like an ox, and you shall be wet
with the dew of heaven, and [b]seven periods of time shall pass over you, till [e]you know
that the Most High rules the kingdom of men and gives it to whom he will. **26** And as
it was commanded [f]to leave the stump of the roots of the tree, your kingdom shall be
confirmed for you from the time that you know that Heaven rules. **27** Therefore, O king,
let my counsel be acceptable to you: break off your sins by [g]practicing righteousness,
[h]and your iniquities by showing mercy to the oppressed, [i]that there may perhaps be a
lengthening of your prosperity."

Nebuchadnezzar's Humiliation

28 All this came upon King Nebuchadnezzar. **29** At the end of twelve months he was
walking on the roof of the royal palace of Babylon, **30** and the king answered and said, [j]"Is
not this great Babylon, which I have built by [k]my mighty power as a royal residence and
for [k]the glory of my majesty?" **31** [l]While the words were still in the king's mouth, there
fell a voice from heaven, "O King Nebuchadnezzar, to you it is spoken: The kingdom has
departed from you, **32** [m]and you shall be driven from among men, and your dwelling shall
be with the beasts of the field. And you shall be made to eat grass like an ox, and seven
periods of time shall pass over you, [m]until you know that the Most High rules the kingdom of men and gives it to whom he will." **33** Immediately the word was fulfilled against
Nebuchadnezzar. [m]He was driven from among men and ate grass like an ox, and his body
was wet with the dew of heaven till his hair grew as long as eagles' feathers, and his nails
were like birds' claws.

19 [u][1 Sam. 25:26; 2 Sam. 18:32]
20 [v][ver. 10, 11]
21 [w][ver. 12]
22 [x][Ezek. 31:3] [y]See Jer. 27:6-8
23 [z]ver. 13 [a]ver. 14, 15 [b]ver. 16
25 [c]ver. 32, 33; [ch. 5:21] [d][Ps. 106:20] [b][See ver. 23 above] [e]ver. 17, 32
26 [f]ver. 15, 23
27 [g]Matt. 6:1 [h]Prov. 16:6; [Matt. 25:35, 36; Luke 11:41] [i][Jer. 18:8; Jonah 3:10; Acts 8:22; 2 Tim. 2:25]
30 [j][ch. 5:20] [k][ver. 36; ch. 2:37]
31 [l][ch. 5:5; Luke 12:20]
32 [m]ver. 17, 25; ch. 5:21
33 [m][See ver. 32 above]

4:22 In his interpretation, Daniel identified the enormous tree as Nebuchadnezzar: **it is you, O king**. The image of a cosmic tree, the center and pivotal point of the universe, acknowledged Nebuchadnezzar's power and might.

4:23 The image of the cosmic tree reaching to the heavens (v. 11) is reminiscent of the Tower of Babel (see Gen. 11:4). Such hubris inevitably ends in disaster, and the divine lumberjack would bring the mighty tree crashing to the ground, removing it from its place of influence and glory. Nebuchadnezzar would not only lose his power and glory but also his rationality (which distinguishes him as human), so that he would behave like the wild animals. The one who thought of himself in godlike terms would become beastlike so he could learn that he is merely human after all. When the tree was cut down, the **stump** and the **roots** were allowed to remain, bound in **iron and bronze**, possibly suggesting that Nebuchadnezzar's kingdom would be protected and then established after he learned to honor the true God.

4:25 There was hope of restoration after Nebuchadnezzar had experienced a full period of judgment, **seven periods of time**, in this animal-like state. When Nebuchadnezzar acknowledged that God controls the universe and human kingdoms and that he (Nebuchadnezzar) does not, his kingdom would be restored to him. Daniel proclaimed God's sovereignty over the affairs of nations, even over Babylon—the greatest nation in the world at that time—by affirming what Nebuchadnezzar had already heard in his dream (v. 17; cf. vv. 32, 35), that **the Most High rules the kingdom of men and gives it to whom he will**.

4:27 Therefore, O king . . . break off your sins by practicing righteousness, and . . . showing mercy to the oppressed. Daniel (a Jew who believed in the one true God) was willing to tell Nebuchadnezzar (a pagan king) that he should conform to moral standards that Daniel had learned from God. This appeal to repentance implied that the fate depicted for Nebuchadnezzar in the dream was not inevitable, and it provided Nebuchadnezzar with an opportunity to repent of his pride. If Nebuchadnezzar humbled himself, God would not need to humble him further. Even pagan rulers are accountable to the God of the Bible (cf. notes on Ps. 82:1–4; Prov. 31:1–9; Mark 6:18; Acts 24:25).

4:28–33 *Nebuchadnezzar's Humbling.* A year went by, but Nebuchadnezzar was unchanged. The view from **the roof of the royal palace of Babylon** (v. 29) included numerous ornate temples, the hanging gardens (one of the Seven Wonders of the ancient world), which he had built for his wife, and the outer wall of the city, wide enough for chariots driven by four horses to pass each other on the top. As he looked at these notable accomplishments, Nebuchadnezzar boasted to himself of his **mighty power** and **glory** (v. 30). Immediately, the sentence of judgment was announced from heaven. His royal authority was taken from him and he was driven away from Babylon. He ate **grass** and lived wild in the open air like the **beasts of the field**, growing his **hair** and **nails** unchecked like the birds of the air (v. 33).

4:34–37 *Nebuchadnezzar's Exaltation.* At the end of God's appointed time of judgment, Nebuchadnezzar raised his **eyes to heaven** and his **reason** was restored. Once brought low by God, he was brought back to the heights and restored to control of his kingdom, demonstrating that the Lord is able

Nebuchadnezzar Restored

34 [n]At the end of the days I, Nebuchadnezzar, lifted my eyes to heaven, and [o]my reason
returned to me, and I blessed the Most High, and praised and honored [p]him who lives
forever,

[q]for his dominion is an everlasting dominion,
and [q]his kingdom endures from generation to generation;
35 [r]all the inhabitants of the earth are accounted as nothing,
and [s]he does according to his will among the host of heaven
and among the inhabitants of the earth;
[t]and none can stay his hand
or [u]say to him, "What have you done?"

36 At the same time [v]my reason returned to me, and for [w]the glory of my kingdom, [w]my
majesty and splendor returned to me. [x]My counselors and [y]my lords sought me, and I
was established in my kingdom, and still more greatness was [z]added to me. 37 Now I,
Nebuchadnezzar, [a]praise and extol and honor the [b]King of heaven, [c]for all his works are
right and his ways are just; and [d]those who walk in pride he is able to humble.

The Handwriting on the Wall

5 [e]King Belshazzar [f]made a great feast for a thousand of his [g]lords and drank wine in
front of the thousand.
2 [e]Belshazzar, when he tasted the wine, commanded that [h]the vessels of gold and of silver
that Nebuchadnezzar his father[1] had taken out of the temple in Jerusalem be brought,
that the king and his lords, his wives, and his concubines might drink from them. 3 Then
they brought in [h]the golden vessels that had been taken out of the temple, the house of
God in Jerusalem, and the king and his lords, his wives, and his concubines drank from
them. 4 They drank wine and [i]praised the [j]gods of gold and silver, bronze, iron, wood,
and stone.
5 [k]Immediately [l]the fingers of a human hand appeared and wrote on the plaster of the
wall of the king's palace, opposite the lampstand. And the king saw [m]the hand as it wrote.
6 [n]Then the king's color changed, [o]and his thoughts alarmed him; [p]his limbs gave way,
and [q]his knees knocked together. 7 [r]The king called loudly to bring in [r]the enchanters, the
[s]Chaldeans, and [t]the astrologers. The king declared[2] to the wise men of Babylon, [u]"Whoever
reads this writing, and shows me its interpretation, shall be clothed with purple and have
a chain of gold around his neck and [v]shall be the third ruler in the kingdom." 8 Then all the
king's wise men came in, but [w]they could not read the writing or make known to the king
the interpretation. 9 Then King Belshazzar was greatly [x]alarmed, and his [n]color changed,
and his [y]lords were perplexed.
10 The queen,[3] because of the words of the king and his lords, came into the banqueting

[1] Or *predecessor*; also verses 11, 13, 18 [2] Aramaic *answered and said*; also verse 10 [3] Or *queen mother*; twice in this verse

34 [n][ver. 26] [o]ver. 36 [p]ch. 6:26; 12:7; Rev. 4:10 [q][Ps. 10:16]; See ch. 2:44
35 [r]Isa. 40:17 [s][Ps. 115:3; Heb. 1:13, 14] [t][Isa. 14:27] [u]Job 9:12; [Isa. 45:9; Rom. 9:20]
36 [v]ver. 34 [w][ver. 30; ch. 5:18] [x]ch. 3:24; 6:7 [y]ch. 5:1; 6:17 [z][Job 42:12; Matt. 6:33]
37 [a]ver. 34 [b][ch. 5:23] [c][Deut. 32:4; Ps. 33:4; Rev. 15:3] [d][ch. 5:20; Prov. 20:23]

Chapter 5

1 [e]ver. 22, 29, 30; ch. 7:1; 8:1 [f]See Esth. 1:3 [g]ch. 4:36; 6:17
2 [e][See ver. 1 above] [h]ver. 23; See ch. 1:2
3 [h][See ver. 2 above]
4 [i]ver. 23; [Judg. 16:24] [j]ver. 23; [Rev. 9:20]; See Ps. 115:4-7
5 [k][ch. 4:31] [l][Ezek. 8:3] [m]ver. 24
6 [n][ver. 10; ch. 7:28] [o][ch. 4:5, 19; 7:28] [p][Ps. 69:23; Isa. 45:1] [q]Nah. 2:10
7 [r][ch. 2:2; 4:6] [s]See ch. 1:4 [t]ch. 2:27 [u]ver. 16, 29; [ch. 2:6] [v]ver. 16, 29
8 [w]ver. 15; ch. 4:7, 18; [ch. 2:27; Gen. 41:8]
9 [x][ch. 2:1] [n][See ver. 6 above] [y]ver. 1

both to humble the proud and to exalt the humble. The great and mighty persecutor of Israel, the destroyer of Jerusalem, was humbled by God's grace and brought to confess God's mercy. He **blessed the Most High, and praised and honored him who lives forever**. God used Daniel's faithfulness to bring light to this Gentile.

5:1–31 *Belshazzar's Feast.* Daniel explains to the last king of Babylon that the writing on the wall is a message that the true God rules over all, and that in his own time he will vindicate his own name against those who defile it, no matter how powerful they are.

5:1–4 *An Idolatrous Feast.* Greek historians recorded many lavish feasts in Babylon. At the center of Belshazzar's **great feast** (v. 1) in 539 B.C. were **the vessels of gold and of silver** (v. 2) that had been taken from the Jerusalem temple by Nebuchadnezzar (cf. 1:2). Nebuchadnezzar was not literally the **father** of **Belshazzar** (5:2); Belshazzar was the son of Nabonidus, with whom he shared co-regency during the closing years of the Babylonian monarchy. The word "father" in Aramaic, like Hebrew, can mean "ancestor" or "predecessor" (v. 2, ESV footnote), but Belshazzar wanted to emphasize his direct connection to this important ruler who had taken Babylon to its peak.

5:5–9 *An Unreadable Message.* The **fingers** of a mysterious **hand** wrote **on the plaster** of the **palace** wall **opposite the lampstand**, where its message could be clearly seen, though not easily understood (v. 5). The king's response was abject terror: literally, the "joints of his loins were loosened," indicating that he lost strength in his hips and legs (v. 6). None of the Babylonian diviners were able to interpret the writing, in spite of the generous reward offered by Belshazzar. Anyone who interpreted the writing would be **clothed with purple**, a fabulously expensive color in the ancient world, and would wear a **chain of gold**, a mark of high rank (v. 7). He would also be **the third ruler in the kingdom** (v. 7), which may refer to being next highest to King Nabonidus and the co-regent Belshazzar, or may be a more general term for a high official.

5:10–12 *A Forgotten Interpreter.* **The queen** most likely refers to the queen mother (v. 10, ESV footnote), since the wives of the king were already present (v. 2). She reminded Belshazzar of the existence of Daniel, whose ability to interpret knotty problems had been repeatedly demonstrated during the time of his illustrious predecessor, Nebuchadnezzar. Nebuchadnezzar had appointed him chief of his wise men, because **the spirit of the holy gods** (or "God"; the Aramaic is ambiguous) indwelt him (v. 11), enabling him to answer difficult questions.

hall, and the queen declared, [z]"O king, live forever! Let not your thoughts alarm you [a]or
your color change. 11 There is a man in your kingdom [b]in whom is the spirit of the holy
gods.[1] In the days of your father, [c]light and understanding and wisdom like the wisdom
of the gods were found in him, and King Nebuchadnezzar, your father—your father the
king—[d]made him chief of the magicians, [r]enchanters, Chaldeans, and astrologers, 12 [e]because
an excellent spirit, knowledge, and [f]understanding [f]to interpret dreams, explain riddles,
and [g]solve problems were found in this Daniel, [h]whom the king named Belteshazzar. Now
let Daniel be called, and he will show the interpretation."

Daniel Interprets the Handwriting

13 Then Daniel was brought in before the king. The king answered and said to Daniel, "You
are that Daniel, one of [i]the exiles of Judah, whom the king my father brought from Judah.
14 I have heard of you that [b]the spirit of the gods[2] is in you, and that [c]light and understanding and excellent wisdom are found in you. 15 Now [j]the wise men, the [k]enchanters, have
been brought in before me to read this writing and make known to me its interpretation,
but [l]they could not show the interpretation of the matter. 16 [m]But I have heard that you
can give interpretations and [n]solve problems. [o]Now if you can read the writing and make
known to me its interpretation, [o]you shall be clothed with purple and have a chain of gold
around your neck and [p]shall be the third ruler in the kingdom."

17 Then Daniel answered and said before the king, [q]"Let your gifts be for yourself, and
give your rewards to another. Nevertheless, I will read the writing to the king and make
known to him the interpretation. 18 O king, the [r]Most High God [s]gave [t]Nebuchadnezzar
your father [u]kingship and greatness and glory and majesty. 19 And because of the greatness
that he gave him, [v]all peoples, nations, and languages [w]trembled and feared before him.
Whom he would, he killed, and whom he would, he kept alive; whom he would, he raised
up, and whom he would, he humbled. 20 But [x]when his heart was lifted up and his spirit
was hardened so that he dealt proudly, [y]he was brought down from his kingly throne, and
his glory was taken from him. 21 [z]He was driven from among the children of mankind,
and his mind was made like that of a beast, and his dwelling was with the wild donkeys.
He was fed grass like an ox, and his body was wet with the dew of heaven, [z]until he knew
that the [r]Most High God rules the kingdom of mankind and sets over it whom he will.
22 And you his son,[3] [a]Belshazzar, [b]have not humbled your heart, though you knew all this,
23 but you have lifted up yourself against [c]the Lord of heaven. And [d]the vessels of his house
have been brought in before you, and you and your lords, your wives, and your concubines
have drunk wine from them. [e]And you have praised the gods of silver and gold, of bronze,
iron, wood, and stone, which do not see or hear or know, [f]but the God in whose hand is
your breath, and [g]whose are all your ways, [h]you have not honored.

24 "Then from his presence [i]the hand was sent, and this writing was inscribed. 25 And
this is the writing that was inscribed: MENE, MENE, TEKEL, and PARSIN. 26 This is the

[1] Or *Spirit of the holy God* [2] Or *Spirit of God* [3] Or *successor*

10 [z]See ch. 2:4 [a][ver. 6, 9]
11 [b]See ch. 4:8 [c][ch. 1:20] [d]ch. 4:9; [ch. 2:48] [r][See ver. 7 above]
12 [e]ch. 6:3 [f]See ch. 1:17 [g]ver. 16 [h]See ch. 1:7
13 [i]See ch. 2:25
14 [b][See ver. 11 above] [c][See ver. 11 above]
15 [j]ver. 7 [k][ch. 2:2; 4:6] [l]See ver. 8
16 [m][ch. 2:26] [n]ver. 12 [o]ver. 7, 29 [p]ver. 7, 29
17 [q][2 Kgs. 5:16]
18 [r]ch. 3:26; 4:2 [s][ch. 2:37; 4:22] [t]ver. 2 [u][ch. 4:36]
19 [v]See ch. 3:4 [w][ch. 6:26]
20 [x][ch. 4:30, 31; Ezek. 31:10, 11] [y]See ch. 2:21
21 [z][ch. 4:25, 32] [r][See ver. 18 above]
22 [a]See ver. 1 [b][2 Chr. 33:23]
23 [c][ch. 4:37] [d]ver. 3; See ch. 1:2 [e]ver. 4 [f]Job 12:10 [g]Jer. 10:23 [h][Acts 12:23; Rev. 16:9]
24 [i]ver. 5

5:12 Daniel's Babylonian name, **Belteshazzar**, probably means "O Lady [wife of the god Bel], protect the king!" It is similar to Belshazzar, which means, "O Bel, protect the king!"

5:13–31 *A Message of Judgment.* Daniel alone is able to decipher the writing on the wall, and he shows that it is a message from the true God, telling of the end of the Babylonian Empire.

5:13–16 Belshazzar addresses him not as the Daniel whom his father made chief of his wise men, but as the Daniel whom his father **brought** as **one of the exiles** from **Judah**. But he does pay Daniel a significant compliment, recognizing that he has heard that Daniel has special insight and can reveal difficult problems.

5:17 Daniel's blunt response omitted the usual deferential politeness of the Babylonian court.

5:18 Daniel contrasted Belshazzar with Nebuchadnezzar, to whom **the Most High God gave . . . kingship and greatness and glory and majesty**. Nebuchadnezzar was given godlike powers to kill and keep alive, to raise up and to humble. Yet when he became proud, God humbled him comprehensively until he confessed the power of God (see ch. 4).

5:23 Belshazzar knew of Nebuchadnezzar's humbling, yet far from humbling himself, he **lifted** himself **up . . . against the Lord of heaven** by using the sacred vessels from the Jerusalem temple for an idolatrous feast.

5:25 Daniel read and interpreted the **writing . . . MENE, MENE, TEKEL, and PARSIN**. The words are clearly Aramaic and form a sequence of weights, decreasing from a mina, to a shekel (1/60th of a mina), to a half-shekel. It was not that the king and wise men could not read them, but they failed to understand their significance for Belshazzar. Read as verbs (with different vowels attached to the Aramaic consonants), the sequence becomes: "Numbered, numbered, weighed, and divided." The Lord had numbered the days of Belshazzar's kingdom and brought it to an end because he had been weighed in the balance and found wanting (v. 27). The repetition of "numbered" may suggest that it will occur quickly.

5:28 As a result, Belshazzar's **kingdom** would be **divided and given to the Medes and** the **Persians** ("**PERES**," the singular of "PARSIN," sounds like the Aramaic for "Persia").

5:30–31 Belshazzar gave Daniel the promised reward (v. 29), but it was an empty gift because **that very night** Belshazzar's rule ended, when

interpretation of the matter: MENE, God has numbered[1] the days of your kingdom and
brought it to an end; 27 TEKEL, [j]you have been weighed[2] in the balances and found wanting;
28 PERES, your kingdom is divided and given to [k]the Medes and [l]Persians."[3]
29 Then [a]Belshazzar gave the command, and Daniel [m]was clothed with purple, a chain
of gold was put around his neck, and a proclamation was made about him, that he should
be the third ruler in the kingdom.
30 [n]That very night [a]Belshazzar the [o]Chaldean king was killed. 31[4] And [p]Darius [k]the
Mede received the kingdom, being about sixty-two years old.

Daniel and the Lions' Den

6 It pleased Darius to set over the kingdom [q]120 [r]satraps, to be throughout the whole
kingdom; 2 and over them [s]three high officials, of whom Daniel was one, to whom
these [r]satraps should give account, so that the king might suffer no loss. 3 Then this Daniel
became [t]distinguished above all [s]the other high officials and [r]satraps, because [u]an excellent spirit was in him. And the king planned [v]to set him over the whole kingdom. 4 Then
[s]the high officials and [r]the satraps [w]sought to find a ground for complaint against Daniel
with regard to the kingdom, [x]but they could find no ground for complaint or any fault,
because he was faithful, [x]and no error or fault was found in him. 5 Then these men said,
"We shall not find any ground for complaint against this Daniel unless we find it in connection with the law of his God."
6 Then these [s]high officials and [r]satraps came by agreement[5] to the king and said to him,
"O [y]King Darius, live forever! 7 All the [s]high officials of the kingdom, the prefects and the
satraps, the [z]counselors and the governors are agreed that the king should establish an
ordinance and enforce an [a]injunction, that whoever makes petition to any god or man
for thirty days, except to you, O king, shall be cast into the den of lions. 8 Now, O king,
establish [a]the injunction and sign the document, so that it cannot be changed, according
to [b]the law of [c]the Medes and the Persians, [d]which cannot be revoked." 9 Therefore King
Darius signed the document and [a]injunction.
10 When Daniel knew that the document had been signed, he went to his house where

[1] MENE sounds like the Aramaic for *numbered* [2] TEKEL sounds like the Aramaic for *weighed* [3] PERES (the singular of *Parsin*) sounds like the Aramaic for *divided* and for *Persia* [4] Ch 6:1 in Aramaic [5] Or *came thronging;* also verses 11, 15

27 [j]Job 31:6; Ps. 62:9
28 [k]ver. 31; [ch. 9:1; Isa. 13:17; 21:2; Jer. 51:28] [l]See ch. 6:28
29 [a][See ver. 22 above] [m][ver. 7, 16]
30 [n]Jer. 50:24; 51:31, 39, 57 [a][See ver. 22 above] [o]ch. 9:1
31 [p]ch. 9:1 [k][See ver. 28 above]

Chapter 6

1 [q][Esth. 1:1] [r]See ch. 3:2
2 [s][ch. 5:7, 16, 29] [r][See ver. 1 above]
3 [t][Esth. 3:1] [s][See ver. 2 above] [r][See ver. 1 above] [u]ch. 5:12 [v][Gen. 41:40; Esth. 10:3]
4 [s][See ver. 2 above] [r][See ver. 1 above] [w][Eccles. 4:4] [x][Ezek. 14:14, 20]
6 [s][See ver. 2 above] [r][See ver. 1 above] [y]ver. 21; See ch. 2:4
7 [s][See ver. 2 above] [z]ch. 3:24; 4:36 [a]ver. 12, 13, 15
8 [a][See ver. 7 above] [b]ver. 12, 15; Esth. 1:19 [c][ch. 8:20] [d][ver. 15; Esth. 8:8]
9 [a][See ver. 7 above]

the Medes and the Persians entered Babylon. Belshazzar **was killed** and replaced as king by **Darius the Mede**. Belshazzar's feast is exposed as the ultimate act of folly: he was feasting on the brink of the grave and either did not know the danger or refused to acknowledge it. The identity of Darius the Mede and the exact nature of his relationship to Cyrus is not certain. It is clear that Cyrus was already king of Persia at the time when Babylon fell to the Persians (539 B.C.), and thus far no reference to "Darius the Mede" has been found in the contemporary documents that have survived. That absence, however, does not prove that the references to Darius in the book of Daniel are a historical anachronism. The book of Daniel recognizes that Cyrus reigned shortly after the fall of Babylon (1:1; 6:28), and knowledge of the history of this period, while substantial, may be incomplete. Until fairly recently there was no cuneiform evidence to prove the existence of Belshazzar either. Some commentators argue that Darius was a Babylonian throne name adopted by Cyrus himself. On this view, 6:28 should be understood as, "during the reign of Darius the Mede, *that is*, the reign of Cyrus the Persian." Others suggest that Darius was actually Cyrus's general, elsewhere named Gubaru or Ugbaru, and credited in the Nabonidus Chronicle with the capture of Babylon.

6:1–28 *The Lions' Den.* In an episode that reminds us of ch. 3, but this time in the Medo-Persian court, Daniel refuses to treat the Persian king as the gods' chief representative. When God delivers him from the lions, Darius learns to respect the God of Daniel.

6:1–3 *Daniel Promoted.* Daniel had served the empire faithfully for almost 70 years, and he continued to serve the new Medo-Persian administration. The **satraps** were provincial rulers, responsible for security and collection of tribute. The **three high officials** oversaw their work, making sure the tribute reached the king's treasury. As one of these three, **Daniel** received the reward promised by Belshazzar (see 5:29), in spite of Belshazzar's demise. Daniel did such an excellent job in this role that **Darius** planned **to set him** in an even higher position, **over the whole kingdom** (6:3).

6:4–15 *The Administrators Plot to Remove Daniel.* The other officials in the Medo-Persian court, jealous of Daniel's successful service, conspire to bring about a royal edict that they know Daniel cannot obey.

6:5 Daniel's faithfulness earned him some powerful enemies, either through jealousy or because his incorruptibility restricted their opportunities to enhance their income. Yet his character was such that they knew that the only way to bring a charge against him was in the area of **the law of his God**.

6:6–7 The high officials and the satraps **came** together **by agreement** (Aramaic *regash*); the equivalent Hebrew (Hb. *ragash*) depicts the nations "noisily assembling" against the Lord and his anointed (Ps. 2:1). They went to **King Darius** with a proposal for a new law: for the next **thirty days** no one was to petition **any god or man . . . except** the **king** himself; all offenders would be **cast into the den of lions**. Darius likely viewed this law as a political rather than a religious edict, seeing it as a means of uniting the realm by identifying himself as the sole mediator between the people and the gods, the source of their every blessing.

6:8 the law of the Medes and the Persians, which cannot be revoked (cf. Est. 1:19; 8:8). This motif does not mean that the Medo-Persian Empire never changed its mind. Yet the concept of the king's word as inflexible and unchanging law underlined the fixed nature of the king's decisions. While it was always possible for the king to issue a contrary counter-edict, to do so would result in an enormous loss of face.

6:10 Daniel continued his practice of prostrating himself **three times** daily **toward Jerusalem**, consciously fulfilling the scenario described in Solomon's prayer at the dedication of the temple in Jerusalem (1 Kings 8:46–50). This practice must have made it easy for the satraps and high officials to gather the evidence necessary to convict Daniel.

[e]he had windows in his upper chamber open [f]toward Jerusalem. He got down on his knees
[g]three times a day and prayed and [h]gave thanks before his God, as he had done previously.
11 Then these men came by agreement and found Daniel making petition and plea before his
God. 12 Then they [i]came near and said before the king, concerning the injunction, "O king!
Did you not sign [j]an injunction, that anyone who makes petition to any god or man within
thirty days except to you, O king, shall be cast into the den of lions?" The king answered
and said, "The thing stands fast, according to the law of [c]the Medes and Persians, [d]which
cannot be revoked." 13 Then they answered and said before the king, [k]"Daniel, who is one
[l]of the exiles [k]from Judah, [m]pays no attention to you, O king, or [j]the injunction you have
signed, but makes his petition [g]three times a day."

14 Then [n]the king, when he heard these words, [n]was much distressed and set his mind
to deliver Daniel. And he labored till the sun went down to rescue him. 15 Then these
men came by agreement to the king and said to the king, "Know, O king, that it is a law
of the Medes and Persians that no [j]injunction or ordinance that the king establishes can
be changed."

16 Then the king commanded, and Daniel was brought and cast into the den of lions.
The king declared[1] to Daniel, "May [o]your God, whom you serve continually, deliver you!"
17 [p]And a stone was brought and laid on the mouth of the den, [q]and the king sealed it [r]with
his own signet and with the signet of his [s]lords, that nothing might be changed concerning Daniel. 18 Then the king went to his palace and spent the night fasting; [t]no diversions
were brought to him, and [u]sleep fled from him.

19 Then, at break of day, the king arose and went in haste to the den of lions. 20 As he came
near to the den where Daniel was, he cried out in a tone of anguish. The king declared to
Daniel, "O Daniel, servant of [v]the living God, [o]has your God, whom you serve continually,
[w]been able to deliver you from the lions?" 21 Then Daniel said to the king, [x]"O king, live
forever! 22 My God [y]sent his angel [z]and shut the lions' mouths, and they have not harmed
me, because I was found blameless [a]before him; [a]and also before you, O king, I have done
no harm." 23 Then the king was exceedingly glad, and commanded that Daniel be taken
up out of the den. So Daniel was taken up out of the den, and [b]no kind of harm was found
on him, because he had trusted in his God. 24 And the king commanded, and [c]those men
who had maliciously accused Daniel were brought and cast into the den of lions—they,
their children, and their wives. And before they reached the bottom of the den, the lions
overpowered them and broke all their bones in pieces.

25 Then King Darius wrote to all [d]the peoples, nations, and languages [e]that dwell in all
the earth: [f]"Peace be multiplied to you. 26 [g]I make a decree, that in all my royal dominion
[h]people are to tremble and fear before the God of Daniel,

> for [i]he is [j]the living God,
> enduring forever;
> his kingdom shall never be destroyed,
> [j]and his dominion shall be [k]to the end.

[1] Aramaic *answered and said;* also verse 20

10 [e][Ps. 137:5] [f][Ps. 28:2; 138:2]; See 1 Kgs. 8:48 [g]Ps. 55:17 [h][ch. 2:23]
12 [i]ch. 3:8 [j]ver. 7, 8, 9 [c][See ver. 8 above] [d][See ver. 8 above]
13 [k]ch. 1:6 [l]See ch. 2:25 [m]ch. 3:12 [j][See ver. 12 above] [g][See ver. 10 above]
14 [n][Matt. 14:9; Mark 6:26]
15 [j][See ver. 12 above]
16 [o][Acts 27:23]
17 [p][Lam. 3:53] [q]Matt. 27:66; Rev. 20:3 [r][Esth. 3:12] [s]ch. 4:36; 5:1
18 [t][Prov. 25:20] [u]Esth. 6:1; [ch. 2:1]
20 [v]ver. 26 [o][See ver. 16 above] [w][ch. 3:15]
21 [x]See ch. 2:4
22 [y]ch. 3:28 [z]Heb. 11:33; [Ps. 22:21; 2 Tim. 4:17] [a][ver. 4]
23 [b][ch. 3:25]
24 [c][Deut. 19:19]
25 [d]See ch. 3:4 [e]ch. 4:1 [f]See ch. 4:1
26 [g]See ch. 3:10 [h][ch. 5:19; Ps. 99:1; Eccles. 12:13] [i]ver. 20 [j]See ch. 4:34 [k]ch. 7:26

6:12 When his officials approached King Darius, they first asked the **king** to reaffirm the unchangeability of the decree, to make it hard for him to circumvent it. In spite of the king's efforts to deliver Daniel, he was forced to acknowledge the fact that his decree condemned Daniel to the den of lions (v. 16).

6:16–24 *Daniel Preserved in the Lions' Den.* An angel protects Daniel from the lions overnight; but the accusers have no such protection.

6:16–18 To make sure that no outside help was given to Daniel, **the mouth of the den** was covered with a **stone**, which was then **sealed** with the **signet** rings of the king and **his lords**. Humanly speaking, Daniel was left all alone to face his fate. Yet Darius's last words to Daniel pointed to a higher source of help: **"May your God, whom you serve continually, deliver you!"**

6:19–23 **At break of day**, Darius arose and hurried to the lions' den, where he discovered that Daniel had spent a far more comfortable night surrounded by wild animals than Darius did in his royal luxury. Because Daniel **trusted in his God** and **was found blameless before him, God sent his angel** and **shut** the **mouths** of the **lions** so that they were unable to hurt him. The meaning of Daniel's name, "God is my Judge," was thus affirmed.

6:24 After Daniel's release, those who had schemed against him were thrown to the same **lions**. This was in accord with the common principle in the ancient Near East that anyone who made a false charge against someone else should be punished by receiving the same fate they had sought for their victim (cf. Deut. 19:16–21). In line with the ruthless practice of the Persians, the sentence was also carried out on the families of the guilty men: **their children, and their wives**. The experience of the conspirators in the den was the exact opposite of Daniel's: they were seized and killed by the lions before they even hit **the bottom of the den**.

6:25–27 *Darius Acknowledges the Power of Daniel's God.* Darius, like Nebuchadnezzar, confesses the awesome power and protection of Daniel's

27[l]ch. 4:2 [m][ch. 3:28, 29]
28[n][ch. 1:21] [o]2 Chr. 36:22, 23; Ezra 1:2; 4:3, 5; 6:3, 14; Isa. 44:28; 45:1; [ch. 1:21; 10:1]
Chapter 7
1[p]See ch. 5:1 [q][ch. 1:17] [r]ver. 15; ch. 2:28; 4:5
2[s]ch. 8:8; 11:4; [Ezek. 37:9; Zech. 2:6; Rev. 7:1]
3[t][Rev. 13:1]

27 He delivers and rescues;
he works [l]signs and wonders
in heaven and on earth,
he who has [m]saved Daniel
from the power of the lions."

28 So this Daniel prospered during the reign of Darius and [n]the reign of [o]Cyrus the Persian.

Daniel's Vision of the Four Beasts

7 In the first year of [p]Belshazzar king of Babylon, [q]Daniel saw a dream and [r]visions
of his head as he lay in his bed. Then he wrote down the dream and told the sum of
the matter. 2 Daniel declared,[1] "I saw in my vision by night, and behold, [s]the four winds
of heaven were stirring up the great sea. 3 And four great beasts [t]came up out of the sea,

[1] Aramaic *answered and said*

God: **he is the living God . . . his kingdom shall never be destroyed** (v. 26).

6:28 *Daniel Preserved Until the End of the Exile.* For the relationship of Darius and Cyrus, see note on 5:30–31. This closing comment rounds off the story of Daniel's life and puts his experience in the lions' den into a broader context. It reminds the reader that Daniel's entire life was spent in exile, in a metaphorical lions' den. Yet God preserved him alive and unharmed throughout the whole of that time, enabling him to prosper under successive kings until the time of King Cyrus, when his prayers for Jerusalem finally began to be answered. **Cyrus** was God's chosen instrument to bring about the return from the exile, when he issued a decree that the Jews could return to their homeland and rebuild Jerusalem (see 2 Chron. 36:22–23; Ezra 1:1–3).

7:1–12:13 *The Visions of Daniel.* These chapters describe Daniel's apocalyptic visions, which reassure God's people that, in spite of exile and persecution, God is still in control of history and will see his purposes through.

7:1–28 *The Vision of Four Great Beasts and the Heavenly Court.* In this vision, four beasts represent four mighty kings (or kingdoms); nevertheless, God's plan to exalt his faithful will be victorious.

7:1–8 *The Four Great Beasts.* The vision, of four wild winds and of four great beasts, is of seemingly uncontrollable forces.

7:1–2 Daniel received the vision during the **first year of Belshazzar** (c. 552 B.C.), when the Babylonians still ruled the world (and thus before the events of ch. 5; see map below). He **saw** the **four winds of heaven** (i.e., each of the four compass points, suggesting winds from all parts of the earth) **stirring up the great sea**, a symbol for chaos and potential rebellion against God (cf. Ps. 89:9; 93:3–4, which show that these are elements of nature still under God's rule), and the home of evil monsters such as the multiheaded monster Leviathan (Ps. 74:13–14).

7:3 This stirred-up **sea** produced **four** startling creatures, one after the other, each more frightening than the preceding one. In v. 17 Daniel is told that the "four great beasts are four kings who shall arise out of the earth." The number four may indicate the literal number of kingdoms or kings, or it may simply describe a complete series (cf. "the four winds of heaven"). Most interpreters see these as representing the same kings (or kingdoms) as the image in Nebuchadnezzar's dream in 2:31–45. On this understanding, the lion (7:4) represents Babylon, and the wings being "plucked off" (v. 4) represent the humbling of Nebuchadnezzar. The bear (v. 5) represents Medo-Persia, with the stronger Persian component being the side that was "raised up" (v. 5). The leopard (v. 6) represents Alexander the Great and his speedy conquest of the civilized world, and the "four heads" represent the division of his kingdom into four parts after his death. The final, terrifying beast (vv. 7–8) then represents the Roman Empire.

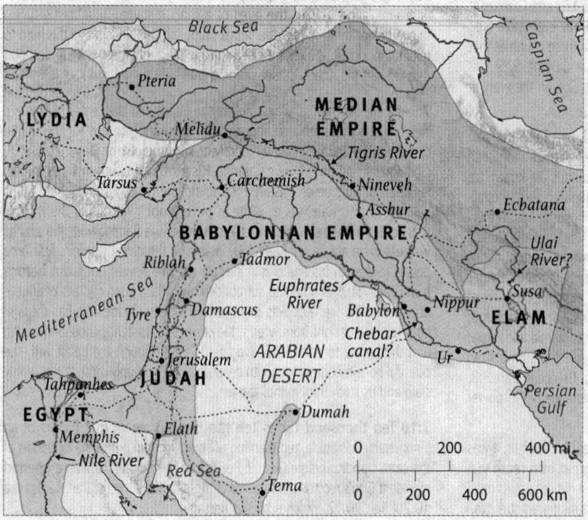

The Empires of Daniel's Visions: The Babylonians
c. 605–538 B.C.

Though their empire was short-lived by comparison with the Assyrians before them and the Persians after them, the Babylonians dominated the Near East during the early days of Daniel, and they were responsible for his initial exile to Babylon. Daniel himself, however, outlived the Babylonian Empire, which fell to the Persians in 538 B.C.

different from one another. 4 The first was like a lion and had eagles' wings. Then as I
looked its wings were plucked off, and it was lifted up from the ground and made to stand
on two feet like a man, and the mind of a man was given to it. 5 And behold, [u]another
beast, a second one, like a bear. It was raised up on one side. It had three ribs in its mouth
between its teeth; and it was told, 'Arise, devour much flesh.' 6 After this I looked, and
behold, another, like a [v]leopard, with four wings of a bird on its back. And the beast had
four heads, and [w]dominion was given to it. 7 After this I saw in the night visions, and
behold, a fourth beast, [x]terrifying and dreadful and exceedingly strong. It had great iron
teeth; [x]it devoured and broke in pieces [x]and stamped what was left with its feet. It was
different from all the beasts that were before it, and [y]it had ten horns. 8 I considered the
horns, and behold, [z]there came up among them another horn, a little one, [z]before which
three of the first horns were plucked up by the roots. And behold, in this horn were eyes
like the eyes of a man, and [a]a mouth speaking great things.

The Ancient of Days Reigns

9 "As I looked,

[b]thrones were placed,
and the [c]Ancient of Days took his seat;
[d]his clothing was white as snow,
and [e]the hair of his head like pure wool;
his throne was fiery flames;
[f]its wheels were burning fire.
10 [g]A stream of fire issued
and came out from before him;
[h]a thousand thousands [i]served him,
[h]and ten thousand times ten thousand [j]stood before him;

5 [u][ch. 2:39]
6 [v][Hab. 1:8; Rev. 13:2] [w][ch. 11:5]
7 [x]ver. 19, 23 [y]ver. 20; [Rev. 12:3; 13:1; 17:12]
8 [z][ver. 20, 21, 24; ch. 8:9] [a]ver. 20; [Rev. 13:5, 6]
9 [b]Rev. 20:4; [Matt. 19:28]; See 1 Kgs. 22:19 [c]ver. 22; [Ps. 90:2] [d]Matt. 28:3 [e]Rev. 1:14 [f][Ezek. 1:16; 10:2]
10 [g][Ps. 21:9] [h]Ps. 68:17; Heb. 12:22; Rev. 5:11 [i]Ps. 103:21 [j][Zech. 3:4]

7:4 The **first** beast was **like a lion** with **eagles' wings**, a mixture of animal and bird. This beast signifies the strength and majesty of a lion combined with the speed and power of an eagle. Both images were used by Jeremiah to depict Nebuchadnezzar (e.g., Jer. 49:19–22). This beast had his wings **plucked off** and was transformed into a **man**, recalling the humbling and restoration of Nebuchadnezzar (cf. Daniel 4).

7:5 The **second** beast was **like a bear**, **raised up on one side**—either poised and ready to spring or grotesquely deformed. Many scholars think the raised up side suggests the unequal power of the two countries combined in the Medo-Persian Empire (cf. 8:3, 20). It had a **mouth** full of the **ribs** of its previous victim(s)—maybe more specifically the people Cyrus conquered to unify his nation (e.g., Astyages [550 B.C.], Anatolia [547], and Croesus of Lydia [c. 547]). However, he was told to **arise** and **devour** even more (i.e., the Babylonians). The **three** ribs could also represent the three countries that Medo-Persia conquered (Babylon, 539 B.C.; Lydia, 546; and Egypt, 525). This empire controlled the land from Egypt and the Aegean Sea on the west to the Indus River on the east.

7:6 The third beast was **like** another composite animal, part **leopard**, part **bird**, **with four wings** and **four heads**. It combined ferocity and speed with the ability to see in all four directions at once. Leopards are known for speed (cf. Hab. 1:8), keen eyesight, and keen hearing, allowing them to stalk their prey and pounce unsuspectingly. But the four wings emphasize even more the element of speed, which corresponds well to Alexander the Great's conquest of the known world by age 32. Alexander invaded Asia Minor in 334 B.C., and within 10 years had conquered the whole Persian Empire. After his death in 323 B.C., his empire was divided among four of his generals: Antipater and later Cassander ruled in Greece and Macedon; Lysimachus in Thrace and much of Asia Minor; Seleucus I Nicator in Mesopotamia and Persia; and Ptolemy I Soter in Egypt and Palestine. These four rulers are symbolized by the four heads (cf. the four horns depicting leaders of Greece in Dan. 8:8, 21–22). Notice that **dominion was given to it**, suggesting a higher power controlling these actions.

7:7 The **fourth beast** cannot be described in terms of earthly animals. It was **terrifying** and **dreadful**, **exceedingly strong**, with **great iron teeth** that **devoured** and crushed, and it trampled down whatever it did not eat. Its head **had ten horns** (cf. ten toes, 2:42), symbolizing at least multiplied strength.

7:8 Even more surprisingly, another small horn **came up** among the horns, uprooting **three** of the 10 others. This horn had **eyes** and a **mouth** that spoke arrogantly. If this vision corresponds to the statue in ch. 2, then it would represent the Roman Empire (cf. iron teeth with iron legs, 2:33; see also *Midrash on Psalms* 80.6) and emphasize its ruthlessness. The Roman Empire was significantly different than the earlier empires, for it far surpassed them in power, longevity, and influence. The world had never before seen anything like it. The 10 horns could emphasize the extreme power of this empire (five times the normal number of two horns), or more likely it signifies 10 rulers or kingdoms (cf. Dan. 7:24; from Julius Caesar to Domitian there are actually 12 Caesars; but two reigned for only a few months). The **little** horn was significantly different than the others, for it had teeth of iron, claws of bronze, and eyes **like the eyes of a man**. It started "little" but grew up to overpower three of the other horns. Some scholars understand this horn to refer to Antiochus IV Epiphanes (see note on 8:23), but many have understood it to refer to the Antichrist (see note on 7:15–27).

7:9–12 *The Ancient of Days Judges the Beasts.* At the center of Daniel's vision was the heavenly courtroom, with **thrones** (perhaps for the saints, cf. Rev. 4:2–4; 20:4) set up for judgment. The **Ancient of Days** (Dan. 7:9), God himself, sat on the central throne. **His clothing was white as snow**, representing uncompromising and radiant purity (cf. Ps. 51:7; Isa. 1:18; Rev. 19:14); his **hair** was as white as **pure wool**, symbolizing the wisdom that comes with great age. His chariot-throne was flaming with fire and its **wheels** were ablaze (cf. Ezekiel 1), images of the divine warrior's fearsome power to destroy his enemies. A **stream of fire** flowed out **from before him** (Dan. 7:10), and he was surrounded by myriads upon myriads of angelic attendants. The scene depicts in powerful imagery a judge who has the *wisdom* to sort out right from wrong, the *purity* to persistently choose the right, and the *power* to enforce his judgments. Even though the beast with the boastful horn continued to mouth defiance at the heavenly court, it was swiftly slain and its body thrown into the fire.

7:10 **Ten thousand times ten thousand** is meant as a picture of an innumerable multitude, representing not one kingdom but all the kingdoms of the earth standing before God (cf. Rev. 5:11). **The books** that **were opened** represent God's records of the deeds of those on the earth (cf. Dan. 12:1; Luke 10:20; Rev. 20:12, which echo this passage).

the [k]court sat in judgment,
and [l]the books were opened.

11 "I looked then because of the sound of [a]the great words that the horn was speaking.
And as I looked, [m]the beast was killed, and its body destroyed [m]and given over to be burned
with fire. 12 As for the rest of the beasts, [n]their dominion was taken away, but their lives
were prolonged for a season and a time.

The Son of Man Is Given Dominion

13 "I saw in the night visions,

and [o]behold, with the clouds of heaven
there came one like a son of man,
and he came to the [c]Ancient of Days
and was presented before him.
14 [p]And to him was given dominion
and glory and a kingdom,
that all [q]peoples, nations, and languages
should serve him;
[r]his dominion is an everlasting dominion,
which shall not pass away,
and his kingdom one
that shall not be destroyed.

Daniel's Vision Interpreted

15 "As for me, Daniel, my spirit within me[1] was anxious, and [s]the visions of my head
alarmed me. 16 I approached one of those who stood there and asked him the truth concerning
all this. So he told me and made known to me the interpretation of the things. 17 [t]'These
four great beasts are four kings who shall arise out of the earth. 18 But [u]the saints of the Most
High shall receive the kingdom and possess the kingdom forever, forever and ever.'

[1] Aramaic *within its sheath*

10 [k]ver. 22, 26; Rev. 11:18; 20:4 [l]Rev. 20:12
11 [a][See ver. 8 above] [m]Rev. 19:20; [Rev. 20:10]
12 [n][ver. 14, 26]
13 [o]Matt. 26:64; Mark 14:62; Rev. 1:7; 14:14 [c][See ver. 9 above]
14 [p]Ps. 110:1, 2; Isa. 9:6, 7; Rev. 11:15 [q]See ch. 3:4 [r]See ch. 2:44
15 [s]See ver. 1
17 [t][ver. 3]
18 [u]ver. 22, 27; Matt. 25:34; [1 Cor. 6:2; Rev. 2:26; 20:4]

7:11–12 As Daniel kept watching, the boastful little **horn** was finally silenced: **the beast was killed, and its body destroyed and given over to be burned with fire** (cf. Rev. 19:20). Daniel looked back at the other **beasts** and **their dominion was taken away**, but they were not destroyed like this last beast. Their kingdoms remained for a time set by God and then were incorporated into the following kingdom.

7:13–14 *The Coming of the Son of Man.* The **one like a son of man** combines in one person both human and divine traits. Elsewhere, this phrase "son of man" often distinguishes mere human beings from God (e.g., Ps. 8:4; Ezek. 2:1). However, this son of man seems also greater than any mere human, for to "come on the **clouds**" is a clear symbol of divine authority (cf. Ps. 104:3; Isa. 19:1). This "son of man" is **given dominion and glory and a kingdom** (Dan. 7:14; cf. ESV footnote at v. 27; this is parallel to God's dominion, 4:34), which at present resides in the hands of human kings such as Nebuchadnezzar (cf. 5:18). But he is far greater than Nebuchadnezzar, because he will rule over the entire world forever: **all peoples, nations, and languages** will **serve** (or worship) **him**, and **his dominion . . . shall not pass away** (7:14). Thus, he must be much more than a personified representative of Israel (cf. vv. 18, 27), and certainly more than a mere angel, for no created being would have the right to rule the entire world forever. Jesus claims he will fulfill this role (cf. Mark 14:61–62), and it is ultimately fulfilled in Rev. 19:11–16 when Jesus comes at the end of the age to judge and rule the nations. Jesus refers to himself as "son of man" more than any other title (see notes on Matt. 8:20; John 1:51). This title was used in the OT in two different ways, first, to refer to a mere human being (see esp. Ezekiel, where it is used over 90 times referring to Ezekiel), and second, to refer to the son of man in Dan. 7:13, who is a divine being dwelling in heaven with the **Ancient of Days**. When people heard Jesus use the term "son of man" for himself, they had to decide which type of "son of man" he was. Technically he was both, but it took faith to believe he was like the "son of man" in Daniel. At the end of Jesus' ministry, when he claimed to be this heavenly "son of man" predicted in Daniel's vision, his opponents said he had committed blasphemy (see notes on Matt. 8:20; 24:30; 26:64).

7:15–27 *The Interpretation of the Vision.* As in ch. 2, many interpreters have identified the four beasts of ch. 7 as Babylon, Medo-Persia, Greece, and Rome (see note on 2:43–44). The beasts in general show the present world order as an ongoing state of violence and lust for power that will continue until the final coming of God's kingdom. The fourth beast will be different from those before it in power and duration, and its 10 horns are 10 kings or kingdoms (7:24). A little horn will grow up afterward and overpower three (if 10 signifies "completeness," then three represents "some") of the kings, which may refer to specific kings. As for the "little" horn (v. 8) who **made war with the saints and prevailed over them** (v. 21) and who **shall wear out the saints** (v. 25), many take this to represent the Antichrist, whom they expect in the end times (see notes on Matt. 24:15; Mark 13:19; 2 Thess. 2:3; 2:4; 2:9–10; 1 John 2:18; Rev. 11:1–2; 12:6; 13:1–10; 13:5). Other interpreters think there is not enough precise data to identify the little horn. It is clear, however, that this king will blaspheme against God (Dan. 7:25), oppress the saints (vv. 21, 25), and try to abolish the calendar and the law (v. 25), which govern how God's people worship. The saints will be handed over into his power for **a time, times, and half a time** (v. 25)—totaling three and a half times, or half of a total period of seven times of judgment (see 4:16; 9:27). To some extent, the description fits several historical tyrants, particularly Antiochus IV Epiphanes (reigned 175–164 B.C.; see note on 8:23), who oppressed God's people in the second century B.C., yet at the same time it is non-specific enough to leave the identity of this horn somewhat uncertain. The angel seems more concerned to drive home his earlier words about the judgment to come and the triumph of the saints than to identify the little horn. The central point of the vision is that the time when the beastly kingdoms of the earth will oppress the saints is limited by God, and beyond it lies the scene of the heavenly court, where the beasts will finally be tamed and destroyed (cf. Rev. 20:1–4, 10).

19 "Then I desired to know the truth about [v]the fourth beast, which was different from
all the rest, exceedingly terrifying, with its teeth of iron and claws of bronze, and which
devoured and broke in pieces and stamped what was left with its feet, 20 [w]and about the
ten horns that were on its head, and the other horn that came up and before which three
of them fell, the horn that had eyes and a mouth that spoke great things, and that seemed
greater than its companions. 21 As I looked, this horn [x]made war with the saints and prevailed
over them, 22 until the [y]Ancient of Days came, and [u]judgment was given for the saints of
the Most High, and the time came when [u]the saints possessed the kingdom.

23 "Thus he said: 'As for [v]the fourth beast,

there shall be a fourth kingdom on earth,
which shall be different from all the kingdoms,
and it shall devour the whole earth,
and trample it down, and break it to pieces.
24 As for the ten horns,
out of this kingdom ten kings shall arise,
and another shall arise after them;
he shall be different from the former ones,
and shall put down three kings.
25 [z]He shall speak words against the Most High,
and shall wear out the saints of the Most High,
and shall think to [a]change the times and the law;
and they shall be given into his hand
for [b]a time, times, and half a time.
26 [c]But the court shall sit in judgment,
and [d]his dominion shall be taken away,
to be consumed and destroyed [e]to the end.
27 [f]And the kingdom and the dominion
and the greatness of the kingdoms under the whole heaven
shall be given to the people of [f]the saints of the Most High;
[g]his kingdom shall be an everlasting kingdom,
and all dominions shall serve and obey him.'[1]

28 "Here is the end of the matter. [h]As for me, Daniel, my [i]thoughts greatly alarmed me,
[j]and my color changed, but [k]I kept the matter in my heart."

Daniel's Vision of the Ram and the Goat

8 In the third year of the reign of [l]King Belshazzar a vision appeared to me, Daniel,
[m]after that which appeared to me [m]at the first. 2 And I saw in the vision; and when I
saw, I was in [n]Susa the citadel, which is in the province of [o]Elam. And [p]I saw in the vision,
[p]and I was at the [q]Ulai canal. 3 I raised my eyes and saw, and behold, [r]a ram standing on

[1] *Or their kingdom shall be an everlasting kingdom, and all dominions shall serve and obey them*

19 [v]ver. 7
20 [w]ver. 8
21 [x][ch. 8:24]
22 [y]ver. 9, 13 [u][See ver. 18 above]
23 [v][See ver. 19 above]
25 [z][ch. 11:36] [a]ch. 2:9, 21 [b]ch. 12:7; Rev. 12:14
26 [c]See ver. 10 [d][ver. 12, 14] [e]ch. 6:26
27 [f]See ver. 18 [g]See ch. 2:44
28 [h]ver. 15; [ch. 8:27; 10:8, 16; Jer. 23:9] [i]ch. 4:5, 19; 5:6 [j][ch. 5:6, 10] [k][Luke 2:19, 51]

Chapter 8

1 [l]See ch. 5:1 [m][ch. 7:1]
2 [n]See Neh. 1:1 [o]See Isa. 11:11 [p]See Ezek. 1:1 [q]ver. 16
3 [r][ver. 20]

7:28 *Daniel's Response.* Daniel, stunned, has strength only to ponder the vision related in this chapter.

8:1–27 *The Vision of the Ram, the Goat, and the Little Horn.* In this vision, Daniel sees what is to come of the Medo-Persian Empire, Alexander the Great's empire, and the Hellenistic empires that succeed it. The upheavals to come will mean terrible times for the people of God, but they must endure, knowing that God rules over it all.

8:1–14 *The Vision of the Ram and the Goat.* Daniel sees a vision of a swift goat defeating a mighty ram, only to be succeeded by four horns. This vision, given **in the third year of the reign of King Belshazzar** (c. 550 B.C.), occurred about the same time that Cyrus conquered the Medes and united the two kingdoms.

8:3 In this vision, Daniel saw an all-powerful **ram** with **two horns, one** of which was longer **than the other**. The ram represents the Medo-Persian Empire (see map, p. 1603), with the **higher** horn representing the stronger, Persian part (see v. 20). (The horns of an animal, which it uses both for defensive and offensive fighting, are frequently found in Scripture as a symbol of the military power of a nation.)

8:5–8 A male **goat** with a single **conspicuous horn** appeared and destroyed the ram, yet at the pinnacle of his power, the single horn was shattered and **four conspicuous horns** replaced it (v. 8). This vision is a striking prediction of the Medo-Persian and Greek empires (see note on vv. 20–22). It is so accurate that some interpreters, who do not think the Bible can contain truly predictive prophecy (and others who think that such specific predictions are not suited to the normal pattern of biblical prophecy), claim that this material was not written in the sixth century by Daniel but had to be written after these events occurred (see Introduction: Date).

8:5 a male goat came from the west. Alexander the Great came from Greece, which was to the "west" of both Babylon and Persia. **without touching the ground**. Alexander conquered the mighty Persian Empire with amazing speed, from 334–331 B.C. (He is also represented as a leopard with four wings in 7:6.)

8:7 he was enraged. Alexander's father was king of Macedonia (a land north of Greece) and brought all of Greece under his control by 336 B.C. Alexander was only 20 when his father was murdered, but managed to consolidate his hold on Greece and to unify the Greeks with "rage" over the way

4[s][Deut. 33:17; Ezek. 34:21] [t][ch. 7:17] [u][ver. 7] [v][ch. 3:15] [w][ch. 11:3, 16, 36] [x]ver. 8
5[y][ver. 21]
6[z][ver. 20] [a][Job 15:26]
7[b]ch. 11:11 [c][ver. 4] [d][Ps. 7:5]
8[y][See ver. 5 above] [e]ver. 4 [f][ver. 5]; See ch. 7:2, 3
9[g]ch. 7:8 [h][ch. 11:25] [i]ch. 11:16, 41; [Ps. 48:2; Ezek. 20:6, 15]
10[j][ch. 11:28] [k]Isa. 14:13 [l][Rev. 12:4] [m]ver. 7
11[n]ver. 25; See ch. 11:36 [o]Josh. 5:14 [p]ch. 11:31; 12:11

the bank of the canal. It had two horns, and both horns were high, but one was higher
than the other, and the higher one came up last. 4 I saw [s]the ram charging westward and
northward and southward. No [t]beast [u]could stand before him, [v]and there was no one who
could rescue from his power. [w]He did as he pleased and [x]became great.
5 As I was considering, behold, a [y]male goat came from the west across the face of the
whole earth, without touching the ground. And the goat had [y]a conspicuous horn between
his eyes. 6 He came to [z]the ram with the two horns, which I had seen standing on the bank
of the canal, [a]and he ran at him in his powerful wrath. 7 I saw him come close to the ram,
[b]and he was enraged against him and struck the ram and broke his two horns. [c]And the
ram had no power to stand before him, but he [d]cast him down to the ground and trampled
on him. And there was no one who could rescue the ram from his power. 8 Then [y]the goat
[e]became exceedingly great, but when he was strong, the great horn was broken, and instead
of it there came up four [f]conspicuous horns toward [f]the four winds of heaven.
9 Out of one of them came [g]a little horn, which grew exceedingly great toward [h]the
south, toward the east, and toward [i]the glorious land. 10 [j]It grew great, [k]even to the host
of heaven. And some of the host [k]and some[1] of [l]the stars it threw down to the ground
and [m]trampled on them. 11 [n]It became great, even as great as [o]the Prince of the host. [p]And

[1] *Or host, that is, some*

the Persians had been attacking them and meddling in their affairs for the previous two centuries.

8:8 the goat became exceedingly great. Alexander the Great's kingdom extended all the way to India, exceeding any kingdom before it in size (approx. 1.5 million square miles/3,885,000 square km). **there came up four conspicuous horns**. After the death of Alexander the Great in 323 B.C., his two sons initially took over the empire, but ultimately, after serious internal struggles, four of his generals divided his kingdom into four parts (cf. v. 22 and 7:6).

8:9–10 A little horn grows out of one of the four horns and expands his realm. Scholars are almost unanimous in recognizing this little horn as the eighth ruler of the Seleucid dynasty, Antiochus IV Epiphanes (ruled 175–164 B.C.; see notes on vv. 23 and 25). The **glorious land** most likely refers to Palestine as God's primary center of operations and the location of his people. This horn **grew great, even to the host of heaven**, and **some of the stars it threw down to the ground**. This almost certainly refers to saints who were killed during Antiochus IV's reign. It began with the assassination of the high priest Onias III in 170 B.C. and continued to the death of Antiochus IV in 164. Within those few years, he executed thousands of Jews.

8:11 the place of his sanctuary was overthrown. According to the Jewish history recorded in *1 Maccabees* (in the Apocrypha), Antiochus IV

The Empires of Daniel's Visions: The Persians

c. 538–331 B.C.

After Cyrus the Great united the Median and Persian empires, he overthrew the Babylonians and established the greatest power the world had ever known. Under later rulers the Persian Empire eventually extended from Egypt and Thrace to the borders of India, and Cyrus himself declared, "the LORD, the God of heaven, has given me all the kingdoms of the earth" (2 Chron. 36:23; Ezra 1:2). Consistent with his regular policies to promote loyalty among his subjugated peoples, Cyrus immediately released the exiled Jews from their captivity in Babylon and even sponsored the rebuilding of the temple.

the regular burnt offering was taken away from him, and the place of his sanctuary was
overthrown. 12 And a host will be given over to it together with the regular burnt offering because of transgression,[1] and it will throw truth to the ground, and [q]it will act and
prosper. 13 Then I heard [r]a holy one speaking, and another holy one said to the one who
spoke, [s]"For how long is the vision concerning the regular burnt offering, [t]the transgression that makes desolate, and the giving over of the sanctuary and host to be trampled
underfoot?" 14 And he said to me,[2] "For 2,300 [u]evenings and mornings. Then the sanctuary
shall be restored to its rightful state."

The Interpretation of the Vision

15 When I, Daniel, had seen the vision, I [v]sought to understand it. And behold, there stood
before me one having [w]the appearance of a man. 16 [x]And I heard a man's voice [x]between the
banks of the [y]Ulai, and it called, [z]"Gabriel, make this man understand the vision." 17 So he
came near where I stood. And when he came, [a]I was frightened [b]and fell on my face. But
he said to me, "Understand, [c]O son of man, that the vision is for [d]the time of the end."
18 And when he had spoken to me, [e]I fell into a deep sleep with my face to the ground.
But [f]he touched me and made me stand up. 19 He said, "Behold, I will make known to
you what shall be at the latter end of [g]the indignation, for it refers to [h]the appointed
time of the end. 20 As for [i]the ram that you saw with the two horns, these are the kings of
[j]Media and Persia. 21 And [k]the goat[3] is the king of Greece. And [k]the great horn between
his eyes is [l]the first king. 22 [m]As for the horn that was broken, in place of which four others
arose, four kingdoms shall arise from his[4] nation, [n]but not with his power. 23 And at the

12 [q]ver. 24; ch. 11:28, 30
13 [r]See ch. 4:13 [s]ch. 12:6; [Rev. 6:10]; See ch. 9:21-27 [t]See ch. 11:31
14 [u][ver. 26]
15 [v][1 Pet. 1:10, 11] [w]ch. 7:13; 10:16, 18; Ezek. 1:26; Rev. 1:13
16 [x]See ch. 12:5-7 [y]ver. 2 [z]ch. 9:21; Luke 1:19, 26
17 [a][Luke 1:12] [b]Ezek. 1:28 [c]See Ezek. 2:1 [d][ver. 19; ch. 11:27, 35, 40; 12:4, 9]
18 [e]ch. 10:9; [Luke 9:32] [f]ch. 9:21; 10:10, 18
19 [g]ch. 11:36 [h][Ps. 102:13]; See ver. 17
20 [i][ver. 3] [j][ch. 6:8]
21 [k][ver. 5] [l]ch. 10:20; 11:3
22 [m]ver. 8 [n]ver. 24

[1] Or *in an act of rebellion* [2] Hebrew; Septuagint, Theodotion, Vulgate *to him* [3] Or *the shaggy goat* [4] Theodotion, Septuagint, Vulgate; Hebrew *the*

tried to unify his realm by forcing the Jews to forsake their law and cultural distinctives, but when they refused he punished them severely (see note on Dan. 8:23). The **Prince of the host** probably refers to God, because of the similar expression "Prince of princes" in v. 25, though some have argued that it is the high priest Onias III.

8:12–14 Because of renewed **transgression** on the part of God's people, the saints and the temple sacrifices were handed over into the hands of Antiochus IV, but only for a limited period: **2,300 evenings and mornings**, or a little over six years (perhaps signifying the period from 170 B.C., the death of Onias III, the high priest, to December 14, 164, when Judas Maccabeus

The Empires of Daniel's Visions: The Greeks

c. 335–303 B.C.

The ascension of Alexander the Great to the throne of the Macedonian kingdom (in northern Greece) spelled the end for the mighty Persian Empire. After gaining the loyalty of the other city-states of Greece, Alexander's astounding military prowess and success enabled him to systematically overtake virtually all of Persia's former territory within 12 years. Soon after he died in Babylon at age 33 (323 B.C.), Alexander's conquered territory was divided among his generals, who constantly vied for power among each other until their territories resembled those shown here (c. 303).

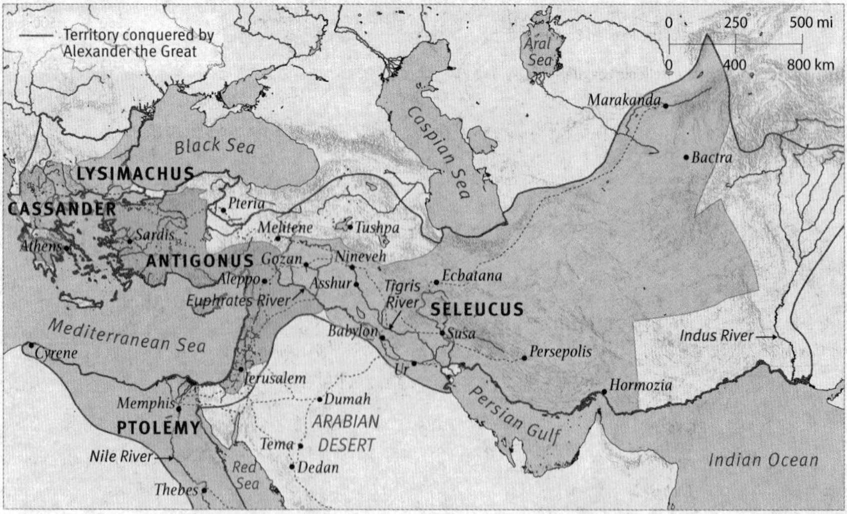

24[o]Rev. 17:17 [p]ver. 12; ch. 11:28, 30 [q][ch. 7:21]
25[r][ch. 11:23] [s]ver. 11 [t][ch. 11:21, 24] [u]See ch. 2:34
26[v][ver. 14] [w][ch. 10:1] [x][ch. 12:4, 9] [y]ch. 10:14
27[z][ch. 7:28] [a][ver. 16]

Chapter 9

1[b]ch. 11:1 [c]See ch. 5:31 [d][ch. 8:20] [e]ch. 5:30
2[f][Ezra 1:1; Jer. 25:12]
3[g]ver. 17, 18, 23; [Neh. 1:4]
4[h]ver. 20; [Ezra 10:1; Neh. 1:6]

latter end of their kingdom, when the transgressors have reached their limit, a king of
bold face, one who understands riddles, shall arise. 24 His power shall be great—[o]but not
by his own power; and he shall cause fearful destruction [p]and shall succeed in what he
does, [q]and destroy mighty men and the people who are the saints. 25 [r]By his cunning he
shall make deceit prosper under his hand, and in his own mind [s]he shall become great.
[t]Without warning he shall destroy many. And he [s]shall even rise up against the Prince of
princes, and he shall be broken—but [u]by no human hand. 26 The vision of [v]the evenings
and the mornings that has been told [w]is true, but [x]seal up the vision, [y]for it refers to many
days from now."

27 And [z]I, Daniel, was overcome and lay sick for some days. Then I rose and went about
the king's business, but I was appalled by the vision [a]and did not understand it.

Daniel's Prayer for His People

9 [b]In the first year of [c]Darius the son of Ahasuerus, by descent a [d]Mede, who was made
king over the realm of the [e]Chaldeans— 2 in the first year of his reign, I, Daniel,
perceived in the books the number of years that, according to [f]the word of the LORD to
Jeremiah the prophet, must pass before the end of the desolations of Jerusalem, namely,
seventy years.

3 Then I turned my face to the Lord God, seeking him by [g]prayer and pleas for mercy
with fasting and sackcloth and ashes. 4 I prayed to the LORD my God and [h]made confession,

cleansed and rededicated the temple; cf. *1 Macc.* 4:52). In the end, the little horn would be judged and the sanctuary **restored to its rightful state**. Unlike the less precise "time, times, and half a time" of Dan. 7:25, this period is measured in days, suggesting that God has a precise calendar for the times of his people's suffering, even though it is utterly inscrutable to human wisdom.

8:15–26 *The Interpretation of the Vision.* The angel Gabriel explains to Daniel that the vision concerns the future of the region, which God rules over for his purposes. The vision is given to prepare God's people for the coming events, even the severe persecutions under Antiochus IV Epiphanes.

8:20–22 Unlike the vision of ch. 7, this vision of 8:3–14 is precisely interpreted by the angel: the two-horned **ram** represents the **kings of Media and Persia**, of whom Cyrus, king of Persia, became the dominant partner (c. 550 B.C.). The **goat** was **the king of Greece** (v. 21), Alexander the Great, who defeated the Persians and conquered most of the then-known world. When he died in 323 B.C., his empire was divided among his four generals, fulfilling the prophecy in v. 22: **four kingdoms shall arise from his nation, but not with his power** (cf. v. 8).

8:23 The "little horn" of v. 9 then corresponds to a **king of bold face**, who was completely wicked (see note on vv. 20–22). This describes Antiochus IV Epiphanes (reigned 175–164 B.C.). He was king of the Seleucid Empire, one of the four kingdoms that emerged from Alexander the Great's former territory (stretching from Asia Minor through Persia). He seized the throne from his nephew and enlarged his kingdom through military power. Antiochus IV was a tyrant who tried to unify his kingdom by forcing all of his subjects to adopt Greek cultural and religious practices. He banned circumcision, ended sacrifice at the temple in Jerusalem (fulfilling v. 11, "the regular burnt offering was taken away"), and deliberately defiled the temple by sacrificing a pig on the altar and placing an object sacred to Zeus in the Holy of Holies (fulfilling v. 13, "the giving over of the sanctuary . . . to be trampled underfoot"; cf. v. 11, and *1 Macc.* 1:37–59; *2 Macc.* 6:2–5). He burned copies of the Scriptures and slaughtered those who remained true to their faith in God (cf. Dan. 8:10, 24–25).

8:25 he shall even rise up against the Prince of princes. This title refers to God and indicates the rebellion of Antiochus IV against even God's legitimate sovereignty. Antiochus IV's coins even have the phrase "god manifest" (Gk. *theos epiphanēs*) on the back of them (see note on 11:37–38), which probably means that he thought he was the gods' representative on earth.

8:27 *Daniel's Response.* Even though Daniel **did not** fully **understand** the **vision**, he was nonetheless **overcome**, **appalled**, and sickened by it, for he recognized and understood the severity of the future suffering coming on his own people. Like the other prophets, he identified with his people when they faced the judgment of God (see Ezek. 3:14–15). Yet in spite of his deep concern for the future, he **went about the king's business**: Daniel did not isolate himself from the culture around him but continued faithfully in his service of Babylonian society.

9:1–27 *Daniel's Prayer and Its Answer.* While reading Jeremiah and realizing that the "seventy years" (v. 2) are almost up, Daniel turns to God in prayer, seeking mercy for Jerusalem. The angel Gabriel (v. 21) appears to him and explains that another period of 70 "sevens" is at hand for God's people. The name Yahweh (represented by LORD, in small capital letters), not used elsewhere in Daniel, is used seven times in this chapter, emphasizing God's covenantal relationship to his people. This vision occurs in Darius's first year (539 B.C.), about 11 years after the one in ch. 8. Daniel appears to be over 80 years old. On the identity of Darius the Mede, see note on 5:30–31.

9:1–19 *Daniel's Prayer Concerning the 70 Years.* Daniel knows why the exile came upon the Jewish people, and he confesses his own and his people's sins and prays for forgiveness and mercy. This prayer occurred shortly after the Babylonian Empire was overthrown by the Medes and the Persians in 539 B.C., thus fulfilling the prophecy of the handwriting on the wall (cf. ch. 5).

9:2 Daniel's prayer was prompted by reading **Jeremiah**, part of the OT canon that had been collected up to that point, where he found a reference to the **desolations of Jerusalem** lasting for **seventy years** (see note on Jer. 25:11). He understood this prophecy to clearly indicate that the desolations were almost over. Some interpreters understand the 70 years to extend from 605 B.C. (cf. note on Dan. 1:1–2) to the first return of the exiles in 538, following Cyrus's decree allowing the Jews to return. Others suggest that the 70 years extend from 586 B.C., when Nebuchadnezzar destroyed Jerusalem, to 515, when the rebuilding of the temple was completed under Zerubbabel (cf. Ezra 6:15). Jeremiah 29:10–14 suggests that at the end of the 70 years Israel will pray to God and he will hear them. This passage may suggest a time when the temple is complete and is being used to call out to God. Both interpretations are reasonable, but Daniel appears to be suggesting the first interpretation, for at the end of the 70 years Babylon would be punished (cf. Jer. 25:12), which fits well with the events of 539 B.C., and God's people would return home (cf. Jer. 29:10).

9:3 Since God was judging the king of Babylon and his nation, as promised (cf. Jer. 25:12), Daniel began to pray for the gracious restoration of God's people to his land (cf. Jer. 29:10). Along with praying, Daniel fasted and clothed himself in **sackcloth and ashes**, signs of intense mourning and repentance for his people's sin.

9:4 Daniel's prayer begins with adoration and an acknowledgment of God's power and his justice, and goes on to plead with him to show his grace to his people. The Lord is a God who **keeps covenant and steadfast love**, faithfully fulfilling his promises to his people. In contrast to God's righteousness and faithfulness, Daniel's own people had been unfaithful, as Daniel confessed.

saying, [i]"O Lord, the [i]great and awesome God, who [j]keeps covenant and steadfast love
with those who love him and keep his commandments, 5 [k]we have sinned and done wrong
and acted wickedly [l]and rebelled, turning aside from your commandments and rules.
6 [m]We have not listened to [n]your servants the prophets, who spoke in your name to [o]our
kings, our princes, and our fathers, and to all the people of the land. 7 To you, [p]O Lord,
belongs righteousness, but to us open shame, as at this day, to the men of Judah, to the
inhabitants of Jerusalem, and to all Israel, [q]those who are near and [q]those who are far
away, in [r]all the lands to which you have driven them, because of [s]the treachery that they
have committed against you. 8 To us, O LORD, belongs open shame, to our kings, to our
princes, and to our fathers, because [k]we have sinned against you. 9 [t]To the Lord our God
belong mercy and forgiveness, for we have rebelled against him 10 [m]and have not obeyed
the voice of the LORD our God by walking in his laws, which he set before us by [n]his
servants the prophets. 11 [u]All Israel has transgressed your law and turned aside, [v]refus-
ing to obey your voice. [w]And the curse and oath [x]that are written in the Law of [y]Moses
the servant of God have been poured out upon us, because [k]we have sinned against him.
12 He has confirmed his words, which he spoke against us and against [z]our rulers who
ruled us,[1] by [a]bringing upon us a great calamity. [b]For under the whole heaven there has
not been done anything like what has been done against Jerusalem. 13 [x]As it is written
in the Law of Moses, all this calamity has come upon us; yet we have not entreated the
favor of the LORD our God, [c]turning from our iniquities and gaining insight by your
truth. 14 [d]Therefore the LORD has kept ready the calamity and has brought it upon us,
[e]for the LORD our God is righteous in all the works that he has done, and [f]we have not
obeyed his voice. 15 And now, O Lord our God, who brought your people out of the land
of Egypt [g]with a mighty hand, and [h]have made a name for yourself, as at this day, [i]we
have sinned, we have done wickedly.

16 "O Lord, [j]according to all your righteous acts, let your anger and your wrath turn
away from your city Jerusalem, [k]your holy hill, [l]because for our sins, and for [m]the iniquities of our fathers, [n]Jerusalem and your people have become [o]a byword among all who
are around us. 17 Now therefore, O our God, listen to the prayer of your servant and to
his pleas for mercy, and for your own sake, O Lord,[2] [p]make your face to shine upon [q]your
sanctuary, which is desolate. 18 [r]O my God, incline your ear and hear. Open your eyes and
see [s]our desolations, and [t]the city that is called by your name. For we do not present our
pleas before you because of our righteousness, but because of your great mercy. 19 O Lord,
hear; O Lord, forgive. O Lord, pay attention and act. [u]Delay not, [v]for your own sake, O my
God, because [t]your city and [w]your people are called by your name."

Gabriel Brings an Answer

20 [x]While I was speaking and praying, confessing my sin and the sin of my people Israel,
and presenting my plea before the LORD my God for [y]the holy hill of my God, 21 while
I was speaking in prayer, the man [z]Gabriel, whom I had seen in the vision at the first,
[a]came to me in swift flight at [b]the time of the evening sacrifice. 22 [c]He made me understand, speaking with me and saying, "O Daniel, I have now come out to give you [d]insight
and understanding. 23 [e]At the beginning of your pleas for mercy a word went out, [f]and I
have come to tell it to you, for [g]you are greatly loved. Therefore consider the word [h]and
understand the vision.

[1] *Or our judges who judged us* [2] Hebrew *for the Lord's sake*

4 [i]Neh. 1:5; 9:32 [j]Deut. 7:9
5 [k]ver. 15 [l]Lam. 3:42
6 [m]2 Chr. 36:15, 16 [n]Ezra 9:11; Zech. 1:6 [o]Ezra 9:7; Neh. 9:34
7 [p][ver. 14; Lam. 1:18] [q][Esth. 9:20] [r]See Jer. 8:3 [s]Lev. 26:40
8 [k][See ver. 5 above]
9 [t]Neh. 9:17; Ps. 86:15
10 [m][See ver. 6 above] [n][See ver. 6 above]
11 [u]See Isa. 1:4-6 [v][Jer. 40:3; 44:23] [w]Jer. 44:22 [x]See Lev. 26:14-45; Deut. 28:15-68 [y]1 Chr. 6:49; 2 Chr. 24:9; Neh. 10:29 [k][See ver. 5 above]
12 [z][Ps. 82:2, 3] [a]Jer. 39:16 [b]Ezek. 5:9; [Lam. 1:12]
13 [x][See ver. 11 above] [c]Hos. 7:10
14 [d][Jer. 1:12] [e]Neh. 9:33; See ver. 7 [f]ver. 10
15 [g]Ex. 32:11; [Ex. 6:1; Neh. 1:10] [h]Ex. 14:18; Neh. 9:10 [i]See ver. 5
16 [j]Ps. 31:1; 71:2 [k]ver. 20; ch. 11:45; Jer. 31:23; Zech. 8:3 [l]Lam. 1:5 [m][Ex. 20:5] [n]Lam. 2:15, 16 [o]Ps. 44:13; 79:4; Ezek. 36:4; Mic. 6:16
17 [p]Num. 6:25 [q]Lam. 5:18
18 [r]2 Kgs. 19:16; Isa. 37:17 [s]ver. 26; See ver. 27 [t]Jer. 25:29
19 [u]Ps. 40:17; 70:5 [v]Ps. 25:11; 79:9 [t][See ver. 18 above] [w]Jer. 14:9
20 [x]Isa. 65:24 [y]See ver. 16
21 [z]See ch. 8:16 [a]See ch. 8:18 [b]Ex. 29:39; [1 Kgs. 18:36; Ezra 9:4, 5]
22 [c][ch. 8:16] [d][ch. 1:4, 17]
23 [e][ver. 20] [f][ch. 10:12, 14] [g]ch. 10:11, 19 [h][Matt. 24:15; Mark 13:14]

9:11 Under the terms of the covenant God established at Mount Sinai, such unfaithfulness as Daniel confesses to in vv. 5–11 of his prayer would result in the destruction and exile of God's people from the Land of Promise: **the curse and oath that are written in the Law of Moses** refers to Lev. 26:14–45 and Deut. 28:15–68. Yet Deuteronomy also speaks of the promise of a new and gracious beginning for Israel beyond sin and judgment. When his people repented of their sins, the Lord would gather them again to the land (Deut. 30:2–3), which was Daniel's hope.

9:17 Daniel asked God to show favor and **make** his **face to shine upon** his desolate **sanctuary** and bring the exile to an end because of God's commitment to his **own sake**—the glory of his own name.

9:20–27 *Gabriel's Answer: 70 Sevens Before the Promised Redemption.* The angel Gabriel, first seen in ch. 8, hastens to Daniel and reveals that there is more to come.

9:21 In response to his **prayer** for the restoration of Jerusalem, Daniel received an angelic messenger, **Gabriel**, with a vision for him. Gabriel's arrival was clear proof that Daniel's prayer had been heard and his request for favor had been honored by the Lord (v. 23).

24[i][Ezek. 4:6] [j]Neh. 11:1 [k]ch. 8:13 [l][Ps. 78:38; Heb. 2:17]; See Jer. 31:34 [m]Rom. 3:25, 26; See Jer. 23:5, 6 [n][Ps. 45:7; Isa. 61:1; Acts 4:26, 27]
25[o][ver. 23] [p][2 Chr. 36:23; Ezra 1:3; 4:24; 6:15; Neh. 6:15] [q][Ps. 51:18] [r]John 1:41 [s]Isa. 55:4 [t]See Neh. 4:7, 8, 16-18

The Seventy Weeks

24 [i]"Seventy weeks[1] are decreed about your people and [j]your holy city, to finish [k]the
transgression, to put an end to sin, [l]and to atone for iniquity, [m]to bring in everlasting righteousness, to seal both vision and prophet, and [n]to anoint a most holy place.[2]
25 [o]Know therefore and understand that [p]from the going out of the word to restore
and [q]build Jerusalem to the coming of an [r]anointed one, a [s]prince, there shall be seven
weeks. Then for sixty-two weeks it shall be built again[3] with squares and moat, [t]but in

[1] Or *sevens;* also twice in verse 25 and once in verse 26 [2] Or *thing, or one* [3] Or *there shall be seven weeks and sixty-two weeks. It shall be built again*

9:24–27 There are many suggested interpretations of the **seventy weeks** (or "seventy sevens," see ESV footnote), but there are three main views: (1) the passage refers to events surrounding Antiochus IV Epiphanes (175–164 B.C.); (2) the 70 sevens are to be understood figuratively; and (3) the passage refers to events around the time of Christ. Most scholars understand the 70 "sevens" to be made up of 70 times seven years, or 490 years, but they apply these years to different periods of time. (See chart, p. 1608.) In any case, the important point is that God has appointed the amount of time, and thus his people should not lose heart.

(1) Those who hold the first view often understand **the word to restore and build Jerusalem** (v. 25) to allude to Jeremiah's prophecy of the "seventy years of captivity" (Jer. 25:1, 11), which began in 605 B.C. (or some start at 586, when the Babylonians destroyed the temple) and extended to the cleansing of the temple by Judas Maccabeus (164) or the death of Antiochus IV Epiphanes (164). These solutions give only an approximate fulfillment for the "seventy weeks" (since 490 years after 605 is 115 B.C., and 490 years after 586 is 96 B.C.). An objection to this view is that it is hard to see how the events around Antiochus IV could fulfill the purpose for the "seventy weeks" (such as, "to finish the transgression," to make "an end to sin," "to bring in everlasting righteousness").

(2) Scholars who hold the second view believe the 490 years (7 + 62 + 1, each multiplied by seven years) to be symbolic periods of time ending in the first century A.D. Support for finding symbolism here comes from the mention of "seventy" in Dan. 9:2, and the connection of "seven" to the weekly Sabbath (Lev. 23:3), to the Feast of Weeks (Lev. 23:11–16, "seven weeks"), to the sabbatical year (Lev. 25:3–4, connected to discipline of the people in Lev. 26:34–35; 2 Chron. 36:21), and to the Jubilee year (Lev. 25:8, "seven weeks/Sabbaths of years"). These numbers can therefore imply God's perfect appointment of time. One approach for this second view is simply to say that 70 x 7 symbolizes the ultimate in completeness, and no further specificity is implied. Another approach is to see three broad periods, with the first period of seven sevens extending from Cyrus's decree allowing the Jews to return and build the temple (538 B.C.) to about the time of Ezra and Nehemiah in the fifth century (c. 458–433). Then the 62 weeks extends from about 400 B.C. to the advent of Christ. The last "seven" goes from the first advent of Christ to sometime after his death, but before the destruction of Jerusalem in A.D. 70. An argument against this view is that the enumeration of 7 + 62 + 1 weeks seems to be intended to give a much more precise chronology rather than just a sequence of three periods of history. In addition, the purposes for the 70 weeks do not appear to be fulfilled in A.D. 70 ("to finish transgression," "to put an end to sin," and "to bring in everlasting righteousness"). Some interpreters who hold a symbolic view have suggested it refers to periods of time ending with Christ's second coming, which would answer this last objection.

(3) The third view sees the "seventy sevens" as a literal period of 490 years, culminating around the time of Christ. But what starting date can be used for this? (a) The starting date for this period of time is not likely to be 538 B.C., when Cyrus gave permission for the Jews to return to Jerusalem and rebuild the temple (2 Chron. 36:23; Ezra 1:2–4), for that was not a decree to build the city, and 490 years from 538 yields 48 B.C., a date of no great significance. (b) One reasonable possibility is the decree of Artaxerxes in Ezra 7:12–26, which occurred in 458 B.C. (see note on Ezra 7:6–7). Though this decree still has much to do with provisions for the temple, it makes provision for "magistrates and judges" (Ezra 7:25) and thus assumes rebuilding of a city would take place. And 490 years after 458 B.C. is exactly A.D. 33, the most likely date of the crucifixion of Christ. (See article on The Date of Jesus' Crucifixion, pp. 1809–1810.) (458 + 33 = 491, but one year must be subtracted since there was no year 0, so from 458 B.C. to A.D. 33 is exactly 490 years, or "seventy sevens.") This calculation also fits Dan. 9:24, for Christ's death accomplished the things mentioned there as what would be done in the 70 weeks: "to finish the transgression, to put an end to sin, and to atone for iniquity, to bring in everlasting righteousness." Possibly a better understanding of this interpretation is that the 7 + 62 = 69 weeks in v. 25 brings us to A.D. 26, and some NT scholars think that Jesus began his ministry in A.D. 26 and died in 30. But v. 26 simply says, "*After* the sixty-two weeks, an anointed one shall be cut off and shall have nothing," and in this interpretation Jesus' death did occur shortly after the 62 weeks. (This understanding of the verse allows for Jesus' death in either A.D. 30 or 33.) (c) A third possibility for the start of the 490 years is 445 B.C., when Artaxerxes gave letters to Nehemiah authorizing him to rebuild the wall and to build a home in Jerusalem (Neh. 2:5–8; cf. Neh. 2:1 for the date, 13 years after Ezra 7:7). But 490 years after 445 B.C. gives A.D. 46, a date well beyond the crucifixion of Christ. An alternative to this view is to see Christ's death occurring in the sixty-ninth week, which would be A.D. 39, but that is still too late. However, some interpreters argue that a "year" in this prophecy should be calculated at 12 months x 30 days = 360 days (cf. Dan. 12:7, 11; Rev. 11:2; 12:6). On that basis, 69 "weeks" of such years equals 483 years of 360 days, and that comes out to A.D. 32 or 33, depending on whether Artaxerxes' letter in Neh. 2:5–8 is dated 445 or 444 B.C. It is difficult to decide among these alternatives.

An additional question is whether Daniel's prophecy allows for a gap between the sixty-ninth and seventieth weeks. Dispensational interpreters understand Dan. 9:26 to allow for the entire church age, and v. 27 to describe the seventieth week, which includes the seven-year great tribulation and the appearance of the Antichrist. Dispensationalists argue that Daniel's vision appears to be dealing primarily with the events regarding the nation of Israel, not the Gentiles. Other interpreters have thought that no such gap is implied by Daniel's words.

There are many difficulties in deciding between these interpretations, which also involve questions of the proper approach to interpreting biblical prophecy. In all of this it is crucial not to miss Daniel's message for his audience, namely, that God has allotted the amount of time for these events, and therefore his people should trust and endure.

9:24 Gabriel's message was that Daniel's requests for a transformation in the state of his **people** and city would be answered. The very year of Daniel's request (cf. v. 1 with 2 Chron. 36:23; Ezra 1:2–4) would be the initial end of the desolations of Jerusalem, for Cyrus fulfilled this when he allowed God's people to return home. But Gabriel surpasses that event and explains when the ultimate desolations of Jerusalem would be over. The **transgression, sin,** and **iniquity** of Israel that had led to their abandonment by God (Dan. 9:7) would ultimately be atoned for. God would bring **everlasting righteousness,** making his people into a holy nation. Because of the past neglect of the words of the prophets by his people (v. 6), the Lord would **seal** their words as an ancient document writer might seal a letter. God would stamp the words of the prophets as authentic expressions of his mind through their fulfillment. **To anoint a most holy place** might refer to the sanctuary in Jerusalem and its reconsecration by Judas Maccabeus in 164 B.C., or to the "anointing" of the heavenly "most holy place" by Christ when he died (cf. Heb. 9:11–14, 23–24); some even take it as the anointing of a future temple, according to their reading of Ezekiel 40–48. The Lord was committed to bring in the promised new covenant of Jer. 31:31–33. However, this promised new covenant would not arrive at the end of the 70 years of the exile. That period of judgment was a small part of a larger plan of God, which would take **seventy weeks** (or "sevens," ESV footnote) rather than 70 years to work itself out.

9:25–26 The promised restoration of God's people and sanctuary would come in three stages. (See note on vv. 24–27 for various views of the actual dates.) The first **seven** sevens would run from the issuing of the decree to restore and rebuild Jerusalem to the time when that rebuilding was complete (perhaps 458–409 B.C., or 445–396). This period of restoration, along with the

a troubled time. 26 And after the sixty-two weeks, an anointed one shall [u]be cut off and
shall have nothing. And the people of the prince who is to come [v]shall destroy the city
and the sanctuary. [w]Its[1] end shall come with a flood, [x]and to the end there shall be war.
[y]Desolations are decreed. 27 And he shall make a strong covenant with many for one
week,[2] and for half of the week he shall put an end to sacrifice and offering. [z]And on
the wing of abominations shall come one who makes desolate, until [a]the decreed end
is poured out on the desolator."

[1] Or *His* [2] Or *seven*; twice in this verse

26 [u]Isa. 53:8; [Mark 9:12; Luke 24:26] [v][Matt. 24:2; Mark 13:2; Luke 19:43, 44] [w]Nah. 1:8; [ch. 11:10, 22, 26, 40] [x]Matt. 24:6, 14 [y]Ver. 18; See ver. 27
27 [z]Matt. 24:15; Mark 13:14; [Luke 21:20] [a]Isa. 10:23

subsequent **sixty-two** sevens after the city had been rebuilt, would be a time of trouble. The messianic ruler would make his appearance at the end of these 69 sevens. Even the appearing of this **anointed one, a prince**, would not immediately usher in the peace and righteousness that Jeremiah anticipated. Instead, the anointed one (Hb. *mashiakh*, from which "Messiah" is derived) would himself **be cut off** (v. 26), leaving him with **nothing**, surely a reference to the crucifixion of Christ. After the cutting off of the anointed one, **the people of the prince** (Hb. *nagid*) **who is to come** would destroy Jerusalem and its sanctuary. Many commentators understand this "coming prince" as a reference to the Roman general Titus, whose army destroyed Jerusalem in A.D. 70, or as a reference to a future antichrist. Other interpreters understand this prince to be the same "anointed prince" (Hb. *mashiakh nagid*) anticipated in v. 25. This person is addressed as "anointed one," where the focus is on his priestly work of offering himself as a sacrifice, and as a "ruler" whose people fail to submit to his rule. The principal cause of the destruction of the city and temple of Jerusalem in A.D. 70 was the transgression of God's people in rejecting the Messiah that God had sent to them (Luke 19:41–44).

9:27 he shall put an end to sacrifice and offering. On one interpretation, this refers to Christ's atonement. With the death of Jesus on the cross, the atoning sacrifices of the OT were abolished (Heb. 10:1–9). His death brought those whom God had chosen into the new covenant relationship with the Lord. On another interpretation, if "the prince who is to come" (Dan. 9:26) is not the Messiah but an opponent of God's people, then "he shall put an end to sacrifice and offering" means he will destroy the temple, and the prediction refers to the destruction of Jerusalem. The final part of v. 27 is extremely difficult to translate. Literally, it reads, "In the middle of that seven, he will put an end to sacrifice and offering, and on account of the extremity [or "wing"] of abominations that cause desolation, until the end that has been decreed, it will be poured out unto desolation." On the connection of "abominations" and "makes desolate," see note on 11:31–32. Yet a third interpretation comes from dispensational scholars, who have argued that 9:27 will be fulfilled at the end of the church age, during the great tribulation. The argument in support of this position is as follows: If the first 69 weeks end with the death of Jesus, and if he comes back after the "seventieth week" to punish the **one who makes desolate**, then there must be a gap or period of time between these weeks (namely, the entire church age). Often this gap is explained as the time when God is dealing with the church and not specifically Israel, and thus it is not part of the "seventy sevens." In the climactic seventieth week,

The 70 Weeks of Daniel 9

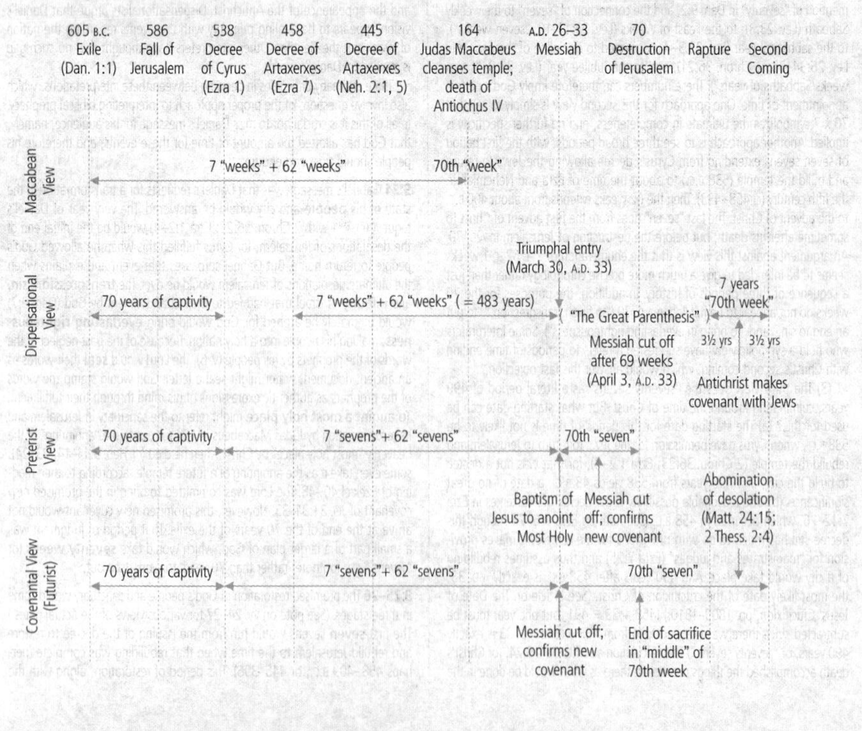

Daniel's Terrifying Vision of a Man

10 [b]In the third year of Cyrus king of Persia a word was revealed to Daniel, [c]who was
named Belteshazzar. And [d]the word was true, and it was a great conflict.[1] And [e]he
understood the word and [e]had understanding of the vision.
2 In those days I, Daniel, was mourning for [f]three weeks. **3** I ate no delicacies, no meat
or wine entered my mouth, nor did I [g]anoint myself at all, for [f]the full three weeks. **4** On
the twenty-fourth day of the first month, as I was standing [h]on the bank of the great
river ([i]that is, the Tigris) **5** [j]I lifted up my eyes and looked, and behold, [k]a man clothed in
linen, [l]with a belt of fine [m]gold from Uphaz around his waist. **6** His body was like [n]beryl,
his face [o]like the appearance of lightning, [p]his eyes like flaming torches, his arms and
[q]legs like the gleam of burnished bronze, and [q]the sound of his words like the sound of
a multitude. **7** [r]And I, Daniel, alone saw the vision, for the men who were with me did not
see the vision, but a great trembling fell upon them, and they fled to hide themselves.
8 So I was left alone and saw this great vision, and [s]no strength was left in me. My radiant
appearance was fearfully changed,[2] [t]and I retained no strength. **9** Then I heard the sound
of his words, [u]and as I heard the sound of his words, I fell on my face in deep sleep [u]with
my face to the ground.
10 And behold, [v]a hand touched me and set me trembling on my hands and knees. **11** And
he said to me, "O Daniel, [w]man greatly loved, [x]understand the words that I speak to you,
and [y]stand upright, for [z]now I have been sent to you." And when he had spoken this
word to me, I stood up trembling. **12** Then he said to me, [a]"Fear not, Daniel, for from the
first day that you [b]set your heart to understand and [b]humbled yourself before your God,
[c]your words have been heard, [d]and I have come because of your words. **13** [e]The prince of
the kingdom of Persia withstood me [f]twenty-one days, but [g]Michael, one of the chief
princes, came to help me, for I was left there with the kings of Persia, **14** [d]and came to
make you understand what is to happen to your people [h]in the latter days. For [i]the vision
is for days yet to come."
15 When he had spoken to me according to these words, [j]I turned my face toward the

[1] *Or and it was about a great conflict* [2] Hebrew *My splendor was changed to ruin*

Chapter 10
1 [b][ch. 1:21]; See ch. 6:28 [c]See ch. 1:7 [d][ch. 8:26] [e]See ch. 1:17
2 [f][ver. 13]
3 [g][Amos 6:6; Matt. 6:17] [f][See ver. 2 above]
4 [h][ch. 12:5] [i]Gen. 2:14
5 [j][Josh. 5:13] [k]Ezek. 9:2 [l][Rev. 1:13; 15:6] [m]Jer. 10:9
6 [n][Ezek. 1:16; 10:9] [o]Ezek. 1:14; Matt. 28:3 [p]Rev. 1:14 [q]Rev. 1:15
7 [r][Acts 9:7]
8 [s][ch. 7:28] [t]ver. 16
9 [u]ch. 8:18
10 [v]See Ezek. 2:9
11 [w]ver. 19; ch. 9:23 [x]See ch. 1:17 [y]Ezek. 2:1 [z][Heb. 1:14]
12 [a]ver. 19; [Judg. 6:23; Rev. 1:17] [b][ch. 9:3] [c][Acts 10:4] [d][ch. 9:23]
13 [e]ver. 20 [f][ver. 2, 3] [g]ver. 21; ch. 12:1; Jude 9; Rev. 12:7
14 [d][See ver. 12 above] [h]ch. 2:28 [i]ch. 8:26; [Hab. 2:3]
15 [j]ver. 9; ch. 8:18

the ruler (taken to be the "Antichrist") makes **a strong covenant** ("treaty or alliance") **with many** (i.e., the Jewish people) for three and a half years and then puts "an end to sacrifice and offering" that he had allowed to be offered in a rebuilt temple (cf. Isa. 66:6; Ezekiel 40–44; 47; Rev. 3:12; 11:1–2). The cutting off of the sacrifices will then usher in the second half of the "great tribulation" (by this reading of Rev. 7:14; cf. Matt. 24:21) because it will be an intense time of persecution. The final part of Dan. 9:27 envisages a climactic abomination that causes the devastating final judgment decreed for the Antichrist (the one who makes desolate). Other interpreters do not see such a specific prediction in v. 27.

10:1–12:13 *Daniel's Vision of the Final Conflict.* Conflicts on earth reflect conflicts in the heavens, and this will continue to the end, when God will ultimately triumph.

10:1–11:1 *A Heavenly Messenger Brings News of Heavenly Conflict.* A heavenly visitor overawes Daniel and explains that he has met resistance from other spiritual powers. He arrives to tell Daniel what is to come.

10:1 Chapters 10–12 form a single vision, received **in the third year of Cyrus king of Persia** (536 B.C.). Two years earlier, the first party of Jewish exiles had returned to Jerusalem in response to Cyrus's decree, but they faced severe opposition and by this point had ceased their rebuilding work. During this time of discouragement, Daniel received his **vision** of a **great conflict**, which exposed the ongoing spiritual warfare in the heavenly realm.

10:2–3 As a sign of identification with the trials of his brothers and sisters in Judah, Daniel was in **mourning**, adopting a deliberately ascetic lifestyle for **three weeks**. He went without choice foods such as **meat or wine** and abstained from the lotions that made life more comfortable in a dry, desert climate.

10:5–6 At the end of Daniel's time of fasting, he received a vision of a heavenly being, dressed in **linen, with a belt of fine gold . . . around his waist**. His **body** glowed with inner light, **like beryl**, a flashing gemstone, and his face shone like **lightning** with **eyes** like **torches** and **arms and legs like** polished **bronze**. **The sound of his words** echoed **like** the roar of a crowd. Yet this glorious figure was unable to complete his task without the help of Michael, one of the chief princes (v. 13), so it is unlikely that this is a physical manifestation of God or Christ. More probably, he is one of the angelic attendants of God, who reflect their master's glory (see Ezekiel 1; 10). The revelation of God's glory shining through this mighty creature was overwhelming, crushing Daniel to the ground and sending his companions scurrying for cover.

10:12 The awe-inspiring messenger encouraged Daniel by telling him that he was "greatly loved" by God (v. 11) and that he had been sent to Daniel in answer to his prayers, to give him insight and understanding and encouragement in response to his mourning and meditation over the situation in Jerusalem.

10:13 The angelic messenger was delayed on his journey **twenty-one days** by the **prince of the kingdom of Persia**, an evil angel associated with the Persian Empire and who resists God's purposes. This information showed that the Jews were not simply facing human opposition and enmity at the earthly court of the Persian king but powerful spiritual beings operating in the heavenly realms. Although this spiritual opponent was powerful enough to delay God's messenger for a period of three weeks, all he could do was delay him. When **Michael, one of the chief princes** (angels), came to help him, the angel was finally able to complete his journey and bring the message of encouragement to Daniel. Michael appears to have a special responsibility to care for the nation of Israel (cf. v. 21; 12:1).

10:15–16 On hearing of the magnitude and power of the spiritual forces ranged against God's people in Jerusalem, Daniel was overtaken again by such an overwhelming sense of weakness that he was bowed to the ground, unable even to speak until the angel **touched** him on the **lips**.

ground [k]and was mute. 16 And behold, [l]one in the likeness of the children of man [m]touched
my lips. Then I opened my mouth and spoke. I said to him who stood before me, "O my
lord, by reason of the vision pains have come upon me, and [n]I retain no strength. 17 How
can my lord's servant talk with my lord? For now no strength remains in me, and no
breath is left in me."
18 Again [l]one having the appearance of a man [m]touched me and strengthened me. 19 And
he said, [o]"O man greatly loved, [p]fear not, peace be with you; be strong and of good courage." And as he spoke to me, I was strengthened and said, "Let my lord speak, for you
have strengthened me." 20 Then he said, "Do you know why I have come to you? But now
I will return to fight against the [q]prince of Persia; and when I go out, behold, the prince
of [r]Greece will come. 21 But I will tell you [s]what is inscribed in the book of truth: there is
none who contends by my side against these except [t]Michael, your prince.

The Kings of the South and the North

11 "And as for me, [u]in the first year of [u]Darius the Mede, I stood up to confirm and
strengthen him.
2 "And now I will show you [v]the truth. Behold, three more kings shall arise in Persia, and
a fourth shall be far richer than all of them. And when he has become strong through his
riches, he shall stir up all against the kingdom of Greece. 3 Then [w]a mighty king shall arise,
who shall rule with great dominion and [x]do as he wills. 4 And as soon as he has arisen, [y]his
kingdom shall be broken and divided [y]toward the [z]four winds of heaven, but [a]not to his
posterity, nor according to the authority with which he ruled, for his kingdom shall be
plucked up and go to others besides these.
5 "Then the king of the south shall be strong, but one of his princes shall be stronger
than he [b]and shall rule, and his authority shall be a great authority. 6 After some years [c]they

15 [k]Ps. 39:2, 9
16 [l]See ch. 8:15 [m]Isa. 6:7 [n]ver. 8
18 [l][See ver. 16 above] [m][See ver. 16 above]
19 [o]ver. 11; ch. 9:23 [p]See ver. 12
20 [q]ver. 13 [r]ch. 8:21
21 [s]ch. 12:1, 4; [Ex. 32:32] [t]See ver. 13

Chapter 11

1 [u]ch. 9:1
2 [v]ch. 10:21
3 [w][ch. 7:6; 8:5, 21] [x]ver. 16, 36; [ch. 8:4]
4 [y][ch. 8:8, 22] [z]See ch. 7:2 [a]Ps. 109:13
5 [b][ch. 7:6]
6 [c][ver. 23]

10:20 The angel declared that he would return to the fray against the **prince of Persia**, and after that against the **prince of Greece**, the spiritual counterpart of the next world power to arise. This information is in preparation for the revelations in ch. 11.

10:21 The **book of truth** most likely refers to the plan that God has for Israel and the world. The conflict against satanic forces continues to this day, though the human adversary constantly changes. Time and again the people of God are bowed to the ground, yet they are not destroyed because God continues to support and sustain them through the strengthening ministry of his own angels (cf. Heb. 1:14).

11:1 Mention of **the first year of Darius the Mede** (539 B.C.) is significant since it was the year when the decree allowing the Jews to return was issued. **I stood up to confirm and strengthen him**. It appears that the interpreting angel had some role in these events.

11:2–45 *A Detailed Vision of Future Earthly Conflicts among Nations.* This passage gives a selective yet detailed overview of the flow of history from the time of Daniel in the late sixth century B.C. until the end of the world, the final climactic conflict and victory of God. Some scholars regard this as a "prophecy after the fact" that was actually written later than the events in the mid-second century B.C. because of the detail and accuracy of its predictions, but Isa. 44:6–7 asserts the Lord's ability and purpose to declare ahead of time what would happen in order to demonstrate his power and sovereignty. (See Introduction: Date.) Such an assurance of God's sovereign control of history would have been profoundly relevant for Daniel's day. Judah was about to be restored from exile (see note on Dan. 11:1), and yet it was not really free. It would be subject to the Persians, and then to Alexander's Greeks; after that it would be caught in the middle between powerful heirs of Alexander's empire, the Seleucids and the Ptolemies (see map, p. 1611). Pious Jews would readily fall into bewilderment: how do these circumstances display God's concern for his people, and how will God ever use his now-insignificant people to bring blessing to the whole world? The vision is therefore reassurance for the faithful.

11:2 Three more kings would **arise in Persia** after Cyrus (Cambyses [530–522 B.C.], Smerdis [522], and Darius I Hystaspes [522–486]), and then a **fourth**, who would be **richer** and more powerful than the others and would enter into conflict with **Greece**. This fourth king was Xerxes I (486–464 B.C.), who invaded Greece, only to be defeated at the Battle of Salamis (480).

11:3 Several other lesser Persian kings are then passed over without mention as the prophecy moves on to the next significant ruler, the **mighty king** who would bring down the Persian Empire and rule a vast realm (a **great dominion**), Alexander the Great (336–323 B.C.).

11:4 as soon as he has arisen, his kingdom shall be broken and divided toward the four winds of heaven. Alexander the Great died in 323 B.C., shortly after establishing an enormous empire that was eventually divided among his four generals—none of whom were **his posterity**, as the prophecy says.

11:5–20 This section contains prophecies concerning the kings of Egypt and Syria. Two of the four kingdoms that came from Alexander's empire were the kingdom of the Ptolemies (based in Egypt) and the kingdom of the Seleucids, (based in Syria and Babylonia). This chapter deals only with these two kingdoms since they will have the most influence on Israel. Many of the specific predictions of this chapter were fulfilled in striking detail.

11:5 Ptolemy I Soter (323–285 B.C., **king of the south**) was a very capable general under Alexander who became ruler of Egypt. About the same time, Seleucus I Nicator (king of the north) started out as a lesser general under Alexander and was given Babylon to rule, but one of the other generals, Antigonus I Monophthalmus, took over Babylon and caused Seleucus to flee (c. 316 B.C.). He fled south to Ptolemy I Soter in Egypt to serve under him. Thus for a short time he became **one of his princes**. Then Antigonus was defeated at Gaza in 312 B.C., and Seleucus returned to Babylon to retake his former **authority**. He increased significantly in power and took over the areas of Babylon, Syria, and Media, so that he was **stronger than** Ptolemy I Soter.

11:6 There was constant conflict between the Ptolemaic (Egyptian) and Seleucid (Syrian) kingdoms, but around 250 B.C. Ptolemy II Philadelphus (285–246, "the king of the south") attempted to make peace with Antiochus II Theos (261–246, "the king of the north") by sending his daughter Berenice to marry him, as Daniel had predicted: **the daughter of the king of the south shall come to the king of the north to make an agreement**. Antiochus II then planned to divorce his first wife, Laodice, and disinherit her sons so that he could marry Berenice and have a child who would then rule over the Seleucid kingdom. But Laodice had Antiochus II and Berenice poisoned, fulfilling the words **she shall not retain the strength of her arm** and **he and his arm shall not endure**. In the same year, Berenice's father (**he who fathered her**) died in Egypt.

The Empires of Daniel's Visions: The Ptolemies and the Seleucids (Early)

c. 323–198 B.C.

The two most powerful successors to Alexander, Ptolemy and Seleucus, continued to expand their domains into territory claimed by other generals of Alexander, and they repeatedly clashed with each other over land along the eastern coast of the Mediterranean Sea, including the land later called Palestine.

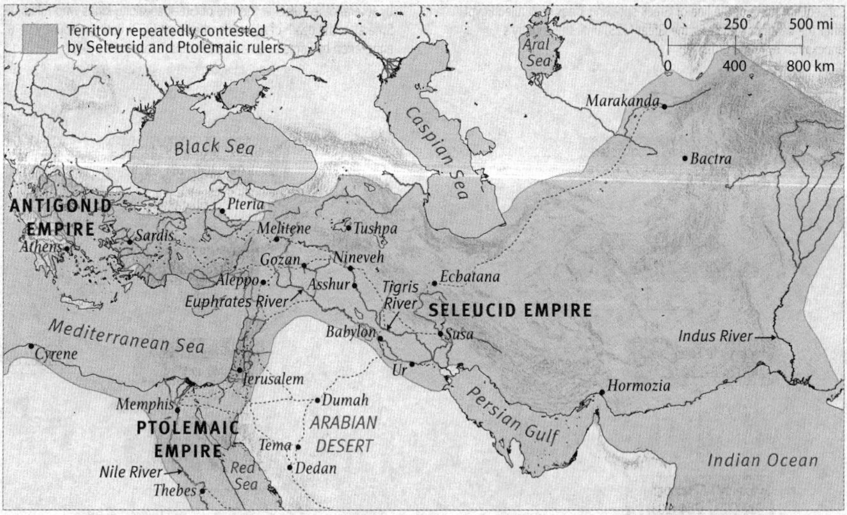

The Empires of Daniel's Visions: The Ptolemies and the Seleucids (Late)

c. 198–133 B.C.

By the second century B.C., the Seleucid Empire was losing its grip on much of its territory, and the Roman Empire was rapidly expanding throughout the Mediterranean world. In an attempt to unite his empire and shore up his defenses against these pressures, Antiochus IV Epiphanes imposed a strict policy of Hellenization over his domain, which now included the land of Israel. His policy proved too abhorrent for many Jews, including the Maccabean (also called Hasmonean) family, and in 167 B.C. they led a revolt that established a new, independent kingdom of Israel.

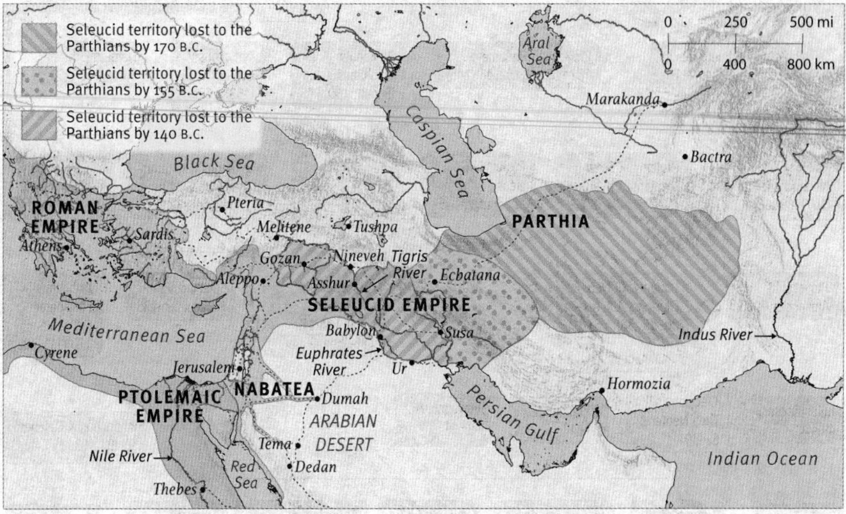

Rulers of Syria, Judea, and Egypt after Alexander the Great

The **Ptolemaic** Dynasty (323–30 B.C.): The name "Ptolemaic" is derived from the name of Ptolemy I Soter (367/66–283 B.C.), one of Alexander the Great's three main succeeding generals, and was borne by all subsequent rulers of the line of Greek-speaking kings who ruled Egypt after the death of Alexander the Great (323) until the country's annexation by Rome (30).

The **Seleucid** Dynasty (312 [305]–80 [66] B.C.): The name "Seleucid" is derived from the name of Seleucus I Nicator (358–281 B.C.), one of Alexander the Great's three main succeeding generals, and was borne by several other rulers in this line of Greek-speaking kings who ruled Syria after the death of Alexander the Great (323) until the country's annexation by Rome as a result of Pompey's conquests (63).

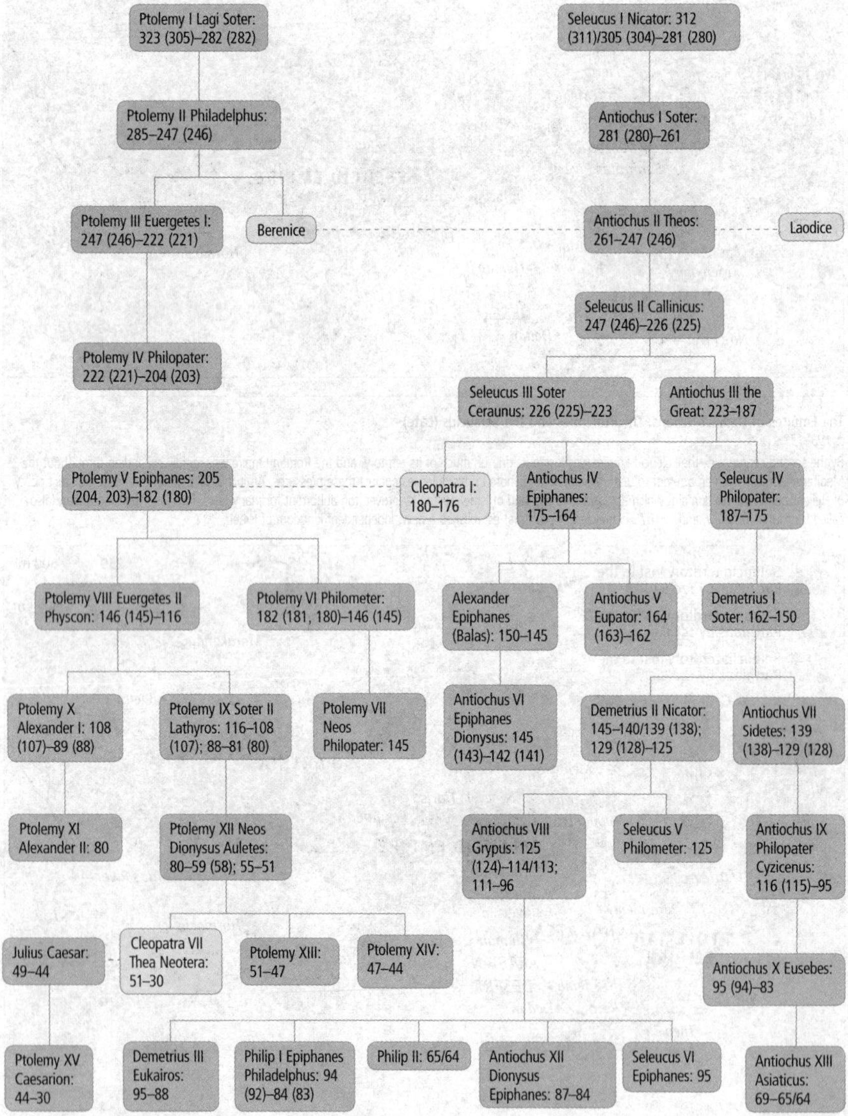

Rulers Foretold in Daniel 11

In the absence of legitimate heirs following the death of Alexander the Great in 323 B.C. (cf. *1 Macc.* 1:5–9), four of his generals divided the conquered territory of his empire into fourths (which then included most of the known world throughout Europe and Asia Minor; see notes on Dan. 7:6; 8:8; 8:20–22; 11:4). By 277 B.C., three Hellenistic kingdoms had stabilized out of the four divisions: (1) the Antigonid dynasty in Macedonia (issuing from Alexander's general Antigonus I Monophthalmus, 382–301 B.C., and beginning with his son Demetrius I Poliorcetes in 294/293); (2) the Ptolemaic dynasty in Egypt (issuing from Alexander's general Ptolemy I Soter, 367–283 B.C.); and (3) the Seleucid dynasty in Syria (issuing from Alexander's general Seleucus I Nicator, c. 358–281 B.C.), which included much of Asia Minor from 312 to 64 (see Dan. 11:4–35 and notes there). Though Judea came under control of the Seleucids in 198 B.C., it was initially under Ptolemaic (Egyptian) rule. Each dynasty continued until it eventually became conquered by and absorbed into the emerging Roman Empire.

Geographically, Judea was wedged in the middle of the aggressive struggle between the kings "of the south" (Egyptian Ptolemies) and "of the north" (Syrian Seleucids) spoken of in Daniel 11. God's people received their most degrading attack when the Seleucid ruler Antiochus IV Epiphanes (175–164 B.C.) set up "the abomination that makes desolate" (Dan. 11:31) in the Jerusalem temple. This event precipitated the Maccabean Revolt (c. 167 B.C.) and the reestablishment of Jewish rule in Judea through the Hasmonean dynasty (Mattathias and his sons). Independent Hasmonean rule lasted over a century until Judea was finally conquered by the Roman general Pompey in 63 B.C.

The Edomite Herod the Great, through his marriage to Mariamne I (d. 29 B.C.), Hasmonean daughter of Alexandra and Alexander, claimed to be a "legitimate" Jewish heir to the Hasmonean throne. The Roman Senate declared Herod the Great "King of the Jews" in 40 B.C., giving him vassal rulership over Palestine (comprised of the provinces Judea and Galilee). His rule did not begin until 37 B.C., however, when he was able to recapture Jerusalem from Antigonus and the Parthians through the help of Roman forces, to whom he had fled for help three years earlier. (See The Herodian Dynasty, pp. 1790–1791.)

Rulers of Judea/Palestine after the Maccabean Revolt

The **Hasmonean** (Maccabean) Dynasty (168–63 [37] B.C.): The name "Hasmonean" is now generally thought to derive from a place name, either Heshmon or Hashmonah. However, Josephus says that the name of Hashman (Gk. *Asamōnaios*; see Josephus, *Jewish Antiquities* 12.265) belonged to the great-grandfather of Mattathias, suggesting that this is the true derivation of "Hasmonean." Mattathias was the father of five sons who were (in order): John (surnamed Gaddi), Simon (called Thassi), Judas (called Maccabeus), Eleazar (called Avaran), and Jonathan (called Apphus) (see *1 Macc.* 2:1–5). Mattathias initiated the Maccabean Revolt in c. 167 B.C.

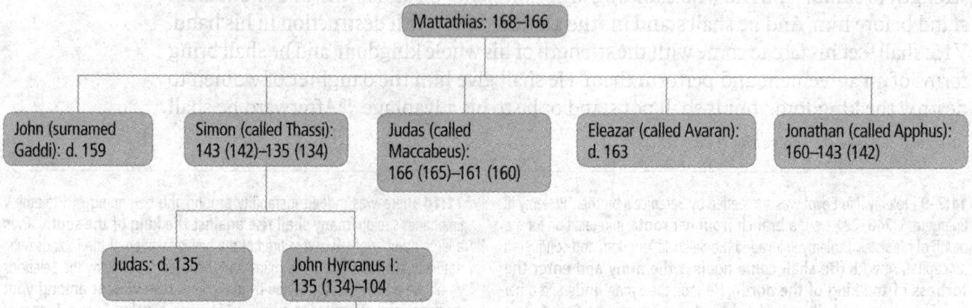

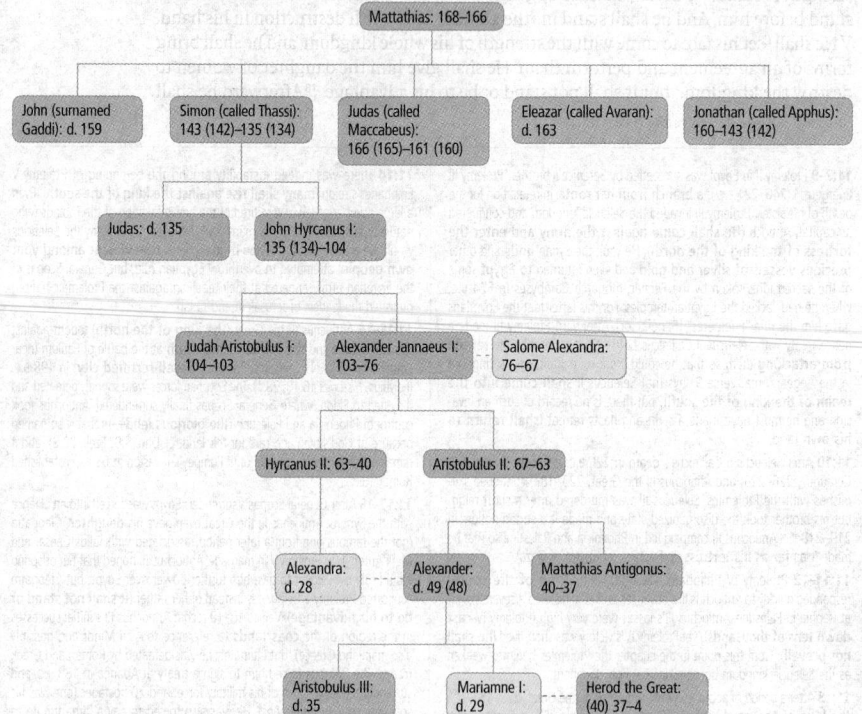

Only the names of the more important rulers have been included on these pages. All the dates are B.C. and indicate years of reign unless otherwise noted. The dates marking the reign of certain rulers are disputed; where possible, alternative beginning or ending regnal dates are indicated in parentheses. A darker background signifies a male, and a lighter background a female; a dotted line signifies a marriage; "d." indicates year of death.

shall make an alliance, and the daughter of the king of the south shall come to the king
of the north to make an agreement. But she shall not retain the strength of her arm, and
he and his arm shall not endure, but she shall be given up, and her attendants, he who
fathered her, and he who supported[1] her in those times.
7 "And from a branch from her roots one shall arise in his place. He shall come against
the army and enter the [d]fortress of the king of the north, and he shall deal with them and
shall prevail. 8 He shall also carry off to Egypt their gods with their metal images and their
precious [e]vessels of silver and gold, and for some years he shall refrain from attacking the
king of the north. 9 Then the latter shall come into the realm of the king of the south but
shall return to his own land.
10 "His sons shall wage war and assemble a multitude of great forces, which shall keep
coming [f]and overflow and pass through, and again shall carry the war as far as his [d]for-
tress. 11 Then the king of the south, [g]moved with rage, shall come out and fight against
the king of the north. [h]And he shall raise a great multitude, but it shall be given into his
hand. 12 And when the multitude is taken away, his heart shall be exalted, and he shall cast
down tens of thousands, but he shall not prevail. 13 For the king of the north shall again
[i]raise a multitude, greater than the first. And [j]after some years[2] he shall come on with a
great army and abundant supplies.
14 "In those times many shall rise against the king of the south, and the violent among
your own people shall lift themselves up in order to fulfill the vision, but [k]they shall fail.
15 Then the king of the north shall come and [l]throw up siegeworks and take a well-fortified
city. And the forces of the south shall not stand, or even his best troops, for there shall be no
strength to stand. 16 But he who comes against him shall [m]do as he wills, and [n]none shall
stand before him. And he shall stand in [o]the glorious land, with destruction in his hand.
17 He shall [p]set his face to come with the strength of his whole kingdom, and he shall bring
terms of an agreement and perform them. He shall give him the daughter of women to
destroy the kingdom,[3] but it shall not stand or be to his advantage. 18 Afterward he shall

[1] Or *obtained* [2] Hebrew *at the end of the times* [3] Hebrew *her*, or *it*

7 [d][ver. 10, 19, 38, 39]
8 [e][ver. 43]
10 [f]ver. 26, 40; Isa. 8:8 [d][See ver. 7 above]
11 [g]ch. 8:7 [h]ver. 13
13 [i]ver. 11 [j][ch. 4:16]
14 [k]ver. 19, 33, 34
15 [l]See Ezek. 4:2
16 [m]ver. 3, 36 [n][Josh. 10:8] [o]ver. 41; See ch. 8:9
17 [p]See Jer. 42:15

11:7–9 Ptolemy II in Egypt was succeeded by Berenice's brother, Ptolemy III Euergetes I (246–221 B.C.), **a branch from her roots**. In retaliation for the death of his sister, Ptolemy III invaded the Seleucid kingdom and conquered its capital, Antioch (**He shall come against the army and enter the fortress of the king of the north**). He took the Syrian **gods** and other **precious vessels of silver and gold** and even returned **to Egypt** some of the sacred idols taken by the Persian monarch Cambyses in 524 B.C. when he had sacked the Egyptian temples. For this latter feat the Egyptians gave him the title "Euergetes" [Benefactor]. Afterward Ptolemy III made a peace treaty with Seleucus II Callinicus (246–226 B.C.) and he did **refrain from attacking** them so that he could work on expanding his kingdom in the Aegean area. Verse 9 says that Seleucus II **shall come into the realm of the king of the south**, but there is no record of such an invasion and he must have made a swift and hasty retreat (**shall return to his own land**).

11:10 After Seleucus II Callinicus's death in 226 B.C. his **sons** (Seleucus III Ceraunus, 226–223; and Antiochus III the Great, 223–187) continued skirmishes with the Ptolemies. Seleucus III was murdered after a short reign, but his brother took the disorganized state and made it a strong nation. In 219–218 B.C. Antiochus III campaigned in Phoenicia and Palestine so that he made it **as far as his fortress** (in Raphia, southwest of Gaza).

11:11–12 Ptolemy IV Philopator (221–204 B.C., **king of the south**) responded quickly to Antiochus III's advances and administered a severe defeat at Raphia in Palestine. Antiochus III's losses were very high (Ptolemy IV **cast down tens of thousands**), yet Ptolemy IV's victory was short-lived (**he shall not prevail**). From this point in the chapter the Ptolemies begin to weaken as the Seleucid kingdom becomes increasingly dominant.

11:13 After a period of about 15 years, Antiochus III (the Great, 223–187 B.C., **the king of the north**) invaded Phoenicia and Syria with a **great army**. Ptolemy IV had just died (203 B.C.), and Antiochus III intended to use the instability around the young king (Ptolemy V Epiphanes [203–180]) to his advantage. It worked, at least initially, and by 201 B.C. the fortress of Gaza had been recaptured, possibly with the help of Philip V of Macedonia.

11:14 There was indeed instability around the beginning of Ptolemy V Epiphanes's reign (**many shall rise against the king of the south**). Even a large number of Jews were tired of the heavy taxation of the Tobiads (who naturally favored Egypt), and many Jews believed that rule by the Seleucids would be preferable. A rebellion by many Jews (**the violent among your own people**) attempted to overthrow Egyptian rule, but General Scopas of the Egyptian army, angered at their rebellion against the Ptolemaic nation, punished the leaders of Jerusalem and Judah.

11:15–16 Antiochus III the Great (**the king of the north**) fought against General Scopas and **the forces of the south** at the battle of Panium (near Paneas, which is NT Caesarea Philippi), **a well-fortified city**, in 198 B.C. (Polybius, *Histories* 16.18; 28.1). The Egyptian forces were soundly defeated and they fled to Sidon, where General Scopas finally surrendered. Antiochus took control of Phoenicia and Palestine (**the glorious land**—probably so named because of God's plan and care for this land, cf. Dan. 8:9; Ezek. 20:6), and it remained under Syrian control until Pompey's invasion in 63 B.C. established Roman rule.

11:17–19 After General Scopas's surrender, Egypt was forced into an alliance with the Syrians. Antiochus III the Great even gave his **daughter**, Cleopatra (not the famous one from a later period, associated with Julius Caesar and Mark Antony), to Ptolemy V in marriage. Antiochus III hoped that her offspring would rule over Egypt to give him further power over Egypt, but Cleopatra supported Ptolemy V Epiphanes instead of her father (**it shall not stand or be to his advantage**). Verses 18–19 record Antiochus III's initial successes in the region of the **coastlands** (a reference to Asia Minor and possibly also mainland Greece), but ultimately he was defeated by Roman and Greek troops. The Romans forced him to sign a treaty at Apanea in 188 B.C. and surrender territory, much of his military force, and 20 hostages (one was his son Antiochus IV Epiphanes). He was also forced to pay a large tribute to Rome. He returned home and was killed by an angry mob (**he shall stumble and fall**) while he was trying to pillage a temple of Zeus in Elymais to pay for the heavy tribute to Rome.

11:20 Antiochus III the Great's son Seleucus IV Philopater (187–175 B.C.) suc-

18 [q][Hos. 12:14]
19 [r][ver. 7, 10, 38, 39] [s]Jer. 46:6 [t]Job 20:8; Ps. 37:36; Ezek. 26:21
20 [u][Isa. 60:17; Zech. 9:8]
21 [v]ver. 24 [w][ver. 34]
22 [x][ver. 10; Jer. 46:7]
24 [y]ver. 21 [z][Gen. 27:28, 39]
25 [a][ch. 8:9]
26 [b]ver. 10, 40
27 [c][ver. 35]
30 [d]Gen. 10:4; Num. 24:24 [e]See ver. 28
31 [f][ch. 12:11]

turn his face to the coastlands and shall capture many of them, but a commander shall
put an end to his insolence. Indeed,[1] he [q]shall turn his insolence back upon him. 19 Then
he shall turn his face back toward the [r]fortresses of his own land, but he shall [s]stumble
and fall, [t]and shall not be found.
20 "Then shall arise in his place one who shall send an [u]exactor of tribute for the glory of
the kingdom. But within a few days he shall be broken, neither in anger nor in battle. 21 In
his place shall arise a contemptible person to whom royal majesty has not been given. [v]He
shall come in without warning and obtain the kingdom [w]by flatteries. 22 Armies shall be
[x]utterly swept away before him and broken, even the prince of the covenant. 23 And from
the time that an alliance is made with him he shall act deceitfully, and he shall become
strong with a small people. 24 [y]Without warning he shall come into [z]the richest parts[2] of
the province, and he shall do what neither his fathers nor his fathers' fathers have done,
scattering among them plunder, spoil, and goods. He shall devise plans against strongholds,
but only for a time. 25 And he shall stir up his power and his heart against [a]the king of the
south with a great army. And the king of the south shall wage war with an exceedingly
great and mighty army, but he shall not stand, for plots shall be devised against him. 26 Even
those who eat his food shall break him. His army shall be [b]swept away, and many shall fall
down slain. 27 And as for the two kings, their hearts shall be bent on doing evil. They shall
speak lies at the same table, but to no avail, for [c]the end is yet to be at the time appointed.
28 And he shall return to his land with great wealth, but his heart shall be set against the
holy covenant. And he shall work his will and return to his own land.
29 "At the time appointed he shall return and come into the south, but it shall not be
this time as it was before. 30 For ships of [d]Kittim shall come against him, and he shall be
afraid and withdraw, and shall turn back and [e]be enraged and [e]take action against the holy
covenant. He shall turn back and pay attention to those who forsake the holy covenant.
31 Forces from him shall appear and [f]profane the temple and fortress, and shall take away

[1] The meaning of the Hebrew is uncertain [2] Or *among the richest men*

ceeded him and sent a "tax collector" (or an **exactor of tribute**), Heliodorus, to collect the money necessary to pay Rome their yearly tribute of 1,000 talents. He even tried to plunder the temple in Jerusalem, but decided against it after being terrified by a dream (cf. *2 Macc.* 3:7–40). Seleucus IV was not killed **in anger** (i.e., by an angry mob like his father), or **in battle**, but was poisoned by his own tax collector, Heliodorus.

11:21–23 In his place shall arise a contemptible person, Antiochus IV Epiphanes (reigned 175–164 B.C.), who is also the "little horn" of ch. 8 (8:9–12, 23–25). He took the name Antiochus "Epiphanes" ("Manifest One"; see note on 8:25), but others called him "Epimanes" ("madman"). Seleucus IV Philopater's son, Demetrius I Soter, was the rightful heir to the throne, but because he was imprisoned in Rome, Antiochus IV Epiphanes took the throne, even though **royal majesty** had **not been given** to him. He paid off important people for supporting him, which is what the phrase to **obtain the kingdom by flatteries** refers to. Ptolemy VI Philometer (181–145 B.C.) of Egypt came against Antiochus IV but was defeated and held as a hostage. Later Ptolemy VI (**the prince of the covenant**) made an **alliance** (a covenant) with Antiochus IV to regain his throne because his brother (Ptolemy VIII Euergetes II Physcon) had taken it while he was imprisoned in Syria. This worked, and he received his throne back, but later he broke this covenant and joined with his brother Ptolemy VIII, to force Antiochus IV out of Pelusium, one of Egypt's fortress cities.

11:24 Without warning, Antiochus IV Epiphanes retaliated and plundered some of **the richest parts of** Egypt's territory (i.e., even Judea). He appeared to divide plunder among his soldiers (cf. Livy, *Roman History* 41.20; *1 Macc.* 3:30; Polybius, *Histories* 26.1), but his grand plans against Egypt's **strongholds** lasted **only for a time** (i.e., a time set by God).

11:25–27 These verses appear to refer to the events of Antiochus IV Epiphanes's first battle with Egypt (cf. v. 22) and explain in more detail why Ptolemy VI Philometer was defeated. Ptolemy VI's own trusted counselors (**those who eat his food**) encouraged him to go against Antiochus IV (his uncle), and he was defeated. Then the **two kings**, Antiochus IV and Ptolemy VI (now the former's prisoner), made a covenant to regain control of Egypt from Ptolemy VI's brother, Ptolemy VIII, but neither king intended to keep the covenant (**they shall speak lies** to each other)—merely intending to use each other for their own advantage. While their alliance had initial success capturing Memphis, it failed to capture all of Egypt, and Ptolemy VIII continued to rule in Alexandria. Later the two brothers, Ptolemy VI and Ptolemy VIII, joined forces and ruled together over all of Egypt.

11:28 Antiochus IV Epiphanes returned **to his land** after plundering Egypt in 169 B.C., and on his way home stopped in Palestine and found an insurrection going on (cf. *1 Macc.* 1:16–28; *2 Macc.* 5:1–11). He dealt ruthlessly with the Jews (**his heart shall be set against the holy covenant**), killing eighty thousand men, women, and children (*2 Macc.* 5:12–14) and plundering the temple (*2 Macc.* 5:15–21). The Jews were infuriated at the brutality of this ruler and began a full-fledged revolt (generally called the Maccabean Revolt; see map, p. 1616).

11:29–30 In 168 B.C. (i.e., the **time appointed** by God) Antiochus IV Epiphanes invaded Egypt again, but this time he met with a humiliating defeat. The Romans had joined forces with the Ptolemies, and Antiochus IV was no match for the Roman army and especially the **ships of Kittim** ("Kittim" is the ancient name for Cyprus, but it came to be used for the lands around the Mediterranean Sea in general, and in this case specifically the Romans). Several early historians (cf. Polybius, *Histories* 29.27; Livy, *Roman History* 45) tell the story of the defeat of Antiochus IV, stating that the Roman commander Gaius Popilius Laenas met Antiochus IV outside Alexandria and handed him a letter from the Roman senate telling him to leave Egypt or risk war with Rome. Next he drew a circle around Antiochus IV and told him to decide before he left the circle. Antiochus IV wisely chose to leave Egypt. In 167 B.C. he turned his anger toward Palestine (**and be enraged and take action against the holy covenant**) and sent his chief tax collector, Apollonius, to Jerusalem. Initially Apollonius appeared to come in peace, but on the Sabbath he began killing people and plundering the city (cf. *1 Macc.* 1:30–32; *2 Macc.* 5:25–26). He also rewarded those Jews who supported the Hellenistic policies, like the high priest Menelaus (he will **pay attention to those who forsake the holy covenant**).

11:31–32 Later in 167 B.C., Syrian forces came back to suppress the Jewish religious practices in earnest. They entered the temple (possibly called the

the regular burnt offering. And [g]they shall set up the abomination that makes desolate.
32 He shall seduce with flattery those who violate the covenant, but the people who know
their God shall stand firm and take action. 33 [h]And the wise among the people shall make
many understand, though for some days they shall stumble by sword and flame, by captivity and plunder. 34 When they stumble, they shall receive a little help. And many shall
join themselves to them with flattery, 35 and some of the wise shall stumble, so that they
may be refined, [i]purified, and [j]made white, until [k]the time of the end, [k]for it still awaits
the appointed time.
36 "And the king shall [l]do as he wills. [m]He shall exalt himself and magnify himself above
every god, [n]and shall speak astonishing things against [o]the God of gods. [p]He shall prosper
[q]till the indignation is accomplished; for what is decreed shall be done. 37 He shall pay no
attention to the gods of his fathers, or to the one beloved by women. He shall not pay attention to any other god, for [m]he shall magnify himself above all. 38 He shall honor the god
of fortresses instead of these. A god whom his fathers did not know he shall honor [r]with
gold and silver, with precious stones and costly gifts. 39 He shall deal with the strongest

31 [g]Matt. 24:15; Mark 13:14; [ch. 8:13; 12:11]
33 [h]ch. 12:3, 10
35 [i][Mal. 3:3, 4] [j][Rev. 7:14] [k][ver. 27, 40]
36 [l]ver. 3, 16 [m][ch. 7:25; 2 Thess. 2:4] [n][ch. 7:25; Rev. 13:5, 6] [o]Deut. 10:17 [p][ch. 8:12] [q][Isa. 10:25]; ch. 9:27
37 [m][See ver. 36 above]
38 [r][Joel 3:5]

temple and fortress because it was the religious strength of the people, or else Antiochus IV Epiphanes profaned the temple and a fortress also). They stopped the **regular burnt offering**, and on the fifteenth day of Chislev (December), 167 B.C. (*1 Macc.* 1:59), they set up an altar or idol devoted to Zeus (Jupiter) in the temple (**the abomination that makes desolate**; cf. Dan. 9:27; 12:11) and shortly afterward offered up sacrifices (likely swine) on the altar (*1 Macc.* 1:47; *2 Macc.* 6:4–5). The Greek for this expression (*bdelygma erēmōseōs*, "abomination of desolation") is applied to this action of Antiochus IV (*1 Macc.* 1:54) and is the background for Jesus' prediction of "the abomination of desolation spoken of by the prophet Daniel" (see notes on Matt. 24:15; Mark 13:14). Antiochus IV's **flattery** enticed some of the Jews to turn against the **covenant** (cf. *1 Macc.* 2:18; *2 Macc.* 7:24). But some faithful Jews (those **who know their God**) chose to **stand** strong and die rather than go against God's laws (*1 Macc.* 1:62–63), and many did die. Some also began to organize a revolt (**take action**), probably referring to the priest Mattathias and his five sons who led the Maccabean Revolt and who in 164 B.C. rededicated the temple (*1 Macc.* 4:52).

The Maccabean Kingdom
c. 167–63 B.C.
The Maccabean kingdom of Israel had its beginnings when the priest Mattathias and his family refused to obey the Seleucid rulers' order to sacrifice to the pagan god Zeus at Modein. They led a revolt that initially controlled only the territory of Judea in the vicinity of Jerusalem. Over the next hundred years, however, the Maccabean rulers slowly added portions of territory to the kingdom until it resembled the borders of the territory allotted to the Israelite tribes by Joshua.

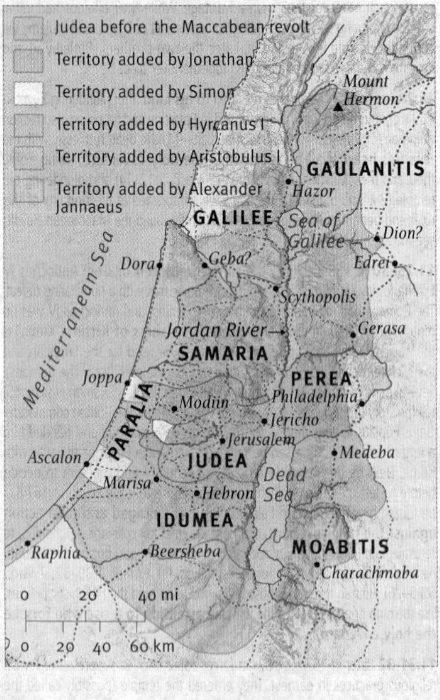

11:33–35 the wise among the people shall make many understand. This likely refers to those who truly fear God and who will encourage others to fight and even die rather than perform abominations before God. This refers primarily to the Maccabean Revolt. In that process many (tens of thousands) would die. In this time of persecution, the nation will **receive a little help**, which probably refers to the small forces that initially rebelled against the Syrians in Modein, 17 miles (27 km) northwest of Jerusalem, led by Mattathias and later his third son Judas Maccabeus (*1 Macc.* 2–4). The rest of Dan. 11:34 probably has in view the **many** who would **join themselves** to the Maccabean rebellion out of necessity to save their lives, though it may more specifically refer to the *Hasidim* who joined with the Maccabeans and killed those who were sympathetic to the Seleucids (cf. *1 Macc.* 2:42–48). **Some of the wise shall stumble** likely describes true believers who would die in this persecution; through this persecution they would be **refined, purified, and made white**. Similarly, church history has shown that the Christian church has flourished under times of intense persecution, which may be what Dan. 11:35b is referring to (**until the time of the end**). But at least it refers to the end of Antiochus IV's persecution, which ended with his death in 164 B.C. while he was on a campaign in Persia.

11:36 Toward the conclusion of the prophecy, the vision seems to shift focus and address a situation that transcends the persecution under Antiochus IV, and thus the remainder of the chapter is often thought to deal with the "Antichrist" (taken by many as the figure in 2 Thess. 2:3–4; Rev. 13:5–8). Though Antiochus IV was powerful, he was able to **do as he wills** only up to a point, since the power of the Romans was far greater than his.

11:37–38 Antiochus IV viewed himself as a god, as his nickname "Epiphanes" ("[god] manifest") and coinage made clear (see note on 8:25). But it is doubtful that he fulfilled the prophecy, **he shall magnify himself above all**. He abandoned **the gods of his fathers**, including Apollo, and showed no regard for the **one beloved by women**, probably the god Adonis or Dionysius. Instead, he worshiped Zeus, a god who embodied military strength, but all these gods were still in the Greek pantheon and thus there is some question as to whether Antiochus IV abandoned "the gods of his fathers." Instead this person will worship **the god of fortresses** (i.e., of military power and might) and will spend lavishly (**gold and silver, with precious stones and costly gifts**) to support this strength.

39[s][Lam. 5:2, 6]
40[t][ver. 27, 35] [u]Zech. 9:14 [v]ver. 10, 26
41[w]ver. 16; See ch. 8:9 [x][Isa. 11:14]
43[y][2 Chr. 12:3] [z]2 Chr. 12:3; Ezek. 30:4, 5; Nah. 3:9

Chapter 12

1[a]See ch. 10:13 [b]Jer. 30:7; Matt. 24:21; Mark 13:19; [Rev. 16:18] [c]Ex. 32:32, 33; [Ezek. 13:9; Luke 10:20; Rev. 20:12]
2[d][Ps. 17:15; John 11:11] [e][Isa. 26:19]; See Ezek. 37:1-10 [f]Matt. 25:46; John 5:28, 29; Acts 24:15; Rev. 20:12, 13
3[g]ch. 11:33 [h]Matt. 13:43 [i][Mal. 2:6]
4[j][ver. 9; ch. 8:26] [k]Isa. 8:16; 29:11; Rev. 5:1; 10:4; 22:10 [l][ver. 13]; See ch. 8:17 [m]Amos 8:12
5[n][ch. 10:4]
6[o]ch. 10:5; Ezek. 9:2 [p]ch. 8:13
7[o][See ver. 6 above] [q]See Gen. 14:22 [r][Rev. 10:6] [s]ch. 7:25 [t][ch. 8:24]
8[u][ch. 8:15]
9[v]ver. 13 [w][ver. 4]

fortresses with the help of a foreign god. Those who acknowledge him he shall load with
honor. He shall make them rulers over many and [s]shall divide the land for a price.[1]
40 [t]"At the time of the end, the king of the south shall attack[2] him, but the king of the
north shall rush upon him [u]like a whirlwind, with chariots and horsemen, and with many
ships. And he shall come into countries and [v]shall overflow and pass through. **41** He shall
come into [w]the glorious land. And tens of thousands shall fall, but these shall be delivered
out of his hand: [x]Edom and [x]Moab and the main part of the [x]Ammonites. **42** He shall stretch
out his hand against the countries, and the land of Egypt shall not escape. **43** He shall
become ruler of the treasures of gold and of silver, and all the precious things of Egypt,
and the [y]Libyans and the [z]Cushites shall follow in his train. **44** But news from the east and
the north shall alarm him, and he shall go out with great fury to destroy and devote many
to destruction. **45** And he shall pitch his palatial tents between the sea and the glorious holy
mountain. Yet he shall come to his end, with none to help him.

The Time of the End

12 "At that time shall arise [a]Michael, the great prince who has charge of your people.
And [b]there shall be a time of trouble, such as never has been since there was a nation
till that time. But at that time your people shall be delivered, [c]everyone whose name shall
be found written in the book. **2** And many of those who [d]sleep in [e]the dust of the earth
shall [e]awake, [f]some to everlasting life, and [f]some to shame and everlasting contempt.
3 [g]And those who are wise [h]shall shine like the brightness of the sky above;[3] and [i]those
who turn many to righteousness, like the stars forever and ever. **4** But you, Daniel, [j]shut
up the words and [k]seal the book, until [l]the time of the end. [m]Many shall run to and fro,
and knowledge shall increase."
5 Then I, Daniel, looked, and behold, two others stood, one on [n]this bank of the stream
and one on that bank of the stream. **6** And someone said to [o]the man clothed in linen, who
was above the waters of the stream,[4] [p]"How long shall it be till the end of these wonders?"
7 And I heard [o]the man clothed in linen, who was above the waters of the stream; [q]he raised
his right hand and his left hand toward heaven and [r]swore by him who lives forever that
it would be for a [s]time, times, and half a time, and that when the shattering of [t]the power
of [t]the holy people comes to an end all these things would be finished. **8** I heard, [u]but I did
not understand. Then I said, "O my lord, what shall be the outcome of these things?" **9** He
said, [v]"Go your way, Daniel, [w]for the words are shut up and sealed until the time of the

[1] Or *land as payment* [2] Hebrew *thrust at* [3] Hebrew *the expanse*; compare Genesis 1:6–8 [4] Or *who was upstream*; also verse 7

11:39 The passage probably speaks of a future king who will be a larger and more ultimate version of Antiochus IV Epiphanes, one who will truly "do as he wills," will **deal with the strongest fortresses**, and will **make** his followers **rulers over many**. Many interpreters see here another prediction of the Antichrist, whom they connect to the "little horn" of ch. 7 and the ruler of 9:26 who is to come. The NT has been taken as referring to him in various ways ("the man of lawlessness," 2 Thess. 2:3–12; "antichrist," 1 John 2:18; "the beast," Revelation 11–20).

11:40–41 **At the time of the end** there will be a major battle where armies will come from the **north** and the **south** to **attack** this powerful ruler in the land of Israel (**the glorious land**). **Edom and Moab and the main part of the Ammonites** will escape from his hand, possibly because of their connection with Israel or because they are out of his way.

11:44–45 One striking difference between Antiochus IV Epiphanes and the Antichrist lies in the events surrounding the king's death, which do not fit what is known of the death of Antiochus IV. He met his end during a relatively minor campaign against Persia in 164 B.C., not **between the sea** and Jerusalem after a grand and successful assault on Egypt. When compared to the precision of fulfillment of the previous verses of ch. 11, these verses may be looking for a greater fulfillment that is yet to come at the time of the end. **the glorious holy mountain**. This is the Temple Mount in Jerusalem, which perhaps here should be connected to the fall of the Antichrist in the battle of Armageddon (cf. Rev. 16:13–16).

12:1–4 *The Promise of Resurrection to Glory or Shame.* God's people will not be left alone in the fiery trials in the times ahead. Their angelic representative, **Michael**, will rise up to deliver them. **A time of trouble** unlike any other is indeed a desperate time; some connect it to the "great tribulation" (cf. Rev. 12:7–14). Sometime afterwards there will be a resurrection of the dead. Those who were faithful in life, **everyone whose name shall be found written in the book** (Dan. 12:1; cf. 7:10), will rise to **everlasting life** in glory, while the others will rise **to shame and everlasting contempt** (12:2; cf. John 5:28–29). This makes present faithfulness worthwhile for the saints, even if it costs them their lives (see Dan. 11:33). Their ultimate outcome will be that they **shine** brightly **like the stars forever and ever** (12:3). However, in the meantime (v. 4), Daniel was instructed to **shut up the words and seal the book**, both because its contents were not fully comprehensible and also to keep them safe for future generations of God's people to read. The wise will know where to find this wisdom, though those around them **run to and fro**, seeking **knowledge** in vain (cf. Amos 8:12).

12:5–13 *How Long Until the End?* Daniel and his angelic companion address two related questions to the divine messenger clothed in linen. The angel's question is a reminder that a heavenly audience is watching with interest the unfolding earthly drama. The questions concern **"How long shall it be till the end of these wonders?"** (v. 6) and **"what shall be the outcome of these things?"** (v. 8). The answer to the question "How long?" has two parts: **"for a time, times, and half a time"** (v. 7), and for "1,290 days" (v. 11, cf. 9:27). Revelation 11:3 and 12:6 apparently look back to this idea, though the number in those two verses is 1,260 days. (Both 1,290 and 1,260 are approximately three and a half years—1,290 in terms of a 365-day year, and 1,260 in terms of a 360-day year.) Yet "a time, times, and half a time"

end. 10 [x]Many shall purify themselves and make themselves white and be refined, but [y]the
wicked shall act wickedly. And none of the wicked shall understand, [g]but those who are
wise shall understand. 11 And from the time that [z]the regular burnt offering is taken away
and [a]the abomination that makes desolate is set up, there shall be 1,290 days. 12 [b]Blessed
is he who waits and arrives at the 1,335 days. 13 [c]But go your way till the end. [d]And you
shall rest and shall stand in your allotted place at [e]the end of the days."

10 [x][ch. 11:35] [y][Rev. 9:20; 22:11] [g][See ver. 3 above]
11 [z]ch. 11:31 [a]See ch. 11:31
12 [b][Matt. 10:22]
13 [c]ver. 9 [d]Isa. 57:2; [Rev. 6:11] [e][Matt. 13:39]

(probably three and a half times) focuses on the limited nature of this period as half of a complete period of judgment, which is seven times (see Dan. 4:25).

12:10 Those who are wise will be able to determine specifically when the three and a half years of the tribulation start (they **shall understand**), namely, "from the time that the regular burnt offering is taken away" (cf. 9:27).

12:11 The specification of **1,290 days** emphasizes the precision with which the period is measured, predetermined by God to the very day (just over three and a half years, however this time is understood). In this time many will "purify themselves" and "be refined" (v. 10), and the Jewish nation will be shattered by their enemies, but then God will step in to vindicate them.

12:12–13 The additional figure of **1,335 days**, 45 days longer than the 1,290-day period, heightens the sense of mystery that surrounds the Lord's timing and emphasizes the need for the saints to persevere faithfully, even when to human wisdom God's arrival seems overdue. The response to the "outcome of these things" is the assurance of continuing persecution to purify and refine the wise (v. 10; cf. 11:33–35) and of continuing wickedness on the part of the wicked. This matches God's consistent pattern of working in this world, moving through suffering to glory, and refining his people through trials and persecution, even to the point of martyrdom. In the meantime, God's people are to go on living faithfully in this corrupt world, confident of the inheritance that is stored up for them **at the end of the days**.

INTRODUCTION TO

HOSEA

Author and Title

The opening verse, "The word of the LORD that came to Hosea, the son of Beeri," identifies Hosea with other OT prophets and follows the same general pattern of naming the book after its author (cf. Joel 1:1; Jonah 1:1; Mic. 1:1; Zeph. 1:1; Mal. 1:1). *Beeri* is a Hittite name in Genesis 26:34, perhaps demonstrating the practice, as today, of naming children from the Scriptures. Because chapters 1–3 of Hosea are quite different from chapters 4–14, Hosea's authorship of the whole book has been questioned. But this is unnecessary. The latter section expands and applies the essential message of God's mercy for his people; the preceding biographical sketch enhances that message, though it employs different literary forms.

Date

The OT prophets commonly dated their ministries in conjunction with reigning kings. In Hosea's day the Judean kings were Uzziah, Jotham, Ahaz, and Hezekiah. The king of Israel (the northern kingdom, also called "Ephraim" in Hosea; see note on 4:17) was Jeroboam, son of Joash. Jeroboam's last year was 753 B.C., and Hezekiah's was 687, so Hosea's ministry was situated in this time period. The prophet's ministry was probably not that long (66 years), though a 35-year ministry is possible. The significant feature is that he ministered during the latter half of the eighth century. This period was the most turbulent and trying time in the history of Israel prior to the captivity.

Theme

Hosea depicts Israel's unfaithfulness with a number of images from family and nature. Israel is like: a promiscuous wife, an indifferent mother, an illegitimate child, an ungrateful son, a stubborn heifer, a silly dove, a luxuriant vine, and grapes in the wilderness. Yet Israel's unfaithfulness and obstinacy are not enough to exhaust God's redeeming love that outstrips the human capacity to comprehend.

Purpose, Occasion, and Background

The purpose, occasion, and background of Hosea all work in tandem. They pertain to the latter half of the eighth century B.C., certain aspects of Baalism, and the ideology of the prophet Hosea.

The latter days of the eighth century B.C. witnessed the rise of the neo-Assyrian king Tiglath-pileser III (745–727). He was followed by several capable kings who extended Assyrian dominance over the entire ancient Near East (eventually including Egypt) for more than a century. Particularly relevant to Hosea were at least six incursions into Palestine and its neighbors by an unstoppable Assyrian army during the prophet's lifetime. Conquest and exile were the most dreaded fate in biblical times. This perennial threat hanging over Israel (specifically the northern kingdom) came with a time of unparalleled political upheaval and instability. The nation had six kings within about 30 years, a period filled with intrigue and violence. Zechariah (753 B.C.) was murdered after only six months in power. The usurper, Shallum, was assassinated one month later. The next king, Menahem (752–742 B.C.) survived for a decade only by paying a burdensome tribute to Tiglath-pileser. His son, Pekahiah (742–740 B.C.), was assassinated by an army officer, Pekah (740–732), after only two years' reign. Subsequently, Pekah was disposed of by Hoshea, whose rebellion against the Assyrians led to the end of the northern kingdom (732–722 B.C.).

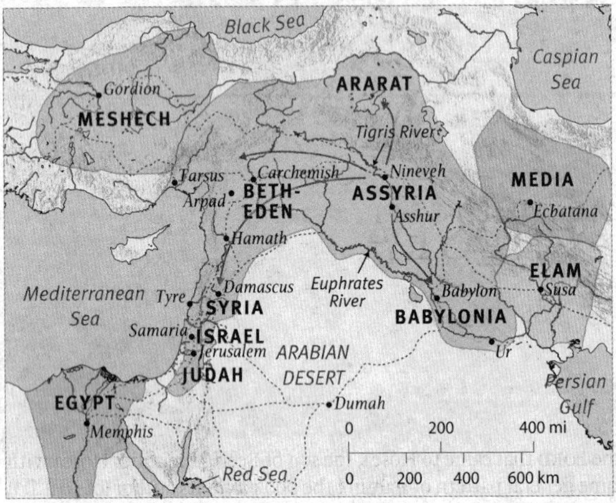

The Near East at the Time of Hosea
c. 740 B.C.
Hosea prophesied to Israel and Judah during the decades surrounding the fall of Samaria to the Assyrian Empire. The resurgence of this ancient empire dominated much of the politics of the ancient Near East from the time of Jeroboam and Azariah until the empire's demise at the end of the seventh century B.C. Assyria would eventually engulf nearly the entire Near East from Ur to Ararat to Egypt.

Within this chaotic 30-year period, external conflicts and failures of international diplomacy repeatedly proved disastrous. These times are reflected in Hosea, whose primary audience was Ephraim (the northern kingdom, Israel), mentioned 35 times in the book. As Hosea reflects these times, it is often difficult to be sure just what specific historical reference he has in mind. Although there is a range of suggestions regarding different passages, most lack consensus. The prophet's messages, however, are not tarnished by the reader's inability to tie down all of the details. His priority was to see Israel turn back to God.

Hosea's major concern was the worship of Baal—an apostasy that he understood to be the reason for Israel's dilemma. Baal was the weather-god worshiped in Syria-Palestine, who had control over agriculture and fertility, rainfall and productivity. Since ancient Israel was always an agricultural society, Baal worship was of unrivaled importance. Baal was localized at different shrines identified by such names as Baal-peor (9:10) and Baal-gad (Josh. 11:17) and hence was sometimes referred to as the Baals (Judg. 2:11; 3:7; 8:33). While a full description of this religion is not possible here, one major aspect of Baalism touches on this prophet's message: the religion's appeal to human sexuality (cf. Isa. 57:3–10). Other aspects—such as drunkenness, bestiality, human sacrifice, mutilations, and incest—may be discerned in the book, but Hosea understands the strength of Baalism's appeal to the sex drive by way of ritual prostitution.

This amounted to sexual intimacy at one of the pagan shrines, understood most probably as an act of imitative magic. That is, sexual behavior at these shrines was expected to cause the Baals to respond in like manner—to follow the worshipers by producing for them fertile seed and rain for a good crop. This intimacy took place with cult prostitutes (Hos. 4:14). When a worshiper selected a prostitute, he prayed, "I beseech the goddess of Astarte to favor you and Baal to favor me." There was also eating and drinking at shrines as an act of worship.

Hosea's approach is dominated by his knowledge that God's people have been joined to the Lord. Hosea makes a number of references to Israel's past to remind them of that. Israel is the Lord's bride, but Israel has instead become joined to the Baals. Worship of Baal is not just a violation of the first of the Ten Commandments (Ex. 20:3), it is a betrayal of that intimate and endearing union that God made with his people. Idolatry, therefore, is depicted as spiritual adultery, transgression against the marriage between the Lord and Israel (cf. Ex. 34:11–16; Lev. 17:7; 20:4–6; Deut. 31:16). The prophet justifies the Lord's coming judgments with a litany of offenses that amount to the radical ingratitude of a wayward wife. But punishment is not ultimately what the Lord wants for his people; he desires that they leave their fornication and return to the One who first loved them and can indeed provide what is for their best.

Key Themes

1. Hosea frequently refers to the Pentateuch, the foundation of Israel's relationship to God (1:10; 2:9–10, 18; 4:3; 6:7, 9; 7:13; 8:4–6; 9:6–10, 14; 10:9–10; 11:1–4, 8; 12:2–5, 9–10, 12–13; 13:4–6, 15).

2. Hosea stresses divine sovereignty, with God speaking in the first person, "I," almost a hundred times in the book.

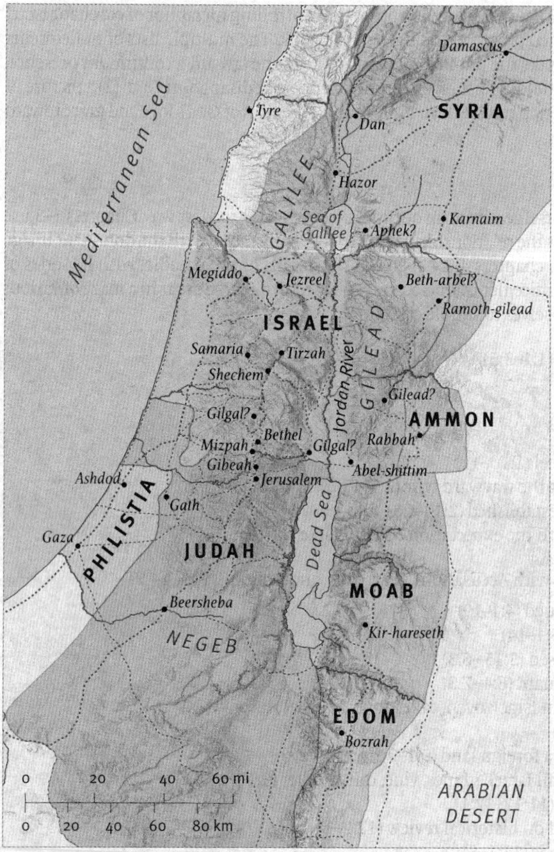

Israel and Judah at the Time of Hosea
c. 740 B.C.
Hosea prophesied during a time of great political turbulence in Israel and Judah. The early part of his ministry witnessed a brief period of resurgence under the reign of Jeroboam II, who captured much of Syria for Israel. Within a couple decades, however, Israel and Syria attacked Judah, but Assyria in turn attacked Israel and captured Galilee and Gilead. Finally, in 722 B.C., the Assyrians captured Samaria itself and annexed the rest of Israel's territory into their empire.

3. Hosea's personal biography exemplifies the Lord's compassion (chs. 1–3).
4. Isolation/exile, which is coming upon Israel, is a means to restoration (1:6–7; 2:14–23; 3:1–3; 5:6–6:3; 11:8–11; 12:9).

History of Salvation Summary

The Lord has yoked himself to Israel and will not give up on her, even in the face of the rampant unfaithfulness of the northern kingdom. He must purify Israel from her unfaithfulness through terrible punishments. For the northern kingdom to return to the Lord, the people must return to the house of David (3:5), which they will do in the "latter days" (the time of the Messiah). (For an explanation of the "History of Salvation," see the Overview of the Bible, pp. 23–26. See also History of Salvation in the Old Testament: Preparing the Way for Christ, pp. 2635–2661.)

Literary Features

The overall genre of the book is prophecy, and most of the book consists of oracles of judgment, with only a few interspersed oracles of salvation. Its main literary form is satire (in this case, sharp and bitter). Virtually the entire book is embodied in poetry. The overall format is that of a legal or judicial indictment, as God presents a detailed case against his covenant people.

The vividness of the poetry and figurative language is a striking feature of the book, as God's people, e.g., are pictured as an oven or a stubborn heifer or wild grapes. Even though the failed and restored marriage of Hosea and Gomer is present only in the first three chapters, the controlling metaphor of covenant Israel as an unfaithful wife exerts an implied presence throughout the book. The multiple lists of indictments that God brings against Israel also make the implied metaphor of a divine lawsuit a continuous presence. Recurrent themes include: (1) the unfolding list of acts and attitudes that disappoint God; (2) a picture of what people who reject God can expect to receive from him; and (3) evidences of God's love and grace toward people who do not deserve them.

Outline

The book of Hosea does not lend itself easily to an outline, except in the broadest way. Chapters 1–3 use Hosea's own marriage as a parable for the relationship between God and Israel—with the dominant image of Israel as an unfaithful wife. Then chapters 4–14 spell out the details of the parable, with its series of accusations, warnings, appeals, and enticements for God's people to return. These occur in a maze of various literary forms that do not lend themselves to simple categories.

I. Biographical: Hosea's Family (1:1–3:5)
   - A. Introduction (1:1)
   - B. Command to marry (1:2)
   - C. Birth of children (1:3–9)
   - D. Covenant renewal at Jezreel (1:10–11)
   - E. Legal proceedings against the wayward wife (2:1–13)
   - F. Covenant relationship reestablished (2:14–23)
   - G. Command to remarry, with the expectation of a king like David (3:1–5)

II. Hosea Spells Out His Parable with Accusations, Warnings, and Promises (4:1–14:9)
   - A. Legal proceedings continued (4:1–19)
   - B. Adultery in high places (5:1–14)
   - C. Appeal: return and be raised (5:15–6:3)
   - D. Transgressors of the covenant (6:4–7:3)
   - E. Four similes for unfaithful Israel: oven, cake, dove, treacherous bow (7:4–16)
   - F. Israel's hypocrisy (8:1–14)
   - G. Warnings: no worship in a foreign land (9:1–9)
   - H. More similes for unfaithful Israel: grapes, vine, calf, toddler (9:10–11:11)
   - I. Dependence on alliances (11:12–12:1)
   - J. Further indictment based on historical review (12:2–14)
   - K. Worship of man-made gods (13:1–8)
   - L. Rejecting the only hope they have (13:9–16)
   - M. Closing appeals (14:1–9)

HOSEA

Chapter 1
1 [a]Isa. 1:1; Amos 1:1; Mic. 1:1 [b]2 Kgs. 14:23; 15:1
2 [c][ch. 3:1] [d]ch. 2:4 [e][ch. 2:5]; See Ezek. 16:15
4 [f][2 Kgs. 10:11] [g][Amos 7:9]
5 [h][2 Kgs. 15:29] [i]Josh. 17:16; Judg. 6:33
6 [j][ver. 9; ch. 2:1, 23; Rom. 9:25; 1 Pet. 2:10] [k]ch. 2:4; 2 Kgs. 17:6, 23
7 [l][ch. 11:12; 2 Kgs. 19:35] [m][ch. 2:18; Zech. 4:6; 9:10]

1 The word of the LORD that came to Hosea, the son of Beeri, [a]in the days of Uzziah,
Jotham, Ahaz, and Hezekiah, kings of Judah, and in the days of [b]Jeroboam the son
of Joash, king of Israel.

Hosea's Wife and Children

2 When the LORD first spoke through Hosea, the LORD said to Hosea, [c]"Go, take to yourself a wife of whoredom and have [d]children of whoredom, for [e]the land commits great
whoredom by forsaking the LORD." 3 So he went and took Gomer, the daughter of Diblaim,
and she conceived and bore him a son.
4 And the LORD said to him, "Call his name Jezreel, for in just a little while [f]I will punish
the house of Jehu for the blood of Jezreel, and [g]I will put an end to the kingdom of the
house of Israel. 5 And on that day [h]I will break the bow of Israel [i]in the Valley of Jezreel."
6 She conceived again and bore a daughter. And the LORD said to him, [j]"Call her name No
Mercy,[1] for [k]I will no more have mercy on the house of Israel, to forgive them at all. 7 But [l]I
will have mercy on the house of Judah, and I will save them by the LORD their God. I [m]will
not save them by bow or by sword or by war or by horses or by horsemen."

[1] Hebrew *Lo-ruhama*, which means *she has not received mercy*

1:1–3:5 *Biographical: Hosea's Family.* Hosea uses his own marriage to Gomer, her unfaithfulness, and their eventual restoration as a parable for the Lord's relationship to Israel.

1:1 *Introduction.* **The word of the LORD that came to Hosea, the son of Beeri**. The name "Hosea" comes from the same verb as "Joshua" and "Jesus," meaning "to save or deliver" (Hb. *yasha'*).

1:2 *Command to Marry.* God instructs Hosea to marry, but foretells that his wife's unfaithfulness will be an image for Israel's unfaithfulness. **take to yourself a wife of whoredom**. Some have supposed that God commands Hosea to marry a prostitute, but this does not suit the words. The word translated "whoredom" throughout the book is a broad term for various kinds of sexual misconduct, and only in certain contexts does it refer to prostitution. In Hosea it generally refers to a married woman being unfaithful to her husband, which is why it serves as a metaphor for Israel's unfaithfulness to the Lord, her husband (**for the land commits great whoredom by forsaking the LORD**; cf. 2:5). Further, one should not think that Gomer was already promiscuous when Hosea married her. As the notes below will show, she seems to have been faithful to Hosea in the begetting of her first child (1:3), and under suspicion in the begetting of her second and third (vv. 6, 8). Thus the second and third children will be **children of whoredom** (the word **and** in "and have children" is taken in the sense, "that is"). This helps explain the legal proceedings in ch. 2, and the specific word "adulteress" in 3:1. Hosea uses marriage and unfaithfulness as a prominent metaphor (cf. Ezekiel 16 and 23 for the extended version of the metaphor; elsewhere the idea is important, but not given extended treatment, e.g., Isa. 1:21). The tragedy of Hosea is the tragedy of a marriage that began well but went bad. And so it was with the Lord and Israel: a good beginning went awry. The book of Hosea refers to Israel's cherished beginnings (e.g., Hos. 2:14–15).

1:3–9 *Birth of Children.* Hosea's wife bears children, and God gives them prophetic names.

1:3 bore him. The first child, Jezreel, is explicitly said to be the son of Hosea. With Gomer's other children, any mention of Hosea's paternity is conspicuously absent (vv. 6, 8). Unlike Jezreel, those children are called "her children" and "children of whoredom" (2:4; cf. 4:6; 5:7).

1:4 Call his name Jezreel. Hosea, like Isaiah, uses children as signs and symbols for prophetic pronouncements (cf. Isa. 7:3; 8:1–3, 18). **the house of Jehu**. Jeroboam II (Hos. 1:1) was the fourth king of the dynasty begun by Jehu in 841 B.C. This dynasty was the longest in the history of the northern kingdom. Many suppose that **the blood of Jezreel** refers to the shedding of blood of the house of Ahab and Ahaziah when Jehu usurped the throne (2 Kings 9:21–28), but this proposal suffers from serious difficulties. First, the kingdom of Israel did not come to an end with Jehu's dynasty. Israel survived for 30 years after Zechariah, the last king of that dynasty. Second, God commanded Jehu to exterminate Ahab's dynasty, and commended his work (2 Kings 9:1–10; 10:30; cf. 2 Chron. 22:7). It seems unlikely that the Lord would punish someone for carrying out his command. It is better to take the phrase "house of Jehu" as parallel to **house of Israel**, and thus another name for Israel. By this reading, "the blood of Jezreel" refers to 1 Kings 21: Ahab, who promoted Baalism as the national religion of Israel, permitted the murder of Naboth, a man loyal to the Lord, in order to seize his vineyard in Jezreel. Appropriately, this verse sets the tenor of the rest of the book: the ongoing confrontation between Baal and the God of Israel.

1:5 The promise to **break the bow of Israel in the Valley of Jezreel** signified the defeat of Baalism at the same place where Baal had seemingly triumphed over the Lord (cf. v. 4). (To break a soldier's bow is a symbol for defeating him.) Israel will be judged at the place where she sinned. That the blood of Ahab was licked up by dogs there should have served as an ominous sign of the Lord's future judgment on followers of Baal (1 Kings 21:19). The judgment at Jezreel joined poetic justice with divine justice.

1:6 The wording here differs from v. 3, in that it does not say she bore *him* the daughter; this suggests that Hosea was not the father, and the name, **No Mercy**, is Hosea's denial of fatherhood. Hosea does not have the natural affection that a father has for his own children, as a father shows **mercy** to his children (cf. 2:4a; Ps. 103:13, "compassion").

1:7 The Lord will **save** Judah, but not by conventional means, i.e., without use of national military prowess (cf. Isa. 37:29).

8 When she had weaned No Mercy, she conceived and bore a son. 9 And the LORD said,
[n]"Call his name Not My People,[1] for [o]you are not my people, and I am not your God."[2]
10[3] Yet [p]the number of the children of Israel shall be [q]like the sand of the sea, which
cannot be measured or numbered. [r]And [s]in the place where it was said to them, [o]"You
are not my people," it shall be said to them, [t]"Children[4] of [u]the living God." 11 And [v]the
children of Judah and the children of Israel shall be gathered together, and [w]they shall
appoint for themselves one head. And they shall go up from the land, for great shall be
the day of Jezreel.

Israel's Unfaithfulness Punished

2[5] Say to your brothers, [x]"You are my people,"[6] and to your sisters, [y]"You have received
mercy."[7]

2 "Plead with your mother, plead—
for [z]she is not my wife,
and I am not her husband—
that she put away [a]her whoring from her face,
and her adultery from between her breasts;
3 lest [b]I strip her naked
and make her as [c]in the day she was born,
and [d]make her like a wilderness,
and make her like a parched land,
and kill her with thirst.
4 [e]Upon her children also I will have no mercy,
[f]because they are children of whoredom.
5 For [g]their mother has played the whore;
she who conceived them has acted shamefully.
For [h]she said, 'I will go after my lovers,
who [i]give me my bread and my water,
my wool and my flax, my oil and my drink.'

[1] Hebrew *Lo-ammi,* which means *not my people* [2] Hebrew *I am not yours* [3] Ch 2:1 in Hebrew [4] Or *Sons* [5] Ch 2:3 in Hebrew [6] Hebrew *ammi,* which means *my people* [7] Hebrew *ruhama,* which means *she has received mercy*

9 [n]ver. 4, 6 [o]ch. 2:23; [Lev. 26:12]
10 [p][Ezek. 36:10, 37] [q]Gen. 22:17; See Gen. 13:16 [r]Cited Rom. 9:26 [s]Isa. 62:4 [o][See ver. 9 above] [t]Deut. 14:1; [2 Cor. 6:18] [u]Ps. 42:2; See Josh. 3:10
11 [v]Isa. 11:12, 13; Jer. 3:18; 50:4; Ezek. 34:23; Zech. 10:6; See Ezek. 37:16-24 [w][ch. 3:5]

Chapter 2

1 [x][ch. 1:9] [y][ch. 1:6]
2 [z][Isa. 50:1] [a][ch. 4:12; Ezek. 16:25]
3 [b][Ezek. 16:39] [c][Ezek. 16:4] [d][ver. 9; Ezek. 19:13]
4 [e]ch. 1:6 [f]ch. 1:2
5 [g][ch. 1:2] [h][ver. 12, 13] [i][ver. 8, 9; Jer. 44:17]

1:8–9 The birth (v. 8) and naming of another child by Gomer reinforces what was seen with regards to the preceding birth. The name **Not My People** makes it explicit: he is not Hosea's son (cf. 2:4). **for you are not my people, and I am not your God**. The phrase "my people" is an expression of endearment. It appears 17 times in the book of Exodus alone. The naming of this son signifies a negation of the marital bond that God made with the nation at Sinai (Ex. 6:7; Lev. 26:12).

1:10–11 *Covenant Renewal at Jezreel.* God does not intend repudiation to be the end of the story for his ancient people.

1:10 In the same breath that the Lord uttered his detachment from physical Israel, he uses the language of the Abrahamic covenant to articulate the basis for restoration: **the number of the children of Israel shall be like the sand of the sea** (Gen. 22:17; 32:12). The failure of Israel to live up to the demands of the covenant at Sinai could not nullify the promises made to Abraham (cf. Gal. 3:17). Israel's salvation must be gained just as Abraham's was: salvation by grace through faith and not by works of the law (Gen. 15:6; Rom. 4:1–3; Gal. 3:6). **In the place** is not a geographical reference but a reference to the event when God and his people bonded at Sinai. The Lord will meet Israel at the same place he met with Israel before, i.e., under the same conditions. It is the place of repentance (cf. also Hos. 2:7, 16). God will take Israel back to the desert and begin his work with them all over again.

1:11 the children of Judah and the children of Israel shall be gathered together. The hostility between "the children of Judah" (the southern kingdom) and the "children of Israel" (the northern kingdom) had a protracted history (beginning in 1 Kings 12:16–24). "Shall be gathered together" is passive; a force outside of Judah and Israel is operative, i.e., God keeping his promises to Abraham. This did not happen in Hosea's time. The prophecy points forward, perhaps to a messianic age when the people would be in such agreement that they would **appoint for themselves one head**. Their reconciliation is depicted in their following the same leader. While it is not explicit here what form this reconciliation would take, the text views the judgment at Jezreel (Hos. 1:5) as working toward that glorious experience, **for great shall be the day of Jezreel**.

2:1–13 *Legal Proceedings against the Wayward Wife.* Hosea uses the legal process of an offended husband against his wife as an image for God's plans to deal with Israel.

2:1 Those addressed are Israelites who, the prophet hopes, will respond to his promise. The verse begins with an imperative, **Say to your brothers**, as does the following verse. Both serve as an enticement for Israel to return to her God. Israel is entreated to anticipate a change in names when unity is restored. No longer will they be "No Mercy" and "Not My People."

2:2 Plead . . . plead. The plea for repentance is repeated twice for emphasis. As commonly understood, **she is not my wife, and I am not her husband** is a repudiation of the marriage bond, which would parallel God's right to repudiate his covenant bond with Israel. But perhaps it should be read as a threat, rather than an actual divorce. Otherwise, Hosea would have no right to issue the warnings and threats that follow. Isaiah likewise expressed God's reluctance to turn finally away from his people (Isa. 50:1). The marriage between God and Israel has not ended; the covenant made with Israel contains provision for restoration, and Israel is urged to respond to that provision: **that she put away her whoring from her face, and her adultery from between her breasts**.

2:3 lest I strip her naked and make her as in the day she was born. Public humiliation of an unfaithful wife was not exceptional during this time. Similar language was used to describe retributions for breaking treaties. Some commentators see this "stripping" as the retrieval of everything a husband had provided for his bride (Ex. 21:10–11; cf. Hos. 2:9).

2:4–5 they are children of whoredom. For their mother has played

6[j]Job 3:23 [k][Job 19:8; Lam. 3:7, 9]
7[l][Luke 15:17, 18] [m][Isa. 54:5, 6]
8[n][ver. 20; Isa. 1:3] [o][Ezek. 16:19] [p]Deut. 7:13 [q]ch. 13:2 [r][Ezek. 16:17, 18]
9[s][ver. 3; Joel 1:10]
10[t]Lam. 1:8; Ezek. 16:37; 23:29
11[u][Jer. 7:34; Amos 8:10] [v][Amos 8:5] [w][ch. 9:5; Isa. 1:13, 14]
12[x][Isa. 5:5] [y][ver. 5] [z][Mic. 1:7] [a][ch. 13:8]
13[b][ch. 4:9] [c][ch. 11:2; 13:1, 2] [d]Ezek. 23:40; [Isa. 61:10]

6 Therefore [j]I will hedge up her[1] way with thorns,
and [k]I will build a wall against her,
so that she cannot find her paths.
7 She shall pursue her lovers
but not overtake them,
and she shall seek them
but shall not find them.
[l]Then she shall say,
'I will go and return to [m]my first husband,
[l]for it was better for me then than now.'
8 And [n]she did not know
that it was [o]I who gave her
[p]the grain, the wine, and the oil,
and who lavished on [q]her silver and gold,
[r]which they used for Baal.
9 Therefore [s]I will take back
my grain in its time,
and my wine in its season,
and [s]I will take away my wool and my flax,
which were to cover her nakedness.
10 Now [t]I will uncover her lewdness
in the sight of her lovers,
and no one shall rescue her out of my hand.
11 [u]And I will put an end to all her mirth,
her feasts, her [v]new moons, her [v]Sabbaths,
and all her [w]appointed feasts.
12 And [x]I will lay waste her vines and her fig trees,
[y]of which she said,
'These are [z]my wages,
which my lovers have given me.'
I will make them a forest,
[a]and the beasts of the field shall devour them.
13 And [b]I will punish her for [c]the feast days of the Baals
when she burned offerings to them
and [d]adorned herself with her ring and jewelry,
and went after her lovers
and forgot me, declares the LORD.

[1] Hebrew *your*

the whore; she who conceived them . . . shamefully. Here is a clear disclaimer of fatherhood. The Lord, like Hosea, proceeds as a husband not only wronged, but injured, by infidelity. **For she said, "I will go after my lovers."** This suggests that it was Gomer/Israel who pursued the lovers, rather than the other way around (cf. Jer. 2:23–24). Israel's "lovers" are other gods.

2:6 Therefore. This is the first of three "therefores" in this chapter (cf. vv. 9, 14). It is spoken in response to the mother's unbridled lust. The eighth-century prophets (including Hosea) truly believed that Israel's sins could be forgiven and the nation restored. The jealous Husband of Israel will put a **hedge** around his wife so that she is prevented from straying (i.e., making pilgrimages to pagan shrines). The intention is redemptive.

2:7 By the obstruction of thorns and a wall, the wayward wife will not be able to find **her lovers**, though she diligently seeks them. Left in limbo, without a husband to provide for her needs, she repeats the same words she said in v. 5: **I will go**. She decides that she should return to her **first husband**. She acknowledges him as her husband and that there was a time in her marriage when things went well.

2:8 In retrospect, **she did not know**. Israel's failure to "know" the Lord and his provision, and the Lord's plan to remedy this, is a key idea in the book (vv. 8, 20; 4:1, 6; 5:3, 4; 6:3; 7:9; 8:2; 11:3; 13:4, 5). The prosperity lavished upon Israel was due to the generosity not of Baal but of the Lord. Particularly hurtful is that the prosperity was used in heathen worship, a slap in God's face. **I who gave her** continues the dominance of the first-person pronoun "I" in the rest of the chapter.

2:9 This second **therefore** is in response to Israel's blind stubbornness in the face of God's goodness. Like Hosea, who threatens to strip his adulterous wife of what he has bestowed upon her, the Lord will strip the land completely bare. **Wool**, **flax**, and linen were the primary sources for weaving cloth for apparel. Thus, the use of these in pagan feasts will come to an end. Verses 9–10 and what follows complement v. 6 as additional descriptions of the Lord's discipline. The disciplines work in tandem, and the condition of the land throughout the OT serves as a barometer of Israel's relationship to the Lord.

2:10 The Lord will expose the Baals' impotency so that Israel will know that **no one shall rescue her out of my hand**, for there is no other god (Deut. 32:39).

2:12–13 These are my wages. Sacrifices presented to the Baals are likened to a fee given to a shrine prostitute (9:1). Adulterous behavior applies literally to the woman, and figuratively to the nation. It is also clear that the **lovers** are the **Baals** (2:13).

The Lord's Mercy on Israel

14 "Therefore, behold, I will allure her,
and [e]bring her into the wilderness,
and [f]speak tenderly to her.
15 And there I will give her her vineyards
and make the Valley of Achor[1] a door of hope.
And there she shall answer [g]as in the days of her youth,
as at the time when she came out of the land of Egypt.

16 "And [h]in that day, declares the LORD, you will call me 'My Husband,' and no longer
will you call me 'My Baal.' 17 For [i]I will remove the names of the Baals from her mouth,
and they shall be remembered by name no more. 18 And [j]I will make for them a covenant
on that day with the beasts of the field, the birds of the heavens, and the creeping things
of the ground. And [k]I will abolish[2] the bow, the sword, and war from the land, and I will
make you lie down in [l]safety. 19 And I will betroth you to me [m]forever. [n]I will betroth you to
me in righteousness and in justice, in steadfast love and in mercy. 20 [n]I will betroth you
to me in faithfulness. And [o]you shall know the LORD.

21 "And [p]in that day [q]I will answer, declares the LORD,
I will answer the heavens,
and they shall answer the earth,
22 and the earth shall answer the grain, the wine, and the oil,
and they shall answer [r]Jezreel,[3]
23 and [s]I will sow her for myself in the land.
And [t]I [u]will have mercy on No Mercy,[4]
and [v]I will say to Not My People,[5] [w]'You are my people';
and he shall say, 'You are my God.'"

Hosea Redeems His Wife

3 And the LORD said to me, [x]"Go again, love a woman who is loved by another man
and is an adulteress, even as the LORD loves the children of Israel, though they turn
to other gods and love cakes of raisins." 2 So I bought her for fifteen shekels of silver and
a [y]homer and a lethech[6] of barley. 3 And I said to her, "You must [z]dwell as mine for many

[1] *Achor* means *trouble*; compare Joshua 7:26 [2] Hebrew *break* [3] *Jezreel* means *God will sow* [4] Hebrew *Lo-ruhama* [5] Hebrew *Lo-ammi* [6] A *shekel* was about 2/5 ounce or 11 grams; a *homer* was about 6 bushels or 220 liters; a *lethech* was about 3 bushels or 110 liters

14 [e][Ezek. 20:35] [f]Isa. 40:2
15 [g][ch. 9:10; 11:1; Jer. 2:2; Ezek. 16:22, 60]
16 [h]ver. 18, 21
17 [i]Zeph. 1:4; Zech. 13:2; [Ex. 23:13]
18 [j]Ezek. 34:25; [Job 5:23] [k]Ps. 46:9; Isa. 2:4; 9:5; Ezek. 39:9, 10 [l]Lev. 26:5; Jer. 23:6
19 [m][Ezek. 43:7] [n][ver. 7, 16; Jer. 3:14, 15; 2 Cor. 11:2]
20 [n][See ver. 19 above] [o]Jer. 31:34; John 17:3
21 [p]ver. 16 [q][Zech. 8:12]
22 [r][ch. 1:4, 11]
23 [s][ch. 1:10]; See Ezek. 36:9-11 [t]Cited Rom. 9:25, 26 [u]ch. 1:6 [v]ch. 1:9; 1 Pet. 2:10 [w]ver. 1; Zech. 13:9; See Lev. 26:12; Jer. 31:33

Chapter 3

1 [x][ch. 1:2, 3]
2 [y]Lev. 27:16; [Ezek. 45:11]
3 [z]Deut. 21:13

2:14–23 *Covenant Relationship Reestablished.* Hosea indicates God's plan to restore his "marriage" with Israel.

2:14 With this third **therefore**, the reason for the punishments for Israel's roaming becomes clear—to bring Israel to repentance. The verb **allure** can have the idea "to entice or seduce" (Judg. 14:15; 16:5), but here it is paralleled with **speak tenderly to her**. The Lord will woo his estranged wife away from her lovers with the language of courtship (Ruth 2:13; Isa. 40:2; cf. 2 Sam. 19:7). **Bring her into the wilderness** depicts the wilderness (see Ex. 19:1–2) as if it were a brighter time in the marriage.

2:15 The **Valley of Achor**, where Achan was cursed (Josh. 7:25–26), will become a place for hope.

2:16–17 And in that day. This is not a reference to a particular time but a description of what the day will be like when God lures Israel back. The act of changing names continues: **you will call me "My Husband," and no longer will you call me "My Baal."** The Israelites had fused the name of the Lord with Baal as though doing so made no difference. In earlier times the Hebrew for "my husband" sounded like "my Baal" (cf. Ex. 21:22; 24:4; 2 Sam. 11:26; Prov. 12:4; 30:23; 31:11, 23, 28), but now Israel must use a different word in order to make clear her exclusive devotion to the Lord, and not to Baal.

2:18 For them refers to the Israelites who are recipients of the covenant announced in 1:10–11. The terms for the animals here evoke Genesis 1–2, where man in his created condition had a proper dominion over them; hence Israel is in its restored condition living out the creational ideal, which was the goal of God's redemption. To **lie down in safety** is the ultimate blessing in a world fraught with persistent threats of aggression.

2:19 Recovery is described as a renewed betrothal. The betrothal, a marriage agreement, is established by the payment of a bride price to the bride's father (2 Sam. 3:14), a practice still found in the Arab world. The bride price paid is **righteousness**, **justice**, **steadfast love**, and **mercy**. These attributes come only from the Lord (Ex. 34:6–7) and are precisely what Israel desperately lacks. This is in harmony with the divine initiative represented by the many "I wills" in Hosea.

2:21–23 And in that day. That is, when the marriage is again consummated. Former adversities suffered by Israel will be reversed; **grain**, **wine**, and **oil** will be replenished (cf. vv. 5, 8–9). **No Mercy** will receive **mercy** (cf. 1:6; 2:4), and **Not My People** will again be God's **people** (cf. 1:9).

3:1–5 *Command to Remarry, with the Expectation of a King Like David.* Hosea returns to his own marriage situation, which is still an image for God and Israel. Israel's hope, like Judah's, lies with the house of David.

3:1 Though the name of this **woman** is not stated, she should be understood as Gomer, Hosea's wife in chs. 1–2; otherwise, the analogy of the woman to Israel breaks down. It is Israel, the **adulteress**, that the Lord pursues, not another people. Hosea is to retrieve his adulterous wife so that Israel will clearly know that the Lord still loves Israel, his spiritually unfaithful wife. **Though they . . . love cakes of raisins** probably refers to some rite in the Canaanite cult.

3:2 The word **bought** refers to some kind of trade (e.g., Deut. 2:6), which traditionally has been understood to mean redeeming Gomer from slavery, though the exact custom is unknown. Some interpreters hold that it is unlikely that Gomer had become a bondservant, as the price for a slave was 30 shekels, not 15 and some barley (Ex. 21:32; Zech. 11:12; cf. Lev. 27:4). Other interpreters, however, think that 15 shekels plus some barley and wine could have been the agreed-upon price for this particular slave, and 30 shekels may not have been the standard price for every slave in every circumstance. In any case, the amount paid is not great, and it shows the desperate condition into which Gomer had fallen.

3:3–4 You must dwell as mine has the force of a command. The segre-

days. You shall not play the whore, or belong to another man; so will I also be to you." 4 For
the children of Israel [z]shall dwell many days [a]without king or prince, [b]without sacrifice or
[c]pillar, without [d]ephod or [e]household gods. 5 Afterward [f]the children of Israel shall return
and [g]seek the LORD their God, and [h]David their king, [i]and they shall come in fear to the
LORD and to his goodness in the [j]latter days.

The LORD Accuses Israel

4

1 [k]Hear the word of the LORD, O children of Israel,
for [l]the LORD has a controversy with the inhabitants of the land.
There is no faithfulness or steadfast love,
and [m]no knowledge of God in the land;
2 [n]there is swearing, lying, murder, stealing, and committing adultery;
they break all bounds, and [o]bloodshed follows bloodshed.
3 Therefore [p]the land mourns,
and all who dwell in it languish,
[q]and also the beasts of the field
and the birds of the heavens,
[r]and even the fish of the sea are taken away.

4 [s]Yet let no one contend,
and let none accuse,
for with you is [t]my contention, O priest.[1]
5 You shall stumble by day;
the prophet also shall stumble with you by night;
and I will destroy [u]your mother.
6 My people are destroyed [v]for lack of knowledge;
[w]because you have rejected knowledge,
I reject you [x]from being a priest to me.

[1] Or *for your people are like those who contend with the priest*

4 [z][See ver. 3 above] [a]ch. 10:3, 7 [b][ch. 9:4] [c][ch. 10:1, 2] [d]See Judg. 8:27 [e]See Gen. 31:19
5 [f][ch. 14:1] [g]Jer. 29:13; 50:4 [h]Ezek. 34:23; [ch. 1:11]; See Jer. 23:5 [i][Mic. 7:17] [j]Isa. 2:2; See Mic. 4:1-3

Chapter 4
1 [k]See ch. 5:1 [l]Isa. 3:13, 14; Jer. 25:31; Mic. 6:2 [m][ver. 6, 14; Jer. 4:22; 5:4]
2 [n][ch. 7:1] [o][ch. 6:9; 12:14; Mic. 3:10; 7:2]
3 [p]Isa. 24:4; Jer. 4:28; Joel 1:10 [q][Joel 1:18; Zeph. 1:3] [r][Ezek. 38:20]
4 [s][ver. 17] [t][Deut. 17:12]
5 [u]ch. 2:2
6 [v][ver. 1; Isa. 5:13] [w][Prov. 1:29] [x][Ex. 19:6]

gation of Gomer/Israel will lead to her purification, rededication, and renewal. This segregation will be an extensive, though undefined, time of the absence of those things that constituted Israel's apostasy, namely, **king** and **prince** (v. 4), who failed in keeping Israel faithful to the Lord (cf. 1:4; 8:4); **sacrifice**, which they offered to the Baals (cf. 11:2; 13:1–2); the cult **pillar** (cf. 10:2), popular in Canaanite religion; the **ephod**, which degenerated into a tool for magical rites; and **household gods**, idols prohibited from Israel's religion (Judg. 17:5; 18:14; 2 Kings 23:24; Zech. 10:2). The Lord's purging, far from being incompatible with his love, is a major aspect of it. During this time the phrase **so will I also be to you** (Hos. 3:3) is reassuring and resonates covenant promises and divine support. The Lord God doggedly persists with his people during these trying times. But Israel must not **play the whore** (v. 3). The lesson having been learned, Israel will be restored beyond all expectation (Deut. 30:5). Romans 11:23 expresses a like sentiment ("they, if they do not continue in their unbelief, will be grafted in").

3:5 To call **David their king** is significant for the northern kingdom, which has been in revolt against the house of David for two centuries. They must **return** in order to be full participants in God's covenant—in other words, God intends to honor the covenant with David (2 Sam. 7:8–16). It is from the house of David that the ultimate king for God's people will come, as indicated in the term **the latter days** (see Isa. 2:2). God has a glorious future in store for his people.

4:1–14:9 *Hosea Spells Out His Parable with Accusations, Warnings, and Promises.* In the rest of the book, Hosea goes into detail about the various aspects of Israel's life that constitute her unfaithfulness to the Lord, urges her to repent, and reveals to his audience God's powerful and passionate commitment to his people, in spite of their unfaithfulness. Throughout these chapters the prophet changes the subject abruptly, without an obvious plan. Perhaps this shows that the sections were once independent oracles that have been stitched together.

4:1–19 *Legal Proceedings Continued.* The Lord continues to prosecute his "controversy" against unfaithful Israel.

4:1–2 Charges against Israel are framed in the vocabulary of a lawsuit (a **controversy**), a setting used by eighth-century contemporaries (cf. Isa. 3:13–15; Mic. 6:2). The charges are offenses against God's law, particularly the Ten Commandments: perjury (false **swearing**), **lying**, **murder**, **stealing**, **adultery**, and all manner of violence (Hos. 4:2). **Faithfulness** and **steadfast love** (v. 1) are attributes of God in Ex. 34:6; genuine **knowledge of God** in the hearts of his people will produce a character like his.

4:3 The whole **land** suffers from the curses of the covenant, because it is the arena in which God's unfaithful people are chastised—small wonder that it **mourns**.

4:4 Yet let no one contend, and let none accuse. While determining the precise meaning is difficult, this is certainly a reprimand.

4:5 The prophet refers to false prophets, the companions of the priests (v. 4). Together they were leading the people astray. **Your mother** is an allusion to Israel (2:4–5). Hosea's symbols of Israel include a mother, children, and a bride.

4:6 The people are the focal point in this chapter (cf. vv. 1, 12, 15) and are referred to as "my people" throughout (cf. vv. 8, 12). The priests had the responsibility of teaching the people God's laws (cf. Lev. 10:11; Mal. 2:6–7), but they had failed miserably, and as a result, the people lacked knowledge of God's laws and his ways. Therefore God says, **My people are destroyed for lack of knowledge**. But he puts the blame squarely on the priests: **because you have rejected knowledge, I reject you from being a priest to me**. On "knowledge," see notes on Hos. 2:8 and 4:1–2. The statements have the air of a judicial decision and sentence. The kind of knowledge the priests had rejected is further specified: **since you have forgotten the law of your God**. The consequences of this neglect of God's Word would be seen in the lives of what was most precious to the priests: **I also will forget your children** (cf. 2:4). The future tense still may indicate a warning, hinting that repentance might avert this judgment. But the great privilege of knowing God was in danger of being forfeited, even for the next generation.

And since you have forgotten the law of your God,
[y]I also will forget your children.
7 [z]The more they increased,
the more they sinned against me;
[a]I will change their glory into shame.
8 [b]They feed on the sin[1] of my people;
they are greedy for their iniquity.
9 [c]And it shall be like people, like priest;
I will punish them for their ways
and repay them for their deeds.
10 [d]They shall eat, but not be satisfied;
they shall play the whore, but not multiply,
because they have forsaken the LORD
to cherish 11 whoredom, wine, and new wine,
which [e]take away the understanding.
12 My people [f]inquire of a piece of wood,
and their walking staff gives them oracles.
For [g]a spirit of whoredom has led them astray,
and they have left their God to play the whore.
13 [h]They sacrifice on the tops of the mountains
and burn offerings on the hills,
[i]under oak, poplar, and terebinth,
because their shade is good.
Therefore your daughters play the whore,
and your brides commit adultery.
14 I will not punish your daughters when they play the whore,
nor your brides when they commit adultery;
for [j]the men themselves go aside with prostitutes
and sacrifice with [k]cult prostitutes,
and a people [l]without understanding shall come to ruin.

15 Though you play the whore, O [m]Israel,
let not [m]Judah become guilty.
[n]Enter not into [o]Gilgal,
nor go up to [p]Beth-aven,
and swear not, "As the LORD lives."
16 Like a stubborn heifer,
Israel is stubborn;

[1] Or *sin offering*

6 [y][Jer. 23:39]
7 [z][ch. 13:6] [a]1 Sam. 2:30; Mal. 2:9
8 [b][Lev. 6:25, 26; 10:17]
9 [c]Isa. 24:2
10 [d]Lev. 26:26; Mic. 6:14; Hag. 1:6
11 [e][1 Kgs. 11:4; Prov. 20:1]
12 [f][Judg. 18:5] [g]ch. 5:4; [ch. 2:2]
13 [h]Ezek. 6:13 [i][Isa. 1:29]
14 [j][ch. 9:10] [k]Deut. 23:17 [l][ver. 1, 6]
15 [m]See ch. 6:4 [n]Amos 4:4, 5; 5:5 [o]ch. 9:15; 12:11 [p]ch. 5:8; 10:5; [ch. 10:8; 1 Kgs. 12:29; Amos 1:5]

4:8 They feed on the sin of my people. "Sin" can mean "sin offering" (see ESV footnote), and perhaps that is what is meant here. It was a most holy offering, intended only for the priests (Lev. 6:25–30). **they are greedy for their iniquity**. Literally, "they lift their soul to their iniquity." This obliterates the strict distinction between the priest and the laity that was required by God's law.

4:10–11 They shall eat, but not be satisfied. If this is still directed to the priests, it means that though they eat the sin offerings, they will be spiritually hungry. But v. 10 may expand the focus to speak of punishment for all the people, in which case God is saying that no food will satisfy their hunger. **they shall play the whore**. An allusion to Baalism. The prophet here makes little distinction between abuses of God's law and Baal worship. **whoredom, wine, and new wine . . . take away the understanding**. In addition to the moral perversion of "whoredom," Hosea warns against the common link between sexual immorality and the effects of alcohol, both of which cloud one's thinking, taking away one's ability to discern good and evil.

4:12–13 These verses describe ritual violations against God's laws, in accordance with Canaanite practices. **inquire of a piece of wood**. They would ask for guidance from an idol carved out of wood. **led them astray**. Like sheep following a wicked shepherd. **Therefore your daughters play the whore**. There is a connection between following a false religion (which is spiritual adultery, vv. 12–13a) and the immoral conduct (physical adultery) of the next generation ("Therefore," v. 13b; cf. v. 6). The parents turned away from God, and as a consequence he allowed their daughters and other young women (**your brides**) to stray into sexual immorality.

4:14 I will not punish your daughters. Perhaps spoken in sarcasm, as if to say, how can anyone blame them when the whole people is unfaithful? **sacrifice with cult prostitutes**. This is the only place in Hosea where shrine prostitutes are mentioned. Hosea's wife is never called that. But here an unfaithful spouse is grouped alongside those who participate in sexual activity at pagan places of worship.

4:15 Judah is warned not to follow Israel's lead, though eventually Judah did. Several shrines that might entice Judah are named. **Gilgal**, near Jericho (9:15; 12:11), is where Israel circumcised the new generation, observed the Passover, and where they camped when they marched around Jericho seven days (Josh. 4:19; 5:10; 6:1–14). **Beth-aven** (cf. Hos. 5:8; 10:5; "Aven" in 10:8) means "house of evil"; here it serves as a pejorative name for Bethel (cf. 10:15; 12:4), which means "house of God" (see Gen. 28:19). They are commanded to **swear not, "As the LORD lives"** at these pagan sites. The name of the Lord is not to be associated in any way with such practices.

17[q][ver. 12; ch. 5:3] [r][Matt. 15:14]
18[s][ch. 9:10]
19[t]ch. 13:15; Jer. 4:11; 51:1; [Zech. 5:9] [u][Isa. 1:29]

Chapter 5

1[v]ch. 4:1; Joel 1:2; Amos 3:1; Mic. 1:2 [w][ch. 6:9; 9:8] [x]Judg. 4:6
2[y][ch. 9:15] [z][ch. 9:9; Isa. 29:15] [a][Ps. 50:21]
3[b][Amos 3:2; 5:12]
4[c][Isa. 59:2] [d]ch. 4:12
5[e]ch. 7:10 [f]See ch. 6:4
6[g]ch. 6:6; Isa. 1:11 [h]ch. 9:12
7[i]ch. 6:7
8[j]ch. 8:1; Jer. 4:5 [k]ch. 9:9; 10:9 [l]Josh. 18:25

can the LORD now feed them
like a lamb in a broad pasture?
17 [q]Ephraim is joined to idols;
[r]leave him alone.
18 When their drink is gone, they give themselves to whoring;
[s]their rulers[1] dearly love shame.
19 [t]A wind has wrapped them[2] in its wings,
and they shall [u]be ashamed because of their sacrifices.

Punishment Coming for Israel and Judah

5

1 [v]Hear this, O priests!
Pay attention, O house of Israel!
Give ear, O house of the king!
For the judgment is for you;
for [w]you have been a snare at Mizpah
and a net spread upon [x]Tabor.
2 And [y]the revolters [z]have gone deep into slaughter,
but [a]I will discipline all of them.

3 [b]I know Ephraim,
and Israel is not hidden from me;
for now, O Ephraim, you have played the whore;
Israel is defiled.
4 [c]Their deeds do not permit them
to return to their God.
For [d]the spirit of whoredom is within them,
and they know not the LORD.

5 [e]The pride of Israel testifies to his face;[3]
Israel and [f]Ephraim shall stumble in his guilt;
[f]Judah also shall stumble with them.
6 [g]With their flocks and herds they shall go
to seek the LORD,
[g]but they will not find him;
[h]he has withdrawn from them.
7 [i]They have dealt faithlessly with the LORD;
for they have borne alien children.
Now the new moon shall devour them with their fields.

8 [j]Blow the horn in [k]Gibeah,
the trumpet in [l]Ramah.

[1] Hebrew *shields* [2] Hebrew *her* [3] Or *in his presence*

These sites violate the Mosaic law, which requires one central sanctuary and a Levitical priesthood (Deut. 12:8–14; cf. 1 Kings 12:26–30).

4:17 This is the first time Hosea uses the name **Ephraim** for Israel (using the prominent and centrally located tribe to stand for the whole). He will use it 34 more times.

4:19 A wind has wrapped them in its wings. The Hebrew word for "wind" can also mean "spirit"; cf. v. 12, where "a spirit of whoredom" has engulfed Israel like a whirlwind.

5:1–14 *Adultery in High Places.* The rulers of Israel have led the way into unfaithfulness.

5:1 Hear this, O priests . . . O house of Israel . . . O house of the king. Both royal and religious leadership are addressed. **Mizpah** in Gilead and **Tabor**, a mountain in the Valley of Jezreel, marked high points in Israel's past. Mizpah was the home of Jephthah (Judg. 10:17; 11:8, 11, 29, 34), and Tabor was the scene of Barak's victory (Judg. 4:14; Tabor is also the traditional site of the transfiguration). These revered sites became a "**net spread upon** Tabor." The image of a net, a device used for catching birds, depicts the Israelites as the prey of priests and royalty.

5:2 Have gone deep into slaughter may refer to child sacrifice (cf. Ps. 106:36–38).

5:3–4 Israel is not hidden from me is a subtle barb directed at idolatry where misdeeds are disregarded and concealed. The Lord knows Israel, though Israel does not **know** the Lord (v. 4).

5:5 Israel and Judah have stumbled in **guilt** (cf. 4:5; 14:1, 9). To **stumble** is not a superficial mishap but a serious or even fatal accident. Presumably Israel had some role in leading Judah astray (cf. 4:15).

5:6–7 Though they bring their sacrifices to places like Mizpah and Tabor (v. 1), they **will not find** the Lord. **He has withdrawn from them**—a reference to the worshipers, not these cult centers (for he was never there; cf. note on 4:15). Thus **they have borne alien children** (5:7; i.e., alien to the Lord), illustrated by the last two children born to Gomer. Sadly, **new moon** festivals (celebrations for Israel to rejoice for an abundant harvest, and now syncretized with the cults of the Canaanites) will **devour** the Israelites who participate in them. They and their inheritance (**fields**) will be swallowed up.

5:8 The **horn** (Hb. *shopar*) originally meant a ram's horn, and is the most frequently mentioned musical instrument in the Bible; the **trumpet** is a bugle

Sound the alarm at [m]Beth-aven;
we follow you,[1] O Benjamin!
9 Ephraim shall become a desolation
in the day of punishment;
among the tribes of Israel
I make known what is sure.
10 The princes of Judah have become
like [n]those who move the landmark;
upon them I will pour out
my wrath like water.
11 Ephraim is [o]oppressed, crushed in judgment,
because he was determined to go after filth.[2]
12 But I am [p]like a moth to Ephraim,
and [p]like dry rot to the house of Judah.

13 When Ephraim saw his sickness,
and Judah [q]his wound,
then Ephraim went [r]to Assyria,
and sent to the great king.[3]
[s]But he is not able to cure you
or heal [q]your wound.
14 For I will be [t]like a lion to [u]Ephraim,
and like a young lion to the house of [u]Judah.
[v]I, even I, will tear and go away;
I will carry off, and no one shall rescue.

15 [w]I will return again to my place,
until they acknowledge their guilt and seek my face,
and [x]in their distress earnestly seek me.

Israel and Judah Are Unrepentant

6
1 "Come, let us [y]return to the LORD;
for [z]he has torn us, that he may heal us;
he has struck us down, and [a]he will bind us up.
2 After two days [b]he will revive us;
on the third day he will raise us up,
that we may live before him.

[1] Or *after you* [2] Or *to follow human precepts* [3] Or *to King Jareb*

8 [m]See ch. 4:15
10 [n]Deut. 19:14
11 [o]Deut. 28:33; Amos 4:1
12 [p][Job 13:28]
13 [q][Isa. 1:5, 6] [r]ch. 7:11; 8:9; 12:1; 2 Kgs. 15:19 [s]ch. 14:3
14 [t]ch. 13:7 [u]See ch. 6:4 [v][Mic. 5:8]
15 [w][Jer. 29:10-12; Ezek. 6:9]; See Lev. 26:40-42 [x]Isa. 26:16

Chapter 6

1 [y]ch. 14:1; [ch. 3:5] [z]ch. 5:14; [ch. 13:7, 8] [a][Isa. 30:26]
2 [b]Ps. 71:20; [Luke 24:27, 44; John 2:22; 20:9; 1 Cor. 15:4]

of beaten silver. Both were used to alert the community to danger and summon it to a religious festival. Both **Gibeah** and **Ramah** were in the path of destruction (cf. Isa. 10:29).

5:10 like those who move the landmark. To move a neighbor's boundary marker is expressly forbidden; it brings a curse (Deut. 19:14; 27:17). Land-grabbing violates the divine intention that all of God's people are to enjoy their inheritance, and creates a wealthy, callous, power-abusing class. **my wrath like water**. The word for "wrath" (Hb. *'ebrah*) carries the image of overflowing fury (cf. Isa. 14:6).

5:12 But I am like a moth . . . and like dry rot. These are unusual similes for the Lord; they emphasize his power to make the people waste away (cf. Isa. 50:9; Ps. 39:11 for the moth; and Isa. 40:20 for dry rot; for both together, see Job 13:28).

5:13 When Ephraim saw his sickness, and Judah his wound. The use of physical infirmities to describe spiritual corruption is common to the OT prophets. (Notice how frequently Hosea puts Israel/Ephraim and Judah together: 1:11; 4:15; 5:12–14; 6:4; 8:14; 10:11; 11:12.) Suggestions as to specifics include Menahem paying heavy tribute to Assyria (2 Kings 15:19) after pacifying Assyria by assassinating Shallum (2 Kings 15:13–15), and Ahaz's frantic appeal for military aid (2 Kings 16:5–9). **The great king** is probably Tiglath-pileser III, also called Pul in the OT (745–727 B.C.). This formidable leader headed the neo-Assyrian Empire that ruthlessly subjugated the ancient Near East for over a century.

5:14 I will be like a lion . . . like a young lion. The repetition of the first person, **I, even I**, reminds the audience that it is solely the Lord who controls the nation's fate and not the "great king" (commonly depicted as a lion). Wounded Israel and Judah are vulnerable to a far superior menace, the unleashed fury of the Lord.

5:15–6:3 *Appeal: Return and Be Raised.* The Lord will "return" to his place, expecting the people to "return" to him.

5:15 I will return again to my place alludes to the immediately preceding figure of the lion returning to its den; it is the Lord speaking, and **until they acknowledge their guilt . . . in their distress** declares what he expects of his people.

6:1 let us return to the LORD. Now the prophet includes himself in his imagining of humble submission to the Almighty's discipline. The OT prophets did not separate themselves from the plight of their people (Isa. 6:5; 53:4–6).

6:2 After two days he will revive us shows that even after this fierce slaying (v. 1) they are not beyond the Lord's healing. Healing is a picture of a complete metamorphosis: a rising from the dead on the third day. The Septuagint's Greek translation for **on the third day he will raise us up** is part of what lay behind Jesus' and the NT writers' statements that Jesus' resurrection "on the third day" was according to the Scriptures (Luke 24:46; 1 Cor. 15:4; cf. also Jonah in Matt. 12:40). Hosea was not writing about the Messiah directly, however, but about the people of Israel. The NT use of this idea depends on seeing a parallel between Israel's resurrection on the third day

3 [c]Let us know; [c]let us press on to know the LORD;
[d]his going out is sure as the dawn;
he will come to us [e]as the showers,
[f]as the spring rains that water the earth."
4 What shall I do with you, [g]O [h]Ephraim?
What shall I do with you, O [h]Judah?
Your love is [i]like a morning cloud,
[i]like the dew that goes early away.
5 Therefore I have hewn them by the prophets;
I have slain them [j]by the words of my mouth,
and my judgment goes forth as the light.
6 For [k]I desire steadfast love[1] and not sacrifice,
[l]the knowledge of God rather than burnt offerings.
7 But [m]like Adam they [n]transgressed the covenant;
[o]there they dealt faithlessly with me.
8 [p]Gilead is a city of evildoers,
[q]tracked with blood.
9 As robbers [r]lie in wait for a man,
so the priests band together;
they murder on the way to [s]Shechem;
they commit villainy.
10 In the house of Israel I have seen a horrible thing;
[t]Ephraim's whoredom is there; [u]Israel is defiled.
11 For you also, O [u]Judah, [v]a harvest is appointed,
when [w]I restore the fortunes of my people.

7

1 [x]When I would heal Israel,
the iniquity of Ephraim is revealed,
and the evil deeds of [y]Samaria;
for [z]they deal falsely;
the thief breaks in,
and the bandits raid outside.

3[c][ch. 4:6] [d]Mic. 5:2 [e][ch. 14:5] [f]Joel 2:23
4[g][ch. 11:8] [h]ver. 10, 11; ch. 4:15; 5:5; 8:14; 10:11; 11:12; 12:1, 2; See ch. 5:9-14 [i]ch. 13:3
5[j]Jer. 23:29; [Heb. 4:12]
6[k]Cited Matt. 9:13; 12:7; [1 Sam. 15:22] [l][ch. 2:20]
7[m][Gen. 3:11; Job 31:33; Rom. 5:14] [n]ch. 8:1; Deut. 17:2 [o]ch. 5:7
8[p][ch. 12:11] [q]See ch. 4:2
9[r][ch. 5:1; 7:6] [s]Josh. 24:1
10[t]ch. 5:3; 7:4; [ch. 4:2, 12, 14; 9:10] [u]See ver. 4
11[u][See ver. 10 above] [v]See Joel 3:13 [w]Ps. 126:1; [Job 42:10]

Chapter 7

1[x][ch. 6:4] [y][Jer. 23:13] [z][ch. 4:2]

[1] Septuagint *mercy*

in this verse, and Jesus as the Messiah representing and embodying his people. The potential of Israel's third-day resurrection is to be ultimately realized in the resurrection of the One who acted in Israel's stead (cf. Matt. 3:13–15). This picture of Israel's death and resurrection thus sets the pattern for what eventually will be accomplished in and through Christ.

6:4–7:3 *Transgressors of the Covenant.* Israel's sins are worse than simply violating the law: they repudiate the gracious covenant that is the foundation of their life and hope.

6:4 What shall I do with you, O Ephraim? . . . O Judah? One must not miss this outburst of emotion, like an anguished father not knowing what to do with his wayward child, or a husband agonizingly frustrated with his promiscuous bride (cf. 11:8; Luke 15:20). Israel's response, as envisaged in Hos. 6:1–3, is described as a **morning cloud** and the **dew that goes early away**, both representing the inconstancy of an adulterous wife.

6:5 My judgment goes forth as the light means that God's light exposes Israel's idolatry.

6:6 rather than burnt offerings. God prefers real participation in the covenant on the part of his people, here expressed as **steadfast love** and **knowledge of God**, to the polluted ceremonies of the northern kingdom that ignore these qualities (cf. notes on 4:15; Amos 4:4–5).

6:7 But like Adam they transgressed the covenant. "Covenant" appears four other times in Hosea (2:18; 8:1; 10:4; 12:1). Twice it refers to the transgressing of covenant (6:7; 8:1). The following phrase, **there they dealt faithlessly with me**, along with 8:1 ("they have transgressed my covenant and rebelled against my law") makes it virtually certain that the "covenant" in view is the Mosaic covenant. In addition, the kinds of sins and curses pronounced in the Sinai covenant dovetail precisely with the warnings of the prophet: the end of agricultural prosperity, military disaster, foreign exile, the demise of their offspring, and a return to slavery in Egypt. In sum, the crisis in Israel was Israel's failure to keep covenant. The hard issue is: to whom or to what does "Adam" refer? Many commentators suggest a geographical locality. The difficulty is that there is no record of covenant breaking at a place called Adam (Josh. 3:16), and it requires a questionable taking of the preposition "like" (Hb. *ke-*) to mean "at" or "in." "There" represents the act wherein Israel was unfaithful to the covenant (cf. Hos. 5:7; 6:10). "Mankind" is another suggestion for "Adam," but that would be a vague statement with no known event indicated, and therefore it would not clarify the sentence. It is best to understand "Adam" as the name of the first man; thus Israel is like Adam, who forgot his covenant obligation to love the Lord, breaking the covenant God made with him (Gen. 2:16–17; 3:17). This also implies that there was a "covenant" relationship between God and Adam, the terms of which were defined in God's words to Adam, though the actual word "covenant" is not used in Genesis 1–3.

6:8 Gilead is another of Hosea's allusions to former glories (Judg. 10:17–11:11).

6:9 On the road to **Shechem**, the priests became involved in a conspiracy to assassinate defenseless people. The word for **villainy** (Hb. *zimmah*) is a powerful term for human depravity.

6:11 a harvest is appointed. A harvest which is supposed to depict joy but which will instead depict tragedy. Thus it is a "harvest" of judgment (cf. Joel 3:13; Rev. 14:18–19), which stands in ironic contrast to the harvest of joy that will come to the faithful, **when I restore the fortunes of my people**.

7:1 When I would heal Israel. Similar motifs link this chapter with the previous chapters (5:13 and 7:1; 6:8 and 7:1; 6:9 and 7:11; 5:15 and 7:2). It is the Lord's generosity, not his threats, that weighs heavy.

2 But they do not consider
that [a]I remember all their evil.
Now [b]their deeds surround them;
[c]they are before my face.
3 By their evil [d]they make [d]the king glad,
and the princes by their treachery.
4 [e]They are all adulterers;
they are like a heated oven
whose baker ceases to stir the fire,
from the kneading of the dough
until it is leavened.
5 On the day of [f]our king, the princes
became sick with the heat of wine;
he stretched out his hand with mockers.
6 For with hearts like an oven [g]they approach their intrigue;
all night their anger smolders;
in the morning it blazes like a flaming fire.
7 All of them are hot as an oven,
and they devour their rulers.
All [h]their kings [i]have fallen,
and none of them calls upon me.

8 Ephraim [j]mixes himself with the peoples;
Ephraim is a cake not turned.
9 [k]Strangers devour his strength,
and [l]he knows it not;
gray hairs are sprinkled upon him,
and [l]he knows it not.
10 [m]The pride of Israel testifies to his face;[1]
[n]yet they do not return to the LORD their God,
nor seek him, for all this.

11 Ephraim is like a dove,
[o]silly and without sense,
calling to [p]Egypt, going to [q]Assyria.
12 As they go, [r]I will spread over them my net;
I will bring them down like birds of the heavens;
[s]I will discipline them [t]according to the report made to their
congregation.

2[a][ch. 5:3] [b]Ps. 9:16; Prov. 5:22 [c]Ps. 90:8
3[d]ver. 5; [Rom. 1:32]
4[e]See ch. 6:10
5[f]ver. 3
6[g]ch. 6:9
7[h]ch. 8:4 [i]2 Kgs. 15:10, 14, 25, 30
8[j]Ps. 106:35
9[k][ch. 8:7] [l]Isa. 42:25
10[m]ch. 5:5 [n]Isa. 9:13
11[o]ch. 4:11 [p][ch. 12:1; 2 Kgs. 17:4] [q]See ch. 5:13
12[r]See Ezek. 12:13 [s]ch. 10:10 [t]See Lev. 26:14-39; Deut. 28:15-68

[1] Or *in his presence*

7:2–3 The actions described in ch. 7 illustrate that any sign of remorse for Israel's guilt is completely absent. **By their evil they make the king glad** describes pleasing royalty, perhaps by assassinating potential rivals.

7:4–16 *Four Similes for Unfaithful Israel: Oven, Cake, Dove, Treacherous Bow.* Hosea compares Israel to an oven (vv. 4–7), a half-baked cake (vv. 8–10), a silly dove (vv. 11–12), and a treacherous bow (vv. 13–16), thus describing their passion for evil, their foolishness, and their uselessness.

7:4–7 The word "oven" (Hb. *tannur*), repeated three times in these verses (vv. 4, 6, 7), can designate either a fixed or portable structure. This oven is made of earthenware and is used especially for bread. The comparisons of **adulterers** with an **oven** are both progressive and overlapping. In v. 4, the **heated oven** represents a quiet passion that does not go out even though the **baker ceases to stir the fire**. In v. 6, the **oven** is a suppressed passion, like anger smoldering, that unexpectedly and violently erupts; **it blazes like a flaming fire**. In v. 7 the oven depicts a consuming passion that will **devour . . . rulers** and **all their kings**. Many relate this to the political intrigue that marked Ephraim's final hours. Four of the last six kings of Israel were assassinated. **None of them calls upon** God (v. 7). Here is a close association between an unquenchable zeal for political control and unbridled lust.

7:8 Difficulties with foreign politics inevitably followed these civil internal upheavals. **mixes himself with the peoples**. "Mixes" (Hb. *balal*) is associated with blending ingredients in cooking and links with the "baker" in v. 4 (cf. Lev. 2:4; 7:10; 14:10). Israel's apostasy has made it indistinguishable from the pagan nations. **a cake not turned**. I.e., half-baked, not fit for eating. Some cakes probably included honey and the juice of grapes and figs, and had to be turned while baking.

7:9 Strangers (i.e., foreigners) **devour his strength, and he knows it not**. Israel is unaware of being manipulated by foreigners' politics. **gray hairs are sprinkled upon him**. The nation is like a man who has suddenly grown older and weaker but does not yet realize it. (Perhaps, cf. v. 8, the "gray hairs" are like mold on food.)

7:10 they do not return . . . nor seek him. This explains the conundrum as to why Israel will be devastated despite the Lord's promises of good (cf. v. 13b; 8:3).

7:11–12 Ephraim is like a dove. The dove, usually noted for admirable qualities (cf. 11:11), here is described as fickle. This probably refers to Israel's oscillating between **Egypt** and **Assyria**. It describes the subterfuge of making secret alliances with two opposing powers at the same time as a guarantee of security. **I will bring them down like birds of the heavens**. Pronouncements of judgment include 7:12, 13, 16.

13[u] ch. 9:12 [v] ch. 13:14 [w] [ch. 11:12; 12:1; Mic. 6:12]
14[x] Ps. 78:36, 37 [y] [Amos 6:4, 5]
15[z] [ch. 11:3]
16[a] [ch. 6:1] [b] Ps. 78:57 [c] Ps. 73:9 [d] ch. 9:3

Chapter 8

1[e] ch. 5:8 [f] See Deut. 28:49 [g] ch. 6:7
2[h] See Matt. 7:21-23
4[i] ch. 7:7; 1 Kgs. 12:20 [j] [2 Chr. 13:5]
5[k] ch. 10:5, 6; [1 Kgs. 12:28] [l] [Jer. 13:27]
6[k] [See ver. 5 above] [m] [Mic. 1:6, 7]
7[n] [ch. 10:12, 13]

13 [u]Woe to them, for they have strayed from me!
Destruction to them, for they have rebelled against me!
[v]I would redeem them,
but [w]they speak lies against me.
14 [x]They do not cry to me from the heart,
but [y]they wail upon their beds;
for grain and wine they gash themselves;
they rebel against me.
15 Although [z]I trained and strengthened their arms,
yet they devise evil against me.
16 They [a]return, but not upward;[1]
they are [b]like a treacherous bow;
their princes shall fall by the sword
because of [c]the insolence of their tongue.
This shall be their derision [d]in the land of Egypt.

Israel Will Reap the Whirlwind

8

1 Set [e]the trumpet to your lips!
One [f]like a vulture is over the house of the LORD,
because [g]they have transgressed my covenant
and rebelled against my law.
2 To me they cry,
[h]"My God, we—Israel—know you."
3 Israel has spurned the good;
the enemy shall pursue him.
4 [i]They made kings, [j]but not through me.
They set up princes, but I knew it not.
With their silver and gold they made idols
for their own destruction.
5 [k]I have[2] spurned your calf, O Samaria.
My anger burns against them.
[l]How long will they be incapable of innocence?
6 For it is from Israel;
a craftsman made it;
it is not God.
[k]The calf of Samaria
[m]shall be broken to pieces.[3]
7 For [n]they sow the wind,
and they shall reap the whirlwind.

[1] *Or to the Most High* [2] *Hebrew He has* [3] *Or shall go up in flames*

7:14–15 gash themselves. Probably as a means of invoking Baal (cf. 1 Kings 18:28). **I trained and strengthened their arms.** Cf. Hos. 2:8 and 11:3.

7:16 Egypt here is a symbolic name for all foreign powers, and is intended as a metaphorical reference to Israel's bondage in Egypt prior to the exodus, rather than a literal reference to a new deportation to Egypt. Like other historical references in Hosea, this name bemoans the reversal of Israel's fortunes. The humiliation and degradation of being taken into captivity is depicted on numerous reliefs from the ancient Near East (cf. Joel 2:17).

8:1–14 *Israel's Hypocrisy.* The people of Israel may claim to know and love the Lord, but their deeds prove otherwise.

8:1 Set the trumpet to your lips. See note on 5:8. The **vulture** is a symbol of an aggressor, possibly the Assyrian. **House of the LORD** does not refer to the temple, since the temple resided in Jerusalem. It probably refers to the Lord's land, a phrase peculiar to Hosea (cf. 9:4, 15). The remarks are obviously ominous from what follows. **because they have transgressed my covenant.** Note that he says "transgressed," not "annulled" (cf. 6:7). The Lord had not "annulled" his covenant with Israel; she was still his estranged wife. While it was a foregone conclusion that Israel would violate the covenant, provisions for reconciliation were put in place (Lev. 26:40–45; Deut. 31:27–29; cf. Deut. 30:1–10).

8:2 Chapter 8 is a response to Israel's **cry**. For the people of Israel to say they **know** God is hypocritical (cf. 2:8; 5:4; 11:3). What follows are accusations that expose Israel's idolatry, politics, and false worship.

8:3 The enemy shall pursue him perhaps refers to the "vulture" in v. 1.

8:4 kings . . . princes. The grievance is twofold. The leaders are not the Lord's choice, and these usurpers are not godly. **I knew it not.** Hosea and his readers were well aware that God knows everything; the point is not whether God was aware of the princes they had set up, but rather, that the people had never asked him for guidance before choosing these leaders.

8:5–6 I have spurned your calf, O Samaria. These verses respond to v. 3, "Israel has spurned the good." Archaeologists have found sculptures of Baal standing on a bull. This calf-idol is reminiscent of the calf-idol made by Aaron (Ex. 32:1–4) and the calf-idol erected at Bethel (1 Kings 12:28–29). As the calf-idol in Aaron's day was pulverized, so this idol **shall be broken to pieces** (cf. also 2 Kings 23:15).

8:7 For they sow the wind, and they shall reap the whirlwind. Trusting flimsy alliances ("sowing the wind") will exacerbate the situation by reaping "the whirlwind" (by bringing on a ruthless invader).

The standing grain has no heads;
it shall yield no flour;
if it were to yield,
[o]strangers would devour it.
8 [p]Israel is swallowed up;
already they are among the nations
as [q]a useless vessel.
9 For [r]they have gone up to Assyria,
[s]a wild donkey wandering alone;
Ephraim has hired lovers.
10 Though they hire allies among the nations,
I will soon gather them up.
And [t]the king and princes [u]shall soon writhe
because of the tribute.

11 Because Ephraim [v]has multiplied altars for sinning,
they have become to him altars for sinning.
12 [w]Were I to write for him my laws by the ten thousands,
they would be regarded as a strange thing.
13 As for my sacrificial offerings,
[x]they sacrifice meat and eat it,
but the LORD does not accept them.
[y]Now he will remember their iniquity
and punish their sins;
[z]they shall return to Egypt.
14 For [a]Israel has forgotten [b]his Maker
and [c]built palaces,
and [a]Judah has multiplied fortified cities;
so [d]I will send a fire upon his cities,
and it shall devour her strongholds.

The LORD Will Punish Israel

9

1 Rejoice not, O Israel!
Exult not like the peoples;
[e]for you have played the whore, forsaking your God.
[f]You have loved a prostitute's wages
on all threshing floors.
2 [g]Threshing floor and wine vat shall not feed them,
and [g]the new wine shall fail them.
3 They shall not remain in [h]the land of the LORD,
but [i]Ephraim shall return to Egypt,
and [j]they shall eat unclean food in Assyria.

4 [k]They shall not pour drink offerings of wine to the LORD,
[l]and their sacrifices shall not please him.
It shall be like [m]mourners' bread to them;
all who eat of it shall be defiled;
for their bread shall be for their hunger only;
[n]it shall not come to the house of the LORD.
5 [o]What will you do on the day of the appointed festival,
and on the day of the feast of the LORD?

7[o][ch. 7:9]
8[p]2 Kgs. 17:6 [q]Jer. 22:28
9[r]See ch. 5:13 [s][Jer. 2:24]
10[t]See Ezek. 26:7 [u][ch. 4:7, 10]
11[v]ch. 10:1; 12:11
12[w][Deut. 4:6, 8]
13[x]Jer. 7:21; [Amos 4:4] [y]ch. 9:9; Amos 8:7 [z]ch. 9:3; Deut. 28:68; [ch. 11:5]
14[a]See ch. 6:4 [b]Isa. 17:7 [c][Amos 5:11] [d]Amos 2:5

Chapter 9

1[e]ch. 1:2 [f]ch. 2:5; Jer. 44:17
2[g][ch. 2:9]
3[h]Jer. 2:7; 16:18; See Lev. 25:23 [i]See ch. 8:13 [j]Ezek. 4:13; Dan. 1:8
4[k][ch. 3:4] [l][ch. 8:13] [m]Deut. 26:14; Ezek. 24:17 [n][Hag. 2:13]
5[o][Isa. 10:3]

8:10 Foreign armies ravaged the land, exacting heavy **tribute** as they went.

8:14 Shall devour her strongholds refers to the most secure place within each city, its citadel (1 Kings 16:18; 2 Kings 15:25; Ps. 48:3; Isa. 25:4). Ephraim trusted religious shrines for security; Judah her armaments. Both will prove to be futile.

9:1–9 *Warnings: No Worship in a Foreign Land.* God will punish Israel by sending her people away from the land, to a place where they will not be able to make sacrifices to the Lord.

9:1 A **prostitute's wages** (cf. 2:12) are scorned by the Lord (Deut. 23:18).

9:3 The failure of crops in the land is not the only outcome of Ephraim's adultery. Expulsion is another consequence. The mention of exile to **Egypt** and **Assyria** reflects the oscillating politics of Israel, trying to play the two against each other (cf. 7:11).

6 For behold, they are going away from destruction;
but [p]Egypt shall gather them;
Memphis shall bury them.
Nettles shall possess [q]their precious things of silver;
[r]thorns shall be in their tents.

7 [s]The days of punishment have come;
the days of recompense have come;
Israel shall know it.
[t]The prophet is a fool;
the man of the spirit is mad,
because of your great iniquity
and great hatred.
8 The prophet is [u]the watchman of Ephraim with my God;
yet [v]a fowler's snare is on all his ways,
and hatred in the house of his God.
9 [w]They have deeply corrupted themselves
as [x]in the days of Gibeah:
[w]he will remember their iniquity;
he will punish their sins.

10 Like grapes in the wilderness,
[y]I found Israel.
Like the first fruit on the fig tree
in its first season,
I saw your fathers.
But [z]they came to Baal-peor
and [a]consecrated themselves to the thing of shame,
and [b]became detestable like the thing they loved.
11 Ephraim's [c]glory shall fly away like a bird—
[d]no birth, no pregnancy, no conception!
12 [e]Even if they bring up children,
I will bereave them till none is left.
[f]Woe to them
when [g]I depart from them!
13 Ephraim, [h]as I have seen, was like a young palm[1] planted in a meadow;
but [e]Ephraim must lead his children out to slaughter.[2]
14 Give them, O LORD—
what will you give?
Give them [i]a miscarrying womb
and dry breasts.

6 [p]See ch. 8:13 [q][ch. 10:8; Isa. 2:20] [r][ch. 10:8]
7 [s]See Isa. 10:3 [t]Ezek. 13:3
8 [u]Ezek. 3:17 [v]Ps. 91:3; [ch. 5:1]
9 [w][ch. 5:2] [x]ch. 10:9; Judg. 19:22
10 [y][Ps. 80:8; Isa. 5:1] [z]Num. 25:3; Ps. 106:28 [a][ch. 4:14] [b][Rom. 1:28, 29]
11 [c]ch. 10:5; [ch. 4:7] [d][Isa. 26:18]
12 [e]ch. 13:16 [f]ch. 7:13 [g]ch. 5:6; 1 Sam. 28:15, 16; Ezek. 10:18
13 [h][Ezek. 27:3] [e][See ver. 12 above]
14 [i][Luke 23:29]

[1] Or *like Tyre* [2] Hebrew *to him who slaughters*

9:4 their sacrifices shall not please him. It shall be like mourners' bread. A description of conditions in exile. Because the food is unclean (v. 3), they **shall be defiled** and therefore not acceptable in God's presence.

9:6 They are going away from destruction is an indication that they think they are safe. Their hope is quickly dashed, however: **but Egypt shall gather them**. Other disasters are described in the rest of the verse.

9:7 Some understand **the prophet is a fool** as Hosea's quotation of Israel's earlier ridicule of the prophet, God's watchman (cf. Jer. 6:16; Ezek. 3:17; 33:2, 6–7)—i.e., that Ephraim's rejection of God's messenger causes them to entrap themselves. By this interpretation, the last two lines would be Hosea's response, showing why the prophets have been prophesying such disaster. Others understand this as Hosea's own statement. By this interpretation, Hosea then says, in the last two lines, that the people's **great iniquity** shows the reason why these prophets' predictions have been so foolish.

9:9 As in the days of Gibeah refers to the events in Judges 19–21, where God brings judgment on Gibeah and the tribe of Benjamin (Judg. 20:35) for their cruel violence (Judg. 19:22–26; cf. Hos. 10:9).

9:10–11:11 *More Similes for Unfaithful Israel: Grapes, Vine, Calf, Toddler.* Hosea uses four more comparisons to describe Israel: grapes in the wilderness (9:10–17), a luxuriant vine (10:1–10), a trained calf (10:11–15), and a toddler (11:1–11), all of which stress God's past care for them, their reckless ingratitude, and the unavoidable consequences.

9:10 Like grapes in the wilderness. . . . Like the first fruit on the fig tree. The unexpected discovery of grapes in the desert or the first figs of the season is absolutely delightful (cf. v. 13). **I saw your fathers** shows this is another reference to the nation's early history. But like Hosea's marriage, that cherished relationship had a surprisingly short life. **they came to Baal-peor** (Num. 25:3, 5, 18; cf. Ps. 106:28). Idolatry and whoredom have also gone hand in hand from Israel's very beginning.

9:11–12 Woe to them when I depart from them. When Israel spurns God's grace, they are left to their own devices. Judgment is dramatic, for there will be **no birth, no pregnancy**, not even **conception**. If the nation does not change, it will soon head toward extinction.

9:14 A **miscarrying womb** would be the opposite of the fruitfulness the people sought in Baal worship (see Introduction: Purpose, Occasion, and Background).

15 Every evil of theirs is in [j]Gilgal;
there I began to hate them.
Because of the wickedness of their deeds
I will drive them out of my house.
I will love them no more;
all [k]their princes are [l]rebels.
16 Ephraim is stricken;
[m]their root is dried up;
they shall bear no fruit.
Even [n]though they give birth,
[e]I will put their beloved children to death.
17 [o]My God will reject them
because they have not listened to him;
[p]they shall be wanderers among the nations.

10

1 [q]Israel is a luxuriant vine
that yields its fruit.
The more his fruit increased,
[r]the more altars he built;
as his country improved,
he improved his pillars.
2 Their heart is false;
now they must bear their guilt.
The LORD[1] will break down their altars
and destroy their pillars.
3 For now they will say:
[s]"We have no king,
for we do not fear the LORD;
and a king—what could he do for us?"
4 They utter [t]mere words;
with empty oaths they make covenants;
so [u]judgment springs up like poisonous weeds
[v]in the furrows of the field.
5 The inhabitants of Samaria tremble
for [w]the calf[2] of [x]Beth-aven.
Its people mourn for it, and so do its idolatrous priests—
those who rejoiced over it and [y]over its glory—
for it has departed[3] from them.
6 [z]The thing itself shall be carried to Assyria
as tribute to [a]the great king.[4]
Ephraim shall be put to shame,
and Israel shall be ashamed [b]of his idol.[5]

15[j]ch. 4:15; 12:11 [k]ch. 8:4 [l][ch. 5:2]
16[m][ver. 11] [n][ver. 12, 13] [e][See ver. 12 above]
17[o][ch. 8:5] [p]Deut. 28:64, 65

Chapter 10

1[q]See Ps. 80:8-11 [r]ch. 8:11
3[s][ver. 7, 15; 1 Sam. 12:12]
4[t][ch. 4:2] [u]Amos 5:7; 6:12 [v]ch. 12:11
5[w]See 1 Kgs. 12:28 [x]See ch. 4:15 [y]ch. 9:11; [1 Sam. 4:21, 22]
6[z][Isa. 46:2] [a]ch. 5:13 [b]ch. 11:6

[1] Hebrew *He* [2] Or *calves* [3] Or *has gone into exile* [4] Or *to King Jareb* [5] Or *counsel*

9:16–17 their root is dried up; they shall bear no fruit. Again (see note on v. 14), this punishment is the opposite of what they sought in worshiping the Baals. **wanderers among the nations.** That is, they will be exiles. **they have not listened to him.** God's people put themselves at risk when they abandon dependency on the Lord and obedience to him.

10:1–2 For the image of Israel as a **vine**, cf. Ps. 80:8–16; Jer. 2:21; Ezek. 15:1–8; 17:1–10. This example suits Hosea's repeated pattern that Israel got off to a good start but then went wrong. The vine's **fruit increased**, and the **country improved**. However, the more Israel prospered, the more Israel sinned. **the more altars he built . . . he improved his pillars**. It was just as Moses had warned (Deut. 8:11–14). Abundance is risky; God's people could not handle it (cf. Prov. 30:7–9).

10:3 We have no king. The prophet foretells the end of the northern monarchy due to the people's unfaithfulness.

10:4 It is difficult to determine whether those who **utter mere words** are Israelites (v. 3) or their kings. If Israelites, it refers to Israel's misplaced reliance on their leaders and the hypocritical or blind claim that they are nevertheless faithful to the Lord (cf. 1 Sam. 8:7; Hos. 7:14). If it refers to the words of kings, their covenants/promises do not stem from integrity but are untrustworthy, **empty oaths**.

10:5 The address moves to the future. **The inhabitants . . . tremble**. Both their king and calf-idol will be removed from Samaria. What the people and the priests once **rejoiced over**, they will mourn for. On **Beth-aven**, see note on 4:15. The term **glory** describes the special presence of God in his sanctuary (cf. Ex. 40:34). Here it is the presumed presence of God at the illegitimate sanctuary. It will depart (or go into exile, ESV footnote), just as the legitimate glory did (1 Sam. 4:21–22).

10:6 The idol they worshiped becomes tribute for the **great king** of **Assyria** (see 5:13).

7 [c]Samaria's king shall perish
like a twig on the face of the waters.
8 The high places of [x]Aven, [d]the sin of Israel,
shall be destroyed.
[e]Thorn and thistle shall grow up
on their altars,
and [f]they shall say to the mountains, "Cover us,"
and to the hills, "Fall on us."

9 From [g]the days of Gibeah, you have sinned, O Israel;
there they have continued.
Shall not the war against the unjust[1] overtake them in Gibeah?
10 [h]When I please, [i]I will discipline them,
and nations shall be gathered against them
when they are bound up for [j]their double iniquity.

11 Ephraim was a trained calf
that [k]loved to thresh,
and I spared her fair neck;
but I will put [l]Ephraim to the yoke;
[l]Judah must plow;
Jacob must harrow for himself.
12 [m]Sow for yourselves righteousness;
reap steadfast love;
[n]break up your fallow ground,
for it is the time to seek the LORD,
that he may come and [o]rain righteousness upon you.

13 [p]You have plowed iniquity;
you have reaped injustice;
you have eaten the fruit of lies.
Because you have trusted in your own way
and in the multitude of your warriors,
14 therefore [q]the tumult of war shall arise among your people,
and all your fortresses shall be destroyed,
as [r]Shalman destroyed Beth-arbel on the day of battle;
[s]mothers were dashed in pieces with their children.
15 Thus it shall be done to you, O [t]Bethel,
because of your great evil.
At dawn [a]the king of Israel
shall be utterly cut off.

The LORD's Love for Israel

11

1 [u]When Israel was a child, [v]I loved him,
and out of Egypt I [w]called [x]my son.

7[c][ver. 3]
8[x][See ver. 5 above] [d]1 Kgs. 12:30; Amos 8:14 [e][ch. 9:6] [f]Luke 23:30; Rev. 6:16; [Isa. 2:19]
9[g]ch. 9:9
10[h][Ex. 32:34] [i]ch. 7:12 [j][1 Kgs. 12:28]
11[k][Deut. 25:4; 1 Cor. 9:9; 1 Tim. 5:18] [l]See ch. 6:4
12[m][ch. 8:7; Gal. 6:8] [n]Jer. 4:3 [o]Isa. 45:8
13[p][ch. 8:7]
14[q][ch. 1:5] [r]2 Kgs. 17:3 [s][ch. 13:16]
15[t][ver. 5] [a][See ver. 6 above]

Chapter 11

1[u][ch. 2:15] [v]Deut. 7:8; [ch. 14:4] [w]Cited Matt. 2:15 [x]Ex. 4:22; [Mal. 1:6]

[1] Hebrew *the children of injustice*

10:7 The imagery **like a twig on the face of the waters** (i.e., tossed about every which way and then swept away) illustrates the helplessness and weakness of the kings that Israel trusted.

10:8 The **thorn and thistle** indicate that the land is unproductive; cf. Gen. 3:18; Matt. 7:16; Heb. 6:8. For **Aven** (another name for Beth-aven), see note on Hos. 4:15.

10:9 the days of Gibeah. See note on 9:9. The idea is that if disaster overtook the Benjaminites at Gibeah, how much more is Israel now in trouble.

10:10 When I please, I will discipline them. While the primary source of Israel's discipline and downfall is the Lord himself, the agency of discipline will be through the **nations** that **shall be gathered against them** (cf. Isa. 10:5). OT prophets frequently linked the first cause (the Lord) with secondary causes (here, the nations).

10:11–13 The passage is punctuated with agrarian images, again alluding to the issue of fertility. **Ephraim was a trained calf**—another allusion to Israel's beginnings. The Lord spared Israel the yoke; she loved to thresh in his field (cf. Deut. 25:4). But that freedom was abused: **you have plowed iniquity . . . reaped injustice** (Hos. 10:13). Therefore, the Lord must harness Ephraim. The idea here is in concert with Hosea restraining his wife, so that Israel would **sow** the seeds of **righteousness** and plow and **reap** a crop of **steadfast love** (v. 12; cf. 8:7). A deaf ear to the prophet's appeals will translate into a military disaster.

10:14 as Shalman destroyed Beth-arbel on the day of battle. "Shalman" is an otherwise unknown name but may refer to the Assyrian king Shalmaneser V (727–722 B.C.), who besieged Samaria from 725 to 723. The location of "Beth-arbel" is unknown. The violence described suits Assyrian barbarity, and the degree of punishment is equal to the size of the offenses.

11:1 When Israel was a child, I loved him, and out of Egypt I called

2 [y]The more they were called,
the more they went away;
[z]they kept sacrificing to the Baals
and burning offerings to idols.

3 Yet it was [a]I who taught Ephraim to walk;
I took them up by their arms,
but they did not know that [b]I healed them.

4 [c]I led them with cords of kindness,[1]
with the bands of love,
and [d]I became to them as one who eases the yoke on their jaws,
and [e]I bent down to them and fed them.

5 [f]They shall not[2] return to the land of Egypt,
but [g]Assyria shall be their king,
[h]because [i]they have refused to return to me.

6 [j]The sword shall rage against their cities,
consume the bars of their gates,
and devour them [k]because of their own counsels.

7 My people are bent [l]on turning away from me,
and though [m]they call out to the Most High,
he shall not raise them up at all.

8 How can I give you up, O Ephraim?
How can I hand you over, O Israel?
[n]How can I make you [o]like Admah?
How can I treat you [o]like Zeboiim?
[p]My heart recoils within me;
my compassion grows warm and tender.

9 I will not execute my burning anger;
I will not again destroy Ephraim;
[q]for I am God and not a man,
[r]the Holy One in your midst,
and I will not come in wrath.[3]

10 [s]They shall go after the LORD;
[t]he will roar like a lion;
when he roars,
his children shall come trembling [u]from the west;

[1] Or *humaneness;* Hebrew *man* [2] Or *surely* [3] Or *into the city*

2[y][ver. 7] [z][ch. 2:13; 13:1, 2]
3[a][ch. 7:15; Deut. 1:31] [b]Ex. 15:26
4[c]Jer. 31:3; [John 6:44; 12:32] [d]Lev. 26:13 [e]See Ps. 78:24-29
5[f][ch. 8:13] [g][ch. 10:3] [h][2 Kgs. 17:13, 14] [i][ch. 4:16; 7:16]
6[j][ch. 10:14] [k]ch. 10:6
7[l]ch. 14:4 [m][ver. 2]
8[n][Gen. 19:24, 25; Jer. 49:18; 50:40; Amos 4:11; Jude 7] [o]Gen. 14:8; Deut. 29:23 [p][Deut. 32:36]
9[q]See Num. 23:19 [r]See Isa. 12:6
10[s][ch. 3:5] [t]Isa. 31:4; Jer. 25:30; Joel 3:16; Amos 1:2 [u]Isa. 11:11; Zech. 8:7

my son. Here is one of the most endearing passages in Hosea. The prophet uses another family metaphor, portraying the Lord not only as a husband but also as a father (cf. Luke 15:11–32). This metaphor was not original to Hosea (cf. Ex. 4:22–23). Matthew 2:15 uses the line "out of Egypt I called my son" to show that Jesus is the "Son of God," i.e., the heir of David who embodies Israel's relationship to God (cf. 2 Sam. 7:14; Ps. 89:26–27).

11:2–4 The Lord loved Israel from the beginning and never stopped loving them. Throughout their history, he **taught Ephraim** (that is, Israel) **to walk** and **healed them** (v. 3), as a father does with his child. Some commentators think the image of a parent and a child continues in v. 4 in **led them with cords of kindness, with the bands of love**. The meaning would be light bands or cords with which a parent supports and guides a toddler who is learning to walk. But most commentators think that in v. 4 the image changes to that of a kind farmer with his animals, who removes the **yoke** and leads the animal, not with harsh ropes and a yoke (as in 10:11), but with light "cords" and "bands" to guide the animals to their food. Then the Lord, like a gentle farmer, even **bent down** and **fed them** (11:4). In all of this manifestation of grace, the Lord was *not* initiating a new basis for a relationship between him and his people, for the relationship from the beginning was never based on law but on redemptive grace. Among other places, this is illustrated by the preamble of the Ten Commandments: "I am the LORD your God, who brought you out of the land of Egypt, out of the house of slavery" (Ex. 20:2). It was God's love that provided and still provides the underpinning for an ultimate relationship of care, guidance, and obedience. Tragically, however, more than anything else, it was the Lord's love that was spurned: **The more they were called, the more they went away** (Hos. 11:2), and "My people are bent on turning away from me" (v. 7).

11:5–7 They shall not return . . . but Assyria. Some read "not" as "surely" (ESV footnote), since 8:13; 9:3; and 11:11 seem to contradict reading a negative here. This is grammatically possible, but not necessary. (See note on 7:16: "Egypt" in those earlier verses may be a name representing all foreign powers, whereas here Hosea says they will not literally return to **Egypt**.) This verse may mean that hope of finding deliverance from Egypt will fail. The Israelites will find themselves subject to a new pharaoh, not in Egypt but in Assyria.

11:8 How can I give you up? In highly anthropomorphic terms, the Lord pours out his irrepressible love; Isa. 49:15 and Jer. 31:20 express the same sentiment. The relationship between God and his chosen must not be viewed as a formality. These emotional outpourings demonstrate that the Lord is a person, filled with compassion—unlike the lifeless Baals. His affection weighs heavier than Israel's ingratitude, and he cannot bring himself to renounce his people, even though they renounce him. **How can I make you like Admah . . . like Zeboiim?** These two cities were totally destroyed (see Deut. 29:23; also Gen. 14:2, 8). The love that the Lord has for his children restrains him from obliterating them. He will preserve Israel through a remnant (cf. Rom. 11:5).

11 [v]See ch. 8:13 [w]Isa. 60:8 [x]Zech. 10:6, 10; [ch. 9:3]
12 [y][ch. 7:13]
Chapter 12
1 [z][ch. 13:15; Jer. 18:17] [y][See ch. 11:12 above] [a]See ch. 5:13 [b][ch. 7:11; 2 Kgs. 17:4]
2 [c]See ch. 4:1
3 [d]Gen. 25:26; [Gen. 27:36]
4 [e]Gen. 28:12, 19; 35:9, 10, 15
5 [f]Ex. 3:15
6 [g]ch. 14:1, 2; Joel 2:12, 13 [h][Mic. 6:8]
7 [i]Amos 8:5; Mic. 6:11; [Prov. 11:1; 20:23] [j]Mic. 2:2
8 [k]Zech. 11:5; Rev. 3:17 [l][Deut. 29:19]
9 [m]ch. 13:4 [n]See Lev. 23:39-43; Neh. 8:14-18
10 [o][2 Kgs. 17:13] [p][Joel 2:28]

11 they shall come trembling like birds [v]from Egypt,
and [w]like doves [x]from the land of Assyria,
and I will return them to their homes, declares the LORD.
12 [1] Ephraim [y]has surrounded me with lies,
and the house of Israel with deceit,
but Judah still walks with God
and is faithful to the Holy One.

12

1 Ephraim feeds on the wind
and pursues [z]the east wind all day long;
they multiply [y]falsehood and violence;
[a]they make a covenant with Assyria,
and [b]oil is carried to Egypt.

The LORD's Indictment of Israel and Judah

2 [c]The LORD has an indictment against Judah
and will punish Jacob according to his ways;
he will repay him according to his deeds.
3 [d]In the womb he took his brother by the heel,
and in his manhood he strove with God.
4 He strove with the angel and prevailed;
he wept and sought his favor.
[e]He met God[2] at Bethel,
and there God spoke with us—
5 the LORD, the God of hosts,
[f]the LORD is his memorial name:
6 "So you, [g]by the help of your God, return,
[h]hold fast to love and justice,
and wait continually for your God."
7 A merchant, in whose hands are [i]false balances,
he loves [j]to oppress.
8 Ephraim has said, "Ah, but [k]I am rich;
I have found wealth for myself;
in all my labors [l]they cannot find in me iniquity or sin."
9 [m]I am the LORD your God
from the land of Egypt;
I will again make you [n]dwell in tents,
as in the days of the appointed feast.
10 [o]I spoke to the prophets;
it was I who multiplied [p]visions,
and through the prophets gave parables.

[1] Ch 12:1 in Hebrew [2] Hebrew *him*

11:10–11 His children shall come trembling . . . I will return them to their homes describes the return of a remnant of God's people from exile.

11:12–12:1 *Dependence on Alliances.* **Ephraim has surrounded me with lies . . . but Judah still walks with God** (11:12). Judah and the northern tribes (Ephraim) both suffered lapses in fidelity to the Lord, but Judah, unlike Ephraim, had some good kings (in particular, Hezekiah). One of the highest points in Judah's history was the victory over the Assyrians when Hezekiah was king (see 2 Kings 18–19, which was 20 years after Samaria fell).

12:1 Ephraim feeds on the wind. Ephraim depends on what is elusive and unprofitable (for wind used as an image this way, cf. Job 6:26; 8:2; 15:2; Ps. 78:39; Eccles. 1:14; 2:11; Isa. 26:18; 41:16). "Wind" graphically describes the duplicity of both Israel and Judah's covenant making. **Oil . . . to Egypt** could refer to an inducement offered to Egypt for relief when Israel was paying tribute to Assyria.

12:2–14 *Further Indictment Based on Historical Review.* Hosea recounts incidents from Israel's past in order to display the Lord's enduring kindness and Israel's stubborn ingratitude.

12:3–4 The references are to events in Jacob's life where he excelled. Jacob **took his brother by the heel** at birth (Gen. 25:26). **He strove with the angel and prevailed** (Hos. 12:4) at Peniel (Gen. 32:24–31). There the angel touched Jacob's hip socket and put it out of joint. That divine wounding of Jacob made him into a new man, Israel. Jacob **met God at Bethel** (Hos. 12:4) when he complied with God's command, and God reassured Jacob of his former promises (Gen. 35:9–15).

12:5–8 The specific mention of **the LORD** by his fuller name is joined with the prevailing of Jacob. (For the **memorial name**, cf. Ex. 3:15.) The prophet once again calls his people to their divine calling and election, ratified by promises to the patriarchs (see note on Hos. 2:8; cf. Rom. 9:10–13). God's election was the origin of Israel's calling and the very reason that Israel can now be restored: by grace, Israel can return and exhibit the qualities of **love and justice** (Hos. 12:6). But Israel's deeds and words (vv. 7–8) show they refuse to **hold fast** and **wait continually for** their **God** (v. 6). **A merchant, in whose hands are false balances**. Their cruel and deceptive business practices **oppress** while they think of themselves as innocent.

12:10 it was I who multiplied visions. The revelations granted to the

11 [q]If there is iniquity in Gilead,
they shall surely come to nothing:
[r]in Gilgal they sacrifice bulls;
[s]their altars also are like stone heaps
[t]on the furrows of the field.
12 [u]Jacob fled to the land of Aram;
there Israel [v]served for a wife,
and for a wife he guarded sheep.
13 By [w]a prophet [x]the LORD brought Israel up from Egypt,
and by a prophet he was guarded.
14 [y]Ephraim has given bitter provocation;
so his Lord [z]will leave his bloodguilt on him
[a]and will repay him for his disgraceful deeds.

The LORD's Relentless Judgment on Israel

13 1 When Ephraim spoke, there was trembling;
[b]he was exalted in Israel,
but he incurred guilt [c]through Baal and died.
2 And now they sin more and more,
and [d]make for themselves metal images,
idols skillfully made of their silver,
[e]all of them the work of craftsmen.
It is said of them,
"Those who offer human sacrifice [f]kiss calves!"
3 Therefore they shall be [g]like the morning mist
or [g]like the dew that goes early away,
[h]like the chaff that swirls from the threshing floor
or [i]like smoke from a window.

4 But [j]I am the LORD your God
from the land of Egypt;
[k]you know no God but me,
and [l]besides me there is no savior.
5 [m]It was I who knew you in the wilderness,
in the land of drought;
6 [n]but when they had grazed,[1] they became full,
[o]they were filled, and their heart was lifted up;
[o]therefore they forgot me.
7 So [p]I am to them like a lion;
[q]like a leopard I will lurk beside the way.
8 I will fall upon them [r]like a bear robbed of her cubs;
I will tear open their breast,

[1] Hebrew *according to their pasture*

11 [q]ch. 6:8 [r]ch. 4:15; 9:15 [s]ch. 8:11 [t]ch. 10:4
12 [u]Gen. 28:5 [v]Gen. 29:20, 28
13 [w][Deut. 18:15] [x]Ex. 12:50, 51; Ps. 77:20; See Isa. 63:11-14
14 [y]2 Kgs. 17:17 [z]See ch. 4:2 [a]ver. 2

Chapter 13
1 [b][Amos 6:13] [c]See ch. 11:2
2 [d]ch. 2:8 [e][Ps. 115:4; Isa. 40:19, 20] [f][1 Kgs. 19:18; Job 31:26, 27]
3 [g]ch. 6:4 [h]See Ps. 1:4 [i]See Ps. 68:2
4 [j]ch. 12:9 [k]See Ex. 20:3 [l]Isa. 43:11; 45:21
5 [m]Deut. 2:7; Amos 3:2
6 [n][ch. 4:7] [o]Deut. 8:12, 14; [Deut. 32:15]
7 [p]ch. 5:14 [q]Jer. 5:6
8 [r]2 Sam. 17:8; Prov. 17:12

Lord's people by the ministry of the Lord's prophets were special and numerous (Deut. 4:5–6, 32–36; Ps. 147:19–20). The visions and **parables** given to the prophets indicate the normal means that God uses to reveal truths to the prophets (cf. Num. 12:6).

12:12–14 The mention again of **Jacob** emphasizes God's grace in preserving his fugitive so that he would father the 12 tribes of Israel. **Aram** is Paddan-Aram (Gen. 28:2, 5). The **prophet** was Moses, who led the nation out of **Egypt** (Deut. 18:15; 34:10). In the face of God's gracious deliverance and preservation of his people, **Ephraim has given bitter provocation**.

13:1–8 *Worship of Man-made Gods.* The man-made gods that Israel worships are nothing compared to their actual God, who is living, active, and true to his word.

13:1 there was trembling. The idea seems to be that at one time Ephraim's word commanded respect.

13:2 who offer human sacrifice. Child sacrifice was a part of Baal worship (Isa. 57:5). **kiss calves**. Kissing is a way of paying homage (1 Kings 19:18). The excavations at Ashkelon have uncovered an example of calf worship in a sanctuary from the sixteenth century B.C. A small, solid bronze calf was discovered, and around it were remains of a pottery shrine that housed the calf. Calf worship, of course, was a problem throughout the history of Israel (see Exodus 32; 1 Kings 12).

13:3 The similes of **mist**, **dew**, **chaff**, and **smoke** liken Israel's end to vapors that quickly dissipate.

13:4–5 But I am the LORD your God from the land of Egypt. In contrast to fleeting vapors, this is a solemn statement that rehearses Ex. 20:2. The passing work of the craftsmen who make idols (Hos. 13:2) stands in vivid disparity to the God who sustained Israel **in the land of drought** by his devoted care.

13:6 but when they had grazed. Their devotion in the wilderness diminished with prosperity (cf. 2:8; 10:1–2).

13:7–8 a lion . . . a leopard . . . a bear. Hosea's contemporary (and fellow prophet to the northern kingdom) Amos also depicts Israel as the prey of wild beasts, an image of God's judgment (Amos 3:12; cf. Hos. 5:14).

8[s][ch. 2:12]
9[t][Deut. 33:26]
10[u][ch. 8:4; 10:3] [v]1 Sam. 8:5, 19
11[w][1 Sam. 8:22] [x][1 Sam. 15:23]
12[y]Job 14:17
13[z]Isa. 13:8; 1 Thess. 5:3 [a][2 Kgs. 19:3]
14[b]Isa. 25:8; 26:19; Ezek. 37:12 [c][1 Cor. 15:55] [d][Ezek. 14:21] [e][Ezek. 9:10]
15[f][Gen. 41:52] [g][Ezek. 19:12; Jonah 4:8; Hab. 1:9] [h][Ezek. 17:10] [i][ch. 12:8]
16[j][Hab. 1:11] [k]2 Kgs. 18:12 [l][ch. 9:12; 10:14] [m][2 Kgs. 8:12; 15:16; Amos 1:13]

Chapter 14

1[n]ch. 6:1; 12:6; [ch. 3:5] [o][ch. 13:9]

and there I will devour them like a lion,
[s]as a wild beast would rip them open.

9 He destroys[1] you, O Israel,
for you are against me, against [t]your helper.
10 [u]Where now is your king, to save you in all your cities?
Where are all your rulers—
those of whom [v]you said,
"Give me a king and princes"?
11 [w]I gave you a king in my anger,
and [x]I took him away in my wrath.

12 The iniquity of Ephraim is [y]bound up;
his sin is [y]kept in store.
13 [z]The pangs of childbirth come for him,
but he is an unwise son,
for at the right time he does not present himself
[a]at the opening of the womb.
14 [b]Shall I ransom them from the power of Sheol?
[b]Shall I redeem them from Death?
[c]O [d]Death, where are your plagues?
[c]O [d]Sheol, where is your sting?
[e]Compassion is hidden from my eyes.

15 Though [f]he may flourish among his brothers,
[g]the east wind, the wind of the LORD, shall come,
rising from the wilderness,
[h]and his fountain shall dry up;
his spring shall be parched;
it shall strip [i]his treasury
of every precious thing.
16[2] Samaria [j]shall bear her guilt,
because [k]she has rebelled against her God;
they shall fall by the sword;
[l]their little ones shall be dashed in pieces,
and their [m]pregnant women ripped open.

A Plea to Return to the LORD

14 1 [n]Return, O Israel, to the LORD your God,
for [o]you have stumbled because of your iniquity.
2 Take with you words
and return to the LORD;

[1]Or *I will destroy* [2]Ch 14:1 in Hebrew

13:9–16 *Rejecting the Only Hope They Have.* Ephraim, by its stubborn refusal to return to the Lord, rejects the only hope that God offers. Three figures of judgment are pronounced in these verses: the incompetent king (vv. 10–11), the unborn child (vv. 13–14), and the withering wind of God (v. 15).

13:9–11 The question **where now is your king**? (v. 10) need not mean that Israel had no king but that the royal leadership was inept to save, for the kings were **against your helper** (v. 9). **I gave you a king in my anger, and I took him away in my wrath** (v. 11) may be a reference to Saul, the first king of Israel; Israel asked for the wrong kind of king (1 Sam. 8:4–9), and still does.

13:12–13 The iniquity of Ephraim is bound up; his sin is kept in store, probably suggests that Ephraim holds on to its sins and will not let the Lord take them away. **he does not present himself**. Ephraim, in its refusal to repent and be healed, is likened to a baby who refuses to be born—which would be most **unwise**, since it would be fatal (cf. v. 14).

13:14 Shall I ransom them from the power of Sheol? In the OT, "Sheol" is a proper name and can be a poetic personification of the grave (e.g., 1 Kings 2:6; Ps. 141:7). But it can also designate the grim destination of the wicked after death (e.g., Ps. 49:14–15). The parallel wording with Ps. 49:15 suggests that Hosea sees Ephraim's "death" as leading to Sheol in the second sense, i.e., as damnation. Thus God asks himself whether he should rescue Ephraim from such consequences. **O Death, where are your plagues?** If the Lord is their strong deliverer, then not even death will be able to terrify them or harm them. In 1 Cor. 15:55 Paul cites part of Hos. 13:14. In that context, he is viewing the general resurrection as God's triumph over not only bodily death but also eternal judgment, for the faithful. Sadly, in Hosea's time Israel is rejecting the only power that can save her. Thus **compassion is hidden from** God's **eyes**, and Israel will perish miserably (vv. 15–16).

14:1–9 *Closing Appeals.* Hosea finishes his book with a series of moving appeals to the wayward northern kingdom to return to the Lord and find healing and covenant renewal.

14:2–3 Take with you words means to know ahead of time what you will say. Hosea then gives the words of repentance and confession that the people should use before the Lord (vv. 2b–3). These verses are peppered with

say to him,
"Take away all iniquity;
accept [p]what is good,
and we will pay with bulls
[q]the vows[1] of our lips.
3 [r]Assyria shall not save us;
[s]we will not ride on horses;
and [t]we will say no more, 'Our God,'
to the work of our hands.
[u]In you the orphan finds mercy."
4 I [v]will heal their apostasy;
[w]I will love them freely,
for my anger has turned from them.
5 [x]I will be like the dew to Israel;
[y]he shall blossom like the lily;
he shall take root like the trees [z]of Lebanon;
6 his shoots shall spread out;
his beauty shall be [a]like the olive,
and his fragrance like Lebanon.
7 They shall return and [b]dwell beneath my[2] shadow;
they shall flourish like the grain;
they shall blossom like the vine;
their fame shall be like the wine of Lebanon.
8 O [c]Ephraim, what have I to do with idols?
It is I who answer and look after you.[3]
I am like an evergreen cypress;
[d]from me comes your fruit.
9 [e]Whoever is wise, let him understand these things;
whoever is discerning, let him know them;
for the ways of the LORD are right,
and [f]the upright walk in them,
[f]but transgressors stumble in them.

[1] Septuagint, Syriac *pay the fruit* [2] Hebrew *his* [3] Hebrew *him*

2 [p][ch. 5:15] [q]Heb. 13:15; [Ps. 50:13, 14; 69:30, 31]
3 [r]ch. 5:13 [s][Isa. 30:16; 31:1] [t][ver. 8] [u]See Ps. 10:14
4 [v]Jer. 3:22; [ch. 6:1] [w][ch. 11:1]
5 [x][ch. 6:3] [y]Isa. 27:6 [z][Ps. 92:12; Isa. 35:2]
6 [a]Ps. 52:8
7 [b]Ps. 91:1
8 [c][ver. 3; Isa. 30:22] [d][ch. 2:8, 23; John 15:4, 5]
9 [e]Ps. 107:43; Jer. 9:12; Dan. 12:10; John 8:47; 18:37 [f][Prov. 10:29; Luke 2:34; 2 Cor. 2:16]

terms from the covenant that express God's grace and the proper response of gratitude: **take away all iniquity** evokes Ex. 34:7 ("forgiving"; cf. Ps. 32:5), while **pay with bulls the vows of our lips** probably describes peace offerings (cf. Ex. 24:5; Num. 7:88), in which the grateful worshiper enjoys a meal in God's presence. This is what Israel can expect, if only they will **return to the LORD**. Also (Hos. 14:3), no longer will they place their trust in foreign princes (such as **Assyria**) or in implements of warfare (**horses**); neither will they worship handmade gods (cf. 13:3–4).

14:4 As so often happens with calls to repentance, there follow astounding promises to entice Israel to return. The Lord **will heal their apostasy**. As noted in 5:13–14, the prophets often depict sin as a sickness and renewal as healing. **I will love them freely**. It is not that the Lord had stopped loving Israel, but now he will love them without the prospect of imminent judgment.

14:5 I will be like the dew. Dew was one of the key sources of water for Israel. It would be vital for the growth of the kind of plants that follow. **like the lily**. The Hebrew term can refer to several different lily-like flowers; all are prized for their beauty. Biblical authors regularly celebrate **the trees of Lebanon** (especially cedars) as the most majestic (e.g., Ps. 104:16).

14:6 his shoots shall spread out. Here the imagery depicts an expanding kingdom like the growth of a great tree: Israel's original calling was to spread its influence through the whole world. **beauty shall be like the olive**. The olive was regarded as a symbol of strength and prosperity (cf. Ps. 52:8). **fragrance like Lebanon**. A reference to the scent of cedars.

14:7 they shall flourish like the grain . . . like the vine . . . like the wine. Israel again becomes a choice vine, which was her design from the beginning (cf. 10:1). The landscape here depicted is an Eden-like paradise, illustrating covenant renewal by the replanting of Israel as a lush garden (cf. 2:14–23).

14:8 I am like an evergreen cypress. Nowhere else in the OT is the Lord likened to a tree, which leads some to suggest that these words are spoken by Israel. However, in 5:12 Hosea uses an equally bold comparison of the Lord with "a moth" and "dry rot," so this suggestion is unnecessary. An "evergreen" tree is ever full of life and strength.

14:9 Hosea has an apt conclusion for his book. The Lord has made his case, and is justified in punishing Israel for ingratitude and covenant breaking. Yet there is a final appeal for the **wise**, who **understand** (the same verb used in 4:14: "people without understanding shall come to ruin"). This verse is full of terms otherwise met in the Psalms and Proverbs, such as "wise," "understand," **discerning, the ways of the LORD**, and the contrast between **the upright** and **transgressors**. Most of the book has addressed Ephraim as a corporate body, but these terms in Hos. 14:9 focus on the moral response of individual Israelites. The positive terms in such a setting refer to those who really grasp the grace of the covenant. They also guide them in their own course of life, even when terrible disaster overtakes the people as a whole.

INTRODUCTION TO

JOEL

Title and Author

"Joel, the son of Pethuel," whose name means "Yahweh is God," gives the book its title. Little is known of Joel except what is learned from the book itself. His references to Judah (3:1, 6, 8, 18, 19, 20) and Jerusalem (2:32; 3:1, 6, 16, 17, 20), along with his knowledge of the activities of priest and temple (1:9, 13–14, 16; 2:14–17), suggest that he was from Judah or perhaps even Jerusalem. His address to priests (1:9, 13; 2:17) and elders (1:2, 14; 2:16) likely eliminates him as a member of either group.

Date

Estimates for dating the book of Joel range from the ninth to the fourth centuries B.C. While no consensus has been reached, most scholars hold to a date after the exile (586 B.C.) for the following reasons: (1) the exile is treated as a past event (3:2–3); (2) the conquest of Jerusalem is mentioned (3:17); (3) no king is mentioned; (4) the temple plays a positive role, while there is no prophetic denunciation against the idolatry and syncretism mentioned in Hosea and Amos; and (5) the anger expressed toward Edom is best explained by its treatment of Judeans during the Babylonian conquest (Joel 3:19; Obad. 1–21).

Theme

The "day of the Lord" is the dominant theme of the book of Joel. Both the nations (3:2–3) and Israel (1:15; 2:1–2) experience this judgment. However, for the repentant community, the "day" also holds out the hope of restoration (2:12–14). Ultimately, the Lord's covenant faithfulness is expressed in his promises of abundance and protection (2:23–26; 3:1), which evidence his dwelling in the midst of his people (2:27; 3:17, 21). This is epitomized in the great promise of "my Spirit" that would be poured out on "all flesh" (2:28, 29; cf. Acts 2:17–21).

Purpose, Occasion, and Background

Joel calls all the inhabitants of Judah and Jerusalem to lament and return to the Lord during a time of national calamity. This crisis is precipitated in the first instance by a locust plague that has destroyed both wine (1:5, 7, 12) and grain (1:10) and therefore threatens the ability of the people of God to present offerings in the temple (1:9, 13, 16). Given this background, Joel may have served as a lament in the ongoing life of God's people during other times of national tragedy.

Key Themes

1. *Day of the Lord.* This is the major theme of Joel. The exact expression, *yom yhwh* (Hb., "day of the LORD"), is found five times in Joel (1:15; 2:1, 11, 31; 3:14) and 13 times in seven other prophetic books (Isa. 13:6, 9; Jer. 46:10; Ezek. 13:5; 30:3; Amos 5:18–20; Obad. 15; Zeph. 1:7, 14; Mal. 4:5; see note on Amos 5:18–20). Other ways of referring to the "day" found throughout prophetic literature (e.g., "a day," "those days," "that day") are used by Joel as well (Joel 2:2; 3:1, 18). Within Joel, the "day" refers not only to a final day of judgment upon the nations (3:2) but also to God's ongoing judgment of Israel, both past and future (1:15; 2:2, 11), and instances of his intervention between Israel and the nations (3:1–2, 12, 14, 16). In each case, the

"day of the Lord" indicates a time when the presence of the Lord brings judgment and/or deliverance and blessing, depending on the circumstances (see note on 1:15). Therefore, although the "day" heralds destruction for the nations, it also functions as a time of salvation for God's people; the Lord remains a refuge amid the chaos of judgment (3:15–16).

2. *Repentance.* If the whole community would cry out to the Lord (1:13–20) and look to him—not merely with external actions but in sincerity with their whole persons (2:12–13)—then judgment may be averted. However, the Lord is not bound by the acts of the community (2:14); it is his prerogative to send or withhold the destruction by the locusts (1:15), just as the army is his to command (2:11).

3. *The Lord in their midst.* It is, of course, crucial that the people have a living faith and repentance; however, the reason the Lord will turn from judgment to blessing is to express his covenant-keeping character (2:13, 18–26; 3:18). His promise to dwell in the midst of his people is prominent not only in Joel (2:27; 3:17, 21) but also throughout the OT (Num. 35:34; Deut. 6:15; 7:21; Isa. 12:6; Hos. 11:9; Zeph. 3:15, 17; Hag. 2:5; Zech. 2:10–11; 8:3). God's restoration of what the locusts have destroyed (Joel 2:27) and his protection of Israel as the cosmos crumbles (3:16–17) both have the same goal: knowledge of his presence. This theme concludes the book (3:21), highlighting its importance for Joel.

4. These themes—the day of the Lord, repentance, and God dwelling amid his people—converge in *the promise of the future outpouring of the Spirit* (2:28–32). This outpouring is associated with the day of the Lord (2:31) in both its judgmental (2:30–31; cf. 2:10; 3:15) and its saving (2:32) manifestations. It is related to repentance in that those who are saved are those who call "on the name of the LORD" (2:32). Finally, the giving of the Spirit, crossing all boundaries of gender, generation, social class, or nationality (2:28–29), is the ultimate evidence of God "in the midst of them" (Isa. 63:11; see Hag. 2:5).

Interpretative Challenge: The Locust Invasion

The relationship between the locust plague and drought (1:1–20) and the onslaught of the Lord's army (2:1–11) provides a major challenge to readers. Scholars provide a number of options, as outlined in the following chart:

If chapter 1 . . .	then chapter 2 . . .
1. describes an actual locust infestation . . .	presents a heightened description of the same invasion.
2. describes an actual locust infestation . . .	issues a warning about a coming military offensive.
3. describes an actual locust infestation functioning as a prophetic forerunner . . .	uses that imagery to portray a human army in terms of a decisive conflict on the day of the Lord.
4. describes a military attack in terms of the metaphor of a locust invasion . . .	represents the coming of an enemy usually viewed as the Assyrians or Babylonians.

While there are serious arguments for each of these options, the third fits best with the overall context. Joel uses the imagery of a dramatic locust plague along with military imagery (2:4–9) to describe the coming of the Lord's army on his great day (2:11). The verbs of chapter 1 are predominantly imperative and past-tense forms, calling the people to act based on past events. The verbs in chapter 2 are in the imperfect and imperative forms, highlighting the fact that, though the judgment is approaching, a return to God is still possible. The lament of 1:15–20 is clearly concerned with the effects of the locusts, while the prayer of 2:17 focuses not upon the destruction of locusts but rather upon the depressed social status of the people of God threatened by foreign rule. Reference to the "northerner" is a typical OT description of enemies (see note on 2:20) but an unusual label if referring to a swarm of locusts. The judgment of the nations in 3:1–21 makes better sense contextually if chapter 2 portrays the threat of an army and a decisive conflict. These and other reasons support option 3.

History of Salvation Summary

God called his ancient people in love and mercy, he preserved them to be the vehicle through which he poured out his Spirit on all kinds of people (2:28–32), and he will preserve them against all who seek to destroy them (ch. 3). In all of his care for them, he aims for "torn" hearts, and not just torn garments, from his people (2:12–14), that they might love him with their whole hearts. (For an explanation of the "History of Salvation," see the Overview of the Bible, pp. 23–26. See also History of Salvation in the Old Testament: Preparing the Way for Christ, pp. 2635–2661.)

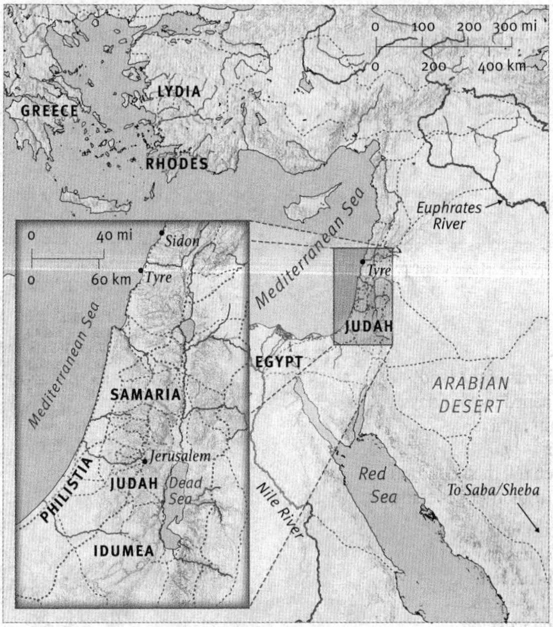

The Setting of Joel
c. 500 B.C.?
Though there is much debate about the date of Joel's prophecies, it is likely that they occurred during a national calamity sometime after Judah returned from exile in Babylon.

Literary Features

As a work of prophecy, the book of Joel relies on the staples of the oracle of judgment and the oracle of salvation. Poetry counts for a lot in the book of Joel, whose author is particularly adept at description. By the time Joel's imagination amplifies the killer locusts into more-than-literal creatures, the book of Joel emerges as almost a horror story. The technique of apostrophe (direct address to entities that are literally absent but treated as though they can hear and respond) is prominent in the first two chapters. Even though the writer is a prophet rather than a nature writer, there are so many pictures of nature in the book that it does rank as nature writing, in a prophetic mode.

The most striking literary feature of the book is the way in which Joel's imagination amplifies literal locusts into images of apocalyptic horror—pictures of God's judgment against human sinfulness. Of course Joel's images are a timeless and universal picture of punishment from God for human evil.

Outline

I. The Judgment against Judah and the Day of the Lord (1:1–2:17)
   A. Locust invasion: forerunner of the day of the Lord (1:1–20)
   B. Army invasion: the arrival of the day of the Lord (2:1–17)

II. The Mercy of the Lord and Judgment against the Nations (2:18–3:21)
   A. Mercy: the Lord responds by restoring his people (2:18–32)
   B. Judgment: the Lord's judgment against the nations and his dwelling with his people (3:1–21)

JOEL

1 The word of the LORD that came to Joel, the son of Pethuel:

An Invasion of Locusts

2 [a]Hear this, [b]you elders;
give ear, [b]all inhabitants of the land!
[c]Has such a thing happened in your days,
or in the days of your fathers?
3 [d]Tell your children of it,
and let your children tell their children,
and their children to another generation.

4 What [e]the cutting locust left,
[f]the swarming locust has eaten.
What the swarming locust left,
[g]the hopping locust has eaten,
and what the hopping locust left,
[h]the destroying locust has eaten.

5 Awake, you drunkards, and weep,
and [i]wail, all you drinkers of wine,
because of [j]the sweet wine,
for it is cut off from your mouth.
6 For [k]a nation has come up against my land,
[k]powerful and beyond number;
[l]its teeth are lions' teeth,
and it has the fangs of a lioness.
7 It has laid waste my vine
and splintered my [m]fig tree;

Chapter 1
2[a][Hos. 5:1] [b]ver. 14 [c][ch. 2:2]
3[d][Ps. 78:4]
4[e]ch. 2:25; Amos 4:9 [f][Amos 7:1]; See Ex. 10:4 [g]ch. 2:25; Ps. 105:34; Nah. 3:15 [h]ch. 2:25; Ps. 78:46
5[i][Isa. 24:11] [j]ch. 3:18; Isa. 49:26; Amos 9:13
6[k]ch. 2:2 [l][Rev. 9:7, 8]
7[m][ver. 12]

1:1–2:17 *The Judgment against Judah and the Day of the Lord.* This first part of Joel introduces the Lord's judgment in the form of a locust infestation, drought, and the coming of a great army. These events on the "day of the LORD" are followed by a call to seek the Lord.

1:1–20 *Locust Invasion: Forerunner of the Day of the Lord.* The first unit (vv. 1–14) describes the devastation that has come upon Judah, providing the reason for the call to lament in the second unit (vv. 15–20).

1:1 The word . . . came to. (See Hos. 1:1; Jonah 1:1; Mic. 1:1; Zeph. 1:1; Zech. 1:1.) This message has a divine source, and the prophet is given the privilege and responsibility of bearing that message to his hearers.

1:2 Elders (see v. 14; 2:16) likely refers to older members of the community rather than a formal office (cf. 2:28; but see also note on 1 Sam. 4:3). Commands are imparted to a wide range of groups (elders, drunkards, priests, farmers) within the community. Verses 2 and 14 of Joel 1 set limits for the first subsection (vv. 2–14) as each mentions "elders" and **all inhabitants**.

1:3 Tell your children. The people of Judah should recount this to four generations (cf. Ex. 10:1–2, 4–6). The telling of the Lord's great deeds and words occurs in the context of the covenant community (Ex. 13:8, 14; Deut. 4:9; 6:4–7, 20–21; Ps. 78:4–6).

1:4 The **locust** is a kind of grasshopper; under the right conditions they travel in large swarms and devastate all plant life in their path. **cutting . . . swarming . . . hopping . . . destroying**. Joel likely uses these terms as names for one kind of locust (perhaps in successive swarms), rather than four different types, in order to emphasize the totality of destruction (note the different sequence in 2:25). The Bible often uses four agents of destruction to stress utter devastation (cf. Jer. 15:2–3; Ezek. 14:21; Rev. 6:1–8; 9:15).

1:5 drunkards, drinkers of wine. Both groups, unaware of the coming chaos, must be aroused from their ignorance. They will have no **sweet wine** to drink when the locusts lay waste to the vines. Sweet wine was intoxicating, though its shorter fermentation time made it less so than wine fermented for a longer period.

1:6 Locusts are compared to a **nation**, equivalent to a great army (cf. Prov. 30:27; Jer. 5:15–17; Joel 2:25; Rev. 9:7). Armies are compared to locusts elsewhere in the OT (Judg. 6:5; 7:12; Isa. 33:4; Jer. 46:23; 51:14, 27) and other ancient Near Eastern texts.

1:7 The **vine** and **fig tree** are symbols of a prosperous and peaceful life for Israel (2 Kings 18:31; Mic. 4:4), which the Lord sees as his property. With the destruction of vine and fig tree, the validity of the "lions' teeth" metaphor (Joel 1:6) becomes clear.

8[n][ver. 13]; See 2 Sam. 3:31
9[o]ver. 13; ch. 2:14 [p]ch. 2:17; [Isa. 61:6; Ezek. 45:4]
10[q]See Hos. 4:3 [r][Hos. 2:9]
11[s][Jer. 14:4] [t]ver. 17
12[u][ver. 7] [v]Isa. 24:11; Jer. 48:33
13[w][ver. 8; Jer. 4:8] [p][See ver. 9 above] [x][ver. 8; Mic. 1:8] [y]ver. 9; ch. 2:14
14[z]ch. 2:15, 16; See 2 Chr. 20:3 [a]ver. 2
15[b]ch. 2:1, 11, 31; 3:14; Isa. 13:6, 9; Jer. 46:10; Ezek. 30:2, 3; Amos 5:18; Obad. 15; Zeph. 1:14, 15; Zech. 14:1; 2 Pet. 3:10

it has stripped off their bark and thrown it down;
their branches are made white.

8 Lament like a virgin[1] [n]wearing sackcloth
for the bridegroom of her youth.
9 [o]The grain offering and the drink offering are cut off
from the house of the LORD.
[p]The priests mourn,
[p] the ministers of the LORD.
10 The fields are destroyed,
[q]the ground mourns,
because [r]the grain is destroyed,
[r] the wine dries up,
the oil languishes.

11 [s]Be ashamed,[2] O tillers of the soil;
wail, O vinedressers,
for the wheat and the barley,
[t]because the harvest of the field has perished.
12 The vine dries up;
[u]the fig tree languishes.
Pomegranate, palm, and apple,
all the trees of the field are dried up,
and [v]gladness dries up
from the children of man.

A Call to Repentance

13 [w]Put on sackcloth and lament, [p]O priests;
[x]wail, O ministers of the altar.
Go in, [w]pass the night in sackcloth,
[p] O ministers of my God!
[y]Because grain offering and drink offering
are withheld from the house of your God.

14 [z]Consecrate a fast;
[z] call a solemn assembly.
Gather [a]the elders
and [a]all the inhabitants of the land
to the house of the LORD your God,
and cry out to the LORD.

15 Alas for the day!
[b]For the day of the LORD is near,
and as destruction from the Almighty[3] it comes.

[1] Or *young woman* [2] The Hebrew words for *dry up* and *be ashamed* in verses 10–12, 17 sound alike [3] *Destruction* sounds like the Hebrew for *Almighty*

1:8 bridegroom of her youth. Or, "husband of her youth." The people are called to a grief as deep as that of a betrothed **virgin** whose promised husband dies before the marriage is consummated. **sackcloth**. A garment of goat or camel hair worn during times of mourning, repentance, or fasting.

1:9 offering. Nothing is left for the offerings that accompany the daily burnt offering (Ex. 29:38–42; Lev. 23:13). **priests mourn**. Their loss is personal since they ate a portion of the offering.

1:10 ground mourns . . . oil languishes. Joel poetically personifies these things as experiencing grief. The presence of **grain**, **wine**, and oil is evidence of God's covenant blessing (Deut. 7:13; 11:14; Joel 2:19, 24), and their absence is evidence of God's judgment (Deut. 28:49–51; Hos. 2:8–9).

1:11–12 Be ashamed (Hb. *hobishu*) sounds like **dries up** (Hb. *hobish*, used to say that "wine dries up" in v. 10 and "gladness dries up" in v. 12; also Hb. *hobishah*, used to say the "vine dries up" in v. 12). The loss of harvest means a loss of joy.

1:13 This is the peak of this section, filled with specific commands to priests. The commands to **put on** and **lament** mimic the actions of the virgin (v. 8). The reason for the priests' lament is that the **offering** is **withheld**.

1:14 Consecrate and **gather** are further tasks for the priests. **a fast . . . cry out**. OT fasts are undertaken as a sign of mourning, repentance, humility, and as a means of seeking God's help, guidance, or forgiveness (Judg. 20:26; 1 Sam. 7:6; 2 Sam. 1:12; Ezra 8:21–23; Neh. 1:4; 9:1; Dan. 9:3).

1:15–20 These verses, forming the second unit of vv. 1–20, comprise the content of the communal "cry" mentioned in v. 14.

1:15 The day of the LORD (see Introduction: Key Themes) is a major theme in Joel; it can refer both to the particular devastation of the locusts (v. 15) and to a final vindication of God and his people (3:18–21). It can refer to a day of destruction and threat for Israel (2:1, 11), or for the nations (3:14). However, for God's people, it is also associated with his presence (2:27), blessing (3:18), and salvation (2:31–32; 3:16). For more on "the day of the

16 Is not the food cut off
before our eyes,
[c]joy and gladness
from the house of our God?
17 [d]The seed shrivels under the clods;[1]
the storehouses are desolate;
the granaries are torn down
because [e]the grain has dried up.
18 How [f]the beasts groan!
The herds of cattle are perplexed
because there is no pasture for them;
even the flocks of sheep suffer.[2]

19 To you, [g]O LORD, I call.
[h]For fire has devoured
the pastures of the wilderness,
[h] and flame has burned
all the trees of the field.
20 Even the beasts of the field [i]pant for you
because the water brooks are dried up,
[h]and fire has devoured
the pastures of the wilderness.

The Day of the LORD

2

1 [j]Blow a trumpet in [k]Zion;
sound an alarm on [k]my holy mountain!
Let all the inhabitants of the land tremble,
for [l]the day of the LORD is coming; it is near,
2 [m]a day of darkness and gloom,
[m] a day of clouds and thick darkness!
Like blackness there is spread upon the mountains
[n]a great and powerful people;
[o]their like has never been before,
nor will be again after them
through the years of all generations.

3 [p]Fire devours before them,
and behind them a flame burns.
The land is like [q]the garden of Eden before them,
but [r]behind them a desolate wilderness,
and nothing escapes them.

[1] The meaning of the Hebrew line is uncertain [2] Or *are made desolate*

16[c][Deut. 12:6, 7; 16:14, 15]
17[d][Mal. 2:3] [e]ver. 11
18[f]ch. 2:22; [Jer. 12:4; Hos. 4:3]
19[g]Ps. 50:15 [h]Jer. 9:10
20[i][Job 38:41; Ps. 104:21; 145:15] [h][See ver. 19 above]

Chapter 2

1[j]ver. 15; Isa. 58:1; Hos. 5:8; Amos 3:6 [k]See ch. 3:17 [l]See ch. 1:15
2[m]Amos 5:18, 20; Zeph. 1:15 [n]ch. 1:6; [ver. 11, 25] [o][ch. 1:2]
3[p]ch. 1:19, 20 [q]Gen. 2:8, 9; See Isa. 51:3 [r]Zech. 7:14

Lord," see note on Amos 5:18–20; and The Day of the Lord in the Prophets, p. 1668. **destruction . . . Almighty**. Joel uses an alliteration with the Hebrew words *shod* . . . *Shadday* (see ESV footnote), which suggests that the wordplay implies something like "destruction of the Destroyer."

1:17 seed shrivels . . . clods. These three words occur only here in the Masoretic text, and thus their precise meaning is uncertain (see ESV footnote). Nevertheless, it is clear from what follows that a drought has also come upon the land (v. 20).

1:18 the flocks of sheep suffer. The Hebrew for "suffer" is *'asham*, and here it means "to suffer punishment" or "to bear guilt." The idea would be that creation suffers for Israel's guilt. It is also possible to read this as a form of *shamem*, "to be desolate" (see ESV footnote).

1:19–20 To you, O LORD, I call (2:32; Ps. 28:1; 30:8). The devastation brought by the Lord can be relieved only by him. **Fire** is sometimes an expression of divine judgment (Gen. 19:24; Num. 11:1; Deut. 32:22; Jer. 4:4; Hos. 8:14; Amos 1:4, 7, 10, 12, 14; Zeph. 1:18; 3:8).

2:1–17 *Army Invasion: The Arrival of the Day of the Lord.* Joel describes the coming of an army, whose arrival may yet be averted by wholehearted return to the Lord. Verses 1–11 describe the coming of this great army, and vv. 12–17 describe the command to return to the Lord.

2:1 Zion is the place of the Lord's throne. The word generally refers to the temple region but could also signify Jerusalem in its entirety.

2:2 Darkness recalls the Lord's appearance at Sinai (Ex. 19:16–19; Deut. 4:11; 5:22–23). God's appearance at Sinai foreshadows his "day" in the future (Amos 5:18–20; Zeph. 1:14–15).

2:3 Fire devours . . . flame burns. In keeping with biblical imagery regarding God's coming (Ps. 50:3; 97:3; Isa. 30:27; 66:15), the army is associated with destructive fire (see Joel 1:19). **like the garden of Eden . . . a desolate wilderness**. The destructive power of this "great . . . people" (Hb. *'am*

4[s]Rev. 9:7
5[t]Rev. 9:9; [Nah. 3:2] [u]Isa. 5:24; 47:14; Obad. 18; Nah. 1:10 [n][See ver. 2 above]
6[v]Nah. 2:10
8[w]Prov. 30:27
9[x]Isa. 33:4 [y][Jer. 9:21] [z][John 10:1]
10[a]ch. 3:16; [Ps. 18:7; Amos 8:8] [b]ch. 3:15; Isa. 13:10; Ezek. 32:7; Matt. 24:29; [Rev. 9:2]
11[c]ch. 3:16; [1 Thess. 4:16] [d]ver. 25 [e]Rev. 18:8 [f]See ch. 1:15 [g]ver. 31 [h]Mal. 3:2; [Num. 24:23]
12[i]Deut. 4:30; 1 Sam. 7:3; Jer. 4:1; Hos. 12:6 [j][1 Sam. 7:6]
13[k][Ps. 34:18] [l]See Gen. 37:29 [m]Ex. 34:6; Ps. 86:5, 15; Jonah 4:2 [n][Num. 23:19; Ezek. 24:14]

4 [s]Their appearance is like the appearance of horses,
and like war horses they run.
5 [t]As with the rumbling of chariots,
they leap on the tops of the mountains,
like the crackling of [u]a flame of fire
devouring the stubble,
[n]like a powerful army
drawn up for battle.

6 Before them peoples are in anguish;
[v]all faces grow pale.
7 Like warriors they charge;
like soldiers they scale the wall.
They march each on his way;
they do not swerve from their paths.
8 They do not jostle one another;
[w]each marches in his path;
they burst through the weapons
and are not halted.
9 [x]They leap upon the city,
they run upon the walls,
[y]they climb up into the houses,
[y]they enter through the windows [z]like a thief.

10 [a]The earth quakes before them;
the heavens tremble.
[b]The sun and the moon are darkened,
and the stars withdraw their shining.
11 [c]The LORD utters his voice
before [d]his army,
for his camp is exceedingly great;
[e]he who executes his word is powerful.
[f]For the day of the LORD is [g]great and very awesome;
[h]who can endure it?

Return to the LORD

12 "Yet even now," declares the LORD,
[i]"return to me with all your heart,
[j]with fasting, with weeping, and with mourning;
13 and [k]rend your hearts and not [l]your garments."
Return to the LORD your God,
[m]for he is gracious and merciful,
slow to anger, and abounding in steadfast love;
[n]and he relents over disaster.

rab, 2:2) can only be compared to the devastation wrought to God's original creation by mankind's fall (Gen. 2:8, 10; 3:17–19; 13:10).

2:4–5 like . . . horses. (Cf. Job 39:19–20; Jer. 51:27.) Locusts and armies have an analogous appearance, movement, and sound; both are used by Joel to capture the presence of the ultimate **powerful army** (lit., "mighty people" [Hb. *'am 'atsum*]).

2:7–9 they do not swerve. . . . They do not jostle. This army cannot be thwarted from its assigned course as every member of the unified ranks advances. It executes its actions (**leap, run, climb, enter**) at will, moving from outside to inside (**city, walls, houses, windows**).

2:10 before them (lit., "before him"; as in vv. 3, 6). **quakes . . . tremble. . . . darkened**. Only the day of the Lord could produce this "cosmic shakedown." In many cases in the Prophets, the Hebrew verb *ra'ash* (here translated "tremble") was associated with the end of the age, the return of chaos, and God's final judgment (Isa. 13:13; 24:18; Jer. 4:23–24; Amos 8:8–9; Nah. 1:5; Hag. 2:6, 21).

2:11 utters his voice. Thunder is associated with the cosmic events of v. 10 (cf. Job 37:4; Ps. 18:13; 77:17; Jer. 10:13). **his army**. The force that brings such dread and terror is under God's command. **he who executes**. The parallelism suggests that "he" refers to the army as executor of the Lord's command (cf. Ezek. 9:1–11).

2:12 Yet even now . . . return. There is still time for the people to return to the Lord, that is, to repent of their coldness toward him. **all your heart**. God calls for undivided devotion.

2:13 Rend your hearts is an expression of internal anguish. This command, coupled with the wholehearted devotion prescribed in v. 12, echoes Deut. 30:6, where a circumcised heart is one that loves God completely. **gracious and merciful**. God's unchanging character, described throughout Scripture, is the grounds for his people's repentance (cf. Ex. 34:6–7).

14 [o]Who knows whether he will not turn and relent,
and [p]leave a blessing behind him,
[q]a grain offering and a drink offering
for the LORD your God?

15 [r]Blow the trumpet in Zion;
[s]consecrate a fast;
call a solemn assembly;
16 gather the people.
[t]Consecrate the congregation;
assemble the elders;
[u]gather the children,
even nursing infants.
[v]Let the bridegroom leave his room,
and the bride her chamber.

17 [w]Between the [x]vestibule and the [y]altar
[z]let the priests, the ministers of the LORD, weep
and say, "Spare your people, O LORD,
and make not your heritage a reproach,
a byword among the nations.[1]
[a]Why should they say among the peoples,
'Where is their God?'"

The LORD Had Pity

18 [b]Then the LORD became jealous for his land
[c]and had pity on his people.
19 The LORD answered and said to his people,
"Behold, [d]I am sending to you
grain, wine, and oil,
[d]and you will be satisfied;
and I will no more make you
a reproach among the nations.

20 "I will remove the northerner far from you,
and drive him into a parched and desolate land,
his vanguard[2] into [e]the eastern sea,
and his rear guard[3] into [f]the western sea;
[g]the stench and foul smell of him will rise,
for he has done great things.

[1] Or *reproach, that the nations should rule over them* [2] Hebrew *face* [3] Hebrew *his end*

14 [o]Jonah 3:9 [p]Hag. 2:19; Mal. 3:10 [q]ch. 1:9, 13
15 [r]See ver. 1 [s]See ch. 1:14
16 [t]See Josh. 3:5 [u][2 Chr. 20:13] [v][Deut. 24:5; Eccles. 3:5; Zech. 12:12-14; 1 Cor. 7:5]
17 [w]Ezek. 8:16 [x]1 Kgs. 6:3; 2 Chr. 3:4 [y]2 Chr. 4:1 [z]See ch. 1:9 [a]Ps. 42:3; 79:10; 115:2
18 [b]Zech. 1:14; 8:2 [c][Ps. 103:13]
19 [d][ch. 1:10; Ps. 4:7]; See Mal. 3:10-12
20 [e]Ezek. 47:18; Zech. 14:8 [f]Zech. 14:8 [g]Isa. 34:3; [Amos 4:10]

2:14 Who knows. The sovereign God acts according to his own purposes. **turn and relent**. The language leaves open the possibility that the Lord, in keeping with his revealed character (cf. Jonah 3:9; 4:2), will bring blessing instead of disaster.

2:16 Consecrate the congregation. As in 1:14, every segment of the religious community assembles for worship, readying themselves to call upon the Lord with a fast (2:15). Even **nursing infants**, i.e., children still being breast-fed, and newlyweds are not exempt.

2:17 The place of prayer was between the entrance hall to the temple (the **vestibule** or portico) and the **altar**. **Your people** is an appeal to God's covenantal care for his people. A **byword** means a "proverb" or "common saying," often used in scorn. An alternative translation is "to rule over them" (see ESV footnote), which makes sense if a foreign, human invasion is in view. **Where is their God?** is a mocking question from those who doubt that God defends his people (Ps. 79:10; 115:2).

2:18–3:21 *The Mercy of the Lord and Judgment against the Nations.* The second part of Joel is signaled by the appearance in 2:18 of the Hebrew narrative tense for the first time in the book.

2:18–32 *Mercy: The Lord Responds by Restoring His People.* The Lord answers the prayer of v. 17. He restores the reputation of his people (vv. 18–20), the land (vv. 21–27), and his presence through pouring out the Spirit (vv. 28–32). Much of this unit is spoken by the Lord himself in the first person.

2:18 jealous. Jealousy here is a deep devotion that leads the Lord to intervene, saving his people for the sake of his own glory (Ezek. 39:25; Zech. 1:14; 8:2).

2:19 answered. The Lord hears the prayers of his people.

2:20 The **northerner** may be the locusts, an invading army, or a final apocalyptic enemy of Israel. Arguments for the third option include: (1) reference to locusts as the "northerner" would be unusual, as they typically came from the south or the east; (2) Jeremiah and Ezekiel portray a great enemy coming from the north (see Jer. 1:14–15; 4:6; 6:1, 22–23; Ezek. 23:24; 26:7; 38:6, 15; 39:2); and (3) the words **vanguard . . . rear guard** (lit., "his face" and "his end") show that destruction is complete and final. **eastern sea . . . western sea**. The Dead Sea and the Mediterranean.

2:21 Ironically, the "foul smell" (v. 20) of corpses is all that remains of the great deeds of this enemy (Isa. 34:3). This contrasts with the **great things** done by the Lord, whose acts of salvation form the basis of the command to **fear not**.

21 “Fear not, O land;
be glad and rejoice,
for [h]the LORD has done great things!
22 Fear not, [i]you beasts of the field,
for [j]the pastures of the wilderness are green;
[k]the tree bears its fruit;
the fig tree and [k]vine give their full yield.
23 [l]“Be glad, O children of Zion,
and [l]rejoice in the LORD your God,
for he has given [m]the early rain for your vindication;
he has poured down for you abundant rain,
[m]the early and [n]the latter rain, as before.
24 “The threshing floors shall be full of grain;
the vats shall overflow with wine and oil.
25 I will restore[1] to you the years
that [o]the swarming locust has eaten,
[o]the hopper, [o]the destroyer, and [o]the cutter,
[p]my great army, which I sent among you.
26 [q]“You shall eat in plenty and be satisfied,
and praise the name of the LORD your God,
who has dealt wondrously with you.
And my people [r]shall never again be put to shame.
27 [s]You shall know that I am [t]in the midst of Israel,
and that [u]I am the LORD your God [v]and there is none else.
And my people [r]shall never again be put to shame.

The LORD Will Pour Out His Spirit

28[2] [w]“And it shall come to pass afterward,
that [x]I will pour out my Spirit on all flesh;
[y]your sons and [z]your daughters shall prophesy,
your old men shall dream dreams,
and your young men shall see visions.
29 [a]Even on the male and female servants
in those days I will pour out my Spirit.

30 “And I will show [b]wonders in the heavens and [b]on the earth, blood and fire and columns of smoke. 31 [c]The sun shall be turned to darkness, [d]and the moon to blood, [e]before

[1] Or *pay back* [2] Ch 3:1 in Hebrew

21 [h]Ps. 126:2, 3
22 [i]See ch. 1:18 [j][ch. 1:19] [k][Zech. 8:12]
23 [l]Ps. 100:1, 2; Hab. 3:18; Zech. 10:7 [m]Deut. 11:14; Jer. 5:24 [n]Hos. 6:3
25 [o]ch. 1:4 [p]ver. 11
26 [q]Lev. 25:19 [r][Isa. 49:23]
27 [s]ch. 3:17 [t]Hos. 11:9; See Ezek. 37:26 [u]See Ex. 20:2 [v][Isa. 44:8] [r][See ver. 26 above]
28 [w]ver. 28-32, cited Acts 2:17-21 [x]Isa. 32:15; Ezek. 39:29; Zech. 12:10; John 7:39 [y][Acts 2:39] [z][Acts 21:9]
29 [a][1 Cor. 12:13]
30 [b][Matt. 24:30; Luke 21:11]
31 [c]See ver. 10 [d]Rev. 6:12 [e]Mal. 4:5

2:22 are green. The underlying Hebrew verb (*dasha'*) is found elsewhere in Scripture only at Gen. 1:11. Perhaps Joel wants his readers to envisage the restoration of the land to an Eden-like state (see Joel 2:3).

2:23 early rain (Hb. *hammoreh*) . . . **vindication** (Hb. *litsdaqah*). The clause by itself can also be understood as “the teacher [Hb. *hammoreh*] for righteousness,” a figure mentioned in the Qumran Scrolls of the Dead Sea. But the word *moreh* in the final line of the verse clearly means “early rain,” and thus the context supports the ESV translation.

2:25 Being human often means bearing loss never to be regained (**the years that the swarming locust has eaten**), and yet the Lord, the bringer of the calamity (Ps. 90:15), is also the Lord of mercy and abundant grace who is fully able to recompense: **I will restore to you**. On “locust,” see Joel 1:4. **my great army . . . I sent**. As at 2:11 and elsewhere (e.g., Amos 4:6–13), those whom the Lord uses to judge his people are under his authority.

2:27 You shall know. The great purpose of the nation's trauma is for them to know God's presence, that he is the covenant-keeping God, and that he will remove their shame. **I am the LORD your God** is a recognition of God's covenantal bond with Israel (Ex. 6:7; Deut. 5:6; Isa. 43:3; Ezek. 20:5). The perpetual removal of **shame** unites God's provision (Joel 2:26) with his presence and peerless nature (v. 27).

2:28–32 Some past Jewish interpreters understood this passage to be referring to the messianic age. The early church followed this line of thinking, as Peter quoted this passage on the day of Pentecost (Acts 2:17–21).

2:28–29 Afterward refers to a time after the assurances of vv. 18–27 and a time that is parallel with **in those days** (v. 29). **pour out my Spirit**. The abundant, life-giving rains (v. 23), which God will shower on his people, illustrate the way in which God will pour out his Spirit on his people in the future (cf. Isa. 32:15; 44:3; Ezek. 39:29). **all flesh**. All God's people will experience the outpouring of the Spirit and intimate communication with the Lord. The sign of this outpouring will be that not just a few but all (**sons and . . . daughters, old . . . and . . . young, male and female**) will **prophesy** and **dream dreams** and **see visions**.

2:30–31 Universal **wonders** related to the day of the Lord are war-like activities on earth (**fire . . . columns of smoke**) and unnatural events in the sky (**darkness**, see 2:10; 3:15; Isa. 13:10; Amos 8:9). Some interpreters hold that these events of judgment, which did not take place at Pentecost (see notes on Acts 2:17; 2:19–21), will still take place sometime in the future, at the return of Christ. These interpreters hold that OT prophecies should often be understood in terms of both a near-term and a long-term fulfillment—with some long-term events being fulfilled when Jesus brought the good news of salvation at his first coming, but with other long-term

the great and awesome day of the LORD comes. **32** And it shall come to pass that [f]everyone
who calls on the name of the LORD shall be saved. [g]For in Mount Zion and in Jerusalem
there shall be those who escape, as the LORD has said, and among [h]the survivors shall be
those whom the LORD calls.

The LORD Judges the Nations

3[1] "For behold, [i]in those days and at that time, when I restore the fortunes of Judah
and Jerusalem, **2** [j]I will gather all the nations and bring them down to the Valley of
Jehoshaphat. And [k]I will enter into judgment with them there, on behalf of my people and
my heritage Israel, because they have scattered them among the nations and have divided
up my land, **3** and [l]have cast lots for my people, and have traded a boy for a prostitute, and
have sold a girl for wine and have drunk it.

4 "What are you to me, [m]O Tyre and Sidon, and all [n]the regions of Philistia? Are you
paying me back for something? If you are paying me back, [o]I will return your payment
on your own head swiftly and speedily. **5** For [p]you have taken my silver and my gold, and
have carried my rich treasures into your temples.[2] **6** You have sold [q]the people of Judah
and Jerusalem to the Greeks in order to remove them far from their own border. **7** Behold,
I will stir them up from the place to which you have sold them, and [o]I will return your
payment on your own head. **8** I will sell your sons and your daughters into the hand of
the people of Judah, and they will sell them to the [r]Sabeans, to a nation far away, for the
LORD has spoken."

9 Proclaim this among the nations:
[s]Consecrate for war;[3]
stir up the mighty men.
Let all the men of war draw near;
let them come up.
10 [t]Beat your plowshares into swords,
and [t]your pruning hooks into spears;
let the weak say, "I am a warrior."

[1] Ch 4:1 in Hebrew [2] Or *palaces* [3] Or *Consecrate a war*

32 [f]Cited Rom. 10:13 [g]Isa. 46:13; 59:20; Obad. 17 [h]Jer. 31:7; Mic. 4:7; Zech. 8:12

Chapter 3

1 [i]Jer. 30:3
2 [j][Zeph. 3:8]; See Zech. 14:2-4 [k]Isa. 66:16; Jer. 25:31
3 [l]Obad. 11; Nah. 3:10
4 [m]Isa. 23:1, 2; Jer. 47:4; Amos 1:9 [n][Ezek. 25:15, 16] [o][Obad. 15]
5 [p][2 Chr. 21:16, 17]
6 [q][ver. 3]
7 [o][See ver. 4 above]
8 [r]See 1 Kgs. 10:1
9 [s][Mic. 3:5]
10 [t][Isa. 2:4]

events being fulfilled when he will return in judgment at his second coming. Other interpreters hold that the language used here should be understood as prophetic symbolism for God's judgment, and that no specific literal fulfillment is intended.

2:32 everyone. Salvation is extended beyond the devastation caused by the locusts. **calls on the name**. This implies exclusive, covenantal worship of the only God who is able to save (Ps. 116:4; Prov. 18:10; Isa. 44:5–8). Paul quotes this in Rom. 10:13 because he, along with other Christians, understood these verses to describe events in the messianic age, when Jews and Gentiles alike would **be saved**. The words **as the LORD has said** may refer to Isa. 4:3; Joel 2:27; or Obad. 17. Those who **escape** are parallel to **survivors . . . whom the LORD calls**. Those whom the Lord calls are those who respond by calling on his name (Gen. 12:8; 13:4; Isa. 51:2).

3:1–21 *Judgment: The Lord's Judgment against the Nations and His Dwelling with His People.* The Lord provides reasons for judgment (vv. 1–8), a description of judgment on the day of the Lord that will be their climax (vv. 9–16), and the certainty of the Lord's dwelling with his people (vv. 17–21).

3:1 in those days. This generic reference recalls the events of 2:28–32 and particularly the day of the Lord (Jer. 33:15; 50:4, 20).

3:2 all the nations. That is, all oppressors of God's people (cf. Ps. 110:6; Isa. 66:18; Jer. 25:31; Ezek. 39:21; Mic. 4:11–12; Zeph. 3:8). **Valley of Jehoshaphat** ("Yahweh has judged") refers to a place of final judgment rather than a known geographical location. **Scattered** refers to deportation associated with exile.

3:3 cast lots for my people. In order to take them away as slaves. See Obad. 11.

3:4–8 As if in a courtroom, the Lord brings the questions, charges, and verdict directly to specific nations.

3:4 Tyre and **Sidon** were Phoenician cities along the Mediterranean coast. Relations between Israel and Phoenicia were occasionally good (cf. 1 Kings 5:1), but sometimes Phoenicia was a polluting influence (1 Kings 16:31). **Philistia**, on the other hand, was a longtime enemy of Israel (Jer. 47:4). **I will return your payment**. Restoration for God's people becomes God's recompense against the nations. Cf. "restore" in Joel 3:1—the same Hebrew verb as "return" in v. 4.

3:6 sold . . . to the Greeks. The Hebrew, *hayyewanim* ("Javan"; see Gen. 10:2; 1 Chron. 1:7; Isa. 66:19), refers to Greek-speakers on both sides of the Aegean Sea. Both the Philistines and the Phoenicians are accused of selling slaves to the Edomites (Amos 1:6–9). Slave trade between Tyre and Javan is mentioned in Ezek. 27:13.

3:7–8 stir them up. Cf. vv. 9, 12. The enslaved (**people of Judah**) will become the enslavers. Sidon was destroyed by Artaxerxes III in 343 B.C., and resistant Tyre was defeated by Alexander the Great in 332. **Sabeans**. Most commentators identify this people as inhabitants of the land of Sheba or Saba located in **far away** southern Arabia (1 Kings 10:1–13; Job 1:15).

3:9 Consecrate. (Cf. 1:14; 2:15.) Warriors were to seek the will of their deity prior to military engagement (e.g., Judg. 20:19–28). Some commentators view this as an ironic statement: the **nations** are told to consecrate themselves for **war**, unaware that the Lord of heaven and earth is their adversary (Isa. 8:9–10; Jer. 46:9–10).

3:10 Beat your plowshares into swords. This is the reverse of Isa. 2:4 and Mic. 4:3. The warfare preparation is so comprehensive that implements of agriculture must be transformed into weapons of warfare. **the weak**. The great need for soldiers means that even those unfit for battle must become warriors.

3:12 sit to judge. The connection between the place (**Valley of Jehoshaphat**) and the action of the Lord (judgment) is made explicit. The

11 [u]Hasten and come,
all you surrounding nations,
and gather yourselves there.
[v]Bring down your warriors, O LORD.
12 Let the nations stir themselves up
and come up to [w]the Valley of Jehoshaphat;
[x]for there I will sit to judge
all the surrounding nations.

13 [y]Put in the sickle,
[z]for the harvest is ripe.
[a]Go in, tread,
[a]for the winepress is full.
The vats overflow,
for their evil is great.

14 Multitudes, multitudes,
in the valley of decision!
For [b]the day of the LORD is near
in the valley of decision.
15 [c]The sun and the moon are darkened,
and the stars withdraw their shining.

16 [d]The LORD roars from Zion,
and [d]utters his voice from Jerusalem,
[e]and the heavens and the earth quake.
But the LORD is [f]a refuge to his people,
a stronghold to the people of Israel.

The Glorious Future of Judah

17 [g]"So you shall know that I am the LORD your God,
[h]who dwells in Zion, [i]my holy mountain.
And Jerusalem shall be holy,
and [j]strangers shall never again pass through it.

18 "And in that day
[k]the mountains shall drip sweet wine,
and the hills shall flow with milk,
and [l]all the streambeds of Judah
shall flow with water;
[m]and a fountain shall come forth from the house of the LORD
and water the Valley of [n]Shittim.

11 [u][Isa. 54:15] [v][Zech. 14:5]
12 [w]ver. 2 [x]Ps. 96:13; 98:9; 110:6; Isa. 2:4; 3:13; Mic. 4:3
13 [y]Rev. 14:15 [z][Jer. 51:33; Hos. 6:11; Matt. 13:30, 39; Mark 4:29; John 4:35; Rev. 14:15, 18] [a]Rev. 14:20; [Isa. 63:2, 3]
14 [b]See ch. 1:15
15 [c]See ch. 2:10
16 [d]ch. 2:11; Amos 1:2; [Jer. 25:30] [e]ch. 2:10 [f]Isa. 4:6; 25:4
17 [g]ch. 2:27; [Ezek. 6:7] [h]ver. 21; [Ezek. 43:7] [i]ch. 2:1; Ps. 48:1; Isa. 65:11; Jer. 31:23 [j]Isa. 52:1; Nah. 1:15; Zech. 14:21; [Rev. 21:27; 22:15]
18 [k]Jer. 31:12; Amos 9:13 [l]Isa. 30:25 [m]Ezek. 47:1 [n]See Num. 25:1

irony of v. 9 is apparent as there is no battle, only the Lord's verdict upon **surrounding nations** (v. 11).

3:13 Lack of **harvest** due to the locusts (1:11) is now a full harvest of the gathered nations cut with a **sickle** like grain (Isa. 17:4–5; Jer. 9:22; 51:33; Mic. 4:11–12). **winepress . . . vats**. The evil of the nations is so great that the vats of judgment are overflowing (Isa. 63:1–6; Rev. 14:14–20). This is an ironic reversal of the promise of Joel 2:24 that the threshing floors and wine vats would be full!

3:14 Multitudes, multitudes is a picture of all the people of the world standing before the Lord for judgment. **valley of decision**. This is the Valley of Jehoshaphat (vv. 2, 12), where the Lord will be the judge. Only the Lord makes decisions in this valley, and his decree is absolute. **the day of the LORD is near**. While the day was near for Israel (1:15; 2:1), the Lord's covenant love and the people's repentance halted his judgment.

3:15 darkened. See note on 2:10.

3:16 roars . . . utters his voice. Cf. Amos 1:2. God thunders as he engages the battle (Jer. 25:30–31; Joel 2:11 and note). **refuge**. Cf. Ps. 73:28; 91:2, 9. **stronghold**. Cf. Ps. 27:1; 37:39; Isa. 25:4. Amid the cosmic and military confusion, the **people** of God are held secure and spared destruction.

3:17 you shall know that I am the LORD your God. Judgment and salvation lead to knowledge of the covenant Lord, his presence, and the removal of the people's shame (see 2:27). **Zion** (cf. 3:21) is the original stronghold (see note on 2:1); here it denotes the promise of God's intimate residence among his people (cf. Rev. 21:3). **strangers**. Those who do not worship the Lord. **Jerusalem shall be holy**. Where God is present, all is purified and even ordinary deeds become acts of holy worship. Nothing unacceptable is found in a place of such holiness (cf. Isa. 35:8; 52:1; Nah. 1:15; Zech. 14:21).

3:18 in that day. I.e., the day of the Lord (2:2; 3:1). **wine . . . milk . . . water**. (Cf. Amos 9:13.) This and other descriptions of God's provision (Joel 2:19, 22–26) recall the earlier scarcity (1:5, 9, 12, 16–20). **a fountain . . . from the house of the LORD**. Cf. Ezek. 47:1–13; Zech. 14:8; Rev. 22:1–2. Abundant waters extend even to the arid-dwelling acacia trees (**Shittim**). The

19 [o]"Egypt shall become a desolation
and [p]Edom a desolate wilderness,
[q]for the violence done to the people of Judah,
because they have shed innocent blood in their land.
20 [r]But Judah shall be inhabited forever,
and Jerusalem to all generations.
21 [s]I will avenge their blood,
blood I have not avenged,[1]
[h]for the LORD dwells in Zion."

[1] Or *I will acquit their bloodguilt that I have not acquitted*

19[o]See Isa. 19:1-17 [p]See Isa. 34:5 [q]Obad. 10
20[r]Ps. 125:1, 2; Ezek. 37:25
21[s]Isa. 4:4; Ezek. 36:25, 29 [h][See ver. 17 above]

location of this "fountain" may be Wadi en-Nar, extending from the Kidron Valley to the Dead Sea.

3:19 The restoration of God's people (v. 18) is contrasted with the judgment upon the nations (2:19–20; 3:1–3). **Egypt** and **Edom** were ancient adversaries representing all of those opposed to the people of God (cf. 1 Kings 14:25–26; 2 Kings 23:29–34; Isa. 34:5–17; Obad. 1–21). **Desolation** was prophesied against Egypt (Ezek. 29:10, 12; 32:15) and Edom (Ezek. 35:3, 4, 7, 9, 14, 15). **shed**. The nations "poured out" (Hb. *shapak*) **blood** but the Lord will "pour out" (Hb. *shapak*) his Spirit (Joel 2:28–29).

3:20 The Lord's residence in Zion (vv. 17, 21) coincides with that of his people living in unending security.

3:21 The first two lines are difficult to interpret; God will either **avenge** what he has **not avenged** (ESV text), or "acquit" what he has "not acquitted" (ESV footnote). The context seems to favor the ESV text. **their blood**. This is a comment on the "innocent blood" of the Judeans in v. 19. The verse brings together the two primary themes of Joel: judgment on the day of the Lord, and the fact that the Lord **dwells in Zion** (2:27; 3:17).

INTRODUCTION TO

AMOS

Author and Title

The first verse of the book identifies it as the work of Amos, one of "the shepherds of Tekoa." Nothing else is known about Amos apart from what he says about himself in 7:14–15. There Amos insists that he is not a prophet by profession, but a "herdsman and a dresser of sycamore figs" whom God entrusted with the special task of carrying a divine message to the people of the northern kingdom.

Date

The first verse of the book also identifies the time period when Amos spoke. It is said to have been during the reigns of "Uzziah king of Judah and . . . Jeroboam . . . king of Israel." Since these were both long reigns, a lengthy time frame emerges when the book could have been written. Jeroboam II began to reign over Israel in 793 B.C., and Uzziah died in 739. Many scholars suggest a date roughly in the middle of the period, about 760 B.C., but there is no conclusive evidence to say that it could not have been earlier or later. One bit of circumstantial evidence is found in 7:17, where Amos seems to predict that the priest Amaziah will be taken into exile and die there. Since Amaziah must have been at least 30 years old to be a practicing priest (if Num. 4:3 was observed in the north), and since the exile of the northern kingdom occurred in 722 B.C., this would suggest a date for this encounter nearer the end of the period 793–739 than the beginning.

Theme

The theme of Amos is the universal justice of God. The Israelites clearly expected a "day of the LORD" when all their enemies would be judged (1:2–2:5). What they were not prepared for was that the judgment of that day would fall on them as well (2:6–9:10). Far from enjoying favored status, they would be held more accountable than their neighbors.

Purpose, Occasion, and Background

From c. 780–745 B.C. the Assyrian Empire was unable to continue the pressure it had put on the nations of the Canaanite coast during the previous century. At this same time, both Judah and Israel were blessed with fairly stable governments. As a result of these two factors, the two nations were experiencing a time of wealth and prosperity unparalleled since the day of Solomon. This was especially true for the northern kingdom, Israel. Judah tended to be more isolated from the world at large and possessed less arable land than did Israel. Thus, when opportunities for amassing wealth and the trappings of prosperity presented themselves, Israel was in a better position to capitalize on those opportunities.

As has tended to be true throughout history, the Israelites took this wealth and prosperity to be unmistakable signs of the blessing of God. Thus, they were reinforced in their belief that "the day of the LORD" would soon dawn in which God would subdue their enemies under their feet and make them the rulers of the world. But in fact, their present wealth and power was not evidence of the blessing of God. As Amos conclusively showed, they were actually under the curse of God because of their egregious breaches of their covenant with him. Much of their wealth had been amassed at the expense of the poor, whom the rich and powerful were systematically oppressing. Their worship of God was little more than attempts at magical manipulation of him, much like the religion of their pagan neighbors. It is no accident that Amos delivered

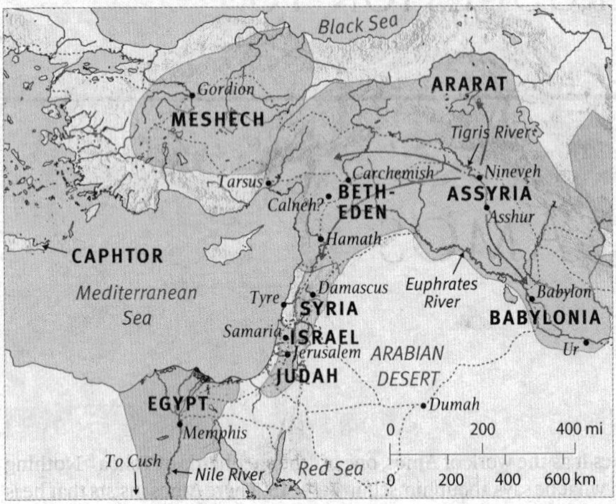

The Near East at the Time of Amos
c. 750 B.C.
Amos likely prophesied to Israel during the decades just prior to the fall of Samaria to the Assyrian Empire. The resurgence of this ancient empire dominated much of the politics of the ancient Near East from the time of Jeroboam and Azariah until the empire's demise at the end of the seventh century B.C. Assyria would eventually engulf nearly the entire Near East from Ur to Ararat to Egypt.

his messages at Bethel, where Jeroboam's namesake (Jeroboam I) had set up a golden calf for Israel to worship in 930 B.C. at the very outset of the northern kingdom.

Thus, what the Israelites saw as the beginning of a new "Golden Age" was really the last flush of a terminal illness. And it was Amos's unhappy task to disabuse them of their foolish expectations. Not only was Israel not going to become ruler of the world, within just a few years they would not exist as a nation at all, and would continue to exist as a people only by the unmerited grace of God (9:11–15). "The day of the LORD," far from being a day of light, was going to be a day of darkness.

As it turned out, Amos was profoundly correct. Though no human could have predicted it, God knew that Assyria was not entering its final decline but was only "catching its breath" before its explosion into its final century of greatness. In 745 B.C. Tiglath-pileser III would ascend the throne of Assyria, and hardly more than 20 years later, in 722, the northern kingdom of Israel would cease to exist.

Structure

The first six chapters of Amos are composed of *judgment oracles*—oral messages from God through Amos to the people of Israel. Among these there seem to be two subgroups. The first is found in 1:2–2:16. These are poetic sayings introduced by "Thus says the LORD" (1:3, 6, 9, 11, 13; 2:1, 4, 6). All of these except the last (2:6–16) are brief and are addressed to Israel's neighbors, from Syria (1:3–5) to Judah (2:4–5). Each of them (with the exception of the one addressed to Judah) deals with cruelty and oppression—basic sins against humanity. Judah is held to a higher standard: rejection of the law of the Lord (2:4–5).

One can imagine that Amos's Israelite hearers were very pleased with him up to this point (2:5). He was reinforcing exactly what they believed: God was going to judge these godless neighbors (including the self-righteous Judeans), and there was every reason to believe that he would use Israel for the task of righteous judgment. But the last, and by far the longest, opening oracle is addressed to Israel. That must have come as a shock. Amos details Israel's sins, ranging from oppression to obscenity to ritualistic religion (2:6–8). And these sins are clearly the worse because they are violations of Israel's covenant with the God who graciously delivered them from Egypt and gave them the land of Canaan (2:9–12). As a result, nothing but destruction awaits them (2:13–16).

The second group of oracles (3:1–6:14) expands on these accusations and the accompanying announcement of judgment. They are lengthier than those in the first group and are characterized by the opening phrase "Hear this word" (3:1; 4:1; 5:1). From 5:18 to 6:14 there are three "woe" oracles, which may be construed as three parts of one longer address, or as a collection of three related addresses. This second group contains two short poems to God as Creator (4:13; 5:8–9). They are variously understood as fragments of a larger hymn that Amos made use of, or simply as an outburst of lyricism on the part of the prophet.

The final section of the book is a group of *visions of the impending judgment* (7:1–9:15). The first vision (7:1–17) shows that if God's justice is to prevail, judgment cannot be averted. After the vision proper (7:1–9), there comes a historical experience in which the point of the vision is reinforced. If the priest of God,

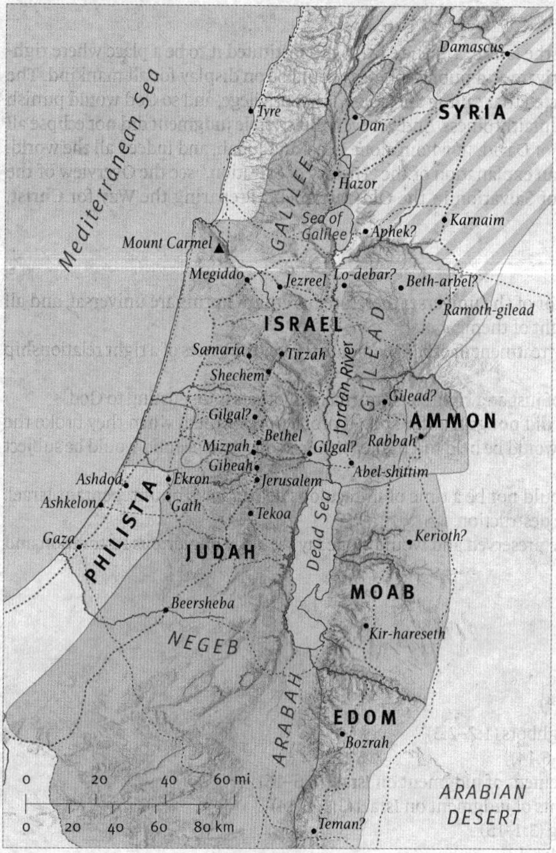

Israel and Judah at the Time of Amos
c. 750 B.C.
Amos, a shepherd from the Judean town of Tekoa, prophesied during a resurgence of political power for Israel and Judah. Under Jeroboam II, Israel had captured much of Syria, though it is not certain how firmly they held it. Likewise, Judah captured several Philistine towns as well as other territory to the south. Within a couple decades, however, the rising Assyrian Empire would capture Syria, Galilee, and Gilead from Israel, and both Israel and Judah would become vassals of the empire.

Amaziah, will not hear and repent (7:10–17), what hope can there be? The second vision (8:1–14) speaks of the imminence of the end. The final vision (9:1–15) describes the sacrifice that the Lord is going to make of Israel and yet of his preservation of the "booth of David" (9:11).

Literary Features

The umbrella under which everything in Amos fits is prophecy, with its attendant oracles of judgment and a concluding oracle of redemption. But the dominant literary form is satire, with the usual elements of objects of attack, a satiric vehicle (very multiple in this book, such as catalogs of "woe" formulas and brief vignettes of bad behavior), a satiric norm or standard by which the criticism is conducted, and a prevailing satiric tone (in this case, biting and sarcastic). In addition to these big literary forms, Amos is a master of smaller forms such as metaphor and simile, epithet ("you cows of Bashan," 4:1), parallelism, rhetorical questions, and parody (in which a conventional literary or rhetorical form such as the priestly call to worship [4:4] is echoed with new or inverted effect from its usual meaning). Other genres that find a place in the book include saying or proverb, doom song, woe formula, and visionary writing.

Amos characterizes himself as the plainspoken satirist (7:14–15), but he is in fact a master of literary technique and rhetoric, seen especially in his management of small units of discourse. The effect is that of a literary collage in which the author dazzles with his imaginative energy and inventiveness and uses the techniques of satire to subject readers to shock treatment with regard to their complicity with evil, especially in its institutionalized forms.

History of Salvation Summary

God "knew" Israel (3:2) out of "all the families of the earth," and instituted it to be a place where righteousness and justice, in both the private and public spheres, would be on display for all mankind. The northern kingdom of Israel had rejected that calling and abused that privilege, and so God would punish them all the more severely for their unfaithfulness. And yet even this terrible judgment did not eclipse all hope: there would still come an heir of David, in whom alone Israel and Judah, and indeed all the world, would find peace and blessing. (For an explanation of the "History of Salvation," see the Overview of the Bible, pp. 23–26. See also History of Salvation in the Old Testament: Preparing the Way for Christ, pp. 2635–2661.)

Key Themes

1. The Lord (Yahweh) is the Creator of the universe; therefore his ethical norms are universal, and all people are subject to judgment in light of them.
2. Justice and righteousness in the treatment of other people are the key evidences of a right relationship to the Lord.
3. Religious ritual in the absence of just and righteous treatment of others is disgusting to God.
4. Israel's covenant with the Lord did not guarantee special protection for them when they broke the covenant. Rather, it meant that they would be held to a higher standard of obedience and would be subject to more scrutiny in judgment.
5. Thus, the "day of the LORD" would not be a time of miraculous deliverance for unrepentant Israel. Rather, it would be a time of terrible destruction.
6. Yet a faithful remnant would be preserved and would someday see a day of glorious restoration and blessing.

Outline

I. Superscription (1:1)

II. Oracles of Judgment (1:2–6:14)
- A. Judgments on Israel's neighbors (1:2–2:5)
- B. Judgments on Israel (2:6–6:14)
  1. Introductory announcement of judgment on Israel (2:6–16)
  2. Detailed announcements of judgment on Israel (3:1–6:14)
     - a. An oracle of warning (3:1–15)
     - b. An oracle of doom (4:1–13)
     - c. An oracle of entreaty (5:1–17)
     - d. An oracle of woe (5:18–6:14)

III. Visions of Judgment (7:1–9:15)
- A. A vision of inescapable judgment (7:1–17)
  1. The vision itself (7:1–9)
  2. An experience reinforcing the vision (7:10–17)
- B. A vision of the terrible end (8:1–14)
- C. A vision of the Lord standing beside the altar (9:1–15)
  1. The thresholds shaken (9:1–10)
  2. The booth of David restored (9:11–15)

AMOS

1 The words of Amos, who was among the [a]shepherds[1] of [b]Tekoa, which he saw concerning Israel [c]in the days of [d]Uzziah king of Judah and in the days of [e]Jeroboam the son
of Joash, king of Israel, two years[2] before [f]the earthquake.

Judgment on Israel's Neighbors

2 And he said:

> [g]"The LORD roars from Zion
> and utters his voice from Jerusalem;
> [h]the pastures of the shepherds mourn,
> and the [i]top of [j]Carmel withers."

3 Thus says the LORD:

> [k]"For three transgressions of [l]Damascus,
> and for four, [l]I will not revoke the punishment,[3]
> because they have threshed [m]Gilead
> with threshing sledges of iron.
> 4 [n]So I will send a fire upon the house of [o]Hazael,
> and it shall devour the strongholds of [o]Ben-hadad.

[1] Or *sheep breeders* [2] Or *during two years* [3] Hebrew *I will not turn it back*; also verses 6, 9, 11, 13

Chapter 1

1 [a]ch. 7:14, 15 [b]2 Sam. 14:2 [c]See Hos. 1:1 [d]2 Kgs. 15:1, 13, 30; 2 Chr. 26:1 [e]ch. 7:10; 2 Kgs. 14:23 [f]Zech. 14:5; [Isa. 29:6]
2 [g]See Joel 3:16 [h][Ps. 65:12] [i]ch. 9:3 [j]See Josh. 19:26
3 [k]ver. 9, 11, 13; ch. 2:1, 4, 6; Prov. 30:15, 18, 21, 29 [l][Isa. 8:4] [m]ver. 13; [2 Kgs. 10:33; Isa. 21:10]
4 [n]Jer. 49:27 [o]2 Kgs. 13:24, 25

1:1 *Superscription.* The first verse identifies the book's speaker, audience, and time frame. **Amos** addresses **Israel** during the time covered in 2 Kings 14:23–15:7, which is the period between the accession of **Jeroboam** II (796 B.C.) and the death of **Uzziah** (739); more specifically, it is **two years before the earthquake**. Zechariah, like Amos, mentions an earthquake "in the days of Uzziah king of Judah" (Zech. 14:5). At the site of Hazor in the eighth century B.C., archaeologists uncovered walls that were tilted (Stratum VI), perhaps pointing to this very earthquake. However, even if it is uncertain when this particular event took place, this statement is significant because it makes unmistakable the genuine historicity of the book and its message. **Shepherds** were at or near the bottom of the social order, which underscores the irony of God's choice of Amos to prophesy against Israel's wealthy, apostate leaders. (If, on the other hand, the ESV footnote ["sheep breeders"] is followed, then Amos may have been a prosperous businessman.) **Tekoa** was a small village southeast of Bethlehem in Judah.

1:2–6:14 *Oracles of Judgment.* Amos delivers a series of messages from God showing that no one can escape the consequences of his actions, neither Israel's neighbors (1:2–2:5) nor Israel herself (2:6–6:14).

1:2–2:5 *Judgments on Israel's Neighbors.* At this time the southeastern coast of the Mediterranean Sea (now called Palestine) was inhabited by seven other small nations besides Israel. All of them were in danger because of Assyria's push toward Egypt. But Amos showed that what was about to befall them would not come from Assyria but from the Creator of all the earth who had revealed himself to Israel in particular. The culpability of these nations demonstrates the biblical principle that one is accountable for what one knows. Thus the first six were judged for sins of common cruelty and brutality, while Judah was judged for failure to keep the Torah (God's covenant instruction). These judgments by God on Israel's Gentile neighbors are similar to pronouncements of judgment on various non-Jewish nations in the writings of other prophets (see chart, p. 1264; cf. Genesis 19). They are a reminder that God's moral standards as revealed in the Bible are not merely for Jewish people, or for Jews and Christians in the NT period, but that God holds all people and all nations and cultures accountable to his moral standards, whether they have them in written form or simply in their hearts and consciences (see also Rom. 1:18–32; 2:14–15; and note on Amos 2:1–3).

1:2 Despite Israel's rejection of **Jerusalem** as the only appropriate place of worship, that was still the place from which God's **voice** of judgment issued to all the earth. **Carmel**. Perhaps an allusion to the encounter between the Lord and Baal, when the Lord struck the top of Mount Carmel with fire, demonstrating that he alone is the true God (1 Kings 18:36–39).

1:3–5 Syria was both a major partner and a rival with Israel in the affairs of the region. It was located north and east of the Sea of Galilee.

1:3 three transgressions . . . four. This poetic expression is used to introduce the judgment upon all seven of the neighboring nations, and upon Israel as well (2:6). It is a way of expressing totality: "three" expresses the plural in Hebrew, and by raising it to "four" the idea of multiplicity is conveyed (see Prov. 30:15, 18, 21). **Gilead** was on the east side of the Jordan River where the tribe of Gad resided. Syria sought to control that area in part because the highway leading south to the Red Sea and its lucrative trade with Sheba went through it. **threshing sledges of iron**. One way of separating grain kernels from their hulls was to put all the grain in a pile and then have an ox pull a heavy wooden sledge around on the pile. Amos says Syria has treated the people of Gilead as though they were nothing but a pile of grain, crushing them into the ground.

1:4 Ben-hadad, the son of **Hazael**, was the king of Syria during the first years of the eighth century B.C. (see 2 Kings 13:24). **Fire** is the judgment meted out on all seven neighboring nations (see Deut. 4:24; 9:3; Isa. 29:6; 30:27, 30; 33:14). Against the fire of God not even the most powerful of human **strongholds** can endure (Amos 1:7, 10, 12, 14; 2:2, 5).

5 I will [p]break the gate-bar of [l]Damascus,
and cut off the inhabitants from the Valley of [q]Aven,[1]
and him who holds the scepter from [r]Beth-eden;
and the people of [s]Syria shall go into exile to [t]Kir,"
says the LORD.

6 Thus says the LORD:

[k]"For three transgressions of [u]Gaza,
and for four, I will not revoke the punishment,
because [v]they carried into exile a whole people
to deliver them up to Edom.
7 So I will send a fire upon the wall of [u]Gaza,
and it shall devour her strongholds.
8 I will cut off the inhabitants from [w]Ashdod,
and him who holds the scepter from Ashkelon;
I will turn my hand against Ekron,
and the remnant of the Philistines shall perish,"
says the Lord GOD.

9 Thus says the LORD:

[k]"For three transgressions of [x]Tyre,
and for four, I will not revoke the punishment,
because they delivered up a whole people to Edom,
and did not remember the covenant of brotherhood.
10 So I will send a fire upon the wall of [x]Tyre,
and it shall devour her strongholds."

11 Thus says the LORD:

[k]"For three transgressions of [y]Edom,
and for four, I will not revoke the punishment,
[y]because he pursued his brother with the sword
[z]and cast off all pity,
[a]and his anger tore perpetually,
[a]and he kept his wrath forever.
12 So I will send a fire upon [b]Teman,
and it shall devour the strongholds of [c]Bozrah."

[1] Or *On*

5 [p]Jer. 51:30 [l][See ver. 3 above] [q]See Hos. 4:15 [r]2 Kgs. 19:12 [s]ch. 9:7; [2 Kgs. 16:9] [t]ch. 9:7; 2 Kgs. 16:9
6 [k][See ver. 3 above] [u]Jer. 47:1, 5; Zeph. 2:4; Zech. 9:5 [v]2 Chr. 28:18; See Joel 3:4-6
7 [u][See ver. 6 above]
8 [w]ch. 3:9; 1 Sam. 5:1
9 [k][See ver. 3 above] [x]See Joel 3:4
10 [x][See ver. 9 above]
11 [k][See ver. 3 above] [y][2 Chr. 28:17] [z]Ps. 137:7; [Joel 3:19; Mal. 1:4] [a]Ezek. 35:5
12 [b]Obad. 9; See 1 Chr. 1:45 [c]Isa. 63:1; See 1 Chr. 1:44

1:5 gate-bar. The wooden city gates were fastened shut with a heavy wood bar across them. If that bar were broken, the city could be entered by an invading army. **Valley of Aven . . . Beth-eden**. Regions in Syria. **Kir** is identified in 9:7 as the ancestral home of the Syrians. It is conjectured to be somewhere to the northeast of Mesopotamia. Thus they were being sent back to where they started, with nothing to show for the intervening years. In 2 Kings 16:9 this is where the Assyrians brought the people of Damascus for exile.

1:6–8 Four of the five cities of the **Philistines** are named in this judgment oracle (Gath is not mentioned). This is because there never was a single enduring capital city of Philistia. Rule of the region went back and forth among the five cities depending on which city's ruler happened to be strongest at the time. Philistia was located southwest of Jerusalem on the Mediterranean coast.

1:6 they carried . . . to Edom. It is not known precisely what event this refers to. It may be a prediction of events at the time of the fall of Jerusalem to Babylon in 586 B.C., when Edom was actively assisting the Babylonians in subduing Judah (see Obad. 12–14). This would then be saying that the Philistines were the partners of the Edomites in that affair. But it may also refer to something that had taken place in Amos's lifetime in the continuing struggles between the Judeans and the Philistines (cf. 2 Chron. 26:6–7). **whole people**. Probably not an entire national group, but an entire community.

1:9–10 Tyre. The great maritime city of **Tyre** was northwest of Israel on the Mediterranean coast. With its fine harbor and easily defended island citadel, it was positioned to dominate the sea trade of the eastern Mediterranean (see Isaiah 23; Ezekiel 26–28). Tyre is accused of the same act of inhumanity as the Philistines (Amos 1:6), but it was more heinous because it involved the repudiation of a **covenant of brotherhood**. This may refer to the covenant that had existed between Solomon and Hiram (1 Kings 5:12), or perhaps to that between Ahab and Eshbaal of Sidon as a result of which Jezebel became Ahab's wife (1 Kings 16:31).

1:11–12 Edom was located south and southeast of Judah around the southern end of the Dead Sea. Descended from Esau, the Edomites maintained enmity toward Israel, extending at least as far back as Israel's journey from the wilderness to the plains of Moab prior to crossing the Jordan (Num. 20:14–21). Here the sin for which Edom is judged is implacability—perpetual **anger**. **Teman** and **Bozrah** are Edomite cities.

1:13–15 The **Ammonites** were located east of the Jordan River between Syria to the north and Moab to the south. Their ancestral territory did not extend all the way west to the Jordan, so they were in constant conflict with the tribes of Reuben and Gad in an effort to extend their **border** westward to gain control of the desirable region of **Gilead** where the two Israelite tribes lived. The sin of the Ammonites was the viciousness and brutality of their attacks, without pity even for **pregnant women**. Ammon's capital city of **Rabbah** (see Deut. 3:11) is present-day Amman, Jordan.

1:15 exile. When Assyria conquered a nation, they deported the leadership and

13 [k][See ver. 3 above] [d]Jer. 49:1, 2; Zeph. 2:8, 9 [e]See Hos. 13:16 [f]ver. 3
14 [g]2 Sam. 11:1; 12:26; See Ezek. 21:20 [h][Ezek. 21:28, 29]
15 [i]Jer. 49:3

Chapter 2

1 [k][See ch. 1:3 above] [j]Zeph. 2:8, 9; See Isa. 15 [k][2 Kgs. 3:27]
2 [l]Jer. 48:24, 41
3 [m][Jer. 48:7]
4 [n]See ch. 1:3 [o]Lev. 26:14, 15; Neh. 1:7; Ezek. 20:13, 16, 24; [Dan. 9:11] [p]Jer. 16:19, 20; Rom. 1:25
5 [q]Jer. 17:27; Hos. 8:14
6 [n][See ver. 4 above]

13 Thus says the LORD:

[k]"For three transgressions of the [d]Ammonites,
and for four, I will not revoke the punishment,
because [e]they have ripped open pregnant women in [f]Gilead,
that they might enlarge their border.
14 So I will kindle a fire in the wall of [g]Rabbah,
[h]and it shall devour her strongholds,
with shouting on the day of battle,
[h]with a tempest in the day of the whirlwind;
15 and [i]their king shall go into exile,
he and his princes[1] together,"
says the LORD.

2 Thus says the LORD:

[k]"For three transgressions of [j]Moab,
and for four, I will not revoke the punishment,[2]
because [k]he burned to lime
the bones of the king of Edom.
2 So I will send a fire upon Moab,
and it shall devour the strongholds of [l]Kerioth,
and Moab shall die amid uproar,
amid shouting and the sound of the trumpet;
3 [m]I will cut off the ruler from its midst,
and will kill [m]all its princes[3] with him,"
says the LORD.

Judgment on Judah

4 Thus says the LORD:

[n]"For three transgressions of Judah,
and for four, I will not revoke the punishment,
because [o]they have rejected the law of the LORD,
and have not kept his statutes,
but [p]their lies have led them astray,
those after which their fathers walked.
5 So [q]I will send a fire upon Judah,
and it shall devour the strongholds of Jerusalem."

Judgment on Israel

6 Thus says the LORD:

[n]"For three transgressions of Israel,
and for four, I will not revoke the punishment,

[1] Or *officials* [2] Hebrew *I will not turn it back*; also verses 4, 6 [3] Or *officials*

imported people from elsewhere into the area. This was both a way of defusing any tendency to rebellion and also of homogenizing their diverse empire.

2:1–3 Moab was Ammon's neighbor to the south, perhaps included here because Moab and Ammon were both descended from Lot through his daughters (Gen. 19:37–38). The fact that Moab's sin was against neither Israel nor Judah, but its southern neighbor **Edom**, demonstrates that these judgments are based not on ethnicity but on the universal justice of God.

2:4–5 Unlike the other nations, **Judah** is not judged for inhumanity to others but according to a higher standard, **the law of the LORD**, which they had sworn with a blood oath to keep (Ex. 24:8).

2:4 lies. Very likely a reference to false gods (see Isa. 44:20; Jer. 16:19–20; Hab. 2:18). The first of the **statutes** of the Mosaic law was the prohibition against worshiping other gods (Ex. 20:3).

2:6–6:14 *Judgments on Israel.* The introduction (2:6–16)—in which Amos demonstrates that Israel, far from being better than its neighbors, is even more worthy of condemnation than they—is followed by four extended addresses: 3:1–15; 4:1–13; 5:1–17; and 5:18–6:14. The first three are each introduced with the words "Hear this word" (3:1; 4:1; 5:1). They show how desperate Israel's condition is. The fourth address is characterized by the repetition of the word "Woe" (5:18; 6:1; 6:4), identifying this as a funeral dirge for the soon-to-be-destroyed nation.

2:6–16 *Introductory Announcement of Judgment on Israel.* It is easy to imagine that up to this point Amos's preaching had met with an enthusiastic response. Not only were the pagan neighbors coming in for judgment, but so also was the sister/rival Judah, and for idolatry at that. But here, with the very same introduction that had been given the others ("for three . . . four"; see note on 1:3), the prophet indicts Israel. Significantly, he does not accuse them of idolatry, although that was manifestly the case. Rather, he condemns them for

because [r]they sell the righteous for [s]silver,
and the needy for a pair of sandals—
7 those who trample the head of the poor [t]into the dust of the earth
and [u]turn aside the way of the afflicted;
[v]a man and his father go in to the same girl,
so that my holy name is profaned;
8 they lay themselves down beside every altar
on garments [w]taken in pledge,
and in the house of their God they drink
the wine of those who have been fined.

9 "Yet [x]it was I who destroyed the Amorite before them,
[y]whose height was like the height of the cedars
and who was as strong as the oaks;
[z]I destroyed his fruit above
and his roots beneath.
10 [a]Also it was I who brought you up out of the land of Egypt
[b]and led you forty years in the wilderness,
[x]to possess the land of the Amorite.
11 And I raised up some of your sons for prophets,
and some of your young men for [c]Nazirites.
Is it not indeed so, O people of Israel?"
declares the LORD.
12 "But you made the Nazirites [d]drink wine,
and commanded the prophets,
saying, [e]'You shall not prophesy.'

13 "Behold, I will press you down in your place,
as a cart full of sheaves presses down.
14 [f]Flight shall perish from the swift,
[f]and the strong shall not retain his strength,
[g]nor shall the mighty save his life;
15 he who handles the bow shall not stand,
and he who is [h]swift of foot shall not save himself,
[i]nor shall he who rides the horse save his life;
16 and he who is stout of heart among the mighty
shall flee away naked in that day,"
declares the LORD.

6[r][Lev. 25:39; 2 Kgs. 4:1] [s]ch. 8:6
7[t]Lam. 2:10 [u]ch. 5:12; Job 24:4; Isa. 10:2 [v][1 Cor. 5:1]; See Ezek. 22:11
8[w]See Ex. 22:26
9[x]Deut. 2:31; Josh. 24:8; See Num. 21:21-25 [y][Num. 13:32, 33; Isa. 10:33] [z][Job 18:16]
10[a]ch. 3:1; Ex. 12:17, 51 [b]See Deut. 8:2 [x][See ver. 9 above]
11[c]Num. 6:2
12[d][Num. 6:3] [e]ch. 7:13, 16; Isa. 30:10; Mic. 2:6
14[f][ch. 9:1; Eccles. 9:11] [g][Ps. 33:16]
15[h][2 Sam. 2:18] [i][Ps. 33:17]

social injustice. Amos 5:18–24 suggests that he considers their entire religious behavior to be terribly corrupted by their sinful conduct, especially by their hard-hearted injustice toward the poor and oppressed. Verses 6–12 of ch. 2 contain the accusation, and vv. 13–16 give the announcement of judgment.

2:6–7a They sell the righteous perhaps refers to giving false witness for money, but it might also speak of selling someone into slavery for indebtedness over something as paltry as a pair of **sandals** (cf. Lev. 25:39–43). Instead of helping the **afflicted** as the law commanded (Ex. 23:6–8), the affluent Israelites were crushing them (see also Amos 8:6).

2:7b–8 a man and his father. It appears that Amos is intentionally linking here the sins of incest (Lev. 18:6–18; Deut. 22:30) and of ritual prostitution (Deut. 23:17–18). God required sexual purity for at least two reasons: faithfulness in heterosexual marriage was an expression of the unique faithfulness of the Creator, and pagan religions sought to use sexual performance as a way of manipulating the divine power of fertility. To make it appear that the Lord was just like the pagan gods—faithless and capable of manipulation—was to profane his **holy name**, to defame his character. **Garments taken in pledge** refers to a poor person's cloak that was given to a money-lender as security for a loan. It was to be returned to the poor person at night since he or she probably had no other covering (Ex. 22:26). In the context it seems likely the **wine** was payment for an unjust fine (Isa. 10:1–2).

2:11–12 Not only had God graciously delivered Israel and given them the land of Canaan (vv. 9–10), he had also raised up from among them **prophets** to warn them, and **Nazirites** to shame them with the example of their commitment (see Jer. 35:1–19 for a similar instance). But instead of being warned and shamed, the Israelites had tried to shut up the prophets and to compromise the Nazirites (Num. 6:3 prohibited Nazirites from drinking wine).

2:13 Behold signals the beginning of the conclusion. Israel will be flattened in the road like an animal run over by a loaded **cart**.

2:14–15 No one will be able to escape the coming destruction. The **swift** will not be able to run away from it, and the **strong** and **mighty** warrior will not be able to stand before it.

3:1–6:14 ***Detailed Announcements of Judgment on Israel.*** Four oracles (3:1–15; 4:1–13; 5:1–17; 5:18–6:14) move from the general to the specific, leaving no doubt that, unless there is true repentance, Israel cannot hope to escape destruction.

3:1–15 ***An Oracle of Warning.*** The sins for which Israel is to be judged are touched upon but not detailed here. Rather, God is simply warning Israel through Amos that judgment is surely coming. The prophet has heard the roar of the lion just as he launches himself on his prey (vv. 4, 8). What can the prophet do but tell what he has heard?

3:1–2 Hear this word introduces the first three messages (3:1; 4:1; 5:1).

Chapter 3
1 [j]ch. 7:16; [ch. 2:10]
2 [k]Deut. 7:6; 10:15; Ps. 147:19, 20; [Hos. 5:3; 13:5; Mic. 2:3] [l][Matt. 10:15; 11:21, 22; Luke 10:13, 14; 12:47; Rom. 2:9]
6 [m]Ezek. 33:4; See Joel 2:1 [n][Isa. 45:7; Lam. 3:38; Mic. 1:12]
7 [o]Gen. 18:17; [Jer. 15:1]
8 [p][Num. 22:38]
9 [q]ch. 1:8 [r]ch. 4:1; 6:1; [1 Kgs. 16:24] [s]Ps. 94:5, 6; 103:6; See 1 Kgs. 21:1-16
10 [t][ch. 6:3; Isa. 3:14, 15]; See Mic. 6:10-12
11 [u][2 Kgs. 17:5, 6]; See 2 Kgs. 18:9-12 [v][Isa. 39:6]

Israel's Guilt and Punishment

3 [j]Hear this word that the LORD has spoken against you, O people of Israel, against the whole family that I brought up out of the land of Egypt:

2 [k]"You only have I known
of all the families of the earth;
[l]therefore I will punish you
for all your iniquities.

3 "Do two walk together,
unless they have agreed to meet?
4 Does a lion roar in the forest,
when he has no prey?
Does a young lion cry out from his den,
if he has taken nothing?
5 Does a bird fall in a snare on the earth,
when there is no trap for it?
Does a snare spring up from the ground,
when it has taken nothing?
6 [m]Is a trumpet blown in a city,
and the people are not afraid?
[n]Does disaster come to a city,
unless the LORD has done it?

7 "For the Lord GOD does nothing
[o]without revealing his secret
to his servants the prophets.
8 The lion has roared;
who will not fear?
[p]The Lord GOD has spoken;
who can but prophesy?"

9 Proclaim to the strongholds in [q]Ashdod
and to the strongholds in the land of Egypt,
and say, "Assemble yourselves on [r]the mountains of Samaria,
and see the great tumults within her,
and [s]the oppressed in her midst."
10 "They do not know how to do right," declares the LORD,
[t]"those who store up violence and robbery in their strongholds."
11 Therefore thus says the Lord GOD:

[u]"An adversary shall surround the land
and bring down[1] your defenses from you,
and [v]your strongholds shall be plundered."

[1] Hebrew *An adversary, one who surrounds the land—he shall bring down*

The God of Israel is the Creator who spoke the world into existence and who is characterized from first to last as the God who speaks (Isa. 45:18–19; John 1:1; Rev. 22:18–19). It seems clear that Israel and Judah believed that their role as the chosen people of God would protect them from harm (see note on Amos 5:18–20). Amos says that the very opposite is true. It is precisely because God has **known** them as he has known no other nation that they are being judged according to a higher standard (see Luke 12:48).

3:3–8 With a series of questions, Amos shows that imminent disaster is for Israel. He points out that in the world of nature, certain sequences of events can lead to predictable outcomes. If a **lion** (vv. 4, 8) roars, then it has taken, or is about to take, its prey. What he, the prophet, is doing is simply telling Israel that the **Lord GOD** (v. 7) has announced judgment and that unless Israel takes immediate corrective action, the outcome is certain. **disaster** (v. 6). The ESV has correctly captured the sense of the Hebrew word *ra'ah* in this verse, a word which has a very broad range of connotations (see chart, p. 1687). Often translated "evil," it is used to express everything from "moral evil" (Gen. 6:5) to "disaster" (as here and also Jonah 3:10). If there is disaster occurring, the people should not attribute it to bad luck but should take note that God is at work, in his sovereign wisdom, and they should respond accordingly to his judgment. **without revealing his secret** (v. 7). Throughout the OT God often showed the prophets his own perspective on the events of history and revealed to them his purposes and actions, so that the prophets could interpret historical events accurately for God's people.

3:9–11 Israel's capital city of **Samaria** was a powerful stronghold, located on a high hill (**mountains**) in a good position of natural defense. It stood just off the great highway that ran along the Mediterranean coast connecting Egypt with Mesopotamia. If Samaria fell to the Assyrians, there was nothing more to prevent the destruction of the Philistine cities (represented by **Ashdod**) and of **Egypt** itself. But Israel would fall, not because of the superior power of Assyria but because of its own spiritual and social corruption. The stronghold

12 Thus says the LORD: [w]"As the shepherd rescues from the mouth of the lion two legs,
or a piece of an ear, [x]so shall the people of Israel [y]who dwell in Samaria be rescued, with
the corner of a couch and part[1] of a bed.

13 "Hear, [z]and testify against the house of Jacob,"
declares the Lord GOD, [a]the God of hosts,
14 "that on the day I punish Israel for his transgressions,
[b]I will punish the altars of Bethel,
and [c]the horns of the altar shall be cut off
and fall to the ground.
15 [d]I will strike [e]the winter house along with [f]the summer house,
and [g]the houses of ivory shall perish,
and the great houses[2] shall come to an end,"
declares the LORD.

4

1 "Hear this word, [h]you cows of Bashan,
who are [i]on the mountain of Samaria,
[j]who oppress the poor, [j]who crush the needy,
who say to your husbands, 'Bring, that we may drink!'
2 [k]The Lord GOD has sworn by his holiness
that, behold, the days are coming upon you,
[l]when they shall take you away with hooks,
[l]even the last of you with fishhooks.
3 [m]And you shall go out through the breaches,
each one straight ahead;
and you shall be cast out into Harmon,"
declares the LORD.

4 [n]"Come to Bethel, and transgress;
to [o]Gilgal, and multiply transgression;
[n]bring your [p]sacrifices every morning,

[1] The meaning of the Hebrew word is uncertain [2] Or *and many houses*

12 [w][Ex. 22:13] [x]See Jer. 31:8, 9 [y][ch. 6:4]
13 [z][Ps. 50:7; 81:8] [a]ch. 4:13; Ps. 80:4, 7, 14
14 [b][Hos. 10:15]; See 1 Kgs. 13:1-3 [c][2 Kgs. 23:15]
15 [d][ch. 6:11] [e]Jer. 36:22 [f]Judg. 3:20 [g]1 Kgs. 22:39; Ps. 45:8

Chapter 4

1 [h]Ps. 22:12 [i]ch. 3:9; 6:1 [j]Hos. 5:11
2 [k]Ps. 89:35 [l][Jer. 16:16; Hab. 1:15]; See 2 Kgs. 19:28
3 [m][Ezek. 12:5, 12]
4 [n][ch. 5:5; Ezek. 20:39; Matt. 23:32] [o][ch. 5:5; Hos. 4:15; 9:15; 12:11] [p]Num. 28:3, 4; [Jer. 7:21]

was filled with oppression, and with **violence and robbery**. Thus, Israel had forfeited God's protection, and without him all their natural **defenses** were useless (see Isa. 5:5–6).

3:12 Picturesque prose expresses the total destruction that was to be visited upon Samaria and Israel, though a tiny "remnant" would be left. See also 5:3.

3:13–15 The conclusion of the message emphasizes in a general way the two factors that would account for the coming destruction: (1) false, ritualistic religion and (2) the accumulation of wealth at the expense of the poor.

3:13 God of hosts. This title for God became increasingly popular among the prophets (cf. chart, p. 1775). "Hosts" in this context refers to troops of soldiers. Thus the image expresses the unlimited power of God. He is a general with an infinite number of troops at his command. The term sometimes refers to hosts of heavenly beings (1 Kings 22:19; Neh. 9:6; Ps. 148:2; see also Matt. 26:53).

3:14 Bethel was not only associated with the patriarch Jacob and his vision (Gen. 28:10–22), it also stood close to the border between Israel and Judah. Thus, Jeroboam I chose it as the site of one of his two golden calves (1 Kings 12:25–33). It was not by accident that this was the place where Amos chose to deliver his prophecies (Amos 7:12–13). It represented the corruption of the true religion (4:4–5). Far from appeasing God's anger against Israel, the religious practices carried out there would seal that anger. See also Hosea 10:5, where "Beth-aven" (house of iniquity) is substituted for "Beth-el" (house of God). The **horns of the altar** were short vertical projections at the four corners of the top of the altar (Ex. 27:2). They had ritual significance as places where God's protection was available (1 Kings 1:50; 2:28), but the horns of Bethel's altar would provide no protection whatsoever.

3:15 All of Israel's social injustice is represented by the sin of amassing property (see also Isa. 5:8). This was a violation of the covenant that said a family's land was a trust from God to be held in perpetuity by that family. There were legal fictions to get around this, but those fictions did not impress God. Here Amos does not condemn wealth in itself, but wealth accompanied by injustice toward the poor (Amos 4:1), fraudulent business practices (5:7, 11, 12; 8:4–6), and living in luxury without care for the needy (5:12; 8:4–6), without concern for sin and evil in the land (6:4–6), and without genuine religious faith (5:21–23). Archaeological excavations at Samaria have uncovered fragmentary remains of rich **ivory** objects, attesting to the luxury built upon the backs of the poor.

4:1–13 *An Oracle of Doom.* The oracle is composed of two parts: vv. 1–5 and vv. 6–13. In the first part, the prophet expands somewhat on the points made in 3:14–15: the sins of self-indulgence built upon oppression (4:1–3) and of false religion (vv. 4–5). In the second part, God details all the ways in which he had appealed to the Israelites to return to him, yet without response (vv. 6–11). There is nothing left but that they must come face to face with the infinite Creator in all his power (vv. 12–13).

4:1 Bashan was rich pastureland northeast of the Sea of Galilee. Cattle that grazed there tended to be plump and healthy. Amos compares the matrons of **Samaria** to those cattle. Not just the husbands, but even these wives **oppress the poor** and **crush the needy**.

4:2–3 A description of what would happen to these wealthy and self-indulgent women when the city fell to the Assyrians: they would be dragged out through the broken-down walls (**breaches**) like a fisherman dragging a fish out of the water with **fishhooks**. But the reference may be literal as well. Some Assyrian illustrations seem to show captives being taken away with ropes attached to rings in the captives' noses. **Harmon**. This location is unknown.

4:4–5 The prophet denounces the religious activity at **Bethel** and also at

5 [q]Lev. 7:13 [r]Ex. 35:29; Lev. 22:18, 21; Deut. 12:6 [s][Ps. 81:11, 12]
6 [t][Deut. 28:57; Lam. 2:12] [u]Jer. 15:7; Hag. 2:17
7 [v]Jer. 3:3; [Joel 2:23] [w][Ex. 9:26]
8 [x][ch. 8:12] [u][See ver. 6 above]
9 [y]Deut. 28:22; Hag. 2:17 [z]Joel 1:4 [u][See ver. 6 above]
10 [a]Deut. 28:27, 60; [Ex. 12:29; Ps. 78:50; Isa. 10:24, 26] [b]2 Kgs. 13:7 [c][Joel 2:20] [u][See ver. 6 above]
11 [d][Isa. 13:19] [e]Zech. 3:2; [Jude 23] [u][See ver. 6 above]

your tithes every three days;
5 offer a sacrifice of thanksgiving of [q]that which is leavened,
and proclaim [r]freewill offerings, publish them;
[s]for so you love to do, O people of Israel!"
declares the Lord God.

Israel Has Not Returned to the Lord

6 "I gave you cleanness of teeth in all your cities,
and [t]lack of bread in all your places,
[u]yet you did not return to me,"
declares the Lord.

7 "I also [v]withheld the rain from you
when there were yet three months to the harvest;
[w]I would send rain on one city,
and send no rain on another city;
one field would have rain,
and the field on which it did not rain would wither;
8 so two or three cities [x]would wander to another city
to drink water, and would not be satisfied;
[u]yet you did not return to me,"
declares the Lord.

9 [y]"I struck you with blight and mildew;
your many gardens and your vineyards,
your fig trees and your olive trees [z]the locust devoured;
[u]yet you did not return to me,"
declares the Lord.

10 "I sent among you a pestilence [a]after the manner of Egypt;
I killed your young men with the sword,
and [b]carried away your horses,[1]
and [c]I made the stench of your camp go up into your nostrils;
[u]yet you did not return to me,"
declares the Lord.

11 "I overthrew some of you,
[d]as when God overthrew Sodom and Gomorrah,
and you were [e]as a brand[2] plucked out of the burning;
[u]yet you did not return to me,"
declares the Lord.

[1] Hebrew *along with the captivity of your horses* [2] That is, a burning stick

the ancient site of **Gilgal** (Josh. 4:20; 10:43) with bitter sarcasm. Far from procuring forgiveness for **transgression**, this activity was itself transgression! The Israelites might **love** to engage in such worship, but it only disgusted God (Amos 5:14–15, 21–24). The prophets often seem to dismiss sacrificial worship, but careful attention to the context shows that they are concerned with faithful use of the divine ordinances and obedience from the heart. Hosea 6:6; Amos 4:4–5; and 5:21–25 are addressed to the northern kingdom, in which the worship practices blatantly defy the Mosaic prescriptions with golden calves, sanctuaries other than the one in Jerusalem, and priests who were not Levites (see 1 Kings 12:26–33). Texts such as Isa. 1:11–17; Jer. 6:20; 7:21–23; and Mic. 6:6–8 are addressed to Judah, where the external form of the sacrifices may be proper, but is not combined with genuine repentance and godly living. In such cases the worship is worse than empty; it is an attempt to manipulate God.

4:5 Although the people could claim that the **thanksgiving** offering and the **freewill offerings** were what God had specified in the Torah (see Lev. 7:12–21), that meant nothing to God because the offerings were not being celebrated in the right place under the Levitical priests, nor were they accompanied by moral obedience (see Amos 5:15, 24).

4:6–11 Even though God had sent various natural and social calamities, the people would not turn back. The repeated refrain is **yet you did not return to me** (vv. 6, 8, 9, 10, 11). In short, the coming destruction of Israel at the hands of the Assyrians would not be a sudden unexpected outbreak by a short-tempered God. It was the final outcome of many patient appeals and warnings that the people should have heeded but did not.

4:6 cleanness of teeth. They had no food to cling to their teeth. **yet you did not return to me**. Stubbornness, like the stubbornness of Pharaoh in the exodus, increases guilt.

4:7 rain . . . yet three months. After the summer dry season, the rains of November and December were absolutely necessary if the seeds of grain were to germinate in the ground and yield a harvest beginning in April.

4:10 The Bible does not describe the **pestilence after the manner of Egypt** elsewhere. However, the reference in Ex. 15:26 supports the idea that

12 "Therefore thus I will do to you, O Israel;
because I will do this to you,
prepare to meet your God, O Israel!"

13 For behold, [f]he who forms the mountains and creates the wind,
and [g]declares to man what is his thought,
[h]who makes the morning darkness,
and [i]treads on the heights of the earth—
[j]the LORD, the God of hosts, is his name!

Seek the LORD and Live

5 Hear this word that I [k]take up over you in lamentation, O house of Israel:

2 " Fallen, no more to rise,
is [l]the virgin Israel;
forsaken on her land,
with none to raise her up."

3 For thus says the Lord GOD:

"The city that went out a thousand
shall have a hundred left,
and that which went out a hundred
shall have ten left
to the house of Israel."

4 For thus says the LORD to the house of Israel:

[m]"Seek me and live;
5 but do not seek [n]Bethel,
and do not enter into [n]Gilgal
or cross over to [o]Beersheba;
for [n]Gilgal shall surely go into exile,
and [n]Bethel shall come to nothing."

6 [m]Seek the LORD and live,
[p]lest he break out like fire in the house of Joseph,
and it devour, with none to quench it for [n]Bethel,
7 O [q]you who turn justice to wormwood[1]
and cast down righteousness to the earth!

[1] Or *to bitter fruit*

13 [f][Ps. 102:25] [g][Ps. 139:2] [h][ch. 5:8; 8:9] [i]Isa. 58:14; Mic. 1:3 [j]ch. 3:13; 5:8; 9:6; See Jer. 10:16

Chapter 5

1 [k]Ezek. 19:1
2 [l]Lam. 2:1; [Isa. 47:1]
4 [m]2 Chr. 15:2; Isa. 55:6; Zeph. 2:3
5 [n]See ch. 4:4 [o]ch. 8:14
6 [m][See ver. 4 above] [p][Isa. 9:18, 19] [n][See ver. 5 above]
7 [q][ch. 6:12]

the swampy areas of the northeast Nile delta where Israel lived in slavery must have been disease-ridden, probably with malaria among other diseases.

4:12 It seems apparent that the Israelites were asking God to appear on their behalf in a great day of vindication, making them the rulers of the world (see 5:18–20). Amos says they are about to **meet . . . God**, but not at all in the way they expect.

4:13 Amos uses lyrical poetry to underline the seriousness of the situation. Israel is not dealing with some local mountain deity. They are about to come face to face with the Creator of the universe, **the LORD, the God of hosts** (see note on 3:13). See also 5:8–9 and 9:5–6 and notes. One of the ways God manifests his greatness over the false gods of the pagans is that he alone knows all thoughts and therefore he **declares to man what is his thought** (cf. Dan. 2:27–28; 1 Cor. 14:24–25).

5:1–17 *An Oracle of Entreaty.* A special feature of this oracle is God's pleading for his people to return to him. Although they face imminent destruction, it is still not too late to seek God and his goodness (vv. 4–6, 14).

5:1 lamentation. Neither the prophet nor God takes delight in these pronouncements of doom. Like mourners at a funeral, they grieve at what lies ahead for the unrepentant people. For the same reaction on the part of Jesus, see Matt. 23:37–39 and Luke 19:41–44.

5:2 Virgin Israel is an image used frequently in the prophets to speak of the special value God places on Israel. She is like a virgin daughter to him, and the thought of her selling herself into prostitution or being raped by an enemy is heartbreaking to him.

5:4–9 This is a powerful plea to **seek the LORD** as he has revealed himself and not in the pagan forms found at **Bethel**, **Gilgal**, and **Beersheba**. Whenever God is identified with the things of this world, there are two results: ethical behavior as a means of expressing devotion to God disappears (v. 7), and any concept of a purposeful Creator is lost (vv. 8–9).

5:5 On **Bethel** and **Gilgal**, see 4:4–5 and note. Since **Beersheba** was in Judah, it is not clear what its significance was for the Israelites. Perhaps people from the northern kingdom made pilgrimage there, remembering its association with the patriarchs (Gen. 21:14–19, 31; 26:23, 33; 46:1–5); perhaps they also felt that there was a special power available there.

5:6 The religious activities carried on at **Bethel** would not quench the **fire** of God's anger. In fact, they would fuel it.

5:7 Wormwood is a plant native to Europe, Asia, and northern Africa, with a bitter-tasting and poisonous extract (also 6:12). True worshipers of God will manifest justice and righteousness (cf. James 1:26–27). See also Amos 5:21–24. **Justice** (Hb. *mishpat*) is much more than legal equity; it refers to the entire scope of God's government of his world. Thus, to "do justice" involves, on the part of government, a fair and just use of power and proper function-

8[r]Job 9:9; 38:31 [s]Ps. 104:20; [ch. 4:13; 8:9] [t]ch. 9:6; [Gen. 6:17; Ps. 104:6, 7] [u]See ch. 4:13
9[v][Jer. 50:32]
10[w]Isa. 29:21; [Prov. 15:5, 10] [x]See Ruth 4:1 [y][1 Kgs. 22:8]
11[z][James 2:6] [a]Deut. 28:30, 39; Mic. 6:15; Zeph. 1:13
12[b]1 Sam. 8:3; 12:3; [Ps. 26:10] [c]ch. 2:7; Isa. 29:21 [x][See ver. 10 above]
13[d][Eccles. 3:7] [e]Mic. 2:3
14[f][Deut. 30:15, 19; Zeph. 2:3] [g]ch. 3:13
15[h]Ps. 97:10; Rom. 12:9 [x][See ver. 10 above] [i]Joel 2:14; [Ex. 32:30]
16[g][See ver. 14 above] [j][Jer. 9:17, 18]

8 He who made the [r]Pleiades and Orion,
and turns deep darkness into the morning
and [s]darkens the day into night,
who [t]calls for the waters of the sea
[t]and pours them out on the surface of the earth,
[u]the LORD is his name;
9 [v]who makes destruction flash forth against the strong,
so that destruction comes upon the fortress.

10 [w]They hate him who reproves [x]in the gate,
and they [y]abhor him who speaks the truth.
11 Therefore because you [z]trample on[1] the poor
and you exact taxes of grain from him,
[a]you have built houses of hewn stone,
but you shall not dwell in them;
[a]you have planted pleasant vineyards,
but you shall not drink their wine.
12 For I know how many are your transgressions
and how great are your sins—
you who afflict the righteous, who [b]take a bribe,
and [c]turn aside the needy [x]in the gate.
13 Therefore he who is prudent will [d]keep silent in such a time,
[e]for it is an evil time.

14 [f]Seek good, and not evil,
that you may live;
and so the LORD, [g]the God of hosts, will be with you,
as you have said.
15 [h]Hate evil, and love good,
and establish justice [x]in the gate;
[i]it may be that the LORD, the God of hosts,
will be gracious to the remnant of Joseph.

16 Therefore thus says the LORD, [g]the God of hosts, the Lord:

"In all the squares [j]there shall be wailing,
and in all the streets they shall say, 'Alas! Alas!'
They shall call the farmers to mourning
and [j]to wailing those who are skilled in lamentation,

[1] Or *you tax*

ing of a fair judicial system, especially to protect the weak from the strong. On the part of individuals, "justice" involves honest and fair business dealings and faithfulness to keep one's word, as well as not taking advantage of the poor or those with less power or protection. **Righteousness** (Hb. *tsedaqah*) involves doing what is right in the sight of God, especially with regard to conduct toward others.

5:8–9 This is another piece of lyrical poetry (cf. 4:13 and 9:5–6) used to contrast the limitless glory of the Creator with the paltry things worshiped in the confines of Bethel, Gilgal, and Beersheba. **Pleiades and Orion**. Constellations of stars. In ancient Near Eastern religions, the stars were often thought to be gods. See also Isa. 40:26. To say that God **calls for the waters of the sea** and then **pours them out on the surface of the earth** is to remind Israel that he alone governs the rainfall, which he can and will use to discipline his people.

5:10 reproves in the gate. The walled cities of the ancient Near East had covered gatehouses in which there were multiple sets of gates. Thus, if the enemy broke through one set, they were immediately confronted with another. During times of peace all these gates would be open and the gatehouse would provide a shady place where the old men of the city could sit to observe the comings and goings, and where they could decide the cases of those who came to them for justice. But in Israel, justice was going to the highest bidder. See also vv. 12, 15.

5:11 Shall not dwell in them and **shall not drink their wine** express frustrated hope; cf. Mic. 6:15; Zeph. 1:13.

5:13 keep silent. The reference is probably to the legal proceedings taking place in the gatehouse (see note on v. 10). If someone were to speak out against the manifest injustice taking place, his own life might be in danger (v. 10), while his objections would do no good because they could not stop the ongoing, entrenched evil.

5:14–15 Speaking through the prophet, God addresses a further appeal to his people (see vv. 4–7). In that evil time (v. 13), they should **seek good** for those around them. If they will, there may be hope for the nation, even at that late hour. **as you have said**. There are two possible explanations. It may be that "God be with you" was a popular form of greeting, as in the original "Goodbye" of English. A more theological explanation is that the religious leaders of the nation may have been saying that the nation could not fall because "God is with us." Amos says that God will only be with them if there is a return to godly behavior in the land. **establish justice**. See note on v. 7. For **God of hosts** (also vv. 15, 16), see note on 3:13.

5:16–17 Although Israel could have returned to God, the fact is that they

17 and in all vineyards there shall be wailing,
for [k]I will pass through your midst,"
says the LORD.

Let Justice Roll Down

18 Woe to you who desire [l]the day of the LORD!
Why would you have the day of the LORD?
[m]It is darkness, and not light,

17[k]Ex. 12:12
18[l]See Joel 1:15 [m]See Joel 2:1, 2

would not. As a result, Amos announces that a great funeral cry of **wailing . . . mourning . . . lamentation** (see v. 1) will go up all over the land from the **streets** of the cities to the **vineyards** in the countryside. **I will pass through your midst**. See 4:12 and note.

5:18–6:14 *An Oracle of Woe.* This fourth message follows closely on the third, because it details the kinds of sins that will provoke the funeral of the nation. Three times the funeral cry of "Woe" appears: 5:18; 6:1; 6:4. Each one introduces another category of sin. The first (5:18–27) is manipulative, paganized religious activity carried on without regard for daily justice and righteousness. The second (6:1–3) is complacency. The third (6:4–7) is self-indulgence. The message ends with an announcement of coming destruction (6:8–14).

5:18–27 The Israelites' religious activities, far from pleasing God, actually alienated him. The recurrence of the pronoun "your" in connection with the several kinds of religious behaviors in these verses gives a clue to the point being made: the **feasts** and **assemblies** as they are celebrating them cannot bring them closer to God. God does not want only religious behavior from his people; he wants their total devotion as shown in the ethical character of their lives (v. 24). See note on 4:4–5.

5:18–20 This is the earliest known use of the prophets' expression, **the day of the LORD**. It also occurs in Isaiah (Isa. 13:6, 9), Jeremiah (Jer. 46:10), Ezekiel (Ezek. 13:5; 30:3), Joel (Joel 1:15; 2:1, 11, 31; 3:14), Obadiah (Obad. 15), Zephaniah (Zeph. 1:7, 14), and Malachi (Mal. 4:5). (See dia-

The Day of the Lord in the Prophets

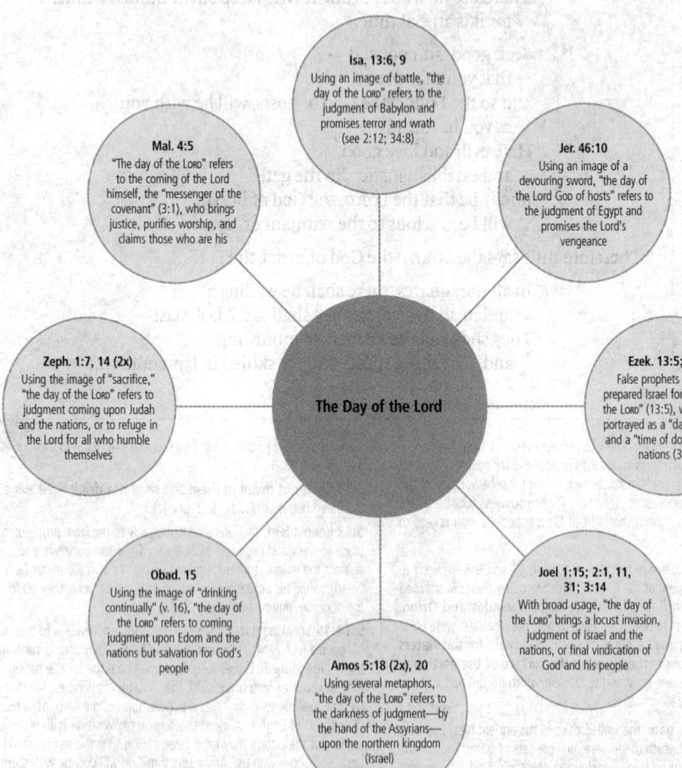
The Day of the Lord
Isa. 13:6, 9
Using an image of battle, "the day of the LORD" refers to the judgment of Babylon and promises terror and wrath (see 2:12; 34:8)
Jer. 46:10
Using an image of a devouring sword, "the day of the Lord GOD of hosts" refers to the judgment of Egypt and promises the Lord's vengeance
Ezek. 13:5; 30:3
False prophets have not prepared Israel for "the day of the LORD" (13:5), which later is portrayed as a "day of clouds" and a "time of doom" for the nations (30:3)
Joel 1:15; 2:1, 11, 31; 3:14
With broad usage, "the day of the LORD" brings a locust invasion, judgment of Israel and the nations, or final vindication of God and his people
Amos 5:18 (2x), 20
Using several metaphors, "the day of the LORD" refers to the darkness of judgment—by the hand of the Assyrians—upon the northern kingdom (Israel)
Obad. 15
Using the image of "drinking continually" (v. 16), "the day of the LORD" refers to coming judgment upon Edom and the nations but salvation for God's people
Zeph. 1:7, 14 (2x)
Using the image of "sacrifice," "the day of the LORD" refers to judgment coming upon Judah and the nations, or to refuge in the Lord for all who humble themselves
Mal. 4:5
"The day of the LORD" refers to the coming of the Lord himself, the "messenger of the covenant" (3:1), who brings justice, purifies worship, and claims those who are his

19[n][Isa. 24:18; Jer. 48:44]
20[m][See ver. 18 above]
21[o]Isa. 1:14; [Jer. 6:20]
22[p]Ps. 51:16, 17; Isa. 1:11
23[q][ch. 6:5; 8:3; Isa. 5:12]
25[r]Cited Acts 7:42, 43
26[s][Deut. 32:17; Ezek. 20:16, 24] [t][Isa. 46:7]
27[u]2 Kgs. 17:6 [g][See ver. 14 above]

Chapter 6

1[w]Isa. 32:9; Zeph. 1:12; Luke 6:24; James 5:1 [x]ch. 3:9; 4:1 [y][Ezek. 22:6] [z]See Ex. 19:5
2[a]Gen. 10:10; Isa. 10:9 [b]1 Kgs. 8:65; 2 Kgs. 18:34; Isa. 10:9 [c]See 1 Sam. 17:4 [d][Nah. 3:8]
3[e][ch. 9:10; Ezek. 12:27] [f]See ch. 3:10

19 [n]as if a man fled from a lion,
and a bear met him,
or went into the house and leaned his hand against the wall,
and a serpent bit him.
20 [m]Is not the day of the LORD darkness, and not light,
and gloom with no brightness in it?

21 [o]"I hate, I despise your feasts,
and I take no delight in your solemn assemblies.
22 [p]Even though you offer me your burnt offerings and grain offerings,
I will not accept them;
and the peace offerings of your fattened animals,
I will not look upon them.
23 Take away from me the noise of your songs;
to [q]the melody of your harps I will not listen.
24 But let justice roll down like waters,
and righteousness like an ever-flowing stream.

25 [r]"Did you bring to me sacrifices and offerings during the forty years in the wilderness,
O house of Israel? 26 [s]You [t]shall take up Sikkuth your king, and Kiyyun your star-god—your
images that you made for yourselves, 27 [u]and I will send you into exile beyond Damascus,"
says the LORD, whose name is [g]the God of hosts.

Woe to Those at Ease in Zion

6

1 [w]"Woe to those who are at ease in Zion,
and to those who feel secure on [x]the mountain of Samaria,
[y]the notable men of [z]the first of the nations,
to whom the house of Israel comes!
2 Pass over to [a]Calneh, and see,
and from there go to [b]Hamath the great;
then go down to [c]Gath of the Philistines.
[d]Are you better than these kingdoms?
Or is their territory greater than your territory,
3 [e]O you who put far away the day of disaster
[f]and bring near the seat of violence?

gram, p. 1668.) Perhaps in Amos's day the term was in popular use for the time when the Lord would intervene and put Israel at the head of the nations (possibly based on Deut. 32:35–37); but Amos, and all prophets after him, clarify what it would mean for the Lord to visit his people: it means judgment upon them if they are unfaithful. In Amos, the term points forward to the coming judgment on the northern kingdom at the hands of the Assyrians (Amos 5:27); in Zephaniah, it points to the coming judgment on Judah at the hands of the Babylonians. Other prophets use the term to signal God's forthcoming punishment of other nations for their brutalities, e.g., Babylon (Isa. 13:6, 9); Egypt (Jer. 46:10); Edom (Obad. 15); and many nations (Joel 3:14; Obad. 15). In some cases the prophet uses the term to denote something farther off in the future (Mal. 4:5; probably in Joel 2:31). All of this indicates that the "day" is not unique, but may be repeated as circumstances call for it. The NT authors apply the term as well to the return of Christ (e.g., 1 Cor. 1:8; 2 Pet. 3:10).

5:21 God hates and despises Israel's religious **feasts** and **solemn assemblies**, their offerings (v. 22) and songs (v. 23) because of their persistent sinful conduct (see note on 3:15) and because of their perversion of worship at Bethel (cf. note on 4:4–5), as well as the absence of "justice" and "righteousness" in their conduct toward one another (5:24). Worshiping God in a way contrary to his Word and without moral integrity in one's life is blatant hypocrisy (cf. Isa. 29:13; Matt. 15:8–9).

5:22 I will not accept them. God graciously extends his fellowship and forgiveness to those who will accept his covenant, as shown by their changed lives. He cannot be manipulated into doing such a thing by ritualism.

5:24 On **justice** and **righteousness**, see note on 5:7.

5:25–26 The Israelites had in fact given such **offerings** in the desert, but since their hearts were not right (note the mention of **Sikkuth** and **Kiyyun**, Mesopotamian astral deities), God nevertheless judged them. Thus the religiosity of the people of Israel in Amos's day will not fool God, either.

5:27 Exile beyond Damascus is just what happened (2 Kings 17:6). This is a startling and significant prediction, as Assyria was comparatively weak in Amos's time. On **God of hosts**, see note on Amos 3:13.

6:1–3 Amos calls on the complacent (those who believe they have no cause for concern) to consider the other kingdoms (stronger than they) that had already fallen to Assyria.

6:1 The prophet did not leave the Judeans out of his diatribe (see 2:4–5). Both **Zion** (Jerusalem), the capital of Judah, and **Samaria**, the capital of Israel, were strong fortresses, easily defended. But pride and self-confidence are never fitting for God's cherished people.

6:2 Stronger cities than either Jerusalem or Samaria had already fallen. Among these were **Calneh**, in south-central Mesopotamia (see Gen. 10:10; Isa. 10:9); **Hamath**, in Syria to the north of Israel; and **Gath**, a Philistine city southwest of Israel. Since the three locations reflect the entire extent of the so-called "Fertile Crescent," they may have been chosen for their representative value. No city in the whole region could claim immunity to destruction.

6:3 The only hope for either Israel or Judah was in the power of God made available through repentance, but Israel, at least, saw no need for such a thing.

4 “Woe to those [g]who lie on [h]beds of ivory
[g]and stretch themselves out on their couches,
and eat lambs from the flock
[i]and calves from the midst of the stall,
5 [j]who sing idle songs to the sound of the harp
and like David [j]invent for themselves instruments of music,
6 [k]who drink wine in bowls
and [l]anoint themselves with the finest oils,
but are not grieved over the ruin of Joseph!
7 [m]Therefore they shall now be the first of those who go into exile,
and the revelry of those who stretch themselves out shall pass away.”

8 [n]The Lord GOD has sworn by himself, declares the LORD, the God of hosts:

“I abhor [o]the pride of Jacob
and hate his strongholds,
[p]and I will deliver up the city and all that is in it.”

9 And [q]if ten men remain in one house, they shall die. 10 And when one’s relative, [r]the
one who anoints him for burial, shall take him up to bring the bones out of the house,
and shall say to him who is in the innermost parts of the house, “Is there still anyone
with you?” he shall say, “No”; and he shall say, [s]“Silence! We must not mention the name
of the LORD.”

11 For behold, the LORD commands,
and [t]the great house shall be struck down into fragments,
and the little house into bits.
12 Do horses run on rocks?
Does one plow there[1] with oxen?
[u]But you have turned justice into [v]poison
[u]and the fruit of righteousness into wormwood[2]—
13 you who rejoice in Lo-debar,[3]
who say, [w]“Have we not by our own strength
captured Karnaim[4] for ourselves?”
14 “For behold, [x]I will raise up against you a nation,
O house of Israel,” declares the LORD, the God of hosts;
“and they shall oppress you from [y]Lebo-hamath
to the Brook of [z]the Arabah.”

4 [g][ch. 3:12] [h][Esth. 1:6] [i][James 5:5]
5 [j]See ch. 5:23
6 [k][Isa. 5:12] [l][Dan. 10:3]
7 [m]ch. 7:11, 17
8 [n]Jer. 22:5; 51:14 [o]ch. 8:7; [Ps. 47:4] [p][Jer. 17:3]
9 [q][ch. 3:3]
10 [r]See 1 Sam. 31:12 [s][ch. 5:13; 8:3]
11 [t][ch. 3:15]
12 [u][ch. 5:7] [v]Deut. 29:18
13 [w][1 Kgs. 22:11; Mic. 4:13]
14 [x][Jer. 5:15] [y]2 Kgs. 14:25 [z]See Deut. 1:1

[1] Or *the sea* [2] Or *into bitter fruit* [3] *Lo-debar* means *nothing* [4] *Karnaim* means *horns* (a symbol of strength)

6:4–7 Instead of mourning and grieving over their sins and those of their nation (v. 6), the Israelites were treating themselves to the very best of life’s pleasures. It was these people, the “cream” of Israelite society, whom the Assyrians would take first into exile (v. 7). On God’s requirements concerning wealth and the wealthy, see note on 3:15.

6:4 Ivory was then, as now, a luxury. These people indulged in tender lamb and veal, not the tougher mutton and beef. On ivory, see note on 3:15.

6:5 Although the Israelite elite emulated **David** in making music, and perhaps congratulated themselves on that, it is clear that they had no real awareness of the deep meaning of the Hebrew psalms with their passion for God and his ways.

6:6 Wine in bowls and **finest oils** are further indications that any trace of moderation or restraint was gone from this complacent upper echelon of society. They cared extravagantly for their own bodies but cared nothing for the needs of others. The two main tribes in Israel were Ephraim and Manasseh, descended from **Joseph**.

6:8–14 Israel’s paganized religion, their strong fortresses, and their decadent culture would be helpless against the enemy that God was raising up.

6:8 sworn by himself. See Gen. 22:16; Isa. 45:23; Jer. 22:5; 51:14. Hebrews 6:13 explains this on the grounds that “he had no one greater by whom to swear.” On **strongholds**, see Amos 3:9–11 and note.

6:9–10 While the general sense of this vignette is clear—nothing would be left of the great houses and families—the specific sense is not as clear. Perhaps it describes a time when the survivors (v. 10) would be so traumatized that they would be afraid of any mention of **the name of the LORD** lest it be done inappropriately and bring yet more disaster upon them.

6:12 horses run on rocks. Even the least-educated farmer understands that there are laws of nature that must be obeyed if life and health are to be preserved. But Israel’s leaders have no such understanding. Perverting **justice** and **righteousness** is ultimately as destructive as trying to get a crop from a rock pile. On both justice and **wormwood**, see note on 5:7.

6:13 Lo-debar and **Karnaim** were two cities on the east side of the Jordan. Lo-debar may be the same as Debir in Josh. 13:26. If so, it was located on the northern border of Gad, near Mahanaim (see also 2 Sam. 9:4–5; 17:27). Karnaim was farther north, in the territory of Bashan (see Amos 4:1). Both cities were in areas that were in constant dispute with Syria. It is likely that Israel had succeeded in recapturing them from Syria during the Assyrian weakness just before Amos’s time, and that this was a cause for Israelite self-confidence.

6:14 Amos says the little victories of the previous verse will be nothing compared to the destruction that is to come. **Lebo-hamath** was in the far north, in the valley between the Lebanon and the Anti-Lebanon Mountains. **The Brook of the Arabah** is in the valley in the far south between the Dead Sea and the Gulf of Aqaba. The Assyrian conquest and oppression would cover the whole land, not just a few isolated cities.

Warning Visions

7 [a]This is what the Lord GOD showed me: behold, [b]he was forming locusts when the
latter growth was just beginning to sprout, and behold, it was the latter growth after
the king's mowings. 2 When they had finished eating the grass of the land, I said,

"O Lord GOD, please forgive!
[c]How can Jacob stand?
He is so small!"
3 [d]The LORD relented concerning this:
"It shall not be," said the LORD.

4 [a]This is what the Lord GOD showed me: behold, the Lord GOD was calling [e]for a judgment by fire, and it devoured the great deep and was eating up the land. 5 Then I said,

"O Lord GOD, please cease!
[c]How can Jacob stand?
He is so small!"
6 [d]The LORD relented concerning this:
"This also shall not be," said the Lord GOD.

7 [a]This is what he showed me: behold, the Lord was standing beside a wall built with
[f]a plumb line, with a plumb line in his hand. 8 And the LORD said to me, [g]"Amos, what do
you see?" And I said, "A plumb line." Then the Lord said,

"Behold, I am setting [f]a plumb line
in the midst of my people Israel;
[g]I will never again pass by them;
9 [h]the high places of Isaac shall be made desolate,
and the sanctuaries of Israel shall be laid waste,
and I will rise against [i]the house of Jeroboam with the sword."

Amos Accused

10 Then Amaziah [j]the priest of Bethel sent to [k]Jeroboam king of Israel, saying, "Amos
has [l]conspired against you in the midst of the house of Israel. The land is not able to bear
all his words. 11 For thus Amos has said,

Chapter 7

1 [a]ch. 8:1 [b][Joel 1:4]; See Ex. 10:4
2 [c][Ps. 130:3]
3 [d][Deut. 32:36; Joel 2:13]
4 [a][See ver. 1 above] [e][Rev. 8:7, 8]
5 [c][See ver. 2 above]
6 [d][See ver. 3 above]
7 [a][See ver. 1 above] [f][ver. 17]; See 2 Kgs. 21:13
8 [g]ch. 8:2 [f][See ver. 7 above]
9 [h]Gen. 26:23, 25 [i]See 2 Kgs. 15:8-12
10 [j]1 Kgs. 12:32 [k]ch. 1:1 [l][Jer. 38:4]

7:1–9:15 *Visions of Judgment.* In the final section of the book, the prophet turns from speech to sight. He now tells of visions he has received from God that leave no doubt of the deadly peril in which the nation stands. The first is a vision of inescapable judgment (7:1–9), a vision frighteningly confirmed by the prophet's experience with the priest of Bethel (7:10–17). The second vision is of Israel's terrible end (8:1–14). The last is of the Lord standing at the altar of sacrifice (9:1–15). But this vision has two parts, the first of which continues the theme of judgment (9:1–10), whereas the second sounds a note of hope (9:11–15).

7:1–17 *A Vision of Inescapable Judgment.* Israel is too far gone to avoid judgment.

7:1–9 *The Vision Itself.* God reveals to Amos in three pictures that there is no hope for Israel. In response to the first two, the prophet pleads for mercy for the nation (vv. 2, 5), and God twice graciously relents (vv. 3, 6). But the third picture is so convincing that the prophet sees there is no hope and therefore makes no intercession. The idea is that God has repeatedly shown mercy to his erring people, only to have them continue in their complacency toward him. Sooner or later, their time will be up.

7:1 Judgment would fall on Israel like a plague of **locusts**. The **latter growth** was the wheat crop harvested after the barley. If it was lost, there would be little to eat in the coming year. The **king's mowings** were the part of the crop paid as a tax to the king.

7:2 please forgive. In spite of the severity of all that Amos had said, there was no element of vindictiveness in him. Unlike Jonah, he did not want what he was predicting to happen. He pleaded earnestly that God would show mercy.

7:3 The LORD relented. Like Amos, God does not desire to destroy his people. He is very patient (see Ex. 34:6). Unlike the capricious gods, who may decide for no reason either to destroy or release, the Lord is utterly reliable: he has promised to relent in response to repentance (see Jer. 8:5–10; cf. Jonah 3:10–4:2).

7:4 Judgment would come upon Israel like a **fire** so intense it would dry up the sea (**the great deep**) and scorch the **land**.

7:7–9 The third picture that God **showed** Amos was of a **plumb line** held against a **wall**. A plumb line is a string with a weight fastened to the end of it. When the string is placed beside a wall and the weight is allowed to hang freely, it will be apparent whether or not the wall is perfectly vertical. If the wall is leaning and it is not fixed, it will eventually collapse. Compared to the standard of the Torah, the plumb line according to which the wall of Israel was **built**, it is clear to Amos that the nation is now so far out of true vertical that the collapse cannot be prevented. Israel is hardened in sin; thus, in this case, Amos does not ask God to relent.

7:9 The reference to **high places** and **sanctuaries** makes it plain that Israel is out of line with reality, particularly regarding her relationship to God. When this situation is laid where it should be, at the foot of the king **Jeroboam** (II), the royal chaplain comes to his defense (vv. 10–17).

7:10–17 *An Experience Reinforcing the Vision.* If the plumb line according to which Israel was constructed was the Torah, then the priesthood should have held Israel accountable to the Torah (Deut. 33:10; Mal. 2:6–7). But the priesthood itself was corrupt (see 1 Kings 12:31 for how Jeroboam I ruined the priesthood for the northern kingdom). Thus, there was no external standard being applied by which Israel's true condition could be recognized and corrected. In such a case, the end truly was at hand.

7:10 The reference to **Amaziah the priest** shows that a representative of the established religious leadership, who had the ear of the king, opposed the prophecies of Amos. His words, **Amos has conspired against you**, were a lie.

"'Jeroboam shall die by the sword,
and [m]Israel must go into exile
away from his land.'"

12 And Amaziah said to Amos, [n]"O seer, go, flee away [o]to the land of Judah, and [p]eat bread
there, and prophesy there, 13 but [q]never again prophesy at Bethel, for [r]it is the king's sanctuary, and it is a temple of the kingdom."
14 Then Amos answered and said to Amaziah, [s]"I was[1] no prophet, nor a prophet's son,
but [t]I was a herdsman and a dresser of sycamore figs. 15 [u]But the LORD took me from following the flock, and the LORD said to me, 'Go, prophesy to my people Israel.' 16 [v]Now
therefore hear the word of the LORD.

"You say, [n]'Do not prophesy against Israel,
and [w]do not preach against the house of [x]Isaac.'

17 [y]Therefore thus says the LORD:

"'Your wife shall be a prostitute in the city,
and your sons and your daughters shall fall by the sword,
and your land [z]shall be divided up with a measuring line;
you yourself shall die in an unclean land,
and [m]Israel shall surely go into exile away from its land.'"

The Coming Day of Bitter Mourning

8 [a]This is what the Lord GOD showed me: behold, a basket of summer fruit. 2 And he
said, [b]"Amos, what do you see?" And I said, [c]"A basket of summer fruit." Then the
LORD said to me,

[d]"The end[2] has come upon my people Israel;
I will never again pass by them.
3 [e]The songs of the temple[3] [f]shall become wailings[4] in that day,"
declares the Lord GOD.
[g]"So many dead bodies!"
"They are thrown everywhere!"
[h]"Silence!"

4 Hear this, [i]you who trample on the needy
and bring the poor of the land to an end,
5 saying, "When will [j]the new moon be over,
that we may sell grain?

[1] *Or am; twice in this verse* [2] *The Hebrew words for end and summer fruit sound alike* [3] *Or palace* [4] *Or The singing women of the palace shall wail*

11 [m]ch. 6:7
12 [n]See 1 Sam. 9:9 [o][ch. 1:1] [p][Mic. 3:5, 11]
13 [q]See ch. 2:12 [r]See 1 Kgs. 12:29–13:1
14 [s]ch. 1:1; [Zech. 13:5] [t]ch. 1:1
15 [u][Ps. 78:71]
16 [v]ch. 3:1 [n][See ver. 12 above] [w]Ezek. 20:46; 21:2; Mic. 2:6 [x][ver. 9]
17 [y][Jer. 28:16; 29:21, 31, 32] [z][ver. 7, 8] [m][See ver. 11 above]

Chapter 8

1 [a]ch. 7:1
2 [b]ch. 7:8 [c][Jer. 24:1; Mic. 7:1] [d]Lam. 4:18
3 [e][ch. 5:23] [f][Jer. 47:2] [g][ch. 6:9] [h][ch. 6:10; Jer. 16:4, 6]
4 [i][Ps. 14:4]
5 [j]See Num. 28:11

7:12–13 When **Amaziah** called Amos a **seer**, his intent may have been contemptuous. This term for a prophet (2 Sam. 24:11) suggests Amos is not a member of the royal guild of prophets (who, since they were paid by the king, would speak to his pleasure), and thus has no standing in **the king's sanctuary**. Note that no mention is made of this being *God's* sanctuary or **temple**. **never again prophesy at Bethel**. Amaziah the priest and those supporting him wanted only to hear messages of God's promises of blessing and success, not messages about sin and obedience and judgment (cf. 2 Tim. 4:3).

7:14–16 Far from being humiliated at his lack of professional standing, Amos takes it as a badge of honor. He is not paid to say what he is saying, but does so solely at the command of the Lord.

7:14 dresser of sycamore figs. Sycamore figs were somewhat like a mulberry. They would only ripen if bruised. They were usually eaten by the very poor.

7:15 the LORD took me . . . the LORD said to me. Amos was not prophesying on his own authority but on God's authority.

7:17 All the honor that Amaziah prized so highly would be taken from him: his wife would belong to other men indiscriminately; he would be deprived of any progeny; he would lose his property; he would lose his profession (because of being defiled by the **unclean land** to which he would be taken as captive); and he would die as an **exile**. These terrible punishments would be heaped on this religious leader (recognized by the king but not by God) for rejecting the words of God that came through the prophet Amos.

8:1–14 *A Vision of the Terrible End.* Amos describes the final end of Israel in powerful imagery.

8:1–2 The Hebrew terms for **summer fruit** (*qayits*) and **end** (*qets*) sound alike. In Hebrew literature this kind of wordplay is very common. Beyond this, "summer fruit" did signify the last of the harvest. See Jer. 8:20, "the summer is ended, and we are not saved." The long summer of God's patience has finally come to an end, and there has been no harvest of repentance.

8:3 dead bodies. See Ezek. 9:7. The paganized worship of Israel will end in a terrible **silence**.

8:4–6 The terrible irony is that the Israelites thought that ritualistic worship could excuse oppression and greed. Even a sincere worship could not have atoned for that. See the notes on 4:4–5 and 5:22.

8:4 you who trample on the needy. The rich and powerful were oppressing the poor and weak rather than helping them. But those who sought to **bring the poor of the land to an end** were themselves going to face a terrible end.

8:5–6 Real worship of God in the **new moon** and **Sabbath** festivals would have created compassion for the **poor** and the **needy**. Throughout the OT,

5[k][Neh. 13:15, 16] [l]Ezek. 45:10; Mic. 6:10, 11; See Hos. 12:7
6[m]ch. 2:6
7[n]ch. 6:8 [o]Hos. 8:13; 9:9
8[p][Hos. 4:3] [q]ch. 9:5 [r][Zech. 10:11]
9[s]Jer. 15:9; Mic. 3:6; Matt. 24:29; [ch. 4:13; 5:8]
10[t][Jer. 7:34; 16:9; Hos. 2:11] [u]Isa. 3:24 [v]Jer. 6:26; Zech. 12:10
11[w][Isa. 8:20, 21] [x][Ps. 74:9; Prov. 29:18; Mic. 3:7]
12[x][See ver. 11 above] [y][ch. 4:8]
13[z]Isa. 51:20 [a][Jonah 4:8]
14[b]Deut. 9:21; 1 Kgs. 12:29, 30; Hos. 10:8 [c][Acts 9:2] [d]ch. 5:5

And [k]the Sabbath,
that we may offer wheat for sale,
that we may make [l]the ephah small and the shekel[1] great
and deal deceitfully with false balances,
6 that we may buy the poor for [m]silver
and the needy for a pair of sandals
and sell the chaff of the wheat?"

7 The LORD has sworn by [n]the pride of Jacob:
"Surely [o]I will never forget any of their deeds.
8 [p]Shall not the land tremble on this account,
and everyone mourn who dwells in it,
[q]and all of it rise like the Nile,
and be tossed about [r]and sink again, like the Nile of Egypt?"

9 "And on that day," declares the Lord GOD,
[s]"I will make the sun go down at noon
and darken the earth in broad daylight.
10 [t]I will turn your feasts into mourning
and all your songs into lamentation;
[u]I will bring sackcloth on every waist
[u]and baldness on every head;
[v]I will make it like the mourning for an only son
and the end of it like a bitter day.

11 "Behold, the days are coming," declares the Lord GOD,
"when [w]I will send a famine on the land—
not a famine of bread, nor a thirst for water,
[x]but of hearing the words of the LORD.
12 [x]They shall wander from sea to sea,
and from north to east;
they shall run to and fro, to seek the word of the LORD,
[y]but they shall not find it.

13 [z]"In that day the lovely virgins and the young men
shall [a]faint for thirst.
14 Those who swear by [b]the Guilt of Samaria,
and say, 'As your god lives, O Dan,'
and, 'As [c]the Way of [d]Beersheba lives,'
they shall fall, and never rise again."

[1] An *ephah* was about 3/5 bushel or 22 liters; a *shekel* was about 2/5 ounce or 11 grams

false balances are a symbol of injustice (Lev. 19:35–36; Prov. 20:10; Mic. 6:10–11). The weight of goods being bought or sold was determined by hanging them on one end of a balance beam while standard weights (such as a **shekel**) were hung on the other end. If the weights were only slightly false in the merchant's favor, considerable profits could be made. The situation was similar if the measure of volume (such as an **ephah**) being used was incorrect.

8:6 buy the poor . . . and the needy. Rather than helping their poor neighbors, the rich and powerful were using their money and power to put these people into slavery.

8:7 The **pride of Jacob** could be taken in two different ways: it could be a reference to God himself (see 6:8), or it could be a literal reference to Israel's insupportable pride in its strength and wealth (see also 6:8).

8:8 rise . . . and sink . . . like the Nile. Amos sees the coming destruction to be like the annual flooding of the Nile. The flood is absolutely inevitable, covering everything and leaving destruction in its wake. See also 9:5.

8:9–10 Israel's destruction will be so terrible that even nature will go into mourning, with the **sun** hiding its face. This is reminiscent of the darkness that covered the earth when God's only Son died for the sins of Israel and the whole world (see Mark 15:33). Darkening can serve as a symbol of judgment (Joel 3:15; see also Rev. 6:12; 8:12).

8:11–12 Israel had rejected the **words of the LORD** from Amos and so they would go into exile, where there would be no word from the Lord at all. In its absence they will find that the revelation from God had been their most precious possession. **they shall not find it**. People who have repeatedly rejected God's words will suddenly be unable to find God's words at all. In 7:17 severe judgment came to a priest for rejecting God's words, but here severe judgment comes upon the people as a whole for the same sin.

8:13–14 Israel had depended on their paganized ideas of Yahweh, represented by the idols at Samaria and **Dan**, or on the ancestral tradition of Yahweh at **Beersheba** (see 5:5 and note), but they would find that these pseudo-Yahwehs were no good at all. **The Guilt of Samaria** might be a mocking wordplay on "Asherah of Samaria," since the Hebrew for "guilt" (*'ashmah*) sounds like Asherah. For a similar wordplay, see the transformation of Eshbaal, "man of Baal" (1 Chron. 8:33), into Ish-bosheth, "man of shame" (2 Sam. 2:8).

The Destruction of Israel

9 I saw the Lord standing beside[1] the altar, and he said:

[e]"Strike the capitals until [e]the thresholds [f]shake,
[g]and shatter them on the heads of all the people;[2]
and those who are left of them I will kill with the sword;
[h]not one of them shall flee away;
not one of them shall escape.

2 [i]"If they dig into Sheol,
from there shall my hand take them;
[i]if they climb up to heaven,
from there I will bring them down.
3 If they hide themselves on [j]the top of Carmel,
from there I will search them out and take them;
[k]and if they hide from my sight at the bottom of the sea,
there I will command the serpent, and it shall bite them.
4 [l]And if they go into captivity before their enemies,
there I will command the sword, and it shall kill them;
[m]and I will fix my eyes upon them
for evil and not for good."

5 The Lord GOD of hosts,
he who touches the earth and [n]it melts,
and all who dwell in it mourn,
[o]and all of it rises like the Nile,
[o]and sinks again, like the Nile of Egypt;
6 [p]who builds his upper chambers in the heavens
and founds his vault upon the earth;
[q]who calls for the waters of the sea
and pours them out upon the surface of the earth—
[r]the LORD is his name.

7 "Are you not like [s]the Cushites to me,
O people of Israel?" declares the LORD.
[t]"Did I not bring up Israel from the land of Egypt,
and [u]the Philistines from [v]Caphtor and the Syrians from [w]Kir?
8 Behold, [x]the eyes of the Lord GOD are upon the sinful kingdom,

[1] Or *on* [2] Hebrew *all of them*

Chapter 9
1 [e]Zeph. 2:14 [f][Isa. 6:4] [g]See Judg. 16:26-30 [h][ch. 2:14]
2 [i][Ps. 139:8-10]
3 [j]ch. 1:2 [k][Job 26:5]
4 [l][Deut. 28:65] [m]See Jer. 21:10
5 [n]Ps. 46:6 [o]ch. 8:8
6 [p][Ps. 104:3, 5] [q]See ch. 5:8 [r]See ch. 4:13
7 [s][Zeph. 3:10] [t]Ex. 20:2 [u]Jer. 47:4 [v]Gen. 10:14 [w]ch. 1:5
8 [x][ver. 4]

9:1–15 *A Vision of the Lord Standing beside the Altar.* This vision has two parts, one negative (vv. 1–10) and the other positive (vv. 11–15). The negative aspect is the culmination of the previous oracles and visions. God renders as worthless all the sacrifices that the Israelites had given in an attempt to manipulate God on their behalf while they brought reproach to his name with their sinful lives. God would shatter (v. 1) their pagan temples and demand their own lives as sacrifices (vv. 9–10). But God's ultimate purpose in judgment is never destruction (v. 8); it is always restoration. So vv. 11–15 depict a day on the other side of judgment when Israel, again recognizing David (v. 11), would be restored to its land.

9:1–10 *The Thresholds Shaken.* The primary theme of this part of the vision is the inescapability of God's judgment. He will search out the sinful Israelites wherever they try to hide from him (vv. 1–4). The final piece of lyrical poetry in the book comes next, emphasizing the sovereign power of the Creator (vv. 5–6; see also 4:13; 5:8–9). The ultimate blow is to the idea that Israel ought to receive special favor from God because they are uniquely chosen (9:10). In fact, says Amos, God had directed the movements of many peoples on the earth (v. 7), and if Israel has any special status, it is a special accountability (vv. 8–10).

9:1 Capitals are the tops of the columns, and **thresholds** are the bases. The two together form a merism expressing the totality of the temple structure. Revelation 20:11–15 uses this image of no escape to describe the last judgment.

9:2–3 Two more merisms: **Sheol** (the underworld) vs. **heaven**; and **Carmel** (the mountaintop) vs. **the bottom of the sea**. In short, there is no place between these extremes to escape God.

9:4 for evil and not for good. This is a terrifying statement, showing that there is no escape anywhere in the entire creation, but it was what God had promised long before (Deut. 28:64–68) if the people were unfaithful. And yet even there, God offers forgiveness and restoration to those who repent (Deut. 30:1–10). As Ps. 103:9 puts it, "nor will he keep his anger forever."

9:5 The Lord GOD of hosts. See 3:13 and note. **rises like the Nile**. See 8:8 and note.

9:6 Heavens, **earth**, and **sea** are all at the beck and call of the One whose **name** is **the LORD**.

9:7 Cushites (or Nubians), who lived south of Egypt, were considered to be living at the end of the world. All peoples are under God's providential care. **Caphtor**. Crete. For **Kir**, see 1:5.

9:9 no pebble shall fall. Israel *will* stand out among the nations, but in the sense that none of the Israelites will be able to hide among the nations.

8[y]Jer. 30:11; [Obad. 17]
9[z][Jer. 15:7; Matt. 3:12; Luke 3:17]
10[a][ch. 6:3]
11[b]Cited Acts 15:16
12[c][Obad. 19] [d]Cited Acts 15:17, 18
13[e]Lev. 26:5 [f]Joel 3:18
14[g]Jer. 30:3 [h]Isa. 61:4 [i]Jer. 31:5
15[j]Jer. 24:6; Ezek. 34:29 [k][Joel 3:20] [l][Jer. 3:18]

and I will destroy it from the surface of the ground,
[y]except that I will not utterly destroy the house of Jacob,"
declares the LORD.

9 "For behold, I will command,
[z]and shake the house of Israel among all the nations
as one shakes with a sieve,
but no pebble shall fall to the earth.
10 All the sinners of my people shall die by the sword,
who say, [a]'Disaster shall not overtake or meet us.'

The Restoration of Israel

11 "In that day [b]I will raise up
the booth of David that is fallen
and repair its breaches,
and raise up its ruins
and rebuild it as in the days of old,
12 [c]that they may possess the remnant of Edom
and [d]all the nations who are called by my name,"[1]
declares the LORD who does this.

13 "Behold, the days are coming," declares the LORD,
[e]"when the plowman shall overtake the reaper
and the treader of grapes him who sows the seed;
[f]the mountains shall drip sweet wine,
and all the hills shall flow with it.
14 [g]I will restore the fortunes of my people Israel,
and [h]they shall rebuild the ruined cities and inhabit them;
[i]they shall plant vineyards and drink their wine,
and they shall make gardens and eat their fruit.
15 [j]I will plant them on their land,
[k]and they shall never again be uprooted
out of the land [l]that I have given them,"
says the LORD your God.

[1] Hebrew; Septuagint (compare Acts 15:17) *that the remnant of mankind and all the nations who are called by my name may seek the Lord*

Isaiah 27:12–13 uses the sieve figure to say that none of the remnant will be lost among the nations.

9:11–15 *The Booth of David Restored.* In contrast to the mighty edifice of Israel that God would smash to the ground (v. 1), the fragile, torn tent of David (v. 11) would be repaired. The reminder that well-being depends on the line of David would come with special force to the northern audience of Amos, who had rejected the Davidic king. God has committed himself to bless his people, and eventually the world, through the family of David (2 Sam. 7:15–16; Ps. 72:17). In that context, Israel's fortunes (Amos 9:14) would be restored. The abundance described in vv. 13–15 stands in stark contrast to the ruin and destruction that fell on Israel after God repeatedly warned them, appealing to them to come to repentance (4:6–11). Again, the point is that God does not intend for judgment on Israel to be final, but to be a tool through which blessing may ultimately come.

9:11 In that day reminds the reader of the day of the Lord that the Israelites confidently expected. If it was to be a day of destruction instead of blessing (5:18–20; see note), that did not mean it was to be God's final word on the subject.

9:12 Just as the "booth" in v. 11 contrasted with the temple of v. 1, so here the "possession" of the **nations . . . called by my name** stands in connection with the nations described in vv. 7–8. Israel does have a special place among the nations, but it is a place of mission, not of privilege. In Acts 15:16–17, James cites Amos 9:11–12, understanding that passage to indicate that in the messianic reign inaugurated by Jesus' resurrection (when David's fallen tent is raised), "all the nations" (i.e., Gentiles) become included in God's blessings, as God had promised to Abraham (Gen. 12:3).

9:13 The abundant productivity of the restored land, under the blessing of God, will be so amazing that the land does not need to lie fallow for a moment, but as soon as the **reaper** has harvested one crop, the **plowman** comes right behind planting another one, and as soon as someone **sows the seed**, the grapes grow so rapidly that the **treader of grapes** comes to pick the ripe grapes and gather them for the winepress. This is a beautiful poetic image of a land like the garden of Eden—with productivity that is free from the curse (Gen. 3:17–19; cf. Amos 4:6–10) and with greater abundance than anything currently known. Some interpreters apply this passage, which in its immediate context describes the fruitfulness of a renewed land of Israel, to a wider renewal of the whole earth in a future age (cf. Rom. 8:19–21).

9:14 I will restore the fortunes. To build **cities** and enjoy food and prosperity, when these things are enjoyed in obedience to the Lord and with thanksgiving to him, is to enjoy God's blessing.

9:15 This final blessing of the people is predicated upon their recognition of their Davidic messiah, something that is yet to occur. See Rom. 11:25–27.

INTRODUCTION TO

OBADIAH

Author and Title

The superscription for the book identifies the genre as a "vision," a prophetic revelation from God spoken through his prophet "Obadiah." Unfortunately, the only thing known about this prophet is his name (a common one in the OT), which means "one who serves Yahweh." It is unlikely that he is the same Obadiah as the official over Ahab's household in 1 Kings 18:3–16 (9th century B.C.), for the book seems to have been written after the fall of Jerusalem (586; see Date).

Date

Because the superscription gives no chronological information, readers can infer only the approximate time of the prophet from the book's contents. Suggested dates range from very early (c. 850 B.C.) to very late (c. 400). Since the book presents the fall of Jerusalem as a past event (v. 11) and the fall of Edom as a future event, a probable date would be after 586 B.C. (the destruction of Jerusalem by Babylon) and before 553 (Babylon's campaign against Edom). Therefore, the most likely situation is the first half of the Babylonian exile. The place of writing is Jerusalem.

Theme

On the one hand, Edom, together with all other nations that oppose Israel's God and his people, will experience God's retributive judgment. On the other hand, God's own covenant people, who have already experienced God's judgment, will receive restoration from their God. The book ends with the promise of the kingdom of God.

Purpose, Occasion, and Background

Obadiah exhibits numerous parallels with other OT texts, especially Jeremiah's Edom prophecy (Jer. 49:7–22). Essentially the message of Obadiah spells out what Lamentations 4:22 announces: restoration for Zion but doom for Edom.

The Jerusalemites experienced God's judgment (Obad. 16a) when enemies invaded and "cast lots for Jerusalem" (v. 11). The Edomites, the descendants of Jacob's brother Esau and one of Israel's neighbors to the southeast, should have assisted their brothers during the Babylonian crisis. Instead they sided with the foreign invaders and even took advantage of Israel's misfortune (vv. 10–14).

Holy Zion had been profaned, and God's people were put to public shame. Edom felt secure in spite of its complicity in Israel's demise. For all intents and purposes it looked as though Edom and the foreign nations were in charge, ruling over the future of Israel. The book of Lamentations reveals the extent to which Israel was devastated by the exile—politically, economically, and theologically. Does Israel have a future? Will Zion be profaned forever? Will the plan for Abraham's offspring to bring blessing to the world come to nothing? Will Edom and the hostile nations triumph? Is God indifferent to all of this?

Into this bleak situation the prophet Obadiah proclaimed the word of Yahweh. The first half of Obadiah (vv. 1–15) addresses Edom with "you" singular. The prophet announces coming judgment against Edom and warns Edom to desist from its anti-Judahite hostilities before it is too late, before "the day of the LORD"

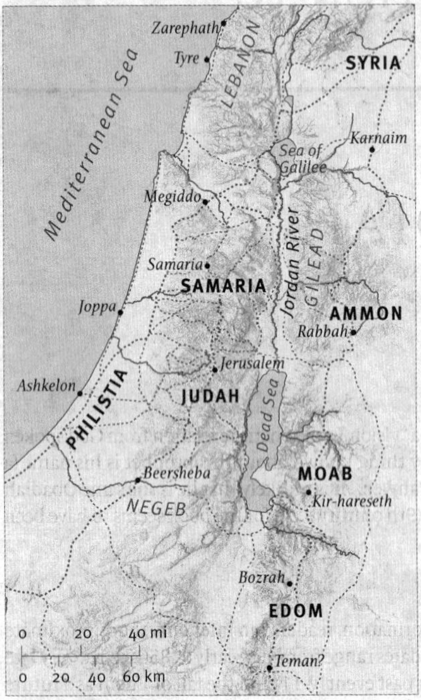

The Setting of Obadiah

c. 570 B.C.

Though various dates have been given for the prophecy of Obadiah, it was most likely written sometime after the fall of Jerusalem to the Babylonians in 586 B.C. but prior to the fall of Edom in 553. Obadiah condemned the Edomites, who were descendants of Jacob's brother Esau, for attacking the Judeans during the Babylonian crisis rather than assisting them.

comes against "all the nations" (v. 15). The standard of the judgment will be strict retributive justice (v. 15).

The second half (vv. 16–21) addresses the people of Jerusalem with "you" plural in verse 16: "you . . . on my holy mountain." Here the prophet gives hope to God's beleaguered people with the good news of the future great reversal. On the terrible day of the Lord the hostile nations will receive God's judgment, but those in Zion will be saved, and Zion will be holy (vv. 16–17a). All Israel will be reunited and given the Promised Land and victory over Edom (vv. 17b–20). The last line expresses God's ultimate goal: to establish his kingly reign over all the earth (v. 21).

Key Themes

1. Enemies will be put to shame because of their enmity against God's people (v. 10).
2. Every proud human effort at self-security will ultimately fail before God's coming judgment (vv. 1–9).
3. God's retributive justice is strict and fair, with the punishment corresponding to the misdeeds (v. 15).
4. Reunited Israel will experience God's deliverance (vv. 16–17), possess the Promised Land, and defeat and rule over Edom (vv. 17–21).
5. In the future, Yahweh will definitively manifest his kingly rule (v. 21).

History of Salvation Summary

Edom is the target of Obadiah's prophecy of doom because it exemplifies hostility toward God's people. The Edomites took delight in bringing disaster to Jerusalem. Even though Jerusalem fell for its unfaithfulness, and even though Edom was one of God's tools for bringing judgment, the Lord has tied himself to his people and will punish those who hurt them. Eventually, Jerusalem will be restored and its blessings will extend to the Gentiles (vv. 19–21). (For an explanation of the "History of Salvation," see the Overview of the Bible, pp. 23–26. See also History of Salvation in the Old Testament: Preparing the Way for Christ, pp. 2635–2661.)

Literary Features

The primary genre is prophecy, and as is customary in prophecy, the predictions of the future are couched in oracles of judgment and an oracle of salvation or deliverance. The oracles of judgment against Edom are examples of satire, with discernible objects of attack and a satiric norm by which Edom and other nations are criticized.

Outline

I. First Announcement of Judgment to Edom (vv. 1–4)

II. Second Announcement of Judgment to Edom (vv. 5–7)

III. Announcement of Judgment, Accusation, and Warning to Edom (vv. 8–15)

IV. Promise of Restoration and Victory to Israel (vv. 16–18)

V. Promise of Restoration and Yahweh's Kingship (vv. 19–21)

OBADIAH

1 The vision of Obadiah.

Edom Will Be Humbled

Thus says the Lord GOD [a]concerning Edom:
[b]We have heard a report from the LORD,
and a messenger has been sent among the nations:
"Rise up! Let us rise against her for battle!"
2 Behold, I will make you small among the nations;
you shall be utterly despised.[1]
3 [c]The pride of your heart has deceived you,
you who live in the clefts of the rock,[2]
in your lofty dwelling,
[d]who say in your heart,
"Who will bring me down to the ground?"
4 Though you soar aloft like the eagle,
though your nest is set among the stars,
from there I will bring you down,
declares the LORD.

5 If [e]thieves came to you,
if plunderers came by night—
how you have been destroyed!—
would they not steal only enough for themselves?
If [e]grape gatherers came to you,
would they not leave gleanings?
6 [f]How Esau has been pillaged,
his treasures sought out!
7 All your allies have driven you to your border;
those at peace with you have deceived you;
they have prevailed against you;
[g]those who eat your bread[3] have set a trap beneath you—
[h]you have[4] no understanding.

1 [a]See Jer. 49:7-22; Ezek. 25:12-14 [b]For ver. 1-4, see Jer. 49:14-16
3 [c][Num. 24:21, 22] [d][Isa. 14:13-15]
5 [e]Jer. 49:9
6 [f][Jer. 49:10]
7 [g][Ps. 41:9] [h][Jer. 49:7]

[1] Or *Behold, I have made you small among the nations; you are utterly despised* [2] Or *Sela* [3] Hebrew lacks *those who eat* [4] Hebrew *he has*

1 Thus says the Lord GOD was a formulaic expression among the prophets, indicating that the prophet reports God's own speech. The prophet as the called and sent messenger of the Lord Yahweh introduces the divine speech that begins in v. 2. But first Obadiah provides background information. The nations are now being recruited by God to rise up against Edom (e.g., Isa. 13:2–5).

2–4 God through his prophet begins to address Edom. Prophetic discourse typically personifies a nation as a collective unity. Edom is insignificant among the nations and in fact is despised. Just as Edom gloated over Judah (vv. 12–13), so other nations hold it in contempt. This is said in contrast to Edom's own pride. The Edomites dwell in the mountainous region east of the Arabah (see map, p. 1678), with elevations up to 5,000 feet (1.5 km) above sea level. Their inaccessible location has given them false hopes of invulnerability. Normally a rhetorical question expects no answer, but God answers it: **Who will bring me down to the ground? . . . I will bring you down** (vv. 3–4). God opposes the proud and arrogant (cf. Prov. 15:25; James 4:6). **Though your nest is set among the stars** is hyperbole even for eagles.

5–6 Normally, thieves and grape gatherers leave something behind. In contrast, Edom will be thoroughly plundered with nothing remaining. Just as Edom acted as a thief (v. 13), so its own hidden treasures will be ransacked. **Destroyed . . . pillaged . . . sought out** are in the "prophetic perfect," speaking about a future event as though it had already been completed. **Esau** is used as a substitute name for Edom (by metonymy) and evokes the Jacob-Esau narratives (Deut. 2:5; Jer. 49:8–10; Mal. 1:3–4). According to Genesis 36, Esau was the father of the Edomites.

7 The past-tense verbs speak about a future event as though it were already completed (see note on vv. 5–6). Just as Edom betrayed its own brother Jacob (vv. 10, 12), so Edom's own allies will turn against it. In the most likely

8 [i][Isa. 29:14] [j][Ezek. 35:2]
9 [k]Amos 1:12; See 1 Chr. 1:45 [j][See ver. 8 above]
10 [l]Num. 20:20, 21 [m][Ezek. 35:9]
11 [n]Ps. 137:7; [Jer. 12:14] [o]See 2 Kgs. 25:10-20 [p]Joel 3:3
12 [q][Ps. 22:17] [r][Mic. 4:11; 7:8] [s][1 Sam. 2:3]
13 [t][Prov. 17:5] [u][Ezek. 35:10]
14 [v][Ezek. 21:21]
15 [w]See Joel 1:15 [x]Jer. 50:29; Ezek. 35:15; Hab. 2:8

8 [i]Will I not on that day, declares the LORD,
destroy the wise men out of Edom,
and understanding out of [j]Mount Esau?
9 And your mighty men shall be dismayed, [k]O Teman,
so that every man from [j]Mount Esau will be cut off by slaughter.

Edom's Violence Against Jacob

10 [l]Because of the violence done to your brother Jacob,
shame shall cover you,
[m]and you shall be cut off forever.
11 [n]On the day that you stood aloof,
[o]on the day that strangers carried off his wealth
and foreigners entered his gates
[p]and cast lots for Jerusalem,
you were like one of them.
12 [q]But do not gloat over the day of your brother
in the day of his misfortune;
[r]do not rejoice over the people of Judah
in the day of their ruin;
[s]do not boast[1]
in the day of distress.
13 [t]Do not enter the gate of my people
in the day of their calamity;
[t]do not gloat over his disaster
in the day of his calamity;
[u]do not loot his wealth
in the day of his calamity.
14 [v]Do not stand at the crossroads
to cut off his fugitives;
do not hand over his survivors
in the day of distress.

The Day of the LORD Is Near

15 For [w]the day of the LORD is near upon all the nations.
[x]As you have done, it shall be done to you;
your deeds shall return on your own head.

[1] Hebrew *do not enlarge your mouth*

historical setting, this would be a reference to the Babylonians (v. 11). In 553 B.C. Babylon campaigned against Edom. During the subsequent Persian period, Edom's land was settled by the Nabateans. **Those who eat your bread** is a term for allies, since covenants and pacts were often sealed by covenant meals (cf. Ps. 41:9).

8–9 On that day synchronizes vv. 8–10 with vv. 1–7 and anticipates "the day of the LORD" in v. 15. Neither Edom's political acumen nor its military strength can provide national security (Jer. 49:7, 22). **Teman** is the name of a grandson of Esau (Gen. 36:9–11). Here it refers either to Edom as a whole or to its southern region. Just as the Edomites "cut off" Judah's fugitives (Obad. 14), so the Edomites **will be cut off** (see vv. 10, 18; Ezek. 25:13; 35:7). **Mount Esau**. Another name for Edom.

10–11 Just as Esau pursued Jacob (Genesis 27–33), so Edom did violence against Judah. And instead of coming to the aid of their brother Jacob, the Edomites acted like the foreign invaders (Babylonians). By having **cast lots for Jerusalem**, the Babylonians treated Jerusalem, Yahweh's "holy mountain" (Obad. 16), like a commodity to be contested (cf. Jer. 51:51; Joel 3:3; Nah. 3:10). **you shall be cut off forever**. Those who harm God's people will eventually be destroyed. **On the day that you stood aloof . . . you were like one of them** rebukes the Edomites, not for actively doing wrong but for failing to do right—i.e., for failing to give military support to neighboring Jerusalem when it was wrongly attacked.

12–14 These verses spell out Edom's deeds of violence: gloating over Judah's demise, looting, capturing fleeing fugitives, and delivering them up to the slave trade. The Edomites took advantage of Judah's plight during the Babylonian crisis (Ps. 137:7; Lam. 4:21–22; Ezek. 25:12–14; 35:1–36:7). But instead of past-tense verbal statements, Obad. 12–14 is written in the form of warnings with eight prohibitions in the form of **do not**. Edom should cease its anti-Judahite hostilities before it is too late. Reconciliation was still available to Edom (see Genesis 33). **do not hand over his survivors**. Apparently Edomites were capturing Judahite survivors and surrendering them to the Babylonian authorities. On Edom's involvement in slave trade, see Amos 1:6, 9.

15 The Edomites should discontinue their enmity against God's people because (**For**) the day of God's universal judgment is near. **The day of the LORD** is a term for events that especially vindicate God's character and purposes (see Ex. 32:34; Deut. 31:16–19; 32:35–38 for background). The term can be used for near-term judgments on God's own people (Amos 5:18–27, the exile of Israel; and Zeph. 1:7, 14, the fall of Jerusalem) or on nations that oppress them (Isa. 13:6, the punishment of Babylon), as well as for events far off with universal significance (Mal. 4:1, 5). The NT applies the term "day of the Lord" to the return of the Lord Jesus Christ in glory (e.g., 1 Cor. 1:8; 2 Pet. 3:10). (On the theme of "the day of the LORD," see note on Amos 5:18–20; see also The Day of the Lord in the Prophets, p. 1668.) **As you have done**. The judgment will

16 [y]For as you have drunk on [z]my holy mountain,
so all the nations shall drink continually;
they shall drink and swallow,
and shall be as though they had never been.
17 [a]But in Mount Zion there shall be those who escape,
and it shall be holy,
[b]and the house of Jacob shall possess their own possessions.
18 [c]The house of Jacob shall be a fire,
and the house of Joseph a flame,
and the house of Esau [d]stubble;
they shall burn them and consume them,
[e]and there shall be no survivor for the house of Esau,
for the LORD has spoken.

The Kingdom of the LORD

19 Those of [f]the Negeb [b]shall possess [g]Mount Esau,
and those of the Shephelah shall possess [h]the land of the Philistines;
they shall possess the land of Ephraim and the land of [i]Samaria,
and Benjamin shall possess Gilead.
20 The exiles of this host of the people of Israel
shall possess the land of the Canaanites as far as [j]Zarephath,
and the exiles of Jerusalem who are in Sepharad
shall possess the cities of the Negeb.
21 [k]Saviors shall go up to Mount Zion
to rule [g]Mount Esau,
and [l]the kingdom shall be the LORD's.

16[y]See Jer. 25:27, 28 [z]See Joel 3:17
17[a][Amos 9:8]; See Joel 2:32 [b][Amos 9:12]
18[c]Zech. 12:6; [Isa. 10:17; Jer. 5:14] [d]See Joel 2:5 [e]Ezek. 25:14
19[f][Josh. 10:40; Judg. 1:9] [b][See ver. 17 above] [g]ver. 8 [h]Jer. 17:26 [i]See Jer. 23:13
20[j]1 Kgs. 17:9; [Luke 4:26]
21[k][2 Kgs. 13:5; Isa. 19:20; 1 Tim. 4:16; James 5:20] [g][See ver. 19 above] [l]Ps. 22:28; Dan. 2:44; 7:14, 27; Zech. 14:9; Luke 1:33; 1 Cor. 15:24; Rev. 11:15; 19:6

be based on retributive justice. Prophetic-judgment texts typically reflect this standard. The correspondence between misdeeds and punishment shows the punishment to be appropriate, fair, and deserved.

16 Many prophetic texts like this one view the nations as enemies of Israel's God and rebellious creatures outside of the saving covenant. In store for them is the all-consuming wrath of their holy Creator and Judge. Other prophetic texts envisage the nations' coming to Zion and enjoying fellowship with Israel's God (e.g., Isa. 25:6–9; 45:22; Mic. 4:1–4). **As you have drunk** is a common biblical metaphor—experiencing God's wrath is likened to getting drunk on wine that does not bring joy but pain and destruction (Isa. 51:17–23; Jer. 25:15–29; Ezek. 23:31–34; Rev. 14:10). Jesus refers to this "cup" in Gethsemane (Matt. 26:39, 42). The people of Jerusalem ("you" plural) drank the cup of God's wrath when Babylon attacked (Obad. 11). In the future day of the Lord, the hostile nations will have to drink the cup (see Jer. 49:12; Lam. 4:21).

17 Mount Zion is the place where Yahweh dwelt among and for his people. Those gathered around his presence and taking refuge in him will be delivered from the coming wrath (Isa. 14:32). In principle, Zion's blessings were available to Gentiles (1 Kings 8:41–43; Isa. 2:2–4); "B.C. Zion" was a foretaste of "A.D. Zion" (Heb. 12:22), i.e., all those gathered around the new and greater temple, God in the flesh (John 2:19–21). **Their own possessions** is a reference to the Promised Land, as clarified in Obad. 19–20.

18 Reunited Israel will defeat Edom (Ezek. 25:14; 37:15–28).

19–20 All of Israel, including the **exiles** far away, will regain the full extent of the Promised Land—both west and east of the Jordan—much of which was lost over the years. The **Negeb** is the desert in the far south, particularly south of Beersheba. **Esau** is to the east, the **Philistines** are to the west, **Gilead** is also to the east, and **Zarephath** is far north, a city on the Phoenician coast between Tyre and Sidon (1 Kings 17). The B.C. Promised Land became an image for the new and greater Promised Land, the new creation (see Heb. 11:16). On Israel's possessing Edom, see Num. 24:18 and Amos 9:12. The location of **Sepharad** is debated, but the most likely place is Sardis in western Turkey. God's people, exiled to the farthest regions, will return to possess the land that had been taken from them.

21 Saviors. Those appointed by God to deliver the people and bring just governance. The Lord has always been the King over the nations (v. 1), but here the prophet promises the future, definitive manifestation of God's kingly rule from **Mount Zion**, i.e., Jerusalem. That end-time redemptive reign will be inaugurated by the ministry, death, and resurrection of Jesus the Messiah (Matt. 12:28) and consummated at his coming in glory (Matt. 25:34).

INTRODUCTION TO JONAH

Author and Title

The title of the book is the name of the main character, Jonah. The book is anonymous, and there are no indicators elsewhere in Scripture to identify the author. The foundational source for the book was likely Jonah's own telling of the story after his return from Nineveh.

Date

Since Jonah prophesied during the reign of Jeroboam II (782–753 B.C.; see 2 Kings 14:23–28), and since *Sirach* 49:10 (from the 2nd century B.C.) refers to the "twelve prophets" (namely, the 12 Minor Prophets, of which Jonah is the fifth), the book of Jonah was written sometime between the middle of the eighth and the end of the third centuries. No compelling evidence leads to a more precise date.

Theme

The Lord is a God of boundless compassion not just for "us" (Jonah and the Israelites) but also for "them" (the pagan sailors and Ninevites).

Purpose, Occasion, and Background

The primary purpose of the book of Jonah is to engage readers in theological reflection on the compassionate character of God, and in self-reflection on the degree to which their own character reflects this compassion, to the end that they become vehicles of this compassion in the world that God has made and so deeply cares about.

Jonah prophesied during the reign of Jeroboam II (2 Kings 14:23–28), who ruled in Israel (the northern kingdom) from 782 to 753 B.C. Jeroboam was the grandson of Jehoahaz, who ruled in Israel from 814 to 798 B.C. Because of the sins of Jehoahaz, Israel was oppressed by the Arameans (2 Kings 13:3). But because of the Lord's great compassion (2 Kings 13:4, 23), Israel was spared destruction and delivered from this oppression (2 Kings 13:5). This deliverance came through a "savior" (2 Kings 13:5), who may have been Adad-nirari III (810–783 B.C.), king of Assyria.

Jeroboam's father, Jehoash (798–782 B.C.), capitalized on this freedom from Aramean oppression and began to expand Israel's boundaries, recapturing towns taken during the reign of Jehoahaz (2 Kings 13:25). Though Jeroboam "did what was evil in the sight of the LORD" (2 Kings 14:24), he nevertheless expanded Israel even farther than his father did, matching the boundaries in the days of David and Solomon (2 Kings 14:25); this was "according to the word of the LORD, the God of Israel, which he spoke by his servant Jonah the son of Amittai, the prophet, who was from Gath-hepher" (2 Kings 14:25). Thus Jonah witnessed firsthand the restorative compassion of God extended to his wayward people.

In God's providence, the expansion by Jeroboam was made easier because of Assyrian weakness. The Assyrians were engaged in conflicts with the Arameans and the Urartians. There was also widespread famine, and numerous revolts within the Assyrian Empire (where regional governors ruled with a fair degree of autonomy). Then there was an auspicious eclipse of the sun during the reign of Ashur-dan III (771–754 B.C.). This convergence of events supports the plausibility of the Ninevites being so responsive to Jonah's call to repent.

It was not until some years later that Tiglath-pileser (745–727 B.C.) would gain control and reestablish Assyrian dominance in the area, and his son Shalmaneser V (727–722) was the king responsible for the conquest of Israel and the destruction of Samaria in 722. Thus Jonah prophesied in an era when Assyria was not an immediate threat to Israel and when Israel enjoyed peace and prosperity because of the compassion of God.

Genre

The genre of Jonah is debated. The book has been read as an *allegory*, using fictional figures to symbolize some other reality. According to this interpretation, Jonah is a symbol of Israel in its refusal to carry out God's mission to the nations. The primary argument against this view is that Jonah is clearly presented as a historical and not a fictional figure (see the specific historical and geographical details in 1:1–3; 3:2–10; 4:11; cf. also 2 Kings 14:25). Another proposal is that the book is a *parable* to teach believers not to be like Jonah. Like allegories, parables are also based on fictional and not historical characters. Parables, however, are typically simple tales that make a single point, whereas the book of Jonah is quite complex and teaches a multiplicity of themes.

The book of Jonah has all the marks of a *prophetic narrative*, like those about Elijah and Elisha found in 1 Kings, which set out to report actual historical events. The phrase that opens the book ("the word of the LORD came to") is also at the beginning of the first two stories told about Elijah (1 Kings 17:2, 8) and is used in other prophetic narratives as well (e.g., 1 Sam. 15:10; 2 Sam. 7:4). Just as the Elijah and Elisha narratives contain extraordinary events, like ravens providing bread and meat for the prophet (1 Kings 17:6), so does the book of Jonah, as when the fish "provides transportation" for the prophet. In fact, the story of Jonah is so much like the stories about Elijah and Elisha that one would hardly think it odd if the story of Jonah were embedded in 2 Kings right after Jonah's prophetic words about the expansion of the kingdom. The story of Jonah is thus presented as historical, like the other prophetic narratives.

There are additional arguments for the historical nature of the book of Jonah. It is difficult to say that the story teaches God's sovereignty over the creation if God did not in fact "appoint" the fish (1:17), the plant (4:6), the worm (4:7), and the east wind (4:8) to do his will. Jesus, moreover, treated the story as historical when he used elements of the story as analogies for other historical events (see Matt. 12:40–41). This is especially clear when Jesus declared that "the men of Nineveh will rise up at the judgment with this generation and condemn it, for they repented at the preaching of Jonah" (Matt. 12:41).

The story of Jonah is not, however, history for history's sake. The book is clearly *didactic* (as the allegorical and parabolic interpretations rightly affirm); that is, the story is told *to teach the reader key lessons*. The didactic character of the book shines through in the repeated use of questions, 11 out of 14 being addressed to Jonah, and the question that closes the narrative leaves readers asking themselves how they will respond to the story.

Key Themes

The primary theme in Jonah is that God's compassion is boundless, not limited just to "us" but also available for "them." This is clear from the flow of the story and its conclusion: (1) Jonah is the object of God's compassion throughout the book, and the pagan sailors and pagan Ninevites are also the benefactors of this compassion. (2) The story ends with the question, "Should I not pity Nineveh . . . ?" (4:11). Tied to this theological teaching is the anthropological question, Do readers of the story have hearts that are like the heart of God? While Jonah was concerned about a plant that "perished" (4:10), he showed no such concern for the Ninevites. Conversely, the pagan sailors (1:14), their captain (1:6), and the king of Nineveh (3:9) all showed concern that human beings, including Jonah, not "perish."

Several other major themes in the book include:

1. God's sovereign control over events on the earth
2. God's determination to get his message to the nations
3. The need for repentance from sin in general
4. The need for repentance from self-centeredness and hypocrisy in particular
5. The full assurance that God will relent when people repent

History of Salvation Summary

Jonah's rescue from death provides an analogy for the resurrection of Christ (Matt. 12:39–40). The repentance of the Ninevites anticipates the wide-scale repentance of Gentiles in the messianic era (Matt. 28:18–20;

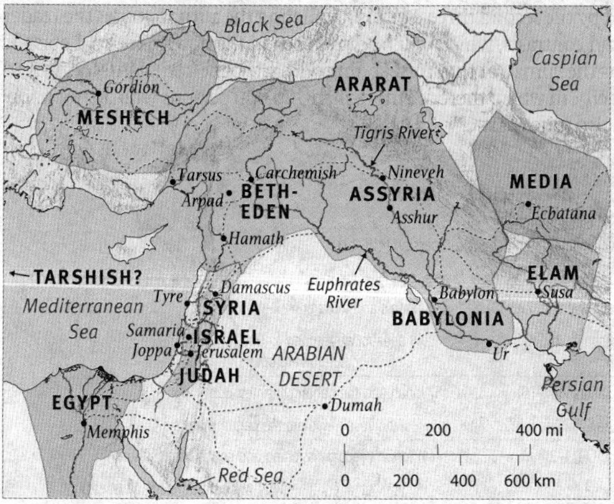

The Setting of Jonah
c. 760 B.C.
Jonah prophesied during the politically prosperous time of Jeroboam II of Israel (2 Kings 14:23–28). During this time the Assyrians were occupied with matters elsewhere in the empire, allowing Jeroboam II to capture much of Syria for Israel. The Lord called Jonah to go to the great Assyrian city of Nineveh to pronounce judgment upon it. Jonah attempted to escape the Lord's calling by sailing from the seaport of Joppa to Tarshish, which was probably in the western Mediterranean. Eventually he obeyed the Lord and traveled overland to Nineveh at the heart of the Assyrian Empire.

Luke 24:47). (For an explanation of the "History of Salvation," see the Overview of the Bible, pp. 23–26. See also History of Salvation in the Old Testament: Preparing the Way for Christ, pp. 2635–2661.)

Literary Features

The book of Jonah is a literary masterpiece. While the story line is so simple that children follow it readily, the story is marked by as high a degree of literary sophistication as any book in the Hebrew Bible. The author employs structure, humor, hyperbole, irony, double entendre, and literary figures like merism to communicate his message with great rhetorical power. The first example of this sophistication is seen in the outline of the book (see below).

The main category for the book is satire—the exposure of human vice or folly. The four elements of satire take the following form in the book of Jonah: (1) the *object of attack* is Jonah and what he represents—a bigotry and ethnocentrism that regarded God as the exclusive property of the believing community (in the OT, the nation of Israel); (2) the *satiric vehicle* is narrative or story; (3) the *satiric norm* or standard by which Jonah's bad attitudes are judged is the character of God, who is portrayed as a God of universal mercy, whose mercy is not limited by national boundaries; (4) the *satiric tone* is laughing, with Jonah emerging as a laughable figure—someone who runs away from God and is caught by a fish, and as a childish and pouting prophet who prefers death over life without his shade tree.

Three stylistic techniques are especially important. (1) The *giantesque motif*—the motif of the unexpectedly large (e.g., the magnitude of the task assigned to Jonah, of the fish that swallows him, and of the repentance that Jonah's eight-word sermon accomplishes). (2) A *pervasive irony* (e.g., the ironic discrepancy between Jonah's prophetic vocation and his ignominious behavior, and the ironic impossibility of fleeing from the presence of God). (3) *Humor*, as Jonah's behavior is not only ignominious but also ridiculous.

Outline

The story of Jonah unfolds in seven episodes (see diagram, p. 1686):

A. Jonah's commissioning and flight (1:1–3)
    B. Jonah and the pagan sailors (1:4–16)
        C. Jonah's grateful prayer (1:17–2:10)
A′. Jonah's recommissioning and compliance (3:1–3a)
    B′. Jonah and the pagan Ninevites (3:3b–10)
        C′. Jonah's angry prayer (4:1–4)
D. Jonah's lesson about compassion (4:5–11)

The first three episodes are paralleled by the second three. By this paralleling the author invites the reader to make a number of comparisons and contrasts, which will be drawn out in the notes. The final episode is unparalleled and thus stands out as the climax of the story, ending with the penetrating question, "And should not I pity Nineveh, that great city, in which there are more than 120,000 persons who do not know their right hand from their left, and also much cattle?"

Seven Episodes in Jonah

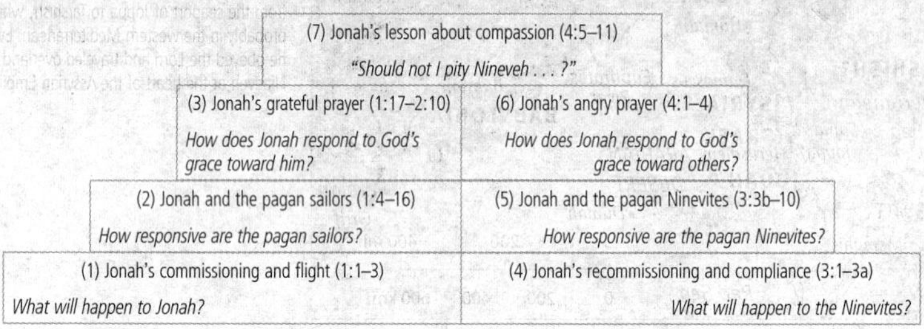

(7) Jonah's lesson about compassion (4:5–11)
"Should not I pity Nineveh . . . ?"
(3) Jonah's grateful prayer (1:17–2:10)
How does Jonah respond to God's grace toward him?
(6) Jonah's angry prayer (4:1–4)
How does Jonah respond to God's grace toward others?
(2) Jonah and the pagan sailors (1:4–16)
How responsive are the pagan sailors?
(5) Jonah and the pagan Ninevites (3:3b–10)
How responsive are the pagan Ninevites?
(1) Jonah's commissioning and flight (1:1–3)
What will happen to Jonah?
(4) Jonah's recommissioning and compliance (3:1–3a)
What will happen to the Ninevites?

JONAH

Chapter 1
1[a]2 Kgs. 14:25
2[b]Gen. 10:11, 12; 2 Kgs. 19:36; Nah. 1:1; Zeph. 2:13; Matt. 12:41; Luke 11:30, 32 [c]ch. 3:3; 4:11 [d]Rev. 18:5
3[e]ch. 4:2 [f]See 1 Kgs. 10:22 [g]See Josh. 19:46 [h]Gen. 4:16; [Ps. 139:9, 10]
4[i][Ps. 107:25] [j]1 Kgs. 22:48; Ps. 48:7
5[k][Ps. 107:28] [l][Acts 27:18, 19, 38]
6[k][See ver. 5 above] [m][ch. 3:9]
7[n][Judg. 20:9]

Jonah Flees the Presence of the Lord

1 Now the word of the LORD came to [a]Jonah the son of Amittai, saying, **2** "Arise, go to
[b]Nineveh, that [c]great city, and call out against it, [d]for their evil[1] has come up before
me." **3** But Jonah [e]rose to flee to [f]Tarshish from the presence of the LORD. He went down
to [g]Joppa and found a ship going to [f]Tarshish. So he paid the fare and went down into it,
to go with them to [f]Tarshish, [h]away from the presence of the LORD.
4 But [i]the LORD hurled a great wind upon the sea, and there was a mighty tempest on the
sea, so that the ship threatened [j]to break up. **5** Then the mariners were afraid, and [k]each cried
out to his god. And [l]they hurled the cargo that was in the ship into the sea to lighten it for
them. But Jonah had gone down into the inner part of the ship and had lain down and was
fast asleep. **6** So the captain came and said to him, "What do you mean, you sleeper? Arise, [k]call
out to your god! [m]Perhaps the god will give a thought to us, that we may not perish."

Jonah Is Thrown into the Sea

7 And they said to one another, "Come, let us [n]cast lots, that we may know on whose
account this evil has come upon us." So they cast lots, and the lot fell on Jonah. **8** Then they

[1] The same Hebrew word can mean *evil* or *disaster*, depending on the context; so throughout Jonah

1:1–3 *Jonah's Commissioning and Flight.* This episode records Jonah's call to prophesy and his flight from that call. Two questions drive the plot: (1) What will happen to the Ninevites? and (2) What will happen to Jonah? (See diagram, p. 1686.)

1:1 Jonah prophesied prosperity for Israel during the reign of Jeroboam II (2 Kings 14:23–28). Jonah means "dove," a symbol for Israel as silly and senseless (Hos. 7:11); Jonah will be true to his name. **Son of Amittai** means "son of my faithfulness"; Jonah will remain the object of God's faithful love.

1:2 Nineveh sat on the east bank of the Tigris River about 220 miles (354 km) north of present-day Baghdad and over 500 miles (805 km) northeast of Israel.

Occurrences of the key word (*ra'ah*; "evil"/"disaster"/"discomfort") in Jonah

1:2	The Lord confronts Jonah with the **evil** of the city Nineveh.
1:7	The sailors decide to cast lots to find the source of the **evil** they experience.
1:8	The sailors confront Jonah, wondering why **evil** has come upon them.
3:8	The Ninevite king calls for inhabitants of the city to turn from **evil**.
3:10	God sees the city turn from **evil**, and he relents from the **disaster** he was sending.
4:1	God's gracious response to Nineveh **displeased** Jonah greatly.
4:2	Jonah's anger arises from the fact that God relents from **disaster**.
4:6	The Lord appoints a plant to save Jonah from his **discomfort**.

Great (Hb. *gadol*) is used 14 times in Jonah. Nineveh was an important ("great") **city** (see 3:3). **evil**. As the ESV footnote indicates, the same Hebrew term (Hb. *ra'ah*; used 9 times in Jonah [see chart to the left]) can mean "evil" or "disaster." The Ninevites were evil, and they were in line for disaster.

1:3 To Tarshish is repeated three times in this verse to underscore that Jonah is not going to Nineveh. Tarshish, an unknown locale associated with distant coastlands, was somewhere in the western Mediterranean—the opposite direction from Nineveh. **From the presence of the LORD** is repeated at the end of this verse to underscore Jonah's purpose in going to Tarshish. **Went down** (twice in this verse; see also v. 5; 2:6) is also a euphemism for death (e.g., Gen. 37:35). The suggestion is that each step away from the presence of the Lord is one step closer to "going down" to death (see notes on Jonah 1:4–5; 2:6).

1:4–16 *Jonah and the Pagan Sailors.* This episode highlights Jonah's encounter with pagan sailors and raises the question, Who fears the Lord—Jonah or the pagans? The key repeated word is "fear": at the beginning and end the sailors "fear" (vv. 5, 16); in the middle Jonah claims to "fear" the Lord (v. 9) while the sailors actually fear (v. 10a).

1:4–5 Hurled is used four times in this episode (vv. 4, 5, 12, 15). Just as God hurled the great wind, the sailors hurled the cargo. **cried out**. The sailors pray, evidently believing that a divine being could come to their aid. **had gone down**. In contrast to the sailors, Jonah goes down below deck, taking yet another step closer to death (see note on v. 3).

1:6 Arise, call out echoes God's commission in v. 2. Ironically, the Israelite prophet has to be summoned to prayer by a pagan sailor. **not perish**. "Perish" is repeated in v. 14; 3:9; 4:10. Ironically, a pagan, not Jonah, is concerned that people not perish.

1:7 cast lots. Casting lots was used in the ancient world to discern the divine will (e.g., Num. 26:55; Josh. 18:6). Israelites believed that God controlled the outcome (Prov. 16:33). **Evil** (Hb. *ra'ah*) may here suggest "disaster" (see chart to the left).

said to him, "Tell us on whose account this evil has come upon us. What is your occupation?
And where do you come from? What is your country? And of what people are you?" 9 And
he said to them, "I am a Hebrew, and I fear [o]the LORD, the God of heaven, [p]who made the
sea and the dry land." 10 Then the men were exceedingly afraid and said to him, "What is
this that you have done!" For the men knew that [h]he was fleeing from the presence of the
LORD, because he had told them.

11 Then they said to him, "What shall we do to you, that the sea may quiet down for
us?" For the sea grew more and more tempestuous. 12 He said to them, "Pick me up and
hurl me into the sea; then the sea will quiet down for you, [q]for I know it is because of
me that this great tempest has come upon you." 13 Nevertheless, the men rowed hard[1] to
get back to dry land, but they could not, for the sea grew more and more tempestuous
against them. 14 Therefore they called out to the LORD, "O LORD, let us not perish for this
man's life, and [r]lay not on us innocent blood, [s]for you, O LORD, have done as it pleased
you." 15 So they picked up Jonah and hurled him into the sea, [t]and the sea ceased from its
raging. 16 Then the men feared the LORD exceedingly, [u]and they offered a sacrifice to the
LORD [v]and made vows.

A Great Fish Swallows Jonah

17[2] And the LORD appointed[3] a great fish to swallow up Jonah. [w]And Jonah was in the
belly of the fish three days and three nights.

Jonah's Prayer

2 Then Jonah prayed to the LORD his God from the belly of the fish, 2 saying,

[x]"I called out to the LORD, out of my distress,
and he answered me;
[y]out of the belly of Sheol I cried,
[z]and you heard my voice.
3 [a]For you cast me into the deep,
into the heart of the seas,

[1] Hebrew *the men dug in* [their oars] [2] Ch 2:1 in Hebrew [3] Or *had appointed*

9 [o]Rev. 11:13 [p]Ps. 146:6
10 [h][See ver. 3 above]
12 [q][Josh. 7:20]
14 [r]Deut. 21:8 [s][Ps. 115:3]
15 [t]Ps. 65:7; Luke 8:24
16 [u][Gen. 8:20; 31:54] [v]See ch. 2:9
17 [w]Matt. 12:40; 16:4; [Luke 11:30]

Chapter 2

2 [x]Ps. 3:4; 120:1; Lam. 3:55 [y]Ps. 118:5 [z]Lam. 3:56
3 [a]Ps. 88:6, 7

1:9–10 Hebrew is an ethnic term used to identify Israelites in international contexts (e.g., Gen. 40:15; Ex. 1:19; 1 Sam. 4:6). Jonah claims to **fear the LORD**, but his actions contradict his confession. **God of heaven** refers to the universal and supreme God (see Ezra 1:2; Neh. 2:20; Dan. 2:37). **made the sea**. Ironically, Jonah confesses to fear the God who controls the sea, which Jonah is crossing to escape from the presence of God (Jonah 1:3). The sailors who were "afraid" (v. 5) are now **exceedingly afraid**.

1:12–13 hurl. See note on vv. 4–5. **rowed hard**. It would have been natural for these pagans to hurl Jonah overboard immediately, but they did not. **The sea grew more and more tempestuous**, for God was not ready to have Jonah delivered to dry land.

1:14–15 called out. Whereas each of the sailors had prayed to his god (v. 5), they now pray **to the LORD**. The pagan sailors, not Jonah, are concerned that people **not perish** (see note on v. 6). **Have done as it pleased you** echoes the liturgical language of Ps. 115:3 and 135:6, and is thus the sailors' confession of faith in the absolute sovereignty of God. The sailors' actions are in harmony with God's: as God had **hurled** the wind onto the **sea** (see note on Jonah 1:4–5) to start the storm, the sailors now hurl **Jonah** to stop the storm (see v. 12).

1:16 feared the LORD exceedingly. What started as a general fear (v. 5) grew into an intense fear (v. 10) and matured into the fear—that is, the reverent worship—of the Lord (v. 16). **sacrifice . . . vows**. The exact response expected from people who fear the Lord (2 Kings 17:32–36; Ps. 22:5; 61:5; 76:11).

1:17–2:10 *Jonah's Grateful Prayer.* Jonah's prayer (2:2b–9) is framed by an introduction (1:17–2:2a) and a conclusion (2:10), both of which mention the "fish."

1:17 appointed. This is the first of four uses of "appoint" that underscore God's sovereign control over creation (cf. 4:6–8). **Fish** (Hb. *dag*) is not limited to what is called "fish" today (generally cold-blooded vertebrate sea creatures with fins and gills) but is a general word for an aquatic beast, which cannot be identified further. However, a large whale such as a sperm whale could easily swallow a man whole. **three days and three nights**. Though this may be a symbolic expression for a time of dying and rising (cf. Hos. 6:2), it more likely describes the actual number of days, or parts of three days, according to accepted reckoning of days at that time (cf. 1 Sam. 30:12; 2 Kings 20:5, 8). In either case it has associations with return from death or near-death—which perhaps is why Jesus likened the time between his own death and resurrection to Jonah's time in the fish (Matt. 12:40).

2:1 Finally, **Jonah prayed**. He did not pray for God to save the *pagan sailors*, but he did thank God for saving *him*.

2:2–9 Jonah's prayer is not a request to be saved *from* the fish but is thanksgiving for being saved *by* the fish. Verse 2 summarizes the prayer: Jonah **called** for help and God **answered**. Verses 3–6a expand on Jonah's call for help; vv. 6b–10 expand on God's answer.

2:2 Sheol refers to the realm of the dead, which one would enter by going through a gate made of "bars" (see v. 6 and Job 17:16; 38:17; Ps. 9:13). Jonah did not literally pray from Sheol but describes his near-death experience (see Ps. 30:2–3).

2:3–4 you cast me. Though it was the sailors who had hurled Jonah into the sea (1:15), he knows that God was working sovereignly through them, and so he can say that God cast him into the sea. **Look upon**, or "look toward," refers to the ancient practice of praying toward the temple (see 2:7; 1 Kings 8:30, 35, 38, 42; Dan. 6:10).

2:6 I went down (see notes on 1:3; 1:4–5). Jonah's descent to death is almost complete as he reaches the **roots of the mountains** at the bottom of the seas, where the gates of Sheol are located. Since the **bars** refer to the gates of Sheol (see note on 2:2), the **land** refers to the realm of the dead (see Ps. 63:9; Ezek. 26:20; 32:18, 24), as does **pit** (see Job 33:22–24; Ps. 49:9;

3[b]Ps. 42:7
4[c]Ps. 31:22 [d][1 Kgs. 8:35, 38]
5[e][Lam. 3:54] [f]Ps. 69:1
7[g][2 Chr. 30:27]
8[h]Ps. 31:6; [2 Kgs. 17:15; Jer. 2:5] [i][Jer. 2:13]
9[j]Ps. 50:14; [Hos. 14:2; Heb. 13:15] [k]Ps. 3:8
Chapter 3
2[l]See ch. 1:2
3[l][See ver. 2 above]

and the flood surrounded me;
[b]all your waves and your billows
passed over me.
4 [c]Then I said, 'I am driven away
from your sight;
[d]yet I shall again look
upon your holy temple.'
5 [e]The waters closed in over me [f]to take my life;
the deep surrounded me;
weeds were wrapped about my head
6 at the roots of the mountains.
I went down to the land
whose bars closed upon me forever;
yet you brought up my life from the pit,
O LORD my God.
7 When my life was fainting away,
I remembered the LORD,
[g]and my prayer came to you,
into your holy temple.
8 [h]Those who pay regard to vain idols
[i]forsake their hope of steadfast love.
9 [j]But I with the voice of thanksgiving
will sacrifice to you;
what I have vowed I will pay.
[k]Salvation belongs to the LORD!"

10 And the LORD spoke to the fish, and it vomited Jonah out upon the dry land.

Jonah Goes to Nineveh

3 Then the word of the LORD came to Jonah the second time, saying, 2 "Arise, go to
[l]Nineveh, that great city, and call out against it the message that I tell you." 3 So Jonah
arose and went to Nineveh, according to the word of the LORD. Now [l]Nineveh was an
exceedingly great city,[1] three days' journey in breadth.[2] 4 Jonah began to go into the city,
going a day's journey. And he called out, "Yet forty days, and Nineveh shall be overthrown!"

[1] Hebrew *a great city to God* [2] Or *a visit was a three days' journey*

103:4). **you brought**. Jonah had done nothing to deserve being rescued; his salvation was by grace alone.

2:8–9 Those who pay regard to vain idols refers to the pagan sailors, who prayed each to his own god (1:5), but it is also a message to Jonah's idolatrous fellow Israelites. Ironically, these sailors ended up experiencing God's **steadfast love**, while Jonah ended up in the sea. **Sacrifice . . . vowed** recalls the actions of the sailors (1:16), whom Jonah is now like. **Salvation belongs to the LORD** is Jonah's confession that God is the sovereign source of salvation, though the rest of the story will show that Jonah believes God is free to save any, as long as they are "us" and not "them" (see 4:1–4).

2:10 Vomited can express disgust (Job 20:15; Prov. 23:8; 25:16), and some interpreters see here an indication that God was still displeased with the hostility toward the Ninevites that was still in Jonah's heart (as revealed in Jonah 4), in spite of the obvious gratitude of his prayer. Nevertheless, the fish's action brought deliverance to Jonah, an indication of God's favor.

3:1–3a *Jonah's Recommissioning and Compliance.* The fourth episode parallels the first (1:1–3) and focuses on the second question raised at the beginning of the story: "What will happen to the Ninevites?" (see note on 1:1–3).

3:1–2 The second time underscores God's determination to get his message to the Ninevites and to use Jonah in the process. **The message that I tell you** replaces "for their evil has come up before me" (1:2).

3:3a Jonah **went to Nineveh** instead of fleeing to Tarshish. He complies with God's will, but whether this compliance is from the heart remains to be seen.

3:3b–10 *Jonah and the Pagan Ninevites.* The fifth episode parallels the second (1:4–16) and focuses on how responsive the pagan Ninevites—like the pagan sailors—are to God's word. The structure follows the pattern of corporate repentance found elsewhere in the OT (cf. 1 Sam. 7:3–14; Joel 1–2): (1) message of divine judgment (Jonah 3:3a–5); (2) account of human repenting (vv. 6–9); and (3) record of divine relenting (v. 10).

3:3b an exceedingly great city (cf. ESV footnote, "a great city to God"; see 1:2; 3:2). Nineveh is *important* to God and will be the recipient of his *great* compassion. **three days' journey in breadth** (cf. ESV footnote, "a visit was a three days' journey"). In Jonah's day neither the circumference nor the diameter of the walled city of **Nineveh** (see plan, p. 1691) was a three-day walk. The phrase may refer to the time it would take Jonah to walk throughout the city, preaching his message. (Nineveh could also refer to the much larger administrative area including the city and the outlying villages, which was 30–56 miles/48–90 km across.)

3:4 Yet forty days, and Nineveh shall be overthrown! "Overthrown"

5 [m]And the people of Nineveh believed God. [n]They called for a fast and [o]put on sackcloth,
from the greatest of them to the least of them.

The People of Nineveh Repent

6 The word reached[1] the king of Nineveh, and [p]he arose from his throne, removed his
robe, covered himself with sackcloth, [q]and sat in ashes. 7 And he issued a proclamation and
published through Nineveh, [r]"By the decree of the king and his nobles: Let neither man
nor [s]beast, herd nor flock, taste anything. Let them not feed or drink water, 8 but let man
and [s]beast be covered with sackcloth, and let them call out mightily to God. [t]Let everyone
turn from his evil way and from [u]the violence that is in his hands. 9 [v]Who knows? God may
turn and relent [w]and turn from his fierce anger, so that we may not perish."

10 When God saw what they did, [x]how they turned from their evil way, [x]God relented of
the disaster that he had said he would do to them, and he did not do it.

Jonah's Anger and the LORD's Compassion

4 But it displeased Jonah exceedingly,[2] and [y]he was angry. 2 And he prayed to the LORD
and said, "O LORD, is not this what I said when I was yet in my country? [z]That is why I
made haste to flee to Tarshish; for I knew that you are a [a]gracious God and merciful, slow
to anger and abounding in steadfast love, and [a]relenting from disaster. 3 [b]Therefore now,
O LORD, please take my life from me, [c]for it is better for me to die than to live." 4 And the
LORD said, [d]"Do you do well to be angry?"

5 Jonah went out of the city and sat to the east of the city and [e]made a booth for himself
there. He sat under it in the shade, till he should see what would become of the city. 6 Now
the LORD God appointed a plant[3] and made it come up over Jonah, that it might be a shade

[1] Or *had reached* [2] Hebrew *it was exceedingly evil to Jonah* [3] Hebrew *qiqayon*, probably the castor oil plant; also verses 7, 9, 10

5 [m][Matt. 12:41; Luke 11:32] [n]See 2 Chr. 20:3 [o]See 2 Sam. 3:31
6 [p][Job 1:20; Ezek. 26:16] [q]Job 2:8
7 [r][Dan. 6:26] [s][ch. 4:11; Ps. 36:6; Joel 1:18, 20]
8 [s][See ver. 7 above] [t]Jer. 18:11; 36:3 [u]Isa. 59:6
9 [v]2 Sam. 12:22; Joel 2:14 [w]Ps. 85:3
10 [x][Jer. 18:8]

Chapter 4

1 [y][ver. 4, 9]
2 [z]ch. 1:3 [a]See Joel 2:13
3 [b][1 Kgs. 19:4] [c][Eccles. 7:1]
4 [d][ver. 1, 9]
5 [e][Neh. 8:15]

is the same verb used for God's destruction of Sodom and Gomorrah (Gen. 19:21, 25, 29). Although the threat sounds unconditional, a condition was implied: If people repent, God will relent (see Jer. 18:7–8). Jonah knows this condition is included (see Jonah 4:2), and the king of Nineveh will hope that it is (see 3:9).

3:5 Believed is the first word in the Hebrew text of the sentence, and the grammar underscores the immediacy of Nineveh's repentance. To **fast** and wear **sackcloth** were ancient demonstrations of mourning (Neh. 9:1; Est. 4:3; Dan. 9:3).

3:6 The **word** that **reached the king of Nineveh** was the "word" of the Lord (see 1:1; 3:1, 3). The "king of Nineveh" was probably not the king of Assyria, since Nineveh was not an Assyrian capital in Jonah's day; he may have been a provincial governor who ruled from Nineveh.

3:7–8 issued a proclamation. It seems odd that the king would tell everyone to fast and put on sackcloth when they had already done so (v. 5). Therefore it is more likely that v. 5 and vv. 6–9 are in topical rather than chronological order. First the king issued the proclamation, and then the people carried it out (see a similar summons to repentance in Joel 1:13–14). By putting the people's response ahead of the king's proclamation, the author underscores the immediacy of the people's response and that they are responding to Jonah's message, not just to the king's command. The Ninevites each **turn from his evil way**, whereas the Israelites did not (cf. 2 Kings 17:13–14).

3:9 Who knows? expresses hope (see 2 Sam. 12:22) that **God may turn and relent**—the exact hope of the prophet Joel for the people of Judah (Joel 2:14). **we may not perish**. This is the third time a pagan has been concerned that people not perish (see Jonah 1:14 and note on 1:6); ironically, Jonah has not expressed any such concern.

3:10 evil . . . disaster. Both terms translate Hebrew *ra'ah* (see note on 1:2). The use of the same word underscores the close connection between human action and divine response. God did not carry out the threatened disaster because the Ninevites repented of their evil (see note on 3:4). From a temporal perspective, God responds to human action; from an eternal perspective, God chooses the means (human repenting) as well as the end (divine relenting). The repentance of Gentiles contrasts with the repeated lack of repentance on the part of Israel (see note on vv. 7–8).

4:1–4 *Jonah's Angry Prayer.* The sixth episode parallels the third (1:17–2:10) and focuses on Jonah's self-centeredness and hypocrisy. Both episodes have the same structure: (1) Jonah "prayed to the LORD" (1:17–2:1a; 4:1–2a); (2) Jonah's prayer (2:1b–9; 4:2b–3); and (3) "the LORD spoke/said" (2:10; 4:4).

4:1 it displeased Jonah exceedingly (cf. the ESV footnote, "it was exceedingly evil to Jonah"). In the previous episode (see 3:10) the pagans got rid of their "evil" and God got rid of the "disaster" he had threatened (both Hb. *ra'ah*). The pagans are in harmony with God, but Jonah is not, as he alone is now characterized by "displeasure" (or "evil"; Hb. *ra'ah*).

4:2 This is Jonah's second prayer; the repetition of **prayed to the LORD** (see 2:1) invites the reader to compare the two. **gracious God . . . relenting from disaster.** These same words occur in Joel 2:13 as the basis for hope (see Ex. 34:6–7; Neh. 9:17; Ps. 145:8). Ironically, this standard confession of the compassionate character of God is the root of Jonah's anger. **Steadfast love**, when extended to Jonah, filled him with thanksgiving (Jonah 2:8), but when extended to the Ninevites, filled him with anger.

4:3 My life translates Hebrew *napshi* ("my soul"), and **to live** translates Hebrew *khayyay* ("my life"). These two expressions occur in Jonah's first prayer, where he is grateful that his "life" was brought up from the pit (2:6) and his fainting "life/soul" was revived (2:7). Ironically, when God extends the same mercy to the Ninevites, Jonah wishes his "life" and "soul" to be taken.

4:5–11 *Jonah's Lesson about Compassion.* The seventh and final episode has no parallel and thus stands out as the climax of the story.

4:5 Jonah went out . . . till he should see. Apparently, Jonah hopes that God still will not relent but will destroy the city after all. **sat under it in the shade**. Jonah is hot—both emotionally (i.e., angry) and physically.

4:6 the LORD God appointed. This is the second use of the verb "appoint" (see 1:17). The kind of **plant** appointed is not known; the term (Hb. *qiqayon*) occurs nowhere else in the Bible, but a castor oil plant or a gourd plant, both of which have large leaves, are the most common suggestions. **Discomfort** (or "evil," Hb. *ra'ah*; see ESV footnote and note on 1:2) refers both to Jonah's outer "discomfort" and to his inner "evil." **Jonah was exceedingly glad**. The grammar of this phrase is identical to that at

8 [f]Jer. 18:17 [g][Ps. 121:6] [h][Amos 8:13] [c][See ver. 3 above]
9 [i][ver. 1, 4]
11 [j]See ch. 1:2 [k][ch. 3:7]

over his head, to save him from his discomfort.[1] So Jonah was exceedingly glad because of
the plant. 7 But when dawn came up the next day, God appointed a worm that attacked the
plant, so that it withered. 8 When the sun rose, God appointed a scorching [f]east wind, [g]and
the sun beat down on the head of Jonah so that he [h]was faint. And he asked that he might
die and said, [c]"It is better for me to die than to live." 9 But God said to Jonah, [i]"Do you do
well to be angry for the plant?" And he said, "Yes, I do well to be angry, angry enough to
die." 10 And the LORD said, "You pity the plant, for which you did not labor, nor did you
make it grow, which came into being in a night and perished in a night. 11 And should not
I pity [j]Nineveh, that great city, in which there are more than 120,000 persons who do not
know their right hand from their left, and also much [k]cattle?"

[1] Or *his evil*

the beginning of 4:1 ("It displeased Jonah exceedingly") and underscores the contrast between Jonah's anger at the salvation of the Ninevites and his joy at his own salvation.

4:7–8 God appointed a worm . . . God appointed a scorching east wind. These are the third and fourth uses of the verb "appoint" (see note on v. 6). The "east wind" is a drying wind from the desert.

4:9 angry for the plant. As God had questioned the justice of Jonah's anger over the salvation of the Ninevites (v. 4), he now questions the justice of Jonah's anger over the destruction of the plant.

4:10–11 perished. Finally Jonah expresses concern over something perishing (see note on 3:9), but ironically it is a plant, not the **120,000** people **who do not know their right hand from their left**, an idiom for being morally and spiritually unaware, that probably refers to the entire population. Jonah's compassion for the plant explains the rather odd expression that translates the final words in the Hebrew text, **and also much cattle**. The ironic question raised by these words is: If Jonah will not allow God to have compassion on Nineveh for the sake of the 120,000 people whom God created and cares for, will Jonah not allow God to have compassion on Nineveh for the sake of the animals, since after all, Jonah was willing to have compassion on a plant? The question is left unanswered so that the readers of the book may answer it for themselves.

The City of Nineveh

Nineveh, which was situated at the confluence of the Tigris and Khoser rivers (modern-day Mosul, Iraq), was first settled in the seventh millennium B.C. According to the Bible, Nimrod was the founder of the city (Gen. 10:11). Major excavations took place under the direction of Henry Layard from 1845 to 1854. The diagram pictures the results of those excavations, especially as they reflect the period of the Assyrian Empire (1420–609 B.C.). Around 1000 B.C. there occurred a great revival of Assyrian power, and Nineveh became a royal city. It was a thriving city during the first half of the first millennium, and contained such luxuries as public squares, parks, botanical gardens, and even a zoo. One of the great archaeological finds of the period is the library of King Ashurbanipal (669–627 B.C.; called Osnappar in Ezra 4:10). The size of the city was approximately 1,850 acres. The book of Jonah reflects the flourishing nature of Nineveh at this time (3:1–5). Nineveh eventually fell to the Medes and Babylonians in 612 B.C. The invading armies dammed the rivers that supplied water to the city, causing a flood that broke through one of the perimeter walls, giving the foreign armies access to the city.

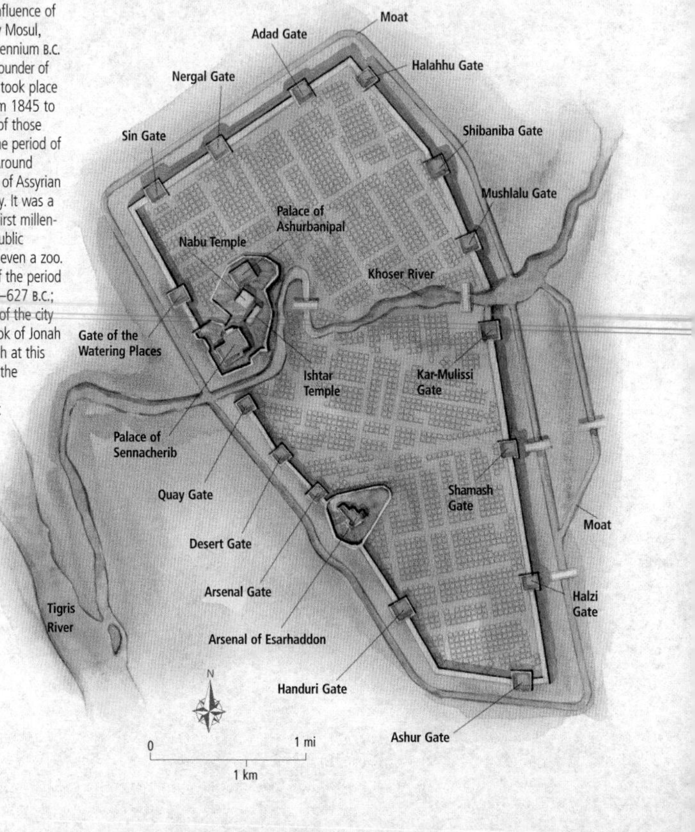

INTRODUCTION TO

MICAH

Author and Title

Rather than being identified by his father or family (cf. Joel "son of Pethuel" [Joel 1:1]; Jonah "son of Amittai" [Jonah 1:1]), this prophet is identified by a location, "Micah of Moresheth" (Mic. 1:1; for Moresheth-gath, see 1:14). It was about 22 miles (35 km) southwest of Jerusalem in the "lowland" or Shephelah region. Unlike the calls to prophetic office of some other prophets (e.g., Isa. 6:1–13; Jeremiah 1), Micah's call is not recorded. Micah is never explicitly referred to as "prophet," but the source of his power is explicitly attributed to the "Spirit of the LORD" (Mic. 3:8; cf. 2 Pet. 1:20–21). The name "Micah" may be translated as a simple rhetorical question: "Who is like Yahweh?" Similarly, the book concludes with an inquiry: "Who is a God like you?" (Mic. 7:18). These questions underscore the unrivaled character and actions of the Lord.

Date

Micah prophesied during the reigns of the Judean kings Jotham (750–735 B.C.), Ahaz (735–715), and Hezekiah (715–687). The time span roughly parallels those of other eighth-century prophets like Hosea (Hos. 1:1) and Isaiah (Isa. 1:1), though Micah 1:1's omission of the name of King Uzziah (767–739 B.C.) may place Micah somewhat later. It is difficult to assess the length of Micah's public activity with any precision. At a minimum, the 16-year reign of Ahaz (2 Kings 16:2), in combination with the presumed transitions at the end of the reign of Jotham and the start of the reign of Hezekiah, provides a ministry length of 20 to 25 years. In Jeremiah 26:18 the elders of the land note the influence of Micah's words on Hezekiah (directly quoting Mic. 3:12).

Theme

The theme of Micah is judgment and forgiveness. The Lord, the Judge who scatters his people for their transgressions and sins, is also the Shepherd-King who in covenant faithfulness gathers, protects, and forgives them.

Purpose, Occasion, and Background

Micah writes in order to bring God's "lawsuit" against his people (3:8). He indicts Samaria and Jerusalem for their sins (1:2–7), with both Assyria (5:5–6) and Babylon (4:10) looming as instruments of the divine sentence.

Free from Assyrian interference in the first half of the eighth century, the reigns of Jeroboam II of Israel (782–753 B.C.) and the Judean kings Uzziah and Jotham (see Date) witnessed the emergence of a wealthy upper class. Yet this brought with it significant corruption. As Amos had condemned the economic and legal injustices prevalent in the northern kingdom in the first half of the eighth century (Amos 2:6–7; 5:10–12; 6:4–5), so Micah catalogs specific sins of both the northern and southern kingdoms. These sins included idolatry (Mic. 1:7; 5:12–14); the seizure of property (2:2, 9); the failure of civil leadership (3:1–3, 9–10; 7:3), religious leadership (3:11), and prophetic leadership (3:5–7, 11); the belief that personal sacrifice satisfies divine justice (6:6–7); and corrupt business practices and violence (6:10–12).

The reigns of Jotham, Ahaz, and Hezekiah, along with the increasing threat of the Neo-Assyrian Empire, provide the broad background for Micah. First, Ahaz stands out among the three Judean kings for his idolatry (2 Kings 16:1–4; Mic. 6:16) as well as for the help he sought from the Assyrian king Tiglath-pileser III

(745–727 B.C.) in the face of Syro-Ephraimite aggression against Jerusalem (2 Kings 16:5–9; 2 Chron. 28:16–21). Second, Samaria, the northern Israelite capital, experienced exile as it fell (2 Kings 17; Mic. 1:6–7) to the Assyrian Shalmaneser V (727–722 B.C.). Finally, Sennacherib (705–681 B.C.) captured numerous cities and villages of the Shephelah controlled by Hezekiah (1:10–16), but ultimately failed to capture Jerusalem in 701 (2 Kings 18:13–19:37).

Key Themes

1. The character of the sovereign Lord and the sins of his people demand judgment (1:2–5; 2:3; 6:1–2, 9–11). The sentence of God's "lawsuit" comes in the form of an oppressor (1:15; 4:11; 5:1, 5–6) and by means of covenant curses (6:13–15) rendered for covenant unfaithfulness (6:16).

2. A Shepherd-King gathers and delivers a remnant (2:12–13; 4:6–8; 7:14, 18). This deliverer, functioning as a new David, will come from the very region under Assyrian control (5:2–5a).

3. Covenant faithfulness consists not merely in ritual but in the proper expression of the primary forms of love: justice, mercy, and faithfulness (6:8; cf. Matt. 23:23).

4. The Lord is the focus of worship. The nations will no longer "flow" to false gods (cf. Jer. 51:44) but to Zion to learn of the true Lord and to live in peace (Mic. 4:1–5; 7:12; cf. Isa. 2:2–5).

5. The liberating light of grace flowing from the Lord's steadfast love (Mic. 7:18–20) overcomes the ominous sentence due to sin (7:8–9). Forgiveness is grounded in God's faithfulness to his promises (7:20).

6. God's saving acts in the past (6:4–5; 7:14–15) are interpretative analogies for his saving acts in the future (7:19–20).

History of Salvation Summary

In every age God wants his people to respond to his love by doing justice, practicing loving-kindness, and walking humbly with God (6:8). This is genuine humanness, and by it Israel was called to commend God's goodness to all mankind. Israel and Judah in Micah's day were corrupted by their refusal to embrace God's purpose, and thus would suffer judgment; but there would yet be a remnant who would experience God's forgiveness and be part of his plan to bless the world through the Messiah's rule. (For an explanation of the "History of Salvation," see Overview of the Bible, pp. 23–26. See also History of Salvation in the Old Testament: Preparing the Way for Christ, pp. 2635–2661.)

Literary Features

Micah comprises a series of oracles (prophetic pronouncements) delivered in a variety of historical and political contexts. The overall genre is prophecy. While Micah uses a variety of forms such as disputation (2:6–11) and lament (1:8–16), the two leading prophetic forms in Micah are the oracle of judgment (2:1–4) and the oracle of salvation or redemption (5:2–5). The oracles of judgment follow the rules of satire: they have one or more objects of attack, a vehicle in which the attack is embodied, a stated or implied norm by which the criticism is conducted, and a prevailing tone that is either biting or laughing. Some of the oracles of salvation picture a future golden age (which can be taken either as messianic visions of the first coming of Christ or as apocalyptic visions of Christ's second coming). Much of the book's content is embodied in poetical language, requiring the reader to unpack the meanings of images and figures of speech such as wordplay (see note on 1:10–15), metaphor, and simile (1:4, 8; 2:12; 3:3, 12; 4:9–10; 5:8; 7:1, 4).

Outline

The current arrangement of the text permits a number of possible outlines. One that has garnered much support, and that is followed here, centers on the pattern of judgment and salvation found throughout the book. In each of three large units, the use of the plural imperative "hear" begins a major section on judgment, and each unit moves toward hope and deliverance (1:2–2:13; 3:1–5:15; 6:1–7:20).

I. Superscription (1:1)

II. The Announcement of Judgment on Israel and Judah (1:2–2:13)

- A. God's punishment of Samaria and Judah (1:2–16)
  1. Judgment on Samaria (1:2–7)
  2. Judgment on Judah (1:8–16)

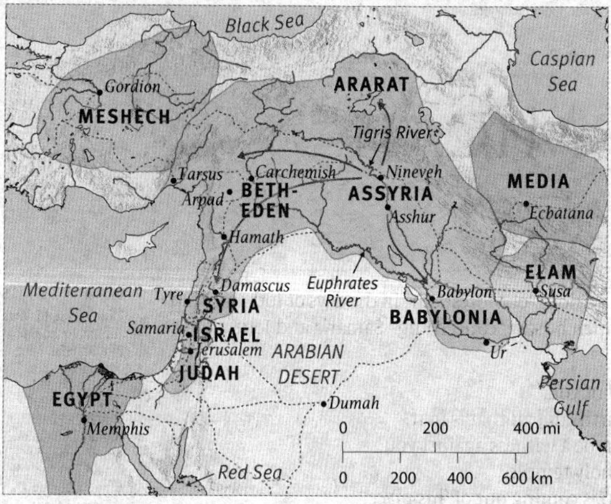

The Near East at the Time of Micah
c. 740 B.C.
Micah prophesied to Israel and Judah during the decades just before the fall of Samaria through the time of King Hezekiah of Judah. Micah witnessed the destruction of Israel by the rising Assyrian empire, yet he probably also witnessed the Lord's dramatic rescue of Jerusalem from the Assyrians during Hezekiah's reign.

- B. Abuses and abusers of Yahweh's land (2:1–11)
  - 1. Indictment and future punishment (2:1–5)
  - 2. Rejection of the prophetic word (2:6–11)
- C. The divine promise to gather Jacob (2:12–13)

III. The Present Injustice and the Future Prospect of Just Rule in Jerusalem (3:1–5:15)
- A. Present leaders denounced (3:1–12)
  - 1. Judgment against the heads of Jacob (3:1–4)
  - 2. Judgment against the prophets (3:5–8)
  - 3. Judgment against the heads of Jacob (3:9–12)
- B. Jerusalem's restoration among the nations—promised (4:1–7)
  - 1. Nations approach Zion in peace (4:1–5)
  - 2. Divine promise to gather Zion (4:6–7)
- C. Jerusalem's restoration among the nations—accomplished (4:8–5:15)
  - 1. Restoration of Zion's dominion (4:8)
  - 2. Nations approach Zion for battle (4:9–13)
  - 3. The Shepherd-King arrives and the remnant is restored (5:1–15)

IV. The Lord's Indictment and Restoration of His People (6:1–7:20)
- A. Israel accused: covenant violation (6:1–8)
  - 1. The prophetic summons (6:1–2)
  - 2. Divine interrogation and saving acts (6:3–5)
  - 3. People's response and prophetic reply (6:6–8)
- B. Crisis in relationship (6:9–7:7)
  - 1. Divine indictment of treachery (6:9–12)
  - 2. Divine sentence for treachery (6:13–16)
  - 3. Consequences of disobedience: social upheaval (7:1–7)
- C. Zion's repentance and renewed faith in Yahweh's help (7:8–13)
- D. Restoration of the relationship between Israel and Yahweh (7:14–20)

MICAH

1 The word of the LORD that came to Micah [a]of Moresheth [b]in the days of Jotham, Ahaz, and Hezekiah, kings of Judah, which he saw [c]concerning [d]Samaria and Jerusalem.

The Coming Destruction

2 [e]Hear, you peoples, all of you;[1]
[f]pay attention, O earth, and all that is in it,
and [g]let the Lord GOD be a witness against you,
[h]the Lord from his holy temple.
3 For behold, [i]the LORD is coming out of [j]his place,
and will come down and [k]tread upon the high places of the earth.
4 And [l]the mountains will melt under him,
and the valleys will split open,
like wax before the fire,
like waters poured down a steep place.
5 All this is for [m]the transgression of Jacob
and for the sins of the house of Israel.
[n]What is the transgression of Jacob?
Is it not [d]Samaria?
And what is [o]the high place of Judah?
Is it not Jerusalem?
6 Therefore I will make [d]Samaria [p]a heap in the open country,
a place for planting vineyards,
and I will pour down her stones [q]into the valley
and [r]uncover her foundations.
7 All [s]her carved images shall be beaten to pieces,
[t]all her wages shall be burned with fire,
and all her idols I will lay waste,
for from [t]the fee of a prostitute she gathered them,
and to the fee of a prostitute they shall return.
8 [u]For this I will lament and wail;
I will go [v]stripped and naked;

[1] Hebrew *all of them*

Chapter 1

1 [a][ver. 14] [b]Isa. 1:1 [c]Amos 1:1 [d]Isa. 7:9; Jer. 23:13
2 [e]ch. 3:1, 9; 6:1, 2; See Hos. 5:1 [f]See Isa. 1:2 [g]Mal. 3:5 [h]Ps. 11:4; Jonah 2:7; Hab. 2:20
3 [i]Isa. 26:21 [j]Ps. 115:3 [k]Amos 4:13; [Deut. 32:13]
4 [l]Ps. 97:5; [Judg. 5:5; Amos 9:5, 13; Nah. 1:5]
5 [m]See ch. 3:8 [n][ver. 13] [d][See ver. 1 above] [o][2 Chr. 28:4]
6 [d][See ver. 1 above] [p][ch. 3:12] [q][1 Kgs. 16:24] [r]Ezek. 13:14
7 [s][Hos. 8:6] [t][Hos. 2:12; 9:1]
8 [u][Isa. 22:4] [v]See Isa. 20:2-4

1:1 *Superscription.* On **Micah of Moresheth**, see Introduction: Author and Title. On **Jotham, Ahaz, and Hezekiah**, see Introduction: Purpose, Occasion, and Background. The sequence **Samaria** and **Jerusalem** anticipates the structure of chs. 1–3.

1:2–2:13 *The Announcement of Judgment on Israel and Judah.* The first major section describes the impending judgment: (1) God's punishment of Samaria and Judah (1:2–16); (2) abuses and abusers of Yahweh's land (2:1–11); and (3) the divine promise to gather Jacob (2:12–13).

1:2–16 *God's Punishment of Samaria and Judah.* The prophecy opens with the pronouncement of judgment on Samaria (vv. 2–7), with Judah following (vv. 8–16).

1:2–7 *Judgment on Samaria.* The coming of the Lord and the reason for his appearing (vv. 2–5a) is followed by four rhetorical questions from the Lord (vv. 5b–7). The undoing of creation (v. 4) anticipates the undoing of Samaria (vv. 6–7).

1:2 Hear. This verb marks the beginning of major divisions (1:2; 3:1; 6:1). As **witness against** Samaria, the Lord will bring accusations and provide evidence (1 Sam. 12:5; Mal. 3:5). **Holy temple** refers to the Lord's dwelling in the heavens (cf. Ps. 11:4; Hab. 2:20). It is parallel to "his place" (Mic. 1:3).

1:3 Coming out implies Yahweh's marching out for battle (cf. Judg. 5:4; Isa. 26:21; Zech. 14:3). **High places** designates either geographical "heights" (cf. Amos 4:13) or the cultic Canaanite shrines located on them.

1:4 mountains will melt. Cf. Ps. 97:5; Nah. 1:5.

1:5 Jacob . . . house of Israel. These terms and the mention of the capital cities of **Samaria** (northern kingdom) and **Jerusalem** (southern kingdom) underscore that the whole nation is in view (2:12; 3:1, 8–9).

8[w]Job 30:29; Ps. 44:19 [x]Isa. 13:21
9[y][Hos. 5:13]
10[z]2 Sam. 1:20 [a]See 1 Sam. 17:4 [b][Jer. 6:26]
11[c][Isa. 20:4; 47:3]
12[d]See Amos 3:6
13[e]Josh. 10:3; 2 Kgs. 18:14, 17; 2 Chr. 32:9

I will make lamentation [w]like the jackals,
and mourning [x]like the ostriches.
9 [y]For her wound is incurable,
and it has come to Judah;
it has reached to the gate of my people,
to Jerusalem.

10 [z]Tell it not in [a]Gath;
weep not at all;
in Beth-le-aphrah
[b]roll yourselves in the dust.
11 Pass on your way,
inhabitants of Shaphir,
[c]in nakedness and shame;
the inhabitants of Zaanan
do not come out;
the lamentation of Beth-ezel
shall take away from you its standing place.
12 For the inhabitants of Maroth
wait anxiously for good,
because disaster has come down [d]from the LORD
to the gate of Jerusalem.
13 Harness the steeds to the chariots,
inhabitants of [e]Lachish;

1:6 I will expresses the Lord's intention to act (1:7, 15; 2:3, 12; 4:6–7, 13; 5:10–15; 6:14; 7:15). **Samaria a heap**. A similar fate awaits Jerusalem (3:12). **uncover her foundations**. The threat speaks of judgment and introduces the concept of public shame (cf. 4:11; 7:10).

1:7 All her carved images . . . wages . . . idols. Yahweh's judgment and destruction will be extensive. **fee of a prostitute**. The spiritual infidelity of the city is likened to the actions of a prostitute, as elsewhere in the OT (Judg. 2:17; Ezek. 16:33–36).

1:8–16 *Judgment on Judah.* Micah's mourning (vv. 8–9) is followed by a list of the cities that will face disaster (vv. 10–15) and the threat of exile (v. 16).

1:8 go stripped and naked. Mourning was usually signified by the wearing of sackcloth (Gen. 37:34; 1 Kings 21:27; Joel 1:8) and head covering (2 Sam. 15:30); hence this may be a more intense mourning, or else an image of going into exile (cf. Isa. 20:3–4). **jackals . . . ostriches**. Judah is pictured as a land laid waste (Isa. 34:13; Jer. 50:39).

1:9 It has reached probably refers to the yet-to-be-identified "disaster" (v. 12). The delayed identification of what exactly has reached **to the gate** spotlights the subject when finally disclosed.

1:10–15 Using the names of towns taken by the Assyrians, Micah's extensive wordplay reflects the various disasters that Judah will face. For the cities identified in vv. 10–15, see map to the right.

1:10 Tell it not in Gath. Micah seeks to prevent either sympathy or rejoicing from outside observers over the coming destruction (cf. note on 2 Sam. 1:20). **Beth-le-aphrah** ("House of Dust") plays on the similar sound of the Hebrew *'apar* (**dust**). **roll yourselves**. Those under judgment must give full expression to their grief.

1:11 Shaphir sounds like a related word for "beautiful" and contrasts with **nakedness and shame**. **Zaanan** sounds like the Hebrew for "come out." In fear, the trembling **inhabitants** do not **come out** for battle. **Beth-ezel** ("House of Taking Away") expresses **lamentation** that the village was "taken away," i.e., destroyed.

1:12 Maroth conveys the concept of bitterness. Thus, a "bitter" town longs **for good**. The word **disaster** (Hb. *ra'*) is a key word in Micah (see ESV footnote at 2:3). The "disaster" from Yahweh, who "will come down" (1:3), **has come down** to Jerusalem's gate (cf. v. 9).

1:13 Steeds (Hb. *larekesh*, lit., "to the steeds") sounds like **Lachish**. Ironically, the people are urged to harness not chariot horses to fight but swift courier horses to flee.

Micah Prophesies Destruction
c. 740 B.C.

Micah foretold the destruction that awaited Jerusalem and the towns that guarded the approach to the city. Though these towns lay to the southwest of Jerusalem, they lay along the route normally traveled by invading forces from the north, who typically followed the Great Trunk Road south until they reached Gath.

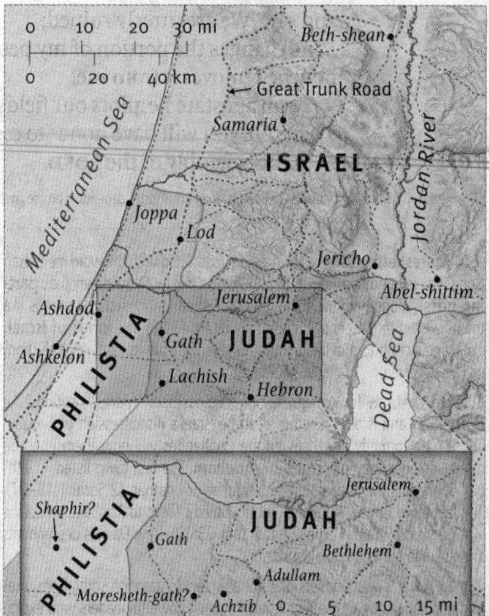

it was the beginning of sin
to the daughter of Zion,
for in you were found
[f]the transgressions of Israel.
14 Therefore you shall give parting gifts[1]
to [g]Moresheth-gath;
the houses of [h]Achzib shall be a deceitful thing
to the kings of Israel.
15 I will again bring [i]a conqueror to you,
inhabitants of [h]Mareshah;
the glory of Israel
shall come to [j]Adullam.
16 [k]Make yourselves bald and cut off your hair,
for the children of your delight;
[k]make yourselves as bald as the eagle,
for they shall go from you into exile.

Woe to the Oppressors

2

1 [l]Woe to those who devise wickedness
and work evil [m]on their beds!
When the morning dawns, they perform it,
because it is in the power of their hand.
2 They covet fields and [n]seize them,
and houses, and take them away;
they oppress a man and his house,
a man and his inheritance.
3 Therefore thus says the LORD:
behold, against [o]this family I am devising disaster,[2]
from which you cannot remove your necks,
and you [p]shall not walk haughtily,
[q]for it will be a time of disaster.
4 In that day [r]they shall take up a taunt song against you
and moan bitterly,
and say, "We are utterly ruined;
[s]he changes the portion of my people;
[s]how he removes it from me!
[t]To an apostate he allots our fields."
5 Therefore you will have none [u]to cast the line by lot
in the assembly of the LORD.

[1] Or *give dowry* [2] The same Hebrew word can mean *evil* or *disaster*, depending on the context

13[f][ver. 5; Hos. 13:1]
14[g][ver. 1] [h]Josh. 15:44
15[i][ch. 2:4; Jer. 6:12] [h][See ver. 14 above] [j]See 1 Sam. 22:1, 2
16[k]See Isa. 22:12

Chapter 2

1[l][Isa. 10:1, 2] [m][Ps. 36:4]
2[n][Isa. 5:8]
3[o][Jer. 8:3; Amos 3:1, 2] [p][Isa. 2:11, 17] [q]Amos 5:13
4[r]Hab. 2:6; See Num. 23:7 [s][ch. 1:15] [t][Ps. 68:6]
5[u]Deut. 32:8, 9; [Josh. 14:1, 2]

1:14 Moresheth-gath. The town is here associated with the word *me'orasah* ("one who is betrothed," Deut. 22:23). Assyria will receive a dowry (i.e., **parting gifts**), along with the bride (i.e., Moresheth-gath). **Achzib** sounds like the noun *'akzab* ("deceptive, deceitful"; cf. Jer. 15:18). The **kings of Israel**, expecting Achzib to provide a source of revenue from its pottery production, will be deceived.

1:15 The Hebrew for **conqueror** or "dispossessor" (*yoresh*) sounds like **Mareshah** and is often used to describe Israel's dispossession of Canaan. Those who formerly dispossessed the Canaanites will now themselves be dispossessed. **glory of Israel . . . Adullam**. The first town listed, "Gath" (v. 10), recalls David's lament over Saul and Jonathan (2 Sam. 1:19–27). The last town listed, "Adullam," recalls David's flight to Adullam, where he was pursued by Saul (1 Sam. 22:1; 2 Sam. 23:13). Now David's descendants likewise flee from a hostile conqueror.

2:1–11 *Abuses and Abusers of Yahweh's Land.* Attention shifts from cities and populations to accusations leveled against powerful leaders who exploit the vulnerable (vv. 1–5) and reject God's message (vv. 6–11).

2:1–5 *Indictment and Future Punishment.* The powerful are accused (vv. 1–2), and their sentence is issued (vv. 3–4). Ultimately, they lose all hope for inheritance among the Lord's people (v. 5).

2:1 in the power of their hand. Those who devise wickedness do evil because they have the authority and ability to carry out their schemes (cf. Gen. 31:29 for the expression).

2:2 covet . . . seize . . . take . . . oppress. The tearing away of land and property (**his inheritance**) from the weak was a flagrant violation of the covenant (Ex. 20:17) and a primary reason for judgment against Ahab's house (1 Kings 21; 2 Kings 9:24–26; cf. Mic. 6:16).

2:3 against this family. The entire community is accountable for the sins of its leaders. **I am devising disaster** reveals the principle of correspondence (Obad. 15b): the "evil" they devised for others (Mic. 2:1) will now be visited on them (see note on 1:12; ESV footnote). **a time of disaster**. See Amos 5:13.

2:4 taunt song. The losses sustained by the land barons will be mocked. These oppressors had seized property from the defenseless (vv. 1–2), so now the **apostate** (the Assyrians?) will seize the land of the oppressors. In the phrase **he changes the portion of my people**, "he" possibly refers to God, but some interpreters understand it to refer to the invading conqueror.

2:5 you will have none. The unscrupulous land-grabbers are excluded from the inheritance they denied to others (v. 2). **assembly**. There yet remains a people to whom land would be distributed after exile.

2:6–11 *Rejection of the Prophetic Word.* This disputation addresses unprin-

6 [v]See Amos 2:12 [w][Amos 8:11, 12] [x][Amos 8:10]
7 [v][See ver. 6 above]
8 [y][2 Chr. 28:8]
10 [z][ch. 1:11, 16] [a]Deut. 12:9; [Heb. 13:14] [b]Lev. 18:25
11 [c]Jer. 5:13 [d][Amos 2:12]
12 [e][2 Kgs. 25:11] [f]See ch. 4:7 [h][Jer. 31:10]
13 [i][2 Kgs. 25:10] [j][ch. 4:10] [k][Isa. 52:12]

Chapter 3

1 [l]See ch. 1:2

6 [v]"Do not preach"—thus they preach—
[w]"one should not preach of such things;
[x]disgrace will not overtake us."
7 Should this be said, O house of Jacob?
[v]Has the LORD grown impatient?[1]
Are these his deeds?
Do not my words do good
to him who walks uprightly?
8 But lately [y]my people have risen up as an enemy;
you strip the rich robe from those who pass by trustingly
with no thought of war.[2]
9 The women of my people you drive out
from their delightful houses;
from their young children you take away
my splendor forever.
10 [z]Arise and go,
for this is no [a]place to rest,
because of [b]uncleanness that destroys
with a grievous destruction.
11 If a man should go about and [c]utter wind and lies,
saying, "I will preach to you [d]of wine and strong drink,"
he would be the preacher for this people!
12 I will surely assemble all of you, O Jacob;
[e]I will gather [f]the remnant of Israel;
I will set them together
like sheep in a fold,
[h]like a flock in its pasture,
a noisy multitude of men.
13 [i]He who opens the breach goes up before them;
they break through and pass the gate,
[j]going out by it.
Their king passes on before them,
[k]the LORD at their head.

Rulers and Prophets Denounced

3 1 And I said:
[l]Hear, you heads of Jacob
and rulers of the house of Israel!

[1] Hebrew *Has the spirit of the LORD grown short?* [2] Or *returning from war*

cipled prophets (cf. 3:5–7). Those who reject Micah are exposed (2:6), and the Lord brings to light further abuses of the powerful (vv. 8–9). Exile is the sentence for the "uncleanness" of their injustice and their willingness to welcome deceptive preaching (vv. 10–11).

2:6 preach. This verb frames the unit (vv. 6, 11) and conveys the idea "to drip," a term used metaphorically for divulging a prophetic message (Ezek. 20:46). The attempt to silence the prophetic voice also appears elsewhere (Amos 2:12; 7:10–16).

2:7 The rhetorical questions expose the misunderstanding of the people, who thought that a God of grace could never devise the disaster of vv. 3–5.

2:8–9 The acts cataloged are similar to the abuses detailed in vv. 1–5. **my people . . . an enemy**. The accusation of hostility is supported by three examples of enemy-like conduct in war.

2:10 Arise and go . . . no place to rest. Widespread injustice has denied rest to others, and so the Lord demands that the people leave their place of rest.

2:11 preach . . . of wine. The people welcomed "preaching" that emphasized overindulgence rather than God's condemnation of unethical behavior.

2:12–13 *The Divine Promise to Gather Jacob.* The first main section ends with the Shepherd of Israel gathering his sheep into the protective fold (v. 12) and leading them out as their triumphant King (v. 13).

2:12 assemble . . . gather . . . set . . . like sheep. The descriptive actions culminate in the image of Yahweh as a protective shepherd. **remnant**. Perhaps a reference to numerous refugees of the Assyrian invasion, gathered in Jerusalem.

2:13 opens the breach. The metaphor shifts to a king leading his army out (**they break through**) from an enclosed city. **Pass the gate** probably refers to Jerusalem's gate (cf. 1:9, 12). **king . . . before them . . . LORD**. The identity of the Shepherd-King who opened the breach and leads the people into battle is fully revealed.

3:1–5:15 *The Present Injustice and the Future Prospect of Just Rule in Jerusalem.* The second section focuses on the corrupt leadership in the house of Israel (3:1–12); Jerusalem's restoration among the nations is promised (4:1–7) and accomplished (4:8–5:15).

3:1–12 *Present Leaders Denounced.* The abuse of power (vv. 1–4) and flagrant misuse of prophetic office (vv. 5–8) is followed by a general indictment of the leadership, followed by the sentence (vv. 9–12).

3:1–4 *Judgment against the Heads of Jacob.* Micah describes the depraved character of the civil leaders using the gruesome imagery of cannibalism.

3:1–2a Is it not for you to know justice? Delighting in God's law and

[m]Is it not for you to know justice?—
2 you [n]who hate the good and love the evil,
[o]who tear the skin from off my people[1]
and their flesh from off their bones,
3 [p]who eat the flesh of my people,
and flay their skin from off them,
and break their bones in pieces
and chop them up like meat in a pot,
like flesh in a cauldron.

4 [q]Then they will cry to the LORD,
but he will not answer them;
[r]he will hide his face from them at that time,
because they have made their deeds evil.

5 Thus says the LORD concerning [s]the prophets
who lead my people astray,
[t]who cry "Peace"
when they have something to eat,
but declare war against him
who puts nothing into their mouths.
6 Therefore [u]it shall be night to you, without vision,
and darkness to you, without divination.
[v]The sun shall go down on the prophets,
and the day shall be black over them;
7 [w]the seers shall be disgraced,
and the diviners put to shame;
[x]they shall all cover their lips,
for [y]there is no answer from God.
8 But as for me, [z]I am filled with power,
with the Spirit of the LORD,
and with justice and might,
to declare to Jacob [a]his transgression
and to Israel his sin.

9 [b]Hear this, you heads of the house of Jacob
and rulers of the house of Israel,
[c]who detest justice
and make crooked all that is straight,
10 [d]who build Zion with blood
and Jerusalem with iniquity.
11 [e]Its heads give judgment for a bribe;
[f]its priests teach for a price;
[g]its prophets practice divination for money;

[1] Hebrew *from off them*

1 [m]Jer. 5:5; [Ezek. 22:6, 27]
2 [n][ver. 9] [o][Ezek. 34:3]
3 [p][Ps. 14:4; Isa. 3:15]
4 [q]See Prov. 1:28 [r]Isa. 1:15; See Deut. 31:17
5 [s]Jer. 23:13, 32; Ezek. 13:10 [t][Jer. 6:14]
6 [u]Ezek. 12:24; 13:23 [v]See Amos 8:9
7 [w]Zech. 13:4; [Jer. 37:19] [x][Lev. 13:45] [y]See Amos 8:11
8 [z][Jer. 6:11] [a]ch. 1:5; Isa. 58:1; [Ezek. 23:36]
9 [b]See ch. 1:2 [c][ver. 2]
10 [d]Jer. 22:13; Ezek. 22:27; Hab. 2:12
11 [e]ch. 7:3; Isa. 1:23 [f]See Jer. 6:13 [g][ver. 5; Ezek. 22:25]

discerning what is right should be the joy of those given judicial responsibility (Isa. 5:20).

3:2b–3 tear . . . eat . . . flay . . . break . . . chop. The imagery of cannibalism is used to symbolize the destructive violence of the leaders against the oppressed (cf. Ps. 14:4; 27:2; Prov. 30:14; Isa. 9:19–21).

3:4 he will not answer . . . he will hide his face. In just retribution (see notes on 2:3; 2:4), those who would not hear the cries of the people will now find that God will not hear them. God's silence is part of their sentence.

3:5–8 *Judgment against the Prophets.* Micah rebukes the false prophets (cf. 2:11). Just as civil leaders will receive no answer from the Lord, so erring prophets will receive no vision.

3:5 when they have something to eat (lit., "who bite [Hb. *nashak*] with their teeth"). The verb in this form generally refers to the deadly bite of a serpent (Gen. 49:17; Num. 21:6); in another form it refers to lending money with interest (Deut. 23:19–20). **Peace . . . war**. Thus, profit-seeking prophets proclaim that all is well with the world, as long as they receive what they ask for.

3:6–7 darkness (Hb. *khashak*) **to you**. The "biting" (Hb. *nashak*, v. 5) of the false prophets results in "blindness." **no answer from God**. As with the civil leaders (cf. v. 4), God's silence is part of their sentence.

3:8 But as for me distinguishes Micah and his unpopular message from that of the false prophets. **to declare**. The true prophet is **filled with** (i.e., empowered by) the **Spirit of the LORD**.

3:9–12 *Judgment against the Heads of Jacob.* This climactic third oracle of judgment adds priests to the previously addressed civil rulers (vv. 1–4) and false prophets (vv. 5–8).

3:9 detest justice. The rulers were meant to know and do justice (cf. vv. 1, 8),

[h]yet they lean on the LORD and [i]say,
"Is not the LORD in the midst of us?
[j]No disaster shall come upon us."
12 Therefore because of you
[k]Zion shall be plowed as a field;
Jerusalem [l]shall become a heap of ruins,
and [m]the mountain of the house [n]a wooded height.

The Mountain of the LORD

4

1 It shall come to pass [o]in the latter days
that the mountain of the house of the LORD
shall be established as the highest of the mountains,
and it shall be lifted up above the hills;
and peoples shall flow to it,
2 and many nations shall come, and say:
"Come, let us go up to the mountain of the LORD,
to the house of the God of Jacob,
that he may teach us his ways
and that we may walk in his paths."
For out of Zion shall go forth the law,[1]
and the word of the LORD from Jerusalem.
3 He shall judge between many peoples,
and shall decide for strong nations far away;
and they shall [p]beat their swords into plowshares,
and their spears into pruning hooks;
nation shall not lift up sword against nation,
neither shall they learn war anymore;
4 [q]but they shall sit every man under his vine and under his fig tree,
[r]and no one shall make them afraid,
[s]for the mouth of the LORD of hosts has spoken.
5 For [t]all the peoples walk
each in the name of its god,
but [u]we will walk in the name of the LORD our God
forever and ever.

The LORD Shall Rescue Zion

6 [v]In that day, declares the LORD,
[w]I will assemble the [x]lame

11 [h]Isa. 48:2 [i]Jer. 7:4; [Amos 5:14] [j][Jer. 23:17; Amos 9:10]
12 [k]Cited Jer. 26:18 [l][ch. 1:6] [m]ch. 4:2 [n][Luke 13:35]

Chapter 4

1 [o]For ver. 1-3, see Isa. 2:2-4
3 [p][Joel 3:10]
4 [q]See 1 Kgs. 4:25 [r]Isa. 17:2 [s]See Isa. 1:20
5 [t][Jer. 2:11] [u][Zech. 10:12]
6 [v][ver. 1] [w]See Ezek. 11:17 [x]Ezek. 34:16; Zeph. 3:19

[1] Or *teaching*

but instead they find it abhorrent. **make crooked.** Leaders who "hate the good and love the evil" (v. 2) continue that pattern with twisted judicial decisions.

3:11 The **heads . . . priests . . . prophets** (all the main groups of leaders) give desired results in exchange for compensation. **lean on the LORD.** Profession of faith without justice is lifeless (James 2:14–18). **No disaster.** There is no basis for their confidence that they will escape that which the Lord has appointed (Mic. 1:12; 2:3).

3:12 This verse is quoted in Jer. 26:16–19. **because of you.** As the leaders had built Jerusalem with injustice and violent acts (Mic. 3:10), so they are responsible for its "unbuilding." **mountain of the house.** This sets up a contrast with "mountain of the house of the LORD" (4:1). The temple without the Lord's presence becomes simply a structure on a hill.

4:1–7 *Jerusalem's Restoration among the Nations—Promised.* Jerusalem and its temple, once destroyed (3:12), are exalted as a source of instruction, justice, and righteousness (4:1–5). The weak become strong under Yahweh's rule (vv. 6–7).

4:1–5 *Nations Approach Zion in Peace.* The mountain of the Lord is now the focal point of the nations. The oracle in Isa. 2:1–5 is almost identical; for more on its details, see notes on Isa. 2:1–5.

4:1 in the latter days. Micah envisions a new epoch in which Jerusalem's fortunes are reversed. **the mountain of the house of the LORD shall be established.** See note on Isa. 2:2 for this concept and for the time of "the latter days." **shall flow to it.** Rather than streaming to false gods (cf. Jer. 51:44), the nations will worship the Lord.

4:2 God of Jacob. The nations' access to the Lord comes through Israel. **out of Zion shall go forth the law.** The teaching of God's ways will flow from Jerusalem outward to all nations (cf. note on Isa. 2:3).

4:3 They shall beat their swords into plowshares looks forward to a time "in the latter days" (v. 1) when the nations of the earth will no longer need armies or weapons to defend against the threat of evil aggressors (see note on Isa. 2:4).

4:4 vine . . . fig tree. A key OT image of peace and prosperity (cf. 1 Kings 4:25; Zech. 3:10). The military title **LORD of hosts** (i.e., of armies) emphasizes God's sovereign right to bring about these events.

4:5 but we will walk . . . forever. In contrast to the pantheon available to the nations, the people of God walk together, united to their King and under his law and word (v. 2) in unending relationship. Such faithfulness is how the members of Judah play their part in bringing the story to the fulfillment of vv. 1–4.

4:6–7 *Divine Promise to Gather Zion.* God expresses his covenant faithfulness.

and gather those who have been driven away
  and those whom I have afflicted;
7 and the lame I will make [y]the remnant,
  and those who were cast off, a strong nation;
and [z]the LORD will reign over them [a]in Mount Zion
  from this time forth and forevermore.

8 And you, O tower of the flock,
  hill of the daughter of Zion,
to you shall it come,
  the former dominion shall come,
  kingship for the daughter of Jerusalem.

9 Now why do you cry aloud?
  [b]Is there no king in you?
[c]Has your counselor perished,
  that [d]pain seized you like a woman in labor?
10 [e]Writhe and groan,[1] O daughter of Zion,
  like a woman in labor,
for [f]now you shall go out from the city
  and dwell in the open country;
  you [g]shall go to Babylon.
There you shall be rescued;
  [h]there the LORD will redeem you
  from the hand of your enemies.

11 Now [i]many nations
  are assembled against you,
saying, "Let her be defiled,
  and [j]let our eyes gaze upon Zion."
12 But [k]they do not know
  the thoughts of the LORD;
they do not understand his plan,
  that [l]he has gathered them as sheaves to the threshing floor.
13 Arise and thresh,
  O daughter of Zion,
for I will make your horn iron,
  and I will make your hoofs bronze;

[1] *Or push*

7 [y]ch. 2:12; 5:7, 8; Joel 2:32; Zeph. 2:7 [z]Isa. 24:23; [Dan. 7:14; Luke 1:33] [a]Ps. 2:6; Heb. 12:22
9 [b]Jer. 8:19 [c][Isa. 3:3] [d]Jer. 6:24
10 [e][John 16:20, 21] [f][ch. 2:13] [g]Isa. 39:6, 7 [h]See Isa. 44:22, 23
11 [i]Zech. 12:3 [j]ch. 7:10; Obad. 12
12 [k][Isa. 10:7] [l][Joel 3:13; Hab. 3:12; Matt. 3:12; Luke 3:17]

These pivotal verses develop the theme of exiles regathered (v. 6), restored, and submissive to the Lord's reign (v. 7) in ongoing fellowship.

4:6 In that day. See v. 1; 5:10. **assemble . . . gather**. Along with "I will make" (4:7), these same verbs are found in 2:12–13. Deliverance from the disaster at Jerusalem's gate (1:12) thus becomes a type of greater salvation. **I have afflicted**. It is the Lord's doing (2:3).

4:7 the LORD will reign . . . forevermore. As at 2:12–13, the shepherd theme ("gather," "assemble") gives way to the royal.

4:8–5:15 *Jerusalem's Restoration among the Nations—Accomplished.* The kingdom is established (4:8). The unit moves from distress and salvation (4:9–5:1) to messianic intervention and victory (5:2–6). The remnant both blesses and curses the nations (5:7–9), and the Lord obliterates idolatries from his people (5:10–15).

4:8 *Restoration of Zion's Dominion.* **And you** (see 5:2). This verse is a transition between 4:6–7 and 4:9–5:6. **tower of the flock . . . former dominion**. As David "shepherded his flock" from Jerusalem, so a new king will rule once more. Again the Shepherd-King language is prominent.

4:9–13 *Nations Approach Zion for Battle.* The word "now" (vv. 9–11) focuses attention on impending exile and siege. Each subunit moves from distress to deliverance.

4:9 Is there no king in you? Zion's daughter must look beyond ineffectual human kings to Yahweh alone for salvation (Jer. 8:19). **your counselor**. The Lord executes his plan (Mic. 4:12; cf. Isa. 9:6).

4:10 go to Babylon. There. The Lord focuses attention on rescue and redemption after the "labor" of exile. **your enemies**. In the context, this refers to the Babylonian captivity (586 B.C.).

4:11 Now marks a new subunit. The **you** against whom the unnamed **nations are assembled** applies to God's people in every age. The specific setting is probably the Assyrian siege in 701 B.C. (cf. 5:5). **defiled . . . gaze**. The gathered forces express their contemptuous desire to desecrate Jerusalem's holy temple and expose it to public scorn.

4:12 his plan . . . he has gathered. The nations have assembled themselves (v. 11), and yet it is Yahweh who brings them to his **threshing floor** (2 Sam. 24:21). War is pictured as harvest, and harvest is used as a figure of judgment (Jer. 51:33; Matt. 13:30; Rev. 14:15).

13[m]Lev. 27:28 [n]Isa. 23:18 [o]Ps. 97:5
Chapter 5
1[p]See 1 Kgs. 22:24
2[q]Cited Matt. 2:6; [John 7:42] [r][Heb. 7:14] [s][Gen. 49:10; Isa. 9:6, 7; Jer. 30:21; Zech. 9:9] [t]Hos. 6:3 [u]Ps. 90:2; [Prov. 8:22, 23; John 1:1]
3[v][ch. 4:9, 10] [w][ch. 4:7]
4[x]Isa. 40:11; [ch. 7:14] [y]See Isa. 11:3-5 [z]Ps. 72:8; Isa. 52:13; Luke 1:32
5[a][Isa. 9:6; Zech. 9:10; Eph. 2:14] [b][2 Kgs. 18:13] [c][Isa. 3:2, 3]
6[d]Gen. 10:8, 10, 11 [b][See ver. 5 above]

you shall beat in pieces many peoples;
and [m]shall devote[1] [n]their gain to the LORD,
their wealth to [o]the Lord of the whole earth.

The Ruler to Be Born in Bethlehem

5[2]
1 Now muster your troops, O daughter[3] of troops;
siege is laid against us;
with a rod [p]they strike the judge of Israel
on the cheek.
2[4] [q]But you, O Bethlehem Ephrathah,
who are too little to be among the clans of [r]Judah,
from you shall come forth for me
one who is to be [s]ruler in Israel,
[t]whose coming forth is [u]from of old,
from ancient days.
3 Therefore he shall give them up [v]until the time
when she who is in labor has given birth;
then [w]the rest of his brothers shall return
to the people of Israel.
4 And he shall stand [x]and shepherd his flock [y]in the strength of the LORD,
in the majesty of the name of the LORD his God.
And they shall dwell secure, for now [z]he shall be great
to the ends of the earth.
5 And he shall be [a]their peace.

[b]When the Assyrian comes into our land
and treads in our palaces,
then we will raise against him seven [c]shepherds
and eight princes of men;
6 they shall shepherd the land of Assyria with the sword,
and the land of [d]Nimrod at its entrances;
and he shall deliver us from the Assyrian
[b]when he comes into our land
and treads within our border.

[1] Hebrew *devote to destruction* [2] Ch 4:14 in Hebrew [3] That is, city [4] Ch 5:1 in Hebrew

4:13 Arise and thresh. Zion is pictured as an unassailable ox treading grain. **Lord of the whole earth**. There is nothing outside of the rule and rights of the sovereign Lord. His afflicting (v. 6) has become his saving (v. 12).

5:1–15 *The Shepherd-King Arrives and the Remnant Is Restored.* A new hope for Israel, and for the whole world, comes by means of a new David. His deeds are praised (vv. 1–6), and the influence of the remnant among the nations is described (vv. 7–9). The chapter concludes with divine removal of all idolatries (vv. 10–15).

5:1 Now. As earlier (4:9, 11), this word signals distress for Zion. The play on words between **muster your troops** (Hb. *titgodedi*) and **daughter of troops** (Hb. *bat-gedud*) suggests Zion's inability to establish an army to defend itself. **siege**. Probably that of Sennacherib (701 B.C.). **strike the judge of Israel**. A metaphor of humiliation for Israel's king now under siege (2 Chron. 32:10).

5:2 But you. Both here and in 4:8, these words signal renewed kingship. **Ephrathah** is the name of the district in which Bethlehem is located and David was born (1 Sam. 17:12). **too little**. The unlikely choice of David as king foreshadows the unlikely choice of Bethlehem as the hometown of the greater David. Matthew 2:6 (combining this with Mic. 5:4) shows that Jewish scholars of Jesus' day read this as a prediction of the Messiah's birthplace (cf. John 7:42). The Messiah's reign is at God's behest (**for me**), and his **coming forth** (or "origins"; plural of Hb. *motsa'ah*, "coming out") is **from of old, from ancient days**. This has been taken to indicate either an ancient (Davidic) lineage or eternal (and therefore divine) origin of the predicted Messiah. The first time-related expression ("from of old"; Hb. *miqqedem*) generally refers to ancient historical times (e.g., Neh. 12:46; Ps. 77:5, 11; 78:2; 143:5; Isa. 45:21; 46:10) but can also refer to eternity past (e.g., Ps. 74:12; Hab. 1:12). The second time-related expression ("from ancient days"; Hb. *mime 'olam*), however, refers to ancient historical times both in Micah (7:14; cf. 7:20) and elsewhere (Deut. 32:7; Isa. 63:9, 11; Amos 9:11; Mal. 3:4); thus this text is referring to the Messiah's ancient Davidic lineage, confirming that the ancient covenantal promises made to David still stand.

5:3 he shall give them up. Israel's loss of king and subjection to enemies will prevail until the birth of the Lord's ruler. **the rest of his brothers shall return**. The statement emphasizes the unity of the people of God under the Messiah's rule.

5:4 he shall stand and shepherd. The Messiah's rule and protection of Yahweh's flock are accomplished by Yahweh's authority and power. **dwell secure . . . ends of the earth**. The breadth of his greatness ensures that those who return (Hb. *yeshubun*, v. 3) will also dwell (Hb. *yashabu*) without fear.

5:5–6 True **peace** among people is achieved by the Messiah, who overcomes conflict (cf. Eph. 2:14). The **Assyrian** of Micah's day represents the enemies of God's people in every age. **seven shepherds . . . eight princes**. This traditional formula (cf. Eccles. 11:2) expresses a parallel between the Messiah's actions and those who faithfully lead in his place. This is evidenced in the main verbs **they shall shepherd . . . he shall deliver**, extending the Messiah's rule even among these Gentiles.

A Remnant Shall Be Delivered

7 Then [w]the remnant of Jacob shall be
in the midst of many peoples
like dew from the LORD,
like showers on the grass,
which delay not for a man
nor wait for the children of man.
8 And [w]the remnant of Jacob shall be among the nations,
in the midst of many peoples,
like a lion among the beasts of the forest,
like a young lion among the flocks of sheep,
[e]which, when it goes through, treads down
and tears in pieces, and there is none to deliver.
9 Your hand shall [f]be lifted up over your adversaries,
and all your enemies shall be cut off.

10 And [g]in that day, declares the LORD,
[h]I will cut off your horses from among you
and will destroy your chariots;
11 [i]and I will cut off the cities of your land
and throw down all your strongholds;
12 and I will cut off [j]sorceries from your hand,
and [k]you shall have no more tellers of fortunes;
13 and [l]I will cut off your carved images
and [m]your pillars from among you,
[n]and you shall bow down no more
to the work of your hands;
14 and I will root out your [o]Asherah images from among you
[i]and destroy your cities.
15 And in anger and wrath [p]I will execute vengeance
on the nations that did not obey.

The Indictment of the LORD

6
1 [q]Hear what the LORD says:
Arise, plead your case before the mountains,
and let the hills hear your voice.

7[w][See ver. 3 above]
8[w][See ver. 3 above] [e][Hos. 5:14]
9[f]Isa. 26:11
10[g][ch. 4:1, 6] [h]Zech. 9:10; [Isa. 2:7; Hag. 2:22]
11[i]ver. 14; Isa. 17:9; 27:10; [Hos. 8:14; Zech. 2:4]
12[j][2 Kgs. 9:22] [k]Deut. 18:10; [Isa. 2:6]
13[l]Zech. 13:2 [m]Hos. 3:4 [n][Isa. 17:8]
14[o]Ex. 34:13; See Deut. 16:21 [i][See ver. 11 above]
15[p][ver. 8; Ps. 149:7; 2 Thess. 1:8]

Chapter 6

1[q]See ch. 1:2

5:7–8 These verses, with parallel structures, describe: (1) the presence of the remnant among the nations; (2) two comparisons; and (3) an explanation of the comparisons. **delay not . . . nor wait**. Like **dew** and rain, the beneficial influence of the remnant is given or withheld by the Lord alone. **goes through, treads . . . tears . . . none to deliver**. The remnant—no longer a gentle rain—is now a destructive lion.

5:9 This verse may be read as a prayer uttered by the remnant. **cut off**. This action of the Lord is featured in the final section (vv. 10–15).

5:10–15 The Lord cleanses his people from military and cultic idols. The paired verses include elements natural (vv. 10–11) and supernatural (vv. 12–13). A summary statement closes the section (vv. 14–15).

5:10–11 in that day. See 4:1, 6. The Lord answers the implicit prayer of 5:9 to **cut off** things that compromise the holiness of his people. **horses . . . strongholds**. Armies and fortifications, rather than the Lord, were often relied on as security against external enemies (cf. Isa. 31:1; Hos. 8:14).

5:12–13 sorceries . . . tellers of fortunes. Seeking occult knowledge was explicitly forbidden to Israel (Deut. 18:10, 14). **your carved images . . . your pillars**. In representing the presence of the deity in this wrongful way, Israel was tempted to **bow down** to created things rather than to the Creator (Mic. 1:7; Rom. 1:22–23).

5:14 Asherah images are wooden images of the female fertility goddess of the Canaanites, regularly denounced by the prophets. (A grim reminder of these pagan ways in Israel has been found at the site of Kuntillat Ajrud, perhaps the southernmost outpost of Judah during the early eighth century B.C. Remarkable discoveries of inscriptions and drawings were made here, including one that reads, "I bless you by Yahweh of Samaria and his Asherah." This refers to the Lord and his consort goddess, an idea that is utterly contrary to the revealed biblical beliefs, and is thus a clear example of pagan influence on God's people.)

5:15 execute vengeance. The Lord alone, as the sovereign ruler, has the right to rescue his people and punish the **nations that did not obey**. The nature of the disobedience is not mentioned, but a contrast is established in the wider context. The nations returning to the Lord receive instruction (4:1–2), while those that will not submit to his rule receive destruction (5:15).

6:1–7:20 *The Lord's Indictment and Restoration of His People.* The Lord's indictment is delivered (6:1–8), and the crisis within the covenantal relationship is described (6:9–7:7). Micah expresses trust that the Lord will bring vindication (7:8–13), and he declares that the Lord will shepherd his flock with compassion (7:14–20).

6:1–8 *Israel Accused: Covenant Violation.* In this "covenant lawsuit," Micah calls creation as a witness (vv. 1–2), and the Lord interrogates his people and provides them an opportunity to respond (v. 3), recounts his past faithfulness to them (vv. 4–5), and establishes the demands of covenantal obedience (vv. 6–8).

6:1–2 *The Prophetic Summons.* **Hear** (see also 1:2; 3:1). Micah summons the participants (Israel, the created order, Yahweh) to the trial. **case . . . indict-**

2[r]Ps. 50:1, 4; Ezek. 36:4 [s]Isa. 1:18; See Hos. 4:1
3[t]Isa. 5:4; [Jer. 2:5, 31] [u]Isa. 43:22, 23; [Mal. 1:13]
4[v]Ex. 12:51; Hos. 12:13; Amos 2:10 [w]2 Sam. 7:23 [x]Ex. 15:20; Num. 12:1, 2
5[y]See Num. 22:5 [z]Num. 25:1 [a][Judg. 5:11]
6[b][Hos. 5:6; Heb. 10:4] [c]Isa. 57:15
7[d]See 1 Sam. 15:22 [e]2 Kgs. 3:27; 16:3; 21:6; 23:10; [Lev. 18:21]
8[f][Deut. 10:12] [g][Gen. 5:22]
9[h]Isa. 30:27 [i]Isa. 10:5; 30:32

2 [r]Hear, you mountains, [s]the indictment of the LORD,
and you enduring foundations of the earth,
for the LORD has an indictment against his people,
and he will contend with Israel.

3 "O my people, [t]what have I done to you?
[u]How have I wearied you? Answer me!
4 For [v]I brought you up from the land of Egypt
and [w]redeemed you from the house of slavery,
and I sent before you Moses,
Aaron, and [x]Miriam.
5 O my people, remember [y]what Balak king of Moab devised,
and what Balaam the son of Beor answered him,
and what happened from [z]Shittim to Gilgal,
that you may know [a]the righteous acts of the LORD."

What Does the LORD Require?

6 [b]"With what shall I come before the LORD,
and bow myself before [c]God on high?
Shall I come before him with burnt offerings,
with calves a year old?
7 [d]Will the LORD be pleased with[1] thousands of rams,
with ten thousands of rivers of oil?
[e]Shall I give my firstborn for my transgression,
the fruit of my body for the sin of my soul?"
8 He has told you, O man, what is good;
and [f]what does the LORD require of you
but to do justice, and to love kindness,[2]
and to [g]walk humbly with your God?

Destruction of the Wicked

9 The voice of the LORD cries to the city—
and it is sound wisdom to fear [h]your name:
"Hear of [i]the rod and of him who appointed it![3]
10 Can I forget any longer the treasures[4] of wickedness in the house of the wicked,
and the scant measure that is accursed?

[1] Or *Will the LORD accept* [2] Or *steadfast love* [3] The meaning of the Hebrew is uncertain [4] Or *Are there still treasures*

ment. These translate the Hebrew word *rib*, which suggests a legal procedure (cf. 7:9; Isa. 41:21; 50:8; Jer. 2:9ff.). The prophet invites the Lord to set forth his case before the created cosmos (**mountains . . . foundations of the earth**), which he does in Mic. 6:3–5.

6:3–5 *Divine Interrogation and Saving Acts.* Two questions from the Lord are followed by examples of his saving acts.

6:3 my people. The Lord reminds Israel of its covenantal relationship with him. The two questions assume that the Israelites believe the Lord has wronged them. **Answer me!** challenges the Israelites to substantiate their complaints.

6:4 I brought you up . . . redeemed you . . . sent before you. The Lord directed the events surrounding the exodus (cf. Amos 3:1–2).

6:5 The mention of **Balak** and **Balaam** (Numbers 22–24) reminds the Israelites that the Lord longs to bless rather than curse them. **remember . . . that you may know**. The faith of God's people is strengthened in the present by recounting his covenant-keeping deliverances of the past. The people of Israel crossed the Jordan from **Shittim to Gilgal** on the final portion of their journey (Joshua 2–4). At Shittim the covenant was broken (Num. 25:1–9), and at Gilgal it was renewed (Joshua 5).

6:6–8 *People's Response and Prophetic Reply.* These words are the direct response to the divine address in vv. 3–5. The unit is composed of questions (vv. 6–7) and a reply (v. 8).

6:6–7 With what shall I come before the LORD? This is *the* question for all people in every age. "LORD . . . **God on high**." The covenantal Lord is also the transcendent God. **Shall I give . . . ?** The values of the sacrifices escalate in an attempt to discern the price for entering God's presence. The way in which the proposals increase in absurdity, ending with an outrage (**ten thousands of rivers of oil . . . my firstborn**), shows that Micah is exposing an attitude that wrongly sees sacrifice as an entry fee, rather than as an avenue for God to administer grace and forgiveness to the penitent (who will express thanks as v. 8 describes). For more on the prophets' approach to sacrifice, see note on Amos 4:4–5.

6:8 The Lord desires the primary forms of love—justice (**do justice**), mercy (**love kindness**), and faithfulness (**walk humbly**)—as the expressed response of his people to his redemptive acts (Matt. 23:23; cf. Deut. 10:12–13; 1 Sam. 15:22; Isa. 1:11–17; Hos. 6:6). On the meaning of "justice," see notes on Isa. 42:1; Jer. 22:3; Amos 5:7. **your God**. The complement to "my people" (Mic. 6:3, 5).

6:9–7:7 *Crisis in Relationship.* The Lord's "lawsuit" continues with the city and its people indicted for specific crimes (6:9–12). The divine sentence is delivered (6:13–16), and the consequences are envisioned (7:1–6).

6:9–12 *Divine Indictment of Treachery.* After an introductory statement, direct charges of injustice, violence, and deception are leveled against the city.

6:9 the city. Probably Jerusalem and its inhabitants, who should be the paradigm of godliness for the world.

6:10–11 treasures of wickedness . . . wicked scales. The difficult Hebrew

11 Shall I acquit the man [j]with wicked scales
and with a bag of deceitful weights?
12 Your[1] rich men are [k]full of violence;
your inhabitants [l]speak lies,
and [m]their tongue is deceitful in their mouth.
13 Therefore I strike you with a grievous blow,
[n]making you desolate because of your sins.
14 [o]You shall eat, but not be satisfied,
and there shall be hunger within you;
you shall put away, but not preserve,
and what you preserve I will give to the sword.
15 [p]You shall sow, but not reap;
you shall tread olives, but not anoint yourselves with oil;
you shall tread grapes, but not drink wine.
16 For you have kept the statutes of [q]Omri,[2]
and all the works of the house of [r]Ahab;
and you have walked in their counsels,
that I may make you [s]a desolation, and your[3] inhabitants [s]a hissing;
so you shall bear [t]the scorn of my people."

Wait for the God of Salvation

7 1 Woe is me! For I have become
[u]as when the summer fruit has been gathered,
as when the grapes have been gleaned:
there is no cluster to eat,
no [v]first-ripe fig that my soul desires.
2 [w]The godly has perished from the earth,
and [x]there is no one upright among mankind;
[y]they all lie in wait for blood,
and [z]each hunts the other with a net.
3 [a]Their hands are on what is evil, to do it well;
[b]the prince and [c]the judge ask for a bribe,
and the great man utters the evil desire of his soul;
thus they weave it together.
4 The best of them is [d]like a brier,
the most upright of them a thorn hedge.

[1] Hebrew *whose* [2] Hebrew *For the statutes of Omri are kept* [3] Hebrew *its*

11 [j]See Hos. 12:7
12 [k]Amos 3:10; Hab. 1:2, 3 [l]Hos. 7:13 [m]Jer. 9:8
13 [n]ch. 7:13
14 [o]Hos. 4:10
15 [p][Zeph. 1:13; Hag. 1:6]
16 [q]1 Kgs. 16:25, 26; [ch. 1:13] [r]See 1 Kgs. 16:30-33; 21:25, 26 [s]See 2 Chr. 29:8 [t]Isa. 25:8

Chapter 7

1 [u]Isa. 24:13; [Isa. 17:6] [v]Hos. 9:10
2 [w][Ps. 12:1; Isa. 57:1] [x]Ps. 14:1, 3 [y][Ps. 10:9; Hos. 6:8, 9] [z]Isa. 9:19
3 [a][Zeph. 3:7] [b][Ps. 82:1, 2] [c]ch. 3:11
4 [d][2 Sam. 23:6, 7; Nah. 1:10]; See Ezek. 2:6

of v. 10a (see ESV footnote) is clarified by the parallel in v. 11: the Lord cannot tolerate his people's gaining wealth by unjust business practices (Prov. 11:1; 16:11; 20:10).

6:12 tongue is deceitful. Deceptive speech corresponds naturally with deceptive scales (v. 11).

6:13–16 *Divine Sentence for Treachery.* A summary judgment (v. 13) is followed by examples of covenant curses (vv. 14–15) and then a fitting concluding statement of the Lord's case (v. 16).

6:13 Therefore I strike you . . . , making you desolate. The Lord himself delivers the sentence. This general statement of judgment connects the previously discussed wickedness (vv. 10–12) with the specific sentence that follows (vv. 14–15).

6:14–15 You shall sow, but not reap. These illustrative covenant curses, focusing attention throughout with the personal pronoun **you**, emphasize the ultimate futility of the people's activities (cf. Deut. 28:30–31, 38–40; Amos 5:11; Zeph. 1:13; Hag. 1:6). God controls their weather and their crops; therefore, the people's turning from God brings severe economic consequences.

6:15 olives. Olive presses from as early as the eighth to seventh centuries B.C. have been discovered at the sites of Gezer, Tell Beit Mirsim, Beth-shemesh, and Tell Dan. Normal operation is that an upper stone is rolled over olives in the depression of a lower stone; the weight of the upper stone squeezes out the oil, which is then saved in a vat.

6:16 Omri and **Ahab** are mentioned only here in all the Minor Prophets. Micah refers to the corrupting influence of these northern kings on the southern kingdom of Judah (cf. 1 Kings 16:25–33). **walked in their counsels**. Replacing the true counselor (Mic. 4:9) with the counsels of these wicked human kings led to **desolation . . . hissing . . . scorn**: the city becomes like its inhabitants, disparaged and belittled. **my people**. Hope remains because they still bear this title.

7:1–7 *Consequences of Disobedience: Social Upheaval.* In light of the curses (6:13–15), Micah laments the loss of godliness (7:1–4) and the grave disloyalty even among the closest of family members (vv. 5–6). The unit concludes with a declaration of hope in God's salvation (v. 7).

7:1–2 summer fruit has been gathered . . . grapes have been gleaned. . . . The godly has perished. In gleaning the fields of the summer harvest, one expects to find leftovers. Micah's search yields no remainder—i.e., no godly remnant—only sorrow and futility (Isa. 17:6; Mic. 6:14–15).

7:3 The "asking" of the **prince** and **judge** and "uttering" of the **great man** highlight the unrelenting demands of corrupt leadership.

7:4 day of your watchmen. As the lookout on the city wall warned of approaching danger, so the prophet announced the approaching judgment (Ezek. 3:16–21; 33:7–9; Hos. 9:8). **your punishment . . . their confusion**. The referents may be the notables of Mic. 7:3. The confusion is illuminated by the examples that follow (vv. 5–6).

The day of [e]your watchmen, of your punishment, has come;
[f]now their confusion is at hand.
5 [g]Put no trust in a neighbor;
have no confidence in a friend;
guard [h]the doors of your mouth
from her who lies in your arms;[1]
6 for [i]the son treats the father with contempt,
the daughter rises up against her mother,
the daughter-in-law against her mother-in-law;
[j]a man's enemies are the men of his own house.
7 But as for me, I will look to the LORD;
[k]I will wait for the God of my salvation;
my God will hear me.

8 [l]Rejoice not over me, O [m]my enemy;
[n]when I fall, I shall rise;
[o]when I sit in darkness,
the LORD will be a light to me.
9 [p]I will bear the indignation of the LORD
because I have sinned against him,
until [q]he pleads my cause
and executes judgment for me.
[r]He will bring me out to the light;
I shall look upon his vindication.
10 Then [s]my enemy will see,
and shame will cover her who [t]said to me,
"Where is the LORD your God?"
[u]My eyes will look upon her;
now she will be trampled down
[v]like the mire of the streets.

11 [w]A day for the building of your walls!
In that day the boundary shall be far extended.
12 In that day they[2] will come to you,
[y]from Assyria and the cities of Egypt,
and from Egypt to [z]the River,
[a]from sea to sea and from mountain to mountain.
13 But [b]the earth will be desolate
because of its inhabitants,
for the fruit of their deeds.

[1] Hebrew *bosom* [2] Hebrew *he*

4 [e]See Ezek. 33:2 [f][ch. 3:6, 7; Isa. 22:5]
5 [g]Jer. 9:4 [h][Ps. 141:3]
6 [i]Ezek. 22:7; [Matt. 10:21, 35; Luke 12:53] [j]Cited Matt. 10:36
7 [k][Lam. 3:26]
8 [l][Jer. 50:11; Lam. 4:21] [m]ver. 10 [n]Ps. 37:24 [o]Ps. 112:4
9 [p][Jer. 10:19] [q]See 1 Sam. 24:15 [r]Ps. 37:6
10 [s]ver. 8 [t]See Joel 2:17 [u]ch. 4:11 [v]Ps. 18:42; See 2 Sam. 22:43
11 [w][Ps. 102:13]
12 [y][Isa. 11:11, 16; 19:23, 24; 27:13; Hos. 11:11; Zech. 10:10] [z]See Gen. 31:21 [a]Zech. 9:10
13 [b]ch. 6:13

7:5–6 Both societal and familial relationships have disintegrated in a city under siege. **daughter-in-law against her mother-in-law**. Cf. Matt. 10:35–36.

7:7 But as for me contrasts Micah with the unfaithful leaders of vv. 3–4 (cf. 3:8), while **I will look** identifies Micah with the watchmen of 7:4. "Look" and "watchmen" are forms of the same Hebrew verb. **I will wait . . . my God will hear me**. This unit, which began with a cry of mourning (vv. 1–2), ends with the quiet confidence that God will act.

7:8–13 *Zion's Repentance and Renewed Faith in Yahweh's Help.* Zion's humiliation is affirmed to be both God's just judgment and his gracious liberation as the roles with the enemy are reversed. The speakers are not identified but are probably personified cities.

7:8 I fall . . . rise . . . I sit in darkness . . . light. The city is likened to a prisoner of war, near death and in a dungeon of gloom, yet the Lord provides the sure hope of freedom.

7:9 indignation of the LORD . . . he pleads my cause. The city recognizes that it suffers the Lord's judgment because of its sin, but now sees the Lord as its advocate in a court case (see note on 6:1–2). **out to the light . . . his vindication**. The rightness and justice of the Lord's action are "seen" in the freeing of the prisoner and the shaming of the enemy. Both sides will "see" it.

7:10 shame will cover. . . . My eyes will look upon her. A reversal of roles takes place: those nations that earlier desired to "see" Zion defiled (4:11) are now open to public scorn. **Where is the LORD your God?** This taunting question disputes not God's existence but his ability to save his people from distress.

7:11–12 Three activities of that future **day** bind these verses together. (1) **building . . . walls**. The enemy "now trampled" (v. 10) contrasts with the rising security (cf. v. 8) of Zion's walls. (2) **boundary . . . extended**. Beyond security, there is a promise of territorial expansion (Ex. 23:31; Isa. 26:15; 54:2–3). (3) **They will come** refers to the gathered remnant (Isa. 11:11–12; Zech. 10:9–10) and the nations (Mic. 4:1–2; Zech. 14:16). **Assyria . . . Egypt . . . sea . . . mountain**. These geographical entities express the extensive scope of salvation going out to all the Gentiles.

7:13 desolate. In this summary expression of the eschatological picture, safety is found only within Jerusalem's wide and secure borders. Outside there is only a wasteland.

14 [c]Shepherd your people [d]with your staff,
the flock of your inheritance,
who dwell alone in a forest
[e]in the midst of [f]a garden land;[1]
let them graze in Bashan and Gilead
as in the days of old.
15 [g]As in the days when you came out of the land of Egypt,
I will show them[2] marvelous things.
16 [h]The nations shall see and be ashamed of all their might;
[i]they shall lay their hands on their mouths;
their ears shall be deaf;
17 [j]they shall lick the dust like a serpent,
like the crawling things of the earth;
[k]they shall come trembling out of their strongholds;
[l]they shall turn in dread to the LORD our God,
and they shall be in fear of you.

God's Steadfast Love and Compassion

18 [m]Who is a God like you, [n]pardoning iniquity
and passing over transgression
[n] for the remnant of his inheritance?
[o]He does not retain his anger forever,
because he delights in steadfast love.
19 He will [p]again have compassion on us;
[q]he will tread our iniquities underfoot.
[r]You will cast all our[3] sins
into the depths of the sea.
20 [s]You will show faithfulness to Jacob
and steadfast love to Abraham,
[t]as you have sworn to our fathers
from the days of old.

[1] Hebrew *of Carmel* [2] Hebrew *him* [3] Hebrew *their*

14[c]Ps. 28:9; [ch. 5:4] [d]Ps. 23:4 [e]Jer. 50:19; [Zech. 10:10] [f]See Josh. 19:26
15[g]Ps. 78:12; See Isa. 11:16
16[h][Isa. 26:11; 52:15] [i]See Judg. 18:19
17[j]Ps. 72:9; Isa. 49:23 [k]Ps. 18:45 [l][ch. 4:1]
18[m]See Ex. 15:11 [n]Jer. 50:20; See Ex. 34:7 [o]Ps. 103:9
19[p]Ps. 80:14 [q][Rom. 6:14] [r][Isa. 38:17]
20[s][Luke 1:72, 73] [t]Ps. 105:9, 10

7:14–20 *Restoration of the Relationship between Israel and Yahweh.* This section begins with a prayer that, in shepherding his flock, the Lord will silence the nations (vv. 14–17). The final words of the prophecy focus on the Lord's faithfulness and compassion expressed in the restoration of the covenant relationship (vv. 18–20).

7:14 Shepherd your people . . . your inheritance is a request that Israel's sole possessor would feed and protect the nation (Deut. 32:9; Ps. 28:9; 78:70–71). **Bashan and Gilead.** These fertile areas east of the Jordan were among the first lands that Israel gained (Josh. 13:19–31) and the first lands lost (2 Kings 10:32–33; Jer. 50:19).

7:15 This statement is the literary "center" of vv. 14–17. The Lord has acted in the past, and he will do so again. **when you came out**. The people of God in all ages are included in the deliverance from Egypt (cf. Deut. 5:3). **marvelous things**. This term is associated with the Lord's acts before Pharaoh (Ex. 3:20).

7:16–17 see and be ashamed. "Sight and shame" describe what the nations experience when they observe God's power (cf. v. 10). **the LORD our God**. The shepherd of v. 14 is now identified. **fear**. The similar sound and spelling of "graze" (Hb. *yir'u*, v. 14), "see" (Hb. *yir'u*, v. 16), and "fear" (Hb. *yire'u*, v. 17) clarify the interaction of the Lord with Israel and the nations. God's people are fed, and the nations fear (cf. Ex. 15:14–16).

7:18 Who is a God like you . . . ? The question underscores the peerless nature of the God who defends and pardons his people (Ex. 15:11; Deut. 3:24; Ps. 35:10; 89:5–8; cf. Mic. 7:10). **because he delights in steadfast love**. This provides the basis for why God forgives and relents of his anger. The divine and prophetic confrontation as a result of Israel's sin (1:5; 3:8) yields to the feeding (7:14) and forgiving of his inheritance (Jer. 50:17–20).

7:19 cast . . . into the depths. As God cast Pharaoh's armies into the sea (Ex. 15:4), so he will deal decisively with the sins of his people (cf. Jer. 31:34).

7:20 faithfulness . . . steadfast love . . . you have sworn. The book rightly concludes by summarizing the foundational attributes and actions of the covenant-keeping Lord (Ex. 34:6–7; Deut. 4:31; 7:12). **the days of old**. God's character (his steadfast love) moves him to keep his word (his faithfulness), and thus the old promises to **our fathers** (Abraham and Jacob) still stand.

INTRODUCTION TO

NAHUM

Author and Title

The book is named after its author, the prophet Nahum of Elkosh. His name means "comfort." The message given to him by God, that Nineveh would be destroyed, brings comfort to Judah. The location of Elkosh is uncertain, although the date (see below) and the address to Judah (1:15) make it likely that Nahum was from Judah.

Date

Nahum refers to the fall of Thebes as a well-known occurrence (3:8–10). The Assyrian king Ashurbanipal took the city in 664/663 B.C. Nahum also predicts the fall of Nineveh, the capital of Assyria, as a future event. Nineveh fell to a coalition of Medes and Babylonians in 612 B.C. (see note on 2:3–4). The book was composed, therefore, between 664/663 and 612 B.C.

This range can be further narrowed. The book implies that Nineveh (and Assyria) was still at or near the height of its power (cf. 1:12a; 2:11–13; 3:1, 4b) and that Judah was still firmly under Assyrian control (from which the Lord would free them; 1:12b–13, 15; 2:2). Assyria remained at the zenith of its might until 640 B.C., after which it began to weaken, and rapid decline set in after the death of the last great Assyrian emperor, Ashurbanipal (669–627).

Further, Josiah, king of Judah (640–609 B.C.), began a religious reformation in the twelfth year of his reign (628/627; cf. 2 Chron. 34:3), about the time that Ashurbanipal died. The extension of Josiah's reforming efforts beyond Judah's borders (2 Chron. 34:6–7) probably indicates that Assyrian control over Judah and neighboring regions had come to an end.

Taking these dates into consideration, the book was likely composed after c. 660 B.C. and before 630.

Theme

Nineveh, the arrogant capital of the Assyrian Empire, would be destroyed.

Purpose, Occasion, and Background

Nahum was God's messenger to announce the fall of Nineveh and the complete overthrow of Assyria. This coming judgment from the Lord was certain and irrevocable, as was Obadiah's message concerning Edom.

Nahum's book is a sequel to, and a dramatic contrast with, the book of Jonah. Jonah's mission to Nineveh was probably sometime in the first half of the eighth century B.C. He was to warn that large city of God's impending judgment because of Nineveh's wickedness. To Jonah's dismay, the Ninevites heeded his message, repented, and were spared God's judgment.

This repentance, however, did not last beyond 745 B.C., when Tiglath-pileser III (745–728/727) made his people the leading military power in the Near East. The vast Assyrian Empire was established by bloodshed and massacre, cruelty and torture, destruction, plundering, and exiling such as has seldom been seen in history. After several campaigns, Tiglath-pileser greatly enlarged the territory paying him homage with annexed land and vassal kingdoms, including the northern kingdom of Israel (reduced in size by the Assyrians) and the southern kingdom of Judah. Succeeding rulers maintained and expanded this empire. In 722 B.C. the Assyrians brought to an end the northern kingdom of Israel.

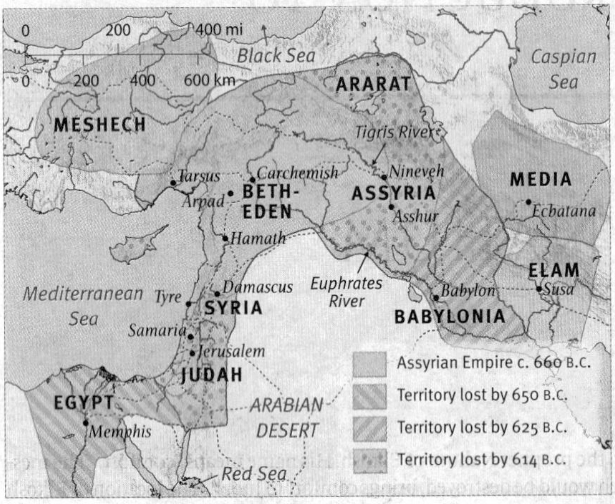

The Near East at the Time of Nahum
c. 660–614 B.C.
Nahum likely prophesied sometime between the zenith of Assyria's power around 664 B.C. and the fall of Nineveh in 612. During this time the Assyrian Empire was in decline as Egypt, Judah, and Babylonia (with the help of the Medes) regained autonomy and eroded the power of Assyria. Nahum foretold of the fall of Nineveh, the capital of the mighty Assyrian Empire.

Sennacherib (reigned 704–681 B.C.) made Nineveh the capital of his kingdom (c. 700). His energetic building program included a splendid palace, water-supply and water-control projects, and a massive wall to surround the expanded city. Nineveh was destroyed in 612 B.C., never to be restored, marking the end of Assyria. A small remnant of Assyrians did escape the city, fleeing to Haran and making Ashur-uballit II "king of Assyria." In 610 B.C., though, Haran fell to the Babylonians and their allies. Ashur-uballit retreated, but in 609 B.C., with Egyptian help, he tried to recapture Haran. That attempt failed, and Ashur-uballit and the Assyrians disappeared from history.

Key Themes

1. Nahum proclaims that the Lord is slow to anger and long-suffering, a jealous God (for his own honor, and for his people), wrathful and avenging (against his enemies), the one who controls nations and history, just, righteous, the majestic ruler of nature, good, merciful, gracious, loving, faithful, and the deliverer and protector of those who trust in him.
2. God had used Assyria as his scourge on unfaithful Israel (both northern and southern kingdoms), but he in turn brought well-deserved judgment on Assyria, according to his timetable and method.
3. Nineveh fell not because it was a large, wealthy, Gentile commercial city, but because it was a godless and idolatrous city, a city of violence, lust, and greed.
4. The Lord of history is a "stronghold" for "those who take refuge in him" (1:7). He can handle any and all problems in their individual lives. He has defeated powers far greater than Assyria. He grants to his own the ultimate deliverance and vindication.

History of Salvation Summary

Although God had used the Assyrians to chasten the wayward southern kingdom, he did not allow Judah to be annihilated. God's plan, that the Messiah would come from the line of David, would not be thwarted. The religious feasts of Judah, which God encouraged them to keep (1:15), would have reminded them of the future Savior. (For an explanation of the "History of Salvation," see the Overview of the Bible, pp. 23–26. See also History of Salvation in the Old Testament: Preparing the Way for Christ, pp. 2635–2661.)

Literary Features

The prophetic book of Nahum consists entirely of oracles of judgment, with no oracles of redemption or blessing, though a future restoration of Judah is indicated in passing. The second half of the book includes taunts, pronouncements of woe (sometimes called "the woe formula"), and vivid narratives of destruction. In a sense, the whole book is an extended taunt. Since the imagery and motifs are consistently military in reference (with God pictured as a divine warrior), the book can be considered war poetry.

The book of Nahum is constructed on a simple two-part plan. Chapter 1 is a prelude to battle. Chapters 2–3 move from preview to actual battle, pictured as a series of oracles of judgment against Nineveh and vivid pictures of her destruction (narrated as if by an eyewitness reporter).

Outline

I. Introduction (1:1)

II. A Psalm Descriptively Praising the Lord (1:2–8)
  A. The Lord takes vengeance on his guilty adversaries (1:2–3a)
  B. The Lord rules creation in majesty, and no one can stand before his wrath (1:3b–6)
  C. The Lord delivers those who take refuge in him (1:7)
  D. The Lord destroys his adversaries (1:8)

III. The Lord's Coming Judgment on Nineveh and Deliverance of Judah (1:9–15)
  A. The destruction of wicked, plotting Nineveh (1:9–12a)
  B. Judah, having been afflicted by the Lord, is freed from Assyrian bondage (1:12b–13)
  C. The termination of vile, idolatrous Nineveh (1:14)
  D. Peace and deliverance for Judah (1:15)

IV. Focus on Nineveh: The Lord's Coming Judgment (2:1–13)
  A. The beginning of the attack on Nineveh (2:1)
  B. Reasons for judgment: the Assyrians' plundering of Judah, though Judah's restoration by God is planned (2:2)
  C. Attacking soldiers and military action at Nineveh (2:3–5)
  D. The fall and plundering of Nineveh (2:6–9)
  E. A taunting song portraying Nineveh's destruction because of the city's lust for conquest (2:10–12)
  F. The Lord speaks a word of judgment (2:13)

V. Again, Focus on Nineveh: More concerning the Lord's Coming Judgment (3:1–19)
  A. Reasons for judgment: the violence, lying, and greed of Nineveh (3:1)
  B. Military action at Nineveh and the ensuing slaughter of the Assyrians (3:2–3)
  C. Reasons for judgment: the wickedness of Nineveh (3:4)
  D. The Lord speaks a word of judgment (3:5–7)
  E. Comparison with the conquest of Thebes (3:8–11)
  F. A taunting song presenting Nineveh's inevitable destruction because of the city's incessant evil (3:12–19)

NAHUM

1 [a]An oracle concerning [b]Nineveh. The book of the vision of Nahum of Elkosh.

God's Wrath Against Nineveh

2 [c]The LORD is a jealous and avenging God;
the LORD is avenging and wrathful;
[d]the LORD takes vengeance on his adversaries
and [e]keeps wrath for his enemies.
3 [f]The LORD is slow to anger and [g]great in power,
and [h]the LORD will by no means clear the guilty.
[i]His way is in whirlwind and storm,
and the clouds are the dust of his feet.
4 [j]He rebukes the sea and makes it dry;
he dries up all the rivers;
[k]Bashan and [l]Carmel wither;
the bloom of [k]Lebanon withers.
5 [m]The mountains quake before him;
[n]the hills melt;
the earth heaves before him,
[o]the world and all who dwell in it.
6 [p]Who can stand before his indignation?
Who can endure the heat of his anger?
His wrath [q]is poured out like fire,
and [r]the rocks are broken into pieces by him.
7 [s]The LORD is good,
[t]a stronghold in the day of trouble;
[u]he knows those who take refuge in him.

Chapter 1

1 [a]See Isa. 13:1 [b]ch. 2:8; 3:7; See Jonah 1:2
2 [c]See Ex. 20:5 [d][Ps. 92:9] [e][Ps. 103:9]
3 [f]See Ex. 34:6 [g]Job 9:4; Ps. 147:5 [h]See Ex. 34:7 [i][Ps. 97:2]; See Ps. 18:9-13
4 [j]Ps. 106:9; [Isa. 50:2] [k]Isa. 33:9 [l]See Josh. 19:26
5 [m][Jer. 4:24; Hab. 3:6] [n]Amos 9:13 [o]Ps. 98:7
6 [p][Mal. 3:2] [q]2 Chr. 34:21; [Ps. 79:6] [r]Ezek. 38:20
7 [s]Jer. 33:11; See Ps. 100:5 [t]Ps. 46:1; Isa. 25:4 [u]Ps. 1:6; John 10:14, 27; 1 Cor. 8:3; 2 Tim. 2:19

1:1 *Introduction.* The double title in this superscription for the book is unique in the OT: **oracle** (Hb. *massa'*) denotes a prophetic utterance or proclamation (see note on Hab. 1:1), and **vision** (Hb. *khazon*) indicates how God communicated the contents of the book to Nahum. In Nahum, the name **Nineveh** occurs again only in 2:8 and 3:7.

1:2–8 *A Psalm Descriptively Praising the Lord.* This praise is general in nature, describing God as he has been and will be throughout world history.

1:2–3a *The Lord Takes Vengeance on His Guilty Adversaries.* The Lord is **jealous** with regard to his own honor and those in covenant fellowship with him. **avenging**. God's holy anger is righteous and just, in defense of his word and his people. **keeps wrath**. God holds back the venting of his anger until an appropriate time (cf. Ps. 103:9). **slow to anger** (Ex. 34:6). God's patience explains why the wicked often do not immediately receive the judgment they deserve (cf. Ezek. 33:11). **great in power**. The delay in deserved judgment is not due to a lack of power or control on God's part. **will by no means clear the guilty** (cf. Ex. 34:7). That the wicked seemingly prosper does not mean God regards them as innocent or has forgotten their iniquity.

1:3b–6 *The Lord Rules Creation in Majesty, and No One Can Stand before His Wrath.* God's interaction with, and his effect on, nature and the natural world is described in figurative language illustrating God's awesome majesty and omnipotence.

1:3b whirlwind and storm. A possible polemic against the storm-god(s) theology of many ancient Near Eastern religions.

1:4–5 rebukes the sea . . . dries up . . . rivers. Cf. the exodus (Exodus 14) and conquest (Joshua 3–4). **Bashan**, a northern Transjordanian region, was famous for its rich pasturelands. **Carmel**, a mountain next to the Mediterranean Sea and close to Lower Galilee, was well known for its beauty and luxuriant countryside. **Lebanon**, a mountainous region just to the north of Israel, was noted for its forests. For a similar reference to these three regions, see Isa. 33:9. **Hills** and **mountains** are symbols of permanence and immovability, but even they cannot stand before God.

1:6 wrath. See v. 2. **Fire** is a frequent image used in the OT to emphasize God's fierce and all-consuming wrath (e.g., Gen. 19:24; Ps. 11:6; Amos 5:6). **Rocks** represent the hardest objects in nature, easily shattered by the Lord.

1:7 *The Lord Delivers Those Who Take Refuge in Him.* In contrast to his anger, God is **good** to his people, blessing those who trust in him. **stronghold**. The Lord is the never-failing protector of his people. He will keep them safe and rescue them from human and spiritual enemies (e.g., Ps. 27:1; 37:39;

8[v][Isa. 30:28] [w]Isa. 8:22
9[x][Isa. 10:7] [y][Jer. 4:27]
10[z]See Mic. 7:4 [a]See Joel 2:5
11[b][ver. 9; 2 Kgs. 19:22, 23]
12[c]Isa. 10:33, 34; [Isa. 37:36] [d]ver. 9; [Isa. 9:1]
13[e][Isa. 9:4; 10:27; 14:25]
14[f][Ps. 109:13] [g][2 Kgs. 19:37] [h][Isa. 30:33]; See Ezek. 32:21-23 [i][ch. 3:6]

8 But [v]with an overflowing flood
he will make a complete end of the adversaries,[1]
and [w]will pursue his enemies into darkness.
9 What [x]do you plot against the LORD?
[y]He will make a complete end;
trouble will not rise up a second time.
10 For they are [z]like entangled thorns,
like drunkards as they drink;
[a]they are consumed like stubble fully dried.
11 From you came one
[b]who plotted evil against the LORD,
a worthless counselor.
12 Thus says the LORD,
"Though they are at full strength and many,
[c]they will be cut down and pass away.
[d]Though I have afflicted you,
I will afflict you no more.
13 And now [e]I will break his yoke from off you
and will burst your bonds apart."
14 The LORD has given commandment about you:
[f]"No more shall your name be perpetuated;
from [g]the house of your gods I will cut off
the carved image and the metal image.
[h]I will make your grave, [i]for you are vile."

[1] Hebrew *of her place*

Isa. 17:10; Jer. 16:19). God **knows** his people with love and affection, which results in his benevolent actions.

1:8 *The Lord Destroys His Adversaries.* A striking contrast to v. 7. This alternation at the end of the first major section (vv. 2–8) sets the pattern for a similar alternation in the next section (vv. 9–15). The description in v. 8 of God dealing with his "enemies" echoes v. 2. Like an **overflowing flood**, God's judgment is overwhelming; Nineveh was to be destroyed by a flood (see 2:6, 8). **complete end . . . darkness**. God's judgment will culminate with removal from this life and everlasting damnation.

1:9–15 *The Lord's Coming Judgment on Nineveh and Deliverance of Judah.* The preceding section (vv. 2–8) presented in a general way the omnipotent cosmic monarch's attitude toward, and action with, his enemies and his people. In this section (vv. 9–15) the focus turns to Nineveh and Judah, alternating between the Lord's coming judgment on Nineveh and his deliverance of Judah.

1:9–12a *The Destruction of Wicked, Plotting Nineveh.* God addresses Nineveh, saying that in spite of her plots and might, she will fall.

1:9 You is masculine plural in Hebrew, presumably addressing the Assyrians (cf. the superscription in v. 1, "concerning Nineveh," the capital of Assyria). **plot**. Plots to harm God's people are ultimately **against the LORD** himself. **complete end**. See v. 8; here it is specifically applied to Nineveh. **Trouble** (cf. v. 7) is what Judah experienced because of oppressive Assyria.

1:10 Entangled thorns can be thrown en masse into the fire, just as the Assyrians as a whole will be wiped out. **Like drunkards**, the Assyrians will be unable to defend themselves successfully against their attackers. The image of burning dry **stubble**, a frequent one in the OT, conveys the sense of quick extermination.

1:11 You is feminine singular in Hebrew and thus refers to the city of Nineveh (see v. 9). **one who . . . worthless counselor**. Either a reference to a particular wicked Assyrian king or to the series of evil Assyrian kings who reigned in Nineveh after Sennacherib made that city the capital (see Introduction: Purpose, Occasion, and Background).

1:12a they. The Assyrians. **full strength**. Assyria was likely at the height of its power when Nahum wrote (see Introduction: Date). **many**. The Assyrian army was large enough to manage a number of extensive conquests (e.g., 2 Kings 19:35) and maintain control of the empire for lengthy periods of time. **will be cut down and pass away**. God would end the military dominance of the Assyrians, and they would pass from the pages of history (see Introduction: Purpose, Occasion, and Background).

1:12b–13 *Judah, Having Been Afflicted by the Lord, Is Freed from Assyrian Bondage.* The Assyrian yoke was only temporary, for God's purposes.

1:12b Though I have afflicted you. Suddenly God addresses Judah (see v. 15). This dramatic change in the flow of v. 12, the direct address, and the initial anonymity of the addressee were attention-getting devices emphasizing the announcement of good news that follows. God had used the Assyrians to chasten wayward Judah. **I will afflict you no more**. Since God would overthrow Nineveh, the Assyrians would never again be Judah's scourge.

1:13 His yoke refers to the burdensome rule of the Assyrian monarchs (cf. v. 11) over Judah. About 734/733 B.C., during the reign of Ahaz (2 Kings 16:7–8), the southern kingdom had become a vassal state of Assyria. This involved paying heavy tribute to the Assyrians (cf. 2 Kings 18:13–16) and other oppressive measures. When Judah revolted under Hezekiah, the Assyrians in 701 B.C. devastated the land (2 Kings 18:13; Isa. 7:18–25; 8:5–8) and took away many people and much plunder. **break . . . burst**. The vassalage of Judah lasted until the reign of Josiah (640–609 B.C.), when Assyria began to decline rapidly and finally ceased to be a nation (see Introduction: Date).

1:14 *The Termination of Vile, Idolatrous Nineveh.* **You** is masculine singular in Hebrew. Nahum suddenly switches to directly addressing the Assyrian king(s) (see v. 11): the Assyrian monarchy would come to a decisive end. This implies the total conquest of Assyria and the irreversible fall of Nineveh. **the house of your gods I will cut off**. Complete defeat of the Assyrian ruler would also be marked by the desecration of his temple and the destruction or removal of his idols, which represented the gods who he believed gave him power, wealth, and descendants. Archaeologists have noted the complete destruction that Nineveh's temples underwent.

15[1] [j]Behold, upon the mountains, [k]the feet of him
who brings good news,
who publishes peace!
[l]Keep your feasts, O Judah;
[m]fulfill your vows,
[n]for never again shall the worthless pass through you;
he is utterly cut off.

15[j]See Isa. 52:7 [k][Rom. 10:15] [l][Isa. 30:29] [m]See Num. 30:2 [n][ver. 12]; See Joel 3:17

[1] Ch 2:1 in Hebrew

1:15 *Peace and Deliverance for Judah.* This verse concludes the second major portion of the book (vv. 9–15). Nahum returns to addressing Judah. What he has foretold with regard to Nineveh, the Assyrian monarchy, and the Assyrians he now considers as good as accomplished. **upon the mountains**. The imagery is that of a messenger bearing the **good news** of the fall and devastation of Nineveh. The people first catch sight of him running along the Judean mountains (cf. Isa. 52:7). **peace**. Judah does not have to be afraid of any more military action and oppression coming from Assyria (on peace in the OT and NT, cf. note on John 14:27). **Keep your feasts**. These festivals would remind the people of the Lord's past acts of deliverance and the future hope of the coming Messiah. At the feasts they would also, as a nation, worship the Lord and give him proper thanks and praise. **fulfill your vows**. Some in Judah voluntarily made vows to the Lord to give him thank offerings. **the worthless**. I.e., the Assyrians (cf. Nah. 1:11).

2:1–13 *Focus on Nineveh: The Lord's Coming Judgment.* In this next major section of the book, the focus falls on Nineveh. Nahum's prediction reads like an eyewitness account of the city being attacked, overrun by the enemy, and plundered.

2:1 *The Beginning of the Attack on Nineveh.* **scatterer**. This word for the enemy (viewed here as a collective whole) foretells the outcome of the siege. Nineveh will be taken, and any Ninevites not slaughtered will flee before the conquerors (see 3:17–18) or be taken into exile. Ultimately, it is God who "scatters." **has come up**. A technical phrase signifying impending hostile military action (e.g., Judg. 1:1; 1 Sam. 7:7; 1 Kings 15:17; 2 Kings 18:13). **Man the ramparts**. Nineveh is told to get ready for battle. Nahum writes as if he were at Nineveh in 612 B.C., speaking to the Ninevites (with underlying sarcasm).

2:2 *Reasons for Judgment: The Assyrians' Plundering of Judah, Though Judah's Restoration by God Is Planned.* Here Nahum gives one reason for the fall of Nineveh: God had used the Assyrians as his scourge of discipline on unfaithful Judah, but this scourge would no longer be needed because **the LORD is restoring the majesty of Jacob**. The true majesty of Judah, basically what was left of the nation **Israel** (the northern tribes having been "lost" in the Assyrian exile), was spiritual, not secular or political. God separated Israel from the nations to be devoted to him; with them he made his covenants; from them would come the Messiah (Rom. 9:4–5). This majesty, then, involved having a covenant relationship with the Lord and giving evidence of that relationship in godly living. **plunderers**. The Assyrians **plundered** Judah (see Nah. 2:13). **Their branches** are the individual clans, families, or members of the southern kingdom, likened to a vineyard (cf. Isa. 5:1–7).

2:3–5 *Attacking Soldiers and Military Action at Nineveh.* Nahum describes how the invading army closes in on the city.

2:3–4 shield . . . red. Either their shields were painted red, or they were permanently stained with the blood of defeated foes from previous military campaigns. **His . . . he** is a reference to the scatterer mentioned in v. 1. The attacking army was a coalition made up of Medes and Babylonians, and possibly Scythians. Cyaxares (625–585 B.C.) was the leader of the Medes (who

Afflictions of Assyria against Israel

The Neo-Assyrian period (935–609 B.C.) brought renewed threats from the Assyrians. God used the Assyrians to chasten wayward Israel. In Nah. 1:12 the Lord tells Judah that "Though I have afflicted you [through the Assyrians], I will afflict you no longer."

Assyrian Ruler	Reign	Affliction	Significance and Biblical References
Shalmaneser III	858–824 B.C.	Exacted tribute from "Jehu, son of Omri" according to the Black Obelisk	Defeated at Qarqar in 853 B.C. by a Syrian coalition that included "Ahab the Israelite"
Adad-nirari III	811–783	Exacted tribute from Jehoash of Israel	His attacks on Damascus enabled Jehoash to recover Israelite cities lost previously to Hazael (2 Kings 13:25)
Tiglath-pileser III (Pul)	745–727	Invaded the land and exacted tribute	To avoid deportation, Menahem paid tribute to Tiglath-pileser III (Pul) (2 Kings 15:19–20); Pul deported the Transjordanian tribes (2 Kings 15:29; 1 Chron. 5:26); Pul aided Ahaz of Judah against Rezin of Damascus and Pekah of Israel (2 Kings 16:5–10; 2 Chron. 28:16–21)
Shalmaneser V	727–722	Exacted tribute from Hoshea of Israel; took the northern kingdom (Israel) into exile	Hoshea refused to pay tribute and sought Egypt for help, the Assyrians besieged Samaria (2 Kings 17:3–6; 18:9–12)
Sargon II	722–705	Took credit for the invasion and exile of the northern kingdom (Israel) that began under Shalmaneser V	Sargon II may be the unnamed king of Assyria in 2 Kings 17:6
Sennacherib	705–681	Invaded Judah	Sennacherib besieged Lachish and forced tribute from Hezekiah (2 Kings 18:13–16); he besieged Jerusalem and demanded Hezekiah's surrender (2 Kings 18:17–19:9); the Lord delivered Jerusalem from Sennacherib (2 Kings 19:10–37). See also 2 Chronicles 32; Isaiah 36–37
Esarhaddon	681–669	Exacted tribute from Manasseh of Judah	Mentioned at 2 Kings 19:37 as successor to Sennacherib (see also Ezra 4:2)
Ashurbanipal	669–627	Exacted tribute	Increasing tensions from Babylonia required Assyria's direct attention. The increased political freedom of the western city-states is reflected in the reforms instituted by Josiah

Chapter 2
1 [o][Jer. 51:20] [p][Jer. 51:12]
2 [q][Isa. 37:31] [r]See Ps. 80:8-13; Isa. 5:1-7
3 [s][Ezek. 23:14, 15]
4 [t][ch. 3:2]
5 [u]ch. 3:18 [v]Jer. 46:12
6 [w][Isa. 45:1] [x][Isa. 14:31]
7 [y][Isa. 22:8] [z]Isa. 38:14
8 [b]See ch. 1:1 [c]Jer. 46:5

2

The Destruction of Nineveh

1 [o]The scatterer has come up against you.
[p]Man the ramparts;
watch the road;
dress for battle;[1]
collect all your strength.

2 For [q]the LORD is restoring the majesty of Jacob
as the majesty of Israel,
for plunderers have plundered them
and [r]ruined their branches.

3 The shield of his mighty men is red;
[s]his soldiers are clothed in scarlet.
The chariots come with flashing metal
on the day he musters them;
the cypress spears are brandished.
4 [t]The chariots race madly through the streets;
they rush to and fro through the squares;
they gleam like torches;
they dart like lightning.
5 He remembers [u]his officers;
[v]they stumble as they go,
they hasten to the wall;
the siege tower[2] is set up.
6 [w]The river gates are opened;
the palace [x]melts away;
7 its mistress[3] is [y]stripped;[4] she is carried off,
her slave girls [z]lamenting,
moaning like doves
and beating their breasts.
8 [b]Nineveh is like a pool
whose waters run away.[5]
"Halt! Halt!" they cry,
but [c]none turns back.
9 Plunder the silver,
plunder the gold!
There is no end of the treasure
or of the wealth of all precious things.

[1] Hebrew *gird your loins* [2] Or *the mantelet* [3] The meaning of the Hebrew word rendered *its mistress* is uncertain [4] Or *exiled* [5] Compare Septuagint; the meaning of the Hebrew is uncertain

played the dominant role in the destruction of Nineveh), and Nabopolassar (626–605) led the Babylonians. The **streets** and **squares** are those of the suburbs surrounding Nineveh, the first areas to be overrun by the attacking army. **flashing metal . . . gleam like torches**. The sunlight reflects off of the metal pieces of the chariots. **dart like lightning**. This could refer again to the light reflecting, or indicate the swift movement of the chariots.

2:5 The attacking army now reaches the wall of Nineveh proper. **He remembers**. "He" (see v. 3) may be so eager to be involved in the attack that he almost forgets to delegate parts of the operation to **his officers**. These officers, eager both to join in the attack themselves and to please their superior(s), so rush into the action that they practically **stumble** over one another. Or, as they move toward Nineveh's wall, they may stumble over the wreckage in the devastated suburbs. **siege tower**. This could also be rendered "mantelet" (see ESV footnote), a covering that protects the attacking soldiers from arrows, spears, and other objects thrown down on them by the defenders on the wall.

2:6–9 *The Fall and Plundering of Nineveh.* Now Nahum takes the reader into the city as it falls to the invaders.

2:6 river gates. The Khoser River flowed through Nineveh; north of the city were dams, most likely with gates to regulate the flow of this river. The besieging coalition could easily have closed the gates (cutting off this water supply), waited until a considerable quantity of water collected, and then opened the gates. The resulting mass of water crashing against and through Nineveh would have done much damage to portions of the city's wall, system of gates, and internal structures, thus greatly aiding the besiegers. Another river that probably flowed through Nineveh was the Tebiltu, which could have been used by the coalition in the same manner. The destruction caused by the waters no doubt was a factor contributing to the short length of the siege—only three months. **The palace melts away** because of the floodwaters.

2:8 like a pool. See v. 6. **Halt . . . they cry**. Nahum places the reader in Nineveh as the city is being entered and overrun by the coalition forces. The reader "sees" the fleeing inhabitants and "hears" some of the Assyrian commanders crying out, "Halt! Stand and fight," **but none turns back** to do so. The Assyrians had terrified many, but now they themselves are filled with terror.

2:9 silver . . . gold. Nineveh was filled with tremendous wealth, due to the plunder seized during numerous military campaigns and the tribute received over the many years Assyria ruled the Near East.

10 [d]Desolate! Desolation and ruin!
[e]Hearts melt and [f]knees tremble;
[g]anguish is in all loins;
[h]all faces grow pale!
11 Where is the lions' den,
the feeding place of [i]the young lions,
where the lion and lioness went,
where his cubs were, with [j]none to disturb?
12 [k]The lion tore enough for his cubs
and [l]strangled prey for his lionesses;
he filled his caves with prey
and his dens with torn flesh.

13 [m]Behold, I am against you, declares the LORD of hosts, and [n]I will burn your[1] chariots
in smoke, and the sword shall devour your young lions. I will cut off your prey from the
earth, and [o]the voice of your messengers shall no longer be heard.

Woe to Nineveh

3

1 Woe to [p]the bloody city,
all full of lies and plunder—
[q]no end to the prey!
2 The crack of the whip, and [r]rumble of the wheel,
[s]galloping horse and [t]bounding chariot!
3 Horsemen charging,
flashing sword and [u]glittering spear,
[v]hosts of slain,
heaps of corpses,
dead bodies without end—
they stumble over the bodies!
4 And all for the countless whorings of the [w]prostitute,
[x]graceful and of deadly charms,
who betrays nations with her whorings,
and peoples with her charms.

[1] Hebrew *her*

10[d]See Zeph. 2:13-15 [e]Ps. 22:14; Isa. 13:7 [f]Dan. 5:6 [g]Isa. 21:3 [h]Joel 2:6
11[i]Isa. 5:29; Jer. 2:15 [j]See Isa. 17:2
12[k][Ezek. 19:3] [l][ver. 9; ch. 3:1]
13[m]ch. 3:5; [Zeph. 2:5]; See Ezek. 13:8 [n][Ps. 46:9] [o][2 Kgs. 19:9, 23]

Chapter 3

1[p]Ezek. 24:9; [Hab. 2:12] [q][ch. 2:12]
2[r][ch. 2:4] [s][Judg. 5:22] [t][Joel 2:5]
3[u]Hab. 3:11 [v][2 Kgs. 19:35]
4[w][Rev. 17:2; 18:3] [x][Isa. 47:9, 12]

2:10–12 *A Taunting Song Portraying Nineveh's Destruction Because of the City's Lust for Conquest.* These verses figuratively portray the obliteration of Nineveh, the extinction of Assyrian nobility, and the termination of Assyrian power.

2:10 Desolate . . . ruin is a description of Nineveh emptied of inhabitants (due to their fleeing, slaughter, or captivity) and destroyed by the victorious invaders (after they have finished their plundering). **Hearts melt . . . pale.** The Assyrians, who previously had been proud of how they terrorized other peoples, now experience extreme terror.

2:11–12 lions. Members of the Assyrian royal house (and perhaps aristocracy), headed by the king. The lion was a symbol for kingship in the ancient Near East (cf. Gen. 49:9); the Assyrian kings exhibited ferocity in their attacking and "devouring" other lands, and called themselves lions. Reliefs on palace walls depicted lions being hunted by the Assyrian rulers. **none to disturb.** During the time of Assyrian might, no other nation dared to, or could, attack Nineveh. There was none to terrify those in the city, and particularly the household of the king. **enough . . . prey . . . torn flesh.** I.e., the vast amounts of plunder taken by the "ravenous" Assyrians from their brutal, bloody conquest of numerous lands.

2:13 *The Lord Speaks a Word of Judgment.* Nahum closes the fourth major portion of the book (vv. 1–13) by quoting God's proclamation of judgment against Nineveh. The city will fall because this is the will of the Lord. In vv. 1 and 13 Nineveh is addressed ("you," "your"), and both verses express the thought "against you." **LORD of hosts.** See note on 1 Sam. 1:3. **burn your chariots.** A striking contrast to the swift chariots of the conquering coalition (Nah. 2:3–4). **sword shall devour.** The devouring pride of **lions** (vv. 11–12) shall now be devoured by the enemy. **voice . . . messengers . . . no longer be heard.** The end of the Assyrian messengers brings about the messenger of peace coming to Judah (1:15).

3:1–19 *Again, Focus on Nineveh: More concerning the Lord's Coming Judgment.* This last major section of the book repeats most of the themes of the preceding section (2:1–13). Absent in ch. 3 is a reference to the plundering of Nineveh (2:9), and new in this section is the comparison of Nineveh's downfall to the destruction of Thebes (3:8–11).

3:1 *Reasons for Judgment: The Violence, Lying, and Greed of Nineveh.* **bloody.** The Assyrians were notorious for the atrocities they committed. **lies.** Second Kings 18:31–32 is an example of lying ultimately being traced back to the king who ruled from Nineveh (cf. 2 Chron. 28:20). **plunder . . . prey.** See Nah. 2:11–13.

3:2–3 *Military Action at Nineveh and the Ensuing Slaughter of the Assyrians.* Nahum quickly flashes to a vivid picture of the coalition forces attacking and entering Nineveh and slaughtering the Assyrians (cf. 2:3–5). Again, the details seem to come from an eyewitness.

3:4 *Reasons for Judgment: The Wickedness of Nineveh.* This verse uses figurative language to present reasons for the destruction of Nineveh. **whorings.** As the capital of idolatrous Assyria, Nineveh continually engaged in many violations of God's will. **graceful . . . deadly charms.** Nineveh, with its power and wealth, exerted a corrupting influence throughout the Near East (cf. 2 Kings 16:18). **betrays.** The monarchy based in Nineveh did not hesitate to use treachery and deceit (see Nah. 3:1) to achieve its aims.

3:5–7 *The Lord Speaks a Word of Judgment.* The seductive prostitute (i.e., Nineveh; see v. 4) will receive a punishment befitting her shameful trade. The figurative language dramatically conveys the message that God will bring

5 [m] Behold, I am against you,
declares the LORD of hosts,
and [y] will lift up your skirts over your face;
and I will make nations look at [z] your nakedness
and kingdoms at your shame.
6 I will throw filth at you
and [a] treat you with contempt
and make you [b] a spectacle.
7 And all who look at you [c] will shrink from you and say,
"Wasted is [d] Nineveh; [e] who will grieve for her?"
[f] Where shall I seek comforters for you?

8 [g] Are you better than [h] Thebes[1]
that sat [i] by the Nile,
with water around her,
her rampart a sea,
and water her wall?
9 [j] Cush was her strength;
Egypt too, and that without limit;
[k] Put and the [l] Libyans were her[2] helpers.

10 [m] Yet she became an exile;
she went into captivity;
[n] her infants were dashed in pieces
at the head of every street;
for her honored men [o] lots were cast,
[p] and all her great men were bound in chains.
11 [q] You also will be drunken;
you will go into hiding;
[r] you will seek a refuge from the enemy.
12 All your fortresses are [s] like fig trees
with first-ripe figs—
if shaken they fall
into the mouth of the eater.

[1] Hebrew *No-amon* [2] Hebrew *your*

5 [m] [See ch. 2:13 above] [y] Jer. 13:22, 26; [Isa. 3:17; 47:3] [z] Hab. 2:16
6 [a] Mal. 2:9; [ch. 1:14] [b] Heb. 10:33; [1 Cor. 4:9]
7 [c] Jer. 51:9; Rev. 18:10 [d] [Zeph. 2:13]; See ch. 1:1 [e] Isa. 51:19; Jer. 15:5 [f] Lam. 1:2, 9, 16, 17, 21
8 [g] [Amos 6:2] [h] Jer. 46:25 [i] [Ezek. 29:3]
9 [j] See Dan. 11:43 [k] Gen. 10:6 [l] See 2 Chr. 12:3
10 [m] Isa. 20:4 [n] Isa. 13:16 [o] Joel 3:3; Obad. 11 [p] [Ps. 149:8]
11 [q] Jer. 25:17, 27; [Ps. 75:8; Isa. 51:17; Obad. 16] [r] [Jer. 4:5, 6]
12 [s] [Rev. 6:13]

Nineveh's wicked activity to an end and utterly humiliate the city by having it conquered and devastated. Its disgrace would be internationally known.

3:5 Behold, I am against you. Cf. 2:13. This repetition emphasizes the certainty of Nineveh's doom.

3:7 who will grieve for her? The answer to the rhetorical question is that no one will grieve or comfort, not even some of those who gave in to the enticements of the alluring prostitute (but had no real love for her). People will **shrink** back, or flee, in horror at the sight of what will happen to Nineveh.

3:8–11 *Comparison with the Conquest of Thebes.* The prophet now recalls an event that was well known in the Near East, especially to the Assyrians, at the time of his writing: the capture and destruction of the Egyptian city of Thebes by the Assyrians in 664/663 B.C. To all who think it is impossible that Nineveh would fall, Nahum says, "Look at what happened to Thebes!"

3:8 Are you better than Thebes . . . ? Nineveh was not better fortified and did not appear more invincible than Thebes, a very important, powerful city located in southern Egypt (about 400 miles/644 km from the Mediterranean). **Nile . . . water around her**. This mighty river, along with canals and channels from the Nile that surrounded most of Thebes, was an aspect of the city's strong defense system and its seeming invulnerability. **Rampart a sea** is a poetic reference to the Nile (cf. Isa. 19:5), which was about half a mile wide at Thebes. The Nile, canals, and channels formed a natural outer **wall** for the city. Nineveh did not have similar protection.

3:9 Cush was the region just south of Egypt. **Egypt** refers to military aid coming from northern Egypt. The location of **Put** is not certain; perhaps it was situated along the north African coastline, just to the west of Libya, which was just to the west of the Nile delta region of Egypt. While Thebes could count on military assistance from these different areas, Assyria could not rely on help from any region.

3:10 Despite these strategic advantages, Thebes was taken by the Assyrians, sacked, and destroyed, and its inhabitants either slaughtered or taken off as exiles. **lots were cast**. The Assyrian soldiers cast lots to determine who would get the more highly prized men (with their education and skills) as slaves.

3:11 This verse directly applies vv. 8–10: "Nineveh, you can expect the same!" Just as a **drunken** man cannot effectively defend himself against an attacker, so Nineveh will not be able to turn back its enemies. **hiding**. Figuratively, Nineveh will be conquered and humiliated such that, if it could, the city would go into hiding from fear and shame. More literally, this could refer to the remnant band of Assyrians who fled to the west and temporarily had their base at Haran (see Introduction: Purpose, Occasion, and Background). Nineveh will find no **refuge**, unlike those who put their trust in the Lord (1:7).

3:12–19 *A Taunting Song Presenting Nineveh's Inevitable Destruction Because of the City's Incessant Evil.* After finishing the analogy with Thebes, the book concludes with a taunting song presenting Nineveh's total defeat because of the city's ceaseless evil.

3:12–13 The Assyrian **fortresses** surrounding Nineveh will be the first to encounter the advancing enemy army. The coalition forces will easily and quickly take these strongholds, with two results: First, the **gates** of Assyria will be **wide open** to the **enemies** since the fortresses which guarded those entrances have been destroyed. Second, the **troops**, i.e., the soldiers within Nineveh, will be demoralized and filled with fear so that they cannot acquit themselves as men in the coming siege. **fire**. See 2:13; 3:15. **Your bars**, that is, the bars or bolts of the gates, which had kept these entrances closed.

13 Behold, your troops
[t]are women in your midst.
The gates of your land
are wide open to your enemies;
fire has devoured your bars.
14 [u]Draw water for the siege;
[r]strengthen your forts;
go into the clay;
tread the mortar;
take hold of the brick mold!
15 There will the fire devour you;
the sword will cut you off.
It will [v]devour you [w]like the locust.
Multiply yourselves [w]like the locust;
multiply [w]like the grasshopper!
16 You increased [x]your merchants
more than the stars of the heavens.
[w]The locust spreads its wings and flies away.
17 Your [z]princes are [w]like grasshoppers,
[a]your scribes[1] like clouds of locusts
settling on the fences
in a day of cold—
when the sun rises, they fly away;
no one knows where they are.
18 Your shepherds [b]are asleep,
O king of Assyria;
[c]your nobles slumber.
Your people [d]are scattered on the mountains
with none to gather them.
19 There is no easing your hurt;
[e]your wound is grievous.
All who hear the news about you
[f]clap their hands over you.
For [g]upon whom has not come
your unceasing evil?

13 [t]Isa. 19:16; Jer. 51:30
14 [u][Isa. 22:11] [r][See ver. 11 above]
15 [v][Joel 2:3] [w][Joel 1:4, 6]
16 [x][Ezek. 27:23, 24] [w][See ver. 15 above]
17 [z][Isa. 10:8] [w][See ver. 15 above] [a]Jer. 51:27
18 [b][Ps. 76:5] [c]ch. 2:5 [d][1 Kgs. 22:17]
19 [e]Jer. 10:19; Mic. 1:9 [f]Lam. 2:15; [Zeph. 2:15] [g][Isa. 37:18]

[1] Or *marshals*

3:14 As the enemy draws close, Nahum tells the city to get ready for the siege (see 2:1). However, any preparations they make will be useless. **Draw water**. The Ninevites can anticipate that the enemy will shut off the city's water supply by closing the river gates (see 2:6) and blocking the aqueduct system built by Sennacherib. Water could be stored inside the city in vessels and cisterns. **forts**. The fortresses and other fortifications at the walls and within the city would be strengthened or repaired with bricks, which were made from **clay**, shaped by molds, and held together with **mortar**.

3:15 No matter how well supplied and fortified Nineveh is, **there** the inhabitants will die. **fire**. Archaeologists have found evidence of a devastating fire at Nineveh. **sword**. Cf. 2:13. There will be mass extermination of the Ninevites, as when a **locust** plague strips the countryside of all vegetation (e.g., Joel 1:4–10). **Multiply . . . locust . . . grasshopper**. Nahum sarcastically tells the Ninevites, in preparation for the siege, to multiply themselves greatly and thus increase their strength.

3:16 You increased your merchants. When Nineveh was the proud capital of a vast empire, her merchants brought enormous wealth to the city. Now, however, these merchants, and the huge treasure in Nineveh, will do the city no good. **The locust . . . flies away**. Cf. v. 15. The enemy, having devoured all that there was in Nineveh through plundering (and slaughter and destruction), will quickly leave the scene.

3:17 Like swarms of **grasshoppers** or **locusts** that quickly **fly away** and disappear, some of the leading men of Nineveh, who for a while had been very prominent, will flee at the appearance of the enemy overrunning the city. **Scribes** were probably a type of official, perhaps "secretaries."

3:18–19 king of Assyria. Cf. 1:11. Nahum, surveying the wreckage of Nineveh, addresses its monarchy with sarcastic language. Many of Nineveh's **shepherds** (leaders and officials) and nobles are sleeping the slumber of death. Many of the **people** are forever dispersed. This verse may imply, since the king is alive to see the aftermath, that a shadow of the Assyrian monarchy would continue (briefly) after the fall of Nineveh (see Introduction: Purpose, Occasion, and Background). The **wound** that is **grievous** is a fatal injury. The Assyrian monarchy has received a mortal blow, and the absolute end is imminent. **unceasing evil**. The reign of the Assyrian emperors from Nineveh had continually caused terror and suffering. Nahum foretells that the Assyrian monarchy, and Nineveh, will experience this same evil that it meted out to other peoples of the Near East. Nahum ends his book with a rhetorical question, joining Jonah as the only other biblical writer to do so.

INTRODUCTION TO
HABAKKUK

Author and Title

Little is known about the prophet Habakkuk. He was likely a contemporary of Zephaniah and Jeremiah, and possibly even of Ezekiel and Daniel, but none of the other prophets mention him. His name appears twice in the book (1:1; 3:1), and he is clearly the main character. God commands Habakkuk to record the vision in chapter 2, and he probably also wrote chapter 3. In the apocryphal book *Bel and the Dragon*, Habakkuk is said to supply nourishment to Daniel when the latter was in the lions' den, but this work is not considered historically reliable.

Date

The only hint of a date for this book is its prediction of the Babylonian invasion of Judah (1:6), but it is unclear how far into the future this event would be (see 2:2–3). The Babylonians do not appear to be an imminent threat when Habakkuk was writing, but he seems to be very aware of their potential threat, and thus Habakkuk's time frame is probably not later than the end of Josiah's reign (640–609 B.C.). Before Josiah, Judah had radically turned away from God under the leadership of the extremely wicked kings Manasseh and Amon, and the nation was ripe for punishment (2 Kings 23:26–27). Judah was morally and spiritually corrupt, worshiping Baal on the high places, offering its children to Molech, dedicating horses to the sun god, and allowing the temple to fall into ruin. Judah experienced a significant, though short-lived, time of revival during Josiah's reign with the restoration of the temple and reinstitution of the Feast of Passover, but returned quickly to its evil ways following his death. It was a politically turbulent time as well. Assyria had ruled Judah with a heavy hand for well over a hundred years, inflicting punishment and tribute; but Assyria was beginning to weaken, and soon Babylon would be the world power. Habakkuk probably lived to see the following events: the destruction of Nineveh by Babylon in 612 B.C.; the battle of Haran in 609 in which Josiah died as he tried to hinder the Egyptians from reaching the battle; the final defeat of the Assyrians at the Battle of Carchemish (605); and possibly the fulfillment of his own prophecy of the Babylonian invasions of Judah in 605, 597, and 586.

Theme

By the end of the book, Habakkuk is a changed person—he has learned to wait and trust in God, who works out all things for his glory. Habakkuk, like Job, questions God's justice, but in the end both realize that God is sovereign and his justice is far beyond their comprehension. Habakkuk's message of judgment on Judah would not have been well accepted, for the nation had been blinded by sin while false prophets were declaring that God would not punish his chosen people. But God's justice demands that wickedness be punished, whether found in pagan nations or in his own people.

Purpose, Occasion, and Background

Habakkuk is unusual as a prophetic book in that it never addresses the people of Judah directly but rather is a dialogue between the prophet and God. The first two chapters are organized around Habakkuk's prayers (or, more correctly, complaints) and the Lord's replies. Habakkuk saw the rapid progress of Judah's moral and spiritual deterioration and this deeply troubled him. Yet God's response puzzled him even more, for "how could a good and just God use a more wicked nation to punish a less wicked one?" God makes it clear that both nations are to be judged and appropriately punished for their evil acts. Although Habakkuk may not fully understand, he has learned to rely totally on the wisdom and justice of God to bring about the proper resolution in ways he could never have imagined. This God is certainly worthy of Habakkuk's praise and worship, which is how the book ends.

The words of this prophet would surely have resonated with many of the righteous in Judah, who wondered what God was doing and struggled with the same issues that Habakkuk struggled with. God's words reassured them that he was in control and would take appropriate measures to deal with the nations. This book continued to have relevance to its readers, as evidenced by a commentary on the first two chapters discovered among the Dead Sea Scrolls.

Key Themes

1. God is just and merciful, even though his people may not always understand his ways (2:4).
2. Wickedness will eventually be punished, and the righteous will ultimately see God's justice (2:5–20).
3. God uses some wicked nations to punish other wicked nations, but ultimately God will judge all nations (1:6; 2:5–20).
4. The key phrase "but the righteous will live by his faith" summarizes the path of life God sets for his people and is quoted three times in the NT (Rom. 1:17; Gal. 3:11; Heb. 10:38), each time highlighting a different aspect of the phrase's meaning.

History of Salvation Summary

God's ways of preserving and purifying his people are mysterious to the believer; and yet God calls his suffering people to show faith that God's purposes for the world will at last prevail (2:4, 14; 3:17–19)—a faith that NT authors develop and commend. (For an explanation of the "History of Salvation," see the Overview of the Bible, pp. 23–26. See also History of Salvation in the Old Testament: Preparing the Way for Christ, pp. 2635–2661.)

Literary Features

The first two chapters fall into the dramatic format of dialogue; more specifically, they are question-and-answer exchanges between the prophet and God. The prophet's vision of God's appearance (3:3–15) is a theophany, and it is followed by a personal testimony (3:17–19). Overall, the first-person format of the dialogue, the visionary theophany, and the testimony make the book read like a personal journal.

Part of the artistry of the book is its patterns. The prophet complains twice, listens to God twice, and prays once (ch. 3). There are two oracles from God (1:5–11; 2:2–20) and one vision of God (3:3–15). In the first two chapters, the prophet's faith is troubled; in chapter 3, it is triumphant. Two chapters tell us what God is doing, followed by a chapter that demonstrates who God is.

Outline

I. Superscription (1:1)

II. First Cycle (1:2–11)
- A. Habakkuk's lament (1:2–4)
- B. God's response (1:5–11)

III. Second Cycle (1:12–2:20)
- A. Habakkuk's lament (1:12–2:1)
- B. God's response (2:2–20)

IV. Habakkuk's Prayer (3:1–19)

HABAKKUK

Chapter 1
1[a]See Nah. 1:1
2[b]Ps. 13:1; 89:46 [c]Mic. 6:12
3[d]See Jer. 9:2-6 [c][See ver. 2 above]
4[e][Mic. 7:3] [f][Job 21:7; Jer. 12:1]
5[g]Cited Acts 13:41 [h][Isa. 28:21; 29:14]
6[i]See Jer. 5:15 [j][ch. 2:5] [k][ch. 2:6]

1 [a]The oracle that Habakkuk the prophet saw.

Habakkuk's Complaint

2 O LORD, [b]how long shall I cry for help,
and you will not hear?
Or cry to you [c]"Violence!"
and you will not save?
3 [d]Why do you make me see iniquity,
and why do you idly look at wrong?
Destruction [c]and violence are before me;
strife and contention arise.
4 [e]So the law is paralyzed,
and justice never goes forth.
[f]For the wicked surround the righteous;
so justice goes forth perverted.

The LORD's Answer

5 [g]"Look among the nations, and see;
wonder and be astounded.
[h]For I am doing a work in your days
that you would not believe if told.
6 For behold, [i]I am raising up the Chaldeans,
that bitter and hasty nation,
[j]who march through the breadth of the earth,
[k]to seize dwellings not their own.

1:1 *Superscription.* "Oracle" translates a common word for "burden" (Hb. *massa'*), but when used in the Prophets it may more specifically signify a prophetic oracle (see Isa. 14:4). Jeremiah 20:9 and Amos 3:8 suggest that once God gives a message, it becomes a "burden" until the prophet announces it. Prophets do not typically use the term "prophet" for themselves, but Habakkuk is called a prophet twice (Hab. 1:1; 3:1), possibly because his message differs significantly from that of most other prophets.

1:2–11 *First Cycle.* Habakkuk is disappointed that God does not seem to be answering his prayers; but God's response indicates that, unknown to the prophet, he has already begun answering them.

1:2–4 *Habakkuk's Lament.* Habakkuk believes that God is letting sin go unpunished and that therefore there is no justice. A major interpretative decision is whether the source of the wrongdoing in these verses is a foreign power that suppresses faithfulness (Assyrians) or the leaders of Judah who oppress their own people. These notes reflect the second position.

1:2 O LORD. Habakkuk uses the covenant name for God, emphasizing the relationship between God and the prophet. **how long**? This is the common form of the formal complaint (cf. Ps. 13:1, 2). **Violence!** During much of the latter seventh century B.C., Judah was morally corrupt (with much wrongful violence) and spiritually apostate. The description of Josiah's reforms underscores the depths of the people's depravity (2 Kings 23).

1:3 idly look at wrong. Habakkuk can hardly believe that his God appears to tolerate sin instead of punishing it (see v. 13).

1:4 the law is paralyzed. The Mosaic law had little impact on the hearts of these people and was not accomplishing its purpose. Instead, they were living according to their own greedy, self-centered desires. **justice never goes forth.** Habakkuk believes that God's inactivity has caused injustice to become worse. The rich were using their power and money to get what they wanted; the rights of the poor were being trampled on. **righteous.** There was still a righteous remnant, but life was hard for them because they fell prey to the wicked and would not break God's laws to get ahead.

1:5–11 *God's Response.* God has already begun to answer Habakkuk's request (the Babylonians are coming to punish the Israelites).

1:5 Look among the nations. Habakkuk lived in a time of political turmoil—the Assyrians were losing power, whereas the Babylonians were gaining it. **you would not believe.** Habakkuk refused to believe that a just God would allow the cruel Babylonians to punish his people.

1:6 I am raising up. God controls the political scene and uses nations for his own purposes (cf. Isa. 44:28; Dan. 2:21). **Chaldeans.** Another name for the Babylonians, but technically they were an ethnically diverse Aramean tribe in southern Babylon that began to take control as the Assyrians weakened. The Babylonians gained independence from Assyria in 626 B.C. and, continuing

7 They are dreaded and fearsome;
[l]their justice and dignity go forth from themselves.
8 [m]Their horses are swifter than leopards,
more fierce than [n]the evening wolves;
their horsemen press proudly on.
Their horsemen come from afar;
[o]they fly like an eagle swift to devour.
9 They all come [p]for violence,
all their faces forward.
They gather captives [r]like sand.
10 At kings they scoff,
and at rulers they laugh.
[s]They laugh at every fortress,
for [t]they pile up earth and take it.
11 Then they sweep by like the wind and go on,
[u]guilty men, [v]whose own might is their god!"

Habakkuk's Second Complaint

12 Are you not [w]from everlasting,
O LORD my God, my Holy One?
[x]We shall not die.
O LORD, [y]you have ordained them as a judgment,
and you, O [z]Rock, have established them for reproof.
13 You who are [a]of purer eyes than to see evil
and cannot look at wrong,
[b]why do you idly look at traitors
and [c]remain silent when the wicked swallows up
the man more righteous than he?
14 You make mankind like the fish of the sea,
like crawling things that have no ruler.
15 [d]He[1] brings all of them up [e]with a hook;
he drags them out with his net;

[1] That is, the wicked foe

7[l][ver. 10, 11]
8[m]Jer. 4:13 [n]Jer. 5:6; Zeph. 3:3 [o]See Deut. 28:49
9[p][ch. 2:17] [r]See Josh. 11:4
10[s][Nah. 3:12] [t][Ezek. 4:2]
11[u][Hos. 13:16] [v][ver. 7]
12[w]Deut. 33:27; Ps. 90:2; 93:2 [x][Mal. 3:6] [y]See Isa. 10:5-7 [z]See Deut. 32:4
13[a][Ps. 5:5] [b]Jer. 12:1 [c]Ps. 35:22
15[d]Jer. 16:16; Amos 4:2 [e][Isa. 19:8]

to increase in power, defeated Assyria in 605. Nebuchadnezzar led the Babylonians in this victory and consolidated the Babylonian Empire. After his father's death in 605 B.C. he became king over the vast empire, which flourished until the Persians defeated it in 539. **bitter and hasty nation**. God knows the Babylonians well and uses their character traits to punish Judah.

1:7 their justice and dignity go forth from themselves. In pursuit of domination, the Babylonians were not bound by Judean legal systems, or even common decency. In their pride and arrogance they abused their power.

1:8 The Babylonians conquered their enemies so quickly that their **horses** seemed to come faster than swift **leopards**. Using horses allowed them to overtake their enemies before they had time to prepare. **eagle**. A bird of prey, depicting the Babylonians' fierceness and voracious appetite for conquest.

1:9 violence. Habakkuk had seen violence in the land (v. 2), but the Babylonians took it to a whole new level. **They gather captives like sand**. The Babylonians continued the Assyrian policy of deporting captives to their land to discourage and disorient them.

1:10 scoff . . . laugh. The powerful Babylonians had little regard for weaker kings or rulers whose meager fortifications offered little resistance. **they pile up earth**. One of the primary means of capturing a walled city was to construct earthen ramps so that movable towers could be pushed close enough to the walls to breach them (see Isa. 29:3; Jer. 32:24).

1:11 whose own might is their god. The Babylonians had become so successful and powerful that they relied on their military might for protection, as others would have relied on their gods.

1:12–2:20 *Second Cycle.* This expresses the age-old dilemma concerning God's justice: "Why does evil seem to go unpunished?" God's vindicating answer is, "I will see to it that all those who are wicked will be punished, but the righteous ones must live by faith."

1:12–2:1 *Habakkuk's Lament.* Habakkuk wonders how God can use a wicked nation to punish a less wicked one.

1:12 Are you not from everlasting? Habakkuk has good theology and knows that God lives forever (see Ps. 90:2). **We shall not die**. Several translations have "You shall not die" at this point, reflecting a later rabbinic tradition. This makes an easier reading than the abrupt change from "you" to "we," but it finds no support in the Hebrew manuscripts or the Septuagint, and should not be considered original. Habakkuk grounds his confidence in God's future for his people in the eternal nature of God. **you . . . have established them**. Habakkuk understands that God has ordained Babylon to be his agent of punishment.

1:13 purer eyes than to see evil. This is a classic statement of the puzzle of how an all-powerful God can allow sin to continue unchecked. Habakkuk cannot understand the justice of allowing wicked Babylon to punish a less wicked nation such as Judah. (He can call Judah **more righteous** because, even though most of its people were unfaithful to God's covenants, some of them actually were faithful.) Habakkuk thinks that God's holiness should have prohibited him from using the corrupt Babylonians.

1:14 Habakkuk's charge against God is that he allows mankind to act like lower creatures (**fish** and **crawling things**) with no rulers or judges, so that wickedness goes unchecked.

1:15 He. That is, the "wicked" one in v. 13, a personification of the nation of Babylon. **hook**. See Amos 4:2. Captives were sometimes taken away with hooks in their noses—an intentionally painful and humiliating treatment.

16[f][ver. 11]
17[g][ch. 2:10]
Chapter 2
1[h]Isa. 21:8 [i]Jer. 6:17; Ezek. 33:2 [j]Ps. 85:8
2[k]Isa. 8:1; 30:8; [Rev. 1:19]
3[l][Dan. 10:14]; See Ezek. 7:5-7 [m]Zeph. 3:8; See Isa. 8:17 [n]Cited Heb. 10:37; [2 Pet. 3:9]

he gathers them in his dragnet;
so he rejoices and is glad.
16 [f]Therefore he sacrifices to his net
and makes offerings to his dragnet;
for by them he lives in luxury,[1]
and his food is rich.
17 Is he then to keep on emptying his net
[g]and mercilessly killing nations forever?

2

1 I will [h]take my stand at my watchpost
and station myself on the tower,
and [i]look out to see [j]what he will say to me,
and what I will answer concerning my complaint.

The Righteous Shall Live by His Faith

2 And the LORD answered me:

[k]"Write the vision;
make it plain on tablets,
so he may run who reads it.
3 For still [l]the vision awaits its appointed time;
it hastens to the end—it will not lie.
If it seems slow, [m]wait for it;
[n]it will surely come; it will not delay.

[1] Hebrew *his portion is fat*

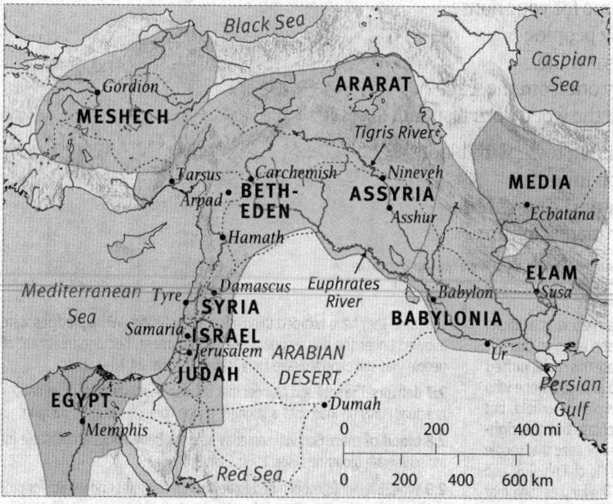

The Near East at the Time of Habakkuk
c. 620 B.C.
Though the exact date of the prophecies of Habakkuk is difficult to determine, it is likely that he prophesied a short time before the Babylonian invasions of Judah, which began in 605 B.C. During this time the Assyrian Empire was in decline, and the Babylonians were rising to replace them as the dominant power in the Near East.

drags them out with his net. The image is that of a fish helplessly caught in a fishing net; Mesopotamian rock reliefs portray prisoners in nets being hauled off to captivity.

1:16 he sacrifices to his net. See note on v. 11. The Babylonians appear quite proud of their weapons of destruction.

1:17 mercilessly killing nations forever? If a righteous God does not step in to end the Babylonians' wicked plan, who will? Where is God's justice, and how can he tolerate this?

2:1 I will take my stand at my watchpost. Similar to a lookout who awaits a coming enemy, Habakkuk waits in the city's watchtower for God to rebuke his direct challenge. **tower**. Probably part of a wall and tower system to protect the city.

2:2–20 *God's Response*. God assures Habakkuk that he will punish all the wicked at the right time.

2:2 Write the vision. This word "vision" commonly refers to the prophetic message from God (see 1 Chron. 17:15; Prov. 29:18). This message was to be a permanent witness, since it would not be imminently fulfilled. The content may be the entire book of Habakkuk, or some shorter portion. **so he may run who reads it**. This may refer to a herald spreading the message throughout the nation, or more generally to anyone fleeing the coming judgment.

2:3 the vision awaits its appointed time. The fulfillment of the message may occur more slowly than expected, but God's timing will be perfect. **wait for it**. While the judgment coming upon Judah will begin quite soon (586 B.C.), the punishment of the Babylonians will not be fulfilled until 539.

4 "Behold, his soul is puffed up; it is not upright within him,
but [o]the righteous shall live by his faith.[1]
5 "Moreover, wine[2] is [p]a traitor,
an arrogant man who is never at rest.[3]
His greed is as wide as Sheol;
like death [q]he has never enough.
[r]He gathers for himself all nations
and collects as his own all peoples."

Woe to the Chaldeans

6 Shall not all these [s]take up their taunt against him, with scoffing and riddles for him,
and say,

[t]"Woe to him [u]who heaps up what is not his own—
for [v]how long?—
and [w]loads himself with pledges!"
7 [x]Will not your debtors suddenly arise,
and those awake who will make you tremble?
Then you will be spoil for them.
8 [y]Because you have plundered many nations,
all the remnant of the peoples shall plunder you,
[z]for the blood of man and [y]violence to the earth,
to cities and all who dwell in them.

9 [t]"Woe to him who gets evil gain for his house,
[a]to [b]set his nest on high,
to be safe from the reach of harm!
10 You have devised shame for your house
[c]by cutting off many peoples;
you have forfeited your life.
11 For [d]the stone will cry out from the wall,
and the beam from the woodwork respond.

12 [t]"Woe to him [e]who builds a town with blood
and founds a city on iniquity!
13 Behold, is it not from the LORD of hosts
that [f]peoples labor merely for fire,

[1] Or *faithfulness* [2] Masoretic Text; Dead Sea Scroll *wealth* [3] The meaning of the Hebrew of these two lines is uncertain

4 [o]Cited Rom. 1:17; Gal. 3:11; Heb. 10:38; [John 3:36]
5 [p]ch. 1:13; Isa. 21:2 [q][Prov. 27:20] [r]Jer. 27:7; [ch. 1:6; Dan. 2:37, 38]
6 [s]Mic. 2:4; See Num. 23:7 [t]ver. 19; Isa. 5:8 [u][ch. 1:6] [v]See Zech. 1:12 [w][Ezek. 18:7]
7 [x]See Isa. 21:5-9
8 [y][Isa. 33:1] [z]ver. 17
9 [t][See ver. 6 above] [a][Isa. 14:13] [b]Jer. 49:16; [Num. 24:21]
10 [c][ch. 1:17]
11 [d][Luke 19:40]
12 [t][See ver. 6 above] [e]See Mic. 3:10
13 [f]Jer. 51:58

2:4 his soul. The singular form refers to the Babylonian nation as a whole, but with a primary reference to the king. A proud person relies on himself, whereas a righteous person relies on God. While the phrase "his soul is **puffed up**" refers primarily to Babylon in this context, it could include anyone who is proud. It will take faith to wait patiently for God's plan to unfold, but the righteous believe that God will accomplish it. The phrase **but the righteous shall live by his faith** is quoted in the NT to emphasize that people are saved by grace through faith (Rom. 1:17; Gal. 3:11; cf. Eph. 2:8) and that Christians should live by faith (Heb. 10:38–39). The kind of faith that Habakkuk describes, and that the NT authors promote, is continuing trust in God and clinging to God's promises, even in the darkest days.

2:5 His greed is as wide as Sheol. Sometimes in the OT, Sheol is the place of the dead where everyone went, yet which never filled up (see Prov. 30:15–16).

2:6–20 The taunt against the Babylonians consists of five "woe oracles" that are divided into two parts (vv. 6–14 and vv. 15–20), both of which end with summary statements declaring the glory and greatness of God. These woe oracles (vv. 6, 9, 12, 15, 19) describe the reasons why Babylon deserves its coming punishment (cf. Isa. 5:8–23). Woe oracles are generally composed of two parts: declaration of the wrong, and pronouncement of impending judgment as a result.

2:6 all these. That is, all the nations that Babylon has destroyed (see Isa. 14:9–11). **Woe**. The Babylonians are condemned for their excessive greed in conquest. They have hoarded things that are not theirs. While **pledges** were allowed under the law as guarantee of repayment, humane treatment of people was still expected (see Ex. 22:26–27; Deut. 24:10–13).

2:7 debtors. The spoil and plunder that Babylon has taken from other nations is actually only on loan until a stronger nation comes to plunder Babylon.

2:8 blood of man. God will someday hold the Babylonians accountable for indiscriminate bloodshed (see 1:17; Gen. 9:6).

2:9 Woe. Babylon is condemned for relying on treasures and wealth for protection. **evil gain**. Amassing stolen goods was prohibited under the law (Ex. 20:13–17; Deut. 5:17–21). **set his nest on high**. Like the eagle that builds its nest in inaccessible spots, the Babylonians attempted to build a city that was inaccessible to their enemies (see Isa. 14:4–15; cf. Obad. 3–4). Herodotus says that Babylon had a huge wall with 100 bronze gates. It was wide enough for a four-horse chariot to run upon it (*History* 1.178–179).

2:10 forfeited your life. God will hold Babylon responsible for killing many people.

2:11 stone will cry out. The stones were plundered from other nations' buildings or purchased with plundered goods and would serve as a witness against Babylon.

2:12 Woe. Babylon is condemned for its violence and injustice.

2:13 LORD of hosts. Yahweh is the commander of the heavenly armies, all of which do his bidding; see note on Amos 3:13. **peoples labor merely**

and nations weary themselves for nothing?
14 [g]For the earth will be filled
with the knowledge of [h]the glory of the LORD
as the waters cover the sea.

15 [t]"Woe to him [i]who makes his neighbors drink—
you pour out your wrath and make them drunk,
in order to gaze [j]at their nakedness!
16 You will have your fill [k]of shame instead of glory.
[l]Drink, yourself, and show your uncircumcision!
[l]The cup in the LORD's right hand
will come around to you,
and [m]utter shame will come upon your glory!
17 [n]The violence [o]done to Lebanon will overwhelm you,
as will the destruction of the beasts that terrified them,
[n]for the blood of man and violence to the earth,
to cities and all who dwell in them.

18 [p]"What profit is an idol
when its maker has shaped it,
a metal image, [q]a teacher of lies?
For its maker trusts in his own creation
when he makes [r]speechless idols!
19 [s]Woe to him [t]who says to a wooden thing, Awake;
to a silent stone, Arise!
Can this teach?
Behold, it is overlaid with gold and silver,
and [u]there is no breath at all in it.
20 But [v]the LORD is in his holy temple;
[w]let all the earth keep silence before him."

Habakkuk's Prayer

3 A prayer of Habakkuk the prophet, according to Shigionoth.

2 O LORD, [x]I have heard the report of you,
and [y]your work, O LORD, do I fear.
In the midst of the years [z]revive it;

14[g]Isa. 11:9 [h]Ps. 72:19
15[t][See ver. 6 above] [i][ver. 5; Jer. 51:7] [j]Lam. 4:21; [Gen. 9:22]
16[k]Nah. 3:5 [l]Jer. 25:15, 26 [m][Nah. 3:6]
17[n]ver. 8 [o][Isa. 14:8; Jer. 22:23]
18[p]Isa. 44:10 [q]Jer. 10:8, 14; Zech. 10:2 [r]Ps. 115:5; 1 Cor. 12:2
19[s]ver. 6, 9, 12, 15 [t]See 1 Kgs. 18:26, 27 [u]Ps. 135:17; Jer. 10:14
20[v]Ps. 11:4; Mic. 1:2 [w][Zeph. 1:7; Zech. 2:13]

Chapter 3

2[x]ver. 16; [Ps. 44:1] [y]Ps. 90:16 [z]Ps. 85:6

for fire. God controls man's destiny and will punish injustice; thus, Babylon's cities will ultimately be destroyed or given to others. Even the people of Judah were chastened for similar practices (Mic. 3:10).

2:14 The glory of the LORD is his special presence with his people, especially at the sanctuary. The glory "filled" the tabernacle and temple (Ex. 40:34–35; 1 Kings 8:11); a number of texts look forward to a day when God's glory fills the whole earth (Num. 14:21; Ps. 72:19; Isa. 6:3 ESV footnote). Israel existed so that the nations might come to know the true God (Gen. 12:2–3; Ex. 19:5–6), and the prophets nurtured the hope that one day the light would indeed reach all the nations. (Christian interpreters dispute whether a prophecy such as this will be fulfilled before or after Christ's return.)

2:15 Woe. Babylon is chastened for violence to its neighbors. **gaze at their nakedness**. That is, to dishonor them (cf. Gen. 9:20–22).

2:16 shame. Babylon will experience the same shame and embarrassment that it inflicted on others (see note on v. 15). **Cup** is a symbol of divine retribution on Babylon (see Isa. 51:17, 22; Jer. 25:15–17; Lam. 4:21; Rev. 14:10; 16:19).

2:17 violence done to Lebanon. Babylon used the famed cedars of Lebanon for its massive building projects (see Isa. 14:8). Nebuchadnezzar's royal annals indicate that he commanded his army to construct a road to bring these cedars to Babylon. The animal population may also have been decimated—Assyrian inscriptions record hunting expeditions in the Lebanese ranges, and the Babylonians probably indulged in the same practices.

2:18 idols. Carved images or likenesses of false gods were often condemned as worthless and lifeless objects unworthy of the faith placed in them (cf. Isa. 41:29; 44:9; Jer. 10:15). **teacher of lies**. This highlights the deceptive nature of worshiping idols (cf. Isa. 44:20).

2:19 Woe. The Babylonians are condemned for their idolatry. Idols were often ornate and covered with valuable metals to enhance their prestige.

2:20 But the LORD. There is a tremendous contrast between silent, inanimate idols and the awesome living God who sits enthroned in heaven and rules over the earth. He is the One who deserves the honor and reverence bestowed on worthless idols (see Isa. 41:1; Zeph. 1:7; Zech. 2:13). **Silence** is commanded so that everyone will consider God's awesome nature and realize his sovereignty over all creation (see Zeph. 1:7).

3:1–19 *Habakkuk's Prayer.* Habakkuk asks for a new demonstration of God's wrath and mercy, such as God demonstrated so powerfully in the past, and closes with a confession of faith and trust in God. This prayer uses terms similar to the Psalms of Trust (compare vv. 1, 3, 9, 13, 19 with Psalms 17; 90).

3:1 The word for **prayer** here usually refers specifically to a prayer of supplication (v. 2) but can also refer to prayer in general, including prayers sung corporately (e.g., Ps. 54:2; 55:1). **Shigionoth** occurs only twice in the OT (once in the singular and once in the plural) and may refer to an instrument or

in the midst of the years make it known;
[a]in wrath remember mercy.
3 God came from [b]Teman,
[c]and the Holy One from Mount Paran. *Selah*
His splendor covered the heavens,
and the earth was full of his praise.
4 [d]His brightness was like the light;
rays flashed from his hand;
and there he veiled his power.
5 [e]Before him went pestilence,
and plague followed [f]at his heels.[1]
6 He stood [g]and measured the earth;
he looked and shook the nations;
then the [h]eternal mountains [i]were scattered;
the everlasting hills sank low.
His were [j]the everlasting ways.
7 I saw the tents of [k]Cushan in affliction;
[l]the curtains of the land of Midian did tremble.
8 [m]Was your wrath against the rivers, O LORD?
Was your anger against the rivers,
[m]or your indignation against the sea,
[n]when you rode on your horses,
[n]on your chariot of salvation?
9 You stripped the sheath from your bow,
calling for many arrows.[2] *Selah*
[p]You split the earth with rivers.
10 [q]The mountains saw you and writhed;
the raging waters swept on;
[r]the deep gave forth its voice;
[s]it lifted its hands on high.
11 [t]The sun and moon stood still in their place
[u]at the light of your arrows as they sped,
at the flash of your glittering spear.
12 [v]You marched through the earth in fury;
[w]you threshed the nations in anger.
13 [v]You went out for the salvation of your people,
for the salvation of [x]your anointed.
[y]You crushed the head of the house of the wicked,

[1] Hebrew *feet* [2] The meaning of the Hebrew line is uncertain

2[a][Ps. 77:9]
3[b]See 1 Chr. 1:45 [c]See Deut. 33:2
4[d]See Ezek. 1:27
5[e][2 Kgs. 19:35]; See Ex. 12:29, 30; 1 Chr. 21:11-15 [f][Job 18:11]
6[g][Ps. 60:6]
6[h]Gen. 49:26; Deut. 33:15 [i]Mic. 1:4; Nah. 1:5 [j][Isa. 51:9]
7[k]Judg. 3:8 [l]See Judg. 8:19-21
8[m][Ps. 114:5] [n]Deut. 33:26, 27; Ps. 18:10; 68:4, 17; 104:3; Isa. 19:1; 66:15
9[p]Ps. 78:15, 16
10[q]Ex. 19:18; See Judg. 5:5 [r]Ps. 93:3 [s][Ex. 14:22; 15:8]
11[t]See Josh. 10:12, 13 [u][ver. 5]; See 2 Sam. 22:15
12[v][Josh. 10:42] [w][Mic. 4:12, 13]
13[v][See ver. 12 above] [x]1 Chr. 16:22; Ps. 105:15 [y]Ps. 68:21; 110:6

a type of psalm. The other usage of the word (Ps. 7:1) favors a type of psalm, and it may be related to Akkadian *shigu*, "a lament."

3:2 I have heard. Habakkuk had heard (perhaps in the temple) of God's great saving acts, which he recounts in vv. 3–15; see the Song of Moses (Ex. 15:1–21). **in wrath remember mercy**. A plea that when God judges, he will also be merciful—a classic statement of how God deals with his people.

3:3 Teman means "south"; with the reference to **Mount Paran** (Num. 13:3, 26; Deut. 33:2), it may suggest the time following Israel's exodus from Egypt. When the biblical authors refer to God's mighty acts in the exodus, they often use images to evoke the fear or awe of God (see Deut. 33:2; Judg. 5:4–5; Ps. 18:7–15; etc.). **Selah** is a term occurring often in the Psalms, of unknown meaning; it is probably some kind of musical direction.

3:4–5 Habakkuk likens God's presence at Mount Sinai to that of a thunderstorm with darkness and flashes of lightning (see Ex. 19:18–20; Ps. 18:9–14). **Pestilence** and **plague** are often used as pictures of divine judgment (Ex. 7:14–12:30; Lev. 26:25; Deut. 28:21–22; Ps. 91:3, 6).

3:6 eternal mountains. Mountains were considered part of the foundation of the earth, and thus their quaking was a sign of divine judgment. Earthquakes are frequently associated with God's power (Ex. 19:18; Ps. 18:7; Isa. 24:1–3; Jer. 4:24–26; 10:10; Mic. 1:3–4; Nah. 1:5).

3:7 Cushan . . . Midian. These Arab tribes living near Edom see God's power and are stricken with fear (see Ex. 15:14–16; Josh. 2:9–10).

3:8 God used his power over the Nile (Ex. 7:14–24) and Jordan Rivers (Josh. 3:14–17), as well as the Red Sea (Ex. 14:2–15:5), to demonstrate his greatness in the exodus. The **chariot of salvation** is a picture of God bringing deliverance to this people.

3:9 many arrows. Probably an image of thunderbolts sent by God. **split the earth**. An image of thunderstorms and floods cutting through the desert landscape.

3:11 sun and moon stood still. A reference to Joshua's victory at Gibeah (Josh. 10:12–13); the victory here will be equally sensational. God is pictured as a great warrior with his bow and spear.

3:12 threshed the nations. See Amos 1:3.

3:13 God fought for his people (**your anointed**) because they were his covenant people, a nation of priests (Ex. 19:6; Ps. 114:2). **The head of the house of the wicked** may refer to the pharaoh of Egypt or the leaders of

15[z][Ps. 77:19]
16[a]ver. 2 [b]Jer. 4:19
[c][Prov. 12:4] [d][Ps. 94:13; Isa. 14:3, 4]
18[e][Job 13:15] [f]Ps. 9:14; 13:5; 21:1; 35:9; Luke 1:47; See Joel 2:23
19[g]See 2 Sam. 2:18
[h]Amos 4:13; Mic. 1:3
[i]Deut. 32:13; 33:29 [j]See Ps. 4 [k]Isa. 38:20

laying him bare from thigh to neck.[1] *Selah*
14 You pierced with his own arrows the heads of his warriors,
who came like a whirlwind to scatter me,
rejoicing as if to devour the poor in secret.
15 [z]You trampled the sea with your horses,
the surging of mighty waters.

16 [a]I hear, and [b]my body trembles;
my lips quiver at the sound;
[c]rottenness enters into my bones;
my legs tremble beneath me.
Yet [d]I will quietly wait for the day of trouble
to come upon people who invade us.

Habakkuk Rejoices in the LORD

17 Though the fig tree should not blossom,
nor fruit be on the vines,
the produce of the olive fail
and the fields yield no food,
the flock be cut off from the fold
and there be no herd in the stalls,
18 [e]yet I will rejoice in the LORD;
[f]I will take joy in the God of my salvation.
19 GOD, the Lord, is my strength;
[g]he makes my feet like the deer's;
he makes me [h]tread on my [i]high places.

[j]To the choirmaster: with [k]stringed[2] instruments.

[1] The meaning of the Hebrew line is uncertain [2] Hebrew *my stringed*

Canaan; both felt God's displeasure. **laying him bare from thigh to neck**. The Hebrew is obscure, but it suggests a thorough defeat.

3:14–15 Another reference to the destruction that God brought on the Egyptians, who had set out to defeat the Israelites.

3:16 I hear. Habakkuk realizes that he must wait patiently for the destruction of his people and that God will then unleash his power against the Babylonians. **people who invade us**. That is, the Babylonians.

3:17–19 Anticipating great destruction at the hands of the Babylonians, Habakkuk has radically changed—he began by informing God how to run his world, and ended by trusting that God knows best and will bring about justice. **Though the fig tree should not blossom**. Verse 17 contains a frequently quoted list of material disasters in which all crops and livestock are lost, and as a result it is unclear how there will be food to eat. Yet even amid suffering and loss, Habakkuk has learned that he can trust God, and with that trust comes great joy, not in circumstances but in God himself: **yet I will rejoice in the LORD; I will take joy in the God of my salvation**. Yahweh has become Habakkuk's strength (see Ps. 18:32, 39).

3:19 he makes my feet like the deer's. Habakkuk can have sure-footed confidence in God and can live on the heights even amid extreme circumstances (see Mal. 4:2). **choirmaster**. Probably the director of the temple musicians (see Psalms 4; 5; 6; 8; 9; 11; etc.). **stringed instruments**. Harps, lyres, etc. (see Ps. 33:2; 92:3; 144:9). This kind of liturgical notation suggests that Habakkuk meant this to be a "prayer" (Hab. 3:1) that the faithful would sing together.

INTRODUCTION TO

ZEPHANIAH

Author and Title

While the originator of the words of this book ultimately was Israel's God ("the LORD"), the prophetic intermediary who delivered them to Judah was Zephaniah, after whom the book is named. Little is known about him apart from his name and pedigree. That the prophet was named "Zephaniah," which means "Yahweh has hidden/protected," could indicate his parents' piety, as they trusted in God during the godless reign of Manasseh. Indeed, the genealogy in 1:1 may indicate that Zephaniah was a descendant of Hezekiah, the pious ruler of Judah before two wicked kings assumed the throne.

Date

The prophecy takes place during the reign of Josiah (640–609 B.C.), a significant Judean king (2 Kings 21:26–23:20; 2 Chron. 33:25–35:27). The northern kingdom of Israel had already been exiled, in 722 B.C., so "Israel" (Zeph. 2:9; 3:13–15) does not refer to it. Rather, these references speak of the remainder of the nation of Israel: little Judah and its capital, Jerusalem.

Josiah was a reforming king, trying to reestablish acceptable worship practices that had fallen out of use since the time of his great-grandfather Hezekiah (2 Kings 21:1–26). Some suggest that the prophecy comes from the beginning of Josiah's reign, since the people are still engaging in condemned pagan practices (Zeph. 1:8–9). This is not compelling evidence, however, since even after a religious reform, not all lives are changed. This is clear from the other prophets preaching during this same time (e.g., Jeremiah, Nahum, and Habakkuk), indicating that no matter how clear the call to repentance, there were always those who refused to respond and who need to hear the prophetic word afresh.

Theme

The theme of Zephaniah, one preached more consistently by him than by any other prophet, is the "day of the LORD" (1:7, etc.). This approaching day shows two faces: one of judgment against those who sin against God, and one of blessing for those who follow him. God will show himself just in both punishment and praise.

Purpose, Occasion, and Background

In spite of having seen the destruction and exile of her sister, Israel, a generation or two previously, Judah refuses to turn back as a nation to her covenant obligations toward God. The reign of pious Josiah provides an ideal opportunity to make this move, and God, through Zephaniah, wants to clarify the decision that lies before Judah, and indeed before all the other nations, along with the consequences of that decision. God is calling for Judah's punishment because she has already shown herself sinful. If she should repent and abandon her evil, "perhaps" God will forgive (2:3).

The book is set against the background of numerous nations, many of which opposed God through opposition to his people, Israel. The Philistines (2:4–7) had been vying against Israel for the same land since the time of the conquest (e.g., Ex. 13:17; Josh. 13:2), while Moab and Ammon (Zeph. 2:8–11), distant relatives of the Israelites (Gen. 19:36–38), had opposed Israel's passage through their land before the conquest (Numbers 22–24). "Cush" (Zeph. 2:12) possibly refers to the Egyptian Twenty-fifth (Ethiopian) Dynasty (see

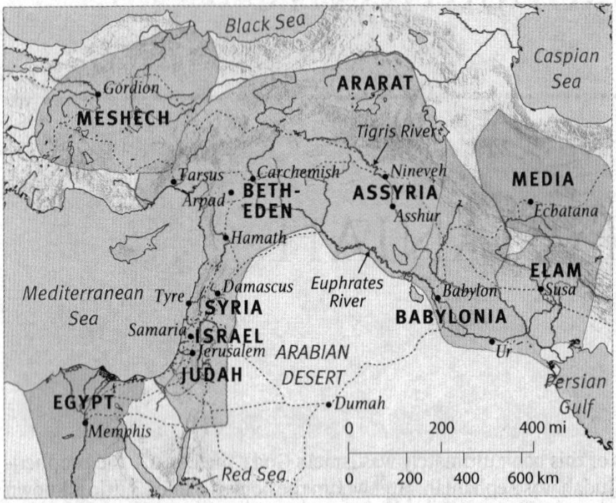

The Near East at the Time of Zephaniah
c. 620 B.C.
Zephaniah prophesied during the reign of Josiah, when Egypt, Judah, and Babylonia (with the help of the Medes) were regaining their autonomy and eroding the power of Assyria. Shortly after this time the Babylonians would replace the Assyrians as the dominant power in the Near East.

Isaiah 18), while Assyria (Zeph. 2:13–15) is the foreign power controlling Judah at the time of the prophecy. Surprisingly, the last among the nations being warned is represented by Jerusalem, the capital of another of God's enemies, Judah (3:1–7). This places the message of God's displeasure right in the face of those who claimed to be his own people.

Key Themes

1. God will judge the whole earth (1:2–3, 17–18; 3:8), Judah (1:4–16; 3:1–7) and her pagan neighbors (2:4–8) alike.
2. God, as covenant keeper, will bless his people when they return to their covenant relationship with him (3:11–20).
3. God wants to extend blessing and grace to all peoples and nations (3:9–10).
4. Judgment and blessing occur both in the near future for the prophet and his audience (1:4–18; 2:3) and also in the more distant future (3:8–9, 11, 13–17).
5. There is no such thing as a second-generation child of God. Every generation must own God's covenant, not relying on the faith of a previous generation.

History of Salvation Summary

God visits judgment on his own people to purge the faithless from their number. At the same time, he preserves the faithful and will use them to bring knowledge of God to all peoples. On the great day of judgment, God will purge the faithless from all mankind and bring the faithful into their full inheritance. (For an explanation of the "History of Salvation," see the Overview of the Bible, pp. 23–26. See also History of Salvation in the Old Testament: Preparing the Way for Christ, pp. 2635–2661.)

Literary Features

The book of Zephaniah is a typical work of prophecy, but with distinctive features woven into the tapestry. The primary genre within this prophetic book is the oracle of judgment, with an oracle of salvation coming at the expected place, namely, at the end. Zephaniah, almost uniquely among the so-called "minor prophets," looks like a "major prophet" in miniature: it has oracles of judgment (1:1–18), oracles against foreign nations (2:4–15), and oracles of hope (3:8–20), with 2:1–3 and 3:1–7 (modulating from foreign to domestic interest, much as Amos does in Amos 2:4ff.) functioning as "transitional" oracles which make pointed application to Jerusalem.

The literary intentions of the book are as follows: to picture God's judgment of sin by means of the motif of a coming day of the Lord; to use the resources of poetry to paint vivid word-pictures of the coming judgment; to evoke fear of the coming judgment with a view to awakening repentance; to embody the possibility of God's blessing in the form of a concluding oracle of restored favor with God; and to identify with the people and show concern for the poor (esp. Zeph. 2:3) while indicting those with position and wealth (1:8–9, 12, 18; 3:3–4), both encapsulated in 3:11–13.

Outline

I. Heading (1:1)

II. Judgment Coming Against Judah (1:2–6)

III. The Day of the Lord (1:7–3:20)
- A. Day of sacrifice and punishment (1:7–9)
- B. The coming wrath (1:10–18)
  1. Against God's people (1:10–16)
  2. Against all humanity (1:17–18)
- C. Repentance is still possible (2:1–3)
- D. Nations warned (2:4–3:8)
  1. Philistines (2:4–7)
  2. Moab and Ammon (2:8–11)
  3. Cush (2:12)
  4. Assyria (2:13–15)
  5. Jerusalem (3:1–7)
  6. Summary (3:8)
- E. Anticipation of hope (3:9–20)
  1. Conversion of the nations (3:9–10)
  2. Judah's return (3:11–13)
  3. Joyful song (3:14–17)
  4. God's promised restoration (3:18–20)

ZEPHANIAH

1 The word of the LORD that came to Zephaniah the son of Cushi, son of Gedaliah, son of
Amariah, son of Hezekiah, [a]in the days of [b]Josiah the son of Amon, king of Judah.

The Coming Judgment on Judah

2 [c]"I will utterly sweep away everything
from the face of the earth," declares the LORD.
3 "I will sweep away [d]man and beast;
I will sweep away the birds of the heavens
and [d]the fish of the sea,
and [e]the rubble[1] with the wicked.
I will [f]cut off mankind
from the face of the earth," declares the LORD.
4 "I will stretch out my hand against Judah
and against all the inhabitants of Jerusalem;
[g]and I will cut off from this place the remnant of Baal
and the name of the idolatrous priests along with the priests,
5 [h]those who bow down on the roofs
to the host of the heavens,
[i]those who bow down and swear to the LORD
and yet swear by [j]Milcom,
6 [k]those who have turned back from following the LORD,
[l]who do not seek the LORD or inquire of him."

[1] Or *stumbling blocks* (that is, idols)

Chapter 1
1[a]Jer. 1:2 [b]2 Kgs. 22:1
2[c]Jer. 8:13; [ver. 18; 2 Kgs. 22:16, 17]
3[d]Hos. 4:3 [e]See Ezek. 7:19 [f]Ezek. 14:17
4[g]See 2 Kgs. 23:4
5[h]Jer. 19:13 [i][1 Kgs. 18:21; 2 Kgs. 17:33, 41] [j]1 Kgs. 11:5, 33
6[k]Jer. 2:13, 17; 15:6 [l][Jer. 5:24; Heb. 11:6]

1:1 *Heading.* This verse introduces the genre, ultimate author, prophetic intermediary, and time period of the prophecy. **Word** opens other prophecies as well (e.g., Hos. 1:1; Joel 1:1; Mic. 1:1). **LORD** is the personal name of Israel's God, Yahweh or Jehovah. See note on Ex. 3:15. **Cushi**, a proper name (Jer. 36:14), is also an ethnic designation for "Cushite, Ethiopian." This could explain the inclusion of the genealogy indicating that Zephaniah is in fact an Israelite. **Hezekiah** is possibly the early, reforming fourteenth king of Judah (2 Kings 18:1–20:21; 2 Chron. 29:1–32:33). **Josiah**, the pious Judean king, reestablished worship of Yahweh (2 Kings 22:1–23:30; 2 Chron. 34:1–35:27; Jer. 1:2). **Amon** was an evil king of Judah like his apostate father Manasseh (2 Kings 21:19–26; 2 Chron. 33:21–25).

1:2–6 *Judgment Coming against Judah.* God first directs his attention against all living beings (vv. 2–3), then more specifically against his own people, Judah, represented by their capital, Jerusalem (vv. 4–6).

1:2 To **sweep away** is to completely remove or destroy something (1 Sam. 15:6; Jer. 16:5). Who and what will be swept away is specified in Zeph. 1:4–6; namely, "the remnant of Baal" and the "idolatrous priests" in Jerusalem (v. 4); all who practice idolatrous worship ("who bow down on the roofs to the host of the heavens" and who "swear by Milcom," v. 5); and all "those who have turned back from following the LORD" (v. 6). In his holiness and his righteous judgment, God zealously destroys evil, sweeping away the lives of all "who do not seek the LORD" (v. 6).

1:3 The listing of **man and beast . . . the birds . . . and the fish** highlights the totality of destruction through terms that occur in the creation account (Gen. 1:20, 24–25, 26–28). God, the Creator of everything, will destroy everything due to the sin of **mankind**, creation's representative.

1:4 Judah alone remained to serve as God's new humanity since her northern neighbor Israel was exiled to Assyria in 722 B.C. Yet the presence of a righteous king such as Josiah (v. 1) was not enough to avert God's judgment from Judah when other officials (v. 8; 3:3–5) and the people (1:9–12) were persisting in evil. **Jerusalem**, Judah's capital, represented the entire nation. **Baal** (lit., lord, master) is the title commonly designating the Canaanite storm god, Hadad, whom Israel was prone to worship (Judg. 6:25; 1 Kings 16:31–32; 18). It could also refer to an Assyrian god, Bel. The term **idolatrous priests** is used only of pagan priests (cf. 2 Kings 23:5; Hos. 10:5).

1:5 Host of the heavens refers to the astral deities worshiped by both Assyrians and Canaanites (Deut. 4:19; Jer. 19:13). **Milcom** is the god of the pagan Ammonites (1 Kings 11:5, 33). The law strictly prohibited mixing worship of God and a pagan deity (Ex. 20:3).

1:6 The people **turned back**, becoming apostate and leaving their first faith (Isa. 59:13).

1:7–3:20 *The Day of the Lord.* The remainder of the prophecy concerns the multifaceted "day of the LORD," which on the one hand holds judgment (1:7–3:8), and on the other, hope (3:9–20). It affects not only God's covenant nation (1:8–13; 2:1–3; 3:1–7) but others as well

7 [m][Hab. 2:20] [n][ver. 14]; See Joel 1:15 [o]Isa. 34:6; Jer. 46:10; Ezek. 39:17, 19 [p]1 Sam. 16:5
8 [q]2 Kgs. 24:12, 14; 25:7 [r][Matt. 22:11]
9 [s][1 Sam. 5:5]
10 [t]See 2 Chr. 33:14 [u]Zech. 11:3 [v]2 Kgs. 22:14
11 [w]Zech. 11:2; James 5:1
12 [x]Amos 9:3 [y]Jer. 48:11; [Amos 6:1] [z]Ps. 94:7; Ezek. 8:12; Mal. 2:17; 3:14, 15
13 [a]Isa. 42:22 [b]See Amos 5:11 [c]See Mic. 6:15

The Day of the Lord Is Near

7 [m]Be silent before the Lord God!
For [n]the day of the Lord is near;
[o]the Lord has prepared a sacrifice
and [p]consecrated his guests.
8 And on the day of the Lord's sacrifice—
[q]"I will punish the officials and the king's sons
and [r]all who array themselves in foreign attire.
9 On that day I will punish
everyone [s]who leaps over the threshold,
and those who fill their master's[1] house
with violence and fraud.

10 "On that day," declares the Lord,
"a cry will be heard from [t]the Fish Gate,
[u]a wail from [v]the Second Quarter,
a loud crash from the hills.
11 [w]Wail, O inhabitants of the Mortar!
For all the traders[2] are no more;
all who weigh out silver are cut off.
12 At that time [x]I will search Jerusalem with lamps,
and I will punish the men
[y]who are complacent,[3]
[z]those who say in their hearts,
'The Lord will not do good,
nor will he do ill.'
13 Their goods shall be [a]plundered,
and their houses laid waste.
[b]Though they build houses,
they shall not inhabit them;
[c]though they plant vineyards,
they shall not drink wine from them."

[1] *Or their Lord's* [2] *Or all the people of Canaan* [3] *Hebrew are thickening on the dregs* [of their wine]

(1:14–18; 2:4–15). Looking to more immediate, historical fulfillment (2:4–15), it also points toward the distant future (1:14–18; 3:8–13; Acts 17:31; 2 Pet. 3:10; Rev. 20:11–15). On the theme of the "day of the Lord," see note on Amos 5:18–20 and chart, p. 1668.

1:7–9 *Day of Sacrifice and Punishment.* After an announcement of the day of the Lord (v. 7), practitioners of specific evil deeds are warned (vv. 8–9).

1:7 The people are commanded to **be silent**, a sign of respect or fear (Amos 6:10; 8:3). The **day of the Lord** is the coming day in which God will judge his enemies (cf. Joel 1:8–3:8) and bless his followers (Zeph. 3:9–20). The **sacrifice** will be prepared by God himself, not dedicated to him as is customary. The guests will be **consecrated**. This either means (1) that they are to eat a holy meal (cf. 1 Sam. 16:5); or possibly (2) that they are themselves the sacrifice, in judgment of their sins.

1:8 Officials and the king's sons are the civil leadership punished for the nation's sin. Those engaged in syncretism (combining service of God with things taken from other religions) during worship (2 Kings 10:22; Mal. 2:11) or in daily life (Neh. 13:30) appear to have worn some undefined **foreign attire**.

1:9 When one **leaps over the threshold**, it is a pagan routine, possibly a Philistine practice (cf. 1 Sam. 5:4–5). **Violence and fraud** are evil acts in opposition to the healing and truth that come from truly worshiping God (cf. Gen. 6:11). "Fraud" (Hb. *mirmah*) can also be translated "deceit," as in Jer. 9:6 (cf. Isa. 53:9).

1:10–18 *The Coming Wrath.* A litany of punishments is leveled against Jerusalem and its inhabitants (vv. 10–16) and against all humanity (vv. 17–18).

1:10–16 *Against God's People.* Inhabitants of specific Jerusalem neighborhoods are noted (vv. 10–11), their chief failing (complacency in sin) is mentioned (v. 12), and their punishment is detailed (vv. 13–16).

1:10 The **Fish Gate** was probably the main northern city gate (2 Chron. 33:14), while the **Second Quarter** was a newer city section north of the temple (2 Kings 22:14). Jerusalem is surrounded by **hills**, but this could be a specific area, probably to the north, known to Zephaniah's hearers.

1:11 The location of the **Mortar** is uncertain, but it was possibly a mortar-shaped, or hollow, quarry (Judg. 15:19). **Traders**, lit., "Canaanites" (Prov. 31:24; Hos. 12:7), who became the later Phoenicians, were important merchants and traders.

1:12 The **complacent** are those who "are thickening on their dregs" (ESV footnote) like undisturbed wine that collects useless sediment. These lethargic people will not rouse themselves enough to save themselves. Since God has not yet judged their sin, perhaps they assume that he never will, not realizing that judgment can come any day (cf. James 5:1–9; 2 Pet. 3:3–4). **The Lord will not do good, nor . . . ill** is an expectation of the apathetic Judeans. Not denying the existence of God, they deny rather his ongoing activity in either blessing or punishing. This negates a core element of biblical theology: God is constantly active in history.

1:13 Goods . . . houses . . . vineyards belong to the rich and powerful; those who can afford their own dwellings and lands will lose everything and do not seem to care. (See further the covenant curses for disobedience in Deut. 28:15–68.) **They shall not inhabit them** implies that, because of their sin, God will not allow them to enjoy the rewards of their work.

14 [d]The great day of the LORD is near,
near and hastening fast;
the sound of the day of the LORD is bitter;
[e]the mighty man cries aloud there.
15 [f]A day of wrath is that day,
a day of distress and anguish,
a day of [g]ruin and devastation,
[h]a day of darkness and gloom,
[h]a day of clouds and thick darkness,
16 [i]a day of trumpet blast and battle cry
[j]against the fortified cities
and against the lofty battlements.

17 [k]I will bring distress on mankind,
so that they shall walk [l]like the blind,
because they have sinned against the LORD;
[m]their blood shall be poured out like dust,
and their flesh [n]like dung.
18 [o]Neither their silver nor their gold
shall be able to deliver them
on the day of the wrath of the LORD.
[p]In the fire of his jealousy,
[q]all the earth shall be consumed;
[r]for a full and sudden end
he will make of all the inhabitants of the earth.

Judgment on Judah's Enemies

2

1 Gather together, yes, gather,
O [s]shameless nation,
2 [t]before the decree takes effect[1]
—before the day passes away [u]like chaff—
[v]before there comes upon you
the burning anger of the LORD,
before there comes upon you
the day of the anger of the LORD.
3 [w]Seek the LORD, [x]all you humble of the land,
who do his just commands;[2]

[1] Hebrew *gives birth* [2] Or *who carry out his judgment*

14[d][ver. 7; Ezek. 7:7, 12] [e][Isa. 33:7]
15[f]See Joel 1:15 [g]Job 30:3 [h]See Joel 2:2
16[i][Jer. 4:19] [j][Isa. 2:15]
17[k]Jer. 10:18 [l]Deut. 28:29; Isa. 59:10 [m]Ps. 79:3 [n][Ps. 83:10]
18[o]Ezek. 7:19; [Prov. 11:4] [p][ch. 3:8] [q]Ezek. 36:5 [r][ver. 2, 3]

Chapter 2

1[s]Jer. 6:15
2[t][ch. 3:8] [u]Ps. 1:4 [v][2 Kgs. 23:26]
3[w]See Amos 5:6 [x]Ps. 76:9; Isa. 11:4

1:14 God's day is **near and hastening fast**. The importance of quickly responding to God is highlighted through emphasizing the impending judgment (v. 7). The **mighty man cries aloud** as the valiant hero lifts his battle cry (Isa. 42:13; cf. Zeph. 3:17) on God's day.

1:15 The description as a **day of wrath** highlights the judgmental nature of the day. It is described by a catalog of frightening terms, many of which accompany theophanies (appearances of God) in other contexts (e.g., Ex. 19:16–19) where God will act against his own people as if they were his enemy.

1:16 Fortified cities speaks of even the most secure of Judah's strongholds; they will prove vulnerable to her almighty God.

1:17–18 *Against All Humanity.* Since sin is universal, so is God's judgment of sinners.

1:17 Instead of walking in God's guidance, Judah will **walk like the blind**, staggering from her spiritual blindness (cf. Deut. 28:28, where blindness is a punishment for unfaithfulness). **Blood . . . like dust . . . like dung** renders the valuable worthless. Though blood carries life itself (Lev. 17:11), it will lose all its value like these two insignificant items (1 Kings 14:10; Zech. 9:3).

1:18 Neither their silver nor their gold means that material valued by humans (cf. vv. 11, 13), which was often formed into idols (Isa. 2:20; 30:22), will not be able to withstand God, whether in its natural or idolatrous form. God's **jealousy** means that he cherishes his position as unique in the affections of his people to such an extent that he makes it the foundation of his covenant with them (Ex. 20:3).

2:1–3 *Repentance Is Still Possible.* While sin is a universal human problem, God still shows grace if his people repent.

2:1 shameless nation. Israel's shameful actions demonstrate that they are not covenant followers; they have no right to be considered God's people unless they repent.

2:2 This verse is difficult to interpret. When grain is winnowed, the light, outer husk, worthless for human or animal food, is allowed to blow quickly away. Something's being **like chaff** refers here either to the quickly coming day or to the quick departure of those worthless people who abandon God. The **day of the anger of the LORD** highlights the judgmental nature of God's coming (3:8), precipitated by Judah's sin.

2:3 Rather than abandoning God, as it had been doing, Judah is called to **seek** diligently for him, the mark of true piety (cf. 1:6; Ps. 27:8; 105:3; Isa. 51:1). Addressing the **humble of the land** indicates that not everyone is apostate. A few rely on God rather than themselves, being "humble and lowly" (Zeph. 3:12; cf. "poor in spirit," Matt. 5:3). The humble realize that they need to turn beyond themselves for help. Another translation for "humble of the land" is "meek of the earth" (cf. Matt. 5:5, using Ps. 37:11). **Righteousness** describes the goal of correct living in relation to God and humanity (Isa. 1:21), following his will as revealed in his commands. **Perhaps** is a theologically

[y]seek righteousness; seek humility;
[y] perhaps [z]you may be hidden
on the day of the anger of the LORD.

4 [a]For Gaza shall be deserted,
and Ashkelon shall become a desolation;
Ashdod's people shall be driven out at noon,
and Ekron shall be uprooted.

5 Woe to [b]you inhabitants of the seacoast,
you nation of [c]the Cherethites!
[d]The word of the LORD is against you,
[e]O Canaan, land of the Philistines;
and I will destroy you [f]until no inhabitant is left.

6 [g]And you, O seacoast, [h]shall be pastures,
with meadows[1] for shepherds
and folds for flocks.

7 [i]The seacoast shall become the possession
of [j]the remnant of the house of Judah,
[h]on which they shall graze,
and in the houses of Ashkelon
they shall lie down at evening.
For the LORD their God [k]will be mindful of them
and [l]restore their fortunes.

8 "I have heard [m]the taunts of Moab
and [n]the revilings of the Ammonites,
how they have taunted my people
and made boasts [o]against their territory.

3[y][Amos 5:14, 15] [z][Isa. 2:10; 26:20, 21]
4[a]Zech. 9:5, 6; [Jer. 47:5]; See Amos 1:6-8
5[b]Jer. 47:7; Ezek. 25:16 [c]See 1 Sam. 30:14 [d][Nah. 2:13] [e][Josh. 13:3] [f]ch. 3:6
6[g]ver. 7 [h]Isa. 65:10
7[i][Josh. 19:29] [j][ch. 3:13; Obad. 19] [h][See ver. 6 above] [k]Zech. 10:3; Luke 1:68 [l]ch. 3:20
8[m][Jer. 48:27] [n]Ezek. 25:3, 6 [o][Jer. 49:1]

[1] Or *caves*

important word, which highlights God's grace and sovereignty (Ex. 32:30; Amos 5:15). God is just, and can and should punish wrongdoing; he is also loving and gracious, willing that none should perish (John 3:17; cf. 2 Pet. 3:9). A sinner can only throw himself on the mercy of God, who has forgiven in the past and might do so again. The fact that God forgives the penitent (1 John 1:9) does not mean that forgiveness should be expected lightly and cheaply, for it should always evoke wonder at God's grace. **You may be hidden** indicates that humble, righteous people may be protected when God's judgment falls on the rest of the nation (cf. Ex. 9:6, 26; 10:23; 12:23; Josh. 6:22–23; Isa. 1:27–28; 2 Pet. 2:5–9).

2:4–3:8 *Nations Warned.* As in Amos's prophecy (Amos 1:3–2:3), the judgment prophecy first focuses on Israel's neighbors and enemies (Zeph. 2:4–15), whom Judah would have heartily joined in condemning. Only then do the people of Judah feel the focus turning on themselves (3:1–7), being just as sinful before the same just God.

2:4–7 *Philistines.* These coastal dwellers, for so long enemies of God's people lying to their north and east, will be taken over by Israel.

2:4 Gaza, **Ashkelon**, **Ashdod**, and **Ekron** are four of the five Philistine city-states lying on the Mediterranean coast and coastal plain, here presented in south-to-north order (see map to the right). These bustling opponents of Israel (see Judges) will soon be gone.

2:5 The **seacoast** indicates the location of the **Philistines**, from which the name "Palestine" is derived. They lived to the southwest of Judah, and are also called **Cherethites** (1 Sam. 30:14; 2 Sam. 15:18), showing historical links with Crete. An unusual title for them is **Canaan**, which more regularly refers to the natives of the territory before the arrival of Israel and the Philistines (Gen. 12:5) but could indicate the traders from the area (Zeph. 1:11).

2:6–7 Remnant is a theologically significant term, showing two sides of God's relationship with his people. His judgment against sin will be so severe that only a few survivors will remain (v. 9; 3:13; Isa. 17:6). All hope is not lost, however, since the destruction is not complete; at least a few refugees will remain, continuing the existence of God's people. **God will be mindful** of Judah, taking note of their need and responding to it (Zech. 10:3). This involves not only thought but also action, since he will **restore** (Zeph. 3:20) the bounty of which they have been deprived. The mention of **pastures** and **shepherds** (2:6) predicts that, after the Philistine cities have been destroyed, the area will be repopulated by God's people (v. 7), who will live in peace.

2:8–11 *Moab and Ammon.* Judah's eastern neighbors, cousins yet enemies, face punishment.

2:8 Taunts and **revilings** are verbal attacks using insults (3:18; Isa. 43:28) against the people of God. These are launched by two of Israel's longtime enemies to the east, **Moab** and the **Ammonites**. They descended from Lot through his incestuous relationship with his daughters (Gen. 19:30–38). Having frequently opposed Israel (Numbers 22–24; 1 Sam. 11:1–11; 2 Kings 1:1), they were a desirable target for Josiah's geographical expansion because of their location just east of the Dead Sea.

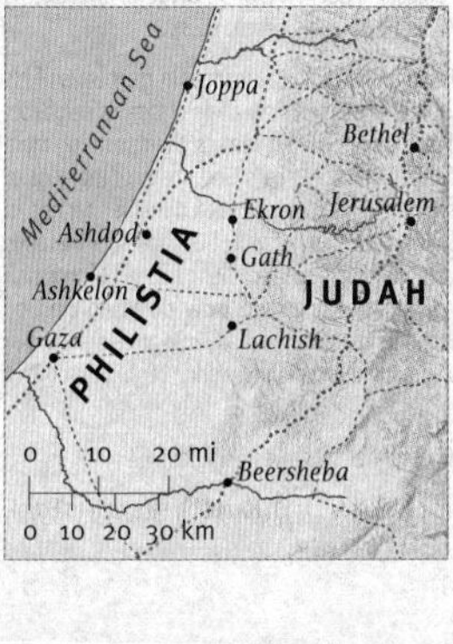

Zephaniah Prophesies against Judah's Neighbors
c. 620 B.C.
Zephaniah prophesied against Judah's longtime enemies in Philistia, to the west of Judah along the coast.

9 Therefore, [p]as I live," declares the LORD of hosts,
the God of Israel,
"Moab shall become [q]like Sodom,
and the Ammonites [q]like Gomorrah,
a land possessed by nettles and salt pits,
and a waste forever.
The remnant of my people shall plunder them,
and the survivors of my nation shall possess them."
10 This shall be their lot in return [r]for their pride,
because they taunted and boasted
against the people of the LORD of hosts.
11 The LORD will be awesome against them;
[s]for he will famish all the gods of the earth,
and [t]to him shall bow down,
each in its place,
all [u]the lands of the nations.

12 [v]You also, O Cushites,
shall be slain by my sword.

13 And he will stretch out his hand against the north
[w]and destroy Assyria,
and he [x]will make Nineveh a desolation,
a dry waste like the desert.
14 [y]Herds shall lie down in her midst,
all kinds of beasts;[1]
[z]even the owl and the hedgehog[2]
shall lodge in her capitals;
a voice shall hoot in the window;
devastation will be on the threshold;
for [a]her cedar work will be laid bare.
15 This is the exultant city
[b]that lived securely,

9 [p]Isa. 49:18; See Ezek. 16:48 [q]Deut. 29:23; See Isa. 13:19
10 [r]Isa. 16:6
11 [s][Isa. 17:4] [t]Ps. 22:27 [u]See Gen. 10:5
12 [v][ch. 3:10]
13 [w][Isa. 10:12] [x]Nah. 3:7
14 [y]Isa. 13:21, 22; 34:14 [z]Isa. 34:11 [a][Jer. 22:14, 15]
15 [b]Isa. 47:8

[1] Hebrew *beasts of every nation* [2] The identity of the animals rendered *owl* and *hedgehog* is uncertain

2:9 As I live strengthens an oath that God makes, in swearing by his own existence (Isa. 49:18; see 1 Sam. 14:39, 45). **Sodom** and **Gomorrah** were two infamous cities near the Dead Sea so completely destroyed by God for their great sins (Gen. 19:24–26; Isa. 1:9) that their exact location is unknown. The peoples mentioned in Zeph. 2:8–9 are probably placed together here because they are also joined in Genesis 19. For people whose livelihood depends on agriculture, it would be devastating to be overrun by **nettles** or weeds (Prov. 24:31) and arid and nonproductive **salt pits** (Gen. 19:26), another reference back to the events in Genesis 19. On the theme of the **remnant** of God's **people**, see notes on Isa. 1:9 and Zeph. 2:6–7.

2:10 In this summary of the preceding poem (vv. 8–9), **pride** or arrogance is contrasted with the humility desired of God's people (v. 3).

2:11 Awesome describes Israel's God, who causes fear in the hearts of his opponents (Ex. 15:11; 34:10). He moves not only against Judah's neighbors but against **all the gods of the earth**. He will **famish** them, causing them to waste away (cf. Isa. 10:16; 17:4). Unlike Israel's God, many of the gods of her neighbors needed nourishment, which was provided through offerings. In one Mesopotamian story about a flood—the myth of Gilgamesh—the gods are famished because there are no people to feed them. Instead of worshiping these powerless pagan deities, foreigners will **bow down** to the God of Israel, either coming to worship in Jerusalem (Isa. 2:3) or else joining in the worship of the true God spreading around the world (Zeph. 3:9; cf. Phil. 2:10–11; Rev. 5:9–10).

2:12 *Cush.* Ethiopia and Egypt, farther southwest, will fall.

2:12 Cushites are Ethiopians (3:10; Isa. 11:11), probably referring to Egypt, Israel's enemy to the south. In the late eighth and early seventh centuries B.C., Egypt was under the control of the Ethiopian Twenty-fifth Dynasty. In 525 B.C. Egypt and Ethiopia were both defeated by the Persians under Cambyses, so this defeat could refer to his campaign.

2:13–15 *Assyria.* The greatest threat to Israel lies farther east and north. A major world power of the time, Assyria cannot withstand God.

2:13 God will **stretch out his hand**, the body part used as an image indicating power and control (cf. Gen. 16:12; Isa. 28:2), in judgment against his people's northern enemy, **Assyria**. The Assyrians, coming especially from one of their greatest cities and onetime capital, **Nineveh** (cf. Jonah; Nahum), conquered the Near East, including Judah's sister, Israel. In 722 B.C. Israel's capital city, Samaria, fell to Assyria, and the leaders of Israel disappeared into exile (2 Kings 17).

2:14 Though the exact translation is uncertain, **the owl and the hedgehog** represent two of the inhabitants of what used to be a major metropolis. Humans will be gone; animals and birds will take their place. The actual buildings themselves will become dilapidated, with the underlying **cedar work** exposed. Cedars from Lebanon were commonly used for main building beams (cf. 1 Kings 6:9; 7:2) because of their size and strength, which will now be of no use.

2:15 Nineveh, formerly known as an **exultant city**, will be deprived of its joyful abandon (Isa. 24:8) as well as its safety and security. Human pride and power are useless in a time of God's judgment. In its pride (Zeph. 2:10; 3:11) Nineveh arrogantly boasted, **"I am, and there is no one else."** This primacy is reserved for God alone (Isa. 45:6; cf. Ex. 20:3), and such pride will

15[c][Ezek. 25:5] [d]Jer. 19:8 [e][Nah. 3:19]

Chapter 3

1[f]Jer. 6:6
2[g]Jer. 5:3 [h][ver. 12]
3[i]Ezek. 22:27; [Mic. 3:9, 10] [j]Hab. 1:8
4[k]Jer. 23:11; Hos. 9:7 [l]Ezek. 22:26
5[m][Jer. 12:1] [n][ch. 2:1]
6[o]See ch. 2:4-15 [p][Zech. 7:14; 9:8]
7[q][Jer. 36:3] [r][ver. 2] [s][Mic. 7:3]

that said in her heart,
"I am, and there is no one else."
What a desolation she has become,
[c]a lair for wild beasts!
[d]Everyone who passes by her
hisses and [e]shakes his fist.

Judgment on Jerusalem and the Nations

3

1 Woe to her who is rebellious and defiled,
[f]the oppressing city!
2 She listens to no voice;
[g]she accepts no correction.
[h]She does not trust in the LORD;
she does not draw near to her God.

3 [i]Her officials within her
are roaring lions;
her judges are [j]evening wolves
that leave nothing till the morning.
4 [k]Her prophets are fickle, treacherous men;
[k]her priests [l]profane what is holy;
they do violence to the law.
5 The LORD within her [m]is righteous;
he does no injustice;
every morning he shows forth his justice;
each dawn he does not fail;
but [n]the unjust knows no shame.

6 [o]"I have cut off nations;
their battlements are in ruins;
I have laid waste their streets
[p]so that no one walks in them;
their cities have been made desolate,
without a man, without an inhabitant.
7 [q]I said, 'Surely you will fear me;
[r]you will accept correction.
Then your[1] dwelling would not be cut off
according to all that I have appointed against you.'[2]
But [s]all the more they were eager
to make all their deeds corrupt.

[1] Hebrew *her* [2] Hebrew *her*

be punished. Anyone who sees the destruction of Nineveh **hisses** (cf. Jer. 19:8) and **shakes his fist**, actions not of aggression but of horror and amazement at how the mighty have fallen.

3:1–7 *Jerusalem.* God's people cannot think that they will emerge unscathed on the day of the Lord. If they sin (vv. 1–4) and are shameless (v. 5), they are also held accountable, especially if they lack repentance (vv. 6–7).

3:1 The city is now described as **defiled** and **oppressing**. It has become ritually polluted (Isa. 59:3; Mal. 1:7) through sins of idolatry and covenant breaking. Rather than showing care, the city has become brutal and overbearing (Jer. 25:38).

3:3 Among those who should lead the city aright, but have in fact turned against her, are its **officials**, the civil authorities (1:8; 1 Chron. 28:1), and **judges**, those in charge of settling legal disputes (Ex. 18:13, 22). Instead of showing benevolence, these leaders were acting as **roaring lions**, ferocious beasts possessing great power, about to seize prey (Amos 3:4), and as **evening** (or desert) **wolves**, known for their ravenous appetite (Gen. 49:27). Leaders, rather than guarding their flock, devour it.

3:4 Religious officials are also condemned, including the **prophets**. Rather than being speakers of God's sure word, they speak their own **fickle** (cf. Gen. 49:4, where "unstable" is the same Hb. word) and even **treacherous** words (cf. Jer. 3:20). **Priests** have two roles, and have failed in both. First, they are to help purify sinners through presenting their offerings before God (Leviticus 1–7), but instead they make them **profane**, unsuitable to be in God's holy presence (Lev. 10:10; 19:8). Second, they are to teach life under the **law** (Lev. 10:11; Deut. 17:8–13; 33:10), but instead they do **violence** (Ezek. 22:26), leading others to do the same.

3:5 Unlike the human leaders, God perpetually shows that he is **righteous** in not breaking the law (Ezek. 18:5–9) and **shows forth his justice** in seeing that all receive fair treatment (cf. Ex. 23:6).

3:7 God calls the city to **fear**, not in panic but in respectful awe at his power (2:11; Ex. 14:31). This is further defined as willingness to **accept correction** (contrast Zeph. 3:2 as well as Jer. 2:30; 5:3), learning from God's reproof in renewed obedience and showing the fear of God in action (Prov. 10:17). If they were to do this, they would not experience God's judgment: **your dwelling would not be cut off**.

8 “Therefore [t]wait for me,” declares the LORD,
“for the day when I rise up to seize the prey.
For my decision is [u]to gather nations,
to assemble kingdoms,
to pour out upon them my indignation,
all my burning anger;
for in the fire of my jealousy
[v]all the earth shall be consumed.

The Conversion of the Nations

9 “For at that time I will change the speech of the peoples
to [w]a pure speech,
that all of them may call upon the name of the LORD
and serve him with one accord.
10 [x]From beyond the rivers [y]of Cush
my worshipers, the daughter of my dispersed ones,
shall bring my offering.

11 [z]“On that day [a]you shall not be put to shame
because of the deeds by which you have rebelled against me;
for then [b]I will remove from your midst
your proudly exultant ones,
and [c]you shall no longer be haughty
in my holy mountain.
12 But I will leave in your midst
a people [d]humble and lowly.
[e]They shall seek refuge in the name of the LORD,
13 [f]those who are left in Israel;
they [g]shall do no injustice
and speak no lies,
[h]nor shall there be found in their mouth
a deceitful tongue.
[i]For they shall graze and lie down,
and none shall make them afraid.”

Israel’s Joy and Restoration

14 [j]Sing aloud, O daughter of Zion;
shout, O Israel!

8 [t]Hab. 2:3; See Isa. 8:17 [u]Joel 3:2 [v][ch. 1:18]
9 [w]Isa. 19:18
10 [x]Ps. 68:31; Isa. 11:11; 60:4 [y][ch. 2:12]
11 [z]Isa. 2:11 [a][Isa. 54:4] [b][Mal. 4:1] [c]Jer. 7:4; [Matt. 3:9]
12 [d]Isa. 14:32; [Matt. 5:3] [e][ver. 2]
13 [f][ch. 2:7] [g]Isa. 60:21 [h][Rev. 14:5] [i]See Mic. 5:4
14 [j]Isa. 12:6; 54:1; Zech. 2:10; 9:9

3:8 *Summary.* The section concludes with a return to worldwide judgment. The people are called to **wait for** God, not for possible blessing (Isa. 30:18) but rather for his coming judgment. But this time it will not be against Judah itself, since he will **gather** (Zeph. 3:18–20) all **nations** of the earth for their judgment.

3:9–20 *Anticipation of Hope.* God the judge is also God the gracious. He intends that the nations should turn to him (vv. 9–10), as well as his own people (vv. 11–13). This will cause rejoicing (vv. 14–17), not least because God alone has accomplished salvation (vv. 18–20).

3:9–10 *Conversion of the Nations.* God the judge also purifies and calls the distant ones to himself.

3:9 In that day, God will alter the **speech** (or lips) **of the peoples** gathered to be punished (Isa. 6:5–7). The nations had polluted speech, worshiping pagan gods, but now they will have **pure speech** (cf. Ps. 24:4), cleansed to **call upon the name of the LORD** in worship (Gen. 4:26). (Some have suggested that this may also allude to the reversal of the Babel syndrome in Gen. 11:1–9.) Worship is not only through word but also through deed, since the nations will **serve him**. The term *'abad* (“work, serve”) designates obedient work for God (Mal. 3:14). This service is universal, done by **all**, and unanimous, “with one accord” (cf. 1 Kings 22:13).

3:10 The Israelite exiles will be restored to their place **from beyond the rivers of Cush** (1:1; 2:12; Isa. 18:1) or Ethiopia. These rivers are the Blue and White Nile. “Beyond the river” more often has an eastward orientation, and it can refer to Assyria (Isa. 7:20), as can Cush (Gen. 10:6–8; see Zeph. 2:12–13). These true worshipers will now move toward Jerusalem, whether from east or west.

3:11–13 *Judah’s Return.* Not ignoring their sin, God speaks of the removal of impurity from Jerusalem so that his people might be restored.

3:11 Jerusalem’s **shame** (Isa. 1:29; 54:4) is over, even though it was deserved because of the people’s godless deeds (Zeph. 3:1–4, 7). They had **rebelled**, flagrantly and purposefully turning against what they knew was right (Hos. 8:1). They were dominated by **proudly exultant ones**, complacent, wealthy people (Zeph. 1:8–13) who, in being **haughty** (Isa. 3:16), thought they were self-sufficient, needing nothing from God. Ironically, this contempt was shown in God’s earthly dwelling place, his **holy mountain**, Zion (Obad. 16), the site of the temple.

3:12 God will especially provide a place for the **humble and lowly** (2:3) who, unlike the arrogant (3:11), know that they are in need. They not only call on God’s name (v. 9) but also **seek refuge** in his name (see the same term in Isa. 57:13; Nah. 1:7).

3:13 Previous sins among God’s people—injustice (v. 5), lying (Ezek. 13:6–9), and a **deceitful tongue** giving words that are not from God (Jer. 14:14)—will be among them no longer.

3:14–17 *Joyful Song.* As in the Psalms, people even in the throes of suffering are called to worship and give thanks for their anticipated salvation.

15[k]Matt. 27:42; John 1:49 [l]Ps. 46:5; Zech. 2:10; [Rev. 21:3]
16[z][See ver. 11 above] [m][Isa. 35:3; Heb. 12:12]
17[l][See ver. 15 above] [n][Isa. 63:1] [o]Isa. 62:5; Jer. 32:41
18[p]Lam. 1:4; 2:6
19[q][Isa. 60:14] [r]Mic. 4:6, 7 [s]Isa. 61:7 [t][Jer. 13:11; 33:9]
20[u]Isa. 11:12; Jer. 32:37; Ezek. 11:17 [v]ch. 2:7

Rejoice and exult with all your heart,
O daughter of Jerusalem!
15 The LORD has taken away the judgments against you;
he has cleared away your enemies.
[k]The King of Israel, [l]the LORD, is in your midst;
you shall never again fear evil.
16 [z]On that day it shall be said to Jerusalem:
"Fear not, O Zion;
[m]let not your hands grow weak.
17 [l]The LORD your God is in your midst,
[n]a mighty one who will save;
[o]he will rejoice over you with gladness;
he will quiet you by his love;
he will exult over you with loud singing.
18 I will gather those of you who mourn [p]for the festival,
so that you will no longer suffer reproach.[1]
19 Behold, at that time [q]I will deal
with all your oppressors.
And [r]I will save the lame
and gather the outcast,
and I will change [s]their shame into [t]praise
and renown in all the earth.
20 [u]At that time I will bring you in,
at the time when I gather you together;
for I will make you renowned and praised
among all the peoples of the earth,
[v]when I restore your fortunes
before your eyes," says the LORD.

[1] The meaning of the Hebrew is uncertain

3:14 The defiled city and nation (v. 1) is raised up by being again called the beloved **daughter of Zion** (Isa. 62:11). Zion is an alternative name for **Jerusalem**, the city of David (2 Sam. 5:7) and home of the temple (Ps. 9:11; 76:2). Jerusalem's inhabitants are called **Israel** since, now that the northern, Israelite tribes are in exile, Judah and its capital, Jerusalem, are the only remaining people who can bear this name as descendants of the first Israel (Jacob; Gen. 28:10–15; 32:28).

3:15 Rejoicing is appropriate because of the presence of the real **King of Israel**, God, among his people. The human kings of Israel and Judah served only as representatives of Israel's true monarch, who here blesses with his presence those who repent and return to him. He is not powerless, as some had claimed (1:12).

3:16 When frightened or dismayed, literally one's **hands grow weak** (Isa. 13:7; Jer. 6:24). Since God is now present and in control, this will not happen.

3:17 The previously weakened nation is in the presence of the **mighty one** (Deut. 10:17; Ps. 24:8; Isa. 10:21; 42:13), God himself, who, unlike human warriors and heroes (Zeph. 1:14), does not lose heart. Instead of fleeing in the face of danger, God can **save** his people from it (Ex. 14:30). This verse remarkably adds that God himself **will rejoice over you with gladness**, indicating that when God's people seek him and follow him (Zeph. 3:12–13), and rejoice in him and trust him (vv. 14–16), then God personally delights in them. This is not an aloof, emotionless contentment, but it bursts forth in joyful divine celebration: **he will exult over you with loud singing**.

3:18–20 *God's Promised Restoration.* Joy is increased through the increased promised blessings from God.

3:18 This verse is very obscure, with numerous translations suggested. This version suggests that those Judean sinners who had been unable to join in the **festival** celebrations that were reserved for God's righteous people (see Numbers 28–29) are now able to do so once again.

3:19 God will act on behalf of all his flock who suffered under exile, taking steps to **save the lame** (Mic. 4:6–7) like a shepherd. Also, the exiles, like **outcast**, scattered animals (Deut. 22:1; 30:4; John 11:52), will no longer suffer **shame** at their plight but will rejoice that it is over.

3:20 God's far-flung people will face restoration at the hand of their King. Instead of being justifiably shamed for their sin, they will be **renowned and praised** (Deut. 26:19) because of the gracious salvation of God.

INTRODUCTION TO

HAGGAI

Author and Title

The book of Haggai contains messages delivered by the prophet Haggai, and thus it is reasonable to consider Haggai its author. The name Haggai, which means "festal," promotes the conjecture that his birth occurred during a festival of Israel, or perhaps links his name with his message, anticipating the restoration of Israel's great feasts within a restored temple. Nothing is known of his genealogy.

Date

The word of the Lord comes to Haggai between late August and mid-December of 520 B.C. There is widespread scholarly consensus on these dates, though this does not preclude the possibility of editorial activity. If such editing did take place, it likely occurred before 515 B.C., when the temple was completed. The dates given are significant for their places in both the liturgical and agricultural calendars of Judah (see notes on 1:1; 1:15b–2:1; 2:10).

Dates of the Oracles in Haggai (All in 520 B.C.)

Oracle	Reference	Date
First	1:1	1st day of 6th month (Aug. 29)
Second	1:15	24th day of 6th month (Sept. 21)
Third	2:1	21st day of 7th month (Oct. 17)
Fourth	2:10	24th day of 9th month (Dec. 18)
Fifth	2:20	24th day of 9th month (Dec. 18)

Theme

The restoration of the Lord's house by the people of God will mediate God's presence.

Purpose, Occasion, and Background

Haggai motivates the leaders (Zerubbabel and Joshua) and the people of God to consider their current economic and spiritual circumstances and to renew their efforts to complete the work of temple restoration.

The historical setting of the book is in the sixth century B.C. among the returned exiles from the Babylonian captivity. The Persian ruler Cyrus the Great (559–530 B.C.) captured Babylon in 539. His edict in 538 B.C. permitted the return of Jews to Jerusalem so that they might rebuild the temple (Ezra 1–2). Initial work stalled, however, when opposition arose (Ezra 3:1–4:5).

The events within the book of Haggai take place during the reign of Darius I (522–486 B.C.), a general who rose to power following the death of Cyrus's son Cambyses (530–522). The specific mention of the "second year of Darius" (Hag. 1:1) places the book firmly in the year 520 B.C. Darius's support was vital for the completion of the temple (Ezra 5–6).

Key Themes

1. *The restoration of God's house.* Temple restoration highlights the Lord's desire to renew a covenant relationship with his people, characterized by his presence (1:13; 2:4–5). A decaying temple signifies a decaying relationship and brings defilement rather than holiness to the people (2:14).

2. *The prophetic word is the divine Word.* The divine message comes "by the hand of Haggai" (1:1, 3; 2:1, 10), is characterized by "thus says the LORD" (1:2, 5, 7; 2:6, 11), is a message "to Haggai" (2:20), is characterized

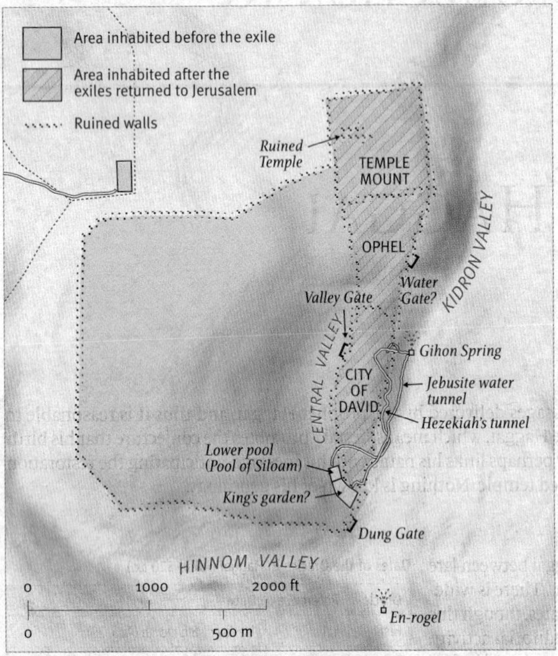

Jerusalem at the Time of Haggai
c. 520 B.C.
Haggai prophesied to the people of Jerusalem after they had returned from Babylon in 538 B.C. and before they had rebuilt the temple in 515. The city of Jerusalem lay in ruins, the walls and the temple having been destroyed by the Babylonians in 586 B.C. Within a year after returning from Babylon, the people had laid the foundation for the new temple, but by Haggai's time they had still not completed it. Haggai, together with Zechariah, called upon the people to stop focusing on their own economic well-being and complete the temple.

by "declares the LORD" (1:9, 13; 2:4 [3x], 8, 9, 14, 17, 23 [3x]), is the "voice of the LORD their God" (1:12), and is the "LORD's message" (1:13).

3. *The Lord is sovereign.* The phrase "LORD of hosts" occurs 14 times in these 38 verses (see 1:2). The Lord gives the divine word, controls the fortunes of his people (1:9; 2:17, 19) and nations (2:6–8), directs nature (1:10), motivates his people to action (1:14; 2:4), and establishes and deposes kingdoms (2:20–23).

4. *The people must work.* A restored house will bring pleasure and glory to the Lord (1:8) and convey blessing to the people (2:19), but there is work to be done. Physical labor (1:14) is urged in the form of numerous imperatives (1:7–8; 2:4–5). But there is also "heart" work to be done, as evidenced by the call to consider past experience in light of the present inaction (1:5–7; 2:15–19).

5. *The restoration of David's house.* Undoubtedly Zerubbabel, the heir of David (see note on 1:1), is promised an elevated status (2:23). The Lord, who had taken off the "ring" of the Davidic house (Jer. 22:24–27), now promises to wear it once again. As in the OT (2 Samuel 7; Ps. 2:6), the NT understanding inextricably unites king and temple. It is only as the temple is rebuilt (Matt. 26:61; 27:40; John 2:18–22) that Christ Jesus, the Davidic heir, is installed as the messianic King (Rom. 1:1–4), thus fulfilling the promises to Zerubbabel (Matt. 1:1, 12–13; Luke 3:27).

History of Salvation Summary

After the exile, the Lord is renewing his promises to his people and calls on them to finish rebuilding the temple so that he might be with them and fulfill his promises to bless the whole world through them (2:9), particularly through the Messiah from the house of David (2:23). (For an explanation of the "History of Salvation," see the Overview of the Bible, pp. 23–26. See also History of Salvation in the Old Testament: Preparing the Way for Christ, pp. 2635–2661.)

Literary Features

Although the book of Haggai falls within the general category of prophecy, it is not a typical prophetic book. It is written in prose instead of the customary poetry. Although there are predictions of promised blessing, there are no oracles of judgment in the usual sense. Instead, God simply calls the nation's attention to its low ebb, as though judgment had already occurred. There are also intermittent golden-age visions, as well as a narrative episode (1:12–15). By means of a specific instance (the rebuilding of the temple), the book of Haggai is a relevant and timeless book on the need to put God's work first in one's life. For the prophet's society, rebuilding the temple would be the visible sign of the people's determination to put God first.

Outline

I. Introduction: Reluctant Rebuilders (1:1–2)
   A. Characters (1:1)
   B. Context (1:2)

II. Consider Your Ways: Fruitless Prosperity (1:3–12)
   A. Work without satisfaction (1:3–11)
   B. General response: obedience and fear (1:12)

III. Promise and Progress (1:13–15a)
   A. God's promise (1:13)
   B. Specific response: work begins (1:14–15a)

IV. The Former and Latter Glory of This House (1:15b–2:9)
   A. Comparing past and present (1:15b–2:3)
   B. Acting based on the past (2:4–5)
   C. An image of God's house restored (2:6–9)

V. Consider Your Ways: Holiness and Defilement; Repentance and Blessing (2:10–19)
   A. Analogy: holiness and defilement (2:10–14)
   B. Consider life before restoration began: you did not turn (2:15–17)
   C. Consider life since restoration began: I will bless (2:18–19)

VI. Zerubbabel: The Signet Ring (2:20–23)
   A. Destruction upon kingdoms (2:20–22)
   B. An image of David's house restored (2:23)

HAGGAI

The Command to Rebuild the Temple

1 [a]In the second year of Darius the king, in the sixth month, on the first day of the month,
the word of the LORD came by the hand of Haggai the prophet to [b]Zerubbabel the son
of [c]Shealtiel, governor of Judah, and to [d]Joshua the son of [e]Jehozadak, the high priest:
2 "Thus says the LORD of hosts: These people say the time has not yet come to rebuild the
house of the LORD." 3 Then the word of the LORD came [f]by the hand of Haggai the prophet,
4 [g]"Is it a time for you yourselves to dwell in your paneled houses, while [h]this house lies
in ruins? 5 Now, therefore, thus says the LORD of hosts: [i]Consider your ways. 6 [j]You have
sown much, and harvested little. [k]You eat, but you never have enough; you drink, but you
never have your fill. You clothe yourselves, but no one is warm. And he who [l]earns wages
does so to put them into a bag with holes.
7 "Thus says the LORD of hosts: [i]Consider your ways. 8 Go up to the hills and bring wood
and build the house, that [m]I may take pleasure in it and that [n]I may be glorified, says the
LORD. 9 [j]You looked for much, and behold, it came to little. And when you brought it home,
[o]I blew it away. Why? declares the LORD of hosts. Because of my house [h]that lies in ruins,
while each of you busies himself with his own house. 10 Therefore [p]the heavens above you
have withheld the dew, and the earth has withheld its produce. 11 And [q]I have called for a
drought on the land and the hills, on [r]the grain, the new wine, the oil, on what the ground
brings forth, on man and beast, and [s]on all their labors."

Chapter 1

1 [a]ver. 15; ch. 2:10; Ezra 4:24; 5:1; Zech. 1:1, 7 [b]See 1 Chr. 3:19 [c]See 1 Chr. 3:17 [d]See Ezra 3:2 [e]1 Chr. 6:15
3 [f]Ezra 5:1
4 [g][2 Sam. 7:2]; See Ps. 132:3-5 [h]Neh. 2:3, 17; Isa. 64:11; Jer. 33:10, 12
5 [i][ch. 2:15, 18]
6 [j]See Mic. 6:15 [k]Hos. 4:10 [l][Zech. 8:10]
7 [i][See ver. 5 above]
8 [m][Ps. 132:13, 14] [n][ch. 2:9]
9 [j][See ver. 6 above] [o][ch. 2:17] [h][See ver. 4 above]
10 [p][Jer. 5:24, 25; Zech. 8:12]; See 1 Kgs. 8:35
11 [q]2 Kgs. 8:1; [Ps. 105:16] [r]Hos. 2:9 [s]ch. 2:17; Ps. 128:2

1:1–2 *Introduction: Reluctant Rebuilders.* The opening establishes the characters and context of the book. The Lord, prophet, king, priest, and people figure prominently as the major problem is presented, namely, that the Lord's house is in ruins and the people do nothing about it.

1:1 *Characters.* **second year . . . sixth month . . . first day**. August 29, 520 B.C. As the first of the month, it is the day of a new moon festival, and thus of public worship (1 Chron. 23:31); it is also three weeks after the anniversary of the destruction of the first temple (2 Kings 25:8; Jer. 52:12). At this point most of the harvesting is finished, with only dates and summer figs left to be harvested. **Darius**. Persian king 522–486 B.C. **by the hand of** (cf. Hag. 1:3; 2:1). A phrase unique to Haggai among the writing prophets, though common in the books of Moses. **Zerubbabel** was a grandson of Jehoiachin, heir to the Davidic throne, and governor of Judah (see Ezra 3:2, 8; 4:2–3; 5:2). **Joshua**. High priest and son of Jehozadak, whose line is traced through Zadok to Aaron (1 Chron. 6:11–15; Zech. 3:1, 8; 6:11).

1:2 *Context.* **LORD of hosts**. Highlights the Lord as the leader of heavenly or earthly armies. Approximately one-third of all biblical occurrences of the phrase are found in Haggai, Zechariah, and Malachi (see chart, p. 1775); it emphasizes the Lord's universal rule (see note on 1 Sam. 1:3). **not yet come**. The people claim that the time for temple restoration has not yet arrived: they want to postpone the work until sometime later.

1:3–12 *Consider Your Ways: Fruitless Prosperity.* In the second word to Haggai, the Lord asks his hearers to consider whether their prosperity, such as it is, brings about the intended satisfaction, and he exhorts them to supply materials for "my house" (vv. 3–11). A general response follows (v. 12).

1:3–11 *Work without Satisfaction.* On the date of this oracle the people can reflect on the disappointing harvest season (cf. vv. 10–11). They struggle mightily for personal gain at the neglect of the Lord's house. God evaporates their gain in order to teach them that the building of his house will bring him glory and must be their priority.

1:4 paneled . . . ruins. The inattentive people focus on comfortable personal dwellings (v. 9) while the Lord remains "homeless" (2 Sam. 7:2; 1 Kings 6:9; Jer. 22:13–15).

1:5 Consider your ways. Ponder your actions and the resulting experiences.

1:6 sown much . . . harvested little. This describes the hard work the people have done, and the frustrating yield. God has not blessed their crops because of their preference for personal comfort over the rebuilding of the temple (v. 4). **eat . . . drink . . . clothe . . . earns wages**. Their efforts to care for themselves and their families lead only to frustration, so the Lord wants them to "consider their ways" (v. 5).

1:8 Go up . . . bring . . . build. The people are commanded to bring wood to build a proper house. As the Lord takes pleasure in acceptable sacrifice (Ps. 51:19), the sacrifice of temple-building will result in his **pleasure** and glory.

1:9 The word "house" is used three times with three different meanings: **home** (a place to store goods); **my house** (the Lord's temple); **his own house** (one's personal dwelling). **busies himself with** (lit., "is running for"). As compared with the implicit critique of v. 4, the misplaced priorities of the people are now made explicit.

1:10–11 Therefore. There is a causal link between the ruin (Hb. *khareb*) of the Lord's house (vv. 4, 9) and the **drought** (Hb. *khoreb*).

The People Obey the LORD

12 [t]Then [u]Zerubbabel the son of Shealtiel, and [u]Joshua the son of Jehozadak, the high
priest, with all [v]the remnant of the people, obeyed the voice of the LORD their God, and
the words of Haggai the prophet, as the LORD their God had sent him. And the people
feared the LORD. 13 Then Haggai, the messenger of the LORD, spoke to the people with the
LORD's message, [w]"I am with you, declares the LORD." 14 And [x]the LORD stirred up the spirit
of [u]Zerubbabel the son of Shealtiel, governor of Judah, and the spirit of [y]Joshua the son
of Jehozadak, the high priest, and the spirit of all [z]the remnant of the people. And they
came and [a]worked on the house of the LORD of hosts, their God, 15 [b]on the twenty-fourth
day of the month, in the sixth month, in the second year of Darius the king.

The Coming Glory of the Temple

2 [c]In the seventh month, on the twenty-first day of the month, the word of the LORD
came by the hand of Haggai the prophet, 2 "Speak now to [d]Zerubbabel the son of
Shealtiel, governor of Judah, and to [d]Joshua the son of Jehozadak, the high priest, and
to all the remnant of the people, and say, 3 [e]'Who is left among you who saw this house
[f]in its former glory? How do you see it now? [g]Is it not as nothing in your eyes? 4 Yet now
[h]be strong, O [d]Zerubbabel, declares the LORD. [h]Be strong, O [d]Joshua, son of Jehozadak,
the high priest. [h]Be strong, all you people of the land, declares the LORD. [i]Work, for [j]I
am with you, declares the LORD of hosts, 5 [k]according to the covenant that I made with
you when you came out of Egypt. [l]My Spirit remains in your midst. [m]Fear not. 6 For thus
says the LORD of hosts: [n]Yet once more, in a little while, [o]I will shake the heavens and the
earth and the sea and the dry land. 7 And I will shake all nations, so that the treasures of all

12 [t]Ezra 5:2 [u]ver. 1 [v]ch. 2:2
13 [w]ch. 2:4; [Isa. 43:5]
14 [x][2 Chr. 36:22; Ezra 1:1] [u][See ver. 12 above] [y]ver. 1 [z]ch. 2:2 [a][ch. 2:4; Ezra 5:8]
15 [b][ver. 1]

Chapter 2

1 [c][Lev. 23:34, 36]
2 [d]ch. 1:1
3 [e][Ezra 3:12] [f][ver. 9] [g][Zech. 4:10]
4 [h]Zech. 8:9; [Zech. 4:6, 7] [d][See ver. 2 above] [i][ch. 1:14] [j]ch. 1:13
5 [k]See Ex. 29:45 [l]Neh. 9:20 [m]Zech. 8:13, 15
6 [n]Cited Heb. 12:26 [o]ver. 21

1:12 *General Response: Obedience and Fear.* To the admonition of vv. 3–11, people render a general response of hearing and alarm. The **remnant** (v. 14; 2:2) is the same as the people addressed in 1:2; 2:4, 14. **feared the LORD.** See note on Acts 9:31.

1:13–15a *Promise and Progress.* The obedience and fear characterizing the general response of v. 12 provokes the third statement from the prophet. The promise of the Lord's presence (v. 13) engenders the actual response of "work" in vv. 14–15a.

1:13–14 messenger (Hb. *mal'ak*) . . . **message** (Hb. *mal'akut*) . . . **worked** (Hb. *mela'kah*). This play on words makes a direct connection between the speaker (Haggai), the content of what was spoken (statement of assurance), and the desired effect upon the people (lit., "and they performed work").

1:13 *God's Promise.* **I am with you** (cf. 2:4). This is the great promise of covenantal assurance (cf. Num. 14:9; Josh. 14:12; Judg. 1:19; Isa. 43:5; cf. Matt. 28:20). The task before them will be undertaken with the promise of God's aid.

1:14–15a *Specific Response: Work Begins.* In this fine example of divine prompting and human response, the Spirit of the Lord moves in the people and the people take action.

1:14 the LORD stirred up the spirit. God awakens in the people an intense desire to work on repairing his house. Progress on the house arises only by means of the enabling power of the sovereign God (Ex. 35:21, 26, 30–35). **their God.** The companion statement of covenantal assurance (e.g., Jer. 24:7; 31:33; Ezek. 11:20; 37:27).

1:15a twenty-fourth day . . . sixth month. September 21, 520 B.C.

1:15b–2:9 *The Former and Latter Glory of This House.* Haggai bolsters flagging spirits in this fourth message. Comparing the past glory of the temple with the present ruins brought inevitable discouragement (2:1–3). The people are called to act based on the past (2:4–5). As God moved Israel to build the tabernacle, so he will now move among the nations to provide for the restoration of his house (2:6–9).

1:15b–2:3 *Comparing Past and Present.* The Lord challenges those who remember to compare the past glory of the temple with its present status.

1:15b–2:1 second year . . . seventh month . . . twenty-first day. October 17, 520 B.C. (cf. 1:1), and the next-to-last day of the Feast of Tabernacles (1 Kings 8:2). It is likely that the people celebrated with limited resources (Hag. 1:10–11).

2:3 Who is left. "Left" translates Hebrew *sha'ar*, a wordplay on "remnant" (Hb. *she'erit*, v. 2, i.e., "what is left"). Among those who remained were some in their 70s or older who could remember Solomon's temple that had been destroyed 66 years earlier (cf. Ezra 3:12). **this house.** The loss of temple and land is evidence for covenant curses for disobedience (1 Kings 9:6–9). **Is it not as nothing in your eyes?** The people could see that the rebuilt temple would be far inferior to Solomon's temple in its wealth and physical beauty. The word **glory** is used in two senses in Haggai: here and in Hag. 1:8 it conveys the idea of "honor, distinction," while in 2:7 it is probably "the glory of the Lord" (his special presence), which is said to "fill" the sanctuary (1 Kings 8:10–11; cf. Ex. 40:34–35).

2:4–5 *Acting Based on the Past.* All of those addressed (both leaders and people) are called to move ahead in God's strength.

2:4 Yet now. This transition moves the people from their past reflection to present action by means of a series of imperatives. As earlier, God's presence (**I am with you**) forms the basis for their ongoing **work** in the face of pessimism (cf. 1:13–14).

2:5 The command **Fear not** is based on an assurance of God's presence: **My Spirit remains in your midst.** This is one of the strongest statements in the entire OT of God's ongoing presence among his people. As the people gave willingly of talent, time, and goods in the building of the tabernacle (Ex. 25:1–3, 8; 28:3; 35:4–5, 10–11), so now they are exhorted to fulfill their covenant obligations in contributing to the current temple restoration.

2:6–9 *An Image of God's House Restored.* The previous promise of the Lord's presence is matched in this section by a promise to provide materially for the temple, even as it looks forward to the decisive presence of God with his people (v. 9).

2:6 LORD of hosts occurs five times in vv. 6–9, emphasizing the Lord's sovereign authority over all things, including the adornment of his house (see note on 1:2). **I will shake.** The same verb form is translated "about to shake" in 2:21 (see note on Joel 2:10; cf. Heb. 12:26–27). In the present context, "shaking" does not primarily involve future judgment but God's immediate intervention in providing for the work at hand (cf. Hag. 2:7–8).

2:7 God promises to **shake all nations** (as well as "the heavens and the earth," v. 6). The result of this shaking will be that the **treasures of all**

nations shall come in, and [p]I will fill this house with glory, says the LORD of hosts. 8 [q]The
silver is mine, and the gold is mine, declares the LORD of hosts. 9 [r]The latter glory of this
house shall be greater than the former, says the LORD of hosts. And [s]in this place I will
give peace, declares the LORD of hosts.'"

Blessings for a Defiled People

10 [t]On the twenty-fourth day of the ninth month, [u]in the second year of Darius, the word
of the LORD came by Haggai the prophet, 11 "Thus says the LORD of hosts: [v]Ask the priests
about the law: 12 'If someone carries [w]holy meat in the fold of his garment and touches
with his fold bread or stew or wine or oil or any kind of food, does it become holy?'"
The priests answered and said, [x]"No." 13 Then Haggai said, [y]"If someone who is unclean
by contact with a dead body [z]touches any of these, does it become unclean?" The priests
answered and said, "It does become unclean." 14 Then Haggai answered and said, [a]"So is
it with this people, and with this nation before me, declares the LORD, and so with every
work of their hands. And what they offer there is unclean. 15 Now then, [b]consider from
this day onward.[1] Before stone was placed upon stone in the temple of the LORD, 16 how
did you fare? [c]When[2] one came to a heap of twenty measures, there were but ten. When
one came to the wine vat to draw fifty measures, there were but twenty. 17 [d]I struck you and
all the products of your toil with blight and with mildew and with hail, [e]yet you did not
turn to me, declares the LORD. 18 [b]Consider from this day onward, [f]from the twenty-fourth
day of the ninth month. Since [g]the day that the foundation of the LORD's temple was laid,

[1] Or *backward*; also verse 18 [2] Probable reading (compare Septuagint); Hebrew *LORD, since they were. When*

7 [p][Isa. 60:1]
8 [q][1 Chr. 29:14, 16]
9 [r][ch. 1:8] [s][Zech. 6:13; Eph. 2:14]
10 [t]ver. 18, 20 [u]ch. 1:1
11 [v]See Lev. 10:10, 11
12 [w]Jer. 11:15 [x][ver. 14]
13 [y]Lev. 22:4, 6 [z][Num. 19:22]
14 [a][Isa. 64:6]
15 [b][ch. 1:5]
16 [c][ch. 1:6]
17 [d]Amos 4:9; [ch. 1:9; Deut. 28:22] [e]Jer. 5:3; Amos 4:6
18 [b][See ver. 15 above] [f]ver. 10 [g]Ezra 3:10; Zech. 8:9

nations will be yielded by the nations to adorn the temple; but the result will also be more than this, for the Lord **will fill** his **house with glory**—that is, with his own presence. The focus of Haggai's oracle in its context is specifically on the immediate fulfillment of this prophecy. In addition, from a NT vantage point, many would see a foreshadowing of events unfolding in the incarnation of Christ and ultimately in his second coming at the end of the age (e.g., when Jesus spoke of his body as "this temple" in John 2:20–21; and when the book of Revelation speaks of the day when the whole city of Jerusalem will be filled with the presence of God, "for its temple is the Lord God the Almighty and the Lamb . . . and the kings of the earth will bring their glory into it," Rev. 21:22, 24).

2:8 God ultimately owns all the wealth of all nations: **the silver is mine, and the gold is mine**. Therefore it should be used in obedience to him.

2:9 The latter glory of this house. The ultimate fulfillment of this passage demands a still wider view of redemptive history. The possessions of Jew and Gentile are enlisted in restoring the temple as a place of *shalom* (**peace**, well-being). Likewise, Ezekiel envisions the temple as a source of healing (Ezek. 47:1, 12; cf. Rev. 22:2). The NT "mystery" is a new spiritual temple composed of people from all nations (1 Cor. 3:9, 16–17), a new community that is the focal point of God's saving work in the world (Eph. 3:8–10). Ultimately, the temple as a sign of God's presence with his people is eclipsed by the presence of the Lord of hosts and the Lamb (Rev. 21:22–26).

2:10–19 *Consider Your Ways: Holiness and Defilement; Repentance and Blessing.* In this fifth message, the Lord uses an analogy of ritual holiness and defilement to compel reflection upon the actual status of the people before him (vv. 10–14), consideration of that status and its relation to past agricultural failures before temple restoration (vv. 15–17), and consideration of their experience since rebuilding of the temple began (vv. 18–19).

2:10–14 *Analogy: Holiness and Defilement.* Haggai uses questions directed to priests (cf. 1:4; 2:3) and an analogy to force reflection upon the uncleanness of the people before the Lord (v. 14).

2:10 twenty-fourth day . . . ninth month . . . second year. December 18, 520 B.C., the three-month anniversary since the work of renewal began. This oracle came during the time for sowing seed.

2:11 priests. It is their duty to give a ruling in matters of ritual and law (Hb. *Torah*; Lev. 10:10–11; Deut. 17:8–13).

2:12 Holy meat is meat dedicated for sacrifice (Jer. 11:15). It was assumed that holiness could be transferred from a consecrated object to a person or other object (Lev. 6:27). Haggai questions whether holiness may be transferred from that second consecrated object to a third.

2:13 dead body. While holiness may not be attained through indirect contact, one defiled by contact with a dead body pollutes all that he contacts (Lev. 22:1–9; Num. 19:11–13, 22). **Any of these** likely refers to the foods mentioned in Hag. 2:12.

2:14 every work of their hands. All that they do is unclean (cf. v. 17). **there**. The temple. The lack of holiness and the presence of defilement is due not to the impropriety of current sacrifices (Ezra 3:3–7) but rather to the fact that they permit a ruinous "corpse" (the unfinished temple) to remain in their midst.

2:15–17 *Consider Life before Restoration Began: You Did Not Turn.* The Lord calls the people to reflect upon their economic situation prior to the start of reconstruction. The past lack of agricultural prosperity did not lead to repentance.

2:15 consider (lit., "set your hearts"; cf. v. 18 [2x]). They are to keep an eye on past experience while looking forward to the new thing that God is presently doing. **Before stone was placed**. The play on this verb (Hb. *sim*, translated both "consider" and "placed") supports a correlation between the current state of the people's hearts and their common experience before construction restarted (vv. 16–17).

2:16 how did you fare? There is a direct correlation between the lack of progress on the temple and the people's shattered agricultural expectations (1:6, 9).

2:17 I struck. A drastic action motivated by the love of a Father for his children, but to no avail (Deut. 8:1–5; 30:1–10; Heb. 12:7–11). **blight . . . mildew**. These examples of covenant curses (Deut. 28:22; 1 Kings 8:37; Amos 4:6–9) represent the spectrum of dangers (heat and moisture) faced by crops. **to me** (lit., "and there is not you to me"; cf. Amos 4:9). The people come "to" (Hb. *'el*) their failed agricultural production (Hag. 2:16) but not "to me" (Hb. *'elay*), i.e., they do not return to God.

2:18–19 *Consider Life Since Restoration Began: I Will Bless.* The Lord calls his people to reflect upon their economic situation since the start of reconstruction. Things still appear bleak, but the mention of four crops essential to the life of the people is now a promise that God's blessing is on the horizon.

2:18 Since the day that the foundation . . . was laid. Probably a reference to the resumption of work in 520 B.C., including an official foundation-laying ceremony (rather than the initial work on the foundation, begun in 538, which subsequently had been abandoned).

18[b][See ver. 15 above]
19[h][Zech. 8:12] [i]Joel 2:14
20[f][See ver. 18 above]
21[j]ch. 1:1; [Zech. 4:6]
[k]ver. 6
22[l]Dan. 2:44; Zech. 12:9; [Matt. 24:7] [m][Mic. 5:10]
[n][Zech. 14:13]
23[j][See ver. 21 above]
[o][Isa. 43:10] [p]ch. 1:1
[q]Jer. 22:24

[b]consider: **19** [h]Is the seed yet in the barn? Indeed, the vine, the fig tree, the pomegranate,
and the olive tree have yielded nothing. But from this day on [i]I will bless you."

Zerubbabel Chosen as a Signet

20 The word of the LORD came a second time to Haggai [f]on the twenty-fourth day of
the month, **21** "Speak to [j]Zerubbabel, governor of Judah, saying, [k]I am about to shake the
heavens and the earth, **22** and [l]to overthrow the throne of kingdoms. I am about to destroy
the strength of the kingdoms of the nations, and [m]overthrow the chariots and their riders. And the horses and their riders shall go down, [n]every one by the sword of his brother.
23 On that day, declares the LORD of hosts, I will take you, O [j]Zerubbabel [o]my servant, the
son of [p]Shealtiel, declares the LORD, and make you [q]like a[1] signet ring, [o]for I have chosen
you, declares the LORD of hosts."

[1] Hebrew *the*

2:19 The late-summer harvest of these essential crops (**vine . . . fig . . . pomegranate . . . olive**) fits well with the late-December date (see v. 10). **Is the seed yet in the barn?** Although God's people had already planted their seeds, the day of harvest is still months away, so the Lord promises that an abundant harvest will in fact come. The work on the temple had been started again, giving evidence of the people's renewed devotion to the Lord and their return to a God-centered lifestyle. Thus they should mark **this day** as the day when the Lord has promised, **I will bless you**. Although God is not obligated by their obedience, the statement heralds a brighter tomorrow than the meager results of previous years (cf. 1:6–11).

2:20–23 *Zerubbabel: The Signet Ring.* The sixth and final message from the Lord to Haggai complements the previous word and comes on the same day (vv. 10, 18, 20). Consideration of the past and present (vv. 10–19) shifts suddenly to a future royal vision of trembling creation, overthrown kingdoms, and perishing armies. Ultimately, the vision comes to focus upon the actions of the divine King whose hand bears, as a signet ring, the promise of David's house restored in the person of Zerubbabel. Seven times in this short section the Lord is the acting subject.

2:20–22 *Destruction upon Kingdoms.* In this section the sovereign Lord warns of a coming destruction of kingdoms and nations.

2:20 a second time. This assumes the same date as vv. 10, 18 and makes a clear connection between vv. 20–23 and vv. 10–19.

2:21 shake. Earlier this was for the purpose of harvesting the wealth of the nations (vv. 6–7), while here it is tied to a wide-ranging sense of impending destruction of the nations.

2:22 overthrow. Complete devastation of political entities by divine action. **chariots . . . riders . . . go down**. An allusion to the destruction of Pharaoh's army (Ex. 14:22–29). **sword of his brother**. The chaos will be so great that the enemies of God's people will destroy themselves (Ezek. 38:21).

2:23 *An Image of David's House Restored.* **On that day**. A phrase common to prophetic contexts. Here it sets the Lord's actions in an unspecified future, i.e., "the day of the LORD" (Isa. 2:11–20; see note on Amos 5:18–20; cf. Joel 2; Zechariah 14; see also The Day of the Lord in the Prophets, p. 1668). **I will take**. The Lord's actions are underscored by the thrice-repeated **declares the LORD** [of hosts]. **my servant**. A title given to individuals selected to accomplish God's appointed task. It is particularly associated with David himself or an ideal Davidic king (2 Sam. 3:18; Ps. 89:3; Isa. 49:5–6; Ezek. 34:23–24). **signet ring**. A ring that provided evidence of royal authority and ownership. Like a king sealing legal documents with his ring, the Lord will set his authentic impression upon the world through his royal representative. Zerubbabel, a descendant of one previously discarded (Jer. 22:24–27), is the ring placed back on the hand of the divine King. God's promise to bless his people and the whole world through the house of David still stands (cf. Matt. 1:1).

Consider: Is the seed yet in the barn? Indeed, the vine, the fig tree, the pomegranate, and the olive tree have yielded nothing. But from this day on I will bless you."

Zerubbabel Chosen as a Signet

20 The word of the LORD came a second time to Haggai on the twenty-fourth day of the month, 21 "Speak to Zerubbabel, governor of Judah, saying, I am about to shake the heavens and the earth, 22 and to overthrow the throne of kingdoms. I am about to destroy the strength of the kingdoms of the nations, and overthrow the chariots and their riders. And the horses and their riders shall go down, every one by the sword of his brother. 23 On that day, declares the LORD of hosts, I will take you, O Zerubbabel my servant, the son of Shealtiel, declares the LORD, and make you like a signet ring, for I have chosen you, declares the LORD of hosts."

[illegible]

[illegible]

INTRODUCTION TO

ZECHARIAH

Author and Date

The prophet Zechariah was a priest, the son of Berechiah and grandson of Iddo. He was a member of a prominent priestly family who returned from Babylon with Zerubbabel in about 538 B.C. (Neh. 12:4). Zechariah began his ministry in 520 B.C., shortly after Haggai had begun his prophetic work, and there are many points of contact between Haggai and Zechariah 1–8. Both contain precise date formulas for their oracles and address the need to rebuild the temple, along with giving reassurance that God will bless his people for their faithfulness. Zechariah 9–14 is different in style and content from the earlier chapters, showing more similarities to the later book of Malachi. Some scholars therefore claim that it was written by a different author at a different time. But the evidence in the text can be explained equally well if Zechariah himself wrote those chapters significantly later, perhaps in the fifth century B.C., when different needs surfaced within the community of God's people.

Theme, Purpose, and Occasion

Nearly 20 years after their return from the Babylonian exile in the time of Cyrus (538 B.C.), discouragement dogged God's people, replacing their earlier enthusiasm. The foundation of the temple had been laid shortly after the initial return, in 536 B.C., but powerful opposition had prevented any further progress on rebuilding the temple. Though Persian foreign policy accorded a significant role to local traditions—unlike the previous overlords, the Babylonians (prior to 538 B.C.)—life was still hard in the province of Judah (often referred to as "Yehud" in this period). Taxes were high, especially as the Persian king, Darius Hystaspes, prepared for a campaign against Egypt. There was little evidence of the kind of transformation of the state of things that the earlier prophets had anticipated, whether externally in a restoration of Jewish sovereignty, or internally in a moral reformation of the people. In particular, the city of Jerusalem was still only partially rebuilt and was on the sidelines of world significance. Under the circumstances, it was easy for the people to conclude that theirs was a "day of small things" (4:10) in which God was absent from his people. In such a context, faithful obedience was viewed by many as useless: pragmatically, it made more sense to pursue the best life possible in spite of the present difficulties.

Zechariah addressed such discouragement by reminding his hearers that, though hidden, God's envoys were watching everything, and that when the time was right, he would act to reorder the universe (1:8–11). Their forefathers had discovered God's faithfulness to judge his people if they failed to heed the words of the prophets (1:4–6). If the people would heed the words of the prophets and turn to the Lord, they would discover him turning to them. He would trouble the nations who were enjoying rest and grant rest to his troubled people, making Jerusalem once again the center of the world, a place of universal pilgrimage (1:14–17). The temple that was being rebuilt and the priesthood that would serve in it were signs of the Lord's commitment to his people, a commitment that would be demonstrated by the ultimate removal of all their sin from the land (3:8–10). This would happen when the promised Davidic king, the Branch, arrived (3:8). The result would be peace, harmony, and prosperity for all the inhabitants of the land, as the Lord once more dwelt in their midst.

The latter chapters of Zechariah also show that the coming of this Davidic ruler will not be without challenge. A new ruler will come to Jerusalem, a ruler who will not be like the existing rulers but will be righteous and humble, bringing salvation (9:9–11). In contrast to the shepherds who feed themselves at

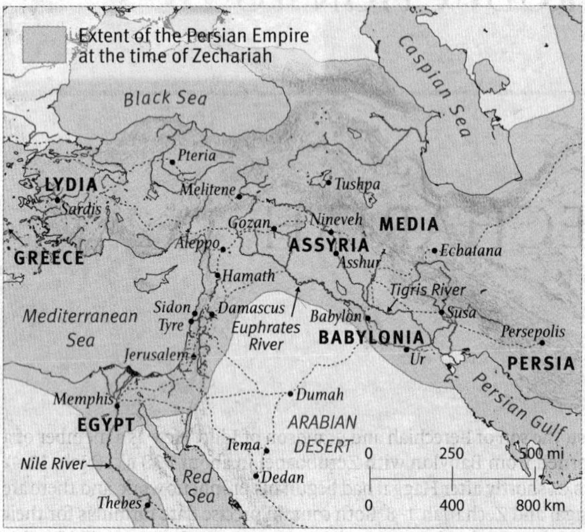

The Near East at the Time of Zechariah
c. 520 B.C.
Zechariah prophesied to the people of Judah soon after they had returned from exile in Babylon. Several years earlier, in 539 B.C., Cyrus the Great, who had united the Persians and the Medes under his rule, conquered Babylon and absorbed its territory into his empire. A year later he permitted the people of Judah to return to their homeland and rebuild the temple. He and his son Cambyses extended the Persian Empire until it stretched from Egypt and Lydia to the borders of India.

the expense of the flock, this good shepherd will take care of the flock and provide for them (9:16). He will cleanse them of all their iniquities (13:1). Yet the flock will themselves reject this good shepherd, and the Lord's own sword will be unleashed against him (11:4–16; 13:7). The sheep will be scattered and left to their oppressors in a time of trial and testing. Yet ultimately God will redeem his flock and rescue his city. Final judgment will come upon all the nations that assaulted God's people, and the end result will be the complete holiness of Jerusalem. It will be restored as God's chosen city, to which the nations will come on pilgrimage (ch. 14).

The book of Zechariah is densely mined for quotations by the NT, whose authors discerned in it several prophecies concerning the Messiah's coming. The clearest instances come from Zechariah 8:16 (in Eph. 4:25), Zechariah 9:9 (in Matt. 21:5 and John 12:15), Zechariah 11:12–13 (in Matt. 27:9–10), Zechariah 12:10 (in John 19:37), and Zechariah 13:7 (in Matt. 26:31 and Mark 14:27). In addition to these are numerous allusions, which are sometimes difficult to assess; one estimate, however, finds about 54 passages from Zechariah echoed in about 67 different places in the NT, with the lion's share of these found in the book of Revelation.

Key Themes

1. The need for repentance and turning to the Lord (1:1–6).
2. The necessity of sincerity in serving the Lord (ch. 7).
3. The Lord's concern and care for the plight of his people (1:8–17; 4:10).
4. The future expansion and blessing of Jerusalem (2:4, 12; 8:1–8; 14:16).
5. The complete and permanent removal of the sin of the people (ch. 3; ch. 5).
6. The removal of false prophecy and idolatry from the land (13:2–6).
7. The centrality of the temple as the source of God's blessing (ch. 4).
8. The Lord's wrath at the nations that plundered Judah and Jerusalem (1:18–21; 14:3–5).
9. The return of the Divine Warrior to terrorize Israel's foes (9:1–8).
10. The coming of the Branch, a Davidic ruler who will save his people, cleanse their sins, and establish peace (3:8; 6:9–15; 9:9–10).
11. The pouring out of God's Spirit, resulting in repentance, and the opening of a fountain for the cleansing of sin (12:10–13:1).
12. Judgment on the wicked shepherds of God's people and their replacement by a good shepherd (11:1–17).
13. The striking of the good shepherd and the scattering of the flock (13:7–9).
14. The final triumph of the Lord over the nations (ch. 14).

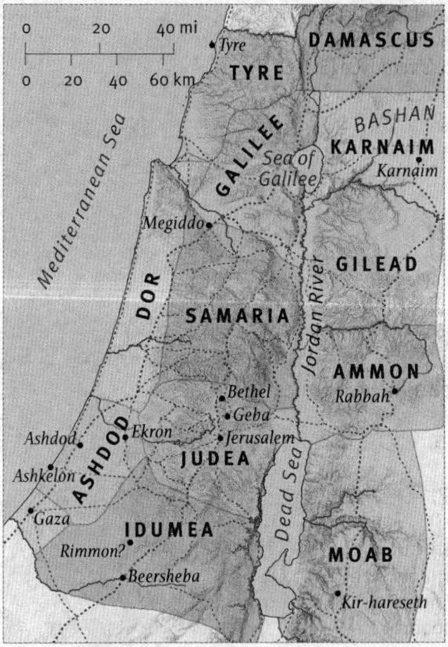

Palestine at the Time of Zechariah
c. 520 B.C.
By Zechariah's time the borders of the land of Israel and Judah, later called Palestine, had been completely redrawn from the days before the Assyrian and Babylonian invasions. The minor Persian province to which exiles of Judah returned from Babylon was now called Judea, and it encompassed only a fraction of the territory that had once belonged to Judah. Edomites had migrated northwest from their traditional homeland just south of Moab into the area immediately south of Judea, and this land was now called Idumea. Territory that had once belonged to the northern kingdom of Israel was divided into several different minor provinces, including Samaria.

History of Salvation Summary

After the horrors of the exile, God is renewing his commitment to restore Judah as his treasured people. They will still suffer more distress, but in the end God will judge the Gentile oppressors and Judah will produce the Messiah, who will rule over the whole world, bringing them to worship the true God. (For an explanation of the "History of Salvation," see the Overview of the Bible, pp. 23–26. See also History of Salvation in the Old Testament: Preparing the Way for Christ, pp. 2635–2661.)

Literary Features

The main genre of Zechariah is futuristic prophecy. Although the second half of the book contains some conventional oracles of judgment and oracles of redemption, in the first half the preferred medium is visions that embody in symbolic form what God plans to do. This part of the book needs to be approached much like the NT book of Revelation—by first allowing the images and symbols to activate the imagination, and then by exploring what those details symbolize. Visions and oracles of salvation predominate over images of judgment. Chapters 1–6 of Zechariah, with their striking otherworldly visions in the company of an angelic interpreter, form an important precursor to later apocalyptic literature.

Like other prophetic books, the book of Zechariah is a collection of individual units. In keeping with its dream format of momentary pictures that follow each other quickly and partly disjointedly, little narrative continuity emerges. The nine visions that open the book are organized like a succession of visual pageants. The oracles that constitute the second half of the book are equally kaleidoscopic in their arrangement, though they are unified by the motif of God's blessing his people.

Outline

I. Oracles and Visions (1:1–8:23)
   A. Introduction: return to me and I will return to you (1:1–6)
   B. Eight night visions and a sign-act (1:7–6:15)
      1. Vision one: the Lord's hidden horsemen (1:7–17)
      2. Vision two: Judah's oppressors oppressed (1:18–21)
      3. Vision three: Jerusalem unwalled (2:1–13)
      4. Vision four: the reclothing of Joshua (3:1–10)

5. Vision five: the olive trees and the lampstand (4:1–14)
6. Vision six: the flying scroll—wickedness judged (5:1–4)
7. Vision seven: the flying ephah—wickedness removed (5:5–11)
8. Vision eight: the Lord's army on the move (6:1–8)
9. A sign-act: the crowning of Joshua (6:9–15)

C. From fasts to feasts (7:1–8:23)
1. Ritual or reality (7:1–14)
2. The promise of the future (8:1–23)

II. The Return of the King (9:1–14:21)

A. The first oracle: leaders and their people (9:1–11:17)
1. The return of the king (9:1–17)
a. The divine warrior comes (9:1–8)
b. The king enters Jerusalem (9:9–11)
c. The king's enemies destroyed and his people redeemed (9:12–17)
2. The shepherds and the flock (10:1–12)
a. Judgment on Judah's shepherds (10:1–5)
b. The restoration of the flock (10:6–12)
3. The shepherds and one shepherd (11:1–17)
a. Judgment on Judah's shepherds (11:1–3)
b. A sign-act: the shepherd rescues his flock but is rejected (11:4–17)

B. The second oracle: the people and their leaders (12:1–14:21)
1. The restoration and renewal of God's people (12:1–13:6)
a. Jerusalem's triumph and the nations' doom (12:1–9)
b. Mourning for sin (12:10–14)
c. Cleansing from sin and idolatry (13:1–6)
2. Judgment and transformation (13:7–14:21)
a. The shepherd struck and the flock scattered (13:7–9)
b. Jerusalem's judgment, deliverance, and exaltation (14:1–11)
c. The nations humbled and brought into submission (14:12–21)

ZECHARIAH

A Call to Return to the LORD

1 In the eighth month, [a]in the second year of Darius, the word of the LORD came to the
prophet [b]Zechariah, the son of [c]Berechiah, son of [d]Iddo, saying, 2 [e]"The LORD was very
angry with your fathers. 3 Therefore say to them, Thus declares the LORD of hosts: [f]Return
to me, says the LORD of hosts, and [g]I will return to you, says the LORD of hosts. 4 [h]Do not
be like your fathers, [i]to whom the former prophets cried out, 'Thus says the LORD of
hosts, [f]Return from your evil ways and from your evil deeds.' But [j]they did not hear or pay
attention to me, declares the LORD. 5 Your fathers, where are they? And [k]the prophets, do
they live forever? 6 [l]But my words and my statutes, which I commanded [m]my servants the
prophets, did they not [n]overtake your fathers? So they repented and said, [o]'As the LORD of
hosts purposed to deal with us for [p]our ways and [p]deeds, so has he dealt with us.'"

A Vision of a Horseman

7 On the twenty-fourth day of the eleventh month, which is the month of Shebat, in the
second year of Darius, the word of the LORD came to the prophet [b]Zechariah, the son of
[c]Berechiah, son of [d]Iddo, saying, 8 "I saw in the night, and behold, [q]a man riding on a red
horse! He was standing among the myrtle trees in the glen, and behind him were [r]red,
sorrel, and white horses. 9 Then I said, 'What are these, my lord?' [s]The angel who talked
with me said to me, 'I will show you what they are.' 10 So [q]the man who was standing

Chapter 1

1 [a]See Hag. 1:1 [b]Ezra 6:14; Matt. 23:35 [c]1 Chr. 6:39 [d]Neh. 12:4, 16
2 [e][Jer. 2:5]
3 [f]Isa. 31:6; Jer. 3:1, 22; Ezek. 18:30; Mal. 3:7 [g]Jer. 12:15; Mic. 7:19
4 [h][Ps. 78:8] [i]See 2 Chr. 36:15 [f][See ver. 3 above] [j]ch. 7:11; 2 Chr. 36:16; See Jer. 35:15
5 [k][John 8:52]
6 [l][Isa. 40:8; Matt. 24:35] [m]See Dan. 9:6 [n]Deut. 28:2, 15 [o]Lam. 2:17 [p][Ezek. 36:31]
7 [b][See ver. 1 above] [c][See ver. 1 above] [d][See ver. 1 above]
8 [q][Rev. 6:4] [r][Rev. 6:4, 5, 8]; See ch. 6:2-7
9 [s][Rev. 22:6]
10 [q][See ver. 8 above]

1:1–8:23 *Oracles and Visions.* The lengthy vision sequence (1:7–6:15) dominates the first half of the book. It is punctuated by an oracle of restoration (2:6–13) after the third vision and concluded by the identification of the high priest Joshua as the pivotal agent of renewal (6:9–15). In the company of the angelic guide, the prophet (and the reader) encounters several tightly interwoven elements: the supernatural agents of God's will, natural powers as tools of the divine plan, the identification and equipping of the community's divinely appointed leaders, and the consistent plea for God's people to repent and cooperate with God's saving actions. In short, God is moving, and the whole of creation is affected. This awareness of heavenly realities now reflected in human affairs was to become the hallmark of later apocalyptic literature. Chapter 7 attends to the ethical state of the community. The trauma and triumph of Zion's restoration frame the whole (1:1–6; 8:1–23), as it also does in the second half of the book (cf. 9:9–13; 14:16–21).

1:1–6 *Introduction: Return to Me and I Will Return to You.* After the exile, God invites his people to renew their commitment to him.

1:1 The second year of Darius is 520 B.C., a time when stability was returning to the Persian Empire after a period of internal unrest. Interest in the old prophecies was stirred by the rebuilding work beginning on the temple under the preaching of Haggai, who had begun his ministry two months earlier. Zechariah's name means "Yahweh remembered."

1:2–3 The LORD was very angry with their **fathers** (v. 2), the generations whose sins caused the exile. Yet that need not be the Lord's attitude to this generation: if they would return to the Lord, then he would **return to** them in favor and blessing (v. 3).

1:6 Their forefathers ignored the words of the Lord's **prophets** and paid the price of God's judgment. Even the prophets themselves died. Yet the Lord's **words** and **statutes** that he spoke through the prophets were effective in bringing their threatened judgment. Now they also bore fruit in the response of the new generation, who **repented** (lit., "returned") and confessed the justice of the Lord's judgments. This is the foundation for the following visions, which speak of the Lord's returning to his people.

1:7–6:15 *Eight Night Visions and a Sign-act.* The eight visions that follow were all received in a single night shortly before the new year, a date often associated in the ancient Near East with temple building.

1:7–17 *Vision One: The Lord's Hidden Horsemen.* In his first vision, Zechariah sees horsemen, who report to God the condition of the earth and prompt the angel of the Lord to intercede for Jerusalem.

1:8 The first vision concerns a **man riding on a red horse**, accompanied by others on **red, sorrel, and white horses**. In Hebrew "red" is actually a conventional color for a horse (dark chestnut), while "sorrel" is a lighter brown. These normal horses are concealed **among the myrtle trees** (evergreens that provide plenty of foliage for cover) **in the glen** (a deep valley or ravine).

1:10–11 These horsemen, **whom the LORD has sent to patrol the earth** (v. 10), are his "special operations" forces, not human beings (who could not

Dates of the Oracles in Zechariah

Reference	Date	
1:1	eighth month of the second year of Darius	October/November 520 B.C.
1:7	24th day of the 11th month (Shebat) of the second year of Darius	February 15, 519
7:1	fourth day of the ninth month (Kislev) of the fourth year of Darius	December 7, 518

among the myrtle trees answered, [t]"These are they whom the LORD has sent to [u]patrol
the earth.' 11 And they answered [s]the angel of the LORD who was standing among the
myrtle trees, and said, [u]'We have patrolled the earth, and behold, all the earth [v]remains
at rest.' 12 Then [s]the angel of the LORD said, [w]'O LORD of hosts, [w]how long will you [x]have
no mercy on Jerusalem and the cities of Judah, against which you have been angry these
[y]seventy years?' 13 And the LORD answered [z]gracious and comforting words to [s]the angel
who talked with me. 14 So [s]the angel who talked with me said to me, 'Cry out, Thus says
the LORD of hosts: [a]I am exceedingly jealous for Jerusalem and for Zion. 15 [b]And I am
exceedingly angry with the nations that are [c]at ease; [d]for while I was angry but a little,
[e]they furthered the disaster. 16 Therefore, thus says the LORD, [f]I have returned to Jerusalem
with mercy; [g]my house shall be built in it, declares the LORD of hosts, and [h]the measuring
line shall be stretched out over Jerusalem. 17 Cry out again, Thus says the LORD of hosts:
[i]My cities shall again overflow with prosperity, [j]and the LORD will again comfort Zion
and again [k]choose Jerusalem.'"

A Vision of Horns and Craftsmen

18 [1] And I lifted my eyes and saw, and behold, [l]four horns! 19 And I said to [s]the angel who
talked with me, "What are these?" And he said to me, [l]"These are the horns that have scattered Judah, Israel, and Jerusalem." 20 Then the LORD showed me four craftsmen. 21 And I
said, "What are these coming to do?" He said, [l]"These are the horns that scattered Judah, so
that no one raised his head. And these have come [m]to terrify them, to cast down the horns
of the nations [n]who lifted up their horns against the land of Judah to scatter it."

A Vision of a Man with a Measuring Line

2 [2] And I lifted my eyes and saw, and behold, [o]a man with a measuring line in his hand!
2 Then I said, "Where are you going?" And he said to me, [p]"To measure Jerusalem, to
see what is its width and what is its length." 3 And behold, [q]the angel who talked with me
came forward, and another angel came forward to meet him 4 and said to him, "Run, say
to that young man, [r]'Jerusalem shall be inhabited [s]as villages without walls, because of
[t]the multitude of people and livestock in it. 5 And I will be to her [u]a wall of fire all around,
declares the LORD, and I will be the glory in her midst.'"
6 Up! Up! [v]Flee from the land of the north, declares the LORD. For I have [w]spread you

[1] Ch 2:1 in Hebrew [2] Ch 2:5 in Hebrew

10 [t][Heb. 1:14] [u]ch. 6:7; [Job 1:7]
11 [s][See ver. 9 above] [u][See ver. 10 above] [v][ver. 15]
12 [s][See ver. 9 above] [w]Ps. 80:4; 89:46; Hab. 2:6; Rev. 6:10 [x]Ps. 102:13 [y]ch. 7:5; Jer. 25:11; 29:10
13 [z]See Jer. 29:10, 11 [s][See ver. 9 above]
14 [s][See ver. 9 above] [a]ch. 8:2; Joel 2:18
15 [b][Joel 3:2] [c][ver. 11] [d][Isa. 54:7, 8] [e][Isa. 47:6]
16 [f]ch. 8:3 [g][ch. 4:9; Ezra 6:14] [h]Jer. 31:39; Ezek. 40:3; 47:3
17 [i]ch. 2:4 [j]Isa. 40:1; 51:3 [k]ch. 2:12
18 [l][1 Kgs. 22:11]
19 [s][See ver. 9 above] [l][See ver. 18 above]
21 [l][See ver. 18 above] [m]Deut. 28:26; Jer. 7:33 [n][Ps. 75:4, 5]

Chapter 2

1 [o]Ezek. 40:3; Rev. 11:1
2 [p][ch. 1:16]
3 [q]ch. 1:9, 19
4 [r][ch. 12:6; 14:10, 11] [s]See Esth. 9:19 [t]Isa. 49:19; Jer. 31:27
5 [u]Isa. 4:5; [ch. 9:8; Ps. 125:2]
6 [v]Isa. 48:20 [w][ch. 7:14; Ezek. 5:10; 17:21]

quickly inspect the whole earth) but angels engaged in secret observation of the world to provide up-to-date and accurate intelligence information for the Lord. Their report states that **all the earth remains at rest** (v. 11).

1:12 For the nations to be at rest while the Lord's people have no rest is a reversal of the proper order. The **angel of the LORD**, God's personal representative, therefore intercedes with the Lord to bring to an end the **seventy years** of judgment (see note on Jer. 25:11).

1:13–14 gracious and comforting words. The Lord's response was positive, and Zechariah was commissioned to spread the good news. The Lord's jealousy toward **Jerusalem** and **Zion** was aroused: this covenantal language implies not merely an emotional change but action in their favor. Though the Lord's anger had been aroused against his own people by their sin (v. 2) and he had summoned the nations to judge them, now it was the turn of the nations to feel the Lord's wrath.

1:17 Since his people had returned to him (v. 6), now the Lord was returning to them. The temple ("my house," v. 16) would be rebuilt and the covenantal blessing of **prosperity** would flow out from it. The Lord would **again choose Jerusalem** as the place of his dwelling with his people.

1:18–21 *Vision Two: Judah's Oppressors Oppressed.* The second vision describes **four horns** (v. 18), which are symbols of military strength. "Four" symbolizes the totality of world powers responsible for the scattering of **Judah, Israel, and Jerusalem** (v. 19). Interpreters differ on the precise identity of these four. The view taken here is that they represent (1) the Assyrians, who exiled the northern kingdom in 722 B.C.; (2) the Babylonians, who exiled Judah and Jerusalem in 586; (3) the Persians, who were their current overlords; and (4a) Greece, by prophetic prediction (see 9:13), or (4b) all other earthly powers that would attack Israel. Another view, commonly held, is that they represent the same kingdoms as those mentioned in Daniel 2 and 7 (Babylonia, Medo-Persia, Greece, Rome). A third view is that no specific kingdoms are in view, but "four" represents all the national enemies of Israel, who would come from the north (Assyria, Babylon, Samaria), south (Egypt), east (Ammon and Moab), and west (or southwest: Philistia). These nations had **scattered** (Zech. 1:21) God's people for their sins, just as the covenant curse of Lev. 26:33 had threatened. The result was that they were bowed down under their oppressors' feet, unable to raise their head. The punishment of the horns fits their crime: those who raised horns against Judah will have their horns cast down by **four craftsmen** (Zech. 1:20), who represent other nations that will cut off the horns of Israel's tormentors and disturb their rest. The Abrahamic covenant promise to curse those who dishonor Abraham and his offspring (Gen. 12:3) is still in force.

2:1–13 *Vision Three: Jerusalem Unwalled.* In this vision Zechariah anticipates a renewed Jerusalem, so full of people that it overspreads its walls. It will attract those Jews who remain in exile, as well as countless Gentiles.

2:1 The third vision is of a **man with a measuring line in his hand.** The focus of this vision is on the future size of the restored city, in contrast to its present unimpressive state.

2:5 Jerusalem will be so large that it will need to be "without walls" (v. 4) because of the numbers of people and animals within it. Yet the lack of a wall will not leave Jerusalem insecure: the Lord himself will provide a **wall of fire** around it, reminiscent of the cherubim and flaming sword that protected the garden of Eden (Gen. 3:24) and of the "horses and chariots of fire" that protected Elisha (2 Kings 6:17). The **glory** of God that had earlier inhabited the tabernacle and temple (Ex. 40:34; 2 Chron. 7:1), and had abandoned it before the destruction of Jerusalem by Nebuchadnezzar (Ezekiel 10), would return to inhabit the entire city (see Ezekiel 43).

2:6–7 Flee from the land of the north. In view of the return of the Lord's glory to Jerusalem and his coming judgment on their former rulers (1:18–20),

abroad as the four winds of the heavens, declares the LORD. **7** [x]Up! Escape to Zion, you who
dwell with the daughter of Babylon. **8** For thus said the LORD of hosts, after his glory sent
me[1] to the nations who plundered you, [y]for he who touches you touches [z]the apple of his
eye: **9** "Behold, [a]I will shake my hand over them, [b]and they shall become plunder for those
who served them. Then [c]you will know that the LORD of hosts has sent me. **10** [d]Sing and
rejoice, O daughter of Zion, for [e]behold, I come [f]and I will dwell in your midst, declares
the LORD. **11** [g]And many nations shall join themselves to the LORD in that day, and shall
be my people. [f]And I will dwell in your midst, and [c]you shall know that the LORD of hosts
has sent me to you. **12** [h]And the LORD will inherit Judah as his portion in the holy land,
and will again [i]choose Jerusalem."

13 Be silent, all flesh, before the LORD, for he has roused himself from his holy
dwelling.

A Vision of Joshua the High Priest

3 Then he showed me [j]Joshua the high priest standing before the angel of the LORD,
and [k]Satan[2] standing at his right hand to accuse him. **2** And the LORD said to Satan,
[l]"The LORD rebuke you, O Satan! The LORD who has [m]chosen Jerusalem rebuke you! Is
not this [n]a brand[3] plucked from the fire?" **3** Now [j]Joshua was standing before the angel,
[o]clothed with filthy garments. **4** And the angel said to [p]those who were standing before
him, [q]"Remove the filthy garments from him." And to him he said, "Behold, [r]I have taken
your iniquity away from you, and [s]I will clothe you with pure vestments." **5** And I said, [t]"Let
them put a clean turban on his head." So they put a clean turban on his head and clothed
him with garments. And the angel of the LORD was standing by.

6 And the angel of the LORD solemnly assured [j]Joshua, **7** "Thus says the LORD of hosts:
If you will walk in my ways and [u]keep my charge, then you shall [v]rule my house and
have charge of my courts, and I will give you the right of access among [w]those who are

[1] *Or he sent me after glory* [2] *Hebrew the Accuser or the Adversary* [3] *That is, a burning stick*

7 [x][Isa. 52:11]
8 [y]Jer. 12:14 [z]See Deut. 32:10
9 [a]Isa. 11:15; 19:16 [b]Ezek. 39:10 [c]ch. 4:9; 6:15; Ezek. 33:33
10 [d]See Zeph. 3:14 [e]Ps. 40:7 [f]ch. 8:3; Isa. 12:6; Ezek. 37:27; Zeph. 3:15; 2 Cor. 6:16; See Lev. 26:12
11 [g]ch. 8:22; See Isa. 2:2 [f][See ver. 10 above] [c][See ver. 9 above]
12 [h]See Deut. 32:9 [i]ch. 1:17; [Hab. 2:20]

Chapter 3

1 [j]ch. 6:11; See Ezra 3:2 [k][1 Chr. 21:1; Ps. 109:6]
2 [l]Jude 9 [m]ch. 1:17; [Rom. 8:33] [n]Amos 4:11
3 [j][See ver. 1 above] [o][Isa. 64:6; Jude 23]
4 [p][ver. 7; Luke 1:19] [q]Rev. 7:14 [r][ver. 9; Isa. 6:7] [s]Isa. 61:10; Luke 15:22; Rev. 19:8
5 [t]Job 29:14; [ch. 6:11]
6 [j][See ver. 1 above]
7 [u]Gen. 26:5; Mal. 3:14; See Lev. 8:35 [v][Deut. 17:9; Mal. 2:7] [w][ver. 4]

those still in exile in **Babylon** should **escape** from there and return to **Zion**, the home of the temple.

2:8 The Hebrew in v. 8 is difficult to understand: it could be rendered "he sent me after glory" (see ESV footnote) or **after his glory sent me**. The rendering in the ESV text is suggested by the parallel clause found at the end of v. 9. Zechariah is thus alluding to his commission as a prophet (cf. Isa. 6:1–5; Ezek. 1:28) as he prepares to fulfill that role. His message is that the Lord is about to bring judgment on those who **plundered** his people (cf. Ezek. 39:25–29). Though once he brought the nations in judgment on Judah, now whoever assaults the Lord's people assaults **the apple of his eye**, that is, the pupil, one of the most sensitive parts of the anatomy.

2:9 The Lord will **shake** his **hand over** Judah's oppressors, thereby giving a signal for their destruction by their former slaves (cf. Isa. 13:2), and the implication of the Hebrew is that this is imminent ("about to shake"). These events would authenticate the validity of the prophet's words.

2:10 The instruction to **sing and rejoice** is paralleled in the Psalms at the conjunction of divine justice (Ps. 35:27; cf. Prov. 29:6) and divine presence (Ps. 90:14). The dramatic return of the Lord to inhabit his rebuilt house is cause for praise for those who have returned to Judah.

2:11 The **nations** too will come and **join themselves to** (enter covenant with) **the LORD in that day** (see Isa. 56:3–5; Jer. 50:3). The result will be Jews and Gentiles together in one nation, **my people**, with the Lord dwelling in their midst (cf. Eph. 2:13–16).

2:12 Though the nations will come to worship the Lord, **Judah** and **Jerusalem** will still be his chosen **portion**.

2:13 Since the Lord **has roused himself from his holy dwelling**, a hushed and reverent awe should descend on **all flesh** (cf. Hab. 2:20).

3:1–10 *Vision Four: The Reclothing of Joshua.* Here Zechariah sees Joshua, the high priest, allowed to represent the people before God and called to live faithfully, with the assurance that God is preserving his people for the messianic Branch.

3:1 The fourth vision is located in the heavenly courtroom, where the **angel of the LORD** is seated as the judge. **Joshua the high priest**, one of the leaders of the returned exiles (Hag. 1:1; spelled "Jeshua" in Ezra and Nehemiah), is the defendant, and **Satan**, whose name means "the Accuser," or "the Adversary," is the prosecutor.

3:2 The Lord's **rebuke** of Satan provides the most likely basis for the reflection on the nature of spiritual authority in 2 Pet. 2:11 (cf. Jude 9).

3:3 Satan has a very strong case, for Joshua was not merely **clothed with filthy garments** but, more precisely, clothed in garments soiled with excrement, which would automatically defile the wearer. Joshua's defilement posed a severe problem for the people, since he was the intermediary through whom their own defilement was to be removed on the Day of Atonement. Yet the Lord ruled Satan's charges inadmissible before he could present them. The Lord's election of Jerusalem and Joshua's position as one "plucked from the fire" (v. 2; i.e., brought safely from the holocaust of exile) means that Joshua is free from any possible condemnation.

3:4 The Lord also acts to cleanse Joshua from his **iniquity**. He commands his servants to **remove the filthy garments**, so removing Joshua's iniquity, and to clothe Joshua in **pure vestments**, garments suitable for him to wear in the presence of the King of kings. Since the filthy garments represent iniquity, these "pure vestments" represent a new righteousness imputed to Joshua.

3:5 Zechariah requests that the reclothing be completed by placing a **clean turban** on Joshua's **head**, an act that has overtones of glory and royalty (Isa. 3:23; 62:3). Joshua's reclothing in ceremonially pure festival garments in the presence of the **angel of the LORD** is a sign of God's gracious acceptance of him and of the people he represented.

3:7 Joshua is charged with a task and granted a promise. The Lord commanded him to **walk in my ways and keep my charge**, language that describes faithful behavior within a covenant context. If he did these things, then he would also **rule my house and have charge of my courts**, which involved ensuring that the worship in the temple was undefiled by idolatry (cf. Ezek. 44:23–24). Joshua would also receive the **right of access among those who are standing here**, that is, in the heavenly council gathered before the Lord. The Lord would not be silent or distant from his people any longer.

standing here. **8**Hear now, O Joshua the high priest, you and your friends who sit before
you, for [x]they are men who are a sign: behold, I will bring [y]my servant [z]the Branch. **9**For
behold, on [a]the stone that I have set before Joshua, on a single stone with [b]seven eyes,[1] I
will [c]engrave its inscription, declares the LORD of hosts, and [d]I will remove the iniquity
of this land in a single day. **10**In that day, declares the LORD of hosts, every one of you will
invite his neighbor to come [e]under his vine and under his fig tree."

A Vision of a Golden Lampstand

4 And [f]the angel who talked with me came again [g]and woke me, like a man who is
awakened out of his sleep. **2**And he said to me, "What do you see?" I said, "I see, and
behold, [h]a lampstand all of gold, with a bowl on the top of it, and [i]seven lamps on it, with
seven lips on each of the lamps that are on the top of it. **3**And there are [j]two olive trees
by it, one on the right of the bowl and the other on its left." **4**And I said to [f]the angel who
talked with me, "What are these, my lord?" **5**Then the angel who talked with me answered

[1] *Or facets*

8 [x][Ezek. 12:11] [y]See Isa. 42:1 [z]ch. 6:12; Isa. 11:1; See Jer. 23:5
9 [a]Ps. 118:22; Isa. 28:16; [ch. 4:7]; See Ezra 3:9-11 [b]ch. 4:10; Rev. 5:6 [c][2 Tim. 2:19] [d][ver. 4]
10 [e]See 1 Kgs. 4:25

Chapter 4

1 [f]ch. 1:9, 19 [g]Dan. 8:18; 10:9, 10
2 [h]See Ex. 25:31 [i]Ex. 25:37; [Rev. 1:12; 4:5]
3 [j][ver. 11; Rev. 11:4]
4 [f][See ver. 1 above]

3:8–9 The promise of divine attentiveness in the present was a shadow of greater things to come. **Joshua** and his **friends**, the priestly class, were **men who are a sign:** their very existence after the exile was an indication of God's commitment to bless his people (v. 8). The future held an even greater blessing, the coming of **my servant the Branch** (v. 8), which would result in the complete and instantaneous removal of the **iniquity of this land** (v. 9). "The Branch" refers back to the prophecies of Jeremiah. The Lord had declared in Jer. 22:30 that none of Jehoiachin's seed would sit on his throne, yet in Jer. 23:5 he nonetheless promised to raise up a righteous "Branch" for David (i.e., the Messiah), who would reign with justice and establish salvation for his people. The engraved **stone** was probably part of the high priest's clothing, a gemstone with seven "facets" (ESV footnote) fastened to the turban and inscribed with an **inscription** (Zech. 3:9). A similar ornament on Aaron's turban was engraved with the words "Holy to the LORD," which enabled Aaron to bear the iniquity of the people before the Lord (Ex. 28:36–38).

3:10 The coming Branch would definitively remove the "iniquity of this land," resulting in the blessing of restored fertility and peace for the land. As at the height of the Solomonic Empire, each man would **invite his neighbor to come under his vine and under his fig tree** (1 Kings 4:25; Mic. 4:4).

4:1–14 *Vision Five: The Olive Trees and the Lampstand.* Zechariah sees lamps on a golden lampstand, a symbol of God's watchfulness and power to fulfill his promises to David's house (represented by Zerubbabel).

4:2 The fifth vision consisted of a solid gold **lampstand** flanked by "two olive trees" (v. 3). A "lampstand" (menorah) is almost always a ritual object, especially one made of gold: there was a single golden lampstand in the tabernacle (Ex. 25:31–40) and 10 in Solomon's temple (2 Chron. 4:7, 20). The lampstand supported a **bowl**, which served as a reservoir for the oil. Arranged around the bowl were **seven lamps**, each of which had **seven lips** (i.e., "spouts"). Individual seven-spouted lamps have been uncovered by archaeologists, but the combination of seven around a single bowl is unmatched. The result would be 49 wicks to give light, a kind of "super-menorah."

4:4 Zechariah asked the angel, **"What are these, my lord?"** and he responded with an oracle explaining the message of the vision.

Zechariah's Visions

Vision	Passage	Content Summary	Zechariah's Question(s) to the Messenger	Promise/Outcome
1	1:7–17	Vision of horsemen who "patrol the earth" and report the condition of the earth; the Lord promises to build his house in Jerusalem	What are these, my lord? (v. 9)	The Lord is jealous for Jerusalem and promises that his house will be built there and that the Lord's cities will overflow with prosperity
2	1:18–21	Vision of four horns and four craftsmen: the horns have scattered Judah, Israel, and Jerusalem, and the craftsmen come to terrify and cast down the horns	What are these? (v. 19) What are these coming to do? (v. 21)	The craftsmen will cast down those who have oppressed Judah, Israel, and Jerusalem
3	2:1–13	Vision of a man with a measuring line in his hand who comes to measure Jerusalem	Where are you going? (v. 2)	Jerusalem will be inhabited, and the Lord will be in the midst of his people
4	3:1–10	Vision of Joshua the high priest and the removal of his iniquity as the representative of the people		Joshua the priest will rule the Lord's house and courts, and the coming of "my servant the Branch" is promised
5	4:1–14	Vision of a lampstand and two olive trees	What are these, my lord? (v. 4) What are these two olive trees . . . ? (v. 11)	The rebuilding of the temple is charged to Zerubbabel and Joshua and will occur by the power of the Lord
6	5:1–4	Vision of a flying scroll		Covenant curses will come upon the covenant breaker, e.g., the one who steals and the one who swears falsely
7	5:5–11	Vision of a woman in the basket (ephah), later carried away by two women	What is it? (v. 6) Where are they taking the basket? (v. 10)	"Wickedness"—symbolized by the presence of the woman—will be removed to Babylon (Shinar)
8	6:1–8	Vision of four chariots pulled by strong horses: red, black, white, dappled	What are these, my lord? (v. 4)	The chariots and horses go north (black and white) and south (dappled) to "patrol the earth"

5 [k]ver. 12
6 [l]See 1 Chr. 3:19 [m][Hos. 1:7]
7 [n][Jer. 51:25] [l][See ver. 6 above] [o]Isa. 40:4 [p]See ch. 3:9
9 [q][Ezra 3:10] [l][See ver. 6 above] [r][ch. 1:16] [s]See ch. 2:9
10 [t][Hag. 2:3] [u][ch. 1:16] [v]ch. 3:9 [w]2 Chr. 16:9; [Prov. 15:3]
11 [j][See ver. 3 above]
12 [j][See ver. 3 above]
13 [x]ver. 5
14 [y]Rev. 11:4 [z]ch. 6:5

Chapter 5

1 [a]Jer. 36:2, 28
2 [a][See ver. 1 above]
3 [b][Jer. 29:18; Ezek. 2:9, 10]; See Deut. 29:27 [c]See Ex. 20:15 [d]Ex. 20:7; [Eccles. 5:2]
4 [e]ch. 8:17; Lev. 19:12; Mal. 3:5 [f]Prov. 3:33 [g][Lev. 14:45]
5 [h]ch. 1:9 [i][ver. 1, 9; ch. 6:1]
6 [j][Ezek. 45:11]

and said to me, [k]"Do you not know what these are?" I said, "No, my lord." 6 Then he said
to me, "This is the word of the LORD to [l]Zerubbabel: [m]Not by might, nor by power, but by
my Spirit, says the LORD of hosts. 7 Who are you, [n]O great mountain? Before [l]Zerubbabel
[o]you shall become a plain. And he shall bring forward [p]the top stone amid shouts of 'Grace,
grace to it!' "

8 Then the word of the LORD came to me, saying, 9 [q]"The hands of [l]Zerubbabel have laid
the foundation of this house; his hands shall also [r]complete it. [s]Then you will know that
the LORD of hosts has sent me to you. 10 [t]For whoever has despised the day of small things
shall rejoice, and shall see [u]the plumb line in the hand of Zerubbabel.

[v]"These seven [v]are the eyes of the LORD, [w]which range through the whole earth." 11 Then
I said to him, "What are these [j]two olive trees on the right and the left of the lampstand?"
12 And a second time I answered and said to him, "What are these [j]two branches of the olive
trees, which are beside the two golden pipes from which the golden oil[1] is poured out?"
13 He said to me, [x]"Do you not know what these are?" I said, "No, my lord." 14 Then he said,
[y]"These are the two anointed ones[2] who stand by [z]the Lord of the whole earth."

A Vision of a Flying Scroll

5 Again I lifted my eyes and saw, and behold, a flying [a]scroll! 2 And he said to me, "What
do you see?" I answered, "I see a flying [a]scroll. Its length is twenty cubits, and its width
ten cubits."[3] 3 Then he said to me, "This is [b]the curse that goes out over the face of the whole
land. For everyone who [c]steals shall be cleaned out according to what is on one side, and
everyone who [d]swears falsely[4] shall be cleaned out according to what is on the other side.
4 I will send it out, declares the LORD of hosts, and it shall enter the house of the thief, and
the house of [e]him who swears falsely by my name. And [f]it shall remain in his house and
[g]consume it, both timber and stones."

A Vision of a Woman in a Basket

5 [h]Then the angel who talked with me came forward and said to me, [i]"Lift your eyes and
see what this is that is going out." 6 And I said, "What is it?" He said, "This is [j]the basket[5]

[1] Hebrew lacks *oil* [2] Hebrew *two sons of new oil* [3] A *cubit* was about 18 inches or 45 centimeters [4] Hebrew lacks *falsely* (supplied from verse 4) [5] Hebrew *ephah*; also verses 7–11. An *ephah* was about 3/5 bushel or 22 liters

4:6 The oracle is addressed to **Zerubbabel**, the governor, who along with Joshua the high priest had been charged by the prophet Haggai with the task of rebuilding the temple (Ezra 5:2; Hag. 1:1). God's word to him is a reminder that the obstacles that face him in the rebuilding task will not be overcome by conventional resources of **might** or **power**. Instead, the resources will come from an outpouring of God's **Spirit** (see Hag. 2:5).

4:7 With that assurance of divine aid, the **great mountain** of difficulties that stands in the way of rebuilding, whether practical, political, or spiritual, is cut down to size. All these obstacles will become a **plain** in front of Zerubbabel (cf. Isa. 40:4).

4:9 As Zerubbabel began the work when he **laid the foundation**, so he would bring it to completion when he brought out the "top stone" (v. 7), or capstone, of the building. The people would respond to Zerubbabel's action by invoking God's blessing upon the building, with shouts of "Grace, grace" (v. 7); its completion would vindicate the prophet's authenticity.

4:10a The growth of the building begun under Zerubbabel would be a challenge to those who thought of their times as a **day of small things**. God's work may start in small and unobtrusive ways, yet reach a glorious conclusion (Matt. 13:31–32).

4:10b A number of the vision's details remain to be clarified. The **seven** lamps on top of the lampstand **are the eyes of the LORD**, representing his watchfulness and awareness of everything that is going on **through the whole earth**. This watchfulness results in blessing for his faithful people (see 2 Chron. 16:9).

4:11–12 Some of the details of how the **two olive trees** (v. 11) on either side of the lampstand are connected to it are obscure. Whatever the precise nature of the branches and the golden pipes, their function is to transmit olive oil from the inexhaustible source of the two olive trees to the bowl of the lampstand, ensuring that the lamps will never go out.

4:14 The two olive trees **are the two anointed ones** (Hb. *bene hayyitshar*; "sons of new oil," ESV footnote). *Yitshar* indicates "new oil," one of the marks of the fertility that flows from God's blessing (Hag. 1:11). These trees are thus characterized by endless fertility, which means unlimited amounts of oil for the lampstand, and they **stand by the Lord of the whole earth** as members of his heavenly court. Most interpreters think these two represent Zerubbabel (the governor, who was descended from David) and Joshua (the high priest). They stand in the Lord's presence and receive his favor and protection. Other possibilities are that they represent Haggai and Zechariah, who as prophets had entrance into the heavenly deliberations; or the angels, who act as God's agents in supplying unlimited divine assistance to the restored temple.

5:1–4 *Vision Six: The Flying Scroll—Wickedness Judged.* The sixth vision is of a gigantic **scroll**, 30 feet by 15 feet (9.1 m by 4.6 m), flying in midair. Its dimensions are those of a large billboard, suggesting that the scroll is unrolled so that its fearful contents may be read. The scroll is a covenant document, written on both sides, like the tablets Moses received from the Lord in Ex. 32:15. Its task is to bring the covenant curses to bear on covenant breakers, using **everyone who steals** and **everyone who swears falsely** as representative examples (Zech. 5:3). Theft was a sin against one's fellow man, while swearing falsely was an offense to God, since the oath was taken in the Lord's **name** (v. 4). All covenant breakers will **be cleaned out** (v. 3) from the community by God's covenant curse. It will **enter the house** of the covenant breaker and **consume it** (v. 4), no matter what building materials have been used.

5:5–11 *Vision Seven: The Flying Ephah—Wickedness Removed.* This vision symbolically describes iniquity's being removed from the land and taken off to Shinar.

5:6–7 The seventh vision is closely linked to the sixth, adding deportation to the threat of destruction. The prophet saw a **basket** (v. 6), or ephah, about three-fifths of a bushel. Inside this small container was **their iniquity in all the land** (v. 6), personified as **a woman** (v. 7). She was trapped in the basket by a circular **leaden cover** (v. 7) weighing roughly 75 pounds (34 kg).

that is going out." And he said, "This is their iniquity[1] in all the land." 7 And behold, the
leaden cover was lifted, and there was a woman sitting in the basket! 8 And he said, "This is
Wickedness." And he thrust her back into the basket, and thrust down [j]the leaden weight
on its opening.

9 Then I lifted my eyes and saw, and behold, two women coming forward! [k]The wind
was in their wings. They had wings like the wings of a stork, and they lifted up the basket
between earth and heaven. 10 Then I said to the angel who talked with me, "Where are they
taking the basket?" 11 He said to me, "To the [l]land of Shinar, to build a house for it. And
when this is prepared, they will set the basket down there on its base."

A Vision of Four Chariots

6 Again I lifted my eyes and saw, and behold, four chariots came out from between two
mountains. And the mountains were mountains of [m]bronze. 2 The first chariot had [n]red
horses, the second [o]black horses, 3 the third [p]white horses, and the fourth chariot dappled
horses—all of them strong.[2] 4 Then I answered and said to [q]the angel who talked with me,
"What are these, my lord?" 5 And the angel answered and said to me, [r]"These are going out
to the four winds of heaven, after [s]presenting themselves before [t]the Lord of all the earth.
6 The chariot with the black horses goes toward [u]the north country, the white ones go after
them, and the dappled ones go toward [v]the south country." 7 When the strong horses came
out, they were impatient to go and [w]patrol the earth. And he said, "Go, [w]patrol the earth."
[w]So they patrolled the earth. 8 Then he cried to me, "Behold, those who go toward [u]the
north country have set my Spirit at rest in [u]the north country."

The Crown and the Temple

9 And the word of the LORD came to me: 10 "Take from the exiles [x]Heldai, Tobijah, and
[y]Jedaiah, who have arrived from Babylon, and go the same day to the house of Josiah, the
son of [z]Zephaniah. 11 Take from them silver and gold, and make a crown, [a]and set it on
the head of [b]Joshua, the son of Jehozadak, the high priest. 12 And say to him, 'Thus says
the LORD of hosts, "Behold, the man whose name is [c]the Branch: for he shall branch out

[1] One Hebrew manuscript, Septuagint, Syriac; most Hebrew manuscripts *eye* [2] Or *and the fourth chariot strong dappled horses*

8 [j][See ver. 6 above]
9 [k][Hos. 4:19]
11 [l]See Gen. 11:2

Chapter 6

1 [m]Dan. 2:39
2 [n]ch. 1:8; Rev. 6:4 [o]Rev. 6:5
3 [p]ch. 1:8; Rev. 6:2
4 [q]ch. 1:9
5 [r]Ps. 104:4; Heb. 1:7 [s]ch. 3:4 [t]ch. 4:14
6 [u]ver. 8; ch. 2:6; Jer. 1:13 [v][ch. 9:14]
7 [w][ch. 1:10]
8 [u][See ver. 6 above]
10 [x][ver. 14] [y]Neh. 7:39 [z]2 Kgs. 25:18
11 [a][ch. 3:5] [b]ch. 3:1
12 [c]See ch. 3:8

5:8 Wickedness personified in female form may represent an idolatrous image of a female deity, perhaps Asherah, and is a comprehensive term for all kinds of sin, both religious and social (Deut. 9:4; 2 Chron. 22:2–3). It is also possible that the woman represents foreign wives (see Ezra 9; Neh. 13:23–27). The two issues were connected, since foreign wives often led the Israelites into idolatry (Neh. 13:26). Yet the vision includes nothing less than the removal of all iniquity from the land (see Zech. 3:9). The angel was careful that the woman did not escape. He **thrust her back into the basket, and thrust down the leaden weight on its opening**. There is no danger of the situation's getting out of control. Wickedness exists under the power and authority of God.

5:9 The wickedness that has been personified in female shape was removed by **two women** with the **wind** (Hb. *ruakh*), the divine agency of motion, **in their wings**. They have **wings like the wings of a stork**, a large bird that migrates northward from Palestine each year, traveling in the same direction as the basket. There is no consensus among interpreters regarding any other symbolic significance of these women. They are God's messengers, perhaps angels or other heavenly beings. (If angels, this would be the only place in Scripture where angels are portrayed as women rather than as men.)

5:11 The basket of wickedness was to be transported to a new location in the **land of Shinar** (Babylon), where a **house**, or temple, would be built for it. All the idolaters would thus be removed, along with the object of their idolatry, to a safe distance from whence they would never again return to trouble God's people by their wickedness.

6:1–8 *Vision Eight: The Lord's Army on the Move.* Zechariah sees four chariots, symbolic of God's power ruling over all the earth.

6:1–3 The eighth vision is clearly similar to the first. Zechariah saw **four chariots** (v. 1) with horses of different colors: **red**, **black** (v. 2), **white**, and **dappled** (v. 3). On red horses, see note on 1:8. The chariots were going out from between **two mountains . . . of bronze** (6:1), whose color reflects a shining appearance. Chariots were the ancient equivalent of tanks, the key symbol of military power. These chariots were pulled by **strong** horses (v. 3), and there were four of them, the number of completeness. The heavenly army is finally on the move.

6:5 The interpreting angel explains that the chariots represent the **four winds of heaven**, stressing the universality of their range: nowhere in the world is outside their reach. The Hebrew word for "wind" (Hb. *ruakh*) is the same as that for "spirit," so these winds also represent the agency of divine power at work in the world (cf. 5:9).

6:6 The "chariots" went in different directions: the **white** and the **black horses** went to the **north country**, while the **dappled ones** went to the **south country**. The red horses were not included in the commission, perhaps being held in reserve. Judah's main enemies always came from the north (Babylon, Assyria, Persia) or the south (Egypt), since to the west is the Mediterranean Sea and to the east is the desert.

6:7 The **strong horses** (with their chariots) moved out at the divine command to **patrol the earth**, asserting and imposing God's sovereign rule over the whole world. The prime target was "the north country," Babylon, which was the objective assigned to two of the four chariots.

6:8 Victory is easily accomplished, and God's **Spirit** (Hb. *ruakh*) is **set . . . at rest in the north country**, the former home of his enemies. This implies the full and final defeat of those opposed to God (cf. Deut. 12:10).

6:9–15 *A Sign-act: The Crowning of Joshua.* This oracle looks forward to the successful building of the temple.

6:11 Joshua, the son of Jehozadak, the high priest is to be crowned with a **crown** of **silver and gold** in a symbolic action. The composite crown reflects the expectation of Hag. 2:8 that both of these elements would come to the temple from afar and fill it with glory. The resources for the sign-act are provided by those "who have arrived from Babylon" (Zech. 6:10), underlining the place of the exiles in the future of the community.

6:12 Joshua is to be crowned as a symbol of the reality to come, **the Branch**, a reference to Jer. 33:15. Zechariah reiterates Jeremiah's promise of a com-

12[d][Matt. 16:18; Heb. 3:3]; See Eph. 2:20-22
13[d][See ver. 12 above] [e]Ps. 21:5; Ezek. 21:27 [f]Ps. 110:4; Heb. 3:1 [g][Hag. 2:9]
14[h]Ex. 12:14; [Matt. 26:13; Mark 14:9] [i][ver. 10] [j]ver. 10
15[k]Isa. 57:19; [Eph. 2:13, 19] [l]Isa. 60:10 [m]See ch. 2:9 [n]See Deut. 30:1-3

Chapter 7

1[o][ch. 1:1, 7] [p]Neh. 1:1
2[q]ch. 8:21, 22; 1 Sam. 13:12; Mal. 1:9
3[r]Mal. 2:7 [s]ch. 8:9; [Ezra 5:1; 6:14] [t][ch. 12:12] [u]ch. 8:19; [2 Kgs. 25:8]
5[u][See ver. 3 above] [v][2 Kgs. 25:25] [w]See ch. 1:12 [x][Isa. 58:4, 5]
6[y][1 Cor. 11:20, 21]
7[z][ch. 1:5, 6] [a]ver. 12 [b]Jer. 17:26
9[c]Isa. 1:17; Jer. 21:12; Mic. 6:8; [Matt. 23:23]
10[d]Isa. 1:23; Jer. 5:28; See Ex. 22:21, 22 [e]Prov. 22:22 [f]ch. 8:17
11[g]ch. 1:4 [h]Neh. 9:29
12[i][Ezek. 11:19; 36:26] [j][Neh. 9:30]

from his place, and [d]he shall build the temple of the LORD. **13** [d]It is he who shall build the
temple of the LORD [e]and shall bear royal honor, and shall sit and rule on his throne. And
there shall be a [f]priest on his throne, [g]and the counsel of peace shall be between them
both."' **14** And the crown shall be in the temple of the LORD as [h]a reminder to [i]Helem,[1]
[j]Tobijah, [j]Jedaiah, and Hen [j]the son of Zephaniah.
15 [k]"And those who are far off shall come and [l]help to build the temple of the LORD.
[m]And you shall know that the LORD of hosts has sent me to you. [n]And this shall come to
pass, if you will diligently obey the voice of the LORD your God."

A Call for Justice and Mercy

7 [o]In the fourth year of King Darius, the word of the LORD came to Zechariah on the
fourth day of the ninth month, which is [p]Chislev. **2** Now the people of Bethel had sent
Sharezer and Regem-melech and their men [q]to entreat the favor of the LORD, **3** [r]saying
to the priests of the house of the LORD of hosts and [s]the prophets, "Should I weep and
[t]abstain in [u]the fifth month, as I have done for so many years?"
4 Then the word of the LORD of hosts came to me: **5** "Say to all the people of the land and
the priests, When you fasted and mourned in [u]the fifth month and in [v]the seventh, for these
[w]seventy years, [x]was it [x]for me that you fasted? **6** [y]And when you eat and when you drink,
do you not eat for yourselves and drink for yourselves? **7** [z]Were not these the words that the
LORD proclaimed [a]by the former prophets, when Jerusalem was inhabited and prosperous,
[b]with her cities around her, and the [b]South and the [b]lowland were inhabited?"
8 And the word of the LORD came to Zechariah, saying, **9** "Thus says the LORD of hosts,
[c]Render true judgments, show kindness and mercy to one another, **10** [d]do not oppress the
widow, the fatherless, the sojourner, [e]or the poor, and [f]let none of you devise evil against
another in your heart." **11** But [g]they refused to pay attention [h]and turned a stubborn shoulder
and stopped their ears that they might not hear.[2] **12** [i]They made their hearts diamond-hard
[j]lest they should hear the law and the words that the LORD of hosts had sent [j]by his Spirit

[1] An alternate spelling of *Heldai* (verse 10) [2] Hebrew *and made their ears too heavy to hear*

ing king who will flourish and branch out and **build the temple of the LORD** and will bear royal honor, reflecting the authority and legitimacy of the king's rule.

6:13 The coming king will sit on his throne, with a **priest** also seated on a **throne** (perhaps next to him). As in Jeremiah 33, the continuance of the Davidic monarchy and the Levitical priesthood are intertwined. The king is necessary to rebuild the temple, while the Levitical priests stand before the Lord in that renewed temple, offering sacrifices (Jer. 33:18). **Between them both**, the future king and the future priest, there will be a **counsel of peace**, and flowing from the peace and harmony between these two offices will be peace and blessing for the nation.

6:14 The oracle ends with the named exiles, underlining their present responsibilities. Two of the names are slightly different, perhaps nicknames. The **crown** is to be stored **in the temple of the LORD as a reminder** for the Lord (cf. Ex. 30:11–16; Num. 10:9–10) and as an assurance, for the people, of God's determination to act.

6:15 Those who are still **far off** will **help** those already in Jerusalem **to build the temple of the LORD**. Some interpreters think these represent Jews still in exile who will come to help; others think they represent future help from Gentiles in building the temple. They must continue **diligently** to **obey the voice of the LORD** their **God**, as they began to do in Hag. 1:12.

7:1–8:23 *From Fasts to Feasts.* This section mentions fasts that commemorate the destruction of Jerusalem, which will be transformed into feasts celebrating its renewal. The renewal gives the people another chance to exhibit a society of justice and love, and to be the vehicle by which light comes to all the world.

7:1–14 *Ritual or Reality.* Like the former prophets before him, Zechariah emphasizes that ritual without obedience and justice is empty.

7:1 The **ninth month** of the **fourth year of King Darius** is two years after Zechariah's earlier prophecies, December 518 B.C., after the ceremony to reestablish the temple but before its completion. The month **Chislev** overlaps with November/December (see The Hebrew Calendar, p. 34).

7:2–3 Sharezer and Regem-melech came from **Bethel** (v. 2) in the north with an inquiry addressed to the **priests** and the **prophets** (v. 3). The dual address may be because the question dealt with an issue of ritual to which there was no obvious answer in the law given to Moses. Weeping and abstaining from food and other luxuries were ritual acts of mourning aimed at demonstrating repentance and thereby changing God's disposition toward the penitent (see 2 Sam. 12:21–22). The **fifth month** (Zech. 7:3) was the month in which the temple in Jerusalem had been destroyed by Nebuchadnezzar nearly 70 years earlier. Now that the temple was being rebuilt, it was natural to question whether there was any need to observe the rite any longer.

7:5 Zechariah's ruling applied not simply to the petitioners but to all the inhabitants of the land, and also included the fast observed in the **seventh** month commemorating the assassination of Gedaliah (Jer. 41:1–3). **seventy years**. See note on Jer. 25:11.

7:7 The **South** is the area to the south of Jerusalem, around Beersheba, while the **lowland** is to the west of Jerusalem. Though the original inquiry reflected a ritual concern, the Lord's response asks a deeper question: "When you fasted and mourned, was it really out of a concern over the loss of my favor? If you stop fasting and return to normal eating and drinking, does that mean an abandonment of that concern?" If the people had learned the lesson that the destruction of the temple was intended to teach, and had truly repented and turned from their sins, then they could stop fasting. The temple was being rebuilt. But if they have simply been fasting for themselves all along, then their fasting was a waste of time.

7:9–10 The test of true repentance is a life of obedience to God, specifically, **true judgments** that **show kindness and mercy** (v. 9) to the **widow** and **fatherless**, the **sojourner** and the **poor** (v. 10). These naturally disadvantaged groups in society were easy targets for the strong to oppress. This concern for the weaker members of society was what the Lord had required of his people in the former days, before Jerusalem's fall.

7:12 The law and the words of the **former prophets** were the two parallel means of God's communicating his will to his people, through the priests and prophets. Yet former generations "refused to pay attention" (v. 11) to God's self-revelation. They turned their backs on the Lord, closing their ears and hardening their hearts, thus incurring his anger (1:2).

through [k]the former prophets. [l]Therefore great anger came from the LORD of hosts. **13** [m]"As
I[1] called, and they would not hear, [m]so they called, and I would not hear," says the LORD
of hosts, **14** [n]"and I scattered them with a whirlwind among all [o]the nations that they had
not known. [p]Thus the land they left was desolate, [q]so that no one went to and fro, [r]and
the pleasant land was made desolate."

The Coming Peace and Prosperity of Zion

8 And the word of the LORD of hosts came, saying, **2** "Thus says the LORD of hosts: [s]I am
jealous for Zion with great jealousy, and I am jealous for her with great wrath. **3** Thus
says the LORD: [t]I have returned to Zion and [u]will dwell in the midst of Jerusalem, [v]and
Jerusalem shall be called the faithful city, [w]and the mountain of the LORD of hosts, the holy
mountain. **4** Thus says the LORD of hosts: [x]Old men and old women shall again sit in the
streets of Jerusalem, each with staff in hand because of great age. **5** And the streets of the
city shall be full of boys and girls playing in its streets. **6** Thus says the LORD of hosts: [y]If
it is marvelous in the sight of the remnant of this people in those days, [z]should it also be
marvelous in my sight, declares the LORD of hosts? **7** Thus says the LORD of hosts: Behold,
[a]I will save my people [b]from the east country and from the west country, **8** and I will bring
them to dwell in the midst of Jerusalem. [c]And they shall be my people, and I will be their
God, [d]in faithfulness and in righteousness."

9 Thus says the LORD of hosts: [e]"Let your hands be strong, you who in these days have
been hearing these words from the mouth of [f]the prophets who were present on [g]the day
that the foundation of the house of the LORD of hosts was laid, that the temple might be
built. **10** For before those days [h]there was no wage for man or any wage for beast, neither was
there any safety from the foe for him who went out or came in, for I set every man against
his neighbor. **11** But now I will not deal with the remnant of this people as in the former
days, declares the LORD of hosts. **12** [i]For there shall be a sowing of peace. The vine shall give
its fruit, and the ground shall give its produce, [j]and the heavens shall give their dew. [k]And
I will cause the remnant of this people to possess all these things. **13** And as [l]you have been
a byword of cursing among the nations, O house of Judah and house of Israel, [m]so will I
save you, and [n]you shall be a blessing. [o]Fear not, but [e]let your hands be strong."

14 For thus says the LORD of hosts: [p]"As I purposed to bring disaster to you when your
fathers provoked me to wrath, and I did not relent, says the LORD of hosts, **15** so again have
I purposed in these days to bring good to Jerusalem and to the house of Judah; [o]fear not.

[1] Hebrew *he*

12 [k]ver. 7 [l][2 Chr. 36:16; 1 Thess. 2:16]
13 [m][Isa. 1:15; Jer. 11:11]; See Prov. 1:24-28
14 [n][ch. 2:6] [o]See Deut. 28:33 [p]Ezek. 12:19 [q]ch. 9:8; [Zeph. 3:6] [r][Jer. 7:34]

Chapter 8
2 [s]ch. 1:14
3 [t]ch. 1:16 [u]See ch. 2:10 [v][Isa. 1:26] [w]See Isa. 2:3
4 [x][Ps. 128:6; Prov. 10:27]
6 [y][Ps. 118:23] [z]See Gen. 18:14
7 [a]ch. 10:6 [b]Ps. 107:3; Isa. 43:5; [Isa. 49:12; Ezek. 37:21]
8 [c]ch. 13:9; See Jer. 31:33 [d]Jer. 4:2
9 [e]2 Sam. 16:21; [Hag. 2:4] [f]ch. 7:3; Ezra 5:1, 2 [g]Hag. 2:18
10 [h][Hag. 1:6]
12 [i]Hos. 2:21, 22; Hag. 2:19 [j][Hag. 1:10] [k]See Jer. 3:18
13 [l][Isa. 43:28; 65:15] [m]ch. 10:6 [n]See Gen. 12:2, 3 [o]Hag. 2:5 [e][See ver. 9 above]
14 [p][Jer. 31:28; 32:42]
15 [o][See ver. 13 above]

7:14 The Lord's judgment came upon his people like a **whirlwind**, scattering them among **nations that they had not known**. Fittingly, they themselves joined the ranks of the vulnerable classes that they had oppressed, and the land was left desolate.

8:1–23 *The Promise of the Future.* God is renewing his presence with his people and reaffirming his purpose to bless the nations through them.

8:3 The somber word of judgment on the former generation is not the end of the story. The time of judgment for God's chosen city is reaching an end, and there will be a new beginning (1:14–16). God has **returned to Zion and will dwell in the midst of Jerusalem**. In the days ahead, Jerusalem will become the **faithful city** (cf. Isa. 1:26) and Zion would again be the **holy mountain**. For God's return to the land to be a blessing, the people must also be transformed, so that the dwelling place of the true and holy God will be peopled by truth-telling, holy inhabitants.

8:4 Old and young, male and female are depicted enjoying their natural habitat. Such an idyllic picture of opposite extremes implies peace and plenty for all ages and both sexes, with images of healthful play and relaxed rest that contrast dramatically with the slave labor, malnutrition, and starvation that had been the fate of former Jerusalem. Certainly, compared with their present impoverished circumstances, the future holds greater blessing.

8:6 Such a transformation may seem a **marvelous** miracle to Zechariah's hearers, but it is the sort of miracle that the Creator God of the universe does routinely.

8:7 The Lord uses opposite extremes to underscore the comprehensiveness of his salvation: he will save his people from the **east country** ("the land of the sunrise") and the **west country** ("the land where the sun sets") and thus from everywhere in between.

8:8 When the Lord returns to Jerusalem, all his people must likewise be brought in, so that the central relationship of the covenant between God and his people can be realized, and they can live together **in faithfulness and in righteousness**. The promise **and they shall be my people, and I will be their God** looks back to Jer. 31:33; 32:38; Ezek. 37:23, 27.

8:9 The assurance of God's transforming work is the basis for the people to **be strong** (cf. Hag. 2:3–9).

8:12–13 With the reestablishment of the temple, the Lord's attitude toward his people has changed. Before its rebuilding, travel was hazardous and agricultural labor was unrewarded. But now, after its reconstruction, there will be a **sowing of peace** (v. 12), resulting in the blessings of agricultural prosperity and security promised in the Sinai covenant (Lev. 26:4). Through the Lord's sovereign act of salvation, the **remnant of this people** (Zech. 8:12), who encompass both the **house of Judah and house of Israel** (v. 13), will receive the peace that unfaithful Israel never possessed. As a result, their name will be transformed from use as a **byword of cursing among the nations** into a formula of **blessing** (v. 13), fulfilling the Lord's purpose for them (Gen. 12:2).

8:15 As surely as the Lord carried through his purpose to judge their disobedient forefathers, so certainly the Lord has planned **good** things for this new generation. The Lord's commitment to bless them should have a twofold

[16] These are the things that you shall do: [q]Speak the truth to one another; [r]render in your
gates judgments [s]that are true and make for peace; [17] [t]do not devise evil in your hearts against
one another, and [u]love no false oath, for all these things I hate, declares the LORD."
[18] And the word of the LORD of hosts came to me, saying, [19] "Thus says the LORD of
hosts: The fast of the [v]fourth month and the fast of the [w]fifth and the fast of the [x]seventh
and the fast of the [y]tenth shall be to the house of Judah [z]seasons of joy and gladness and
cheerful feasts. Therefore love [a]truth and peace.
[20] "Thus says the LORD of hosts: Peoples shall yet come, even the inhabitants of many
cities. [21] The inhabitants of one city shall go to another, saying, [b]'Let us go at once [c]to entreat
the favor of the LORD and to seek the LORD of hosts; I myself am going.' [22] [b]Many peoples
and strong nations shall come to seek the LORD of hosts in Jerusalem and [c]to entreat the
favor of the LORD. [23] Thus says the LORD of hosts: In those days [d]ten men [e]from the nations
of every tongue shall take hold of the robe of a Jew, saying, 'Let us go with you, for [f]we
have heard that God is with you.'"

Judgment on Israel's Enemies

9

[1] The oracle of the word of the LORD is against the land of Hadrach
and [g]Damascus is its resting place.
For the LORD has an eye on mankind
and on all the tribes of Israel,[1]
[2] [h]and on Hamath also, which borders on it,
[i]Tyre and [i]Sidon, though [j]they are very wise.
[3] Tyre has built herself [k]a rampart
and [l]heaped up silver like dust,
and fine gold like the mud of the streets.
[4] But behold, the Lord will strip her of her possessions
and strike down [m]her power on the sea,
and [n]she shall be devoured by fire.

[1] Or *For the eye of mankind, especially of all the tribes of Israel, is toward the LORD*

16[q]Cited Eph. 4:25; See Ps. 15:2 [r]See ch. 7:9 [s]ver. 19
17[t]ch. 7:10 [u]See ch. 5:4
19[v][Jer. 39:2] [w]ch. 7:3 [x]ch. 7:5 [y]2 Kgs. 25:1 [z]Isa. 35:10 [a]ver. 16
21[b][ch. 2:11; 14:16; Isa. 2:3] [c]See ch. 7:2
22[b][See ver. 21 above] [c][See ver. 21 above]
23[d]See Gen. 31:7 [e][Isa. 66:18; Rev. 5:9] [f][1 Cor. 14:25]

Chapter 9

1[g]See Isa. 17:1
2[h]Jer. 49:23; See 1 Kgs. 8:65 [i]Josh. 19:28, 29; Isa. 23:1, 2 [j]See Ezek. 28:3-5
3[k][Josh. 19:29] [l]Ezek. 28:4, 5
4[m]Ezek. 26:17 [n]Ezek. 28:18

impact: it should free them from **fear** and motivate them to lives of new obedience toward one another in truth, justice, and grace.

8:19 Formerly, the people fasted in the **fourth month**, when the walls of Jerusalem were breached (2 Kings 25:3–4; Jer. 39:2; 52:6–7); in the **fifth**, when the city fell (Jer. 52:12–15); in the **seventh**, when Gedaliah was assassinated (2 Kings 25:25; Jer. 41:1–3); and in the **tenth**, when the siege of the city first began (2 Kings 25:1; Ezek. 24:1–2). Yet in the days ahead, these fast days would be turned to feast days, **seasons of joy and gladness**, celebrating the salvation and transformation that the Lord had accomplished for them. In view of this, the people are called to **love truth and peace**: "love" implies commitment and devotion rather than being simply an emotional response.

8:20–22 This blessing will extend beyond Jerusalem and Judah to include others as well, the **inhabitants of many cities** (v. 20). Like the people of Bethel in 7:2, they will come to Jerusalem to **entreat the favor of the LORD** (8:21). It will extend beyond God's own people to include the Gentiles: **Many peoples and strong nations shall come** (v. 22).

8:23 **Ten men** represents a complete group **from the nations of every tongue** who recognize that God is with his people and therefore who come to Jerusalem to seek the Lord. This prophecy found its fulfillment on the day of Pentecost (Acts 2).

9:1–14:21 *The Return of the King.* Reference to the surrounding nations in 8:20–23 and 9:1–8 links the book's main parts (chs. 1–8 and chs. 9–14). In the second half of the book, visions recede as does interest in Joshua and Zerubbabel as the named leaders of the community. These latter chapters comprise two blocks of oracles, both introduced as the "oracle of the word of the LORD" (9:1; 12:1; cf. also Mal. 1:1). The twin themes of the purity of God's people and the fidelity of their leaders—often termed "shepherds"—run throughout these oracles. The community and its leaders suffer turmoil: this turn to the Lord faces opposition, tearing at the fabric of society and the natural world. Ultimately, the jubilant "return of the king" (Zech. 9:9) issues in the triumph of God's purposes and the restoration of God's people now joined by all nations (14:9, 16; cf. 8:20–23), for salvation belongs to the Lord (12:7).

9:1–11:17 *The First Oracle: Leaders and Their People.* Judgment on Jerusalem's neighbors contributes to its security (9:1–8), but the arrival of a saving king completes it (9:9–17). While this remains the community's only hope, it still must recover from destructive leaders (10:1–12) who themselves come under judgment (11:1–17).

9:1–17 *The Return of the King.* Zechariah tells restored Judah that its current circumstances are only temporary: God will bring judgment on those who oppress his people, and will bring forth the promised king, who will rule Israel and the nations.

9:1–8 *The Divine Warrior Comes.* **Oracle**. Cf. 12:1; Mal. 1:1. As in Zech. 1:12, the issue is the nations that are wrongfully at rest, and that will now be subject to the Lord's judgment. The oracle starts with **Hadrach** (9:1), an area in northern Syria that encompassed **Damascus** and neighboring **Hamath** (v. 2), after which it moves south along the coast through **Tyre and Sidon** (v. 2) to four of the five cities of the Philistines: **Ashkelon**, **Gaza**, **Ekron** (v. 5), and **Ashdod** (v. 6). In spite of all its natural resources, this whole region will experience the fiery judgment of God that will leave it desolate. Yet even from the destruction of those nations, a **remnant** (v. 7) will emerge who will attach themselves to the Lord and become part of his people (see 8:22–23). In this way, the Lord will eliminate any future threats to the peace and safety of his **house** (9:8) and his people. They will no longer have to fear that an **oppressor** (v. 8) would invade from the north, as they had so often in the past.

5 [o]Ashkelon shall see it, and be afraid;
Gaza too, and shall writhe in anguish;
Ekron also, because its hopes are confounded.
The king shall perish from Gaza;
Ashkelon shall be uninhabited;
6 [p]a mixed people[1] shall dwell in Ashdod,
and I will cut off the pride of Philistia.
7 I will take away [q]its blood from its mouth,
and [r]its abominations from between its teeth;
[s]it too shall be a remnant for our God;
it shall be like [t]a clan in Judah,
and Ekron shall be like the Jebusites.
8 Then [u]I will encamp at my house as a guard,
[v]so that none shall march to and fro;
[w]no oppressor shall again march over them,
[x]for now I see with my own eyes.

The Coming King of Zion

9 [y]Rejoice greatly, O daughter of Zion!
Shout aloud, O daughter of Jerusalem!
[z]Behold, [a]your king is coming to you;
righteous and having salvation is he,
[b]humble and mounted on a donkey,
on a colt, the foal of a donkey.
10 [c]I will cut off the chariot from Ephraim
and [d]the war horse from Jerusalem;
and the battle bow shall be cut off,
and [e]he shall speak peace to the nations;
[f]his rule shall be from sea to sea,
and from [g]the River to the ends of the earth.
11 As for you also, because of [h]the blood of my covenant with you,
[i]I will set your prisoners free from [j]the waterless pit.

5 [o]See Zeph. 2:4
6 [p][Deut. 23:2]
7 [q]See Lev. 3:17 [r][Isa. 66:17] [s][Isa. 14:1] [t]ch. 12:5, 6
8 [u][ch. 2:5] [v]ch. 7:14 [w]ch. 10:4; [Isa. 60:17] [x][ch. 12:4]
9 [y]See Zeph. 3:14 [z]Cited Matt. 21:5; [John 12:15] [a]See Jer. 23:5 [b][Matt. 11:29]
10 [c]See Hos. 1:7 [d]See Mic. 5:10 [e]See Mic. 5:5 [f]Ps. 72:8 [g]See Ex. 23:31
11 [h]Ex. 24:8 [i]Isa. 42:7; 51:14; 61:1 [j][Gen. 37:24; Jer. 38:6]

[1] *Or a foreign people;* Hebrew *a bastard*

9:8 for now I see with my own eyes. The Lord has now observed the severe affliction of his people, and he will act to deliver them. The mention of "eyes" ties the end of this oracle to the beginning, where the Lord's "eye" was mentioned (v. 1).

9:9–11 *The King Enters Jerusalem.* The coming king will bring peace for his people and for the nations.

9:9 This campaign over Israel's enemies would culminate in the triumphal entry of its **king** to **Jerusalem**. The people are summoned to acclaim their coming king. He is described as "righteous," like the ideal ruler of Psalm 72. He will ensure God's blessing on his people, thereby bringing about their "salvation." He is also **humble** (cf. Deut. 17:18–20), hinting that this king is still obedient to the King of kings, and he comes riding **on a donkey**, the mount of one who comes to bring peace, not on the standard military mount, a horse. This prophecy famously finds its counterpart in Jesus' triumphal entry into Jerusalem, when Jesus clearly signals his messianic identity. This verse is directly quoted at Matt. 21:5 and John 12:15, but both evangelists abbreviate the quotation. **righteous and having salvation is he**. As Jesus enters Jerusalem, this work is still to be accomplished. **daughter of Zion**. See note on 2 Kings 19:21.

9:10 The Lord will bring to an end Israel's need for the traditional instruments of war: **chariot, war horse**, and **battle bow**. The coming ruler will rule the whole earth, from **sea to sea** and from the Euphrates **River** to the ends of the earth, just as Ps. 72:8 anticipated. The result of his rule will be universal **peace**.

9:11 The **prisoners**, those of God's people remaining in exile, would be set free from the **waterless pit** (v. 11), a dry well that could be used as a temporary prison (see Gen. 37:24; Jer. 38:6). This salvation would come because of the **blood of my covenant** (Zech. 9:11), that is, the blood of the sacrifices offered to ratify the covenant (see Ex. 24:8). This blood testified to the seriousness of the covenant bond between God and his people. As a result of this hope, they should return to Jerusalem, their "stronghold" (Zech. 9:12;

Zechariah Texts Quoted in the New Testament Regarding Jesus' Ministry

Zechariah Text	Content Summary	NT Passages
9:9	the king comes to Zion humble and riding a donkey	Matt. 21:5; John 12:15
11:13	30 pieces of silver thrown into the house of the Lord	Matt. 27:9
12:10	looking on him whom they have pierced	John 19:37; Rev. 1:7
13:7	the shepherd is struck and the sheep scattered	Matt. 26:31; Mark 14:27

12 [k][Jer. 31:17] [l]Isa. 61:7
13 [m][ch. 10:3, 4] [n]Gen. 10:2; Ezek. 27:13
14 [o]See 2 Sam. 22:15 [p][Isa. 27:13] [q]Isa. 21:1 [r][ch. 6:6]
15 [s]ch. 12:8; [ch. 10:5] [t]ch. 12:6 [u][ch. 10:5] [v]ch. 10:7 [w][Lev. 4:18, 25]
16 [x]Ps. 100:3 [y]Isa. 62:3; [Mal. 3:17]
17 [z][Isa. 62:3, 4] [a][Isa. 62:8, 9; Jer. 31:12]

Chapter 10

1 [b]Jer. 14:22 [c]See Deut. 11:14 [d]Ps. 135:7 [e]Ezek. 34:26
2 [f]See Gen. 31:19 [g]Hab. 2:18

12 Return to your stronghold, O [k]prisoners of hope;
today I declare that [l]I will restore to you double.
13 For [m]I have bent Judah as my bow;
I have made Ephraim its arrow.
I will stir up your sons, O Zion,
against your sons, [n]O Greece,
and wield you like a warrior's sword.

The LORD Will Save His People

14 Then the LORD will appear over them,
and [o]his arrow will go forth like lightning;
[p]the Lord GOD will sound the trumpet
and will march forth in [q]the whirlwinds [r]of the south.
15 The LORD of hosts [s]will protect them,
and [t]they shall devour, [u]and tread down the sling stones,
and [v]they shall drink and roar as if drunk with wine,
and be full like a bowl,
drenched [w]like the corners of the altar.

16 On that day the LORD their God will save them,
as [x]the flock of his people;
for [y]like the jewels of a crown
they shall shine on his land.
17 [z]For how great is his goodness, and how great his beauty!
[a]Grain shall make the young men flourish,
and new wine the young women.

The Restoration for Judah and Israel

10

1 Ask rain [b]from the LORD
in the season of [c]the spring rain,
from the LORD [d]who makes the storm clouds,
and [e]he will give them showers of rain,
to everyone the vegetation in the field.
2 For [f]the household gods [g]utter nonsense,
and the diviners see lies;

see 2:6–7), for the Lord had committed himself to "double" his people's former prosperity (9:12; cf. Isa. 40:2).

9:12–17 *The King's Enemies Destroyed and His People Redeemed.* The prisoners of war are not the only ones who need to hear the news of the coming king. The day of those who are oppressing God's people will soon be over. Instead of the breaking of threatening bows and removal of chariots, God will make his people themselves into a bow against their oppressors (v. 13). He will make Zion's sons into a "warrior's sword" (v. 13). The Lord will appear as the Divine Warrior, sounding the trumpet to advance, shooting his deadly arrow (v. 14), destroying and pouring out blood, just as it is poured out in the sacrificial ritual in which it drenches the altar. By destroying their enemies, he will rescue his people and shepherd his flock (v. 16). They will be "like the jewels of a crown" (v. 16), his treasured possession. They will never again go hungry and thirsty, but will receive the covenantal blessings of grain and new wine (v. 17).

9:13 The oppressors of the **sons** of **Zion** (or Israel) are identified as the **sons** of **Greece** (v. 13). God promises to make Zion **like a warrior's sword**, defeating the Greeks. This is best understood as a predictive prophecy regarding future events, much like the mention of "the king of Greece" in Dan. 8:21. Zechariah was writing between 520 and perhaps 480 B.C., but the Greek ruler Alexander the Great did not conquer Palestine until 333. Then the Jewish people did not successfully rebel against domination by the Seleucids (the Greek-speaking successors to Alexander's rule) until the Maccabean period (the revolt was 166–160 B.C.; they gained full independence in 142). Some interpreters, not allowing the possibility of such predictive prophecy, see this as a later insertion added into the text, but there is no manuscript support for this idea, and it is not necessary. The name "Greece" (Hb. *Yawan*) was known at the time of Zechariah, for the Greeks had defeated the invading Persian armies of King Darius at the battle of Marathon in 490 B.C., but Greece was never an enemy of Israel or a conquering world power until Alexander the Great.

9:15–16 tread down the sling stones. The reference is to stones hurled by slings in battle, but these stones are also a poetic representation of the enemies themselves. The army of Israel will simply trample on them and continue moving forward to conquer. By contrast, God's people are immensely valuable, **like the jewels of a crown**.

10:1–12 *The Shepherds and the Flock.* In this section Zechariah uses the image of Judah's leaders as "shepherds"; the current leaders are unfaithful and greedy, and God must rescue his people from them.

10:1–5 *Judgment on Judah's Shepherds.* Those who currently lead Judah lead them astray, and must be replaced.

10:1 In view of the Lord's promise to provide the grain and new wine for his people (9:17), they should look to him in faith for "rain." The Israelite agricultural economy was dependent on rain for its success, especially the **spring rain**. Since pagan gods such as Baal also claimed to make the **storm clouds** that controlled the rainfall, a crucial test of Israel's faithfulness to the Lord was, from whom would they seek the rain?

10:2 In the past, the leaders sought help from the **household gods**, like those that Rachel stole from Laban (Gen. 31:34), or from pagan **diviners**. Yet these sources had yielded only **empty consolation**, and the people had been left leaderless, like **sheep** without a **shepherd**.

[h]they tell false dreams
and give empty consolation.
Therefore [i]the people wander like sheep;
they are afflicted for lack of a shepherd.

3 [j]"My anger is hot against the shepherds,
and [k]I will punish the leaders;[1]
for [l]the LORD of hosts cares for his flock, the house of Judah,
and will make them like his majestic steed in battle.
4 From him shall come [m]the cornerstone,
from him [n]the tent peg,
from him the battle bow,
from him every ruler—[o]all of them together.
5 They shall be like mighty men in battle,
[p]trampling the foe in the mud of the streets;
they shall fight because the LORD is with them,
and they shall put to shame [q]the riders on horses.

6 [r]"I will strengthen the house of Judah,
and [s]I will save the house of Joseph.
[t]I will bring them back [u]because I have compassion on them,
and they shall be as though I had not rejected them,
for [v]I am the LORD their God and I will answer them.
7 Then Ephraim shall become like a mighty warrior,
and [w]their hearts shall be glad as with wine.
Their children shall see it and be glad;
their hearts shall rejoice in the LORD.

8 [x]"I will whistle for them and [y]gather them in,
for I have redeemed them,
and [z]they shall be as many as they were before.
9 [a]Though I scattered them among the nations,
yet in far countries [b]they shall remember me,
and with their children they shall live and return.
10 [c]I will bring them home from the land of Egypt,
and gather them from Assyria,
and [d]I will bring them to the land of Gilead and to Lebanon,
[e]till there is no room for them.

[1] Hebrew *the male goats*

2 [h]Jer. 23:25 [i]Ezek. 34:5, 6
3 [j][Ezek. 34:10] [k][Ezek. 34:17] [l]Zeph. 2:7
4 [m][Ps. 118:22] [n]Isa. 22:23 [o][ch. 9:8]
5 [p][ch. 9:15] [q][Ps. 20:7]
6 [r][ver. 12] [s]ch. 8:7, 13 [t][Jer. 3:18] [u]Isa. 14:1 [v]ch. 13:9
7 [w]ch. 9:15
8 [x]Isa. 5:26 [y]Jer. 31:10, 11; See Hos. 1:11 [z]Ezek. 36:10, 11, 37
9 [a][Hos. 2:23] [b]Ezek. 6:9; See Deut. 30:1-3
10 [c]Isa. 11:11; 27:13; Hos. 11:11 [d][Mic. 7:14] [e]Isa. 49:20

10:3 The Lord's **anger** was kindled against the **leaders** of his people, described as the **shepherds** and "male goats" (ESV footnote; cf. Jer. 50:8), an image of abusive power (see Ezekiel 34). As a result, he would remove them and provide a new shepherd for his flock.

10:4 The flock would be transformed from wandering sheep into a majestic warhorse, while the new leadership that the Lord would provide for them is described metaphorically as a **cornerstone** (the foundation around which a building was constructed; see Isa. 28:16), a **tent peg** (an image of solid stability; see Isa. 22:20–23), and a **battle bow** (representing military power; see Zech. 9:10). These images have royal associations, but the renovation of leadership extends down to the lower level of overseer (**ruler**; cf. 9:8, where these were Israel's oppressors). These new leaders would be triumphant against all foes because of the Lord's presence with them.

10:6–12 *The Restoration of the Flock.* God will care for the remnant of both Judah and Ephraim, restoring them as his people after the exile.

10:6 The Lord's intervention for his people will result in their strengthening and deliverance. Whereas they were once like sheep without a shepherd, **rejected** by the Lord, he will now **have compassion on them**, completing the process of restoration begun when he brought Judah back from exile. This restoration will extend beyond Judah to include the **house of Joseph**, the northern kingdom, which was scattered by the Assyrians in 722 B.C. When these people cry out to him in exile, he **will answer them** and bring them home, resulting in strength and joy for all of God's people.

10:7 **Ephraim**, as one of the most prominent and centrally located tribes, is named here as standing for the entire northern kingdom (cf. note on Hos. 4:17).

10:8–12 As a shepherd whistles for his flock, the Lord will **whistle** for his people (v. 8), bringing them back from the nations where he scattered them. Earlier, he used the same signal to summon **Egypt** and **Assyria** (v. 10) to judge Israel (see Isa. 5:26; 7:18). Now it will be the signal for their restoration. This involves a second exodus, in which the Lord will pass through the **sea of troubles** (Zech. 10:11) and strike down the **waves of the sea**, representing all the forces of chaos arrayed against God's people. The Lord will also gather his people from their more recent adversary, Assyria, bringing their bondage to an end. Egypt and Assyria are geographical opposites, with Egypt as the major military threat to the south of Israel and Assyria to the north. Both of these historical adversaries will be laid low by the Lord, when he restores his people to himself and brings them to the historical centers of fertility, **Gilead** and **Lebanon** (v. 10).

11 [f]He shall pass through the sea of troubles
and strike down the waves of the sea,
[g]and all the depths of the Nile shall be dried up.
The pride of Assyria shall be laid low,
and [h]the scepter of Egypt shall depart.
12 [i]I will make them strong in the LORD,
and [j]they shall walk in his name,"
declares the LORD.

The Flock Doomed to Slaughter

11

1 Open your doors, [k]O Lebanon,
that the fire may devour your cedars!
2 Wail, O cypress, for the cedar has fallen,
for the glorious trees are ruined!
Wail, [k]oaks of Bashan,
for the thick forest has been felled!
3 The sound of [l]the wail of [l]the shepherds,
for their glory is ruined!
The sound of the roar of [m]the lions,
[n]for the thicket of the Jordan is ruined!

4 Thus said the LORD my God: [o]"Become shepherd of the flock doomed to slaughter.
5 [p]Those who buy them slaughter them and go unpunished, and those who sell them say,
'Blessed be the LORD, [q]I have become rich,' and their own shepherds have no pity on them.
6 For [r]I will no longer have pity on the inhabitants of this land, declares the LORD. Behold,
I will cause each of them to fall into the hand of his neighbor, and each into the hand of
his king, and they shall crush the land, and I will deliver none from their hand."
7 [s]So I became the shepherd of the flock doomed to be slaughtered by the sheep traders.
And I took two staffs, one I named [u]Favor, the other I named [v]Union. [s]And I tended the
sheep. 8 In one month [w]I destroyed the three shepherds. But I became impatient with them,
and they also detested me. 9 So I said, "I will not be your shepherd. [x]What is to die, let it
die. What is to be destroyed, let it be destroyed. And let those who are left devour the flesh

11 [f]Isa. 11:15 [g][Amos 8:8] [h]Ezek. 30:13
12 [i][ver. 6] [j]Mic. 4:5

Chapter 11

1 [k][Isa. 2:12, 13]
2 [k][See ver. 1 above]
3 [l]Jer. 25:34 [m]See Ezek. 19:1-3 [n][Jer. 12:5]
4 [o][ver. 7]
5 [p]Ezek. 34:3 [q]Hos. 12:8
6 [r]Jer. 13:14
7 [s][ver. 4] [u]ver. 10 [v]ver. 14
8 [w][ver. 3, 16; ch. 10:3; Jer. 22:11, 18, 24]
9 [x]Jer. 15:2

11:1–17 *The Shepherds and One Shepherd.* Zechariah's focus turns from the flock back to the shepherds. The fable of vv. 1–3 conveys impending destruction, but of what or whom? Interpreters differ on this question and on several details in the rest of this difficult section. The regions described may be the primary referent—just as Egypt and Assyria were in the preceding verses (cf. Ezek. 31:3)—in which case the metaphors anticipate the destruction following the fall of the **shepherds** of Judah (Zech. 11:3). The alternative view—that the metaphors portray the devastation of the shepherds themselves—is covered in the notes on ch. 11. From a plurality of shepherds, attention turns in vv. 4–17 to a single **shepherd** who, once appointed (vv. 4–7), acts briefly on behalf of the flock before abandoning them (vv. 8–14). He is equipped with two staffs, one symbolizing an international covenant (v. 10) and the other a national covenant between **Judah and Israel** (v. 14), both broken in succession. Verses 15–17 see the reappointment (**once more**, Hb. *'od*) of a **foolish shepherd,** whose carelessness results in the devastation of the flock and who thus stands condemned. The allusive and symbolic language poses problems for interpretation. Were the actions assigned to the shepherd carried out as sign-acts, or are the instructions more parable-like, themselves communicating the divine message? Who is the single shepherd who receives these instructions: simply Zechariah, or is a different figure envisaged in vv. 15–16? Is it possible, or desirable, to identify the three **destroyed** shepherds of v. 8? While one coherent line of interpretation is followed below, such questions occasion caution at the level of detail. They also have the effect of promoting the fundamental truths enshrined in the text: that the fate of the community for good or ill lies in God's sovereign hands; that God reveals his will to his people; and that God's agents remain responsible for their own actions in response to the divine word.

11:1–3 *Judgment on Judah's Shepherds.* The **glory** of Israel's **shepherds,** the subjects of the Lord's judgment in 10:3, will be brought low. They are pictured in three horticultural images as (1) massive **cedar** trees, for which **Lebanon** was famous (11:1); then as (2) the mighty **oaks of Bashan** (v. 2), a fertile region in the Transjordan; and then as (3) the lush **thicket of the Jordan** (v. 3). As glorious and prosperous as these trees are, they could be devoured by fire, or felled and brought low, or made worthless by the presence of a fierce lion; so too, Israel's shepherds will lose their glory when the Lord acts to deliver his people.

11:4–17 *A Sign-act: The Shepherd Rescues His Flock but Is Rejected.* Zechariah himself acts out the role of a shepherd whom the sheep come to detest, and who then leaves the flock to a worthless shepherd.

11:4 These verses record a prophetic sign-act that Zechariah was instructed to perform. He was to **become** the **shepherd** to a flock symbolically described as **doomed to slaughter**, for neither their owners nor their shepherds cared about them as anything other than a means of acquiring wealth. This represented the Lord's attitude toward his people in the past, abandoning them without pity to suffer abuse from their Persian overlords (their "king") and their fellow citizens (their "neighbor," v. 6).

11:7 The reason for the Lord's lack of compassion becomes clear as the sign-act unfolds. Zechariah tended his flock with the staffs, **Favor** and **Union**, symbolizing his positive intentions for them.

11:8 In a very short period Zechariah removed **three** other **shepherds** and became the shepherd to this flock, symbolizing a complete purging of the defective leadership. Yet instead of developing a positive relationship between himself and his flock, he **became impatient with them** and they **detested** him. Interpreters have suggested many specific identifications of these three shepherds, but there is no consensus, and they probably represent either leaders well known to readers at that time ("*the* three shepherds"), or else leaders in general whom God has rejected.

11:9 Zechariah resigned from his position, leaving the flock to **devour** itself.

of one another." 10 And I took [y]my staff Favor, and I broke it, annulling the covenant that
I had made with all the peoples. 11 So it was annulled on that day, and the sheep traders,
who were watching me, knew that it was the word of the LORD. 12 Then I said to them, "If
it seems good to you, give me my wages; but if not, keep them." And they weighed out as
my wages [z]thirty pieces of silver. 13 Then the LORD said to me, "Throw it to the potter"—
[a]the lordly price at which I was priced by them. So I took the [z]thirty pieces of silver and
threw them into the house of the LORD, to the potter. 14 Then I broke [b]my second staff
Union, annulling the brotherhood between Judah and Israel.
15 Then the LORD said to me, "Take once more the equipment of [c]a foolish shepherd.
16 For behold, I am raising up in the land a shepherd [d]who does not care for those being
destroyed, or seek the young or heal the maimed or nourish the healthy, but [e]devours the
flesh of the fat ones, tearing off even their hoofs.

17 [f]"Woe to my worthless shepherd,
[g]who deserts the flock!
May the sword strike his arm
and [h]his right eye!
Let his arm be wholly withered,
his right eye utterly blinded!"

The LORD Will Give Salvation

12 [i]The oracle of the word of the LORD concerning Israel: Thus declares the LORD,
[j]who stretched out the heavens and [k]founded the earth and [j]formed the spirit of
man within him: 2 "Behold, I am about to make Jerusalem [l]a cup of staggering to [m]all the
surrounding peoples. The siege of Jerusalem [n]will also be against Judah. 3 [o]On that day I will
make Jerusalem a heavy stone for all the peoples. [p]All who lift it will surely hurt themselves.
And [m]all the nations of the earth will gather against it. 4 [o]On that day, declares the LORD,
[q]I will strike every horse [r]with panic, and its rider [r]with madness. But for the sake of the
house of Judah I will keep my eyes open, when I strike every horse of the peoples [r]with
blindness. 5 Then the clans of Judah shall say to themselves, 'The inhabitants of Jerusalem
have strength through the LORD of hosts, their God.'

10 [y]ver. 7
12 [z][Ex. 21:32; Matt. 26:15]
13 [a][Matt. 27:9, 10] [z][See ver. 12 above]
14 [b]ver. 7
15 [c]See 2 Kgs. 24:18-20
16 [d][Ezek. 34:4; John 10:13] [e]Ezek. 34:3
17 [f]Jer. 23:1 [g]John 10:12 [h][2 Kgs. 25:7]

Chapter 12

1 [i]See Nah. 1:1 [j]See Isa. 42:5 [k]Isa. 48:13
2 [l]Isa. 51:17, 22, 23 [m][ch. 14:2] [n][ch. 14:14]
3 [o]ch. 13:1, 2, 4; 14:4, 6, 8; Isa. 2:11 [p][Matt. 21:44; Luke 20:18] [m][See ver. 2 above]
4 [o][See ver. 3 above] [q][Ps. 76:6] [r][Deut. 28:28]

11:10 Zechariah **broke** his staff, **Favor**, breaking his **covenant** with the nations around Israel, leaving the flock exposed to their predation.

11:12–13 Zechariah received as his pitifully inadequate wages **thirty pieces of silver** (v. 12), the price of a slave, which he rejected, throwing it to the **potter** (v. 13). This potter worked at the **house of the LORD** (v. 13), suggesting the Lord's rejection of the temple activities as well.

11:14 At this point, Zechariah broke the **second staff**, **Union**, destroying the unity between the northern and southern kingdoms of **Judah and Israel**.

11:17 Zechariah then left the **flock** to the mercies of a **worthless shepherd** who would not care for the flock but would exploit it for his own benefit. This sign-act reverses the pictures of Ezekiel 34 and 37, in which the Lord promised to be Israel's shepherd, judging their present bad shepherds and providing a good shepherd, a new David, to reunite his people. Instead, because of their failure to respond to the shepherd he provided, the Lord declares that they will be given over to false shepherds, returning to the situation that led up to the exile. The NT sees in the rejection of the shepherd by the flock and the pitifully inadequate wages a connection to the rejection and betrayal of Jesus (Matt. 27:3–10; John 10:25–27). Yet the handing over of the Lord's people to a worthless shepherd cannot be the end of the story. The Lord will ultimately act to bring judgment on the worthless shepherd, striking his **right eye** and his **arm**, parts of the body essential to carrying out warfare and exerting control over the flock.

12:1–14:21 *The Second Oracle: The People and Their Leaders.* In this last section of the book, hope for Judah is now tied explicitly to the "house of David" as various scenarios relating to the future of Jerusalem unfold, signaled by the distinctive phrase "on that day" (17 times in these chapters). The assertion of divine deliverance (12:1–9) is followed by its impact on different constituents within the community (12:10–13:9). Chapter 14 develops these themes in connection with the "day of the Lord," so familiar throughout the Minor Prophets (see note on Amos 5:18–20).

12:1–13:6 *The Restoration and Renewal of God's People.* Not only will God protect his people, he will lead them to true repentance and will cleanse them from their sin and idolatry.

12:1–9 *Jerusalem's Triumph and the Nations' Doom.* In time God will punish the nations that seek to harm Judah, and will elevate the house of David.

12:1 The phrase **The oracle of the word of the LORD** marks this as beginning a new section in Zechariah's prophecy (see 9:1; Mal. 1:1), describing the complete restoration and renewal of the Lord's people. Foundational to that transformation is the identity of the Lord as the Creator of the universe and of humanity. As Creator, the Lord is able to re-create a new society out of the existing chaos. Because God does all this, his promises of judgment and redemption are sure, and can be trusted.

12:2 Jerusalem will be the instrument of God's judgment on the nations, a **cup of staggering**, i.e., a cup filled with intoxicating liquor whose consumption results in shame, disorientation, and destruction (cf. Jer. 25:15–29).

12:3 The phrase **on that day** initiates a series of nine such statements, the last coming at 13:4. Although the phrase is common, such long sequences are rare, with the best parallel coming in Isa. 19:16–25. The Hebrew prophets' future statements tend to have an imminent time frame, but these sequences look rather to a more distant temporal horizon, probably to be associated with "the day of the Lord." **Jerusalem** will also become a **heavy stone** that will **hurt** (the same Hb. word in Lev. 21:5 has the more specific sense "cut") the nations that try to move it.

12:4 When the nations of the earth gather against Jerusalem, the Lord will **strike** their elite cavalry troops with **blindness** and **panic**, images drawn from the covenant curses of Deut. 28:28. Regarding the **house of Judah** (the Jewish people), the Lord says, **"I will keep my eyes open,"** meaning that he will watch out for them and protect them.

12:5–6 The **clans of Judah** take the momentary focus: they recognize that the indestructible strength of Jerusalem comes not from themselves but from the **LORD of hosts** (v. 5; God's military title), while they themselves will be like a **blazing** fire under a cooking **pot** or a **flaming torch** among the intensely

6 [o]“On that day I will make the clans of Judah [s]like a blazing pot in the midst of wood, like
a flaming torch among sheaves. And [t]they shall devour to the right and to the left all the surrounding peoples, while [u]Jerusalem shall again be inhabited in its place, in Jerusalem.
7 “And the LORD will give salvation to the tents of Judah first, that the glory of the house
of David and the glory of the inhabitants of Jerusalem may not surpass that of Judah. 8 [o]On
that day [v]the LORD will protect the inhabitants of Jerusalem, so that [w]the feeblest among
them on that day shall be like David, and the house of David shall be like God, [x]like the
angel of the LORD, going before them. 9 [o]And on that day [y]I will seek to destroy all the
nations that come against Jerusalem.

Him Whom They Have Pierced

10 “And [z]I will pour out on the house of David and the inhabitants of Jerusalem a spirit
of grace and [z]pleas for mercy, so that, [a]when they look on me, on him whom they have
pierced, [b]they shall mourn for him, [c]as one mourns for an only child, and weep bitterly
over him, as one weeps over a firstborn. 11 [o]On that day [d]the mourning in Jerusalem will
be as great [e]as the mourning for Hadad-rimmon in the plain of Megiddo. 12 The land shall
mourn, [f]each family[1] by itself: the family of the house of David by itself, and their wives
by themselves; the family of the house of [g]Nathan by itself, and their wives by themselves;
13 the family of the house of Levi by itself, and their wives by themselves; the family of [h]the
Shimeites by itself, and their wives by themselves; 14 and all the families that are left, each
by itself, and their wives by themselves.

13 [i]“On that day there shall be [j]a fountain opened for the house of David and the
inhabitants of Jerusalem, to cleanse them from sin and uncleanness.

Idolatry Cut Off

2 “And [i]on that day, declares the LORD of hosts, [k]I will cut off the names of the idols
from the land, so that [l]they shall be remembered no more. And also [m]I will remove from
the land the prophets and the spirit of uncleanness. 3 And if anyone again prophesies,

[1] Or *clan*; also verses 13, 14

6 [o][See ver. 3 above] [s][Jer. 5:14; Obad. 18] [t]ch. 9:15 [u]ch. 2:4; 14:10, 11
8 [o][See ver. 3 above] [v]ch. 9:15 [w][Isa. 60:22] [x][1 Sam. 29:9; 2 Sam. 14:17, 20; 19:27]
9 [o][See ver. 3 above] [y][ch. 14:3]
10 [z][Jer. 31:9] [a]Cited John 19:37; [Rev. 1:7] [b]Jer. 50:4 [c]Jer. 6:26; Amos 8:10
11 [o][See ver. 3 above] [d][Acts 2:37] [e][2 Chr. 35:24]
12 [f][ch. 7:3] [g]2 Sam. 5:14; Luke 3:31
13 [h]Num. 3:18

Chapter 13

1 [i]See ch. 12:3 [j][Ezek. 36:25]
2 [i][See ver. 1 above] [k]Mic. 5:13; [Jer. 10:11; Ezek. 30:13] [l]Ex. 23:13 [m][ch. 10:2]

flammable **sheaves** of grain (v. 6; cf. Judg. 15:1–8), devouring the nations all around them as Jerusalem is restored.

12:7 The promise of the Abrahamic covenant will be fulfilled (see Gen. 12:1–3), with resulting **glory** for **Jerusalem** and the whole of **Judah**, and destruction for the nations that come against it. **Salvation** will come **to the tents of Judah first**, even before Jerusalem, meaning that either the soldiers in tents or the poorer people living in tents outside Jerusalem would first experience the Lord's deliverance, so that the people in Jerusalem would not become proud over their privileged location.

12:8 All of Jerusalem's **inhabitants** will be raised to the highest human glory, **like David**, the man after God's own heart (1 Sam. 13:14), while the line of David will attain an even greater, godlike glory. (The text does not say that they will become God, or become equal to God, but become **like God**.) **On that day** the descendant of **David** will lead them into battle as the **angel of the LORD** did in days of old (see Josh. 5:14).

12:9 The Lord will bring judgment on **all the nations that come against Jerusalem**, and with this summary statement the sequence begun in v. 3 reaches closure. The fate of "all the nations," first introduced by "all . . . peoples" and "all . . . nations" in v. 3, is settled.

12:10–14 *Mourning for Sin.* Interest in Judah recedes as these verses focus primarily on the **house of David** and **Jerusalem**. The "pouring out" of the **spirit** elsewhere in the OT always indicates the pouring out of God's Spirit (v. 10; see Ezek. 39:29; Joel 2:28–29). The Spirit will give **grace and pleas for mercy** (Zech. 12:10), which implies both repentance on the part of the people and forgiveness from the Lord. They will **mourn** because of the one **whom they have pierced** (v. 10), a word that usually connotes being stabbed to death by a sword or spear (see Num. 25:8). The mourning will be like that for a **firstborn** son, an only child on whom all hope for continuation of the family line rested, or like the **mourning for** (or at) **Hadad-rimmon** (Zech. 12:11). Under one interpretation, Hadad-rimmon is a name for the Canaanite god, Baal, whose worship involved lament for his death and descent into the underworld. But it is doubtful that Zechariah would be predicting a day of blessing when Jerusalem's mourning would resemble the mourning of those in a pagan worship ceremony. A better interpretation is that Hadad-rimmon could be the name of a town near **Megiddo**, making this a reference to the deep mourning that followed King Josiah's death in a battle there (v. 11; see 2 Chron. 35:24). The identity of the one who is "pierced" (Zech. 12:10) and on whom the **inhabitants of Jerusalem . . . look** is difficult to discern. If **on me** is defined by the following phrase ("whom they have pierced"), then the reference is to God himself, perhaps in the person of the shepherd who will be struck in 13:7, a prophecy that John 19:37 sees fulfilled in the person of Jesus. The mourning will affect the entire community, family by family, men and women alike. Two particular lines are singled out: the royal line of **David**, by way of his son **Nathan** (Zech. 12:12; cf. 1 Chron. 14:4), and the priestly line of **Levi** (Zech. 12:13), by way of his grandson Shimei (1 Chron. 6:16–17).

13:1–6 *Cleansing from Sin and Idolatry.* The repentant people need to be cleansed from their iniquity, so God will open up for them a **fountain** (v. 1), or spring, from which will flow the running water necessary for ritual purification (see Lev. 14:5; cf. Ezek. 47:1–12; Rev. 22:1–2). The people's uncleanness comes from their devotion to **idols** (Zech. 13:2; cf. Ezek. 36:25). This is the sin that "pierced" the Lord in Zech. 12:10, metaphorically in its original context and really in the person of Jesus. The Lord promises to excise the **names** of the idols from the land, terminating their influence and even their memory (13:2). The influence of the idols was exercised through false prophets, who told the people what they wanted to hear (see 10:1–3), so they too will be removed from the land (13:2), executed by their own parents in line with Deut. 13:6–10. The punishment of "piercing" fits the impact of their sin in "piercing" the Lord (Zech. 12:10). This will make the false prophets eager to conceal their activities (13:4–6). They will no longer dress in a **hairy cloak**, as did Elijah (v. 4; see 1 Kings 19:13). They will explicitly deny that they are prophets: instead, each one will claim to be a **worker of the soil** (Zech. 13:5; cf. Gen. 4:2). Yet the true nature of the false prophet will be exposed by the **wounds on** his **back**, ritual scars related to pagan practices that he will confess to having received at the **house of** his **friends** (or "lovers"), the idolaters with whom he practiced pagan worship (Zech. 13:6; cf. Ezek. 16:33–37).

his father and mother who bore him will say to him, [n]'You shall not live, for you speak
lies in the name of the LORD.' And his father and mother who bore him shall pierce him
through when he prophesies.
4 "On that day [o]every prophet will be ashamed of his vision when he prophesies. He
will not put on a hairy cloak in order to deceive, 5 but he will say, [p]'I am no prophet, I am a
worker of the soil, for a man sold me in my youth.'[1] 6 And if one asks him, 'What are these
wounds on your back?'[2] he will say, 'The wounds I received in the house of my friends.'

The Shepherd Struck

7 "Awake, O sword, against [q]my shepherd,
against the man who stands next to me,"
declares the LORD of hosts.
[r]"Strike the shepherd, and the sheep will be scattered;
I will turn my hand against the little ones.
8 In the whole land, declares the LORD,
two thirds shall be cut off and perish,
[s]and one third shall be left alive.
9 And [t]I will put this third into the fire,
and refine them as one refines silver,
and test them as gold is tested.
[u]They will call upon my name,
and [v]I will answer them.
[w]I will say, 'They are my people';
and they will say, 'The LORD is my God.'"

The Coming Day of the LORD

14 Behold, [x]a day is coming for the LORD, when the spoil taken from you will be divided
in your midst. 2 For [y]I will gather all the nations against Jerusalem to battle, and
[z]the city shall be taken [a]and the houses plundered [b]and the women raped. [c]Half of the city

3 [n]See Deut. 13:1-11
4 [o][Mic. 3:7]
5 [p]Amos 7:14
7 [q][Isa. 40:11; Heb. 13:20] [r][Matt. 26:31; Mark 14:27]
8 [s][ch. 14:2]
9 [t]Ps. 66:10, 12; Isa. 48:10; Mal. 3:2, 3; 1 Pet. 1:7 [u][Ps. 50:15] [v]ch. 10:6 [w]ch. 8:8; See Ezek. 11:20

Chapter 14

1 [x]See Joel 1:15
2 [y]Joel 3:2 [z][Luke 21:24] [a]Isa. 13:16 [b]Lam. 5:11 [c]ch. 13:8; [Matt. 24:40, 41]

[1] *Or for the land has been my possession since my youth* [2] *Or on your chest; Hebrew wounds between your hands*

13:7–14:21 *Judgment and Transformation.* Fearsome conflicts await the people of God, but God will intervene and usher in a day in which Jerusalem is supreme and all the world worships the true God.

13:7–9 *The Shepherd Struck and the Flock Scattered.* The **sword** of the Lord's judgment goes out against a shepherd (v. 7), as in 11:17, but this time against the good shepherd. His death will result in the scattering of the flock and a time of great trial and testing for God's people, during which many will **perish** (13:8). Yet the result of that period of testing is the refining of the Lord's people, culminating in the expression by the Lord and his people of their mutual commitment to one another (v. 9).

14:1–11 *Jerusalem's Judgment, Deliverance, and Exaltation.* Terrible times are yet in store for the people of Jerusalem, but God will visit them and make Jerusalem secure and prominent.

14:2 I will gather all the nations against Jerusalem to battle predicts a future time that is not specified in Zechariah.

14:4 The trials for Jerusalem are spelled out in the beginning of ch. 14. Judah's possessions will be divided by her enemies in front of her, and Jerusalem will again be captured, with horrific consequences including rape, plunder, and the exile of a significant portion of her population. Yet at the height of her distress, the Lord will go out once more as a warrior, arriving by way of the **Mount of Olives**, across the Kidron Valley to the east of Jerusalem, the same route by which he abandoned the Jerusalem temple in Ezek. 11:23. In a manner typical of such appearances of God (e.g., Ps. 29:1–11; 50:3; Isa. 29:6; Mic. 1:3–4; Habakkuk 3), this theophany will shake the natural order, splitting the mountain in two, creating a **valley** aligned **from east to west** along the sacred axis of the temple. Zechariah's vision thus resonates with the upheaval of the earth at the coming of the Lord depicted elsewhere at Isa. 40:4 and Ezek. 43:2.

14:5 This valley will provide a way of escape for the inhabitants of Jerusalem to **Azal**, an unknown location, and an access road for the Divine Warrior to return to his city. He comes accompanied by **all the holy ones**, either his angelic army or the exiles who return under his protection. The **earthquake in the days of Uzziah** was a traumatic event also mentioned in Amos 1:1–2.

14:6 On that day. It is difficult to determine what period of time is being indicated by the remarkable prophecies in this entire chapter, whether a future time in this present age, or a future millennial kingdom and the rebellion that follows it, or the events that surround Christ's return and the beginning of the eternal state (see note on Ezek. 40:1–48:35; see also 1 Pet. 1:10–11).

14:7 The transformation of the natural order at the coming of the Lord continues with a return to the primordial conditions (vv. 6–8). That day will be like the first day of history (lit., "day one"; or "one [single] day," cf. v. 9; see ESV footnote), a **unique day, which is known to the LORD**. Just as on the first day, when light and darkness had not yet been separated (Gen. 1:3–4), so on that day there will be **neither day nor night, but at evening time there shall be light**. Instead of alternating light and darkness, permanent light will prevail.

14:8 A perpetual supply of **living** (or flowing) **waters** will also emanate from Jerusalem, reaching out both east and west, to the Dead Sea and to the Mediterranean. Such a life-giving river is a common feature in describing sanctuaries, from the garden of Eden to the new Jerusalem (Gen. 2:10; Ps. 46:4; Ezek. 47:1–12; Joel 3:18; Rev. 22:1; cf. John 4:10; Rev. 21:6).

14:9 The LORD will be king over all the earth points to a time that far exceeds the simple idea of a Messiah who will give Israel deliverance from oppression and bring the people God's presence and blessing, for this predicts a worldwide earthly reign of the Lord himself. Some interpreters see this fulfilled in the reign of Christ in a future 1,000-year millennial kingdom (see note on Rev. 20:1–6), while others see it fulfilled after the final judgment, in the new heaven and new earth (see notes on Revelation 21–22). Still others see this as the Lord's reign as exercised by the Messiah, who is regularly expected in the OT to bring the Gentiles into his empire (e.g., Isa. 11:1–10). **The LORD will be one** echoes the fundamental confession of the OT, "Hear, O Israel: The LORD our God, the LORD is one" (Deut. 6:4). As the Lord's sole kingship is

3[d][ch. 12:9]
4[e][ver. 1]; See ch. 12:3 [f][Ezek. 11:23] [g]2 Sam. 15:30 [h][ver. 10]
5[i]Amos 1:1
6[e][See ver. 4 above] [j][Isa. 60:19; Rev. 21:23]
7[k]Rev. 21:25 [l]Matt. 24:36 [m][Isa. 30:26]
8[e][See ver. 4 above] [n]John 4:10; Rev. 22:1; [Isa. 33:21; Ezek. 47:1; Joel 3:18] [o]Joel 2:20 [p][Isa. 33:16]
9[q]Ps. 47:7; [ver. 16, 17; Mal. 1:14] [r][ver. 1]; See ch. 12:3 [s]Eph. 4:5, 6 [t][ch. 13:2]
10[u][ver. 4; Isa. 40:4] [v]Josh. 18:24 [w]Josh. 15:32 [x]Isa. 2:2 [y]ch. 12:6; [ch. 2:4] [z]See Jer. 37:13 [a]Jer. 31:38 [b]Neh. 3:1; Jer. 31:38
11[c]Rev. 22:3 [d][Jer. 23:6]

shall go out into exile, but the rest of the people shall not be cut off from the city. **3** [d]Then
the LORD will go out and fight against those nations as when he fights on a day of battle.
4 [e]On that day his feet shall stand [f]on [g]the Mount of Olives that lies before Jerusalem on the
east, and [g]the Mount of Olives shall be split in two from east to west by [h]a very wide valley,
so that one half of the Mount shall move northward, and the other half southward. **5** And
you shall flee to the valley of my mountains, for the valley of the mountains shall reach
to Azal. And you shall flee as you fled from [i]the earthquake in the days of Uzziah king of
Judah. Then the LORD my God will come, and all the holy ones with him.

6 [e]On that day [j]there shall be [j]no light, cold, or frost.[1] **7** [k]And there shall be a unique[2] day,
[l]which is known to the LORD, neither day nor night, but [m]at evening time there shall be
light.

8 [e]On that day [n]living waters shall flow out from Jerusalem, half of them to [o]the eastern
sea[3] and half of them to [o]the western sea.[4] [p]It shall continue in summer as in winter.

9 And [q]the LORD will be king over all the earth. [r]On that day the LORD will be [s]one and
[t]his name one.

10 [u]The whole land shall be turned into a plain from [v]Geba to [w]Rimmon south of
Jerusalem. But [x]Jerusalem shall remain aloft [y]on its site from [z]the Gate of Benjamin to
the place of the former gate, to [a]the Corner Gate, and from [b]the Tower of Hananel to the
king's winepresses. **11** And it shall be inhabited, for [c]there shall never again be a decree of
utter destruction.[5] [d]Jerusalem shall dwell in security.

[1] Compare Septuagint, Syriac, Vulgate, Targum; the meaning of the Hebrew is uncertain [2] Hebrew *one* [3] That is, the Dead Sea [4] That is, the Mediterranean Sea [5] The Hebrew term rendered *decree of utter destruction* refers to things devoted (or set apart) to the Lord (or by the Lord) for destruction

established, so too he becomes the sole object of worship (cf. Zech. 8:20–23). **And his name one**, that is, the Lord's name remains, unlike the names of the idols that were cut off (cf. 13:2; Deut. 6:13). Just as there was *one* day of the Lord (Zech. 14:7), so there is one Lord, with one name.

14:10 The territory of Judah will be turned into a flat **plain**, from **Geba** on its northern border to **Rimmon**, 35 miles (56 km) to the southwest of Jerusalem, in order that the city of Jerusalem can tower over its surrounding countryside (cf. Isa. 2:2–4).

14:11 Jerusalem will be fully **inhabited** and secure, without fear of a further **decree of utter destruction** from the Lord because of its sins.

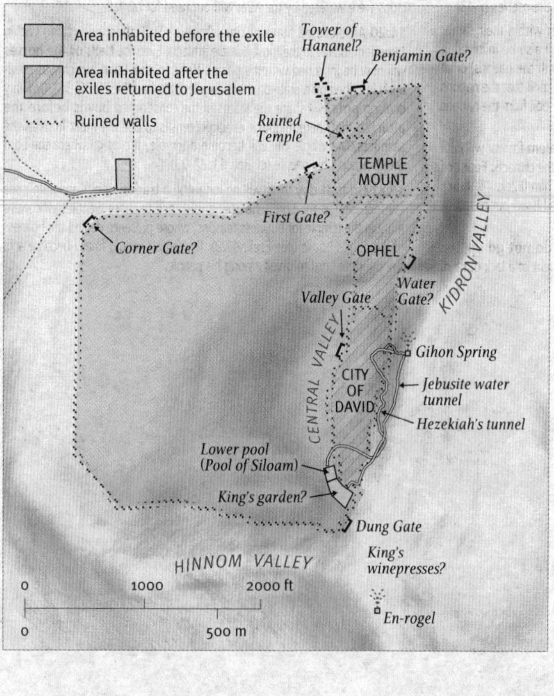

Jerusalem at the Time of Zechariah

c. 520 B.C.

Zechariah prophesied to the people of Jerusalem after they returned from Babylon in 538 B.C. and before they rebuilt the temple in 515. The city of Jerusalem lay in ruins, the walls and the temple having been destroyed by the Babylonians in 586 B.C. Within a year after returning from Babylon, the people had laid the foundation for the new temple, but by Zechariah's time they had still not completed it. Zechariah, together with Haggai, encouraged the people to complete the temple.

12 And this shall be [e]the plague with which the LORD will strike all the peoples that wage
war against Jerusalem: their flesh will rot while they are still standing on their feet, their
eyes will rot in their sockets, and their tongues will rot in their mouths.
13 And [f]on that day a great panic from the LORD shall fall on them, so that [g]each will
seize the hand of another, and the hand of the one will be raised against the hand of the
other. 14 Even [h]Judah will fight at Jerusalem. And [i]the wealth of all the surrounding nations
shall be collected, gold, silver, and garments in great abundance. 15 And [j]a plague like this
plague shall fall on the horses, the mules, the camels, the donkeys, and whatever beasts
may be in those camps.
16 Then everyone who survives of all the nations that have come against Jerusalem [k]shall
go up year after year to worship [l]the King, the LORD of hosts, and [m]to keep [n]the Feast of
Booths. 17 And if [o]any of the families of the earth do not go up to Jerusalem to worship
[l]the King, the LORD of hosts, [p]there will be no rain on them. 18 And if the family of Egypt
does not go up and present themselves, then on them there shall be no rain;[1] there shall
be [j]the plague with which the LORD afflicts the nations that do not go up [m]to keep the
Feast of Booths. 19 This shall be the punishment to Egypt and the punishment to all the
nations that do not go up [m]to keep the Feast of Booths.
20 And [q]on that day there shall be inscribed on the bells of the horses, [r]"Holy to the LORD."
And the pots in the house of the LORD shall be as the bowls before the altar. 21 And every
pot in Jerusalem and Judah shall be [r]holy to the LORD of hosts, so that all who sacrifice
may come and take of them and boil the meat of the sacrifice in them. And [s]there shall
no longer be [t]a trader[2] in the house of the LORD of hosts [q]on that day.

[1] Hebrew lacks *rain* [2] Or *Canaanite*

12 [e][ver. 15, 18]
13 [f]See ch. 12:3 [g]Hag. 2:22; [1 Sam. 14:20]
14 [h][ch. 12:2] [i][Ezek. 39:10]
15 [j][ver. 12]
16 [k]See ch. 8:21 [l][ver. 9] [m][Nah. 1:15]; See Lev. 23:34 [n]See Lev. 23:39-43
17 [o]Isa. 60:12 [l][See ver. 16 above] [p]See 1 Kgs. 17:1
18 [j][See ver. 15 above] [m][See ver. 16 above]
19 [m][See ver. 16 above]
20 [q]See ch. 12:3 [r]Ex. 28:36; Isa. 23:18; Mic. 4:13
21 [r][See ver. 20 above] [s]Ezek. 44:9; See Joel 3:17 [t][Deut. 7:1, 2] [q][See ver. 20 above]

14:12–21 *The Nations Humbled and Brought into Submission.* After the nations have suffered a gruesome defeat, they will dedicate themselves to worshiping the true God in Jerusalem.

14:12–13 Instead of judging his own city, the Lord will now curse the nations that have come against it. Their bodies will instantaneously **rot** under the effects of this hideous curse, and they will fight among themselves (v. 13).

14:15 The same curse will affect the military animals within their camp: the **horses**, **mules**, **camels**, and **donkeys**. Judah will also be involved in this conflict, fighting either against Jerusalem (along with the nations) or at Jerusalem (against the other nations). In contrast to the spoil that the nations took from Jerusalem in v. 1, now Judah will collect vast spoil from the nations who assaulted it.

14:16 The nations that once came up **against Jerusalem** for war will now come to the city for the three annual festivals, especially the climactic **Feast of Booths**, or Tabernacles, in the fall. Like Ezekiel before him (Ezek. 46:9–12), Zechariah envisages ongoing festival worship in renewed Israel but broadens this to include those from beyond Israel's bounds.

14:17 And if any of the families of the earth do not go up. This requirement will be enforced by the threat of the judgment of a lack of **rain**, which would cripple their harvests. While Ezekiel seemed to have understood that foreigners could become members of the covenant community (e.g., Ezek. 44:9; but cf. 37:28), Zechariah depicts them as simultaneously retaining their distinctive identities (cf. Zech. 8:20–23; also Isa. 19:23–25).

14:18 Egypt is singled out for mention with a separate **plague**, since its crops were watered by the Nile, without need for rainfall.

14:20 An elevated state of ritual holiness will affect everything within Jerusalem, down to the most humble artifacts. Even the **bells of the horses** will now be inscribed with the phrase **Holy to the LORD**, which was previously inscribed on a plate on the high priest's turban (Ex. 28:36–38). Ordinary cooking **pots** will share the status of the consecrated **bowls before the altar**, so that there might be enough utensils to boil the meat from all the sacrifices. The whole city will become a temple, the place where the Lord dwells among his people (cf. Rev. 21:22–23).

14:21 On that day there will no longer be a **trader** (or a "Canaanite"; see ESV footnote) in the Lord's **house**, a reference to those Gentiles who were there in the temple for business reasons, whose presence defiled the holiness of the Lord's house (see Ezek. 44:9). The temple would finally become a fit place for the Lord to dwell among his people.

INTRODUCTION TO

MALACHI

Author and Title

The Hebrew name "Malachi" means "my messenger," or perhaps "messenger of (the LORD)" if "Malachi" is a shortened form of "Malachiah" (*2 Esd.* 1:40). Based on the LXX and Targum Jonathan, some scholars have argued that "Malachi" in 1:1 ought to be understood as a title, "my messenger," rather than as a proper name. It appears more likely, however, that "Malachi" is a proper name, as it is interpreted by many other ancient sources (*2 Esd.* 1:40, the Gk. translations by Symmachus and Theodotion, the Syriac Peshitta translation, etc.). If so, the book of Malachi follows the pattern of 14 other prophetic books in the Hebrew Bible (Isaiah, Jeremiah, Ezekiel, and the other 11 Minor Prophets), where the author is introduced by name in the opening verses using language similar to Malachi 1:1. Accordingly, 3:1 offers an important wordplay on the prophet's name: "Behold, I send *my messenger*, and he will prepare the way before me." This wordplay suggests that Malachi's own ministry was intended to foreshadow that of the coming messenger, who is identified in the NT as John the Baptist (see notes on 3:1 and 4:4–6).

Date

The book of Malachi offers no clear pointer to the date of its composition. Nevertheless, most scholars agree that Malachi was probably a contemporary of Ezra and Nehemiah in the mid-fifth century B.C. This is supported by the implied existence of the temple (Mal. 1:10; 3:1, 8), which requires a date after its reconstruction c. 516 B.C. Further support is offered by the reference to a "governor" (1:8), since this term is often used for regional officials during the Persian period (539–332 B.C.). The most compelling evidence for dating Malachi, however, is the substantial parallel between the sins reproved by Malachi and those reproved by Ezra and Nehemiah. These include corruption of the priesthood (Neh. 13:4–9, 29–31; Mal. 1:6–2:9), marriage to idolaters (Ezra 9–10; Neh. 10:30; 13:1–3, 23–27; Mal. 2:10–12), abuse of the disadvantaged (Neh. 5:1–13; Mal. 3:5), and failure to pay tithes (Neh. 10:32–39; 13:10–13; Mal. 3:8–10).

Theme

Malachi's contemporaries may have been free from blatant idolatry (though see 2:11) and relatively orthodox in their beliefs, but theirs had become a dead orthodoxy. They were all too ready to make ethical compromises and to dilute the strenuous demands of proper worship. In response to the cynicism and religious malaise of his contemporaries, Malachi's prophecy comes as a wake-up call to renewed covenant fidelity (see Key Themes).

Purpose, Occasion, and Background

Malachi's ministry took place nearly a hundred years after the decree of Cyrus in 538 B.C., which ended the Babylonian captivity and allowed the Jews to return to their homeland and rebuild the temple (2 Chron. 36:23). This was some 80 years after Haggai and Zechariah encouraged the rebuilding of that temple with promises of God's blessing, the engrafting of the nations, prosperity, expansion, peace, and the return of God's own glorious presence (cf. Haggai 2; Zech. 1:16–17; 2:1–13; 8:1–9:17). To Malachi's disillusioned contemporaries, these predictions must have seemed a cruel mockery. In contrast to the glowing promises, the harsh reality was one of economic privation, prolonged drought, crop failure, and pestilence (Mal. 3:10ff.).

After the return from exile, Judah remained an almost insignificant territory of about 20 by 30 miles (32 by 48 km), inhabited by a population of perhaps 150,000. Although they enjoyed the benefits of Persia's enlightened policy of religious toleration and limited self-rule, the Jews acutely felt their subjugation to a foreign power (Neh. 1:3; 9:36ff.), and they suffered persistent opposition from their neighbors (Ezra 4:23; Dan. 9:25). Judah was no longer an independent nation and was no longer ruled by a Davidic king.

Worst of all, in spite of the promises of the coming Messiah and God's own glorious presence (e.g., Zech. 1:16ff.; 2:4, 10–13; 8:3–17, 23; 9:9–13), Israel experienced only spiritual destitution. Unlike Bible books from earlier periods, the postexilic books of Ezra, Nehemiah, and Esther are remarkably candid in their description of Judah as generally lacking miraculous evidences of God's presence. In contrast to both Solomon's temple and the prophetic promise of the restored temple (Ezekiel 40–43), the actual postexilic temple was physically and spiritually inferior. As Malachi 3:1 implies, the Most Holy Place in this second temple had no visible manifestation of the glory of God. Though God was certainly alive and well (as revealed, e.g., by his remarkable providences in the book of Esther), it was a period in which God's people had to live more by faith than by sight.

Key Themes: Malachi's Sixfold Wake-up Call to Renewed Covenant Fidelity

Disputation	Reference	Summary	Focus
Disputation 1	1:2–5	Malachi begins by defending the reality of God's elective love for Israel, a love which calls for robust covenantal obedience and sincere worship as its proper response. Instead, the people were dishonoring God by their worthless offerings and the hypocritical formalism of their worship.	Israel is to remember the Law of Moses.
Disputation 2	1:6–2:9	Malachi exposes these offenses and rebukes the priests for condoning them and thereby violating the Lord's covenant with Levi.	
Disputation 3	2:10–16	Malachi condemns marriage to an idolater as infidelity against Israel's covenant with the Lord, and he condemns unauthorized divorce as infidelity against the marriage covenant between a husband and his wife, to which the Lord is witness.	
Disputation 4	2:17–3:5	Malachi broadens his indictment as he promises that the Lord will vindicate his justice. This will take place when "the messenger of the covenant" comes to judge the wicked (when the Lord will function as a witness not only against adulterers, as in 2:10–16, but also against other offenders) and to purify his people so that their offerings will be acceptable at last.	Israel is to remember the promise of Elijah and the coming day of the Lord.
Disputation 5	3:6–12	Malachi returns to the subject of Israel's begrudging offerings. The people experienced material adversity and were under a curse—not in spite of their behavior, but because of it. Accordingly, Malachi challenges them to conscientious tithing, which will be rewarded with divine blessing.	
Disputation 6	3:13–4:3	Malachi assures his grumbling contemporaries that evildoers, who seem to escape divine justice because of their prosperity, will yet be judged, while the Lord will deliver those who fear him.	
Summary	4:4–6	Malachi summarizes the main points of his prophecy: remember the Law of Moses (the focus of disputations 1–3), and remember the promise of Elijah and the coming day of the Lord (the focus of disputations 4–6).	

History of Salvation Summary

Even though God has disciplined his people severely by means of the exile, he still intends for his name to be honored among the Gentiles (1:11, 14). God's chosen vehicle for bringing his name to the Gentiles is his people loving him faithfully. This is therefore the time for Israel to renew its commitment to the covenant. (For an explanation of the "History of Salvation," see the Overview of the Bible, pp. 23–26. See also History of Salvation in the Old Testament: Preparing the Way for Christ, pp. 2635–2661.)

Literary Features

The content of the book of Malachi places it in the category of prophecy, but the form in which that content is packaged is out of the norm for OT prophecy. The book is written entirely in prose. Further, the material is not embodied in the conventional format of oracles of judgment and salvation. The dominant genre is satire—an attack on vice in a discernible literary form, and with a satiric norm by which the criticism is conducted. The object of attack is halfhearted and negligent religious service, which in the prophet's day took multiple forms (e.g., inappropriate offerings, untruth promoted by the priests, and the prevalence of divorce). The satiric norm is God's law. The primary vehicle in which the satire is embodied is a rhetoric of question and answer, as the people of Judah are pictured as asking a series of questions that God answers in an accusatory and condemning way.

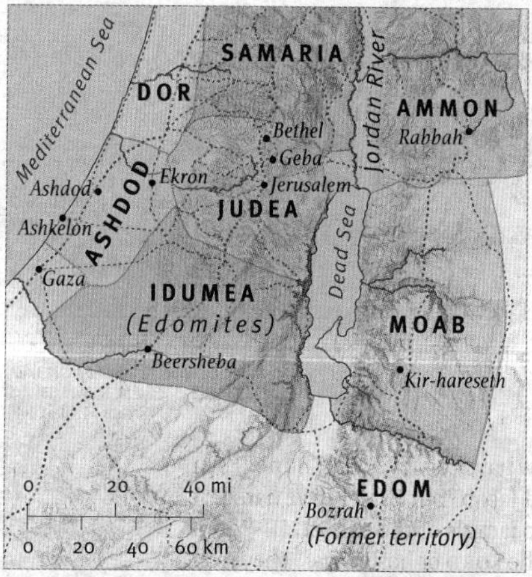

The Setting of Malachi
c. 460 B.C.
Malachi likely prophesied several decades after the first exiles of Judah, now under Persian rule, had returned from Babylon to the minor province of Judea and rebuilt the temple. Edomites had migrated northwest from their traditional homeland just south of Moab into the area immediately south of Judea, and this land was now called Idumea. Territory that once belonged to the northern kingdom of Israel had been divided into several different minor provinces, including Samaria.

One of the organizing patterns is an accumulating litany of attitudes and actions that are offensive to God. Another is an expanding portrait of the coming Messiah and the blessings that he will bring. Finally, a common repeated pattern is as follows: (1) God voices an indictment of his people for bad behavior; (2) the people are pictured as asking God how his charge is true; (3) God replies to the question, in the process of which he expands the charge. God's indictments are sometimes phrased as rhetorical questions (e.g., 1:6 and 8; 2:10 and 15).

Outline

The book of Malachi is carefully structured in terms of a heading (1:1), followed by six pericopes or disputations (1:2–5; 1:6–2:9; 2:10–16; 2:17–3:5; 3:6–12; 3:13–4:3) and a conclusion (4:4–6). Each disputation is relatively coherent and is introduced by an assertion from either the Lord or the prophet. This is followed by an anticipated challenge from those being addressed, which is invariably introduced by the expression, "But you say" (1:2, 6, 7, 13; 2:14, 17; 3:7, 8, 13). Each challenge, in turn, is answered with fuller substantiation by the Lord or by the prophet speaking on the Lord's behalf.

The book also has an unobtrusive concentric (chiasmic) structure. One conspicuous literary indicator of this pattern is the double introductory assertion ("But you say") and the anticipated response, which are found only in the parallel second (1:6–2:9) and fifth (3:6–12) disputations (the "B" sections below).

Heading (1:1)

A. *First disputation*: Does God make a distinction between the good and the arrogantly wicked? God's elective love vindicated in his judgment (1:2–5)

B. *Second disputation*: Israel's begrudging offerings condemned (1:6–2:9)

C. *Third disputation*: Marriage to an idolater—and divorce based on aversion—condemned by the Lord, who is witness to the covenant of marriage (2:10–16)

C′. *Fourth disputation*: The Lord is a witness against adultery and other moral offenses (2:17–3:5)

B′. *Fifth disputation*: Israel's begrudging offerings condemned (3:6–12)

A′. *Sixth disputation*: Does God make a distinction between the good and the arrogantly wicked? God's elective love vindicated in his judgment (3:13–4:3)

Conclusion (4:4–6)

MALACHI

1 The oracle of the word of the LORD to Israel by Malachi.[1]

The LORD's Love for Israel

2 [a]"I have loved you," says the LORD. [b]But you say, "How have you loved us?" "Is not Esau
[c]Jacob's brother?" declares the LORD. "Yet [d]I have loved Jacob 3 but Esau I have hated. [e]I
have laid waste his hill country and left his heritage to jackals of the desert." 4 If Edom
says, "We are shattered but we will rebuild the ruins," the LORD of hosts says, "They may
build, but I will tear down, and they will be called 'the wicked country,' and 'the people
with whom the LORD is angry forever.'" 5 [f]Your own eyes shall see this, and you shall say,
"Great is the LORD beyond the border of Israel!"

The Priests' Polluted Offerings

6 [g]"A son honors his father, and a servant his master. If then I am [h]a father, where is my
honor? And if I am [i]a master, where is my fear? says the LORD of hosts to you, O priests,

[1] *Malachi* means *my messenger*

Chapter 1

2 [a]Deut. 7:8; Jer. 31:3 [b][ch. 2:14, 17; 3:7, 8, 13] [c][Amos 1:11; Obad. 10] [d]Cited Rom. 9:13
3 [e]Isa. 34:13; Jer. 49:10, 18; Ezek. 35:3, 4; Joel 3:19
5 [f]Ps. 91:8
6 [g]See Ex. 20:12 [h]Ex. 4:22; Hos. 11:1 [i][Luke 6:46]

1:1 *Heading.* **Malachi** acknowledges his role as a prophetic intermediary and explicitly identifies his book as the **word of the LORD**. In keeping with this, nearly half of the remaining 54 verses of this concise and profound book are punctuated with "says the LORD of hosts," "says the LORD," etc. (On the phrase "LORD of hosts," see chart, p. 1775.) Similar to the headings found in Zech. 9:1 and 12:1 (cf. Hab. 1:1), Mal. 1:1 identifies the contents of this work as an **oracle** or a "burden," with implications of urgent responsibility and even dread (Jer. 23:33–40; see note on Hab. 1:1). While Malachi directs his message to the postexilic remnant state of Judah, in Mal. 1:1 the prophet boldly confers on this people the ancient comprehensive designation of "**Israel**," thereby identifying them as accountable for all the covenant obligations and as heirs of all the covenant promises of God.

1:2–5 *First Disputation: Does God Make a Distinction between the Good and the Arrogantly Wicked? God's Elective Love Vindicated in His Judgment.* Malachi exposes and answers the doubts of his contemporaries who question God's love because of their political, economic, and spiritual destitution.

1:2–3 In a classic text, which Paul quotes in Rom. 9:13, Malachi appeals to God's elective and unconditional love of **Jacob** and corresponding hatred of **Esau**. In this context **loved** refers to choice rather than affection, and **hated** refers to rejection rather than animosity (which was explicitly prohibited against Edomites, Esau's descendants, in Deut. 23:7). For a similar use of these terms, see Prov. 29:24; Luke 14:26; 16:13. Although Jacob and Esau were brothers, Jacob experienced God's sovereign favor by which he was granted a privileged role in redemptive history as a bearer of the messianic promise, while Esau experienced God's rejection in terms of this same role. Malachi's concern, however, is primarily with the nations of Israel and Edom, of which Jacob and Esau were the representatives and progenitors. To Malachi's contemporaries, it must have seemed that the prophet had committed a terrible blunder by citing the contrasting national fates of Israel and Edom as proof of Israel's favored status. If God had chosen Jacob/Israel over Esau/Edom, why did he allow his people to suffer the total devastation of their country in 586 B.C. by Nebuchadnezzar and 70 years of Babylonian captivity, while Edom remained intact and seemed only to benefit from Israel's loss? Malachi makes his point, however, by alluding to Jer. 9:11. Two centuries earlier Jeremiah announced the Lord's impending judgment against Judah: "I will make Jerusalem a heap of ruins, a lair of jackals, and I will make the cities of Judah a desolation, without inhabitant." By applying this same threat to Edom, Malachi makes clear that, like Judah, Edom would not escape God's judgment. It is likely that this judgment came through the agency of Nabatean Arabs, who gradually forced the Edomites from their homeland between 550 and 400 B.C., causing them to resettle in an area later called Idumea. Being semi-nomadic, the Nabateans allowed the cities of Edom to go to ruin while their herds overgrazed and destroyed previously arable land. Whereas Judah was graciously restored after her punishment, reflecting the Lord's love for his people, Edom's judgment was to be permanent and irreversible (Mal. 1:4). There would continue to be individual Edomites (implied by 1:4; cf. Mark 3:8), but they had forfeited their national identity.

1:5 beyond the border of Israel. A chastened Israel will acknowledge the Lord's universal sovereignty. This universal perspective, sometimes misunderstood as if it implied God's acceptance of the religions of other nations, is a subtheme to which the prophet returns in vv. 11, 14, and 3:12.

1:6–2:9 *Second Disputation: Israel's Begrudging Offerings Condemned.* In his second disputation Malachi turns the tables on the complaint treated in the first. What should be questioned is not God's love for Israel but Israel's love for God. Malachi recognizes that all the people were guilty of dishonoring God, as revealed in their begrudging offerings (1:14). Nevertheless, he focuses on Israel's priests (2:1–9) because it is their responsibility to guard the sanctuary from defilement and to inspect all sacrifices so as to exclude, for example, blind, lame, or sick animals (1:8; Lev. 22:17–25; Deut. 15:21; 17:1).

6[b][See ver. 2 above]
7[j][ver. 8; ch. 2:12; 3:3] [b][See ver. 2 above] [k][ver. 12]
8[l][ver. 13]; See Lev. 22:22
9[m]See Zech. 7:2 [n]See Deut. 10:17
10[o][Isa. 1:13] [p][Isa. 1:11; Jer. 6:20; Amos 5:21]
11[q][Isa. 2:2; 56:7; 60:3; 66:19]
12[r][ver. 7]
13[s]Isa. 43:23; [ch. 3:14; Mic. 6:3] [t][ver. 8; Lev. 22:20]
14[u]See Ex. 12:5 [v][Lev. 22:21] [w]See Zech. 14:9 [x]Ps. 47:2; 76:12

Chapter 2

1[y]ch. 1:6 [z]ver. 4
2[a]Lev. 26:14; See Deut. 28:15 [b][ch. 3:9] [c][Ps. 69:22]

who despise my name. [b]But you say, 'How have we despised your name?' **7** [j]By offering
polluted food upon my altar. [b]But you say, 'How have we polluted you?' By saying that
[k]the LORD's table may be despised. **8** [l]When you offer blind animals in sacrifice, is that
not evil? And when you offer those that are lame or sick, is that not evil? Present that to
your governor; will he accept you or show you favor? says the LORD of hosts. **9** And now
[m]entreat the favor of God, that he may be gracious to us. With such a gift from your
hand, [n]will he show favor to any of you? says the LORD of hosts. **10** [o]Oh that there were
one among you who would shut the doors, that you might not kindle fire on my altar in
vain! I have no pleasure in you, says the LORD of hosts, [p]and I will not accept an offering
from your hand. **11** For from the rising of the sun to its setting my name [q]will be[1] great
among the nations, and in every place incense will be offered to my name, and a pure
offering. For my name [q]will be great among the nations, says the LORD of hosts. **12** But
you profane it when you say that [r]the Lord's table is polluted, and its fruit, that is, its food
may be despised. **13** But you say, [s]'What a weariness this is,' and you snort at it, says the
LORD of hosts. [t]You bring what has been taken by violence or is lame or sick, and this you
bring as your offering! Shall I accept that from your hand? says the LORD. **14** Cursed be
the cheat who has [u]a male in his flock, and [v]vows it, and yet sacrifices to the Lord what is
blemished. For [w]I am a great King, says the LORD of hosts, and my name [x]will be feared
among the nations.

The LORD Rebukes the Priests

2 "And now, [y]O priests, [z]this command is for you. **2** [a]If you will not listen, if you will
not take it to heart to give honor to my name, says the LORD of hosts, then I will
send [b]the curse upon you and I will curse [c]your blessings. Indeed, I have already cursed

[1] Or *is* (three times in verse 11; also verse 14)

1:11 Surprisingly, Malachi refers to the presentation of incense and pure offerings in many places, even **among the nations**, rather than exclusively in the temple in Jerusalem as Deuteronomy 12 requires (cf. Mal. 3:3–4; 4:4). A key to this controversial verse is to recognize that **from the rising of the sun to its setting** is standard predictive language regarding a future age of great blessing (e.g., Ps. 50:1; 113:3). Isaiah 45:6 and 59:19 include with this phrase a reference to the ultimate engrafting of the nations, suggesting that a similar meaning is implied in Malachi. This finds further definition in such texts as Isa. 19:19–25 and 66:1–21, where the nations will be made to be "Levites" and will offer acceptable offerings on approved altars to the true God. For the engrafting of converted Gentiles into Israel, cf. Ruth 1:16–17; Est. 8:17; Psalm 87; Isa. 56:6–8; Zech. 2:11; 8:23.

2:2–9 Since the priests failed to guard the purity of the temple, the Lord threatens to punish them in a manner that fits their crime. Because they "despised" (1:6) and failed **to give honor to** the Lord's **name**, they will be **despised and abased before all the people**. Because they "polluted" God (1:7), he will figuratively pollute and disqualify them for service at the altar by spreading on their faces the **dung** taken from their rejected sacrifices (2:3). Since that dung was to be taken away from the sanctuary and burned (e.g., Ex. 29:14; Lev. 4:11ff.), so they too will be **taken away**. Because they presumed to bless the people of

The LORD of Hosts: Frequency and Use in the OT

Why does the title "LORD of hosts" appear more frequently in Malachi than in any other OT book, and in the time of prophetic books more than during other time periods? In the period of Isaiah, the northern kingdom was overrun and destroyed and the southern kingdom almost destroyed by the "hosts" (armies) of Assyria. God's people had so few troops that the Assyrian King Sennacherib could mockingly challenge King Hezekiah with the offer of a gift of 2,000 horses if Hezekiah could find enough soldiers to ride them (Isa. 36:8). Similarly, in the period of Jeremiah, the southern kingdom was wiped out by the hosts (armies) of Babylon.

In the postexilic period of Malachi, the postage-stamp-sized Judah, as a tiny province within the vast Persian Empire, had no army of its own. It is precisely in such times, when God's people are painfully aware of how limited their own resources are, that there is no greater comfort than the fact that the Lord has his invincible heavenly armies standing at the ready. It is like the comfort that Elisha prayed for his servant at Dothan when they were surrounded by the Syrian armies: "'O LORD, please open his eyes that he may see.' So the LORD opened the eyes of the young man, and he saw, and behold, the mountain was full of horses and chariots of fire all around Elisha" (2 Kings 6:17). Perhaps it is like the comfort felt by Jesus before the cross: "Do you think that I cannot appeal to my Father, and he will at once send me more than twelve legions of angels?" (Matt. 26:53).

The following chart shows the percentages of verses in a book containing at least one occurrence of the phrase, "LORD of hosts" (or related variation):

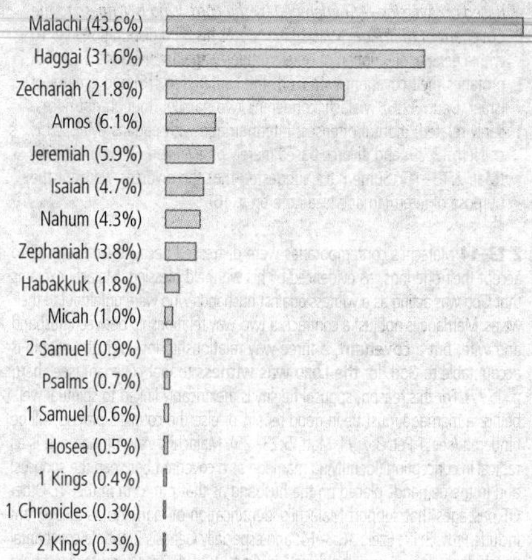

them, because you do not lay it to heart. 3 Behold, [d]I will rebuke your offspring,[1] and
[e]spread dung on your faces, the [f]dung of your offerings, and you shall be taken away
with it.[2] 4 So shall you know that I have sent [g]this command to you, that [h]my covenant
with Levi may stand, says the LORD of hosts. 5 My covenant with him was one of life and
[i]peace, and I gave them to him. [j]It was a covenant of fear, and he feared me. He stood in
awe of my name. 6 [k]True instruction[3] was in his mouth, and no wrong was found on his
lips. He walked with me in peace and uprightness, and he [l]turned many from iniquity.
7 For [m]the lips of a priest should guard knowledge, and people[4] should seek instruction
from his mouth, for he is the messenger of the LORD of hosts. 8 But you have turned
aside from the way. [n]You have caused many to stumble by your instruction. You have
corrupted [o]the covenant of Levi, says the LORD of hosts, 9 and so [p]I make you despised
and abased before all the people, inasmuch as you do not keep my ways but [q]show partiality in your instruction."

Judah Profaned the Covenant

10 Have we not all [r]one Father? Has not [s]one God created us? Why then are we [t]faithless
to one another, profaning the covenant of our fathers? 11 Judah has been [t]faithless, and
abomination has been committed in Israel and in Jerusalem. For [u]Judah has profaned the
sanctuary of the LORD, which he loves, and has married the daughter of a foreign god.
12 May the LORD cut off from the tents of Jacob any descendant[5] of the man who does this,
who [v]brings an offering to the LORD of hosts!

13 And this second thing you do. [w]You cover the LORD's altar with tears, with weeping
and groaning because he no longer regards the offering or accepts it with favor from your
hand. 14 [x]But you say, "Why does he not?" Because the LORD [y]was witness between you and
the wife of your youth, [z]to whom [t]you have been faithless, though she is your companion
and your wife by covenant. 15 [a]Did he not make them one, with a portion of the Spirit in
their union?[6] And what was the one God[7] seeking?[8] [b]Godly offspring. So guard yourselves[9]
in your spirit, and let none of you be [t]faithless to the wife of your youth. 16 "For [c]the man

[1] Hebrew *seed* [2] Or *to it* [3] Or *law*; also verses 7, 8, 9 [4] Hebrew *they* [5] Hebrew *any who wakes and answers* [6] Hebrew *in it* [7] Hebrew *the one* [8] Or *And not one has done this who has a portion of the Spirit. And what was that one seeking?* [9] Or *So take care*; also verse 16

3 [d][Joel 1:17; Hag. 2:17] [e]Nah. 3:6 [f][Ex. 29:14]
4 [g]ver. 1 [h]ver. 8; Num. 25:12, 13; Neh. 13:29; [Num. 3:45]
5 [i]See Isa. 54:10 [j][Lev. 16:2]
6 [k][Deut. 33:10] [l][Dan. 12:3; James 5:20]
7 [m]Deut. 17:9; See Lev. 10:11
8 [n][1 Sam. 2:17; Jer. 18:15; Ezek. 22:26] [o]See ver. 4
9 [p][1 Sam. 2:30] [q]Deut. 1:17; 16:19
10 [r]1 Cor. 8:6; Eph. 4:6 [s]Acts 17:26 [t][Isa. 21:2; 24:16; 33:1]
11 [t][See ver. 10 above] [u]See Ezra 9:2
12 [v][ch. 1:7]
13 [w][Zech. 7:3]
14 [x][ch. 1:2] [y]ch. 3:5 [z][ver. 11; Isa. 54:6] [t][See ver. 10 above]
15 [a]Matt. 19:4, 5; See Gen. 2:24 [b][Ezra 9:2] [t][See ver. 10 above]
16 [c]Matt. 5:32; Mark 10:9, 11; Luke 16:18; 1 Cor. 7:10

God, as if Israel's sacrifices had been accepted and atonement made, God will now **curse** their **blessings**. As Matthew Henry put it, "Nothing profanes the name of God more than the misconduct of those whose business it is to do honor to it." On the phrase **guard knowledge**, see note on Prov. 5:2–3.

2:10–16 *Third Disputation: Marriage to an Idolater—and Divorce Based on Aversion—Condemned by the Lord, Who Is Witness to the Covenant of Marriage.* Malachi introduces his third disputation in v. 10 with a general description of Israel's infidelity against one another, which profanes their covenant with God, the Father (see 1:6) and Creator of Israel (Deut. 32:6). Malachi condemns two parallel (though not necessarily related) marital offenses: intermarriage with pagans (Mal. 2:11; cf. Neh. 13:29) and divorce based merely on aversion or incompatibility (Mal. 2:13–16). Some have suggested that the divorces were for the purpose of intermarriage (see note on v. 16).

2:13–14 Malachi's contemporaries were distressed because God refused to accept their offerings, as evidenced by his withheld blessing. Malachi explains that God was acting as a witness against husbands who were unfaithful to their wives. Marriage is not just a contract, a two-way relationship between husband and wife, but a **covenant**, a three-way relationship in which the couple is accountable to God, for **the LORD was witness** to that covenant (see chart, p. 1777). For this reason, spousal fidelity is inextricably linked to spiritual well-being: a marriage must be in good repair, or else the couple's prayers will be hindered (see 1 Pet. 3:7; cf. Matt. 5:23–25). Malachi's view of marriage is as radical in conception (identifying marriage as a covenant between the spouses) and in the demands placed on the husband as that put forth in the NT. Other OT passages that support Malachi's identification of marriage as a covenant include Prov. 2:17; Ezek. 16:8–14; and especially Genesis 2, where covenantal vocabulary ("leave" and "hold fast" in Gen. 2:24) is employed to describe a husband's duty (cf. the covenantal use of "leave" and "hold fast" in, e.g., Deut. 4:4; 10:20; Josh. 1:5), and where Adam commits himself to Eve before God by employing a formula which is attested elsewhere in covenant-ratifying contexts: "this at last is bone of my bones" (Gen. 2:23; cf., e.g., 2 Sam. 5:1).

2:15 Make them one may be a reference to Gen. 2:24; if so, then perhaps Malachi derived his understanding of marriage as a covenant and the primacy of the husband's obligation from the exemplary marriage of Adam and Eve. The translation and meaning of this verse are obscure, and various translations have rendered the verse differently, but the approach taken by the ESV does account for the dire warnings in Mal. 2:15b and 16b. There is, then, a remarkable similarity between the logic of v. 15 and the teaching of Jesus in Matt. 19:5–9, namely, that it is God who joins a couple together; Malachi says there was **a portion of the Spirit in their union**. Furthermore, this verse asserts that the Lord intends marriage to produce **godly offspring** (lit., "a seed of God"). In Malachi's view, divorce may frustrate this purpose in a manner analogous to marriage to an idolater (Ezra 10:3, 44; Neh. 13:23–27). The expression "a seed of God" reflects the imagery established in Mal. 2:10 (and 1:6) of God as a "Father" to his people, in virtue of his redemptive acts and covenant, and it offers an intentional contrast to the phrase in 2:11, "the daughter of a foreign god."

2:16 The Hebrew text of this verse is one of the most difficult passages in the OT to translate, with the result that the two main alternative translations proposed for this verse are strongly disputed. The ESV translation team has included in a footnote the other most common translation. Given the complexity of the linguistic issues involved, both alternatives are simply summarized briefly as follows, rather than presenting comprehensive arguments for each.

1. The ESV text reads, **the man who does not love his wife but divorces her**. This rendering understands the Hebrew (and the Gk. of the Septuagint) in the sense of, "For he hates (or "does not love") [and] he divorces." The action of "hating" and thus "divorcing" is seen also in Deut. 24:3; further, the idea of a man "hating" his wife appears in Gen. 29:31; Deut. 21:15–17; 22:13; each case in the sense of "loving less" or "ceasing to love." The expression **covers his garment with violence** is probably a figure of speech referring to the defiling of one's character with violent wrongdoing

16[t][See ver. 10 above]
17[d]Isa. 43:24 [x][See ver. 14 above] [e][ch. 3:15; Isa. 5:20] [f][ch. 3:1; 2 Pet. 3:4]
Chapter 3
1[g]Cited Matt. 11:10; Mark 1:2; Luke 7:27; [ch. 4:5; Luke 1:76] [h]See ch. 2:7 [i]See Isa. 40:3 [j][ch. 2:17] [k][ch. 4:5]
2[l]Joel 2:11 [m]Isa. 4:4

who does not love his wife but divorces her,[1] says the LORD, the God of Israel, covers[2] his garment with violence, says the LORD of hosts. So guard yourselves in your spirit, and [t]do not be faithless."

The Messenger of the LORD

17 [d]You have wearied the LORD with your words. [x]But you say, "How have we wearied him?" [e]By saying, "Everyone who does evil is good in the sight of the LORD, and he delights in them." Or by asking, [f]"Where is the God of justice?"

3 [g]"Behold, I send [h]my messenger, and [i]he will prepare the way before me. And the Lord
[j]whom you seek will suddenly come to his temple; and [k]the messenger of the covenant
in whom you delight, behold, he is coming, says the LORD of hosts. **2** But [l]who can endure
the day of his coming, and who can stand when he appears? For [m]he is like a refiner's fire

[1] Hebrew *who hates and divorces* [2] Probable meaning (compare Septuagint and Deuteronomy 24:1–4); or *"The LORD, the God of Israel, says that he hates divorce, and him who covers*

(see the similar image in Ps. 73:6; 109:18; Rev. 3:4; and see the opposite in Job 29:14; Ps. 132:9; Isa. 59:17; 61:10). Although divorce based on loss of affection was recognized under the OT civic law, it is nowhere morally approved (unlike divorce based on a spouse's sexual infidelity or desertion). This is so, as Malachi stresses, because divorce based merely on the loss of affection breaks the marriage covenant and defiles one's character, since it is untrue to the creation ideal of faithfulness (Gen. 2:24; see note on Deut. 24:1–4).

2. The ESV footnote reads, "The LORD, the God of Israel, says that he hates divorce, and him who covers [his garment with violence]." This is similar to the rendering that originally appeared in English in the King James Version of 1611. If this alternative rendering is followed, the focus is on *God's hatred of the practice of divorce*, rather than on *the hatred of the divorcing man toward his wife*. Also following this alternative rendering, the phrase "covers his garment with violence" is understood either: (a) with reference to a second thing that God hates in addition to divorce, namely, the person "who covers his garment with violence"; or, as some hold, (b) that God hates divorce because the act of divorce itself "covers [one's] garment with violence."

In either case, this passage is clear in its recognition that the biblical standard for marriage derives from the creation account (see notes on Gen. 2:23–24), which establishes the covenantal nature of marriage. (Jesus, when discussing a question about divorce, began with creation; Matt. 19:3–9.) Malachi starts from this creational base: he refers to creation (Mal. 2:10), calls marriage a covenant (v. 14), refers to the oneness of Gen. 2:24 ("union," Mal. 2:15), and reminds the community of the purpose of marriage ("godly offspring," v. 15). The man who would divorce the Israelite wife of his youth (perhaps even for the purpose of taking a pagan girl as his wife) thus commits a grievous offense: he violates the creation order, he breaks his covenantal relationship with his wife—and, in so doing, he deeply damages his character ("covers his garment with violence"). But the impact of divorce reaches far beyond the individual, for divorce has a ruinous effect on the vitality of the whole community (vv. 13–15) and on its ability to fulfill its calling as God's holy people.

Again, in either case, God is opposed to the kind of divorce that is in view because of the destructiveness and pain that inevitably results when "faithless" husbands send away their wives, as mentioned in Mal. 2:13, 15. (See also the notes on Matt. 5:31–32; 19:3–9; Mark 10:10–12; 1 Cor. 7:15; and Divorce and Remarriage, pp. 2545–2547.)

2:17–3:5 *Fourth Disputation: The Lord Is a Witness against Adultery and Other Moral Offenses.* The prophet begins by accusing the people of wearying the Lord with their cynical complaints: "Everyone who does evil is good in the sight of the LORD, and he delights in them" and "Where is the God of justice?" Now that they had returned to the Promised Land and the temple had been rebuilt, many were distressed at the apparent failure of the prophetic promises of restored prosperity, international prominence, and wealth (Haggai 2; Zech. 1:16ff.; 2:1–13; 8:1–9:17). Instead, Israel was experiencing only continued social and political oppression and economic privation (Neh. 1:3; 9:36ff.; Mal. 3:10ff.). Still worse, it had been promised that God would return to Jerusalem and to his temple, which he would again inhabit with his own glorious presence (e.g., Zech. 1:16ff.; 2:4ff., 10–13; 8:3–8; 9:9–17). Since Moses' tabernacle and Solomon's temple were filled with the visible glory of God as soon as they were completed, it was hoped that the same would happen with the rebuilt temple (Ex. 40:34ff.; 1 Kings 8:10ff.; Ezek. 43:1–12). Indeed, Hag. 2:9 promised that the rebuilt temple would be filled with an even greater measure of glory than Solomon's. But far from enjoying such radiant glory, the temple of Malachi's day was devoid of any visible manifestation of God. Yet it would not always be so, for Malachi promised, "the Lord whom you seek will suddenly come to his temple" (Mal. 3:1). Simeon witnessed at least a partial fulfillment of this prophecy when he encountered in the temple the infant Jesus, who had come "for glory to your people Israel" (Luke 2:32). The NT unfolds further fulfillment, for only the glory of God in the person of Jesus Christ would be this greater glory (Luke 2:29–32; John 1:14; 2 Cor. 4:6).

3:1 From the "delight" mentioned in this verse, it appears that Israel had repeated the error of their forebears in the days of Amos (Amos 5:18) by supposing that the Lord's appearance would be unmitigated good news. When he comes, it will be not only for blessing, as they assume, but also

Covenant in Malachi

The word "covenant" (Hb. *berit*) in the OT entails four essential components: (1) a relationship (2) with a nonrelative that (3) involves obligations and (4) is established through an oath. It is used seven times in Malachi (out of a mere 1,193 words): a rate 10 times greater than almost every other OT book (except for Deuteronomy, Joshua, Hosea, and Obadiah). This may explain why Malachi goes out of his way to identify marriage as a "covenant" (Proverbs is the only other book to do so explicitly). Malachi is also the only book to use the designation, "the messenger [or angel] of the covenant."

Reference	Partners in Covenant	Qualities in Covenant
2:4–5, 8	Covenant between the Lord and Levi, of perpetual priesthood; corrupted in 2:8	A covenant of life, peace, and reverence for the Lord (cf. Num. 25:12–13); broken covenant resulted in abasement of priesthood
2:10	Covenant of "our fathers" with the Lord	Expectation of fidelity of Judah, Israel, Jerusalem to an exclusive relationship with the Lord, implicates community relationships
2:14	Marital covenant between husband and wife	The Lord as witness, involving faithful relationship, the Spirit, and godly offspring
3:1	The messenger of the covenant (between God and his people)	The Lord as witness; future orientation, as the Lord's longed-for presence results in purity in the community

and like fullers' soap. 3 He will sit [n]as a refiner and purifier of silver, and he will purify
the sons of Levi and refine them like gold and silver, and they will bring [o]offerings in
righteousness to the LORD.[1] 4 [p]Then the offering of Judah and Jerusalem will be pleasing
to the LORD as in the days of old and as in former years.
5 "Then I will draw near to you for judgment. I will be [q]a swift witness against the sorcerers, against the adulterers, against those who swear falsely, against those [r]who oppress
the hired worker in his wages, [s]the widow and the fatherless, against those who thrust
aside the sojourner, and do not fear me, says the LORD of hosts.

Robbing God

6 "For [t]I the LORD do not change; [u]therefore you, O children of Jacob, are not consumed.
7 [v]From the days of your fathers you have turned aside from my statutes and have not kept
them. [w]Return to me, and I will return to you, says the LORD of hosts. [x]But you say, 'How
shall we return?' 8 Will man rob God? Yet you are robbing me. [x]But you say, 'How have
we robbed you?' [y]In your tithes and contributions. 9 [z]You are cursed with a curse, for you
are robbing me, the whole nation of you. 10 [a]Bring the full tithe into the storehouse, that
there may be food in my house. And thereby [b]put me to the test, says the LORD of hosts,

[1] *Or and they will belong to the LORD, bringers of an offering in righteousness*

3 [n]Isa. 1:25; Zech. 13:9 [o][ch. 1:7]
4 [p]Ezek. 20:40
5 [q]ch. 2:14; Jer. 29:23 [r]See Lev. 19:13 [s]See Deut. 24:17
6 [t]Ps. 102:27; See Num. 23:19 [u]Lam. 3:22
7 [v]Acts 7:51 [w]See Zech. 1:3 [x][ch. 1:2]
8 [x][See ver. 7 above] [y][Neh. 13:10]
9 [z][ch. 2:2]
10 [a][Prov. 3:9, 10] [b]See 2 Cor. 9:6-8

for judgment—he will come to be a "witness" (the term in Mal. 3:5 is the same as in 2:14) against all evildoers, including these blasphemous cynics! In preparation for this fearful epiphany, the Lord promises, **"Behold, I send my messenger, and he will prepare the way before me."** "My messenger," who "will prepare the way," is distinguished in 3:1a from the divine **LORD of hosts**, who is the speaker and to whom the pronouns "I," "my," and "me" refer. So the messenger in v. 1a is someone different from the Lord of hosts. And despite the fact that "my messenger" and "Malachi" are the same in Hebrew, the future-oriented context of vv. 1–5 and the parallel between 3:1 and 4:5 make clear that "my messenger" is not Malachi. Nevertheless, the play on Malachi's name suggests that his own ministry of preparation was intended to foreshadow the work of this promised messenger in 3:1a. But in v. 1b, another idea is in view, for v. 1b speaks in poetic parallelism, in which two lines express the same idea in different words. Therefore, **the Lord whom you seek** is the same person as **the messenger of the covenant in whom you delight**, and thus this coming "messenger of the covenant" is the same divine being as "the Lord," who also is desired and will come. Then in the following verses, the ministry described in vv. 2–4 also indicates the divine nature of this coming Lord. The NT confirms this interpretation by its identification of John the Baptist as the promised messenger of v. 1a, who prepares the way for the Lord who is predicted in v. 1b (see Matt. 11:10–14 par.).

3:2–5 When the Lord comes, he will perform two complementary works: he will purify some sinners (vv. 2–4) and judge others (v. 5). The images used for that purifying work, the **refiner's fire** and **fullers' soap**, stress both its thoroughness and its severity. The heat of the refiner's fire was intense in order to separate the dross from the molten pure metal. Similarly, the fuller washed clothes using strong lye soap, after which the clothes would be placed on rocks and beaten with sticks. If sinners prefer the Lord's cleansing work to his judgment, this is the price that must be paid (cf. Heb. 12:7–11).

3:6–12 *Fifth Disputation: Israel's Begrudging Offerings Condemned.* The prophet returns to Israel's begrudging offerings, a subject treated in the parallel second disputation (1:6–2:9). There the emphasis was on the priests' failure, but here Malachi's concern expands to include the whole nation (3:9). Perhaps the reference to Jacob serves as a reminder of Jacob's return from exile in Paddan Aram; upon coming back both to the Promised Land and to the Lord, he built an altar at Bethel and offered a tithe according to his vow in Gen. 28:20–22 (cf. Gen. 35:1–7). Similarly, when Jacob's descendants returned from their exile, they rebuilt the altar at Jerusalem, but they were grossly negligent in offering their tithes (cf. Neh. 13:10–13). This negligence may have seemed justified because of crop failure, drought, and pestilence (Mal. 3:10–11). The Lord reveals, however, that these natural disasters were not the *cause* of the nation's disobedience, but the cursed *result* (3:8; cf. Hag. 1:6, 9–11; 2:16–19).

3:6 I the LORD do not change implies that God's character and eternal purposes do not change, which gives a solid foundation for his people's faith and hope. However, unchangeableness in *character* does not mean that the Lord is unchanging in his *actions*, for the very next verse, "Return to me and I will return to you" (v. 7), shows that God acts differently in response to different situations. **Therefore** implies that God's purpose to bring blessing to the world through Abraham's descendants and through a Davidic Messiah will not be defeated, and thus the **children of Jacob** are **not consumed**: their existence as the restored community is evidence of God's faithfulness.

3:8 you are robbing me. When the people did not give the "tithe" (see note on vv. 10–12), they were keeping wealth that rightly belonged to God.

3:10–12 As an evidence of wholehearted repentance (v. 7), God promises that if his people become faithful in presenting their **full tithe** (the Hb. word means "a tenth"), then the desperately needed rain will come (v. 10), pestilence and crop failure will cease (v. 11), and the Abrahamic promise that **all nations will call you blessed** (v. 12; Ps. 72:17) will be fulfilled. The tithes were given to support the priests and Levites (see Neh. 10:38; 12:44), whose ministry was essential if Israel was to be faithful to its calling. By saying, **"put me to the test,"** God is challenging the people to give the tithe that they owed him and then watch to see if he would be faithful to his promise. God promises to meet all their needs, but not necessarily all their "greeds," and to **pour down for you a blessing until there is no more need.**

3:13–4:3 *Sixth Disputation: Does God Make a Distinction between the Good and the Arrogantly Wicked? God's Elective Love Vindicated in His Judgment.* This section echoes the first disputation; there, the focus was on his people and "not-his-people" (see note on 1:2–3; cf. Hos. 1:9), while here it is on those of his own people who do and do not embrace the covenant.

3:13–15 The sixth disputation begins with Israel's audacious and blasphemous complaint that **it is vain to serve God**. It looks like **keeping his charge** and **walking as in mourning** are parallel statements, which suggests that they refer to ceremonial or liturgical requirements such as the ritual mourning about which Israel boasts in Zech. 7:1–6. Because of their hypocrisy, these acts had degenerated into meaningless formalities (Isa. 58:3–9; Mal. 2:13).

3:16 In sharp contrast to the fault-finding cynics, a second group is now mentioned, **those who feared the LORD and esteemed his name**. Just as the Lord recounts the contemptuous blasphemies of the first group (vv. 13–15), so he overhears the faithful conversation of the second. Similar to the honor roll kept by King Xerxes, which recorded the long-unrewarded faithfulness of Mordecai (Est. 6:1–3), a **book of remembrance** is written in God's presence concerning these faithful believers. Similar books of significant deeds were kept by kings in the ancient world (see Est. 2:23; 6:1). This image of God's record book, which appears throughout Scripture (see e.g., Ex. 32:32–33; Ps.

if I will not open [c]the windows of heaven for you and pour down for you a blessing until
there is no more need. **11** I will rebuke [d]the devourer[1] for you, so that it will not destroy
the fruits of your soil, and your vine in the field shall not fail to bear, says the LORD of
hosts. **12** Then [e]all nations will call you blessed, for you will be [f]a land of delight, says the
LORD of hosts.

13 [g]"Your words have been hard against me, says the LORD. [h]But you say, 'How have we
spoken against you?' **14** You have said, [i]'It is vain to serve God. [j]What is the profit of our
keeping his charge or of walking as in mourning before the LORD of hosts? **15** And now
we call [k]the arrogant blessed. [k]Evildoers not only prosper but [l]they put God to the test
and they escape.'"

The Book of Remembrance

16 Then those who feared the LORD [m]spoke with one another. The LORD paid attention
and heard them, and [n]a book of remembrance was written before him of those who feared
the LORD and esteemed his name. **17** "They shall be mine, says the LORD of hosts, [o]in the
day when I make up [p]my treasured possession, and I will spare them as a man spares his
son who serves him. **18** Then once more you shall [q]see the distinction between the righteous
and the wicked, between one who serves God and one who does not serve him.

The Great Day of the LORD

4[2] "For behold, [r]the day is coming, [s]burning like an oven, when [t]all the arrogant and
[t]all evildoers [u]will be stubble. The day that is coming [u]shall set them ablaze, says the
LORD of hosts, so that it will leave them neither root nor branch. **2** But for you [v]who fear
my name, [w]the sun [x]of righteousness shall rise [y]with healing in its wings. You shall go out
[z]leaping like calves from the stall. **3** And you shall tread down the wicked, for they will be
ashes under the soles of your feet, [a]on the day when I act, says the LORD of hosts.

4 [b]"Remember [c]the law of my servant Moses, the statutes and rules[3] that I commanded
him at Horeb for all Israel.

5 [d]"Behold, I will send you [e]Elijah the prophet [f]before the great and awesome day

[1] Probably a name for some crop-destroying pest or pests [2] Ch 4:1–6 is ch 3:19–24 in Hebrew [3] Or *and just decrees*

10 [c]See Gen. 7:11
11 [d][Joel 1:4]
12 [e]Zeph. 3:19 [f][Isa. 62:4]
13 [g][ch. 2:17] [h][ch. 1:2]
14 [i][Zeph. 1:12] [j][Job 21:15]
15 [k][ch. 4:1] [l][Ps. 95:9]
16 [m][Deut. 6:6, 7] [n]See Ex. 32:32
17 [o][ch. 4:3; Acts 17:31] [p]Ex. 19:5; 1 Pet. 2:9
18 [q][ch. 4:1]

Chapter 4

1 [r][ver. 5; ch. 3:2] [s][2 Thess. 1:7, 8] [t]ch. 3:15 [u]Isa. 47:14; [Matt. 3:12; Luke 3:17]
2 [v]ch. 3:16 [w]Ps. 84:11; Luke 1:78; John 1:4; 8:12; 9:5; 12:46 [x][Jer. 23:6] [y]Isa. 53:5 [z][Jer. 50:11]
3 [a]See ch. 3:17
4 [b][Deut. 4:9, 10] [c]See Ex. 20:3-17; Deut. 4:10
5 [d][ch. 3:1] [e][Matt. 11:14; Mark 9:11; Luke 1:17] [f]Joel 2:31

56:8; 139:16; Dan. 7:10; 12:1; Rev. 20:12), indicates that God will never forget and will rightly judge both the good deeds of the righteous and the evil deeds of the wicked.

3:17–4:3 The insolent complainers had charged that "evildoers not only prosper but they put God to the test and they escape" (3:15). But in 3:17–4:3 the Lord promises that a day is coming when these complainers will see how wrong they were. For those faithful believers listed in the "book of remembrance" (3:16), it will be a day when God will say, **"They shall be mine,"** his **treasured possession** (3:17; cf. Ex. 19:5), and they will be spared **as a man spares his son who serves him**. Although for **the arrogant and all evildoers** it will be a day when they are burned up like **stubble**, for those **who fear** God's **name** it will be a day when **the sun of righteousness shall rise with healing in its wings** (Mal. 4:2; cf. Isa. 60:1–3; Luke 1:78), and they will subdue the **wicked**.

4:2 Just as the sun drives away darkness and clouds, bringing light and joy, so the **sun of righteousness** will appear to dispel gloom, oppression, and injustice. For the image of the rising sun applied to a great visitation from God, cf. Isa. 60:1–2; for the recognition that the birth of John the Baptist had ushered in this expected era, see Luke 1:78. The "righteousness" brought by this "sun" includes both judgment on evildoers and reward for those who are righteous in their deeds. Its **wings** are a poetic image for the rays of this sun, bringing **healing** to all who come under its influence. Some suggest that ancient Near Eastern depictions of a winged sun disk are reflected in the image. Malachi's readers probably would have thought this image predicted the sudden appearance of God himself, who is elsewhere compared to the sun (Ps. 84:11; Isa. 60:19–20; cf. Ps. 27:1; Isa. 60:1; Rev. 21:23). But Christian interpreters throughout the history of the church have understood this prophecy to be fulfilled in Christ, who is "the light of the world" (John 8:12; cf. John 1:4–6).

4:4–6 *Conclusion.* These closing appeals summarize the main points of Malachi's prophecy: **Remember the law of my servant Moses** (the focus of the first three disputations) and the promised sending of **Elijah the prophet** before the coming **day of the LORD** (the focus of the last three disputations). **Horeb** is another name for Mount Sinai (cf. Exodus 19–20; Deut. 5:2). Malachi's own thoroughgoing dependence on the Law of Moses and many allusions to Pentateuchal texts prepare the reader for the first climactic charge. In the second charge, the reason for the identification of the coming prophet as "Elijah" is less obvious. Perhaps the need for an Elijah-like ministry was suggested by a long-standing drought (Mal. 3:10; cf. 1 Kings 17:1; James 5:17). Alternatively, Malachi's concern with the corrosive effects of marriage to an idolater (Mal. 2:10–12) may have brought to mind Ahab's notorious interfaith marriage to Jezebel, which proved so troublesome to Elijah and so disastrous to Israel (1 Kings 16:31; 18:4, 19; 19:2). No doubt Malachi would have welcomed an Elijah-like challenge to religious compromise and complacency (1 Kings 18). It seems most likely, however, that Malachi recognized that of all the OT prophets, Elijah best fit the portrait of the messianic prophet "like Moses" predicted in Deut. 18:15 and 34:10–12. As such, Elijah stands alongside Moses in Mal. 4:4–6 as the representative of the entire OT line of prophets, much as he functions on the Mount of Transfiguration (Mark 9:4 and parallels). The promise to send Elijah the prophet **before the great and awesome** "day of the LORD" confirms the interpretation given here of Mal. 3:1–5, that the promised messenger is not Malachi himself but some future prophet. It is likely that this future prophet is identified with Elijah not because Elijah was spared from death, as if this might permit a literal return to life, but because the future messenger would have a prophetic ministry similar to that of the historical Elijah. Compare the many OT predictions of a future "David" that do not suggest David's literal return to life (Jer. 30:9; Ezek. 34:23–25; 37:24). The NT identifies John the Baptist as the fulfillment of Malachi's prophesied Elijah (Matt. 11:10–14; 17:10–13; etc.). When John the Baptist denied that he was Elijah (John 1:21, 25), it is possible either that he was denying that he was Elijah in person, or that he rejected not the ministry predicted in Malachi but misguided

of the LORD comes. 6 And he will [g]turn the hearts of fathers to their children and the hearts of children to their fathers, lest I come and [h]strike the land with a decree of utter destruction."[1]

[1] The Hebrew term rendered *decree of utter destruction* refers to things devoted (or set apart) to the Lord (or by the Lord) for destruction

6[g][Luke 1:17] [h]Isa. 11:4; [Zech. 5:3]

popular elaborations of this promise based on other notable features in the original Elijah's ministry, especially his many miracles, which pointed more to Christ than to John (John 10:41; see note on Matt. 11:14). (For more on "the day of the LORD," see note on Amos 5:18–20.)

Background to the New Testament

The Time between the Testaments

Most of the writers of the NT grew up in the world of "Second Temple Judaism," the time between the temple's reconstruction (516 B.C.) and its final destruction (A.D. 70). This period introduced changes into the political structure, culture, and religion of the OT world.

Sources of Information

Among the many resources about Second Temple Judaism, the most substantial are the Apocrypha and the pseudepigrapha of the OT, the writings of Josephus (c. A.D. 37–100), and the writings of the Jewish philosopher Philo (c. 20 B.C.–A.D. 50). The 1946–1947 discovery of the Dead Sea Scrolls not only provided new documents from the Second Temple era but also led to different ways of reading and understanding previously known material. The Targums (Aramaic translations and paraphrases of the Bible) and rabbinic literature (which developed over centuries but attained its current written form after the time of the NT) also provide some indirect evidence of this period. Because Second Temple Judaism overlaps with the first century, the NT itself is a primary source of information about the life, thought, conditions, and situations of that time.

The Apocrypha and Pseudepigrapha

The Apocrypha and pseudepigrapha are collections of Jewish writings from the period of Second Temple Judaism. Most of the 15 (or 14) books of the Apocrypha are included in the canon of the Orthodox and Roman Catholic traditions, and excerpts from them are still read regularly in some Anglican churches. (For more information, see The Apocrypha, pp. 2581–2583.)

The word "pseudepigrapha" means "false inscription" or "false title" (referring to the name of the supposed "author" attached to each one). "False" is more a judgment of the names with which the writings are traditionally associated than of their content. Most of these writings represent the beliefs of distinctive groups or schools (or in some cases just individuals) connecting themselves with the name of a notable person of antiquity, such as Enoch, Noah, Moses, or Ezra. Modern collections of the pseudepigrapha contain more than 60 titles.

The Dead Sea Scrolls

Thousands of documents and fragments make up the Dead Sea Scrolls. They contain parts of all OT books except Esther, as well as parts of some apocryphal and pseudepigraphal writings. "Sectarian documents" are related to the organization, worship, and thought of the group that collected and wrote them.

History

Second Temple Judaism emerged in the fifth century B.C. during the Persian Empire, which was the dominant power at the end of OT history. The Hebrews, both living in their own land and scattered elsewhere, seem to have had a fairly ordinary existence, apart from events such as rebuilding the temple and the walls of Jerusalem. The book of Esther, however, demonstrates how quickly serious crises could develop for the Jews.

The Hellenistic Period (331–164 B.C.)

In the 330s B.C. the Persians were supplanted by the Greeks under Alexander the Great (ruled 334–323). In addition to military conquest and political control, Alexander was intent to spread Greek (Hellenistic) culture, including use of the Greek language.

The Jews simply shifted allegiance to Alexander and, at first, were generally left alone. Following Alexander's death and the ensuing struggles, his empire was divided among four of his generals.

From 320 to 198 B.C., the Jews were controlled by the Egyptian Ptolemaic Empire. A sizable Jewish community also grew in Egypt, and a large Jewish colony in Alexandria was influential well past the time of Christ (cf. Apollos, Acts 18:24). A Greek translation of the Pentateuch was made in Egypt c. 250 B.C., and of the rest of the OT by about 130 B.C. (together commonly called the Septuagint). Most of Palestine's countryside, outside Jerusalem, adopted Greek culture (Hellenism).

In about 198 B.C., the Seleucid (Syrian) Empire to the north of Palestine gained control over the Jews. The Seleucids attempted to spread Hellenism throughout their empire. The Jews were forbidden, on pain of death, to practice their traditional way of life, including their religion. The Jerusalem temple was turned into a pagan shrine, and persecution became prevalent.

Mattathias, an aged priest, along with his five sons, led a revolt. After Mattathias's death, leadership fell to one of his sons, Judas (called "Maccabeus"). Judas and his successors eventually won independence. In 164 B.C. the temple was

Major Periods within Second Temple Judaism

Second Temple Judaism developed as political authority changed hands from the Persians to the Greeks, to the Jewish Hasmoneans, and finally to the Romans.

539–331 B.C.	331–164 B.C.	164–63 B.C.	63 B.C.–A.D. 70
The Persian Period	The Hellenistic Period Ptolemaic (Egyptian) Period (320–198) Seleucid (Syrian) Period (198–164)	The Hasmonean (Maccabean) Period	The Roman Period

cleansed, and the daily burnt offering and other religious ceremonies resumed. The event is still commemorated by Jews each December as Hanukkah, the "Feast of Lights."

The Hasmonean (Maccabean) Period (164–63 B.C.)

During the Maccabean period (164–63 B.C.) all rulers were from the same family of Jewish priests (also called the "Hasmonean" family after the Hebrew name of Simon, an early Maccabean leader). Nine rulers followed Judas Maccabeus to the throne, including two of his brothers. From the second generation onward, the Maccabean rulers became progressively dictatorial, corrupt, immoral, and even pagan. Internal strife led Jewish leaders to ask the Roman general Pompey to come and restore order. Pompey did so, but he also brought Roman rule, which began in 63 B.C. and lasted into the fourth century A.D.

The Roman Period (63 B.C.–A.D. 135)

When Pompey took Jerusalem, he entered the temple and even the Most Holy Place. To the Jews, this was the ultimate insult and sacrilege. The Romans could not understand why the Jews resented the various exercises of privilege and control by their conqueror. Hence, deep suspicion and ill will began growing, lasting over a century until the Jews rebelled and the Romans destroyed the Jewish state. The NT reader must remain aware of this seething undercurrent that colors much of what takes place, even during the ministry of Jesus.

In the centuries before this, Greece had conquered the ancient world and left its intellectual and cultural mark. The Romans built on this through political achievements. Paul and other travelers made good use of the vast system of Roman roads. Roman government, organization, law, money, taxation, culture, religion, army, and demands were everywhere. "Roman Peace" (*Pax Romana*) was enforced by arms but brought a measure of security and stability to the empire. The levels of its society were clearly understood, and the higher levels often oppressed the lowest. In most strata of society, morals were degenerate. Some captured peoples were restless, yearning to be free from Rome—none more than the Jews. Many, like the prophetess Anna, were patiently "waiting for the redemption of Jerusalem" (Luke 2:38).

Roman influence, good and bad, was an ever-present reality in the NT world. Zechariah, the father of John the Baptist, prayed for a salvation that combined deliverance "from our enemies" with increased religious fervor, "that we might . . . serve him [the Lord] without fear, in holiness and righteousness" (Luke 1:70–75). One Jewish group, the Zealots, sought violent, armed rebellion for religious reasons. The dominion of the Romans over the land where Jesus lived was most evident through the governmental structures they established, the rulers they appointed, and the actions they carried out. The Jewish Sanhedrin, or Council (a combination civil-religious body), predated the coming of the Romans. It retained broad authority, but always under the watchful eye of Rome. The high priest was the head of these 70 (or 72) officials, but rulers under the Romans removed and appointed high priests at will (in spite of the OT provision that the high priesthood was for life). Tax collectors collected taxes for Rome. They were given, and many used, wide freedom in the amount they collected. The Jews hated them for collaborating with the Romans; they suspected that these tax collectors collected enough to satisfy not only their Roman masters but also their own greed.

In 37 B.C. the Roman senate appointed Herod the Great to be "king" of all Palestine. Until his death in 4 B.C., he maintained this position by cooperating with whatever Roman group or emperor happened to be in power. He was king when Jesus was born (c. 5 B.C.). It was Herod who killed the boy babies in Bethlehem (Matt. 2:16–18), an unsurprising atrocity, similar in character to his treatment of friends and family.

Herod carried out great building projects. About 20/19 B.C. he began enlarging and reconstructing the temple in Jerusalem. The main work was completed fairly quickly, but additional improvements continued until A.D. 64 (cf. John 2:20).

Herod's will divided his kingdom between three sons. After changing and ratifying Herod's will, Roman authorities made Archelaus the ethnarch (ruler of half a "kingdom") of Judea, Samaria, and Idumea. Mismanagement led to his banishment in A.D. 6 (see Matt. 2:22). He was succeeded by governors, the best known being Pontius Pilate, who ruled from A.D. 26 to 36. Pilate was governor during (1) the ministry of Jesus (c. A.D. 27–30 or 30–33), (2) Pentecost, (3) the earliest days of the church, (4) Stephen's speech and death, and (5) the beginnings of Christian missions.

The second of Herod's sons, Philip, ruled as tetrarch (ruler of a fourth of a "kingdom") over Ituraea and Trachonitis, areas northeast of Galilee (Luke 3:1). At his death (A.D. 34) his territory was briefly assigned to the governors who also ruled Judea. Agrippa I (Herod the Great's grandson) was given this territory, with the title "king," in A.D. 37.

The third of Herod the Great's sons, Herod Antipas (often simply called "Herod" or "Herod the tetrarch" in the Gospels and Acts; see chart of Herodian Dynasty, pp. 1790–1791) was tetrarch of Galilee and Perea from 4 B.C. until A.D. 39. While visiting his half brother Herod Philip (not the tetrarch), Antipas became infatuated with Philip's wife, Herodias, daughter of another half brother, Aristobulus, and mother of Philip's daughter Salome (cf. Mark 6:22ff.). Contrary to OT law (Lev. 18:16; 20:21), Antipas married her. The denunciation of this union precipitated Herodias's anger against John the Baptist and eventually his imprisonment and death (Matt. 14:4; Mark 6:17–19; Luke 3:19–20).

Antipas (at Herodias's request) asked Emperor Gaius to give him the title of "king," the same as that given to Herodias's brother, Agrippa I. Agrippa charged Herod Antipas with plotting insurrection. Antipas, accompanied by Herodias, was exiled to Gaul (modern France) in A.D. 39. Antipas's former territory was then given to Agrippa.

In A.D. 41 the former territory of Archelaus was added to that of Agrippa, thus giving him the same title and virtually the same territory that his grandfather (Herod the Great) had held. During his kingship James, the brother of John, was beheaded (Acts 12:2), and Peter was imprisoned but freed by an angel (Acts 12:3–19). Agrippa was struck by an angel and died in Caesarea in A.D. 44 (Acts 12:23). Roman governors again ruled after this time. In A.D. 53 Herod Agrippa II (son of Agrippa I) became "king" of Ituraea and Trachonitis. Galilee and Perea were added to his domain in A.D. 56 or 61.

Two other Roman governors, Felix (A.D. 52–60) and Festus (60–62), appear in the biblical account. Paul was held prisoner and given judicial hearings by both (Acts 24:10–27; 25:8). While King Agrippa II and his sister Bernice were visiting Festus, Paul was again called on to make a defense (Acts 25:13–26:31). Festus transferred Paul to Rome for trial (Acts 26:32–28:16).

Adjustment after 586 B.C.

With the Babylonian victory of 586 B.C., the Hebrews faced loss of land, monarchy, the city of Jerusalem, and their temple. They lived under the direct control of foreign rulers, without national identity. Bereft of their own rulers, the Jews found their religious system without political support for protection, implementation, or financial backing.

From this date onward, the majority of the Hebrews were scattered throughout the world. This scattering—the Diaspora, or "Dispersion"—presented a continual threat to racial, ethnic, and cultural identity. The latter included problems related to their distinctive religious outlook, including its ceremonial, dietary, and other practices pertaining to ritual purity. Wherever they lived immediately after 586 B.C. the Hebrews faced a "theological crisis." Why had the Lord permitted his people to be conquered? Was he still good, loving, caring, and able to protect them?

By the mid-300s B.C., the Hebrews had been back in their own land for two centuries. The second temple was functioning. But then the arrival of Hellenism, with the coming of Alexander the Great in 333 B.C. and the subsequent reign of his successors, intensified the crisis and introduced new threats.

The OT law, the Torah, had established twin foundational pillars for the proper response to the Lord with whom the Hebrews were in covenant relationship. These were (1) the *temple-centered, ceremonial* pillar and (2) the pillar of *observance of ethical and moral instructions*. Before the Babylonian exile in 586 B.C. Hebrew religion had been largely temple-centered and ceremonial; it was denounced by the OT prophets when not combined with a proper effect on life and behavior. The prophets insisted on obedience to God and condemned false trust in the temple and abuses of external forms. Unless the people showed the type of repentance that resulted in a godly life and a true relationship with God, the prophets warned that they would experience God's judgment, marked by the loss of their nation and land.

With the captivity of Judah (586 B.C.) the prophets had been vindicated. The corporate life of the nation was gone, and the temple was in rubble and ashes. Ceremonial worship was all but impossible. Under similar circumstances, most other ancient religions simply disappeared.

After the return from captivity (538 B.C.) the temple was rebuilt (516) and the priest-led ceremonial worship was reestablished in Jerusalem. But some Hebrews had decided that their religion could survive without it. At the moment, they most needed an inspired message from the Lord, yet the prophets were silent (*1 Macc.* 4:44–46; 9:27; 14:41–42; Josephus, *Against Apion* 1.38–42; Babylonian Talmud, *Sanhedrin* 11a; *Prayer of Azariah* 15; Dead Sea Scrolls, *Rule of the Community* 11). Even so, the Hebrew religion had begun a remarkable adjustment.

Though the Jewish people retained both the ceremonial pillar of their response to God and the moral-ethical pillar as well, the primary emphasis shifted away from the ceremonial to the moral-ethical. But to obey the law, one needed to know its content, which required study. As a result, the center of worship was no longer exclusively the temple with its liturgy but also the place of learning, the assembly, the local synagogue. The major religious leader was no longer only the priest but also the teacher-rabbi. Such adjustments required careful, detailed study. This resulted in new and different forms of interpretation and the birth of traditions, often additional laws, which supposedly expanded and clarified the written Torah. During the NT period these additional laws were taught and passed on both orally and in written form (note the frequent mention of "scribes" in the NT). Many people regarded these rabbinic traditions as having a divine origin, equal to the laws in the written Scriptures, but Jesus pronounced them "the tradition of men" (Mark 7:1–23, esp. v. 8).

Divisions grew within the Judaism of the Second Temple era. Some Jews lived in their ancestral land, others did not; some adopted Hellenistic culture, while others clung to the Hebraic one. (Such culturally oriented conflicts are behind the complaint of Acts 6:1.) The new interpretative methods and the additional traditions increasingly became the subject of disagreement. Groups competed for religious prestige and authority, political power, recognition as being wise, wealth, the satisfaction that they were really in the "right," etc. Thus arose numerous parties, denominations, or sects. The best known are the Sadducees, Pharisees, Zealots, and Essenes. (See the article on Jewish Groups at the Time of the NT, pp. 1799–1800.) Most of their differences resulted from their distinctive traditions. One example of such differences is seen in the tensions between the Sadducees and Pharisees in Acts 23:6–9 and elsewhere.

Most people in the land of Israel belonged to none of these groups, being too busy earning a living and caring for their families. According to Josephus (*Jewish Antiquities* 18.11–17), the Pharisees were the most influential on the general public; the Sadducees came from aristocratic priestly families and were not generally popular. Most ordinary Jews were devoted to their nation and religion, and some (it is hard to know how many) were genuinely devoted to God (such as Zechariah and Elizabeth, Joseph and Mary, Simeon, and Anna; see Luke 1–2). From such as these came most of Jesus' early followers. With contempt, the Jewish leaders regarded them as "this crowd that does not know the law" (John 7:49).

Conclusion

The Jews revolted against the Romans in A.D. 66. Before the overthrow of the city and temple in A.D. 70, Jerusalem Christians fled to the Decapolis city of Pella (probably in response to Jesus' warning and instruction, Matt. 24:15–16; Mark 13:14; Luke 21:20–24; cf. 19:43). Afterward, Jewish Christian activity during the first century in Jerusalem was limited, but seems to have continued in Galilee.

Roman victory over this Jewish revolt brought "The Time between the Testaments" to its end. The third era of Hebrew history, Rabbinic Judaism, began about A.D. 90, under Roman rule, and continues to this day. (See the article on The Bible and Contemporary Judaism, pp. 2623–2625.)

From the second century on, Jerusalem was a Gentile city, and Christianity became largely a Gentile movement. ◀

Jewish and Roman Rulers

Date	Roman Emperors	Roman Prefects/Procurators of Judea and Samaria	Roman Prefects/ Procurators of All Israel	Herodian Dynasty (37 B.C.–A.D. 93)
40 B.C.				
38				Herod the Great (37 B.C.–4 B.C.)
36				
34				
32				
30				
28	Augustus (31 B.C.–A.D. 14)			
26				
24				
22				
20				
18				
16				
14				
12				
10				
8				
6				Philip (4 B.C.–A.D. 34)
4				
2				
A.D. 2				
4				
6		Coponius (A.D. 6–9)		
8		Marcus Ambibulus (A.D. 9–12)		
10				
12		Annius Rufus (A.D. 12–15)		
14	Tiberius (A.D. 14–37)			
16		Valerius Gratus (A.D. 15–26)		
18				
20				
22				
24				
26		Pontius Pilate (A.D. 26–36/37)		
28				
30				
32				
34				
36		Marcellus (A.D. 36/37)		Agrippa I (A.D. 37, 41–44)
38	Gaius (A.D. 37–41)	Marullus (A.D. 37–41)		
40				
42	Claudius (A.D. 41–54)			
44			Fadus (A.D. 44–46)	Agrippa II (A.D. 44–92/93)
46			Tiberius Alexander (A.D. 46–48)	
48			Ventidius Cumanus (A.D. 48–52)	
50				
52			Felix (A.D. 52–60)	
54	Nero (A.D. 54–68)			
56				
58				
60			Porcius Festus (A.D. 60–62)	
62			Albinus (A.D. 62–64)	
64			Gesius Florus (A.D. 64–66)	
66				
68	Galba/Otho/Vitellius (A.D. 68)			
70	Vespasian (A.D. 69–79)			
72				
74				
76				
78	Titus (A.D. 79–81)			
80	Domitian (A.D. 81–96)			
90	Nerva (A.D. 96–98)			
100	Trajan (A.D. 98–117)			
120	Hadrian (A.D. 117–138)			
140	Antonius Pius (A.D. 138–161)			
160	Marcus Aurelius (A.D. 161–180) with Lucius Verus (A.D. 161–169)			

Date	Herodian Dynasty (37 B.C.–A.D. 93)		Jewish High Priests	
40 B.C.				
38				
36				
34				
32				
30				
28				
26				
24				
22				
20				
18				
16				
14				
12				
10				
8				
6				
4	Archelaus (4 B.C.–A.D. 6)	Antipas (4 B.C.–A.D. 39)	Joazar son of Boethus (4 B.C.)	Eleazar son of Boethus (4 B.C.–?)
2			Jesus son of Sie (3 B.C.–A.D. 6)	
A.D. 2				
4				
6			Annas (A.D. 6–15)	
8				
10				
12				
14			Ishmael son of Phiabi (A.D. 15–16)	
16			Eleazar son of Annas (A.D. 16–17)	
18			Simon son of Camithus (A.D. 17–18)	Josephus Caiaphas son-in-law of Annas (A.D. 18–36)
20				
22				
24				
26				
28				
30				
32				
34				
36			Jonathan son of Annas (A.D. 36–37)	Theophilus son of Annas (A.D. 37–41)
38				
40			Simon Cantheras son of Boethus (A.D. 41)	Matthias son of Annas (A.D. 41–44)
42				
44			Elionaeus son of Cantheras (A.D. 44–46)	
46			Ananias son of Nedebaeus (A.D. 47–58)	
48				
50				
52				
54				
56				
58				
60				
62			Ananus son of Annas (A.D. 62)	
64				
66				
68				
70				
72				
74				
76				
78				
80				
90				
100				
120				
140				
160				

Intertestamental Events Timeline

334–330 B.C.	Alexander the Great (356–323 B.C.) sweeps through Asia Minor and conquers the Persian Empire, including Egypt and Mesopotamia (see notes on Dan. 7:3; 7:6; 8:5; 8:8; 8:20–22; 11:3; cf. *1 Macc.* 1:1–7). Alexander imposes the Greek language and culture on all the nations he conquers, marking the beginning of the Hellenistic Age (ranging approximately from the death of Alexander the Great in 323 to the establishment of Roman Imperial rule around 30 B.C.). As a result of Alexander's imposition of the Greek language on conquered kingdoms, the entire NT will later be written in Greek, and will be understandable throughout the ancient world.
333	Alexander the Great passes through Palestine (comprised of Judea and Galilee), extending the influence of Greek thought and culture throughout the region and also into the Judaism of the period. ("Palestine" derives from a Latin name the conquering Romans later gave to this province [c. 63 B.C.] on the east coast of the Mediterranean Sea, comprising parts of modern Israel, Jordan, and Egypt.)
323–281	In the absence of legitimate heirs, following Alexander the Great's death in 323 B.C. (cf. *1 Macc.* 1:5–9) four of his generals (called the *Diadochoi*, "successors") divide the conquered territory of his empire into fourths (which then included most of the known world throughout Europe and Asia Minor; see notes on Dan. 7:6; 8:8; 8:20–22; 11:4): (1) Antipater (and later Cassander and then Antigonus I Monophthalmus) ruled in Greece and Macedon; (2) Lysimachus took control in Thrace and much of Asia Minor; (3) Seleucus I Nicator assumed power in Mesopotamia and Persia; and (4) Ptolemy I Lagi Soter became sovereign of Egypt and Palestine.
310*	Zeno of Citium (c. 334–262 B.C.) founds Stoicism in Athens, a philosophy which prizes logic, reason, and indifference toward pleasure and pain alike. Paul later encounters Stoics and Epicureans in Athens (see Acts 17:18).
307*	Epicurus (c. 341–270 B.C.) founds the Garden, an egalitarian community based upon friendship, in Athens (see Acts 17:18). The philosophical system of Epicureans stands somewhat opposite Stoicism in its pursuit of pleasure, especially emphasizing the importance of friendships and the luxurious enjoyment of eating, drinking, and other comforts.
277	By 277 B.C. three Hellenistic kingdoms stabilize out of the four divisions of Alexander the Great's kingdom: (1) the Antigonid dynasty in Macedonia (issuing from Alexander's general Antigonus I Monophthalmus, 382–301, and beginning with his son Demetrius I Poliorcetes in 294/293); (2) the Ptolemaic dynasty in Egypt (issuing from the general Ptolemy I Lagi Soter, 367–283); and (3) the Seleucid dynasty in Syria (issuing from the general Seleucus I Nicator, c. 358–281), the latter which also ruled much of Asia Minor from 312 to 64 (see Dan. 11:4–35 and notes there). Though Judea will later become controlled by the Seleucids in 198 B.C., it is initially under Ptolemaic (Egyptian) rule, with little disturbance.
198	The Seleucids gain control over Judea from the Ptolemies after the battle at Panium (see note on Dan. 11:15–16). They are led in victory by their king, Antiochus III the Great (reigned 223–187 B.C.; see notes on Dan. 11:10; 11:11–12; 11:13; 11:15–16; 11:17–19), the father of Antiochus IV Epiphanes (reigned 175–164/163; see notes on Dan. 8:9–10; 8:23; 8:25; 9:24–27; 11:21–23; 11:24; 11:25–27; 11:29–30; 11:33–35; 11:37–38).
190	Antiochus III the Great and the Seleucids are defeated by the Romans at the Battle of Magnesia (fought on the plains of Lydia, in modern Turkey) and forced to pay an indemnity in 12 annual payments. The Seleucids continue to rule over Judea, however.
176*	The Teacher of Righteousness, the founder of the Qumran community (perhaps the Essenes) which produced many of the so-called Dead Sea Scrolls, becomes active.
174	The Seleucid king Antiochus IV Epiphanes (who reigned from 175 to 164/163 B.C. and was the son of Antiochus III the Great and brother of Seleucus IV Philopator) deposes the Zadokite high priest Onias III (*2 Macc.* 3:1–4:6), the son of Simon the Just (cf. *Sir.* 50:1–21). Onias III, who had functioned as the effective head of state for the Jewish people to that time, was replaced with his brother Jason (*2 Macc.* 4:7–22; see also note on Dan. 8:9–10). Jason in turn would be supplanted by Menelaus (*2 Macc.* 4:23–26), who was eventually put to death about 162 B.C. following a 10-year reign (*2 Macc.* 13:1–8). ("Zadokite" refers to the descendants of Zadok, a high priest during King David's reign. Zadokites held a monopoly on the Jerusalem priesthood from the time of Solomon forward.) Antiochus IV takes on the name "Epiphanes," meaning "[god] manifest" (cf. *1 Macc.* 1:10), however his enemies would call him "Epimanes," meaning "madman."
168/167	Antiochus IV Epiphanes, led into the sanctuary by the high priest Menelaus, loots and desecrates the temple in Jerusalem (*1 Macc.* 1:20–24; 1:37–64; *2 Macc.* 5:11–26; 6:2–5; see also notes on Dan. 11:28; 11:31–32). On Kislev (Nov.–Dec.) 25, 167 B.C. (*1 Macc.* 1:59), an idol devoted to Zeus (Jupiter) was erected in the temple ("the abomination that makes desolate"; cf. Dan. 11:31; 12:11) and shortly afterwards sacrifices (likely swine) were offered up on the altar in the "Most Holy Place."
167/166	Mattathias, father of Judas and his brothers, leads the Maccabean Revolt against Seleucid king Antiochus IV Epiphanes (cf. *1 Macc.* 2:1–48; see also notes on Dan. 11:28; 11:31–32; 11:33–35), and dies (*1 Macc.* 2:49–70). See Rulers Foretold in Daniel 11, pp. 1612–1613.
164	Judas "Maccabeus," third son of Mattathias and second leader of the revolt and later the Jewish government during 166/165–161/160 B.C. (*1 Macc.* 3:1–5:68; 6:18–54; 7:26–9:22; cf. *2 Maccabees* 8; 10:14–38; 11:1–15; 12; 13:9–22; 14–15) purifies the temple—an event still remembered by Jews at Hanukkah (*1 Macc.* 4:36–61; see also notes on Dan. 8:12–14; 9:24).
161*	The Zadokite priest Onias IV migrates to Egypt and founds a rival temple at Leontopolis.
152	Jonathan (assumed leadership during 160–143/142 B.C.; cf. *1 Maccabees* 9–12), brother of Judas Maccabeus, fifth son of Mattathias, and third leader of the revolt, accepts the high priesthood as a gift from Alexander Epiphanes (Balas) (*1 Macc.* 10:1–21), the son of Antiochus IV Epiphanes and pretender to the Seleucid throne. Three distinct sects within Judaism become active at this time: the Essenes (or perhaps Qumran community—the sect with which the Dead Sea Scrolls are most closely connected), the Pharisees (see note on John 1:24), and the Sadducees (see note on Matt. 3:7). See also Jewish Groups at the Time of the New Testament, pp. 1799–1800.

142	Jewish independence is recognized by Seleucid king Demetrius II Nicator (d. 125 B.C.; cf. *1 Macc*. 13:31–42). Simon, brother of Judas Maccabeus and second son of Mattathias, is named "high priest and commander and leader" of the Judeans (*1 Macc*. 13:42; cf. 14:35, 41), effectively establishing the Hasmonean Dynasty. Simon rules 142–135 B.C. (cf. *1 Maccabees* 13–16). ("Hasmonean" is derived from the name of Hashman [see Josephus, *Jewish Antiquities* 12.265], great-grandfather of Mattathias.)
135/134–104	John Hyrcanus I, son of Simon, rules following his father's murder (cf. *1 Macc*. 16:11–24).
113	The Hasmonean king John Hyrcanus I destroys the Samaritan temple.
104–103	Judah Aristobulus I, oldest son of John Hyrcanus I, rules.
103–76	Alexander Jannaeus, youngest son of John Hyrcanus I, rules.
88	The Seleucid king Demetrius III Eukairos (son of Antiochus VIII Grypus) is invited by the opponents of Alexander Jannaeus to invade Palestine.
76–67	Salome Alexandra, wife of Alexander Jannaeus, rules.
73–71	Spartacus, a gladiator-slave, leads an ultimately unsuccessful slave revolt (known as the Third Servile War) against the Roman Republic.
67	Civil war breaks out in Judea between supporters of Hyrcanus II and Aristobulus II, Hasmonean brothers. Hyrcanus II, older son of Alexander Jannaeus, rules from 67 to 63 B.C. Aristobulus II, younger son of Alexander Jannaeus, rules from 63 to 40 B.C. Herod the Great would eventually marry into the Hasmonean Dynasty through his union with the granddaughter of Aristobulus II, Mariamne I.
64	Syria becomes a Roman province, effectively establishing Roman rule on Palestine's northern boundaries.
63	Aemelius Scaurus leads Pompey's armies into Palestine, leading to Roman control over Palestine and thus marking the definitive end of Jewish political independence.
47	The Library of Alexandria is burned. Once the largest library in the world, probably containing half a million scrolls or volumes, it suffers the loss of many primary sources of ancient Greek literary texts, as well as translations or adaptations of important works written in other languages. According to the *Letter of Aristeas*, the Greek translation of the OT called the Septuagint (LXX) was begun for the needs of this library. No works housed in this once great library survived antiquity.
44 (March 15)	Julius Caesar is murdered.
43–40	Parthian invasion and interregnum: Phasael, Herod's brother and tetrarch of Judea ("tetrarch" is a ruler of one of four divisions of a Roman country or province), is killed when the last Hasmonean, Antigonus, the son of Aristobulus II and nephew of Hyrcanus II, gains the support of the Parthians to the east and invades Judea.
40–37	Mattathias Antigonus, son of Aristobulus II, rules from Jerusalem.
40	The Roman Senate declares Herod the Great "King of the Jews," giving him vassal rulership over Palestine (comprised of the provinces Judea and Galilee). His rule does not truly begin until 37 B.C., however, when he is able to recapture Jerusalem from Antigonus.
37–4	Herod the Great rules from 37 to 4 B.C. and is the "legitimate" successor to the Hasmonean Dynasty through his marriage to Mariamne I, granddaughter of both Aristobulus II and Hyrcanus II (her parents were first cousins). Herod recaptures Jerusalem from Antigonus and the Parthians in 37 B.C. through the help of Roman forces, to whom he had fled for help three years earlier.
37–31	Herod the Great fortifies Masada, a mountaintop fortress in southeast Israel on the southwest shore of the Dead Sea, as a refuge in case of revolt. (Masada would be the site of the last stand of the Zealot Jewish community against the Romans during the revolt of A.D. 66–73. After a two-year siege, the Zealots chose to commit mass suicide rather than surrender to the Romans.)
31	Octavian (later called Caesar Augustus) defeats Antony and Cleopatra in the Battle of Actium, effectively consolidating his de facto power as the sole ruler of the Roman Empire. His reign lasted until his death in A.D. 14, with Tiberius assuming power after him.
30	Egypt becomes a Roman province.
20/19	Herod the Great begins rebuilding the temple proper in Jerusalem.
5*	Jesus of Nazareth is born within the province of Judea in the town of Bethlehem during the final years of the reign of Herod the Great (cf. notes on Matt. 2:1; Luke 1:5–7; 2:2).
4	Herod the Great dies, and his kingdom is divided between his three surviving sons: (1) Herod Archelaus ("Herod the Ethnarch") became ethnarch of Judea, Samaria, and Idumea (or Edom; ruled 4 B.C.–A.D. 6; "ethnarch" refers to ruler of a people under the Roman Empire); (2) Herod Antipas became tetrarch of Galilee and Perea (ruled 4 B.C.–A.D. 39); and (3) Herod Philip II became tetrarch of Iturea and Trachonitis (ruled 4 B.C.–A.D. 34).

** denotes approximate date; / signifies either/or*

The Herodian Dynasty

This simplified version of the Herodian family tree focuses on those most relevant to NT study. Dates indicate period of reign, unless marked otherwise. Solid lines signify descent; dotted lines signify marriage. Abbreviations: d. = died; c. = circa (around, about).

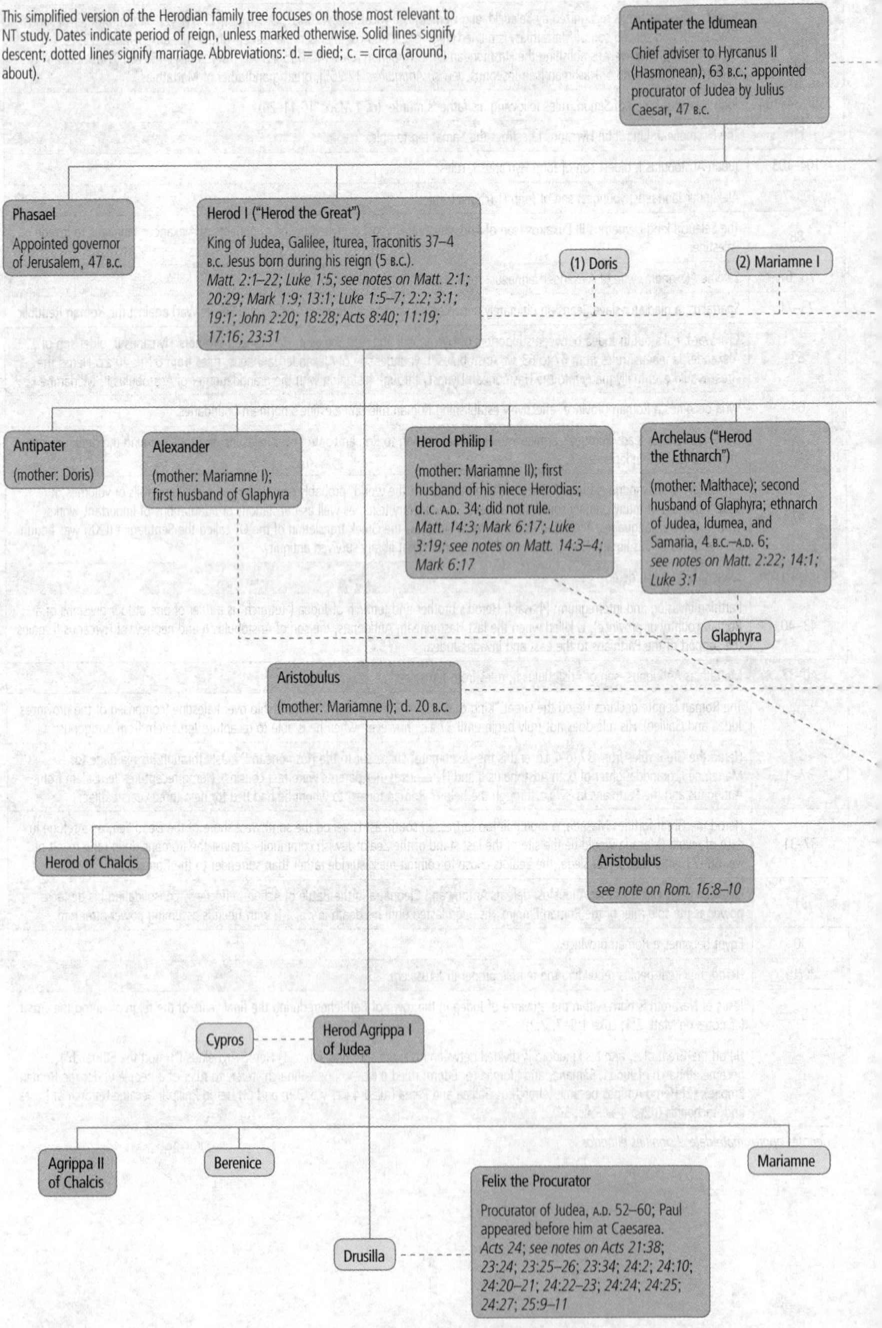
Antipater the Idumean
Chief adviser to Hyrcanus II (Hasmonean), 63 B.C.; appointed procurator of Judea by Julius Caesar, 47 B.C.
Phasael
Appointed governor of Jerusalem, 47 B.C.
Herod I ("Herod the Great")
King of Judea, Galilee, Iturea, Traconitis 37–4 B.C. Jesus born during his reign (5 B.C.).
Matt. 2:1–22; Luke 1:5; see notes on Matt. 2:1; 20:29; Mark 1:9; 13:1; Luke 1:5–7; 2:2; 3:1; 19:1; John 2:20; 18:28; Acts 8:40; 11:19; 17:16; 23:31
(1) Doris
(2) Mariamne I
Antipater
(mother: Doris)
Alexander
(mother: Mariamne I); first husband of Glaphyra
Herod Philip I
(mother: Mariamne II); first husband of his niece Herodias; d. c. A.D. 34; did not rule.
Matt. 14:3; Mark 6:17; Luke 3:19; see notes on Matt. 14:3–4; Mark 6:17
Archelaus ("Herod the Ethnarch")
(mother: Malthace); second husband of Glaphyra; ethnarch of Judea, Idumea, and Samaria, 4 B.C.–A.D. 6;
see notes on Matt. 2:22; 14:1; Luke 3:1
Glaphyra
Aristobulus
(mother: Mariamne I); d. 20 B.C.
Herod of Chalcis
Aristobulus
see note on Rom. 16:8–10
Cypros
Herod Agrippa I of Judea
Agrippa II of Chalcis
Berenice
Mariamne
Felix the Procurator
Procurator of Judea, A.D. 52–60; Paul appeared before him at Caesarea.
Acts 24; see notes on Acts 21:38; 23:24; 23:25–26; 23:34; 24:2; 24:10; 24:20–21; 24:22–23; 24:24; 24:25; 24:27; 25:9–11
Drusilla

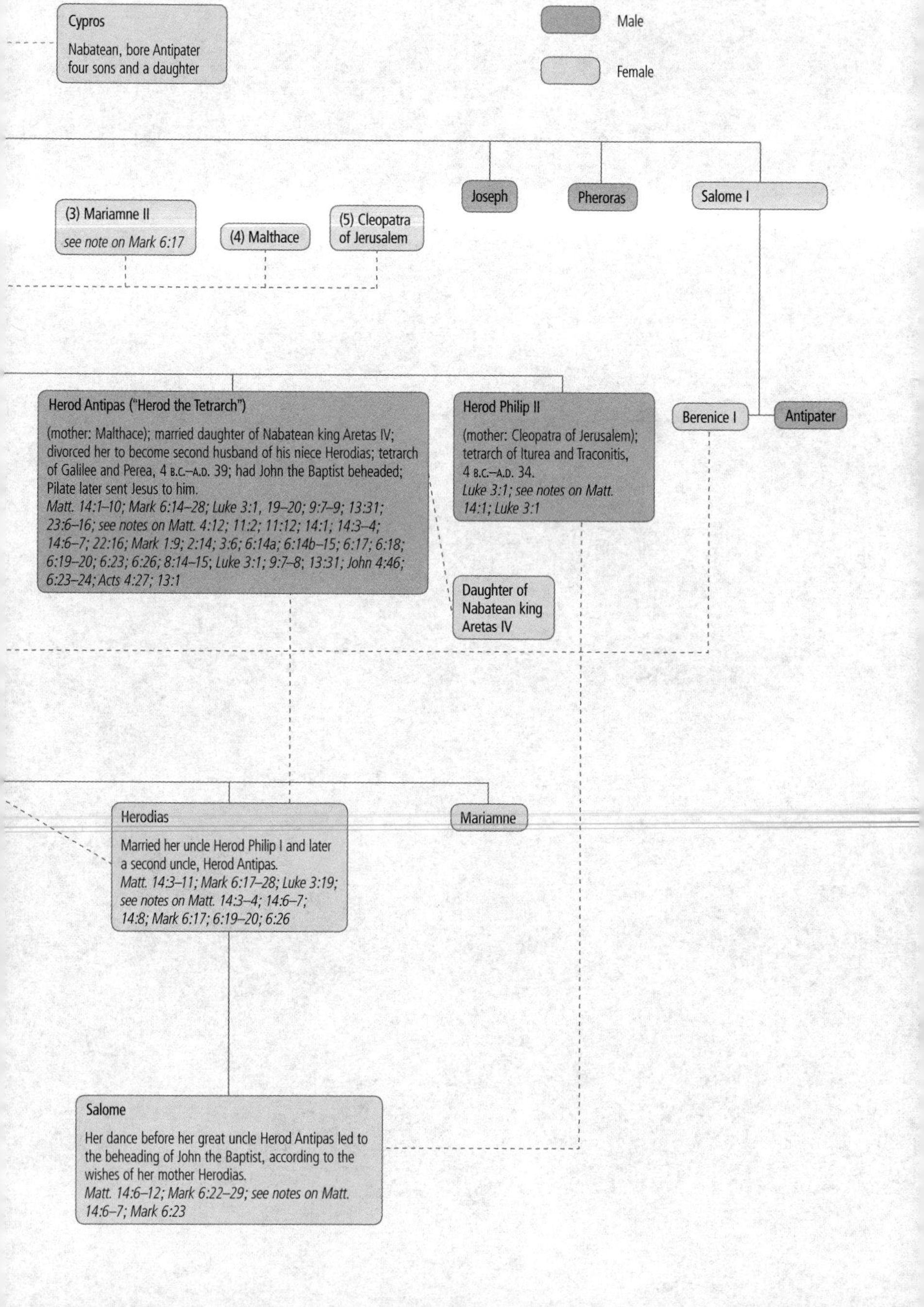
Cypros
Nabatean, bore Antipater four sons and a daughter
Male
Female
Joseph
Pheroras
Salome I
(3) Mariamne II
see note on Mark 6:17
(4) Malthace
(5) Cleopatra of Jerusalem
Herod Antipas ("Herod the Tetrarch")
(mother: Malthace); married daughter of Nabatean king Aretas IV; divorced her to become second husband of his niece Herodias; tetrarch of Galilee and Perea, 4 B.C.–A.D. 39; had John the Baptist beheaded; Pilate later sent Jesus to him.
Matt. 14:1–10; Mark 6:14–28; Luke 3:1, 19–20; 9:7–9; 13:31; 23:6–16; see notes on Matt. 4:12; 11:2; 11:12; 14:1; 14:3–4; 14:6–7; 22:16; Mark 1:9; 2:14; 3:6; 6:14a; 6:14b–15; 6:17; 6:18; 6:19–20; 6:23; 6:26; 8:14–15; Luke 3:1; 9:7–8; 13:31; John 4:46; 6:23–24; Acts 4:27; 13:1
Herod Philip II
(mother: Cleopatra of Jerusalem); tetrarch of Iturea and Traconitis, 4 B.C.–A.D. 34.
Luke 3:1; see notes on Matt. 14:1; Luke 3:1
Berenice I
Antipater
Daughter of Nabatean king Aretas IV
Herodias
Married her uncle Herod Philip I and later a second uncle, Herod Antipas.
Matt. 14:3–11; Mark 6:17–28; Luke 3:19; see notes on Matt. 14:3–4; 14:6–7; 14:8; Mark 6:17; 6:19–20; 6:26
Mariamne
Salome
Her dance before her great uncle Herod Antipas led to the beheading of John the Baptist, according to the wishes of her mother Herodias.
Matt. 14:6–12; Mark 6:22–29; see notes on Matt. 14:6–7; Mark 6:23

The Roman Empire and the Greco-Roman World at the Time of the New Testament

The first-century Roman world of the NT lay culturally at the intersection of Hellenism (Greek language and culture) and Roman imperial rule. Hence, to understand this world, it is important first to explore the spread of Hellenism and the rise of Roman might.

History

Although the Greeks had settled and conducted commerce throughout the Mediterranean world long before Alexander the Great (356–323 B.C.), this Macedonian conqueror is most associated with the spread of Hellenistic (i.e., Greek) culture. Alexander, tutored in Greek philosophy and culture by Aristotle, inherited the reins of Macedonian and Greek leadership from his father, Philip, in 336 B.C. In short order, Alexander marched through Asia Minor, continued south through Syria and Palestine, was welcomed as ruler of Egypt, and conquered the forces of Persia. Alexander was received with awe in many of these lands, which led their inhabitants (esp. members of the various ruling elites) to accelerate their reception of Hellenistic culture—including Greek language, education, and religion.

In 330 B.C. Alexander received the title of "Great King" of Persia. Yet his short life ended in 323 B.C. without a clear successor. Eventually a few of Alexander's generals (later termed the *Diadochoi*, meaning "successors") claimed different portions of his former territory, establishing their own dynastic lines—the Ptolemies of Egypt, the Seleucids of Persia (and portions of Asia Minor), and the Antigonids of Macedon (see map, The Empires of Daniel's Visions: The Greeks, p. 1604).

As it had so frequently before, Judea again lay between the competing powers of Egypt and Mesopotamia. Although first under Ptolemaic control, Judea was absorbed into the Seleucid Empire (198 B.C.) during the reign of Antiochus III "the Great" (see maps, The Empires of Daniel's Visions: The Ptolemies and the Seleucids, p. 1611). The appeal of Hellenism was not lost on the Judeans, and some

The Rise of the Roman Empire

c. 753 B.C.–A.D. 117

From its earliest beginnings as a small kingdom centered in Rome, the Roman Empire eventually grew to become one of the most powerful empires the world has ever known. After solidifying control over the Italian peninsula, the Romans fought a series of wars (the Punic Wars) with the growing Carthaginian Empire and absorbed their territory in Africa and Hispania. Pushing eastward into Greece, Asia, and Syria, and westward into Gallia (Gaul) and western Hispania, the Romans continued to expand their territory until they ruled the entire Mediterranean region by A.D. 117.

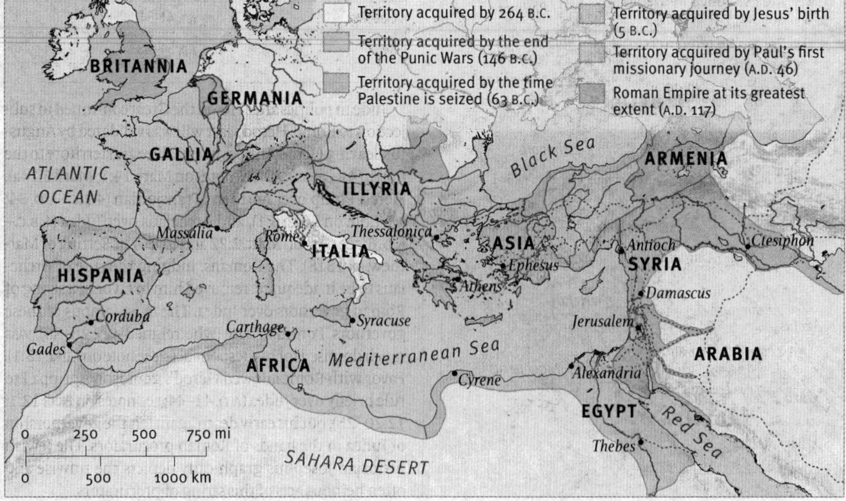

sought a wholesale adoption of Greek practices through sending their sons to Greek secondary schools. Pro- and anti-Hellenistic factions formed in Judea. Meanwhile, the Seleucid ruler Antiochus IV "Epiphanes," desiring a subservient and financially supportive Judea, decided to force Hellenistic religious practices on the Jewish people. Circumcision was declared illegal, scriptural texts were destroyed, and pagan worship was instituted. In 168/167 B.C. the Jerusalem temple was despoiled, as prophesied in Daniel (Dan. 11:31; cf. 9:27; 12:11; *1 Macc.* 1:54); Jesus draws on this image of the "abomination of desolation" in reference to future events (Matt. 24:15–16).

In reaction to the policies of Antiochus IV, the Hasmonean family (also known as the Maccabees) launched an uprising led by Mattathias and his sons (esp. Judas Maccabeus, Jonathan, and Simon). A combination of guerilla warfare and larger geopolitics (esp. Seleucid losses in Asia Minor and internal coups) led to the success of this Jewish rebellion (see map, The Maccabean Kingdom, p. 1616). For several decades Jews regained autonomy over Judea. The Hasmoneans established their own royal dynasty, with Jonathan also proclaiming himself high priest (152 B.C.) although he was not of the proper Zadokite lineage. Many of the Jewish factions known during the time of the NT (e.g., Pharisees, Essenes, etc.) likely stem from reactions pro and con to the Hasmonean reign.

Meanwhile, in the west, Roman power was growing. Successive wars with Carthage and Macedon left Rome victorious over the western Mediterranean by 146 B.C. Roman expansion continued eastward toward Syria (see map, The Rise of the Roman Empire, p. 1793). In 63 B.C. Pompey marched into Jerusalem and entered the temple. Feuding Judean leaders found that the surest way to secure the Judean crown was to align oneself with Rome. Herod the Great, who was not even fully Jewish, befriended Rome and thus captured for himself the kingship of Judea and surrounding territories (37–4 B.C.; see note on Matt. 2:1 and map, The Setting of Matthew, p. 1818).

However, Roman internal politics were far from stable in the first century B.C. The historic rule of the Roman senate was diminishing with Roman military expansion. The senate attempted to play various generals (notably Julius and Pompey) off one another. In 49 B.C. Julius crossed the Rubicon River beyond his allotted territory, won handily against Pompey, and assumed dictatorial power. A later senatorial revolt led to the assassination of Julius Caesar (44 B.C.). Quickly a new alliance was formed as Antony and Octavian defeated the senatorial rebels at Philippi (42 B.C.). Friction arose between these men, and eventually Octavian destroyed the forces of Antony and Cleopatra at Actium (31 B.C.). By 27 B.C. Octavian received the title "Augustus," and the lifelong tribuneship was his in 23. The empire had begun. Throughout much of the NT period the family of Augustus held the imperial title (see chart).

Augustus	31 B.C.–A.D. 14
Tiberius	A.D. 14–37
Gaius Caligula	A.D. 37–41
Claudius	A.D. 41–54
Nero	A.D. 54–68

Judean politics after Herod the Great continued in subjection to Rome. Herod's last will was validated by Augustus, leaving Herod Antipas over Galilee and territory to the north (4 B.C.–A.D. 39; see notes on Matt. 14:1; Mark 6:14a), Herod Philip over northern Transjordan (4 B.C.–A.D. 34; see note on Luke 3:1), and Archelaus over Judea (4 B.C.–A.D. 6; see note on Matt. 2:22 and map, The Setting of Matthew, p. 1818). The Romans, judging the rule of Archelaus to be inadequate, removed him in favor of a string of Roman governors over Judea. The most famous of these governors, Pontius Pilate (who reigned A.D. 26–36), was much despised for his despotic acts (see note on Luke 23:1). Favor with Rome allowed Herod's grandson Agrippa I to rule briefly over Judea (A.D. 41–44; see notes on Acts 12:1; 12:20–25), but his early death again left the governorship of Judea in the hands of Roman procurators. The Jewish historian Josephus graphically depicts the unwise and often heinous acts of this string of procurators.

The First Jewish Revolt

A.D. 66–73

Years of growing Jewish resentment toward Roman rule and paganism eventually erupted in full-scale revolt in A.D. 66. The revolt was ignited in Caesarea and quickly spread to Jerusalem, Judea, Idumea, parts of Samaria, and Galilee. The following spring, the Roman general Vespasian began his systematic campaign to crush the rebellion, beginning in Galilee and then moving south into Samaria and along the coast. Meanwhile, Jewish forces began to fight among themselves in a bitter power struggle between various Zealots and aristocratic leaders, thus weakening their ability to fend off the Romans as they advanced into Judea. In A.D. 70 the Romans captured Jerusalem and destroyed the temple, but isolated resistance still continued even as late as A.D. 73, when the stronghold of Masada was finally taken by the Romans.

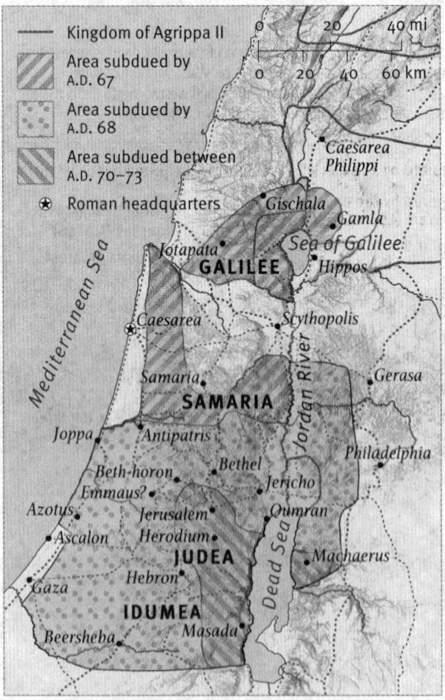

Eventually anger with Rome spilled over into the Jewish revolt (A.D. 66–73/74). The Romans could not permit rebellion in any of their territories, let alone in an important commercial trade center such as Palestine. Thus Vespasian and his son Titus (both future emperors) were sent as generals to suppress the rebellion, which they accomplished with precision and cruelty (see map, The First Jewish Revolt, p. 1794). The destruction of Jerusalem and the Jewish temple (A.D. 70) transformed Jewish religion forever. Subsequently, there was a suppressed uprising of Diaspora Jews (esp. in Egypt, A.D. 115–117) during the reign of Trajan. Some Jews hoped for a rebuild of the Jerusalem temple, but the ineffective Second Jewish Revolt in Judea under Bar Kochba (A.D. 132–135, during the emperorship of Hadrian; see map, The Bar Kochba Revolt, below) resulted instead both in a ban on Jews entering Jerusalem and in the building of a temple to Zeus on the former Temple Mount.

Amid this history, Jesus Christ launched his ministry in a Galilee governed by a Roman client king, a Judea under Roman procurators, and a Judaism tinged with Hellenism. After his crucifixion by the Romans and his resurrection, his gospel was carried by the apostles directly into the heart of Greek culture and Roman power.

Social Structure, Economics, Politics, and Law

The social structure of the Roman world differed in some important ways from modern life. For example, it is debated whether ancient Rome had a "middle class." Outside the cities, agrarian life largely consisted of either subsistence farming or of great estate farms. Commerce was key to the life of the empire, and the *Pax Romana* ("peace of Rome") largely relied on safe, well-guarded trade routes (both by land and by sea). Cities thrived with commercial enterprise, as well as with artisan, religious, and intellectual life. Public entertainment included theater, musical performance, rhetorical contests, athletics, and gladiatorial combat.

The central Greco-Roman social unit was the family. Marriage was deemed of great importance, even if sexual activity outside of marriage was prevalent (especially on the part of husbands) and divorce was widely practiced. Patriarchal assumptions were strong, with the father possessing control over, and legal responsibility for, the family. Inheritances were normally passed substantially to male

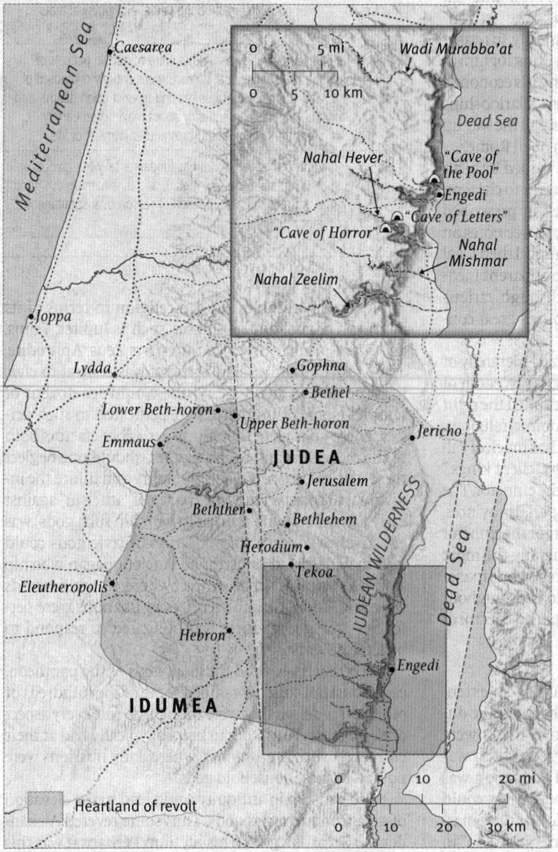

The Bar Kochba Revolt

A.D. 132–135

News of Hadrian's plans to transform Jerusalem into a thoroughly Roman city, complete with pagan temples, dashed Jewish hopes of one day rebuilding the temple of the Lord. In response, Jewish leaders prepared for revolt by stockpiling weapons and supplies in various underground caverns and other fortresses. The leader of this new revolt, Simeon Bar Kochba, was supported by the Sanhedrin and was even hailed as the "Messiah" by many prominent Jews. Resistance, however, was limited primarily to Judea, and eventually the Romans systematically reclaimed all territory in revolt. After the fall of the Sanhedrin fortress of Bethther, the last vestiges of resistance fled from Engedi to nearby caves, where some survived but most perished at the hands of the Romans.

children (whether biological or adopted for purposes of inheritance). The role of women varied throughout the empire: some had great autonomy and wealth while others were cloistered and rarely appeared in public. Children were commonly seen as a blessing, though infanticide and abortion were sometimes practiced. Most households, aside from the poorest, included slaves.

The Roman economy was highly dependent on slavery. Slaves came from conquest in war, voluntary entrance into slavery, or birth into a slave family. There was thus no single racial profile for a slave. The lives of slaves also varied considerably. State-owned slaves who worked in the brutal conditions of the mines had a short life expectancy. Agricultural slaves toiled in the fields. Household slaves served as cooks, hairdressers, servants, and concubines; yet, they could also be trained to positions of significant authority, even administrating businesses for their owners. Such slaves could be granted their freedom, thus achieving the status of "freedmen" and earning the economic benefits of a continued patronage relationship with their former owners. For this reason, some people voluntarily entered into a set period of slavery to wealthy aristocrats (for more on this, see note on 1 Cor. 7:21).

Patronage relationships were central to economic and political life. The wealthy would agree to be the "patron" of certain "clients," assisting them economically. In return the clients would support their patron by voting for him in his run for political office and by furthering his economic interests. In theory, a chain of patron/client relationships extended from the less prosperous in society all the way up to the emperor, who was the great patron of all Rome.

Citizenship in the NT-era empire was gained by birth to citizen parents, emancipation from slavery to citizens, military service, or special edict. Laws generally prescribed less severe punishments for Roman citizens (see notes on Acts 16:37; 22:22–29), and citizens could appeal their legal cases to Rome (cf. Acts 25:10–12). Despite apparent inequities, a clear legal code, administered through various political officials, is often considered Rome's great contribution to Western society.

Roman government applied a centralized hierarchy of control, while simultaneously granting some freedom of local self-government. Large cities often retained the right to vote for their leaders, who served in economic, religious, and political civic duties. Some regions (such as much of Palestine in the 1st century) were governed by "client kings," whose monarchical rule was validated by the emperor. The empire was divided into senatorial and imperial provinces, depending upon whether the Roman senate or the emperor appointed the provincial governors. Generally the more outlying (and less militarily secure) provinces were imperial appointments (such as Syria and the regions throughout Palestine), although the emperors also retained control of some important agricultural regions (esp. Egypt).

Education and Philosophy

Most people in antiquity could not afford an extensive education. Slaves were trained for their specific duties; the poor continued in family agrarian life or were apprenticed to a specific craft. However, education was central to the Hellenistic ideal. Formal education was generally private. Certain slaves, called *pedagogues*, could be responsible for overseeing the education of their master's children through hiring teachers (see "guardian" in Gal. 3:24–25). That teacher would educate the children in a set curriculum, including reading and writing, literature, mathematics, Greek and/or Latin, rhetoric, and philosophy. Rhetoric (the study of verbal persuasion) was necessary for political and legal life, and philosophy was considered the highest expression of learning.

Philosophy involved investigation into the physical and conceptual makeup of the world (metaphysics as well as science) and into ethics. Most religions in antiquity did not substantively address ethical matters (Judaism and Christianity were significant exceptions); rather, this was the realm of philosophy. Various competing philosophical systems were taught around the first century (see chart).

Middle Platonists	Expanded and dogmatized upon Plato's concept of the realm of ideas/forms as more substantial than their individual physical expression.
Sophists	Enamored with the successful execution of rhetorical argumentation (sometimes regardless of the particular position taken in the argument).
Cynics	Contended for a more naturalistic way of pious living, often engaging in shocking verbal and physical feats to make their points.
Epicureans	Believed that all that exists were miniscule packets of matter (atoms), that humans were entirely composed of aggregate matter (thus ceasing to exist upon death), and that life was consequently about maximizing earthly pleasure through friendships and enjoyment of life.
Stoics	Argued that the world was fundamentally the expression of a rational force (the *logos*), and that harmonious good living required an exaltation of reason over spontaneous emotions in all of life.

Religion and Magic

Most today think of Roman religion in terms of its pantheon of gods and goddesses, such as Jupiter, Venus, and Mars (or their Greek counterparts Zeus, Aphrodite, and Ares). Certainly, this pantheon was central to civic life. Touring an ancient city, one would see dozens of temples (some of immense size) dedicated to such deities. These gods were thought to act as benefactors both to the individual and to the city. Yet, should one neglect these deities, they could become angry and injure the individual or society. Thus, the charge of "atheism" against early Christians (who refused to worship such gods) was effectively a concern that rejection of civic gods could lead to widespread catastrophe. Ancient pagan worship assumed a kind of ritual contract where, if specific words were said, and if certain sacrifices or libations were performed, the god/goddess was obligated to respond to benefit the worshiper.

Nevertheless, beyond the great gods of the pantheon, each household also worshiped some of the hundreds of other lesser deities that were thought to rule every aspect of human life. Thus Roman houses typically had at their entrance a shrine, a *lararium*, where daily libations were poured to these household gods.

Hero worship in antiquity could lead to the elevation of great conquerors as gods. Thus some revered Alexander the Great as a god in his lifetime. Perhaps it was this tendency that allowed the emperor, as patron of the whole empire, to be received as a god, especially in Asia Minor where extravagant temples to the emperors were built even before the NT period. Some emperors (esp. Gaius Caligula, Nero, and Domitian) were known to encourage their own worship.

By the first century A.D. mystery religions had become widespread throughout the empire, conducting secret ceremonies to gods and goddesses of Asian or Egyptian origin. The inductees learned the mysteries and participated in secretive worship practices.

Magic, though often viewed with suspicion, still played a central role in Roman life (e.g., Acts 13:6; 19:13–20). Alongside the worship of gods of healing (such as Asklepies), magic provided healing remedies, as well as promoting potions, incantations, and charms to provide material and physical blessings or curses. The Romans were also concerned with knowing the future through dreams, prophetic oracles, and various forms of divination (i.e., the reading of portents such as animal entrails, astrological signs, etc.; cf. Acts 16:16).

Most people in antiquity were involved in syncretistic worship of multiple deities. Yet some were attracted to monotheistic beliefs, especially those of Judaism and Christianity. Judaism had been granted official legitimacy by Rome, and evidences of Diaspora Jewish communities abound throughout the Mediterranean and Mesopotamia. While some admired Judaism's worship of a single god and its high ethical ideals, others believed its practices (esp. circumcision, Sabbath, and food laws) to be ridiculous. Christianity was often suspected and persecuted for its "atheistic" beliefs (since it rejected all other gods), its worship of a crucified Lord, its practice of the Lord's Supper, and its view of all Christians as "brothers and sisters." Nonetheless, the Christian hope thrived; it was declared a legitimate religion under Constantine in the fourth century and eventually grew to become the dominant faith of people throughout the Roman Empire. ◀

Jewish Groups at the Time of the New Testament

When Jesus began to proclaim the gospel, the Sadducees, Essenes, and Pharisees were also laying claim to Israel's heritage. Josephus (*Jewish Antiquities* 13.171) mentions the groups for the first time during the high priesthood of Jonathan (152–142 B.C.) after the demise of the Zadokite priesthood, which had dominated the religious life of Judea for centuries. The Essenes eventually dropped out of public life and became a network of close-knit communities. It is probably for this reason that the NT does not mention them. The Sadducees and Pharisees continued to compete for control of the temple and Sanhedrin. By the first century, the Sadducees were dominant (cf. Acts 5:17). However, the Pharisees remained an influential minority in Jerusalem, and had mounted a successful campaign to win the hearts of the people.

The Sadducees

The Sadducees, including the high priest Caiaphas (A.D. 18–36), were primarily of wealthy, priestly families in Jerusalem. Josephus claims they were unfriendly—even to one another—and were unpopular (*Jewish War* 2.166; *Jewish Antiquities* 13.298). They could be cruel judges (Josephus, *Jewish Antiquities* 20.199; Mishnah, *Sanhedrin* 7.2; *Makkot* 1.6). When Jesus disrupted their financial interests in the temple, he was arrested and condemned (Mark 11:15–19; 14:53–65). James, the brother of the Lord, was later killed by a Sadducean high priest (Josephus, *Jewish Antiquities* 20.200).

The Sadducees rejected the extrabiblical traditions of the Pharisees, perhaps embracing only the Pentateuch as canonical (Josephus, *Jewish Antiquities* 13.297; 18.16). This narrow canon may explain why they did not believe in the general resurrection of the dead (Mark 12:18; Acts 4:1–2; 23:6–8), since it is not explicitly mentioned in the Pentateuch. Perhaps for the same reason, they embraced human responsibility, which is emphasized in the Law of Moses (e.g., Gen. 4:7; Deut. 30:19–20), in contrast to the determinism of the Essenes (Josephus, *Jewish War* 2.164; *Jewish Antiquities* 13.173). Jesus, when arguing for the resurrection (Mark 12:18–27), meets the Sadducees on their own ground by showing the implications of Exodus 3:6 instead of appealing to a more straightforward passage (e.g., Dan. 12:2).

The Essenes

The Essenes lived communally in villages and cities throughout Palestine and Syria (Josephus, *Jewish War* 2.124; 11.1; Philo, *Hypothetica* 11.1). According to Pliny the Elder, an Essene community resided near the Dead Sea (*Natural History* 5.15.73). Some of the Dead Sea Scrolls, which were discovered in caves at Qumran, probably reflect the ideology of this community.

The Essene communities shared all things in common, including food and clothing (Josephus, *Jewish War* 2.122, 127; Philo, *Good Person* 86). Wages were given to a steward, who would purchase and distribute goods to those in need (Josephus, *Jewish War* 2.123; Philo, *Hypothetica* 11.10). They cared for their elderly and sick (Philo, *Good Person* 87). The Jerusalem church adopted a similar way of life (Acts 2:44–45; 4:34–35; James 1:27), except that giving was voluntary (Acts 5:4).

Many of the Essenes did not marry (Josephus, *Jewish War* 2.120; Philo, *Hypothetica* 11.14; Pliny, *Natural History* 5.15.73; but see *Jewish War* 2.160). The group survived by attracting converts. Pliny claims they drew large crowds (*Natural History* 5.15.73). A convert would follow their way of life for a year (Josephus, *Jewish War* 2.137). He could then be baptized, but was not allowed to live with them for another two years (*Jewish War* 2.138). Followers of Jesus were similarly baptized into the church, but without a probationary period (cf. Acts 2:37–47; 8:37–38).

The Essenes believed God was the cause of all things (Josephus, *Jewish Antiquities* 13.172; 18.18; Philo, *Good Person* 84). Consequently, they viewed all government as divinely ordained (Josephus, *Jewish War* 2.140). However, the Dead Sea Scrolls assume belief in two spirits—one divine, the other satanic—that will be in conflict until the end of the age (e.g., 1QS Col. 3.17–19; Col. 4.16–17). Paul similarly ties spiritual warfare with God's ultimate sovereignty over all things, including government (Rom. 13:1–7; Eph. 2:1–3).

The Essenes were especially scrupulous about maintaining purity. They dressed only in white linen (Josephus, *Jewish War* 2.123). They no longer participated in the sacrifices of the temple, because, in their view, the priests were defiling the sanctuary (Dead Sea Scrolls, *Damascus Document* 5.6–7, 14–15). Josephus claims they offered their own sacrifices (*Jewish Antiquities* 18.19), while Philo assumes they abstained from animal sacrifice altogether (*Good Person* 75). The Dead Sea Scrolls claim prayer is an acceptable sacrifice (Dead Sea Scrolls, *Damascus Document* 11.21; 1QS Col. 9.3–5). They also strictly observed the Sabbath. Whereas Jesus assumes most Jews would pull an ox out of a well on the Sabbath (Luke 14:5), the Dead Sea Scrolls forbid it (*Damascus Document* 11.13).

The Pharisees

The Pharisees resided primarily in Jerusalem (but see Luke 5:17) and were divided into at least three schools: the disciples of Shammai, Hillel, and Gamaliel. These schools were especially concerned about the proper administration of the temple.

The disciples of Shammai, who represented the more conservative wing of the group, were dominant before the destruction of the temple in A.D. 70 (Mishnah, *Shabbat* 1.4). But Hillel, representing a more liberal interpretation of the Jewish Scriptures, had moved from Babylon to Jerusalem about a generation before Jesus, and gained wide influence as well.

Gamaliel, the son (or grandson) of Hillel, was a renowned teacher of the law in Jerusalem. The apostle Paul had been a disciple of Gamaliel (Acts 22:3). Gamaliel is remembered for his wisdom (Acts 5:34) and careful management of the Jewish calendar. Most Jews followed a lunisolar calendar, which consisted of 12 lunar months, totaling 354 days. Every three years or so a thirteenth month had to be added, in order to bring the average total days of the year up to the 365.25 days of the solar year. Otherwise, the seasons would not have matched the festivals and sacrifices in the temple. Gamaliel determined when to add the thirteenth month (Mishnah, *Rosh Hashshanah* 2.8; *Sanhedrin* 2.6). Ironically, if the Galatian Christians had adopted the calendar of Jewish religious holidays advocated by Paul's opponents (Gal. 4:10), they would have found themselves under the authority of his old teacher!

These three schools attempted to shape the religious life of the ordinary Jew through the dissemination of their traditions (Matt. 23:15; Mark 7:1–13; Josephus, *Jewish Antiquities* 13.297). Galilee was also a part of their mission. The Jerusalem Talmud (*Shabbat* 15d) claims that Johanan ben Zakkai, a disciple of Hillel, spent 18 years—probably from A.D. 20 to about 40—teaching in the Galilean town of Araba (or Gabara). So Johanan and Jesus were teaching in Galilee at the same time.

The Pharisees also had considerable influence over local scribes, who would preach in the synagogue according to their interpretations (Matt. 7:29; 23:1–2; Mark 2:16). When the Pharisees in Jerusalem were alerted by some scribes that Jesus was preaching a new teaching with authority, they sent a delegation, which, after observing some alarming behaviors, attributed his miraculous power to Beelzebul (Mark 3:22; 7:1). Since the Pharisees were highly respected by the people, the accusation may have had devastating consequences for Jesus' mission (cf. Matt. 11:20–24).

The Pharisaic tradition was pragmatic and relevant to the needs of the time. For instance, the Law of Moses requires all loans to be forgiven in the sabbatical (seventh) year (Deut. 15:2). The intention was to provide relief for borrowers, but the reality was that lenders refused to give loans near the seventh year. Hillel addressed the problem by establishing the *prosbol*, a contract that requires a borrower to pay back a lender even in the seventh year (Mishnah, *Shabbat* 7.1). His school was also highly pragmatic (at least for husbands wanting a divorce) when it came to rules for divorce, interpreting the ambiguous phrase in Deuteronomy 24:1—"some indecency in her"—as allowing a husband to divorce his wife for almost any reason, including burning his dinner (Mishnah, *Gittin* 9.10). However, the school of Shammai interpreted the law more narrowly, allowing divorce only in the case of adultery.

The Dead Sea Scrolls accuse the Pharisees of being "Seekers of Smooth Things," that is, passing on easy interpretations to the people (e.g., 4Q169 Fragment 1; cf. Isa. 30:10). While Jesus too was vulnerable to this criticism in some areas of his teaching, especially his indifference to matters of ritual purity and Sabbath observance, he is even more stringent than Moses when it comes to justice. Instead of recommending the *prosbol*, he flatly commands his disciples, "do not refuse the one who would borrow from you" (Matt. 5:42). Concerning divorce, he adopts a similar position to the school of Shammai, but also notes that divorce was not God's original plan and is not required (Matt. 5:31–32; 19:9).

The difference in stringency can be further illustrated by the summations of the law provided by Hillel and Jesus. Hillel says, "What is hateful to you, do not to your neighbor: that is the whole Torah, while the rest is commentary thereof; go and learn it" (Babylonian Talmud, *Shabbat* 31a). Jesus says, "So whatever you wish that others would do to you, do also to them, for this is the Law and the Prophets" (Matt. 7:12). We find the negative wording of Hillel's teaching in earlier Jewish writings (*Tobit* 4:15; Philo, *Hypothetica* 7.6–8). Jesus' summation is more challenging, requiring nothing less than a universal love for all people, including one's enemies (Matt. 5:44).

However, despite the curious quality of some of their tradition, the Pharisees were especially scrupulous to maintain a righteous status before God. Many were probably like Paul, who claimed that as a Pharisee he was "blameless" as to the Law of Moses (Phil. 3:6). While many Jews tithed, Pharisees even tithed their garden herbs (Matt. 23:23). While others fasted periodically, they fasted twice a week (Mark 2:18; Luke 18:12). They also maintained purity at their meals to the point of "straining out a gnat" from a cup (Matt. 23:24; cf. Mark 7:4), and they avoided sharing a table with "sinners," those like tax collectors who habitually broke the law (Mark 2:16; Luke 7:39).

All three expressions of piety come together in the parable of the Pharisee and the tax collector (Luke 18:9–14). Jesus depicts the Pharisee as distinguishing himself from the tax collector because he fasted and tithed in order to retain a righteous status before God. Elsewhere, Jesus affirms tithing but claims the Pharisees neglect the "weightier matters of the law"—justice, mercy, and faithfulness (Matt. 23:23).

The Pharisees took their personal relationship with God seriously, in part because they believed that the resurrection of the dead was a reward for living a righteous life (Josephus, *Jewish War* 2.163; *Jewish Antiquities* 18.14; Acts 23:8; *Aboth of Rabbi Nathan* 5A). But Jesus says, "For I tell you, unless your righteousness exceeds that of the scribes and Pharisees, you will never enter the kingdom of heaven" (Matt. 5:20). On another occasion, he tells the Pharisaic teacher Nicodemus that he needs to be "born again," or "born from above" (*anōthen*, John 3:3). Despite the blameless way of life many Pharisees pursued, such effort, in Jesus' view, was not enough: like all people, they needed to repent and believe in the gospel. From this perspective, Paul could anticipate being found by God, at the resurrection, "not having a righteousness of my own that comes from the law, but that which comes through faith in Christ" (Phil. 3:9). ◀

THE NEW TESTAMENT

The Theology of the New Testament

New Testament theology as a discipline is a branch of what scholars call "biblical theology." Systematic theology and biblical theology overlap considerably, since both explore the theology found in the Bible. Biblical theology, however, concentrates on the historical story line of the Bible and explains the various steps in the progressive outworking of God's plan in redemptive history. In this article some of the main themes of NT theology are presented.

Already but Not Yet

The message of the NT cannot be separated from that of the OT. The OT promised that God would save his people, beginning with the promise that the seed of the woman would triumph over the seed of the Serpent (Gen. 3:15). God's saving promises were developed especially in the covenants he made with his people: (1) the covenant with Abraham promised God's people land, seed, and universal blessing (Gen. 12:1–3); (2) the Mosaic covenant pledged blessing if Israel obeyed the Lord (Exodus 19–24); (3) the Davidic covenant promised a king in the Davidic line forever, and that through this king the promises originally made to Abraham would become a reality (2 Samuel 7; Psalm 89; 132); and (4) the new covenant promised that God would give his Spirit to his people and write his law on their hearts, so that they would obey his will (Jer. 31:31–34; Ezek. 36:26–27).

As John the Baptist and Jesus arrived on the scene, it was obvious that God's saving promises had not yet been realized. The Romans ruled over Israel, and a Davidic king did not reign in the land. The universal blessing promised to Abraham was scarcely a reality, for even in Israel it was sin, not righteousness, that reigned. John the Baptist therefore summoned the people of Israel to repent and to receive baptism for the forgiveness of their sins, so that they would be prepared for a coming One who would pour out the Spirit and judge the wicked.

Jesus of Nazareth represents the fulfillment of what John the Baptist prophesied. Jesus, like John, announced the imminent arrival of the kingdom of God (Mark 1:15), which is another way of saying that the saving promises found in the OT were about to be realized. The kingdom of God, however, came in a most unexpected way. The Jews had anticipated that when the kingdom arrived, the enemies of God would be immediately wiped out and a new creation would dawn (Isa. 65:17). Jesus taught, however, that the kingdom was present in his person and ministry (Luke 17:20–21)—and yet the foes of the kingdom were not instantly annihilated. The kingdom did not come with apocalyptic power but in a small and almost imperceptible form. It was as small as a mustard seed, and yet it would grow into a great tree that would tower over the entire earth. It was as undetectable as leaven mixed into flour, but the leaven would eventually transform the entire batch of dough (Matt. 13:31–33). In other words, the kingdom was *already* present in Jesus and his ministry, but it was *not yet* present in its entirety. It was "already—but not yet." It was inaugurated but not consummated. Jesus fulfilled the role of the servant of the Lord in Isaiah 53, taking upon himself the sins of his people and suffering death for the forgiveness of their sins. The day of judgment was still to come in the future, even though there would be an interval between God's beginning to fulfill his promises in Jesus (the kingdom inaugurated) and the final realization of his promises (the kingdom consummated). Jesus, who has been reigning since he rose from the dead, will return and sit on his glorious throne and judge between the sheep and the goats (Matt. 25:31–46). Hence, believers pray both for the progressive growth and for the final consummation of the kingdom in the words "your kingdom come" (Matt. 6:10).

The Synoptic Gospels (Matthew, Mark, and Luke) focus on the promise of the kingdom, and John expresses a similar truth with the phrase "eternal life." Eternal life is the life of the age to come, which will be realized when the new creation dawns. Remarkable in John's Gospel is the claim that those who believe in the Son enjoy the life of the coming age *now*. Those who have put their faith in Jesus have *already* passed from death to life (John 5:24–25), for he is the resurrection and the life (John 11:25). Still, John also looks ahead to the day of the final resurrection, when every person will be judged for what he or she has done (John 5:28–29). While the focus in John is on the initial fulfillment of God's saving promises now, the future and final fulfillment is in view as well.

The already-not-yet theme dominates the entire NT and functions as a key to grasping the whole story (see chart, p. 1804). The resurrection of Jesus indicates that the age to come has arrived, that now is the day of salvation. In the same way the gift of the Holy Spirit represents one of God's end-time promises. NT writers joyously proclaim that the promise of the outpouring of the Holy Spirit has been fulfilled (e.g., Acts 2:16–21; Rom. 8:9–16; Eph. 1:13–14). The last days have come through Jesus Christ (Heb. 1:1–2), through whom we have received God's final and definitive word. Since the resurrection has penetrated history and the Spirit has been given, we might think that salvation history has been completed—but there is still the "not yet." Jesus has been raised from the dead, but believers await the resurrection of their bodies and must battle against sin until the day of redemption (Rom. 8:10–13, 23; 1 Cor. 15:12–28; 1 Pet. 2:11). Jesus reigns on high at the right hand of God, but all things have not yet been subjected to him (Heb. 2:5–9).

Fulfillment through Jesus Christ, the Son of God

The NT highlights the fulfillment of God's saving promises, but it particularly stresses that those promises and covenants are realized through his Son, Jesus the Christ.

Who is Jesus? According to the NT, he is the new and better Moses, declaring God's word as the sovereign interpreter of the Mosaic law (Matt. 5:17–48; Heb. 3:1–6). Indeed, the Law and the Prophets point to him and find their fulfillment in him. Jesus is the new Joshua who gives final rest to his people (Heb. 3:7–4:13). He is the true wisdom of God, fulfilling and transcending wisdom themes from the OT (Col. 2:1–3). In the Gospels, Jesus is often recognized as a prophet. Indeed, Jesus is the final prophet predicted by Moses (Deut. 18:15; Acts 3:22–23; 7:37). Jesus' miracles, healings, and authority over demons indicate that the promises of the kingdom are fulfilled in him (Matt. 12:28), but his miracles also indicate that he shares God's authority and is himself divine, for only the Creator-Lord can walk on water and calm the sea (Matt. 8:23–27; cf. Ps. 107:29). Jesus is the Messiah, who brings to realization the promise that One would sit on David's throne forever. Recognizing Jesus as the Messiah is fundamental to all the Gospels and the missionary preaching of Acts, and is an accepted truth in the Epistles and Revelation.

The stature of Jesus shines out in the NT narrative, for he authoritatively calls on others to be his disciples, summoning them to follow him (Matt. 4:18–22; Luke 9:57–62). Indeed, a person's response to Jesus determines his or her final destiny (Matt. 10:32–33; cf. 1 Cor. 16:22). Jesus is the Son of Man who will receive the kingdom from the Ancient of Days (Dan. 7:13–14) and will reign forever. The Gospels emphasize, however, that his reign has been realized through suffering, for he is also the servant of the Lord who has atoned for the sins of his people (Isa. 52:13–53:12; Mark 14:24; Rom. 4:25; 1 Pet. 2:21–25).

This One who atones for sin is fully God and divine. (See The Person of Christ, pp. 2515–2519.) He has the authority to forgive sins (Mark 2:7). Various NT occurrences of the word "name" indicate Jesus' divine status: people prophesy in his name (Matt. 7:22) and are to hope in his name (Matt. 12:21), and salvation comes in his name alone (Acts 4:12). But the OT establishes that human beings are to prophesy only in God's name, hope only in the Lord, and find salvation only in him; thus, such use of Jesus' name indicates his divinity.

The Greek translation of the OT (the Septuagint) identifies Yahweh as "the Lord." In quoting or alluding to OT texts that refer to Yahweh, the NT authors often apply the title "Lord" to Jesus and evidently use it in that strong OT sense (e.g., Acts 2:21; Phil. 2:10–11; Heb. 1:10–12). The title is therefore another clear piece of evidence supporting Christ's divinity. Jesus is the image of God (Col. 1:15; cf. Heb. 1:3), is in the very form of God, and is equal to God, though he temporarily surrendered some of the privileges of deity by being clothed with humanity so that human beings could be saved (Phil. 2:6–8). Jesus as the Son of God enjoys a unique and eternal relationship with God (cf. Matt. 28:18; John 20:31; Rom. 8:32), and he is worshiped just as the Father is (cf. Revelation 4–5). His majestic stature is memorialized by a meal celebrated in his memory (Mark 14:22–25) and by people being baptized in his name (Acts 2:38; 10:48). The Son of God is the eternal divine Word (Gk. *Logos*) who has become flesh and has been identified as the man who is God's Son (John 1:1, 14). Finally, in a number of texts Jesus is specifically called "God" (e.g., John 1:1, 18; 20:28; Rom. 9:5; Titus 2:13; Heb. 1:8; 2 Pet. 1:1). Such texts involve no trace of the heresy of either modalism or tritheism. Rather, such statements contain the raw materials from which the doctrine of the Trinity was rightly formulated. (See The Trinity, pp. 2513–2515.)

New Testament theology, then, is Christ-centered and God-focused, for what Christ does on earth brings glory to God (John 17:1; Phil. 2:11). The NT particularly focuses on Jesus' work on the cross, by which he redeemed and saved his people. The story line in each of the Gospels culminates in and focuses on Jesus' death and resurrection. Indeed, the

The Already and Not Yet of the Last Days

The OT prophets, writing from the vantage point of their present age (the time of promise), spoke of "the last days" as being the time of fulfillment in the distant future (e.g., Jer. 23:20; 49:39; Ezek. 38:16; Hos. 3:5; Mic. 4:1).

The Structure of the OT Expectation of the Last Days

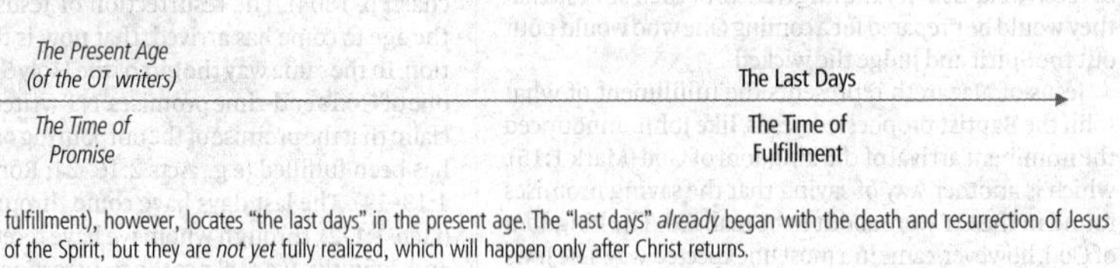

The NT (the time of fulfillment), however, locates "the last days" in the present age. The "last days" *already* began with the death and resurrection of Jesus and the outpouring of the Spirit, but they are *not yet* fully realized, which will happen only after Christ returns.

The NT Restructuring of the OT Expectation of the Last Days

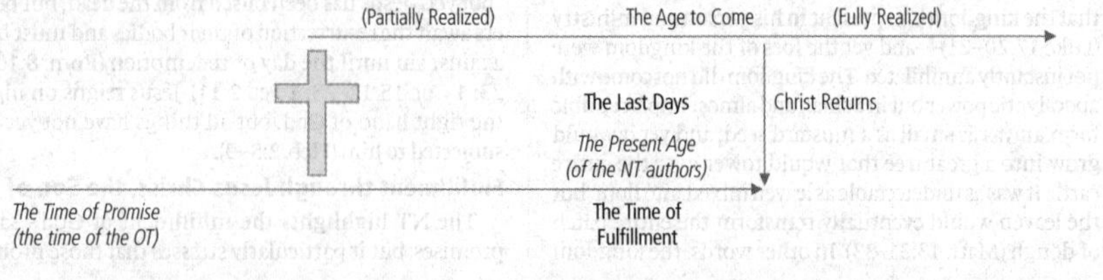

narrative of Jesus' suffering and death consumes a significant amount of space in the Gospels, indicating that the cross and resurrection are the point of the story. In Acts we see the growth of the church and the expansion of the mission, as the apostles and others proclaim the crucified and resurrected Lord. The Epistles explain the significance of Jesus' work on the cross and his resurrection, so that believers are enabled to grasp the height, depth, breadth, and width of the love of God (Rom. 8:39). The significance of the cross is explained in relation to themes such as new creation, adoption, forgiveness of sins, justification, reconciliation, redemption, sanctification, and propitiation. Woven together, these themes teach that salvation comes from the Lord, and that Jesus as the Christ has redeemed his people from the guilt and bondage of sin.

The Promise of the Holy Spirit

Bound up with the work of Christ is the work of the Holy Spirit. Jesus promised to send the Spirit to those who are truly his disciples (John 14:16–17, 26; 15:26), and he poured out the Spirit on his people at Pentecost (Acts 2:1–4, 33) after he had been exalted to the right hand of the Father. The Spirit was given to bring glory to Jesus Christ (John 16:14), so that Christ would be magnified as the great Savior and Redeemer. Luke and Acts in particular emphasize that the Spirit is given for ministry, so that the church is empowered to bear witness to Jesus Christ. At the same time, having the Spirit within is the mark of a person belonging to the people of God (Acts 10:44–48; 15:7–9; Rom. 8:9; Gal. 3:1–5). The Spirit also strengthens believers, so that they are enabled to live in a way that is pleasing to God. Transformation into Christlikeness is the Spirit's work (Rom. 8:2, 4, 13–14; 2 Cor. 3:18; Gal. 5:16, 18).

The Human Response

Because of sin, all humanity stands in need of the salvation that Christ brings. The power of sin is reflected in the biblical story line, for even Israel as the chosen people of the Lord lived under the dominion of sin, showing that the written law of God by its own power cannot deliver human beings from bondage to sin. Paul emphasizes that sin and death are twin powers that rule over all people, so that they stand in need of the redemption Christ brings (see Rom. 1:18–3:20; 5:1–7:25). Sin does not merely constitute failure to keep the law of God, but represents personal rebellion against God's lordship (1 John 3:4). The essence of sin is idolatry, in which people refuse to give thanks and praise to the one and only God, and worship the creature rather than the Creator (Rom. 1:18–25).

But sin is not the last word, since Jesus Christ came to save sinners, thereby highlighting the mercy and grace of God. The fundamental response demanded by God is faith and repentance (see note on Acts 2:38). The call to faith and repentance is evident in the ministry of John the Baptist, in Jesus' announcement of the kingdom (Mark 1:15), in the speeches in Acts, in the Pauline letters, and throughout the NT. Those who desire to be part of Jesus' new community (the church) and part of the kingdom of God (God's rule in people's hearts and lives) must forsake false gods, renounce self-worship and evil, and turn to Jesus as Lord and Master. The call to repentance is nothing less than a summons to abandonment of sin and to personal faith, whereby people are called to trust in the saving work of the Lord on their behalf instead of thinking that they can save themselves. All people everywhere have violated God's will and must look outside of themselves to the saving work of Christ for deliverance from God's wrath. Indeed, the whole of the NT can be understood as a call to repentance and faith (cf. Hebrews 11). Even those who are already believers are to exert themselves in faith and repentance as long as life lasts, for this is the mark of Christ's true disciples. The NT writers constantly encourage their readers to persevere in faith until the end, and warn of the dangers of rejecting Jesus as Lord at any stage. True believers testify that salvation is of the Lord, and that Jesus Christ is the One who has delivered them from the coming wrath.

The People of God

The saving promises of God, then, have begun to be fulfilled in a new community, the church of Jesus Christ. The church is composed of believers in Jesus Christ, both Jews and Gentiles, for the laws in the OT that separated Jews from Gentiles (e.g., circumcision, purity laws, and special festivals and holidays) are no longer in force. The church is God's new temple, indwelt by the Holy Spirit, and is called to live out the beauty of the gospel by showing the supreme mark of Christ's disciples: love for one another (John 13:34–35).

The church recognizes, however, that she exists in an interim state. She eagerly awaits the return of Jesus Christ, and the consummation of all of God's purposes. In the interim, the church is to live out her life in holiness and godliness as the radiant bride of Christ, and to herald the good news of salvation to the ends of the earth, so that others who live in the darkness of sin may be transferred from Satan's kingdom to the kingdom of the Lord. The church longs for the day when she will behold God face-to-face and worship Jesus Christ forever. The new creation will be a full reality, all things will be new, and the Lord will be praised forever for his love and mercy and grace—for NT theology is ultimately about glorifying and praising God. ◀

New Testament Timeline

5 B.C.*	Jesus is born in Bethlehem.
4 B.C.	Jesus' family flees to Egypt to escape from Herod's plan to kill Jesus (Matt. 2:13–18); Herod dies; Judas (of Sepphoris) and others rebel, requiring the Syrian Governor Varus to intervene throughout Palestine; Sepphoris, a city four miles from Nazareth, is destroyed by Roman soldiers; Judea, Samaria, and Idumea are given to Herod's son, Archelaus; Galilee and Perea are given to his son Antipas; Jesus' family, after returning from Egypt, resides in Nazareth (Matt. 2:19–23), a small village in southern Galilee.
A.D. 6	Archelaus is exiled for incompetence; Judea becomes a Roman province; Judas the Galilean (of Gamla) leads a revolt against the tax census; the governor of Syria, Quirinius (A.D. 6–7), appoints Annas high priest (6–15).
8*	Jesus (age 12) interacts with the teachers in the temple (Luke 2:41–50).
8*–28/30	Jesus works as a carpenter in Nazareth (Matt. 13:55; Mark 6:3) and probably in neighboring villages and Sepphoris, which was being rebuilt.
28–29*	John the Baptist begins his ministry around the Jordan River (John 1:19).
28–30*	Jesus begins his ministry in Judea, but soon focuses his efforts in Galilee. In Jerusalem, Pharisees (like Gamaliel) train disciples (like Paul) in their tradition. They send a delegation to Galilee, but the delegation rejects Jesus' teaching. In Alexandria, Philo (20 B.C.–A.D. 50) attempts to unify Greek philosophy with Hebrew Scripture.
33 (or 30)	Jesus returns to Judea, is crucified, and resurrected. James the brother of Jesus becomes a believer after witnessing the resurrected Jesus (1 Cor. 15:7; Acts 12:17). Jesus ascends to the Father's right hand (Acts 1). Jesus' first followers receive the Holy Spirit at Pentecost and begin to proclaim the gospel (Acts 2).
33/34*	Paul witnesses the resurrected Lord on the way to Damascus and is commissioned as an apostle to the nations (Acts 9; Gal. 1:15–16).
34–37	Paul ministers in Damascus and Arabia (Acts 9:19–22; 26:20; Gal. 1:16–18).
36	Pilate loses his position for incompetence.
36/37*	Paul meets with Peter in Jerusalem (Acts 9:26–30; Gal. 1:18).
37–45	Paul ministers in Syria, Tarsus, and Cilicia (Acts 9:30; Gal. 1:21).
38*	Peter witnesses to Cornelius (Acts 10).
39	Antipas is exiled.
40–45*	James writes his letter to believers outside Palestine (cf. James 1:1).
41–44	Agrippa, Herod the Great's grandson, rules Palestine; he kills James the brother of John (Acts 12:2) and imprisons Peter (Acts 12:3).
42–44	Paul receives his "thorn in the flesh" (2 Cor. 12:7).
44	Peter leaves Jerusalem; Agrippa is killed by an "angel of the Lord" (Acts 12:23).
44–46	Theudas persuades many Jews to sell their possessions and follow him into the wilderness where he claimed he would miraculously divide the Jordan River; Roman procurator Fadus dispatches his cavalry and beheads the would-be messiah.
44–47*	Paul's Second Visit to Jerusalem; time of famine (Acts 11:27–30; Gal. 2:1–10).
46–47	Paul's First Missionary Journey (with Barnabas) from Antioch to Cyprus, Antioch in Pisidia, Iconium, and Lystra (Acts 13:4–14:26).
46–48	Roman procurator Tiberius Alexander crucifies two sons (Jacob and Simon) of Judas the Galilean.
48*	Paul writes *Galatians*, perhaps from Antioch (cf. Acts 14:26–28).
48–49*	Paul and Peter return to Jerusalem for the Apostolic Council, which, with the assistance of James, frees Gentile believers from the requirement of circumcision in opposition to Pharisaic believers (Acts 15:1–29); Paul and Barnabas return to Antioch (Acts 15:30) but split over a dispute about John Mark (Acts 15:36–40).
48/49–51*	Paul's Second Missionary Journey (with Silas) from Antioch to Syria, Cilicia, southern Galatia, Macedonia, notably Philippi, Thessalonica, and Berea; and then on to Achaia, notably Athens and Corinth (Acts 15:36–18:22).
49	Claudius expels Jews from Rome because of conflicts about Jesus (Acts 18:2); Paul befriends two refugees, Priscilla and Aquila, in Corinth (Acts 18:2–3).
49–51*	Paul writes *1–2 Thessalonians* from Corinth (Acts 18:1, 11; also cf. Acts 18:5 with 1 Thess. 1:8).
51	Paul appears before Gallio, proconsul of Achaia (Acts 18:12–17).
50–54*	Peter comes to Rome.
52–57*	Paul's Third Missionary Journey from Antioch to Galatia, Phrygia, Ephesus, Macedonia, Greece (Acts 18:23–21:17).
52–55	Paul ministers in Ephesus (Acts 19:1–20).
53–55*	Mark writes his Gospel, containing Peter's memories of Jesus; perhaps within a decade, Matthew publishes his Gospel, which relies on Mark and other sources. Paul writes *1 Corinthians* from Ephesus (Acts 19:10).

54	Claudius dies (edict exiling Jews repealed); Priscilla and Aquila return to Rome and host a church in their home (cf. Rom. 16:3–5).
54–68	Nero reigns.
55–56*	Paul writes *2 Corinthians* from Macedonia (Acts 20:1, 3; 2 Cor. 1:16; 2:13; 7:5; 8:1; 9:2, 4; cf. 1 Cor. 16:5).
57*	Paul winters in Corinth and writes *Romans* (Acts 20:3; cf. Rom. 16:1–2; also cf. Rom. 16:23 with 1 Cor. 1:14); travels to Jerusalem (Acts 21:1–16), visits with James the brother of Jesus (Acts 21:17–26), and is arrested (Acts 21:27–36; 22:22–29).
57–59	Paul is imprisoned and transferred to Caesarea (Acts 23:23–24, 33–34).
60	Paul begins voyage to Rome (Acts 27:1–2); he is shipwrecked for three months on the island of Malta (Acts 27:39–28:10).
60–70*	Letter to the *Hebrews* is written.
62	James the brother of the Lord is executed by the Sadducean high priest Ananus.
62–63*	Peter writes his first letter (*1 Peter*) from Rome (1 Pet. 5:13).
62*	Paul arrives in Rome and remains under house arrest (Acts 28:16–31); he writes *Ephesians* (see verses for Colossians), *Philippians* (Phil. 1:7, 13, 17; 4:22), *Colossians* (Col. 4:3, 10, 18; cf. Acts 27:2 with Col. 4:10), *Philemon* (cf. Philem. 23 with Col. 1:7; Philem. 2 with Col. 4:17; Philem. 24 with Col. 4:10; also cf. Col. 4:9). Luke, Paul's physician and companion (cf. Col. 4:14), writes *Luke* and *Acts*.
62–64	Paul is released, extends his mission (probably reaching Spain), writes *1 Timothy* from Macedonia (cf. 1 Tim. 1:3) and *Titus* from Nicopolis (Titus 3:12); he is rearrested in Rome (2 Tim. 1:16–17).
63–64	Work on the temple complex is completed.
64 (July 19)	Fire in Rome; Nero blames and kills many Christians.
64–67*	Peter writes his second letter (*2 Peter*). Jude writes his letter. Paul writes *2 Timothy* (cf. 2 Tim. 4:6–8). Paul and Peter are martyred in Rome.
66	First Jewish-Roman War begins with a riot between Greeks and Jews at Caesarea; Roman procurator Gesius Florus (A.D. 64–66) is murdered and a Roman garrison wiped out; Menahem, son or grandson of Judas the Galilean, murders the high priest Ananias and seizes control of the temple; Nero dispatches Vespasian with three legions.
67*	Romans destroy the Qumran community, who beforehand hid the so-called Dead Sea Scrolls in nearby caves; the church in Jerusalem flees to Pella (Matt. 24:15–16; Mark 13:14; Luke 21:20–22); John migrates to Ephesus with Mary, Jesus' mother.
68	Nero commits suicide; year of the three emperors.
69	Rebellion quelled in Galilee and Samaria; Vespasian summoned back to Rome to become emperor.
70 (Aug. 30)	Titus, Vespasian's son, after a five-month siege of Jerusalem, destroys the temple after desecrating it; the temple's menorah, Torah, and veil are removed and later put on display in a victory parade in Rome; the influence of the Sadducees ends; the Pharisee Johanan ben Zakkai escapes and convinces the Romans to allow him and others to settle in Jamnia, where they found a school.
73 (May 2)*	Before Roman general Silva breaches the fortress atop Masada following a two-year siege, 936 Jewish rebels commit suicide.
75	Titus has an affair with the Jewish princess Berenice, sister of Agrippa II (Acts 25:13, 23), whom he later abandons because of the scandal.
77	Pliny the Elder writes *Natural History*.
77–78	Josephus publishes *Jewish War* in Rome.
79	Pompeii and Herculaneum are destroyed by eruption of Vesuvias; Pliny the Elder dies attempting to investigate.
81	The Arch of Titus, celebrating his destruction of the temple, is erected in Rome.
81–96	Domitian, Titus's brother, persecutes Christians among the Roman nobility, including his own relatives Clemens and Domitilla.
85–95*	John writes his letters (*1–3 John*), probably in Ephesus.
89–95*	John writes his Gospel, probably in Ephesus.
93–94	Josephus publishes *Jewish Antiquities* in Rome.
94	Domitian exiles philosophers from Rome.
95*	Amidst persecution, Clement, a leader in the Roman church, writes his *Letter to the Corinthians* (*1 Clement*) appealing for peace between the young men and elders.
95–96*	Exiled by Domitian to Patmos, John writes *Revelation* (Rev. 1:9).
96–98	Nerva, the first of five "good" emperors, ends official persecution.

** denotes approximate date; / signifies either/or*

The Date of Jesus' Crucifixion

Scholars continue to debate the year and date of Jesus' crucifixion. Several pieces of evidence, both inside and outside the Bible, help historians to calculate and determine this date, and are described below.

John the Baptist's Ministry Begins: The 15th Year of Tiberius Caesar

Luke ties the beginning of John the Baptist's ministry to "the fifteenth year of the reign of Tiberius Caesar" (Luke 3:1). Through confirmation of the Roman Senate, Tiberius succeeded Augustus as emperor on August 19 in A.D. 14. The "fifteenth year" has been calculated in various ways, but the most likely possibilities are that his reign was counted either from the day he took office in A.D. 14 or from January 1 of A.D. 15. This means that the earliest beginning of the "fifteenth year" of Tiberius Caesar, during which John the Baptist began his ministry, would be August 19, A.D. 28, and the latest end of that 15th year would be December 31, A.D. 29.

If Jesus began his ministry shortly after John the Baptist, at the very earliest it would have begun in late A.D. 28 and at the latest sometime in A.D. 30. If Jesus was born in 5/4 B.C. (see notes on Luke 1:5–7; 2:2), and he began his ministry sometime in A.D. 28–30, then he would be 31–34 years old when he began his ministry (5 B.C.–A.D. 30 would make him 34, while 4 B.C.–A.D. 28 would make him 31, since there was no year 0). Any age between 31 and 34 would fit with Luke 3:23: "Jesus, when he began his ministry, was about thirty years of age."

Jesus Is Crucified on the Day of Preparation: Friday, Nisan 14, in A.D. 30 or 33

The Gospel of John (19:31) notes that Jesus was crucified on "the day of Preparation," a phrase referring to Friday (cf. Mark 15:42), the day before the Sabbath (Saturday). But this was also a Passover week (see Mark 14:12), and Jesus had eaten a Passover meal with his disciples the night before (Thursday). Passover is always on the 14th day of the Jewish month of Nisan, and Nisan 14 (by Jewish reckoning) would have extended from Thursday sundown to Friday sundown. If the Pharisaic-Rabbinic lunar-solar calendar (the one in common use by Jews at that time) was followed, the only plausible years for such a Friday corresponding to Nisan 14 are A.D. 30 or 33. The question then becomes, does A.D. 30 or A.D. 33 best fit with other evidence regarding the years of Jesus' ministry?

Arguments for A.D. 30

A number of NT scholars believe that Jesus died in A.D. 30, advancing the following arguments.

Tiberius's 15th year. Although Tiberius became emperor in A.D. 14, some have suggested that he may have begun as a co-emperor with his stepfather, Caesar Augustus, in A.D. 11/12. If so, and if Luke counts Tiberius's "fifteenth year" from the beginning of such a co-regency, then John the Baptist could have begun his public ministry in A.D. 25/26, and Jesus sometime in A.D. 27 or 28, hence giving enough time for Jesus' ministry as reported in the Gospels and fitting with a crucifixion in A.D. 30.

The 46 years of building the temple. When Jesus says to his Jewish opponents, "Destroy this temple [Gk. *naos*], and in three days I will raise it up" (John 2:19), the Jews respond by referring to the "forty-six years" of building Herod's temple (John 2:20). According to Josephus (*Jewish Antiquities* 15.380, 421), Herod the Great began to restore the temple sanctuary (Gk. *naos*) in the 18th year of his reign (20/19 B.C.). If the Jews are saying that it has been 46 years since construction of the temple sanctuary *began* in 20/19 B.C., this would place Jesus' first Passover in A.D. 27/28 (20 B.C. plus 46 years equals A.D. 27) and hence would fit with a date of his death in A.D. 30.

Passovers in John. Another way to reach a date of A.D. 30 for Jesus' death is to argue that there are only two Passovers in John, not three, because the Passover mentioned in John 2:13 did not occur at the beginning of Jesus' ministry but was actually the same Passover as in John 11:55 at the end of Jesus' ministry. Those who hold this view say that Jesus cleansed the temple only once, and this cleansing reported in John 2 is the same as the one mentioned in the Synoptics at the end of Jesus' ministry (Matt. 21:12–13; Mark 11:15–17; Luke 19:45–46), and that John placed it at John 2:13–17 for topical and thematic reasons. This gives Jesus a two-year public ministry, from A.D. 28 to 30, and Jesus' death could then be on Nisan 14, A.D. 30.

Evidence for A.D. 33

The other possible date for Jesus' crucifixion is A.D. 33. The following arguments can be made for this date.

Tiberius's 15th year. The ancient sources unequivocally state that Tiberius began his reign upon the death of Emperor Augustus in August of A.D. 14. While some scholars, as noted above, propose that there was a co-regency of Augustus and Tiberius between A.D. 11/12 and 14, no reliable ancient evidence for such a co-regency has ever been found. While Tiberius may have been given charge of certain provinces prior to Augustus's death, this co-administration was most likely not empire-wide, and ancient sources universally reckon the beginning of Tiberius's reign from A.D. 14. But even if, for argument's sake, such a co-regency did in fact occur, it is still much more likely that the calculation of Tiberius's reign would have begun in A.D. 14, and therefore Jesus' ministry began sometime between late A.D. 28 and A.D. 30 (see first section above).

The 46 years of building the temple. In seeking to understand the references to the temple in Jesus' interchange with the Jewish leaders in John 2:20, it is important to recognize that "temple" in this passage refers to Greek *naos*, the sanctuary or temple proper (see Herod's Temple in the Time of Jesus, p. 1943), not the surrounding temple complex (Gk. *hieron*) (see Herod's Temple Complex in the Time of Jesus, pp. 1950–1951). Josephus (*Jewish Antiquities* 15.380, 421) does not merely refer to the beginning of renovation of the temple sanctuary in 20/19 B.C. but also to its completion one and a half years later in 18/17 B.C. (The wider temple area, however, continued to be renovated.) Therefore, when Jesus and the Jewish leaders are speaking of the construction of the temple proper (*naos*) in John 2:20, they cannot be talking about that renovation as still ongoing, because, as Josephus makes clear, that renovation had in fact been completed decades prior to that time (46 years, to be exact).

For this reason it is much more likely that the Jews are saying that the construction of the temple sanctuary was *completed* 46 years ago (18/17 B.C.). (The Gk. expression in John 2:20 can legitimately be translated, "This temple was built forty-six years ago." This makes better sense of the Gk. grammar: the dative case of "forty-six years" is most likely a reference to a point in time [it is not accusative, which would indicate length of time or duration], and the aorist verb for "built" most likely fits with a completed action [if it were referring to a continuing process of 46 years, the imperfect tense would have been better suited].) If this is the case (as seems much more likely), then 46 years later than 18/17 B.C. yields A.D. 29/30, which, in turn, comports well with a three-year ministry of Jesus and a crucifixion date of A.D. 33. Thus, John 2:20 occurred at the Passover on Nisan 14 of A.D. 30, and Jesus was crucified three years later, in A.D. 33.

Passovers in John. John seems to assume that Jesus' ministry coincided with at least three or possibly four Passovers, which he mentions at different points in Jesus' ministry (John 2:13//23; 6:4; 11:55//12:1). These make an A.D. 30 crucifixion difficult to maintain, because even if Jesus began his ministry in late A.D. 28 (the earliest date likely from Luke 3:1, see first section, above), the first of these Passovers (at the beginning of Jesus' ministry; John 2:13) would fall on Nisan 14 in A.D. 29 (because Nisan is in March/April, near the beginning of a year). The second would fall in A.D. 30 at the earliest, and the third would fall in 31 at the earliest. This means that if Jesus' ministry coincided with at least three Passovers, and if the first Passover was in A.D. 29, he could not have been crucified in A.D. 30.

But if John the Baptist began his ministry in A.D. 29, then Jesus probably began his ministry in late A.D. 29 or early A.D. 30. Then the Passovers in John would occur on Nisan 14 in A.D. 30 (John 2:13), Nisan 14 in A.D. 31 (either the unnamed feast in John 5:1 or else a Passover that John does not mention), Nisan 14 in A.D. 32 (John 6:4), and Nisan 14 in A.D. 33 (John 11:55, the Passover at which Jesus was crucified). If this reckoning is correct, then Jesus was probably crucified on April 3 (Nisan 14) in A.D. 33.

These references to Passover in John, then, most naturally suggest that during Jesus' ministry he attended at least three, and possibly four, Passovers (perhaps including a Passover alluded to only in the Synoptics), resulting in a three-year ministry. Together with the reference to Tiberius's 15th year—which, starting from A.D. 14/15 (see above), brings us to A.D. 29/30 for the beginning of Jesus' ministry—the three-year ministry of Jesus indicated by John yields a crucifixion date of A.D. 33.

As noted in the arguments for A.D. 30, some have proposed that the *first* Passover mentioned in John (at the occasion of Jesus' cleansing of the temple) is the same Passover mentioned by the Synoptics at the *end* of Jesus' ministry, and that John transposed it for theological reasons. This would result in only two Passovers in John, and a crucifixion date of A.D. 30 would still be possible. But this is problematic in light of the explicit time markers in both John and the Synoptics with regard to the respective temple cleansing they record. The Synoptics all agree that the temple cleansing took place at the end of Jesus' public ministry (Matt. 21:12–17 par.). John, on the other hand, says in 2:12 that "after this" (the miracle at Cana), Jesus went with his mother and disciples to Capernaum "for a few days," and that then "the Passover of the Jews was at hand, and Jesus went up to Jerusalem" (2:13). These specific time markers make it difficult to conclude that John transferred an event that actually took place at the end of Jesus' ministry to the beginning of his account of Jesus' ministry merely for theological reasons. In addition, there are other differences in detail between the respective temple cleansings recorded by the Synoptics and John. For this reason many (though not all) conservative evangelical interpreters believe that the temple cleansing recorded in John 2:13–22 is different from that recorded in the Synoptics and took place, as John seems to indicate, at the beginning of Jesus' ministry, most likely in A.D. 30.

Conclusion

Given the arguments above, the evidence for a date of A.D. 33 for Jesus' crucifixion seems much stronger. However, because the date of A.D. 30 is held by a number of respected NT scholars, both dates are included in the various chronologies herein. ◀

Reading the Gospels and Acts

The Gospels and Acts were designed to be read as full accounts, each in their own right, even as they seek to tell about Jesus and his followers. The main obstacle in the Gospels continues into Acts: many in Israel have rejected a message and promise originally intended for them. A key to understanding these accounts is to trace the negative reaction and what it teaches about how people respond to God, and how God still moves to draw people to himself.

Genre

The Gospels have a genre parallel in the ancient world that was called the *bios*. This was ancient biography. Rather than focusing on physical description and tracing psychological thinking and personal development like modern biographies, a *bios* highlighted the key events that surrounded a person and his teaching. That is very much what the Gospels do. The key characters are Jesus and God, as Jesus carries out the plan of the Father.

Acts belongs to a different kind of genre. It is a *legitimization* document: its goal is to explain and legitimate the early church and its roots. This was necessary because in the ancient world what counted in religion was its age and time-tested quality. Since Christianity was new, it needed to explain how it could be new and still be of merit. The answer was that, although the *form* of Christianity was new, the *faith itself* was old, rooted in promises and commitments made to Israel. In fact, the new movement did not seek to make itself into a new entity but was moved in a new direction only when official Judaism rejected it and expelled it from the synagogue, with the result that (in accord with God's plan, as Acts clarifies) the gospel was taken to the Gentiles also. Acts tells this story as it presents how the promise of God expanded as far as Rome.

Though the Gospels are historical writings, they are not always presented in a strict chronology, since some of their scenes are organized topically. For example, Mark 2:1–3:6 reports five controversies in a row that Matthew spreads out over chapters 8–12.

Perspectives

Even though the Gospels each offer varying accounts, they all share the view that Jesus is the promised Messiah, uniquely related to God to bring his promise and salvation. Three of the Gospels (called the Synoptics because they overlap at many places) tell the story of Jesus "from the earth up," gradually depicting how one can see his unique relationship to the Father. Mark starts with John the Baptist, while Matthew and Luke start with Jesus' unique birth. John, however, tells the story very much "from heaven down." He starts with the preincarnate Word becoming flesh. His presentation of Jesus as Son of God is more direct and explicit. The Synoptics allow the reader to gradually see this idea, much in the manner people come to realize gradually who Jesus is. This difference in how the story unfolds does not represent a conflicting account of Jesus, but simply a distinct perspective on how to highlight who he is and what he has done.

Acts chronicles the expansion of Jesus' newly formed community from Jerusalem to Rome. Here God and Jesus are the key figures, directing the action through the Spirit, with the key human figures being Peter, Stephen, Philip, and Paul. Acts is not a defense of Paul, as many argue, but is a defense of what Paul's ministry to the Gentiles represents: the realization of God's promise to reconcile all people groups to himself and to one another through Jesus.

Distinctives of Matthew

Matthew's major concerns include Jesus' relationship to Israel and explaining Israel's rejection of him. Those who were Christians did not seek a break with Judaism but had separated from Judaism because the nation rejected the completion of the divine and scriptural promise Jesus brought and offered. However, that rejection did not stop the arrival of the promise; it raised the stakes of discipleship and led to the creation of a new entity, the church. The message was not limited to Israel but included the whole world. Five discourse units consisting of six discourses (long sections of teaching by Jesus) are the backbone of the book (chs. 5–7; 10; 13; 18; 24–25 [eschatological discourse followed by a parables section]). As with all the Gospels, there is an interaction and interchange between Jesus' word and deeds. Jesus' actions support what he preaches. Jesus' death was an act of the divine plan that led to his vindication and mission. Disciples are those who come to Jesus in personal relationship and trust, seeking forgiveness and the righteousness that God so graciously offers.

A brief listing of major Matthean themes shows the variety of his interests. (Italics identify the key themes, which in some cases overlap with other Gospels and in other cases are unique.) Matthew's Christology presents a *royal, messianic understanding of Jesus*, who as *Son of God* comes to be seen as the revealer of God's will and the bearer of divine authority. As the promised King of the Jews, Jesus heals, teaches *the real meaning of the OT in all its dimensions*, calls for a *practical righteousness*, inaugurates the kingdom, and teaches about the *mystery* elements of God's promise. Matthew associates all of this with a program he calls the *kingdom of heaven*. This kingdom is both present and yet to come (12:28; 13:1–52; 24:1–25:46). Jesus proclaims its hope throughout the nation to the lost sheep of *Israel*. He *calls on them to repent, challenges their current practices, expresses his authority over sin and the Sabbath*, and *calls them to read the law with mercy*. Most of Israel rejects the message, but the mystery is that the promise comes despite that rejection. One day that kingdom will encompass the entire world (cf. the parables of ch. 13). At the consummation, the authority of Jesus in that kingdom will be evident to all in a *judgment* rendered on the entire creation (chs. 24–25). Thus, for Matthew the kingdom program, eschatology, and salvation history are all bound together.

Distinctives of Mark

Mark is generally regarded today as the first Gospel to have been written, although a minority of scholars regard Matthew as first. Thus, Mark's outline of Jesus' ministry has become the basic structure through which his life has been traced, even though sections of it are probably given in topical rather than chronological arrangement (e.g., the conflicts of chs. 2–3). The first major section of this Gospel (1:16–8:26) cycles through a consistent structure in each of its three parts. There is a story about disciples at the start (1:16–20; 3:13–19; 6:7–13) and a note about rejection or a summary at the end (3:7–12; 6:1–6; 8:22–26). The turning point of the Gospel is the confession in 8:27–31 that Jesus is the Christ. Half of the Gospel treats the movement toward the final week of Jesus' ministry, while a full quarter of it is on the last week alone. For Mark, the events of the final week are central to the story.

The key themes are also evident in how the account proceeds. It begins with a note that what is being told is *the gospel*. Though to a lesser degree than Matthew or Luke, Mark also traces the *kingdom of God* as a theme. For Mark, it has elements that indicate its initial presence, while the bulk of the emphasis is that it will come in fullness one day in the future. The *mystery of the kingdom* is that it starts out small but will accomplish all that God has called it to be. It will grow into a full harvest.

Mark is more a Gospel of *action* than of teaching. Things happen *immediately*, one of Mark's favorite expressions. Mark has only two discourses, the parables of the kingdom (4:1–33) and the eschatological discourse (13:1–37). Miracles abound. Mark has 20 *miracle accounts*. Combined with healing summaries, these units comprise a third of the Gospel and are nearly one-half of the first 10 chapters. These pictures of Jesus' authority are important to Mark, as he presents Jesus as one who teaches with authority. The authority underscores that Jesus is *the Christ, the Son of God* (1:1; 8:29; 15:39). Mark's Christology presents Jesus as this promised figure. His claims of authority over sin, human relationships, and practices tied to purity, Sabbath, and temple get him into trouble with the Jewish leaders, who early on determine they must stop him. This *conflict raised by Jesus' claims* is also a central feature of the Gospel.

However, Jesus' authority is not one of raw power. In terms of proportion, Mark highlights Jesus as *the suffering Son of Man and suffering servant* more than the other Gospels. His mission is to come and give his life *as a ransom for many* (10:45). The importance of understanding the suffering role probably explains the *commands for silence* given to those, including demons, who recognize Jesus as Messiah (1:44; 3:11; 5:43; 9:9). Without an appreciation of his suffering, Jesus' messianic calling is not understood. It is here that the pastoral *demands of discipleship* appear as well (10:35–45; cf. 8:31–38; 9:33–37). Mark is like Matthew here. After the suffering come glory and vindication. The same Son of Man will return one day to render judgment, as the eschatological discourse reveals (Mark 13). The need for discipleship and really listening to Jesus is clear as Mark notes without hesitation *the failures of the disciples*. Their instincts will not take them in the right direction. Instead, they must trust in God and his ways. In addition, Mark notes *the emotions of Jesus and the disciples* more than any of the other Gospels.

Distinctives of Luke

The third Gospel is the longest. It has a mix of teaching, miracles, and parables. Luke gives more parables than any other Gospel. Whereas Matthew presents teaching in discourse blocks, Luke scatters his teaching throughout his Gospel, usually in smaller units. Many key discourses happen in meal scenes (7:36–50; 11:37–52; 14:1–24; 22:1–38; 24:36–49), which recall Greek symposia where "wisdom" is presented.

Key themes center on *God's plan*. Things "*must be*" (Gk. *dei*) in Luke (2:49; 4:43; 9:22; 24:7, 26, 44–47). God has designed a plan to reach and deliver *the poor, the oppressed, and those caught in Satan's oppressive grip* (4:16–18; 11:14–23). The plan reflects a *promise and fulfillment* structure, where key figures express scriptural realization of the plan (7:28; 16:16). The opening infancy section does this through the use of hymns decorated in scriptural language, underscoring the note of *joy* that works through the Gospel. Things also happen with an immediacy, as many texts speak of what is happening "*today*" (2:11; 4:21; 5:26; 19:9; 22:34; 23:43). The gospel marches forward, as is indicated by *the geographic progression* in the story from Galilee to Jerusalem (9:52–19:44).

Jesus appears as the *Messiah-Servant-Lord*. The basic category is messianic (1:31–35; 3:21–22; 4:16–30; 9:18–20), but as the story proceeds it is clear that this role is one of great authority that can be summarized by the image of *the judging Son of Man* or by the concept of *Lord* (5:24; 20:41–44; 21:27; 22:69). All of these connections reflect what Scripture has said about the plan. Jesus also functions as a *prophet* like Moses, a leader-deliverer-prophet who is to be heard (4:20–30; 9:35). Jesus' miracles provide evidence for the inaugurated presence of the *kingdom*. Ultimately the kingdom brings with its deliverance the *defeat of Satan* (11:14–23; 17:20–21). Yet there also is a future to that kingdom, which will see Jesus return to reign over both Israel and the nations, visibly expressing the sovereignty he now claims (ch. 21). Thus Jesus' deliverance looks to the realization of covenantal promises made to Abraham, David, and the nation (1:45–54).

The national leadership is steadfast in its rejection of the message. Nevertheless, the plan proceeds. *Israel* will experience judgment for her unfaithfulness (19:41–44; 21:20–24). Her city will be destroyed as a picture of what final judgment is like and as an assurance that God's program is taking place. Efforts to call Israel to faithfulness continue despite her refusal to embrace God's care and Promised One.

In the meantime, Jesus forms a *new community* (called "the Way" in the book of Acts). This community is made up of those who *turn* to embrace Jesus' message and follow in *faith*. Acts is really the second half of Luke's story, telling how God led the gospel into the heart of the Roman Empire, despite stiff opposition, through the boldness of exemplary witnesses drawing on God's Spirit.

Distinctives of John

The fourth Gospel's account emphasizes Jesus as the Sent One from God, who acts in unity with the Father. John highlights Jesus' uniqueness from the declaration of the incarnation, through a narration of seven signs, to the use of multiple discourse-dialogues. This Gospel's explicit portrayal of Jesus gives it its literary power.

John's themes focus on *Christology*. Unlike the Synoptics, he speaks little of the kingdom. Rather, it is *eternal life* that is the key theme to express what the Synoptics call the kingdom promise. The emphasis in the term "eternal life" is not only the duration of the life (eternal) but also its quality (i.e., *real, unending life*). Thus, to know the Father and Jesus Christ whom the Father sent is eternal life (17:3). This life is available now (5:24–26). Along with the opportunity is also the prospect of judgment for those who refuse it (3:16–21, 36).

The promise is brought by the *Word/Logos* sent from God in the form of human flesh. The *"I Am" sayings* convey various ways in which Jesus represents the way of God. Each image (light of the world, the resurrection and the life, the good shepherd, the bread of life, the vine) specifies some central role that belongs to Jesus. As *Son*, Jesus only does that which the *Father* shows him. It is the *unity with the Father* in mission that John highlights. Jesus is the hoped-for *Messiah*, as well as the *Son of Man* who ascends and descends between earth and heaven. In this role, he will judge (5:27), be lifted up (3:14), and serve in mediating salvation (3:13; 6:27). Even when Jesus is seen as a *prophet*, it is as a *leader*-prophet like Moses (6:14; 7:40).

Seven *signs* dominate the first two-thirds of the Gospel. The response to them covers the range from rejection (12:37–39) to openness (9:25). Interestingly, unlike the Synoptics, there is no casting out of demons in John. He focuses on acts of healing, restoration, and provision. What these signs especially highlight is *Jesus' superiority to Jewish institutions* (1:17; 2:19–21; 7:37–39; 9:38; 10:1–18). Most of the miracles take place in a setting of Jewish celebrations and underscore how Jesus provides what the feasts celebrate. At the end of the Gospel, blessing comes to those who have faith without the need for such signs (20:29).

Jesus is seen as the *revelator* of God. He makes the Father and his way known, functioning as light (1:14–18). Jesus' death shows the love of the Father for his own people and is an example to disciples of how they should love (13:1, 11–17). Jesus' death also serves to gather God's people together (10:1–18) and is a means by which the Son and Father are glorified as life is made available through him (3:14–16).

Also of great importance to John is *the Spirit*, also called the Helper (Gk. *paraklētos*; see John 14:16–18, 26; 15:26; 16:7–14; 20:22), the one Jesus sends after his death, a point Acts also highlights. This encourager-enabler leads the disciples into the truth, empowers them for ministry and mission, and convicts the world of sin, righteousness, and judgment (John 14:25–31; 16:8–11). He is the one who sustains life (4:8–10; 7:37–39).

Distinctives of Acts

Acts teaches that the new community is rooted in old promises. It does this by telling how God directed the inclusion of Gentiles and took the message from Jerusalem to Rome. The central figures in the book are Peter (chs. 1–5; 10–12); evangelists from the Hellenistic believing community, such as Stephen and Philip (chs. 6–8); and Paul (chs. 9; 13–28). Discourses are important to the book, whether they be *missionary speeches* to call people to belief or *defense speeches* where the Christian mission is explained. In the end, the book makes it clear how an originally Jewish movement came to include Gentiles. The gospel can go to all the world because (1) Jesus is Lord and (2) God directed that the gospel go into all the world. The book ends on a note of triumph as the gospel comes to Rome, even though believers suffered in terms of injustice and physical persecution in an effort to get the gospel there. ◂

INTRODUCTION TO

THE GOSPEL ACCORDING TO

MATTHEW

Author and Title

Since none of the four Gospels includes the names of their authors in the original manuscripts, they are all technically anonymous. This is not surprising, since the authors likely compiled their Gospel accounts for members of their own churches, to whom they were already well known. However, historical documents from early church history provide significant insight into the Gospels' authorship. The earliest traditions of the church are unanimous in attributing the first Gospel to Matthew, the former tax collector who followed Jesus and became one of his 12 disciples. The earliest and most important of these traditions comes from the second century in the writings of Papias, bishop of Hierapolis in Asia Minor (c. A.D. 135), and Irenaeus, bishop of Lyons in Gaul (c. 175). Because these early church leaders had either direct or indirect contact with the apostolic community, they would have been very familiar with the Gospels' origins. Moreover, no competing traditions now exist (if they ever did) attributing Matthew's Gospel to any other author. If Matthew did not write the book, it is hard to see why the false ascription would bear the name of a relatively obscure apostle when more well-known and popular figures could have been chosen (e.g., Philip, Thomas, or James).

Matthean authorship is denied by some modern scholars, especially on the view that the author of Matthew borrowed much of his material from Mark's Gospel. Given that Matthew was an apostle while Mark was not, it is assumed that Matthew would not have needed (or chosen) to depend on Mark's material. But even if Matthew did borrow from Mark's Gospel, it would only have added to Matthew's apostolic credibility since the evidence suggests that Mark himself relied extensively on the testimony of the apostle Peter.

When Jesus called him, Matthew was sitting in the tax collector's booth (9:9), collecting taxes for Herod Antipas, and this may have been along a commercial trading route about 4 miles (6.4 km) from Capernaum. However, since the narrative surrounding Matthew's call is set in Capernaum (9:1, 7, 10; cf. 4:13), the tax booth may have been on the Sea of Galilee at Capernaum, since Herod also taxed fishermen. At his calling in the first Gospel he is referred to as "Matthew" (9:9), while Mark's and Luke's Gospels describe him as "Levi the son of Alphaeus" (Mark 2:14) and "Levi" (Luke 5:27). The reason for the variation in names has elicited much discussion, but most scholars believe that the tax collector had two names, Matthew Levi, which he either possessed from birth or took on following his conversion. His occupation as a tax collector implies that he had training in scribal techniques and was thus able to write, while his identity as a Galilean Jewish Christian suggests his ability to interpret the words and actions of Jesus in light of OT messianic expectations.

Date

The precise date of the writing of Matthew's Gospel is not known. Some scholars argue for a date later than the destruction of Jerusalem in A.D. 70, since Jesus alludes to this event in 24:1–28. Of course, such a conclusion is warranted only if one denies Jesus' ability to predict the future. In light of Irenaeus's assertion (c. A.D. 175) that Matthew composed his Gospel while Peter and Paul were still living (Irenaeus, *Against Heresies* 3.1.1), it is traditionally dated to the late 50s or early 60s.

Theme

This is the story of Jesus of Nazareth, recorded by the apostle Matthew as a compelling witness that Jesus is the long-anticipated Messiah, who brought the kingdom of God to earth and is the prophesied fulfillment of God's promise of true peace and deliverance for both Jew and Gentile.

Purpose, Occasion, and Background

Matthew crafted his account to demonstrate Jesus' messianic identity, his inheritance of the Davidic kingship over Israel, and his fulfillment of the promise made to his ancestor Abraham (Matt. 1:1) to be a blessing to all the nations (Gen. 12:1–3). Thus in large part Matthew's Gospel is an evangelistic tool aimed at his fellow Jews, persuading them to recognize Jesus as their long-awaited Messiah. At the same time, the Gospel reveals clearly to Gentiles that salvation through Jesus the Messiah is available to all nations. For Jewish Christians, Matthew's Gospel provides encouragement to stand steadfast amid opposition from their own countrymen, as well as Gentile pagans, secure in the knowledge of their citizenship in God's kingdom.

Against the backdrop of such opposition to Jesus' message, Matthew establishes the identity of Christ's church as the true people of God, who now find their unity in service to Jesus despite previous racial, class, and religious barriers. His Gospel provides necessary instruction for all future disciples, Jew and Gentile, who form a new community centered upon devotion and obedience to Jesus the Messiah amid significant opposition.

Many scholars have suggested that the prominent church in Antioch of Syria, whose members included both Jewish and Gentile Christians (cf. Acts 11:19–26; 13:1–3), was the intended audience of Matthew's Gospel. They point to the Gospel's influence on Ignatius, an early bishop of Antioch. At the same time, Matthew's message spoke to all of the fledgling churches of his day, and the Gospel appears to have circulated rapidly and widely.

Timeline

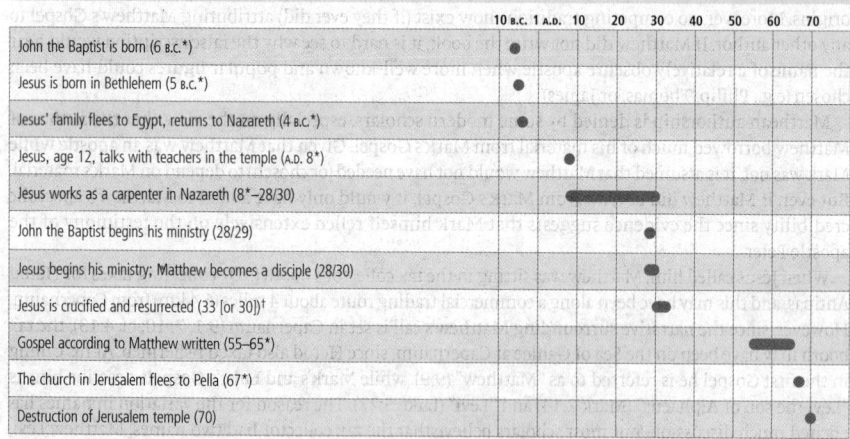

Event	10 B.C. · 1 A.D. · 10 · 20 · 30 · 40 · 50 · 60 · 70
John the Baptist is born (6 B.C.*)	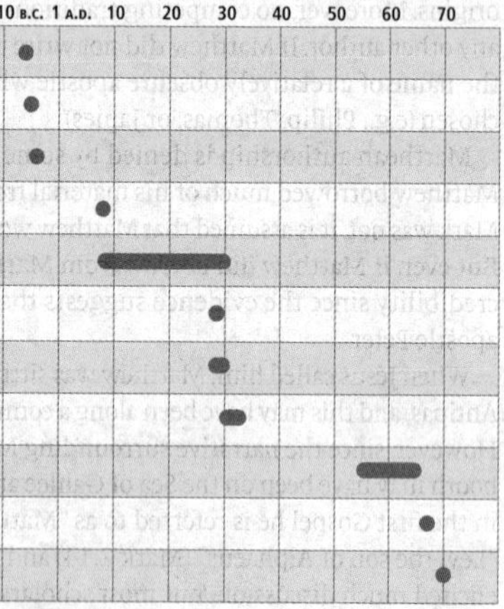
Jesus is born in Bethlehem (5 B.C.*)	
Jesus' family flees to Egypt, returns to Nazareth (4 B.C.*)	
Jesus, age 12, talks with teachers in the temple (A.D. 8*)	
Jesus works as a carpenter in Nazareth (8*–28/30)	
John the Baptist begins his ministry (28/29)	
Jesus begins his ministry; Matthew becomes a disciple (28/30)	
Jesus is crucified and resurrected (33 [or 30])†	
Gospel according to Matthew written (55–65*)	
The church in Jerusalem flees to Pella (67*)	
Destruction of Jerusalem temple (70)	

** denotes approximate date; / signifies either/or; † see The Date of Jesus' Crucifixion, pp. 1809–1810*

History of Salvation Summary

Jesus comes as the messianic King in the line of David to fulfill the OT, especially its promises of everlasting salvation. The ultimate fulfillment comes with his crucifixion and resurrection. (For an explanation of the "History of Salvation," see the Overview of the Bible, pp. 23–26.)

Literary Features

The primary genre of Matthew is the Gospel, and the organizing framework of all four Gospels is narrative or story. However, with the narrative framework of Matthew's Gospel, a major amount of space is devoted to Jesus' discourses. Beyond that, the usual array of subtypes are found: birth stories, calling or vocation stories, miracle stories, parables, pronouncement stories, encounter stories, passion stories, and resurrection stories.

The most notable literary feature of the book's format is the alternating pattern around which the book is organized. The material in Matthew's Gospel is based on a rhythmic, back-and-forth movement between blocks of narrative material and blocks of discourse material. There are five passages of discourse, which can be viewed as corresponding to the five digits on the human hand and can be easily remembered if one lists the questions that Jesus in effect answers in each unit: (1) How are citizens of the kingdom to live (chs. 5–7)? (2) How are traveling disciples to conduct themselves on their evangelistic journeys (ch. 10)? (3) What parables did Jesus tell (ch. 13)? (4) What warning did Jesus give about not hindering entrance into the kingdom and on forgiveness (chs. 18–20)? (5) How will human history end (chs. 24–25)? Matthew even used a set formula to signal these units, ending them with the statement "when Jesus had finished [these sayings]" (7:28; 11:1; 13:53; 19:1; 26:1).

Matthew's distinguishing stylistic features include recurrent quotation and citation from the OT and an emphasis on Jesus as being kingly or royal (even the opening genealogy places Jesus' father Joseph in the Davidic line). Additionally, Matthew is fond of the term "Son of David" as a title for Christ, statements to the effect that "this was done that it might be fulfilled as the prophets had said," and the formula "the kingdom of heaven is like . . ."

Key Themes

1. *Portrait of Jesus.* Jesus is the true Messiah, Immanuel (God incarnate with his people), Son of God, King of Israel, and Lord of the church.	1:1, 23; 2:2; 14:33; 16:16; 18:20; 21:5–9
2. *The bridge between Old and New Testaments.* Jesus fulfills the hopes and promises of the OT through his messianic genealogy, fulfillment of OT prophecies, and fulfillment of the OT law. These bridging qualities may have been one reason Matthew was chosen to begin the NT canon. Another possible reason is that many in the early church thought that Matthew was the first Gospel written, and another is that it was personally written by an apostle, in contrast to Mark and Luke.	1:1–17, 22–23; 2:4–5, 15, 17, 23; 5:17–20
3. *Salvation-historical "particularism" and "universalism."* Matthew's Gospel traces God's continuing work of salvation within Israel ("particularism") and extends this saving work to all the peoples of the earth ("universalism"), through the person and work of Christ.	10:5–6; 28:19
4. *The new community of faith.* The early church included both Jewish and Gentile Christians. Matthew's Gospel would have encouraged them to transcend ethnic and cultural barriers to find unity in service to Jesus the Messiah as members of his universal church.	11:28; 16:18–19; 28:19
5. *The church is built and maintained by Jesus' continuing presence.* God's saving work in the present age is carried out chiefly by and through the church, which Jesus continues to build and inhabit. Anyone who responds to Jesus' call—whether Jew or Gentile, male or female, rich or poor, slave or free—is brought into the fellowship of his church to enjoy him and participate in the community of his kingdom.	16:18; 18:15–20; 22:10; 28:20
6. *A "great commission" for evangelism and mission.* Jesus' command to "make disciples of all nations" is found only in Matthew and has motivated countless believers to reach out to the lost with the good news of the gospel. As Jesus made disciples in his earthly ministry, he commissions his church to follow his example.	28:19
7. *Jesus' five discourses recorded in Matthew can be viewed as a manual on discipleship.* The presentation of five of Jesus' major discourses, addressed at least in part to his disciples, forms the most comprehensive collection of Jesus' instructional ministry found anywhere in Scripture. They paint a holistic picture of life lived in obedience to Christ, and the church has used them to instruct disciples through the ages.	chs. 5–7; 10; 13; 18–20; 24–25

Outline

I. The Arrival in History of Jesus the Messiah (1:1–2:23)
- A. The genealogy of Jesus the Messiah (1:1–17)
- B. The angelic announcement of the conception of Jesus the Messiah (1:18–25)
- C. Magi report the star-sign of the birth of "the King of the Jews" (2:1–12)
- D. OT prophecies are fulfilled in Jesus the Messiah (2:13–23)

II. John the Baptist Prepares for the Appearance of the Messianic Kingdom (3:1–17)

III. Jesus the Messiah Begins to Advance the Messianic Kingdom (4:1–25)
- A. Temptations of the Messiah (4:1–11)
- B. Jesus the Messiah begins his Galilean ministry (4:12–25)

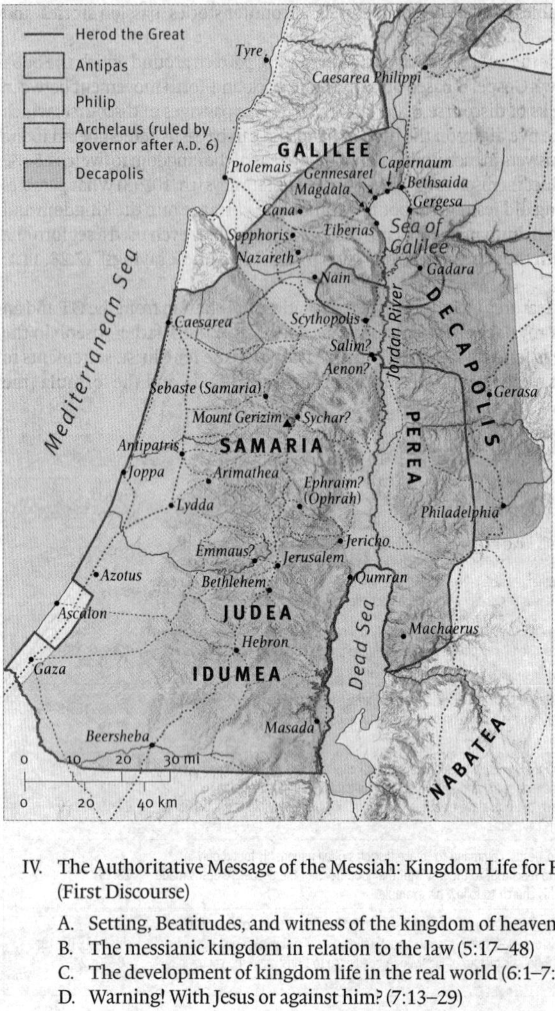

The Setting of Matthew
The events in the book of Matthew take place almost entirely within the vicinity of Palestine, an area extending roughly from Caesarea Philippi in the north to Beersheba in the south. During this time it was ruled by the Roman Empire. The opening chapters describe events surrounding Jesus' birth in Judea, where Herod had been appointed king by the Romans. The closing chapters end with Jesus' death, resurrection, and ascension during the rule of Pontius Pilate and the tetrarchs Antipas and Philip.

IV. The Authoritative Message of the Messiah: Kingdom Life for His Disciples (5:1–7:29) (First Discourse)
   A. Setting, Beatitudes, and witness of the kingdom of heaven (5:1–16)
   B. The messianic kingdom in relation to the law (5:17–48)
   C. The development of kingdom life in the real world (6:1–7:12)
   D. Warning! With Jesus or against him? (7:13–29)

V. The Authoritative Power of the Messiah: Kingdom Power Demonstrated (8:1–9:38)
   A. Healings, discipleship, and overpowering Satan's strongholds (8:1–9:8)
   B. Unexpected discipleship, miracles, and workers (9:9–38)

VI. The Authoritative Mission of the Messiah's Messengers (10:1–42) (Second Discourse)
   A. Commissioning and instructions for the short-term mission to Israel (10:1–15)
   B. Instructions for the long-term mission to the world (10:16–23)
   C. Characteristics of missionary disciples (10:24–42)

VII. Opposition to the Messiah Emerges (11:1–12:50)
   A. Jesus, John the Baptist, and ministry in Galilee (11:1–30)
   B. Confrontations with the Pharisees (12:1–45)
   C. Jesus' disciples are his true family (12:46–50)

VIII. Mysteries of the Messianic Kingdom Revealed in Parables (13:1–53) (Third Discourse)
  A. The opening of the Parabolic Discourse (13:1–23)
  B. Further parables told to the crowds (13:24–35)
  C. Explanations and parables told to the disciples (13:36–53)

IX. The Identity of the Messiah Revealed (13:54–16:20)
  A. Prophet(s) without honor (13:54–14:12)
  B. Compassionate healer and supplier for Israel (14:13–21)
  C. The Son of God worshiped (14:22–36)
  D. Teacher of the Word of God and compassionate healer (15:1–39)
  E. Peter confesses Jesus as the Christ, the Son of the living God (16:1–20)

X. The Suffering of the Messiah Revealed (16:21–17:27)
  A. The suffering sacrifice (16:21–28)
  B. The beloved, transfigured Son (17:1–13)
  C. Sons of the kingdom (17:14–27)

XI. The Community of the Messiah Revealed (18:1–20:34) (Fourth Discourse)
  A. Characteristics of life in the kingdom community (18:1–35)
  B. Valuing the kingdom community (19:1–20:34)

XII. The Messiah Asserts His Authority over Jerusalem (21:1–23:39)
  A. The triumphal entry into Jerusalem: Jesus' authority as Messiah (21:1–11)
  B. The temple actions: Jesus' pronouncement on the temple establishment (21:12–17)
  C. Cursing the fig tree: Jesus' judgment of the nation (21:18–22)
  D. Controversies in the temple court over Jesus' authority (21:23–22:46)
  E. Warnings against the teachers of the law and the Pharisees (23:1–12)
  F. Woes of judgment against the teachers of the law and the Pharisees (23:13–36)
  G. Lament over Jerusalem (23:37–39)

XIII. The Delay, Return, and Judgment of Messiah (24:1–25:46) (Fifth [Olivet] Discourse)
  A. The beginning of birth pains (24:1–14)
  B. "Great tribulation" and the coming of the Son of Man (24:15–31)
  C. The nearness and time of Jesus' coming (24:32–41)
  D. Parabolic exhortations to watch and be prepared for the coming of the Son of Man (24:42–25:30)
  E. Judgment at the end (25:31–46)

XIV. The Crucified Messiah (26:1–27:66)
  A. Plot, anointing, and betrayal to the religious leaders (26:1–16)
  B. The Passover and the Lord's Supper (26:17–35)
  C. Gethsemane: Jesus' agonizing prayers (26:36–46)
  D. Jesus arrested (26:47–56)
  E. The Jewish trial of Jesus (26:57–27:10)
  F. The Roman trial of Jesus (27:11–26)
  G. Jesus the Messiah crucified (27:27–44)
  H. The death of Jesus the Messiah (27:45–50)
  I. Testimonies, women followers, and burial (27:51–66)

XV. The Resurrection and Commission of the Messiah (28:1–20)
  A. An empty tomb and the risen Jesus (28:1–10)
  B. The conspiracy to deny the truth of Jesus' resurrection (28:11–15)
  C. The risen Jesus' Great Commission (28:16–20)

THE GOSPEL ACCORDING TO

MATTHEW

The Genealogy of Jesus Christ

1 [a]The book of the genealogy of Jesus Christ, [b]the son of David, [c]the son of Abraham.
2 [d]Abraham was the father of Isaac, and [e]Isaac the father of Jacob, and [f]Jacob the father
of Judah and his brothers, 3 and [g]Judah the father of Perez and Zerah by Tamar, and Perez
the father of Hezron, and Hezron the father of Ram,[1] 4 and Ram the father of Amminadab,
and Amminadab the father of Nahshon, and Nahshon the father of Salmon, 5 and Salmon
the father of Boaz by [h]Rahab, and Boaz the father of Obed by Ruth, and Obed the father
of Jesse, 6 and [i]Jesse the father of David the king.
And [j]David was the father of Solomon by [k]the wife of Uriah, 7 and [l]Solomon the father
of Rehoboam, and Rehoboam the father of Abijah, and Abijah the father of Asaph,[2] 8 and
Asaph the father of Jehoshaphat, and Jehoshaphat the father of Joram, [m]and Joram the
father of Uzziah, 9 and Uzziah the father of Jotham, and Jotham the father of Ahaz, and
Ahaz the father of Hezekiah, 10 and Hezekiah the father of Manasseh, and Manasseh the
father of Amos,[3] and Amos the father of Josiah, 11 and [n]Josiah the father of [o]Jechoniah and
his brothers, at the time of the deportation to Babylon.
12 And after the deportation to Babylon: [p]Jechoniah was the father of [q]Shealtiel,[4] and
[r]Shealtiel the father of Zerubbabel, 13 and Zerubbabel the father of Abiud, and Abiud the
father of Eliakim, and Eliakim the father of Azor, 14 and Azor the father of Zadok, and Zadok
the father of Achim, and Achim the father of Eliud, 15 and Eliud the father of Eleazar, and
Eleazar the father of Matthan, and Matthan the father of Jacob, 16 and Jacob the father of
[s]Joseph the husband of Mary, of whom Jesus was born, who is called Christ.

[1] Greek *Aram*; also verse 4 [2] *Asaph* is probably an alternate spelling of *Asa*; some manuscripts *Asa*; also verse 8 [3] *Amos* is probably an alternate spelling of *Amon*; some manuscripts *Amon*; twice in this verse [4] Greek *Salathiel*; twice in this verse

Chapter 1
1 [a][Luke 3:23-38] [b]2 Sam. 7:12-16; Ps. 132:11; Isa. 11:1; Jer. 23:5; Luke 1:32, 69; John 7:42; Acts 2:30; 13:23; Rom. 1:3; 2 Tim. 2:8; Rev. 22:16 [c]Gen. 22:18; Gal. 3:16
2 [d]Gen. 21:3 [e]Gen. 25:26 [f]Gen. 29:35
3 [g][Ruth 4:18-22; 1 Chr. 2:1-15]
5 [h]Josh. 6:25
6 [i]1 Sam. 16:1; 17:12 [j]2 Sam. 12:24 [k]2 Sam. 12:10
7 [l]For ver. 7-10, see 1 Chr. 3:10-14
8 [m][2 Kgs. 15:1; 1 Chr. 3:11, 12]
11 [n]1 Chr. 3:15, 16 [o]Esth. 2:6; Jer. 24:1; 27:20
12 [p]1 Chr. 3:17-19 [q]Luke 3:27 [r]Ezra 3:2
16 [s]Luke 3:23

1:1–2:23 *The Arrival in History of Jesus the Messiah.* Matthew's introduction echoes the language of Genesis. The word rendered "genealogy" (1:1) is Greek *genesis* ("beginning, origin, birth, genealogy"), and this is also the title of the Greek translation of Genesis, implying that it is a book of "beginnings." "The book of the genealogy" appears to function not only as a heading for the genealogy itself (1:2–17) but also as a title for the entire story to follow: a new beginning with the arrival of Jesus the Messiah and the kingdom of God (cf. note on Gen. 2:4).

1:1–17 *The Genealogy of Jesus the Messiah.* Jews kept extensive genealogies to establish a person's heritage, inheritance, legitimacy, and rights (cf. Josephus, *Life of Josephus* 1–6). Matthew likely draws on the genealogies of the OT, with some omissions (see note on Matt. 1:17). He demonstrates Jesus' legal claim to the throne of David, emphasizing Jesus' legal descent from David and Abraham, while Luke's genealogical record (Luke 3:23–38) emphasizes Jesus' biological descent from David and Adam.

1:1 The book of the genealogy. The Gospel's opening words carried special significance for a Jewish audience, whose ancestry was inseparably intertwined with the covenants God made with Israel. **Jesus** (Gk. *Iēsous*) was the historical, everyday name, and is *Yeshua'*/*Yehoshua'* (Joshua) in Hebrew, meaning "Yahweh saves" (Neh. 7:7; cf. Matt. 1:21). **Christ** (Gk. *Christos*, from Hb. *mashiakh*, "anointed") points back to David as the anointed king of Israel. The designation "Messiah" came to summarize several strands of OT expectation, especially the promise of an "anointed one" who would righteously rule God's people (2 Sam. 7:11b–16). **Son of David** evoked images of a Messiah with a royal lineage who would reestablish the throne in Jerusalem and the kingdom of Israel. **son of Abraham**. God's covenant with Abraham established Israel as a chosen people and also affirmed that the whole world would be blessed through his line (Gen. 12:1–3; 22:18).

1:2–6a The four generations between **Perez** and **Amminadab** encompass approximately 450 years. The six generations from **Nahshon** to the rise of the monarchy with **David** total about 400 more.

1:3 Tamar. The inclusion of five women in Jesus' genealogy—Tamar, Rahab (v. 5), Ruth (v. 5), Bathsheba ("the wife of Uriah," v. 6), and Mary (v. 16)—is unusual, since descent was usually traced through men as the head of the family. Rahab and Ruth were Gentiles, and Tamar, Rahab, and Bathsheba were women of questionable character. The lineage is comprised of men, women, adulterers, prostitutes, heroes, and Gentiles—and Jesus will be Savior of all.

1:6b–11 Matthew may have drawn from 1 Chron. 3:10–14, since both genealogies omit several kings found in the narrative of Kings and Chronicles. Omitting names in a genealogy was common to make for ease of memorization. One is struck in this section by the alternately godly and wicked kings who ruled Israel.

1:12–13 Zerubbabel led the first group given permission to return to Israel from the exile.

1:12 The evil of **Jechoniah** (2 Kings 24:8–9) was so great that his line was cursed (Jer. 22:30). While a natural, biological son could not therefore inherit the throne, the legal claim could still come through Jechoniah's line.

1:16–17 Jesus is the rightful legal heir to the covenant promises associated

17[t]ch. 2:4; 11:2; 16:16; 22:42; 23:10; Mark 8:29; Luke 3:15; [John 1:41; 4:25]
18[u]ver. 1; Mark 1:1; John 1:17; 17:3; [ver. 16] [v]Luke 1:27 [w]Luke 1:35
19[x][Deut. 24:1]
20[y]ch. 2:13, 19; [ch. 2:12, 22]
21[z]ver. 25; Luke 1:31; 2:21 [a]Luke 2:11; Acts 4:12; 5:31; 13:23, 38; [Acts 3:26]
22[b]ch. 21:4; 26:56; John 19:36 [c]ch. 2:15, 23; 4:14; Mark 14:49
23[d]Cited from Isa. 7:14 [e]Isa. 8:8, 10

17 So all the generations from Abraham to David were fourteen generations, and from
David to the deportation to Babylon fourteen generations, and from the deportation to
Babylon to [t]the Christ fourteen generations.

The Birth of Jesus Christ

18 Now the birth of [u]Jesus Christ[1] took place in this way. [v]When his mother Mary had
been betrothed[2] to Joseph, before they came together she was found to be with child [w]from
the Holy Spirit. 19 And her husband Joseph, being a just man and unwilling [x]to put her
to shame, resolved to divorce her quietly. 20 But as he considered these things, behold, [y]an
angel of the Lord appeared to him in a dream, saying, "Joseph, son of David, do not fear
to take Mary as your wife, for that which is conceived in her is from the Holy Spirit. 21 She
will bear a son, and [z]you shall call his name Jesus, [a]for he will save his people from their
sins." 22 [b]All this took place [c]to fulfill what the Lord had spoken by the prophet:

23 [d]"Behold, the virgin shall conceive and bear a son,
and they shall call his name [e]Immanuel"

[1] Some manuscripts *of the Christ* [2] That is, legally pledged to be married

with the Davidic throne (v. 6) as well as the rightful legal heir to the covenant promises related to the Abrahamic seed and land (vv. 1–2).

1:17 fourteen generations. Matthew does not mean **all** the generations that had lived during those times but "all" that he included in his list (for he evidently skipped some, such as three generations between Joram and Uzziah [Azariah] in v. 8; cf. 1 Chron. 3:10–12); cf. note on Matt. 1:6b–11. Perhaps for ease of memorization, or perhaps for literary or symbolic symmetry, Matthew structures the genealogy to count 14 generations from each major section. (According to the Jewish practice of *gematria*, the giving of a numeric value to the consonants in a word, David's name would add to D + V + D or 4 + 6 + 4 = 14, and David is the 14th name on the list.)

1:18–25 *The Angelic Announcement of the Conception of Jesus the Messiah.* A new era in Israel's history begins with the story of Jesus' conception in the little town of Nazareth. The angel announces his conception (vv. 18–21), explaining that he is the prophesied Immanuel (vv. 22–23). Joseph immediately obeys the angel's directive (vv. 24–25).

1:18 Mary had been betrothed to Joseph. The custom of betrothal was different from "engagement" in modern society. Customarily the parents of a young man chose a young woman to be engaged to their son. A second stage of betrothal involved official arrangements and a prenuptial agreement before witnesses, which was a legally binding contract and could be broken only by a formal process of divorce. **found to be with child**. Mary is about four months pregnant, having spent three months with Elizabeth, her "relative" (Luke 1:36, 56).

1:19 Betrothed partners were referred to as **husband** and "wife" (v. 20), though they were not yet considered to be married, and having sexual relations during that period was considered immoral. **put her to shame**. Sexual unfaithfulness during betrothal was considered adultery, and under the Mosaic law carried the death penalty by stoning. **divorce her quietly**. Joseph intended to maintain his personal righteousness, yet he desired to show compassion even though Mary appeared to be an adulteress.

1:20 Behold represents Greek *idou*, used frequently by Matthew to signal emphasis, prompt the reader to pay special attention, or introduce something new or unusual. The **angel of the Lord** is Gabriel (cf. Luke 1:26).

1:21 The name **Jesus** was given to sons as a symbolic hope for the Lord's anticipated sending of salvation through a Messiah who would purify his people and save them from oppression (see note on v. 1). But the angel points to a more important theme: to **save his people from their sins**. Salvation from sins was a repeated promise in OT prophets (e.g., Isa. 40:2; 53:6; Jer. 31:31–34; Ezek. 36:25–27; Dan. 9:24; Zech. 13:1).

1:22 All this took place to fulfill. This is Matthew's "fulfillment formula," by which he points to an event or teaching of Jesus that fulfills an OT passage, indicating: (1) a direct prediction-fulfillment (e.g., vv. 22–23); (2) the intended full meaning of the OT Scripture (e.g., 5:17–20); or (3) a divinely orchestrated analogical/typological correspondence to Israel's history (e.g., 2:15, 17–18).

1:23 the virgin. The Greek word *parthenos* ("virgin") corresponds to the Hebrew term *'almah*, which is used in the prophecy of Isa. 7:14 regarding the virgin birth of the coming Savior (see note on Isa. 7:14). The Hebrew word *'almah* ("virgin" or "maiden") generally denotes an unmarried woman who is a virgin (e.g., Gen. 24:43; Ex. 2:8; Ps. 68:25). The prophecy in Isaiah 7:14

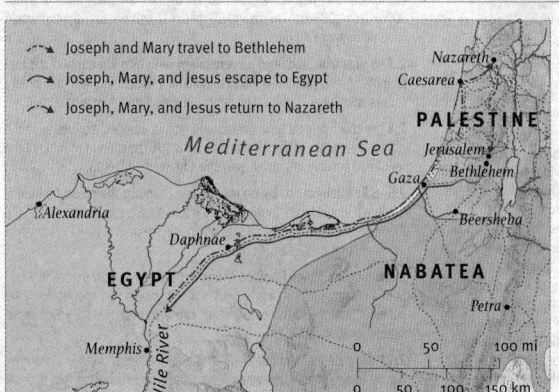

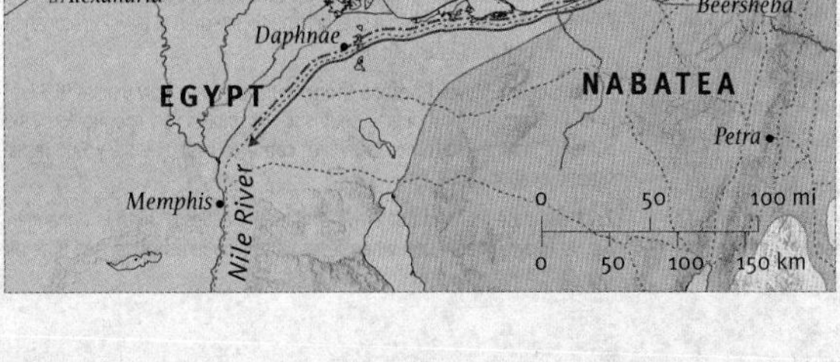

Jesus' Birth and Flight to Egypt

As the time drew near for Jesus to be born, a mandatory Roman census made it necessary for Joseph to return to his ancestral home of Bethlehem. There Mary gave birth to Jesus, and later, wise men from the east came to worship him. The wise men's recognition of a new king, however, troubled King Herod and the ruling establishment in Jerusalem, and Herod sought to kill Jesus. Joseph and his family escaped to Egypt and remained there until Herod died. When they returned to Palestine, they settled in the remote district of Galilee, where Jesus grew up in the northern village of Nazareth, to avoid the attention of the rulers in Jerusalem.

(which means, God [f]with us). 24 When Joseph woke from sleep, he did as the angel of the
Lord commanded him: he took his wife, 25 but knew her not until she had given birth to
a son. And [g]he called his name Jesus.

The Visit of the Wise Men

2 Now [h]after Jesus was born in [i]Bethlehem of Judea [j]in the days of Herod the king,
behold, wise men[1] from [k]the east came to Jerusalem, 2 saying, "Where is he who has
been born [l]king of the Jews? For we saw [m]his star when it rose[2] and have come to [n]wor-
ship him." 3 When Herod the king heard this, he was troubled, and all Jerusalem with
him; 4 and assembling all the chief priests and scribes of the people, he inquired of them
where [o]the Christ was to be born. 5 They told him, "In Bethlehem of Judea, for so it is
written by the prophet:

6 [p]"'And you, O Bethlehem, in the land of Judah,
  are by no means least among the rulers of Judah;
for from you shall come a ruler
  who will [q]shepherd my people Israel.'"

7 Then Herod summoned the wise men secretly and ascertained from them what time
the star had appeared. 8 And he sent them to Bethlehem, saying, "Go and search diligently
for the child, and when you have found him, bring me word, that I too may come and worship him." 9 After listening to the king, they went on their way. And behold, the star that
they had seen when it rose went before them until it came to rest over the place where the
child was. 10 When they saw the star, they rejoiced exceedingly with great joy. 11 And going

[1] Greek *magi*; also verses 7, 16 [2] Or *in the east*; also verse 9

23 [f]See ch. 28:20
25 [g]ver. 21

Chapter 2

1 [h]Luke 2:4-7 [i]Luke 2:15; John 7:42 [j]Luke 1:5 [k][Gen. 25:6; 1 Kgs. 4:30]
2 [l]ch. 27:11, 37; Jer. 23:5; 30:9; Zech. 9:9 [m][Num. 24:17; Rev. 22:16] [n]See ch. 8:2
4 [o]See ch. 1:17
6 [p]Cited from Mic. 5:2 [q]Ezek. 34:23; John 21:15-17; [2 Sam. 5:2; Rev. 7:17]

(occasioned by threat of attack on Judah in the time of Isaiah; see notes on Isa. 7:10–17), points to God's enduring promise for the line of David. Matthew thus presents the virgin birth of Jesus as God's miraculous fulfillment of this promise in the person of Jesus the Messiah. This brings further affirmation of the promise that **God** (**Immanuel**) will be **with** his disciples in every age, to empower them in their commission to "make disciples of all nations"—as Jesus reaffirms in the closing words of Matthew's Gospel: "behold, I am with you always, to the end of the age" (cf. Matt. 28:20).

1:24 he took his wife. Mary, being betrothed to Joseph, was already considered to be his wife (cf. notes on vv. 18, 19).

1:25 The name "**Jesus**" specifies what he does ("God saves"), while the messianic title "Immanuel" (v. 23) specifies who he is ("God with us"). Matthew concludes his Gospel with the same theme: "I am with you always" (28:20).

2:1–12 *Magi Report the Star-sign of the Birth of "the King of the Jews."* As much as two years have passed since the events of ch. 1. Matthew highlights God's sovereign care in this infancy account of Jesus the King.

2:1 Jesus' birth in **Bethlehem of Judea**, about 6 miles (9.7 km) south of Jerusalem, marks him as being from the tribe of Judah and from the city that produced the Davidic kings (Ruth 1:1, 19; 2:4; 1 Sam. 17:12, 15; see note on Luke 2:4). **Herod the king** (also commonly Herod I or Herod the Great) ruled Israel and Judah 37–4 B.C. He was an Idumean, appointed king of the Jews under the authority of Rome. He ruled firmly and at times ruthlessly, murdering his own wife, several sons, and other relatives. He was a master builder who restored the temple in **Jerusalem** and built many theaters, cities, palaces, and fortresses. Herod's building programs included his palace at Jericho, the fortresses of Herodium, Machaerus, Sebaste, and Masada, the harbor and city of Caesarea Maritima (see note on Acts 8:40), and especially the Jerusalem temple (cf. John 2:14). He also financed structures (including pagan temples) throughout the Roman Empire—e.g., at Antioch (cf. Acts 11:19), Nicopolis (cf. Titus 3:12), and Athens (cf. Acts 17:16). Herod, ravaged by disease, died in his palace at Jericho (see note on Luke 19:1) and was buried at Herodium (Josephus, *Jewish Antiquities* 6.168–181). Excavations at Herodium since the 1960s have revealed the circular palace-fortress built atop its mountain, as well as the monumental buildings and huge pool below; in 2007 the excavator announced the discovery of Herod's mausoleum and sarcophagus. In earlier times, **wise men** (Gk. *magoi*, plural of *magos*) referred to priests and experts in mysteries in Persia and Babylon (cf. Septuagint of Dan. 1:20; 2:2, 10, 27; etc.), but by this time it applied to a wide range of people whose practices included astrology, dream interpretation, study of sacred writings, the pursuit of wisdom, and magic.

2:2 we saw his star when it rose. The wise men would likely have been familiar with OT prophecy through interaction with Jews in Babylon, and they may have remembered Balaam's prophecy that "A star shall come out of Jacob, and a scepter shall rise out of Israel" (Num. 24:17). This was understood by Jews to point to a messianic deliverer (e.g., Dead Sea Scrolls, *Damascus Document* 7.18–21; *Testimonia* 9–13). The movement of the star (Matt. 2:9) suggests that it is not a natural phenomenon (e.g., a comet, supernova, or conjunction of planets) but was supernatural, perhaps a guiding angel that appeared as a star, or perhaps some specially created heavenly phenomenon that had the brightness of a star. **have come to worship him**. The wise men likely traveled with a large number of attendants and guards for the long journey, which would have taken several weeks. For example, if they had come from Babylon by the main trade route of about 800 miles (1,288 km), averaging 20 miles (32 km) per day, the trip would have taken about 40 days.

2:3 he was troubled, and all Jerusalem with him. The arrival of this true King of the Jews presents a threat to Herod the Great's throne and to Israel's corrupt religious and political leadership in Jerusalem (cf. note on 21:10).

2:4 The **chief priests** gave oversight to temple activities; **scribes** were the official interpreters of the OT (see note on 8:19). The concept of "King of the Jews" had become associated with **the Christ**, the Messiah.

2:5–6 Bethlehem was **by no means least among the rulers of Judah**, because it would be the birthplace of the future ruler, the Messiah (Mic. 5:2). The quotation also alludes to a shepherding theme cited at David's coronation as king over Israel (2 Sam. 5:2).

2:9 the star . . . went before them. Bethlehem was only 6 miles (9.7 km) from Jerusalem, almost directly south, so this implies very specific, localized guidance from the traveling star, which **came to rest** over the young Jesus' specific location.

2:11 The wise men did not arrive at the time of Jesus' birth in a manger, but up to two years later, when Jesus was living in a **house** (see note on

11 [r][1 Sam. 9:7; Ps. 72:10] [s]Isa. 60:6 [t]Rev. 18:13 [u]Ex. 30:23; Ps. 45:8; John 19:39
12 [v]ver. 22; [ver. 13, 19] [w][ch. 27:19; Gen. 20:6; 31:11; Num. 12:6; Job 33:15]
13 [x]ver. 19; ch. 1:20; [ver. 12, 22]
15 [y]See ch. 1:22 [z]Cited from Hos. 11:1
17 [a]ch. 27:9; [ch. 1:22]
18 [b]Cited from Jer. 31:15 [c]Gen. 42:13, 36; Lam. 5:7
20 [d][Ex. 4:19]
22 [e]See ver. 12
23 [f]ch. 4:13; Mark 1:9; Luke 1:26; 2:39; 4:16; John 1:45 [g]See ch. 1:22

into the house they saw the child with Mary his mother, and they fell down and worshiped
him. Then, opening their treasures, [r]they offered him gifts, [s]gold and [t]frankincense and
[u]myrrh. 12 And [v]being warned [w]in a dream not to return to Herod, they departed to their
own country by another way.

The Flight to Egypt

13 Now when they had departed, behold, [x]an angel of the Lord appeared to Joseph in a
dream and said, "Rise, take the child and his mother, and flee to Egypt, and remain there
until I tell you, for Herod is about to search for the child, to destroy him." 14 And he rose
and took the child and his mother by night and departed to Egypt 15 and remained there
until the death of Herod. [y]This was to fulfill what the Lord had spoken by the prophet,
[z]"Out of Egypt I called my son."

Herod Kills the Children

16 Then Herod, when he saw that he had been tricked by the wise men, became furious,
and he sent and killed all the male children in Bethlehem and in all that region who were
two years old or under, according to the time that he had ascertained from the wise men.
17 [a]Then was fulfilled what was spoken by the prophet Jeremiah:

18 [b]"A voice was heard in Ramah,
weeping and loud lamentation,
Rachel weeping for her children;
she refused to be comforted, because they [c]are no more."

The Return to Nazareth

19 But when Herod died, behold, an angel of the Lord appeared in a dream to Joseph
in Egypt, 20 saying, "Rise, take the child and his mother and go to the land of Israel, for
[d]those who sought the child's life are dead." 21 And he rose and took the child and his
mother and went to the land of Israel. 22 But when he heard that Archelaus was reigning
over Judea in place of his father Herod, he was afraid to go there, and [e]being warned in
a dream he withdrew to the district of Galilee. 23 And he went and lived in a city called
[f]Nazareth, so [g]that what was spoken by the prophets might be fulfilled, that he would
be called a Nazarene.

v. 16). **worshiped him**. It is doubtful that these quasi-pagan religious men understood Jesus' divine nature, but their actions were unknowingly appropriate and wonderfully foreshadowed the worship of Jesus by all the Gentile nations (cf. 28:19; Rom. 1:5; Phil. 2:9–11; Rev. 7:9–10; 21:24). **gold and frankincense and myrrh**. The number of gifts contributed to the tradition that there were three men, but the actual number is unknown. Frankincense is resin used ceremonially for the only incense permitted on the altar (Ex. 30:9, 34–38). Myrrh is sap used in incense and perfume and as a stimulant tonic. The gifts were likely used providentially to support the family in their flight to Egypt (Matt. 2:13–15).

2:13–23 *OT Prophecies Are Fulfilled in Jesus the Messiah.* Matthew explains how Jesus' personal history repeats certain aspects of Israel's national history.

2:13 flee to Egypt. The Egyptian border lay approximately 90 miles (146 km) from Bethlehem (see map, p. 1821). Jesus and his family would be safe from Herod the Great in Egypt, since it was outside his jurisdiction.

2:15 fulfill. The prophet Hosea recounted how God had faithfully brought Israel out of Egypt in the exodus (Hos. 2:15), which Matthew cites in comparing Israel, God's "son," being rescued and delivered, to Jesus, the One who will be revealed as God's true Son.

2:16 all the male children in Bethlehem . . . two years old or under. The small village may have had 10 to 30 boys of that age. Herod the Great's earlier query to the wise men about the time of the appearing of the star (v. 7) gave him an estimated time of birth for his potential challenger.

2:17–18 Jeremiah used personification to describe the mothers of Israel (**Rachel**) mourning for their **children** who had been removed from the land and carried off into exile, leaving Israel no longer a nation and considered dead (Jer. 31:15). Like the exile, the attempt on Jesus' life was intended to wipe out the chosen one of God.

2:22 Archelaus, one of Herod the Great's sons, succeeded Herod's throne over Judea, Samaria, and Idumea and ruled 4 B.C.–A.D. 6 (see Jewish and Roman Rulers, pp. 1786–1787). He was hated by the Jews and displayed the same kind of cruelty that had characterized his father's reign. Caesar Augustus, fearing a revolution from the people, deposed and banished him to Gaul.

2:23 Nazareth, in the lower Galilean hills halfway between the Mediterranean Sea and the Sea of Galilee, was a relatively small village (population estimates vary from 200 to 1,600). Luke 1:26–27 and 2:39 indicate that Joseph and Mary had earlier come from Nazareth. **he would be called a Nazarene**. Matthew is not quoting any specific OT prophecy but is referring to a general theme in the OT **prophets** (plural). Thus Matthew is saying that the OT prophets foretold that the Messiah would be despised (see Ps. 22:6; Isa. 49:7; 53:3; cf. Dan. 9:26), comparable to the way in which the town of Nazareth was despised in the time of Jesus (cf. John 1:46; 7:41, 52). Matthew may also have intended a wordplay connecting the word "Nazareth" to the OT messianic prophecy in Isa. 11:1, since "Nazareth" sounds like the word for "branch" in Hebrew, which was a designation for the Messiah. "Nazarene" has no evident connection with the OT "Nazirite" vow (Num. 6:2; Judg. 13:5), which is spelled differently, has no messianic significance, and has no connection with the town of Nazareth.

John the Baptist Prepares the Way

3 [h]In those days [i]John the Baptist came preaching in [j]the wilderness of Judea, 2 [k]"Repent,
for [l]the kingdom of heaven is at hand." 3 For this is he who was spoken of by the prophet
Isaiah when he said,

> [m]"The voice of one crying in the wilderness:
> [n]'Prepare[1] the way of the Lord;
> make his paths straight.'"

4 Now John wore [o]a garment of camel's hair and a leather belt around his waist, and his
food was [p]locusts and [q]wild honey. 5 Then Jerusalem and all Judea and all the region about
the Jordan were going out to him, 6 and they were baptized by him in the river Jordan,
[r]confessing their sins.

7 But when he saw many of [s]the Pharisees and [t]Sadducees coming to his baptism, he said
to them, [u]"You brood of [v]vipers! Who warned you to flee from [w]the wrath to come? 8 Bear
fruit [x]in keeping with repentance. 9 And do not presume to say to yourselves, [y]'We have
Abraham as our father,' for I tell you, God is able from [z]these stones to raise up children
for Abraham. 10 Even now the axe is laid to the root of the trees. [a]Every tree therefore that
does not bear good fruit is cut down and thrown into the fire.

11 [b]"I baptize you with water [c]for repentance, but [d]he who is coming after me is mightier
than I, whose sandals I am not worthy to carry. He will baptize you [e]with the Holy Spirit
and [f]fire. 12 His [g]winnowing fork is in his hand, and he will clear his threshing floor and
[h]gather his wheat into the barn, [i]but the chaff he will burn with [j]unquenchable fire."

The Baptism of Jesus

13 [k]Then Jesus came [l]from Galilee to the Jordan to John, to be baptized by him. 14 [m]John
would have prevented him, saying, "I need to be baptized by you, and do you come to

[1] *Or crying: Prepare in the wilderness*

Chapter 3

1 [h]For ver. 1-12, see Mark 1:2-8; Luke 3:2-17 [i]John 1:6, 7 [j]Josh. 15:61; [Judg. 1:16]
2 [k]ch. 4:17; Mark 1:15 [l]ch. 10:7; Dan. 2:44; [ch. 6:10]
3 [m]John 1:23; Cited from Isa. 40:3 [n]Luke 1:76
4 [o]2 Kgs. 1:8; Zech. 13:4; [Heb. 11:37] [p]Lev. 11:22 [q]1 Sam. 14:26
6 [r]Acts 19:18
7 [s]ch. 23:13, 15 [t]ch. 22:23 [u]ch. 12:34; 23:33 [v]Ps. 140:3 [w]Rom. 5:9; Eph. 5:6; Col. 3:6; 1 Thess. 1:10
8 [x]Acts 26:20
9 [y]John 8:39 [z][ch. 4:3]
10 [a]ch. 7:19; Luke 13:7, 9; John 15:2, 6
11 [b]John 1:26; Acts 1:5 [c]Acts 13:24; 19:4 [d]John 1:15, 27; 3:30, 31; Acts 13:25 [e]John 1:33; Acts 11:16 [f][Isa. 4:4; Mal. 3:2, 3; Acts 2:3]
12 [g]Isa. 30:24 [h]ch. 13:30 [i]Mal. 4:1 [j]Mark 9:43, 48
13 [k]For ver. 13-17, see Mark 1:9-11; Luke 3:21, 22; [John 1:32-34] [l]ch. 2:22
14 [m][John 13:6]

3:1–17 *John the Baptist Prepares for the Appearance of the Messianic Kingdom.* John now appears, preaching in the Judean desert. It is more than 25 years since Joseph and his family moved back to Nazareth. The focus of Matthew's Gospel now shifts to Jesus' public ministry.

3:1 John the Baptist was born around 6 B.C. to devout parents who were both of the priestly line and well advanced in age (Luke 1:5–25, 39–80). John will play an important historical role in linking God's saving activity in the OT and his saving activity in the person and work of Jesus.

3:2 To **repent**, or "change one's mind," in the OT called for a change in a person's attitude toward God that impacted one's actions and life choices; it involved the idea of "turning," that is, from one way of thinking and living to a different way. Common external signs of repentance included prayers of remorse and confession and renouncing of sin. The term **kingdom of heaven** is found only in Matthew's Gospel but is interchangeable with "kingdom of God," found in the other Gospels (cf. Matt. 19:14 and Mark 10:14). **is at hand**. The kingdom of heaven has come near to people in the person of Jesus (the Messiah), who was soon to be revealed as the "beloved Son" of the Father (Matt. 3:17), and who himself was soon to begin proclaiming that message of repentance, because "the kingdom of heaven is at hand" (see note on 4:17). Here John calls for the people to remove the obstacles from their lives that might hinder their reception of the Messiah and his kingdom.

3:3 John the Baptist fulfills Isa. 40:3 and also the prophecies in Malachi about the messenger who prepares the way before the Lord (Mal. 3:1; cf. Matt. 11:10) and about Elijah (Mal. 4:5–6; cf. Matt. 11:14; 17:10–13; Luke 1:17).

3:4 a garment of camel's hair. John's appearance would have evoked images of prophecies about "Elijah," who was to return to prepare the way for God's wrathful appearance (cf. 2 Kings 1:8; Mal. 3:1; 4:5–6). John's garments were common to nomadic desert dwellers and thus were associated with poorer people. **Locusts and wild honey** were not an unusual source of food for people living in the desert (on locusts, see Dead Sea Scrolls, *Damascus Document* 12.14–15). The desert locust (Gk. *akris*) is a large grasshopper, still eaten today by poorer people in the Middle East and Africa.

3:5–6 going out to him. John's startling declaration of the nearness of God's kingdom draws even city dwellers out into the wilderness. "Baptize" (Gk. *baptizō*) means "to plunge, dip, immerse," and John was immersing people **in the river Jordan**. When people **were baptized by him**, going under the water symbolized both the cleansing away of sin and a passing safely through the waters of judgment and death (cf. Gen. 7:6–24; Ex. 14:26–29; Jonah 1:7–16; see notes on Rom. 6:4; 1 Pet. 3:21). Christians today differ over whether full bodily immersion is required for the symbolism of baptism. Having made the difficult journey from Jerusalem, the people demonstrate their repentance by **confessing their sins**.

3:7 Pharisees. A laymen's fellowship, popular with the common people and connected to local synagogues, chiefly characterized by adherence to extensive extrabiblical traditions, which they rigorously obeyed as a means of applying the law to daily life. **Sadducees**. A small group who derived their authority from the activities of the temple. They were removed from the common people by aristocratic and priestly influence as well as by their cooperation with Rome's rule. (See Jewish Groups at the Time of the New Testament, pp. 1799–1800.) **brood of vipers**. Vipers were well known for their subtle movements and lethal strikes. **the wrath to come**. The coming Messiah will bring punishment for those who do not repent.

3:11 He who is coming after me expresses strong messianic expectation. **is mightier than I**. John announces the nearness of the kingdom, but the Coming One will arrive with the power of God to inaugurate messianic rule. **baptize you with the Holy Spirit and fire**. John's water baptism will be superseded by the baptism associated with the Coming One (see note on 1 Cor. 12:13). Those who repent and trust in him will receive the blessing of the Holy Spirit (cf. Joel 2:28–29; Acts 2:16–21), while the unrepentant will receive the judgment of eternal fire, and even the repentant may undergo a purifying fire.

3:12 Winnowing fork (cf. Ruth 3:2) is used figuratively for the separation of the repentant from the unrepentant. The harvest has begun.

3:13 The precise location of Jesus' baptism is disputed, and today competing venues vie for visitors. The traditional baptism site is Qasr el-Yahud, on the western bank of the Jordan River. However, the scene might instead be identified with "Bethany across [i.e., on the eastern side of] the Jordan" as

me?" 15 But Jesus answered him, "Let it be so now, for thus it is fitting for us to fulfill all
righteousness." Then he consented. 16 And when Jesus was baptized, immediately he went
up from the water, and behold, [o]the heavens were opened to him,[1] and he [p]saw the Spirit
of God descending like a dove and coming to rest on him; 17 and behold, [q]a voice from
heaven said, [r]"This is my beloved Son,[2] with whom I am well pleased."

The Temptation of Jesus

4 [s]Then Jesus was led up by the Spirit into the wilderness [t]to be tempted by the devil.
2 And after fasting [u]forty days and forty nights, he [v]was hungry. 3 And [w]the tempter
came and said to him, "If you are [x]the Son of God, command [y]these stones to become loaves
of bread." 4 But he answered, [z]"It is written,

> [a]'Man shall not live by bread alone,
> but by every word that comes from the mouth of God.'"

5 [b]Then the devil took him to [c]the holy city and set him on the pinnacle of the temple 6 and
said to him, "If you are the Son of God, throw yourself down, for it is written,

> [d]'He will command his angels concerning you,'

and

> "'On their hands they will bear you up,
> lest you strike your foot against a stone.'"

7 Jesus said to him, "Again [e]it is written, [f]'You shall not [g]put the Lord your God to the test.'"
8 [h]Again, the devil took him to a very high mountain and showed him all the kingdoms
of the world and their glory. 9 And he said to him, "All these I will give you, if you will fall
down and worship me." 10 Then Jesus said to him, "Be gone, [i]Satan! For [j]it is written,

[1] Some manuscripts omit *to him* [2] Or *my Son, my* (or *the*) *Beloved*

16 [o]Acts 7:56 [p]John 1:32, 33; [Luke 4:18, 21; Acts 10:38]
17 [q]John 12:28 [r]ch. 17:5; 2 Pet. 1:17; [Ps. 2:7; Isa. 42:1; Eph. 1:6; Col. 1:13; 1 John 5:9]

Chapter 4

1 [s]For ver. 1-11, see Mark 1:12, 13; Luke 4:1-13 [t][Heb. 2:18; 4:15]
2 [u][Deut. 9:9, 18; 1 Kgs. 19:8] [v][John 4:6, 7]
3 [w]1 Thess. 3:5 [x]See ch. 14:33 [y][ch. 3:9]
4 [z]ver. 7, 10; Eph. 6:17 [a]Cited from Deut. 8:3; [John 4:34]
5 [b]Luke 4:9 [c]ch. 27:53; Neh. 11:18; Isa. 48:2; 52:1; Rev. 11:2; [Ps. 46:4; 48:1; Rev. 21:2; 22:19]
6 [d]Cited from Ps. 91:11, 12
7 [e]ver. 4, 10 [f]Cited from Deut. 6:16 [g][Isa. 7:12]
8 [h]Luke 4:5
10 [i]See 1 Chr. 21:1 [j]ver. 4, 7

noted in John 1:28 (though this text may imply that John had baptized Jesus earlier and perhaps in a different locale). It is likely that John baptized people in more than one location (cf. Luke 3:3; John 3:23; 10:40).

3:14 Jesus goes to the desert to be baptized by John, but **John would have prevented him**, because he knows Jesus' identity as the mightier one who brings messianic baptism.

3:15 for us to fulfill all righteousness. Jesus' baptism inaugurates his ministry and fulfills God's saving activity prophesied throughout the OT, culminating with his death on the cross (cf. John 1:31–34). In so doing, Jesus also endorses John's ministry and message and links his mission to John's. Although he needed no repentance or cleansing, Jesus identifies with the sinful people he came to save through his substitutionary life and death (cf. 2 Cor. 5:21).

3:16 The **Spirit of God** anoints Jesus as Israel's King and Messiah and commissions him as God's righteous "servant" (cf. Isa. 42:1).

3:17 The **voice from heaven** confirms the eternally existing relationship of divine love that the Son and Father share as well as Jesus' identity as the messianic Son of God (Ps. 2:7). This **beloved Son** is the triumphant messianic King, yet he is also the humble "servant" into whose hands the Father is **well pleased** to place the mission to bring salvation to the nations (Isa. 42:1–4).

4:1–25 *Jesus the Messiah Begins to Advance the Messianic Kingdom.* Jesus triumphs over the devil in the wilderness (vv. 1–11), proclaims the kingdom of God (vv. 12–17), and calls disciples to follow him (vv. 18–22).

4:1–11 *Temptations of the Messiah.* The temptations are a diabolical attempt to subvert God's plan for human redemption by causing Jesus to fall into sin and disobedience, thus disqualifying him as the sinless Savior.

4:1 Jesus was led up by the Spirit. The Holy Spirit guided Jesus in his earthly life, providing a pattern for Jesus' followers to be empowered and led by the Holy Spirit (cf. notes on Gal. 5:16; 5:17; 5:18). The Greek for **tempted** (*peirazō*) can also mean "test." While God clearly never tempts anyone to do evil (see note on James 1:13), he does use circumstances to test a person's character (e.g., Heb. 11:17). **by the devil.** *Diabolos* (Gk. "slanderer, accuser") is here preceded by the definite article to indicate that this one who tempts Jesus is uniquely "the devil" (see also Matt. 4:5, 8, 11; 13:39; 25:41). Although the devil intends to thwart God's plan and purposes, the Father uses his evil intention for the good purpose of strengthening Jesus in his messianic role.

4:2 fasting forty days and forty nights. Jesus' experience of 40 days of fasting in the wilderness corresponds to Israel's experience of 40 years of testing in the wilderness (Deut. 8:2–3). Jesus endured his testing victoriously and obediently. Moses also fasted and prayed for 40 days and nights on two occasions (Ex. 24:18; 34:28; Deut. 9:9, 11, 18, 25; 10:10; cf. Elijah in 1 Kings 19:8). Fasting was a means of focusing intently on prayer. Forty days is about the longest a human can fast without permanent bodily harm.

4:3 If you are the Son of God. Jesus, of course, was (and is) the Son of God, but he refused to be tricked by the devil into using his divine prerogatives to make the trial any easier for himself. Jesus obeyed as a man, as the representative for all who believe, so as to "fulfill all righteousness" (3:15) on behalf of his people.

4:4 It is written. Jesus responds to each temptation by quoting from Deuteronomy, linking his experience to Israel's in the desert. In Deut. 8:2 Moses reminds the Israelites of God's testing through hunger and his miraculous provision of manna.

4:5 The holy city is Jerusalem, and the **pinnacle of the temple** is probably the southeast corner of the temple area, the top of which was some 300 feet (91 m) above the floor of the Kidron Valley (cf. Josephus, *Jewish Antiquities* 15.411–412). See The Temple Mount in the Time of Jesus, pp. 1924–1925.

4:6–7 for it is written. The devil's quotation of Psalm 91 is a blatant misuse of Scripture in an effort to manipulate Jesus. Such a spectacular display as jumping from this great height unharmed would have gained him an enthusiastic following, but it would not have followed the Father's messianic and redemptive plan of suffering and proclaiming the kingdom of heaven.

4:9 fall down and worship me. The devil offers a shortcut to Jesus' future reign in God's kingdom—a shortcut that side-steps Jesus' redemptive work on the cross and comes at the cost of exchanging the love of the Father for the worship of Satan. **All these I will give you** was a lie (see note on Luke 4:5–8; cf. John 8:44.)

[k]"'You shall worship the Lord your God
and [l]him only shall you serve.'"

11 Then the devil left him, and behold, [m]angels came and were ministering to him.

Jesus Begins His Ministry

12 Now when he heard that [n]John had been arrested, [o]he withdrew into Galilee. 13 And
leaving [p]Nazareth he went and lived in [q]Capernaum by [r]the sea, in the territory of [s]Zebulun
and Naphtali, 14 [t]so that what was spoken by the prophet Isaiah might be fulfilled:

15 [u]"The land of Zebulun and the land of Naphtali,
the way of the sea, beyond the Jordan, Galilee of the Gentiles—
16 [v]the people dwelling in darkness
have seen a great light,
and for those dwelling in the region and [w]shadow of death,
on them a light has dawned."

17 [x]From that time Jesus began to preach, saying, [z]"Repent, for the kingdom of heaven is
at hand."

Jesus Calls the First Disciples

18 [a]While walking by [b]the Sea of Galilee, he saw two brothers, Simon (who is called
Peter) and Andrew his brother, casting a net into the sea, for they were fishermen. 19 And
he said to them, "Follow me, and I will make you [c]fishers of men."[1] 20 Immediately they
left their nets and followed him. 21 And going on from there he saw two other brothers,
James the son of Zebedee and John his brother, in the boat with Zebedee their father,

[1] The Greek word *anthropoi* refers here to both men and women

10 [k]Cited from Deut. 6:13 [l]1 Sam. 7:3
11 [m]ch. 26:53; Luke 22:43
12 [n]ch. 14:3; Mark 1:14; Luke 3:19, 20; [John 3:24] [o]Luke 4:14
13 [p]See ch. 2:23 [q][ch. 9:1] [r]John 6:1 [s]Josh. 19:32-34
14 [t]See ch. 1:22
15 [u]Cited from Isa. 9:1, 2
16 [v]Isa. 42:7; Luke 1:79 [w]Job 3:5; Ps. 23:4; Amos 5:8
17 [x]Mark 1:14 [z]ch. 3:2
18 [a]For ver. 18-22, see Mark 1:16-20; [Luke 5:2-11; John 1:40-42] [b]ver. 13
19 [c]ch. 13:47

4:11 Then the devil left him. Jesus resisted the devil by standing firm on God's Word, setting an example for his followers (cf. James 4:7; 1 Pet. 5:9). **angels came and were ministering to him**. Their ministering probably included much needed physical sustenance. All of heaven knew the significance of Jesus' initial victory in this cosmic battle.

Jesus' Ministry in Galilee

Jesus spent most of his life and ministry in the region of Galilee, a mountainous area in northern Palestine. He grew up in the hill town of Nazareth, about 3.5 miles (5.6 km) south of the Gentile administrative center of Sepphoris. Soon after he began his public ministry, Jesus relocated to Capernaum on the Sea of Galilee. By Jesus' time, a thriving fishing industry had developed around the Sea, and several of Jesus' disciples were fishermen.

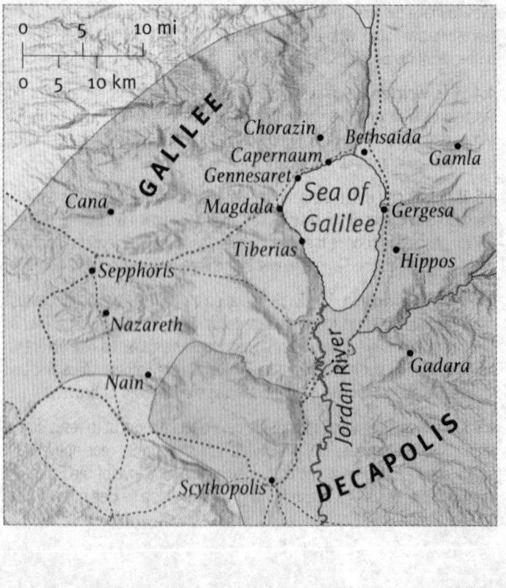

4:12–25 *Jesus the Messiah Begins His Galilean Ministry.* The duration of Jesus' ministry has traditionally been thought to have been three years: a year of obscurity, a year of popularity, and a year of increasing rejection. Matthew and the other Synoptic Gospels (Mark and Luke) largely omit discussing the first, obscure year, but it is recounted in John's Gospel (cf. John 1–4).

4:12 John had been arrested. Jesus returns to Galilee amid a gathering storm over the imprisonment of John the Baptist by Herod Antipas, one of the sons of Herod the Great (cf. 11:2; 14:1–12; see Jewish and Roman Rulers, pp. 1786–1787).

4:13 Capernaum, on the northern shore of the Sea of Galilee (see note on Mark 1:21), will remain Jesus' base of operations and his new hometown for the duration of his ministry in Galilee.

4:16 darkness . . . light. The region of Zebulun and Naphtali (v. 13) had experienced turmoil under Assyrian domination (2 Kings 15:29) and the Jewish inhabitants had longed for liberation from Gentile rule. They are now the first to see the great light of God's deliverance in Jesus.

4:17 From that time marks a significant turning point in Matthew's narrative (cf. 16:21), indicating that the preparations for Jesus' messianic ministry are complete. **Repent, for the kingdom of heaven is at hand**. Jesus' message builds on that of John the Baptist (see note on 3:2).

4:18–22 Peter, **James**, and **John** will become the inner circle among Jesus' 12 disciples.

4:18–19 two brothers, Simon (who is called Peter) and Andrew. These brothers had been followers of Jesus for about a year (cf. John 1:35–42) but apparently had returned for a time to their normal work. **casting a net into the sea**. A circular cast net, 20–25 feet (6.1–7.6 m) in diameter with lead sinkers attached to the outer edge, enveloped fish as it sank. **Follow me**. Jesus calls them to abandon their ordinary occupations (Matt. 4:20) and accompany him full-time.

4:21 A **boat**, dated from around or before the first century A.D. by radiocarbon analysis and associated pottery, was found in the Sea of Galilee south of Kibbutz Ginnosar in 1986 (see Galilean Fishing Boat, p. 1851). It is consistent with boat representations in mosaics from Migdal/Magdala (also on the Sea of Galilee). Approximately 26.5 feet long and 7.5 feet wide (8 by 2.3 m), it could hold about 15 people (including four rowers and a helmsman). It probably had both fore and aft decks and a central mast and sail, with positions for two sets of oars on both sides.

mending their nets, and he called them. 22 Immediately they left the boat and their father
and followed him.

Jesus Ministers to Great Crowds

23 [d]And he went throughout all Galilee, [e]teaching in their synagogues and [f]proclaim-
ing the gospel of the kingdom and [g]healing every disease and every affliction among the
people. 24 So his fame spread throughout all [h]Syria, and [g]they brought him all the sick,
those afflicted with various diseases and [i]pains, [j]those oppressed by demons, [k]epileptics,
and [l]paralytics, and he healed them. 25 [m]And great crowds followed him from Galilee and
the [n]Decapolis, and from Jerusalem and Judea, and from beyond the Jordan.

The Sermon on the Mount

5 Seeing the crowds, [o]he went up on the mountain, and when he [p]sat down, his disciples
came to him.

The Beatitudes

2 And [q]he opened his mouth and taught them, saying:
3 [r]"Blessed are [s]the poor in spirit, for [u]theirs is the kingdom of heaven.

23 [d]Mark 1:39 [e]ch. 9:35; 13:54; Mark 1:21; Luke 4:15; John 18:20 [f]ch. 24:14; Luke 4:43; [ch. 13:19] [g]ch. 8:16; 14:35, 36; Mark 1:34; 6:55, 56
24 [h]Luke 2:2 [g][See ver. 23 above] [i]ch. 8:6 [j][John 10:21] [k]ch. 17:15 [l]ch. 9:2, 6
25 [m]Mark 3:7, 8; Luke 6:17 [n]Mark 5:20

Chapter 5

1 [o]ch. 15:29 [p]Luke 4:20
2 [q]Ps. 78:2
3 [r]For ver. 3-12, [Luke 6:20-23] [s][Isa. 61:1; 66:2] [u][Luke 12:32]

4:22 left the boat and their father. They relinquished commitment to the family business and their livelihood to join Jesus' messianic mission.

4:23 The **Galilee** region had a population of about 300,000 in 200 or more villages and towns, with no major cities in the area. Jesus' ministry included **teaching** disciples and those already familiar with his message, **proclaiming** truth to those unfamiliar with the message, and **healing** physical, emotional, and spiritual infirmities. Healing of **every disease and every affliction** gives an amazing foretaste of the age to come, where there will be no more disease (1 Cor. 15:42–43; Phil. 3:21; Rev. 21:4). Jesus combined ministry that met people's physical needs with ministry to their minds and hearts (proclaiming **the gospel of the kingdom**). On **synagogues**, see note on Luke 4:16 and The Synagogue and Jewish Worship, pp. 1956–1957.

4:24 Syria. A Gentile region north of Galilee, between Damascus and the Mediterranean Sea.

4:25 The **great crowds** that **followed** Jesus had responded in some sense to his teaching and healing ministry but had not yet become his disciples (cf. 5:1). **Decapolis** (Gk. "ten cities") is the Roman and generally Gentile district to the south and east of the Sea of Galilee. **Beyond the Jordan** commonly referred to the region of Perea, or more generally the territory east of the Jordan River.

5:1–7:29 *The Authoritative Message of the Messiah: Kingdom Life for His Disciples.* This is the first of five major discourses in Matthew (chs. 5–7; 10; 13; 18–20; 24–25). Speaking to his disciples (5:1), Jesus expounds the reality of discipleship lived in the presence and power of the kingdom of God but within the everyday world. Some interpreters have thought the purpose of this sermon was to describe a moral standard so impossibly high that it is relevant only for a future millennial kingdom. Others have thought its primary purpose was to portray the absoluteness of God's moral perfection and thereby to drive people to despair of their own righteousness, so they will trust in the imputed righteousness of Christ. Both views fail to recognize that these teachings, rightly understood, form a challenging but practical ethic that Jesus expects his followers to live by in this present age. The sermon, commonly called the "Sermon on the Mount," is probably a summary of a longer message, but the structure is a unified whole. It has similarities to the "Sermon on the Plain" in Luke 6:17–49, but there are also significant differences. The three main theories about their relationship are: (1) they record the same sermon but Matthew and Luke give summaries that report different sections and emphases; (2) they record two different sermons, given on different occasions but repeating much of the same content, as itinerant preachers often do; and (3) either Matthew or Luke, or both, have collected sayings that Jesus gave on different occasions and put them together in a sermon format. View (3) seems to make Matthew's presentation of this as a single historical event untruthful (cf. Matt. 5:1–2 with 7:28–29; 8:1; and Luke 6:17, 20 with Luke 7:1), and evangelical commentators have not generally adopted it. Views (1) and (2) are both possible, and it is difficult to decide between them.

5:1–16 *Setting, Beatitudes, and Witness of the Kingdom of Heaven.* In his Beatitudes, Jesus makes pronouncements to the crowds and religious leaders and gives instructions to his disciples concerning the nature of life in the kingdom (vv. 3–12). He follows this with two piercing metaphors on salt and light to illustrate the impact that the disciples will have on the world around them (vv. 13–16).

5:1 mountain. The traditional site of this sermon (though Matthew does not pinpoint the location) is above Tabgha, near Capernaum, on a ridge of hills northwest of the town, with a magnificent view of the Sea of Galilee. A twentieth-century church marks this site today, although down the hill in Tabgha there are remains of a small Byzantine chapel (probably from the 4th century) commemorating the sermon. This ridge is likely also where Jesus went "to a desolate place" (14:13; cf. Mark 1:35) and where he went "up on the mountain" (Matt. 14:23; 28:16). **he sat down.** Teachers in Judaism typically taught while sitting (cf. 23:2), a position Jesus takes regularly (cf. 13:1–2; 15:29; 24:3–4; 26:55).

5:2 While Jesus was seated, **he opened his mouth** (a Jewish idiom) **and taught them**, i.e., his disciples who had come to him (v. 1). "Disciples" (Gk. "learners") were those who had made a commitment to Jesus as the Messiah; the "crowds" (v. 1) were those who were curious and often astounded by his teaching and ministry (7:28–29) yet for the most part remained neutral and uncommitted.

5:3–12 The Beatitudes all begin with "Blessed are . . ." They are called "beatitudes" from Latin *beatus*, "blessed, happy" (but see note on v. 3). These short statements summarize the essence of the Sermon on the Mount.

5:3 Blessed. More than a temporary or circumstantial feeling of happiness, this is a state of well-being in relationship to God that belongs to those who respond to Jesus' ministry. The **poor in spirit** are those who recognize they are in need of God's help. **theirs is the kingdom of heaven.** It belongs to those who confess their spiritual bankruptcy. On a contrast with the first seven beatitudes, see note on 23:13–36.

Jesus' Five Discourses

The authoritative message of the Messiah (Sermon on the Mount)	chs. 5–7
The authoritative mission of the Messiah's messengers	ch. 10
The mysteries of the messianic kingdom revealed in parables	ch. 13
The community of the Messiah revealed	chs. 18–20
The delay, return, and judgment of the Messiah (Olivet Discourse)	chs. 24–25

4 “Blessed are [v]those who mourn, for they shall be comforted.
5 “Blessed are the [w]meek, for they [w]shall inherit the earth.
6 “Blessed are those who hunger and [x]thirst [y]for righteousness, for they shall be
satisfied.
7 “Blessed are [z]the merciful, for they shall receive mercy.
8 “Blessed are [a]the pure in heart, for [b]they shall see God.
9 “Blessed are [c]the peacemakers, for [d]they shall be called [e]sons[1] of God.
10 [f]“Blessed are those who are persecuted for righteousness’ sake, for [u]theirs is the kingdom of heaven.
11 [g]“Blessed are you when others revile you and persecute you and utter all kinds of
evil against you falsely [h]on my account. 12 [i]Rejoice and be glad, for your reward is great in
heaven, for [j]so they persecuted the prophets who were before you.

Salt and Light

13 “You are the salt of the earth, [k]but if salt has lost its taste, how shall its saltiness be
restored? It is no longer good for anything except to be thrown out and trampled under
people’s feet.
14 [l]“You are the light of the world. A city set on a hill cannot be hidden. 15 [m]Nor do people
light a lamp and put it under a basket, but on a stand, and it gives light to all in the house.
16 In the same way, let your light shine before others, so [n]that[2] they may see your good
works and [o]give glory to your Father who is in heaven.

Christ Came to Fulfill the Law

17 [p]“Do not think that I have come to abolish [q]the Law or the Prophets; I have not come
to abolish them but [r]to fulfill them. 18 For truly, I say to you, [s]until heaven and earth pass
away, not an iota, not a dot, will pass from the Law until all is accomplished. 19 [t]Therefore
whoever relaxes [u]one of the least of these commandments and teaches others to do the same

4 [v]Isa. 61:2, 3; John 16:20; 2 Cor. 1:7; 7:10; Rev. 21:4; [James 4:9, 10]
5 [w]Ps. 37:11
6 [x]Ps. 42:2; Isa. 55:1, 2; John 7:37 [y]2 Tim. 2:22; [ch. 6:33]
7 [z]ch. 18:33; 25:34-36; Prov. 19:17; Luke 6:36; 2 Tim. 1:16; Heb. 6:10
8 [a]Ps. 24:4; 2 Tim. 2:22; [1 Pet. 1:22] [b]Heb. 12:14; 1 John 3:2, 3; Rev. 22:4; [1 Cor. 13:12]
9 [c]James 3:18 [d]1 John 3:1 [e]Rom. 8:14
10 [f]2 Tim. 2:12; James 5:11; 1 Pet. 3:14 [u][See ver. 3 above]
11 [g]Heb. 11:26; 1 Pet. 4:14 [h]John 15:21
12 [i]Acts 5:41; Rom. 5:3; 2 Cor. 12:10; Col. 1:11, 24; Heb. 10:34; James 1:2; 1 Pet. 4:13 [j]See ch. 21:35
13 [k]Mark 9:50; Luke 14:34
14 [l]Eph. 5:8; Phil. 2:15; [John 8:12]
15 [m]Mark 4:21; Luke 8:16; 11:33
16 [n]Philem. 6; 1 Pet. 2:12 [o]John 15:8; 2 Cor. 9:13; Phil. 1:11; [ch. 9:8]
17 [p]Rom. 3:31 [q]ch. 7:12 [r][Rom. 10:4; 13:8; Gal. 3:24]
18 [s]Luke 16:17; [ch. 24:35]
19 [t][1 Cor. 3:12-15] [u][Gal. 3:10; James 2:10]

[1] Greek *huioi*; see Preface [2] Or *house*. [16] *Let your light so shine before others that*

5:4 those who mourn. The spiritual, emotional, or financial loss resulting from sin should lead to mourning and a longing for God’s forgiveness and healing (cf. 2 Cor. 7:10).

5:5 The **meek** are the “gentle” (cf. 11:29), those who do not assert themselves over others in order to further their own agendas in their own strength, but who will nonetheless **inherit the earth** because they trust in God to direct the outcome of events. Cf. Ps. 37:11.

5:6 Those who hunger and thirst for righteousness recognize that God is the ultimate source of real righteousness, so they long for his righteous character to be evident in people’s lives on earth. They **shall be satisfied** by responding to his invitation to be in relationship with him.

5:7 The kindness and forgiveness that the **merciful** show to others will also be shown to them.

5:8 The pure in heart are those whose pursuit of purity and uprightness affects every area of life. **they shall see God**. Note the ultimate fulfillment in Rev. 22:4; cf. note on John 1:18. In contrast to Jewish traditions that overemphasized external ritual purity, Jesus taught that purity of heart was most important (cf. note on Matt. 5:28).

5:9 peacemakers. Those who promote God’s messianic peace (Hb. *shalom*, total well-being both personally and communally) will receive the ultimate reward of being called **sons of God** (see note on Gal. 3:26) as they reflect the character of their heavenly Father.

5:10 Those who are persecuted are those who have been wrongly treated because of their faith. God is pleased when his people show that they value him above everything in the world, and this happens when they courageously remain faithful amid opposition **for righteousness’ sake**.

5:11–12 Blessed are you when others revile you and persecute you . . . on my account. Just as Jesus experienced opposition and persecution, his disciples can expect the same. Their reward may not come on earth, but it surely will be theirs **in heaven**. **so they persecuted the prophets**. Throughout history, beginning with Cain’s murder of Abel (Gen. 4:8; cf. 1 John 3:12), there have been those who oppose God’s people.

5:13 As **salt** is beneficial in a number of ways (as a preservative, seasoning, etc.), so are disciples of Jesus who influence the world for good.

5:14 light of the world. Jesus’ disciples have the kingdom life within them as a living testimony to those in the world who do not yet have the light.

5:15 The typical **lamp** in a Jewish home was fairly small and was placed on a **stand** to give maximum illumination.

5:16 The world will see the **light** of the kingdom through the **good works** done by Jesus’ disciples (and believers today), with the result that the **Father who is in heaven** will be glorified.

5:17–48 *The Messianic Kingdom in Relation to the Law.* Verses 17–20 explain how Jesus and the kingdom fulfill the law of Moses; this is the key to interpreting the Sermon on the Mount and indeed the whole of Jesus’ ministry. Jesus then offers six antitheses (vv. 21–48) that contrast proper and false interpretation and application of the OT.

5:17 abolish the Law or the Prophets. The “Law” or “Torah” refers to the first five books of the OT, while the “Prophets” includes the rest of the OT, all of which was held to have been written by prophets (cf. Matt. 13:35, which cites Ps. 78:2; on “Law [and the] Prophets,” cf. Matt. 7:12; 11:13; 22:40; Rom. 3:21). **but to fulfill them**. Jesus “fulfills” all of the OT in that it all points to him, not only in its specific predictions of a Messiah but also in its sacrificial system, which looked forward to his great sacrifice of himself, in many events in the history of Israel which foreshadowed his life as God’s true Son, in the laws which only he perfectly obeyed, and in the Wisdom Literature, which sets forth a behavioral pattern that his life exemplified (cf. Matt. 2:15; 11:13; 12:3–6, 39–41, 42; also Luke 24:27). Jesus’ gospel of the kingdom does not replace the OT but rather fulfills it as Jesus’ life and ministry, coupled with his interpretation, complete and clarify God’s intent and meaning in the entire OT.

5:18 until heaven and earth pass away. Jesus confirms the full authority of the OT as Scripture for all time (cf. 2 Tim. 3:15–16), even down to the smallest components of the written text: the **iota** is the smallest letter of the Greek alphabet (or the *yod* of the Hb. alphabet) and the **dot** likely refers to a tiny stroke or a part of a letter used to differentiate between Hebrew letters. **pass from the Law**. The OT remains an authoritative compendium of divine testimony and teaching, within which some elements (such as sacrifices

will be called least [v]in the kingdom of heaven, but whoever does them and teaches them will
be called great [v]in the kingdom of heaven. 20 For I tell you, unless your righteousness exceeds
[w]that of the scribes and Pharisees, you [x]will never enter the kingdom of heaven.

Anger

21 [y]"You have heard that it was said to those of old, [z]'You shall not murder; and whoever
murders will be liable [a]to judgment.' 22 But I say to you that [b]everyone who is angry with
his brother[1] will be liable [a]to judgment; whoever insults[2] his brother will be liable to the
council; and whoever says, 'You fool!' will be liable to [c]the hell[3] of fire. 23 [d]So if [e]you are
offering your gift at the altar and there remember that your brother has something against
you, 24 leave your gift there before the altar and go. First be reconciled to your brother,
and then come and offer your gift. 25 [f]Come to terms quickly with your accuser while you
are going with him to court, lest your accuser hand you over to the judge, and the judge
to the guard, and you be put in prison. 26 Truly, I say to you, [g]you will never get out until
you have paid the last penny.[4]

Lust

27 [h]"You have heard that it was said, [i]'You shall not commit adultery.' 28 But I say to you
that [j]everyone who looks at a woman with lustful intent has already committed adultery
with her in his heart. 29 [k]If your right eye [l]causes you to sin, tear it out and throw it away.
For it is better that you lose one of your members than that your whole body be thrown
into [m]hell. 30 [k]And if your right hand [l]causes you to sin, cut it off and throw it away. For it
is better that you lose one of your members than that your whole body go into [m]hell.

Divorce

31 [h]"It was also said, [n]'Whoever divorces his wife, let him give her a certificate of divorce.'
32 [o]But I say to you that everyone who divorces his wife, except on the ground of sexual

[1] Some manuscripts insert *without cause* [2] Greek *says Raca to* (a term of abuse) [3] Greek *Gehenna;* also verses 29, 30 [4] Greek *kodrantes,* Roman copper coin (Latin *quadrans*) worth about 1/64 of a *denarius* (which was a day's wage for a laborer)

19 [v]ch. 11:11; 18:1-4
20 [w][Rom. 10:3; Phil. 3:9] [x]John 3:5
21 [y]ver. 33; [ver. 27, 31, 38, 43] [z]Cited from Ex. 20:13; Deut. 5:17; [ch. 19:18; Mark 10:19; Luke 18:20; Rom. 13:9; James 2:11] [a][Deut. 16:18]
22 [b]1 John 3:15 [a][See ver. 21 above] [c]ch. 18:9; Mark 9:43; James 3:6; [ver. 29]
23 [d][ch. 6:15; Mark 11:25] [e]ch. 8:4; 23:18
25 [f]Luke 12:58, 59
26 [g][ch. 18:34, 35]
27 [h]See ver. 21 [i]Cited from Ex. 20:14; Deut. 5:18
28 [j]Job 31:1; Prov. 6:25; [2 Sam. 11:2]
29 [k]ch. 18:8, 9; Mark 9:43-48 [l][ch. 13:41; Luke 17:1] [m]ch. 10:28; 23:15, 33; Luke 12:5; [ver. 22]
30 [k][See ver. 29 above] [l][See ver. 29 above] [m][See ver. 29 above]
31 [h][See ver. 27 above] [n]ch. 19:7; Jer. 3:1; Cited from Deut. 24:1
32 [o]ch. 19:9; Mark 10:11, 12; Luke 16:18; [1 Cor. 7:10, 11]

and other ceremonial laws) predicted or foreshadowed events that would be accomplished in Jesus' ministry (see notes on Gal. 4:10; 5:1) and so are not now models for Christian behavior. **Until all is accomplished** points to Jesus' fulfillment of specific OT hopes, partly through his earthly life, death, and resurrection, and then more fully after his second coming.

5:19 These commandments refers to all the commands in the OT (although many will be applied differently once their purpose has been "fulfilled" in Christ; v. 17). The rabbis recognized a distinction between "light" commandments (such as tithing garden produce) and "weighty" commandments (such as those concerning idolatry, murder, etc.). **relaxes one of the least**. Jesus demands a commitment to both the least and the greatest commandments yet condemns those who confuse the two (cf. 23:23–24). The entire OT is the expression of God's will but is now to be taught according to Jesus' interpretation of its intent and meaning.

5:20 Jesus calls his disciples to a different kind and quality of **righteousness** than that of **the scribes and Pharisees**. They took pride in outward conformity to many extrabiblical regulations but still had impure hearts (see 23:5, 23, 27–28). But **kingdom** righteousness works from the inside out because it first produces changed hearts and new motivations (Rom. 6:17; 2 Cor. 5:17; Gal. 5:22–23; Phil. 2:12; Heb. 8:10), so that the actual conduct of Jesus' followers does in fact "[exceed] the righteousness of the scribes and Pharisees."

5:21–48 These verses demonstrate that Jesus' interpretation of the OT is the antithesis of faulty interpretations and applications by the religious leaders. Repeatedly introducing his comments with "You have heard that it was said" (vv. 21, 27, 33, 38, 43), Jesus corrects not the OT (see note on v. 43) but the misunderstandings of the OT that were prevalent at the time.

5:21 Premeditated **murder** is prohibited by the sixth commandment (Ex. 20:13) and under OT law carried the death penalty (Num. 35:31). The prohibition is grounded in the fact that humans are created in the image of God (Gen. 1:26–27; 9:6). Concerning unpremeditated murder (manslaughter), see notes on Deut. 19:4–6 and 19:8–10.

5:22 angry. The dangerous and destructive effect of human anger is likewise stressed throughout Scripture (e.g., Prov. 20:2; 22:3; 29:22; 2 Cor. 12:20; Gal. 5:20; Eph. 4:31; Col. 3:8; James 1:20). Anger typically entails a desire to damage or destroy the other person, either in some personal way or literally in the form of murder (cf. Matt. 5:21 and James 4:1–2). Calling someone a **fool** is closely related to anger, in that it represents a destructive attack on one's character and identity. Thus Jesus warns that the person who violates another person in this grievous way is **liable to the hell of fire**.

5:23–24 First be reconciled. Reconciliation with the person who has **something against you** must take precedence even over **offering** one's **gift** in worship. The one who initiates the reconciliation here is the one who has wronged the other person.

5:25–26 Come to terms quickly. The importance of reconciliation is illustrated by the example of the person who is about to be judged in **court**. Not to be reconciled will have disastrous consequences on a human level but much more so if one is not reconciled to God. (Regarding the question of Christians and lawsuits, see note on 1 Cor. 6:1.)

5:27 Adultery was considered an extremely serious offense (cf. Ex. 20:14) because, in addition to violating another person, it broke the marriage covenant (Mal. 2:14) that was a reflection of the relationship between God and his people.

5:28 with lustful intent (Gk. *pros to epithymēsai autēn*, lit., "for the purpose of lusting for her"). Lust begins in the **heart**, the center of a person's identity and will. It is not enough to maintain physical purity alone; one must also guard against engaging mentally in an act of unfaithfulness. Jesus is not adding to OT law but correctly interpreting it, for even in the Ten Commandments God had required purity of heart (Ex. 20:17; cf. 1 Sam. 16:7; Ps. 19:14; 24:4).

5:29–30 right eye . . . right hand. The right side often stood for the more powerful or important. The eye is the medium through which one is tempted to lust, and the hand represents the physical actions that result from lusting. **cut it off**. Jesus uses deliberate overstatement to emphasize the importance of maintaining exclusive devotion to one's spouse. Even things of great value should be given up if they are leading a person to sin. See note on Mark 9:43–48.

5:31–32 A certificate of divorce in the ancient world gave a woman the

immorality, makes her commit adultery, and [p]whoever marries a divorced woman commits adultery.

Oaths

33 "Again [h]you have heard that it was said to those of old, [q]'You shall not swear falsely, but
[r]shall perform to the Lord what you have sworn.' 34 But I say to you, [s]Do not take an oath at
all, either by heaven, for [t]it is the throne of God, 35 or by the earth, for it is his footstool, or
by Jerusalem, for it is [u]the city of the great King. 36 And do not take an oath by your head,
for you cannot make one hair white or black. 37 Let what you say be simply 'Yes' or 'No';
[v]anything more than this comes from evil.[1]

Retaliation

38 [h]"You have heard that it was said, [y]'An eye for an eye and a tooth for a tooth.' 39 But I say
to you, [z]Do not resist the one who is evil. But [a]if anyone [b]slaps you on the right cheek, turn to
him the other also. 40 And [z]if anyone would sue you and take your tunic,[2] let him have your
cloak as well. 41 And if anyone [c]forces you to go one mile, go with him two miles. 42 [d]Give to
the one who begs from you, and [e]do not refuse the one who would borrow from you.

Love Your Enemies

43 [f]"You have heard that it was said, [g]'You shall love your neighbor and hate your enemy.'
44 But I say to you, [i]Love your enemies and [j]pray for those who persecute you, 45 [k]so that you
may be sons of your Father who is in heaven. For he makes his sun rise on the evil and on

[1] Or *the evil one* [2] Greek *chiton*, a long garment worn under the cloak next to the skin

32 [p]Rom. 7:3
33 [h][See ver. 27 above] [q]Lev. 19:12; 1 Tim. 1:10 [r]Num. 30:2; Deut. 23:21; Eccles. 5:4
34 [s]James 5:12 [t]ch. 23:22; Isa. 66:1; Acts 7:49; See Rev. 4:2
35 [u]Ps. 48:2
37 [v][Prov. 10:19]
38 [h][See ver. 27 above] [y]Cited from Ex. 21:24; Lev. 24:20; Deut. 19:21
39 [z]1 Pet. 2:23 [a]For ver. 39-42, see Luke 6:29, 30; [Rom. 12:17] [b]ch. 26:67; Isa. 50:6; Lam. 3:30
40 [z][See ver. 39 above]
41 [c]ch. 27:32
42 [d]Ps. 37:21; Prov. 21:26 [e]Deut. 15:8; Ps. 37:26; 112:5; Luke 6:34, 35
43 [f]See ver. 21 [g]Cited from Lev. 19:18; See ch. 19:19
44 [i]Luke 6:27, 28; Rom. 12:20; [Ex. 23:4; Job 31:29, 30; Ps. 7:4] [j]Luke 23:34; Acts 7:60; 2 Tim. 4:16; 1 Pet. 3:9
45 [k]Luke 6:35; [Eph. 5:1; Phil. 2:15]

right to remarry (e.g., Mishnah, *Gittin* 9.3: "The essential formula in the bill of divorce is 'Lo, thou art free to marry any man'") and reflects the fact that divorce and remarriage were widely accepted and practiced in the first century world. **But I say to you** indicates that Jesus does not accept the practice of easy divorce represented in v. 31. Because divorce was widespread in ancient times, God had instituted a regulation through Moses that was intended to uphold the sanctity of marriage and to protect women from being divorced for no reason. (See notes on Deut. 24:1–4; Matt. 19:8.) Here and in 19:3–9, Jesus bases his teaching on God's original intention that marriage should be a permanent union of a man and woman as "one flesh" (Mark 10:8). Divorce breaks that union. **Sexual immorality** (Gk. *porneia*) can refer to adultery (Jer. 3:9; see also the use of the term in *Sir.* 23:23), prostitution (Nah. 3:4; 1 Cor. 6:13, 18), incest (1 Cor. 5:1), or fornication (Gen. 38:24; John 8:41). Scripture prohibits any kind of sexual intercourse outside of marriage (thus forbidding the practice of homosexuality and bestiality as well). **Except on the ground** of sexual immorality. This implies that when a divorce is obtained (by the injured party) *because of* the sexual immorality of one's spouse, then such a divorce is not morally wrong. But when a man divorces his wife wrongly (i.e., when his wife has not been sexually immoral), the husband thus **makes her commit adultery**. Even though some female Jewish divorcees would have gone back to live with their parents in shame, many would have sought to remarry (which seems to be the typical situation that Jesus is addressing here). Jesus is thus indicating that such second marriages begin with committing adultery, since the divorce would not have been valid in God's eyes. (On whether the adultery is onetime or continual, see note on Matt. 19:9.) But Jesus places primary blame on the husband who has wrongly divorced his wife, by stating that he (the husband) "makes her commit adultery." **Whoever marries a divorced woman** is not an isolated statement that applies to all divorced women, or it would contradict the "except" clause that Jesus had just given (as well as the further exception in 1 Cor. 7:15). The statement rather continues the same subject that Jesus had mentioned earlier in the sentence, and thus means, "whoever marries *such a wrongly divorced woman* commits adultery." See also the notes on Matt. 19:3–9; Mark 10:2–12; Luke 16:18; 1 Cor. 7:15; and Divorce and Remarriage, pp. 2545–2547.

5:33–37 An **oath** involved invoking God's name, or substitutes for it, to guarantee the truth of one's statements (cf. Num. 30:2). Jesus' disciples are not to swear **at all**. Instead, their character should be of such integrity that their words can be believed without an oath.

5:38 eye for an eye. This "law of retaliation" (Latin *lex talionis*) was God's means of maintaining justice and purging evil from among his people (see Deut. 19:20–21). It was intended to prevent inappropriate punishment (the punishment should fit the crime) and was imposed by civil authorities rather than individuals.

5:39 Do not resist the one who is evil. Jesus is not prohibiting the use of force by governments, police, or soldiers when combating evil (see notes on Luke 3:12–14; Rom. 13:1–4; 1 Pet. 2:13–14). Rather, Jesus' focus here is on individual conduct, as indicated by the contrast with Matt. 5:38, which shows that he is prohibiting the universal human tendency to seek personal revenge (see note on Rom. 12:19). **If anyone slaps you on the right cheek** pictures a backhanded slap given as an insult (a right-handed person would use the back of the hand to slap someone on the right cheek; cf. Mishnah, *Baba Kamma* 8.6). The word "slaps" translates Gk. *rhapizō*, "to slap, to strike with the open hand." **turn to him the other also**. One should not return an insulting slap, which would lead to escalating violence. In the case of a more serious assault, Jesus' words should not be taken to prohibit self-defense (see Luke 12:11; 22:36–38; Acts 22:1; 24:10) or fleeing from evil (see 1 Sam. 19:10; Luke 4:29–30; John 8:59; 10:39; 2 Cor. 11:32–33), for often a failure to resist a violent attack leads to even more serious abuse. Acting in love toward an attacker (Matt. 5:44; 22:39) will often include taking steps to prevent him from attempting further attacks. Jesus' teaching must be applied with wisdom in the light of related Scriptures that address similar situations (cf. note on 5:42).

5:42 Give to the one who begs from you. Christians should help those who are truly needy (and therefore forced to beg), but they are not required to give foolishly (cf. 7:6) or to a lazy person who is not in need (2 Thess. 3:10), or where giving would bring harm rather than benefit.

5:43 You have heard that it was said . . . hate your enemy. The OT never says that anyone should hate his or her enemy. This shows that, in his "you have heard" statements (vv. 21, 27, 33, 38, 43), Jesus is correcting not the OT itself but only misinterpretations of the OT. God's hatred of evil was a central theme in the OT (e.g., Ps. 5:4–5). Consequently, those who embodied evil were understood to be God's enemies, and it was natural to hate them (cf. Ps. 26:4–5; 139:21–22), but such hatred is never commanded by God.

5:44 Love your enemies. God hates evil, but he still brings many blessings in this life even to his enemies (v. 45) by means of "common grace" (the favor that he gives to all people and not just to believers). These blessings are intended to lead unbelievers to repentance (Acts 14:17; Rom. 2:4). Of course there is a sense in which God hates those who are resolutely and impenitently wicked (cf. Ps. 5:5; 11:5; Eph. 2:3), but God's blessings of common grace constitute his primary providential action toward mankind here and now.

5:45 sons. The children of the heavenly **Father** are those who respond to

the good, and [l]sends rain on the just and on the unjust. **46** [m]For if you love those who love
you, what reward do you have? Do not even the tax collectors do the same? **47** And if you
greet only your brothers,[1] what more are you doing than others? Do not even [n]the Gentiles
do the same? **48** [o]You therefore must be [p]perfect, [q]as your heavenly Father is perfect.

Giving to the Needy

6 "Beware of [r]practicing your righteousness before other people in order [s]to be seen by
them, for then you will have no reward from your Father who is in heaven.
2 [t]"Thus, when you give to the needy, sound no trumpet before you, as the hypocrites
do in the synagogues and in the streets, that they may [u]be praised by others. Truly, I say
to you, they have [v]received their reward. **3** But when you give to the needy, do not let your
left hand know what your right hand is doing, **4** so that your giving may be in secret. [w]And
your Father who sees in secret will reward you.

The Lord's Prayer

5 "And when you pray, you must not be like the hypocrites. For they love [x]to stand and
pray in the synagogues and at the street corners, that they may be seen by others. [y]Truly,
I say to you, they have received their reward. **6** But when you pray, [z]go into your room
and shut the door and pray to your Father who is in secret. [a]And your Father who sees in
secret will reward you.
7 "And when you pray, do not heap up empty phrases as [b]the Gentiles do, for [c]they think
that they will be heard [d]for their many words. **8** Do not be like them, [e]for your Father knows
what you need before you ask him. **9** [f]Pray then like this:

[g]"Our Father in heaven,
[h]hallowed be [i]your name.[2]
10 [j]Your kingdom come,

[1] Or *brothers and sisters*. The plural Greek word *adelphoi* (translated "brothers") refers to siblings in a family. In New Testament usage, depending on the context, *adelphoi* may refer either to *brothers* or to *brothers and sisters* [2] Or *Let your name be kept holy*, or *Let your name be treated with reverence*

45 [l]Acts 14:17
46 [m]Luke 6:32
47 [n]ch. 6:7, 32
48 [o][Luke 6:36] [p]ch. 19:21; 1 Cor. 2:6 (Gk.); Phil. 3:15 (Gk.); Col. 1:28; 4:12 (Gk.); James 1:4; 3:2; See Gen. 17:1 [q][Lev. 19:2; 1 Pet. 1:15]

Chapter 6

1 [r]1 John 2:29 [s]ver. 16; ch. 23:5
2 [t][1 Cor. 13:3] [u]John 5:44 [v]Luke 6:24
4 [w]ver. 6, 18
5 [x]Mark 11:25; Luke 18:11 [y]ver. 2, 16
6 [z]2 Kgs. 4:33; Isa. 26:20 [a]ver. 4, 18
7 [b]ver. 32; ch. 5:47 [c]1 Kgs. 18:26 [d]Prov. 10:19; Eccles. 5:2
8 [e]ver. 32
9 [f]For ver. 9-13, [Luke 11:2-4] [g]ver. 1 [h]Isa. 29:23; [Luke 1:49; 1 Pet. 3:15] [i]John 17:6
10 [j][ch. 3:2; 4:17]

his will as expressed in the ministry of Jesus (cf. 12:48–50). (Regarding "sons" [Gk. *huioi*], see ESV Preface, pp. 19–22.) **sun . . . rain**. God shows grace and care for all of his creatures; therefore Jesus' disciples are to imitate God and love both neighbor and enemy.

5:46–47 In Palestine, **tax collectors** were representatives of the Roman governing authorities. Their tendency to resort to extortion made them despised and hated by their own people (cf. Luke 19:8). Christians should not merely **do the same** as unbelievers; their transformed lives should result in behavior that shows significantly greater love.

5:48 be perfect, as your heavenly Father is perfect. Scripture is a reflection of God himself as he has made his will and character known to his people. As Christians seek to live in conformity to Scripture, they are in fact pursuing the very perfection of God. This verse provides the conclusion and summary to the antithesis section (vv. 21–48), showing that all of the Law and the Prophets find their perfect (Gk. *teleios*) fulfillment in the perfection of the Father, which is what all Jesus' disciples are called to pursue.

6:1–7:12 *The Development of Kingdom Life in the Real World.* Jesus sets forth principles for spirituality in religious life (6:1–18), everyday life (6:19–34), and community relationships (7:1–12).

6:1–18 Jesus gives examples of how a person's faith can be expressed in a hypocritical way, when giving to the needy (vv. 2–4), praying (vv. 5–15), and fasting (vv. 16–18).

6:1 before other people. Public acts of obedience are valuable and honorable, but if they are done merely for the sake of public recognition, there will be no reward from God (cf. vv. 2, 5, 16).

6:2–4 Hypocrites originally referred to Greek actors who wore different masks to play various roles. Jesus criticizes the religious leaders, most notably the Pharisees, for a particular form of hypocrisy: doing right things for the wrong reasons. To **give to the needy** was one of the pillars of piety, but the religious leaders gave to the needy in order to be **praised** by others. The tragic irony was that they had **received their reward** of public and professional acclaim, but that was all the reward they would ever receive, and such fleeting human adulation precludes satisfaction of the deep longing of people's hearts to stand approved by their **Father who sees in secret**.

6:5–15 Prayer was a pillar of Jewish piety. Public prayer, said aloud in the morning, afternoon, and evening, was common.

6:5–6 stand and pray in the synagogues. At the set time of prayer, pious Jews would stop what they were doing and pray, some discreetly, but others with pretentious display. Jesus did not condemn all public prayer, as indicated by his own prayers in public (e.g., 14:19; 15:36). One's internal motivation is the central concern. **shut the door**. Though public prayer has value, prayer completely away from public view allows a person (or group) to focus more exclusively on God.

6:7–8 heap up empty phrases. Pagans repeated the names of their gods or the same words over and over without thinking (cf. 1 Kings 18:26; Acts 19:34). Jesus is prohibiting mindless, mechanical repetition, not the earnest repetition that flows from the imploring heart (Mark 14:39; 2 Cor. 12:8; cf. Psalm 136; Isa. 6:3).

6:9–13 Jesus gives his disciples an example to follow when praying. The prayer has a beginning invocation and six petitions that give proper priorities. The first three petitions focus on the preeminence of God while the final three focus on personal needs in a community context.

6:9 Father (Gk. *patēr*, "father") would have been "Abba" in Aramaic, the everyday language spoken by Jesus (cf. Mark 14:36; Rom. 8:15; Gal. 4:6). It was the word used by Jewish children for their earthly fathers. However, since the term in both Aramaic and Greek was also used by adults to address their fathers, the claim that "Abba" meant "Daddy" is misleading and runs the risk of irreverence. Nevertheless, the idea of praying to God as "Our Father" conveys the authority, warmth, and intimacy of a loving father's care, while **in heaven** reminds believers of God's sovereign rule over all things. The theme of "heavenly Father" is found throughout the OT (Deut. 14:1; 32:6; Ps. 103:13; Jer. 3:4; 31:9; Hos. 11:1). Jesus' disciples are invited into the intimacy of God the Son with his Father. The concern of this first petition (see note on Matt. 6:9–13) is that God's **name** would be **hallowed**—that God would be treated with the highest honor and set apart as holy.

6:10 Christians are called to pray and work for the continual advance of God's **kingdom** on earth (the second petition; see note on vv. 9–13). The presence of God's kingdom in this age refers to the reign of Christ in the hearts and lives

[k] your will be done,[1]
[l] on earth as it is in heaven.
11 [m] Give us [n]this day our daily bread,[2]
12 and forgive us our debts,
as we also have forgiven our debtors.
13 And [o]lead us not into temptation,
but [p]deliver us from [q]evil.[3]

14 [r]For if you forgive others their trespasses, your heavenly Father will also forgive you,
15 [s]but if you do not forgive others their trespasses, neither will your Father forgive your
trespasses.

Fasting

16 "And [t]when you fast, do not look gloomy like the hypocrites, for they disfigure their
faces that their fasting may be seen by others. [u]Truly, I say to you, they have received their
reward. 17 But when you fast, [v]anoint your head and wash your face, 18 that your fasting
may not be seen by others but by your Father who is in secret. [w]And your Father who sees
in secret will reward you.

Lay Up Treasures in Heaven

19 [x]"Do not lay up for yourselves treasures on earth, where [y]moth and rust[4] destroy and
where thieves [z]break in and steal, 20 [x]but lay up for yourselves treasures in heaven, where
neither moth nor rust destroys and where thieves do not break in and steal. 21 For where
your treasure is, there your heart will be also.

[1] Or *Let your kingdom come, let your will be done* [2] Or *our bread for tomorrow* [3] Or *the evil one; some manuscripts add For yours is the kingdom and the power and the glory, forever. Amen* [4] Or *worm*; also verse 20

10 [k]ch. 26:42; Luke 22:42; Acts 21:14; [ch. 12:50; Heb. 13:21] [l]Ps. 103:20, 21; Dan. 4:35
11 [m]Prov. 30:8 [n][ver. 34]
13 [o]ch. 26:41; Mark 14:38; Luke 22:40, 46; [1 Cor. 10:13] [p]John 17:15; 2 Thess. 3:3; [2 Tim. 4:18] [q]See ch. 13:19
14 [r]Mark 11:25; Luke 6:37; Eph. 4:32; Col. 3:13
15 [s]ch. 18:35; See James 2:13
16 [t]Isa. 58:5 [u]ver. 2, 5
17 [v]Ruth 3:3; 2 Sam. 12:20
18 [w]ver. 4, 6
19 [x]ch. 19:21; Luke 12:21, 33, 34; 18:22; 1 Tim. 6:9, 10, 17-19; Heb. 13:5 [y]James 5:2, 3 [z]ch. 24:43
20 [x][See ver. 19 above]

of believers, and to the reigning presence of Christ in his body, the church—so that they increasingly reflect his love, obey his laws, honor him, do good for all people, and proclaim the good news of the kingdom. The third petition speaks of God's **will**. This means God's "revealed will" (see note on Eph. 5:17), which involves conduct that is pleasing to him as revealed in Scripture. Just as God's will is perfectly experienced in heaven, Jesus prays that it will be experienced on earth. The will of God will be expressed in its fullness only when God's kingdom comes in its final form, when Christ returns in power and great glory (see Matt. 24:30; cf. Rom. 8:18–25; Rev. 20:1–10), but it will increasingly be seen in this age as well (Matt. 13:31–33).

6:11 The fourth petition (see note on vv. 9–13) focuses on the disciples' **daily bread**, a necessity of life which by implication includes all of the believer's daily physical needs.

6:12 Forgive us our debts (the fifth petition) does not mean that believers need to ask daily for justification, since believers are justified forever from the moment of initial saving faith (Rom. 5:1, 9; 8:1; 10:10). Rather, this is a prayer for the restoration of personal fellowship with God when fellowship has been hindered by sin (cf. Eph. 4:30). Those who have received such forgiveness are so moved with gratitude toward God that they also eagerly forgive those who are **debtors** to them. On sin as a "debt" owed to God, see note on Col. 2:14.

6:13 This final (sixth) petition addresses the disciples' battle with sin and evil. **Lead us not into temptation**. The word translated "temptation" (Gk. *peirasmos*) can indicate either temptation or testing (see notes on 4:1; James 1:13). The meaning here most likely carries the sense, "Allow us to be spared from difficult circumstances that would tempt us to sin" (cf. Matt. 26:41). Although God never directly tempts believers (James 1:13), he does sometimes lead them into situations that "test" them (cf. Matt. 4:1; also Job 1; 1 Pet. 1:6; 4:12). In fact, trials and hardships will inevitably come to believers' lives, and believers should "count it all joy" (James 1:2) when trials come, for they are strengthened by them (James 1:3–4). Nonetheless, believers should never pray to be brought into such situations but should pray to be delivered from them, for hardship and temptation make obedience more difficult and will sometimes result in sin. Believers should pray to be delivered from temptation (cf. Matt. 26:41; Luke 22:40, 46; 2 Pet. 2:9; Rev. 3:10) and led in "paths of righteousness" (Ps. 23:3). **deliver us from evil**. The phrase translated "evil" (Gk. *tou ponērou*) can mean either "evil" or "the evil one," namely, Satan. The best protection from sin and temptation is to turn to God and to depend on his direction. "For yours is the kingdom and the power and the glory, forever. Amen" (ESV footnote) is evidently a later scribal addition, since the most reliable and oldest Greek manuscripts all lack these words, which is the reason why these words are omitted from most modern translations. However, there is nothing theologically incorrect about the wording (cf. 1 Chron. 29:11–13), nor is it inappropriate to include these words in public prayers.

6:14–15 forgive others. Jesus reemphasizes the importance of forgiving others, indicating that there is a direct relationship between having been forgiven by God and the forgiveness that his disciples of necessity must extend to others. As in v. 12, **forgive your trespasses** here refers to restoration of personal relationship with God, not to initial justification (cf. note on v. 12).

6:16–18 Various kinds of fasts were commonly practiced in OT times, though the law required only one fast a year, on the Day of Atonement (though fasting is probably implied by the command to "afflict yourselves"; Lev. 16:29–34; 23:26–32). In addition to abstaining from food, people were to humble themselves by praying, mourning, and wearing sackcloth. As with giving (Matt. 6:2–4) and praying (vv. 5–15), fasting is to be a matter of the heart between the Christian and God. **when you fast**. Jesus assumes that his disciples will fast. **Disfigure** indicates leaving one's face unwashed and sprinkled with ashes, with the intention of publicizing the physical hardships of fasting. **their reward**. See note on vv. 2–4. Anointing and washing (v. 17) signify preparations to enjoy life (cf. Eccles. 9:7–8).

6:19–34 The righteousness of the kingdom of heaven works out in the details of one's personal life. Jesus calls his followers to choose their master, either God or wealth (vv. 19–24), and to choose their outlook on life, either faith or worry (vv. 25–34).

6:19 moth . . . rust . . . thieves. See note on Luke 12:33–34.

6:20 But lay up for yourselves treasures in heaven implies that people often have a choice between activities that lead to greater earthly reward in the present (cf. vv. 2, 5, 16) and those that store up greater future reward in heaven. Elsewhere in the Gospels the consequences of making the wrong choice are shown to be eternally disastrous (see Mark 8:36; Luke 12:20–21).

6:21 Throughout Scripture, the **heart** refers to the center of one's being, involving one's emotions, reason, and will.

22 [a]"The eye is the lamp of the body. So, if your eye is healthy, your whole body will be
full of light, **23** [a]but if [b]your eye is bad, your whole body will be full of darkness. If then the
light in you is darkness, how great is the darkness!

24 [c]"No one can serve two masters, for either he will hate the one and love the other, or
he will be devoted to the one and despise the other. You cannot serve God and [d]money.[1]

Do Not Be Anxious

25 [e]"Therefore I tell you, [f]do not be anxious about your life, what you will eat or what
you will drink, nor about your body, what you will put on. Is not life more than food, and
the body more than clothing? **26** [g]Look at the birds of the air: they neither sow nor reap
nor gather into barns, and yet your heavenly Father feeds them. [h]Are you not of more
value than they? **27** And which of you by being anxious can add a single hour to his [i]span
of life?[2] **28** And why are you anxious about clothing? Consider the lilies of the field, how
they grow: they neither toil nor spin, **29** yet I tell you, [j]even Solomon in all his glory was
not arrayed like one of these. **30** But if God so clothes the grass of the field, which today is
alive and tomorrow is thrown into the oven, will he not much more clothe you, [k]O you of
little faith? **31** Therefore do not be anxious, saying, 'What shall we eat?' or 'What shall we
drink?' or 'What shall we wear?' **32** For [l]the Gentiles seek after all these things, and [m]your
heavenly Father knows that you need them all. **33** But [n]seek first [o]the kingdom of God and
his righteousness, [p]and all these things will be added to you.

34 [q]"Therefore do not be anxious about tomorrow, for tomorrow will be anxious for
itself. Sufficient for the day is its own trouble.

Judging Others

7 [r]"Judge not, that you be not judged. **2** [s]For with the judgment you pronounce you will
be judged, and [t]with the measure you use it will be measured to you. **3** Why do you see
the speck that is in your brother's eye, but [u]do not notice the log that is in your own eye?
4 Or how can you say to your brother, 'Let me take the speck out of your eye,' when there is
the log in your own eye? **5** You hypocrite, first take the log out of your own eye, and then
you will see clearly to take the speck out of your brother's eye.

6 [v]"Do not give [w]dogs what is holy, and do not throw your [x]pearls before pigs, lest they
trample them underfoot and turn to attack you.

[1] Greek *mammon*, a Semitic word for money or possessions [2] Or *a single cubit to his stature*; a *cubit* was about 18 inches or 45 centimeters

22 [a]Luke 11:34, 35
23 [a][See ver. 22 above] [b]ch. 20:15; Deut. 15:9; Prov. 28:22
24 [c]Luke 16:13; [Rom. 6:16; James 4:4] [d]Luke 16:9, 11, 13
25 [e]For ver. 25-33, see Luke 12:22-31 [f]ver. 27, 28, 31, 34; ch. 10:19; 13:22 (Gk.); 1 Cor. 7:32 (Gk.); Phil. 4:6; 1 Pet. 5:7
26 [g][Job 38:41; Ps. 147:9] [h]ch. 10:31
27 [i]Luke 2:52
29 [j]1 Kgs. 10:4-7
30 [k]ch. 8:26; 14:31; 16:8; [ch. 17:20]
32 [l]ver. 7 [m]ver. 8
33 [n][ch. 5:6, 20] [o]ver. 10 [p][1 Kgs. 3:11-14; Mark 10:29, 30; 1 Tim. 4:8; 1 Pet. 3:9]
34 [q][James 4:13, 14]

Chapter 7

1 [r]For ver. 1-5, see Luke 6:37, 38, 41, 42; [Rom. 14:13; 1 Cor. 4:5; James 5:9]
2 [s]Rom. 2:1, 3; 14:10; James 2:13; 4:11, 12 [t]Mark 4:24; [Judg. 1:7]
3 [u][John 8:7-9]
6 [v]ch. 15:26; [Prov. 9:7, 8; 23:9] [w][Phil. 3:2; Rev. 22:15] [x]ch. 13:46

6:22–23 The **eye** (similar to the "heart" in Jewish literature) is a **lamp** that reveals the quality of a person's inner life. A **healthy** eye (clear vision) suggests loyal devotion to God, while a **bad** eye (impaired vision) connotes moral corruption.

6:24 Serve (Gk. *douleuō*) indicates the work of a slave, not an employee. Since a slave is the sole property of one master, he must give the master exclusive service. A disciple's loyalties cannot be divided—that is, one is either a slave to **God** or to **money**.

6:25 Therefore . . . do not be anxious. If one makes the right choices (see vv. 19–24), there is ("therefore") no reason that one should be anxious. Jesus gives two *a fortiori* ("how much more") examples—"look at the birds" (v. 26), "consider the lilies" (v. 28)—to show that, since God cares even for the birds and the lilies, how much more will he care for his own. To be anxious, then, demonstrates a lack of trust in God, who promises that he will graciously care for "all these things" (v. 33; cf. Rom. 8:32). See also Phil. 4:5–6.

6:26 Human beings are of **more value** than animals (cf. 10:31; 12:12) because only humans, out of all God's creatures, are created "in the image of God" (Gen. 1:27), because God gave the human race dominion over all the earth and all its creatures (Gen. 1:28), and because God loved human beings so much "that he gave his only Son" to die for our sins (John 3:16).

6:30 Grass was a natural source of fuel for fire and a common biblical metaphor for human frailty (e.g., Ps. 37:2; 102:4). **Little faith** implies a deficiency rather than an absence of faith (cf. Matt. 8:26).

7:1–12 Jesus moves from personal temptations to interpersonal temptations. He warns against inappropriate judging (vv. 1–5) and commends appropriate evaluation (v. 6). He then looks at God's guidance as the source of the believer's stability in relationship to others (vv. 7–12).

7:1–2 Judge not forbids pronouncing another person guilty before God. But see note on vv. 3–5. **For with the judgment you pronounce you will be judged**. Undue harshness and a judgmental attitude toward others will result in being treated in much the same way by God.

7:3–5 Jesus may have drawn on his background as a carpenter (13:55; Mark 6:3) for his metaphor of a **log in your own eye**, which of course was hyperbole (intentional overstatement; cf. Matt. 5:29–30). **then you will see clearly to take the speck out of your brother's eye**. Jesus does not forbid all evaluation or even judgment of others, for ultimately the one who feels grieved and humbled over his own sin can help remove the "speck" from others. What Jesus does rule out is pride that views oneself as better than others (cf. Gal. 6:1).

7:6 In the ancient world, **dogs** lived in squalor and scavenged the streets for food (Ps. 59:14–15). Jews considered them unclean and used the term to describe those apart from, or enemies of, Israel's covenant community (cf. 1 Sam. 17:43; Ps. 22:16; Prov. 26:11). **Pigs** were rejected by Jews, probably because they too were scavenging animals, and they were unclean according to OT law. **Pearls** symbolize the great value of the message of the kingdom of heaven (cf. Matt. 13:45–46). Believers are to be merciful, forgiving, and slow to judge (7:1–5), yet they should wisely discern the true character of people and not indefinitely continue proclaiming the gospel to those who adamantly reject it, so that they can move on and proclaim the gospel to others (cf. 10:14; also Acts 13:46; 18:6; Titus 3:10–11).

Ask, and It Will Be Given

7 [y]"Ask, [z]and it will be given to you; [a]seek, and you will find; [b]knock, and it will be opened
to you. 8 For everyone who asks receives, and the one who seeks finds, and to the one who
knocks it will be opened. 9 Or which one of you, if his son asks him for [c]bread, will give
him [c]a stone? 10 Or if he asks for a fish, will give him a serpent? 11 If you then, [d]who are evil,
know how to give good gifts to your children, how much more will [z]your Father who is
in heaven give good things to those who ask him!

The Golden Rule

12 "So [e]whatever you wish that others would do to you, do also to them, for this is [f]the
Law and the Prophets.
13 [g]"Enter by the narrow gate. For the gate is wide and the way is easy[1] that leads to
destruction, and those who enter by it are many. 14 For the gate is narrow and [h]the way is
hard that leads to life, and [i]those who find it are few.

A Tree and Its Fruit

15 [j]"Beware of false prophets, who come to you in sheep's clothing but inwardly are
[k]ravenous wolves. 16 You will recognize them [l]by their fruits. Are grapes gathered from
thornbushes, or figs from thistles? 17 So, [m]every healthy tree bears good fruit, but the diseased tree bears bad fruit. 18 A healthy tree cannot bear bad fruit, nor can a diseased tree
bear good fruit. 19 [n]Every tree that does not bear good fruit is cut down and thrown into
the fire. 20 Thus you will recognize them [l]by their fruits.

I Never Knew You

21 [o]"Not everyone who [p]says to me, 'Lord, Lord,' will [q]enter the kingdom of heaven, but
the one who [r]does the will of my Father who is in heaven. 22 [s]On that day [t]many will say to
me, 'Lord, Lord, did we not [u]prophesy in your name, and cast out demons [v]in your name,
and do many mighty works in your name?' 23 [t]And then will I declare to them, 'I [w]never
knew you; [x]depart from me, [y]you workers of lawlessness.'

Build Your House on the Rock

24 [z]"Everyone then who hears these words of mine and does them will be like [a]a wise
man who built his house on the rock. 25 And the rain fell, and the floods came, and the

[1] Some manuscripts *For the way is wide and easy*

7 [y]For ver. 7-11, see Luke 11:9-13 [z]ch. 18:19; 21:22; Mark 11:24; John 14:13; 15:7, 16; 16:23, 24; James 1:5, 6, 17; 1 John 3:22; 5:14, 15 [a]1 Chr. 28:9; 2 Chr. 15:2; Prov. 8:17; Jer. 29:13; [Isa. 55:6] [b][Rev. 3:20]
9 [c]ch. 4:3
11 [d]ch. 12:34; Gen. 6:5; 8:21 [z][See ver. 7 above]
12 [e]Luke 6:31 [f]See ch. 22:40
13 [g]Luke 13:24
14 [h]Ps. 16:11; [ch. 18:8; John 14:6] [i][Luke 13:23]
15 [j]ch. 24:11, 24; Deut. 13:1-3; Jer. 14:14; 23:16; Mark 13:22; Luke 6:26; Acts 13:6; 2 Pet. 2:1; 1 John 4:1 [k]Ezek. 22:27; Acts 20:29; [Mic. 3:5; John 10:12]
16 [l]Luke 6:43, 44; James 2:18
17 [m]ch. 12:33-35
19 [n]See ch. 3:10
20 [l][See ver. 16 above]
21 [o]Luke 6:46; Rom. 2:13; James 1:22 [p][Hos. 8:2] [q][John 3:3, 5] [r]ch. 12:50
22 [s]ch. 25:11, 12; Luke 13:25-27 [t]Mal. 3:17, 18 [u][Num. 24:4; John 11:51; 1 Cor. 13:2] [v]See Mark 9:38
23 [t][See ver. 22 above] [w]ch. 10:33; [Ps. 101:4] [x]ch. 25:41; Ps. 6:8 [y]ch. 13:41; Ps. 5:5
24 [z]For ver. 24-27, see Luke 6:47-49 [a]ch. 25:2; [Ezek. 13:10-14]

7:7–11 Ask. Disciples should come to God in humility and awareness of need. **Seek** connects one's prayer with responsible action in pursuing the will of God. **Knock** suggests perseverance. Disciples are to persist in prayer, confident that their Father will provide whatever is best for them, according to his sovereign, gracious will.

7:11 you . . . who are evil. Earthly parents have an innate impulse to do what is best for their children, yet they are flawed as a result of sin's corruption of all humanity through the fall of Adam and Eve (cf. Rom. 5:12–14), and the quality of their parenting does not match God's. This is an example of a "how much more" argument frequently used in Matthew and Luke (e.g., Matt. 10:25; 12:12; Luke 11:13; 12:24; cf. Heb. 9:14).

7:12 do also to them. Known as "the Golden Rule," this verse summarizes the teaching of **the Law and the Prophets** (see note on 5:17). The way in which one wants to be treated should determine the way that one treats others. This should come naturally for believers who love God with all their heart and soul and mind, and who love their neighbor as themselves (22:37–40). See note on 5:17.

7:13–29 *Warning! With Jesus or Against Him?* Jesus concludes the Sermon on the Mount by giving the disciples, the crowd, and the religious leaders four basic warnings: they must choose between two gates and roads (vv. 13–14), two kinds of prophets (vv. 15–20), two kinds of disciples (vv. 21–23), and two foundations (vv. 24–27). They are either with Jesus or against him.

7:13–14 narrow gate. The way to eternal life is "narrow" in that it is through Jesus alone (cf. note on Acts 4:12). Though the way is **hard**, those who choose the **way** that **is easy** (by seeking the approval of man rather than God) will find that the easy way only **leads to destruction**—ultimately to eternal punishment and separation from God.

7:15–20 Beware of false prophets. Maintaining the earlier balance of not judging (vv. 1–5) yet not being naively accepting (v. 6), Jesus teaches his disciples that they must be wisely discerning when professed prophets come into their midst. The life of the prophet and the results of his influence on others are the **fruits** that will indicate whether or not his message is consistent with the kingdom life of righteousness. **fire.** The only thing bad trees are good for is firewood, a striking metaphor of the future judgment for false prophets.

7:21–23 The **kingdom** community must guard against not only false prophets (vv. 15–20) but also false disciples. **Lord, Lord.** An oral confession of Jesus as Lord does not always indicate a repentant heart.

7:22 False disciples may exercise power in Jesus' **name** but their activities are meaningless because they deceive themselves and other believers, desiring attention for their own spectacular displays. **Mighty works** are not proof of the Father's will since they can come from sources other than God, including demons and human contrivance (cf. Acts 19:13–16; 2 Thess. 2:9–12; Rev. 13:13–14).

7:23 then will I declare to them. Jesus says that he will one day exercise the prerogative of condemning people to hell, something that only God can do (cf. note on John 5:22). Though these condemned prophets appeared to belong to Jesus, they were never truly saved, for Jesus **never knew** them (cf. note on Matt. 7:21–23).

7:24–27 hears these words of mine and does them. A parable brings the Sermon on the Mount to a close as Jesus calls for his audience to decide between himself and the religious establishment, drawing a dividing line between himself and any other foundation for life. The evidence of whether one is truly a believer is in whether one **does** the words of Jesus (cf. James 1:22–23 and 2:20–22 and notes on these verses). **wise man.** Disciples who build their lives on the bedrock of Jesus and his message of the kingdom of heaven are truly wise, regardless of the shifting cultural or religious fashions.

7:25 the rain fell, and the floods came. During the hot summer months,

26[a][See ver. 24 above]
28[b]ch. 13:54; 22:33; Mark 1:22; 6:2; 11:18; Luke 4:32; [Acts 13:12]
29[c]John 7:46

Chapter 8

1[d]ch. 4:25
2[e]For ver. 2-4, see Mark 1:40-44; Luke 5:12-14 [f][ch. 18:26; Acts 10:25]
4[g]ch. 9:30; 17:9; Mark 1:34; 5:43; 7:36; 8:26; See ch. 12:16 [h]Luke 17:14 [i]Lev. 14:2-32 [j]ch. 10:18; 24:14; Mark 6:11; Luke 9:5; James 5:3
5[k]For ver. 5-13, see Luke 7:1-10
8[l]Ps. 107:20; [ver. 16]
10[m][Mark 6:6] [n]See ch. 9:2
11[o]Luke 13:29; Eph. 3:6; [Isa. 59:19; Mal. 1:11]
12[p]Luke 13:28; [ch. 19:30; 21:41, 43] [q]ch. 22:13; 25:30 [r]ch. 13:42, 50; 22:13; 24:51; 25:30; Luke 13:28
13[s]ch. 9:29 [t]John 4:53; [ch. 9:22]

winds blew and beat on that house, but it did not fall, because it had been founded on the
rock. 26 And everyone who hears these words of mine and does not do them will be like [a]a
foolish man who built his house on the sand. 27 And the rain fell, and the floods came, and
the winds blew and beat against that house, and it fell, and great was the fall of it."

The Authority of Jesus

28 And when Jesus finished these sayings, [b]the crowds were astonished at his teaching,
29 [c]for he was teaching them as one who had authority, and not as their scribes.

Jesus Cleanses a Leper

8 When he came down from the mountain, [d]great crowds followed him. 2 [e]And behold,
a leper[1] came to him and [f]knelt before him, saying, "Lord, if you will, you can make me
clean." 3 And Jesus[2] stretched out his hand and touched him, saying, "I will; be clean." And
immediately his leprosy was cleansed. 4 And Jesus said to him, [g]"See that you say nothing
to anyone, but go, [h]show yourself to the priest and [i]offer the gift that Moses commanded,
[j]for a proof to them."

The Faith of a Centurion

5 [k]When he had entered Capernaum, a centurion came forward to him, appealing to him,
6 "Lord, my servant is lying paralyzed at home, suffering terribly." 7 And he said to him, "I
will come and heal him." 8 But the centurion replied, "Lord, I am not worthy to have you
come under my roof, but [l]only say the word, and my servant will be healed. 9 For I too am
a man under authority, with soldiers under me. And I say to one, 'Go,' and he goes, and to
another, 'Come,' and he comes, and to my servant,[3] 'Do this,' and he does it." 10 When Jesus
heard this, [m]he marveled and said to those who followed him, "Truly, I tell you, with [n]no
one in Israel[4] have I found such faith. 11 I tell you, [o]many will come from east and west and
recline at table with Abraham, Isaac, and Jacob in the kingdom of heaven, 12 [p]while the
sons of the kingdom [q]will be thrown into the outer darkness. In that place [r]there will be
weeping and gnashing of teeth." 13 And to the centurion Jesus said, "Go; let it be done for
you [s]as you have believed." [t]And the servant was healed at that very moment.

[1] *Leprosy* was a term for several skin diseases; see Leviticus 13 [2] Greek *he* [3] Greek *bondservant* [4] Some manuscripts *not even in Israel*

the sand around the Sea of Galilee was hard on the surface. But a wise builder knew that he needed to dig several feet below the surface to the bedrock in order to establish the foundation for his house.

7:26–27 on the sand. The religious establishment had embraced a mere surface righteousness built on an unstable foundation of religious pretense.

7:28–29 Astonished suggests a variety of emotional reactions to Jesus' words, but not a commitment of faith. While the **scribes** cite other rabbis, Jesus has inherent divine **authority**.

8:1–9:38 *The Authoritative Power of the Messiah: Kingdom Power Demonstrated.* Jesus has shown himself as the Messiah in word through his teaching (chs. 5–7) and now shows himself to be the Messiah in deed through the performance of many miracles, demonstrating that the kingdom of God truly has arrived.

8:1–9:8 *Healings, Discipleship, and Overpowering Satan's Strongholds.* Jesus' mission involves ministering to the marginalized (8:1–17), disappointing the messianic expectations of some who wanted to follow him (8:18–22), and overthrowing Satan's strongholds (8:23–9:8).

8:2–3 leper. The OT provided specific guidelines for the examination and treatment of those with a variety of skin diseases, generally called leprosy, many of which were highly contagious (see Leviticus 13–14). **Lord** (Gk. *kyrios*) is the title of respect (similar to "Sir") that people commonly used when they came to Jesus for aid, though in contexts that show knowledge of its OT background it can be an affirmation of deity (see note on 1 Cor. 12:4–6). **make me clean**. Not only was leprosy a disease, it made the leper as well as anyone who touched him ceremonially unclean (Lev. 13:45–46; Num. 5:2–4; cf. Leviticus 15). But when Jesus **touched him**, he was healed, and Jesus did not become unclean.

8:4 show yourself to the priest. Jesus instructs the man to do what the law required for lepers to return to society. **say nothing to anyone**. Jesus carefully avoids stirring up a misunderstanding of his messianic identity. Although miracles attest to the authenticity of his message concerning the kingdom's arrival, he does not want to draw crowds who come simply for the sake of miracles. For other instances of what some have called the "messianic secret," see 9:30; 12:16; 16:20; 17:9.

8:5–7 centurion. A Roman officer in charge of a hundred men. In Luke's account (Luke 7:1–5), others came to Jesus on his behalf, but Matthew does not mention them. The accounts are not contradictory; Matthew, as is often the case, simply abbreviates the story. He actually reports what the centurion said *through* his messengers, based on the idea that what a person does through an agent is what the person himself does (cf. note on John 3:17).

8:8 Addressing Jesus as **Lord** (cf. v. 2), the Roman centurion reveals a remarkable sensitivity for Jewish traditions, saying that he is unworthy of receiving Jesus into his Gentile home. A Jew who entered the home of a Gentile became ceremonially unclean (see Acts 10:28).

8:10 The centurion seems to understand what **no one in Israel** understands: Jesus is the long-awaited Messiah. Jesus **marveled**, commending the centurion for his exemplary faith and censuring Israel for lack of faith.

8:11–12 recline at table. The peoples of the earth who respond to Jesus' ministry will join the patriarchs at the end-time messianic banquet in the kingdom of heaven (Rev. 19:9), fulfilling God's promise to Abraham (Gen. 12:3). But the **sons of the kingdom** (a Semitic term for national Israel) will lose their claim to the kingdom unless they follow the centurion's example of faith. **weeping and gnashing of teeth**. This description of terrible suffering

Jesus Heals Many

14 [u]And when Jesus entered Peter's house, he saw [v]his mother-in-law lying sick with a
fever. 15 He [w]touched her hand, and the fever left her, and she rose and began to serve him.
16 That evening they brought to him many who were [x]oppressed by demons, and he cast
out the spirits [y]with a word and healed all who were sick. 17 [z]This was to fulfill what was
spoken by the prophet Isaiah: [a]"He took our illnesses and bore our diseases."

The Cost of Following Jesus

18 Now [b]when Jesus saw a crowd around him, [c]he gave orders to go over to the other
side. 19 [d]And a scribe came up and said to him, "Teacher, I will follow you wherever you
go." 20 And Jesus said to him, "Foxes have holes, and birds of the air have nests, but the
Son of Man has nowhere to lay his head." 21 Another of the disciples said to him, "Lord,
let me first go and bury my father." 22 And Jesus said to him, "Follow me, and leave [e]the
dead to bury their own dead."

Jesus Calms a Storm

23 [f]And when he got into the boat, his disciples followed him. 24 And behold, there arose
a great storm on the sea, so that the boat was being swamped by the waves; but [g]he was
asleep. 25 And they went and woke him, saying, [h]"Save us, Lord; we are perishing." 26 And
he said to them, "Why are you [i]afraid, [j]O you of little faith?" Then he rose and [k]rebuked
the winds and the sea, and [l]there was a great calm. 27 And the men [m]marveled, saying,
"What sort of man is this, that even [n]winds and sea obey him?"

Jesus Heals Two Men with Demons

28 [o]And when he came to the other side, to the country of the Gadarenes,[1] two [p]demon-
possessed[2] men met him, coming out of the tombs, so fierce that no one could pass that
way. 29 And behold, they [q]cried out, "What have you to do with us, [r]O Son of God? Have
you come here to torment us [s]before the time?" 30 Now a herd of many pigs was feeding at
some distance from them. 31 And the demons begged him, saying, "If you cast us out, send
us away into the herd of pigs." 32 And he said to them, "Go." So they came out and went into
the pigs, and behold, the whole herd rushed down the steep bank into the sea and drowned
in the waters. 33 The herdsmen fled, and going into the city they told everything, especially

[1] Some manuscripts *Gergesenes*; some *Gerasenes* [2] Greek *daimonizomai*; also verse 33; elsewhere rendered *oppressed by demons*

14 [u]For ver. 14-16, see Mark 1:29-34; Luke 4:38-41 [v]1 Cor. 9:5
15 [w][ch. 9:25]
16 [x]ver. 28, 33; See ch. 4:24 [y][ver. 8]
17 [z]See ch. 1:22 [a]Cited from Isa. 53:4
18 [b][ch. 14:22; John 6:15-17] [c]Mark 4:35; Luke 8:22
19 [d]For ver. 19-22, see Luke 9:57-60
22 [e][John 5:25]
23 [f]For ver. 23-27, see Mark 4:36-41; Luke 8:22-25; [John 6:16-21]
24 [g][John 4:6, 7]
25 [h][ch. 14:30]
26 [i]John 14:27 [j]See ch. 6:30 [k]Ps. 104:6, 7; [Luke 4:39] [l]Job 38:11; Ps. 65:7; [ch. 14:32]
27 [m][Mark 1:27] [n][Luke 5:9]
28 [o]For ch. 8:28–9:1, see Mark 5:1-21; Luke 8:26-40 [p]ver. 16; [Rev. 18:2]
29 [q]Mark 1:23, 24, 26; Luke 4:34; Acts 8:7 [r][ch. 4:3, 6]; See ch. 14:33 [s][Rev. 12:12]

in hell appears several times in Matthew (cf. Matt. 13:42, 50; 22:13; 24:51; 25:30) and in Luke 13:28.

8:14 The home belonged to both Peter and his brother Andrew (Mark 1:29). Peter's **mother-in-law** was afflicted with a **fever**, perhaps malaria.

8:16–17 He took our illnesses and bore our diseases. A reference to Isaiah's prophecy of the servant (Isaiah 53), focusing on Jesus' messianic role as healer (see Isa. 53:5; cf. note on Matt. 11:3–5). The fact that not all sicknesses have a demonic origin is seen in the distinction between the healings of the **sick** and the casting out of spirits from those **oppressed by demons**.

8:19 scribe. An expert in handling written documents. In Israel, scribes' duties included teaching, interpretation, and regulation of the law (see note on 2:4).

8:20 Son of Man (see note on John 1:51; cf. Dan. 7:13) is Jesus' favorite self-designation, indicating the true meaning of his identity and ministry: (1) the humble servant who has come to forgive common sinners (cf. Matt. 9:6); (2) the suffering servant whose atoning death and resurrection will redeem his people (16:13, 27–28); and (3) the glorious King and Judge who will return to establish God's kingdom on earth (25:31; 26:64). **nowhere to lay his head**. Since believers can expect to be treated as Jesus was (John 15:18; cf. 16:33), the Christian life will not be one of ease and comfort.

8:22 leave the dead to bury their own dead. While Jesus clearly upholds the biblical command to honor father and mother (see 15:1–9), the call to follow him rises above all other allegiances. Anything that hinders unqualified commitment to him and to the new covenant family of faith must be set aside.

8:23–24 great storm (Gk. *seismos*, "violent shaking, earthquake"). Although the Sea of Galilee is located in the earthquake-prone Jordan Rift Valley, Matthew also mentions "winds" (v. 26), which points in the direction of a powerful storm that created large **waves** that shook the boat. This boat may have been similar to the one discovered in Galilee in 1986 (see note on 4:21 and illustration, p. 1851).

8:26 Little faith (Gk. *oligopistos*) is not "no faith" (Gk. *apistos*), but "ineffective," "defective," or "deficient" faith (cf. 6:30). Jesus calls the disciples to a clearer understanding of who he is. **rebuked**. Jesus is able to command even the forces of nature, just as God in the OT "rebukes" the sea, showing his sovereign control over the natural world (2 Sam. 22:16; Ps. 18:15).

8:27 Marveled (Gk. *thaumazō*, "to wonder, be amazed") is different from the term used to describe the reaction of the crowds ("astonished," 7:28), yet even the disciples do not yet fully grasp Jesus' identity.

8:28 Other side often marks the movement from a Jewish to a Gentile territory and vice versa (e.g., 14:22; 16:5). **Gadarenes** refers to both the town of Gadara (modern Umm Qais), about 6 miles (9.7 km) southeast of the Sea of Galilee, and also the surrounding region (see Mark 5:1).

8:29 Son of God. The demons recognize that one of Satan's strongholds, the spirit world, is being invaded and overpowered. **before the time**. The demons know that they will be judged and punished at God's appointed time.

8:30–34 The **herd of pigs** would have been raised for food in this Gentile region on the east shore of the Sea of Galilee, and the local people were very upset (**all the city . . . begged him to leave**) at the loss of this large herd (about 2,000, Mark 5:13). The pigs' fate in the sea prefigures and pictures the final fate of demons, when God defeats Satan and throws him into the lake of fire (Rev. 20:10). Jesus accomplished the decisive defeat of Satan in his earthly ministry (Matt. 4:1–11; Luke 10:18–19), and ultimately in his crucifixion and resurrection (John 12:31; Col. 2:15; Heb. 2:14–15).

what had happened to the [t]demon-possessed men. 34 And behold, all the city came out to
meet Jesus, and when they saw him, [u]they begged him to leave their region.

Jesus Heals a Paralytic

9 And getting into a boat he crossed over and came to [v]his own city. 2 [w]And behold, some
people brought to him a paralytic, lying on a bed. And when Jesus [x]saw their faith, he
said to the paralytic, [y]"Take heart, my son; [z]your sins are forgiven." 3 And behold, some of
the scribes said to themselves, [a]"This man is blaspheming." 4 But Jesus, [b]knowing[1] their
thoughts, said, "Why do you think evil in your hearts? 5 For which is easier, to say, 'Your
sins are forgiven,' or to say, 'Rise and walk'? 6 But that you may know that the Son of Man
has authority on earth to forgive sins"—he then said to the paralytic—"Rise, pick up your
bed and go home." 7 And he rose and went home. 8 When the crowds saw it, [c]they were
afraid, and [c]they glorified God, who had [d]given such authority to men.

Jesus Calls Matthew

9 [e]As Jesus passed on from there, he saw a man called [f]Matthew sitting at the tax booth,
and he said to him, "Follow me." And he rose and followed him.
10 And as Jesus[2] reclined at table in the house, behold, many [g]tax collectors and sinners
came and were reclining with Jesus and his disciples. 11 And when the Pharisees saw this,
they said to his disciples, [h]"Why does your teacher eat with [g]tax collectors and sinners?"
12 But when he heard it, he said, "Those who are well have no need of a physician, but those
who are sick. 13 Go and learn [i]what this means, [j]'I desire mercy, and not sacrifice.' For [k]I
came not to call the righteous, [l]but sinners."

A Question About Fasting

14 Then [m]the disciples of John came to him, saying, [n]"Why do we and [o]the Pharisees
fast,[3] but your disciples do not fast?" 15 And Jesus said to them, [p]"Can the wedding guests
mourn as long as the bridegroom is with them? [q]The days will come when the bridegroom
is taken away from them, and [r]then they will fast. 16 No one puts a piece of unshrunk
cloth on an old garment, for the patch tears away from the garment, and a worse tear is
made. 17 Neither is new wine put into old [s]wineskins. If it is, the skins burst and the wine
is spilled and the skins are destroyed. But new wine is put into fresh wineskins, and so
both are preserved."

[1] Some manuscripts *perceiving* [2] Greek *he* [3] Some manuscripts add *much,* or *often*

33 [t]ver. 16
34 [u][1 Kgs. 17:18; Luke 5:8; Acts 16:39]

Chapter 9

1 [v]ch. 4:13; [Mark 2:1]
2 [w]For ver. 2-8, see Mark 2:3-12; Luke 5:18-26 [x]ver. 22, 29; ch. 8:10, 13; 15:28; Mark 10:52; Luke 7:9, 50; 17:19; 18:42; Acts 3:16; 14:9; James 5:15 [y]ver. 22 [z]Luke 7:48; [John 5:14]
3 [a]ch. 26:65; John 10:36
4 [b]ch. 12:25; John 2:24, 25
8 [c]See Luke 7:16 [d]ch. 28:18
9 [e]For ver. 9-17, see Mark 2:14-22; Luke 5:27-38 [f]ch. 10:3; Mark 3:18; Luke 6:15; Acts 1:13
10 [g]ch. 11:19; See ch. 5:46
11 [h][Luke 15:2] [g][See ver. 10 above]
13 [i]ch. 12:7 [j]Cited from Hos. 6:6; [ch. 23:23; Mark 12:33] [k][Luke 15:7; John 9:39] [l]1 Tim. 1:15
14 [m]ch. 11:2; 14:12; Luke 11:1; John 1:35; 3:25; 4:1; [Acts 18:25; 19:3] [n][ch. 15:2] [o]Luke 18:12
15 [p]John 3:29 [q]See Luke 17:22 [r][John 16:20]
17 [s]Josh. 9:4

9:1 Jesus returned to **his own city**, Capernaum, the home base of his ministry in Galilee. The healing probably took place in Peter's home (cf. 8:14–15).

9:2 paralytic. Jesus had already cured paralysis (4:24; 8:6), and these people had no doubt heard of his miraculous powers. **Your sins are forgiven** implies that in this case sin and sickness are related but also that, of the two, sin is the more fundamental problem. Though individual sin is not always the direct cause of a person's disease or illness (John 9:2–3), ultimately all corruption and death result from the entrance of sin into the world (see Gen. 2:17; 3:16–19).

9:3 blaspheming. The scribes believed Jesus was dishonoring God by taking upon himself the prerogative to forgive sins, which only God can do (cf. Mark 2:7; Luke 5:21).

9:5 which is easier. The implied answer is that it is easier to say "Your sins are forgiven," for there is no way to verify whether or not this has happened.

9:6–7 Son of Man. See note on 8:20. Jesus' **authority on earth to forgive sins** is an explicit evidence of his divinity, since only God has that prerogative. That the man **rose and went home** is visible evidence of Jesus' authority.

9:9–38 *Unexpected Discipleship, Miracles, and Workers.* Jesus reveals his unexpected definition of discipleship (vv. 9–17) and demonstrates extraordinary compassion through his unexpected miracles (vv. 18–34). The underappreciated are called to follow him, while the religious leaders continue to resist him.

9:9 Matthew. See Introduction: Author and Title. **sitting at the tax booth**. The Jews probably considered Matthew a traitor, since collecting taxes entailed cooperation with the Roman occupiers of Palestine. **rose and followed him**. Matthew had likely witnessed Jesus' public teaching and healings and was now ready to join him.

9:10 tax collectors. See notes on v. 9 and 5:46–47. Pharisees would have regarded as **sinners** anyone who failed to keep God's law as they interpreted it, and the term here seems to reflect a commonly understood meaning by which it included both people guilty of publicly known sin and others who did not keep the strict purity requirements of the Pharisees.

9:11 Pharisees. See note on 3:7.

9:12 those who are well . . . those who are sick. The Pharisees considered themselves "healthy" before God because of their observance of the law, and thus they were blind to their spiritual sickness. Jesus' point is that only those who realize their need come to him to receive the help they need.

9:13 I came not to call the righteous, but sinners. Jesus' offer of salvation to sinners threatens the Pharisees' way of life, yet it is at the heart of the gospel he came announcing. **"I desire mercy, and not sacrifice"** is a quotation from Hos. 6:6 (see note). "Sacrifice" summarized observance of religious rituals. More important to God was "mercy" (the Septuagint rendering of Hb. *hesed*, meaning "steadfast love"), which would have led the Pharisees to care for these sinners as Jesus did.

9:14 fast. See note on 6:16–18.

9:15 The **bridegroom** in the OT was Yahweh (cf. Isa. 62:5; Hos. 2:19–20). The arrival of the kingdom of heaven is cause for a time of rejoicing, similar to what is experienced during marriage ceremonies (cf. Matt. 25:10).

9:16–17 unshrunk cloth on an old garment. Rather than patching up the traditional practices of righteousness within religious Judaism, Jesus has come to offer real growth in kingdom righteousness, which is like when **new wine is put into fresh wineskins**.

A Girl Restored to Life and a Woman Healed

18 [t]While he was saying these things to them, behold, a ruler came in and [u]knelt before
him, saying, "My daughter has just died, but come and lay your hand on her, and she will
live." 19 And Jesus rose and followed him, with his disciples. 20 And behold, a woman [v]who
had suffered from a discharge of blood for twelve years came up behind him and touched
[w]the fringe of his garment, 21 for she said to herself, "If I only touch his garment, I will be
made well." 22 Jesus turned, and seeing her he said, [x]"Take heart, daughter; your faith has
made you well." [y]And instantly[1] the woman was made well. 23 And when Jesus came to the
ruler's house and saw [z]the flute players and the crowd making a commotion, 24 he said,
"Go away, for [a]the girl is not dead but [b]sleeping." And they laughed at him. 25 But [c]when
the crowd had been put outside, he went in and [d]took her by the hand, and the girl arose.
26 And the report of this went through all that district.

Jesus Heals Two Blind Men

27 [e]And as Jesus passed on from there, two blind men followed him, crying aloud, "Have
mercy on us, [f]Son of David." 28 When he entered the house, the blind men came to him,
and Jesus said to them, "Do you believe that I am able to do this?" They said to him, "Yes,
Lord." 29 [g]Then he touched their eyes, saying, [h]"According to your faith be it done to you."
30 And their eyes were opened. And Jesus sternly warned them, [i]"See that no one knows
about it." 31 [j]But they went away and spread his fame through all that district.

Jesus Heals a Man Unable to Speak

32 As they were going away, behold, a [k]demon-oppressed man who was mute [l]was brought
to him. 33 And when the demon had been cast out, the mute man spoke. And the crowds
[m]marveled, saying, "Never was anything like this seen in Israel." 34 But the Pharisees said,
"He casts out demons by the prince of demons."

The Harvest Is Plentiful, the Laborers Few

35 [n]And Jesus went throughout all the cities and villages, teaching in their synagogues
and proclaiming the gospel of the kingdom and healing every disease and every affliction.
36 [o]When he saw the crowds, [p]he had compassion for them, because they were harassed and
helpless, [q]like sheep without a shepherd. 37 [r]Then he said to his disciples, "The harvest is

[1] Greek *from that hour*

18 [t]For ver. 18-26, see Mark 5:22-43; Luke 8:41-56 [u]See ch. 8:2
20 [v]Lev. 15:25 [w]ch. 14:36; 23:5; [Num. 15:38, 39; Deut. 22:12]
22 [x]ver. 2; See Luke 7:50 [y]ch. 15:28; 17:18; [ch. 8:13]
23 [z]Rev. 18:22
24 [a][Acts 20:10] [b]John 11:4, 11
25 [c]Acts 9:40 [d]Mark 9:27; Acts 3:7; 9:41
27 [e][ch. 20:30-34] [f]ch. 12:23; 15:22; 20:30, 31; 22:42; See ch. 1:1
29 [g]Mark 8:25; John 9:6 [h]See ver. 2
30 [i]See ch. 8:4
31 [j]Mark 1:45; 7:36
32 [k][ch. 12:22-24; Luke 11:14, 15] [l]See ch. 4:24
33 [m][Mark 1:27]
35 [n]See ch. 4:23, 24
36 [o][ch. 14:14] [p]Mark 6:34 [q]Num. 27:17; 1 Kgs. 22:17; Ezek. 34:5
37 [r]Luke 10:2; John 4:35

9:18 Though Jairus was a **ruler** (cf. Mark 5:22 and Luke 8:41) and a man of considerable influence, he **knelt before** Jesus, the appropriate position to take before God. **she will live**. Evidence of Jairus's deep faith in Jesus, in the face of death.

9:20 discharge of blood. Her plight is heightened by its duration (**twelve years**), leaving her hopeless and in an anemic, weakened condition. Moreover, her hemorrhaging would have made her ceremonially unclean, which would have excluded her from normal social and religious relations.

9:22 your faith has made you well. Faith itself does not do the healing; God does. But the woman's faith was the divinely appointed means for her bodily healing, as well as for her spiritual salvation.

9:23 flute players and the crowd. Professional mourners were customarily hired to assist at funerals, usually including flutists and wailing women (**making a commotion**). Since bodies decomposed quickly in Palestine, mourners had to assemble fairly soon after a death.

9:24–26 took her by the hand. Touching a corpse rendered a person unclean for seven days (Num. 19:11–21), but Jesus brings the **girl** to life, transforming uncleanness into purity. Jesus' power over death anticipates his later raising of Lazarus and his own resurrection (Matt. 28:1–10; John 10:17–18; 11:25–26; etc.).

9:27 This account of the healing of **two blind men** has significant differences from the healing of Bartimaeus (20:29–34; Mark 10:46–52; Luke 18:35–43) and should not be thought of as the same event. Jesus no doubt healed many blind people over the course of his ministry. **Son of David**. A reference to the promised messianic deliverer from the line of David whose kingdom will continue forever (2 Sam. 7:12–16), and the first of several times in Matthew that people refer to Jesus by this title (see Matt. 12:23; 15:22; 20:30, 31; 21:9, 15; 22:42; cf. 1:1). The messianic age was to bring healing to the blind (Isa. 29:18; 35:5).

9:30 See that no one knows about it. See note on 8:4. Cf. 12:16; 16:20; 17:9.

9:32–33 a demon-oppressed man. Demonic influence manifests itself in a variety of forms; here it prevents the man from speaking (see also 12:22).

9:34 He casts out demons by the prince of demons. The Pharisees were unable to recognize that God was doing something unique in the teaching and works of Jesus, so they attributed his powers to the only other existing source, since they could not deny the reality of the miraculous works that Jesus had done. But the truthfulness of Jesus' teachings, the moral excellence of his character, and his ministry of doing good should have convinced them otherwise (cf. 7:16; John 3:2; 9:31–33).

9:36–38 The **compassion** of Jesus is a repeated theme in Matthew (cf. 14:14; 15:32) and throughout both the OT (e.g., Deut. 30:3; 1 Sam. 23:21; Ps. 103:13; Isa. 49:15; 54:8; Lam. 4:10) and the NT, where Christians are especially admonished to show compassion to those in need (e.g., Col. 3:12; Heb. 10:34; cf. James 5:11). **like sheep without a shepherd**. The leaders have failed in their responsibility, but Mic. 5:4 predicted that the Messiah would "shepherd" his people. Given the helplessness and the need of the crowds, Jesus' disciples are urged to **pray earnestly** that the Lord (shifting metaphors) would **send out laborers into his harvest**, since many

38[s][2 Thess. 3:1] [t]ch. 20:2; [Mark 1:12]
Chapter 10
1[u]Mark 3:13-15; 6:7-13; Luke 6:13; 9:1, 2
2[v]For ver. 2-4, see Mark 3:16-19; Luke 6:14-16; Acts 1:13 [w]ch. 16:18; John 1:42 [x]ch. 4:18, 21
3[y]ch. 9:9

plentiful, but the laborers are few; **38** therefore [s]pray earnestly to the Lord of the harvest to [t]send out laborers into his harvest."

The Twelve Apostles

10 [u]And he called to him his twelve disciples and gave them authority over unclean spirits, to cast them out, and to heal every disease and every affliction. **2** [v]The names of the twelve apostles are these: first, Simon, [w]who is called Peter, and [x]Andrew his brother; [x]James the son of Zebedee, and John his brother; **3** Philip and Bartholomew; Thomas and [y]Matthew the tax collector; James the son of Alphaeus, and Thaddaeus;[1] **4** Simon the Zealot,[2] and Judas Iscariot, who betrayed him.

[1] Some manuscripts *Lebbaeus*, or *Lebbaeus called Thaddaeus* [2] Greek *kananaios*, meaning zealot

are ready to receive the good news of the kingdom—a prayer that is as urgent today as it was when Jesus' original disciples heard his words.

10:1–42 *The Authoritative Mission of the Messiah's Messengers.* This second major discourse of Jesus (see Introduction: Key Themes; Literary Features) focuses on the disciples' mission to Israel (vv. 1–15), preparation for a worldwide mission among the Gentiles (vv. 16–23), and characteristics that Jesus' disciples will need to embody as they carry out that mission (vv. 24–42).

10:1–15 *Commissioning and Instructions for the Short-term Mission to Israel.* Jesus commissions (vv. 1–4) and instructs (vv. 5–15) the Twelve, sending them out with his message and power.

10:1 Jesus calls the disciples to him as an initial answer to the prayer for the Lord to send workers (9:38). **twelve**. Probably reflective of the 12 tribes of Israel and symbolic of the continuity of God's plan of salvation. The disciples will have **authority . . . to heal every disease** just as Jesus did (e.g., 4:23; 9:35).

10:2 Apostles (plural of Gk. *apostolos*; used only here in Matthew; see note on Rom. 1:1) describes those commissioned to be Jesus' special representatives, while "disciples" (Matt. 10:1) was also used more broadly to refer to anyone who believed in Jesus. **Peter** heads all the lists of the Twelve (cf. Mark 3:16–19; Luke 6:13–16; Acts 1:13) and serves as their spokesman. Peter, along with **James** and **John**, made up Jesus' inner circle.

10:3–4 There is remarkable diversity among the 12 apostles, including fishermen, a tax collector (**Matthew**), and a zealous revolutionary (**Simon the Zealot**). **Judas Iscariot** is always listed last; "Iscariot" most likely denotes where he was from. He was the treasurer for the group (John 12:6) and the betrayer of Jesus. See notes on Luke 6:14; 6:15; 6:16 for additional information on the 12 disciples.

The Twelve Apostles*

Matthew 10:2–4	Mark 3:16–19	Luke 6:14–16	John (various verses)	Acts 1:13
1. Simon, who is called Peter	1. Simon (to whom he gave the name Peter)	1. Simon, whom he named Peter	Simon Peter (1:40–42)	1. Peter
2. Andrew his [Simon Peter's] brother	4. Andrew	2. Andrew his [Simon Peter's] brother	Andrew, Simon Peter's brother (1:40)	4. Andrew
3. James the son of Zebedee	2. James the son of Zebedee	3. James	unnamed son of Zebedee (21:2)	3. James
4. John his [James's] brother	3. John the brother of James	4. John	unnamed son of Zebedee (21:2)	2. John
5. Philip	5. Philip	5. Philip	Philip of Bethsaida (1:43–44)	5. Philip
6. Bartholomew	6. Bartholomew	6. Bartholomew	Nathanael of Cana (1:45–49; 21:2)**	7. Bartholomew
7. Thomas	8. Thomas	8. Thomas	Thomas called the Twin (11:16)	6. Thomas
8. Matthew the tax collector	7. Matthew (Levi, son of Alphaeus, a tax collector, 2:14)	7. Matthew (Levi, tax collector, 5:27)		8. Matthew
9. James the son of Alphaeus	9. James the son of Alphaeus	9. James the son of Alphaeus		9. James the son of Alphaeus
10. Thaddaeus	10. Thaddaeus	11. Judas the son of James	Judas (not Iscariot) (14:22)	11. Judas the son of James
11. Simon the Zealot	11. Simon the Zealot	10. Simon who was called the Zealot		10. Simon the Zealot
12. Judas Iscariot	12. Judas Iscariot	12. Judas Iscariot	Judas the son of Simon Iscariot (6:71)	12. Matthias replaces Judas [who had died] (Acts 1:26)

**Others in the NT are regarded as apostles besides the Twelve, notably James the brother of Jesus (Acts 15:12–21; 1 Cor. 15:7; Gal. 1:19), Paul (Acts 14:4, 14; 1 Cor. 9:1; 15:8–9), and Barnabas (Acts 14:4, 14).*

***Nathanael is probably Bartholomew, since he is closely associated with Philip. He is certainly not Levi/Matthew, who already has two names and who was from Capernaum. It is possible but unlikely that he is Thaddeus/Judas or Simon the Zealot.*

Jesus Sends Out the Twelve Apostles

5 [u]These twelve Jesus sent out, instructing them, "Go nowhere among the Gentiles and
enter no town of [z]the Samaritans, 6 [a]but go rather to [b]the lost sheep of [c]the house of Israel.
7 And proclaim as you go, saying, [d]'The kingdom of heaven is at hand.' 8 [e]Heal the sick,
raise the dead, cleanse lepers,[1] cast out demons. [f]You received without paying; give without pay. 9 [g]Acquire no gold or silver or copper for your belts, 10 no bag for your journey, or
two tunics[2] or sandals or a staff, for [h]the laborer deserves his food. 11 And whatever town
or village you enter, find out who is worthy in it and stay there until you depart. 12 As
you enter the house, [i]greet it. 13 And if the house is [j]worthy, let [i]your peace come upon it,
but if it is not worthy, let [i]your peace return to you. 14 And if anyone will not receive you
or listen to your words, [l]shake off the dust from your feet when you leave that house or
town. 15 Truly, I say to you, [m]it will be more bearable on the day of judgment for [n]the land
of Sodom and Gomorrah than for that town.

Persecution Will Come

16 [o]"Behold, I am sending you out as sheep in the midst of wolves, so be [p]wise as serpents
and [q]innocent as doves. 17 Beware of men, for [r]they will deliver you over to courts and
flog you [s]in their synagogues, 18 [r]and you will be dragged before governors and kings
for my sake, [t]to bear witness before them and the Gentiles. 19 [r]When [u]they deliver you
over, [v]do not be anxious how you are to speak or what you are to say, for [w]what you are
to say will be given to you in that hour. 20 [x]For it is not you who speak, but [y]the Spirit of
your Father speaking through you. 21 [z]Brother will deliver brother over to death, and
the father his child, and children will rise against parents and have them put to death,
22 [a]and you will be hated by all for my name's sake. [b]But the one who endures to the
end will be saved. 23 When they [c]persecute you in one town, [d]flee to the next, for truly,
I say to you, you will not have gone through all the towns of Israel [e]before the Son of
Man comes.

[1] *Leprosy* was a term for several skin diseases; see Leviticus 13 [2] Greek *chiton*, a long garment worn under the cloak next to the skin

5 [u][See ver. 1 above] [z]2 Kgs. 17:24; Ezra 4:10; Luke 9:52; 10:33; 17:16; John 4:9, 39, 40; 8:48; Acts 8:25; [Acts 1:8]
6 [a]ch. 15:24; [Acts 3:25, 26; 13:46] [b]Ps. 119:176; Isa. 53:6; Jer. 50:6; [ch. 9:36; 18:12] [c]Acts 2:36; 7:42; Heb. 8:8, 10
7 [d]ch. 3:2; 4:17; Luke 10:9
8 [e][ch. 11:5] [f][Isa. 55:1; Acts 3:6; 20:33, 35]
9 [g]For ver. 9-15, see Mark 6:8-11; Luke 9:3-5; [Luke 10:4-12; 22:35]
10 [h]1 Tim. 5:18; [1 Cor. 9:4, 7-14]
12 [i][1 Sam. 25:6; 1 Chr. 12:18]
13 [j][ch. 8:8; Acts 16:15] [i][See ver. 12 above]
14 [l]Acts 13:51; [Neh. 5:13; Acts 18:6]
15 [m]ch. 11:24 [n]Gen. 18:20; 19:28; 2 Pet. 2:6
16 [o]Luke 10:3; [John 17:18] [p]Gen. 3:1 [q]Rom. 16:19 (Gk.); Phil. 2:15; [1 Cor. 14:20]
17 [r]See Mark 13:9, 11; Luke 12:11, 12 [s]See ch. 23:34
18 [r][See ver. 17 above] [t]See ch. 8:4
19 [r][See ver. 17 above] [u]For ver. 19-22, [Mark 13:11-13; Luke 21:12-19; 2 Tim. 4:16, 17] [v]See ch. 6:25 [w]Deut. 18:18; [Num. 23:5]; See Ex. 4:12
20 [x]Luke 12:12; Acts 4:8; 6:10; 13:9; 1 Cor. 15:10; 2 Cor. 13:3; [ver. 40; 1 Thess. 2:13; Heb. 1:1] [y][John 15:26] **21** [z]ver. 35, 36 **22** [a]ch. 24:9; John 15:18-21 [b]ch. 24:13; Mark 13:13; [Dan. 12:12, 13; James 5:11; Rev. 2:10]; See Heb. 3:6 **23** [c]ch. 23:34 [d][ch. 12:15; Acts 8:1; 9:25, 30; 14:6; 17:10, 14] [e]ch. 16:28

10:5 Go nowhere among the Gentiles and enter no town of the Samaritans. The mission was restricted to Jewish Galilee, which was surrounded on all sides by Gentile territory except for Samaria to the south (see note on John 4:4). Though the gospel would later go to the whole world (see Acts 1:8), Jesus' initial ministry was to the Jewish people.

10:6 Lost sheep of the house of Israel denotes the whole lost nation of Israel rather than just part of it. God's plan is that the gospel would be proclaimed first to the Jew, then to the Gentile (cf. Acts 1:8; Rom. 1:16; 2:9–10).

10:7–8a And proclaim . . . "The kingdom of heaven is at hand." Heal the sick . . . Jesus instructed the 12 disciples to minister to both the spiritual and the physical needs of the lost. Thus the apostles' message (the kingdom of heaven) is the same as that of Jesus (3:2; 10:1), and their power is an extension of Jesus' own power ("authority," v. 1), enabling them to do the same works he has done.

10:8b You received without paying; give without pay. The disciples have received the gift of the kingdom of heaven, and they are likewise to share this gospel freely. But see note on vv. 9–10.

10:9–10 Acquire no gold or silver . . . or sandals or a staff. Jesus is not prohibiting the Twelve from owning any of these items; rather, he is stressing the specific requirements of this particular mission. This is to be a relatively quick preaching journey, so they are not to spend time procuring extra supplies; those to whom they minister must support their mission (**for the laborer deserves his food**). Although some have seen a contradiction between the commissioning of the 12 disciples in Matthew (and Luke 9:3) as compared to a similar commissioning account in Mark 6:8–9, it seems best to understand the two accounts as being complementary—that is, that they report two different parts of a longer set of instructions, in which Jesus told the Twelve not to acquire new supplies, but that they could take the essential supplies needed for the journey, i.e., the staff and sandals that they already had. See also note on Luke 9:3.

10:11 Worthy indicates someone who responds positively to the disciples' message.

10:13 Individuals (v. 14), homes (v. 13), or cities (v. 11) that receive the greeting, "**peace** be to this house" (cf. Luke 10:5), show that they recognize the Twelve as God's emissaries.

10:14 shake off the dust from your feet. A sign used by Jews after leaving a Gentile region. For the missionaries it is a sign of judgment on those rejecting the gospel (cf. Acts 13:51).

10:15 it will be more bearable on the day of judgment. Increased understanding of God's revelation means increased responsibility.

10:16–23 *Instructions for the Long-term Mission to the World.* Jesus prepares his disciples for a worldwide mission to the Gentiles and for the persecution that will inevitably accompany their mission.

10:16 sheep in the midst of wolves. Jesus warns the disciples about the persecution that missionary disciples will endure. **wise as serpents and innocent as doves**. The serpent was the symbol of shrewdness and intellectual cunning (Gen. 3:1; Ps. 58:4–5), while the dove was emblematic of simple innocence (Hos. 7:11).

10:17 Synagogues were not only places of worship but also places where discipline was carried out (**flog**).

10:18 to bear witness before them and the Gentiles. As Jesus foretold, the early church leaders would be called before Jewish officials (Acts 4:1–22), the secular authorities of Israel (Acts 12:1–4), and Rome (Acts 14:5).

10:19–20 Jesus encourages the disciples not to be **anxious** because the same **Spirit** who has guided and empowered Jesus (4:1; cf. 1:18, 20; 3:1) will speak through his disciples amid their most difficult challenges.

10:22 hated by all for my name's sake. Jesus' disciples have the privilege of carrying his name, but the antagonism and hatred that is directed toward him will naturally shift to them (cf. 24:9). **endures . . . will be saved**. Cf. notes on 2 Tim. 2:11–13 and Jude 21.

10:23 you will not have gone through all the towns of Israel before the Son of Man comes. Several interpretations have been suggested: the coming of the Son of Man may refer to (1) Jesus' resurrection,

24 [f]"A disciple is not above his teacher, nor a servant[1] above his master. 25 It is enough
for the disciple to be like his teacher, and the servant like his master. [g]If they have called
the master of the house Beelzebul, how much more will they malign[2] those of his
household.

Have No Fear

26 "So have no fear of them, [i]for nothing is covered that will not be revealed, or hidden
that will not be known. 27 What I tell you in the dark, say in the light, and what you hear
whispered, proclaim on [j]the housetops. 28 And [k]do not fear those who kill the body but
cannot kill the soul. Rather fear him [l]who can destroy both soul and body in hell.[3] 29 Are
not two sparrows sold for a penny?[4] And not one of them will fall to the ground apart from
your Father. 30 But [m]even the hairs of your head are all numbered. 31 Fear not, therefore;
[n]you are of more value than many sparrows. 32 [o]So everyone who acknowledges me before
men, I also will acknowledge before my Father who is in heaven, 33 but [p]whoever denies
me before men, [q]I also will deny before my Father who is in heaven.

Not Peace, but a Sword

34 [r]"Do not think that I have come to bring peace to the earth. [s]I have not come to bring
peace, but a sword. 35 [r]For I have come [t]to set a man against his father, and a daughter against
her mother, and a daughter-in-law against her mother-in-law. 36 [u]And a person's enemies
will be those of his own household. 37 [v]Whoever loves father or mother more than me is
not worthy of me, and whoever loves son or daughter more than me is not worthy of me.
38 And [w]whoever does not take his cross and [x]follow me is not worthy of me. 39 [y]Whoever
finds his life will lose it, and whoever loses his life for my sake will find it.

Rewards

40 [z]"Whoever receives you receives me, and [a]whoever receives me receives him who sent
me. 41 [b]The one who receives a prophet because he is a prophet will receive a prophet's
reward, and the one who receives a righteous person because he is a righteous person

[1] Greek *bondservant*; also verse 25 [2] Greek lacks *will they malign* [3] Greek *Gehenna* [4] Greek *assarion*, Roman copper coin (Latin *quadrans*) worth about 1/16 of a *denarius* (which was a day's wage for a laborer)

24 [f]Luke 6:40; John 13:16; 15:20; [Heb. 12:3]
25 [g]ch. 9:34; 12:24; Mark 3:22; Luke 11:15; See John 7:20
26 [i]Mark 4:22; Luke 8:17; [1 Tim. 5:25]; For ver. 26-33, see Luke 12:2-9
27 [j]See Luke 5:19
28 [k]Isa. 8:12, 13; 51:12, 13; Jer. 1:8; 1 Pet. 3:14 [l]James 4:12
30 [m]See 1 Sam. 14:45
31 [n]ch. 6:26; 12:12
32 [o][Rom. 10:9, 10; Heb. 10:35; Rev. 3:5]
33 [p]2 Tim. 2:12; 2 Pet. 2:1; 1 John 2:23; [Mark 8:38] [q]ch. 7:23; 25:12; Luke 13:25
34 [r]See Luke 12:51-53 [s][Rev. 6:4]
35 [r][See ver. 34 above] [t]ver. 21; [Mic. 7:6]
36 [u]Cited from Mic. 7:6; [Ps. 41:9; 55:12, 13; John 13:18]
37 [v]Luke 14:26
38 [w]ch. 16:24; Mark 8:34; Luke 9:23; 14:27 [x]ch. 9:9; John 8:12; 12:26; 21:19
39 [y]ch. 16:25; Mark 8:35; Luke 9:24; 17:33; John 12:25
40 [z]Luke 10:16; John 13:20; Gal. 4:14; [ver. 20; ch. 18:5; 25:40] [a]Mark 9:37; Luke 9:48; [John 12:44, 45]
41 [b]1 Kgs. 17:10-15; 18:4; 2 Kgs. 4:8; [3 John 5-8]

when he came back from the dead, (2) his sending of the Spirit at Pentecost, (3) his coming in judgment on Jerusalem when it was destroyed in A.D. 70, or (4) the second coming of Christ at the end of the age. Option (4) helps make sense of the larger fact: that the mission to Israel must continue alongside the mission to the nations until Jesus returns. But interpretations (1) and (3) also have significant arguments to support them, and they give a more natural explanation for the need for haste in reaching "all the towns of Israel." In the case of (4), v. 23 is understood in light of the preceding verses (vv. 16–22), as a reference to the widespread persecution that occurred prior to the fall of Jerusalem and the destruction of the Jewish temple in A.D. 70. In this case, the judgment on Israel reflected in these events is pictured as a foreshadowing of the final judgment that will come upon all who reject Christ as their Savior, when Christ comes in power and great glory at the end of the age.

10:24–42 *Characteristics of Missionary Disciples.* These characteristics are to guide all disciples as they carry out Jesus' mission to the world.

10:24 A disciple is not above his teacher. The ultimate goal of a disciple is to be like his master—a well-established belief in Judaism and the Greco-Roman world.

10:25 Beelzebul (cf. 12:24, 27) means "master of the house" and refers to Satan. The accusation that Jesus (the real "master of all") was really Satan is shockingly perverse; **how much more,** then, should Jesus' own disciples expect to be falsely accused and maligned.

10:27 proclaim on the housetops. Up to now Jesus has consistently called for secrecy (see note on 8:4), but the time is approaching when the secret will be proclaimed universally.

10:29 Sparrows were customarily thought of as the smallest of creatures, and the **penny** was one of the least valuable Roman coins (cf. 5:26). **apart from your Father.** God is sovereign over even the most insignificant events.

10:30–31 Fear not, therefore. Since the heavenly Father gives constant sovereign supervision even to seemingly insignificant creatures, surely he will also care for his disciples in their mission to proclaim the good news of the kingdom. **more value.** See note on 6:26.

10:32–33 everyone who acknowledges me before men. A Christian can easily avoid persecution by denying that he or she is Jesus' disciple. But the true disciple does not fear death (v. 28) and will publicly acknowledge and confess Jesus. **whoever denies me.** The eternal consequences for those who deny Christ, in fact, will be far worse than the persecution that they sought to avoid.

10:34–37 Sword is a metaphor for the inevitable separation between those who believe in Christ and those who do not, even within a family (i.e., faith in Christ may **set a man against his father**). Jesus' own family opposed him before they came to recognize his true identity (13:53–58; Mark 3:21; John 7:3–5). Thus, **whoever loves father or mother more than me is not worthy of me.** Jesus asked for unqualified allegiance, something even the most esteemed rabbi did not demand. The central point of Matt. 10:34–37 is that love of God and his kingdom must take precedence over every other human relationship.

10:38 take his cross (cf. 16:24). Crucifixion is a shocking metaphor for discipleship. A disciple must deny himself (die to self-will), take up his cross (embrace God's will, no matter the cost), and follow Christ.

10:40 Whoever receives you receives me. Christ's disciples bear his message and his authority (cf. v. 1), so to receive them is to receive Jesus.

10:41–42 prophet. One who speaks for God. **will receive a prophet's reward.** Will share in the reward God gives the prophet, for the helper also played a part in the prophet's work. **righteous person.** One who has the righteousness that comes from obeying Jesus. **one of these little ones.** That is, anyone in need, especially those of "little" standing, who may be overlooked as leaders focus on those more prominent in the community (cf. James 2:1–7).

will receive a righteous person's reward. 42 And [c]whoever gives one of [d]these little ones
even a cup of cold water because he is a disciple, truly, I say to you, he will by no means
lose his reward."

Messengers from John the Baptist

11 When Jesus had finished instructing his twelve disciples, he went on from there to
teach and preach in their cities.
2 [e]Now when John heard [f]in prison about the deeds of [g]the Christ, he sent word by [h]his
disciples 3 and said to him, "Are you [i]the one who is to come, or shall we [j]look for another?"
4 And Jesus answered them, "Go and tell John what you hear and see: 5 [k]the blind receive
their sight and the lame walk, lepers[1] are cleansed and the deaf hear, and the dead are
raised up, and [l]the poor have good news preached to them. 6 And blessed is the one who
[m]is not offended by me."
7 As they went away, Jesus began to speak to the crowds concerning John: "What did
you go out [n]into the wilderness to see? [o]A reed shaken by the wind? 8 What then did you
go out to see? A man[2] dressed in soft clothing? Behold, those who wear soft clothing are
in kings' houses. 9 What then did you go out to see? [p]A prophet?[3] Yes, I tell you, and more
than a prophet. 10 This is he of whom it is written,

[q]"'Behold, I send my messenger before your face,
who will prepare your way before you.'

11 Truly, I say to you, among those born of women there has arisen no one greater than
John the Baptist. Yet the one who is least in the kingdom of heaven is greater than he.
12 [r]From the days of John the Baptist until now the kingdom of heaven has suffered violence,[4] and the violent take it by force. 13 [r]For all the Prophets and the Law prophesied
until John, 14 and if you are willing to accept it, he is [s]Elijah who is to come. 15 [t]He who has
ears to hear,[5] let him hear.

[1] *Leprosy was a term for several skin diseases; see Leviticus 13* [2] Or *Why then did you go out? To see a man . . .* [3] Some manuscripts *Why then did you go out? To see a prophet?* [4] Or *has been coming violently* [5] Some manuscripts omit *to hear*

42 [c]ch. 25:35, 40; Mark 9:41; Heb. 6:10 [d]ch. 18:10

Chapter 11

2 [e]For ver. 2-19, see Luke 7:18-35 [f]ch. 14:3; [ch. 4:12] [g]See ch. 1:17 [h]See ch. 9:14
3 [i]John 4:25; 6:14; 11:27 [j][Luke 3:15]
5 [k]See Luke 7:22 [l]Luke 4:18; [ch. 5:3; James 2:5]
6 [m]Isa. 8:14, 15; John 6:61
7 [n]ch. 3:1; Luke 1:80 [o][Eph. 4:14; James 1:6]
9 [p]ch. 14:5; 21:26; Luke 1:76
10 [q]Mark 1:2; Cited from Mal. 3:1
12 [r]Luke 16:16
13 [r][See ver. 12 above]
14 [s]ch. 17:10-13; Mal. 4:5; Mark 9:11-13; Luke 1:17; [John 1:21]
15 [t]ch. 13:9, 43; Luke 8:8; 14:35

11:1–12:50 *Opposition to the Messiah Emerges.* Resistance to Jesus' ministry has appeared occasionally (e.g., 9:3–4) but now begins to build significantly, occasioned first by the innocuous questions of John the Baptist (11:2–19), then through the overt hostility of the Jewish religious leaders (12:1–45).

11:1–30 *Jesus, John the Baptist, and Ministry in Galilee.* Jesus responds to John the Baptist's questions (vv. 2–6) with a mild rebuke and a glowing tribute (vv. 7–19). He then speaks words of judgment on the unrepentant (vv. 20–24) and words of invitation to those who would find their rest in him (vv. 25–30).

11:1 When Jesus had finished signals the conclusion of the Mission Discourse (ch. 10) and provides a transition to the next section. **he went on from there to teach and preach in their cities.** Jesus carried on his mission while the Twelve went on theirs (ch. 10).

11:2 when John heard in prison. John had been imprisoned by Herod Antipas, and as he awaited death (see 14:1–12) he presumably heard about Jesus' ministry.

11:3–5 Are you the one who is to come? John is probably concerned because his present imprisonment does not match his understanding of the Coming One's arrival, which was to bring blessing on those who repented and judgment on those who did not (see note on 3:11). Jesus' ministry, however, is in line with prophetic promises about the time of salvation, as seen especially in these descriptions that recall the words of Isaiah: **the blind receive** sight (cf. 9:27–31; Isa. 29:18; 35:5), **the lame walk** (Isa. 35:6; cf. Matt. 15:30–31), **lepers** are cured (Isa. 53:4; cf. Matt. 8:1–4), **the deaf hear** (Isa. 29:18–19; 35:5; cf. Mark 7:32–37), **the dead are raised** (Isa. 26:18–19; cf. Matt. 10:8; Luke 7:11–17; John 11:1–44), and the **good news** is preached to the **poor** (Isa. 61:1; cf. Matt. 5:3; Luke 14:13, 21). Jesus' deeds gave sufficient proof of who he was and that the prophesied time of salvation had come ("the year of the Lord's favor"; Isa. 61:1; cf. Isa. 62:1).

11:6 blessed is the one who is not offended by me. The beatitude is a mild rebuke; John and his disciples must be open to God's unfolding plan, even though Jesus' ministry did not exactly match their messianic expectations (see note on vv. 3–5).

11:10 who will prepare your way. See note on 3:3.

11:11 Those born of women is a Jewish idiom for ordinary human birth (cf. Job 14:1; 15:14; 25:4), and Jesus implicitly contrasts this with the new birth into the kingdom of heaven. **no one greater.** John's mission was uniquely privileged because he prepared the way for the Messiah and the kingdom. **greater than he.** But those **in the kingdom of heaven** have the greater privilege because they have actually entered the kingdom (in its new covenant reality) and become partakers in the new covenant through the blood of Christ. (On the salvation of believers in the OT, see Romans 4; see also notes on Matt. 22:31–32; Rom. 10:14–15; Heb. 11:4.)

11:12 That the kingdom has **suffered violence** (Gk. *biazō*) probably indicates opposition from the religious establishment, and **the violent take it by force** probably refers to the actions of specific evil people like Herod Antipas, who had arrested John.

11:13 all the Prophets and the Law prophesied until John. John the Baptist was the last of a long history of OT prophets that looked forward to the coming of Christ.

11:14 he is Elijah who is to come. Malachi had prophesied that "Elijah" would prepare the way for the Messiah (Mal. 3:1; 4:5; see note on Mal. 4:4–6). He did not actually imply only a literal reappearance of Elijah, and John's earlier denial that he was Elijah (John 1:21) was probably an attempt to correct a popular belief that Elijah himself would reappear. Before John's birth,

18[u]ch. 3:4; Mark 1:6 [v]Luke 1:15
19[w]ch. 9:10; Luke 7:36; 14:1; John 2:1; 12:2 [x]ch. 9:11; Luke 15:2; 19:7 [y]ch. 18:17
20[z][Ps. 81:11-13; Isa. 1:2-5]
21[a]For ver. 21-24, see Luke 10:12-15 [b]ch. 15:21; Mark 3:8; [Isa. 23; Ezek. 28:2-24; Amos 1:9, 10]
22[c][Luke 12:47, 48] [d]See Acts 17:31 [b][See ver. 21 above]
23[e]Cited from Isa. 14:13-15 [f]ch. 16:18 (Gk.); Luke 16:23; Acts 2:27
24[c][See ver. 22 above] [g]ch. 10:15 [d][See ver. 22 above]
25[h]For ver. 25-27, see Luke 10:21, 22 [i]See Acts 17:24 [j]Job 37:24; 1 Cor. 1:19-27; 2 Cor. 3:14 [k]ch. 21:16; Ps. 8:2; [ch. 13:11; 16:17]
26[l]Luke 12:32; Gal. 1:15
27[m]See ch. 28:18 [n][John 1:18; 6:46; 7:29; 8:19; 10:15; 17:25] [o][John 17:26]
28[p]John 7:37; [John 6:37] [q][ver. 3] [r][ch. 23:4; Luke 11:46]
29[s]John 13:15; Eph. 4:20; Phil. 2:5; 1 Pet. 2:21; 1 John 2:6 [t]Zech. 9:9; 2 Cor. 10:1; Phil. 2:7, 8; [ch. 5:5] [u]Jer. 6:16
30[v]1 John 5:3

16 “But to what shall I compare this generation? It is like children sitting in the marketplaces and calling to their playmates,

> **17** “‘We played the flute for you, and you did not dance;
> we sang a dirge, and you did not mourn.’

18 For John came [u]neither eating [v]nor drinking, and they say, ‘He has a demon.’ **19** The Son
of Man came [w]eating and drinking, and they say, ‘Look at him! A glutton and a drunkard,
[x]a friend of [y]tax collectors and sinners!’ Yet wisdom is justified by her deeds.”[1]

Woe to Unrepentant Cities

20 [z]Then he began to denounce the cities where most of his mighty works had been
done, because they did not repent. **21** [a]“Woe to you, Chorazin! Woe to you, Bethsaida! For
if the mighty works done in you had been done in [b]Tyre and Sidon, they would have
repented long ago in sackcloth and ashes. **22** [c]But I tell you, it will be more bearable on
[d]the day of judgment for [b]Tyre and Sidon than for you. **23** And you, [e]Capernaum, will
you be exalted to heaven? You will be brought down to [f]Hades. For if the mighty works
done in you had been done in Sodom, it would have remained until this day. **24** [c]But I
tell you that [g]it will be more tolerable on [d]the day of judgment for the land of Sodom
than for you.”

Come to Me, and I Will Give You Rest

25 [h]At that time Jesus declared, “I thank you, Father, [i]Lord of heaven and earth, that [j]you
have hidden these things from the wise and understanding and [k]revealed them to little
children; **26** yes, Father, for such was your [l]gracious will.[2] **27** [m]All things have been handed
over to me by my Father, and no one knows the Son [n]except the Father, and no one knows
the Father except the Son and anyone [o]to whom the Son chooses to reveal him. **28** [p]Come
to [q]me, all who labor and are [r]heavy laden, and I will give you rest. **29** Take my yoke upon
you, and [s]learn from me, for I am [t]gentle and lowly in heart, and [u]you will find rest for
your souls. **30** For [v]my yoke is easy, and my burden is light.”

[1] Some manuscripts *children* (compare Luke 7:35) [2] Or *for so it pleased you well*

he was designated as the one who would minister in the “spirit and power of Elijah” (Luke 1:17), thereby fulfilling Malachi’s prophecy.

11:16 this generation. The crowds and the religious leaders who have rejected John’s and Jesus’ ministries. They are like selfish and stubborn **children**, always insisting on their own way.

11:17 We played the flute . . . and you did not dance. The people reject the gospel because John and Jesus do not conform to their expectations and do what they want.

11:18–19 neither eating nor drinking. Some apparently accused John of demonic influence because of his appearance and ascetic lifestyle. **Son of Man came eating and drinking**. Jesus’ association with those in need of spiritual healing, and his refusal to fast according to Pharisaic expectations (see 9:14–17), was turned into an accusation of his being **a glutton and a drunkard**. However, God’s **wisdom** (Gk. *sophia*) would be **justified** (vindicated) by the righteous fruit of John’s and Jesus’ life and ministry.

11:20–24 Chorazin, **Bethsaida**, and **Capernaum** were **the cities** in which most of Jesus’ miracles were performed, and yet their occupants rejected Jesus’ mission and remained unrepentant. For Bethsaida and Capernaum, see notes on Mark 1:21; Luke 9:10. Chorazin has been identified with Khirbet Karazeh, just northwest of Capernaum. **Tyre and Sidon** were Gentile cities in Phoenicia (see Mark 7:24) and were often the object of condemnation by OT prophets for their Baal worship and arrogant materialism. **Sodom** was the epitome of a “city of sin.” Yet, Jesus says, even Sodom would have repented if it had witnessed his miracles and the reality of the kingdom.

11:25–26 these things. The message and activities of the kingdom of heaven, which require faith and humility to grasp. **wise and understanding**. Those who are wise in the world’s eyes but are unrepentant and stubbornly refuse to accept the gospel. **little children**. Those who receive the gospel in simple faith (cf. 18:1–5).

11:27 All things have been handed over to me by my Father. This reveals the profound divine self-consciousness of Jesus, as well as the supreme authority of the Father within the Trinity, by which he has delegated authority over “all things” to the Son. “All things” probably refers to everything needed with respect to the carrying out of Christ’s ministry of redemption, including the revelation of salvation to those to whom he **chooses to reveal** the Father. **no one knows the Son except the Father**. In both Jesus’ incarnate state and his eternal state as Son, the Father and the Son share an exclusive relationship, including a direct and immediate knowledge of each other.

11:28 Come to me is an invitation to trust Jesus personally, not merely to believe historical facts about him. **All who labor and are heavy laden** refers in the immediate context to those oppressed by the burden of religious legalism imposed on people by the scribes and Pharisees. But the wider application is that Jesus provides “rest for your souls” (v. 29)—that is, eternal rest for all who seek forgiveness of their sins and freedom from the crushing legalistic burden and guilt of trying to earn salvation by good works.

11:29 yoke. The wooden frame joining two animals (usually oxen) for pulling heavy loads was a metaphor for one person’s subjection to another, and a common metaphor in Judaism for the law. The Pharisaic interpretation of the law, with its extensive list of proscriptions, had become a crushing burden (cf. 23:4) but was believed by the people to be of divine origin. Jesus’ yoke of discipleship, on the other hand, brings **rest** through simple commitment to him (cf. 1 John 5:3).

Jesus Is Lord of the Sabbath

12 At that time [w]Jesus went through the grainfields on the Sabbath. His disciples
were hungry, and [x]they began to pluck heads of grain and to eat. 2 But when the
Pharisees saw it, they said to him, [y]"Look, your disciples are doing [z]what is not lawful to
do on the Sabbath." 3 He said to them, [a]"Have you not read what David did when he was
hungry, and those who were with him: 4 how he entered the house of God and ate [b]the
bread of the Presence, which it was not lawful for him to eat nor for those who were with
him, but only for the priests? 5 Or have you not read [c]in the Law how on the Sabbath the
priests in the temple profane the Sabbath and are guiltless? 6 I tell you, [d]something greater
than the temple is here. 7 And if you had known [e]what this means, [f]'I desire mercy, and
not sacrifice,' you would not have condemned the guiltless. 8 For [g]the Son of Man is lord
of the Sabbath."

A Man with a Withered Hand

9 He went on from there and [h]entered their synagogue. 10 And a man was there with a
withered hand. And they asked him, [i]"Is it lawful to heal on the Sabbath?"—[j]so that they
might accuse him. 11 He said to them, "Which one of you who has a sheep, [k]if it falls into a
pit on the Sabbath, will not take hold of it and lift it out? 12 [l]Of how much more value is a
man than a sheep! So [m]it is lawful to do good on the Sabbath." 13 Then he said to the man,
"Stretch out your hand." And [n]the man stretched it out, and it was restored, healthy like
the other. 14 But the Pharisees went out and conspired against him, how to destroy him.

God's Chosen Servant

15 Jesus, aware of this, [o]withdrew from there. And [p]many followed him, and he healed
them all 16 and [q]ordered them not to make him known. 17 [r]This was to fulfill what was
spoken by the prophet Isaiah:

18 [s]"Behold, my [t]servant whom I have chosen,
my beloved with whom my soul is well pleased.

Chapter 12
1 [w]For ver. 1-8, see Mark 2:23-28; Luke 6:1-5 [x]Deut. 23:25
2 [y][ver. 10; Luke 13:14; 14:3; John 5:10; 7:23; 9:16] [z][Ex. 20:9-11]
3 [a]1 Sam. 21:1-6; See ch. 21:16
4 [b]Ex. 25:30; Lev. 24:5-9
5 [c]Num. 28:9, 10; [1 Chr. 9:32; John 7:22, 23]
6 [d]ver. 41, 42; [ver. 8; Hag. 2:9; Mal. 3:1]
7 [e]ch. 9:13 [f]Cited from Hos. 6:6; [Mic. 6:6-8]
8 [g][ch. 9:6]
9 [h]For ver. 9-14, see Mark 3:1-6; Luke 6:6-11
10 [i][Luke 14:3]; See ver. 2 [j][Luke 11:54; 20:20; John 8:6]
11 [k][Ex. 23:4, 5; Deut. 22:4]
12 [l]ch. 6:26; 10:31 [m][John 5:16, 17]
13 [n][1 Kgs. 13:4]
15 [o]Mark 3:7; John 10:39; See ch. 10:23 [p]ch. 19:2
16 [q]Mark 1:25 (Gk.); 3:12; 8:30; Luke 4:41 (Gk.); 9:21; See ch. 8:4
17 [r]See ch. 1:22
18 [s]Cited from Isa. 42:1-3 [t]Acts 4:27, 30

12:1–45 *Confrontations with the Pharisees.* The Pharisees accuse Jesus of violating the Sabbath (vv. 1–14), suggest he is in league with Satan (vv. 22–37), and demand a cosmic sign (vv. 38–42). Jesus vindicates himself as lord of the Sabbath (v. 8), divine servant of justice (v. 18), and the Spirit-empowered inaugurator of the kingdom of God (v. 28). Judgment will come upon the hard-hearted blasphemers (vv. 30–45), but those who follow Jesus are his true family (see vv. 46–50).

12:1 pluck heads of grain. The edges of a field were not normally harvested, so that the poor and hungry, foreigners, orphans, and widows could gather food for themselves (see Lev. 19:9; 23:22). This law showed the compassion of God for those in need.

12:2 Pharisees. See note on 3:7.

12:4 ate the bread of the Presence. Twelve loaves of bread, representing God's covenant with the 12 tribes of Israel, were to be baked and placed in the tabernacle on each Sabbath as an offering. The bread was only to be eaten by **the priests** (Lev. 24:5–9), but Scripture does not condemn David for eating the bread during his escape from Saul. The law was intended to serve God's people, rather than God's people being intended to serve the law (cf. Mark 2:27).

12:5 The fact that priests, in carrying out their duties, had to work on (and thus **"profane"**) the Sabbath, but were **guiltless** in doing so, shows that God made allowances within the law.

12:6 something greater. The Sabbath points to Christ (see v. 8) and to the "rest" he gives from the impossible task of earning salvation by good works (cf. 11:28).

12:7 I desire mercy, and not sacrifice. See note on 9:13.

12:8 the Son of Man is lord of the Sabbath. Jesus does not challenge the Sabbath law itself but rather the Pharisees' interpretation of it. As Messiah, Jesus authoritatively interprets every aspect of the law (cf. 5:17–48) and here points out the Pharisees' blindness to the actual intent of the Sabbath—to bring rest and well-being. This final argument in response to the Pharisees' challenge (12:2) is the decisive argument—that because of who Jesus is, he has the authority to interpret the law.

12:9–10 heal on the Sabbath. In rabbinic teaching, numerous regulations defined minute categories of "work" that were prohibited on the Sabbath, but these legalistic regulations were never God's intent for the OT law. (See the 39 things prohibited on the Sabbath in Mishnah, *Shabbat* 7.2.) Jesus' opponents believed that the Sabbath could be broken only in extreme cases of life and death. Since the life of the man with the **withered hand** was not in danger, they believed his healing should wait until after the Sabbath.

12:11–12 Of how much more value is a man than a sheep! Jesus contrasts the value of an animal to that of a human (see note on 6:26) and asserts that the higher principle is not simply refraining from activity on the Sabbath but doing **good on the Sabbath**.

12:13 it was restored, healthy. The miracle confirms Jesus' authority to interpret laws relating to the Sabbath (vv. 1–12) and further validates his claim to be the messianic Son of Man (cf. 9:1–8; 12:8).

12:14 conspired against him. The religious leaders see clearly that Jesus' claim concerning authority to interpret the law was in fact a claim to messianic authority, which they judged to be a heresy worthy of death.

12:15 Jesus . . . withdrew from there (cf. 2:14, 22; 4:12, 13), not trying to escape all opposition but to prevent its escalation until the time comes for his predicted betrayal and death.

12:16 ordered them not to make him known. See note on 8:4; cf. 9:30; 16:20; 17:9.

12:17 to fulfill what was spoken by the prophet Isaiah. Matthew's typical fulfillment formula (see note on 1:22) introduces his longest OT quotation (Isa. 42:1–4). It comes from the "Servant Songs" (Isaiah 42–53), in which the "servant" represents alternately the nation of Israel and the gentle, Spirit-endowed, suffering servant, whose mission is to bring justice to the nations.

12:18–20 my servant whom I have chosen, my beloved. The Father expresses the same delight in his Son at Jesus' baptism (3:17) and at his transfiguration (17:5). **he will proclaim justice**. The servant brings the good news of the arrival of the kingdom but also pronounces judgment on the rulers of this world who reject him. **will not quarrel or cry aloud**. He did

18[u][Isa. 61:1; Luke 4:18; John 3:34; Acts 10:38]
21[v]Isa. 42:4 (Gk.); [Isa. 11:10; Rom. 15:12]
22[w]For ver. 22-24, see Luke 11:14, 15; [ch. 9:32-34]
23[x]John 4:29; 7:26, 31; See ch. 9:27
24[y]Mark 3:22; See ch. 10:25
25[z]See ch. 9:4 [a]For ver. 25-29, see Mark 3:23-27; Luke 11:17-22
27[b][Acts 19:13] [c][2 Kgs. 2:7]
28[d][ver. 18] [e]ch. 19:24; 21:31, 43; Luke 17:21
29[f]Isa. 49:24 [g][Isa. 53:12]
30[h]Luke 11:23; [Mark 9:40; Luke 9:50]
31[i]For ver. 31, 32, see Mark 3:28-30; [Luke 12:10; Heb. 6:4-6; 10:26; 1 John 5:16] [j][Acts 7:51; Heb. 10:29]
32[k]ch. 11:19; John 7:12; 9:24 [l]1 Tim. 1:12, 13 [j][See ver. 31 above] [m][Eph. 1:21]
33[n]ch. 7:16-20 [o]Luke 6:43, 44
34[p]ch. 3:7; 23:33 [q]ch. 7:11 [r]ch. 15:18, 19; Luke 6:45; [ch. 13:52; Eph. 4:29]
35[r][See ver. 34 above]
36[s][Eph. 5:4, 11; 2 Pet. 1:8] [t]Eccles. 12:14; Rom. 14:12; 1 Pet. 4:5 [u]See Acts 17:31

[u]I will put my Spirit upon him,
and he will proclaim justice to the Gentiles.
19 He will not quarrel or cry aloud,
nor will anyone hear his voice in the streets;
20 a bruised reed he will not break,
and a smoldering wick he will not quench,
until he brings justice to victory;
21 [v]and in his name the Gentiles will hope."

Blasphemy Against the Holy Spirit

22 [w]Then a demon-oppressed man who was blind and mute was brought to him, and he
healed him, so that the man spoke and saw. 23 [x]And all the people were amazed, and said,
[x]"Can this be the Son of David?" 24 But when the Pharisees heard it, they said, [y]"It is only
by Beelzebul, the prince of demons, that this man casts out demons." 25 [z]Knowing their
thoughts, [a]he said to them, "Every kingdom divided against itself is laid waste, and no
city or house divided against itself will stand. 26 And if Satan casts out Satan, he is divided
against himself. How then will his kingdom stand? 27 And if I cast out demons by Beelzebul,
[b]by whom do [c]your sons cast them out? Therefore they will be your judges. 28 But if it is
[d]by the Spirit of God that I cast out demons, then [e]the kingdom of God has come upon
you. 29 Or [f]how can someone enter a strong man's house and plunder his goods, unless he
first binds the strong man? Then indeed [g]he may plunder his house. 30 [h]Whoever is not
with me is against me, and whoever does not gather with me scatters. 31 [i]Therefore I tell
you, every sin and blasphemy will be forgiven people, but [j]the blasphemy against the
Spirit will not be forgiven. 32 And whoever speaks a word [k]against the Son of Man [l]will be
forgiven, but [j]whoever speaks against the Holy Spirit will not be forgiven, either in [m]this
age or in the age to come.

A Tree Is Known by Its Fruit

33 [n]"Either make the tree good and its fruit good, or make the tree bad and its fruit bad,
[o]for the tree is known by its fruit. 34 [p]You brood of vipers! How can you speak good, [q]when
you are evil? [r]For out of the abundance of the heart the mouth speaks. 35 [r]The good person
out of his good treasure brings forth good, and the evil person out of his evil treasure
brings forth evil. 36 I tell you, [s]on the day of judgment [t]people will give account for [u]every

not come the first time as a conquering warrior. **bruised reed . . . smoldering wick**. Jesus the servant compassionately cares for those who have been abused (cf. 9:36; 11:28).

12:23 Can this be the Son of David? See note on 9:27. The people thought of David as a warrior and king and believed the Son of David would be a liberator. It was difficult for them to comprehend that this gentle healer could indeed be David's promised Son.

12:24 only by Beelzebul, the prince of demons. See note on 10:25. Practicing magic by Satan's power was a capital offense, punishable by stoning. This view of Jesus as a sorcerer was common among Jews even into the early centuries of Christianity.

12:25–26 Knowing their thoughts indicates Jesus' omniscience and therefore his deity. **kingdom divided against itself**. Satan would not work against himself by exorcising demons, who were part of his attempt to control the world.

12:27 your sons. Possibly associates or disciples of the Pharisees. Extrabiblical Jewish literature contains stories about strange rituals for casting out evil spirits (see Josephus, *Jewish Antiquities* 8.45–48; *Tobit* 8:2–3; *Testament of Solomon* throughout), but it is unclear that they were successful (see Acts 19:13–16). The amazement of the crowd in Luke 4:36 indicates that Jesus' authoritative casting out of demons "with a word" (Matt. 8:16) was unprecedented. No example of people casting out demons is found in the OT (but see 1 Sam. 16:14–23).

12:28 by the Spirit of God . . . I cast out demons. Jesus' amazing power over demons was due to the power of the Holy Spirit working through him (cf. 3:16). The **kingdom of God** is inaugurated, though not completely realized, in the ministry of Jesus. "Kingdom of God" occurs only five times in Matthew, compared to 32 occurrences of "kingdom of heaven," which occurs in none of the other Gospel accounts. Jesus is not only the messianic Son of David (12:23) but the King who exercises God's own kingdom power against Satan and his agents and overcomes the kingdom of Satan through his much greater power (see Isa. 59:17; Eph. 6:10–20; Rev. 19:11–21).

12:29 Jesus was able to expel demons because he had bound Satan, **the strong man**. Beginning with Jesus' victory over Satan during the temptation in the wilderness (4:1–11), Jesus demonstrated that Satan was powerless to prevent him from proclaiming the good news of the kingdom and demonstrating the reality of its presence through his work and his words. Satan's **house** represents the sinful world over which, until the coming of Christ, he had such power. Jesus has come to **plunder his house** and rescue people for the kingdom of God (see Col. 1:13).

12:30 Whoever is not with me is against me. Jesus does not allow anyone to remain neutral about him. (But see further Mark 9:38–41, esp. v. 40, where Jesus' followers cannot make such demands about loyalty to themselves.)

12:31–32 blasphemy against the Spirit will not be forgiven. The sin is attributing to Satan what is accomplished by the power of God, and doing this through the flagrant, willful, and persistent rejection of God and his commands. This sin is committed today only by unbelievers who deliberately and unchangeably reject the ministry of the Holy Spirit in calling them to salvation. (See further the extended note on Luke 12:10.)

12:33–35 abundance of the heart. The Pharisees' attempt to label Jesus a blasphemer (v. 24) is itself blasphemy against the Holy Spirit. Their wicked words reveal the evil within their own hearts; they were bad trees (v. 33) in need of radical conversion.

12:36–37 the day of judgment. Christ's second coming (see note on 7:23).

careless word they speak, 37 for [v]by your words you will be justified, and by your words
you will be condemned."

The Sign of Jonah

38 Then some of the scribes and Pharisees answered him, saying, "Teacher, [w]we wish to
see a sign from you." 39 But he answered them, [x]"An evil and [y]adulterous generation seeks
for a sign, but no sign will be given to it except the sign of the prophet Jonah. 40 For [z]just
as Jonah was three days and three nights in the belly of the great fish, [a]so will the Son of
Man be three days and three nights in the heart of the earth. 41 [b]The men of Nineveh will
rise up at the judgment with this generation and [c]condemn it, for [d]they repented at the
preaching of Jonah, and behold, [e]something greater than Jonah is here. 42 [f]The queen
of the South will rise up at the judgment with this generation and condemn it, for she
came from the ends of the earth to hear the wisdom of Solomon, and behold, [e]something
greater than Solomon is here.

Return of an Unclean Spirit

43 "When [g]the unclean spirit has gone out of a person, it passes through [h]waterless
places seeking rest, but finds none. 44 Then it says, 'I will return to my house from which
I came.' And when it comes, it finds the house empty, swept, and put in order. 45 Then it
goes and brings with it seven other spirits more evil than itself, and they enter and dwell
there, and [i]the last state of that person is worse than the first. So also will it be with this
[j]evil generation."

Jesus' Mother and Brothers

46 While he was still speaking to the people, behold, [k]his mother and his [l]brothers stood
outside, asking to speak to him.[1] 48 But he replied to the man who told him, "Who is my
mother, and who are my brothers?" 49 And stretching out his hand toward his disciples, he
said, "Here are my mother and my brothers! 50 For [m]whoever [n]does the will of my Father
in heaven is my brother and sister and mother."

[1] Some manuscripts insert verse 47: *Someone told him, "Your mother and your brothers are standing outside, asking to speak to you"*

37 [v][ch. 5:22; James 3:2-12]
38 [w]ch. 16:1; Mark 8:11, 12; Luke 11:16; 23:8; John 2:18; 4:48; 6:30; 1 Cor. 1:22
39 [x]ch. 16:4; For ver. 39-42, see Luke 11:29-32; [Mark 8:11, 12] [y]Isa. 57:3; Mark 8:38; James 4:4
40 [z]Jonah 1:17 [a][ch. 17:22, 23]
41 [b]Jonah 1:2 [c]Heb. 11:7; [Jer. 3:11; Ezek. 16:51, 52; Rom. 2:27] [d]Jonah 3:5 [e]ver. 6
42 [f]1 Kgs. 10:1; 2 Chr. 9:1 [e][See ver. 41 above]
43 [g]For ver. 43-45, see Luke 11:24-26 [h][Ps. 63:1; Jer. 2:6]
45 [i]2 Pet. 2:20-22; [John 5:14] [j]ver. 39
46 [k]For ver. 46-50, see Mark 3:31-35; Luke 8:19-21 [l]ch. 13:55; Mark 6:3; John 2:12; 7:3, 5, 10; Acts 1:14; 1 Cor. 9:5; Gal. 1:19
50 [m][John 15:14; Heb. 2:11] [n]ch. 7:21; [Luke 11:28]

every careless word. Eternal judgment awaits any who attempt to turn the people against Jesus by slanderous accusations of blasphemy. **By your words you will be justified** means people's words will be outward evidence of their inward character. "Justified" here means "shown to be righteous." This verse does not use "justified" in the Pauline sense of "declared righteous by God" (see notes on Gal. 2:16; James 2:21). Similarly, evil people's evil words will be evidence by which they **will be condemned**.

12:38 a sign. Jesus had already performed many miracles ("signs") that validated his messianic identity. These men were asking for a sign that they could use against him.

12:39 Adulterous refers to spiritual adultery, i.e., unfaithfulness to God. Jesus never rebukes people who seek healing out of genuine need, but he knows these opponents have malicious motives (cf. 16:1). Jonah's being rescued by God was a **sign** to the people of Nineveh that his message was from God. Jesus' death and resurrection (see 12:40) will likewise be God's sign to the present generation.

12:40 Three days and three nights in Jewish reckoning is inclusive, meaning no more than three days or the combination of any part of three separate days. Jesus was raised "in three days" although he was buried Friday afternoon and resurrected Sunday morning (i.e., part of Friday is day one, all of Saturday is day two, and part of Sunday is day three).

12:41 Jesus' words affirm the historicity of the story of Jonah: he says that **the men of Nineveh will rise up at the judgment**, thus predicting an actual future event; and that these same men **repented at the preaching of Jonah** (Jonah 3:5), indicating that Jonah's preaching in Nineveh was an actual historical event.

12:42 queen of the South. The queen of Sheba (1 Kings 10:1–29). Sheba was most likely the home of the Sabaeans in southwestern Arabia, in present-day Yemen. Jesus claims that he is **greater than** the temple (Matt. 12:6), the prophet Jonah (v. 41), and the wise king **Solomon**. He thus elevates himself and his message of the kingdom to be greater than, and the fulfillment of, the three greatest institutions in Israel—priest, prophet, and king.

12:43 Demons were often associated with **waterless places**, apparently because deserts were thought of as being devoid of the blessing of God that came with rainfall and abundant crops (cf. Isa. 13:19–22; 34:13–14; Jer. 17:6; 22:6; 50:12; 51:43; Zeph. 2:13; Mal. 1:3).

12:44 my house from which I came. Demons are persistent in seeking ownership of a person's entire material and immaterial self.

12:45 seven. Linked in Scripture with completion or perfection, here perhaps signifying the completeness of demon possession once the demon returns. If **this evil generation** continues to reject Jesus, even after witnessing his divine authority over demons, their condition will be **worse than** if they had never seen him.

12:46–50 *Jesus' Disciples Are His True Family.* Jesus calls for a new spiritual family in relationship to him and his Father, united in the defining characteristic of Jesus' life and ministry: obedience to the will of the Father (v. 50).

12:46 mother and . . . brothers. There is no mention of "father," which may indicate that Joseph had died by this time (Joseph is never mentioned after the trip to Jerusalem when Jesus was 12; see Luke 2:41–51). Jesus' family may have been trying to bring him to his senses (cf. Mark 3:21); as the eldest son, Jesus would have been responsible for the care of the family after Joseph's death.

12:49 Here are my mother and my brothers. Jesus' messianic mission takes priority even over familial loyalties. Rather than negating the importance of one's biological family (cf. 15:3–9), Jesus is demonstrating the preeminence of a person's commitment to him and the kingdom of heaven.

Chapter 13
1 [o]For ver. 1-15, see Mark 4:1-12; Luke 8:4-10
2 [p][Mark 3:9; Luke 5:1-3]
3 [q]ver. 34 [r][Isa. 55:10; Amos 9:13]
6 [s]James 1:11 [t]John 15:6
7 [u]Jer. 4:3
8 [v]ver. 23; Gen. 26:12
9 [w]See ch. 11:15
11 [x]ch. 19:11; Col. 1:27; [1 Cor. 2:6-10; 1 John 2:20, 27]; See ch. 11:25 [y]See Rom. 16:25
12 [z]ch. 25:29; Mark 4:25; Luke 8:18; 19:26; [John 15:2; James 4:6]

The Parable of the Sower

13 That same day Jesus went out of the house [o]and sat beside the sea. 2 And great
crowds gathered about him, [p]so that he got into a boat and sat down. And the
whole crowd stood on the beach. 3 And [q]he told them many things in parables, saying: [r]"A
sower went out to sow. 4 And as he sowed, some seeds fell along the path, and the birds
came and devoured them. 5 Other seeds fell on rocky ground, where they did not have
much soil, and immediately they sprang up, since they had no depth of soil, 6 but [s]when
the sun rose they were scorched. And since they had no root, [t]they withered away. 7 Other
seeds fell among [u]thorns, and the thorns grew up and choked them. 8 Other seeds fell on
good soil and produced grain, some [v]a hundredfold, some sixty, some thirty. 9 [w]He who
has ears,[1] let him hear."

The Purpose of the Parables

10 Then the disciples came and said to him, "Why do you speak to them in parables?"
11 And he answered them, [x]"To you it has been given to know [y]the secrets of the kingdom
of heaven, but to them it has not been given. 12 [z]For to the one who has, more will be given,

[1] Some manuscripts add here and in verse 43 *to hear*

13:1–53 *Mysteries of the Messianic Kingdom Revealed in Parables.* This is the third of Jesus' five major discourses (see Introduction: Key Themes; Literary Features), called the Parabolic Discourse because of its collection of parables.

13:1–23 *The Opening of the Parabolic Discourse.* Jesus gives the parable of the sower and soils (vv. 3b–9), explains his purpose in speaking in parables (vv. 10–17), then interprets the parable (vv. 18–23).

13:1–2 sat beside the sea. The Sea of Galilee. Sitting was the typical posture for teachers. Local tradition locates this discourse at the "Cove of the Parables," a natural horseshoe-shaped amphitheater whose environmental acoustics could have carried Jesus' voice over 300 feet (91 m) from the **boat** to a crowd of hundreds on the shore.

13:3 Parables are Jesus' means of communicating truth through a narrative analogy in order to teach a moral or spiritual lesson. His parables produce very different results in different people: they hide truth from the "crowd" (v. 2; see note on 5:2), while they communicate truth to the disciples.

13:4–7 seeds fell along the path. As seed was scattered in all directions while the farmer walked up and down the field, some would fall accidentally on the hard paths that surrounded the field. **rocky ground.** The terrain in Palestine was uneven and rocky, covered by a thin layer of soil. **among thorns.** Competing for nutrients from the soil, weeds choke out the good plants, which are then unable to reach maturity and bear fruit.

13:8 hundredfold, some sixty, some thirty. Typical agricultural yields ranged from about fivefold to fifteenfold, with a tenfold return considered a good crop, though some historical reports tell of extraordinary yields up to a hundredfold (one is in Gen. 26:12).

13:10–11 secrets (plural of Gk. *mystērion*, "mystery, secret"). The mysteries of how the kingdom of heaven would operate are revealed to the disciples but withheld from the spiritually unresponsive crowd. In particular, these secrets **of the kingdom of heaven** explained its partial and preliminary manifestations in Jesus' day as it was breaking into the world in advance of its full and final appearing at the end of the age.

13:12–13 seeing they do not see. God sovereignly uses the parables to

The Parables of Jesus

Parable	Matthew	Mark	Luke
The Purpose of the Parables	13:10–17	4:10–12	8:9–10
The Sower	13:1–9, 18–23	4:1–9, 13–20	8:4–8, 11–15
The Weeds	13:24–30, 36–43	4:26–29	
The Mustard Seed	13:31–32	4:30–32	13:18–19
The Leaven	13:33		13:20–21
The Hidden Treasure	13:44		
The Pearl of Great Value	13:45–46		
The Net	13:47–50		
The Lost Sheep	18:10–14		15:3–7
The Unforgiving Servant	18:23–35		
The Two Sons	21:28–32		
The Tenants	21:33–44	12:1–11	20:9–18
The Wedding Feast	22:1–14		14:16–24

Parable	Matthew	Mark	Luke
The Ten Virgins	25:1–13		
The Talents	25:14–30		19:11–27
The Good Samaritan			10:29–37
The Rich Fool			12:16–21
The Barren Fig Tree			13:6–9
The Wedding Feast			14:7–11
The Lost Coin			15:8–10
The Prodigal Son			15:11–32
The Dishonest Manager			16:1–9
The Rich Man and Lazarus			16:19–31
The Persistent Widow			18:1–8
The Pharisee and the Tax Collector			18:9–14

and he will have an abundance, but from the one who has not, [a]even what he has will be
taken away. 13 This is why I speak to them in parables, because [b]seeing they do not see, and
hearing they do not hear, [c]nor do they understand. 14 Indeed, in their case the prophecy
of Isaiah is fulfilled that says:

[d]"'You will indeed hear but never understand,
and you will indeed see but never perceive.'
15 For this people's heart has grown dull,
and with their ears [e]they can barely hear,
and [f]their eyes they have closed,
lest they should see with their eyes
and hear with their ears
and [g]understand with their heart
and [h]turn, and I would heal them.'

16 But [i]blessed are your eyes, for they see, and your ears, for they hear. 17 [i]For truly, I say to
you, [j]many prophets and righteous people longed to see what you see, and did not see it,
and to hear what you hear, and did not hear it.

The Parable of the Sower Explained

18 [k]"Hear then the parable of the sower: 19 When anyone hears the word of [l]the kingdom
and [m]does not understand it, [n]the evil one comes and snatches away what has been sown in
his heart. This is what was sown along the path. 20 As for what was sown on rocky ground,
this is the one who hears the word and immediately [o]receives it with joy, 21 yet he has no
root in himself, but [p]endures for a while, and when tribulation or persecution arises on
account of the word, immediately [q]he falls away.[1] 22 As for what was sown among thorns,
this is the one who hears the word, but [r]the cares of [s]the world and [t]the deceitfulness of
riches choke the word, and it proves unfruitful. 23 As for what was sown on good soil, this
is the one who hears the word and [m]understands it. He indeed [u]bears fruit and yields, in
one case [v]a hundredfold, in another sixty, and in another thirty."

The Parable of the Weeds

24 He put another parable before them, saying, [w]"The kingdom of heaven may be compared to a man who sowed good seed in his field, 25 but while his men were sleeping, his
enemy came and sowed weeds[2] among the wheat and went away. 26 So when the plants
came up and bore grain, then the weeds appeared also. 27 And the servants[3] of the master
of the house came and said to him, 'Master, did you not sow good seed in your field? How
then does it have weeds?' 28 He said to them, 'An enemy has done this.' So the servants said
to him, 'Then do you want us to go and gather them?' 29 But he said, [x]'No, lest in gathering the weeds you root up the wheat along with them. 30 Let both grow together until the
harvest, and at harvest time I will tell the reapers, [y]Gather the weeds first and bind them
in bundles to be burned, but gather the wheat into my barn.'"

[1] Or *stumbles* [2] Probably *darnel*, a wheat-like weed [3] Greek *bondservants*; also verse 28

12 [a][Rev. 2:5]
13 [b]Deut. 29:4; Jer. 5:21; Ezek. 12:2; Rom. 11:8; 2 Cor. 3:14; 4:4; [Isa. 42:19, 20] [c]ver. 19, 51; ch. 15:10; 16:12; Mark 8:21
14 [d]John 12:40; Acts 28:26, 27; Cited from Isa. 6:9, 10
15 [e][Heb. 5:11] [f][John 9:39, 41] [g][Rom. 10:10] [h]See Luke 22:32
16 [i]Luke 10:23, 24; [ch. 16:17]
17 [i][See ver. 16 above] [j]Heb. 11:13; 1 Pet. 1:10-12; [John 8:56]
18 [k]For ver. 18-23, see Mark 4:13-20; Luke 8:11-15
19 [l]ver. 38; ch. 4:23; 8:12 [m]See ver. 13 [n]John 17:15; Eph. 6:16; 2 Thess. 3:3; 1 John 2:13, 14; 3:12; 5:18, 19
20 [o][Isa. 58:2; Ezek. 33:31, 32; Mark 6:20; John 5:35]
21 [p]Gal. 1:6; [Hos. 6:4; Gal. 5:7] [q]See ch. 11:6
22 [r]See ch. 6:25 [s]2 Tim. 4:10 [t]1 Tim. 6:9, 10, 17; [ch. 19:23; Mark 10:23; Acts 5:1-11; Heb. 3:13]
23 [m][See ver. 19 above] [u]Hos. 14:8; John 15:5, 16; Phil. 1:11; Col. 1:6 [v]ver. 8
24 [w]ver. 37-42; [Mark 4:26-29]
29 [x][1 Cor. 4:5]
30 [y]ch. 3:12

either harden a person's heart so that he or she will be unable to respond (v. 15), or to elicit the positive response of coming to Jesus, asking for an explanation, and accepting his message (cf. v. 10).

13:18 Hear then the parable of the sower. Jesus explains the parable in response to the disciples' receptive hearts that lead them to ask him for clarification (cf. v. 10). (For additional notes on the parable of the sower, see Luke 8:11–15.)

13:19 The seed in the parable (vv. 3–9) represents **the word of the kingdom** (i.e., "the gospel of the kingdom," cf. 4:23; 9:35; 24:14). All of Jesus' "seeds" are good, so the emphasis is on the various types of soil (13:19–23). **The evil one** is Satan, the devil (see note on 4:1). **sown along the path**. Hearts that are hardened, like the scribes and Pharisees.

13:20–23 Sown on rocky ground depicts a heart that is immediately receptive, but hardened, so that the gospel never takes **root** and thus fails to bear fruit. The seed **sown among thorns** likewise is **unfruitful**, choked out by a heart weighed down with the **cares of the world and the deceitfulness of riches**. The good soil depicts the heart that has been prepared to receive the gospel, yielding an abundant harvest according to individual potential.

13:24–35 *Further Parables Told to the Crowds.* Jesus presents the parables of the wheat and the weeds (vv. 24–30), the mustard seed (vv. 31–32), and the leaven (v. 33).

13:24 The kingdom of heaven may be compared to. Jesus draws on various common experiences to describe the arrival and activity of the kingdom. Cf. "the kingdom of heaven is like" (vv. 31, 33, 44, 45, 47; 20:1; see also 18:23; 22:1; 25:1).

13:25–30 Weeds (plural of Gk. *zizanion*, only here in the NT) are probably darnel, a weedy rye grass with poisonous black seeds which resembles wheat in its early growth but is easily distinguished from it at maturity. Any attempt to **gather** the weeds would only endanger the wheat, because the roots of the weeds would be intertwined with those of the wheat. **Let both grow together** (v. 30). God allows both believers and unbelievers to live in the world until the day of judgment; see note on v. 38.

The Mustard Seed and the Leaven

31 He put another parable before them, saying, [z]"The kingdom of heaven is like [a]a grain
of mustard seed that a man took and sowed in his field. 32 It is the smallest of all seeds, but
when it has grown it is larger than all the garden plants and becomes a tree, so that the
birds of the air come and make nests in its branches."

33 He told them another parable. [b]"The kingdom of heaven is like leaven that a woman
took and hid in [c]three measures of flour, till it was [d]all leavened."

Prophecy and Parables

34 [e]All these things Jesus said to the crowds in parables; indeed, he said nothing to them
without a parable. 35 This was to fulfill what was spoken by the prophet:[1]

[f]"I will open my mouth in parables;
[g]I will utter what has been hidden [h]since the foundation of the world."

The Parable of the Weeds Explained

36 Then he left the crowds and went into [i]the house. And his disciples came to him, saying, [j]"Explain to us the parable of the weeds of the field." 37 He answered, "The one who
sows the good seed is the Son of Man. 38 The field is the world, and the good seed is [k]the
sons of the kingdom. The weeds are [l]the sons of the evil one, 39 and the enemy who sowed
them is the devil. [m]The harvest is [n]the end of the age, and the reapers are angels. 40 Just as
the weeds [o]are gathered and burned with fire, so will it be at [n]the end of the age. 41 [p]The
Son of Man will send his angels, and they will gather out of his kingdom all [q]causes of sin
and [r]all law-breakers, 42 [s]and throw them into the fiery furnace. In that place [t]there will
be weeping and gnashing of teeth. 43 Then [u]the righteous will shine like the sun [v]in the
kingdom of their Father. [w]He who has ears, let him hear.

The Parable of the Hidden Treasure

44 "The kingdom of heaven [x]is like treasure hidden in a field, which a man found and
covered up. Then in his joy [y]he goes and sells all that he has and [z]buys that field.

The Parable of the Pearl of Great Value

45 "Again, the kingdom of heaven is like a merchant in search of fine pearls, 46 who, on
finding [a]one pearl of great value, [y]went and sold all that he had and [z]bought it.

The Parable of the Net

47 "Again, the kingdom of heaven is [b]like a net that was thrown into the sea and [c]gathered
fish of every kind. 48 When it was full, [d]men drew it ashore and sat down and sorted the

[1] Some manuscripts *Isaiah the prophet*

31 [z]For ver. 31, 32, see Mark 4:30-32; Luke 13:18, 19 [a]ch. 17:20; Luke 17:6
33 [b]Luke 13:20, 21 [c]Gen. 18:6 [d]1 Cor. 5:6; Gal. 5:9
34 [e]ver. 3; Mark 4:33, 34; [John 16:25, 29]
35 [f]Cited from Ps. 78:2 [g][ver. 11; Rom. 16:25, 26; 1 Cor. 2:7] [h]ch. 25:34; Luke 11:50; [John 17:24; Eph. 1:4; 1 Pet. 1:20]
36 [i]ver. 1 [j]ver. 24-30; [ch. 15:15]
38 [k][ver. 43] [l]John 8:44; Acts 13:10; 1 John 3:10; [ch. 23:15]; See ver. 19
39 [m]Joel 3:13; Rev. 14:15 [n]ver. 49; ch. 24:3; 28:20; [Dan. 12:13; Heb. 9:26]
40 [o]John 15:6; [ch. 3:12] [n][See ver. 39 above]
41 [p]ch. 24:31 [q]ch. 18:7; [Zeph. 1:3] [r]ch. 7:23
42 [s]ver. 50; Rev. 9:2; [Rev. 19:20; 20:10] [t]See ch. 8:12
43 [u]Prov. 4:18; Dan. 12:3; [1 Cor. 15:41, 42] [v][ver. 38; ch. 25:34; 26:29; Luke 12:32] [w]See ch. 11:15
44 [x]Prov. 2:4 [y][ch. 25:9; Prov. 23:23; Phil. 3:7, 8] [z][Isa. 55:1; Rev. 3:18]
46 [a]ch. 7:6 [y][See ver. 44 above] [z][See ver. 44 above]
47 [b]ch. 4:19 [c][ver. 38; ch. 22:10; 25:2]
48 [d]John 21:11

13:31–32 The remarkable contrast between the small beginnings of the **mustard seed** and its final, large mustard plant had earned it proverbial status in Judaism (cf. 17:20). It was the **smallest of all** agricultural **seeds** in Palestine. **becomes a tree**. The mustard "tree" grows to a height of 8 to 12 feet (2.4 to 3.7 m). Israel was not prepared for an insignificant beginning to the kingdom of God, so this image would have shocked the listeners. (See also note on Luke 13:19.)

13:33 Jesus uses the metaphor of **leaven**, which usually has a negative connotation in Scripture (cf. 16:6; 1 Cor. 5:6–7), to symbolize the positive, hidden permeation of the kingdom of heaven in this world. The kingdom is indeed active though not fully visible to the world, because it begins with an inner transformation of the heart. **Three measures** was probably about 50 pounds (39 liters) and would have produced enough bread to feed a hundred people.

13:36–53 *Explanations and Parables Told to the Disciples.* Jesus explains the parable of the wheat and weeds (vv. 36–43) and then gives the disciples the parables of the hidden treasure (v. 44), the costly pearl (vv. 45–46), the dragnet (vv. 47–48), and the householder's treasure (vv. 51–52).

13:38 The parable describes the activity of God's kingdom in the **world** rather than within the church. The enemies of the kingdom (**weeds**) will always coexist with the sons of the kingdom (**good seed**) in this age.

13:39–40 harvest. The judgment that will follow the Son of Man's return at the end of the age (see note on 24:3) to establish his kingdom in its fully realized form.

13:41–42 fiery furnace . . . weeping and gnashing of teeth. Jesus' typical description of eternal judgment in Matthew's Gospel (cf. 8:12; 13:50; 22:13; 24:51; 25:30).

13:43 The righteous will shine like the sun, thus reflecting in some lesser way the brightness of the glory of God (cf. Ex. 34:35; Dan. 12:3; Matt. 17:2; 1 Cor. 15:49).

13:44 Treasure was often **hidden** in fields, since formal banks did not exist (the "bankers" of 25:27 were money-changers who exchanged currency and also seem to have loaned money at interest). **Buys that field** does not suggest earning one's salvation; instead, the parable emphasizes the supreme value of the hidden treasure (**the kingdom of heaven**), which is worth far more than any sacrifice one could make to acquire it (**sells all that he has**).

13:45–46 Unlike the man who stumbled upon the hidden treasure (v. 44), this **merchant** searched diligently for the **fine pearls**. But when he found the **one pearl of great value** (**the kingdom of heaven**), his reaction was the same: he sacrificed all that he had and **bought it** (see note on v. 44).

13:47–50 The **net**, shaped like a long wall, was dragged toward shore by both ends, trapping fish of every kind. **sorted**. Fish without scales and fins, e.g., were considered **bad** and unclean (cf. Lev. 11:9–12). Evil will not be totally removed from the world until **the end of the age**.

good into containers but threw away the bad. 49 So it will be at [e]the end of the age. The
angels will come out and [f]separate the evil from the righteous 50 [g]and throw them into the
fiery furnace. In that place [g]there will be weeping and gnashing of teeth.

New and Old Treasures

51 [h]"Have you understood all these things?" They said to him, "Yes." 52 And he said to
them, "Therefore every [i]scribe [j]who has been trained for the kingdom of heaven is like a
master of a house, who [k]brings out of his treasure what is new and what is old."

Jesus Rejected at Nazareth

53 And when Jesus had finished these parables, he went away from there, 54 [l]and coming
to [m]his hometown [n]he taught them in their synagogue, so that [o]they were astonished, and
said, "Where did this man get this wisdom and these mighty works? 55 [p]Is not this [q]the
carpenter's son? Is not his mother called Mary? And are not [r]his brothers James and Joseph
and Simon and Judas? 56 And are not all his sisters with us? Where then did this man get
all these things?" 57 And [s]they took offense at him. But Jesus said to them, [t]"A prophet is
not without honor except in his hometown and in his own household." 58 And he did not
do many mighty works there, [u]because of their unbelief.

The Death of John the Baptist

14 [v]At that time [w]Herod the tetrarch heard about the fame of Jesus, 2 and he said to his
servants, [x]"This is John the Baptist. He has been raised from the dead; that is why
these miraculous powers are at work in him." 3 For [y]Herod had seized John and bound him
and [z]put him in prison for the sake of Herodias, his brother Philip's wife,[1] 4 because John
had been saying to him, [a]"It is not lawful for you to have her." 5 And though he wanted
to put him to death, [b]he feared the people, because they held him to be [c]a prophet. 6 But
when Herod's [d]birthday came, the daughter of Herodias danced before the company and
pleased Herod, 7 so that he promised with an oath to give her whatever she might ask.
8 Prompted by her mother, she said, "Give me the head of John the Baptist here on a plat-

[1] Some manuscripts *his brother's wife*

49 [e]See ver. 39 [f]ch. 25:32; [ver. 41]
50 [g]See ver. 42
51 [h]ver. 10-16; [John 10:6; 16:29]
52 [i]ch. 23:34 [j]ch. 28:19 [k][ch. 12:35]
54 [l]For ver. 54-58, see Mark 6:1-6; [Luke 4:16-30] [m]ch. 2:23; Luke 4:23 [n]See ch. 4:23 [o]See ch. 7:28
55 [p][Luke 4:22; John 6:42] [q][Mark 6:3] [r]See ch. 12:46
57 [s]See ch. 11:6 [t]Luke 4:24; John 4:44; [Jer. 11:21; 12:6; John 7:5]
58 [u][ch. 17:20]

Chapter 14

1 [v]For ver. 1-12, see Mark 6:14-29; Luke 9:7-9 [w]Luke 3:1; Acts 13:1
2 [x]ch. 16:14
3 [y]Luke 3:19, 20 [z]ch. 11:2; John 3:24
4 [a]Lev. 18:16; 20:21
5 [b]ch. 21:26; [ch. 21:46] [c]See ch. 11:9
6 [d]Gen. 40:20

13:51–52 Have you understood . . . Yes. True disciples grow in understanding through Jesus' teaching (cf. 28:20). They are like the man who **brings out of his treasure what is new and what is old**, in that they understand both the "new" revelation from Jesus and how it fulfills the "old" promises in the OT.

13:54–16:20 *The Identity of the Messiah Revealed.* This section marks a major new emphasis in Matthew's narrative as Jesus' messianic identity is increasingly clarified.

13:54–14:12 *Prophet(s) without Honor.* Jesus is rejected at Nazareth (13:54–58); John the Baptist is beheaded by Herod Antipas (14:1–12).

13:54 Although Capernaum had become Jesus' "own city" during his Galilean ministry (4:13; 9:1), **his hometown** is Nazareth, the village of his family and where he spent his childhood (see note on 2:23). Perhaps he is responding to a request from his mother and brothers to return home (see note on 12:46).

13:55–56 Since they know Jesus' human roots, the people of Nazareth assume he cannot be anything special. He is a hometown son making fantastic claims for himself. **His brothers** and **his sisters** refers to other children born to Joseph and Mary after the birth of Jesus. Some interpreters, seeking to defend a doctrine of the "perpetual virginity of Mary," have suggested that these were cousins, or children of Joseph from another marriage, but no evidence in the Greek words *adelphoi* ("brothers") and *adelphai* ("sisters"), or in any other historical information, gives support to that view. For Mary to have sexual relations with her husband, Joseph, and to bear children, would contribute to her holiness, not detract from it (cf. Gen. 1:28; 1 Cor. 7:3–5; 1 Tim. 5:14). On Jesus' family, see note on Mark 6:3.

13:57 took offense. See note on 11:6. **prophet**. Jesus aligns himself with the OT prophets who had revealed God's will for the people of Israel but had consistently been rejected by them.

13:58 not . . . many mighty works . . . because of their unbelief. Hard-heartedness and rejection of Jesus prevent the Spirit's healing ministry, just as they prevent forgiveness of sin (see note on 12:31–32). The Holy Spirit does not force his miracles on a hostile, skeptical audience.

14:1 Herod the tetrarch. Herod Antipas was the Roman ruler over the region where Jesus ministered. He was only 17 years old when his father, Herod the Great, died. The kingdom was divided among three of Herod's sons—Archelaus, Antipas, and Philip II (see note on 2:22). Herod Antipas was made tetrarch (the ruler of a fourth part of a kingdom) of Galilee and Perea and had a long rule (4 B.C.–A.D. 39).

14:2 This is John the Baptist. He has been raised from the dead. Herod Antipas's reaction at hearing of Jesus' ministry reveals a curious blend of theology and superstition, based partly on semi-pagan ideas of returning spirits.

14:3–4 For Herod had seized John. Verses 3–12 are a historical flashback. Herod Antipas had fallen in love with **Herodias**, the wife of his half brother Herod Philip I (not the tetrarch Philip mentioned in Luke 3:1), even though both were married at the time. Herodias divorced Herod Philip I and Herod Antipas divorced his wife (the daughter of the Nabatean king, Aretas IV), and they were married. John the Baptist had publicly condemned Herod Antipas for his actions (**It is not lawful for you to have her**). Josephus reports that John the Baptist was imprisoned at Herod Antipas's fortress-palace called Machaerus (*Jewish Antiquities* 18.116–119; cf. the description in *Jewish War* 7.164–177), which was a fortress built atop a steep hill east of the Dead Sea. It had been fortified by the Hasmonean Jewish kings (2nd century B.C.), destroyed by the Romans (c. 56 B.C.), and rebuilt as a palace by Herod the Great. Archaeological investigation has delineated the Herodian palace enclosure, including a cistern from this era.

14:6–7 When Herod's birthday came a great celebration was held in his honor at the palace at Machaerus. Herodias had her daughter (named Salome in Josephus, *Jewish Antiquities* 18.136) perform a dance for Herod Antipas. She was only 12 to 14 years old, but in that debased setting it likely was a sensual dance, which **pleased Herod**.

14:8 Prompted by her mother. Herodias steps in to eliminate the accusing voice of John the Baptist, a threat to her husband's reign.

12[e] See ch. 9:14
13[f] For ver. 13-21, see Mark 6:32-44; Luke 9:10-17; John 6:1-13; [ch. 15:32-38; 16:9; Mark 8:2-9]
14[g] [ch. 9:36]
15[h] ver. 22; [ch. 15:23]
16[i] [2 Kgs. 4:42-44]
19[j] Mark 7:34; John 11:41; 17:1 [k] ch. 26:26; 1 Sam. 9:13; Mark 8:7; 14:22; Luke 24:30; [1 Cor. 14:16]
22[l] For ver. 22-33, see Mark 6:45-51; John 6:15-21 [m] [ch. 8:18]
23[n] Luke 6:12; 9:28; [Mark 1:35; Luke 5:16] [o] [Mark 13:35]

ter." 9 And the king was sorry, but because of his oaths and his guests he commanded it to
be given. 10 He sent and had John beheaded in the prison, 11 and his head was brought on
a platter and given to the girl, and she brought it to her mother. 12 And [e]his disciples came
and took the body and buried it, and they went and told Jesus.

Jesus Feeds the Five Thousand

13 Now when Jesus heard this, [f]he withdrew from there in a boat to a desolate place by
himself. But when the crowds heard it, they followed him on foot from the towns. 14 When
he went ashore he [g]saw a great crowd, and [g]he had compassion on them and healed their
sick. 15 Now when it was evening, the disciples came to him and said, "This is a desolate
place, and the day is now over; [h]send the crowds away to go into the villages and buy food
for themselves." 16 But Jesus said, "They need not go away; [i]you give them something to
eat." 17 They said to him, "We have only five loaves here and two fish." 18 And he said, "Bring
them here to me." 19 Then he ordered the crowds to sit down on the grass, and taking the
five loaves and the two fish, [j]he looked up to heaven and [k]said a blessing. Then he broke
the loaves and gave them to the disciples, and the disciples gave them to the crowds. 20 And
they all ate and were satisfied. And they took up twelve baskets full of the broken pieces left
over. 21 And those who ate were about five thousand men, besides women and children.

Jesus Walks on the Water

22 [l]Immediately he [m]made the disciples get into the boat and go before him to the other
side, while he dismissed the crowds. 23 And after he had dismissed the crowds, [n]he went up
on the mountain by himself to pray. When [o]evening came, he was there alone, 24 but the
boat by this time was a long way[1] from the land,[2] beaten by the waves, for the wind was

[1] Greek *many stadia*, a *stadion* was about 607 feet or 185 meters [2] Some manuscripts *was out on the sea*

14:12 disciples. John's disciples had remained loyal to him throughout his imprisonment. They now devotedly cared for his burial, since all of John's family was quite likely deceased by this time (cf. "advanced in years," Luke 1:7).

14:13–21 *Compassionate Healer and Supplier for Israel.* Jesus begins his withdrawal from Galilee (vv. 13–14) and feeds the 5,000 (vv. 15–21)—the only miracle from Jesus' earthly ministry recorded in all four Gospels.

14:13 withdrew. See note on 12:15.

14:15–21 Having followed Jesus to a **desolate place**, the great crowd (v. 14) is stranded late in the day without food. The scene recalls the nation of Israel wandering in the wilderness after the exodus, and God's gracious provision of manna for his people. The explicit mention of **twelve baskets** left over may symbolize the 12 tribes of Israel as well as the abundance of God's provision. **They all ate and were satisfied** may also be a prefiguring of the messianic banquet in the kingdom at the end of the age (cf. 8:11). **loaves . . . fish**. Staple foods of bread and dried or pickled fish, ideal for short journeys into the hills. The loaves were small cakes sufficient for one person's afternoon meal. **looked up to heaven**. A typical posture for prayer (cf. John 17:1). Jesus **said a blessing** for the meal miraculously provided by God the Father—a fitting practice for all who trust the Father for the daily provision of their needs (see Matt. 6:11). **five thousand men, besides women and children**. The total number may have included 10,000 or more. Jesus is the new and better Moses, who supplies the needs of his people.

14:22–36 *The Son of God Worshiped.* Jesus walks on the water (vv. 22–27), saving Peter and calming the storm (vv. 28–32), with the result that the disciples worship Jesus as the Son of God (v. 33). After the storm, the Son of God heals at Gennesaret (vv. 34–36).

14:22 other side. See note on 8:28.

14:23 by himself to pray. In preparation for his mission into Gentile regions (see 15:21), and with his trials in Jerusalem impending, Jesus spends the evening and night in concentrated prayer with his heavenly Father.

14:24 long way from the land. The disciples are probably about 3 miles (4.8 km) out into the lake (cf. John 6:19), which would have been 4–5 miles (6.4–8.0 km) wide at that point, depending on exactly where they crossed (cf. Matt. 14:34; also John 6:17).

Galilean Fishing Boat

This illustration shows the type of boat that Jesus and his disciples probably used, based on the remains of an approximately 2,000-year-old fishing boat found on the northwestern shore of the Sea of Galilee. It could hold 15 men, and was 26.5 feet long, 7.5 feet wide, and 4.5 feet high (8.1 x 2.3 x 1.4 m).

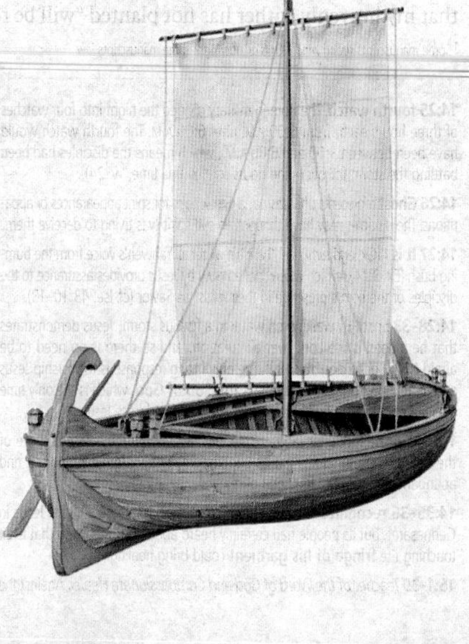

against them. **25** And [l]in the fourth watch of the night he came to them, walking on the
sea. **26** But when the disciples saw him walking on the sea, [p]they were terrified, and said,
"It is a ghost!" and they cried out in fear. **27** But immediately Jesus spoke to them, saying,
[q]"Take heart; it is I. [q]Do not be afraid."

28 And Peter answered him, "Lord, if it is you, command me to come to you on the water."
29 He said, "Come." So Peter got out of the boat and [r]walked on the water and came to Jesus.
30 But when he saw the wind,[1] he was afraid, and beginning to sink he cried out, [s]"Lord, save
me." **31** Jesus immediately reached out his hand and took hold of him, saying to him, [t]"O you
of little faith, why did you [u]doubt?" **32** And when they got into the boat, [s]the wind ceased.
33 And [v]those in the boat [w]worshiped him, saying, [x]"Truly you are [y]the Son of God."

Jesus Heals the Sick in Gennesaret

34 [z]And when they had crossed over, they came to land at [a]Gennesaret. **35** And when the
men of that place recognized him, they sent around to all that region and [b]brought to
him all who were sick **36** and implored him that they might only touch [c]the fringe of his
garment. And [d]as many as touched it were made well.

Traditions and Commandments

15 [e]Then Pharisees and [f]scribes came to Jesus [f]from Jerusalem and said, **2** [g]"Why do
your disciples break [h]the tradition of the elders? [j]For they do not wash their hands
when they eat." **3** He answered them, "And why do you break the commandment of God for
the sake of your tradition? **4** For God commanded, [k]'Honor your father and your mother,'
and, [l]'Whoever reviles father or mother must surely die.' **5** But you say, 'If anyone tells his
father or his mother, "What you would have gained from me is given to God,"[2] **6** he need
not honor his father.' So for the sake of your tradition you have [m]made void the word[3] of
God. **7** [n]You hypocrites! Well did Isaiah prophesy of you, when he said:

> **8** [o]"'This people honors me with their lips,
> but their heart is far from me;
> **9** in vain do they worship me,
> teaching as [p]doctrines the commandments of men.'"

What Defiles a Person

10 And he called the people to him and said to them, [q]"Hear and understand: **11** [r]it is
not what goes into the mouth that defiles a person, but what comes out of the mouth;
this defiles a person." **12** Then the disciples came and said to him, "Do you know that the
Pharisees were [s]offended when they heard this saying?" **13** He answered, [t]"Every plant
that my heavenly Father has not planted [u]will be rooted up. **14** Let them alone; [v]they are

[1] Some manuscripts *strong wind* [2] Or *is an offering* [3] Some manuscripts *law*

25 [l][See ver. 22 above]
26 [p][Luke 24:37]
27 [q]ch. 17:7; [Deut. 31:6; Isa. 41:13; 43:1, 2; John 16:33]
29 [r][John 21:7]
30 [s][ch. 8:25, 26]
31 [t]See ch. 6:30 [u][James 1:6]
32 [s][See ver. 30 above]
33 [v]ver. 22 [w]See ch. 8:2 [x][John 6:14] [y]ch. 16:16; 26:63; Ps. 2:7; Mark 1:1; Luke 1:35; 4:41; John 1:49; 10:36; 11:27; 20:31; [ch. 3:17]
34 [z]For ver. 34-36, see Mark 6:53-56; [John 6:24, 25] [a]Luke 5:1
35 [b]ch. 4:24
36 [c]See ch. 9:20 [d]Mark 3:10; Luke 6:19; [Acts 5:15]

Chapter 15

1 [e]For ver. 1-20, see Mark 7:1-23 [f]Mark 3:22
2 [g][ch. 9:11] [h]Gal. 1:14; Col. 2:8 [j]Luke 11:38
4 [k]Cited from Ex. 20:12 [l]Cited from Ex. 21:17
6 [m]Gal. 3:17 (Gk.); [Rom. 2:23]
7 [n]ch. 23:13
8 [o]Cited from Isa. 29:13; [Ezek. 33:31]
9 [p]Col. 2:22; Titus 1:14
10 [q]ch. 13:51
11 [r]See Acts 10:14, 15
12 [s][ch. 13:57; Luke 7:23]
13 [t][Isa. 60:21; 61:3; John 15:1, 2; 1 Cor. 3:9] [u]Jude 12
14 [v]ch. 23:16, 24; [Isa. 56:10; Mal. 2:8]

14:25 fourth watch. The Roman military divided the night into four watches of three hours each, from 6:00 P.M. until 6:00 A.M. The fourth watch would have been between 3:00 and 6:00 A.M., which means the disciples had been battling the storm for over nine hours (cf. "by this time," v. 24).

14:26 Ghost represents *phantasma*, a Greek term for spirit appearances or apparitions. The disciples may have thought an evil spirit was trying to deceive them.

14:27 It is I (Gk. *egō eimi*, lit., "I am") may recall Yahweh's voice from the burning bush (Ex. 3:14), which when spoken now by Jesus provides assurance to the disciples of the Lord's presence in their midst as Savior (cf. Isa. 43:10–13).

14:28–33 Lord. By walking on water in a furious storm, Jesus demonstrates that he indeed is the Lord over all creation, and so there is no need to be afraid (v. 27) or to **doubt** (v. 32). The only fitting response is to worship Jesus and to acknowledge that **truly** he is **the Son of God**, which is the only time in Matthew that the disciples use this full title to address Jesus.

14:34 Gennesaret. Either the town or the plain on the western shore of the Sea of Galilee, southwest of Capernaum, known for its fertile soil and abundance of walnuts, figs, and olives.

14:35–36 recognized. There is no record of any prior ministry by Jesus in Gennesaret, but its people had certainly heard about him, knowing that even touching the **fringe of his garment** could bring healing.

15:1–39 *Teacher of the Word of God and Compassionate Healer.* Against the traditions of the Jewish elders (vv. 1–9), Jesus teaches on purity and impurity of the heart, showing himself to be the true teacher of God's Word (vv. 10–20) and the compassionate healer and provider for Gentiles (vv. 21–39).

15:1 from Jerusalem. The highest-ranking **Pharisees and scribes** arrive to confront Jesus.

15:2 tradition of the elders. Interpretations of Scripture handed down from esteemed rabbis. **they do not wash their hands**. Priests were required to wash their hands and feet prior to performing their duties. The Pharisees made this a matter of ceremonial purity and, in their desire to meticulously avoid any possibility of becoming unclean, applied it to all Israelites.

15:3 Jesus makes a clear distinction between the OT, which was the **commandment of God**, and the Pharisaic **tradition**, which consisted of merely human pronouncements.

15:5 Given to God reflects a technical term for a formal vow (cf. "Corban," Mark 7:11). This allowed a person to be released from other responsibilities, such as caring for aging parents.

15:6 The Pharisees have **made void the word of God** with their traditions and rulings: anyone who broke a vow (human law) in order to help needy parents (God's law) would have committed a serious transgression, according to the Pharisees.

15:7–9 The Pharisees are **hypocrites** for two reasons: (1) their actions are

14[w]Luke 6:39
15[x][ch. 13:36]
16[y]ch. 16:9
17[z][1 Cor. 6:13]
18[a]ch. 12:34; James 3:6
19[b]James 2:4 [c]ch. 5:22, 28; See Ex. 20:13-16 [d]Eph. 4:31; Col. 3:8; 1 Tim. 6:4
20[e]1 Cor. 6:9, 10 [f]Mark 7:2, 5
21[g]For ver. 21-28, see Mark 7:24-30
22[h]Gen. 10:15, 19; Judg. 1:30-33 [i]See ch. 9:27
23[j][ch. 14:15]
24[k]Rom. 15:8; See ch. 10:5, 6
25[l]See ch. 8:2
26[m]ch. 7:6
27[n][Luke 16:21]
28[o]See ch. 9:2 [p][ch. 8:13] [q]ch. 9:22; 17:18; [John 4:52, 53]
29[r]For ver. 29-31, [Mark 7:31-37] [s]ch. 4:18; John 6:1 [t]ch. 5:1
30[u]See ch. 11:5

blind guides.[1] And [w]"if the blind lead the blind, both will fall into a pit." **15** But Peter said to
him, [x]"Explain the parable to us." **16** And he said, [y]"Are you also still without understanding? **17** Do you not see that [z]whatever goes into the mouth passes into the stomach and is
expelled?[2] **18** But [a]what comes out of the mouth proceeds from the heart, and this defiles a
person. **19** For out of the heart come [b]evil thoughts, [c]murder, adultery, sexual immorality,
theft, false witness, [d]slander. **20** [e]These are what defile a person. But [f]to eat with unwashed
hands does not defile anyone."

The Faith of a Canaanite Woman

21 [g]And Jesus went away from there and withdrew to the district of Tyre and Sidon. **22** And
behold, [h]a Canaanite woman from that region came out and was crying, [i]"Have mercy on
me, O Lord, Son of David; my daughter is severely oppressed by a demon." **23** But he did
not answer her a word. And his disciples came and begged him, saying, [j]"Send her away,
for she is crying out after us." **24** He answered, [k]"I was sent only to the lost sheep of the
house of Israel." **25** But she came and [l]knelt before him, saying, "Lord, help me." **26** And he
answered, "It is not right to take the children's bread and [m]throw it to the dogs." **27** She said,
"Yes, Lord, yet even the dogs eat [n]the crumbs that fall from their masters' table." **28** Then
Jesus answered her, "O woman, [o]great is your faith! [p]Be it done for you as you desire." [q]And
her daughter was [p]healed instantly.[3]

Jesus Heals Many

29 [r]Jesus went on from there and walked [s]beside the Sea of Galilee. And he [t]went up on
the mountain and sat down there. **30** And great crowds came to him, bringing with them
[u]the lame, the blind, the crippled, the mute, and many others, and they put them at his

[1] Some manuscripts add *of the blind* [2] Greek *is expelled into the latrine* [3] Greek *from that hour*

merely external and do not come from their hearts, and (2) their teachings are not from God but reflect human tradition (cf. vv. 2–3).

15:11 not what goes into . . . but what comes out. Cf. notes on Mark 7:19; 7:20–23.

15:13 The Pharisees have not been **planted** by the Father, therefore they **will be rooted up**.

15:14 blind guides. The Pharisees are both blind to their own hypocrisy and blindly leading the people astray because they cannot see the true intent of God's will in the OT.

15:17–20 whatever goes into the mouth. Cf. notes on Mark 7:19 and 7:20–23.

15:21 Tyre and Sidon. See note on 11:20–24; see map to the right. Jesus completed his Galilean ministry and **withdrew** to Gentile regions.

15:22 For this **Canaanite woman**, the title **Lord** is probably just an expression of great respect; she does not fully realize what she is saying, though her use of **Son of David** shows some knowledge of Jewish thoughts about him (but see note on v. 27). She probably knows about Eshmun, a pagan god of healing, whose temple was just 3 miles (4.8 km) northeast of Sidon, but she has heard of Jesus and goes to him instead. "Canaanite" here means a non-Jewish pagan person living in that region (the term occurs only here in the NT).

15:24 only to the lost sheep of the house of Israel. Later, through the apostles, the message of the gospel is to go to the Gentiles (Acts 1:8; 22:21; 26:17–18, 23; cf. Luke 24:47; John 10:16), but at this point in the unfolding of God's purpose, the focus is on the Jews and their spiritual need. See Matt. 10:6 and note on 22:9.

15:26–27 Jews frequently insulted Gentiles by calling them **dogs**, which in ancient Palestine were wild, homeless scavengers. But the form Jesus uses here (Gk. *kynarion*, "little dog") suggests a more affectionate term for domestic pets. Jesus is not insulting the woman but testing her faith.

15:27 The woman presses Jesus by alluding to the extended blessings promised to the Gentiles through Abraham (cf. Gen. 12:3), which she knows about. See note on Matt. 1:1.

15:28 Although God's plan was to bring salvation first to his chosen Israel and then to Gentiles (see note on v. 24), he responds to all who call on him in true **faith**. This Gentile woman's attitude of humble faith allowed Jesus' healing ministry to operate.

Jesus' Ministry beyond Israel

Almost all of Jesus' ministry took place within the traditional borders of Israel in areas dominated by Jews. Yet Jesus also traveled to the region of Tyre and Sidon, where he healed a Gentile woman's daughter, and to the region of Decapolis, where he healed many people. It was also at the extreme northern border of Israel at Caesarea Philippi that Peter made his confession that "You are the Christ, the son of the living God," and Jesus declared "on this rock I will build my church" (Matt. 16:18).

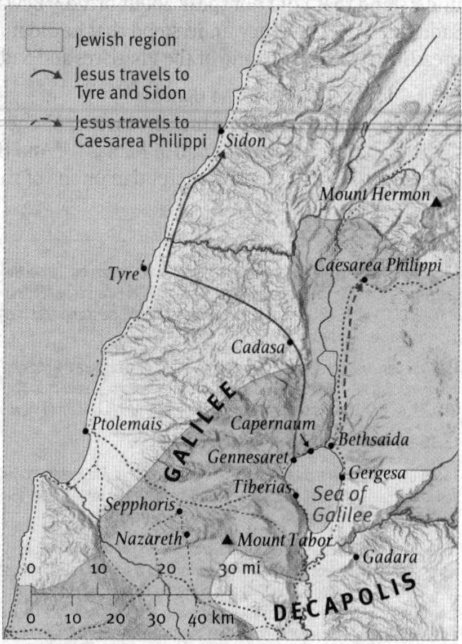

feet, and he healed them, 31 [v]so that the crowd wondered, when they saw the mute speaking, [w]the crippled healthy, the lame walking, and the blind seeing. And [x]they glorified
[y]the God of Israel.

Jesus Feeds the Four Thousand

32 [z]Then Jesus called his disciples to him and said, [a]"I have compassion on the crowd
because they have been with me now three days and have nothing to eat. And I am unwilling to send them away hungry, lest they faint on the way." 33 And the disciples said to him,
"Where are we to get enough bread in such a desolate place to feed so great a crowd?" 34 And
Jesus said to them, "How many loaves do you have?" They said, [b]"Seven, and a few small
fish." 35 And directing the crowd to sit down on the ground, 36 he took the seven loaves and
the fish, and [c]having given thanks he broke them and gave them to the disciples, and the
disciples gave them to the crowds. 37 And [d]they all ate and were satisfied. And they took
up seven baskets full of the broken pieces left over. 38 Those who ate were four thousand
men, besides women and children. 39 And after sending away the crowds, he got into the
boat and went to the region of [e]Magadan.

The Pharisees and Sadducees Demand Signs

16 [f]And the Pharisees and Sadducees came, and [g]to test him [h]they asked him to show
them [i]a sign from heaven. 2 He answered them,[1] [j]"When it is evening, you say, 'It
will be fair weather, for the sky is red.' 3 And in the morning, 'It will be stormy today, for
the sky is red and threatening.' [k]You know how to interpret the appearance of the sky, but
you cannot interpret [l]the signs of the times. 4 [m]An evil and adulterous generation seeks
for a sign, but no sign will be given to it except the sign of Jonah." So [n]he left them and
departed.

The Leaven of the Pharisees and Sadducees

5 When the disciples reached the other side, they had forgotten to bring any bread. 6 Jesus
said to them, "Watch and [o]beware of [p]the leaven of the Pharisees and Sadducees." 7 And
they began discussing it among themselves, saying, "We brought no bread." 8 But [q]Jesus,
aware of this, said, [r]"O you of little faith, why are you discussing among yourselves the
fact that you have no bread? 9 [s]Do you not yet perceive? Do you not remember [t]the five
loaves for the five thousand, and how many baskets you gathered? 10 Or [u]the seven loaves
for the four thousand, and how many baskets you gathered? 11 How is it that you fail to
understand that I did not speak about bread? [o]Beware of the leaven of the Pharisees and
Sadducees." 12 [v]Then they understood that he did not tell them to beware of the leaven of
bread, but of [w]the teaching of the Pharisees and Sadducees.

Peter Confesses Jesus as the Christ

13 [x]Now when Jesus came into the district of Caesarea Philippi, he asked his disciples,
"Who do people say that the Son of Man is?" 14 And they said, "Some say [y]John the Baptist,
others say [z]Elijah, and others Jeremiah or one of the prophets." 15 He said to them, "But

[1] Some manuscripts omit the following words to the end of verse 3

31 [v]See ch. 9:33 [w]ch. 18:8; Mark 9:43 [x]ch. 9:8 [y]Isa. 29:23; Luke 1:68; Acts 13:17
32 [z]For ver. 32-39, see Mark 8:1-10; [ch. 14:14-21] [a][ch. 9:36]
34 [b]ch. 16:10
36 [c]ch. 26:27; Mark 14:23; Luke 22:17, 19; John 6:11, 23; Acts 27:35; Rom. 14:6; 1 Cor. 10:30; 11:24; 14:16; 1 Tim. 4:3, 4
37 [d][2 Kgs. 4:42-44]
39 [e][Mark 8:10]

Chapter 16

1 [f]For ver. 1-12, see Mark 8:11-21 [g]John 8:6 [h]1 Cor. 1:22; See ch. 12:38 [i]Luke 11:16; 21:11
2 [j][Luke 12:54, 55]
3 [k]Luke 12:56 [l][ch. 12:28; Luke 19:44]
4 [m]See ch. 12:39 [n]ch. 4:13; 21:17
6 [o]Luke 12:1 [p]1 Cor. 5:6-8; Gal. 5:9
8 [q]ch. 26:10 [r]See ch. 6:30
9 [s]ch. 15:16 [t]ch. 14:17-21
10 [u]ch. 15:34-38
11 [o][See ver. 6 above]
12 [v]ch. 17:13 [w][ch. 5:20; 23:3]
13 [x]For ver. 13-16, see Mark 8:27-29; Luke 9:18-20
14 [y]ch. 14:2; Mark 6:14; Luke 9:7 [z]Mark 6:15; Luke 9:8; [ch. 17:10; Mark 9:11; John 1:21]

15:32 Jesus goes to the Decapolis, a primarily Gentile region on the southeastern coast of the Sea of Galilee (see map, p. 1826). As in the feeding of the 5,000 (14:13–21), Jesus feels **compassion** for the crowd that has gathered to seek his healing.

15:34 seven. Usually symbolic of perfection or completion; here the number may symbolize the fullness of God's provision for all peoples, now including Gentiles. As Israel rejects the kingdom, Gentiles increasingly come into view.

15:35–38 For a similar instance, see notes on 14:13–21.

15:39 There are no historical or archaeological records of **Magadan**, mentioned only here in the NT. Most likely it is a variant spelling for Magdala, the residence of Mary Magdalene, in Jewish territory (see map, p. 1826).

16:1–20 *Peter Confesses Jesus as the Christ, the Son of the Living God.* In response to the Pharisees and Sadducees' demand for a sign, Jesus announces he will give no more signs (vv. 1–4) and warns his disciples about the spiritual "leaven" of the Pharisees and Sadducees (vv. 5–12). Jesus then asks his disciples about the identity of the Son of Man (vv. 13–14). Peter rightly confesses Jesus (vv. 15–16), and Jesus in turn makes a pronouncement about Peter (vv. 17–20).

16:1 The **Pharisees and Sadducees** (see note on 3:7) were often bitter opponents, but they joined forces against Jesus, whom they saw as a threat to their leadership and power. They came to Jesus not out of need or genuine faith but **to test him**. They were seeking a **sign** or miracle to use against him. See note on 12:38.

16:4–5 sign of Jonah. See note on 12:39. **other side**. See note on 8:28.

16:6–12 In contrast to 13:33, here **leaven** is a negative metaphor to indicate how the evil of corruption can infiltrate and ruin what is good. Cf. Ex. 12:8, 15–20. **We brought no bread**. The disciples are so preoccupied with their physical needs that they fail to understand that Jesus' reference to leaven is figurative, intended as a spiritual lesson. Following Jesus' rebuke, they finally **understood**.

16:13 Caesarea Philippi, some 25 miles (40 km) north of the Sea of Galilee, had been a center of the worship of (1) Baal, then of (2) the Greek god Pan, and then of (3) Caesar. At this time it was an important Greco-

16 [a]John 11:27 [b]See ch. 1:17 [c]See ch. 14:33 [d]Deut. 5:26; Josh. 3:10; Ps. 42:2; Jer. 10:10; Dan. 6:20; Hos. 1:10; Acts 14:15; 2 Cor. 3:3; 1 Tim. 4:10
17 [e][ch. 13:16] [f]John 1:42; 21:15-17] [g]1 Cor. 15:50; Gal. 1:16 (Gk.); Eph. 6:12; Heb. 2:14 [h]1 Cor. 2:10; 12:3; [ch. 11:25; John 6:45]
18 [i][ch. 10:2; John 1:42] [j]Eph. 2:20; Rev. 21:14; [ch. 7:24] [k]Job 38:17; Isa. 38:10 [l]See ch. 11:23
19 [m][Isa. 22:22; Rev. 1:18; 3:7] [n][ch. 18:18; John 20:23]
20 [o]Mark 8:30; Luke 9:21; [ch. 17:9]; See ch. 12:16
21 [p]For ver. 21-28, see Mark 8:31–9:1; Luke 9:22-27; [ch. 17:12, 22, 23; 20:17-19] [q]ch. 20:18; [Luke 13:33] [r]ch. 17:12, 22, 23; Luke 24:7

who do you say that I am?" 16 Simon Peter replied, [a]"You are [b]the Christ, [c]the Son of [d]the
living God." 17 And Jesus answered him, [e]"Blessed are you, [f]Simon Bar-Jonah! For [g]flesh
and blood has not revealed this to you, [h]but my Father who is in heaven. 18 And I tell you,
[i]you are Peter, and [j]on this rock[1] I will build my church, and [k]the gates of [l]hell[2] shall not
prevail against it. 19 I will give you [m]the keys of the kingdom of heaven, and [n]whatever
you bind on earth shall be bound in heaven, and whatever you loose on earth shall be
loosed[3] in heaven." 20 [o]Then he strictly charged the disciples to tell no one that he was
the Christ.

Jesus Foretells His Death and Resurrection

21 [p]From that time Jesus began to show his disciples that [q]he must go to Jerusalem and
[r]suffer many things from the elders and chief priests and scribes, and be killed, and on

[1] The Greek words for *Peter* and *rock* sound similar [2] Greek *the gates of Hades* [3] Or *shall have been bound . . . shall have been loosed*

Roman city, with a primarily pagan Syrian and Greek population. In fact, its name had recently been changed from Paneas to Caesarea Philippi by Philip the Tetrarch (one of Herod the Great's sons), in honor of himself and Augustus Caesar. Excavations at the site have revealed coins minted to depict the temple built to honor Augustus Caesar, and a pagan cave dedicated to Pan, with shrines and cult niches that are still visible today. Regarding the title **Son of Man**, see note on 8:20.

16:14 John the Baptist . . . Elijah . . . Jeremiah . . . one of the prophets. The responses are in line with the popular messianic expectations held in Israel, arising from a strand of OT predictions about a great prophet who was to come (cf. Deut. 18:15–18; Mal. 4:5).

16:16 Simon Peter replied. Peter acts once again as spokesman for the Twelve (cf. 15:15). **Christ** means "Messiah" or "Anointed One" (see note on 1:1). **Son of the living God**. Jesus is the Son of the God who is alive, unlike the pagan gods of Caesarea Philippi (see note on 16:13). Jesus is God's unique Son (cf. 1:21–23; 2:15; 3:17; 4:4, 5; 7:21; 8:29; 10:32–33; 11:25–27; 12:50; 15:13; 18:35; 20:23; 24:36; 25:34; 26:39, 42, 53; 28:19), the fulfillment of the OT promise of a divine son as anointed king (2 Sam. 7:14; Ps. 2:7).

16:17 Jesus answered him. Although Peter spoke for the group, Jesus' reply is directed at Peter himself. **Blessed** (Gk. *makarios*; see note on 5:3). Jesus is not *conferring* blessing so much as *acknowledging* Peter's condition of being privileged to benefit from God's personal revelation. **Simon Bar-Jonah** (Aramaic for "Simon son of Jonah"). Simon has a natural father, Jonah, but his ability to confess Jesus (16:16) came not from any **flesh and blood** source but from **my Father who is in heaven**.

16:18 you are Peter, and on this rock I will build my church. This is one of the most controversial and debated passages in all of Scripture. Roman Catholics have appealed to this passage to defend the idea that Peter was the first pope. The key question concerns Peter's relationship to "this rock." In Greek, "Peter" is *Petros* ("stone"), which is related to *petra* ("rock"). The other NT name of Peter, Cephas (cf. John 1:42; 1 Cor. 1:12), is the Aramaic equivalent: *kepha'* means "rock," and translates in Greek as *Kēphas*. "This rock" has been variously interpreted as referring to (1) Peter himself; (2) Peter's confession; or (3) Christ and his teachings. For several reasons, the first option is the strongest. Jesus' entire pronouncement is directed toward Peter, and the connecting word "and" (Gk. *kai*) most naturally identifies the rock with Peter himself. But even if "this rock" refers to Peter, the question remains as to what that means. Protestants generally have thought that it refers to Peter *in his role of confessing Jesus as the Messiah*, and that the other disciples would share in that role as they made a similar confession (see Eph. 2:20, where the church is built on all the apostles; cf. Rev. 21:14). Jesus' statement did not mean that Peter would have greater authority than the other apostles (indeed, Paul corrects him publicly in Gal. 2:11–14), nor did it mean that he would be infallible in his teaching (Jesus rebukes him in Matt. 16:23), nor did it imply anything about a special office for Peter or successors to such an office. Certainly in the first half of Acts Peter appears as the spokesman and leader of the Jerusalem church, but he is still "sent" by other apostles to Samaria (Acts 8:14), and he has to give an account of his actions to the Jerusalem church (Acts 11:1–18). Peter is presented as having only one voice at the Jerusalem council, and James has the decisive final word (Acts 15:7–21). And, though Peter certainly has a central role in the establishment of the church, he disappears from the Acts narrative after Acts 15. "Church" (Gk. *ekklēsia*) is used only here and in Matt. 18:17 in the Gospels. Jesus points ahead to the time when his disciples, his family of faith (12:48–50), will be called "my church." Jesus will build his church, and though it is founded on the apostles and the prophets, "Christ Jesus himself [is] the cornerstone" (Eph. 2:20). Some scholars object that Jesus could not have foreseen the later emergence of the "church" at this time, but the use of Greek *ekklēsia* to refer to God's "called out" people has substantial background in the Septuagint (e.g., Deut. 9:10; 31:30; 1 Sam. 17:47; 1 Kings 8:14). Jesus is predicting that he will build a community of believers who follow him. This "called out" community would soon become known as "the church," a separate community of believers, as described in the book of Acts. **gates of hell** (Gk. *hadēs*, "Hades"; cf. "gates of Sheol" [Isa. 38:10]; "gates of death" [Job 38:17; Ps. 9:13; 107:18]). "Gates" were essential for a city's security and power. Hades, or Sheol, is the realm of the dead. Death will not overpower the church.

16:19 keys of the kingdom of heaven. Peter is given the authority to admit entrance into the kingdom through preaching the gospel, an authority that is subsequently granted to all who are called to proclaim the gospel. (Note the contrast with the scribes and Pharisees, who shut the kingdom in people's faces, neither entering themselves nor allowing others to enter; see 23:13.) In Acts, Peter is the apostle who first preaches the message of the kingdom to the Jews at Pentecost (Acts 2), to the Samaritans (Acts 8), and to the Gentiles (Acts 10). **whatever you bind . . . whatever you loose**. Peter also has authority to exercise discipline concerning right and wrong conduct for those in the kingdom, an authority that is not exclusive to Peter but is extended to the church as a whole in Matt. 18:18; cf. John 20:23. Jesus delegates authority to human leaders in the church who are called to govern his church on earth, under his ultimate authority, through the application of his Word.

16:20 Jesus warned his disciples against telling anyone **that he was the Christ**, since the concept of Christ/Messiah was widely misunderstood by the crowds—and often by the disciples themselves. See note on 8:4; cf. 9:30; 12:16; 17:9.

16:21–17:27 *The Suffering of the Messiah Revealed.* Jesus reveals the nature of his messiahship. He is a suffering Messiah, and those who are his disciples must suffer with him (16:21–28). Still, the transfiguration (17:1–13) discloses who Jesus really is: the Son of God. And believers, who are themselves sons of the kingdom, are free from the old era of the law (17:14–27).

16:21–28 *The Suffering Sacrifice.* Jesus predicts his suffering and resurrection (vv. 21–23), and reveals the cost of discipleship (vv. 24–28).

16:21 From that time marks the conclusion of Jesus' Galilean ministry and the beginning of his journey to **Jerusalem** to face the cross. This is the first of four times (v. 21; 17:22–23; 20:17–19; 26:2) that Jesus predicts his arrest and crucifixion.

[s]the third day be raised. **22** And Peter took him aside and began to rebuke him, saying, "Far
be it from you, Lord![1] This shall never happen to you." **23** But he turned and said to Peter,
[t]"Get behind me, Satan! You are [u]a hindrance[2] to me. For you [v]are not setting your mind
on the things of God, but on the things of man."

Take Up Your Cross and Follow Jesus

24 Then Jesus told his disciples, "If anyone would come after me, let him [w]deny himself
and [x]take up his cross and follow me. **25** For [x]whoever would save his life[3] will lose it, but
whoever loses his life for my sake will find it. **26** For [y]what will it profit a man if he gains
the whole world and forfeits his soul? Or [z]what shall a man give in return for his soul?
27 [a]For the Son of Man is going to come with [b]his angels in the glory of his Father, and
[c]then he will repay each person according to what he has done. **28** Truly, I say to you, there
are some standing here who will not [d]taste death [e]until they see the Son of Man [f]coming
in his kingdom."

The Transfiguration

17 [g]And after six days Jesus took with him [h]Peter and James, and John his brother, and
led them up a high mountain by themselves. **2** And he was [i]transfigured before them,
and [j]his face shone like the sun, and [k]his clothes became white as light. **3** And behold, there
appeared to them Moses and Elijah, talking with him. **4** And Peter said to Jesus, "Lord, it
is good that we are here. If you wish, I will make three tents here, one for you and one for
Moses and one for [l]Elijah." **5** He was still speaking when, behold, [m]a bright cloud overshadowed them, and [m]a voice from the cloud said, [n]"This is my beloved Son,[4] with whom I am
well pleased; [o]listen to him." **6** When [p]the disciples heard this, [q]they fell on their faces and
were terrified. **7** But Jesus came and [r]touched them, saying, "Rise, and [s]have no fear." **8** And
when they lifted up their eyes, they saw no one but Jesus only.

9 [t]And as they were coming down the mountain, Jesus commanded them, [u]"Tell no
one the vision, until the Son of Man is raised from the dead." **10** And the disciples asked
him, "Then why do the scribes say [v]that first Elijah must come?" **11** He answered, "Elijah

[1] Or "[May God be] *merciful to you, Lord!*" [2] Greek *stumbling block* [3] The same Greek word can mean either *soul* or *life*, depending on the context; twice in this verse and twice in verse 26 [4] Or *my Son, my* (or *the*) *Beloved*

21 [s]See ch. 27:63; John 2:19
23 [t][ch. 4:10] [u]See ch. 13:41 [v]Rom. 8:5; Phil. 3:19; Col. 3:2; [Phil. 2:5]
24 [w][2 Tim. 2:12, 13] [x]See ch. 10:38, 39
25 [x][See ver. 24 above]
26 [y][Luke 12:20] [z][Ps. 49:7, 8]
27 [a]ch. 24:30; 25:31; 26:64; Dan. 7:10, 13; Zech. 14:5; John 1:51; Acts 1:11; 1 Thess. 1:10; 4:16; Jude 14; Rev. 1:7; [Deut. 33:2] [b]ch. 13:41 [c]Rom. 2:6; 14:12; 2 Cor. 5:10; Heb. 9:27; 1 Pet. 1:17; Rev. 2:23; 20:12; 22:12; See Acts 10:42; 1 Cor. 3:8
28 [d]John 8:52; Heb. 2:9 [e][ch. 10:23; 23:36; 24:34] [f]Luke 23:42

Chapter 17

1 [g]For ver. 1-8, see Mark 9:2-8; Luke 9:28-36 [h]ch. 26:37; Mark 5:37
2 [i][2 Cor. 3:18 (Gk.)] [j]Rev. 1:16; 10:1 [k]Dan. 7:9; [ch. 28:3; Ps. 104:2]
4 [l][Mal. 4:5]
5 [m]2 Pet. 1:17; [Ex. 24:15, 16] [n]See ch. 3:17 [o]Acts 3:22
6 [p]2 Pet. 1:18 [q][Gen. 17:3; Ezek. 1:28; Rev. 1:17]
7 [r]Dan. 8:18; 10:10, 18 [s]ch. 14:27
9 [t]For ver. 9-13, see Mark 9:9-13 [u]See ch. 8:4; 12:16
10 [v]See ch. 11:14; Mal. 4:5, 6

16:22 In the context of the Jewish master-disciple relationship, it would have been audacious for a disciple to correct his master, let alone **rebuke** him. **This shall never happen to you.** Peter, like most of his fellow Jews, resisted the idea that the Messiah must suffer, even though it is found in the OT (e.g., Psalm 22; Isaiah 53; Zech. 12:10; 13:7).

16:23 Satan attempts to hinder Jesus' mission through Peter, who must change his human-centered ideas about the mission of the Messiah (see note on v. 22). Peter still does not understand that Jesus' messianic role must include suffering and death.

16:24 take up his cross. See note on 10:38.

16:25 Verses 25–27, each beginning with **for** (Gk. *gar*), provide three related reasons why a disciple must let go of his earthly life and take up his cross. **whoever would save his life.** The person who rejects God's will and instead pursues his own will for his life ultimately loses eternally every earthly good he is trying to protect.

16:26 gains the whole world. Acquiring all of the money, pleasure, and power of this world brings no lasting benefit if one **forfeits his soul** to spiritual death and separation from God (cf. Phil. 3:7–9).

16:27 Son of Man is going to come. See note on 8:20. The second coming of Christ with **his angels in the glory of his Father** will bring judgment for those who have chosen to follow their own will, and reward only for those who have taken up the cross.

16:28 Some of the Twelve who were **standing** there with Jesus in Caesarea Philippi would live to **see the Son of Man coming in his kingdom.** This predicted event has been variously interpreted as referring to: (1) Jesus' transfiguration (17:1–8); (2) his resurrection; (3) the coming of the Spirit at Pentecost; (4) the spread of the kingdom through the preaching of the early church; (5) the destruction of the temple and Jerusalem in A.D. 70; or (6) the second coming and final establishment of the kingdom. The immediate context seems to indicate the first view, the transfiguration, which immediately follows (see also Mark 9:2–10; Luke 9:28–36). There, "some" of Jesus' disciples "saw" what Jesus will be like when he comes in the power of his kingdom. This interpretation is also supported by 2 Pet. 1:16–18, where Peter equates Jesus' "glory" with his transfiguration, of which Peter was an eyewitness. At the same time, interpretations (2), (3), and (4) are also quite possible, for they are all instances where Jesus "came" in the powerful advance of his kingdom, which was partially but not yet fully realized. Some interpreters think that Jesus is more generally speaking of many or all of the events in views (2) through (4). View (5) is less persuasive because the judgment on Jerusalem does not reflect the positive growth of the kingdom. View (6) is unacceptable, for it would imply that Jesus was mistaken about the timing of his return.

17:1–13 *The Beloved, Transfigured Son.* Jesus reveals his divine glory in the transfiguration (vv. 1–8) and explains how John the Baptist's ministry fulfills the prophecy of Elijah's return (vv. 9–13).

17:1 After six days probably indicates that they are still in Caesarea Philippi. **Peter and James, and John.** The inner circle of disciples (cf. 26:37). **high mountain.** Church tradition identifies this as Mount Tabor, about 12 miles (19 km) from the Sea of Galilee, but most scholars favor Mount Hermon, outside of Galilee and rising 9,166 feet (2,794 m) above sea level.

17:2 was transfigured. Jesus' physical transformation was a reminder of the glory he had before he became man (John 1:14; 17:5; Phil. 2:6–7) and a preview of his future exaltation (2 Pet. 1:16–18; Rev. 1:16).

17:3 The appearance of **Moses and Elijah** represents the Law and the Prophets, which witness to Jesus as the Messiah, the one who fulfills the OT (cf. 5:17). Elijah was considered the prophetic forerunner of the Messiah (Mal. 4:5–6; cf. Matt. 3:1–3; 11:7–10).

11 [w]Luke 1:16, 17; [Acts 1:6; 3:21]
12 [x]ch. 14:3, 10 [y]ch. 16:21
13 [z]ch. 16:12
14 [a]For ver. 14-19, see Mark 9:14-28; Luke 9:37-42
15 [b]ch. 4:24
16 [c][ch. 10:1; Mark 6:7; Luke 10:17]
17 [d]Phil. 2:15; [John 20:27] [e][John 14:9]
18 [f]ch. 8:26; Zech. 3:2; Mark 1:25; Luke 4:35, 39; Jude 9 [g]See ch. 9:22
20 [h][John 11:40]; See ch. 6:30 [i]ch. 21:21, 22; Mark 11:23 [j]Luke 17:6; [ch. 13:31] [k]ver. 9; [1 Cor. 13:2] [l]Mark 9:23
22 [m]For ver. 22, 23, see Mark 9:30-32; Luke 9:43-45; [ch. 16:21-28; 20:17-19]
23 [n]See Mark 8:31

does come, and [w]he will restore all things. 12 But I tell you that Elijah has already come,
and they did not recognize him, but [x]did to him whatever they pleased. [y]So also the Son
of Man will certainly suffer at their hands." 13 [z]Then the disciples understood that he was
speaking to them of John the Baptist.

Jesus Heals a Boy with a Demon

14 [a]And when they came to the crowd, a man came up to him and, kneeling before him,
15 said, "Lord, have mercy on my son, for he is [b]an epileptic and he suffers terribly. For often
he falls into the fire, and often into the water. 16 And I brought him to your disciples, and
[c]they could not heal him." 17 And Jesus answered, "O faithless and [d]twisted generation, how
long am I to be with you? [e]How long am I to bear with you? Bring him here to me." 18 And
Jesus [f]rebuked the demon,[1] and it[2] came out of him, and [g]the boy was healed instantly.[3]
19 Then the disciples came to Jesus privately and said, "Why could we not cast it out?" 20 He
said to them, [h]"Because of your little faith. For [i]truly, I say to you, [j]if you have faith like a
grain of mustard seed, [k]you will say to this mountain, 'Move from here to there,' and it
will move, and [l]nothing will be impossible for you."[4]

Jesus Again Foretells Death, Resurrection

22 [m]As they were gathering[5] in Galilee, Jesus said to them, "The Son of Man is about to
be delivered into the hands of men, 23 and they will kill him, and he will be raised on [n]the
third day." And they were greatly distressed.

[1] Greek *it* [2] Greek *the demon* [3] Greek *from that hour* [4] Some manuscripts insert verse 21: *But this kind never comes out except by prayer and fasting* [5] Some manuscripts *remained*

17:4 three tents. Peter wishes to make some sort of fitting memorial for this glorious event.

17:5 bright cloud. Reminiscent of the cloud of God's presence and glory that appeared at various times in the OT (e.g., Ex. 13:21–22; 34:5–7; 1 Kings 8:10–13). **voice**. God the Father's public endorsement of Jesus his **beloved Son** echoes that given at Jesus' baptism (Matt. 3:17). Jesus is the incarnate Son of God, superior to Moses and Elijah, so the disciples must **listen to him** in order to understand his messianic purpose.

17:6 terrified. Fear was a common experience of people in the OT who witnessed the awesome reality of God's presence (e.g., Ex. 19:16; Deut. 5:5).

17:9 Tell no one the vision. See note on 8:4; cf. 9:30; 12:16; 16:20.

17:10–13 Elijah has already come. See notes on Mal. 4:4–6 and Matt. 11:14. Jesus indicates that the ministry of **John the Baptist** fulfilled Malachi's prophecy.

17:13 Then the disciples understood. "Understanding" is a key theme in Matthew's Gospel, and it comes here as a result of Jesus' teaching (cf. notes on 13:51–52; 16:6–12).

17:14–27 ***Sons of the Kingdom.*** Through the healing and exorcism of an epileptic boy, Jesus shows the contrast between defective and effective faith (vv. 14–20). Jesus also teaches that his impending death will come through betrayal (vv. 22–23) and that the OT law has no claim on him or his disciples (vv. 24–27).

17:15 By calling him **Lord**, the man shows respect for Jesus as an esteemed, righteous teacher, but he goes beyond that by believing that Jesus will show **mercy** and heal his son.

17:17 faithless. In spite of the miracles and teaching of Jesus, the majority of people did not place their faith in him as the Messiah. **Twisted** indicates people's distorted perception of Jesus and spiritual truth.

17:20 little faith. The disciples are not, of course, devoid of faith, but their faith is not functioning properly. Faith can be stronger or weaker (cf. 6:30; 8:26; 14:31; 16:8; Rom. 14:1). Moving a **mountain** was a common metaphor in Jewish literature for doing what was seemingly **impossible** (cf. Isa. 40:4; 49:11; 54:10; Matt. 21:21–22).

17:22–23 to be delivered. This second prediction of Jesus' passion (cf. 16:21), has an ominous new detail: Jesus will not only be handed over to his enemies, he will be betrayed.

Jesus' Final Journey to Jerusalem

Though John mentions several trips to Jerusalem by Jesus during his ministry, Matthew, Mark, and Luke recount only one, which occurred as Jesus prepared for his triumphal entry and subsequent death and resurrection. Beginning at Capernaum, Jesus was apparently diverted from the more direct route when Samaritans refused him access (Luke 9:51–56), so he may have crossed the Jordan and traveled through Perea. Jesus then passed through Jericho and proceeded to Jerusalem.

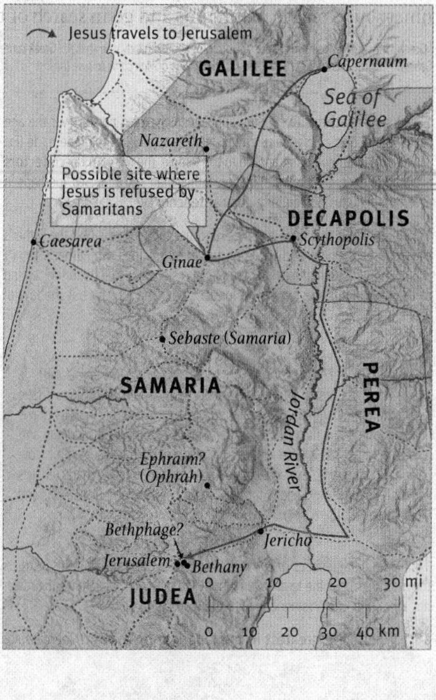

The Temple Tax

24 [o]When they came to Capernaum, the collectors of [p]the two-drachma tax went up to
Peter and said, "Does your teacher not pay the tax?" 25 He said, "Yes." And when he came
into the house, Jesus spoke to him first, saying, [q]"What do you think, Simon? From whom
do kings of the earth take toll or [r]tax? From their sons or from others?" 26 And when he
said, "From others," Jesus said to him, "Then the sons are free. 27 However, not to give
offense to them, go to the sea and cast a hook and take the first fish that comes up, and
when you open its mouth you will find a shekel.[1] Take that and give it to them for me
and for yourself."

Who Is the Greatest?

18 [t]At that time the disciples came to Jesus, saying, "Who is the greatest in the kingdom of heaven?" 2 And calling to him a child, he put him in the midst of them 3 and
said, "Truly, I say to you, unless you [u]turn and [v]become like children, you [w]will never enter
the kingdom of heaven. 4 [x]Whoever humbles himself like this child is the [w]greatest in the
kingdom of heaven.

5 [y]"Whoever receives one such child in my name receives me, 6 but [z]whoever causes one
of these [a]little ones who believe in me to sin,[2] it would be better for him to have a great
millstone fastened around his neck and to be drowned in the depth of the sea.

Temptations to Sin

7 "Woe to the world for [b]temptations to sin![3] [c]For it is necessary that temptations come,
[d]but woe to the one by whom the temptation comes! 8 [e]And if your hand or your foot
causes you to sin, cut it off and throw it away. It is better for you to enter life crippled or
lame than with two hands or two feet to be thrown into [f]the eternal fire. 9 [e]And if your eye
causes you to sin, tear it out and throw it away. It is better for you to enter life with one
eye than with two eyes to be thrown into the [f]hell[4] of fire.

The Parable of the Lost Sheep

10 "See that you do not despise [g]one of these little ones. For I tell you that in heaven
[h]their angels always [i]see the face of my Father who is in heaven.[5] 12 [j]What do you think?
[k]If a man has a hundred sheep, and one of them has gone astray, does he not leave the
ninety-nine on the mountains and go in search of the one that went astray? 13 And if he

[1] Greek *stater*, a silver coin worth four drachmas or approximately one shekel [2] Greek *causes . . . to stumble*; also verses 8, 9 [3] Greek *stumbling blocks* [4] Greek *Gehenna* [5] Some manuscripts add verse 11: *For the Son of Man came to save the lost*

24 [o]Mark 9:33 [p]Ex. 30:13; 38:26
25 [q]ch. 18:12; 21:28 [r]ch. 22:17, 19; Mark 12:14; Rom. 13:7

Chapter 18

1 [t]ch. 17:24; For ver. 1-5, see Mark 9:33-37; Luke 9:46-48; [ch. 20:20-28]
3 [u]See Luke 22:32 [v]ch. 19:14; Mark 10:15; Luke 18:17; [Ps. 131:2; 1 Cor. 14:20; 1 Pet. 2:2] [w][ch. 5:19, 20]
4 [x]ch. 20:27; 23:11, 12 [w][See ver. 3 above]
5 [y][ch. 10:40, 42]
6 [z]Mark 9:42 [a]Luke 17:2; [1 Cor. 8:12]
7 [b]See ch. 13:41 [c]Luke 17:1; See 1 Cor. 11:19 [d]ch. 26:24
8 [e]ch. 5:29, 30; Mark 9:43-48 [f]See ch. 25:41
9 [e][See ver. 8 above] [f][See ver. 8 above]
10 [g][ch. 6:29; 25:40, 45; Luke 15:7, 10] [h]Acts 12:15; [Ps. 34:7; 91:11; Heb. 1:14] [i]Luke 1:19; Rev. 8:2; [Esth. 1:14]
12 [j]ch. 17:25; 21:28 [k]For ver. 12-14, [Luke 15:4-7]

17:24 two-drachma tax. At the annual census, each person over the age of 20 was to give a half-shekel offering for the support of the tabernacle (Ex. 30:11–16), which was later applied to the temple. The religious tax **collectors** approach **Peter**, the disciples' leader, rather than Jesus himself, perhaps in deference to Jesus' esteem as a popular **teacher**.

17:25–26 Then the sons are free. Because the temple is God the Father's own house, the Son and those he has brought into the Father's family (12:48–50) are exempt from the temple **tax**, signaling that, with the coming of the kingdom, believers are no longer under the OT law but the law of Christ (see Gal. 6:2).

18:1–20:34 *The Community of the Messiah Revealed*. This is the fourth of Jesus' five major discourses in Matthew's Gospel (see Introduction: Key Themes; Literary Features). As his earthly ministry draws to a close, Jesus has spent considerable time clarifying his identity and mission (chs. 14–17). He instructs his disciples on the nature of his covenant community, explaining the kingdom community's characteristics (18:1–35), its implications for the sanctity of marriage (19:1–12), and its value (19:13–20:34).

18:1–35 *Characteristics of Life in the Kingdom Community*. Jesus instructs the disciples about the kind of community life that will characterize their relationships with one another and with the world at large.

18:1 Who is the greatest in the kingdom of heaven? The disciples misunderstand greatness in terms of human endeavor, accomplishment, and status.

18:2–4 Whoever humbles himself like this child. The humility of a child consists of childlike trust, vulnerability, and the inability to advance his or her own cause apart from the help, direction, and resources of a parent.

18:5–6 One such child (see vv. 2–4) and **these little ones who believe in me** both refer to Christ's disciples (cf. 10:40–42).

18:6–9 drowned in the depth of the sea . . . foot causes you to sin, cut it off . . . eye causes you to sin, tear it out. Jesus uses hyperbole (intentional overstatement) to emphasize the necessity of rigorous self-discipline and radically removing sin from the disciple's life before it leads to judgment; see note on 5:29–30. The Greek for **hell** in 18:9 is *gehenna*, a name derived from the Valley of the Son of Hinnom near Jerusalem (cf. 2 Kings 23:10; Jer. 7:31; 19:2; etc.), where rubbish was constantly burned so that it came to be seen as a metaphor for the **fire** of hell (cf. Matt. 3:12; Rev. 20:15; etc.).

18:10 The heavenly Father uses angels to care for his childlike disciples (cf. Heb. 1:14), but **their angels** does not imply that each disciple has one assigned "guardian angel." **always see the face of my Father**. These angels do, however, have continuous and open communication with God.

18:12 a hundred sheep, and one of them has gone astray. Here the wandering sheep represents a believer, but in a similar parable in Luke 15:3–7 it is an unbeliever. Jesus draws upon the OT images of God's people as both secure sheep (e.g., Psalm 23; Isa. 53:6; Jer. 13:17; Zech. 10:3; 13:7) and straying sheep (e.g., Ps. 119:176; Jer. 23:1–4; 50:6; Ezek. 34:1–30). Cf. also John 10:7–8; 1 Pet. 5:2–4; Rev. 7:17.

finds it, truly, I say to you, he rejoices over it more than over the ninety-nine that never
went astray. 14 So [l]it is not the will of my[1] Father who is in heaven that one of these little
ones should perish.

If Your Brother Sins Against You

15 [m]"If your brother sins against you, [n]go and tell him his fault, between you and him
alone. If he listens to you, you have [o]gained your brother. 16 But if he does not listen, take
one or two others along with you, that every charge may be established [p]by the evidence
of two or three witnesses. 17 If he refuses to listen to them, [q]tell it to the church. And if he
refuses to listen even to the church, [r]let him be to you as [s]a Gentile and [s]a tax collector.
18 Truly, I say to you, [t]whatever you bind on earth shall be bound in heaven, and whatever
you loose on earth shall be loosed[2] in heaven. 19 Again I say to you, if two of you [u]agree
on earth about anything they ask, [v]it will be done for them by my Father in heaven. 20 For
where two or three are [w]gathered in my name, [x]there am I among them."

The Parable of the Unforgiving Servant

21 Then Peter came up and said to him, "Lord, how often [y]will my brother sin against
me, and I forgive him? [z]As many as seven times?" 22 Jesus said to him, "I do not say to you
seven times, but seventy-seven times.

23 "Therefore the kingdom of heaven may be compared to a king who wished [a]to settle
accounts with his servants.[3] 24 When he began to settle, one was brought to him who owed
him [b]ten thousand [c]talents.[4] 25 [d]And since he could not pay, his master ordered him [e]to
be sold, with his wife and [f]children and all that he had, and payment to be made. 26 So
the servant[5] [g]fell on his knees, imploring him, 'Have patience with me, and I will pay
you everything.' 27 And out of pity for him, the master of that servant released him and
[d]forgave him the debt. 28 But when that same servant went out, he found one of his fellow
servants who owed him a hundred [h]denarii,[6] and seizing him, he began to choke him,

[1] Some manuscripts *your* [2] Or *shall have been bound . . . shall have been loosed* [3] Greek *bondservants;* also verses 28, 31 [4] A *talent* was a monetary unit worth about twenty years' wages for a laborer [5] Greek *bondservant;* also verses 27, 28, 29, 32, 33 [6] A *denarius* was a day's wage for a laborer

14 [l]John 6:39; 10:28; [John 17:12]
15 [m]Luke 17:3 [n]2 Thess. 3:15; [Titus 3:10; James 5:19]; See Lev. 19:17 [o]1 Cor. 9:19-22; 1 Pet. 3:1
16 [p]Deut. 19:15; 2 Cor. 13:1; [Num. 35:30; John 8:17; 1 Tim. 5:19; Heb. 10:28]
17 [q][1 Cor. 5:4, 5; 6:1-6] [r][Rom. 16:17; 1 Cor. 5:9-13; 2 Thess. 3:6, 14; 2 John 10] [s]ch. 5:46, 47
18 [t][ch. 16:19; John 20:23]
19 [u][Acts 12:5, 12; Philem. 22] [v]See ch. 7:7
20 [w][Acts 4:30, 31; 1 Cor. 5:4] [x][ch. 28:20; John 12:26; 20:20, 26]
21 [y]ver. 15 [z]Luke 17:3, 4; [Col. 3:13]
23 [a]ch. 25:19
24 [b]Esth. 3:9 [c]ch. 25:15
25 [d][Luke 7:42] [e]Ex. 21:2; Lev. 25:39 [f]2 Kgs. 4:1; Neh. 5:5
26 [g]Acts 10:25; See ch. 8:2
27 [d][See ver. 25 above]
28 [h]ch. 20:2; 22:19; Mark 6:37; 14:5; Luke 7:41; 10:35; John 6:7

18:14 little ones should perish. A dangerous yet real possibility is that apparent followers of Jesus may not be true disciples at all but only professing believers (e.g., Judas Iscariot).

18:15 go and tell him his fault, between you and him alone. If a matter can be settled without getting others involved, that will keep rumors and misunderstandings from multiplying and will keep the conflict from spreading (cf. Prov. 25:9). **gained**. The ultimate objective is restoration of the offending brother or sister to the path of discipleship.

18:16 Evidence of two or three witnesses follows the guideline in Deut. 19:15 and refers to witnesses of the subsequent confrontation described in this verse, not necessarily eyewitnesses to the original offense (Matt. 18:15).

18:17 If the offending party of vv. 15–16 will not repent after the matter has been brought before the entire **church**, then he or she is to be excluded from the fellowship and thought of as an unbeliever. **Gentile** and **tax collector** describes those who are deliberately rebellious against God.

18:18 whatever you bind on earth shall be bound in heaven. Peter's foundational authority is extended to the entire community of disciples, giving them the authority to declare the terms under which God forgives or refuses to forgive the sin of wayward disciples (see note on 16:19).

18:20 there am I among them. Jesus affirms that he will be divinely present among his disciples as they seek unity in rendering decisions, which is rightly understood also as an affirmation of omnipresence and therefore of deity.

18:21–22 how often will . . . I forgive him? Within Judaism, three times was sufficient to show a forgiving spirit (based on Job 33:29, 30; Amos 1:3; 2:6), thus **Peter** (**seven**) believes he has shown generosity. But true disciples of Jesus are to forgive without keeping count (**seventy-seven times**). This may echo and reverse Lamech's boast of vengeance in Gen. 4:24.

18:24 ten thousand talents. In OT times, a talent was a unit of weight equaling about 75 pounds (34 kg). In NT times, it was a unit of monetary reckoning (though not an actual coin), valued at about 6,000 drachmas, the equivalent of about 20 years' wages for a laborer. (A common laborer earned about one denarius per day.) In approximate modern equivalents, if a laborer earns $15 per hour, at 2,000 hours per year he would earn $30,000 per year, and a talent would equal $600,000 (USD). Hence, "ten thousand talents" hyperbolically represents an incalculable debt—in today's terms, about $6 billion.

18:25 sold, with his wife and children. A practice common in the ancient world (cf. Ex. 21:2–11; Deut. 15:12–18; 2 Kings 4:1; Neh. 5:4–8), often as punishment for those whose debts could not possibly be repaid.

18:27 forgave him the debt. The forgiveness of such a massive debt (equivalent to $6 billion; see note on v. 24) is a dramatic illustration of (1) the massive debt that people owe, because of their sins, to the holy, righteous God; (2) their complete inability ever to pay such a debt ("For the wages of sin is death . . . ," Rom. 6:23a); (3) God's great mercy and patience (Matt. 18:26, 29) in withholding his immediate righteous judgment that all people deserve for their sins; and (4) God's gracious provision of Christ's death and resurrection to pay the debt for sins and to break the power of sin ("but the free gift of God is eternal life in Christ Jesus our Lord," Rom. 6:23b). The two central points of the parable are: *first*, that the gift of salvation is immeasurably great ("how shall we escape if we neglect such a great salvation?" Heb. 2:3); and, *second*, that unless a person is comparably merciful to others, (a) God's mercy has not had a saving effect upon him (Matt. 18:32–33), and (b) he will be liable to pay the consequences himself (vv. 34–35).

18:28–32 a hundred denarii. This was still a large amount (equivalent to about 20 weeks of common labor, or about $12,000 in today's terms), but compared to the debt that the wicked servant himself owed ($6 billion), it was a relatively small amount. The servant's unwillingness to forgive even this amount, though having been forgiven his own insurmountable debt, revealed the servant's true **wicked** character (v. 32) and that he had not in fact been transformed by the forgiveness that his **master** had extended to him.

saying, 'Pay what you owe.' 29 So his fellow servant fell down and pleaded with him, 'Have
patience with me, and I will pay you.' 30 He refused and went and put him in prison until
he should pay the debt. 31 When his fellow servants saw what had taken place, they were
greatly distressed, and they went and reported to their master all that had taken place.
32 Then his master summoned him and said to him, 'You wicked servant! I forgave you all
that debt because you pleaded with me. 33 [i]And should not you have had mercy on your
fellow servant, as I had mercy on you?' 34 [j]And in anger his master delivered him to the
jailers,[1] [k]until he should pay all his debt. 35 [l]So also my heavenly Father will do to every
one of you, if you do not forgive your brother [m]from your heart."

Teaching About Divorce

19 Now when Jesus had finished these sayings, he went away from [n]Galilee and [o]entered
[p]the region of Judea beyond the Jordan. 2 And [q]large crowds followed him, and he
healed them there.
3 And Pharisees came up to him and [r]tested him by asking, [s]"Is it lawful to divorce one's
wife for any cause?" 4 He answered, [t]"Have you not read that he who created them from
the beginning made them male and female, 5 and said, [u]'Therefore a man shall leave his
father and his mother and hold fast to his wife, and [v]the two shall become one flesh'? 6 So
they are no longer two but one flesh. [w]What therefore God has joined together, let not man
separate." 7 They said to him, [x]"Why then did Moses command one to give a certificate
of divorce and to send her away?" 8 He said to them, "Because of your [y]hardness of heart
Moses allowed you to divorce your wives, but from the beginning it was not so. 9 [z]And I

[1] Greek *torturers*

33 [i][ch. 6:12; Eph. 4:32; Col. 3:13; 1 John 4:11]
34 [j]See James 2:13 [k]ver. 30; [ch. 5:25, 26]
35 [l]ch. 6:15; [Prov. 21:13] [m]1 Pet. 1:22; [Rom. 6:17]

Chapter 19

1 [n]ch. 17:24 [o]For ver. 1-9, see Mark 10:1-12 [p]Luke 9:51; 17:11; John 10:40; [ch. 4:25]
2 [q]ch. 12:15
3 [r]John 8:6 [s]ch. 5:31
4 [t]Gen. 1:27; 2:18, 21-23; 5:2; [ch. 21:16]
5 [u]Eph. 5:31; Cited from Gen. 2:24 [v]1 Cor. 6:16; [Mal. 2:15]
6 [w]1 Cor. 7:10
7 [x]Deut. 24:1-4
8 [y]Mark 16:14; [Mark 3:5; 6:52; Heb. 3:8]
9 [z]See ch. 5:32

18:34 delivered him to the jailers. A metaphorical allusion to eternal punishment that the wicked servant justly deserves (cf. 8:12; 10:28; 13:42, 49–50; 22:13; 24:51).

18:35 not forgive your brother from your heart. A transformed heart must result in a changed life that offers the same mercy and forgiveness as has been received from God (cf. Isa. 40:2). Someone who does not grant forgiveness to others shows that his own heart has not experienced God's forgiveness. Throughout Scripture, the heart refers to the center of one's being, including one's reason, emotions, and will.

19:1–20:34 *Valuing the Kingdom Community.* The great Galilean ministry has now ended, and Jesus and his disciples begin the momentous journey to Jerusalem. Jesus explains the sanctity of marriage (19:3–12) and reveals the tragedy of the rich young man (19:16–22), in contrast to the gracious reward awaiting those who follow him (19:23–30). This leads to the parable of the vineyard workers (20:1–16). Jesus then gives his third prediction of his death (20:17–19) and sets an example for community sacrifice, suffering, and service (20:20–28). As he and his disciples begin their ascent to Jerusalem, Jesus mercifully heals two blind men in Jericho (20:29–34).

19:1 Judea beyond the Jordan. Most likely Perea, the area just east of the Jordan River between Samaria and the Decapolis, whose population was largely Jewish (see map, p. 1857).

19:2 large crowds followed him. Jesus' fame has quickly spread, due to his healing ministry in Galilee.

19:3 Pharisees . . . tested him. See note on 3:7. The religious leaders try to get Jesus to incriminate himself through misinterpreting the law. **divorce**. There was a significant debate between Pharisaical parties on the correct interpretation of Moses' divorce regulations (Deut. 24:1), as noted in this excerpt from the Mishnah, *Gittin* 9.10: "The school of Shammai says: A man may not divorce his wife unless he has found unchastity in her. . . . And the school of Hillel says: [He may divorce her] even if she spoiled a dish for him. . . . Rabbi Akiba says, [he may divorce her] even if he found another fairer than she" (see Mishnah, *Gittin* 9 for an example of a Jewish certificate of divorce and the terms required for remarriage; see also Josephus, *Jewish Antiquities* 4.253 for the phrase "whatsoever cause").

19:4–5 He who created them . . . said is a strong affirmation of the divine inspiration of the OT Scriptures, because Jesus goes on to quote words from Genesis that are not attributed to any speaker (**"Therefore a man . . ."** cf. Gen. 2:24) and attributes those words to God.

19:6 What . . . God has joined together implies that marriage is not merely a human agreement but a relationship in which God changes the status of a man and a woman from being single (**they are no longer two**) to being married (**one flesh**). From the moment they are married, they are unified in a mysterious way that belongs to no other human relationship, having all the God-given rights and responsibilities of marriage that they did not have before. Being "one flesh" includes the sexual union of a husband and wife (see Gen. 2:24), but it is more than that because it means that they have left their parents' household ("a man shall leave his father and his mother," Gen. 2:24) and have established a new family, such that their primary human loyalty is now to each other, before anyone else. **let not man separate**. Jesus avoids the Pharisaic argument about reasons for divorce and goes back to the beginning of creation to demonstrate God's intention for the institution of marriage. It is to be a permanent bond between a man and a woman that joins them into one new union that is consecrated by physical intercourse (Gen. 2:24).

19:8 Because of your hardness of heart should not be understood to mean that only "hard-hearted" people would ever initiate a divorce. Rather, it means, "because there was hard-hearted rebellion against God among you, leading to serious defilement of marriages." The presence of sin in the community meant that some marriages would be seriously defiled and irretrievably damaged, and God therefore provided divorce as a solution in those cases. **Moses allowed you to divorce**. The Pharisees had asked why Moses commanded divorce (v. 7), but Jesus corrects them, showing that divorce is not what God intended from the beginning, and that even when it is allowed, it is permitted only on very specific grounds but never required. See note on Deut. 24:1–4. **From the beginning it was not so** points back to God's original intent that marriage would be lifelong.

19:9 Every phrase in this verse is important for understanding Jesus' teaching on divorce. **whoever divorces his wife**. "Divorces" is Greek *apoluō*, which always means "divorce" in contexts concerning marriage. Some commentators have claimed that *apoluō* means "separates from, sends away" in this verse (implying separation but not divorce), but this is not persuasive because (a) this word has not been shown to include the sense of "separate" in any other contexts concerning marriage and (b) the same word clearly means "divorce" in the Pharisees' question in v. 3 (the current dispute among Jewish rabbis was about divorce, not separation), and therefore it should be understood to have the same meaning in Jesus' response to their question in vv. 8 and 9. **except for sexual immorality** (Gk. *porneia*). (1) This implies that divorce and remarriage on the grounds of sexual immorality are not prohibited and thus *do not* constitute adultery. This is the one exception Jesus makes to the requirement that marriage be lifelong, for sexual immorality grievously defiles

11[a]1 Cor. 7:2, 7-9, 17 [b][ch. 20:23] [c]ch. 13:11
12[d][1 Cor. 7:32]
13[e]For ver. 13-15, see Mark 10:13-16; Luke 18:15-17 [f]Mark 10:48
14[g]ch. 18:3 [h][Mark 9:39]
16[i]For ver. 16-29, see Mark 10:17-30; Luke 18:18-30; [Luke 10:25-28] [j][ver. 29] [k]ch. 25:46; [ch. 18:8]
17[l]Lev. 18:5; Neh. 9:29; Ezek. 20:11, 13, 21; Rom. 10:5; Gal. 3:12
18[m]Rom. 13:9; Cited from Ex. 20:12-16; Deut. 5:16-20; [ch. 5:21, 27]
19[n]ch. 5:43; 22:39; Mark 12:31; Luke 10:27; Gal. 5:14; James 2:8; Cited from Lev. 19:18

say to you: whoever divorces his wife, except for sexual immorality, and marries another,
commits adultery."[1]
10 The disciples said to him, "If such is the case of a man with his wife, it is better not
to marry." 11 But he said to them, [a]"Not everyone can receive this saying, but only [b]those
to [c]whom it is given. 12 For there are eunuchs who have been so from birth, and there are
eunuchs who have been made eunuchs by men, and there are eunuchs who have made
themselves eunuchs [d]for the sake of the kingdom of heaven. Let the one who is able to
receive this receive it."

Let the Children Come to Me

13 [e]Then children were brought to him that he might lay his hands on them and pray.
The disciples [f]rebuked the people, 14 but Jesus said, [g]"Let the little children [h]come to me
and do not hinder them, for to such belongs the kingdom of heaven." 15 And he laid his
hands on them and went away.

The Rich Young Man

16 [i]And behold, a man came up to him, saying, "Teacher, what good deed must I do to
[j]have [k]eternal life?" 17 And he said to him, "Why do you ask me about what is good? There is
only one who is good. [l]If you would enter life, keep the commandments." 18 He said to him,
"Which ones?" And Jesus said, [m]"You shall not murder, You shall not commit adultery, You
shall not steal, You shall not bear false witness, 19 Honor your father and mother, and, [n]You

[1] Some manuscripts add *and whoever marries a divorced woman commits adultery;* other manuscripts *except for sexual immorality, makes her commit adultery, and whoever marries a divorced woman commits adultery*

and indeed corrupts the "one flesh" union (v. 5). (2) The parallel passages in Mark 10:11–12 and Luke 16:18 omit "except for sexual immorality," but that was probably because everyone, whatever their position in Jewish disputes over divorce (see note on Matt. 19:3), assumed that divorce was allowed in the case of adultery (i.e., the question of divorce because of adultery was not at issue in the immediate context in Mark 10 and Luke 16). But Matthew includes this fuller account of Jesus' words, with the exception clause, perhaps to prevent any possible misunderstanding in other contexts, and perhaps to explicitly situate Jesus' teaching within the context of the Jewish debates, for the benefit of his Jewish-Christian audience. (Also note that Matthew sometimes includes clarifying exceptions not included by Mark and Luke; e.g., Mark 8:12 quotes Jesus saying "no sign will be given to this generation," whereas Matt. 16:4 says "no sign will be given to [this generation] *except the sign of Jonah*.") (3) Some have claimed that *porneia* in this context refers to a very narrow, specific kind of sexual immorality, either sexual relations among close relatives or sexual immorality discovered during the betrothal period. Those who hold this position then argue that divorce in any other case is always prohibited, or else if divorce is allowed, remarriage is never allowed. But *porneia* had a broader range of meaning in ordinary usage, referring to any sexual intercourse that was contrary to the moral standards of Scripture, and nothing in this context would indicate that this should be understood in such a restricted sense (see note on 5:31–32). **and marries another, commits adultery**. (1) If a divorce is obtained for any reason other than ("except for") sexual immorality, then the second marriage begins with adultery. Jesus is prohibiting divorce for the many trivial reasons that were used so frequently in the first century, leading to widespread injustice, especially for women whose husbands suddenly divorced them. (2) "And marries another" implies that the second marriage, though it begins with adultery, is still a marriage. Once a second marriage has occurred, it would be further sin to break it up. The second marriage should not be thought of as continually living in adultery, for the man and woman are now married to each other, not to anyone else. (3) If the exception ("sexual immorality") occurs, then the implication is that remarriage to "another" does not constitute adultery and is therefore permissible. (4) Divorce, it must be remembered, is *permitted* but *not required* in the case of sexual immorality. Since God's intention is that marriage should be for life (19:4–8), this provides good reason to make every reasonable effort to achieve restoration and forgiveness in marriage before taking steps to dissolve a marriage through divorce. This makes Jesus' teaching fundamentally different from all of first-century Judaism, which *required* divorce in the case of adultery. (On the question of divorce and desertion, see 1 Cor. 7:15 and note.)

19:10–12 After hearing Jesus nullify most of the currently popular grounds for divorce, the disciples overreact and say, **it is better not to marry** (than to run the risk of a lifelong unhappy marriage). **This saying** is best understood as referring to that statement ("it is better not to marry"). Jesus explains that what they have said is true, but **only** for **those to whom it is given**, namely, for **eunuchs**. This would include those without the capacity for sexual relations either through a birth defect or castration, and those who have chosen a life of abstinence. Celibacy is an acceptable alternative to marriage (cf. 1 Cor. 7:6–9; and note on 1 Cor. 7:6–7).

19:13 lay his hands on them. A traditional manner of blessing children in Israel, especially when passing on a blessing from one generation to the next (cf. Gen. 48:14; Num. 27:18).

19:14 to such belongs the kingdom of heaven. See notes on 18:2–4; 18:5–6. **Children** serve as a metaphor of the humility necessary for entrance into the kingdom of heaven.

19:16 a man came up to him. Verses 16–22 have been called the story of the "rich young ruler" since he is rich (v. 22), young (v. 20), and a ruler (cf. Luke 18:18). He may have been a religious lay leader, quite possibly a Pharisee (because of the diligence he displays in following the law). After addressing Jesus as **Teacher**, a title of respect, he asks **what good deed** he must do **to have eternal life**. "Eternal life" is virtually synonymous with expressions such as "entering the kingdom of heaven" (Matt. 5:20) and being "saved" (19:25–26); it is the first occurrence of this expression in Matthew (cf. v. 29; 25:46). In the parallel accounts (Mark 10:17–22; Luke 18:18–23), the wording of the question and answer differs somewhat, but there is no contradiction, and it seems to be a case of different Gospels reporting different parts of the same conversation.

19:17 There is only one who is good. Only in understanding God as infinitely good can the young man discover that human good deeds cannot earn eternal life. **keep the commandments**. Jesus is not teaching that good works can earn eternal life, for in vv. 21–22 he will show the man how far short he falls of keeping the first commandment (cf. Ex. 20:3) and the first of the two greatest commandments (cf. Deut. 6:5; Matt. 22:36–40). But obedience to the law is also an expression of belief in the truly good God who is the source of all good, including eternal life. Scripture elsewhere clearly affirms that salvation is a gift of God's grace received through faith, and not by works (see notes on Eph. 2:8; 2:9–10).

19:18–19 Which ones? Jesus gives a representative list of laws, including five commandments from the second half of the Decalogue (cf. Ex. 20:1–17; Deut. 5:7–21), and the second of the two greatest commandments (Lev. 19:18; cf. Matt. 22:36–40).

shall love your neighbor as yourself." 20 The young man said to him, [o]"All these I have kept.
What do I still lack?" 21 Jesus said to him, "If you would be [p]perfect, go, [q]sell what you possess
and give to the poor, and you will have [r]treasure in heaven; and come, follow me." 22 [s]When
the young man heard this he went away sorrowful, for he had great possessions.
23 And Jesus said to his disciples, "Truly, I say to you, [t]only with difficulty will a rich
person enter the kingdom of heaven. 24 [u]Again I tell you, it is easier for a camel to go
through the eye of a needle than for a rich person to enter [v]the kingdom of God." 25 When
the disciples heard this, they were greatly astonished, saying, "Who then can be saved?"
26 But Jesus [w]looked at them and said, [x]"With man this is impossible, but with God all
things are possible." 27 Then Peter said in reply, "See, [y]we have left everything and followed
you. What then will we have?" 28 Jesus said to them, "Truly, I say to you, in the new world,[1]
[z]when the Son of Man will sit on his glorious throne, you who have followed me [a]will also
sit on twelve thrones, [b]judging the twelve tribes of Israel. 29 [c]And everyone who has left
houses or brothers or sisters or father or mother or children or lands, for my name's sake,
will receive a hundredfold[2] and will [d]inherit eternal life. 30 But [e]many who are [f]first will
be last, and the last first.

Laborers in the Vineyard

20 "For the kingdom of heaven is like a master of a house who went out early in the
morning to hire laborers for his vineyard. 2 After agreeing with the laborers for
a denarius[3] a day, he sent them into his vineyard. 3 And going out about the third hour he
saw others standing idle in the marketplace, 4 and to them he said, 'You go into the vineyard too, and whatever is right I will give you.' 5 So they went. Going out again about
the sixth hour and the ninth hour, he did the same. 6 And [g]about the eleventh hour he
went out and found others standing. And he said to them, 'Why do you stand here idle

[1] Greek *in the regeneration* [2] Some manuscripts *manifold* [3] A *denarius* was a day's wage for a laborer

20 [o][Phil. 3:6]
21 [p]See ch. 5:48 [q]Luke 12:33; [Luke 16:9; 19:8; Acts 2:45; 4:34, 35; 1 Tim. 6:18, 19] [r]ch. 6:19, 20
22 [s][Ezek. 33:31]
23 [t][1 Cor. 1:26]; See ch. 13:22
24 [u][Mark 10:24] [v]See ch. 12:28
26 [w]Mark 10:21; Luke 22:61 [x]Gen. 18:14; Job 42:2; Jer. 32:17, 27; Zech. 8:6; Mark 14:36; Luke 1:37
27 [y]ch. 4:20, 22; Mark 1:18, 20
28 [z]See ch. 16:27 [a]Luke 22:30; Rev. 3:21 [b][1 Cor. 6:2]
29 [c][Luke 14:26] [d][ver. 16]; See ch. 25:34
30 [e]ch. 20:16; Mark 10:31; Luke 13:30 [f][ch. 21:31, 32]

Chapter 20

6 [g][1 Cor. 15:8]

19:20 All these I have kept. The man implies he has kept not only these, but the entire law, which they represent. He views his obedience to the law as complete, but he still senses that something is lacking.

19:21 If you would be perfect. Jesus knows the man's wealth has become his means to personal identity, power, and a sense of meaning in life—that it has become the idolatrous god of his life (cf. note on v. 17). Jesus' strategy is to turn this man from focusing on external conformity to the law to examining his heart, revealing his ruling god. **give to the poor.** The man had no doubt given some money to the poor, as the giving of alms was considered a pious duty, especially among the Pharisees. But Jesus calls him to give everything away, exchanging the god of wealth for the eternal **treasure** found in following Jesus as the one true God. Jesus' ultimate answer to the question posed in v. 16 ("What . . . must I do to have eternal life?") is to **follow** him.

19:22 went away sorrowful. Even though he wants "eternal life" (v. 16), the young man cannot bring himself to cease worshiping the ruling force in his life, his **great possessions.**

19:23 only with difficulty will a rich person enter the kingdom of heaven. Wealth is both deceptive and intoxicating: it fools a person into thinking that he or she is self-sufficient apart from God; and the rich person wants desperately to hold on to that supposed self-sufficiency. The general attributes of the "rich" are the opposite of those of a "child" (cf. 18:1–5; 19:13–15).

19:24 camel. The largest land animal in Palestine. **the eye of a needle.** The smallest opening found in the home. Jesus paints a picture of something impossible in order to illustrate that even the seemingly impossible is possible with God. There is no evidence for the popular interpretation that there was a gate in Jerusalem called "the eye of the needle," which camels had to stoop to their knees to enter. Such an interpretation would miss the point: it is not merely *difficult* for the wealthy to be saved; without God's grace it is *impossible* (cf. v. 26).

19:25 astonished. Wealth was often equated with God's favor and blessing (cf. Deut. 28:1–14).

19:26 For the wealthy to shift their primary allegiance to God is humanly impossible, but **with God all things are possible**, as evidenced by the conversions of rich men like Joseph of Arimathea (27:57) and Zacchaeus (Luke 19:9–10).

19:27 we have left everything and followed you. What then will we have? In response to Peter's self-seeking and perhaps self-pity, Jesus acknowledges the rewards that his disciples will receive. But his parable in 20:1–15 will be a subtle rebuke.

19:28 the new world (Gk. *palingenesia*, lit., "renewal" or "regeneration"). The term occurs in the NT only here and in Titus 3:5. In Titus it refers to present, individual regeneration, but here it looks forward to the future end-time renewal of the world (cf. 2 Pet. 3:10–13; Revelation 21–22). **judging.** In this new world, the **twelve** apostles (except for Judas, see Acts 1:12–26) will participate in the final establishment of the kingdom of God on the earth.

19:29 receive a hundredfold. Cf. 13:8. Those who have given up the god of their lives to follow Jesus will receive abundant reward (the other Synoptics add "in this time"; cf. Mark 10:29–30 and note; Luke 18:30) and **will inherit eternal life.** Eternal life (which is a gift) is an inheritance, not an earned reward.

19:30 But many who are first will be last, and the last first. See note on 20:16.

20:1 the kingdom of heaven is like. See note on 13:24. **vineyard.** Grapes were one of ancient Israel's most important crops, and thus Israel was often referred to as the "vine" or "vineyard" of God (e.g., Isa. 5:1–7; Jer. 2:21; Hos. 10:1; cf. Matt. 21:28–46). "Vineyard" represents the activity of the kingdom in this world (cf. Matt. 21:28–46).

20:2–15 denarius. A typical day's wage for a laborer. **third hour.** 9:00 A.M. The workday was typically divided into four three-hour increments, running from approximately 6:00 A.M. to 6:00 P.M. **eleventh hour.** 5:00 P.M., near the end of the workday. These workers are desperate enough to continue waiting for work. **each of them received a denarius.** Surprisingly, the last laborers to be hired are paid a complete denarius, the same as those who had worked all day. **Friend, I am doing you no wrong.** The landowner addresses the worker gently, explaining the fairness of his actions. **do you begrudge.** Literally, "Is your eye evil?" The laborer failed to be thankful for his

8 [h]Lev. 19:13; Deut. 24:15 [i]Luke 8:3; [ch. 24:45]
12 [j]Luke 12:55; James 1:11 (Gk.)
13 [k]ch. 22:12; 26:50
14 [l]ch. 25:25
15 [m][Rom. 9:15-24] [n]ch. 6:23; Deut. 15:9; Prov. 23:6
16 [o]See ch. 19:30
17 [p]For ver. 17-19, see Mark 10:32-34; Luke 18:31-33; [ch. 16:21-28; 17:12, 22, 23]
18 [q]See ch. 16:21 [r]ch. 26:66; John 19:7
19 [s]ch. 27:2; John 18:30, 31; Acts 3:13; [Acts 2:23; 4:27; 21:11] [t]ch. 27:26-31 [u]ch. 26:2; Luke 24:7; John 12:32, 33; 18:32 [v]ch. 16:21; 27:63
20 [w]For ver. 20-28, see Mark 10:35-45 [x]ch. 4:21; 27:56 [y]See ch. 8:2
21 [z][ch. 19:28] [a]ch. 16:28; 25:31, 34; Luke 23:42
22 [b][Luke 9:33; 23:34] [c]ch. 26:29, 42; Mark 14:36; Luke 22:42; John 18:11; [Isa. 51:22]
23 [d][Rom. 8:17; Phil. 3:10] [e]Acts 12:2; Rev. 1:9 [f][ch. 19:11] [g]ch. 25:34
25 [h]For ver. 25-28, [ch. 18:1-4; Luke 22:25-27] [i]1 Pet. 5:3
26 [j]ch. 23:11; [Luke 9:48]

all day?' 7 They said to him, 'Because no one has hired us.' He said to them, 'You go into
the vineyard too.' 8 And [h]when evening came, the owner of the vineyard said to his [i]fore-
man, 'Call the laborers and pay them their wages, beginning with the last, up to the first.'
9 And when those hired about the eleventh hour came, each of them received a denarius.
10 Now when those hired first came, they thought they would receive more, but each of
them also received a denarius. 11 And on receiving it they grumbled at the master of the
house, 12 saying, 'These last worked only one hour, and you have made them equal to us
who have borne the burden of the day and [j]the scorching heat.' 13 But he replied to one
of them, [k]'Friend, I am doing you no wrong. Did you not agree with me for a denarius?
14 Take [l]what belongs to you and go. I choose to give to this last worker as I give to you.
15 [m]Am I not allowed to do what I choose with what belongs to me? Or [n]do you begrudge
my generosity?'[1] 16 So [o]the last will be first, and the first last."

Jesus Foretells His Death a Third Time

17 [p]And as Jesus was going up to Jerusalem, he took the twelve disciples aside, and on
the way he said to them, 18 "See, [q]we are going up to Jerusalem. And the Son of Man will
be delivered over to the chief priests and scribes, and they will [r]condemn him to death
19 and [s]deliver him over to the Gentiles [t]to be mocked and flogged and [u]crucified, and he
will be raised on [v]the third day."

A Mother's Request

20 [w]Then [x]the mother of the sons of Zebedee came up to him with her sons, and [y]kneeling
before him she asked him for something. 21 And he said to her, "What do you want?" She
said to him, "Say that these two sons of mine [z]are to sit, one at your right hand and one at
your left, [a]in your kingdom." 22 Jesus answered, [b]"You do not know what you are asking.
Are you able [c]to drink the cup that I am to drink?" They said to him, "We are able." 23 He
said to them, [d]"You will drink [e]my cup, but to sit at my right hand and at my left is not
mine to grant, [f]but it is for those for whom it has been [g]prepared by my Father." 24 And
when the ten heard it, they were indignant at the two brothers. 25 But Jesus called them to
him and said, [h]"You know that the rulers of the Gentiles [i]lord it over them, and their great
ones exercise authority over them. 26 [j]It shall not be so among you. But whoever would be
great among you must be your servant,[2] 27 and whoever would be first among you must

[1] *Or is your eye bad because I am good?* [2] Greek *diakonos*

own wage because he was blinded by his self-interested lack of compassion for his fellow worker.

20:16 So the last will be first, and the first last. A disciple of Jesus should not measure his or her worth by comparing it with the accomplishments and sacrifices of others, but should focus on serving from a heart of gratitude in response to God's grace. Jesus is not denying degrees of reward in heaven (see note on 1 Cor. 3:14–15) but is affirming that God's generosity is more abundant than anyone would expect: all the laborers except the very first got more than they deserved. It is probably correct also to see here a warning that Jesus' early followers (such as the Twelve) should not despise those who would come later.

20:17–19 the Son of Man will be delivered over. This is the third of four predictions of Jesus' arrest and crucifixion. See note on 16:21; cf. 17:22–23 and 26:2. The reference to **Jerusalem**, the religious leaders, and the **Gentiles** heightens the drama; for the first time in the narrative, Jesus gives additional clues about his betrayal and who will carry out his arrest and crucifixion.

20:20 Salome (cf. 27:56; Mark 15:40; 16:1) was not only the **mother of the sons of Zebedee**, she was also in all probability the sister of Mary, Jesus' mother (cf. John 19:25), so that James and John were in fact Jesus' cousins. She was among the women who stayed with Jesus at the cross and later witnessed the empty tomb. **with her sons.** Mark 10:35–37 focuses on the sons themselves and reports her request as their words. Two solutions to this apparent inconsistency are possible: (1) Based on the principle that an agent of a person counts as the person himself (see note on John 3:17), Mark may be reporting the mother's words as the words of James and John, who had told her to ask this; or (2) Matthew and Mark may be reporting different aspects of a longer conversation, in which the mother first asked Jesus the question and then Jesus asked the brothers if that was actually what they wanted. In either case, beginning in Matt. 20:22, the plural "you" shows that Jesus is speaking directly to James and John, as well as to their mother. **kneeling.** Salome shows respect to Jesus as her messianic Master, but she also evidently hopes to use her and her sons' earthly kinship with Jesus to her sons' advantage.

20:21 these two sons of mine are to sit. Salome's petition was likely inspired by Jesus' remarks in 19:28, where he had announced the Twelve's rulership with him in his future kingdom. **right hand.** A place of honor (1 Kings 2:19; Ps. 16:11; 110:1, 5; cf. Matt. 22:44).

20:22–23 You. The plural pronoun indicates that Jesus addressed the mother and the brothers directly. The **cup** in Scripture is symbolic of one's divinely determined destiny, whether blessing (Ps. 16:5) or disaster (Jer. 25:15), salvation (Ps. 116:13) or wrath (Isa. 51:17). Here it refers to Jesus' forthcoming suffering (Matt. 26:39).

20:23 You will drink my cup. James became the first apostolic martyr (Acts 12:2), and John suffered persecution and exile (Rev. 1:9). **for whom it has been prepared by my Father.** They must submit to the Father's will for their future, just as Jesus does.

20:24 indignant. They were perhaps not as upset by the immodesty of the request as by the brothers' attempt to use their family relationship to Jesus to gain an unfair advantage in obtaining what they themselves also wanted.

20:26–27 A **servant** was a hired worker who maintained the master's household, and a **slave** was someone forced into service. These were two of the lowest positions in Jewish society, yet Jesus reverses their status in the community of disciples to indicate prominence and greatness.

be your slave,[1] 28 even as the Son of Man came not to be served but [k]to serve, and [l]to give
his life as a ransom for [m]many."

Jesus Heals Two Blind Men

29 [n]And as they went out of Jericho, a great crowd followed him. 30 And behold, there
were two blind men sitting by the roadside, and when they heard that Jesus was passing
by, they cried out, "Lord,[2] have mercy on us, [o]Son of David!" 31 The crowd [p]rebuked them,
telling them to be silent, but they cried out all the more, "Lord, have mercy on us, Son of
David!" 32 And stopping, Jesus called them and said, "What do you want me to do for you?"
33 They said to him, "Lord, let our eyes be opened." 34 And Jesus in pity touched their eyes,
and immediately they recovered their sight and followed him.

The Triumphal Entry

21 [q]Now when they drew near to Jerusalem and came to Bethphage, to [r]the Mount
of Olives, then Jesus [s]sent two disciples, 2 saying to them, "Go into the village in
front of you, and immediately you will find a donkey tied, and a colt with her. Untie them

[1] Greek *bondservant* (*doulos*) [2] Some manuscripts omit *Lord*

28 [k]John 13:4, 13-15; Phil. 2:7; [2 Cor. 8:9] [l]Isa. 53:10; Dan. 9:26; John 10:15; 11:51, 52; Rom. 4:25; Gal. 1:4; 2:20; 1 Tim. 2:6; Titus 2:14; 1 Pet. 1:18, 19 [m]ch. 26:28; Isa. 53:11, 12; Heb. 2:10; 9:28; [Rom. 5:15; Rev. 5:9]
29 [n]For ver. 29-34, see Mark 10:46-52; Luke 18:35-43; [ch. 9:27-31]
30 [o]ch. 21:9; 22:42; See ch. 1:1
31 [p]ch. 19:13

Chapter 21

1 [q]For ver. 1-9, see Mark 11:1-10; Luke 19:29-38; John 12:12-15 [r]ch. 24:3; 26:30; Zech. 14:4; [John 8:1]; [Acts 1:12] [s][Mark 14:13]

20:28 Son of Man. See note on 8:20. **came not to be served but to serve**. Jesus himself is the primary example of servanthood. Jesus will give his life as a **ransom** (Gk. *lutron*, the price of release, often used of the money paid to release slaves) **for many**. "For" (Gk. *anti*) means "in place of" and signifies the notion of the exchange and substitution of Jesus' life on the cross for all those who accept his payment for their sins (see notes on 1 Pet. 2:24; 3:18).

20:29 Jericho. Not the ancient city of OT fame (e.g., Joshua 5–6), but the new Jericho nearby, about a mile (1.6 km) to the south. This new Jericho surrounded a huge palace complex first built by the Hasmoneans (2nd century B.C.), which Herod the Great expanded. Matthew says the healing of the blind men took place **as they went out** of Jericho (and Mark 10:46 agrees), but Luke 18:35 says it was "as he drew near to Jericho." It is possible that Matthew and Mark refer to the new Jericho, and Luke to the old Jericho nearby, or vice versa. Another possibility is that the blind men cried out to Jesus first as he was entering the city (Luke 18:35), but he did not respond and heal them until he was leaving the city. Since none of the accounts tells everything about the event, this may simply reflect the selection of different details about the event by the different Gospel writers. None of the accounts tells everything about the event.

20:30–31 two blind men. Mark 10:46 and Luke 18:35 mention only one blind man, and Mark gives his name ("Bartimaeus"). This does not mean that Matthew's report of two blind men is inaccurate, only that Mark and Luke focused on the one. The blind men recognize Jesus as the **Son of David** (cf. note on Matt. 9:27).

20:34 Jesus in pity touched their eyes. In the face of rejection by his own people, and impending betrayal as he enters Jerusalem, Jesus continues to show compassion for those in great need.

21:1–23:39 *The Messiah Asserts His Authority over Jerusalem.* Jesus' authority over Jerusalem is revealed in his triumphal entry (21:1–11), actions in the temple (21:12–17), cursing the fig tree (21:18–22), debates with religious leaders (21:23–22:46), and woes pronounced on the teachers of the law and the Pharisees (23:1–39).

21:1–11 *The Triumphal Entry into Jerusalem: Jesus' Authority as Messiah.* As he enters Jerusalem, Jesus is acclaimed as the Messiah; but he enters humbly, riding on a donkey.

21:1 Jerusalem is the city of the Great King (Ps. 48:1–2), the center of

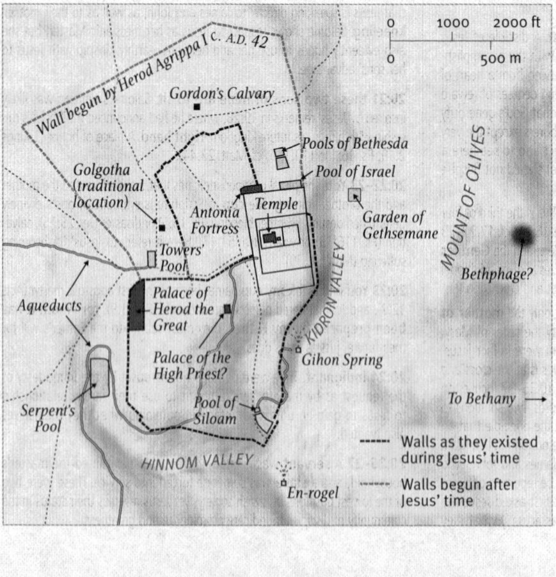

Jerusalem at the Time of Jesus

By the time of Jesus, Jerusalem had grown from a modest military fortress to a world-class city with a newly renovated temple that rivaled nearly any in the ancient world. Public pools were fed by the Gihon Spring and by two aqueducts that brought water to the city from as far as 7 miles (11 km) away. The towns of Bethphage and Bethany were located on the eastern slope of the Mount of Olives, which lay to the east of Jerusalem. See also Jerusalem in the Time of Jesus, pp. 1878–1879.

4[t]See ch. 1:22
5[u]Cited from Zech. 9:9; [Isa. 62:11] [v]ch. 11:29
8[w]2 Kgs. 9:13
9[x][Rev. 7:10]; See Ps. 118:25 (Heb.) [y]ch. 20:30 [z]ch. 23:39; Cited from Ps. 118:26 [a]Luke 2:14; [Ps. 148:1]
10[b]Mark 11:11
11[c]ver. 46; Luke 7:16; 13:33; 24:19; John 4:19; 6:14; 7:40; 9:17; [Mark 6:15; Luke 9:8, 19; John 1:21] [d]See ch. 2:23
12[e]For ver. 12-16, see Mark 11:15-18; Luke 19:45-47; [John 2:14-16] [f][Ex. 30:13] [g]Lev. 1:14; 5:7; 12:8; Luke 2:24
13[h]Cited from Isa. 56:7 [i]Jer. 7:11
14[j]ch. 11:5; 15:31
15[k][Luke 19:39, 40] [x][See ver. 9 above]

and bring them to me. **3** If anyone says anything to you, you shall say, 'The Lord needs
them,' and he will send them at once." **4** This took place [t]to fulfill what was spoken by the
prophet, saying,

> **5** [u]"Say to the daughter of Zion,
> 'Behold, your king is coming to you,
> [v]humble, and mounted on a donkey,
> on a colt,[1] the foal of a beast of burden.'"

6 The disciples went and did as Jesus had directed them. **7** They brought the donkey
and the colt and put on them their cloaks, and he sat on them. **8** Most of the crowd
[w]spread their cloaks on the road, and others cut branches from the trees and spread
them on the road. **9** And the crowds that went before him and that followed him were
shouting, [x]"Hosanna to [y]the Son of David! [z]Blessed is he who comes in the name of the
Lord! Hosanna [a]in the highest!" **10** And [b]when he entered Jerusalem, the whole city was
stirred up, saying, "Who is this?" **11** And the crowds said, "This is [c]the prophet Jesus,
[d]from Nazareth of Galilee."

Jesus Cleanses the Temple

12 [e]And Jesus entered the temple[2] and drove out all who sold and bought in the temple,
and he overturned the tables of [f]the money-changers and the seats of those who sold
[g]pigeons. **13** He said to them, "It is written, [h]'My house shall be called a house of prayer,'
but [i]you make it a den of robbers."
14 [j]And the blind and the lame came to him in the temple, and he healed them. **15** [k]But
when the chief priests and the scribes saw the wonderful things that he did, and the children crying out in the temple, [x]"Hosanna to the Son of David!" they were indignant, **16** and

[1] Or *donkey, and on a colt,* [2] Some manuscripts add *of God*

Israel's religious life and messianic expectations. **Bethphage** (see note on Luke 19:29) is traditionally located less than a mile east of Jerusalem on the southeast slope of the **Mount of Olives** (see note on Mark 13:3), which rises 2,660 feet (811 m) above sea level and lies to the east of Jerusalem, directly overlooking the temple area.

21:3 Jesus plainly refers to himself as **the Lord**, the sovereign orchestrator of these events.

21:4–5 This took place to fulfill. Matthew specifies that Jesus' entrance into Jerusalem upon a colt fulfills the prophecy of Zech. 9:9. Jesus' action is an open declaration that he is the righteous Davidic Messiah, for the prophecy says, **"your king is coming to you."** Matthew could also be alluding to Gen. 49:8–12, where Jacob prophesies about a kingly descendant of Judah whose rule will extend to the nations. The first line of the OT quotation, however, is from Isa. 62:11 and uses the phrase **daughter of Zion** to refer to the inhabitants of Jerusalem. **On a colt** can also mean "and on a colt" (see ESV footnote); cf. Matt. 21:7. In Zechariah it is an example of Hebrew poetic parallelism, where an idea is stated twice, in successive lines, using slightly different wording.

21:6–7 the donkey and the colt. Matthew alone mentions two animals, which Zechariah's prophecy allows. Having the mother donkey move alongside her unbroken colt would be the best way to calm it during the noisy entrance into Jerusalem. **and he sat on them**. "Them" refers to the cloaks (which is the closest antecedent in Gk.), not to the two animals.

21:8 Cloaks on the road symbolized the crowd's submission to Jesus as king (cf. 2 Kings 9:13). **Branches** (palms) symbolized Jewish nationalism and victory (see John 12:13). They were connected with prominent Jewish victories (e.g., *1 Macc.* 13:51) and with the Festival of Tabernacles; palm motifs were common on both Jewish coinage and synagogue decoration.

21:9 Hosanna. Hebrew, meaning "O save" (cf. 2 Sam. 14:4). **Son of David**. The crowd acknowledges that Jesus is the Davidic Messiah (see note on Matt. 9:27).

21:10 whole city. Just as "all Jerusalem" was "troubled" in 2:3 when the King of the Jews was born, so here the religious establishment is once again **stirred up**, fearing that Jesus may usurp their power.

21:11 the prophet Jesus, from Nazareth of Galilee. Although Moses had predicted the coming of a "prophet like me," to whom "you shall listen" (Deut. 18:15–18; see note on John 6:14), there is no indication that the crowds here in Jerusalem recognized Jesus as that prophet.

21:12–17 *The Temple Actions: Jesus' Pronouncement on the Temple Establishment.* John's Gospel records a similar cleansing of the temple at the beginning of Jesus' ministry (John 2:13–17). Interpreters have proposed two explanations: (1) there was only one cleansing, but John narrated the action at the beginning for thematic/theological purposes, while the Synoptic Gospels narrate the actual historical chronology; (2) there were indeed two similar but distinctly different temple cleansings. The differences of detail seem to indicate the latter, for while the initial action is similar, Jesus' statement (Matt. 21:13) and the challenge from the Jewish leaders (vv. 15–16) are entirely different from what John records. In addition, John places the event so early in his Gospel that it would be difficult to think he wanted readers to take it as anything but an event that happened early in Jesus' ministry. Thus Jesus cleansed the temple at the beginning as a warning, and at the end of his ministry as a statement of judgment on the leadership of Israel.

21:12 And Jesus entered the temple might seem to suggest that this cleansing of the temple took place immediately after Christ's entry into Jerusalem on Sunday (vv. 1–11), but Mark clearly places the incident on Monday morning (Mark 11:12–19). At times Matthew condenses some of the narrative of Jesus' activities during Holy Week and arranges it topically, which is the case here. Once Matthew tells readers that Jesus entered Jerusalem (Matt. 21:1–11), he recounts what else Jesus did in Jerusalem (vv. 12–17) without specifying that it was the next day. **all who sold and bought**. Within the temple was a sort of market where commercial activity enabled pilgrims from throughout the Diaspora (see note on John 7:35) to participate in temple activities, exchange their own currency for temple currency (Matt. 17:24–27; cf. Ex. 30:11–16), and purchase animals and other items for sacrifices.

21:13 Jesus compares the temple and its keepers to a **den of robbers**. Thieves often used caves to store their ill-gotten wealth and to plot future crimes.

21:15–16 Hosanna to the Son of David! Jesus acknowledges the children's praise and links it to Ps. 8:2, which the religious leaders should have known applied such praise to God, thus confirming Jesus as the divine Messiah.

they said to him, "Do you hear what these are saying?" And Jesus said to them, "Yes; [l]have
you never read,

[m]"'Out of the mouth of [n]infants and nursing babies
you have prepared praise'?"

17 And [o]leaving them, he [p]went out of the city to [q]Bethany and lodged there.

Jesus Curses the Fig Tree

18 [r]In the morning, as he was returning to the city, [s]he became hungry. 19 [t]And seeing a
fig tree by the wayside, he went to it and found nothing on it but only leaves. And he said
to it, "May no fruit ever come from you again!" And the fig tree withered at once.
20 When the disciples saw it, they marveled, saying, "How did the fig tree wither at once?"

16 [l]ver. 42; ch. 12:3, 5; 19:4; 22:31 [m]Cited from Ps. 8:2 (Gk.) [n]ch. 11:25
17 [o]ch. 16:4 [p]Mark 11:19; [Luke 21:37] [q]Mark 11:1; Luke 19:29; 24:50; John 11:18
18 [r]For ver. 18-22, see Mark 11:12-14, 20-24 [s]ch. 4:2
19 [t][Luke 13:6-9]

Harmony of the Events of Holy Week

Day	Event	Matthew	Mark	Luke	John
Friday/Saturday	Jesus arrives in Bethany				12:1
	Mary anoints Jesus				12:2–8
	Crowd comes to see Jesus				12:9–11
Sunday	Triumphal entry into Jerusalem	21:1–11	11:1–10	19:28–44	12:12–18
	Some Greeks seek Jesus				12:20–36
	Enters temple		11:11		
	Returns to Bethany	21:17	11:11		
Monday	Jesus curses the fig tree	21:18–19	11:12–14		
	Clears the temple	21:12–13	11:15–17	19:45–46	
	Returns to Bethany with the Twelve		11:19		
Tuesday	Disciples see the withered fig tree on the return to Jerusalem	21:20–22	11:20–21		
	Temple controversies in Jerusalem	21:23–23:39	11:27–12:44	20:1–21:4	
	Olivet Discourse on the return to Bethany	24:1–25:46	13:1–37	21:5–36	
Wednesday	Jesus continues daily teaching in the temple			21:37–38	
	Sanhedrin plots to kill Jesus	26:3–5	14:1–2	22:1–2	
Wednesday/Thursday	Preparations for the Passover	26:17–19	14:12–16	22:7–13	
Thursday	Passover meal/Last Supper	26:20–35	14:17–26	22:14–30	
	Upper Room Discourse				13:1–17:26
	Jesus prays in Gethsemane	26:36–46	14:32–42	22:39–46	
Friday	Betrayal and arrest *(after midnight?)*	26:47–56	14:43–52	22:47–53	18:2–12
	Jewish trial:				
	—before Annas				18:13–24
	—before Caiaphas and part of the Sanhedrin	26:57–75	14:53–72	22:54–65	18:19–24
	—before full Sanhedrin *(after sunrise?)*	27:1–2	15:1	22:66–71	
	Roman trials:				
	—before Pilate	27:2–14	15:2–5	23:1–5	
	—before Herod			23:6–12	
	—before Pilate	27:15–26	15:6–15	23:13–25	18:28–19:16
	Crucifixion (*approx. 9:00 A.M. to 3:00 P.M.*)	27:27–54	15:16–39	23:26–49	19:16–37
	Burial (*evening*)	27:57–61	15:42–47	23:50–54	19:38–42
Sunday	Empty-tomb witnesses	28:1–8	16:1–8	24:1–12	
	Resurrection appearances	28:9–20	16:9–20	24:13–53	20:1–21:25

21 And Jesus answered them, [u]"Truly, I say to you, [v]if you have faith and [w]do not doubt, you
will not only do what has been done to the fig tree, but even if you say to this mountain,
[x]'Be taken up and thrown into the sea,' it will happen. 22 And [v]whatever you ask in prayer,
you will receive, [y]if you have faith."

The Authority of Jesus Challenged

23 [z]And when he entered the temple, the chief priests and the elders of the people
came up to him [a]as he was teaching, and said, [b]"By what authority are you doing these
things, and who gave you this authority?" 24 Jesus answered them, "I also will ask you
one question, and if you tell me the answer, then I also will tell you by what authority
I do these things. 25 The baptism of John, [c]from where did it come? [d]From heaven or
from man?" And they discussed it among themselves, saying, "If we say, 'From heaven,'
he will say to us, [e]'Why then did you not believe him?' 26 But if we say, 'From man,' [f]we
are afraid of the crowd, for they all hold that John was [g]a prophet." 27 So they answered
Jesus, "We do not know." And he said to them, "Neither will I tell you by what authority I do these things.

The Parable of the Two Sons

28 [h]"What do you think? A man had two sons. And he went to the first and said, 'Son,
go and work in [i]the vineyard today.' 29 And he answered, 'I will not,' but afterward he
[j]changed his mind and went. 30 And he went to the other son and said the same. And he
answered, 'I go, sir,' but did not go. 31 Which of the two did the will of his father?" They
said, "The first." Jesus said to them, "Truly, I say to you, [k]the tax collectors and [l]the prostitutes go into [m]the kingdom of God before you. 32 For John came to you [n]in the way of
righteousness, and [o]you did not believe him, but [p]the tax collectors and the prostitutes
believed him. And even when you saw it, you did not afterward [j]change your minds and
believe him.

The Parable of the Tenants

33 [q]"Hear another parable. There was a master of a house who planted [r]a vineyard [s]and
put a fence around it and dug a winepress in it and built a tower and [t]leased it to tenants,
and [u]went into another country. 34 When the season for fruit drew near, he sent his servants[1]
to the tenants [t]to get his fruit. 35 [v]And the tenants took his servants and beat one, killed

[1] Greek *bondservants*; also verses 35, 36

21 [u]ch. 17:20 [v][John 14:12] [w]Acts 10:20; Rom. 4:20; 14:23; James 1:6 [x][Ps. 46:2; 1 Cor. 13:2; Rev. 8:8]
22 [v][See ver. 21 above] [y]See ch. 7:7
23 [z]For ver. 23-27, see Mark 11:27-33; Luke 20:1-8 [a]See ch. 26:55 [b][Ex. 2:14; John 1:25; Acts 4:7]
25 [c][ch. 13:54] [d]Luke 15:18, 21; John 3:27 [e]ver. 32; Luke 7:30
26 [f]ver. 46; ch. 14:5 [g][John 5:35]; See ch. 11:9
28 [h]ch. 17:25; 18:12 [i]ver. 33; ch. 20:1
29 [j]ver. 32; ch. 27:3; Heb. 7:21
31 [k]Luke 7:29 [l]Luke 7:37-50 [m]See ch. 12:28
32 [n][ch. 3:8-12, 15; Prov. 8:20; 2 Pet. 2:21] [o]ver. 25; ch. 11:18 [p]Luke 3:12, 13 [j][See ver. 29 above]
33 [q]For ver. 33-46, see Mark 12:1-12; Luke 20:9-19 [r]ver. 28; Ps. 80:8; Isa. 5:1 [s]Isa. 5:2 [t]Song 8:11, 12 [u]ch. 25:14, 15; [Mark 13:34]
34 [t][See ver. 33 above]
35 [v]ch. 5:12; 22:6; 23:34, 37; [2 Chr. 24:19; 36:15, 16; Neh. 9:26; Jer. 37:15; 38:6; Acts 7:52; 2 Cor. 11:24-26; 1 Thess. 2:15; Heb. 11:36, 37]

21:17 to Bethany. A village about 2 miles (3.2 km) from Jerusalem on the eastern slope of the Mount of Olives. Perhaps Jesus **lodged** at the home of Lazarus and his sisters Mary and Martha, with whom he had close association (Luke 10:38–42; John 11:1–44; 12:1–3).

21:18–22 *Cursing the Fig Tree: Jesus' Judgment of the Nation.* Matthew discusses the cursing of the fig tree and the disciples' reaction together, treating the events topically just as he did the triumphal entry and the cleansing of the temple (see note on v. 12). Mark gives the probable chronological order, while Matthew gives a literary compression of the account. Thus the tree was cursed most likely on Monday morning on the way into the city, and on Tuesday morning the disciples react to the withering on their way back to Jerusalem (cf. Mark 11:12–14, 20–26).

21:19 found nothing on it but only leaves. Since the fruit of the fig tree begins to appear about the same time as the leaves (or a little thereafter), the appearance of leaves in full bloom should have indicated that fruit (in the form of green figs) was already growing. Jesus' actions here have symbolic importance, signifying the hypocrisy of all who have the appearance that they are bearing fruit but in fact are not (cf. Hos. 9:10–17).

21:21–22 if you have faith . . . say to this mountain. See note on 17:20.

21:23–22:46 *Controversies in the Temple Court over Jesus' Authority.* On Tuesday of Holy Week, Jesus presents three extended parables showing God's judgment on the leaders for not encouraging the people to accept Jesus' invitation to the kingdom of heaven (21:28–22:14). This is followed by a series of four interactions as the religious leaders try to trap Jesus, who in turn reveals his true identity as the Son of God (22:15–46).

21:23 These things most likely refers to Jesus' disrupting of the commercial activities of the temple the previous day (vv. 12–13), and also to his authority to heal (vv. 14–16) and to teach in the temple (v. 23), because he is neither an official priestly nor scribal authority.

21:25–27 From heaven or from man? The leaders' refusal to answer this question shows their dishonesty, but Jesus also traps them, for as religious leaders they must now profess their ignorance. And if they do not know whether John was from God, how can they judge whether Jesus is?

21:28–32 The parable of the **two sons** demonstrates the religious leaders' failure to respond rightly to John the Baptist's prophetic ministry. They hypocritically did not live up to their talk. The fruit of one's life ultimately proves whether or not one is obedient to God's message. A person's actions ultimately prove whether or not he is obedient to God.

21:33–46 The parable of the wicked tenants continues the vineyard metaphor to show that God is taking away the kingdom from Israel.

21:33 master of a house. Large farming estates owned either by foreigners or by wealthy Jews were common in Palestine (see note on Mark 12:1). The landowners frequently rented their vineyards to farmers so they could attend to other interests.

21:34–37 beat, killed, stoned. The treatment of the **servants** brings to mind what God's prophets had experienced throughout OT history (e.g., 1 Kings 18:4; Jer. 20:1–2). **son**. An unmistakable allusion to the Father sending his own Son, Jesus. The parable publicly declares Jesus' divine Sonship.

another, and [w]stoned another. 36 [x]Again he sent other servants, more than the first. And
they did the same to them. 37 Finally he sent his son to them, saying, 'They will respect
my son.' 38 But when the tenants saw the son, they said to themselves, [y]'This is the heir.
Come, [z]let us kill him and have his inheritance.' 39 And they took him and [a]threw him
out of the vineyard and killed him. 40 [b]When therefore the owner of the vineyard comes,
what will he do to those tenants?" 41 They said to him, [c]"He will put those wretches to a
miserable death and [d]let out the vineyard to other tenants who will give him the fruits
in their seasons."

42 Jesus said to them, [e]"Have you never read in the Scriptures:

> [f]" 'The stone that the builders rejected
> has become the cornerstone;[1]
> this was the Lord's doing,
> and it is marvelous in our eyes'?

43 Therefore I tell you, the kingdom of God [g]will be taken away from you and given to a
people [h]producing its fruits. 44 And [i]the one who falls on this stone will be broken to pieces;
and [j]when it falls on anyone, it will crush him."[2]

45 When the chief priests and the Pharisees heard his parables, they perceived that he
was speaking about them. 46 And [l]although they were seeking to arrest him, [m]they feared
the crowds, because they held him to be [n]a prophet.

The Parable of the Wedding Feast

22 And again Jesus [o]spoke to them in parables, saying, 2 [p]"The kingdom of heaven
may be compared to a king who gave [q]a wedding feast for his son, 3 and [r]sent his
servants[3] to call those who were invited to the wedding feast, but they would not come.
4 [s]Again he sent other servants, saying, 'Tell those who are invited, "See, I have prepared
my [t]dinner, [u]my oxen and my fat calves have been slaughtered, and everything is ready.
Come to the wedding feast." ' 5 But [v]they paid no attention and went off, one to his farm,
another to his business, 6 while the rest seized his servants, [w]treated them shamefully, and
[x]killed them. 7 The king was angry, and he sent his troops and [y]destroyed those murderers
and burned their city. 8 Then he said to his servants, 'The wedding feast is ready, but those
invited were not [z]worthy. 9 Go therefore to the main roads and invite to the wedding feast
as many as you find.' 10 And those servants went out into the roads and [b]gathered all whom
they found, both bad and good. So the wedding hall was filled with guests.

11 "But when the king came in to look at the guests, he saw there [c]a man who had no
wedding garment. 12 And he said to him, [d]'Friend, how did you get in here without a wedding garment?' And he was speechless. 13 Then the king said to the attendants, 'Bind him

[1] Greek *the head of the corner* [2] Some manuscripts omit verse 44 [3] Greek *bondservants*; also verses 4, 6, 8, 10

35 [w][2 Chr. 24:21; John 10:31-33; Acts 7:59]
36 [x]ch. 22:4
38 [y]Heb. 1:2; [John 1:11; Rom. 8:17] [z][1 Kgs. 21:19]
39 [a]Heb. 13:12
40 [b][ch. 24:50; 25:19]
41 [c]Luke 19:27 [d]ver. 43; Acts 13:46; 18:6; 28:28; [ch. 8:11, 12]
42 [e]ver. 16 [f]Acts 4:11; 1 Pet. 2:7; Cited from Ps. 118:22, 23
43 [g][Luke 14:24] [h][ch. 3:10; Isa. 5:4, 7]
44 [i]Isa. 8:14, 15; Rom. 9:32, 33; 1 Pet. 2:8 [j]Dan. 2:34, 35, 44, 45
46 [l]Mark 11:18; Luke 19:47, 48; John 7:25, 30, 44; [ch. 26:4] [m]ver. 26 [n][ver. 11]

Chapter 22

1 [o]ch. 13:34
2 [p]For ver. 2-14, [Luke 14:16-24] [q]See Rev. 19:7
3 [r][Esth. 6:14; Prov. 9:3, 5]
4 [s]ch. 21:36 [t]Luke 11:38; John 21:12, 15 (Gk.) [u]Prov. 9:2
5 [v][Heb. 2:3]
6 [w]Luke 18:32; Acts 14:5; 1 Thess. 2:2 [x]See ch. 21:35
7 [y]ch. 21:41; Luke 19:27
8 [z]ch. 10:11; Acts 13:46; Rev. 3:4; [Luke 20:35]
10 [b]See ch. 13:47
11 [c][Rev. 19:8; 22:14]
12 [d]ch. 20:13; 26:50

21:42 cornerstone (cf. Ps. 118:22). The **rejected** Son will receive the position of ultimate prominence and importance.

21:43 kingdom of God will be taken away. The leaders have failed to carry out their obligations to God both in their personal lives and in leading the nation of Israel. Their privileged role in caring for God's vineyard/kingdom is now being taken away and **given to a people producing its fruits**. The church will be a new "people" (Gk. *ethnos*, "nation, people") consisting of disciples, both Jews and Gentiles, gathered out of many "nations" (28:19; plural of Gk. *ethnos*) and brought together as one new "nation" (1 Pet. 2:9; singular of Gk. *ethnos*) in the unfolding of God's kingdom in the present age.

22:1–14 The parable of the **wedding feast** describes the consequences that will befall the derelict religious leaders.

22:1–2 wedding feast. In this case, a countrywide celebration that would have continued for several days. This "feast" represents enjoying fellowship with God in his kingdom, and coming to the feast thus represents entering the kingdom.

22:3 they would not come. To refuse a direct invitation from the king would be an extreme insult and a dangerous affront to his authority.

22:7 burned their city. An extreme punishment reserved for serious treason and revolt against the king; possibly an allusion to the forthcoming destruction of Jerusalem in A.D. 70.

22:9 The wedding invitation to those not previously invited anticipates the spread of the gospel to the Gentiles (28:18–20; Acts 1:8; Rom. 1:16). Cf. note on Matt. 15:24.

22:11 a man who had no wedding garment. Everyone was invited, but proper wedding attire was still expected. There are two possibilities for what this means: (1) There is some evidence in the ancient world for a king supplying garments for his guests (cf. Gen. 45:22; Est. 6:8–9), and, more broadly, there is the story of God clothing his unworthy people in beautiful garments (Ezek. 16:10–13). Jesus could thus be alluding to imputed righteousness, which Paul elaborates later (e.g., Rom. 3:21–31; 4:22–25). Thus by not wearing the garments provided, this guest has highly insulted the host. (2) The wedding garment may refer to a clean garment, symbolizing evidence of righteous works (see note on Matt. 5:20). In either case, the man lacks something that is essential for being accepted at the wedding feast.

22:13 weeping and gnashing of teeth. A common description of eternal judgment (cf. 8:12; 13:42, 50; 24:51; 25:30).

13[e]See ch. 8:12
14[f]Rev. 17:14
15[g]For ver. 15-32, see Mark 12:13-27; Luke 20:20-38 [h][Luke 11:54]
16[i]Mark 2:18 [j]Mark 3:6; [Mark 8:15] [k][John 3:2] [l]Acts 18:26; [Acts 13:10] [m]See Acts 10:34
17[n]ch. 17:25 [o]Luke 2:1; 3:1
18[p]See John 8:6
21[q]Rom. 13:7
22[r]Mark 12:12
23[s]ver. 34; ch. 3:7; 16:1; Acts 4:1; 5:17; 23:6 [t]Acts 23:8; [Acts 4:2]
24[u][Deut. 25:5]
29[v]John 20:9

hand and foot and [e]cast him into the outer darkness. In that place [e]there will be weeping
and gnashing of teeth.' **14** For many are [f]called, but few are [f]chosen."

Paying Taxes to Caesar

15 [g]Then the Pharisees went and plotted how [h]to entangle him in his words. **16** And they
sent [i]their disciples to him, along with [j]the Herodians, saying, "Teacher, [k]we know that
you are true and teach [l]the way of God truthfully, and you do not care about anyone's
opinion, for [m]you are not swayed by appearances.[1] **17** Tell us, then, what you think. Is it
lawful to pay [n]taxes to [o]Caesar, or not?" **18** But Jesus, aware of their malice, said, "Why [p]put
me to the test, you hypocrites? **19** Show me the coin for the tax." And they brought him a
denarius.[2] **20** And Jesus said to them, "Whose likeness and inscription is this?" **21** They said,
"Caesar's." Then he said to them, [q]"Therefore render to Caesar the things that are Caesar's,
and to God the things that are God's." **22** When they heard it, they marveled. And they [r]left
him and went away.

Sadducees Ask About the Resurrection

23 The same day [s]Sadducees came to him, [t]who say that there is no resurrection, and they
asked him a question, **24** saying, "Teacher, Moses said, [u]'If a man dies having no children,
his brother must marry the widow and raise up offspring for his brother.' **25** Now there
were seven brothers among us. The first married and died, and having no offspring left
his wife to his brother. **26** So too the second and third, down to the seventh. **27** After them
all, the woman died. **28** In the resurrection, therefore, of the seven, whose wife will she be?
For they all had her."

29 But Jesus answered them, "You are wrong, [v]because you know neither the Scriptures

[1] Greek *for you do not look at people's faces* [2] A *denarius* was a day's wage for a laborer

22:14 Many (Gk. *polloi*) **are called** means that many have been invited to the wedding feast. But not all those invited are actually the ones who are supposed to be there, because **few are chosen**. This has been described as the doctrine of a "general calling": the gospel is proclaimed to all people everywhere, both those who will believe and those who will not. However, Paul also mentions another kind of calling, an effective calling from God that comes powerfully to individuals and brings a positive response. When the gospel is proclaimed, only some are effectively called—that is, those who are the elect, who respond with true faith (1 Cor. 1:24, 26–28). This is consistent with Jesus' statement that "few are chosen," for the ones "chosen" (Gk. *eklektos*, "selected, chosen") are "the elect," a term used by Jesus to refer to his true disciples (cf. Matt. 11:27; 24:22, 24, 31; on the theme of election, see note on Rom. 9:11).

22:15 entangle. The Pharisees hope that Jesus will say something to incriminate himself, which they can use to bring him before the Romans for execution.

22:16 their disciples. Probably those in training to become full members of the brotherhood of the Pharisees, and perhaps deceptively **sent** to appear as less of a threat than their masters. **Herodians**. A loosely organized group that sought to advance the political and economic influence of the Herodian family (c. 37 B.C.–A.D. 93). Although the Herodians and the Pharisees were adversaries in regard to many political and religious issues, they join forces here to combat the perceived threat to their power and status.

22:17 Is it lawful to pay taxes to Caesar, or not? Taxes were a volatile issue in Israel. All of Rome's subjects, including the people of Israel, labored under the empire's heavy taxation. Some Jews believed that paying any tax to pagan rulers contradicted God's lordship over his people.

22:18 Why put me to the test, you hypocrites? Jesus' questioners reasoned that if he answered that it was right to pay taxes, he would lose favor with the tax-burdened people, but if he answered that it was wrong, they could accuse him of insurrection.

22:19 On one side of the silver **denarius** was a profile of Tiberius Caesar, with the Latin inscription "Tiberius Caesar, son of the divine Augustus" around the coin's perimeter. On the opposite side was a picture of the Roman goddess of peace, Pax, with the Latin inscription "High Priest."

22:21 render to Caesar . . . and to God. Jesus is not establishing a political kingdom in opposition to Caesar, so his followers should pay taxes and obey civil laws. There are matters that belong to the realm of civil government, and there are other matters that belong to God's realm. Jesus does not here specify which matters belong in which realm, but many Christian ethicists today teach that, in general, *civil government* should allow freedom in matters of religious doctrine, worship, and beliefs about God, and the *church* should not attempt to use the power of government to enforce allegiance to any specific religious viewpoint. All forms of the Christian church throughout the world today support some kind of separation between matters of church and matters of state. By contrast, totalitarian governments usually try to suppress the church and subsume everything under the realm of the state. And some extreme Islamic movements have tried to abolish independent civil government and subsume everything under the control of Islamic religious leaders. Historically, when the church and state have become too closely aligned, the result most often has been the compromise of the church.

22:23 Sadducees (see note on 3:7) drew mainly or exclusively on the Pentateuch for doctrine (see Jewish Groups at the Time of the New Testament, pp. 1799–1800), so they did not believe in the resurrection, a theme developed more clearly in later OT books (cf. Isa. 26:19; Dan. 12:2). They **asked him a question** in order to trap him theologically. They assumed that those who believe in a resurrection life think it is like the present life, suggesting that a woman who has been married more than once will be found guilty of adultery after the resurrection. They hope hereby to show that the idea of resurrection is really absurd.

22:24 Moses said. The Sadducees cite the OT law of what is later called "levirate marriage" (from Latin *levir*, "brother-in-law"), in which the surviving brother of a childless, deceased man was obligated to marry his sister-in-law in order to provide for her needs and to preserve the deceased brother's family line (Deut. 25:5–10; cf. Gen. 38:8).

22:29–30 The Sadducees are making two errors: (1) they do not **know . . . the Scriptures** well enough to know that Scripture teaches the reality of the resurrection, and (2) they do not know the **power of God** to create a much more wonderful world than anyone can now imagine. **They neither marry nor are given in marriage** implies that the present institution of marriage will not continue in heaven. **But are like angels in heaven** means living without an exclusive lifelong marriage commitment to one person. This teaching might at first seem discouraging to married couples who are deeply in love with each other in this life, but surely people will know their loved ones in heaven (cf. 8:11; Luke 9:30, 33), and the joy and love of close relationships in heaven will be more rather than less than it is here on earth.

nor [w]the power of God. 30 For in the resurrection they neither [x]marry nor [x]are given in
marriage, but are like angels in heaven. 31 And as for the resurrection of the dead, [y]have
you not read what was said to you by God: 32 [z]'I am the God of Abraham, and the God of
Isaac, and the God of Jacob'? He is not God of the dead, but of the living." 33 And when the
crowd heard it, [a]they were astonished at his teaching.

The Great Commandment

34 [b]But when the Pharisees heard that he had silenced [c]the Sadducees, they gathered
together. 35 [d]And one of them, [e]a lawyer, asked him a question [f]to test him. 36 "Teacher,
which is the great commandment in the Law?" 37 And he said to him, [g]"You shall love the
Lord your God with all your heart and with all your soul and with all your mind. 38 This is
the great and first commandment. 39 And [h]a second is like it: [i]You shall love your neighbor
as yourself. 40 [j]On these two commandments depend [k]all the Law and the Prophets."

Whose Son Is the Christ?

41 [l]Now while the Pharisees [m]were gathered together, Jesus asked them a question, 42 saying,
"What do you think about [n]the Christ? Whose son is he?" They said to him, [n]"The
son of David." 43 He said to them, "How is it then that David, [o]in the Spirit, calls him Lord,
saying,

44 [p]"'The Lord said to my Lord,
"Sit at my right hand,
until I put your enemies under your feet"'?

45 If then David calls him Lord, [q]how is he his son?" 46 [r]And no one was able to answer him
a word, [s]nor from that day did anyone dare to ask him any more questions.

Seven Woes to the Scribes and Pharisees

23 Then Jesus [t]said to the crowds and to his disciples, 2 [u]"The scribes and the Pharisees
[v]sit on Moses' seat, 3 so do and observe whatever they tell you, [w]but not the works
they do. [x]For they preach, but do not practice. 4 [y]They tie up heavy burdens, hard to bear,[1]

[1] Some manuscripts omit *hard to bear*

29 [w]1 Cor. 6:14
30 [x]ch. 24:38; Luke 17:27
31 [y]See ch. 21:16
32 [z]Acts 7:32; Cited from Ex. 3:6
33 [a]See ch. 7:28
34 [b]For ver. 34-40, see Mark 12:28-33 [c]ver. 23
35 [d][Luke 10:25-28] [e]See Luke 7:30 [f]ver. 18
37 [g]Luke 10:27; Cited from Deut. 6:5
39 [h][1 John 4:21] [i]Cited from Lev. 19:18; See ch. 19:19
40 [j][Rom. 13:8, 10] [k]ch. 7:12; [Gal. 5:14]
41 [l]For ver. 41-45, see Mark 12:35-37; Luke 20:41-44 [m]ver. 34
42 [n]See ch. 1:1, 17
43 [o]Rev. 1:10; 4:2; [2 Sam. 23:2]
44 [p]Acts 2:34, 35; Heb. 1:13; Cited from Ps. 110:1; [1 Cor. 15:25; Heb. 10:13]
45 [q][Rom. 1:3, 4]
46 [r][Luke 14:6] [s]Mark 12:34; Luke 20:40

Chapter 23

1 [t]For ver. 1, 2, 5-7, see Mark 12:38, 39; Luke 20:45, 46; [Luke 11:43]
2 [u][Ezra 7:6, 10, 25; Neh. 8:4] [v][Deut. 17:10, 11; John 9:28, 29]
3 [w][ch. 5:20; 15:3-13] [x]Rom. 2:17-23
4 [y]Luke 11:46; [ch. 11:28-30; Acts 15:10]

Jesus' reference to "the power of God" suggests that God is able to establish relationships of even deeper friendship, joy, and love in the life to come. God has not revealed anything more about this, though Scripture indicates that the eternal glories awaiting the redeemed will be more splendid than anyone can begin to ask or think (cf. 1 Cor. 2:9; Eph. 3:20).

22:31–32 I am the God of Abraham, and . . . Isaac, and . . . Jacob. The present tense in the quotation from Ex. 3:6 logically implies that when God spoke these words to Moses, God was still in covenant relationship with the patriarchs, even though they had been dead for centuries. If the Pentateuch thus implies that the patriarchs are still alive, and if the rest of the OT points to the resurrection (as it does), then the Sadducees should recognize God's power to raise the patriarchs and all of God's people to enjoy his eternal covenant in a life beyond this one.

22:35 A lawyer is an expert in the law; this is another expression for "scribes of the Pharisees" (Mark 2:16; cf. Acts 23:9; and Jewish Groups at the Time of the New Testament, pp. 1799–1800).

22:36 the great commandment. The rabbis engaged in an ongoing debate to determine which commandments were "light" and which were "weighty" (cf. 23:23; and note on 5:19). **The Law** refers here to the entire OT.

22:37–38 love the Lord your God . . . heart . . . soul . . . mind. This command from Deut. 6:5, repeated twice daily by faithful Jews, encapsulates the idea of total devotion to God and includes the duty to obey the rest of God's commandments (cf. Matt. 5:16–20). "Heart," "soul," and "mind" do not represent rigid compartments of human existence but rather together refer to the whole person.

22:39 You shall love your neighbor as yourself. See Lev. 19:18, 34. Love signifies a concrete responsibility to seek the greatest good of one's neighbors, both Jew and Gentile.

22:40 The kingdom life that Jesus initiated—summarized in these **two commandments**—fulfills the deepest longings of human beings created in the image of God to display his glory. **the Law and the Prophets**. See note on 5:17.

22:41–46 Having dealt with malicious questions from his adversaries, Jesus now **asked them**, concerning the long-awaited Messiah (**the Christ**), **Whose son is he?** Their reply, **"The son of David,"** reflected the common understanding that the Messiah would be a royal descendant of David (cf. 2 Sam. 7:12–14; Ps. 89:4; Isa. 11:1, 10; Jer. 23:5). Jesus then quotes from Ps. 110:1, one of the most important messianic texts in the OT and the one most quoted in the NT. The Pharisees would have recognized this psalm of David as a divinely inspired messianic prophecy. In the psalm, David said that the coming Messiah (i.e., David's "son") will not be just a special human descended from David; he will be David's **Lord**. Because the Pharisees acknowledged the messianic import of the psalm, they did not **dare to ask** Jesus **any more questions**. The fact that David's descendant (Jesus) would have a more prominent role and title than the ancestor (David) further indicates the uniqueness of the Messiah and the greater honor that is due him as the Son of God. Matthew does not say how exalted a person Jesus was claiming to be in his use of Ps. 110:1; but the psalm itself may well imply the deity of the Messiah (see note on Ps. 110:5), i.e., that the Messiah is to be Yahweh incarnate (cf. John 1:14).

23:1–12 *Warnings against the Teachers of the Law and the Pharisees.* Jesus warns the crowd and his disciples not to follow the false leadership of the Pharisees (vv. 1–12), then directly pronounces woes upon those leaders for their deadly actions (see vv. 13–39).

23:2 The scribes and the Pharisees were two distinct groups, though there was some overlap between them: the scribes were the professional interpretative experts on the Torah itself, while the Pharisees were experts in theological matters that the Torah raised. **Moses' seat**. Traditionally understood as referring symbolically to the authority of Moses. However, recent archaeological evidence has revealed a literal chair found in early synagogues. Whether literal or figurative, it refers to a place from which experts on the law taught.

5 [t][See ver. 1 above] [z]ch. 6:1, 16; [John 5:44] [a]Ex. 13:9; Deut. 6:8; 11:18 [b]See ch. 9:20
6 [c]Luke 14:7, 8 [d]Luke 11:43
7 [d][See ver. 6 above] [e]ch. 11:16; 20:3 [f]See John 1:38
8 [g]James 3:1 [h]Luke 22:32; John 21:23; See Philem. 16
9 [i][1 Cor. 1:12; 3:4] [j]ch. 6:9; Mal. 1:6; See ch. 7:11
10 [k]See ch. 1:17
11 [l]ch. 20:26
12 [m]Luke 14:11; 18:14; [ch. 18:4; Prov. 29:23; Ezek. 21:26; James 4:6, 10; 1 Pet. 5:5, 6]
13 [n]Luke 11:52 [o][ch. 16:19] [p][ch. 5:20; 21:31; Luke 7:30]
15 [q]Acts 2:10; 6:5; 13:43 [r][John 17:12; 2 Thess. 2:3] [s]See ch. 5:29
16 [t]See ch. 15:14 [u]ver. 17, 19, 26; John 9:39-41; Rom. 2:19; 2 Pet. 1:9; Rev. 3:17 [v][ch. 5:33-35]
17 [w]Ex. 30:29
18 [x]ch. 5:23
19 [y]Ex. 29:37
21 [z]1 Kgs. 8:13; 2 Chr. 6:2; Ps. 26:8; 132:14
22 [a][ch. 21:25] [b]See ch. 5:34 [c]See Rev. 4:2
23 [d]Luke 11:42 [e]Deut. 14:22; [Luke 18:12] [f]Isa. 28:25, 27

and lay them on people's shoulders, but they themselves are not willing to move them
with their finger. 5 [t]They do all their deeds [z]to be seen by others. For they make [a]their
phylacteries broad and [b]their fringes long, 6 and they [c]love the place of honor at feasts and
[d]the best seats in the synagogues 7 and [d]greetings in [e]the marketplaces and being called
[f]rabbi[1] by others. 8 [g]But you are not to be called rabbi, for you have one teacher, and you
are [h]all brothers.[2] 9 [i]And call no man your father on earth, for [j]you have one Father, who is
in heaven. 10 Neither be called instructors, for you have one instructor, [k]the Christ. 11 [l]The
greatest among you shall be your servant. 12 [m]Whoever exalts himself will be humbled,
and whoever humbles himself will be exalted.

13 "But woe [n]to you, scribes and Pharisees, hypocrites! For you [o]shut the kingdom of
heaven in people's faces. For you [p]neither enter yourselves nor allow those who would
enter to go in.[3] 15 Woe to you, scribes and Pharisees, hypocrites! For you travel across sea
and land to make a single [q]proselyte, and when he becomes a proselyte, you make him
twice as much a [r]child of [s]hell[4] as yourselves.

16 "Woe to [t]you, [u]blind guides, who say, [v]'If anyone swears by the temple, it is nothing,
but if anyone swears by the gold of the temple, he is bound by his oath.' 17 You blind fools!
For which is greater, the gold or [w]the temple that has made the gold sacred? 18 And you
say, 'If anyone swears by the altar, it is nothing, but if anyone swears by [x]the gift that is
on the altar, he is bound by his oath.' 19 You blind men! For which is greater, the gift or
[y]the altar that makes the gift sacred? 20 So whoever swears by the altar swears by it and
by everything on it. 21 And whoever swears by the temple swears by it and by [z]him who
dwells in it. 22 And whoever swears by [a]heaven swears by [b]the throne of God and by [c]him
who sits upon it.

23 [d]"Woe to you, scribes and Pharisees, hypocrites! For [e]you tithe mint and dill and [f]cumin,

[1] *Rabbi* means *my teacher*, or *my master*; also verse 8 [2] Or *brothers and sisters* [3] Some manuscripts add here (or after verse 12) verse 14: *Woe to you, scribes and Pharisees, hypocrites! For you devour widows' houses and for a pretense you make long prayers; therefore you will receive the greater condemnation* [4] Greek *Gehenna*; also verse 33

23:3 so practice and observe whatever they tell you. Jesus recognized the Pharisees' official function as interpreters of the Law of Moses, and insofar as they accurately interpreted Scripture, they were to be obeyed. However, "so" (Gk. *oun*) connects this verse with v. 2 and the mention of Moses, and therefore "whatever they tell you" should probably be limited to "whatever they tell you about the Law of Moses" and does not include the Pharisees' later extensive additions to Mosaic laws which rabbinic teachers made. **but not what they do.** Jesus is about to show that much of the Pharisees' **practice** and their extrabiblical tradition is wrong.

23:4 Heavy burdens describes the extrabiblical tradition of the rabbis that was a pillar of the Pharisaic branch of Judaism. It was intended as a means of making the OT relevant to new life situations, but its massive obligations had become burdensome and oppressive.

23:5 phylacteries. Small cube-shaped cases made of leather, containing Scripture passages written on parchment. They were worn on the left arm and forehead as a literal way to obey the admonition of Deut. 11:18 (cf. Ex. 13:9; Deut. 6:8). **fringes.** Tassels with a blue cord that were attached to the four corners of a man's garment (Num. 15:37–41; Deut. 22:12), reminding the people to obey God's commandments and to be holy (Num. 15:40).

23:6 place of honor. Seating at banquets was assigned to guests based on their rank or status. **best seats in the synagogues.** Excavations at early Galilean synagogues indicate that bench seats were built along the sides of the synagogue (see note on Luke 4:16; and The Synagogue and Jewish Worship, pp. 1956–1957). In any meeting place, some seats are regarded as better than others.

23:7 Rabbi (Hb. *rabbi*) literally meant "my lord," but it was used generally for outstanding teachers of the law, most frequently heads of rabbinical schools.

23:8–10 not to be called rabbi, . . . call no man your father . . . Neither be called instructors. Jesus' disciples should not try to gain authority over one another as teachers or masters, since Jesus is ultimately each disciple's teacher and master (**you have one teacher . . . one instructor**), to whom the disciple is accountable. Jesus does not literally forbid use of the titles "teacher," "doctor," or "father" for all time in all circumstances, but he prohibits his disciples from using these terms in the way the Pharisees used them, in a spirit that wrongly exalted leaders and reinforced human pride.

23:13–36 *Woes of Judgment against the Teachers of the Law and the Pharisees.* Jesus now addresses the scribes and Pharisees directly, declaring a series of seven "woes" upon them that echoes the criticisms he has repeated throughout his ministry. These seven woes stand in contrast to the first seven "blessings" that introduce the Sermon on the Mount and describe Jesus' true disciples (5:3–9). (For a similar list of woes, see Luke 11:37–54.)

23:13 *First woe: the shut door.* The woes are a mixture of condemnation, regret, and sorrow. The teachers of the law and the Pharisees are false leaders who have drawn the people away from the kingdom of heaven instead of toward it.

23:15 *Second woe: entrapped converts.* Jesus does not criticize proselytism per se, but the manner in which the Pharisees zealously sought converts, only to place them under the burdensome weight of the many requirements in their extrabiblical traditions. **child of hell.** Literally, "child of Gehenna," a reference to the Valley of the Son of Hinnom, just south of Jerusalem, where refuse was burned. Jewish and NT writings used it as a metaphorical picture of eternal punishment (see note on 18:6–9).

23:16–19 *Third woe: binding oaths.* The Pharisees distinguished between oaths made **by the temple** and those made **by the gold of the temple**, and between oaths made **by the altar** and those made **by the gift** on it. As in much of their belief system, they focus on misguided superficial distinctions and overlook the higher principles of the law.

23:20–22 whoever swears. Those with faith in God who recognize their constant accountability in his presence need only give a simple "yes" or "no" as a binding oath (see 5:23, 34–37).

23:23 *Fourth woe: neglecting the weighty matters of the law.* **tithe.** The Mosaic law required giving a tenth of all that one produced for the ongoing work of the Lord through the Levites and priests (e.g., Lev. 27:30–33). **mint, dill, cumin.** The Pharisees were so scrupulous in following this injunction that they paid a tithe even from their smallest garden crops. Jesus does not say that they were wrong in this (**"These you ought to have done"**), but that they should do this **without neglecting** the far more important matters.

and have neglected the weightier matters of the law: [g]justice and mercy and faithfulness.
[h]These you ought to have done, without neglecting the others. 24 You blind guides, straining out a gnat and swallowing [i]a camel!
25 [j]"Woe to you, scribes and Pharisees, hypocrites! For [k]you clean the outside of [l]the cup
and the plate, but inside they are full of [m]greed and self-indulgence. 26 You blind Pharisee!
First clean the inside of [l]the cup and the plate, that the outside also may be clean.
27 [n]"Woe to you, scribes and Pharisees, hypocrites! For you are like [o]whitewashed tombs,
which outwardly appear beautiful, but within are full of dead people's bones and [p]all
uncleanness. 28 So you also [q]outwardly appear righteous to others, but within you are full
of [r]hypocrisy and lawlessness.
29 [s]"Woe to you, scribes and Pharisees, hypocrites! For you build the tombs of the prophets and decorate the monuments of the righteous, 30 saying, 'If we had lived in the days
of our fathers, we would not have taken part with them in shedding the blood of the
prophets.' 31 Thus you witness against yourselves that you are [t]sons of those who murdered
the prophets. 32 [u]Fill up, then, the measure of your fathers. 33 You serpents, [v]you brood of
vipers, how are you to escape being sentenced to [w]hell? 34 [x]Therefore [y]I send you [z]prophets
and wise men and [a]scribes, [b]some of whom you will kill and crucify, and [b]some you will
[c]flog in your synagogues and [d]persecute from town to town, 35 so that on you may come
all [e]the righteous blood shed on earth, from the blood of righteous [f]Abel to the blood of
[g]Zechariah the son of Barachiah,[1] whom you murdered between [h]the sanctuary and [i]the
altar. 36 Truly, I say to you, [j]all these things will come upon this generation.

Lament over Jerusalem

37 [k]"O Jerusalem, Jerusalem, the city that [l]kills the prophets and stones those who are
sent to it! How often would I have [m]gathered [n]your children together [o]as a hen gathers
her brood [p]under her wings, and [q]you were not willing! 38 See, [r]your house is left to you
desolate. 39 For I tell you, you will not see me again, until you say, [s]'Blessed is he who comes
in the name of the Lord.'"

[1] Some manuscripts omit *the son of Barachiah*

23 [g]Ps. 33:5; Jer. 5:1; Mic. 6:8; Zech. 7:9 [h][1 Sam. 15:22]
24 [i]ch. 19:24
25 [j]For ver. 25-28, [ch. 15:11-20] [k]Luke 11:39, 40 [l]Mark 7:4 [m]Luke 16:14; 20:47
26 [l][See ver. 25 above]
27 [n]Luke 11:44 [o][Acts 23:3] [p]Eph. 5:3; [Num. 19:16; 2 Kgs. 23:16]
28 [q]ver. 5 [r]Luke 12:1
29 [s]Luke 11:47, 48
31 [t]Acts 7:51, 52
32 [u]Gen. 15:16; Dan. 8:23; 1 Thess. 2:15, 16
33 [v]ch. 3:7; 12:34 [w]ver. 15
34 [x]For ver. 34-36, [Luke 11:49-51] [y]ch. 10:16 [z]See Acts 13:1; 1 Cor. 12:28 [a]ch. 13:52 [b]See ch. 21:35 [c]ch. 10:17; Mark 13:9; Luke 21:12; Acts 22:19; 26:11; [Luke 12:11] [d]ch. 10:23
35 [e]Rev. 18:24 [f]Gen. 4:4, 8; Heb. 11:4; 1 John 3:12 [g][Zech. 1:1] [h]See Luke 1:9 [i]Ex. 40:6; 2 Kgs. 16:14; Ezek. 40:47
36 [j][ch. 10:23; 16:28; 24:34]
37 [k]For ver. 37-39, see Luke 13:34, 35; [Luke 19:41-44] [l]See ch. 21:35 [m][Ps. 147:2; Prov. 1:24] [n]Luke 23:28 [o][Deut. 32:11, 12] [p]Ruth 2:12 [q]John 5:40
38 [r][Isa. 64:11; Jer. 12:7; 22:5]
39 [s]ch. 21:9; Cited from Ps. 118:26

23:24 straining out a gnat. The rabbis strained wine to remove even small, unclean insects (cf. Lev. 11:23, 41) that could contaminate it. **swallowing a camel**. The camel was the largest land animal in Palestine (cf. Matt. 19:24), also ceremonially unclean (Lev. 11:4). Jesus is speaking in obvious hyperbole (an intended overstatement to make a point). The Pharisees had become lost in the minute details, while neglecting the law's overarching intent.

23:26 *Fifth woe: clean outside, filthy inside.* **clean the inside**. While seeking external purity, the Pharisees were oblivious to the corrupt internal condition of their hearts.

23:27–28 *Sixth woe: whitewashed tombs.* The Pharisees were like **tombs**, which in Jesus' day could be **outwardly** very **beautiful** but **within** held nothing but death and decay. These tombs were customarily **whitewashed** to identify them clearly to passersby, since people would be rendered unclean for seven days through any contact with them (Num. 19:16; cf. Luke 11:44).

23:29–32 *Seventh woe: descendants of murderers of the prophets.* In scheming to have Jesus executed, the religious leaders show that they are following in the footsteps of their ancestors, who had persecuted and **murdered** God's **prophets**.

23:29 tombs . . . monuments. Funerary art became rich and varied around this time, with widespread ornamentation of tomb facades, ossuaries, and stone coffins, as well as wall paintings and graffiti.

23:33 serpents . . . brood of vipers. Virtually synonymous terms that magnify the guilt of these religious leaders (see notes on 3:7; 12:33–35).

23:35 The interval from the blood of righteous **Abel** (Gen. 4:8–11) to the blood of **Zechariah** (2 Chron. 24:20–22) encompasses all of OT biblical history. Abel was the first person murdered in the OT and Zechariah is the last murdered, since 2 Chronicles (where the murder of Zechariah is recorded) is the last book in the Hebrew canon (see 2 Chron. 24:20–22). There is a difficulty with the phrase **son of Barachiah**, however, since in 2 Chron. 24:20 Zechariah is called the "son of Jehoiada," while the more famous prophet who wrote the book of Zechariah is "Zechariah, the son of Berechiah" (Zech. 1:1). Several solutions have been proposed: (1) Just as Zechariah the prophet can be called either "the son of Berechiah" (Zech. 1:1) or "the son of Iddo" (Ezra 6:14; Iddo was his grandfather), so the Zechariah in 2 Chron. 24:20 could have been the son of an otherwise unrecorded "Barachiah," with "Jehoiada" (who lived 130 years; 2 Chron. 24:15) being Zechariah's grandfather. (2) As was the case with a number of people in the OT, the father of Zechariah mentioned in 2 Chron. 24:20 could have been known by more than one name—i.e., Jehoiada and Barachiah. (3) The reference may not be to the Zechariah in 2 Chron. 24:20–22 but to Zechariah the prophet, as is suggested by some extrabiblical Jewish literature that includes a tradition telling about the murder of Zechariah the prophet (who comes near the end of the OT prophets). (4) The phrase "son of Barachiah" may have been a very early textual addition by a scribe who thought "Zechariah the son of Barachiah" was intended (one significant early manuscript, Sinaiticus, in fact, omits the words "the son of Barachiah"). Each of these proposed solutions presents a plausible possibility, though there is not enough information to determine which is most likely.

23:36 Rather than respond to the unique opportunity they had to receive their Messiah and participate in the kingdom of heaven, the religious people of **this generation** would continue to spill righteous blood—now that of Jesus and his followers—and so face God's wrath.

23:37–39 *Lament over Jerusalem.* **Jerusalem** apparently refers to the whole nation of Israel, for whom Jesus deeply laments.

23:38 house. In the OT, this is an expression for the temple; possibly here it has broader reference to Jerusalem's leadership. All Jewish religious authority will collapse with the destruction of the temple in A.D. 70.

23:39 As Jesus cites Ps. 118:26 (cf. Matt. 21:9), he identifies himself with God's Messiah and Savior who will once again come to his people, but only after a time of great judgment, when they are finally ready to receive him.

Chapter 24
1 [t][ch. 21:23]; For ver. 1-51, see Mark 13:1-37; Luke 21:5-36
2 [u]Luke 19:44
3 [v]See ch. 21:1 [w][Mark 4:34] [x][Acts 1:6, 7] [y]ver. 27, 37, 39; See 1 Thess. 2:19 [z]See ch. 13:39
4 [a]Jer. 29:8; Eph. 5:6; Col. 2:8; 2 Thess. 2:3; 1 John 3:7
5 [b]ver. 11, 24; Jer. 14:14; 1 John 2:18 [c]See ch. 1:17
6 [d]2 Thess. 2:2 [e]Rev. 1:1
7 [f]2 Chr. 15:6; [Rev. 6:4] [g]Isa. 19:2 [h]Acts 11:28; Rev. 6:8, 12
8 [i]John 16:21; Acts 2:24 (Gk.); Rom. 8:22
9 [j]ch. 10:17, 21 [k]ver. 21, 29; Rev. 2:10 [l]ch. 23:34; John 16:2 [m]See ch. 10:22
10 [n]ch. 10:21
11 [o]See ch. 7:15 [p]ver. 5, 24
12 [q][Rev. 2:4]
13 [r]See ch. 10:22
14 [s]Rom. 10:18; Col. 1:6, 23; [Mark 14:9] [t]ch. 10:18 [u]ch. 28:19 [v][ver. 6]
15 [w]Dan. 9:27; 11:31; 12:11 [x][John 11:48; Acts 6:13; 21:28] [y][Dan. 9:22, 23, 25; Rev. 1:3]

Jesus Foretells Destruction of the Temple

24 [t]Jesus left the temple and was going away, when his disciples came to point out
to him the buildings of the temple. 2 But he answered them, "You see all these, do
you not? Truly, I say to you, [u]there will not be left here one stone upon another that will
not be thrown down."

Signs of the End of the Age

3 As he sat on [v]the Mount of Olives, the disciples came to him [w]privately, saying, "Tell
us, [x]when will these things be, and what will be the sign of your [y]coming and of [z]the end
of the age?" 4 And Jesus answered them, [a]"See that no one leads you astray. 5 For [b]many
will come in my name, saying, 'I am [c]the Christ,' and they will lead many astray. 6 And you
will hear of wars and rumors of wars. See that you [d]are not alarmed, for this [e]must take
place, but the end is not yet. 7 For [f]nation will rise against nation, and [g]kingdom against
kingdom, and there will be [h]famines and earthquakes in various places. 8 All these are but
the beginning of [i]the birth pains.
9 "Then [j]they will deliver you up [k]to tribulation and [l]put you to death, and [m]you will be
hated by all nations for my name's sake. 10 And then many will fall away[1] and [n]betray one
another and hate one another. 11 And many [o]false prophets will arise [p]and lead many astray.
12 And because lawlessness will be increased, [q]the love of many will grow cold. 13 [r]But the one
who endures to the end will be saved. 14 And this gospel of the kingdom [s]will be proclaimed
throughout the whole world [t]as a testimony [u]to all nations, and [v]then the end will come.

The Abomination of Desolation

15 "So when you see the abomination of desolation [w]spoken of by the prophet Daniel,
standing in [x]the holy place ([y]let the reader understand), 16 then let those who are in Judea

[1] Or *stumble*

24:1–25:46 *The Delay, Return, and Judgment of Messiah.* These two chapters are often called the "Olivet Discourse" because Jesus "sat on the Mount of Olives" (24:3) when he spoke these words. It is the fifth of Jesus' five major discourses recorded in the Gospel of Matthew (see Introduction: Key Themes; Literary Features). Addressed to his disciples, it is intended to give them a prophetic overview of the events to transpire in both the near and distant future.

24:1–14 *The Beginning of Birth Pains.* Jesus previews the general conditions of the earth, which in some sense characterize the entire age, before he returns: sufferings throughout the world (vv. 4–8), the suffering of his disciples (vv. 9–13), and the preaching of the gospel to all nations (v. 14).

24:1 left the temple. The road from Jerusalem to Bethany, where Jesus and his disciples stay each evening, takes one alongside the Mount of Olives, which affords a spectacular view of the temple in the distance.

24:2 Jesus' prophecy of the destruction of the temple was fulfilled in A.D. 70 when the Roman army under Titus destroyed Jerusalem and the temple. **Not . . . one stone upon another** may be intended as a metaphor for total destruction, or it may be understood as something that was literally fulfilled in the destruction of the temple building itself (but not the entire Temple Mount, some of which remains to this day).

24:3 The disciples ask two questions: (1) **when will these things be**, and (2) **what will be the sign of your coming and of the end of the age?** Jesus' answer to these questions apparently intertwines prophecy concerning the destruction of Jerusalem and his second coming. The near event (the destruction of Jerusalem) serves as a symbol and foreshadowing of the more distant event (the second coming). The discourse can be divided into three parts: (1) a generally chronological description of events preceding Christ's return (vv. 4–31); (2) lessons on watching, waiting, and being prepared for Christ's return (24:36–25:30); and (3) a warning of judgment and a promise of reward at the time of Christ's return (25:31–46). On the **Mount of Olives,** see notes on 21:1 and 24:1. Matthew's version of this question, with explicit mention of the second coming, is more developed and detailed than the question in the parallel passages in Mark 13:4 and Luke 21:7.

24:5 saying, "I am the Christ." Throughout the history of the church, and even today, many have made claims to messianic identity. Jesus' disciples must be on their guard against such people.

24:6–7 wars . . . famines and earthquakes. Such cataclysmic events will be a regular part of this age until the return of Jesus to redeem all of creation.

24:8 Birth pains indicates that there will be a time of suffering prior to the messianic age (cf. Rom. 8:22–23). OT prophets use the metaphor to depict terrible suffering in general (cf. Isa. 13:8; 21:3; 42:14; Jer. 30:5–7; Hos. 13:13) as well as suffering that Israel will endure prior to her deliverance (cf. Isa. 26:17–19; 66:7–11; Jer. 22:23; Mic. 4:9–10).

24:11 false prophets. Deception both from the world and from within the church will be prevalent (1 John 2:18–27; 4:1–6). Disciples must "test the spirits" to determine whether or not they acknowledge that Jesus is the Messiah (1 John 2:22; 4:2–3).

24:13 end. Either the end of the persecution when the Son of Man returns (cf. 10:23), or the end of one's life. **will be saved**. Not from physical death (cf. 24:21–22), but from divine wrath and human persecution, to experience the full blessing and peace of salvation when Jesus returns.

24:14 One distinct indicator that will signify the nearness of Christ's return is when the **gospel of the kingdom** is **proclaimed throughout the whole world**, that is, **to all nations** (plural of Gk. *ethnos*, "nation, people"), a task that began with Jesus' command in 28:19.

24:15–31 *"Great Tribulation" and the Coming of the Son of Man.* Jesus moves from the general characteristics of this age to describe the "great tribulation" (vv. 15–28) that will precede the coming of the Son of Man (vv. 29–31).

24:15 Daniel 9:27 tells of the **abomination of desolation**. Several times in Jewish history it was thought that this prophecy was being fulfilled—most notably during the days of the Maccabees when Antiochus IV Epiphanes, the Seleucid king, ordered that an altar to the Greek god Zeus be constructed in the temple (167 B.C.). He also decreed that swine and other unclean animals were to be sacrificed there, that the Sabbath was to be profaned, and that circumcision was to be abolished. But Jesus clarifies that the complete fulfillment of Daniel's prophecy will be found in (1) the Roman destruction of the temple in A.D. 70 and (2) the image of the Antichrist being set up in the last days (cf. 2 Thess. 2:4; Rev. 13:14).

24:16 flee to the mountains. The ancient church historian Eusebius reports that, during the Jewish revolt (A.D. 67), Jesus' warning was fulfilled when

flee to the mountains. **17** [z]Let the one who is on [a]the housetop not go down to take what
is in his house, **18** and let the one who is in the field not turn back to take his cloak. **19** And
[b]alas for women who are pregnant and for those who are nursing infants in those days!
20 Pray that your flight may not be in winter or on a Sabbath. **21** For then there will be [c]great
tribulation, [d]such as has not been from the beginning of the world until now, no, and never
will be. **22** And if those days had not been cut short, no human being would be saved. But
for [e]the sake of the elect those days will be cut short. **23** [f]Then if anyone says to you, 'Look,
here is the Christ!' or 'There he is!' do not believe it. **24** For [g]false christs and [h]false prophets
will arise and [i]perform great signs and wonders, [h]so as to lead astray, if possible, even the
elect. **25** See, [j]I have told you beforehand. **26** So, if they say to you, 'Look, [k]he is in the wilderness,' do not go out. If they say, 'Look, he is in the inner rooms,' do not believe it. **27** [l]For as
the lightning comes from the east and shines as far as the west, so will be [m]the coming of
the Son of Man. **28** [n]Wherever the corpse is, there the vultures will gather.

The Coming of the Son of Man

29 "Immediately after [o]the tribulation of those days [p]the sun will be darkened, and the
moon will not give its light, and [q]the stars will fall from heaven, and the powers of the
heavens will be shaken. **30** Then [r]will appear in heaven [s]the sign of the Son of Man, and
then [t]all the tribes of the earth will mourn, and [u]they will see the Son of Man coming on
the clouds of heaven [v]with power and great glory. **31** And [w]he will send out his angels with
a loud [x]trumpet call, and they will [y]gather [z]his elect from [a]the four winds, [b]from one end
of heaven to the other.

The Lesson of the Fig Tree

32 "From the fig tree learn its lesson: as soon as its branch becomes tender and puts out
its leaves, you know that summer is near. **33** So also, when you see all these things, you

17 [z]Luke 17:31 [a]See Luke 5:19
19 [b]Luke 23:29
21 [c]ver. 29; Dan. 12:1; [Rev. 7:14] [d]Rev. 16:18
22 [e]ver. 24, 31; Isa. 65:8, 9; Luke 18:7; [ch. 22:14]
23 [f]Luke 17:23; [ver. 5, 26]
24 [g][1 John 2:18] [h]ver. 11 [i]Deut. 13:1-3; 2 Thess. 2:9-11; Rev. 13:13, 14; 16:14; 19:20; [Acts 8:9]
25 [j]John 13:19; 14:29; [2 Pet. 3:17]
26 [k]Acts 21:38
27 [l]Luke 17:24 [m]ver. 3, 37, 39
28 [n]Luke 17:37; [Job 39:30]
29 [o]ver. 21 [p]Isa. 13:10; 24:23; Ezek. 32:7; Joel 2:10, 31; 3:15; Acts 2:20; [Amos 5:20; 8:9; Zeph. 1:15; Rev. 6:12; 8:12] [q]Rev. 6:13; [Isa. 14:12; 34:4]
30 [r]Dan. 7:13 [s][ver. 3] [t]Rev. 1:7; [Zech. 12:12] [u]See ch. 16:27 [v]ch. 26:64; Mark 9:1; [ch. 25:31]
31 [w]ch. 13:41 [x]1 Cor. 15:52; 1 Thess. 4:16 [y][ch. 23:37; 2 Thess. 2:1] [z]ver. 22, 24 [a]Dan. 7:2; Zech. 2:6; Rev. 7:1 [b]Deut. 4:32; 30:4

Christians fled to the mountains of Pella (Eusebius, *Ecclesiastical History* 3.5.3).

24:17 on the housetop not go down. There will be no time to gather provisions.

24:20 not . . . in winter or on a Sabbath. They should pray that the harshest conditions and most revered traditions not be a hindrance to fleeing.

24:21 great tribulation. The time of the siege and destruction of Jerusalem in A.D. 70 was horrible, but the vision Jesus paints will have an even more horrific fulfillment in the future (see note on 24:1–25:46).

24:22 if those days had not been cut short, no human being would be saved. Some suggest this means that, if God's wrath were to continue unchecked against the wickedness of humanity, no one would survive the eventual destruction. Others see in this a reference to a cutting short of either the seventieth "seven" (week) of Dan. 9:27 or the 42 months of Rev. 11:2. It is evident that the reference is not to the destruction of Jerusalem in A.D. 70, since the unprecedented destruction described in Matt. 24:21 did not take place in 70. **The elect** includes all those who follow Christ during this period (cf. vv. 24, 31).

24:24 signs and wonders. Supernatural signs and miracles will have the appearance of coming from God but that will actually be the work of Satan and his evil forces. (On testing false prophets, see notes on 7:15–20; 9:34; 1 John 4:1.)

24:26–27 Look, he is in the wilderness . . . Look, he is in the inner rooms. The Messiah will not come secretly to a select group and stay hidden from public view. Rather, he will appear like a flash of **lightning**—sudden and visible to all.

24:28 Wherever the corpse is, there the vultures will gather. It seems best not to "over-interpret" this striking proverbial expression. It probably means simply that, just as people from far away can see vultures circling high in the air, Christ's return in judgment will be visible and predictable. A similar view is that the vultures suggest the widespread death that will accompany the return of Christ to judge those who have rejected his kingdom. In either case, it will be impossible for people not to see and recognize the return of Christ.

24:29 sun . . . moon . . . stars . . . powers. It is possible that this is entirely literal language (with "stars" perhaps referring to a large meteor shower). Others take it as a mixture of literal and figurative language, and still others take it as entirely figurative, pointing to political judgment on nations and governments. The argument in favor of a figurative interpretation is that this verse echoes possibly figurative language about heavenly disturbances in the OT prophets, such as Isa. 13:10; 34:4; Ezek. 32:7; Joel 2:10; and Amos 8:9. Those arguing for a literal interpretation point to biblical accounts of actual darkness: cf. Ex. 10:21–23 and Matt. 27:45. The idea of the stars falling and the heavens being rolled up is mentioned elsewhere in the NT as well (see Heb. 1:12; 2 Pet. 3:7, 10, 12; Rev. 6:13–14). Whether these events are to be understood as being primarily literal or primarily figurative, it is clear that these will be "earth-shattering" events, through which all creation will be radically transformed at the return of Christ. (Regarding the "new heavens and the new earth," see Isa. 65:17; 2 Pet. 3:13; Rev. 21:1.)

24:30 sign of the Son of Man. Some suggest that this is a type of heavenly standard or banner that unfurls in the heavens as Christ returns in "power and great glory," while others understand it to be the arrival of the Son of Man himself as the sign of the end-time consummation of the age (cf. 16:27; 26:64). **mourn.** Either a sorrow that produces repentance, or a great sadness of regret in light of coming judgment. **they will see the Son of Man** (see note on 8:20) **coming on the clouds of heaven.** This most clearly is end-time language that recalls Daniel's prophecy (Dan. 7:13–14) and points to Jesus' return at the end of the age (cf. 2 Thess. 1:7–10; Rev. 19:11–16). **with power and great glory.** Christ will be revealed as the eternal ruler of the kingdom of God, designated by the Ancient of Days to receive worship and to exercise dominion over the earth and all of its inhabitants (cf. Dan. 7:13–14). The return of Christ is a literal event, in which Christ "will come in the same way" that the disciples "saw him go into heaven" (Acts 1:11).

24:31 A **trumpet call** is associated in Jewish end-time thought (Isa. 18:3; 27:13) and also in Christian writings (1 Cor. 15:51–52; 1 Thess. 4:16) with the appearance of the Messiah. **his angels . . . will gather his elect from the four winds, from one end of heaven to the other.** The involvement of angels probably indicates that, when Jesus returns, he will not only gather to himself all believers alive on the earth but will also bring with him all the redeemed who are in heaven (cf. 1 Thess. 4:14; Rev. 19:11–16).

24:32–41 *The Nearness and Time of Jesus' Coming.* Jesus moves from describing future events to dealing with the attitudes that should character-

33[c]James 5:9; Rev. 3:20
34[d]See ch. 16:28
35[e]Ps. 102:26; Isa. 51:6; 2 Pet. 3:10; [ch. 5:18; Heb. 12:27] [f]Ps. 119:89; Isa. 40:8; 1 Pet. 1:23, 25
36[g]ch. 25:13; 1 Thess. 5:1, 2 [h][Phil. 2:6, 7] [i][Zech. 14:7; Acts 1:7]
37[j]Luke 17:26, 27 [k]ver. 27
38[j][See ver. 37 above] [l]ch. 22:30 [m]Gen. 7:7-16
39[k][See ver. 37 above]
41[n]Luke 17:35 [o]Ex. 11:5; Isa. 47:2
42[p]Mark 14:34-38; Luke 12:37; 21:36; Acts 20:31; 1 Thess. 5:6 [q]John 13:13
43[r]For ver. 43-51, [Luke 12:39-46] [s][1 Thess. 5:2; 2 Pet. 3:10; Rev. 3:3]
44[t]ch. 25:10 [u]ver. 27
45[v]ch. 25:21; 1 Cor. 4:2; Heb. 3:5 [w]ch. 7:24; 10:16; 25:2
46[x]John 13:17; Rev. 16:15
47[y]ch. 25:21, 23
48[z]ch. 25:5
49[a]1 Thess. 5:7
50[b]2 Pet. 3:12; [ch. 25:13]
51[c]See ch. 8:12

know that he is near, [c]at the very gates. **34** [d]Truly, I say to you, this generation will not pass
away until all these things take place. **35** [e]Heaven and earth will pass away, but [f]my words
will not pass away.

No One Knows That Day and Hour

36 "But concerning that day and hour [g]no one knows, not even the angels of heaven,
[h]nor the Son,[1] [i]but the Father only. **37** [j]For as were the days of Noah, [k]so will be the coming of the Son of Man. **38** [j]For as in those days before the flood they were eating and
drinking, [l]marrying and giving in marriage, until [m]the day when Noah entered the
ark, **39** and they were unaware until the flood came and swept them all away, [k]so will be
the coming of the Son of Man. **40** Then two men will be in the field; one will be taken
and one left. **41** [n]Two women will be grinding [o]at the mill; one will be taken and one
left. **42** Therefore, [p]stay awake, for you do not know on what day [q]your Lord is coming.
43 [r]But know this, that if the master of the house had known in what part of the night
[s]the thief was coming, he would have stayed awake and would not have let his house
be broken into. **44** Therefore you also must be [t]ready, for [u]the Son of Man is coming at
an hour you do not expect.

45 "Who then is [v]the faithful and [w]wise servant,[2] whom his master has set over his household, to give them their food at the proper time? **46** [x]Blessed is that servant whom his
master will find so doing when he comes. **47** Truly, I say to you, [y]he will set him over all
his possessions. **48** But if that wicked servant says to himself, 'My master [z]is delayed,' **49** and
begins to beat his fellow servants[3] and eats and drinks with [a]drunkards, **50** the master of
that servant will come [b]on a day when he does not expect him and at an hour he does not
know **51** and will cut him in pieces and put him with the hypocrites. In that place [c]there
will be weeping and gnashing of teeth.

[1] Some manuscripts omit *nor the Son* [2] Greek *bondservant*; also verses 46, 48, 50 [3] Greek *bondservants*

ize his followers as they prepare for the end (vv. 32–35), knowing that his return is imminent (vv. 36–41).

24:34 this generation will not pass away until all these things take place. Several interpretations have been offered for this difficult passage: (1) Some think "this generation" refers to the disciples who were alive when Jesus was speaking, and "all these things" refers to the beginning but not the completion of the sufferings described in vv. 4–25. (2) Others see in "all these things" a prediction with multiple fulfillments, so that Jesus' disciples will be both "this generation" that sees the destruction of the temple in A.D. 70 and also those at the end of the age who see the events surrounding the "abomination of desolation" (v. 15). (3) Since "the generation of . . ." in the OT can mean people who have a certain quality (cf. Ps. 14:5; 24:6; cf. Gk. *genea* in Luke 16:8), others understand "this generation" to refer either (a) to "this generation of believers" throughout the entire present age, or (b) to "this evil generation" that will remain until Christ returns to establish his kingdom (cf. Matt. 12:45; Luke 11:29). (4) Others, particularly some dispensational interpreters, understand "generation" to mean "race" (this is another sense of Gk. *genea*) and think it refers to the Jewish people, who will not pass away until Christ returns. (5) Others understand "this generation" to mean the generation that sees "all these things" (Matt. 24:33), namely, the generation alive when the final period of great tribulation begins. According to this view, the illustration of the fig tree (v. 32) shows that when the final events begin, Christ will come soon. Just as "all these things" in v. 33 refers to events leading up to but not including Christ's return, so in v. 34 "all these things" refers to the same events (that is, the events described in vv. 4–25).

24:35 my words will not pass away. Jesus attributes divine authority and permanence to his own teaching—it is greater even than **heaven and earth**.

24:36 In response to the disciples asking, "when will these things be?" (v. 3), Jesus says **no one knows, not even . . . the Son, but the Father only**. In his incarnate life, Jesus learned things as other human beings learn them (cf. Luke 2:52; Heb. 5:8). On the other hand, Jesus was also fully God, and, as God, he had infinite knowledge (cf. John 2:25; 16:30; 21:17). Here he is apparently speaking in terms of his human nature. This is similar to other statements about Jesus which could be true of his human nature only, and not of his divine nature (he grew and became strong, Luke 2:40; increased in stature, Luke 2:52; was about 30 years old, Luke 3:23; was weary, John 4:6; was thirsty, John 19:28; was hungry, Matt. 4:2; was crucified, 1 Cor. 2:8). Taking account of these verses, together with many verses that affirm Christ's deity, the Council of Chalcedon in A.D. 451 affirmed that Christ was "perfect in Godhead and also perfect in manhood; truly God and truly man." Yet it also affirmed that Jesus was "one Person and one Subsistence." With regard to the properties of his human nature and his divine nature, the Chalcedonian Creed affirmed that Christ was to be "acknowledged in two natures, inconfusedly, unchangeably, indivisibly, inseparably; the distinction of natures being by no means taken away by the union, but rather the property of each nature being preserved." That meant the properties of deity and the properties of humanity were both preserved. How Jesus could have limited knowledge and yet know all things is difficult, and much remains a mystery, for nobody else has ever been both God and man. One possibility is that Jesus regularly lived on the basis of his human knowledge but could at any time call to mind anything from his infinite knowledge.

24:40–41 taken . . . left. The description may indicate that one is taken away to final judgment (cf. v. 39) while the other remains to experience salvation at Christ's return. Or possibly the one who is taken is among the elect that the Son of Man will "gather . . . from the four winds" (v. 31).

24:42–25:30 *Parabolic Exhortations to Watch and Be Prepared for the Coming of the Son of Man.* Jesus gives four parables to explain to his disciples how and why they should be prepared for his coming: the homeowner and the thief (24:42–44), the good and wicked servants (24:45–51), the 10 virgins (25:1–13), and the talents (25:14–30).

24:42 stay awake. Christians should not merely keep looking for the coming of the Son of Man. Instead they should be completing the work of the Great Commission (28:19–20), as well as being prepared and expectant, because the time of Christ's return is unknown (24:36). On readiness for Christ's return; cf. 1 Thess. 5:1–11; 1 Pet. 4:7; 2 Pet. 3:2–18.

24:48–51 delayed. The behavior of the **wicked servant** indicates he is a false disciple (cf. Gal. 5:19–21) and is deserving of **that place** where **there will be weeping and gnashing of teeth**, a description of hell (cf. note on Matt. 8:11–12).

The Parable of the Ten Virgins

25 "Then the kingdom of heaven will be like [d]ten virgins who took their lamps[1] and
went to meet [e]the bridegroom.[2] 2 Five of them were foolish, and five were [w]wise.
3 For when the foolish took their lamps, they took no oil with them, 4 but the wise took
flasks of oil with their lamps. 5 As the bridegroom [f]was delayed, they all became drowsy
and slept. 6 But [g]at midnight there was a cry, 'Here is the bridegroom! Come out to meet
him.' 7 Then all those virgins rose and [h]trimmed their lamps. 8 And the foolish said to the
wise, 'Give us some of your oil, for our lamps are going out.' 9 But the wise answered, saying, 'Since there will not be enough for us and for you, go rather to the dealers and buy
for yourselves.' 10 And while they were going to buy, the bridegroom came, and [i]those who
were ready went in with him to [j]the marriage feast, and [k]the door was shut. 11 Afterward
the other virgins came also, saying, [l]'Lord, lord, open to us.' 12 [l]But he answered, 'Truly, I
say to you, [m]I do not know you.' 13 [n]Watch therefore, for you [o]know neither the day nor
the hour.

The Parable of the Talents

14 [p]"For [q]it will be like a man [r]going on a journey, who called his servants[3] and entrusted
to them his property. 15 To one he gave five [s]talents,[4] to another two, to another one, [t]to
each according to his ability. Then he [r]went away. 16 He who had received the five talents
went at once and traded with them, and he made five talents more. 17 So also he who had
the two talents made two talents more. 18 But he who had received the one talent went
and [u]dug in the ground and hid his master's money. 19 Now [v]after a long time the master
of those servants came and [w]settled accounts with them. 20 And he who had received
the five talents came forward, bringing five talents more, saying, 'Master, you delivered
to me five talents; here I have made five talents more.' 21 His master said to him, 'Well
done, good and [x]faithful servant.[5] [y]You have been faithful over a little; [z]I will set you over
much. Enter into [a]the joy of your master.' 22 And he also who had the two talents came
forward, saying, 'Master, you delivered to me two talents; here I have made two talents
more.' 23 His master said to him, 'Well done, good and faithful servant. You have been
faithful over a little; I will set you over much. Enter into the joy of your master.' 24 He
also who had received the one talent came forward, saying, 'Master, I knew you to be [b]a
hard man, reaping [c]where you did not sow, and gathering where you scattered no seed,
25 so I was afraid, and I went and hid your talent in the ground. Here [d]you have what is
yours.' 26 But his master answered him, 'You [e]wicked and [e]slothful servant! You knew that
I reap where I have not sown and gather where I scattered no seed? 27 Then you ought

[1] *Or torches* [2] Some manuscripts add *and the bride* [3] Greek *bondservants;* also verse 19 [4] A *talent* was a monetary unit worth about twenty years' wages for a laborer [5] Greek *bondservant;* also verses 23, 26, 30

Chapter 25
1 [d]Luke 19:13 [e]ch. 9:15; John 3:29; Rev. 19:7; 21:2, 9
2 [w][See ch. 24:45 above]
5 [f]ch. 24:48; [ver. 19; Heb. 10:37; 2 Pet. 3:4, 9]
6 [g]Mark 13:35
7 [h][Luke 12:35]
10 [i]ch. 24:44 [j]ch. 22:2 [k]For ver. 10-12, [Luke 13:25-27]
11 [l][ch. 7:22, 23]
12 [l][See ver. 11 above] [m]ch. 10:33; [2 Tim. 2:19]
13 [n]ch. 24:42 [o][ch. 24:50]
14 [p]For ver. 14-30, [Luke 19:12-27] [q][Mark 13:34] [r]ch. 21:33
15 [s]ch. 18:24 [t][Rom. 12:6; 1 Cor. 12:11; Eph. 4:7; 1 Pet. 4:10] [r][See ver. 14 above]
18 [u][ch. 13:44]
19 [v][ver. 5] [w]ch. 18:23; Rom. 14:12; [Luke 16:2]
21 [x]ver. 23; ch. 24:45 [y]Luke 16:10; 1 Cor. 4:2; [1 Tim. 3:13] [z]ch. 24:47 [a]Heb. 12:2; [John 15:11]
24 [b]1 Sam. 25:3 [c][2 Cor. 8:12]
25 [d]ch. 20:14
26 [e]ch. 18:32; Prov. 20:4; Rom. 12:11

25:1 the kingdom of heaven will be like. See notes on 3:2; 13:24. **ten virgins**. Bridesmaids. **bridegroom**. As God referred to himself as the "husband" of Israel in the OT (e.g., Isa. 54:4–6), so Jesus pictures himself here as a bridegroom (cf. Matt. 9:14–15). It was the Jewish marriage custom (cf. 1:18) for the groom and his friends to leave his home and proceed to the home of the bride, where the marriage ceremony was conducted, often at night. After this, the entire wedding party returned to the groom's home for a celebratory banquet.

25:3–4 lamps. Large dome-shaped torches, fueled by rags soaked in oil and used for walking outside. **oil**. With extra containers of oil, the torches could last for several hours.

25:9–10 not be enough for us and for you. Torches required regular refilling. **those who were ready**. It was the responsibility of each person to be prepared individually to go with the bridegroom to the wedding banquet.

25:11–12 I do not know you. The OT speaks of God "knowing" his chosen people (Jer. 1:5; Hos. 13:5; Amos 3:2). The same theme continues in the NT, where it describes a saving relationship with God through Jesus Christ (cf. Gal. 4:8–9; 2 Tim. 2:19).

25:13 Watch therefore. The point of the parable is that disciples must "watch correctly" in order to be properly prepared and ready to accompany the Son of Man when he returns. **you know neither the day nor the hour**. See note on 24:42.

25:15 talents. See note on 18:24.

25:16–17 The first and second servants acted industriously and earned a return on their entrusted amounts, probably by setting up some kind of business.

25:18 dug in the ground. Since there were no banks in ancient times, it was common practice to bury valuables (see note on 13:44).

25:19 after a long time. Cf. "delayed" in the previous two parables (24:48; 25:5).

25:20–23 Well done, good and faithful servant. The master's identical statements of praise to both servants show that what was important was not the total amount earned but faithfulness in utilizing their gifts and potential. **You have been faithful over a little; I will set you over much**. Faithful stewardship in this life will result in being given greater responsibility and stewardship in the life to come.

25:24–25 Master, I knew you to be a hard man. The third servant's actions result from his apparent misperception of his master, which manifests itself in laziness and bad stewardship.

25:27 you ought to have invested my money with the bankers. In

to have invested my money with the bankers, and at my coming I should have received
what was my own with interest. **28** So take the talent from him and give it to him who
has the ten talents. **29** [f]For to everyone who has will more be given, and he will have an
abundance. But from the one who has not, even what he has will be taken away. **30** And
[g]cast [h]the worthless servant into the outer darkness. In that place [g]there will be weeping
and gnashing of teeth.'

The Final Judgment

31 [i]"When the Son of Man comes in his glory, and all the angels with him, [j]then he will
sit on his glorious throne. **32** Before him [k]will be gathered [l]all the nations, and [m]he will
separate people one from another as a shepherd separates [n]the sheep from the goats. **33** And
he will place the sheep on his right, but the goats on the left. **34** Then [o]the King will say
to [p]those on his right, 'Come, you [q]who are blessed by my Father, [r]inherit [s]the kingdom
[t]prepared for you [u]from the foundation of the world. **35** For [v]I was hungry and you gave
me food, I was thirsty and you [w]gave me drink, [x]I was a stranger and you welcomed me,
36 [v]I was naked and you clothed me, [y]I was sick and you [z]visited me, [a]I was in prison and
you came to me.' **37** Then the righteous will answer him, saying, 'Lord, when did we see you
hungry and feed you, or thirsty and give you drink? **38** And when did we see you a stranger
and welcome you, or naked and clothe you? **39** And when did we see you sick or in prison
and visit you?' **40** And [b]the King will answer them, [c]'Truly, I say to you, as you did it to one
of the least of these [d]my brothers,[1] you did it to me.'

41 "Then he will say to those on his left, [e]'Depart from me, you [f]cursed, into [g]the eternal
fire prepared for [h]the devil and his angels. **42** For [i]I was hungry and you gave me no food,
I was thirsty and you gave me no drink, **43** I was a stranger and you did not welcome me,
naked and you did not clothe me, sick and in prison and you did not visit me.' **44** Then
they also will answer, saying, 'Lord, when did we see you hungry or thirsty or a stranger
or naked or sick or in prison, and did not minister to you?' **45** Then he will answer them,
saying, 'Truly, I say to you, as you did not do it to one of the least of these, [j]you did not
do it to me.' **46** And these will go away [k]into eternal punishment, but the righteous [k]into
[l]eternal life."

[1] Or *brothers and sisters*

29 [f][Luke 12:48]; See ch. 13:12
30 [g]See ch. 8:12 [h][Luke 17:10]
31 [i]See ch. 16:27, 28 [j]ch. 19:28
32 [k][ch. 24:31] [l]Joel 3:12; [ch. 24:14; 28:19] [m]ch. 13:49 [n]Ezek. 34:17
34 [o]ver. 40; Luke 19:38; Rev. 17:14; 19:16; [Isa. 6:5] [p]1 Kgs. 2:19; Ps. 45:9; 110:1 [q][Ps. 37:22; Isa. 65:23; Eph. 1:3] [r]ch. 19:29; Rev. 21:7 [s]Luke 12:32; 22:29 [t]ch. 20:23; [1 Cor. 2:9; Heb. 11:16] [u]See ch. 13:35
35 [v]Isa. 58:7; Ezek. 18:7, 16; [James 2:15, 16] [w]ch. 10:42 [x]Job 31:32; Rom. 12:13; Heb. 13:1, 2; 3 John 5
36 [v][See ver. 35 above] [y][Luke 10:33, 34] [z]James 1:27 [a]2 Tim. 1:16; [Heb. 10:34; 13:3]
40 [b]ver. 34 [c]See ch. 10:40, 42 [d]ch. 28:10; John 20:17; Rom. 8:29; Heb. 2:11; [ch. 12:50]
41 [e]ch. 7:23 [f][Heb. 6:8] [g]ch. 13:40, 42; 18:8; Mark 9:43, 48; Jude 7; [Luke 16:24]; See 2 Thess. 1:8 [h]2 Pet. 2:4; Jude 6; Rev. 12:7
42 [i]Job 22:7
45 [j][Luke 10:16; Acts 9:5; 1 Cor. 8:12]
46 [k]Dan. 12:2; [John 5:29; Acts 24:15] [l]Rom. 2:7; 5:21; 6:23

the OT, Israelites were forbidden from charging interest to other Israelites (Ex. 22:25; Lev. 25:35–37; Deut. 23:19), but it was permissible to charge interest on money loaned to Gentiles (Deut. 23:20). In any case, the central point of the parable concerns the importance of being a faithful servant of all that God has entrusted to one's care.

25:29 to everyone who has will more be given. Using one's God-given abilities wisely and productively is a vital aspect of discipleship and will be rewarded with additional opportunities to serve God faithfully and fruitfully.

25:30 outer darkness . . . weeping and gnashing of teeth. A typical description of hell and eternal damnation, occurring six times in Matthew and once in Luke. See note on Matt. 8:11–12.

25:31–46 *Judgment at the End.* Jesus' disciples are to wait patiently in anticipation of reward at his return, when the unprepared and unrepentant will receive only judgment.

25:31 Son of Man. See note on 8:20. **angels with him**. See 13:41–42; 2 Thess. 1:7; Rev. 14:17–20. **sit on his glorious throne**. As both Judge and King.

25:32 all the nations. Both Jews and Gentiles, who are the object of the Great Commission throughout this age (see note on 28:19). **he will separate people one from another**. See 7:21–23; 13:40–43.

25:34 King. The Son of Man upon his throne (v. 31) recalls the prophecy of Dan. 7:13–14, in which the Ancient of Days bestows the kingdom upon "one like a son of man." **blessed by my Father**. The blessing to the "sheep" (Matt. 25:32) consists of their inheritance of the Father's kingdom, given not as a reward for good works but because of their saving relationship with the Father and the Son.

25:40 In the context of the parable the **least of these** refers to those who are most needy among Jesus' **brothers**—a reference most likely to Jesus' disciples and by extension all believers. The "sheep" are commended for their great compassion for those in need—for the hungry, the thirsty, the stranger; for those who are naked, sick, or in prison. The righteous will inherit the kingdom *not because of* the compassionate works that they have done but because their righteousness comes from their transformed hearts in response to Jesus' proclamation of the kingdom, *as evidenced by* their compassion for the "least of these." In caring for those in need, the righteous discover that their acts of compassion for the needy are the same as if done for Jesus himself (**you did it to me**).

25:41–46 Then he will say to those on his left. In contrast to the sheep (who will "inherit the kingdom"; v. 34), the goats are condemned to the **eternal fire prepared for the devil and his angels**. The reason for their condemnation is that they are guilty of sins of omission—that is, they have refused to show compassion to the **least of these**, which is the same as if they failed to have any care for Jesus himself. Given the evident unrighteousness of their hearts, they are condemned to **eternal punishment**. Some interpreters hold that this judgment (**these will go away**) will occur prior to the inauguration of Jesus' earthly millennial kingdom, and that the "sheep" (v. 33) are those blessed to enter and live under Jesus' dominion. Others equate this judgment scene with that which closes the earthly age, just prior to the eternal state (Rev. 20:11–13). The most important point, however, is that judgment will come.

1 The **Gate of the Essenes** allowed the Essenes to access latrines outside the city walls in accordance with their strict laws of hygiene.

2 **Herod's Palace** was the Jerusalem home of Herod the Great from 23 to 4 B.C. Pilate, who normally resided in Caesarea Maritima, resided in this palace during his visits to Jerusalem, including his visit for the Passover preceding Christ's crucifixion.

3 The **Praetorium** was in Herod's Palace (Matt. 27:27; Mark 15:16), which served as Pilate's official headquarters and as a fortress. A raised stone pavement, used for official judgments, stood outside the palace and was the site of Jesus' condemnation under Pilate (John 19:13).

4 5 6 Herod the Great fortified three towers to protect his palace: from west to east there was the **Tower of Hippicus** (155 feet/47 m tall), the **Tower of Phasael** (138 feet/42 m tall), and the **Tower of Mariamne** (95 feet/29 m tall).

7 The two-level **Palatial Mansion** (6,500 sq. feet/604 sq. m) may have been the Palace of Annas, who served as high priest from A.D. 6 to 15. Annas's son-in-law Caiaphas held this office from A.D. 18 to 36 and presided at the trial of Jesus (Matt. 26:57).

8 This is often considered the most likely location of **Golgotha,** the place of Jesus' death. It was on a hill overlooking a quarry, outside the Second Wall of the city and near the Gennath (Garden) Gate.

9 Herod the Great lived in the luxurious **Hasmonean Palace** from the mid-30s to 23 B.C. while awaiting the building of his own new palace. Herod Antipas ("Herod the Tetrarch") lived in this palace during his reign, 4 B.C.–A.D. 39. Jesus appeared before him here in either A.D. 30 or 33.

10 The **Archives** building contained the public registers (including genealogies) as well as bonds taken by moneylenders, which allowed the recovery of debts.

11 The **Xystus,** built on the site of the former Greek Gymnasium, was a place of mass assembly.

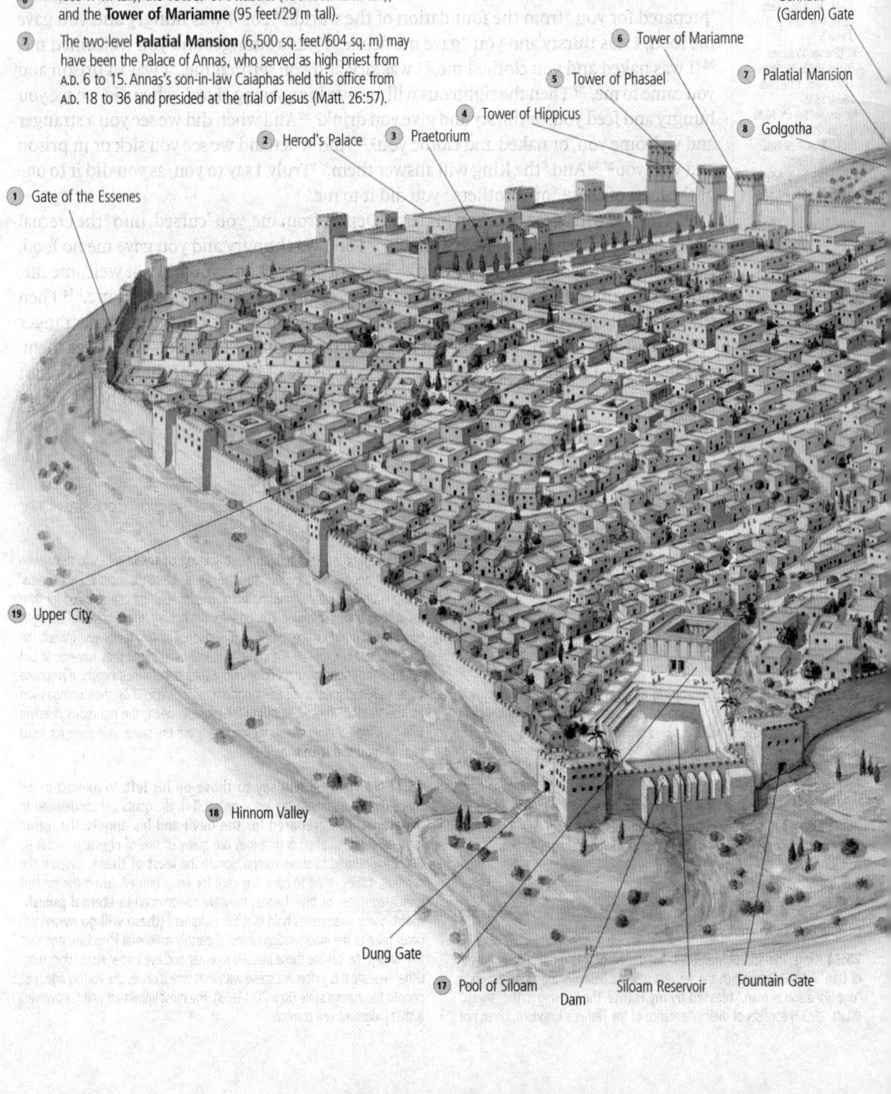

12 The **Council House** was a public building, perhaps functioning as a municipal office.

13 **The Temple** was reconstructed by Herod the Great, beginning in 20/19 B.C.

14 The **Bethesda Pools** (see John 5:2) were twin pools, each measuring c. 312 by 164–196 feet (95 by 50–60 m), and c. 50 feet (15 m) deep. A small Roman temple dedicated to Aesculapius stood to the east of the pools.

15 The **Garden of Gethsemane** was located approximately 300 yards (274 m) from Jerusalem and the Temple Mount. The Mount of Olives was "a Sabbath day's journey away" from Jerusalem (Acts 1:12), approximately 1,100 yards, or 3/5 of a mile.

16 The ravine of the **Kidron Valley** has always served as Jerusalem's eastern boundary.

17 The **Pool of Siloam** (cf. John 9:7), a focal point of Jerusalem, adjoined a large dam and reservoir, and received water from the Gihon Spring.

18 The **Hinnom Valley** was to the south of the hill that was the original city of David.

19 The **Upper City** housed luxurious villas of wealthy residents in the Herodian period.

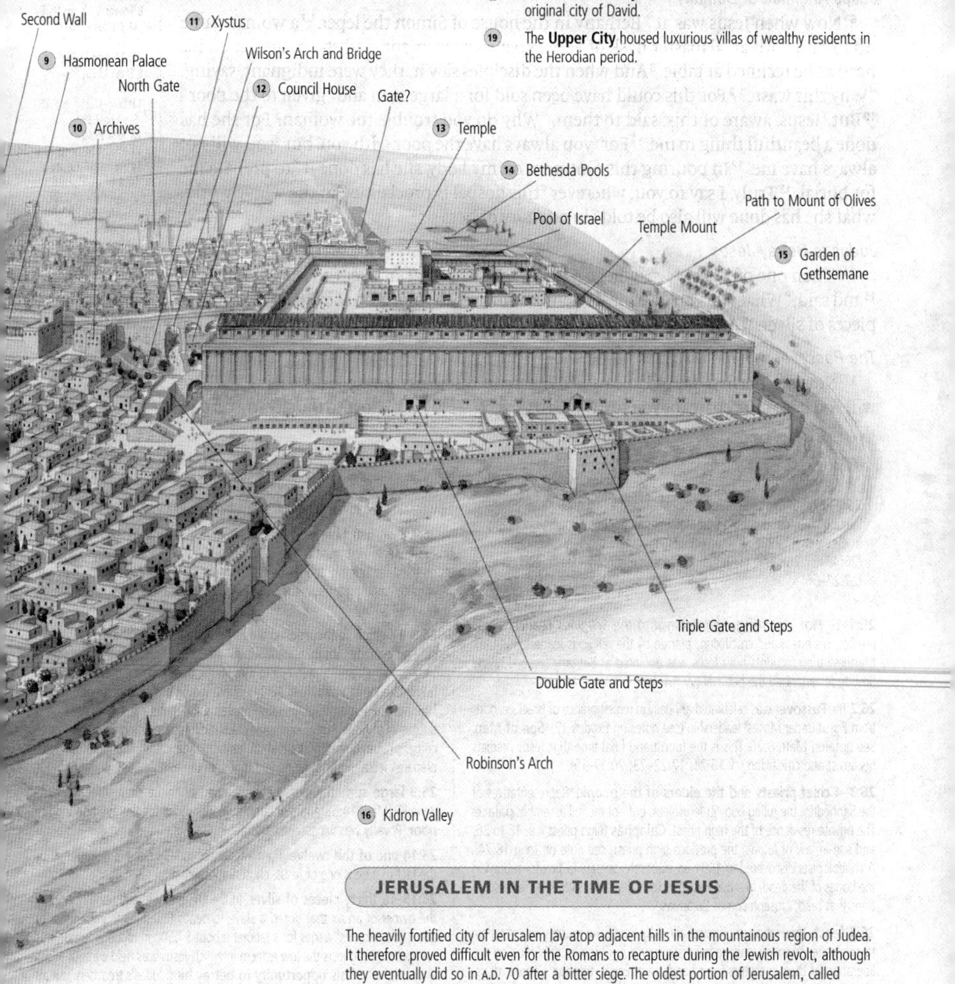

JERUSALEM IN THE TIME OF JESUS

The heavily fortified city of Jerusalem lay atop adjacent hills in the mountainous region of Judea. It therefore proved difficult even for the Romans to recapture during the Jewish revolt, although they eventually did so in A.D. 70 after a bitter siege. The oldest portion of Jerusalem, called "the city of David" and "Mount Zion," lay to the south of the temple, but the city walls in the first century also encompassed the newer Upper City to the west of the temple. To the east, across the Kidron Valley (John 18:1), stood the Mount of Olives (Mark 13:3). To the south of Zion lay the Hinnom Valley. The reconstruction above depicts Jerusalem around A.D. 30, and the general direction of the drawing is looking north.

The Plot to Kill Jesus

26 When Jesus had finished all these sayings, he said to his disciples, 2 [m]“You know
that after two days [n]the Passover is coming, and [o]the Son of Man [p]will be delivered
up to be crucified.”
3 [q]Then the chief priests and the elders of the people gathered in [r]the palace of the
high priest, whose name was [s]Caiaphas, 4 [t]and plotted together in order to arrest Jesus
by stealth and kill him. 5 But they said, “Not during the feast, [u]lest there be an uproar
among the people.”

Jesus Anointed at Bethany

6 [v]Now when Jesus was at [w]Bethany in the house of Simon the leper,[1] 7 a woman came
up to him with an alabaster flask of very expensive ointment, and she poured it on his
head as he reclined at table. 8 And when the disciples saw it, they were indignant, saying,
“Why this waste? 9 For this could have been sold for a large sum and [x]given to the poor.”
10 But [y]Jesus, aware of this, said to them, “Why do you trouble the woman? For she has
done a beautiful thing to me. 11 For [z]you always have the poor with you, but [a]you will not
always have me. 12 In pouring this ointment on my body, she has done it [b]to prepare me
for burial. 13 Truly, I say to you, wherever [c]this gospel is proclaimed in the whole world,
what she has done will also be told [d]in memory of her.”

Judas to Betray Jesus

14 [e]Then one of the twelve, whose name was [f]Judas Iscariot, went to the chief priests
15 and said, “What will you give me if I deliver him over to you?” And they [g]paid him [h]thirty
pieces of silver. 16 And from that moment he sought an opportunity [i]to betray him.

The Passover with the Disciples

17 [j]Now on [k]the first day of Unleavened Bread the disciples came to Jesus, saying, “Where
will you have us prepare for you to eat the Passover?” 18 He said, “Go into the city to a certain

[1] *Leprosy* was a term for several skin diseases; see Leviticus 13

Chapter 26
2 [m]For ver. 2-5, see Mark 14:1, 2; Luke 22:1, 2 [n]See John 6:4 [o]ver. 24 [p]See ch. 20:18, 19
3 [q][Ps. 2:2; John 11:47; Acts 4:27] [r]ver. 58, 69; Luke 11:21; John 18:15; [Rev. 11:2] [s]ver. 57; Luke 3:2; John 11:49; 18:13; Acts 4:6
4 [t]John 11:53; See ch. 21:46
5 [u]ch. 27:24
6 [v]For ver. 6-13, see Mark 14:3-9; John 12:1-8; [Luke 7:37-39] [w]ch. 21:17; John 11:18
9 [x][John 13:29]
10 [y]ch. 16:8
11 [z]Deut. 15:11 [a]ch. 9:15; See John 7:33
12 [b]John 19:40
13 [c][ch. 24:14] [d]Acts 10:4
14 [e]For ver. 14-16, see Mark 14:10, 11; Luke 22:3-6; [John 13:2, 27, 30] [f]ch. 10:4; 27:3; Acts 1:16; [John 6:71; 12:4]
15 [g]Zech. 11:12; [Gen. 23:16; Jer. 32:9] [h]ch. 27:3, 9; Ex. 21:32
16 [i]See ch. 20:18, 19
17 [j]For ver. 17-19, see Mark 14:12-16; Luke 22:7-13 [k]Ex. 12:18

26:1–27:66 *The Crucified Messiah.* Matthew narrates the events leading to Jesus' death: (1) the Passover and Lord's Supper and events in Gethsemane (26:1–46); (2) Jesus' arrest, trials, and conviction (26:47–27:26); and (3) Jesus' flogging, crucifixion, death, and burial (27:27–66).

26:1–16 *Plot, Anointing, and Betrayal to the Religious Leaders.* Jesus predicts his arrest and crucifixion, plotted by the religious leaders (vv. 1–5). Matthew then recounts how Jesus was anointed at Bethany (vv. 6–13) and how Judas arranged the betrayal (vv. 14–16).

26:2 The **Passover** was celebrated annually in remembrance of Israel's exodus from Egypt under Moses' leadership (see notes on Exodus 12). **Son of Man**. See note on Matt. 8:20. This is the fourth and final time that Jesus predicts his arrest and crucifixion (cf. 16:21; 17:22–23; 20:17–19).

26:3–4 chief priests and the elders of the people. Representatives of the Sanhedrin, the ruling body in Jerusalem, but not the full assembly. **palace**. The private residence of the high priest. **Caiaphas** (high priest A.D. 18 to 36, and son-in-law of Annas, the previous high priest; see note on John 18:24). Archaeologists discovered in 1991 an elaborate ossuary (a box for reburying the bones of the dead) in a burial cave in Jerusalem with slightly varied inscriptions that read, “Joseph son of Caiaphas.”

26:5 feast. Thousands of pilgrims annually made the journey to Jerusalem to celebrate Passover, and nationalistic fervor ran high as they recalled the liberation of their ancestors from bondage in Egypt. **uproar**. Popular uprisings were increasingly common especially during such feast periods, and the chief priests and elders were reluctant to arrest Jesus openly because of his popularity with the people.

26:6–13 Matthew thematically organizes this account of Jesus' anointing at Bethany, while John (John 12:1–11) places it chronologically on Saturday night before Jesus' triumphal entry.

26:6 Bethany. See note on 21:17. **Simon the leper** had most likely been healed by Jesus, since the meal is hosted in Simon's home even though lepers were required to live apart from the general population.

26:7 a woman. Identified in John 12:3 as Mary, sister of Martha and Lazarus. **expensive ointment**. “Pure nard” (cf. Mark 14:3; John 12:3), a perfume oil used for solemn acts of devotion. More common household oils were used to anoint guests, for medicine, and for other purposes (see note on Mark 14:3–5).

26:8–12 given to the poor. What seems like a **waste** to the disciples, Jesus calls **a beautiful thing**. If the disciples' real concern was for the poor, there would always be an opportunity to care for the poor because they will **always have the poor with** them (v. 11). There would not be much opportunity, however, to demonstrate their love for Jesus. Given his impending death, the anointing of Jesus' body becomes a dramatic foreshadowing of the events to come. **prepare me for burial**. In her act of devotion, Mary unknowingly prepares Jesus' body for being laid to rest in the tomb.

26:9 large sum. The perfume was valued at “more than three hundred denarii” (Mark 14:5), approximately a year's wages for the average worker. **poor**. Poverty was widespread in Israel.

26:14 one of the twelve. The treachery of Judas's deed is heightened by the fact that he is one of Jesus' chosen apostles.

26:15–16 thirty pieces of silver. In the OT, this was the penalty paid by the owner of an ox that gored a slave to death (Ex. 21:32). Equivalent to about four months' wages for a laborer (about $7,500 in modern terms), this meager sum suggests the low esteem in which Jesus was held by both Judas and the chief priests. **opportunity to betray him**. Judas's treachery reveals that he was not a true believer (cf. Luke 22:3–4).

26:17–35 *The Passover and the Lord's Supper.* Jesus and his disciples prepare for, and then partake in, the Passover meal. Jesus reveals his betrayer and institutes the Lord's Supper.

26:17 first day of Unleavened Bread. The Festival of Unleavened Bread lasted seven days, from Nisan (March/April) 15 to 21 (cf. Lev. 23:5–6). **prepare for you to eat the Passover**. Preparations for the Passover were

18[l]See John 11:28 [m][ver. 45; John 7:6, 8, 30; 8:20; 13:1; 17:1]
20[n]For ver. 20-24, see Mark 14:17-21; [Luke 22:14, 21-23; John 13:21-26]
21[o][John 6:70, 71]
23[p][John 13:18]
24[q]ver. 54, 56; Mark 9:12; Luke 18:31; 24:25-27, 46; Acts 17:2, 3; 26:22, 23; 1 Cor. 15:3; 1 Pet. 1:10, 11 [r]ch. 18:7 [s]John 17:12
25[t]ver. 49; See John 1:38 [u]ver. 64; See Luke 22:70
26[v]For ver. 26-29, see Mark 14:22-25; Luke 22:18-20; 1 Cor. 11:23-25 [w]See ch. 14:19 [x]1 Cor. 10:16; [John 6:53]
27[y]See ch. 15:36
28[x][See ver. 26 above] [z]Ex. 24:8; [Zech. 9:11; Heb. 13:20] [a]See ch. 20:28 [b]Mark 1:4; [Luke 1:77]
29[c][ch. 13:43]
30[d]For ver. 30-35, see Mark 14:26-31 [e]Luke 22:39; John 18:1 [f]See ch. 21:1
31[g]Cited from Zech. 13:7; [John 16:32]

man and say to him, [l]"The Teacher says, [m]My time is at hand. I will keep the Passover at
your house with my disciples.'" 19 And the disciples did as Jesus had directed them, and
they prepared the Passover.

20 [n]When it was evening, he reclined at table with the twelve.[1] 21 And as they were eating,
[o]he said, "Truly, I say to you, one of you will betray me." 22 And they were very sorrowful
and began to say to him one after another, "Is it I, Lord?" 23 He answered, [p]"He who has
dipped his hand in the dish with me will betray me. 24 The Son of Man goes [q]as it is written
of him, but [r]woe to that man by whom the Son of Man is betrayed! [s]It would have been
better for that man if he had not been born." 25 Judas, who would betray him, answered,
"Is it I, [t]Rabbi?" He said to him, [u]"You have said so."

Institution of the Lord's Supper

26 [v]Now as they were eating, Jesus took bread, and [w]after blessing it broke it and gave
it to the disciples, and said, "Take, eat; [x]this is my body." 27 And he took a cup, and when
he [y]had given thanks he gave it to them, saying, "Drink of it, all of you, 28 for [x]this is my
[z]blood of the[2] covenant, which is poured out for [a]many [b]for the forgiveness of sins. 29 I tell
you I will not drink again of this fruit of the vine until that day when I drink it new with
you [c]in my Father's kingdom."

Jesus Foretells Peter's Denial

30 [d]And when they had sung a hymn, [e]they went out to [f]the Mount of Olives. 31 Then
Jesus said to them, "You will all fall away because of me this night. For it is written, 'I will
[g]strike the shepherd, and the sheep of the flock will be scattered.' 32 But after I am raised up,

[1] Some manuscripts add *disciples* [2] Some manuscripts insert *new*

made on Thursday afternoon (Nisan 14). Jesus and the disciples ate the Passover meal after sundown on Thursday evening (now Nisan 15), with Jesus instituting the Lord's Supper later that evening. Jesus was crucified the following afternoon, Friday (still Nisan 15).

26:18 Go . . . to a certain man and say to him, . . . "I will keep the Passover at your house." Either Jesus had made prior arrangements with friends in Jerusalem in order to avoid the Jewish authorities, or the encounter was a miraculous work of God.

26:20 reclined at table. In formal dining, guests reclined on a couch that stretched around three sides of a room. The host took the center seat at a U-shaped series of low tables, surrounded by the most honored guests on either side, with the guests' heads reclining toward the tables and their feet toward the wall.

26:23 he who has dipped his hand in the dish with me. The custom was to take a piece of bread or a piece of meat in bread and dip it into a common bowl of sauce on the table. Each of those around the room had done so, therefore at this point the betrayer could have been any of the Twelve. **will betray me.** The height of disloyalty and betrayal is sharing a meal with a friend before turning on him.

26:24 as it is written. A reference to the suffering servant prophecies in Isaiah 42–53. **woe.** The certainty of divine judgment that will fall upon the one who betrays Jesus.

26:25 Rabbi. The larger group around the table address Jesus as "Lord" (v. 22), but Judas addresses him as "Rabbi," or "Teacher." There is no record of Judas ever calling Jesus "Lord." **You have said so.** A Greek expression that deflects responsibility back upon the one asking a question (cf. v. 64).

26:26 bread . . . this is my body. Jesus' body will be the once-and-for-all fulfillment of the ceremonies surrounding the Passover lamb and other OT sacrifices, as he will become the sacrificial atonement for the sins of the people.

26:27 cup. Most likely the third of four cups at the Passover—the cup of blessing, or the cup of redemption—corresponding to God's third promise in Ex. 6:6: "I will redeem you with an outstretched arm and with great acts of judgment."

26:28 blood of the covenant. The cup foreshadows the shedding of Jesus' blood and the absorbing of God's wrath, which opens the way for the redemption of all peoples through the new covenant relationship with God that was promised to the people of Israel (cf. Jer. 31:31, 34).

26:29 drink it new with you in my Father's kingdom. The messianic banquet (cf. 8:11; Rev. 19:9).

26:30 hymn. Perhaps the Hallel (Psalms 113–118), or perhaps the last great Hallel psalm (Psalm 136).

26:31 You will all fall away. Not just Peter, but all the disciples will forsake Jesus and run (v. 56). They will not cease being his disciples, but they will fail to stand with him in the face of persecution.

26:32 I will go before you to Galilee. Jesus will graciously restore the disciples back to fellowship with himself following their failure to stand.

The Last Supper

After Jesus and his disciples ate the Passover meal, they crossed the Kidron Valley and entered a garden called Gethsemane (meaning "oil press"), where they often spent time while visiting Jerusalem (cf. Luke 22:39).

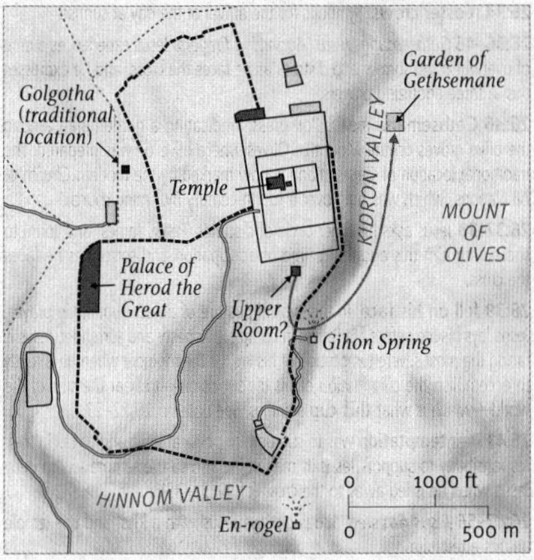

[h]I will go before you to Galilee." 33 [i]Peter answered him, "Though they all fall away because
of you, I will never fall away." 34 [j]Jesus said to him, "Truly, I tell you, this very night, [k]before
the rooster crows, you will deny me three times." 35 [l]Peter said to him, "Even if I must die
with you, I will not deny you!" And all the disciples said the same.

Jesus Prays in Gethsemane

36 [m]Then Jesus went with them [e]to a place called Gethsemane, and he said to his disciples,
"Sit here, while I go over there and pray." 37 And taking with him [n]Peter and [o]the two sons
of Zebedee, he began to be sorrowful and troubled. 38 Then he said to them, [p]"My soul
is very sorrowful, even to death; remain here, and [q]watch[1] with me." 39 And going a little
farther he fell on his face [r]and prayed, saying, "My Father, if it be possible, let [s]this cup
pass from me; [t]nevertheless, not as I will, but as you will." 40 And he came to the disciples
and found them sleeping. And he said to Peter, "So, could you not watch with me one
hour? 41 [q]Watch and [u]pray that you [v]may not enter into temptation. The spirit indeed is
willing, but the flesh is weak." 42 Again, for the second time, he went away and prayed,
"My Father, if this cannot pass unless I drink it, [w]your will be done." 43 And again he came
and found them sleeping, for [x]their eyes were heavy. 44 So, leaving them again, he went
away and prayed for [y]the third time, saying the same words again. 45 Then he came to the
disciples and said to them, "Sleep and take your rest later on.[2] See, [z]the hour is at hand,
and [a]the Son of Man is betrayed into the hands of sinners. 46 Rise, let us be going; see, my
betrayer is at hand."

Betrayal and Arrest of Jesus

47 [b]While he was still speaking, [c]Judas came, one of the twelve, and with him a great
crowd with swords and clubs, from the chief priests and the elders of the people. 48 Now
the betrayer had given them a sign, saying, "The one I will kiss is the man; seize him."
49 And he came up to Jesus at once and said, "Greetings, [d]Rabbi!" And he kissed him. 50 Jesus
said to him, [e]"Friend, [f]do what you came to do."[3] Then they came up and laid hands on
Jesus and seized him. 51 And behold, one of those who were with Jesus stretched out
his hand and drew his [g]sword and struck the servant[4] of the high priest and cut off his
ear. 52 Then Jesus said to him, "Put your sword back into its place. For [h]all who take the
sword will perish by the sword. 53 [i]Do you think that I cannot appeal to my Father, and
he will at once send me [j]more than twelve [k]legions of angels? 54 [l]But how then should
the Scriptures be fulfilled, that it must be so?" 55 At that hour Jesus said to the crowds,

32 [h]ch. 28:7, 10, 16; Mark 16:7
33 [i][Luke 22:31, 33]
34 [j]Luke 22:34; John 13:38 [k]ver. 75
35 [l]Luke 22:33; John 13:37
36 [m]For ver. 36-46, see Mark 14:32-42; Luke 22:40-46 [e][See ver. 30 above]
37 [n]ch. 17:1 [o]ch. 4:21
38 [p][Ps. 42:5, 6; John 12:27] [q]See ch. 24:42
39 [r]Heb. 5:7 [s]See ch. 20:22 [t]ver. 42; John 5:30; 6:38; Phil. 2:8
41 [q][See ver. 38 above] [u]1 Pet. 4:7 [v]ch. 6:13
42 [w]ver. 39; See ch. 6:10
43 [x]Luke 9:32
44 [y][2 Cor. 12:8]
45 [z]John 12:23, 27; 13:1; 17:1; [ver. 18; Luke 22:53] [a]ch. 17:22; 20:18
47 [b]For ver. 47-56, see Mark 14:43-50; Luke 22:47-53; John 18:3-11 [c]ver. 14; Acts 1:16
49 [d]ver. 25
50 [e]ch. 20:13; 22:12 [f][John 13:27]
51 [g][Luke 22:38]
52 [h]Rev. 13:10; [Gen. 9:6; Ezek. 35:6]
53 [i][John 10:18] [j][ch. 4:11; 2 Kgs. 6:17; Dan. 7:10; Luke 22:43; John 18:36] [k]Luke 8:30
54 [l]See ver. 24; ch. 1:22

[1] Or *keep awake*; also verses 40, 41 [2] Or *Are you still sleeping and taking your rest?* [3] Or *Friend, why are you here?* [4] Greek *bondservant*

26:33–35 Peter fails to heed Jesus' warning and underestimates the extreme test of faith they will all soon encounter. **all the disciples said the same**. They are swayed by Peter's bravado.

26:34 rooster crows. Symbolic for the arrival of the day at sunrise.

26:36–46 *Gethsemane: Jesus' Agonizing Prayers.* Jesus experiences a time of overwhelming sorrow and distress as he faces the cross, and he expresses this in three agonizing prayers.

26:36 Gethsemane means "oil press," indicating a garden area among the olive groves on the Mount of Olives where olive oil was prepared. The traditional location of Gethsemane is now marked by the modern Church of All Nations, which was built over a fourth-century Byzantine church.

26:37–38 Jesus asks his inner circle of disciples (Peter, James, and John) to share with him this agonizing time of anticipation and sorrow as he faces the cross.

26:39 fell on his face. In this typical posture of abject humility in prayer, Jesus lays his life before his Father in complete honesty and surrender. Jesus is facing the most severe temptation of his life, at the moment when he is ready to accomplish the culmination of his life's mission—to bear the sins of the world—which is what **this cup** signifies. See note on 20:22–23.

26:41 Their **temptation** was to succumb to physical sleep and so fail in their responsibility to support Jesus. It may point also to the temptation to deny Jesus when he is led away to the cross (cf. vv. 31–35).

26:47–56 *Jesus Arrested.* Judas betrays Jesus with a kiss, and the temple guards arrest him.

26:47 Matthew emphasizes Judas's treachery by referring to him as **one of the twelve**. The **great crowd** consisted of a detachment of Roman soldiers assigned by Pilate to the temple for security, who were carrying **swords**, and Levitical temple police and personal security of the **chief priests** and Sanhedrin (**elders**), carrying **clubs**.

26:48 kiss. A customary way for friends in ancient (and modern) Israel to greet one another now becomes the means of betrayal.

26:49 Rabbi. See note on v. 25.

26:50 Friend represents Greek *hetairos*, implying not the closeness and affection of the usual word for friend (*philos*) but only acquaintance and association. It was used previously by Jesus in parables concerning someone who has taken advantage of a privileged relationship (see 20:13; 22:12).

26:51 one of those who were with Jesus. Simon Peter (John 18:10–11). **servant of the high priest**. Malchus (John 18:10).

26:52 Put your sword back. True disciples of Jesus do not seek to advance or impose God's will on others through violent means.

26:53 twelve legions. 72,000. A Roman legion at full strength had 6,000 soldiers.

26:56 Their scheme had been predicted in the **Scriptures of the prophets** (cf. esp. Psalm 22; Isaiah 53; Zechariah 12–13).

26:57–27:10 *The Jewish Trial of Jesus.* Matthew narrates the events surrounding the trial of Jesus by the Jewish authorities: his stand before the

"Have you come out as against a robber, with swords and clubs to capture me? Day after
day [m]I sat in the temple [n]teaching, and you did not seize me. 56 But [l]all this has taken
place that the Scriptures of the prophets might be fulfilled." [o]Then all the disciples left
him and fled.

Jesus Before Caiaphas and the Council

57 [p]Then [q]those who had seized Jesus led him to [r]Caiaphas the high priest, where the
scribes and the elders had gathered. 58 And [s]Peter was following him at a distance, as far
as [r]the courtyard of the high priest, and going inside he sat with [t]the guards to see the
end. 59 Now the chief priests and the whole council[1] [u]were seeking false testimony against
Jesus that they might put him to death, 60 but they found none, [v]though many false witnesses came forward. At last [w]two came forward 61 and said, "This man said, [x]'I am able to
[y]destroy the temple of God, and to rebuild it in three days.'" 62 And the high priest stood
up and said, "Have you no answer to make? What is it that these men testify against you?"[2]
63 [z]But Jesus remained silent. [a]And the high priest said to him, [b]"I adjure you by [c]the living
God, [d]tell us if you are [e]the Christ, [f]the Son of God." 64 Jesus said to him, [g]"You have said
so. But I tell you, from now on [h]you will see the Son of Man [i]seated at the right hand of
Power and [h]coming on the clouds of heaven." 65 Then the high priest [j]tore his robes and
said, [k]"He has uttered blasphemy. What further witnesses do we need? You have now heard
his blasphemy. 66 What is your judgment?" They answered, [l]"He deserves death." 67 Then
[m]they spit in his face [n]and [o]struck him. And some slapped him, 68 saying, "Prophesy to us,
you [p]Christ! Who is it that struck you?"

[1] Greek *Sanhedrin* [2] Or *Have you no answer to what these men testify against you?*

55 [m][John 8:2]; [Luke 2:46; John 18:20] [n]ch. 21:23; [ch. 4:23]
56 [l][See ver. 54] [o]ver. 31; [Ps. 88:8, 18; John 16:32]
57 [p]Luke 22:54 [q]For ver. 57-68, see Mark 14:53-65; [John 18:12, 13, 19-24] [r]ver. 3
58 [s][John 18:15] [r][See ver. 57 above] [t]John 7:32; 18:3
59 [u]See Acts 6:11
60 [v]Ps. 27:12; 35:11 [w]Deut. 19:15
61 [x][Acts 6:14]; See John 2:19 [y]ch. 27:40
63 [z]ch. 27:12, 14; Isa. 53:7; John 19:9 [a]For ver. 63-66, [Luke 22:67-71] [b][Lev. 5:1; 1 Sam. 14:24, 26; Mark 5:7] [c]See ch. 16:16 [d]John 10:24 [e][ch. 22:42-45]; See ch. 1:17 [f]See ch. 14:33
64 [g]ver. 25 [h]See ch. 16:27; 24:30 [i]Ps. 110:1; Heb. 1:3; [Mark 16:19]
65 [j]Num. 14:6; Acts 14:14 [k]ch. 9:3; John 10:36
66 [l]See Lev. 24:16
67 [m]ch. 27:30; Isa. 50:6; Mark 10:34 [n][Luke 22:63-65; John 18:22] [o]ch. 5:39; Acts 23:2
68 [p]ver. 63

Sanhedrin (26:57–68), Peter's denials (26:69–75), the condemnation and deliverance of Jesus to Pilate (27:1–2), and Judas's remorse and suicide (27:3–10).

26:57–58 The headquarters of **Caiaphas the high priest** was likely a palatial mansion, probably on the eastern slope of the "upper city" of Jerusalem overlooking the temple area (see note on John 18:24).

26:59–60 The Sanhedrin tried to find **false witnesses** who would credibly testify that Jesus had violated the law, so that they could find him guilty as quickly as possible.

26:59 The whole council ("Sanhedrin") need not denote all 70 members but may just indicate those hastily assembled in the middle of the night (23 members made a quorum). "Sanhedrin" (Gk. *synedrion*) could refer either to a local Jewish tribunal (e.g., "council," 5:22; "courts," 10:17) or, as here, to the supreme ecclesiastical court ("council") of the Jews, centered in Jerusalem. The Romans were ultimately in control of all judicial proceedings but allowed their subjects some freedom to try their own cases.

26:61–62 I am able to destroy the temple of God. This saying, misquoted and taken out of context (cf. John 2:19–21), was easily distorted by Jesus' opponents.

26:63 silent. Jesus' silence fulfills Isa. 53:7 and places the responsibility for his death squarely on his accusers. **tell us if you are the Christ**. Caiaphas wants Jesus to admit to this charge so that he can be accused of insurrection against Rome and tried before Pilate for treason.

26:64 You have said so. See note on v. 25. Jesus declares that he is not only the human Messiah anticipated by the Jews but also the divine **Son of Man** (see Dan. 7:13–14; note on Matt. 8:20) who sits at the **right hand** of God (Ps. 110:1–2) and who will come **on the clouds** in power to reign over the earth.

26:65 tore his robes. Normally prohibited for the high priest (Lev. 10:6; 21:10), but this astounding claim by Jesus evokes a vehement response. **blasphemy**. A reference to Jesus' claim of divine status as the Son of Man.

26:66 If Jesus is lying by claiming to be divine, then indeed he **deserves death** from the standpoint of the Jewish law (see Lev. 24:10–23). The irony is that he will be executed for telling the truth.

26:67–68 The Jewish leaders' physical abuse of Jesus and their mocking question, **"Who is it that struck you?"** demonstrate their disbelief in his prophetic gifts and thus their scorn for his claims to divinity (v. 64).

Jesus' Arrest, Trial, and Crucifixion

The path from Jesus' arrest to his crucifixion (part of which is often called the Via Dolorosa, "Way of Sorrows") is difficult to retrace with certainty. According to a possible harmony of the Gospel accounts, after the Passover meal Judas led a contingent of soldiers to Gethsemane to arrest Jesus (1). From there Jesus was led to Annas (location unknown), who sent him to his son-in-law Caiaphas, the high priest (2). The Jewish leaders then appealed to the Roman governor Pilate to have Jesus put to death (3). Luke records that Pilate sent Jesus to Herod Antipas (4), who questioned Jesus but returned him to Pilate without rendering any judgment (5). Pilate then sent Jesus to be crucified at Golgotha (6).

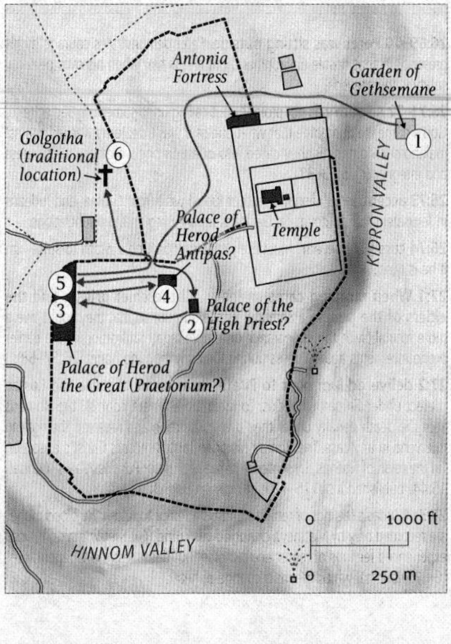

Peter Denies Jesus

69 [q]Now Peter was sitting outside [r]in the courtyard. And a servant girl came up to him
and said, "You also were with Jesus the Galilean." 70 But he denied it before them all, saying,
"I do not know what you mean." 71 And when he went out to the entrance, another servant
girl saw him, and she said to the bystanders, "This man was with Jesus [s]of Nazareth."
72 And again he denied it with an oath: "I do not know the man." 73 After a little while the
bystanders came up and said to Peter, "Certainly you too are one of them, for [t]your accent
betrays you." 74 Then he began to invoke a curse on himself and to swear, "I do not know
the man." And immediately the rooster crowed. 75 And Peter remembered the saying of
Jesus, [u]"Before the rooster crows, you will [v]deny me three times." And he went out and
wept bitterly.

Jesus Delivered to Pilate

27 [w]When morning came, all the chief priests and the elders of the people [x]took counsel
against Jesus to put him to death. 2 And they bound him and [y]led him away and
[z]delivered him over to [a]Pilate the governor.

Judas Hangs Himself

3 Then when [b]Judas, his betrayer, saw that Jesus[1] was condemned, [c]he changed his mind
and brought back [d]the thirty pieces of silver to the chief priests and the elders, 4 saying,
"I have sinned by betraying innocent blood." They said, "What is that to us? [e]See to it
yourself." 5 And throwing down the pieces of silver into the temple, [f]he departed, and he
went and hanged himself. 6 But the chief priests, taking the pieces of silver, said, "It is not
lawful to put them into [g]the treasury, since it is blood money." 7 So they took counsel and
bought with them the potter's field as a burial place for strangers. 8 Therefore [h]that field
has been called the Field of Blood [i]to this day. 9 [j]Then was fulfilled what had been spoken
by the prophet Jeremiah, saying, [k]"And they took the thirty pieces of silver, the price of
him on whom a price had been set by some of the sons of Israel, 10 and they gave them for
the potter's field, as the Lord directed me."

Jesus Before Pilate

11 [l]Now Jesus stood before the governor, and the governor asked him, "Are you [m]the
King of the Jews?" Jesus said, [n]"You have said so." 12 [o]But when he was accused by the chief

[1] Greek *he*

69 [q]For ver. 69-75, see Mark 14:66-72; Luke 22:55-62; John 18:16-18, 25-27 [r]ver. 3
71 [s]ch. 2:23
73 [t][Judg. 12:6]
75 [u]ver. 34 [v][Acts 3:13, 14]

Chapter 27

1 [w]Mark 15:1; Luke 22:66 [x]See ch. 26:4
2 [y]Luke 23:1; John 18:28 [z]See ch. 20:19 [a]Luke 3:1; 13:1; Acts 3:13; 4:27; 1 Tim. 6:13
3 [b]See ch. 26:14 [c]ch. 21:29 [d]ch. 26:15
4 [e]ver. 24
5 [f][2 Sam. 17:23; Acts 1:18]
6 [g]Mark 12:41, 43; Luke 21:1; John 8:20
8 [h]Acts 1:19 [i]ch. 28:15
9 [j]See ch. 1:22 [k]Cited from Zech. 11:13
11 [l]For ver. 11-14, see Mark 15:2-5; Luke 23:2, 3; John 18:29-38 [m]ver. 29, 37; ch. 2:2; John 18:39; 19:3; [ver. 42] [n][1 Tim. 6:13]; See Luke 22:70
12 [o]See ch. 26:63

26:69–70 Peter was sitting outside. Peter demonstrates courage by his presence in that hostile environment, but it fails him when his own personal safety is threatened.

26:71–72 An **oath** was not profanity but calling upon something sacred (e.g., God's name) to guarantee that what one said was true. Jesus warned against making such oaths, as they called into question one's ordinary truthfulness and integrity (cf. 5:33–37).

26:73 accent. Jesus' disciples (except Judas) were from Galilee, and Judeans in Jerusalem looked down on Galileans for their regional pronunciations.

26:74 curse . . . swear. Most likely calling upon God's wrath to strike him if he is lying.

27:1 When morning came on Friday, **all the chief priests and the elders of the people** assembled with a quorum so that they could give a more formal (with the appearance of a more legal) ratification of the earlier pronouncements against Jesus during the early morning hours (26:57–68).

27:2 delivered him over to Pilate. The governor of Judea and Roman prefect under Emperor Tiberius. To maintain ultimate control, the Romans kept the death penalty under their own jurisdiction and reserved the right to intervene in any case. The Roman historian Tacitus records Christ's execution "in the reign of Tiberius, by sentence of the procurator Pontius Pilatus" (*Annals* 15.44, published A.D. 115–120; cf. note on Luke 3:1).

27:3–4 Judas's feelings of remorse and his attempt to return the blood money are recorded only by Matthew. **changed his mind** (Gk. *metamelomai*). Judas experienced feelings of regret and remorse, but this is less than "repentance" (Gk. *metanoia*), which means a change of heart.

27:5 Showing no sign of repentance, Judas **hanged himself** rather than face his crushing guilt. The account in Acts 1:18–19 is complementary, not contradictory; see note on Acts 1:18.

27:6 blood money. Based on precepts found in Deut. 23:18.

27:7–8 The name **Field of Blood** arose from its association with the violent death of Judas (cf. Acts 1:18–19) and perhaps also with the "blood money" (Matt. 27:6) paid for his betrayal of Jesus. Most church traditions from at least the fourth century place this in the Hinnom Valley south of Jerusalem (cf. note on 18:6–9), although it is difficult to confirm the precise location.

27:9–10 the prophet Jeremiah. While drawing on a combination of words from Jeremiah (Jer. 19:1–13) and Zechariah (Zech. 11:11–13), Matthew attributes the prophecy to Jeremiah as the more prominent prophet. In the same way, Mark combines quotations from Isaiah and Malachi but cites only Isaiah as the more prominent prophet (see Mark 1:2; cf. Isa. 40:3; Mal. 3:1).

27:11–26 *The Roman Trial of Jesus.* The Jewish religious leaders lacked the final authority to impose the death penalty, and the charge of blasphemy was insufficient for a death sentence under Roman rule. So Jesus was sent to the Roman governor, Pilate, for trial.

27:11 governor. Pontius Pilate (see note on v. 2). **King of the Jews**. Since blasphemy is not sufficient to warrant the death penalty under Roman rule, the Jewish leaders restate the charges when they hand Jesus over to Pilate (cf. Luke 23:2). Such a claim to kingship would be a direct challenge to Caesar. **You have said so**. See note on Matt. 26:25; cf. 26:64.

27:12–14 he gave no answer . . . he gave him no answer. Jesus has

priests and elders, he gave no answer. 13 Then Pilate said to him, [p]"Do you not hear how
many things they testify against you?" 14 But he gave him no answer, not even to a single
charge, so that the governor was greatly amazed.

The Crowd Chooses Barabbas

15 [q]Now at the feast the governor was accustomed to release for the crowd any one prisoner whom they wanted. 16 And they had then a notorious prisoner called Barabbas. 17 So
when they had gathered, Pilate said to them, "Whom do you want me to release for you:
Barabbas, or [r]Jesus who is called Christ?" 18 For he knew that it was out [s]of envy that they
had delivered him up. 19 Besides, while he was sitting on [t]the judgment seat, his wife sent
word to him, "Have nothing to do with [u]that righteous man, for I have suffered much
because of him today [v]in a dream." 20 Now the chief priests and the elders persuaded the
crowd to [w]ask for Barabbas and destroy Jesus. 21 The governor again said to them, "Which
of the two do you want me to release for you?" And they said, "Barabbas." 22 Pilate said to
them, "Then what shall I do with Jesus who is called Christ?" [x]They all said, "Let him be
crucified!" 23 And he said, "Why, [y]what evil has he done?" But they shouted all the more,
"Let him be crucified!"

Pilate Delivers Jesus to Be Crucified

24 So when Pilate saw that he was gaining nothing, but rather that [z]a riot was beginning,
he took water and [a]washed his hands before the crowd, saying, "I am innocent of [b]this
man's blood;[1] [c]see to it yourselves." 25 And all the people answered, [d]"His blood be on us
and [e]on our children!" 26 Then he released for them Barabbas, and having [f]scourged[2] Jesus,
delivered him to be crucified.

Jesus Is Mocked

27 [g]Then the soldiers of the governor took Jesus into the [h]governor's headquarters,[3] and
they gathered the whole [i]battalion[4] before him. 28 And they stripped him and put [j]a scarlet
robe on him, 29 and twisting together a crown of thorns, they put it on his head and put a
reed in his right hand. And kneeling before him, they [k]mocked him, saying, "Hail, [l]King of
the Jews!" 30 And [m]they spit on him and took the reed and struck him on the head. 31 And
when they had mocked him, they stripped him of the robe and put his own clothes on
him and [n]led him away to crucify him.

[1] Some manuscripts *this righteous blood*, or *this righteous man's blood* [2] A Roman judicial penalty, consisting of a severe beating with a multi-lashed whip containing imbedded pieces of bone and metal [3] Greek *the praetorium* [4] Greek *cohort*; a tenth of a Roman legion, usually about 600 men

13 [p]John 19:10
15 [q]For ver. 15-26, see Mark 15:6-15; Luke 23:18-25; John 18:39, 40; 19:16
17 [r]ver. 22
18 [s][John 12:19]
19 [t]John 19:13 [u]ver. 24; [Luke 23:47] [v]See ch. 2:12
20 [w]Acts 3:14
22 [x]Acts 13:28
23 [y][Luke 23:41; John 8:46]
24 [z]ch. 26:5 [a][Deut. 21:6-8; Ps. 26:6; 73:13] [b]ver. 19 [c]ver. 4
25 [d][ch. 23:35, 36; Josh. 2:19; Acts 5:28] [e][Ex. 20:5; Lam. 5:7]
26 [f]ch. 20:19; Isa. 50:6; 53:5; [Luke 23:16; John 19:1]
27 [g]For ver. 27-31, see Mark 15:16-20; John 19:2, 3 [h]John 18:28, 33; 19:9; Acts 23:35; Phil. 1:13 (Gk.) [i]See Acts 10:1 (Gk.)
28 [j]Rev. 18:12, 16; [Luke 23:11]
29 [k]ch. 20:19 [l]See ver. 11
30 [m]See ch. 26:67
31 [n]Isa. 53:7

sufficiently answered Pilate's original question (v. 11), and there was nothing more to say that would change Pilate's mind. See further Isa. 53:7.

27:14 Pilate **was greatly amazed** at Jesus' refusal to defend himself.

27:15–18 release for the crowd. Pilate had apparently instituted this custom as a means of winning favor with the masses. **Barabbas**. A notorious criminal who had committed robbery (see note on John 18:40), insurrection, and murder (Mark 15:7; Luke 23:18–19). He may have belonged to one of the rural guerilla bands that victimized the wealthy upper class of Israel as well as the Romans and were therefore popular with the common people.

27:18 envy. Pilate knows the high priest and the Sanhedrin are not concerned about threats to Roman rule; rather, they are envious of Jesus' popularity and feel threatened by his authoritative ministry.

27:19 dream. Romans often viewed dreams as omens. The dream was probably given by God as a sign of Jesus' innocence.

27:20–22 A few days earlier the people of Jerusalem had shouted "Hosanna!" at Jesus' entry. Now they cry, **"Let him be crucified!"**

27:24 washed his hands. Not an attempt to purge himself of sin but a public demonstration that he finds no grounds for giving Jesus the death penalty.

27:25 People (Gk. *laos*) is Matthew's normal term for Israel as a nation. **His blood be on us** (cf. "Your blood be on your own heads!" Acts 18:6) was a common idiom denoting culpability for someone's death. The people placed the responsibility for Jesus' crucifixion directly on themselves, and they were judged with the destruction of Jerusalem in A.D. 70. However, future generations should not be held responsible for the sins of their ancestors, for that would be unjust (cf. Deut. 24:16; Jer. 31:29–30).

27:26 scourged. Roman flogging was a horrifically cruel punishment. Those condemned to it were tied to a post and beaten with a leather whip that was interwoven with pieces of bone and metal, which tore through skin and tissue, often exposing bones and intestines. In many cases, the flogging itself was fatal. The Romans scourged Jesus nearly to death so that he would not remain alive on the cross after sundown.

27:27–44 *Jesus the Messiah Crucified.* Matthew now takes readers to the very heart of his Gospel: the fulfillment of OT prophecies about the suffering servant (Isa. 42:1–4; 52:13–53:12) and Jesus' own predictions (Matt. 16:21; 17:22–23; 20:17–19; 26:2) about his death.

27:27 the governor's headquarters. The Praetorium, Pilate's official headquarters, doubled as a fortress (see note on John 18:28). **whole battalion**. Probably a maniple (a third of a cohort), which was 120–200 soldiers.

27:28–31 put a scarlet robe on him. Roman soldiers in Jerusalem were infamous for playing cruel games with condemned prisoners, particularly insurrectionists, including dressing them in costumes and moving them around a huge game board as a "game piece." Still, their actions spoke louder than they knew. The one they dressed and hailed as a king was truly the crucified **King**. Mark and John describe the same cloak as "purple," but colors were not as clearly distinguished as they are today, and dyes varied, so a violet-red cloak might be called scarlet by some and purple by others.

The Crucifixion

32 [o], [p]As they went out, they found a man of Cyrene, Simon by name. They compelled this
man to [o]carry his cross. **33** [q]And when they came to a place called Golgotha (which means
Place of a Skull), **34** [r]they offered him wine to drink, mixed with [s]gall, but when he tasted
it, he would not drink it. **35** And when they had crucified him, [t]they divided his garments
among them by casting lots. **36** Then they sat down and [u]kept watch over him there. **37** And
over his head they put the charge against him, which read, "This is Jesus, [v]the King of the
Jews." **38** Then two [w]robbers were crucified with him, [x]one on the right and one on the left.
39 And [y]those who passed by [z]derided him, [a]wagging their heads **40** and saying, [b]"You who
would destroy the temple and rebuild it in three days, save yourself! [c]If you are [d]the Son
of God, come down from the cross." **41** So also the chief priests, with the scribes and elders,
mocked him, saying, **42** [e]"He saved others; [f]he cannot save himself. [g]He is the King of Israel;
let him come down now from the cross, and we will believe in him. **43** [h]He trusts in God;
let God deliver him now, if he desires him. For he said, 'I am the Son of God.'" **44** [i]And the
robbers who were crucified with him also reviled him in the same way.

The Death of Jesus

45 Now from the sixth hour[1] there was darkness over all the land[2] until the ninth hour.[3]
46 And about the ninth hour Jesus [j]cried out with a loud voice, saying, [k]"Eli, Eli, lema
sabachthani?" that is, "My God, my God, why have you forsaken me?" **47** And some of the

[1] That is, noon [2] Or *earth* [3] That is, 3 P.M.

32 [o]Mark 15:21; Luke 23:26; [John 19:17] [p]Heb. 13:12; [ch. 21:39; Num. 15:35]
33 [q]For ver. 33-51, see Mark 15:22-38; Luke 23:32-38, 44-46; John 19:17-19, 23, 24, 28-30
34 [r][Ps. 69:21] [s]Acts 8:23
35 [t]Ps. 22:18
36 [u]ver. 54; [Ps. 22:17]
37 [v]ver. 11, 29
38 [w][John 18:40] [x][ch. 20:21]
39 [y]Ps. 22:7; 109:25; [Lam. 1:12] [z]Luke 22:65; 23:39; [James 2:7] [a]Job 16:4; Isa. 37:22; Jer. 18:16; Lam. 2:15
40 [b]ch. 26:61 [c]ch. 4:3, 6 [d]ver. 43; ch. 26:63; See ch. 14:33
42 [e][Luke 4:23] [f][ch. 26:53, 54; John 10:18] [g]John 1:49; 12:13; [ver. 37]
43 [h]Cited from Ps. 22:8
44 [i][Luke 23:39-43]
46 [j][Heb. 5:7] [k]Cited from Ps. 22:1

27:32 man of Cyrene. Cyrene was a region in North Africa (see note on Acts 13:1) with a large Jewish population. **Simon** was likely a Jew who had traveled to Jerusalem for the Passover. **carry his cross**. Jesus was severely weakened from the scourging and loss of blood (see note on Matt. 27:26) and was therefore unable to carry his cross (see note on v. 35), which weighed 30 to 40 pounds. The skin and muscles of his back would have been severely lacerated, and he could have suffered severe injury to his internal organs. The most common Greek word for "cross" (*stauros*), though originally designating a "sharpened pole," became associated before the NT with various penal means of suspending bodies (before or after death), including those employing a *crux*, or cross-shaped device, for crucifixion.

27:33 Golgotha. Transliteration of the Aramaic word for "skull." It may have been given this name because it was a place of execution, or because the area had a number of tombs, or possibly because the site in some way resembled a skull (see Mark 15:22).

27:34 This was one more mockery in that the **wine** they offered was **mixed with gall**, a bitter herb that could even be poisonous.

27:35 crucified him. Crucifixion was widely practiced by the Romans, and the early Jewish historian Josephus mentions thousands of people crucified in first-century Palestine (mostly during rebellions against Rome). There are stories of Roman soldiers cruelly playing with different postures for crucified victims (e.g., Josephus, *Jewish War* 5.449–551), though the use of nails and a crossbar appear to have been common. Modern medical explanations for the cause of death on a cross have focused on either asphyxiation or shock. Crucifixion was widely believed to be the worst form of execution, due to the excruciating pain and public shame. Hanging suspended by one's arms eventually caused great difficulty in breathing, which could be alleviated only by pushing up with one's feet to take the weight off the arms. But that motion itself would cause severe pain in the feet, arms, legs, and back, causing the exhausted victim to slump down again, only to be nearly unable to breathe once more. Eventually, the victim would succumb to suffocation, if he had not already died as a result of the cumulative effect of the physical trauma inflicted on him. **They divided his garments among them by casting lots** is a clear reference to Ps. 22:18. Matthew alludes to Psalm 22 throughout much of the narrative without his typical fulfillment formula (see note on Matt. 1:22). His readers would know that the soldiers' actions fulfill Scripture.

27:37 charge. Written on a placard above Jesus' head as a deterrent against any who would dare rise up against Rome. It was written "in Aramaic, in Latin, and in Greek" (John 19:20).

27:38 Robbers (Gk. *lēstēs*) is sometimes rendered "insurrectionist," which is possible, but the alleged examples in extrabiblical literature are not conclusive, and the meaning "robber" is appropriate in all 24 examples of *lēstēs* in the NT and Septuagint; see note on John 18:40. Nothing more is known about the background of these men. Jesus' crucifixion with criminals fulfills Isa. 53:12.

27:39–40 Since Heb. 13:12 says that Jesus was crucified "outside the gate" (the city gate), **those who passed by** probably included many pilgrims who had come to Jerusalem for the Passover. **derided**. They mocked Jesus' claim of supernatural power. **wagging their heads**. An allusion to Ps. 22:7; see notes on Ps. 22:6–8 and Matt. 27:35.

27:41–43 chief priests, with the scribes and elders, mocked him. The highest levels of Israel's establishment seek one more opportunity to insult Jesus. The religious leaders do not address Jesus directly, but turn to one another as they mock him. **let God deliver him**. An allusion to Ps. 22:8; see note on Matt. 27:35.

27:45–50 *The Death of Jesus the Messiah.* After being on the cross for about six hours (cf. v. 45 with Mark 15:25), Jesus dies.

27:45 sixth hour . . . until the ninth hour. From noon until 3:00 P.M. Josephus says that the ninth hour was the time when Jews offered the daily evening sacrifice (*Jewish Antiquities* 14.65). **darkness**. Not a solar eclipse, since Passover occurred during a full moon, and a solar eclipse can occur only during a new moon; rather, it is a supernatural act of God, displaying his displeasure and judgment upon humanity for crucifying his Son.

27:46 Eli, Eli, lema sabachthani? Jesus quotes Ps. 22:1 (see note on Matt. 27:35). The last two words are Aramaic (the everyday language spoken by Jesus), and the first two could be either Aramaic or Hebrew. **My God, my God, why have you forsaken me?** Some of the most profoundly mysterious words in the entire Bible. In some sense Jesus had to be cut off from the favor of and fellowship with the Father that had been his eternally, because he was bearing the sins of his people and therefore enduring God's wrath (cf. Isa. 53:6, 10; Hab. 1:13; Rom. 3:25; 2 Cor. 5:21; Gal. 3:13; 1 John 2:2). And yet, in quoting Ps. 22:1 Jesus probably has in mind the remainder of the psalm as well, which moves on to a cry of victory (Ps. 22:21–31); and he expresses faith, calling God "my God." Surely he knows why he is dying, for this was the purpose of his coming to earth (cf. Matt. 16:21; 20:18–19, 28). And surely his cry, uttered **with a loud voice**, is expressing, not bewilderment at his plight, but witness to the bystanders, and through them to the world, that he was experiencing God-forsakenness not for anything in himself but for the salvation of others. Surely Matthew, understanding this, quotes Jesus' words to challenge his readers. Jesus' torment, despite his anticipations of it in Gethsemane, was surely inconceivable in advance (cf. note on 24:36).

27:47 Elijah. Jesus' call to God in Aramaic (*'Eli, 'Eli*) sounds similar to the Hebrew name for Elijah (*'Eliyahu*), which the bystanders misunderstand as a summons to the prophet.

bystanders, hearing it, said, "This man is calling Elijah." **48** And one of them at once ran
and took a sponge, filled it with [l]sour wine, and put it on a reed and [m]gave it to him to
drink. **49** But the others said, "Wait, let us see whether Elijah will come to save him." **50** And
Jesus [n]cried out again with a loud voice and [o]yielded up his spirit.
51 And behold, [p]the curtain of the temple was torn in two, from top to bottom. And [q]the
earth shook, and the rocks were split. **52** The tombs also were opened. And many bodies
of [r]the saints [s]who had fallen asleep were raised, **53** and coming out of the tombs after his
resurrection they went into [t]the holy city and appeared to many. **54** [u]When the centurion
and those who were with him, [v]keeping watch over Jesus, saw the earthquake and what
took place, they were filled with awe and said, [w]"Truly this was the Son[1] of God!"
55 There were also [x]many women there, looking on [y]from a distance, who had followed
Jesus from Galilee, [z]ministering to him, **56** among whom were [z]Mary Magdalene and Mary
the mother of James and Joseph and [a]the mother of the sons of Zebedee.

Jesus Is Buried

57 [b]When it was evening, there came a rich man from Arimathea, named Joseph, who
also was a disciple of Jesus. **58** He went to Pilate and asked for the body of Jesus. Then Pilate
ordered it to be given to him. **59** And Joseph took the body and wrapped it in a clean linen
shroud **60** and [c]laid it in his own new tomb, [d]which he had cut in the rock. And he rolled [e]a
great stone to the entrance of the tomb and went away. **61** Mary Magdalene and [f]the other
Mary were there, sitting opposite the tomb.

The Guard at the Tomb

62 The next day, that is, after the day of [g]Preparation, the chief priests and the Pharisees
gathered before Pilate **63** and said, "Sir, we remember how [h]that impostor said, while he
was still alive, [i]'After three days I will rise.' **64** Therefore order the tomb to be made secure
until the third day, [j]lest his disciples go and steal him away and tell the people, 'He has
risen from the dead,' and the last fraud will be worse than the first." **65** Pilate said to them,
"You have [k]a guard[2] of soldiers. Go, make it as secure as you can." **66** So they went and made
the tomb secure by [l]sealing the stone and setting a guard.

[1] Or *a son* [2] Or *Take a guard*

48 [l]Ruth 2:14 [m]Ps. 69:21
50 [n]ver. 46 [o][John 10:18]
51 [p]Ex. 26:31-33; 2 Chr. 3:14 [q]ver. 54
52 [r][Dan. 7:18, 22] [s]John 11:11-13; Acts 7:60; 13:36; 1 Cor. 15:6, 18, 20; 1 Thess. 4:13-15; 2 Pet. 3:4
53 [t]See ch. 4:5
54 [u]For ver. 54-56, see Mark 15:39-41; Luke 23:47, 49 [v]ver. 36 [w]ver. 43
55 [x]John 19:25 [y]Ps. 38:11 [z]See Luke 8:2, 3
56 [z][See ver. 55 above] [a]ch. 20:20; [Mark 15:40]
57 [b]For ver. 57-61, see Mark 15:42-47; Luke 23:50-56; John 19:38-42
60 [c][Isa. 53:9] [d]Isa. 22:16 [e]Mark 16:4; [John 11:38]
61 [f]ver. 56; ch. 28:1
62 [g]Mark 15:42; Luke 23:54; John 19:14, 31, 42
63 [h][ver. 64; John 7:12] [i]ch. 16:21; 17:23; 20:19; 28:6; Mark 8:31; 10:34; Luke 9:22; 18:33; 24:6, 7; [ch. 26:61; John 2:19]
64 [j][ch. 28:13]
65 [k]ch. 28:11
66 [l]Dan. 6:17

27:48 sour wine. Used as a daily drink with meals by common people and soldiers. It was cheaper than regular wine and effectively quenched thirst. Cf. Ps. 69:21.

27:50 yielded up his spirit. Even in death, Jesus maintains authoritative control over his destiny (cf. John 10:17–18; Heb. 7:16). "His spirit" means his human spirit. While Jesus' body remained on the cross and was then put in the tomb, his spirit went into the presence of God his Father (cf. Luke 23:43, 46; also Eccles. 12:7) and in this way he became the pattern for believers who would die after him (2 Cor. 5:8; Phil. 1:23; Heb. 12:23).

27:51–66 *Testimonies, Women Followers, and Burial.* A series of testimonies—from the temple (v. 51), the dead (vv. 51b–53), and Gentiles (v. 54)—indicate the historical and theological impact of Jesus' death. Matthew mentions the women who watched these scenes unfold (vv. 55–56) and recounts the burial of Jesus and the posting of the guard at his tomb (vv. 57–66).

27:51 curtain of the temple. The curtain between the Holy Place and the Most Holy Place was an elaborately woven fabric of 72 twisted plaits of 24 threads each. It was 60 feet (18 m) high and 30 feet (9.1 m) wide. No one was allowed to enter the Most Holy Place behind the curtain except the high priest, and he only once a year, on the Day of Atonement (Heb. 9:2–7). **Torn in two** signifies the removal of the separation between God and the people. An extended commentary on this event, and the heavenly reality that it symbolized, is found in Heb. 9:11–10:22; see especially Heb. 9:12, 24; 10:19–20. **earth shook**. Palestine sits on a major seismic rift, so earthquakes were not uncommon, but the splitting of rocks and opening of tombs (Matt. 27:52) make this a major testimony to the meaning of Jesus' resurrection.

27:52–53 saints who had fallen asleep. Probably pious OT figures and godly intertestamental Jews, reembodied to witness to the new order of things that was now in the process of dawning. This shows that the resurrection of people who died looking forward to the Messiah depends on Christ's actual death and resurrection, just as does the future resurrection of Jesus' disciples today. **coming out of the tombs after his resurrection they went into the holy city**. Matthew apparently jumps ahead here (treating materials topically, as he often does) and begins to speak of events that would happen after the resurrection. The wording suggests that these saints were not merely brought back to life (like Lazarus; John 11:44) but were "raised" (Matt. 27:52) with new, resurrection bodies, a foretaste of what would happen to all believers at Christ's return. No other historical information about this event has been found, but it is natural to suppose that if they had resurrection bodies, they would not have died again. They may have been taken up to heaven at or after Jesus' ascension (Acts 1:1–11).

27:54 The **centurion** and his guards were accustomed to seeing crucifixions, but these cataclysmic events, coupled with the extraordinary self-control, purity, and love shown by Jesus in his death, made the centurion realize that Jesus was **the Son of God**.

27:55–56 These **women** accompanied Jesus as his disciples (see Mark 15:41; Luke 8:1–3; 23:49), witnessed the crucifixion, and will be the first witnesses to his resurrection.

27:57–60 Joseph was a member of the Sanhedrin who did not consent to the actions against Jesus (Luke 23:50–51). His high standing within the Jewish community gave him access to **Pilate**. The location of **Arimathea** is uncertain—perhaps Ramathaim in the hill country of Ephraim, 20 miles (32 km) northwest of Jerusalem. **asked for the body of Jesus**. Jewish custom dictated that crucified bodies should be taken down before evening, especially before the Sabbath, which began at sundown on Friday. **new tomb**. A rectangular chamber cut into rock. It was accessed through a low entry room and blocked with a **stone** that could be rolled back and forth, mainly to protect the body from wild animals (see illustration of The Tomb of Jesus, p. 2069). The use of a rich man's tomb fulfills Isa. 53:9.

27:61 the other Mary (cf. 28:1). Most likely the mother of Joses (cf. Mark 15:40, 47; he was probably the same person as "Joseph," Matt. 27:56).

27:62 The next day, . . . after the day of Preparation is the Sabbath.

27:65–66 guard. This was the same Roman military guard assigned to oversee temple security.

The Resurrection

28 [m]Now after the Sabbath, toward the dawn of the first day of the week, Mary Magdalene and [n]the other Mary went to see the tomb. 2 And behold, there was a great earthquake, for [o]an angel of the Lord descended from heaven and came and rolled back the stone and sat on it. 3 [p]His appearance was like lightning, and [q]his clothing white as snow. 4 And for fear of him the guards trembled and [r]became like dead men. 5 But the angel said to the women, "Do not be afraid, for I know that you seek Jesus who was crucified. 6 He is not here, for he has risen, [s]as he said. Come, see the place where he[1] lay. 7 Then go quickly and tell his disciples that he has risen from the dead, and behold, [t]he is going before you to Galilee; there you will see him. See, I have told you." 8 So they departed quickly from the tomb [u]with fear and great joy, and ran to tell his disciples. 9 And behold, Jesus [v]met them and said, "Greetings!" And they came up and [w]took hold of his feet and [x]worshiped him. 10 Then Jesus said to them, "Do not be afraid; [y]go and tell [z]my brothers to go to Galilee, and there they will see me."

The Report of the Guard

11 While they were going, behold, some of [a]the guard went into the city and told the chief priests all that had taken place. 12 And when they had assembled with the elders and taken counsel, they gave a sufficient sum of money to the soldiers 13 and said, "Tell people, [b]'His disciples came by night and stole him away while we were asleep.' 14 And if this comes to [c]the governor's ears, we will [d]satisfy him and keep you out of trouble." 15 So they took the money and did as they were directed. And this story has been spread among the Jews [e]to this day.

The Great Commission

16 Now the eleven disciples [f]went to Galilee, to the mountain to which Jesus had directed them. 17 And when they saw him they [g]worshiped him, but some doubted. 18 And Jesus came and said to them, [h]"All authority [i]in heaven and on earth has been given to me. 19 [j]Go therefore and [k]make disciples of [l]all nations, [j]baptizing them [m]in[2] [n]the name of the Father and of the Son and of the Holy Spirit, 20 teaching them [o]to observe all that [p]I have commanded you. And behold, [q]I am with you always, to [r]the end of the age."

[1] Some manuscripts *the Lord* [2] Or *into*

Chapter 28
1 [m]For ver. 1-8, see Mark 16:1-8; Luke 24:1-10; John 20:1 [n]ch. 27:56, 61
2 [o][John 20:12]
3 [p]Dan. 10:6 [q][Dan. 7:9; Mark 9:3; John 20:12; Acts 1:10]
4 [r][Rev. 1:17]
6 [s]ch. 27:63
7 [t]ver. 10, 16; ch. 26:32
8 [u][Ps. 2:11]
9 [v][Mark 16:9; John 20:14] [w]2 Kgs. 4:27 [x]ver. 17; Luke 24:52
10 [y]See John 20:18 [z]John 20:17; [Ps. 22:22; Rom. 8:29; Heb. 2:11, 12, 17]
11 [a]ch. 27:65, 66
13 [b][ch. 27:64]
14 [c]ch. 27:2 [d]See Acts 12:20 (Gk.)
15 [e]ch. 27:8
16 [f]ver. 7
17 [g]ver. 9
18 [h]ch. 11:27; Dan. 7:13, 14; John 3:35; 13:3; 17:2; Acts 2:36; Rom. 14:9; 1 Cor. 15:27; Eph. 1:10, 20-22; Phil. 2:9, 10; Col. 2:10; Heb. 1:2; 2:8; 1 Pet. 3:22; [ch. 9:6; John 5:27] [i][ch. 6:10; Luke 2:14]
19 [j]Mark 16:15, 16 [k]ch. 13:52 [l]Luke 24:47; [ch. 24:14; Mark 11:17; Rom. 1:5] [m]See Acts 8:16 [n][2 Cor. 13:14]
20 [o]John 14:15 [p][Acts 1:2] [q][ch. 1:23; 18:20; John 12:26; 14:3; 17:24; Acts 18:10] [r]See ch. 13:39

28:1–20 *The Resurrection and Commission of the Messiah.* Matthew's concluding chapter recounts Jesus' resurrection from the dead. His resurrection confirms his identity and that his accomplishment at the cross was accepted by God the Father. Jesus now lives as the faithful companion, master, and Lord of those who respond to his great commission (vv. 16–20).

28:1–10 *An Empty Tomb and the Risen Jesus.* The female disciples of Jesus discover an empty tomb (vv. 1–4). After an angel announces Jesus' resurrection and instructs them (vv. 5–7), they meet the risen Jesus (vv. 8–10).

28:1 first day of the week. Sunday morning. **Mary Magdalene and the other Mary** (cf. 27:61). The women remain courageously faithful. Cf. note on 26:31.

28:2 great earthquake, for an angel of the Lord. The earthquake either occurred simultaneously with the appearance of the angel or was the means the angel used to roll away the stone.

28:3–4 fear of him. The appearance of angels often produced fear (cf. Judg. 13:19–20). The guards are probably battle-hardened soldiers, but they have never witnessed anything like this.

28:7 his disciples. Probably the Eleven. **Galilee**. The central location of Jesus' earthly ministry continues in importance during his post-resurrection ministry.

28:9 Took hold of his feet shows that this is no mere vision or hallucination but a physical resurrection. By allowing this act of worship, here and in v. 17, Jesus accepts the acknowledgment of his deity, as only God is to be worshiped.

28:10 my brothers. Perhaps the Eleven, but more likely the broader group of disciples who had followed Jesus (cf. "my brothers" in 12:49–50; 25:40). If so, this is the larger group of disciples who will see the risen Lord (e.g., 1 Cor. 15:6).

28:11–15 *The Conspiracy to Deny the Truth of Jesus' Resurrection.* **taken counsel**. Faced with the reality of Jesus' resurrection, the religious leaders are forced once again (cf. 26:3–5) to conspire together in order to preserve their religious and political influence. The **soldiers** faced possible execution for dereliction of guard duty, one of the most severe offenses while occupying foreign territory. In cooperating with the Jewish religious leaders, they at least have a chance to save themselves.

28:16–20 *The Risen Jesus' Great Commission.* As the resurrected Lord, Jesus calls upon his followers to make disciples of all people groups through the preaching of the gospel of the kingdom.

28:17 Some doubted probably refers to people other than the 11 disciples (see note on 28:10).

28:18 All authority. In his risen state, Jesus exercises absolute authority throughout heaven and earth, which shows his deity. His authority **has been given** by the Father, which indicates that he remains subject to the Father (see note on 1 Cor. 15:28).

28:19 The imperative (**make disciples**, that is, call individuals to commit to Jesus as Master and Lord) explains the central focus of the Great Commission, while the Greek participles (translated **go**, **baptizing**, and "teaching" [v. 20]) describe aspects of the process. **all nations**. Jesus' ministry in Israel was to be the beginning point of what would later be a proclamation of the gospel to all the peoples of the earth, including not only Jews but also Gentiles. The **name** (singular, not plural) of the Father, Son, and Holy Spirit is an early indication of the Trinitarian Godhead and an overt proclamation of Jesus' deity.

28:20 Teaching is a means by which disciples of Jesus are continually transformed in order to become more like Christ (cf. 10:24–25; Rom. 8:29; 2 Cor. 3:18). **observe**. Obey. **I am with you always**. Jesus concludes the commission, and Matthew his Gospel, with the crucial element of discipleship: the presence of the Master, who is "God with us" (cf. Matt. 1:23).

INTRODUCTION TO

THE GOSPEL ACCORDING TO

MARK

Author and Title

Widespread evidence from the early church fathers affirms that Peter passed on reports of the words and deeds of Jesus to his attendant and writer, John Mark. Of particular significance in this regard are the brief statements by Papias (Bishop of Hierapolis; c. A.D. 120), preserved by Eusebius of Caesarea (260–340). Papias states that he received oral tradition from John the elder and apostle, and he passes on the following regarding Mark: (1) he was the writer for Peter; (2) he wrote down accurately as much as he could remember of Peter's words, which the latter had adapted to the needs of the moment; (3) he was not an eyewitness of Jesus, nor a disciple (but see note on Mark 14:52); and (4) it was his desire not to omit or misrepresent anything. Papias concluded that the Gospel of Mark gains its apostolic and reliable character from its Petrine origin (Eusebius, *Ecclesiastical History* 2.15.1–2; 3.39.14–16).

Internal evidence also supports the Patristic testimony that Peter stands behind Mark's Gospel. Mark's account is especially vivid when recounting incidents involving Peter. It presents the weaknesses of Peter, as well as the disciples as a whole, and omits praiseworthy or noticeable references to Peter reported in Matthew and Luke. It has also been observed that there exists a certain structural proximity between Peter's Caesarea speech (Acts 10:34–43) and the Gospel of Mark.

Date and Location

The external and internal data most convincingly point to Rome as the place of composition and a date for Mark in the mid- to late-50s A.D. (but some scholars date it in the mid- or late-60s; see below). The argument in favor of the mid- to late-50s is that the book of Acts ends with Paul in prison c. A.D. 62, leading many scholars to believe that Acts was written around that time. (Others suggest that Acts does not end at the point it was written because the key point of Acts is that the gospel had made it to Rome.) If Acts was written in the early 60s, then Luke's Gospel was written before Acts (cf. Luke 1:3 with Acts 1:1), sometime in the early 60s. And if Luke depends on Mark's Gospel for much of his material and overall structure (the clear majority view among scholars today), then Mark was written before Luke. This would place Mark in the mid- to late-50s. In fact, such a date fits with an early church tradition that Peter was in Rome in the early- to mid-50s. Eusebius (writing c. A.D. 325) says, "in the same reign of Claudius [who died in A.D. 54] the Providence of the universe . . . guided to Rome the great and mighty Peter . . . preaching the gospel. . . . But . . . the hearers of Peter . . . were not satisfied with a single hearing . . . but with every kind of exhortation besought Mark . . . seeing that he was Peter's follower, to leave them a written statement of the teaching given them verbally, nor did they cease until they had persuaded him, and so became the cause of the Scripture called the Gospel of Mark" (Eusebius, *Ecclesiastical History* 2.14.6–2.15.1; cf. a similar tradition in 6.14.6–7, quoting Clement of Alexandria, who lived c. 155–220). The *Anti-Marcionite Prologue* to Mark (late 2nd century A.D.) also places the writing during Peter's lifetime, for it says that Mark "wrote this gospel in parts of Italy. When Peter heard this, he approved and affirmed it by his own authority for the reading of the church."

However, if a somewhat later date for Luke–Acts is adopted, or if the similarities between Mark and Luke do not demonstrate that Luke used a completed written copy of Mark, then a date for Mark in the mid- to late-60s is possible. Some find support for this in a statement from Irenaeus (d. c. A.D. 195) that, "After their [Peter and Paul's] departure, Mark, the disciple and interpreter of Peter, did also hand down to us in writing what had been preached by Peter" (*Against Heresies* 3.1.2). If Peter's "departure" refers to his death, and Peter died in A.D. 64, then the Gospel of Mark would have been written after 64, the year Peter died. On the other hand, this may refer not to the writing but to the publication of Mark, or may speak of Peter and Paul's "departure" from Rome, not their death. So a date in the mid- to late-50s is most likely, but a date in the mid-60s is possible.

Theme

The ultimate purpose and theme of Mark is *to present and defend Jesus' universal call to discipleship*. Mark returns often to this theme, and as the narrative unfolds he categorizes his main audience as either followers or opponents of Jesus. The outline (pp. 1891–1892) demonstrates that Mark's central effort in presenting and supporting this call is *to narrate the identity and teaching of Jesus*. This fact implies that discipleship for Mark is essentially a relationship with Jesus, not merely following a certain code of conduct. Fellowship with Jesus marks the heart of the disciple's life, and this fellowship includes trusting him, confessing him, taking note of his conduct, following his teaching, and being shaped by a relationship to him. Discipleship also means being prepared to face the kind of rejection that Jesus faced.

Purpose, Occasion, and Background

Though Mark wrote from Rome, the Gospel of Mark was composed for the wider church as the record of the apostolic testimony of Peter. Even during the early Patristic period, Gentile Christians were frequently mentioned as the recipients of this Gospel. Mark addresses an audience that is largely unfamiliar with Jewish customs. He intends to familiarize them with those customs, because only then will they understand the coming of Jesus as the culmination of God's work with Israel and the entire world.

Key Themes

1. Jesus seeks to correct messianic expectations and misunderstandings.	1:25, 34, 44; 3:12; 4:10–12; 5:18–19, 43; 8:30; 9:9
2. Jesus is man.	3:5; 4:38; 6:6; 7:34; 8:12, 33; 10:14; 11:12; 14:33–42
3. Jesus is the Son of God.	1:11; 3:11; 5:7; 8:38; 9:7; 12:6–8; 13:32; 14:36, 61; 15:39
4. Jesus is the Son of Man with all power and authority.	1:16–34; 2:3–12, 23–28; 3:11; 4:35–41; 6:45–52; 7:1–23; 10:1–12
5. Jesus as the Son of Man must suffer.	8:31; 10:45; 14:21, 36
6. Jesus is Lord.	2:28; 12:35–37; 14:62
7. Jesus calls his followers to imitate him in humble service, self-denial, and suffering.	8:34–38; 9:35–37; 10:35–45
8. Jesus teaches on the kingdom of God, and implies that God continues to call a people to himself.	ch. 4; cf. 1:15; 9:1; 14:25; 15:43

History of Salvation Summary

Mark tells of Jesus' coming to bring everlasting salvation, as prophesied in the OT, and to triumph over sin and Satan. The ultimate fulfillment comes with his crucifixion and resurrection. (For an explanation of the "History of Salvation," see the Overview of the Bible, pp. 23–26.)

Literary Features

Of the four Gospels, Mark is most overtly a "docudrama," consisting of noteworthy "clips" as well as typical or representative events; snatches of speeches or dialogues; and commentary by the narrator. Mark's approach to the biographical data is that of a careful recorder. Mark's Gospel, however, is not a biography in the modern sense, as there is no attempt to describe Jesus physically, treat his family origins, or portray Jesus' inner life. Rather, like other ancient biographies (which were called a *bios* or "life"), Mark's purpose is to speak about the actions and teachings of Jesus that present his ministry and mission. Of course, the book is at the same time an implied proclamation and apologetic work that hints at the redemptive meaning of the events recorded. All of the Gospels are hero stories. Additionally, Mark's Gospel is made up of the usual array of subgenres found in the NT Gospels, including calling stories, recognition stories, witness/testimony stories, encounter stories, conflict or controversy stories, pronouncement stories, miracle stories, parables, discourses and sermons, proverbs or sayings, passion stories, and resurrection stories.

Even though the overall format of Mark's Gospel is narrative, it does not possess a continuous story line but is a collection of discrete units. There are crowd scenes, small-group scenes, public scenes, and private scenes. The resulting book is a collage or mosaic of the life of Jesus. The best way to negotiate this format is to regard oneself as Mark's traveling companion as he assembles his documentary on the life of Christ. The main unifying element in the mosaic is the protagonist, Christ himself.

Mark's Gospel (the shortest of the four) is a fast-paced narrative. Mark tends to include vivid descriptive details, and he prefers Greek verbs that portray an action in process. He often records people's responses to what Jesus did and said. Like all storytellers, Mark selected his material by two criteria: he chose events that were *typical* or representative in the life of Jesus (such as miracles of healing and the telling of parables), and *unique*, once-only events (esp. those connected with the crucifixion and resurrection of Jesus).

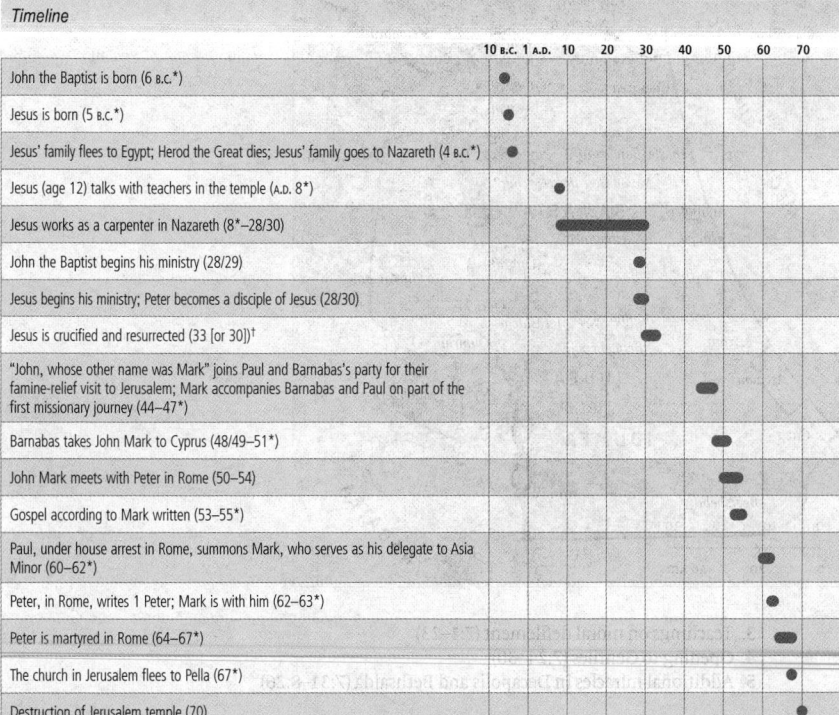

Timeline

Event	10 B.C. – 70 A.D.
John the Baptist is born (6 B.C.*)	●
Jesus is born (5 B.C.*)	●
Jesus' family flees to Egypt; Herod the Great dies; Jesus' family goes to Nazareth (4 B.C.*)	●
Jesus (age 12) talks with teachers in the temple (A.D. 8*)	●
Jesus works as a carpenter in Nazareth (8*–28/30)	▬
John the Baptist begins his ministry (28/29)	●
Jesus begins his ministry; Peter becomes a disciple of Jesus (28/30)	●
Jesus is crucified and resurrected (33 [or 30])†	●
"John, whose other name was Mark" joins Paul and Barnabas's party for their famine-relief visit to Jerusalem; Mark accompanies Barnabas and Paul on part of the first missionary journey (44–47*)	▬
Barnabas takes John Mark to Cyprus (48/49–51*)	▬
John Mark meets with Peter in Rome (50–54)	▬
Gospel according to Mark written (53–55*)	●
Paul, under house arrest in Rome, summons Mark, who serves as his delegate to Asia Minor (60–62*)	●
Peter, in Rome, writes 1 Peter; Mark is with him (62–63*)	●
Peter is martyred in Rome (64–67*)	▬
The church in Jerusalem flees to Pella (67*)	●
Destruction of Jerusalem temple (70)	●

** denotes approximate date; / signifies either/or; † see The Date of Jesus' Crucifixion, pp. 1809–1810*

Outline

I. Introduction (1:1–15)

II. Demonstration of Jesus' Authority (1:16–8:26)
   - A. Jesus' early Galilean ministry (1:16–3:12)
   - B. Jesus' later Galilean ministry (3:13–6:6)
     1. Calling of the Twelve (3:13–35)
     2. Parables (4:1–34)
     3. Nature miracle, exorcism, and healing (4:35–5:43)
     4. Rejection at Nazareth (6:1–6)
   - C. Work beyond Galilee (6:7–8:26)
     1. Sending of the Twelve (6:7–13)
     2. Death of John the Baptist (6:14–56)

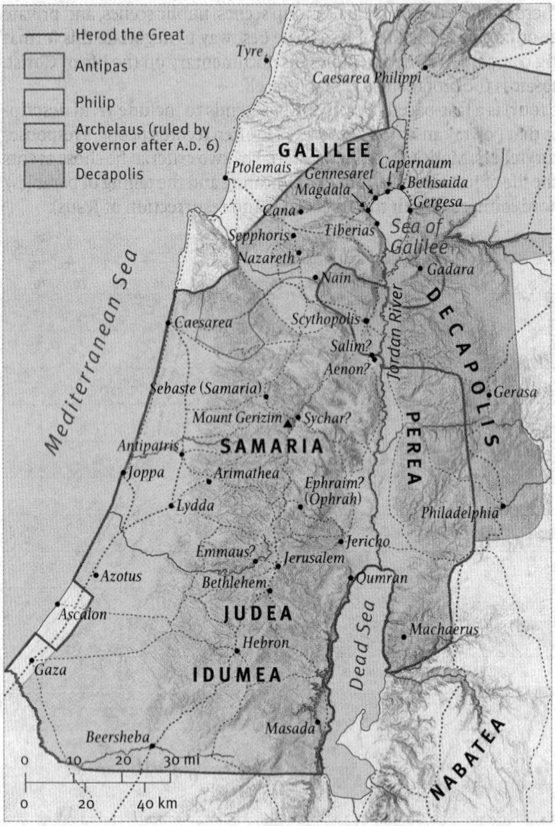

The Setting of Mark
The events in the book of Mark take place almost entirely within the vicinity of Palestine, an area extending roughly from Caesarea Philippi in the north to Beersheba in the south. During this time it was ruled by the Roman Empire. The book opens with Jesus' baptism by John during the rule of Pontius Pilate and the tetrarchs Antipas and Philip, and it closes with Jesus' death and resurrection about three years later.

3. Teachings on moral defilement (7:1–23)
4. Opening to Gentiles (7:24–30)
5. Additional miracles in Decapolis and Bethsaida (7:31–8:26)

III. Testing Jesus' Authority in Suffering (8:27–16:8)
- A. Journey to Jerusalem (8:27–10:52)
  1. Peter's confession (8:27–33)
  2. Call to discipleship (8:34–9:1)
  3. Transfiguration and healing (9:2–29)
  4. Instruction on discipleship: putting others first (9:30–50)
  5. Instruction on discipleship: divorce, wealth, humility (10:1–52)
- B. Entering and judging Jerusalem (11:1–13:37)
  1. Triumphal entry to Jerusalem (11:1–11)
  2. Jesus' judgment on religious leaders (11:12–12:44)
  3. Jesus and the coming judgment (13:1–37)
- C. Death and resurrection in Jerusalem (14:1–16:8)
  1. Betrayal (14:1–52)
  2. Trial (14:53–15:20)
  3. Crucifixion and resurrection (15:21–16:8)
  [4. "Longer ending of Mark" (16:9–20; see note)]

THE GOSPEL ACCORDING TO

MARK

Chapter 1

1 [a]See Matt. 14:33
2 [b]For ver. 2-8, see Matt. 3:1-11; Luke 3:2-16 [c]Matt. 11:10; Luke 1:17, 76; 7:27; Cited from Mal. 3:1
3 [d]John 1:23; Cited from Isa. 40:3 [e]Luke 1:76
4 [f]John 1:6, 7 [g]Josh. 15:61; [Judg. 1:16] [h]Acts 2:38 [i]ver. 15 [j]Matt. 26:28; [Luke 1:77]
5 [k]Acts 19:18
6 [l][2 Kgs. 1:8; Zech. 13:4; Heb. 11:37] [m]Lev. 11:22 [n]1 Sam. 14:26
7 [o]John 1:15, 27; 3:30, 31; Acts 13:25
8 [p]John 1:26; Acts 1:5; 11:16 [q]See John 1:33
9 [r]For ver. 9-11, see Matt. 3:13-17; Luke 3:21, 22; [John 1:32-34] [s]Matt. 2:23
10 [t]Acts 7:56 [u]Isa. 64:1

John the Baptist Prepares the Way

1 The beginning of the gospel of Jesus Christ, [a]the Son of God.[1]
2 [b]As it is written in Isaiah the prophet,[2]

> [c]"Behold, I send my messenger before your face,
> who will prepare your way,
> 3 [d]the voice of one crying in the wilderness:
> [e]'Prepare[3] the way of the Lord,
> make his paths straight,'"

4 [f]John appeared, baptizing in [g]the wilderness and proclaiming [h]a baptism of [i]repentance
[j]for the forgiveness of sins. 5 And all the country of Judea and all Jerusalem were going out to
him and were being baptized by him in the river Jordan, [k]confessing their sins. 6 Now John
was [l]clothed with camel's hair and [l]wore a leather belt around his waist and ate [m]locusts
and [n]wild honey. 7 And he preached, saying, [o]"After me comes he who is mightier than I,
the strap of whose sandals I am not worthy to stoop down and untie. 8 [p]I have baptized
you with water, but [q]he will baptize you with the Holy Spirit."

The Baptism of Jesus

9 [r]In those days Jesus [s]came from Nazareth of Galilee and was baptized by John in the
Jordan. 10 And when he came up out of the water, immediately he [t]saw [u]the heavens being

[1] Some manuscripts omit *the Son of God* [2] Some manuscripts *in the prophets* [3] Or *crying: Prepare in the wilderness*

1:1–15 *Introduction.* Mark begins his account with the public ministry of John the Baptist, the forerunner of Jesus (see note on Matt. 3:1). There is a contrasting parallelism between Mark's presentation of John and of Jesus: both are characterized by a word from the Lord (Mark 1:2–3 and v. 11); both are described in their person and function (vv. 4–6 and vv. 12–13); and both of their messages are summarized (vv. 7–8 and vv. 14–15).

1:1 Rather than emphasizing the events leading up to Jesus' public ministry in terms of his genealogy and family roots (as do Matthew and Luke) or in terms of its theological foundation (as does John), Mark focuses on its actual **beginning**. The **gospel** is the good news of the fulfillment of God's promises. In the OT (Isa. 40:9; 52:7; Nah. 1:15) "good news" is connected with the saving intervention of God to help his people. **of Jesus Christ**. The gospel is proclaimed *by* Jesus, the Messiah, but in a secondary sense the good news is the report *about* Jesus. Mark communicates both at the beginning and end of his Gospel (Mark 1:1; 15:39) that Jesus is **the Son of God**.

1:2–3 Mark identifies John the Baptist as the predicted one who prepares **the way of the Lord** (cf. Isa. 40:3; Mal. 3:1). **Isaiah the prophet** is named because he was more prominent and more of the quoted material comes from him. When the text is expounded in the following verses, Mark refers only to the Isaiah citation. John will be identified by Jesus as the one who comes in the spirit of Elijah (Mal. 4:5; Matt. 11:13–14; Mark 9:11–13; cf. also note on Luke 3:2). The path or "way" is to be readied for "the Lord," and surprisingly the one who comes after John is both the Lord and the Messiah (Mark 8:29). The following Gospel account demonstrates that Jesus, the Messiah, is also a member of the Godhead.

1:4 John prepares the way by calling people to **repentance** (see notes on Matt. 3:2; 3:5–6): turning away from sin and turning to God for **forgiveness of sins**. Repentance had to precede baptism, and thus baptism was not the means by which sins were forgiven but rather was a sign indicating that one had truly repented. John labors in the **wilderness** as a place of purification and fulfillment of prophecy (Isa. 40:3).

1:5 all the country of Judea and all Jerusalem. John's ministry represents a fulfillment of the promise of a new exodus (cf. Isa. 11:11–15; 40:3–11; 42:16; 43:2, 5–7, 16–19; 48:20–49:11; 51:10) in which Israel is delivered from the wilderness, and, so to speak, enters into **the river Jordan** again (as in Josh. 3:1–4:24) to receive God's promises of end-time salvation. **confessing their sins**. God was working in people's hearts, calling them to turn back to himself, in preparation for the coming Messiah.

1:6 John's clothing and food correspond to that of other preachers in the desert (cf. 1 Kings 17:4, 9; Mal. 3:1; 4:5–6). On **locusts**, see note on Matt. 3:4.

1:7–8 John's expectation of the **mightier** one is connected with Isa. 40:3. The coming one (Isa. 40:3; Mal. 3:1) is both human (**sandals**) and divine ("the LORD," Isa. 40:3) and **will baptize . . . with the Holy Spirit** (see note on Matt. 3:11). Untying the straps of sandals can be the responsibility of a low servant, but it was something that a Jewish person was not supposed to do. The baptism with the Spirit represents the fulfillment of God's promises in the OT (see Isa. 32:15; 44:3; Ezek. 11:18–19; Joel 2:28).

1:9 was baptized. Jesus identifies with the sins of his people, even though he himself is free from sin (10:45). On **Nazareth**, see Luke 1:26. **Galilee** is the region west of the Jordan and the Sea of Galilee and north of Samaria. In the NT era Galilee was successively ruled by Herod the Great (see note on Matt. 2:1), his son Herod Antipas (Matt. 14:1; Mark 6:14), and then by Herod Antipas's nephew Herod Agrippa I. **Jordan.** See note on Matt. 3:13.

1:10–11 Immediately is a favorite word of Mark's (he uses Gk. *euthys*, "immediately, at once," 41 times). It imparts a sense of speed and urgency and often introduces a new incident or a surprising turn of events within an

torn open [v]and the Spirit descending on him like a dove. 11 And [w]a voice came from heaven,
[x]"You are my beloved Son;[1] with you I am well pleased."

The Temptation of Jesus

12 [y]The Spirit immediately drove him out into the wilderness. 13 [y]And he was in the
wilderness forty days, being [z]tempted by [a]Satan. And he was with the wild animals, and
[b]the angels were ministering to him.

Jesus Begins His Ministry

14 [c]Now after John was arrested, Jesus [d]came into Galilee, proclaiming the gospel of
God, 15 and saying, [e]"The time is fulfilled, and [f]the kingdom of God is at hand; [g]repent
and believe in the gospel."

Jesus Calls the First Disciples

16 [h]Passing alongside the Sea of Galilee, he saw Simon and Andrew the brother of Simon
casting a net into the sea, for they were fishermen. 17 And Jesus said to them, "Follow
me, and I will make you become [i]fishers of men."[2] 18 And immediately they left their
nets and followed him. 19 And going on a little farther, he saw James the son of Zebedee
and John his brother, who were in their boat mending the nets. 20 And immediately he
called them, and they left their father Zebedee in the boat with the hired servants and
followed him.

[1] *Or my Son, my* (or *the*) *Beloved* [2] The Greek word *anthropoi* refers here to both men and women

10 [v]John 1:32, 33; [Luke 4:18, 21; Acts 10:38]
11 [w]John 12:28 [x][ch. 9:7; Ps. 2:7; Isa. 42:1; Eph. 1:6; Col. 1:13; 2 Pet. 1:17; 1 John 5:9]
12 [y]See Matt. 4:1-11; Luke 4:1-13
13 [y][See ver. 12 above] [z][Heb. 2:18; 4:15] [a]See 1 Chr. 21:1 [b]Matt. 26:53; Luke 22:43
14 [c]Matt. 4:12; 14:3; Luke 3:20; [John 3:24] [d]Matt. 4:17, 23
15 [e]Dan. 9:25; Gal. 4:4; Eph. 1:10; [Luke 21:8; John 7:8] [f]See Matt. 3:2 [g]Acts 19:4; 20:21; Heb. 6:1
16 [h]For ver. 16-20, see Matt. 4:18-22; [Luke 5:2-11; John 1:40-42]
17 [i]Matt. 13:47

incident. The **Spirit** of God descends upon Jesus in his baptism (see notes on Matt. 3:16; Luke 3:22). Jesus is thus commissioned for a unique service (cf. Isa. 11:2; 42:1; 61:1). Mark's allusions to the OT here involve Jesus' claim to be the Son of God (Ps. 2:7) and the servant of God (Isa. 42:1). The heavenly **voice** confirms the eternal, love-filled Sonship of Jesus (see note on Matt. 3:17). Note that all three persons of the Godhead—the Spirit, the Father, and the Son—are involved here.

1:12–13 At the commencement of Jesus' public ministry, God the **Spirit** paradoxically drives him **into the wilderness** to be **tempted by Satan** (see note on Matt. 4:1). Jesus' battle against the powers of darkness has begun. "Being tempted" indicates that the temptations happened over the 40-day period and were not confined to the three temptations mentioned by Matthew (Matt. 4:1–11) and Luke (Luke 4:1–13). Surrounded by evil and in danger from **wild animals**, Jesus is nevertheless not abandoned, for he has the presence of the Holy Spirit, and **the angels were ministering to him** (see note on Matt. 4:11).

Jesus' Ministry in Galilee

Jesus spent most of his life and ministry in the region of Galilee, a mountainous area in northern Palestine. Jesus grew up in the hill town of Nazareth, about 3.5 miles (5.6 km) south of the Gentile administrative center of Sepphoris. Soon after he began his public ministry, Jesus relocated to Capernaum on the Sea of Galilee. By Jesus' time, a thriving fishing industry had developed around the Sea of Galilee, and several of Jesus' disciples were fishermen.

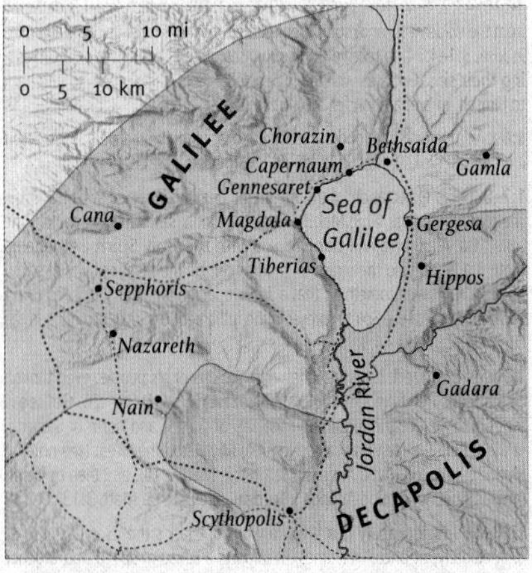

1:14–15 These verses summarize Jesus' preaching ministry. The **gospel** (see note on v. 1) is the "good news" that **the kingdom of God is at hand**, meaning that God's rule over people's hearts and lives is now being established, and people should **repent and believe in the gospel** (on repentance and faith, see notes on Matt. 3:2; Acts 2:38). The kingdom is more than simply the rule of the Spirit within people, since the kingdom will ultimately include the restoration of all creation (see Rev. 21:1). However, Jesus has not yet revealed the fact that the kingdom will come in stages. How Jesus relates to this kingdom will be seen in the following chapters. Initially, he is the one who proclaims the coming saving rule of God.

1:16–8:26 *Demonstration of Jesus' Authority.* The first half of Mark's Gospel is dedicated to the demonstration of Jesus' authority over sickness, laws of nature, and the demonic world. He also calls, appoints, and sends out his disciples while regularly teaching in a unique and authoritative way.

1:16–3:12 *Jesus' Early Galilean Ministry.* The call of the disciples is intertwined with narrative descriptions of Jesus' authority over demons and sickness, as well as with authoritative teaching (see note on Matt. 4:12–25).

1:17 Jesus calls his disciples to be **fishers of men**, an assignment they will fulfill as they have continual fellowship with him and carry out the mission that Jesus gives them (3:14). Jesus' words recall Jer. 16:15–17, where "fishers" and "hunters" of men will call people back from idols to God after judgment has occurred. This call happens in a context of purification (Jer. 16:17) and will include Gentiles (Jer. 16:19).

1:20 they left their father . . . with the hired servants. Several of Jesus' first disciples were not poor but were self-employed fishermen or, as in this case (James and John), were part of a family business. Levi (2:14) was a fairly well-to-do tax collector.

1:21 Excavations at **Capernaum** (Talhum) have revealed residential structures, a **synagogue**, and an octagonal Christian site. Capernaum's prominent, well-preserved synagogue has been dated (based on thousands of coins found below its pavement) to the fourth or fifth century A.D.

Jesus Heals a Man with an Unclean Spirit

21 [j]And they went into Capernaum, and immediately [k]on the Sabbath [l]he entered the
synagogue and was teaching. 22 And [m]they were astonished at his teaching, [m]for he taught
them as one who had authority, and not as the scribes. 23 And immediately there was in
their synagogue a man with an unclean spirit. And he cried out, 24 [n]"What have you to do
with us, Jesus of Nazareth? Have you come to destroy us? [o]I know who you are—[p]the Holy
One of God." 25 But Jesus [q]rebuked him, saying, "Be silent, and come out of him!" 26 And
the unclean spirit, [r]convulsing him and [s]crying out with a loud voice, came out of him.
27 And they were all [t]amazed, so that they questioned among themselves, saying, "What
is this? [u]A new teaching with authority! He commands even the unclean spirits, and they
obey him." 28 And at once his fame spread everywhere throughout all the surrounding
region of Galilee.

Jesus Heals Many

29 [v]And immediately he[1] [w]left the synagogue and entered the house of Simon and Andrew,
with James and John. 30 Now [x]Simon's mother-in-law lay ill with a fever, and immediately
they told him about her. 31 And he came and [y]took her by the hand and lifted her up, and
the fever left her, and she began to serve them.
32 That evening at sundown they brought to him all who were sick or [z]oppressed by
demons. 33 And the whole city was gathered together at the door. 34 [a]And he healed many
who were sick with various diseases, and cast out many demons. And [b]he would not permit
the demons to speak, because they knew him.

Jesus Preaches in Galilee

35 [c]And rising very early in the morning, while it was still dark, he departed and went
out to a desolate place, and [d]there he prayed. 36 And Simon and those who were with him
searched for him, 37 and they found him and said to him, [e]"Everyone is looking for you."
38 And he said to them, "Let us go on to the next towns, that I may preach there also, for
[f]that is why I came out." 39 [g]And [h]he went throughout all Galilee, preaching in their synagogues and casting out demons.

Jesus Cleanses a Leper

40 [i]And a leper[2] came to him, imploring him, and [j]kneeling said to him, [k]"If you will,
you can make me clean." 41 Moved with pity, he stretched out his hand and touched him
and said to him, "I will; be clean." 42 And immediately the leprosy left him, and he was
made clean. 43 And [l]Jesus[3] sternly charged him and sent him away at once, 44 and said to
him, [m]"See that you say nothing to anyone, but go, [n]show yourself to the priest and [o]offer

[1] Some manuscripts *they* [2] *Leprosy* was a term for several skin diseases; see Leviticus 13 [3] Greek *he*; also verse 45

21 [j]Matt. 4:13; For ver. 21-28, see Luke 4:31-37 [k]See ch. 6:2 [l]ver. 39; See Matt. 4:23
22 [m]See Matt. 7:28, 29
24 [n]See Matt. 8:29 [o][ver. 34; Acts 19:15; James 2:19] [p]John 6:69; Acts 3:14; Rev. 3:7; [Luke 1:35; Heb. 7:26; 1 John 2:20]
25 [q]See Matt. 12:16
26 [r]ch. 9:26 [s]ch. 5:7; Acts 8:7
27 [t][Matt. 8:27] [u]Acts 17:19
29 [v]For ver. 29-34, see Matt. 8:14-16; Luke 4:38-41 [w]ver. 21, 23
30 [x]1 Cor. 9:5
31 [y]ch. 9:27; Acts 3:7; 9:41
32 [z]See Matt. 4:24
34 [a]See Matt. 4:23 [b]ch. 3:11, 12; [Acts 16:17, 18]
35 [c]For ver. 35-38, see Luke 4:42, 43 [d]Luke 5:16; See Matt. 14:23
37 [e][John 12:19]
38 [f]Isa. 61:1
39 [g][Luke 4:44] [h]ver. 21
40 [i]For ver. 40-44, see Matt. 8:2-4; Luke 5:12-14 [j]ch. 10:17; Matt. 17:14; 27:29 [k][ch. 9:22, 23; Matt. 9:28]
43 [l]Matt. 9:30
44 [m]ver. 34; ch. 5:43; 7:36; 8:26; Matt. 9:30; 17:9; See Matt. 12:16 [n]Luke 17:14 [o]Lev. 14:2-32

(though some argue it is earlier); however, beneath this were found walls of a previous structure, which is very likely the synagogue of Jesus' day. The fifth-century octagonal building, designed like many Byzantine commemorative Christian holy places, stands over a fourth-century church built by modifying a first-century house. This marks the traditional site of Peter's home.

1:22 The core purpose of Jesus' earthly ministry was **teaching**, rather than performing miracles or casting out demons—actions which accompanied his teaching and attested to God's presence with him (see v. 15; 2:1–12; 3:1–6; 7:1–13). The **scribes** mentioned here may have been a local group of pious, literate men who taught in the synagogues, in distinction from the higher-ranking scribes who "came down from Jerusalem" and were bold enough to challenge Jesus directly (3:22). Jesus taught with his own divine **authority**, not simply repeating the traditions of others.

1:23–25 An unclean spirit tries to resist Jesus' power and his teaching on the kingdom of God, but he correctly fears that Jesus has come to **destroy** him. The act of naming Jesus as **the Holy One of God** may display the demon's attempt at exercising power over Jesus. But Jesus resists and tells the unclean spirit, **"Be silent."**

1:26–28 they were all amazed. Casting out this demon reinforces Jesus' authority to teach. See notes on Matt. 12:27; 12:28; 12:29.

1:32–34 Sundown marks the end of the Sabbath (roughly 6:00 P.M. Saturday); people are now permitted to move about and to come to Jesus with their needs. Jesus heals mercifully and casts out **demons**, thereby substantiating the authority given him by his heavenly **Father**. (On the difference between demonic oppression and illness, see note on Matt. 8:16–17.) When Jesus casts out demons, it shows that the kingdom of God is advancing, driving back the power of the enemy over people's lives.

1:35 Four verbs (**rising/departed/went/prayed**) emphasize Jesus' resolve to have fellowship with his Father. Jesus prayed at a very early hour: **while it was still dark**.

1:37–38 Everyone is looking for you. Peter and the others only see the needs and therefore do not understand why Jesus went away to pray (v. 35). Jesus intentionally removes himself from the crowds and then goes on **to the next towns**, obeying the Father's call to **preach** the gospel.

1:40 A **leper** is ceremonially unclean (Lev. 13:45–46; see also note on Matt. 8:2–3). As an outcast, he is financially and socially isolated, dependent on charity.

1:41–42 touched him. Jesus' love, mercy, and power are such that his touch, instead of making Jesus unclean, actually makes the leper **clean**.

1:44 say nothing. This is Mark's first report of Jesus telling a healed person not to tell anyone of his being healed (see note on Matt. 8:4). **Show yourself**

for your cleansing what Moses commanded, [p]for a proof to them." **45** [q]But he went out
and began to talk freely about it, and to spread the news, so that Jesus could no longer
openly enter [ʹ]a town, but was out in [ʹ]desolate places, and [s]people were coming to him
from every quarter.

Jesus Heals a Paralytic

2 And when he returned to [t]Capernaum after some days, it was reported that he was
at home. **2** And many were gathered together, so that there was no more room, not
even at the door. And he was preaching the word to them. **3** [u]And they came, bringing to
him a paralytic carried by four men. **4** And when they could not get near him because of
the crowd, [v]they removed the roof above him, and when they had made an opening, they
let down the bed on which the paralytic lay. **5** And when Jesus [w]saw their faith, he said to
the paralytic, "Son, [x]your sins are forgiven." **6** Now some of the scribes were sitting there,
questioning in their hearts, **7** "Why does this man speak like that? [y]He is blaspheming!
[z]Who can forgive sins but God alone?" **8** And immediately Jesus, [a]perceiving in his spirit
that they thus questioned within themselves, said to them, "Why do you question these
things in your hearts? **9** Which is easier, to say to the paralytic, 'Your sins are forgiven,' or
to say, 'Rise, take up your bed and walk'? **10** But that you may know that [b]the Son of Man
has authority on earth to forgive sins"—he said to the paralytic— **11** "I say to you, rise,
pick up your bed, and go home." **12** And he rose and immediately picked up his bed and
went out before them all, so that they were all amazed and [c]glorified God, saying, "We
never saw anything like this!"

Jesus Calls Levi

13 He went out again beside the sea, and [d]all the crowd was coming to him, and he was
teaching them. **14** [e]And as he passed by, he saw [f]Levi the son of Alphaeus sitting at the tax
booth, and he said to him, "Follow me." And he rose and followed him.
15 And as he reclined at table in his house, many [g]tax collectors and sinners were reclining
with Jesus and his disciples, for there were many who followed him. **16** And [h]the scribes

44 [p]ch. 6:11; Luke 9:5; James 5:3
45 [q]ch. 7:36; Matt. 9:31; [Luke 5:15, 16] [r]2 Cor. 11:26 [s]ch. 2:2, 13; 3:7; [John 6:2]

Chapter 2

1 [t][Matt. 9:1]
3 [u]For ver. 3-12, see Matt. 9:2-8; Luke 5:18-26
4 [v][Luke 5:19]
5 [w]ch. 10:52; Matt. 8:10, 13; 9:22, 29; 15:28; Luke 7:9, 50; 17:19; 18:42; Acts 3:16; 14:9; James 5:15 [x]Luke 7:48; [John 5:14]
7 [y]ch. 14:64; John 10:36 [z]Ps. 32:5; Isa. 43:25
8 [a]See John 2:25
10 [b][ver. 28]
12 [c]See Luke 7:16
13 [d]See ch. 1:45
14 [e]For ver. 14-22, see Matt. 9:9-17; Luke 5:27-38 [f][Matt. 9:9]
15 [g]Matt. 11:19; Luke 15:2
16 [h]Acts 4:5; 23:9

to the priest is commanded so that the healed person will be declared ceremonially clean and will be socially rehabilitated (Lev. 14:2–31). It may be commanded in a secondary sense to bear witness to the priest (**for a proof to them**) of his having been healed by Jesus.

1:45 The joy of the healed man overrides Jesus' injunction to silence and therefore **Jesus could no longer openly enter a town**, lest he be mobbed. So Jesus cannot stay hidden (e.g., v. 45; 3:7–12, 20; 6:31–33). Mark often emphasizes how the crowds' excessive attention to Jesus' miracles is a frequent problem, causing the crowds to miss the true purpose of his ministry (i.e., to proclaim the good news of the kingdom).

2:1 Jesus returns from his time of preaching and ministry throughout Galilee (see 1:38–45) to **Capernaum** (c. 20 miles [32 km] northeast of Nazareth; see map, p. 1894), which serves as the base for his Galilean ministry. **at home**. Jesus seems to be living now in Capernaum.

2:2 no more room. At the most, perhaps 50 people could come into the house; the rest must listen from outside. Jesus' core concern is to proclaim the **word** (e.g., 1:38–39; 3:14; 6:12; 13:10; 14:9), including his teaching about the imminent rule of God and the need for repentance and trust in him (see note on 1:14–15; also 4:14–20, 33; 7:13; 8:38; 10:24; 13:31).

2:3 paralytic. See note on Matt. 9:2.

2:4 A flat **roof** could be accessed from the outside. It consisted of branches or sticks, combined with clay, and Luke adds the detail that this roof also had clay "tiles" (see note on Luke 5:19), which were used on some houses at that time.

2:5–7 their faith. "Their" is plural and most naturally refers to the faith of the friends who brought the paralytic to Jesus but may include the faith of the paralytic as well (see note on James 5:15). **your sins are forgiven**. An OT prophet might declare, "The LORD also has put away your sin" (2 Sam. 12:13). Jesus, however, claims to be able to forgive sins directly, as **God alone** can. The opponents reason therefore that Jesus is guilty of blasphemy, which is punishable by death (Lev. 24:10–23; Num. 15:30–31; see Mark 14:62–64).

2:8 perceiving . . . that they thus questioned within themselves. Jesus' divine nature is revealed in his ability to read their thoughts. (Cf. note on Matt. 24:36 concerning the limits and extent of Jesus' knowledge in his human and divine nature as the incarnate Son of God.)

2:9–11 Which is easier . . . ? On the surface, of course, it is easier to say the words, "**Your sins are forgiven**," because that is something invisible and impossible to disprove. But it is harder to say, "**take up your bed and walk**" because, if the man does not get up, the one who said the words will be shown to have no authority to heal. On a deeper level, however, it is harder to forgive sins, because only God can forgive sins—at the cost of Christ's death on the cross. The logic here is that, since Jesus can do the visible miracle (heal the paralytic), this is evidence that he also has the power to do the invisible miracle (forgive sins).

2:10 Jesus' healing of the **paralytic** verifies that he also has divine **authority . . . to forgive sins**. That Jesus is the **Son of Man**, when fully understood, will communicate his exalted authority (see note on Matt. 8:20; also Dan. 7:13–14; Mark 2:28; 8:38; 14:62), but in Mark's Gospel, Jesus only gradually reveals the full meaning of this term. Drawing specifically on the imagery in Daniel, the title "Son of Man" is Jesus' favorite way of referring to himself in Mark's Gospel, bearing witness to both his human and his divine nature (see esp. 8:38; 13:26; and 14:62, in comparison with Dan. 7:13–14).

2:14 Jesus continues to focus on "teaching" (v. 13; see note on 1:14–15). **Levi** (called "Matthew" in 3:18; see Matt. 9:9) collected taxes and thus collaborated with Herod Antipas who, in turn, collaborated with the Roman Empire. As the occupying political force in the Jewish land of Palestine, Rome and all who collaborated with Rome were despised by pious Jews. The taxation system was corrupt, and most tax collectors skimmed money from the taxes for themselves. "Beside the sea" (Mark 2:13) and "in his house" (v. 15) suggest that the **tax booth** used by Levi was by the Sea of Galilee and was used for taxing fishermen (see Introduction to Matthew: Author and Title).

2:15–16 To recline **at table** indicates personal acceptance and cordiality. When dining formally in a home, guests reclined on a couch that stretched

16[g][See ver. 15 above]
17[i][Luke 15:7; John 9:39] [j]1 Tim. 1:15
18[k]Matt. 11:2; 14:12; Luke 11:1; John 1:35; 3:25; 4:1; [Acts 18:25; 19:3] [l][ch. 7:5] [m]Luke 18:12
19[n]John 3:29
20[o]See Luke 17:22 [p][John 16:20]
22[q]Josh. 9:4
23[r]For ver. 23-28, see Matt. 12:1-8; Luke 6:1-5 [s]Deut. 23:25
24[t][Matt. 9:11] [u][Ex. 20:9-11]
25[v]See Matt. 21:16 [w]1 Sam. 21:1-6
26[x]1 Chr. 24:6; [1 Sam. 21:1; 2 Sam. 8:17] [y]Ex. 25:30; Lev. 24:5-9
27[z]Ex. 23:12; Deut. 5:14 [a]Col. 2:16
28[b][ver. 10]

of[1] the Pharisees, when they saw that he was eating with sinners and tax collectors, said
to his disciples, [g]"Why does he eat[2] with tax collectors and sinners?" **17** And when Jesus
heard it, he said to them, "Those who are well have no need of a physician, but those who
are sick. [i]I came not to call the righteous, [j]but sinners."

A Question About Fasting

18 Now [k]John's disciples and the Pharisees were fasting. And people came and said to him,
[l]"Why do John's disciples and [m]the disciples of the Pharisees fast, but your disciples do not
fast?" **19** And Jesus said to them, [n]"Can the wedding guests fast while the bridegroom is
with them? As long as they have the bridegroom with them, they cannot fast. **20** [o]The days
will come when the bridegroom is taken away from them, and [p]then they will fast in that
day. **21** No one sews a piece of unshrunk cloth on an old garment. If he does, the patch tears
away from it, the new from the old, and a worse tear is made. **22** And no one puts new wine
into old [q]wineskins. If he does, the wine will burst the skins—and the wine is destroyed,
and so are the skins. But new wine is for fresh wineskins."[3]

Jesus Is Lord of the Sabbath

23 [r]One Sabbath he was going through the grainfields, and as they made their way, his
disciples [s]began to pluck heads of grain. **24** And the Pharisees were saying to him, "Look,
[t]why are they doing [u]what is not lawful on the Sabbath?" **25** And he said to them, [v]"Have
you never read [w]what David did, when he was in need and was hungry, he and those who
were with him: **26** how he entered the house of God, in the time of[4] [x]Abiathar the high
priest, and ate [y]the bread of the Presence, which it is not lawful for any but the priests to
eat, and also gave it to those who were with him?" **27** And he said to them, [z]"The Sabbath
was made for man, [a]not man for the Sabbath. **28** So [b]the Son of Man is lord even of the
Sabbath."

[1] Some manuscripts *and* [2] Some manuscripts add *and drink* [3] Some manuscripts omit *But new wine is for fresh wineskins* [4] Or *in the passage about*

around three sides of a room. The host took the central place surrounded by a U-shaped series of tables. The most honored guests reclined on either side of the host, with the guests' heads toward the tables and their feet toward the wall. **Tax collectors and sinners** conveys the Pharisaic perspective that both groups disregard the Law of Moses (on the **Pharisees**, see note on John 1:24). According to Pharisaic interpretation, Jesus is to keep himself "clean" from such people (see Lev. 10:10; 12:1–15:33). Jesus pursues a third path: personal purity *and* the fellowship of mercy (see also note on Luke 5:30).

2:17 Jesus likens those who are **well** to those who are **righteous**, and those who are **sick** to **sinners**; Jesus' opponents must judge for themselves which ones they are. On account of their lack of mercy, they are in fact "sick" and sinners (see vv. 23–27; 3:1–5; 7:1–15; note on Matt. 9:13).

2:18 fasting. See note on Matt. 6:16–18.

2:19–20 Jesus refers to himself as **the bridegroom**, who in the OT was the Lord (cf. Isa. 62:5; Hos. 2:19–20). While Jesus is present with his disciples, they are to rejoice; when he is **taken away from them . . . then they will fast**. They will then return to the practice of fasting to seek the presence of God, but they need not do that when Jesus, the Son of God (see Mark 1:1; 15:39), is with them. "Taken away" is an indirect prediction of Jesus' death (see Isa. 53:8).

2:21–22 Just as new, **unshrunk cloth** cannot coexist with an **old garment**, the kingdom of God cannot be regarded merely as a patch over the regulations of the Mosaic law and extrabiblical traditions. **New wine** vs. **old wineskins** illustrates the same truth—that Jesus brings a new era with new ways.

2:23–24 Deuteronomy 23:25 implies that, in the case of hunger, it was permissible to eat **heads of grain** from any field one might pass by. Work, however, was not permitted on the **Sabbath** (Ex. 34:21). Pharisaic interpretation sought to guard against work on the Sabbath by prohibiting even the minimal "work" involved in thus satisfying one's hunger.

2:25–26 Jesus initially emphasizes that the restrictive Pharisaic interpretation of the law does not take into account the situation of need in which David and his men found themselves (1 Sam. 21:1–6). David ate the **bread of the Presence**, so it follows that, at least in the case of need, actions are allowed on a Sabbath that otherwise might not be permitted. **in the time of Abiathar the high priest**. The incident with David actually occurred when Ahimelech, not his son Abiathar, was high priest (1 Sam. 21:1). "In the time of Abiathar" could mean: (1) "In the time of Abiathar, who later became high priest" (naming Abiathar because he was a more prominent person in the OT narrative, remaining high priest for many years of David's reign); (2) "In [the Scripture section of] Abiathar, the high priest" (taking Gk. *epi* plus the genitive to indicate a location in Scripture, as in Mark 12:26). Abiathar, the only son of Ahimelech to survive the slaughter by Doeg (1 Samuel 22), is the best-known high priest in this larger section of 1 Samuel.

2:27–28 The Sabbath was made for man. Jesus next (see note on vv. 25–26) emphasizes that man is not to be confined by the Sabbath but rather that the Sabbath is given as a gift to man (for spiritual and physical refreshment). Again Jesus emphasizes his authority as **Son of Man** (see Introduction: Key Themes; and note on Matt. 8:20). If the Sabbath is for the benefit of mankind, and if the Son of Man is Lord over all mankind, then the Son of Man is surely **lord even of the Sabbath**.

Five Controversies from Mark 2:1–3:6

Reference	Point of Conflict
2:1–12	forgiveness
2:15–17	eating with sinners
2:18–22	fasting
2:23–28	Sabbath
3:1–6	Sabbath, and the decision to kill Jesus

A Man with a Withered Hand

3 [c]Again [d]he entered the synagogue, and a man was there with a withered hand. 2 And
[e]they watched Jesus,[1] to see whether he would heal him on the Sabbath, so that they
might accuse him. 3 And he said to the man with the withered hand, "Come here." 4 And
he said to them, [f]"Is it lawful on the Sabbath to do good or to do harm, to save life or to
kill?" But they were silent. 5 And he [g]looked around at them with anger, grieved at [h]their
hardness of heart, and said to the man, "Stretch out your hand." [i]He stretched it out, and
his hand was restored. 6 [j]The Pharisees went out and immediately [j]held counsel with [k]the
Herodians against him, how to destroy him.

A Great Crowd Follows Jesus

7 [l]Jesus withdrew with his disciples to the sea, and [m]a great crowd followed, from Galilee
and Judea 8 and Jerusalem and [n]Idumea and from beyond the Jordan and from around
[o]Tyre and Sidon. When the great crowd heard all that he was doing, they came to him.
9 And he told his disciples to [p]have a boat ready for him because of the crowd, lest they
[q]crush him, 10 for [r]he had healed many, so that all who had [s]diseases pressed around him
[t]to touch him. 11 [u]And whenever the unclean spirits saw him, they [v]fell down before him
and cried out, "You are [w]the Son of God." 12 And [x]he strictly ordered them not to make
him known.

The Twelve Apostles

13 [y]And he went up on the mountain and called to him those [z]whom he desired, and
they came to him. 14 [y]And he appointed twelve (whom he also named apostles) so that they
might be with him and he might send them out to preach 15 [y]and have authority to cast out
demons. 16 He appointed the twelve: [a]Simon (to whom [b]he gave the name Peter); 17 [c]James
the son of Zebedee and John the brother of James (to whom he gave the name Boanerges,
that is, Sons of Thunder); 18 Andrew, and Philip, and Bartholomew, and [d]Matthew, and
Thomas, and James the son of Alphaeus, and Thaddaeus, and Simon the Zealot,[2] 19 and
Judas Iscariot, who betrayed him.

Chapter 3
1 [c]For ver. 1-6, see Matt. 12:9-14; Luke 6:6-11 [d]ch. 1:29
2 [e]Luke 14:1; 20:20; [Luke 11:54; John 8:6]
4 [f][Luke 14:3]
5 [g]ver. 34; ch. 5:32; 10:23; [ch. 10:21] [h]ch. 6:52; Rom. 11:25; Eph. 4:18 [i][1 Kgs. 13:4]
6 [j]See Matt. 12:14 [k]ch. 12:13; Matt. 22:16; [ch. 8:15]
7 [l]Matt. 12:15 [m]Matt. 4:25; Luke 6:17
8 [n]Isa. 34:5; Ezek. 35:15 [o]See Matt. 11:21
9 [p]ch. 6:32, 45 (Gk.); 8:10 (Gk.) [q]ch. 5:24, 31
10 [r]See Matt. 4:23 [s]ch. 5:29, 34 [t]ch. 6:56; Matt. 9:20, 21; 14:36; Luke 6:19
11 [u]ch. 1:26, 34; Luke 4:41 [v]Luke 8:28 [w]See Matt. 14:33
12 [x]See Matt. 12:16
13 [y]Matt. 10:1; Luke 6:12, 13; [ch. 6:7-13; Luke 9:1, 2] [z]John 13:18; 15:16, 19
14 [y][See ver. 13 above]
15 [y][See ver. 13 above]
16 [a]For ver. 16-19, see Matt. 10:2-4; Luke 6:14-16; Acts 1:13 [b]Matt. 16:18; John 1:42
17 [c]Matt. 4:21
18 [d]Matt. 9:9

[1] Greek *him* [2] Greek *kananaios,* meaning *zealot*

3:2 The scribes believe that healing is a form of work and is thus not permitted on a **Sabbath**. **Accuse** (Gk. *katēgoreō*, "accuse, bring charges") is a technical term: they seek to mount a legal case against Jesus by collecting evidence against him.

3:3–5 Jesus is not intimidated by his opponents; he makes the Sabbath healing (cf. v. 2) an intentionally public incident. **they were silent**. The silence of the opponents displays **their hardness of heart**, and Jesus' **anger** shows that his question, **"Is it lawful on the Sabbath to do good or to do harm . . . ?"** should have been answered: "to do good." This would not violate the OT law, but it *would* violate the opponents' extrabiblical, mostly Pharisaic tradition. Their tradition misses the point of the Mosaic law: to love God and one's neighbor (cf. 12:29–31). **Stretch out your hand**. See note on Luke 6:10.

3:6 The **Pharisees** were quite different from the **Herodians** (supporters and associates of Herod Antipas of Galilee and the Herodian family dynasty; see note on Matt. 22:16). However, these two groups **held counsel** together (cf. Ps. 2:2) in order to **destroy** their common enemy, Jesus (Mark 14:1–2).

3:7–8 Despite serious opposition, **Jesus** is now known in **Galilee**, in **Judea** (including **Jerusalem**) and **Idumea** (to the south), in the area **beyond the Jordan** (to the east; see note on Matt. 4:25), and in **Tyre and Sidon** (to the north). All of these regions had belonged to Israel during the time of the judges, and descendants of the 12 tribes have now resettled in these regions following the Babylonian exile.

3:9–10 have a boat ready . . . because of the crowd. The popularity of Jesus grows especially on account of his healings and casting out demons. His chief goal, however, is to teach about, and to call people to, the kingdom of God (1:14–15).

3:11–12 Jesus does not permit **unclean spirits** to speak about him, for even when they make true statements, unwillingly acknowledging his greater authority, their intent is still evil, and they would divulge Jesus' true identity, which would lead to much misunderstanding, before he wants to **make** himself **known**.

3:13–6:6 *Jesus' Later Galilean Ministry.* Jesus appoints his disciples to teach what he teaches and to do what he does. Parables, nature miracles, and healings expand the range of his authority, which is met with rejection in Nazareth.

3:13–35 *Calling of the Twelve.* The appointment of his disciples to do the will of God constitutes a further movement toward the formation of the messianic people of God.

3:14–15 As is often the case, Mark presupposes further actions of Jesus without narrating them. Here it becomes evident that Jesus had, in the meantime, selected and appointed the **twelve**, whom he called out of the larger crowd that had been following him (vv. 7–9; cf. v. 16; 4:10; 14:10, 17, 20, 43). The Twelve have a specific, twofold task: (1) that **they might be with him** (reinforcing the call to discipleship [see 1:17, 20; 2:14; 3:13] and to being shaped by Jesus [4:33]), and (2) that **he might send them out** (1:17; 9:37; thus suggesting the sense of the term **apostles** as those who are "sent out"; see note on Rom. 1:1). In their function of serving as Jesus-dependent emissaries, they are to do what Jesus did and taught them: (1) **preach** (Mark 1:14, 39; 6:12) the word of the kingdom of God, and (2) **cast out demons** (1:34, 39). Mark 6:13 will clarify that (3) healing is also part of their commission. This commission is put into action in 6:7–12. Initially, Jesus proclaims the kingdom of God to descendants of the 12 tribes of Israel, and the selection of the 12 apostles probably represents these tribes (Rev. 21:14). The disciples' experience of being under the immediate oversight of Jesus will be important for them, as they themselves will soon oversee the ministry of others after Jesus' death, resurrection, and ascension.

3:16–17 The core group of three disciples (cf. 5:37; 9:2; 14:33) is mentioned first: (**Simon**) **Peter**, **James**, and **John**. Then the others are named (3:18–19). See also note on Matt. 10:2.

3:19 Judas Iscariot, who betrayed him (14:10, 18, 20–21, 41–44), is mentioned last. Judas was called to be with Jesus, to be one of the Twelve,

20 Then he went [e]home, and the crowd gathered again, [f]so that they could not even eat.
21 [g]And when [h]his family heard it, they went out to seize him, for they were saying, "He
[i]is out of his mind."

Blasphemy Against the Holy Spirit

22 And [j]the scribes who came down from Jerusalem were saying, [k]"He is possessed by
Beelzebul," and "by the prince of demons he casts out the demons." **23** [l]And he called them
to him and said to them in parables, "How can Satan cast out Satan? **24** If a kingdom is
divided against itself, that kingdom cannot stand. **25** And if a house is divided against
itself, that house will not be able to stand. **26** And if Satan has risen up against himself
and is divided, he cannot stand, but is coming to an end. **27** But [m]no one can enter a strong
man's house and plunder his goods, unless he first binds the strong man. [n]Then indeed
he may plunder his house.

28 [o]"Truly, I say to you, all sins will be forgiven the children of man, and whatever blasphemies they utter, **29** but whoever [p]blasphemes against the Holy Spirit never has forgiveness,
but is guilty of an eternal sin"— **30** for they were saying, "He has an unclean spirit."

Jesus' Mother and Brothers

31 [q]And his mother and his [r]brothers came, and standing outside they sent to him and
called him. **32** And a crowd was sitting around him, and they said to him, "Your mother and
your brothers[1] are outside, seeking you." **33** And he answered them, "Who are my mother
and my brothers?" **34** And [s]looking about at those who sat around him, he said, "Here are
my mother and my brothers! **35** [t]For whoever [u]does the will of God, he is my brother and
sister and mother."

The Parable of the Sower

4 Again [v]he began to teach beside the sea. And a very large crowd gathered about him,
[w]so that he got into a boat and sat in it on the sea, and the whole crowd was beside the
sea on the land. **2** And [x]he was teaching them many things in parables, and in his teaching
he said to them: **3** "Listen! Behold, [y]a sower went out to sow. **4** And as he sowed, some seed
fell along the path, and the birds came and devoured it. **5** Other seed fell on rocky ground,
where it did not have much soil, and immediately it sprang up, since it had no depth of
soil. **6** And [z]when the sun rose, it was scorched, and since it had no root, [a]it withered away.
7 Other seed fell among [b]thorns, and the thorns grew up and choked it, and it yielded no
grain. **8** And other seeds fell into good soil and produced grain, growing up and increasing

[1] Other early manuscripts add *and your sisters*

20 [e]ch. 7:17; 9:28 [f]ch. 6:31
21 [g][John 7:5] [h][ver. 31] [i]2 Cor. 5:13; [John 10:20; Acts 26:24]
22 [j]ch. 7:1; Matt. 15:1 [k]Matt. 9:34; 12:24; Luke 11:15; [Matt. 10:25]; See John 7:20
23 [l]For ver. 23-27, see Matt. 12:25-29; Luke 11:17-22
27 [m]Isa. 49:24 [n][Isa. 53:12]
28 [o]For ver. 28-30, see Matt. 12:31, 32; [Luke 12:10; Heb. 6:4-6; 10:26; 1 John 5:16]
29 [p][Acts 7:51; Heb. 10:29]
31 [q]For ver. 31-35, see Matt. 12:46-50; Luke 8:19-21 [r]ch. 6:3; Matt. 13:55; John 2:12; 7:3, 5, 10; Acts 1:14; 1 Cor. 9:5; Gal. 1:19
34 [s]ver. 5
35 [t][John 15:14; Heb. 2:11] [u]Matt. 7:21; [Luke 11:28]

Chapter 4

1 [v]For ver. 1-12, see Matt. 13:1-15; Luke 8:4-10 [w][ch. 3:9; Luke 5:1-3]
2 [x]ver. 33
3 [y][Isa. 55:10; Amos 9:13]
6 [z]James 1:11 [a]John 15:6
7 [b]Jer. 4:3

to proclaim, to heal, and to cast out demons; he is loved and warned—but not trusted—by Jesus (John 2:24; 6:64, 70).

3:20 Jesus returns **home**, i.e., to the place where he stayed in Capernaum (see note on 2:1).

3:21 The members of Jesus' earthly **family** (his mother and half brothers and sisters) believe **he is out of his mind** (see John 7:5) on account of all that has happened. Besides his opponents, Jesus now also has to contend with unbelieving family members. He will never forsake his relationship with his physical family, yet he will always pursue the call of God above all else (see Mark 3:31–35). (Some of Jesus' brothers did later come to faith in him; see note on 1 Cor. 9:4–5.)

3:22 Scribes . . . from Jerusalem now accuse Jesus; he has come to the attention of the Jewish leaders in Jerusalem. They implicitly acknowledge his undeniable powers but label them as satanic. **Beelzebul**. See note on Matt. 10:25. **by the prince of demons he casts out the demons**. See notes on Matt. 9:34 and 12:24.

3:23 Jesus uses two illustrations (**parables**) to show that the scribes' accusations are false: (1) if the satanic sphere of power were internally divided, then it could not stand (vv. 24–26); and (2) Satan must be bound before his sphere of power can be challenged (v. 27; see note on Matt. 12:29).

3:29 The opponents' accusation against Jesus is the unforgivable, **eternal sin** of blasphemy **against the Holy Spirit** (cf. Matt. 12:31–37; Luke 12:10). Mark 3:28 emphasizes that "all sins will be forgiven," anticipating the eternally valid, substitutionary atonement of Jesus (cf. 10:45). However, if a person persistently attributes to Satan what is accomplished by the power of God—that is, if one makes a flagrant, willful, decisive judgment that the Spirit's testimony about Jesus is satanic—then such a person **never has forgiveness**. (See further the extended note on blasphemy against the Holy Spirit at Luke 12:10.)

3:35 In the midst of Jesus' teaching, his mother and half brothers are "seeking" him (v. 32); they presumably now try to "seize" him (see v. 21). Without severing his relationship with his earthly family (e.g., John 19:26–27; Acts 1:14; 1 Cor. 15:7), Jesus emphasizes the priority of the messianic community of faith (Ex. 32:25–29; Deut. 33:8–9) as the core family of God: **whoever does the will of God** (see Matt. 6:10; John 7:17; Rom. 12:2; 1 Pet. 4:2), **he is my brother and sister and mother** (see Ps. 22:23; Heb. 2:11–12).

4:1–34 *Parables.* Jesus teaches in parables both as judgment against those "outside" and as a means of instruction for those "inside" his newly formed messianic community of faith.

4:2 Mark provides several examples of Jesus **teaching** in **parables**. To the hard-hearted, parables are a warning; to those who are open-hearted, parables illustrate principles of the messianic rule of God. A parable consists of a story and its corresponding intended message.

4:3–7 a sower went out to sow. Using a common farming method of the time, the sower sows the seed without first plowing the ground. Thus the seed fell on various kinds of ground that had not been prepared to receive the seed.

4:8 The **good soil** facilitates the **growing, increasing,** and **yielding** of much fruit. **thirtyfold and sixtyfold and a hundredfold**. Typical

and yielding thirtyfold and sixtyfold and [c]a hundredfold." 9 And he said, [d]"He who has
ears to hear, let him hear."

The Purpose of the Parables

10 And [e]when he was alone, those around him with the twelve asked him about the
parables. 11 And he said to them, [f]"To you has been given [g]the secret of the kingdom of
God, but for [h]those outside everything is in parables, 12 [i]so that

"they [j]may indeed see but not perceive,
and may indeed hear but not understand,
lest they [k]should turn and be forgiven."

13 [l]And he said to them, "Do you not understand this parable? How then will you understand all the parables? 14 [m]The sower sows [n]the word. 15 And these are the ones along the
path, where the word is sown: when they hear, Satan immediately comes and takes away
the word that is sown in them. 16 And these are the ones sown on rocky ground: the ones
who, when they hear the word, immediately receive it [o]with joy. 17 And they have no root
in themselves, but [p]endure for a while; then, when tribulation or persecution arises on
account of the word, immediately [q]they fall away.[1] 18 And others are the ones sown among
thorns. They are those who hear the word, 19 but [r]the cares of [s]the world and [t]the deceitfulness of riches and the desires for other things enter in and choke the word, and it proves
unfruitful. 20 But those that were sown on the good soil are the ones who hear the word
and accept it and [u]bear fruit, [v]thirtyfold and sixtyfold and a hundredfold."

A Lamp Under a Basket

21 [w]And he said to them, [x]"Is a lamp brought in to be put under a basket, or under a bed,
and not on a stand? 22 [y]For nothing is hidden except to be made manifest; nor is anything
secret except to come to light. 23 [z]If anyone has ears to hear, let him hear." 24 And he said
to them, "Pay attention to what you hear: [a]with the measure you use, it will be measured
to you, and still more will be added to you. 25 [b]For to the one who has, more will be given,
and from the one who has not, even what he has will be taken away."

The Parable of the Seed Growing

26 And he said, [c]"The kingdom of God is as if a man should scatter seed on the ground.
27 He sleeps and rises night and day, and the seed sprouts and grows; [d]he knows not how.

[1] *Or stumble*

8 [c]ver. 20; Gen. 26:12
9 [d]See Matt. 11:15
10 [e]ver. 34
11 [f]Matt. 19:11; Col. 1:27; [1 Cor. 2:6-10; 1 John 2:20, 27]; See Matt. 11:25 [g]See Rom. 16:25 [h]1 Cor. 5:12, 13; Col. 4:5; 1 Thess. 4:12; 1 Tim. 3:7
12 [i]Isa. 6:9, 10 [j]Deut. 29:4; Jer. 5:21; Ezek. 12:2; Rom. 11:8; 2 Cor. 3:14; 4:4; [Isa. 42:19, 20] [k]See Luke 22:32
13 [l]For ver. 13-20, see Matt. 13:18-23; Luke 8:11-15
14 [m][Matt. 13:37; John 4:36, 37] [n]ver. 33; ch. 2:2; Luke 1:2; Acts 8:4; James 1:21
16 [o][ch. 6:20; Isa. 58:2; Ezek. 33:31, 32; John 5:35]
17 [p]Gal. 1:6; [Hos. 6:4; Gal. 5:7] [q]See Matt. 11:6
19 [r]See Matt. 6:25 [s]2 Tim. 4:10 [t]1 Tim. 6:9, 10, 17; [ch. 10:23; Matt. 19:23; Acts 5:1-11; Heb. 3:13]
20 [u]Hos. 14:8; John 15:5, 16; Phil. 1:11; Col. 1:6 [v]ver. 8
21 [w]For ver. 21-25, see Luke 8:16-18 [x]Matt. 5:15; Luke 11:33
22 [y]Matt. 10:26; Luke 12:2; [1 Tim. 5:25]
23 [z]ver. 9
24 [a]Matt. 7:2; Luke 6:38
25 [b]See Matt. 13:12
26 [c][Matt. 13:24-30]
27 [d][Eccles. 11:5, 6]

agricultural yields ranged from about fivefold to fifteenfold, with a tenfold return considered a good crop, though some historical reports tell of extraordinary yields up to a hundredfold (see Gen. 26:12, where hundredfold fruit represents the blessing of God).

4:9 Having **ears to hear** involves surrender of proud self-reliance and submission to God (cf. Isa. 6:10; 43:8; 44:18).

4:10 Those who are **with the twelve** disciples (see 3:14) receive insight into the content of Jesus' **parables**.

4:11 Many parables illustrate aspects of **the secret of the kingdom of God**, i.e., the nature of the rule of God over individuals and the community of God (see note on Matt. 13:10–11). Those who do not (yet) participate in the messianic community are **outside**.

4:12 hear but not understand. Since Isa. 6:9–10 describes the hard-heartedness of Israel, its citation here emphasizes the fact that Jesus speaks the parables to outsiders as a form of prophetic warning. Jesus warns of the serious consequences for all, both Gentiles and Jews, who do not open their hearts to him. And yet, there is still room for repentance (see note on Mark 4:33).

4:13 How then will you understand. Jesus hints that even the disciples may suffer from hard hearts (see 8:17–18).

4:14–20 The **sower** in the parable (vv. 4–8) primarily represents Jesus but in a secondary sense every faithful preacher of the gospel. The various soils represent human hearts. The inhospitable hearts in the parable gradually become more receptive (from indifferent, to opportunistic, to very interested), but nevertheless remain preoccupied with the **cares** of their present life in rebellion against God's true purposes. The **good soil** represents a consistently attentive and accepting heart. (See further the extended explanation in the note on Luke 8:15.)

4:21–22 The proclamation of the kingdom of God (his rule and presence) is like bringing an oil **lamp** into a room (see Matt. 5:15; Luke 8:16); the coming messianic rule of God makes **hidden** things (e.g., a hard heart, hidden sin) apparent.

4:23 ears to hear. Cf. note on v. 9.

4:24 Measure refers to the attitude with which the word of Jesus is being received (cf. Matt. 7:2; Luke 6:38). If the hearer embraces Jesus' message of the kingdom in a rich and profound way, then **still more will be added to you**—that is, God will take up residence in that heart and give increased understanding and blessing, both in this age and in the age to come.

4:25 The paradox in this verse reinforces the point in the previous one: the person who welcomes God's rule and presence will **be given** more of God's intended fruit (vv. 13–20); the one who depends on his own resources without receiving the word (**the one who has not**) will lose even that (**what he has will be taken away**). See also notes on Matt. 25:29; Luke 8:16–18; 12:41–48.

4:26–29 As the farmer **sleeps and rises**, the fruit grows **by itself** (Gk. *automatē*, lit., "automatically," "by itself"; that is, without human effort). Fruit for God's kingdom grows from soil that is hospitable to his Word. **First the blade, then the ear** goes against the popular expectation at the time of Jesus that God's kingdom would come suddenly and all at once. Jesus teaches that the messianic rule of God commences inconspicuously (see note on vv. 30–32), grows slowly but steadily in the midst of much adversity, and

29 [e]Joel 3:13; Rev. 14:15
30 [f]For ver. 30-32, see Matt. 13:31, 32; Luke 13:18, 19
31 [g]Matt. 17:20; Luke 17:6
33 [h]Matt. 13:34 [i]See ver. 14 [j]John 16:12; 1 Cor. 3:2; Heb. 5:12
34 [k][John 16:25] [l]ver. 10; [ch. 13:3] [m][2 Pet. 1:20]
35 [n]For ver. 35-41, see Matt. 8:18, 23-27; Luke 8:22-25; [John 6:16-21]
37 [o][Acts 27:14]
39 [p]Ps. 104:7; [Luke 4:39] [q]Job 38:11; Ps. 65:7; [ch. 6:51; Matt. 14:32]
40 [r]John 14:27
41 [s][ch. 1:27] [t][Luke 5:9]
Chapter 5
1 [u]For ver. 1-21, see Matt. 8:28–9:1; Luke 8:26-40
3 [v][Rev. 18:2]

28 The earth produces by itself, first the blade, then the ear, then the full grain in the ear. **29** But
when the grain is ripe, at once [e]he puts in the sickle, because the harvest has come."

The Parable of the Mustard Seed

30 [f]And he said, "With what can we compare the kingdom of God, or what parable shall
we use for it? **31** It is like [g]a grain of mustard seed, which, when sown on the ground, is the
smallest of all the seeds on earth, **32** yet when it is sown it grows up and becomes larger
than all the garden plants and puts out large branches, so that the birds of the air can
make nests in its shade."
33 [h]With many such parables he spoke [i]the word to them, [j]as they were able to hear
it. **34** He did not speak to them [k]without a parable, but [l]privately to his own disciples he
[m]explained everything.

Jesus Calms a Storm

35 [n]On that day, when evening had come, he said to them, "Let us go across to the other
side." **36** And leaving the crowd, they took him with them in the boat, just as he was. And
other boats were with him. **37** And a great windstorm arose, and the waves [o]were breaking
into the boat, so that the boat was already filling. **38** But he was in the stern, asleep on the
cushion. And they woke him and said to him, "Teacher, do you not care that we are perishing?"
39 And he awoke and [p]rebuked the wind and said to the sea, "Peace! Be still!" And
the wind ceased, and [q]there was a great calm. **40** He said to them, "Why are you [r]so afraid?
Have you still no faith?" **41** And they were filled with great fear and said to one another,
[s]"Who then is this, that even [t]the wind and the sea obey him?"

Jesus Heals a Man with a Demon

5 [u]They came to the other side of the sea, to the country of the Gerasenes.[1] **2** And when
Jesus[2] had stepped out of the boat, immediately there met him out of the tombs a man
with an unclean spirit. **3** [v]He lived among the tombs. And no one could bind him anymore,
not even with a chain, **4** for he had often been bound with shackles and chains, but he
wrenched the chains apart, and he broke the shackles in pieces. No one had the strength
to subdue him. **5** Night and day among the tombs and on the mountains he was always
crying out and cutting himself with stones. **6** And when he saw Jesus from afar, he ran and

[1] Some manuscripts *Gergesenes*; some *Gadarenes* [2] Greek *he*; also verse 9

reaches its glorious culmination point at the second coming of Jesus (see also v. 32). There is great hope here. Cf. note on vv. 30–32.

4:29 Sickle and **harvest** are metaphors for the last judgment (cf. Joel 3:13).

4:30–32 A third and final **parable** of the **kingdom** points out that the messianic rule of God begins in a small and unnoticed way, which is different from what was popularly expected (see note on vv. 26–29). Its beginning is likened to a **mustard seed**, which was **the smallest of all the seeds** (see note on Matt. 13:31–32) but could produce a bush as large as 3 by 12 feet (0.9 by 3.7 m). The metaphor emphasizes small beginnings and gradual but remarkable growth (cf. note on Luke 17:20). The nesting of **birds** in the shadow of the grown bush points to divine blessing (cf. Judg. 9:8–15; Ps. 91:1–2; Ezek. 17:22–24).

4:33 Mark provides mere excerpts of Jesus' parabolic teaching on the **word** of the messianic kingdom of God (cf. 1:45; 2:2; 8:32). Jesus uses parables to warn his opponents, who might yet turn to him (**as they were able to hear it**).

4:34 Privately, Jesus helps his **disciples** to understand and receive what he is teaching (see vv. 10–12). **He did not speak to them without a parable** is a broad generalization meaning that he regularly included parables whenever he taught; it does not mean he spoke only in parables.

4:35–5:43 *Nature Miracle, Exorcism, and Healing.* Jesus continues to demonstrate his authority over laws of nature, the demonic world, and sickness.

4:36 On Galilean **boats**, see note on Matt. 4:21 and illustration, p. 1851.

4:37 The Sea of Galilee is 696 feet (212 m) below sea level, resulting in violent downdrafts and sudden storms (**windstorm**; cf. 6:48).

4:38 Asleep on the cushion is an eyewitness detail included only in Mark, no doubt conveyed to him personally by Peter (see Introduction: Author and Title). Jesus' sleeping indicates lack of fear and also great fatigue, a reminder of his true humanity. There are possible echoes of Jonah. However, Jonah is fleeing from God, while Jesus is restoring people to God. The disciples' fear of **perishing** is greater than their confidence in the presence of Jesus (see v. 40).

4:39 Peace! Be still! Jesus displays his divine power over nature. In the OT, God calms the waves (Job 12:15; Ps. 33:7) and the storm (Job 28:25; Ps. 107:25–30; Amos 4:13).

4:40 Jesus chides the disciples for being **afraid** (cf. 7:18; 8:17–18, 21). The antidote to fear is **faith**, i.e., trust in Jesus (see also note on Matt. 8:26). They are right in turning to Jesus, but they are exhorted regarding their fear and feeling of being forsaken by God.

4:41 Who then is this? The disciples ask the right question, for the calming of the storm gives evidence that this man is also truly God.

5:1 Gerasenes. The incident occurs near Gerasa, a small town by the sea (to be distinguished from the larger Gerasa [Jerash], which is 34 miles [54 km] away from the sea). Matthew 8:28 specifies that this was in the region of Gadara. A fifth-century church excavated in Kursi possibly marks the traditional location of this event, on the eastern shore of Galilee.

5:5 cutting himself. The goal of demons is to destroy the person created in the image of God. The man's demonization is evident in his social isolation, superhuman strength, and self-destructive tendencies.

5:6–7 When the man **ran and fell down before** Jesus, it may indicate an involuntary submission of the demons to Jesus' greater power, or that the man himself longed to be free of the demonic influence, or some of both. In either case, the demon immediately takes over the man's voice.

[w]fell down before him. 7 And [x]crying out with a loud voice, he said, "What have you to do
with me, Jesus, [y]Son of [z]the Most High God? [a]I adjure you by God, do not torment me."
8 For he was saying to him, "Come out of the man, you unclean spirit!" 9 And Jesus asked
him, "What is your name?" He replied, "My name is [b]Legion, for we are many." 10 And he
begged him earnestly not to send them out of the country. 11 Now a great herd of pigs was
feeding there on the hillside, 12 and they begged him, saying, "Send us to the pigs; let us
enter them." 13 So he gave them permission. And the unclean spirits came out and entered
the pigs; and the herd, numbering about two thousand, rushed down the steep bank into
the sea and drowned in the sea.
14 The herdsmen fled and told it in the city and in the country. And people came to see
what it was that had happened. 15 And they came to Jesus and saw the demon-possessed[1]
man, the one who had had [c]the legion, sitting there, [d]clothed and in his right mind, and
they were afraid. 16 And those who had seen it described to them what had happened to the
demon-possessed man and to the pigs. 17 And [e]they began to beg Jesus[2] to depart from their
region. 18 As he was getting into the boat, the man who had been possessed with demons
begged him that he might be with him. 19 And he did not permit him but said to him,
"Go home to your friends and [f]tell them how much the Lord has done for you, and how
he has had mercy on you." 20 And he went away and began to proclaim in [g]the Decapolis
how much Jesus had done for him, and everyone marveled.

Jesus Heals a Woman and Jairus's Daughter

21 And when Jesus had crossed again in the boat to the other side, a great crowd gathered
about him, and he was beside the sea. 22 [h]Then came one of [i]the rulers of the synagogue,
Jairus by name, and seeing him, he fell at his feet 23 and implored him earnestly, saying,
"My little daughter is at the point of death. Come and [j]lay your hands on her, so that she
may be made well and live." 24 And he went with him.
And a great crowd followed him and [k]thronged about him. 25 And there was a woman
[l]who had had a discharge of blood for twelve years, 26 and who had suffered much under
many physicians, and had spent all that she had, and was no better but rather grew worse.
27 She had heard the reports about Jesus and came up behind him in the crowd and touched
his garment. 28 For she said, "If I touch even his garments, I will be made well." 29 [m]And
immediately the flow of blood dried up, and she felt in her body that she was healed
of her [n]disease. 30 And Jesus, perceiving in himself that [o]power had gone out from him,
immediately turned about in the crowd and said, "Who touched my garments?" 31 And

[1] Greek *daimonizomai*; also verses 16, 18; elsewhere rendered *oppressed by demons* [2] Greek *him*

6 [w]See Matt. 8:2
7 [x]ch. 1:26; Acts 8:7 [y][Matt. 4:3, 6]; See Matt. 14:33 [z]Gen. 14:18; Num. 24:16; Ps. 57:2; Dan. 3:26; Luke 1:32; 6:35; Acts 16:17 [a]Matt. 26:63; Acts 19:13; [James 2:19]
9 [b]Matt. 26:53
15 [c][Luke 8:27] [d]ver. 9
17 [e][Luke 5:8; Acts 16:39]
19 [f]Ps. 66:16; [ch. 1:44]
20 [g]ch. 7:31; Matt. 4:25
22 [h]For ver. 22-43, see Matt. 9:18-26; Luke 8:41-56 [i]Luke 13:14; Acts 13:15; 18:8, 17
23 [j]ch. 6:5; 7:32; 8:23, 25; 16:18; Matt. 9:18; Luke 4:40; 13:13; Acts 9:12, 17; 28:8
24 [k]ver. 31; ch. 3:9
25 [l]Lev. 15:25
29 [m]Matt. 15:28; 17:18 [n]See ch. 3:10
30 [o]Luke 5:17; 6:19; 8:46; [Acts 10:38]

5:8 Was saying (imperfect tense) indicates that Jesus had told the demon more than once to **come out of the man**, but it had not obeyed.

5:9 My name is Legion. A legion was the largest unit of the Roman army and at full strength had 6,000 soldiers. This does not necessarily mean that there were 6,000 demons in the man, only that there were a great **many**.

5:11 Due to Hellenistic influence, ceremonially unclean **pigs** are no surprise in the Gentile Decapolis region.

5:13 The great number of **pigs** that perished verified the claim that many demons inhabited the man (v. 9). If the demons cannot destroy the man, they will destroy the pigs, another part of God's creation. See also note on Matt. 8:30–34.

5:15 The (formerly) **demon-possessed** man is now **in his right mind**, i.e., properly functioning again as an image-bearer of God (see note on Luke 8:35). **they were afraid**. See note on Luke 8:37.

5:18–20 did not permit him. Jesus did not allow the restored and thankful man (v. 15) to join him. It is possible that he was asking Jesus for permission to belong to the closer circle of disciples (**that he might be with him** recalls 3:14). Jesus wanted the restored man to be a witness to God's power **in the Decapolis**—an example of Jesus intentionally instructing a restored person to proclaim what had happened to him, in contrast to his call for secrecy in other cases (see 1:44; 5:43; 9:9). Jewish and Gentile people in the Decapolis did not yet pose the same danger of misunderstanding Jesus as a political or military messiah, as was the case in Galilee. Note that the work of the **Lord** in 5:19 is described as the work of **Jesus** in v. 20, indicating that Jesus shares the same nature as God himself.

5:21 to the other side (see note on Matt. 8:28). Jesus returns to the Galilean side of the sea, where his popularity has constantly grown.

5:22 The laymen who were **rulers of the synagogue** presided over the affairs of the synagogue, including organizing and teaching in synagogue services. Most of them were Pharisees. The Greek term, *archisynagōgos*, has been found on many inscriptions from Palestine and throughout the Roman world (on synagogues, see note on Luke 4:16 and The Synagogue and Jewish Worship, pp. 1956–1957). The fact that **Jairus . . . fell at** Jesus' **feet** demonstrates his real need and his sincerity.

5:25–27 While Jesus is on his way to heal Jairus's daughter, Mark interjects the simultaneous event of the healing of the woman with a constant **discharge of blood** (vv. 25–34; see note on Matt. 9:20). On account of her condition, she is ceremonially unclean (cf. Lev. 15:25–28) and is not permitted to enter the temple section reserved for women; nor is she permitted to be in public without making people aware that she is unclean. By touching Jesus' **garment**, she technically renders him ceremonially unclean (cf. Lev. 15:19–23), but Jesus is greater than any purity laws, for he makes her clean by his power instead of becoming unclean himself (cf. Mark 1:41; 5:41).

5:30 Jesus senses **in himself**, probably indicating some physical sensation in his body, **that power had gone out from him**, not merely by being **touched** but by being touched by someone who has faith that he can heal her.

5:31–33 When Jesus asked, **"Who touched me?"** the woman responded

34[p]See Luke 7:50 [n][See ver. 29 above]
35[q]ver. 22 [r]Luke 7:6 [s]See John 11:28
36[q][See ver. 35 above]
37[t]ch. 9:2; 14:33 [u]ch. 3:17
39[v][Acts 20:10] [w]John 11:4, 11
40[x]Acts 9:40
41[y]See ch. 1:31 [z]Luke 7:14, 22; [Matt. 11:5; John 11:43]
43[a]ch. 9:9; See Matt. 8:4
Chapter 6
1[b]For ver. 1-6, see Matt. 13:54-58; [Luke 4:16-30] [c]Matt. 2:23; Luke 4:23
2[d]ch. 1:21; Luke 4:31; 6:6; 13:10; [Acts 13:14]; See Matt. 4:23 [e]See Matt. 7:28
3[f][Luke 4:22; John 6:42] [g][Matt. 13:55] [h]See ch. 3:31 [i]See Matt. 11:6
4[j]Luke 4:24; John 4:44; [Jer. 11:21; 12:6; John 7:5]

his disciples said to him, "You see the crowd pressing around you, and yet you say, 'Who
touched me?'" 32 And he looked around to see who had done it. 33 But the woman, knowing what had happened to her, came in fear and trembling and fell down before him and
told him the whole truth. 34 And he said to her, "Daughter, [p]your faith has made you well;
[p]go in peace, and be healed of your [n]disease."
35 While he was still speaking, there came from [q]the ruler's house some who said, "Your
daughter is dead. Why [r]trouble [s]the Teacher any further?" 36 But overhearing[1] what they
said, Jesus said to [q]the ruler of the synagogue, "Do not fear, only believe." 37 And he allowed
no one to follow him except [t]Peter and James and [u]John the brother of James. 38 They came
to the house of the ruler of the synagogue, and Jesus[2] saw a commotion, people weeping
and wailing loudly. 39 And when he had entered, he said to them, [v]"Why are you making
a commotion and weeping? The child is not dead but [w]sleeping." 40 And they laughed at
him. But he [x]put them all outside and took the child's father and mother and those who
were with him and went in where the child was. 41 [y]Taking her by the hand he said to her,
"Talitha cumi," which means, "Little girl, I say to you, [z]arise." 42 And immediately the girl
got up and began walking (for she was twelve years of age), and they were immediately
overcome with amazement. 43 And [a]he strictly charged them that no one should know
this, and told them to give her something to eat.

Jesus Rejected at Nazareth

6 [b]He went away from there and came to [c]his hometown, and his disciples followed
him. 2 And [d]on the Sabbath he began to teach in the synagogue, and [e]many who heard
him were astonished, saying, "Where did this man get these things? What is the wisdom
given to him? How are such mighty works done by his hands? 3 [f]Is not this [g]the carpenter,
the son of Mary and [h]brother of James and Joses and Judas and Simon? And are not his
sisters here with us?" And [i]they took offense at him. 4 And Jesus said to them, [j]"A prophet
is not without honor, except in his hometown and among his relatives and in his own

[1] Or *ignoring*; some manuscripts *hearing* [2] Greek *he*

with **fear and trembling**. Her fear may have been partly because, in working her way through the crowd to get to Jesus, she would have touched many other people and thus rendered them ceremonially unclean (cf. Lev. 15:19–27). Again Mark notes the theme of fear and shows how it leads to faith. More importantly, the woman felt deep awe (Gk. *phobeomai* can be rendered "be afraid" or "feel awe and reverence") at the powerful presence of God who has healed her: she **fell down before him and told him the whole truth**, which testifies to her confidence in and sincere gratitude toward Jesus.

5:34 Daughter. Having been on the fringes of the crowd surrounding Jesus, the woman now finds herself welcomed into the family of God. **Your faith has made you well** would suggest both physical and spiritual healing, for Greek *sōzō* can mean either "heal" or "save." The woman's faith in Jesus for physical healing at the same time became faith in him for salvation from sin (cf. note on Matt. 9:22).

5:35 Verses 35–43 resume the account of Jairus's daughter (vv. 22–24) by showing the stark contrast between the words in v. 34 ("Daughter, your faith has made you well") and the fact that now Jairus's **daughter is dead**.

5:36 Do not fear, only believe. Again, Jesus defines faith as the antidote to fear (cf. 2:5; 4:40; 5:34). In the face of death, this is a supreme challenge for Jairus.

5:37 Peter and James and John. Only the inner circle of disciples is permitted to join Jesus (cf. 1:29; 9:2; and note on 3:16–17).

5:38–40 The **commotion** with **weeping and wailing loudly** reflects deep grief in the face of death. However, some in the crowd are professional mourners, who were a required presence even at funerals for the poor (see note on Matt. 9:23). Amid the mourning, Jesus proclaims that **the child is not dead but sleeping**. The mocking and laughing crowd takes Jesus' statement literally (cf. Mark 9:26), supposing that Jesus cannot accept the reality of death. The child had indeed died (see Luke 8:55), but from Jesus' viewpoint her real death is but sleep. **put them all outside**. The unbelieving crowd would only be a distraction (see note on Mark 6:5–6), so Jesus allows only the girl's closest family members and his closest followers to witness the miracle.

5:41 Touching a dead person renders one ceremonially unclean (Lev. 22:4; Num. 19:11), but once again (cf. note on Mark 5:25–27) Jesus overcomes uncleanness, for the girl comes back to life (cf. 2 Kings 4:17–37; Acts 9:39–41). **Talitha cumi**. At times, Mark reports Jesus' statements in Aramaic, reinforcing the eyewitness quality of this Gospel account.

5:42 The **amazement** of those who witnessed the miracle does not necessarily indicate faith in Jesus. No doubt some believed, but others remained puzzled.

5:43 no one should know this. See notes on vv. 18–20; Matt. 8:4.

6:1–6 *Rejection at Nazareth*. This story closes the larger section (3:13–6:6) with the theme of the rejection of Jesus in Nazareth, where Jesus is not accepted in his hometown.

6:1–2 Jesus goes to his **hometown** of Nazareth (see note on Matt. 13:54) despite tensions with his natural family (see Mark 3:21, 31–35). As is so often the case, Jesus begins to **teach** (see 1:21, 39; 3:1; 4:1; 6:34; 8:31; etc.). On **synagogue**, see note on Luke 4:16 and The Synagogue and Jewish Worship, pp. 1956–1957. Jesus was most likely asked to give a message following the reading of Scripture (cf. Luke 4:16–30, which most commentators understand to be the same incident, though this is not certain; see notes on Luke 4:17; 4:18–19). **Where did this man get these things?** This verse testifies to the genuine humanity of Jesus. Until he began his ministry, his deity was so hidden that even people in his hometown, who had known him well since childhood, had no idea that he was also fully God.

6:3 The questions of v. 2 are followed by skeptical, slightly derogatory questions: is not Jesus a simple **carpenter**, the **son of Mary**? The latter comment may hint that Jesus was rumored to be an illegitimate child. Joseph must have had at least four sons, among whom were **James** (see Acts 12:17; Gal. 1:19; 2:9, 12; and Introduction to James: Author and Title) and **Judas** (not the betrayer; see Jude 1 and Introduction to Jude: Author and Title), as well as at least two daughters (on Jesus' brothers and sisters, see note on Matt. 13:55–56). Because of the tension between Jesus' obvious wisdom and power and his simple origins, the people take **offense at him**.

6:4 Like other prophets before him (e.g., 2 Chron. 36:16; Jer. 11:21; Mark 6:17; 12:1–12), Jesus is not honored by his own family and his **hometown**.

household." **5** And [k]he could do no mighty work there, except that [l]he laid his hands on a
few sick people and healed them. **6** And [m]he marveled because of their unbelief.
[n]And he went about among the villages teaching.

Jesus Sends Out the Twelve Apostles

7 [o]And he called the twelve and began to send them out two by two, and gave them
authority over the unclean spirits. **8** He charged them to take nothing for their journey
except a staff—no bread, no bag, no money in their belts— **9** but to [p]wear sandals and not
put on two tunics.[1] **10** And he said to them, "Whenever you enter a house, stay there until
you depart from there. **11** And if any place will not receive you and they will not listen to
you, when you leave, [q]shake off the dust that is on your feet [r]as a testimony against them."
12 [s]So they went out and [t]proclaimed [u]that people should repent. **13** [t]And they cast out many
demons and [v]anointed with oil many who were sick and healed them.

The Death of John the Baptist

14 [w]King Herod heard of it, for Jesus'[2] name had become known. Some[3] said, [x]"John the
Baptist[4] has been raised from the dead. That is why these miraculous powers are at work
in him." **15** [x]But others said, "He is Elijah." And others said, "He is [y]a prophet, like one of
the prophets of old." **16** But when Herod heard of it, he said, "John, whom I beheaded,
has been raised." **17** [z]For it was Herod who had sent and seized John and [a]bound him in
prison for the sake of Herodias, his brother Philip's wife, because he had married her.
18 [z]For John had been saying to Herod, [b]"It is not lawful for you to have your brother's
wife." **19** And Herodias had a grudge against him and wanted to put him to death. But
she could not, **20** for Herod [c]feared John, knowing that he was a righteous and holy man,
and he kept him safe. When he heard him, he was greatly perplexed, and yet he [d]heard
him gladly.
21 But an opportunity came when Herod [e]on his birthday [f]gave a banquet for his nobles
and military commanders and the leading men of Galilee. **22** For when Herodias's daughter
came in and danced, she pleased Herod and his guests. And the king said to the girl, "Ask
me for whatever you wish, and I will give it to you." **23** And he vowed to her, "Whatever
you ask me, I will give you, [g]up to half of my kingdom." **24** And she went out and said to
her mother, "For what should I ask?" And she said, "The head of John the Baptist." **25** And

[1] Greek *chiton*, a long garment worn under the cloak next to the skin [2] Greek *his* [3] Some manuscripts *He* [4] Greek *baptizer*; also verse 24

5 [k][ch. 9:23; Gen. 19:22] [l]See ch. 5:23
6 [m][Matt. 8:10] [n]Matt. 9:35; 11:1; Luke 8:1; 13:22
7 [o]ch. 3:13-15; For ver. 7-11, see Matt. 10:1, 5, 9-14; Luke 9:1, 3-5; [Luke 10:4-11; 22:35]
9 [p]Acts 12:8
11 [q]Acts 13:51; [Neh. 5:13; Acts 18:6] [r]See ch. 1:44
12 [s]Luke 9:6 [t]Matt. 10:7, 8 [u]Matt. 3:2; 4:17
13 [t][See ver. 12 above] [v]James 5:14
14 [w]For ver. 14-29, see Matt. 14:1-12; Luke 9:7-9 [x]ch. 8:28; Matt. 16:14
15 [x][See ver. 14 above] [y]See Matt. 21:11
17 [z]Luke 3:19, 20 [a]Matt. 11:2; John 3:24
18 [z][See ver. 17 above] [b]Lev. 18:16; 20:21
20 [c][Matt. 14:5; 21:26] [d]ch. 12:37; [ch. 4:16]
21 [e]Gen. 40:20 [f]1 Kgs. 3:15; Esth. 1:3; 2:18
23 [g]Esth. 5:3; 7:2

This rejection foreshadows Jesus' ultimate rejection in Jerusalem. Jesus indirectly acknowledges that he sees himself at least as a **prophet** of God.

6:5–6 With some exceptions, Jesus **could do no mighty work there**. Jesus will not force his miracles on a hostile, skeptical audience. It stands in contradiction to the character and will of Jesus to heal where there is fundamental rejection of him (**unbelief**); see note on Matt. 13:58. Nevertheless, Jesus continues **teaching** (see Mark 1:22; 4:1, 2; 6:2, etc.).

6:7–8:26 *Work beyond Galilee.* The systematically trained disciples are sent out to spread the message of God's kingdom, to heal, and to cast out demons. Jesus again demonstrates his authority and warns his disciples against hard hearts.

6:7–13 *Sending of the Twelve.* What was anticipated in 3:14–15 now happens. The Twelve are by now trained emissaries of Jesus' message (see 1:14–15): like Jesus, they are to proclaim repentance (6:10–12), cast out unclean spirits (v. 7), and heal (v. 13). The message of the kingdom is thus spread even further. (On the significance of there being 12 disciples, see note on Matt. 10:1.)

6:8–9 The travel instructions are unique and specific for the disciples (in contrast to the more general teaching in 8:34–38). These unique instructions serve as signs to Jewish people of peace, defenselessness, trust in God, and urgency. The scene echoes the first exodus (cf. Ex. 12:11). In both instances there is liberation from servitude. **Bread**, **bag**, **money in their belts**, and **two tunics** all represent that which secures life; the provisions are to come from people who repent upon hearing the disciples' message. **nothing . . . except a staff . . . but to wear sandals**. Various explanations have been proposed to reconcile these words with Matt. 10:9–10 and Luke 9:3. The best solution is probably that in Matthew and Luke Jesus tells the disciples not to acquire a new staff or sandals for their journey, but in Mark he adds that they can take the sandals and staff they already have (see note on Matt. 10:9–10). Some interpreters have proposed that the disciples were permitted to take a walking staff while the staff prohibited in Matt. 10:10 and Luke 9:3 was for self-defense.

6:11 Later rabbinic sources note that Jews who returned from Gentile regions were to **shake off the dust that is on** their **feet** as a form of cleansing. Here it also serves as a sign **against them**. But there is no human militancy in the proclamation of Jesus' message. God is the sole judge (cf. note on Matt. 10:14). The act of shaking off the dust is an illustration of the fact that their rejection of God's message leaves the town accountable to God.

6:13 Oil was commonly used in prayer for healing (cf. note on James 5:13–14).

6:14–56 *Death of John the Baptist.* The death of John the Baptist casts an ominous shadow on Jesus' future (cf. 3:1–6; 6:1–6). Jesus' life is in danger, partly on account of his authoritative, miraculous deeds.

6:14a Herod Antipas, seventh son of Herod the Great, was tetrarch of Galilee and Perea (4 B.C.–A.D. 39), serving as an administrator under Rome (see note on Matt. 14:1). Antipas was not technically a **King**, although his contemporaries may have referred to him as such (cf. his statement in Mark 6:23: "half of my kingdom"). He lost his position in A.D. 39 after trying to gain complete sovereignty.

6:14b–15 The list of popular beliefs (see also 8:27–28) about Jesus includes that he is (1) the revived **John the Baptist**, (2) the expected **Elijah** (from Mal. 4:5), or (3) **one of the prophets**. The first belief, held by Herod Antipas (see Mark 6:16), is clearly false. The second opinion reflects the widespread expectation in Judaism (Mal. 3:1–2; 4:5–6) that Elijah, who was caught up to heaven without dying (2 Kings 2:11), would return at the end of time.

29 [h]See Matt. 9:14
30 [i]Luke 9:10 [j]Matt. 10:2; Luke 6:13; 17:5; 22:14; 24:10
31 [k]ch. 3:20
32 [l]For ver. 32-44, see Matt. 14:13-21; Luke 9:10-17; John 6:1-13; [ch. 8:2-9] [m]See ch. 3:9
33 [n]ver. 54
34 [o][Matt. 9:36]
36 [p]ver. 45; [Matt. 15:23]
37 [q][2 Kgs. 4:42-44] [r][John 6:7] [s][Num. 11:13, 21, 22]
38 [t]ch. 8:19
41 [u]ch. 7:34; John 11:41; 17:1 [v]ch. 8:7; 14:22; 1 Sam. 9:13; Matt. 26:26; Luke 24:30; [1 Cor. 14:16]

she came in immediately with haste to the king and asked, saying, "I want you to give me
at once the head of John the Baptist on a platter." **26** And the king was exceedingly sorry,
but because of his oaths and his guests he did not want to break his word to her. **27** And
immediately the king sent an executioner with orders to bring John's[1] head. He went and
beheaded him in the prison **28** and brought his head on a platter and gave it to the girl,
and the girl gave it to her mother. **29** When his [h]disciples heard of it, they came and took
his body and laid it in a tomb.

Jesus Feeds the Five Thousand

30 [i, j]The apostles returned to Jesus and told him all that they had done and taught. **31** And
he said to them, "Come away by yourselves to a desolate place and rest a while." For many
were coming and going, and [k]they had no leisure even to eat. **32** [l]And they went away in
[m]the boat to a desolate place by themselves. **33** Now many saw them going and [n]recognized
them, and they ran there on foot from all the towns and got there ahead of them. **34** When
he went ashore he [o]saw a great crowd, and [o]he had compassion on them, because they were
like sheep without a shepherd. And he began to teach them many things. **35** And when it
grew late, his disciples came to him and said, "This is a desolate place, and the hour is
now late. **36** [p]Send them away to go into the surrounding countryside and villages and
buy themselves something to eat." **37** But he answered them, [q]"You give them something
to eat." And [r]they said to him, [s]"Shall we go and buy two hundred denarii[2] worth of bread
and give it to them to eat?" **38** And he said to them, "How many loaves do you have? Go
and see." And when they had found out, they said, [t]"Five, and two fish." **39** Then he commanded them all to sit down in groups on the green grass. **40** So they sat down in groups,
by hundreds and by fifties. **41** And taking the five loaves and the two fish he [u]looked up
to heaven and [v]said a blessing and broke the loaves and gave them to the disciples to set
before the people. And he divided the two fish among them all. **42** And they all ate and were

[1] Greek *his* [2] A *denarius* was a day's wage for a laborer

Contrary to popular speculation that Jesus might be the expected Elijah, Jesus himself describes John the Baptist as having come "in the spirit and power of Elijah" (Luke 1:17; cf. Mark 9:11–13). The third proposal—"a prophet, like one of the prophets of old"—might have arisen from Deut. 18:15, 18. Jesus was far greater than any of these theories, something that Peter's confession at Caesarea Philippi will show (cf. Mark 8:27–30).

6:17 John the Baptist had publicly charged **Herod** Antipas with breaking the law (Lev. 18:16; 20:21) by marrying **Herodias**, the former **wife** of his (still living) half brother Herod Philip I (son of Mariamne II and Herod the Great), in A.D. 27; as a result, Herod had put John **in prison** (see note on Matt. 14:3–4).

6:18 It is not lawful for you to have your brother's wife. Herod Antipas was not a Jew, yet John did not hesitate to tell him that he had violated the moral law of God (cf. Lev. 18:16). Similarly, the gospel message that people should "repent" (Mark 1:15; 6:12), which would eventually go to Gentiles as well as Jews, assumes that God holds all people in the world accountable to his moral laws as revealed in Scripture.

6:19–20 Herodias thus (see v. 18) held **a grudge against** John and intended to put him **to death**. But **Herod** Antipas **feared John** and resisted this plan. Perhaps he feared an uprising on account of John's popularity (1:5) and also held a superstitious fear of some kind of divine punishment. The Jewish historian Josephus notes that people viewed Antipas's death as God's judgment for slaying John the Baptist (*Jewish Antiquities* 18.116–118). Antipas also saw John's innocence and godliness and thus had conflicting thoughts about him (**he was greatly perplexed, and yet he heard him gladly**).

6:21 Leaders of three societal groups are invited to celebrate the birthday of **Herod** Antipas: (1) **nobles**, or high-ranking governmental leaders of Galilee; (2) **military** officers; and (3) **leading men**, wealthy and prominent Galileans.

6:23 Foolishly, Herod Antipas not only offers to fulfill the wish of Herodias's daughter Salome (cf. note on Matt. 14:6–7) but reinforces his statement by means of a public oath (see Mark 6:26). **Up to half of my kingdom** is to be understood more as a figure of speech than a literal promise.

6:26 was exceedingly sorry. Herod Antipas was grieved because he did not relish putting John to death. However, Herodias had maneuvered Antipas into a public oath in the presence of his most important subjects. His reputation and authority were at stake.

6:30 Mark refers back to Jesus' sending of the disciples in vv. 7–13. The disciples learn Jesus' message by listening to his teaching, by proclaiming what he proclaims, and by reporting upon their return **all that they had done and taught** (5:14, 19).

6:34 Despite his need for rest, Jesus has **compassion**; he sees the people as being **like sheep without a shepherd** (cf. Num. 27:17; Ezek. 34:4–5). In Ezekiel 34:10–16, God promises to shepherd the people again directly, since Israel's leaders have failed. Jesus continues to **teach them**, functioning as the good shepherd (Gen. 48:15; Ps. 23:1–4; Isa. 40:11; Jer. 23:4) who calls for repentant submission to the messianic rule of God (see John 10:14).

6:36–37 The disciples' plausible request (**Send them away to . . . buy themselves something to eat**) is met with Jesus' thought-provoking response (**You give them something to eat**). The disciples in turn respond with mild sarcasm. **Two hundred denarii** represented 200 days' wages for a laborer.

6:38 How many loaves do you have? Jesus clearly intends for the disciples to do what he says and to trust him for the outcome.

6:39–40 commanded them all to sit down. Cf. Ps. 23:2. **by hundreds and by fifties**. Cf. Ex. 18:21, 25.

6:41–42 he looked up to heaven. Jesus depends on his heavenly Father in this miracle of multiplying food. As the true shepherd, he satisfies them. As God provided manna in the desert (cf. Deut. 8:3, 16), so Jesus provides food in a deserted place (Mark 6:35). The focus is thus not on the miracle itself but on the one who worked it. Jesus is not merely a prophet; he acts as God acts. The feeding of the 5,000 reinforces Jesus' proclamation: after feeding them the Word of God (v. 34), they now miraculously receive bread and fish (basic foods; see Luke 24:42; John 21:9). Once again the question of Jesus' true identity is raised; and once again (on account of their hard-heartedness), the disciples do not understand (see Mark 6:52; 8:18–21).

satisfied. 43 And they took up twelve baskets full of broken pieces and of the fish. 44 And
those who ate the loaves were five thousand men.

Jesus Walks on the Water

45 [w]Immediately he [x]made his disciples get into [y]the boat and go before him to the other
side, [z]to Bethsaida, while he dismissed the crowd. 46 And after he had taken leave of them,
[a]he went up on the mountain to pray. 47 And when [b]evening came, the boat was out on the
sea, and he was alone on the land. 48 And he saw that they were making headway painfully,
for the wind was against them. And about [b]the fourth watch of the night[1] he came to them,
walking on the sea. [c]He meant to pass by them, 49 but when they saw him walking on the
sea they thought it was a ghost, and cried out, 50 for they all saw him and [d]were terrified.
But immediately he spoke to them and said, [e]"Take heart; it is I. [e]Do not be afraid." 51 And
he got into the boat with them, and the wind ceased. And they were utterly astounded,
52 for [f]they did not understand about the loaves, but their hearts [g]were hardened.

Jesus Heals the Sick in Gennesaret

53 [h]When they had crossed over, they came to land at [i]Gennesaret and moored to the
shore. 54 And when they got out of the boat, the people immediately [j]recognized him 55 and
ran about the whole region and began to bring [k]the sick people [l]on their beds to wherever
they heard he was. 56 And wherever he came, in villages, cities, or countryside, [m]they laid
the sick in the marketplaces and implored him that they might touch even [n]the fringe of
his garment. And [o]as many as touched it were made well.

Traditions and Commandments

7 [p]Now when the Pharisees gathered to him, with some of the scribes [q]who had come
from Jerusalem, 2 they saw that some of his disciples ate with hands that were [r]defiled,
that is, unwashed. 3 (For the Pharisees and all the Jews do not eat unless they wash their
hands properly,[2] holding to [s]the tradition of [t]the elders, 4 and when they come from the
marketplace, they do not eat unless they wash.[3] And there are many other traditions that
they observe, such as [u]the washing of [v]cups and pots and copper vessels and dining couches.[4])
5 And the Pharisees and the scribes asked him, "Why do your disciples not walk according
to [s]the tradition of [t]the elders, [w]but eat with [r]defiled hands?" 6 And he said to them, "Well
did Isaiah prophesy of you [x]hypocrites, as it is written,

[1] That is, between 3 A.M. and 6 A.M. [2] Greek *unless they wash the hands with a fist*, probably indicating a kind of ceremonial washing [3] Greek *unless they baptize*; some manuscripts *unless they purify themselves* [4] Some manuscripts omit *and dining couches*

45 [w]For ver. 45-51, see Matt. 14:22-32; John 6:15-21 [x][Matt. 8:18] [y]ver. 32 [z]ch. 8:22; [Luke 9:10]
46 [a]Luke 6:12; 9:28; [ch. 1:35; Luke 5:16]
47 [b][ch. 13:35]
48 [b][See ver. 47 above] [c][Luke 24:28]
50 [d][Luke 24:37] [e]Matt. 17:7; [Deut. 31:6; Isa. 41:13; 43:1, 2; John 16:33]
52 [f]ch. 8:17-21 [g]John 12:40; Rom. 11:7; 2 Cor. 3:14; See ch. 3:5
53 [h]For ver. 53-56, see Matt. 14:34-36; [John 6:24, 25] [i]Luke 5:1
54 [j]ver. 33
55 [k]Matt. 4:24 [l]Luke 5:18
56 [m]Acts 5:15 [n]See Matt. 9:20 [o]ch. 3:10; Luke 6:19

Chapter 7

1 [p]For ver. 1-30, see Matt. 15:1-28 [q]ch. 3:22
2 [r][Acts 10:14; Rom. 14:14 (Gk.)]
3 [s]Gal. 1:14; Col. 2:8 [t]Heb. 11:2
4 [u]Heb. 9:10; [John 2:6] [v]Matt. 23:25; Luke 11:39
5 [s][See ver. 3 above] [t][See ver. 3 above] [w]Luke 11:38 [r][See ver. 2 above]
6 [x]Matt. 23:13

6:43 they took up twelve baskets full. As with the miracles of Elijah and Elisha (see 1 Kings 17:16; 2 Kings 4:7, 42–44; Luke 5:6–7; John 21:6, 11), much food is left over. Jesus did not want any food to be wasted.

6:45 Jesus sends **his disciples** ahead (to **Bethsaida**, see note on Luke 9:10) in order to retreat for personal prayer (Mark 6:46; see 1:35–39; 14:26–42).

6:48 The **fourth watch** is the time between 3:00 A.M. and 6:00 A.M. The Sea of Galilee is 696 feet (212 m) below sea level, resulting in violent downdrafts and sudden windstorms (cf. 4:37). Jesus sees their need and walks on water toward them (see Job 9:8; Ps. 77:20; Isa. 43:16). **He meant to pass by them,** not so that they would fail to see him (in which case he would have stayed farther away from them), but so that they would see him "pass by" (Gk. *parerchomai*), walking on the water, thus giving visible evidence of his deity (and thus answering the question they asked after he stilled the sea in Mark 4:41: "Who then is this . . . ?"). The passage echoes the incident where God "passed" before Moses (the same verb, *parerchomai*, occurs in the Septuagint of Ex. 33:19, 22; 34:6), giving a glimpse of his glory. But it also echoes Job 9, where Job says that it is God who "trampled the waves of the sea" (Job 9:8; the Septuagint has *peripatōn . . . epi thalassēs*, "walking on the sea," using the same words as Mark 6:48, *peripatōn epi tēs thalassēs*) and then also says, "he *passes by* me" (Job 9:11, Gk. *parerchomai*). There is an implicit claim to divinity in Jesus' actions.

6:49–50 The disciples are overwhelmed by what appears to be a **ghost** (see note on Matt. 14:26). Like God in the OT, Jesus calms their troubled hearts by identifying himself (**"It is I"** echoes Ex. 3:14).

6:51–52 the wind ceased. Cf. 4:35–41. **their hearts were hardened**. When Jesus calmed the storm earlier, the disciples had struggled with faith vs. fear (4:40); now, they struggled with faith vs. fear plus hard-heartedness. Mark explains that multiplying the **loaves** should have demonstrated Jesus' true identity to them (cf. 8:18–21), but neither that miracle nor the appearance of Jesus on the water could open their hearts to the reality of his divine nature.

6:53 The northeasterly wind had caused the ship to drift southwestward, bringing them to **Gennesaret** (see note on Matt. 14:34) instead of their intended destination of Bethsaida (see Mark 6:45 and map, p. 1908).

6:54–55 By this time Jesus is well known in Galilee. Whenever he enters that region, great multitudes gather.

6:56 Jesus continues to pursue his core calling to preach in **villages** (e.g., vv. 6, 36), **cities** (see 1:33, 45; 5:14; 6:33), and the **countryside** (5:14; 6:36). The healing power of God is so strongly present that **as many as touched** the **fringe** of **his garment . . . were made well**.

7:1–23 *Teachings on Moral Defilement.* Conflict ensues between the Pharisees and Jesus over the issue of true moral purity.

7:5 Scribes are sent from Jerusalem (v. 1) to investigate the situation brought about by Jesus' popularity. In 2:15–28 and 3:6, 20–30 as well as here, it is evident that many **Pharisees** and **scribes** merely intend to convict Jesus of breaking the written Law of Moses (i.e., aspects of the ceremonial law in Ex. 30:19; 40:12) as interpreted by the later **tradition of the elders** and thus to discredit his authority with the people. **eat with defiled hands.** The disciples are not breaking the Mosaic law but rather later Jewish traditions that prescribed ritual washing of hands, utensils, and furniture (see Mark 7:2–4). By his example, Jesus implies that his disciples can ignore these traditions (see Luke 11:37–38).

7:6–8 The Pharisees are **hypocrites** for two reasons: (1) their actions are

[y]"'This people honors me with their lips,
but their heart is far from me;
7 in vain do they worship me,
teaching as [z]doctrines the commandments of men.'

8 You leave the commandment of God and hold to the tradition of men."
9 And he said to them, "You have a fine way of [a]rejecting the commandment of God in
order to establish your tradition! **10** For Moses said, [b]'Honor your father and your mother';
and, [c]'Whoever reviles father or mother must surely die.' **11** But you say, 'If a man tells
his father or his mother, "Whatever you would have gained from me is Corban"' (that is,
given to God)[1]— **12** then you no longer permit him to do anything for his father or mother,
13 thus [d]making void the word of God by your tradition that you have handed down. And
many such things you do."

What Defiles a Person

14 And he called the people to him again and said to them, [e]"Hear me, all of you, and
understand: **15** [f]There is nothing outside a person that by going into him can defile him,
but the things that come out of a person are what defile him."[2] **17** And when he had entered
[g]the house and left the people, [h]his disciples asked him about the parable. **18** And he said to
them, "Then [i]are you also without understanding? Do you not see that whatever goes into a
person from outside cannot defile him, **19** since it enters not his heart [j]but his stomach, and is
expelled?"[3] ([k]Thus he declared all foods clean.) **20** And he said, [l]"What comes out of a person
is what defiles him. **21** For from within, out of the heart of man, come evil thoughts, sexual
immorality, theft, [m]murder, adultery, **22** coveting, wickedness, deceit, [n]sensuality, [o]envy, [p]slander,
[q]pride, [r]foolishness. **23** [s]All these evil things come from within, and they defile a person."

The Syrophoenician Woman's Faith

24 And from there he arose and went away to the region of Tyre and Sidon.[4] And he
entered a house and did not want anyone to know, yet he could not be hidden. **25** But
immediately a woman whose little daughter had an unclean spirit heard of him and came
and fell down at his feet. **26** [t]Now the woman was a [u]Gentile, [v]a Syrophoenician by birth.

[1] Or *an offering* [2] Some manuscripts add verse 16: *If anyone has ears to hear, let him hear* [3] Greek *goes out into the latrine* [4] Some manuscripts omit *and Sidon*

6 [y]Cited from Isa. 29:13; [Ezek. 33:31]
7 [z]Col. 2:22; Titus 1:14
9 [a]Luke 7:30; Gal. 2:21 (Gk.); Heb. 10:28 (Gk.)
10 [b]Cited from Ex. 20:12 [c]Cited from Ex. 21:17
13 [d]Gal. 3:17 (Gk.); [Rom. 2:23]
14 [e]Matt. 13:51
15 [f]See Acts 10:14, 15
17 [g]ch. 9:28 [h][Matt. 13:36; 15:15]
18 [i]ch. 8:17, 18
19 [j][1 Cor. 6:13] [k][Luke 11:41; Acts 10:15; 11:9]
20 [l]Matt. 12:34; James 3:6
21 [m]Matt. 5:22, 28; See Ex. 20:13, 14, 17
22 [n]2 Cor. 12:21; Gal. 5:19; Eph. 4:19; 2 Pet. 2:7; Jude 4 [o]See Matt. 6:23 (Gk.) [p]Eph. 4:31; Col. 3:8; 1 Tim. 6:4 [q]See Luke 1:51 [r][Eph. 5:17]
23 [s]1 Cor. 6:9, 10
26 [t][John 12:20, 21] [u][1 Cor. 12:13] [v][Acts 21:2, 3]

merely external and do not come from their hearts, which are **far from** God; and (2) their teachings are not from God but reflect **the tradition of men**.

7:9 rejecting the commandment of God. Not only are human traditions ineffective for cleansing the heart, they actually lead to disregard for God's Word (see v. 13; 10:5, 19; 12:28, 31).

7:10–13 honor your father and your mother (cf. Ex. 20:12; 21:17; Deut. 5:16). No one questions the importance of this law in the Ten Commandments; disregarding it was punishable with death in ancient Israel. Part of honoring father and mother is to care for them, both financially and personally, in their old age. However, Jewish tradition allowed that funds originally dedicated to the care of parents could be declared **Corban** (Hebrew/Aramaic for legally "dedicated to God"; cf. Lev. 1:2; 2:1; etc.), meaning that the person would no longer be required to do anything **for . . . father or mother**. These funds could now be given to the temple, if so desired. Such human traditions thus allow room for the depravity of the human heart, directly opposing the Law of Moses which so often serves to protect the weak and helpless, in this case, parents in their feeble old age (**making void the word of God**). The "Corban" tradition is an example (along with **many such things you do**) of disregarding and rejecting the more important aspects of the Mosaic law.

7:15 can defile him. The problem of the defiled human heart is much deeper than one might assume (see Isa. 29:13–16; Jer. 17:9–10) and significantly more serious than mere ceremonial impurity (see Mark 7:19b). The core problem of defilement is what resides in the heart (**things that come out**), not things **going into** a person. Throughout Scripture, the heart refers to the center of one's being, including the mind, emotions, and will.

7:17–18 Alone with his disciples, Jesus gives further instruction on the importance of a pure heart (cf. note on v. 15). The disciples lack **understanding** (cf. 4:10–13, 40; 6:52; 8:14–21, 32–33), but they remain with Jesus, and they are gradually learning.

7:19 Mark notes that Jesus' teaching, in essence, **declared all foods clean**. The Mosaic ceremonial laws distinguished between "clean" and "unclean" foods (see Lev. 11:1–47). Their purpose was to instill an awareness of God's holiness and of the reality of sin as a barrier to fellowship with God. But once defilement of the heart is thoroughly removed and full fellowship with God becomes a reality (through the atoning death of Jesus; see Mark 10:45; Rom. 14:14; Heb. 8:6–13; 9:10, 14), the ceremonial laws have fulfilled their purpose and are no longer required—though as seen in Acts 10–11, it took several years for the disciples to understand this. (On Christian freedom from ceremonial laws, see notes on Acts 15:1; 15:19–21; Gal. 2:11–12; 4:10; 5:1; on food laws in particular, see 1 Tim. 4:3–5.)

7:20–23 What comes out of a person repeats Jesus' earlier teaching (v. 15). Here he mentions specific sinful thoughts and actions, and characteristics of a defiled heart, summarizing his teaching in v. 23: **all these evil things come from within**.

7:24–30 *Opening to Gentiles.* Jesus went first to the people of Israel. However, these verses foreshadow the future ministry of the disciples to the Gentiles.

7:24 Tyre and Sidon. Jesus travels to a Hellenistic Gentile region where he is already known (esp. among its resettled Jewish residents; cf. 3:8). Jesus is called first to bring the news of God's kingdom to the people of Israel. However, he foresees a later mission to the Gentiles through his disciples (7:27; 13:10; 14:9). Excavations have unearthed many remarkable finds at both Tyre and Sidon. Tyre evidences both Roman and Byzantine structures, including (largely from after Jesus' time) a hippodrome, an immense bathhouse, a forum, a theater, and tombs. Tyre was originally an offshore island, later connected to the mainland during a siege in the days of Alexander the Great (4th century B.C.).

7:26 Elijah had also aided a non-Jewish woman in this area (1 Kings 17:8, 17–24). Mark emphasizes that this woman was a **Gentile** and in great need.

And she begged him to cast the demon out of her daughter. 27 And he said to her, "Let
the children be [w]fed first, for it is not right to take the children's bread and [x]throw it to
the dogs." 28 But she answered him, "Yes, Lord; yet even the dogs under the table eat the
children's [y]crumbs." 29 And he said to her, "For this statement you may [z]go your way; the
demon has left your daughter." 30 And she went home and found the child lying in bed
and the demon gone.

Jesus Heals a Deaf Man

31 [a]Then he returned from the region of Tyre and went through Sidon to [b]the Sea of
Galilee, in the region of the [c]Decapolis. 32 And they brought to him [d]a man who was deaf
and [d]had a speech impediment, and they begged him to [e]lay his hand on him. 33 And [f]tak-
ing him aside from the crowd privately, he put his fingers into his ears, and [f]after spitting
touched his tongue. 34 And [g]looking up to heaven, [h]he sighed and said to him, "Ephphatha,"
that is, "Be opened." 35 [d]And his ears were opened, his tongue was released, and he spoke
plainly. 36 And [i]Jesus[1] charged them to tell no one. But [j]the more he charged them, the more
zealously they proclaimed it. 37 And they were [k]astonished beyond measure, saying, "He
has done all things well. He even makes the deaf hear and the mute speak."

Jesus Feeds the Four Thousand

8 [l]In those days, when again a great crowd had gathered, and they had nothing to eat,
he called his disciples to him and said to them, 2 [m]"I have compassion on the crowd,
because they have been with me now three days and have nothing to eat. 3 And if I send
them away hungry to their homes, they will faint on the way. And some of them have come
from far away." 4 And his disciples answered him, "How can one feed these people with

[1] Greek *he*

27 [w][Acts 3:26; Rom. 1:16] [x]Matt. 7:6
28 [y][Luke 16:21]
29 [z]John 4:50
31 [a]For ver. 31-37, [Matt. 15:29-31] [b]Matt. 4:18; John 6:1 [c]ch. 5:20; Matt. 4:25
32 [d]Isa. 35:5, 6 [e]See ch. 5:23
33 [f]ch. 8:23
34 [g]See ch. 6:41 [h]ch. 8:12; [John 11:33]
35 [d][See ver. 32 above]
36 [i]ch. 9:9; See Matt. 8:4 [j]ch. 1:45; Matt. 9:31
37 [k]ch. 10:26

Chapter 8

1 [l]For ver. 1-10, see Matt. 15:32-39; [ch. 6:32-44]
2 [m][Matt. 9:36]

Jesus' Ministry beyond Israel
Almost all of Jesus' ministry took place within the traditional borders of Israel in areas dominated by Jews. Yet Jesus also traveled to the region of Tyre and Sidon, where he healed a Gentile woman's daughter, and to the region of Decapolis, where he healed many people. It was also at the extreme northern border of Israel at Caesarea Philippi that Peter made his confession that "You are the Christ, the son of the living God," and Jesus declared, "on this rock I will build my church."

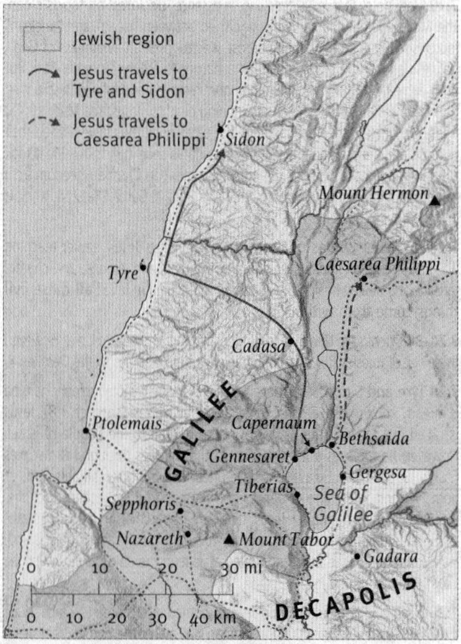

Syrophoenician indicates that she was a native of Phoenicia, which included Tyre and Sidon (cf. "Canaanite" in Matt. 15:22).

7:27 Jesus' noncommittal response is surprising and may seem offensive. He gives three comparisons: **bread**/his message; **children**/the Jewish people; and **dogs**/Gentiles. **First** holds out the hope, however, that Gentiles will also become the recipients of God's grace. Taking into account vv. 29–30, it is reasonable to conclude that Jesus spoke as he did merely to test the woman's faith.

7:28–30 yet even the dogs. The woman's response to Jesus' surprising statement (v. 27) is both humble and persistent. Perhaps she understands and humbly accepts that God called Israel first for a particular purpose (cf. Ex. 4:22). **For this statement**. Jesus honors the woman's simple faith, so that upon returning home, she finds that **the demon** is **gone** out of her **daughter**.

7:31–8:26 *Additional Miracles in Decapolis and Bethsaida.* As Jesus continues his ministry of teaching and healing, the disciples' hearts remain hard (8:17–21). They fail to understand who Jesus really is.

7:31 Jesus preached far and wide to Galilean and Judean Jews, as well as to the remnant people of Israel who by this time had resettled in the Hellenistic regions of **Tyre**, **Sidon**, and the **Decapolis**.

7:33 Jesus takes the deaf man (see Isa. 35:5–6) **aside** so as not to make a spectacle of his healing (see Mark 5:37, 40). Unlike his other healings, Jesus uses physical means to heal the man. The healing not only demonstrates Jesus' power; it also allows him to confront his disciples by word and deed with the problem of spiritual deafness and blindness (see 7:32–8:26; esp. 8:17–18, 21).

7:34 Jesus **sighed** over the hard-heartedness (cf. 8:12, 17; 9:19) and physical weaknesses that had arisen on account of mankind's fall (Genesis 3).

7:36 to tell no one. Jesus' injunction to silence (cf. 1:45; 5:20, 34; 8:26) is addressed to all who witnessed the healing, on account of the fact that he has now become more widely known in the Decapolis (cf. 5:19). However, the healed man and the witnesses disregard Jesus' prohibition and go out and proclaim the miracle.

7:37 The people are **astonished** in the sense that they wonder whether Jesus is the Messiah (see Isa. 35:5–6). They are not expecting a suffering Messiah but rather a political liberator along the lines of the earlier Maccabean uprising (166–160 B.C.).

8:1–10 The feeding of the 4,000 shows that Jesus is the living bread for Gentiles, since it likely occurred in Gentile territory.

bread here in this desolate place?" 5 And he asked them, "How many loaves do you have?"
They said, [n]"Seven." 6 And he directed the crowd to sit down on the ground. And he took
the seven loaves, and [o]having given thanks, he broke them and gave them to his disciples to
set before the people; and they set them before the crowd. 7 And they had a few small fish.
And [p]having blessed them, he said that these also should be set before them. 8 And [q]they
ate and were satisfied. And they took up the broken pieces left over, [n]seven baskets full.
9 And there were about four thousand people. And he sent them away. 10 And immediately
he got into [r]the boat with his disciples and went to the district of [s]Dalmanutha.[1]

The Pharisees Demand a Sign

11 [t]The Pharisees came and began to argue with him, [u]seeking from him [v]a sign from
heaven [w]to test him. 12 And [x]he sighed deeply [y]in his spirit and said, "Why does this generation seek a sign? Truly, I say to you, no sign will be given to this generation." 13 And [z]he
left them, got into the boat again, and went to the other side.

The Leaven of the Pharisees and Herod

14 Now they had forgotten to bring bread, and they had only one loaf with them in the
boat. 15 And he cautioned them, saying, "Watch out; [a]beware of [b]the leaven of the Pharisees
and the leaven of [c]Herod."[2] 16 And they began discussing with one another the fact that
they had no bread. 17 And [d]Jesus, aware of this, said to them, "Why are you discussing the
fact that you have no bread? [e]Do you not yet perceive [f]or understand? [f]Are your hearts
hardened? 18 [g]Having eyes do you not see, and having ears do you not hear? And do you
not remember? 19 When I broke [h]the five loaves for the five thousand, how many baskets
full of broken pieces did you take up?" They said to him, "Twelve." 20 "And [i]the seven for
the four thousand, how many baskets full of broken pieces did you take up?" And they
said to him, "Seven." 21 And he said to them, "Do you not yet understand?"

Jesus Heals a Blind Man at Bethsaida

22 And they came [j]to Bethsaida. And some people brought to him a blind man and begged
him to touch him. 23 And [k]he took the blind man by the hand and led him out of the village,

[1] Some manuscripts *Magadan*, or *Magdala* [2] Some manuscripts *the Herodians*

5 [n]Matt. 16:10
6 [o]ch. 14:23; Matt. 26:27; Luke 22:17, 19; John 6:11, 23; Acts 27:35; Rom. 14:6; 1 Cor. 10:30; 11:24; 14:16; 1 Tim. 4:3, 4
7 [p]See Matt. 14:19
8 [q][2 Kgs. 4:42-44] [n][See ver. 5 above]
10 [r]See ch. 3:9 [s][Matt. 15:39]
11 [t]For ver. 11-21, see Matt. 16:1-12 [u]1 Cor. 1:22; See Matt. 12:38 [v]Luke 11:16; 21:11 [w]John 8:6
12 [x]ch. 7:34 [y]John 11:33
13 [z]Matt. 4:13; 21:17
15 [a]Luke 12:1 [b]1 Cor. 5:6-8; Gal. 5:9 [c][ch. 3:6; 12:13]
17 [d]Matt. 26:10 [e]ch. 7:18 [f]ch. 6:52
18 [g]Jer. 5:21; Ezek. 12:2; [Isa. 42:18, 19; 43:8; Matt. 13:13]
19 [h]ch. 6:41, 44
20 [i]ver. 6, 9
22 [j]See ch. 6:45
23 [k]ch. 7:33

8:2 three days. At times, Jesus' teaching ministries lasted several days.

8:4 The disciples probably remember Jesus' previous miracle of feeding the 5,000 (see 6:31–44; 8:19–20; note also "again," v. 1). According to v. 17 and vv. 32–33, however, they are constantly captive to their own very limited frame of reference (cf. Ps. 81:10–13).

8:5 Seven. See note on Matt. 15:34. The determination of how little food is available makes the contrast of the multiplication all the greater.

8:6 Giving **thanks**, breaking bread, and distributing it are common elements in a Jewish meal. The disciples are personally involved in passing on that which Jesus multiplies.

8:8 The great surplus (cf. 6:43; John 6:12) underscores the fact that Jesus is capable of providing beyond satisfaction.

8:10 Jesus crosses the Sea of Galilee, traveling westward to **Dalmanutha** (Magdala).

8:11 The Pharisees demand to be given a **sign from heaven**—not just a miracle, but a conclusive sign directly from God, to confirm that the promise had been fulfilled. Their demand for a sign, however, excludes the one essential demand that Jesus required: a fundamental change of heart. See note on Matt. 12:39.

8:12 Jesus **sighed** on account of the attitude underlying and driving the demand of v. 11. (For other examples of Jesus expressing emotions, see 1:41; 3:5; 7:34.) **this generation**. Cf. Deut. 32:5, 20; Ps. 95:10; Mark 9:19. **no sign**. See note on Matt. 12:39. An open heart, together with Jesus' demonstrations of divine authority, should be more than enough for seeing that he truly is the Messiah.

8:13 Once again Jesus crosses the Sea of Galilee (cf. v. 10), this time traveling east.

8:14–15 The mention of **bread** introduces a discussion between Jesus and his disciples (vv. 15–21). **Leaven** (see note on 1 Cor. 5:6–7) is a figurative description of the self-centered self-reliance of both the **Pharisees** and **Herod** Antipas (see Luke 12:1; 1 Cor. 5:6–8; Gal. 5:9). Jesus warns his disciples against such an attitude.

8:16 had no bread. The disciples take the term "leaven" (v. 15) literally, showing their ongoing inability to grasp spiritual truths (cf. vv. 17–21).

8:17–18 The disciples' **hearts** are still partially closed to the depth of Jesus' teaching and person, for he asks if they do **not yet perceive or understand**. Although Jesus does not rebuke them as hard-hearted "hypocrites" like the Pharisees and scribes (7:6), they still lack full understanding of who Jesus is. While the Pharisees reject Jesus' teaching outright, the disciples are slow to appreciate it. The figurative reference to **eyes** and **ears** echoes the healings of the deaf man (7:31–35) and the blind man (8:22–26). Jesus wants to open the "ears" and "eyes" of the disciples' hearts.

8:21 When Jesus had twice multiplied food, the disciples were supposed to **understand** the significance of these miracles: he who stands before them is none other than the eternal creator and giver of life (cf. Col. 1:15–20).

8:22 Jesus remains on the east side of the Sea of Galilee (see note on v. 13); he travels to **Bethsaida** (see note on Luke 9:10) and eventually to Caesarea Philippi (Mark 8:27). The details of the two-stage healing of the **blind man** (vv. 22–26) are unique to Mark.

8:23–25 Jesus **led** the blind man **out of the village**, perhaps to be away from elements of unbelief and hostility (cf. 5:40; 6:6). **Do you see anything**? In the context of 7:31–8:26, and especially in light of Jesus' focus on the disciples' lack of understanding (8:17–21), the man's answer may be analogous to their limited apprehension of Jesus. They see him vaguely (see v. 29), just as the blind man now sees people merely **like trees, walking**. Jesus' healing of the man in two stages may have been intended to emphasize this fact. This interpretation is supported by the fact that vv. 22–26 contain no less than nine terms related to "seeing." The disciples will soon understand that Jesus is the Messiah (vv. 27–30), but they will not yet fully grasp that he is to be a suffering Messiah (8:31–9:1).

and when [k]he had [l]spit on his eyes and [m]laid his hands on him, he asked him, "Do you
see anything?" **24** And he looked up and said, "I see people, but they look like trees, walking." **25** Then Jesus[1] laid his hands on his eyes again; and he opened his eyes, his sight was
restored, and he saw everything clearly. **26** And he sent him to his home, saying, [n]"Do not
even enter the village."

Peter Confesses Jesus as the Christ

27 [o]And Jesus went on with his disciples to the villages of Caesarea Philippi. And on the
way he asked his disciples, "Who do people say that I am?" **28** And they told him, [p]"John
the Baptist; and others say, [q]Elijah; and others, one of the prophets." **29** And he asked them,
"But who do you say that I am?" Peter answered him, [r]"You are [s]the Christ." **30** [t]And he
strictly charged them to tell no one about him.

Jesus Foretells His Death and Resurrection

31 [u]And he began to teach them that [v]the Son of Man must [w]suffer many things and
[x]be rejected by the elders and the chief priests and the scribes and be killed, and [y]after
three days rise again. **32** And he said this [z]plainly. And Peter took him aside and began
to rebuke him. **33** But turning and seeing his disciples, he rebuked Peter and said, [a]"Get
behind me, Satan! For you [b]are not setting your mind on the things of God, but on the
things of man."

34 And calling the crowd to him with his disciples, he said to them, "If anyone would
come after me, let him [c]deny himself and [d]take up his cross and follow me. **35** For [d]whoever

[1] Greek *he*

23 [k]ch. 7:33 [l]John 9:6 [m]See ch. 5:23
26 [n]ver. 23; [Matt. 8:4]
27 [o]For ver. 27-29, see Matt. 16:13-16; Luke 9:18-20
28 [p]ch. 6:14; Matt. 14:2; Luke 9:7 [q]Luke 9:8; [ch. 9:11; Matt. 17:10; John 1:21]
29 [r]John 11:27 [s]ch. 14:61, 62; See Matt. 1:17
30 [t]Matt. 16:20; Luke 9:21; See Matt. 12:16
31 [u]For ch. 8:31–9:1, see Matt. 16:21-28; Luke 9:22-27 [v]ch. 10:33; [Luke 13:33] [w]ch. 9:30, 31; Matt. 17:12, 22, 23; Luke 24:7 [x]Luke 17:25; 1 Pet. 2:4; [ch. 12:10] [y]ch. 10:34; Matt. 27:63; [Matt. 12:40]; See John 2:19
32 [z]John 16:25
33 [a][Matt. 4:10] [b]Rom. 8:5; Phil. 3:19; Col. 3:2; [Phil. 2:5]
34 [c][2 Tim. 2:12, 13] [d]See Matt. 10:38, 39
35 [d][See ver. 34 above]

8:27–16:8 *Testing Jesus' Authority in Suffering.* Having displayed his messianic authority and power (1:1–8:26), Jesus is now tested as the Messiah of God.

8:27–10:52 *Journey to Jerusalem.* Three predictions of Jesus' death and resurrection are followed by instruction about the cost of discipleship.

8:27–33 *Peter's Confession.* Near the source of the Jordan River, Jesus begins to teach his disciples that the Messiah of God must die and be raised again (v. 31). Each of the major predictions of Jesus' death and resurrection (see chart below) is followed by teaching on discipleship (vv. 32–38; 9:32–50; 10:34–45).

8:27–29a Caesarea Philippi was some 25 miles (40 km) north of the Sea of Galilee, and had been a center of the worship of Baal, then of the Greek god Pan, and then of Caesar (see note on Matt. 16:13). **Who do people say that I am?** Jesus' questions (Mark 8:27, 29) prepare for his teaching. He must clarify that the Messiah of God is to be humbled (v. 31; 10:45) and exalted (8:38) for the sake of his people. This goes against popular expectations. On **John the Baptist** and **Elijah**, see note on 6:14b–15.

8:29b–30 Peter speaks for the Twelve (cf. 1:36; 8:32; 9:5; 10:28; 14:29) and confesses Jesus as **the Christ**, i.e., the divinely anointed leader and Messiah (2 Sam. 7:14–16; Psalm 2; Jer. 23:5–6) who they expect will liberate the Jewish people from the oppressive yoke of Rome (see John 6:15). Peter's confession is God-given (Matt. 16:17) but incomplete (Mark 8:31–33), for the messianic Son of Man is both divine (Ps. 110:1, 5; Dan. 7:13–14; Mark 8:38; 12:35–37) and destined to suffer (Isa. 53:1–12; Mark 8:31; 10:45). This is why Jesus charges his disciples to **tell no one about him**.

8:31 Jesus corrects the disciples' messianic expectation by stressing that the **Son of Man must** (cf. 9:12; 14:21, 41) **be killed** (cf. 9:9, 12, 31; 10:34, 45; 14:21, 41) and **rise again** (cf. Isa. 53:1–12). Christ's death is necessary because the eternal, messianic rule of God begins with atonement for sin, i.e., the sacrifice that will bring about reconciliation between God and man. **and be rejected by the elders and the chief priests and the scribes**. The leaders, who will reject Jesus, belong to factions of the Sanhedrin, the highest Jewish court in Israel (e.g., Mark 10:33; 11:18; 14:1; 15:1). While the opponents seek to kill Jesus (3:6), God's appointed will is that the Messiah atone for sins. To "rise" again must puzzle the disciples. They expect only the general resurrection of all mankind at the end of the age, prior to judgment (Dan. 12:2).

8:33 turning and seeing his disciples, he rebuked Peter. The fact that Jesus looked at all the disciples implies that his rebuke of Peter was intended for all of them. **"Get behind me, Satan!"** It is only Peter's thought, not him personally, that Jesus rejects as satanic. **not . . . on the things of God, but on the things of man**. Peter does not recognize that the messianic ruler of God's eternal kingdom has come to die for his sins (cf. note on v. 31).

8:34–9:1 *Call to Discipleship.* The cost of discipleship includes being able to follow Jesus and to confess him courageously.

8:34 Following the first major prediction of his death and resurrection (v. 31), Jesus instructs in discipleship all those who **would come after me**. The goal of self-denial (cf. 14:30, 31, 72) and taking up one's **cross** is not pathological self-abasement or a martyr complex but being free to **follow** the Messiah (1:18; 2:13). Self-denial means letting go of self-determination (cf. Ps. 49:6–8) and replacing it with obedience to and dependence on the Messiah.

8:35 Jesus' paradoxical statement demands two different senses of the word

The Three Major Passion Predictions in Mark

Three times in Mark 8–10 Jesus predicts his death, the disciples fail to understand or to respond appropriately, and he then teaches them about discipleship.

Announcement of Jesus' Death	Failure on the Part of the Disciples	Jesus Teaches on Discipleship
Jesus will suffer, be rejected, killed, and will rise after three days (8:31)	Peter rebukes Jesus (8:32–33)	Jesus commands them to deny themselves, take up their cross, and follow him (8:33–9:1)
Jesus will be delivered, killed, and will rise after three days (9:30–31)	The disciples do not understand the saying and are afraid to ask him about it (9:32)	Jesus teaches that the first must be last and that those who receive children in his name receive him (9:33–50)
Jesus will be delivered, condemned, mocked, flogged, killed, and will rise after three days (10:33–34)	James and John ask that they may sit next to Jesus in his glory (10:35–37)	Jesus teaches that, to be great, they must become servants; to be first, they must become slaves; and that he came to serve by giving his life as a ransom for many (10:38–45)

would save his life[1] will lose it, but whoever loses his life for my sake [e]and the gospel's
will save it. 36 [f]For what does it profit a man to gain the whole world and forfeit his soul?
37 For [g]what can a man give in return for his soul? 38 For [h]whoever is ashamed of me and
of my words in this [i]adulterous and sinful generation, of him will the Son of Man also be
ashamed [j]when he comes in the glory of his Father with [k]the holy angels."

9 And he said to them, "Truly, I say to you, there are some standing here who will not
[l]taste death [m]until they see the kingdom of God after it has come [n]with power."

The Transfiguration

2 [o]And after six days Jesus took with him [p]Peter and James and John, and led them
up a high mountain by themselves. And he was [q]transfigured before them, 3 and [r]his
clothes became radiant, intensely white, as no one[2] on earth could bleach them. 4 And
there appeared to them Elijah with Moses, and they were talking with Jesus. 5 And Peter
said to Jesus, [s]"Rabbi,[3] it is good that we are here. Let us make three [t]tents, one for you
and one for Moses and one for Elijah." 6 For [u]he did not know what to say, for they were
terrified. 7 And [v]a cloud overshadowed them, and [v]a voice came out of the cloud, [w]"This
is my beloved Son;[4] [x]listen to him." 8 And suddenly, looking around, they no longer saw
anyone with them but Jesus only.

9 [y]And as they were coming down the mountain, [z]he charged them to tell no one
what they had seen, [a]until the Son of Man had risen from the dead. 10 [b]So they kept
the matter to themselves, [c]questioning what this rising from the dead might mean.
11 And they asked him, "Why do the scribes say [d]that first Elijah must come?" 12 And
he said to them, "Elijah does come first [e]to restore all things. And [f]how is it written
of the Son of Man that he should [g]suffer many things and [h]be treated with contempt?
13 But I tell you that Elijah has come, and [i]they did to him whatever they pleased, as it
is written of him."

[1] The same Greek word can mean either *soul* or *life*, depending on the context; twice in this verse and once in verse 36 and once in verse 37
[2] Greek *launderer (gnapheus)* [3] *Rabbi* means *my teacher*, or *my master* [4] Or *my Son, my (*or *the) Beloved*

35 [e]ch. 10:29; [1 Cor. 9:23; 2 Tim. 1:8; Philem. 13]
36 [f][Luke 12:20]
37 [g][Ps. 49:7, 8]
38 [h]Rom. 1:16; 2 Tim. 1:8, 12, 16; Heb. 11:16; 1 John 2:28; [Matt. 10:33] [i]Isa. 57:3; Matt. 12:39; James 4:4 [j]Dan. 7:10, 13; Zech. 14:5; Matt. 24:30; 25:31; 26:64; Acts 1:11; 1 Thess. 1:10; 4:16; Jude 14; Rev. 1:7; [Deut. 33:2] [k]Acts 10:22; Rev. 14:10; [Matt. 13:41; 16:27]

Chapter 9

1 [l]John 8:52; Heb. 2:9 [m][ch. 13:30; Matt. 10:23; 23:36; 24:34] [n]ch. 13:26; 14:62; [Matt. 25:31]
2 [o]For ver. 2-8, see Matt. 17:1-8; Luke 9:28-36 [p]ch. 5:37; 14:33 [q][2 Cor. 3:18 (Gk.)]
3 [r]Dan. 7:9; [Ps. 104:2; Matt. 28:3]
5 [s]See John 1:38 [t][Neh. 8:15]
6 [u][ch. 14:40; Luke 9:33]
7 [v]2 Pet. 1:17; [Ex. 24:15, 16] [w]ch. 12:6; See Matt. 3:17 [x]Acts 3:22
9 [y]For ver. 9-13, see Matt. 17:9-13 [z]ch. 5:43; See Matt. 8:4 [a]ch. 8:31
10 [b]Luke 9:36 [c][John 16:17]
11 [d]See Matt. 11:14
12 [e]Mal. 4:6; Luke 1:16, 17; [Acts 1:6; 3:21] [f]Ps. 22:6, 7; Isa. 53:2, 3; Dan. 9:26; Zech. 13:7; [Phil. 2:7]; See Matt. 26:24 [g]See ch. 8:31 [h]Luke 23:11; Acts 4:11
13 [i]ch. 6:17, 27

"life": whoever lives a self-centered life focused on this present world (i.e., **would save his life**) will not find eternal life with God (**will lose it**); whoever gives up his self-centered life of rebellion against God (**loses his life**) for the **sake** of Christ and the gospel will find everlasting communion with God (**will save it**; see v. 38).

8:38 of him will the Son of Man also be ashamed. Jesus claims divine authority in final judgment.

9:1 Some standing here who will not taste death probably points toward the three disciples who will accompany Jesus to the Mount of Transfiguration. To **see** the coming of **the kingdom of God . . . with power** refers to an anticipation of this future event in the transfiguration (see 2 Pet. 1:16–18), which prefigures the overwhelming glory of Christ in his return (Dan. 7:13–27; Matt. 16:28; Mark 8:38; 13:26–27). For various interpretations of Jesus' statement, see note on Matt. 16:28. Letting go of self-centered self-determination (Mark 8:34) leads to glimpses of future glory (9:1–8), just as the death (8:31) and glory (8:38) of the Messiah are to be seen together.

9:2–29 *Transfiguration and Healing.* Jesus' transfiguration affords a glimpse into his divine nature. It is followed by continued struggle against evil, as Jesus heals a boy who has an unclean spirit.

9:2 high mountain. Probably Mount Hermon (see note on Matt. 17:1).

9:3 The transfiguration offers a glimpse into the **radiant** and divine glory of Jesus (Heb. 1:3; see also note on Luke 9:29), who is God's Son and the judge of all. On **white** as heavenly brightness, cf. Dan. 7:9; Luke 24:4; Acts 1:10; Rev. 1:14; 20:11.

9:4 Jesus is greater than both **Moses** (who represents the Law; see Ex. 24:1, 9) and **Elijah** (who represents the Prophets; see 1 Kings 19:8); Jesus thus fulfills both the Law and the Prophets (cf. Matt. 5:17). Whereas Moses' radiance reflects God's glory (Ex. 34:33–35), Jesus radiates light "from the inside." Moses and Elijah are not reincarnations but rather come from being in the presence of God. Luke adds the detail that they discuss Jesus' imminent "departure" (Luke 9:31).

9:5 Once more, Peter and his companions do not grasp the greatness of the Messiah (cf. 4:40; 6:52; 7:18; 8:17–21, 32–33; 9:32; 14:26–42). Peter sees Jesus merely as someone similar to **Moses** and **Elijah** and wishes to raise **tents** (as earthly habitations for heavenly beings) for them, perhaps because he wants to prolong the experience. Peter does not know what he is saying, for he is speaking out of fear (9:6).

9:7 The **voice . . . out of the cloud** echoes Ex. 24:15–16. **This is my beloved Son; listen to him** is uttered for the benefit (cf. Mark 9:2, 4, 7, 12–13) of the three disciples (cf. 4:34; 6:31–44; 9:28; 13:3; 2 Pet. 1:16–18). Jesus, with all his claims, is endorsed by the Father (see Ps. 2:7; Isa. 42:1; Mark 1:11). "Listen to him" echoes Deut. 18:15, 18, where Moses is shown to be a leader-prophet. Anyone who does not listen to the Messiah of God rejects God, who sent him. The three disciples see the glory of Jesus; they see his greatness over Moses and Elijah; and they hear the divine authentication of Jesus as the eternal Son.

9:9 tell no one (cf. note on 7:36). Jesus commands silence in order to avoid a popular movement that would make him into a political "freedom fighter" (John 6:15) and block his path to suffering and dying to save his people.

9:10 The disciples do not understand what **rising from the dead** means, as they expect simply the resurrection of all mankind at the end of this age, after the coming of Elijah (v. 12; see Dan. 12:2).

9:12 John the Baptist restored **all things** by preparing the way (Mal. 3:1) for the coming of the ultimate Restorer (cf. Luke 1:17; Acts 3:21). On John the Baptist as Elijah, see also notes on Mal. 4:4–6 and Matt. 11:14. Both John the Baptist and Jesus experience suffering and **contempt** in the process of restoration (cf. Isa. 53:3). According to Jesus, Isa. 53:1–12 and Mal. 4:4–6 have to be understood together.

9:13 Referring to John the Baptist, Jesus states that **Elijah has come**; both were preachers of repentance, and John came in Elijah's "spirit and . . .

Jesus Heals a Boy with an Unclean Spirit

14 [j]And when they came to the disciples, they saw a great crowd around them, and scribes
arguing with them. 15 And immediately all the crowd, when they saw him, [k]were greatly
amazed and ran up to him and greeted him. 16 And he asked them, "What are you arguing
about with them?" 17 And someone from the crowd answered him, "Teacher, I brought
my son to you, for he has [l]a spirit that makes him mute. 18 And whenever it seizes him, it
throws him down, and he foams and grinds his teeth and becomes rigid. So I asked your
disciples to cast it out, and [m]they were not able." 19 And he answered them, "O [n]faithless
generation, [n]how long am I to be with you? How long am I to bear with you? Bring him
to me." 20 And they brought the boy to him. And when the spirit saw him, immediately
it [o]convulsed the boy, and he fell on the ground and rolled about, foaming at the mouth.
21 And Jesus asked his father, "How long has this been happening to him?" And he said,
"From childhood. 22 And it has often cast him into fire and into water, to destroy him. But
[p]if you can do anything, have compassion on us and help us." 23 And Jesus said to him,
[p]"'If you can'! [q]All things are possible for one who believes." 24 Immediately the father of
the child cried out[1] and said, "I believe; [r]help my unbelief!" 25 And when Jesus saw that
[s]a crowd came running together, he rebuked the unclean spirit, saying to it, [t]"You mute
and deaf spirit, I command you, come out of him and never enter him again." 26 And after
crying out and [o]convulsing him terribly, it came out, and the boy was like a corpse, so that
most of them said, "He is dead." 27 But Jesus [u]took him by the hand and lifted him up,
and he arose. 28 And when he had [v]entered the house, his disciples asked him privately,
"Why could we not cast it out?" 29 And he said to them, "This kind cannot be driven out
by anything but prayer."[2]

Jesus Again Foretells Death, Resurrection

30 [w]They went on from there and passed through Galilee. And he did not want anyone
to know, 31 for he was teaching his disciples, saying to them, "The Son of Man is going to
be delivered into the hands of men, and they will kill him. And when he is killed, [x]after
three days he will rise." 32 [y]But they did not understand the saying, and were afraid to
ask him.

Who Is the Greatest?

33 And [z]they came to Capernaum. And when he was in the house [a]he asked them, "What
were you discussing on the way?" 34 But they kept silent, for on the way [b]they had argued

14 [j]For ver. 14-28, see Matt. 17:14-19; Luke 9:37-42
15 [k][ch. 10:32]
17 [l]ver. 25; Luke 11:14
18 [m][ch. 6:7; Matt. 10:1; Luke 10:17]
19 [n][John 14:9; 20:27]
20 [o]ch. 1:26
22 [p][ch. 1:40; Matt. 9:28]
23 [p][See ver. 22 above] [q][ch. 6:5, 6; Matt. 17:20]
24 [r][Luke 17:5]
25 [s]ver. 15 [t]ver. 17
26 [o][See ver. 20 above]
27 [u]See ch. 1:31
28 [v]ch. 7:17
30 [w]For ver. 30-32, see Matt. 17:22, 23; Luke 9:43-45; [ch. 8:31; 10:32-34]
31 [x]See ch. 8:31
32 [y]ch. 6:52; Luke 2:50; 18:34; 24:25; John 10:6; 12:16; 16:17-19; [ver. 10]
33 [z]Matt. 17:24 [a]For ver. 33-37, see Matt. 18:1-5; Luke 9:46-48; [ch. 10:35-45]
34 [b]Luke 22:24; [ver. 50]

[1] Some manuscripts add *with tears* [2] Some manuscripts add *and fasting*

power" (cf. Luke 1:17). Jesus thus contradicted popular expectation (Mark 9:11), which hoped for the literal return of Elijah.

9:18 Both the "scribes" (v. 14) and the father of the possessed son expect to find Jesus, and they transfer this expectation to the **disciples**, who are learning to represent Jesus (see 6:7–13). The evil "spirit" (9:17) seeks to "destroy" the boy (vv. 20, 22), and he cries out (v. 26). Due to their lack of prayer, the disciples are **not able** to heal him (cf. vv. 28–29).

9:19 The fundamental problem of the people (the opponents, the spiritually oppressed, and even the disciples) is that they are **faithless** (cf. 6:6; 9:23). Jesus' burdened expression echoes that of the prophets (e.g., Deut. 32:5, 20; Isa. 6:11; Jer. 5:21–22; cf. note on Mark 8:12).

9:22b–24 The father merely seeks help through Jesus' miraculous powers: **if you can do anything**. Jesus corrects the father's statement by calling him to put his trust in God. **I believe; help my unbelief!** The father immediately confesses that he has some faith but also acknowledges his spiritual weakness and appeals to Jesus to create in him a heart that believes more firmly.

9:28–29 "Why could we not cast it out?" Besides lacking understanding (8:17–18, 21; 9:5), the disciples lack the ability to fully carry out their commission from Jesus (cf. 6:7, 13; 9:18). Their failure is an occasion for encouragement to more **prayer** (cf. 4:10; 7:17; 10:10), implying that more time and effort in prayer (and therefore in closer fellowship with God) leads to growth in faith.

9:30–50 *Instruction on Discipleship: Putting Others First.* The second prediction of Jesus' death and resurrection is followed by the second instruction in discipleship, which focuses on childlike trust and an attitude of service that places others first.

9:30–31 he did not want anyone to know. Jesus seeks privacy in order to continue **teaching his disciples** about his impending suffering in Jerusalem. While the disciples still do not understand, they will later remember the wordplay, **Son of Man . . . hands of men** (see 14:41; cf. 2 Sam. 24:14). By the plan of God the Father, Jesus would be intentionally "delivered into the hands" of Jewish leaders (Mark 8:31) and Gentiles. The paradox is profound: the murderous intent of Jesus' opponents succeeds, because God the Father hands him over to achieve the atonement planned through his death (10:45; cf. Isa. 53:6, 11–12; Acts 2:23; 4:27–28).

9:32 The disciples **understand** neither the necessity of the Messiah's death (they still expect a political liberator) nor the idea of the resurrection of an individual (they expect the resurrection of mankind at the last judgment; cf. Dan. 12:2; see notes on Mark 9:9; 9:10). Yet they understand enough of what Jesus is saying that they do not want to know more, so they are **afraid to ask him**. Perhaps they remember that Peter's earlier attempt to express disapproval of Jesus' predictions of suffering led to a harsh rebuke (8:33).

9:33 in the house. See note on 2:1. As is so often the case, Jesus instructs the disciples in the privacy of the home (see 4:10, 34; 7:17; 9:28; 10:10). Jesus' question—**What were you discussing**—does not display his ignorance but rather triggers the following lesson on discipleship (9:33–37; cf. 8:27, 29, 31, 34–38). They "kept silent" (9:34) because they were ashamed.

9:34 who was the greatest. In conjunction with their messianic expectation of a political liberator, the disciples dream of status, honor, and power, along the lines of the Maccabean revolt (166–160 B.C.; cf. 8:34–38).

with one another about who was the greatest. **35** And he sat down and called the twelve.
And he said to them, [c]"If anyone would be first, he must be last of all and servant of all."
36 And he took a child and put him in the midst of them, and [d]taking him in his arms, he
said to them, **37** [e]"Whoever receives one such child in my name receives me, and [e]whoever
receives me, receives not me but him who sent me."

Anyone Not Against Us Is for Us

38 [f]John said to him, "Teacher, we saw someone [g]casting out demons in your name,[1]
and [h]we tried to stop him, because he was not following us." **39** But Jesus said, "Do not
stop him, for no one who does a mighty work in my name will be able soon afterward
to speak evil of me. **40** [i]For the one who is not against us is for us. **41** For truly, I say to you,
[j]whoever gives you a cup of water to drink because you belong to Christ will by no means
lose his reward.

Temptations to Sin

42 [k]"Whoever causes one of [l]these little ones who believe in me to sin,[2] [m]it would be better
for him if a great millstone were hung around his neck and he were thrown into the sea.
43 [n]And if your hand causes you to sin, cut it off. It is better for you to enter life crippled
than with two hands to go to [o]hell,[3] to [p]the unquenchable fire.[4] **45** [q]And if your foot causes
you to sin, cut it off. It is better for you to enter life lame than with two feet to be thrown
into [o]hell. **47** [r]And if your eye causes you to sin, tear it out. It is better for you to enter the
kingdom of God with one eye than with two eyes to be thrown into [s]hell, **48** 'where [t]their
worm does not die and the fire is not quenched.' **49** For everyone will be salted with fire.[5]
50 [v]Salt is good, [w]but if the salt has lost its saltiness, how will you make it salty again? [x]Have
salt in yourselves, and [y]be at peace with one another."

35 [c]ch. 10:43, 44; Matt. 20:26, 27; 23:11, 12; Luke 22:26
36 [d]ch. 10:16
37 [e][Matt. 10:40, 42]
38 [f]For ver. 38-40, see Luke 9:49, 50 [g]ch. 16:17; Matt. 7:22; Luke 10:17; Acts 19:13; [Matt. 12:27] [h][Num. 11:28]
40 [i][Matt. 12:30; Luke 11:23]
41 [j]See Matt. 10:42
42 [k]Matt. 18:6; Luke 17:2; [1 Cor. 8:12] [l][Zech. 13:7] [m][ch. 14:21]
43 [n]Matt. 5:30; 18:8 [o]See Matt. 5:22, 29 [p]ver. 48; Matt. 3:12; See Matt. 25:41
45 [q]Matt. 18:8 [o][See ver. 43 above]
47 [r]Matt. 5:29; 18:9 [s]See Matt. 5:22, 29
48 [t]Isa. 66:24
50 [v]Luke 14:34 [w]Matt. 5:13 [x]Ezek. 43:24; Col. 4:6; [Eph. 4:29] [y]Rom. 12:18; 2 Cor. 13:11; 1 Thess. 5:13; [ver. 34]; See Rom. 14:19

[1] Some manuscripts add *who does not follow us* [2] Greek *to stumble*; also verses 43, 45, 47 [3] Greek *Gehenna*; also verse 47 [4] Some manuscripts add verses 44 and 46 (which are identical with verse 48) [5] Some manuscripts add *and every sacrifice will be salted with salt*

9:35 he sat down. Teachers often sat in order to teach. Just as the Messiah of God leads by suffering, each disciple is to lead (**be first**) by becoming a **servant of all**. The suffering of Jesus not only marks the beginning of the messianic rule of God but characterizes patterns of conduct (such as humility, faith, and love) that are required in the kingdom (Phil. 2:1–11).

9:36–37 taking him in his arms. The attitude of heart Jesus is teaching does not even overlook a lowly **child** (at times marginalized in ancient societies) but **receives,** and thereby cares for, such a little one in Christ's **name**. In contrast to the status-seeking of the disciples (v. 34), Jesus is showing them they should willingly take on lowly, often unnoticed tasks and care for those who have little status in the world. Anyone who does this, Jesus says, **receives me** and in so doing also receives the Father (**him who sent me**). (**Receives not me** should be understood as an idiom meaning "receives not only me"; see note on Luke 9:48.) Humbly caring for people of lowly status out of obedience to Christ ("in my name") will be rewarded by rich personal fellowship with both the Son and the Father (see note on Matt. 25:40).

9:40 the one who is not against us is for us. Paul makes a similar argument in Phil. 1:17–18. The disciples are to focus on their task and leave the rest up to God, not being quick to criticize others who also follow Christ but who do not belong to their group. (Such generous acceptance, however, does not apply to those who do not follow Christ at all; see Matt. 12:30.)

9:41 will by no means lose his reward. God notices the smallest of deeds, and the giving of **water** to those who proclaim the gospel will be rewarded by God himself.

9:42 Jesus has emphasized that receiving lowly persons in Christ's name means receiving him (v. 37). Now he warns against causing such people **who believe in me to sin**, that is, to lead them to disbelief or to transgression of God's moral laws. Any who do this will receive severe punishment from God (**thrown into the sea**). This warning applies to anyone who would seek to destroy the faith of a child or a new Christian.

9:43–48 Jesus uses hyperbole (intentional overstatement) to show the seriousness of **sin** and the fact that nothing, even things of greatest importance to humans such as a **hand**, **foot**, or **eye**, can be more important than God. "Hand," "foot," and "eye" probably also serve as metonymies (where one thing stands for something related to it) for sins that can be committed with these body parts. (E.g., the "hand" may represent theft or murder done by the hand; the "foot" may represent going somewhere to undertake a sinful act; the "eye" may represent coveting, lust, or adultery, as in Matt. 5:27–30.) Of course, Jesus does not mean that people should literally cut off those body parts, for the literal removal of them cannot remove the root of sin in the heart (see Mark 7:20–23; 9:45). Jesus' words serve as a sober warning concerning the severity of sin, which can lead to **hell** (Gk. *gehenna*; see Isa. 66:24) and **fire** that **is not quenched** (Mark 8:35–37; 9:47–48).

9:49 For everyone will be salted with fire is a puzzling statement that occurs only in Mark, and many interpretations have been proposed: (1) Against the background of Lev. 2:13, "with all your offerings you shall offer salt" (see also Ezek. 43:24), some think Jesus means that believers themselves are now what is being offered to God (cf. Rom. 12:1), and the "salt" that is in them is the purifying "fire" of God's Holy Spirit. The cleansing and purifying properties of salt support this idea, but this is surely an obscure way to refer to the Holy Spirit, and the connection to the larger context of Mark 9:43–48 is unclear. (2) A second interpretation also views believers as a sacrifice to God against that same OT background but understands the salt to represent purification by the "fire" of suffering and hardship, which is related to the costliness of discipleship implied in the willingness to give up even a hand or an eye (vv. 43–48). In other words, "Be willing to give up anything (vv. 43–48), and also to suffer for Christ's sake, for something costly and painful will come into everyone's life (v. 49)." But the "salt" and the "fire" also make the sacrifice pleasing to God and have a purifying effect on the believer. And as salt does not destroy but preserves food, so the suffering will not destroy the believer. (3) Others think that "everyone" means both believers and unbelievers, and thus the verse teaches that unbelievers will undergo the terrible fire of God's judgment (cf. vv. 47–48), but believers, while not experiencing hell, will still in this life undergo the purifying, cleansing fire of God that comes through hardship and suffering. Interpretations (2) and (3) are similar, (2) being perhaps the best.

9:50 lost its saltiness. See note on Luke 14:34.

Teaching About Divorce

10 [z]And he left there and went [a]to the region of Judea and beyond the Jordan, and
crowds gathered to him again. And again, as was his custom, he taught them.
2 And Pharisees came up and in order [b]to test him asked, [c]"Is it lawful for a man to
divorce his wife?" **3** He answered them, "What did Moses command you?" **4** They said,
[d]"Moses allowed a man to write a certificate of divorce and to send her away." **5** And Jesus
said to them, "Because of your [e]hardness of heart he wrote you this commandment. **6** But
[f]from the beginning of creation, 'God made them [g]male and female.' **7** [h]'Therefore a man
shall leave his father and mother and hold fast to his wife,[1] **8** and [i]the two shall become one
flesh.' So they are no longer two but one flesh. **9** [j]What therefore God has joined together,
let not man separate."
10 And in the house the disciples asked him again about this matter. **11** And he said to
them, [k]"Whoever divorces his wife and marries another commits adultery against her,
12 and [l]if she divorces her husband and marries another, she commits adultery."

Let the Children Come to Me

13 [m]And they were bringing children to him that he might touch them, and the disciples [n]rebuked them. **14** But when Jesus saw it, he was indignant and said to them,
[o]"Let the children come to me; [p]do not hinder them, for to such belongs the kingdom
of God. **15** [q]Truly, I say to you, whoever does not [r]receive the kingdom of God like a
child shall not enter it." **16** And [s]he took them in his arms and blessed them, [t]laying his
hands on them.

[1] Some manuscripts omit *and hold fast to his wife*

Chapter 10

1 [z]For ver. 1-12, see Matt. 19:1-9 [a]Luke 9:51; 17:11; John 10:40; [Matt. 4:25]
2 [b]See John 8:6 [c]Matt. 5:31
4 [d]Deut. 24:1-4
5 [e]ch. 16:14; [ch. 3:5; 6:52; Heb. 3:8]
6 [f]ch. 13:19; 2 Pet. 3:4; [Rom. 1:20] [g]Cited from Gen. 1:27; 5:2
7 [h]Eph. 5:31; Cited from Gen. 2:24
8 [i]1 Cor. 6:16; [Mal. 2:15]
9 [j]1 Cor. 7:10
11 [k]See Matt. 5:32
12 [l]1 Cor. 7:11, 13
13 [m]For ver. 13-16, see Matt. 19:13-15; Luke 18:15-17 [n]ver. 48
14 [o]Matt. 18:3 [p][ch. 9:39]
15 [q][John 3:3, 5] [r][Luke 8:13; James 1:21]
16 [s]ch. 9:36 [t]Rev. 1:17

Jesus' Final Journey to Jerusalem

Though John mentions several trips to Jerusalem by Jesus during his ministry, Matthew, Mark, and Luke recount only one, which occurred as Jesus prepared for his triumphal entry and subsequent death and resurrection. Beginning at Capernaum, Jesus was apparently diverted from the more direct route when Samaritans refused him access (Luke 9:51–56), so he may have crossed the Jordan and traveled through Perea. Jesus then passed through Jericho and proceeded to Jerusalem.

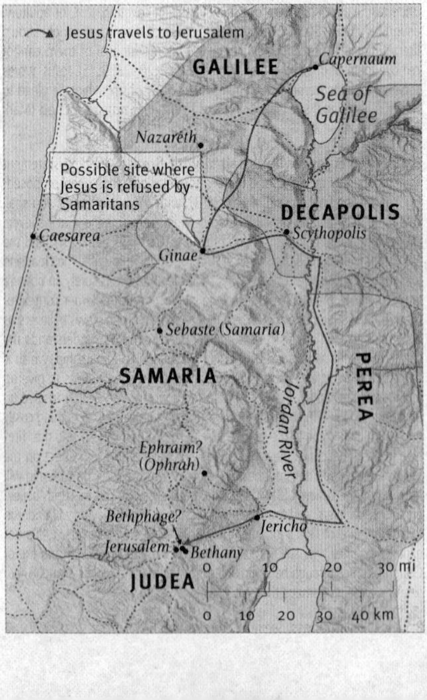

10:1–52 *Instruction on Discipleship: Divorce, Wealth, Humility.* Jesus continues instruction in the context of controversy with his opponents and discussions with his disciples, dealing first with the topic of divorce. His encounter with the rich young man then reveals the barrier that wealth can be to finding entrance to the kingdom of God. The third prediction of Jesus' death and resurrection (vv. 33–34) is followed by instruction on humility, culminating in Jesus' affirmation of his own substitutionary atonement (v. 45). Finally, Jesus heals blind Bartimaeus near the town of Jericho.

10:1 And he left there. Jesus sets out on his final journey from Galilee to Jerusalem (vv. 17, 32, 46; 11:1). He returns to the area north of Jericho where his ministry began. He continues to focus his ministry on teaching, **as was his custom**.

10:2 Once again, Jesus' Pharisaic opponents seek to **test him** (cf. 8:11; 12:15) with a question, this time concerning the legality of **divorce**. They hope to expose him as an opponent of the Law of Moses (cf. note on Matt. 19:3).

10:4 Certificate of divorce refers to the provisions about divorce in Deut. 24:1–4.

10:5–6 Jesus emphasizes that marriage, as a permanent relationship between a man and a woman, goes back to God's purpose at the **beginning of creation** (Gen. 1:27; 2:24; Ex. 20:14). Moses' regulations on divorce (Deut. 24:1–3) were not part of God's original ("beginning") plan but were instituted **because of your hardness of heart** (see note on Matt. 19:8).

10:10–11 in the house. Again, Jesus gives his disciples further instruction in private (cf. 4:10; 9:33). **Whoever divorces his wife and marries another**. Here and in Luke 16:18 Jesus does not include the phrase "except for sexual immorality" as in Matt. 5:32 and 19:9. The most likely reason is that there was no dispute or disagreement among Jews, or in Greek or Roman culture, that **adultery** was a legitimate ground for divorce, and Jesus is not addressing that issue here. The disputes were over the many other causes for divorce, so Jesus gave a blanket statement about all the other causes without explicitly specifying what everyone already agreed was true. For further discussion, see notes on Matt. 5:31–32; 19:6; 19:8; 19:9; 19:10–12.

10:12 And if she divorces her husband is the only time in the Gospels where it is assumed that a woman also has a right to initiate a divorce (a right upheld by Roman law; cf. note on 1 Cor. 7:10–11).

10:13–15 rebuked them. The disciples consider **children** to be an annoying distraction (cf. 9:36–37, 42). Jesus reacts emphatically. To Jesus, **children** are as important as adults, and equally worthy of love (9:36–37; 10:16). **to such**

17[u]For ver. 17-30, see Matt. 19:16-29; Luke 18:18-30; [Luke 10:25-28] [v]See ch. 1:40 [w][Matt. 19:16]; See Matt. 25:34
19[x]Rom. 13:9; Cited from Ex. 20:12-16; Deut. 5:16-20; [Matt. 5:21, 27]
20[y][Phil. 3:6]
21[z]ver. 27; Luke 22:61; John 1:42; [ch. 3:5] [a][John 11:5; 13:23] [b]Luke 12:33; [Luke 16:9; 19:8; Acts 2:45; 4:34, 35; 1 Tim. 6:18, 19] [c]Matt. 6:19, 20
22[d][Ezek. 33:31]
23[e]See ch. 3:5 [f][1 Cor. 1:26]; See Matt. 13:22 [g]See Matt. 12:28
24[h]ver. 32 [i]ch. 2:5 (Gk.); [John 13:33; 21:5] [j]Job 31:24; Ps. 49:6; 52:7; Prov. 11:28; 1 Tim. 6:17 [g][See ver. 23 above]
25[g][See ver. 23 above]
27[k]ver. 23 [l]ch. 14:36; Gen. 18:14; Job 42:2; Jer. 32:17, 27; Luke 1:37
28[m]ch. 1:18, 20; Matt. 4:20, 22
29[n][Luke 14:26] [o]See ch. 8:35
30[p][Matt. 6:33] [q]2 Cor. 12:10; 2 Thess. 1:4; 2 Tim. 3:11, 12; [John 15:20; Acts 14:22] [r]Matt. 12:32; Eph. 1:21; [Luke 20:35]
31[s]See Matt. 19:30
32[t]For ver. 32-34, see Matt. 20:17-19; Luke 18:31-33 [u]Luke 9:51; 19:28 [v]ver. 24

The Rich Young Man

17 [u]And as he was setting out on his journey, a man ran up and [v]knelt before him and
asked him, "Good Teacher, what must I do to [w]inherit eternal life?" 18 And Jesus said to
him, "Why do you call me good? No one is good except God alone. 19 You know the commandments: [x]'Do not murder, Do not commit adultery, Do not steal, Do not bear false
witness, Do not defraud, Honor your father and mother.'" 20 And he said to him, "Teacher,
[y]all these I have kept from my youth." 21 And Jesus, [z]looking at him, [a]loved him, and said
to him, "You lack one thing: go, [b]sell all that you have and give to the poor, and you will
have [c]treasure in heaven; and come, follow me." 22 [d]Disheartened by the saying, he went
away sorrowful, for he had great possessions.

23 And Jesus [e]looked around and said to his disciples, [f]"How difficult it will be for those
who have wealth to enter [g]the kingdom of God!" 24 And the disciples [h]were amazed at his
words. But Jesus said to them again, [i]"Children, [j]how difficult it is[1] to enter [g]the kingdom
of God! 25 It is easier for a camel to go through the eye of a needle than for a rich person to
enter [g]the kingdom of God." 26 And they were exceedingly astonished, and said to him,[2]
"Then who can be saved?" 27 Jesus [k]looked at them and said, [l]"With man it is impossible,
but not with God. For all things are possible with God." 28 Peter began to say to him, "See,
[m]we have left everything and followed you." 29 Jesus said, "Truly, I say to you, [n]there is no
one who has left house or brothers or sisters or mother or father or children or lands, for
my sake and [o]for the gospel, 30 who will not receive a hundredfold [p]now in this time, houses
and brothers and sisters and mothers and children and lands, [q]with persecutions, and in
[r]the age to come eternal life. 31 But [s]many who are first will be last, and the last first."

Jesus Foretells His Death a Third Time

32 [t]And they were on the road, going up to Jerusalem, and [u]Jesus was walking ahead
of them. And [v]they were amazed, and those who followed were afraid. And taking the

[1] Some manuscripts add *for those who trust in riches* [2] Some manuscripts *to one another*

belongs the kingdom of God. Children do not belong automatically to the kingdom but must **come to** Jesus and **receive** him the same as adults.

10:17–27 Contrary to childlike trust (vv. 13–16), the rich young **man** relies on his **possessions** (v. 22) and his self-righteousness (v. 20) to **inherit eternal life**. The accounts of this incident in Matthew (Matt. 19:16–22) and Luke (Luke 18:18–23) are supplementary rather than contradictory.

10:18 Why do you call me good? To ask this question, Jesus assumes the perspective of the rich young man. **No one is** completely **good except God alone**, therefore it is not proper for the young man to address Jesus as "Good Teacher" until he is ready to acknowledge that Jesus is God. On the deity of Christ, see notes on John 5:21; 5:22; 5:23; 20:28.

10:19 You know the commandments. Jesus initially seems to agree with the young man's framework (cf. note on v. 18), which is essentially, "do well, and you will inherit the kingdom." But he is about to show the man how far short he falls of keeping the most important commandment (see note on v. 21). **Do not defraud** probably combines the eighth (not stealing) and ninth (not bearing false witness) commandments.

10:20 all these I have kept. The rich man answers Jesus' challenge (v. 19) in the affirmative (cf. Paul, prior to his conversion, Phil. 3:6). From a human perspective, his answer is plausible. However, once the righteousness of God sheds light on the human condition (see Rom. 3:21–26; Phil. 3:7–11), human righteousness is seen to be no more than a thin cover-up for mankind's basic hostility toward God (Col. 1:21).

10:21 Jesus . . . loved him. Jesus speaks lovingly to the man's heart. **You lack one thing**. The man has replaced direct trust in God and its reward (**treasure in heaven**) with earthly riches. He thus fails the first commandment, "You shall have no other gods before me" (Ex. 20:3). This does not mean that every disciple of Christ must **sell all** that he has; rather, the heart must be focused on God, and every possession yielded to God, with the result that possessions will be handled as a form of stewardship.

10:22 he went away sorrowful. The man's true state has been laid bare, but he does not repent.

10:23 How difficult. Material possessions can be a dangerous instrument for reinforcing self-sufficiency and independence from God.

10:24 The **disciples** are **amazed**, because at least some of them had possessions, such as Peter, who was a fisherman.

10:25 Anyone who trusts in riches (as an idolatrous replacement for God; Matt. 6:24) cannot **enter the kingdom of God**; his life disposition is diametrically opposed to submitting to God's will. The hyperbole of a large **camel** having to fit through the small **eye of a needle** stresses that such a thing is humanly impossible (but see Mark 10:27). For other hyperboles in Jesus' teaching, see Matt. 7:3–5; 23:24; on the "eye of a needle," see note on Matt. 19:24.

10:29–30 The person who leaves **house**, **lands**, and family **for** Jesus' **sake** (cf. 8:35, 38; Matt. 5:11; Luke 12:8–9; 18:29) **and for the gospel** can expect in this life (**now in this time**) to enjoy fellowship with other believers and to find a welcome in the **houses** and **lands** of other believers (see also note on Luke 18:29–30). But in this life these blessings will also be mixed with **persecutions** (cf. Mark 8:34–38). The future will yield an even better reward: **eternal life**. By answering in this way, Jesus assures the disciples that they have answered the call and are blessed.

10:31 The context suggests that it is an inconspicuous, obedient disciple, not much recognized in this life (**last**), who will receive the greatest honor (**first**).

10:32–45 Each of Jesus' major predictions of his death and resurrection (8:31; 9:30–32; 10:32–34) is followed by instruction in discipleship (8:32–38; 9:35–37; 10:35–45). As Jesus walks the path of surrender, so should his disciples.

10:32 Jesus is aware of his impending death (cf. 8:31; 9:31; Isa. 53:1–12) but proceeds resolutely toward **Jerusalem**, like the servant of the Lord in Isa. 50:7 who set his face "like a flint" (cf. Luke 9:53, "his face was set"). The Twelve **were amazed** to see Jesus' solemn determination in light of what he had already told them about his forthcoming suffering and death (Mark 8:31; 9:31). In addition to the Twelve, others **followed** along, but Mark says that they **were afraid**. This fear might have arisen from their belief that Jesus was a political messiah; if so, they might be facing fierce battles in Jerusalem, as in the earlier Maccabean revolt. It is more likely that the larger group of followers

twelve again, he began to tell them what was to happen to him, **33** saying, "See, [w]we are
going up to Jerusalem, and the Son of Man will be delivered over to the chief priests and
the scribes, and they will [x]condemn him to death and [y]deliver him over to the Gentiles.
34 And they will [z]mock him and [a]spit on him, and flog him and kill him. And [b]after three
days he will rise."

The Request of James and John

35 [c]And James and John, [d]the sons of Zebedee, came up to him and said to him, "Teacher,
we want you to do for us [e]whatever we ask of you." **36** And he said to them, [f]"What do you
want me to do for you?" **37** And they said to him, "Grant us [g]to sit, one at your right hand
and one at your left, [h]in your glory." **38** Jesus said to them, [i]"You do not know what you are
asking. Are you able [j]to drink the cup that I drink, or [k]to be baptized with the baptism
with which I am baptized?" **39** And they said to him, "We are able." And Jesus said to them,
[l]"The cup that I drink [m]you will drink, and with the baptism with which I am baptized,
[n]you will be baptized, **40** but to sit at my right hand or at my left is not mine to grant, [o]but
it is for those for whom it has been [p]prepared." **41** And when the ten heard it, they began to
be indignant at James and John. **42** [q]And Jesus called them to him and said to them, "You
know that those who are considered rulers of the Gentiles [r]lord it over them, and their
great ones exercise authority over them. **43** But [s]it shall not be so among you. But whoever
would be great among you must be your servant,[1] **44** and whoever would be first among
you must be [t]slave[2] of all. **45** For even the Son of Man came not to be served but [u]to serve,
and [v]to give his life as a ransom for [w]many."

Jesus Heals Blind Bartimaeus

46 [x]And they came to Jericho. And [y]as he was leaving Jericho with his disciples and a great
crowd, Bartimaeus, [z]a blind beggar, the son of Timaeus, was sitting by the roadside. **47** And

[1] Greek *diakonos* [2] Greek *bondservant (doulos)*

Luke 18:35-43 [y][Luke 18:35; 19:1] [z]John 9:1, 8

33 [w]See Matt. 16:21 [x]Matt. 26:66; John 19:7 [y]Matt. 27:2; John 18:30, 31; Acts 3:13; [Acts 2:23; 4:27; 21:11]
34 [z]Matt. 27:26-31 [a]ch. 14:65; 15:19; See Matt. 26:67 [b]See ch. 8:31
35 [c]For ver. 35-45, see Matt. 20:20-28 [d]ch. 1:19 [e][Matt. 18:19]
36 [f]ver. 51
37 [g][Matt. 19:28] [h][Luke 9:26]
38 [i][Luke 9:33; 23:34] [j]ch. 14:36; Matt. 26:29, 42; Luke 22:42; John 18:11; [Isa. 51:22] [k]Luke 12:50
39 [l][Rom. 8:17; Phil. 3:10] [m]Acts 12:2; Rev. 1:9 [n][Rom. 6:3]
40 [o][Matt. 19:11] [p]Matt. 25:34
42 [q]For ver. 42-45, [ch. 9:33-36; Luke 22:25-27] [r]1 Pet. 5:3
43 [s]Matt. 23:11; [Luke 9:48]
44 [t]2 Cor. 4:5
45 [u]John 13:4, 13-15; Phil. 2:7; [2 Cor. 8:9] [v]Isa. 53:10; Dan. 9:26; John 10:15; 11:51, 52; Rom. 4:25; Gal. 1:4; 2:20; 1 Tim. 2:6; Titus 2:14; 1 Pet. 1:18, 19 [w]ch. 14:24; Isa. 53:11, 12; Heb. 2:10; 9:28; [Rom. 5:15; Rev. 5:9]
46 [x]For ver. 46-52, see Matt. 20:29-34;

saw Jesus' sober, deliberate progress toward Jerusalem, and had heard from the Twelve something of his predictions of suffering, and thus concluded that by following Jesus they might face a similar fate.

10:33 will be delivered. Jesus speaks of a double deliverance: God will hand him over to the Jewish leaders, who, in turn, must hand **him over to the Gentiles** (the Roman authorities). The details of mistreatment in v. 34 were well known to Jews living under Roman occupation.

10:35–37 James and John belonged to Jesus' "inner circle" (cf. 1:19, 29; 3:17; 5:37; 9:2). If Jesus was going to die and be raised in Jerusalem, they may have thought this journey was their last opportunity to put in a request for future assignments. They falsely envisioned special places of honor (**one at your right hand and one at your left**) when Jesus (as a strictly political messiah) would rule in Jerusalem on the throne of David (**in your glory**; see note on Matt. 20:20).

10:38 There would indeed be a future time of glory (8:38; 13:26), but the path there would be through severe, divine judgment for Jesus. The **cup** that he was to drink was the cup of God's wrath that would be poured out on him, bearing God's wrath in the place of sinful mankind (see 14:36; Isa. 51:17, 22; Jer. 25:15; and notes on Luke 22:42; John 18:11). His **baptism** was his suffering and death, which would pour over him like a flood (cf. Ps. 88:7; Jonah 2:3; Luke 12:50; and note on 1 Pet. 3:21).

10:39 The disciples understand Jesus' question ("Are you able to drink the cup that I drink?" v. 38) to mean that they will need to fight alongside Jesus, and they bravely answer, **"We are able."** Jesus, however, teaches them that they too will undergo a form of suffering: **you will drink . . . you will be baptized**. Since only Jesus will bear the divine judgment in a substitutionary way (v. 45), the disciples' suffering will be for their own purification and for God's glory (8:34–38; 1 Pet. 4:13).

10:40 is not mine to grant. Though Jesus is fully God, yet there are differences of authority within the Trinity (cf. note on John 3:35), and the Son throughout Scripture is always subject to the authority and direction of the Father, who will ultimately determine who exactly receives such positions of honor. Jesus both defers authority to his heavenly Father and implies that he will himself be exalted.

10:41 The other disciples become **indignant at James and John**, perhaps on account of their own ambition and jealousy (vv. 42–45).

10:42 The disciples are to be marked by humility of service, not by wanting to **lord it over** those for whom they are responsible. Jesus does not deny all use of human authority (cf. Matt. 16:19; 18:18) but exposes its oppressive misuse.

10:43 must be your servant. Leadership among God's people should be characterized by serving the people and acting for their best interests, not by assuming that the people are to serve the leaders. These principles apply not only to leadership in the church but also in all relations (e.g., in civil government, the civil authority is to be "God's servant for your good" [Rom. 13:4; cf. 1 Sam. 8:11–20; 12:3–5]).

10:45 not to be served but to serve. The messianic rule of God is inaugurated by the greatest example of service: Jesus' death as a substitutionary atonement (**ransom for many**; cf. Lev. 5:14–6:7; Isa. 52:14, 15; 53:8–12; Mark 14:24; Rom. 4:25; 1 Cor. 15:3; and note on 1 Tim. 2:6), offered by the future ruler (**Son of Man**; cf. Dan. 7:13–14; Mark 8:38; 14:62; and note on Matt. 8:20). This quality of humility and love for others, flowing from the infinite love of God for his people, will also characterize Christ's eternal rule. The "ransom" of Christ's life was paid to God the Father, who accepted it as just payment for the sins of "many" (all who would be saved).

10:46–52 Both 8:22–26 and 10:46–52 narrate the healing of a blind man. These two stories serve as literary bookends surrounding the three major predictions of Jesus' death and resurrection (8:31; 9:30–32; 10:32–34), as well as the major instructions on discipleship. The disciples' blindness regarding the true mission of Jesus is thus also being emphasized, but as Jesus teaches them, he is healing this spiritual blindness as well.

10:46 The old **Jericho** near the pilgrimage path to Jerusalem may no longer have been populated at the time of Jesus. The newer, Herodian Jericho was situated southeast of the pilgrimage path, serving as a meeting place for pilgrims. To reach this new Jericho from the pilgrimage road, one had to travel the same road there and back. This might explain the slight differences between Mark's account and those of Matt. 20:29 and Luke 18:35 (see also the notes

47[a]ch. 1:24
48[b]Matt. 19:13
49[c]John 16:33
50[d]ch. 13:16 (Gk.)
51[e]ver. 36 [f]John 20:16
52[g]ch. 5:34; Matt. 9:22; Luke 7:50; 8:48; 17:19 [h]ch. 5:23, 28; 6:56

Chapter 11

1[i]For ver. 1-10, see Matt. 21:1-9; Luke 19:29-38; John 12:12-15; [Zech. 9:9] [j]Matt. 21:17; Luke 24:50; John 11:18 [k]Zech. 14:4; Matt. 24:3; 26:30; John 8:1; [Acts 1:12] [l][ch. 14:13]
2[m][Luke 23:53]

when he heard that it was [a]Jesus of Nazareth, he began to cry out and say, "Jesus, Son of
David, have mercy on me!" **48** And many [b]rebuked him, telling him to be silent. But he
cried out all the more, "Son of David, have mercy on me!" **49** And Jesus stopped and said,
"Call him." And they called the blind man, saying to him, [c]"Take heart. Get up; he is calling
you." **50** And throwing off his [d]cloak, he sprang up and came to Jesus. **51** And Jesus said to
him, [e]"What do you want me to do for you?" And the blind man said to him, [f]"Rabbi, let
me recover my sight." **52** And Jesus said to him, "Go your way; [g]your faith has [h]made you
well." And immediately he recovered his sight and followed him on the way.

The Triumphal Entry

11 [i]Now when they drew near to Jerusalem, to [j]Bethphage and Bethany, at [k]the Mount
of Olives, Jesus[1] sent [l]two of his disciples **2** and said to them, "Go into the village
in front of you, and immediately as you enter it you will find a colt tied, [m]on which no
one has ever sat. Untie it and bring it. **3** If anyone says to you, 'Why are you doing this?'
say, 'The Lord has need of it and will send it back here immediately.' " **4** And they went
away and found a colt tied at a door outside in the street, and they untied it. **5** And some
of those standing there said to them, "What are you doing, untying the colt?" **6** And they

[1] Greek *he*

on Matt. 20:29 and Luke 19:1). The healing occurs when Jesus heads back to the pilgrimage road from Jericho (cf. Matt. 20:29; Luke 18:38).

10:47 Jesus will later identify the cry of the blind man (**Jesus, Son of David, have mercy on me**) as expressing "faith" (v. 52; Matthew notes there were actually two blind men, but Mark and Luke [Luke 18:35–43] only tell about one of them; see note on Matt. 20:30–31). "Son of David" is a messianic acclamation (see Mark 12:35–37).

10:48 many rebuked him. Given the popularity of Jesus, a socially insignificant blind man is considered an interruption.

10:49 The attitude of some in the crowd changes from rebuke (v. 48) to encouragement (**Take heart**) as soon as Jesus pays attention to Bartimaeus. Though Jesus himself is facing suffering in Jerusalem, he still considers the marginalized (cf. vv. 43–45).

10:51 What do you want me to do for you? Jesus asks the obvious question in order to give the blind man the opportunity to express his trust in Jesus.

10:52 Your faith has made you well also hints at spiritual salvation; see note on the same expression in 5:34. **and followed him**. Bartimaeus joins Jesus and the other pilgrims on their final journey to Jerusalem, indicating that he has become one of Jesus' disciples.

11:1–13:37 *Entering and Judging Jerusalem.* Jesus enters Jerusalem triumphantly, he cleanses the temple, and he authoritatively teaches both opponents and disciples.

11:1–11 *Triumphal Entry to Jerusalem.* Jesus enters Jerusalem upon a colt and is hailed as the triumphant Messiah of Israel.

11:1 Jesus and the pilgrims head for **Bethphage and Bethany**. Jesus enters **Jerusalem** (see map below) by way of the **Mount of Olives** (see note on Mark 13:3) and the Kidron Valley.

11:2 a colt tied. Matthew 21:2 also mentions that a donkey was with the colt, but Mark only mentions the colt, which was most important because Jesus would ride on it.

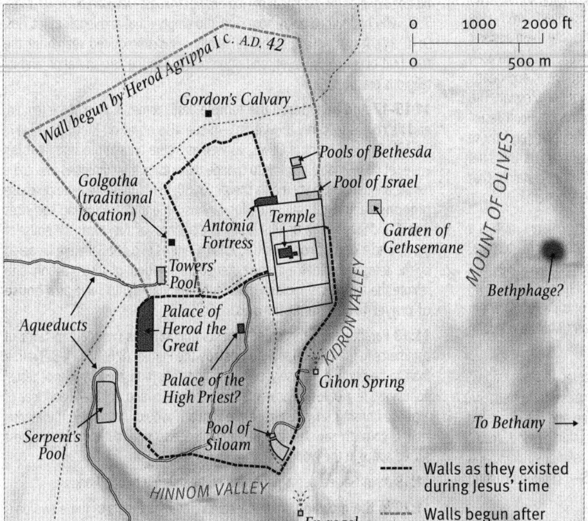

Jerusalem at the Time of Jesus
By the time of Jesus, Jerusalem had grown from a modest military fortress to a world-class city with a newly renovated temple that rivaled nearly any in the ancient world. Public pools were fed by the Gihon Spring and by two aqueducts that brought water to the city from as far as 7 miles (11 km) away. The towns of Bethphage and Bethany were located on the eastern slopes of the Mount of Olives, which lay to the east of Jerusalem. See also Jerusalem in the Time of Jesus, pp. 1878–1879.

told them what Jesus had said, and they let them go. 7 And they brought the colt to Jesus
and threw their cloaks on it, and he sat on it. 8 And many [n]spread their cloaks on the road,
and others spread leafy branches that they had cut from the fields. 9 And those who went
before and those who followed were shouting, [o]"Hosanna! [p]Blessed is he who comes in
the name of the Lord! 10 Blessed is [q]the coming [r]kingdom of [s]our father [r]David! [o]Hosanna
[t]in the highest!"

11 [u]And he entered Jerusalem and went into the temple. And when he had looked around
at everything, as it was already late, [v]he went out to Bethany with the twelve.

Jesus Curses the Fig Tree

12 [w]On the following day, when they came from Bethany, [x]he was hungry. 13 [y]And seeing
in the distance a fig tree in leaf, he went to see if he could find anything on it. When he
came to it, he found nothing but leaves, for [z]it was not the season for figs. 14 And he said
to it, "May no one ever eat fruit from you again." And his disciples heard it.

Jesus Cleanses the Temple

15 [a]And they came to Jerusalem. And he entered the temple and began to drive out those
who sold and those who bought in the temple, and he overturned the tables of [b]the money-
changers and the seats of those who sold [c]pigeons. 16 And he would not allow anyone to
carry anything through the temple. 17 And he was teaching them and saying to them, "Is
it not written, [d]'My house shall be called a house of prayer for all the nations'? But [e]you
have made it a den of robbers." 18 And the chief priests and the scribes heard it and [f]were
seeking a way to destroy him, for they feared him, because [g]all the crowd was astonished
at his teaching. 19 [h]And when evening came they[1] went out of the city.

[1] Some manuscripts *he*

8 [n]2 Kgs. 9:13
9 [o]See Ps. 118:25 (Heb.) [p]Matt. 23:39; Cited from Ps. 118:26
10 [q]See Luke 1:32 [r][Ezek. 37:24, 25] [s][Acts 2:29] [o][See ver. 9 above] [t]Luke 2:14; [Ps. 148:1]
11 [u]Matt. 21:10 [v]ver. 19; Matt. 21:17
12 [w]For ver. 12-14, see Matt. 21:18, 19 [x]Matt. 4:2
13 [y][Luke 13:6-9] [z]ch. 13:28
15 [a]For ver. 15-18, see Matt. 21:12-16; Luke 19:45-47; [John 2:14-16] [b][Ex. 30:13] [c]Lev. 1:14; 5:7; 12:8; Luke 2:24
17 [d]Cited from Isa. 56:7 [e]Jer. 7:11
18 [f]See Matt. 21:46 [g]See Matt. 7:28
19 [h]Luke 21:37; [ver. 11]

11:7 Jesus fulfills a prophecy about the Messiah in Zech. 9:9 by riding on a donkey; see notes on Matt. 21:4–5 and John 12:15.

11:8 On the significance of **cloaks** and **branches**, see 2 Kings 9:12–13 and notes on Matt. 21:8; John 12:13.

11:9 Hosanna (Hb. "Save!" or "Please save!"; see Ps. 118:25). Here "Hosanna" points to the celebration of Jesus as a political, Davidic messiah (cf. 2 Sam. 7:14; Isa. 9:1–21; 11:1–16; Jer. 23:1–8). **Blessed is he who comes in the name of the Lord** is from Ps. 118:25–26, a prayer of blessing for the coming messianic kingdom (but see also notes on Matt. 23:39; Luke 13:35). The Triumphal Entry takes place at the beginning of Passover week, which recalls the Jewish people's liberation from Egyptian slavery (see notes on Mark 14:17; John 2:13); the pilgrims now anticipate the messianic liberation from Rome's oppression. The claims of the disciples are ultimately true, but it will not be Rome that is defeated now but Satan, sin, and death. All enemies of righteousness will one day see the authority of Messiah. This is the only time in Mark where there is no evident tension between Jesus' messianic identity, the messianic expectations of his disciples, and those of the people (cf. Mark 2:8–10; 8:27–31; 10:45). Jesus tolerates this brief period of celebration in fulfillment of Zech. 9:9, but with the certainty that nothing will obstruct the divinely ordained death of the Messiah.

11:11 Jesus **looked around at everything** in the temple area, not as a pilgrim but as the sovereign Lord who "will suddenly come to his temple" (Mal. 3:1). He looks around this center of Jewish religious life to see if it is fulfilling its purpose of leading people to true worship of God. During this week, Jesus and the Twelve stay a short distance outside Jerusalem in **Bethany**, probably with their friends Lazarus, Mary, and Martha (cf. John 12:2–3).

11:12–12:44 *Jesus' Judgment on Religious Leaders.* Jesus' first actions, after being hailed by the people as King, are to pass judgment on Jerusalem figuratively through the cursing of the fig tree and the cleansing of the temple, which highlight Jesus' zeal for true worship of God. Jesus' teaching is bold and authoritative in confronting the religious rulers, and is both introduced (11:20–25) and concluded (12:38–44) by instruction of his disciples.

11:12–21 The way in which Mark organizes his material in these verses (fig tree/cleansing of temple/fig tree) suggests a connection between the cleansing of the temple and the cursing of the fig tree.

11:13–14 found nothing but leaves. Since the fruit of the fig tree begins to appear about the same time as the leaves (or a little after), the appearance of leaves in full bloom should have indicated that fruit (in the form of green figs) was already growing. Jesus' actions here have symbolic importance, signifying the hypocrisy of all who have the appearance that they are bearing fruit but in fact are not. The specific reference, though, is to Israel, since in the OT the **fig tree** often serves as a metaphor for Israel and its standing before God (e.g., Jer. 8:13; Hos. 9:10, 16; Joel 1:7). Here the cursing of the fig tree signifies the judgment of God on the "fruitless" Jewish people (cf. Mark 7:6), who had turned away from God into empty ritual and legalism (cf. Hos. 9:10–17). It is a visual parable to signify Jesus' unrequited search for the true fruit of worship, prayer, and righteousness in the Jewish nation and its religious practices.

11:15–17 And he entered the temple. Jesus comes as Lord of the temple, and he comes to purify it (Mal. 3:1–4; see also notes on Matt. 21:12–17; 21:12). On the Mount of Olives, as well as in the temple precincts, **tables** were set up to enable pilgrims to change their respective currencies into coins for the annual temple tax (half a shekel; Ex. 30:13–16), as well as to purchase **pigeons**, lambs, oil, salt, etc., for various sin and thanksgiving sacrifices (Lev. 1:14; 5:7, 11; 12:8; 14:22, 30). The business activity turns the house of prayer into a **den of robbers** (Jer. 7:11). Gentiles in particular were hindered by the temple commerce in the outer court. The goal of Jesus' action is to restore the temple (temporarily) to its function, namely, to serve as **a house of prayer for all the nations** (Isa. 56:7).

11:18 Paradoxically, the **chief priests** and **scribes** (who are in favor of commerce in the temple) seek to **destroy** the Purifier (3:6; 15:31–32) rather than to be purified themselves. Their actions are motivated by fear of Jesus' popularity, fear of losing power (social, economic, and political), and fear of a public uprising (in which case the Romans would intervene). The Jewish leaders correctly saw Jesus' act as a challenge to their authority in the most sacred space in the world.

11:19 As in Galilee, Jesus periodically retreats from public work.

11:20 in the morning. Matthew compresses the events of these two days into a single narrative and does not specify that the disciples did not see the

20[i] For ver. 20-24, see Matt. 21:19-22
21[j] See John 1:38
22[k] Eph. 3:12; Phil. 3:9
23[l] Matt. 17:20 [m] [Ps. 46:2; 1 Cor. 13:2; Rev. 8:8] [n] Rom. 4:20; 14:23; James 1:6 [o] [ch. 16:17; John 14:12]
24[p] See Matt. 7:7 [o] [See ver. 23 above] [q] [Isa. 65:24; Matt. 6:8]
25[r] Matt. 6:5; Luke 18:11 [s] See Matt. 6:14 [t] Col. 3:13; [Matt. 5:23; 6:15] [u] Matt. 7:11
27[v] For ver. 27-33, see Matt. 21:23-27; Luke 20:1-8
28[w] [Ex. 2:14; John 1:25; Acts 4:7]
30[x] Luke 15:18, 21; John 3:27
31[y] Matt. 21:32; Luke 7:30
32[z] Matt. 14:5; 21:46 [a] [John 5:35]; See Matt. 11:9

Chapter 12

1[b] For ver. 1-12, see Matt. 21:33-46; Luke 20:9-19 [c] Ps. 80:8; Isa. 5:1; Matt. 21:28 [d] Isa. 5:2 [e] Song 8:11, 12 [f] ch. 13:34; Matt. 25:14, 15

The Lesson from the Withered Fig Tree

20 [i]As they passed by in the morning, they saw the fig tree withered away to its roots.
21 And Peter remembered and said to him, [j]"Rabbi, look! The fig tree that you cursed has
withered." 22 And Jesus answered them, "Have [k]faith in God. 23 [l]Truly, I say to you, whoever
says to this mountain, [m]'Be taken up and thrown into the sea,' and does not [n]doubt in his
heart, but [o]believes that what he says will come to pass, it will be done for him. 24 Therefore
I tell you, [p]whatever you ask in prayer, [o]believe that you [q]have received[1] it, and it will be
yours. 25 And whenever [r]you stand praying, [s]forgive, [t]if you have anything against anyone,
so that [u]your Father also who is in heaven may forgive you your trespasses."[2]

The Authority of Jesus Challenged

27 [v]And they came again to Jerusalem. And as he was walking in the temple, the chief
priests and the scribes and the elders came to him, 28 and they said to him, [w]"By what
authority are you doing these things, or who gave you this authority to do them?" 29 Jesus
said to them, "I will ask you one question; answer me, and I will tell you by what authority I do these things. 30 Was the baptism of John [x]from heaven or from man? Answer me."
31 And they discussed it with one another, saying, "If we say, 'From heaven,' he will say,
[y]'Why then did you not believe him?' 32 But shall we say, 'From man'?"—[z]they were afraid
of the people, for they all held that John really was [a]a prophet. 33 So they answered Jesus,
"We do not know." And Jesus said to them, "Neither will I tell you by what authority I do
these things."

The Parable of the Tenants

12 [b]And he began to speak to them in parables. "A man planted [c]a vineyard [d]and put
a fence around it and dug a pit for the winepress and built a tower, and [e]leased it
to tenants and [f]went into another country. 2 When the season came, he sent a servant[3] to

[1] Some manuscripts *are receiving* [2] Some manuscripts add verse 26: *But if you do not forgive, neither will your Father who is in heaven forgive your trespasses*
[3] Greek *bondservant*; also verse 4

withered **fig tree** until the next day. Mark gives more detailed chronological information, while Matthew treats the event topically (Matt. 21:18–22).

11:21 The **fig tree** had **withered** within 24 hours, perhaps sooner (Matt. 21:19). It represents the judgment of God on Israel (Isa. 34:4; Joel 1:7–12; Amos 4:9; see note on Mark 11:13–14).

11:22–23 Have faith in God. Jesus' response must have surprised the disciples. (What does faith have to do with the cursing of the fig tree?) His point is that they should trust God to remove whatever hinders them from bearing fruit for God. Moving a **mountain** was a metaphor in Jewish literature for doing what was seemingly impossible (Isa. 40:4; 49:11; 54:10; cf. Matt. 21:21–22). Those who believe in God can have confidence that he will accomplish even the impossible, according to his sovereign will.

11:24–25 whatever you ask. God delights to "give good things to those who ask him" (Matt. 7:11) and is capable of granting any **prayer**, though we must ask with godly motives (James 4:3) and according to God's will (1 John 5:14). **believe that you have received it, and it will be yours.** Those who trust God for the right things in the right way can have confidence that God will "supply every need . . . according to his riches in glory in Christ Jesus" (Phil. 4:19), knowing that he will work "all things together for good" and will "graciously give us all things" (Rom. 8:28, 32). Some have misused this verse by telling people that if they pray for physical healing (or for some other specific request) and if they just have enough faith, then they can have confidence that God has already done (or will do) whatever they ask. But we must always have the same perspective that Jesus had—that is, confidence in God's power but also submission to his will: "Father, all things are possible for you. . . . Yet not what I will, but what you will" (Mark 14:36).

11:28–33 The official leaders of Israel inquire of Jesus **by what authority** he is **doing these things**. The question relates immediately to the cleansing of the temple (vv. 15–19) but also to his healing and teaching in the temple (and throughout his ministry), because Jesus is neither an official priestly nor a scribal authority according to the official standards of his questioners. **Was the baptism** (i.e., the ministry) **of John from heaven** (i.e., from God) **or from man** (i.e., did it have a merely human origin)? To avoid the dilemma posed by the question, Jesus' opponents say that they **do not know**, because they feared the consequences of speaking against John the Baptist, whose divinely authorized ministry was also carried out apart from the official Jewish authority. Their confession of ignorance, however, demonstrates that they have no basis on which to assess Jesus' ministry. If they do not know whether John the Baptist was from God, they cannot know whether Jesus is, either. Faced with such hostility, Jesus refuses to answer his opponents' question and exposes their ignorance and lack of sincerity.

12:1–12 This parable of judgment is addressed primarily to the religious leaders of Israel (vv. 1, 12). The story draws on everyday life. Disputes between absentee landlords, their representatives (in this case, a **servant**), and **tenants** were common (vv. 3–5). The attempt to seize the land by killing the rightful heir is bold but plausible (vv. 6–8). The key to understanding the story lies in v. 12 (see also vv. 1, 5); the opponents of Jesus understand his story to be an accusation against them, yet they do not take Jesus' words to heart. The **vineyard** is a well-known metaphor for Israel (cf. Neh. 9:16–37; Isa. 5:1–5; John 15:1–27). The son of the landlord (**beloved son**) is rejected as the "messianic stone" (Ps. 118:22; Mark 12:10). The **builders** (v. 10; a metaphor for "leaders of Israel") kill the "messianic stone" (vv. 7, 10). This interpretation corresponds to the current tension between Jesus and his opponents and the overall saving work of God despite the rebellion of his people (Neh. 9:6, 26, 28–31, 33–35; Acts 7:2–53). Jesus' parabolic teaching either instructs (Mark 4:1–20) or hardens (4:10–12; 12:1–12) its hearers.

12:1 The landlord goes to great expense, which justifies his rightful expectation for a share in the profit. The allusion to Isa. 5:1–5 (**vineyard, fence, tower**) suggests that Jesus continues the theme of "fruit of worship and righteousness for God" (see note on Mark 11:13–14). Immense Herodian-era manor houses with walls, towers, and a winepress have been excavated near Caesarea Maritima.

12:2 At the time of harvest, a representative of the landlord (in this case, his **servant**) comes to receive the landlord's share (**some of the fruit of the vineyard**).

the tenants to get from them some of the fruit of the vineyard. 3 [g]And they took him and
beat him and sent him away empty-handed. 4 [g]Again [h]he sent to them another servant,
and [i]they struck him on the head and [j]treated him shamefully. 5 [g]And he sent another, and
him they killed. And so with many others: some they beat, and some they killed. 6 He had
still one other, [k]a beloved son. [l]Finally he sent him to them, saying, 'They will respect my
son.' 7 But those tenants said to one another, [m]'This is the heir. Come, [n]let us kill him, and
the inheritance will be ours.' 8 And they took him and killed him and [o]threw him out of
the vineyard. 9 What will the owner of the vineyard do? [p]He will [q]come and destroy the
tenants and [r]give the vineyard to others. 10 [s]Have you not read [t]this Scripture:

[u]"'The stone that the builders rejected
has become the cornerstone;[1]
11 this was the Lord's doing,
and it is marvelous in our eyes'?"

12 And [v]they were seeking to arrest him [w]but feared the people, for they perceived that
he had told the parable against them. So they [x]left him and went away.

Paying Taxes to Caesar

13 [y]And they sent to him some of [z]the Pharisees and some of [z]the Herodians, to [a]trap him
in his talk. 14 And they came and said to him, "Teacher, [b]we know that you are true and
do not care about anyone's opinion. For [c]you are not swayed by appearances,[2] but truly
teach [d]the way of God. Is it lawful to pay [e]taxes to [f]Caesar, or not? Should we pay them,
or should we not?" 15 But, knowing [g]their hypocrisy, he said to them, "Why [h]put me to the
test? Bring me [i]a denarius[3] and let me look at it." 16 And they brought one. And he said to
them, "Whose likeness and inscription is this?" They said to him, "Caesar's." 17 Jesus said
to them, [j]"Render to Caesar the things that are Caesar's, and to God the things that are
God's." And they marveled at him.

The Sadducees Ask About the Resurrection

18 And [k]Sadducees came to him, [l]who say that there is no resurrection. And they asked
him a question, saying, 19 "Teacher, Moses wrote for us that [m]if a man's brother dies and

3 [g]Matt. 5:12; 22:6; 23:34, 37; [2 Chr. 24:19; 36:15, 16; Neh. 9:26; Jer. 37:15; 38:6; Acts 7:52; 2 Cor. 11:24-26; 1 Thess. 2:15; Heb. 11:36, 37]
4 [g][See ver. 3 above] [h]Matt. 22:4 [i][Acts 14:19] [j]Acts 5:41 (Gk.)
5 [g][See ver. 3 above]
6 [k]See Matt. 3:17 [l][Heb. 1:1]
7 [m]Heb. 1:2; [John 1:11; Rom. 8:17] [n][1 Kgs. 21:19]
8 [o]Heb. 13:12
9 [p][Luke 19:27] [q][Matt. 24:50; 25:19] [r]Matt. 21:43; Acts 13:46; 18:6; 28:28; [Matt. 8:11, 12]
10 [s]See Matt. 21:16 [t]Luke 4:21; Acts 8:35 [u]Acts 4:11; 1 Pet. 2:7; Cited from Ps. 118:22, 23
12 [v]ch. 11:18; Luke 19:47, 48; John 7:25, 30, 44; [Matt. 26:4] [w]ch. 11:32 [x]Matt. 22:22
13 [y]For ver. 13-27, see Matt. 22:15-32; Luke 20:20-38 [z]ch. 3:6; [ch. 8:15] [a]Luke 11:54
14 [b][John 3:2] [c]See Acts 10:34 [d]Acts 18:25, 26; [Acts 13:10] [e]Matt. 17:25 [f]Luke 2:1; 3:1
15 [g]Matt. 23:28; Luke 12:1 [h]See John 8:6 [i]See Matt. 18:28
17 [j]Rom. 13:7
18 [k]Matt. 3:7; 16:1; 22:34; Acts 4:1; 5:17; 23:6 [l]Acts 23:8; [Acts 4:2]
19 [m][Deut. 25:5]

[1] Greek *the head of the corner* [2] Greek *you do not look at people's faces* [3] A *denarius* was a day's wage for a laborer

12:3–5 There is an escalation in the mistreatment of the landlord's servants: they are beaten, **struck . . . on the head** (v. 4), and **killed** (v. 5). The repetition of these events (**and so with many others**) reinforces the injustice. While Israel might have borne fruit, the leaders of Israel by their misleading leadership hinder the fruit from being given to God.

12:6 still one other, a beloved son (see note on Luke 20:13). The tenants' attitude toward the landlord will be directly reflected in their **respect**, or lack of it, for his son, who represents Jesus (Ex. 10:3; Lev. 26:41; 2 Chron. 36:11–16; see the echo of this theme in Mark 1:11; 9:7).

12:7 The **tenants** display disrespect for the landlord by seeking to **kill** his heir. They may be assuming that the heir's arrival means the landlord has died.

12:9 Finally the **owner of the vineyard** (God) punishes the evil tenants (leaders of Israel; Isa. 5:3, 5) and seeks new tenants (**give the vineyard to others**). Israel (and the Son sent to her) belongs to God. Israel's leaders disrespect the possessions of God (Mark 11:27–12:12) and thus incur the judgment of God.

12:10 At the time of Jesus, Ps. 118:22–23 was already known as a messianic psalm (cf. Acts 4:11). The opponents of Jesus can thus understand what he means: the "stone" refers to the Messiah. **Builders** refers to the leaders of Israel. **Rejected** echoes the theme of the persecution of the prophets of God (Neh. 9:9–35; Acts 7:1–53). The new Israel (or faithful Israel) will accept the Son as the rightful messenger, heir, and **cornerstone** of the messianic kingdom (Jer. 31:26; Zech. 4:7). Both Mark 12:9 and 12:10 speak of reversal: in v. 9 God transfers responsibility for his people to "others," and in v. 10 the rejected messianic "stone" is divinely vindicated and established as the cornerstone of a new building (see notes on 1 Pet. 2:4–8).

12:12 The opponents of Jesus have long determined to kill him (11:18). From their vantage point, only his popularity hinders them (11:32; 14:1–2).

12:13 The opponents of Jesus attempt **to trap him** by means of difficult questions (cf. 8:11; 10:2; 11:27–28). Different groups in Palestinian Judaism, both **Pharisees** and **Herodians** (see note on Matt. 22:16; and the article on Jewish Groups at the Time of the New Testament, pp. 1799–1800), collaborate against Jesus.

12:14 we know that you are true. Jesus rightly labels his opponents' kind words as "hypocrisy" (v. 15). Since Jesus purports to be teaching **the way of God**, they figure that he must have an opinion on whether it is **lawful to pay** poll **taxes** or property taxes to the oppressive Roman emperor. A rejection of paying taxes would seem to entail rebellion against Caesar; a willingness to pay taxes appears to compromise devotion to God (on civic duties and the relationship between church and state, see note on Matt. 22:21).

12:16 The **likeness** (of Tiberius Caesar) and **inscription** on the denarius (valued as the wage of a day's labor) represent the person of Caesar and his authority (see note on Matt. 22:19). By carrying the coin, Jesus' opponents show that they already participate in the Roman social order.

12:17 the things that are Caesar's . . . the things that are God's. See notes on Matt. 22:21 and Luke 20:25. Jesus does not discuss the question of whether the current Roman governance is just or unjust, but he does imply that it is right to pay taxes to **Caesar**. God's kingdom, however, transcends all of these "things."

12:18–23 The overstated and theoretical question (**seven** successive levirate marriages; see note on Matt. 22:24) assumes a tension between the Mosaic law (Gen. 38:8; Deut. 25:5–6; Ruth 4) and belief in the **resurrection**, which the party of the **Sadducees** rejects (on Saddducees, see note on Matt. 3:7). How can one woman and seven men be married in heaven?

leaves a wife, but leaves no child, the man[1] must take the widow and raise up offspring
for his brother. 20 There were seven brothers; the first took a wife, and when he died left no
offspring. 21 And the second took her, and died, leaving no offspring. And the third likewise.
22 And the seven left no offspring. Last of all the woman also died. 23 In the resurrection,
when they rise again, whose wife will she be? For the seven had her as wife."
24 Jesus said to them, "Is this not the reason you are wrong, because [n]you know neither
the Scriptures nor [o]the power of God? 25 For when they rise from the dead, they neither
[p]marry nor [p]are given in marriage, but are like angels in heaven. 26 And as for the dead
being raised, [q]have you not read in [r]the book of Moses, in [s]the passage about the bush,
how God spoke to him, saying, [t]'I am the God of Abraham, and the God of Isaac, and the
God of Jacob'? 27 He is not God of the dead, but of the living. You are quite wrong."

The Great Commandment

28 [u]And one of the scribes came up and heard them disputing with one another, and seeing that he answered them well, asked him, "Which commandment is the most important
of all?" 29 Jesus answered, "The most important is, [v]'Hear, O Israel: The Lord our God, [w]the
Lord is one. 30 And you shall love the Lord your God with all your heart and with all your
soul and with all your mind and with all your strength.' 31 [x]The second is this: [y]'You shall
love your neighbor as yourself.' There is no other commandment [z]greater than these."
32 And the scribe said to him, "You are right, Teacher. You have truly said that [w]he is one,
and [a]there is no other besides him. 33 And to love him with all the heart and with all [b]the
understanding and with all the strength, and to love one's neighbor as oneself, [c]is much
more than all [d]whole burnt offerings and sacrifices." 34 And when Jesus saw that he answered
wisely, he said to him, "You are not far from the kingdom of God." [e]And after that no one
dared to ask him any more questions.

Whose Son Is the Christ?

35 [f]And as [g]Jesus taught in the temple, he said, "How can the scribes say that [h]the Christ
is the son of David? 36 David himself, [i]in the Holy Spirit, declared,

[j]"'The Lord said to my Lord,
"Sit at my right hand,
until I put your enemies [k]under your feet."'

37 David himself calls him Lord. So [l]how is he his son?" And the great throng [m]heard him
gladly.

Beware of the Scribes

38 [n]And in his teaching he said, "Beware of the scribes, who like to walk around in long
robes and like greetings in the marketplaces 39 and have the best seats in the synagogues

[1] Greek *his brother*

24 [n]John 20:9 [o]1 Cor. 6:14
25 [p]Matt. 24:38; Luke 17:27
26 [q]See Matt. 21:16 [r][Luke 3:4; 20:42; Acts 1:20; 7:42] [s]Ex. 3:1-4, 17 [t]Acts 7:32; Cited from Ex. 3:6
28 [u]For ver. 28-34, see Matt. 22:34-40, 46; [Luke 10:25-28]
29 [v]Luke 10:27; Cited from Deut. 6:4, 5 [w]Rom. 3:30; 1 Cor. 8:4, 6; Gal. 3:20; Eph. 4:6; 1 Tim. 1:17; 2:5; James 2:19; 4:12; Jude 25; [Matt. 19:17; 23:9]
31 [x][1 John 4:21] [y]Cited from Lev. 19:18; See Matt. 19:19 [z][Matt. 23:23]
32 [w][See ver. 29 above] [a]Cited from Deut. 4:35 (Gk.)
33 [b]Deut. 4:6; Luke 2:47; Col. 1:9; 2:2 [c]1 Sam. 15:22; Hos. 6:6; Mic. 6:6-8; Matt. 9:13; 12:7 [d]Ps. 40:6; Heb. 10:6, 8
34 [e]Luke 20:40
35 [f]For ver. 35-37, see Matt. 22:41-45; Luke 20:41-44 [g]See Matt. 26:55 [h]See Matt. 1:1, 17
36 [i][Luke 10:21; 1 Cor. 12:3] [j]Acts 2:34, 35; Heb. 1:13; Cited from Ps. 110:1; [1 Cor. 15:25; Heb. 10:13] [k][Acts 7:49]
37 [l][Rom. 1:3, 4] [m]ch. 6:20
38 [n]For ver. 38, 39, see Matt. 23:1, 2, 5-7; Luke 20:45, 46; [Luke 11:43]

12:24 In asking their question (vv. 18–23), the Sadducees **are wrong** on two counts: they **know neither the Scriptures nor the power of God** (see note on vv. 26–27).

12:25 The Sadducees falsely assume marriage in **heaven**. Interpersonal relationships in heaven are similar to the relationships of **angels** (whose existence the Sadducees likewise deny; see Acts 23:8). See note on Matt. 22:29–30.

12:26–27 Citing the OT "Scriptures," Jesus explains the full "power of God" when it comes to **the dead being raised**. Exodus 3:6 cannot mean that God makes himself known to Moses as the **God of the dead**. Rather, as **the God of Abraham . . . Isaac, and . . . Jacob** (i.e., the faithful, covenant-keeping God), he is the God **of the living** (Ex. 3:15–16; 4:5). Abraham therefore continues to exist and to enjoy the blessings of God's covenant (cf. Rom. 8:35–39), and hence will also be raised from the dead.

12:28–31 A teachable scribe (a theological scholar, probably of the Pharisaic faction) holds a friendly dialogue with Jesus. He asks which **commandment** of God is of fundamental importance and central to everything else. Jesus answers directly: the **most important** commandment, introduced by Deut. 6:4, is to **love the Lord your God** completely (Deut. 6:5; cf. notes on Matt. 22:37–38 and Luke 10:27). **Second** to this is to **love your neighbor as yourself** (Lev. 19:18, 34). The faithful, covenant-keeping God asks the objects of his love to love him and other human beings too (Rom. 13:8–10; Gal. 5:14; 1 John 4:10–11, 19).

12:34 not far. This inquisitive scribe is separated from the present **kingdom of God** simply by his ignorance of Jesus as the beloved Son (9:7), as the one to be confessed (8:38), and as the one who will suffer a substitutionary death on his behalf (10:45; see 12:35–37).

12:35–37 While in the **temple**, Jesus publicly raises a question that he has already discussed in private with his disciples: who is the Messiah of God—is he essentially the **son** of David or the **Lord** of **David**? Jesus' point is not to deny that the Messiah is a descendant of David (e.g., Ps. 2:1–12; 89:1–52; Isa. 9:1–7; Jer. 23:5–6; Ezek. 34:23–24). The issue is that, in *this* passage (i.e., Ps. 110:1–5), there is no mention of the Messiah being the son of David; rather, the Messiah is here the "Lord of David" (see note on Matt. 22:41–46). Jesus affirms the divine inspiration of the Psalm through the **Holy Spirit**. **The Lord** (Hb. *Yahweh*) grants to David's **Lord** (Hb. *'Adonay*) an exclusive place of honor at his **right hand** and helps David's Lord overcome his **enemies**. Jesus anticipates being exalted to the right hand of God, and thus he far transcends any expectation of a merely political, Davidic messiah.

12:38 scribes. See note on Matt. 8:19.

12:39 Many scribes seek public recognition by means of their clothing and

and [o]the places of honor at feasts, 40 [p]who devour widows' houses and [q]for a pretense make long prayers. They will receive the greater condemnation."

The Widow's Offering

41 [r]And he sat down opposite [s]the treasury and watched the people [t]putting money into the offering box. Many rich people put in large sums. 42 And a poor widow came and put in two [u]small copper coins, which make a penny.[1] 43 And he called his disciples to him and said to them, "Truly, I say to you, [v]this poor widow has put in more than all those who are contributing to the offering box. 44 For they all contributed out of their abundance, but she out of her [w]poverty has put in everything she had, all [x]she had to live on."

Jesus Foretells Destruction of the Temple

13 [y]And as he came out of the temple, one of his disciples said to him, "Look, Teacher, what wonderful stones and what wonderful buildings!" 2 And Jesus said to him, "Do you see these great buildings? [z]There will not be left here one stone upon another that will not be thrown down."

Signs of the Close of the Age

3 And as he sat on [a]the Mount of Olives opposite the temple, [b]Peter and James and John and [c]Andrew asked him [d]privately, 4 "Tell us, [e]when will these things be, and what will be the sign when all these things are about to be accomplished?" 5 And Jesus began to say to them, [f]"See that no one leads you astray. 6 [g]Many will come in my name, saying, [h]'I am he!' and they will lead many astray. 7 And when you hear of wars and rumors of wars, [i]do not be alarmed. This [j]must take place, but the end is not yet. 8 For [k]nation will rise against nation, and [l]kingdom against kingdom. There will be [m]earthquakes in various places; there will be [n]famines. These are but the beginning of the birth pains.

9 [o]"But [p]be on your guard. For they will deliver you over to councils, and you will be beaten [q]in synagogues, and you will stand before [r]governors and [s]kings for my sake, [t]to bear witness before them. 10 And the gospel must first be proclaimed [u]to all nations. 11 And when they bring you to trial and deliver you over, [v]do not be anxious beforehand what you are to say, but say [w]whatever is given you in that hour, [x]for it is not you who speak, but the Holy Spirit. 12 [y]And brother will deliver brother over to death, and the father his child, and children will rise against parents and have them put to death. 13 [z]And you will be hated by all for my name's sake. [a]But the one who endures to the end will be saved.

[1] Greek *two lepta*, which make a *kodrantes*; a *kodrantes* (Latin *quadrans*) was a Roman copper coin worth about 1/64 of a *denarius* (which was a day's wage for a laborer)

39 [o]Luke 14:7, 8
40 [p][Luke 11:39; 16:14] [q][Matt. 6:5, 7]
41 [r]For ver. 41-44, see Luke 21:1-4 [s]Matt. 27:6; John 8:20 [t]2 Kgs. 12:9
42 [u]Luke 12:59
43 [v][2 Cor. 8:2, 12]
44 [w]Phil. 4:11 [x]Luke 8:43

Chapter 13

1 [y]For ver. 1-37, see Matt. 24:1-51; Luke 21:5-36
2 [z]Luke 19:44
3 [a]See Matt. 21:1 [b]Matt. 17:1 [c]ch. 1:16, 29 [d][ch. 4:34]
4 [e][Acts 1:6, 7]
5 [f]ver. 9, 23, 33; Jer. 29:8; Eph. 5:6; Col. 2:8; 1 Thess. 2:3; 1 John 3:7
6 [g]ver. 22; Jer. 14:14; 1 John 2:18 [h]See John 8:24
7 [i]2 Thess. 2:2 [j]Rev. 1:1
8 [k]2 Chr. 15:6; [Rev. 6:4] [l]Isa. 19:2 [m]Rev. 6:12 [n]Acts 11:28; Rev. 6:8
9 [o]For ver. 9, 11-13, [Matt. 10:17-22; Luke 12:11, 12] [p]ver. 5; 2 John 8 [q]See Matt. 23:34 [r]Acts 17:6; 18:12; 24:1; 25:6 [s][Acts 27:24] [t]See Matt. 8:4
10 [u]Matt. 28:19; Rom. 10:18; Col. 1:6, 23; [ch. 14:9]
11 [v]See Matt. 6:25 [w]Deut. 18:18; [Num. 23:5]; See Ex. 4:12 [x]Acts 4:8; 6:10; 13:9; 1 Cor. 15:10; 2 Cor. 13:3; [1 Thess. 2:13; Heb. 1:1]
12 [y]Matt. 10:35, 36
13 [z]John 15:18-21; [Luke 6:22] [a][Dan. 12:12, 13; James 5:11; Rev. 2:10]; See Heb. 3:6

---

places of honor (see note on Matt. 23:6). As lawyers, they exploit widows while pretending to be pious (Mark 12:40). For Jesus, true devotion to God includes a concern for social justice.

12:42–44 Small copper coins (Gk. *lepta* [plural]; a *lepton* was a Jewish coin worth about 1/128th of a denarius, which was a day's wage for a laborer) are valued at a fraction of a cent. The **poor widow** gave **more than all** the rich people, according to God's evaluation, for she gave **everything she had**, while the rich gave from their surplus.

13:1–37 *Jesus and the Coming Judgment.* Jesus' discourse about the end times focuses the attention of the disciples on preparedness, on readiness to suffer, and on trust.

13:1 Herod the Great expanded the second **temple** to about double the size of the Solomonic temple (cf. note on Luke 21:5–6).

13:2 The future destruction of the temple (and Jerusalem) would occur on account of its misuse by the leaders (12:9; Luke 19:41–44). (The sacrificial system of the temple cannot, in any case, make sufficient atonement for the sinfulness of mankind; Heb. 10:4.) **not . . . one stone upon another**. See note on Matt. 24:2. Titus, son of the emperor Vespasian, led the destruction of Jerusalem and the temple in A.D. 66–70.

13:3 The **Mount of Olives** (Olivet), with its spectacular view of the Temple Mount, stands just east of Jerusalem across the Kidron Valley (see note on John 18:1). Jesus and his disciples regularly crossed over Olivet on their way from Jerusalem through Bethphage (Luke 19:29) to Bethany (John 11:1), which lay on the mountain's eastern slope. The traditional site of Gethsemane lies on Olivet's western slope (Matt. 26:36).

13:4–37 In response to Jesus' statement about the future destruction of the temple (v. 2), the disciples ask him, **"When will these things be, and what will be the sign when all these things are about to be accomplished?"** Jesus' answer deals primarily with the second part of their question ("what will be the sign"), but he also addresses the timing of the coming events ("when"). Verses 5–23 focus on local and world events (destruction of the temple, persecution, and universal evangelism); vv. 24–27 focus on cosmic events (the transformation of the known cosmos and the coming of the Son of Man). The disciples assume that the destruction of the temple will coincide with the end of time, but Jesus corrects their thinking (vv. 7, 13). Since Jesus predicts these events, believers must not lose heart. The destruction of Jerusalem (which came in A.D. 70) functions as a type of the last judgment, which will occur when Jesus returns. God already knows about them, and the elect (vv. 20, 22, 27) will be preserved.

13:8 The metaphor of **birth pains** (see note on Matt. 24:8) describes the increase in frequency and duration of these events.

13:9–13 Amid these troubles, including family divisions (v. 12; cf. Luke 12:50–53), the disciples are to be worldwide (Mark 7:27; 8:35; 10:29; 13:27), Spirit-led witnesses before both Jewish and Gentile authorities (v. 9).

The Abomination of Desolation

14 "But when you see [b]the abomination of desolation standing where he ought not
to be ([c]let the reader understand), then let those who are in Judea flee to the mountains. **15** [d]Let the one who is on [e]the housetop not go down, nor enter his house, to
take anything out, **16** and let the one who is in the field not turn back to take his cloak.
17 And [f]alas for women who are pregnant and for those who are nursing infants in those
days! **18** Pray that it may not happen in winter. **19** For in those days there will be [g]such
[h]tribulation as has not been [i]from the beginning of the creation that [j]God created until
now, and never will be. **20** And if the Lord had not cut short the days, no human being
would be saved. But for [k]the sake of the elect, whom [l]he chose, he shortened the days.
21 And [m]then if anyone says to you, 'Look, here is the Christ!' or 'Look, there he is!' do
not believe it. **22** [n]For false christs and false prophets will arise and [o]perform signs and
wonders, [p]to lead astray, if possible, [q]the elect. **23** But [r]be on guard; [s]I have told you all
things beforehand.

The Coming of the Son of Man

24 "But in those days, after [t]that tribulation, [u]the sun will be darkened, and the moon
will not give its light, **25** and [v]the stars will be falling from heaven, and the powers in the
heavens will be shaken. **26** And then they will see [w]the Son of Man coming in clouds [x]with
great power and glory. **27** And then [y]he will send out the angels and [z]gather [a]his elect from
[b]the four winds, from [c]the ends of the earth [d]to the ends of heaven.

The Lesson of the Fig Tree

28 "From the fig tree learn its lesson: as soon as its branch becomes tender and puts out
its leaves, you know that summer is near. **29** So also, when you see these things taking place,
you know that he is near, [e]at the very gates. **30** [f]Truly, I say to you, this generation will not
pass away until all these things take place. **31** [g]Heaven and earth will pass away, but [h]my
words will not pass away.

14 [b]Dan. 9:27; 11:31; 12:11 [c][Dan. 9:23, 25; Rev. 1:3]
15 [d]Luke 17:31 [e]See Luke 5:19
17 [f]Luke 23:29
19 [g]Rev. 16:18 [h]ver. 24; Dan. 12:1; [Rev. 7:14] [i]See ch. 10:6; [Deut. 4:32] [j]Gen. 1:1
20 [k]ver. 22, 27; Isa. 65:8, 9; Luke 18:7; [Matt. 22:14] [l]John 13:18; 15:19; Eph. 1:4
21 [m]Luke 17:23; [ver. 6]
22 [n][1 John 2:18] [o]Deut. 13:1-3; 2 Thess. 2:9-11; Rev. 13:13, 14; 16:14; 19:20; [Acts 8:9] [p]ver. 6 [q]ver. 20, 27
23 [r]ver. 5 [s]John 13:19; 14:29; [2 Pet. 3:17]
24 [t]ver. 19 [u]Isa. 13:10; 24:23; Ezek. 32:7; Joel 2:10, 31; 3:15; Acts 2:20; [Amos 5:20; 8:9; Zeph. 1:15; Rev. 6:12; 8:12]
25 [v]Rev. 6:13; [Isa. 14:12; 34:4]
26 [w]See Dan. 7:13 [x]ch. 9:1; Matt. 26:64; [Matt. 25:31]
27 [y]Matt. 13:41 [z][Matt. 23:37; 2 Thess. 2:1] [a]ver. 20, 22 [b]Dan. 7:2; Zech. 2:6; Rev. 7:1 [c][Acts 1:8] [d]Deut. 4:32; 30:4
29 [e][James 5:9; Rev. 3:20]
30 [f]See ch. 9:1
31 [g]Ps. 102:26; Isa. 51:6; 2 Pet. 3:10; [Matt. 5:18; Heb. 12:27] [h]Ps. 119:89; Isa. 40:8; 1 Pet. 1:23, 25

13:14 The abomination of desolation (cf. Dan. 9:27; 11:31; 12:11) points to the Antichrist's ultimate desecration of God's temple (**where he ought not to be**, which some understand as a literal, rebuilt temple, and others understand as the people of God; see 2 Thess. 2:1–12; 1 John 2:18). This event was anticipated in the destruction of the temple in Jerusalem (see note on Matt. 24:15). **flee to the mountains**. See note on Matt. 24:16.

13:19 Tribulation will occur in conjunction with the Antichrist's desecration (v. 14). This tribulation will not be confined to Judea and will be on a scale unprecedented since the **beginning of the creation**. The flight of Christians from Jerusalem in A.D. 67 anticipated this universal tribulation (see note on Matt. 24:16).

13:20 The universal extent of tribulations is **cut short** by the **Lord**. The **elect** (see also vv. 22, 27) are not a proud elite but recipients of God's gracious and undeserved call and protection (see note on Matt. 22:14).

13:22 The tribulation (v. 19) is accompanied by **false christs and false prophets** (on testing false prophets, see notes on Matt. 7:15–20; 9:34; 1 John 4:1). They **lead astray** by performing **signs and wonders** (cf. the actions of the Antichrist in 2 Thess. 2:3, 7–12; 1 John 2:18). Unlike Scripture, signs and wonders are not clear indicators of God's presence and will. Jesus' remark that even **the elect** (see note on Matt. 22:14) could be led astray emphasizes the stunning character of the false prophets' miracles. But God will protect his own, so that they will not believe in a false messiah or prophet.

13:24–26 After that tribulation clearly sets the further statements of Jesus apart from the preceding verses. **sun . . . moon . . . stars**. Jesus now describes cosmic events (see note on Matt. 24:29) in anticipation of the **coming** of the enthroned (Mark 14:62) **Son of Man** (see 8:38; Rev. 1:7; note on Matt. 24:30).

13:28–29 Some have understood **fig tree** here as a symbol for the nation of Israel (see note on 11:13–14), but it is more likely that in this case Jesus is just using a familiar event in nature as another illustration: just as the fig tree's branches put forth **leaves**, giving a sure sign that **summer** would soon follow, so **when you see these things taking place, you know** that Christ will come soon. "These things" probably refers not to the events of 13:24–27 (for they *are* the end) but the events of vv. 5–23.

13:30 this generation will not pass away until all these things take place. Several interpretations have been offered for this difficult passage: (1) Some think "this generation" refers to the disciples who were alive when Jesus was speaking, and "all these things" refers to the beginning but not the completion of the sufferings described in vv. 3–13. (2) Others see in "all these things" a prediction with multiple fulfillments, so that Jesus' disciples will be both "this generation" that sees the destruction of the temple in A.D. 70 and also those at the end of the age who see the events surrounding the "abomination of desolation" (v. 14). (3) Since "the generation of . . ." in the OT can mean people who have a certain quality (cf. Ps. 14:5; 24:6; cf. Gk. *genea* in Luke 16:8), others understand "this generation" to refer either (a) to "this generation of believers" throughout the entire present age, or (b) to "this evil generation" that will remain until Christ returns to establish his kingdom (cf. Matt. 12:45; Luke 11:29). (4) Others, particularly dispensational interpreters, understand "generation" to mean "race" (this is another sense of Gk. *genea*), and think it refers to the Jewish people, who will not pass away until Christ returns. (5) Others understand "this generation" to mean the generation that sees "all these things" (Matt. 24:33), namely, the generation alive when the final period of great tribulation begins. According to this view, the illustration of the fig tree (Mark 13:28) shows that when the final events begin, Christ will come soon. Just as "these things" in v. 29 refers to events leading up to but not including Christ's return, so in v. 30 "all these things" refers to the same events (that is, the events described in vv. 3–13).

13:31 my words will not pass away. Jesus claims that his words (like those of the OT, see Matt. 5:18) are more enduring than creation and are in truth the revealed Word of God (cf. Isa. 51:6; Jer. 31:35–37).

THE TEMPLE MOUNT IN THE TIME OF JESUS

Herod's Temple Mount was the focal point of Jerusalem during the time of Jesus. Sitting atop Jerusalem's north-eastern ridge, it occupied one-sixth of the city's area. Under Herod the Great, the Temple Mount's foundation was expanded to encompass approximately 1.5 million square feet (140,000 square meters). Its foundational walls were constructed using gigantic stones, the largest found being 45 feet long, 11.5 feet high, and 12 feet thick (13.7 m by 3.5 m by 3.7 m).

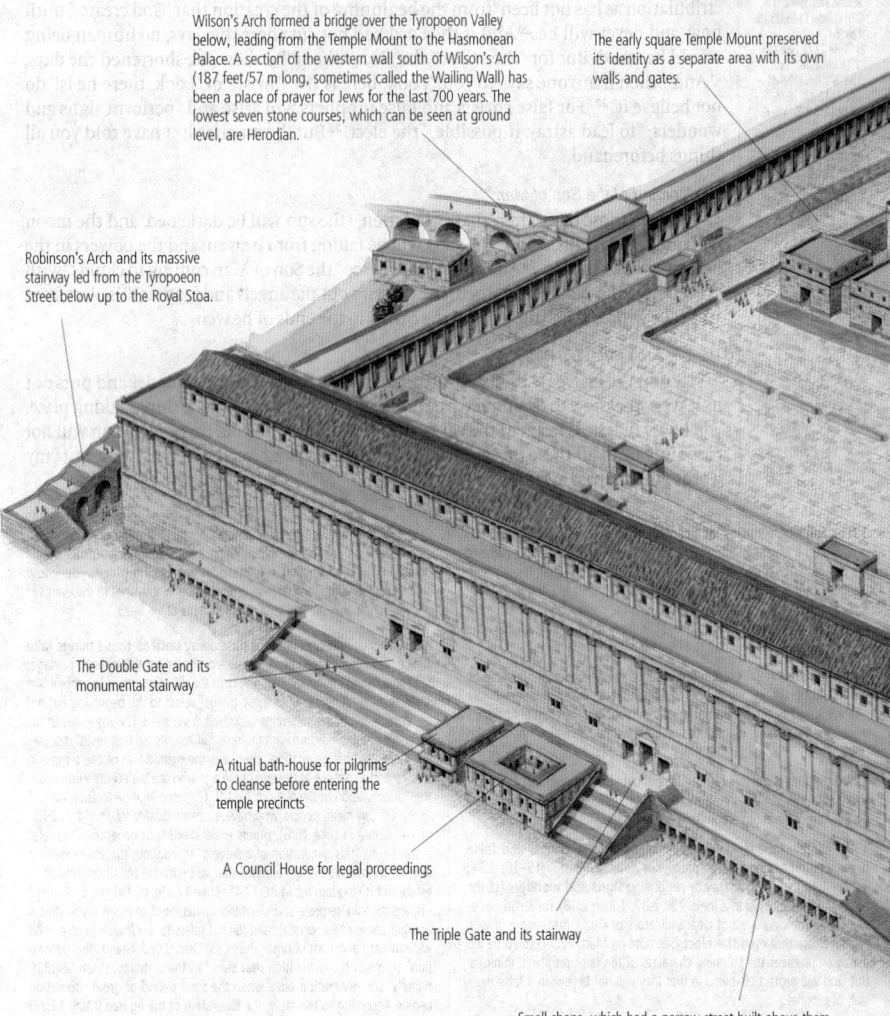

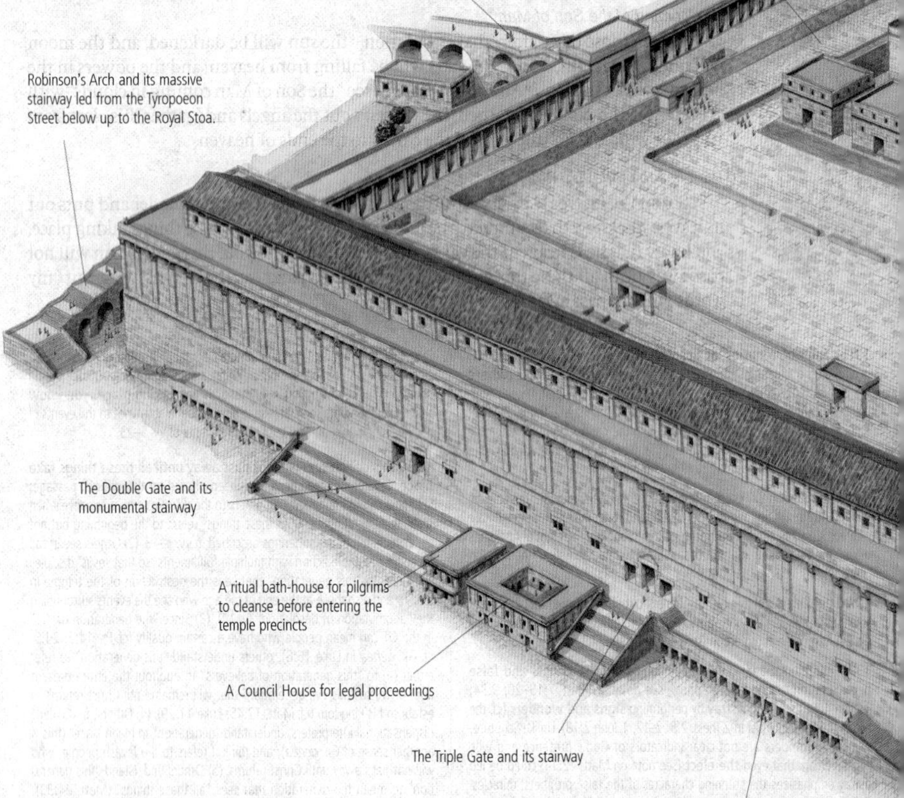

Wilson's Arch formed a bridge over the Tyropoeon Valley below, leading from the Temple Mount to the Hasmonean Palace. A section of the western wall south of Wilson's Arch (187 feet/57 m long, sometimes called the Wailing Wall) has been a place of prayer for Jews for the last 700 years. The lowest seven stone courses, which can be seen at ground level, are Herodian.
The early square Temple Mount preserved its identity as a separate area with its own walls and gates.
Robinson's Arch and its massive stairway led from the Tyropoeon Street below up to the Royal Stoa.
The Double Gate and its monumental stairway
A ritual bath-house for pilgrims to cleanse before entering the temple precincts
A Council House for legal proceedings
The Triple Gate and its stairway
Small shops, which had a narrow street built above them, were built along the southern wall of the Temple Mount.

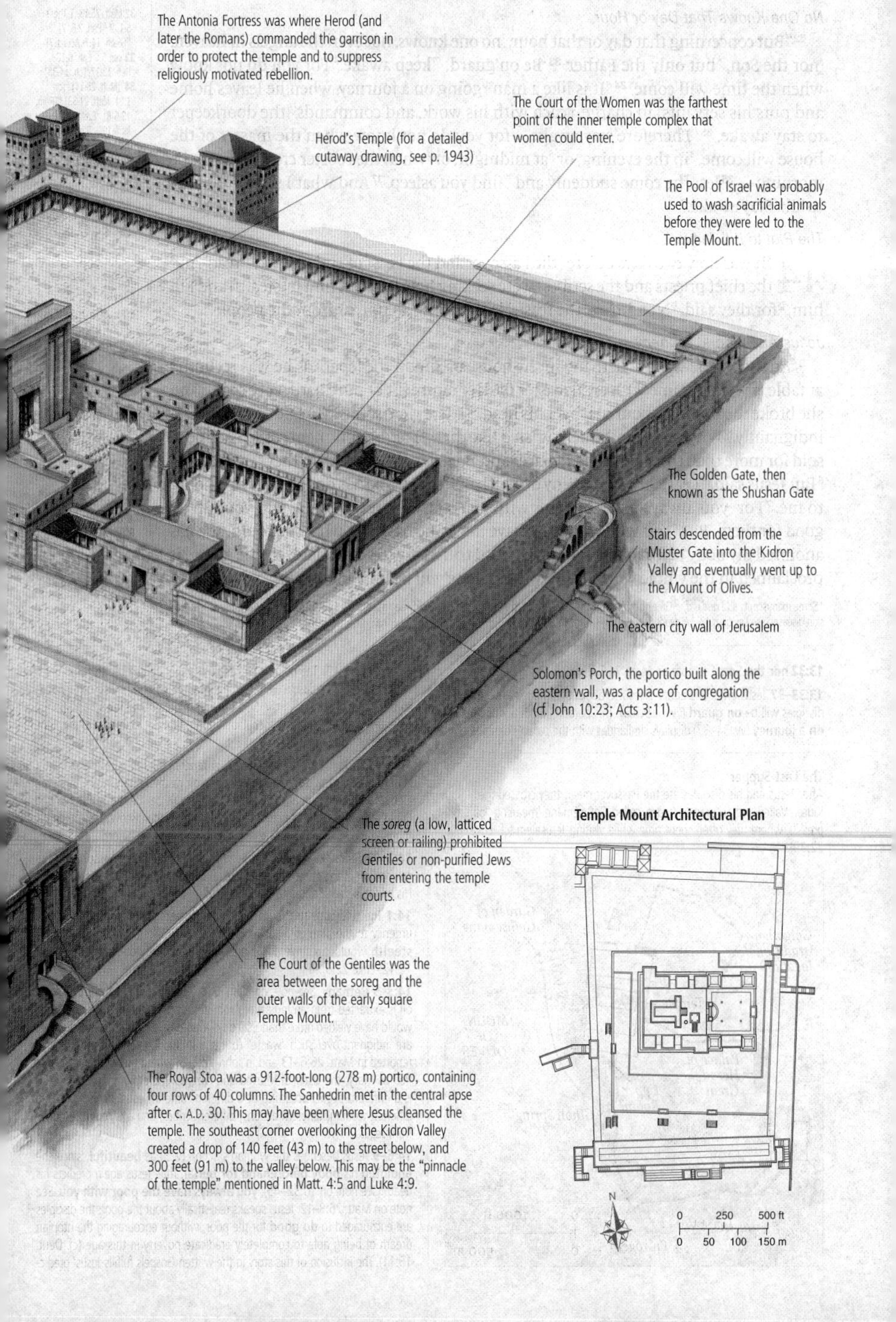
The Antonia Fortress was where Herod (and later the Romans) commanded the garrison in order to protect the temple and to suppress religiously motivated rebellion.
The Court of the Women was the farthest point of the inner temple complex that women could enter.
Herod's Temple (for a detailed cutaway drawing, see p. 1943)
The Pool of Israel was probably used to wash sacrificial animals before they were led to the Temple Mount.
The Golden Gate, then known as the Shushan Gate
Stairs descended from the Muster Gate into the Kidron Valley and eventually went up to the Mount of Olives.
The eastern city wall of Jerusalem
Solomon's Porch, the portico built along the eastern wall, was a place of congregation (cf. John 10:23; Acts 3:11).
The *soreg* (a low, latticed screen or railing) prohibited Gentiles or non-purified Jews from entering the temple courts.
The Court of the Gentiles was the area between the soreg and the outer walls of the early square Temple Mount.
The Royal Stoa was a 912-foot-long (278 m) portico, containing four rows of 40 columns. The Sanhedrin met in the central apse after c. A.D. 30. This may have been where Jesus cleansed the temple. The southeast corner overlooking the Kidron Valley created a drop of 140 feet (43 m) to the street below, and 300 feet (91 m) to the valley below. This may be the "pinnacle of the temple" mentioned in Matt. 4:5 and Luke 4:9.

Temple Mount Architectural Plan

N
0 250 500 ft
0 50 100 150 m

No One Knows That Day or Hour

32 "But concerning that day or that hour, [i]no one knows, not even the angels in heaven,
[j]nor the Son, [k]but only the Father. 33 [l]Be on guard, [m]keep awake.[1] For you do not know
when the time will come. 34 [n]It is like a man [o]going on a journey, when he leaves home
and puts his servants[2] in charge, [p]each with his work, and commands [q]the doorkeeper
to stay awake. 35 [r]Therefore stay awake—for you do not know when the master of the
house will come, [s]in the evening, or [s]at midnight, or [t]when the rooster crows,[3] or [u]in the
morning— 36 lest [v]he come suddenly and [w]find you asleep. 37 And what I say to you I say
to all: [r]Stay awake."

The Plot to Kill Jesus

14 [x]It was now two days before [y]the Passover and the Feast of Unleavened Bread. And
the chief priests and the scribes [z]were seeking how to arrest him by stealth and kill
him, 2 for they said, "Not during the feast, [a]lest there be an uproar from the people."

Jesus Anointed at Bethany

3 [b]And while he was at [c]Bethany in the house of Simon the leper,[4] as he was reclining
at table, a woman came with an alabaster flask of ointment of pure nard, very costly, and
she broke the flask and poured it over his head. 4 There were some who said to themselves
indignantly, "Why was the ointment wasted like that? 5 For this ointment could have been
sold for more than three hundred denarii[5] and [d]given to the poor." And they [e]scolded her.
6 But Jesus said, "Leave her alone. Why do you trouble her? She has done a beautiful thing
to me. 7 For [f]you always have the poor with you, and whenever [g]you want, you can do
good for them. But [h]you will not always have me. 8 [i]She has done what she could; she has
anointed my body beforehand [j]for burial. 9 And truly, I say to you, wherever [k]the gospel is
proclaimed in the whole world, what she has done will be told [l]in memory of her."

[1] Some manuscripts add *and pray* [2] Greek *bondservants* [3] That is, the third watch of the night, between midnight and 3 A.M. [4] *Leprosy* was a term for several skin diseases; see Leviticus 13 [5] A *denarius* was a day's wage for a laborer

32 [i]Matt. 25:13; 1 Thess. 5:1, 2 [j][Phil. 2:6, 7] [k][Zech. 14:7; Acts 1:7]
33 [l]ver. 5 [m]Eph. 6:18; Heb. 13:17; [ch. 14:38]
34 [n][Matt. 25:14] [o][ch. 12:1; Matt. 21:33] [p][Rom. 12:6-8] [q]Ezek. 44:11; John 10:3; [Luke 12:36]
35 [r]ch. 14:34-38; Matt. 25:13; 26:41; Luke 12:37; 21:36; Acts 20:31; 1 Cor. 16:13; 1 Thess. 5:6; 1 Pet. 5:8 [s]ch. 1:32; Luke 12:38 [t]ch. 14:30, 68, 72 [u][ch. 6:48; Ex. 14:24]
36 [v][1 Thess. 5:1-6] [w]ch. 14:40
37 [r][See ver. 35 above]

Chapter 14

1 [x]For ver. 1, 2, see Matt. 26:2-5; Luke 22:1, 2 [y]See John 6:4 [z]John 11:53; See Matt. 21:46
2 [a]Matt. 27:24
3 [b]For ver. 3-9, see Matt. 26:6-13; John 12:1-8; [Luke 7:37-39] [c]Matt. 21:17; John 11:18
5 [d][John 13:29] [e]John 11:33, 38 (Gk.)
7 [f]Deut. 15:11 [g][2 Cor. 9:7] [h]ch. 2:20; See John 7:33
8 [i][ch. 12:43; Luke 21:3; 2 Cor. 8:12] [j]John 19:40
9 [k][Matt. 24:14] [l]Acts 10:4

13:32 nor the Son. See note on Matt. 24:36.

13:33–37 Jesus gives this entire discourse about the end times so that the disciples will be **on guard** (vv. 5, 9, 23). This parable about **a man going on a journey** (vv. 34–37) displays similarities with the parable of the wicked tenants (12:1–12). The point is perpetual readiness while bearing God-given responsibilities. The sudden return of the **master of the house** corresponds to the sudden coming of the Son of Man (**find you asleep**, 13:36; see Luke 17:24–32). Instead of speculating about the specific timing of end-time events, **all** disciples are to be vigilant.

The Last Supper
After Jesus and his disciples ate the Passover meal, they crossed the Kidron Valley and entered a garden called Gethsemane (meaning "oil press"), where they often spent time while visiting Jerusalem (cf. Luke 22:39).

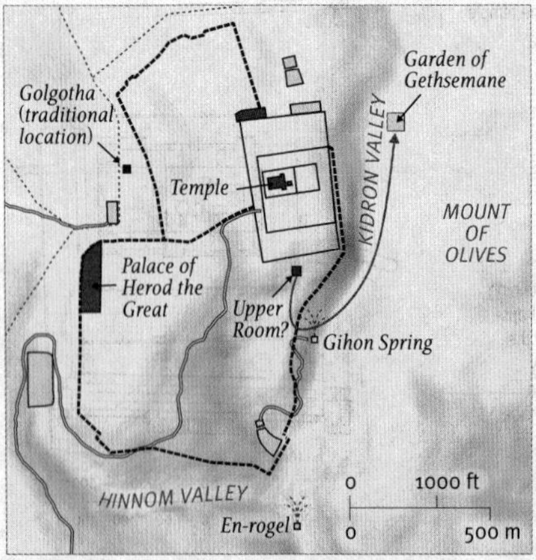

14:1–16:8 *Death and Resurrection in Jerusalem.* The narrative of Jesus' suffering moves quickly from the celebration of the Passover, the betrayal, Gethsemane, and the arrest of Jesus to his trials before the Sanhedrin and Pilate. It culminates in the crucifixion of Jesus and the discovery of the empty tomb, complemented by the announcement of Jesus' resurrection.

14:1–52 *Betrayal.* Jesus is betrayed by one of his closest associates. The celebration of the Passover anticipates his impending substitutionary death. His arrest is the first step toward that end.

14:1 The reference to the upcoming **Passover** feast renders a sense of urgency to the plan of Jesus' opponents. Their efforts to capture him **by stealth** would circumvent the protective popularity of Jesus (cf. 11:18; 12:12; Luke 22:6).

14:3–5 Bethany. See note on Matt. 21:17. The aromatic and **pure nard** oil is extracted from an Indian or Arabian root. The sale of such **costly** oil would have yielded more than 300 days' wages of a laborer. **Some** disciples are indignant over such "waste" (but see John 12:4–6). This story is also reported in Matt. 26:6–13 and in John 12:1–8, where the woman is identified as Mary, the sister of Martha and Lazarus. The story in Luke 7:36–50 is a different event, occurring at a different time in Jesus' ministry, with a different woman, different actions, different critics, and a different response from Jesus.

14:6–9 Jesus describes the woman's action (v. 3) as **beautiful**, since she **anointed** his **body beforehand for burial**. Thus Jesus again predicts his death (see note on 10:32–45). **you always have the poor with you**. See note on Matt. 26:8–12. Jesus speaks realistically about the poor: the disciples are encouraged to **do good** for the poor, without encouraging the utopian dream of being able to completely eradicate poverty in this age (cf. Deut. 15:11). The inclusion of this story in the written Gospels fulfills Jesus' predic-

Judas to Betray Jesus

10 [m]Then [n]Judas Iscariot, who was one of the twelve, [n]went to the chief priests in order
to betray him to them. **11** And when they heard it, they were glad and promised to give
him money. And he sought an opportunity to [o]betray him.

The Passover with the Disciples

12 [p]And on [q]the first day of Unleavened Bread, when they [r]sacrificed the Passover lamb, his
disciples said to him, "Where will you have us go and prepare for you to eat the Passover?"
13 And he sent [s]two of his disciples and said to them, "Go into the city, and a man carrying
a jar of water will meet you. Follow him, **14** and wherever he enters, say to the master of the
house, [t]'The Teacher says, Where is [u]my guest room, where I may eat the Passover with my
disciples?' **15** And he will show you [v]a large upper room furnished and ready; there prepare
for us." **16** And the disciples set out and went to the city and found it just as he had told
them, and they prepared the Passover.

17 [w]And when it was evening, he came with the twelve. **18** And as they were reclining
at table and eating, [x]Jesus said, "Truly, I say to you, one of you will betray me, [y]one who
is eating with me." **19** They began to be sorrowful and to say to him one after another,
"Is it I?" **20** He said to them, "It is [z]one of the twelve, [y]one who is dipping bread into the
dish with me. **21** For the Son of Man goes [a]as it is written of him, but [b]woe to that man
by whom the Son of Man is betrayed! [c]It would have been better for that man if he had
not been born."

Institution of the Lord's Supper

22 [d]And as they were eating, he took bread, and after [e]blessing it broke it and gave it
to them, and said, "Take; [f]this is my body." **23** And he took a cup, and when he had [g]given
thanks he gave it to them, and they all drank of it. **24** And he said to them, [f]"This is my
[h]blood of the[1] covenant, which is poured out for [i]many. **25** Truly, I say to you, I will not
drink again of the fruit of the vine until that day when I drink it new in the kingdom
of God."

[1] Some manuscripts insert *new*

10 [m]For ver. 10, 11, see Matt. 26:14-16; Luke 22:3-6; [John 13:2, 27, 30] [n]ch. 3:19; Matt. 27:3; Acts 1:16; [John 6:71; 12:4]
11 [o]See Matt. 20:18, 19
12 [p]For ver. 12-16, see Matt. 26:17-19; Luke 22:7-13 [q]Ex. 12:18 [r]1 Cor. 5:7
13 [s][ch. 11:1]
14 [t]See John 11:28 [u]Luke 2:7 (Gk.)
15 [v][Acts 1:13]
17 [w]For ver. 17-21, see Matt. 26:20-24; [Luke 22:14, 21-23; John 13:21-26]
18 [x][John 6:70, 71] [y][Ps. 41:9; John 13:18]
20 [z]ver. 10 [y][See ver. 18 above]
21 [a]ver. 49; ch. 9:12; Luke 18:31; 24:25, 27, 46; Acts 17:2, 3; 26:22, 23; 1 Cor. 15:3; 1 Pet. 1:10, 11 [b]Matt. 18:7 [c][See John 17:12]
22 [d]For ver. 22-25, see Matt. 26:26-29; Luke 22:18-20; 1 Cor. 11:23-25 [e]See Matt. 14:19 [f]1 Cor. 10:16; [John 6:53]
23 [g]See Matt. 15:36
24 [f][See ver. 22 above] [h]Ex. 24:8; [Zech. 9:11; Heb. 13:20] [i]See Matt. 20:28

tion that the story would be told **wherever the gospel is proclaimed in the whole world**.

14:10 The Jewish authorities had issued orders seeking the (inconspicuous) arrest of Jesus (John 11:57). **Judas Iscariot** could help them because he was one of the Twelve and would be able to tell them where Jesus could be found (fulfilling Ps. 41:9) when there were no crowds present. Judas is to identify Jesus to his opponents by night. Without modern lighting systems, finding and identifying someone at night would be a difficult task.

14:11 Mark, like Luke (Luke 22:5), is more general in his report and simply says Judas was given **money** in exchange for betraying Jesus, but Matthew records the exact amount: "thirty pieces of silver" (Matt. 26:15). In the OT, this was the price of a slave accidentally gored to death by an ox (Ex. 21:32), probably equivalent to about four months' wages. See note on Luke 22:3.

14:12 The first day of Unleavened Bread (Ex. 12:15, 18) could refer either to Nisan 14 or Nisan 15 according to Jewish reckoning in the NT era, and **Passover** lambs were apparently killed on both days, but here Mark is referring to Nisan 14 (Thursday). (Nisan usually falls somewhere in March/April in the Gregorian calendar; cf. note on Matt. 26:17; and The Hebrew Calendar, p. 34.) The Passover lamb is to be eaten within the walls of Jerusalem. Preparations for the meal have to be made inconspicuously, as Jesus is already a marked target.

14:13 a man carrying a jar of water. See note on Luke 22:7–13.

14:16 just as he had told them. Either Jesus had made prior arrangements with friends in Jerusalem in order to avoid the Jewish authorities, or the encounter was a miraculous work of God. **the Passover**. On the significance of this Passover meal, see note on Luke 22:15.

14:17 After sunset, with the beginning of Nisan 15 (see note on v. 12), the Passover meal begins. The celebrants remember the beginning of Israel's deliverance from slavery, when the Lord brought judgment by killing the firstborn in every Egyptian house but "passed over" the Israelite houses where the blood of the Passover lamb had been applied (Ex. 12:7, 12–13, 22–28). Those who celebrate the Passover also look forward to the ultimate liberation (Ex. 12:42; cf. note on John 2:13). From now on, Jesus' blood will protect from judgment those who take refuge in him (1 Cor. 5:7).

14:18 reclining at table. See note on Matt. 26:20. Despite intimate fellowship, Judas will **betray** his master (Ps. 41:9).

14:21 Jesus confirms that **the Son of Man goes as it is written** (cf. Ps. 55:13–14; Isa. 53:1–12; Dan. 9:25–26; Mark 8:31). **but woe to that man**. Despite the fact that the Scriptures have predicted that Jesus would suffer a substitutionary death, Judas is responsible for his evil deed. This is one of many scriptures that simultaneously affirm God's sovereign ordering of events and also human responsibility for those events (see notes on Gen. 50:18–21; Acts 2:23; 4:28; 18:9–11; 2 Tim. 2:10).

14:22 Jesus declares **this is my body** while he is still *in* his body, thus establishing a particular connection with **bread** as representing his own, once-and-for-all sacrifice. On the differing views regarding the significance of the communion elements, see notes on Luke 22:19 and 1 Cor. 11:24.

14:23–24 he took a cup. See note on Matt. 26:27. The communion wine corresponds to the covenant-establishing, once-and-for-all shed blood of Jesus as atonement **for many** (Mark 10:45; cf. Ex. 24:8; Isa. 53:12; Jer. 31:31–34).

14:25 that day when I drink it new. Jesus is confident that his impending death does not jeopardize his celebration (as exalted Lord of David; cf. 12:35–37; Ps. 110:1, 5) in the future **kingdom of God**.

Jesus Foretells Peter's Denial

26 [j]And when they had sung a hymn, [k]they went out to [l]the Mount of Olives. 27 And
Jesus said to them, "You will all fall away, for it is written, 'I will [m]strike the shepherd, and
the sheep will be scattered.' 28 But after I am raised up, [n]I will go before you to Galilee."
29 [o]Peter said to him, "Even though they all fall away, I will not." 30 And [p]Jesus said to him,
"Truly, I tell you, this very night, before [q]the rooster crows twice, you will deny me three
times." 31 But [r]he said emphatically, "If I must die with you, I will not deny you." And they
all said the same.

Jesus Prays in Gethsemane

32 [s]And they went [k]to a place called Gethsemane. And he said to his disciples, "Sit here
while I pray." 33 And he took with him [t]Peter and James and John, and began [u]to be greatly
distressed and troubled. 34 And he said to them, [v]"My soul is very sorrowful, even to death.
Remain here and [w]watch."[1] 35 And going a little farther, he fell on the ground [x]and prayed
that, if it were possible, [y]the hour might pass from him. 36 And he said, [z]"Abba, Father,
[a]all things are possible for you. Remove [b]this cup from me. [c]Yet not what I will, but what
you will." 37 And he came and found them sleeping, and he said to Peter, "Simon, are you
asleep? Could you not watch one hour? 38 [w]Watch and [d]pray that you may not [e]enter into
temptation. The spirit indeed is willing, but the flesh is weak." 39 And again he went away
and prayed, [f]saying the same words. 40 And again he came and found them sleeping, for
[g]their eyes were very heavy, and [h]they did not know what to answer him. 41 And he came
the third time and said to them, "Are you still sleeping and taking your rest? [i]It is enough;
[j]the hour has come. [k]The Son of Man is betrayed into the hands of sinners. 42 Rise, let us
be going; see, my betrayer is at hand."

Betrayal and Arrest of Jesus

43 [l]And immediately, while he was still speaking, [m]Judas came, one of the twelve, and
with him a crowd with swords and clubs, from the chief priests and the scribes and the
elders. 44 Now the betrayer had given them a sign, saying, "The one I will kiss is the man.
Seize him and lead him away under guard." 45 And when he came, he went up to him at
once and said, [n]"Rabbi!" And he [o]kissed him. 46 And they laid hands on him and seized
him. 47 But one of those who stood by drew his [p]sword and struck the servant[2] of the high
priest and cut off his ear. 48 And Jesus said to them, "Have you come out as against a robber, with swords and clubs to capture me? 49 [q]Day after day I was with you in the temple

[1] Or *keep awake*; also verses 37, 38 [2] Greek *bondservant*

26 [j]For ver. 26-31, see Matt. 26:30-35 [k]Luke 22:39; John 18:1 [l]See Matt. 21:1
27 [m]Cited from Zech. 13:7; [John 16:32]
28 [n]ch. 16:7; Matt. 28:7, 10, 16
29 [o][Luke 22:31, 33]
30 [p]Luke 22:34; John 13:38 [q]ver. 68, 72
31 [r]John 13:37
32 [s]For ver. 32-42, see Matt. 26:36-46; Luke 22:40-46 [k][See ver. 26 above]
33 [t]ch. 5:37; 9:2 [u][Matt. 17:23]
34 [v][Ps. 42:5, 6; John 12:27] [w]See Matt. 24:42
35 [x]Heb. 5:7 [y]ver. 41; John 12:23, 27; 13:1; 17:1; [Luke 22:53; John 16:4]
36 [z]Rom. 8:15; Gal. 4:6 [a]See Matt. 19:26 [b]See ch. 10:38 [c]John 5:30; 6:38; Phil. 2:8
38 [w][See ver. 34 above] [d]1 Pet. 4:7 [e]Matt. 6:13
39 [f]ver. 36
40 [g]Luke 9:32 [h][ch. 9:6; Luke 9:33]
41 [i][Luke 22:38] [j]See ver. 35 [k]ch. 9:31; 10:33
43 [l]For ver. 43-50, see Matt. 26:47-56; Luke 22:47-53; John 18:3-11 [m]ver. 10; Acts 1:16
45 [n]See John 1:38 [o]Luke 7:38, 45; 15:20; Acts 20:37 (Gk.)
47 [p][Luke 22:38]
49 [q][John 8:2]; [Luke 2:46; John 18:20]

14:26 hymn. See note on Matt. 26:30. **went out to the Mount of Olives**. Passover celebrants were to remain in Jerusalem for this night (Deut. 16:7); therefore Jesus did not return to Bethany.

14:27–28 You will all fall away. Jesus interprets the impending desertion by all of his disciples (v. 50; cf. John 16:32) in light of Zech. 13:7 (**strike the shepherd, and the sheep will be scattered**; cf. Mark 6:34). The striking of the shepherd, who "stands next to" God (Zech. 13:7), occurs in order to purify the people (Zech. 13:1, 7, 9). Jesus is confident that, following this dispersion, he will once again gather his flock (**after I am raised up**; see Mark 16:7). It is unclear why Jesus chooses **Galilee** as the place for this post-resurrection gathering—perhaps it is to draw the disciples' attention away from expecting a revolutionary event in Jerusalem (cf. Acts 1:6). At any rate, the disciples would naturally return to their home region of Galilee.

14:30 before the rooster crows twice. Each morning, roosters would crow a number of times separated by a few minutes. Jesus here specifies the first two individual crowings (cf. v. 72). Matthew, Luke, and John, however, refer to the entire time of several crowings.

14:31 I will not deny you. . . . they all said the same. See note on Matt. 26:33–35.

14:32 On **Gethsemane**, see note on Matt. 26:36. **while I pray**. Jesus prays, aware of his impending arrest and the weight of bearing the judgment of God (Mark 10:38).

14:36 The **cup** is a metaphor for the wrath of God, which he would pour out on sinners in righteous judgment (see note on 10:38; also Isa. 51:17–23; Jer. 25:15–18; and notes on Luke 22:42; John 18:11; Rom. 3:25; 1 John 2:2). Since Jesus satisfies God's wrath by becoming a propitiation for sin (see note on Rom. 3:25), the continued passing of the cup to the disciples (Mark 10:38–39: "The cup that I drink you will drink") turns judgment on Jesus into purification for them. In this intense time of trial, Jesus entrusts himself into the personal hands of his **Father**. On the word **Abba**, see note on Matt. 6:9.

14:37 Jesus is totally forsaken; his disciples are **sleeping** (contrast this with Peter's statement in v. 29). **Could you not watch**? Despite his own suffering, Jesus still calls his disciples to trusting prayer and watchfulness in the midst of temptation (cf. vv. 50–52, 66–72).

14:38 The spirit indeed is willing is not a reference to the Holy Spirit but to the disciples' human spirits, which desired to follow Jesus and be faithful (see v. 31). But they quickly gave in to physical fatigue: **the flesh is weak**. Well-intentioned believers can easily fail to fulfill their calling by merely giving in to various physical needs or desires.

14:39 Saying the same words does not mean the "empty phrases" that Jesus had taught against (Matt. 6:7); this was earnest repetition expressing the deep longing of his heart (for repetition in prayer, cf. Ps. 136:1–26; Isa. 6:3; 2 Cor. 12:8; Rev. 4:8).

14:41 It is enough may mean (1) enough prayer and wrestling with God—it is settled, and Jesus is going to the cross; (2) enough time—the end has come; or (3) enough sleep—it is time for the disciples to awake. **The hour** refers here to the time of Jesus' death and of his bearing divine judgment (as in vv. 35–36). This is also the time of his being given **into the hands of**

[r]teaching, and you did not seize me. But [s]let the Scriptures be fulfilled." **50** [t]And they all
left him and fled.

A Young Man Flees

51 And a young man followed him, with nothing but [u]a linen cloth about his body. And
they seized him, **52** but he left the linen cloth and ran away naked.

Jesus Before the Council

53 [v]And [w]they led Jesus to the high priest. And all the chief priests and the elders and
the scribes came together. **54** [w]And [x]Peter had followed him at a distance, [y]right into [z]the
courtyard of the high priest. And he was sitting with [a]the guards and [b]warming himself
at the fire. **55** Now the chief priests and the whole council[1] were seeking testimony against
Jesus to put him to death, but they found none. **56** [c]For many bore false witness against
him, but their testimony [d]did not agree. **57** And some stood up and bore false witness
against him, saying, **58** [e]"We heard him say, [f]'I will destroy this temple [g]that is made with
hands, and in three days I will build another, [h]not made with hands.'" **59** Yet even about
this their testimony did not agree. **60** And the high priest stood up in the midst and asked
Jesus, "Have you no answer to make? What is it that these men testify against you?"[2] **61** But
[i]he remained silent and made no answer. [j]Again the high priest asked him, "Are you [k]the
Christ, the Son of [l]the Blessed?" **62** And Jesus said, "I am, and [m]you will see the Son of Man
[n]seated at the right hand of Power, and [m]coming with the clouds of heaven." **63** And the
high priest [o]tore his garments and said, "What further witnesses do we need? **64** You have
heard [p]his blasphemy. What is your decision?" And they [q]all condemned him as [r]deserving

[1] Greek *Sanhedrin* [2] Or *Have you no answer to what these men testify against you?*

49 [r]Matt. 21:23; [Matt. 4:23] [s]See ver. 21; Matt. 1:22
50 [t]ver. 27; [Ps. 88:8, 18; John 16:32]
51 [u]ch. 15:46; Judg. 14:12; Prov. 31:24
53 [v]For ver. 53-65, see Matt. 26:57-68; [John 18:12, 13, 19-24] [w]Luke 22:54, 55
54 [w][See ver. 53 above] [x][John 18:15] [y][ver. 68] [z]See Matt. 26:3 [a]John 7:32; 18:3 [b]ver. 67; John 18:18
56 [c]Ps. 27:12; 35:11 [d][Deut. 17:6; 19:15]
58 [e][Acts 6:14] [f]ch. 15:29; See John 2:19 [g]Acts 7:48; 17:24; Heb. 9:11, 24 [h]2 Cor. 5:1
61 [i]ch. 15:4, 5; Isa. 53:7; John 19:9 [j]For ver. 61-63, [Luke 22:67-71] [k]ch. 8:29; See Matt. 1:17 [l][Rom. 1:25]
62 [m]See Matt. 16:27; 24:30 [n]Ps. 110:1; Heb. 1:3; [ch. 16:19]
63 [o]Num. 14:6; Acts 14:14
64 [p]Matt. 9:3; John 10:36 [q][Luke 23:50, 51] [r]See Lev. 24:16

sinners (cf. 9:31). Jesus accepts the reality of his coming death (cf. 10:45; Isa. 53:1–12).

14:43–46 Armed temple officials, employed by the Jewish leaders, arrest Jesus (vv. 46, 53). As a traitor, **Judas** misuses familiar actions of respect and friendship: he calls Jesus **Rabbi** and greets him with a **kiss**. Though it is dark, Judas knows Jesus well enough to pick him out from the group.

14:47 cut off his ear. See note on John 18:10.

14:50 they all left him. See note on vv. 27–28.

14:52 he left the linen cloth. This incident is recorded only in Mark's Gospel, leading many commentators to think that Mark himself, the author of this Gospel, was this young man, but that out of modesty he did not include his own name.

14:53–15:20 *Trial.* The trial before the Jewish Sanhedrin leads to the verdict of blasphemy, requiring the death penalty. But only the Roman governor Pilate has the authority to execute Jesus.

14:53 Before daybreak on Friday, Nisan 15, Jesus is brought before the **high priest** Caiaphas (see notes on Matt. 26:57–58; John 18:24) and the Sanhedrin (consisting of prominent Sadducees and Pharisees; see note on Matt. 26:59) for prosecution.

14:56 their testimony did not agree. The testimony of the many witnesses is contradictory (cf. Ex. 20:16; Deut. 5:20) and thus could not be used in a formal charge (Deut. 17:6).

14:58 Jesus never stated that *he* would **destroy** the **temple** (cf. John 2:19). He is innocent of this charge, as the high priest, acting as judge, is surely aware.

14:61–62 he remained silent. Jesus' silence complicates the high priest's task. He thus assumes the role of prosecutor. **Are you the Christ, the Son of the Blessed?** This question may be drawn from Jesus' public teaching in the temple (12:1–12, 35–37; cf. 3:5–11), in which he claimed to be the Son of the God of Israel and the messianic Lord of David, who shares exclusive honor with God himself. **I am**. Jesus answers affirmatively and then applies to himself messianic prophecies from Ps. 110:1 (cf. Mark 12:35–37) and Dan. 7:13–14.

14:64 Jesus' statement is considered **blasphemy** in that he claims divine Sonship and an exclusively exalted position at the right hand of God. Following the high priest's lead, they **all condemned him as deserving death**. The one option they fatally disregard is that Jesus is indeed speaking the truth

Jesus' Arrest, Trial, and Crucifixion

The path from Jesus' arrest to his crucifixion (part of which is often called the Via Dolorosa, "Way of Sorrows") is difficult to retrace with certainty. According to a possible harmony of the Gospel accounts, after the Passover meal Judas led a contingent of soldiers to Gethsemane to arrest Jesus (1). From there Jesus was led to Annas (location unknown), who sent him to his son-in-law Caiaphas, the high priest (2). The Jewish leaders then appealed to the Roman governor Pilate to have Jesus put to death (3). Luke records that Pilate sent Jesus to Herod Antipas (4), who questioned Jesus but returned him to Pilate without rendering any judgment (5). Pilate then sent Jesus to be crucified at Golgotha (6).

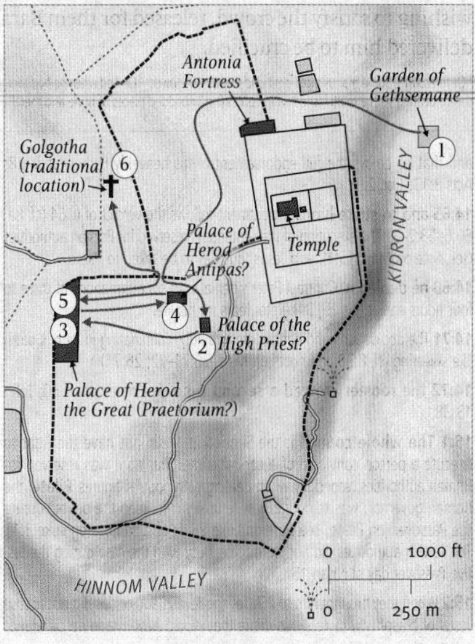

death. 65 [s]And some began [t]to spit on him and [u]to cover his face and to strike him, saying
to him, "Prophesy!" And the guards received him [v]with blows.

Peter Denies Jesus

66 [w]And as Peter was below in the courtyard, one of the servant girls of the high priest
came, 67 and seeing Peter [x]warming himself, she looked at him and said, "You also were
with the Nazarene, Jesus." 68 But he denied it, saying, "I neither know nor understand
what you mean." And he went out into the gateway[1] and [y]the rooster crowed.[2] 69 And
the servant girl saw him and began again to say to the bystanders, "This man is one
of them." 70 But again he denied it. And after a little while the bystanders again said to
Peter, "Certainly you are one of them, for you are a Galilean." 71 But he began to invoke
a curse on himself and to swear, "I do not know this man of whom you speak." 72 And
immediately the rooster crowed [z]a second time. And Peter remembered how Jesus had
said to him, [a]"Before the rooster crows twice, you will [b]deny me three times." And he
broke down and wept.[3]

Jesus Delivered to Pilate

15 [c]And as soon as it was morning, the chief priests [d]held a consultation with the elders
and scribes and the whole council. And [e]they bound Jesus and [f]led him away and
[g]delivered him over to [h]Pilate. 2 [i]And Pilate asked him, [j]"Are you the King of the Jews?" And
he answered him, [k]"You have said so." 3 And the chief priests accused him of many things.
4 And Pilate again asked him, [l]"Have you no answer to make? See how many charges they
bring against you." 5 But Jesus [l]made no further answer, so that Pilate was amazed.

Pilate Delivers Jesus to Be Crucified

6 [m]Now at the feast he used to release for them one prisoner for whom they asked. 7 And
among the rebels in prison, who had [n]committed murder [o]in the insurrection, there was a
man called Barabbas. 8 And the crowd came up and began to ask Pilate to do as he usually
did for them. 9 And he answered them, saying, "Do you want me to release for you the King
of the Jews?" 10 For he perceived that [p]it was out of envy that the chief priests had delivered
him up. 11 But the chief priests stirred up the crowd to have him release for them Barabbas
instead. 12 And Pilate again said to them, "Then what shall I do with [q]the man you call the
King of the Jews?" 13 And they cried out again, "Crucify him." 14 And Pilate said to them,
"Why, [r]what evil has he done?" But they shouted all the more, "Crucify him." 15 So Pilate,
wishing to satisfy the crowd, released for them Barabbas, and having [s]scourged[4] Jesus, he
delivered him to be crucified.

[1] Or *forecourt* [2] Some manuscripts omit *and the rooster crowed* [3] Or *And when he had thought about it, he wept* [4] A Roman judicial penalty, consisting of a severe beating with a multi-lashed whip containing imbedded pieces of bone and metal

65 [s]Luke 22:63, 64 [t]ch. 10:34; 15:19; Isa. 50:6 [u][Esth. 7:8] [v]Matt. 5:39; [Acts 23:2]
66 [w]For ver. 66-72, see Matt. 26:69-75; Luke 22:55-62; John 18:16-18, 25-27
67 [x]ver. 54
68 [y]ver. 30, 72
72 [z]ver. 68 [a]ver. 30 [b][Acts 3:13, 14]

Chapter 15

1 [c]Matt. 27:1; Luke 22:66 [d]ch. 3:6 [e]Matt. 27:2 [f]Luke 23:1; John 18:28 [g]See ch. 10:33 [h]Luke 3:1; 13:1; Acts 3:13; 4:27; 1 Tim. 6:13
2 [i]For ver. 2-5, see Matt. 27:11-14; Luke 23:2, 3; John 18:29-38 [j]ver. 9, 12, 18, 26; Matt. 2:2; John 18:39; 19:3; [ver. 32] [k][1 Tim. 6:13]; See Luke 22:70
4 [l][John 19:10]; See Matt. 26:63
5 [l][See ver. 4 above]
6 [m]For ver. 6-15, see Matt. 27:15-26; Luke 23:18-25; John 18:39, 40; 19:16
7 [n]Acts 3:14 [o][Acts 5:36, 37]
10 [p][John 12:19]
12 [q][John 19:15]
14 [r][Luke 23:41; John 8:46]
15 [s]ch. 10:34; Isa. 50:6; 53:5; [Luke 23:16; John 19:1]

and that he enjoys the full endorsement of his heavenly Father (cf. v. 28; Acts 3:13; Col. 2:9).

14:65 and to strike him. Mistreatment follows the verdict of v. 64 (cf. Isa. 50:6; 53:2–3). The execution of the sentence is reserved for Roman authorities (see note on Mark 15:1), and Jesus thus has to be taken to Pilate.

14:68 he denied it. Contrast Peter's denial with his affirmations of three to four hours earlier (vv. 29, 31). Peter fears for his life.

14:71 The accusations and denials grow rapidly, culminating in Peter's oath-like swearing (cf. 8:38 and notes on Matt. 26:71–72; 26:74).

14:72 the rooster crowed a second time. See notes on v. 30; John 13:38.

15:1 The whole council is the Sanhedrin. It did not have the right to execute a person convicted of a capital crime. That right was reserved for Roman authorities, especially when dealing with popular figures. **Pilate**, the Roman governor, was temporarily in Jerusalem "to keep the peace" during the Passover (on Pilate, see note on Luke 23:1; cf. also note on Luke 3:1). The Jewish authorities did not want to be busy with the case during the festive Passover day of Nisan 15.

15:2 When they brought him to **Pilate**, the Jewish authorities did not accuse Jesus of blasphemy (a religious crime that would have made no difference to Pilate) but rather of claiming to be **King of the Jews**, thus challenging Caesar's rule (in the eyes of Rome, a capital crime).

15:5 No further answer fulfills Isa. 53:7.

15:6–7 release . . . one prisoner . . . Barabbas. See note on Matt. 27:15–18.

15:10 Pilate realizes that the Jewish leaders are motivated by **envy**, and thus that their accusation of Jesus is ill-founded. However, he does not understand the theological issues at stake (i.e., blasphemy; see note on 14:64).

15:11–13 release . . . Barabbas instead. Ironically, Pilate will free a convicted rebel against Rome instead of a righteous man who has not spoken against Rome. **Crucify him**. Pilate is in a precarious position; he will execute Jesus in Roman fashion (crucifixion) based on a Jewish verdict.

15:14 what evil has he done? Pilate's last recourse is to protest that Jesus has been accused of nothing worthy of death (cf. Ps. 38:20–21; Isa. 53:9; Acts 3:13). While Pilate thus tried to make the Jewish authorities solely responsible for the death of Jesus, the fact remains that it occurred under his jurisdiction.

15:15 Pilate condemned Jesus to crucifixion, which was the means of executing criminals convicted of high treason. **having scourged Jesus**. Scourging, by itself, could lead to death (see note on Matt. 27:26; cf. note on John 19:1).

Jesus Is Mocked

16 [t]And the soldiers led him away inside [u]the palace (that is, [v]the governor's headquarters),[1] and they called together the whole [w]battalion.[2] **17** And they clothed him in [x]a purple
cloak, and twisting together a crown of thorns, they put it on him. **18** And they began to
salute him, [y]"Hail, King of the Jews!" **19** And they were striking his head with a reed and
[z]spitting on him and [a]kneeling down in homage to him. **20** And when they had [b]mocked
him, they stripped him of [x]the purple cloak and put his own clothes on him. And they
[c]led him out to crucify him.

The Crucifixion

21 [d]And they compelled a passerby, Simon of Cyrene, who was coming in from the country, the father of Alexander and Rufus, to carry his cross. **22** [e]And they brought him to the
place called Golgotha (which means Place of a Skull). **23** And they offered him wine mixed
with [f]myrrh, but he did not take it. **24** And they crucified him and [g]divided his garments
among them, casting lots for them, to decide what each should take. **25** And [h]it was the third
hour[3] when they crucified him. **26** And the inscription of the charge against him read, [i]"The
King of the Jews." **27** And with him they crucified two [j]robbers, [k]one on his right and one
on his left.[4] **29** And [l]those who passed by derided him, [m]wagging their heads and saying,
[n]"Aha! [o]You who would destroy the temple and rebuild it in three days, **30** save yourself,
and come down from the cross!" **31** So also the chief priests with the scribes mocked him
to one another, saying, [p]"He saved others; [q]he cannot save himself. **32** Let [r]the Christ, [s]the
King of Israel, come down now from the cross that we may [t]see and believe." [u]Those who
were crucified with him also reviled him.

The Death of Jesus

33 And when the sixth hour[5] had come, there was darkness over the whole land until
the ninth hour.[6] **34** And at the ninth hour Jesus [v]cried with a loud voice, [w]"Eloi, Eloi, lema
sabachthani?" which means, "My God, my God, why have you forsaken me?" **35** And some
of the bystanders hearing it said, "Behold, he is calling Elijah." **36** And someone ran and
filled a sponge with [x]sour wine, put it on a reed [y]and gave it to him to drink, saying, "Wait,
let us see whether Elijah will come to take him down." **37** And Jesus [z]uttered a loud cry and

[1] Greek *the praetorium* [2] Greek *cohort*; a tenth of a Roman legion, usually about 600 men [3] That is, 9 A.M. [4] Some manuscripts insert verse 28: *And the Scripture was fulfilled that says, "He was numbered with the transgressors"* [5] That is, noon [6] That is, 3 P.M.

16 [t]For ver. 16-20, see Matt. 27:27-31; John 19:2, 3 [u]See Matt. 26:3 [v]John 18:28, 33; 19:9; Acts 23:35; Phil. 1:13 (Gk.) [w]See Acts 10:1
17 [x]Rev. 18:12, 16; [Luke 23:11]
18 [y]See ver. 2
19 [z]See ch. 14:65 [a]See Matt. 8:2
20 [b]ch. 10:34 [x][See ver. 17 above] [c]Isa. 53:7
21 [d]Matt. 27:32; Luke 23:26; [John 19:17]
22 [e]For ver. 22-38, see Matt. 27:33-51; Luke 23:32-38, 44-46; John 19:17-19, 23, 24, 28-30
23 [f]Matt. 2:11; See John 19:39
24 [g]Ps. 22:18
25 [h][John 19:14]
26 [i]ver. 2
27 [j][John 18:40] [k][ch. 10:37]
29 [l]Ps. 22:7; 109:25; [Lam. 1:12] [m]Job 16:4; Jer. 18:16; Lam. 2:15 [n]Ps. 35:25; 40:15 [o]ch. 14:58
31 [p][Luke 4:23] [q][Matt. 26:53, 54; John 10:18]
32 [r]See Matt. 1:17 [s]John 1:49; 12:13; [ver. 26] [t]John 20:29 [u][Luke 23:39-43]
34 [v][Heb. 5:7] [w]Cited from Ps. 22:1
36 [x]Ruth 2:14 [y]Ps. 69:21
37 [z]ver. 34

15:16–19 On the **governor's headquarters**, see note on John 18:28. The presence of **the whole battalion** (about 600 men at full strength) assumes that Jesus is a rebel against Rome. Therefore the soldiers dress, mock, and mistreat him as **King of the Jews** (Matt. 27:28; Mark 15:9, 12, 26), which, contrary to their view, he truly was. The sarcastic **homage** paid to Jesus imitates what various emperors in Rome expected of their subjects (see also note on Matt. 27:28–31).

15:21–16:8 *Crucifixion and Resurrection.* In Mark's narrative, Jesus' death separates the group of scoffers (speaking before his death) from his followers and admirers (speaking after his death). The empty tomb is part of the fulfillment of Jesus' prediction of his resurrection (8:31; 9:30–32; 10:32–34).

15:21 According to both Jewish and Roman custom, Jesus had to be taken outside the city walls to be crucified. It was the morning of Nisan 15. As allowed by Roman law, **Simon of Cyrene** was forced to **carry** Jesus' **cross** (see note on Matt. 27:32). Crucifixion was the final public deterrent to warn people not to rebel against Rome. The mention of **Alexander and Rufus** leads many to conclude that they were believers known in the early church at the time that Mark wrote his Gospel. See note on Rom. 16:13.

15:23 Wine mixed with myrrh is intended to have a mildly numbing effect. Jesus would not take this mixture.

15:24 And they crucified him. Jesus' hands were nailed above the wrist on the horizontal beam, and his feet were placed with one above the other and then nailed to the vertical beam (on crucifixion, see notes on Matt. 27:35; John 18:32). **Casting lots** fulfilled the prophecy in Ps. 22:18.

15:25 it was the third hour. John has "about the sixth hour," but he is not attempting to pinpoint the exact time; the time references should not be seen as contradictory (see note on John 19:14).

15:26 The inscription of the charge against him (see note on John 19:19) is posted above Jesus' head, so that all can see why he was so shamefully executed. **"The King of the Jews."** With this inscription, Pilate justified his actions (Jesus was crucified as a political rebel) and also provoked the Jewish authorities (John 19:19–22; cf. Mark 15:10).

15:27 The **two robbers** crucified with Jesus fulfill the prophecy, "he was numbered with the transgressors" (Isa. 53:12). On "robbers," see note on Matt. 27:38. Luke alone records that, sometime later, one of the two robbers repented and expressed faith in Jesus (Luke 23:39–43).

15:29–31 Because it was Passover, many **passed by** the place of Christ's crucifixion. **wagging their heads**. See Ps. 22:7–8. **You who would destroy the temple**. See note on Mark 14:58. Jesus' opponents conceded that he **saved others** (as in 5:23, 28, 34; 6:56; 10:52), but they believed that all of his authority, power, and claims had been nailed to the cross. Jesus appeared to have been silenced and divinely condemned for his blasphemy (cf. Deut. 21:23).

15:33 Between noon and 3:00 P.M. there was **darkness**. This was not a solar eclipse (see note on Matt. 27:45). Darkness represents lament (Amos 8:9–10) and divine judgment (Ex. 10:21–23; cf. note on Luke 23:44–45).

15:34 My God, my God, why have you forsaken me? See note on Matt. 27:46. Jesus utters the opening words of Psalm 22 and in so doing cries out to God in the immense pain of divine abandonment (see Isa. 59:2; Hab. 1:13), which he suffers as a substitute for sinful mankind (see note on Mark 10:45). Yet the following verses of Psalm 22 also anticipate divine intervention on his behalf (cf. Heb. 5:7–9). Jesus knows why he is experiencing God-forsakenness, just as he knows his death will not be the end of his story.

15:35 he is calling Elijah. See note on Matt. 27:47.

15:36 sour wine. Cf. note on Luke 23:36.

15:37 The final **loud cry** is probably the cry of victory, "It is finished" (John

[a]breathed his last. **38** And [b]the curtain of the temple was torn in two, from top to bottom.
39 [c]And when the centurion, who stood facing him, saw that in this way he[1] breathed his
last, he said, [d]"Truly this man was the Son[2] of God!"
40 There were also [e]women looking on [f]from a distance, among whom were [g]Mary
Magdalene, and Mary the mother of James the younger and of Joses, and [i]Salome. **41** When
he was in Galilee, they followed him and [g]ministered to him, and there were also many
other women who [j]came up with him to Jerusalem.

Jesus Is Buried

42 [k]And when evening had come, since it was [l]the day of Preparation, that is, the day
before the Sabbath, **43** Joseph of Arimathea, [m]a respected member of the council, who [n]was
also himself looking for the kingdom of God, took courage and went to Pilate and asked
for the body of Jesus. **44** Pilate was surprised to hear that he should have already died.[3] And
summoning [o]the centurion, he asked him whether he was already dead. **45** And when he
learned from [o]the centurion that he was dead, he granted the corpse to Joseph. **46** And
Joseph[4] bought [p]a linen shroud, and taking him down, wrapped him in the linen shroud
and [q]laid him in a tomb [r]that had been cut out of the rock. And he rolled [s]a stone against
the entrance of the tomb. **47** [t]Mary Magdalene and Mary the mother of Joses saw where
he was laid.

The Resurrection

16 [u, v]When the Sabbath was past, [w]Mary Magdalene, [w]Mary the mother of James,
and [i]Salome [x]bought spices, so that they might go and anoint him. **2** And very early
on the first day of the week, when the sun had risen, they went to the tomb. **3** And they
were saying to one another, "Who will roll away [y]the stone for us from the entrance of
the tomb?" **4** And looking up, they saw that the stone had been rolled back—[z]it was very
large. **5** And [a]entering the tomb, they saw a young man sitting on the right side, [b]dressed
in [c]a white robe, and [d]they were alarmed. **6** And he said to them, [d]"Do not be alarmed.

[1] Some manuscripts insert *cried out and* [2] Or *a son* [3] Or *Pilate wondered whether he had already died* [4] Greek *he*

37 [a][John 10:18]
38 [b]Ex. 26:31-33; 2 Chr. 3:14
39 [c]For ver. 39-41, see Matt. 27:54-56; Luke 23:47, 49 [d]Matt. 27:43
40 [e]John 19:25 [f]Ps. 38:11 [g]See Luke 8:2, 3 [i]ch. 16:1; [Matt. 27:56]
41 [g][See ver. 40 above] [j]Luke 2:4
42 [k]For ver. 42-47, see Matt. 27:57-61; Luke 23:50-56; John 19:38-42 [l]See Matt. 27:62
43 [m]Acts 13:50; 17:12 [n]Luke 2:25, 38
44 [o]ver. 39
45 [o][See ver. 44 above]
46 [p]See ch. 14:51 [q][Isa. 53:9] [r]Isa. 22:16 [s]ch. 16:4; [John 11:38]
47 [t]ver. 40

Chapter 16

1 [u]For ver. 1-8, see Matt. 28:1-8; Luke 24:1-10; John 20:1 [v][ch. 1:32] [w]ch. 15:40 [i][See ch. 15:40 above] [x]Luke 23:56; [John 19:39, 40]
3 [y]ch. 15:46
4 [z]Matt. 27:60
5 [a][John 20:11, 12] [b][ch. 9:3; Dan. 7:9; John 20:12; Acts 1:10] [c]Rev. 6:11; 7:9 [d]ch. 9:15 (Gk.)
6 [d][See ver. 5 above]

19:30). Once Jesus dies, all mocking ceases in Mark's account. Subsequently, only the voices of the respectful (centurion) and the mourners (women) are heard. Jesus died around the time of the daily afternoon sacrifice in the temple (see note on Matt. 27:45).

15:38 The inner **curtain of the temple was torn in two, from top to bottom,** removing the separation between the Holy Place and the Most Holy Place (see Heb. 9:2–3, 12, 24; 10:19–20; note on Matt. 27:51). Access to God is now provided by the unique sacrifice of Jesus, rendering the temple sacrifices obsolete.

15:39 The **centurion** has observed the death of many crucified criminals; he recognizes the purity and power of Jesus (**in this way**) and rightly sees that he is **the Son of God** (cf. note on Luke 23:47). Like the thief on the cross who expressed faith in Jesus (Luke 23:39–43), the centurion may have had incomplete understanding of Jesus' identity and mission, but Mark seems to record this testimony as an indication of the centurion's faith and the truth about Jesus' identity.

15:40 women looking on. See note on Luke 23:49. **Mary Magdalene**. See note on Luke 8:2.

15:42 Deuteronomy 21:23 mandates the burial of a corpse on the day of death (taking priority over Passover; see John 19:40). The **day of Preparation** (see notes on John 19:14; 19:31; 19:42) is idiomatic for "the day before a regular Sabbath."

15:43 Joseph of Arimathea (see note on Matt. 27:57–60), **a respected member of the** Jewish **council** (or "Sanhedrin"; see note on Matt. 26:59), courageously intended to bury Jesus before the Sabbath began at sundown (Nisan 16). He was **looking for the kingdom of God**, and Matt. 27:57 calls him "a disciple of Jesus."

15:44–45 Pilate had jurisdiction over whether or not the corpse should be buried. Once he ascertained that Jesus was indeed **dead**, Pilate agreed to it as a benevolent concession.

15:46 Joseph wrapped the corpse in a **linen shroud** (complemented by Nicodemus's burial spices; see John 19:39–40) and placed it **in a tomb . . . cut out of the rock** (John 19:41). According to Jewish custom (in part due to Deut. 21:22–23), proper burials were to take place within 24 hours. The main options for Judean burial included shallow trench graves, sarcophagi (coffin-like stone boxes, rarely used above ground), and rock-cut tombs (such as the one described here; see The Tomb of Jesus, p. 2069). Rock-cut tombs were much more expensive than trench graves since they required extensive excavation into existing or manufactured caves; they are thought to have generally belonged to single extended families. Therefore, this tomb would most probably have been Joseph of Arimathea's family tomb. Inside rock-cut tombs, burials would occur in *loculi* (beds cut into the rock) or *arcosolia* (beds cut sideways into the rock like ledges with an arched top). Sarcophagi and wooden coffins were also occasionally used in the tombs. After a body had decayed, its bones were removed to allow reuse of the *loculus* or *arcosolium*. These bones could be piled elsewhere in the tomb or reinterred in a specially designed box (ossuary), which held one or two bodies. The two main locations where Jesus is thought to have been buried (the Church of the Holy Sepulchre, west of the temple; and the Garden Tomb, north of the ancient city) were rock-cut tombs with rolling stone doors. Both would have been outside the first-century city walls. Early church tradition strongly favors the Holy Sepulchre site, and the area around the Garden Tomb consists largely of Iron Age (OT-era) tombs, thus also favoring the Holy Sepulchre site for a NT-era burial. The Holy Sepulchre Church originally dated from the time of Constantine (dedicated in A.D. 335), though the present structure is largely medieval.

15:47 Mary Magdalene and Mary the mother of James and **Joses** (v. 40) were eyewitnesses to Jesus' burial.

16:1–2 Once the **Sabbath** is over (at sundown on Saturday evening), the women can buy oils for (delayed) embalming of the corpse after sunrise on Sunday morning (**the first day of the week**). This occurred on the "third day" (8:31; 10:34).

16:5 they saw a young man. An angel. Luke 24:4 and John 20:12 give additional information, specifying two angels, but Mark and Matthew (Matt. 28:2–5) mention only one.

16:6 He has risen; he is not here. The heavenly messenger confirms that

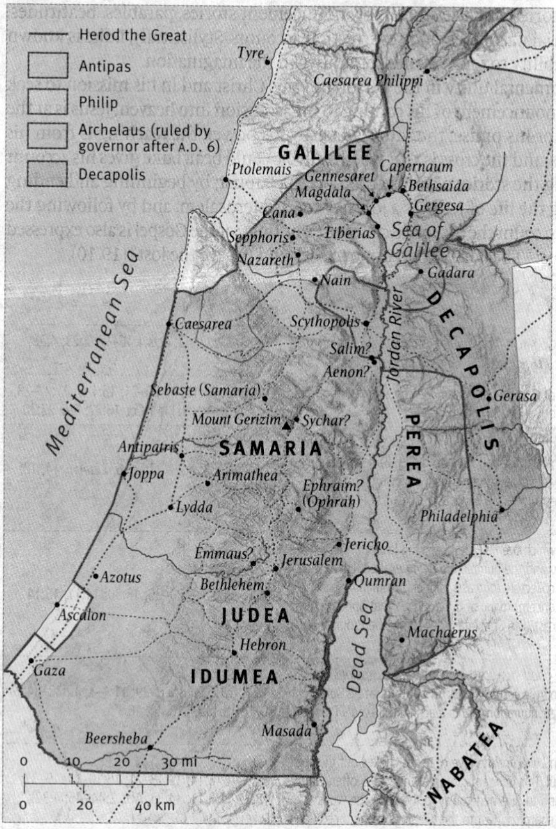

The Setting of Luke
The events in the book of Luke take place almost entirely within the vicinity of Palestine, an area extending roughly from Caesarea Philippi in the north to Beersheba in the south. During this time it was ruled by the Roman Empire. The opening chapters describe events surrounding Jesus' birth in Judea, where Herod had been appointed king by the Romans. The closing chapters end with Jesus' death, resurrection, and ascension during the rule of Pontius Pilate and the tetrarchs Antipas and Philip.

parousia (return of Christ) would come immediately but that there would be a period between his resurrection and his return (9:27; 19:11; 21:20–24; 22:69; Acts 1:6–9). Nevertheless, Jesus would return (Luke 3:9, 17; 12:38–48; 18:8; 21:32) in bodily form (Acts 1:11), and believers should live in watchful expectation (Luke 21:34–36).

4. *To emphasize that his readers need not fear Rome.* Luke hints at this theme by highlighting Herod's and Pilate's desire to release Jesus and the Roman centurion's recognition of his innocence. Luke also records (in Acts) several occasions where Roman authorities came to Paul's rescue. When Roman officials *did* persecute, Luke explains that it was due to error and that the persecution ceased immediately when the error was discovered (cf. Acts 16:22–39).

History of Salvation Summary

Jesus comes as the messianic King to deliver the poor and needy and downcast (4:18–19). He fulfills the whole OT (24:44–47), especially its promises of everlasting salvation. The fulfillment of his mission comes with his crucifixion and resurrection. (For an explanation of the "History of Salvation," see Overview of the Bible, pp. 23–26.)

Literary Features

The narrative of Luke as a whole follows the chronology of Christ's life and death. No Gospel encompasses such a complete range of subgenres as Luke: annunciation stories, birth narratives, lyric praise psalms, Christmas carols, prophecies, genealogies, preparation stories, temptation stories, calling stories, recognition stories, conflict stories, encounter stories, miracle stories, pronouncement stories, parables, beatitudes, sermons, proverbs, passion stories, trial narratives, and resurrection accounts. Stylistically, Luke is known for his vivid descriptive details and ability to make scenes come alive in the imagination.

The Gospel of Luke finds its fundamental unity in the person of Jesus Christ and in his mission to seek and to save the lost. From the first announcement of his coming to his ascension into heaven, Jesus is at the center of everything: the songs are for his praise, the miracles are by his power, the teaching is from his wisdom, the conflict is over his claims, and the cross is that which only he could bear. Luke gives his account further literary unity by intertwining the stories of Jesus and John the Baptist; by beginning and ending his story at the temple; by presenting the life of Jesus as a journey toward Jerusalem; and by following the progress of the disciples as they learn to count the cost of discipleship. The unity of the Gospel is also expressed in Jesus' pronouncement to Zacchaeus: "The Son of Man came to seek and to save the lost" (19:10).

Key Themes

1. *God's sovereign rule over history.* The promises God made through the prophets are already being fulfilled.	13:33; 22:22, 42; Acts 1:16–17; 2:23; 4:28; etc.
2. *The arrival and actual presence of the kingdom of God.* Nevertheless, the consummation of the kingdom is still a future event, a blessed hope for which the church prays.	11:2, 20; 16:16; 17:20–21; 18:1–8; 21:27–28, 34–36; cf. Acts 1:11; 1 Cor. 16:22; Rev. 22:20
3. *The coming and indwelling of the Holy Spirit upon Jesus and his followers.* The Spirit is present in the Gospel of Luke, from the births of John the Baptist and Jesus to the end. The Spirit is present at Jesus' dedication in the temple, his baptism, temptation, early ministry, and first sermon. The Holy Spirit is central to the message of John the Baptist, and Jesus at his ascension promises the Spirit's future coming in power.	1:15–17, 35; 2:25–27; 3:16, 22; 4:1, 14, 18; 5:17; 24:49
4. *The great reversal taking place in the world,* in which the first are becoming last and the last are becoming first, the proud are being brought low and the humble are being exalted. Luke places great emphasis on God's love for the poor, tax collectors, outcasts, sinners, women, Samaritans, and Gentiles. In keeping with this concern, many of the episodes that appear only in Luke's Gospel feature the welcome of an outcast (the Christmas shepherds, the Prodigal Son, the persistent widow, Zacchaeus, etc.).	1:48, 52–53; 6:20–26; 13:30; 14:11; 18:14
5. *Believers are to live a life of prayer and practice good stewardship with their possessions.* In Luke's narrative, prayer occurs at every major point in Jesus' life: at his baptism; at his selection of the Twelve; at Peter's confession; at Jesus' transfiguration; in his teaching the Lord's Prayer; before Peter's denial; etc.	3:21; 6:12; 9:18, 28–29; 11:1–4; 12:33–34; 16:9; 18:1; 22:32, 40, 46
6. *The danger of riches* is constantly emphasized in Luke, for the love of riches chokes out the seed of the gospel and keeps it from becoming fruitful. This danger is so great that Jesus often warns his readers not to set their hearts upon riches and to give generously to the poor. The woes pronounced upon haughty rich people stand in sharp contrast to the blessings pronounced upon the humble poor.	6:20–26; 8:14; 12:13–21; 16:10–13, 19–31; 18:22 (cf. 5:11; 14:33; Acts 2:44–45; 4:32); Luke 21:3–4

Outline

I. The Prologue (1:1–4)

II. The Infancy Narrative (1:5–2:52)
- A. The birth of John the Baptist foretold (1:5–25)
- B. The birth of Jesus foretold (1:26–38)
- C. Mary visits Elizabeth (1:39–56)
- D. The birth of John the Baptist (1:57–80)
- E. The birth of Jesus Christ (2:1–52)
  1. Jesus is born (2:1–20)
  2. Jesus presented in the temple (2:21–40)
  3. The boy Jesus in the temple (2:41–52)

III. Preparation for the Ministry of Jesus (3:1–4:15)
- A. John the Baptist prepares the way (3:1–20)
- B. Jesus' baptism, genealogy, and temptation (3:21–4:15)
  1. Jesus' baptism (3:21–22)
  2. The genealogy of Jesus Christ (3:23–38)
  3. The temptation of Jesus (4:1–15)

IV. The Ministry of Jesus in Galilee (4:16–9:50)
   A. The beginning (4:16–5:16)
      1. Jesus rejected at Nazareth (4:16–30)
      2. Jesus begins his healing ministry (4:31–41)
      3. Jesus preaches in synagogues (4:42–44)
      4. Jesus calls the first disciples (5:1–11)
      5. Jesus cleanses a leper (5:12–16)
   B. The beginning of controversy (5:17–6:11)
      1. Jesus heals a paralytic (5:17–26)
      2. Jesus calls Levi (5:27–32)
      3. A question about fasting (5:33–39)
      4. Jesus is lord of the Sabbath (6:1–5)
      5. A man with a withered hand (6:6–11)
   C. Jesus teaches the disciples (6:12–49)
      1. Jesus appoints twelve apostles (6:12–16)
      2. Jesus ministers to a great multitude (6:17–19)
      3. The Beatitudes (6:20–23)
      4. Jesus pronounces woes (6:24–26)
      5. Love your enemies (6:27–36)
      6. Judging others (6:37–42)
      7. A tree and its fruit (6:43–45)
      8. Build your house on the rock (6:46–49)
   D. Who is this Jesus? (7:1–50)
      1. Jesus heals a centurion's servant (7:1–10)
      2. Jesus raises a widow's son (7:11–17)
      3. Messengers from John the Baptist (7:18–35)
      4. A sinful woman forgiven (7:36–50)
   E. Jesus teaches in parables (8:1–21)
      1. Women accompanying Jesus (8:1–3)
      2. The parable of the sower (8:4–8)
      3. The purpose of the parables (8:9–15)
      4. A lamp under a jar (8:16–18)
      5. Jesus' mother and brothers (8:19–21)
   F. Jesus, Lord of nature, demons, disease, and death (8:22–56)
      1. Jesus calms a storm (8:22–25)
      2. Jesus heals a demon-possessed man (8:26–39)
      3. Jesus heals a woman and Jairus's daughter (8:40–56)
   G. Jesus and the Twelve (9:1–50)
      1. Jesus sends out the Twelve (9:1–6)
      2. Herod Antipas is perplexed by Jesus (9:7–9)
      3. Jesus feeds the 5,000 (9:10–17)
      4. Peter confesses Jesus as the Christ (9:18–20)
      5. Jesus foretells his death (9:21–22)
      6. Jesus teaches the disciples (9:23–27)
      7. The transfiguration (9:28–36)
      8. The healing of a boy with an unclean spirit (9:37–43a)
      9. Jesus again foretells his death (9:43b–45)
      10. Who is the greatest? (9:46–48)
      11. Anyone not against us is for us (9:49–50)

V. The Journey to Jerusalem (9:51–19:27)
   A. The first mention of the journey to Jerusalem (9:51–13:21)
      1. The mission to Samaria (9:51–56)
      2. The cost of following Jesus (9:57–62)
      3. The mission of the seventy-two (10:1–24)
      4. The parable of the good Samaritan (10:25–37)

THE GOSPEL ACCORDING TO
LUKE

Dedication to Theophilus

1 Inasmuch as many have undertaken to compile a narrative of the things that [a]have
been accomplished among us, 2 [b]just as those who [c]from the beginning were [d]eyewit-
nesses and [e]ministers of [f]the word [g]have delivered them to us, 3 it seemed good to me also,
having followed all things closely for some time past, to write [h]an orderly account for
you, [i]most excellent [j]Theophilus, 4 that you may have [k]certainty concerning the things
[l]you have been taught.

Birth of John the Baptist Foretold

5 [m]In the days of Herod, king of Judea, there was a priest named Zechariah,[1] [n]of [o]the
division of Abijah. And he had a wife from the daughters of Aaron, and her name was
Elizabeth. 6 And they were both [p]righteous before God, walking [q]blamelessly in all the
commandments and statutes of the Lord. 7 But they had no child, because [r]Elizabeth was
barren, and [s]both were advanced in years.
8 Now [t]while he was serving as priest before God when [u]his division was on duty, 9 according to the custom of the priesthood, he was chosen by lot [v]to enter [w]the temple of the Lord
and burn incense. 10 And the whole multitude of the people [x]were praying [y]outside at the
hour of incense. 11 And there appeared to him an angel of the Lord standing on the right
side of [z]the altar of incense. 12 And Zechariah was troubled when he saw him, and [a]fear
fell upon him. 13 But the angel said to him, "Do not be afraid, Zechariah, for [b]your prayer

[1] Greek *Zacharias*

12 [a]Acts 19:17 **13** [b][Acts 10:4, 31]

Chapter 1

1 [a]2 Tim. 4:5, 17 (Gk.); [Acts 3:18]
2 [b][Heb. 2:3] [c]John 15:27; 16:4; [Mark 1:1; Acts 11:15] [d]2 Pet. 1:16; 1 John 1:1, 3; [Acts 4:20; 1 Pet. 5:1] [e]Acts 26:16; 1 Cor. 4:1 [f]See Mark 4:14 [g]1 Cor. 11:2, 23
3 [h]Acts 11:4 [i]Acts 23:26; 24:3; 26:25 [j]Acts 1:1
4 [k]Acts 2:36 (Gk.); [2 Pet. 1:16, 19] [l]Acts 18:25; Rom. 2:18; 1 Cor. 14:19; Gal. 6:6 (Gk.)
5 [m]Matt. 2:1 [n]1 Chr. 24:10 [o]ver. 8
6 [p]ch. 2:25 [q]Phil. 2:15; 3:6; 1 Thess. 2:10; 3:13; 5:23; [Acts 23:1; 24:16]
7 [r]ver. 36; [Judg. 13:2; 1 Sam. 1:2] [s][Gen. 18:11; Heb. 11:11, 12]
8 [t]1 Chr. 24:19; 2 Chr. 8:14; 31:2; [ver. 23] [u]ver. 5
9 [v]Ex. 30:7, 8; 1 Sam. 2:28; 1 Chr. 23:13; 2 Chr. 29:11 [w]ver. 21, 22; Rev. 11:2, 19; [Heb. 9:2, 3]
10 [x]Ps. 141:2; [Rev. 5:8; 8:3, 4] [y][Lev. 16:17]
11 [z]Ex. 30:1-10; 40:26, 27

1:1–4 *The Prologue.* The prologue to Luke's Gospel, comprised of a single sentence, ranks among the finest Greek writing of the first century and demonstrates Luke's skill and credentials as a writer (cf. 3:1–2; Acts 1:1–2).

1:1 Inasmuch introduces the purpose of Luke's writing. **Many** may include more than just the authors of the Gospels. **Accomplished** emphasizes that Jesus' ministry constitutes the realization or fulfillment of what is prophesied in the OT.

1:2–3 The sources for these narratives were the **eyewitnesses and ministers**, especially the 12 apostles (6:13–16). **delivered.** A technical Greek term for passing on tradition. **word.** Divine revelation. Luke's credentials as a writer involve **having followed** (or investigated) **all things closely** (or carefully) **for some time past. Orderly** refers to logical orderliness (cf. Acts 11:4). **most excellent.** An address for officials (cf. Acts 23:26; 24:2; 26:25) and people of high social standing.

1:4 Luke's purpose in writing is so **that** Theophilus might know the **certainty** of what he has **been taught**. Written Scripture gives believers more certainty than the memory of an oral proclamation can give.

1:5–2:52 *The Infancy Narrative.* The opening (1:8–23) and conclusion (2:21–52) of this section take place in the temple and form literary "bookends," indicating its unity.

1:5–25 *The Birth of John the Baptist Foretold.* In Jesus' day most Jews believed that for more than 400 years the Holy Spirit had not been active in Israel, because there had been no more prophets since Malachi. Now God once again visits his people.

1:5–7 John the Baptist's birth is foretold during the reign of **Herod** the Great, who is described as the **king of Judea** (see note on Matt. 2:1). After being granted kingship from Rome in 40 B.C., Herod ruled Judea, Galilee, Samaria, Perea, and Idumea from 37–4. "Judea" is used broadly here to describe the land of the Jews rather than narrowly to refer to the Roman province. **division of Abijah.** To provide service for the temple, the priests were divided into 24 divisions, each of which served for a week, twice a year. During major festivals (Passover, Pentecost, the Feast of Tabernacles) all the divisions served. Luke focuses on one priest, **Zechariah**, and his wife, **Elizabeth**. Luke records both that they were **righteous** and blameless **in all the commandments** and that they **had no child**, for **Elizabeth was barren**. Their childlessness was not due to any personal sin on their part but to God's sovereign and wise plan.

1:8–10 Zechariah—**chosen by lot**—is serving in the temple sanctuary. Outside the temple sanctuary **the people were praying** (see Introduction: Key Themes).

1:12 fear fell upon him. A typical reaction to an angelic or divine presence (cf. vv. 29–30, 65; 2:9).

1:13–14 your prayer has been heard. Though the specific content of Zechariah's prayer is not given, it most likely would have included at least two petitions: Zechariah would have been interceding on behalf of Israel as a nation, and he apparently also raised a second petition, for a child, as indicated by v. 13b (cf. Gen. 25:21; 30:22; 1 Sam. 1:10–17). Zechariah must have prayed for a child hundreds of times over many years, and now at last the answer has come. **Joy and gladness** come to Zechariah and Elizabeth

HEROD'S TEMPLE IN THE TIME OF JESUS

Herod began construction of this magnificent temple in 20/19 B.C., during the 18th year of his reign. The main construction phase was completed within about a decade. Detailed descriptions of the temple exist in Josephus (*Jewish Antiquities* 15.380–425; *Jewish War* 5.184–247) and in early rabbinic writings (esp. Mishnah, *Middot*). The Roman army under Titus destroyed the temple during the capture of Jerusalem in A.D. 70. The temple was 172 feet (52 m) long, wide, and high (about 16 to 20 stories tall).

Temple Architectural Plan

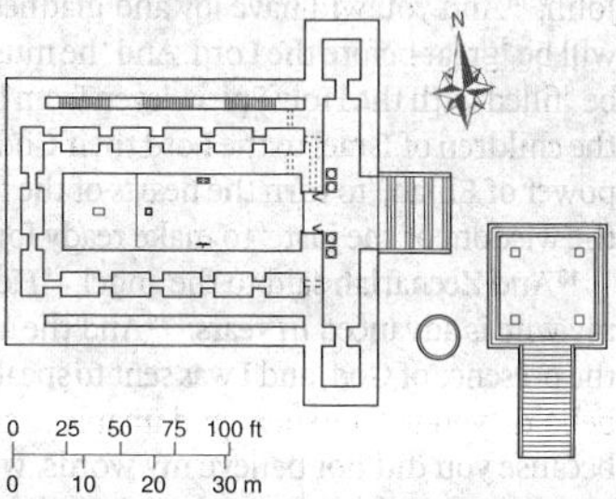
N
0 25 50 75 100 ft
0 10 20 30 m

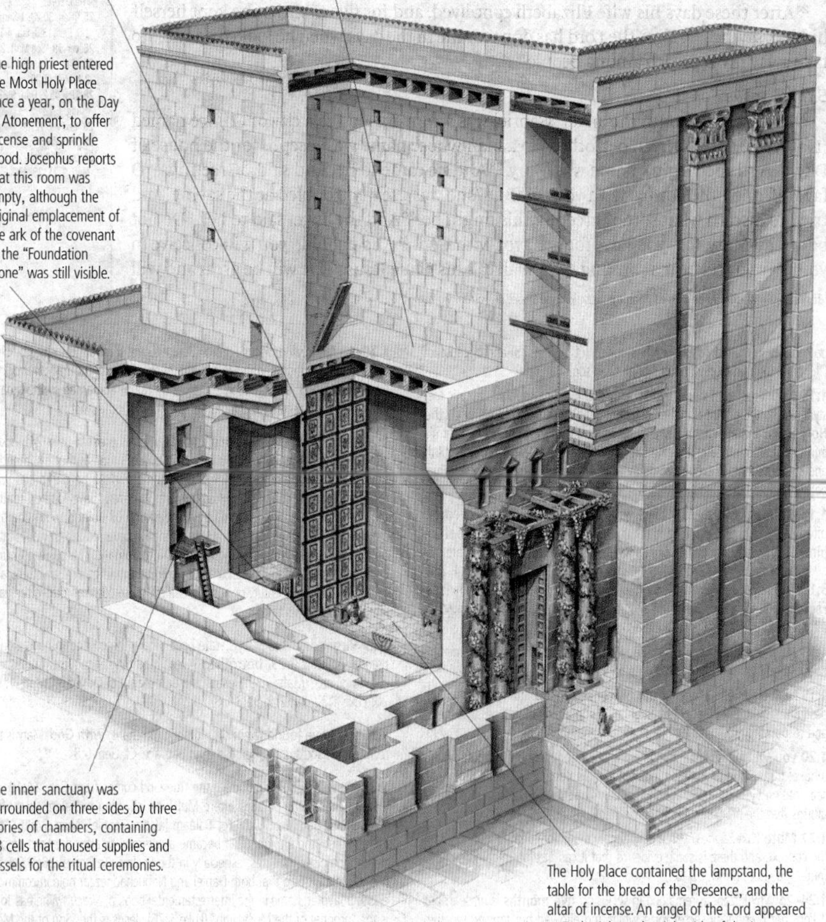
There was an upper chamber above the sanctuary, which allowed access (through holes in the floor) for cleaning of the gold-covered walls below. A ladder (shown partly cut away in this section) gave access to the upper roof level.
A massive curtain separated the Holy Place from the Most Holy Place. When Jesus died, this curtain was torn in two from top to bottom (Matt. 27:51; Mark 15:38; Luke 23:45).
The high priest entered the Most Holy Place once a year, on the Day of Atonement, to offer incense and sprinkle blood. Josephus reports that this room was empty, although the original emplacement of the ark of the covenant in the "Foundation Stone" was still visible.
The inner sanctuary was surrounded on three sides by three stories of chambers, containing 38 cells that housed supplies and vessels for the ritual ceremonies.
The Holy Place contained the lampstand, the table for the bread of the Presence, and the altar of incense. An angel of the Lord appeared to Zechariah on the right side of the incense altar (Luke 1:11).

has been heard, and your wife Elizabeth will bear you a son, and [c]you shall call his name
John. 14 And you will have joy and gladness, and many will [d]rejoice at his birth, 15 for he
will be [e]great before the Lord. And [f]he must not drink wine or strong [g]drink, and [g]he will
be [h]filled with the Holy Spirit, [i]even from his mother's womb. 16 And he will turn many of
the children of Israel to the Lord their God, 17 and [j]he will go before him [k]in the spirit and
power of Elijah, [l]to turn the hearts of the fathers to the children, and [m]the disobedient to
the wisdom of the just, [n]to make ready for the Lord a people prepared."
18 And Zechariah said to the angel, [o]"How shall I know this? For I am an old man, and
my wife is advanced in years." 19 And the angel answered him, "I am [p]Gabriel. [q]I stand in
the presence of God, and I was sent to speak to you and to bring you this good news. 20 And
behold, [r]you will be silent and unable to speak until the day that these things take place,
because you did not believe my words, which will be fulfilled in their time." 21 And the
people were waiting for Zechariah, and they were wondering at his delay in [s]the temple.
22 And when he came out, he was unable to speak to them, and they realized that he had
seen a vision in [s]the temple. And [t]he kept making signs to them and remained mute.
23 And [u]when his time of [v]service was ended, he went to his home.
24 After these days his wife Elizabeth conceived, and for five months she kept herself
hidden, saying, 25 "Thus the Lord has done for me in the days when he looked on me, [w]to
take away my reproach among people."

Birth of Jesus Foretold

26 In the sixth month the angel [x]Gabriel was sent from God to a city of Galilee named
[y]Nazareth, 27 [z]to a virgin betrothed[1] to a man whose name was Joseph, [a]of the house of
David. And the virgin's name was Mary. 28 And he came to her and said, "Greetings, [b]O
favored one, [c]the Lord is with you!"[2] 29 But [d]she was greatly troubled at the saying, and
tried to discern what sort of greeting this might be. 30 And the angel said to her, "Do not
be afraid, Mary, for [e]you have found favor with God. 31 And behold, [f]you will conceive in
your womb and bear a son, and [g]you shall call his name Jesus. 32 He will be great and will

[1] That is, legally pledged to be married [2] Some manuscripts add *Blessed are you among women!*

13 [c]ver. 60, 63
14 [d][ver. 58]
15 [e]ch. 7:28; Matt. 11:11 [f]ch. 7:33; Num. 6:3; Judg. 13:4, 7, 14; Matt. 11:18 [g][Acts 2:15, 17; Eph. 5:18] [h]ver. 41, 67; See Acts 2:4 [i]Isa. 49:1, 5; Jer. 1:5; Gal. 1:15
17 [j]ver. 76; John 3:28 [k]See Matt. 11:14 [l]Cited from Mal. 4:6 [m]Rom. 10:21 [n]ch. 7:27; Mal. 3:1; Matt. 11:10; Mark 1:2
18 [o]Gen. 15:8; [Gen. 17:17]
19 [p]ver. 26; Dan. 8:16; 9:21 [q]Rev. 8:2; [1 Kgs. 17:1; Job 1:6; Isa. 63:9; Matt. 18:10]
20 [r][Ezek. 3:26; 24:27]
21 [s]See ver. 9
22 [s][See ver. 21 above] [t]ver. 62
23 [u]2 Chr. 23:8; [ver. 8; 2 Kgs. 11:5; 1 Chr. 9:25] [v]Heb. 10:11
25 [w][Gen. 30:23; 1 Sam. 1:6; Ps. 113:9; Isa. 4:1]
26 [x]ver. 19 [y]See Matt. 2:23
27 [z]Matt. 1:16, 18 [a]ch. 2:4; Matt. 1:20
28 [b][Ps. 45:2; Dan. 9:23] [c]Judg. 6:12
29 [d]See ver. 12
30 [e]Acts 7:46
31 [f]Isa. 7:14 [g]ch. 2:21; Matt. 1:21, 25

both because their childlessness has ended (cf. Luke 1:25) and because of ("for," v. 15) what God will do through their son.

1:15 Abstinence from **wine** and **strong drink** indicates John's ascetic lifestyle akin to the Nazirites in the OT (Num. 6:1–3). His being **filled with the Holy Spirit** in the **womb** (Luke 1:41) reveals God's equipping him for his ministry. It also indicates that he was a distinct human person before birth and suggests that, in an uncommon way, God imparted regeneration to him before he was born.

1:16–17 Turn, used twice in these verses, describes a change in direction, often in the sense of conversion (cf. Acts 9:35; 11:21; 14:15). **go before him**. Cf. "Prepare the way," Luke 3:4. The terms **spirit** and **power** are frequently associated (e.g., 4:14; Acts 1:8; 10:38; Rom. 15:13; 1 Cor. 2:4; Eph. 3:16; 1 Thess. 1:5; 2 Tim. 1:7), for the Holy Spirit imparts power for ministry. For John's association with **Elijah**, cf. Luke 9:8–9, 19; and notes on Matt. 11:14; 17:1–13; 17:10–13; John 1:20–21.

1:18 How shall I know this? Zechariah requests a sign confirming the angel's prediction (see v. 13 and note on v. 20).

1:19 I am Gabriel. I stand in the presence of God. This astounding "job description" identifies Gabriel as an angel of surpassing faithfulness, holiness, and responsibility (cf. Dan. 9:21).

1:20 you will be silent. The sign given by Gabriel is both gracious and a rebuke; it results in muteness (and probably also deafness, implied by v. 62; see note on vv. 62–63). But **until the day that these things take place** affirms that the promise will still be fulfilled.

1:22 Mute (Gk. *kōphos*) can mean either "mute" or "deaf," depending on the context, and there is some evidence that it can at times mean "deaf and mute" (see note on vv. 62–63).

1:24–25 Why Elizabeth remained in seclusion **five months** is unclear, but it kept her pregnancy secret for a while and allowed her time to worship God (v. 25) and prepare for this special child. **to take away my reproach**. Childlessness was considered a disgrace (cf. Gen. 30:23; Isa. 4:1).

1:26–38 *The Birth of Jesus Foretold.* Luke moves from announcing the birth of John the Baptist to announcing the birth of Jesus. The mighty work of God through John's conception and ministry will be surpassed by the greater miracle of virginal conception and the greater work of Christ.

1:26 sixth month. The sixth month of Elizabeth's pregnancy (v. 24). Luke's specifying that **Nazareth** was a **city of Galilee** suggests that his intended readers were not from Palestine and would therefore be unfamiliar with the city's location (cf. 4:31). Excavations at Nazareth have located tombs, olive presses, wells, and vaulted cells for wine and oil storage, indicating that the village was a small agricultural settlement. However, Nazareth was located on a road leading from nearby Sepphoris into Samaria. The current Church of the Annunciation lies atop previous early Byzantine church structures and caves (from the 4th century or possibly earlier); these commemorated the early life of Jesus and his family.

1:27 Virgin describes Mary's state both before the conception and during pregnancy (Matt. 1:25). **betrothed**. A legally binding engagement breakable only by divorce (Matt. 1:19). Joseph is a descendant of **David** (cf. Matt. 1:16, 20; Luke 1:32–33; 2:4; 3:23–38).

1:30 you have found favor (lit., "grace"; Gk. *charis*) **with God**. Mary is the recipient of God's grace, not the giver of grace. Cf. Gen. 6:8.

1:32 Most High. This name for the true God comes from Gen. 14:18–22 (see note on Gen. 14:18), where Melchizedek, king of Salem, identifies Yahweh as "God Most High" (cf. Balaam [also a Gentile], Num. 24:16: "the Most High"; "the Almighty"). It became a common title for the Lord among the monotheistic Israelites, especially in the Psalms. (In Dan. 3:26; 4:24, 34 it is the title for God that both Daniel and Nebuchadnezzar hold in common, and is a favored name in the intertestamental book of *Sirach*.) Whereas John is the "prophet of the Most High" (Luke 1:76), Jesus is the "Son of the Most High." He is the promised successor to the **throne** of **David** (see 2 Sam. 7:12–13, 16).

be called the Son of [h]the Most High. And the Lord God [i]will give to him the throne of [j]his
father David, 33 and he will reign over the house of Jacob [k]forever, and of his kingdom
there will be no end."
34 And Mary said to the angel, "How will this be, since I am a virgin?"[1]
35 And the angel answered her, [l]"The Holy Spirit will come upon you, and the power of
[h]the Most High will overshadow you; therefore the child to be born[2] will be called [m]holy—
[n]the Son of God. 36 And behold, your relative Elizabeth in her old age has also conceived a
son, and this is the sixth month with her [o]who was called barren. 37 For [p]nothing will be
impossible with God." 38 And Mary said, "Behold, I am the servant[3] of the Lord; let it be
to me according to your word." And [q]the angel departed from her.

Mary Visits Elizabeth

39 In those days Mary arose and went with haste into [r]the hill country, to a town in Judah,
40 and she entered the house of Zechariah and greeted Elizabeth. 41 And when Elizabeth
heard the greeting of Mary, the baby leaped in her womb. And Elizabeth [s]was filled with
the Holy Spirit, 42 and she exclaimed with a loud cry, [t]"Blessed are you among women, and
[u]blessed is [v]the fruit of your womb! 43 And why is this granted to me that the mother of
[w]my Lord should come to me? 44 For behold, when the sound of your greeting came to my
ears, the baby in my womb leaped for joy. 45 And [x]blessed is she who believed that there
would be[4] a fulfillment of what was spoken to her from the Lord."

Mary's Song of Praise: The Magnificat

46 And Mary said,

[y]"My [z]soul [a]magnifies the Lord,
47 [b]and my [z]spirit rejoices in [c]God my Savior,
48 for [d]he has looked on the humble estate of his servant.
For behold, from now on all generations [e]will call me blessed;
49 for [f]he who is mighty [g]has done great things for me,
and [h]holy is his name.
50 And [i]his mercy is for those who fear him
from generation to generation.
51 [j]He has shown strength with his arm;

[1] Greek *since I do not know a man* [2] Some manuscripts add *of you* [3] Greek *bondservant*; also verse 48 [4] Or *believed, for there will be*

32 [h]ver. 76; ch. 6:35; Acts 7:48; See Mark 5:7 [i]ver. 69; 2 Sam. 7:11-13, 16; Ps. 89:4; 132:11; Isa. 9:6, 7; 16:5; Acts 2:30; [Rev. 3:7] [j]See Matt. 1:1
33 [k]Dan. 2:44; 7:14, 18, 27; Heb. 1:8; Rev. 11:15; [John 12:34]
35 [l]Matt. 1:18, 20 [h][See ver. 32 above] [m]John 6:69 [n]See Matt. 14:33
36 [o]ver. 7
37 [p]Cited from Gen. 18:14 (Gk.); See Matt. 19:26
38 [q][Judg. 6:21; Acts 12:10]
39 [r]ver. 65; Josh. 20:7; 21:11
41 [s]ver. 15, 67
42 [t][Judg. 5:24] [u][Deut. 28:4] [v]Ps. 127:3
43 [w]ch. 20:42; John 20:28; [ch. 2:11]
45 [x]John 20:29; [ver. 20]
46 [y]For ver. 46-53, [1 Sam. 2:1-10] [z]1 Thess. 5:23 [a]Ps. 34:2, 3; 69:30; Acts 10:46; 19:17
47 [b]Ps. 35:9; Isa. 61:10; Hab. 3:18; [Acts 16:34] [z][See ver. 46 above] [c]Ps. 106:21; 1 Tim. 1:1; 2:3; Titus 1:3; 2:10; 3:4; Jude 25; [2 Tim. 1:9]
48 [d]1 Sam. 1:11; Ps. 138:6; [ch. 9:38] [e]ch. 11:27; Ps. 72:17; [Mal. 3:12]
49 [f]Ps. 89:8; Zeph. 3:17 [g]Ps. 71:19; 126:2, 3 [h]Ps. 99:3; 111:9; Isa. 57:15
50 [i]Deut. 5:10; 7:9; Ps. 89:1, 2; 103:17
51 [j]Ps. 89:10; 98:1; 118:16; Isa. 51:9

1:34 since I am a virgin (lit., "since I know no man"). Mary assumes that she will conceive (v. 31) while still a virgin.

1:35 The **Holy Spirit** will perform this great miracle, so that Mary will become pregnant without having sexual relations with a man. **Therefore** indicates that Jesus' holiness derives from his being conceived by the Holy Spirit. Though Jesus was a genuine human being, he did not inherit a sinful nature and disposition from Adam, as all other human beings do (cf. 2 Cor. 5:21; Heb. 4:15; 1 Pet. 2:22; 1 John 3:5; by contrast, Ps. 143:2; Eph. 2:3).

1:38 Behold, I am the servant of the Lord. The section ends with Mary's example of true discipleship, in submission to God's word and promise.

1:39–56 *Mary Visits Elizabeth.* This section builds upon the previous two and contains an introductory narrative (vv. 39–41), two hymns (vv. 42–45, 46–55), and a conclusion (v. 56).

1:39–41 In those days (cf. 6:12; Acts 1:15) links the present account with the preceding. It is likely that both the **hill country** and **Judah** refer to the (largely hilly) region of Judea. **The baby leaped** could be seen as the prophetic first instance of John preparing the way for Jesus (see Luke 1:17, 76). John's prophetic role is evidenced even as an unborn child in the womb. Elizabeth, **filled with the Holy Spirit**, explains the baby's leaping (vv. 42–45).

1:42–45 Blessed are you among women. The reason for Mary's blessedness is located in the second **blessed is**, i.e., because of the blessedness of the child she will bear (lit., **the fruit of your womb**).

1:44 The baby in my womb leaped for joy pictures the unborn child at the sixth month of pregnancy as a distinct person, able to feel "joy."

1:45 Mary is **blessed** for her faith, but she is most blessed for the privilege of bearing the Son of God (see note on vv. 42–45).

1:46–55 Mary's song of praise in these verses traditionally has been called the "Magnificat," a title derived from the opening word (*magnificat*, **magnifies**) in the Latin Vulgate translation. The Magnificat is the first of three hymns in Luke 1–2, the other two being the "Benedictus" (1:68–79) and the "Nunc Dimittis" (2:29–32).

1:46–47 My soul magnifies the Lord. Mary's hymn of praise (the Magnificat) follows the common form of Psalms of Thanksgiving, which begin by thanking God and then telling why one is thankful. The Magnificat carries echoes of the content and form of Ps. 103:1. **my spirit rejoices.** Mary's entire being is caught up in praise to God. **God my Savior.** Mary herself is not free from sin but is in need of a Savior.

1:48 For indicates that Mary is about to present the grounds or foundation of her praise (vv. 46–47). **he has looked.** This first ground for Mary's praise recalls Hannah's hymn (1 Sam. 2:1–10). **humble estate.** Cf. Luke 1:52; 1 Cor. 1:26–29. God often uses people who are not great in the world's eyes to work his great purposes on the earth. **from now on.** Cf. Luke 12:52; 22:18, 69; Acts 18:6. **All generations . . . blessed** recalls Luke 1:42.

1:50–55 The hymn moves from Mary to what her son's birth means for believing Israelites. **fear.** Reverent, humble obedience that seeks to please God. The second ground for Mary's praise is introduced by **He has shown strength with his arm**, an anthropomorphism for God's might. **has scattered . . . has brought.** Luke's use of the aorist tense expresses Mary's certainty of what God will do. **To Abraham and to his offspring** emphasizes the fulfillment of salvation history.

[k]he has scattered the proud in the thoughts of their hearts;
52 [j]he has brought down the mighty from their thrones
[l]and exalted those of humble estate;
53 he has filled [m]the hungry with good things,
and the rich [n]he has sent away empty.
54 He has [o]helped [p]his servant Israel,
[q]in remembrance of his mercy,
55 [r]as he spoke to our fathers,
[q]to Abraham and to his offspring forever."

56 And Mary remained with her about three months and returned to her home.

The Birth of John the Baptist

57 Now the time came for Elizabeth to give birth, and she bore a son. 58 And her neighbors
and relatives heard that the Lord [s]had shown great mercy to her, and they rejoiced with
her. 59 And [t]on the eighth day they came to circumcise the child. And they would have
called him Zechariah after his father, 60 but his mother answered, "No; [u]he shall be called
John." 61 And they said to her, "None of your relatives is called by this name." 62 And [v]they
made signs to his father, inquiring what he wanted him to be called. 63 And he asked for [w]a
writing tablet and wrote, [u]"His name is John." And they all wondered. 64 [x]And immediately
his mouth was opened and his tongue [y]loosed, and he spoke, [z]blessing God. 65 And [a]fear
came on all their neighbors. And all these things were talked about through all [b]the hill
country of Judea, 66 and all who heard them [c]laid them up in their hearts, saying, "What
then will this child be?" For [d]the hand of the Lord was with him.

Zechariah's Prophecy

67 And his father Zechariah [e]was filled with the Holy Spirit and [f]prophesied, saying,

68 [g]"Blessed be the Lord [h]God of Israel,
for he has [i]visited and [j]redeemed his people
69 and [k]has raised up [l]a horn of salvation for us
[m]in the house of his servant David,
70 [n]as [o]he spoke by the mouth of his holy prophets from of old,
71 [p]that we should be saved from our enemies
and from the hand of all who hate us;
72 [q]to show the mercy promised to our fathers
and [r]to remember his holy [s]covenant,
73 [t]the oath that he swore to our father Abraham, to grant us
74 that we, being delivered from the hand of our enemies,
might serve him [u]without fear,
75 [v]in holiness and righteousness before him [w]all our days.
76 And you, child, will be called [x]the prophet of [y]the Most High;

51 [k]Dan. 4:37; See James 4:6
52 [j][See ver. 51 above] [l]Job 5:11; Ps. 75:7; 107:40, 41; 113:7, 8; 147:6; Ezek. 21:26; [James 4:10]
53 [m]Ps. 34:10; 107:9; [ch. 6:21, 24, 25] [n]Job 22:9
54 [o]Isa. 41:8, 9; Heb. 2:16 [p]Isa. 44:21; 49:3 [q]Ps. 98:3; Mic. 7:20; [ver. 72, 73]
55 [r]Gen. 17:19; Ps. 132:11; Gal. 3:16 [q][See ver. 54 above]
58 [s]Gen. 19:19
59 [t]ch. 2:21; Gen. 17:12; Lev. 12:3; Phil. 3:5
60 [u]ver. 13
62 [v]ver. 22
63 [w]Isa. 8:1; 30:8 [u][See ver. 60 above]
64 [x]ver. 20 [y]Mark 7:35 [z]ch. 2:28; 24:53
65 [a]ch. 7:16 [b]See ver. 39
66 [c][ch. 2:19, 51] [d]Acts 11:21; 13:11
67 [e]ver. 15, 41 [f]Joel 2:28
68 [g]1 Kgs. 1:48; 1 Chr. 29:10; Ezra 7:27; Ps. 41:13; 72:18; 106:48 [h]Isa. 29:23; Matt. 15:31; Acts 13:17 [i]ch. 7:16; Ex. 4:31; [ver. 78; Acts 15:14; Heb. 2:6] [j]ch. 2:38; Ps. 111:9; 130:7, 8; [ch. 24:21; Isa. 43:1; 59:20]
69 [k]1 Sam. 2:1, 10; Ps. 132:17; Ezek. 29:21 [l]2 Sam. 22:3; Ps. 18:2 [m]ver. 32
70 [n]Rom. 1:2; [Jer. 23:5, 6] [o]Acts 3:21
71 [p]Ps. 106:10
72 [q]Mic. 7:20 [r]Lev. 26:42; Ps. 105:8, 9; [ver. 54, 55] [s]See Rom. 9:4
73 [t]Gen. 22:16-18; 26:3; Heb. 6:13, 14
74 [u]Zeph. 3:15
75 [v]Eph. 4:24; [1 Thess. 2:10; Titus 2:12] [w][Jer. 32:39 (Heb.); Matt. 28:20 (Gk.)]
76 [x]ch. 7:26; 20:6; Matt. 11:9; 14:5 [y]See ver. 32

1:57–80 *The Birth of John the Baptist.* This section includes Luke's account of John's birth (vv. 57–66) and Zechariah's hymn of praise (vv. 67–79).

1:58 shown great mercy. Cf. v. 25. **Rejoiced with her** is a partial fulfillment of v. 14 (cf. 2:10).

1:59 Circumcision on the **eighth day** is commanded in Gen. 17:12–14; 21:4; Lev. 12:3.

1:60 Elizabeth names her son **John** as the angel instructed (v. 13), but the choice is questioned (v. 61).

1:62–63 They made signs to his father indicates that Zechariah was deaf as well as mute, or else they would simply have spoken to him (see note on v. 22). This is confirmed by the people's amazement (v. 63) that he chose the same name as Elizabeth chose, something that would not have been surprising if he had been able to hear her. Zechariah, using a **writing tablet** (a wooden tablet covered with wax), affirms Elizabeth's choice.

1:65–66 Fear comes upon all the neighbors of Zechariah and Elizabeth (cf. v. 12), for they suddenly realize that God is working among them. Luke emphasizes the greatness of John's fame by his expressions **all their neighbors, all the hill country of Judea**, and **all who heard**.

1:67 Zechariah, **filled with the Holy Spirit**, like Elizabeth (v. 41), gives a prophecy (vv. 68–79), a single sentence in the Greek text. It is often called the "Benedictus," from its first word in the Latin Vulgate.

1:68 Like the Magnificat (vv. 46–55), the Benedictus begins with a word of praise: **Blessed be the Lord God of Israel. For** indicates that all of the following (vv. 68–79) is the cause of Zechariah's praise. **he has visited and redeemed his people**. With the events of vv. 5–67, the promised time of salvation has begun. (Cf. v. 78, which also speaks of God "visiting" his people with the dawning of the "sunrise . . . from on high"—that is, with the coming of Christ.)

1:69 The **horn**, symbolizing an animal's strength, refers to Jesus. **David**. Cf. v. 27.

1:70 As he spoke . . . from of old emphasizes the fulfillment and continuity between the old and new covenants (cf. vv. 72–73).

1:73–75 swore to our father Abraham. The content of the **oath** (v. 73) is given in vv. 74–75, that is, to bless the world through Abraham's offspring. The Benedictus proper ends at v. 75.

1:76–77 This **knowledge**, brought by John the Baptist, prepares the way for

76[z]ver. 17; ch. 3:4; 7:27; Mal. 3:1; Matt. 3:3; Mark 1:2, 3
77[a][Matt. 26:28; Mark 1:4]
78[b]Col. 3:12 (Gk.) [c]Mal. 4:2; Eph. 5:14; 2 Pet. 1:19 [d]See ver. 68 [e]ch. 24:49
79[f]Isa. 9:2; Matt. 4:16; [Acts 26:18]; See John 8:12 [g]Ps. 107:10; Isa. 42:7 [h]Rom. 3:17 [i]See ch. 2:14
80[j]ch. 2:40 [k]Matt. 3:1; 11:7

Chapter 2

1[l]Acts 17:7 [m][ch. 3:1] [n][Acts 5:37]
2[n][See ver. 1 above] [o]ch. 3:1

for [z]you will go before the Lord to prepare his ways,
77 to give knowledge of salvation to his people
[a]in the forgiveness of their sins,
78 because of the [b]tender mercy of our God,
whereby [c]the sunrise shall [d]visit us[1] [e]from on high
79 to [f]give light to [g]those who sit in darkness and in the shadow of death,
to guide our feet into [h]the way of [i]peace."

80 [j]And the child grew and became strong in spirit, and he was [k]in the wilderness until the day of his public appearance to Israel.

The Birth of Jesus Christ

2 In those days [l]a decree went out from [m]Caesar Augustus that all the world should
be [n]registered. 2 This was the first [n]registration when[2] Quirinius [o]was governor of
Syria. 3 And all went to be registered, each to his own town. 4 And Joseph also went up

[1] *Or when the sunrise shall dawn upon us; some manuscripts since the sunrise has visited us* [2] *Or This was the registration before*

the coming of Jesus. Such knowledge is not merely theoretical or cognitive but deeply experiential, resulting in a fundamental change of heart and behavior (e.g., "repentance"; cf. 3:7–8). **Salvation** and the **forgiveness of . . . sins** (cf. 3:3) reveal the nature of the redemption brought by the Christ.

1:78–79 the sunrise shall visit us . . . to give light. Probably a metaphor referring to the coming of the Messiah (cf. Isa. 60:2–3; Mal. 4:2; and perhaps Num. 24:17).

1:80 the child grew and became strong in spirit. Cf. 2:40.

2:1–52 *The Birth of Jesus Christ.* This section includes three parts: Jesus' birth (vv. 1–20); his presentation in the temple (vv. 21–40); and his presence as a boy in the temple (vv. 41–52).

2:1–20 *Jesus Is Born.* Whereas the birth of John is described in two verses (1:57–58), the birth of Jesus (the "greater" one) covers 20 verses.

2:1 The fact that Jesus was born in Bethlehem rather than in Nazareth (cf. 1:26) was due to a **decree**, i.e., an imperial edict (cf. Acts 17:7), from **Caesar Augustus** (reigned 31 B.C.–A.D. 14). **In those days** is an imprecise date (contrast Luke 3:1–2), suggesting that Luke did not know the exact year (cf. 3:23). **All the world** (Gk. *oikoumenē*) means all of the known, inhabited world that was subject to the civilization and governance of Rome. People were **registered** for the purpose of taxation.

2:2 the first registration when Quirinius was governor. According to Josephus, Quirinius was governor of Syria A.D. 6–7 and conducted a census in A.D. 6 (which Luke is aware of and mentions in Acts 5:37). But this cannot be the census Luke is referencing here, since it occurred *after* the death of Herod the Great in 4 B.C., and it is known that Jesus was born *during* Herod's reign (cf. Matt. 2:1; Luke 1:5). Various plausible solutions have been proposed. Some interpreters believe that because "governor" (participle of Gk. *hēgemoneuō*) was a very general term for "ruler," it may be that Quirinius was the *administrator* of the census, but not the governor proper. Another solution is to translate the verse, "This was the registration *before* Quirinius was governor of Syria" (see ESV footnote), which is grammatically possible (taking Gk. *prōtos* as "before" rather than "first"; the Greek construction is somewhat unusual on any reading). This would make sense because Luke would then be clarifying that this was before the well-known, troublesome census of A.D. 6 (Acts 5:37). (One additional proposal is that Quirinius was governor for two separate terms, though this lacks confirming historical evidence.) Though the year cannot be determined with complete certainty, there are several reasonable possibilities which correspond well to Luke's carefully researched investigation (Luke 1:3–4) and to the historical and geographical accuracy evidenced throughout Luke and Acts. The most reasonable date is late in the year of 6 B.C. or early 5. See further The Date of Jesus' Crucifixion, pp. 1809–1810.

2:3–4 Although Joseph was at this time living in Nazareth (vv. 4, 39), his ancestral home (**own town**) was **Bethlehem**. They **went up . . . to Judea**, since Bethlehem (in Judea) lies on a mountain 2,654 feet (809 m) high. The references to **David** (1:27, 32–33; 2:11; cf. 1 Sam. 16:4, 13) explain why Jesus was born in Bethlehem (cf. Mic. 5:2).

2:4 The traditional site for Jesus' birth, a cave/grotto in **Bethlehem**, was made into a pagan shrine to Adonis in the second century A.D. (under Hadrian). The Constantinian basilica-style Church of the Nativity replaced this shrine in the fourth century, with an octagonal room providing views of the grotto. The fourth-century church, however, was destroyed and rebuilt as the present-day structure in the sixth century.

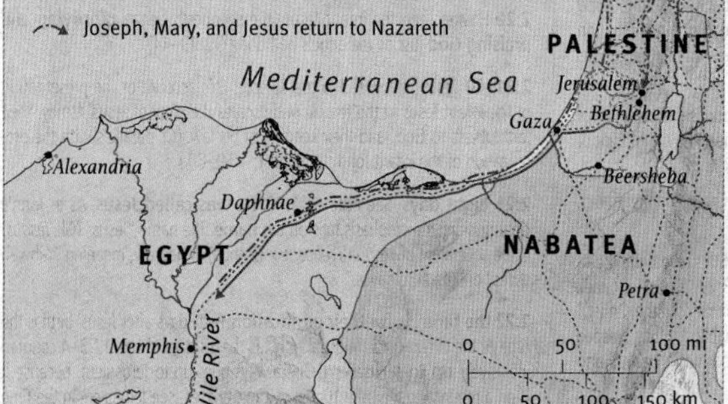

Jesus' Birth and Flight to Egypt
As the time drew near for Jesus to be born, a mandatory Roman registration made it necessary for Joseph to return to his ancestral home of Bethlehem. There Mary gave birth to Jesus, and later, wise men from the East came to worship him. The wise men's recognition of a new king, however, troubled King Herod and the ruling establishment in Jerusalem, and Herod the Great sought to kill Jesus. Joseph and his family escaped to Egypt and stayed there until Herod died. When they returned to Palestine, they settled in the remote district of Galilee, where Jesus grew up in the village of Nazareth, to avoid the attention of the rulers in Jerusalem.

[p]from Galilee, from the town of [q]Nazareth, to Judea, to [r]the city of David, which is called
[s]Bethlehem, [t]because he was of the house and lineage of David, **5** to be registered with
Mary, his betrothed,[1] who was with child. **6** And [t]while they were there, the time came for
her to give birth. **7** And she gave birth to her firstborn son and [u]wrapped him in swaddling
cloths and [v]laid him in a manger, because there was no place for them in [w]the inn.

The Shepherds and the Angels

8 And in the same region there were shepherds out in the field, keeping watch over their
flock by night. **9** And an angel of the Lord [x]appeared to them, and [y]the glory of the Lord
shone around them, and they were filled with great fear. **10** And the angel said to them,
"Fear not, for behold, I bring you good news of great joy that will be for all [z]the people.
11 For [a]unto you is born this day in [b]the city of David [c]a Savior, who is [d]Christ [e]the Lord.
12 And [f]this will be a sign for you: you will find a baby [g]wrapped in swaddling cloths and
lying in a manger." **13** And suddenly there was with the angel [h]a multitude of the heavenly
host praising God and saying,

14 [i]"Glory to God [j]in the highest,
[j]and on earth [k]peace [l]among those with whom he is pleased!"[2]

15 When the angels went away from them into heaven, the shepherds said to one another,
"Let us go over to Bethlehem and see this thing that has happened, which the Lord has
made known to us." **16** And they went with haste and found Mary and Joseph, and the baby
[m]lying in a manger. **17** And when they saw it, they made known the saying that had been
told them concerning this child. **18** And all who heard it wondered at what the shepherds
told them. **19** But [n]Mary treasured up all these things, pondering them in her heart. **20** And
the shepherds returned, [o]glorifying and praising God for all they had heard and seen, as
it had been told them.

21 And [p]at the end of eight days, when he was circumcised, [q]he was called Jesus, the name
given by the angel before he was conceived in the womb.

Jesus Presented at the Temple

22 And [r]when the time came for their purification according to the Law of Moses, they
brought him up to Jerusalem [s]to present him to the Lord **23** (as it is written in [t]the Law of

[1] That is, one legally pledged to be married [2] Some manuscripts *peace, good will among men*

4 [p]ch. 1:26 [q]See Matt. 2:23 [r]ver. 11; John 7:42; [1 Sam. 16:1] [s]Matt. 2:1 [t]ch. 1:27
6 [t][See ver. 4 above]
7 [u]ver. 12 [v]ver. 16 [w]ch. 22:11 (Gk.)
9 [x]ch. 24:4; Acts 12:7 [y]ch. 9:31; Acts 7:55; 2 Cor. 3:18
10 [z]ver. 32; John 11:50; [Zech. 9:9]
11 [a]Isa. 9:6 [b]ver. 4 [c]Matt. 1:21; John 4:42 [d]Acts 2:36; 10:36; [ch. 23:2]; See Matt. 1:17 [e][ch. 1:43]
12 [f]1 Sam. 2:34; 2 Kgs. 19:29; 20:8, 9; Isa. 7:11, 14 [g]ver. 7
13 [h]Gen. 28:12; 32:1, 2; 1 Kgs. 22:19; 2 Chr. 18:18; Ps. 103:21; 148:2; Dan. 7:10; Rev. 5:11
14 [i]ch. 19:38; [Ps. 148:1; Matt. 21:9] [j][ch. 10:21; Matt. 6:10; 28:18; John 17:4; Acts 7:49; Eph. 3:15; Col. 1:16, 20; Rev. 5:13] [k]ch. 1:79; Ps. 85:10; Isa. 9:6, 7; Hag. 2:9; Acts 10:36; Rom. 5:1; Eph. 2:14, 17; Col. 1:20 [l][ch. 3:22; 12:32; Eph. 1:5, 9; Phil. 2:13]
16 [m]ver. 7, 12
19 [n]ver. 51; [ch. 1:66; Gen. 37:11]
20 [o]See ch. 7:16
21 [p]See ch. 1:59 [q]ch. 1:31; Matt. 1:21, 25
22 [r]Lev. 12; [ver. 21, 27; Gal. 4:4] [s][1 Sam. 1:22, 24]
23 [t]ver. 39; Ex. 13:9; 2 Chr. 31:3

2:5 betrothed. See note on 1:27.

2:6 the time came. See 1:57. On the surface, political reasons determine where Jesus is born, but the ultimate cause is the God who controls history and who guarantees that the Messiah will be born in Bethlehem, in accordance with OT prophecy (cf. Mic. 5:2; Matt. 2:1–6).

2:7 And she gave birth to her firstborn son. The greatest miracle in the history of the world, the eternal Son of God being born as a man, happens quietly in a stable in an obscure village in Judea. Luke's description is restrained, giving only a very few details. **swaddling cloths**. In ancient times strips of cloth were used to wrap babies to keep them warm and secure. **manger**. A feeding trough for animals. **The inn**, with the definite article ("the"), indicates that this was a specific, publicly known lodging place for individual travelers and caravans. **no place for them**. The inn was full, since many had come to Bethlehem to register for the census (see note on v. 2).

2:9 the glory of the Lord. The bright light that surrounds the presence of God himself, sometimes appearing as a cloud, sometimes as a bright light or burning fire (cf. Ex. 16:10; 24:17; 40:34; Ezek. 1:28; Rev. 21:23).

2:10 fear not. Cf. 1:13. **I bring you good news** is Greek *euangelizomai*, the verbal form of "gospel." **great joy**. Cf. 1:14.

2:11 a Savior, who is Christ the Lord. These three titles reveal the greatness of Mary's son. For "Savior," cf. 1:69; Acts 5:31; 13:23. "Christ" is Greek for the Hebrew "Messiah." It is a title rather than a name (cf. "the Christ," Acts 5:42; 17:3). The astonishing announcement, probably not fully grasped by the shepherds, is that this Messiah who has been born as a baby is also the Lord God himself.

2:13 a multitude of the heavenly host. Thousands of angels.

2:14 Glory to God in the highest. The angels proclaim the news about Jesus: the eternal, omnipotent Son of God has just taken "the form of a servant, being born in the likeness of men" (Phil. 2:7), for "the fullness of time" has now come, and God has "sent forth his Son, born of woman, born under the law, to redeem those who were under the law" (Gal. 4:4–5). **peace**. The peace of salvation that God gives through his Son (see note on John 14:27). Jesus is the "Prince of Peace" prophesied by Isaiah (Isa. 9:6). **among those with whom he is pleased**. God's gift of "peace" will come not to all humanity but to those whom God is pleased to call to himself.

2:15 the Lord has made known. The Lord himself, not the angelic intermediary (v. 9), is the ultimate source of the revelation.

2:20 Having seen the infant Jesus, the shepherds began **glorifying and praising God** just as the angels had done (vv. 13–14).

2:21–40 *Jesus Presented in the Temple*. This account of the presentation of the infant Jesus in the temple underscores the piety of Jesus' family, their faithfulness to God, and their keeping of his law. (Cf. parallels with the presentation of the infant John the Baptist; 1:59–80.)

2:21 eight days. See note on 1:59. **he was called Jesus**. As in John's circumcision, the emphasis falls on the **name**. The name "Jesus" (Gk. *Iēsous*) is the equivalent of *Yeshua'*/*Yehoshua'* (Joshua) in Hebrew, meaning "Yahweh saves" or "the Lord saves."

2:22 the time . . . for their purification. Forty days after Jesus' birth is the time of the circumcision (eight days) plus the 33 days of Lev. 12:3–4 counted inclusively. **up to Jerusalem**. One always goes up to Jerusalem, because it is on a mountain (see Luke 10:30; on the city itself, see Jerusalem in the Time of Jesus, pp. 1878–1879).

the Lord, [u]"Every male who first opens the womb shall be called holy to the Lord") 24 and to
offer a sacrifice according to what is said in [t]the Law of the Lord, [v]"a pair of turtledoves, or
two young pigeons." 25 Now there was a man in Jerusalem, whose name was Simeon, and
this man was [w]righteous and [x]devout, [y]waiting for [z]the consolation of Israel, and the Holy
Spirit was upon him. 26 And it had been revealed to him by the Holy Spirit that he would
not [a]see death before he had seen [b]the Lord's Christ. 27 And he came in the Spirit into the
temple, and when [c]the parents brought in the child Jesus, to do for him according to the
custom of the Law, 28 he took him up in his arms and [d]blessed God and said,

29 "Lord, now you are letting your servant[1] depart [e]in peace,
[f]according to your word;
30 for [g]my eyes have seen your [h]salvation
31 [i]that you have prepared in the presence of all peoples,
32 [j]a light for revelation to the Gentiles,
and [k]for glory to [l]your people Israel."

33 And [m]his father and his mother marveled at what was said about him. 34 And Simeon
blessed them and said to Mary his mother, "Behold, this child is appointed [n]for the fall and
rising of many in Israel, and for a sign [o]that is opposed 35 (and a sword will pierce through
your own soul also), so that thoughts from many hearts may be revealed."
36 And there was [p]a prophetess, Anna, the daughter of Phanuel, of the tribe of Asher.
She was advanced in years, having lived with her husband seven years from when she
was a virgin, 37 and then as a widow until she was eighty-four.[2] She did not depart from
the temple, [q]worshiping with [r]fasting and prayer night and day. 38 And coming up at that
very hour she began to give thanks to God and to speak of him to all who were [s]waiting
for the redemption of Jerusalem.

The Return to Nazareth

39 And when they had performed everything according to [t]the Law of the Lord, they
returned into Galilee, to their own town of [u]Nazareth. 40 [v]And the child grew and became
strong, filled with wisdom. And the favor of God was upon him.

The Boy Jesus in the Temple

41 Now [w]his parents went [x]to Jerusalem every year at [y]the Feast of the Passover. 42 And
when he was twelve years old, [z]they went up according to custom. 43 And when the feast
[a]was ended, as they were returning, the boy Jesus stayed behind in Jerusalem. [w]His parents

[1] Greek *bondservant* [2] Or *as a widow for eighty-four years*

23 [u][Ex. 13:2, 12]
24 [t][See ver. 23 above] [v]Cited from Lev. 12:8
25 [w]ch. 1:6 [x]Acts 2:5; 8:2; 22:12 [y]ver. 38; ch. 23:51; Isa. 25:9; Mark 15:43; [Gen. 49:18] [z]Isa. 40:1; 57:18
26 [a]Ps. 89:48; John 8:51; Heb. 11:5; [Acts 2:27] [b][ch. 9:20; 23:35; 1 Sam. 24:6]
27 [c]ver. 33, 41, 43, 48-51
28 [d]ch. 1:64
29 [e]Gen. 15:15 [f]ver. 26
30 [g]Isa. 52:10 [h]See ch. 3:6
31 [i]Ps. 98:2; See ch. 24:47
32 [j]Isa. 42:6; 49:6; 52:10; 60:3; John 8:12; Acts 13:47; 26:23 [k][Isa. 45:25; 46:13] [l]ver. 10
33 [m]ver. 27
34 [n][Isa. 8:14; Matt. 21:44; John 9:39; 1 Cor. 1:23, 24; 2 Cor. 2:16; 1 Pet. 2:8, 9] [o]Acts 28:22
36 [p]See Ex. 15:20
37 [q]1 Tim. 5:5 [r]ch. 5:33; Matt. 6:16-18; Acts 13:2; 14:23; 2 Cor. 6:5; 11:27
38 [s]ver. 25; See ch. 1:68
39 [t]ver. 23 [u]ver. 4
40 [v]ch. 1:80
41 [w]ver. 27 [x][1 Sam. 1:3] [y]Ex. 23:15; Deut. 16:1; John 2:13
42 [z]John 11:55
43 [a]Ex. 12:15; Lev. 23:8; Deut. 16:3 [w][See ver. 41 above]

2:24 A pair of turtledoves, or two young pigeons indicates that Joseph and Mary were poor, or of modest means (cf. Lev. 12:8), at least not among the more well-to-do who could afford to offer a lamb.

2:25–26 Nothing else is known historically concerning **Simeon**. He is **waiting for the consolation of Israel**. "Consolation" (Gk. *paraklēsis*, "consolation," "comfort") is the hope that God would come to rescue and comfort his people. Others also eagerly waited with a similar expectation (cf. v. 38; 23:50–51; Mark 15:43; Acts 10:22), and Luke's expression ties in with the wording of messianic prophecies in Isaiah (Isa. 40:1; 49:13; 51:3; 57:18; 61:2). This hope involves salvation (Luke 2:30), the "forgiveness of . . . sins" (1:77), and the saving of the lost (19:10). **The Holy Spirit was upon** Simeon, indicating the powerful anointing and manifest presence of the Holy Spirit (see Introduction: Key Themes).

2:27 in the Spirit. Under the guidance and direction of the Holy Spirit (cf. Matt. 22:43; Luke 10:21; Acts 19:21; Eph. 6:18; Rev. 1:10; 4:2). The scene of the encounter is the **temple** complex, not the temple sanctuary (see illustration, pp. 1950–1951).

2:30–32 all peoples. Both Israel and the Gentiles (cf. v. 10). **A light** (v. 32) is parallel to **your salvation** in vv. 30–31 (cf. Isa. 49:6). Whereas this salvation gives light **for revelation to the Gentiles** (cf. Acts 26:17–18), it brings **glory** for **Israel**, who already possessed God's revelation and are the people through whom the Savior came.

2:34–35 Fall refers to the judgment of the haughty and arrogant (cf. 1:50–53; 6:24–26); **rising** refers to the salvation of the humble and meek (4:18–19; 6:20–23). **A sign that is opposed** foretells future opposition to Jesus. **Sword** refers to Mary's future sorrow at Jesus' crucifixion (see John 19:25).

2:36–37 worshiping with fasting and prayer night and day. God reveals his secret purposes in history to humble servants who continually live in his presence (cf. Amos 3:7; Luke 24:53).

2:39 Joseph and Mary **performed everything according to the Law of the Lord** and thus demonstrated that they were part of the pious remnant in Israel like Zechariah and Elizabeth (cf. 1:6). **own town of Nazareth**. I.e., where they currently lived (see notes on 1:26; 2:3–4).

2:40 grew and became strong, filled with wisdom . . . the favor of God. The fourfold description of Jesus' growth parallels the twofold description of John in 1:80 but shows that Jesus is greater. Jesus experienced physical and intellectual growth as any ordinary human child would, but he also experienced "the favor of God" in his everyday life in an unusual and increasing (2:52) measure (cf. 3:22).

2:41–52 *The Boy Jesus in the Temple*. The stories of Jesus' birth and childhood end with one final story that takes place where the infancy narrative began, in the temple (cf. 1:5–23).

2:41 Every year reveals the piety of Joseph and Mary (see Deut. 16:16). The **Passover** was the opening-day **feast** of the seven-day Feast of Unleavened Bread (Lev. 23:5–6).

2:43–44 His parents did not know. They assumed that Jesus was proceeding home to Nazareth in the pilgrim caravan, perhaps with the family of a relative or neighbor. **a day's journey**. About 20 miles (32 km).

HEROD'S TEMPLE COMPLEX IN THE TIME OF JESUS

When the Gospels and the book of Acts refer to entering the temple or teaching in the temple, it is often not a reference to Herod's temple itself, but rather to this temple complex, including a number of courts and chambers that surrounded the temple. These latter structures were the great and wonderful buildings referred to by the disciples in Matt. 24:1; Mark 13:1–2.

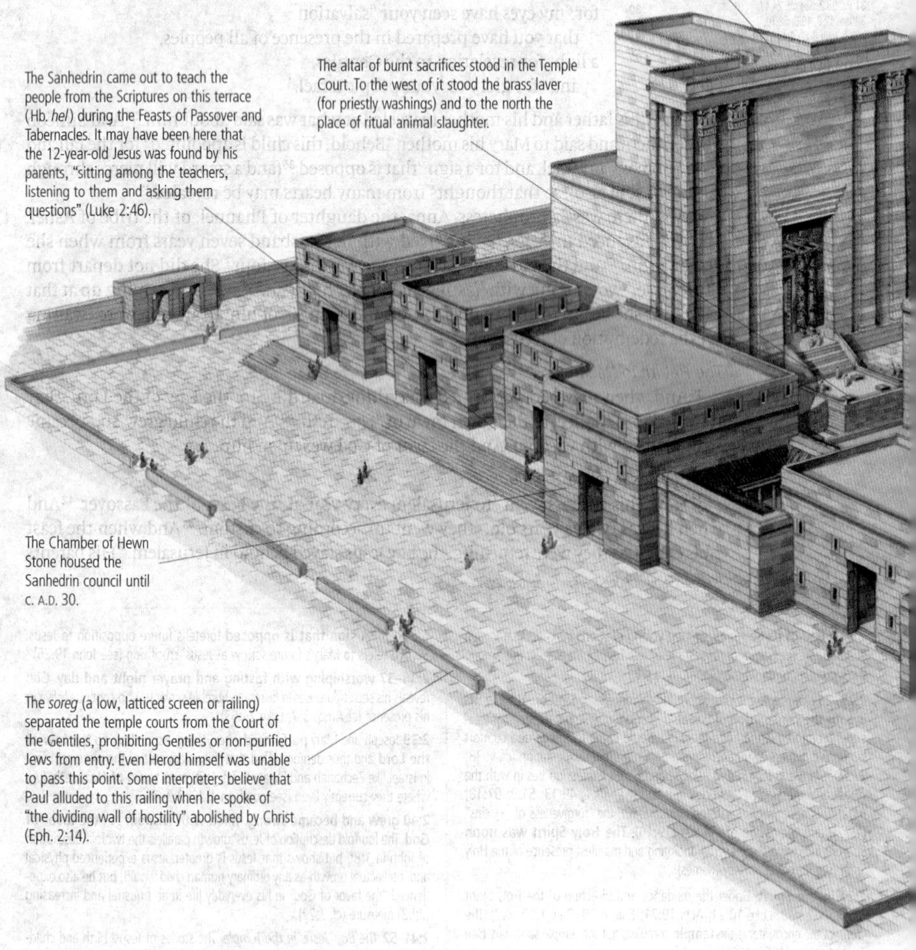

Herod's Temple
The Sanhedrin came out to teach the people from the Scriptures on this terrace (Hb. *hel*) during the Feasts of Passover and Tabernacles. It may have been here that the 12-year-old Jesus was found by his parents, "sitting among the teachers, listening to them and asking them questions" (Luke 2:46).
The altar of burnt sacrifices stood in the Temple Court. To the west of it stood the brass laver (for priestly washings) and to the north the place of ritual animal slaughter.
The Chamber of Hewn Stone housed the Sanhedrin council until c. A.D. 30.
The *soreg* (a low, latticed screen or railing) separated the temple courts from the Court of the Gentiles, prohibiting Gentiles or non-purified Jews from entry. Even Herod himself was unable to pass this point. Some interpreters believe that Paul alluded to this railing when he spoke of "the dividing wall of hostility" abolished by Christ (Eph. 2:14).

Temple Complex Architectural Plan

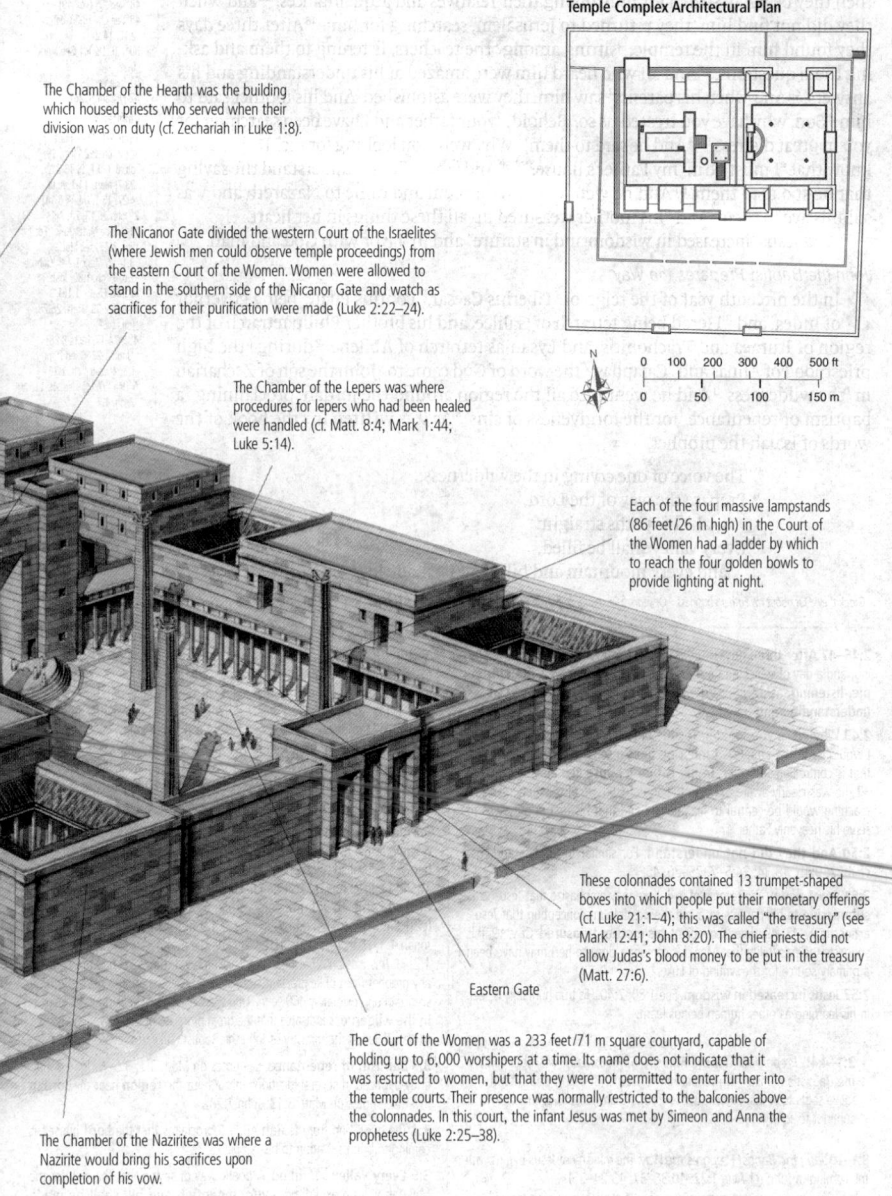

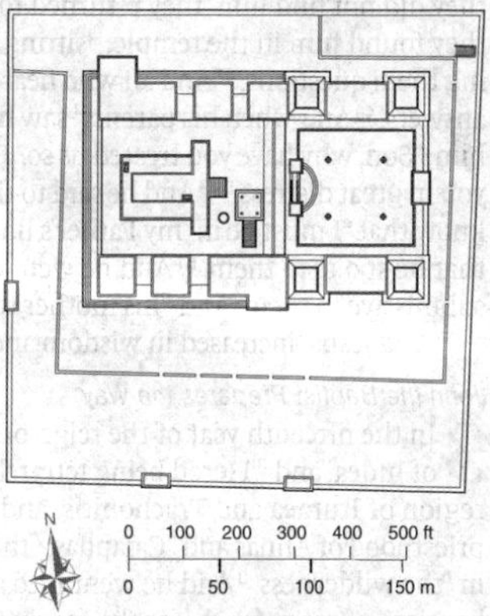
N
0 100 200 300 400 500 ft
0 50 100 150 m

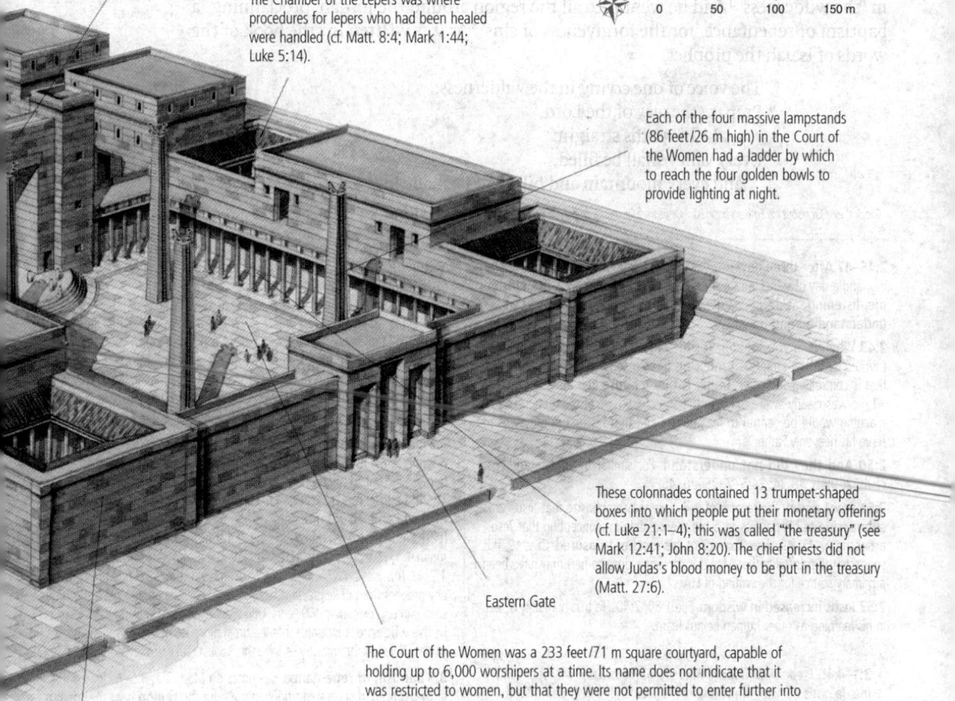
The Chamber of the Hearth was the building which housed priests who served when their division was on duty (cf. Zechariah in Luke 1:8).
The Nicanor Gate divided the western Court of the Israelites (where Jewish men could observe temple proceedings) from the eastern Court of the Women. Women were allowed to stand in the southern side of the Nicanor Gate and watch as sacrifices for their purification were made (Luke 2:22–24).
The Chamber of the Lepers was where procedures for lepers who had been healed were handled (cf. Matt. 8:4; Mark 1:44; Luke 5:14).
Each of the four massive lampstands (86 feet/26 m high) in the Court of the Women had a ladder by which to reach the four golden bowls to provide lighting at night.
These colonnades contained 13 trumpet-shaped boxes into which people put their monetary offerings (cf. Luke 21:1–4); this was called "the treasury" (see Mark 12:41; John 8:20). The chief priests did not allow Judas's blood money to be put in the treasury (Matt. 27:6).
Eastern Gate
The Court of the Women was a 233 feet/71 m square courtyard, capable of holding up to 6,000 worshipers at a time. Its name does not indicate that it was restricted to women, but that they were not permitted to enter further into the temple courts. Their presence was normally restricted to the balconies above the colonnades. In this court, the infant Jesus was met by Simeon and Anna the prophetess (Luke 2:25–38).
The Chamber of the Nazirites was where a Nazirite would bring his sacrifices upon completion of his vow.

did not know it, 44 but supposing him to be in the group they went a day's journey, but
then they began to search for him among their relatives and acquaintances, 45 and when
they did not find him, they returned to Jerusalem, searching for him. 46 After three days
they found him in the temple, [b]sitting among [c]the teachers, listening to them and asking them questions. 47 And all who heard him were amazed at his understanding and his
answers. 48 And when his parents[1] saw him, they were astonished. And his mother said to
him, "Son, why have you treated us so? Behold, [d]your father and I have been searching for
you in great distress." 49 And he said to them, "Why were you looking for me? Did you not
know that [e]I must be in [f]my Father's house?"[2] 50 And [g]they did not understand the saying
that he spoke to them. 51 And he went down with them and came to Nazareth and was
submissive to them. And [h]his mother treasured up all these things in her heart.
52 And Jesus [i]increased in wisdom and in stature[3] and in [i]favor with God and man.

John the Baptist Prepares the Way

3 In the fifteenth year of the reign of [j]Tiberius Caesar, [k]Pontius Pilate [l]being governor
of Judea, and [m]Herod being tetrarch of Galilee, and his brother Philip tetrarch of the
region of Ituraea and Trachonitis, and Lysanias tetrarch of Abilene, 2 during [n]the high
priesthood of Annas and [o]Caiaphas, [p]the word of God came to [q]John the son of Zechariah
in [r]the wilderness. 3 And he went into all the region around the Jordan, proclaiming [s]a
baptism of repentance [t]for the forgiveness of sins. 4 As it is written in [u]the book of the
words of Isaiah the prophet,

> [v]"The voice of one crying in the wilderness:
> [w]'Prepare the way of the Lord,[4]
> make his paths straight.
> 5 [x]Every valley shall be filled,
> [y]and every mountain and hill shall be made low,

[1] Greek *they* [2] Or *about my Father's business* [3] Or *years* [4] Or *crying, Prepare in the wilderness the way of the Lord*

46 [b]See Matt. 26:55 [c]ch. 5:17
48 [d]ver. 27; [ver. 49]
49 [e]See ch. 13:33 [f]John 2:16; 14:2
50 [g][ch. 18:34]; See Mark 9:32
51 [h]See ver. 19
52 [i][1 Sam. 2:26]

Chapter 3

1 [j][ch. 2:1] [k]See Matt. 27:2 [l]ch. 2:2 [m]ver. 19; ch. 8:3; 9:7, 9; 13:31; 23:7; Matt. 14:1; Acts 4:27; 13:1; [Mark 6:14]
2 [n]John 18:13, 24; Acts 4:6 [o]See Matt. 26:3 [p]For ver. 2-17, see Matt. 3:1-12; Mark 1:2-8 [q]John 1:6, 7 [r]ch. 1:80; Josh. 15:61; [Judg. 1:16]
3 [s]Acts 2:38 [t]Matt. 26:28; [ch. 1:77]
4 [u]ch. 4:17; [Acts 8:28] [v]John 1:23; Cited from Isa. 40:3-5 [w]ch. 1:76
5 [x][Isa. 57:14] [y]Isa. 49:11; Zech. 4:7

2:46–47 After three days—a day's journey from Jerusalem, a day returning, and a day of searching for Jesus—his parents found Jesus **in the temple, listening, asking . . . questions**, and amazing those present **at his understanding and his answers**. On the temple, see note on John 2:14.

2:49 Why were you looking for me probably means, "Didn't you know I would be in the temple?" **I must be** gives a sense of obligation to God that is controlling Jesus' life. **In my Father's house** indicates that, at age 12, he was clearly aware of being the Son of God. He also understood that teaching would be central to his ministry and that his first priority was to serve his heavenly Father.

2:50 And they did not understand. For similar misunderstandings, cf. 4:22; 9:45; 18:34; 24:5–7, 25–26, 45.

2:51 went down. The reverse of v. 4. Luke may emphasize that Jesus **was submissive** to his parents to avoid the possible misconception that Jesus' actions in vv. 43–49 were disobedient. **his mother treasured**. Cf. v. 19. This suggests the possibility that Mary (or someone close to her) may have been a primary source for the writing of Luke.

2:52 Jesus increased in wisdom. See 1:80; 2:40. His true humanity is seen in his learning as other human beings learn.

3:1–4:15 *Preparation for the Ministry of Jesus.* Luke describes John the Baptist's ministry of preparation for Jesus (3:1–20), and then the focus shifts to Jesus himself (3:21–4:15). Again, Jesus is seen as being superior to John (3:16–17).

3:1–20 *John the Baptist Prepares the Way.* The ministry of Jesus begins with the coming of John (cf. Acts 1:22; 10:36–37; 13:24–25).

3:1 In the fifteenth year of . . . Tiberius Caesar is probably A.D. 29 (plus or minus a year). Tiberius became emperor in A.D. 14, though he may have been in charge of certain provinces prior to that time. **Pontius Pilate . . . governor of Judea**. Pilate reigned over Judea A.D. 26–36 (see note on 23:1). **Herod** Antipas was a **tetrarch**, ruling **Galilee** and Perea from 4 B.C. to A.D. 39 (see Matt. 14:1). Herod **Philip** II was **tetrarch** of the northern Transjordanian territories (east of the Jordan River and largely north of the Yarmuk River) known as **Ituraea**, Batanaea, **Trachonitis**, Auranitis, and Gaulonitis, from 4 B.C. to A.D. 34. Antipas and Philip II were both sons of Herod the Great (on Herod see note on Matt. 2:1) and were designated as Herod's heirs upon his death in 4 B.C. along with their brother Archelaus (who reigned as ethnarch of Judea until A.D. 6; see Matt. 2:22). It is likely that **Lysanias** ruled a territory near Damascus, and that this region was given to Herod Agrippa I around A.D. 37. See The Herodian Dynasty, pp. 1790–1791. Luke's precision in naming five Roman officials with their specific titles shows concern for detailed historical accuracy, and his accuracy is confirmed by historical records outside of the Bible.

3:2 high priesthood of Annas and Caiaphas. Caiaphas (served A.D. 18–36) was the actual high priest at this time. Annas had been high priest A.D. 6–15 but was still called "high priest" after he left office (see notes on John 18:13; 18:24; cf. Josephus, *Jewish Antiquities* 20.197–200, 244–251). **The word of God came to John** designates him as a prophet like the OT prophets (cf. 1 Sam. 15:10; 2 Sam. 7:4; 24:11; 1 Kings 12:22; Jer. 1:4; Ezek. 1:3; Jonah 1:1; Hag. 1:1; Zech. 1:1; Mal. 1:1; see also notes on Matt. 3:1; Mark 1:2–3). This was an amazing event since "the word of God" had not come to any prophet (for public proclamation) since Malachi in about 460 B.C. After a silence of approximately 460 years, God was once again speaking to his people. **In the wilderness** indicates that the great promises of Isaiah were beginning to be fulfilled in the ministry of John the Baptist (Luke 3:4; cf. Isa. 40:3).

3:3 baptism of repentance. See notes on Matt. 3:2; 3:5–6. John apparently baptized in several locations throughout the **region** near the **Jordan** River (see notes on Matt. 3:13; John 1:28).

3:4 The quotation from **Isaiah** 40:3–5 proclaims that the **Lord** himself is coming to bring salvation to his people.

3:5 Every valley . . . filled. A poetic way of saying that the way for the Messiah will be expedited. **every mountain and hill shall be made low**. Obstacles will be removed. But these images are also metaphors that have ethical overtones: the proud and arrogant will be humbled (1:52; 14:11; 18:14), the humble and lowly will be exalted, and the **crooked** (cf. Acts 2:40) will be changed.

3:6 All flesh shall see predicts the salvation also of the Gentiles (cf. 2:30–32).

5[z]Isa. 42:16; 45:2
6[a]Isa. 52:10; [Ps. 98:2, 3] [b]ch. 2:30; Acts 28:28; [ch. 1:69, 71, 77; Titus 2:11]
7[c]Matt. 12:34; 23:33 [d]Ps. 140:3 [e]Rom. 5:9; Eph. 5:6; Col. 3:6; 1 Thess. 1:10
8[f]Acts 26:20 [g]John 8:39 [h][ch. 4:3]
9[i]ch. 13:7, 9; Matt. 7:19; John 15:2, 6
10[j]Acts 2:37; 16:30; 22:10
11[k]Isa. 58:7; Dan. 4:27; Eph. 4:28; James 2:15, 16; 1 John 3:17; [ch. 18:22]
12[l]ch. 7:29; Matt. 21:32 [j][See ver. 10 above]
13[m]ch. 19:8
14[j][See ver. 10 above] [m][See ver. 13 above] [n]1 Cor. 9:7 (Gk.)
15[o]John 1:19, 20 [p]See Matt. 1:17
16[q]John 1:26; Acts 1:5 [r]John 1:15, 27; 3:30, 31; Acts 13:25 [s]Isa. 5:27 [t]John 1:33; Acts 11:16 [u][Mal. 3:2, 3; Acts 2:3]
17[v]Isa. 30:24 [w]Matt. 13:30 [x]Mal. 4:1 [y]Mark 9:43, 48
18[z][John 20:30; 21:25]
19[a]Matt. 14:3; Mark 6:17, 18; See ver. 1
20[b][John 3:24]
21[c]For ver. 21, 22, see Matt. 3:13-17; Mark 1:9-11; [John 1:32-34] [d]Acts 7:56
22[e][ch. 4:18, 21; Acts 10:38]

[z]and the crooked shall become straight,
and the rough places shall become level ways,
6 [a]and all flesh shall see [b]the salvation of God.'"

7 He said therefore to the crowds that came out to be baptized by him, [c]"You brood of
[d]vipers! Who warned you to flee from [e]the wrath to come? 8 Bear fruits [f]in keeping with
repentance. And do not begin to say to yourselves, [g]'We have Abraham as our father.' For
I tell you, God is able from [h]these stones to raise up children for Abraham. 9 Even now the
axe is laid to the root of the trees. [i]Every tree therefore that does not bear good fruit is cut
down and thrown into the fire."

10 And the crowds asked him, [j]"What then shall we do?" 11 And he answered them,
[k]"Whoever has two tunics[1] is to share with him who has none, and whoever has food is
to do likewise." 12 [l]Tax collectors also came to be baptized and said to him, "Teacher, [j]what
shall we do?" 13 And he said to them, [m]"Collect no more than you are authorized to do."
14 Soldiers also asked him, "And we, [j]what shall we do?" And he said to them, [m]"Do not extort
money from anyone by threats or by false accusation, and be content with your [n]wages."

15 As the people were in expectation, and all were questioning in their hearts concerning
John, [o]whether he might be [p]the Christ, 16 [q]John answered them all, saying, "I baptize you
with water, but [r]he who is mightier than I is coming, [s]the strap of whose sandals I am not
worthy to untie. He will baptize you [t]with the Holy Spirit and [u]fire. 17 His [v]winnowing
fork is in his hand, to clear his threshing floor and to [w]gather the wheat into his barn, [x]but
the chaff he will burn with [y]unquenchable fire."

18 So [z]with many other exhortations he preached good news to the people. 19 But [a]Herod the
tetrarch, who had been reproved by him for Herodias, his brother's wife, and for all the evil
things that Herod had done, 20 added this to them all, that [b]he locked up John in prison.

21 Now when all the people were baptized, and when [c]Jesus also had been baptized
and was praying, [d]the heavens were opened, 22 and [e]the Holy Spirit descended on him in

[1] Greek *chiton*, a long garment worn under the cloak next to the skin

3:7 vipers. A general term for any of a number of poisonous snakes in Israel, showing that the people had become the seed of the Serpent (Gen. 3:15). **Who warned you to flee . . . ?** I.e., "Who has told you to flee the coming wrath by merely submitting to a rite of baptism?"

3:8 do not begin to say. They are not even to think of saying "**We have Abraham as our father.**" Cf. John 8:39, 53. One is not a member of God's family by natural descent but by responding personally to God and his call.

3:9 Even now. The kingdom of God is not a remote future event but was revealed in a new and decisive way in the ministry of Jesus, for which John the Baptist was preparing the way. **the axe . . . trees**. A warning that the coming judgment is very close at hand (cf. 13:6–9).

3:10 What then (in light of vv. 7–9) **shall we do?** The frequency of this question in Luke–Acts indicates its importance. Cf. Luke 3:12, 14; 10:25; Acts 2:37; 22:10. True repentance requires a change in ethical behavior, as is indicated by the examples in Luke 3:10–14 (cf. "bear fruit in keeping with repentance," v. 8).

3:11 tunics. Garments worn under the cloak (cf. 6:29).

3:12–14 Tax collectors. See note on Matt. 5:46–47. They collected tolls, tariffs, and customs, and were notoriously dishonest (cf. Luke 15:1–2; 19:8) and despised. They are not told to quit their profession but to be honest in carrying out their duties. Similarly, **soldiers** are not told to resign but to avoid the moral temptations of their profession. John does not say that working for the Roman government or serving as a soldier is in itself morally wrong, but he insists that God expects upright conduct from his people.

3:16 In the two phrases (1) **he who is mightier than I is coming** and (2) **He will baptize you with the Holy Spirit and fire**, the Greek word order emphasizes the pronoun "he," pointing to Jesus (cf. John 3:30). John the Baptist's answer indicates that people will know that the Christ has come when he baptizes with the Holy Spirit—which took place at Pentecost in Acts 2. Whether being baptized "with the Holy Spirit and fire" will be positive (involving the coming of the purifying fire of the Spirit at Pentecost; Acts 1:8; 2:3) or negative (involving the divine judgment of fire; Luke 9:54; 12:49; 17:29) depends on the response of the individual person. See notes on Matt. 3:11 and Acts 2:3.

3:17 winnowing fork. A wooden pitchfork used to throw the chaff and grain into the air to separate them. The **wheat** (or grain) would be gathered and the **chaff** burned as fuel in the oven (Matt. 6:30). **Unquenchable fire** portrays the horrible nature of the final judgment.

3:18–20 John preaches the **good news** ("gospel"), indicating that he is different from the OT prophets because he is the first preacher of the good news of the kingdom of God (see 16:16).

3:21–4:15 *Jesus' Baptism, Genealogy, and Temptation.* The description of Jesus as God's Son (1:31–35) is confirmed: at his baptism by a voice from heaven (3:22) and his anointing by the Spirit (3:22; 4:1, 18); by his genealogy (3:38); and by Satan's acknowledgment of him as the Son of God at his temptation (4:3, 9).

3:21–22 *Jesus' Baptism.* Jesus submits to John's baptism of repentance to identify with Israel's sin, foreshadowing the judgment he will endure at the cross. (Luke does not explicitly mention John's role in Jesus' baptism, though he acknowledges it in Acts 1:22.)

3:21 On the location of Jesus' baptism, see note on Matt. 3:13. **was praying**. See Introduction: Key Themes. **The heavens were opened** to show visible evidence of God's action.

3:22 the Holy Spirit descended on him. Jesus is anointed and empowered by the Holy Spirit for his ministry. This will be an important theme in the following chapters (cf. 4:1, 14, esp. vv. 18–19). **like a dove**. This simile does not necessarily mean that the Spirit actually assumed the form of a dove, but it does indicate a bodily form of something like a dove. **voice came from heaven**. God speaks (cf. Isa. 6:4, 8). **You are my beloved Son**. Jesus is not only a man; he is also the uniquely loved Son of the Father (see note on John 1:14). This divine affirmation (cf. Luke 1:31–35; 2:49) will be repeated at the transfiguration (9:35). **Well pleased** shows that the Father takes delight in all that Jesus is and all that he has done in his life. It may also indicate that Jesus is the servant of the Lord by alluding to Isa. 42:1, in which case it would be forecasting the death of Jesus for his people.

bodily form, like a dove; and [f]a voice came from heaven, [g]"You are my beloved Son;[1] with
you I am well pleased."[2]

The Genealogy of Jesus Christ

23 Jesus, [h]when he began his ministry, was about [i]thirty years of age, being [j]the son
(as was supposed) of Joseph, the son of Heli, **24** the son of Matthat, the son of Levi, the
son of Melchi, the son of Jannai, the son of Joseph, **25** the son of Mattathias, the son of
Amos, the son of Nahum, the son of Esli, the son of Naggai, **26** the son of Maath, the
son of Mattathias, the son of Semein, the son of Josech, the son of Joda, **27** the son of
Joanan, the son of Rhesa, [k]the son of Zerubbabel, the son [l]of Shealtiel,[3] the son of Neri,
28 the son of Melchi, the son of Addi, the son of Cosam, the son of Elmadam, the son
of Er, **29** the son of Joshua, the son of Eliezer, the son of Jorim, the son of Matthat, the
son of Levi, **30** the son of Simeon, the son of Judah, the son of Joseph, the son of Jonam,
the son of Eliakim, **31** the son of Melea, the son of Menna, the son of Mattatha, the son
of [m]Nathan, the son of David, **32** [n]the son of Jesse, the son of Obed, the son of Boaz, the
son of Sala, the son of Nahshon, **33** the son of Amminadab, the son of Admin, the son of
Arni, the son of Hezron, the son of Perez, the son of Judah, **34** [o]the son of Jacob, [p]the son
of Isaac, [q]the son of Abraham, [r]the son of Terah, the son of Nahor, **35** the son of Serug,
the son of Reu, the son of Peleg, the son of Eber, the son of Shelah, **36** the son of Cainan,
the son of Arphaxad, the son of Shem, the son of Noah, the son of Lamech, **37** the son of
Methuselah, the son of Enoch, the son of Jared, the son of Mahalaleel, the son of Cainan,
38 the son of Enos, the son of Seth, the son of Adam, the son of God.

The Temptation of Jesus

4 [s]And Jesus, [t]full of the Holy Spirit, [u]returned from the Jordan and was led [v]by the
Spirit in the wilderness **2** for [w]forty days, [x]being tempted by the devil. [w]And he ate
nothing during those days. And when they were ended, [y]he was hungry. **3** The devil said
to him, "If you are [z]the Son of God, command [a]this stone to become bread." **4** And Jesus
answered him, [b]"It is written, [c]'Man shall not live by bread alone.'" **5** [d]And the devil took

[1] Or *my Son, my* (or *the*) *Beloved* [2] Some manuscripts *beloved Son; today I have begotten you* [3] Greek *Salathiel*

22 [f]John 12:28 [g][ch. 9:35; Ps. 2:7; Isa. 42:1; Eph. 1:6; Col. 1:13; 2 Pet. 1:17; 1 John 5:9]
23 [h]Matt. 4:17; Acts 1:1, 22 [i][Num. 4:3] [j]ch. 4:22; Matt. 13:55; John 1:45; 6:42; For ver. 23-38, [Matt. 1:1-16]
27 [k]Matt. 1:12 [l]Ezra 3:2
31 [m]2 Sam. 5:14; 1 Chr. 3:5; 14:4; Zech. 12:12
32 [n]1 Sam. 16:1; 17:12; [Ruth 4:18-22; 1 Chr. 2:1-15]
34 [o]Gen. 29:35 [p]Gen. 25:26 [q]Gen. 21:3 [r]For ver. 34-38, see Gen. 5:3-32; 11:10-26; 1 Chr. 1:1-4, 24-27

Chapter 4

1 [s]For ver. 1-13, see Matt. 4:1-11; Mark 1:12, 13 [t]ver. 18; ch. 3:22; John 1:33; 3:34; Acts 10:38; [ch. 1:15; Acts 6:5] [u]ch. 3:3, 21 [v]ver. 14
2 [w][Deut. 9:9, 18; 1 Kgs. 19:8] [x][Heb. 2:18; 4:15] [y][John 4:6, 7]
3 [z]See Matt. 14:33 [a][ch. 3:8]
4 [b]ver. 8, 10; Eph. 6:17 [c]Cited from Deut. 8:3; [John 4:34]
5 [d]Matt. 4:8

3:23–38 *The Genealogy of Jesus Christ.* Whereas Matthew (see notes on Matt. 1:1–17) traces Jesus' lineage from Abraham to emphasize Jesus' Jewish heritage, Luke traces it back to Adam to show that Jesus is the fulfillment of the hopes of all people (cf. Acts 17:26). In addition to some minor differences and gaps (see note on Matt. 1:17), the genealogies in Matthew and Luke differ significantly in the period from David to Jesus, even naming different fathers for Joseph (Jacob in Matt. 1:16; Heli in Luke 3:23). Both Matthew and Luke are evidently depending on detailed historical records, and various suggestions have been proposed to explain the differences: (1) An old suggestion is that Matthew traces Joseph's ancestry while Luke traces Mary's ancestry. But very few commentators defend this solution today, because 1:27 refers to Joseph, not Mary, and taking 3:23 as a reference to Mary's ancestry requires the unlikely step of inserting Mary into the text where she is not mentioned but Joseph *is* mentioned. (2) The most commonly accepted suggestion is that Matthew traces the line of *royal succession* (moving from David to Solomon; Matt. 1:6) while Luke traces Joseph's actual *physical descent* (moving from David to Nathan, a little-known son mentioned in 2 Sam. 5:14; Luke 3:31), and both lines converge at Joseph. Then there are various explanations for the two different people named as Joseph's father (Jacob in Matthew; Heli in Luke). In most proposed solutions, they are thought to be different people and a second marriage is assumed (sometimes a levirate marriage; see note on Matt. 22:24), so that Joseph was the legal son of one but the physical son of the other, and thus there are two lines of ancestry for the two men. (3) Some commentators have suggested that Heli was Mary's father, but that there were no male heirs in the family, so Heli adopted Joseph as his "son" when Mary and Joseph were married (cf. 1 Chron. 2:34–35; Ezra 2:61; Neh. 7:63; also Num. 27:1–11 for inheritance through daughters when there is no son). Although the genealogies in Matthew and Luke differ in their organizing principles, both of these genealogies emphasize that Jesus was the "son of David" (Luke 3:31; cf. Matt. 1:6). Luke further emphasizes the virgin birth (cf. 1:34–35) with the phrase "being the son (as was supposed) of Joseph" (3:23).

3:23 If Jesus was born sometime before Herod the Great's death in 4 B.C. (cf. Matt. 2:16) and **began his ministry** C. A.D. 28 (see Luke 3:1), he would have been **about thirty years** old (or in his early 30s).

3:38 For **the son of God**, cf. 1:31–35; 2:11; 3:22.

4:1–15 *The Temptation of Jesus.* The temptation is the last preparatory event before Jesus' public ministry begins. It is tied intimately with the declaration of his sonship at his baptism (3:22; cf. 4:3, 9).

4:1 Jesus, having been anointed by the Spirit at his baptism (3:22) and **full of the Holy Spirit** (see 1:41), is **led by the Spirit** to face Satan. See note on Matt. 4:1.

4:2 Forty days is reminiscent of Israel's 40 years of wilderness wandering (Num. 14:34) and the 40-day fasts by Moses (Ex. 34:28; Deut. 9:9) and Elijah (1 Kings 19:8). See note on Matt. 4:2. **Being tempted** (a present participle) indicates Jesus was tempted the entire 40 days and that the three temptations mentioned were the culmination. **devil**. A Greek term (*diabolos*) used seven times in Luke–Acts. It commonly translates Hebrew *satan* ("Satan") in the Septuagint. See note on Matt. 4:1. He is the supreme adversary of God.

4:3–4 If you are the Son of God implies a challenge for Jesus to demonstrate his divine power. Satan is asking, in essence, "Why should the very Son of God have to suffer in the wilderness in this way?" See note on Matt. 4:3. **command this stone . . . bread**. Satan tempted Jesus to use his power to satisfy his own desires rather than trusting in God to supply all that he needed during this temptation. Jesus' reply here (and in the following temptations) begins with **It is written** followed by a quotation from Deuteronomy that tells what the people of Israel should have learned in the wilderness: **Man shall not live by bread alone** (Deut. 8:3). Satisfying one's need for food is not as important as trusting and obeying God.

4:5–8 And the devil took him up introduces another temptation but does not imply that the temptations occurred in this order (Matthew has a different order, and more indications of chronological sequence). This temptation involves being shown **kingdoms of the world in a moment of time**. **To you I will give**. Though Satan claims that **all this authority and their glory** (of the kingdoms) **has been delivered to me**, and though in some

him up and showed him all the kingdoms of the world in a moment of time, 6 and said
to him, “To you [e]I will give all this authority and their glory, [e]for it has been delivered to
me, and I give it to whom I will. 7 If you, then, will worship me, it will all be yours.” 8 And
Jesus answered him, [f]“It is written,

> [g]“ ‘You shall worship the Lord your God,
> and [h]him only shall you serve.’ ”

9 [i]And he took him to Jerusalem and set him on the pinnacle of the temple and said to him,
“If you are [j]the Son of God, throw yourself down from here, 10 for it is written,

> [k]“ ‘He will command his angels concerning you,
> to guard you,’

11 and

> [k]“ ‘On their hands they will bear you up,
> lest you strike your foot against a stone.’ ”

12 And Jesus answered him, “It is said, [l]‘You shall not [m]put the Lord your God to the test.’ ”
13 And when the devil had ended every temptation, he departed from him [n]until an opportune time.

Jesus Begins His Ministry

14 [o]And Jesus returned [p]in the power of the Spirit to Galilee, and [q]a report about him
went out through all the surrounding country. 15 And [r]he taught in their synagogues,
being glorified by all.

Jesus Rejected at Nazareth

16 [s]And he came to [t]Nazareth, where he had been brought up. And [u]as was his custom,
[v]he went to the synagogue on the Sabbath day, and he stood up [w]to read. 17 And [x]the scroll

6 [e]Rev. 13:2
8 [f]ver. 4; [ver. 12] [g]Cited from Deut. 6:13 [h]1 Sam. 7:3
9 [i]Matt. 4:5 [j]ver. 3
10 [k]Cited from Ps. 91:11, 12
11 [k][See ver. 10 above]
12 [l]Cited from Deut. 6:16 [m][Isa. 7:12]
13 [n][ch. 22:53; John 14:30]
14 [o]Matt. 4:12 [p]ver. 1; [Acts 1:8] [q]ver. 37
15 [r]See Matt. 4:23
16 [s]For ver. 16-30, [Matt. 13:54-58; Mark 6:1-6] [t]ch. 2:39, 51 [u][Acts 17:2] [v]ver. 31; See Mark 6:2 [w]Acts 13:15, 27; 15:21
17 [x]ch. 3:4; [Acts 8:28]

sense Satan is the “ruler of this world” (John 12:31; cf. 1 John 5:19), the claim should not be accepted as fully true. Satan is “a liar and the father of lies” (John 8:44), and in the final analysis, all authority belongs to God (see Rom. 13:1–4; cf. Ps. 24:1; Dan. 4:17). Because of common grace (see notes on Matt. 5:44; 5:45), even a fallen world still gives glory to God (Isa. 6:3). This is a temptation to break the first commandment (Ex. 20:3). Jesus replies that worship belongs to the **Lord your God** alone.

4:9–12 The next temptation takes place on the **pinnacle of the temple**, the southeastern corner of the Temple Mount, overlooking the Kidron Valley (see note on Matt. 4:5). **He will . . . guard you**. This time the Devil quotes Scripture (Ps. 91:11–12), but incorrectly, for the psalmist did not mean that a person should attempt to force God to protect him (see also note on Matt. 4:6–7). Jesus replies, **You shall not put the Lord your God to the test** (Deut. 6:16). All of Jesus’ answers come from God’s Word, specifically from the book of Deuteronomy, which was highly respected in Jesus’ time. By quoting Scripture back to Satan, Jesus demonstrates the centrality of God’s Word in defeating Satan’s attacks and temptations (cf. Eph. 6:17).

4:13–15 he departed from him. Although the Devil will remain active in opposing Jesus’ ministry, Jesus will not experience such a direct confrontation again until his crucifixion. Having experienced divine confirmation and anointing by the Spirit at his baptism and now through his victory over the Devil in the wilderness, **Jesus returned in the power of the Spirit to Galilee** to begin his ministry (cf. 23:5; Acts 1:22; 10:37). For the connection between “power” and “Spirit,” see note on Luke 1:16–17. That Luke describes Jesus as **being glorified by all** indicates Luke’s strong belief in Jesus’ deity.

4:16–9:50 *The Ministry of Jesus in Galilee.* Except for 8:22–39, this next section of Luke centers on Galilee.

4:16–5:16 *The Beginning.* Jesus began his ministry by preaching in his hometown of Nazareth. Soon thereafter he was preaching in many places, healing many people, and calling disciples to work with him.

4:16–30 *Jesus Rejected at Nazareth.* Jesus’ sermon reveals the nature of his messiahship.

4:16 Nazareth. Cf. 1:26; 2:4, 39, 51. **where he had been brought up** (cf. 2:39–51). **As was his custom** reveals Jesus’ faithful attendance at the **synagogue**. Ever-increasing archaeological evidence exists for the importance of the synagogue in early Jewish communities. Many synagogues have been

Jesus’ Ministry in Galilee

Jesus spent most of his life and ministry in the region of Galilee, a mountainous area in northern Palestine. Jesus grew up in the small hill town of Nazareth, about 3.5 miles (5.6 km) south of the Gentile administrative center of Sepphoris. Soon after he began his public ministry, Jesus relocated to Capernaum on the Sea of Galilee. By Jesus’ time, a thriving fishing industry had developed around the Sea of Galilee, and several of Jesus’ disciples were fishermen.

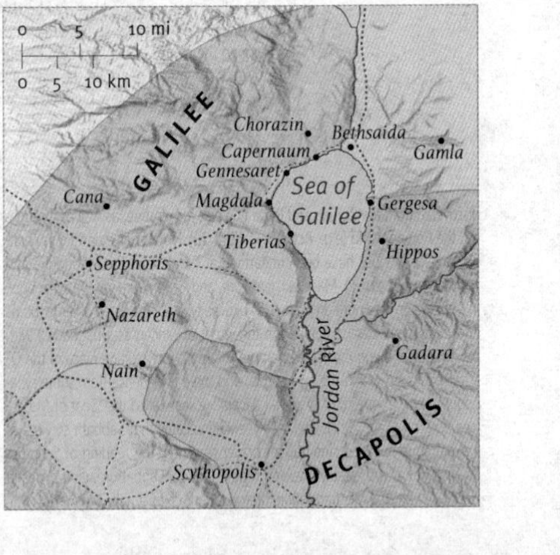

of the prophet Isaiah was given to him. He unrolled the scroll and found the place where it was written,

18 [y]"The Spirit of the Lord [z]is upon me,
because he has anointed me
to [a]proclaim good news to the poor.
[b]He has sent me to proclaim liberty to the captives
and [c]recovering of sight to the blind,
[d]to set at liberty those who are oppressed,
19 [e]to proclaim the year of the Lord's favor."

20 And he rolled up the scroll and gave it back to the attendant and [f]sat down. And the eyes

18 [y]Cited from Isa. 61:1, 2 [z]ver. 1; [Acts 1:2] [a]Matt. 11:5; [ch. 6:20] [b]Ps. 146:7, 8 [c][Isa. 42:7; John 9:39; Acts 26:18] [d]Isa. 58:6
19 [e]Lev. 25:10; [Isa. 49:8; 2 Cor. 6:2]
20 [f]Matt. 26:55; [John 8:2]; [Matt. 5:1; 13:2]

THE SYNAGOGUE AND JEWISH WORSHIP

In cities other than Jerusalem, the synagogue was the center of Jewish worship during the time of Christ. Synagogues were located in most of the leading towns of Israel. Although very little remains of the original first-century synagogue at Nazareth, extensive archaeological evidence exists for a typical Jewish synagogue in the town of Gamla, which would have had much in common with the synagogues Jesus visited in Nazareth and other cities.

This illustration is based on the excavation of the Gamla synagogue, one of the oldest in Israel. The city of Gamla was 6 miles (9.7 km) northeast of the Sea of Galilee. It was destroyed by the Romans in A.D. 67, early in the Jewish Revolt.

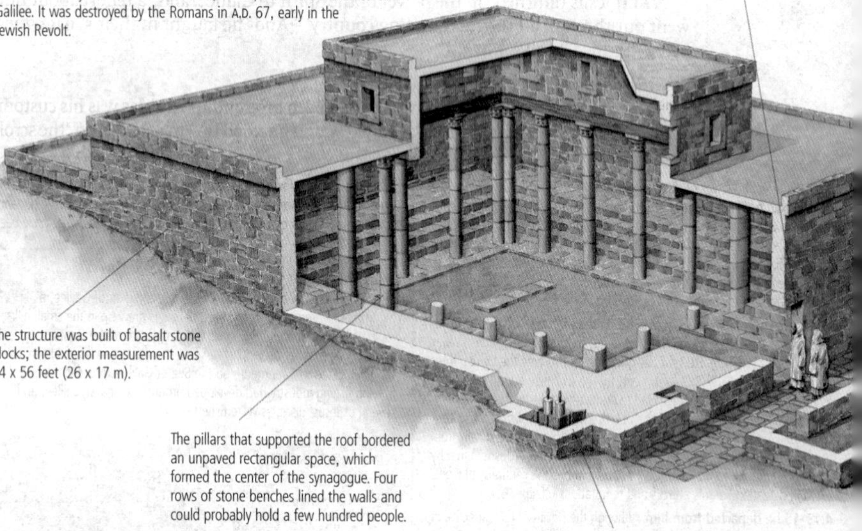

discovered from the Roman and Byzantine eras in Palestine, as well as throughout the Roman world (e.g., Acts 17:1; 18:4, 26). From Galilee and Judea, first-century synagogues have been unearthed at Gamla (see The Synagogue and Jewish Worship above), Masada, Herodium, and Capernaum (on the synagogue in Capernaum, see note on Mark 1:21). These typically consisted of large rooms (including some basilicas built with the intent of serving as synagogues) with bench seating along the wall. Often the Torah ark (the storage place of the OT scrolls) is found within the synagogue; and there is evidence from some synagogues (e.g., Chorazin) of a special decorative seat called the "Seat of Moses" (see note on Matt. 23:2). Literary evidence indicates that Sabbath services at a synagogue involved singing, set prayer readings, the reading of Scripture (in Palestine this probably involved regular annual Sabbath reading cycles in Hebrew, with Aramaic translation/interpretation; cf. Mishnah, *Megillah* 4.1–5, 10), an interpretative homily on the weekly Scripture reading, and a priestly blessing. The leadership of the synagogue fell to the elders of the congregation and to officials such as the *archisynagōgos* ("ruler of the synagogue"; cf. note on Mark 5:22). Also evidenced was the practice of "putting out of the synagogue" those who were at variance with accepted belief and practice (e.g., John 9:22).

The entrance to the synagogue faced southwest, toward Jerus
The structure was built of basalt stone blocks; the exterior measurement was 84 x 56 feet (26 x 17 m).
The pillars that supported the roof bordered an unpaved rectangular space, which formed the center of the synagogue. Four rows of stone benches lined the walls and could probably hold a few hundred people.
A closet held the scrolls of the Law and the Prophets.

4:17 He . . . found the place. Jesus chooses to read Isa. 61:1–2a, but also quotes from Isa. 58:6.

4:18–19 The Spirit of the Lord is upon me. Jesus is aware of his anointing (Luke 3:22; cf. Acts 4:26–27; 10:38) and claims to be the messianic servant of the Lord who is speaking in this passage from Isaiah 61 ("Today this Scripture has been fulfilled," Luke 4:21). Jesus' mission involves proclaiming **good news to the poor** (see 6:20) and **liberty to the captives** (in the

20[g] Acts 3:4; [ch. 19:48]
21[h] Mark 12:10; Acts 8:35 [i] See Matt. 1:22
22[j] Ps. 45:2 [k] [Matt. 13:55; John 6:42] [l] ch. 3:23
23[m] [ch. 23:39; Matt. 27:42] [n] Matt. 11:23; Mark 2:1-12; John 4:46-53
24[o] See Matt. 13:57
25[p] 1 Kgs. 17:1; 18:1; James 5:17; [Rev. 11:6]
26[q] 1 Kgs. 17:9
27[r] [2 Kgs. 7:3] [s] 2 Kgs. 5:1-14

of all in the synagogue were [g]fixed on him. 21 And he began to say to them, "Today [h]this
Scripture [i]has been fulfilled in your hearing." 22 And all spoke well of him and marveled at
[j]the gracious words that were coming from his mouth. And they said, [k]"Is not this [l]Joseph's
son?" 23 And he said to them, "Doubtless you will quote to me this proverb, [m]'Physician,
heal yourself.' What we have heard you did [n]at Capernaum, do here in your hometown
as well." 24 And he said, "Truly, I say to you, [o]no prophet is acceptable in his hometown.
25 But in truth, I tell you, there were many widows in Israel in the days of Elijah, when [p]the
heavens were shut up three years and six months, and a great famine came over all the
land, 26 and Elijah was sent to none of them [q]but only to Zarephath, in the land of Sidon,
to a woman who was a widow. 27 And [r]there were many lepers[1] in Israel in the time of the
prophet Elisha, and none of them was cleansed, [s]but only Naaman the Syrian." 28 When
they heard these things, all in the synagogue were filled with wrath. 29 And they rose up

[1] *Leprosy* was a term for several skin diseases; see Leviticus 13

Synagogue Architectural Plan

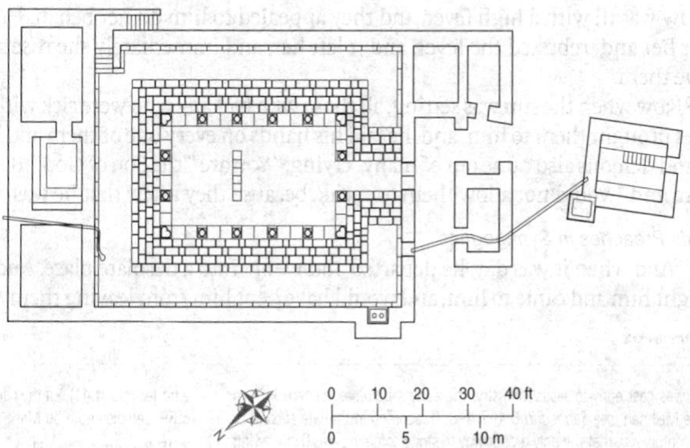

A covered water channel ran to the mikveh, which was a stone ritual bath with seven steps. The mikveh held just enough water for the complete immersion of people and items needing purification, such as jars and utensils used in worship.

OT this meant release for those enslaved in exile, but more is included here, since "liberty" elsewhere in Luke–Acts refers to forgiveness of sins). **Sight to the blind** includes both the physically blind and the spiritually blind. **Liberty** for **those who are oppressed** included, in Jesus' ministry, healing the sick, casting out demons, forgiving sins, and ethical teachings that promote social justice. **Proclaim the year of the Lord's favor** quotes Isa. 61:2, but the background of the Year of Jubilee (Lev. 25:10) is also in view in this entire passage. Jesus carries out the role of a prophet by proclaiming the "good news," but he also carries out the role of Deliverer (or "Savior," Luke 1:74) as the one who saves his people (Matt. 1:21).

4:20 The eyes of all . . . on him is a literary attention-getting device that focuses the reader on what Jesus is about to say.

4:21 On **Scripture** being **fulfilled**, cf. 24:44.

4:23 proverb. For a similar proverb, cf. 23:35. For Jesus' awareness of people's thoughts (an indication of deity), cf. 5:22; 6:8; 7:40; 9:47; 11:17.

4:24 Truly (Gk. *amēn*), used over 70 times in the Gospels, was placed by Jesus at the beginning of statements, rather than at the end. It emphasizes the truth of what follows. **no prophet**. Cf. 7:16.

4:25–27 Citing examples from the ministries of **Elijah and Elisha**, Jesus reminds the people of Nazareth that when Israel rejects God's prophets, God sends them elsewhere, even to Gentiles. At this the crowd becomes angry (v. 28; cf. Acts 22:21–22).

4:28–29 The attempt to kill Jesus (cf. 2:35) reveals that the shadow of the

and [t]drove him out of the town and brought him to the brow of the hill on which their
town was built, so that they could throw him down the cliff. 30 But [u]passing through their
midst, he went away.

Jesus Heals a Man with an Unclean Demon

31 [v]And he [w]went down to Capernaum, a city of Galilee. And [x]he was teaching them [y]on
the Sabbath, 32 and [z]they were astonished at his teaching, [z]for his word possessed authority.
33 And [x]in the synagogue there was a man who had the spirit of an unclean demon, and
he cried out with a loud voice, 34 "Ha![1] [a]What have you to do with us, Jesus of Nazareth?
Have you come to destroy us? [b]I know who you are—[c]the Holy One of God." 35 But Jesus
[d]rebuked him, saying, "Be silent and come out of him!" And when the demon had thrown
him down in their midst, he came out of him, having done him no harm. 36 And [e]they were
all amazed and said to one another, "What is this word? [e]For with authority and power he
commands the unclean spirits, and they come out!" 37 And [f]reports about him went out
into every place in the surrounding region.

Jesus Heals Many

38 [g]And he arose and left the synagogue and entered Simon's house. Now [h]Simon's mother-
in-law was ill with a high fever, and they appealed to him on her behalf. 39 And he stood
over her and [i]rebuked the fever, and it left her, and immediately she rose and began to
serve them.

40 Now when the sun was setting, all those who had any who were sick with various diseases brought them to him, and [j]he laid his hands on every one of them and healed them.
41 [k]And demons also came out of many, [l]crying, "You are [m]the Son of God!" But he rebuked
them and [k]would not allow them to speak, because they knew that he was [n]the Christ.

Jesus Preaches in Synagogues

42 [o]And when it was day, he departed and went [p]into a desolate place. And [q]the people
sought him and came to him, and would have kept him from leaving them, 43 but he said

[1] Or *Leave us alone*

29 [t][Num. 15:35; Acts 7:58]
30 [u]John 8:59; 10:39
31 [v]For ver. 31-37, see Mark 1:21-28 [w]Matt. 4:13 [x]ver. 15, 16; See Matt. 4:23 [y]See Mark 6:2
32 [z]ver. 36; See Matt. 7:28, 29
33 [x][See ver. 31 above]
34 [a]See Matt. 8:29 [b][Acts 19:15; James 2:19] [c]John 6:69; Acts 3:14; Rev. 3:7; [ch. 1:35; Heb. 7:26; 1 John 2:20]
35 [d]ver. 41; See Matt. 12:16
36 [e]ver. 32; [Matt. 8:27]
37 [f]ver. 14
38 [g]For ver. 38-41, see Matt. 8:14-16; Mark 1:29-34 [h]1 Cor. 9:5
39 [i]ch. 8:24; 9:42; Matt. 8:26; 17:18; Mark 4:39; 9:25
40 [j]See Mark 5:23
41 [k]Mark 3:11, 12; [Acts 16:17, 18] [l]ver. 33 [m]See Matt. 14:33 [n]See Matt. 1:17
42 [o]For ver. 42, 43, see Mark 1:35-38 [p]ch. 5:16 [q][Mark 1:36]

cross was cast early in Jesus' ministry. The early rabbinic document known as the Mishnah (see *Sanhedrin* 6.4; 7:4–8:7) recorded in the late second or third century A.D. that the only proper way to stone someone was by throwing the person **down the cliff**. However, it is likely that official death penalty practices were in flux during the first century. Like other stoning incidents in the NT, which more typically involved pelting someone with rocks, this action is a mob activity (under Roman rule, only government officials could carry out a death penalty). Properly, at least two reliable eyewitnesses were required (see Num. 35:30; Deut. 17:6–7), and the rabbis later taught that, after the court's careful verdict, the witnesses should act on behalf of the court to execute the criminal. The body of the stoned person was then to be hung up on a stake until sundown (following Deut. 21:22–23). The rabbis considered stoning a legitimate death penalty, especially for those whose sins included adultery, blasphemy, idolatry, witchcraft, persistent rebellion against parents, or Sabbath breaking.

4:30 passing through their midst. Luke does not explain how Jesus did this, but, since an entire mob was arrayed against him, some miraculous deliverance by the power of the Holy Spirit would seem to be the case. It was not yet Jesus' time to die, because his "hour" had not come (22:53; John 7:30).

4:31–41 *Jesus Begins His Healing Ministry.* The healing of the man with a demon (vv. 31–37) will be the first of 21 miracles recorded in Luke.

4:31 Capernaum. See note on Mark 1:21. **a city of Galilee**. See note on Luke 1:26.

4:32 The people were **astonished at** Jesus' **teaching** (cf. 2:48; 4:22; 9:43) because **his word possessed authority**. In contrast to their rabbis, who merely cited the opinions of other rabbis, Jesus' teachings had inherent authority, the authority of God himself (cf. Matt. 5:22). His authority is also seen in the following triumphs over demons (Luke 4:36, 41), and in his healings (vv. 39, 40).

4:34 come to destroy us. The demon recognizes Jesus as **the Holy One of God** who has come in the power of the Holy Spirit to triumph over demonic powers (10:17–18; 11:20; cf. 8:31). **I know who you are**. The demons know who Jesus is (4:41) but they do not believe in him with personal trust (cf. John 6:69; see also note on Mark 1:23–25).

4:35 Be silent. Cf. v. 41.

4:36 They were all amazed because Jesus was able to cast out demons with a word. Jesus' triumph over demons was a clear indication that God's kingdom was breaking into the present age in a new and decisive way, driving back demonic forces and setting people free to serve God (see Matt. 12:28; see also notes on Matt. 12:27–29).

4:37 every place in the surrounding region. Jesus' fame spreads "even more" (5:15): great crowds gather "from every village of Galilee and Judea and from Jerusalem" (5:17), from "the seacoast of Tyre and Sidon" (6:17), and "the whole of Judea and all the surrounding country" (7:17).

4:38 The fact that **Simon's mother-in-law** had a **high fever** underscores the miraculous nature of the healing (cf. Mark 1:30). Simon was also called "Peter" (Luke 6:14).

4:39 rebuked the fever. The only instance in the Gospels where Jesus' words are addressed to a disease. **And immediately** emphasizes the power of Jesus.

4:40 the sun was setting. See note on Mark 1:32–34. **Sick with various diseases** reveals the breadth of Jesus' healings. For laying on hands, cf. Luke 5:13; 13:13. **All those who had any** indicates a large crowd of people waiting to be healed. Though it was late and the sun was setting, Jesus did not miraculously perform an instantaneous "group healing" but paid individual attention to each person: **he laid his hands on every one of them and healed them**.

4:41 And demons also. Luke clearly distinguishes between the casting out of demons and healing, showing that not all diseases are due to demonic power, though some diseases do have a demonic origin (cf. 13:10–17; note on Matt. 8:16–17).

4:42–44 *Jesus Preaches in Synagogues.* Jesus is called not just to heal but to preach and teach the good news. **to the other towns as well**. Neither

to them, “[r]I must [s]preach the good news of the kingdom of God to the other towns as well;
for I was sent for this purpose.” **44** And he was preaching [t]in the synagogues of Judea.[1]

Jesus Calls the First Disciples

5 On one occasion, while the crowd was pressing in on him to hear the word of God,
he was standing by [u]the lake of Gennesaret, **2** [v]and he saw two boats by the lake, but
the fishermen had gone out of them and were [w]washing their nets. **3** Getting into one of
the boats, which was Simon's, he asked him to put out a little from the land. And [x]he sat
down and taught the people from the boat. **4** And when he had finished speaking, he said to
Simon, [y]“Put out into the deep and let down your nets for a catch.” **5** And Simon answered,
“Master, [z]we toiled all night and took nothing! But at your word I will let down the nets.”
6 And when they had done this, [a]they enclosed a large number of fish, and [a]their nets were
breaking. **7** They signaled to their partners in the other boat to come and help them. [b]And
they came and filled both the boats, so that they began to sink. **8** But when Simon Peter saw
it, he fell down at Jesus' knees, saying, [c]“Depart from me, for [d]I am a sinful man, O Lord.”
9 For he and all who were with him were astonished at the catch of fish that they had taken,
10 and so also were James and John, sons of Zebedee, who were partners with Simon. And
Jesus said to Simon, “Do not be afraid; from now on you will be catching men.”[2] **11** And
when they had brought their boats to land, [e]they left everything and followed him.

Jesus Cleanses a Leper

12 While he was in one of the cities, [f]there came a man full of leprosy.[3] And when he saw
Jesus, he [g]fell on his face and begged him, “Lord, [h]if you will, you can make me clean.” **13** And
Jesus[4] stretched out his hand and touched him, saying, “I will; be clean.” And immediately
the leprosy left him. **14** And he charged him [i]to tell no one, but “go and show [j]yourself to
the priest, and [k]make an offering for your cleansing, as Moses commanded, [l]for a proof
to them.” **15** [m]But now even more the report about him went abroad, and great crowds
gathered to hear him and to be healed of their infirmities. **16** But [n]he would withdraw to
desolate places and [n]pray.

[1] Some manuscripts *Galilee* [2] The Greek word *anthropoi* refers here to both men and women [3] *Leprosy* was a term for several skin diseases; see Leviticus 13 [4] Greek *he*

43 [r]See ch. 13:33 [s]ch. 8:1; 16:16; Matt. 4:23; 24:14; Acts 8:12
44 [t][Mark 1:39]
Chapter 5
1 [u]Num. 34:11; Deut. 3:17; Josh. 12:3; John 6:1; [Matt. 14:34]
2 [v]For ver. 2-11, [Matt. 4:18-22; Mark 1:16-20; John 1:40-42] [w][Mark 1:19]
3 [x][Matt. 5:1]
4 [y][John 21:6]
5 [z][John 21:3]
6 [a][John 21:11]
7 [b]See John 21:4-8
8 [c]See Matt. 8:34 [d]Isa. 6:5
11 [e]ch. 18:28; Matt. 19:27; [ver. 28]
12 [f]For ver. 12-14, see Matt. 8:2-4; Mark 1:40-44 [g]See ch. 17:16 [h][Matt. 9:28; Mark 9:22, 23]
14 [i]Matt. 9:30; 17:9; Mark 1:34; 5:43; 7:36; 8:26; See Matt. 12:16 [j]ch. 17:14 [k]Lev. 14:2-32 [l]ch. 9:5; Mark 6:11; James 5:3
15 [m][Mark 1:45]
16 [n]Mark 1:35; See Matt. 14:23

Nazareth nor Capernaum had “exclusive rights” to Jesus' time and ministry (see vv. 25–27). Luke often refers to what **must** be, emphasizing the necessity of God's providential plan being fulfilled. **Preach . . . the kingdom of God** is the first of 31 such references in Luke. “Kingdom” should be interpreted dynamically as “reign,” not statically as a territory (see Introduction: Key Themes). Jesus **was sent** by God.

5:1–11 *Jesus Calls the First Disciples.* Jesus calls common fishermen to leave everything and become his disciples as fishers of men (cf. v. 10). Jesus precedes the call by demonstrating his authority through the miraculous catch of fish.

5:1 lake of Gennesaret. The Sea of Galilee.

5:3 Getting into one of the boats . . . he . . . taught. Cf. Mark 4:1–2.

5:4–5 let down your nets. . . . Master, we toiled all night and took nothing. Simon's reply to Jesus' command should not be seen as one of disrespect, in light of his addressing him as “Master” (cf. 8:24, 45; 9:33, 49; 17:13), and then immediately adding, **But at your word I will let down the nets**.

5:6–7 A large number of fish is dramatized by **their nets . . . breaking** and their signaling **to their partners . . . to come and help them**. That both ships **began to sink** further emphasizes the great catch of fish. Jesus' miracle demonstrates that he is Lord of the sea and all that is in it.

5:8–9 Simon's reaction is appropriate for times when God himself appears to someone (cf. Isa. 6:1–8; Ezek. 1:28): **he fell down at Jesus' knees** (in the midst of the fish!), asking the **Lord** to **depart from** him, lest he be judged as a **sinful man**. Peter was **astonished** by the miracle as a demonstration of the presence of God, which was the first step in understanding who Jesus is. At this point Peter simply understands that God works through Jesus, though he will come to a much deeper understanding, as this unfolds only over a period of time (see Mark 8:29). But it is only after the resurrection that Peter and the disciples fully understand who Jesus is (cf. Luke 24:31, 36–43, 52).

5:10 Do not be afraid. See 1:13. **Catching men** builds on the analogy of catching fish. It means bringing people into the kingdom of God, and into relationship with Jesus.

5:12–16 *Jesus Cleanses a Leper.* Luke may have placed this account here due to the similarity between the events described in vv. 8 and 12.

5:12 leprosy. See note on Matt. 8:2–3. This term (Gk. *lepra*) included a variety of serious skin diseases and was not limited to what is today called “leprosy” (Hansen's disease). **fell on his face**. A position of reverence (cf. Luke 17:16). **if you will, you can make me clean**. The miracle reveals Jesus' authority to cure the ritual uncleanness of the leper. (Cf. 5:17–26 regarding Jesus' authority to forgive the “spiritual uncleanness” of sin.)

5:13 be clean. Only a single word (Gk. *katharisthēti*) is required to effect the miracle. Jesus is not made unclean by touching the leper. Instead, the leper is cleansed by Jesus' touch.

5:14 tell no one. See note on Matt. 8:4. **go . . . to the priest** (cf. Luke 17:14), as **Moses commanded**. The rationale for this instruction is found in Lev. 14:2–32. This was to serve as a **proof to them**, i.e., the people (and probably the priests as well). As a result of Jesus' healing, the (former) leper is brought back into full participation and fellowship in the Jewish community according to the provisions of the Mosaic law.

5:15 now even more. Jesus' fame spreads (see 4:37). **to hear him and to be healed**. Luke places Jesus' preaching ministry before his healing ministry (cf. 6:18).

5:16 But he would withdraw . . . and pray. The Greek construction indicates a continual practice and could also be translated “was regularly withdrawing and praying” (Gk. imperfect verb plus two present participles); see Introduction: Key Themes. The increasing crowds, the unceasing demands

Jesus Heals a Paralytic

17 On one of those days, as he was teaching, Pharisees and [o]teachers of the law were
sitting there, who had come from every village of Galilee and Judea and from Jerusalem.
And [p]the power of the Lord was with him to heal.[1]
18 [q]And behold, some men were bring-
ing [r]on a bed a man who was paralyzed, and they were seeking to bring him in and lay
him before Jesus,
19 but finding no way to bring him in, because of the crowd, they went
up on [s]the roof and let him down with his bed [t]through the tiles into the midst before
Jesus.
20 And [u]when he saw their faith, he said, "Man, [v]your sins are forgiven you."
21 And
the scribes and the Pharisees began to question, saying, "Who is this who speaks [w]blas-
phemies? [x]Who can forgive sins but God alone?"
22 When Jesus [y]perceived their thoughts,
he answered them, "Why do you question in your hearts?
23 Which is easier, to say, 'Your
sins are forgiven you,' or to say, 'Rise and walk'?
24 But that you may know that [z]the Son of
Man has authority on earth to forgive sins"—he said to the man who was paralyzed—"I
say to you, rise, pick up your bed and go home."
25 And immediately he rose up before
them and picked up what he had been lying on and went home, [a]glorifying God.
26 And
amazement seized them all, and they [a]glorified God and were filled [a]with awe, saying,
"We have seen extraordinary things today."

Jesus Calls Levi

27 [b]After this he went out and saw [c]a tax collector named [d]Levi, sitting at the tax
booth. And he said to him, "Follow me."
28 And [e]leaving everything, he rose and followed him.

29 And Levi made him a great feast in his house, and there was a large company [f]of
tax collectors and others reclining at table with them.
30 And the Pharisees and [g]their
scribes grumbled at his disciples, saying, [h]"Why do you eat and drink with tax collectors and sinners?"
31 And Jesus answered them, "Those who are well have no need of a
physician, but those who are sick.
32 [i]I have not come to call the righteous [j]but sinners
[k]to repentance."

A Question About Fasting

33 And they said to him, [l]"The disciples of John [m]fast often and [m]offer prayers, [n]and
so do the disciples of the Pharisees, but yours eat and drink."
34 And Jesus said to them,

17 [o]ch. 2:46; Acts 5:34; 1 Tim. 1:7 (Gk.); [Matt. 22:35] [p]See ch. 8:46
18 [q]For ver. 18-26, see Matt. 9:2-8; Mark 2:3-12 [r]Mark 6:55
19 [s]Deut. 22:8; 1 Sam. 9:25; Neh. 8:16; Matt. 10:27; 24:17; Acts 10:9 [t][Mark 2:4]
20 [u]ch. 7:9, 50; 17:19; 18:42; Matt. 8:10, 13; 9:22, 29; 15:28; Mark 10:52; Acts 3:16; 14:9; James 5:15 [v]ch. 7:48; [John 5:14]
21 [w]Matt. 26:65; John 10:36 [x]Ps. 32:5; Isa. 43:25
22 [y]See John 2:25
24 [z][ch. 6:5]
25 [a]See ch. 7:16
26 [a][See ver. 25 above]
27 [b]For ver. 27-38, see Matt. 9:9-17; Mark 2:14-22 [c]Matt. 11:19; See Matt. 5:46 [d][Matt. 9:9]
28 [e][ver. 11]
29 [f][ch. 15:1, 2]
30 [g]Acts 4:5; 23:9 [h]ch. 15:2; Matt. 11:19
32 [i][ch. 15:7; John 9:39] [j]1 Tim. 1:15 [k]ch. 13:3, 5; 15:10; 24:47; Matt. 4:17; 11:20; Mark 1:15; Acts 5:31
33 [l]ch. 11:1; Matt. 11:2; 14:12; John 1:35; 3:25; 4:1; [Acts 18:25; 19:3] [m]ch. 2:37 [n]ch. 18:12

[1] Some manuscripts *was present to heal them*

on Jesus' time, and the fact that no one else could duplicate his ministry did not deter Jesus from spending extensive times in prayer.

5:17–6:11 *The Beginning of Controversy.* Luke returns to the theme of opposition to Jesus (cf. Luke 4:28–30) by including five accounts of controversy (cf. Mark 2:1–3:6).

5:17–26 *Jesus Heals a Paralytic.* Jesus provides divine proof that he has not only the power to heal but also the authority to forgive sins.

5:17 The **Pharisees** were the most influential of the three major Jewish sects. (See note on John 1:24; also Jewish Groups at the Time of the New Testament, pp. 1799–1800.) **teachers of the law**. A synonym for "scribes" (Luke 5:21; cf. note on Matt. 8:19). **From every village** indicates Jesus' great fame.

5:19 they went up on the roof. Houses in ancient Palestine often had external stairs leading up to a flat roof. **through the tiles**. Some have claimed that Luke erred in saying that the roof had tiles. Though tiles were not widely used at this time, evidence exists that they were in fact used for some roof construction in Palestine, suggesting that this may have been a wealthy person's house. In addition, typical mud roofs were made from slabs of mud first baked in the sun, then carried to the roof, and Luke may have called these "tiles" (plural of Gk. *keramos*).

5:20 their faith. See note on Mark 2:5–7. **your sins are forgiven**. By proclaiming that the man's "sins are forgiven," Jesus is announcing that he has the authority to forgive sins; he then demonstrates this authority by healing the man (Luke 5:24).

5:21–22 The scribes and the Pharisees are often paired together in the Gospels (see notes on Matt. 5:20; Mark 7:5). Jesus does not deny that **God alone** can forgive sins, but claims that he has the authority (as the "Son of Man," Luke 5:24) to forgive sins. If this were not true, then Jesus would be guilty of blasphemy. **Jesus perceived their thoughts**, an indication of divine omniscience (cf. Matt. 9:4; Mark 2:8).

5:23–24 Jesus' counter-question involves the difference between "saying" and "doing." It is easier to say that a person's sins are forgiven (which *cannot* be disproved) than to tell him to rise up and walk (which *can* be disproved). Jesus' healing of the paralytic thus serves as proof (**that you may know**) that he, as the **Son of Man**, has the authority to forgive sins. (On "Son of Man," see notes on Matt. 8:20 and Mark 2:10.)

5:27–32 *Jesus Calls Levi.* Jesus now brings forgiveness to a despised tax collector.

5:27–28 tax collector. See note on Matt. 5:46–47. **Levi**. In Matt. 9:9 he is called "Matthew" (see note). **tax booth**. See note on Mark 2:14. **Follow me**. An invitation to a total commitment to Christ. Levi responded by **leaving everything** (cf. the "rich ruler," Luke 18:18–30).

5:29 reclining at table. See note on Matt. 26:20.

5:30 Why do you eat and drink with tax collectors and sinners? Such table fellowship implies welcoming these people into extended interpersonal association, which the Pharisees thought would make a person "unclean." But just as Jesus would cleanse the leper rather than being made unclean by the leper (see note on v. 13), so Jesus will bring sinners to repentance (v. 32) and forgiveness rather than being defiled by association with the sinners.

5:31–32 Those who are well . . . those who are sick. See notes on Matt. 9:13 and Mark 2:17.

5:33–39 *A Question about Fasting.* This account contrasts the "new" situ-

34[o]John 3:29
35[p]See ch. 17:22 [q][John 16:20]
37[r]Josh. 9:4

Chapter 6

1[s]For ver. 1-5, see Matt. 12:1-8; Mark 2:23-28 [t]Deut. 23:25
2[u][Matt. 9:11] [v][Ex. 20:9-11]
3[w]See Matt. 21:16 [x]1 Sam. 21:1-6
4[y]Ex. 25:30; Lev. 24:5-9
5[z][ch. 5:24]
6[a]For ver. 6-11, see Matt. 12:9-14; Mark 3:1-6 [b]See Mark 6:2
7[c]ch. 14:1; 20:20; [ch. 11:54] [d][John 8:6]
8[e]See Matt. 9:4
9[f]ch. 14:3
10[g]Mark 3:34; 5:32; 10:23; [Mark 10:21] [h][1 Kgs. 13:4]
11[i]2 Tim. 3:9 (Gk.)

[o]"Can you make wedding guests fast while the bridegroom is with them? **35** [p]The days will
come when the bridegroom is taken away from them, and [q]then they will fast in those
days." **36** He also told them a parable: "No one tears a piece from a new garment and puts
it on an old garment. If he does, he will tear the new, and the piece from the new will not
match the old. **37** And no one puts new wine into old [r]wineskins. If he does, the new wine
will burst the skins and it will be spilled, and the skins will be destroyed. **38** But new wine
must be put into fresh wineskins. **39** And no one after drinking old wine desires new, for
he says, 'The old is good.'"[1]

Jesus Is Lord of the Sabbath

6 [s]On a Sabbath,[2] while he was going through the grainfields, his disciples [t]plucked
and ate some heads of grain, rubbing them in their hands. **2** But some of the Pharisees
said, [u]"Why are you doing [v]what is not lawful to do on the Sabbath?" **3** And Jesus answered
them, [w]"Have you not read [x]what David did when he was hungry, he and those who were
with him: **4** how he entered the house of God and took and ate [y]the bread of the Presence,
[y]which is not lawful for any but the priests to eat, and also gave it to those with him?"
5 And he said to them, [z]"The Son of Man is lord of the Sabbath."

A Man with a Withered Hand

6 On another Sabbath, [a]he entered the synagogue [b]and was teaching, and a man was
there whose right hand was withered. **7** And the scribes and the Pharisees [c]watched him,
to see whether he would heal on the Sabbath, [d]so that they might find a reason to accuse
him. **8** But [e]he knew their thoughts, and he said to the man with the withered hand, "Come
and stand here." And he rose and stood there. **9** And Jesus said to them, "I ask you, [f]is it
lawful on the Sabbath to do good or to do harm, to save life or to destroy it?" **10** And [g]after
looking around at them all he said to him, "Stretch out your hand." And [h]he did so, and
his hand was restored. **11** But they were filled with [i]fury and discussed with one another
what they might do to Jesus.

[1] Some manuscripts *better* [2] Some manuscripts *On the second first Sabbath* (that is, on the second Sabbath after the first)

ation of the kingdom of God with the previous, "old" situation under the Mosaic law.

5:33–34 Can (they) **fast while the bridegroom is with them?** See note on Mark 2:19–20. On fasting, see note on Matt. 6:16–18.

5:35 days will come. Jesus is fully aware of his coming death. **when the bridegroom is taken away**. Although a riddle for Jesus' audience, Luke's readers would have understood this as referring to Jesus' death. **In those days**, that is, in the time between Jesus' death and resurrection, and also after he has returned to heaven, fasting will be appropriate for his followers.

5:36–39 Jesus concludes his response to the question about fasting (v. 33) with a parable consisting of two main metaphors: (1) A **new** patch cannot be put on an **old garment**, for upon washing it will shrink and, pulling on the already shrunken, old garment, will tear it. (2) One does not put **new wine into old wineskins**. New, fermenting wine would stretch the old, inelastic wineskins and cause them to burst. New wine needs newer, more elastic skins. **No one** is best understood as an ironical condemnation of the Pharisees, who favored the past and rejected the arrival of the kingdom and the "new covenant" (22:20) it brought. The point of these two metaphors is that one cannot mix the old and the new covenant, and that the new covenant era inaugurated by Jesus' coming will require repentance (Matt. 4:17), regeneration (cf. John 3:3), and new forms of worship (cf. John 4:24).

6:1–5 *Jesus Is Lord of the Sabbath.* In this first Sabbath controversy (cf. vv. 6–11; 13:10–17; 14:1–6), Jesus announces that he is lord of the Sabbath.

6:1 On a Sabbath . . . plucked and ate some heads of grain. The law permitted plucking grain from another person's field, but no instrument like a sickle could be used (Deut. 23:24–25). **Rubbing them** removed the outer chaff.

6:2 Some . . . Pharisees considered plucking grain on the Sabbath as work and therefore forbidden. **You** (plural) includes Jesus in his disciples' activity, because a teacher was responsible for his disciples' actions.

6:3–4 what David did. The Sabbath is not mentioned in 1 Sam. 21:1–6, but the point is that David did something **not lawful** (cf. Lev. 24:5–9) by eating the **bread of the Presence** (i.e., the consecrated sanctuary bread). Jesus points out that both David and his followers did this unlawful act because of David's authority (cf. notes on Matt. 12:4; Mark 2:25–26): how much more, therefore, can David's Lord (cf. Luke 20:41–44) and his followers do something that meets a human need even though it violated the Pharisees' interpretation of the law.

6:5 Jesus argument, essentially, is that the **Son of Man**—not the Pharisees through their regulations—ultimately rules over and interprets the **Sabbath**. See note on Mark 2:27–28.

6:6–11 *A Man with a Withered Hand.* In a second Sabbath controversy (cf. vv. 1–5; 13:10–17; 14:1–6) Jesus exercises his power (4:14, 34; 5:17) and authority (4:32, 36; 5:24) to heal on the Sabbath.

6:6 withered. Paralyzed or atrophied.

6:7 The scribes and the Pharisees (see 5:21) **watched** Jesus, not to gain insight but **to accuse him**. They would have conceded that life-threatening situations allowed for breaking the Sabbath, but this was not such a situation (13:14).

6:8 he knew their thoughts. See note on 4:23.

6:9 is it lawful on the Sabbath to do good or to do harm . . . ? Jesus had acted out of compassion to heal the man with the withered hand. His opponents, however, finding themselves in a dilemma, refuse to answer (cf. 13:15–17; 14:5–6; 20:3–7).

6:10 Stretch out your hand. Jesus pointedly did not do anything in this situation that could be called "work": he did not even touch the man, but simply spoke a word (and surely *speaking* is not prohibited on the Sabbath!). Nor did the disabled man do any forbidden "work," for he simply stretched out his hand. Jesus' accusers were silenced, and they were furious (v. 11). **his hand was restored**. This is proof that Jesus is lord of the Sabbath (cf. v. 5).

6:11 they were filled with fury. Even a mighty miracle cannot change their hardened hearts. **What they might do to Jesus** serves as the conclusion of vv. 1–10 and foreshadows his suffering and death.

The Twelve Apostles

12 In these days [j]he went out to the mountain to pray, and all night he continued in
prayer to God. 13 And when day came, [k]he called his disciples [l]and [m]chose from them twelve,
whom he named [n]apostles: 14 Simon, [o]whom he named Peter, and [p]Andrew his brother,
and [p]James and John, and Philip, and Bartholomew, 15 and [q]Matthew, and Thomas, and
James the son of Alphaeus, and Simon who was called [r]the Zealot, 16 and [s]Judas the son of
James, and Judas Iscariot, who became a traitor.

Jesus Ministers to a Great Multitude

17 And [t]he came down with them and stood on a level place, with [u]a great crowd of his
disciples and a great multitude of people from all Judea and Jerusalem and the seacoast
of [v]Tyre and Sidon, 18 who came to hear him and to be healed of their diseases. [w]And those
who were troubled with unclean spirits were cured. 19 And all the crowd [x]sought to touch
him, for [y]power came out from him and healed them all.

The Beatitudes

20 And [z]he lifted up his eyes on his disciples, [a]and said:
"Blessed are you who are poor, for [b]yours is the kingdom of God.
21 [c]"Blessed are you who are hungry now, for you shall be satisfied.
[d]"Blessed are you who weep now, for you shall laugh.

12 [j]See Matt. 14:23
13 [k]ch. 9:1; Matt. 10:1; Mark 3:13; 6:7 [l]For ver. 13-16, see Matt. 10:2-4; Mark 3:16-19; Acts 1:13 [m]See John 13:18 [n]See Mark 6:30
14 [o]Matt. 16:18; John 1:42 [p]Matt. 4:18, 21
15 [q]Matt. 9:9 [r][Acts 21:20]
16 [s]John 14:22
17 [t][ver. 12; Matt. 5:1] [u]Matt. 4:25; Mark 3:7, 8 [v]See Matt. 11:21
18 [w]Matt. 4:24
19 [x]Matt. 14:36; Mark 3:10; [Acts 5:15] [y]See ch. 8:46
20 [z]John 6:5 [a]For ver. 20-23, [Matt. 5:3-12] [b][ch. 12:32]
21 [c][ch. 1:53] [d]Isa. 25:8; 57:18; See Matt. 5:4

6:12–49 *Jesus Teaches the Disciples.* Jesus appoints 12 apostles, then gives extended teaching to a large group of disciples, including what is often called the "Sermon on the Plain" (vv. 20–49; cf. the "Sermon on the Mount," Matthew 5–7).

6:12–16 *Jesus Appoints Twelve Apostles.* From among his many disciples, Jesus chooses 12 apostles (Gk. *apostolos*, "messenger, one who is sent out"). On the office of apostle, see note on Rom. 1:1.

6:12 he went . . . to pray. Luke alone mentions Jesus praying before choosing the apostles (see Introduction: Key Themes). **All night he continued in prayer** underscores the importance that Jesus placed on prayer, especially here before making the crucial choice of who should be his disciples.

6:13 disciples . . . apostles. See note on vv. 12–16.

6:14 Simon, whom he named Peter. The most prominent disciple heads each listing of the disciples. Henceforth Luke will use the name "Peter" (except in 22:31 and 24:34). **Andrew**, the brother of Peter, is also mentioned in Acts 1:13. **James and John**. A second set of brothers, who were also Galilean fishermen (Luke 5:10–11) and partners (5:7) of Peter and Andrew. **Philip**. From Bethsaida, the same city (or birthplace) as Peter and Andrew (John 1:44). **Bartholomew** is a family name (*patronym*) that occurs in each of the lists in the Synoptic Gospels. He is probably the same person as Nathanael listed in John's Gospel (cf. note on John 1:45).

6:15 Matthew. See 5:27. **Thomas**. Called the "Twin" (Gk. *Didymos*) in John 11:16; 20:24; 21:2. **James the son of Alphaeus**. Not to be confused with James the brother of John, James the brother of Jesus, or the James of Mark 15:40. **Simon . . . the Zealot**. (Cf. Matt. 10:4; Mark 3:18.) "Zealot" comes from the Greek word *zēlōtēs*. The Zealots were political activists who were radically opposed to Roman rule. Apart from Jesus' call and influence on their lives, Matthew and Simon would have had deep animosity toward each other, with Matthew (as a tax collector) working in the service of Rome, and Simon (as a Zealot) seeking to overthrow Rome.

6:16 Judas the son of James does not appear in the parallel accounts in Matthew (10:3) and Mark (3:18); in his place is "Thaddaeus," which is probably his other name (many of the apostles had double names). The name for the other **Judas** was qualified by **Iscariot**, which probably means "man from Kerioth," a town in Judea (see John 6:71; 13:26). **who became a traitor**. Cf. Luke 22:3–6, 47–48; Acts 1:16–20.

6:17–19 *Jesus Ministers to a Great Multitude.* Luke introduces Jesus' "Sermon on the Plain" (see note on vv. 20–23) with a summary of his activities (cf. Mark 3:7–12).

6:17 he came down. Jesus had been on a mountain (v. 12). Now he preaches on a **level place** (hence "the Sermon on the Plain"). Among the listeners are three groups: **them** (the apostles); **a great crowd of his disciples; and a great multitude of people**. "A great multitude" emphasizes Jesus' ever-growing popularity (see 4:37). People from **Tyre and Sidon** would likely have included Gentiles. Cf. 10:13–14.

6:18–19 The crowd's purpose is **to hear** Jesus and **to be healed of their diseases**. In addition, those with unclean spirits come and are cured. For the distinction between disease and demon possession, see 4:40–41 and the note on 4:41. **sought to touch**. Cf. 8:44–47; 18:15. For the association of **power** and healing, see 5:17.

6:20–23 *The Beatitudes.* (See note on Matt. 5:3–12.) Luke's first record of a sermon by Jesus was in Luke 4:16–30; his second sermon is here in 6:20–49. The Beatitudes are not conditions for entering the kingdom of God but blessings pronounced on those who have already entered. The main theme of the Beatitudes and the following "woes" involves the "great reversal" (see Introduction: Key Themes). On the relationship between this "Sermon on the Plain" (vv. 20–49) and the "Sermon on the Mount" (Matthew 5–7), see note on Matt. 5:1–7:29.

6:20 Blessed are you who are poor. This means "blessed are those of you who are poor in material things and who are also my disciples and thus are putting your trust in God." In the OT, "the poor" (the same Gk. word, *ptōchos*, in the Septuagint) frequently referred to the pious poor who looked to and depended on God. Jesus is not saying that poverty in itself is a state of happiness or blessing; it is a blessing only when accompanied by trust in God. Jesus' statement elsewhere that he was anointed "to proclaim good news to the poor" (4:18) is a quotation from Isa. 61:1, which has a strong spiritual dimension as well: good news would come to the poor who long and wait for God. **for yours is the kingdom of God**. Such people belong to the kingdom and will receive the blessings of the kingdom (cf. note on Matt. 5:3). Jesus consistently gave special care to those on the fringes of society—people who bear God's image but who are treated as trivial and the objects of oppression (see Luke 14:13, 21; 18:22; cf. James 2:3–6; 5:1–6).

6:21 In a way similar to v. 20 (see note), **you who are hungry** refers to those among Jesus' disciples who are physically hungry and also hungry for God's help and presence. (Cf. Matt. 5:6, "who hunger and thirst for righteousness.") **Now** implies that the hunger will not last forever, **for you shall be satisfied**. God will supply their needs, first with his abundant presence in this life (Ps. 107:9), and then also with meeting their physical needs, perhaps quickly in this age (Matt. 25:35–40; Mark 10:30; James 2:15–17; 1 John 3:17–18), but certainly in the abundance of the age to come (Luke 13:29; cf. note on Matt. 5:6). **who weep now**. Cf. "mourn" in Matt. 5:4 and note. "Now" indicates that in the consummated kingdom God will wipe away every tear (Rev. 7:17; 21:4). Instead of weeping there will be laughter (Ps. 126:1–2).

22 [e]See Matt. 10:22 [f][John 9:22; 12:42; 16:2] [g]Heb. 11:26; 1 Pet. 4:14 [h]John 15:21
23 [i]See Matt. 5:12 [j]See Matt. 21:35
24 [k]Amos 6:1; James 5:1; [ch. 12:21] [l][ch. 16:25] [m]Matt. 6:2
25 [n]Isa. 65:13 [o]Isa. 65:14; [Prov. 14:13; James 4:9]
26 [p][John 15:19; 17:14; James 4:4; 1 John 4:5] [q]Jer. 5:31; [Isa. 30:10; Mic. 2:11] [r]See Matt. 7:15
27 [s]See Matt. 5:44 [t]Prov. 25:21, 22; Rom. 12:20, 21
28 [u]1 Pet. 3:9 [s][See ver. 27 above]
29 [v]For ver. 29, 30, see Matt. 5:39-42; [Rom. 12:17] [w]Isa. 50:6; Lam. 3:30; Matt. 26:67
30 [x]Ps. 37:21; Prov. 21:26
31 [y]Matt. 7:12
32 [z]Matt. 5:46
34 [a][ch. 14:12-14; Prov. 19:17; Matt. 5:42] [b]Ps. 37:26
35 [c]ver. 27 [d]Matt. 5:45 [e]ch. 1:32; See Mark 5:7 [f][James 1:5]
36 [g][Matt. 5:7, 48; Eph. 5:1, 2; James 3:17] [h]James 5:11
37 [i]For ver. 37, 38, 41, 42, see Matt. 7:1-5; [Rom. 14:13; 1 Cor. 4:5; James 5:9] [j][Matt. 6:14; 18:23-35]
38 [k]2 Cor. 9:6-8

22 "Blessed are you when [e]people hate you and when they [f]exclude you and revile you and
[g]spurn your name as evil, [h]on account of the Son of Man! 23 [i]Rejoice in that day, and leap for
joy, for behold, your reward is great in heaven; for [j]so their fathers did to the prophets.

Jesus Pronounces Woes

24 [k]"But woe to you who are rich, [l]for you [m]have received your consolation.
25 "Woe to you who are full now, for [n]you shall be hungry.
"Woe to [o]you who laugh now, [o]for you shall mourn and weep.
26 "Woe to you, [p]when all people speak well of you, for [q]so their fathers did to [r]the false
prophets.

Love Your Enemies

27 "But I say to you who hear, [s]Love your enemies, [t]do good to those who hate you,
28 [u]bless those who curse you, [s]pray for those who abuse you. 29 [v]To one who [w]strikes you
on the cheek, offer the other also, and from one who takes away your cloak do not withhold your tunic[1] either. 30 [x]Give to everyone who begs from you, and from one who takes
away your goods do not demand them back. 31 And [y]as you wish that others would do to
you, do so to them.
32 [z]"If you love those who love you, what benefit is that to you? For even sinners love those
who love them. 33 And if you do good to those who do good to you, what benefit is that to
you? For even sinners do the same. 34 And [a]if you [b]lend to those from whom you expect
to receive, what credit is that to you? Even sinners lend to sinners, to get back the same
amount. 35 But [c]love your enemies, and do good, and lend, expecting nothing in return,
and your reward will be great, and [d]you will be sons of [e]the Most High, for [f]he is kind to
the ungrateful and the evil. 36 [g]Be merciful, even as [h]your Father is merciful.

Judging Others

37 [i, j]"Judge not, and you will not be judged; condemn not, and you will not be condemned;
[j]forgive, and you will be forgiven; 38 [k]give, and it will be given to you. Good measure, pressed

[1] Greek *chiton*, a long garment worn under the cloak next to the skin

6:22–23 Whenever enemies **hate, exclude, revile,** or **spurn** Christians (cf. note on Matt. 5:11–12), the response should be to **rejoice** (Acts 5:41; 16:25; 21:13ff.), because their **reward is great in heaven.**

6:24–26 *Jesus Pronounces Woes.* "Blessed" is now followed by "woe" (cf. the warning in Isa. 65:13–14 to those who forsake the Lord).

6:24 Woe to you who are rich is a solemn warning to those who are rich against the tendency to delight in and trust the things of this life more than God, **for you have received your consolation.** Care for the poor and the dangers of riches are common themes in Luke (cf. 1:53; 12:13–21; 16:19–31; also notes on James 2:1–7; 5:1–6).

6:25 Woe to you who are full now continues describing the rich, who have no worldly cares but are not rich in faith (cf. 1:53; James 5:1). **Woe to you who laugh now** is not a condemnation of all joy and laughter, only the condescending, boastful, or mocking laughter of the callous, complacent rich, who care little for others or for God. They shall **mourn and weep** when God's judgment comes.

6:26 The fourth woe warns that, while true prophets were hated, excluded, reviled, spurned, beaten, tortured, and killed (cf. Heb. 11:32–38), **false prophets** were well spoken of, for they prophesied what people wanted to hear. This is a warning against seeking the approval of the world rather than being faithful to God.

6:27–36 *Love Your Enemies.* Resuming the theme of his disciples being hated (v. 22), Jesus gives several examples of what it means to **love your enemies.**

6:28 For blessing **those who curse you,** see 1 Cor. 4:12. For examples of praying for one's abusers, cf. Luke 23:34; Acts 7:59–60. The ability to bless those who do this depends on confident trust in God's care and sovereign direction of the events of life.

6:29 strikes you on the cheek. An insulting slap (cf. note on Matt. 5:39). **Offer the other also** is not intended as a command for every circumstance (Luke 6:30) but is a vivid illustration of how love for one's enemies should look. This verse should not be understood as a prohibition against governments using military or police force, since in this context Jesus is addressing individual conduct. **takes away your cloak.** The point of both examples is that, even though believers will often be subject to abuse or taken advantage of, they are to face such rejection differently from the world, that is, by being generous and compassionate rather than retaliating.

6:30 Give to everyone who begs from you. Jesus again stresses that believers must be "generous to a fault," even when someone **takes away your goods** (cf. note on Matt. 5:42). The standards by which Jesus' disciples are to live are higher than the standards of the world.

6:31 The "Golden Rule" is to be practiced with respect to both friends and enemies alike. See note on Matt. 7:12.

6:32–33 In vv. 32–35, Jesus gives three examples of the Golden Rule (v. 31). Reciprocity is insufficient (cf. 14:12–14), because **even sinners** practice reciprocity. The first two examples (**If you love** and **if you do good**) correspond to the first two commands in 6:27 ("Love your enemies, do good to those who hate you").

6:35 love your enemies. See notes on Matt. 5:44–45 and Luke 23:34. Keeping the commands of 6:35a results in **your reward** being **great** (cf. v. 23). **You will be sons** does not mean "you will become sons" but "you will demonstrate that you are sons" by imitating God's care and compassion even for those who are evil. For **Most High** as an expression for God, cf. note on 1:32.

6:37–42 *Judging Others.* This section begins with two negative (v. 37a, b) and two positive (vv. 37c, 38a) commands.

6:37–38 Judge not . . . condemn not. Lit., "Stop judging . . . condemning." Jesus is not ruling out the legitimate use of discernment, church discipline, and law courts, but is rather admonishing his listeners to discontinue their tendency to criticize and find fault with others (see notes on Matt. 7:1–5). **be judged . . . condemned** (by God). **Forgive** and **give** emphasize the continual nature of these commands and go beyond not judging and not condemning to seeking the positive well-being of others. The result is **it will be given** (by God) in **good measure** (not meagerly), **pressed down** (filling all the space in the container), **shaken** (so that grain will settle and fill

down, shaken together, running over, will be put [l]into your lap. For [m]with the measure
you use it will be measured back to you."
39 He also told them a parable: [n]"Can a blind man lead a blind man? Will they not both
fall into a pit? 40 [o]A disciple is not above his teacher, but everyone when he is [p]fully trained
will be like his teacher. 41 [i]Why do you see the speck that is in your brother's eye, but [q]do
not notice the log that is in your own eye? 42 How can you say to your brother, 'Brother,
let me take out the speck that is in your eye,' when you yourself do not see the log that is
in your own eye? You hypocrite, first take the log out of your own eye, and then you will
see clearly to take out the speck that is in your brother's eye.

A Tree and Its Fruit

43 "For [r]no good tree bears bad fruit, nor again does a bad tree bear good fruit, 44 for
[s]each tree is known by its own fruit. For figs are not gathered from thornbushes, nor are
grapes picked from a bramble bush. 45 [t]The good person out of the good treasure of his
heart produces good, and the evil person out of his evil treasure produces [u]evil, [v]for out
of the abundance of the heart his mouth speaks.

Build Your House on the Rock

46 [w]"Why [x]do you call me 'Lord, Lord,' and not do what I tell you? 47 [y]Everyone who comes
to me and hears my words and does them, I will show you what he is like: 48 he is like a man
building a house, who dug deep and laid the foundation on the rock. And when a flood
arose, the stream broke against that house and could not shake it, because it had been well
built.[1] 49 [z]But the one who hears and does not do them is like a man who built a house on
the ground without a foundation. When the stream broke against it, immediately it fell,
and [a]the ruin of that house was great."

Jesus Heals a Centurion's Servant

7 After he had finished all his sayings in the hearing of the people, [b]he entered Capernaum.
2 Now a centurion had a servant[2] who was sick and at the point of death, who was
highly valued by him. 3 When the centurion[3] heard about Jesus, [c]he sent to him elders of
the Jews, asking him to come and heal his servant. 4 And when they came to Jesus, they
pleaded with him earnestly, saying, [d]"He is worthy to have you do this for him, 5 for he loves
our nation, and he is the one who built us [e]our synagogue." 6 And Jesus went with them.
When he was not far from the house, the centurion sent friends, saying to him, "Lord, [f]do
not trouble yourself, for I am not worthy to have you come under my roof. 7 Therefore I did
not presume to come to you. But [g]say the word, and let my servant be healed. 8 For I too

[1] Some manuscripts *founded upon the rock* [2] Greek *bondservant*; also verses 3, 8, 10 [3] Greek *he*

38 [l]Ps. 79:12; Isa. 65:6, 7 [m]Mark 4:24; [Judg. 1:7]
39 [n]Matt. 15:14
40 [o]See Matt. 10:24 [p]2 Cor. 13:11; Heb. 13:21; 1 Pet. 5:10; [1 Cor. 1:10; 2 Tim. 3:17]
41 [i][See ver. 37 above] [q][John 8:7-9]
43 [r]For ver. 43, 44, see Matt. 7:16, 20
44 [s]Matt. 12:33
45 [t]Matt. 12:35; 15:18, 19; [Matt. 13:52; Eph. 4:29] [u][Matt. 5:37] [v]Matt. 12:34
46 [w][Mal. 1:6]; See Matt. 7:21 [x]John 13:13
47 [y]For ver. 47-49, see Matt. 7:24-27
49 [z][Ezek. 13:10-16] [a]Amos 6:11

Chapter 7

1 [b]For ver. 1-10, see Matt. 8:5-13
3 [c][Matt. 8:5]
4 [d][Acts 10:22]
5 [e]ch. 4:31, 33
6 [f]ch. 8:49; Mark 5:35; [Matt. 9:36 (Gk.)]
7 [g]Ps. 107:20; [Matt. 8:16]

the container even more fully), **running over** (so that a rounded heap will form at the top). **your lap**. The folding of a man's cloak with his arms underneath, forming a "container." **For with the measure you use it will be measured back to you**. In other words, God richly blesses such an attitude. Cf. Matt. 7:2; Mark 4:24.

6:39 The **parable** speaks of being **blind** to one's own faults while judging others (cf. Matt. 23:23–24; Rom. 2:19–21).

6:40 A disciple is not above his teacher. See note on Matt. 10:24. **Fully trained** means being like Jesus in every way.

6:41–42 speck . . . log. The hyperbolic nature of these verses (see note on Matt. 7:3–5) refers back to the judgmental attitude of Luke 6:37. It is clear that not all judging is excluded, for when one sees one's own sinfulness, then others can be helped with the specks in their eyes. At the same time, Christians need to take great care concerning their own faults, not censuring others for things that they are guilty of doing themselves.

6:43–45 *A Tree and Its Fruit.* This teaching can be taken in either of two ways. In one sense, observing good and bad fruit allows one to judge wisely in dealing with others (cf. v. 42; that is the context also of Matt. 7:15–20; see note). In another sense, it applies to the disciples themselves, for the **fruit** of a **bad tree** involves judging and condemning others while the **fruit** of a **good tree** involves forgiving and giving to others and loving one's enemies (cf. Luke 8:8, 15; 13:6–9). Either way, the difference between a good and a bad tree involves the **heart** (6:45). **evil person**. Cf. note on Matt. 6:13. **out of the abundance of the heart his mouth speaks**. The true nature of people's hearts can often be seen when they speak off-the-cuff, without reflection.

6:46–49 *Build Your House on the Rock.* Two examples illustrate what it means to hear and to do Jesus' words (vv. 47–48) and to hear but not do them (v. 49). Confession apart from obedience is worthless (cf. Matt. 7:21; Luke 8:21; 11:28).

7:1–50 *Who Is This Jesus?* Luke helps his readers answer the question "Who is this . . . ?" (v. 49) by recounting two healing miracles (vv. 1–10, 11–17), John's testimony to Jesus (vv. 18–35), and another example of Jesus forgiving sins (vv. 36–50).

7:1–10 *Jesus Heals a Centurion's Servant.* This account is also recorded in Matt. 8:5–13, but John 4:46–53 appears to be a different incident.

7:2 centurion. A Roman officer in charge of a hundred men.

7:3 elders of the Jews. Local Jewish officials. The villages of Galilee had their own elders, who presided as local judges (see Apocrypha, *Judith* 6:14–16).

7:4–5 The Jewish officials were saying, in effect, "He is a kind man who loves our people and helped build our synagogue. Please help him." The "synagogue" in Capernaum is the same as the one mentioned in 4:33.

7:6–7 I am not worthy reveals the centurion's humility. **Say the word** reveals his great faith.

7:8 The centurion responds, in effect, "I too can do things because of the authority given me, so how much more can you!"

am a man set under authority, with soldiers under me: and I say to one, 'Go,' and he goes;
and to another, 'Come,' and he comes; and to my servant, 'Do this,' and he does it." 9 When
Jesus heard these things, [h]he marveled at him, and turning to the crowd that followed
him, said, "I tell you, not even in Israel have I found such [i]faith." 10 And when those who
had been sent returned to the house, they found the servant well.

Jesus Raises a Widow's Son

11 Soon afterward[1] he went to a town called Nain, and his disciples and a great crowd
went with him. 12 As he drew near to the gate of the town, behold, a man who had died
was being carried out, [j]the only son of his mother, and she was a widow, and a considerable
crowd from the town was with her. 13 And when the Lord saw her, [k]he had compassion
on her and [l]said to her, "Do not weep." 14 Then he came up and touched [m]the bier, and the
bearers stood still. And he said, "Young man, I say to you, [n]arise." 15 And the dead man sat
up and began to speak, and Jesus[2] [o]gave him to his mother. 16 Fear seized them all, and
[p]they glorified God, saying, [q]"A great prophet has arisen among us!" and [r]"God has visited
his people!" 17 And this report about him spread through the whole of Judea and all the
surrounding country.

Messengers from John the Baptist

18 [s, t]The disciples of John reported all these things to him. And John, 19 calling two of
his disciples to him, sent them to the Lord, saying, "Are you the one [u]who is to come, or
[v]shall we look for another?" 20 And when the men had come to him, they said, "John the
Baptist has sent us to you, saying, 'Are you the one [u]who is to come, or [v]shall we look for
another?'" 21 In that hour [w]he healed many people of diseases and plagues and evil spirits,
and [x]on many who were blind he bestowed sight. 22 And he answered them, "Go and tell
John what you have seen and heard: [y]the blind receive their sight, the lame walk, [z]lepers[3]
are cleansed, and [a]the deaf hear, [b]the dead are raised up, [c]the poor have good news preached
to them. 23 And blessed is the one who is [d]not offended by me."
24 When John's messengers had gone, Jesus[4] began to speak to the crowds concerning

[1] Some manuscripts *The next day* [2] Greek *he* [3] *Leprosy* was a term for several skin diseases; see Leviticus 13 [4] Greek *he*

9 [h][Mark 6:6] [i]See Matt. 9:2
12 [j][ch. 8:42; 9:38; Judg. 11:34; Heb. 11:17]
13 [k]Matt. 20:34 [l]ch. 8:52
14 [m]2 Sam. 3:31 [n]ch. 8:54; Mark 5:41; [ver. 22; Matt. 11:5; John 11:43; Acts 9:40]
15 [o][1 Kgs. 17:23; 2 Kgs. 4:36; Heb. 11:35]
16 [p]ch. 2:20; Matt. 9:8; 15:31; Acts 11:18; 21:20; [Matt. 5:16]; See ch. 13:13 [q]ver. 39; See Deut. 18:15; Matt. 21:11 [r]See ch. 1:68
18 [s]For ver. 18-35, see Matt. 11:2-19 [t]See Matt. 9:14
19 [u]John 4:25; 6:14; 11:27 [v][ch. 3:15]
20 [u][See ver. 19 above] [v][See ver. 19 above]
21 [w]Mark 1:34 [x]ch. 18:42; Matt. 9:30; 12:22; 15:31; 20:34; 21:14; Mark 8:25; John 9:7
22 [y]Isa. 29:18; 35:5, 6; Matt. 15:30 [z]ch. 17:14 [a]Mark 7:35 [b]See ver. 14 [c]ch. 4:18; [Matt. 5:3; James 2:5]
23 [d]Isa. 8:14, 15; John 6:61

7:9 Not even in Israel foreshadows the entry of Gentiles into the kingdom of God. **such faith**. Jesus commends the centurion (who is a Gentile) for his humble faith (v. 6)—one of the few places where Jesus commends the way in which someone approaches him.

7:10 they found the servant well. As in all healing miracles in Scripture, the proof of the miracle is described.

7:11–17 *Jesus Raises a Widow's Son.* Jesus' power to heal is now demonstrated by a greater miracle: raising the dead (cf. 8:40–56; John 11:1–44; Acts 9:36–43). This miracle, involving a widow's son, recalls a similar miracle by Elijah (1 Kings 17:17–24).

7:11 Nain is commonly identified with a modern village (Nein) southeast of Nazareth, though other locations have also been suggested.

7:12 The only son of his mother . . . a widow reveals the desperate economic situation of the woman.

7:13 Do not weep indicates that Jesus will do something. Although not intended as a sign but as an act of **compassion**, this miracle will nevertheless provide evidence for answering the question "Who is this . . . ?" (v. 49).

7:14 Jesus **touched the bier** (a plank that served as an open coffin, used to carry the dead body outside the city to its burial place). Jesus is unconcerned about ceremonial uncleanness (cf. Num. 19:11, 16), for he is not made unclean when he touches the dead. Instead, the dead man comes to life.

7:15 sat up and began to speak. Proof of the miracle (cf. note on v. 10). **gave him to his mother**. These are the exact words found in the Septuagint of 1 Kings 17:23, describing the raising of a widow's son by Elijah.

7:16 In recognition of God's powerful presence, the people's **fear** immediately leads to worship: **they glorified God** (cf. 2:20). A **great prophet** is a correct description of Jesus (4:23–24; 7:39; 9:8, 19; 13:33; 24:19) but an inadequate one unless one adds: Christ; Son of God; Son of Man; Lord; etc. **God has visited his people**. God is making known his presence in Jesus, bringing salvation to the Jewish people who had waited so long for him (cf. 1:68; 19:44; Acts 15:14).

7:18–35 *Messengers from John the Baptist.* Luke records John's question to Jesus (vv. 18–23), Jesus' testimony to John (vv. 24–30), and the judgment on Israel for rejecting both John and Jesus (vv. 31–35).

7:18 All these things refers to the mighty miracles Jesus has been doing, as well as to his remarkable teaching.

7:19–20 the one . . . to come. John's question indicates his doubt as to whether Jesus was the "mightier one" who would baptize with the Holy Spirit and fire (see 3:16). For some reason, Jesus did not seem to be exactly the kind of Messiah John was expecting, perhaps because it did not appear that Jesus was going to overthrow the Roman rulers, and probably also because Jesus was not immediately bringing judgment on evildoers. John's concern was probably aggravated by his being in prison.

7:21 Luke prefaces Jesus' response to John with a summary of his ministry of healing (cf. 4:40–41; 5:15; 6:18–19). Luke mentions separately the restoring of **sight** to the **blind**, possibly to emphasize the greatness of such a miracle.

7:22 tell John. Jesus does not answer John's question directly but gives evidence demonstrating that he is the "coming one." From the following report, John can come to his own conclusion. **blind receive . . . sight** (see 4:18; 18:35–43); **lame walk** (5:17–25); **lepers are cleansed** (5:12–16; 17:11–19); **deaf hear** (cf. Isa. 29:18; 35:5; 42:18); **dead are raised** (Luke 7:11–17; 8:40–56; cf. Acts 9:36–43); **poor have good news preached to them** (Luke 4:18; 6:20; 14:13, 21). In other words, Jesus is indeed the coming one predicted in the OT. The days of salvation foretold by Isaiah have begun, even though they will not be consummated until Christ returns to establish the eternal kingdom.

7:23 Jesus' exhortation, **blessed is the one who is not offended**, is surely directed to John and his disciples.

7:24–27 Reed shaken by the wind suggests something flimsy and uncertain—far from an accurate description of John the Baptist (cf. Mark 1:6). John was **more than a prophet**: he was *the* prophet sent to fulfill Mal. 3:1.

John: "What did you go out [e]into the wilderness to see? [f]A reed shaken by the wind? **25** What
then did you go out to see? A man dressed in soft clothing? Behold, those who are dressed in
splendid clothing and live in luxury are in kings' courts. **26** What then did you go out to see?
[g]A prophet? Yes, I tell you, and more than a prophet. **27** This is he of whom it is written,

> [h]"'Behold, I send my messenger before your face,
> who will prepare your way before you.'

28 I tell you, among those born of women none is greater than John. Yet the one who is least
in the kingdom of God is greater than he." **29** ([i]When all the people heard this, and [j]the tax
collectors too, they declared God just,[1] [j]having been baptized with [k]the baptism of John,
30 [l]but the Pharisees and [m]the lawyers [n]rejected [o]the purpose of God for themselves, not
having been baptized by him.)
31 "To what then shall I compare the people of this generation, and what are they like?
32 They are like children sitting in the marketplace and calling to one another,

> "'We played the flute for you, and you did not dance;
> we sang a dirge, and you did not weep.'

33 For John the Baptist has come [p]eating no bread and [q]drinking no wine, and you say,
'He has a demon.' **34** The Son of Man has come [r]eating and drinking, and you say, 'Look at
him! A glutton and a drunkard, [s]a friend of tax collectors and sinners!' **35** Yet [t]wisdom is
justified by all her children."

A Sinful Woman Forgiven

36 [u]One of the Pharisees asked him to eat with him, and he went into the Pharisee's house
and reclined at the table. **37** [v]And behold, a woman of the city, who was a sinner, when she
learned that he was reclining at table in the Pharisee's house, brought an alabaster flask
of ointment, **38** and standing behind him at his feet, weeping, she began to wet his feet
with her tears and [w]wiped them with the hair of her head and kissed his feet and anointed
them with the ointment. **39** Now when the Pharisee who had invited him saw this, he said
to himself, "If [x]this man were [y]a prophet, he [z]would have known who and what sort of
woman this is who is touching him, for she is a sinner." **40** And Jesus answering said to him,
"Simon, I have something to say to you." And he answered, "Say it, Teacher."
41 "A certain moneylender had two debtors. One owed five hundred [a]denarii, and the other
fifty. **42** [b]When they could not pay, he [c]cancelled the debt of both. Now which of them will
love him more?" **43** Simon answered, "The one, I suppose, for whom he cancelled the larger

[1] Greek *they justified God*

24 [e]ch. 1:80; 3:2 [f][Eph. 4:14; James 1:6]
26 [g]ch. 1:76; 20:6; Matt. 14:5
27 [h]Mark 1:2; Cited from Mal. 3:1; [ch. 1:17, 76]
29 [i][ch. 20:6] [j]ch. 3:12; Matt. 21:32 [k]Acts 18:25; 19:3
30 [l][Matt. 21:25, 32; 23:13] [m]ch. 10:25; 11:45, 46, 52; 14:3; Matt. 22:35 [n]See Mark 7:9 [o]Acts 2:23; 13:36
33 [p]Matt. 3:4; Mark 1:6 [q]ch. 1:15
34 [r]ver. 36; ch. 14:1; Matt. 9:10; John 2:1; 12:2 [s]ch. 15:2; 19:7; Matt. 9:11
35 [t][ch. 11:49; Prov. 8:1-36]
36 [u]ch. 11:37; 14:1
37 [v]For ver. 37-39, [Matt. 26:6-13; Mark 14:3-9; John 12:1-8]
38 [w]ver. 44; John 11:2
39 [x][ch. 15:2] [y]ver. 16; John 4:19 [z][ch. 22:64]
41 [a]See Matt. 18:28
42 [b]Matt. 18:25 [c][Rom. 8:32 (Gk.)]

7:28 none is greater. John's greatness among all the OT prophets, all those who came before the arrival of the kingdom of God, comes from his function as direct forerunner of Jesus the Messiah. But John was not part of the kingdom of God that Jesus was proclaiming and bringing to reality, for he was still part of the old covenant system. Therefore **the one who is least in the kingdom of God** (one who has believed in Jesus and has become a member of the new covenant kingdom) is actually **greater than** John, for those who come after John live in the age of fulfillment, following the coming of Jesus. This underscores the qualitative difference between the old age and the dawning of the new kingdom age (cf. note on Matt. 11:11).

7:29–30 Jesus' hearers rightly take his words in vv. 24–28 as a commendation of John, not a criticism. God was working through John for his purposes in his time. Therefore, those who had been **baptized with the baptism of John** were glad, and they **declared God just**.

7:31–34 This generation does not refer to everyone then living but to the leaders and others who rejected both John the Baptist and Jesus, and who were still the dominant force in the culture. In their rejection of both the "ascetic" John and the "non-ascetic" Jesus, they were like **children** refusing to play either a sad or a happy game.

7:35 Wisdom (God's way, v. 29) **is justified** (shown to be right) **by all her children** (the followers of John and Jesus).

7:36–50 *A Sinful Woman Forgiven.* This is the culmination of vv. 1–35 and answers the question "Who is this . . . ?" (v. 49). This and the similar accounts in Matt. 26:6–13, Mark 14:3–9, and John 12:1–8 probably involved two separate incidents (see note on Mark 14:3–5).

7:36 Pharisees. See note on 5:17.

7:37–38 a woman. Unnamed; cf. note on Mark 14:3–5. **Alabaster** is a soft stone frequently used as a perfume container. **Reclining** toward a low center table(s), the feet of the participants would have faced outward like spokes from a hub. **With her tears** she washed Jesus' **feet** (an act of hospitality omitted by Simon; Luke 7:44) and **wiped them** with her **hair**. Her tears are tears both of thankfulness and also of reverent awe as she senses the presence of God in the person of Jesus. Her act would have been considered improper, therefore it took great courage to honor Jesus in this way.

7:39–40 If this man were a prophet. The Pharisee charges that Jesus is not a prophet (contrast v. 16) because a true prophet would not allow a sinful woman to touch him. **said to himself . . . Jesus answering**. Jesus knows Simon's thoughts, showing that he is indeed a prophet.

7:41 five hundred denarii. Equivalent to about 20 months' wages. **Fifty** denarii is about two months' wages.

7:42 cancelled the debt. For the analogy of sin with debt, cf. 11:4; Matt. 6:12; 18:21–35.

7:43–46 Simon's answer (**The one** [who owed] **the larger debt**) leads to the comparison of Simon's lack of hospitality (**no water for my feet . . . no kiss . . . did not anoint my head with oil**; cf. Ps. 23:5; 141:5) with the greater love of the woman (washing his feet with her tears, continually kissing his feet, and anointing them with expensive ointment).

debt." And he said to him, "You have judged rightly." **44** Then turning toward the woman
he said to Simon, "Do you see this woman? I entered your house; [d]you gave me no water
for my feet, but [e]she has wet my feet with her tears and wiped them with her hair. **45** [f]You
gave me no kiss, but from the time I came in she has not ceased to [g]kiss my feet. **46** [h]You did
not anoint my head with oil, but she has anointed my feet with ointment. **47** Therefore I tell
you, her sins, [i]which are many, are forgiven—for she loved much. But he who is forgiven
little, loves little." **48** And he said to her, [j]"Your sins are forgiven." **49** Then those who were
at table with him began to say among[1] themselves, [k]"Who is this, who even forgives sins?"
50 And he said to the woman, [l]"Your faith has saved you; [m]go in peace."

Women Accompanying Jesus

8 Soon afterward he went on [n]through cities and villages, proclaiming and [o]bringing
the good news of the kingdom of God. And the twelve were with him, **2** and also [p]some
women who had been healed of evil spirits and infirmities: [q]Mary, called Magdalene, [r]from
whom seven demons had gone out, **3** and [s]Joanna, the wife of Chuza, Herod's household
manager, and Susanna, and many others, who provided for them[2] out of their means.

The Parable of the Sower

4 [t]And when a great crowd was gathering and people from town after town came to
him, he said in a parable, **5** [u]"A sower went out to sow his seed. And as he sowed, some fell
along the path and was trampled underfoot, and the birds of the air devoured it. **6** And
some fell on the rock, and as it grew up, [v]it withered away, because it had no moisture.
7 And some fell among [w]thorns, and the thorns grew up with it and choked it. **8** And some
fell into good soil and grew and yielded [x]a hundredfold." As he said these things, he called
out, [y]"He who has ears to hear, let him hear."

The Purpose of the Parables

9 And when his disciples asked him what this parable meant, **10** he said, [z]"To you it
has been given to know [a]the secrets of the kingdom of God, but for others they are

[1] Or *to* [2] Some manuscripts *him*

44 [d]1 Tim. 5:10; See Gen. 18:4 [e]ver. 38
45 [f]2 Sam. 15:5; 19:39; 20:9 [g]ver. 38
46 [h]Ps. 23:5; 141:5; Eccles. 9:8; Matt. 6:17
47 [i][ver. 39]
48 [j]ch. 5:20; Matt. 9:2; Mark 2:5; James 5:15; 1 John 2:12; [John 20:23]
49 [k]ch. 5:21
50 [l]ver. 9; [ver. 47; 1 Tim. 1:14]; See Mark 10:52; Eph. 2:8 [m]ch. 8:48; 1 Sam. 1:17; Mark 5:34

Chapter 8

1 [n]See Mark 6:6 [o]See ch. 4:43
2 [p]ch. 23:49, 55; Matt. 27:55; Mark 15:40, 41; Acts 1:14 [q]ch. 24:10; Matt. 27:56, 61; 28:1; John 19:25; 20:1, 18 [r]Mark 16:9
3 [s]ch. 24:10
4 [t]For ver. 4-10, see Matt. 13:1-15; Mark 4:1-12
5 [u][Isa. 55:10; Amos 9:13]
6 [v]John 15:6
7 [w]Jer. 4:3
8 [x]Gen. 26:12 [y]See Matt. 11:15
10 [z]Matt. 19:11; Col. 1:27; [1 Cor. 2:6-10; 1 John 2:20, 27]; See Matt. 11:25 [a]See Rom. 16:25

7:47 For she loved much refers not to the cause of the woman's forgiveness but the result of it (cf. note on v. 50; cf. also "which of them will love him more," v. 42).

7:48–49 Your sins are forgiven (cf. 5:20). As in 5:20–25, Jesus' statement is understood as exercising the divine prerogative of forgiving sins and is followed by a similar question: **Who is this, who even forgives sins?** Luke intentionally raises this question for his readers to reflect on the significance and implications of who Jesus is.

7:50 Your faith has saved you. Cf. 8:48; 17:19; 18:42. The woman experienced the forgiveness of her sins not because of love (see note on 7:47) but through faith, which was evidenced in the way she honored Jesus in her act of washing his feet.

8:1–21 *Jesus Teaches in Parables.* Included in this section are the parables of the sower (vv. 4–15) and of the lamp (vv. 16–18).

8:1–3 *Women Accompanying Jesus.* Luke has more references to the role of women in Jesus' ministry than any other Gospel. Here he mentions several by name. It is noteworthy that the women come from a wide array of social levels, from the highest levels of the social order in Herod's palace, to a demon-possessed woman who would have been a social outcast. Cf. 23:49; 24:1–11; Acts 1:14.

8:1 On the **good news of the kingdom of God**, see Introduction: Key Themes.

8:2 Mary was **called Magdalene** because she was from Magdala (a city on the western shore of Galilee, identified with modern Migdal). Later writers in church history connected Mary Magdalene to the sinful woman of 7:37, calling her a former prostitute. There is no evidence for this in the biblical text or in early church history. This mistaken identification arose from erroneously combining the two separate accounts found in John 12:1–8 and Luke 7:36–50 with this passage in Luke 8. On the other hand, heterodox Gnostic writers from the late-second century and afterward promoted their own interpretation of Mary (along with other minor NT figures such as Thomas, Philip, and Judas), considering her a special possessor of secret knowledge from the Savior. Contrary to various popular media accounts, no ancient source (whether orthodox or heterodox) says that Mary was married to Jesus, let alone had a son with him. In fact, there is no source anywhere that says that Jesus was married to anyone. The NT simply informs readers that Jesus healed her of demonic possession, and that she gratefully followed him to the foot of the cross and the empty tomb (Matt. 27:56, 61; 28:1; Mark 15:40, 47; 16:1; Luke 24:10). **Seven demons** reveals the greatness of her healing (cf. 11:26).

8:3 Both the mention of **Joanna**, wife of **Herod's household manager**, and the report that these women **provided for them out of their means** indicate that although Jesus' ministry was directed primarily to the "poor" (4:18), some of the wealthy and powerful supported and welcomed it. The phrase **many others** and the relative pronoun **who** are both feminine in Greek, referring to women who supported Jesus and his disciples.

8:4–8 *The Parable of the Sower.* Although referred to as the parable of the sower, the sower is the least important component and is only referred to once (v. 5; cf. its omission in v. 11 with Mark 4:14). The focus, rather, is on the various kinds of soil on which the sower sows his seed. **parable**. See notes on Matt. 13:3; Mark 4:2. For **birds of the air**, cf. Luke 9:58; 13:19; Acts 10:12; 11:6. **Some fell on the rock** lying beneath a thin layer of soil. **ears to hear** (cf. Matt. 11:15; 13:9, 43; Mark 4:9; Luke 14:35). An exhortation to understand and heed the parable. **hundredfold**. See note on Mark 4:8.

8:9–15 *The Purpose of the Parables.* In his explanation of the parable of the sower, Jesus also explains that parables blind those who have resisted God's revelation while helping those who have believed it.

8:10 To you it has been given to know. For the disciples' unique access to Jesus' teachings, cf. 10:21–22; 12:32; 22:29. **secrets**. See also note on Matt. 13:10–11. **So that** indicates the purpose of Jesus' teaching in parables (cf. notes on Matt. 13:12–13; Mark 4:12).

in parables, so [b]that 'seeing they may not see, and hearing they may not understand.'
11 [c]Now the parable is this: The seed is [d]the word of God. 12 The ones along the path are
those who have heard; then the devil comes and takes away the word from their hearts,
so that they may not [e]believe and be saved. 13 And the ones on the rock are those who,
when they hear the word, receive it [f]with joy. But these have no root; they [g]believe for
a while, and in time of testing [h]fall away. 14 And as for what fell among the thorns, they
are those who hear, but [i]as they go on their way they are choked by the [j]cares and riches
and pleasures of life, and their fruit does not mature. 15 As for that in the good soil, they
are those who, hearing the word, hold it fast in an honest and good heart, and [k]bear
fruit [l]with patience.

A Lamp Under a Jar

16 [m], [n]"No one after lighting a lamp covers it with a jar or puts it under a bed, but puts
it on a stand, so that those who enter may see the light. 17 [o]For nothing is hidden that will
not be made manifest, nor is anything secret that will not be known and come to light.
18 [p]Take care then how you hear, [q]for to the one who has, more will be given, and from the
one who has not, even what he thinks that he has will be taken away."

Jesus' Mother and Brothers

19 [r]Then his mother and [s]his brothers came to him, but they could not reach him because
of the crowd. 20 And he was told, "Your mother and your brothers are standing outside,
desiring to see you." 21 But he answered them, "My mother and my brothers are those [t]who
hear the word of God and do it."

Jesus Calms a Storm

22 [u]One day he got into a boat with his disciples, and he said to them, "Let us go across
to the other side of [v]the lake." So they set out, 23 and as they sailed he fell asleep. And a
windstorm came down on [v]the lake, and they were filling with water and were in danger. 24 And they went and woke him, saying, "Master, Master, we are perishing!" And he
awoke and [w]rebuked the wind and the raging waves, and they ceased, [x]and there was a
calm. 25 He said to them, "Where is your faith?" And they [y]were afraid, and they [z]marveled,
saying to one another, "Who then is this, that [a]he commands even winds and water, and
they obey him?"

10 [b]Isa. 6:9, 10; See Matt. 13:13
11 [c]For ver. 11-15, see Matt. 13:18-23; Mark 4:13-20 [d]ch. 1:2; Mark 2:2; 4:33; Acts 8:4; James 1:21
12 [e]See Mark 16:16
13 [f][Isa. 58:2; Ezek. 33:31, 32; Mark 6:20; John 5:35] [g]Gal. 1:6; [Hos. 6:4; Gal. 5:7] [h]1 Tim. 4:1; Heb. 3:12
14 [i][James 1:11] [j]See Matt. 6:25
15 [k]Hos. 14:8; John 15:5, 6; Phil. 1:11; Col. 1:6 [l]James 5:7; See Heb. 10:36
16 [m]For ver. 16-18, see Mark 4:21-25 [n]ch. 11:33; Matt. 5:15
17 [o]ch. 12:2; Matt. 10:26; [1 Tim. 5:25]
18 [p][ver. 11-15] [q]See Matt. 13:12
19 [r]For ver. 19-21, see Matt. 12:46-50; Mark 3:31-35 [s]Matt. 13:55; Mark 6:3; John 2:12; 7:3, 5, 10; Acts 1:14; 1 Cor. 9:5; Gal. 1:19
21 [t]ch. 11:28; See James 1:22
22 [u]For ver. 22-25, see Matt. 8:23-27; Mark 4:36-41; [John 6:16-21] [v]ver. 33; See ch. 5:1
23 [v][See ver. 22 above]
24 [w]ch. 4:39; Ps. 104:7 [x]Ps. 65:7; [Matt. 14:32; Mark 6:51]
25 [y]John 14:27 [z][Mark 1:27] [a][ch. 5:9]

8:11 the parable is this. See note on Mark 4:14–20.

8:12 The seeds **along the path** (through the field) represent one group of hearers. **So that they may not believe and be saved** assumes that faith is the means of salvation.

8:13 The second group of hearers **receive** the word **with joy** and **believe**. A few interpreters think this is saving faith because these people "believe," and though they "fall away" (from fellowship?), this is not an ultimate rejection of Christ. But it is more likely that this is temporary, merely intellectual "faith" (cf. James 2:17) that is not saving faith, for these plants **have no root** (see Mark 4:17), they bear no fruit, and they do not persevere but last only **for a while** (on perseverance, see notes on John 6:40; Rom. 8:29; 8:30; 2 Tim. 2:11–13; Jude 21).

8:14 The third kind of soil, containing **thorns**, describes those who initially embrace the message (start **on their way**) but do not persevere to maturity and so fail to produce mature **fruit** because of the **cares** (cf. 12:22–34; 21:34), **riches** (6:24; 12:15; 16:1–13), and **pleasures of life**.

8:15 The fourth group hears with an **honest and good heart**. They **hold it fast** and **bear** ("much," cf. v. 8) **fruit**. **With patience** can also be translated "with perseverance" (cf. 21:19; Acts 14:22), showing that fruit-bearing in God's kingdom often requires much work before significant results are seen.

8:16–18 *A Lamp under a Jar.* If believers do not hide the **light** (message) they have heard (vv. 8, 15, 18) but proclaim it for others to **see**, then what is **hidden** (cf. v. 10) will **be made manifest**, and what is **secret** will **come to light**. Jesus is ultimately speaking about the final judgment, but gospel proclamation and gospel ministry in this age are like a "lamp" (v. 16) that illumines and drives away dark areas of sin before the final judgment. **The one who** [already] **has** a knowledge of God's Word will understand it better (**more will be given**), whereas the one who does not listen carefully (**has not**) will lose even what he has heard (cf. Acts 13:46; 18:6; 28:25–28; and notes on Matt. 25:29; Mark 4:24; 4:25; Luke 12:41–48).

8:19–21 *Jesus' Mother and Brothers.* The **brothers** of Jesus are most naturally understood as the sons born to Joseph and Mary after Jesus' birth. **My mother and my brothers are those**. For Jesus, spiritual relationships were more important than physical ones. Thus his real family is made up of those **who hear the word of God and do it** (see notes on Matt. 12:46; 12:49; 13:55–56; Mark 3:35).

8:22–56 *Jesus, Lord of Nature, Demons, Disease, and Death.* In the following accounts Luke helps his readers answer the question "Who then is this?" (v. 25; cf. note on 7:1–50). The sequence of this section shows the extent of Jesus' authority—over nature, demons, disease, and even death.

8:22–25 *Jesus Calms a Storm.* **windstorm**. See notes on Matt. 8:23–24; Mark 4:37. On the similarities to Jonah 1:4–5, see note on Mark 4:38. Although rebuked for lack of faith (Luke 8:25), the disciples were aware that, whereas they were helpless in the storm, Jesus was not, so **they went** to **him**. Jesus **rebuked the wind and . . . waves**, revealing that he has authority over nature, just as the Lord God does (cf. Ps. 107:29). **Where is your faith?** See notes on Matt. 8:26; Mark 4:40. For **were afraid, and . . . marveled**, see Luke 1:21 and note on Matt. 8:27. The account culminates with the question, **Who then is this** who exercises lordship over nature itself? (Luke 8:25; cf. note on 7:1–50).

26[b]For ver. 26-40, see Matt. 8:28–9:1; Mark 5:1-21
27[c][Rev. 18:2]
28[d]ch. 4:33, 34; Mark 1:23; 24, 26; Acts 8:7 [e][ch. 4:3, 9]; See Matt. 14:33 [f]ch. 1:32; 6:35; Gen. 14:18; Num. 24:16; Ps. 57:2; Isa. 14:14; Dan. 3:26; Acts 16:17
29[g][ch. 11:24; Matt. 12:43]
30[h]Matt. 26:53
31[i]See Rev. 9:1
33[j]ver. 22, 23
35[k]ch. 10:39 [l][ver. 27]
37[m][ch. 5:8; Acts 16:39]
39[n]Ps. 66:16; [ch. 5:14]
40[o]ch. 9:11
41[p]For ver. 41-56, see Matt. 9:18-26; Mark 5:22-43 [q]ch. 13:14; Acts 13:15; 18:8, 17
42[r]See ch. 7:12

Jesus Heals a Man with a Demon

26 [b]Then they sailed to the country of the Gerasenes,[1] which is opposite Galilee. **27** When
Jesus[2] had stepped out on land, there met him a man from the city who had demons. For a
long time he had worn no clothes, and he had not lived in a house [c]but among the tombs.
28 When he saw Jesus, he [d]cried out and fell down before him and said [d]with a loud voice,
"What have you to do with me, Jesus, [e]Son of [f]the Most High God? I beg you, do not torment me." **29** For he had commanded the unclean spirit to come out of the man. (For many
a time it had seized him. He was kept under guard and bound with chains and shackles,
but he would break the bonds and be driven by the demon [g]into the desert.) **30** Jesus then
asked him, "What is your name?" And he said, [h]"Legion," for many demons had entered
him. **31** And they begged him not to command them to depart into [i]the abyss. **32** Now a
large herd of pigs was feeding there on the hillside, and they begged him to let them enter
these. So he gave them permission. **33** Then the demons came out of the man and entered
the pigs, and the herd rushed down the steep bank into [j]the lake and drowned.

34 When the herdsmen saw what had happened, they fled and told it in the city and in
the country. **35** Then people went out to see what had happened, and they came to Jesus and
found the man from whom the demons had gone, sitting [k]at the feet of Jesus, [l]clothed and
in his right mind, and they were afraid. **36** And those who had seen it told them how the
demon-possessed[3] man had been healed. **37** Then all the people of the surrounding country
of the Gerasenes [m]asked him to depart from them, for they were seized with great fear. So
he got into the boat and returned. **38** The man from whom the demons had gone begged
that he might be with him, but Jesus sent him away, saying, **39** "Return to your home, and
[n]declare how much God has done for you." And he went away, proclaiming throughout
the whole city how much Jesus had done for him.

Jesus Heals a Woman and Jairus's Daughter

40 Now when Jesus returned, the crowd [o]welcomed him, for they were all waiting for
him. **41** [p]And there came a man named Jairus, who was [q]a ruler of the synagogue. And falling at Jesus' feet, he implored him to come to his house, **42** for he had [r]an only daughter,
about twelve years of age, and she was dying.

[1] Some manuscripts *Gadarenes*; others *Gergesenes*; also verse 37 [2] Greek *he*; also verses 38, 42 [3] Greek *daimonizomai*; elsewhere rendered *oppressed by demons*

8:26–39 *Jesus Heals a Demon-Possessed Man.* Jesus demonstrates his greatness through his mastery over the demonic realm.

8:26 the country of the Gerasenes. See notes on Matt. 8:28 and Mark 5:1.

8:27 The description of the **man . . . who had demons** in vv. 27–30 underscores his terrible plight and the greatness of Jesus, who can cast out so many (a legion, v. 30) powerful demons. The use of "he" (vv. 27–30) and "they" (vv. 31–33) is determined primarily by whether the demons are seen as acting in unity with the man or apart from him.

8:28 When he saw Jesus, he . . . fell down before him. See note on Mark 5:6–7. For the demons' knowledge of Jesus' identity, see Luke 4:41 and note on Matt. 8:29. **I beg you** reveals the subservience of the demons. The significance of **do not torment me** becomes clear in Luke 8:31.

8:29 For many a time heightens the man's plight. **He had commanded** indicates that the demon did not come out the first time Jesus commanded it to (see note on Mark 5:8).

8:30 Legion indicates thousands of demons but may be an intentional overstatement. Cf. note on Mark 5:9. Mary Magdalene's plight of being possessed by seven demons (see Luke 8:2) is exponentially exceeded by this man's situation.

8:31 abyss. The final destination of Satan and his angels; cf. Matt. 25:41; 2 Pet. 2:4; Rev. 20:3; see also note on Matt. 8:30–34.

8:32–33 A **large herd of pigs** reveals that this is a Gentile region, since pigs were forbidden for Jews (Lev. 11:7; Deut. 14:8; cf. note on Matt. 8:30–34).

8:35 The demoniac's salvation is confirmed by: the drowning of the pigs; his **sitting at the feet of Jesus** instead of being among the tombs, bound with chains and shackles (vv. 27, 29); his being **clothed** rather than naked (v. 27); and his being **in his right mind** (cf. Mark 5:15). **afraid.** See notes on Luke 1:65–66; 7:16; 8:47. The drowning of so many pigs also verifies that a large number of demons were in the man.

8:36 The man is described as **healed**, which can also be translated "saved" (Gk. *sōzō*).

8:37 So he . . . returned. In "orderly" (1:3) fashion, Luke completes the story concerning the townspeople before completing the story of the demoniac. **for they were seized with great fear.** While fearful reverence and awe are appropriate in the presence of Jesus (see note on 8:35), the fear of these townspeople is negative and seems to be a wrongful, superstitious fear of Jesus' mysterious power, and perhaps a fear of further loss of their property, for their fear does not draw them to Jesus.

8:38–39 The parallel statements **Return . . . and declare how much God has done for you** and **went away, proclaiming . . . how much Jesus had done for him** should be noted (cf. 9:42–43), indicating that Jesus has the same status as God. Following Jesus involves the responsibility to evangelize ("he went . . . proclaiming"; see note on Mark 5:18–20).

8:40–56 *Jesus Heals a Woman and Jairus's Daughter.* Jesus raises Jairus's daughter (vv. 40–42a, 49–56) after being interrupted by another person needing his attention (vv. 42b–48).

8:40 returned. See note on Mark 5:21. **The crowd welcomed him** refers back to Luke 8:1–21 and the "crowd" of vv. 4 and 19.

8:41–42a a ruler of the synagogue. See note on Mark 5:22. A board member of the synagogue, or more likely the official in charge of arranging services (cf. Luke 8:49; Acts 13:15; 18:8). **Falling at Jesus' feet, he implored.** The description reveals Jairus's desperation, as does **only daughter** (cf. Luke 7:12; 9:38).

8:42b–48 While Jesus heals someone else, Jairus's daughter dies.

As Jesus went, the people [s]pressed around him. **43** And there was a woman [t]who had
had a discharge of blood for twelve years, and though she had spent all her [u]living on
physicians,[1] she could not be healed by anyone. **44** She came up behind him and touched
[v]the fringe of his garment, and [w]immediately her discharge of blood ceased. **45** And Jesus
said, "Who was it that touched me?" When all denied it, Peter[2] said, "Master, the crowds
surround you and are pressing in on you!" **46** But Jesus said, "Someone touched me, for I
perceive that [x]power has gone out from me." **47** And when the woman saw that she was not
hidden, she came trembling, and falling down before him declared in the presence of all
the people why she had touched him, and how she had been immediately healed. **48** And
he said to her, "Daughter, [y]your faith has made you well; [y]go in peace."

49 While he was still speaking, someone from [z]the ruler's house came and said, "Your daughter is dead; [a]do not trouble [b]the Teacher any more." **50** But Jesus on hearing this answered
him, "Do not fear; only believe, and she will be well." **51** And when he came to the house,
he allowed no one to enter with him, except [c]Peter and [d]John and James, and the father
and mother of the child. **52** And all were weeping and [e]mourning for her, but he [f]said, "Do
not weep, for [g]she is not dead but [h]sleeping." **53** And they laughed at him, knowing that she
was dead. **54** But [i]taking her by the hand he called, saying, "Child, [j]arise." **55** And [k]her spirit
returned, and she got up at once. And he directed that something should be given her to eat.
56 And her parents were amazed, but [l]he charged them to tell no one what had happened.

Jesus Sends Out the Twelve Apostles

9 [m]And he called the twelve together and gave them power and authority over all demons
and to cure diseases, **2** [n]and he sent them out to [o]proclaim the kingdom of God and to
heal. **3** [p]And he said to them, "Take nothing for your journey, [q]no staff, nor bag, nor bread,

[1] Some manuscripts omit *and though she had spent all her living on physicians,* [2] Some manuscripts add *and those who were with him*

42 [s]ver. 45; Mark 3:9
43 [t]Lev. 15:25 [u]ch. 21:4; Mark 12:44
44 [v]Matt. 14:36; 23:5; [Num. 15:38, 39; Deut. 22:12] [w]Matt. 15:28; 17:18
46 [x]ch. 5:17; 6:19; [Acts 10:38]
48 [y]See ch. 7:50
49 [z]ver. 41 [a]ch. 7:6 [b]See John 11:28
51 [c]ch. 9:28; Mark 14:33 [d]Mark 3:17
52 [e]ch. 23:27; Matt. 11:17 [f]ch. 7:13 [g][Acts 20:10] [h]John 11:4, 11
54 [i]See Mark 1:31 [j]ch. 7:14, 22; [Matt. 11:5; John 11:43]
55 [k][Judg. 15:19; 1 Sam. 30:12]
56 [l]See Matt. 8:4

Chapter 9

1 [m]Matt. 10:1; Mark 3:13-15; 6:7
2 [n]Matt. 10:5, 7, 8; [ver. 11; ch. 10:1, 9] [o]ver. 11, 60; See ch. 4:43
3 [p]For ver. 3-5, see Matt. 10:9-14; Mark 6:8-11; [ch. 10:4-11; 22:35] [q][Mark 6:8]

8:43 discharge of blood. See note on Matt. 9:20. Her plight is heightened by its duration (**twelve years**) and hopelessness (**she could not be healed by anyone**). Moreover, her hemorrhaging would also have made her ceremonially unclean, which would have cut her off from many social and religious relationships (cf. Lev. 15:25).

8:44 touched the fringe of his garment. See note on Mark 5:25–27. In contrast to the 12 years of hemorrhaging and failure to be healed by human means, the miraculous healing that comes from God happens **immediately** (cf. Luke 18:43).

8:45–46 Who . . . touched me? Jesus is aware that one of the many people touching him had been healed (cf. note on Mark 5:30).

8:47 The healed woman **came trembling**. In Luke, fear is appropriate when experiencing God's presence (see v. 35 and notes on 1:65–66; 7:16; 8:37). The woman **declared . . . why she had touched him**. Cf. Mark 5:33 and note on Mark 5:31–33.

8:48 Jesus' addressing her as **daughter** probably reassures the woman, as does his statement that **your faith has made you well** (in the sense of both physical and spiritual healing, for the verb here is "saved" [Gk. *sōzō*]; see notes on v. 36 and Matt. 9:22; also, Jesus' final words to her, **go in peace**, suggest that she has been saved).

8:49 While he was still speaking marks a change back to the story of Jairus. **Do not trouble the Teacher any more** assumes that while Jesus could heal the sick, the girl's death placed her beyond his ability to heal (cf. John 11:21, 32, 37, 39).

8:50 Do not fear (see 1:13); **only believe**. Words of reassurance. The two exhortations are followed by the promise **she will be well** (again this is Gk. *sōzō*, which can mean either "heal" or "save," but several times in these miracle accounts it seems to mean that both physical healing and spiritual salvation have taken place).

8:51 Peter and John and James. This is the first mention of this inner group of disciples in Luke (cf. 9:28).

8:52–53 weeping and mourning. See note on Matt. 9:23 (cf. Luke 7:13). **She is not dead but sleeping** must be understood in light of 8:49, 53. The ridicule Jesus receives affirms the girl's death but misunderstands his metaphorical use of "sleeping" (see note on Mark 5:38–40).

8:54–55 taking her by the hand. See note on Mark 5:41. **Child, arise**. Cf. Luke 7:14. **And her spirit returned**. The reuniting of the girl's spirit and body resulted in the return to her former earthly life. **she got up at once**. Along with the fact of her eating, this offers immediate proof of the miracle (see note on 7:10).

8:56 he charged them to tell no one. A sharp contrast to v. 39, for Jesus is now back in a Jewish region where mistaken expectations about a political and revolutionary messiah could make Jesus' ministry much more difficult.

9:1–50 *Jesus and the Twelve.* Jesus interacts with his 12 apostles in various ministry and teaching situations.

9:1–6 *Jesus Sends Out the Twelve.* The mission of the 12 apostles serves as a time of apprenticeship for their ultimate mission after Jesus' ascension (1:2; 24:45–49; Acts 1:8).

9:1–2 And he called the twelve together. See 6:13. For **power and authority**, see 4:36; for power to **heal**, see 5:17. Some think this power and authority was for the duration of this mission, as its absence in 9:40 and the equipping in 24:49 and Acts 1:8 suggest. It is manifested in their casting out **demons**, curing **diseases**, and proclaiming the **kingdom of God**. The close relationship between "the kingdom of God" and "the gospel" is shown in

Parallels in the Ministries of Jesus, Peter, and Paul in Luke–Acts

Luke shows Peter and Paul continuing the ministry of Jesus in the book of Acts. Representative examples are cited on the chart below.

Type of Ministry	Jesus	Peter	Paul
Preaching that the OT is fulfilled in Jesus the Messiah	Luke 4; 24	Acts 2; 3	Acts 13; 17
Casting out unclean spirits	Luke 4:31–37	Acts 5:16	Acts 16:16–18
Healing the lame	Luke 6:6–11	Acts 3:1–10	Acts 14:8–10
Raising the dead	Luke 7:11–17	Acts 9:36–43	Acts 20:7–12
Healing by a touch, a shadow, or cloths	Luke 8:42–48	Acts 5:15	Acts 19:11–12

5 [r]Acts 13:51; [Neh. 5:13; Acts 18:6] [s]See Mark 1:44 [t]James 5:3
6 [u]Mark 6:12
7 [v]For ver. 7-9, see Matt. 14:1-12; Mark 6:14-29 [w]ch. 3:1, 19; Acts 13:1 [x]ver. 19
8 [x][See ver. 7 above]
9 [y]ch. 23:8
10 [z]Mark 6:30 [a]For ver. 10-17, see Matt. 14:13-21; Mark 6:32-44; John 6:1-13; [Matt. 15:32-38; Mark 8:2-9]
11 [b]ch. 8:40 [c]ver. 2
12 [d]ch. 24:29 (Gk.); Jer. 6:4 [e][Matt. 15:23]
13 [f][2 Kgs. 4:42-44] [g]Matt. 16:9; Mark 8:19
16 [h]Mark 7:34; John 11:41; 17:1 [i]ch. 24:30; 1 Sam. 9:13; Matt. 26:26; Mark 8:7; 14:22; [1 Cor. 14:16]

nor money; and do not have two tunics.[1] **4** And whatever house you enter, stay there, and
from there depart. **5** And wherever they do not receive you, when you leave that town [r]shake
off the dust from your feet [s]as a testimony [t]against them." **6** [u]And they departed and went
through the villages, preaching the gospel and healing everywhere.

Herod Is Perplexed by Jesus

7 [v]Now [w]Herod the tetrarch heard about all that was happening, and he was perplexed,
because it was said by some that [x]John had been raised from the dead, **8** [x]by some that
Elijah had appeared, and [x]by others that one of the prophets of old had risen. **9** Herod
said, "John I beheaded, but who is this about whom I hear such things?" And [y]he sought
to see him.

Jesus Feeds the Five Thousand

10 On their return [z]the apostles told him all that they had done. [a]And he took them and
withdrew apart to a town called Bethsaida. **11** When the crowds learned it, they followed
him, and he [b]welcomed them and [c]spoke to them of the kingdom of God and [c]cured those
who had need of healing. **12** Now [d]the day began to wear away, and the twelve came and
said to him, [e]"Send the crowd away to go into the surrounding villages and countryside to
find lodging and get provisions, for we are here in a desolate place." **13** But he said to them,
[f]"You give them something to eat." They said, "We have no more than [g]five loaves and two
fish—unless we are to go and buy food for all these people." **14** For there were about five
thousand men. And he said to his disciples, "Have them sit down in groups of about fifty
each." **15** And they did so, and had them all sit down. **16** And taking the five loaves and the
two fish, [h]he looked up to heaven and [i]said a blessing over them. Then he broke the loaves
and gave them to the disciples to set before the crowd. **17** And they all ate and were satisfied.
And what was left over was picked up, twelve baskets of broken pieces.

[1] Greek *chiton*, a long garment worn under the cloak next to the skin

Luke 9:6, where the work of the disciples is described as "preaching the gospel and healing" (for the meaning of "the kingdom of God," see Introduction: Key Themes). **he sent them out**. The verbal form (Gk. *apostellō*) of the noun "apostle" (Gk. *apostolos*).

9:3 Take nothing for your journey. See notes on Matt. 10:9–10 and Mark 6:8–9. Perhaps this is due to the brevity of their mission and to teach them to trust God to supply their needs (Luke 12:22–31). **no staff**. According to Mark 6:8, the disciples *were* allowed to take a staff. Here in Luke's account, Jesus is probably not prohibiting a staff altogether but prohibiting taking an extra one (as Luke 10:4 prohibits extra sandals). **bag**. A knapsack for carrying provisions.

9:4 whatever house. The Twelve were not to go from house to house, possibly to seek better housing (cf. 10:7), but were to establish their headquarters within the hospitality of one home, as a base for ministering in the community.

9:5 wherever they do not receive you. "Receive" is used elsewhere with respect to welcoming and receiving God's word (8:13), Jesus (9:48, 53), Jesus' followers (vv. 5, 48), and the kingdom of God (18:17). **shake off the dust from your feet** (cf. 10:11; Acts 13:51; notes on Matt. 10:14 and Mark 6:11). This visibly illustrates the future judgment of those who reject Christ's messengers (Luke 10:11–15).

9:7–9 *Herod Antipas Is Perplexed by Jesus.* This section picks up the question of 8:25 ("Who then is this?") and provides an interlude to Luke's report of the mission of the Twelve (9:1–6, 10).

9:7–8 Herod the tetrarch (see 3:1 and note on Matt. 14:1). As a careful historian (see note on Luke 1:2–3), Luke uses the proper title ("tetrarch") to describe Herod Antipas rather than the less precise, general term "king" (Matt. 14:9; Mark 6:14, 25). Herod **heard about all that was happening**, perhaps due to the mission of the Twelve (Luke 9:1–6). **it was said by some**. On the various misunderstandings of Jesus' identity, see note on Mark 6:14b–15.

9:8 Elijah had appeared. See note on Mark 6:14b–15. **one of the prophets**. Like Moses (Deut. 18:15) or Jeremiah (Matt. 16:14). Cf. John 6:14. **had risen**. The term is used to describe Jesus' resurrection (Luke 16:31; 18:33; 24:7, 46; Acts 2:24), which would indicate that a literal return from the dead is probably meant.

9:9 John I beheaded. For a fuller account of this story, see Matt. 14:1–12; Mark 6:14–29; and notes. **And he sought to see him** foreshadows Luke 13:31 and 23:6–12 and refers to either Herod Antipas's desire to see Jesus perform a miracle (23:8) or his desire to kill him (13:31).

9:10–17 *Jesus Feeds the 5,000.* When the Twelve returned from their mission (cf. vv. 1–6), Jesus sought to spend some time with them in private (v. 10). But they were soon found by "the crowds" (v. 11). Jesus performed many miracles of healing, then miraculously provided a meal.

9:10 The **apostles** (cf. note on Rom. 1:1), the "twelve" (Luke 9:12), and the "disciples" (vv. 14, 16) are used interchangeably here. **All that they had done** refers to their use of Jesus' delegated power and authority in the casting out of demons, healings, and preaching (vv. 1–2). **Bethsaida** was just northeast of where the Jordan flows into the Sea of Galilee from the north. Research since the 1980s has focused on et-Tell as the site for Bethsaida. This site does have residential remains from around NT times (including an apparent "fisherman's house" with ancient fishing equipment) atop an earlier Iron Age (OT-era) settlement. Excavation geologists suggest that the Sea of Galilee originally extended closer to this site than it does today.

9:11 kingdom of God. Jesus' and the apostles' message was identical (cf. vv. 2, 6 with 4:43; 8:1). **cured those who had need of healing**. As in 9:6, "healing" receives more emphasis than casting out demons; probably the need for exorcism was less common than the need for healing.

9:12 Send the crowd away. The disciples manifest a sincere concern for the crowd but have forgotten Jesus' miracles in 8:22–56 and their own in 9:6.

9:14 about five thousand men. See note on John 6:10–11.

9:15 And they did so. As in 5:5, the disciples' obedience precedes understanding.

9:16 looked up to heaven. See note on Mark 6:41–42. With the exception of "looked up," a praying gesture, all of these actions (**taking, said a blessing, broke, gave**) are found in the accounts of the Last Supper (Matt. 26:26; Mark 14:22; Luke 22:19; cf. also 1 Cor. 11:23–24).

9:17 twelve baskets. See note on Mark 6:43.

Peter Confesses Jesus as the Christ

18 [j]Now it happened that as he was praying alone, the disciples were with him. And
he asked them, "Who do the crowds say that I am?" 19 And they answered, [k]"John the
Baptist. But others say, [l]Elijah, and others, that one of the prophets of old has risen."
20 Then he said to them, "But who do you say that I am?" And Peter answered, [m]"The
Christ of God."

Jesus Foretells His Death

21 [n]And he strictly charged and commanded them to tell this to no one, 22 [o]saying, [p]"The
Son of Man must [q]suffer many things and [r]be rejected by the elders and chief priests and
scribes, and be killed, and on [s]the third day be raised."

Take Up Your Cross and Follow Jesus

23 And he said to all, "If anyone would come after me, let him [t]deny himself and [u]take up
his cross [v]daily and follow me. 24 For [u]whoever would save his life will lose it, but whoever
loses his life for my sake will save it. 25 [w]For what does it profit a man if he gains the whole
world and loses or forfeits himself? 26 For [x]whoever is ashamed of me and of my words,
of him will the Son of Man be ashamed [y]when he comes in [z]his glory and the glory of the
Father and of [a]the holy angels. 27 But I tell you truly, there are some standing here who
will not [b]taste death [c]until they see the kingdom of God."

18 [j]For ver. 18-20, see Matt. 16:13-16; Mark 8:27-29
19 [k]ver. 7; Matt. 14:2; Mark 6:14 [l]ver. 8; Mark 6:15; [Matt. 17:10; Mark 9:11; John 1:21]
20 [m]ch. 23:35; Acts 3:18; Rev. 12:10; See Matt. 1:17
21 [n]Matt. 16:20; Mark 8:30; See Matt. 12:16
22 [o]For ver. 22-27, see Matt. 16:21-28; Mark 8:31–9:1 [p]ch. 18:31; [ch. 13:33] [q]ch. 24:7; Matt. 17:12, 22, 23; Mark 9:30, 31 [r]ch. 17:25; 1 Pet. 2:4; [ch. 20:17] [s]ch. 18:33; 24:7, 46; See Matt. 27:63; John 2:19
23 [t][2 Tim. 2:12, 13] [u]See Matt. 10:38, 39 [v]1 Cor. 15:31
24 [u][See ver. 23 above]
25 [w][ch. 12:20]
26 [x]Rom. 1:16; 2 Tim. 1:8, 12, 16; Heb. 11:16; 1 John 2:28; [Matt. 10:33] [y]Dan. 7:10, 13; Zech. 14:5; Matt. 24:30; 25:31; 26:64; John 1:51; Acts 1:11; 1 Thess. 1:10; 4:16; Jude 14; Rev. 1:7; [Deut. 33:2] [z]Matt. 19:28; 25:31; Mark 10:37; John 17:24 [a]Acts 10:22; Rev. 14:10; [Matt. 13:41; 16:27] **27** [b]John 8:52; Heb. 2:9 [c][ch. 21:31, 32; Matt. 10:23; 23:36; 24:34; Mark 13:30]

9:18–20 *Peter Confesses Jesus as the Christ.* **praying alone**. For Jesus praying before important events, see Introduction: Key Themes. Here he may have prayed that his disciples would truly grasp who he is. **John the Baptist**. The disciples repeat the same possibilities mentioned in vv. 7–8 (cf. note on Matt. 16:14). **But who do you say**. "You" is plural and is emphasized in the Greek. **Peter**, spokesman for the disciples, **answered, "The Christ of God."** (On Peter's confession, see notes on Matt. 16:16 and Mark 8:29b–30.) Jesus' identity as the "Christ"—confessed by angels (Luke 2:11); by the Gospel narrator (2:26); by demons (4:41); and by Jesus himself (4:18)—is now confessed for the first time by the Twelve. For "Christ," see note on 2:11. Even with this confession, the disciples still have more to learn about the kind of Messiah Jesus will be, as the next passage shows (9:21–22). What the disciples do understand at this point is that Jesus is more than a prophet—that is, that Jesus' role as the Messiah is central to the inauguration of the new era of the kingdom.

Predictions, Reminders, and Proofs of the Death and Resurrection of Jesus in the Gospel of Luke

9:22	"The Son of Man must suffer many things and be rejected . . . and be killed, and on the third day be raised."
9:44	"The Son of Man is about to be delivered into the hands of men."
12:50	"I have a baptism to be baptized with."
13:32	"I cast out demons and perform cures today and tomorrow, and the third day I finish my course."
13:33	"for it cannot be that a prophet should perish away from Jerusalem."
17:25	"But first he must suffer many things and be rejected by this generation."
18:32	"he will be delivered over to the Gentiles and will be mocked and shamefully treated and spit upon."
18:33	"after flogging him, they will kill him, and on the third day he will rise."
24:6–7	"Remember how he told you, while he was still in Galilee, that the Son of Man must be delivered into the hands of sinful men and be crucified and on the third day rise."
24:25–26	". . . slow of heart to believe all that the prophets have spoken! Was it not necessary that the Christ should suffer these things and enter into his glory?"
24:46	"Thus it is written, that the Christ should suffer and on the third day rise from the dead."

9:21–22 *Jesus Foretells His Death.* For the first time (cf. vv. 43b–45), Jesus clearly teaches the Twelve that his role as God's anointed Messiah (Christ) involves suffering and death. **tell this to no one**. Peter's confession (v. 20) is correct, but proclaiming it widely at this time would be misunderstood because of Jewish nationalistic expectations and would make Jesus' ministry more difficult, as people tried to force him into the role of a political and military leader against the Roman army. That Jesus **must suffer** refers to the necessity of God's providential plan being fulfilled in his death. For the **Son of Man**, see note on Matt. 8:20. **by the elders and chief priests and scribes**. The use of a single article (in English, "the") emphasizes in Greek the unity of this group. The "chief priests" are not the high priests but members of the most prominent priestly families. Jesus will be **raised** to life by God.

9:23–27 *Jesus Teaches the Disciples.* The following teachings on discipleship are addressed not just to the Twelve but to "all" (v. 23).

9:23 Come after me means to become a disciple (cf. 14:27) and requires that a disciple: (1) **deny himself** (not simply denying certain things but denying personal control of one's life); (2) **take up his cross** (cf. 14:27; notes on Matt. 10:38 and Mark 8:34; make a commitment that will lead to rejection and possibly even death); and (3) **follow me** (following the example and teachings of Jesus). In Jesus' day, "follow me" also meant joining the company of his disciples who traveled in ministry with Jesus around Palestine.

9:24 save his life . . . lose it. See note on Mark 8:35.

9:25 Gaining even the **whole world** is infinitely less valuable than one's eternal destiny in relation to God (see note on Mark 8:35).

9:26 Being **ashamed** of Jesus means to deny any link with him (cf. 22:54–61) and is the opposite of acknowledging him as one's Lord and teacher (12:8–9; see note on Mark 8:38). The person and message of Jesus (**me** and **my words**) are indivisible. **When he comes in his glory** refers to the second coming. Luke emphasizes the glory of Jesus (cf. Luke 21:27; 24:26).

9:27 truly. See note on 4:24. **Some standing here** refers to Peter, John, and James, who will witness the transfiguration. See note on Matt. 16:28.

The Transfiguration

28 [d]Now about eight days after these sayings he took with him [e]Peter and John and
James and [f]went up on the mountain to pray. 29 And as he was praying, the appearance
of his face was [g]altered, and [h]his clothing became dazzling white. 30 And behold, two
men were talking with him, Moses and Elijah, 31 who appeared in glory and spoke of
his departure,[1] which he was about to accomplish at Jerusalem. 32 Now Peter and those
who were with him [i]were heavy with sleep, but when they became fully awake [j]they
saw his glory and the two men who stood with him. 33 And as the men were parting
from him, Peter said to Jesus, "Master, it is good that we are here. Let us make three
[k]tents, one for you and one for Moses and one for Elijah"—[l]not knowing what he said.
34 As he was saying these things, [m]a cloud came and overshadowed them, and they were
afraid as they entered the cloud. 35 And [m]a voice came out of the cloud, saying, "This
is my Son, [n]my Chosen One;[2] [o]listen to him!" 36 And when the voice had spoken, Jesus
was found alone. [p]And they kept silent and told no one in those days anything of what
they had seen.

Jesus Heals a Boy with an Unclean Spirit

37 [q]On the next day, when they had come down from the mountain, a great crowd met
him. 38 And behold, a man from the crowd cried out, "Teacher, I beg you to look at my
son, for [r]he is my only child. 39 And behold, a spirit seizes him, and he suddenly cries out.
It convulses him so that he foams at the mouth, and shatters him, and will hardly leave
him. 40 And I begged your disciples to cast it out, but [s]they could not." 41 Jesus answered,
"O [t]faithless and twisted generation, [u]how long am I to be with you and bear with you?
Bring your son here." 42 While he was coming, the demon threw him to the ground and
convulsed him. But Jesus [v]rebuked the unclean spirit and healed the boy, and [w]gave him
back to his father. 43 And all were astonished at [x]the majesty of God.

[1] Greek *exodus* [2] Some manuscripts *my Beloved*

28 [d]For ver. 28-36, see Matt. 17:1-8; Mark 9:2-8 [e]ch. 8:51; Mark 14:33 [f]See Matt. 14:23
29 [g]Mark 16:12 (Gk.) [h]Dan. 7:9; [Ps. 104:2; Matt. 28:3]
32 [i]Dan. 8:18; Matt. 26:43 [j]See John 1:14
33 [k][Neh. 8:15] [l][Mark 9:6; 14:40]
34 [m]2 Pet. 1:17; [Ex. 24:15, 16]
35 [m][See ver. 34 above] [n]ch. 23:35; Isa. 42:1; [Ps. 89:3; Isa. 49:7] [o]Acts 3:22
36 [p]Matt. 17:9; Mark 9:9, 10
37 [q]For ver. 37-42, see Matt. 17:14-19; Mark 9:14-28
38 [r]See ch. 7:12
40 [s][ver. 1; ch. 10:17; Matt. 10:1; Mark 6:7]
41 [t]Phil. 2:15; [John 20:27] [u][John 14:9]
42 [v]ch. 4:35, 39; Zech. 3:2; Matt. 8:26; Mark 1:25; Jude 9 [w]See ch. 7:15
43 [x]2 Pet. 1:16

9:28–36 *The Transfiguration.* The question "Who [then] is this?" (8:25; 9:9), answered by Peter in v. 20, is now answered decisively by God himself.

9:28 About eight days after (probably an inclusive reckoning of time; cf. Mark 9:2) indicates that this account should be understood in light of Luke 9:20–27. Peter, John, and James see the kingdom coming in power at the transfiguration. **Peter and John and James**. Cf. 8:51. **mountain**. See note on Matt. 17:1. **to pray**. Perhaps Jesus prayed that the three disciples would see him in his glory. See Introduction: Key Themes.

9:29 his face was altered. The transfiguration is not an illumination of Jesus from the outside (cf. Ex. 34:29–35) but from the inside. **dazzling white** (lit., "bright as a flash of lightning"). The transfiguration provides a glimpse of the future glory of the Christ (Luke 9:20), the Son of Man, at his second coming (vv. 26–27) when he comes in the cloud of the glory of God. Cf. v. 26; 21:27; 2 Pet. 1:16–18; Rev. 1:7. It likewise gives a glimpse into the reality that Christ is the transcendent Son of God, sent by the Father for the salvation of his people—i.e., for all who believe in him, both Jews and Gentiles.

9:30 Moses and Elijah represent the Law and the Prophets; their appearance refutes the incorrect guesses of vv. 8, 19, indicating that Jesus is the fulfillment of both (cf. note on Mark 9:4).

9:31 Jesus' **departure** (Gk. *exodos*) is his future death, resurrection, and ascension (all of which would take place **at Jerusalem**).

9:33–34 Let us make three tents. This suggestion is a mistake, as indicated by Luke's comment (**not knowing what he said**) and the Father's pronouncement ("this is my Son, my Chosen One," v. 35, confirming v. 20). The **cloud** is a manifestation of God's presence (see note on Matt. 17:5).

9:35 This is my Son. Cf. 3:22 and note on Mark 9:7. **Listen to him** means to give attention to Jesus' teaching above all else, even above the Law (Moses) and the Prophets (Elijah) of the OT (not that they are any less the Word of God, but that Jesus' teaching supersedes and rightly interprets the OT for the new age of the kingdom of God and the new covenant). Jesus is not merely equal to Moses and Elijah; he is far greater. All the OT pointed to him (see Luke 24:27). "Listen to him" also alludes to Deut. 18:15, indicating that Jesus is the prophet that Moses predicted "the LORD your God will raise up for you."

9:36 Kept silent . . . in those days contrasts the situation in Jesus' day with that of Luke's day, the time after Pentecost when Peter, James, and John freely proclaimed this event (e.g., 2 Pet. 1:17).

9:37–43a *The Healing of a Boy with an Unclean Spirit.* This is an abbreviated version (7 verses) of Mark 9:14–29 (16 verses), also recounted in Matt. 17:14–20.

9:37 the next day. This close tie with vv. 28–36 suggests that the account provides an example of Jesus' glory in v. 32 (cf. v. 43a).

9:39 a spirit seizes him. In the parallel account in Matt. 17:15, 18 the demon is associated with epilepsy; but see Matt. 4:24, where epilepsy is distinguished from demon possession. **will hardly leave him**. The demon continually plagued the child.

9:40 they could not. The disciples' inability to heal highlights Jesus' greater ability. Mark more explicitly points to the weak faith of the disciples (see notes on Mark 9:18–29).

9:41 O faithless and twisted generation. See note on Mark 9:19. The first of several such references (cf. Luke 11:30–32, 50–51; 17:25). It is addressed to the disciples (9:40) and the "all" of v. 43a. For "generation," see note on 7:31–34.

9:43a all were astonished. Cf. 2:48; 4:32; cf. also 8:25; 11:14. The healing performed by Jesus (9:37–42) is credited to the **majesty of God**. Compare the close tie between the glory of the Son and of the Father (v. 26), the interchangeableness of declaring what God has done and what Jesus has done (8:39), and being astonished/marveling with respect to God and Jesus (9:43).

9:43b–45 *Jesus Again Foretells His Death.* Once again (cf. vv. 21–22) Jesus warns his disciples of his impending, violent death.

9:43b The **marveling** of the "crowd" (cf. v. 37) is not necessarily due to faith (cf. vv. 41, 43a).

Jesus Again Foretells His Death

[y]But while they were all marveling at everything he was doing, Jesus[1] said [z]to his disciples,
44"Let these words sink into your ears: [z]The Son of Man is about to be delivered into the
hands of men." **45** [a]But they did not understand this saying, and [b]it was concealed from them,
so that they might not perceive it. And they were afraid to ask him about this saying.

Who Is the Greatest?

46 [c]An argument arose among them as to which of them was the greatest. **47** But Jesus,
knowing the reasoning of their hearts, took a child and put him by his side **48** and said to
them, [d]"Whoever receives this child in my name receives me, and [d]whoever receives me
receives him who sent me. For [e]he who is least among you all is the one who is great."

Anyone Not Against Us Is For Us

49 [f]John answered, "Master, we saw someone [g]casting out demons in your name, and
[h]we tried to stop him, because he does not follow with us." **50** But Jesus said to him, "Do
not stop him, [i]for the one who is not against you is for you."

A Samaritan Village Rejects Jesus

51 When the days drew near for [j]him to be taken up, [k]he set his face [l]to go to Jerusalem.
52 And [m]he sent messengers ahead of him, who went and entered a village of [n]the Samaritans,
to make preparations for him. **53** But [o]the people did not receive him, because [p]his face was
set toward Jerusalem. **54** And when his disciples James and John saw it, they said, "Lord, do
you want us to tell [q]fire to come down from heaven and consume them?"[2] **55** But he turned
and rebuked them.[3] **56** And they went on to another village.

The Cost of Following Jesus

57 As they were going [r]along the road, [s]someone said to him, "I will follow you wherever
you go." **58** And Jesus said to him, "Foxes have holes, and birds of the air have nests, but the

[1] Greek *he* [2] Some manuscripts add *as Elijah did* [3] Some manuscripts add *and he said, "You do not know what manner of spirit you are of; for the Son of Man came not to destroy people's lives but to save them"*

43 [y]For ver. 43-45, see Matt. 17:22, 23; Mark 9:30-32 [z]ver. 22
44 [z][See ver. 43 above]
45 [a]ch. 2:50; 18:34; Mark 6:52; John 10:6; 12:16; 16:17-19; [Matt. 17:13; Mark 9:10] [b]ch. 18:34; [ch. 24:16]
46 [c]For ver. 46-48, see Matt. 18:1-5; Mark 9:33-37; [Matt. 20:20-28; Mark 10:35-45]
48 [d][Matt. 10:40, 42] [e]ch. 22:26
49 [f]For ver. 49, 50, see Mark 9:38-40 [g]ch. 10:17; Matt. 7:22; Mark 16:17; Acts 19:13; [Matt. 12:27] [h][Num. 11:28]
50 [i][ch. 11:23; Matt. 12:30]
51 [j]See Mark 16:19 [k]2 Kgs. 12:17; Isa. 50:7; Jer. 42:15 [l]ch. 13:22; 17:11; 18:31; 19:11, 28
52 [m][ch. 10:1] [n]See Matt. 10:5
53 [o]John 4:9; [ch. 10:33] [p]John 4:20
54 [q]See Rev. 13:13
57 [r]ver. 51 [s]For ver. 57-60, see Matt. 8:19-22

9:44 [You] **let these words**. The subject "you" is emphasized in the Greek, underscoring the importance of heeding Jesus' second prediction of his suffering. **The Son of Man is about to be delivered** (by God) **into the hands of men**. See note on Mark 9:30–31.

9:45 The disciples' lack of understanding is due to the meaning of Jesus' words being **concealed from them** by God. Compare an almost identical statement in 18:34. **And they were afraid to ask him**, probably because they could comprehend enough of what he was saying that they did not want to know more.

9:46–48 *Who Is the Greatest?* The disciples' inability to understand Jesus' forthcoming suffering is linked to their own desire for greatness.

9:46 Which . . . was the greatest can refer to having the greatest authority, deserving the most preferential treatment, being most valuable, or being most favored by God (cf. note on Mark 9:34). Any such comparison, however, was wrong.

9:47 Jesus, knowing . . . their hearts. See note on 4:23. **took a child . . . by his side**. See note on Mark 9:36–37.

9:48 receives this child . . . receives me; receives me receives him who sent me. An example of "step parallelism" (cf. 10:16), in which the first thought is raised a step higher in the second thought: a child is received as a representative of Jesus; Jesus is received as a representative of God. **he who is least**. The one who is servant of all and thus has lowly status (Mark 9:35). **who is great**. In God's eyes (cf. Luke 14:11; 18:14; 22:26), not according to the disciples' mistaken understanding of greatness (e.g., 9:46).

9:49–50 *Anyone Not against Us Is for Us.* **Because he does not follow with us** probably refers to a believer outside the circle of the Twelve. **The one who is not against you is for you** is the reverse of 11:23. The two sayings should be seen as complementary. Those who cast out demons in the name of Jesus are his friends; those who attribute Jesus' casting out of demons to Beelzebul, and thus do not believe in him, are his enemies (11:15, 23). Cf. note on Mark 9:40.

9:51–19:27 *The Journey to Jerusalem.* Amid all the activities of his ministry of teaching, healing, and making disciples, Jesus "set his face" (9:51) for his final journey to Jerusalem.

9:51–13:21 *The First Mention of the Journey to Jerusalem.* Jesus resolves to fulfill the mission for which God sent him into the world ("set his face," 9:51; cf. "must" in 9:22; also Mark 10:45) and accomplish his "exodus" in Jerusalem (see note on Luke 9:31).

9:51–56 *The Mission to Samaria.* As Jesus and his disciples go south from Galilee to Jerusalem, they enter and minister in Samaria.

9:51 Taken up means "taken up to heaven." The Greek noun used here (*analēmpsis*) corresponds to the verb (*analambanō*) translated "taken up" in Acts 1:2, 11, 22; 1 Tim. 3:16; all instances refer to Christ's ascension. **He set his face to go to Jerusalem** provides the theme for Luke 9:51–19:27, the largest section of Luke's Gospel, and points toward Jesus' cross (23:33), resurrection (24:6), and ascension into heaven (24:51). Cf. "set my face like flint," Isa. 50:7.

9:52 a village of the Samaritans. For Jewish-Samaritan relations, see notes on John 4:4 and 4:9; cf. John 8:48. **to make preparations**. To arrange housing.

9:53 did not receive him, because his face was set toward Jerusalem (cf. v. 51). The Samaritans rejected the messengers most likely because the Samaritans did not accept Jerusalem as the place where God should be worshiped (see John 4:20), and also because Jesus was going there to die, and the cost of following him was high.

9:54–55 Jesus rejects the suggestion of **James and John ("tell fire to come down")**, for his ministry at his first coming is not to bring judgment (cf. John 3:17), and not to compel people to follow him through threat of immediate punishment, but to bring the free offer of the gospel (cf. Matt. 11:28).

9:57–62 *The Cost of Following Jesus.* Jesus encounters three would-be disciples. The word "follow" plays a key role in each encounter (vv. 57, 59, 61).

9:58 The Son of Man has nowhere to lay his head is Jesus' challenge

60 [t][John 5:25] [u]ver. 2
61 [v][1 Kgs. 19:20]
62 [w][Phil. 3:13]

Chapter 10

1 [x]Ex. 24:1, 9; Num. 11:16 [y][ch. 9:2, 52]
2 [z]Matt. 9:37, 38; John 4:35 [a][2 Thess. 3:1]
3 [b]Matt. 10:16; [John 17:18]
4 [c]For ver. 4-12, [ch. 9:1-5; 22:35; Matt. 10:9-15; Mark 6:8-11] [d]2 Kgs. 4:29
5 [e]1 Sam. 25:6
6 [f][Ps. 35:13 (Heb.)]
7 [g]See 1 Tim. 5:18
9 [h]ver. 11; See Matt. 3:2
11 [i]Acts 13:51; [Neh. 5:13; Acts 18:6] [j]ver. 9
12 [k]See Matt. 10:15 [l]Matt. 7:22
13 [m]For ver. 13-15, see Matt. 11:21-23 [n][Isa. 23; Ezek. 28:2-24; Amos 1:9, 10]

Son of Man has nowhere to lay his head." 59 To another he said, "Follow me." But he said,
"Lord, let me first go and bury my father." 60 And Jesus[1] said to him, "Leave [t]the dead to bury
their own dead. But as for you, go and [u]proclaim the kingdom of God." 61 Yet another said, "I
will follow you, Lord, [v]but let me first say farewell to those at my home." 62 Jesus said to him,
[w]"No one who puts his hand to the plow and looks back is fit for the kingdom of God."

Jesus Sends Out the Seventy-Two

10 After this the Lord appointed [x]seventy-two[2] others and [y]sent them on ahead of him,
two by two, into every town and place where he himself was about to go. 2 [z]And he
said to them, "The harvest is plentiful, but the laborers are few. [a]Therefore pray earnestly
to the Lord of the harvest to send out laborers into his harvest. 3 Go your way; [b]behold, I
am sending you out as lambs in the midst of wolves. 4 [c]Carry no moneybag, no knapsack,
no sandals, and [d]greet no one on the road. 5 Whatever house you enter, first say, [e]'Peace be
to this house!' 6 And if a son of peace is there, your peace will rest upon him. But if not, [f]it
will return to you. 7 And remain in the same house, eating and drinking what they provide,
for [g]the laborer deserves his wages. Do not go from house to house. 8 Whenever you enter a
town and they receive you, eat what is set before you. 9 Heal the sick in it and say to them,
[h]'The kingdom of God has come near to you.' 10 But whenever you enter a town and they do
not receive you, go into its streets and say, 11 [i]'Even the dust of your town that clings to our
feet we wipe off against you. Nevertheless know this, that [j]the kingdom of God has come
near.' 12 I tell you, [k]it will be more bearable on [l]that day for Sodom than for that town.

Woe to Unrepentant Cities

13 [m]"Woe to you, Chorazin! Woe to you, Bethsaida! For if the mighty works done in you
had been done in [n]Tyre and Sidon, they would have repented long ago, sitting in sackcloth

[1] Greek *he* [2] Some manuscripts *seventy;* also verse 17

to a would-be follower, reminding him that the path of following Jesus is not easy and comfortable, for ultimately Jesus is not at home in this world. In this and the following two brief stories (vv. 59–62), Luke does not tell his readers how the person responded.

9:59 To **go and bury** a deceased parent was an important duty, and Jesus clearly upholds honoring one's parents (Matt. 15:1–9). The request seems reasonable on the surface, but this man's first response was not to obey Jesus immediately (as others did, cf. Luke 5:21, 28) but to make an excuse for not following him. Burial at this time in Judaism often involved a year-long period from the time when the body was first buried until a year later when the bones of the deceased were placed in an ossuary box. Though this was a basic family obligation, Jesus is teaching the priority of the kingdom over family.

9:60 Leave the dead to bury their own dead constitutes a pun in which "dead" means both "spiritually dead" (cf. 15:24, 32) and "physically dead." Here (as in 14:25–26) Jesus insists that following him must take precedence over every other relationship and obligation. This does not imply that Jesus' followers can never care for their family obligations, but when they do, it must be out of obedience to Jesus, not *instead of* obedience to Jesus. In this man's case, Jesus was clearly not his highest commitment (see 9:59).

9:61 As in v. 59, this man's halfhearted discipleship begins with a "but": **I will follow you, Lord, but**. This recalls 1 Kings 19:19–21, where Elijah permitted Elisha to **say farewell**; but Jesus does not permit this. Jesus' summons to discipleship takes precedence over everything else.

9:62 Anyone who **puts his hand to the plow** has to keep looking forward to guide the plow, for if he **looks back** the plow will quickly veer off course.

10:1–24 *The Mission of the Seventy-two.* Having sent out the Twelve (9:1–6), Jesus now sends 72 of his disciples on a mission of healing and gospel proclamation.

10:1 seventy-two. Many very old and reliable Greek manuscripts have "seventy-two" here and in v. 17, while many other old and reliable manuscripts have "seventy," and all interpreters agree that it is difficult to decide about which number was in the original of Luke's Gospel. Most modern translations have decided in favor of "seventy-two," based on basic principles for determining manuscript readings. In any case, no doctrinal issue is at stake, and the number probably has symbolic significance representing the number of nations in the world (cf. Genesis 10). Sending them out two by two fulfills the OT requirement for two witnesses (Deut. 17:6; 19:15).

10:3 I am sending (Gk. *apostellō*) **you**. Although only the Twelve are named "apostles" (6:13; 9:10; 22:14; Acts 1:26), others are also "sent ones." **as lambs in the midst of wolves**. See note on Matt. 10:16; also John 10:12. "Lambs" implies that the disciples should not attempt to gain converts by force; the spread of the gospel is to come through preaching the "good news" of Jesus Christ and inviting hearers to respond willingly (cf. Matt. 11:28; John 1:11–12; Acts 3:19; Rom. 10:14–17; Rev. 22:17). The principle that genuine religious commitment cannot be compelled by force sets Christianity in clear contrast to significant segments of Islam, Hinduism, and many tribal religions.

10:4 No sandals probably means not to take an extra pair, since Jesus is telling them what they should not **carry**. They are to **greet no one**. Such greetings were lengthy and time-consuming (cf. 2 Kings 4:29).

10:5 Peace. See notes on Matt. 10:13 and John 14:27.

10:6 son of peace. One who has found the peace that comes with salvation. **it will return to you**. If faith is not present, the blessing will be nullified.

10:7 eating and drinking what they provide. Accept whatever food they offer. **for the laborer deserves his wages**. Paul alludes to this saying in 1 Cor. 9:14 and quotes it as "Scripture" in 1 Tim. 5:18.

10:9 Heal the sick assumes the same bestowal of power and authority as in 9:1 (cf. 10:19). **The kingdom of God has come**. See 9:2; 11:20; 16:16; 17:21. See also Introduction: Key Themes. The "kingdom of God" in this present age is not an earthly, military, or political kingdom but is the rule and reign of God in people's hearts and lives, and it is manifested both in people following Jesus and his teaching, and in the miraculous healings that God brought through the disciples, giving a foretaste of resurrected life in the age to come.

10:10 go into its streets. The symbolic act of judgment against a town will be visible and public (cf. 9:5).

10:11 the dust of your town that clings to our feet we wipe off against you. See notes on Matt. 10:14 and Mark 6:11. Jesus repeats for emphasis the heart of the message: **the kingdom of God has come near** (cf. Luke 10:9).

10:12 more bearable on that day. See note on Matt. 10:15.

10:13–14 The judgment of **Tyre and Sidon** will be less severe than that of **Chorazin** and **Bethsaida** (9:10–17), for the former cities would have repented had they experienced Jesus' ministry (on these cities, see notes

and ashes. 14 [o]But it will be more bearable in the judgment for [n]Tyre and Sidon than for
you. 15 And you, Capernaum, [p]will you be exalted to heaven? You shall be brought down
to [q]Hades.

16 [r]"The one who hears you hears me, and [s]the one who rejects you rejects me, and [t]the
one who rejects me rejects him who sent me."

The Return of the Seventy-Two

17 [u]The seventy-two returned with joy, saying, "Lord, [v]even the demons are subject to
us in your name!" 18 And he said to them, [w]"I saw Satan [x]fall like lightning from heaven.
19 Behold, I have given you authority [y]to tread on serpents and scorpions, and over all the
power of [z]the enemy, and [a]nothing shall hurt you. 20 [b]Nevertheless, do not rejoice in this,
that the spirits are subject to you, but rejoice that [c]your names are written in heaven."

Jesus Rejoices in the Father's Will

21 [d]In that same hour [e]he rejoiced [f]in the Holy Spirit and said, "I thank you, Father, [g]Lord
of heaven and earth, that [h]you have hidden these things from the wise and understanding and [i]revealed them to little children; yes, Father, for [j]such was your gracious will.[1]
22 [k]All things have been handed over to me by my Father, and no one knows who the Son
is [k]except the Father, or who the Father is [k]except the Son and anyone [l]to whom the Son
chooses to reveal him."

23 Then turning to the disciples he said privately, [m]"Blessed are the eyes that see what
you see! 24 For I tell you [n]that many prophets and kings desired to see what you see, and
did not see it, and to hear what you hear, and did not hear it."

The Parable of the Good Samaritan

25 [o]And behold, a [p]lawyer stood up to [q]put him to the test, saying, "Teacher, what shall I
do to [r]inherit eternal life?" 26 He said to him, "What is written in the Law? How do you read
it?" 27 And he answered, [s]"You shall love the Lord your God with all your heart and with all
your soul and with all your strength and with all your mind, and [t]your neighbor as yourself."
28 And he said to him, "You have answered correctly; [u]do this, and you will live."

[1] *Or for so it pleased you well*

28 [u]Lev. 18:5; Neh. 9:29; Ezek. 20:11; Rom. 10:5; Gal. 3:12

14 [o][ch. 12:47, 48] [n][See ver. 13 above]
15 [p]Cited from Isa. 14:13-15 [q]ch. 16:23; Acts 2:27
16 [r]See Matt. 10:40 [s]John 12:48; 1 Thess. 4:8; [Matt. 25:45] [t]John 5:23
17 [u]ver. 1 [v]See Mark 16:17
18 [w][John 12:31; 16:11; Col. 2:15; Rev. 12:8, 9] [x][Isa. 14:12; Rev. 9:1]
19 [y]Ps. 91:13; Mark 16:18; Acts 28:5 [z]Matt. 13:39 [a]ch. 21:18; [Rom. 8:28, 39]
20 [b][Matt. 7:22, 23] [c]Ex. 32:32, 33; Ps. 69:28; Isa. 4:3; Ezek. 13:9; Dan. 12:1; Phil. 4:3; Heb. 12:23
21 [d]For ver. 21, 22, see Matt. 11:25-27 [e][Isa. 53:11] [f][Mark 12:36] [g]See Acts 17:24 [h]Job 37:24; 1 Cor. 1:19-27; 2 Cor. 3:14 [i]Ps. 8:2; Matt. 21:16; [ch. 8:10; Matt. 16:17] [j][ch. 12:32]
22 [k]John 1:18; 6:46; 7:29; 8:19; 10:15; 17:25; See Matt. 28:18 [l][John 17:26]
23 [m]Matt. 13:16, 17; [Matt. 16:17]
24 [n]Heb. 11:13; 1 Pet. 1:10-12; [John 8:56]
25 [o]For ver. 25-28, [ch. 18:18-20; Matt. 19:16-19; 22:34-39; Mark 10:17-19] [p]See ch. 7:30 [q]See John 8:6 [r]Matt. 19:29; 25:34, 46
27 [s]Matt. 22:37; Mark 12:30; Cited from Deut. 6:5 [t]Cited from Lev. 19:18; See Matt. 19:19

on Matt. 11:20–24; Mark 6:45; 7:24; Luke 9:10). **sitting in sackcloth and ashes**. An expression of mourning and repentance. "Sackcloth" is rough cloth made from goat's hair; "ashes" were either placed on the head (2 Sam. 13:19) or sat upon (Job 2:8; Jonah 3:6).

10:15 Capernaum will receive the severest judgment because they witnessed Jesus' ministry and miracles to such a great extent (4:23; 7:1–10; cf. Matt. 4:13; on the city, see note on Mark 1:21). **will you be exalted to heaven?** Due to having witnessed and rejected Jesus' ministry, they will be **brought down to Hades**, the place of the unrighteous dead (Luke 16:22–26).

10:16 The one who hears you hears me emphasizes the solidarity of Jesus and his disciples (cf. 9:48; Matt. 9:16).

10:17 Having completed their mission (cf. vv. 1–12), the **seventy-two** disciples are filled **with joy** at seeing the kingdom of God advance and people being set free from their bondage to demonic oppression. **even the demons are subject**. See v. 19.

10:18 I saw Satan fall can also be translated, "I was watching Satan fall" (imperfect tense of Gk. *theōreō*, "to see"). It is not clear whether Jesus is speaking of a vision by which he saw something in the spiritual realm or if this is simply a graphic declaration of what has been happening, but in either case Jesus indicates that Satan's authority and power over people has been decisively broken. **Like lightning** describes the suddenness of the fall (cf. Isa. 14:12).

10:19 I have given you authority. Cf. 9:1. Jesus' great power over demons has been delegated to his disciples. **Serpents and scorpions** are physical dangers that the disciples will face in their preaching, and also symbols of demonic opposition. **nothing shall hurt you**. Cf. 21:18; Acts 28:3–5.

10:20 Nevertheless. Jesus warns against rejoicing too much in what God has done through them, for an even greater blessing is their eternal salvation: **your names are written** (by God) **in heaven** (cf. Phil. 4:3; Rev. 3:5; 20:15).

10:21 rejoiced in the Holy Spirit. Cf. 3:22; 4:1, 14, 18; and Introduction: Key Themes. **Father**. See notes on 11:2 and Matt. 6:9. **Lord of heaven and earth**. Cf. Acts 17:24. Jesus' rejoicing is primarily due to God's having **revealed** (Luke 10:22) the presence of the kingdom and Satan's fall (vv. 17–18) to **little children**, that is, to the disciples, who have childlike faith themselves (v. 23). Jesus notes with irony the **wise and understanding** of this world who nonetheless have rejected the gospel (see note on Matt. 11:25–26; cf. Luke 1:51–52; 1 Cor. 1:19).

10:22 All things . . . handed over to me. See note on Matt. 11:27. **anyone to whom the Son chooses to reveal him**. Salvation is offered only through Jesus (John 14:6; Acts 4:12).

10:25–37 *The Parable of the Good Samaritan.* This parable is an example of how the "wise and understanding" (v. 21) do not understand even the simplest commands of Scripture (cf. v. 27c with Lev. 19:18).

10:25 The **lawyer** desired only "to justify himself" (v. 29). He was not genuinely seeking to be taught by Jesus. **what shall I do . . . ?** A good question, as 18:18; Acts 2:37; 16:30 reveal (cf. also Luke 3:10, 12, 14). **Eternal life** (cf. 18:18, 30; Acts 13:46, 48) is a synonym for "entering the kingdom of God" (see note on John 3:16).

10:26 What is written in the Law? For Jesus, the OT is the definitive, unerring standard of faith and practice (cf. 18:19–20).

10:27 To **love the Lord your God** involves having faith in him and also delighting in him above all else. All the Synoptic Gospels (Matthew, Mark, and Luke) include the words **heart** (emotions, will, and deepest convictions), **soul** (the immaterial part of a person's being), and **mind** (reason; however, this term is lacking in Deut. 6:5). Matthew (22:37) alone lacks the term **strength** (how a person uses the abilities and powers that he has), an indication of the total devotion of one's entire being that is required. (See notes on Matt. 22:37–38 and Mark 12:28–31.)

29[v]ch. 16:15
30[w][ch. 18:31; 19:28]
31[x]John 1:19; [Num. 8:19]
32[x][See ver. 31 above]
33[y]See Matt. 10:5
34[z]Isa. 1:6
35[a]See Matt. 18:28
38[b]John 11:1, 19, 20; 12:2, 3 [c]ch. 19:6
39[b][See ver. 38 above] [d]ch. 8:35; [Acts 22:3]
41[e][1 Cor. 7:32-34]; See ch. 12:22
42[f]Ps. 16:5

Chapter 11

1[g]See ch. 5:33
2[h]For ver. 2-4, [Matt. 6:9-13]

29 But he, [v]desiring to justify himself, said to Jesus, "And who is my neighbor?" 30 Jesus replied, "A man [w]was going down from Jerusalem to Jericho, and he fell among robbers, who stripped him and beat him and departed, leaving him half dead. 31 Now by chance a [x]priest was going down that road, and when he saw him he passed by on the other side. 32 So likewise [x]a Levite, when he came to the place and saw him, passed by on the other side. 33 But a [y]Samaritan, as he journeyed, came to where he was, and when he saw him, he had compassion. 34 He went to him and [z]bound up his wounds, pouring on [z]oil and wine. Then he set him on his own animal and brought him to an inn and took care of him. 35 And the next day he took out two [a]denarii[1] and gave them to the innkeeper, saying, 'Take care of him, and whatever more you spend, I will repay you when I come back.' 36 Which of these three, do you think, proved to be a neighbor to the man who fell among the robbers?" 37 He said, "The one who showed him mercy." And Jesus said to him, "You go, and do likewise."

Martha and Mary

38 Now as they went on their way, Jesus[2] entered a village. And a woman named [b]Martha [c]welcomed him into her house. 39 And she had a sister called [b]Mary, who [d]sat at the Lord's feet and listened to his teaching. 40 But Martha was distracted with much serving. And she went up to him and said, "Lord, do you not care that my sister has left me to serve alone? Tell her then to help me." 41 But the Lord answered her, "Martha, Martha, you are [e]anxious and troubled about many things, 42 but one thing is necessary.[3] Mary has chosen [f]the good portion, which will not be taken away from her."

The Lord's Prayer

11 Now Jesus[4] was praying in a certain place, and when he finished, one of his disciples said to him, "Lord, teach us to pray, [g]as John taught his disciples." 2 And he said to them, [h]"When you pray, say:

[1] A *denarius* was a day's wage for a laborer [2] Greek *he* [3] Some manuscripts *few things are necessary, or only one* [4] Greek *he*

10:28 You have answered correctly. There is nothing wrong with the lawyer's answer. **do this, and you will live**. Knowledge of "What shall I do to inherit eternal life?" is insufficient. One must "do this." Jesus is about to show the lawyer that he falls far short of following these commands (see note on Mark 10:19).

10:29 Desiring to justify himself reveals the lawyer's insincerity. **who is my neighbor?** An improper question, because the lawyer was trying to exclude responsibility for others by making some people "non-neighbors." A more appropriate question would be, "How can I be a loving neighbor?"

10:30 Jericho. See notes on Matt. 20:29 and Mark 10:46. The route of the Jericho road, still visible today, included long stretches of rocky terrain that made it a useful base of operations for **robbers**. The road descended (**down**) about 3,200 feet (975 m) from Jerusalem to Jericho along this 18-mile (29-km) route.

10:31 priest. A descendant of Aaron who had priestly responsibilities in the Jerusalem temple. **passed by on the other side**. A tangible way of describing his unwillingness to love his neighbor.

10:32 Levite. A member of the tribe of Levi but not a descendant of Aaron and therefore not a priest. The Levites assisted the priests.

10:33 Samaritan. Culturally, it would have been unthinkable for a Samaritan to help a Jew (cf. John 4:9; 8:48; see note on John 4:4). Thus Jesus makes the additional point that to love one's neighbor involves showing care and compassion even to those with whom one would not normally have any relationship (cf. Jesus' command to "love your enemies"; Luke 6:27, 35).

10:34–35 The Samaritan ministers to the injured and suffering robbery victim. **set him on his own animal**. The man was too injured to walk. The Samaritan **brought him to an inn**, where he cared for him, and gave the innkeeper **two denarii** (the equivalent of two days' salary) to continue caring for him. Jesus underscores the Samaritan's compassionate care, extending to **whatever more** cost and care may be needed.

10:36 Which of these . . . proved to be a neighbor? Jesus' question corrects the lawyer's improper question (v. 29). The question is not "who is my neighbor?" but "how can I be a neighbor?"

10:38–42 *Martha and Mary*. **village**. Bethany (cf. John 12:1; see note on John 11:1). **who sat at the Lord's feet**. A disciple's proper place (cf. Luke 8:35; Acts 22:3); unlike some in his culture, Jesus encouraged women to study the Scriptures. **you are anxious . . . about many things**. Cf. Luke 8:14; 12:11, 22–30; 21:34. **Mary has chosen the good portion** echoes OT passages where the greatest possession is close fellowship with the Lord as one's "portion" in life (cf. Ps. 16:5; 27:4; 73:26; 119:57; 142:5; also Josh. 18:7). Mary has chosen this, and it **will not be taken away from her**—neither now to help Martha in the kitchen, nor for all eternity.

11:1–13 *The Lord's Prayer*. These verses include a prayer Jesus taught his disciples (vv. 1–4), a parable about prayer (vv. 5–8), and various encouragements to pray (vv. 9–13).

11:1 Now Jesus was praying. See Introduction: Key Themes. **Lord, teach us to pray**. The request of the disciples is for a distinctive prayer that they can pray as his disciples. Usually referred to as "The Lord's Prayer," it would be better to understand this as "The Disciples' Prayer"—i.e., as the prayer that uniquely binds them together in a community of worship and intercession—and as such it is therefore a distinctively Christian prayer. The prayer underscores the unique relationship of Christian believers to God as their "Father" (cf. Rom. 8:14–17; Gal. 4:4–7).

11:2 Father is *Patēr* in Greek and *'Abba* in Aramaic (Mark 14:36; Rom. 8:15–16; Gal. 4:6–7; see note on Matt. 6:9). **Hallowed be your name** is a request that God's name would be honored and treated with reverence. His name includes his reputation and all that is said about him. **Your kingdom come** has a twofold emphasis: (1) it is first a prayer that God's rule and reign would continually advance in people's hearts and lives until the day Jesus returns and brings the kingdom in perfect fullness (see note on Matt. 6:10); (2) thus it also refers to the future consummation of the kingdom already realized in part by Jesus' coming (Luke 11:20; see Introduction: Key Themes and note on Matt. 6:10).

[i]"Father, [j]hallowed be [k]your name.
[l]Your kingdom come.
3 [m]Give us [n]each day our daily bread,[1]
4 and [o]forgive us our sins,
for we ourselves forgive everyone who is indebted to us.
And [p]lead us not into temptation."

5 And he said to them, "Which of you who has a friend will go to him at midnight and
say to him, 'Friend, lend me three loaves, 6 for a friend of mine has arrived on a journey,
and I have nothing to set before him'; 7 and he will answer from within, 'Do not bother me;

[1] *Or our bread for tomorrow*

2 [i]John 20:17; 1 Pet. 1:17 [j]Isa. 29:23; [ch. 1:49; 1 Pet. 3:15] [k]John 17:6 [l][Matt. 3:2; 4:17]
3 [m]Prov. 30:8 [n][Matt. 6:34]
4 [o]See ch. 7:48 [p]ch. 22:40, 46; Matt. 26:41; Mark 14:38; [1 Cor. 10:13]

Jesus and Prayer in the Gospel of Luke

References	The Prayers of Jesus
3:21	Jesus is praying as the heavens are opened at his baptism
5:16	Jesus would often withdraw to desolate places and pray
6:12	Jesus goes to the mountain to pray and continues all night in prayer before he chooses the Twelve
9:18	Jesus is praying alone before asking who the crowds say he is
9:28–36	Jesus goes with Peter, James, and John up on the mountain to pray and is transfigured
10:21–22	Jesus prays to thank God the Father in the Holy Spirit for concealing and revealing
11:1–4	Jesus is praying and then teaches his disciples to pray
22:17, 19	Jesus prays to give thanks to God for the cup and for the bread
22:32	Jesus tells Peter that he has prayed that Peter's faith may not fail
22:41	Jesus prays about "the cup"
22:44	Jesus prays more earnestly

References	Jesus' Teachings on Prayer and Exhortations to Pray
6:28	Jesus teaches people to pray for those who abuse them
10:2	Jesus teaches people to pray earnestly for the Lord of the harvest to send out laborers
11:5–13	Jesus teaches the disciples to persist in prayer and assures them the Father will give the Holy Spirit
18:1	Jesus tells the parable of the unjust judge to teach his disciples always to pray and not to lose heart
18:9–14	Jesus tells the parable of the Pharisee and the tax collector, contrasting their prayers
19:46	Jesus says that the temple is to be a house of prayer
20:47	Jesus warns against the scribes, who make long prayers for show
21:36	Jesus warns his disciples to pray for strength to escape the things that will take place at the end and to stand before the Son of Man
22:40, 46	Jesus tells his disciples to pray that they may not enter into temptation

11:3 Daily bread includes all of the believer's physical needs, which the Lord supplies not once for all but day by day.

11:4 Forgive us our sins refers not to initial salvation but to the continual confession of sins (cf. 1 John 1:9) needed to maintain one's relationship with God (see note on Matt. 6:12). **for we ourselves**. Asking God's forgiveness requires forgiving others. "Sins" and **indebted to us** are synonyms (cf. Luke 7:41–43, 47–49). **lead us not into temptation**. See note on Matt. 6:13. The use of the first person plural ("us") throughout emphasizes that the petitions of "The Disciples' Prayer" are not primarily for the individual but for the entire community of believers.

11:6 Having **nothing to set before** a guest was unthinkable for a host in Jesus' day.

11:7 Do not bother me. The omission of "friend" (cf. v. 5) reveals the man's aggravation. **my children . . . in bed**. The entire family is sleeping, and opening the door to the guest would probably awaken everyone. This friend's unwillingness to help is in contrast to God's great desire to help his children (vv. 9–10; cf. 18:1–8).

11:8 Impudence is Greek *anaideia*, which occurs only here in the NT. In all of its other known uses in ancient literature, the term means "lack of sensitivity to what is proper," "impertinence," "impudence"; it describes being without *aidōs* ("respect," "modesty"). "Impudence," then, would indicate that the friend is shamelessly and boldly awakening his neighbor, and of course the neighbor will give him whatever he needs. On this interpretation, Jesus' point is that if even a human being will respond to his neighbor in that way, then Christians should go boldly before God with any need they face, for God is more gracious and caring than any human neighbor. Some other interpreters believe that *anaideia* means "persistence" here, even though there are no other known occurrences of that meaning. Such a reading does fit the context, however, for the very next verses emphasize that believers must keep seeking, asking, and knocking (vv. 9–10). This would make the parable similar to 18:1–8. Both ideas—a kind of shameless persistence—are possibly intended by this unusual term.

11:9–10 Jesus tells his followers to **ask** God (a common term for "pray"), **seek** God (Deut. 4:29; Isa. 55:6; 65:1), and **knock** at the gates of God for mercy (cf. Luke 11:5–8 and note on Matt. 7:7–11). The three verbs are all present imperatives, and in this context of teaching a general principle, they encourage prayer as a continual habit of life (cf. 1 Thess. 5:17). The promised result is that **it will be given** and **opened** (by God). **Everyone who asks receives** does not mean that believers always receive what they ask for, because God is wiser than they are and has better plans for his children than they could imagine (cf. Rom. 8:28; 1 Cor. 2:9).

11:11–13 This concluding example in Jesus' teaching on prayer (vv. 1–13) is a "lesser to greater" argument: granted the truth of vv. 11–12, the concluding statement (v. 13) must be even more true (cf. notes on 12:6–7; 12:25–27; 13:15–16; 18:1–8). **If you then, who are evil**. Human sinfulness would be readily acknowledged by Jesus' audience (Genesis 3; Rom. 3:10–23; cf. note on Matt. 7:11). Fish and eggs were common foods in Palestine, while serpents and scorpions were regular hazards. A far more important gift than material blessings is the powerful anointing and guidance of the **Holy Spirit** in a believer's life (see Matt. 12:28; Luke 4:1, 14; Acts 1:8; Rom. 8:13–14, 26; 1 Cor. 12:11; Gal. 5:18).

8[q][ch. 18:1-6]
9[r]For ver. 9-13, see Matt. 7:7-11 [s]Matt. 18:19; 21:22; Mark 11:24; John 14:13; 15:7, 16; 16:23, 24; James 1:5, 6, 17; 1 John 3:22; 5:14, 15 [t]1 Chr. 28:9; 2 Chr. 15:2; Prov. 8:17; Jer. 29:13; [Isa. 55:6] [u][Rev. 3:20]
13[w]Gen. 6:5; 8:21; Matt. 12:34 [x][John 4:10; Acts 2:38]
14[y]For ver. 14, 15, see Matt. 12:22-24; [Matt. 9:32-34]
15[z]See Matt. 10:25
16[a]See John 8:6
17[b]For ver. 17-22, see Matt. 12:25-29; Mark 3:23-27 [c]See Matt. 9:4
19[d][Acts 19:13] [e][2 Kgs. 2:7]
20[f]Ex. 8:19; 31:18; Deut. 9:10; Ps. 8:3 [g]ch. 17:21; Matt. 19:24; 21:31, 43
22[h]Isa. 49:24-26 [i][John 16:33] [j]Eph. 6:11 [k][Isa. 53:12]
23[l]Matt. 12:30; [ch. 9:50; Mark 9:40]
24[m]For ver. 24-26, see Matt. 12:43-45 [n][Ps. 63:1; Jer. 2:6]
26[o]2 Pet. 2:20-22; [John 5:14]
27[p]ch. 12:13 [q][2 Chr. 9:7]; See ch. 1:48
28[r][Rev. 1:3; 22:7] [s]ch. 8:21; See James 1:22 [t]Lev. 22:31

the door is now shut, and my children are with me in bed. I cannot get up and give you
anything'? 8 I tell you, though he will not get up and give him anything [q]because he is his
friend, yet because of his impudence[1] he will rise and give him whatever he needs. 9 And
I tell you, [r]ask, and [s]it will be given to you; [t]seek, and you will find; [u]knock, and it will be
opened to you. 10 For everyone who asks receives, and the one who seeks finds, and to the
one who knocks it will be opened. 11 What father among you, if his son asks for[2] a fish, will
instead of a fish give him a serpent; 12 or if he asks for an egg, will give him a scorpion? 13 If
you then, [w]who are evil, know how to give good gifts to your children, how much more
will the heavenly Father [x]give the Holy Spirit to those who ask him!"

Jesus and Beelzebul

14 [y]Now he was casting out a demon that was mute. When the demon had gone out,
the mute man spoke, and the people marveled. 15 But some of them said, "He casts out
demons [z]by Beelzebul, the prince of demons," 16 while others, [a]to test him, kept seeking
from him a sign from heaven. 17 [b]But he, [c]knowing their thoughts, said to them, "Every
kingdom divided against itself is laid waste, and a divided household falls. 18 And if Satan
also is divided against himself, how will his kingdom stand? For you say that I cast out
demons by Beelzebul. 19 And if I cast out demons by Beelzebul, [d]by whom do [e]your sons
cast them out? Therefore they will be your judges. 20 But if it is by [f]the finger of God that
I cast out demons, then [g]the kingdom of God has come upon you. 21 When a strong man,
fully armed, guards his own palace, his goods are safe; 22 [h]but when one stronger than
he attacks him and [i]overcomes him, he takes away his [j]armor in which he trusted and
[k]divides his spoil. 23 [l]Whoever is not with me is against me, and whoever does not gather
with me scatters.

Return of an Unclean Spirit

24 [m]"When the unclean spirit has gone out of a person, it passes through [n]waterless places
seeking rest, and finding none it says, 'I will return to my house from which I came.' 25 And
when it comes, it finds the house swept and put in order. 26 Then it goes and brings seven
other spirits more evil than itself, and they enter and dwell there. And [o]the last state of
that person is worse than the first."

True Blessedness

27 As he said these things, [p]a woman in the crowd raised her voice and said to him,
[q]"Blessed is the womb that bore you, and the breasts at which you nursed!" 28 But he said,
[r]"Blessed rather are those [s]who hear the word of God and [t]keep it!"

[1] Or *persistence* [2] Some manuscripts insert *bread, will give him a stone; or if he asks for*

11:14–23 *Jesus and Beelzebul.* Jesus is accused of collusion with Satan.

11:14 a demon that was mute. The demon in some way prohibited the man from speaking. The demon is distinguished from "Satan" (v. 18), who is the prince of demons. **the mute man spoke**. Proof that the demon has been cast out.

11:15 He casts out demons by . . . the prince of demons. See notes on Matt. 9:34 and 12:24. **Beelzebul**. See note on Matt. 10:25.

11:16 kept seeking . . . a sign. Jesus knew that no sign would overcome an unwillingness to believe (see note on Matt. 13:58).

11:17–19 Knowing their thoughts is an indication of Jesus' deity. Jesus' defense consists of two arguments. The first involves two analogies: a **kingdom divided against itself is laid waste** (i.e., through civil war) and likewise a **divided household falls**. Thus the idea that Satan was working through Jesus to undermine his own work was absurd (v. 18). The second argument (v. 19) indicates that the same charge (v. 15) could be leveled against the casting out of demons by **your sons**, i.e., "your followers" (see note on Matt. 12:27).

11:20 Jesus explains that his casting out demons reveals that the **kingdom of God has come** (see Introduction: Key Themes and note on Matt. 12:28). Jesus was plundering Satan's kingdom (Luke 11:21–22; cf. 10:17–19) by transferring people into his own new kingdom. Jesus' miracles, taken as a whole, indicate that the kingdom of God has broken into this specific time and place in history, as demonstrated by his life and work (cf. Mark 1:14–15; Gal. 4:4).

11:22 The **one stronger** is Jesus, and the "strong man" in v. 21 is Satan. Jesus has overcome him. See note on Matt. 12:29.

11:23 This verse combines the metaphors of fighting (**with me . . . against me**) and farming (**does not gather with me scatters**). Neutrality with respect to Jesus is not possible (see note on 9:49–50).

11:24–26 *The Return of an Unclean Spirit.* Cleansing from sin must be followed by obedience to God's word, not complacency. **unclean spirit**. A demon. **waterless places**. For the desert as a place inhabited by demons, cf. Lev. 16:10; Luke 8:29; and note on Matt. 12:43. **the house swept and put in order**. The demon has been cast out. **seven other spirits**. A full contingent of demons (cf. Luke 8:2). On the significance of "seven," see note on Matt. 12:45.

11:27–13:9 *Various Warnings and Teachings.* As they continue their journey toward Jerusalem (cf. note on 9:51–19:27) Jesus gives his disciples additional instruction.

11:27 Blessed (see 6:20) **is the womb**. An example of synecdoche

The Sign of Jonah

29 [u]When the crowds were increasing, he began to say, [v]"This generation is an evil generation. [w]It seeks for a sign, but no sign will be given to it except the sign of Jonah. **30** For as
[x]Jonah became a sign to the people of Nineveh, so will the Son of Man be to this generation. **31** [y]The queen of the South will rise up at the judgment with the men of this generation and [z]condemn them, for she came from the ends of the earth to hear the wisdom of
Solomon, and behold, [a]something greater than Solomon is here. **32** [b]The men of Nineveh
will rise up at the judgment with this generation and [z]condemn it, for [c]they repented at
the preaching of Jonah, and behold, [a]something greater than Jonah is here.

The Light in You

33 [d]"No one after lighting a lamp puts it in a cellar or under a basket, but on a stand, so
that those who enter may see the light. **34** Your eye is [e]the lamp of your body. When your
eye is healthy, your whole body is full of light, but when it is [f]bad, your body is full of
darkness. **35** [e]Therefore be careful lest the light in you be darkness. **36** If then your whole
body is full of light, having no part dark, it will be wholly bright, [g]as when a lamp with
its rays gives you light."

Woes to the Pharisees and Lawyers

37 While Jesus[1] was speaking, [h]a Pharisee asked him to dine with him, so he went in and
reclined at table. **38** The Pharisee was astonished to see [i]that he did not first wash before
dinner. **39** And the Lord said to him, [j]"Now you Pharisees cleanse the outside of the cup
and of the dish, but inside you are full of [k]greed and wickedness. **40** [l]You fools! [j]Did not
he who made the outside make the inside also? **41** But [m]give as alms those things that are
within, and behold, [n]everything is clean for you.

42 [o]"But woe to you Pharisees! For [p]you tithe mint and rue and every herb, and neglect
[q]justice and [r]the love of God. [s]These you ought to have done, without neglecting the others. **43** Woe to you Pharisees! For [t]you love the best seat in the synagogues and greetings
in the marketplaces. **44** Woe to you! [u]For you are like unmarked graves, and people walk
over them without knowing it."

45 One of [v]the lawyers answered him, "Teacher, in saying these things you insult us

[1] Greek *he*

29 [u]ch. 12:1 [v]For ver. 29-32, see Matt. 12:39-42; [Mark 8:11, 12] [w]ver. 16; See Matt. 12:38
30 [x]Jonah 1:17
31 [y]1 Kgs. 10:1; 2 Chr. 9:1 [z]Heb. 11:7; [Jer. 3:11; Ezek. 16:51, 52; Rom. 2:27] [a][Matt. 12:6]
32 [b]Jonah 1:2 [z][See ver. 31 above] [c]Jonah 3:5 [a][See ver. 31 above]
33 [d]ch. 8:16; Matt. 5:15; Mark 4:21
34 [e]Matt. 6:22, 23 [f]Deut. 15:9
35 [e][See ver. 34 above]
36 [g][Matt. 5:16]
37 [h]ch. 7:36; 14:1
38 [i]Matt. 15:2; Mark 7:3, 4
39 [j]Matt. 23:25, 26; [ch. 20:47] [k][ch. 16:14]
40 [l]ch. 12:20 [j][See ver. 39 above]
41 [m]ch. 12:33; [ch. 16:9; Dan. 4:27] [n][Titus 1:15]
42 [o]Matt. 23:23 [p]ch. 18:12; Deut. 14:22 [q]Ps. 33:5; Jer. 5:1; Mic. 6:8; Zech. 7:9 [r][1 John 3:17] [s][1 Sam. 15:22]
43 [t]ch. 20:46; Matt. 23:6, 7; Mark 12:38, 39; [ch. 14:7]
44 [u]Matt. 23:27
45 [v]ver. 46, 52; See ch. 7:30

(a literary device in which a part of something stands for the whole); here "womb" represents "mother" (cf. Gen. 49:25).

11:29 The account in vv. 29–32 answers the request of v. 16 from those who were testing Jesus by seeking a cosmic sign, in spite of already having seen many miracles. For **evil generation**, see notes on 7:31–34 and Matt. 12:39. **no sign will be given**. For the meaninglessness of a sign when hearts are hardened, cf. Luke 16:31; John 12:9–11. The **sign of Jonah** refers first to Jonah's "three days and nights in the belly of the great fish" (cf. note on Matt. 12:40), which foreshadows "the Son of Man" being "three days and three nights in the heart of the earth," i.e., a reference to Jesus' death and resurrection (cf. Luke 16:30–31). Additionally, "the sign of Jonah" draws attention to the need for a concrete response of repentance, as was the case of Nineveh in response to Jonah's message.

11:31 The **queen of the South** (the queen of Sheba; 1 Kings 10:1–13; 2 Chron. 9:1–12) will **condemn** this **generation** because **she came** a long distance to see Solomon and **hear** his **wisdom** (1 Kings 10:1–4, 7), whereas **something greater than Solomon** (the Son of God and his wisdom; cf. note on Matt. 12:42) has come to them and the people reject this and ask for a sign.

11:32 Even though the Ninevites were wicked, they at least **repented at the preaching of Jonah** (see note on Matt. 12:41). How much greater condemnation, then, for those who refuse to repent at the teaching of Jonah's Lord, who is **greater than Jonah**. Jesus is both the ultimate wise man (Luke 11:31) and the ultimate prophet (v. 32).

11:33 lamp. Probably a metaphor for Jesus and his mission.

11:34 An **eye** that is **healthy** describes a spiritually healthy way of looking at things. A **bad** eye, or evil way of looking at things, results in a life **full of** moral and spiritual **darkness**.

11:36 When a person is filled with the **light** of Christ, it will affect his or her whole being (**wholly bright**).

11:37 Pharisee. See note on 5:17. **reclined at table**. The usual posture at a banquet or Sabbath meal (see note on Matt. 26:20).

11:38 wash before dinner. An extrabiblical tradition (cf. note on Mark 7:5) involving ceremonial cleanness, not ordinary hygienic practices.

11:39–41 you Pharisees cleanse. Keeping the traditions that they had added to Scripture was like cleansing the **outside of the cup** but leaving the **inside . . . full of greed and wickedness** (cf. note on Matt. 23:26); for "greed," cf. Luke 16:14; 20:47. **Those things that are within** are the things in a person's heart. If the believer first offers his heart to God, then **everything is clean**; that is, God will accept the good he does ("alms . . . that are within") even if he does not follow the outward ceremonial washing required by Jewish traditions.

11:42–44 Jesus directs three woes against the Pharisees (see note on Matt. 23:13). The first **woe** targets their hypocrisy in tithing **every herb** (such specific detail is not mentioned in Lev. 27:30–33; Deut. 14:22–29; 2 Chron. 31:5–12; see note on Matt. 23:23), but neglecting **justice and the love of God**. The second **woe** focuses on their **love** of the **best seat** (as illustrated in Luke 14:7–11; cf. note on Matt. 23:6). The third **woe** compares them to **unmarked graves**. According to OT law, coming in contact with a grave made a person unclean (see Num. 19:16; cf. note on Matt. 23:27–28). But if the grave was in the ground and had no marking, people might **walk over** it and become unclean **without knowing it**. Likewise people who follow the Pharisees are deceived, for they become "unclean" before God without even knowing that the Pharisees have led them astray.

11:45 The second set of woes (vv. 46–52) is directed at **lawyers** (experts in the law, another expression for "scribes of the Pharisees"; Mark 2:16; cf. Luke 11:53 and note on Matt. 23:2).

also." 46 And he said, "Woe to you [w]lawyers also! For [x]you load people with burdens hard
to bear, and you yourselves do not touch the burdens with one of your fingers. 47 [y]Woe
to you! For you build the tombs of the prophets whom your fathers killed. 48 [z]So you are
witnesses and you [a]consent to the deeds of [b]your fathers, for they killed them, and you
build their tombs. 49 Therefore also [c]the Wisdom of God said, [d]'I will send them [e]prophets
and apostles, [f]some of whom they will [g]kill and persecute,' 50 so that [h]the blood of all the
prophets, shed [i]from the foundation of the world, may be [j]charged against this generation,
51 from the blood of [k]Abel to the blood of [l]Zechariah, who perished between [m]the altar and
the sanctuary. Yes, I tell you, it will be [j]required of this generation. 52 Woe to you [n]lawyers!
[o]For you have taken away the key of [p]knowledge. You [q]did not enter yourselves, and you
hindered those who were entering."
53 As he went away from there, the scribes and the Pharisees began to press him hard
and to provoke him to speak about many things, 54 [r]lying in wait for him, [s]to catch him
in something he might say.

Beware of the Leaven of the Pharisees

12 In the meantime, [t]when so many thousands of the people had gathered together
that they were trampling one another, he began to say to his disciples first, [u]"Beware
of [v]the leaven of the Pharisees, [w]which is hypocrisy. 2 [x]Nothing is covered up that will not
be revealed, or hidden that will not be known. 3 Therefore whatever you have said in the
dark shall be heard in the light, and what you have whispered in [y]private rooms shall be
proclaimed on [z]the housetops.

Have No Fear

4 "I tell you, my friends, [a]do not fear those who kill the body, and after that have nothing more that they can do. 5 But I will warn you whom to fear: fear him [b]who, after he has
killed, has authority to cast into hell.[1] Yes, I tell you, fear him! 6 Are not five sparrows sold
for two pennies?[2] And [c]not one of them is forgotten before God. 7 Why, [d]even the hairs of
your head are all numbered. Fear not; [e]you are of more value than many sparrows.

Acknowledge Christ Before Men

8 "And I tell you, [f]everyone who acknowledges me before men, the Son of Man also
will acknowledge [g]before the angels of God, 9 but [h]the one who denies me before men
[i]will be denied [g]before the angels of God. 10 And [j]everyone who speaks a word [k]against

[1] Greek *Gehenna* [2] Greek *two assaria*; an *assarion* was a Roman copper coin worth about 1/16 of a *denarius* (which was a day's wage for a laborer)

46 [w]ver. 45, 52 [x]Matt. 23:4; [Matt. 11:28-30; Acts 15:10]
47 [y]Matt. 23:29, 30
48 [z]Matt. 23:31 [a]See Rom. 1:32 [b]Acts 7:51, 52
49 [c][ch. 7:35; Prov. 8:12, 22, 23, 30; Matt. 11:19; 1 Cor. 1:24, 30; Col. 2:3] [d]For ver. 49-51, [Matt. 23:34-36] [e]See Acts 13:1; 1 Cor. 12:28 [f]See Matt. 21:35 [g]1 Thess. 2:15 (Gk.)
50 [h]Rev. 18:24 [i]See Matt. 13:35 [j]Gen. 42:22; 2 Chr. 24:22; Ezek. 3:18
51 [k]Gen. 4:4, 8; Heb. 11:4; 1 John 3:12 [l]2 Chr. 24:20, 21 [m]Ex. 40:6; 2 Kgs. 16:14; Ezek. 40:47 [j][See ver. 50 above]
52 [n]ver. 45, 46 [o]Matt. 23:13; [Mal. 2:7, 8] [p]Rom. 2:20 [q][ch. 7:30; Matt. 5:20; 21:31]
54 [r]ch. 20:20; Mark 3:2; John 8:6; [Isa. 29:21] [s]Matt. 22:15; Mark 12:13

Chapter 12

1 [t]ch. 11:29 [u]Matt. 16:6, 11, 12; Mark 8:15 [v]1 Cor. 5:6-8; Gal. 5:9 [w]Matt. 23:28; Mark 12:15
2 [x]ch. 8:17; Mark 4:22; [1 Tim. 5:25]; For ver. 2-9, see Matt. 10:26-33
3 [y]Matt. 6:6 [z]See ch. 5:19
4 [a]Isa. 8:12, 13; 51:12, 13; Jer. 1:8; 1 Pet. 3:14
5 [b]James 4:12
6 [c][Ps. 50:11]
7 [d]See 1 Sam. 14:45 [e]Matt. 6:26; 12:12
8 [f][Rom. 10:9, 10; Heb. 10:35; Rev. 3:5] [g][ch. 15:10; Matt. 25:31; 1 Tim. 5:21; Rev. 3:5]
9 [h]2 Tim. 2:12; 2 Pet. 2:1; 1 John 2:23; [Mark 8:38] [i]ch. 13:25; Matt. 7:23; 25:12 [g][See ver. 8 above]
10 [j][Matt. 12:31, 32; Mark 3:28-30; Heb. 6:4-6; 10:26; 1 John 5:16] [k]Matt. 11:19; John 7:12; 9:24

11:46 The first **woe** involves the lawyers (cf. v. 45) loading **people with burdens** by interpreting the law in light of their extrabiblical traditions and making it **hard to bear**. Worse still, they **do not touch the burdens** themselves, i.e., they make no effort to help people keep these laws (see notes on Matt. 23:3, 4).

11:47–51 The second woe involves the lawyers' hypocrisy in building monuments to the prophets, although it was their **fathers** who **killed** those same prophets, and they themselves continue to "kill and persecute" them (v. 49). The unusual expression **Wisdom of God** probably means "God in his wisdom" or "God, speaking to express his wisdom." **From the blood of Abel** (Genesis 4) **to the blood of Zechariah** (2 Chron. 24:20–22), i.e., from the beginning of the first book to the end of the last book in the Hebrew Bible. See note on Matt. 23:35.

11:52–54 The last woe condemns the lawyers for their interpretations of Scripture that deprive the people of the **key of knowledge** needed to understand God's plan of salvation. Not only do they refuse to enter into God's plan and be saved, but their distorted interpretations keep others from truly knowing God. **To press . . . hard and to provoke him** describes a continual attempt to "ambush" Jesus (**lying in wait . . . to catch him**; cf. Acts 23:21). **something he might say**. Something that could be used to condemn him (cf. Luke 22:66–23:25).

12:1 many thousands of the people. The crowds continue to increase and provide proof that Jesus "is of God" (Acts 5:33–39). **Beware of the leaven of the Pharisees**. Leaven (see note on 1 Cor. 5:6–7) is a metaphor for the self-centered, hypocritical approaches of the Pharisees in Luke 11:37–54 (see also note on Mark 8:14–15).

12:2–3 Everything will **be revealed** and **be** (made) **known** by God (cf. 8:17)—a reference to future judgment (Acts 17:31). Because Luke 12:2 is true, v. 3 will take place. **Housetops** were commonly flat and were used as living space (see Acts 10:9–10).

12:4 Do not fear those who kill the body, as the prophets experienced (11:47) and as Christ's followers would experience as well (11:49), for physical death cannot affect the believer's ultimate destiny (cf. Rom. 8:35–39).

12:5 The second **fear** refers to God (**him**), who at the final judgment **has authority to cast into hell**. Repetition (**fear him**) gives this command additional emphasis.

12:6–7 The observations about **sparrows** and the **hairs of your head** show God's providential care over the smallest details of life. **Of more value** signals a "lesser to greater" argument: if A (the lesser) is true, then how much more B (the greater) must be true. That is, if God even cares about sparrows, how much greater is his care for every one of his own children, whose value is so much greater (cf. vv. 22–31; see also note on Matt. 6:26). **Fear not**. Fear of God (Luke 12:5) results in not needing to fear anyone or anything else.

12:9 denies me before men. See note on Matt. 10:32–33.

12:10 Speaks a word against . . . will be forgiven versus **blasphemes against . . . will not be forgiven**. Jesus closes this occasion of teaching his disciples (v. 1) with one of the most enigmatic, debated, and misunderstood

the Son of Man [l]will be forgiven, but the one who [m]blasphemes against the Holy Spirit
will not be forgiven. **11** [n]And when they [o]bring you before the synagogues and [p]the rulers and [p]the authorities, [q]do not be anxious about how you should defend yourself or
what you should say, **12** [r]for the Holy Spirit will teach you in that very hour what you
ought to say."

The Parable of the Rich Fool

13 [s]Someone in the crowd said to him, "Teacher, tell my brother to divide the inheritance
with me." **14** But he said to him, [t]"Man, [u]who made me a judge or arbitrator over you?"
15 And he said to them, [v]"Take care, and be on your guard against all covetousness, for one's
life does not consist in the abundance of his possessions." **16** And he told them a parable,
saying, [w]"The land of a rich man produced plentifully, **17** and he thought to himself, [x]'What
shall I do, for I have nowhere to store my crops?' **18** And he said, 'I will do this: I will tear
down my [y]barns and build larger ones, and there I will store all my grain and my goods.
19 And I will say to my soul, "Soul, you have ample goods laid up [z]for many years; relax,
[a]eat, drink, be merry."' **20** But God said to him, [b]'Fool! [z]This night [c]your soul is required
of you, and the things you have prepared, [d]whose will they be?' **21** So is the one [e]who lays
up treasure for himself and is not rich toward God."

Do Not Be Anxious

22 And he said to his disciples, [f]"Therefore I tell you, [g]do not be anxious about your life,
what you will eat, nor about your body, what you will put on. **23** For life is more than food,
and the body more than clothing. **24** [h]Consider the ravens: they neither sow nor reap, they
have neither storehouse nor barn, and yet God feeds them. [i]Of how much more value are
you than the birds! **25** And which of you by being anxious can add a single hour to his [j]span
of life?[1] **26** If then you are not able to do as small a thing as that, why are you anxious about
the rest? **27** Consider the lilies, how they grow: they neither toil nor spin,[2] yet I tell you,
[k]even Solomon in all his glory was not arrayed like one of these. **28** But if God so clothes the
grass, which is alive in the field today, and tomorrow is thrown into the oven, how much
more will he clothe you, [l]O you of little faith! **29** And do not seek what you are to eat and
what you are to drink, nor [m]be worried. **30** For [n]all the nations of the world seek after these

[1] Or *a single cubit to his stature*; a *cubit* was about 18 inches or 45 centimeters [2] Some manuscripts *Consider the lilies; they neither spin nor weave*

10 [l]1 Tim. 1:12, 13 [m][Acts 7:51; Heb. 10:29]
11 [n]Matt. 10:17, 19; [ch. 21:12, 14; Mark 13:11] [o]See Matt. 23:34 [p]Titus 3:1 [q]See ver. 22
12 [r]See Matt. 10:19, 20
13 [s]ch. 11:27
14 [t]Mic. 6:8; Rom. 2:1, 3; 9:20 [u][Ex. 2:14; Acts 7:27]
15 [v]1 Tim. 6:6-11; [Heb. 13:5]
16 [w][Ps. 49:16-20]
17 [x][Eccles. 5:10]
18 [y]ver. 24
19 [z][Prov. 27:1; James 4:13-15] [a]Eccles. 2:24; 11:9; 1 Cor. 15:32; [ch. 15:23]
20 [b]Jer. 17:11; [Matt. 16:26] [z][See ver. 19 above] [c]Job 27:8 [d]Ps. 39:6; [Job 27:17-22; Eccles. 2:18, 21]
21 [e]Matt. 6:19, 20
22 [f]For ver. 22-31, see Matt. 6:25-33 [g]ver. 11; ch. 10:41; Matt. 10:19; 13:22 (Gk.); 1 Cor. 7:32 (Gk.); Phil. 4:6; 1 Pet. 5:7
24 [h][Job 38:41; Ps. 147:9] [i]See ver. 7
25 [j]ch. 2:52 (Gk.)
27 [k]1 Kgs. 10:4-7
28 [l]Matt. 8:26; 14:31; 16:8; [ch. 17:6]
29 [m][James 1:6]
30 [n]Matt. 6:8

sayings of his ministry. Key to understanding this passage is the distinction Jesus makes between, on one hand, the extreme case of blasphemy against "the Holy Spirit" and, on the other hand, the lesser case of speaking in a dishonorable way against "the Son of Man." One who asks to be forgiven for disrespectful words hastily spoken against Jesus (the Son of Man) will be forgiven. (Note, e.g., Peter's rejection of Jesus [see 22:54–62] and his subsequent restoration [John 21:15–19].) But blasphemy against the Holy Spirit—that is, the persistent and unrepentant resistance against the work of the Holy Spirit and his message concerning Jesus (cf. Acts 7:51)—this, Jesus says, will not be forgiven. The person who persists in hardening his heart against God, against the work of the Holy Spirit, and against the provision of Christ as Savior, is outside the reach of God's provision for forgiveness and salvation. Christians often worry that they have committed this sin, but such a concern is itself evidence of an openness to the work of the Spirit (see also notes on Matt. 12:31–32 and Mark 3:29).

12:11–12 Before the synagogues, i.e., before the Jewish authorities. The **rulers and the authorities**, i.e., before Gentile courts. **Do not be anxious** because the **Holy Spirit** will guide at such times (21:14–15; cf. notes on Matt. 10:19–20 and Gal. 5:18).

12:13–15 tell my brother to divide. Because of Jesus' teaching on covetousness, which immediately follows this request, this man is probably speaking from personal greed. **who made me a judge . . . ?** Though Jesus was Lord of the entire universe, he was careful not to become involved in matters that did not directly pertain to his earthly work and ministry, and he expected people to work out such things on their own. **life does not consist in . . . abundance**. Cf. 9:24–25; 12:22–34.

12:19–21 Fool! Ironically, the man who took such great care to prepare for his own (earthly) needs turns out to be a fool. Instead of fulfilling his moral responsibility to care for the needs of others, he is rebuked for laying **up treasure for himself** and for not being **rich toward God**. Though this verse does not prohibit wealth, Jesus clearly warns his hearers concerning the dangerous eternal implications of wealth, with its seductive tendency toward complacency, self-sufficiency, and covetousness. Though the rich fool anticipates years of ease—a time to **eat, drink, be merry**—instead an eternal destiny apart from God awaits him. As Jesus' condemning words confirm, "**This night your soul is required of you.**"

12:22–25 Therefore, i.e., because of the truths taught in vv. 13–21, **do not be anxious**. The first reason why believers should not be anxious is given in v. 23 (**for life is more than . . .**); the second in v. 24 (**of how much more value are you**; cf. note on Matt. 6:26); and the third in Luke 12:25 (because no one has enough control over his own life even to **add a single hour to his span of life**). **Life** (or "soul"; Gk. *psychē*) and **body** refer to the whole person. (Regarding "add a single hour to his span of life," see ESV footnote; "hour" is literally "cubit" [Gk. *pēchys*], and most commentators take it to be a metaphor for adding a standard unit of measure to the length of one's life.)

12:25–27 Jesus employs two "lesser to greater" arguments (vv. 25–26 and v. 27; cf. notes on 11:11–13; 12:6–7; 13:15–16; 18:1–8) to affirm God's care for his children. **Solomon in all his glory**. Cf. 1 Kings 10:4–5; 2 Chron. 9:5.

12:28 the grass . . . is thrown into the oven. Due to the scarcity of wood in ancient Palestine, dry grass was used as fuel. **O you of little faith** implies a deficiency rather than an absence of faith (cf. Matt. 6:30; 8:2b; 14:31; 16:8).

12:29 Do not seek does not mean that people should neglect to work and support themselves (cf. 1 Thess. 4:11–12), but is a warning against worrying and continually seeking after **what . . . to eat** and **what . . . to drink**. Cf. Luke 12:31 for what *should* be sought after.

things, and [n]your Father knows that you need them. 31 Instead, [o]seek [p]his[1] kingdom, [q]and
these things will be added to you.
32 [r]"Fear not, little [s]flock, for [t]it is your Father's good pleasure to give you [u]the kingdom.
33 [v]Sell your possessions, and [w]give to the needy. [x]Provide yourselves with moneybags that do
not grow old, with [y]a treasure in the heavens that does not fail, where no thief approaches
and no moth destroys. 34 [z]For where your treasure is, there will your heart be also.

You Must Be Ready

35 [a]"Stay dressed for action[2] and [b]keep your lamps burning, 36 and be like men who are
[c]waiting for their master to come home from the wedding feast, so that they may open the
door to him at once when he comes and [d]knocks. 37 [e]Blessed are those servants[3] whom the
master finds [e]awake when he comes. Truly, I say to you, [f]he will dress himself for service
and [g]have them recline at table, and he will come and serve them. 38 If he comes in the
second watch, or in the third, and finds them awake, blessed are those servants! 39 [h]But
know this, that if the master of the house had known at what hour [i]the thief was coming,
he[4] would not have left his house to be broken into. 40 You also must be [j]ready, for [k]the Son
of Man is coming at an hour you do not expect."
41 Peter said, "Lord, [l]are you telling this parable for us or for all?" 42 And the Lord said,
"Who then is [m]the faithful and [m]wise [n]manager, whom his master will set over his household,
to give them their portion of food at the proper time? 43 [o]Blessed is that servant[5]
whom his master will find so doing when he comes. 44 Truly, I say to you, [p]he will set him
over all his possessions. 45 But if that servant says to himself, 'My master [q]is delayed in
coming,' and begins to beat the male and female servants, and to eat and drink and [r]get
drunk, 46 the master of that servant will come [s]on a day when he does not expect him and
[s]at an hour he does not know, and will cut him in pieces and put him with the unfaithful.
47 [t]And that servant who [u]knew his master's will but [v]did not get ready [u]or act according
to his will, will receive a [w]severe beating. 48 [x]But the one who did not know, and did what
deserved a beating, [y]will receive a light beating. [z]Everyone to whom much was given,
of him much will be required, and from him to whom they entrusted much, they will
demand the more.

Not Peace, but Division

49 [a]"I came to cast fire on the earth, and would that it were already kindled! 50 [b]I have a
baptism to be baptized with, and how [c]great is my distress until it is accomplished! 51 [d]Do

[1] Some manuscripts *God's* [2] Greek *Let your loins stay girded;* compare Exodus 12:11 [3] Greek *bondservants* [4] Some manuscripts add *would have stayed awake and* [5] Greek *bondservant;* also verses 45, 46, 47

30 [n]Matt. 6:8
31 [o][Matt. 5:6, 20] [p]ch. 11:2 [q][1 Kgs. 3:11-14; Mark 10:29, 30; 1 Tim. 4:8; 1 Pet. 3:9]
32 [r]Isa. 41:14; 44:2 [s]Isa. 40:11; Matt. 26:31; John 10:16; 21:15-17; Acts 20:28, 29; 1 Pet. 5:2, 3 [t][ch. 10:21; Matt. 11:26; Eph. 1:5, 9; Phil. 2:13] [u]ch. 22:29; See Matt. 13:19
33 [v]See Matt. 19:21 [w]ch. 11:41 [x][ch. 16:9] [y]Matt. 6:20; [ver. 21; 1 Pet. 1:4]
34 [z]Matt. 6:21
35 [a]Eph. 6:14; 1 Pet. 1:13 [b][Matt. 25:7]
36 [c]See 2 Pet. 3:12 [d]Rev. 3:20
37 [e]See Matt. 24:42, 46 [f]John 13:4; [ver. 35; ch. 17:8] [g][ch. 22:27]
39 [h]For ver. 39-46, [Matt. 24:43-51] [i][1 Thess. 5:2; 2 Pet. 3:10; Rev. 3:3]
40 [j]ver. 47; Matt. 25:10 [k]ch. 21:27
41 [l][Mark 13:37]
42 [m]See Matt. 24:45 [n]ch. 16:1
43 [o]John 13:17; Rev. 16:15
44 [p]Matt. 25:21, 23
45 [q]Matt. 25:5; [Heb. 10:37; 2 Pet. 3:4, 9] [r]1 Thess. 5:7
46 [s]2 Pet. 3:12; [ver. 40]
47 [t][Matt. 11:24; John 15:22, 24] [u][James 4:17; 2 Pet. 2:21] [v]ver. 40 [w][Deut. 25:2, 3]
48 [x]Lev. 5:17; [Num. 15:29, 30] [y]Rom. 1:19, 20; 2:14, 15; [1 Tim. 1:13] [z][Matt. 25:29]; See Matt. 13:12
49 [a][Matt. 3:11]
50 [b]Mark 10:38 [c]2 Cor. 5:14 (Gk.)
51 [d]For ver. 51-53, see Matt. 10:34, 35

12:33–34 Sell your possessions, and give to the needy is a strong emphasis in Luke (see Introduction: Key Themes). **Moneybags that do not grow old** is a metaphor for the place where one stores one's treasures. Because the believer's treasures are stored in heaven, the believer's "moneybag" (the heavenly storehouse of his treasure) will never wear out, will **not fail**, and is safe from being stolen by thieves and destroyed by moths (cf. Matt. 6:19–21). In contrast to the world's preoccupation with possessions, the disciples are to be characterized by exceedingly great generosity, especially in giving to those in need (lit., "to give alms"). This even has eternal implications—**for**, as Jesus solemnly warns, **where your treasure is** (whether on earth or in heaven,) **there will your heart be also**. This concluding proverb (Luke 12:34) emphasizes the importance of the disposition of one's heart, which throughout Scripture represents the center of one's being and one's deepest desires, including one's reason, convictions, emotions, and will. The nature of one's heart is reflected in the things that one values most.

12:35 Stay dressed for action (lit., "Let your loins stay girded," ESV footnote) depicts a man prepared to run, with his long robe tucked under his belt.

12:37–38 awake. Believers should be continually expecting and ready for Christ's return, because the time of his coming is unknown (see note on Matt. 24:36). **Recline at table** has in view the end-time messianic banquet (Luke 13:29; 14:15–24; 22:27–30; Rev. 19:9). **second watch, or in the third**. Most interpreters think Jesus is using a Jewish understanding of "three watches of the night" (6:00–10:00 P.M., 10:00 P.M.–2:00 A.M., 2:00–6:00 A.M.). However, others think he is using a Roman understanding of four watches (6:00–9:00 P.M., 9:00 P.M.–12:00 A.M., 12:00–3:00 A.M., 3:00–6:00 A.M.). In either case, the point that Jesus is making is that "the master" could come at any time, even when one is not normally prepared.

12:39–40 This parable, similar to but separate from vv. 37–38, uses the imagery of a **thief** to indicate the unexpected nature of Christ's second coming.

12:41–48 are you telling this parable for us or for all? Jesus does not actually answer Peter's question, which would seem to indicate that the application is for "everyone" to whom much has been given (see v. 48). The **faithful and wise manager** is the person who faithfully and fairly cares for those for whom he is responsible, giving them **their portion . . . at the proper time**. When the master returns, the faithful manager will be rewarded—a metaphorical picture of the rewards that will be given to faithful believers at the return of Christ. The faithful manager is then contrasted with the unfaithful **servant** who beats the household **servants** and gets **drunk**. To the surprise of the unfaithful servant, however, the master will return **at an hour he does not know** (v. 46), resulting in swift and harsh judgment: he will **cut him in pieces** (cf. Jer. 34:18) **and put him with the unfaithful**—a metaphorical reference to the punishment that awaits the unbeliever at the return of Christ. The latter description (cf. Luke 13:27–28 and esp. the parallel in Matt. 24:51) indicates eternal judgment and separation from God (cf. Luke 8:13). **much will be required**. People who have been entrusted by God with many abilities and responsibilities will be held to a higher standard on the last day (cf. notes on Matt. 25:29; Mark 4:24, 25).

12:49–53 Jesus came not only to bring salvation but also to become the "Great Divider" of humanity, as people decide whether or not to follow him. **Cast fire on the earth** probably refers not to final judgment but to the

you think that I have come to give peace on earth? [e]No, I tell you, but rather division. 52 For
from now on in one house there will be five divided, three against two and two against
three. 53 They will be divided, [f]father against son and son against father, mother against
daughter and daughter against mother, mother-in-law against her daughter-in-law and
daughter-in-law against mother-in-law."

Interpreting the Time

54 He also said to the crowds, [g]"When you see [h]a cloud rising in the west, you say at once,
'A shower is coming.' And so it happens. 55 And [g]when you see the south wind blowing,
you say, 'There will be [i]scorching heat,' and it happens. 56 You hypocrites! [j]You know how
to interpret the appearance of earth and sky, but why do you not know how to interpret
the present time?

Settle with Your Accuser

57 "And why [k]do you not judge [l]for yourselves what is right? 58 [m]As you go with your
accuser before the magistrate, make an effort to settle with him on the way, lest he drag you
to the judge, and the judge hand you over to the officer, and the officer put you in prison.
59 I tell you, [n]you will never get out until you have paid the very last [o]penny."[1]

Repent or Perish

13 There were some present at that very time who told him about the Galileans whose
blood [p]Pilate had mingled with their sacrifices. 2 And he answered them, [q]"Do you
think that these Galileans were worse sinners than all the other Galileans, because they
suffered in this way? 3 No, I tell you; but unless you [r]repent, you will all likewise perish.
4 Or those eighteen on whom the tower in [s]Siloam fell and killed them: do you think that
they were worse offenders than all the others who lived in Jerusalem? 5 No, I tell you; but
unless you [r]repent, you will all likewise perish."

The Parable of the Barren Fig Tree

6 And he told this parable: "A man had [t]a fig tree planted in his vineyard, and he came
seeking fruit on it and found none. 7 And he said to the vinedresser, 'Look, for three years
now I have come seeking fruit on this fig tree, and I find none. [u]Cut it down. Why should
it use up the ground?' 8 And he answered him, 'Sir, let it alone this year also, until I dig
around it and put on manure. 9 Then if it should bear fruit next year, well and good; but
if not, you can cut it down.'"

A Woman with a Disabling Spirit

10 Now [v]he was teaching in one of the synagogues on the Sabbath. 11 And behold, there was
a woman who had had [w]a disabling spirit for eighteen years. She was bent over and could not

51 [e][Rev. 6:4]
53 [f]Matt. 10:21; [Mic. 7:6]
54 [g][Matt. 16:2, 3] [h]1 Kgs. 18:43, 44
55 [g][See ver. 54 above] [i]See Matt. 20:12
56 [j]Matt. 16:3
57 [k]ch. 21:30 [l]John 7:24; 1 Cor. 11:13
58 [m]Matt. 5:25, 26; [Prov. 25:8]
59 [n][Matt. 18:34, 35] [o]ch. 21:2; Mark 12:42

Chapter 13

1 [p]ch. 3:1
2 [q][Job 4:7; John 9:2; Acts 28:4]
3 [r]See ch. 5:32
4 [s]John 9:7, 11
5 [r][See ver. 3 above]
6 [t]Matt. 21:19; Mark 11:13; [Isa. 5:2]
7 [u]ch. 3:9; Matt. 7:19
10 [v]See Matt. 4:23; Mark 6:2
11 [w]Acts 16:16; [ver. 16]

[1] Greek *lepton*, a Jewish bronze or copper coin worth about 1/128 of a *denarius* (which was a day's wage for a laborer)

refining fire of division between believers and unbelievers (see vv. 51–53). **I have a baptism**. Whereas the "fire" affects the world, this "baptism" is Christ's own suffering and death, which would pour over him like a flood (cf. Ps. 88:7; Jonah 2:3; and notes on Mark 10:38 and 1 Pet. 3:21). **great is my distress until**. Even though it would mean suffering and death (cf. Luke 13:32–33), Jesus earnestly sought to fulfill the divine plan. Though in many ways Jesus did bring peace to the world (see note on John 14:27), it could also be said that he brought not **peace . . . but rather division**, involving even **father against son** (see note on Matt. 10:34–37) as one chose to follow Jesus and the other chose to reject him.

12:54–56 A **cloud rising in the west** over the Mediterranean would have brought moist air that condensed (a **shower**) as it climbed the cooler hills of Palestine (cf. 1 Kings 18:44). The **south wind blowing** involved a sirocco (hot, dry wind) blowing in from the desert, bringing scorching heat. The crowd could **interpret** these signs, but the spiritual emptiness of their hypocrisy blinded them from understanding the signs announcing the arrival of the kingdom of God in Jesus' teaching and ministry (cf. Luke 11:20).

12:57–59 This parable offers practical advice; it is better to settle with one's **accuser** before the dispute is brought before a **judge** (see notes on Matt. 5:25–26 and 1 Cor. 6:1). But within its broader context, the parable seems also to have in view the arrival of the kingdom—that is, the need to be in right standing with God, the Judge of the universe, before it is too late.

13:1–5 The incidents concerning Pilate killing the **Galileans** and the fall of the tower in Siloam are not recorded elsewhere in Scripture. **whose blood Pilate had mingled**. Nothing more is known about this incident, but Pilate had apparently put people to death when they were trying to offer sacrifices (see note on 23:1). **Do you think . . . worse sinners?** Jesus' rhetorical question reflects a popular view that tragedies and physical ailments were due to personal sin (see note on John 9:2), but his answer (**No**) denies any such connection in this case. **unless you repent, you will all likewise perish**. Though Jesus regularly has compassion on those who suffer, here he draws a broader lesson: this tragic event is a warning that final judgment is coming to the entire world. The **tower in Siloam** was probably part of the wall of Jerusalem near the pool of Siloam.

13:6–9 This parable symbolizes Israel's last opportunity to repent before experiencing God's judgment. **Three years** signifies that Israel has had enough time to repent. **Sir, let it alone this year**. The period of grace and opportunity is extended, but only for a limited time. **Dig around it** implies loosening the soil so that water can flow easily to the roots; if the fig tree does not respond, it will be **cut . . . down** (cf. vv. 34–35; 19:41–44). The Greek construction suggests that this last attempt will also result in failure. God's graciousness and patience should not be presumed upon.

13:10–17 *Jesus Heals on the Sabbath*. Whereas the incidents recorded

fully straighten herself. 12 When Jesus saw her, he called her over and said to her, "Woman,
you are freed from your disability." 13 And he [x]laid his hands on her, and immediately she was
made straight, and she [y]glorified God. 14 But [z]the ruler of the synagogue, indignant because
Jesus [a]had healed on the Sabbath, said to the people, [b]"There are six days in which work
ought to be done. Come on those days and be healed, and not on the Sabbath day." 15 Then
the Lord answered him, "You hypocrites! [c]Does not each of you on the Sabbath untie his ox
or his donkey from the manger and lead it away to water it? 16 And ought not this woman,
[d]a daughter of Abraham whom [e]Satan bound for eighteen years, be loosed from this bond
on the Sabbath day?" 17 As he said these things, [f]all his adversaries were put to shame, and
[g]all the people rejoiced at all the glorious things that were done by him.

The Mustard Seed and the Leaven

18 [h]He said therefore, "What is the kingdom of God like? And to what shall I compare it?
19 It is like [i]a grain of mustard seed that a man took and sowed in his garden, and it grew
and became a tree, and the birds of the air made nests in its branches."
20 And again he said, "To what shall I compare the kingdom of God? 21 [j]It is like leaven
that a woman took and hid in [k]three measures of flour, until it was [l]all leavened."

The Narrow Door

22 [m]He went on his way through towns and villages, teaching and [n]journeying toward
Jerusalem. 23 And someone said to him, "Lord, [o]will those who are saved be few?" And he said
to them, 24 [p]"Strive [q]to enter through the narrow door. For many, I tell you, will seek to enter
and will not be able. 25 [r]When once the master of the house has risen and shut the door, and
you begin to stand outside and to knock at the door, saying, [s]'Lord, open to us,' then he will
answer you, [t]'I do not know where you come from.' 26 Then you will begin to say, [u]'We ate
and drank in your presence, and you taught in our streets.' 27 But he will say, 'I tell you, [t]I do
not know where you come from. [v]Depart from me, all you workers of evil!' 28 [w]In that place

13 [x]See Mark 5:23 [y]ch. 5:25; 18:43; See ch. 7:16
14 [z]See ch. 8:41 [a]See Matt. 12:2 [b]Ex. 20:9; Ezek. 46:1
15 [c]ch. 14:5; [Matt. 12:11]
16 [d]ch. 19:9 [e][ver. 11; Acts 10:38; 1 Cor. 5:5; 2 Cor. 12:7]; See 1 Chr. 21:1
17 [f]Ps. 132:18; 1 Pet. 3:16 [g]ch. 18:43
18 [h]For ver. 18, 19, see Matt. 13:31, 32; Mark 4:30-32
19 [i]ch. 17:6; Matt. 17:20
21 [j]Matt. 13:33 [k]Gen. 18:6 [l]1 Cor. 5:6; Gal. 5:9
22 [m]See Mark 6:6 [n][ver. 33]; See ch. 9:51
23 [o]Acts 2:47; 1 Cor. 1:18; 2 Cor. 2:15
24 [p]1 Tim. 4:10; Heb. 12:4; [1 Tim. 6:12 (Gk.)]; See 1 Cor. 9:25 [q]Matt. 7:13
25 [r]For ver. 25-27, [Matt. 25:10-12] [s]Matt. 7:22, 23 [t]Matt. 10:33; 25:12; [2 Tim. 2:19]
26 [u][Ex. 24:11]
27 [t][See ver. 25 above] [v]See Ps. 6:8
28 [w]See Matt. 8:11, 12

in 6:1–5 and 6:6–11 involve Jesus' *lordship* over the Sabbath, this account involves the *meaning* of the Sabbath.

13:11 disabling spirit. For other examples of demons being associated with physical ailments, see 11:14; but see also note on 4:41.

13:13 immediately. The contrast with the 18 years of disability magnifies Jesus' miracle-working power (cf. 18:43).

13:14 For **ruler of the synagogue**, see notes on 8:41–42a; Mark 5:22. Because **Jesus had healed on the Sabbath**, the ruler's indignation was aroused, completely ignoring the woman's being freed from 18 years of suffering. Jesus was not violating any OT commandment; later Jewish traditions had added many more commandments and prohibitions than God had ever given in his Word.

13:15–16 You hypocrites. Cf. 6:42; 12:56. **Does not each of you** introduces a "lesser to greater" argument (cf. notes on 11:11–13; 12:6–7; 12:25–27; 18:1–8) in which the generally accepted practice of caring for animals on the Sabbath underscores the greater need to show such concern for a **daughter of Abraham**. **Untie** and **loosed** are the same word in Greek (*luō*).

13:18–21 *The Parables of the Mustard Seed and the Leaven.* Luke concludes his first section on Jesus' journey to Jerusalem (9:51–13:21) with two parables emphasizing the arrival of the kingdom (see Introduction: Key Themes). They contrast the kingdom's modest beginning and its glorious final state.

13:19 The **mustard seed** (see notes on Matt. 13:31–32 and Mark 4:30–32) would have been the smallest known seed to Jesus' audience. **became a tree**. The mustard "tree" refers to a large herbal plant that grows to the height of 8 to 12 feet (2.4 to 3.7 m). **The birds . . . made nests** emphasizes the surprising supernatural result—i.e., the enormous size of the final plant in comparison to the very small seed from which it grew. The Jews expected the kingdom to come with apocalyptic power, bringing God's judgment on all evil, and hence Jesus' teaching that it would arrive in such an "insignificant" way was surprising (cf. note on Luke 17:20).

13:21 Similar to the mustard seed (v. 19), a minute quantity of yeast can permeate a large amount of dough to produce a large amount of bread (cf. note on 1 Cor. 5:6–7). **Three measures** would have produced enough bread to feed 100 people. Some think these parables teach only the contrast between the small beginning and large end result, and not the gradual growth process of the kingdom between start and finish. Others argue that the growth process is also in view. Both sides agree that the parables contrast the apparently small and unnoticed arrival of the kingdom (the "already now") with its extensive and glorious consummation when the Son of Man returns (the "not yet"). See The Already and Not Yet of the Last Days, p. 1804.

13:22–17:10 *The Second Mention of the Journey to Jerusalem.* This next section begins with a second mention of Jesus' intention to go to Jerusalem ("journeying toward Jerusalem," v. 22; cf. "set his face," 9:51), where he will die for the sins of his people.

13:22–30 *The Narrow Door.* This account from Jesus' ministry opens with a summary (v. 22) and a question (v. 23), followed by a series of warnings (vv. 24, 25–27, 28–29) and a concluding summary (v. 30).

13:22 He went on his way . . . teaching (cf. 4:15, 31–32, 43–44) **and journeying toward Jerusalem**. Cf. 9:51–53.

13:23 Jesus' response to the question—**will those who are saved be few?**—does not speculate on God's plans and actions but states what individuals should do to be "saved." For a similar question, cf. 18:26.

13:24 To be "saved," one should **strive to enter through the narrow door**. This involves repentance (vv. 3, 5) and faith (8:12). **For many . . . will seek to enter and will not be able**. There will eventually be a time when the opportunity to trust in Christ will be taken away. (But see note on John 6:37.)

13:25–26 The second warning and analogy has to do with entering the **house** (i.e., the kingdom of God, v. 28) and warns that people may be shut out by the **Lord** (Jesus), in whose presence they **ate and drank** and whose teachings they heard. Listening to Jesus' teachings and sharing fellowship with his people are not by themselves any guarantee of eternal life, for that comes only through personal faith in Christ.

13:27 I do not know . . . depart from me. Jesus is not only the Savior but also the final Judge of all mankind (see note on 2 Cor. 5:10).

13:28 Abraham and Isaac and Jacob (cf. 20:37; Matt. 8:11; Acts 3:13;

there will be weeping and gnashing of teeth, when you see [w]Abraham and Isaac and Jacob
and all the prophets in the kingdom of God but [w]you yourselves cast out. 29 And [w]people will
come from east and west, and from north and south, and [x]recline at table in the kingdom of
God. 30 And behold, [y]some are last who will be first, and some are first who will be last."

Lament over Jerusalem

31 At that very hour some Pharisees came and said to him, "Get away from [z]here, for
[a]Herod wants to kill you." 32 And he said to them, "Go and tell that fox, 'Behold, I cast out
demons and perform cures today and tomorrow, and the third day [b]I finish my course.
33 Nevertheless, [c]I [d]must go on my way today and tomorrow and the day following, for it
cannot be that [e]a prophet should perish away from Jerusalem.' 34 [f]O Jerusalem, Jerusalem,
the city that [g]kills the prophets and stones those who are sent to it! [h]How often would I
have [i]gathered [j]your children together [k]as a hen gathers her brood [l]under her wings, and
[m]you were not willing! 35 Behold, [n]your house is forsaken. And I tell you, you will not see
me until you say, [o]'Blessed is he who comes in the name of the Lord!'"

Healing of a Man on the Sabbath

14 One Sabbath, [p]when he went to dine at the house of a ruler of the Pharisees, they
were [q]watching him carefully. 2 And behold, there was a man before him who had
dropsy. 3 And Jesus responded to [r]the lawyers and Pharisees, saying, [s]"Is it lawful to heal
on the Sabbath, or not?" 4 But they remained silent. Then he took him and healed him
and sent him away. 5 And he said to them, [t]"Which of you, having a son[1] or an ox that has
fallen into a well on a Sabbath day, will not immediately pull him out?" 6 [u]And they could
not reply to these things.

[1] Some manuscripts *a donkey*

29 [w][See ver. 28 above] [x][ch. 14:15; 22:30]
30 [y]See Matt. 19:30
31 [z][Matt. 19:1; Mark 10:1] [a]See ch. 3:1
32 [b][See Heb. 2:10; 5:9; 7:28]
33 [c][John 11:9] [d]Acts 3:21; 17:3 [e]See Matt. 21:11
34 [f]For ver. 34, 35, see Matt. 23:37-39; [ch. 19:41-44] [g]See Matt. 21:35 [h][Matt. 26:55] [i][Ps. 147:2; Prov. 1:24] [j]ch. 23:28 [k][Deut. 32:11, 12] [l]Ruth 2:12 [m]John 5:40
35 [n][Isa. 64:11; Jer. 12:7; 22:5] [o]ch. 19:38; Cited from Ps. 118:26

Chapter 14

1 [p]ch. 7:36; 11:37 [q]ch. 20:20; Mark 3:2
3 [r]See ch. 7:30 [s]ch. 13:14; Matt. 12:10
5 [t]ch. 13:15; [Deut. 22:4; Matt. 12:11]
6 [u][Matt. 22:46]

7:32) **and all the prophets** (Luke 11:50; 24:27; Acts 3:18, 24; 10:43) represent believing Israel **in the kingdom of God**. But those listening who did not believe in Jesus will be **cast out** or excluded.

13:29 In addition to believing Israelites (v. 28), believing Gentiles (people from the **east**, **west**, **north**, and **south**; cf. Ps. 107:3) will enter the kingdom (cf. Luke 24:47; Acts 1:8).

13:30 will be first . . . will be last. See Introduction: Key Themes; and notes on Matt. 19:30; 20:16.

13:31–35 *Lament over Jerusalem.* As he warns his disciples about Herod Antipas and laments over Jerusalem, Jesus again emphasizes that many Israelites will be excluded from the kingdom (cf. vv. 24, 25–28, 30).

13:31 At that very hour ties the present account closely with the preceding. **Herod** is Herod Antipas, tetrarch of Galilee and Perea, where Jesus likely was teaching; see notes on 3:1 and Matt. 14:1.

13:32 fox. A metaphor for deceitful cunning. **I cast . . . perform cures** (see 4:40–41) **. . . finish**. The present tenses emphasize Jesus' continuing ministry. **third day**. The day of Jesus' resurrection (see 9:22).

13:33 I must go. Jesus was committed to finishing his course. **Today and tomorrow** indicate a limited time (cf. Ex. 19:10). **for it cannot be**. Herod Antipas's plotting (Luke 13:31) could not interfere with God's plan. **that a prophet should perish away from Jerusalem**. Jesus did not mean that no prophet had ever died outside of Jerusalem, for some had (see 2 Chron. 24:20–22; Jer. 26:20–23; 38:4–6). Rather, he was employing irony: Jerusalem, the center of Jewish religion and worship, was more dangerous to a true prophet of God than any threats from Herod in Galilee. From the time of David onward, Jerusalem was chosen by God to be the center of worship for Israel, and the center of God's unique presence and redeeming work in the world ("the city of the great King," Matt. 5:35; cf. Ps. 48:1–3). Jerusalem boasted of its religious heritage as the former seat of the Davidic throne and the Solomonic temple. In the first century A.D., Herod the Great's monumental temple, along with the adjacent Antonia Fortress, served as the focal point of the city (see Jerusalem in the Time of Jesus, pp. 1878–1879). Under Herod, and later at the pleasure of the Romans, the Jewish high priest and Sanhedrin retained key aspects of religious leadership in the city. Herod built himself a palace at the Jaffa gate to the west. Nonetheless, after the dethroning of Herod's son Archelaus (A.D. 6; see Matt. 2:22) the city of Jerusalem was formally controlled by the Romans through their legate (except for a brief period under Agrippa I in 41–44) until the Jewish revolt (66–73).

13:34 O Jerusalem, Jerusalem (see 10:41). Jesus bemoaned the fate of Jerusalem, with its inhabitants at the time being around 25,000 to 30,000 (cf. the lament in Psalm 137). His lament, however, also applied to all of Israel, since Jerusalem was the religious and political center of the nation. **as a hen gathers her brood under her wings**. A common metaphor for loving care (cf. Deut. 32:11; Ruth 2:12; Ps. 17:8; 36:7; see note on Luke 19:41).

13:35 you will not see me until you say, "Blessed . . ." The quoted blessing is from Ps. 118:26; it was chanted to incoming pilgrims on feast days. This is not an allusion to Palm Sunday (Luke 19:38) because in Matthew's account (Matt. 23:39) the saying occurs after Palm Sunday, and therefore it must refer to a later event. Some interpreters understand this to refer in a negative way to a coerced, forced confession of Jesus as Lord at the time of the second coming, but the quotation from Ps. 118:26 is in a positive context of welcome and worship, and the phrase "Blessed is he" implies worship. Therefore other interpreters understand this to be a prediction that a large number of Jews will trust in Jesus before his second coming (cf. Rom. 11:12, 14, 24–27, 31–32).

14:1–6 *The Healing of a Man on the Sabbath.* This is Jesus' third and last Sabbath healing (cf. 6:6–11; 13:10–17).

14:2 dropsy (Gk. *hydrōpikos*). The man probably had edema, where excess fluid gathers in various parts of the body.

14:3 Is it lawful to heal on the Sabbath, or not? Cf. 6:9; 13:16. See note on Matt. 12:9–10.

14:4 they remained silent. By now the Pharisees have learned that they can never win when they get into an argument with Jesus (see, e.g., 5:30–6:11).

14:5 a son or an ox. See note on Matt. 12:11–12.

14:6 They could not reply emphasizes Jesus' mastery in debate. He has silenced all the Pharisees' objections and yet they will not believe in him or follow him (see notes on 6:10, 11).

7 [v] See ch. 11:43
10 [w] Prov. 25:6, 7
11 [x] ch. 18:14; [Prov. 29:23; Ezek. 21:26; Matt. 18:4; James 4:6, 10; 1 Pet. 5:5, 6]
12 [y] John 21:12 (Gk.) [z] [ch. 6:34]
13 [a] [Neh. 8:10, 12; Esth. 9:22] [b] ver. 21
14 [c] 1 Cor. 15:23; 1 Thess. 4:16; [John 11:24; Rev. 20:4, 5] [d] Acts 24:15
15 [e] Rev. 19:9 [f] [ch. 13:29; 22:16, 30]
16 [g] For ver. 16-24, [Matt. 22:2-14] [h] [Isa. 25:6]
17 [i] [Esth. 6:14; Prov. 9:3, 5]
20 [j] Deut. 24:5
21 [k] ver. 13
24 [m] Matt. 21:43; Acts 13:46

The Parable of the Wedding Feast

7 Now he told a parable to those who were invited, when he noticed [v] how they chose
the places of honor, saying to them, 8 "When you are invited by someone to a wedding
feast, do not sit down in a place of honor, lest someone more distinguished than you be
invited by him, 9 and he who invited you both will come and say to you, 'Give your place
to this person,' and then you will begin with shame to take the lowest place. 10 But when
you are invited, go and sit in the lowest place, [w] so that when your host comes he may say
to you, 'Friend, move up higher.' Then you will be honored in the presence of all who sit at
table with you. 11 For [x] everyone who exalts himself will be humbled, and he who humbles
himself will be exalted."

The Parable of the Great Banquet

12 He said also to the man who had invited him, "When you give [y] a dinner or a banquet,
do not invite your friends or your brothers[1] or your relatives or rich neighbors, [z] lest they
also invite you in return and you be repaid. 13 But when you give a feast, [a] invite [b] the poor,
the crippled, the lame, the blind, 14 and you will be blessed, because they cannot repay you.
For you will be repaid [c] at [d] the resurrection of the just."

15 When one of those who reclined at table with him heard these things, he said to
him, [e] "Blessed is everyone who will [f] eat bread in the kingdom of God!" 16 But he said
to him, [g] "A man once [h] gave a great banquet and invited many. 17 And at the time for the
banquet he [i] sent his servant[2] to say to those who had been invited, 'Come, for everything is now ready.' 18 But they all alike began to make excuses. The first said to him,
'I have bought a field, and I must go out and see it. Please have me excused.' 19 And
another said, 'I have bought five yoke of oxen, and I go to examine them. Please have
me excused.' 20 And another said, [j] 'I have married a wife, and therefore I cannot come.'
21 So the servant came and reported these things to his master. Then the master of the
house became angry and said to his servant, 'Go out quickly to the streets and lanes of
the city, and bring in [k] the poor and crippled and blind and lame.' 22 And the servant
said, 'Sir, what you commanded has been done, and still there is room.' 23 And the master
said to the servant, 'Go out to the highways and hedges and compel people to come in,
that my house may be filled. 24 For I tell you,[3] [m] none of those men who were invited
shall taste my banquet.'"

[1] Or *your brothers and sisters*. The plural Greek word *adelphoi* (translated "brothers") refers to siblings in a family. In New Testament usage, depending on the context, *adelphoi* may refer either to *brothers* or to *brothers and sisters* [2] Greek *bondservant;* also verses 21, 22, 23 [3] The Greek word for *you* here is plural

14:7–17:10 *Various Teachings and Parables.* Jesus teaches on discipleship and God's love.

14:7–11 The parable of the wedding feast was directed to **those who were invited** to the dinner at the house of the Pharisee (v. 1); similarly, the parable of the great banquet (see vv. 12–24) was directed to "the man who had invited him" to that dinner (v. 12). **when he noticed**. Here (as in 18:1, 9; 19:11), Luke states at the beginning Jesus' purpose in telling the parable. The parable teaches the wisdom of humility: it is better to be humble than humiliated (**lowest place . . . move up higher**; cf. Prov. 25:6–7). **will be humbled . . . will be exalted** (cf. Luke 18:14). As the parable shows, sometimes this happens even in this life, but it will take place most fully at the final judgment (cf. James 4:6, 10; 1 Pet. 5:5–6).

14:12–14 do not invite your friends (but do) **invite the poor, the crippled, the lame, the blind**. Jesus again emphasizes the radical generosity and care that his disciples are to show toward those who are physically impaired and economically deprived.

14:15 Blessed is everyone who will eat seems to be a common saying, possibly intended here to change the uncomfortable subject—i.e., to shift the focus away from the need to care for the poor and the infirm. **In the kingdom of God** points to the future messianic banquet, to which the people of Jesus' day would have understood only godly Jews would be invited. Jesus, however, uses the parable to teach his listeners, contrary to their expectations, that the guests invited originally will miss the banquet (v. 24) and will be replaced instead by "the poor and crippled and blind and lame" and the outsiders (the Gentiles) found in the "highways and hedges" (vv. 21, 23).

14:16–20 A **great banquet** refers to the arrival of the kingdom in the ministry of Jesus, with its initial present taste of the joyful fellowship with God that will be fully realized in the coming age. **invited many**. Two invitations would have been involved. The first would have concerned reservations for the banquet and would have been given well in advance. The second invitation would have been given on the day of the banquet, announcing that the **time for the banquet** had come and **everything** was **ready**. Although the guests had been invited well in advance, they **began to make excuses**—failing to see that the kingdom is now here, and that God is inviting people to participate in its great blessings. **Bought a field . . . bought five yoke of oxen . . . have married a wife** shows that these people have put the business of everyday life ahead of the claims of God and his kingdom, and they are therefore not worthy to enter it (Jesus taught on similar themes in 8:19–21; 9:23–24, 59–62; 10:41–42; 12:31; cf. 14:26–27).

14:21–24 Streets and lanes, within the city, were where the outcasts of Israelite society (the **poor, crippled, blind**, and **lame**; cf. v. 13) would be found. The **highways and hedges**, outside the city, represent Gentiles being invited into the kingdom. **compel people to come in**. The Greek (*anagkazō*) usually means to "compel" or "force" someone, but a number of interpreters understand a weaker sense here: "strongly urge, persuade." That sense seems better suited to the context and is supported in other examples in Greek literature. The kingdom will be **filled**, but many of those originally invited will be excluded.

The Cost of Discipleship

25 Now great crowds accompanied him, and he turned and said to them, 26 [n]"If anyone
comes to me and [o]does not hate his own father and mother and wife and children and
brothers and sisters, [p]yes, and even his own life, he cannot be my disciple. 27 [q]Whoever
does not [r]bear his own cross and come after me cannot be my disciple. 28 For which of
you, desiring to build a tower, does not [s]first sit down and count the cost, whether he
has enough to complete it? 29 Otherwise, when he has laid a foundation and is not able to
finish, all who see it begin to mock him, 30 saying, 'This man began to build and was not
able to finish.' 31 Or what king, going out to encounter another king in war, will not [t]sit
down first and deliberate whether he is able with ten thousand to meet him who comes
against him with twenty thousand? 32 And if not, while the other is yet a great way off, he
sends a delegation and asks for terms of peace. 33 [u]So therefore, any one of you who [v]does
not renounce all that he has cannot be my disciple.

Salt Without Taste Is Worthless

34 [w]"Salt is good, [x]but if salt has lost its taste, how shall its saltiness be restored? 35 It is
of no use either for the soil or for the manure pile. It is thrown away. [y]He who has ears to
hear, let him hear."

The Parable of the Lost Sheep

15 Now [z]the tax collectors and sinners were all drawing near to hear him. 2 And the
Pharisees and the scribes [a]grumbled, saying, [b]"This man receives sinners and [c]eats
with them."
3 So he told them this parable: 4 [d]"What man of you, having a hundred sheep, [e]if he has
lost one of them, does not leave the ninety-nine [f]in the open country, and [g]go after the
one that is lost, until he finds it? 5 And when he has found it, [h]he lays it on his shoulders,
rejoicing. 6 And when he comes home, he calls together his friends and his neighbors,
saying to them, 'Rejoice with me, for [i]I have found my sheep that was lost.' 7 Just so, I tell
you, there will be more joy in heaven over one sinner who [j]repents than over ninety-nine
[k]righteous persons who need no repentance.

The Parable of the Lost Coin

8 "Or what woman, having ten silver coins,[1] if she loses one coin, does not light a lamp
and sweep the house and seek diligently until she finds it? 9 And when she has found it,

[1] Greek *ten drachmas*; a *drachma* was a Greek coin approximately equal in value to a Roman *denarius*, worth about a day's wage for a laborer

26 [n]ver. 33; Matt. 10:37; [Deut. 33:9] [o]ch. 16:13 [p]John 12:25; Acts 20:24; Rev. 12:11
27 [q]ch. 9:23; Matt. 10:38; 16:24; Mark 8:34 [r]John 19:17
28 [s][Prov. 24:27]
31 [t]ver. 28
33 [u][Phil. 3:7] [v][ver. 26; ch. 18:28]
34 [w]Mark 9:50 [x]Matt. 5:13
35 [y]See Matt. 11:15

Chapter 15

1 [z]See Matt. 11:19
2 [a]ch. 19:7; [Ex. 16:2, 7, 8; Num. 14:2; Josh. 9:18] [b][ch. 7:39] [c]ch. 5:30; Matt. 9:11; 11:19; Mark 2:16; [Acts 11:3; 1 Cor. 5:11; Gal. 2:12]
4 [d]For ver. 4-7, [Matt. 18:12-14] [e]Ezek. 34:6; [1 Pet. 2:25] [f][Ex. 3:1; 1 Sam. 17:28] [g]Ezek. 34:4, 11, 12, 16; [ch. 19:10]
5 [h][Isa. 40:11; 49:22; 60:4; 66:12]
6 [i]1 Pet. 2:25
7 [j]ver. 10; See ch. 5:32 [k][ch. 5:32; Matt. 9:13]

14:25 Great crowds continue to follow Jesus (see 4:37).

14:26 If anyone comes to me. Cf. 9:23–24. Those who would be Christ's disciples must (1) love their family less than they love Christ (14:26); (2) bear the cross and follow Christ (v. 27); and (3) relinquish everything (v. 33). These are complementary ways of describing complete commitment. The first condition for discipleship is to **hate** one's **father, mother, wife, children, brothers, sisters,** and **life** (cf. 18:29; see 6:20–22). "Hating" is a Semitic expression for loving less (cf. Gen. 29:30–31; Deut. 21:15–17; Matt. 10:37).

14:27 For the second condition for discipleship, **bear his own cross and come after me**, see notes on Matt. 10:38 and Mark 8:34.

14:28–32 Two parabolic illustrations involving building (vv. 28–30) and going to war (vv. 31–32) both warn against making a hasty decision to follow Jesus. Potential disciples must first **count the cost** to see if they will persevere in the faith (cf. 8:15; 21:19).

14:33 The third condition for discipleship (see note on v. 26) involves renouncing **all** (cf. 5:11, 28; 12:33; 18:22).

14:34 if salt has lost its taste. Most salt came from the Dead Sea and contained impurities (carnallite and gypsum). If not processed properly, it would have a poor taste and would be worse than useless, being unusable for food and creating a disposal problem. If the conditions of discipleship (vv. 26–27, 33) are not kept, the disciples likewise will become less than worthless (cf. Rev. 3:15–17).

15:1 Tax collectors (see notes on 3:12–14 and Matt. 5:46–47) **and sinners** (see note on Matt. 9:10) are also associated together in Luke 5:30; 7:34; 19:7. **Were all drawing near to hear him** reveals Jesus' popularity with the outcasts of society who had "ears to hear" (14:35).

15:2 Pharisees and the scribes. See notes on 5:17, 21–22; also Matt. 5:20; Mark 7:5. **grumbled**. See note on Luke 5:30; cf. 19:7. **Receives sinners and eats with them** again reflects Jesus' concern for the outsider. For similar criticisms, cf. 5:27–32; 7:39; 19:7. For the implications of eating with sinners, see note on 5:30.

15:3 So he told them. The following parables are directed to the Pharisees and scribes. The lost sheep (vv. 4–7), lost coin (vv. 8–10), and prodigal son (vv. 11–32) all correspond to lost sinners being found by Jesus (i.e., entering the kingdom of God).

15:4 The man leaves the **ninety-nine in the open country** to **go after** the one **lost** (cf. 19:10; John 10:11, 14).

15:5 lays it on his shoulders. The sheep is too weak to return on its own.

15:6 calls together his friends and his neighbors. Cf. v. 9. The Pharisees and scribes should **rejoice** that the lost sheep of Israel are entering the kingdom.

15:7 Joy in heaven contrasts with the grumbling of Jesus' opponents. It apparently means that both God and all the heavenly beings, including the angels, rejoice greatly (cf. v. 10). **righteous persons who need no repentance** (cf. 5:31–32). In light of the emphasis in Luke–Acts on the universal need of repentance (see Luke 3:3) and the evil of humanity (11:13; cf. Rom. 3:10–20), this is best understood as ironic for "those who think they are righteous and have no need to repent."

15:8 ten silver coins. Lit., "ten *drachmas*" (perhaps about 10 denarii, hence 10 days' wages for a laborer).

10[l] See ch. 12:8
12[m] Deut. 21:17 [n] ver. 30; Mark 12:44
13[o] [Eph. 5:18; Titus 1:6; 1 Pet. 4:4]
16[p] [ch. 16:21]
17[q] [1 Kgs. 8:47] [r] [Acts 12:11]
18[s] [Ex. 10:16] [t] Matt. 21:25; John 3:27
19[u] [ch. 7:6, 7]
20[v] [James 4:8] [w] Gen. 33:4; Acts 20:37 [x] 2 Sam. 14:33
21[u] [See ver. 19 above]
22[y] Zech. 3:3-5 [z] Gen. 41:42; Esth. 3:10; 8:2 [a] Ezek. 16:10
23[b] [1 Sam. 28:24] [c] [ch. 12:19]
24[d] ver. 32; [Rom. 11:15; Eph. 2:1; Col. 2:13; Rev. 3:1]
29[e] ver. 23
30[f] Prov. 29:3 [g] ver. 12

she calls together her friends and neighbors, saying, 'Rejoice with me, for I have found
the coin that I had lost.' **10** Just so, I tell you, there is joy before [l]the angels of God over one
sinner who repents."

The Parable of the Prodigal Son

11 And he said, "There was a man who had two sons. **12** And the younger of them said to
his father, 'Father, give me [m]the share of property that is coming to me.' And he divided
[n]his property between them. **13** Not many days later, the younger son gathered all he had
and took a journey into a far country, and there he squandered his property in [o]reckless
living. **14** And when he had spent everything, a severe famine arose in that country, and
he began to be in need. **15** So he went and hired himself out to[1] one of the citizens of that
country, who sent him into his fields to feed pigs. **16** And he [p]was longing to be fed with
the pods that the pigs ate, and no one gave him anything.

17 "But [q]when he [r]came to himself, he said, 'How many of my father's hired servants
have more than enough bread, but I perish here with hunger! **18** I will arise and go to my
father, and I will say to him, "Father, [s]I have sinned against [t]heaven and before you. **19** [u]I
am no longer worthy to be called your son. Treat me as one of your hired servants."' **20** And
he arose and came to his father. But while he was still a long way off, his father saw him
and felt compassion, and [v]ran and [w]embraced him and [x]kissed him. **21** And the son said
to him, 'Father, I have sinned against heaven and before you. [u]I am no longer worthy to
be called your son.'[2] **22** But the father said to his servants,[3] 'Bring quickly [y]the best robe,
and put it on him, and put [z]a ring on his hand, and [a]shoes on his feet. **23** And bring [b]the
fattened calf and kill it, and [c]let us eat and celebrate. **24** For this my son [d]was dead, and is
alive again; he was lost, and is found.' And they began to celebrate.

25 "Now his older son was in the field, and as he came and drew near to the house, he
heard music and dancing. **26** And he called one of the servants and asked what these things
meant. **27** And he said to him, 'Your brother has come, and your father has killed the fattened
calf, because he has received him back safe and sound.' **28** But he was angry and refused to
go in. His father came out and entreated him, **29** but he answered his father, 'Look, these
many years I have served you, and I never disobeyed your command, yet you never gave
me a young goat, that I might [e]celebrate with my friends. **30** But when this son of yours
came, [f]who has devoured [g]your property with prostitutes, you killed the fattened calf for

[1] Greek *joined himself to* [2] Some manuscripts add *treat me as one of your hired servants* [3] Greek *bondservants*

15:12 give me . . . property . . . coming to me. The younger son does not want to wait for his father's death to receive his inheritance. He was probably a teenager, since he was unmarried. His share would have been half of what the older brother would receive, or one-third of the estate (cf. Deut. 21:17). **He divided** indicates that the father responded to his younger son's request and allowed him to make his own choice to go his own way.

15:13 Gathered all indicates that the son converted into cash all of his inheritance, which may have included land or cattle, which he then foolishly **squandered . . . in reckless living**.

15:15 In desperation the son **hired himself out** to a Gentile **to feed pigs** (unclean animals; Lev. 11:7; Deut. 14:8) that would have been repugnant to him.

15:16 no one gave him anything. His worldly friends all deserted him.

15:17–18 When the son **came to himself** he realized that his sin was not only against his earthly father but in the deepest sense **against heaven**, that is, against God himself.

15:20 A long way off emphasizes the father's great love; he must have been watching for the son. **ran**. The father cast aside all behavioral conventions of the time, as running was considered to be undignified for an older person, especially a wealthy landowner such as this man. **embraced him**. Literally "fell on his neck"; cf. Gen. 33:4; 45:14; 46:29.

15:21 The prodigal repeats his prepared speech (cf. vv. 18–19), but the father cuts him short before he finishes, showing that he has forgiven him.

15:22 The **best robe** and **ring** and **shoes** give a picture of the finest clothing, so that the son is ornately dressed. The ring may have contained a seal, indicating that he has been reconciled and welcomed back as a full member of the family.

15:23 fattened calf. Kept for special occasions (Gen. 18:7; Amos 6:4). They will **eat and celebrate** in thanksgiving to God and not godless self-indulgence (contrast Luke 12:19).

15:24 The **son was** (assumed to be) **dead**, but is now **alive** (united with the family) **again**: a picture of membership in God's kingdom.

15:25 While the younger son represents tax collectors and sinners, the **older son** represents the Pharisees. Both groups were listening to the parables of this chapter (see vv. 1–3), but the Pharisees were probably the primary intended audience of this parable (see note on v. 3).

15:27 Safe in the protection of the father's household and **sound** in terms of both spiritual and physical health.

15:28 He was angry mirrors the grumbling of the Pharisees and scribes (v. 2).

15:29 but he answered his father. The older brother protests that the welcome extended to the returning younger son is not fair, likening life with his father to years of servitude without celebration. The picture offers a sharp contrast between, on one hand, the mercy and grace extended by the father (representing God the Father) and, on the other hand, the self-righteous resentment (**never disobeyed . . . yet you never gave me**) of the older brother (exemplified by the Pharisees).

15:30 this son of yours. The older brother refuses to acknowledge the prodigal as his brother.

him!' 31 And he said to him, 'Son, [h]you are always with me, and all that is mine is yours.
32 It was fitting [e]to celebrate and be glad, for this your brother [i]was dead, and is alive; he
was lost, and is found.' "

The Parable of the Dishonest Manager

16 He also said to the disciples, "There was a rich man who had [j]a manager, and charges
were brought to him that this man was wasting his possessions. 2 And he called him
and said to him, 'What is this that I hear about you? Turn in the account of your [k]manage-
ment, for you can no longer be manager.' 3 And the manager said to himself, 'What shall
I do, since my master is taking the management away from me? I am not strong enough
to dig, and I am ashamed to beg. 4 I have decided what to do, so that when I am removed
from management, people may receive me into their houses.' 5 So, summoning his master's
debtors one by one, he said to the first, 'How much do you owe my master?' 6 He said, 'A
hundred measures[1] of oil.' He said to him, 'Take your bill, and sit down quickly and write
fifty.' 7 Then he said to another, 'And how much do you owe?' He said, 'A hundred measures[2]
of wheat.' He said to him, 'Take your bill, and write eighty.' 8 The master commended the
dishonest manager for his [l]shrewdness. For [m]the sons of this world[3] are [l]more shrewd in
dealing with their own generation than [n]the sons of light. 9 And I tell you, [o]make friends
for yourselves by means of [p]unrighteous wealth,[4] so that when it fails they may receive
you into the eternal dwellings.

10 [q]"One who is [r]faithful in a very little is also faithful in much, and one who is dishonest
in a very little is also dishonest in much. 11 If then you have not been faithful in the unrighteous wealth, who will entrust to you the true riches? 12 And if you have not been faithful
in [s]that which is another's, who will give you that which is your own? 13 [p]No servant can

[1] About 875 gallons or 3,200 liters [2] Between 1,000 and 1,200 bushels or 37,000 or 45,000 liters [3] Greek *age* [4] Greek *mammon*, a Semitic word for money or possessions; also verse 11; rendered *money* in verse 13

31 [h]John 8:35
32 [e][See ver. 29 above] [i]ver. 24

Chapter 16

1 [j]ch. 12:42
2 [k]See 1 Cor. 9:17
8 [l]See Matt. 25:2 [m]ch. 20:34; See ch. 10:6 [n]John 12:36; 1 Thess. 5:5; [Eph. 5:8]
9 [o][ch. 12:33; Matt. 6:20; 19:21; 1 Tim. 6:10, 17-19] [p]ver. 11, 13; Matt. 6:24
10 [q]Matt. 25:21, 23 [r]ch. 19:17
12 [s][1 Chr. 29:14, 16]
13 [p][See ver. 9 above]

15:31 Son. An affectionate appeal by the father, showing that he still loved the older son and wanted him to join in the celebration. By implication, Jesus is still inviting the Pharisees to repent and accept the good news.

16:1 The audience for the parable of the dishonest manager (vv. 1–8a) included Christ's disciples (v. 1) and also the Pharisees (v. 14). The **manager** is the steward in charge of the estate, a trusted servant who exercised the chief responsibility for the management and distribution of the household goods. The manager acted as the agent for his master, and had full authority to transact business on behalf of his master. **wasting his possessions**. The manager's dishonesty is a central theme woven throughout the parable. The manager is clearly guilty as charged, because when the master fired him (v. 2), the manager made no attempt to defend himself (v. 3).

16:4–7 The dishonest manager **decided** that, in his last few moments as manager, he would seek to ingratiate himself with his master's debtors **so that** they would still owe him favors, thus assuring his future well-being (**may receive me into their houses**). The reduction of both bills would have amounted to about 500 denarii (about 20 months' wages).

16:8a The master commended the dishonest manager. Various explanations have been suggested for this seemingly undeserved commendation: (1) In giving the discounts, the manager had excluded any commission for himself; but the discounts seem too high for that to have been the case. (2) The debts were hard to collect and, by reducing the amounts, the manager provided a sudden influx of cash for his master. (3) The master commended the manager for his shrewdness in looking out for himself (but this does not mean that the master praises him for his evil). In any case, the details of the parable should not be pressed, for a parable often makes only one major point, and here the main point is that the manager had great foresight to anticipate his financial needs after his dismissal, thus using his financial expertise to make friends for himself (see note on v. 9).

16:8b Verses 8b–13 constitute a series of teachings related to the parable of the dishonest manager (vv. 1–8a). Jesus applies the parable both as a comparison and as a contrast. In contrast to the manager, Jesus' disciples must not use their money unrighteously, but like the manager they must use their money in such a way that they prepare for their future life. The **sons of this world** (or, "this age") often show more concern and skill in taking care of their earthly well-being than do the **sons of light** (i.e., believers) in taking care of eternal matters.

16:9 And I tell you is a solemn expression stressing the importance of the application, which Jesus now states by admonishing his disciples to be generous in their use of money and possessions. **Unrighteous wealth** probably refers to the way in which the pursuit of money may often involve: (1) unrighteous means in acquiring wealth by taking advantage of others; (2) unrighteous desires in the use of wealth for personal gratification and selfish purposes, rather than for the care and well-being of others; and (3) the corrupting influence of wealth that often leads people into unrighteousness. The word translated here as "wealth" is a Hebrew and Aramaic term (Hb. and Aramaic *mamon*; Gk. *mamōnas*; English "mammon") for wealth and possessions (including money) and is the same word translated "money" in v. 13 (see ESV footnote). **so that when it fails**. Because wealth will inevitably fail both to satisfy and to provide for eternal needs, Jesus exhorts his disciples to **make friends for yourselves** in the generous use of wealth and possessions for the care and well-being of others, so that when wealth does fail, **they may receive you into the eternal dwellings**. "They" probably refers to the "friends" who have been helped by such generous giving. Believers who use their wealth and possessions generously in this way give evidence of their faith and commitment to God and of their understanding that God will give eternal rewards to those who are generous in their use of the resources he has entrusted to them.

16:11 Unrighteous wealth here refers to earthly money and possessions (see note on v. 9). **True riches** means spiritual stewardship and responsibility in God's kingdom, and ultimately heavenly reward as well (cf. 12:33; 18:22; Matt. 6:19–21, 24).

16:12 Not . . . faithful in that which is another's means faithfulness with respect to worldly possessions that God entrusts to his people for their stewardship during their lifetime (cf. 19:11–27). **Your own** refers back to the "true riches" of 16:11 regarding spiritual responsibility in God's kingdom and heavenly reward.

16:13 You cannot serve God and money. Jesus does not say "*should not* serve" but "*cannot* serve"; see note on Matt. 6:24. Those who are Jesus' true disciples must make an either/or choice between serving God and serving money. "Money" is personified here in parallel with "God," indicating the way

serve two masters, for either he will hate the one and love the other, or he will be devoted
to the one and despise the other. You cannot serve God and money."

The Law and the Kingdom of God

14 [t]The Pharisees, who were [u]lovers of money, heard all these things, and they [v]ridiculed him.
15 And he said to them, "You are those who [w]justify yourselves before men, but [x]God knows
your hearts. For what is exalted among men [y]is an abomination in the sight of God.
16 [z]"The Law and the Prophets were until John; since then [a]the good news of the kingdom
of God is preached, and [b]everyone forces his way into it.[1] **17** But [c]it is easier for heaven and
earth to pass away than for one dot of the Law to become void.

Divorce and Remarriage

18 [d]"Everyone who divorces his wife and marries another commits adultery, and he who
marries a woman divorced from her husband commits adultery.

The Rich Man and Lazarus

19 "There was a rich man who was clothed in [e]purple and fine linen and [f]who feasted
sumptuously every day. **20** And at his gate [g]was laid a poor man named Lazarus, covered
with sores, **21** who desired to be fed with [h]what fell from the rich man's table. Moreover,
even the dogs came and licked his sores. **22** The poor man died and was carried by [i]the
angels [j]to Abraham's side.[2] The rich man also died and was buried, **23** and in [k]Hades, being
in torment, he lifted up his eyes and [l]saw Abraham far off and Lazarus [j]at his side. **24** And
he called out, [m]'Father Abraham, have mercy on me, and send Lazarus to dip the end of

[1] *Or everyone is forcefully urged into it* [2] Greek *bosom*; also verse 23

14 [t][ch. 11:39; 20:47] [u]2 Tim. 3:2; [1 Tim. 6:10] [v]ch. 23:35
15 [w]ch. 10:29 [x]1 Sam. 16:7; 1 Chr. 28:9; Prov. 21:2 [y]Prov. 16:5
16 [z]Matt. 11:12, 13 [a]See ch. 4:43 [b][ch. 15:1]
17 [c]Matt. 5:18
18 [d]See Matt. 5:32
19 [e]Esth. 8:15; Rev. 18:16 [f][James 5:5]
20 [g][Acts 3:2]
21 [h][Matt. 15:27]
22 [i]ch. 15:10; Matt. 18:10; Acts 12:15; Heb. 1:13, 14; See ch. 12:8 [j][John 13:23 (Gk.)]
23 [k]See Matt. 11:23 [l]Matt. 8:11, 12 [j][See ver. 22 above]
24 [m]ver. 30; John 8:33, 39, 53

in which money can often take on an idolatrous place in one's life. The way to serve God rather than money is to put one's resources to the service of others and the work of the kingdom.

16:14 For the Pharisees as **lovers of money**, cf. 11:39; 20:46–47. **ridiculed**. The opposition of the Pharisees now escalates from grumbling (15:2) to ridicule.

16:15 justify yourselves. Cf. 10:29. People who seek to appear righteous before others typically are not righteous before God, for **God knows your hearts**. **What is exalted among men** includes any kind of human achievement not done for the glory of God. Cf. 18:9–14.

16:16 The Law and the Prophets is the old covenant age, now superseded by the kingdom of God. **until John**. John the Baptist was still part of the old covenant age, so that his ministry served as the culmination of a long history of OT prophecy that looked forward to the coming of the messianic kingdom. **Since then** (since John's ministry, which overlapped with the beginning of Jesus' ministry), the new covenant period has begun. **Everyone forces his way into it** is a puzzling and much debated statement. Greek *biazō* means "to use force," but the verb form here (*biazetai*) could be either in the middle voice ("everyone is using force" to enter into it) or in the passive voice ("everyone is being forced [or forcefully urged]" to enter into it). The meaning in the ESV text, "everyone forces his way into it," is possible grammatically and fits the meaning of the same verb when used in Matt. 11:12. By this interpretation, the verse suggests that exercising the faith that brings one into the kingdom and keeps one there involves a kind of holy "violence" toward oneself in the form of repentance and self-denial. Some interpreters object, however, that this view does not fit well in the context, for *not everyone* is forcing their way into the kingdom and in fact *many are rejecting it*. In addition, there is arguably some tension between forcing one's way into the kingdom and the emphasis throughout the Gospels on entering the kingdom of God by faith. These interpreters have favored the meaning in the ESV footnote, "everyone is forcefully urged into it." The verb takes that sense elsewhere (see Gen. 33:11; 2 Sam. 13:25, 27; *parabiazomai* has this meaning in Luke 24:29; Acts 16:15). This is similar to the idea of Luke 14:23 (see note on 14:21–24). On this view, the meaning of *biazō* would be different from its sense in Matt. 11:12, but the verses appear in different contexts and the meaning may be different as well (cf. note on Matt. 11:12).

16:17 But suggests that Jesus is seeking to correct a possible misunderstanding of v. 16a, showing that the OT moral law still has validity as the Word of God (see note on Matt. 5:18). Those laws will never become **void** since they reflect the very person and character of God, who will never **pass away**. (In Luke 21:33, Jesus ascribes to his own teaching the same permanence and authority.)

16:18 Everyone who divorces . . . and marries another commits adultery. No exception is mentioned in Mark or Luke, but Matthew adds "except on the ground of sexual immorality" (Matt. 5:32; 19:9) and Paul allows for divorce in the case of desertion by an unbelieving partner (1 Cor. 7:10–11). For more on divorce and remarriage, see notes on Matt. 5:31–32; 19:3–9; Mark 10:10–12; 1 Cor. 7:15; and Divorce and Remarriage, pp. 2545–2547.

16:19–20 There was a rich man. Jesus continues to address and repudiate the abusive use of riches with this additional dramatic parable contrasting the excesses of the rich man and the destitute condition of Lazarus. The rich man is dressed in regal splendor (**clothed in purple**), feasting **sumptuously every day**, while the **poor man named Lazarus** lies at his gate, starving and **covered with sores**—a picture that conveys the utter disregard of the rich man for the poverty-stricken person living in the shadow of the rich man's own opulent self-indulgence.

16:21 Though Lazarus would have eaten even **what fell from the rich man's table**, there is no indication that the rich man gave him anything. **dogs came and licked his sores**. The culmination of the poor man's misery; the reference here is not to friendly household pets but to dangerous unclean dogs that ran wild in the streets.

16:22–23 The **poor man died** and received no burial, in contrast to the **rich man** who **was buried**. The poor man **was carried . . . to Abraham's side** (lit., "bosom"), which means he was welcomed into the fellowship of other believers already in heaven, particularly Abraham, the father of the Jewish people. But the rich man went to **Hades** (the place of the wicked, the dead, or "hell"), a place of **torment**. That the rich man **saw Abraham far off** indicates the unbridgeable gulf between heaven and hell. The previous earthly situations of the rich man and Lazarus are completely reversed. As in 13:28, the unbelieving dead seem to have some awareness of the blessedness of believers in heaven. Though this is a parable, and thus it is unclear how far the actual details should be pressed, the story seems clearly to teach that, immediately after death, both believers and unbelievers have a conscious awareness of their eternal status and enter at once into either suffering or blessing.

16:24 have mercy. The merciless one now seeks mercy but will not receive it

his finger in water and [n]cool my tongue, for [o]I am in anguish in this flame.' **25** But Abraham
said, 'Child, remember that [p]you in your lifetime received your good things, and Lazarus
in like manner bad things; but now he is comforted here, and you are in anguish. **26** And
besides all this, between us and you a great chasm has been fixed, in order that those
who would pass from here to you may not be able, and none may cross from there to us.'
27 And he said, 'Then I beg you, father, to send him to my father's house— **28** for I have five
brothers[1]—so that he may warn them, lest they also come into this place of torment.' **29** But
Abraham said, 'They have [q]Moses and the Prophets; [r]let them hear them.' **30** And he said,
'No, [s]father Abraham, but if someone goes to them from the dead, they will repent.' **31** He
said to him, 'If they do not hear [q]Moses and the Prophets, [t]neither will they be convinced
if someone should rise from the dead.' "

Temptations to Sin

17 And he said to his disciples, [u]"Temptations to sin[2] are [v]sure to come, but [w]woe to
the one through whom they come! **2** [x]It would be better for him if a millstone were
hung around his neck and he were cast into the sea than that he should cause one of these
little ones to sin.[3] **3** Pay attention to yourselves! [y]If your brother sins, [z]rebuke him, and if
he repents, [a]forgive him, **4** and if he sins against you [b]seven times in the day, and turns to
you seven times, saying, 'I repent,' you must forgive him."

Increase Our Faith

5 [c]The apostles said to the Lord, [d]"Increase our faith!" **6** And the Lord said, [e]"If you had
faith like [f]a grain of mustard seed, you could say to this [g]mulberry tree, 'Be uprooted and
planted in the sea,' and it would obey you.

Unworthy Servants

7 "Will any one of you who has a servant[4] plowing or keeping sheep say to him when
he has come in from the field, 'Come at once and recline at table'? **8** Will he not rather say
to him, 'Prepare supper for me, and [h]dress properly,[5] and serve me while I eat and drink,
and afterward you will eat and drink'? **9** Does he thank the servant because he did what
was commanded? **10** So you also, when you have done all that you were commanded, say,
'We are [i]unworthy servants;[6] we have done only what was our duty.' "

[1] *Or brothers and sisters* [2] Greek *Stumbling blocks* [3] Greek *stumble* [4] Greek *bondservant;* also verse 9 [5] Greek *gird yourself* [6] Greek *bondservants*

24 [n][Zech. 14:12] [o][Isa. 66:24]; See Matt. 25:41
25 [p][ch. 6:24; Job 21:13; Ps. 17:14]
29 [q]ver. 31; ch. 24:27; Acts 26:22; 28:23 [r][John 5:45-47]
30 [s]ver. 24
31 [q][See ver. 29 above] [t][Matt. 28:11-15; John 12:10, 11]

Chapter 17

1 [u]Matt. 18:7 [v]See Matt. 13:41 [w]ch. 22:22
2 [x]Matt. 18:6; Mark 9:42
3 [y]Matt. 18:15, 21, 22 [z]Lev. 19:17 [a]See Matt. 6:14
4 [b][Matt. 18:21]
5 [c]See Mark 6:30 [d][Mark 9:24]
6 [e]Matt. 17:20 [f]Matt. 13:31 [g][ch. 19:4 (Gk.)]
8 [h]John 13:4; [ch. 12:35, 37]
10 [i]Matt. 25:30; [Job 22:2, 3; 35:7; Rom. 11:35]

(vv. 25–26) because the "year of the Lord's favor" (4:19) has passed. **send Lazarus**. The rich man knows Lazarus's name and thus knew his plight, though he had ignored it. The conversation between the rich man and Abraham may be one of those details of the parable that should not be pressed for doctrinal significance, for nowhere else in Scripture is there any indication that there will be personal communication between those in heaven and those in hell.

16:25 Although physically a **"child** of Abraham," the rich man was not one of Abraham's true offspring (cf. John 8:39) because he lacked Abraham's faith (cf. Rom. 9:6ff.; Gal. 3:9, 29). **good . . . bad . . . but now**. For this great reversal, see Introduction: Key Themes.

16:26 A **great chasm has been fixed** by God between heaven and hell so that the fate of the dead is irreversible.

16:27–31 but if someone . . . from the dead. The rich man believes that if Lazarus returns from the dead he will be a sign confirming what the OT says and therefore his brothers **will repent**. As seen by the context and the content of the parable, such repentance would need to include a change of heart and a change in behavior, involving the use of the brothers' wealth and possessions for the care and well-being of those who are destitute and impoverished like Lazarus. But the refusal to repent and the corresponding refusal to believe the gospel is not primarily due to lack of evidence but to a hardened heart (cf. Mark 8:17; John 11:37–40; Heb. 3:7–11, 15; 4:7). Luke will later point out that **Moses and the Prophets** all testify to Jesus as the true Messiah (Luke 24:27).

17:1 God has ordained that **temptations** to sin **are sure to come**, but that does not excuse any individual from being the cause of temptations to others, for Jesus says, **woe to the one through whom they come** (cf. 22:22; Acts 2:23; 4:27–28).

17:2 millstone. A round stone used for grinding grain (here probably weighing hundreds of pounds, propelled by a donkey walking in circles on a track). **better for him . . . than that**. Drowning with a millstone around one's neck has less serious consequences (because they may not be eternal consequences) than causing **one of these little ones** (who believe in Christ or who have begun to follow him in some way) **to sin** (cf. Matt. 18:6; see note on Mark 9:42).

17:3–4 If your brother sins refers here to individual acts of sin. **rebuke him**. Sin cannot be overlooked but must be rebuked so that repentance and restoration can occur. **if he repents, forgive him . . . seven times**. In Judaism it was considered honorable to forgive three times; the disciples, as part of the new covenant community, were to exceed that standard. (Cf. note on Matt. 18:21–22.)

17:5–6 Increase our faith! See note on Matt. 17:20. Jesus' reply indicates that even a very small amount of faith, if it is genuine trust in God, can lead to remarkable results. The issue is not the size of faith, but its presence. This verse must be understood in connection with other passages that talk about prayer and the nature of genuine faith (see notes on John 15:7; James 1:6; 1:7–8; 1 John 5:21). **uprooted and planted in the sea**. In practice, the apostles' faith would not manifest itself in such dramatic signs but in their preaching, healing, and perseverance.

17:7–10 The question of v. 9 (**Does he thank the servant**?) implies an answer of "no." Jesus is not, however, encouraging anyone to be inconsiderate or rude. Rather, it is a vivid example to illustrate the point of v. 10—namely, that **we are unworthy servants**. Like the tax collector (18:13) and unlike the Pharisee (18:11–12), Christians should acknowledge that God owes them nothing and that they owe him everything, even their very lives (cf. 1 Cor. 4:7).

11[j] See ch. 9:51 [k][John 4:3, 4]; See Matt. 19:1
12[l] See Lev. 13:45, 46
14[m] ch. 5:14; Lev. 13:2–14:32; Matt. 8:4
15[n] See ch. 13:13
16[o] ch. 5:12; Num. 16:22; [Matt. 26:39] [p] See Matt. 10:5
17[q] ver. 12
18[r] See John 9:24 [s] Isa. 66:5
19[t] See Mark 10:52
20[u] ch. 19:11; Acts 1:6 [v][ch. 12:39]
21[w] [ver. 23]
22[x] ch. 5:35; 21:6; Matt. 9:15; Mark 2:20; [ch. 19:43; 23:29; John 4:21] [y] John 8:56; [Amos 5:18]
23[z] ch. 21:8; Matt. 24:23; Mark 13:21; [ver. 21]
24[a] Matt. 24:27 [b] See 1 Cor. 1:8
25[c] See ch. 13:33; Matt. 16:21; 17:22; Mark 8:31
26[d] Gen. 6:5; 7:7; Matt. 24:37; [1 Thess. 5:3] [e] Heb. 11:7; 1 Pet. 3:20; 2 Pet. 2:5
27[f] Matt. 24:38, 39
28[g] 2 Pet. 2:7
29[h] Gen. 19:16, 24; 2 Pet. 2:6
30[i] 1 Cor. 1:7; 2 Thess. 1:7; 1 Pet. 1:7, 13; 4:13; [Matt. 16:27; 24:44]
31[j] ch. 21:21; Matt. 24:17, 18; Mark 13:15, 16

Jesus Cleanses Ten Lepers

11 [j]On the way to Jerusalem [k]he was passing along between Samaria and Galilee. 12 And
as he entered a village, he was met by ten lepers,[1] [l]who stood at a distance 13 and lifted
up their voices, saying, "Jesus, Master, have mercy on us." 14 When he saw them he said
to them, "Go and [m]show yourselves to the priests." And as they went they were cleansed.
15 Then one of them, when he saw that he was healed, turned back, [n]praising God with
a loud voice; 16 and [o]he fell on his face at Jesus' feet, giving him thanks. Now he was [p]a
Samaritan. 17 Then Jesus answered, "Were not [q]ten cleansed? Where are the nine? 18 Was
no one found to return and [r]give praise to God except this [s]foreigner?" 19 And he said to
him, "Rise and go your way; [t]your faith has [t]made you well."[2]

The Coming of the Kingdom

20 Being asked by the Pharisees [u]when the kingdom of God would come, he answered
them, "The kingdom of God [v]is not coming in ways that can be observed, 21 nor [w]will they
say, 'Look, here it is!' or 'There!' for behold, the kingdom of God is in the midst of you."[3]
22 And he said to the disciples, [x]"The days are coming when you will desire [y]to see one
of the days of the Son of Man, and you will not see it. 23 [z]And they will say to you, 'Look,
there!' or 'Look, here!' Do not go out or follow them. 24 [a]For as the lightning flashes and
lights up the sky from one side to the other, so will the Son of Man be [b]in his day.[4] 25 But
first [c]he must suffer many things and [c]be rejected by this generation. 26 [d]Just as it was in the
days of [e]Noah, so will it be in the days of the Son of Man. 27 [f]They were eating and drinking
and marrying and being given in marriage, until the day when Noah entered the ark, and
the flood came and destroyed them all. 28 Likewise, just as it was in the days of [g]Lot—they
were eating and drinking, buying and selling, planting and building, 29 [h]but on the day
when Lot went out from Sodom, fire and sulfur rained from heaven and destroyed them
all— 30 so will it be [i]on the day when the Son of Man is revealed. 31 On that day, [j]let the

[1] *Leprosy was a term for several skin diseases; see Leviticus 13* [2] *Or has saved you* [3] *Or within you, or within your grasp* [4] *Some manuscripts omit in his day*

17:11–19:27 *The Third Mention of the Journey to Jerusalem.* This section begins with the third mention of Jesus' intention of completing his final journey to Jerusalem ("On the way to Jerusalem," 17:11; cf. "set his face," 9:51; and "journeying toward Jerusalem," 13:22).

17:11–19 *Jesus Cleanses Ten Lepers.* Jesus heals 10 lepers, of whom only one (a Samaritan) expresses thanks.

17:11 On the way to Jerusalem. Cf. 9:51 and 13:22. For **Samaria**, see notes on 10:33 and John 4:4.

17:12–13 ten lepers (see note on 5:12) . . . **stood at a distance** (cf. Num. 5:2–4; 2 Kings 7:3). The law required lepers not to mingle with other people (Lev. 13:45–46; Num. 5:2–4). **have mercy**. Cf. Luke 16:24; 18:38–39.

17:14 show yourselves to the priests. See note on 5:14. **As they went they were cleansed**, i.e., healed. The priests would declare them clean. They had to begin to obey Jesus' command to go to the priests before they were actually healed (cf. 5:5; 2 Kings 5:13–14).

17:15–16a One leper **turned back** (cf. 2 Kings 5:15), **praising God with a loud voice** (a favorite Lukan expression; cf. Luke 4:33; 8:28; 19:37, etc.). The leper **fell on his face** (cf. 5:12), **giving** Jesus **thanks**. Elsewhere in the NT such giving of thanks (Gk. *eucharisteō*) is always directed to God (in every one of 37 other occurrences of this verb).

17:16b Now he was a Samaritan. The noun "he" is emphasized in the Greek; placing this statement later in the story also serves to emphasize that the only grateful leper was a Samaritan (on Samaritans, see 9:52; 10:33; and notes on John 4:4; 4:9).

17:19 The Samaritan's **faith has made** him **well** (lit., "saved" him; cf. the same Gk. verb in 7:50; 8:48; 18:42), so that the healing here was more than physical.

17:20–37 *The Coming of the Kingdom.* This account consists of two sections involving the "already now" (vv. 20–21) and the "not yet" (vv. 22–37) of the kingdom.

17:20 The **Pharisees** apparently desire to know the cosmic signs preceding the coming of the **kingdom** so that they can be sure not to miss it. Jesus replies that the kingdom will not come **in ways that can be observed** (a phrase that translates a Greek word *paratērēsis* that occurs only here in the entire Bible). In light of vv. 21–37, Jesus apparently means that the arrival of the kingdom of God will not be accompanied by spectacular signs in the heavens but rather that the kingdom will come quietly, evident only in the change in people's lives. See notes on 19:11; Acts 1:6.

17:21 The Pharisees repeat their mistake of 14:15 in not recognizing that the **kingdom of God** has already come. It is **in the midst of you**, in the person of Jesus and in the reign of God manifested in those who are already following Jesus. Some understand Jesus to say here that the kingdom is "within you," but he would not say that to disbelieving Pharisees.

17:22 For **Son of Man**, see note on Matt. 8:20. **One of the days** probably means they will long to see a day when Jesus has already returned to the earth and is with them again, but some take it to mean they will long for the time when Jesus was with them on earth. **You will not see it** because he will no longer be on earth and will not yet have returned.

17:23 Believers should not **follow** people who claim that Jesus has come in a secret or hidden way, for he will come in a way that is dramatic and visible to all.

17:24 The coming of the kingdom, inaugurated by Christ's return, will be as bright, unmistakable, and sudden as **lightning**; just as lightning **lights up the sky**, all will see it.

17:25 first he must suffer. The consummation of the kingdom requires that a divine event "must" first take place—that is, the obligation that Jesus must first die according to God's plan to redeem a people for himself. **this generation**. See note on 7:31–34.

17:26–29 Eating and drinking is not a description of specific evils in the **days of Noah** and **Lot**. It means, rather, that life went on as normal, and people were caught unprepared.

17:31 On the housetop envisions a Palestinian home with a flat roof and outside stairs. **in the house . . . in the field**. These analogies, using imagery familiar to the original listeners, stress that there will be no time to prepare when the Son of Man comes. Some interpreters argue from the Palestinian

one who is on [k]the housetop, with his goods in the house, not come down to take them
away, and likewise let the one who is in the field not turn back. **32** [l]Remember Lot's wife.
33 [m]Whoever seeks to preserve his life will lose it, but whoever loses his life will [n]keep it.
34 I tell you, in that night there will be two in one bed. One will be taken and the other left.
35 [o]There will be two women [p]grinding together. One will be taken and the other left."[1]
37 And they said to him, "Where, Lord?" He said to them, [q]"Where the corpse[2] is, there the
vultures[3] will gather."

The Parable of the Persistent Widow

18 And he told them a parable to the effect that they ought [r]always to pray and not
[s]lose heart. **2** He said, "In a certain city there was a judge who [t]neither feared God
nor respected man. **3** And there was a widow in that city who kept coming to him and saying, 'Give me justice against my adversary.' **4** For a while he refused, but afterward he said
to himself, [u]'Though I neither fear God nor respect man, **5** yet because this widow keeps
bothering me, I will give her justice, so that she will not beat me down by her continual
coming.'" **6** And the Lord said, "Hear what the unrighteous judge says. **7** And [v]will not God
give justice to [w]his elect, [x]who cry to him day and night? [y, z]Will he delay long over them? **8** I
tell you, he will give justice to them [a]speedily. Nevertheless, when the Son of Man comes,
[b]will he find faith on earth?"

The Pharisee and the Tax Collector

9 He also told this parable to some [c]who trusted [d]in themselves that they were righteous,
[e]and treated others with contempt: **10** "Two men [f]went up into the temple to pray, one a
Pharisee and the other a tax collector. **11** The Pharisee, [g]standing by himself, prayed[4] [h]thus:
'God, I thank you that I am not like other men, extortioners, unjust, adulterers, or even
like this tax collector. **12** [i]I fast twice a week; [j]I give tithes of all that I get.' **13** But the tax

[1] Some manuscripts add verse 36: *Two men will be in the field; one will be taken and the other left* [2] Greek *body* [3] Or *eagles* [4] Or *standing, prayed to himself*

31 [k]See ch. 5:19
32 [l]Gen. 19:26
33 [m]See Matt. 10:39 [n]Acts 7:19 (Gk.)
35 [o]Matt. 24:41 [p]Ex. 11:5; Isa. 47:2
37 [q]Matt. 24:28; [Job 39:30]

Chapter 18

1 [r]ch. 21:36; Rom. 12:12; Eph. 6:18; Col. 4:2; 1 Thess. 5:17; [ch. 11:5-9] [s]2 Cor. 4:1, 16; 2 Thess. 3:13 (Gk.)
2 [t][2 Cor. 8:21]
4 [u][ch. 11:8]
7 [v]Rev. 6:10; [Isa. 63:4] [w]Rom. 8:33; Col. 3:12; Titus 1:1; See Mark 13:20 [x]Ps. 88:1 [y]James 5:7 (Gk.) [z]2 Pet. 3:9
8 [a]Heb. 10:37 [b]ch. 17:26-30; [Matt. 24:12]
9 [c]ch. 16:15; [Matt. 5:20] [d]2 Cor. 1:9 [e]Prov. 30:12; Isa. 65:5; John 7:48, 49
10 [f]2 Kgs. 20:5, 8; Acts 3:1; [ver. 14]
11 [g]Matt. 6:5; Mark 11:25 [h][Rev. 3:17]
12 [i]Matt. 9:14 [j]ch. 11:42

details of this illustration that Jesus is referring to the destruction of Jerusalem in A.D. 70.

17:32 Lot's wife turned back, looking longingly at Sodom (see Gen. 19:17, 26). Her death is an example of divine judgment that comes quickly on those who do not wholeheartedly obey the Lord's commands.

17:33 Cf. 9:24 and note on Mark 8:35.

17:34–35 taken . . . left. One is caught up to be with Christ, while the other is left (cf. Matt. 24:31).

17:37 corpse . . . vultures. See note on Matt. 24:28.

18:1–8 *The Parable of the Persistent Widow.* The parable consists of a "lesser to greater" argument—i.e., if A (the lesser) is true, then how much more B (the greater) must be true (cf. notes on 11:11–13; 12:6–7; 12:25–27; 13:15–16). The comparison here is between the reluctant action of an unjust judge (the lesser) and "how much more" just will be the action of a just God (the greater).

18:1 And he told them (the disciples, 17:22) **. . . always to pray** (cf. Introduction: Key Themes; 1 Thess. 5:17) **and not lose heart** (because of delay in the Lord's return; cf. Luke 17:20–37). As in 18:9 and 19:11, the introduction of the parable serves as the guide to its interpretation—i.e., to pray persistently for justice for God's people, as the woman did who pleaded with the judge for justice.

18:2 nor respected man. He showed no special deference toward anyone, whether great or small.

18:3 The **widow** represents the poor, needy, and oppressed (cf. 20:47). **kept coming**. Persistence is her only asset in seeking **justice** from the "unjust" judge (18:6).

18:7 If an unjust judge finally grants the widow's "prayer," how much more will God hear the prayers of his elect? Cf. 12:22–31; see also how God cared for his people Israel, the "apple of his eye," Deut. 32:10; Ps. 17:8. **day and night**. I.e., "always" (Luke 18:1; cf. 2:37; Acts 9:24; 20:31; 26:7). **Justice to his elect** refers primarily to God rescuing his people from suffering and injustice in the world (cf. Luke 1:68–74). **Will he delay long over them** probably means, "Will God be patient much longer as he sees his elect suffer?" The implied answer is no.

18:8 From God's perspective, **justice** will come to his elect (cf. v. 7) **speedily**. From a human perspective, of course, justice may seem to be a long time coming. Therefore God's people must persist in prayer, as the widow persisted until she received justice (vv. 2–5). **will he find faith on earth?** The answer, of course, is "yes," but Jesus poses this as a question in order to encourage his disciples to constant watchfulness and prayer (cf. vv. 1, 7). When he returns, Jesus will be looking for those who are praying and watching for him.

18:9–14 *The Parable of the Pharisee and the Tax Collector.* This parable contrasts a Pharisee boasting in his self-righteousness and a tax collector confessing his sins and seeking God's mercy.

18:9 Again, as in v. 1, Luke interprets the parable before the parable itself is given. **to some who trusted . . . that they were righteous**. The audience addressed by the parable (probably Pharisees) had an unrealistic sense of self-worth (see note on Matt. 5:20). Falsely confident of their own righteousness, they **treated others with contempt**.

18:10 Two men (cf. 15:11; 17:34–35) **went up into the temple**. Even if a person is in Jerusalem, he or she still must go "up" to the temple and "down" from there (see 18:14) because the temple was situated on an elevated mount with the rest of Jerusalem below it (on the temple, see note on John 2:14). **Pharisee**. See note on Luke 5:17. For **tax collector**, see notes on 3:12–14; Matt. 5:46–47.

18:11 The Pharisee, standing. The normal posture of prayer. **God, I thank you that I**. The five "I's" in this passage reveal the egocentricity of the Pharisee. Rather than thanking God for what God has done for him, the Pharisee arrogantly brags to God about his own moral purity and religious piety.

18:12 I fast twice a week. The OT law did not require this much fasting, but apparently only one fast a year, on the Day of Atonement (see note on Matt. 6:16–18). **tithes of all that I get**. See Deut. 14:22–27, which required a tithe of the crops; see also Lev. 27:30–32; Num. 18:21–24.

18:13 Because of shame the **tax collector . . . would not even lift up his eyes to heaven**, but **beat his breast**, which was a sign of sorrow and contrition (cf. 23:48), and said, **God, be merciful to me, a sinner**. The "sinner's prayer" (cf. Ps. 51:1) seeks God's mercy. The stark contrast between the contrition of the sinner and the self-righteousness of the Pharisee is key to understanding the central point of the parable.

collector, [g]standing far off, [k]would not even lift up his eyes to heaven, but [l]beat his breast,
saying, 'God, [m]be merciful to me, a sinner!' 14 I tell you, this man went down to his house
justified, rather than the other. For [n]everyone who exalts himself will be humbled, but
the one who humbles himself will be exalted."

Let the Children Come to Me

15 [o]Now they were bringing even infants to him that he might touch them. And when
the disciples saw it, they [p]rebuked them. 16 But Jesus called them to him, saying, [q]"Let
the children come to me, and [r]do not hinder them, [q]for to such belongs the kingdom
of God. 17 [s]Truly, I say to you, whoever does not [t]receive the kingdom of God like a child
shall not enter it."

The Rich Ruler

18 [u]And a ruler asked him, "Good Teacher, what must I do to [v]inherit eternal life?"
19 And Jesus said to him, "Why do you call me good? No one is good except God alone.
20 You know the commandments: [w]'Do not commit adultery, Do not murder, Do not steal,
Do not bear false witness, Honor your father and mother.'" 21 And he said, [x]"All these
I have kept from my youth." 22 When Jesus heard this, he said to him, "One thing you
still lack. [y]Sell all that you have and distribute to the poor, and you will have [z]treasure
in heaven; and come, follow me." 23 [a]But when he heard these things, he became very
sad, for he was extremely rich. 24 Jesus, seeing that he had become sad, said, [b]"How difficult it is for those who have wealth to enter [c]the kingdom of God! 25 For it is easier for
a camel to go through the eye of a needle than for a rich person to enter [c]the kingdom
of God." 26 Those who heard it said, "Then who can be saved?" 27 But he said, [d]"What
is impossible with man is possible with God." 28 And Peter said, "See, [e]we have left our

13 [g][See ver. 11 above] [k]Ezra 9:6 [l]ch. 23:48 [m]Ps. 79:9; Ezek. 16:63; Dan. 9:19
14 [n]See ch. 14:11
15 [o]For ver. 15-17, see Matt. 19:13-15; Mark 10:13-16 [p]ver. 39
16 [q]Matt. 18:3 [r][Mark 9:39]
17 [s][John 3:3, 5] [t][ch. 8:13; James 1:21]
18 [u]For ver. 18-30, see Matt. 19:16-29; Mark 10:17-30; [ch. 10:25-28] [v][Matt. 19:16]; See Matt. 25:34
20 [w]Rom. 13:9; Cited from Ex. 20:12-16; Deut. 5:16-20; [Matt. 5:21, 27]
21 [x][Phil. 3:6]
22 [y]ch. 12:33; [ch. 16:9; 19:8; Acts 2:45; 4:34, 35; 1 Tim. 6:18, 19] [z]Matt. 6:19, 20
23 [a][Ezek. 33:31]
24 [b][1 Cor. 1:26]; See Matt. 13:22 [c]See Matt. 12:28
25 [c][See ver. 24 above]
27 [d]ch. 1:37; Gen. 18:14; Job 42:2; Jer. 32:17, 27
28 [e]Matt. 4:20, 22; Mark 1:18, 20

18:14 Jesus pronounces a shocking reversal of common expectations (cf. 14:11 and Introduction: Key Themes). The Pharisee thought that he was "righteous" (18:9) and tried to justify himself (cf. 16:15), but the tax collector depended on God's mercy and as a result received God's gift of righteousness and was pronounced **justified**.

18:15–17 *Jesus Blesses the Children.* Only those who humble themselves like children shall enter the kingdom.

18:15 People brought **even infants** to Jesus in order that **he might touch them**, i.e., bless them (cf. 5:13; 6:19). **Were bringing** suggests that this was a frequent occurrence in Jesus' ministry.

18:16–17 Let the children come. Jesus' attitude toward children contrasted significantly with that of other religious leaders in Judaism. In most ancient cultures children were regarded as a burden until they were physically strong enough to contribute to the family. **For to such belongs** does not mean children automatically belong to the kingdom but that the kingdom belongs to "such"—that is, to those who possess childlike trust (see note on Mark 10:13–15; cf. Matt. 18:4). **like a child**. That is, in childlike faith and trust in Jesus.

18:18–30 *The Rich Ruler.* The report of Jesus' encounter with the rich ruler answers the question with which it begins: "What must I do to inherit eternal life?" (v. 18).

18:18 ruler. See note on Matt. 19:16. Probably a ruler of a synagogue (Luke 8:41) or member of the Sanhedrin (23:13, 35; 24:20; John 3:1). **Good Teacher, what must I do . . . ?** A good question (see note on Luke 10:25). For inheriting (not meriting) eternal life, cf. 18:30; Acts 13:46, 48.

18:19 Why do you call me good? Jesus does not let the ruler's superficial view of "goodness" go unchallenged (see note on Mark 10:18). **No one is good except God alone** directs the ruler's attention to God, in whom ultimate goodness resides. Only in understanding God as infinitely good can he discover that human good deeds cannot earn eternal life.

18:20 You know the commandments. See note on Matt. 19:17. **Do not**. Although only the second table of the law is mentioned (commandments 6–10; see Ex. 20:13–16), Luke expects his readers to assume that the first table (Ex. 20:1–12) is also included (cf. Luke 10:25–28).

18:21 All these I have kept from my youth. See note on Mark 10:20; cf. Paul's righteous keeping of the law from his youth (Acts 26:4; Phil. 3:6).

18:22 One thing you still lack refers not to higher piety but to the kingdom of God (vv. 24–25), salvation (v. 26), and eternal life (v. 18). **Sell all that you have**. See notes on Matt. 19:21 and Mark 10:21. Cf. Luke 5:11, 28; 14:33; 18:28. Jesus shows that the ruler has not really kept the commandments, and he clarifies the meaning of true repentance. **treasure in heaven**. In 12:33 this refers to the rewards believers will receive in heaven, but here it means eternal life itself (cf. 18:24–25). **Follow me** involves denying oneself, taking up one's cross, and following Jesus (cf. 9:23).

18:23 The ruler was **very sad** because **he was extremely rich**; he loved his riches more than God, showing that he had kept neither the first commandment nor the tenth, for riches were his god and he desired them more than God.

18:25 it is easier for a camel. An example of hyperbole (see note on Matt. 19:24). It is simply impossible for those who are rich (and for anyone else) to enter God's kingdom on the basis of their works, or to have the desire to seek God above all else apart from God's grace.

18:26 who can be saved? Since riches were supposedly a sign of God's favor, Jesus' listeners must have wondered: if a rich man who could freely offer alms and sacrifices could not be saved, who could be?

18:27 What is impossible (Gk. *adynatos*) **with man is possible** (Gk. *dynatos*) **with God** (cf. 1:37; Gen. 18:14). Because of God's power and grace, repenting and following Jesus is possible (see Luke 18:28–30), even for a rich man (19:1–10). Salvation is the work of the Lord, who does himself what would otherwise be impossible.

18:29–30 who has left house or wife or brothers or parents or children. Jesus is not encouraging his disciples to abandon familial responsibilities (cf. Eph. 5:25; 6:4). But sometimes family members turn against a believer, or there may be times of temporary separation due to Christian ministry. Only Luke mentions "wife"; see note on Matt. 19:10–12. Whatever someone has to sacrifice **for the sake of the kingdom** will be repaid **many times more** by God. Regarding "for the sake of the kingdom of God," see further "for my sake and for the gospel" (Mark 10:29) and "for my name's sake" (Matt. 19:29). **in this time**. See note on Mark 10:29–30. **eternal life**. The scene ends where it began, with the question of eternal life (Luke 18:18) and Jesus' final answer (v. 30).

homes and followed you." 29 And he said to them, "Truly, I say to you, [f]there is no one
who has left house or wife or brothers[1] or parents or children, for the sake of the kingdom of God, 30 who will not receive [g]many times more [h]in this time, and in [i]the age to
come eternal life."

Jesus Foretells His Death a Third Time

31 [j]And taking the twelve, he said to them, "See, [k]we are going up to Jerusalem, and
[l]everything that is written about the Son of Man by the prophets will be accomplished.
32 For he will be [m]delivered over to the Gentiles and will be [n]mocked and shamefully treated
and [o]spit upon. 33 And after flogging him, they will kill him, and on [p]the third day he will
rise." 34 [q]But they understood none of these things. [r]This saying was hidden from them,
and they did not grasp what was said.

Jesus Heals a Blind Beggar

35 [s]As he drew near to Jericho, [t]a blind man was sitting by the roadside begging. 36 And
hearing a crowd going by, he inquired what this meant. 37 They told him, [u]"Jesus of
Nazareth is passing by." 38 And he cried out, "Jesus, [v]Son of David, have mercy on me!"
39 And those who were in front [w]rebuked him, telling him to be silent. But he cried out
all the more, "Son of David, have mercy on me!" 40 And Jesus stopped and commanded
him to be brought to him. And when he came near, he asked him, 41 [x]"What do you want
me to do for you?" He said, "Lord, let me recover my sight." 42 And Jesus said to him,
"Recover your sight; [y]your faith has [z]made you well." 43 And immediately he recovered

[1] *Or wife or brothers and sisters*

29 [f][ch. 14:26]
30 [g][Job 42:10] [h][Matt. 6:33] [i]Matt. 12:32; Eph. 1:21; [ch. 20:35]
31 [j]For ver. 31-33, see Matt. 20:17-19; Mark 10:32-34 [k]See ch. 9:51 [l]Ps. 22; See Matt. 1:22; 26:24
32 [m]Matt. 27:2; John 18:30, 31; Acts 3:13; [Acts 2:23; 4:27; 21:11] [n]Matt. 27:26-31 [o]Mark 14:65; 15:19; See Matt. 26:67
33 [p]See ch. 9:22
34 [q]See Mark 9:32 [r]ch. 9:45; [ch. 24:16]
35 [s]For ver. 35-43, see Matt. 20:29-34; Mark 10:46-52 [t]John 9:1, 8
37 [u]Matt. 2:23
38 [v]See Matt. 1:1; 9:27
39 [w]ver. 15
41 [x]Mark 10:36
42 [y]ch. 7:50; 8:48; 17:19; Matt. 9:22; Mark 5:34 [z]ch. 7:3; 8:36, 50

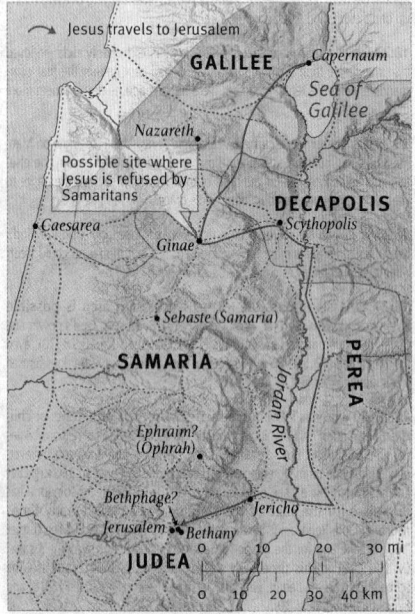

Jesus Travels to Jerusalem

Though John mentions several trips to Jerusalem by Jesus during his ministry, Matthew, Mark, and Luke recount only one, which occurred as Jesus prepared for his triumphal entry and subsequent death and resurrection. Beginning at Capernaum, Jesus was apparently diverted from the more direct route when Samaritans refused him access (Luke 9:51–56), so he may have crossed the Jordan and traveled through Perea. Jesus then passed through Jericho and proceeded to Jerusalem.

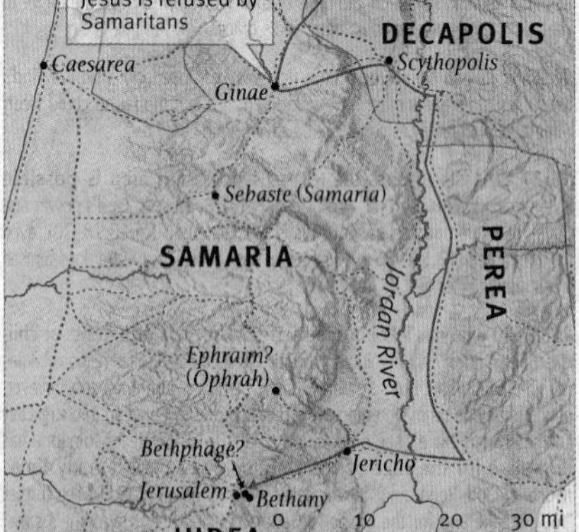

18:31–34 *Jesus Foretells His Death a Third Time.* Having predicted his suffering and death twice before (9:22, 43b–45), Jesus again reminds his followers that the way to Jerusalem will be the way to the cross.

18:31 we are going up to Jerusalem. See note on Mark 10:32; cf. Luke 9:51–53; 13:33; 19:28. **will be accomplished**. The cross is to be seen as the fulfillment of prophecy, not a horrible accident.

18:32 Jesus **will be delivered over to the Gentiles**. See note on Mark 10:33. Just as Israel was handed over to Gentiles for punishment of their sin in the OT, so Jesus was handed over to bear God's wrath for the sins of his people. Cf. Luke 20:20; 23:2; Acts 2:23; 13:28.

18:34 But they (the Twelve) **understood none of these things**. Although they understood the meaning of Jesus' words, they could not understand why Jesus was predicting this or how it could possibly fit into God's plans for the Messiah. The fact that the Messiah must first suffer and die was still **hidden from them**.

18:35–43 *Jesus Heals a Blind Beggar.* This and 19:1–10 are the last two reported incidents before Jesus' entry into Jerusalem (19:28).

18:35 For **Jericho**, see notes on 10:30; 19:1; Matt. 20:29; Mark 10:46. **a blind man**. Named Bartimaeus in Mark 10:46. **sitting by the roadside**. A good place to beg, for pilgrims heading to Jerusalem would tend to be generous.

18:38 The blind man **cried out**, which indicates that he had heard of Jesus. (Matthew reports two blind beggars; see note on Matt. 20:30–31.) **Jesus, Son of David, have mercy on me**. See Luke 17:13. The blind man acknowledges that Jesus is the Messiah.

18:39 he cried out all the more. An example of persevering faith (see 8:15; cf. 18:1–8; 21:19).

18:41 Let me recover my sight confirms the man's great faith (see note on v. 38). Rather than continuing to beg for money (see v. 35), he seeks a miracle.

18:42 Recover your sight. A single word in Greek (*anablepson*, "see"). For Jesus, only a brief command is necessary. **your faith has made you well**. Literally, "saved you"; cf. the same Greek verb in 7:50; 8:48. The blind man was healed both physically and spiritually.

18:43 More than healing takes place, as indicated by the beggar's following Jesus in discipleship (cf. 9:23). **glorifying God**. See 4:15 and note on 4:13–15. **all the people**. For Jesus' popularity among the people, see note on 4:37.

19:1–10 *Jesus and Zacchaeus.* Jesus' encounter with Zacchaeus is an example of the kingdom of God bringing salvation to the outcasts. It also provides a lesson on the proper kingdom use of money and possessions.

43[a]See ch. 7:16; 13:13 [b][ch. 19:37]
Chapter 19
1[c]ch. 18:35; [Matt. 20:29; Mark 10:46]
3[d][John 12:21]
4[e]1 Kgs. 10:27; 1 Chr. 27:28; Ps. 78:47; Isa. 9:10
5[f][ch. 13:33]
6[g]ch. 10:38
7[h]See ch. 15:2
8[i][ch. 18:22] [j]ch. 3:14 [k]Ex. 22:1; 2 Sam. 12:6
9[l]John 8:33; Rom. 4:11, 12, 16; Gal. 3:7
10[m]Ezek. 34:11, 16; [ch. 15:4; Matt. 9:13; 10:6; 15:24; 18:12]
11[n][ch. 17:20; Acts 1:6]
12[o]For ver. 12-27, [Matt. 25:14-30; Mark 13:34]
13[p]Matt. 25:1 [q][John 21:22, 23]
14[r][John 1:14]

his sight and followed him, [a]glorifying God. And [b]all the people, when they saw it, gave
praise to God.

Jesus and Zacchaeus

19 [c]He entered Jericho and was passing through. 2 And behold, there was a man named
Zacchaeus. He was a chief tax collector and was rich. 3 And [d]he was seeking to see who
Jesus was, but on account of the crowd he could not, because he was small in stature. 4 So
he ran on ahead and climbed up into [e]a sycamore tree to see him, for he was about to pass
that way. 5 And when Jesus came to the place, he looked up and said to him, "Zacchaeus,
hurry and come down, for [f]I must stay at your house today." 6 So he hurried and came
down and [g]received him joyfully. 7 And when they saw it, they all [h]grumbled, "He has gone
in to be the guest of a man who is a sinner." 8 And Zacchaeus stood and said to the Lord,
"Behold, Lord, the half of my goods [i]I give to the poor. And if I have [j]defrauded anyone
of anything, I restore it [k]fourfold." 9 And Jesus said to him, "Today salvation has come to
this house, since [l]he also is a son of Abraham. 10 For [m]the Son of Man came to seek and to
save the lost."

The Parable of the Ten Minas

11 As they heard these things, he proceeded to tell a parable, because he was near to
Jerusalem, and because [n]they supposed that the kingdom of God was to appear immediately. 12 He said therefore, [o]"A nobleman went into a far country to receive for himself a
kingdom and then return. 13 Calling [p]ten of his servants,[1] he gave them ten minas,[2] and
said to them, 'Engage in business [q]until I come.' 14 But [r]his citizens hated him and sent a
delegation after him, saying, 'We do not want this man to reign over us.' 15 When he returned,

[1] Greek *bondservants*; also verse 15 [2] A *mina* was about three months' wages for a laborer

19:1 He entered Jericho ties this account closely with the preceding (see 18:35). Jericho in this period was quite different from the OT city. Herod the Great had obtained Jericho from Caesar Augustus and proceeded to build aqueducts, a fortress, a monumental winter palace, and a hippodrome in the vicinity of the more ancient town. Excavations have revealed much of the Herodian palace structures; they were built in stages, by expanding on a previous Hasmonean palace. One striking feature of the palace site is its huge pools, in one of which Herod probably had his own son drowned. Jericho boasted a tropical climate and excellent access to water for agriculture.

19:2 chief tax collector. This title is found nowhere else in the NT. Jericho was a major toll collection point for goods passing east and west.

19:5 Zacchaeus, . . . I must stay at your house today shows the divine necessity of Jesus' bringing salvation to Zacchaeus's home (vv. 9–10).

19:6 Joyfully may imply that Zacchaeus had already come to faith.

19:7 All grumbled is in sharp contrast to "glorified by all" (4:15). Zacchaeus symbolized the authority of a government that was taking the people's money and oppressing them. For the symbolism of Jesus' eating with tax collectors and sinners, see note on 5:30; also 4:18; 5:32; 15:1–2.

19:8 Half of my goods includes Zacchaeus's possessions (cf. 12:15, 33), not just his salary. **I** (shall) **give to the poor** (cf. 11:41; 12:33; 18:22). **if I have defrauded . . . I** (shall) **restore it fourfold** (cf. Ex. 22:1; 2 Sam. 12:6). Zacchaeus's actions reveal that his repentance and faith are genuine (see Luke 3:8). The example of Zacchaeus, who gave away half of his goods, underscores the kind of openhanded generosity that characterizes those whose hearts have been transformed by the gospel. (See note on Acts 2:44.)

19:9 Jesus said to him. Although spoken to Zacchaeus, Jesus' statement is directed to the grumbling "all" (v. 7). **Today salvation has come** indicates that with God all things are possible, and a rich man can be saved (cf. 18:26–27). By his actions, Zacchaeus reveals that he **also** is a true **son of Abraham** (cf. Gal. 3:7) and not just his physical descendant (cf. Luke 3:8).

19:10 To seek and to save the lost summarizes Jesus' mission (cf. 5:32; 15:4, 6–7, 10, 24, 32).

19:11–27 *The Parable of the Ten Minas.* This parable concludes Luke's account of Jesus' journey to Jerusalem (begun in 9:51). It is distinct from the parable of the talents in Matt. 25:14–30, since most of the key elements are different, but there are also some similarities in wording. Jesus would sometimes modify his teachings to fit different situations and emphasize slightly different truths.

19:11 The key to the meaning of this parable is given at the beginning (cf. note on 18:1). Jesus gave the parable in response to those who **supposed that the kingdom of God was to appear immediately**. This was probably a concern especially **because he was near to Jerusalem**, where expectations of a political messiah may have been extra high. The parable will show that the kingdom will not be seen in its fullness until Christ returns; it begins in a small way and grows gradually until then (cf. 13:18–21).

19:12 To receive for himself a kingdom means to receive authority over a kingdom. The kingdom that he is going to receive is not the **far country** to which he is traveling but the land from which he started out. Into a "far country" implies that the return of the nobleman (i.e., the second coming of the Son of Man) will not take place immediately. Luke's readers should not be troubled over this delay, because Jesus had already taught that he would not return immediately. From here to the end of the Gospel, Luke frequently emphasizes the kingship of Jesus.

19:13 The rounded number **ten** shows that Jesus' parable applies to all his disciples, not just the Twelve. **Minas** were about three months' wages for a laborer, about 100 drachmas. "Until I come" refers to the time between Jesus' ascension and return at the end of the age. **Engage in business until I come** is one of several examples where Jesus uses business activity in a positive way in his parables and teachings (however, Gk. *pragmateuomai*, "do business, trade, be engaged in a business," occurs only here in the NT). Though the main point of the parable is stewardship rather than business per se, the NT in general (as is the case here) views work and business activity in a positive way (see Matt. 25:14–30; Luke 10:7; 19:13–23; Col. 3:23–4:1; James 4:13–15), but also as an area where there are substantial temptations to sin (see Matt. 6:19–21; 1 Tim. 6:9–10) and to exploit others (James 5:1–6).

19:14 His citizens represents the Jews who **hated** Jesus. **sent a delegation**. This image would be familiar to the Jews since they had sent delegations to Rome protesting some of their local rulers.

19:15 When he returned represents the time of Jesus' second coming.

having received the kingdom, he ordered these servants to whom he had given the money
to be called to him, that he might know what they had gained by doing business. 16 The
first came before him, saying, 'Lord, your mina has made ten minas more.' 17 And he said
to him, 'Well done, good servant![1] Because you have been [s]faithful in a very little, [t]you
shall have authority over ten cities.' 18 And the second came, saying, 'Lord, your mina has
made five minas.' 19 And he said to him, 'And you are to be over five cities.' 20 Then another
came, saying, 'Lord, here is your mina, which I kept laid away in [u]a handkerchief; 21 for I
was afraid of you, because you are [v]a severe man. You take [w]what you did not deposit, and
reap what you did not sow.' 22 He said to him, [x]"I will condemn you with your own words,
[y]you wicked servant! You knew that I was [v]a severe man, taking what I did not deposit
and reaping what I did not sow? 23 Why then did you not put my money in the bank, and
at my coming I might have collected it with interest?' 24 And he said to those who stood
by, 'Take the mina from him, and give it to the one who has the ten minas.' 25 And they
said to him, 'Lord, he has ten minas!' 26 'I tell you that [z]to everyone who has, more will be
given, but from the one who has not, even what he has will be taken away. 27 But [r]as for
these enemies of mine, who did not want me to reign over them, bring them here and
[a]slaughter them before me.'"

The Triumphal Entry

28 And when he had said these things, [b]he went on ahead, [c]going up to Jerusalem. 29 [d]When
he drew near to Bethphage and [e]Bethany, at [f]the mount that is called Olivet, he sent [g]two
of the disciples, 30 saying, "Go into the village in front of you, where on entering you will
find a colt tied, [h]on which no one has ever yet sat. Untie it and bring it here. 31 If anyone asks
you, 'Why are you untying it?' you shall say this: 'The Lord has need of it.'" 32 So those who
were sent went away and found it [i]just as he had told them. 33 And as they were untying the
colt, its owners said to them, "Why are you untying the colt?" 34 And they said, "The Lord
has need of it." 35 And they brought it to Jesus, and throwing their cloaks on the colt, they
set Jesus on it. 36 And as he rode along, they [j]spread their cloaks on the road. 37 As he was
drawing near—already on the way down the Mount of Olives—[k]the whole multitude of
his disciples began to rejoice and praise God with a loud voice [l]for all the mighty works

17 [s]ch. 16:10; 1 Cor. 4:2; [1 Tim. 3:13] [t][Matt. 24:47]
20 [u]John 11:44; 20:7; Acts 19:12 (Gk.)
21 [v][1 Sam. 25:3] [w][2 Cor. 8:12]
22 [x]2 Sam. 1:16; Job 9:20; 15:6 [y]Matt. 18:32 [v][See ver. 21 above]
26 [z][ch. 12:48]; See Matt. 13:12
27 [r][See ver. 14 above] [a]ch. 20:16; Matt. 22:7; [1 Sam. 15:33]
28 [b]Mark 10:32 [c]See ch. 9:51; 10:30
29 [d]For ver. 29-38, see Matt. 21:1-9; Mark 11:1-10; John 12:12-15; [Zech. 9:9] [e]ch. 24:50; Matt. 21:17; John 11:18 [f]Zech. 14:4; Matt. 24:3; 26:30; [John 8:1]; [Acts 1:12] [g][Mark 14:13]
30 [h][ch. 23:53]
32 [i]ch. 22:13
36 [j]2 Kgs. 9:13
37 [k][ch. 18:43] [l][John 12:17, 18]

[1] Greek *bondservant*; also verse 22

19:16 your mina has made ten minas more. An unusually high return in real life, indicating unusual wisdom and faithfulness on the part of the servant.

19:17 Well done, good servant! See note on Matt. 25:20–23. **faithful in a very little.** Cf. Luke 16:10. **you shall have authority over ten cities.** Faithful carrying out of stewardship responsibilities in this life will result in being given greater responsibility and stewardship in the life to come. This is one of a number of passages that teach degrees of reward and responsibility in heaven (see notes on Matt. 6:20; 1 Cor. 3:8; 3:14–15; 1 Tim. 6:17–19).

19:20 Lord, here is your mina. The third servant has not labored or conducted business with the mina but has hidden it **away** where it did no good for anyone and did not gain additional value. Those who fail to do anything useful with the resources, talents, and opportunities God has given them will fall under his displeasure and may thereby indicate that they are not even true believers (cf. Matt. 25:30).

19:21 Severe man does not mean selfish or unfair but, rather, strict and holding to high standards, or austere, like the Greek word it comes from (Gk. *austēros*, "strict in requirements," "exacting"; cf. Matt. 25:24). This is not intended as a description of Christ, for Luke 19:17, 19 show him to be abundantly generous and gracious. This servant does not know his master well, or else he is simply making up an excuse for his own failure.

19:22–23 The servant is condemned by his **own words**, for if he believed what he said, he would at least have put the **money in the bank** to earn **interest** (see note on Matt. 25:27). This would have required minimal effort by the servant, and the money would have been useful to others, as the bankers used it to make loans.

19:26 given . . . taken away. See note on Mark 4:25.

19:27 But as for these enemies of mine may allude to the destruction of Jerusalem in A.D. 70, but it also forecasts the final judgment of those who reject Jesus.

19:28–21:38 *The Ministry of Jesus in Jerusalem.* In this section, Luke's Gospel is closely parallel to Mark 11:1–13:37.

19:28–40 *The Triumphal Entry.* The Son of David enters Jerusalem riding on a colt.

19:28 Jerusalem. See Jerusalem in the Time of Jesus, pp. 1878–1879.

19:29 The location of **Bethany** on the eastern slopes of the Mount of Olives is well established (see note on John 11:1). Although the location of **Bethphage** has not been certainly identified, it was clearly farther along the road from Bethany.

19:30 Go . . . on entering you will find. Either an example of Jesus' foreknowledge or a prearrangement (cf. 22:13). **A colt tied, on which no one has ever yet sat** implies a kind of purity that destines an animal for a sacred task (cf. animals offered to the Lord in Num. 19:2 and Deut. 21:3). Matthew 21:2 mentions that a donkey was with the colt, but Luke mentions only the colt, which was most important because Jesus would ride on it (see also note on Matt. 21:5–7).

19:32 They **found it** (v. 30; cf. 22:13), as Jesus had said.

19:35 set Jesus on it. Jesus fulfills a prophecy about the Messiah in Zech. 9:9 by riding on the donkey (see notes on Matt. 21:4–5; John 12:15; cf. 1 Kings 1:33).

19:36 spread . . . cloaks on the road. An act of homage (see note on Matt. 21:8; cf. 2 Kings 9:13).

19:37 On the **Mount of Olives**, see note on Mark 13:3. **began to rejoice** (cf. Zech. 9:9) **and praise God.** This came primarily from Jesus' disciples. **all the mighty works that they had seen.** The miracles they had seen recently (e.g., in Luke 9:51–19:27), and many more as well.

38[m] ch. 13:35; Cited from Ps. 118:26 [n] See Matt. 25:34; John 1:49 [o] ch. 2:14; [Ps. 148:1]
39[p] [Matt. 21:15, 16]
40[q] Hab. 2:11
41[r] For ver. 41-44, [ch. 13:34, 35; 23:28-31] [s] [John 11:35; Heb. 5:7]
42[t] [Deut. 32:29] [u] [John 12:40]
43[v] See ch. 17:22 [w] Isa. 29:3; 37:33; Jer. 6:6; Ezek. 4:2; 26:8 [x] ch. 21:20
44[y] [Ps. 137:9; Hos. 13:16; Nah. 3:10] [z] ch. 21:6 [a] [Dan. 9:24] [b] 1 Pet. 2:12
45[c] For ver. 45-47, see Matt. 21:12-16; Mark 11:15-18; [John 2:14-16]
46[d] Cited from Isa. 56:7 [e] Jer. 7:11
47[f] ch. 20:1; See Matt. 26:55 [g] See Matt. 21:46

that they had seen, 38 saying, [m]"Blessed is [n]the King who comes in the name of the Lord!
Peace in heaven and [o]glory in the highest!" 39 [p]And some of the Pharisees in the crowd said
to him, "Teacher, rebuke your disciples." 40 He answered, "I tell you, if these were silent,
[q]the very stones would cry out."

Jesus Weeps over Jerusalem

41 [r]And when he drew near and saw the city, [s]he wept over it, 42 saying, [t]"Would that
you, even you, had known on this day the things that make for peace! But now [u]they are
hidden from your eyes. 43 For [v]the days will come upon you, when your enemies [w]will set
up a barricade around you and [x]surround you and hem you in on every side 44 [y]and tear
you down to the ground, you and your children within you. And [z]they will not leave one
stone upon another in you, because you did not know [a]the time of your [b]visitation."

Jesus Cleanses the Temple

45 [c]And he entered the temple and began to drive out those who sold, 46 saying to
them, "It is written, [d]'My house shall be a house of prayer,' but [e]you have made it a den
of robbers."
47 [f]And he was teaching daily in the temple. [g]The chief priests and the scribes and the

19:38 Blessed . . . in the name of the Lord! A blessing from Ps. 118:26 that pilgrims traveling to Jerusalem received (cf. note on Mark 11:9).

19:39–40 These verses illustrate v. 14. The Pharisees' attempt to squelch the joy of the occasion is rebuked, for if the disciples stopped expressing their praise, **the very stones would cry out**. All creation was made to worship this King who is Lord of all.

19:41–44 *Jesus Weeps over Jerusalem.* This account occurs only in Luke.

19:41 he wept over it. See notes on 13:34 and John 11:35. Though the rejection of Jesus by many of the Jews was predicted in the OT (see note on John 12:37–40), Jesus still feels great sorrow over their rejection, surely reflecting the heart of God as he contemplates the Jewish people rejecting his prophets and his Son.

19:42 this day. That is, the day when the true Messiah and King came, "the time of your visitation" (v. 44). Broadly speaking, this refers to the coming of the kingdom; more narrowly, it means the coming of Jesus as Israel's King. **The things that make for peace** are the things that would lead the Jewish people to salvation (see note on John 14:27). **But now they** (the things that make for peace) **are hidden** (see note on John 12:37–40).

19:43–44 days will come. See note on 21:5–6. **a barricade around you**. Earthworks constructed by the Romans. **tear you down . . . and your children**. A result of the siege. **not leave one stone**. See note on Matt. 24:2; also Luke 21:6; cf. 2 Sam. 17:13; Ps. 137:7; Mic. 3:12. **Because** explains the reason for this divine judgment.

19:45–48 *Jesus Cleanses the Temple.* Luke's account of this incident is greatly abbreviated (cf. Matt. 21:12–16; Mark 11:15–18). **he entered the temple**. See notes on Matt. 21:12–17; Mark 11:15–17; cf. Mal. 3:1. **began to drive out those who sold**. See note on Matt. 21:12. This probably occurred in the Royal Stoa, though it may have been in the Court of the Gentiles. **den of robbers**. See note on Matt. 21:13; cf. Jer. 7:11. **chief priests**. See note on Luke 9:21–22. **Scribes** (see notes on 5:17; 5:21–22) are often associated with the Pharisees (see note on Mark 11:18). **were** (continually) **seeking to destroy him**. Luke's first explicit mention of a plot against Jesus' life.

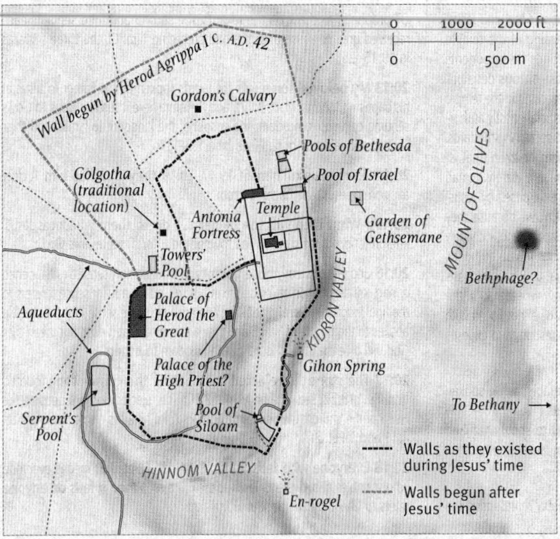

Jerusalem at the Time of Jesus
By the time of Jesus, the city of Jerusalem had grown from a modest military fortress to a world-class city with a newly renovated temple that rivaled nearly any in the ancient world. Public pools were fed by the Gihon Spring and by two aqueducts that brought water to the city from as far as 7 miles (11 km) away. The towns of Bethphage and Bethany were located on the eastern slopes of the Mount of Olives, which lay to the east of Jerusalem. See also Jerusalem in the Time of Jesus, pp. 1878–1879.

principal men of the people were seeking to destroy him, 48 but they did not find anything
they could do, for all the people were hanging on his words.

The Authority of Jesus Challenged

20 [h]One day, [i]as Jesus[1] was teaching the people in the temple and preaching the gospel,
[j]the chief priests and the scribes with the elders came up 2 and said to him, "Tell
us [k]by what authority you do these things, or who it is that gave you this authority." 3 He
answered them, "I also will ask you a question. Now tell me, 4 was the baptism of John [l]from
heaven or from man?" 5 And they discussed it with one another, saying, "If we say, 'From
heaven,' he will say, [m]'Why did you not believe him?' 6 But if we say, 'From man,' all the
people will stone us to death, for they are convinced that John was [n]a prophet." 7 So they
answered that they did not know where it came from. 8 And Jesus said to them, "Neither
will I tell you by what authority I do these things."

The Parable of the Wicked Tenants

9 [o]And he began to tell the people this parable: "A man planted [p]a vineyard and [q]let it
out to tenants and [r]went into another country for a long while. 10 When the time came,
he sent a servant[2] to the tenants, so that [q]they would give him some of the fruit of the
vineyard. [s]But the tenants beat him and sent him away empty-handed. 11 [t]And [s]he sent
another servant. But they also beat and [u]treated him shamefully, and sent him away empty-
handed. 12 [s]And he sent yet a third. This one also they wounded and cast out. 13 Then the
owner of the vineyard said, 'What shall I do? I will send my [v]beloved son; perhaps they
will respect him.' 14 But when the tenants saw him, they said to themselves, [w]'This is the
heir. [x]Let us kill him, so that the inheritance may be ours.' 15 And they [y]threw him out of
the vineyard and killed him. What then will the owner of the vineyard do to them? 16 [z]He
will [a]come and destroy those tenants and [b]give the vineyard to others." When they heard
this, they said, "Surely not!" 17 But he [c]looked directly at them and said, "What then is
this that is written:

> [d]"'The stone that the builders rejected
> has become the cornerstone'?[3]

18 [e]Everyone who falls on that stone will be broken to pieces, and when it falls [f]on anyone,
it will crush him."

[1] Greek *he* [2] Greek *bondservant*; also verse 11 [3] Greek *the head of the corner*

Chapter 20
1 [h]For ver. 1-8, see Matt. 21:23-27; Mark 11:27-33 [i]ch. 19:47 [j]Acts 4:1; 6:12
2 [k][Ex. 2:14; John 1:25; Acts 4:7]
4 [l]ch. 15:18, 21; John 3:27
5 [m]ch. 7:30; Matt. 21:32
6 [n][John 5:35]; See Matt. 11:9
9 [o]For ver. 9-19, see Matt. 21:33-46; Mark 12:1-12 [p]Ps. 80:8; Isa. 5:1; Matt. 21:28 [q]Song 8:11, 12 [r]Matt. 25:14, 15; [Mark 13:34]
10 [q][See ver. 9 above] [s]Matt. 5:12; 22:6; 23:34, 37; [2 Chr. 24:19; 36:15, 16; Neh. 9:26; Jer. 37:15; 38:6; Acts 7:52; 2 Cor. 11:24-26; 1 Thess. 2:15; Heb. 11:36, 37]
11 [t]Matt. 22:4 [s][See ver. 10 above] [u]Acts 5:41 (Gk.)
12 [s][See ver. 10 above]
13 [v]See Matt. 3:17
14 [w]Heb. 1:2; [John 1:11; Rom. 8:17] [x][1 Kgs. 21:19]
15 [y]Heb. 13:12
16 [z][ch. 19:27] [a][Matt. 24:50; 25:19] [b]Matt. 21:43; Acts 13:46; 18:6; 28:28; [Matt. 8:11, 12]
17 [c]See Mark 10:21 [d]Acts 4:11; 1 Pet. 2:7; Cited from Ps. 118:22
18 [e]Isa. 8:14, 15; Rom. 9:32, 33; 1 Pet. 2:8 [f]Dan. 2:34, 35, 44, 45

20:1–8 *The Authority of Jesus Challenged.* The question concerning Jesus' authority (vv. 1–2) is closely associated with his cleansing of the temple (19:45–48). Jesus' counter-question (20:3–4) confounds his opponents (vv. 5–7). **as Jesus was teaching**. Cf. 19:47. **Do these things** describes Jesus' cleansing of the temple, but also his healing and teaching in the temple (and throughout his ministry), because he is neither an official priestly authority nor a scribal authority, according to his questioners' sectarian standards. **Was the baptism** (i.e., the ministry) **of John . . . from heaven** (that is, "from God"; 15:7, 18, 21) **or from man**, i.e., did it have a merely human origin (cf. note on Matt. 21:25–27)? To avoid the dilemma posed by Jesus' question (Luke 20:4), his opponents say they do **not know**, because they feared the consequences of speaking against John the Baptist whose divinely authorized ministry was also carried out apart from official Jewish authority. Their confession of ignorance, however, demonstrates that they have no basis upon which to assess Jesus' ministry. If they do not know whether John the Baptist was from God, they do not know whether Jesus is, either. Faced with such hostility, Jesus refuses to answer his opponents' question, and exposes their ignorance.

20:9–18 *The Parable of the Wicked Tenants.* This parable, while spoken to the people (vv. 1, 9), is directed to Jesus' opponents (19:47; 20:1, 19) and is intended as an analogy (with many referents) to show that God (the "owner," v. 13) is taking away the kingdom from Israel (see note on Mark 12:1–12).

20:10–12 he sent. The man sent three servants, probably representing the OT prophets, to check on the tenants. The second and third servants each received greater abuse than the one preceding him. Cf. the three servants in 19:15–25.

20:13 My beloved son recalls the words spoken by the Father to Jesus at his baptism (3:22; cf. Matt. 3:17), and therefore here it surely alludes to God's sending of Jesus to proclaim the gospel of the kingdom to Israel, and their widespread rejection of him (see John 1:9–11).

20:14–15a Let us kill him. Cf. 19:47; 20:19. **they . . . killed him**. A clear allusion to Jesus' approaching death.

20:15b What then will the owner . . . do to them introduces Jesus' interpretation of the parable. The "owner" (lit., "lord") represents God.

20:16 God will **destroy those tenants**. In a preliminary sense this happened during the destruction of Jerusalem in A.D. 70, but in a fuller sense it refers to the final judgment. **Surely not!** The hearers have some sense that the parable applies to the people of Israel, and they are hoping that it does not mean that God will give the land of Israel or the kingdom to **others**.

20:17 The stone . . . rejected has become the cornerstone (quoted from Ps. 118:22; see note on Mark 12:10). The rejected Son will become the Head of the church, the people of God. Psalm 118:22 is also quoted in Acts 4:11 and 1 Pet. 2:7.

20:18 Everyone who falls (cf. Isa. 8:14–15; 1 Pet. 2:8) means everyone who stumbles at and rejects Jesus as the Messiah. **When it falls on anyone** refers to Christ coming back in judgment.

19 [h]ch. 19:47, 48
20 [i]For ver. 20-38, see Matt. 22:15-32; Mark 12:13-27 [j]ch. 14:1; Mark 3:2 [k][1 Kgs. 14:6] [l]ver. 26; ch. 11:54 [m]Matt. 27:2, 11; 28:14; See Acts 23:24
21 [o]See Acts 10:34 [p]Acts 18:25, 26; [Acts 13:10]
22 [q]Matt. 17:25 [r]ch. 2:1; 3:1
23 [s]1 Cor. 3:19; 2 Cor. 4:2; 11:3; Eph. 4:14; [2 Cor. 12:16]
24 [t]See Matt. 18:28
25 [u]Rom. 13:7
26 [v]ver. 20
27 [w]Matt. 3:7; 16:1; 22:34; Acts 4:1; 5:17; 23:6 [x]Acts 23:8; [Acts 4:2]
28 [y][Deut. 25:5]
34 [z]ch. 16:8; See ch. 10:6 [a]ch. 17:27; Matt. 24:38; [ver. 35]
35 [b]Acts 5:41; 2 Thess. 1:5, 11; See Matt. 22:8 [c][ch. 18:30]; See Mark 10:30 [d][ver. 34]
36 [e]1 Cor. 15:54, 55; Rev. 21:4 [f][Heb. 2:7, 9] [g][Gen. 1:26; Ps. 82:6] [h][Rom. 8:19, 23; 1 Cor. 15:52] [i]See ch. 10:6
37 [j]ver. 28 [k]Ex. 3:1–4:17 [l]Acts 7:32; Cited from Ex. 3:15; [Ex. 3:6]
38 [m]Rom. 6:11; 14:7, 8; 2 Cor. 5:15; Gal. 2:19; 1 Thess. 5:10; 1 Pet. 4:2; [Heb. 9:14]
39 [n]Mark 12:28; [Matt. 22:34]
40 [o]Matt. 22:46; Mark 12:34

Paying Taxes to Caesar

19 [h]The scribes and the chief priests sought to lay hands on him at that very hour, for
they perceived that he had told this parable against them, but they feared the people. 20 [i]So
they [j]watched him and sent spies, who [k]pretended to be sincere, that they might [l]catch
him in something he said, so as to deliver him up to the authority and jurisdiction of [m]the
governor. 21 So they asked him, “Teacher, we know that you speak and teach rightly, and
[o]show no partiality,[1] but truly teach [p]the way of God. 22 Is it lawful for us to give [q]tribute
to [r]Caesar, or not?” 23 But he perceived their [s]craftiness, and said to them, 24 “Show me [t]a
denarius.[2] Whose likeness and inscription does it have?” They said, “Caesar’s.” 25 He said
to them, “Then [u]render to Caesar the things that are Caesar’s, and to God the things that
are God’s.” 26 And they were not able in the presence of the people [v]to catch him in what
he said, but marveling at his answer they became silent.

Sadducees Ask About the Resurrection

27 There came to him [w]some Sadducees, [x]those who deny that there is a resurrection,
28 and they asked him a question, saying, “Teacher, Moses wrote for us [y]that if a man’s
brother dies, having a wife but no children, the man[3] must take the widow and raise up
offspring for his brother. 29 Now there were seven brothers. The first took a wife, and died
without children. 30 And the second 31 and the third took her, and likewise all seven left
no children and died. 32 Afterward the woman also died. 33 In the resurrection, therefore,
whose wife will the woman be? For the seven had her as wife.”
34 And Jesus said to them, [z]“The sons of this age [a]marry and [a]are given in marriage,
35 but those who are [b]considered worthy to attain to [c]that age and to the resurrection
from the dead [d]neither marry [d]nor are given in marriage, 36 for [e]they cannot die anymore,
because they are [f]equal to angels and [g]are [h]sons of God, being [i]sons[4] of the resurrection.
37 But that the dead are raised, [j]even Moses showed, in [k]the passage about the bush,
where he calls [l]the Lord the God of Abraham and the God of Isaac and the God of Jacob.
38 Now he is not God of the dead, but of the living, for all [m]live to him.” 39 Then some of
the scribes [n]answered, “Teacher, you have spoken well.” 40 For [o]they no longer dared to
ask him any question.

[1] Greek *and do not receive a face* [2] A *denarius* was a day’s wage for a laborer [3] Greek *his brother* [4] Greek *huioi*; see Preface

20:19–26 *Paying Taxes to Caesar.* Realizing that the parable of the wicked tenants (vv. 9–18) was spoken “against them” (v. 19), the Jewish leaders try to entrap Jesus in his words.

20:20 Governor can refer to a procurator or prefect (see 3:1). Here it refers to Pontius Pilate.

20:21 You speak and teach rightly is an insincere compliment (see v. 20).

20:22 Is it lawful . . . ? See notes on Matt. 22:17; Mark 12:14.

20:25 render to Caesar. See note on Matt. 22:21. The denarius has Caesar’s image and represents the tribute they should give to him. Jesus adds a more important command: people should give **to God** that which bears his image and likeness, namely, themselves (cf. note on Rom. 12:1).

20:26 The wisdom of the one “greater than Solomon” (11:31) thwarts this attempt to **catch him** in his speech. Even Christ’s opponents were **marveling** and were reduced to silence (cf. 14:4, 6).

20:27–40 *Sadducees Ask about the Resurrection.* The second and last attempt to entrap Jesus involves a well-crafted, hypothetical example that the Sadducees believe refutes the doctrine of the resurrection.

20:27 Sadducees. See notes on Matt. 3:7; 22:23. This is the only mention of this Jewish sect in Luke (cf., however, Acts 4:1; 5:17; 23:6–8). They were a priestly sect, and one view is that they claimed descent from Zadok, the high priest under David (1 Kings 1:26; see Jewish Groups at the Time of the New Testament, pp. 1799–1800). **who deny . . . a resurrection**. This is the main issue in the following discussion.

20:28–31 Moses wrote. The Sadducees’ puzzle is based on the OT command that if a man dies leaving no children, his brother is to marry the widow and take care of her (see note on Matt. 22:24). **all seven left no children and died**. The example is carefully worked out so that no brother has a special claim to the woman.

20:33 In the resurrection . . . whose wife . . . ? Since neither Jesus nor the Pharisees could reply that she would equally be the wife of all seven, the Sadducees believed this illustration refuted belief in the resurrection.

20:34–35 Jesus first demonstrates the flaw of equating the coming age with this age. Whereas the **sons of this age** (cf. “sons of this world,” 16:8) **marry**, those **considered worthy to attain to that age and to the resurrection from the dead** (cf. Acts 4:2 and 1 Pet. 1:3 for another description of “that age”) **neither marry nor are given in marriage**. Marriage is not a permanent fixture in God’s eternal purpose (see note on Matt. 22:29–30).

20:36 Equal to angels explains why resurrected believers **cannot die** (since angels are immortal). **sons of God . . . sons of the resurrection**. The believer’s relationship as a child of God becomes fully realized at the resurrection after Christ’s return (cf. Rom. 8:23; 1 Cor. 15:53–54).

20:37–38 in the passage about the bush. Since the OT at that time did not have verses or chapters, Jesus refers to the passage (Ex. 3:1–4:17) in this manner (cf. Rom. 11:2). When the **Lord** calls himself the **God of Abraham and . . . of Jacob** after their death, this indicates that he is still their God, and since only living people can have a God (**he is not God of the dead, but of the living**), then there must be a resurrection. Cf. notes on Matt. 22:31–32; Mark 12:26–27.

20:39–40 Jesus’ argument is such that even some of the scribes remark, **you have spoken well** (cf. Acts 23:6–10); his opponents are silenced (cf. Luke 13:17; 19:48; 20:19, 26).

Whose Son Is the Christ?

41 [p]But he said to them, "How can they say that [q]the Christ is [q]David's son? **42** For David
himself says in the Book of Psalms,

> [r]"'The Lord said to my Lord,
> "Sit at my right hand,
> **43** until I make your enemies [s]your footstool."'

44 David thus calls him Lord, so [t]how is he his son?"

Beware of the Scribes

45 [u]And in the hearing of all the people he said to his disciples, **46** "Beware of the scribes,
who like to walk around in long robes, and love greetings in the marketplaces and the best
seats in the synagogues and [v]the places of honor at feasts, **47** [w]who devour widows' houses
and [x]for a pretense make long prayers. They will receive the greater condemnation."

The Widow's Offering

21 [y]Jesus[1] looked up and saw the rich [z]putting their gifts into [a]the offering box, **2** and
he saw a poor widow put in two [b]small copper coins.[2] **3** And he said, "Truly, I tell
you, [c]this poor widow has put in more than all of them. **4** For they all contributed out of
their abundance, but she out of her [d]poverty put in all [e]she had to live on."

Jesus Foretells Destruction of the Temple

5 [f]And while some were speaking of the temple, how it was adorned with noble stones
and offerings, he said, **6** "As for these things that you see, [g]the days will come when there
will not be left here one stone upon another that will not be thrown down." **7** And they
asked him, "Teacher, [h]when will these things be, and what will be the sign when these
things are about to take place?" **8** And he said, [i]"See that you are not led astray. For [j]many
will come in my name, saying, [k]'I am he!' and, [l]'The time is at hand!' Do not go after them.
9 And when you hear of wars and tumults, do not be [m]terrified, for these things [n]must first
take place, but the end will not be at once."

Jesus Foretells Wars and Persecution

10 Then he said to them, [o]"Nation will rise against nation, and [p]kingdom against kingdom. **11** There will be great [q]earthquakes, and in various places [r]famines and pestilences.

[1] Greek *He* [2] Greek *two lepta*; a *lepton* was a Jewish bronze or copper coin worth about 1/128 of a *denarius* (which was a day's wage for a laborer)

41 [p]For ver. 41-44, see Matt. 22:41-45; Mark 12:35-37 [q]See Matt. 1:1, 17
42 [r]Acts 2:34, 35; Heb. 1:13; Cited from Ps. 110:1; [1 Cor. 15:25; Heb. 10:13]
43 [s][Acts 7:49]
44 [t][Rom. 1:3, 4]
45 [u]For ver. 45, 46, see Matt. 23:1, 2, 5-7; Mark 12:38, 39; [ch. 11:43]
46 [v]ch. 14:7, 8
47 [w][ch. 11:39; 16:14] [x][Matt. 6:5, 7]

Chapter 21

1 [y]For ver. 1-4, see Mark 12:41-44 [z]2 Kgs. 12:9 [a]John 8:20 (Gk.)
2 [b]ch. 12:59
3 [c][2 Cor. 8:2, 12]
4 [d][Phil. 4:11] [e]ch. 8:43
5 [f]For ver. 5-36, see Matt. 24:1-51; Mark 13:1-37
6 [g]ch. 19:43, 44; See ch. 17:22
7 [h][Acts 1:6, 7]
8 [i]Jer. 29:8; Eph. 5:6; Col. 2:8; 2 Thess. 2:3; 1 John 3:7 [j]Jer. 14:14; 1 John 2:18 [k]See John 8:24 [l][Matt. 3:2; 4:17; Mark 1:15]
9 [m]ch. 24:37 [n]Rev. 1:1
10 [o]2 Chr. 15:6; [Rev. 6:4] [p]Isa. 19:2
11 [q]Rev. 6:12 [r]Acts 11:28; Rev. 6:8

20:41–44 *Whose Son Is the Christ?* **How can they say that the Christ is David's son?** Jesus answers his own question: Scripture teaches that Jesus is *more* than David's son. Jesus quotes Ps. 110:1: **David . . . says . . . The Lord** (the God of Israel) **said to my Lord** (the Messiah). See note on Mark 12:35–37. **Sit at my right hand.** The Lord (Messiah) is given the place of honor. See note on Matt. 22:41–46. Since David calls the Messiah his Lord, **how is he his son?** (that is, how can Jesus be *only* David's son?). The Messiah is, in fact, greater than his father David, and thus David calls him Lord (see note on Matt. 22:41–46).

20:45–47 *Beware of the Scribes.* Luke concludes the preceding "debates" with a warning about the hypocrisy of the scribes. **Beware of the scribes.** Although not all scribes deserved the following condemnation (cf. v. 39; Mark 12:34), the majority of them did (cf. Luke 11:45–53; 12:1). They **walk . . . in long** (ostentatious) **robes** (cf. note on Matt. 23:5); they **love greetings** and **places of honor** (cf. Luke 11:43; 14:7–8; notes on Matt. 23:6; 23:7). While doing this, they **devour widows' houses** (probably while serving as executors of their estates) **and for a pretense make long prayers** (cf. Matt. 6:5–6). As a consequence, **they will receive the greater condemnation** (cf. Matt. 23:13–36; Luke 11:37–52).

21:1–4 *The Widow's Offering.* The point of this story is that God measures gifts not by their size but on the basis of how much of a sacrifice it was to give them and how sincere and selfless the heart was that gave the gift. **offering box.** One of the 13 collection chests in the temple, with trumpet-like openings (Mishnah, *Shekalim* 6.5). The **two small copper coins** were about one centimeter in diameter.

21:5–24 *Jesus Foretells the Destruction of the Temple and Jerusalem.* The teaching of Jesus in the temple begun in 19:45 now concludes with his foretelling the destruction of the temple and Jerusalem (21:5–24) and the coming of the Son of Man (vv. 25–38). Most of this material is found also in Mark, but (assuming that Luke built on Mark's account) Luke has added vv. 12, 15, 18, 20–22, 23b–26a, 28. As is also the case earlier in Luke (cf. 17:22; 19:43–44), the destruction of Jerusalem in A.D. 70 is used by Jesus as a pattern or a "type" (a typological example) that points to the ultimate destruction that will come at the end of the age when Christ returns.

21:5–6 *Jesus Foretells the Destruction of the Temple.* Jesus corrects a number of misconceptions regarding the destruction of Jerusalem and the end of the world. **how it was adorned.** The beauty and size of Herod the Great's Temple Mount exceeded that of most of the seven wonders of the world. It was more than twice the size of the Acropolis in Athens. Its perimeter was 0.96 miles (1.55 km) and enclosed a space equivalent to one-sixth of the entire city. **noble stones.** One of the stones of the temple complex still remaining measures 45 x 11.5 x 12 feet (13.7 x 3.2 x 4 m) and is estimated to weigh 570 tons. **offerings.** Tapestries, gold and bronze doors, golden grape clusters, etc. **The days will come** refers not to the second coming but to a time in history before that (cf. 5:35; 17:22; 19:43; 23:29). **not . . . one stone upon another.** See note on Matt. 24:2.

21:7–9 *Signs before the Destruction.* **when will these things be, and what will be the sign . . . ?** See notes on Matt. 24:3 and Mark 13:4–37. **For many** introduces what the disciples should not be **led astray** by. **in my name.** People claiming the title "Messiah." These imposters will say **I am he**, i.e., "I am the Messiah," and therefore **the time is at hand!** (cf. Dan. 7:22; Rev. 1:3; 22:10). **Do not go after them**, for these pretenders are not Christ himself (cf. Luke 17:23). **when you hear of wars and tumults.** See note on Matt. 24:6–7.

And there will be [s]terrors and great [t]signs from heaven. 12 But before all this [u]they will lay
their hands on you and persecute you, delivering you up to [v]the synagogues and [w]prisons,
and you [x]will be brought before [y]kings and [z]governors for my name's sake. 13 [a]This will
be your opportunity to bear witness. 14 Settle it therefore in your minds [b]not to meditate
beforehand how to answer, 15 for [c]I will give you a mouth and [d]wisdom, which none of
your adversaries will be able to withstand or [e]contradict. 16 You will be delivered up [f]even
by parents and brothers[1] and relatives and friends, and some of you they will put to death.
17 [g]You will be hated by all for my name's sake. 18 But [h]not a hair of your head will perish.
19 By your [i]endurance you will gain your lives.

Jesus Foretells Destruction of Jerusalem

20 "But [j]when you see Jerusalem surrounded by armies, then know that [k]its desolation
has come near. 21 Then let those who are in Judea flee to the mountains, and let those who
are inside the city depart, and let not those who are out in the country enter it, 22 for these
are [l]days of [m]vengeance, to fulfill [n]all that is written. 23 [o]Alas for women who are pregnant
and for those who are nursing infants in those days! For there will be great distress upon
the earth and [p]wrath against this people. 24 They will fall by the edge of the sword and [q]be
led captive among all nations, and [r]Jerusalem will be trampled underfoot by the Gentiles,
[s]until the times of the Gentiles are fulfilled.

The Coming of the Son of Man

25 "And [t]there will be signs in sun and moon [u]and stars, and on the earth [v]distress of
nations in perplexity because of the roaring of the sea and the waves, 26 people fainting
with fear and with foreboding of what is coming on the world. For [w]the powers of the
heavens will be shaken. 27 And then they will see [x]the Son of Man coming in a cloud [y]with
power and great glory. 28 Now when these things begin to take place, straighten up and
[z]raise your heads, because [a]your redemption is drawing near."

The Lesson of the Fig Tree

29 And he told them a parable: "Look at the fig tree, and all the trees. 30 As soon as they
come out in leaf, you see [b]for yourselves and know that the summer is already near. 31 So

[1] *Or parents and brothers and sisters*

11 [s]Isa. 19:17 [t]ch. 11:16; Matt. 16:1; Mark 8:11; [ver. 25; Rev. 12:1, 3; 13:13; 15:1]
12 [u]For ver. 12-17, [Matt. 10:17-22] [v]Acts 22:19; 26:11 [w]Acts 4:3; 5:18; 8:3; 12:4; 16:24; 24:27; 2 Cor. 11:23 [x]See Acts 16:19 [y][Acts 27:24] [z]Acts 17:6; 18:12; 24:1; 25:6
13 [a][Phil. 1:13, 14, 19]
14 [b]ch. 12:11
15 [c][Ex. 4:12; Jer. 1:9] [d]Acts 6:10 [e][Acts 4:14]
16 [f][ch. 12:53; Matt. 10:35]
17 [g]John 15:18-21; [ch. 6:22]
18 [h][ver. 16; John 10:28]; See 1 Sam. 14:45
19 [i]Rom. 5:3; [Matt. 10:22; 24:13]; See Heb. 10:36
20 [j]See ch. 19:43 [k]Dan. 9:27
22 [l]Isa. 34:8; 63:4; Hos. 9:7 [m][ch. 18:7, 8] [n]See Matt. 1:22
23 [o]ch. 23:29 [p]1 Thess. 2:16
24 [q][Deut. 28:64] [r]Rev. 11:2; [Ps. 79:1; Isa. 63:3, 18; Dan. 8:13; Zech. 12:3] [s][Dan. 12:7; Rom. 11:25]
25 [t]Isa. 13:10; 24:23; Ezek. 32:7; Joel 2:10, 31; 3:15; Acts 2:20; [Amos 5:20; 8:9; Zeph. 1:15; Rev. 6:12; 8:12] [u]Rev. 6:13; [Isa. 14:12; 34:4] [v][Ps. 65:7]
26 [w][Isa. 34:4]
27 [x]See Dan. 7:13 [y]Matt. 26:64; Mark 9:1; [Matt. 25:31]
28 [z]Job 10:15 [a]Rom. 8:23; Eph. 4:30; [Rom. 13:11]; See ch. 1:68
30 [b]ch. 12:57; [Matt. 16:3]

21:10–19 *Nation Will Rise against Nation.* Jesus warns of calamities caused by nature and by humanity (vv. 10–11) and of persecution from government (vv. 12–15) and family (vv. 16–17). He also offers words of encouragement (vv. 13, 14–15, 18–19).

21:12 before all this. Before the events of vv. 6–11.

21:13 opportunity to bear witness. Cf. 24:48; Acts 1:8.

21:14 not to meditate beforehand how to answer. Cf. 12:11–12.

21:16 You will be delivered up even by parents intensifies 12:53; 14:26; 18:29. **Some of you** suggests that martyrdom will be the exception.

21:18 In light of the prediction that some disciples will be "put to death" (v. 16), it is best to take **not a hair of your head will perish** as a metaphorical way of saying that God's people will suffer no eternal spiritual harm.

21:19 Through **endurance** (Gk. *hypomonē*, "endurance, steadfastness, perseverance, patience") believers will **gain** their **lives** (that is, will be enabled to partake of the full benefits of final salvation in the end times; see 9:24).

21:20–24 *Jesus Foretells the Destruction of Jerusalem.* Whereas vv. 8–19 describe what will occur before Jerusalem's destruction, Luke now describes the destruction itself. In vv. 8–19 the audience is Jesus' followers ("you"); here it is described as "those," "women," "this people," and "they," indicating that Jesus' followers are not in immediate view.

21:20 Jerusalem surrounded by armies. The first fulfillment of this was the destruction of Jerusalem in A.D. 70, and this destruction may also foreshadow a greater judgment at the end of the age, so that some of what Jesus predicted in vv. 5–24 may also find fulfillment in events that precede Christ's second coming. Cf. also note on 19:43–44.

21:21 Then (while there is still time) **. . . flee to the mountains** (see note on Matt. 24:16). **Those who are inside the city** (should) **depart** before the Roman siege occurs.

21:22 days of vengeance. "Vengeance" refers to God's vengeance and judgment, not Rome's. **to fulfill all that is written**. Cf. 18:31; 24:44; Acts 13:29.

21:23 women who are pregnant and . . . nursing. In war, they are the most vulnerable; thus what was normally a blessing would now present a great difficulty.

21:24 the edge of the sword. Cf. Jer. 21:7; Heb. 11:37. **Until the times of the Gentiles are fulfilled** may suggest a time when Israel/Jerusalem will repent and be restored to God's favor (see Rom. 11:11–32).

21:25–38 *Jesus Foretells the Coming of the Son of Man.* Having warned of the approaching destruction of the temple and Jerusalem (vv. 5–24), Jesus turns now to the more distant future and foretells his second coming.

21:25–28 *The Coming of the Son of Man.* Jesus turns next to teachings about the consummation of all things and his return. **signs in sun and moon and stars**. See note on Matt. 24:29. **The powers of the heavens will be shaken** describes great changes in the skies (see note on Matt. 24:29). **they will see**. The second coming involves the visible return of the Son of Man from heaven (Acts 1:11; see notes on Matt. 8:20 and 24:30), bringing history to its end. **These things . . . take place** refers to Luke 21:25–27. **straighten up and raise your heads**. A posture of hope and confidence. **Redemption** refers to the time of Christ's return, when mortality puts on immortality (1 Cor. 15:53) and the redemption of the body takes place (Rom. 8:23).

21:29–33 *The Lesson of the Fig Tree.* The analogy of the fig tree (vv. 29–30) indicates that, when the signs of vv. 25–26 take place, the return of the Son of Man is at hand.

21:31 So also introduces the reality to which the fig tree analogy of

also, when you see these things taking place, you know that the kingdom of God is near.
32 [c]Truly, I say to you, this generation will not pass away until all has taken place. 33 [d]Heaven
and earth will pass away, but [e]my words will not pass away.

Watch Yourselves

34 "But watch yourselves [f]lest [g]your hearts be weighed down with dissipation and drunkenness and [h]cares of this life, and [i]that day come upon you suddenly [j]like a trap. 35 For it
will come upon all who dwell on the face of the whole earth. 36 But [k]stay awake at all times,
[l]praying that you may [m]have strength to escape all these things that are going to take place,
and [n]to stand before the Son of Man."

37 And [o]every day he was teaching in the temple, but [p]at night he went out and lodged
on [q]the mount called Olivet. 38 And early in the morning [o]all the people came to him in
the temple to hear him.

The Plot to Kill Jesus

22 [r]Now the Feast of Unleavened Bread drew near, which is called [s]the Passover. 2 And
the chief priests and the scribes [t]were seeking how to put him to death, for they
feared the people.

Judas to Betray Jesus

3 [u]Then [v]Satan entered into [w]Judas called Iscariot, who was of the number of the twelve.
4 He went away and conferred with the chief priests and [x]officers how he might betray
him to them. 5 And they were glad, and agreed to give him money. 6 So he consented and
sought an opportunity to [y]betray him to them in the absence of a crowd.

The Passover with the Disciples

7 [z]Then came [a]the day of Unleavened Bread, on which the Passover lamb had to be
sacrificed. 8 So Jesus[1] sent Peter and John, saying, "Go and prepare the Passover for us, that

32 [c]See ch. 9:27
33 [d]Ps. 102:26; Isa. 51:6; 2 Pet. 3:10; [Matt. 5:18; Heb. 12:27] [e]Ps. 119:89; Isa. 40:8; 1 Pet. 1:23, 25
34 [f][Rom. 13:13; 1 Thess. 5:6, 7; 1 Pet. 4:7] [g]James 5:5 [h][Matt. 13:22] [i]1 Thess. 5:3, 4; [ch. 12:40] [j]Eccles. 9:12; Isa. 24:17
36 [k]ch. 12:37; Matt. 25:13; 26:41; Mark 14:34-38; Acts 20:31; 1 Cor. 16:13; 1 Thess. 5:6; 1 Pet. 5:8 [l]See ch. 18:1 [m][Hos. 12:4] [n]See Rev. 6:17
37 [o]See Matt. 26:55 [p]ch. 22:39; Matt. 21:17; Mark 11:19; [John 8:1; 18:2] [q]See Matt. 21:1
38 [o][See ver. 37 above]

Chapter 22

1 [r]For ver. 1, 2, see Matt. 26:2-5; Mark 14:1, 2 [s]See John 6:4
2 [t]John 11:53; See Matt. 21:46
3 [u]For ver. 3-6, see Matt. 26:14-16; Mark 14:10, 11; [John 13:2, 27, 30] [v][Acts 5:3] [w]ch. 6:16; Matt. 27:3; Acts 1:16; [John 6:71; 12:4]
4 [x]Acts 4:1; 5:24, 26
6 [y]See Matt. 20:18, 19
7 [z]For ver. 7-14, see Matt. 26:17-19; Mark 14:12-16 [a]Ex. 12:18; 1 Cor. 5:7

[1] Greek *he*

vv. 29–30 points. **These things** refers to the second coming (vv. 25–28). **The kingdom of God is near** means the consummation of the kingdom (see Introduction: Key Themes), when the Son of Man returns.

21:32 this generation will not pass away. See notes on Matt. 24:34 and Mark 13:30.

21:33 my words will not pass away. Jesus emphasizes the permanence, certainty, and truth of his words and his teaching—more permanent, in fact, than even **heaven and earth**. This applies to all of Jesus' teaching, but specifically in this context to his teaching about the certainty and truth of his return and the events leading up to this. (Cf. the note on 16:17, where Jesus also claims that his teaching has the same divine authority and permanence as the Mosaic law.)

21:34–38 *Watch Yourselves.* Luke ends this section (19:28–21:38) with two warnings from Jesus concerning his return (21:34–36), and a summary conclusion (vv. 37–38).

21:34 watch yourselves. This and the next warning ("stay awake," v. 36) involve being prepared and remaining faithful (cf. 12:35–48; 1 Thess. 5:2–4) for **that day** when the Son of Man comes (Luke 21:27) and the kingdom comes in its fullness (v. 31).

21:35 The warnings of vv. 34 and 36 apply to people throughout the **whole earth**, not just "those who are in Judea" (v. 21).

21:36 Stay awake at all times means spiritual alertness, made possible especially by **praying** (see Introduction: Key Themes). Such prayer will enable the believer **to escape all these things** (i.e., to avoid being harmed by the tumultuous times and circumstances before Christ's return) and not to "lose heart" (18:1) but to keep the faith (18:8; see note on Matt. 24:36). **to stand before the Son of Man**. They should pray to escape judgment and hear him say, "Well done" (Luke 19:17).

22:1–23:56 *The Suffering and Death of Jesus.* As the time of Jesus' death draws near, Luke's focus shifts from the temple to the broader city of Jerusalem, and from the teachings of Jesus to increasingly fast-moving events.

22:1–38 *The Plot to Kill Jesus and the Passover Meal.* As Jesus has his last meal with his disciples, he once again discusses with them his approaching death. Meanwhile, plans are set in motion against him.

22:1–6 *The Plot to Kill Jesus.* As the people gathered in Jerusalem to celebrate the Passover, some of their leaders plotted in secret to kill Jesus.

22:1 The **Feast of Unleavened Bread** spanned the 15th to the 21st of Nisan, the first month in the Jewish calendar (March/April in the Gregorian calendar). See notes on Matt. 26:17; Mark 14:12; and The Hebrew Calendar, p. 34. **Passover**. See note on Luke 2:41.

22:2 chief priests. See notes on 9:21–22 and Matt. 26:3–4. For **scribes**, see note on Matt. 8:19. **were seeking how**. Their verdict about Jesus is already decided; the only remaining issue is how to get rid of him (cf. Luke 19:47–48).

22:3 Judas had never truly believed in Jesus, and Jesus was aware of this (see John 6:64, 70), though apparently none of his other disciples realized it (see note on Luke 22:23). Judas's pattern of dishonest behavior was evidence of his unbelief (see John 12:6). But here (with the consent of Judas's sinful heart) **Satan entered into Judas** and thereby he exercises much greater influence over his actions, prompting him to go to the chief priests with a plot (Luke 22:4). John mentions that Satan entered into Judas again at the time of the Last Supper (John 13:27).

22:4–6 officers. Leaders of the temple police (cf. v. 52; Acts 4:1; 5:24). **how he might betray him**. Judas planned that Jesus would be seized apart from the crowd (cf. Luke 22:53 and notes on Matt. 26:15–16; Mark 14:10; 14:11).

22:7–13 *Preparations for the Passover Meal.* As in Mark 14:12–16, the Passover account follows the plot against Jesus. **day of Unleavened Bread**. See notes on Mark 14:12 and Luke 22:1. **on which the Passover lamb had to be sacrificed**. See note on Matt. 26:17. The Passover meal had to be eaten within the walls of Jerusalem (Deut. 16:5–6). **Go and prepare** involved

11 [b]See John 11:28 [c]ch. 2:7 (Gk.)
12 [d][Acts 1:13]
13 [e]ch. 19:32
14 [f]Matt. 26:20; Mark 14:17
16 [g][ver. 30; ch. 14:15; Rev. 19:9]
17 [h]See Matt. 15:36
18 [i]Matt. 26:29; Mark 14:25 [g][See ver. 16 above]
19 [j]For ver. 19, 20, see Matt. 26:26-28; Mark 14:22-24; 1 Cor. 11:23-25 [h][See ver. 17 above] [k]1 Cor. 10:16; [John 6:53]
20 [k][See ver. 19 above] [l]See 2 Cor. 3:6 [m]Ex. 24:8; [Zech. 9:11; Heb. 13:20]
21 [n]For ver. 21-23, see Matt. 26:21-24; Mark 14:18-21; [John 13:21-26]

we may eat it." **9** They said to him, "Where will you have us prepare it?" **10** He said to them,
"Behold, when you have entered the city, a man carrying a jar of water will meet you. Follow
him into the house that he enters **11** and tell the master of the house, [b]'The Teacher says
to you, Where is [c]the guest room, where I may eat the Passover with my disciples?' **12** And
he will show you [d]a large upper room furnished; prepare it there." **13** And they went and
found it [e]just as he had told them, and they prepared the Passover.

Institution of the Lord's Supper

14 [f]And when the hour came, he reclined at table, and the apostles with him. **15** And he
said to them, "I have earnestly desired to eat this Passover with you before I suffer. **16** For I
tell you I will not eat it[1] [g]until it is fulfilled in the kingdom of God." **17** And he took a cup,
and [h]when he had given thanks he said, "Take this, and divide it among yourselves. **18** [i]For
I tell you that from now on I will not drink of the fruit of the vine [g]until the kingdom of
God comes." **19** [j]And he took bread, and [h]when he had given thanks, he broke it and gave
it to them, saying, [k]"This is my body, which is given for you. Do this in remembrance of
me." **20** And likewise the cup after they had eaten, saying, [k]"This cup that is poured out for
you is [l]the new [m]covenant in my blood.[2] **21** [n]But behold, the hand of him who betrays me

[1] Some manuscripts *never eat it again* [2] Some manuscripts omit, in whole or in part, verses 19b-20 (*which is given . . . in my blood*)

having the lamb sacrificed at the temple, roasting it, preparing the room for the meal, and preparing various side dishes. The disciples would be met by a **man** recognized by his **carrying a jar of water**—something one would expect a woman to be doing. The man would be looking for them and would lead them to the place for their Passover meal. The secretive nature of the meeting suggests that Jesus was seeking privacy. Everything takes place **just as he had told them** (cf. Luke 19:32), suggesting either a prearrangement or a miraculous work of God.

22:14–23 *The Passover Meal and the Institution of the Lord's Supper.* Luke's version of Jesus' final Passover meal with his disciples differs in two ways from Matthew and Mark: he places Jesus' statement about his betrayal after the meal rather than before (probably an arrangement by topic), and he refers to two cups (vv. 17–18, 20) rather than one.

22:14 when the hour came. The "hour" to celebrate the Passover (v. 15) and, in a broader sense, the "hour" of Jesus' suffering and death (v. 53; John 13:1; 17:1). **he reclined at table**. The Passover was eaten in a reclining position, as were other festive meals (Luke 11:37; 14:10; 17:7; cf. note on Matt. 26:20).

22:15 Jesus **earnestly desired** to eat this meal with his disciples for several reasons: (1) it represented the founding of the nation of Israel (see note on Mark 14:17); (2) Jesus himself was now about to become the true Passover Lamb who would be sacrificed for the sins of his people, and thus this Passover meal was the last in long centuries of celebrating it while looking forward to the Messiah; (3) Jesus knew the meal would richly symbolize the giving of his body and blood for the disciples to earn salvation for them; and (4) this Passover meal itself looked forward to the "marriage supper of the Lamb" in heaven (see note on Rev. 19:9–10).

22:16 I will not eat it implies "I will not eat it again" (some manuscripts make this more explicit; see ESV footnote). **Until it is fulfilled** refers to the future messianic banquet (see note on Rev. 19:9–10).

22:17 took a cup. See note on Matt. 26:27. **had given thanks**. Greek *eucharisteō*, from which comes "Eucharist."

22:19 took bread. For parallels with the feeding of the 5,000, see note on 9:16. The expression **This is my body** has been subject to widely varying interpretations throughout the history of the church. Roman Catholics understand it literally, and claim that the bread and wine actually become the body and blood of Christ. Lutherans hold that the literal body and blood of Christ are present "in, with, and under" the bread and wine (something like the way water is present in a sponge). Some Anglicans refer to the "real presence" of Christ in the bread and wine. Most other Protestants have argued that the body and blood of Christ are not literally, physically, or "really" present, but that Christ is present "symbolically"; most would also add that Christ is present spiritually, with and in the believing recipients of the bread and wine, strengthening their faith and fellowship in him and thereby feeding their souls. Christ's spiritual presence can be supported from Matt. 18:20; 28:20. **given for you**. This same verb (Gk. *didōmi*, "give") is used with respect to sacrifice in Mark 10:45; Luke 2:24; Gal. 1:4. The Greek construction translated "for you" (Gk. *hyper* plus genitive) often has a vicarious sense, where one person does something in place of someone else. As represented and predicted in this celebration of the Lord's Supper, Jesus' body will be the once-and-for-all fulfillment of the ceremonies surrounding the Passover lamb, as he will become the sacrificial atonement on the basis of which God will "pass over" the sins of the people. **Do this in remembrance of me**. Cf. note on 1 Cor. 11:24.

22:20 this cup. See notes on Matt. 26:28 and Luke 22:42. **New covenant in my blood** (cf. "blood of the covenant," Ex. 24:8; see also Lev. 17:11–14) indicates that Jesus' blood is sacrificial blood, sealing a new covenant. **Poured out**, i.e., in death. **For you** (cf. Luke 22:19) makes explicit the "for many" of Mark 14:24.

22:21 the hand of him who betrays me. See note on Matt. 26:23.

The Last Supper

After Jesus and his disciples ate the Passover meal, they crossed the Kidron Valley and entered a garden called Gethsemane (meaning "oil press"), where they often spent time while visiting Jerusalem (cf. 22:39).

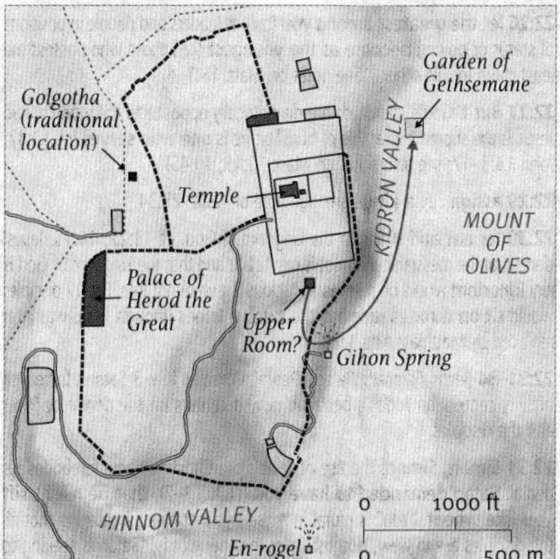

is [o]with me on the table. 22 For the Son of Man goes [p]as it has been determined, but woe
to that man by whom he is betrayed!" 23 And they began to question one another, which
of them it could be who was going to do this.

Who Is the Greatest?

24 [q]A dispute also arose among them, as to which of them was to be regarded as the greatest. 25 [r]And he said to them, "The kings of the Gentiles [s]exercise lordship over them, and
those in authority over them are called benefactors. 26 [t]But not so with you. Rather, let [s]the
greatest among you become as the youngest, and the leader as one who serves. 27 For who
is the greater, [u]one who reclines at table or one who serves? Is it not the one who reclines
at table? But [v]I am among you as the one who serves.

28 "You are those who have stayed with me [w]in my trials, 29 and [x]I assign to you, as my
Father assigned to me, a kingdom, 30 [y]that you may eat and drink at my table in my kingdom and [z]sit on thrones judging [a]the twelve tribes of Israel.

Jesus Foretells Peter's Denial

31 "Simon, Simon, behold, [b]Satan demanded to have you,[1] [c]that he might sift you like
wheat, 32 but [d]I have prayed for you that your faith may not fail. And when you have turned
again, [e]strengthen your brothers." 33 Peter[2] said to him, "Lord, I am ready to go with you
both [f]to prison and [g]to death." 34 [h]Jesus[3] said, "I tell you, Peter, the rooster will not crow
this day, until you deny three times that you know me."

Scripture Must Be Fulfilled in Jesus

35 And he said to them, [i]"When I sent you out with no moneybag or knapsack or sandals,
did you lack anything?" They said, "Nothing." 36 He said to them, "But now let the one who
has a moneybag take it, and likewise a knapsack. And let the one who has no sword sell his

[1] The Greek word for *you* (twice in this verse) is plural; in verse 32, all four instances are singular [2] Greek *He* [3] Greek *He*

21 [o][Ps. 41:9; John 13:18]
22 [p]Acts 2:23
24 [q]ch. 9:46; Mark 9:34
25 [r]For ver. 25-27, [Matt. 18:1-4; 20:25-28; Mark 10:42-45] [s]1 Pet. 5:3
26 [t]ch. 9:48; [Matt. 23:11] [s][See ver. 25 above]
27 [u][ch. 12:37] [v]See Matt. 20:28
28 [w][See Heb. 2:18; 4:15]
29 [x]2 Tim. 2:12; [John 17:18]; See Matt. 25:34; 28:18; Acts 14:22; Rev. 1:6
30 [y][ver. 16; ch. 13:29; 14:15; Matt. 8:11] [z]See Matt. 19:28 [a]Acts 26:7; James 1:1; Rev. 21:12
31 [b]Job 1:6-12; 2:1-6; [2 Cor. 2:11; 1 Pet. 5:8]; See 1 Cor. 5:5 [c]Amos 9:9; [John 16:32]
32 [d]John 17:9, 11, 15 [e][Ps. 51:13; John 21:15-17]
33 [f][Acts 12:4] [g][John 21:19]
34 [h][Matt. 26:33-35; Mark 14:29-31; John 13:37, 38]
35 [i]ch. 9:3; 10:4; Matt. 10:9, 10; Mark 6:8

22:22 The coming events for the **Son of Man** have been **determined** by God; however, **woe to that man by whom he is betrayed** refutes all attempts to justify Judas's action (see note on Mark 14:21).

22:23 which of them it could be. Judas is still present, and his outward behavior, like his previous conduct, apparently did not give him away (see note on John 13:22).

22:24–30 *Who Is the Greatest?* Jesus takes the opportunity raised by a dispute of the disciples to teach about true greatness. Just as membership in the kingdom is the opposite of what humans might think, so greatness in the kingdom is also the opposite (v. 26).

22:24 greatest. In conjunction with their messianic expectation of a political liberator, the disciples dream of status, honor, and power, perhaps recalling the Maccabean revolt (166–160 B.C.). Cf. Mark 8:34–38.

22:26 let the greatest among you (church leaders and people in positions of status or power) **become as the youngest** (i.e., those who possess the least claim to rule others). See notes on Matt. 18:1–4.

22:27 But I. God's standards are diametrically opposite to the world's, and Jesus is the supreme example of humility: he is **one who serves** (cf. 12:37; John 13:3–17; see also notes on Mark 10:43; 10:45).

22:29 assign . . . a kingdom. See note on Matt. 25:34.

22:30 For **eat and drink** in the kingdom of God, cf. 13:29; 14:15. Jesus' claim that the messianic banquet is **my table** and that the kingdom of God is **my kingdom** would be seen as audacious if it were not true. The 12 disciples would **sit on thrones judging the twelve tribes** (though Judas was later replaced by Matthias; Acts 1:26).

22:31–34 *Jesus Foretells Peter's Denial.* Whereas in v. 3 Satan's increased activity centers on Judas's betrayal, now it centers on the denial by Peter and the disciples.

22:31 Simon, Simon. The use of Peter's pre-Christian name forebodes his denial. **Satan demanded to have you** (cf. Job 1–2), **that he might sift you like wheat**. "You" is plural in these two instances, indicating that all the disciples are in view, not just Peter. In other words, "Satan is seeking to shake you all violently, as one does wheat, to cause you to fall" (cf. Amos 9:9). In Peter's case, the shaking was to be his panic-prompted, thrice-repeated denial that he knew Christ.

22:32 I have prayed . . . that your faith may not fail. "Your" here is singular, so Peter alone is addressed. "Not fail" must mean "not fail completely." Peter's subsequently restored faith was not his own accomplishment but a result of the Holy Spirit's work in response to Jesus' prayer for him. The Greek for **turned** (*epistrephō*, "turn around, go back, return") is often used in contexts of repenting or turning back to God (e.g., Acts 3:19; 9:35; 2 Cor. 3:16).

22:34 rooster . . . crow. See notes on Mark 14:30 and John 13:38. **deny three times**. Cf. Luke 22:54–62.

22:35–38 *Scripture Must Be Fulfilled in Jesus.* Jesus prepares the disciples for their postresurrection mission (24:45–49; Acts 1:8).

22:35–36 Earlier in his ministry, Jesus sent his disciples out **with no moneybag** (see 9:3; 10:4). **moneybag . . . knapsack**. Now, however, they will need extra provisions and supplies. **let the one who has no sword . . . buy one**. Many interpreters take this to be a metaphorical statement commanding the disciples to be armed spiritually to fight spiritual foes (cf. Eph. 6:10–17). In favor of this view: (1) In Luke 22:38 the disciples misunderstand Jesus' command and produce literal swords (v. 38); on this view, Jesus' response that "It is enough" is a rebuke, saying essentially, "Enough of this talk about swords." (2) Just a few minutes later Jesus will again prohibit the use of a literal sword (vv. 49–51; cf. Matt. 26:51–52; John 18:10–11). Others take this as a command to have a literal sword for self-defense and protection from robbers. In support of this view: (a) The moneybag and knapsack and cloak in this same verse are literal, and so the sword must be taken literally as well. (b) Jesus' response that "It is enough" (Luke 22:38) actually approves the swords the disciples have as being enough, and Jesus' later rebuke in vv. 49–51 only prohibits them from blocking his arrest and suffering (cf. John 18:11), that is, from seeking to advance the kingdom of God by force. (c) The very fact that the disciples possess swords (Luke 22:38) suggests that Jesus has not prohibited them from carrying swords up to this point (cf. John 18:10–11), and Jesus never prohibited self-defense (see note on Matt. 5:39). Both views have some merit. See note on Luke 22:49–51.

37[j][Acts 1:16]; See ch. 13:33; Matt. 1:22 [k]Cited from Isa. 53:12 [l][John 17:4; 19:30]
38[m][ver. 49] [n][Deut. 3:26; Mark 14:41]
39[o]Matt. 26:30; Mark 14:26; [John 18:1] [p]ch. 21:37; John 18:2 [q]See Matt. 21:1
40[r]For ver. 40-46, see Matt. 26:36-46; Mark 14:32-42 [s]John 18:2 [t]1 Pet. 4:7 [u]Matt. 6:13
41[v]See Acts 7:60
42[w]Heb. 5:7 [x]See Matt. 20:22 [y]See Matt. 6:10
43[z]Matt. 4:11; [Heb. 1:14]
44[w][See ver. 42 above]
46[a]ver. 40
47[b]For ver. 47-53, see Matt. 26:47-56; Mark 14:43-50; John 18:3-11 [c]ver. 3

cloak and buy one. **37** For I tell you that [j]this Scripture must be fulfilled in me: [k]'And he was
numbered with the transgressors.' For [l]what is written about me has its fulfillment." **38** And
they said, "Look, Lord, here are two [m]swords." And he said to them, [n]"It is enough."

Jesus Prays on the Mount of Olives

39 [o]And he came out and went, [p]as was his custom, to [q]the Mount of Olives, and the
disciples followed him. **40** [r]And when he came to [s]the place, he said to them, [t]"Pray that
you may not [u]enter into temptation." **41** And he withdrew from them about a stone's
throw, and [v]knelt down and prayed, **42** saying, [w]"Father, if you are willing, remove [x]this
cup from me. [y]Nevertheless, not my will, but yours, be done." **43** And there appeared to
him [z]an angel from heaven, strengthening him. **44** And [w]being in an agony he prayed more
earnestly; and his sweat became like great drops of blood falling down to the ground.[1]
45 And when he rose from prayer, he came to the disciples and found them sleeping for
sorrow, **46** and he said to them, "Why are you sleeping? Rise and [a]pray that you may not
enter into temptation."

Betrayal and Arrest of Jesus

47 [b]While he was still speaking, there came a crowd, and the man called [c]Judas, one of the
twelve, was leading them. He drew near to Jesus to kiss him, **48** but Jesus said to him, "Judas,

[1] Some manuscripts omit verses 43 and 44

22:37 Scripture must be fulfilled. Jesus' coming suffering and death are a "divine necessity"; God's providential plan *must* be fulfilled. **he was numbered with the transgressors**. See 23:32–33, 39–43; Isa. 53:12.

22:38 Lord, here are two swords. See note on vv. 35–36.

22:39–23:56 *The Arrest and Trial.* This second part of the passion narrative recounts the events surrounding the trial and execution of Jesus.

22:39–46 *Jesus Prays on the Mount of Olives.* The second part of the account of Christ's suffering and death opens with a change in scene.

22:39 The Passover evening had to be spent in "greater Jerusalem" (cf. Deut. 16:1–7), which included the **Mount of Olives** (see note on Mark 13:3; and Jerusalem in the Time of Jesus, pp. 1878–1879).

22:40 when he came to the place. Luke assumes his readers knew that "the place" was the garden of Gethsemane (on Gethsemane, see note on Matt. 26:36). **Pray that you may not enter into temptation**. See notes on Matt. 6:13 and Luke 11:4. The temptation was to succumb to physical sleep (see 22:45–46) and thus fail in their responsibility to support Jesus. It may point also to the temptation to deny Jesus when he is led away to the cross (cf. vv. 54–62).

22:41 Jesus **withdrew . . . about a stone's throw**, enough to be alone but close enough for the disciples to overhear him praying. **knelt down**. See note on Matt. 26:39.

22:42 On **Father**, see note on Matt. 6:9. **this cup**. A metaphor for Jesus' future suffering (cf. Matt. 20:22–23; Mark 10:38–39). It is clear from the OT that the taking of the cup denotes that Jesus took upon himself the wrath of God (cf. Isa. 51:17, 22; Jer. 25:15, 17, 28; 49:12; Lam. 4:21; Ezek. 23:31–33; Hab. 2:16; Zech. 12:2), so that he died for the sake of and instead of his people (cf. notes on Mark 14:36; John 18:11; Rom. 3:25; 1 John 2:2). **Nevertheless, not my will, but yours, be done**. Jesus consciously, voluntarily, and obediently "endured the cross, despising the shame" (Heb. 12:2).

22:44 Jesus was in **agony** (Gk. *agōnia*) in anticipation of bearing "our sins in his own body on the tree" (1 Pet. 2:24), and therefore he **prayed more earnestly**. **his sweat became like great drops of blood falling down to the ground**. Though the word "like" may indicate that this is to be understood metaphorically, there are both ancient and modern accounts on record of people sweating blood—a condition known as *hematidrosis*, where extreme anguish or physical strain causes one's capillary blood vessels to dilate and burst, mixing sweat and blood. In either case, Luke's main purpose is to highlight the intensity of Jesus' emotional and physical trauma.

22:45 sleeping for sorrow. It had been a long day, and the disciples were emotionally and physically exhausted.

22:46 that you may not enter into temptation. See note on v. 40.

22:47–53 *The Betrayal and Arrest of Jesus.* This section is closely tied to the preceding narrative by "While he was still speaking" (v. 47).

22:47 Usually the **"crowd"** is positive toward Jesus, but this is not an ordinary crowd (cf. v. 52; see note on Matt. 26:47). **Judas** led them to Jesus and gave him a **kiss**. Whereas it was customary for a disciple to greet his teacher

Jesus' Arrest, Trial, and Crucifixion

The path from Jesus' arrest to his crucifixion (part of which is often called the Via Dolorosa, "Way of Sorrows") is difficult to retrace with certainty. According to a possible harmony of the Gospel accounts, after the Passover meal Judas led a contingent of soldiers to Gethsemane to arrest Jesus (1). From there Jesus was led to Annas (location unknown), who sent him to his son-in-law Caiaphas, the high priest (2). The Jewish leaders then appealed to the Roman governor Pilate to have Jesus put to death (3). Luke records that Pilate sent Jesus to Herod Antipas (4), who questioned Jesus but returned him to Pilate without rendering any judgment (5). Pilate then sent Jesus to be crucified at Golgotha (6).

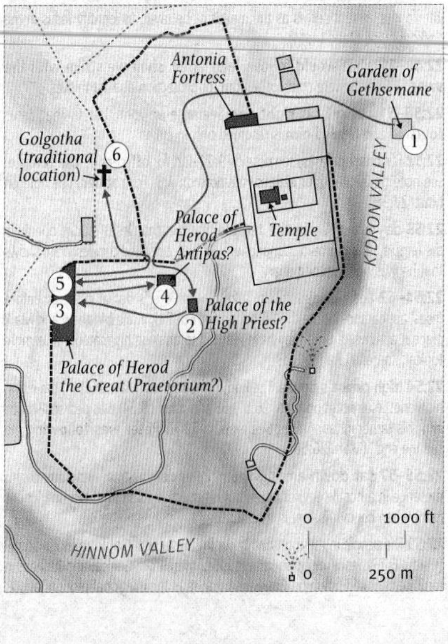

would you betray the Son of Man with a kiss?" **49** And when those who were around him saw
what would follow, they said, "Lord, shall we strike [d]with the sword?" **50** And one of them
struck the servant[1] of the high priest and cut off his right ear. **51** But Jesus said, "No more
of this!" And he touched his ear and healed him. **52** Then Jesus said to the chief priests and
[e]officers of the temple and elders, who had come out against him, "Have you come out as
against a robber, with swords and clubs? **53** When [f]I was with you day after day in the temple,
you did not lay hands on me. But this is [g]your hour, and [h]the power of darkness."

Peter Denies Jesus

54 [i]Then they seized him and led him away, bringing him into the high priest's house,
[j]and Peter was following at a distance. **55** [k]And when they had kindled a fire in the middle
of [l]the courtyard and sat down together, Peter sat down among them. **56** Then a servant
girl, seeing him as he sat in the light and looking closely at him, said, "This man also was
with him." **57** But he denied it, saying, "Woman, I do not know him." **58** And a little later
someone else saw him and said, "You also are one of them." But Peter said, "Man, I am
not." **59** And after an interval of about an hour still another [m]insisted, saying, "Certainly
this man also was with him, for he too is a Galilean." **60** But Peter said, "Man, I do not know
what you are talking about." And immediately, while he was still speaking, the rooster
crowed. **61** And the Lord turned and [n]looked at Peter. And Peter remembered the saying
of the Lord, how he had said to him, [o]"Before the rooster crows today, you will [p]deny me
three times." **62** And he went out and wept bitterly.

Jesus Is Mocked

63 [q]Now the men who were holding Jesus in custody were mocking him as they beat
him. **64** [q]They also blindfolded him and kept asking him, [r]"Prophesy! Who is it that struck
you?" **65** And they said many other things against him, [s]blaspheming him.

Jesus Before the Council

66 [t]When day came, [u]the assembly of the elders of the people gathered together, both
chief priests and scribes. And they led him away to their [v]council, and they [w]said, **67** [x]"If
you are [y]the Christ, tell us." But he said to them, "If I tell you, you will not believe, **68** and
if I ask you, you will not answer. **69** But from now on the Son of Man shall be seated [z]at
the right hand of the power of God." **70** So they all said, "Are you [a]the Son of God, then?"

[1] Greek *bondservant*

49 [d]ver. 38
52 [e]See ver. 4
53 [f][John 8:2]; [ch. 2:46; John 18:20] [g][Mark 14:35, 41; John 12:27; 16:4] [h]Eph. 6:12; [Acts 26:18]
54 [i]Matt. 26:57; Mark 14:53 [j]Matt. 26:58; Mark 14:54; John 18:15
55 [k]For ver. 55-62, see Matt. 26:69-75; Mark 14:66-72; John 18:16-18, 25-27 [l]See Matt. 26:3
59 [m]Acts 12:15
61 [n]See Mark 10:21 [o]ver. 34 [p][Acts 3:13, 14]
63 [q][Matt. 26:67, 68; Mark 14:65; John 18:22, 23]
64 [q][See ver. 63 above] [r][ch. 7:39]
65 [s]See Matt. 27:39
66 [t]Matt. 27:1; Mark 15:1; John 18:28 [u]Acts 22:5 (Gk.) [v]See Matt. 5:22 [w]For ver. 67-71, [Matt. 26:63-66; Mark 14:61-64; John 18:19-21]
67 [x]John 10:24, 25 [y]See Matt. 1:17
69 [z]Mark 16:19; Acts 7:56; Heb. 1:3
70 [a]See Matt. 14:33

with a kiss, here it serves as the means of betrayal, to identify Jesus in the darkness (see Mark 14:44).

22:49–51 what would follow. Jesus' arrest. **shall we strike with the sword?** Swords were commonly worn for protection against thieves.

22:50–51 cut off his right ear. See note on John 18:10. That Jesus **touched** and **healed him** is recorded only in Luke.

22:52 For **chief priests**, see note on 9:21–22; for **officers of the temple**, see note on 22:4–6; for **elders**, see note on 7:3. For **robber**, see note on Matt. 27:38.

22:53 day after day in the temple. The fact that Jesus taught openly in the temple, whereas revolutionaries would have operated clandestinely, shows that he was not a revolutionary.

22:54–62 *Peter Denies Jesus.* Luke places Peter's denial of Jesus before Jesus' appearance before the Sanhedrin (vv. 66–71), while Matthew and Mark place it afterward. Luke may have wanted to arrange his material in a more topical, "orderly" way (cf. 1:3).

22:54 high priest's house. The home of Caiaphas (Matt. 26:57), the ruling high priest (see notes on Matt. 26:57–58 and John 18:24) was perhaps shared with his father-in-law Annas. See map, p. 2007. **Peter was following** "to see the end" (Matt. 26:58).

22:55–57 sat down among them. Peter demonstrates courage by his presence in a hostile environment, but his courage fails him (**I do not know him**) when his own safety is threatened.

22:59 The people in the courtyard know that Peter **is a Galilean** by his accent (Matt. 26:73). Jesus' disciples (except Judas) were from Galilee, and Judeans in Jerusalem looked down on Galileans because of their regional pronunciations.

22:60 Upon Peter's third denial, the **rooster crowed** (see v. 34 and note).

22:63–65 *Jesus Is Mocked.* Before his trial, Jesus is mocked and beaten, just as he had predicted (9:22; 17:25; 18:32–33).

22:63 The **men . . . holding Jesus** were probably "officers" (vv. 4, 52), that is, leaders of the temple police, rather than actual members of the Sanhedrin.

22:64 blindfolded him . . . Prophesy! Jesus is challenged to prove that he is a prophet by identifying who **struck** him.

22:65 blaspheming him. Whereas Jesus is accused of blasphemy (23:39; Matt. 26:65; Mark 14:64), here he is the object of blasphemy.

22:66–71 *Jesus before the Council.* Luke's account of Jesus' trial is considerably shorter than Matthew's and Mark's.

22:66 When day came. Luke combines the first (Mark 14:53–65) and second (Mark 15:1) meetings of the Sanhedrin. **assembly of the elders**. A synonym for the Sanhedrin (cf. Acts 22:5; see note on Matt. 26:59). **Both chief priests and scribes** describes the makeup of the Sanhedrin.

22:67–68 If you are the Christ, tell us. This was the key issue of the trial. Jesus answers with a qualified yes (22:67–23:3). **If I tell you . . . if I ask you**. Jesus knows that it would be futile to enter into dialogue with those whose minds are already made up (cf. 20:3–8).

22:69 the Son of Man shall be seated at the right hand . . . of God. The crucifixion of Jesus is not the end but his "exodus" (cf. "departure," 9:31; see ESV footnote) leading to glory (24:26; Acts 3:13). Jesus declares that he is not only the human Messiah anticipated by the Jews but also the divine Son of Man (Dan. 7:13–14) who sits at the right hand of God (Ps. 110:1–2) and who will come in power to reign over the earth (cf. note on Matt. 8:20).

22:70 Son of God, "the Christ" (the Messiah; v. 67), and "Son of Man" all

70 [b]ch. 23:3; Matt. 27:11; Mark 15:2; [Matt. 26:25]

Chapter 23

1 [c]Matt. 27:2; Mark 15:1; John 18:28
2 [d]ver. 14; [Acts 17:6, 7; 24:5] [e][ch. 20:25] [f]ch. 2:1; 3:1 [g]John 18:33, 36, 37; 19:12; [Acts 17:7]
3 [h]Matt. 27:11; Mark 15:2 [i]ver. 37, 38; Matt. 2:2; John 18:39; 19:3 [j]See ch. 22:70
4 [k]ver. 14, 22; John 18:38; 19:4, 6; [Matt. 27:24; 1 Pet. 2:22]
5 [l]ch. 4:14; Matt. 4:12, 23; Mark 1:14; John 1:43; 2:11
7 [m]See ch. 3:1
8 [n]ch. 9:9 [o]Matt. 14:1; Mark 6:14 [p]See Matt. 12:38
11 [q]Mark 9:12; Acts 4:11 [r]ch. 18:32 [s][Matt. 27:28; Mark 15:17]
12 [t]Acts 4:27; [Ps. 2:2]
13 [u]See ch. 24:20
14 [v]ver. 2 [w]Acts 3:13 [x]ver. 4
15 [y]ver. 11
16 [z]ver. 22; John 19:1; [Acts 5:40]

And he said to them, [b]"You say that I am." 71 Then they said, "What further testimony do
we need? We have heard it ourselves from his own lips."

Jesus Before Pilate

23 [c]Then the whole company of them arose and brought him before Pilate. 2 And they
began to accuse him, saying, "We found this man [d]misleading our nation and [e]for-
bidding us to give tribute to [f]Caesar, and saying that he himself is Christ, [g]a king." 3 [h]And
Pilate asked him, [i]"Are you the King of the Jews?" And he answered him, [j]"You have said
so." 4 Then Pilate said to the chief priests and the crowds, [k]"I find no guilt in this man."
5 But they were urgent, saying, "He stirs up the people, teaching throughout all Judea,
[l]from Galilee even to this place."

Jesus Before Herod

6 When Pilate heard this, he asked whether the man was a Galilean. 7 And when he learned
that he belonged to [m]Herod's jurisdiction, he sent him over to Herod, who was himself in
Jerusalem at that time. 8 When Herod saw Jesus, he was very glad, [n]for he had long desired
to see him, [o]because he had heard about him, and he was hoping [p]to see some sign done
by him. 9 So he questioned him at some length, but he made no answer. 10 The chief priests
and the scribes stood by, vehemently accusing him. 11 And Herod with his soldiers [q]treated
him with contempt and [r]mocked him. Then, [s]arraying him in splendid clothing, he sent
him back to Pilate. 12 And [t]Herod and Pilate became friends with each other that very day,
for before this they had been at enmity with each other.
13 Pilate then called together the chief priests and [u]the rulers and the people, 14 and said
to them, "You brought me this man [v]as one who was misleading the people. And [w]after
examining him before you, behold, I [x]did not find this man guilty of any of your charges
against him. 15 Neither did Herod, for [y]he sent him back to us. Look, nothing deserving
death has been done by him. 16 [z]I will therefore punish and release him."[1]

[1] Here, or after verse 19, some manuscripts add verse 17: *Now he was obliged to release one man to them at the festival*

refer to Jesus, emphasizing different aspects of his person and role. "Son of God" points to Jesus' unique relationship to God and (when rightly understood) his equality with God the Father in his very being. The term "Christ" indicates that Jesus claimed to be the Son of David, the Messiah. "Son of Man" points to the person identified in Dan. 7:13–14, who will rule the kingdom of God. **You say that I am.** A Greek expression that deflects responsibility back upon the one asking the question (cf. Matt. 26:25, 64).

22:71 What further testimony do we need? The desire to catch Jesus in something he might say (11:54; 20:20, 26) has been achieved. **We have heard . . . from his own lips** indicates that the members of the Sanhedrin considered Jesus' Christological claims (22:68–70) to be sufficient justification for condemning him.

23:1–5 *Jesus before Pilate.* Since only Rome possessed authority to impose capital punishment (John 18:31), the Sanhedrin brought Jesus to Pilate (see note on Luke 23:1). The charges are now recast from religious ("blasphemy") to political ones (v. 2).

23:1 the whole company of them. The "assembly" (Sanhedrin) of 22:66. **before Pilate.** See 3:1. Normally the seat of the Roman government in Judea was Caesarea, not Jerusalem. Pilate was in Jerusalem at Passover to prevent rebellious activities. Pilate had certainly witnessed disturbances in Jerusalem, some of his own making, and he ultimately lost his position by mishandling a disturbance in Samaria. Pilate's willingness to execute Jesus is credited in the Gospels to his desire to maintain public calm rather than to follow the dictates of justice. Jewish sources considered Pilate's reign (A.D. 26–36) to have been quite harsh, charging him with greed and cruelty (cf. 13:1). As examples of his disregard for Jewish religion, Josephus mentions Pilate bringing pagan Roman legionary standards into Jerusalem and appropriating temple funds to build an aqueduct (*Jewish Antiquities* 18.55–62; see also Philo, *Embassy to Gaius* 299–306). An inscription found at Caesarea indicates that Pilate dedicated a structure there to the imperial cult of Tiberius (see note on Acts 8:40).

23:2 They **began to accuse** (bring charges against) **him** (cf. Acts 24:2–21; 25:5–22). The religious grounds of Jesus' condemnation would be of little interest to Rome, so the Sanhedrin changed them to political ones. The first charge, **misleading our nation**, involves seducing the nation away from loyalty to Rome. The second, **forbidding . . . tribute to Caesar**, is clearly false (see Luke 20:20–26). The third is **that he himself is Christ, a king** (cf. John 18:33, 36, 37). This new charge focuses on insurrection: Jesus' claims to kingship would be a direct challenge to Caesar. (See note on Matt. 27:11–26.)

23:3 Ignoring the first two charges (the first was too ambiguous and the second false), Pilate focuses on the third and asks, **Are you the King of the Jews?** Jesus' answer, **You have said so**, is affirmative and repeats his earlier reply (see note on 22:70).

23:4–5 These verses are unique to Luke and emphasize Jesus' innocence. Pilate's verdict **I find no guilt** is repeated in vv. 14–16 and 22, and his crucifixion of Jesus (vv. 23–24) does not alter his official verdict that Jesus was innocent. **But they** (the chief priests and crowds) continue to insist that Jesus is guilty of fomenting revolution **throughout all Judea**.

23:6–16 *Jesus before Herod Antipas.* This account is found only in Luke (cf. Acts 4:27–28). Luke recounts this incident to reveal that both Pilate and Herod Antipas found Jesus innocent (Luke 23:15).

23:7 On **Herod** Antipas, see notes on 3:1 and Matt. 14:1.

23:8 Herod . . . was very glad. Not because he still wanted to kill Jesus (see 13:31), for he returns him back to Pilate, but because he longed to see Jesus perform **some sign** (cf. 11:16, 29).

23:9 Jesus **made no answer**. Jesus' silence fulfills Isa. 53:7 and places the responsibility for his death squarely on his accusers (cf. note on Mark 14:61–62).

23:11 Herod and his soldiers dressed Jesus in **splendid clothing** (cf. Mark 15:17–20) to mock his claim to kingship.

23:14 Examining implies a legal examination. **did not find this man guilty.** For the second time, Pilate acknowledges Jesus' innocence.

23:15 Neither did Herod. Both Pilate and Herod agreed that Jesus was innocent.

Pilate Delivers Jesus to Be Crucified

18 [a]But they all cried out together, [b]"Away with this man, and release to us Barabbas"—
19 a man who had been thrown into prison for an insurrection started in the city and [c]for
murder. 20 Pilate addressed them once more, desiring to release Jesus, 21 but they kept shouting, "Crucify, crucify him!" 22 A third time he said to them, "Why, [d]what evil has he done?
[e]I have found in him no guilt deserving death. [f]I will therefore punish and release him."
23 But they were urgent, demanding with loud cries that he should be crucified. And their
voices prevailed. 24 So Pilate decided that their demand should be granted. 25 He released
the man who had been thrown into prison [g]for insurrection and murder, for whom they
asked, [h]but he delivered Jesus over to their will.

The Crucifixion

26 [i]And as they led him away, they seized one Simon of Cyrene, who was coming in from
the country, and laid on him the cross, to carry it behind Jesus. 27 And there followed him
a great multitude of the people and of women who were [j]mourning and lamenting for
him. 28 But turning to them Jesus said, "Daughters of Jerusalem, do not weep for me,
but weep for yourselves and for your children. 29 For behold, [k]the days are coming when
they will say, [l]'Blessed are the barren and the wombs that never bore and the breasts that
never nursed!' 30 [m]Then they will begin to say to the mountains, 'Fall on us,' and to the
hills, 'Cover us.' 31 For [n]if they do these things when [o]the wood is green, what will happen
[o]when it is dry?"
32 [p]Two others, who were criminals, were led away to be put to death with him. 33 [q]And
when they came to the place that is called The Skull, there they crucified him, and the
criminals, [p]one on his right and one on his left. 34 And Jesus said, "Father, [r]forgive them,

18 [a]For ver. 18-25, see Matt. 27:15-26; Mark 15:6-15; John 18:39, 40; 19:16 [b][Acts 21:36; 22:22]
19 [c]Acts 3:14
22 [d][ver. 41; John 8:46] [e]ver. 14, 15 [f]ver. 16
25 [g]ver. 19 [h]John 19:16
26 [i]Matt. 27:32; Mark 15:21; [John 19:17]
27 [j]ch. 8:52; Matt. 11:17
29 [k]See ch. 17:22 [l]ch. 21:23; Matt. 24:19; Mark 13:17
30 [m]Hos. 10:8; Rev. 6:16; [Isa. 2:19]
31 [n][Prov. 11:31; 1 Pet. 4:17] [o]Ezek. 20:47
32 [p]Matt. 27:38; Mark 15:27; John 19:18; [Matt. 20:21]
33 [q]Matt. 27:33; Mark 15:22; John 19:17 [p][See ver. 32 above]
34 [r]Isa. 53:12; See Matt. 5:44

23:18–25 *Pilate Delivers Jesus to Be Crucified.* Pilate continues to seek Jesus' release by a custom of releasing at the Passover a prisoner chosen by the people. When the people chose Barabbas instead of Jesus, however, Pilate delivered Jesus to them to be crucified.

23:18 they all cried out together. "They" are the chief priests, the rulers, and the crowd of ordinary people who have been stirred up by them. **Away with this man, and release . . . Barabbas** assumes that the readers know of the custom of releasing a prisoner at the Passover (see Matt. 27:15; Mark 15:6; and the ESV footnote on Luke 23:16). "Away with him" essentially means "crucify him" (cf. John 19:15; Acts 21:36; 22:22; cf. also Luke 23:21). Barabbas was a notorious criminal who had committed robbery, insurrection, and murder (see notes on Matt. 27:15–18 and John 18:40).

23:22 For the **third time** Pilate affirms Jesus' innocence: **Why, what evil has he done?** (vv. 4, 14–15). The last recourse for Pilate is to declare that Jesus has not received any accusation worthy of death (cf. Ps. 38:20–21; Isa. 53:9; Acts 3:13). While Pilate might have attempted to make the Jewish authorities solely responsible for the death of Jesus, it remains a fact that it occurred under his jurisdiction. **therefore**. Pilate seeks to appease the crowd by beating Jesus and then releasing him (cf. Luke 23:16).

23:23 But they were urgent. The crowd's animosity is so great that only Jesus' crucifixion will satisfy them.

23:24 Pilate does not declare Jesus guilty; nevertheless he grants the desire of Jesus' opponents.

23:25 Luke emphasizes that choosing Barabbas involved releasing one guilty of **insurrection and murder** and condemning Jesus, whom Luke will later call "the Holy and Righteous One" (Acts 3:14), who "went about doing good and healing all who were oppressed by the devil" (Acts 10:38). **he delivered Jesus over to their will**. Cf. Luke 9:44; 18:32; 24:7. Pilate acquiesced to the wishes of the bloodthirsty crowd and condemned Jesus to crucifixion, the Roman means of executing criminals convicted of high treason. Though Luke and John do not mention it, prior to crucifixion the prisoner was first "scourged" (see Mark 15:15; also notes on Matt. 27:26 and John 19:1). Luke (23:16) and John (19:1) do call attention to the lighter flogging Jesus received after being detained and questioned by Pilate, but omit his scourging, a punishment which in and of itself could cause death.

23:26–43 *The Crucifixion.* Jesus is led out to be crucified, and Simon of Cyrene carries his cross. Luke alone records Jesus' following lament over the fate of Jerusalem (vv. 27–31). The crucifixion is described succinctly, and the account concludes with the story of the repentant thief (vv. 39–43).

23:26 they (the Roman soldiers) **. . . seized one Simon of Cyrene**. See notes on Matt. 27:32; Mark 15:21; Acts 13:1. Since scourging preceded crucifixion (see note on Luke 23:25; cf. Matt. 27:26; Mark 15:15; note on John 19:1), Jesus' physical condition may have prevented him from carrying the **cross** (the *patibulum* or crossbeam; on the cross, see note on Matt. 27:32).

23:27–31 The sympathetic **mourning and lamenting** of the women leads Jesus to quote from the prophet Zechariah (cf. Zech. 12:10–14). **the days are coming**. See Luke 19:43; 21:6, 22–24. **Blessed are the barren**. See note on 21:23. In those days, the "reproach" of childlessness (see 1:25) will be a blessing. **Fall on us**. A request (cf. Hos. 10:8; Rev. 6:16) to be put out of their misery. **green . . . dry**. If God did not spare his innocent son ("green" wood), how much worse will it be when he allows the Romans to unleash his wrath on a sinful nation ("dry" wood)?

23:32 Two others . . . criminals fulfills the prophecy of Isa. 53:12 (cf. Luke 22:37) that Jesus in his death would be "numbered with the transgressors."

23:33 The Skull. (Gk. *Kranion*). In Matthew it is also called Golgotha (in Latin, *Calvariae*), a transliteration of the Aramaic word for "skull." See notes on Matt. 27:33; John 19:17. **they crucified him**. All the Gospels have a similar, brief statement (on crucifixion, see notes on Matt. 27:35; Mark 15:24; John 18:32). In Matt. 27:38 and Mark 15:27 the **criminals** are called "robbers"; see note on Matt. 27:38.

23:34 They cast lots to divide his garments is a clear reference to Ps. 22:18. Casting lots was sometimes used in the OT to discover God's will, but here it is a form of gambling by the Roman guards. **Father, forgive them, for they know not what they do**. Jesus fulfills his own teaching about loving one's enemies (see Luke 6:35) and highlights the fact that his death was providing the very basis upon which those who crucified him could be forgiven (see Isa. 53:12). Jesus thus provides an example for all believers who would follow him (see Acts 7:60; 1 Pet. 2:21–24). "They know not what they do" does not absolve either the Jews or the Romans of their responsibility in Jesus' death, but it shows that they did not fully understand the horrible evil that they were doing in crucifying the "Holy and Righteous One" (Acts 3:14) who was both the true Messiah and the Son of God.

[s]for they know not what they do."[1] And they cast lots [t]to divide his garments. 35 And [u]the
people stood by, watching, [v]but [w]the rulers [x]scoffed at him, saying, [y]"He saved others;
[z]let him save himself, [a]if he is [b]the Christ of God, [c]his Chosen One!" 36 The soldiers also
mocked him, coming up and [d]offering him sour wine 37 and saying, [e]"If you are [f]the King
of the Jews, save yourself!" 38 [g]There was also an inscription over him,[2] "This is [f]the King
of the Jews."

39 [h]One of the criminals who were hanged [i]railed at him,[3] saying, "Are you not [j]the
Christ? Save yourself and us!" 40 But the other rebuked him, saying, "Do you not fear God,
since you are under the same sentence of condemnation? 41 And we indeed justly, for we
are receiving the due reward of our deeds; but this man has done nothing wrong." 42 And
he said, "Jesus, remember me [k]when you come into your kingdom." 43 And he said to him,
"Truly, I say to you, today you will be with me in [l]Paradise."

The Death of Jesus

44 [m]It was now about the sixth hour,[4] and there was darkness over the whole land
until the ninth hour,[5] 45 while the sun's light failed. And [n]the curtain of the temple
was torn in two. 46 Then Jesus, [o]calling out with a loud voice, said, "Father, [p]into your
hands I [q]commit my spirit!" And having said this [r]he breathed his last. 47 Now [s]when the
centurion saw what had taken place, [t]he praised God, saying, "Certainly this man was
innocent!" 48 And all the crowds that had assembled for this spectacle, when they saw
what had taken place, returned home [u]beating their breasts. 49 And all [v]his acquaintances
and [w]the women who had followed him from Galilee [x]stood at a distance watching
these things.

Jesus Is Buried

50 [y]Now there was a man named Joseph, from the Jewish town of Arimathea. He was
a member of the council, a good and righteous man, 51 who had not consented to their

34 [s][Mark 10:38]; See Acts 3:17 [t]Ps. 22:18; Matt. 27:35; Mark 15:24; John 19:23
35 [u]Ps. 22:7, 17 [v]Matt. 27:41, 42; Mark 15:31, 32 [w]See ch. 24:20 [x]ch. 16:14 [y][ch. 4:23] [z][Matt. 26:53, 54; John 10:18] [a][ch. 4:3, 9] [b]See ch. 9:20; Matt. 1:17 [c]ch. 9:35; Isa. 42:1; [Matt. 12:18; 1 Pet. 2:4]
36 [d][Ps. 69:21; Matt. 27:48; Mark 15:36; John 19:29]
37 [e]ver. 35 [f]See ver. 3
38 [g]Matt. 27:37; Mark 15:26; John 19:19; [John 19:21, 22] [f][See ver. 37 above]
39 [h][Matt. 27:44; Mark 15:32] [i]See Matt. 27:39 [j]ver. 35, 37
42 [k][Matt. 16:28]
43 [l]2 Cor. 12:3; Rev. 2:7
44 [m]Matt. 27:45; Mark 15:33; [John 19:14]
45 [n]Ex. 26:31-33; 2 Chr. 3:14
46 [o][Matt. 27:50; Mark 15:37; John 19:30] [p]Cited from Ps. 31:5; [Acts 7:59] [q]1 Pet. 4:19 [r][John 10:18]
47 [s]Matt. 27:54; Mark 15:39 [t]See ch. 7:16
48 [u]ch. 18:13
49 [v]Ps. 88:8 [w]ver. 55; John 19:25; See ch. 8:2 [x]Ps. 38:11
50 [y]For ver. 50-56, see Matt. 27:57-61; Mark 15:42-47; John 19:38-42

[1] Some manuscripts omit the sentence *And Jesus . . . what they do* [2] Some manuscripts add *in letters of Greek and Latin and Hebrew* [3] Or *blasphemed him*
[4] That is, noon [5] That is, 3 P.M.

23:35 the people stood by . . . but the rulers scoffed. Luke contrasts the behavior of the Jewish crowds (cf. v. 48) and the Sanhedrin. The highest levels of Israel's establishment seek one more opportunity to insult Jesus. They do not address Jesus directly but turn to one another as they mock him. For **He saved others; let him save himself,** cf. Ps. 22:7–8. This is the first of three similar taunts (cf. Luke 23:37, 39). For **Christ of God**, cf. note on 9:18–20. For **Chosen One**, cf. note on 9:35.

23:36 The soldiers (cf. John 18:12) **also mocked him . . . offering him sour wine.** This "wine vinegar" was the ordinary wine soldiers drank. The gesture is best interpreted as seeking to prolong Jesus' suffering by quenching his thirst.

23:38 There was also an inscription. It was customary for the charge against an executed person to be displayed prominently (see notes on Matt. 27:37; Mark 15:26; John 19:20). **Over him** suggests the shape of the cross was not an "X" or "T," but the traditional "t." **King of the Jews.** Jesus was crucified on political grounds for claiming to be the Messiah, the King of the Jews. The inscription, considered a condemnation by the Romans, has become for Christians a confession of truth.

23:39–43 These verses are unique to Luke. **Hanged** is a synonym for "crucified" (cf. Acts 5:30; 10:39; Gal. 3:13; also Deut. 21:22–23). **Jesus, remember me when you come into your kingdom** is both a plea and a confession of faith. **Paradise** is another name for heaven, the dwelling place of God and the eternal home of the righteous (cf. 2 Cor. 12:3; Rev. 2:7). The Septuagint uses the same Greek word to refer to the "garden of Eden" (cf. note on Gen. 2:8–9). Jesus' words therefore may hint at a restoration of the intimate, personal fellowship with God that existed in Eden before the fall.

23:44–49 *The Death of Jesus.* This section narrating the death of the Messiah is the culmination of Luke's emphasis on his innocence.

23:44–45 about the sixth hour . . . until the ninth hour. Noon until 3:00 P.M. (cf. Matt. 27:45; Mark 15:33; see note on Matt. 27:45). Often a sign of an eschatological event taking place, **darkness** represents lament (Amos 8:9–10) and divine judgment (Ex. 10:21–23). Here it is both literal (**the sun's light failed**) and figurative (cf. Acts 2:20), probably signifying that Jesus was bearing God's wrath for his people (cf. Joel 2:2; Amos 5:18, 20; Zeph. 1:15), and also expressive of God's displeasure and judgment upon humanity for crucifying his Son. The darkness was not caused by a solar eclipse (see note on Matt. 27:45). **the curtain of the temple was torn in two.** The curtain leading from the Holy Place into the Most Holy Place (see note on Matt. 27:51); see Herod's Temple in the Time of Jesus, p. 1943.

23:46 I commit my spirit! Jesus' own human spirit returned to the presence of God the Father (see v. 43 and note on John 19:30; also Ps. 31:5; Eccles. 12:7; Acts 7:59; 1 Pet. 4:19). **having said this he breathed his last.** Even in death, Jesus is still in control of things (see note on John 10:17).

23:47 A **centurion** is a Roman officer in charge of a hundred men. What he **saw** includes: Jesus' behavior toward his enemies (v. 34), the words spoken to the repentant criminal (v. 43), the supernatural darkness (v. 44), Jesus' prayer to God (v. 46), and his giving up his life (v. 46). **Certainly this man was innocent.** Although this is not as theologically profound as Matt. 27:54 and Mark 15:39 (see notes there), for Luke this confession is important and serves as the culminating expression of Jesus' innocence (see Luke 23:41).

23:48 beating their breasts. Symbolic of grief and repentance (cf. 18:13).

23:49 all his acquaintances. Jesus' relatives, friends, and disciples. The **women** (cf. 8:1–3) are singled out because of their role in the resurrection account (23:55–56; 24:1–12; cf. John 19:25–27 and note on John 19:25).

23:50–56 *Jesus Is Buried.* As Jesus is buried in the tomb of a wealthy disciple, other disciples prepare spices to complete the burial process.

23:50–51 a man named Joseph. See note on Matt. 27:57–60. He is unknown except for this incident, recorded in all four Gospels. The location of **Arimathea** has not been conclusively determined, though Eusebius in his fourth-century list of place-names believed it was identical to Ramah (or Ramathaim-Zophim; cf. 1 Sam. 1:19). **From the Jewish town** implies that Luke's readers were Gentiles (see Luke 1:26; 4:31). **a member of the council.** The Sanhedrin. **A good and righteous man** (cf. 1:6; 2:25; Acts 10:22) and **looking for the kingdom of God** imply that Joseph was a believer (Matt. 27:57 calls him "a disciple of Jesus").

decision and action; and he [z]was looking for the kingdom of God. 52 This man went to
Pilate and asked for the body of Jesus. 53 Then he took it down and wrapped it in a linen
shroud and [a]laid him in a tomb cut in stone, [b]where no one had ever yet been laid. 54 It was
the day of [c]Preparation, and the Sabbath was beginning.[1] 55 [d]The women [e]who had come
with him from Galilee followed and saw the tomb and how his body was laid. 56 Then they
returned and [f]prepared spices and ointments.
On the Sabbath they rested [g]according to the commandment.

The Resurrection

24 [h]But on the first day of the week, at early dawn, they went to the tomb, [i]taking the
spices they had prepared. 2 And they found [j]the stone rolled away from the tomb, 3 but
when they went in they did not find the body of the Lord Jesus. 4 While they were perplexed
about this, behold, [k]two [l]men stood by them in dazzling apparel. 5 And as they were [m]fright-
ened and bowed their faces to the ground, the men said to them, "Why do you seek the living
among the dead? 6 He is not here, but has risen. Remember how he told you, [n]while he was
still in Galilee, 7 [n]that the Son of Man [o]must be delivered into the hands of sinful men and
[p]be crucified and on [q]the third day rise." 8 And [r]they remembered his words, 9 and returning
from the tomb they [s]told all these things to the eleven and to all the rest. 10 Now it was [t]Mary
Magdalene and [u]Joanna and Mary the mother of James and the other women with them who
told these things to the apostles, 11 but these words seemed to them an idle tale, and [v]they did
not believe them. 12 But [w]Peter rose and ran to the tomb; stooping and looking in, he saw [x]the
linen cloths by themselves; and he went home marveling at what had happened.

On the Road to Emmaus

13 That very day [y]two of them were going to a village named Emmaus, about seven miles[2]
from Jerusalem, 14 and they were talking with each other about all these things that had happened. 15 While they were talking and discussing together, Jesus himself drew near and went

[1] Greek *was dawning* [2] Greek *sixty stadia;* a *stadion* was about 607 feet or 185 meters

51 [z]ch. 2:25, 38
53 [a][Isa. 53:9] [b][Mark 11:2]
54 [c]See Matt. 27:62
55 [d]Matt. 28:1 [e]ver. 49
56 [f]ch. 24:1; Mark 16:1; [John 19:39] [g]Ex. 20:10; Deut. 5:14

Chapter 24

1 [h]For ver. 1-10, see Matt. 28:1-8; Mark 16:1-8; John 20:1 [i]ch. 23:56
2 [j]Matt. 27:60; Mark 15:46; [John 11]
4 [k]John 20:12 [l][Acts 1:10; 10:30]
5 [m]ver. 37
6 [n]ch. 9:22, 44; Matt. 17:22, 23; Mark 9:30, 31; [ver. 44]
7 [n][See ver. 6 above] [o]See ch. 13:33 [p]See Matt. 20:19 [q]See ch. 9:22
8 [r]John 2:22; 12:1
9 [s][John 20:18]
10 [t]Matt. 27:56; Mark 15:40, 41 [u]ch. 8:3
11 [v]Mark 16:11; See Mark 16:16
12 [w]John 20:3-6 [x]John 19:40
13 [y]Mark 16:12

23:52 went to Pilate and asked. As a member of the Sanhedrin, Joseph had greater access to the governor and would raise less suspicion and hostility than Jesus' family or the disciples (see note on Mark 15:46).

23:53 Then he took it down. Joseph supervised Jesus' body being taken down. **a tomb cut in stone.** Joseph's own tomb (Matt. 27:60; see note on Mark 15:46; and illustration, p. 2069). Thus Jesus is buried in a rich man's tomb (remarkably fulfilling Isa. 53:9). **where no one had . . . been laid.** Cf. John 19:41; see Luke 19:30.

23:54 The **day of Preparation** was the day before the **Sabbath**, and was Friday (cf. notes on John 19:14; 19:31; 19:42).

23:55 The women . . . followed and saw the tomb, so that they could return (see 24:1).

23:56 Because they thought the body was inadequately prepared, the women (whom Mark 16:1 identifies as "Mary Magdalene and Mary the mother of James and Salome") **prepared spices and ointments. On the Sabbath they rested according to the commandment.** Like Zechariah and Elizabeth, they walked "blamelessly in all the commandments" (Luke 1:6).

24:1–53 *The Resurrection of Jesus.* Luke's Gospel began in the temple (1:5–23) and, after Jesus has risen from the dead, it will conclude in the temple as well (24:52–53).

24:1–12 *The Empty Tomb.* Returning to the tomb, the women find it empty and are told by two angels that Jesus is risen and they should tell the disciples. Hearing this, Peter goes to the tomb and finds it empty.

24:1 on the first day of the week. All four Gospels state that the resurrection took place on Sunday.

24:3 The earthly **Lord Jesus** is no longer in the tomb. He is now the risen Lord (cf. Acts 2:34; Rom. 1:4).

24:4 two men. Angels (v. 23; cf. Matt. 28:2, 5). For the women, the empty tomb was at first perplexing; for Luke and his readers, it is a proof of Jesus' resurrection and confirmation that Jesus' claims to be the Son of God were in fact true (cf. Luke 22:70).

24:5 They were frightened (cf. v. 37; Acts 10:4) refers to fear that can lead to reverence (see Luke 1:12). The appearance of angels often produced such fear (cf. Judg. 13:19–20). For **the living,** cf. Luke 24:23; Acts 1:3; 3:15; Rom. 14:9.

24:6 Remember how he told you. Cf. 9:22, 44; 18:32–33.

24:7 Must emphasizes the necessity of God's providential plan being fulfilled (see 9:22). **third day.** See 9:22.

24:8 They remembered his words, i.e., his prophecies of 9:22, 44; 18:32–33.

24:9 the eleven. Judas is now missing (cf. v. 33; Matt. 28:16; Acts 1:26). **And to all the rest** includes the two disciples of Luke 24:13–25 and the 120 of Acts 1:15.

24:10 It was Mary . . . and the other women indicates that at least five women went to the tomb. On women as the first witnesses to the resurrection, see note on Mark 16:7. For **apostles,** see Luke 6:13 and note on Rom. 1:1.

24:11 They (the apostles) **did not** initially **believe** the women.

24:12 Peter rose and ran. Cf. John 20:3–6. For **the linen cloths by themselves,** see note on John 20:6. **he went home marveling.** This can be associated with unbelief (Luke 11:38; Acts 13:41) but usually involves a positive response (see Luke 1:21). Cf. 24:34.

24:13–35 *Jesus' Appearance on the Road to Emmaus.* This is the first of three resurrection appearances found in Luke and is one of the longest stories in the Gospel.

24:13 That very day is the first day of the week, Sunday (see v. 1). **two of them.** One is unnamed; the other is named Cleopas (v. 18). They **were going** to **Emmaus,** possibly after having celebrated the Passover in Jerusalem. The location of Emmaus is uncertain, but it was in Judea **seven miles** (lit., Gk. "sixty *stadia*"; 11 km) **from Jerusalem.** A *stadion* was about 607 feet (185 m).

24:14 All these things that had happened is explained in vv. 20–24.

24:16 But their eyes were kept (by God; cf. 9:45; 18:34) **from recognizing him.** Cf. John 20:14–15; 21:4.

16[z]John 20:14; 21:4; [ver. 31; ch. 9:45; 18:34]
19[a]See Matt. 21:11 [b]Acts 2:22; [Acts 7:22]
20[c]Acts 2:23; 5:30; 13:27, 28; 1 Thess. 2:15 [d]ch. 23:13, 35; John 3:1; 7:26, 48; 12:42; Acts 3:17; 4:5, 8; 13:27; [1 Cor. 2:8]
21[e]See ch. 1:68; 1 Pet. 1:18 [f]ver. 7
22[g]ver. 1
23[h]ver. 3 [i]ver. 4, 5, 9
24[j]ver. 12; John 20:3
26[k]ver. 7, 44, 46; Heb. 2:10; 12:2; 1 Pet. 1:11; See Acts 3:18 [l]See Matt. 1:17 [m]See ch. 9:26
27[n]Acts 8:35 [o]Gen. 3:15; 12:3; 22:18; Num. 21:9; 24:17; [John 1:45; 5:46] [p]2 Sam. 7:12-16; Isa. 7:14; 9:6; 50:6; 52:13–53:12; 61:1; Jer. 23:5, 6; Dan. 7:13, 14; 9:24-27; Mic. 5:2; Zech. 6:12; 9:9; 12:10; 13:7; [Acts 13:27]
28[q][Mark 6:48]
29[r]ch. 9:12 (Gk.)
30[s]See Matt. 14:19
31[t][ver. 16] [u][ch. 4:30]
32[v]Ps. 39:3 [w]ver. 45

with them. 16 [z]But their eyes were kept from recognizing him. 17 And he said to them, "What
is this conversation that you are holding with each other as you walk?" And they stood still,
looking sad. 18 Then one of them, named Cleopas, answered him, "Are you the only visitor to
Jerusalem who does not know the things that have happened there in these days?" 19 And he
said to them, "What things?" And they said to him, "Concerning Jesus of Nazareth, a man
who was [a]a prophet [b]mighty in deed and word before God and all the people, 20 and [c]how
our chief priests and [d]rulers delivered him up to be condemned to death, and crucified
him. 21 But we had hoped that he was [e]the one to redeem Israel. Yes, and besides all this, it is
now [f]the third day since these things happened. 22 Moreover, some women of our company
amazed us. [g]They were at the tomb early in the morning, 23 and [h]when they did not find his
body, they came back saying that [i]they had even seen a vision of angels, who said that he was
alive. 24 [j]Some of those who were with us went to the tomb and found it just as the women
had said, but him they did not see." 25 And he said to them, "O foolish ones, and slow of heart
to believe all that the prophets have spoken! 26 [k]Was it not necessary that [l]the Christ should
suffer these things and enter into [m]his glory?" 27 And [n]beginning with [o]Moses and [p]all the
Prophets, he interpreted to them in all the Scriptures the things concerning himself.

28 So they drew near to the village to which they were going. [q]He acted as if he were going
farther, 29 but they urged him strongly, saying, "Stay with us, for it is toward evening and [r]the
day is now far spent." So he went in to stay with them. 30 When he was at table with them, he
took the bread and [s]blessed and broke it and gave it to them. 31 [t]And their eyes were opened,
and they recognized him. And [u]he vanished from their sight. 32 They said to each other, [v]"Did
not our hearts burn within us while he talked to us on the road, while he [w]opened to us the

24:19–20 Prophet is a correct but inadequate designation (see 7:16). **Mighty in deed and word**, as shown in his casting out of demons, performing healing and nature miracles, his divine authority to forgive sins, and his extensive teaching with divine authority. **Before God and all the people** (24:19) stands in contrast with **chief priests and rulers** (v. 20). **delivered him up**. What Judas did in delivering Jesus over to the chief priests and rulers, they in turn did by delivering him over to Pilate (23:1). **crucified him**. While the physical act of crucifixion was by the Romans, Luke places the human responsibility of Jesus' crucifixion primarily on the religious leadership.

24:21 But we had hoped contrasts the people's view of Jesus with that of the religious leadership.

24:24 Some of those . . . went to the tomb assumes that, after Peter's visit, other disciples went (cf. John 20:2–10) and also found it empty.

24:25 O foolish ones is a more precise translation than "O foolish men," because the Greek text does not specify whether these were two men or a man and a woman (perhaps a husband and a wife) walking together.

24:26 Was it not necessary refers to the fact that the entire OT had shown how God brought his chosen leaders first through suffering and then to glory. Therefore the Messiah himself, in fulfillment of this extensive pattern and in fulfillment of many prophecies, would also first suffer before entering **into his glory** (see 9:22; cf. 24:44). This glory, foreshadowed in 9:32, comes at his resurrection and then more fully at his ascension into heaven (22:69; Acts 2:33; 7:55; 22:6–11; Phil. 2:8–11; Heb. 1:3).

24:27 Moses and all the Prophets refers to the entire OT, also summarized as **all the Scriptures**. Jesus explained to them how not only the explicit prophecies about the Messiah but also the historical patterns of God's activity again and again throughout the OT looked forward to Jesus himself. (See Overview of the Bible, pp. 23–26.)

24:30 For other resurrection appearances associated with eating, cf. vv. 41–43; John 21:9–15; Acts 10:41. **he took the bread and blessed and broke it and gave it to them**. There is striking similarity between this, the Last Supper (Luke 22:19), and the feeding of the 5,000 (see 9:16).

24:31 Their eyes were opened when Jesus broke the bread, suggesting that they recognized him as the crucified one who died for the redemption of Israel (see v. 21). Jesus **vanished**. Cf. v. 36; John 20:19, 26.

24:32 Did not our hearts burn within us. Even before the two disciples recognized Jesus, the fact that he **opened** (interpreted) the **Scriptures** (cf. v. 27; Acts 17:2–3) gave them hope and began convincing them of the resurrection.

Jesus' Appearances after His Resurrection

Each of the Gospels and a few other NT books mention various appearances by Jesus after his resurrection, but only Luke notes that Jesus ascended to heaven from the Mount of Olives just outside Jerusalem. Luke also recounts Jesus' discussion with the two disciples on the road to Emmaus (likely modern Qaluniyah, not the Emmaus of the intertestamental period, which lay too far west). Matthew and John note that Jesus also appeared to his disciples in the region of Galilee.

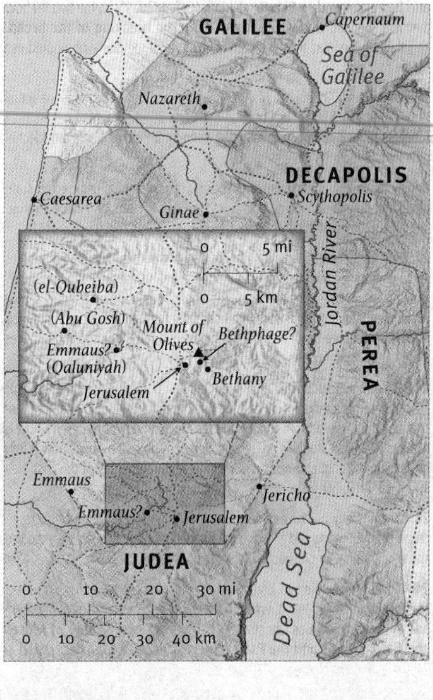

Scriptures?" 33 And they rose that same hour and returned to Jerusalem. And they [x]found
the eleven and [y]those who were with them gathered together, 34 saying, "The Lord has risen
indeed, and [z]has appeared to Simon!" 35 Then they told what had happened on the road,
and [a]how he was known to them in [b]the breaking of the bread.

Jesus Appears to His Disciples

36 As they were talking about these things, [c]Jesus himself stood among them, and said
to them, "Peace to you!" 37 But they were [d]startled and [e]frightened and [f]thought they saw
a spirit. 38 And he said to them, "Why are you troubled, and why do doubts arise in your
hearts? 39 See my hands and my feet, that it is I myself. [g]Touch me, and see. For a spirit
does not have flesh and bones as you see that I have." 40 And when he had said this, [h]he
showed them his hands and his feet. 41 And while they still disbelieved [i]for joy and were
marveling, [j]he said to them, "Have you anything here to eat?" 42 They gave him a piece of
broiled fish,[1] 43 and he took it and ate before them.

44 Then he said to them, [k]"These are my words that I spoke to you while I was still with
you, [l]that everything written about me in the Law of Moses and the Prophets and the
Psalms must be fulfilled." 45 Then [m]he opened their minds to understand the Scriptures,
46 and said to them, "Thus [n]it is written, [o]that the Christ should suffer and on the third
day [p]rise from the dead, 47 and that [q]repentance and[2] forgiveness of sins should be proclaimed [r]in his name [s]to all nations, [t]beginning from Jerusalem. 48 [u]You are witnesses of
these things. 49 And behold, I am sending [v]the promise of my Father upon you. But stay
in the city until you [w]are clothed with [x]power [y]from on high."

The Ascension

50 Then [z]he led them out as far as [a]Bethany, and lifting up his hands he blessed them.
51 While he blessed them, [b]he parted from them and was carried up into heaven. 52 And
they [c]worshiped him and [z]returned to Jerusalem [d]with great joy, 53 and [e]were continually
in the temple [f]blessing God.

[1] Some manuscripts add *and some honeycomb* [2] Some manuscripts *for*

33 [x]Mark 16:13; Acts 17:3 [y][Acts 1:14]
34 [z]1 Cor. 15:5
35 [a]ver. 30, 31 [b]See Acts 2:42
36 [c]Mark 16:14; John 20:19
37 [d]ch. 21:9 [e]ver. 5 [f][Matt. 14:26; Mark 6:49]
39 [g]1 John 1:1; [John 20:27]
40 [h]John 20:20
41 [i]Acts 12:14; [Gen. 45:26] [j]John 21:5
44 [k]See ver. 6 [l]See ver. 27
45 [m]ver. 32; [Job 33:16; Ps. 119:18; Acts 16:14; 1 John 5:20]
46 [n]See Matt. 26:24 [o]See ver. 7, 26 [p]John 20:9
47 [q]Acts 5:31; See Acts 2:38 [r]See Acts 4:12 [s]ch. 2:32; Gen. 12:3; Ps. 22:27; Isa. 2:2; 49:6; Hos. 2:23; Mal. 1:11; Matt. 28:19 [t]Acts 10:37; Gal. 3:8
48 [u]Acts 1:8, 22; 2:32; 3:15; 5:32; 10:39, 41; 13:31; 1 Pet. 5:1; [John 15:27; 1 Cor. 15:15]
49 [v]John 14:26; Acts 1:4; [Acts 2:33; Eph. 1:13]; See Acts 2:16, 17 [w]Job 29:14; Ps. 132:9 [x]Acts 1:8 [y]ch. 1:78; Isa. 32:15
50 [z]Acts 1:12 [a]Matt. 21:17; John 11:18
51 [b]See Mark 16:19
52 [c]Matt. 28:9 [z][See ver. 50 above] [d]See John 16:22
53 [e]Acts 2:46; 3:1; 5:21, 42 [f]ch. 1:64; 2:28

24:34–35 After being told by the Eleven that **the Lord has risen indeed, and has appeared to Simon** (cf. Mark 16:7; 1 Cor. 15:5), the two tell how they met the Lord who **was known . . . in the breaking of the bread**. I.e., they understood that the risen one was also the one who poured out his life for them.

24:36–49 *Jesus Appears to His Disciples.* This account emphasizes the actual physical reality of Jesus' resurrection body (vv. 36–43) and the necessity of Jesus' death and resurrection taking place in fulfillment of God's providential plan (vv. 44–49).

24:36 Jesus . . . stood among them. For Jesus in his resurrected state being able to appear and disappear, cf. note on John 20:19. **Peace to you**. See John 20:19 and note on John 14:27.

24:38 In light of what Jesus says in vv. 39–40, their **doubts** at least includes some confusion about the actual physical reality of Jesus' resurrection body, and continuing questions about the reality of the resurrection itself. But Jesus will prove that it is really he who has risen from the dead by appealing to their sight (they can see him), hearing (they hear him talk), and touch (he invites them to touch him to see that he is real).

24:39 See . . . Touch me, and see (cf. John 20:25, 27; 1 John 1:1). Jesus is not a disembodied spirit. **it is I**. The risen Christ and Jesus of Nazareth are one and the same person, though the resurrected body of the risen Christ is gloriously different from his pre-resurrection body, in that his body now is fully healed, and strong, and not subject to the death and decay of the flesh (see 1 Cor. 15:1–19, 50–58).

24:41 anything . . . to eat. Jesus proves the corporeal nature of his resurrected body by eating and allowing the disciples to touch him, for disembodied spirits cannot eat or be touched (cf. note on 24:39).

24:44 My words refers to Jesus' teaching concerning his death and resurrection (see note on 9:21–22). **while I was still with you**. Jesus of Nazareth and the risen Lord Jesus Christ are one and the same. The **Law of Moses and the Prophets and the Psalms** refers to the three divisions of the OT in Jesus' day. "Psalms" is an example of synecdoche, in which one of the books in the Writings represents the whole.

24:45 he opened their minds to understand. True understanding of the Scriptures, so that one understands how all of redemptive history fits together, is a gift of God (cf. 9:45; 18:34).

24:46 The Christ should suffer repeats v. 26 and emphasizes that Jesus' death and resurrection were necessary in order to fulfill God's providential plan.

24:47 repentance and forgiveness of sins. See note on Acts 2:38. **in his name**. See notes on Acts 2:38; 10:48. **to all nations, beginning from Jerusalem**. See Acts 1:8 and note on Matt. 28:19.

24:48 witnesses of these things. As eyewitnesses, the disciples served as guardians of the gospel tradition (1:2).

24:49 The promise of my Father refers to the Holy Spirit, who had been promised by the Father (see note on Acts 2:33). The coming of the Holy Spirit had been announced by John the Baptist as a sign that the Messiah had come (Luke 3:15–17). The Holy Spirit would enable the disciples to fulfill their commission as Jesus' witnesses (cf. Acts 1:8). The futuristic present ("I am sending") emphasizes the certainty of the Spirit's coming. **But stay in the city until** (cf. Acts 1:4). For the tie between **power** and the Spirit, see note on Luke 1:16–17.

24:50–53 *The Ascension of Jesus.* Luke's Gospel ends with Jesus bestowing a blessing upon the disciples and ascending into heaven, and the disciples going to the temple and praising God.

24:50 Jesus **led them out as far as Bethany** on the Mount of Olives (see notes on 19:29 and John 11:1).

24:51 While he blessed them (indicating that the blessing of v. 50 lasted for a period of time), **he parted from them and was carried up into heaven** (cf. Acts 1:9, 11, 22). In John 20:17 Jesus states that he was "ascending" to his Father. See note on Acts 1:9.

24:52–53 And they worshiped him (cf. note on Matt. 28:9). The Gospel ends where it began, with God's people **in the temple** (cf. Luke 1:5–17; 24:53) blessing God with **great joy**, "for he has visited and redeemed his people" (1:68).

INTRODUCTION TO

THE GOSPEL ACCORDING TO

JOHN

Author and Title

The title says that the Gospel was written by John, and other evidence identifies this John as the son of Zebedee. The internal evidence indicates that the author was (1) an apostle (1:14; cf. 2:11; 19:35), (2) one of the 12 disciples ("the disciple whom Jesus loved"; 13:23; 19:26; 20:2; 21:20; cf. 21:24–25), and, still more specifically, (3) John the son of Zebedee (note the association of "the disciple whom Jesus loved" with Peter in 13:23–24; 18:15–16; 20:2–9; 21:2–23; cf. Luke 22:8; Acts 1:13; 3:1–4:37; 8:14–25; Gal. 2:9). The external evidence from the church fathers supports this identification (e.g., Irenaeus, *Against Heresies* 3.1.2).

Date and Place of Writing

The most likely date of writing is the period between A.D. 70 (the date of the destruction of the temple) and A.D. 100 (the end of John's lifetime), but there is not enough evidence to be much more precise. A date subsequent to A.D. 70 is suggested, among other things, by the references in 6:1 and 21:1 to the Sea of Tiberias (a name widely used for the Sea of Galilee only toward the end of the 1st century), the reference in 21:19 to Peter's martyrdom (probably between A.D. 64 and 66), and the lack of reference to the Sadducees (who ceased to be a Jewish religious party after A.D. 70). The testimony of the early church also favors a date after A.D. 70. Thus Clement of Alexandria stated, "Last of all, John, perceiving that the external facts had been made plain [in the other canonical Gospels] . . . composed a spiritual gospel" (cited in Eusebius, *Ecclesiastical History* 6.14.7).

The most likely place of writing is Ephesus in Asia Minor (modern-day Turkey), which was one of the most important urban centers of the Roman Empire at the time (Irenaeus, *Against Heresies* 3.1.2; cf. Eusebius, *Ecclesiastical History* 3.1.1). However, the readership envisioned by John's Gospel transcends any one historical setting.

Theme

The theme of John's Gospel is that Jesus is the promised Messiah and Son of God. By believing in Jesus, people can have eternal life (cf. 20:30–31).

Purpose, Occasion, and Background

The Gospel of John was written by the apostle John, the son of Zebedee, a Palestinian Jew and a member of Jesus' inner apostolic circle during his earthly ministry. John's original audience consisted of both Jews and Gentiles living in the larger Greco-Roman world in Ephesus and beyond toward the close of the first century A.D. He frequently explains Jewish customs and Palestinian geography and translates Aramaic terms into Greek (see note on 1:38), thus showing awareness of non-Jewish readers. He also presents Jesus as the Word become flesh against the backdrop of Greek thought that included Stoicism and early Gnosticism. But John also shows awareness of Jewish readers as he demonstrates Jesus to be the Jewish Messiah, the fulfillment of many OT themes, and the Son of God who was sent by God the Father to reveal the only true God and to provide redemption for humanity.

The purpose statement in 20:30–31 makes it appear that John wrote with an evangelistic intent. However, his depth of teaching shows that he wanted readers not only to come to initial saving faith in Jesus but also to grow into a rich, well-informed faith. John's central contention is that Jesus is the long-awaited Messiah and Son of God, and that by believing in him people may have eternal life. To this end, he marshals the evidence of several selected messianic signs performed by Jesus and of a series of witnesses to Jesus—including the Scriptures, John the Baptist, Jesus himself, God the Father, Jesus' works, the Spirit, and John himself. It is also likely that John sought to present Jesus as the new temple and center of worship for God's people, a concept that would be especially forceful if the date of composition (as seems likely) was subsequent to A.D. 70 (the time of the destruction of the Jerusalem temple).

Key Themes

1. Jesus is God.	1:1–2, 18; 5:17–18; 8:58–59; 10:30–33; 20:28
2. Jesus existed before the creation of the world.	1:1–2; 8:58; 17:5, 24
3. Jesus has supernatural knowledge.	1:48; 2:4, 19, 23–25; 3:14; 4:17–18; 6:51, 70; 8:28; 9:3; 10:15, 17–18; 11:4, 14; 12:24, 32; 13:10–11, 38; 21:18–19
4. Jesus is the Messiah and the Son of God.	1:36, 41, 49; 3:18; 4:25, 29; 5:25; 7:26, 27, 31, 41, 42; 9:22; 10:24, 36; 11:4, 27; 12:34; 19:7; 20:30–31
5. Jesus is the "I am."	4:26; 6:20, 35, 48, 51; 8:12, 18, 24, 28, 58; 9:5; 10:7, 9, 11, 14; 11:25; 13:19; 14:6; 15:1; 18:5–6 (cf. Ex. 3:14–15; Isa. 41:4; 43:10–13, 25; 45:18; 51:12; 52:6)
6. Jesus, the sent Son, reflects the sender.	3:17, 35–36; 5:19–26; 6:40; 8:35–36; 14:13; 17:1
7. Jesus is the fulfillment of Jewish festivals and institutions (including the temple).	1:29, 36; 2:14–22, esp. v. 21; 4:23–24; 8:12; 9:5; 19:14
8. Jesus is the giver of eternal life.	1:4; 3:15–16, 36; 4:14, 36; 5:24, 26, 39–40; 6:27, 33, 35, 40, 47–48, 51, 53–54, 68; 8:12; 10:10, 25, 28; 11:25; 12:25, 50; 14:6; 17:2–3; 20:31
9. The signs of Jesus show that he is the Messiah (cf. also Jesus as the Messiah and Son of God, above).	2:1–11, 13–22; 4:46–54; 5:1–15; 6:1–15; 9:1–41; 11:1–44
10. The witnesses to Jesus testify that he is the Messiah.	1:7–8, 15, 19, 32, 34; 3:11, 32–33; 4:39; 5:31–39; 8:14, 18; 10:25; 15:26–27; 18:37; 19:35; 21:24
11. Father, Son, and Spirit are united in their work of revelation and redemption.	14:17–18, 23, 26; 15:26; 20:21–22
12. Jesus' death is the basis of salvation.	1:29; 3:14–15; 6:51–58; 10:15; 11:50–52; 12:24; 15:13
13. God is sovereign in salvation.	3:21; 5:21; 6:37–45, 64–65; 10:16, 26–30; 15:16; 17:2, 6, 9
14. Salvation is obtained through believing in Jesus as the Messiah and the Son of God.	1:12; 3:15, 16; 5:24; 6:29, 35; 8:24; 11:25–27, 42; 12:44; 17:8, 21; 20:31
15. Believers can experience the benefits of salvation already in the here and now, during this present evil age.	3:18, 36; 4:23; 5:24; 6:39–40; 10:10, 26–29; 11:25–26
16. Believers are called to continue Jesus' mission (cf. also Jesus as the sent Son, above).	4:38; 15:16; 17:18; 20:21–22

History of Salvation Summary

Jesus comes as God in the flesh (1:14), the revealer of the Father (14:9), and the messianic King (1:41, 49; 4:25; 6:15). He fulfills the OT and its symbols, especially its promises of everlasting salvation. The ultimate fulfillment comes with his crucifixion and resurrection. (For an explanation of the "History of Salvation," see the Overview of the Bible, pp. 23–26.)

Literary Features

The main genre is gospel, which combines three ingredients—what Jesus did, what Jesus said (discourse and dialogue), and people's responses to Jesus. Within this format the usual gospel subgenres are found: calling stories, recognition stories, witness stories, conflict stories, encounter stories, miracle stories, discourses, proverbs or sayings, passion stories, resurrection stories, and post-resurrection appearances.

Balancing the narrative richness are expanded discourses by Jesus. The Gospel of John also frequently employs symbolism, especially with reference to Christ, who is portrayed by images such as light, bread, water, and a shepherd. As an extension of this, the first half of the book is built around seven great "signs" that Jesus performed as proof of his messianic identity (see 2:1–11; 4:46–54; 5:1–15; 6:5–13; 6:16–21; 9:1–7; 11:1–44).

Then, in a further intricacy, John often links a "sign" or other great symbol with a corresponding statement made by Jesus in the form of either a conversation or full-fledged discourse. For example, Jesus feeds 5,000 (6:1–13), which is followed a few verses later by Jesus' discourse on being the bread of life (6:25–40).

Literary motifs include: (1) statements that are misunderstood—in which Jesus makes a pronouncement, a bystander expresses an unduly literal understanding of Jesus' words, and Jesus explains the true, spiritual meaning of his original statement (nine instances: 3:3–8; 4:10–15; 4:31–38; 6:47–58; 7:33–36; 8:21–30; 8:31–47; 8:56–58; 11:11–15), (2) events or statements that occur in threes (e.g., three denials of Jesus; three utterances from the cross) and statements that occur in sevens (including seven great signs and seven "I am" statements by Jesus; see notes on 2:11; 6:35), and (3) heightened contrasts scattered throughout the book (e.g., light vs. darkness; life vs. death; the fleeting vs. the eternal; disease vs. health; love vs. hate).

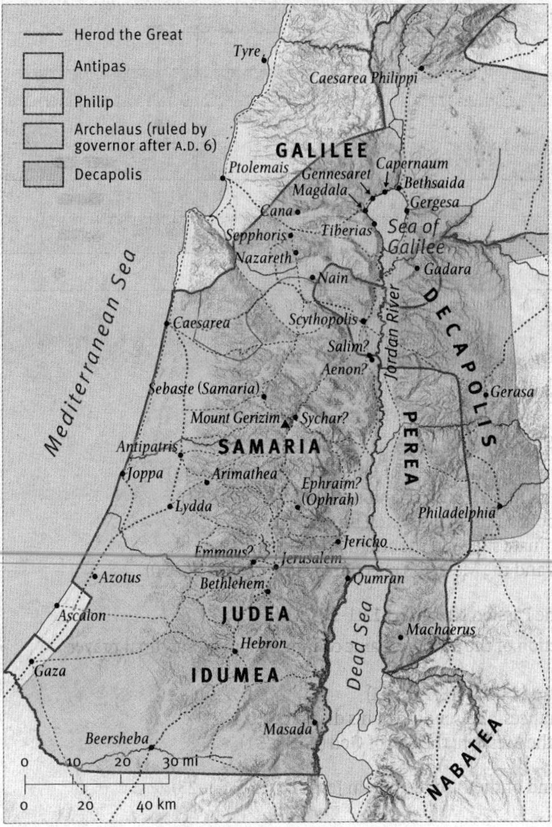

The Setting of John

The events of the Gospel of John take place in Palestine, incorporated into the Roman Empire in 63 B.C. Appointed by the Romans as king over the Jews in 37 B.C., Herod the Great ruled until his death in 4 B.C. The Romans divided his kingdom among his descendants. The predominantly Gentile region of the Decapolis, or "Ten Cities," was a loose confederation of semiautonomous cities administered by the Roman legate of Syria.

Timeline

Event
John the Baptist born (6 B.C.*)
Jesus born (5 B.C.*)
Flight to Egypt; death of Herod; return to Nazareth (4 B.C.*)
Jesus, age 12, talks with teachers in temple (A.D. 8*)
Jesus works as carpenter in Nazareth (8*–28/30)
John the Baptist begins ministry (28/29)
Jesus begins ministry; John becomes disciple (28/30)
Jesus crucified and resurrected (33 [or 30])†
Jerusalem church flees to Pella (67*)
Destruction of Jerusalem temple (70)
Domitian's reign (81–96)
Gospel according to John written (85–95*)
John writes 1–3 John, probably from Ephesus (85–95*)
John writes Revelation from Patmos (95–96*)

** denotes approximate date; / signifies either/or; † see The Date of Jesus' Crucifixion, pp. 1809–1810*

Outline

I. Prologue: The Incarnate Word (1:1–18)

II. The Signs of the Messiah (1:19–12:50)
- A. John the Baptist's witness and the first week of Jesus' ministry (1:19–2:11)
- B. Jesus' ministry in Jerusalem, Judea, Samaria, and to Gentiles (2:12–4:54)
- C. Mounting Jewish opposition, additional signs (5:1–10:42)
- D. The final Passover: the ultimate sign and the aftermath (11:1–12:19)
- E. The approaching Gentiles and the Messiah's rejection by the Jews (12:20–50)

III. The Farewell Discourse and the Passion Narrative (13:1–20:31)
- A. The cleansing and instruction of the new messianic community and Jesus' final prayer (13:1–17:26)
- B. Jesus' arrest, trials, death, and burial (18:1–19:42)
- C. Jesus' resurrection, appearances, and sending of his disciples (20:1–29)
- D. Purpose statement: Jesus the Messiah, the Son of God (20:30–31)

IV. Epilogue: The Roles of Peter and of the Disciple Whom Jesus Loved (21:1–25)

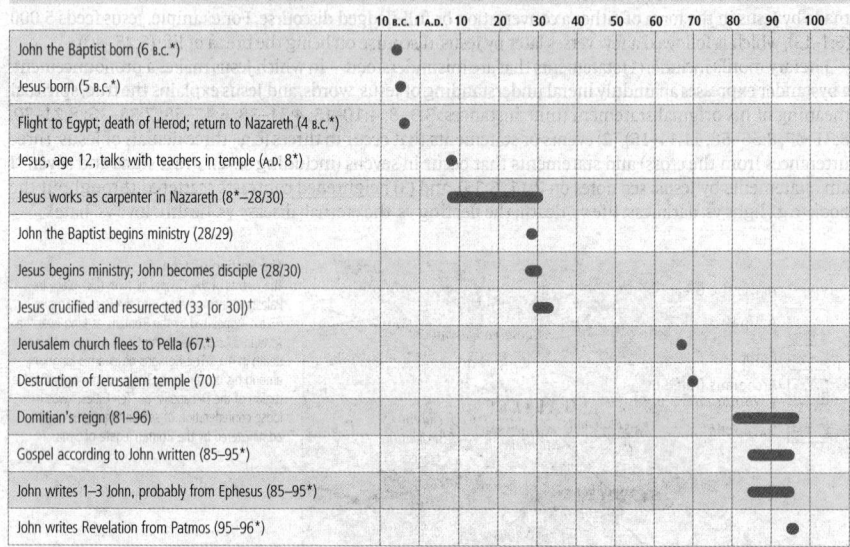

THE GOSPEL ACCORDING TO

JOHN

The Word Became Flesh

1 [a]In the beginning was [b]the Word, and [c]the Word was with God, and [d]the Word was
God. **2** He was in the beginning with God. **3** [e]All things were made through him,
and without him was not any thing made that was made. **4** [f]In him was life,[1] and [g]the
life was the light of men. **5** [h]The light shines in the darkness, and the darkness has not
overcome it.

6 There was a man [i]sent from God, whose name was [j]John. **7** He came as a [k]witness, to
bear witness about the light, [l]that all might believe through him. **8** [m]He was not the light,
but came to bear witness about the light.

9 [n]The true light, which gives light to everyone, was coming into the world. **10** He was in
the world, and the world was made through him, yet [o]the world did not know him. **11** He
came to [p]his own,[2] and [q]his own people[3] [r]did not receive him. **12** But to all who did receive

[1] *Or was not any thing made. That which has been made was life in him* [2] *Greek to his own things*; that is, to his own domain, or to his own people [3] *People* is implied in Greek

Chapter 1

1 [a]Gen. 1:1; [Col. 1:17; 1 John 1:1; Rev. 1:4, 8, 17; 3:14; 21:6; 22:13] [b]Rev. 19:13; [Heb. 4:12; 1 John 1:1] [c]1 John 1:2; [ch. 17:5] [d]Phil. 2:6
3 [e]ver. 10; Ps. 33:6; 1 Cor. 8:6; Col. 1:16; Heb. 1:2
4 [f]ch. 5:26; 11:25; 1 John 1:2; 5:11 [g]ch. 8:12; 9:5; 12:46
5 [h][ch. 3:19]
6 [i]ver. 33; ch. 3:28; Mal. 3:1 [j]Matt. 3:1; Mark 1:4; Luke 3:2
7 [k]ch. 3:26; 5:33 [l]Acts 19:4
8 [m]ver. 20
9 [n]Isa. 49:6; 1 John 2:8
10 [o][ch. 16:3; 1 John 3:1]
11 [p]Matt. 21:38 [q]ch. 13:1 [r]ch. 5:43; [ch. 3:11, 32]

1:1–18 *Prologue: The Incarnate Word.* In the prologue John presents Jesus as the eternal, preexistent, now incarnate Word (vv. 1, 14) and as the one-of-a-kind Son of the Father who is himself God (vv. 1, 18). God's revelation and redemption in and through Jesus are shown to form the culmination of the history of salvation, which previously included God's giving of the law through Moses (v. 17), his dwelling among his people in the tabernacle and the temple (v. 14), and the sending of the forerunner, John the Baptist (vv. 6–8, 15). The prologue also introduces many of the major themes developed later in the Gospel, such as Jesus as the life (v. 4), the light (vv. 5–9), and the truth (vv. 14, 16–17); believers as God's children (vv. 12–13); and the world's rejection of Jesus (vv. 10–11).

1:1 In the beginning was the Word echoes the opening phrase of the book of Genesis, "In the beginning, God created the heavens and the earth." John will soon identify this Word as Jesus (v. 14), but here he locates Jesus' existence in eternity past with God. The term "the Word" (Gk. *Logos*) conveys the notion of divine self-expression or speech and has a rich OT background. God's Word is effective: God speaks, and things come into being (Gen. 1:3, 9; Ps. 33:6; 107:20; Isa. 55:10–11), and by speech he relates personally to his people (e.g., Gen. 15:1). John also shows how this concept of "the Word" is superior to a Greek philosophical concept of "Word" (*logos*) as an impersonal principle of Reason that gave order to the universe. **And the Word was with God** indicates interpersonal relationship "with" God, but then **and the Word was God** affirms that this Word was also the same God who created the universe "in the beginning." Here are the building blocks that go into the doctrine of the Trinity: the one true God consists of more than one person, they relate to each other, and they have always existed. From the Patristic period (Arius, c. A.D. 256–336) until the present day (Jehovah's Witnesses), some have claimed that "the Word was God" merely identifies Jesus as *a* god rather than identifying Jesus as *God*, because the Greek word for God, *Theos*, is not preceded by a definite article. However, in Greek grammar, Colwell's Rule indicates that the translation "a god" is not required, for lack of an article does not necessarily indicate indefiniteness ("a god") but rather specifies that a given term ("God") is the predicate nominative of a definite subject ("the Word"). This means that the context must determine the meaning of *Theos* here, and the context clearly indicates that this "God" that John is talking about ("the Word") is the one true God who created all things (see also John 1:6, 12, 13, 18 for other examples of *Theos* without a definite article but clearly meaning "God").

1:3 All things includes the whole universe, indicating that (except for God) everything that exists was created and that (except for God) nothing has existed eternally. **Made through him** follows the consistent pattern of Scripture in saying that God the Father carried out his creative works through the activity of the Son (cf. 1 Cor. 8:6; Col. 1:16; Heb. 1:2). This verse disproves any suggestion that the Word (or the Son, John 1:14) was created, for the Father would have had to do this by himself, and John says that nothing was created that way, for **without him was not any thing made that was made.**

1:4–5 The references to **life, light**, and **darkness** continue to draw on Genesis motifs (cf. Gen. 1:3–5, 14–18, 20–31; 2:7; 3:20; cf. also Isa. 9:2; 42:6–7; 49:6; 60:1–5; Mal. 4:2; Luke 1:78–79). Against this background, Jesus as the "light" brings to this dark world true knowledge, moral purity, and the light that shows the very presence of God (cf. John 8:12; 1 John 1:5).

1:7–9 light. See note on vv. 4–5. **witness**. See note on 5:31–47.

1:11 John moves from **his own** things (see ESV footnote)—that is, creation—to **his own people**, the Jews. The Jewish rejection of the Messiah, despite convincing proofs of his messianic identity (esp. the "signs"), is one of the major emphases of the Gospel (see esp. 12:37–40).

1:12–13 Receive him implies not merely intellectual agreement with some facts about Jesus but also welcoming and submitting to him in a personal relationship. "Believed in" (Gk. *pisteuō eis*) implies personal trust. **His name** refers to all that is true about him, and therefore the totality of his person. **Born, not of blood . . . , but of God** makes clear that neither physical birth nor ethnic descent nor human effort can make people children of God, but only God's supernatural work (8:41–47; cf. 3:16). This extends the possibility of becoming God's children to Gentiles and not just Jews (11:51–52; cf. 10:16). See also 3:3–8. **To all . . . who believed . . . he gave the right** indicates that saving faith precedes becoming members of God's family through adoption as his children.

him, [s]who believed in his name, [t]he gave the right [u]to become [v]children of God, 13 who
[w]were born, [x]not of blood [y]nor of the will of the flesh nor of the will of man, but of God.
14 And [z]the Word [a]became flesh and [b]dwelt among us, [c]and we have seen his glory, glory
as of the only Son from the Father, full of [d]grace and [e]truth. 15 ([f]John bore witness about
him, and cried out, "This was he of whom I said, [g]'He who comes after me ranks before
me, because he was before me.'") 16 For from [h]his fullness we have all received, [i]grace upon
grace.[1] 17 For [j]the law was given through Moses; [k]grace and truth came through Jesus
Christ. 18 [l]No one has ever seen God; [m]the only God,[2] who is at the Father's side,[3] [n]he has
made him known.

The Testimony of John the Baptist

19 And this is the [o]testimony of John, when the Jews sent priests and Levites from
Jerusalem to ask him, [p]"Who are you?" 20 [q]He confessed, and did not deny, but confessed,

[1] Or *grace in place of grace* [2] Or *the only One, who is God;* some manuscripts *the only Son* [3] Greek *in the bosom of the Father*

18 [l]ch. 5:37; 6:46; Ex. 33:20; Col. 1:15; 1 Tim. 6:16; 1 John 4:12, 20; [ch. 12:45] [m]ver. 14; See ch. 3:16 [n][Matt. 11:27]; See ch. 3:32 **19** [o]ch. 3:26 [p][ch. 8:25] **20** [q]ver. 8; ch. 3:28; Acts 13:25; [Luke 3:15]

12 [s]See 1 John 5:13 [t]1 John 5:1 [u]1 John 3:1; [Matt. 5:45] [v][Gal. 3:26]; See ch. 11:52
13 [w]James 1:18; [ch. 3:3; 1 Pet. 1:3] [x]1 Pet. 1:23 [y]ch. 3:6
14 [z]ver. 1 [a]Rom. 1:3; 8:3; Gal. 4:4; Phil. 2:7, 8; Col. 1:22; 1 Tim. 3:16; Heb. 2:14; 1 John 4:2; 2 John 7; [ch. 6:51] [b]Rev. 7:15; 21:3 [c]ch. 2:11; Luke 9:32; 2 Pet. 1:16, 17; 1 John 1:1; 4:14 [d]See ver. 7 [e][ch. 14:6]
15 [f]See ver. 7 [g]ver. 27, 30; See Matt. 3:11
16 [h]Eph. 1:23; 3:19; 4:13; Col. 1:19; 2:9 [i][Matt. 25:29]
17 [j]ch. 7:19; Ex. 20:1 [k]ver. 14; [Rom. 5:21]

1:14 The Word continues the opening words of the prologue in v. 1. **Became flesh** does not mean the Word ceased being God; rather, the Word, who was God, also took on humanity (cf. Phil. 2:6–7). This is the most amazing event in all of history: the eternal, omnipotent, omnipresent, infinitely holy Son of God took on a human nature and lived among humanity as one who was both God and man at the same time, in one person. **Dwelt among us** means more literally "pitched his tent" (Gk. *skēnoō*), an allusion to God's dwelling among the Israelites in the tabernacle (cf. Ex. 25:8–9; 33:7). In the past, God had manifested his presence to his people in the tabernacle and the temple. Now God takes up residence among his people in the incarnate Word, Jesus Christ (cf. John 1:17). Thus, the coming of Christ fulfills the OT symbolism for God's dwelling with man in the tabernacle and the temple. Later, through the Holy Spirit, Christ will make into a temple both the church (1 Cor. 3:16) and a Christian's body (1 Cor. 6:19). The references to God's **glory** refer back to OT passages narrating the manifestation of the presence and glory of God in theophanies (appearances of God), the tabernacle, or the temple (e.g., Ex. 33:22; Num. 14:10; Deut. 5:22). **the only Son from the Father**. Jesus is the "Son of God," not in the sense of being created or born (see John 1:3), but in the sense of being a Son who is exactly like his Father in all attributes, and in the sense of having a Father-Son relationship with God the Father. The Greek word underlying "only," *monogenēs*, means "one of a kind, unique," as in the case of Isaac, who is called Abraham's "one-of-a-kind" son in Heb. 11:17 (in contrast to Ishmael; cf. Gen. 22:2, 12, 16). Thus "only" is a better translation than "only begotten" (made familiar through its use in the KJV). On **grace and truth**, see note on John 1:16–17.

1:15 bore witness. See note on 5:31–47. **he was before me**. See note on 1:1.

1:16–17 Grace indicates God's (unmerited) favor that brings blessing and joy. **Grace and truth** most likely recalls the Hebrew behind the phrase "steadfast love [Hb. *hesed*] and faithfulness [Hb. *'emet*]" in Ex. 34:6 (cf. Ex. 33:18–19), where the expression refers to God's covenant faithfulness to his people Israel. According to John, God's covenant faithfulness found ultimate expression in his sending of his one-of-a-kind Son, Jesus Christ (see note on John 1:14). The contrast is not that the Mosaic law was bad and Jesus is good. Rather, both the giving of the law and the coming of Jesus Christ mark decisive events in the history of salvation. In the law, God graciously revealed his character and righteous requirements to the nation of Israel. Jesus, however, marked the final, definitive revelation of God's grace and truth. He was superior to Abraham (8:53), Jacob (4:12), and Moses (5:46–47; cf. 9:28).

1:18 No one has ever seen God, that is, in a full and complete way (cf. 6:46), but some people did see partial revelations of God in the OT. To see God in Christ would be far better (see 14:6). Some ancient manuscripts say "the only Son" here (see ESV footnote), but the earliest manuscripts say **the only God** (using the same word for "only" as 1:14, meaning "unique, one-of-a-kind"). John refers to two different persons here as "God," as he did in v. 1. John concludes the prologue by emphasizing what he taught in v. 1: Jesus as the Word is God, and he has revealed and explained God to humanity.

1:19–12:50 *The Signs of the Messiah.* The first half of John's Gospel features Jesus' demonstration of his messianic identity by way of several selected "signs" (cf. 20:30–31), such as the changing of water into wine (2:1–11), many signs in Jerusalem (2:23; cf. 7:31; 9:16; 11:47), the healing of the official's son (4:46–54), the healing of the invalid (5:1–15), the feeding of the multitude (6:1–15), the healing of the man born blind (9:1–41), and the raising of Lazarus (11:1–44; cf. 12:18). (Regarding John's use of the word "signs," see Introduction: Literary Features.) This section ends with a reference to the Jewish nation's rejection of the Messiah (12:36b–37).

1:19–2:11 *John the Baptist's Witness and the First Week of Jesus' Ministry.* This introductory section of John's Gospel narrates the course of the first week of Jesus' ministry. He is hailed by John the Baptist as "God's lamb" (1:29, 36), is followed by his first disciples (1:37–51), and performs his first "sign" (see Introduction: Literary Features), turning water into wine at the wedding at Cana (2:1–11).

1:19 testimony. See note on 5:31–47. **The Jews** is an expression used 68 times in the Greek text of John, sometimes in a neutral (2:6) or positive (4:22) sense, but often to refer to hostile Jewish opponents of Jesus among the Jewish leaders and the ordinary people who followed them. The phrase does not usually mean all the Jews, for Jesus and John the Baptist were also Jews, as was the author, John. John wants Jewish readers in his own time to realize that opposition to Jesus by many Jewish leaders goes back to the very beginning of Jesus' ministry, but that did not deter many other Jews from following him anyway. In many places in John, "the Jews" seems to be a shorthand expression for "the Jews who opposed Jesus" (see ESV footnotes on 5:10, etc.). **Jerusalem**. See Jerusalem in the Time of Jesus, pp. 1878–1879.

1:20–21 John denies being the Christ (cf. v. 8, 15; 3:28), Elijah, or the Prophet. **the Christ**. See note on 1:41. **Elijah**, who never died (2 Kings 2:11), was expected to return in the end times (Mal. 4:5) to "restore all things" (Matt. 17:11; cf. Luke 1:17). Though the Baptist resembled Elijah in his rugged lifestyle (Matt. 3:4; cf. 2 Kings 1:8), he denied that he himself was Elijah (though Jesus, understanding more about this than John, saw John

The First Week of Jesus' Ministry

Day 1	John the Baptist's witness concerning Jesus	1:19–28
Day 2	John the Baptist's encounter with Jesus	1:29–34
Day 3	John the Baptist's referral of disciples to Jesus	1:35–39
Day 4	Andrew's introduction of his brother Peter to Jesus	1:40–42
Day 5	The recruitment of Philip and Nathanael	1:43–51
Day 6		
Day 7	The wedding at Cana	2:1–11

21[r][Matt. 11:14; 16:14] [s]See Deut. 18:15, 18
23[t]Cited from Isa. 40:3; See Matt. 3:3
25[u]Matt. 3:6; Mark 1:4; Luke 3:3, 7
26[v]Matt. 3:11; Mark 1:7, 8; Luke 3:16; Acts 1:5; 13:25
27[w]ver. 15, 30
29[x]ver. 36; Ex. 12:3; Isa. 53:7; Acts 8:32; 1 Pet. 1:19; [Gen. 22:8; Rev. 5:6] [y]1 John 3:5; [Heb. 10:4, 11] [z][ch. 3:16, 17; 4:42; 12:47; 1 John 2:2; 4:14]
30[a]ver. 15, 27
31[b]Luke 1:17, 76, 77
32[c]See ver. 7 [d]Matt. 3:16; Mark 1:10; Luke 3:22 [e][Isa. 11:2; Acts 10:38]
33[f]ver. 6; Luke 3:2 [g][ch. 3:5] [h]Matt. 3:11; Mark 1:8; Luke 3:16; Acts 1:5
36[i]See ver. 29

"I am not the Christ." **21** And they asked him, "What then? [r]Are you Elijah?" He said, "I am
not." "Are you [s]the Prophet?" And he answered, "No." **22** So they said to him, "Who are you?
We need to give an answer to those who sent us. What do you say about yourself?" **23** He
said, "I am [t]the voice of one crying out in the wilderness, 'Make straight[1] the way of the
Lord,' as the prophet Isaiah said."

24 (Now they had been sent from the Pharisees.) **25** They asked him, [u]"Then why are you
baptizing, if you are neither the Christ, nor Elijah, nor the Prophet?" **26** John answered
them, [v]"I baptize with water, but among you stands one you do not know, **27** even [w]he who
comes after me, the strap of whose sandal I am not worthy to untie." **28** These things took
place in Bethany across the Jordan, where John was baptizing.

Behold, the Lamb of God

29 The next day he saw Jesus coming toward him, and said, "Behold, [x]the Lamb of God,
who [y]takes away the sin [z]of the world! **30** This is he of whom I said, [a]'After me comes a man
who ranks before me, because he was before me.' **31** I myself did not know him, but [b]for
this purpose I came baptizing with water, that he might be revealed to Israel." **32** And John
[c]bore witness: [d]"I saw the Spirit descend from heaven like a dove, and [e]it remained on him.
33 I myself did not know him, but [f]he who sent me to baptize [g]with water said to me, 'He
on whom you see the Spirit descend and remain, [h]this is he who baptizes [g]with the Holy
Spirit.' **34** And I have seen and have borne witness that this is the Son of God."

Jesus Calls the First Disciples

35 The next day again John was standing with two of his disciples, **36** and he looked at
Jesus as he walked by and said, "Behold, [i]the Lamb of God!" **37** The two disciples heard him

[1] *Or crying out, 'In the wilderness make straight*

as fulfilling the prophecy about Elijah; cf. Matt. 11:14). The coming of **the Prophet** was predicted by Moses in Deut. 18:15, 18 (cf. Acts 3:22; 7:37) and was expected in Jesus' day (John 6:14; 7:40). John denied being this Prophet as well (though he was a prophet; see Matt. 11:11–14; John 10:40–41).

1:23 John is **the voice of one crying out in the wilderness**, in keeping with the prophet Isaiah's words (Isa. 40:3; cf. Matt. 3:3; Mark 1:3; Luke 3:4). By preaching a word of repentance and divine judgment, this messenger of God was to prepare the way for the **Lord** God of the OT (Yahweh himself) to come to his people through the wilderness.

1:24 Pharisees. A relatively small but highly influential group of Jews who emphasized meticulous observance of God's law (as understood both from the OT laws and from their accumulated extrabiblical traditions) as the means by which one attains righteousness before God and retains his favor. Many Pharisees opposed Jesus (see Matt. 23:1–36, where Jesus condemns their hypocrisy), but some followed him (John 3:1–5; 7:50; 19:38–40; cf. Acts 23:6; Phil. 3:5). See note on Matt. 3:7.

1:27 sandal. Leather sandals with ties are pictured in ancient art representing Judeans from various eras. Some archaeological examples of sandals are known from this period (e.g., from the Cave of Letters in the Judean desert).

1:28 John was baptizing. Cf. Luke 3:3. John's baptism was an outward sign of cleansing reflecting inward repentance from sins (see Matt. 3:6; cf. later Christian baptisms at Matt. 28:19; Rom. 6:3; 1 Pet. 3:21). The **Bethany across the Jordan** (cf. John 10:40) is different from the village near Jerusalem where Lazarus was raised (cf. 11:1, 18); this Bethany is designated as "across" (i.e., east of) the Jordan River (cf. 3:26; 10:40).

1:29 Cf. v. 36. Regarding **the next day**, see note on 2:1. **Jesus**, by his sacrifice, fulfills the symbolism of the Passover lamb and other OT sacrifices (Lev. 1:1–5:19; 1 Cor. 5:7; Eph. 5:2; Heb. 10:1–14). Deliverance through the blood of a lamb prefigured the coming of Jesus as the **Lamb of God** to obtain final salvation for God's people through his death, which in turn redeemed them from death, sin, and Satan (Col. 1:13–14; Heb. 2:14–15). See also Isa. 53:7 and other OT passages about sacrifices for sins (Gen. 22:8; Lev. 14:25; 16:15–22). This lamb imagery will later culminate in John's vision of Jesus as the apocalyptic warrior Lamb who will bring judgment and universal victory (Rev. 5:6–13; 7:17; 21:22–23; 22:1–3). **Takes away the sin of the world** refers to Jesus' sacrificial, substitutionary death and his appeasement of the divine wrath by way of atonement for sin (his propitiation; cf. Rom. 3:25; Heb. 2:17; 1 John 2:2; 4:10; and notes on 1 Pet. 2:24; 3:18).

1:31 I myself did not know him. John probably means that he did not know that Jesus was the Messiah until he saw the sign mentioned in vv. 32–33.

1:32–34 The Spirit did not merely **descend** on Jesus, he **remained on him** (cf. 3:34), a sign of Jesus' divine anointing. In the OT, the Spirit came upon people to enable them to accomplish certain God-given tasks. But Isaiah predicted that the Messiah would be full of the Spirit at all times (Isa. 11:2; 61:1; cf. Luke 4:18). Jesus is God himself, the second person of the Trinity, with an eternal relation of sonship to God the Father (cf. John 5:18; 17:5; Gal. 4:4). See note on John 5:31–47.

1:36 Lamb of God. See note on v. 29.

Jesus Is God: Specific Examples Where Greek *Theos* ("God") Is Applied to Jesus

John 1:1	In the beginning was the Word, and the Word was with God, and the Word was *God*.
John 1:18	No one has ever seen God; the only *God*, who is at the Father's side, he has made him known.
John 20:28	Thomas answered him, "My Lord and my *God*!"
Rom. 9:5	To them belong the patriarchs, and from their race, according to the flesh, is the Christ who is *God* over all, blessed forever. Amen.
Titus 2:13	. . . waiting for our blessed hope, the appearing of the glory of our great *God* and Savior Jesus Christ . . .
Heb. 1:8	But of the Son he says, "Your throne, O *God*, is forever and ever, the scepter of uprightness is the scepter of your kingdom."
2 Pet. 1:1	To those who have obtained a faith of equal standing with ours by the righteousness of our *God* and Savior Jesus Christ . . .

say this, and they followed Jesus. **38** Jesus turned and saw them following and said to them,
[j]"What are you seeking?" And they said to him, [k]"Rabbi" (which means Teacher), "where
are you staying?" **39** He said to them, "Come and you will see." So they came and saw where
he was staying, and they stayed with him that day, for it was about the tenth hour.[1] **40** [l]One
of the two who heard John speak and followed Jesus[2] was Andrew, Simon Peter's brother.
41 He first found his own brother Simon and said to him, "We have found [m]the Messiah"
(which means Christ). **42** He brought him to Jesus. Jesus looked at him and said, "You are
Simon the son of [n]John. You shall be called [o]Cephas" (which means [p]Peter[3]).

Jesus Calls Philip and Nathanael

43 [q]The next day Jesus decided [r]to go to Galilee. He found Philip and said to him, "Follow
me." **44** Now [s]Philip was from Bethsaida, the city of Andrew and Peter. **45** Philip found
[t]Nathanael and said to him, "We have found him of whom [u]Moses in the Law and also
the prophets wrote, Jesus [v]of Nazareth, [w]the son of Joseph." **46** Nathanael said to him, [x]"Can
anything good come out of Nazareth?" Philip said to him, "Come and see." **47** Jesus saw
Nathanael coming toward him and said of him, "Behold, [y]an Israelite indeed, [z]in whom
there is no deceit!" **48** Nathanael said to him, "How [a]do you know me?" Jesus answered
him, "Before Philip called you, when you were under the fig tree, I saw you." **49** Nathanael
answered him, [b]"Rabbi, [c]you are the Son of God! You are the [d]King of Israel!" **50** Jesus
answered him, "Because I said to you, 'I saw you under the fig tree,' do you believe? You
will see greater things than these." **51** And he said to him, "Truly, truly, I say to you,[4] you
will see [e]heaven opened, and [f]the angels of God ascending and descending on [g]the Son
of Man."

The Wedding at Cana

2 On [h]the third day there was a wedding at [i]Cana in Galilee, and the mother of Jesus
was there. **2** Jesus also was invited to the wedding with [j]his disciples. **3** When the wine
ran out, the mother of Jesus said to him, "They have no wine." **4** And Jesus said to her,

38 [j]ch. 18:4, 7; 20:15 [k]ver. 49; ch. 3:2, 26; 6:25; [ch. 20:16; Mark 10:51]
40 [l]For ver. 40-42, [Matt. 4:18-22; Mark 1:16-20; Luke 5:2-11]
41 [m]ch. 4:25
42 [n]ch. 21:15-17 [o]1 Cor. 1:12; 3:22 [p]Matt. 16:18
43 [q][ver. 35; ch. 2:1] [r][ver. 28]
44 [s]ch. 12:21
45 [t]ch. 21:2 [u]See Luke 16:16; 24:27 [v]See Matt. 2:23 [w]ch. 6:42; Luke 3:23
46 [x][ch. 7:41, 52]
47 [y]Ps. 73:1; Rom. 9:4, 6 [z]Ps. 32:2; [Zeph. 3:13; Rev. 14:5]
48 [a]ch. 2:24, 25
49 [b]See ver. 38 [c][ch. 6:69; 11:27; 20:28] [d]ch. 12:13; Zeph. 3:15; Matt. 27:11, 42; [Zech. 9:9]
51 [e]Ezek. 1:1; Matt. 3:16; Luke 3:21 [f][Gen. 28:12] [g]See Dan. 7:13

Chapter 2

1 [h][ch. 1:29, 35, 43] [i]ch. 4:46; 21:2
2 [j]ch. 1:40-49

[1] That is, about 4 P.M. [2] Greek *him* [3] *Cephas* and *Peter* are from the word for *rock* in Aramaic and Greek, respectively [4] The Greek for *you* is plural; twice in this verse

1:38 "Rabbi" (which means Teacher) is one of seven Hebrew/Aramaic terms translated by John for his readers.

1:40 One of the two . . . was Andrew. The name of the other disciple is not stated. Most likely, he was John the son of Zebedee (see Introduction: Author and Title).

1:41 The terms **Messiah** (Hb.) and **Christ** (Gk.) both mean "anointed" (usually by God). In the NT and early Judaism, "Messiah" is a summary term that gathers up many strands of OT expectations about a coming "anointed one" who would lead and teach and save God's people, especially the great King and Savior in the line of David whom the OT promised (see, e.g., 2 Sam. 7:5–16; Ps. 110:1–4; Isa. 9:6–7).

1:42 Cephas is an Aramaic word meaning "rock" (cf. Matt. 16:16–18; cf. also note on John 1:38). In Bible times, God frequently changed people's names to indicate their special calling, as was the case with Abram (Abraham) and Jacob (Israel); see Gen. 17:5; 32:28.

1:43 Galilee. See note on Mark 1:9.

1:44 Bethsaida. See note on Luke 9:10.

1:45 Nathanael is also mentioned in 21:2. "Nathanael" may be the personal name of Bartholomew (Bar-Tholomaios, "son of Tholomaios"), who is linked with Philip in all three Synoptic lists of apostles (Matt. 10:3; Mark 3:18; Luke 6:14). **The Law and . . . the prophets** commonly referred to the Jewish Scriptures (i.e., the OT) in their entirety (e.g., Matt. 5:17; 7:12).

1:46 Nazareth. Not mentioned in the OT, Nazareth was a small town of no more than 2,000 people in Jesus' day. See note on Luke 1:26.

1:48 I saw you. Jesus here displays supernatural knowledge, thus identifying himself as the Messiah. **fig tree**. See note on Mark 11:13–14.

1:49 Son of God designates Jesus as the Messiah predicted in the OT (2 Sam. 7:14; Ps. 2:7; see note on John 1:14). **King of Israel** likewise is an OT designation for the Messiah (e.g., Zeph. 3:15). The two terms are also found side by side in Matt. 27:42–43.

1:51 Truly, truly, I say to you is a solemn affirmation stressing the authoritative nature and importance of Jesus' pronouncements. The expression is found 25 times in this Gospel. The two references to "you" here are plural. **See heaven opened, and the angels of God ascending and descending** recalls the story of Jacob in Genesis 28 (see esp. v. 12). Jesus will be a greater way of access to God than the heavenly ladder on which angels traveled between God and Jacob (Gen. 28:12; cf. Heb. 10:19–20), and wherever Jesus is, that place will become the "New Bethel" where God is revealed. Jesus is not merely "a son of man" (an ordinary male human being), but he repeatedly (over 80 times in the Gospels) calls himself **the Son of Man**, suggesting the greatest, most notable son of man of all time. "The Son of Man" is thus a messianic title that refers back to the mysterious, human-divine figure of "one like a son of man" in Dan. 7:13–14, one who would be given rule over all the nations of the earth forever (cf. Matt. 26:64). The Son of Man will be "lifted up" by being crucified (see note on John 3:14), will provide divine revelation (6:27), and will act with end-time authority (5:27; 9:39).

2:1 This is the **third day**—that is, two days after Jesus' encounter with Nathanael (1:43–51). This continues the narration of Jesus' activities spanning an entire week (see the references to "the next day" in 1:29, 35, 43). **Cana in Galilee**. Archaeological attention has focused on the excavation site of Khirbet Kana, 8.3 miles (13 km) north of Nazareth, as the most likely locale for the Roman town of Cana. Excavation of this site has revealed substantial quantities of Roman potsherds, thus confirming Roman-era occupation; it also features a prime location on the Roman road from Ptolemais to Magdala.

2:3 The wedding party's running out of wine may be seen as symbolizing the spiritual barrenness of first-century Judaism, especially against an OT background that viewed wine (but never drunkenness) as a sign of joy and God's blessing (Ps. 104:15; Prov. 3:10; cf. Matt. 26:29).

2:4 Jesus' address for his mother, **Woman**, is an expression of polite distance, as is his question to her. **My hour has not yet come**. In John, Jesus' "hour" is the time of his crucifixion, at which time his saving work is accomplished in his atoning death (see 7:30; 8:20; 12:23, 27; 13:1; 17:1; also note on 7:30). At this point in his ministry, because of people's misconceptions about the

4 [k]ch. 19:26 [l]See 2 Sam. 16:10 [m]ch. 7:30; 8:20; 13:1
6 [n]ch. 3:25; [Mark 7:3, 4] [o]2 Chr. 4:5 (Gk.)
9 [p]ch. 4:46
11 [q]See ch. 1:14 [r]ver. 2
12 [s]See Matt. 12:46
13 [t]ch. 11:55; See ch. 6:4 [u]ver. 23; Deut. 16:1-6; Luke 2:41
14 [v]For ver. 14-17, [Matt. 21:12, 13; Mark 11:15-17; Luke 19:45, 46, with Mal. 3:1-3]
16 [w][ch. 14:2; Luke 2:49]
17 [x]Cited from Ps. 69:9

[k]"Woman, [l]what does this have to do with me? [m]My hour has not yet come." **5** His mother
said to the servants, "Do whatever he tells you."
6 Now there were six stone water jars there [n]for the Jewish rites of purification, each
holding twenty or thirty [o]gallons.[1] **7** Jesus said to the servants, "Fill the jars with water."
And they filled them up to the brim. **8** And he said to them, "Now draw some out and take
it to the master of the feast." So they took it. **9** When the master of the feast tasted [p]the water
now become wine, and did not know where it came from (though the servants who had
drawn the water knew), the master of the feast called the bridegroom **10** and said to him,
"Everyone serves the good wine first, and when people have drunk freely, then the poor
wine. But you have kept the good wine until now." **11** This, the first of his signs, Jesus did
at Cana in Galilee, and manifested [q]his glory. And [r]his disciples believed in him.
12 After this he went down to Capernaum, with his mother and [s]his brothers[2] and his
disciples, and they stayed there for a few days.

Jesus Cleanses the Temple

13 [t]The Passover of the Jews was at hand, and Jesus [u]went up to Jerusalem. **14** [v]In the temple
he found those who were selling oxen and sheep and pigeons, and the money-changers
sitting there. **15** And making a whip of cords, he drove them all out of the temple, with
the sheep and oxen. And he poured out the coins of the money-changers and overturned
their tables. **16** And he told those who sold the pigeons, "Take these things away; do not
make [w]my Father's house a house of trade." **17** His disciples remembered that it was written, [x]"Zeal for your house will consume me."

[1] Greek *two or three measures* (*metrētas*); a *metrētēs* was about 10 gallons or 35 liters [2] Or *brothers and sisters*. The plural Greek word *adelphoi* (translated "brothers") refers to siblings in a family. In New Testament usage, depending on the context, *adelphoi* may refer either to *brothers* or to *brothers and sisters*

coming Messiah, Jesus chooses not to reveal himself openly to Israel (though he does perform numerous messianic "signs"; see note on 2:11). Even this miracle is done quietly. Compared to the other Gospels, John places less emphasis on Jesus' public ministry and more emphasis on his private ministry to specific individuals.

2:6 six stone water jars. Archaeologists have found large goblet-shaped stone storage jars from this period in Jerusalem and elsewhere. The examples were lathe-cut from sizable single blocks of stone.

2:11 signs. Miracles that attest to Jesus' identity as Messiah and Son of God and lead unbelievers to faith. John specifies that after this sign, Jesus' **disciples believed in him** (cf. v. 23). The statement that this was **the first** of his signs indicates that Jesus did not do any miracles during his childhood or early manhood (contrary to dozens of apocryphal "gospel stories" outside the NT) but lived as an ordinary man with his divine identity hidden (cf. 7:5). In each of the signs that John includes, the emphasis is on the way in which the "sign" reveals Jesus' messianic character (cf. 12:37–40; 20:30–31) and on the exceptional and striking nature of the feat accomplished by Jesus—such as the large quantity and high quality of wine (2:6, 10), the fact that the official's son is healed a long distance away by the sheer power of Jesus' word (4:47, 49–50), the invalid's recovery from a 38-year-long ordeal (5:5), the large quantity of food produced by Jesus (6:13), the man's recovery from lifelong blindness (9:1–2), and the raising of Lazarus after four days in the tomb (11:17, 39). **and manifested his glory**. This miracle showed the glory of Jesus as the sovereign Creator and ruler of the material universe and also as the merciful God who provides abundantly for his people's needs (cf. 1:14).

2:12–4:54 *Jesus' Ministry in Jerusalem, Judea, Samaria, and to Gentiles.* Jesus' Jerusalem ministry commences with the clearing of the temple. The bulk of chs. 3 and 4 features two major encounters, one with a representative of the Jewish religious establishment (Nicodemus, 3:1–21), and one with the Samaritan religion (a Samaritan woman, 4:1–26). The section concludes with Jesus' ministry to a Gentile official (4:43–54).

2:12 Jesus **went down** from Cana to Capernaum, since Cana was in the hill country while Capernaum was at the Sea of Galilee. **Capernaum** is about 16 miles (26 km) to the northeast of Cana and could easily be reached in a day's journey (see note on Mark 1:21). Capernaum served as Jesus' headquarters after the Baptist's imprisonment (Matt. 4:12–13; Luke 4:28–31; cf. Matt. 9:1).

2:13–22 The first major confrontation with the Jewish leaders in John's Gospel takes place on the occasion of Jesus' clearing of the Jerusalem temple at the Jewish Passover. (The Synoptic Gospels record a second, later temple clearing,

Seven Signs Pointing to Jesus as the Messiah

The first half of John's Gospel features Jesus' demonstration of his messianic identity by way of seven selected signs (cf. 20:30–31):

Changing water into wine	2:1–11
Healing the official's son	4:46–54
Healing the invalid	5:1–15
Feeding the multitude	6:5–13
Walking on the water*	6:16–21
Healing the man born blind	9:1–7
Raising Lazarus	11:1–44

**John does not explicitly identify this event as a sign.*

just prior to the crucifixion; see Mark 11:15–19 par.) By clearing the temple, Jesus displays prophetic zeal for God's house (John 2:17; cf. Ps. 69:9) and foreshadows judgment on the Jewish leaders who had allowed worship to deteriorate into commerce, rendering prayer difficult in the temple (see note on John 2:14).

2:13 Here and in v. 23 are the first references to a Jewish festival in John's Gospel and the first references to the Jewish **Passover** (see Ex. 12:1–28). Later, John refers to two more Passovers—at John 6:4 (Jesus in Galilee) and 11:55; 12:1 (Jesus' final Passover in Jerusalem). Apart from these Passover references, John also mentions Jesus' activities at an unnamed Jewish festival in 5:1 (possibly Tabernacles), at the Feast of Tabernacles (or Booths) in 7:2, and at the Feast of Dedication (or Hanukkah) in 10:22. People **went up** to Jerusalem because it was located at a higher elevation than Galilee and because it was the capital.

2:14 Temple (Gk. *hieron*) denotes the area surrounding the temple, including the Court of the Gentiles, in distinction from the temple building proper (Gk. *naos*), from which non-Jews were excluded. By selling **oxen**, **sheep**, and **pigeons**, the merchants, as well as the **money-changers**, rendered a service to those who had traveled to Jerusalem from afar, enabling them to buy the animals on-site rather than having to carry them for long distances. By conducting their business in the temple complex, however, these individuals disrupted the worship of non-Jewish God-fearers (see note on 12:20) and thus obstructed the very purpose for which the temple existed.

18So the Jews said to him, [y]"What sign do you show us for doing these things?" 19Jesus
answered them, [z]"Destroy this temple, and in three days [a]I will raise it up." 20The Jews
then said, "It has taken forty-six years to build this temple,[1] and will you raise it up in
three days?" 21But he was speaking about [b]the temple of his body. 22When therefore he was
raised from the dead, [c]his disciples remembered that he had said this, and they believed
[d]the Scripture and the word that Jesus had spoken.

Jesus Knows What Is in Man

23Now when he was in Jerusalem at the Passover Feast, many believed in his name [e]when
they saw the signs that he was doing. 24But Jesus [f]on his part did not entrust himself to
them, because [g]he knew all people 25and needed no one to bear witness about man, for
[g]he himself knew what was in man.

You Must Be Born Again

3 Now there was a man of the Pharisees named [h]Nicodemus, [i]a ruler of the Jews. 2This
man came to Jesus[2] [j]by night and said to him, [k]"Rabbi, [l]we know that you are a teacher
come from God, for no one can do these signs that you do [m]unless God is with him." 3Jesus

[1] Or *This temple was built forty-six years ago* [2] Greek *him*

18 [y]ch. 4:48; 6:30; [Ex. 4:1, 8; 7:9]; See Matt. 12:38
19 [z][Matt. 26:61; 27:40; Mark 14:58; 15:29] [a]ch. 10:18
21 [b][ch. 1:14; 1 Cor. 6:19; Col. 2:9]
22 [c]ch. 12:16; Luke 24:8 [d]ch. 20:9; Ps. 16:10
23 [e]ch. 11:45
24 [f][ch. 6:14, 15] [g]ch. 1:48; 5:42; 16:30; [ch. 6:61, 64]; See Matt. 9:4
25 [g][See ver. 24 above]

Chapter 3

1 [h]ch. 7:50; 19:39 [i]See Luke 24:20
2 [j][ch. 12:42] [k]See ch. 1:38 [l][ch. 9:29; Matt. 22:16] [m]Acts 10:38; [ch. 5:36; 9:33; Acts 2:22]

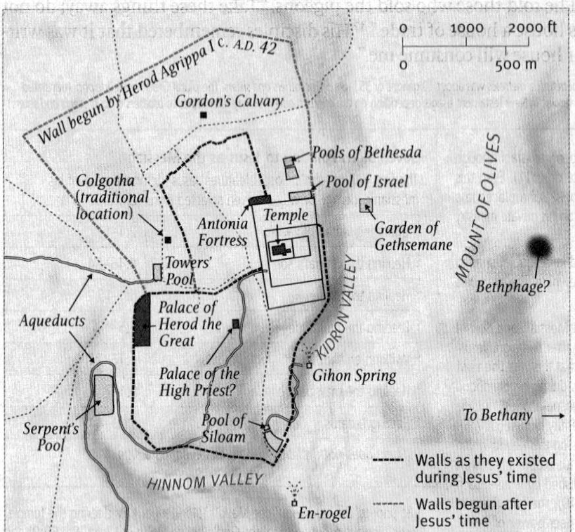

Jerusalem at the Time of Jesus
Herod the Great and his successors renovated the city of Jerusalem and the temple. Public pools were fed by the Gihon Spring and by two aqueducts that brought water from as far as 7 miles (11 km) away. The towns of Bethphage and Bethany were located on the eastern slopes of the Mount of Olives, to the east of Jerusalem. See also Jerusalem in the Time of Jesus, pp. 1878–1879.

2:19 I will raise it up implies that Jesus himself would have a part in raising himself from the dead, though other verses mention that the Father and the Holy Spirit were also involved (see Acts 2:24; Rom. 6:4; 1 Cor. 6:14; Gal. 1:1; Eph. 1:20; also Rom. 1:4; 8:11; and note on John 10:17). In fact, Jesus says that he is "the resurrection and the life" (11:25).

2:20 forty-six years. Herod the Great's construction of the **temple** proper (Gk. *naos*; see note on v. 14) lasted from 20/19 to 18/17 B.C., but the larger temple area (Gk. *hieron*) was not finished until A.D. 66. Some scholars favor an alternative translation: "This temple (Gk. *naos*) was built forty-six years ago," which would date this statement in A.D. 29/30, since there was no year "0" (see The Date of Jesus' Crucifixion, pp. 1809–1810).

2:23–25 This section serves as an introduction to Jesus' encounter with Nicodemus in ch. 3. **Believed** and **did not entrust himself** constitutes a wordplay in Greek (both use the verb *pisteuō*). Jesus **knew all people**, an affirmation of divine omniscience. His knowledge of people's hearts is displayed in his encounters with Nicodemus and the Samaritan woman in chs. 3 and 4.

3:1 Ruler of the Jews refers to a member of the Jewish governing body called the Sanhedrin.

3:2 Nicodemus comes to Jesus **by night**, which usually carries a symbolic overtone of spiritual darkness elsewhere in John (9:4; 11:10; 13:30; but not 21:3). Coming from the "teacher of Israel" (3:10), the address **Rabbi** (meaning "teacher") denotes respect, especially since it was known that Jesus did not have formal rabbinic training (cf. 7:15). The **signs** presumably include many miracles performed by Jesus in Jerusalem (cf. 2:23).

3:3–6 This discussion of the need for spiritual rebirth further develops the earlier reference to the "children of God" who are "born of God" (1:12–13; cf. 8:39–58; 11:51–52). The phrase **born of water and the Spirit** in 3:5 refers to spiritual birth, which cleanses from sin and brings spiritual transformation and renewal. Water here does not refer to the water of physical birth, nor is it likely that it refers to baptism. The background is probably Ezek. 36:25–27, where God promises, "I will sprinkle clean water on you, and you shall be clean. . . . And I will give you a new heart. . . . And I will put my Spirit within you." For further discussion of being **born again**, see 1 John 2:29; 3:9; 4:7; 5:1, 4, 18. The

answered him, "Truly, truly, I say to you, unless one is [n]born [o]again[1] he cannot [p]see the
kingdom of God." **4** Nicodemus said to him, "How can a man be born when he is old? Can
he enter a second time into his mother's womb and be born?" **5** Jesus answered, "Truly,
truly, I say to you, unless one is born [q]of water and the Spirit, he cannot enter the kingdom
of God. **6** [r]That which is born of the flesh is [s]flesh, and that which is born of the Spirit is
spirit.[2] **7** [t]Do not marvel that I said to you, 'You[3] must be born [u]again.' **8** [v]The wind[4] blows
[w]where it wishes, and you hear its sound, but you do not know where it comes from or
where it goes. So it is with everyone who is born of the Spirit."

9 Nicodemus said to him, [x]"How can these things be?" **10** Jesus answered him, "Are you
the teacher of Israel [y]and yet you do not understand these things? **11** Truly, truly, I say to
you, [z]we speak of what we know, and bear witness to what we have seen, but [z]you[5] do
not receive our testimony. **12** If I have told you earthly things and you do not believe, how
can you believe if I tell you heavenly things? **13** [a]No one has [b]ascended into heaven except
[c]he who descended from heaven, the Son of Man.[6] **14** And [d]as Moses lifted up the serpent
in the wilderness, so must the Son of Man [e]be lifted up, **15** that whoever believes [f]in him
[g]may have eternal life.[7]

For God So Loved the World

16 "For [h]God so loved [i]the world,[8] [j]that he gave his only Son, that whoever believes in
him should not [k]perish but have eternal life. **17** For [l]God did not send his Son into the
world [m]to condemn the world, but in order that the world might be saved through him.
18 [n]Whoever believes in him is not condemned, but whoever does not believe is condemned
already, because he has not [o]believed in the name of the only Son of God. **19** [p]And this is the
judgment: [q]the light has come into the world, and [r]people loved the darkness rather than

3 [n]See ch. 1:13 [o][2 Cor. 5:17; Gal. 6:15; 1 Pet. 1:3, 23] [p]ver. 36
5 [q][Ezek. 36:25-27; Mark 16:16; Acts 2:38; Eph. 5:26; Titus 3:5; Heb. 10:22]
6 [r]1 Cor. 15:50 [s]ch. 6:63
7 [t]ch. 5:28 [u]See ver. 3
8 [v][Eccles. 11:5; Ezek. 37:9] [w]1 Cor. 12:11
9 [x]ch. 6:52, 60
10 [y][ch. 9:30]
11 [z]See ver. 32
13 [a]Prov. 30:4; [Acts 2:34; Eph. 4:9] [b][ch. 7:34] [c]ver. 31; ch. 6:38, 42, 62; 1 Cor. 15:47; [Rom. 10:6]
14 [d]Num. 21:9 [e]ch. 8:28; 12:32, 34
15 [f][ch. 15:4; 16:33; 1 John 5:12, 20] [g]ver. 36
16 [h]Rom. 5:8; Eph. 2:4; 2 Thess. 2:16; 1 John 3:1; 4:9, 10 [i]See ch. 1:29 [j]Rom. 8:32 [k]ch. 10:28
17 [l]ch. 5:36, 38; 6:29, 57; 7:29; 8:42; 10:36; 11:42; 17:3; 20:21; Rom. 8:3; 1 John 4:9, 10, 14 [m]ch. 5:45; 8:15; 12:47
18 [n]ch. 5:24; [Mark 16:16] [o]See 1 John 5:13
19 [p][ch. 9:39] [q]See ch. 1:4, 5, 9 [r][Isa. 30:10; Jer. 5:31]

[1] Or *from above*; the Greek is purposely ambiguous and can mean both *again* and *from above*; also verse 7 [2] The same Greek word means both *wind* and *spirit* [3] The Greek for *you* is plural here [4] The same Greek word means both *wind* and *spirit* [5] The Greek for *you* is plural here; also four times in verse 12 [6] Some manuscripts add *who is in heaven* [7] Some interpreters hold that the quotation ends at verse 15 [8] Or *For this is how God loved the world*

kingdom of God, a major topic in the other Gospels, is mentioned in John only in 3:3, 5 (see the reference to Jesus' kingdom in John 18:36).

3:7–8 The change from singular to plural in **I said to you** [singular], **"You** [plural] **must be born again,"** probably is meant to include Nicodemus and his fellow Sanhedrin members (cf. "we" in v. 2), but the plural also carries broader application to all people: everyone "must be born again." **Wind** and **Spirit** translate the same Greek and Hebrew words.

3:10 As a prominent teacher (**the teacher of Israel**), Nicodemus should be able to understand Jesus, since this new life is like the resurrection depicted in Ezekiel 37 and the new heart in Deut. 30:6; Jer. 31:33; and Ezek. 36:26.

3:11–12 Earthly things probably refers to Jesus' teaching about the new birth, which takes place in a person's life on earth. If Nicodemus as a teacher cannot even understand this, then Jesus cannot convey deeper truths to him. **You** is plural (in Gk.) in the second instance in v. 11, and all four times in v. 12.

3:13 Ascended into heaven probably means "entered into the counsels of God in heaven and remained there." When Jesus **descended from heaven** it does not mean that in his omnipresent, divine personhood he completely left all fellowship with the Father, but rather that the focus of his activity became his earthly life as one who was now both God and man.

3:14 The reference to the Son of Man being **lifted up** is the first of three "lifted up" sayings in John's Gospel (cf. 8:28; 12:32). All three sayings speak of the future "lifting up" of the Son of Man in a typical Johannine double meaning (see notes on 4:10; 8:24; 11:50–51; 19:19; cf. also 3:7–8), so that it refers to both Jesus' death and his resurrection and exaltation to glory in heaven (cf. Acts 2:33; 5:31). Regarding the **serpent in the wilderness**, see Num. 21:9; but cf. Isa. 52:13 also.

3:16 Here is the most famous summary of the gospel in the entire Bible. **For** connects to v. 15 and explains what happened to make it possible that someone can "have eternal life" (v. 15), that is, through believing in Christ. **God so loved the world** was an astounding statement in that context because the OT and other Jewish writings had spoken only of God's love for his people Israel. God's love for "the world" made it possible for "whoever" (v. 15) believes in Christ, not Jews alone, to have eternal life. God's love for the world was not mere sentiment but led to a specific action: he **gave his only Son**, which John elsewhere explains as sending him to earth as a man (v. 17) to suffer and die and thereby to bear the penalty for sins (see note on 1 John 2:2; cf. Rom. 3:25). On "only Son," see note on John 1:14, which contains the same Greek phrase. The purpose of giving his Son was to make God's great gift of eternal life available to anyone—to **whoever believes in him**, that is, whoever personally trusts in him (see note on 11:25). **Not perish** means not perish in eternal judgment, in contrast to having **eternal life**, the life of abundant joy and immeasurable blessing in the presence of God forever. Those who "believe in" Christ **have** that "eternal life" and already experience its blessings in this present time, not yet fully, but in some significant measure.

3:17 send his Son. John's favorite designation of Jesus is that of the Son "sent" by the Father (see also vv. 34–36; 5:19–26; 6:40; 8:35–36; 14:13; 17:1). There was a familiar concept in Jewish life that the messenger is like the sender himself (Mishnah, *Berakoth* 5.5; cf. John 13:16, 20). Jesus is that Sent One par excellence (cf. 9:7), and in 20:21–22 he in turn sends his disciples (see note there). Being sent (in the case of both Jesus and his followers) implies that the commission, charge, and message are issued by the sender rather than originating with the one who is sent. This verse refers to Christ's first coming. He will return to judge the world at his second coming (5:27–29).

3:18 Those who do **not believe** and trust in Christ have neither a positive nor a neutral standing before God. They stand **condemned already** before God for their sins because they have not trusted God's solution for guilt, **the only Son of God**. This verse also refutes the assertion that a sincere person following any religion can have eternal life with God (cf. 14:6; Acts 4:12; Rom. 10:13–17; 1 Tim. 2:5–6; regarding OT believers who looked forward to Christ, see John 8:56; Rom. 4:1–24; Heb. 11:13, 26).

3:19–21 This elaborates on the prologue's reference to the world's darkness and unbelief (1:5, 10–11). See also note on 8:12. The evil of human beings is reflected in their fleeing from the light; at the same time, anything good is the product of God's work.

the light because [s]their works were evil. 20 [t]For everyone who does wicked things hates the
light and does not come to the light, [u]lest his works should be exposed. 21 But whoever
[v]does what is true [w]comes to the light, so that it may be clearly seen that his works have
been carried out in God."

John the Baptist Exalts Christ

22 After this Jesus and his disciples went into the Judean countryside, and he remained
there with them and [x]was baptizing. 23 John also was baptizing at Aenon near Salim, because
water was plentiful there, and people were coming and being baptized 24 (for [y]John had
not yet been put in prison).

25 Now a discussion arose between some of John's disciples and a Jew over [z]purification.
26 And they came to John and said to him, [a]"Rabbi, he who was with you across the Jordan,
[b]to whom you bore witness—look, he is baptizing, and [c]all are going to him." 27 John
answered, [d]"A person cannot receive even one thing [e]unless it is given him [f]from heaven.
28 You yourselves bear me witness, that I said, [g]'I am not the Christ, but [h]I have been sent
before him.' 29 [i]The one who has the bride is the bridegroom. [j]The friend of the bridegroom,
who stands and hears him, [k]rejoices greatly at the bridegroom's voice. Therefore this joy
of mine is now complete. 30 [l]He must increase, but I must decrease."[1]

31 [m]He who comes from above [n]is above all. He who is of the earth belongs to the earth
and [o]speaks in an earthly way. [p]He who comes from heaven [n]is above all. 32 [q]He bears witness
to what he has seen and heard, [r]yet no one receives his testimony. 33 Whoever receives his
testimony [s]sets his seal to this, [t]that God is true. 34 For he whom [u]God has sent utters the
words of God, for he gives the Spirit [v]without measure. 35 [w]The Father loves the Son and
[x]has given all things into his hand. 36 [y]Whoever believes in the Son has eternal life; [z]whoever
does not obey the Son shall not [a]see life, but the wrath of God remains on him.

[1] Some interpreters hold that the quotation continues through verse 36

19 [s]ch. 7:7
20 [t][Job 24:13; Rom. 13:12; Eph. 5:13] [u]Eph. 5:11, 13
21 [v]1 John 1:6 [w]Ps. 139:23, 24
22 [x]ver. 26; ch. 4:1, 2
24 [y][ch. 5:35]; See Matt. 4:12
25 [z]ch. 2:6
26 [a]ver. 2 [b]See ch. 1:7 [c]ch. 12:19
27 [d]1 Cor. 4:7; Heb. 5:4 [e]ch. 6:65; [James 1:17] [f]See Matt. 21:25
28 [g]See ch. 1:20 [h]Mal. 3:1; Mark 1:2; Luke 1:17; Acts 19:4
29 [i]See Matt. 25:1 [j]Judg. 14:20; Song 5:1 [k]Matt. 9:15
30 [l]Matt. 3:11
31 [m]ch. 8:23 [n]Rom. 9:5; Eph. 1:21 [o][1 John 4:5] [p]See ver. 13
32 [q]ver. 11 [r][ver. 19; ch. 1:11; 5:43; 12:37]
33 [s][ch. 6:27; 2 Cor. 1:22; Eph. 1:13; Rev. 7:3-8] [t][1 John 5:10]
34 [u]See ver. 17 [v][Ezek. 4:11, 16]
35 [w]See ch. 5:20 [x]See Matt. 28:18
36 [y]ver. 15, 16; ch. 5:24; 6:40, 47, 54; 1 John 5:12, 13; [ch. 11:25, 26; 20:31]; See Matt. 19:16 [z][Rom. 2:8; Eph. 5:6; Col. 3:6] [a]ver. 3

3:22 Jesus **was baptizing**, that is, overseeing his disciples (see 4:2) as they continued administering the baptism of John, which was based on repentance and which symbolized purification from sin (see note on 1:28).

3:24 John had not yet been put in prison alerts readers to the fact that everything that has happened up to this point in John's Gospel takes place prior to Mark 1:14 ("after John was arrested").

3:28 The Baptist's assertion that he has been **sent before** the Messiah alludes to Mal. 3:1, which is directly applied to the Baptist in Matt. 11:10; Mark 1:2; and Luke 7:27.

3:29 The Baptist's reference to Jesus as **the bridegroom** (cf. Matt. 9:15 par.) identifies Jesus as Israel's long-awaited King and Messiah. In the OT, Israel is frequently depicted as God's "bride" (e.g., Isa. 62:4–5; Jer. 2:2; Hos. 2:16–20). The Baptist's role is that of the bridegroom's **friend**, who selflessly rejoices with the groom (cf. John 1:6–9, 15, 19–36). On Christ as bridegroom, see Eph. 5:25–27; Rev. 19:7–8.

3:30 He must increase, but I must decrease. At this point in salvation history, now that the light has come (1:6–9), the "lamp" has done its work (5:35).

3:32 What he has seen and heard refers to Jesus' eternal existence in heaven and his infinite knowledge of God's nature and counsels. **No one receives his testimony** likely means that very few people (at least to that point) had received it (but some had; see v. 33). See 1:10, 11 for similar generalizations.

3:33 sets his seal. See note on 6:27.

3:34 Cf. 1:32–33. See also Rev. 3:1; 5:6. In this context about the Father sending the Son, John is saying that the Father gives to Jesus the Spirit **without measure**. Others had been and will be empowered by the Spirit to some extent, but Jesus has a measureless anointing from the Spirit.

3:35 The Father . . . has given all things into his hand indicates supreme authority for the Father in the counsels of the Trinity, and a delegated authority over the whole created universe for the Son, as is indicated also in many other NT passages (1:3; 3:16, 17; 5:22; 6:38; 14:16, 28; Acts 2:33; 5:31; Rom. 8:29, 34; 1 Cor. 8:6; 15:28; Eph. 1:4–5; Heb. 1:2, 3, 13; 1 Pet. 3:22).

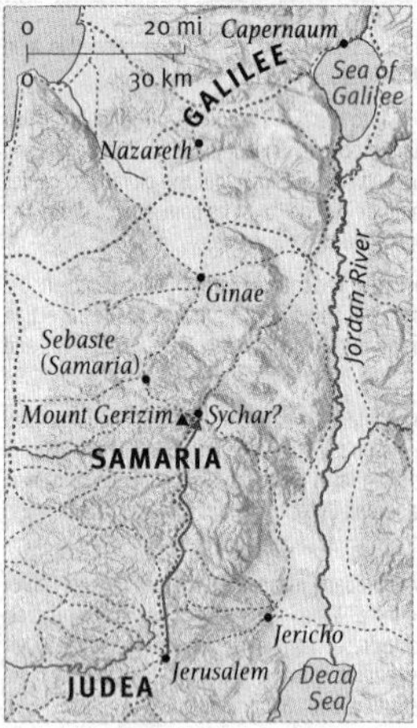

Jesus Travels through Samaria
As they returned from Jerusalem to Galilee, Jesus and his disciples followed the expedient route and passed through Samaria, stopping to rest at the village of Sychar, near the ancient city of Shechem (which no longer existed in NT times). Here Jesus spoke with a Samaritan woman at a well.

Yet at the same time, the Father, Son, and Spirit are fully God in the unity of a single divine being.

3:36 Has eternal life indicates that eternal life is not merely a future expectation but already a present experience. (This is sometimes called John's "realized eschatology," where "eschatology" means the events of the end times and the life of the age to come. In John, this kind of life is partially "realized" or partially made the believer's possession even now in this present age.) **The wrath of God remains on him** makes clear that unless a person believes in Jesus the Messiah, he or she remains under God's judgment (cf. vv. 19–21; Rom. 1:18–25).

Jesus and the Woman of Samaria

4 Now when Jesus learned that the Pharisees had heard that Jesus was making and
[b]baptizing more disciples than John **2**(although Jesus himself did not baptize, but
only his disciples), **3**he left Judea and departed [c]again for Galilee. **4** [d]And he had to pass
through Samaria. **5**So he came to a town of Samaria called Sychar, near the field [e]that Jacob
had given to his son Joseph. **6**Jacob's well was there; so Jesus, [f]wearied as he was from his
journey, was sitting beside the well. It was about the sixth hour.[1]
7A woman from Samaria came to draw water. Jesus said to her, [f]"Give me a drink." **8**(For
his disciples had gone away into the city to buy food.) **9**The Samaritan woman said to him,
"How is it that you, a Jew, ask for a drink from me, a woman of Samaria?" ([g]For Jews have
no dealings with Samaritans.) **10**Jesus answered her, "If you knew the gift of God, and
who it is that is saying to you, 'Give me a drink,' you would have asked him, and he would
have given you [h]living water." **11**The woman said to him, "Sir, you have nothing to draw
water with, and the well is deep. Where do you get that living water? **12** [i]Are you greater
than our father Jacob? [j]He gave us the well and drank from it himself, as did his sons and
his livestock." **13**Jesus said to her, "Everyone who drinks of this water will be thirsty again,
14but [k]whoever drinks of the water that I will give him [l]will never be thirsty again.[2] The
water that I will give him will become [m]in him a spring of water welling up to eternal life."

[1] That is, about noon [2] Greek *forever*

Chapter 4
1 [b]ch. 3:22, 26
3 [c]ch. 2:11, 12
4 [d][Luke 13:33]
5 [e]ver. 12; Gen. 33:19; 48:22; Josh. 24:32
6 [f]ch. 19:28; [Matt. 4:2; 8:24; 21:18]
7 [f][See ver. 6 above]
9 [g]Luke 9:53; [ch. 8:48; Ezra 4:3, 10]; See Matt. 10:5
10 [h]ch. 7:38; Jer. 2:13; 17:13
12 [i][ch. 8:53] [j]ver. 5
14 [k][ch. 6:35, 51, 58; 7:37] [l][Isa. 49:10; Rev. 7:16] [m]ch. 7:38

4:4 Jesus **had to pass** this way because of geography (it was the shortest route), but the words may also indicate that Jesus' itinerary was subject to the sovereign and providential plan of God ("had to" translates Gk. *dei*, "to be necessary," which always indicates divine necessity or requirement elsewhere in John: 3:7, 14, 30; 9:4; 10:16; 12:34; 20:9). **Through Samaria** was the usual route taken by travelers from Judea to Galilee, though strict Jews, in order to avoid defilement, could bypass Samaria by opting for a longer route that involved crossing the Jordan and traveling on the east side. The Samaritans were a racially mixed group of partly Jewish and partly Gentile ancestry, who were disdained by both Jews and non-Jews (see Luke 10:33; 17:16; John 8:48; see also 2 Kings 17:24–31, which describes how the king of Assyria brought foreign people to settle in Samaria in 722 B.C.; over time they had intermarried with some Jews who had remained in the area). See also note on John 4:20–21. Many inhabitants of this region between Judea and Galilee were descendants of the OT northern kingdom of Israel, although from the Jewish perspective these Samaritans had assimilated strongly into non-Jewish culture and had intermarried with Mesopotamian colonists. The Samaritans had their own version of the Pentateuch, their own temple on Mount Gerizim (see 4:20), and their own rendering of Israelite history. Copies of their Pentateuch in Hebrew (and in Targumic Aramaic) remain extant, as do their basic historical narratives. Tensions often ran high between Jews and Samaritans; thus Josephus recounts fighting between Jews and Samaritans during Claudius's reign in the first century A.D. being so intense that Roman soldiers were called in to pacify (and to crucify) many of the rebels (*Jewish War* 2.232–246).

4:5 The village of **Sychar** is usually identified with Askar, which is approximately 0.7 miles (1.2 km) from Jacob's well and on the slope of Mount Ebal. Roman-era tombs are known in this area. The reference to **the field that Jacob had given to his son Joseph** reflects the customary inference from Gen. 48:21–22 and Josh. 24:32 that Jacob gave his son Joseph the land at Shechem, which he had bought from the sons of Hamor (Gen. 33:18–19) and which later served as Joseph's burial place (Ex. 13:19; Josh. 24:32).

4:6 Jacob's well. The probable location for this well lies in modern Nablus—known in the Roman period as Flavia Neapolis and called in the OT by the name Shechem. This well was once covered with vaulted stone and a Byzantine (4th–7th century A.D.) church. It is quite deep (as described in v. 11), although measurements have varied over the years (possibly due to debris in the well). It was also at a juncture of major ancient roads and near the traditional sacred site of Joseph's tomb. The reference to Jesus being **wearied . . . from his journey** underscores his full humanity (see also 11:35; 19:28). Jesus' human nature could be weak and tired, though his divine nature was omnipotent (cf. 1:3, 10). **Sixth hour** refers to noon, when it would have been hot and time to rest, and travelers would be thirsty. Normally, women would come to draw water in the morning or evening when it was cooler (Gen. 24:11; cf. 29:7–8); the immoral woman comes at a time when no one else would be at the well.

4:7 Jesus took the initiative in speaking to a Samaritan woman—an astonishing break with culture and tradition, showing his desire to save the lost.

4:9 The comment that **Jews have no dealings with Samaritans** explains to John's readers outside the land of Palestine that Samaritans were considered by many Jews to be in a continual state of uncleanness, thus they would have thought that drinking water from this woman's water jar would make a person ceremonially unclean. The verb in the phrase rendered "have no dealings" can also have a more specific meaning of "share use of [things]."

4:10 Jesus' words about **living water** again involve double meaning (see notes on 3:14; 8:24; 11:50–51; 19:19; cf. also 3:7–8). Literally, the phrase refers to fresh spring water (Gen. 26:19; Lev. 14:6), but John 7:38–39 identifies this "living water" as the Holy Spirit dwelling within a believer (cf. Jer. 2:13; Ezek. 47:1–6; Zech. 14:8; also Isa. 12:3).

4:11 The **well** today is still over 100 feet (31 m) **deep** and was probably deeper at that time.

4:12 By referring to **our father Jacob** the woman shows that she and her people still think of themselves as true descendants of Jacob (Israel, Gen. 32:28). Clearly the woman does not understand who Jesus is, for then she would understand that he is greater even than Jacob, the father of the 12 tribes of Israel (see Gen. 49:1–28).

4:14 The water that I will give him is the "living water" of v. 10, identified in 7:37–39 as the Holy Spirit dwelling within believers. **never be thirsty again**. A person's deepest spiritual longing to know God personally will, amazingly, be satisfied forever. The phrase **will become in him a spring of water welling up to eternal life** is reminiscent of Isa. 12:3 (see also Isa. 44:3; 55:1–3).

Tangible Images of Believing

John vividly illustrates what it is to believe in Jesus through the use of a number of physical images.

Drinking living water	4:10–14; 7:37–38
Eating the bread of life	6:35, 47–48, 50–51, 53–58
Eating Jesus' flesh and drinking his blood	6:53–56
Walking in and having the light	8:12; 12:35–36
Abiding/remaining in Jesus and his Word	6:56; 8:31; 15:7

15 The woman said to him, "Sir, [n]give me this water, so that I will not be thirsty or have to
come here to draw water."
16 Jesus said to her, "Go, [o]call your husband, and come here." 17 The woman answered him,
"I have no husband." Jesus said to her, "You are right in saying, 'I have no husband'; 18 for you
have had five husbands, and the one you now have is not your husband. What you have said
is true." 19 The woman said to him, "Sir, I perceive that [p]you are [q]a prophet. 20 [r]Our fathers
worshiped on [s]this mountain, but you say that [t]in Jerusalem is [u]the place where people
ought to worship." 21 Jesus said to her, [v]"Woman, believe me, [w]the hour is coming when
[x]neither on this mountain nor in Jerusalem will you worship the Father. 22 [y]You worship
what you do not know; [z]we worship what we know, for [z]salvation is [a]from the Jews. 23 But
[b]the hour is coming, and is now here, when the true worshipers will worship the Father
[c]in spirit and [d]truth, for the Father [e]is seeking such people to worship him. 24 God is spirit,

15 [n][ch. 6:34]
16 [o]ch. 16:8
19 [p]ch. 9:17; [ch. 6:14] [q]Luke 7:16, 39; See Matt. 21:11
20 [r]Gen. 12:6, 7; 33:18, 20; Deut. 11:29; 27:12; Josh. 8:33 [s]Judg. 9:7 [t]See Deut. 12:5 [u][ch. 11:48]
21 [v]ch. 2:4 [w]ver. 23; ch. 5:25, 28; 16:2, 25, 32 [x]Zeph. 2:11; Mal. 1:11; 1 Tim. 2:8
22 [y][2 Kgs. 17:28-34; Acts 17:23] [z]Ps. 147:19, 20; Isa. 2:3; Rom. 3:1, 2; 9:4, 5 [a]Matt. 2:4, 5; Acts 13:23; Rom. 11:26
23 [b]ver. 21 [c][Rom. 8:15; Eph. 2:18; 6:18; Phil. 3:3] [d]Ps. 145:18; [ch. 1:17] [e][ch. 6:44]

4:15 The woman takes Jesus literally and misunderstands him, just as Nicodemus did (see 3:4). In John's Gospel, Jesus frequently speaks in terms of the visible, physical world (birth, water, bread, his body, light) to teach about the unseen spiritual world (see chart below).

4:17 no husband. While technically truthful, the woman's curt statement is probably intended to close the subject. But Jesus, with gentleness and compassion, reveals both her sin and his omniscient knowledge of her life.

4:18 The woman had had **five husbands** who had either died or divorced her. When Jesus says **the one you now have is not your husband**, he implies that merely living together does not constitute a marriage. A marriage requires some kind of official sanction and public ceremony at which a man and woman commit to the obligations of marriage and the community then recognizes that a marriage has begun (see 2:1; also Song 3:11; Mal. 2:14; Matt. 9:15). Sexual relationships prior to marriage were without question thought to be morally wrong (Gen. 38:24; Ex. 22:16; Deut. 22:13–29; Matt. 15:19; John 8:41; Acts 15:20; 1 Cor. 6:18; 7:2, 9; 1 Thess. 4:3; cf. the imagery in 2 Cor. 11:2).

4:20–21 Our fathers worshiped on this mountain. Mount Gerizim (Deut. 11:29; 27:12) was the OT setting for the pronouncement of blessings for keeping the covenant. The Samaritans' version (see note on v. 4) of Deut. 27:4 named Mount Gerizim (rather than Ebal) as the place for the altar; this is where the Samaritans had built their temple. When the woman mentioned the "fathers" who "worshiped" on Mount Gerizim, she may well have included Abraham (Gen. 12:7) and Jacob (Gen. 33:18–20), who built altars in that region. A Samaritan temple on Mount Gerizim was recorded in Josephus (*Jewish Antiquities* 11.310, 346–347; 12:257–264; cf. *2 Macc.* 6:2). It was destroyed by the Hasmonean leader John Hyrcanus during his reign (134–104 B.C.). This temple has been identified by some with a large Hellenistic-era structure made with unhewn stones atop Tel er-Ras at the northern spur of the mountain, although many have suggested that a more probable location is beneath the old Byzantine (4th–7th century A.D.) church atop the mountain itself. Despite the destruction of this temple, Samaritan sacrificial worship has continued atop Mount Gerizim even until the modern era.

4:21 neither on this mountain nor in Jerusalem will you worship the Father. Jesus is inaugurating a new age in which people will not have to travel to a physical temple in one city to worship but will be able to worship God in every place, because the Holy Spirit will dwell in them, and therefore God's people everywhere will become the new temple where God dwells (cf. 1 Cor. 3:16–17; Eph. 2:19–22).

4:22 You is plural, implying "You Samaritans." In saying **we worship what we know** Jesus identifies himself as a Jew. The verse shows that John's Gospel is not anti-Semitic. **Salvation is from the Jews** in the sense that the whole OT, which taught about salvation, was from the Jewish people, and the Messiah himself came from the Jews and not from the Samaritans or (by implication) from the Gentiles.

4:24 God is spirit means that God is not made of any physical matter and does not have a material body but has a more wonderful kind of existence that is everywhere present (hence worship is not confined to one place, v. 21), is not perceived by the bodily senses (cf. 3:6, 8), and yet is so powerful that

Physical Items Used by Jesus to Teach Spiritual Truths

Though often misunderstood by Jesus' hearers, the use of these tangible metaphors helps readers of John's Gospel understand its message as they meditate on the analogies between these physical realities and spiritual truths.

Physical Item	Spiritual Truth	References
Light	true knowledge and presence of God; moral purity	1:4–5, 7–9; 3:19–21; 8:12; 9:5; 11:9–10; 12:35–36, 46; cf. 1 John 2:8–10
Jerusalem temple	Christ's physical body	2:19–22
Physical birth	spiritual birth: being "born again"	1:13; 3:3–8; cf. 6:63; 1 John 3:9; 4:7; 5:1, 18
Wind	the Holy Spirit	3:8
Water	the Holy Spirit within believers	4:7–15; 7:37–39; cf. 1 John 5:6, 8
Food	doing the will of God	4:31–34
Bread	Jesus himself, his life and death	6:32–51, 58
Flesh and blood	Jesus' death	6:53–56; cf. 1 John 1:7; 5:6, 8
Door	path to eternal life in Jesus	10:1–9
Shepherd	Jesus' sacrifice and care for his people	10:11–18, 26–28; 21:15–17
Vine	Jesus in relationship to his followers	15:1–11
Cup	God's wrath toward sin	18:11
Breath	the Holy Spirit coming upon the disciples	20:22

and those who worship him must worship in spirit and truth." 25 The woman said to him,
"I know that [f]Messiah is coming (he who is called Christ). When he comes, [g]he will tell us
all things." 26 Jesus said to her, [h]"I who speak to you am he."
27 Just then [i]his disciples came back. They marveled that he was talking with a woman,
but no one said, "What do you seek?" or, "Why are you talking with her?" 28 So the woman
left her water jar and went away into town and said to the people, 29 "Come, see a man
[j]who told me all that I ever did. Can this be the Christ?" 30 They went out of the town and
were coming to him.
31 Meanwhile the disciples were urging him, saying, [k]"Rabbi, eat." 32 But he said to them,
"I have food to eat that you do not know about." 33 So the disciples said to one another,
[l]"Has anyone brought him something to eat?" 34 Jesus said to them, [m]"My food is [n]to do
the will of him who sent me and [o]to accomplish his work. 35 Do you not say, 'There are yet
four months, then comes the harvest'? Look, I tell you, lift up your eyes, and see that [p]the
fields are white for harvest. 36 Already the one who reaps is receiving wages and gathering
fruit for eternal life, so that [q]sower and [r]reaper [s]may rejoice together. 37 For here the saying
holds true, [t]'One sows and another reaps.' 38 I sent you to reap [u]that for which you did not
labor. Others have labored, [v]and you have entered into their labor."
39 Many Samaritans [w]from that town believed in him [x]because of [y]the woman's testimony,
"He told me all that I ever did." 40 So when the Samaritans came to him, they asked him to
stay with them, and he stayed there two days. 41 And many more believed [z]because of his
word. 42 They said to the woman, "It is no longer because of what you said that we believe, for
we have heard for ourselves, [a]and we know that this is indeed [b]the Savior [c]of the world."
43 After [d]the two days he departed for Galilee. 44 (For Jesus himself had testified [e]that a
prophet has no honor in his own hometown.) 45 So when he came to Galilee, the Galileans
welcomed him, [f]having seen all that he had done in Jerusalem at the feast. For [g]they too
had gone to the feast.

Jesus Heals an Official's Son

46 So he came again to [h]Cana in Galilee, [i]where he had made the water wine. And at
Capernaum there was an official whose son was ill. 47 When this man heard that Jesus
[j]had come from Judea to Galilee, he went to him and asked him to come down and heal
his son, for he was at the point of death. 48 So Jesus said to him, [k]"Unless you[1] see signs

[1] The Greek for *you* is plural; twice in this verse

25 [f]See ch. 1:41 [g]Deut. 18:18; [ver. 29]
26 [h]ch. 9:35-37
27 [i]ver. 8
29 [j]ver. 17, 18; [ver. 25]
31 [k]See ch. 1:38
33 [l][ver. 11, 15; ch. 3:4; 6:34, 52]
34 [m][Job 23:12] [n]ch. 5:30; 6:38; 14:31 [o]ch. 5:36; 17:4
35 [p]Matt. 9:37; Luke 10:2; [ver. 25, 30]
36 [q][Matt. 13:37; Mark 4:14] [r]ver. 38 [s]Isa. 9:3; [Amos 9:13]
37 [t][Job 31:8]
38 [u]Josh. 24:13 [v][Acts 8:5-17, 25]
39 [w]ver. 5, 8 [x][ch. 17:20] [y]ver. 29
41 [z]ch. 8:30
42 [a][1 John 5:20] [b]1 John 4:14; [ch. 3:17; 12:47; 1 Tim. 4:10] [c]See ch. 1:29
43 [d]ver. 40
44 [e]See Matt. 13:57
45 [f]ch. 2:23; 3:2 [g]ver. 20
46 [h]ch. 2:1 [i]ch. 2:9
47 [j]ver. 3, 54
48 [k]ch. 2:18; 6:30; [ch. 20:29]

he brought the universe into existence (cf. 1:1–3, 10; 17:5). Because "God is spirit," the Israelites were not to make idols "in the form of anything" in creation as did the surrounding nations (Ex. 20:4).

4:25–26 Messiah . . . (he who is called Christ). See note on 1:38. Jesus does not often identify himself directly as the Messiah (see note on 1:41) since most would then think he had come to bring instant political deliverance, but he departs from that pattern here in Samaria, which is removed from the centers of Judaism.

4:28 The woman's **water jar** was probably a large earthenware pitcher, carried either on the shoulder or the hip.

4:32–34 food to eat. Jesus again speaks in terms of the physical world to teach about different realities in the unseen spiritual world (see note on v. 15). The accomplishment of Jesus' mission is more important to him than physical food (cf. Deut. 8:3; Matt. 4:4; Luke 4:4; also Matt. 6:25; Mark 3:20–21). **work.** See note on John 14:12.

4:35 In the physical realm, there is a period of time between sowing and harvesting. But in the spiritual realm, Jesus' coming has already ushered in the end-time harvest in which sowing and reaping paradoxically coincide, so that the "crop" of believers is now being gathered into God's kingdom. The immediate reference may be to the approaching Samaritans who are going to believe in Jesus (cf. vv. 39–42).

4:36 This statement is reminiscent of Amos 9:13, where the "treader of grapes" overtakes "him who sows the seed," depicting the abundance and prosperity of the new age. Hence Jesus claims that he is ushering in the messianic age in which sowing and reaping coincide. **rejoice.** There is a unique joy that comes from seeing others come to faith.

4:37–38 The **others** who have labored are Jesus and his predecessors, especially John the Baptist and his followers, but in a broader sense all the OT writers and prophets. Jesus' followers are the beneficiaries of their work and will bring in the harvest.

4:41–42 Savior of the world. Not just of Jews. Jesus' large-scale harvest among the Samaritans marks the first indication of the universal scope of his saving mission (cf. 10:16; 11:51–52). The early church engaged in a Samaritan mission as well (Acts 8:4–25). Hence the pattern of Jesus' mission according to John—from Judea (Nicodemus, John 3:1–15), to Samaria (4:1–42), to the Gentiles (4:46–54; cf. 12:20–33)—anticipates the post-Pentecost mission of the early church (cf. Acts 1:8).

4:43–54 The healing of the official's son resembles that of the Gentile centurion's servant in Matt. 8:5–13 and Luke 7:2–10, but this is not the same incident.

4:43 Jesus **departed for** and arrived in **Galilee** (v. 45). It is at least 49 miles (79 km) by road from Sychar to Cana (v. 46), a journey that, by foot, would have taken at least two or three days.

4:44 For . . . a prophet has no honor tells the reason Jesus is now going to Galilee: he is going to minister where he does not yet have honor, so that people would then come to believe in him. The wording of the proverb is different in Matt. 13:57, Mark 6:4, and Luke 4:24, and the application there is also different.

4:46 Cana. See note on 2:1. **Capernaum.** See note on Mark 1:21. The **official** was probably a Gentile centurion, possibly in the service of Herod Antipas (cf. Mark 6:14). John shows Jesus bringing the gospel to a respected Jewish teacher (John 3:1–21), then to an outcast Samaritan woman (4:1–42), then to an official working for the Roman government (4:46–54), and thus, by implication from these examples, to everyone in the world.

4:48 Unless you see signs and wonders you will not believe is a

and wonders you will not believe." 49 The official said to him, "Sir, come down [l]before my
child dies." 50 Jesus said to him, "Go; your son will live." The man believed the word that
Jesus spoke to him and went on his way. 51 As he was going down, his servants[1] met him
and told him that his son was recovering. 52 So he asked them the hour when he began to
get better, and they said to him, "Yesterday at the seventh hour[2] the fever left him." 53 The
father knew that was the hour when Jesus had said to him, "Your son will live." And he
himself believed, [m]and all his household. 54 [n]This was now the second sign that Jesus did
when he had come from Judea to Galilee.

The Healing at the Pool on the Sabbath

5 After this there was a [o]feast of the Jews, and Jesus went up to Jerusalem.
2 Now there is in Jerusalem by [p]the Sheep Gate a pool, in Aramaic[3] called Bethesda,[4]
which has five roofed colonnades. 3 In these lay a multitude of invalids—blind, lame, and
[q]paralyzed.[5] 5 One man was there who had been an invalid for thirty-eight years. 6 When
Jesus saw him lying there and knew that he had already been there a long time, he said to
him, "Do you want to be healed?" 7 The sick man answered him, "Sir, I have no one to put

49 [l][ch. 11:21, 32; Mark 5:35; Luke 8:49]
53 [m]Acts 16:34; 18:8; See Acts 11:14
54 [n][ch. 2:11 with ver. 45, 46]

Chapter 5

1 [o]See ch. 6:4
2 [p]Neh. 3:1, 32; 12:39
3 [q]Matt. 12:10

[1] *Greek bondservants* [2] That is, at 1 P.M. [3] Or *Hebrew* [4] Some manuscripts *Bethsaida* [5] Some manuscripts insert, wholly or in part, *waiting for the moving of the water; [4]for an angel of the Lord went down at certain seasons into the pool, and stirred the water: whoever stepped in first after the stirring of the water was healed of whatever disease he had*

challenge not only to the royal official (**Jesus said to him**), but also to the Galilean people ("you" is plural). Some may become entranced with signs and wonders and fail to see that they point to Jesus and hence fail to believe in him (cf. 6:2, 26, 30). However, this does not mean that John views "signs" in and of themselves negatively. To the contrary, Jesus' miracles are one of the primary means God uses to bring people to faith in him; they often lead people to follow Jesus or place their faith in him as the Messiah (2:11, 23; 3:2; 4:53–54; 6:2, 14; 7:31; 11:47–48; 12:11, 18; 20:31).

4:49–50 Your son will live indicates not just that Jesus knew that a miracle had happened, but that Jesus himself had healed the son, for John calls this a miracle "that Jesus did" (v. 54). A similar but different incident is narrated in Matt. 8:5–13 (cf. Luke 7:1–10).

Jesus' Ministry in Galilee

Jesus spent most of his life and ministry in the region of Galilee, a mountainous area in northern Palestine. Jesus grew up in the hill town of Nazareth, about 3.5 miles (5.6 km) south of the Gentile administrative center of Sepphoris. Soon after he began his public ministry, Jesus relocated to Capernaum on the Sea of Galilee. By Jesus' time, a thriving fishing industry had developed around the Sea, and several of Jesus' disciples were fishermen.

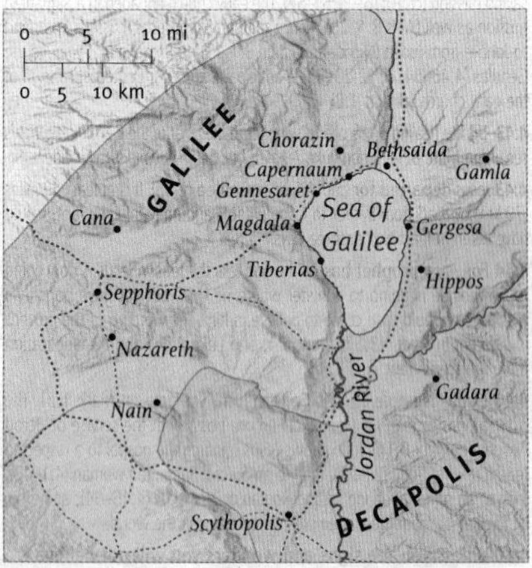

4:54 This was the **second sign** following the first sign done in Cana (cf. 2:11); in the interim, Jesus had also performed signs in Jerusalem (cf. 2:23; 3:2; 4:45).

5:1–10:42 *Mounting Jewish Opposition, Additional Signs.* The "festival cycle" in John's Gospel, which spans chs. 5–10, is characterized by escalating conflict between Jesus and the Jewish authorities. In the course of Jesus' defense of his ministry, he cites several major witnesses on his behalf (see note on 5:31–47).

5:1 After this marks the passing of an indefinite period of time (cf. 6:1; 21:1). There is no way to be certain which feast is indicated by the unnamed **feast of the Jews.**

5:2 pool, in Aramaic called Bethesda. "Bethesda" means "house of mercy," a fitting term given the desperate state of the people lying there in hope of a miracle cure. See also note on 1:38. Various spellings of the name of this pool are found in the Greek manuscripts (see ESV footnote). Nonetheless, there remains strong reason to identify this pool with a single large two-pool complex near the Sheep Gate in Jerusalem and adjacent to the modern Church of St. Anne. The two pools are separated from each other by a partition. The remains of columns found around this site help confirm that the partition between the pools, along with each of the four sides surrounding the pool complex, likely contained the **five roofed colonnades** (i.e., five stoas, which are covered walkways; a "colonnade" is a row of columns). A fifth-century Byzantine basilica was built over this site.

5:3 The statement in the ESV footnote about an angel of the Lord stirring the water and the first person who stepped in being healed is found in some early manuscripts, but not the earliest. Therefore the omitted verse 4 should not be considered part of Scripture, although v. 7 (which is in all manuscripts) shows that people believed something like what this statement reports.

5:5 Invalid (Gk. *astheneia*), in light of v. 7, probably means "paralyzed," "lame," or "extremely weak" (the Greek term is the general expression for a "disabled" condition). He had been an invalid for **thirty-eight years**, longer than many people in antiquity lived. For a similar healing see Matt. 9:1–8.

5:6 Knew probably indicates Jesus' divine knowledge of the man's situation, similar to Jesus' knowledge of Nathanael (1:48) and the Samaritan woman (4:18).

Jewish Festivals Mentioned in John

Jewish Passover	2:13, 23; 6:4; 11:55; 12:1
Unnamed (possibly Tabernacles)	5:1
Feast of Tabernacles (or Booths)	7:2
Feast of Dedication (or Hanukkah)	10:22

me into the pool when the water is stirred up, and while I am going another steps down
before me." 8 Jesus said to him, [r]"Get up, take up your bed, and walk." 9 [r]And at once the
man was healed, and he took up his bed and walked.

[s]Now that day was the Sabbath. 10 So the Jews[1] said to the man who had been healed, "It
is the Sabbath, and [t]it is not lawful for you to take up your bed." 11 But he answered them,
"The man who healed me, that man said to me, 'Take up your bed, and walk.'" 12 They
asked him, "Who is the man who said to you, 'Take up your bed and walk'?" 13 Now the
man who had been healed did not know who it was, for [u]Jesus had withdrawn, as there
was a crowd in the place. 14 Afterward Jesus found him in the temple and said to him, "See,
you are well! [v]Sin no more, [w]that nothing worse may happen to you." 15 The man went
away and told the Jews that it was Jesus who had healed him. 16 And this was why the Jews
[x]were persecuting Jesus, [y]because he was doing these things on the Sabbath. 17 But Jesus
answered them, "My Father is working until now, and I am working."

Jesus Is Equal with God

18 This was why the Jews [z]were seeking all the more to kill him, [a]because not only was
he [b]breaking the Sabbath, but he was even calling God [c]his own Father, [d]making himself
equal with God.

The Authority of the Son

19 So Jesus said to them, "Truly, truly, I say to you, [e]the Son [f]can do nothing of his own
accord, but only what he sees the Father doing. For whatever the Father[2] does, that the
Son does likewise. 20 For [g]the Father loves the Son and shows him all that he himself is
doing. And [h]greater works than these will he show him, so that [i]you may marvel. 21 For
as the Father [j]raises the dead and [k]gives them life, so [l]also the Son gives life [m]to whom he
will. 22 [n]The Father judges no one, but [o]has given all judgment to the Son, 23 that all may

[1] The Greek word *Ioudaioi* refers specifically here to Jewish religious leaders, and others under their influence, who opposed Jesus in that time; also verses 15, 16, 18 [2] Greek *he*

8 [r]Matt. 9:6, 7; Mark 2:9, 11, 12; Luke 5:24, 25
9 [r][See ver. 8 above] [s]ch. 9:14
10 [t]Ex. 20:10; Neh. 13:19; Jer. 17:21, 22; [ch. 7:23; 9:16; Matt. 12:2; Mark 2:24; 3:4; Luke 6:2; 13:14]
13 [u][ch. 6:15]
14 [v][ch. 8:11] [w][Ezra 9:14]
16 [x]ch. 15:20; [Acts 9:4, 5] [y]ch. 7:23; 9:16
18 [z]See ch. 7:1 [a]See ch. 10:33 [b]ver. 16 [c][Rom. 8:32] [d]Phil. 2:6
19 [e]See ver. 30 [f][ch. 16:13]
20 [g]ch. 3:35; 10:17; 15:9, 10; 17:23-26; [Matt. 3:17] [h][ch. 14:12] [i]ch. 7:21
21 [j][Deut. 32:39; 2 Cor. 1:9] [k]Rom. 4:17; 8:11 [l][ch. 6:33; 11:25]; See 1 Cor. 15:45 [m][Rom. 9:18]
22 [n][Acts 17:31] [o]ver. 27; ch. 9:39; Acts 10:42; [ch. 3:17]; See ch. 17:2

5:7 When the water is stirred up indicates that people thought at least the first person entering the troubled water would be healed.

5:10 It is the Sabbath. Nothing in the OT specifically prohibited such an innocent activity as carrying one's bedroll on the Sabbath day (cf. Ex. 20:8–11), but the man was violating later Jewish traditions that had developed hundreds of minutely detailed and burdensome rules about what kind of "work" was prohibited, including a code that forbade carrying an object "from one domain into another" (Mishnah, *Shabbat* 7.2). Nonetheless, Jesus does not defend himself by getting into a rabbinic discussion on the nature of work. Rather, he claims he is *working*, just like God (John 5:17), and hence is, as the Synoptics teach, the lord of the Sabbath (cf. Matt. 12:8; Mark 2:28; Luke 6:5).

5:14 Jesus meets the man again in the **temple**, that is, the larger temple complex rather than the actual building (see note on 2:14), a short distance from where the original healing had taken place (the pool of Bethesda is located just north of the Temple Mount). **Sin no more** may imply that the man's suffering was due to sin, without suggesting that all suffering is due to personal sin (see note on 9:2).

5:16 Jesus' Jewish opponents were putting their merely human religious tradition above genuine love and compassion for others, which the OT commanded (e.g., Lev. 19:18) and Jesus exemplified. It was Jesus, not these Jews, who was truly obeying the Scriptures.

5:17 My Father suggests a far closer relationship with God than other people had (see 20:17). When Jesus says, "My Father **is working until now, and I am working**," he implies that he, like the Father, is lord over the Sabbath. Therefore this is a claim to deity. These Jews recognize what he is claiming (see 5:18). While Gen. 2:2–3 teaches that God rested (Hb. *shabat*) on the seventh day of creation, Jewish rabbis agreed that God continually upholds the universe, yet without breaking the Sabbath. (In John 7:22–23 Jesus makes a different argument about healing on the Sabbath; see also note on 9:14.)

5:18 making himself equal with God. Jesus was claiming to be the Son of God, not in the way that ordinary human believers are sons of God but in the sense of one who was equal to God in his nature and in every way, yet who related to God in a Father-Son relationship (see note on 1:14). If Jesus had been merely a man (as his Jewish opponents thought), then this claim would have been blasphemy on Jesus' part.

5:19 Jesus' claim that **the Son can do nothing of his own accord,** taken with vv. 17–18, affirms two themes: (1) Jesus is equal to God, i.e., he is fully divine (vv. 17–18); (2) the Father and the Son have different functions and roles (v. 19), and the Son is subject to the Father in everything he does, yet this does not deny their fundamental equality. See notes on vv. 21, 22, 23; 20:28. **Only what he sees the Father doing** may imply that Jesus had a unique ability to see the Father's providential activities in the events of everyday life, activities that are ordinarily invisible to human beings.

5:20 The Father shows to Jesus **all that he himself is doing**—i.e., Jesus perceives God's hand and purpose in every event in this world. The **greater works** are initially the raising of the dead (11:1–45). Even more, they include Jesus' own death and resurrection (chs. 18–20), then the voice of this same Jesus summoning all mankind to final resurrection and judgment (5:27–30).

5:21 Jesus' statement that **the Son** also **gives life to whom he will** is another claim to deity, showing that Jesus does what only God can do, for the OT makes clear that raising the dead and giving life are the sole prerogatives of God (cf. Deut. 32:39; 1 Sam. 2:6; 2 Kings 5:7). This "life" is both the new "life" now given to believers (John 5:24; 11:25–26; 2 Cor. 5:17) and the resurrection of the body at Christ's second coming (1 Cor. 15:42–57; 1 Thess. 4:13–18; see Dan. 12:2).

5:22 Jesus' assertion that **the Father . . . has given all judgment to the Son** is yet another claim to deity, since judgment is the exclusive prerogative of God (e.g., Gen. 18:25; Judg. 11:27). The Father has delegated the work of final judgment to the Son.

5:23 The statement **that all may honor the Son, just as they honor the Father** in effect establishes Jesus' right to be worshiped and also amounts to a claim to deity. **Whoever does not honor the Son does not honor the Father who sent him** shows that religions such as Judaism and Islam that consider Jesus merely a great prophet do not represent the truth about God, because they fail to worship and honor Jesus.

honor the Son, just as they [p]honor the Father. [q]Whoever does not honor the Son does not
honor the Father who sent him. 24 Truly, truly, I say to you, [r]whoever hears my word and
[s]believes him who sent me has eternal life. He [t]does not come into judgment, but [u]has
passed from death to life.
25 "Truly, truly, I say to you, [v]an hour is coming, and is now here, when [w]the dead will
hear [x]the voice of the Son of God, and those who hear [w]will live. 26 [y]For as the Father has
life in himself, [z]so he has granted the Son also to have life in himself. 27 And he [a]has given
him authority to execute judgment, because he is the Son of Man. 28 Do not marvel at this,
for [v]an hour is coming when [b]all who are in the tombs will hear his voice 29 and come out,
[c]those who have done good to the resurrection of life, and those who have done evil to
the resurrection of judgment.

Witnesses to Jesus

30 [d]"I can do nothing on my own. As I hear, I judge, and [e]my judgment is just, because
[f]I seek not my own will [g]but the will of him who sent me. 31 [h]If I alone bear witness about
myself, my testimony is not true. 32 There is [i]another who bears witness about me, and [j]I
know that the testimony that he bears about me is true. 33 [k]You sent to John, and he has
borne witness to the truth. 34 Not that [l]the testimony that I receive is from man, but I say
these things so that you may be saved. 35 He was a burning and [m]shining lamp, and [n]you
were willing to rejoice for a while in his light. 36 But [l]the testimony that I have is greater
than that of John. For [o]the works that the Father has given me [p]to accomplish, the very
works that I am doing, [q]bear witness about me that [r]the Father has sent me. 37 And the
Father who sent me [s]has himself borne witness about me. His voice you have never heard,
[t]his form you have never seen, 38 and [u]you do not have his word abiding in you, for you do
not believe the one whom he has sent. 39 [v]You search the Scriptures because you think that

23 [p]ch. 8:49 [q]Luke 10:16; [ch. 15:23; 1 John 2:23]
24 [r][ch. 8:51] [s]ch. 20:31; 1 John 5:9-13; [ch. 3:15, 36; 12:44] [t]ch. 3:18; [ver. 29] [u]1 John 3:14
25 [v]See ch. 4:21, 23 [w]See Eph. 2:1, 5 [x][ch. 11:43]
26 [y][ch. 6:57] [z]See ch. 1:4; 17:2
27 [a]ver. 22
28 [v][See ver. 25 above] [b]ch. 11:24; 1 Cor. 15:52; [ch. 11:44, 45]
29 [c]See Dan. 12:2
30 [d]ver. 19; ch. 8:28; 14:10 [e]ch. 8:16 [f]ch. 4:34; 6:38; [ch. 7:18; Rom. 15:3] [g]See Matt. 26:39
31 [h][ch. 8:13, 14, 18, 54; 18:21]
32 [i]ver. 37 [j]ch. 7:28, 29
33 [k]See ch. 1:7, 19
34 [l]1 John 5:9
35 [m]2 Pet. 1:19 [n][Matt. 13:20; 21:26]
36 [l][See ver. 34 above] [o]ch. 10:25, 38; 14:11; 15:24; [ch. 2:23; Matt. 11:4] [p]See ch. 4:34 [q][ch. 3:2] [r]See ch. 3:17
37 [s]ch. 8:18; [Matt. 3:17] [t]See ch. 1:18
38 [u][1 John 2:14; 4:13, 14; 5:10]
39 [v][Acts 17:11; 2 Tim. 3:15]

5:24 Has eternal life is one of the most striking statements in John regarding the present possession of eternal life. Eternal life begins immediately, in a partially realized but significant way, when one believes in Jesus. Those who believe can face the last judgment with confidence (cf. 1 John 5:11–13).

5:25 Here Jesus is not emphasizing the final resurrection but the present reality and experience of eternal life, for he says the hour is **now here**. The phrase **the dead** refers to the spiritually dead who hear Jesus' message and believe.

5:26 For. This verse explains why the voice of Jesus is able to speak to dead people and grant them life. Just as **the Father** was never created and was never given his life by someone else, but **has life in himself** so that he can impart that life to others, so the Son has **life in himself** and is able to call the dead to life. **He has granted the Son** does not mean that the Father created the Son (see 1:3 and note) but that the Father authorized the Son to be able to give life to other people (thus this verse explains 5:25). This statement about "life in himself" echoes the affirmation in the prologue that "in him [Jesus] was life" (1:4; see also 3:15–16; 11:25; and note on 14:6).

5:27 Because he is the Son of Man echoes Dan. 7:13; see note on John 1:51. Because Jesus is not only the divine Son of God but also the truly human "Son of Man" who is the eternal world ruler prophesied in Dan. 7:13–14, the Father has given him authority to carry out the final judgment of every human being.

5:28–29 Jesus reaffirms the resurrection on the last day. Cf. Dan. 12:2. **Those who have done good . . . those who have done evil** does not imply that people's deeds in this life are the basis on which judgment is pronounced (for that would contradict John's strong emphasis on belief in Jesus as the way to gain eternal life: see John 3:16; 5:24–25; etc.). Instead, good works function as evidence of true faith, and if good works are lacking they show an absence of true faith. All those who truly believe will be brought "from death to life" (v. 24) and as a consequence will do good and will therefore enjoy **the resurrection of life**.

5:30 nothing on my own. See notes on vv. 19, 22.

5:31–47 In this section, Jesus speaks of several witnesses who bear testimony concerning him (see chart, this page). The Johannine "witness" theme, in turn, is part of the larger "trial motif," according to which it was not Jesus who was put on trial and condemned by the world but rather the world that was put on trial by Jesus. In order to demonstrate Jesus' innocence and the world's guilt, John parades before the reader a multitude of witnesses who bear testimony to Jesus' true messianic identity and hence establish the world's guilt in rejecting Jesus.

5:31 Jesus' statement is in keeping with OT teaching regarding the need for multiple witnesses (Deut. 17:6; 19:15; cf. Num. 35:30). **I alone** represents the inclusion of the pronoun *egō* in Greek, which makes **bear witness** emphatic; such witness is not considered **true** in court.

5:32 The Jews may think **another** refers to the Baptist (cf. vv. 33–35), but Jesus is talking about God the Father (v. 37).

5:33 the truth. See note on 14:6.

5:35 Jesus' characterization of the Baptist as a **burning and shining lamp** echoes Ps. 132:17, where it is said that God has "prepared a lamp" for his anointed. John the Baptist was a "lamp," but not the light (John 1:7–9); his witness was small (though important) and of a temporary nature. The past tense may imply that John is now dead or at least in prison. See also notes on 3:28–30. On "lamp," see note on Matt. 25:3–4.

5:37 The Father . . . has himself borne witness refers to the whole of the Father's witness, including all of Jesus' miracles and teaching as directed by the Father (3:2; 5:19–20) and all of God's witness in Scripture (cf. vv. 45–47; Luke 24:27, 44; Acts 13:27; 1 John 5:9).

5:39 The study of Scripture does not by itself impart life. The Scriptures rather bear witness to the One who gives life, namely, Jesus (cf. vv. 46–47).

Witnesses to Jesus

1. John the Baptist	5:32–36; cf. 1:7–8, 15, 19, 32–34; 3:26
2. Jesus' own works	5:36; cf. 10:25, 32, 37–38; 15:24
3. God the Father	5:37–38; 8:18
4. The Scriptures, esp. by Moses	5:39, 45–47
5. Jesus himself	3:11, 32; 8:14, 18; 18:37
6. The Spirit	14:26; 15:26; 16:8–11, 13–14
7. The disciples, esp. John	15:27; 19:35; 21:24

in them you have eternal life; and [w]it is they that bear witness about me, 40 yet [x]you refuse
to come to me that you may have life. 41 [y]I do not receive glory from people. 42 But [z]I know
that you do not have [a]the love of God within you. 43 I have come [b]in my Father's name, and
[c]you do not receive me. [d]If another comes in his own name, you will receive him. 44 How
can you believe, when you receive glory from one another and [e]do not seek the glory that
comes from [f]the only God? 45 Do not think that I will accuse you to the Father. There is one
who accuses you: Moses, [g]on whom you have set your hope. 46 For if you believed Moses,
you would believe me; for [h]he wrote of me. 47 But [i]if you do not believe his writings, how
will you believe my words?"

Jesus Feeds the Five Thousand

6 After this [j]Jesus went away to the other side of [k]the Sea of Galilee, which is [l]the Sea of
Tiberias. 2 And a large crowd was following him, because they saw the signs that he
was doing on the sick. 3 Jesus went up on [m]the mountain, and there he sat down with his
disciples. 4 Now [n]the Passover, the [o]feast of the Jews, was at hand. 5 [p]Lifting up his eyes,
then, and seeing that a large crowd was coming toward him, Jesus said to [q]Philip, "Where
are we to buy bread, so that these people may eat?" 6 He said this to test him, for he himself
knew what he would do. 7 [r]Philip answered him, "Two hundred denarii[1] worth of bread
would not be enough for each of them to get a little." 8 One of his disciples, [s]Andrew, Simon
Peter's brother, said to him, 9 "There is a boy here who has five [t]barley loaves and two fish,
but [t]what are they for so many?" 10 Jesus said, "Have the people sit down." [u]Now there was
much grass in the place. So the men sat down, about five thousand in number. 11 Jesus then
took the loaves, and [v]when he had given thanks, he distributed them to those who were
seated. So also the fish, as much as they wanted. 12 And when they had eaten their fill, he
told his disciples, "Gather up the leftover fragments, that nothing may be lost." 13 So they
gathered them up and filled twelve baskets with fragments from the five barley loaves

39 [w]See Luke 24:27
40 [x]ver. 43; ch. 3:19; 7:17; [Matt. 23:37; Luke 13:34]
41 [y]ver. 34; [Matt. 6:1, 2; 1 Thess. 2:6]
42 [z]See ch. 2:24, 25 [a]Luke 11:42; See Jude 21
43 [b]ch. 10:25; 12:13; 17:12 [c]ch. 1:11; 3:11, 32 [d][Matt. 24:5]
44 [e]Rom. 2:29 [f]ch. 17:3
45 [g][ch. 9:28, 29; Rom. 2:17]
46 [h]ver. 47; Num. 21:9; Deut. 18:15; Luke 24:27; [ch. 12:41]
47 [i][Luke 16:31]

Chapter 6

1 [j]For ver. 1-13, see Matt. 14:13-21; Mark 6:32-44; Luke 9:10-17 [k]See Matt. 4:18 [l]ch. 21:1
3 [m]ver. 15
4 [n]ch. 2:13; 11:55; See Ex. 12 [o]ch. 5:1; 7:2
5 [p]Luke 6:20 [q]ch. 1:44
7 [r][Mark 6:37]
8 [s]ch. 1:40, 44
9 [t]2 Kgs. 4:42, 43
10 [u][Mark 6:39]
11 [v]ver. 23; See Matt. 15:36

[1] A *denarius* was a day's wage for a laborer

Consequently, the study of the Bible ought to result in genuine faith in Jesus, followed by obedient action and transformed lives, not merely acquisition of Bible knowledge. **it is they that bear witness about me.** People who (like Jesus' Jewish opponents) read the OT without seeing that it all points to Jesus fail to understand its message. See also Overview of the Bible, pp. 23–26.

5:43 I have come in my Father's name means that Jesus came in the authority of the Father and, in a deeper sense, represented the entire character of the Father (his "name" in an OT sense represented all that was true about him). **If another comes.** Jesus predicted the proliferation of false christs (Matt. 24:24 par.) as a sign of the end times (Matt. 24:5 par.), and the first-century Jewish historian Josephus reports a whole string of messianic pretenders before A.D. 70.

5:44 One reason people fail to believe is that they long for the approval and favor of others instead of seeking the approval and favor of God.

5:46 If you believed Moses, you would believe me assumes that genuine believers have a heart that is receptive to the true words of God, and therefore those who believe the words of God as written by Moses (that is, Genesis–Deuteronomy) will also recognize and eagerly receive the words of God as spoken by Jesus. Those who disbelieve Moses' writings will also disbelieve Jesus. **For he wrote of me** applies not only to specific predictions like Deut. 18:15 but also to all the ways in which the history of salvation in these writings pointed to Christ (e.g., Luke 24:27, 44; John 1:45; 3:14; 8:56; Acts 26:22; 28:23; 1 Cor. 10:4; Heb. 11:23–26; 1 Pet. 1:10–12; Jude 5; and Overview of the Bible, pp. 23–26).

6:1–15 The feeding of the multitude (recorded in all four Gospels; cf. Matt. 14:13–21; Mark 6:30–44; Luke 9:10–17) constitutes another of Jesus' messianic "signs" (see note on John 2:11). The sign shows that Jesus fulfills symbolism related to God's provision of manna to Israel in the wilderness through Moses (see 6:30–31).

6:1 After this again indicates the passing of an unspecified period of time (cf. 5:1). As much as half a year may have passed since the previous event. **Sea of Galilee, which is the Sea of Tiberias** (cf. 21:1). This lake (also known as the Kinneret) is fed from the Jordan to the north and spills out again to the Jordan in the south. It currently measures approximately 7 miles (11.3 km) wide and 13 miles (21 km) long. Archaeological discoveries in and around this lake include a first-century boat (see note on Matt. 4:21) and excavations in various coastal cities (including Capernaum and Tiberias). On the location of the feeding of the 5,000, see note on Luke 9:10. On the city of Tiberias, see note on John 6:23–24.

6:3 Mountain may refer not to any specific mountain but to the hill country east of the lake, known today as the Golan Heights (cf. Matt. 14:23; Mark 6:46).

6:4 This is the second of three Passovers mentioned by John (cf. 2:13; 11:55), and the only one during Jesus' ministry that finds him in Galilee. See also note on 2:13.

6:7 Two hundred denarii constitute roughly eight months' wages, since one denarius was about one day's pay (Matt. 20:2; cf. John 12:5).

6:9 Barley was common food for the poor (the more well-to-do preferred wheat bread). The **fish** were probably dried or preserved, possibly pickled.

6:10–11 The men numbered **about five thousand,** plus women and children (cf. Matt. 14:21), totaling perhaps as many as 20,000 people.

Parallels between John 6 and Numbers 11

Where are we to get meat/bread?	John 6:5; Num. 11:13
The striking disproportion between the existing need and the available resources	John 6:7–9 ; Num. 11:22
The description of the manna	John 6:31; Num. 11:7–9
The people's grumbling	John 6:41, 43; Num. 11:1
The reference to the eating of meat/Jesus' "flesh"	John 6:51; Num. 11:13

left by those who had eaten. 14 When the people saw the sign that he had done, they said,
[w]"This is indeed [x]the Prophet [y]who is to come into the world!"
15 [z]Perceiving then that they were about to come and take him by force to make him
king, Jesus [a]withdrew again to [b]the mountain by himself.

Jesus Walks on Water

16 When evening came, his disciples went down to the sea, 17 got into a boat, and started
across the sea to Capernaum. It was now dark, and Jesus had not yet come to them. 18 The
sea became rough because a strong wind was blowing. 19 When they had rowed about three
or four miles,[1] they saw Jesus walking on the sea and coming near the boat, and they were
frightened. 20 [c]But he said to them, "It is I; do not be afraid." 21 Then they were glad to take
him into the boat, and immediately the boat was at the land to which they were going.

I Am the Bread of Life

22 On the next day the crowd that remained on the other side of the sea saw that there
had been only [d]one boat there, and that Jesus had not entered the boat with his disciples,
but that his disciples had gone away alone. 23 Other boats from Tiberias came near the
place where they had eaten the bread after the Lord [e]had given thanks. 24 [f]So when the
crowd saw that Jesus was not there, nor his disciples, they themselves got into the boats
and [g]went to Capernaum, seeking Jesus.
25 When they found him on the other side of the sea, they said to him, [h]"Rabbi, when
did you come here?" 26 Jesus answered them, "Truly, truly, I say to you, [i]you are seeking
me, not because you saw [j]signs, but because you ate your fill of the loaves. 27 [k]Do not work
for the food that perishes, but for [l]the food that endures to eternal life, which [m]the Son
of Man will give to you. For on [n]him God the Father has [o]set his seal." 28 Then they said to
him, "What must we do, to be doing [p]the works of God?" 29 Jesus answered them, "This
is the work of God, [q]that you believe in him whom [r]he has sent." 30 So they said to him,
[s]"Then what sign do you do, that we may see and believe you? What work do you perform?
31 [t]Our fathers ate the manna in the wilderness; as it is written, [u]'He gave them bread from
heaven to eat.'" 32 Jesus then said to them, "Truly, truly, I say to you, it was not Moses who

14 [w]See ch. 4:19 [x]ch. 1:21; 7:40; See Matt. 21:11 [y]ch. 11:27; See Matt. 11:3
15 [z][ch. 12:12-15] [a]For ver. 15-21, see Matt. 14:22-33; Mark 6:45-51; [Matt. 8:18] [b]ver. 3
20 [c][Luke 24:38, 39]
22 [d]ch. 21:8
23 [e]ver. 11
24 [f]For ver. 24, 25, [Matt. 14:34-36; Mark 6:53-56] [g]ver. 17, 59
25 [h]See ch. 1:38
26 [i]ver. 24 [j]ver. 2
27 [k]Isa. 55:2 [l][ver. 35, 50, 51, 54, 58] [m]See Dan. 7:13 [n][ch. 5:36, 37; 10:36] [o][Ezek. 9:4; Rom. 4:11; 1 Cor. 9:2; 2 Tim. 2:19]; See ch. 3:33
28 [p]1 Cor. 15:58; Rev. 2:26
29 [q]1 John 3:23 [r]See ch. 3:17
30 [s]See Matt. 12:38
31 [t]ver. 49, 58; Ex. 16:15; Num. 11:7-9 [u]Cited from Neh. 9:15; [Ps. 78:24, 25; 105:40; 1 Cor. 10:3]

[1] Greek *twenty-five or thirty stadia*; a *stadion* was about 607 feet or 185 meters

6:14 the Prophet. The people here see Jesus as fulfilling the prediction of a prophet like Moses who was promised in Deut. 18:15, 18. (Cf. notes on John 1:20–21; 7:40–41. In Acts 3:22–23 Peter identifies Jesus as the fulfillment of this prophecy; cf. Acts 7:37.) However, "prophet" is not a common title for Jesus and is more often used by those who know little about him (e.g., Matt. 16:14; John 4:19), since Jesus is much more than a prophet.

6:15 to make him king. Jesus did not want to be pushed into the middle of an unruly mob that would march to begin a futile, spontaneous uprising against the Roman authorities. The people did not understand that Jesus' kingship at his first coming was spiritual (see 18:36).

6:17 boat. See note on Matt. 4:21.

6:19 They **had rowed about three or four miles**. If the feeding of the multitude took place at the eastern shore of the Sea of Galilee, the shortest distance to Capernaum would be 5–6 miles (8–10 km). **Walking on the sea** is not something Jesus did just to amaze the disciples, but rather it is a powerful, visible demonstration of Jesus' sovereignty over the world that he created (Heb. 1:3, 10). In the OT, God alone rules over the seas (Ps. 29:10–11; 89:9; 107:28–30).

6:20 Jesus' words, **"It is I,"** represent the Greek phrase *egō eimi*, which in other contexts can be translated "I am." Here it may allude to God's self-identification as "I AM WHO I AM" (Ex. 3:14) and may thus be an indication of Jesus' divinity. This connection becomes more clear when the phrase is repeated in later verses (see notes on John 6:35; 8:24; 8:58).

6:21 Immediately the boat was at the land is a miraculous instance of what is taught in Ps. 107:23–32 (esp. vv. 29–30): God alone stills the storm, and he is the one who brings those who travel the sea safely to their destination.

6:23–24 Tiberias. This chief and largest city on the west shore of the Sea of Galilee (see note on v. 1) was founded early in the first century by Herod Antipas in honor of his patron, the Roman emperor Tiberius (A.D. 14–37); it subsequently continued as the Galilean royal city under Agrippa I (A.D. 39–44). The city was built upon an old cemetery, and thus was considered unclean by many Jews until the second century, when it became the center of Palestinian rabbinic Judaism. The ancient city boasts a rich archaeological heritage, including evidence of a first-century city gate, although many of the exposed structures are from a period just after the NT (such as the 2nd-century basilica and theater, the 4th-century synagogue and nearby bath complex, and many Byzantine ruins from the 4th–7th century A.D.). While **Capernaum** (see note on Mark 1:21) is located on the northwest edge of the Sea of Galilee, Tiberias is several miles to the south.

6:26 But because you ate your fill of the loaves implies that people were seeking Jesus only for the physical or material benefit that he gave, whereas they should have sought him **because** they **saw signs**, that is, miraculous signs that pointed to Jesus' divine nature and identity as the true Messiah.

6:27 set his seal. A seal made of wax, clay, or various kinds of soft metal would signify either ownership or authentication of an item or a document; the second sense is probably in view here.

6:28–29 Doing the works represents the same word that is translated "labor" in v. 27 (Gk. *ergazomai*). Jesus tells them to work "for the food that endures to eternal life" (v. 27), but the people misunderstand Jesus' statement and ask about the works required by God. Jesus replies that the **work** God requires is that people **believe** in the Messiah.

6:31 The OT reference seems to involve several passages, with Ps. 78:23–24 being the most prominent (see also Ex. 16:4, 15; Neh. 9:15; Ps. 105:40). The passage sustains links with (1) the exodus and Passover motifs, (2) the characterization of Jesus as the Prophet like Moses, and (3) the expectation that God would provide manna once again in the messianic age.

6:32 The true bread from heaven would be something that nourishes people eternally and spiritually and thus is infinitely superior to the manna

gave you the bread from heaven, but my Father gives you the true bread from heaven.
33 For the bread of God is [v]he who comes down from heaven and gives life to the world."
34 They said to him, [w]"Sir, give us this bread always."
35 Jesus said to them, [x]"I am the bread of life; [y]whoever comes to me shall not hunger,
and whoever believes in me shall never thirst. **36** But I said to you that you have seen me and
yet do not believe. **37** [z]All that [a]the Father gives me will come to me, and [b]whoever comes to
me I will never cast out. **38** For [c]I have come down from heaven, not to do [d]my own will but
[d]the will of him [e]who sent me. **39** And [f]this is the will of him who sent me, [g]that I should
lose nothing of [h]all that he has given me, but [i]raise it up on the last day. **40** For this is the
will of my Father, that everyone who [j]looks on the Son and [k]believes in him [l]should have
eternal life, and I will raise him up on the last day."
41 So the Jews grumbled about him, because he said, [m]"I am the bread that came down
from heaven." **42** They said, [n]"Is not this Jesus, [o]the son of Joseph, whose father and mother
[p]we know? How does he now say, 'I have come down from heaven'?" **43** Jesus answered them,
"Do not grumble among yourselves. **44** No one can come to me unless the Father who sent
me [q]draws him. And [r]I will raise him up on the last day. **45** It is written in the Prophets, [s]'And
they will all be [t]taught by God.' [u]Everyone who has heard and learned from the Father
comes to me— **46** [v]not that anyone has seen the Father except [w]he who is from God; he
[x]has seen the Father. **47** Truly, truly, I say to you, [y]whoever believes has eternal life. **48** [z]I am
the bread of life. **49** [a]Your fathers ate the manna in the wilderness, and [b]they died. **50** [c]This
is the bread that comes down from heaven, so that one may eat of it [d]and not die. **51** I am
the living bread [e]that came down from heaven. If anyone eats of this bread, he will live
forever. And the bread that I will give [f]for the life of the world is [g]my flesh."
52 The Jews then [h]disputed among themselves, saying, [i]"How can this man give us his
flesh to eat?" **53** So Jesus said to them, "Truly, truly, I say to you, unless you eat the flesh
of [j]the Son of Man and drink his blood, you [k]have no life in you. **54** Whoever feeds on my
flesh and drinks my blood [l]has eternal life, and [m]I will raise him up on the last day. **55** For

33[v]ver. 50
34[w]See ch. 4:15, 33
35[x]ver. 41, 48, 51; [ver. 58] [y]ch. 4:14; 7:37; [ch. 5:40; Matt. 11:28; Rev. 7:16]
37[z]ver. 39; ch. 17:2 [a]ch. 10:29; 17:6, 9, 24 [b]ch. 10:28; 17:12
38[c]See ch. 3:13 [d]See ch. 5:30 [e]See ch. 4:34
39[f]ch. 10:28, 29; Matt. 18:14 [g]ch. 17:12; 18:9 [h]ver. 37 [i]ver. 40, 44, 54; [ch. 11:25; 1 Cor. 6:14]
40[j]ch. 12:45; 14:17, 19 [k]ver. 47; ch. 3:15, 16 [l]ver. 27, 54; ch. 4:14
41[m]ver. 33, 35, 38
42[n]See Matt. 13:55 [o]See ch. 1:45 [p]ch. 7:27, 28
44[q]ch. 12:32; Jer. 31:3; Hos. 11:4; [ver. 65; ch. 4:23] [r]ver. 39
45[s]Cited from Isa. 54:13; [Jer. 31:33, 34; Heb. 8:10, 11] [t]1 Cor. 2:13; 1 Thess. 4:9; 1 John 2:20 [u][ver. 37]
46[v]See ch. 1:18 [w]See ch. 7:29 [x][ch. 3:32; 8:38]
47[y]See ch. 3:36
48[z]See ver. 35
49[a]See ver. 31 [b]ver. 58
50[c]ver. 33 [d]ver. 51, 58
51[e]ch. 3:13 [f]ver. 57; Luke 22:19 [g]ver. 53-56; [ch. 1:14]
52[h]ch. 9:16; 10:19 [i]ver. 60; ch. 3:9
53[j]ver. 27 [k]See ch. 20:31 **54**[l]See ver. 40 [m]ver. 39

given to Israel in OT times, which was able to meet only temporal, physical needs. Jesus identifies himself as this "true bread" in v. 35.

6:35 Jesus' claim, **"I am the bread of life,"** constitutes the first of seven "I am" sayings recorded in this Gospel (see chart, p. 2041). Apart from these sayings there are also several absolute statements where Jesus refers to himself as "I am" (e.g., v. 20; 8:24, 28, 58; 18:5), in keeping with the reference to God as "I AM" in Ex. 3:14 and the book of Isaiah (e.g., Isa. 41:4; 43:10, 25). Jesus is the "bread of life" in the sense that he nourishes people spiritually and satisfies the deep spiritual longings of their souls. In that sense, those who trust in him **shall not hunger**; that is, their spiritual longing to know God will be satisfied (cf. John 4:14 for a similar discussion of satisfying people's spiritual thirst).

6:37 Whoever comes to me I will never cast out implies that people should never think, "Maybe I am not chosen by God, and therefore maybe Jesus will reject me when I come to him." Jesus promises to receive everyone who comes to him and trusts him for salvation. Yet, a few verses later (v. 44) Jesus states the paradoxical and corresponding truth that once people come to Jesus, they will realize that behind their willing decision to come and believe lies the mysterious, invisible work of the Father who all along was drawing them to Christ. See Romans 9; Eph. 1:3–6.

6:39 All that he has given me implies that everyone who has been chosen by the Father and has been "given" by the Father to the Son for salvation will in fact be saved. In v. 40 Jesus further explains that these people whom the Father has "given" him are also those who believe in the Son and have "eternal life."

6:40 everyone who . . . believes in him. See notes on 3:16; 3:18. This verse implies that no true believer will ever lose his or her salvation, since everyone who believes in the Son will also **have eternal life** and will continue as a believer until the final judgment (**the last day**), when Jesus **will raise him up** into the fullness of eternal life.

6:43 The grumbling is reminiscent of the pattern of grumbling against God in the OT (e.g., Ex. 16:8; Num. 14:27; Ps. 95:8–9).

6:44 No one can come to me means "no one is able to come to me" (Gk. *dynamai* means "to be able"). This implies that no human being in the world, on his own, has the moral and spiritual ability to come to Christ unless God the Father **draws him**, that is, gives him the desire and inclination to come and the ability to place trust in Christ (see notes on v. 37; 12:32).

6:46 seen the Father. See note on 1:18.

6:51 living bread. The "bread" Jesus gives is his flesh (a reference to Jesus' death on the cross). Jesus' statement intermingles physical and spiritual truth. Jesus is not talking about literal "bread," but he is the true "living bread" in the sense that those who believe in him have their spiritual hunger satisfied. He becomes this spiritually satisfying "bread" by sacrificing his own physical body in his death on the cross, and in that sense he can say that this spiritual bread is **my flesh**.

6:52 Another example of misunderstanding in which Jesus' hearers take him literally (cf. 3:4; 4:15). Jesus teaches spiritual truths by referring to physical objects, and people frequently misunderstand.

6:53 Unless you eat the flesh of the Son of Man and drink his blood cannot be intended literally, for no one ever did that. As Jesus has done frequently in this Gospel, he is speaking in terms of physical items in this world to teach about spiritual realities. Here, to "eat" Jesus' flesh has the spiritual meaning of trusting or believing in him, especially in his death for the sins of mankind. (See also v. 35, where Jesus speaks of coming to him as satisfying "hunger" and believing in him as satisfying "thirst.") Similarly, to "drink his blood" means to trust in his atoning death, which is represented by the shedding of his blood. Although Jesus is not speaking specifically about the Lord's Supper here, there is a parallel theme, because the receiving of eternal life through being united with "the Son of Man" is represented in the Lord's Supper (where Jesus' followers symbolically eat his flesh and drink his blood; cf. 1 Cor. 11:23–32). This is anticipated in OT feasts (see 1 Cor. 5:7) and consummated in the marriage supper of the Lamb (Rev. 19:9).

my flesh is true food, and my blood is true drink. 56 Whoever feeds on my flesh and drinks
my blood [n]abides in me, and I in him. 57 As [o]the living Father [p]sent me, and [q]I live because
of the Father, so whoever feeds on me, he also will live because of me. 58 [r]This is the bread
that came down from heaven, not like the bread[1] the fathers ate, and died. Whoever feeds
on this bread will live forever." 59 Jesus[2] said these things in the synagogue, as he taught
[s]at Capernaum.

The Words of Eternal Life

60 [t]When many of his disciples heard it, they said, "This is a hard saying; who can listen
to it?" 61 But Jesus, [v]knowing in himself that his disciples were grumbling about this, said
to them, "Do you take offense at this? 62 Then what if you were to see [w]the Son of Man
[x]ascending to [y]where he was before? 63 [z]It is the Spirit who gives life; [a]the flesh is no help
at all. [b]The words that I have spoken to you are spirit and life. 64 But [c]there are some of
you who do not believe." (For Jesus [v]knew from the beginning who those were who did
not believe, and [d]who it was who would betray him.) 65 And he said, "This is why I told
you [e]that no one can come to me unless it is granted him by the Father."
66 [f]After this many of his disciples turned back and no longer walked with him. 67 So Jesus
said to [g]the Twelve, "Do you want to go away as well?" 68 Simon Peter answered him, "Lord,
to whom shall we go? You have [h]the words of eternal life, 69 and [i]we have believed, and
have come to know, that [j]you are [k]the Holy One of God." 70 Jesus answered them, [l]"Did I
not choose you, [g]the Twelve? And yet one of you is [m]a devil." 71 He spoke of Judas [n]the son
of Simon Iscariot, for [o]he, one of the Twelve, was going to betray him.

Jesus at the Feast of Booths

7 After this Jesus went about in Galilee. He would not go about in Judea, because [p]the
Jews[3] were seeking to kill him. 2 Now [q]the Jews' Feast of [r]Booths was at hand. 3 [s]So his
brothers[4] said to him, "Leave here and go to Judea, that your disciples also may see the
works you are doing. 4 For no one works in secret if he seeks to be known openly. If you do
these things, [t]show yourself to the world." 5 [u]For not even [v]his brothers believed in him.
6 Jesus said to them, [w]"My time has not yet come, but your time is always here. 7 The world

[1] Greek lacks *the bread* [2] Greek *He* [3] Or *Judeans*; Greek *Ioudaioi* probably refers here to Jewish religious leaders, and others under their influence, in that time [4] Or *brothers and sisters*; also verses 5, 10

56 [n]ch. 15:4, 5; 1 John 3:24; 4:13, 15, 16
57 [o][ch. 5:26]; See Matt. 16:16 [p]See ch. 3:17 [q]ch. 11:25; Rev. 1:18
58 [r]ver. 31, 33, 49-51
59 [s]ver. 24
60 [t]ver. 66; [ver. 64]
61 [v][ch. 2:24, 25]
62 [w]ver. 27 [x]See Mark 16:19 [y][ch. 17:5]; See ch. 3:13
63 [z][1 Cor. 15:45; 2 Cor. 3:6] [a]ch. 3:6 [b]ver. 68
64 [c]ver. 66 [v][See ver. 61 above] [d]ver. 71; ch. 13:11
65 [e]ver. 44, 45; ch. 3:27
66 [f]ver. 60, 64
67 [g]ver. 70, 71
68 [h]Acts 5:20; [ch. 12:50; 17:8]
69 [i][ch. 11:27; 1 John 4:16] [j]See ch. 1:49 [k]See Mark 1:24
70 [l]See ch. 13:18 [g][See ver. 67 above] [m]ch. 13:2, 27; 17:12
71 [n]ch. 13:26 [o]ver. 64, 67

Chapter 7

1 [p]ch. 5:18; 8:37, 40; 11:53
2 [q]ch. 5:1; 6:4 [r]See Lev. 23:34
3 [s]ver. 5, 10; See Matt. 12:46
4 [t][ch. 14:22; 18:20]
5 [u][Matt. 13:57; Mark 3:21] [v]ver. 3, 10
6 [w][ver. 8, 30]; See ch. 2:4

6:59 synagogue. See note on Luke 4:16.

6:60 It was a **hard saying** because they wrongly interpreted Jesus' statements literally (see note on v. 53).

6:63 The **flesh** (i.e., human nature including emotions, will, and intellect) is completely incapable of producing genuine spiritual life (see Rom. 7:14–25), for this can only be done by **the Spirit**. But the Holy Spirit works powerfully in and through the **words** that Jesus speaks, and those words **are spirit and life** in the sense that they work in the unseen spiritual realm and awaken genuine spiritual life.

6:64 Jesus' divine omniscience is shown by the fact that he knew the status of everyone's heart and therefore he knew **who those were who did not believe**. He also knew the future because he knew **who it was who would betray him**. Only God could know these things.

6:66 Many of these early **disciples** were not genuine disciples of Christ, for they **turned back**. Their initial "faith" was not genuine and they were perhaps following Jesus only because of the physical benefits he gave, such as healing and multiplying food.

6:67 This is the first reference to **the Twelve** in this Gospel (cf. vv. 70, 71; 20:24). Their existence and appointment are assumed from the Synoptics (cf. the reference to Andrew as "Simon Peter's brother" in 1:40).

6:68 To whom shall we go rightly implies that there is no other teacher who can lead people to eternal life and to true fellowship with God himself.

6:69 We have believed implies that Jesus' disciples at this point had genuine, saving faith (though they would still have to learn much more about Jesus' death and resurrection and the meaning of these things for them). Peter's confession of Jesus as **the Holy One of God** anticipates later references to Jesus being consecrated, or set apart for service to God (10:36; 17:19). In the OT, God was called "the Holy One of Israel" (Ps. 71:22; Isa. 43:3; 54:5). See the similar confessions of Jesus as the Christ by Peter in the Synoptics (Matt. 16:16; Mark 8:29; Luke 9:20).

7:2 The Jewish **Feast of Booths**, also called Tabernacles, was celebrated in September or October, two months prior to the Feast of Dedication (see note on 10:22). It is called the "Feast of Booths" because people lived in leafy shelters to remember God's faithfulness to Israel during her wilderness wanderings (Lev. 23:42–43; cf. Matt. 17:4 par.). It was also a time of celebration and thanksgiving for the harvest (Lev. 23:39–41; Deut. 16:13–15; cf. Ex. 23:16; 34:22). See also note on John 2:13.

7:3–4 Jesus' brothers (cf. Matt. 13:55; Mark 6:3) are best understood to be other naturally born sons of Mary, for that is the ordinary and natural sense of the Greek *adelphoi* ("brothers"). However, Roman Catholics believe that Mary remained a "perpetual virgin" and did not have other naturally born children, so they commonly explain this verse by saying that Joseph must have had other children from a previous marriage (or, less frequently, by saying that these must be Jesus' cousins). (But cf. Matt. 1:25; Luke 2:7.) Jesus' brothers' advice stems from unbelief (cf. John 7:5) and reveals a fundamental misunderstanding of Jesus' messianic identity (cf. Matt. 4:5–7 par.).

7:5 So real and genuine was Jesus' humanity, and so well hidden was his deity before he began his earthly ministry, that even those who had lived in the same house with him for nearly 30 years did not know who he was: **not even his brothers believed in him**. They lived and ate and slept in the same rooms as the eternal Son of God and did not know it.

7:6 My time in John probably refers to the cross (see note on 2:4). Jesus speaks at a deeper level that is misunderstood by his brothers. **Your time** then refers to "your time to go up to the feast with the crowds who are going to Jerusalem." In both cases the word "time" is *kairos* in Greek, meaning time that is suitable, right, or opportune.

7:7 The world **cannot hate** Jesus' brothers because they themselves belonged to the world; they did not yet believe in Jesus.

7[x]ch. 15:18, 24 [y]ch. 3:19; [Col. 1:21; 1 John 3:12]
8[z]See ch. 2:4
10[a]ver. 3, 5
11[b]ver. 1 [c]ch. 11:56
12[d]ver. 32 [e][ver. 40-43] [f]ver. 47
13[g]ch. 19:38; 20:19; [ch. 9:22; 12:42]
14[h]ver. 28
15[i][ver. 46; Luke 2:47; 4:22; Acts 4:13]
16[j]ch. 8:28; 12:49; 14:10, 24; [ch. 3:34] [k]See ch. 3:17
17[l][ch. 8:31, 32; 14:21, 23] [m][ch. 8:43; Ps. 25:9; Dan. 12:10; Phil. 3:15] [n]See ch. 5:30
18[o]ch. 5:41; 8:50
19[p]ver. 23; See ch. 1:17 [q]ver. 1
20[r]ch. 8:48, 52; 10:20; [Matt. 11:18; Mark 3:22; Luke 7:33]
21[s]ver. 23; ch. 5:2-9
22[t]Lev. 12:3 [u]Gen. 17:10
23[v]ch. 5:16; See Matt. 12:2
24[w]ch. 8:15; [Isa. 11:3; 2 Cor. 10:7]; See Deut. 1:16, 17
25[x]ver. 1
26[y]ch. 18:20 [z]ver. 48
27[a][ch. 6:42; 8:14, 19; 9:29] [b]ch. 19:9 [c][ver. 42]
28[d]ver. 14 [a][See ver. 27 above] [e]ch. 8:42; [ch. 5:43] [f]See ch. 8:26 [g]ch. 8:19; 15:21; [ch. 4:22; 8:55]
29[h]ch. 8:55; See Matt. 11:27 [i]ch. 6:46; 9:16, 33; [ch. 1:14] [j]See ch. 3:17
30[k]ver. 44; ch. 10:39; [Matt. 21:46] [l]ch. 8:20 [m]ver. 6

cannot hate you, but [x]it hates me because I testify about it that [y]its works are evil. **8** You go
up to the feast. I am not[1] going up to this feast, for [z]my time has not yet fully come." **9** After
saying this, he remained in Galilee.

10 But after [a]his brothers had gone up to the feast, then he also went up, not publicly
but in private. **11** [b]The Jews [c]were looking for him at the feast, and saying, "Where is he?"
12 And there was much [d]muttering about him among the people. [e]While some said, "He is
a good man," others said, "No, [f]he is leading the people astray." **13** Yet [g]for fear of the Jews
no one spoke openly of him.

14 About the middle of the feast Jesus went up [h]into the temple and began teaching.
15 The Jews therefore [i]marveled, saying, "How is it that this man has learning,[2] when he
has never studied?" **16** So Jesus answered them, [j]"My teaching is not mine, but his [k]who
sent me. **17** [l]If anyone's will is to do God's[3] will, [m]he will know whether the teaching is
from God or whether I [n]am speaking on my own authority. **18** The one who speaks on his
own authority [o]seeks his own glory; but the one who seeks the glory of him who sent him
is true, and in him there is no falsehood. **19** [p]Has not Moses given you the law? Yet none
of you keeps the law. [q]Why do you seek to kill me?" **20** The crowd answered, [r]"You have
a demon! Who is seeking to kill you?" **21** Jesus answered them, "I did [s]one work, and you
all marvel at it. **22** [t]Moses gave you circumcision (not that it is from Moses, but [u]from the
fathers), and you circumcise a man on the Sabbath. **23** If on the Sabbath a man receives
circumcision, so that the law of Moses may not be broken, [v]are you angry with me because
on the Sabbath I made a man's whole body well? **24** [w]Do not judge by appearances, but
judge with right judgment."

Can This Be the Christ?

25 Some of the people of Jerusalem therefore said, "Is not this the man whom [x]they seek
to kill? **26** And here he is, [y]speaking openly, and they say nothing to him! Can it be that [z]the
authorities really know that this is the Christ? **27** But [a]we know [b]where this man comes
from, and when the Christ appears, [c]no one will know where he comes from." **28** So Jesus
proclaimed, [d]as he taught in the temple, [a]"You know me, and you know where I come
from. But [e]I have not come of my own accord. [f]He who sent me is true, [g]and him you do
not know. **29** [h]I know him, for I come [i]from him, and [j]he sent me." **30** [k]So they were seeking
to arrest him, but [l]no one laid a hand on him, [m]because his hour had not yet come. **31** Yet

[1] Some manuscripts add *yet* [2] Or *this man knows his letters* [3] Greek *his*

7:8 Jesus' statement, "**I am not going up to this feast**," should not be taken as a mistake by John or a falsehood by Jesus, even though John then records that Jesus did go up to the feast (v. 10). The Greek present tense in v. 8 can legitimately have the sense, "I am not now going," indicating that Jesus did not go up to the feast in the way the brothers suggested, for they wanted Jesus to manifest himself to his contemporaries for secular reasons. In fact, many of the oldest and best manuscripts have *oupō* (Gk. "not yet") rather than simply *ouk* (Gk. "not"), and that might have been the original reading, though the reading "not" seems more likely to be original.

7:12 leading the people astray. Later Jewish literature likewise calls Jesus a deceiver.

7:14 temple. See note on 2:14.

7:15 The Jews may include both the Judean crowds and the Jewish authorities. **he has never studied**. Jesus lacked formal rabbinic training (as did his disciples, Acts 4:13), but his teaching and authority came from God (John 7:16; 8:28; cf. Matt. 5:21ff.; 7:28–29).

7:17 Whether people follow Jesus depends on whether they are willing to obey him. Those who are morally willing to follow Jesus will be intellectually convinced that he is the way, the truth, and the life (cf. 14:6).

7:20 This is one of several instances where Jesus is falsely charged with **demon** possession (cf. 8:48; 10:20; Matt. 12:24 par.). The same charge was leveled against John the Baptist (Matt. 11:18). Other false accusations include breaking the Sabbath (John 5:16, 18; 9:16), blasphemy (5:18; 8:59; 10:31, 33, 39; 19:7), deceiving the people (7:12, 47), being a Samaritan (8:48), madness (10:20), and criminal activity (18:30).

7:21 This **one work** is probably the healing of the invalid in 5:1–15.

7:22 This recalls Gen. 17:9–14 (**the fathers**, i.e., Abraham), Ex. 12:44, 48–49, and Lev. 12:3 (**Moses**). Jesus' argument is "from the lesser to the greater": the Jews were to circumcise their males on the eighth day even if that day fell on the Sabbath (the "lesser" issue); if "perfecting" one part of the human body on the Sabbath was legitimate, how much more the healing of an entire person (the "greater" issue).

7:26 The authorities probably refers to the Sanhedrin (cf. v. 48; 12:42; see note on 3:1).

7:27 But we know. Some rabbis taught that the Messiah would be wholly unknown until he set out to procure salvation for Israel. Others, however, were sure about his birthplace (v. 42; cf. Matt. 2:1–6).

7:28 temple. See note on 2:14.

7:30 Because his hour had not yet come shows Jesus' strong awareness of God's providential direction of the circumstances of his life; his enemies could not capture or harm him until "the hour" of his arrest, crucifixion, and death, as ordained by God. God the Father would not allow these things to happen until the earthly ministry of Jesus (God the Son) was complete. (See note on 2:4; also 8:20; 12:23, 27; 13:1; 17:1.)

7:31 Since the Messiah would be a prophet like Moses (Deut. 18:15, 18) and Moses performed many miraculous signs at the exodus (Exodus 7–11), the Messiah was expected to perform miracles as well (cf. John 6:30–31). In any case, it would have been natural for people to wonder, after witnessing Jesus' miracles, if he was the Messiah.

[n]many of the people believed in him. They said, [o]"When the Christ appears, will he do
more signs than this man has done?"

Officers Sent to Arrest Jesus

32 The Pharisees heard the crowd [p]muttering these things about him, and the chief
priests and Pharisees sent [q]officers to arrest him. 33 Jesus then said, [r]"I will be with you a
little longer, and then [s]I am going to him who sent me. 34 [t]You will seek me and you will
not find me. Where I am you cannot come." 35 The Jews said to one another, "Where does
this man intend to go that we will not find him? [u]Does he intend to go to [v]the Dispersion
among [w]the Greeks and teach the Greeks? 36 What does he mean by saying, [x]'You will seek
me and you will not find me,' and, 'Where I am you cannot come'?"

Rivers of Living Water

37 [y]On the last day of the feast, the great day, Jesus stood up and cried out, [z]"If anyone
thirsts, let him [a]come to me and drink. 38 Whoever believes in me, [b]as[1] the Scripture has
said, [c]'Out of his heart will flow rivers of [d]living water.'" 39 Now [e]this he said about the
Spirit, [f]whom those who believed in him were to receive, [g]for as yet the Spirit had not
been [h]given, [i]because Jesus was not yet glorified.

Division Among the People

40 When they heard these words, [j]some of the people said, "This really is [k]the Prophet."
41 Others said, "This is [l]the Christ." But some said, [m]"Is the Christ to come from Galilee?
42 Has not the Scripture said that the Christ comes [n]from the offspring of David, and
comes [o]from Bethlehem, the village [p]where David was?" 43 So there was [q]a division
among the people over him. 44 [r]Some of them wanted to arrest him, but no one laid
hands on him.

45 [s]The officers then came to the chief priests and Pharisees, who said to them, "Why did
you not bring him?" 46 The officers answered, [t]"No one ever spoke like this man!" 47 The
Pharisees answered them, [u]"Have you also been deceived? 48 [v]Have any of the authorities
or the Pharisees believed in him? 49 But this crowd that does not know the law is accursed."
50 [w]Nicodemus, who had gone to him before, and who was one of them, said to them,
51 [x]"Does our law judge a man without first [y]giving him a hearing and learning what he
does?" 52 They replied, [z]"Are you from Galilee too? Search and see that [a]no prophet arises
from Galilee."

[1] *Or let him come to me, and let him who believes in me drink. As*

31 [n]ch. 8:30; 10:42; 11:45; 12:11; [ch. 2:23; 12:42; Matt. 21:11] [o]Matt. 12:23
32 [p]ver. 12 [q]ver. 45, 46
33 [r]ch. 12:35; 13:33; 14:19; 16:16-19 [s]ch. 16:5
34 [t]ch. 8:21; 13:33
35 [u][ch. 8:22] [v]James 1:1; 1 Pet. 1:1; [Isa. 11:12; Zeph. 3:10] [w]ch. 12:20
36 [x]ver. 34
37 [y]Lev. 23:36; Num. 29:35; Neh. 8:18 [z]Isa. 55:1; See ch. 4:14 [a]See ch. 6:35
38 [b][Isa. 12:3; Ezek. 47:1] [c]ch. 4:14; [Prov. 18:4] [d]See ch. 4:10
39 [e]Isa. 44:3; [1 Cor. 12:13; Gal. 3:14] [f]Joel 2:28; Acts 2:16-18; [ch. 1:33; 20:22; Luke 24:49] [g]Acts 2:4, 33 [h]ch. 3:34; Luke 11:13 [i]ch. 14:16, 17; 16:7
40 [j]See ver. 31 [k]ch. 1:21; 6:14; See Matt. 21:11
41 [l]ver. 26 [m][ver. 52; ch. 1:46]
42 [n][Ps. 89:3, 4]; See Matt. 1:1 [o]Mic. 5:2; Matt. 2:1, 5; Luke 2:4 [p]1 Sam. 16:1
43 [q]ch. 9:16; 10:19; [ver. 12]
44 [r]ver. 30
45 [s]ver. 32
46 [t]See Matt. 7:29
47 [u]ver. 12
48 [v]1 Cor. 1:20, 26; 2:8; [ch. 12:42]
50 [w]ch. 3:1; 19:39
51 [x]Deut. 17:6; 19:15; [Acts 23:3] [y]Deut. 1:16; Prov. 18:13
52 [z]ver. 41 [a][2 Kgs. 14:25 with Josh. 19:13]

7:32 The **chief priests and Pharisees**, representing the Sanhedrin, deployed **officers** (or temple police) to arrest Jesus. The temple police were drawn from the Levites and were charged with maintaining order in the temple precincts. The order to **arrest** Jesus implies that they planned to allege criminal activity on his part (but see further vv. 45–52).

7:35 People misunderstand Jesus' statement in v. 34 (see also 3:4; 4:15; 6:52). **The Dispersion** (Gk. *diaspora*) was a common Jewish expression to refer to all the Jewish people scattered throughout the Roman Empire, and even beyond the bounds of the empire, but not living in Palestine itself.

7:37 While v. 14 makes reference to "the middle of the feast," this is now the last and greatest day of the Feast of Tabernacles. Jesus' invitation refers back to OT prophetic passages such as Isa. 55:1 (see also Isa. 12:3). **thirsts.** That is, "thirsts" for God (see note on John 4:14). To **come** to Jesus **and drink** means to believe in him, to enter into a trusting, ongoing personal relationship with him. Both the image of "coming" to Jesus as one would come to a person and the image of "drinking" imply not mere intellectual assent but a wholehearted personal involvement and participation.

7:38 Although there is no specific **Scripture** passage from the OT that matches Jesus' words here, he is apparently giving a summary of the teaching and implication of several passages that picture the inward work of God in a believer as a river of water flowing out to bring blessing to others (see Prov. 4:23; Isa. 58:11).

7:39 As yet the Spirit had not been given does not mean that there was no work of the Holy Spirit in the world prior to Jesus' resurrection, for already in Gen. 1:2 the Holy Spirit was present in the world, "hovering over the face of the waters" (see also Gen. 6:3; 41:38; Ex. 31:3; Num. 11:25). Some OT verses even speak of the Spirit of God at work within believers prior to the coming of Christ (see Num. 27:18; Deut. 34:9; Ezek. 2:2; 3:24; Dan. 4:8–9, 18; 5:11; Mic. 3:8; cf. Luke 1:15, 41, 67). This verse must therefore mean that "the Spirit had not been given" in the full and powerful sense that was promised for the new covenant age (see Ezek. 36:26, 27; 37:14; Joel 2:28–29; cf. John 20:22; Acts 2:1–13).

7:40–41 The Prophet is the figure referenced in Deut. 18:15–18 (see notes on John 1:20–21; 6:14). This "Prophet" and the Messiah were held to be different persons by some in first-century Judaism. Jesus is both.

7:42 Bethlehem, a village south of Jerusalem in the heart of Judea, is clearly predicted as the Messiah's birthplace in Mic. 5:2 (cf. Matt. 2:5–6; see also notes on John 7:27 and Matt. 2:1). **the Christ . . . comes from** (Bethlehem). The irony is apparent, for they did not realize that Bethlehem was in fact Jesus' birthplace.

7:45–46 officers. See note on v. 32. **No one ever spoke like this man** is more profoundly true than these officers could have realized, for no other man in history has been fully God as well and thus able to speak with the infinite knowledge and authority of God himself.

7:50 Nicodemus. See 3:1–15.

7:52 Contrary to the Pharisees' implication, prophets occasionally did arise **from Galilee**, such as Jonah (2 Kings 14:25), and possibly Elijah (1 Kings 17:1) and Nahum (Nah. 1:1). The Pharisees may simply have been reflecting current bias against Galileans, or John may be reporting their willingness even to distort the facts in order to make their arguments against Jesus (see John 8:44, 55).

[THE EARLIEST MANUSCRIPTS DO NOT INCLUDE 7:53–8:11.][1]

The Woman Caught in Adultery

8 **53**[[They went each to his own house, **1**but Jesus went to the Mount of Olives. **2**[b]Early
in the morning he came again to the temple. All the people came to him, and [c]he
sat down and taught them. **3**The scribes and the Pharisees brought a woman who had
been caught in adultery, and placing her in the midst **4**they said to him, "Teacher, this
woman has been caught in the act of adultery. **5**Now [d]in the Law Moses commanded us
[e]to stone such women. So what do you say?" **6**This they said [f]to test him, [g]that they might
have some charge to bring against him. Jesus bent down and wrote with his finger on the
ground. **7**And as they continued to ask him, he stood up and said to them, [h]"Let him who
is without sin among you [i]be the first to throw a stone at her." **8**And once more he bent
down and wrote on the ground. **9**But when they heard it, they went away one by one,
beginning with the older ones, and Jesus was left alone with the woman standing before
him. **10**Jesus stood up and said to her, "Woman, where are they? Has no one condemned
you?" **11**She said, "No one, Lord." And Jesus said, [j]"Neither do I condemn you; go, and from
now on [k]sin no more."]]

I Am the Light of the World

12[l]Again Jesus spoke to them, saying, [m]"I am the light of the world. Whoever [n]follows me
will not [o]walk in darkness, but will have the light of life." **13**So the Pharisees said to him,
[p]"You are bearing witness about yourself; your testimony is not true." **14**Jesus answered,
"Even if I do bear witness about myself, [q]my testimony is true, for I know [r]where I came
from and [s]where I am going, but [t]you do not know where I come from or where I am
going. **15**[u]You judge according to the flesh; [v]I judge no one. **16**Yet even if I do judge, [w]my
judgment is true, for [x]it is not I alone who judge, but I and the Father[2] who sent me. **17**[y]In
your Law it is written that the testimony of two people is true. **18**I am the one who bears
witness about myself, and [z]the Father who sent me bears witness about me." **19**They said
to him therefore, "Where is your Father?" Jesus answered, [a]"You know neither me nor
my Father. [b]If you knew me, you would know my Father also." **20**These words he spoke
in [c]the treasury, as he taught in the temple; but [d]no one arrested him, because [e]his hour
had not yet come.

21So he said to them again, [f]"I am going away, and [g]you will seek me, and [h]you will
die in your sin. Where I am going, you cannot come." **22**So the Jews said, [i]"Will he kill
himself, since he says, 'Where I am going, you cannot come'?" **23**He said to them, [j]"You
are from below; I am from above. [k]You are of this world; [l]I am not of this world. **24**I told

Chapter 8
2[b][Luke 21:38] [c]Matt. 5:1; Luke 4:20
5[d]Lev. 20:10; Deut. 22:22 [e]Deut. 22:24; Ezek. 16:38, 40
6[f]Matt. 16:1; 19:3; 22:18, 35; Mark 8:11; 10:2; 12:15; Luke 10:25; 11:16 [g]See Luke 11:54
7[h]Rom. 2:1, 22 [i]Deut. 17:7
11[j]ver. 15; [ch. 3:17; Luke 12:14] [k]ch. 5:14
12[l]ch. 7:37, 38 [m][Ps. 36:9; Isa. 42:6; 49:6; Mal. 4:2]; See ch. 1:4, 9 [n]ch. 12:26; 21:19 [o]See ch. 12:35
13[p]ch. 5:31
14[q][Rev. 3:14] [r]ch. 13:3; 16:28 [s]ver. 21; ch. 7:33 [t][ch. 7:28; 9:29]
15[u]ch. 7:24; 1 Sam. 16:7; [Job 10:4] [v]ch. 12:47; [ver. 11]
16[w]ch. 5:30 [x]ver. 29; ch. 16:32
17[y]See Num. 35:30
18[z]ch. 5:37
19[a]ver. 55; ch. 16:3 [b]ch. 14:7
20[c]See Matt. 27:6 [d]ch. 7:30 [e]ch. 7:8
21[f]ch. 14:28; [ch. 14:2, 3; 16:7] [g]See ch. 7:34 [h]ver. 24; Ezek. 3:18; 33:8
22[i][ch. 7:35]
23[j][ver. 44; ch. 3:31] [k]1 John 4:5 [l]ch. 17:14, 16

[1] Some manuscripts do not include 7:53–8:11; others add the passage here or after 7:36 or after 21:25 or after Luke 21:38, with variations in the text
[2] Some manuscripts *he*

7:53–8:11 There is considerable doubt that this story is part of John's original Gospel, for it is absent from all of the oldest manuscripts. But there is nothing in it unworthy of sound doctrine. It seems best to view the story as something that probably happened during Jesus' ministry but that was not originally part of what John wrote in his Gospel. Therefore it should not be considered as part of Scripture and should not be used as the basis for building any point of doctrine unless confirmed in Scripture.

8:12 I am. See note on 6:35. Jesus is **the light of the world** (see note on 1:4–5; also 3:19–21; 12:35–36, 46). Jesus fulfills OT promises of the coming of the "light" of salvation and the "light" of God (e.g., Ex. 25:37; Lev. 24:2; Ps. 27:1; Isa. 9:2; 42:6; 49:6; John 9:5; Acts 13:47; 26:18, 23; Eph. 5:8–14; 1 John 1:5–7).

8:13–14 The Pharisees' challenge continues the dispute of 5:31–47 (see note on 5:31).

8:15 according to the flesh. That is, according to the natural understanding and human standards of this world. When Jesus says, "**I judge no one**," he means that during his earthly ministry he did not come as judge of the world but as its Savior (see 3:17; 12:47). However, Jesus' coming does itself provide a basis for division and thus "judgment" in another sense (see 3:19; 9:39), and at a later time Jesus will come to judge the entire world (see 5:22, 27, 29; 12:48). In yet another sense, where "judge" means "rightly evaluate," Jesus does judge events and people throughout his earthly ministry (see 5:30; 7:24; 8:16, 26).

8:20 The **treasury** as a structure is mentioned in Josephus (*Jewish Antiquities* 19.294; *Jewish War* 6.282) and likely was located adjacent to the Court of the Women (Josephus, *Jewish War* 5.200; cf. Mark 12:41–44; Luke 21:1–4). The NT occurrences of this Greek term may indicate either a collection box for the treasury or the treasury structure itself. Furthermore, in John 8:20 the Greek preposition (*en*), translated as "*in* the treasury," can mean "in the vicinity of" (i.e., "at" or "by"); thus it need not be assumed that Jesus and the disciples had access to the secured halls that stored the immense wealth of the temple. **hour**. See notes on 2:4; 7:30.

8:21 Where I am going refers to heaven, in the presence of the Father.

8:23 From below means belonging to this natural world; **from above** means from heaven, from God the Father, and also following his will and speaking his truth.

8:24 I am he at one level may simply mean "I am the Messiah" or the one "sent" by the Father (or, in view of v. 12, "I am the light of the world"). The Greek phrase *egō eimi* simply means "I am" and is used in an ordinary sense in 9:9 by a man Jesus healed. However, John is fond of using words with a double meaning (see notes on 3:14; 4:10; 11:50–51; 19:19; cf. also 3:7–8) and this verse is one of several that hint at a connection with God's statement

you that you [m]would die in your sins, for [n]unless you believe that [o]I am he you will die
in your sins." 25 So they said to him, [p]"Who are you?" Jesus said to them, "Just what I
have been telling you from the beginning. 26 I have much to say about you and much
to judge, but [q]he who sent me is true, and I declare [r]to the world [s]what I have heard
from him." 27 They did not understand that [t]he had been speaking to them about the
Father. 28 So Jesus said to them, "When you have [u]lifted up the Son of Man, [v]then you
will know that [w]I am he, and that [x]I do nothing on my own authority, but [y]speak just
as the Father taught me. 29 And [z]he who sent me is with me. [z]He has not left me alone,
for [a]I always do the things that are pleasing to him." 30 As he was saying these things,
[b]many believed in him.

The Truth Will Set You Free

31 So Jesus said to the Jews who had believed him, [c]"If you abide in my word, you are
truly my disciples, 32 and you will [d]know the truth, and the truth [e]will set you free." 33 They
answered him, [f]"We are offspring of Abraham and have never been enslaved to anyone.
How is it that you say, 'You will become free'?"

34 Jesus answered them, "Truly, truly, I say to you, [g]everyone who practices sin is a slave[1]
to sin. 35 [h]The slave does not remain in the house forever; [i]the son remains forever. 36 So if
the Son sets you free, you will be free indeed. 37 I know that you are offspring of Abraham;
yet [j]you seek to kill me because my word finds no place in you. 38 [k]I speak of what I have
seen with my Father, and you do what you have heard [l]from your father."

You Are of Your Father the Devil

39 They answered him, [m]"Abraham is our father." Jesus said to them, [n]"If you were
Abraham's children, you would be doing the works Abraham did, 40 but now [o]you seek
to kill me, a man who has told you the truth [p]that I heard from God. This is not what
Abraham did. 41 You are doing the works your father did." They said to him, [q]"We were
not born of sexual immorality. We have [r]one Father—even God." 42 Jesus said to them, [s]"If
God were your Father, you would love me, for [t]I came from God and [u]I am here. [v]I came
not of my own accord, but [w]he sent me. 43 [x]Why do you not understand what I say? It is
because you cannot [y]bear to hear my word. 44 [z]You are of your father the devil, and your
will is to do your father's desires. [a]He was a murderer from the beginning, and [b]does not
stand in the truth, because there is no truth in him. [c]When he lies, he speaks out of his
own character, for he is a liar and the father of lies. 45 But because I tell the truth, you do
not believe me. 46 Which one of you convicts me of sin? If I tell the truth, why do you not

[1] Greek *bondservant*; also verse 35

24 [m]ver. 21 [n]ch. 16:9 [o]Mark 13:6; Luke 21:8
25 [p][ch. 1:19]
26 [q]ch. 3:33; 7:28; Rom. 3:4 [r][ch. 18:20] [s]ver. 40; ch. 15:15; [ch. 3:32; Rev. 1:1]
27 [t]ver. 18, 26
28 [u]ch. 3:14; 12:32, 34 [v][ch. 16:8-11] [w]See ver. 24 [x]See ch. 5:30 [y]See ch. 7:16
29 [z]ver. 16; ch. 16:32; Acts 10:38; See ch. 10:38 [a]ch. 4:34; 5:30; 6:38; [1 John 3:22]
30 [b]See ch. 7:31
31 [c]ch. 15:7, 8; 2 John 9
32 [d]2 John 1 [e]ver. 36; Rom. 6:18, 22; 8:2; 1 Cor. 7:22; 2 Cor. 3:17; Gal. 5:1, 13; James 1:25; 2:12; 1 Pet. 2:16
33 [f]ver. 37, 39; Matt. 3:9; [Luke 19:9; Rom. 9:7]
34 [g]Rom. 6:16-20; Titus 3:3; 2 Pet. 2:19
35 [h]Gen. 21:10; Gal. 4:30 [i]Luke 15:31
37 [j]ver. 40; See ch. 7:1
38 [k]ch. 3:32; 5:19; 6:46 [l]ver. 41, 44
39 [m]ver. 33, 56 [n][Gal. 3:7, 9]
40 [o]ver. 37 [p]ver. 26
41 [q][Hos. 2:4] [r]Deut. 32:6; Isa. 63:16; 64:8; [ver. 47]
42 [s][1 John 5:1] [t]1 John 5:20; [Heb. 10:9] [u]ch. 16:28; 17:8 [v]ch. 7:28 [w]See ch. 3:17
43 [x]ch. 7:17 [y]Jer. 6:10; [1 Cor. 2:14]
44 [z]1 John 3:8, 12; [ver. 23]; See Matt. 13:38 [a]Gen. 4:8, 9; 1 John 3:12, 15; [Rom. 5:12] [b][1 John 2:4] [c]Gen. 3:4; 2 Cor. 11:3; Rev. 12:9

to Moses in Ex. 3:14, "I AM [Gk. Septuagint: *Egō eimi*] WHO I AM." See notes on John 6:20; 8:58.

8:28 lifted up. See note on 3:14.

8:29 This verse affirms not only Jesus' lack and avoidance of sin but also that he is always doing positive things that are **pleasing** to God.

8:31 Their "belief" is shown to be false in the course of the story (see vv. 33–47). To **abide in** Jesus' word means to continue believing what Jesus has said and walking in obedience to him (see note on 15:4; also 6:56; 1 John 2:6, 28; 3:6). This verse shows that continuing to trust Jesus and obey him is one test of who are **truly my disciples**.

8:32 This verse is frequently quoted out of context, but the connection with v. 31 shows that Jesus is only talking about one way to **know the truth**, and that is by continuing to believe and obey his word. **set you free**. From the guilt and enslaving power of sinful patterns of conduct (see note on v. 34).

8:34 A slave to sin (see also notes on Rom. 6:16 and 1 Cor. 7:21) means unable to escape from sinful patterns of conduct without the help of Jesus to set a person free (see John 8:36).

8:36 Sets you free from both the guilt and the life-controlling power of sin (and probably also from the accompanying influence of demonic activity, as Jesus mentions in v. 44).

8:37 my word finds no place in you. It was not the persuasiveness or power of Jesus' words that determined how people responded to him, but the spiritual condition of their own hearts.

8:39–58 our father. See note on 3:3–6.

8:39–40 Jesus had just agreed that they were physically descended from Abraham (v. 37), but now he denies that they are truly **Abraham's children**, for their behavior contradicts their claim. This implies that Abraham's true children are only those who believe in Jesus (cf. Rom. 2:28–29; 9:6–8). **What Abraham did** most prominently was believe God (Gen. 15:6; Rom. 4:3; Gal. 3:6; James 2:23). Similarly, the Jews who are speaking here should believe in Jesus, for he comes from God and is speaking the very words of God.

8:42–44 Their response to Jesus shows they are not truly God's children, but children of the Devil. The clear implication is that not all religious people are children of God—not even Jewish people who reject Jesus—but only those who believe in Jesus as the Messiah.

8:43 not understand. Throughout this Gospel many people misunderstand Jesus and his teaching. Here he gives the reason: it is **because you cannot bear** (or, "you are not able," Gk. *dynamai*) **to hear my word**, where "hear" should be taken in the sense of "hear and receive," or "hear and accept."

8:44 The Devil was **a murderer from the beginning**: that is, the Devil incited Cain to kill Abel (cf. 1 John 3:12). He **does not stand in the truth**, i.e., it is not the realm that he lives and acts and thinks in. He is **the father of lies**: at the fall, the Devil blatantly contradicted God's word (Gen. 3:3–4; cf. Gen. 2:17).

47[d][ch. 18:37; 1 John 4:6] [e][ch. 10:26] [f][ver. 41]
48[g]See ch. 7:20
49[h]ch. 5:23; [ch. 7:18]
50[i]ver. 54; ch. 5:41
51[j]ch. 5:24; 11:26 [k]See Luke 2:26
52[l][Zech. 1:5] [m]ver. 51 [n]Matt. 16:28; Heb. 2:9
53[o][ch. 4:12]
54[p]ver. 50 [q]ch. 13:32; 17:1; Acts 3:13; Heb. 5:5; 2 Pet. 1:17 [r]ver. 41
55[s]ver. 19; ch. 7:28 [t]ch. 7:29; See Matt. 11:27 [u]1 John 1:6 [v]ver. 44
56[w]ver. 39 [x]See Matt. 13:17 [y]Luke 17:22 [z][Heb. 11:13]
58[a]See Ex. 3:14
59[b]ch. 10:31

Chapter 9

2[c]See ch. 1:38 [d][Luke 13:2, 4] [e][ver. 34] [f]Ex. 20:5
3[g][ch. 11:4]
4[h]See ch. 4:34 [i]ch. 11:9; 12:35; [Rom. 13:12; Gal. 6:10]
5[j]See ch. 1:4, 5, 9; 8:12
6[k]Mark 7:33; 8:23 [l]See Matt. 9:29

believe me? **47** [d]Whoever is of God hears the words of God. [e]The reason why you do not
hear them is that [f]you are not of God."

Before Abraham Was, I Am

48 The Jews answered him, "Are we not right in saying that you are a Samaritan and
[g]have a demon?" **49** Jesus answered, "I do not have a demon, but [h]I honor my Father, and
you dishonor me. **50** Yet [i]I do not seek my own glory; there is One who seeks it, and he is
the judge. **51** Truly, truly, [j]I say to you, if anyone keeps my word, he will never [k]see death."
52 The Jews said to him, "Now we know that you have a demon! [l]Abraham died, as did the
prophets, yet [m]you say, 'If anyone keeps my word, he will never [n]taste death.' **53** [o]Are you
greater than our father Abraham, who died? And the prophets died! Who do you make
yourself out to be?" **54** Jesus answered, [p]"If I glorify myself, my glory is nothing. [q]It is my
Father who glorifies me, [r]of whom you say, 'He is our God.'[1] **55** But [s]you have not known
him. [t]I know him. If I were to say that I do not know him, I would be [u]a liar [v]like you, but
I do know him and I keep his word. **56** [w]Your father Abraham [x]rejoiced [y]that he would see
my day. [z]He saw it and was glad." **57** So the Jews said to him, "You are not yet fifty years
old, and have you seen Abraham?"[2] **58** Jesus said to them, "Truly, truly, I say to you, before
Abraham was, [a]I am." **59** So [b]they picked up stones to throw at him, but Jesus hid himself
and went out of the temple.

Jesus Heals a Man Born Blind

9 As he passed by, he saw a man blind from birth. **2** And his disciples asked him, [c]"Rabbi,
[d]who sinned, [e]this man or [f]his parents, that he was born blind?" **3** Jesus answered, "It
was not that this man sinned, or his parents, but [g]that the works of God might be displayed
in him. **4** We must [h]work the works of him who sent me [i]while it is day; night is coming,
when no one can work. **5** As long as I am in the world, [j]I am the light of the world." **6** Having
said these things, [k]he spit on the ground and made mud with the saliva. [l]Then he anointed

[1] Some manuscripts *your God* [2] Some manuscripts *has Abraham seen you?*

8:47 You do not hear in the sense of hearing, believing, and following (see note on v. 43).

8:48 Samaritan. See note on 4:4.

8:56 Abraham rejoiced that he would see the day of Christ; he **saw it and was glad**. Jesus is possibly referring to a whole pattern of joyful and confident faith in Abraham's life, rather than one specific event. If the reference is to one event, some possibilities are Gen. 12:1–3; or 17:17, 20; or 22:8, 13–18; cf. Rom. 4:13–21.

8:58 If there had been any uncertainty about Jesus' identity in other passages where he said, **"I am"** (e.g., 6:35; 9:5; 11:25), there was no confusion here because Jesus is claiming to be the one who was alive **before Abraham was**, that is, more than 2,000 years earlier. Jesus does not simply say, "Before Abraham was, I was," which would simply mean that he is more than 2,000 years old. Rather, he uses the present tense "I am" in speaking of existence more than 2,000 years earlier, thus claiming a kind of transcendence over time that could only be true of God. The words "I am" in Greek use the same expression (*Egō eimi*) found in the Septuagint in the first half of God's self-identification in Ex. 3:14, "I AM WHO I AM." Jesus is thus claiming not only to be eternal but also to be the God who appeared to Moses at the burning bush. His Jewish opponents understood his meaning immediately and they "picked up stones" to stone him to death for blasphemy (see John 8:59). See notes on 6:20; 8:24.

8:59 picked up stones. See note on Acts 7:58. Stoning was the prescribed punishment for blasphemy (Lev. 24:16; cf. Deut. 13:6–11; John 10:31–33; 11:8). However, this punishment was supposed to be the result of righteous judgment, not mob violence (Deut. 17:2–7).

9:2 The disciples' question reflects the assumption, customary in ancient Judaism, that suffering could be traced to sin. The underlying concern—well-intentioned, but misguided—was not to charge God with perpetrating evil on innocent people (cf. Ex. 20:5; Num. 14:18; Deut. 5:9). Yet the NT makes clear that suffering is not always a direct result of a person's sin (e.g., Luke 13:2–3a; 2 Cor. 12:7; Gal. 4:13; and Jesus' crucifixion; see also John 12:28, 37–41; 17:1, 5).

9:3 That the works of God might be displayed in him indicates that God in his mysterious and wise providence sometimes allows his children to go through hardship and suffering so that they can experience God's mercy and power in delivering them.

9:4 While it is day refers to the time when Jesus is here in his earthly ministry, for he is "the light of the world" (8:12; 9:5) whose presence makes everything "day." **Night** would then be the time of Jesus' crucifixion and death. Jesus shows an intense awareness of the need to fulfill all that the Father sent him to accomplish during his earthly ministry; **we** indicates that he is involving his disciples in that work as well.

9:5 I am. See note on 6:35. **the light of the world**. See note on 1:4–5.

9:6 It is unclear why Jesus **made mud** and put it on the man's eyes. There may be an echo of God's creative activity in Gen. 2:7 (cf. John 20:22): the Creator is now re-creating.

Jesus' "I Am" Statements

Absolute "I am" statements	6:20; 8:24, 28, 58; 18:5
Metaphorical "I am" statements	
1. I am the bread of life	6:35, 48, 51
2. I am the light of the world	8:12; 9:5
3. I am the door of the sheep	10:7, 9
4. I am the good shepherd	10:11, 14
5. I am the resurrection and the life	11:25
6. I am the way, the truth, and the life	14:6
7. I am the true vine	15:1

the man's eyes with the mud 7 and said to him, "Go, wash in [m]the pool of Siloam" (which
means Sent). So he went and washed and [n]came back seeing.
8 The neighbors and those who had seen him before as a beggar were saying, [o]"Is this
not the man who used to sit and beg?" 9 Some said, "It is he." Others said, "No, but he is
like him." He kept saying, "I am the man." 10 So they said to him, "Then how were your
eyes opened?" 11 He answered, [p]"The man called Jesus made mud and anointed my eyes
and said to me, 'Go to Siloam and wash.' So I went and washed and received my sight."
12 They said to him, "Where is he?" He said, "I do not know."
13 They brought to the Pharisees the man who had formerly been blind. 14 [q]Now it was a
Sabbath day when Jesus made the mud and opened his eyes. 15 [r]So the Pharisees again asked
him how he had received his sight. And he said to them, "He put mud on my eyes, and I
washed, and I see." 16 Some of the Pharisees said, "This man is not [s]from God, [t]for he does
not keep the Sabbath." But others said, [u]"How can a man who is a sinner do such signs?"
And [v]there was a division among them. 17 So they said again to the blind man, "What do
you say about him, since he has opened your eyes?" He said, [w]"He is a prophet."
18 [x]The Jews[1] did not believe that he had been blind and had received his sight, until they
called the parents of the man who had received his sight 19 and asked them, "Is this your
son, who you say was born blind? How then does he now see?" 20 His parents answered,
"We know that this is our son and that he was born blind. 21 But how he now sees we do
not know, nor do we know who opened his eyes. Ask him; he is of age. He will speak for
himself." 22 (His parents said these things [y]because they feared the Jews, for [z]the Jews had
already agreed that if anyone should [a]confess Jesus[2] to be Christ, [b]he was to be put out of
the synagogue.) 23 Therefore his parents said, [c]"He is of age; ask him."
24 So for the second time they called the man who had been blind and said to him,
[d]"Give glory to God. We know that [e]this man is a sinner." 25 He answered, "Whether he is
a sinner I do not know. One thing I do know, that though I [f]was blind, now I see." 26 They
said to him, "What did he do to you? How did he open your eyes?" 27 He answered them,
[g]"I have told you already, and you would not listen. Why do you want to hear it again?
Do you also want to become his disciples?" 28 And they reviled him, saying, "You are his
disciple, but [h]we are disciples of Moses. 29 We know that God has spoken to Moses, but as
for this man, [i]we do not know where he comes from." 30 The man answered, "Why, this is
[j]an amazing thing! [k]You do not know where he comes from, and yet he opened my eyes.
31 We know that [l]God does not listen to sinners, but [m]if anyone is a worshiper of God and
does his will, God listens to him. 32 Never since the world began has it been heard that
anyone opened the eyes of a man born blind. 33 [n]If this man were not from God, he could
do nothing." 34 They answered him, [o]"You were born in utter sin, and would you teach
us?" And they [p]cast him out.
35 Jesus heard that they had cast him out, and having found him he said, "Do you believe

7 [m]Luke 13:4 [n]ch. 11:37
8 [o][Acts 3:2, 10]
11 [p]ver. 6, 7
14 [q]ch. 5:9
15 [r]ver. 10
16 [s]See ch. 7:29 [t]See Matt. 12:2 [u]ver. 33 [v]ch. 7:43; 10:19
17 [w]See ch. 4:19; 6:14
18 [x]ver. 22; [ver. 13]
22 [y]See ch. 7:13 [z][ch. 7:45-52] [a][Rom. 10:9] [b]ch. 12:42; 16:2
23 [c]ver. 21
24 [d]Josh. 7:19; Jer. 13:16; [1 Sam. 6:5; Isa. 42:12; Acts 12:23] [e]ver. 16
25 [f]ver. 18, 24
27 [g]ver. 15
28 [h][ch. 5:45]
29 [i]See ch. 8:14
30 [j][ch. 12:37] [k][ch. 3:10]
31 [l]Job 27:9; Ps. 66:18; Prov. 28:9 [m]Ps. 34:15, 16; 145:19; Prov. 15:20; [James 5:16]
33 [n]ver. 16; [ch. 1:21; 3:2]
34 [o][ver. 2] [p][ver. 22]

[1] Greek *Ioudaioi* probably refers here to Jewish religious leaders, and others under their influence, in that time; also verse 22 [2] Greek *him*

9:7 pool of Siloam. This site had been associated in both scholarly and tourist literature with a pool connected with the remains of a Byzantine (4th–7th century A.D.) church toward the south of the Temple Mount at the terminus of Hezekiah's tunnel, which brings water from the Gihon Spring. However, additional work just southeast of the traditional site has unearthed a much larger pool (225 feet [69 m] long on one side) with steps leading down into it. This larger pool contains Hasmonean-era (c. 165–63 B.C.) coins embedded in the plaster and remains of late Second Temple (pre-A.D. 70) artifacts resting in the pool itself, dating the large pool to the time before and during the NT. It seems most likely that this is the location of the pool of Siloam referred to here. This miracle is one of several events in John in which the events in the physical world are a "sign" that points to a deeper spiritual meaning. Here Jesus gives sight to a man born blind, but this is also an evident symbol that Jesus, "the light of the world" (v. 5), brings the light of the knowledge of God.

9:14 The belated mention of the **Sabbath** (cf. 5:9 and note on Matt. 12:8) recalls the earlier Sabbath controversy in John 5. Jesus had kneaded the clay with his saliva to make mud, and kneading dough (and by analogy, clay) was included among the 39 classes of work forbidden on the Sabbath (Mishnah, *Shabbat* 7.2). Jesus' frequent conflicts with the Jews over the Sabbath suggest that by his coming he is changing the Sabbath requirements (see John 5:17).

9:18–23 The fear of the parents highlights one of the fundamental reasons in John why many do not believe. They fear people more than God (see 5:44; 12:42–43).

9:22 because they feared the Jews. This does not refer to all Jews, for the parents were Jews themselves. The expression, as often in John, refers here to the Jewish leaders who were opposed to Jesus, and to the ordinary people who followed their lead. **synagogue.** See note on Luke 4:16.

9:31–33 The man's major premise, that **God does not listen to sinners**, reflects a theme in several OT passages (e.g., Ps. 34:15; 66:18; 109:7; 145:19). The man's minor premise, that there was no precedent for the opening of **the eyes** of a person **born blind**, is also confirmed by the absence of similar instances in the OT or extrabiblical sources. The man's conclusion (cf. John 3:2) concurs with the common Jewish view that miracles were performed in answer to prayer.

9:34 Cast him out refers to expulsion from the synagogue (see note on v. 22). The way this is done suggests an impulsive action rather than excommunication based on a formal procedure.

9:35–38 The man continues to be responsive to the revelation of who Jesus is. He confesses him as **the Son of Man** (see note on 1:51) and worships him.

in [q]the Son of Man?"[1] 36 He answered, [r]"And who is he, sir, that I may believe in him?"
37 Jesus said to him, "You have seen him, and [s]it is he who is speaking to you." 38 He said,
"Lord, I believe," and he worshiped him. 39 Jesus said, [t]"For judgment I came into this world,
[u]that those who do not see may see, and [v]those who see may become blind." 40 Some of
the Pharisees near him heard these things, and said to him, [w]"Are we also blind?" 41 Jesus
said to them, "If you were blind, [x]you would have no guilt;[2] but now that you say, 'We
see,' your guilt remains.

I Am the Good Shepherd

10 "Truly, truly, I say to you, he who does not enter the sheepfold by the door but
climbs in by another way, that man is a thief and a robber. 2 But he who enters by
the door is the shepherd of the sheep. 3 To him the gatekeeper opens. The sheep hear his
voice, and he calls his own sheep by name and leads them out. 4 When he has brought out
all his own, he goes before them, and the sheep follow him, for they know his voice. 5 [y]A
stranger they will not follow, but they will flee from him, for they do not know the voice
of strangers." 6 This figure of speech Jesus [z]used with them, but they [a]did not understand
what he was saying to them.
7 So Jesus again said to them, "Truly, truly, I say to you, [b]I am the door of the sheep.
8 All who came before me are thieves and robbers, but the sheep did not listen to them.
9 I am the door. If anyone enters by me, [c]he will be saved and will go in and out and [d]find
pasture. 10 The thief comes only to steal and [e]kill and destroy. I came that they may have
life and have it abundantly. 11 [f]I am the good shepherd. The good shepherd [g]lays down his
life for the sheep. 12 He who is [h]a hired hand and not a shepherd, who does not own the
sheep, sees the wolf coming and [i]leaves the sheep and flees, and the wolf snatches them
and [j]scatters them. 13 He flees because [k]he is a hired hand and [l]cares nothing for the sheep.
14 [m]I am the good shepherd. [n]I know my own and [o]my own know me, 15 [p]just as the Father
knows me and I know the Father; and [q]I lay down my life for the sheep. 16 And [r]I have
other sheep that are not of this fold. [s]I must bring them also, and [t]they will listen to my
voice. So there will be [u]one flock, [v]one shepherd. 17 [w]"For this reason the Father loves me,

[1] Some manuscripts *the Son of God* [2] Greek *you would not have sin*

35 [q]ch. 10:36
36 [r][Rom. 10:14]
37 [s]ch. 4:26
39 [t]See ch. 5:22 [u][Matt. 11:25; Luke 4:18] [v][Matt. 9:13; 13:13; Mark 4:12; 2 Cor. 2:16]
40 [w]Rom. 2:19
41 [x]ch. 15:22, 24; [ch. 19:11; 1 John 1:8]

Chapter 10

5 [y][ver. 12, 13]
6 [z]ch. 9:40 [a]See Mark 9:32
7 [b]ver. 9; [ch. 14:6; Eph. 2:18]
9 [c][ch. 5:34] [d]Ps. 23:2; Ezek. 34:14
10 [e][Jer. 23:1; Ezek. 34:3]
11 [f]Isa. 40:11; Ezek. 34:12, 23; 37:24; Zech. 13:7; Heb. 13:20; 1 Pet. 2:25; 5:4; [ch. 21:15-17; Ps. 23; Rev. 7:17] [g]ver. 15, 17; ch. 15:13; 1 John 3:16; [Matt. 20:28; Mark 10:45]
12 [h][Ezek. 34:2-6] [i]Zech. 11:17; 13:7 [j][Jer. 23:1-3]
13 [k][1 Pet. 5:2] [l]Zech. 11:16
14 [m]See ver. 11 [n]ver. 27; Nah. 1:7; 2 Tim. 2:19 [o]ver. 4
15 [p]See Matt. 11:27 [q]See ver. 11
16 [r]Isa. 56:8 [s][Ezek. 34:11-13; Matt. 8:11, 12; Eph. 2:13-18; 1 Pet. 2:25] [t]ch. 5:25; 18:37; [Acts 28:28] [u][ch. 11:52; 12:32; 17:11, 21, 22] [v]Ezek. 34:23; 37:24
17 [w]Phil. 2:9; See ch. 5:20

9:41 If you were blind means if they had no knowledge at all about God's words or his laws, and no knowledge about who Jesus is. **You would have no guilt** (or sin, see ESV footnote) does not mean that they would be free of a sinful nature inherited from Adam, but that they would have no "guilt" for violating specific teachings or commands that they had received. Paul makes a similar argument in Rom. 1:18–3:20, namely, that all have received some knowledge of God (see Rom. 1:18–20, 32; 2:14–15).

10:1 The **sheepfold** was commonly a courtyard near or beside a house and bordered by a stone wall, in which one or several families kept their sheep, although caves and other natural formations were also used. Such sheepfolds may or may not have a formal **door** and would be guarded at the entrance by a "gatekeeper" (v. 3), who would be hired to stand watch, or by the shepherd himself (cf. vv. 7–10). The word **thief** may focus on entering by covert means and **robber** on the use of violence (cf. Luke 10:30, 36).

10:3–4 gatekeeper. See note on v. 1. Jesus' phrases **the sheep hear his voice** (v. 3) and **they know his voice** (v. 4) repeat a common theme in John: people who truly belong to God listen to and believe in the words of Jesus (cf. 5:46–47; 8:37, 45, 47). On God's appointing of human leaders to be "shepherds" of his people, see Num. 27:15–23; Isa. 63:11; Ezek. 34:1–24. Israel's exodus from Egypt is at times portrayed in terms of a flock being led by its shepherd (Ps. 77:20; Isa. 63:11, 14; cf. Ps. 78:52). OT prophetic literature envisioned a similar mode of end-time deliverance for God's people (Mic. 2:12–13). On Christ as the true shepherd, see note on John 10:11.

10:7 I am the door of the sheep. Jesus is the only way by which one can become part of the people of God (i.e., Jesus' flock). See also Ps. 118:20 and note on John 6:35.

10:8 All who came before me may hint at messianic pretenders who promised their followers freedom but instead led them into armed conflict and doom (cf. Acts 5:36–37; 21:38). **thieves and robbers**. See Ezek. 34:2–4 on Israel's shepherds who have been feeding themselves but not the sheep; see also note on John 10:1.

10:9 door. The NT elsewhere speaks of "entering" God's kingdom as through a door (e.g., Matt. 7:7, 13; 18:8–9; 25:10 par.; Acts 14:22). Jesus' language, **will go in and out**, echoes covenant terminology, especially the blessings for obedience in Deut. 28:6 (cf. Num. 27:16–17; Ps. 121:8). **Find pasture** conveys the assurance of God's provision (cf. 1 Chron. 4:40; Ps. 23:2; Isa. 49:9–10; Ezek. 34:12–15).

10:10 Jesus' promise of abundant life, which begins already in the here and now, brings to mind OT prophecies about abundant blessing (e.g., Ezek. 34:12–15, 25–31). Jesus calls his followers, not to a dour, lifeless, miserable existence that squashes human potential, but to a rich, full, joyful life, one overflowing with meaningful activities under the personal favor and blessing of God and in continual fellowship with his people.

10:11 I am the good shepherd. Another "I am" saying; see note on 6:35. In the OT, God as the true shepherd is contrasted with unfaithful shepherds who will be judged by him (Psalm 23; Isa. 40:11; Jer. 23:1–4; Ezekiel 34; Zech. 11:4–17; see note on John 10:8). But David or the Davidic Messiah is also depicted as a (good) shepherd (2 Sam. 5:2; Ps. 78:70–72; Ezek. 37:24; Mic. 5:4), as is Moses (Isa. 63:11; cf. Ps. 77:20). Jesus as God and man is the fulfillment of both of these themes. The reference to the "good shepherd" who **lays down his life for the sheep** calls to mind young David, who literally risked his life for his sheep (1 Sam. 17:34–37). But Jesus surpassed David in that he gave his life on the cross for his sheep. See also John 10:15.

10:16 The **other sheep that are not of this fold** (cf. v. 1) are Gentiles (cf. Isa. 56:8). The phrase **one flock, one shepherd** alludes to Ezek. 34:23; 37:24; but here Jesus applies it more broadly, as Jews and Gentiles will be united in one messianic community (cf. Matt. 28:18–20; Eph. 2:11–22).

10:17 I lay down my life that I may take it up again implies that Jesus voluntarily yielded up his life when he knew that his suffering was completed

[x]because [y]I lay down my life that I may take it up again. 18 [z]No one takes it from me, but
[y]I lay it down [a]of my own accord. I have authority to lay it down, and [b]I have authority to
take it up again. [c]This charge I have received from my Father."
19 [d]There was again a division among the Jews because of these words. 20 Many of
them said, [e]"He has a demon, and [f]is insane; why listen to him?" 21 Others said, "These
are not the words of one who is oppressed by a demon. [g]Can a demon open the eyes of
the blind?"

I and the Father Are One

22 At that time the Feast of Dedication took place at Jerusalem. It was winter, 23 and Jesus
was walking in the temple, [h]in the colonnade of Solomon. 24 So the Jews gathered around
him and said to him, "How long will you keep us in suspense? If you are [i]the Christ, [j]tell
us plainly." 25 Jesus answered them, "I told you, and you do not believe. [k]The works that
I do [l]in my Father's name bear witness about me, 26 but [m]you do not believe because you
are not among my sheep. 27 [n]My sheep hear my voice, and I know them, and they follow
me. 28 [o]I give them eternal life, and [p]they will never perish, and [q]no one will snatch them
out of my hand. 29 My Father, [r]who has given them to me,[1] [s]is greater than all, and no one
is able to snatch them out of [t]the Father's hand. 30 [u]I and the Father are one."
31 [v]The Jews picked up stones again to stone him. 32 Jesus answered them, "I have shown
you many good works from the Father; for which of them are you going to stone me?"
33 The Jews answered him, "It is not for a good work that we are going to stone you but
[w]for blasphemy, because you, being a man, [x]make yourself God." 34 Jesus answered them,
"Is it not written in [y]your Law, [z]'I said, you are gods'? 35 If he called them gods to whom
the word of God came—and Scripture cannot be [a]broken— 36 do you say of him whom
[b]the Father consecrated and [c]sent into the world, 'You are blaspheming,' because [d]I said,
'I am the Son of God'? 37 [e]If I am not doing the works of my Father, then do not believe
me; 38 but if I do them, [f]even though you do not believe me, believe the works, that you
may know and understand that [g]the Father is in me and I am in the Father." 39 [h]Again they
sought to arrest him, but he escaped from their hands.
40 He went away again across the Jordan to the place [i]where John had been baptizing
at first, and there he remained. 41 And many came to him. And they said, "John did no

[1] Some manuscripts *What my Father has given to me*

17 [x]Isa. 53:7, 8, 12; Heb. 2:9 [y]ver. 11
18 [z][Matt. 26:53] [y][See ver. 17 above] [a][ch. 5:30] [b]ch. 2:19; [Phil. 2:7] [c]ch. 12:49; 14:31; 15:10
19 [d]ch. 7:43; 9:16
20 [e]See ch. 7:20 [f][Mark 3:21]
21 [g][Ex. 4:11; Ps. 146:8]; See ch. 9:33
23 [h]Acts 3:11; 5:12
24 [i]ch. 1:41 [j]Matt. 26:63; Luke 22:67
25 [k]ver. 38; See ch. 5:36 [l]See ch. 5:43
26 [m][ch. 8:47]
27 [n]ver. 14, 16
28 [o][1 John 2:25; 5:11] [p]ch. 17:12; 18:9 [q]ch. 6:37
29 [r]ch. 6:37; 17:2 [s][ch. 14:28] [t][Deut. 32:39; Isa. 49:2; 51:16]
30 [u]ch. 17:11, 22; [ch. 5:19; 14:9]
31 [v]ch. 8:59
33 [w]See Lev. 24:16; Matt. 9:3 [x]ch. 5:18
34 [y][ch. 12:34; 15:25; 1 Cor. 14:21] [z]Cited from Ps. 82:6
35 [a][Matt. 5:17, 19]
36 [b][ch. 6:27] [c]See ch. 3:17 [d]ch. 5:17, 18; [ver. 30]
37 [e]ch. 15:24
38 [f]ver. 25; [ch. 14:11] [g]ch. 14:10, 11, 20; 17:21, 23; [ch. 8:29]
39 [h]ch. 7:30, 44
40 [i]ch. 1:28

(see 19:30). It also implies that the divine nature of Christ was active in his resurrection: he was able to "take up" his life again.

10:20–21 The charge of demon possession (see note on 7:20) is contradicted by OT teaching that it is the Lord who gives sight to the blind (Ps. 146:8; cf. Ex. 4:11).

10:22 The eight-day **Feast of Dedication** celebrates the rededication of the Jewish temple in December 164 B.C., after its desecration by the Seleucid ruler Antiochus Epiphanes IV in 167 (*1 Macc.* 1:59).

10:23 On **temple** denoting the larger temple area, see note on 2:14. Probably because of the cold winter weather (see 10:22), Jesus did not teach out in the open but in the area called **the colonnade** (see note on 5:2) **of Solomon.** While this structure is not mentioned by name in other existing sources, it is likely that this should be identified with the stoa (covered walkway) on the eastern side of the Temple Mount, for it is here that the older parts of the temple were still remembered as Solomonic (cf. Josephus, *Jewish Antiquities* 20.220–221). Cf. Acts 3:11.

10:24–25 works. See note on 14:12. **bear witness**. See note on 5:31–47.

10:26–29 Those who belong to Jesus' flock (i.e., those who are chosen by him) are those who believe. The reason people do not believe is **because** they **are not among** Jesus' **sheep,** implying that God must first give them the ability to believe and make them part of his people with a new heart (see 1:13; 6:44). **Eternal life** (10:28) by definition can never be taken away (see note on 6:40), especially when Jesus' sheep belong to him and to his Father. **Snatch** in 10:28 and 29 denotes the use of force (see note on v. 1). Note the contrast with the "hired hand" in vv. 12–13 who abandons the flock in times of danger (cf. Isa. 43:13).

10:30 Jesus' claim that **I and the Father are one** (i.e., one entity—the Gk. is neuter; cf. 5:17–18; 10:33–38) echoes the *Shema*, the basic confession of Judaism, whose first word in Deut. 6:4 is *shema'* (Hb. "hear"). Jesus' words thus amount to a claim to deity. Hence, the Jews pick up stones to put him to death. Jesus' unity with the Father is later said to constitute the basis on which Jesus' followers are to be unified (John 17:22). As in 1:1, here again the basic building blocks of the doctrine of the Trinity emerge: "I and the Father" implies more than one person in the Godhead, but "are one" implies that God is one being.

10:31 picked up stones again to stone him. See notes on 8:59; Acts 7:58.

10:32 For the "trial motif" in John, see note on 5:31–47.

10:34 Jesus' point in quoting Ps. 82:6 is that if human judges (Ps. 82:2–4) can in some sense be called **gods** (in light of their role as representatives of God), this designation is even more appropriate for the one who truly is the Son of God (John 10:33, 35–36).

10:35 Scripture cannot be broken. Jesus is depending on just one word ("gods") in the OT for his argument. When he says that Scripture "cannot be broken," he implies that every single word in Scripture is completely true and reliable. His opponents do not differ with this high view of Scripture, either here or anywhere else in the Gospels.

10:36 The reference to Jesus having been **consecrated** for his mission echoes OT language regarding those appointed to an office, such as Jeremiah (Jer. 1:5) or the Aaronic priests (Ex. 28:41; 40:13; Lev. 8:30).

10:37–38 For Jesus' works as witnesses to his deity, see note on 5:31–47.

10:40 across the Jordan. See note on 1:28.

sign, but [l]everything that John said about this man was true." 42 And [k]many believed in
him there.

The Death of Lazarus

11 Now a certain man was ill, Lazarus of Bethany, the village of [l]Mary and her sister
Martha. 2 [m]It was Mary who anointed the Lord with ointment and wiped his feet
with her hair, whose brother Lazarus was ill. 3 So the sisters sent to him, saying, "Lord, [n]he
whom you love is ill." 4 But when Jesus heard it he said, [o]"This illness does not lead to death.
It is for [p]the glory of God, so that the Son of God may be glorified through it."
5 Now [q]Jesus loved Martha and her sister and Lazarus. 6 So, when he heard that Lazarus[1]
was ill, [r]he stayed two days longer in the place where he was. 7 Then after this he said to
the disciples, [s]"Let us go to Judea again." 8 The disciples said to him, [t]"Rabbi, [u]the Jews
were just now seeking to stone you, and are you going there again?" 9 Jesus answered,
[v]"Are there not twelve hours in the day? [w]If anyone walks in the day, he does not stumble,
because he sees the light of this world. 10 But [x]if anyone walks in the night, he stumbles,
because the light is not [x]in him." 11 After saying these things, he said to them, "Our friend
Lazarus [y]has fallen asleep, but I go to awaken him." 12 The disciples said to him, "Lord,
if he has fallen asleep, he will recover." 13 Now Jesus had spoken of his death, but they
thought that he meant taking rest in sleep. 14 Then Jesus told them plainly, "Lazarus has
died, 15 and for your sake I am glad that I was not there, so that you may believe. But let
us go to him." 16 [z]So Thomas, called the Twin,[2] said to his fellow disciples, "Let us also go,
[a]that we may die with him."

I Am the Resurrection and the Life

17 Now when Jesus came, he found that Lazarus had already been in the tomb [b]four
days. 18 Bethany was near Jerusalem, about two miles[3] off, 19 and many of the Jews had
come to Martha and Mary [c]to console them concerning their brother. 20 [d]So when Martha
heard that Jesus was coming, she went and met him, but Mary remained seated in the
house. 21 Martha said to [e]Jesus, "Lord, [f]if you had been here, my brother would not have
died. 22 But even now I know that whatever you ask from God, [g]God will give you." 23 Jesus
said to her, "Your brother will rise again." 24 [h]Martha said to him, "I know that he will
rise again in [i]the resurrection on the last day." 25 Jesus said to her, [j]"I am the resurrection

[1] Greek *he*; also verse 17 [2] Greek *Didymus* [3] Greek *fifteen stadia*; a *stadion* was about 607 feet or 185 meters

41 [l]ch. 1:7, 29-34; 3:27-30; 5:33
42 [k]See ch. 7:31

Chapter 11

1 [l]See Luke 10:38, 39
2 [m]ch. 12:3
3 [n]ver. 5, 11, 36
4 [o][ver. 11; Matt. 9:24] [p]ver. 40; [ch. 9:3; 13:31]
5 [q]ver. 3
6 [r][ch. 2:4; 7:6, 8]
7 [s]ch. 10:40
8 [t]See ch. 1:38 [u]ch. 8:59; 10:31
9 [v][Luke 13:33] [w]See ch. 9:4; 1 John 2:10
10 [x]Jer. 13:16
11 [y]See Matt. 27:52
16 [z]ch. 14:5; 20:24, 26-28; 21:2; Matt. 10:3; Mark 3:18; Luke 6:15; Acts 1:13 [a][ch. 13:37]
17 [b]ver. 39
19 [c]ver. 31; Job 2:11
20 [d][Luke 10:38, 39]
21 [e]ver. 32 [f][ver. 37]
22 [g][ver. 42; ch. 9:31]
24 [h][ver. 39] [i]ch. 5:29; Luke 14:14; See ch. 6:39
25 [j][ch. 5:21; 6:40, 44; 1 Cor. 15:21]

11:1–12:19 *The Final Passover: The Ultimate Sign and the Aftermath.* The raising of Lazarus constitutes the final and ultimate messianic "sign" of Jesus in this Gospel (see note on 2:11). This spectacular miracle (recorded only by John) anticipates Jesus' own resurrection and reveals Jesus as "the resurrection and the life" (11:25). The raising of Lazarus also serves as a final event triggering the Jewish leaders' resolve to have Jesus arrested and tried for blasphemy (11:45–57).

11:1 Bethany. Identified in v. 18 as being 2 miles (3.2 km) from Jerusalem, this village is the Bethany most commonly mentioned in the Gospels (see Mark 11:1; 14:3 par.; also Luke 24:50), but it is different from the Bethany mentioned in John 1:28. This is almost certainly the modern village of El-Azariyeh (an Arabic place-name which likely recalls the name of Lazarus) on the eastern slopes of the Mount of Olives. A fourth-century chapel was built over a rock-cut tomb traditionally thought to have been the tomb of Lazarus. Other first-century tombs are found in the hillside around this chapel.

11:4 Jesus could say that Lazarus's illness **does not lead to death** in the sense that it did not lead ultimately to death, but it did lead *through* death to being raised from the dead a few days later. Jesus makes a similar statement in Mark 5:39. Jesus knew what was going to happen, and in John 11:11–14 he tells his disciples clearly that Lazarus has already died.

11:5–6 So (Gk. *oun*, "so, therefore") shows the reason why Jesus **stayed two days longer**: he allowed his friends to go through the sorrow and hardship of the death and mourning of Lazarus because he **loved** them and wanted them to witness an amazing demonstration of Jesus' power over death, thus seeing "his glory, glory as of the only Son from the Father" (1:14). The Lord does not always answer prayers as expected.

11:9–10 If Jesus is the "light of the world" (8:12), then to walk **in the day** means to walk in the light that Jesus gives; that is, to walk in fellowship with him, believing and obeying his words. In contrast, **walks in the night** means to walk apart from Jesus, not believing him and not obeying him. This is an indication that the person has no spiritual life, for **the light is not in him.** Most people at this time worked as long as there was daylight; once it was dark, it was time to stop working. Jesus is divinely called to go to Judea; it is part of what constituted walking "in the day" for him, even though he is heading toward the cross (11:7–8).

11:11 Fallen asleep means "died," as the following conversation (vv. 12–14) makes clear. The OT equivalent is "slept with his fathers" (see, e.g., 1 Kings 2:10 and throughout 1–2 Kings and 1–2 Chronicles). Occasionally, death is compared to a deep sleep from which people will one day be awakened (e.g., Dan. 12:2).

11:15 So that you may believe indicates that Jesus knows raising Lazarus from the dead will lead to deeper faith on the part of the disciples who witness this miracle.

11:16 The Aramaic name **Thomas** means **the Twin** (cf. note on 1:38).

11:17 four days. Though burial usually followed soon after death (see Acts 5:6, 10), some later Jewish sources indicate a belief that the soul hovered over the body for three days, hoping to reenter it, but then gave up and departed.

11:18 Bethany. See note on v. 1.

11:24 Martha's affirmation of end-time resurrection was in keeping with the beliefs of the Pharisees (Acts 23:8) and the majority of first-century Jews, as well as the teaching of Jesus (John 5:21, 25–29; 6:39–44, 54). Martha misunderstood the full import of Jesus' promise (11:23), thinking he was merely speaking of the final resurrection, while Jesus meant much more.

11:25 Jesus does not merely say that he will bring about the resurrection or that he will be the cause of the resurrection (both of which are true), but

and [k]the life.[1] Whoever believes in me, [l]though he die, [m]yet shall he live, **26** and everyone
who lives and believes in me [n]shall never die. Do you believe this?" **27** She said to him,
"Yes, Lord; [o]I believe that [p]you are the Christ, the Son of God, [q]who is coming into the
world."

Jesus Weeps

28 When she had said this, she went and called her sister Mary, saying in private, [r]"The
Teacher is here and is calling for you." **29** And when she heard it, she rose quickly and went
to him. **30** Now Jesus had not yet come into the village, but was still in the place where
Martha had met him. **31** When the Jews [s]who were with her in the house, consoling her,
saw Mary rise quickly and go out, they followed her, supposing that she was going to the
tomb to weep there. **32** Now when Mary came to where Jesus was and saw him, she fell at
his feet, saying to him, [t]"Lord, if you had been here, my brother would not have died."
33 When Jesus saw her weeping, and the Jews who had come with her also weeping, he
[u]was deeply moved[2] in his spirit and [v]greatly troubled. **34** And he said, "Where have you
laid him?" They said to him, "Lord, come and see." **35** [w]Jesus wept. **36** So the Jews said, "See
[x]how he loved him!" **37** But some of them said, "Could not he [y]who opened the eyes of the
blind man [z]also have kept this man from dying?"

Jesus Raises Lazarus

38 Then Jesus, [a]deeply moved again, came to the tomb. It was [b]a cave, and [c]a stone lay
against it. **39** Jesus said, "Take away the stone." Martha, the sister of the dead man, said to
him, "Lord, by this time there will be an odor, for [d]he has been dead four days." **40** Jesus
said to her, [e]"Did I not tell you that if you believed you would see [f]the glory of God?" **41** So
they took away the stone. And Jesus [g]lifted up his eyes and said, "Father, I thank you that
you have heard me. **42** [h]I knew that you always hear me, but I said this [i]on account of the
people standing around, [j]that they may believe that you sent me." **43** When he had said
these things, he cried out with a loud voice, "Lazarus, come out." **44** [k]The man who had
died came out, [l]his hands and feet bound with linen strips, and [m]his face wrapped with a
cloth. Jesus said to them, "Unbind him, and let him go."

The Plot to Kill Jesus

45 [n]Many of the Jews therefore, [o]who had come with Mary and [p]had seen what he
did, believed in him, **46** but some of them went to the Pharisees and told them what
Jesus had done. **47** So the chief priests and the Pharisees [q]gathered [r]the council and said,
[s]"What are we to do? For this man performs many signs. **48** If we let him go on like this,

[1] Some manuscripts omit *and the life* [2] Or *was indignant*; also verse 38

25 [k]ch. 14:6; [ch. 6:57; Col. 3:4]; See ch. 1:4 [l][ch. 12:25] [m]See ch. 3:36
26 [n]ch. 6:50, 51; 8:51
27 [o]ch. 6:69; 20:31; 1 John 5:1, 5; [ch. 8:24; 13:19; 1 John 4:16] [p]Matt. 16:16 [q]ch. 6:14; See Matt. 11:3
28 [r]Matt. 26:18; Mark 14:14; Luke 22:11; See ch. 13:13
31 [s]ver. 19
32 [t]ver. 21
33 [u]ver. 38; Mark 14:5 (Gk.) [v]ch. 12:27; 13:21
35 [w][Luke 19:41]
36 [x]ver. 3
37 [y]ch. 9:6, 7 [z][ver. 21, 32]
38 [a]ver. 33 [b]Isa. 22:16 [c]ch. 20:1; Matt. 27:60; Mark 15:46; Luke 24:2
39 [d]ver. 17
40 [e]ver. 25, 26 [f]ver. 4; [Rom. 6:4]
41 [g]ch. 17:1
42 [h][ver. 22; Matt. 26:53] [i]ch. 12:29, 30 [j]ch. 17:8, 21; See ch. 3:17
44 [k]ch. 5:28, 29 [l]ch. 19:40 [m][ch. 20:7]
45 [n]ch. 12:11; [Acts 9:42] [o]ver. 19 [p]ch. 2:23
47 [q]See Matt. 26:3 [r]See Matt. 5:22 [s]ch. 12:19; [Acts 4:16]

something much stronger: **I am the resurrection and the life**. Resurrection from the dead and genuine eternal life in fellowship with God are so closely tied to Jesus that they are embodied in him and can be found only in relationship to him. Therefore **believes in me** implies personal trust in Christ. The preposition translated "in" (Gk. *eis*) is striking, for *eis* ordinarily means "into," giving the sense that genuine faith in Christ in a sense brings people "into" Christ, so that they rest in and become united with Christ. (This same expression is found in 3:16, 18, 36; 6:35; 7:38; 12:44, 46; 14:12; 1 John 5:10.) The "I am" statement here represents a claim to deity.

11:26 Lives refers to those who have spiritual life now (see note on 3:36). Those who believe **shall never die**, in that they will ultimately triumph over death.

11:27 Martha's reference to the one **who is coming into the world** takes up the messianic expression derived from Ps. 118:26 (cf. John 12:13 par.).

11:28 The Teacher was a natural way of referring to Jesus for any disciple prior to his resurrection (1:38, 49; 3:2; 4:31; 6:25; 9:2; 11:8; cf. 20:16).

11:33 The Greek word underlying **deeply moved**, *embrimaomai* (elsewhere in the NT only in v. 38; Matt. 9:30 ["sternly warned"]; Mark 1:43 ["sternly charged"]; and Mark 14:5 ["scolded"]), means to feel something deeply and strongly. Jesus was moved with profound sorrow at the death of his friend and at the grief that his other friends had suffered. In addition, this sorrow was intermixed with anger (see ESV footnote) at the evil of death (the final enemy; see 1 Cor. 15:26; Rev. 21:4), and also with a deep sense of awe at the power of God that was about to flow through him to triumph over death (in anticipation of his voice summoning the whole world to the resurrection on the last day). **In his spirit** does not refer to the Holy Spirit but to Jesus' own human spirit.

11:35 Jesus wept. Jesus joins his friends' sadness with heartfelt sorrow, yet underlying it is the knowledge that resurrection and joy will soon follow (cf. 1 Thess. 4:13). Jesus' example shows that heartfelt mourning in the face of death does not indicate lack of faith but honest sorrow at the reality of suffering and death.

11:38 deeply moved. See note on v. 33.

11:43 come out. The voice of the omnipotent Creator (1:3, 10) speaks, and even Lazarus's dead body obeys (cf. 4:50; 5:8).

11:44 Remarkably, John does not record Lazarus's reaction or any of the aftermath of his raising (cf. Luke 8:55–56), except for the fact that "many of the Jews . . . believed in him" (i.e., Jesus) as a result of seeing this miracle (John 11:45; see also 12:9–11). The focus is on Jesus, not Lazarus.

11:45 Here John uses the phrase **the Jews** in a positive way, to refer to those Jews who **believed in him** (cf. note on 1:19).

11:47 Council represents the Greek word *synedrion* ("Sanhedrin"); cf. 7:45–52 and note on 3:1.

11:48 Our place almost certainly refers to the temple (cf. Acts 6:13–14; 21:28). **Take away . . . our nation** may refer to the feared removal of the Jews' semiautonomous status by the Romans (cf. *1 Macc.* 5:19). Ironically, what the Sanhedrin sought to prevent by killing Jesus still came to pass when

48[t][ch. 6:15; 18:36, 37] [u]Acts 21:28
49[v]See Matt. 26:3 [w]ver. 51; ch. 18:13
50[x]ch. 18:14
51[y]ver. 49 [z][Ex. 28:30; Num. 27:21; 1 Sam. 23:9; 30:7; Ezra 2:63; Neh. 7:65]
52[a]Isa. 49:6; 1 John 2:2 [b]See ch. 10:16
53[c]See ch. 7:1
54[d]ch. 7:1, 4
55[e]See ch. 6:4 [f]Luke 2:42 [g]2 Chr. 30:17, 18; [ch. 18:28; Acts 21:24]
56[h]See ch. 7:11

Chapter 12

1[i]ver. 12, 20; ch. 11:55 [j]For ver. 1-8, see Matt. 26:6-11; Mark 14:3-8 [k]ch. 11:1
2[l]Luke 10:38, 40
3[m][Luke 7:37, 38]
5[n]ch. 13:29
6[n][See ver. 5 above]

everyone will believe in him, and [t]the Romans will come and take away both our [u]place
and our nation." **49** But one of them, [v]Caiaphas, [w]who was high priest that year, said to
them, "You know nothing at all. **50** Nor do you understand that [x]it is better for you that
one man should die for the people, not that the whole nation should perish." **51** He did
not say this of his own accord, but [y]being high priest that year [z]he prophesied that Jesus
would die for the nation, **52** and [a]not for the nation only, but also [b]to gather into one the
children of God who are scattered abroad. **53** So from that day on they [c]made plans to
put him to death.

54 Jesus therefore [d]no longer walked openly among the Jews, but went from there to
the region near the wilderness, to a town called Ephraim, and there he stayed with the
disciples.

55 Now [e]the Passover of the Jews was at hand, and [f]many went up from the country
to Jerusalem before the Passover [g]to purify themselves. **56** [h]They were looking for[1] Jesus
and saying to one another as they stood in the temple, "What do you think? That he
will not come to the feast at all?" **57** Now the chief priests and the Pharisees had given
orders that if anyone knew where he was, he should let them know, so that they might
arrest him.

Mary Anoints Jesus at Bethany

12 Six days before [i]the Passover, [j]Jesus therefore came to Bethany, [k]where Lazarus was,
whom Jesus had raised from the dead. **2** So they gave a dinner for him there. [l]Martha
served, and Lazarus was one of those reclining with him at table. **3** [m]Mary therefore took a
pound[2] of expensive ointment made from pure nard, and anointed the feet of Jesus and
wiped his feet with her hair. The house was filled with the fragrance of the perfume. **4** But
Judas Iscariot, one of his disciples (he who was about to betray him), said, **5** "Why was this
ointment not sold for three hundred denarii[3] and [n]given to the poor?" **6** He said this, not
because he cared about the poor, but because he was a thief, and [n]having charge of the
moneybag he used to help himself to what was put into it. **7** Jesus said, "Leave her alone,
so that she may keep it[4] for the day of my burial. **8** For the poor you always have with you,
but you do not always have me."

[1] Greek *were seeking for* [2] Greek *litra;* a *litra* (or Roman pound) was equal to about 11 1/2 ounces or 327 grams [3] A *denarius* was a day's wage for a laborer
[4] Or *Leave her alone; she intended to keep it*

the Romans razed the temple and captured Jerusalem in A.D. 70 (see note on John 2:13–22).

11:49 that year. In fact, **Caiaphas** (see note on 18:24) was high priest for 18 years (A.D. 18–36), longer than any other high priest in the first century. **You know nothing at all** displays the rudeness allegedly characteristic of many Sadducees (as confirmed by Josephus).

11:50–51 Die for the people invokes the memory of the Maccabean martyrs (*2 Macc.* 7:37–38). With a typical Johannine double meaning (see notes on John 3:14; 4:10; 8:24; 19:19; cf. also 3:7–8), Caiaphas's pronouncement anticipates Jesus' substitutionary atonement.

11:52 The **children of God . . . scattered**, as referred to here, are the Gentiles (cf. 10:16; see also note on 3:3–6). John is not suggesting that they are already God's children but anticipates their future inclusion into God's people.

11:55 This is the third and final **Passover** mentioned by John; see note on 2:13. People went up early **to purify themselves** from any ceremonial uncleanness that would have prevented them from celebrating the Passover (e.g., Num. 9:4–14; 19:11–12).

12:1–11 The anointing of Jesus by Mary of Bethany (also recorded in Matt. 26:6–13 and Mark 14:3–9) casts a long shadow forward over Jesus' imminent arrest, trial, condemnation, crucifixion, and burial (John 12:7–8). The story in Luke 7:36–50 involves a different woman, a different place, a different reaction from Jesus, and a different time in Jesus' ministry.

12:1 Therefore (Gk. *oun*) ties this verse to the previous one and is a reminder that John is constantly aware of God's providential ordering of all these events and of Jesus' obedience in following the path that he knew would lead to the cross. Regarding **the Passover**, cf. 11:55 and note on 2:13. **Six days before** the Passover most likely refers to Saturday, since the Passover began Friday evening at sundown. **Bethany**. See note on 11:1.

12:2 Dinner (Gk. *deipnon*) refers to the main meal of the day, which was usually held toward evening (cf. Luke 14:12). **Reclining . . . at table** may imply a banquet rather than a regular meal (cf. John 13:2–5, 23). People at special feasts would lie with their heads near a low table and their feet pointing out away from it, resting on one elbow and eating with the other hand.

12:3 Cf. 11:2. A **pound** (or half a liter) is a very large amount of fragrant oil or **perfume. Pure** and expensive **nard** was imported from northern India and used by the Romans for anointing the head. The Synoptics indicate that the perfume was kept in an alabaster jar (Matt. 26:7; Mark 14:3). It is recorded here that Mary **anointed the feet of Jesus**, while Matt. 26:7 and Mark 14:3 mention that she anointed Jesus' "head." Considering the large quantity of ointment, Mary apparently anointed both Jesus' head and his feet. Attending to the feet was the work of servants (cf. John 1:27; 13:5), so Mary's actions show humility and devotion. Her wiping of Jesus' feet **with her hair** is also remarkable, since Jewish women rarely unbound their hair in public. Mary's action indicates an expression of intense personal devotion to Christ, but no hint of immoral thoughts or conduct should be read into her actions.

12:5 Three hundred denarii represents the equivalent of about a year's wages (see note on 6:7).

12:6 Judas's motivation was anything but pure. Before he betrayed Jesus, he had already been a **thief**.

12:7 So that she may keep it may mean "keep the rest of the perfume," but Mark 14:3 says the flask was broken, and Judas complains that it was already wasted. Other interpretations are "so that she may keep (the memory of this)" or "Leave her alone, (for she has saved the perfume) so that she could keep it for the day of my burial."

12:8 the poor. Jesus' response alludes to Deut. 15:11, and therefore he is not discouraging helping the poor. **You do not always have me**

The Plot to Kill Lazarus

9 When the large crowd of the Jews learned that Jesus[1] was there, they came, not only
on account of him but also to see Lazarus, [o]whom he had raised from the dead. 10 [p]So the
chief priests made plans to put Lazarus to death as well, 11 because [q]on account of him
many of the Jews were going away and believing in Jesus.

The Triumphal Entry

12 The next day [r]the large crowd that had come to the feast heard that Jesus was coming
to Jerusalem. 13 So they took branches of [s]palm trees and went out to meet him, crying out,
[t]"Hosanna! Blessed is [u]he who comes in the name of the Lord, even [v]the King of Israel!"
14 And Jesus found a young donkey and sat on it, just as it is written,

15 [w]"Fear not, daughter of Zion;
behold, your king is coming,
sitting on a donkey's colt!"

16 [x]His disciples did not understand these things at first, but [y]when Jesus was glorified,
then [z]they remembered that these things had been written about him and had been
done to him. 17 [a]The crowd that had been with him when he called Lazarus out of the
tomb and raised him from the dead continued to bear witness. 18 The reason why the
crowd went to meet him [b]was that they heard he had done this sign. 19 So the Pharisees
said to one another, [c]"You see that you are gaining nothing. Look, [d]the world has gone
after him."

Some Greeks Seek Jesus

20 Now [e]among those who went up to worship at the feast were some [f]Greeks. 21 So these
came to [g]Philip, who was from Bethsaida in Galilee, and asked him, "Sir, we wish to see
Jesus." 22 Philip went and told [h]Andrew; Andrew and Philip went and told Jesus. 23 And Jesus
answered them, [i]"The hour has come [j]for the Son of Man to be glorified. 24 Truly, truly, I say
to you, [k]unless a grain of wheat falls into the earth and dies, it remains alone; but if it dies, it
bears much fruit. 25 [l]Whoever loves his life loses it, and [m]whoever [n]hates his life in this world

[1] Greek *he*

9 [o]ch. 11:44
10 [p][Luke 16:31]
11 [q]ver. 18; ch. 11:45
12 [r]For ver. 12-15, see Matt. 21:4-9; Mark 11:7-10; Luke 19:35-38
13 [s][Rev. 7:9] [t]Ps. 118:25, 26 [u][ch. 5:43] [v]See ch. 1:49
15 [w]Cited from Zech. 9:9
16 [x][ch. 13:7]; See Mark 9:32 [y]ver. 23; See ch. 7:39 [z]ch. 2:22
17 [a][Luke 19:37]
18 [b]ver. 9-11
19 [c]ch. 11:47 [d][ch. 3:26]
20 [e][1 Kgs. 8:41-43; Acts 8:27] [f]Acts 17:4; [Mark 7:26]; See ch. 7:35
21 [g]ch. 1:44
22 [h]See Mark 13:3
23 [i]ch. 17:1; [ver. 27; ch. 13:31, 32; Mark 14:41]; See ch. 2:4 [j]ver. 16
24 [k]1 Cor. 15:36
25 [l]See Matt. 10:39 [m][ch. 11:25] [n]See Luke 14:26

foreshadows Jesus' impending death on the cross and subsequent resurrection and ascension, as well as the shortness of time remaining for the disciples to have a part in his earthly ministry.

12:10 When the chief priests **made plans to put Lazarus to death**, it betrayed an astounding refusal to allow their beliefs to be changed by undeniable facts. They would rather destroy the evidence than change their minds. This is not rational behavior, but sin produces irrational action.

12:11 the Jews. John uses this expression in a positive way to speak of those who are coming to faith in Christ (cf. 11:45), indicating a hope that many of his Jewish readers will do the same.

12:12–19 Jesus' triumphal entry, with people waving palm branches to greet him, is celebrated in Christian tradition as "Palm Sunday." His riding into Jerusalem mounted on a donkey fulfills OT Scripture (Zech. 9:9; see also Ps. 118:25–26). The waving of palm branches, which symbolically conveyed the notion of victory over one's enemy, probably indicates that the people (mistakenly) thought that Jesus would then and there bring national deliverance from Israel's political enemies, the Romans. Yet Jesus' popular acclaim would not last; within a mere five days, the shouts of praise would turn to angry calls for his crucifixion.

12:12 The next day is probably Sunday of Passion Week, called "Palm Sunday" in Christian tradition. See note on v. 1. **The feast** is Passover.

12:13 By waving **palm** branches (a Jewish national symbol) the people hail Jesus as the Davidic king and echo the language of Ps. 118:25–26, hoping that Jesus is the promised Messiah. Most of the crowd probably understood the title **King of Israel** in a political and military sense, still hoping that Jesus would use his amazing powers to resist Roman rule and lead the nation to independence. Like Caiaphas (John 11:49–52), however, they spoke better than they knew, as his disciples later understood (12:16).

12:15 Jesus is depicted as the humble shepherd-king of Zech. 9:9, who comes to the Holy City to take his rightful place. An early messianic prophecy speaks of a ruler from Judah who, riding on a donkey, will command the obedience of nations (Gen. 49:10–11). **Fear not** may be taken from Isa. 40:9, where the reference is to the one who brings good tidings to Zion (cf. Isa. 44:2).

12:16 An important verse on the misunderstanding motif in John, indicating that many of the things Jesus said and did were understood only after the cross and resurrection.

12:19 The world is an obvious overstatement, highlighting the Pharisees' exasperation (cf. Acts 17:6).

12:20–50 *The Approaching Gentiles and the Messiah's Rejection by the Jews.* The present section concludes the first major part of John's Gospel, which narrates Jesus' mission to the Jews. The arrival of some Greeks signals to Jesus that this mission is about to come to an end. But before Jesus can reach out to the Gentiles, he first must die (cf. 10:16; 11:52). His hour is now at hand (12:23–26; see notes on 2:4; 7:30).

12:20 Greeks refers to Gentiles, not necessarily to people from Greece (see note on 7:35). They are "God-fearers," non-Jews who had come to Jerusalem to worship at the Jewish festival.

12:21 Bethsaida. See note on Luke 9:10.

12:23 hour. See notes on 2:4 and 7:30.

12:25 Here again Jesus speaks in absolute terms to emphasize a point: **loves his life** means "delights in his life in this world more than in God," and **hates his life in this world** means, by contrast, "thinks so little of his life, and so

will keep it for eternal life. **26** If anyone serves me, he must [o]follow me; and [p]where I am, there
will my servant be also. [q]If anyone serves me, [r]the Father will honor him.

The Son of Man Must Be Lifted Up

27 [s]"Now is my soul troubled. And what shall I say? 'Father, [t]save me from [u]this hour'?
But [v]for this purpose I have come to [u]this hour. **28** Father, glorify your name." Then [w]a voice
came from heaven: "I have glorified it, and I will glorify it again." **29** The crowd that stood
there and heard it said that it had thundered. Others said, [x]"An angel has spoken to him."
30 Jesus answered, [y]"This voice has come for your sake, not mine. **31** [z]Now is the judgment
of this world; now will [a]the ruler of this world [b]be cast out. **32** And I, [c]when I am lifted up
from the earth, [d]will draw [e]all people to myself." **33** He said this [f]to show by what kind of
death he was going to die. **34** So the crowd answered him, "We have heard from the Law
that [g]the Christ remains forever. How can you say that [h]the Son of Man must be lifted up?
Who is this Son of Man?" **35** So Jesus said to them, [i]"The light is among you [j]for a little while
longer. [k]Walk while you have the light, lest darkness [l]overtake you. [m]The one who walks
in the darkness does not know where he is going. **36** While you have the light, believe in
the light, that you may become [n]sons of light."

The Unbelief of the People

When Jesus had said these things, he departed and hid himself from them. **37** Though
he had done so many signs before them, they still did not believe in him, **38** [o]so that the
word spoken by the prophet Isaiah might be fulfilled:

> [p]"Lord, who has believed what he heard from us,
> and to whom has the arm of the Lord been revealed?"

39 Therefore they [q]could not believe. For again Isaiah said,

> **40** [r]"He has blinded their eyes
> and [s]hardened their heart,
> lest they see with their eyes,
> and understand with their heart, and turn,
> and I would heal them."

26 [o]ch. 8:12; 21:18 [p]ch. 14:3; 17:24; [2 Cor. 5:8; 1 Thess. 4:17] [q][ch. 14:21, 23; 16:27] [r]1 Sam. 2:30; Ps. 91:15
27 [s]ch. 11:33; 13:21; [Luke 22:44] [t]Mark 14:35; [Heb. 5:7] [u]ver. 23 [v][ch. 18:37]
28 [w]Matt. 3:17; 17:5; Mark 1:11; 9:7; Luke 3:22; 9:35; 2 Pet. 1:17
29 [x]Acts 23:9
30 [y]ch. 11:42
31 [z]ch. 16:11; [ch. 16:33] [a]ch. 14:30; 2 Cor. 4:4; Eph. 2:2; 6:12; [Matt. 13:19; Luke 4:6; 1 John 4:4; 5:19] [b][Luke 10:18; Col. 2:15; 1 John 3:8]
32 [c]ch. 3:14; 8:28 [d]See ch. 6:44 [e]Rom. 5:18; 8:32; 2 Cor. 5:15; 1 Tim. 2:6; Heb. 2:9; 1 John 2:2
33 [f]ch. 18:32
34 [g]Ps. 89:4; 110:4; Isa. 9:7; Ezek. 37:25; Luke 1:33 [h]ver. 32
35 [i]ver. 46; See ch. 1:4, 9; 8:12 [j]See ch. 7:33 [k]Jer. 13:16; Eph. 5:8 [l]1 Thess. 5:4 [m]Isa. 9:2; 1 John 1:6; 2:11; [ch. 11:10]
36 [n]See Luke 10:6
38 [o][Matt. 1:22] [p]Rom. 10:16; Cited from Isa. 53:1
39 [q][ch. 5:44]
40 [r][Isa. 6:10]; See Matt. 13:14, 15 [s]See Mark 6:52

much of God, that he is willing to sacrifice it all for God." Following Christ entails self-sacrifice, shown supremely at the cross.

12:27 Troubled (Gk. *tarassō*) means "to be stirred up, unsettled"; the word or a related compound is found in the Septuagint in Davidic psalms (such as Ps. 6:3; 42:11).

12:28 This is one of three instances during Jesus' earthly ministry where a heavenly voice attests to his identity (the other two are his baptism and the transfiguration; Matt. 3:17; 17:5).

12:29 crowd . . . said that it had thundered. Events of eternal consequence are occurring in the unseen spiritual realm, but when unbelievers see or hear a manifestation of them (even the very voice of God speaking from heaven), they misinterpret them as natural events, showing their spiritual blindness.

12:31 The **ruler of this world** in its present fallen, sinful state is Satan (cf. 14:30; 16:11; 1 John 5:19). **Now**, at the cross, the Devil will **be cast out**, that is, decisively defeated (cf. Luke 10:18; Col. 2:14–15; Heb. 2:14–15). Jesus' triumph over Satan in his death and resurrection is the basis for his final triumph in the consummation (Rev. 20:10).

12:32 This most explicit "lifted up" saying in John complements the earlier references in 3:14 (see note) and 8:28, and echoes Isa. 52:13. **All people**, in context, means "all *kinds of* people," that is, both Jews and Gentiles (John 10:16; 11:52; cf. 12:20–21). The drawing, as in 6:44, is effective.

12:33 what kind of death. Cf. 21:19.

12:34 This is the final of several messianic misunderstandings featured in this Gospel (cf. 7:27, 31, 41–42). The people have some inkling here that Jesus is predicting his death. What is probably meant by **the Law** is the entire Hebrew Scriptures, in which there are several passages that speak of the perpetual existence of the Davidic Messiah (2 Sam. 7:13; Ps. 61:6–7; 89:3–4, 35–37; Isa. 9:7; Dan. 7:13–14; for later Jewish expectations see *1 Enoch* 49.1; 62.14; *Psalms of Solomon* 17.4).

12:35–36 Jesus' answer is indirect; in view of the fact that the **light** will be with people only **for a little while longer**, his crucifixion is near (cf. v. 46; also 7:33; 16:16–19). He urges the people to **believe in the light** (see note on 8:12; see also 9:4 and 11:9–10) while there is still time. On the words **walk while you have the light**, see 9:4–5.

12:36 When Jesus **hid himself from them**, he indicated God's imminent judgment and the completion of his revelatory work to the people of Israel (1:18).

12:37 Though he had done so many signs . . . they still did not believe indicates the culpability of people who had seen these miracles but still did not believe. The purpose of the miracles was to lead them to faith, and the miracles provided abundant proof of Jesus' deity and messiahship, but people in their hardness of heart still rejected this evidence.

12:37–40 John cites Isa. 53:1 and 6:10 to indicate that the Jewish rejection of Jesus as Messiah was predicted by Scripture and thus serves to confirm (rather than thwart) God's sovereign plan. Isaiah 53:1 refers to the servant of the Lord who was rejected by the people but exalted by God; Isa. 6:10 attributes people's hardening ultimately to God himself (similar to Pharaoh's, see Rom. 9:17–18). The present verses are the first in a series of fulfillment quotations in the second half of John's Gospel. Seen here is John's emphasis on divine sovereignty and human responsibility. On the one hand, the people should have believed and are held guilty for disbelieving ("they still did not believe in him," John 12:37). On the other hand, God blinded their eyes so that they did not have the spiritual ability to believe, and John can even say **they could not believe** (v. 39). (On the need for God to first give people the ability to believe, see 1:13; 6:44.) See note on Eph. 1:11.

41 Isaiah said these things because [t]he saw his glory and [u]spoke of him. 42 Nevertheless,
[v]many even of the authorities believed in him, but [w]for fear of the Pharisees they did not
[x]confess it, so that they would not be [x]put out of the synagogue; 43 [y]for they loved the glory
that comes from man more than the glory that comes from God.

Jesus Came to Save the World

44 And Jesus cried out and said, [z]"Whoever believes in me, believes not in me but [a]in
him who sent me. 45 And [b]whoever [c]sees me sees him who sent me. 46 [d]I have come into
the world as light, so that whoever believes in me may not remain in darkness. 47 If anyone
[e]hears my words and does not keep them, [f]I do not judge him; for [g]I did not come to judge
the world but to save the world. 48 [h]The one who rejects me and does not receive my words
has a judge; [i]the word that I have spoken will judge him [j]on the last day. 49 For [k]I have
not spoken on my own authority, but the Father [l]who sent me has himself given me [m]a
commandment—what to say and what to speak. 50 And I know that his commandment
is eternal life. What I say, therefore, I say as the Father has told me."

Jesus Washes the Disciples' Feet

13 Now [n]before [o]the Feast of the Passover, when Jesus knew that [p]his hour had come
[q]to depart out of this world to the Father, [r]having loved [s]his own who were in the
world, he loved them to the end. 2 During supper, when [t]the devil had already put it into
the heart of Judas Iscariot, Simon's son, to betray him, 3 Jesus, knowing [u]that the Father
had given all things into his hands, and that [v]he had come from God and [w]was going back
to God, 4 rose from supper. He laid aside his outer garments, and taking a towel, [x]tied it
around his waist. 5 Then he [y]poured water into a basin and began to wash the disciples'
feet and to wipe them with the towel that was wrapped around him. 6 He came to Simon
Peter, who said to him, "Lord, do you wash my feet?" 7 [z]Jesus answered him, "What I am
doing [a]you do not understand now, but afterward you will understand." 8 [b]Peter said to
him, "You shall never wash my feet." Jesus answered him, [c]"If I do not wash you, you have
no share with me." 9 Simon Peter said to him, "Lord, not my feet only but also my hands

41 [t]Isa. 6:1 [u][ch. 5:46]
42 [v]ch. 3:1; [ch. 7:48] [w]See ch. 7:13 [x]See ch. 9:22
43 [y]ch. 5:44
44 [z][ch. 13:20]; See Matt. 10:40 [a]ch. 14:1; [ch. 5:24; 1 Pet. 1:21]
45 [b]ch. 14:9 [c]ch. 6:40
46 [d]ver. 35, 36; See ch. 1:4, 5, 9; 8:12
47 [e][ch. 3:36] [f]ch. 8:15 [g]See ch. 3:17; 4:42
48 [h]Luke 10:16 [i]Deut. 18:18, 19 [j][Rom. 2:16]
49 [k]See ch. 5:19, 30 [l]See ch. 3:17 [m]ch. 15:10

Chapter 13

1 [n]ch. 12:1 [o]See ch. 6:4 [p]See ch. 12:23 [q]ver. 3; ch. 16:28 [r]ver. 34 [s]ch. 1:11; 17:6, 9-11
2 [t]ver. 11, 27; [Acts 5:3]; See ch. 6:70, 71
3 [u]See ch. 17:2; Matt. 11:27; Rev. 2:27 [v]ch. 8:42; 16:28 [w]See ch. 14:12
4 [x][ch. 21:7; Luke 22:27]
5 [y][2 Kgs. 3:11]
7 [z][ver. 36] [a]ver. 12; [ch. 12:16; 15:15]
8 [b][Matt. 16:22] [c][1 Cor. 6:11; Eph. 5:26; Titus 3:5; Heb. 10:22]

12:41 Isaiah said these things is a strong argument for the entire book of Isaiah being written by one person, the prophet Isaiah (see Introduction to Isaiah: Date). The plural "these things" most likely refers to the two specific passages that John quotes (Isa. 53:1 and Isa. 6:10), but the wider context of both passages is probably also in view. John seems to be claiming that when Isaiah saw the exalted King and the suffering servant, he saw Jesus' glory.

12:42–43 The opposition of the Jewish leaders to Jesus was not at all monolithic; an increasing number of the leaders themselves had come to faith, for **many even of the authorities believed in him.** However, their **fear of the Pharisees** was still strong, and hence they did not confess Jesus publicly. In v. 43 John penetrates the human heart, showing again that the desire for human commendation kept them from following Jesus in a public way. See notes on 5:44; 9:22. **synagogue**. See note on Luke 4:16.

12:44 Believes not in me means "believes not only, not ultimately, in me."

12:46 light. See note on 1:4–5.

12:47 I did not come to judge the world refers to Jesus' first coming, for he will come to judge the world when he returns (see v. 48; 5:22, 27–30).

12:49 Not . . . on my own authority indicates again that supreme authority in the Trinity belongs to the Father, and delegated authority to the Son, though they are equal in deity.

13:1–20:31 *The Farewell Discourse and the Passion Narrative.* The second half of John's Gospel consists of Jesus' Farewell Discourse (chs. 13–17) and the passion narrative (chs. 18–20). Now that Jesus has been rejected by the Jews, he turns his attention to his new messianic community. After the community is cleansed and instructed, Jesus prays, is arrested, and is subjected to Jewish and Roman trials, crucified, and buried. This is followed by the resurrection, resurrection appearances, and Jesus' commissioning of his disciples. The section concludes with a purpose statement (20:30–31).

13:1–17:26 *The Cleansing and Instruction of the New Messianic Community and Jesus' Final Prayer.* In the second major section of John's Gospel, Jesus prepares his new messianic community, represented by the Twelve (minus Judas), for the time subsequent to his exaltation to the Father. The community is first cleansed both literally and symbolically through the footwashing (13:1–17), and then figuratively through the removal of the betrayer (13:18–30). The Farewell Discourse proper extends from 13:31 to 16:33 and contains Jesus' final instructions to his followers before his arrest and crucifixion. The discourse (unique to John's Gospel) concludes with Jesus' final prayer (ch. 17).

13:1–17 With his crucifixion imminent, Jesus washes his disciples' feet as a final proof of his love for them, setting an example of humility and servanthood and signifying the washing away of sins through his death. In a striking demonstration of love for his enemies, Jesus washes *all* of his disciples' feet, including those of Judas. Jesus' act is all the more remarkable, as washing people's feet was considered to be a task reserved for non-Jewish slaves. In a culture where people walked long distances on dusty roads in sandals, it was customary for the host to arrange for water to be available for the washing of feet. Normally, this was done upon arrival, not during the meal.

13:1 Jesus' **own** are now the Twelve, the representatives of his new messianic community (cf. 1:11). Though Jesus was about to die an agonizing death, he continued to love his disciples. **to depart out of this world**. In several places John says that Jesus is leaving the world and going to the Father (see 13:3; also 7:33; 16:28; 17:11). Yet in other places Jesus can say that he will always be present with his disciples, even after his ascension into heaven (see 14:23; Matt. 18:20; 28:20; Rev. 3:20). Both are true: Jesus in his human nature is no longer here on earth but has returned to heaven and will come again one day, but in his divine nature Jesus is omnipresent and is with believers "always" (Matt. 28:20).

13:7 Another instance of misunderstanding (cf. notes on 6:52; 12:16).

13:8 To have **no share** with Jesus means that one does not belong to him. Here the footwashing symbolizes the washing necessary for the forgiveness of sins, in anticipation of Jesus' death for his people, by which sins are washed away.

13:9–11 Jesus applies the footwashing in another way. Those who have been

10[d]See Gen. 18:4 [e]ch. 15:3 [f]ver. 18
11[g]ver. 2; ch. 6:64; See ch. 2:24, 25
12[h]ver. 4 [i]ver. 7
13[j]Luke 6:46 [k]Matt. 23:8, 10; 1 Cor. 8:6; 12:3; Phil. 2:11
14[l]1 Tim. 5:10; [1 Pet. 5:5]
15[m]See Matt. 11:29
16[n]ch. 15:20; Matt. 10:24
17[o]See Luke 11:28; James 1:22
18[p]ver. 10, 11 [q]ch. 6:70; 15:16, 19; [Mark 3:13; Luke 6:13; Acts 1:2] [r][ch. 17:12]; See Matt. 1:22 [s]Cited from Ps. 41:9; [ver. 26; Matt. 26:23]
19[t]ch. 14:29; 16:4
20[u]See Matt. 10:40
21[v]ch. 12:27 [w]Matt. 26:21; Mark 14:18; Luke 22:21 [x]Acts 1:17
22[y]Luke 22:23
23[z]ch. 19:26; 20:2; 21:7, 20 [a][Luke 16:22 (Gk.)]
25[b]Mark 4:36 [c]ch. 21:20 (Gk.)
26[d]Matt. 26:23; Mark 14:20 [e]Ruth 2:14 [f][Matt. 26:25] [g]ch. 6:71
27[h]Luke 22:3; [ver. 2; 1 Cor. 11:27] [i][Luke 12:50]
29[j]ch. 12:6 [k]ver. 1 [l]ch. 12:5
30[m][1 Sam. 28:8]
31[n]See ch. 7:39 [o]ch. 14:13; 15:8; 17:1, 4; 1 Pet. 4:11
32[p]ch. 17:1, 5 [q]See ch. 12:23

and my head!" 10 Jesus said to him, "The one who has bathed does not need to wash, [d]except
for his feet,[1] but is completely clean. And [e]you[2] are clean, [f]but not every one of you." 11 [g]For
he knew who was to betray him; that was why he said, "Not all of you are clean."

12 When he had washed their feet and [h]put on his outer garments and resumed his place,
he said to them, [i]"Do you understand what I have done to you? 13 [j]You call me [k]Teacher and
Lord, and you are right, for so I am. 14 If I then, your Lord and Teacher, have washed your
feet, [l]you also ought to wash one another's feet. 15 For I have given you an example, [m]that
you also should do just as I have done to you. 16 Truly, truly, I say to you, [n]a servant[3] is not
greater than his master, nor is a messenger greater than the one who sent him. 17 If you
know these things, [o]blessed are you if you do them. 18 [p]I am not speaking of all of you; I
know [q]whom I have chosen. But [r]the Scripture will be fulfilled,[4] [s]'He who ate my bread has
lifted his heel against me.' 19 [t]I am telling you this now, before it takes place, that when it
does take place you may believe that I am he. 20 Truly, truly, I say to you, [u]whoever receives
the one I send receives me, and whoever receives me receives the one who sent me."

One of You Will Betray Me

21 After saying these things, [v]Jesus was troubled in his spirit, and testified, [w]"Truly, truly,
I say to you, [x]one of you will betray me." 22 [y]The disciples looked at one another, uncertain
of whom he spoke. 23 [z]One of his disciples, whom Jesus loved, was reclining at table [a]at
Jesus' side,[5] 24 so Simon Peter motioned to him to ask Jesus[6] of whom he was speaking. 25 [b]So
that disciple, [c]leaning back against Jesus, said to him, "Lord, who is it?" 26 Jesus answered,
[d]"It is he to whom I will give this morsel of bread [e]when I have dipped it." So when he
had dipped the morsel, [f]he gave it to Judas, [g]the son of Simon Iscariot. 27 Then after he
had taken the morsel, [h]Satan entered into him. Jesus said to him, [i]"What you are going to
do, do quickly." 28 Now no one at the table knew why he said this to him. 29 Some thought
that, [j]because Judas had the moneybag, Jesus was telling him, "Buy what we need [k]for the
feast," or that he should [l]give something to the poor. 30 So, after receiving the morsel of
bread, he immediately went out. [m]And it was night.

A New Commandment

31 When he had gone out, Jesus said, [n]"Now is the Son of Man glorified, and [o]God is glorified in him. 32 If God is glorified in him, [p]God will also glorify him in himself, and [q]glorify

[1] Some manuscripts omit *except for his feet* [2] The Greek words for *you* in this verse are plural [3] Greek *bondservant* [4] Greek *But in order that the Scripture may be fulfilled* [5] Greek *in the bosom of Jesus* [6] Greek lacks *Jesus*

washed through Jesus' once-for-all death also need daily cleansing of their sins (symbolized by their frequent need to wash their feet). It is apparent that Jesus applies the footwashing figuratively since he says not all are clean, referring to Judas, but clearly he cleaned Judas's feet as well. Because Judas is not spiritually cleansed, unlike Peter, he does not have a "share" (v. 8) with Jesus.

13:12–17 The disciples will understand fully only after the cross, though they do grasp in part Jesus' amazing humility, which serves as a model for all of his disciples.

13:14 Footwashing continues as a regular ceremony in a number of modern denominations, which literally obey Jesus' command, **you also ought to wash one another's feet**. Others believe the language is figurative for the importance of serving one another, and that the act itself is not required.

13:16 messenger (Gk. *apostolos*). This is one of a few places in the NT where this Greek word does not refer to the office of "apostle of Jesus Christ" but simply to a "messenger" in general (it is also used this way in 2 Cor. 8:23 and Phil. 2:25).

13:18 I know whom I have chosen does not refer to choosing for salvation but to Jesus' choosing of the Twelve, including Judas, to be disciples (this is the same sense given to "choose" in 6:70, where it clearly includes Judas). Jesus cites Ps. 41:9, dealing with Absalom's rebellion against King David; the "faithless friend" there may be Ahithophel (2 Sam. 16:23). Judas's lifting **his heel against** Jesus brings out the treacherous and faithless nature of Judas's deed.

13:19 Jesus' statement is one of several references to his foreknowledge in this section (cf. 14:29; 16:1, 4, 32, 33; see also previous note). The statement **I am he** very likely has overtones of a claim to deity (see note on 8:24; also 8:28, 58; 18:5, 6, 8).

13:20 The one I send refers first of all to the disciples whom Jesus would specifically send out at 20:22. But more broadly it applies to all messengers of Christ, in every age, who bring the gospel of Christ to others. **receives**. To truly "receive" such a messenger is to accept and believe the gospel and to trust in Christ. (The same word for "receive" [Gk. *lambanō*] is also used in 1:12; 3:32–33; 5:43; 12:48.) This and similar verses (e.g., 20:22; Luke 18:17; Rom. 3:25) give the basis for using the language of "receiving Christ as Savior" in reference to hearing the gospel message and believing it.

13:21 troubled in his spirit. See note on 12:27; cf. also Ps. 31:9–10; 38:10; 55:2–14.

13:22 uncertain of whom he spoke. Judas's outward behavior conformed so nearly to that of the other disciples that they did not immediately assume that Jesus was talking about Judas.

13:23 This is the first reference to the disciple **whom Jesus loved** (see Introduction: Author and Title). On **reclining**, see note on 12:2. In such a situation it would be easy for John to lean back a bit and whisper privately to Jesus, as he does in 13:25. See also 21:20.

13:27 Satan entered into him. Though Satan had earlier put the desire to betray Christ into Judas's heart (see v. 2), Satan himself now enters into Judas, suggesting a more dominant influence in the actions to follow.

13:30 And it was night strikes an ominous note (cf. Luke 22:53: "this is your hour, and the power of darkness"). See also Matt. 26:20; Mark 14:17; 1 Cor. 11:23.

13:31–32 The passage echoes Isa. 49:3. Again Jesus' glorification is tied to his death.

him at once. **33** Little children, [r]yet a little while I am with you. You will seek me, and just
[s]as I said to the Jews, so now I also say to you, ‘Where I am going you cannot come.’ **34** [t]A
new commandment [u]I give to you, [v]that you love one another: [w]just as I have loved you,
you also are to love one another. **35** [x]By this all people will know that you are my disciples,
if you have love for one another.”

Jesus Foretells Peter’s Denial

36 Simon Peter said to him, “Lord, where are you going?” [y]Jesus answered him, “Where I
am going [z]you cannot follow me now, [a]but you will follow afterward.” **37** [b]Peter said to him,
“Lord, why can I not follow you now? I will lay down my life for you.” **38** Jesus answered,
“Will you lay down your life for me? Truly, truly, I say to you, [c]the rooster will not crow
till you have denied me three times.

I Am the Way, and the Truth, and the Life

14 [d]“Let not your hearts be troubled. [e]Believe in God;[1] believe also in me. **2** In [f]my Father’s
house are many rooms. If it were not so, would I have told you that [g]I go to prepare
a place for you?[2] **3** And if I go and prepare a place for you, I will come again and will take
you [h]to myself, that [i]where I am you may be also. **4** And you know the way to where I am
going.”[3] **5** [j]Thomas said to him, “Lord, [k]we do not know where you are going. How can we
know the way?” **6** Jesus said to him, “I am [l]the way, and [m]the truth, and [n]the life. No one
comes to the Father except through me. **7** [o]If you had known me, you would have [p]known
my Father also.[4] From now on you do know him and [q]have seen him.”
8 [r]Philip said to him, “Lord, [s]show us the Father, and it is enough for us.” **9** Jesus said to
him, “Have I been with you so long, and you still do not know me, Philip? [t]Whoever has seen
me has seen the Father. How can you say, ‘Show us the Father’? **10** Do you not believe that [u]I
am in the Father and the Father is in me? The words that I say to you [v]I do not speak on my
own authority, but the Father who dwells in me does his works. **11** Believe me that [u]I am in
the Father and the Father is in me, or else [w]believe on account of the works themselves.
12 “Truly, truly, I say to you, [x]whoever believes in me will also do the works that I do;

[1] Or *You believe in God* [2] Or *In my Father’s house are many rooms; if it were not so, I would have told you; for I go to prepare a place for you* [3] Some manuscripts *Where I am going you know, and the way you know* [4] Or *If you know me, you will know my Father also*, or *If you have known me, you will know my Father also*

33 [r]See ch. 7:33 [s]ch. 7:34; 8:21
34 [t]1 John 2:7, 8; 3:11; 2 John 5 [u]ch. 15:12, 17; 1 John 3:23; 4:21 [v]Lev. 19:18; Rom. 13:8; Col. 3:14; 1 Thess. 4:9; 1 Tim. 1:5; 1 Pet. 1:22 [w]ch. 15:12; Eph. 5:2; 1 John 4:10, 11
35 [x][1 John 3:14; 4:20]
36 [y][ver. 7] [z][ch. 7:34; 14:2] [a]ch. 21:18, 19; 2 Pet. 1:14
37 [b]Matt. 26:33-35; Mark 14:29-31; Luke 22:33, 34
38 [c]ch. 18:27

Chapter 14

1 [d]ver. 27; [ch. 16:22, 23; 1 Pet. 3:14] [e]See ch. 12:44
2 [f][ch. 2:16] [g]ch. 16:7; [ch. 8:21, 22; 13:33, 36]
3 [h]ver. 18, 28; [ch. 21:22, 23] [i]See ch. 12:26
5 [j]See ch. 11:16 [k]ch. 13:36
6 [l]Heb. 9:8; 10:20; [Eph. 2:18] [m]ch. 1:14, 17; [1 John 5:20] [n]See ch. 11:25
7 [o]ch. 8:19 [p]1 John 2:13, 14 [q][ch. 6:46]
8 [r]ch. 1:43, 44; 12:21 [s][Ex. 33:18]
9 [t]ch. 12:45; [ch. 10:30; 15:24; Col. 1:15; Heb. 1:3]
10 [u]See ch. 10:38 [v]See ch. 5:19, 20
11 [u][See ver. 10 above] [w]See ch. 5:36
12 [x][Matt. 17:20; 21:21; Mark 11:23; 16:17]

13:34–35 Love must be the distinguishing mark of Jesus’ disciples. Jesus’ “new command” takes its point of departure from the Mosaic commands to love the Lord with all one’s powers and to love one’s neighbor as oneself (Lev. 19:18; cf. Deut. 6:5; Mark 12:28–33), but Jesus’ own love and teaching deepen and transform these commands. Jesus even taught love for one’s enemies (Matt. 5:43–48). The command to love one’s neighbor was not new; the newness was found in loving one another as Jesus had loved his disciples (cf. John 13:1; 15:13). In light of Jesus’ subsequent death, **just as** implies a love that is even willing to lay down one’s life for another (see 15:13).

13:38 the rooster will not crow. See also Matt. 26:34; Mark 14:30; Luke 22:34. In a number of manuscripts of Mark’s Gospel, though not all, Mark mentions the rooster crowing “twice” (Mark 14:30, 68, 72), but roosters could crow a number of times separated by a few minutes. Mark specifies the first two individual crowings (as evidently Jesus did), while Matthew, Luke, and John focus on the shameful fact of Peter’s denial. They therefore drop this detail and report Jesus as referring to the entire set of crowings as the time the rooster crows.

14:1 Believe in God is translated as an imperative (or command), but the Greek could also be rendered as a statement, “You believe in God.” The imperative is probably better in light of the previous sentence. What troubles the disciples is Jesus’ imminent departure (see 13:36). “Believe,” in keeping with OT usage (e.g., Isa. 28:16), denotes personal, relational trust.

14:2–3 In light of the context (Jesus going to the Father; 13:1, 3; 14:28), it is best to understand **my Father’s house** as referring to heaven. In keeping with this image, the **many rooms** (or “dwelling places,” Gk. *monē*) are places to live within that large house. The translation “rooms” is not meant to convey the idea of small spaces, but only to keep consistency in the metaphor of heaven as God’s “house.” In a similar passage, Jesus speaks of his followers being received into the “eternal dwellings” (Luke 16:9; cf. 1 Cor. 2:9).

14:6 Jesus as **the** one **way** to **the Father** fulfills the OT symbols and teachings that show the exclusiveness of God’s claim (see note on 3:18), such as the curtain (Ex. 26:33) barring access to God’s presence from all except the Levitical high priest (Leviticus 16), the rejection of human inventions as means to approach God (Lev. 10:2), and the choice of Aaron alone to represent Israel before God in his sanctuary (Num. 17:5). Jesus is the only “way” to God (Acts 4:12), and he alone can provide access to God. Jesus as **the truth** fulfills the teaching of the OT (John 1:17) and reveals the true God (cf. 1:14, 17; 5:33; 18:37; also 8:40, 45–46; 14:9). Jesus alone is **the life** who fulfills the OT promises of “life” given by God (11:25–26), having life in himself (1:4; 5:26), and he is thus able to confer eternal life to all those who believe in him (e.g., 3:16). This is another “I am” saying that makes a claim to deity (see note on 6:35).

14:8–11 Philip apparently asks for some sort of appearance by God. In the OT, Moses asked for and was given a limited vision of God’s glory (Ex. 33:18; cf. Ex. 24:10). Isaiah, too, received a vision of God (Isa. 6:1; see note on John 12:41). Jesus is the greater fulfillment of these limited OT events (see also Ezek. 1:26–28). In keeping with OT teaching, Jesus denied the possibility of a direct vision of God (John 5:37; 6:46; cf. 1:18), yet he makes the stunning assertion that those who have seen him have seen the Father—a clear claim to deity. Philip’s request shows that he has not yet understood the point of Jesus’ coming, namely, to reveal the Father (1:14, 18).

14:10 I am in the Father and the Father is in me. Though there is a complete mutual indwelling of the Father and the Son, the Father and the Son remain distinct persons within the Trinity, as does the Holy Spirit (Matt. 28:19; 2 Cor. 13:14), and the three of them still constitute only one Being in three persons.

14:11 The works themselves includes the miracles of Jesus and also the other actions and teachings that he did and gave (see note on v. 12).

14:12 the works that I do. In John’s Gospel, the term “works” (Gk. *ergon*), both in singular and in plural, is a broader term than “signs.” While “signs” in John are characteristically miracles that attest to Jesus’ identity as Messiah

and greater works than these will he do, because I [y]am going to the Father. **13** [z]Whatever
you ask in my name, this I will do, that [a]the Father may be glorified in the Son. **14** [z]If you
ask me[1] anything in my name, I will do it.

Jesus Promises the Holy Spirit

15 [b]"If you love me, you will [c]keep my commandments. **16** And I will ask the Father, and
he will give you another [d]Helper,[2] to be with you forever, **17** even [e]the Spirit of truth, [f]whom
the world cannot receive, because it neither sees him nor knows him. You know him, for
he dwells with you and [g]will be[3] in you.

18 "I will not leave you as orphans; [h]I will come to you. **19** [i]Yet a little while and the world
will see me no more, but [j]you will see me. [k]Because I live, you also will live. **20** [l]In that day
you will know that [m]I am in my Father, and [n]you in me, and [o]I in you. **21** [p]Whoever has my
commandments and [q]keeps them, he it is who loves me. And [r]he who loves me [s]will be loved
by my Father, and I will love him and [t]manifest myself to him." **22** [u]Judas (not Iscariot) said
to him, "Lord, how is it [v]that you will manifest yourself to us, and not to the world?" **23** Jesus
answered him, [w]"If anyone loves me, he will keep my word, and my Father will love him, and
[x]we will come to him and [y]make our home with him. **24** Whoever does not love me does not
keep my words. And [z]the word that you hear is not mine but the Father's who sent me.

25 "These things I have spoken to you while I am still with you. **26** But the [a]Helper, the Holy
Spirit, [b]whom the Father will send in my name, [c]he will teach you all things and [d]bring to
your remembrance all that I have said to you. **27** [e]Peace I leave with you; [f]my peace I give to

[1] Some manuscripts omit *me* [2] Or *Advocate*, or *Counselor*; also 14:26; 15:26; 16:7 [3] Some manuscripts *and is*

12 [y]ver. 28; ch. 16:28; [ch. 7:33; 13:1, 3; 16:5, 10, 17; 17:11, 13; 20:17]
13 [z]ch. 15:16; 16:23, 24; See Matt. 7:7 [a]See ch. 13:31
14 [z][See ver. 13 above]
15 [b]ver. 21, 23; ch. 15:10; 1 John 5:3; 2 John 6 [c]See 1 John 2:3
16 [d]ver. 26; ch. 15:26; 16:7
17 [e]ch. 15:26; 16:13; [1 Cor. 2:12-14; 1 John 2:27; 4:6; 5:6] [f]1 Cor. 2:14 [g]Acts 2:4; [1 John 2:27; 2 John 2]; See Rom. 8:9
18 [h]ver. 3, 28
19 [i]See ch. 7:33 [j][ch. 12:45; 16:16] [k][Rom. 5:10; Eph. 2:5; Rev. 20:4]
20 [l]ch. 16:23, 26 [m]ver. 10 [n][ch. 15:4-7]; See 1 John 2:28 [o]ch. 17:21, 23, 26
21 [p][ch. 7:17; 8:31, 32] [q]ver. 15; 1 John 2:5 [r]ch. 16:27 [s][ch. 12:26] [t]See ch. 7:4
22 [u]Luke 6:16; Acts 1:13 [v][Acts 10:40, 41]
23 [w]See ver. 15, 21 [x]Rev. 3:20 [y][2 Cor. 6:16; 1 John 2:24]
24 [z][ver. 10]; See ch. 7:16
26 [a]See ver. 16 [b][Luke 24:49; Acts 2:33, with ch. 15:26; 16:7] [c]ch. 16:13; 1 Cor. 2:10; 1 John 2:20, 27 [d]See ch. 2:22
27 [e]ch. 20:19, 21, 26; Luke 24:36 [f]ch. 16:33; Col. 3:15; [Eph. 2:17; Phil. 4:7]

and Son of God, and that lead unbelievers to faith (see note on 2:11), Jesus' "works" include both his miracles (see 7:21) and his other activities and teachings, including the whole of his ministry (see 4:34; 5:36; 10:32; 17:4). These are all manifestations of the activity of God the Father, for Jesus said, "The Father who dwells in me does his works" (14:10). Here Jesus is teaching his disciples to imitate the things he did in his life and ministry. The disciples' **greater works** will be possible because Jesus is **going to the Father**, subsequent to his finished work on the cross (12:24; 15:13; 19:30); this indicates that the "greater works" will be possible because of the power of the Holy Spirit who would be sent after Jesus goes to the Father (see 16:7; also 7:39; 14:16, 26). The expression "greater works" could also be translated more broadly as "greater things," since the Greek *meizona* is simply a neuter adjective and the noun "works" (Gk. *erga*, plural) is not included here as it is in the earlier part of the verse. These "greater works" include evangelism, teaching, and deeds of mercy and compassion—in short, the entire ministry of the church to the entire world, beginning from Pentecost. (E.g., on the day of Pentecost alone, more believers were added to Jesus' followers than during his entire earthly ministry up to that time; cf. Acts 2:41.) These works are "greater" not because they are more amazing miracles but because they will be greater in their worldwide scope and will result in the transformation of individual lives and of whole cultures and societies.

14:13 Praying in Jesus' **name** means praying in a way consistent with his character and his will (a person's name in the ancient world represented what the person was like); it also means coming to God in the authority of Jesus. Probably both senses are intended here. Adding "in Jesus' name" at the end of every prayer is neither required nor wrong. Effective prayer must ask for and desire what Jesus delights in. See also note on 1 John 5:15.

14:14 If you ask me gives warrant for praying directly to Jesus (but see ESV footnote). Many other verses encourage prayer to God the Father (see 15:16).

14:15 Jesus' words echo the demands of the Deuteronomic covenant (cf. Deut. 5:10; 6:5–6; 7:9; 10:12–13; 11:13, 22) and reflect his unique authority. True love manifests itself in willing obedience.

14:16–17 The Holy Spirit (cf. v. 26), the **Spirit of truth** who will guide the disciples into all truth (16:13), will serve as **another Helper** (or "helping Presence"; see also ESV footnote). He will indwell Jesus' followers forever, functioning as Jesus' emissary in his physical absence. The promise of the divine presence with Jesus' followers in 14:15–24 includes the Spirit (vv. 15–17), Jesus (vv. 18–21), and the Father (vv. 22–24). **he dwells with you and will be in you**. This does not mean that there was no work of the Spirit of God within believers prior to this time (see note on 7:39) but rather that the Holy Spirit "will be in you" in a new and more powerful sense after Pentecost.

14:18 I will come to you most likely means that Jesus will appear to the disciples after his resurrection (chs. 20–21). Some interpreters have taken this as a reference to the Holy Spirit's coming, which Jesus does promise (14:16–17), but both Jesus and John always use precise wording in maintaining a distinction between Jesus and the Spirit.

14:21 keeps (i.e., follows and obeys) **them**. Obedience to Christ is an indication of genuine love for him.

14:22 The **Judas** referred to here is probably "Judas the son of James" mentioned in Luke 6:16 and Acts 1:13, not Judas the half brother of Jesus (Matt. 13:55; Mark 6:3).

14:23 Home (Gk. *monē*, "room, dwelling place") is the same word used in a different context in v. 2. Just as the Father and the Son now make their home with Christians in this age, Jesus is preparing for them a place in heaven where they will one day live with God (vv. 2–3). On the theme of God's dwelling among his people, see note on 1:14.

14:26 He will teach you uses the masculine Greek pronoun *ekeinos* ("he") instead of the neuter pronoun *ekeino* ("it"), which would have been expected for grammatical agreement with the grammatically neuter antecedent *Pneuma* (**Spirit**). Many interpreters have seen this as a deliberate choice on John's part, indicating an awareness of the distinct personhood of the Holy Spirit (though others disagree, suggesting that the pronoun is masculine in order to agree with the masculine noun **Helper** earlier in the sentence). John follows the same usage in 15:26 and 16:13–14. That he will teach the disciples **all things and bring to your remembrance all that I have said to you** is an important promise regarding the disciples' future role in writing the words of Scripture; see also 16:13–15. Jesus' promise here is specifically to these disciples (who would become the apostles after Pentecost), though there is of course a broader teaching and guiding ministry of the Holy Spirit generally in the lives of believers, as is taught elsewhere in Scripture (Rom. 8:14; Gal. 5:16, 18). On the work of the Trinity, see chart, p. 2055.

14:27 The expression **peace** (Hb. *shalom*) had a much richer connotation than the English word does since it conveyed not merely the absence of conflict and turmoil but also the notion of positive blessing, especially in terms of a right relationship with God (e.g., Num. 6:24–26; cf. Ps. 29:11; Hag. 2:9, and also, as a result, the idea that "all is well" in one's life). This may be manifested most clearly amid persecution and tribulation; see also John 15:18–19; 16:33.

you. Not as the world gives do I give to you. [g]Let not your hearts be troubled, neither [h]let
them be afraid. 28 [i]You heard me say to you, [j]'I am going away, and I will come to you.' If
you loved me, you would have rejoiced, because I [k]am going to the Father, for [l]the Father
is greater than I. 29 And [m]now I have told you before it takes place, so that when it does take
place you may believe. 30 I will no longer talk much with you, for [n]the ruler of this world
is coming. [o]He has no claim on me, 31 but I do [p]as the Father has commanded me, [q]so that
the world may know that I love the Father. Rise, let us go from here.

I Am the True Vine

15 "I am the [r]true vine, and my Father is [s]the vinedresser. 2 [t]Every branch in me that
does not bear fruit [u]he takes away, and every branch that does bear fruit he prunes,
[v]that it may bear more fruit. 3 Already [w]you are clean [x]because of the word that I have spoken to you. 4 [y]Abide [z]in me, and I in you. As the branch cannot bear fruit by itself, unless
it abides in the vine, neither can you, unless you abide in me. 5 I am the vine; [a]you are the
branches. Whoever abides in me and I in him, he it is that [b]bears much fruit, for apart
from me you can do nothing. 6 If anyone does not abide in me [c]he is thrown away like a
branch and withers; [d]and the branches are gathered, thrown into the fire, and burned.
7 If [e]you abide in me, and my words abide in you, [f]ask whatever you wish, and it will be

27 [g]ver. 1 [h]2 Tim. 1:7
28 [i]ver. 2-4 [j]See ch. 8:21 [k]See ver. 12 [l][ch. 10:29; Phil. 2:6]
29 [m]ch. 13:19; 16:4
30 [n]See ch. 12:31 [o][ch. 17:14; 18:36; Heb. 4:15]
31 [p]ch. 12:49, 50; Phil. 2:8; Heb. 5:8 [q]ch. 17:21, 23

Chapter 15

1 [r][Jer. 2:21] [s][1 Cor. 3:9]
2 [t]ver. 6; Matt. 3:10; 7:19; [Rom. 11:17; 2 Pet. 1:8] [u][Matt. 15:13; Rom. 11:22] [v][Matt. 13:12]
3 [w]ch. 13:10 [x]ch. 17:17; [ver. 7; Eph. 5:26]
4 [y]ver. 5-7; 1 John 2:6; [Phil. 1:11; Col. 1:23]; See ch. 6:56 [z]See ch. 3:15
5 [a]Rom. 6:5 [b]ver. 16; Col. 1:6, 10
6 [c]See ver. 2 [d]Matt. 13:40-42; [Ezek. 15:4]
7 [e]See ch. 8:31 [f]See ch. 14:13

14:28 In saying that **the Father is greater than I**, Jesus means that the Father as the one who sends and commands is "greater" (in authority or leadership) than the Son. However, this does not mean that Jesus is inferior in his being and essence to the Father, as 1:1, 10:30, and 20:28 clearly show.

14:30 On the **ruler of this world**, see note on 12:31. Those who do not follow Christ are not autonomous. They are serving Satan, whether they are aware of this or not. Satan **is coming** in the person of Judas and those with him (see ch. 18), and this is why in a short time Jesus will **no longer talk much** with them. But Jesus is not subject to Satan, for Satan **has no claim on** Jesus. Satan cannot force Jesus to do anything, but Jesus willingly submits to the suffering that is to come, out of obedience to his Father (see 14:31).

14:31 Jesus' obedience to the Father signifies his love for the Father. The transition from 14:31 to 15:1 is at times viewed as a "literary seam" (i.e., an indication that John's Gospel is pieced together from different sources). More likely, John is implying that Jesus and his followers are leaving the upper room, making their way to the Kidron Valley, and arriving in the Garden of Gethsemane (18:1).

15:1–17 Jesus' allegory of the vine and the branches is at the very heart of the Farewell Discourse (13:31–16:33). The OT frequently uses the vineyard or vine as a symbol for Israel, God's covenant people, especially in two "vineyard songs" in Isaiah (Isa. 5:1–7; 27:2–6). However, Israel's failure to produce fruit resulted in divine judgment. Jesus, by contrast, is "the true vine," and his followers abide in him and produce fruit.

15:1 This is the last of Jesus' seven **I am** sayings in this Gospel (see note on 6:35). **True** contrasts Jesus with OT Israel (see previous note), reinforcing John's theme that Jesus is the true Israel. The **vinedresser** refers back to Isaiah's first vineyard song, where God is depicted as tending his vineyard, only to be rewarded with wild grapes (Isa. 5:1–7; cf. Ps. 80:8–9). The fruitfulness of those in Christ contrasts with the fruitlessness of Israel.

15:2 The divine vinedresser does two things to ensure maximum fruit production: (1) he removes unfruitful branches, and (2) **he prunes** all the others (cf. Heb. 6:7–8). **Does not bear fruit** seems to indicate that the person symbolized by such a branch is not a true believer (see John 15:6, 8). In that case, **in me** is just a loose connection needed to make the metaphor of a vine work, reflecting a claim to be Christ's that is not genuine and not implying actual regeneration or true belief. This then would be one of several verses in John showing that not all who follow Jesus for a time and hear his teaching are genuine believers (cf. 6:66; also 13:10–11 on Judas). Others understand these branches to represent true believers who are "unfruitful" for various reasons. In favor of this view is the fact that Jesus says such branches are "in me," and that seems parallel to being "in Christ," as only believers are. However, these unfruitful branches appear to be the same branches that are "thrown away" and "burned" in 15:6, which seems clearly to be a picture of final judgment. **Fruit** is an image for good results coming from the life of a believer, probably in terms of bringing benefit to the lives of others and advancing the work of God in the world (see Matt. 13:8; cf. Gal. 5:22–23 for a different image of "fruit" as changed character). **he takes away**. The Greek verb *airō* can also mean "lifts up" in certain contexts, and some use this to argue that this means God "lifts up" unfruitful branches from the ground so that they will become more fruitful. This interpretation is taken by those who think the branches represent true believers who are not fruitful. But this sense seems less likely because the unfruitful branches in John 15:6 are "thrown into the fire, and burned," which is an image of final judgment. "He prunes" gives a picture of painful but necessary removal of some interests and activities in order that the remaining branches may bear even more fruit. The word translated "prunes" (Gk. *kathairō*) often means "to clean," and has the same root as the adjective *katharos*, translated "clean" in 15:3.

15:3 clean. See 13:10–11.

15:4 Abide in me means to continue in a daily, personal relationship with Jesus, characterized by trust, prayer, obedience (see v. 10), and joy. **And I in you** is a phrase without an explicit verb, but it probably is an abbreviated way of saying, "See that I abide in you"; that is, "Safeguard your relationship with me so that I continue to abide fully in you." (See notes on 8:31; 1 John 2:6.) The "in" terminology in the present passage refers back to OT covenant theology, including prophetic texts regarding a future new covenant (see Ex. 25:8; 29:45; Lev. 26:11–12; Ezek. 37:27–28; 43:9). The repeated references to fruit bearing (also John 15:5, 8) underscore that this is God's primary purpose in creation (Gen. 1:11–12, 22, 28) and in redemption (cf. John 15:8, 16). The OT prophets envisioned a time when God's people would "blossom and put forth shoots and fill the whole world with fruit" (Isa. 27:6; cf. Hos. 14:4–8).

15:5 Apart from me you can do nothing does not mean "nothing at all," for unbelievers of course carry on their ordinary activities of life apart from Christ. Rather, it means "nothing of eternal value," or an inability to produce spiritual fruit.

15:6 The person who **does not abide in me** is an unbeliever who does not have a personal faith in Christ (see note on v. 4). The verse echoes Ezek. 15:1–8, where a vine failing to produce fruit is said to be good for nothing but the fire (see Heb. 6:7–8). **Fire** is a common Jewish and biblical symbol for divine judgment (e.g., Isa. 30:27; Matt. 3:12 par.; 5:22; 18:8; 25:41). Some take this "fire" to imply loss of reward for true believers, not eternal judgment for unbelievers, but this does not fit as well with the image of branches being entirely burned up by a fire. See also note on John 15:2.

15:7 Two conditions are given for answered prayer: abiding in Jesus, and his words abiding in believers (thus transforming their thinking). Elsewhere Jesus says that believers must ask in his name (i.e., in accord with his character and for his glory; see 14:13–14; 16:23–24). If God's people truly **abide in** Jesus (see note on 15:4), they will desire what he desires and will pray according to his words, and those prayers will be pleasing to him.

done for you. **8** [g]By this my Father is glorified, that you [h]bear much fruit and so prove to
be my disciples. **9** [i]As the Father has loved me, [j]so have I loved you. Abide in my love. **10** [k]If
you keep my commandments, you will abide in my love, just as [l]I have kept [m]my Father's
commandments and abide in his love. **11** These things I have spoken to you, [n]that my joy
may be in you, and that [o]your joy may be full.

12 [p]"This is my commandment, that you love one another as I have loved you. **13** [q]Greater
love has no one than this, [r]that someone lay down his life for his friends. **14** You are [s]my
friends [t]if you do what I command you. **15** [u]No longer do I call you servants,[1] for the servant[2]
[w]does not know what his master is doing; but I have called you friends, for [x]all that I have

[1] Greek *bondservants* [2] Greek *bondservant*; also verse 20

8 [g]Isa. 61:3; Matt. 5:16; 2 Cor. 9:13; Phil. 1:11 [h]ver. 5
9 [i]See ch. 5:20 [j]See ch. 13:34
10 [k][ch. 14:15, 23] [l]ch. 8:55; 17:4; Phil. 2:8 [m]See ch. 10:18
11 [n][2 Cor. 2:3] [o]ch. 3:29; 16:24; 17:13; 1 John 1:4; 2 John 12
12 [p]See ch. 13:34
13 [q]Rom. 5:7, 8; Eph. 5:2 [r]See ch. 10:11
14 [s]Luke 12:4 [t][ver. 10; Matt. 12:50]
15 [u][ver. 20] [w][ch. 13:7, 12] [x]ch. 3:32; 8:26, 40; [ch. 16:13]

15:8 God is **glorified** not by praise and worship alone but by his followers also bearing **much fruit** for the advancement of his kingdom on earth. Here again, fruit bearing is evidence of being true believers, or being Jesus' **disciples**.

15:9 Abide in my love. Mutual love between believers and Christ is another element of this "abiding" relationship (see note on v. 4).

15:10–11 Obedience is not to be equated with drudgery; it is all about **joy**. The OT prophets envisioned a period of great end-time rejoicing (e.g., Isa. 25:9; 35:10; 51:3; 61:10; 66:10; Zeph. 3:14–17; Zech. 9:9). God threatened judgment if his people would not serve him "with joyfulness and gladness of heart" (Deut. 28:47–48). **that my joy may be in you**. Just as Jesus had great joy in obeying his Father even in the midst of opposition, so Christians will have joy in obedience.

15:12 love one another. On Jesus' "love commandment" (vv. 12–17), see note on 13:34–35.

15:13–14 You are my friends implies a stunning level of comfortable personal interaction with one who is also the eternal, omnipotent Creator of the universe (see 1:1–3, 10). In the OT, only Abraham (2 Chron. 20:7; Isa. 41:8) and by implication Moses (Ex. 33:11) are called "friends of God." Here Jesus extends this privilege to all obedient believers.

The Work of the Trinity

Though the word "Trinity" does not appear in the Bible, by presenting the Father, Son, and Spirit all doing what no one else ever does, the Gospel of John gives us the raw material on which this doctrine is based. Observing what God says and does helps us to know him, and observing which actions are done by which members of the Godhead helps us to see which roles they play.

Action	Father	Son	Spirit
Give life	5:21, 26; (6:33); 17:3	5:21, 25–26, 40; 6:33; 17:3	3:6, 8; 6:63
Proclaim future	1:33	13:19, 26, 36–38; 14:3, 29; 16:1–4, 16–28, 32; 20:18	16:13
Indwell believers	14:23	14:20, 23; (15:4–7); 17:23, 26	14:17
Teach	6:45; 7:16, 17; 8:28	7:14; (8:2); 8:20; 13:13–14	14:26
Testify to Jesus	5:32, 37; 6:27; 8:18	8:12–14, 18	15:26
Glorify Jesus	5:22–23; 8:50, 54; 13:31–32; 17:1, 22	(1:14); 2:11; 13:31–32; 17:5, 24	16:14

Actions Common to Father and Son

Action	Father	Son
Glorify the Father	4:23; 12:28; 13:31–32	(2:16); (9:3–4); 11:40; 12:28; 13:31–32; 14:13; 17:1, 4–5
Give the Spirit	3:34; 14:16	(4:10–14); (7:37–39); 20:22
Send the Spirit	14:26	15:26; 16:7

Actions Common to Son and Spirit

Action	Son	Spirit
Be given by the Father	3:16	(4:10–14); 14:16
Be sent by the Father	3:17; 4:34; 5:23–24, 36; 6:29, 57; 7:28–29, 33; 8:16, 26, 29, 42; 9:4; 10:36; 11:42; 12:44–45; 13:20; 15:21; 17:3, 8, 18, 23, 25; 20:21	14:26; 15:26
Speak not from himself	(5:19); 5:30; (6:38); 7:16; 12:49–50	16:13
Speak only what he hears	3:32; (3:34); (5:30); 8:26, 40; 12:50; 15:15	16:13
Convict	3:19–20; 4:16, 18; (5:27); (8:7); 8:34, 40; 11:40; 12:7–8; 13:8	16:7–11
Be received	1:12 (cf. 1:10–11)	7:39 (cf. 14:17)
Disclose what belongs to God	1:18	16:13–14

heard from my Father [y]I have made known to you. 16 You did not choose me, but [z]I chose
you and appointed you that you should go and [a]bear fruit and that your fruit should abide,
so that [b]whatever you ask the Father in my name, he may give it to you. 17 These things I
command you, [c]so that you will love one another.

The Hatred of the World

18 [d]"If the world hates you, know that it has hated me before it hated you. 19 [e]If you were
of the world, the world would love you as its own; but because [f]you are not of the world,
but I chose you out of the world, therefore the world hates you. 20 Remember the word
that I said to you: [g]'A servant is not greater than his master.' If they persecuted me, [h]they
will also persecute you. [i]If they kept my word, they will also keep yours. 21 But [j]all these
things they will do to you [k]on account of my name, [l]because they do not know him who
sent me. 22 If I had not come and spoken to them, [m]they would not have been guilty of sin,[1]
but now they have no excuse for their sin. 23 [n]Whoever hates me hates my Father also. 24 [o]If
I had not done among them the works that no one else did, [m]they would not be guilty of
sin, but now they have [p]seen and hated both me and my Father. 25 But [q]the word that is
written in their Law must be fulfilled: [r]'They hated me without a cause.'

26 "But [s]when the Helper comes, whom I will send to you from the Father, the Spirit of
truth, who proceeds from the Father, [t]he will bear witness about me. 27 And [u]you also will
bear witness, [v]because you have been with me [w]from the beginning.

16 "I have said all these things to you to keep you from falling away. 2 [x]They will put
you out of the synagogues. Indeed, [y]the hour is coming when [z]whoever kills you
will think he is offering service to God. 3 And they will do these things [a]because they have
not known the Father, nor me. 4 But [b]I have said these things to you, that when [c]their hour
comes you may remember that I told them to you.

The Work of the Holy Spirit

"I did not say these things to you from the beginning, [d]because I was with you. 5 But
now [e]I am going to him who sent me, and [f]none of you asks me, 'Where are you going?'
6 But because I have said these things to you, [g]sorrow has filled your heart. 7 Nevertheless,

[1] Greek *they would not have sin*; also verse 24

[c]See Luke 22:53 [d][Matt. 9:15] **5** [e]See ch. 14:12 [f][ch. 13:36; 14:5] **6** [g]ver. 22; ch. 14:1

15 [y]ch. 17:26; [Gen. 18:17; 1 Cor. 2:16; 13:9, 10]
16 [z]See ch. 13:18 [a][2 John 8] [b][ver. 7]; See ch. 14:13
17 [c]ver. 12
18 [d]ch. 7:7; 1 John 3:13; [ver. 23, 24]
19 [e][1 John 4:5] [f]ch. 17:14, 16; [Luke 6:26; Gal. 1:4; James 4:4]
20 [g]ch. 13:16; Matt. 10:24; [ver. 15] [h]ch. 16:33; 1 Cor. 4:12; 2 Cor. 4:9; 1 Thess. 2:15; 2 Tim. 3:12 [i][Ezek. 3:7]; See ch. 8:51
21 [j]ch. 16:3 [k]Matt. 10:22; 24:9; Rev. 2:3; [Acts 5:41; 1 Pet. 4:14, 16] [l]See Acts 3:17
22 [m][Matt. 11:22, 24; Luke 12:47, 48]; See ch. 9:41
23 [n]See ch. 5:23
24 [o]ch. 3:2; 7:31; 9:32; Matt. 9:33; [ch. 10:32, 37] [m][See ver. 22 above] [p]See ch. 14:9
25 [q]See ch. 10:34; 12:38 [r]Cited from Ps. 35:19 or 69:4
26 [s]See ch. 14:16, 17, 26 [t]1 Cor. 12:3; 1 John 5:7
27 [u]ch. 19:35; 21:24; 1 John 1:2; 4:14; [3 John 12]; See Luke 24:48 [v]See Acts 4:20 [w][Luke 1:2; Acts 1:21, 22; 1 John 2:7]

Chapter 16

2 [x]ch. 9:22; 12:42 [y]See ch. 4:21 [z]Acts 8:1; 9:1; 26:9-11
3 [a]ch. 8:19, 55; 15:21; 17:25
4 [b]ch. 13:19; 14:29

15:16 You did not choose me does not negate the disciples' willing decision to follow Jesus when he called them. Jesus is emphasizing that the ultimate factor in determining who would follow him was Jesus' own choice. The Greek *eklegomai* has the sense of "to choose or pick out from a group," and it clearly has that sense also in v. 19. **That you should go and bear fruit** implies that the purpose of Christ's choosing people is not merely that their sins be forgiven and they have eternal life but also that their lives be fruitful and productive in fulfilling God's purposes. For key passages on the doctrine of election, see Romans 9 and Ephesians 1.

15:19 therefore the world hates you. Christians should not be surprised that unbelievers in the world hate them. It follows a pattern seen in the world since Cain murdered Abel (see Gen. 4:8; Heb. 11:4; 1 John 3:12), and it is seen in the world's reactions to Christ himself (see John 15:18).

15:22 They would not have been guilty of sin does not mean all sin (see Rom. 3:23), but the specific sin of rejecting the supreme revelation of God that came in Christ himself, a sin that is particularly manifested in hating Christ (see John 15:18, 23, 24). **their sin**. See note on 5:31–47.

15:25 Jesus declares that the Jews' hatred of him fulfills OT Scripture, specifically Ps. 69:4 (cf. Ps. 35:19; also note on Isa. 6:9–10). This Davidic psalm depicts the figure of a righteous sufferer who is zealous for God but is persecuted by God's enemies for no good reason. Thus Jesus found a precedent for his enemies' hatred toward him in the antagonism encountered by David. **Without a cause** reminds believers that hatred and persecution against Jesus and his followers is often not because of any wrong that they have done but simply because of irrational evil in the hearts of the persecutors.

15:26 The Helper is the Holy Spirit; see notes on 14:16–17; 14:26. **Whom I will send** indicates that the Holy Spirit will come in new power into the world in obedience to God the Son. But **who proceeds from the Father** indicates that the Holy Spirit will also come in obedience to the directions of God the Father. Both the Father and the Son will send the Holy Spirit into the world in new fullness at Pentecost (see Acts 2:1–33; also notes on John 7:39; 14:16–17). **He will bear witness about me** reminds believers that when they bear witness about Christ, the Holy Spirit is working silently and invisibly through their words. On "he" as masculine and personal, see note on 14:26.

16:1 Jesus uses his words (now recorded in Scripture) as the means **to keep** believers **from falling away**.

16:2 Whoever kills you will think he is offering service to God implies a deep deception, ultimately inspired by Satan, who is a murderer and the father of lies (see 8:44). Not all "religions" are good, for some religions will teach their followers that they are doing good when in fact they are doing the horribly evil act of murdering true followers of the Son of God. The apostle Paul himself, prior to his conversion, thought he was serving God by persecuting Christians (see Acts 8:1–3 [where Paul is called Saul]; Gal. 1:13–14; 1 Tim. 1:13).

16:4 Believers may think opposition means that God opposes them, but Jesus emphasizes that persecution is to be expected (see also v. 1).

16:5 none of you asks me. But Peter did ask this exact question in 13:36 (cf. 14:5), so the present tense of "asks" probably has the sense, "none of you at the present time is asking me" (this was some time after 13:36; see the indication of change of location in 14:31).

16:7 it is to your advantage that I go away. This is because while Jesus was on earth he could be in only one place at a time, but the Holy Spirit would carry on Jesus' ministry over the entire world at all times. In addition, in God's sovereign plan for the unfolding of history, the Holy Spirit would not come in new covenant power and fullness until Jesus returned to heaven (see notes on 7:39; 14:16–17; 15:26). **The Helper** (see notes on 14:16–17; 14:26) refers back to the anticipation of the pouring out of the Spirit and

I tell you the truth: it is to your advantage that I go away, for [h]if I do not go away, [i]the
Helper will not come to you. But [j]if [k]I go, [l]I will send him to you. **8** [m]And when he comes,
he will [n]convict the world concerning sin and righteousness and judgment: **9** concerning
sin, [o]because they do not believe in me; **10** [p]concerning righteousness, [q]because I go to the
Father, and you will see me no longer; **11** [r]concerning judgment, because the ruler of this
world [s]is judged.
12 "I still have many things to say to you, but you cannot bear them now. **13** When [t]the
Spirit of truth comes, [u]he will [v]guide you into all the truth, for he will not speak on his
own authority, but [w]whatever he hears he will speak, and he will declare to you the things
that are to come. **14** He will [x]glorify me, for he will take what is mine and declare it to you.
15 [y]All that the Father has is mine; [z]therefore I said that he will take what is mine and
declare it to you.

Your Sorrow Will Turn into Joy

16 [a]"A little while, and you will see me no longer; and [b]again a little while, and you will
see me." **17** So [c]some of his disciples said to one another, "What is this that he says to us,
[d]'A little while, and you will not see me, and again a little while, and you will see me'; and,
[e]'because I am going to the Father'?" **18** So they were saying, "What does he mean by 'a little
while'? [f]We do not know what he is talking about." **19** [g]Jesus knew that they wanted to ask
him, so he said to them, "Is this what you are asking yourselves, what I meant by saying, 'A
little while and you will not see me, and again a little while and you will see me'? **20** Truly,
truly, I say to you, [h]you will weep and lament, but [i]the world will rejoice. You will be sorrowful, but [j]your sorrow will turn into joy. **21** [k]When a woman is giving birth, she has sorrow
because her hour has come, but when she has delivered the baby, she no longer remembers
the anguish, for joy that a human being has been born into the world. **22** [l]So also you have
sorrow now, but [m]I will see you again, and [n]your hearts will rejoice, and no one will take
your joy from you. **23** [o]In that day you will [p]ask nothing of me. Truly, truly, I say to you,
[q]whatever you ask of the Father in my name, [r]he will give it to you. **24** Until now you have
asked nothing in my name. [s]Ask, and you will receive, [t]that your joy may be full.

I Have Overcome the World

25 "I have said these things to you in figures of speech. [u]The hour is coming when I will
no longer speak to you in figures of speech but will tell you plainly about the Father. **26** In
that day you will ask in my name, and I do not say to you that I will ask the Father on your
behalf; **27** [v]for the Father himself loves you, because [w]you have loved me and [x]have believed

7 [h]ch. 7:39 [i]ch. 15:26; [ch. 14:16] [j][Acts 2:33] [k]ch. 14:2 [l]See ch. 14:26
8 [m][ch. 8:28] [n][ch. 8:46]
9 [o]ch. 8:24; [Acts 2:36, 37; 1 Cor. 12:3]
10 [p][Acts 17:31] [q]ver. 16, 17, 19
11 [r]See ch. 12:31 [s][Col. 2:15; Heb. 2:14]
13 [t]See ch. 14:17 [u]See ch. 14:26 [v]Acts 8:31; [ch. 1:17; 14:6; Ps. 25:5] [w][ch. 15:15]
14 [x]See ch. 7:39
15 [y]ch. 17:10 [z]ver. 14
16 [a]See ch. 7:33 [b][ver. 22]
17 [c][Mark 9:10, 32] [d]ver. 16 [e]ver. 10
18 [f][ch. 14:5]
19 [g][ver. 30]; See ch. 2:24, 25
20 [h]Matt. 9:15; Mark 16:10; Luke 23:27 [i][Rev. 11:10] [j]Jer. 31:13; See Matt. 5:4
21 [k]Isa. 26:17; [Ps. 48:6; Isa. 13:8; 1 Thess. 5:3; Rev. 12:2]
22 [l]ver. 6; [2 Cor. 6:10] [m][ver. 16] [n]Ps. 33:21; Isa. 66:14; Luke 24:52; Acts 2:46; 8:8, 39; 13:52
23 [o]ver. 26; ch. 14:20 [p]ver. 19, 30 [q]See ch. 14:13 [r]ch. 15:16; [Eph. 1:3]
24 [s]See Matt. 7:7 [t]See ch. 15:11
25 [u]ver. 2
27 [v][ch. 14:21, 23; 17:23] [w]ch. 21:15-17; [1 Cor. 16:22] [x]ver. 30; ch. 17:8

the inauguration of the kingdom spoken of in OT prophetic literature (e.g., Isa. 11:1–10; 32:14–18; 42:1–4; 44:1–5; Jer. 31:31–34; Ezek. 11:17–20; 36:24–27; 37:1–14; Joel 2:28–32).

16:8 He will convict the world gives hope that many who are in "the world" (and currently opposed to Jesus) will not be part of "the world" forever but will repent of their sins and believe in Christ.

16:10 Because I go to the Father means that Jesus will no longer be in the world to teach about true righteousness, and so the Holy Spirit will come to carry on that function, through illumination (v. 13) and through the words of believers who bear witness to the gospel.

16:11 Because the ruler of this world (i.e., Satan; see notes on 12:31; 14:30) **is judged** could also be translated "has been judged"; the perfect-tense verb *kekritai* (Gk.) has the sense of "has been judged and continues in the state resulting from that judgment."

16:13 On the **Spirit of truth**, see note on 14:16–17. The Spirit's ministry of guiding Jesus' followers **into all the truth** is a promise especially directed toward these 11 disciples, and it finds particular fulfillment in the subsequent work of these disciples in personally writing or overseeing the writing of the books of the NT (see note on 14:26). The promise, like the other things that Jesus says in these chapters, also has a broader application to all believers as the Holy Spirit leads and guides them (see Rom. 8:14; Gal. 5:18). The activity of the Holy Spirit in declaring the **things that are to come** suggests that he knows the future, something that is true of God alone; this gives evidence of the full deity of the Holy Spirit. The word **declare** (Gk. *anangellō*) occurs over 40 times in the Septuagint translation of Isaiah, where declaring things to come is said to be the exclusive domain of God (Isa. 48:14) and where God challenges anyone to declare the things that are to come (Isa. 42:9; 44:7; 46:10; cf. 41:21–29, esp. vv. 22–23; 45:19).

16:16–19 A little while . . . again a little while (v. 16). The first reference is plainly to the brief period between the crucifixion and the resurrection of Jesus, and the second reference is to the resurrection appearances (the "little while" after which the disciples will see Jesus again). The phrase is repeated by both Jesus and the disciples (vv. 17–19), recalling four previous instances of "a little while" in John's Gospel (cf. 7:33; 12:35; 13:33; 14:19).

16:23 In that day (that is, after Jesus' resurrection) **you will ask nothing of me** probably means that Jesus' disciples will not have to ask him questions about the meaning of his death and resurrection, because they will understand and because the Holy Spirit will be present to guide them "into all the truth" (v. 13).

16:24 Until now you have asked nothing in my name. While Jesus was on earth the disciples had not prayed to the Father in the name of Jesus. But now he was saying that they should do so. Regarding the meaning of praying "in Jesus' name," see notes on 1:12–13; 14:13. **Ask, and you will receive** reminds believers that frequent answers to prayer will give Jesus' followers great **joy** as they see God actively at work in the world in answer to their prayers.

16:25 The hour is coming refers to the time after Jesus' resurrection when he would explain much more directly to them the meaning of all that he had done (see Luke 24:27; Acts 1:3).

that I came from God.[1] 28 [y]I came from the Father and have come into the world, and now
[z]I am leaving the world and going to the Father."
29 His disciples said, "Ah, now you are speaking plainly and not [a]using figurative speech!
30 Now we know that [b]you know all things and do not need anyone to question you; this is
why we believe that [c]you came from God." 31 Jesus answered them, "Do you now believe?
32 Behold, [d]the hour is coming, indeed it has come, when [e]you will be scattered, each to
his own home, and [f]will leave me alone. [g]Yet I am not alone, for the Father is with me. 33 I
have said these things to you, that [h]in me you may have peace. [i]In the world you will have
[j]tribulation. But [k]take heart; [l]I have overcome the world."

The High Priestly Prayer

17 When Jesus had spoken these words, [m]he lifted up his eyes to heaven, and said,
"Father, [n]the hour has come; [o]glorify your Son that the Son may [p]glorify you, 2 since
[q]you have given him authority over all flesh, [r]to give eternal life to all [s]whom you have
given him. 3 [t]And this is eternal life, [u]that they know you [v]the only [w]true God, and [x]Jesus
Christ whom you have sent. 4 I [y]glorified you on earth, [z]having accomplished the work
that you gave me to do. 5 And now, Father, [a]glorify me in your own presence with the glory
[b]that I had with you [c]before the world existed.
6 [d]"I have manifested your name to the people [e]whom you gave me out of the world.
[f]Yours they were, and you gave them to me, and they have kept your word. 7 Now they
know that everything [f]that you have given me is from you. 8 For I have given them [g]the
words that you gave me, and they have received them and have come to know in truth
that [h]I came from you; and [i]they have believed that you sent me. 9 I am praying for them. [j]I
am not praying for the world but for those [k]whom you have given me, for [l]they are yours.
10 [m]All mine are yours, and yours are mine, and [n]I am glorified in them. 11 And I am no

[1] Some manuscripts *from the Father*

28 [y]ch. 8:14; 13:3 [z]See ch. 14:12
29 [a]ver. 25
30 [b]ch. 21:17; See ch. 2:24, 25 [c][ver. 27, 28; ch. 3:2]
32 [d][ch. 4:21, 23] [e]Matt. 26:31; Mark 14:27 [f][Isa. 63:5] [g]See ch. 8:16, 29
33 [h]See ch. 14:27; Col. 3:15 [i][ch. 15:18-21] [j]Rev. 1:9; See Acts 14:22 [k]ch. 14:1, 27 [l][Rom. 8:37; 1 John 4:4; 5:4, 5; Rev. 3:21; 12:11]

Chapter 17

1 [m]ch. 11:41 [n][ch. 7:30]; See ch. 12:23 [o]See ch. 7:39 [p]ver. 4
2 [q]See Matt. 28:18; Rev. 2:26, 27 [r]ch. 10:28; 1 John 2:25 [s]ver. 6, 9, 24; ch. 6:37, 39; 10:29; 18:9; Heb. 2:13
3 [t][1 John 5:20] [u]Hos. 2:20; 6:3; 2 Pet. 1:2, 3 [v]ch. 5:44 [w]1 Thess. 1:9; 1 John 5:20; [Jer. 10:10] [x]See ch. 3:17
4 [y]ver. 1; See ch. 13:31 [z][ch. 19:30; Luke 22:37]
5 [a]ch. 13:32 [b]ch. 1:1, 2; [Rev. 3:21] [c]ver. 24; Prov. 8:23; See ch. 8:58
6 [d]ver. 26; Ps. 22:22 [e]See ver. 2 [f]ver. 9
7 [f][See ver. 6 above]
8 [g]ver. 14; ch. 15:15; [ch. 8:26; 12:49] [h]ch. 8:42; 16:27 [i]ver. 21, 25; ch. 11:42; 16:30 **9** [j][ver. 20, 21] [k]See ver. 2 [l]ver. 6 **10** [m]ch. 16:15 [n]2 Thess. 1:10

16:28 Now I am leaving the world and going to the Father might have an initial reference to Jesus' spirit returning to heaven when his body died and remained on the earth, prior to his resurrection (see Luke 23:43, 46; John 19:30), but more likely refers to his ascension into heaven 40 days after his resurrection (Luke 24:50–51; Acts 1:3, 9). The parallel truths that Jesus was going to leave the world and go to the Father but also that he promised to come and dwell with all who love him (see John 14:21, 23) reflect Jesus' humanity (which is in one place at one time) and his deity (which is everywhere present)—both of which are true of Jesus as one divine-human person.

16:32 Jesus' prediction of a coming **hour** at which each of his followers **will be scattered, each to his own home** (cf. 19:27) probably alludes to Zech. 13:7 (quoted in Matt. 26:31 par.; cf. Matt. 26:56b). The shepherd will be deserted by his sheep.

16:33 On **peace**, see note on 14:27. In the midst of the suffering and hardship that was to come, Jesus' disciples, and all following them, can have such "peace" in fellowship with Christ. Fittingly, Jesus' Farewell Discourse (13:31–16:33) ends on a note of triumph (cf. 1 John 2:13–14; 4:4; 5:4–5).

17:1–26 In his final prayer, Jesus gives an account of his earthly mission to the Father who sent him. He prays, first for himself (vv. 1–5), then for his disciples (vv. 6–19), and finally for later believers (vv. 20–26).

17:1 Jesus **lifted up his eyes to heaven**, striking a customary posture in prayer (cf. Ps. 123:1; Mark 7:34; Luke 18:13). **the hour has come**. See notes on John 2:4; 7:30. The opening petition **glorify your Son** implies a claim to deity, since the OT affirms that God will not give his glory to another (e.g., Isa. 42:8; 48:11; on Jesus as the sent Son, see also John 3:16–18). As usual in John, God is glorified particularly through the cross of Christ.

17:2–3 Eternal life comes from knowing God and Jesus the sent Son (cf. 1:4; 5:26; 20:31). Knowing God is not confined to intellectual knowledge but entails living in fellowship with him. **That they know you** implies an intimate relationship that involves actually knowing God as a person. That God is the **only true God** is affirmed supremely in Deut. 6:4 (cf. John 5:44; 1 John 5:20). Jesus, in turn, is the "one-of-a-kind" Son sent by the Father (cf. John 1:14, 18; 3:16, 18) and the only way to him (14:6).

17:2 The Father's granting of **authority over all flesh** to Jesus (cf. 5:27) marks the start of a new era (cf. Isa. 9:6–7; Dan. 7:13–14; see also Matt. 11:27; 28:18). "All flesh" means the whole human race.

17:5 Jesus again claims that he existed **before the world existed** (or "before the world was"; cf. 1:1, 14; 3:13; 6:62; 8:58; 16:28; 17:24). This implies that the material universe is not eternal but was brought into being by God. Before that, nothing material existed. But God existed eternally as Father, Son, and Holy Spirit, and here Jesus speaks of a sharing of glory between the Father and the Son prior to creation, implying that there was mutual giving of honor in the interpersonal relationships of the Trinity from all eternity.

17:6 Jesus' revelation of God's **name** entails making known the Father in his whole person, both his works and words (cf. 1:18; 8:19, 27; 10:38; 12:45; 14:9–11).

17:9 Those whom you have given me are those who have believed or who would come to believe in Christ (see vv. 2, 6, 12; also 6:37, 39; 10:29).

17:11 I am no longer in the world. See note on 16:28. **keep them**. Jesus asks that those who have been specially given to him will be kept to the end (i.e., preserved from denying Christ). And since it is Jesus who intercedes for his disciples, his petition will most certainly be answered. The word "holy" in **Holy Father** echoes the assertion of God's awesome purity as described in Lev. 11:44 (cf. Ps. 71:22; 111:9; Isa. 6:3); this is the only time in the NT that this form of address is used with reference to the first person of the Godhead. **that they may be one, even as we are one**. Jesus shows the kind of profound unity that should be the norm among genuine believers. As the following verses indicate (through John 17:26), this is to be a reflection of the unity that has existed eternally between the Father and the Son (v. 11), namely, the unity of a common mind and purpose, an unqualified mutual love, and a sustained comprehensive togetherness in mission, as revealed in the Father-Son relationship characterized by Jesus' own ministry. Such unity is the result of Jesus' active work of "keeping" (vv. 12,

longer in the world, but [o]they are in the world, and [p]I am coming to you. [q]Holy Father,
[r]keep them in your name, [s]which you have given me, [t]that they may be one, [u]even as we
are one. **12** [v]While I was with them, I kept them in your name, which you have given me.
I have [w]guarded them, and [x]not one of them has been lost except [y]the son of destruction,
[z]that the Scripture might be fulfilled. **13** But now [a]I am coming to you, and these things
I speak in the world, that they may have [b]my joy fulfilled in themselves. **14** [c]I have given
them your word, and [d]the world has hated them [e]because they are not of the world, [f]just
as I am not of the world. **15** I [g]do not ask that you [h]take them out of the world, but that you
[i]keep them from [j]the evil one.[1] **16** [k]They are not of the world, just as I am not of the world.
17 [l]Sanctify them[2] in the truth; [m]your word is truth. **18** [n]As you sent me into the world, so I

[1] Or *from evil* [2] Greek *Set them apart* (for holy service to God)

11 [o]ch. 13:1 [p]See ch. 14:12 [q][ver. 25] [r]ver. 12, 15; Jude 1 [s][Ex. 23:21; Phil. 2:9; Rev. 19:12] [t]ver. 21, 22; [ch. 10:16; Rom. 12:5; Gal. 3:28; Eph. 1:10; 4:4] [u]ch. 10:30
12 [v]See ch. 14:25 [w]2 Thess. 3:3; Jude 24 [x]ch. 18:9; [ch. 6:39; 10:28] [y]2 Thess. 2:3 [z]Ps. 109:8; Acts 1:16-20; [ch. 13:18]
13 [a]See ch. 14:12 [b]See ch. 15:11
14 [c]ver. 3 [d]See ch. 15:19 [e]ver. 16 [f]ch. 8:23
15 [g]ver. 9 [h][1 Cor. 5:10] [i]ver. 11 [j]See Matt. 13:19
16 [k]ver. 14
17 [l][1 Thess. 5:23; 2 Thess. 2:13; 1 Pet. 1:22]; See ch. 15:3 [m]2 Sam. 7:28; Ps. 119:160 **18** [n]ch. 20:21; [ch. 4:38; Matt. 10:5]

15) and "guarding" (v. 12); it results in believers being filled with joy (v. 13; see also 3:29; 15:11; 16:24; 1 John 1:4); it is rooted in the truth of God's word (John 17:14, 17, 20); it involves "sanctification," that is, in the sense of consecration to serve (vv. 17, 19); it becomes a witness to the world so that "the world may believe" (v. 21); it is for the revelation of God's glory (v. 24); and it results in the experience of the indwelling love of God and the presence of Christ (v. 26). The kind of unity that is central to Jesus' high priestly prayer is not organizational but is an all-encompassing relational reality that binds believers together with each other and with their Lord—a unity that can be achieved only through the regenerating and sanctifying work of the Father, Son, and Holy Spirit. Although individual Christians, and the church in general, tend to fall short of the fullness of unity that the Lord intends, whenever such unity is even partially realized (never at the expense of truth or holiness; v. 17) the result will always be deep joy (v. 13), a persuasive witness to the world (vv. 21, 23), and a display of God's glory (v. 22).

17:12 name. See note on 5:43. **fulfilled**. Even Judas's betrayal took place in fulfillment of Scripture. The antecedent passage is primarily Ps. 41:9 (applied to Jesus in John 13:18; cf. note). Other Scriptures fulfilled through Judas are Ps. 69:25 and 109:8 (both are cited in Acts 1:20).

17:14 your word. Not the OT Scriptures, but Jesus' own teachings, and more broadly, the whole of his life, which is the revelation of himself as the Word of God (1:1, 14). **the world has hated them**. See note on 15:19.

17:15 Even though God's people in the midst of hardship may sometimes want to be taken **out of the world** (see Num. 11:15; 1 Kings 19:4; Jonah 4:3, 8), Jesus does **not ask** for that. The place of believers during this lifetime is not to withdraw from the world but to remain in the world and to influence it continually for good, as difficult as that may be. **keep them**. The central request of the prayer is repeated again (see John 17:11). Jesus prays that his own will be guarded from the **evil one**, that is, Satan, who would attack them to destroy their lives and their ministries. But the Greek phrase *ek tou ponērou* can also mean "from evil" (see ESV footnote), since Greek nouns denoting abstract qualities often take a definite article, in which case it would be a prayer that their lives and ministries not be overcome by Satan or by any other kind of evil, and that they be kept from doing evil as well (see 1 John 5:19).

17:16 Those who believe in Christ **are not of the world**, meaning that they have an entirely different nature (see 3:3–8), including different heart desires, different fundamental goals, and ultimately a different God. The common saying that Christians are "in the world but not of the world" is not found exactly anywhere in Scripture, but the idea is true and is taken from 17:15–16.

17:17 Sanctify them. The sanctification of Christians is a lifelong process. It involves both a relational component (separation from participating in and being influenced by evil) and a moral component (growth in holiness or moral purity in attitudes, thoughts, and actions). This occurs **in the truth**, that is, as Christians believe, think, and live according to "the truth" in relation to God, themselves, and the world. This truth comprises the entire Bible, for Jesus says, **your word is truth**. The Greek word is surprisingly not an adjective (meaning "your word is *true*") but a noun (*alētheia*, "truth"). This implies that God's Word does not simply conform to some other external standard of "truth," but that it is truth itself; that is, it embodies truth and it therefore is the standard of truth against which everything else must be tested and compared.

17:18 I have sent them into the world probably refers to the teaching that Jesus had just been giving to his disciples, teaching that assumed that they would remain in the world and minister to the world and bear fruit for

The High Priestly Prayer

The Father Gave the Son . . .	John 17
authority to give eternal life	v. 2
people out of this world	vv. 2, 6, 9, 24
work to accomplish	v. 4
words	v. 8
his name	vv. 11, 12
glory	vv. 22, 24

The Son Gives Believers . . .	John 17
eternal life	v. 2
the Father's word	vv. 8, 14
manifestation of the Father's name	vv. 6, 26
glory	v. 22

The Son Asks the Father to . . .	John 17
glorify him	vv. 1, 5
keep believers in the Father's name	v. 11
keep believers from the evil one	v. 15
sanctify believers in the truth	v. 17
make believers one	v. 21

Jesus' Followers and the World	John 17
they are sent into the world	v. 18
they are in the world	v. 11
they are not of the world	v. 16
the world has hated them	v. 14
their unity with each other and union with God may cause the world to believe the Father sent the Son	v. 21

have sent them into the world. 19 And [o]for their sake [p]I consecrate myself,[1] that they also
[q]may be sanctified[2] in truth.
20 "I do not [r]ask for these only, but also for those [s]who will believe in me through
their word, 21 [t]that they may all be one, just as you, Father, are in me, and I in you, that
[u]they also may be in [v]us, so that the world [w]may believe that you have sent me. 22 [x]The
glory that you have given me [y]I have given to them, [t]that they may be one even as we
are one, 23 [z]I in them and you in me, [a]that they may become perfectly one, [b]so that the
world may know that you sent me and [c]loved them even as [d]you loved me. 24 Father, I
desire that they also, whom you have given me, may be [e]with me [f]where I am, [g]to see
my glory that you have given me because you loved me [h]before the foundation of the
world. 25 [i]O righteous Father, even though [j]the world does not know you, I know you,
and these know that you have sent me. 26 [k]I made known to them your name, and I will
continue to make it known, that the love [l]with which you have loved me may be in
them, and [m]I in them."

Betrayal and Arrest of Jesus

18 When Jesus had spoken these words, [n]he went out with his disciples across [o]the
brook Kidron, where there was a garden, which he and his disciples entered. 2 Now
Judas, who betrayed him, also knew [p]the place, for [q]Jesus often met there with his disciples. 3 [r]So Judas, having procured a band of soldiers and some officers from the chief
priests and the Pharisees, went there with lanterns and torches and weapons. 4 Then Jesus,
[s]knowing all that would happen to him, came forward and said to them, [t]"Whom do you
seek?" 5 They answered him, "Jesus of Nazareth." Jesus said to them, "I am he."[3] Judas, who
betrayed him, was standing with them. 6 [u]When Jesus[4] said to them, "I am he," they drew

[1] Or *I sanctify myself*; or *I set myself apart* (for holy service to God) [2] Greek *may be set apart* (for holy service to God) [3] Greek *I am*; also verses 6, 8 [4] Greek *he*

4 [s]ch. 13:1 [t]ver. 7; ch. 1:38; 20:15 **6** [u][ch. 10:18; Matt. 26:53; Rev. 1:17]

19 [o][Titus 2:14] [p]ch. 10:36 [q][1 Cor. 1:2, 30; 6:11; Heb. 2:11; 10:10]
20 [r]ver. 9 [s][ch. 4:39; Rom. 10:14; 1 Cor. 3:5]
21 [t]See ver. 11; [1 Cor. 6:17] [u]1 John 1:3; 3:24; 5:20 [v]ch. 14:23 [w]See ver. 8
22 [x]ver. 24; [ch. 1:14; Luke 9:26] [y]Rom. 8:30 [t][See ver. 21 above]
23 [z]ver. 26; ch. 14:20; Rom. 8:10; 2 Cor. 13:5 [a]1 John 2:5; [Col. 3:14; 1 John 4:12, 17] [b]ver. 21; ch. 14:31 [c]ch. 16:27 [d]ver. 24, 26; See ch. 5:20
24 [e]2 Tim. 2:11, 12 [f]See ch. 12:26 [g]ch. 1:14; 2 Cor. 3:18; [1 John 3:2] [h]Eph. 1:4; 1 Pet. 1:20; See ver. 5
25 [i]Jer. 12:1; [ver. 11; Rev. 16:5]; See 1 John 1:9 [j]See ch. 8:55; 10:15
26 [k]ver. 6; ch. 15:15 [l]ver. 23; ch. 15:9 [m]See ver. 23

Chapter 18

1 [n]Matt. 26:30, 36; Mark 14:26, 32; Luke 22:39 [o]See 2 Sam. 15:23
2 [p]Luke 22:40 [q][Luke 21:37; 22:39]
3 [r]For ver. 3-11, see Matt. 26:47-56; Mark 14:43-50; Luke 22:47-53

the kingdom (see 13:16, 20, 35; 14:12–13, 26; 15:2, 5, 8, 16, 20, 27; 16:2, 8, 33), although Jesus would more formally declare that he is sending them in 20:21, and would repeat that commission at his ascension into heaven (Matt. 28:19–20; on the timing see also Acts 1:4, 8).

17:20–26 Jesus does not stop at praying for himself (vv. 1–5) and his disciples (vv. 6–19) but now prays for **those who will believe in me** in the future. Jesus' concern is for his followers' unity (vv. 21–23) and love (v. 26). The vision of a unified people of God has previously been expressed in 10:16 and 11:52. Believers' unity results from being united in God (cf. 10:38; 14:10–11, 20, 23; 15:4–5). Once unified, they will be able to bear witness to the true identity of Jesus as the Sent One of God.

17:21 that they may all be one. Concerning the unity that Jesus prays for and that he intends for his own, see note on v. 11 (cf. v. 22). **In us** refers to spiritual union with God and also the personal fellowship resulting from that union.

17:22 Glory probably refers to the manifestation of the excellence of God's entire character in Jesus' life (see 1:14). Jesus has **given** this to all believers (see 17:20): his entire life revealed the glory of God and therefore he imparted it to his followers, and Christians now reflect God's excellency in their own lives, in imitation of Christ.

17:23 The Father's love for believers is comparable to his love for Jesus Christ.

17:24 The whole purpose of salvation is communicated in this verse. The foretaste of this is now, but the fullness of it lies beyond this present age. **See** represents the Greek word *theōreō*, "to observe with sustained attention," and includes the idea of entering into and experiencing something. **You loved me before the foundation of the world** implies that love and interpersonal interaction among the members of the Trinity did not begin at any point in time but has existed eternally (cf. v. 5).

17:25 The OT teaches that God is **righteous** and just (e.g., Ps. 116:5; 119:137; Jer. 12:1). With Jesus' betrayal and innocent suffering imminent, he affirms the righteousness of God his Father.

17:26 your name. See note on 5:43. The phrase **I in them** is filled with covenantal overtones (cf. 14:20; 17:23). After the giving of the law at Sinai, God came to dwell in the midst of Israel in the tabernacle (Ex. 40:34). As they moved toward the Promised Land, God frequently assured his people that he was in their midst (Ex. 29:45–46; Deut. 7:21; 23:14).

18:1–19:42 *Jesus' Arrest, Trials, Death, and Burial.* The familiar sequence of events starts with Jesus' betrayal by Judas (18:1–11), his informal hearing before Annas (18:12–27), his Roman trial before Pilate (18:28–19:16a), and his crucifixion and burial (19:16b–42). Only John features Jesus' appearance before Annas, and the Roman trial is covered in more detail. John does not provide an account of Jesus' formal Jewish trial before Caiaphas and the Sanhedrin. John particularly highlights that everything in the passion fulfills Scripture and occurs in accordance with God's plan.

18:1 The **brook Kidron** is mentioned frequently in the Septuagint (though in the Gospels only in John; see 2 Sam. 15:23; 1 Kings 2:37; 15:13; 2 Kings 23:4, 6, 12). The Greek text indicates a wadi (sporadic brook) named Kidron, which occasionally runs during the rainy season in the Kidron Valley east of Jerusalem between the city and the Mount of Olives. The **garden** is likely to be identified with the orchard of "Gethsemane" on the Mount of Olives (see note on Matt. 26:36), which is how it is identified in the Synoptics (Matt. 26:36; Mark 14:32). The verse mentions that Jesus and his disciples **entered**, which may suggest Gethsemane was a walled garden.

18:3 The **band of soldiers** was dispatched to prevent a riot during the festival. The **officers from the chief priests and the Pharisees** (i.e., the temple police) were the primary arresting officers (cf. notes on 7:32; 7:45–46). **Lanterns** and **torches** were needed to track down a suspect thought to be hiding in the dark corners of the garden, and **weapons** were needed to overcome any armed resistance.

18:4 Jesus, confident of God's sovereign control, hands himself over to his captors. See also vv. 7–8.

18:5 Jesus' self-identification, **"I am he,"** has connotations of deity (see notes on 6:20; 6:35; 8:24; 8:58). This is suggested by the soldiers' reaction in the following verse.

18:6 Falling to the ground is a common reaction to divine revelation (Ezek. 1:28; 44:4; Dan. 2:46; 8:18; 10:9; Acts 9:4; 22:7; 26:14; Rev. 1:17; 19:10; 22:8).

7[t][See ver. 4 above]
9[v]ch. 17:12
10[w][Luke 22:38]
11[x]Matt. 20:22; 26:39, 42; [Isa. 51:22]
13[y][Matt. 26:57] [z]ver. 24; Luke 3:2; Acts 4:6 [a]ver. 24, 28; See Matt. 26:3

back and fell to the ground. 7 So he asked them again, [t]"Whom do you seek?" And they
said, "Jesus of Nazareth." 8 Jesus answered, "I told you that I am he. So, if you seek me, let
these men go." 9 [v]This was to fulfill the word that he had spoken: "Of those whom you
gave me I have lost not one." 10 Then Simon Peter, [w]having a sword, drew it and struck
the high priest's servant[1] and cut off his right ear. (The servant's name was Malchus.)
11 So Jesus said to Peter, "Put your sword into its sheath; [x]shall I not drink the cup that
the Father has given me?"

Jesus Faces Annas and Caiaphas

12 So the band of soldiers and their captain and the officers of the Jews[2] arrested Jesus
and bound him. 13 First they [y]led him to [z]Annas, for he was the father-in-law of [a]Caiaphas,

[1] Greek *bondservant*; twice in this verse [2] Greek *Ioudaioi* probably refers here to Jewish religious leaders, and others under their influence, in that time; also verses 14, 31, 36, 38

The Last Supper
After Jesus and his disciples ate the Passover meal, they crossed the Kidron Valley and entered a garden called Gethsemane (meaning "oil press"), where they often spent time while visiting Jerusalem (cf. Luke 22:39).

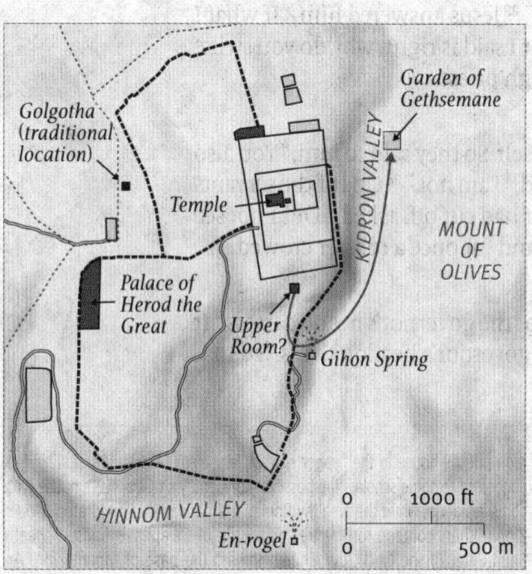

controlled the extremely important position of high priest. **Annas** (also known as "Ananus") was the patriarch of one of these powerful families of high priests (cf. Acts 4:6). He served as high priest during A.D. 6–15, and the high priesthood was subsequently held by five of his sons, including his son-in-law **Caiaphas** (see note on John 18:24). Annas's past stature merited his continued designation as "high priest" (Acts 4:6), and even after his deposition he retained significant control over his family's exercise of this position (so that Luke 3:2 can speak of "the high priesthood of Annas and Caiaphas"). Josephus mentions a monument of Annas (*Jewish War* 5.506), which has been plausibly identified with a highly decorated tomb found near the Kidron Valley.

Jesus' Arrest, Trial, and Crucifixion
The path from Jesus' arrest to his crucifixion (part of which is often called the Via Dolorosa, "Way of Sorrows") is difficult to retrace with certainty; the traditional route was fixed by Franciscan monks in the fourteenth century. The Bible records that after the Passover meal, Judas led a contingent of soldiers to Gethsemane to arrest Jesus (1). From there Jesus was led to Annas (location unknown), who sent him to his son-in-law Caiaphas, the high priest (2). The Jewish leaders then appealed to the Roman governor Pilate to have Jesus put to death (3). Luke records that Pilate sent Jesus to Herod Antipas (4), who questioned Jesus but returned him to Pilate without rendering any judgment (5). Pilate then sent Jesus to be crucified at Golgotha (6).

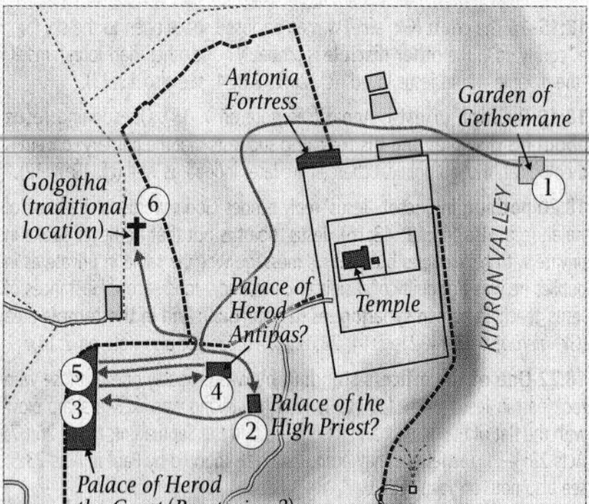

18:8–9 Jesus' statement summarizes 17:12, which in turn refers back to 6:39 and 10:28. Jesus is portrayed as the "good shepherd" who voluntarily chooses death to save the life of his "sheep" (cf. 10:11, 15, 17–18, 28). Their physical preservation symbolizes their spiritual preservation.

18:10 Peter's **sword** was likely the Roman short sword (*gladius*) that could be hidden under a person's garment (cf. Luke 22:38). **ear**. The short sword was for stabbing, not slicing, thus Peter probably intended to kill the soldier with a lethal blow to the head, but the servant was able to evade the sword, suffering only the loss of his ear. Luke adds that Jesus immediately healed the ear (Luke 22:51). **Malchus**. The name of this slave is recorded only in John's Gospel (cf. Luke 22:50–51 par.). However, the name Malchus is known in Josephus (from an earlier period) and in Nabatean and Palmyrene inscriptions. These occurrences make it likely that it was an Arab name.

18:11 Drink the cup serves as a metaphor for death and symbolizes God's wrath (see Ps. 75:8; Isa. 51:17, 22; Jer. 25:15–17, 28–29; 49:12; also Rev. 14:10; 16:19). Note that the cup given to Jesus is from the Father, and hence Jesus is prepared to drink it. In addition to the physical suffering of the cross, Jesus suffered the agony of bearing God's wrath, which was poured out on him as a substitute sacrifice and in payment for sins (see also notes on Rom. 3:25; 1 John 2:2; cf. Heb. 2:17; 1 John 4:10).

18:13 Under the Roman procurators three wealthy priestly families largely

who was high priest that year. **14** It was Caiaphas who had advised the Jews [b]that it would
be expedient that one man should die for the people.

Peter Denies Jesus

15 [c]Simon Peter followed Jesus, and so did another disciple. Since that disciple was known
to the high priest, he entered with Jesus into the courtyard of the high priest, **16** [d]but Peter
stood outside at the door. So the other disciple, who was known to the high priest, went
out and spoke to the servant girl who kept watch at the door, and brought Peter in. **17** [e]The
servant girl at the door said to Peter, "You also are not one of this man's disciples, are you?"
He said, "I am not." **18** Now the servants[1] and officers had made a charcoal fire, because it
was cold, and they were standing and warming themselves. [f]Peter also was with them,
standing and warming himself.

The High Priest Questions Jesus

19 [g]The high priest then questioned Jesus about his disciples and his teaching. **20** Jesus
answered him, "I have spoken [h]openly [i]to the world. I have always taught in synagogues
and in the temple, where all Jews come together. [j]I have said nothing in secret. **21** Why do
you ask me? Ask those who have heard me what I said to them; they know what I said."
22 When he had said these things, one of the officers standing by struck Jesus with his
hand, saying, [k]"Is that how you answer the high priest?" **23** Jesus answered him, "If what I
said is wrong, bear witness about the wrong; but if what I said is right, why do you strike
me?" **24** [l]Annas then sent him bound to [l]Caiaphas the high priest.

Peter Denies Jesus Again

25 [m]Now Simon Peter was standing and warming himself. So they said to him, "You also
are not one of his disciples, are you?" He denied it and said, "I am not." **26** One of the servants
of the high priest, a relative of [n]the man whose ear Peter had cut off, asked, "Did I not see
you [o]in the garden with him?" **27** Peter again denied it, and [p]at once a rooster crowed.

Jesus Before Pilate

28 [q]Then they led Jesus [r]from the house of Caiaphas to [s]the governor's headquarters.[2] It
was early morning. They themselves did not enter the governor's headquarters, [t]so that

[1] Greek *bondservants*; also verse 26 [2] Greek *the praetorium*

14 [b]ch. 11:50
15 [c]Matt. 26:58; Mark 14:54; Luke 22:54
16 [d]For ver. 16-18, see Matt. 26:69, 70; Mark 14:66-68; Luke 22:55-57
17 [e]Acts 12:13
18 [f]ver. 25; Mark 14:54
19 [g]For ver. 19-24, [Matt. 26:59-68; Mark 14:55-65; Luke 22:63-71]
20 [h]ch. 7:26; [Matt. 26:55] [i][ch. 8:26] [j]Isa. 45:19; 48:16; [ch. 7:4]
22 [k][Acts 23:4]
24 [l]ver. 13
25 [m]For ver. 25-27, see Matt. 26:71-75; Mark 14:69-72; Luke 22:58-62
26 [n]ver. 10 [o]ver. 1
27 [p]ch. 13:38
28 [q]Matt. 27:2; Mark 15:1; Luke 23:1 [r]ver. 24 [s]ver. 33; ch. 19:9; See Matt. 27:27 [t]Acts 10:28; 11:3; [ch. 11:55]

18:14 Caiaphas. See 11:49–52.

18:15–16 The **court** (Gk. *aulē*) was an enclosed space open to the sky (i.e., a "courtyard"). The **other disciple** is probably none other than John himself, "the disciple whom Jesus loved" (cf. 20:2; 21:24; see also 13:23).

18:19 The **high priest** is Annas (see note on v. 13). Questioning **Jesus about his disciples and his teaching** suggests that the primary concern is theological, though political charges are later lodged as well (cf. 19:7, 12).

18:20 nothing in secret. Jesus' reply echoes God's words in the book of Isaiah (e.g., Isa. 45:19; 48:16). Jesus' point is not that he never spoke in private with his disciples but that his message was the same in private as in public; he was not guilty of a sinister conspiracy. John records instances of Jesus' teaching both **in synagogues** (cf. John 6:59) **and in the temple** area (Gk. *hieron*; cf. 2:14–21; 7:14, 28; 8:20; 10:23; see also note on 2:14).

18:22 One of the officers standing by was probably one of those who took part in Jesus' arrest (cf. vv. 3, 12). The striking was likely a sharp blow with the flat of the man's hand (cf. Isa. 50:6 in the Septuagint; Matt. 26:67; Acts 23:1–5). The rebuke may echo Ex. 22:28 (quoted by Paul in Acts 23:5; see also note on John 18:23).

18:23 When challenged regarding his response to the high priest, Jesus alludes to the law of Ex. 22:28 and denies having violated it. Truthful self-defense is not sinful but righteous.

18:24 Before Jesus can be brought to the Roman governor, charges must be confirmed by the official high priest, **Caiaphas**, who presided over the Sanhedrin (see note on 3:1). Caiaphas managed to retain control of the high priesthood for nearly 18 years (c. A.D. 18–36)—longer than anyone else in the first century (cf. Josephus, *Jewish Antiquities* 18.35, 95). He was certainly the high priest during Jesus' ministry, although he also consulted frequently with his father-in-law Annas (John 18:13; cf. Luke 3:2). Josephus's depiction of a high priestly house in the "upper city" of Jerusalem (*Jewish War* 2.426) has suggested to some scholars the possibility of identifying Caiaphas's house with some residence amid the wealthy Roman-era houses excavated atop Mount Zion. Others contend for the traditional site of Caiaphas's house beneath Saint Peter of the Cockcrow Church toward the base of Mount Zion. An archaeological find in 1990 raised the possibility that an elaborately decorated ossuary (a box for reburying the bones of the dead), which has the name "Joseph Caiaphas" crudely etched into its side, once contained Caiaphas's bones. This ossuary was found in a relatively modest tomb complex south of Jerusalem.

18:26 the man whose ear Peter had cut off. Cf. v. 10 and note.

18:27 rooster crowed. Cf. 13:38.

18:28 governor's headquarters. The location of this praetorium (the residence of a Roman governor) has long been identified with the Antonia Fortress on the northwest corner of the Temple Mount; this large fortress allowed immediate access to the temple in order to suppress any disturbance. Only portions of the walls of the original Antonia Fortress remain. However, many argue that the Palace of Herod (once the Jerusalem home of Herod the Great, but later in Roman hands—see Philo, *Embassy to Gaius* 299) was more lavish and afforded better accommodations for the Roman governor. It was used later by the governor Florus (Josephus, *Jewish War* 2.301). This palace fortress (today called the Citadel), which was located at the prominent Jaffa Gate at the western entrance to the old city, has since Jesus' day been through many rounds of destruction and rebuilding (beginning with the capture of Jerusalem in A.D. 70 and continuing until after the Crusader period [11th–13th centuries]). However, some original Herodian portions of the palace do still exist. **Early morning** probably means shortly after sunrise, when the Sanhedrin met in formal session and pronounced its verdict on Jesus (Matt. 27:1–2 par.). **not be defiled.** Jews could go inside a Gentile courtyard open to the sky (see

28[u][ch. 19:14]
29[v]For ver. 29-38, see Matt. 27:11-14; Mark 15:2-5; Luke 23:2, 3
31[w][ch. 19:6]
32[x][ch. 13:18] [y]ch. 12:32, 33; Matt. 20:19; 26:2; Mark 10:33; Luke 18:32
33[z]ch. 19:9 [a][ch. 19:12]
36[b][ch. 6:15; Dan. 2:44; 7:14, 27; Luke 17:21] [c]ch. 8:23; [ch. 15:19; 17:14, 16; 1 John 2:16; 4:5] [d][Matt. 26:53] [e]ch. 19:16
37[f]See Luke 22:70 [g][ch. 12:27; Rom. 14:9] [h]ch. 16:28 [i]ch. 3:11, 32; 5:31; 8:13, 14, 18 [j]1 John 4:6; [ch. 8:47] [k]1 John 2:21; 3:19 [l]ch. 10:16, 27
38[m]ch. 19:4 [n]ch. 19:4, 6; See Luke 23:4
39[o]For ver. 39, 40, see Matt. 27:15-18, 20-23; Mark 15:6-14; Luke 23:18-23
40[p]Acts 3:14

they would not be defiled, [u]but could eat the Passover. **29** [v]So Pilate went outside to them
and said, "What accusation do you bring against this man?" **30** They answered him, "If this
man were not doing evil, we would not have delivered him over to you." **31** Pilate said to
them, [w]"Take him yourselves and judge him by your own law." The Jews said to him, "It
is not lawful for us to put anyone to death." **32** [x]This was to fulfill the word that Jesus had
spoken [y]to show by what kind of death he was going to die.

My Kingdom Is Not of This World

33 [z]So Pilate entered his headquarters again and called Jesus and said to him, [a]"Are you the
King of the Jews?" **34** Jesus answered, "Do you say this of your own accord, or did others say
it to you about me?" **35** Pilate answered, "Am I a Jew? Your own nation and the chief priests
have delivered you over to me. What have you done?" **36** Jesus answered, [b]"My kingdom
[c]is not of this world. If my kingdom were of this world, [d]my servants would have been
fighting, that [e]I might not be delivered over to the Jews. But my kingdom is not from the
world." **37** Then Pilate said to him, "So you are a king?" Jesus answered, [f]"You say that I am
a king. [g]For this purpose I was born and for this purpose [h]I have come into the world—[i]to
bear witness to the truth. [j]Everyone who is [k]of the truth [l]listens to my voice." **38** Pilate said
to him, "What is truth?"

After he had said this, [m]he went back outside to the Jews and told them, [n]"I find no guilt
in him. **39** [o]But you have a custom that I should release one man for you at the Passover.
So do you want me to release to you the King of the Jews?" **40** They cried out again, [p]"Not
this man, but Barabbas!" Now Barabbas was a robber.[1]

[1] Or *an insurrectionist*

John 18:15), but they could not go into a Gentile building or home with a roof on it without becoming ceremonially unclean. The reference to **Passover** may be to the entire Feast of Unleavened Bread, which lasted seven days (cf. Luke 22:1: "the Feast of Unleavened Bread . . . called the Passover"), and so "**eat** the Passover" probably means "continue to celebrate the ongoing feast" (cf. 2 Chron. 30:21). See also note on John 18:39. The other Gospels state that Jesus had already eaten the Passover Feast with his disciples (Matt. 26:17–29; Luke 22:1–23; see also John 13:1), but the current verse seems to refer to the Jewish leaders' desire to continue in the ongoing celebrations.

18:29 Pilate was appointed by the emperor Tiberius and served as governor of Judea A.D. 26–36 (see note on Luke 23:1). The famous "Pilate inscription," found in Caesarea in 1961, identifies Pilate as "prefect" (a senior Roman governmental official) of Judea. Pilate **went outside**, respecting the religious sensitivities of the Jews (see John 18:28). This sets up a dramatic sequence in which Pilate goes outside to face the Jews and the crowds (v. 29), then goes inside to speak to Jesus (v. 33), then goes outside to the Jews again (v. 38), then goes back inside to Jesus (19:1), then goes outside again to the Jews and the crowds, bringing Jesus with him (19:4–5), then goes back inside with Jesus to speak to him privately (19:9–11), then comes back outside once again with Jesus (19:13), then finally yields to the Jews and gives Jesus to them to be crucified (19:16). Therefore many of Jesus' statements about himself in this section are uttered "backstage," out of the hearing of his Jewish opponents.

18:31 Like Gallio after him (Acts 18:14–15), **Pilate** is not interested in judging internal Jewish disputes. **It is not lawful for us to put anyone to death**. Prior to Jesus' execution, the Romans reportedly revoked the Sanhedrin's right to impose capital punishment (see Babylonian Talmud, *Sanhedrin* 1.1; 7.2; Palestinian Talmud, *Sanhedrin* 41a). Known exceptions to this judicial restraint on the Sanhedrin are explicable either as unofficial mob actions (cf. Stephen in Acts 7 and also previous attempts to stone Jesus) or as official Jewish actions when Roman oversight was weak (Josephus, *Jewish Antiquities* 20.200ff.). Aside from these events, the one other execution in Palestine reported in the NT was based on regal authority rather than on the authority of the Sanhedrin (Acts 12:1–2). The Sanhedrin clearly desired that Jesus' execution be done officially in keeping with Roman law. Therefore the Jewish leaders had to get approval from Pilate. But this presented a problem for them, since Pilate would not be interested in condemning someone for a religious crime such as blasphemy or claiming to be God (see Matt. 26:64; Luke 22:69–71; John 8:58–59; 10:33; 19:7). This meant they needed to bring a political charge against Jesus, so they essentially accused him of treason by saying that he claimed to be king in opposition to Caesar (see 18:33, 37; 19:3, 12, 15, 19).

18:32 By what kind of death he was going to die is reminiscent of the wording in 12:33 (regarding the death of Jesus) and is later echoed in 21:19 (regarding the death of Peter). Crucifixion was looked upon with horror by the Jews. It was considered the same as hanging (Acts 5:30; 10:39), for which Mosaic law enunciated the principle, "A hanged man is cursed by God" (Deut. 21:23; cf. Gal. 3:13). If Jesus had been put to death by the Sanhedrin, he would have been stoned, the OT sanction for blasphemy (Lev. 24:16; cf. John 10:33; Acts 7:57–58).

18:33 Regarding the **headquarters**, see note on v. 28. **King of the Jews** has clear political overtones. Pilate's question aims to determine whether Jesus constitutes a threat to Rome's imperial power.

18:36 Jesus' description of the nature of his **kingdom** echoes similar passages in Daniel (e.g., Dan. 2:44; 7:14, 27). See also John 6:15.

18:37 On **the truth**, see note on 14:6.

18:38 What is truth? Ironically, the one charged with determining the truth in the matter glibly dismisses the relevance of truth in the very presence of the one who *is* truth incarnate (see note on 14:6). Pilate apparently decides that Jesus is a teacher of abstract philosophical questions to which no one can find an answer, and thus decides that Jesus poses no threat to the Roman government. He seeks no answer from the only one who could give him the answer. **he went back outside**. See note on 18:29. **I find no guilt in him**. Pilate's exoneration of Jesus, repeated three times (cf. 19:4, 6; cf. Luke 23:4), sharply contrasts with the death sentence later pronounced on Jesus due to extensive Jewish pressure (cf. John 19:12–16) and is an example of John's skillful use of irony. See also note on 5:31–47.

18:39 As in v. 28 (see note), **at the Passover** refers to the entire festival.

18:40 Barabbas means "son of the father" (Gk. *bar-abbas*). Ironically, the people wanted Barabbas released rather than the true Son of the Father, Jesus. The word translated **robber** (Gk. *lēstēs*) sometimes means "insurrectionist," but the meaning "robber" is much more common in the NT (see 10:1, 8; also Matt. 21:13; 27:38; Luke 10:30; 2 Cor. 11:26). Each Gospel contributes something to the picture of Barabbas as a man who had committed multiple crimes, including robbery, insurrection, and murder (see Matt. 27:16; Mark 15:7; Luke 23:18–19).

Jesus Delivered to Be Crucified

19 Then Pilate took Jesus and [q]flogged him. **2** [r]And the soldiers twisted together a crown
of thorns and put it on his head and arrayed him in a purple robe. **3** They came up
to him, saying, "Hail, King of the Jews!" and struck him with their hands. **4** Pilate went
out again and said to them, "See, I am bringing him out to you that you may know that
[s]I find no guilt in him." **5** So Jesus came out, wearing [t]the crown of thorns and the purple
robe. Pilate said to them, [u]"Behold the man!" **6** When the chief priests and the officers saw
him, they cried out, "Crucify him, crucify him!" Pilate said to them, [v]"Take him yourselves
and crucify him, for [w]I find no guilt in him." **7** The Jews[1] answered him, "We have a law,
and [x]according to that law he ought to die because [y]he has made himself the Son of God."
8 When Pilate heard this statement, [z]he was even more afraid. **9** [a]He entered his headquarters
again and said to Jesus, [b]"Where are you from?" But [c]Jesus gave him no answer. **10** So Pilate
said to him, "You will not speak to me? Do you not know that I have authority to release
you and authority to crucify you?" **11** Jesus answered him, [d]"You would have no authority
over me at all unless it had been given you from above. Therefore [e]he who delivered me
over to you [f]has the greater sin."

12 From then on [g]Pilate sought to release him, but the Jews cried out, "If you release this
man, you are not Caesar's friend. [h]Everyone who makes himself a king opposes Caesar."
13 So when Pilate heard these words, he brought Jesus out and sat down on [i]the judgment
seat at a place called The Stone Pavement, and in Aramaic[2] Gabbatha. **14** Now it was [j]the day

[1] Greek *Ioudaioi* probably refers here to Jewish religious leaders, and others under their influence, in that time; also verses 12, 14, 31, 38 [2] Or *Hebrew*; also verses 17, 20

Chapter 19

1 [q]Matt. 20:19; 27:26; Mark 15:15; Luke 23:16
2 [r]Matt. 27:27-30; Mark 15:16-19
4 [s]ver. 6; ch. 18:38
5 [t]ver. 2 [u][ver. 14]
6 [v][ch. 18:31] [w]ver. 4
7 [x]Lev. 24:16; [ch. 10:33] [y]ch. 5:17, 18; 10:36; Matt. 26:63; Luke 22:70
8 [z][Matt. 27:19]
9 [a]ch. 18:33 [b]ch. 7:27 [c][ch. 18:37]; See Matt. 26:63
11 [d][Rom. 13:1] [e][ch. 18:14, 28-32; Matt. 27:2] [f]See ch. 9:41
12 [g]Acts 3:13 [h]See Luke 23:2
13 [i]Matt. 27:19
14 [j][ch. 18:28]; See Matt. 27:62

19:1 After the Jewish phase of the trial and the interrogation by **Pilate**, Jesus' sentencing begins. On "Pilate," see note on 18:29. **flogged him**. Jesus was beaten both before being sentenced (19:1) and after being sentenced to death (e.g., Matt. 27:26; Mark 15:15). Some interpreters think this first beating is the same as the severe "scourging" that Jesus received in Matt. 27:26 and Mark 15:15. However, it seems unlikely that Pilate would have administered so violent and severe a punishment to someone who had not yet been condemned to death (see John 19:16) and whom Pilate was still trying to release (see vv. 4, 10, 12). It seems more likely, therefore, that this flogging was what the Romans called *fustigatio*, the lightest form of flogging administered for minor crimes. Thus John 19:1 and Luke 23:16 use the verbs *mastigoō* and *paideuō* (respectively) to refer to this lighter flogging, whereas Matt. 27:26 and Mark 15:15 use a different word, *phragelloō* ("scourged") to refer to the much more severe beating that Jesus received after Pilate pronounced the sentence of death (the Roman *verberatio*, which was the most horrible kind of beating, administered in connection with capital punishments, including crucifixion).

19:2 The **crown of thorns** represents a mock crown ridiculing Jesus' claim of being a king. The thorns would sink into the victim's skull, causing blood to gush out and distorting a person's face. The **purple robe** (cf. Matt. 27:28; Mark 15:17) similarly represents a mock royal robe. Purple is the imperial color (*1 Macc.* 8:14). The soldiers' actions are in stark, ironic contrast to the fact that Jesus truly is the King.

19:3 Hail, King of the Jews! mimics the "*Ave Caesar!*" ("Hail, Caesar!") extended to the Roman emperor.

19:4 went out. See note on 18:29.

19:5 Behold the man! (Latin *Ecce homo!*) probably conveys the sense, "Look at the poor fellow!" (In other words, "What possible threat could this man pose to the government or to anyone else?") In his mock regal garments, Jesus must have been a heartrending sight. But in the context of John's Gospel, the statement may also highlight Jesus' identity as one who is truly the perfect man, and in that case Pilate's words are recorded to show the irony of the situation. Traditionally the location of this event has been identified with the Ecce Homo Arch, which marks the traditional site for the Antonia Fortress on the Via Dolorosa in Jerusalem. However, most scholars believe the pavement in this locale to be later than the time of Jesus and the arch to be Hadrianic (i.e., 2nd century). See also note on v. 13.

19:6 Crucify him, crucify him. On crucifixion, see note on Matt. 27:35. **Take him yourselves**. Pilate uses sarcasm, being fully aware that the Jews do not have the authority to impose the death penalty (see note on John 18:31).

19:7 The Jews' comment recalls Lev. 24:16: "when he blasphemes the name, [he] shall surely be put to death." See also note on John 5:18, as well as 8:59; 10:31, 33.

19:8 Pilate **was even more afraid**. Cf. the reference to Pilate's wife's dream (Matt. 27:19).

19:9 his headquarters. See note on 18:28. **Where are you from?** Jesus' origins were frequently at issue in his dealings with his opponents (e.g., 7:27–28; 8:14; 9:29–30). For John, there are clear spiritual overtones to Pilate's question (cf. 18:36–37). Jesus' silence before Pilate is reminiscent of the depiction of the servant of the Lord in Isa. 53:7 (cf. Mark 14:61; 15:5; 1 Pet. 2:22–23).

19:11 In typical Jewish fashion, Jesus uses **from above** as a circumlocution for God (see note on 5:32). Jesus instructs Pilate that God rules over all, and that Pilate's authority is derived from God. **He who delivered me over to you** probably refers to Caiaphas, the high priest (see 18:24, 28). **Greater sin** implies that there are also lesser sins (cf. Lev. 4:2, 13; 5:17; Num. 15:30; Ezek. 8:6, 13; Matt. 5:19; 23:23).

19:12 Pilate remained unconvinced of Jesus' guilt and sentenced him to die only after intense Jewish pressure (vv. 13–16). **Caesar's friend**. "Friend" here is likely a technical term suggesting that Pilate, in his role as an imperial procurator, was not responding as a good "client" to his "patron" Caesar. "Caesar," originally the last name of Gaius Julius Caesar (d. 44 B.C.), became the title of subsequent Roman emperors (cf. v. 15; Matt. 22:17, 21).

19:13 The Greek for **judgment seat** here (*bēma*) implies a raised area used for official judgments (cf. Matt. 27:19); also, the name **Gabbatha** plausibly indicates a "raised place." The exact locations of the **Stone Pavement** and the judgment seat, however, are uncertain.

19:14 The day of Preparation of the Passover may refer to the day preceding the Sabbath of Passover week (cf. Matt. 27:62; Mark 15:42; Luke 23:54; see notes on John 18:28; 18:39). Thus all four canonical Gospels concur that Jesus' Last Supper was a Passover meal eaten on Thursday evening (by Jewish reckoning, the onset of Friday). **About the sixth hour** means about noon, but it is only an approximate statement since people did not keep precise time. Mark 15:25 has "the third hour" for the crucifixion, and various solutions have been proposed. The answer may simply be that the actual time was around 9:30–10:00 A.M. and John knew this, but his intention here was not to pinpoint the exact time but to note that it was nearing the time ("about" the middle of the day on "the day of Preparation") when the Passover lambs would begin to be sacrificed in Jerusalem, thus highlighting a direct connection with Jesus as "the Lamb of God, who takes away the sin of the world" (John 1:29). **Behold your King!** Pilate's words again show the stark irony of the situation (cf. note on 19:5).

of Preparation of the Passover. It was about the sixth hour.[1] He said to the Jews, [k]"Behold
your King!" 15 They cried out, [l]"Away with him, away with him, crucify him!" Pilate said
to them, "Shall I crucify your King?" The chief priests answered, "We have no king but
Caesar." 16 [m]So he [n]delivered him over to them to be crucified.

The Crucifixion

So they took Jesus, 17 and [o]he went out, [p]bearing his own cross, to the place called The
Place of a Skull, which in Aramaic is called Golgotha. 18 [q]There they crucified him, and
with him two others, one on either side, and Jesus between them. 19 Pilate [r]also wrote
an inscription and put it on the cross. It read, "Jesus of Nazareth, the King of the Jews."
20 Many of the Jews read this inscription, for [s]the place where Jesus was crucified was near
the city, and it was written in Aramaic, in Latin, and in Greek. 21 So the chief priests of the
Jews said to Pilate, "Do not write, 'The King of the Jews,' but rather, 'This man said, I am
King of the Jews.'" 22 Pilate answered, [t]"What I have written I have written."

23 [u]When the soldiers had crucified Jesus, they took his garments and divided them into
four parts, one part for each soldier; also his tunic.[2] But the tunic was seamless, woven in
one piece from top to bottom, 24 so they said to one another, "Let us not tear it, but cast lots
for it to see whose it shall be." [v]This was to fulfill the Scripture which says,

> [w]"They divided my garments among them,
> and for my clothing they cast lots."

So the soldiers did these things, 25 [x]but standing by the cross of Jesus were his mother and
his mother's sister, Mary the wife of Clopas, and Mary Magdalene. 26 When Jesus saw his
mother and [y]the disciple whom he loved standing nearby, he said to his mother, [z]"Woman,
behold, your son!" 27 Then he said to the disciple, "Behold, your mother!" And from that
hour the disciple took her to [a]his own home.

The Death of Jesus

28 After this, Jesus, knowing that all was now [b]finished, said ([v]to fulfill the Scripture),
[c]"I thirst." 29 A jar full of sour wine stood there, [d]so they put a sponge full of the sour wine

[1] That is, about noon [2] Greek *chiton*, a long garment worn under the cloak next to the skin

14 [k][ver. 5]
15 [l]Luke 23:18; [Acts 21:36]
16 [m]Matt. 27:26; Mark 15:15; Luke 23:25 [n]ch. 18:36-40
17 [o]Matt. 27:33; Mark 15:22; Luke 23:33 [p]Luke 14:27; [Matt. 27:32; Mark 15:21; Luke 23:26]
18 [q]Matt. 27:38; Mark 15:24, 27; Luke 23:32, 33
19 [r][Matt. 27:37; Mark 15:26; Luke 23:38]
20 [s]ver. 17; [Num. 15:35, 36; Heb. 13:12]
22 [t][Gen. 43:14; Esth. 4:16]
23 [u]Matt. 27:35; Mark 15:24; Luke 23:34
24 [v]See ch. 13:18 [w]Cited from Ps. 22:18
25 [x]Matt. 27:55, 56; Mark 15:40, 41; Luke 23:49
26 [y]See ch. 13:23 [z]ch. 2:4
27 [a][ch. 16:32]
28 [b][ver. 30] [v][See ver. 24 above] [c]Ps. 69:21; See ch. 4:6, 7
29 [d]Matt. 27:48; Mark 15:36; [Luke 23:36]

19:15 By professing to acknowledge Caesar alone as their king, the Jewish leaders betray their national heritage (in which God himself is their ultimate King; cf. Judg. 8:23; 1 Sam. 8:7) and deny their own messianic expectations based on the promises of Scripture. See also note on John 19:12.

19:16 Upon pronouncement of the sentence, the person was first scourged (see note on v. 1) and then executed.

19:17 Jesus set out carrying **his own cross** until he collapsed on the way, whereupon Simon of Cyrene was pressed into service (cf. Matt. 27:32 par.). **He went out** is in keeping with the Jewish requirement that executions take place outside the camp or city (Lev. 24:14, 23; Num. 15:35–36; Deut. 17:5; 21:19–21; 22:24; cf. Heb. 13:12). **Place of a Skull** translates the Aramaic *Gulgulta*; the Latin equivalent used in the Vulgate is "Calvary." See also note on Matt. 27:33.

19:18 On crucifixion, see notes on 18:32; Matt. 27:35. Jesus' crucifixion between two criminals is reminiscent of Ps. 22:16 ("a company of evildoers encircles me") and Isa. 53:12 ("numbered with the transgressors").

19:19 The purpose of the **inscription** was to indicate a person's specific crime, presumably to deter others from committing similar acts. **the King of the Jews**. Pilate's words again are true in a much more profound way than he or the Jewish people realized, which is another example of John's frequent use of double meaning and irony (see notes on 3:14; 4:10; 8:24; 11:50–51; cf. also 3:7–8).

19:20 the place . . . was near the city. See note on v. 17. **Aramaic** was the language most widely understood by the Jewish population of Palestine; **Latin** was the official language of the Roman occupying force; and **Greek** was the "international language" of the empire, understood by both Jews and Gentiles. The trilingual nature of the inscription thus ensured the widest possible awareness of the official reason why Jesus was being crucified.

19:23 Similar to several later events related to the crucifixion (see vv. 28–37), the soldiers' actions fulfilled Scripture (see note on v. 24; cf. note on 12:37–40).

19:24 John quotes Psalm 22 (the psalm most frequently quoted in the NT), in which the psalmist David provides numerous prophetic details of the execution scene that are fulfilled in Jesus' crucifixion nearly 1,000 years later. This is the first of several references to Jesus as the righteous sufferer in keeping with the experience of the psalmist (cf. John 19:28, 36, 37). By dividing Jesus' garments among them and by casting lots for his tunic, the Roman soldiers unwittingly fulfilled Scripture, continuing John's theme of Jesus' enemies unknowingly participating in God's plan of redemption. The soldiers' reasoning was that they did not want to tear Jesus' tunic, which was formed out of one piece of cloth (vv. 23–24). John's account of Jesus' crucifixion reflects several details of Ps. 22:15–18, which mentions the sufferer's thirst (v. 15), his "pierced . . . hands and feet" (v. 16), and his bones (v. 17). (Cf. Matt. 27:35–43.) This cluster of references strikes a strong note of prophetic fulfillment.

19:25 On Jesus' **mother**, see vv. 26–27 and 2:1–5. **His mother's sister** may be Salome, the mother of the sons of Zebedee mentioned in Matthew and Mark. On Mary the wife of **Clopas**, cf. Luke 24:18. Regarding **Mary Magdalene**, see John 20:1–18 (cf. Luke 8:2–3).

19:26–27 In keeping with biblical injunctions to honor one's parents (Ex. 20:12; Deut. 5:16), Jesus made provision for his mother, who was almost certainly widowed and probably in her late 40s or early 50s, with little or no personal income. On the address **Woman**, see note on John 2:4.

19:28–29 The reference to Scripture being fulfilled builds on v. 24 (see note there), most likely in allusion to Ps. 69:21: "for my thirst they gave me sour wine to drink" (cf. Matt. 27:34, 48; see also Ps. 22:15). The **sour wine** (Mark 15:36) Jesus is offered here was used by soldiers to quench their thirst and is different from the "wine mixed with myrrh," a sedative that Jesus was offered (and refused) on the way to the cross (Mark 15:23). **Hyssop** was a plant classified in 1 Kings 4:33 as a simple shrub that could grow from the crack of a wall. It was used for the sprinkling of blood on the doorposts at the original Passover (Ex. 12:22).

GOLGOTHA AND THE TEMPLE MOUNT

For many centuries, Christians have worshiped at the Church of the Holy Sepulcher in the belief that this was the place where Jesus was crucified, buried, and rose from the dead. This view was challenged in 1883 by General Charles Gordon, who argued that the Garden Tomb, a site just north of the Old City of Jerusalem, was the true site of Calvary.

According to the biblical writers, the requirements of the site were that it was outside the walls of Jerusalem at the time (Heb. 13:12), in a garden (John 19:41), near the city (John 19:20), and called Golgotha, meaning "place of a skull" (Matt. 27:33).

In the 1960s, excavations were carried out below the Church of the Holy Sepulcher, showing that it was built on an isolated mass of rock in the middle of an extensive quarry (which was in use from the eighth until the first century B.C.). This spur of rock was left unquarried in ancient times, because of the poor quality of the limestone. In the sides of the quarry and of this rock, a series of rock-cut tombs of the style of the first century A.D. were found.

This would indicate that the area was not then included within the city walls, as the dead were always buried outside the city. In support of the second and third points, some fortified remains found in the northern part of the nearby Jewish Quarter excavations have been identified as the Gennath (Garden) Gate mentioned by Josephus in his description of the Second Wall (*Jewish War* 5.146). It is assumed that this gate derived its name from a garden which lay just to the north outside the gate. Indeed, a layer of arable soil was found above the quarry fill.

The claim that the site could have been known as "the place of the skull" is said to be based on an ancient Jewish tradition reported by early Christian writers, such as Origen and Epiphanius, that the skull of Adam is preserved in this hill.

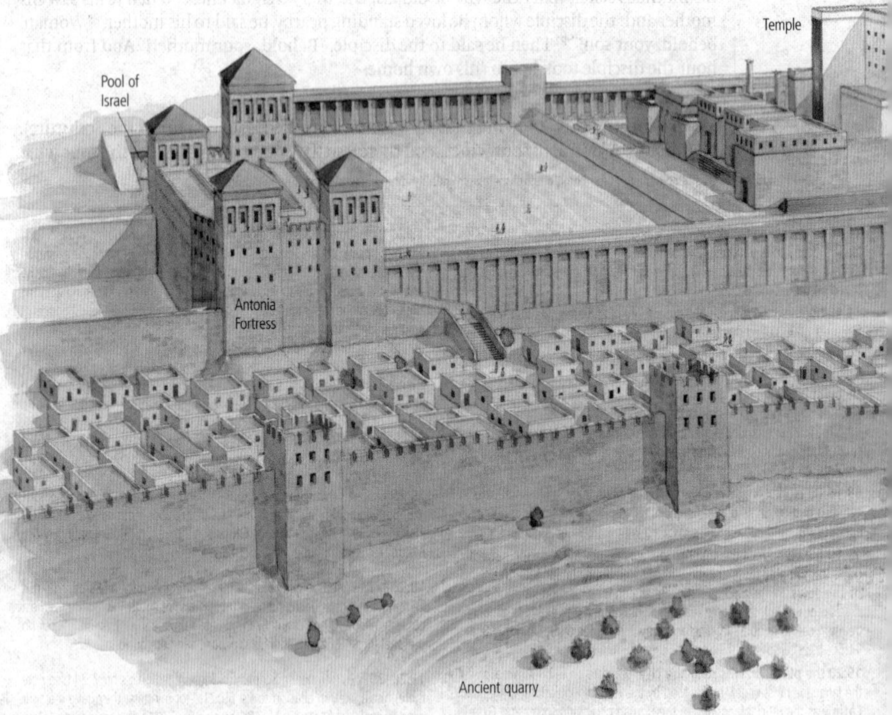

General Gordon's identification of the Garden Tomb with that of Christ was based on his discernment of the shape of a skull in the contours of the hill on the western escarpment of which the Garden Tomb is located. It has since been proven that this tomb was, in fact, a typical tomb of the First Temple period and could never have been called a "new tomb" in the time of Christ. Because of its tranquility, however, and its contrast to the bustle of the Holy Sepulcher, the site is today still regarded by many as the tomb of Christ.

The reconstruction drawing shows the traditional site of the crucifixion (i.e., the Holy Sepulcher). Three crosses are shown on the Hill of Golgotha. The Second Wall of Jerusalem was built above the quarry face. The Temple Mount forms the backdrop to this view, with the Antonia Fortress on the left, the temple in the center, and the Royal Stoa on the far right.

Architectural Plan of the Temple Mount

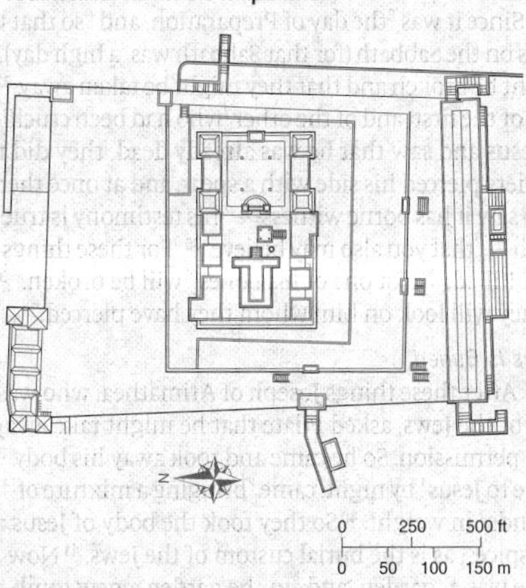

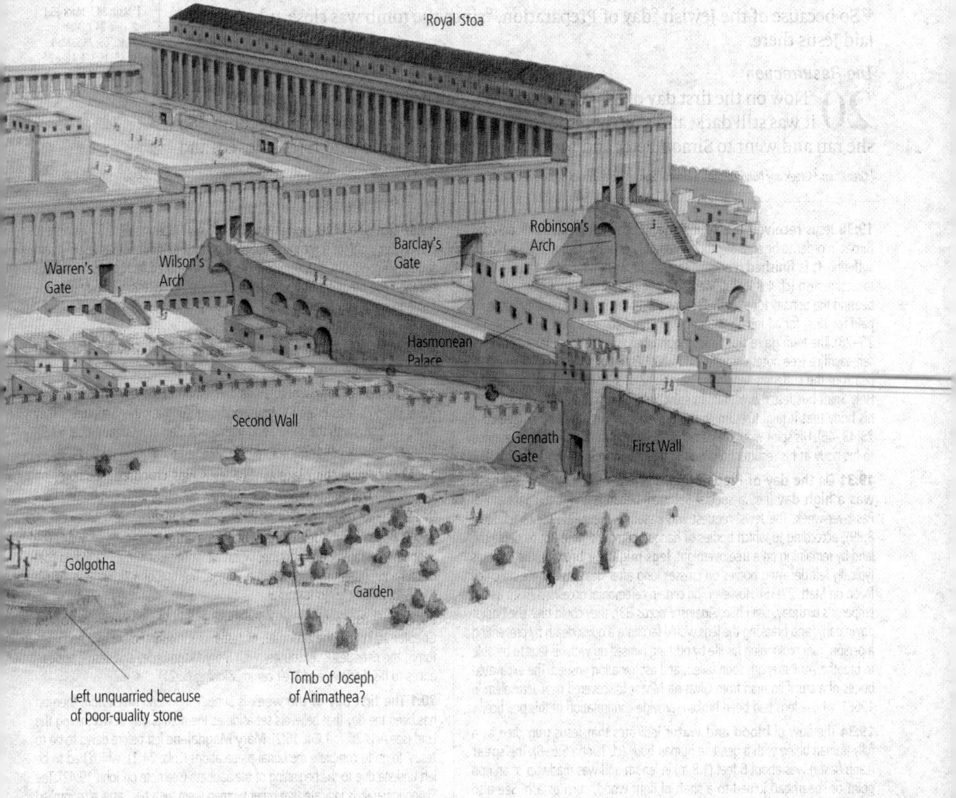

on a hyssop branch and held it to his mouth. **30** When Jesus had received the sour wine, he
said, [e]"It is finished," and he bowed his head and [f]gave up his spirit.

Jesus' Side Is Pierced

31 Since it was [g]the day of Preparation, and [h]so that the bodies would not remain on the
cross on the Sabbath (for that Sabbath was [i]a high day), the Jews asked Pilate that their legs
might be broken and that they might be taken away. **32** So the soldiers came and broke the
legs of the first, and of the other [j]who had been crucified with him. **33** But when they came
to Jesus and saw that he was already dead, they did not break his legs. **34** But one of the
soldiers pierced his side with a spear, and at once there came out [k]blood and water. **35** [l]He
who saw it has borne witness—[m]his testimony is true, and he knows that he is telling the
truth—[n]that you also may believe. **36** [o]For these things took place that the Scripture might
be fulfilled: [p]"Not one of his bones [q]will be broken." **37** And again another Scripture says,
[r]"They will look on him whom they have pierced."

Jesus Is Buried

38 [s]After these things Joseph of Arimathea, who was a disciple of Jesus, but secretly [t]for
fear of the Jews, asked Pilate that he might take away the body of Jesus, and Pilate gave
him permission. So he came and took away his body. **39** [u]Nicodemus also, who earlier had
come to Jesus[1] by night, came [v]bringing a mixture of [w]myrrh and aloes, about seventy-five
pounds[2] in weight. **40** So they took the body of Jesus and [x]bound it in [y]linen cloths with
the spices, as is the burial custom of the Jews. **41** Now in the place where he was crucified
there was a [z]garden, and [a]in the garden a new tomb [b]in which no one had yet been laid.
42 So because of the Jewish [c]day of Preparation, [d]since the tomb was close at hand, they
laid Jesus there.

The Resurrection

20 [e]Now on the first day of the week Mary Magdalene came to the tomb early, while
it was still dark, and saw that [f]the stone had been taken away from the tomb. **2** So
she ran and went to Simon Peter and the other disciple, [g]the one whom Jesus loved, and

[1] Greek *him* [2] Greek *one hundred litras*; a *litra* (or Roman pound) was equal to about 11 1/2 ounces or 327 grams

30 [e][ver. 28; Acts 13:29]; See ch. 17:4 [f]Matt. 27:50; Mark 15:37; Luke 23:46
31 [g]ver. 14 [h]Deut. 21:23; Josh. 8:29; 10:26, 27 [i]Ex. 12:16
32 [j]ver. 18
34 [k]1 John 5:6, 8
35 [l]1 John 1:1-3; Rev. 1:2; See ch. 15:27 [m][ch. 21:24] [n][ch. 20:31]
36 [o]See Matt. 1:22 [p]Cited from Ex. 12:46; Num. 9:12; [1 Cor. 5:7] [q]Ps. 34:20
37 [r]Cited from Zech. 12:10; [Rev. 1:7]
38 [s]For ver. 38-42, see Matt. 27:57-61; Mark 15:42-47; Luke 23:50-56 [t]See ch. 7:13
39 [u]ch. 3:1, 2; 7:50 [v][Mark 16:1; Luke 24:1] [w]Ps. 45:8; Prov. 7:17; Song 4:14
40 [x]ch. 11:44; [2 Chr. 16:14; Acts 5:6] [y]ch. 20:5-7; Luke 24:12
41 [z][ch. 20:15] [a]2 Kgs. 21:18, 26 [b]Luke 23:53; [Mark 11:2]
42 [c]ver. 14, 31 [d]ver. 41

Chapter 20

1 [e]Matt. 28:1; Mark 16:1, 2; Luke 24:1 [f]Matt. 27:60, 66; 28:2; Mark 15:46; 16:3, 4; Luke 24:2
2 [g]See ch. 13:23

19:30 Jesus **received the sour wine**, probably to moisten his parched throat in order to be able to proclaim a loud cry of triumph at the end of his suffering. **It is finished** proclaims that all the work the Father had sent him to accomplish (cf. 4:34; 9:4) was now completed, particularly his work of bearing the penalty for sins. This means there was no more penalty left to be paid for sins, for all Jesus' suffering was "finished" (see Heb. 1:3; 9:11–12, 25–28). The term **gave up**, which emphasizes the voluntary nature of Jesus' self-sacrifice (see notes on John 2:19; 10:17), echoes the description of the death of the suffering servant in Isa. 53:12. **His spirit** does not mean the Holy Spirit but Jesus' own human spirit, which he voluntarily released from his body that it might return to the presence of God the Father (see Luke 23:43, 46). His spirit would remain in heaven with the Father until it returned to his body at his resurrection "on the first day of the week" (John 20:1).

19:31 On **the day of Preparation**, see note on v. 14. **That Sabbath was a high day** (i.e., a special Sabbath) because it was the Sabbath of Passover week. The Jews' request was based on Deut. 21:22–23 (cf. Josh. 8:29), according to which bodies of hanged criminals were not to defile the land by remaining on a tree overnight. **legs might be broken**. The Romans typically left decaying bodies on crosses long after death (see note on crucifixion on Matt. 27:35). However, on certain ceremonial occasions (such as the emperor's birthday, see Philo, *Against Flaccus* 83), they could take the bodies down early, and breaking the legs would facilitate a quick death by preventing a person from prolonging his life by pushing himself up with his legs to be able to breathe. Arm strength soon failed, and asphyxiation ensued. The excavated bones of a crucified man from Givat ha-Mivtar (discovered near Jerusalem in 1968), whose legs had been broken, provide confirmation of this practice.

19:34 The flow of **blood and water** indicates that Jesus truly died as a fully human being with a genuine human body (cf. 1 John 5:6–8). The **spear** (Latin *hasta*) was about 6 feet (1.8 m) in length and was made up of an iron point or spearhead joined to a shaft of light wood, such as ash. See also note on John 19:36.

19:35 See notes on 5:31–47; 13:23; 21:24.

19:36 Not one of his bones will be broken. After vv. 24, 28 (see notes), this is now the third scriptural proof cited by John to indicate that Jesus' death fulfills Scripture (Ps. 34:20; also Ex. 12:46, reiterated in Num. 9:12). Jesus escaped the breaking of his legs, and the spear piercing his body likewise failed to break any bones.

19:37 The second of two texts fulfilled by the Roman soldiers' actions in v. 34 is Zech. 12:10: **They will look on him whom they have pierced** (also cited in Rev. 1:7).

19:38 Joseph of Arimathea, a wealthy member of the Jewish ruling council (Matt. 27:57), asks Pilate for Jesus' body, fulfilling another Scripture: "they made his grave with the wicked and with a rich man in his death" (Isa. 53:9). On Arimathea, see note on Luke 23:50–51.

19:41 Regarding **the place where** Jesus **was crucified**, see notes on vv. 17, 20. **Garden** points to an elaborate structure (cf. note on 18:1); a gardener is mentioned in 20:15. **tomb**. See note on Mark 15:46.

19:42 Regarding the **Jewish day of Preparation**, see note on v. 14. The Sabbath was rapidly approaching, when all work must cease, including that of carrying spices or transporting a corpse. The use of a rich man's **tomb** (cf. Matt. 27:57) fulfills Isa. 53:9.

20:1–29 *Jesus' Resurrection, Appearances, and Sending of His Disciples.* Chapter 20 covers the aftermath of Jesus' crucifixion and burial: the empty tomb, the risen Jesus' encounter with Mary Magdalene, and Jesus' appearances to his disciples and their commissioning (v. 21).

20:1 The first day of the week is Sunday morning, which from then on has been the day that believers set aside as the normal day of worshiping the Lord (see Acts 20:7; 1 Cor. 16:2). **Mary Magdalene** left before dawn to go to Jesus' tomb to complete the burial preparations (Luke 24:1), which had to be left undone due to the beginning of the Sabbath (see note on John 19:42). The Synoptic parallels indicate that other women were with her, as is also implied by the "we" in 20:2. **while it was still dark**. Cf. the slightly different points in time of the process depicted in Matt. 28:1; Mark 16:2; and Luke 24:1. Matthew's

2 [h]ver. 13
3 [i]Luke 24:12
5 [j]ch. 19:40
7 [k]ch. 11:44

said to them, "They have taken the Lord out of the tomb, and [h]we do not know where they
have laid him." 3 [i]So Peter went out with the other disciple, and they were going toward
the tomb. 4 Both of them were running together, but the other disciple outran Peter and
reached the tomb first. 5 And stooping to look in, he saw [j]the linen cloths lying there, but
he did not go in. 6 Then Simon Peter came, following him, and went into the tomb. He
saw the linen cloths lying there, 7 and [k]the face cloth, which had been on Jesus'[1] head, not

[1] Greek *his*

The Tomb of Jesus

The Gospel writers tell us that after his death, Jesus' body was taken to a garden and laid in a newly hewn tomb (Matt. 27:60; Luke 23:53; John 19:41). This is important archaeological information. Tombs from this period usually consisted of several burial chambers, which had *loculi* (burial niches) cut in the side walls in which to place the body of the deceased, and also *arcosolia* (arched niches) where ossuaries (chests for bones) were placed.

The fact that some women saw where the body of Jesus was laid (Mark 15:47) and that also, after the resurrection of Jesus, the disciple John could see the grave clothes lying and the face cloth folded (John 20:5–6), indicates that the body of Jesus was laid on a bench opposite the tomb opening.

The truth of this information can be confirmed by archaeology, in particular by tomb architecture. Newly hewn tombs usually consisted of a simple chamber which had three benches around an excavated pit. This pit allowed the workmen to stand upright while working.

Additional chambers with *loculi* and *arcosolia* were added later after the initial benches were removed. A newly hewn tomb could be used for the "primary burial," which is the first part of the ritual of ossilegium. (This simply means that the body of the deceased, after having been wrapped in linen grave clothes, was placed on a shelf, a bench, or in a niche. About a year later, after the soft tissues had decomposed, the bones were placed in an ossuary. This is called the "secondary burial.") It would appear, therefore, that the body of Jesus was indeed laid in a tomb that was newly hewn out of the rock.

The entrance to the tomb would have been low, causing the disciples to stoop down in order to look inside and enter it (cf. Luke 24:12; John 20:5). Only very few of the almost 1,000 excavated tombs of this period in and around Jerusalem had rolling stones to close off the entrance to the tomb. This luxury was restricted to the wealthy. Usually, tomb entrances had square or rectangular closing stones. These stones fit like a cork in a bottle in the tomb opening. The narrow part fit exactly in the inner opening, while the wider part closed off the outer opening.

However, the biblical record does say that the stone was rolled away (Matt. 27:60; Mark 15:46; Luke 24:2), and therefore a massive rolling stone (4.5 feet/1.4 m in diameter) is shown in this reconstruction drawing. The rare rolling stone entrance would be consistent with the idea that Joseph of Arimathea was "a rich man" (cf. Matt. 27:57).

Gospel explains that the stone had been "rolled back" by "an angel of the Lord" (Matt. 28:2). On the identity of Mary Magdalene, see also note on John 19:25.

20:2 At this point Mary has no thought of resurrection. The plural **we** suggests the presence of other women besides Mary. On the **other disciple**, see vv. 3–4 and note on 18:15–16.

20:5 stooping to look in, he saw. Apparently by now there is enough daylight to see inside the burial chamber through the small, low opening in the cave tomb. **He** (the "other disciple," vv. 2–4) **did not go in**, presumably in deference to the status of Simon Peter among the Twelve (e.g., 6:67–69).

20:6 The linen cloths lying there are clear evidence that Jesus' body had not been taken by grave robbers (cf. Matt. 28:11–15) or by his disciples attempting to steal the body (cf. Matt. 27:62–66) or by his enemies, who would not have taken the time to remove these cloths (see John 19:40). The Greek text simply says that the cloths were "lying" (*keimai*, a common word). Though it is sometimes suggested otherwise, nothing in the text indicates that Jesus' body passed through the cloths or that the cloths were lying in the shape of Jesus' body. The NT elsewhere affirms the real physical materiality of Jesus' resurrection body (see Matt. 28:9; Luke 24:30, 39, 42; John 20:17, 20, 27; Acts 10:41). Most likely Jesus unwrapped these cloths from his body when he awakened from death and left them behind.

20:7 The reference to the **face cloth** being **folded up in a place by itself** suggests that Jesus himself had taken it off and folded it neatly.

lying with the linen cloths but folded up in a place by itself. 8 Then the other disciple,
[l]who had reached the tomb first, also went in, and he saw and believed; 9 for as yet [m]they
did not understand the Scripture, [n]that he must rise from the dead. 10 Then the disciples
went back to their homes.

Jesus Appears to Mary Magdalene

11 But Mary stood weeping outside the tomb, and as she wept she stooped to look into
the tomb. 12 And [o]she saw [p]two angels in white, sitting where the body of Jesus had lain,
one at the head and one at the feet. 13 They said to her, [q]"Woman, why are you weeping?"
She said to them, [r]"They have taken away my Lord, and I do not know where they have
laid him." 14 Having said this, she turned around and [s]saw Jesus standing, [t]but she did not
know that it was Jesus. 15 Jesus said to her, [u]"Woman, why are you weeping? [v]Whom are
you seeking?" Supposing him to be [w]the gardener, she said to him, "Sir, if you have carried him away, tell me where you have laid him, and I will take him away." 16 Jesus said to
her, "Mary." She turned and said to him in Aramaic,[1] [x]"Rabboni!" (which means Teacher).
17 Jesus said to her, "Do not cling to me, for I have not yet ascended to the Father; but go
to [y]my brothers and say to them, [z]'I am ascending to my Father and your Father, to [a]my
God and your God.'" 18 Mary Magdalene [b]went and announced to the disciples, "I have
seen the Lord"—and that he had said these things to her.

Jesus Appears to the Disciples

19 [c]On the evening [d]of that day, the first day of the week, [e]the doors being locked where
the disciples were [f]for fear of the Jews,[2] Jesus came and stood among them and said to
them, [g]"Peace be with you." 20 When he had said this, [h]he showed them his hands and his
side. Then [i]the disciples were glad when they saw the Lord. 21 Jesus said to them again,
"Peace be with you. As [j]the Father has sent me, [k]even so I am sending you." 22 And when
he had said this, he [l]breathed on them and said to them, [m]"Receive the Holy Spirit. 23 [n]If
you forgive the sins of any, they are forgiven them; if you withhold forgiveness from any,
it is withheld."

[1] Or *Hebrew* [2] Greek *Ioudaioi* probably refers here to Jewish religious leaders, and others under their influence, in that time

8 [l]ver. 4
9 [m]Matt. 22:29 [n]Ps. 16:10; Luke 24:46; Acts 2:25-31; 13:34, 35; 17:3; 1 Cor. 15:4
12 [o][Mark 16:5] [p]Luke 24:4
13 [q]ver. 15; [ch. 2:4] [r]ver. 2
14 [s]Mark 16:9; [Matt. 28:9] [t]ch. 21:4; Luke 24:16, 31
15 [u]ver. 13 [v]ch. 1:38; 18:4, 7 [w][ch. 19:41]
16 [x]See ch. 1:38
17 [y]See Matt. 28:10 [z][Mark 16:19]; See ch. 14:12 [a]Matt. 27:46; Eph. 1:17; Rev. 3:2, 12; [1 Cor. 3:23]
18 [b]Mark 16:10; [Matt. 28:10; Luke 24:10, 22, 23]
19 [c]1 Cor. 15:5; [ver. 26] [d]Luke 24:33, 36 [e]ver. 26 [f]See ch. 7:13 [g]See ch. 14:27
20 [h]Luke 24:40 [i]ch. 16:22
21 [j]ch. 17:18; See ch. 3:17 [k]ch. 13:20; See Acts 1:2
22 [l]Gen. 2:7 [m][Acts 2:4]; See ch. 7:39
23 [n][Matt. 16:19; 18:18; 1 Cor. 5:4, 5]

20:8–9 The presence of two male witnesses rendered the evidence admissible under Jewish law (cf. Deut. 17:6; 19:15). **As yet they did not understand the Scripture** proves that the disciples did not fabricate a story to fit their preconceived notions of what was predicted. Rather, they were confronted with certain facts, which they were initially unable to relate to Scripture. Only later, aided by the Spirit's teaching ministry (see notes on John 14:26; 16:13), were they able to do so. In referring to "the Scripture," John may be thinking of specific OT passages (such as Ps. 16:10; Isa. 53:10–12; Hos. 6:2) or of broader themes in the entire scope of Scripture (cf. Luke 24:25–27, 32, 44–47).

20:10 When **the disciples went back to their homes**, John ("the disciple whom Jesus loved") in all likelihood brought the good news of Jesus' resurrection to Jesus' mother, whom he had taken "to his own home" (19:27).

20:11–12 Mary (Magdalene, cf. vv. 1, 18) saw **two angels in white**. Angels often appeared in pairs (e.g., Acts 1:10) and are often depicted as clad in white (cf. Ezek. 9:2; Dan. 10:5–6; Rev. 15:6).

20:15 Mary mistook Jesus for the **gardener**, perhaps because it was not fully light (see v. 1) and perhaps because she had turned and seen someone there but had then turned immediately back toward the tomb as she spoke (in v. 16 she "turned" again to speak directly to Jesus). At other times after his resurrection the disciples did not immediately recognize Jesus (see Luke 24:16, 31). His body also would have looked somewhat different, for he now had his original youthful appearance of perfect health, in contrast to what he had become through his tremendous suffering and disfigurement (cf. Isa. 52:2–3).

20:16 Jesus said to her, "Mary." Hearing only her name, Mary recognizes the voice of Jesus. As Jesus had taught prior to his crucifixion, "He calls his own sheep by name. . . . and the sheep follow him, for they know his voice" (10:3–4).

20:17 I have not yet ascended does not deny the fact that Jesus' spirit went to the presence of the Father in heaven at the moment of his death (see note on 19:30) but affirms that his bodily ascension after his resurrection had not yet occurred (see Luke 24:51; Acts 1:9–11). **To my Father and your Father** maintains a distinction as to the sense in which God is Christ's God and Father and the sense in which this is true for the disciples (see note on John 1:14). But he also calls believers his **brothers**, implying a personal relationship (see note on 15:13–14; also Heb. 2:12, 17).

20:19 Some interpreters understand **the doors being locked** to imply that Jesus miraculously passed through the door or the walls of the room, though the text does not explicitly say this. Since Jesus clearly had a real physical body with flesh and bones after he rose from the dead (see note on v. 6 and verses mentioned there), one possibility is that the door was miraculously opened so that the physical body of Jesus could enter, which is consistent with the passage about Peter going through a locked door some time later (see Acts 12:10).

20:21–22 These verses contain the Johannine "Great Commission," which serves as the culmination of the entire Gospel's presentation of Jesus as the one sent from the Father (see note on 3:17). The Sent One (Jesus) has now become the Sender, commissioning his followers to serve as his messengers and representatives (cf. 17:18). All three persons of the Godhead are involved in this commissioning: as the Father sent Jesus, so Jesus sends his disciples (20:21), equipping them with the Holy Spirit (v. 22). When Jesus **breathed on them** and said, **"Receive the Holy Spirit,"** it is best understood as a foretaste of what would happen when the Holy Spirit was given at Pentecost (see Acts 2). This does not mean that the Holy Spirit had no presence in the disciples' lives prior to this point (see notes on John 7:39; 14:16–17).

20:23 The expressions **they are forgiven** and **it is withheld** both represent perfect-tense verbs in Greek and could also be translated, "they have been forgiven" and "it has been withheld," since the perfect gives the sense of completed past action with continuing results in the present. The idea is not that individual Christians or churches have authority on their own to forgive or not forgive people, but rather that as the church proclaims the gospel message of forgiveness of sins in the power of the Holy Spirit (see v. 22), it proclaims that those who believe in Jesus have their sins forgiven, and that those who

Jesus and Thomas

24 Now [o]Thomas, one of the Twelve, called the Twin,[1] was not with them when Jesus
came. 25 So the other disciples told him, “We have seen the Lord.” But he said to them,
[p]“Unless I see in his hands the mark of the nails, and place my finger into the mark of the
nails, and place my hand into his side, I will never believe.”
26 Eight days later, his disciples were inside again, and Thomas was with them. [q]Although
the doors were locked, Jesus came and stood among them and said, [q]“Peace be with you.”
27 Then he said to Thomas, [r]“Put your finger here, and see my hands; and put out your
hand, and place it in my side. Do not disbelieve, but believe.” 28 Thomas answered him,
[s]“My Lord and my God!” 29 Jesus said to him, “Have you believed because you have seen
me? [t]Blessed are those who have not seen and yet have believed.”

The Purpose of This Book

30 [u]Now Jesus did many other signs [v]in the presence of the disciples, which are not written in this book; 31 [w]but these are written so that you may [x]believe that Jesus is the Christ,
[y]the Son of God, and that by believing [z]you may have life [a]in his name.

Jesus Appears to Seven Disciples

21 After this Jesus [b]revealed himself [c]again to the disciples by [d]the Sea of Tiberias, and
he revealed himself in this way. 2 Simon Peter, [e]Thomas (called the Twin), Nathanael
of [f]Cana in Galilee, [g]the sons of Zebedee, and two others of his disciples were together.
3 Simon Peter said to them, “I am going fishing.” They said to him, “We will go with you.”
They went out and got into the boat, but [h]that night they caught nothing.
4 Just as day was breaking, Jesus stood on the shore; yet the disciples [i]did not know
that it was Jesus. 5 [j]Jesus said to them, “Children, do you have any fish?” They answered
him, “No.” 6 [k]He said to them, “Cast the net on the right side of the boat, and you will
find some.” So they cast it, and now they were not able to haul it in, because of the
quantity of fish. 7 That disciple [l]whom Jesus loved therefore said to Peter, “It is the Lord!”
When Simon Peter heard that it was the Lord, [m]he put on his outer garment, for he
was [n]stripped for work, and [o]threw himself into the sea. 8 The other disciples came in
the boat, dragging the net full of fish, for they were not far from the land, but about a
hundred yards[2] off.

[1] Greek *Didymus* [2] Greek *two hundred cubits; a cubit* was about 18 inches or 45 centimeters

24 [o]See ch. 11:16
25 [p]ver. 20; [Ps. 22:16]
26 [q]ver. 19
27 [r]ver. 20; 1 John 1:1; [Luke 24:39]
28 [s][ch. 1:1, 49]
29 [t]1 Pet. 1:8; [2 Cor. 5:7]
30 [u]ch. 21:25 [v]Acts 10:41
31 [w]1 John 5:13 [x]See ch. 11:27 [y]See Matt. 14:33 [z]ch. 3:15, 16; 5:40; 6:53; 10:10 [a][Acts 10:43; 1 Cor. 6:11]; See Acts 3:6

Chapter 21

1 [b]ver. 14; [Mark 16:12, 14]; See ch. 7:4 [c]ch. 20:19, 26 [d]ch. 6:1
2 [e]See ch. 11:16 [f]ch. 2:1; 4:46 [g]Matt. 4:21; Luke 5:10
3 [h][Luke 5:5]
4 [i]ch. 20:14
5 [j]Luke 24:41
6 [k][Luke 5:4, 6, 7]
7 [l]See ch. 13:23 [m]ver. 18; [ch. 13:4] [n]1 Sam. 19:24; Isa. 20:2; Mic. 1:8 [o][Matt. 14:29]

do not believe in him do not have their sins forgiven—which simply reflects what God in heaven has already done (cf. note on Matt. 16:19).

20:24 Thomas. Cf. 11:16. See also note on 1:38.

20:25 Apparently, Thomas thinks the disciples may have seen a ghost (cf. Matt. 14:26). Yet John is careful to affirm that Jesus is the incarnate Word (John 1:14; cf. 1 John 4:2–3; 2 John 7), which entails that his resurrection body is not a phantom or spirit apparition but a real (albeit glorified) body.

20:26 Eight days later refers to the following Sunday, one week after Easter (cf. v. 19), because the starting day was also included in counting the number of days. Now that the festival of Unleavened Bread was over, the disciples would soon be returning to Galilee. **the doors were locked**. See note on v. 19.

20:28 Thomas's confession of Jesus as his **Lord** (Gk. *Kyrios*) and **God** (Gk. *Theos*) provides a literary link with the references to Jesus as God in the prologue (1:1, 18). This is one of the strongest texts in the NT on the deity of Christ (see 1:1). Some cults try to explain away this clear affirmation of Jesus' deity by arguing that Thomas's statement was merely an exclamation of astonishment that, in effect, took God's name in vain. Such an explanation is unthinkable, however, given the strong Jewish moral convictions of the day and because it is not consistent with the text, which explicitly says that Thomas said these words to **him**, that is, to Jesus. Thomas's statement is in fact a clear confession of his newly found faith in Jesus as his Lord and God. John's entire purpose in writing this book is that all readers come to confess Jesus as their Lord and God in the same way that Thomas did.

20:29 The readers of John's Gospel are at no disadvantage as compared to Jesus' first followers. Note the possible echo of this text in 1 Pet. 1:8; cf. 2 Cor. 5:7.

20:30–31 *Purpose Statement: Jesus the Messiah, the Son of God.* John's purpose statement and conclusion of the Gospel proper rehearse the major themes of the Gospel: Jesus' identity as **the Christ** and **Son of God** (see 1:41, 34), his selected messianic "signs" (see notes on 1:19–12:50; 2:11), the importance of believing in Jesus, and the gift of eternal **life** (see 1:12; 3:16; 17:3). On Jesus' unique status as "Son of God," see note on 1:14.

21:1–25 *Epilogue: The Roles of Peter and of the Disciple Whom Jesus Loved.* Chapter 21 narrates Jesus' third and final resurrection appearance recorded in this Gospel while also comparing the respective callings of Peter and "the disciple [John] whom Jesus loved."

21:1 After this (cf. 5:1; 6:1). With the weeklong festival of Unleavened Bread now past, the disciples have left Jerusalem and returned to Galilee (see note on 20:26; cf. Luke 2:43). Regarding the reference to the **Sea of Tiberias,** see note on John 6:1.

21:2 The names of the **sons of Zebedee** are given in the Synoptics as James and John (e.g., Matt. 4:21 par.). Luke mentions that they were "partners with Simon" in fishing prior to being called by Jesus (Luke 5:10). See also note on John 1:40.

21:3 boat. See note on Matt. 4:21. **Night** was the preferred time of day for fishing in ancient times (e.g., Luke 5:5). Fish caught during the night could be sold fresh in the morning.

21:7 The **disciple whom Jesus loved** must be one of the seven mentioned in v. 2 above, which includes the sons of Zebedee, and is almost certainly John the son of Zebedee, the author of the Gospel (see Introduction: Author and Title; and note on v. 24).

9 When they got out on land, they saw a charcoal fire in place, with fish laid out on it, and
bread. 10 Jesus said to them, "Bring some of the fish that you have just caught." 11 So Simon
Peter went aboard and hauled the net ashore, full of large fish, 153 of them. And although
there were so many, the net was not torn. 12 Jesus said to them, [p]"Come and [q]have breakfast."
Now [r]none of the disciples dared ask him, "Who are you?" They knew it was the Lord. 13 Jesus
came and [s]took the bread and gave it to them, and so with the fish. 14 [t]This was now the
third time that Jesus was revealed to the disciples after he was raised from the dead.

Jesus and Peter

15 When they had [u]finished breakfast, Jesus said to Simon Peter, [v]"Simon, [w]son of John,
[x]do you love me more than these?" He said to him, "Yes, Lord; you know that I love you."
He said to him, "Feed [y]my lambs." 16 He said to him a second time, "Simon, son of John, do
you love me?" He said to him, "Yes, Lord; you know that I love you." He said to him, [z]"Tend
[y]my sheep." 17 He said to him the third time, "Simon, son of John, do you love me?" Peter
was grieved because he said to him [a]the third time, "Do you love me?" and he said to him,
"Lord, [b]you know everything; you know that I love you." Jesus said to him, "Feed [c]my sheep.
18 [d]Truly, truly, I say to you, when you were young, [e]you used to dress yourself and walk
wherever you wanted, but when you are old, you will stretch out your hands, and another
will dress you and carry you where you do not want to go." 19 (This he said to show [f]by what
kind of death he was to glorify God.) And after saying this he said to him, [g]"Follow me."

Jesus and the Beloved Apostle

20 Peter turned and saw [h]the disciple whom Jesus loved following them, [i]the one who
also had leaned back against him during the supper and had said, "Lord, who is it that is
going to betray you?" 21 When Peter saw him, he said to Jesus, "Lord, what about this man?"
22 Jesus said to him, "If it is my will that he remain [j]until [k]I come, what is that to you? [l]You
follow me!" 23 So the saying spread abroad among [m]the brothers[1] that this disciple was
not to die; yet Jesus did not say to him that he was not to die, but, "If it is my will that he
remain until I come, what is that to you?"

24 This is the disciple [n]who is bearing witness about these things, and who has written
these things, and [o]we know [p]that his testimony is true.

25 Now [q]there are also many other things that Jesus did. Were every one of them to be written, I suppose that [r]the world itself could not contain the books that would be written.

[1] Or *brothers and sisters*

12 [p]Acts 10:41 [q]ver. 15 [r][ch. 4:27]
13 [s]ver. 9
14 [t]ver. 1; ch. 20:19, 26
15 [u]ver. 12 [v][Matt. 16:17; Luke 22:31] [w]ch. 1:42 [x][Matt. 26:33; Mark 14:29] [y]ch. 10:11-16; [Isa. 40:11]
16 [z]Acts 20:28; 1 Pet. 5:2; Rev. 7:17 (Gk.) [y][See ver. 15 above]
17 [a][ch. 13:38] [b]See ch. 2:25 [c]ver. 16
18 [d][ch. 13:36] [e]ver. 7
19 [f]2 Pet. 1:14 [g]ver. 22; Matt. 16:24; [ch. 13:36]; See ch. 8:12
20 [h]ver. 7 [i]ch. 13:25
22 [j]Matt. 10:23; 16:28; 1 Cor. 4:5; 11:26; James 5:7; Rev. 2:25 [k][ch. 14:3, 18, 28; Heb. 10:37; Rev. 2:5, 16; 3:3, 11; 16:15; 22:7, 12, 20]; See Matt. 16:27 [l]ver. 19
23 [m]Acts 1:15; 9:30; 11:1; 12:17; 15:1; 16:2, 40; 21:7, 17; 1 John 3:14, 16
24 [n]See ch. 15:27 [o]1 John 3:2, 14; 5:15, 18-20; [ch. 19:35] [p]3 John 12
25 [q]ch. 20:30 [r][Amos 7:10]

21:9 charcoal fire. See 18:18.

21:11 Various attempts have been made to interpret the number **153** symbolically, but more likely it simply represents the number of fish counted. Fishermen routinely counted the number of fish prior to selling them fresh at the market (see note on v. 3).

21:15–17 On **Simon, son of John**, see 1:42. Peter has denied Jesus three times (18:15–18, 25–27); now Jesus asks him three times to reaffirm his love for him and recommissions him. Jesus' question, "**do you love me more than these?**" probably means, "Do you love me more than these other disciples do?" rather than, "Do you love me more than these fish [i.e., his profession]?" or "Do you love me more than you love these men?"—though all three senses are, of course, important. In these three questions and answers, Peter uses the same verb for "love" all three times (Gk. *phileō*), but Jesus uses a different verb for "love" in the first two questions (Gk. *agapaō*) and then switches to Peter's word *phileō* in the third question. There may be a slight difference in nuance between the verbs (Peter seems to see a difference in the related nouns in 2 Pet. 1:7), and many older commentators have argued for a difference, often seeing *agapaō* as representing a higher and purer form of love. However, most modern commentators are not persuaded that there is any clearly intended difference of meaning here because the two words are often used interchangeably in similar contexts and because John frequently uses different words where little discernible difference in meaning can be determined, perhaps for stylistic reasons. While there may be no difference in the meanings of the two verbs, Peter is nonetheless grieved because Jesus kept asking him if he loved him. **You know everything**, taken in its full sense, is an affirmation of Christ's omniscience, consistent with his deity. If he knows everything, then of course he knows Peter's heart. **Feed my lambs**. Jesus as the true shepherd (John 10:11, 14; see note on 10:11) appoints Peter and other apostles to be subordinate shepherds (see 1 Pet. 5:1–4). Peter will demonstrate his love for Jesus by loving God's people and feeding them with his Word.

21:18–19 Stretch out your hands was a way to convey the notion of crucifixion. Early evidence shortly after the NT mentions Peter's martyrdom without telling how it happened. There are some later accounts that say Peter was crucified upside down, refusing to die the same kind of death as his Lord, but some of these are overlaid with legendary material that many scholars consider unreliable, so this tradition is uncertain.

21:20 disciple whom Jesus loved. See note on 13:23.

21:24 This is the disciple is typical of the way in which John, as the author of the Gospel, refers to himself indirectly or in the third person (cf. 20:2–3). Other examples include: "the disciple whom Jesus loved" (cf. 21:7; see note on 13:23), "one" of the Twelve (cf. 21:20), and one of the "sons of Zebedee" (see Introduction: Author and Title). Hence the author is identified as the apostle John, who refers to himself by the modest epithet "the beloved disciple." **We know**. Like the third person singular self-reference ("This is the disciple") earlier in the verse, and the phrase "I suppose" in v. 25, "we know" represents a self-reference on the part of the author, most likely including his readers and/or associates in the affirmation that John's **testimony is true**. See also note on 5:31.

21:25 John's closing observation, **the world itself could not contain the books**, emphasizes the limitless magnitude of all that Jesus accomplished for mankind's salvation as the eternal Son of God (see 1:1–3) through his incarnation, life, death, resurrection, and ascension.

INTRODUCTION TO

THE

ACTS

OF THE APOSTLES

Acts is unique among the NT writings, in that its main purpose is to record a selective history of the early church following the resurrection of Christ. It is the second part of a two-volume work, with the Gospel of Luke being the first volume. Both books are dedicated to a person named Theophilus, and Acts 1:1 explicitly refers back to Luke's Gospel.

Author

Both the Gospel of Luke and Acts are anonymous, but the earliest discussions attribute them to Luke. The name "Luke" appears only three times in the NT: Colossians 4:14; 2 Timothy 4:11; Philemon 24. All three references are in epistles written by Paul from prison, and all three mention Luke's presence with Paul.

The earliest discussion of the authorship of Luke and Acts is from Irenaeus, the bishop of Lyons in Gaul, writing in the late second century. He attributes the books to Luke, the coworker of Paul, and notes that the occurrence of the first-person narrative ("we") throughout the later chapters of Acts (starting at 16:10) indicates that the author of Acts was a companion of Paul and present with him on these occasions. These "we" passages in Acts are the key to the authorship of both Acts and the Gospel of Luke.

Colossians 4:14 indicates that Luke was a physician, and attempts have been made to bolster Lukan authorship by arguing that Luke and Acts use technical medical language. This does not seem to be the case, as Luke seems to have avoided technical language in order to communicate plainly to his readers, but his detailed description of illnesses perhaps reflects his interests as a physician (cf. Acts 28:8). In addition, all the external evidence refers to Luke as the author.

Other than the three NT references, nothing certain is known of Luke. Early traditions link him with Antioch, but that is probably based on the reference in Acts 13:1 to "Lucius," which is a Latin name. "Luke" is a Greek name, and both books are written in excellent Greek. His thorough acquaintance with the OT may reflect that Luke was a converted God-fearer (a Gentile who attended the Jewish synagogue) or Jewish proselyte (convert), though he could have gained his biblical knowledge after becoming a Christian.

Date

Some scholars date Acts c. A.D. 70. This assumes that Acts was written *after* the Gospel of Luke (Acts 1:1) and that Luke used the Gospel of Mark as one of his sources (Luke 1:1–2). (Early tradition has Mark's Gospel written after Peter's death, which most likely occurred in the mid-60s.) Others date Acts in the 70s or 80s. They hold that the primary purpose of Acts was to give an account of how and where the gospel spread, rather than to be a defense of Paul's ministry (thus accounting for the omission of the events at the end of his life). Thus the gospel spread to "the end of the earth" (1:8)—that is, to Rome, which represented the end of the earth as the center of world power. But a number of scholars date Acts as early as A.D. 62, basing their view primarily on the abrupt ending of the book. Since Acts ends with Paul in Rome under house arrest, awaiting his trial before Caesar (28:30–31), it would seem strange if Luke knew about Paul's release (a proof of his innocence), possibly about his defense before Caesar (fulfilling 27:24), and about his preaching the gospel as far as Spain (cf. note on 28:30–31), but then did not mention these events at the end of Acts. It seems most likely, then, that the abrupt ending is an indication that Luke wrote Acts c. A.D. 62, before these events occurred.

Theme

In Acts, believers are empowered by the Holy Spirit to bear witness to the good news of Jesus Christ among both Jews and Gentiles, and in doing this they establish the church. In addition to this, Acts explains how Christianity, although it is new, is in reality the one true religion, rooted in God's promises from the beginning of time. In the ancient world it was important that a religion be shown to have stood the test of time. Thus Luke presents the church as the fulfillment and extension of God's promises.

Timeline

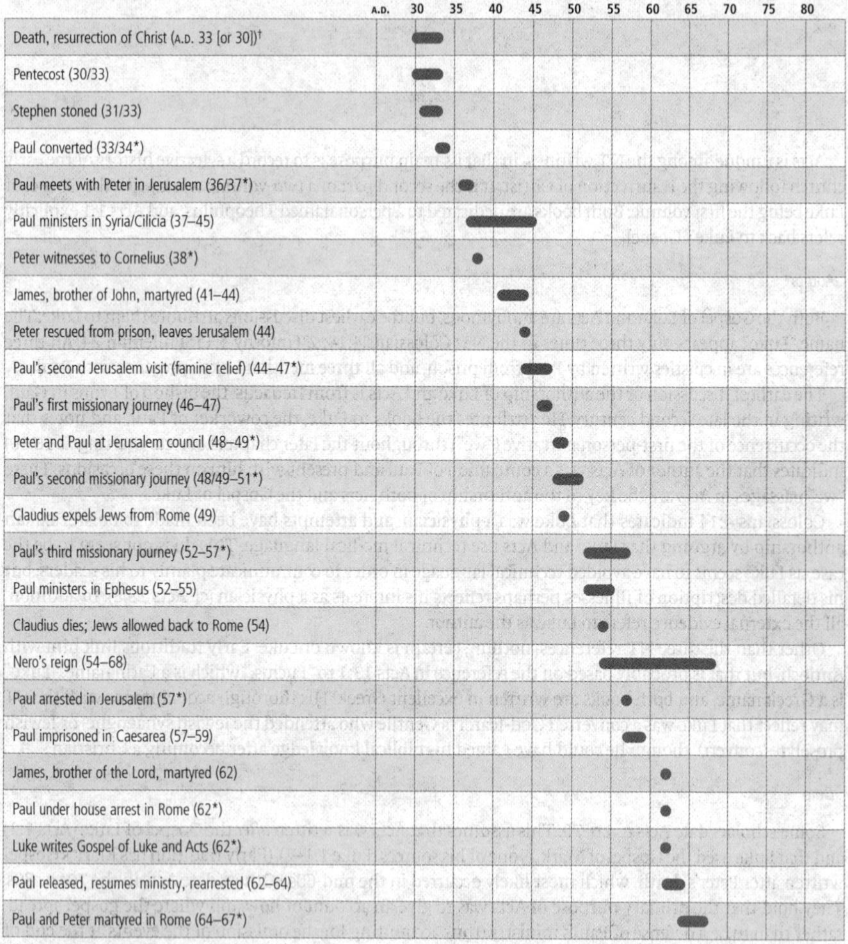

A.D. 30 35 40 45 50 55 60 65 70 75 80
Death, resurrection of Christ (A.D. 33 [or 30])†
Pentecost (30/33)
Stephen stoned (31/33)
Paul converted (33/34*)
Paul meets with Peter in Jerusalem (36/37*)
Paul ministers in Syria/Cilicia (37–45)
Peter witnesses to Cornelius (38*)
James, brother of John, martyred (41–44)
Peter rescued from prison, leaves Jerusalem (44)
Paul's second Jerusalem visit (famine relief) (44–47*)
Paul's first missionary journey (46–47)
Peter and Paul at Jerusalem council (48–49*)
Paul's second missionary journey (48/49–51*)
Claudius expels Jews from Rome (49)
Paul's third missionary journey (52–57*)
Paul ministers in Ephesus (52–55)
Claudius dies; Jews allowed back to Rome (54)
Nero's reign (54–68)
Paul arrested in Jerusalem (57*)
Paul imprisoned in Caesarea (57–59)
James, brother of the Lord, martyred (62)
Paul under house arrest in Rome (62*)
Luke writes Gospel of Luke and Acts (62*)
Paul released, resumes ministry, rearrested (62–64)
Paul and Peter martyred in Rome (64–67*)

** denotes approximate date; / signifies either/or; † see The Date of Jesus' Crucifixion, pp. 1809–1810*

Text

The early manuscripts of Acts have a greater variety of readings than any other NT book. This is reflected in the ESV footnotes that provide alternative readings, as well as the absence of whole verses in some instances (8:37; 15:34; 24:7; 28:29). The greatest diversity is shown by a group of manuscripts that scholars refer to as the "Western text," an early version of Acts that is about ten percent longer than the other texts. Its main difference from the others is in providing additional detail and smoothing out the narrative. No

The Setting of Acts
c. A.D. 30–60
The book of Acts records the spread of the gospel from Jerusalem to Rome, thus fulfilling the risen Christ's words to his apostles in Acts 1:8.

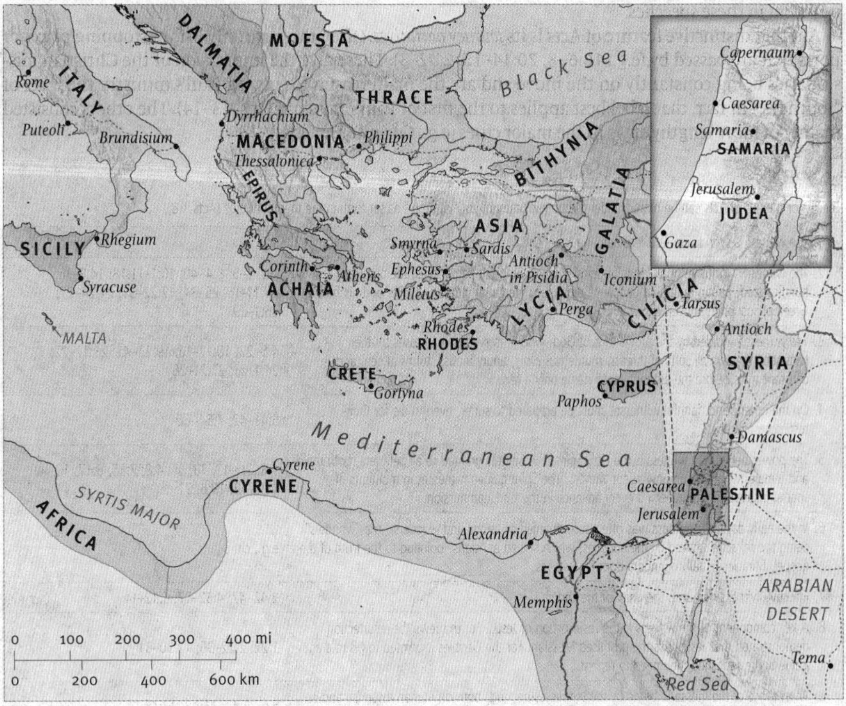

standard English translation follows the Western text. Some of its more interesting readings are provided in the ESV footnotes, such as the note about the hours when Paul preached in the hall of Tyrannus in Ephesus (19:9).

Distinctive Features

Though Acts has much in common with the Gospels, it has a number of unique features. One of these is its genre: it is the only NT book that tells about the ministry of the apostles, hence its traditional name, "The Acts of the Apostles." It deals primarily with two of them, Peter and Paul. Often Luke shows how events in their ministries parallel each other and the ministry of Jesus as well.

Among the unique features of Acts are the frequent *summaries,* where Luke provides a broad generalization about the life of the church at a particular time or place, such as the common life after Pentecost (2:42–47), the early Christian sharing of goods (4:32–35), and the apostolic miracles (5:12–16). Sometimes the summaries are much briefer, such as the single verse that sums up Paul's ministry of more than two years in Ephesus (19:10). Luke's usual method of presenting the Christians' ministry is more "episodic," highlighting individual incidents that illustrate their work, giving it greater liveliness and interest. For instance, at Ephesus this includes the conversion of some disciples of John the Baptist (19:1–7), the "backfiring" exorcism of the sons of Sceva (19:13–16), and the riot occasioned by the silversmith Demetrius (19:23–41).

The most distinctive feature in Acts is the speeches or sermons, constituting nearly a third of the total text of Acts (see chart, p. 2120). Ten of these are major: three by Peter (2:14–36; 3:11–26; 10:34–43), one by Stephen (7:1–53), and six by Paul. Three of Paul's are defense speeches in Jerusalem and Caesarea (22:1–21; 24:10–21; 26:1–29). The other three consist of one speech on each of Paul's missionary journeys, each to a different type of assembly: to Jews on his first journey (13:16–47), to Gentiles on his second (17:22–31), and to Christians on his third (20:18–35). Many shorter testimonies run throughout Acts (e.g., 5:29–32; 14:15–17). All are primarily a witness to Christ in one form or another. Much of the theological material of Acts is to be found in these speeches.

Another distinctive feature of Acts is its *journey narratives*. Often these are only lists of stopping places or ports that are passed by (e.g., 16:6–8; 20:14–15; 21:2–3). These give the impression of the Christian missionaries being constantly on the move and are the main reason for giving Paul's ministry the label of "journeys." In fact, that label best applies to the first of Paul's missions (chs. 13–14). The others consisted mainly of more lengthy stays in the major cities (e.g., Corinth, Ephesus).

Key Themes

The major themes of Acts can be placed under the general category of "witness," as set forth in the thematic verse (Acts 1:8).

1. The witness is worldwide—Judea, Samaria, the "end of the earth."	1:8
2. The witness is inclusive of all kinds of people: Jews, Gentiles, Samaritans, the physically handicapped, pagan mountain people, a prominent merchant woman, a jailer and his family, Greek philosophers, governors, and kings.	chs. 2–5; 8:4–40; 10:1–11:18; 14:8–18; 16:11–15, 25–34; 17:22–31; 24:24–27; 26:1–29
3. The witness is guided by the providence of God, who preserves his witnesses for their testimony through all sorts of threats: murderous plots, angry mobs, storms at sea, and constant trials before the authorities, to name only a few.	4:5–22; 18:12–16; 19:23–41; 23:12–22; 24:1–23; 27:21–26
4. On the other hand, faithful witnesses must be prepared to suffer, even to die for their testimony to Christ.	5:41–42; 7:54–60
5. The power behind the witness is the Holy Spirit. The Spirit is granted to all believers, both male and female, whom he empowers for witness. The Spirit guides witnesses in moments of special inspiration and is behind every advance in the Christian mission.	1:8; 2:1–13, 18, 38; 4:8; 7:55; 8:17; 10:44; 13:2–12; 19:6, 21
6. In the early days, the witness was often accompanied by "signs and wonders," the "wonders" being the miracles worked by the apostles, which served as "signs" pointing to the truth of the gospel. Miracles usually opened a door for witness.	e.g., ch. 3
7. Effective witness demands the unity of the church.	2:42–47; 4:32–37; 5:12–14
8. A key component of the witness is the resurrection of Jesus. For the Jews the resurrection demonstrated that Jesus was the promised Messiah. For the Gentiles it pointed to his role as judge and established their need to repent.	1:22; 2:22–36; 17:30–31
9. Acceptance of the message borne by the witnesses depends both on human response and on the divine sovereignty behind the response.	e.g., 2:47; 11:18; 13:48
10. The OT Scriptures point to the death and resurrection of Christ, and the prophecies that point to Christ and to his followers must be fulfilled (1:16).	(The numerous OT citations in the sermons of Acts illustrate this point.)
11. The witness to the gospel calls for a response. Most speeches in Acts end with some sort of invitation. Representative of this is Paul's exchange with Agrippa II.	26:27–29
12. The response called for is repentance of one's sins in the name of Christ, which brings forgiveness of sins.	e.g., 2:38
13. Witnesses must always maintain integrity before the world. In Acts this is illustrated by the many remarks from the authorities about the Christians giving no evidence of any wrongdoing.	18:12–15; 23:29; 25:18; 26:31–32
14. Christian witnesses continue the ministry that Christ "began" (1:1). This is illustrated throughout Acts with the many implicit parallels between the experiences of the apostles and those of Christ: his miracles, the forebodings of his journey to Jerusalem, the cry of the angry Jewish mob for his death, and his trial before the governor and the king.	20:36–21:16 (cf. Luke 9:22; 13:31–34; 18:31–34); 21:36; 22:21 (cf. Luke 23:18); 24:1–26:32 (cf. Luke 23:1–25)
15. Faithful witness brings great results. Acts is all about the victory of the Christian gospel. The witness brings results among both Jews and Gentiles. The book ends on this note, with Paul bearing his faithful witness to "all" who came to him in Rome.	4:4; 11:20–21; 13:48–49; 17:4; 18:6–11; 21:20; 28:30–31

Purpose, Occasion, and Background

Luke's stated purpose for both of his books is provided at the beginning of the first (Luke 1:1–4). He had a historian's interest in providing an "orderly account" of "the things that have been accomplished among us." One would assume the latter statement applied both to the ministry of Jesus (the gospel) and to that of the early church (Acts). Dedicating the work to Theophilus, he wanted him to have "certainty" (a firm foundation) for what he had been taught. The exact nature of Luke's purpose depends on how one identifies Theophilus. He evidently had already been instructed in the Christian way and may have been a new convert or a seeker on the verge of commitment. Since "Theophilus" means "lover of God," it is also possible that Luke is challenging the devotion of his readers rather than addressing his book to just one of them.

Luke probably had a number of purposes for writing Acts. These are best determined through the emphases or themes found throughout the book.

History of Salvation Summary

After his ascension (1:9; cf. Ps. 68:18; Eph. 4:9–10) Jesus sends the Holy Spirit (Joel 2:28–32) to empower the apostles as witnesses (Acts 1:8), to spread the message of the gospel (Isa. 52:7), and to draw to himself people from the nations (Matt. 28:19). (For an explanation of the "History of Salvation," see the Overview of the Bible, pp. 23–26.)

Literary Features

The book of Acts is a small anthology of individual literary genres. The list includes hero story, adventure story, travel story, conversion story, and miracle story. Drama also figures prominently: there are 32 speeches in Acts.

Following the story line becomes easy when one realizes that the book of Acts is structured on a cyclic principle in which a common pattern keeps getting repeated: (1) Christian leaders arise and preach the gospel; (2) listeners are converted and added to the church; (3) opponents (often Jewish but sometimes Gentile) begin to persecute the Christian leaders; and (4) God intervenes to rescue the leaders or otherwise protect the church. While this pattern is most obvious in the first half of the book, it extends in modified form to the journeys of Paul, whose repeated buffetings are followed by the expansion of the church.

The book of Acts is noteworthy for its narrative qualities. It is the report of an adventure, replete with arrests, imprisonments, beatings, riots, narrow escapes, a resurrection from death, a shipwreck, trial scenes, and rescues.

Places play a key role in Acts. The places that matter most are the great cities of the Mediterranean region in the first century. Geography assumes a symbolic as well as literal importance, as Jerusalem, where the story begins, symbolizes the Jewish religion from which Christianity emerged, and Rome, where the story ends, symbolizes the Gentile world to which Christianity gravitates as the early history of the church unfolds.

Out of a large body of available data, storytellers select the details that fit their design and purpose. It is a plausible premise that sometimes Luke chose to give *representative examples* of categories of experiences: examples of miraculous healings that were no doubt duplicated many times (e.g., 3:1–10; 19:11–12), a specimen of preaching in the temple (3:11–26) and preaching to Greek intellectuals (17:16–34), an example of a martyrdom (ch. 7), and instances of individuals being converted (e.g., a Jew in 9:1–19 and an Ethiopian in 8:26–38) and of groups being converted (e.g., in Jerusalem in 2:37–41 and in Greek Ephesus in 19:17–20).

Outline

I. Preparation for Witness (1:1–2:13)
   A. Jesus prepares the disciples (1:1–5)
   B. Jesus ascends (1:6–11)
   C. Matthias replaces Judas (1:12–26)
   D. The Spirit descends at Pentecost (2:1–13)

II. The Witness in Jerusalem (2:14–5:42)
   A. Peter preaches at Pentecost (2:14–41)
   B. The Christian community shares a life in common (2:42–47)
   C. Peter heals a lame man (3:1–10)
   D. Peter preaches in the temple square (3:11–26)
   E. Peter and John witness before the Jewish council (4:1–22)
   F. The Christian community prays for boldness in witness (4:23–31)
   G. The community shares together (4:32–5:16)
   H. The apostles appear before the council (5:17–42)

III. The Witness beyond Jerusalem (6:1–12:25)
   A. Seven chosen to serve the Hellenist widows (6:1–7)
   B. Stephen bears the ultimate witness (6:8–8:3)
      1. The arrest of Stephen (6:8–15)
      2. Stephen's address before the Sanhedrin (7:1–53)
      3. The martyrdom of Stephen (7:54–8:3)
   C. Philip witnesses beyond Jerusalem (8:4–40)
      1. Witness to the Samaritans (8:4–25)
      2. Witness to an Ethiopian eunuch (8:26–40)
   D. The conversion of Saul (9:1–31)
      1. Saul's encounter with Christ (9:1–9)
      2. Saul's encounter with Ananias (9:10–19a)
      3. Saul's witness in Damascus and Jerusalem (9:19b–31)
   E. Peter preaches in the coastal towns (9:32–11:18)
      1. Healing of Aeneas and Dorcas (9:32–43)
      2. Conversion of Cornelius (10:1–48)
      3. Peter's testimony in Jerusalem (11:1–18)
   F. The Antioch church witnesses to Gentiles (11:19–26)
   G. The offering for Jerusalem (11:27–30)
   H. The Jerusalem church is persecuted (12:1–25)
      1. The death of James (12:1–5)
      2. Peter's deliverance from prison (12:6–19)
      3. The death of Herod Agrippa I (12:20–25)

IV. The Witness in Cyprus and Southern Galatia (13:1–14:28)
   A. The Antioch church commissions Paul and Barnabas (13:1–3)
   B. Paul and Barnabas witness on Cyprus (13:4–12)
   C. Paul preaches in the synagogue of Pisidian Antioch (13:13–41)
   D. Paul turns to the Gentiles (13:42–52)
   E. Paul and Barnabas are rejected at Iconium (14:1–7)
   F. The two missionaries witness in Lystra (14:8–23)
   G. Paul and Barnabas return to Antioch (14:24–28)

V. The Jerusalem Council (15:1–35)
   A. The circumcision party criticizes the Gentile mission (15:1–5)
   B. Peter defends Paul (15:6–11)
   C. James proposes a solution (15:12–21)
   D. A letter is sent to Antioch (15:22–35)

VI. The Witness in Greece (15:36–18:22)
   A. Paul and Barnabas differ over Mark (15:36–41)
   B. Timothy joins Paul and is circumcised (16:1–5)
   C. Paul is called to Macedonia (16:6–10)
   D. Paul witnesses in Philippi (16:11–40)
      1. Conversion of Lydia (16:11–15)
      2. Imprisonment of Paul and Silas (16:16–24)
      3. Conversion of the jailer (16:25–34)
      4. Release of Paul and Silas (16:35–40)
   E. Paul witnesses in Thessalonica (17:1–9)
   F. Paul witnesses in Berea (17:10–15)
   G. Paul witnesses in Athens (17:16–34)
      1. Witness in the marketplace (17:16–21)
      2. Witness before the Areopagus (17:22–34)
   H. Paul witnesses in Corinth (18:1–22)

VII. The Witness in Ephesus (18:23–21:16)

A. Priscilla and Aquila instruct Apollos (18:23–28)
B. Paul encounters disciples of John (19:1–10)
C. Paul encounters false religion at Ephesus (19:11–22)
D. Paul experiences violent opposition at Ephesus (19:23–41)
E. Paul completes his ministry in Greece (20:1–6)
F. Paul travels to Miletus (20:7–16)
G. Paul addresses the Ephesian elders at Miletus (20:17–35)
H. Paul journeys to Jerusalem (20:36–21:16)

VIII. The Arrest in Jerusalem (21:17–23:35)

A. Paul participates in a Nazirite ceremony (21:17–26)
B. An angry mob attacks Paul (21:27–39)
C. Paul addresses the Jewish crowd (21:40–22:21)
D. Paul reveals his Roman citizenship (22:22–29)
E. Paul appears before the Sanhedrin (22:30–23:11)
F. Zealous Jews plot against Paul (23:12–22)
G. Paul is delivered to the governor Felix (23:23–35)

IX. The Witness in Caesarea (24:1–26:32)

A. Paul appears before Felix (24:1–27)
B. Paul appeals to Caesar (25:1–12)
C. Festus presents the case to King Agrippa II (25:13–22)
D. Paul witnesses to Agrippa II (25:23–26:32)

X. The Witness in Rome (27:1–28:31)

A. Paul journeys to Rome by sea (27:1–44)
B. Paul witnesses on Malta (28:1–10)
C. Paul arrives in Rome (28:11–16)
D. Paul witnesses to the Jews in Rome (28:17–31)

THE

ACTS

OF THE APOSTLES

The Promise of the Holy Spirit

1 In the first book, O [a]Theophilus, I have dealt with all that Jesus began [b]to do and teach,
2 until the day when [c]he was taken up, after he [d]had given commands [e]through the
Holy Spirit to the apostles whom he had chosen. 3 [f]He presented himself alive to them
after his suffering by many proofs, appearing to them during forty days and speaking
about the kingdom of God.
4 And while staying[1] with them [g]he ordered them not to depart from Jerusalem, but to
wait for the promise of the Father, which, he said, "you heard from me; 5 for [h]John baptized
with water, [h]but you will be baptized [i]with[2] the Holy Spirit not many days from now."

The Ascension

6 So when they had come together, they asked him, "Lord, [j]will you at this time [k]restore
the kingdom to Israel?" 7 He said to them, [l]"It is not for you to know [m]times or seasons

[1] Or *eating* [2] Or *in*

Chapter 1
1 [a]Luke 1:3 [b]Luke 24:19
2 [c]See Mark 16:19 [d][ch. 10:42; Matt. 28:19, 20; Mark 16:15; Luke 24:47; John 20:21] [e][ch. 10:38; Luke 4:1, 18; John 20:22]
3 [f]ch. 10:40, 41; 13:31; Matt. 28:17; Mark 16:14; Luke 24:34, 36-51; John 20:19-29; 21; 1 Cor. 15:5-7
4 [g]Luke 24:49
5 [h]ch. 11:16; See Matt. 3:11 [i]ch. 2:1-4
6 [j]See Luke 17:20 [k][Mic. 4:8; Matt. 17:11; Mark 9:12; Luke 19:11]
7 [l][Matt. 24:36; Mark 13:32] [m]Dan. 2:21; 1 Thess. 5:1

1:1–2:13 *Preparation for Witness.* Acts opens with the account of the Spirit's descent at Pentecost. Chapter 1 relates the preparation of the disciples for that event, which is covered in 2:1–13.

1:1–5 *Jesus Prepares the Disciples.* After a brief introduction (vv. 1–2), Luke reviews the 40-day period when Jesus prepared the disciples for their witness (vv. 3–5).

1:1 Luke's **first book** is the Gospel of Luke, which gives an account of what Jesus **began to do and teach**. This suggests that the book of Acts is going to be about what Jesus *continued* "to do and teach" in the world. Though physically he had ascended into heaven (v. 9), yet spiritually he was still present on earth (cf. Matt. 28:20). When one realizes that the term "Lord" (Gk. *Kyrios*) in Acts usually refers to Jesus, it becomes evident that the entire book tells how Jesus was building his church: selecting an apostle to replace Judas (Acts 1:24), pouring out the Holy Spirit in new power (2:33), adding people to the church day by day (2:47), appearing to Ananias (9:10) and to Paul (9:5; 18:9), healing a paralyzed man (9:34), receiving worship from the church (13:2), stopping a magician who was opposing the gospel (13:11), and opening people's hearts to believe the gospel (16:14). (See also 1:2 on the Holy Spirit's role.) It is the execution of the divine program that Jesus directs and mediates. Luke's Gospel was also dedicated to **Theophilus**, either an actual person or a symbolic name for any Christian seeker or convert.

1:2 The day when he was taken up refers to Jesus' ascension into heaven (Luke 24:51). The beginning of Acts parallels the conclusion of Luke's Gospel (Luke 24:36–53). **Through the Holy Spirit** means that as Jesus gave instructions and commands to his disciples, the Holy Spirit accompanied his teaching, empowering the disciples so that they would rightly understand it and obey it. **apostles**. See notes on Acts 1:20; Rom. 1:1.

1:3 Jesus appeared multiple times to his disciples and gave them **many proofs** to strengthen their faith. Solid evidence and knowledge of facts increase faith (an idea contrary to some modern views of "faith"). Only Acts provides the specific time reference of a 40-day period for the resurrection appearances, a number that evokes thoughts of many biblical events, such as the wilderness wanderings of Israel and the temptations of Jesus. Though common in the Gospels as the main theme of Jesus' preaching, the phrase **kingdom of God** occurs only six times in Acts (1:3; 8:12; 14:22; 19:8; 28:23, 31). Significantly, two of the six are at the beginning and end of Acts, indicating that the proclamation of the gospel in Acts represents the beginning of the fulfillment of God's kingdom promises. The "kingdom of God" means not an earthly political or military kingdom but the present spiritually directed reign of God, gradually transforming individual lives and entire cultures through the power of the Holy Spirit. Cf. Matt. 6:33.

1:4 The **promise of the Father** refers to the gift that was promised by the Father, namely, the new and greater empowering of the Holy Spirit that the disciples were to await in Jerusalem (see Luke 3:15–17; 24:49).

1:5 Baptized with the Holy Spirit looks forward to Pentecost (see ch. 2). John had contrasted his "repentance" baptism with Jesus' "Holy Spirit" baptism (Mark 1:8). Throughout Acts, baptism and the gift of the Spirit are closely related. Repentance, forgiveness, water baptism, and reception of the Spirit comprise the basic pattern of conversion.

1:6–11 *Jesus Ascends.* At the end of the 40 days (v. 3), Jesus took his disciples to the Mount of Olives and ascended visibly (vv. 9–11). Before doing so he commissioned them to be his witnesses (v. 8).

1:6 The place of the disciples' assembly was the Mount of Olives (v. 12), at the foot of which lay Bethany (Luke 24:50). The disciples asked Jesus when he would **restore the kingdom to Israel** because they concluded from his resurrection and the promise of the Spirit that the messianic era had dawned and the final salvation of Israel was imminent. However, they were probably still expecting the restoration of a military and political kingdom that would drive out the Roman armies and restore national sovereignty to Israel, as had happened numerous times in the OT. Jesus corrected them, not by rejecting the question, but by telling them (Acts 1:8) that they would receive power from the Holy Spirit, not in order to triumph over Roman armies but to spread the good news of the gospel throughout the world. In other words, the return is in God's timing; in the meantime, there are other key things believers are to do.

1:7 the Father has fixed by his own authority. Ultimate authority in determining the events of history is consistently ascribed to God the Father among the persons of the Trinity.

1:8 Jesus corrected the disciples' questions (v. 6) with a commission: "this time" (v. 6) would be for them a time of witnessing for the gospel, and the scope of their witness was not to be just Israel but the world. Verse 8 is the

8 [n]ch. 4:33; Luke 24:49; 1 Thess. 1:5; [ch. 10:38; Luke 4:14] [o]ver. 5 [p][ver. 22]; See Luke 24:48 [q][Isa. 43:12] [r]ch. 8:1, 14; [Matt. 10:5] [s]ch. 13:47; [Mark 16:15; Col. 1:23]
9 [t]ver. 2 [u]See 1 Thess. 4:17
10 [v][Luke 24:4] [w]Josh. 5:13; Dan. 9:21; 10:5; 12:6, 7; Zech. 1:8-11 [x]Matt. 28:3; Mark 16:5; John 20:12
11 [y]ch. 2:7; 13:31 [z][Phil. 3:20; 1 Thess. 1:10]; See Matt. 16:27 [a]2 Thess. 1:10
12 [b]Luke 24:50, 52
13 [c]ch. 9:37, 39; 20:8 [d]See Matt. 10:2-4; Mark 3:16-19; Luke 6:14-16 [e][ch. 21:20]
14 [f]ch. 2:46; 4:24; 5:12; 15:25; Rom. 15:6 [g]ch. 2:42; 6:4; Rom. 12:12; Col. 4:2; [Eph. 6:18] [h]Luke 8:2, 3 [i]See Matt. 12:46
15 [j]See John 21:23
16 [k]Luke 24:44; [Luke 22:37] [l]Matt. 26:47; Mark 14:43; Luke 22:47; John 18:3
17 [m]John 6:71; 13:21 [n]ver. 25; ch. 20:24; 21:19; Rom. 11:13; 2 Cor. 4:1

that the Father has fixed by his own authority. 8 But you will receive [n]power [o]when the
Holy Spirit has come upon you, and [p]you will be [q]my witnesses in Jerusalem and in all
Judea and [r]Samaria, and [s]to the end of the earth." 9 And when he had said these things, as
they were looking on, [t]he was lifted up, and [u]a cloud took him out of their sight. 10 And
while they were gazing into heaven as he went, behold, [v]two [w]men stood by them in
[x]white robes, 11 and said, [y]"Men of Galilee, why do you stand looking into heaven? This
Jesus, who was taken up from you into heaven, [z]will [a]come in the same way as you saw
him go into heaven."

Matthias Chosen to Replace Judas

12 Then [b]they returned to Jerusalem from the mount called Olivet, which is near Jerusalem,
a Sabbath day's journey away. 13 And when they had entered, they went up to [c]the upper
room, where they were staying, [d]Peter and John and James and Andrew, Philip and Thomas,
Bartholomew and Matthew, James the son of Alphaeus and Simon [e]the Zealot and Judas
the son of James. 14 All these [f]with one accord [g]were devoting themselves to prayer, together
with [h]the women and Mary the mother of Jesus, and [i]his brothers.[1]
15 In those days Peter stood up among [j]the brothers (the company of persons was in all
about 120) and said, 16 "Brothers, [k]the Scripture had to be fulfilled, which the Holy Spirit
spoke beforehand by the mouth of David concerning Judas, [l]who became a guide to those
who arrested Jesus. 17 For [m]he was numbered among us and was allotted his share in [n]this
ministry." 18 (Now this man [o]acquired a field with [p]the reward of his wickedness, and falling

[1] Or *brothers and sisters*. The plural Greek word *adelphoi* (translated "brothers") refers to siblings in a family. In New Testament usage, depending on the context, *adelphoi* may refer either to men or to both men and women who are siblings (brothers and sisters) in God's family, the church; also verse 15

18 [o][Matt. 27:5-8] [p][Matt. 26:14-16]

thematic statement for all of Acts. It begins with the Spirit's power that stands behind and drives the witness to Jesus. Then it provides a rough outline of the book: **Jerusalem** (chs. 1–7), **Judea and Samaria** (chs. 8–12), and the **end of the earth** (chs. 13–28). **you will receive power**. Interpreters differ over whether the Holy Spirit was at work in the lives of ordinary believers prior to Pentecost in a lesser way or not at all, except for empowering for special tasks. On either view, something new that needed to be waited for was here. This powerful new work of the Holy Spirit after Pentecost brought several beneficial results: more effectiveness in witness and ministry (1:8), effective proclamation of the gospel (cf. Matt. 28:19), power for victory over sin (Acts 2:42–46; Rom. 6:11–14; 8:13–14; Gal. 2:20; Phil. 3:10), power for victory over Satan and demonic forces (Acts 2:42–46; 16:16–18; 2 Cor. 10:3–4; Eph. 6:10–18; 1 John 4:4), and a wide distribution of gifts for ministry (Acts 2:16–18; 1 Cor. 12:7, 11; 1 Pet. 4:10; cf. Num. 11:17, 24–29). The disciples likely understood "power" in this context to include both the power to preach the gospel effectively and also the power (through the Holy Spirit) to work miracles confirming the message. The same word (Gk. *dynamis*) is used at least seven other times in Acts to refer to power to work miracles in connection with gospel proclamation (see Acts 2:22; 3:12; 4:7; 6:8; 8:10; 10:38; 19:11).

1:9 Elsewhere in Scripture a **cloud** is often associated with a manifestation of God's presence (Luke 9:28–36). This was not an ordinary rain cloud but the cloud of glory that surrounds the very presence of God. **as they were looking on, he was lifted up**. This visible ascension of Jesus into heaven indicates that Jesus retains a physical human body, as a man, though he is exalted to the right hand of God, i.e., given direct executive rule in God's spiritual kingdom (Matt. 28:18). When coupled with Acts 1:11, it also indicates that he will someday return in the same physical body. The amazing miracle of the incarnation is not only that the eternal Son of God took human nature on himself and became a person who is simultaneously God and man, but also that he will remain both fully God and fully man forever.

1:10 The pair of "men" were angels in human form, as their **white robes** attest (see Matt. 28:3; Luke 24:4; John 20:12).

1:11 will come in the same way as you saw him go. Jesus' return, like his ascension, will be bodily and visible. (See note on v. 9.)

1:12–26 *Matthias Replaces Judas.* The remainder of ch. 1 focuses on two events preparatory to Pentecost: the gathering of the band of followers to pray for the coming gift of the Spirit (vv. 12–14) and the selection of Matthias to replace Judas (vv. 15–26).

1:12 A **Sabbath day's journey** was the maximum distance one could travel on the Sabbath without it constituting work. This was not an explicit OT law but a later Jewish tradition. The rabbis set the limit at 2,000 cubits (about 0.6 miles or 1 km). Jews at Qumran had a lower travel limit.

1:14 The **women** in the upper room likely included those who ministered to Jesus' followers (Luke 8:2–3), accompanied them from Galilee (Luke 23:55), and witnessed the crucifixion and empty tomb (Luke 23:49, 55–56; 24:2–11). Jesus had four **brothers**—James, Joses, Judas, and Simon (Mark 6:3). The main activity in the upper room was **prayer**. Jesus had told them "to wait for the promise of the Father" (Acts 1:4), but "waiting" on God and prayer are closely related in several places in the OT, and therefore it is likely that they were praying constantly that the promised Spirit would descend.

1:15 Throughout chs. 1–15 **Peter** is the spokesman for the apostles.

1:16 The Holy Spirit spoke beforehand by the mouth of David is one of the clearest affirmations in Scripture that the Bible is the inspired word of God. The Holy Spirit "spoke" through David's mouth in the sense that David's written words were inspired by the third person of the Trinity (God the Holy Spirit) foretelling events that took place a thousand years later (see v. 20; cf. Ps. 69:25; 109:8).

1:18 this man acquired a field. That is, the field was acquired indirectly by Judas, through the agency of the chief priests. As Matt. 27:3–7 records, Judas brought the 30 pieces of silver back to the chief priests and elders. The chief priests then purchased the potter's field with Judas's money, with the same effect as if Judas had himself made the purchase. **he burst open**. The two accounts of Judas's death are complementary retellings of the same event, each focusing in different ways on the same details. Both accounts involve: Judas's remorse, the purchase of a field with his ill-gotten money, its

Acts 1:8

Text	Region Named	Narrative of Ministry There
Acts 1:8: you will be my witnesses	in Jerusalem	Acts 1–7
	in all Judea and Samaria	Acts 8–12
	to the end of the earth	Acts 13–28

headlong[1] he burst open in the middle and all his bowels gushed out. **19** And it became
known to all the inhabitants of Jerusalem, so that the field was called [q]in their own language
Akeldama, that is, Field of Blood.) **20** "For it is written in the Book of Psalms,

[r]"'May his camp become desolate,
and let there be no one to dwell in it';

and

[s]"'Let another take his office.'

21 So one of the men who have accompanied us during [t]all the time that the Lord Jesus
[u]went in and out among us, **22** [v]beginning from the baptism of John until the day when
[w]he was taken up from us—one of these men must become with us [x]a witness to his
resurrection." **23** And they put forward two, Joseph called [y]Barsabbas, who was also called
[z]Justus, and [a]Matthias. **24** And [b]they prayed and said, "You, Lord, [c]who know the hearts of
all, show which one of these two you have chosen **25** to take the place in [d]this ministry and
[e]apostleship from which Judas turned aside to go to his own place." **26** And they cast lots
for them, and the lot fell on Matthias, and he was numbered with the eleven apostles.

The Coming of the Holy Spirit

2 When [f]the day of Pentecost arrived, they were all together in one place. **2** And suddenly
there came from heaven a sound like [g]a mighty rushing wind, and [h]it filled the entire
house where they were sitting. **3** And divided tongues [i]as of fire appeared to them and
rested[2] on each one of them. **4** And they were all [j]filled with the Holy Spirit and began [k]to
speak in other tongues [l]as the Spirit gave them utterance.

[1] Or *swelling up* [2] Or *And tongues as of fire appeared to them, distributed among them, and rested*

19 [q][ch. 21:40]
20 [r]Cited from Ps. 69:25 [s]Cited from Ps. 109:8
21 [t][John 15:27] [u]Num. 27:17; Deut. 31:2; 1 Sam. 18:13
22 [v]ch. 13:24; Mark 1:1-4 [w]ver. 2, 9 [x]ch. 4:33; [ver. 8; 1 Pet. 1:3]; See Luke 24:48
23 [y][ch. 15:22] [z][ch. 18:7; Col. 4:11] [a]ver. 26
24 [b]ch. 6:6; 13:3 [c]See 1 Sam. 16:7; Rom. 8:27
25 [d]See ver. 17 [e]Rom. 1:5; 1 Cor. 9:2; Gal. 2:8

Chapter 2

1 [f]ch. 20:16; 1 Cor. 16:8; [Lev. 23:15]
2 [g][1 Kgs. 19:11; Job 38:1; Ezek. 1:4] [h][ch. 4:31; 16:26]
3 [i]Matt. 3:11
4 [j]ch. 4:31; 13:52 [k]See Mark 16:17 [l][1 Cor. 12:10, 11]

reputation as "the Field of Blood," and Judas's gory death (for the location of "the Field of Blood," see note on Matt. 27:7–8). The main difference is that Matt. 27:5 speaks of Judas hanging himself, while Acts speaks of his body **falling headlong** and bursting open with all his entrails spilling out. One possible explanation suggests that the field overlooked a cliff, and as Judas hanged himself, the rope (or the branch) may have broken, with his body falling headlong over the edge of the cliff onto jagged rocks below. Others have suggested that Judas's body may have remained hanging for some time decaying and decomposing ("swelling up," ESV footnote), eventually falling to the ground and bursting open in its decomposed condition. In either case, there is no reason to see the two accounts as contradictory, since they focus on complementary details of the same event. In both accounts the effect of Satan's control over Judas's life is clear, demonstrating the general principle that Satan brings total destruction and disgrace to the person who comes under his control, for "he was a murderer from the beginning" (John 8:44).

1:20 Judas's death was the fulfillment of Ps. 69:25, and his place among the disciples was now empty. **Let another take his office.** The selection of Matthias (Acts 1:26) as the twelfth apostle was a direct fulfillment of prophecy (cf. v. 16; Ps. 109:8), carried out under the direction of the Lord. The addition of this new twelfth apostle would complete the new nucleus for the people of God, parallel to the heads of the 12 tribes of Israel in the OT. Though these 12 would remain the core group of the apostles (see Luke 22:30; 1 Cor. 15:5; Rev. 21:12, 14), a few more later became "apostles," including at least Paul and Barnabas (Acts 14:4, 14) and James, the Lord's brother (Gal. 1:19). However, apostles were not replaced from this point onward: in Acts 12, James the brother of John was not replaced after his execution. See also note on Rom. 1:1.

1:23–24 Two men, **Joseph** and **Matthias**, met the necessary requirements to be considered for apostleship. The group turned the matter over to the "Lord" (v. 24; that is, the Lord Jesus, who had chosen all the other apostles), praying that he would make his choice known.

1:26 The **lots** were probably marked stones that were placed in a pot and then shaken out (cf. 1 Chron. 26:13–16). This does not imply that people should cast lots to make their decisions today, for there is no such command in any NT letter or in any of Jesus' earthly teachings. The appointment of a twelfth apostle was a unique situation, a choice that was made by Jesus himself. In the rest of the NT, the elders and deacons and other church leaders are chosen according to decisions made by human beings, whether by an apostle or by others in the churches (see Acts 6:3–6; 14:23; 15:22; 2 Cor. 8:19; cf. 1 Tim. 3:1–13; Titus 1:5–9). On the 12 **apostles**, see note on Matt. 10:1.

2:1–13 *The Spirit Descends at Pentecost.* The promise of the Spirit (cf. 1:5; Joel 2:28–32; Matt. 3:11) is fulfilled at the feast of Pentecost. The event is narrated in two parts: the coming of the Spirit on the believers (Acts 2:1–4), and the reaction of the Jewish crowd to the Spirit-filled Christians (vv. 5–13).

2:1 Pentecost was the second of the annual harvest festivals, coming 50 days after Passover. **All** most likely included the entire 120 assembled in the upper room (1:15).

2:2 Jesus had compared the Holy Spirit's work to the wind (John 3:8), but here the Holy Spirit is coming in greatly increased power, and it was appropriate that this event be accompanied by **a sound** that was not like a gentle breeze but **like a mighty rushing wind**. The **house where they were sitting** probably was the upper room (Acts 1:13), which must have been located close to the temple grounds.

2:3 The **divided tongues as of fire** were not literal flames (for Luke says "as of") but looked enough like fire that this was the best description that could be given. "Fire" in the OT often indicates the presence of God, especially in his burning holiness and purity, consuming everything that is impure (see Ex. 3:2; 13:21; 19:18; 40:38; Isa. 4:5; Ezek. 1:4). These tongues may therefore portray both the purity and the power of the speech of these disciples as they proclaimed "the mighty works of God" (Acts 2:11), as well as the holy presence of God.

2:4 filled with the Holy Spirit. This is a fulfillment of what Jesus promised (see notes on 1:5; 1:8). It does not mean that the Holy Spirit was completely inactive prior to this time (for the Spirit of God was active in the world from Gen. 1:2 onward), but now the Spirit was coming to people in a new, more powerful way, signifying the beginning of the new covenant age (the time from Christ's death until he returns at some time in the future). **to speak in other tongues**. The word translated "tongues" (Gk. *glōssa*, plural) can also be translated "languages," and that is the sense that it has in this verse. In this case the other languages were understood by various people present in Jerusalem, but in 1 Corinthians 14 Paul expects that no one present in the church at Corinth will understand the languages being spoken "in tongues" (see 1 Cor. 14:2). Acts and 1 Corinthians are probably not speaking of different types of gifts but different kinds of audiences: people who understood the languages were present in Jerusalem but were not expected to be present in Corinth (see notes on 1 Cor. 12:10; 12:29–30; 14:2). This is clearly a

6 [m]ver. 2
7 [n]ver. 12 [o]ch. 1:11; [Matt. 26:73]
9 [p]2 Kgs. 17:6 [q]Gen. 14:1, 9; Isa. 11:11; Dan. 8:2
11 [r]ch. 6:5; 13:43; Matt. 23:15
12 [s]ver. 7
13 [t][ch. 17:32; 1 Cor. 14:23]

5 Now there were dwelling in Jerusalem Jews, devout men from every nation under
heaven. 6 And [m]at this sound the multitude came together, and they were bewildered,
because each one was hearing them speak in his own language. 7 And [n]they were amazed and
astonished, saying, "Are not all these who are speaking [o]Galileans? 8 And how is it that we
hear, each of us in his own native language? 9 Parthians and [p]Medes and [q]Elamites and residents of Mesopotamia, Judea and Cappadocia, Pontus and Asia, 10 Phrygia and Pamphylia,
Egypt and the parts of Libya belonging to Cyrene, and visitors from Rome, 11 both Jews and
[r]proselytes, Cretans and Arabians—we hear them telling in our own tongues the mighty
works of God." 12 And [s]all were amazed and perplexed, saying to one another, "What does
this mean?" 13 But others [t]mocking said, "They are filled with new wine."

Peter's Sermon at Pentecost

14 But Peter, standing with the eleven, lifted up his voice and addressed them: "Men of
Judea and all who dwell in Jerusalem, let this be known to you, and give ear to my words.

miracle of speaking, not of hearing, for the disciples began "*to speak* in other tongues." **As the Spirit gave them utterance** indicates that the Holy Spirit was directing the syllables they spoke. Speaking in tongues in this way also seems to be the phenomenon experienced by those at Cornelius's house (Acts 10:45–46) and the disciples of John at Ephesus (19:6).

2:5 The presence of the crowd indicates that the setting must be the temple grounds, the only place in Jerusalem that could accommodate more than 3,000 persons (v. 41). The fact that they were **dwelling in Jerusalem** suggests not only Jewish pilgrims but local residents as well.

2:6 hearing them speak. They spoke the "mighty works of God" (v. 11), the language of praise.

2:9–11 The long list of nations covers most of the first-century Roman world, particularly areas where Jewish communities existed (see map below). It provides one of the most comprehensive ancient catalogs of the Jewish Diaspora (Jews living outside Palestine) and is confirmed by other ancient lists (esp. Philo, *Embassy to Gaius* 281–284), by early Jewish archaeological remains, and by many ancient literary sources. It is only natural that first-century Jerusalem would be filled with devout Jews "from every nation under heaven" (Acts 2:5). The list also demonstrates that already at Pentecost the Christians were starting their worldwide witness. At this point the converts were mainly Jewish. The only Gentiles at Pentecost were **proselytes** (v. 11), Gentiles who had become full converts to Judaism.

2:14–5:42 *The Witness in Jerusalem.* Beginning with Peter's sermon at Pentecost and continuing through ch. 5, the witness of the Christians is confined to the city of Jerusalem and restricted to Jews.

2:14–41 *Peter Preaches at Pentecost.* Peter's sermon is the first in a series of speeches and discourses in Acts (see chart, p. 2120). As a sermon to Jews it consists primarily of scriptural proofs: vv. 14–21 interpret the miracle of tongues as a fulfillment of Joel 2:28–32; Acts 2:22–36 presents Christ as Messiah in fulfillment of Ps. 16:8–11 and Ps. 110:1; and Acts 2:37–41 concludes the sermon with a call to repentance and baptism. There also is an allusion to Ps. 132:10, which itself alludes to 2 Sam. 7:6–16.

Nations at Pentecost

c. a.d. 30/33

Pentecost attracted Jews from all over the world to Jerusalem to celebrate the annual festival. Those who heard the apostles' message in their native languages at Pentecost came from various regions within the two great competing empires of the day—the Roman Empire and the Parthian Empire—with Jerusalem near the center.

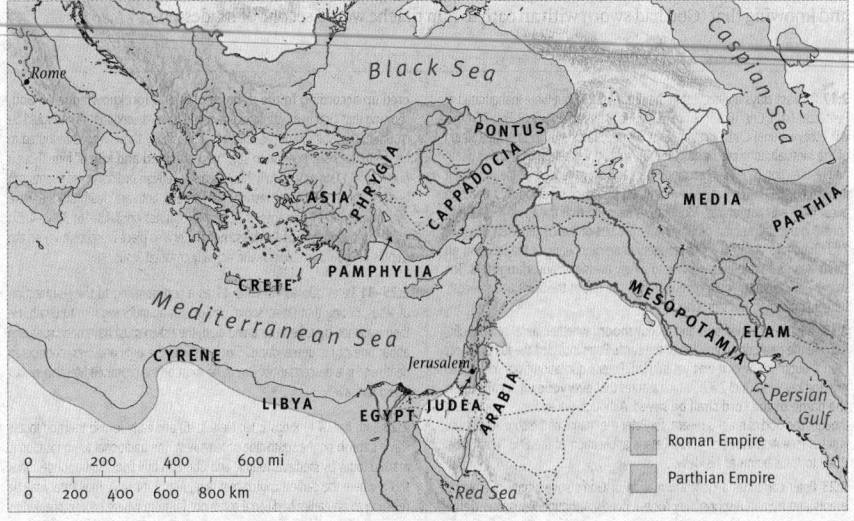

15 For these people are not drunk, as you suppose, [u]since it is only the third hour of the
day.[1] 16 But this is what was uttered through the prophet Joel:

17 [v]"'And in the last days it shall be, God declares,
[w]that I will pour out my Spirit [x]on all flesh,
and your sons and [y]your daughters shall prophesy,
and your young men shall see visions,
and your old men shall dream dreams;
18 even on my male servants[2] and female servants
in those days I will pour out my Spirit, and [z]they shall prophesy.
19 And I will show wonders in the heavens above
and signs on the earth below,
blood, and fire, and vapor of smoke;
20 [a]the sun shall be turned to darkness
and the moon to blood,
before [b]the day of the Lord comes, the great and magnificent day.
21 And it shall come to pass that [c]everyone who calls upon the name of the
Lord shall be saved.'

22 "Men of Israel, hear these words: Jesus of Nazareth, [d]a man attested to you by God
[e]with [f]mighty works and wonders and signs that [g]God did through him in your midst,
as you yourselves know— 23 this Jesus,[3] [h]delivered up according to [i]the definite plan and
[j]foreknowledge of God, [k]you crucified and killed by the hands of lawless men. 24 [l]God
raised him up, loosing the pangs of death, because [m]it was not possible for him to be held
by it. 25 For David says concerning him,

[n]"'I saw the Lord always before me,
for he is at my right hand that I may not be shaken;
26 therefore my heart was glad, and my tongue rejoiced;
my flesh also will dwell [o]in hope.
27 For you will not abandon my soul to [p]Hades,
[q]or let your [r]Holy One [s]see corruption.
28 You have made known to me the paths of life;
you will make me full of gladness with your presence.'

29 "Brothers, I may say to you with confidence about [t]the patriarch David [u]that he both
died and [v]was buried, and [w]his tomb is with us to this day. 30 [x]Being therefore a prophet,
and knowing that [y]God had sworn with an oath to him that he would set one of his descen-

[1] That is, 9 A.M. [2] Greek *bondservants;* twice in this verse [3] Greek *this one*

15 [u][1 Thess. 5:7]
17 [v]Cited from Joel 2:28-32 [w]ver. 18, 33; Isa. 32:15; 44:3; Ezek. 36:27; See Rom. 5:5 [x][ch. 10:45; Titus 3:6] [y]ch. 21:9
18 [z]ch. 11:28; 21:10; 1 Cor. 12:10
20 [a]See Matt. 24:29 [b][1 Thess. 5:2; Rev. 16:14]
21 [c]Rom. 10:13; [ch. 16:31]
22 [d]See John 3:2 [e]ch. 10:38; Luke 24:19 [f]2 Cor. 12:12; 2 Thess. 2:9; Heb. 2:4 [g][Matt. 12:28]
23 [h]Matt. 26:24; [ch. 3:13; Matt. 20:19]; See Luke 24:20 [i]Luke 22:22; [ch. 3:18; 4:28; 13:27] [j]1 Pet. 1:2; [1 Pet. 1:20; Rev. 13:8] [k]See ch. 5:30
24 [l]ver. 32; ch. 3:15; 4:10; 10:40; 13:30, 33, 34, 37; 17:31; Rom. 4:24; 6:4; 8:11; 10:9; 1 Cor. 6:14; 15:15; 2 Cor. 4:14; Gal. 1:1; Eph. 1:20; Col. 2:12; 1 Thess. 1:10; Heb. 13:20; 1 Pet. 1:21; [Eph. 2:5] [m][Luke 24:5; John 10:18; 2 Tim. 1:10; Heb. 2:14; Rev. 1:17, 18]
25 [n]Cited from Ps. 16:8-11
26 [o]Rom. 4:18
27 [p]ver. 31; See Matt. 11:23 [q]ch. 13:35 [r]See Heb. 7:26 [s][Luke 2:26]
29 [t]ch. 7:8, 9; Heb. 7:4 [u][ch. 13:36] [v]1 Kgs. 2:10 [w]Neh. 3:16
30 [x][2 Sam. 23:2; Matt. 22:43; Heb. 11:32] [y]See Luke 1:32

2:17 The **last days** are not just in the distant future but were inaugurated at Pentecost (cf. 1 Cor. 10:11; 2 Tim. 3:1; Heb. 1:2; James 5:3; 2 Pet. 3:3) and will continue until Christ's return. They are the "last days" in that the coming of the Messiah, long predicted in the OT, has now occurred. His saving death and resurrection have been accomplished, and now the work of the Holy Spirit in building the church is a key event in the history of salvation that needs to occur before Christ returns. Most rabbis believed that the Spirit had ceased speaking through human prophets with the last of the OT prophets (Haggai, Zechariah, and Malachi). Joel's prophecy of an outpouring of the Spirit **on all flesh** was understood as referring to a new messianic age. **daughters**. The women in the upper room participated in the gift of the Spirit at Pentecost, further confirming Joel's prophecy.

2:19–21 The darkened **sun** and bloody **moon**, whether literal or symbolic, indicate the final consummation of the earth. Peter included the full prophecy even though not all of it was yet fulfilled. Peter's quotation from Joel ended with the key verse (Joel 2:32), which assures that **everyone who calls upon the name of the Lord shall be saved**. Although the audience would have thought the God of Israel is meant, for Peter the "name of the Lord" that saves is Jesus (see Acts 2:36; cf. 4:12). Peter's application of the title "Lord" (Joel 2:32) to Jesus points to his deity.

2:23 Peter combines a clear affirmation of God's sovereignty over world events and human responsibility for evil deeds. Although Jesus was **delivered up according to the definite plan and foreknowledge of God**, showing that God had both foreknown and foreordained that Jesus would be crucified, that still did not absolve of responsibility those who contributed to his death, for Peter goes on to say, **"you crucified and killed"** him. Though one may not understand fully how God's sovereign ordination of events can be compatible with human responsibility for evil, both are clearly affirmed here and in many other passages of Scripture (cf. notes on 3:13–16; 3:17; 4:27; 4:28). **by the hands of lawless men**. Peter also places responsibility on the Gentile officials and soldiers who actually crucified Jesus.

2:25–31 Peter quoted Ps. 16:8–11 as a text pointing to the resurrection of Jesus, noting that David spoke of God not abandoning him to death. He then reasoned that, because David died, the psalm must have been speaking about one of his descendants. Since Jesus is the only one who conquered death and is a descendant of David, he must be the promised Messiah whom David foresaw.

2:29 Both the OT (1 Kings 2:10; Neh. 3:16) and early Jewish tradition locate David's **tomb** on the south side of Jerusalem. The traditional tomb location is marked today by medieval Islamic and Christian buildings. Some suggest that this is where the earliest church met (e.g., Acts 2:44–45). Thus Peter may be referring to an earlier traditional tomb not far from where he was speaking.

dants on his throne, 31 he foresaw and spoke about the resurrection of the Christ, that [z]he
was not abandoned to Hades, nor did his flesh see corruption. 32 This Jesus [a]God raised up,
[b]and of that we all are witnesses. 33 [c]Being therefore [d]exalted at the right hand of God, and
having received from [e]the Father [f]the promise of the Holy Spirit, [g]he has poured out this
that you yourselves are seeing and hearing. 34 For [h]David did not ascend into the heavens,
but he himself says,

[i]"'The Lord said to my Lord,
"Sit at my right hand,
35 until I make your enemies your footstool."'

36 Let all the house of Israel therefore know for certain that [j]God has made him [k]both Lord
and Christ, this Jesus [l]whom you crucified."
37 Now when [m]they heard this they were cut to the heart, and said to Peter and the rest
of the apostles, "Brothers, [n]what shall we do?" 38 And Peter said to them, [o]"Repent and [p]be
baptized every one of you [q]in the name of Jesus Christ [r]for the forgiveness of your sins,
and you will receive [s]the gift of the Holy Spirit. 39 For [t]the promise is for you and [u]for your
children and for all [v]who are far off, everyone [w]whom the Lord our God calls to himself."
40 And with many other words he bore witness and continued to exhort them, saying,
[x]"Save yourselves from this [y]crooked generation." 41 So those who received his word were
baptized, and [z]there were added that day about three thousand souls.

The Fellowship of the Believers

42 And [a]they devoted themselves to the apostles' [b]teaching and the [c]fellowship, to [d]the
breaking of bread and the prayers. 43 And awe[1] came upon every soul, and [e]many wonders
and signs were being done through the apostles. 44 And all who believed were together

31 [z]ver. 27
32 [a]ver. 24 [b]ch. 1:22; 4:33
33 [c]ch. 5:31; Eph. 1:20; Phil. 2:9; Heb. 2:9; 1 Pet. 3:22 [d]Ex. 15:6; Ps. 98:1 [e]ch. 1:4; [John 16:7] [f]Gal. 3:14 [g]ver. 17
34 [h][John 3:13] [i]Cited from Ps. 110:1
36 [j]See Matt. 28:18 [k]Rom. 14:9; 2 Cor. 4:5 [l]ver. 23
37 [m][ch. 5:33; 7:54] [n]ch. 16:30; Luke 3:10
38 [o]ch. 3:19; 20:21; 26:18, 20; Luke 24:47 [p]ch. 22:16; [ch. 8:12]; See Mark 16:16 [q]ch. 10:48; See ch. 8:16 [r]See Mark 1:4 [s]ch. 10:45; [ch. 8:15, 20; 11:17]; See John 7:39
39 [t]Rom. 9:4 [u]ch. 3:25; Isa. 54:13; [Isa. 44:3] [v]ch. 22:21; Isa. 57:19; Eph. 2:13, 17 [w]Joel 2:32; Rom. 8:30
40 [x][ver. 21, 47] [y]Deut. 32:5; Matt. 17:17; Phil. 2:15
41 [z]ver. 47
42 [a][Heb. 10:25]; See ch. 1:14 [b]See 1 Cor. 14:6 [c]Gal. 2:9; Phil. 1:5; 1 John 1:3 [d]Luke 24:35; [ver. 46]; See ch. 20:7
43 [e]See Mark 16:20

[1] Or *fear*

2:31 he foresaw and spoke about the resurrection of the Christ. Peter affirms that David, who was not only a king but also "a prophet" (v. 30), was able to foresee that Christ would be raised from the dead. Throughout the OT God was leading his prophets to predict the events of Christ's earthly life (cf. Luke 24:25–27; Acts 3:18; 1 Pet. 1:18–20). Acts 2:30–31 looks back to the citation in v. 27 and forward to the seating in v. 34, linking Peter's argument together by an allusion to Psalm 132 and God's promise to David.

2:33 The interactive and differentiated relationship among the persons of the Trinity is clearly evident in this verse. Thus God the Father first gave **the promise** that **the Holy Spirit** would come in a greater, more powerful way to accomplish his work in people's lives (as indicated in Peter's quote from Joel 2 in Acts 2:17–19). Then, when Christ's work on earth was accomplished, Christ was **exalted** to the second highest position of authority in the universe, namely, **at the right hand of God**, with ruling power delegated to him by God the Father. Then Christ **received** authority **from the Father** to send the Holy Spirit in this new fullness. Finally, on the day of Pentecost, Jesus himself **poured out** the Holy Spirit on the disciples in a new and more powerful way (cf. vv. 1–11); the image of pouring suggests overflowing abundance and fullness.

2:34 When Peter says that David **did not ascend into the heavens**, he is referring to his body, not his soul (cf. John 20:17).

2:38 repent and be baptized. This does not imply that people can be saved without having faith in Christ as Savior, because the need to believe is implied both in the command to "repent" and also in the command to "be baptized . . . **in the name of Jesus Christ for the forgiveness of your sins.**" The willingness to submit to baptism is an outward expression of inward faith in Christ (cf. 1 Pet. 3:21). (On baptism "in the name of Jesus Christ," see note on Acts 10:48.) The gospel can be summarized in different ways. Sometimes faith alone is named as the one thing necessary for salvation (see John 3:16; Acts 16:31; Rom. 10:9; Eph. 2:8–9), other times repentance alone is named (Luke 24:47; Acts 3:19; 5:31; 17:30; 2 Cor. 7:10), and sometimes both are named (Acts 20:21). Genuine faith always involves repentance, and vice versa. Repentance includes a change of mind that ends up trusting God (i.e., having faith). On repentance, see notes on Matt. 3:2; 3:5–6. **The gift of the Holy Spirit** does not mean some specific spiritual "gift" as in 1 Corinthians 12–14 but rather the gift of the Spirit himself, coming to dwell within the believer.

2:39 Peter's word that the promise was not just for the Jews who were listening but **for all who are far off** implies the inclusion of Gentiles (cf. Eph. 2:13, 17). **Everyone whom the Lord our God calls to himself** indicates that salvation is ultimately God's work, and comes to those whom the Lord effectively calls into personal relationship with him.

2:40 many other words. Luke was able to provide only a small portion of Peter's sermon.

2:41 The **three thousand** converts at Pentecost were **added** to the initial body of 120 believers.

2:42–47 *The Christian Community Shares a Life in Common.* This is the first extensive "summary" in Acts. It depicts a number of activities characteristic of the earliest church (see note on v. 42).

2:42 The early church was devoted to the **apostles' teaching**, which would have included Jesus' earthly teaching plus what he taught the apostles in his 40 days of resurrection appearances. **Fellowship** (Gk. *koinōnia*, "participation, sharing") included the sharing of material goods (v. 44), the **breaking of bread** (vv. 42, 46), which likely covers both the Lord's Supper and a larger fellowship meal, and **prayers** in house meetings and likely also in the temple (vv. 42, 46).

2:43 The church experienced **awe** (reverent fear) in response to miracles (**wonders**), which served as **signs** of the Spirit's power and presence among them (v. 43). Miracles were occurring regularly (**many . . . were being done**), many more than the few that Luke records in detail.

2:44 all things in common. Though some people have referred to this situation as "early communism," this is clearly not the case, since (1) the giving was voluntary and not compelled by the government, and (2) people still had personal possessions, because they still met in "their homes" (v. 46) and many other Christians after this still owned homes (see 12:12; 17:5; 18:7; 20:20; 21:8, 16; Rom. 16:5; 1 Cor. 16:19; Col. 4:15; Philem. 2; 2 John 10). Further, Peter told Ananias and Sapphira that they did not have any obligation to sell their property and give away the money (Acts 5:4). In contrast to communist theory, the abolition of private property is not commanded or implied here.

and [f]had all things in common. 45 And [f]they were selling their possessions and belongings
and distributing the proceeds to all, as any had need. 46 And day by day, [g]attending the
temple [h]together and [i]breaking bread in their homes, they received their food [j]with glad
and generous hearts, 47 praising God and [k]having favor with all the people. And the Lord
[l]added to their number [m]day by day those who [n]were being saved.

The Lame Beggar Healed

3 Now Peter and John were [o]going up to the temple at [p]the hour of prayer, [q]the ninth
hour.[1] 2 And a man [r]lame from birth was being carried, [s]whom they laid daily at the gate
of the temple that is called the Beautiful Gate [t]to ask alms of those entering the temple.
3 Seeing Peter and John about to go into the temple, he asked to receive alms. 4 And Peter
directed his gaze at him, as did John, and said, "Look at us." 5 And he fixed his attention
on them, expecting to receive something from them. 6 But Peter said, [u]"I have no silver
and gold, but what I do have I give to you. [v]In the name of Jesus Christ of Nazareth, rise
up and walk!" 7 And he took him by the right hand and raised him up, and immediately
his feet and ankles were made strong. 8 And [w]leaping up he stood and began to walk,
and entered the temple with them, walking and leaping and praising God. 9 And [x]all the
people saw him walking and praising God, 10 and recognized him as the one who sat at
the Beautiful Gate of the temple, asking for alms. And they were filled with wonder and
amazement at what had happened to him.

Peter Speaks in Solomon's Portico

11 [y]While he clung to Peter and John, all the people, utterly astounded, ran together to
them in [z]the portico called Solomon's. 12 And when Peter saw it he addressed the people:
"Men of Israel, why do you wonder at this, or why do you stare at us, as though by our
own power or piety we have made him walk? 13 [a]The God of Abraham, the God of Isaac,
and the God of Jacob, [b]the God of our fathers, [c]glorified his servant[2] Jesus, whom [d]you
delivered over and [e]denied in the presence of Pilate, [f]when he had decided to release him.
14 But you denied [g]the Holy and [h]Righteous One, and [i]asked for a murderer to be granted
to you, 15 and you killed [j]the Author of life, [k]whom God raised from the dead. To this we
are witnesses. 16 And [l]his name—by [m]faith in his name—has made this man strong whom
you see and know, and the faith that is [n]through Jesus[3] has given the man this perfect
health in the presence of you all.
17 "And now, brothers, I know that [o]you acted in ignorance, as did also your rulers. 18 But
what God [p]foretold [q]by the mouth of all the prophets, that [r]his Christ would [s]suffer, he

[1] That is, 3 P.M. [2] Or *child*; also verse 26 [3] Greek *him*

44 [f]ch. 4:32, 34, 35; [Matt. 19:21]
45 [f][See ver. 44 above]
46 [g]ch. 3:1; 5:21, 42; Luke 24:53 [h]See ch. 1:14 [i][ver. 42] [j][ch. 16:34]; See John 16:22
47 [k]ch. 5:13 [l]ver. 41; ch. 5:14; 11:24 [m]ch. 16:5 [n]1 Cor. 1:18; [ver. 21, 40; ch. 16:31]

Chapter 3

1 [o]See Luke 18:10 [p]Ps. 55:17 [q]ch. 10:3, 30; Matt. 27:46; [1 Kgs. 18:29]
2 [r]ch. 14:8 [s][Luke 16:20] [t][John 9:8]
6 [u]2 Cor. 6:10 [v][ch. 9:34]
8 [w]ch. 14:10; Isa. 35:6
9 [x]ch. 4:16, 21
11 [y]ch. 4:14 [z]ch. 5:12; John 10:23
13 [a]Matt. 22:32 [b]ch. 5:30; 22:14; [ch. 7:32] [c]Isa. 55:5; [Isa. 52:13]; See John 8:54 [d]See Matt. 20:19 [e]ch. 13:28; John 19:7, 12, 15 [f]Luke 23:14, 16; John 19:12
14 [g][ch. 4:27, 30]; See Mark 1:24 [h]ch. 7:52; 22:14; 1 Pet. 3:18; 1 John 2:1; 3:7; [James 5:6] [i]Luke 23:18, 19, 25
15 [j]ch. 5:31 [k]See ch. 2:24
16 [l][ver. 6] [m][John 1:12] [n][1 Pet. 1:21]
17 [o]ch. 13:27; [ch. 26:9; Luke 23:34; John 16:3; 1 Cor. 2:8; 1 Tim. 1:13]
18 [p]See ch. 2:23 [q]ch. 17:3; 26:22, 23; [Heb. 2:10]; See Luke 24:26, 27 [r]See Luke 9:20 [s]Matt. 17:12; Luke 22:15; 24:46; Heb. 13:12

(See 1 Tim. 6:17–19; but also 1 Tim. 6:6–10.) On the other hand, there is a voluntary generosity in sharing possessions that is seen as commendable.

2:45 On generosity among Christians, cf. 2 Cor. 8:9–15.

2:47 praising God. One of the characteristics of true revival is a desire to spend much time in worship. **And the Lord added to their number** is again an affirmation of God's sovereignty in salvation, since he alone can change the human heart to enable true repentance and faith.

3:1–10 *Peter Heals a Lame Man.* The healing of a lame man at the temple gate provides an example of an apostolic miracle (2:43) and attracts a crowd to hear Peter's second sermon in the temple area. In Acts, actions often lead to an explanation about what God is doing; word and deed go together.

3:2 alms. Gifts of money or goods given to the poor.

3:6 To heal **in the name of Jesus** was to invoke his power and presence.

3:8 The reference to the man's leaping employs a rare word (Gk. *hallomai*), which is found in the Septuagint (Greek OT) of Isa. 35:6 with reference to the messianic age.

3:11–26 *Peter Preaches in the Temple Square.* As with his first, Peter's second sermon took place in the temple precincts. His Pentecost sermon emphasized Jesus' messianic status. This one was primarily a call for Jews to repent of their rejection of Jesus as Messiah and focuses the argument on the Torah.

3:11 Solomon's **portico** was a colonnaded area along the eastern wall of the temple area. See also 5:12.

3:13–16 For the Jews' refusal to take Pilate's advice and their request for a murderer instead, see Luke 23:13–25. The reference to Jesus as God's **servant** (Acts 3:13) recalls Isa. 52:13–53:12. **you delivered over and denied . . . you denied . . . you killed**. Peter directly and repeatedly tells these Jewish people that they were responsible for Jesus' nonrelease and consequent death, and that they needed to repent (but see also Acts 3:17).

3:14 Holy One and **Righteous One** are messianic terms (cf. Isa. 53:11; Mark 1:24).

3:15 you killed . . . God raised . . . we are witnesses. Peter's emphasis on the veracity of Jesus' death and resurrection is a recurring theme in the speeches of Acts (see 2:23–24; 4:10; 5:30–32; 10:39–41; 13:28–29; see also 1 Cor. 15:1–4).

3:16 His name, in the full biblical sense of "name," means everything that is true about the person, and therefore, in a sense, the person himself. **By faith in his name** refers to Peter's faith rather than to any faith on the part of the lame man. Jesus healed the man, and faith (or trust) in Jesus also healed the man, because Jesus worked through Peter's faith. **the faith that is through Jesus**. Jesus himself imparts this kind of miracle-working faith to people's hearts.

3:17 you acted in ignorance, as did also your rulers (cf. 1 Cor. 2:8). "In ignorance" probably means that they did not fully understand that Jesus was the true Messiah and also the true Son of God. But such ignorance, in Scripture, while it may diminish punishment, does not fully absolve people of responsibility for their actions.

3:18 Foretold by the mouth of all the prophets and **fulfilled** by God

thus fulfilled. **19** [t]Repent therefore, and [u]turn back, that [v]your sins may be blotted out, **20** that
times of refreshing may come from the presence of the Lord, and that he may send the
Christ [w]appointed for you, Jesus, **21** [x]whom heaven must receive until the time for [y]restor-
ing all the things about which [z]God spoke by the mouth of his holy prophets long ago.
22 Moses said, 'The Lord God will raise up for you [a]a prophet like me from your brothers.
You shall listen [b]to him in whatever he tells you. **23** And it shall be that every soul who does
not listen to that prophet [c]shall be destroyed from the people.' **24** And [d]all the prophets
who have spoken, from Samuel and those who came after him, also proclaimed these days.
25 [e]You are the sons of the prophets and of [f]the covenant that God made with your fathers,
saying to Abraham, [g]'And in your offspring shall all the families of the earth be blessed.'
26 [h]God, [i]having raised up his servant, sent him to you first, [j]to bless you [k]by turning every
one of you from your wickedness."

Peter and John Before the Council

4 And as they were speaking to the people, the priests and [l]the captain of the temple
and [m]the Sadducees came upon them, **2** greatly annoyed because they were teaching
the people and proclaiming [n]in Jesus the resurrection from the dead. **3** And they arrested
them and [o]put them in custody until the next day, for it was already evening. **4** But many
of those who had heard the word believed, and [p]the number of the men came to about
five thousand.

5 On the next day their rulers and elders and scribes gathered together in Jerusalem,
6 with [q]Annas the high priest and [r]Caiaphas and John and Alexander, and all who were
of the high-priestly family. **7** And when they had set them in the midst, they inquired,
[s]"By what power or [t]by what name did you do this?" **8** Then Peter, [u]filled with the Holy
Spirit, said to them, "Rulers of the people and elders, **9** if we are being examined today
[v]concerning a good deed done to a crippled man, by what means this man has been
healed, **10** let it be known to all of you and to all the people of Israel that [w]by the name

19 [t]See ch. 2:38 [u]See Luke 22:32 [v]Ps. 51:1, 9; Isa. 43:25; 44:22; Col. 2:14
20 [w]ch. 22:14; 26:16
21 [x][ch. 1:11; Luke 24:26] [y][Matt. 17:11; Rom. 8:21] [z]Luke 1:70
22 [a]ch. 7:37, cited from Deut. 18:15, 18, 19 [b]Matt. 17:5
23 [c]Lev. 23:29
24 [d]ch. 13:20; 1 Sam. 3:20; Heb. 11:32
25 [e]See ch. 2:39 [f]See Rom. 9:4, 5 [g]Cited from Gen. 22:18; See Gen. 12:3
26 [h]Rom. 1:16; 2:9; 15:8; [Mark 7:27] [i]ver. 22 [j]ver. 25 [k]Rom. 11:26; [Ezek. 3:19]; See Matt. 1:21

Chapter 4

1 [l]ch. 5:24, 26; Luke 22:4, 52; [1 Chr. 9:11; Neh. 11:11] [m]See Matt. 22:23
2 [n]ch. 17:18; [ch. 3:15]
3 [o]See Luke 21:12
4 [p][ch. 2:41]
6 [q]Luke 3:2; John 18:13, 24 [r]See Matt. 26:3
7 [s][Matt. 21:23] [t][ver. 10]
8 [u]See Matt. 10:20
9 [v]ch. 3:7, 8
10 [w]ch. 3:6

indicates that there is no contradiction between divine sovereignty and human responsibility (cf. notes on 2:23; 3:13–16; 3:17; 4:27; 4:28).

3:19 Turn back. I.e. turn back to God instead of continuing to turn away from him.

3:20 Peter promised three results of repentance: (1) The forgiveness of sins (v. 19). (2) **Times of refreshing** (a mark of the messianic age), as people are "refreshed" in their spirits when the Holy Spirit comes to dwell within them. (This "refreshing" comes also to the world in general as it is affected by believers who are changed by the power of the Spirit.) (3) **That he may send the Christ** is a clear reference to the second coming of Christ, since the next verse looks forward to that time.

3:21 The time for restoring all the things looks forward to when Christ will return and his kingdom will be established on earth, and the earth itself will be renewed even beyond the more abundant and productive state it had before Adam and Eve's fall (see note on Rom. 8:20–21).

3:22–23 Peter quoted Deut. 18:15 to establish that Jesus was the **prophet like me** (i.e., like Moses, a comparison that points to a leader prophet) that God had promised to send. In Acts 3:23 Peter quotes Deut. 18:19 to point out the danger of rejecting the coming prophet (i.e., Jesus).

3:24 Samuel was considered the next prophet after Moses, and Peter declared that he and the rest of the prophets consistently pointed to Christ. **All the prophets . . . proclaimed these days** affirms that all of the OT prophets (including Moses, which implies all of the OT from Genesis onward) were predicting the coming of Christ and the new covenant age that had begun at Pentecost.

3:25–26 Peter noted that the covenant promised to Abraham applied to **all the families of the earth**. The servant Messiah was for all, only being sent to Israel "first" (v. 26). The worldwide mission was already implicit in Peter's message; only later, however, would he fully assimilate its meaning (see 10:1–11:18).

4:1–22 *Peter and John Witness before the Jewish Council.* Provoked by Peter's sermon, the Sadducean leaders had the two apostles arrested and held for trial before the Sanhedrin. The section falls into three parts: the arrest (vv. 1–4), the hearing (vv. 5–12), and the warning (vv. 13–22).

4:1 The captain of the temple was second in rank to the high priest. **The Sadducees** may have accepted only the Pentateuch as Scripture; they also denied the resurrection (see 23:8), and represented the privileged aristocracy who worked closely with the Romans to protect their own political and economic interests. (See Josephus, *Jewish Antiquities* 13.297; 18.17–18; see also Jewish Groups at the Time of the New Testament, pp. 1799–1800.)

4:2 Though the Sadducees did not themselves believe in a resurrection, most other Jews did, including the Pharisees (Josephus, *Jewish Antiquities* 18.14). The Sadducees were upset with Peter's preaching that **in Jesus** the general **resurrection** had begun, a message with definite messianic implications that was liable to be viewed by the Romans as revolutionary.

4:3 The Jewish high court, the Sanhedrin, met in the mornings. Since it was evening, the two apostles were placed in detention for the night.

4:4 Luke continues his catalog of Christian growth: 120 (1:15); then 3,000 (2:41); and now the **men** alone were **about five thousand**, suggesting that the total number of Christians would have been well in excess of 10,000. The incredible growth of the church occurred in response to two activities empowered by the Holy Spirit: the powerful preaching of the gospel message about Jesus and the "many wonders and signs" (2:43; cf. 4:14, 16).

4:5 The Jewish high court consisted of 71 members—70 elders according to the pattern of Num. 11:16 plus the high priest as presiding officer. It was dominated by the priestly Sadducees with a Pharisaic minority, represented mainly by the **scribes** (lawyers) of the court.

4:6 Annas is designated as **high priest**. (Much like U.S. presidents, high priests seem to have retained their title for life.) He had served in that role earlier (A.D. 6–15) and was the controlling figure in the high-priestly circle, which may also explain why he is given the title here. His son-in-law **Caiaphas** was the official high priest at this time (serving A.D. 18–36), and Annas's son **John** would serve in the role later (36–37). See also note on John 18:13.

4:8 filled with the Holy Spirit, said. Cf. Luke 12:11–12.

4:10 whom you crucified. As he had accused the Jews in his two temple sermons (2:23; 3:15), Peter now accused the Sanhedrin judges of their role in Jesus' death and pointed to the divine power that had raised him from the dead.

of Jesus Christ of Nazareth, whom you crucified, [x]whom God raised from the dead—by
him this man is standing before you well. 11 [y]This Jesus[1] is the stone that was [z]rejected
by you, the builders, which has become the cornerstone.[2] 12 And there is [a]salvation [b]in
no one else, for [c]there is no other [d]name under heaven given among men[3] by which we
must be saved."

13 [e]Now when they saw the boldness of Peter and John, and perceived that they were
uneducated, common men, they were astonished. And they recognized that they had
been with Jesus. 14 But seeing the man who was healed [f]standing beside them, [g]they
had nothing to say in opposition. 15 But when they had commanded them to leave the
council, they conferred with one another, 16 saying, [h]"What shall we do with these men?
For that [i]a notable sign has been performed through them is evident to all the inhabitants of Jerusalem, and we cannot deny it. 17 But in order that it may spread no further
among the people, let us warn them [j]to speak no more to anyone in this name." 18 So they
called them and charged them not to speak or teach at all in the name of Jesus. 19 But
Peter and John answered them, [k]"Whether it is right in the sight of God to listen to you
rather than to God, you must judge, 20 for [l]we cannot but speak of what [m]we have seen
and heard." 21 And when they had further threatened them, they let them go, finding
no way to punish them, [n]because of the people, for all were praising God [o]for what had
happened. 22 For the man on whom this sign of healing was performed was more than
forty years old.

The Believers Pray for Boldness

23 When they were released, they went to their friends and reported what the chief
priests and the elders had said to them. 24 And when they heard it, they lifted their voices
[p]together to God and said, "Sovereign Lord, [q]who made the heaven and the earth and the
sea and everything in them, 25 who through the mouth of our father David, your servant,[4]
said by the Holy Spirit,

> [r]"'Why did the Gentiles rage,
> and the peoples plot in vain?
> 26 The kings of the earth set themselves,
> and [s]the rulers were gathered together,
> against the Lord and against his [t]Anointed'[5]—

10 [x]See ch. 2:24
11 [y]See Ps. 118:22 [z]Mark 9:12; Luke 23:11
12 [a]ch. 13:26; 28:28; John 4:22; Heb. 2:3; Jude 3 [b][1 Tim. 2:5] [c][Gal. 1:7] [d]ch. 10:43; Luke 24:47; John 20:31
13 [e][John 7:15]
14 [f]ch. 3:11 [g][Luke 21:15]
16 [h][John 11:47; 12:19] [i]ver. 21; ch. 3:9, 10
17 [j]ch. 5:28, 40
19 [k]ch. 5:29
20 [l][Amos 3:8; John 15:27; 1 Cor. 9:16] [m]ch. 22:15; 1 John 1:1, 3
21 [n]ch. 5:13, 26; [Matt. 21:26, 46; Mark 11:32; Luke 20:6, 19; 22:2] [o]ch. 3:7, 8
24 [p]See ch. 1:14 [q]Ex. 20:11; 2 Chr. 2:12; Neh. 9:6; Ps. 102:25; 124:8; 134:3; 146:6
25 [r]Cited from Ps. 2:1, 2
26 [s]ver. 5 [t]ch. 10:38; Luke 4:18; Heb. 1:9; [Dan. 9:24; Rev. 11:15]

[1] Greek *This one* [2] Greek *the head of the corner* [3] The Greek word *anthropoi* refers here to both men and women [4] Or *child*; also verses 27, 30 [5] Or *Christ*

4:11 cornerstone. Cf. Ps. 118:22; Isa. 28:16.

4:12 Peter's statement that there was salvation in **no other name** was an implicit invitation to the Sanhedrin to place their faith in Jesus. It was Jesus' name that brought physical deliverance to the lame man (3:1–10)—the same powerful and exclusive name that brings eternal salvation to all who call upon him. Peter emphasizes this by saying that it is the only name **under heaven** (that is, throughout the whole earth) by which a person can be saved. Further, there is no other name **among men** (that is, in all of human society) that saves. On Christ as the exclusive way of salvation, see also Matt. 11:27; John 3:18; 14:6; 1 John 5:12. This verse also suggests that salvation comes only through conscious faith in Jesus.

4:13 Boldness (Gk. *parrēsia*) is an important word in Acts which depicts Spirit-inspired courage and confidence to speak in spite of any danger or threat. It also occurs at 2:29; 4:29, 31; 28:31; cf. 2 Cor. 3:12. **Uneducated** and **common** ("nonprofessional") men like Peter and John were not expected to speak so confidently before the supreme court of the land. The two words do not mean that they were illiterate or unintelligent but rather that they had not gone through the advanced training of the rabbinic schools. **they had been with Jesus**. It is impossible to imagine how much the disciples would have learned from spending three years in close association with the Son of God living on earth, listening to him teach, hearing him pray, and watching him interact with the most difficult challenges. They knew Jesus, and in knowing him they knew much more than all the learned scribes of the Sanhedrin.

4:16 What shall we do with these men? The religious leaders didn't know what action to take, since the healing of the man was well known and punishing his healers would displease the populace. Official leaders often act from fear of the people rather than from fear of God: see Matt. 14:5; 21:26, 46; Luke 19:48; 22:2; Acts 4:21; 5:26; cf. John 12:42–43.

4:17 in order that it may spread no further among the people. Sadly, the leaders were motivated by fear of losing power and influence rather than by a desire to glorify God, to be faithful to his Word, or to spread the true knowledge of salvation.

4:18–20 Though the leaders of the council **charged them not to speak or teach . . . in the name of Jesus**, Peter realized the impossibility of abiding by this prohibition, thus demonstrating that believers have the responsibility not to obey authorities when such authorities prohibit preaching the gospel or otherwise require Christians to disobey God's explicit commandments (cf. 5:29).

4:23–31 *The Christian Community Prays for Boldness in Witness.* Peter and John returned to their fellow Christians and reported the Sanhedrin's injunction against preaching the gospel. In response the Christians prayed, asking for power to witness even more boldly.

4:24 After praising God, the believers prayed, quoting Ps. 2:1–2 (Acts 4:25–26), which they treated as a messianic prophecy inspired by the Spirit speaking through David.

4:25 who through the mouth of our father David . . . said. Scripture is truly and totally the word of God even though it comes through flawed men like David. Even as they are persecuted, they address God as master and are in service to his will.

4:27 The psalm is interpreted in light of Jesus' death. The "kings" and "rulers" of v. 26 correspond to **Herod** Antipas (see note on Matt. 14:1) and

27 for truly in this city there were gathered together against your [u]holy servant Jesus,
[v]whom you anointed, both [w]Herod and [x]Pontius Pilate, along [y]with the Gentiles and [z]the
peoples of Israel, 28 [a]to do whatever your hand and [b]your plan had predestined to take
place. 29 And now, Lord, [c]look upon their threats and grant to your servants[1] to continue
to speak your word with all [d]boldness, 30 while [e]you stretch out your hand to heal, and
signs and wonders are performed [f]through the name of your [g]holy servant Jesus." 31 And
when they had prayed, [h]the place in which they were gathered together was shaken,
and [i]they were all filled with the Holy Spirit and [j]continued to speak the word of God
with boldness.

They Had Everything in Common

32 Now the full number of those who believed were of [k]one heart and [l]soul, and no one
said that any of the things that belonged to him was his own, but [m]they had everything
in common. 33 And with great [n]power the apostles were giving their testimony to the
resurrection of the Lord Jesus, and [o]great grace was upon them all. 34 [p]There was not a
needy person among them, for [q]as many as were owners of lands or houses sold them
and brought the proceeds of what was sold 35 and [r]laid it at the apostles' feet, and [s]it was
distributed to each as any had need. 36 Thus Joseph, who was also called by the apostles
Barnabas (which means [t]son of encouragement), a Levite, a native of Cyprus, 37 sold a field
that belonged to him and brought the money and [u]laid it at the apostles' feet.

Ananias and Sapphira

5 But a man named Ananias, with his wife Sapphira, sold a piece of property, 2 and with
his wife's knowledge [v]he kept back for himself some of the proceeds and brought only
a part of it and [w]laid it at the apostles' feet. 3 But Peter said, "Ananias, why has [x]Satan filled

[1] Greek *bondservants*

27 [u]ver. 30 [v]ver. 26 [w]Luke 23:7-11 [x]Matt. 27:2 [y]See Matt. 20:19 [z]Matt. 26:3
28 [a][Isa. 46:10] [b]See ch. 2:23
29 [c][2 Kgs. 19:16] [d]ver. 13, 31; ch. 9:27, 29; 13:46; 14:3; 18:26; 19:8; 28:31; Eph. 6:19
30 [e][Ps. 138:7; Prov. 31:20; Isa. 1:25; Zeph. 1:4] [f]ch. 3:6; [Matt. 7:22; Mark 9:39; 16:17] [g]ver. 27
31 [h][ch. 2:2; 16:26; Ps. 77:18] [i]See ch. 2:4 [j][Phil. 1:14]
32 [k]2 Chr. 30:12; Ezek. 11:19 [l]Phil. 1:27 [m]ch. 2:44
33 [n]See ch. 1:8, 22 [o][ch. 11:23]
34 [p][2 Cor. 8:14, 15] [q]ch. 2:45
35 [r]ver. 37; ch. 5:2 [s][ch. 6:1]
36 [t][Mark 3:17]
37 [u]ver. 35

Chapter 5

2 [v]ver. 3 [w]ch. 4:35, 37
3 [x][Luke 22:3; John 13:2, 27]

Pilate (see note on Matt. 27:2), while the **Gentiles** and **peoples of Israel** exemplify those who participated in the crucifixion (Acts 2:23). Much as in Peter's second temple sermon (3:18), this is viewed as being planned by God. Human responsibility is compatible with divine predestination (cf. notes on 2:23; 3:13–16; 3:17).

4:28 In their prayer, reported with approval by Luke, the believers affirm both God's sovereignty and human responsibility. **Whatever** includes all of the evil rejection, false accusation, miscarriage of justice, wrongful beatings, mockery, and crucifixion that both Jews and Gentiles poured out against Jesus. These things were **predestined** by God, yet the human beings who did them were morally "lawless" (see 2:23, 36); they were responsible for their evil deeds (see 3:13–15); and they needed to "repent" (see 2:38; 3:19). This prayer reflects both a deep acknowledgment of human responsibility and a deep trust in God's wisdom in his sovereign direction of the detailed events of history.

4:29 Their prayer for **boldness** in witness shows a determination to directly disobey the command of the Sanhedrin. They do not pray against those who persecute them but pray for their own faithfulness in witness.

4:30 and signs and wonders are performed. The believers do not hesitate to pray that God would work more miracles as they continued proclaiming the gospel. Such a prayer does not indicate deficient faith but is rather an evidence of their strong belief that God would work in their midst in an immediate way that authenticates the gospel.

4:31 God answered the believers' prayer. The place where they were gathered **was shaken** as if by an earthquake, and the Spirit descended upon them in a way they could perceive. **They were all filled with the Holy Spirit** indicates that people could be "filled" with the Holy Spirit more than once, for Peter was among them and he had already been "filled with the Holy Spirit" (v. 8), and all the disciples present at Pentecost had been "filled" with the Spirit as well (2:4). The Holy Spirit's power did not come on them automatically but in answer to their expectant, believing prayer.

4:32–5:16 *The Community Shares Together.* The second extensive "summary" in Acts deals with the practice of fellow believers sharing goods (see 2:43–44). Luke describes their practice and holds forth Barnabas as a model (4:32–37), followed by the account of the abuse of the practice by Ananias and Sapphira (5:1–11). A final summary highlights the growth of the community and its experience with the Spirit's power (5:12–16).

4:32 everything in common. See note on 2:44.

4:34 The believers' sharing exemplified the OT ideal of there not being a **needy person among them**—that is, there should be no poor in the community of faith (cf. Deut. 15:4–11). To realize this ideal the Christians would sell some of their goods and bring the proceeds to the apostles for distribution to the needy. Neither their sharing nor their bringing offerings should be seen as any sort of communal ownership such as was practiced by the Essenes and by later Christian monks, for the practice was strictly voluntary (see Acts 5:4 and note on 2:44). Such sacrifice and giving is seen as exemplary.

4:36 Barnabas would not have been cited as an example of sharing if the practice had not been voluntary. Barnabas is introduced in the Acts narrative at this point; he is a major character in later chapters, particularly as Paul's companion on his first mission. That mission began on **Cyprus** (13:4b–6), the home of Barnabas. The nickname **son of encouragement** fits his personality well. He introduced the newly converted Paul to the apostolic circle when everyone else was suspicious of him (9:27). He brought Paul to Antioch to participate in the outreach to the Gentiles (11:25–26). And he stood up for the young John Mark when Paul did not want to take him with them (15:36–39).

5:1–11 The positive picture of the community's sharing is marred by the account of a couple who abused the practice by holding back a portion of a gift while claiming to be giving it totally to the church. The context is important to note: the incident is bracketed by references to the Spirit's power (4:31, 33; 5:12–16). The Spirit was closely linked to the unity of the fellowship manifested in their sharing. Ananias and Sapphira abused the fellowship through their deception and thereby threatened its unity.

5:2 The couple **kept back . . . some of the proceeds**. "Kept back" (Gk. *nosphizō*) means "to put aside for oneself, to keep back" in a secret and dishonest way. It is an uncommon word, which was used also in the Septuagint in the story of Achan (Josh. 7:1), who received a sentence of death for holding back some of the spoils from Jericho that were dedicated to God.

5:3 Satan was the instigator behind the couple's deed, "filling" their hearts just as the Spirit had "filled" the community for witness (4:31). Twice Ananias

your heart to lie [y]to the Holy Spirit and [z]to keep back for yourself part of the proceeds of
the land? 4 While it remained unsold, did it not remain your own? And after it was sold,
was it not at your disposal? Why is it that you have contrived this deed in your heart? You
have not lied to man but [a]to God." 5 When Ananias heard these words, he [b]fell down and
breathed his last. And [c]great fear came upon all who heard of it. 6 The young men rose and
[d]wrapped him up and carried him out and buried him.

7 After an interval of about three hours his wife came in, not knowing what had happened. 8 And Peter said to her, "Tell me whether you[1] sold the land for so much." And she
said, "Yes, for so much." 9 But Peter said to her, "How is it that you have agreed together
[e]to test [f]the Spirit of the Lord? Behold, the feet of those who have buried your husband
are at the door, and they will carry you out." 10 Immediately she fell down at his feet and
breathed her last. When the young men came in they found her dead, and they carried her
out and buried her beside her husband. 11 And [g]great fear came upon the whole church
and upon all who heard of these things.

Many Signs and Wonders Done

12 Now many signs and wonders were regularly done among the people [h]by the hands
of the apostles. And they were all [i]together in [j]Solomon's Portico. 13 None of the rest dared
join them, but [k]the people held them in high esteem. 14 And [l]more than ever believers
were added to the Lord, multitudes of both men and women, 15 [m]so that they even [n]car-
ried out the sick into the streets and laid them on cots and mats, that as Peter came by [o]at
least his shadow might fall on some of them. 16 The people also gathered from the towns
around Jerusalem, [p]bringing the sick and those afflicted with unclean spirits, and they
were all healed.

The Apostles Arrested and Freed

17 But the high priest rose up, and all who were with him (that is, the party of [q]the
Sadducees), and filled with [r]jealousy 18 they arrested the apostles and [s]put them in the
public prison. 19 But during the night [t]an angel of the Lord [u]opened the prison doors
and brought them out, and said, 20 "Go and stand in the temple and speak to the people
all [v]the words of [w]this [x]Life." 21 And when they heard this, [y]they entered the temple [z]at
daybreak and began to teach.

[1] The Greek for *you* is plural here

3 [y][ver. 4, 9] [z]ver. 2
4 [a][ver. 3, 9]
5 [b][Ezek. 11:13] [c]ver. 11
6 [d][ch. 8:2; Ezek. 29:5; John 19:40]
9 [e][ch. 15:10; 1 Cor. 10:9] [f][ver. 3, 4]
11 [g]ver. 5
12 [h]ch. 2:43; 4:30; 14:3; 19:11; Mark 16:20; Rom. 15:19; 2 Cor. 12:12; Heb. 2:4 [i]See ch. 1:14 [j]ch. 3:11; John 10:23
13 [k]ver. 26; ch. 2:47; 4:21
14 [l][ch. 6:1, 2]
15 [m][ch. 19:12] [n]Mark 6:55, 56 [o][2 Kgs. 4:29; Matt. 14:36]
16 [p]Mark 16:17, 18
17 [q]See Matt. 22:23 [r]ch. 13:45; James 3:14, 16; [ch. 7:9; 17:5]
18 [s]See Luke 21:12
19 [t]See ch. 8:26 [u]ch. 12:10; 16:26
20 [v][John 6:63, 68; Phil. 2:16] [w][ch. 13:46; 22:4; 28:28] [x]ch. 3:15; 11:18
21 [y]ver. 25, 42 [z][John 8:2]

was charged with keeping **part of** the income from the land (5:2, 3), indicating that he must have claimed that he was dedicating the whole to the Lord's work. His sin was the **lie**, claiming to be doing more than he did.

5:4 Peter made clear the voluntary nature of the church's charity: Ananias did not have to give anything. Note that whereas Peter accused Ananias of lying to the Holy Spirit in v. 3, here he says that he has **lied . . . to God**, showing that the Holy Spirit is a person and that he is himself divine. Lying is characteristic of Satan (see John 8:44) and exactly opposite the character of God, who cannot lie (cf. Num. 23:19; Prov. 30:5; Titus 1:2; Heb. 6:18).

5:5 great fear (Gk. *phobos*). Fear in response to a manifestation of God's presence involves both reverent awe and a healthy fear of God's displeasure and discipline.

5:8 When Peter asked Sapphira whether she **sold the land for so much**, she repeated the lie, stating the partial amount the couple had given.

5:9 Peter accused Sapphira of testing **the Spirit** (cf. Ex. 17:2; Deut. 6:16; Matt. 4:7; Luke 4:12), an expression that echoes OT passages about testing the **Lord**. This is another indication of the Spirit's deity (cf. note on Acts 5:4).

5:10 Peter informed Sapphira of her impending death before it happened; the note of divine judgment is unmistakable. The text does not give enough information to know if Ananias and Sapphira were "false" believers or if they truly belonged to the Lord despite their egregious sin. One could view the event as God's removal from the young Christian community of the distrust and disunity provoked by the couple's dishonesty. It was a time when the Spirit was especially present in the community, blessing it with unity of fellowship (4:32) and the power of miracles (5:12–16). That same power brought judgment to those who by their actions denied this unity and power. Satan (v. 3) was no match for the Holy Spirit.

5:12–16 This summary centers on the Holy Spirit's activity in the apostles' healing ministry.

5:12 The Christians had prayed for God to grant them the power to perform **signs and wonders** (cf. 4:30). This was mightily fulfilled through the apostles, especially in the temple area of **Solomon's Portico**, where the Christians often witnessed (3:11). A "portico" (Gk. *stoa*) is a covered walkway (cf. 3:11; John 5:2; 10:23).

5:13 None of the rest dared join them. Some take the antecedent of "them" to be "the whole church" in v. 13 and understand "they" in v. 12 as referring to all the believers. Others understand "them" to be "the apostles" in v. 13 and understand "they" in v. 12 to refer to the apostles as well. The Greek grammar allows for either interpretation. The first interpretation would show that unbelievers were afraid to attach themselves to the church unless they were truly converted. The second interpretation would show the unique authority and miraculous power of the apostles.

5:15 his shadow might fall on some of them. Though this may seem strange to modern readers, it indicates that the Holy Spirit was so powerfully manifested in and around Peter that even those who only came near him experienced the healing of the Holy Spirit (cf. 19:12).

5:17–42 ***The Apostles Appear before the Council.*** Just as Peter's healing of the lame man provoked a trial before the Sanhedrin (3:1–4:22), once again the apostolic miracles precipitated a trial, this time of all the apostles.

Now when the high priest came, and those who were with him, they called together the
council, all the senate of the people of Israel, and sent to the prison to have them brought.
22 But when the officers came, they did not find them in the prison, so they returned and
reported, 23 "We found the prison securely locked and the guards standing at the doors,
but when we opened them we found no one inside." 24 Now when [a]the captain of the
temple and the chief priests heard these words, they were greatly perplexed about them,
wondering what this would come to. 25 And someone came and told them, "Look! The men
whom you put in prison [b]are standing in the temple and teaching the people." 26 Then [c]the
captain with the officers went and brought them, but not by force, for [d]they were afraid
of being stoned by the people.

27 And when they had brought them, they set them before the council. And the high
priest questioned them, 28 saying, [e]"We strictly charged you not to teach in this name, yet
here you have filled Jerusalem with your teaching, and you [f]intend to bring this man's
blood upon us." 29 But Peter and the apostles answered, [g]"We must obey God rather than
men. 30 [h]The God of our fathers [i]raised Jesus, [j]whom you killed by hanging him on [k]a tree.
31 God exalted [l]him at his right hand as [m]Leader and [n]Savior, [o]to give [p]repentance to Israel
and [o]forgiveness of sins. 32 And [q]we are witnesses to these things, and [r]so is the Holy Spirit,
[s]whom God has given to those who obey him."

33 When they heard this, they [t]were enraged and wanted to kill them. 34 But a Pharisee in
the council named [u]Gamaliel, [v]a teacher of the law held in honor by all the people, stood
up and gave orders to put the men outside for a little while. 35 And he said to them, "Men
of Israel, take care what you are about to do with these men. 36 For [w]before these days
Theudas rose up, [x]claiming to be somebody, and a number of men, about four hundred,
joined him. He was killed, and all who followed him were dispersed and came to nothing. 37 After him Judas the Galilean rose up in the days of [y]the census and drew away some
of the people after him. He too perished, and all who followed him were scattered. 38 So
in the present case I tell you, keep away from these men and let them alone, for [z]if this
plan or this undertaking is of man, it will fail; 39 but [a]if it is of God, you will not be able
to overthrow them. You [b]might even be found opposing God!" So they took his advice,
40 and [c]when they had called in the apostles, [d]they beat them and charged them not to
speak in the name of Jesus, and let them go. 41 Then they left the presence of the council,
[e]rejoicing that they were counted worthy [f]to suffer dishonor for [g]the name. 42 And every
day, [h]in the temple and from house to house, they did not cease teaching and [i]preaching
[j]that the Christ is Jesus.

24 [a]ver. 26; See ch. 4:1
25 [b]ver. 21
26 [c]ver. 24 [d]ver. 13; See ch. 4:21
28 [e]ch. 4:18 [f]ch. 2:23, 36; 3:15; 4:10; 7:52; Matt. 27:25
29 [g][ch. 4:19, 20]
30 [h]See ch. 3:13 [i]See ch. 2:24 [j]ch. 10:39; Gal. 3:13; See Luke 24:20 [k]ch. 13:29; 1 Pet. 2:24
31 [l]See ch. 2:33 [m]See ch. 3:15 [n]See Luke 2:11 [o]Luke 24:47; See Luke 5:32 [p]ch. 11:18; 2 Tim. 2:25; [Rom. 2:4]
32 [q]See Luke 24:48 [r][ch. 15:28; John 15:26, 27; Heb. 2:4; 1 John 5:7] [s]See ch. 2:4
33 [t]ch. 7:54; [ch. 2:37]
34 [u]ch. 22:3 [v]See Luke 5:17
36 [w][ch. 21:38] [x]ch. 8:9; [Gal. 2:6; 6:3]
37 [y][Luke 2:2]
38 [z]Lam. 3:37
39 [a]Prov. 21:30; Isa. 8:9, 10; Nah. 1:9 [b]2 Chr. 13:12; [ch. 11:17]
40 [c]ch. 4:18 [d][ch. 22:19; Mark 13:9; Luke 23:16]
41 [e]1 Pet. 4:13, 14, 16; See Matt. 5:12 [f]ch. 9:16; 21:13; [Rom. 1:5]; See John 15:21 [g]Lev. 24:11, 16; Phil. 2:9; 3 John 7
42 [h]ch. 2:46 [i]ch. 8:35; 11:20; 17:18 [j]See ch. 18:5

5:17 filled with jealousy. These Sadducees were "jealous" not for God's honor or for the advancement of his kingdom but for retaining their own influence and power (this theme is repeated later; see 7:9; 13:45; 17:5; and note on 12:3).

5:20 The **words of this Life** means the words of salvation and eternal life. It seems that early Christianity may also have been called "the Life," as well as "the Way" (see note on 9:1–2).

5:21 It was **daybreak**, and a crowd would be gathering at the temple for the morning sacrifices. The **council** and **all the senate** are two names for the same group, the Sanhedrin ("council" translates Gk. *synedrion*, "Sanhedrin").

5:30 hanging him on a tree. See note on 10:39. The allusion is to Deut. 21:22–23.

5:33 On the Jews' pattern of resistance (cf. 7:51; 12:1–3; 13:45; 25:7; 28:24), see note on Amos 4:6.

5:34 The lone voice in the Sanhedrin to speak against an immediate death sentence was that of **Gamaliel**. He was the most prominent rabbi of his day and the teacher of Paul (22:3). He belonged to the Pharisaic minority on the Sanhedrin but had considerable influence.

5:36 Gamaliel cited two examples from Jewish history to support his basic argument that movements not backed by God always come to nothing. Both examples were failed movements, the first being that of a revolutionary named **Theudas**, and the second that of "Judas the Galilean" (v. 37), who is said to have come "after him." Judas the Galilean is well known, having led a tax revolt in A.D. 6 (Josephus, *Jewish Antiquities* 18.23), and this is evidently the person to whom Gamaliel is referring. Although there is no historical record of the "Theudas" mentioned here (other than this statement by Gamaliel), most likely this "Theudas" was one of many otherwise unknown leaders of such movements following the death of Herod the Great in 4 B.C. Although Jewish historian Josephus (writing in A.D. 95 in *Jewish Antiquities* 20.97) mentions someone named "Theudas" who led a movement at a later date (A.D. 44–46), it is clear that Josephus's reference is to a different person, since the movement to which he refers occurred many years after the speech by Gamaliel (c. A.D. 30 or 33).

5:40 This time the Sanhedrin enforced their command by scourging the **apostles**. The text does not say whether it was with the maximum of 39 stripes prescribed by Jewish law (see 2 Cor. 11:24) or with fewer stripes. The lashing consisted of striking the victim's bare skin with a tripled strip of calf's hide. The victim received two blows to the back, then one to the chest. Thus each cycle had to be divisible by three, which explains the maximum limit of 39—one less than the 40 prescribed in Deut. 25:3.

5:41 The apostles left **rejoicing** at being considered **worthy to suffer** for their witness in Jesus' name, which they boldly resumed despite the Sanhedrin's threat. Their suffering paradoxically resulted in the growth of the church (6:1). Suffering for the name of Jesus is a characteristic theme in Acts.

Seven Chosen to Serve

6 Now in these days [k]when the disciples were increasing in number, a complaint by the
Hellenists[1] arose against the Hebrews because their widows were being neglected in
[l]the daily distribution. 2 And the twelve summoned the full number of the disciples and
said, "It is not right that we should give up preaching the word of God to serve tables.
3 [m]Therefore, brothers,[2] pick out from among you seven men [n]of good repute, [o]full of the
Spirit and of wisdom, whom we will appoint to this duty. 4 But [p]we will devote ourselves
to prayer and to the ministry of the word." 5 And what they said pleased the whole gathering, and they chose Stephen, [q]a man full of faith and [r]of the Holy Spirit, and [s]Philip, and
Prochorus, and Nicanor, and Timon, and Parmenas, and Nicolaus, [t]a proselyte of Antioch.
6 These they set before the apostles, and [u]they prayed and [v]laid their hands on them.
7 And [w]the word of God continued to increase, and the number of the disciples multiplied
greatly in Jerusalem, and a great many of the priests [x]became obedient to [y]the faith.

Stephen Is Seized

8 And Stephen, full of grace and [z]power, was doing great wonders and signs among the
people. 9 Then some of those who belonged to the synagogue of the Freedmen (as it was
called), and of the Cyrenians, and of the Alexandrians, and of those from Cilicia and Asia,

[1] That is, Greek-speaking Jews [2] Or *brothers and sisters*

Chapter 6

1 [k]ch. 2:41, 47; 4:4; 5:14; [ver. 7] [l][ch. 4:35]
3 [m][Deut. 1:13] [n][1 Tim. 3:7] [o]ver. 5; ch. 7:55; 11:24; [Luke 1:15; 4:1]
4 [p]See ch. 1:14
5 [q]ch. 11:24 [r]ver. 3 [s]ch. 8:5; 21:8 [t]ch. 2:11; 13:43; Matt. 23:15
6 [u]ch. 1:24; 13:3 [v]1 Tim. 4:14; 5:22; 2 Tim. 1:6; [ch. 8:17; 9:17; 19:6; Heb. 6:2]
7 [w]ch. 12:24; 19:20; [Col. 1:5, 6] [x]See Rom. 1:5 [y]ch. 13:8; 14:22; 16:5
8 [z]See ch. 1:8

6:1–12:25 *The Witness beyond Jerusalem.* Beginning with Greek-speaking Jewish Christians in Jerusalem (6:1–7), the Christian gospel was proclaimed to an ever-widening circle—to Samaria (8:4–25), to an Ethiopian (8:26–40), to a Gentile God-fearer (10:1–48), and to the Gentiles of Antioch (11:19–30). Key figures in the outreach were the Hellenists Stephen and Philip, the apostle Peter, and eventually Paul and Barnabas. The stage was then set for Paul's ministry that would go to the "end of the earth" (1:8).

6:1–7 *Seven Chosen to Serve the Hellenist Widows.* The growth of the church created problems when a number of Hellenistic (i.e., Greek-speaking) Jews responded to the gospel. The resulting language barrier led to the neglect of some needy widows, and the apostles called upon the Greek-speaking community to choose leaders to meet the need.

6:1 The **Hellenists** were Greek-speaking Jews from the Diaspora ("dispersed" Jews living outside Palestine). Their primary language was Greek. The **Hebrews** were native Palestinian Jews who spoke Aramaic as their primary language and had attended the Hebrew-speaking synagogues. Not as fluent in Greek, they seem to have overlooked the Hellenist widows unintentionally. Some scholars claim this verse is just the "tip of the iceberg" indicating serious theological frictions between these two groups in the Jerusalem church, and that they had major differences over observance of the OT law and the proper role of the Jerusalem temple. But the text itself indicates just the opposite, for several places show essential unity in doctrinal understanding among the apostles and those who followed them (see 15:1–35; Gal. 1:18–19; 2:1–10). Any differences in emphasis were not major, but it does appear the Hellenists were less drawn to the temple, as Stephen's speech in Acts 7 suggests. **the daily distribution**. That is, of provisions for the needy.

6:4 Essential to the work of the apostles was their devotion **to prayer and to the ministry of the word**. The burgeoning ministry of charity was distracting them from this calling. The Greek-speaking Hellenists from whom the seven were selected were better equipped to serve and communicate with the widows.

The Progress of God's Word in Acts

6:7	And the word of God continued to increase.
12:24	But the word of God increased and multiplied.
13:49	And the word of the Lord was spreading throughout the whole region.
19:20	So the word of the Lord continued to increase and prevail mightily.

6:5 Stephen and **Philip** will become prominent in the Acts narrative; the NT makes no further mention of the other five.

6:6 The apostles confirmed the congregational election when **they prayed and laid their hands on them**. Laying on of hands is done in connection with several things in Acts: healing (9:17), the gift of the Spirit (8:18; 9:17; 19:6), and commissioning to a ministry (both here and at 13:3). Interpreters differ over whether these seven men should be considered the first "deacons" in the church. On the one hand, the noun "deacon" (Gk. *diakonos*) does not occur here. On the other hand, the corresponding verb (Gk. *diakoneō*, "to serve, help, render assistance") is used in 6:2, and this same verb is used of those who serve as deacons in 1 Tim. 3:10, 13. However, this is a common verb for "service." It could well be these men were called to deal with this issue and any like it.

6:7 the number of the disciples multiplied greatly in Jerusalem. In spite of suffering and persecution (5:41), in spite of sin in the church (5:1–11), and in spite of conflict (6:1), the church continued to grow. It grew in the context of remarkable love among the Christians in Jerusalem (4:32, 35), frequent miracles (5:12), and the courageous proclamation of the gospel in the power of the Holy Spirit (5:29–32). **The word of God continued to increase** in spite of widespread opposition. **A great many of the priests** became Christians. The lower ranks of the priesthood numbered in the thousands, of whom many were poor and may have first been attracted to Christians by their charity, under the guidance of the newly appointed deacons (6:1–6).

6:8–8:3 *Stephen Bears the Ultimate Witness.* The Greek word for "witness" is *martys*, which came to be associated with witnessing to the point of death, from which the word "martyr" derives. Stephen became the first such "ultimate" witness in the early church (c. A.D. 31/34).

6:8–15 *The Arrest of Stephen.* Stephen was the first listed of the seven Hellenists selected to minister to the widows (v. 5). Like the apostles, he not only ministered to the needy but was primarily concerned with the ministry of the Word. He preached Christ in the Greek-speaking synagogues of Jerusalem, where he was seized and dragged before the Sanhedrin.

6:8 Stephen is described as being filled with faith, the Holy Spirit (v. 5), **grace, power**, and wisdom (v. 10). He is the first person after the apostles said to have performed **wonders and signs**. His "power" was not physical strength or worldly knowledge or influence but the power of the Holy Spirit (see 1:8).

6:9 Those to whom Stephen preached were Diaspora Jews (see note on v. 1) and Greek-speakers like himself. There may have been only the one **synagogue of the Freedmen**, with the various names designating its constituency, or those names may represent individual synagogues. "Freedmen" would refer to Jews who had been enslaved and then granted freedom. The place names all point to the Diaspora: **Cyrenians** and **Alexandrians** represent

rose up and disputed with Stephen. 10 But [a]they could not withstand the wisdom and the
Spirit with which he was speaking. 11 Then [b]they secretly instigated men who said, "We
have heard him speak blasphemous words against Moses and God." 12 And they stirred up
the people and the elders and the scribes, and they came upon him and seized him and
brought him before the council, 13 and they [c]set up false [d]witnesses who said, "This man
never ceases to speak words against [e]this holy place and the law, 14 for we have heard him
say that this Jesus of Nazareth [f]will destroy this place and will [g]change [h]the customs that
Moses delivered to us." 15 And gazing at him, all who sat in the council saw that his face
[i]was like the face of an angel.

Stephen's Speech

7 And the high priest said, "Are these things so?" 2 And Stephen said:
[j]"Brothers and fathers, hear me. [k]The God [l]of glory appeared to our father Abraham
when he was in Mesopotamia, [m]before he lived in Haran, 3 and said to him, [n]'Go out from
your land and from your kindred and go into the land that I will show you.' 4 [m]Then he
went out from the land of the Chaldeans and lived in Haran. And [o]after his father died,
[p]God removed him from there into this land in which you are now living. 5 Yet he gave
him no inheritance in it, not even a foot's length, but promised [q]to give it to him as a possession and to his offspring after him, [r]though he had no child. 6 And God spoke to this
effect—that [s]his offspring would [t]be sojourners in a land belonging to others, who would
enslave them and afflict them [u]four hundred years. 7 'But [v]I will judge the nation that they
serve,' said God, 'and after that they shall come out [w]and worship me in this place.' 8 And
[x]he gave him the covenant of circumcision. And [y]so Abraham became the father of Isaac,
and [z]circumcised him on the eighth day, and [a]Isaac became the father of Jacob, and [b]Jacob
of the twelve patriarchs.
9 "And the patriarchs, [c]jealous of Joseph, [d]sold him into Egypt; but [e]God was with him
10 and rescued him out of all his afflictions and [f]gave him favor and wisdom before Pharaoh,
king of Egypt, [g]who made him ruler over Egypt and over all his household. 11 Now [h]there
came a famine throughout all Egypt and Canaan, and great affliction, and our fathers
could find no food. 12 [i]But when Jacob heard that there was grain in Egypt, he sent out
our fathers on their first visit. 13 And [j]on the second visit [k]Joseph made himself known
to his brothers, and [l]Joseph's family became known to Pharaoh. 14 And [m]Joseph sent and
summoned Jacob his father and all his kindred, [n]seventy-five persons in all. 15 And [o]Jacob
went down into Egypt, and [p]he died, he [q]and our fathers, 16 and [r]they were carried back

10 [a]See Luke 21:14, 15
11 [b][1 Kgs. 21:10, 13; Matt. 26:59, 60]
13 [c]ver. 11 [d]ch. 7:58 [e][ch. 21:28; 25:8; Matt. 24:15]
14 [f][Dan. 9:26; Matt. 26:61] [g][Matt. 5:17] [h]ch. 15:1; 21:21
15 [i][Judg. 13:6; Eccles. 8:1]

Chapter 7

2 [j]ch. 22:1 [k][Gen. 15:7; Josh. 24:3; Neh. 9:7] [l]Ps. 29:3; [1 Cor. 2:8; James 2:1] [m]Gen. 11:31
3 [n]Cited from Gen. 12:1
4 [m][See ver. 2 above] [o]Gen. 11:32 [p]Gen. 12:4, 5
5 [q]Gen. 12:7; 13:15; 15:18; 17:8; 48:4; Heb. 11:8, 9 [r]Gen. 15:3; 18:10
6 [s]Cited from Gen. 15:13, 14 [t][Ex. 2:22; Heb. 11:9] [u]ver. 17; See Ex. 12:40
7 [v][Jer. 25:12; 30:20] [w][Ex. 3:12]
8 [x]Gen. 17:9-12 [y]Gen. 21:2-4 [z]See Luke 1:59 [a]Gen. 25:26 [b]Gen. 29:31-35; 30:5-24; 35:18, 23-26
9 [c]Gen. 37:11 [d]Gen. 37:28; 45:4; Ps. 105:17 [e]Gen. 39:2, 21, 23
10 [f]Gen. 41:37-40 [g]Gen. 41:41, 43, 46; 42:6; Ps. 105:21
11 [h]Gen. 41:54, 55; 42:5; Ps. 105:16
12 [i]Gen. 42:1-3
13 [j]Gen. 43:2-15 [k]Gen. 45:1-4 [l]Gen. 45:16
14 [m]Gen. 45:9, 10, 27 [n][Gen. 46:26, 27; Ex. 1:5; Deut. 10:22]
15 [o]Gen. 46:5, 28; Ps. 105:23 [p]Gen. 49:33 [q]Ex. 1:6
16 [r]Gen. 50:25; Ex. 13:19; Josh. 24:32

North Africa, while those in **Cilicia and Asia** represent the area covered by modern Turkey, also a part of the Diaspora.

6:11 Secretly instigated (Gk. *hypoballō*) implies putting words in someone's mouth or making false suggestions. The basic charge was blasphemy, speaking against **Moses** (the Law) and against **God** (that is, against the temple, God's dwelling place; cf. vv. 13–14). Jesus was accused of the same thing (Mark 14:63–64).

6:13 The use of false witnesses is reminiscent of what happened at Jesus' trial (Matt. 26:59–60) and confirms Jesus' prediction that his followers would be persecuted as he was (John 15:18–21).

6:14 Stephen must have referred to what Jesus said about destroying the temple and rebuilding it in three days (Mark 14:58), which John clarified as referring to the temple of Jesus' body (John 2:19–21).

6:15 Stephen's face is described as being **like the face of an angel**. There was apparently a visible manifestation of the brightness of the glory of God on his face, as there had been with Moses (Ex. 34:29–30, 35) and, to an even greater extent, with Jesus at his transfiguration (Matt. 17:2).

7:1–53 *Stephen's Address before the Sanhedrin.* Stephen's defense is the longest discourse in Acts. It is a selective recital of OT history, including sections on Abraham (vv. 2–8), Joseph (vv. 9–16), Moses (vv. 17–34), and Israel's apostasy (vv. 35–50). It was cut short when Stephen applied his history lesson to Israel's present rejection of the Messiah (vv. 51–53). Stephen responded to the charges by turning them on his accusers: *they* were the ones who were really disobeying God because they rejected his appointed leaders.

7:4 after his father died. See note on Gen. 11:32.

7:5 Abraham himself was given no possession in the Promised Land, not even the **length** of a foot, showing that God was working even when a temple did not yet exist.

7:6 four hundred years. That is, the time Israel spent in Egypt.

7:7 Combining Gen. 15:13–14 with Ex. 3:12, Stephen spoke of God's assurances to Abraham that even after a long exile his descendants would come to Canaan and worship God **in this place**. Stephen's emphasis was on how God revealed himself outside the holy land and how he promised a place of true worship to come.

7:9 The **Joseph** history contrasts how the **patriarchs** were blessed by the brother whom they rejected. Israel's rejection of God's chosen leaders is a theme that runs throughout Stephen's speech, culminating in the rejection of Jesus. **God was with him**. God's presence with Joseph in **Egypt** shows that God can bless those outside the Promised Land, and therefore a physical temple is not crucial for his saving purposes.

7:14 When Stephen cites the number of Jacob's **kindred** at **seventy-five**, he is following the Septuagint rather than Hebrew text for Ex. 1:5, which follows a different calculation and arrives at the number 70. The different texts were apparently based on different decisions regarding whether to include Jacob and his wife and the additional descendants born to Ephraim and Manasseh in Egypt.

7:15 Israel's presence in **Egypt** for 400 years (v. 6) again indicates that the Lord is with his people even when they are not in the Promised Land (cf. notes on vv. 5, 9).

7:16 the tomb that Abraham had bought . . . from the sons of Hamor in Shechem. The OT shows that it was actually Jacob who bought a tomb

to Shechem and laid in the tomb that [s]Abraham had bought for a sum of silver from the
sons of Hamor in Shechem.
17 "But [t]as the time of the promise drew near, which God had granted to Abraham, [u]the
people increased and multiplied in Egypt 18 until there arose over Egypt another king [v]who
did not know Joseph. 19 [w]He dealt shrewdly with our race and forced our fathers to expose
their infants, [x]so that they would not be kept alive. 20 [y]At this time Moses was born; and
he was beautiful in God's sight. And he was brought up for three months in his father's
house, 21 and [z]when he was exposed, Pharaoh's daughter adopted him and brought him
up as her own son. 22 And Moses [a]was instructed in [b]all the wisdom of the Egyptians, and
he was [c]mighty in his words and deeds.
23 "When he was forty years old, it came into his heart [d]to visit his brothers, the children of Israel. 24 And seeing one of them being wronged, he defended the oppressed man
and avenged him by striking down the Egyptian. 25 He supposed that his brothers would
understand that God was giving them salvation by his hand, but they did not understand.
26 [e]And on the following day he appeared to them as they were quarreling and tried to
reconcile them, saying, 'Men, you are brothers. Why do you wrong each other?' 27 But the
man who was wronging his neighbor thrust him aside, saying, [f]'Who made you a ruler
and a judge over us? 28 Do you want to kill me as you killed the Egyptian yesterday?' 29 At
this retort [g]Moses fled and became an exile in the land of Midian, [h]where he became the
father of two sons.
30 "Now when forty years had passed, [i]an angel appeared to him [j]in the wilderness of
Mount Sinai, in a flame of fire in a bush. 31 When Moses saw it, he was amazed at the
sight, and as he drew near to look, there came the voice of the Lord: 32 [k]'I am the God of
your fathers, the God of Abraham and of Isaac and of Jacob.' And Moses trembled and did
not dare to look. 33 Then the Lord said to him, [l]'Take off the sandals from your feet, for
the place where you are standing is holy ground. 34 [m]I have surely seen the affliction of
my people who are in Egypt, and [n]have heard their groaning, and [o]I have come down to
deliver them. [p]And now come, I will send you to Egypt.'
35 "This Moses, whom they rejected, [q]saying, 'Who made you a ruler and a judge?'—
this man God sent as both ruler and redeemer [r]by the hand of the angel who appeared
to him in the bush. 36 [s]This man led them out, performing [t]wonders and signs [u]in Egypt
and [v]at the Red Sea and [w]in the wilderness for [x]forty years. 37 This is the Moses who said
to the Israelites, 'God will raise up for you [y]a prophet like me from your brothers.' 38 This
is the one [z]who was in the congregation in the wilderness with [a]the angel who spoke to
him at Mount Sinai, and with our fathers. [b]He received [c]living [d]oracles to give to us. 39 Our
fathers refused to obey him, but thrust him aside, and [e]in their hearts they turned to Egypt,
40 saying to Aaron, [f]'Make for us gods who will go before us. As for this Moses who led us

16 [s][Gen. 23:16 with Gen. 33:19; Josh. 24:32]
17 [t]ver. 5-7 [u]ch. 13:17; Ex. 1:7, 12; Ps. 105:24
18 [v]Cited from Ex. 1:8
19 [w]Ex. 1:9, 10; Ps. 105:25 [x]Ex. 1:16-18, 22
20 [y]Ex. 2:2; Heb. 11:23
21 [z]Ex. 2:3-10
22 [a][Dan. 1:4, 17] [b]1 Kgs. 4:30; [Isa. 19:11] [c][Luke 24:19]
23 [d]Ex. 2:11, 12
26 [e]Ex. 2:13, 14
27 [f]ver. 35; [Luke 12:14]
29 [g]Ex. 2:15 [h]Ex. 2:22; 18:3, 4
30 [i]Ex. 3:2 [j][Ex. 3:1]
32 [k]Cited from Ex. 3:6
33 [l]Ex. 3:5; Josh. 5:15
34 [m]Ex. 3:7 [n]Ex. 2:24 [o]Ex. 3:8 [p]Ex. 3:10
35 [q]ver. 27 [r][Ex. 3:2; 14:19; 23:20; Num. 20:16]
36 [s]Ex. 12:41; 33:1; Heb. 8:9 [t]Ex. 7:3 [u]Ex. 7-12; Ps. 78:43-51; 105:27-36 [v]Ex. 14:21, 27-31; Ps. 78:53; 106:9 [w]Ex. 16:1, 35; 17:1-6; Ps. 78:15 [x]ver. 42; ch. 13:18; Ex. 16:35; Num. 14:33, 34; Ps. 95:10; Heb. 3:10, 17
37 [y]ch. 3:22; Cited from Deut. 18:15
38 [z]Ex. 19:3, 17, 18 [a][ver. 53; Isa. 63:9] [b]Deut. 5:27, 31; 33:4; See John 1:17 [c][Deut. 32:47] [d]Rom. 3:2; Heb. 5:12; 1 Pet. 4:11
39 [e]Ex. 16:3; Num. 11:4, 5; 14:3, 4; Ezek. 20:8, 24
40 [f]Cited from Ex. 32:1, 23

"from the sons of Hamor" in Shechem (Gen. 33:19) and this is where Joseph was buried (Josh. 24:32). It seems that Stephen is using the name "Abraham" to refer to all of Abraham's family or descendants, including Jacob (cf. Heb. 7:9–10). Another possible explanation is that Abraham had earlier bought the same piece of land when he built an altar in Shechem (Gen. 12:6–7), but Jacob later had to repurchase it just as Isaac had needed to renegotiate his rights to a well that Abraham had earlier bought in Beersheba (cf. Gen. 21:27–31 with Gen. 26:23–33).

7:20 Stephen's recital of the story of **Moses** is in three parts, covering 40 years each: birth and years in Pharaoh's court (vv. 17–22), flight from Egypt and sojourn in Midian (vv. 23–29), and divine commissioning at Sinai and wandering in the wilderness (vv. 30–43).

7:22 Moses' education in Egyptian wisdom is not mentioned in the OT but was well established in Jewish tradition. Stephen emphasizes that the one who delivered Israel was educated in a secular setting, hence God accomplished salvation in an unexpected way, as he has now done through Jesus of Nazareth.

7:23 Stephen highlighted Moses' middle years by relating his avenging of an abused Israelite and the subsequent rejection of his attempt to reconcile two quarreling Israelites (Ex. 2:11–15). The 40-year period was spent primarily in Midian (Acts 7:29), but Stephen chose to emphasize the single incident because it illustrated Israel's constant rejection of its God-sent leaders (see v. 35).

7:30 After spending the middle **forty years** of his life in exile in Midian (cf. vv. 23, 29), Moses began his final 40 years, covered in vv. 30–43.

7:35–36 Stephen continued the story of **Moses**, emphasizing Israel's rejection of his leadership. He implicitly presented Moses as a type of Christ: both were men whom **God sent**, both served as a **redeemer** (see Luke 24:21), and both performed **wonders and signs** (see Acts 2:22).

7:37 Christ is the **prophet** whom Moses predicted (see Deut. 18:15; Acts 3:22).

7:38 The Greek word for **congregation** is *ekklēsia*, the characteristic NT word for "church," and it provides a comparison between Moses' presence with the Israelites and Christ's presence in the church. The word refers to an assembled group. The idea that the law was mediated by angels was well established in Judaism and is repeated in v. 53 and also by Paul in Gal. 3:19 and the author of Hebrews in Heb. 2:2. Stephen employed the Moses/Christ typology to show how both were God-sent deliverers and how Israel rejected the message of both.

7:40–41 The golden **calf** incident illustrates Israel's continuing rejection of Moses' leadership (**we do not know what has become of him**) and their sinful idolatry.

out from the land of Egypt, we do not know what has become of him.' 41 And [g]they made
a calf in those days, and offered a sacrifice to the idol and [h]were rejoicing in [i]the works of
their hands. 42 But [j]God turned away and [k]gave them over to worship [l]the host of heaven,
as it is written in the book of the prophets:

> [m]"'Did you bring to me slain beasts and sacrifices,
> [n]during the forty years in the wilderness, O house of Israel?
> 43 You took up the tent of [o]Moloch
> and the star of your god Rephan,
> the images that you made to worship;
> and I will send you into exile beyond Babylon.'

44 "Our fathers had [p]the tent of witness in the wilderness, just as he who spoke to Moses
[q]directed him to make it, according to the pattern that he had seen. 45 Our fathers in turn
[r]brought it in with Joshua when they [s]dispossessed the nations [t]that God drove out before
our fathers. So it was [u]until the days of David, 46 [v]who found favor in the sight of God and
[w]asked to find a dwelling place for [x]the God of Jacob.[1] 47 But it was [y]Solomon who built
a house for him. 48 [z]Yet the Most High does not dwell [a]in houses made by hands, as the
prophet says,

> 49 [b]"'Heaven is my throne,
> [c]and the earth is my footstool.
> What kind of house will you build for me, says the Lord,
> or what is the place of my rest?
> 50 Did not my hand make all these things?'

51 [d]"You stiff-necked people, [e]uncircumcised in heart and ears, you always resist the
Holy Spirit. [f]As your fathers did, so do you. 52 [g]Which of the prophets did your fathers not
persecute? And they killed those who announced beforehand the coming of [h]the Righteous
One, [i]whom you have now betrayed and murdered, 53 you who received the law [j]as delivered
by angels and [k]did not keep it."

The Stoning of Stephen

54 Now when they heard these things [l]they were enraged, and they [m]ground their teeth
at him. 55 But he, [n]full of the Holy Spirit, gazed into heaven and saw [o]the glory of God, and
Jesus standing [p]at the right hand of God. 56 And he said, "Behold, I see [q]the heavens opened,
and [r]the Son of Man standing [p]at the right hand of God." 57 But they cried out with a loud
voice and stopped their ears and rushed together[2] at him. 58 Then [s]they cast him out of the

[1] Some manuscripts *for the house of Jacob* [2] Or *rushed with one mind*

41 [g]Ex. 32:4-6, 35; Deut. 9:16; Ps. 106:19 [h]Amos 6:13 [i]Isa. 2:8; Jer. 1:16; 25:6, 7
42 [j][Josh. 24:20; Isa. 63:10] [k]Ps. 81:12; Ezek. 20:39; Rom. 1:28 [l]Deut. 4:19; 2 Kgs. 17:16; 21:3; 23:5; Jer. 19:13; Zeph. 1:5 [m]Cited from Amos 5:25-27 [n]See ver. 36
43 [o]See 1 Kgs. 11:7
44 [p]Rev. 15:5; See Ex. 38:21 [q]See Ex. 25:40
45 [r]Josh. 3:14-17 [s]Num. 32:5; Deut. 32:49 [t]ch. 13:19; Josh. 3:10; 23:9; 24:18; 2 Chr. 20:7 [u]2 Sam. 7:1
46 [v]ch. 13:22; 1 Sam. 16:1; Ps. 89:19 [w]1 Kgs. 8:17; 1 Chr. 22:7; Ps. 132:5 [x][Gen. 49:24; Isa. 49:26]
47 [y]2 Sam. 7:13; 1 Kgs. 6:1, 2; 8:20; 2 Chr. 3:1
48 [z][1 Kgs. 8:27; 2 Chr. 2:6] [a]ch. 17:24
49 [b][Ps. 11:4] [c]Matt. 5:34, 35; Cited from Isa. 66:1, 2
51 [d]Deut. 10:16; See Ex. 32:9 [e]Lev. 26:41; Jer. 6:10; 9:26; Ezek. 44:7, 9 [f]Mal. 3:7
52 [g]1 Kgs. 19:10; 2 Chr. 36:16; Jer. 2:30; Matt. 23:31, 37; See Matt. 5:12; 21:35 [h]See ch. 3:14 [i]See ch. 5:28
53 [j]Gal. 3:19; Heb. 2:2; [ver. 38; Deut. 33:2] [k]John 7:19
54 [l]ch. 5:33; [ch. 2:37] [m]Job 16:9; Ps. 35:16; 37:12
55 [n]ch. 6:5 [o]Ex. 24:16; Luke 2:9; John 12:41 [p]Ps. 110:1; See Mark 16:19
56 [q]See John 1:51 [r]See Dan. 7:13 [p][See ver. 55 above]
58 [s]Lev. 24:14-16; Num. 15:35; 1 Kgs. 21:13; [Luke 4:29; Heb. 13:12]

7:42–43 Stephen carried the accusation of Israel's idolatry on down to their occupation of the Promised Land, when they began worshiping heavenly bodies (**the host of heaven**). To establish this he quoted the Greek (Septuagint) version of Amos 5:25–27. **Moloch** was the Canaanite sun god. The identity of **Rephan** is uncertain, but it possibly refers to Repa, the Egyptian name for Saturn.

7:44 Stephen turned to the charge made against him regarding the temple (6:12–14). He contrasted the tabernacle (or **tent**) with the temple. The temple is not necessary for God's purposes, for in the wilderness God directed the construction of the tabernacle (Ex. 25:40). In distinction from the temple, it was movable, and it contained the **witness**, the stone tablets inscribed with God's law. It continued as Israel's place of worship through the period of the conquest on down to the time of David, who was the first to request a temple (2 Sam. 7:1–17). However, Stephen should not be understood as saying that the building of the temple was wrong, for he narrates this event without any hint of disapproval. (Acts 7:48 merely affirms that God cannot be contained in or confined to any earthly temple; cf. 17:24–25.) His point was not to make too much of the temple.

7:48 Stephen quoted Isa. 66:1–2 to establish that God does not dwell **in houses**, a point Solomon himself made in 1 Kings 8:27. Israel's error was in confining God to the temple. Further, Stephen suggested that neither the tabernacle nor the temple were intended to last forever. Both pointed to something greater that was to come.

7:51 Stephen concluded with a direct attack on Israel for rejecting the Messiah. While this may seem harsh, Luke will soon say that Stephen was "full of the Holy Spirit" (v. 55; cf. 6:10, 15) and he was no doubt led by the Spirit, who knew the hearts of Stephen's listeners, to make this accusation. Using the language of the OT he accused them of being **stiff-necked** (see Ex. 33:3, 5; 34:9; Deut. 9:6, 13), **uncircumcised in heart and ears** (Lev. 26:41; Deut. 10:16; Jer. 4:4, 6:10, 9:26; Ezek. 44:7, 9), and resisting the **Holy Spirit** (Isa. 63:10). In fact, the repeated rejection of God's will is the point of his story, justifying the charge that prophets also made against the nation.

7:52 Like Jesus, Stephen accused his Jewish listeners of killing the prophets (cf. Luke 11:47–51; 13:34) and now rejecting their ultimate God-sent deliverer, the **Righteous One** (see Acts 3:14–15).

7:53 It was not Stephen but his accusers who were the ultimate rejecters of the law. In rejecting their God-sent deliverers they rejected God himself.

7:54–8:3 *The Martyrdom of Stephen.* Stephen's testimony was cut short as the enraged Sanhedrin turned on him (7:54). Their anger intensified as he shared his vision of the exalted Christ (7:55–57). They stoned him (7:58), and he died praying for them (7:59–8:1a). His martyrdom triggered a general persecution against the church (8:1b–3).

7:56 On the **Son of Man** and the theme of vindication, see Dan. 7:13; Matt. 26:64.

7:58 It is debated whether Stephen was formally stoned by order of the

city and [t]stoned him. And [u]the witnesses laid down their garments [v]at the feet of a young
man named Saul. **59** And as they were stoning Stephen, [w]he called out, "Lord Jesus, [x]receive
my spirit." **60** And [y]falling to his knees he cried out with a loud voice, [z]"Lord, do not hold
this sin against them." And when he had said this, [a]he fell asleep.

Saul Ravages the Church

8 And [b]Saul [c]approved of his execution.
And there arose on that day a great persecution against the church in Jerusalem, and
[d]they were all scattered throughout the regions of Judea and Samaria, except the apostles.
2 Devout men buried Stephen and made great lamentation over him. **3** But [e]Saul was ravaging the church, and entering house after house, he [f]dragged off men and women and
committed them to prison.

Philip Proclaims Christ in Samaria

4 Now [g]those who were scattered went about preaching the word. **5** [h]Philip went down to
the city[1] of Samaria and proclaimed to them the Christ. **6** [i]And the crowds with one accord
paid attention to what was being said by Philip when they heard him [j]and saw the signs that
he did. **7** For [k]unclean spirits, crying out with a loud voice, came out of many who had them,
and many who were paralyzed or lame were healed. **8** So [l]there was much joy in that city.

Simon the Magician Believes

9 But there was a man named Simon, [m]who had previously practiced magic in the
city and amazed the people of Samaria, [n]saying that he himself was somebody great.
10 They all paid attention to him, from the least to the greatest, saying, [o]"This man is
the power of God that is called [p]Great." **11** And they paid attention to him because for
a long time he had [q]amazed them with his magic. **12** But when [r]they believed Philip as
he preached good news [s]about the kingdom of God and the name of Jesus Christ, [r]they
were baptized, both men and women. **13** Even Simon himself believed, and after being
baptized he continued with Philip. And [t]seeing signs and [u]great miracles[2] performed,
[v]he was amazed.

[1] Some manuscripts *a city* [2] Greek *works of power*

58 [t]Matt. 21:35; 23:37; Heb. 11:37 [u]ch. 6:13; [Deut. 13:9, 10; 17:7] [v]ch. 8:1; 22:20; [ch. 22:4]
59 [w]ch. 9:14 [x]Ps. 31:5; Luke 23:46
60 [y]ch. 9:40; 20:36; 21:5; Luke 22:41; Eph. 3:14 [z]See Matt. 5:44 [a]See Matt. 27:52

Chapter 8

1 [b]ch. 7:58; 22:20 [c]See Rom. 1:32 [d]ch. 11:19; See Matt. 10:23
3 [e]ch. 9:1, 13, 21; 22:4, 19; 26:10, 11; 1 Cor. 15:9; Gal. 1:13; Phil. 3:6; 1 Tim. 1:13 [f][James 2:6]
4 [g]ver. 1
5 [h]ch. 6:5
6 [i][John 4:39] [j]John 2:23
7 [k]See Mark 16:17, 18
8 [l]ver. 39; See John 16:22
9 [m]ver. 11; ch. 13:6 [n]See ch. 5:36
10 [o]ch. 14:11; 28:6 [p][ch. 19:27, 28]
11 [q]ver. 9; [ver. 13; Gal. 3:1]
12 [r]ch. 16:33, 34; 18:8; Mark 16:16 [s]ch. 1:3
13 [t]ver. 6, 7 [u]ch. 19:11 [v][ver. 9]

Sanhedrin or killed by mob violence. The fact that he was appearing before that body (6:12) would favor the former, but the precipitous nature of the stoning suggests mob behavior. Also, under Roman rule the Sanhedrin did not have the legal right to execute without Roman concurrence (see John 18:31).

7:60 Stephen died with two prayers on his lips. The first ("Lord Jesus, receive my spirit," v. 59) recalls Jesus' dying words from the cross (Luke 23:46), and the second (**Lord, do not hold this sin against them**) recalls Jesus' earlier prayer for the forgiveness of those responsible for his death (Luke 23:34). **Fell asleep** is a Christian expression for death, reflecting assurance of a future resurrection. Stephen's death surely had a profound influence on Paul, who later alluded to that experience (Acts 22:20).

The Ministry of Philip the Evangelist
C. A.D. 34?
Philip, a leader in the church in Jerusalem, began his evangelistic ministry in Sebaste (also called Samaria). God then led him south toward Gaza, where he explained the gospel to a God-fearing Ethiopian royal official. Afterwards Philip was transported by God to Azotus, where he preached and continued his ministry up to Caesarea.

8:1 they were all scattered. The scattering or "dispersion" (Gk. *diaspeirō*, "to scatter, disperse") of the believers **throughout the regions of Judea and Samaria** was similar to the earlier *diaspora* ("dispersion") of Jews throughout the world (see note on John 7:35), but this "dispersion" led to the fulfillment of the promise in Acts 1:8 that the gospel would go to the end of the earth (cf. James 1:1; 1 Pet. 1:1).

8:3 Saul was instrumental in the persecution, as he testifies later in Acts (22:4–5; 26:10–11) and in his epistles (1 Cor. 15:9; Gal. 1:13, 23; Phil. 3:6; 1 Tim. 1:13).

8:4–40 *Philip Witnesses beyond Jerusalem.* With his message of a God not bound to one people or place, Stephen had laid the foundation for a worldwide mission. Philip, who like Stephen was a Hellenist, was the first to put Stephen's vision into practice, witnessing to the Samaritans (vv. 4–25) and to a God-fearing Ethiopian (vv. 26–40).

8:4–25 *Witness to the Samaritans.* The gospel spreads to the Samaritans through the witness of Philip and the apostles Peter and John.

8:5 Philip most likely visited ancient Sebaste, the main city of the Samaritans, lying at the foot of their holy mountain Gerizim. The Samaritans were a racially mixed group of partly Jewish and partly Gentile ancestry, disdained by both Jews and non-Jews (see notes on John 4:4; 4:20–21). They believed in Israel's God and in many respects maintained their Jewish heritage but were not considered Jews by those from Judah.

8:6 The Samaritans would have been prepared for Philip's message about the Christ (Messiah). They had their own expectation of a prophetic Messiah called the Taheb, who they believed would come to their holy mountain (see John 4:20). John the Baptist and Jesus had previously ministered in this area (John 3:23; 4:4–42). Like the apostles, **Philip** had received the Holy Spirit's power to cast out demons and to heal, which served as a sign confirming the truth of his message.

14[w]ver. 1 [x]ch. 1:8
15[y]ch. 2:38
16[z][ch. 19:2] [a]ch. 10:44; 11:15 [b]ch. 19:5; [ch. 2:38; 10:47, 48; Matt. 28:19; 1 Cor. 1:13, 15; Gal. 3:27]
17[c]ch. 9:17; 19:6; [ch. 6:6; Heb. 6:2] [d]See ch. 2:4
20[e][2 Kgs. 5:16; Dan. 5:17] [f]Isa. 55:1
21[g]2 Kgs. 10:15; Ps. 78:37
22[h]Dan. 4:27; 2 Tim. 2:25
23[i]Deut. 29:18; 32:32; Heb. 12:15 [j]Isa. 58:6; [Eph. 4:3; Col. 3:14]
24[k][Ex. 8:8; 9:28; 10:17]
25[l][ver. 6-8; John 4:39]
26[m]ch. 5:19; 10:3; 11:13; 12:7, 23; 27:23; [Judg. 6:12; 13:3]
27[n]Ps. 68:31; 87:4; Zeph. 3:10 [o][Jer. 38:7] [p]Ezra 7:21 [q][1 Kgs. 8:41, 42; John 12:20]
31[r]See Rom. 10:14 [s]John 16:13 [t][1 Kgs. 20:33; 2 Kgs. 10:15]

14 Now when [w]the apostles at Jerusalem heard that [x]Samaria had received the word
of God, they sent to them Peter and John, **15** who came down and prayed for them [y]that
they might receive the Holy Spirit, **16** for [z]he had not yet [a]fallen on any of them, but [b]they
had only been baptized in the name of the Lord Jesus. **17** Then [c]they laid their hands on
them and [d]they received the Holy Spirit. **18** Now when Simon saw that the Spirit was
given through the laying on of the apostles' hands, he offered them money, **19** saying,
"Give me this power also, so that anyone on whom I lay my hands may receive the Holy
Spirit." **20** But Peter said to him, [e]"May your silver perish with you, because you thought
you could obtain the gift of God [f]with money! **21** You have neither part nor lot in this
matter, for [g]your heart is not right before God. **22** Repent, therefore, of this wickedness
of yours, and pray to the Lord that, [h]if possible, the intent of your heart may be forgiven
you. **23** For I see that you are in [i]the gall[1] of bitterness and in [j]the bond of iniquity." **24** And
Simon answered, [k]"Pray for me to the Lord, that nothing of what you have said may
come upon me."

25 Now when they had testified and spoken the word of the Lord, they returned to
Jerusalem, [l]preaching the gospel to many villages of the Samaritans.

Philip and the Ethiopian Eunuch

26 Now [m]an angel of the Lord said to Philip, "Rise and go toward the south[2] to the road
that goes down from Jerusalem to Gaza." This is a desert place. **27** And he rose and went. And
there was an [n]Ethiopian, a [o]eunuch, a court official of Candace, queen of the Ethiopians,
[p]who was in charge of all her treasure. [q]He had come to Jerusalem to worship **28** and was
returning, seated in his chariot, and he was reading the prophet Isaiah. **29** And the Spirit
said to Philip, "Go over and join this chariot." **30** So Philip ran to him and heard him reading Isaiah the prophet and asked, "Do you understand what you are reading?" **31** And he
said, [r]"How can I, unless someone [s]guides me?" And [t]he invited Philip to come up and sit
with him. **32** Now the passage of the Scripture that he was reading was this:

[1] That is, a bitter fluid secreted by the liver; bile [2] Or *go at about noon*

8:9 Simon claimed to have divine powers, calling himself "the Great One." (On ancient magic, see note on 13:6.)

8:13 Not only the Samaritans but Simon also **believed** and was **baptized**. Commentators differ over whether Simon had genuine saving faith. Peter's strong rebuke to Simon soon after would suggest that Simon did not have genuine saving faith (see vv. 20–21).

8:14 The apostles at Jerusalem retained their authority over the entire church. When they heard of Philip's Samaritan mission, they sent Peter and John to verify its legitimacy.

8:17 they received the Holy Spirit. Apparently in this unique case, where the gospel was first moving beyond the bounds of Judaism, the Lord sovereignly waited to give any manifestation of the full power of the Holy Spirit (cf. vv. 15–16) until some of the apostles themselves could be present (Philip was not an apostle), and therefore there would be no question at all that the Samaritans had received the new covenant empowering of the Holy Spirit in the same way that the Jewish Christians had. This would show that the Samaritans should be counted full members of the one true church, the new covenant community of God's people, founded and based at that time in Jerusalem. It would also guarantee that the Samaritans, who for many generations had been hostile toward the Jews, would not establish a separate Christian church or be excluded from the church by Jewish believers. The Spirit was given only at the hands of the apostles, to show convincingly to Samaritan and other later, non-Jewish leaders of the church that both Jews and non-Jews who believed in Jesus now had full membership status among God's people (see Rom. 11:13–24; Eph. 2:11–22).

8:18 Simon saw that the Spirit was given. Since this was outwardly evident to Simon and no doubt to others as well, there must have been some outward manifestation of the Spirit. This may have been speaking in tongues, prophesying, or both (see 10:46; 19:6), and it was an evident sign to the apostles that the Holy Spirit had fallen on the Samaritans in a similar way to what had happened to the apostles and those with them at Pentecost. **offered them money**. Simon was acting in character, because magicians often exchanged secrets for money.

8:21 Neither part nor lot is OT language for having no share in something (see Deut. 12:12; 14:27), and this seems to indicate that Simon has now disclosed the condition of his heart and that he did not truly belong to the people of God. The strong language in Acts 8:23 also seems to class Simon as an unbeliever (but see note on v. 13).

8:24 Whether Simon was truly repentant or not is unclear. Against that possibility is the tradition tied to Simon that he was the "first heretic" and the fact that he does not indicate he will do anything to show repentance.

8:25 This transitional verse shows the apostles preaching in **many villages of the Samaritans** along their route back **to Jerusalem**—a fulfillment of 1:8 concerning expansion of the gospel into Samaritan territory.

8:26–40 *Witness to an Ethiopian Eunuch.* Philip was next led to witness to an Ethiopian. This passage strongly emphasizes the Spirit's leading.

8:26–27 Gaza was the last watering place before the desert on the road from Jerusalem to Egypt. Ethiopia was the ancient Nubian Kingdom, south of Aswan on the Nile. The designation **eunuch** could have been a mere title (for a "treasurer" or trusted royal servant), or could refer to his having been emasculated. Since he had been **to Jerusalem to worship**, the eunuch was probably a "God-fearer," a Gentile who worshiped Israel's God but had not become a full convert ("proselyte"). As a eunuch, he would have been barred from the inner courts of the temple, which makes his reading "the prophet Isaiah" (v. 28) especially significant. Isaiah held out the promise that God would grant devout eunuchs a heritage "better than sons and daughters" (Isa. 56:3–5).

8:30 The Holy Spirit directed Philip to approach the eunuch. People usually read aloud in those days, so Philip was probably aware that the eunuch was reading Isa. 53:7–8. A more appropriate passage could not have been chosen as a witness to Christ, attesting to the Holy Spirit's leading. The passage cited focuses on the injustice done to Jesus, something that reflects Luke's presentation of the cross (see Luke 23), as well as the death of Stephen, who followed in his way.

[u]"Like a sheep he was led to the slaughter
and like a lamb before its shearer is silent,
so he opens not his mouth.
33 In his [v]humiliation justice was denied him.
Who can describe his generation?
For his life is taken away from the earth."

34 And the eunuch said to Philip, "About whom, I ask you, does the prophet say this,
about himself or about someone else?" 35 Then Philip opened his mouth, and [w]begin-
ning with this Scripture [x]he told him the good news about Jesus. 36 And as they were
going along the road they came to some water, and the eunuch said, "See, here is water!
[y]What prevents me from being baptized?"[1] 38 And he commanded the chariot to stop,
and they both went down into the water, Philip and the eunuch, and he baptized him.
39 And when they came up out of the water, [z]the Spirit of the Lord [a]carried Philip away,
and the eunuch saw him no more, and went on his way rejoicing. 40 But Philip found
himself at Azotus, and as he passed through he preached the gospel to all the towns
until he came to Caesarea.

The Conversion of Saul

9 But Saul, [b]still [c]breathing threats and murder against the disciples of the Lord,
went to [d]the high priest 2 and asked him for letters [e]to the synagogues at Damascus,
so that if he found any belonging to [f]the Way, men or women, he might bring them
bound to Jerusalem. 3 [g]Now as he went on his way, he approached Damascus, and suddenly a light from heaven shone around him. 4 And falling to the ground he heard a
voice saying to him, "Saul, Saul, why are you persecuting [h]me?" 5 And he said, "Who
are you, Lord?" And he said, "I am Jesus, [h]whom you are persecuting. 6 But [i]rise and
enter the city, and you will be told [j]what you are to do." 7 [k]The men who were traveling

[1] Some manuscripts add all or most of verse 37: *And Philip said, "If you believe with all your heart, you may." And he replied, "I believe that Jesus Christ is the Son of God."*

32 [u]Cited from Isa. 53:7, 8
33 [v][Phil. 2:8]
35 [w]Luke 24:27; [ch. 17:2; 18:28] [x]See ch. 5:42
36 [y]ch. 10:47
39 [z]1 Kgs. 18:12; 2 Kgs. 2:16; Ezek. 3:12, 14; 8:3; 11:1, 24; 43:5 [a]See 2 Cor. 12:2

Chapter 9

1 [b]ver. 13, 21; See ch. 8:3 [c][Ps. 27:12] [d]ch. 22:5; 26:10
2 [e]ch. 22:19; [Luke 12:11; 21:12] [f]ch. 19:9, 23; 24:14, 22; [ch. 16:17; 18:25, 26; 22:4; Isa. 30:21; 35:8; Amos 8:14]
3 [g]For ver. 3-8, see ch. 22:6-11; 26:12-18; [1 Cor. 15:8]
4 [h][Isa. 63:9; Zech. 2:8]
5 [h][See ver. 4 above]
6 [i][Ezek. 3:22; Gal. 1:1] [j]ver. 16; [1 Cor. 9:16]
7 [k][Dan. 10:7]

8:36 The direction of the Holy Spirit in this incident is apparent again as Philip and the eunuch arrive at a rare watering place in the desert precisely when the eunuch requested baptism.

8:39 Philip was snatched up and **carried . . . away**, much like Elijah was (2 Kings 2:11).

8:40 Philip was then taken to witness in the coastal region, first in **Azotus** (OT Ashdod), then in **Caesarea**, where he seems to have settled (see 21:8). Caesarea was a city with a large Greek-speaking population. Originally a small harbor town known as Strato's Tower, it was rebuilt by Herod the Great in magnificent Hellenistic style with a greatly improved harbor. In Philip's day it was the seat of the Roman government of Judea. Excavations have yielded significant finds, including the Herodian port and theater, an "amphitheater" shaped like a hippodrome for horse races, a palace built on a promontory out into the sea (frequently identified as Herod's palace), and a great raised aqueduct. Herod built a temple to Augustus here, and an inscription found in the theater mentions Pontius Pilate's dedication of a *Tiberium* (a sacred site devoted to the emperor Tiberius). Tense relations existed between the mixed Jewish and Gentile inhabitants, and one cause of the First Jewish Revolt (A.D. 66–73) was the Gentile desecration of the Jewish synagogue in Caesarea.

9:1–31 *The Conversion of Saul.* The conversion of Saul may seem like something of an interruption in the Acts narrative, since in this section of Acts (chs. 6–12) Luke deals primarily with the witness of the Jerusalem church through the dispersed Hellenists (Greek-speaking Jews) and the apostle Peter. Paul's conversion fits into this time frame, however, and as a Greek-speaking Diaspora Jew he was a "Hellenist" himself and eventually the prime leader in their outreach to the Gentiles. His conversion is related in detail three times in Acts: here in narrative form, and twice subsequently in Paul's testimony before a Jewish mob (22:3–11) and before King Agrippa II (26:2–18). Luke does not record the date of Paul's conversion, but a reasonable estimate is c. A.D. 33–34.

9:1–9 *Saul's Encounter with Christ.* While traveling to Damascus to arrest any Christians who might be there, Saul encountered the risen Christ and, blinded by a dazzling light, was led into the city to await further instructions.

9:1–2 The account of **Saul** resumes from 8:3. Saul's papers from the high priest may have been official extradition documents or **letters** of introduction to the **synagogues at Damascus**. It is not known how Christianity had come to Damascus—perhaps through converts at Pentecost or by some of those "scattered" following Stephen's martyrdom (8:1). This is the first time in Acts that Christians are described as **belonging to the Way** (Gk. *hodos*, "road, highway, way of life"), meaning either the way of salvation (16:17; cf. Jesus' teachings in Matt. 7:14; John 14:6) or the true way of life in relation to God (cf. Acts 18:25–26; cf. Ps. 1:1, 6; 27:11). The expression also occurs at Acts 19:9, 23; 22:4; 24:14, 22.

9:3 Damascus was 135 miles (217 km) northeast of Jerusalem, a six-day journey by foot. Settled as early as the second millennium B.C., Damascus was an oasis on the border of the Arabian desert and on the main route from Mesopotamia to Egypt. The Nabatean king Aretas IV maintained an ethnarch (i.e., governor) in Damascus (2 Cor. 11:32). Although the modern city of Damascus stands atop the ancient remains, one can still see the "street called Straight" (Acts 9:11) running east to west with its East Gate and monumental arch. Also visible are the ancient theater and the concentric courts of its temple to Jupiter (now replaced by a mosque). Jewish presence in Damascus (assumed by the mention of synagogues in vv. 2, 20) is confirmed in Josephus's record that many thousands of Jewish people were killed in Damascus during the time of the First Jewish Revolt (A.D. 66–73; see *Jewish War* 2.559–561). For the brilliance of the **light**, see Acts 22:6 and 26:13, where it is described as exceeding the midday sun.

9:4 Jesus' reference to Saul's "**persecuting me**" shows his close identity with his followers: to persecute Christians was to persecute Christ.

with him stood speechless, [l]hearing the voice but seeing no one. 8 Saul rose from the
ground, and although his eyes were opened, [m]he saw nothing. So they led him by the
hand and brought him into Damascus. 9 And for three days he was without sight, and
neither ate nor drank.
10 Now there was a disciple at Damascus named [n]Ananias. The Lord said to him in a
vision, "Ananias." And he said, [o]"Here I am, Lord." 11 And the Lord said to him, "Rise and
go to the street called Straight, and at the house of Judas look for a man [p]of Tarsus named
Saul, for behold, he is praying, 12 and he has seen in a vision a man named Ananias come
in and [q]lay his hands on him so that he might regain his sight." 13 But Ananias answered,
"Lord, I have heard from many about this man, [r]how much evil he has done to [s]your [t]saints
at Jerusalem. 14 And here he has authority from [u]the chief priests to bind all who [v]call on
your name." 15 But the Lord said to him, "Go, for [w]he is a chosen instrument of mine to
carry my name [x]before the Gentiles and [y]kings and the children of Israel. 16 For [z]I will show
him how much [a]he must suffer [b]for the sake of my name." 17 So [c]Ananias departed and
entered the house. And [d]laying his hands on him he said, "Brother Saul, the Lord Jesus
who appeared to you on the road by which you came has sent me so that you may regain
your sight and [e]be filled with the Holy Spirit." 18 And immediately something like scales

7 [l][ch. 22:9 with John 12:29]
8 [m][ch. 22:11]
10 [n]ch. 22:12 [o]Gen. 22:1; Isa. 6:8
11 [p]ch. 21:39; 22:3
12 [q]ver. 17; See Mark 5:23
13 [r]ver. 1, 2 [s]1 Thess. 3:13; 2 Thess. 1:10 [t]Rom. 15:25, 26, 31
14 [u]ver. 21 [v]ch. 22:16; Rom. 10:13; 1 Cor. 1:2; [ch. 7:59; 2 Tim. 2:22]
15 [w][ch. 13:2; Rom. 1:1; Gal. 1:15; Eph. 3:7] [x]Rom. 1:5 (Gk.); 11:13; 15:16; Gal. 1:16; 2:2, 7-9; Eph. 3:7, 8; 1 Tim. 2:7; 2 Tim. 4:17 [y]ch. 25:22, 23; 26:1, 32; 2 Tim. 4:16
16 [z]ch. 20:23; 21:4, 11; 1 Thess. 3:3 [a]ver. 6; [ch. 14:22; 2 Cor. 6:4, 5; 11:23-28] [b]See ch. 5:41
17 [c]ch. 22:12-14 [d]ver. 12 [e]See ch. 2:4

9:5 "Who are you, Lord?" Though Paul was ultimately blinded by the bright light (cf. vv. 3, 8–9), he indicates elsewhere that he actually saw the risen Christ on this occasion (see 1 Cor. 9:1; 15:8; Gal. 1:16; cf. Acts 9:27). The scene is significant not only because of Saul's conversion but also because it shows that he would have known of the resurrection from direct experience of Jesus and thus could come to appreciate why this was a key part of the Christian message (see 1 Corinthians 15).

9:7 Saul's companions heard the **voice** but saw **no one**. In his later testimony to the Jews, Paul spoke of them seeing the light but not understanding the voice (22:9). They had no vision of Jesus nor did they hear the message to Saul, but they could testify to a brilliant light and a sound, which pointed to an objective event that was not a matter of Saul's imagination.

9:9 Saul's blindness and his fasting should not be seen as punishment but as a result of the intensity of his encounter with Christ. However, like the deaf-muteness of Zechariah in Luke 1, it was designed to produce a time of reflection.

9:10–19a *Saul's Encounter with Ananias.* Jesus appeared to a believer in Damascus, instructing him to go to Saul, assist him in recovery of his sight, and inform him of his special calling.

9:10 The Lord is Jesus and not the Father (see v. 17). Ananias's response, **Here I am**, is reminiscent of OT predecessors such as Abraham (Gen. 22:1, 11), Jacob (Gen. 31:11; 46:2), Moses (Ex. 3:11), Samuel (1 Sam. 3:4–8), and Isaiah (Isa. 6:8).

9:11 The street called Straight is one of the world's oldest continually occupied streets, still existing today (see note on v. 3). **Tarsus**. See note on v. 30.

9:15 In the remainder of Acts, Saul (later called Paul) preaches to Gentiles and also to **kings** (Agrippa II, ch. 26) as well as to the **children of Israel**, since in each city he always goes first to Jewish synagogues.

9:17 Ananias's **laying his hands** (see note on 6:6) on Saul was a physical symbol of the invisible power of the Holy Spirit coming to heal Saul from his blindness and dwell within him in new covenant fullness (see note on 2:4).

9:18 something like scales fell from his eyes. This physical event was also a symbol that Saul's spiritual blindness had been overcome and he could now see and understand the truth (cf. 2 Cor. 3:14 for a related image). (Note that the change of Saul's name to Paul [which will be first reported in Acts 13:9] is not connected with his conversion; he continues having a right to both names, the first Jewish, the second Roman; Paul continues to call himself [and to be called] Saul until his ministry in Cyprus [13:9].) **was baptized**. Through baptism Saul made an immediate public declaration of his faith in Jesus as the Messiah.

Paul's (Saul's) Conversion and Early Travels

C. A.D. 35–39

As Paul approached Damascus to arrest followers of the Way, Jesus appeared to him (1). Galatians 1:17 makes it clear that soon after this Paul spent time in Arabia (2, 3) before going to meet church leaders in Jerusalem (4). When some believers learned of a plot to kill Paul in Jerusalem, they took him to Caesarea, and he returned to his hometown of Tarsus (5).

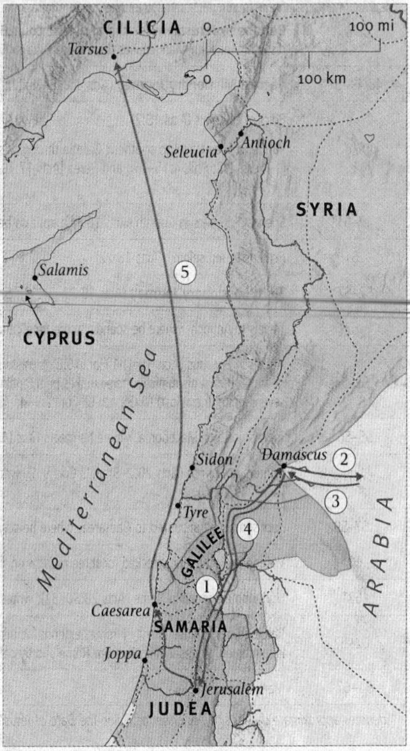

Major Events in the Life of the Apostle Paul

A.D. 5–10?	Born in Tarsus as an Israelite from the tribe of Benjamin and a Roman citizen (Acts 22:3, 28; Rom. 11:1; Phil. 3:5); raised in either Jerusalem (Acts 22:3?) or Tarsus
15–20?	Trained as a Pharisee by Gamaliel I (Acts 22:3; 26:5; Gal. 1:14; Phil. 3:5–6)
30/33†	Death, resurrection of Christ
31–34	Present at Stephen's stoning; persecuted Christians (Acts 7:58; 8:1; 22:4a; 26:9–11; 1 Cor. 15:9; Gal. 1:13; Phil. 3:6)
33/34*	**Converted, called, and commissioned on the way to Damascus** (Acts 9:1–19; 22:6–11; 26:12–18; Gal. 1:15–16)
33/34–36/37	Stays in Damascus a short time (Acts 9:19b); leaves for "Arabia" (i.e., Nabataean Kingdom; 2 Cor. 11:32; Gal. 1:17); returns to Damascus (Gal. 1:17; Acts 9:20–22?); Jews and the governor under King Aretas try to arrest and kill him; Paul escapes through the city wall (Acts 9:23–24; 2 Cor. 11:32–33)
36/37*	**Meets with Peter (and sees James) in Jerusalem** (Acts 9:26–30; Gal. 1:18) Hellenists seek to kill him and he flees to Tarsus (Acts 9:28–30; Gal. 1:21)
37–45	Ministers in Syria/Cilicia (2 Cor. 11:22–27?)
42–44	Receives his "thorn in the flesh" (2 Cor. 12:7–9)
44	Herod Agrippa I dies (Acts 12:20–23)
44–47*	Spends a year ministering with Barnabas in Antioch (Acts 11:25–26) **Second Visit to Jerusalem**; time of famine (Acts 11:27–30; Gal. 2:1–10)
46–47	**First Missionary Journey** (Acts 13:4–14:26): 1.5 years?
48*	Paul and Barnabas spend "no little time" in Antioch (Acts 14:28; cf. Gal. 2:11–14); Paul writes letter to the Galatians
48–49*	**Returns to Jerusalem for the apostolic council** (Acts 15); Paul and Barnabas return to Antioch (Acts 15:30–33), but a dispute over John Mark causes them to part ways (Acts 15:36–41)
48/49–51*	**Second Missionary Journey** (Acts 15:36–18:22): 2.5 years?
49	Edict of Claudius (Acts 18:2) Paul and Silas travel to southern Galatia through Asia Minor, on to Macedonia (notably Philippi [1 Thess. 2:2]); Thessalonica [1 Thess. 2:2; Phil. 4:15–16]; and Berea [Acts 17:10–15]), and then Achaia (notably Athens [1 Thess. 3:1] and Corinth [2 Cor. 11:7–9])
49–51*	Spends 1.5 years in Corinth (Acts 18:11); appears before Gallio (Acts 18:12–17); writes 1 and 2 Thessalonians
51	Returns to Jerusalem? (Acts 18:22)
52–57*	**Third Missionary Journey** (Acts 18:23–21:17): 5 years?
52	Travels to Antioch, where he spends "some time"; then travels through Galatia and Phrygia (Acts 18:23)
52–55	Arrives in Ephesus (Acts 19:1; 1 Cor. 16:8); ministers there for three years (Acts 20:31) and writes 1 Corinthians in the spring, near the end of his ministry there; makes brief, "painful visit" to Corinth (2 Cor. 2:1), then returns to Ephesus and writes "tearful, severe letter" (now lost) to Corinth (2 Cor. 2:3–4; 7:8–16)
55–56*	Travels north to Macedonia, where he meets Titus (Acts 20:1; cf. 2 Cor. 2:12–13); writes 2 Corinthians
57*	Winters in Corinth (Acts 20:2–3; cf. 2 Cor. 9:4), writes letter to the Romans from Corinth; travels to Jerusalem and is arrested (Acts 21:27–36)
57–59	Imprisonment transferred to Caesarea, where he stays for two years (Acts 24:27)
60*	Voyage to Rome; shipwrecked for three months on the island of Malta (Acts 28:11); finally arrives in Rome
62*	Under house-arrest in Rome (Acts 28:30–31), writes Ephesians, Philippians, Colossians, Philemon
62–67	Released from house-arrest in Rome, extends his mission (Spain?), writes 1 Timothy (from Macedonia?) and Titus (from Nicopolis); is rearrested, writes 2 Timothy from Rome shortly before his execution
64–67*	Martyred in Rome

** denotes approximate date; / signifies either/or; † See The Date of Jesus' Crucifixion, pp. 1809–1810*

18[f]ch. 22:13 [g]ch. 22:16
19[h][ver. 9] [i]ch. 26:20
20[j][ver. 22]
21[k]ver. 13, 14 [l]Gal. 1:13, 23
22[m]See 1 Tim. 1:12 [n]ch. 18:28 [o][ver. 20]
23[p][Gal. 1:17, 18]
24[q]ch. 20:3, 19; 23:30; [ch. 23:12; 25:3] [r]2 Cor. 11:32
25[s]2 Cor. 11:33; [Josh. 2:15; 1 Sam. 19:12]
26[t]ch. 22:17-20; 26:20
27[u]ch. 4:36 [v][Gal. 1:18, 19] [w]ver. 3-6 [x]ver. 19, 20, 22 [y]See ch. 4:29
28[z]ch. 1:21
29[a]See ch. 6:1 [b][ch. 22:18]
30[c]See John 21:23 [d][ch. 11:25; Gal. 1:21]
31[e][ch. 8:1; 16:5] [f][Neh. 5:9] [g]ver. 35, 42

fell from his eyes, and [f]he regained his sight. Then [g]he rose and was baptized; **19** and [h]tak-
ing food, he was strengthened.

Saul Proclaims Jesus in Synagogues

For [i]some days he was with the disciples at Damascus. **20** And immediately he proclaimed
Jesus in the synagogues, saying, [j]"He is the Son of God." **21** And all who heard him were
amazed and said, "Is not this the man who [k]made havoc [l]in Jerusalem of those who called
upon this name? And has he not come here for this purpose, to bring them bound before
the chief priests?" **22** But Saul [m]increased all the more in strength, and [n]confounded the
Jews who lived in Damascus by proving [o]that Jesus was the Christ.

Saul Escapes from Damascus

23 [p]When many days had passed, the Jews[1] plotted to kill him, **24** but their [q]plot became
known to Saul. [r]They were watching the gates day and night in order to kill him, **25** but his
disciples took him by night and [s]let him down through an opening in the wall,[2] lowering
him in a basket.

Saul in Jerusalem

26 And [t]when he had come to Jerusalem, he attempted to join the disciples. And they
were all afraid of him, for they did not believe that he was a disciple. **27** But [u]Barnabas
took him and [v]brought him to the apostles and declared to them [w]how on the road he
had seen the Lord, who spoke to him, and [x]how at Damascus he had [y]preached boldly in
the name of Jesus. **28** So he went [z]in and out among them at Jerusalem, preaching boldly
in the name of the Lord. **29** And he spoke and disputed against [a]the Hellenists.[3] But [b]they
were seeking to kill him. **30** And when [c]the brothers learned this, they brought him down
to Caesarea and sent him off [d]to Tarsus.

31 So [e]the church throughout all Judea and Galilee and Samaria had peace and was being
built up. And [f]walking in the fear of the Lord and in the comfort of the Holy Spirit, [g]it
multiplied.

[1] The Greek word *Ioudaioi* refers specifically here to Jewish religious leaders, and others under their influence, who opposed the Christian faith in that time
[2] Greek *through the wall* [3] That is, Greek-speaking Jews

9:19b–31 *Saul's Witness in Damascus and Jerusalem.* This section reports Saul's witness to Christ in Damascus and Jerusalem. In Gal. 1:11–24, Paul provides an account of this same period.

9:19b–20 Saul likely received instruction in the Christian "way" from the **disciples at Damascus**. In Galatians, Paul notes that during this time he "went away into Arabia, and returned again to Damascus" (Gal. 1:17). ("Arabia" here means the Nabatean Kingdom, northeast of the Dead Sea, not the Arabian Peninsula.) **synagogues**. The pattern of Paul's beginning his witness in the synagogues occurs throughout Acts, as does the pattern of opposition developing there (Acts 9:23).

9:23 The Jews does not mean all Jews, of course, since many Jews had believed in Jesus and Paul himself was a Jew. But from this point forward in Acts, Luke often uses the phrase "the Jews" as a shorthand expression to refer to Jewish people who opposed the gospel (see ESV footnote; see also 12:3; 13:45, 50; 14:4; 17:5, 13; 18:12; etc.). Often it is the leaders of communities who are involved in this rejection. **plotted to kill him**. Enemies of the gospel cannot defeat it by free and open debate, so they often resort to force, falsehood, murder, and governmental suppression (cf. 9:29). But the gospel is from God and cannot be stopped. Elsewhere Paul specifies that "the governor under King Aretas" was helping in the attempt to kill him (see 2 Cor. 11:32–33).

9:24 their plot became known to Saul. The Holy Spirit intervenes again and again to protect Saul (cf. 23:16–22).

9:25 Sometimes God does not call his people to stand and lose their lives but rather to escape from the danger that he has revealed to them. Because **his disciples took** decisive action, Paul's life was preserved for his future ministry, for at this point he had not begun his major missionary journeys or written any of his letters.

9:27 Barnabas, "son of encouragement" (4:36), interceded for Saul, introducing him **to the apostles** (in Jerusalem), who were initially skeptical about his conversion. According to Gal. 1:18–19, this visit took place three years (see note on Acts 11:27–30) after his conversion (which could make this c. A.D. 37), and Paul met with Peter for 15 days but had no substantial interaction with the other apostles, except for meeting James, the brother of Jesus.

9:29 The **Hellenists** here are not the same as the Jewish believers called "Hellenists" in 6:1; in this instance they were Jews and not Christians, perhaps some of the same who had seized Stephen (6:8–14). (For the term "Hellenist," see note on 6:1.)

9:30 On **Caesarea**, see note on 8:40. Paul's hometown of Tarsus was a strategically important Cilician city in southeast Asia Minor on the road from Syria into central Asia Minor. Paul calls it "no obscure city" (21:39). Founded on the banks of the river Cydnus, it oversaw the important harbor on Lake Rhegma (approximately 5 miles/8 km south on the Cydnus). The vital Cilician Gates, which allowed passage across the Taurus Mountains, were approximately 25 miles (40 km) north. Alexander the Great had stayed in Tarsus, Pompey had based his campaign against sea pirates on the city, and Antony first met Cleopatra in Tarsus. Tarsus was known as a home to philosophers, especially those of the Stoic school. Archaeologists have uncovered a basalt street with limestone gutters from the NT period, and one can also see the foundations of a huge second-century-A.D. temple (known as the Donuktash). **to Tarsus**. This corresponds to Gal. 1:21, where Paul says he went to "Cilicia," the province in which Tarsus was located. Paul would be based in Tarsus and minister in Syria-Cilicia for the next eight years (c. A.D. 37–45). Some of the events of 2 Cor. 11:23–27 perhaps occurred during this time, and probably also his intense vision of heaven (2 Cor. 12:2–4). Saul is not mentioned again in Acts until Barnabas goes to Tarsus to find him in Acts 11:25. Saul will begin to be called Paul in 13:9.

9:31 the church throughout all Judea and Galilee and Samaria. There must have been hundreds of churches in the small cities and towns throughout this large region, but all of them together can be called a "church" (Gk. *ekklēsia*, singular in the earliest and best manuscripts of this verse, though some later manuscripts have the plural). The NT can apply the singular word "church" to the church meeting in a home (Rom. 16:5; 1 Cor. 16:19), in an entire city (1 Cor. 1:2; 2 Cor. 1:1), in a large region (as here), or throughout the whole world (1 Cor. 12:28; Eph. 5:25). **Peace** came to the church after

The Healing of Aeneas

[32]Now [h]as Peter went here and there among them all, he came down also to the saints
who lived at Lydda. [33]There he found a man named Aeneas, bedridden for eight years,
who was paralyzed. [34]And Peter said to him, "Aeneas, [i]Jesus Christ heals you; rise and
make your bed." And immediately he rose. [35][j]And all the residents of Lydda and [k]Sharon
saw him, and [l]they turned to the Lord.

Dorcas Restored to Life

[36]Now there was in [m]Joppa a disciple named Tabitha, which, translated, means Dorcas.[1]
She was full of [n]good works and acts of charity. [37]In those days she became ill and died, and
when they had washed her, they laid her in [o]an upper room. [38]Since Lydda was near Joppa,
the disciples, hearing that Peter was there, sent two men to him, urging him, [p]"Please come
to us without delay." [39]So Peter rose and went with them. And when he arrived, they took
him to [q]the upper room. All the widows stood beside him weeping and showing tunics[2]
and other garments that Dorcas made while she was with them. [40]But Peter [r]put them all
outside, and [s]knelt down and prayed; and turning to the body [t]he said, "Tabitha, arise."
And she opened her eyes, and when she saw Peter she sat up. [41]And he gave her his hand
and raised her up. Then calling the saints and widows, he presented her alive. [42]And it
became known throughout all Joppa, and [u]many believed in the Lord. [43]And he stayed
in Joppa for many days [v]with one Simon, a tanner.

Peter and Cornelius

10 At Caesarea there was a man named Cornelius, a centurion of [w]what was known
as the Italian Cohort, [2]a devout man [x]who feared God with all his household, gave
alms generously to the people, and prayed continually to God. [3][y]About the ninth hour of

[1] The Aramaic name *Tabitha* and the Greek name *Dorcas* both mean *gazelle* [2] Greek *chiton*, a long garment worn under the cloak next to the skin

32 [h][ch. 8:25]
34 [i][ch. 3:6]
35 [j][ver. 31, 42] [k]1 Chr. 5:16; 27:29; Song 2:1 [l]ch. 11:21; 2 Cor. 3:16
36 [m]See Josh. 19:46 [n]1 Tim. 2:10
37 [o]ver. 39; ch. 1:13; 20:8
38 [p]Num. 22:16 (Heb.; Gk.)
39 [q]ver. 37
40 [r]Matt. 9:25 [s]See ch. 7:60 [t][Mark 5:41; John 11:43]
42 [u][John 11:45; 12:11]
43 [v]ch. 10:6

Chapter 10

1 [w]Matt. 27:27; Mark 15:16; John 18:3, 12
2 [x]ver. 22; ch. 13:16, 26
3 [y]See ch. 3:1

the conversion of its prime persecutor (see also Gal. 1:22–24). **Fear of the Lord** does not mean fear of final judgment but is a common theme in Acts referring either to fear as godly awe, reverence, and devotion (as in Acts 2:43; 10:2; 13:26) or fear of God's displeasure and fatherly discipline (as in 5:5, 11; 16:29; 19:17; see also Heb. 12:7–10).

9:32–11:18 *Peter Preaches in the Coastal Towns.* Peter began to witness outside Jerusalem in the coastal plain of Judea, healing the lame Aeneas (9:32–35) and restoring life to Dorcas (9:36–43). God then led him to witness to a group of Gentiles at Caesarea (10:1–11:18).

9:32–43 *Healing of Aeneas and Dorcas.* Peter was last mentioned in his witness to the Samaritans (8:25). Now he turned to the fertile coastal plain of Sharon, where the next two recorded miracles took place.

9:32 Saints refers to Christians. **Lydda** is the OT Lod, 23 miles (37 km) northwest of Jerusalem on the road to Joppa. Lydda served as a regional

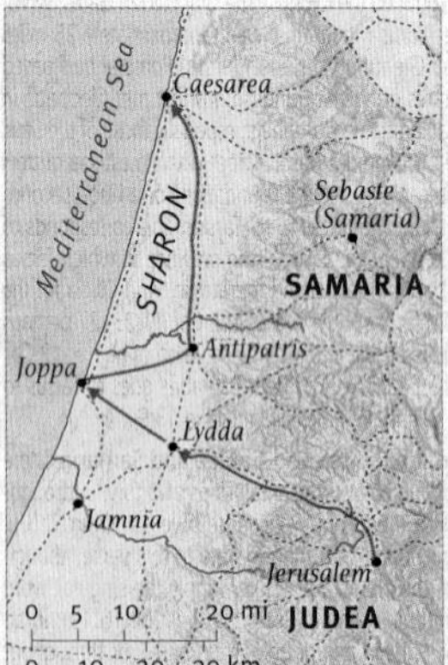

Peter's Early Ministry
C. A.D. 39?
The apostle Peter traveled to the crossroads town of Lydda and healed a paralyzed man, leading many in that region to turn to the Lord. Later Peter traveled to Joppa and raised a woman from the dead. While Peter was staying at the house of Simon, a tanner in Joppa, the Roman centurion Cornelius sent for him to come to Caesarea.

administrative town (toparchy) for Judea, and was on an important trade route.

9:33 Eight years points to the severity of his paralysis.

9:34 Jesus Christ heals you. See note on 3:6. Peter understands that Jesus is invisibly working to build his church. **Make your bed** probably refers to folding the mat on which he was lying.

9:35 they turned to the Lord. As is often the case in Acts, miracles such as this healing (cf. ch. 3) led to the advancement of the gospel. The news spread beyond the town of **Lydda** to the whole coastal plain of **Sharon**.

9:36 Joppa was on the coast, 11 miles (18 km) northwest of Lydda. The port city of Joppa (modern Jaffa/Yafa, just south of Tel Aviv) was captured by the Jewish Hasmoneans (2nd century B.C.) and contained a substantial Jewish population prior to the First Jewish Revolt (A.D. 66–73). Excavations under portions of the modern city have revealed evidence of first-century residences and an early fortress.

9:38 Hearing that Peter was there reflects an understanding that an unusual level of the Holy Spirit's power was present in the apostles.

9:40 Tabitha, arise. See note on 3:6. Peter had no supernatural power in his own words, but the Lord had showed him what he was going to do in response to Peter's prayer, and he imparted to Peter's heart the knowledge and faith that he was going to restore Tabitha to life as Peter spoke.

9:41 The Greek verb for **raised her up** is the same word used throughout the NT for Jesus' resurrection (Gk. *anistēmi*). Though her restoration to life was not permanent, it served to remind Christians of their promised resurrection in Christ.

9:42 many believed in the Lord. Once again there is the pattern that remarkable miracles lead to many more genuine conversions as the gospel spreads.

9:43 As a **tanner**, **Simon** worked with animal hides, which would explain his location close to the ocean breezes (10:6). This meant he was often left in an unclean state, but this was less significant since he is not in Jerusalem.

10:1–48 *Conversion of Cornelius.* The conversion of a Gentile soldier and his relatives and close friends is the longest narrative in Acts. The importance of the story is highlighted through repetition. The visions of Cornelius and Peter are repeated several times, and 11:1–18 is a detailed retelling of the events of ch. 10. The incident put Peter at the center of the mission to the Gentiles.

3[z]ver. 17, 19 [a]See ch. 8:26
4[b]Rev. 8:4; [Ps. 141:2; Dan. 10:12] [c]Matt. 26:13; Mark 14:9; [ver. 31; Heb. 6:10]
6[d]ch. 9:43
9[e]For ver. 9-32, see ch. 11:5-14 [f][2 Kgs. 23:12; Jer. 19:13; 32:29; Zeph. 1:5]; See 1 Sam. 9:25 [g]Ps. 55:17
10[h]ch. 22:17
11[i]See John 1:51
14[j]Ezek. 4:14; Dan. 1:8 [k]ver. 28 [l]Lev. 11:2-47; 20:25; Deut. 14:4-20
15[m]Rom. 14:2, 14, 20; 1 Tim. 4:4; Titus 1:15; [Matt. 15:11; Mark 7:15, 19; 1 Cor. 10:25]
17[n]ver. 3 [o]ver. 7, 8
19[n][See ver. 17 above] [p]See ch. 8:29
20[q][ch. 15:7-9]
22[r]See ver. 2 [s]See Mark 8:38 [t]ch. 11:14
23[u]ver. 45; [ch. 11:12] [v]See John 21:23
25[w]ch. 16:29; Dan. 2:46 [x]See Matt. 8:2
26[y]Rev. 19:10; 22:8, 9; [ch. 14:15]
28[z][ch. 11:3; John 4:9; 18:28; Gal. 2:12] [a][ver. 35]; See ver. 14, 15
30[b]ver. 9, 23, 24 [c]See ch. 3:1

the day[1] [z]he saw clearly in a vision [a]an angel of God come in and say to him, "Cornelius."
4 And he stared at him in terror and said, "What is it, Lord?" And he said to him, "Your
prayers and your alms [b]have ascended [c]as a memorial before God. **5** And now send men to
Joppa and bring one Simon who is called Peter. **6** He is lodging [d]with one Simon, a tanner,
whose house is by the sea." **7** When the angel who spoke to him had departed, he called two
of his servants and a devout soldier from among those who attended him, **8** and having
related everything to them, he sent them to Joppa.

Peter's Vision

9 The next day, as they were on their journey and approaching the city, [e]Peter went up
[f]on the housetop about [g]the sixth hour[2] to pray. **10** And he became hungry and wanted
something to eat, but while they were preparing it, he fell into [h]a trance **11** and saw [i]the
heavens opened and something like a great sheet descending, being let down by its four
corners upon the earth. **12** In it were all kinds of animals and reptiles and birds of the air.
13 And there came a voice to him: "Rise, Peter; kill and eat." **14** But Peter said, "By no means,
Lord; [j]for I have never eaten anything that is [k]common or [l]unclean." **15** And the voice came
to him again a second time, [m]"What God has made clean, do not call common." **16** This
happened three times, and the thing was taken up at once to heaven.

17 Now while Peter was inwardly perplexed as to what [n]the vision that he had seen
might mean, behold, [o]the men who were sent by Cornelius, having made inquiry for
Simon's house, stood at the gate **18** and called out to ask whether Simon who was called
Peter was lodging there. **19** And while Peter was pondering [n]the vision, [p]the Spirit said to
him, "Behold, three men are looking for you. **20** Rise and go down and [q]accompany them
without hesitation,[3] for I have sent them." **21** And Peter went down to the men and said,
"I am the one you are looking for. What is the reason for your coming?" **22** And they said,
"Cornelius, a centurion, an upright and [r]God-fearing man, who is well spoken of by the
whole Jewish nation, was directed by [s]a holy angel to send for you to come to his house
and [t]to hear what you have to say." **23** So he invited them in to be his guests.

The next day he rose and went away with them, and [u]some of [v]the brothers from Joppa
accompanied him. **24** And on the following day they entered Caesarea. Cornelius was expecting them and had called together his relatives and close friends. **25** When Peter entered,
Cornelius met him and [w]fell down at his feet and [x]worshiped him. **26** But Peter lifted him
up, saying, [y]"Stand up; I too am a man." **27** And as he talked with him, he went in and found
many persons gathered. **28** And he said to them, "You yourselves know how unlawful it is
for a Jew [z]to associate with or to visit anyone of another nation, but [a]God has shown me
that I should not call any person common or unclean. **29** So when I was sent for, I came
without objection. I ask then why you sent for me."

30 And Cornelius said, [b]"Four days ago, about this hour, I was praying in my house at [c]the

[1] That is, 3 P.M. [2] That is, noon [3] Or *accompany them, making no distinction*

10:1 Cornelius resided at **Caesarea**, a city on the coast 31 miles (50 km) north of Joppa; Caesarea was the seat of the Roman government of Judea (see note on 8:40). Cornelius was a **centurion**, a commander of 100 men, and a member of the **Italian Cohort**. (A "cohort" consisted of 600 men under the command of six centurions, but with auxiliary forces in remote areas such as Judea a "cohort" might have as many as 1,000 men.) Ten cohorts formed a "legion." Centurions were paid very well (as much as five times the pay of an ordinary soldier), so Cornelius would have been socially prominent and wealthy.

10:2 Devout man who feared God identifies Cornelius as a "God-fearer" (cf. v. 22; 13:16, 26), a Gentile who worshiped Israel's God and was in some way attached to a synagogue but who had not submitted to Jewish conversion rites (esp. circumcision). He followed two of the primary expressions of Jewish piety—prayer and almsgiving. **Alms** are gifts to the poor.

10:3–4 The **ninth hour** is 3:00 P.M. This was a set hour of prayer for Jews, not according to the OT but according to later tradition.

10:4 The designation of Cornelius's piety as a **memorial** is sacrificial language (cf. Lev. 2:2, 9, 16), indicating that something has been "remembered" by God (see Phil. 4:18).

10:5 Joppa was about 31 miles (50 km) south of Caesarea, along the coast.

10:7 Cornelius sent two of his most trusted **servants** and a **soldier**, whose description as being **devout** likely indicates he was a God-fearer himself.

10:9 housetop. Houses in Judea typically had flat roofs accessible by ladders or stairs.

10:12 All kinds of animals and reptiles and birds would include both clean and unclean animals. Jewish law forbade the consumption of unclean animals (see Lev. 11:2–47).

10:13 The command from Jesus to **kill and eat** made no sense to Peter, since it would have violated Jewish food laws. Verse 15 is the key: God was overturning the old clean/unclean distinctions and dietary laws in general, along with all other "ceremonial" laws in the Mosaic covenant (including laws about sacrifices, festivals and special days, and circumcision). Nothing like this was to get in the way of fellowship with Gentiles, as Galatians 2 also shows.

10:26 I too am a man. Compare Herod's opposite response in 12:20–23; cf. Rev. 19:10; 22:8–9.

10:28 unlawful. Not in terms of violating OT commands but in the sense of not following the later customs of strict Jewish traditions about uncleanness. The Jewish traditions of purity made it virtually impossible for them to associate with Gentiles without becoming ritually unclean. **God has shown me** refers to the vision of vv. 10–16. This shows how Peter understood his vision.

ninth hour,[1] and behold, [d]a man stood before me in bright clothing **31** and said, 'Cornelius,
[e]your prayer has been heard and your alms have been remembered before God. **32** Send
therefore to Joppa and ask for Simon who is called Peter. He is lodging in the house of
Simon, a tanner, by the sea.' **33** So I sent for you at once, and you have been kind enough to
come. Now therefore we are all here in the presence of God to hear all that you have been
commanded by the Lord."

Gentiles Hear the Good News

34 So Peter opened his mouth and said: "Truly I understand that [f]God [g]shows no partiality,
35 but [f]in every nation anyone who fears him and [h]does what is right is acceptable to him.
36 As for [i]the word that he sent to Israel, [j]preaching good news of [k]peace through Jesus
Christ ([l]he is Lord of all), **37** you yourselves know what happened throughout all Judea,
[m]beginning [n]from Galilee after the baptism that John proclaimed: **38** how [o]God anointed
Jesus of Nazareth [p]with the Holy Spirit and with [q]power. He went about doing good and
healing all [r]who were oppressed by the devil, [s]for God was with him. **39** And [t]we are witnesses of all that he did both in the country of the Jews and in Jerusalem. [u]They put him to
death by hanging him on a tree, **40** but [v]God raised him on [w]the third day and made him to
[x]appear, **41** [y]not to all the people but to us who had been chosen by God as [z]witnesses, who
ate and drank with him after he rose from the dead. **42** And [a]he commanded us to preach
to the people and to testify [b]that he is the one appointed by God to be judge [c]of the living
and the dead. **43** [d]To him [e]all the prophets bear witness that [f]everyone who believes in him
receives [g]forgiveness of sins [h]through his name."

The Holy Spirit Falls on the Gentiles

44 While Peter was still saying these things, [i]the Holy Spirit fell on all who heard the
word. **45** And the believers from among [j]the circumcised who had come with Peter were
amazed, because [k]the gift of the Holy Spirit [l]was poured out even on the Gentiles. **46** For
they were hearing them [m]speaking in tongues and extolling God. Then Peter declared,
47 [n]"Can anyone withhold water for baptizing these people, who have received the Holy
Spirit [o]just as we have?" **48** And he [p]commanded them [q]to be baptized in the name of Jesus
Christ. Then they asked him to remain for some days.

[1] That is, 3 P.M.

47 [n]ch. 8:36 [o]ch. 2:4; 11:17; 15:8 **48** [p][1 Cor. 1:14-17] [q]ch. 2:38; See ch. 8:12, 16

30 [d][ch. 1:10]
31 [e]See ver. 4
34 [f][ver. 28; ch. 15:19; Deut. 1:17; Rom. 3:29]; See Deut. 10:17 [g]Prov. 24:23; James 2:1, 9; [Jude 16]
35 [f][See ver. 34 above] [h]Isa. 64:5
36 [i]ch. 13:26; Ps. 107:20; 147:18, 19 [j]Isa. 52:7; Nah. 1:15; Eph. 2:17 [k]See Luke 2:14 [l]Rom. 10:12; [Rev. 17:14; 19:16]; See ch. 2:36; Matt. 28:18
37 [m]Luke 24:47 [n]Matt. 4:12; Mark 1:14
38 [o][Matt. 3:16; John 1:32, 33]; See ch. 4:26 [p][ch. 1:2; 2:22; Matt. 12:28; Luke 4:18; Rom. 1:4] [q][Luke 6:19] [r]See Matt. 4:24; Luke 13:16 [s]See John 8:29; 10:38
39 [t]ver. 41; See ch. 2:32; Luke 24:48 [u]ch. 5:30
40 [v]See ch. 2:24 [w]See Luke 9:22 [x]ch. 1:3
41 [y][John 14:21, 22] [z]ver. 39
42 [a]See ch. 1:2 [b]ch. 17:31; 24:25; John 5:22, 27; 2 Cor. 5:10; See Matt. 16:27 [c]2 Tim. 4:1; 1 Pet. 4:5; [Rom. 14:9, 10; 1 Thess. 4:15, 17]
43 [d]ch. 26:22; Rom. 3:21; [Jer. 31:34] [e]ch. 3:18, 24; Luke 24:27 [f]ch. 11:17; 13:38; 15:9; Rom. 9:33; 10:11; Gal. 3:22 [g]ch. 5:31 [h]ch. 2:38; 4:12; John 20:31; 1 John 2:12
44 [i]ch. 11:15; 15:8; 1 Thess. 1:5; See ch. 2:4
45 [j]ver. 23; [ch. 11:2] [k]See ch. 2:38 [l]See ch. 2:17
46 [m]See Mark 16:17

10:34–43 This message to the Gentiles is unique among the sermons of Acts in providing a summary of Jesus' ministry. It contains no scriptural proofs and was cut short before Peter could give an invitation to trust in Christ. It is quite likely, of course, that the speech was an extended one, of which Luke gives an abbreviated account.

10:35 in every nation. Not just among Jews. **acceptable to him**. The word used here (Gk. *dektos*, "acceptable, welcome") does not refer to legal justification before God (for which the NT uses Gk. *dikaioō* and related terms), nor is Peter talking about the basis for justification. Rather, the question here is whether God's favor is made available to Jews only ("partiality," v. 34) or is now available to Gentiles also (those "in every nation"). **fears him and does what is right**. This expression summarizes the behavior of someone whose life is pleasing to God. Although Peter does not explicitly mention saving faith (as he will in v. 43), it would likely be included or implied in the meaning of these two terms in this context (see note on v. 2). After all, faith is trusting God and responding to him.

10:36 The references to the **good news of peace** and to Christ being **Lord of all** echo Isa. 52:7 and 57:19: the gospel is for all people, including Cornelius and his fellow Gentiles.

10:38 The simple statement **he went about doing good and healing** is a profound summary of Jesus' life, and an ideal to which all Christians would do well to aspire.

10:39 The cross is referred to as **a tree**, making a clear connection with the use of the same word (Gk. *xylon*) in the Septuagint translation of Deut. 21:23, "cursed by God is everyone who is hanged on a tree." Jesus was put in a position that the OT says is "cursed by God," thus taking on himself the penalty for sin. See Gal. 3:13.

10:41 Who ate and drank with him shows that Jesus was not a ghost or a spirit but had a real physical body after his resurrection. Eating and drinking are signs of sharing close personal fellowship.

10:43 all the prophets. See note on 3:18. **everyone who believes**. See note on 2:38.

10:44 The **Holy Spirit fell** in a way that was visible and audible from the response of the people on whom he fell (see v. 46). These Gentiles had come to genuine saving faith in Christ and had received the new covenant power and fullness of the Holy Spirit, which was a sign that they had been accepted by God as full and equal members of his people. The fact that they had not followed any Mosaic ceremonial laws (such as those concerning circumcision, sacrifice, and dietary restrictions) before receiving the gift of the Spirit is an important point, as soon becomes evident (see 11:15–17).

10:46 Speaking in tongues and praise of God outwardly demonstrated the Spirit's presence and God's acceptance of Gentiles without circumcision (which had been required for conversion to Judaism).

10:47 Baptizing these people would be an outward sign of an inward work of God in their hearts and of their personal commitment to Christ. **Just as we have** is a reference to the reception of the Spirit at Pentecost. Speaking in tongues also occurred at Pentecost (2:4), later with the Ephesian 12 (19:6), and perhaps also among the Samaritans (8:18). In every case speaking in tongues validates that those in view belong to the people of God and have received the Holy Spirit in new covenant fullness.

10:48 To be **baptized in the name of Jesus Christ** (see also 2:38; 8:16) is not different from being baptized "in the name of the Father and of the Son and of the Holy Spirit" (Matt. 28:19). Even though different words are used here in Acts, the meaning is the same because in biblical usage a person's

Chapter 11

1 [r]ver. 29; See John 21:23
2 [s]ch. 10:45; Gal. 2:12; Col. 4:11; Titus 1:10; [Rom. 4:12]
3 [t]Gal. 2:12, 14; [ch. 10:28] [u][Luke 15:2]
5 [v]For ver. 5-14, see ch. 10:9-32
12 [w]ch. 15:9 [x]ch. 10:23, 45
14 [y]ch. 10:22 [z]ch. 10:2; 16:15, 31-34; 18:8; John 4:53
15 [a]ch. 10:44 [b]ch. 2:4
16 [c]ch. 1:5; [ch. 19:2]; See Matt. 3:11
17 [d]See ch. 10:47 [e]See ch. 2:38 [f]Eph. 1:13; See ch. 10:43 [g][Rom. 9:20] [h]ch. 10:47; See ch. 5:39
18 [i]ch. 21:20 [j][ch. 13:47; Matt. 8:11]; See ch. 10:34, 35 [k]See ch. 5:31 [l][2 Cor. 7:10]
19 [m]ch. 8:1, 4

Peter Reports to the Church

11 Now the apostles and [r]the brothers[1] who were throughout Judea heard that the
Gentiles also had received the word of God. 2 So when Peter went up to Jerusalem,
[s]the circumcision party[2] criticized him, saying, 3 [t]"You went to uncircumcised men and
[u]ate with them." 4 But Peter began and explained it to them in order: 5 [v]"I was in the city
of Joppa praying, and in a trance I saw a vision, something like a great sheet descending,
being let down from heaven by its four corners, and it came down to me. 6 Looking at it
closely, I observed animals and beasts of prey and reptiles and birds of the air. 7 And I heard
a voice saying to me, 'Rise, Peter; kill and eat.' 8 But I said, 'By no means, Lord; for nothing
common or unclean has ever entered my mouth.' 9 But the voice answered a second time
from heaven, 'What God has made clean, do not call common.' 10 This happened three
times, and all was drawn up again into heaven. 11 And behold, at that very moment three
men arrived at the house in which we were, sent to me from Caesarea. 12 And the Spirit
told me to go with them, [w]making no distinction. [x]These six brothers also accompanied
me, and we entered the man's house. 13 And he told us how he had seen the angel stand in
his house and say, 'Send to Joppa and bring Simon who is called Peter; 14 [y]he will declare
to you a message by which [z]you will be saved, you and all your household.' 15 As I began to
speak, [a]the Holy Spirit fell on them [b]just as on us at the beginning. 16 And I remembered
the word of the Lord, how he said, [c]'John baptized with water, but you will be baptized
with the Holy Spirit.' 17 If then [d]God gave [e]the same gift to them as he gave to us [f]when we
believed in the Lord Jesus Christ, [g]who was I [h]that I could stand in God's way?" 18 When
they heard these things they fell silent. And they [i]glorified God, saying, [j]"Then to the
Gentiles also God has [k]granted [l]repentance that leads to life."

The Church in Antioch

19 [m]Now those who were scattered because of the persecution that arose over Stephen
traveled as far as Phoenicia and Cyprus and Antioch, speaking the word to no one except

[1] *Or brothers and sisters* [2] *Or Jerusalem, those of the circumcision*

"name" represents the person's character, everything that is true about the person. The "name" (character and attributes) of the Father and the Son and the Holy Spirit is the same as the "name" (character and attributes) of Jesus Christ. In fact, in Matt. 28:19, the word "name" (Gk. *onoma*) is singular, indicating that Father, Son, and Holy Spirit share one "name" (i.e., one character). To be baptized into that name is a sign of identifying with that name and taking on Christ's character, as well as committing to live one's life from that point on as a representative of that name. **remain for some days**. Peter's willingness to stay with them likely involved his sharing meals with the Gentiles, a bold step for one who formerly was so concerned about clean and unclean foods (see also notes on Gal. 2:11–21).

11:1–18 *Peter's Testimony in Jerusalem.* The final scene of the Cornelius narrative takes place in Jerusalem, where some of Peter's fellow Jewish Christians questioned his acceptance of the Gentiles. Peter defended his action by retelling the events of the Gentile conversions with an emphasis on God's leading. This is basically a summary of ch. 10, with only a few added details.

11:1 The **apostles and the brothers** do not seem to have raised objection to the inclusion of Cornelius and his fellow Gentiles. The issue was raised by "the circumcision party" (v. 2), a group of strict Jewish Christians, perhaps of a Pharisaic background (see 15:1, 5). They probably held the position that Gentiles who wished to become Christians must first become converts to Judaism, which included circumcision and living by the ritual laws.

11:3 On eating with **uncircumcised men**, see note on 10:28.

11:12 Peter was to make **no distinction** or discrimination between Jews and Gentiles.

11:14 a message by which you will be saved. Some think this implies that Cornelius was saved for the first time here. Others think he previously had saving faith (as a Gentile "God-fearer" looking forward to the Messiah), but that this meant he would experience the fullness of new covenant salvation in Christ when he heard the gospel message (see notes on 10:2; 10:35).

11:15 Just as on us refers to Pentecost, apparently meaning that these Gentile believers began to speak in tongues and praise God, giving convincing evidence that they had received the Holy Spirit in the same sense as did those at Pentecost. See also 10:44–48 and note on 10:47. The fact that the Spirit came to Cornelius and other Gentiles without them having done anything in relationship to the Law is God's answer to the debate and settled matters as far as Peter was concerned.

11:17 stand in God's way. Here Peter used the same word (Gk. *kōlyō*) as in the earlier account of Cornelius's conversion (10:47, "withhold"), and the Ethiopian eunuch used the same word at the time of his conversion (8:36). As these three examples demonstrate, God was expanding the church to include Gentiles, and no one should try to "prevent" or "stand in the way" of that. Though Peter did not explicitly refer to baptism, it was probably implicit in the use of this word: Peter knew he could not refuse to allow these new believers to be baptized and thereby give outward evidence that they were full members of the church.

11:18 they glorified God. Though it is taken for granted today that Gentiles can become Christians, it was an astounding realization for these Jewish Christians in Jerusalem that **to the Gentiles also God has granted repentance that leads to life**. On repentance, see note on 2:38. This move was significant given the history of tension between Gentiles and Jews, especially in light of the Maccabean War. Reconciliation is a key theme of the gospel.

11:19–26 *The Antioch Church Witnesses to Gentiles.* The Jerusalem church was the center of the Christian witness to the Gentiles in its earliest days. With the establishing of a church at Antioch and their outreach to Gentiles, the focus in Acts shifts to that congregation.

11:19 The **persecution that arose over Stephen** (see 8:1, 4) caused believers to be **scattered** and led to the spread of the word among Jews in various outlying regions. **Phoenicia** was in the area of present-day Lebanon, its primary cities being Tyre, Sidon, and Ptolemais. (For Christian communities there, see 21:3–7.) **Cyprus** was 100 miles (161 km) off the coast. The primary language of these areas was Greek, as it was for **Antioch** (modern Antakya), the largest city of the area and capital of the Roman province of Syria, with a population of a half million or more. Only Rome and Alexandria were larger in ancient times. At Antioch, an island bearing a palace and a hippodrome

Jews. 20 But there were some of them, men of Cyprus and Cyrene, who on coming to Antioch
spoke to the Hellenists[1] also, [n]preaching the Lord Jesus. 21 And [o]the hand of the Lord was
with them, and a great number who believed [p]turned to the Lord. 22 The report of this came
to the ears of the church in Jerusalem, and they sent Barnabas to Antioch. 23 When he came
and saw [q]the grace of God, he was glad, and he exhorted them all to remain faithful to
the Lord [r]with steadfast purpose, 24 for he was a good man, [s]full of the Holy Spirit and of
faith. And a great many people [t]were added to the Lord. 25 So Barnabas went to [u]Tarsus to
look for Saul, 26 and when he had found him, he brought him to Antioch. For a whole year
they met with the church and taught a great many people. And in Antioch the disciples
were first called [v]Christians.

27 Now in these days [w]prophets came down from Jerusalem to Antioch. 28 And one of them
named [x]Agabus stood up and foretold [y]by the Spirit that there would be a great [z]famine
over all the world (this took place in the days of [a]Claudius). 29 So the disciples determined,
every one according to his ability, [b]to send relief to [c]the brothers[2] living in Judea. 30 [d]And
they did so, sending it to [e]the elders by the hand of Barnabas and Saul.

James Killed and Peter Imprisoned

12 About that time Herod the king laid violent hands on some who belonged to the
church. 2 He killed [f]James the brother of John [g]with the sword, 3 and when he saw
[h]that it pleased the Jews, he proceeded to arrest Peter also. This was during [i]the days of

[1] Or *Greeks* (that is, Greek-speaking non-Jews) [2] Or *brothers and sisters*
[i]ch. 20:6; Ex. 12:14, 15; 23:15

20 [n]See John 7:35; See ch. 5:42
21 [o]ch. 13:11; Luke 1:66; [Ps. 80:17; 89:21] [p]ch. 9:35
23 [q]ch. 13:43; 14:26; 20:24, 32; Rom. 5:15; 2 Cor. 6:1; Eph. 3:2, 7; Col. 1:6; Titus 2:11; Heb. 12:15; 1 Pet. 5:12; [ch. 4:33; 15:40] [r]2 Tim. 3:10
24 [s]ch. 6:5 [t]ch. 5:14; [ver. 26]
25 [u]ch. 9:30
26 [v]ch. 26:28; 1 Pet. 4:16
27 [w]See ch. 13:1
28 [x]ch. 21:10 [y]See ch. 2:18; 8:29 [z]Matt. 24:7 [a]ch. 18:2
29 [b][ch. 24:17; Rom. 15:26] [c]ver. 1
30 [d]ch. 12:25 [e]ch. 14:23; 15:2, 4, 6; 16:4; 20:17; 21:18; 1 Tim. 5:17, 19; Titus 1:5; James 5:14; 2 John 1; 3 John 1

Chapter 12
2 [f]Matt. 4:21; 20:23 [g]Heb. 11:37
3 [h][ch. 24:27; 25:9]

stood in the middle of the Orontes River. Bridges connected the island to the main city. In the first century the main city contained an aqueduct, baths, two theaters, temples (e.g., to Artemis and to Herakles), the Pantheon, and the Kaisareion (a basilica dedicated to the imperial cult). Prior to Paul's arrival, an earthquake in 37 B.C. had devastated Antioch, but the emperor Gaius (Caligula) helped rebuild it. Antioch periodically hosted Olympic-style games. Its great colonnaded and marble-paved road had been sponsored in part by Herod the Great. **speaking the word to no one except Jews**. These people had not yet heard about the events of 10:1–11:18.

11:20 men of Cyprus and Cyrene. They were Diaspora Jews, natives of the nearby island of Cyprus and of the northern African region of Cyrene (see note on 13:1). There is ample archaeological evidence of Jewish inhabitants in these areas. **Hellenists** here means not just people from Greece but Greek-speaking Gentiles who lived in Antioch. (See notes on 6:1 [where "Hellenists" are Greek-speaking Jewish Christians] and 9:29 [where "Hellenists" are Greek-speaking Jews].) Some of the Greek-speaking Jewish Christians who settled in Antioch began witnessing to the Gentiles.

11:21 The hand of the Lord was with them is another reminder that this remarkable expansion of the church came about only by God's power, not by human wisdom or skill.

11:22 they sent Barnabas to Antioch. When the "mother church" in Jerusalem heard of Antioch's witness to the Gentiles, they sent Barnabas to validate the new outreach, much as they had sent Peter and John to approve the Samaritan mission (8:14).

11:24 full of the Holy Spirit and of faith. This does not describe a single experience but a general characteristic of Barnabas's life. The persecution by Herod (12:1–19) and Herod's death (12:20–23) would have been inserted at this point in the narrative if Luke had been writing everything in exact chronological order, because Herod died in A.D. 44 (see 12:23), and Paul apparently stayed in Tarsus until A.D. 45, when Barnabas went there and summoned him to Antioch (11:25–26). But Luke here departs from strict chronological order because he is telling the story of the church in Antioch. He continues on this topic until v. 30 and then turns to discuss what happened to Herod at "about that time" (12:1). Cf. notes on Gal. 1:18; 2:1.

11:26 Paul had gone to his native Tarsus (v. 25) after his conversion (9:30). As a Diaspora Jew, he was particularly suited for the Gentile outreach. His **year** of participation in this mission in Antioch (probably in A.D. 45) prepared him and Barnabas for a much greater mission that would follow (13:1ff.). The fact that **the disciples** were first called **Christians** in Antioch probably reflects a label applied by the unbelieving public in Antioch and shows that the disciples were beginning to have an identity of their own apart from other Jews. Cf. also 26:28 and 1 Pet. 4:16.

11:27–30 *The Offering for Jerusalem.* Paul and Barnabas represented the Antioch church by conveying its offering to the Jerusalem church in a time of need. This offering may have inspired Paul for his own organizing of an offering for Jerusalem sometime later (see notes on 20:3; Rom. 15:25–28). Paul says in Gal. 2:1 that this second visit to Jerusalem (Acts 11:30) took place "after fourteen years" (presumably 14 years after his conversion), which would place this visit in either A.D. 45, 46, or 47. Most commentators believe that these calculations of years were not made according to modern standards of counting (which would require 14 full years) but by ancient "inclusive" methods, in which part of a year was still counted as a year. Paul's "fourteen years" could have been as little as a month or two from the first year, plus 12 whole years, plus a month or two from the final year, giving about twelve and a half years by modern reckoning. Likewise, the "after three years" of Gal. 1:18 could be as little as one and a half years.

11:27 Christian **prophets** are mentioned elsewhere in Acts (13:1; 15:32; 21:9). Their role involved edification and encouragement as they spoke things that had been revealed to them by the Holy Spirit. Sometimes such prophecies foretold the future, as Agabus did here (see also 21:4, 10–11). On the gift of prophecy, see note on 1 Cor. 12:10 and other notes on 1 Corinthians 12–14.

11:28 a great famine. There were several famines in various parts of the Roman Empire during the reign of **Claudius** (A.D. 41–54) including several in Judea in the early years of his reign. Historians believe that this famine took place in the years A.D. 45–46 or else 47. **Over all the world** is a general prediction of the many regional famines that took place during Claudius's reign.

11:30 The reference to **elders** marks a transition in day-to-day leadership of the Jerusalem church (cf. 4:35–37; 6:1–6).

12:1–25 *The Jerusalem Church Is Persecuted.* Chapter 12 is the last chapter in Acts that tells of the Jerusalem church without reference to Paul's ministry.

12:1–5 *The Death of James.* Herod executed the apostle James and imprisoned Peter, intending to do the same to him.

12:1 about that time. See note on 11:24. **Herod** was Herod Agrippa I, a grandson of Herod the Great (see note on Matt. 2:1). He was reared in Rome, and because of boyhood playmates who later became emperors he was granted rule over various territories in Judea until his kingdom reached the full extent of his grandfather's territory (A.D. 41–44). See map, p. 2107. His persecution of the Christians may have been an attempt to curry favor with the Jews (cf. Acts 12:3).

12:2 The martyred **James** was Jesus' disciple, son of Zebedee and brother of

4[j]See Luke 21:12 [k][John 19:23]
5[l]2 Cor. 1:11; Eph. 6:18
6[m]ch. 21:33
7[n]See ch. 8:26 [o]Luke 2:9; 24:4 [p][1 Kgs. 19:7] [q]ch. 16:26
8[r]Mark 6:9

Unleavened Bread. 4 And when he had seized him, he put him [j]in prison, delivering him
over to four [k]squads of soldiers to guard him, intending after the Passover to bring him
out to the people. 5 So Peter was kept in prison, but earnest [l]prayer for him was made to
God by the church.

Peter Is Rescued

6 Now when Herod was about to bring him out, on that very night, Peter was sleeping
between two soldiers, [m]bound with two chains, and sentries before the door were guarding the prison. 7 And behold, [n]an angel of the Lord [o]stood next to him, and a light shone
in the cell. [p]He struck Peter on the side and woke him, saying, "Get up quickly." And [q]the
chains fell off his hands. 8 And the angel said to him, "Dress yourself and [r]put on your

John, not to be confused with James, the brother of Jesus and author of the book of James, who became a prominent leader in the Jerusalem church (see note on v. 17). Jesus had predicted his suffering (Mark 10:39).

12:3 Why this **pleased the Jews** is not specified. Perhaps the persecution following Stephen's death (8:1) had escalated. The **days of Unleavened Bread**, the seven days following the Passover meal, were considered holy and not to be desecrated by an execution.

12:4 The **prison** was probably the Tower of Antonia, which was at the northwestern corner of the temple complex and was the quarters of the Roman garrison. The use of **four squads of soldiers** reflects Roman practice: one squad of four soldiers for each of the four three-hour watches of the night. **Passover** refers to the entire spring festival that unites Passover and the Feast of Unleavened Bread.

12:5 The mention of **earnest prayer** continues Luke's emphasis that every step in building the church is due to God's blessing and supernatural intervention.

12:6–19 *Peter's Deliverance from Prison.* Peter was half asleep throughout his "escape" from prison. The angel had to rouse him and direct him (vv. 7–8), and he remained in a stupor until the angel led him through the gates and into a side street (vv. 9–11).

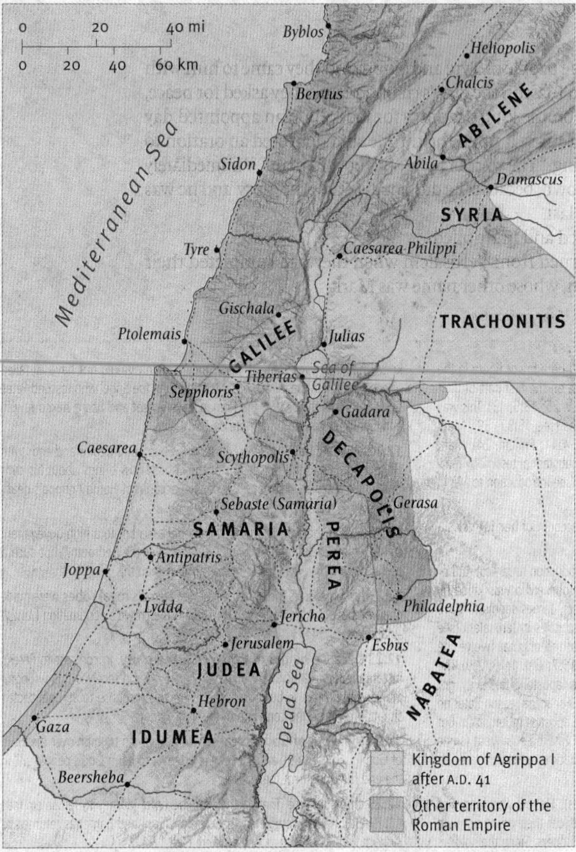

The Kingdom of Herod Agrippa I

C. A.D. 41

Largely due to his influential friendships with the Roman emperors Gaius (Caligula) and Claudius, Herod Agrippa I, a grandson of Herod the Great, pieced together what was essentially his grandfather's old kingdom plus the region of Abilene to the north. He wielded great power over the whole region of Palestine, as well as Syria, including Tyre and Sidon.

sandals." And he did so. And he said to him, "Wrap your cloak around you and follow me."
9 And he went out and followed him. He did not know that what was being done by the
angel was real, but [s]thought he was seeing a vision. 10 When they had passed the first and
the second guard, they came to the iron gate leading into the city. [t]It opened for them of
its own accord, and they went out and went along one street, and immediately the angel
left him. 11 When Peter [u]came to himself, he said, "Now I am sure that [v]the Lord has sent
his angel and [w]rescued me from the hand of Herod and from all that the Jewish people
were expecting."

12 When he realized this, he went to the house of Mary, the mother of [x]John whose
other name was Mark, where many were gathered together and [y]were praying. 13 And
when he knocked at the door of the gateway, [z]a servant girl named Rhoda came to answer.
14 Recognizing Peter's voice, [a]in her joy she did not open the gate but ran in and reported
that Peter was standing at the gate. 15 They said to her, "You are out of your mind." But she
kept insisting that it was so, and they kept saying, "It is [b]his angel!" 16 But Peter continued
knocking, and when they opened, they saw him and were amazed. 17 But [c]motioning to
them with his hand to be silent, he described to them how the Lord had brought him
out of the prison. And he said, "Tell these things to [d]James and to [e]the brothers."[1] Then
he departed and went to another place.

18 Now when day came, there was no little disturbance among the soldiers over what had
become of Peter. 19 And after Herod searched for him and did not find him, he examined
the sentries and [f]ordered that they should be put to death. Then he went down from Judea
to Caesarea and spent time there.

The Death of Herod

20 Now Herod was angry with the people of Tyre and Sidon, and they came to him with
one accord, and [g]having persuaded Blastus, the king's chamberlain,[2] they asked for peace,
because [h]their country depended on the king's country for food. 21 On an appointed day
Herod put on his royal robes, took his seat upon the throne, and delivered an oration to
them. 22 And the people were shouting, "The voice of a god, and not of a man!" 23 Immediately
[i]an angel of the Lord struck him down, because [j]he did not give God the glory, and he was
eaten by worms and breathed his last.

24 But [k]the word of God increased and multiplied.

25 [l]And Barnabas and Saul returned from[3] Jerusalem when they had completed their
service, bringing with them [m]John, whose other name was Mark.

[1] Or *brothers and sisters* [2] That is, trusted personal attendant [3] Some manuscripts *to*

9 [s]Ps. 126:1
10 [t]ch. 5:19; 16:26
11 [u][Luke 15:17] [v]Ps. 34:7; 91:11; Dan. 3:28; 6:22 [w]Ps. 33:18, 19; 2 Cor. 1:10
12 [x]ver. 25; ch. 13:5, 13; 15:37, 39; Col. 4:10; 2 Tim. 4:11; Philem. 24; 1 Pet. 5:13 [y]ver. 5
13 [z]John 18:16, 17
14 [a]Luke 24:41; [Gen. 45:26]
15 [b]Matt. 18:10; See Heb. 1:14
17 [c]ch. 13:16; 19:33; 21:40 [d]ch. 15:13; 21:18; [Gal. 1:19; 2:9, 12] [e]See John 21:23
19 [f][ch. 16:27; 27:42]
20 [g]Matt. 28:14 (Gk.) [h][1 Kgs. 5:9; Ezra 3:7; Ezek. 27:17]
23 [i][2 Sam. 24:16; 2 Kgs. 19:35]; See ch. 8:26 [j]Ps. 115:1
24 [k]See ch. 6:7
25 [l]ch. 11:29, 30 [m]See ver. 12

12:12 John whose other name was Mark will be a major figure in the next three chapters, going with Paul and Barnabas on the first part of their first missionary journey but then leaving them (see v. 25; 13:5, 13). This was a cause of contention between Paul and Barnabas (see 15:37, 39). Mark regained Paul's favor later (see Col. 4:10; 2 Tim. 4:11; Philem. 24). Mark accompanied Peter (see 1 Pet. 5:13), and there is substantial testimony from the early church that he wrote the Gospel of Mark (see Introduction to Mark: Author and Title).

12:13–14 Rhoda's failure to **open the gate** on account of **her joy** adds a touch of humor and heightens the suspense.

12:17 James here is the brother of Jesus (see Introduction to James: Author and Title; Gal. 1:19), not James the brother of John (who was killed by Herod, Acts 12:2). From this point forward in Acts, James seems to have the most prominent leadership role among the apostles in Jerusalem (see 15:13–21; 21:18). Though James was not one of the original Twelve, he apparently became an apostle as well (cf. 1 Cor. 15:7; Gal. 1:19; 2:9). The book of James also seems to be written on his own (apostolic) authority, not as a spokesman for someone else (see James 1:1). For some reason Peter no longer remained the leader and spokesman for the apostles in Jerusalem but **went to another place**. Luke does not specify where Peter went (some have suggested either Rome or Antioch); he was back in Jerusalem later for a conference (Acts 15:7–21).

12:18–19 In executing the **sentries** (i.e., guards), **Herod** was following Roman practice, which specified that soldiers who lost their prisoners were subject to the same penalty as that due to the prisoners. Since the soldiers knew that their lives were at stake, they certainly would not have all fallen asleep apart from the miraculous intervention of the angel who rescued Peter. **Caesarea** was the seat of the Roman government and had a mixed Jewish and Gentile population (see note on 8:40).

12:20–25 *The Death of Herod Agrippa I.* Chapter 12 begins and ends with **Herod** Agrippa I: the persecutor of the church now brings about his own death (see note on 11:24 and the parallel account of Herod Agrippa's death in Josephus, *Jewish Antiquities* 19.343–350).

12:20 A **chamberlain** is a trusted personal assistant to a high government official; the Greek literally means "the one over the bedroom," but such a person would have had wider responsibilities than this.

12:21 Josephus gives the added detail that Herod's **royal robes** were made of silver that sparkled in the sun, provoking the crowd's acclamation (*Jewish Antiquities* 19.344).

12:23 because he did not give God the glory. In contrast to Peter's instantaneous rejection of worship in 10:26, Herod receives this wrongful praise with delight. In both cases the instinctive response to an unexpected situation revealed the condition of the man's heart.

12:24 the word of God increased. No power can triumph over the word of God (cf. 6:7; 13:49), and those who attempt to harm God's people will in the end face judgment themselves.

12:25 their service. That is, their famine relief journey to Jerusalem (see 11:29–30). Having completed that mission, Paul and Barnabas returned to Antioch with Mark accompanying them (see 12:12).

Barnabas and Saul Sent Off

13 Now there were in the church at Antioch [n]prophets and [n]teachers, [o]Barnabas, Simeon
who was called Niger,[1] Lucius of Cyrene, Manaen a lifelong friend of [p]Herod the
tetrarch, and Saul. 2 While they were worshiping the Lord and fasting, [q]the Holy Spirit
said, [r]"Set apart for me Barnabas and Saul [s]for the work to which I have called them."
3 Then after fasting and [t]praying they laid their hands on them and [u]sent them off.

Barnabas and Saul on Cyprus

4 So, being sent out [v]by the Holy Spirit, they went down to Seleucia, and from there
they sailed to Cyprus. 5 When they arrived at Salamis, they proclaimed the word of God
[w]in the synagogues of the Jews. And they had [x]John to [y]assist them. 6 When they had gone
through the whole island as far as Paphos, they came upon a certain [z]magician, [a]a Jewish
false prophet named Bar-Jesus. 7 He was with [b]the proconsul, Sergius Paulus, a man of
intelligence, who summoned Barnabas and Saul and sought to hear the word of God.
8 But Elymas the [z]magician (for that is the meaning of his name) [c]opposed them, seeking
to turn [d]the proconsul away from the faith. 9 But Saul, who was also called Paul, [e]filled
with the Holy Spirit, looked intently at him 10 and said, "You [f]son of the devil, you enemy
of all righteousness, full of all deceit and [g]villainy, will you not stop [h]making crooked
[i]the straight paths of the Lord? 11 And now, behold, [j]the hand of the Lord is upon you,
and you will be blind and unable to see the sun for a time." Immediately mist and darkness fell upon him, and he went about seeking [k]people to lead him by the hand. 12 Then

[1] *Niger* is a Latin word meaning *black, or dark*

Chapter 13
1 [n]ch. 11:27; 15:32; 19:6; 21:9, 10; Rom. 12:6, 7; See 1 Cor. 12:28, 29 [o]ch. 11:22-26 [p]See Luke 3:1
2 [q][ch. 20:28]; See ch. 8:29 [r]Rom. 1:1; Gal. 1:15 [s]See ch. 9:15
3 [t]See ch. 6:6 [u]ch. 14:26
4 [v]ver. 2; [ch. 16:6, 7]
5 [w]ver. 14; ch. 9:20; 14:1; 17:1, 2, 10, 17; 18:4, 19; 19:8; [ver. 46]; See Mark 6:2 [x]See ch. 12:12 [y][ch. 19:22]
6 [z]ch. 8:9, 11 [a]See Matt. 7:15
7 [b]ver. 8, 12; ch. 18:12; 19:38
8 [z][See ver. 6 above] [c][Ex. 7:11; 2 Tim. 3:8] [d]ver. 7, 12
9 [e]ch. 4:8
10 [f]See Matt. 13:38 [g][ch. 18:14] [h]Mic. 3:9 [i]Hos. 14:9; 2 Pet. 2:15; [ch. 18:25, 26]
11 [j]ch. 11:21; Ex. 9:3; 1 Sam. 5:6, 7, 11; Ps. 32:4; [Heb. 10:31; 1 Pet. 5:6] [k][ch. 9:8; 22:11]

13:1–14:28 *The Witness in Cyprus and Southern Galatia.* Chapters 13 and 14 relate Paul's "first missionary journey" (see map, p. 2110). Commissioned by the Antioch church, Paul and Barnabas witnessed on the island of Cyprus and in the southern cities of the Roman province of Galatia.

13:1–3 *The Antioch Church Commissions Paul and Barnabas.* The church in Antioch had already been proclaiming the gospel to the Gentiles nearby, and Paul and Barnabas had participated (11:19–26). Now the Spirit led the church to send them on a wider mission, well beyond the borders of Syria.

13:1 Prophets and teachers are always distinct offices in the NT church. See note on 1 Cor. 12:10 and other notes on 1 Corinthians 12–14. **Niger** is Latin for "black," indicating he likely came from Africa, as did the Cyrenean **Lucius.** (Cyrene was the capital city of Cyrene [sometimes called Cyrenaica], a Roman province in Libya, on the north coast of Africa; see Acts 2:10.) Some have identified Lucius with Luke, but this is unlikely, since Luke is Greek and Lucius is Latin. **Herod the tetrarch** is Herod Antipas, who is mentioned frequently in the Gospels and who reigned in Galilee during Jesus' ministry (cf. Matt. 14:1; Luke 3:1; 23:8; Acts 4:27) 4 B.C. to A.D. 39. He was a son of Herod the Great (Matt. 2:1), and his nephew Herod Agrippa I, grandson of Herod the Great, reigned as king in Judea A.D. 41–44 (Acts 12:1–23). **Lifelong friend** translates Greek *syntrophos*, indicating that **Manaen** was a close friend of Herod Antipas and had been brought up with him from childhood.

13:2 While they were worshiping the Lord and fasting. Though there were recognized "prophets" in the church (v. 1), that did not guarantee that the Holy Spirit would speak to them apart from their spending such extended time in worship, fasting, and prayer. "They" likely refers to the whole congregation at worship, although the five prophets may well have mediated the Spirit's message.

13:3 They again probably refers to the entire congregation rather than just the five "prophets and teachers" (v. 1), since Paul and Barnabas were a part of that latter group. The laying on of hands was a "commissioning," indicating the church's support of the two in their mission, and providing a physical indication of imparting the Holy Spirit's power to them (see 6:6; 8:17; 9:17; 19:6).

13:4–12 *Paul and Barnabas Witness on Cyprus.* The two missionaries worked first on the island of Cyprus, Barnabas's home (4:36). This first of Paul's three missionary journeys is narrated in 13:4–14:26. It likely began in A.D. 46 or 47 and lasted perhaps a year and a half.

13:4 sent out by the Holy Spirit. Luke continues his emphasis on the divine direction of all that is happening in the growth of the church. Setting out from Antioch (v. 1), Paul and Barnabas traveled about 16 miles (26 km) **down to** the port city of **Seleucia.**

13:5 Salamis was the closest port of Cyprus (about 130 miles [209 km] southwest of Seleucia). **John** (John Mark) was an assistant to Paul and Barnabas (see note on 12:12). They began their witness in the **synagogues of the Jews**, a pattern regularly followed by Paul (Acts 17:1–2). This was a natural starting point, since the Jewish people already believed that the OT Scriptures were the absolutely authoritative and truthful words of God.

13:6 Paphos was 90 miles (145 km) southwest of Salamis and was the seat of the Roman government of Cyprus. Paphos here likely refers to the port city of Nea Paphos rather than nearby Old Paphos (with its famous ancient temple of Aphrodite). First-century remains in Nea Paphos include an odeion (a small covered theater), a larger theater, and the Sanctuary of Apollo. **Bar-Jesus** was a **magician** (Gk. *magos*), similar to Simon (8:9–13), and a Jew. He was also a **false prophet.** Paul's subsequent characterization of him as a "son of the devil" suggests that his "magic" was assisted by demonic powers. Magic in antiquity was practiced by both pagan and Jewish people with the goals of healing diseases, bringing physical blessings, cursing or otherwise harming others, and guarding against both curses and demons. Magicians also claimed to foretell the future. Ancient literature (e.g., Pliny, *Natural History*) and discovered magical books (cf. Acts 19:19) indicate that magic often involved special incantations (frequently invoking magical names of deities and demons), potions, and the use of magical objects such as amulets, incantation bowls, or figurines.

13:7 The proconsul was the highest-ranking official in a Roman senatorial province. A few inscriptions have been found around the Mediterranean bearing the name **Sergius Paulus**, but it is difficult to be certain which, if any, relate to the proconsul mentioned here.

13:8 Bar-Jesus, also known as **Elymas**, opposed the missionaries because he viewed them as a threat to his profitable relationship with the proconsul.

13:9 This verse marks the transition in Acts from **Saul** to **Paul**. Now that he is working in Gentile territory, the Hebrew Saul becomes known by his Roman name, Paul. He will be so named throughout the rest of Acts, except in 22:7, 13, and 26:14, which recall earlier events.

13:11–12 When Elymas was miraculously struck blind, the **proconsul believed.** Throughout Acts, miracles have a significant role in bringing unbelievers to genuine faith (cf. notes on ch. 3; etc.).

the proconsul believed, when he saw what had occurred, for he was astonished at [l]the
teaching of the Lord.

Paul and Barnabas at Antioch in Pisidia

13 Now Paul and his companions set sail from Paphos and came to Perga in Pamphylia.
And [m]John left them and returned [n]to Jerusalem, 14 but they went on from Perga and came
to Antioch in Pisidia. And [o]on the Sabbath day [p]they went into the synagogue and sat
down. 15 After [q]the reading from [r]the Law and the Prophets, [s]the rulers of the synagogue
sent a message to them, saying, "Brothers, if you have any [t]word of encouragement for the
people, say it." 16 So Paul stood up, and [u]motioning with his hand said:

"Men of Israel and [v]you who fear God, listen. 17 [w]The God of this people Israel [x]chose
our fathers and [y]made the people great [z]during their stay in the land of Egypt, and [a]with
uplifted arm he led them out of it. 18 And for about [b]forty years [c]he put up with[1] them
in the wilderness. 19 And [d]after destroying [e]seven nations in the land of Canaan, [f]he gave

[1] Some manuscripts *he carried* (compare Deuteronomy 1:31)

12 [l][ver. 49; ch. 15:35]
13 [m]ver. 5 [n]ch. 12:12
14 [o]ver. 42, 44; ch. 16:13; 17:2; 18:4 [p]See ver. 5
15 [q]ch. 15:21 [r]See Luke 16:16 [s]See Mark 5:22 [t]Heb. 13:22
16 [u]See ch. 12:17 [v]ver. 26; ch. 10:2, 22
17 [w]See Matt. 15:31 [x]Deut. 7:6-8 [y]Num. 24:7 [z]ch. 7:17; Ex. 1:1, 7, 12; Ps. 105:23, 24 [a]Ex. 6:6; 13:14, 16
18 [b]See ch. 7:36 [c][Deut. 9:5-24]
19 [d]See ch. 7:45 [e]Deut. 7:1 [f]Josh. 14:1, 2; 19:51; Ps. 78:55; 136:21, 22

13:13–41 *Paul Preaches in the Synagogue of Pisidian Antioch.* From Cyprus the missionaries sailed to the southern coast of what today is Turkey.

13:13 Perga was 8 miles (13 km) inland. Paul does not seem to have remained there long but witnessed there on his return journey (14:25). The reason for John Mark's departure is not specified, though Paul's later conflict with Barnabas (15:36–41) shows it did not sit well with Paul. Among the extensive archaeological remains at Perga, the city gates, theater, sports arena, and an unidentified temple date to the time of Paul.

13:14 Antioch in Pisidia was one of 16 cities that the Syrian king Seleucus had named for his father Antiochus. The city had a large Jewish population and the high status of being a Roman "colony." It is to be distinguished from Antioch in Syria, from which Paul and Barnabas had begun their journey (see v. 1). Excavations at Pisidian Antioch have revealed much from Paul's day: city walls, a theater, large streets, a temple to the Anatolian god Men Askaenos, and a large temple platform probably related to emperor worship. **synagogue**. See notes on v. 5; Rom. 1:16.

13:15 The regular synagogue service centered around the reading of Scriptures from the **Law and the Prophets** (see note on Matt. 3:17). **rulers**. Worship was led by the ruling elder.

13:16–41 Paul's sermon (vv. 16–41) consisted of three parts: a sketch of OT history (vv. 16b–25), God's ultimate provision in Jesus Christ (vv. 26–37), and an invitation (vv. 38–41). With its historical sketch, the sermon is reminiscent of Stephen's. Both sermons emphasize God's raising up leaders for Israel, but with a major (though complementary) difference: Stephen pointed to Israel's rejection of its God-sent leaders, while Paul stressed God's grace in providing the leaders. **You who fear God** (v. 16) is a reference to the "God-fearers" in the synagogue (see note on 10:2).

Paul's First Missionary Journey (Acts 13:4–14:26)

c. A.D. 46–47

Barnabas and Paul first visited Barnabas's home region of Cyprus before sailing to the southern region of Asia Minor. When they reached Perga in Pamphylia, John Mark left the group and returned to Jerusalem. Making their way to Antioch (in Pisidia), Iconium, Lystra, and Derbe, Paul and Barnabas were driven out of each city by jealous Jewish religious leaders. Later they returned by the same route, strengthening the new churches as they went. From Attalia they set sail for their home in Antioch of Syria.

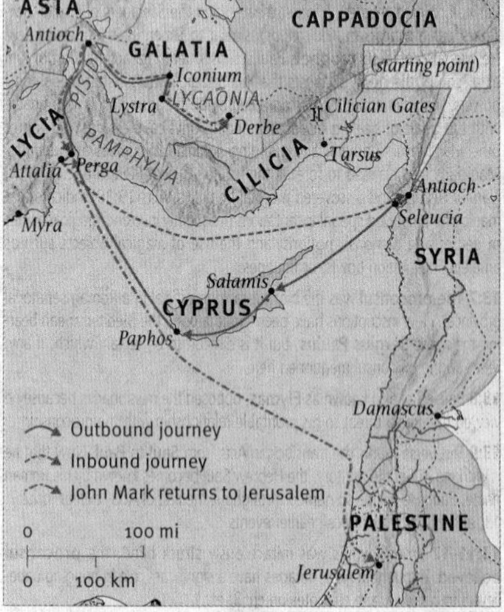

Itinerary of Paul's First Journey

City	Province/Region	Reference
Antioch	Syria	13:1–3
Seleucia	Syria	13:4
Salamis	Cyprus	13:5
Paphos	Cyprus	13:6–12
Perga	Lycia *(region of Pamphylia)*	13:13
Antioch	Galatia *(region of Pisidia)*	13:14–52
Iconium	Galatia	14:1–6
Lystra	Galatia *(region of Lycaonia)*	14:6, 8–19
Derbe	Galatia *(region of Lycaonia)*	14:6, 20–21
Lystra	Galatia *(region of Lycaonia)*	14:21–23
Iconium	Galatia	14:21–23
Antioch	Galatia *(region of Pisidia)*	14:24
Perga	Lycia *(region of Pamphylia)*	14:24–25
Attalia	Lycia	14:25
Antioch	Syria	14:26–28

them their land as an inheritance. 20 All this took about 450 years. And after that [g]he gave
them judges until [h]Samuel the prophet. 21 Then [i]they asked for a king, and God gave them
Saul [j]the son of Kish, a man of the tribe of Benjamin, for forty years. 22 And [k]when he had
removed him, [l]he raised up David to be their king, of whom he testified and said, [m]‘I have
found in David the son of Jesse [n]a man after my heart, [o]who will do all my will.’ 23 [p]Of this
man’s offspring God has brought to Israel [q]a Savior, Jesus, [r]as he promised. 24 Before his
coming, [s]John had proclaimed [t]a baptism of repentance to all the people of Israel. 25 And as
John was finishing his course, [u]he said, ‘What do you suppose that I am? I am not he. No,
but behold, after me one is coming, the sandals of whose feet I am not worthy to untie.’

26 “Brothers, sons of the family of Abraham, and those among you [v]who fear God, to us has
been sent [w]the message of [x]this salvation. 27 For those who live in Jerusalem and their rulers,
because [y]they did not recognize him nor understand [z]the utterances of the prophets, which
are read every Sabbath, [a]fulfilled them by condemning him. 28 And [b]though they found in
him no guilt worthy of death, [c]they asked Pilate to have him executed. 29 And when [d]they
had carried out all that was written of him, [e]they took him down from [f]the tree and laid him
in a tomb. 30 But [g]God raised him from the dead, 31 and for many days [h]he appeared to those
[i]who had come up with him [j]from Galilee to Jerusalem, [k]who are now [l]his witnesses to the
people. 32 And we bring you the good news [m]that what God promised to the fathers, 33 [n]this he
has fulfilled to us their children by raising Jesus, as also it is written in the second Psalm,

[o]“‘You are my Son,
today I have begotten you.’

34 And as for the fact that he raised him from the dead, [p, q]no more to return to corruption,
he has spoken in this way,

“‘I will give you [r]the holy and sure blessings of David.’

35 Therefore he says also in another psalm,

[s]“‘You will not let your Holy One see corruption.’

36 For David, after he had [t]served the purpose of God in his own generation, [u]fell asleep
and [v]was laid with his fathers and saw corruption, 37 but he whom [w]God raised up did not
see corruption. 38 Let it be known to you therefore, brothers, [x]that through this man [y]for-
giveness of sins is proclaimed to you, 39 and by him [z]everyone who believes is freed[1] from
everything [a]from which you could not be freed by the law of Moses. 40 Beware, therefore,
lest what is said in the Prophets should come about:

41 [b]“‘Look, you scoffers,
be astounded and perish;
for I am doing a work in your days,
a work that you will not believe, even if one tells it to you.’ ”

42 As they went out, the people begged that these things might be told them the next
Sabbath. 43 And after the meeting of the synagogue broke up, many Jews and [c]devout

[1] Greek *justified*; twice in this verse

20 [g]Judg. 2:16; 3:9 [h]See ch. 3:24
21 [i]1 Sam. 8:5; 10:1 [j]1 Sam. 9:1, 2
22 [k]1 Sam. 15:23, 26, 28; 16:1; [Hos. 13:11] [l]1 Sam. 16:13; 2 Sam. 2:4; 5:3 [m]Cited from Ps. 89:20 [n]ch. 7:46; Cited from 1 Sam. 13:14 [o]ver. 36
23 [p]See Matt. 1:1 [q]See Luke 2:11 [r]Ps. 132:11; [ver. 32, 33]
24 [s]ch. 1:22; Matt. 3:1 [t]ch. 19:4; Mark 1:4; Luke 3:3; [ch. 2:38; Matt. 3:11]
25 [u]John 1:20, 27; [Matt. 3:11; Mark 1:7; Luke 3:16]
26 [v]ver. 16 [w]ch. 10:36; [Eph. 1:13] [x][ch. 5:20]; See ch. 4:12
27 [y][2 Cor. 3:14, 15]; See ch. 3:17 [z]ver. 15; [ch. 15:21] [a]See Luke 24:20, 26, 27, 44
28 [b][Mark 14:55; Luke 23:22] [c]ch. 2:23; 3:14, 15; Luke 23:23
29 [d]Luke 18:31; 24:44; John 19:28, 30, 36, 37 [e]Matt. 27:59, 60; Mark 15:46; Luke 23:53; John 19:38, 41, 42 [f]See ch. 5:30
30 [g]See ch. 2:24
31 [h]See ch. 1:3 [i]Mark 15:41 [j]ch. 1:11; 2:7 [k]See Luke 24:48 [l]See ch. 1:8
32 [m]ch. 26:6; Rom. 4:13; 15:8; Gal. 3:16; [Rom. 9:4]
33 [n][ver. 23; Luke 1:69-73] [o]Heb. 1:5; 5:5; Cited from Ps. 2:7
34 [p]Rom. 6:9; [Heb. 9:25-28] [q]ver. 35-37 [r]Cited from Isa. 55:3
35 [s]ch. 2:27; Cited from Ps. 16:10
36 [t]ver. 22; ch. 20:27 [u]2 Sam. 7:12; 1 Kgs. 2:10; [ch. 2:29] [v]Judg. 2:10
37 [w]ver. 30
38 [x]Luke 24:47; 1 John 2:12 [y]ch. 5:31
39 [z]Rom. 3:28; See ch. 10:43 [a]Rom. 2:13; 3:20; 8:3; Gal. 2:16; 3:11; Eph. 2:9; 2 Tim. 1:9; Titus 3:5; [Heb. 7:19]
41 [b]Cited from Hab. 1:5; [Isa. 29:14]
43 [c]ver. 50; ch. 17:4, 17; [ch. 16:14]

13:17–21 A quick summary of Israel’s history from the exodus to King Saul emphasized God’s merciful provision for his people.

13:20 The reference to **about 450 years** seems to cover the period from Israel’s time in Egypt (400 years) through the wilderness (40 years) and conquest (about 10 years), to the judges. This brief summary of Israel’s history thus shows the step-by-step unfolding of God’s plan first realized in King David but later fulfilled in the promised Son of David, the promised “Savior, Jesus” (v. 23).

13:31 For many days he appeared suggests that there were more resurrection appearances of Jesus than are recorded in the Gospels.

13:36 After he had served the purpose of God in his own generation reveals a confidence in God’s sovereign direction of history: David’s kingdom was not meant to be final or ultimate but served a specific purpose for its time, as it anticipated the greater Messiah to come. Though he was not sinless, David was for the most part faithful to God, and thus he fulfilled God’s purpose for his life. Faithfulness should be the goal of every Christian in every generation.

13:38–39 freed. The Greek (*dikaioō*) is often translated “justified” and means “to declare innocent, to justify.” Jews sought to deal with their sin through living by the **law of Moses**. But the law cannot free a person from sin, not only because all people fail to keep it but also because it was never designed to bring about effective atonement for sins (Gal. 3:10–14; Heb. 10:1–14); only the one who **believes** in Christ and his saving sacrifice is free from sin and acceptable to God.

13:42–52 *Paul Turns to the Gentiles.* Although the response at the synagogue was favorable, with Paul being asked to preach again, the Jews turned against him the next Sabbath when a large group of Gentiles showed up. Paul responded by turning to the Gentiles, a pattern he would continue in every city he visited: beginning with the Jews, then turning to the Gentiles when opposition forced him from the synagogue.

13:43 converts. The Greek (*prosēlytos*) is sometimes translated “proselyte.”

[d]converts to Judaism followed Paul and Barnabas, who, as they spoke with them, urged
them [e]to continue in [f]the grace of God.
44 The next Sabbath almost the whole city gathered to hear the word of the Lord. **45** [g]But
[h]when the Jews saw the crowds, they were filled with [i]jealousy and began to contradict
what was spoken by Paul, [j]reviling him. **46** And Paul and Barnabas spoke out boldly, saying,
"It was necessary that the word of God [k]be spoken first to you. [l]Since you thrust it aside
and judge yourselves [m]unworthy of eternal life, behold, we [n]are turning to the Gentiles.
47 [o]For so the Lord has commanded us, saying,

> [p]"'I have made you [q]a light for the Gentiles,
> that you may [r]bring salvation to the ends of the earth.'"

48 And when the Gentiles heard this, they began rejoicing and [s]glorifying the word of
the Lord, and as many as were appointed to eternal life believed. **49** And the word of the
Lord was spreading throughout the whole region. **50** [t]But the Jews[1] incited the devout
[u]women of high standing and the leading men of the city, [v]stirred up persecution against
Paul and Barnabas, and [w]drove them out of their district. **51** But they [x]shook off the dust
from their feet against them and went to Iconium. **52** And the disciples were filled [y]with
joy and [z]with the Holy Spirit.

Paul and Barnabas at Iconium

14 Now at Iconium [a]they entered together into the Jewish synagogue and spoke in such
a way that a great number of both Jews and Greeks believed. **2** [b]But the [c]unbeliev-
ing Jews stirred up the Gentiles and poisoned their minds against [d]the brothers.[2] **3** So they
remained for a long time, speaking boldly for [e]the Lord, who bore witness to [f]the word
of his grace, [g]granting signs and wonders to be done by their hands. **4** But the people of
the city [h]were divided; [i]some sided with the Jews and some with the apostles. **5** When an

[1] Greek *Ioudaioi* probably refers here to Jewish religious leaders, and others under their influence, in that time [2] Or *brothers and sisters*

43 [d]ch. 2:11; 6:5; Matt. 23:15 [e][Jude 21] [f]Jude 4; See ch. 11:23
45 [g][ch. 19:9] [h][1 Thess. 2:16] [i]See ch. 5:17 [j]ch. 18:6; 26:11; 1 Tim. 1:20
46 [k]ver. 5, 14; See ch. 3:26 [l]See Matt. 21:43 [m]See Matt. 22:8 [n]ch. 18:6; 22:21; 26:17, 18, 20; 28:28; See ch. 9:15
47 [o][ch. 11:18] [p]Cited from Isa. 49:6; [Isa. 45:22] [q]Isa. 42:6; Luke 2:32 [r][ver. 26; ch. 1:8]
48 [s][2 Thess. 1:12]
50 [t][ch. 14:2, 19; 17:5, 13; 18:12; 20:3, 19; 21:27] [u]ch. 17:12 [v]2 Tim. 3:11 [w]1 Thess. 2:15
51 [x]Matt. 10:14; Mark 6:11; Luke 9:5; [ch. 18:6]
52 [y][1 Thess. 1:6]; See Matt. 5:12; John 16:22 [z]See ch. 2:4

Chapter 14

1 [a]See ch. 13:5
2 [b]See ch. 13:50 [c]ch. 19:9; John 3:36; Rom. 15:31 [d]See John 21:23
3 [e]ch. 15:8; Heb. 2:4; [Mark 16:20] [f]ch. 20:32 [g]ch. 4:29, 30
4 [h][ch. 23:7] [i][ch. 17:4, 5; 19:9; 28:24]

God's Sovereignty in Salvation as Seen in Acts

God ordained the cross	God calls, adds, and appoints many to eternal life	God gives faith and repentance; God cleanses and opens hearts
2:23 "Jesus, delivered up according to the definite plan and foreknowledge of God"	2:39 "the promise is to . . . everyone whom the Lord our God calls to himself"	3:16 "the faith that is through Jesus"
	2:41 "there were added that day about three thousand souls"	5:31 "God exalted him . . . to give repentance to Israel"
3:18 "what God foretold by the mouth of all the prophets, that his Christ would suffer, he thus fulfilled"	2:47 "the Lord added to their number day by day those who were being saved"	11:18 "to the Gentiles also God has granted repentance that leads to life"
4:27–28 "there were gathered together . . . Herod and Pontius Pilate, along with the Gentiles and the people of Israel, to do whatever your hand . . . had predestined to take place"	5:14 "believers were added to the Lord, multitudes of both men and women"	15:8–9 "God . . . having cleansed their hearts by faith"
	11:24 "a great many people were added to the Lord"	16:14 "The Lord opened her heart to pay attention to what was said by Paul"
	13:48 "as many as were appointed to eternal life believed"	18:27 "those who through grace had believed"

13:44 Since the population of Antioch was mainly Gentile, **almost the whole city** indicates that the majority who showed up were Gentiles.

13:46–47 Citing Isa. 49:6, Paul stated he was now turning to the Gentiles. Paul and Barnabas can be seen as doing the work of the Servant because of their connection to Jesus. **It was necessary** to begin with the Jews since they were God's chosen people and had priority in salvation history (see note on Rom. 1:16). **unworthy**. Their stubborn resistance showed Paul that it would not be worthwhile for him to spend any more time trying to reason with them.

13:48 as many as were appointed to eternal life believed. Throughout Acts, Luke affirms the sovereignty of God over all of life while at the same time affirming the significance of human activity, as evidenced by the remarkable human effort and sacrifice involved in proclaiming the gospel. Thus Luke, without contradiction, maintains a dual emphasis on divine election ("appointed") and on human response ("believed") (cf. notes on 2:23; 3:13–16; 3:17; 4:27; 4:28). The emphasis here in 13:48 is on the way in which divine sovereignty (appointment) results in the belief of the Gentiles, demonstrating that their belief was due to God's grace alone.

13:51 shook off the dust from their feet. See note on Matt. 10:14. **Iconium** was 90 miles (145 km) by road southeast from Pisidian Antioch.

14:1–7 *Paul and Barnabas Are Rejected at Iconium.* Forced to leave Antioch, the two missionaries went to Iconium (modern Konya); see note on 13:51. In Iconium, a great many Jews and Greeks believed, but there was much opposition.

14:1 Paul's witness in Iconium followed the pattern in Pisidian Antioch. He began his witness again in the **synagogue** (see notes on 13:5; Rom. 1:16).

14:2–3 In Iconium, Paul and Barnabas again faced opposition. **So they remained for a long time**. In spite of strong opposition, they were able, by the power of the Spirit, to speak **boldly** and perform **signs and wonders**, which once again confirmed the truth of the gospel.

14:4 Both Paul and Barnabas are referred to as **apostles** (vv. 4 and 14). The word (Gk. *apostolos*) carries the general meaning of "one who is sent" but it is often used throughout the NT as a more technical term for someone specifically chosen and commissioned by Christ for the proclamation of the gospel, as in the case of the original 12 apostles (e.g., Matt. 10:2; 19:28; Mark 3:14;

attempt was made by both Gentiles and Jews, with their rulers, [j]to mistreat them and [k]to
stone them, 6 they learned of it and [l]fled to [m]Lystra and Derbe, cities of Lycaonia, and to
the surrounding country, 7 and there they continued to preach the gospel.

Paul and Barnabas at Lystra

8 Now at Lystra there was a man sitting who could not use his feet. He was [n]crippled from
birth and had never walked. 9 He listened to Paul speaking. And Paul, looking intently at
him and [o]seeing that he had faith to be made well,[1] 10 said in a loud voice, "Stand upright
on your feet." And he [p]sprang up and began walking. 11 And when the crowds saw what
Paul had done, they lifted up their voices, saying in Lycaonian, [q]"The gods have come down
to us in the likeness of men!" 12 Barnabas they called [r]Zeus, and Paul, Hermes, because he
was the chief speaker. 13 And the priest of [r]Zeus, whose temple was at the entrance to the
city, brought oxen and garlands to the gates and [s]wanted to offer sacrifice with the crowds.
14 But when the apostles Barnabas and Paul heard of it, they [t]tore their garments and rushed
out into the crowd, crying out, 15 "Men, [u]why are you doing these things? We also are men,
[v]of like nature with you, and we bring you good news, that [w]you should turn from these
[x]vain things to [y]a living God, [z]who made the heaven and the earth and the sea and all that
is in them. 16 In past generations he [a]allowed all the nations [b]to walk in their own ways.
17 Yet [c]he did not leave himself without witness, for he [d]did good by [e]giving you rains from
heaven and [f]fruitful seasons, satisfying your hearts with [g]food and [h]gladness." 18 Even with
these words they scarcely restrained the people from offering sacrifice to them.

Paul Stoned at Lystra

19 [i]But Jews came from Antioch and Iconium, and having persuaded the crowds, [j]they
stoned Paul and dragged him out of the city, supposing that he was dead. 20 But when
the disciples gathered about him, he rose up and entered the city, and on the next day
he went on with Barnabas to Derbe. 21 When they had preached the gospel to that city
and had [k]made many disciples, they returned to Lystra and to Iconium and to Antioch,

[1] Or *be saved*

5 [j]1 Thess. 2:2; [2 Cor. 12:10] [k][ver. 19]
6 [l]See Matt. 10:23 [m]2 Tim. 3:11
8 [n]ch. 3:2
9 [o]See Matt. 9:2
10 [p]ch. 3:8; Isa. 35:6
11 [q]ch. 8:10; 28:6
12 [r][ch. 19:35; 28:11 (Gk.)]
13 [r][See ver. 12 above] [s][Dan. 2:46]
14 [t]See Gen. 37:29
15 [u]See ch. 10:26 [v]James 5:17 [w]ch. 15:19; 26:18, 20; Luke 1:16; 1 Thess. 1:9; [ch. 15:3; James 5:19, 20]; See ch. 9:35 [x]Deut. 32:21; 1 Sam. 12:21; Jer. 14:22; [1 Cor. 8:4] [y]See Matt. 16:16 [z]ch. 17:24; Gen. 1:1; Ex. 20:11; Ps. 146:6; Rev. 4:11; 10:6; 14:7
16 [a][ch. 17:30; 1 Pet. 4:3] [b][Ps. 81:13; Mic. 4:5]
17 [c][ch. 17:27; Rom. 1:19, 20] [d]Num. 10:32 [e]Lev. 26:4; Deut. 11:14; 28:12; Job 5:10; Ps. 65:10; 147:8, 18; Ezek. 34:26; Joel 2:23 [f]Ps. 67:6; 85:12; Ezek. 34:27; Joel 2:24; Zech. 8:12 [g]Ps. 104:27 [h]Ps. 104:15
19 [i]See ch. 13:45, 50 [j]2 Cor. 11:25; [ver. 5; 2 Tim. 3:11]; See ch. 7:58
21 [k]Matt. 28:19

Luke 9:1; Acts 1:2, 15–26). The apostle Paul understood his calling as an apostle to be comparable to the calling of the original Twelve in this technical sense, that is, as one who had seen Christ and who had been specifically chosen and appointed by Christ. This was based on the fact that Paul, on the road to Damascus, had in fact personally seen the risen Christ and had been chosen by Christ (9:15), and that he had been appointed by Christ and sent by Christ (26:16–17) to proclaim the gospel to the Gentiles. (See also Paul's defense of his apostolic calling in 1 Cor. 9:2; 15:7–9; and Gal. 1:1, 12, 16.) Commentators differ as to whether the word "apostles" in Acts 14:4 and 14 refers to Paul and Barnabas as being apostles in the same technical sense as the original Twelve, or whether this is intended in the general sense of "ones who are sent" (cf. 13:2–3, where Paul and Barnabas are "set apart" by the Holy Spirit and "sent . . . off" by the church in Antioch).

14:6 they learned of it and fled. See note on 9:25. **Lystra** was 20 miles (32 km) southwest of Iconium and **Derbe** another 58 miles (93 km) southeast. Both were in the district of **Lycaonia** within the Galatian province. This verse likely implies that Iconium was not a city of Lycaonia (but rather of Phrygia and/or of the province of Galatia); this claim is supported by inscriptions from Iconium in the Phrygian language.

14:8–23 *The Two Missionaries Witness in Lystra.* Lystra was populated mainly by Gentiles and had no synagogue. The ministry of Paul and Barnabas there centered around the healing of a lame man and the attempt of the populace to worship them.

14:9 seeing that he had faith to be made well. The Holy Spirit gave Paul the ability somehow to see what was happening in the invisible, spiritual realm.

14:11–13 The gods have come down to us in the likeness of men. Since the people were speaking in their native **Lycaonian** language, Paul and Barnabas were probably unaware of what was transpiring. They realized the gravity of the situation, however, when the local priest began to **offer sacrifice**. The crowd's acclamation was based on a local myth that the gods **Hermes** and **Zeus** had once visited their region in human form.

14:14–15 tore their garments. Contrast the response of Herod (12:21–23). **who made the heaven and the earth**. Since the Lystrans were polytheists, it was necessary to begin with the basic message that God is the creator of all that exists.

14:17 rains . . . and fruitful seasons. Paul tells these Gentiles who had no knowledge of the Jewish Scriptures that their regular harvests, the **food** they eat every day, and the **gladness** they experience in the ordinary activities of life are all a **witness** from God of his existence, wisdom, and goodness. They should not think that these things "just happen" or that they are the work of some local deities, for they are from the one true God "who made the heaven and the earth" (v. 15). The themes of this short speech will be developed in the speech at Mars Hill (17:16–34). These are the two occasions where Paul speaks to Gentiles who worship idols.

14:19 The **Jews** again stirred up opposition, this time coming from **Iconium** and **Antioch**, over 100 miles (161 km) distant by road. **they stoned Paul**. The action was so brutal that they could see no sign of life in Paul. Later, in recounting his sufferings for the gospel, Paul says, "Once I was stoned" (2 Cor. 11:25; cf. 2 Tim. 3:11). **supposing that he was dead**. Those who stoned Paul apparently thought they had succeeded in killing him. But as "supposing" indicates, they were mistaken in thinking that, even though Paul was indeed gravely injured.

14:20 The presence of **disciples** indicates that despite the opposition, a nucleus of believers was established at Lystra (including Timothy, 16:1). They **gathered about** Paul, perhaps at first to mourn, but then, with some sign of life, to pray for his recovery. Amazingly, and apparently miraculously, he **rose up and entered the city**, apparently under his own strength.

14:21 Derbe, about 58 miles (93 km) southeast of Lystra, marked the farthest point in Paul's first journey. The account is brief, noting only that Paul made a number of converts there. From **that city** (Derbe) Paul could have continued on south to his starting point of Syrian Antioch on foot, a much easier journey than backtracking through **Lystra**, **Iconium**, and Pisidian **Antioch** (see map, p. 2110). The decision to take this longer route shows the importance Paul attached to maintaining contact with his churches and establishing local elders. It also shows tremendous courage that he would return to the cities from which he had been driven by such violent opposition.

22 [l]strengthening the souls of the disciples, encouraging them [m]to continue in [n]the faith,
and saying that [o]through many tribulations we must enter the kingdom of God. 23 And
when they had [p]appointed [q]elders for them in every church, with prayer and fasting [r]they
committed them to the Lord in whom they had believed.

Paul and Barnabas Return to Antioch in Syria

24 Then they passed through Pisidia and came to Pamphylia. 25 And when they had spoken the word in Perga, they went down to Attalia, 26 and from there they sailed to Antioch,
[s]where they had been [t]commended to the grace of God for the work that they had fulfilled.
27 And when they arrived and gathered the church together, [u]they declared all that God
had done with them, and [v]how he had [w]opened [x]a door of faith to the Gentiles. 28 And they
remained no little time with the disciples.

The Jerusalem Council

15 [y]But some men came down from Judea and were teaching [z]the brothers, "Unless you
are [a]circumcised [b]according to the custom of Moses, you cannot be saved." 2 And after
Paul and Barnabas had no small dissension and [c]debate with them, Paul and Barnabas and
[d]some of the others were appointed to go up to Jerusalem to [e]the apostles and the elders
about this question. 3 So, [f]being sent on their way by the church, they passed through both
Phoenicia and Samaria, [g]describing in detail the conversion of the Gentiles, and [h]brought
great joy to all [i]the brothers.[1] 4 [j]When they came to Jerusalem, they were welcomed by the
church and [k]the apostles and the elders, and [g]they declared all that God had done with
them. 5 But some believers who belonged to [l]the party of the Pharisees rose up and said,
[m]"It is necessary [n]to circumcise them and to order them to keep the law of Moses."
6 [o]The [k]apostles and the elders were gathered together to consider this matter. 7 And after

[1] *Or brothers and sisters; also verse 22*

6 [o][ver. 12, 25] [k][See ver. 4 above]

22 [l]ch. 15:32, 41; [ch. 18:23; 1 Thess. 3:2, 13] [m]ch. 13:43; Col. 1:23 [n]See ch. 6:7 [o]John 15:20; 16:33; 1 Thess. 3:3; 2 Tim. 3:12; [ch. 9:16; Mark 10:30; Luke 22:28, 29; Rom. 8:17; Phil. 1:20; 2 Thess. 1:5; 2 Tim. 2:12; 1 Pet. 5:10; Rev. 1:9]
23 [p][Titus 1:5] [q]See ch. 11:30 [r]ch. 20:32
26 [s]ch. 13:3 [t]ch. 15:40
27 [u]ch. 15:4; [ch. 15:3, 12; 21:19] [v][ch. 11:18] [w]1 Cor. 16:9; 2 Cor. 2:12; Col. 4:3; Rev. 3:8 [x][Hos. 2:15]

Chapter 15

1 [y]ver. 24 [z]ver. 3, 22, 23, 36, 40; See John 21:23 [a]ver. 5; Gal. 5:2; [1 Cor. 7:18; Gal. 2:11, 14] [b]ch. 6:14; Lev. 12:3
2 [c]ver. 7 [d][Gal. 2:1, 2] [e]ver. 4, 6, 22, 23; ch. 16:4; See ch. 5:12; 11:30
3 [f]ch. 21:5; Rom. 15:24; 1 Cor. 16:6, 11; 2 Cor. 1:16; Titus 3:13; 3 John 6; [ch. 17:15] [g]See ch. 14:27 [h]ch. 11:18 [i]ver. 1
4 [j][ch. 21:17] [k]ver. 2 [g][See ver. 3 above]
5 [l]See ch. 24:5 [m]ver. 1 [n]Gal. 5:3

Debates surround the exact location of ancient Derbe, but many associate it with the unexcavated mound of Kerti Hüyük since inscriptions mentioning Derbe were found in the area.

14:22 Paul's telling the Christians of those cities to expect **many tribulations** is echoed in his own account of his persecutions there (2 Tim. 3:10–12; cf. Rom. 8:17). Often in Acts new believers are exhorted to persevere in the faith (Acts 11:23; 13:43), and the reference to "tribulations" indicates that the Christian's life is often beset by difficulties.

14:23 Paul's churches followed the synagogue pattern of leadership by **elders**. It is significant that elders were appointed from the beginning for such young churches (cf. James 5:14, which dates to sometime between A.D. 40 and 50). The language here indicates a plurality of elders in every church (cf. also Acts 11:30; 15:2, 4, 6, 22–23; 16:4; 20:17; 21:18; 1 Tim. 5:17; Titus 1:5; 1 Pet. 5:1, 5). See also note on 1 Sam. 4:3.

14:24–28 *Paul and Barnabas Return to Antioch.* Paul and Barnabas summarize God's work among the Gentiles.

14:24–26 Paul and Barnabas retraced their steps south through the regions of Pisidia and Pamphylia to **Perga** and the port city of **Attalia**, then sailed home to their sponsoring congregation in Syrian **Antioch**. This time they shared the gospel in Perga (cf. note on 13:13). Attalia (modern Antalya) continues to serve as a marina to this day, and the remains of an ancient mausoleum still overlook the harbor. The reference to having fulfilled the **work** links up with the Spirit's original commission at Antioch (13:2). It was perhaps during this time in Antioch that Paul penned his letter to the Galatians (c. A.D. 48).

14:27 opened a door. An expression Paul used elsewhere (1 Cor. 16:9; 2 Cor. 2:12; Col. 4:3).

15:1–35 *The Jerusalem Council.* A conference was held in Jerusalem (c. A.D. 48 or 49) to discuss conditions for Gentile membership in the church. The issue was raised by the "Pharisaic" wing of the Jerusalem church (vv. 1–5); the Gentile mission was defended by Peter (vv. 6–11); a solution was proposed by James (vv. 12–21); and an official agreement was reached (vv. 22–35). The fact that James is key to the resolution shows that the Jewish and Gentile believers were less divided than some try to make them. Those who complained here were on the fringe of the church, and their hard line view was rejected.

15:1–5 *The Circumcision Party Criticizes the Gentile Mission.* The Antioch church had reached out to many Gentiles (11:20–21), and God had given Paul and Barnabas great success among the Gentiles on their mission (14:27). No evidence exists that these Gentiles had been circumcised or required to live by all the Mosaic law. In fact, the Spirit had come on them without such an act, as Peter will argue. Some conservative Jewish Christians argued that Gentiles should undergo these things since they were required of all converts to Judaism. The issue was whether Gentiles needed to become Jews and follow Jewish ceremonial laws in order to be Christians. Though some scholars think that Paul is referring to this meeting in Gal. 2:1–10, it is better to see that passage as referring to private contacts made during his famine relief visit to Jerusalem (see note on Acts 11:27–30).

15:1 The Jewish law contained not only basic moral provisions but many aspects of a more "ceremonial" nature, such as circumcision, the kosher food laws, and many requirements involving external purity and various kinds of sacrifices and festivals. These laws presented a problem for Gentiles: to live by them would make it virtually impossible to continue in their Gentile communities. But according to the OT, one had to be circumcised to belong to the people of God (Gen. 17:9–14), and it seemed to many of the Jewish Christians that the church should also require this of male believers. Paul addresses the issue of circumcision in Rom. 2:25–29; 4:9–16; Gal. 2:3–5; 5:2–12; 6:12–15.

15:5 Those from the **Pharisees** were likely the same group as those insisting on circumcision in v. 2 and 11:2. They not only argued that Gentiles had to be circumcised to be saved but also that they were required to **keep** the whole Mosaic **law** as well, for circumcision represented a commitment to observe the law.

15:6–11 *Peter Defends Paul.* Peter, first to speak, defended Paul's Gentile mission.

15:6 The **apostles and the elders** provided the main leadership at the council, but v. 22 indicates that "the whole church" was present for the occasion and apparently also gave consent to the decision.

7 [p]ver. 2 [q]ch. 10:20 [r][Eph. 1:13; Col. 1:5; 1 Thess. 1:5] [s]ch. 20:24
8 [t]ch. 1:24 [u]ch. 14:3 [v]ch. 10:44, 47; 11:15, 17; [ver. 28; Gal. 3:2]
9 [w]ch. 11:12; Rom. 3:22-24; Eph. 3:6; [ch. 10:28, 34] [x]Ps. 51:10; [ch. 26:18; 2 Cor. 7:1; 1 Pet. 1:22] [y]See ch. 10:43
10 [z]Ps. 106:14; Isa. 7:12 [a]Gal. 5:1; [ver. 28] [b][Matt. 11:28; 23:4; Luke 11:46]
11 [c][ch. 16:31] [d]Eph. 2:5, 8; 2 Tim. 1:9; Titus 2:11; 3:7; [Rom. 3:24; 1 Thess. 5:9] [e]Rom. 5:15 [w][See ver. 9 above]
12 [f]ver. 4; See ch. 14:27
13 [g]See ch. 12:17
14 [h][ver. 7] [i][ch. 18:10; Deut. 7:6; Isa. 43:21; Rom. 9:24-26]
16 [j]Cited from Amos 9:11, 12; [Jer. 12:15]
17 [k][ch. 17:27] [l]Isa. 43:7; Jer. 14:9; Dan. 9:19
18 [m][Isa. 45:21]
19 [n][ver. 28] [o]See ch. 14:15
20 [p]ch. 21:25 [q][ver. 29; Ezek. 4:13, 14; Dan. 1:8; Mal. 1:7, 12] [r]1 Cor. 10:7, 8; Rev. 2:14, 20; See 1 Cor. 6:18 [s]See Lev. 3:17

there had been much [p]debate, Peter stood up and said to them, "Brothers, you know that
in the early days God made a choice among you, [q]that by my mouth the Gentiles should
hear [r]the word of [s]the gospel and believe. 8 And God, [t]who knows the heart, [u]bore witness
to them, [v]by giving them the Holy Spirit just as he did to us, 9 and [w]he made no distinction
between us and them, [x]having cleansed their hearts [y]by faith. 10 Now, therefore, why [z]are
you putting God to the test [a]by placing a yoke on the neck of the disciples [b]that neither
our fathers nor we have been able to bear? 11 But we [c]believe that we will be [d]saved through
[e]the grace of the Lord Jesus, [w]just as they will."

12 And all the assembly fell silent, and they listened to Barnabas and Paul [f]as they related
what signs and wonders God had done through them among the Gentiles. 13 After they
finished speaking, [g]James replied, "Brothers, listen to me. 14 [h]Simeon has related how God
first visited the Gentiles, to take from them [i]a people for his name. 15 And with this the
words of the prophets agree, just as it is written,

16 [j]"'After this I will return,
and I will rebuild the tent of David that has fallen;
I will rebuild its ruins,
and I will restore it,
17 that the remnant[1] of mankind [k]may seek the Lord,
and all the Gentiles [l]who are called by my name,
says the Lord, who makes these things 18 [m]known from of old.'

19 Therefore [n]my judgment is that we should not trouble those of the Gentiles who [o]turn
to God, 20 but should write to them [p]to abstain from [q]the things polluted by idols, and
from [r]sexual immorality, and from [s]what has been strangled, and from [s]blood. 21 For from

[1] *Or rest*

15:7 and after there had been much debate. This important theological issue in the early history of the church was not decided by a sudden decree spoken by a prophet but by careful reasoning and thoughtful argumentation based on Scripture. Peter's reference to the Gentiles hearing the **gospel . . . by my mouth . . . in the early days** refers to his witness at the house of Cornelius (10:34–43), c. A.D. 38, as many as 10 years before the Jerusalem council.

15:9 Peter's reference to God having **cleansed their hearts by faith** may allude to the content of his vision prior to visiting Cornelius (see v. 7): "What God has made clean, do not call common" (10:15; 11:9). The faith of the Gentiles at Cornelius's house is only implicit in chs. 10–11, but Peter referred to it explicitly here: they were saved by faith in their hearts, not by circumcision in their flesh. The argument here recalls points made in Acts 11:15–17.

15:10–11 The rabbis often used the metaphor of a **yoke** with reference to the law, and Peter's reference to "yoke" here refers not just to circumcision but to the whole of the Mosaic law (see note on v. 1). By speaking of the law as an unbearable yoke, Peter was not denying that the law was God's gift to Israel. Rather, he was arguing that Israel was unable to fulfill it perfectly and that salvation could not be obtained through the law (cf. Rom. 2:17–24). Only one means of salvation exists for both Jew and Gentile: God's "grace" (Acts 15:11) in Jesus Christ. Paul also refers to any requirement to keep the OT laws as "a yoke of slavery" (Gal. 5:1). By contrast, Jesus calls people to take his new "yoke" upon them, a yoke that is easy (see note on Matt. 11:29).

15:12–21 *James Proposes a Solution.* When some apostles had begun to leave Jerusalem for a wider witness, the Jerusalem leadership was assumed by others, with Jesus' brother James in a prominent role (see 12:17; 21:18–25). At the Jerusalem council, James endorsed Peter's conclusions about a "circumcision-free" Gentile mission and offered a suggestion for establishing fellowship between Jewish and Gentile Christians.

15:13 James was noted for his scrupulous keeping of the Jewish law (cf. Josephus, *Jewish Antiquities* 20.200; Eusebius, *Ecclesiastical History* 2.23).

15:14 Simeon. A different spelling for the name of Simon Peter. James presented scriptural backing (vv. 15–17) to support Peter's contention that God was now including the Gentiles as a **people for his name**. This means "for himself" (since someone's "name" represented all that was true about him and his character) and also seems to imply "for his reputation and his glory."

15:16–18 James refers to "prophets" (v. 15), showing that he could appeal to more than one OT text to defend the inclusion of Gentiles by faith alone. See the allusion to Isa. 45:21 in Acts 15:18, and the context of the Isaiah prophecy. James concentrated on Amos 9:11–12, which looked to the time when God would restore the house of David. Luke provides the Septuagint (Greek) translation of the text, which speaks of the Gentiles (Gk. *ethnē*) seeking the Lord. But even the Masoretic (Hebrew) Text fits with what James argued, since it speaks of a people **called by my name** (Amos 9:12), and those called by God's name are in a saving relationship with him. Amos looked to a time when God would claim a people for himself from among the **Gentiles**. James concurred with Peter that the time of Gentile inclusion in God's people had now arrived.

15:19–21 James agreed with Peter that they should not **trouble** the Gentiles with the ritual laws. But he knew that Gentile Christians would have contact with Jewish Christians who still kept the ceremonial provisions, including laws about sacrifices, festivals, unclean foods, and circumcision. He offered a proposal by which Gentile Christians could have fellowship with Jewish Christians and avoid giving unnecessary offense. The word **for** (Gk. *gar*) at the beginning of v. 21 gives the reason for James's proposal: the Gentile Christians should abstain from certain things *because* "in every city" there are still Jews who observe these ceremonial laws and think them to be important. The first three requirements (see v. 29) seem to be contextually sensitive and designed for these specific circumstances: abstention from food offered to **idols**, from **blood** (meat with the blood in it), and from **strangled** meat (which would also have blood in it). (But Paul in other circumstances permitted believers to eat food offered to idols; see 1 Cor. 8:1–11:1.) The fourth requirement, dealing with **sexual immorality**, was of course not a contextual or optional standard of obedience like the other three. It may have needed special emphasis and clarification because many Gentiles' consciences were so corrupted that they did not hold to a high standard of sexual purity. This reaffirmation of the believer's need to maintain sexual purity also serves as a reminder that the moral standards of the OT still need to be obeyed. James concludes his appeal (v. 21) by noting the widespread (**in every city**) teaching and affirmation of the Mosaic law, thus suggesting that there is no need to give unnecessary offense either to Jewish believers or to unbelieving Jews who might otherwise consider becoming Christians in the future.

ancient generations Moses has had in every city those who proclaim him, [t]for he is read
every Sabbath in the synagogues."

The Council's Letter to Gentile Believers

22 Then it seemed good to [u]the apostles and the elders, with the whole church, to choose
men from among them and send them to Antioch with Paul and Barnabas. They sent Judas
called [v]Barsabbas, and [w]Silas, leading men among [x]the brothers, 23 with the following letter:
[x]"The brothers, both [u]the apostles and the elders, to the brothers[1] who are of the Gentiles
in Antioch and Syria and Cilicia, [y]greetings. 24 Since we have heard that [z]some persons
have gone out from us and [a]troubled you[2] with words, unsettling your minds, although
we gave them no instructions, 25 it has seemed good to us, having come [b]to one accord,
to choose men and send them to you with our [c]beloved Barnabas and Paul, 26 [d]men who
have [e]risked their lives for the name of our Lord Jesus Christ. 27 We have therefore sent
[f]Judas and Silas, who themselves will tell you the same things by word of mouth. 28 For it
has seemed good [g]to the Holy Spirit and [h]to us [i]to lay on you no greater burden than these
requirements: 29 [j]that you abstain from [k]what has been sacrificed to idols, and from blood,
and from what has been strangled, and from sexual immorality. If you keep yourselves
from these, you will do well. Farewell."

30 So when they were sent off, they went down to Antioch, and having gathered the
congregation together, they delivered the letter. 31 And when they had read it, they rejoiced
because of its encouragement. 32 And Judas and Silas, who were themselves [l]prophets,
encouraged and [m]strengthened [n]the brothers with many words. 33 And after they had
spent some time, they were sent off [o]in peace by [n]the brothers to those who had sent
them.[3] 35 But [p]Paul and Barnabas remained in Antioch, teaching and preaching the word
of the Lord, with many others also.

Paul and Barnabas Separate

36 And after some days Paul said to Barnabas, "Let us return and visit [n]the brothers
[q]in every city where we proclaimed the word of the Lord, and see how they are." 37 Now
Barnabas wanted to take with them [r]John called Mark. 38 But Paul thought best not to
take with them one [s]who had withdrawn from them in Pamphylia and had not gone with
them to the work. 39 And there arose [t]a sharp disagreement, so that they separated from
each other. [u]Barnabas took Mark with him and sailed away to Cyprus, 40 but Paul chose
Silas and departed, [v]having been commended by [w]the brothers to [x]the grace of the Lord.
41 And he went through Syria and Cilicia, [y]strengthening the churches.

21 [t]ch. 13:15; 2 Cor. 3:14, 15; [ch. 13:27]
22 [u]ver. 2 [v][ch. 1:23] [w]See 1 Pet. 5:12 [x]ver. 1
23 [x][See ver. 22 above] [u][See ver. 22 above] [y]ch. 23:26; James 1:1; [2 John 10, 11]
24 [z]ver. 1; [Gal. 2:4; 5:12; Titus 1:10] [a]Gal. 1:7; 5:10
25 [b]See ch. 1:14 [c][2 Pet. 3:15]
26 [d]ch. 9:23-25; 14:19 [e][ch. 20:24; 21:13; 2 Cor. 4:11; 1 John 3:16]
27 [f]ver. 22, 32
28 [g][ver. 8; ch. 5:32; John 16:13; 1 Cor. 7:40] [h][ver. 19] [i][ver. 10; Rev. 2:24]
29 [j]See ver. 20 [k]ch. 21:25; 1 Cor. 8:1, 4, 7, 10; 10:19; Rev. 2:14, 20
32 [l]See ch. 13:1 [m]See ch. 14:22 [n]ver. 1
33 [o]Gen. 26:29; Heb. 11:31; [1 Cor. 16:11] [n][See ver. 32 above]
35 [p]ch. 13:1
36 [n][See ver. 32 above] [q]ch. 13:4, 13, 14, 51; 14:6, 24, 25
37 [r]See ch. 12:12
38 [s]ch. 13:13
39 [t][ch. 17:16 (Gk.)] [u][Col. 4:10]
40 [v]ch. 14:26 [w]ver. 1 [x]ver. 11; [ch. 11:23]; See Rom. 16:20
41 [y]ver. 32; ch. 16:5

[1] *Or brothers and sisters; also verses 32, 33, 36* [2] Some manuscripts *some persons from us have troubled you* [3] Some manuscripts insert verse 34: *But it seemed good to Silas to remain there*

15:22–35 *A Letter Is Sent to Antioch.* When the entire assembly agreed to James's provisions, a letter was drafted to inform the Antioch church of their decision.

15:22 it seemed good. Mature Christian wisdom and reasoning, in dependence on the Lord, resulted in a unanimous corporate decision. (See also v. 28.) The letter was accompanied by representatives of the Jerusalem church who could testify to the reasoning that the consensus expressed. Nothing more is known of **Judas called Barsabbas**, but **Silas** soon became Paul's missionary companion (v. 40). Silas is a shortened form of the Greek name Silvanus (the name by which he is known in the NT epistles).

15:23 The Roman province of **Syria** included **Cilicia**, with **Antioch** as its provincial capital.

15:24 unsettling your minds. Those insisting that Gentile converts should be circumcised neither represented the Jerusalem leadership nor had their approval (cf. vv. 1–2, 5).

15:28 it has seemed good to the Holy Spirit and to us. The apostles and elders were confident that the Holy Spirit had guided their decision making process. **no greater burden.** They were not requiring circumcision and observance of the entire Mosaic law (v. 10), for salvation is by grace alone (v. 11).

15:32 Prophets were gifted to speak what the Holy Spirit revealed to them, here resulting in encouragement and strength (see notes on 13:1; 1 Cor. 12:10; and other notes on 1 Corinthians 14).

15:33 They were sent off in peace suggests that Judas and Silas returned to Jerusalem.

15:36–18:22 *The Witness in Greece.* Paul's second missionary journey centered on the cities of the Greek provinces of Macedonia and Achaia, including Philippi, Thessalonica, Berea, Athens, and Corinth. This second journey (see map, p. 2118) probably began in A.D. 48 or 49 and ended in 51.

15:36–41 *Paul and Barnabas Differ over Mark.* Before setting out on his new mission, Paul asked Barnabas to accompany him. A sharp disagreement arose between them over whether to take Mark, resulting in Barnabas taking Mark on a separate mission and Paul choosing Silas as his companion.

15:37 John called Mark. See note on 12:12.

15:39 a sharp disagreement. In the sovereignty of God, out of this disagreement came a doubling of their labor, for Barnabas went to strengthen the churches in Cyprus and Paul went to the churches in Syria, Cilicia, and then Galatia. In addition, both of their assistants (Mark and Silas) went on to have significant ministries themselves.

15:41 Paul's route took him by foot to the churches of his first missionary journey in reverse order.

Chapter 16

1[z]ch. 17:14; 18:5; 19:22; 20:4; Rom. 16:21; 1 Cor. 4:17; Phil. 2:19; Col. 1:1; 1 Thess. 3:2; 2 Thess. 1:1; 1 Tim. 1:2, 18; 2 Tim. 1:2
[a]2 Tim. 1:5; 3:15
2[b]See John 21:23
3[c][Gal. 2:3]
4[d]ch. 17:7 [e]ch. 15:28, 29 [f]See ch. 15:2
5[g][ch. 9:31] [h]See ch. 6:7 [i]ch. 2:47
6[j]ch. 18:23; [Gal. 4:13]
7[k]Rom. 8:9; Gal. 4:6; Phil. 1:19; 1 Pet. 1:11; [ver. 6; ch. 8:29]
8[l]ch. 20:5, 6; 2 Cor. 2:12; 2 Tim. 4:13
10[m]ver. 11-17; ch. 20:5-8, 13-15; 21:1-18; 27:1–28:16
11[n]ch. 21:1
12[o]Phil. 1:1; 1 Thess. 2:2 [p][ver. 21]
13[q]See ch. 13:14

Timothy Joins Paul and Silas

16 Paul[1] came also to Derbe and to Lystra. A disciple was there, named [z]Timothy, [a]the
son of a Jewish woman who was a believer, but his father was a Greek. 2 He was well
spoken of by [b]the brothers[2] at Lystra and Iconium. 3 Paul wanted Timothy to accompany
him, and he [c]took him and circumcised him because of the Jews who were in those places,
for they all knew that his father was a Greek. 4 As they went on their way through the cities, they delivered to them for observance [d]the decisions [e]that had been reached by [f]the
apostles and elders who were in Jerusalem. 5 [g]So the churches were strengthened in [h]the
faith, and they increased in numbers [i]daily.

The Macedonian Call

6 And [j]they went through the region of Phrygia and Galatia, having been forbidden by
the Holy Spirit to speak the word in Asia. 7 And when they had come up to Mysia, they
attempted to go into Bithynia, but [k]the Spirit of Jesus did not allow them. 8 So, passing
by Mysia, they went down [l]to Troas. 9 And a vision appeared to Paul in the night: a man
of Macedonia was standing there, urging him and saying, "Come over to Macedonia and
help us." 10 And when Paul[3] had seen the vision, immediately [m]we sought to go on into
Macedonia, concluding that God had called us to preach the gospel to them.

The Conversion of Lydia

11 So, setting sail from Troas, we [n]made a direct voyage to Samothrace, and the following day to Neapolis, 12 and from there to [o]Philippi, which is a leading city of the[4] district
of Macedonia and [p]a Roman colony. We remained in this city some days. 13 And [q]on the

[1] Greek *He* [2] Or *brothers and sisters;* also verse 40 [3] Greek *he* [4] Or *that*

16:1–5 *Timothy Joins Paul and Is Circumcised.* Timothy joined Paul and Silas at Lystra. Because Timothy's mother was Jewish, Paul had him circumcised. They continued on their way, revisiting the churches of the first mission.

16:1 Probably Timothy, his mother, and his grandmother had been led to Christ upon Paul's first witness in Lystra (14:8–23; cf. 2 Tim. 1:5). Having a Greek father, Timothy had not been circumcised, though by Jewish law the child of a Gentile father and Jewish mother was considered Jewish.

16:3 because of the Jews who were in those places. Paul never abandoned his Jewish heritage, and so he circumcised Timothy. It was all the more necessary if Timothy was to join his mission. He did not want to fight on nonessentials (1 Cor. 9:19–21). Paul always began in the synagogues, and to have an uncircumcised Jew with him would have made any witness to Jews much more difficult. (Since Timothy had grown up in this region, the Jews would have known of his mixed family background.)

16:4 The **decisions** of the Jerusalem council were addressed specifically to believers in Antioch and throughout Syria and Cilicia (15:23), but since the issue of Gentile converts affected all the churches, Paul reported those decisions as he traveled **through** other **cities** as well.

16:5 As is frequent in Acts, the section ends with reference to the growth of the church.

16:6–10 *Paul Is Called to Macedonia.* Through divine direction Paul was led to the town of Troas, where he received a vision directing him to witness in the Greek province of Macedonia.

16:6–7 Paul's route is not altogether clear. After revisiting his earlier field, undoubtedly traveling on the Via Sebaste (a Roman military road), he proceeded farther west into **Phrygia**. Had he continued in that direction he would have traveled through **Asia** with its prosperous coastal cities like Ephesus. **The Spirit of Jesus** prevented this, and he went north through **Mysia**. He was also prevented from witnessing in **Bithynia**.

16:6 having been forbidden by the Holy Spirit to speak the word in Asia. From Antioch in Pisidia Paul and Timothy traveled far northward, and then westward. Natural human wisdom would have led them to think they should preach the gospel in all the cities that they passed through, but instead the Holy Spirit directed them on a 400-mile (644-km) journey by foot to Troas (v. 8). They must have had a strong sense of the Spirit's direct guidance and concluded that he would guide others to preach the gospel in the northern regions of Asia and in Bithynia (cf. 1 Pet. 1:1, where Peter writes to churches in that region).

16:7 the Spirit of Jesus. Another name for the Holy Spirit, who had been sent by Jesus to the church in new power at Pentecost (2:33; cf. John 15:26).

16:8 Troas was a major Aegean port 14 miles (23 km) south of ancient Troy, and the primary Asian harbor for ships destined for Macedonia. The harbor of Troas is still visible, although it is silted over. Ongoing excavations at the site of Troas have yielded a pagan temple and an adjacent agora (marketplace) from the time of Paul. Though not very distant in nautical miles, Macedonia was a different part of the world—Europe—instead of the East, to which the gospel had hitherto been confined.

16:9 a vision . . . a man. Some kind of visible image of a man came in such a forceful way, accompanied by such a strong sense of God's presence, that Paul concluded that God was guiding him. God also spoke to people in visions (Gk. *horama*) elsewhere, as recorded in both Acts and the rest of Scripture (see 7:31; 9:10; 10:3; 12:9; 18:9; cf. Gen. 15:1; 46:2; Ex. 3:3; Dan. 7:1, 13; Matt. 17:9).

16:10 The occurrence of **we** is the first time in the narrative that the first person plural occurs in Acts and most likely indicates that at this point Luke, the author of Acts, joined the missionary group as they set out for Macedonia.

16:11–40 *Paul Witnesses in Philippi.* Philippi was the first Macedonian city in which Paul witnessed. His ministry there is related in four parts: the conversion of Lydia (vv. 11–15), the arrest of Paul and Silas (vv. 16–24), the conversion of the Philippian jailer (vv. 25–34), and the release of Paul and Silas by the magistrates (vv. 35–40).

16:11–15 *Conversion of Lydia.* Finding no synagogue in Philippi, Paul began his witness in the closest thing to one: a group of women gathered outside the city for prayer. One of them, Lydia, responded to the gospel and was baptized along with her household.

16:11 Samothrace was an island on the direct route between **Troas** and **Neapolis**, the port for Philippi, which lay 8.5 miles (14 km) inland. Paul's ship would likely have stopped (probably simply to anchor offshore for the night) on the north side of Samothrace. Neapolis (most plausibly modern Kavalla) was built on a natural harbor still in use today.

16:12 Philippi was a **Roman colony**, the most privileged status for provincial cities (see Introduction to Philippians: The Ancient City of Philippi).

16:13 Philippi seems to have had no significant Jewish population. Like Lydia, the women who attended the prayer meeting may have been God-fearers and not Jews. At least three locations among the remains of Philippi have been suggested for this **place of prayer**.

Sabbath day we went outside the gate [r]to the riverside, where we supposed there was a
place of prayer, and we [s]sat down and spoke to the women who had come together. **14** One
who heard us was a woman named Lydia, from the city of Thyatira, a seller of purple goods,
[t]who was a worshiper of God. The Lord [u]opened her heart to pay attention to what was
said by Paul. **15** And after she was baptized, [v]and her household as well, she urged us, saying, "If you have judged me to be faithful to the Lord, come to my house and stay." And
she [w]prevailed upon us.

Paul and Silas in Prison

16 As we were going to [x]the place of prayer, we were met by a slave girl who had [y]a spirit
of [z]divination and [a]brought her owners much gain by fortune-telling. **17** She followed Paul
and us, [b]crying out, "These men are [c]servants[1] of [d]the Most High God, who proclaim to
you [e]the way of salvation." **18** And this she kept doing for many days. Paul, having become
greatly annoyed, turned and said to the spirit, [f]"I command you [g]in the name of Jesus
Christ to come out of her." And [h]it came out that very hour.

[1] Greek *bondservants*

13 [r][Ezra 8:15, 21; Ps. 137:1] [s]Matt. 5:1
14 [t]ch. 18:7 [u]See Luke 24:45
15 [v]See ch. 11:14 [w]Gen. 19:3; Luke 24:29
16 [x]ver. 13 [y]Luke 13:11 [z]See Lev. 19:31 [a]ver. 19
17 [b]See James 2:19 [c]Dan. 3:26 [d]See Mark 5:7 [e][ch. 9:2; Matt. 7:14]
18 [f][Mark 1:25, 34] [g]See Mark 9:38 [h][Matt. 17:18]

16:14 Lydia came from **Thyatira** (cf. notes on Rev. 2:18–29), a city of the province of Asia in the district of Lydia, for which she may have been named. As a **seller of purple goods**, she would have had some wealth. (Thyatira was famous for its expensive purple dyes.) **The Lord opened her heart.** It is the supernatural work of God, not the wisdom or persuasiveness of the preacher, that ultimately draws people to Christ.

16:15 Lydia's **household** likely included servants as well. Her house eventually became the gathering place for the Christians (v. 40).

Paul's Second Missionary Journey (Acts 15:36–18:22)

c. A.D. 49–51

Paul and Silas revisited the places in Asia Minor where Paul had preached on his first journey (cf. map, p. 2110), while Barnabas took John Mark and sailed to Cyprus. Paul and Silas visited Derbe, Lystra, and Antioch in Pisidia. From there Paul and Silas traveled to Troas, where Paul received a vision of a man from Macedonia calling to them. Crossing into Europe, they passed through several towns along the Egnatian Way and traveled to the cities of Athens and Corinth in southern Greece. Then, sailing to Ephesus and Caesarea, they visited the church in Jerusalem before returning to Antioch of Syria.

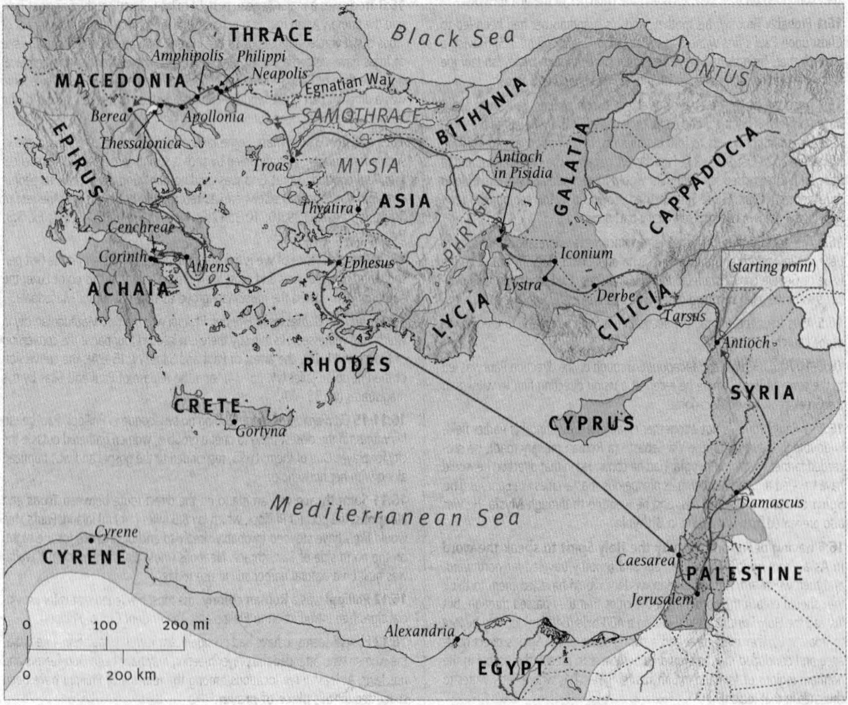

19[i]ver. 16; [ch. 19:25, 26] [j]ch. 17:6-8; 21:30; James 2:6; [ch. 8:3; 18:12; Matt. 10:18]
21[k][Esth. 3:8] [l][ver. 12]
22[m]2 Cor. 6:5; 11:23-25; 1 Thess. 2:2
24[n]See Luke 21:12 [o]Job 13:27; 33:11; Jer. 20:2, 3; 29:26
25[p]Job 35:10; Ps. 42:8; 77:6; 119:62
26[q]See ch. 4:31 [r]ch. 5:19; 12:10 [s]ch. 12:7
27[t][ch. 12:19; 27:42; 1 Kgs. 20:39]
29[u]ch. 10:25
30[v]ch. 2:37; 22:10; Luke 3:10, 12, 14; [John 6:28, 29] [w][ver. 17]
31[x]See Mark 16:16

19 But [i]when her owners saw that their hope of gain was gone, they seized Paul and Silas
and [j]dragged them into the marketplace before the rulers. 20 And when they had brought
them to the magistrates, they said, "These men are Jews, and they are disturbing our city.
21 They [k]advocate customs that are not lawful for us [l]as Romans to accept or practice." 22 The
crowd joined in attacking them, and the magistrates tore the garments off them and gave
orders [m]to beat them with rods. 23 And when they had inflicted many blows upon them,
they threw them into prison, ordering the jailer to keep them safely. 24 Having received
this order, he put them into the inner [n]prison and fastened their feet in [o]the stocks.

The Philippian Jailer Converted

25 [p]About midnight Paul and Silas were praying and singing hymns to God, and the
prisoners were listening to them, 26 and suddenly [q]there was a great earthquake, so that
the foundations of the prison were shaken. And immediately [r]all the doors were opened,
and [s]everyone's bonds were unfastened. 27 When the jailer woke and saw that the prison
doors were open, he drew his sword and [t]was about to kill himself, supposing that the
prisoners had escaped. 28 But Paul cried with a loud voice, "Do not harm yourself, for we
are all here." 29 And the jailer[1] called for lights and rushed in, and trembling with fear he
[u]fell down before Paul and Silas. 30 Then he brought them out and said, "Sirs, [v]what must
I do to be [w]saved?" 31 And they said, [x]"Believe in the Lord Jesus, and you will be saved, you

[1] Greek *he*

16:16–24 *Imprisonment of Paul and Silas.* Paul cast out a spirit that possessed a slave girl and gave her predictive powers. Losing their means of profit, her owners brought Paul and Silas before the magistrates, who had them flogged and jailed.

16:16 a spirit of divination. A demonic spirit who gave information to the slave girl so that she could tell people secrets about their lives. **Fortune-telling** was forbidden to God's people in the OT (cf. Deut. 18:10; 1 Sam. 28:8; 2 Kings 17:17; Mic. 3:11). The Greek OT (Septuagint) uses the same Greek verb for fortune-telling (*manteuomai*) that is used in this verse.

16:18 The words of the fortune-telling girl (v. 17) were true in a formal sense, but Paul was **greatly annoyed**, probably because he did not want it to appear that she was his partner in the gospel. **I command you in the name of Jesus Christ to come out of her**. Rather than praying to God, Paul speaks directly to the spirit and commands it to leave. Such a verbal command is consistent with the authority over demons that Jesus himself had (cf. Matt. 8:16; 12:28) and that he had given to his disciples (Matt. 10:8; Luke 10:17). The NT Epistles elsewhere discuss spiritual battles against the forces of evil (cf. 2 Cor. 10:3–4; Eph. 6:12; James 4:7; 1 Pet. 5:8–9).

16:19 The slave girl's owners were upset by their loss of profit. Throughout Acts, the profit motive often works against the gospel—with Simon the magician (8:18–24), Elymas (13:8–12), and Demetrius the silversmith (19:24).

16:20 The **magistrates** (Gk. *stratēgoi*), responsible for maintaining civil order, were the standard officials for a Roman colony, with two appointed to each colony.

16:22 Responding to the unruly **crowd, the magistrates** had Paul and Silas stripped **and gave orders to beat them with rods**. The magistrates in Roman cities were served by attendants who carried bundles of wooden rods bound together as symbols of the magistrates' authority and their right to inflict corporal punishment. Paul and Silas were severely beaten with these wooden rods (v. 23; cf. 2 Cor. 11:25). The entire process was a miscarriage of justice, since there was no fair hearing to ascertain the facts or to allow Paul and Silas to speak in their own defense. In 1 Thess. 2:2, Paul says he was "shamefully treated at Philippi."

16:23 prison. The stone structure often designated as Paul's prison in tourist literature on Philippi was so designated only in later church tradition.

16:25–34 *Conversion of the Jailer.* Paul and Silas were miraculously freed from their confinement. They did not view their freedom as a means of escape, however, but as an opportunity for witness (cf. 5:17–21). As a result, the jailer and his household became believers.

16:25 praying and singing hymns to God. Amid their suffering Paul and Silas experienced the strong presence of the Holy Spirit, filling their hearts with joy and praise (cf. 1 Pet. 2:19–21; 4:12–14). Joy for the honor of suffering is a common theme in Acts (Acts 4:24–30).

16:30 what must I do to be saved. The jailer's question most likely refers to being saved from the judgment of God, which he would have heard about through listening to his prisoners' prayers and songs.

16:31 For belief in Christ as the key to salvation, cf. 10:43; John 3:16; Rom. 1:16; 10:10–11; etc.

Itinerary of Paul's Second Journey

City	Province/Region	Reference
Antioch	Syria	15:35
	Cilicia	15:41
Derbe	Galatia *(region of Lycaonia)*	16:1
Lystra	Galatia *(region of Lycaonia)*	16:1–5
	Asia *(region of Phrygia)*	16:6
	Galatia	16:6
Troas	Asia *(region of Mysia)*	16:7–10
Samothrace	Thrace	16:11
Neapolis	Macedonia	16:11
Philippi	Macedonia	16:12–40
Amphipolis	Macedonia	17:1
Apollonia	Macedonia	17:1
Thessalonica	Macedonia	17:1–9
Berea	Macedonia	17:10–14
Athens	Achaia	17:15–32
Corinth	Achaia	18:1–17
Cenchreae	Achaia	18:18
Ephesus	Asia	18:19–21
Caesarea	Palestine	18:22
Jerusalem?	Palestine	18:22
Antioch	Syria	18:22

[y]and your household." 32 And they spoke the word of the Lord to him and to all who were
in his house. 33 And he took them [z]the same hour of the night and washed their wounds;
and he [a]was baptized at once, he and all his family. 34 Then he brought them up into his
house and set food before them. And he [b]rejoiced along with his entire household that
he had believed in God.
35 But when it was day, the magistrates sent the police, saying, "Let those men go." 36 And
the jailer reported these words to Paul, saying, "The magistrates have sent to let you go.
Therefore come out now and go in peace." 37 But Paul said to them, "They have beaten us
publicly, [c]uncondemned, men who are Roman citizens, and have thrown us into prison; and
do they now throw us out secretly? No! Let them come themselves and take us out." 38 The
police reported these words to the magistrates, and [c]they were afraid when they heard that
they were Roman citizens. 39 So they came and apologized to them. And they took them
out and [d]asked them to leave the city. 40 So they went out of the prison and visited [e]Lydia.
And when they had seen [f]the brothers, they encouraged them and departed.

Paul and Silas in Thessalonica

17 Now when they had passed through Amphipolis and Apollonia, they came to
[g]Thessalonica, where there was a synagogue of the Jews. 2 And Paul went in, [h]as
was his custom, and on three Sabbath days he reasoned with them [i]from the Scriptures,
3 [j]explaining and proving that it was necessary for [k]the Christ to suffer and [l]to rise from
the dead, and saying, "This Jesus, whom I proclaim to you, is the Christ." 4 And [m]some of
them were persuaded and joined Paul and Silas, as did [n]a great many of the devout [o]Greeks
and not a few of the leading women. 5 [p]But the Jews[1] [q]were jealous, and taking [r]some
wicked men of the rabble, they formed a mob, set the city in an uproar, and attacked the
house of Jason, seeking to bring them out to the crowd. 6 And when they could not find

31 [y]See ch. 11:14
33 [z]ver. 25 [a]See ch. 8:12
34 [b]Ps. 9:14; 13:5; Isa. 25:9; Luke 1:47; 1 Pet. 1:6, 8; [ch. 2:46]
37 [c]ch. 22:25, 29
38 [c][See ver. 37 above]
39 [d][Matt. 8:34]
40 [e]ver. 14 [f]See John 21:23

Chapter 17

1 [g]ch. 20:4; Phil. 4:16; 1 Thess. 1:1
2 [h]See ch. 13:5 [i]See ch. 8:35
3 [j]Luke 24:26, 32 [k]See ch. 3:18 [l]See John 20:9
4 [m][1 Thess. 2:1, 2]; See ch. 14:4 [n]ver. 12 [o]See John 7:35
5 [p]1 Thess. 2:14-16; See ch. 13:50 [q]See ch. 5:17 [r][Judg. 9:4; 11:3; 2 Chr. 13:7]

[1] Greek *Ioudaioi* probably refers here to Jewish religious leaders, and others under their influence, in that time; also verse 13

16:33 The jailer **washed their wounds**, leading Chrysostom (c. 347–407) to comment, "He washed and was washed; he washed them from their stripes, and was himself washed from his sins" (*Homilies on Acts* 36.2). **baptized . . . he and all his family**. The jailer seems to have called forth his whole household to listen to Paul's message. Christians disagree as to whether the baptism of household members included infants or was confined to older members of the household who were capable of believing.

16:34 Rejoiced translates Greek *agalliaō*, a word not used by secular Greek writers and which always in the NT signifies a deep spiritual joy (cf. Matt. 5:12; Luke 1:46–47; 10:21; John 8:56; Acts 2:26; 1 Pet. 4:13; Rev. 19:7).

16:35–40 *Release of Paul and Silas.* When the magistrates secretly ordered their release, Paul insisted that they come to the prison in person to release them, in deference to their Roman citizenship.

16:35 Let those men go. Why the magistrates decided to release the two prisoners is not specified. Perhaps the jailer had told them about the night's events or they had been alarmed by the earthquake, or perhaps they thought that the beating and overnight imprisonment was enough punishment and that Paul and Silas would leave the city.

16:37 do they now throw us out secretly? No! Paul was concerned for the public reputation of his gospel message and also, no doubt, for the good standing of the church that was being established at Philippi. Thus he insisted on public vindication lest the people of Philippi continue to believe that he was a troublemaker and a lawbreaker, ideas that would have presented barriers to the gospel in Philippi for years to come. Paul wanted to make it clear that a mistake had been made. Christianity is no threat to Rome. **citizens**. Roman law forbade scourging or imprisoning a Roman citizen without a formal hearing.

17:1–9 *Paul Witnesses in Thessalonica.* From Philippi Paul traveled the 94 miles (151 km) to Thessalonica, capital of Macedonia (see Introduction to 1 Thessalonians: Purpose, Occasion, and Background). In 1 Thess. 2:2, Paul recounts that they "had boldness in our God to declare to you the gospel of God in the midst of much conflict." He also mentions in Phil. 4:16 that the Philippian church helped him with his material needs during this time.

17:1 Philippi, **Amphipolis**, **Apollonia**, and **Thessalonica** were all cities on the main east-west Roman highway called the "Egnatian Way." These cities were separated from each other by about a day's journey by foot.

17:2 The reference to Paul preaching on **three Sabbath days** gives the impression of a brief stay in Thessalonica, but this was only the period of his synagogue preaching. Paul's first letter to the Thessalonians reflects a longer ministry (see 1 Thess. 2:9; 5:12; also Phil. 4:16).

17:3 necessary for the Christ to suffer. The Jews resisted the idea that the Messiah had to suffer, even though this is found in the OT (Psalm 22; Isaiah 53; Zech. 12:10; 13:7).

17:4 In the Greco-Roman world **women** often held prominent positions (see 13:50; 17:12). Some of them were among the **devout Greeks** (God-fearers) who attended the synagogues.

17:5 The Jews were jealous because they were losing power and influence (cf. 5:17; 13:45); see also 16:19 and 19:23–28, where the opponents to the gospel were stirred up because of their loss of financial gain. On the expression "the Jews," see notes on John 1:19; Acts 9:23.

17:6 men who have turned the world upside down. These hostile opponents spoke better than they knew, for the spread of the gospel through-

Major Sermons in Acts

Speaker	Text	Audience
Peter	2:14–36	Jews in Jerusalem
	3:11–26	Jews in Jerusalem
	10:34–43	Cornelius's household
Stephen	7:1–53	Jews in Jerusalem
Paul	13:16–47	Jews in Pisidian Antioch
	17:22–31	Greeks in Athens
	20:18–35	Church elders in Ephesus
	22:1–21	Jews in Jerusalem
	24:10–21	Felix and his court
	26:1–29	Agrippa and his court

6 [s]ch. 16:19-21
7 [t]ch. 16:4; Luke 2:1 [u]See Luke 23:2
10 [v]ver. 14; See John 21:23 [w]ver. 2
11 [x][Isa. 34:16; John 5:39]
12 [y]ver. 4 [z]ch. 13:50
13 [a]ver. 8
14 [b]ver. 10; See Matt. 10:23 [c]See ch. 16:1
15 [d][ch. 15:3] [e]ch. 18:1; 1 Thess. 3:1 [f]ch. 18:5
16 [g][2 Pet. 2:8] [h][Isa. 2:8]
17 [i]See ch. 13:5

them, [s]they dragged Jason and some of the brothers before the city authorities, shouting,
"These men who have turned the world upside down have come here also, 7 and Jason has
received them, and they are all acting against [t]the decrees of Caesar, saying that there is
[u]another king, Jesus." 8 And the people and the city authorities were disturbed when they
heard these things. 9 And when they had taken money as security from Jason and the rest,
they let them go.

Paul and Silas in Berea

10 [v]The brothers[1] immediately sent Paul and Silas away by night to Berea, and when they
arrived they [w]went into the Jewish synagogue. 11 Now these Jews were more noble than
those in Thessalonica; they received the word with all eagerness, [x]examining the Scriptures
daily to see if these things were so. 12 [y]Many of them therefore believed, with not a few
Greek [z]women of high standing as well as men. 13 But when the Jews from Thessalonica
learned that the word of God was proclaimed by Paul at Berea also, they came there too,
[a]agitating and stirring up the crowds. 14 Then the brothers [b]immediately sent Paul off on
his way to the sea, but Silas and [c]Timothy remained there. 15 [d]Those who conducted Paul
brought him as far as [e]Athens, and after receiving a command [f]for Silas and Timothy to
come to him as soon as possible, they departed.

Paul in Athens

16 Now while Paul was waiting for them at Athens, his spirit was [g]provoked within him
as he saw that the city was [h]full of idols. 17 So [i]he reasoned in the synagogue with the Jews
and the devout persons, and in the marketplace every day with those who happened to

[1] Or *brothers and sisters;* also verse 14

out the Roman Empire was the beginning of a movement that would change the course of history forever.

17:9 The **money as security** was given as a guarantee that there would be no more disturbance of the peace as a result of Paul's preaching. As a practical matter, this probably meant that Paul would have to leave Thessalonica, since his Jewish opponents would continue to stir up trouble. This may have been "Satan's hindrance" (1 Thess. 2:18), which Paul said prevented his return to Thessalonica.

17:10–15 *Paul Witnesses in Berea.* Paul and Silas fled to Berea, 50 miles (81 km) by road southwest of Thessalonica.

17:10 Berea. At least two inscriptions confirm a Jewish presence in Berea after the time of Paul.

17:11 Noble translates the Greek *eugenēs*, which originally meant "of noble birth" or "well born." The word was also applied to people who exhibited noble behavior, in that they were open-minded, fair, and thoughtful. Thus Luke saw the Bereans as "more noble" in their receiving Paul's message **with all eagerness**, and then in looking to the written words of the OT as their final authority, **examining the Scriptures daily to see if these things were so**. By commending this activity, Luke encourages this searching of the Scriptures as a pattern for all believers and also gives support to the doctrine of the clarity of Scripture, the idea that the Bible can be understood rightly, not only by scholars but also by ordinary people who read it eagerly and diligently, with conscious dependence on God for help.

17:14 immediately sent Paul off. Apparently most of the opposition was directed against Paul, who was the main spokesman, so the believers sent him away, while allowing Silas and Timothy to remain among them. The phrase **to the sea** indicates that they took Paul as far as the coast, but the text does not specify whether Paul then traveled to Athens by ship or by land, along the coastal road (a distance of 222 miles or 357 km).

17:15 a command for Silas and Timothy to come to him as soon as possible. Luke does not at this point give many details about the travels of Silas and Timothy, but Paul gives more information in 1 Thessalonians 3, and Luke gives more details at Acts 18:1, 5. These passages reveal the following sequence: (1) Paul traveled to Athens, leaving Silas and Timothy in Berea (17:14–15). (2) Paul summoned Silas and Timothy to join him in Athens (v. 15). (3) Silas and Timothy joined Paul in Athens (v. 16; 1 Thess. 3:1–2). (4) Paul became concerned for the churches he had just founded in Macedonia (in Philippi, Thessalonica, and Berea), so he sent Timothy to Thessalonica to find out how that church was doing amid its persecution and opposition (1 Thess. 3:1–2). At the same time he must have sent Silas somewhere else in Macedonia (Acts 18:5), being willing to be left at Athens "alone" (1 Thess. 3:1). It is likely that Silas went at least to Philippi but possibly also to Berea. (5) Paul "left Athens and went to Corinth" (Acts 18:1). (6) Silas and Timothy joined Paul again in Corinth, bringing good news from the churches of Macedonia (18:5; 1 Thess. 3:6). (7) From Corinth, Paul wrote his two letters to the church at Thessalonica (1 Thess. 1:1; 2 Thess. 1:1; both of these letters come from "Paul, Silvanus [= Silas], and Timothy").

17:16–34 *Paul Witnesses in Athens.* Paul's ministry in Athens began in the marketplace, where he encountered some Athenian philosophers (vv. 16–21). This led to a more formal presentation to the Areopagus (vv. 22–34).

17:16–21 *Witness in the Marketplace.* Paul proclaims the gospel to the Athenians.

17:16 Athens was filled with examples of artistic beauty, particularly its statues of the Greek gods and the architectural magnificence of its temples. Paul, however, was deeply troubled by the idolatry that the art represented. **his spirit was provoked within him**. "His spirit" does not mean the Holy Spirit but Paul's human spirit (cf. Rom. 8:16). He was deeply troubled to see the entire city devoted to false gods represented by **idols**. (Elsewhere Paul would write, "what pagans sacrifice they offer to demons and not to God," 1 Cor. 10:20.) Large portions of central Athens have been excavated. Paul would probably have been speaking in the Roman Forum (used as a marketplace; cf. Acts 17:17) and in the Greek Agora (largely filled with civic structures). These were surrounded by great stoas, one of which (the Stoa of Attalos) has been reconstructed for modern viewers. In Paul's day Athens boasted a stadium, a large theater, and an odeion known as the Agrippeion. Some of Athens's most prominent features were its numerous pagan temples. The great temple to Athena (the Parthenon), the Erechtheion (dedicated to multiple deities), and the temple to the goddess Roma and the emperor Augustus stood atop the acropolis overlooking the city. Many other pagan sacred sites have also been found, confirming Petronius's satirical assertion that it was easier to find a god than a man in Athens. Multiple inscriptions also indicate a Jewish presence in Athens, and Herod the Great was honored by the Athenians for his generosity to the city.

17:17 he reasoned. Witnessing for Christ was a matter of patient persuasion. Although Paul saw a few people come to faith here in Athens (v. 34), he had no helpers with him, there is no record of any miracles being done, and there is no record of a church being established. **Devout persons** means God-fearing Gentiles (see note on 8:26–27).

be there. 18 Some of the Epicurean and Stoic philosophers also conversed with him. And
some said, [j]"What does this babbler wish to say?" Others said, "He seems to be a preacher
of foreign divinities"—because [k]he was preaching [l]Jesus and the resurrection. 19 And they
took him and brought him to [m]the Areopagus, saying, "May we know what this [n]new
teaching is that you are presenting? 20 For you bring some [o]strange things to our ears.
We wish to know therefore what these things mean." 21 Now all the Athenians and the
foreigners who lived there would spend their time in nothing except telling or hearing
something new.

Paul Addresses the Areopagus

22 So Paul, standing in the midst of the Areopagus, said: "Men of Athens, I perceive that
in every way you are very religious. 23 For as I passed along and observed the objects of
your worship, I found also an altar with this inscription, [p]'To the unknown god.' [p]What
therefore you worship [q]as unknown, this I proclaim to you. 24 [r]The God who made the
world and everything in it, being [s]Lord of heaven and earth, [t]does not live in temples
made by man,[1] 25 nor is he served by human hands, [u]as though he needed anything, since
he himself [v]gives to all mankind [w]life and breath and everything. 26 And [x]he made from
one man every nation of mankind to live [y]on all the face of the earth, [z]having determined
allotted periods and [a]the boundaries of their dwelling place, 27 [b]that they should seek God,
[c]and perhaps feel their way toward him and find him. [d]Yet he is actually not far from each
one of us, 28 for

> [e]"'In him we live and move and have our being';[2]

as even some of [f]your own poets have said,

> "'For we are indeed his offspring.'[3]

29 [g]Being then God's offspring, [h]we ought not to think that the divine being is like gold
or silver or stone, an image formed by the art and imagination of man. 30 [i]The times of

18 [j][1 Cor. 4:10] [k]See ch. 5:42 [l]ver. 31, 32; ch. 4:2; [1 Cor. 15:12]
19 [m]ver. 22; [ver. 34] [n]Mark 1:27; [John 7:16; Heb. 13:9]
20 [o]1 Pet. 4:4, 12; [Hos. 8:12]
23 [p][John 4:22; 1 Cor. 15:34] [q][ver. 30]
24 [r]Isa. 42:5; See ch. 14:15 [s]Matt. 11:25; [Deut. 10:14; Ps. 115:16] [t]See ch. 7:48
25 [u]Ps. 50:8-12; [1 Chr. 29:14, 16; Job 22:2] [v]1 Tim. 6:17; James 1:5, 17 [w]Gen. 2:7; 7:22; Job 33:4; [Job 27:3; Eccles. 12:7; Zech. 12:1]; See ver. 28
26 [x][Gen. 3:20; Mal. 2:10] [y]Gen. 11:8; Luke 21:35 [z][Job 12:23; 14:5] [a]Deut. 32:8; [Ps. 74:17]
27 [b][ch. 15:17] [c][Job 23:3, 8, 9] [d][Deut. 4:7; Ps. 145:18; Jer. 23:23, 24]; See ch. 14:17
28 [e]Job 12:10; Dan. 5:23; [Heb. 2:11] [f][Titus 1:12]
29 [g][Luke 3:38; Heb. 12:9] [h]Isa. 40:18, 19, 25; 46:5; [Rom. 1:23]
30 [i]Eph. 4:18; 1 Pet. 1:14; [ver. 23]

[1] Greek *made by hands* [2] Probably from Epimenides of Crete [3] From Aratus's poem "Phainomena"

17:18 Paul conversed with representatives of two of the most popular philosophies of the day, Stoicism and Epicureanism. They called Paul a **babbler** (Gk. *spermologos*, lit., "one who picks up seeds," derived from an older and less common meaning of *legō*, "pick up"). The term thus suggested one who pecks at ideas like a chicken pecks at seeds and then spouts them off without fully understanding them.

17:19 The **Areopagus** is the "hill of Ares" (Ares being the Greek god of war). The Court of the Areopagus was a long-established body with extensive authority over the civil and religious life of Athens. In Paul's day, it exercised jurisdiction especially in matters of religion and morality. In speaking before the group of Epicurean and Stoic philosophers (v. 18), Paul would have addressed them either on the "hill of Ares" (i.e., Mars Hill), located below the acropolis, or northwest of the acropolis in the northwest corner of the Agora, where at the time of Paul the group held its ordinary meetings in the Royal Colonnade.

17:22–34 *Witness before the Areopagus.* Paul's Areopagus address is the prime example in Acts of preaching to Gentiles. Although rooted in OT ideas, it appealed to the Greek philosophers by interacting with their thought, even quoting their own writers in a well-informed, respectful way. Its main subject was the error of idolatry. Paul began with and returned to the theme of idolatry (vv. 23, 29), in a well-informed manner, clearing the way for a full statement of the gospel, but he was interrupted before he could achieve this.

17:22–23 Religious (Gk. *deisidaimōn*) could be taken either positively ("pious") or negatively ("superstitious").

17:23 To the unknown god. In the second century A.D., the Greek geographer Pausanias recorded "altars of the gods named Unknown" in Athens (*Description of Greece* 1.1.4). He also mentioned such an altar at Olympia (*Description of Greece* 5.14.8), and an inscription found at Pergamum has been restored to read "to unknown gods."

17:24–25 Paul speaks of **the God who made the world and everything in it**, including mankind. He identifies this one true God as superior to all the lesser, competing deities that might be worshiped in Athens, with all their foibles and weaknesses. When Paul says that "God . . . **does not live in temples made by man, nor is he served by human hands**" (cf. 7:48), it is easy to imagine him gesturing toward the magnificent temple, the Parthenon, that stood just above him and his hearers on the acropolis. Paul was claiming that the true God of heaven and earth does not live in temples like the Parthenon and is not served by the sacrifices which the Athenians regularly brought to their temples.

17:26 One man refers to Adam, in whom all people find their ancestral unity, an idea that would appeal to the Stoics' strong sense of human brotherhood. Paul thus affirms the historicity of Adam and the descent of the entire human race from him. This also rules out any kind of racism, since the various ethnic groups come from one man. **Having determined allotted periods and the boundaries of their dwelling place** indicates God's sovereignty over the histories of nations.

17:27 Feel their way toward him implies a kind of groping around in darkness, without really knowing how to find God, though they hoped that they would. The verbs translated "feel their way" and "find" are in the optative mood in Greek, suggesting possibilities considered uncertain of realization. **Not far from each one of us** implies God's omnipresence and also implies that God hears people's prayers and knows their hearts (including these philosophers in Athens). God's providence leads people to **seek God**, with the goal that they might **perhaps . . . find** (i.e., worship) **him**, but all people fall short of seeking God wholeheartedly and successfully, as Rom. 1:18–3:20 teaches. Paul is being inviting here. There is a God to find, and he is not hard to find, having revealed himself to us through the story Paul prepares to tell.

17:28 some of your own poets. Instead of the OT, Paul quoted some statements from pagan Greek writers who would be familiar to his audience. Though he quotes them with approval, this does not imply that he approves of other things that these writers said or wrote. The first quotation (**in him we live . . .**) appears to be from a hymn to Zeus by Epimenides of Crete (c. 600 B.C.); the words are found just two lines later than the quotation Paul takes from the same poem in Titus 1:12. The second quotation here is from the poem *Phainomena* by the Stoic poet Aratus (c. 315–240 B.C.).

17:29 God is not **like gold or silver or stone**, of which idols are made. God made us (we are **God's offspring**), and we are much more complex

ignorance [j]God overlooked, but [k]now he [l]commands all people everywhere to repent,
31 because he has fixed [m]a day on which [n]he will judge the world [o]in righteousness by a
man whom he has appointed; and [p]of this he has given assurance to all [q]by raising him
from the dead."
32 Now when they heard of [r]the resurrection of the dead, [s]some mocked. But others said,
[t]"We will hear you again about this." 33 So Paul went out from their midst. 34 But some men
joined him and believed, among whom also were Dionysius [u]the Areopagite and a woman
named Damaris and others with them.

Paul in Corinth

18 After this Paul[1] left Athens and went to Corinth. 2 And he found a Jew named [v]Aquila,
a native of Pontus, recently come from Italy with his wife [v]Priscilla, because [w]Claudius
had commanded all the Jews to leave Rome. And he went to see them, 3 and [x]because he was
of the same trade he stayed with them and worked, for they were tentmakers by trade. 4 And
[y]he reasoned in the synagogue [y]every Sabbath, and tried to persuade Jews and Greeks.
5 [z]When Silas and Timothy arrived from Macedonia, Paul [a]was occupied with the word,
[b]testifying to the Jews that the Christ was [c]Jesus. 6 And when they opposed and reviled
him, [d]he shook out his garments and said to them, [e]"Your blood be on your own heads! [f]I
am innocent. [g]From now on I will go to the Gentiles." 7 And he left there and went to the
house of a man named Titius [h]Justus, [i]a worshiper of God. His house was next door to the
synagogue. 8 [j]Crispus, the ruler of the synagogue, believed in the Lord, together [k]with his
entire household. And many of the Corinthians hearing Paul believed and were baptized.
9 And the Lord said to Paul [l]one night in [m]a vision, [n]"Do not be afraid, but go on speaking

[1] Greek *he*

8 [j]1 Cor. 1:14 [k]See ch. 11:14 **9** [l]ch. 23:11; 27:23 [m][ch. 26:16; 2 Cor. 12:1-4] [n]ch. 27:24; Josh. 1:5, 6; Jer. 1:8; Matt. 28:20

30 [j][Rom. 3:25]; See ch. 14:16 [k][Mark 1:15; Titus 2:11, 12; 1 Pet. 4:3] [l]Mark 6:12
31 [m]Matt. 12:36; Rom. 2:16; 1 Cor. 3:13; 2 Pet. 2:9; 1 John 4:17; [Isa. 2:12] [n]2 Tim. 4:8; See ch. 10:42 [o]Ps. 9:8; 96:13; 98:9; 1 Pet. 2:23; [Rom. 3:6] [p][John 16:10, 11; Rom. 1:4] [q]See ch. 2:24
32 [r]Heb. 6:2; See ver. 18 [s][ch. 2:13; 26:8] [t]ch. 24:25
34 [u]ver. 19, 22

Chapter 18

2 [v]ver. 18, 26; Rom. 16:3; 1 Cor. 16:19; 2 Tim. 4:19 [w]ch. 11:28
3 [x]ch. 20:34; 1 Cor. 4:12; 9:15; 2 Cor. 11:7; 12:13; 1 Thess. 2:9; 2 Thess. 3:8
4 [y]ch. 17:17; See ch. 13:5, 14
5 [z]ch. 17:15; 1 Thess. 3:6 [a]2 Cor. 5:14; [Job 32:18; Jer. 6:11; 20:9; Amos 3:8] [b]ch. 20:21 [c]ver. 28; ch. 2:36; 5:42; 17:3; [ch. 3:20; 8:5; 9:22]
6 [d]Neh. 5:13; [ch. 13:51] [e]Ezek. 18:13; 33:4; [2 Sam. 1:16; Matt. 27:25] [f]ch. 20:26 (Gk.); [Ezek. 3:18, 19] [g]See ch. 13:46
7 [h][ch. 1:23; Col. 4:11] [i]ch. 16:14

and wonderful than these lifeless material substances. Therefore God himself must also be much more wonderful than these things. With this observation Paul returns to the critique of idolatry with which he began and sets up the basis for the need to repent.

17:30 Paul moved to his distinctly Christian appeal, at this point distancing himself from the philosophers. **God overlooked**. That is, God did not bring immediate judgment to the world in previous times (but Paul warns of coming judgment in the next verse).

17:31 He will judge the world means that God will hold all people accountable, even these philosophers in Athens. **raising him from the dead**. Jesus is not just a religious teacher. The resurrection of Jesus is at the center of God's plan for history and is the basis for hope in the future resurrection of the body (1 Cor. 15:42–57; Rev. 21:4). It is also a central evidence to persuade people to believe in Christ (Acts 2:24, 32). Most importantly, the resurrection placed Jesus at God's right hand, showing his authority to be the judge and the giver of salvation that Paul is describing (2:30–36).

17:34 As a result of Paul's address to the Areopagus, Luke notes that **some men** believed (Gk. *andres*, "men" referring to male human beings, as would have been the case for members of the Areopagus; see v. 22). In addition to these men who initially believed, some others **also** (Gk. *kai*, "and, also") believed, including **Dionysius . . . and a woman named Damaris**, as well as **others with them** (i.e., with Dionysius and Damaris).

18:1–22 *Paul Witnesses in Corinth.* Corinth was Paul's last major place of witness on his second journey. His initial establishment of work there (vv. 1–11) is followed by an account of a specific incident when the Jews brought him for trial before the proconsul (vv. 12–17). But Paul was able to stay "many days longer" (v. 18). Then, after completing his Corinthian ministry, Paul returned to Antioch, making a brief stop at Ephesus (vv. 18–22).

18:1 Corinth was 46 miles (74 km) west of Athens. A Roman colony, it was the most influential city of the province of Achaia, both politically and economically (see Introduction to 1 Corinthians: The Ancient City of Corinth).

18:2 Claudius's expulsion of the **Jews** from **Rome** in A.D. 49 seems to have resulted from a disturbance in the Jewish synagogues created by the Christian message. **Aquila** and **Priscilla** had much in common with Paul, being Jews, tentmakers, and possibly already Christians when they fled from Rome.

18:3 First Corinthians 9 may reflect this period of Paul's ministry in Corinth, when he supported himself rather than receiving assistance from the Corinthians.

18:4 he reasoned . . . and tried to persuade. See note on 17:17. **synagogue**. The first-century-A.D. Jewish philosopher Philo emphasized the city of Corinth as a home for Jewish people (*Embassy to Gaius* 281; cf. neighboring Sicyon in *1 Macc.* 15:23). Several funerary epigraphs also confirm a later Jewish presence, as does a rather crude post-Pauline inscription found near the road to Lechaion designating the "Synagogue of the Hebrews." **Greeks** in a synagogue context are God-fearers.

18:5 Paul apparently had sent **Silas and Timothy** from Athens to visit the Macedonian churches (see note on 17:15). When they again joined Paul in Corinth, they probably were the ones who brought a contribution for Paul's ministry from the Macedonian churches (see 2 Cor. 11:9).

18:6 when they opposed and reviled him. Paul will spend much time with audiences where there is interest and response, even if they don't immediately believe (see v. 4), but he will not spend time where he simply faces hostile opposition. Shaking garments was a gesture of rejection, much like shaking the dust from one's feet (cf. 13:51). **Your blood be on your own heads** reflects Ezekiel's words about God's prophetic watchman (Ezek. 33:1–7). "Blood" means "the responsibility for your judgment by God." Paul had faithfully discharged his responsibility, so that at the final judgment no part of these Jews' failure to believe could be attributed to his failure to tell them about Christ (but cf. note on Acts 18:7).

18:7 Paul did not completely give up on witnessing to the Jews of Corinth, as his relocating **next door to the synagogue** indicates. Paul's Jewish opponents cannot have been very pleased about his choice of a new location in such close proximity to the synagogue. Nothing more is known of **Titius Justus**. He is not the Titus who was with Paul long before the founding of the Corinthian church (Gal. 2:1).

18:8 Both Jews and Gentiles were won to the Lord, **Crispus** (see 1 Cor. 1:14) representing the former and **many of the Corinthians** the latter. **believed and were baptized**. Baptism seems to have followed closely after each person's profession of faith.

18:9–11 Up to this point, opposition to his ministry had usually forced Paul to leave a place of witness. But the Lord in a vision assured him that he would have a successful ministry in Corinth and would suffer no further harm. In obedience Paul remained there for 18 months (c. A.D. 49–51, during which time he wrote 1–2 Thessalonians). God's assurance was immediately confirmed by Paul's deliverance from an attempt to condemn him before the

and do not be silent, **10** [n]for I am with you, and [o]no one will attack you to harm you, for [p]I
have many in this city who are my people." **11** And he stayed a year and six months, teaching the word of God among them.

12 But when Gallio was [q]proconsul of Achaia, [r]the Jews[1] made a united attack on Paul and
[s]brought him before the tribunal, **13** saying, "This man is persuading people to worship
God contrary to [t]the law." **14** But when Paul was about to open his mouth, Gallio said to the
Jews, "If it were a matter of wrongdoing or vicious [u]crime, O Jews, I would have reason to
accept your complaint. **15** But [v]since it is a matter of questions about words and names and
[w]your own law, see to it yourselves. I refuse to be a judge of these things." **16** And he drove
them from the tribunal. **17** And they all seized Sosthenes, the ruler of the synagogue, and
beat him in front of the tribunal. But Gallio paid no attention to any of this.

Paul Returns to Antioch

18 After this, Paul stayed many days longer and then took leave of [x]the brothers[2] and set
sail for Syria, and with him [y]Priscilla and Aquila. At [z]Cenchreae [a]he had cut his hair, for he
was under a vow. **19** And they came to [b]Ephesus, and he left them there, but [c]he himself
went into the synagogue and reasoned with the Jews. **20** When they asked him to stay for
a longer period, he declined. **21** But on taking leave of them he said, "I will return to you
[d]if God wills," and he set sail from Ephesus.

22 When he had landed at Caesarea, he [e]went up and greeted the church, and then went
down to Antioch. **23** After spending some time there, he departed and [f]went from one place
to the next through the region of Galatia and Phrygia, [g]strengthening all the disciples.

Apollos Speaks Boldly in Ephesus

24 Now a Jew named [h]Apollos, a native of Alexandria, came to Ephesus. He was an eloquent man, [i]competent in the Scriptures. **25** He had been instructed in [j]the way of the Lord.

10 [n][See ver. 9 above] [o][Luke 21:18; 2 Thess. 3:2] [p][John 10:16]
12 [q]See ch. 13:7 [r]See ch. 13:50 [s]See ch. 16:19
13 [t]ver. 15
14 [u][ch. 13:10]
15 [v]ch. 23:29; 25:19; [1 Tim. 6:4; 2 Tim. 2:14] [w]ver. 13
18 [x]See John 21:23 [y]ver. 2 [z]Rom. 16:1 [a][ch. 21:23, 24; Num. 6:2, 18]
19 [b]ch. 19:1; 20:16, 17; 1 Cor. 15:32; 16:8; Eph. 1:1; 1 Tim. 1:3; 2 Tim. 1:18 [c]ver. 4
21 [d]1 Cor. 4:19; 16:7; Heb. 6:3; James 4:15; [Rom. 15:32; 1 Pet. 3:17]
22 [e]ch. 11:2; 21:15
23 [f]ch. 16:6 [g]See ch. 14:22
24 [h]ch. 19:1; 1 Cor. 1:12; 3:5, 6; 4:6; 16:12; Titus 3:13 [i][Ezra 7:6]
25 [j]See ch. 9:2

[1] Greek *Ioudaioi* probably refers here to Jewish religious leaders, and others under their influence, in that time; also verses 14 (twice), 28 [2] Or *brothers and sisters*; also verse 27

proconsul. Acts 18:10–11 gives helpful insight into Paul's understanding of God's providence and predestination in relation to human responsibility for preaching the gospel. Though God had told Paul, "**I have many in this city who are my people**," indicating that many in Corinth would come to faith in Christ, this did not lead Paul to conclude that he had no further part to play. Rather, Paul **stayed a year and six months**, longer than he stayed at any city except Ephesus, preaching the gospel *in order that through his preaching* those whom God had chosen would come to faith (cf. note on 27:30). Predestination implied successful evangelism.

18:12 The **proconsul** of a province was its chief judicial officer. Since **Gallio** served in this role A.D. 51–52, this provides one of the key dates used in computing dates for Paul's various missionary journeys. The **tribunal** (Gk. *bēma*) was the proconsul's judgment seat. It has been excavated in Corinth and was located in the open air in the marketplace.

18:14 Gallio's judgment—that the Jewish accusations against the Christians concerned only matters of their own religion—established the important legal precedent that Christians were innocent of transgressing Roman law when merely teaching and following Christian doctrine. A similar judgment comes later, in 25:19.

18:17 Sosthenes may have been a Jewish convert to Christianity, for Paul mentions someone by that name as his "coauthor" in 1 Cor. 1:1. In Acts 18:8, Crispus had been called "the ruler of the synagogue," but Sosthenes may have succeeded him when Crispus became a Christian, or there may have been more than one person with this office in that synagogue.

18:18 The **many days longer** that Paul continued in Corinth seems to be in addition to the 18 months of v. 11. **Syria** refers to his sponsoring church of Antioch in Syria. **Cenchreae** was about 6.5 miles (10.5 km) east of Corinth and was Corinth's main port to the Aegean Sea. The Roman harbor of Cenchreae is still visible (though largely submerged), and excavators have identified warehouses, fish tanks, and what they believe may be temples to Isis and Aphrodite. Paul left **Priscilla and Aquila** at Ephesus (v. 19) to establish the ministry there. The cutting of Paul's hair probably indicates he had completed a vow (see Num. 6:1–21; Acts 21:20–24). Besides not cutting the hair, such a vow mandated strict purity and refraining from strong drink. One would have undergone such a vow in seeking divine blessing for an undertaking or to express thanksgiving.

18:19 On the **synagogue** see note on v. 26.

18:21 Paul declines to stay in Ephesus but **will return . . . if God wills**, affirming that his plans are ultimately in God's hands (cf. 1 Cor. 4:19; James 4:15). Paul's brief appearance in the synagogue prepared the way for his later ministry in Ephesus (Acts 19). Indeed, his promise to return if God wills sets the stage and provides the main destination for his third missionary journey.

18:22 Leaving from the main Palestinian port of **Caesarea** (cf. 8:40; 9:30; 21:8) in the spring of A.D. 51, Paul **went up and greeted the church**, which most interpreters understand to mean the church in Jerusalem, which in that region could be called "the church" without further specification, and which was the location to which one would "go up" from Caesarea, given the higher altitude of Jerusalem. Then Paul **went down** (from Jerusalem) **to Antioch** (cf. 13:1–3; 14:26–28; 15:30–35; and see note on 11:19).

18:23–21:16 *The Witness in Ephesus.* This section reports Paul's third missionary journey (c. A.D. 52–57; see map, p. 2126), which took place primarily in Ephesus, the capital of the Roman province of Asia, a major commercial center and home of the famous temple of the goddess Artemis (see Introduction to Ephesians: The Ancient City of Ephesus).

18:23–28 *Priscilla and Aquila Instruct Apollos.* In Ephesus Priscilla and Aquila taught the Christian way "more accurately" to an Alexandrian disciple named Apollos.

18:23 Again sponsored by Antioch in Syria, Paul began his third missionary journey in the spring of A.D. 52, traveling by foot through the region of his first mission on into **Galatia and Phrygia**. On the second missionary journey the Spirit had prevented him from continuing west into Asia (16:6), but that did not happen this time, for Paul was headed directly toward the west, in order to reach Ephesus according to his promise in 18:21.

18:24 Alexandria was an intellectual center in Egypt with a world-renowned library. Apollos's eloquence (Gk. *logios*, "learned, skilled, eloquent") was undoubtedly accompanied by great learning, particularly in the OT Scriptures. He is described as being **competent** (or "powerful," Gk. *dynatos*) in his use

And [k]being fervent in spirit,[1] he spoke and taught accurately the things concerning Jesus,
though he knew only [l]the baptism of John. 26 He began to speak boldly in the synagogue,
but when [m]Priscilla and Aquila heard him, they took him aside and explained to him
[n]the way of God more accurately. 27 And when he wished to cross to [o]Achaia, [p]the brothers
encouraged him and [q]wrote to the disciples to welcome him. When he arrived, [r]he greatly
helped those who through grace had believed, 28 for he powerfully refuted the Jews in
public, showing by the Scriptures [s]that the Christ was Jesus.

Paul in Ephesus

19 And it happened that while [t]Apollos was at Corinth, Paul passed [u]through the inland[2]
country and came to Ephesus. There he found some disciples. 2 And he said to them,
[v]"Did you receive the Holy Spirit when you believed?" And they said, "No, [w]we have not
even heard that there is a Holy Spirit." 3 And he said, [x]"Into what then were you baptized?"
They said, "Into [y]John's baptism." 4 And Paul said, [y]"John baptized with the baptism of
repentance, telling the people [z]to believe in the one who was to come after him, that is,
Jesus." 5 On hearing this, [a]they were baptized in[3] the name of the Lord Jesus. 6 And [b]when
Paul had laid his hands on them, the Holy Spirit came on them, and [c]they began speaking
in tongues and [d]prophesying. 7 There were about twelve men in all.
8 And [e]he entered the synagogue and for three months spoke boldly, reasoning and persuading them [f]about the kingdom of God. 9 [g]But when some became stubborn and [h]continued in
unbelief, speaking evil of [i]the Way before the congregation, he withdrew from them and took
the disciples with him, reasoning daily in the hall of Tyrannus.[4] 10 This continued for [j]two
years, so that [k]all the residents of Asia heard the word of the Lord, both Jews and Greeks.

25 [k]Rom. 12:11 [l]ch. 19:3; Luke 7:29
26 [m]See ver. 2 [n]Matt. 22:16; [ver. 25]
27 [o][ch. 19:1] [p]ver. 18 [q][2 Cor. 3:1] [r]1 Cor. 3:6; [ch. 11:21, 23; 15:11; Eph. 2:8]
28 [s]See ver. 5

Chapter 19

1 [t]See ch. 18:24 [u][ch. 18:23]
2 [v][ch. 11:16, 17] [w][ch. 8:16; John 7:39]
3 [x]See ch. 8:16 [y]ch. 18:25; [Heb. 6:2]; See ch. 13:24, 25
4 [y][See ver. 3 above] [z]John 1:7
5 [a]See ch. 8:12, 16
6 [b]See ch. 8:17 [c]ch. 10:46; See Mark 16:17 [d]See ch. 13:1
8 [e]See ch. 13:5 [f]ch. 1:3; 28:23
9 [g][ch. 13:45, 46; 1 Cor. 16:9] [h]See ch. 14:2 [i]ver. 23; See ch. 9:2
10 [j][ver. 8; ch. 20:31] [k][2 Tim. 1:15]

[1] Or *in the Spirit* [2] Greek *upper* (that is, highland) [3] Or *into* [4] Some manuscripts add *from the fifth hour to the tenth* (that is, from 11 A.M. to 4 P.M.)

of the OT Scriptures in public preaching and debate, no doubt accompanied by the power of the Holy Spirit.

18:25 Apollos **knew only the baptism of John**, which suggests that he had not heard about the baptism that Jesus commanded after his resurrection (see Matt. 28:19), and which began to be administered to all believers in Christ on and after the day of Pentecost (see Acts 2:41; 8:12; etc.). Therefore Apollos's knowledge of the Christian gospel must have been deficient in some ways, though he **taught accurately the things concerning Jesus** as far as he knew them. He certainly knew about Jesus' life and teachings, but he may not have known about Jesus' death and resurrection, or about the outpouring of the Holy Spirit at Pentecost.

18:26 The presence of a **synagogue** in Ephesus (also in v. 19; 19:8) is further evidenced in an ancient inscription mentioning "the leaders of the synagogue and the elders" (on Jewish presence in Ephesus, see Introduction to Ephesians: The Ancient City of Ephesus). Presumably **Priscilla and Aquila . . . explained** the things about Jesus that Apollos did not yet know (see note on Acts 18:25). It is noteworthy that *both* of them "explained" (the verb *exethento* is a plural form of *ektithēmi*, "explain, elaborate, expound") to Apollos **the way of God more accurately**. **They took him** means they did not correct him publicly but took him aside and talked to him privately (Gk. *proslambanō*; cf. Matt. 16:22; Mark 8:32). As an example of the Holy Spirit's work in bringing about the growth of the church in Acts, this verse provides positive support for the idea that both men and women can explain God's Word to each other in private or informal settings (such as personal conversation or a small group Bible study) without violating the prohibition in 1 Tim. 2:12 against women teaching an assembled group of men.

18:27 Achaia refers particularly to Corinth (in the province of Achaia), where Paul had already established a church. Aquila and Priscilla were well known there, and a letter from them on Apollos's behalf would carry great weight. Later, in his first letter to Corinth, Paul acknowledged Apollos's ministry there (1 Cor. 1:12; 3:4–6, 22; 4:6). Apollos evidently returned to Ephesus after his time at Corinth, for he was with Paul when Paul wrote 1 Corinthians, which was written from Ephesus (1 Cor. 16:12) sometime during Paul's ministry there (Acts 19:1–20:1).

18:28 he powerfully refuted the Jews in public. Though Paul had been in Corinth one and a half years, the church still benefited greatly from this help from a skilled scholar and speaker (Apollos) who apparently had advanced academic knowledge accompanied by the power of the Holy Spirit and the Word of God.

19:1–10 *Paul Encounters Disciples of John.* At Ephesus Paul led some disciples of John the Baptist to Christ (vv. 1–7). His Ephesian ministry then extended throughout the entire Asian province (vv. 8–10).

19:1 while Apollos was at Corinth. See 18:27. **Inland country** refers to the main highway that went westward through the mountainous region from Phrygia into Asia and on to Ephesus on the coast. **Disciples** here refers to followers of John the Baptist; they did not know of Jesus (19:4).

19:2 That they had **not even heard that there is a Holy Spirit** indicates they had not heard of the outpouring of the Spirit at Pentecost (ch. 2), and therefore they probably had not heard much of Jesus' life and ministry, and certainly not of his death and resurrection. (Cf. note on 18:25.) They had evidently relocated from Palestine to Ephesus before Jesus' own ministry began. As followers of John they would have known his message that the Messiah would bring the Spirit (Luke 3:16).

19:5 Having learned how Jesus had fulfilled the message of John the Baptist, these disciples of John submitted to baptism **in the name of the Lord Jesus** (in contrast to their former baptism of "repentance" only, v. 4). On baptism in the name of Jesus, see note on 10:48.

19:6 The Holy Spirit came on them means they received the new covenant fullness and power of the Holy Spirit, something that happened to Jesus' disciples for the first time on the day of Pentecost (see notes on 1:8; 2:4; 8:17). They had not previously known about Jesus' death and resurrection, so their earlier belief (19:2) was one of looking forward to the Messiah to come, a state similar to that of OT believers. Their **speaking in tongues and prophesying** was an outward demonstration and verification of their receiving the Spirit. (See discussion of these gifts in note on 1 Cor. 12:10 and notes elsewhere on 1 Corinthians 12–14.)

19:9 the Way. See note on 9:1–2. **the hall of Tyrannus**. Some Greek manuscripts in the "Western text" tradition add that the daily lectures were held between the hours of 11:00 A.M. and 4:00 P.M., which included the hottest part of the day, when people would take off work for a midday nap. **reasoning daily**. See note on 17:17.

19:10 Paul ministered in Ephesus for about three years (c. A.D. 52–55; see 20:31). That he reached **all the residents of Asia** reflects his missionary strategy of setting up in the major cities and sending coworkers into the surrounding region to establish churches. Paul wrote 1 Corinthians near the end of his time at Ephesus (see note on Acts 19:22).

The Sons of Sceva

11 And [l]God was doing extraordinary miracles by the hands of Paul, 12 [l]so that even
handkerchiefs or aprons that had touched his skin were carried away to the sick, and their
diseases left them and [m]the evil spirits came out of them. 13 Then some of the itinerant
Jewish [n]exorcists [o]undertook to invoke the name of the Lord Jesus over those who had
evil spirits, saying, [p]"I adjure you by the Jesus whom Paul proclaims." 14 Seven sons of
a Jewish high priest named Sceva were doing this. 15 But the evil spirit answered them,
[q]"Jesus I know, and Paul I recognize, but who are you?" 16 And the man in whom was the
evil spirit leaped on them, mastered all[1] of them and overpowered them, so that they fled
out of that house naked and wounded. 17 And this became known to all the residents of
Ephesus, both Jews and Greeks. And fear fell upon them all, and [r]the name of the Lord

[1] Or *both*

11 [l][ch. 5:15]; See ch. 5:12
12 [l][See ver. 11 above] [m]See Mark 16:17
13 [n][Matt. 12:27; Luke 11:19] [o]See Mark 9:38 [p]Matt. 26:63; Mark 5:7
15 [q]See James 2:19
17 [r][2 Thess. 1:12]

19:11–22 *Paul Encounters False Religion at Ephesus.* Paul worked many miracles at Ephesus (vv. 11–12), but he encountered others who pursued a false way of working "miracles," including some would-be Jewish exorcists (vv. 13–16) and persons who had a background of faith in magical spells (vv. 17–20).

19:11 God was doing extraordinary miracles by the hands of Paul. As previously in Acts, miracles opened the door for hearing the gospel and gave confirmation that God himself was working through Paul and his message (cf. notes on 3:1–26; etc.).

19:12 handkerchiefs or aprons. These were not magical objects. Rather, the Holy Spirit was pleased to manifest his powerful presence so strongly through Paul that the Spirit's presence sometimes remained evident in connection with objects that Paul had touched (cf. note on 5:15). As had happened at Samaria (8:9–13), Cyprus (13:6–11), and Philippi (16:16–18), the powerful forces of pagan magic (19:19) and religion connected to demonic activity (vv. 12, 15; cf. 1 Cor. 10:20; Eph. 6:12) were confronted by the far more powerful work of the Holy Spirit ministering through Paul.

19:13 itinerant Jewish exorcists. There are records of extensive ceremonies

Paul's Third Missionary Journey (Acts 18:22–21:17)
c. A.D. 52–57

Paul's third missionary journey traversed much the same ground as his second (cf. map, p. 2118). Passing through Galatia and Phrygia, he proceeded directly to the great port city of Ephesus. After three years of preaching and teaching there, Paul traveled again through Macedonia and Achaia, strengthening the believers, and then finished with a visit to Jerusalem.

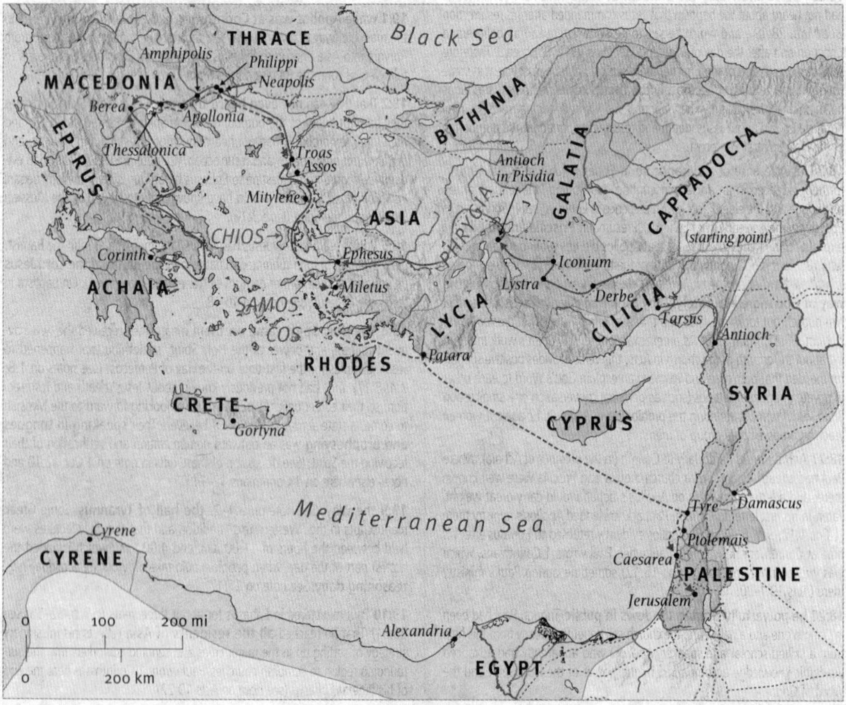

18[s]Matt. 3:6; Mark 1:5; Rom. 14:11; James 5:16
20[t]ch. 6:7; 12:24
21[u]1 Cor. 16:5; [ch. 20:1] [v]Rom. 15:26; 1 Thess. 1:7, 8 [w]ch. 20:16, 22; Rom. 15:25; 2 Cor. 1:16; [1 Cor. 16:3, 4] [x]Rom. 15:24, 28; [ch. 23:11; Rom. 1:13]
22[y]Col. 4:7; 2 Tim. 1:18; 4:11; Philem. 13; [ver. 29; ch. 13:5] [z]See ch. 16:1 [a][1 Cor. 16:8, 9]
23[b][2 Cor. 1:8] [c]ver. 9
24[d][ch. 16:16, 19]
25[d][See ver. 24 above]
26[e]ch. 14:15; 17:29; 1 Cor. 8:4 [f]Deut. 4:28; 2 Kgs. 19:18; Ps. 115:4; Isa. 44:10-20; Jer. 10:3-6; Rev. 9:20
27[g][ch. 8:10]

Jesus was extolled. 18 Also many of those who were now believers came, [s]confessing and
divulging their practices. 19 And a number of those who had practiced magic arts brought
their books together and burned them in the sight of all. And they counted the value
of them and found it came to fifty thousand pieces of silver. 20 So the word of the Lord
[t]continued to increase and prevail mightily.

A Riot at Ephesus

21 Now after these events Paul resolved in the Spirit [u]to pass through [v]Macedonia and
Achaia and [w]go to Jerusalem, saying, "After I have been there, [x]I must also see Rome."
22 And having sent into Macedonia two of [y]his helpers, [z]Timothy and Erastus, he himself
stayed in Asia [a]for a while.

23 About that time [b]there arose no little disturbance concerning [c]the Way. 24 For a man
named Demetrius, a silversmith, who made silver shrines of Artemis, [d]brought no little
business to the craftsmen. 25 [d]These he gathered together, with the workmen in similar
trades, and said, "Men, you know that from this business we have our wealth. 26 And you
see and hear that not only in Ephesus but in almost all of Asia this Paul has persuaded and
turned away a great many people, [e]saying that [f]gods made with hands are not gods. 27 And
there is danger not only that this trade of ours may come into disrepute but also that the
temple of the [g]great goddess Artemis may be counted as nothing, and that she may even
be deposed from her magnificence, she whom all Asia and the world worship."

and spoken formulas that Jewish people in the first century used to try to free themselves from the influence of evil spirits, but it is unlikely that these were very effective, since the people were astounded when Jesus was able to cast out demons with "authority and power" (Luke 4:36).

19:15–16 Not only was the name of **Jesus** important in casting out evil spirits, but so was true faith in Jesus on the part of the one uttering his name. Here, a "reverse exorcism" occurred, with the demon driving out the exorcists. Their nudity enhanced their humiliation.

Itinerary of Paul's Third Journey

City/Island	Province/Region	Reference
Antioch	Syria	18:22
	Galatia	18:23
	Asia *(region of Phrygia)*	18:23
Ephesus	Asia	19:1–40
	Macedonia	20:1–2
Corinth?	Achaia	20:2–3
	Macedonia	20:3
Philippi	Macedonia	20:6
Troas	Asia	20:6–12
Assos	Asia	20:13–14
Mitylene	Asia	20:14
Chios/Samos	Asia	20:15
Miletus	Asia	20:15–38
Cos	Asia	21:1
Rhodes	Rhodes	21:1
Patara	Lycia	21:1
Tyre	Syria	21:3–6
Ptolemais	Syria	21:7
Caesarea	Palestine	21:8–14
Jerusalem	Palestine	21:15–17

19:19 The Greco-Roman world put great stock in magical incantations and spells, often collecting them into books that sold for large sums (see note on 13:6). Converts in Ephesus brought these relics of their pagan past and held a massive book burning. **Pieces of silver** probably refers to the Greek *drachma*, which represented a laborer's average daily wage. At $15 (U.S.) per hour, or $120 per day, 50,000 *drachmas* would equal approximately $6 million in today's currency.

19:20 Luke again emphasizes the inherent power of the **word of the Lord**, showing that the gospel triumphs over all demonic powers. In these summary statements, Luke continues to give glory to God and his word rather than to any human skill, knowledge, or effort.

19:21 Macedonia included the churches in Philippi, Thessalonica, and Berea. **Achaia** included the church in Corinth. This verse provides an outline for the remainder of Acts, for after leaving Ephesus Paul returned to the churches in "Macedonia" and "Achaia" (or Greece, 20:1–2) and from there went to **Jerusalem** (21:17) and then eventually to **Rome** (28:14).

19:22 having sent into Macedonia . . . Timothy and Erastus. Paul apparently wrote 1 Corinthians during the springtime, near the end of his time in Ephesus (cf. v. 21; also 1 Cor. 16:5–10). Paul sent the letter to Corinth with Timothy and Erastus (see 1 Cor. 16:10), and then later left Ephesus to go through Macedonia and eventually to Corinth himself as well (see Acts 20:1–2; 1 Cor. 16:5, 8–9). Erastus was a Corinthian and is included in Paul's greetings in Rom. 16:23 and 2 Tim. 4:20.

19:23–41 *Paul Experiences Violent Opposition at Ephesus.* The account of Paul's Ephesian ministry concludes with a riot against Paul that was provoked by a silversmith named Demetrius.

19:23 The Way refers to Christianity (19:9; 22:4; 24:14, 22; see note on 9:1–2).

19:24 Demetrius was a skilled demagogue. His real problem was that Paul's polemic against idolatry was hurting his business, but he added more volatile accusations that aroused civic and religious pride. **Silver shrines** were replicas of the temple of **Artemis** that were used for home altars or as offerings to be presented to the goddess as often as daily.

19:25–27 Demetrius's statements were basically accurate. Paul *did* preach against idolatry (Acts 17:29), and people from **all Asia and the world** *did* flock to Ephesus to worship Artemis, particularly in the week-long spring festival dedicated to the goddess. Demetrius was not wrong in linking Artemis with the civic, economic, and religious interests of the city.

28 When they heard this they were enraged and were crying out, [g]"Great is Artemis of
the Ephesians!" 29 So the city was filled with the confusion, and they rushed together into
the theater, dragging with them Gaius and [h]Aristarchus, Macedonians who were Paul's
[i]companions in travel. 30 But when Paul wished to go in among the crowd, the disciples
would not let him. 31 And even some of the Asiarchs,[1] who were friends of his, sent to him
and were urging him not to venture into the theater. 32 [j]Now some cried out one thing,
some another, for the assembly was in confusion, and most of them did not know why
they had come together. 33 Some of the crowd prompted Alexander, whom the Jews had
put forward. And Alexander, [k]motioning with his hand, wanted to make a defense to the
crowd. 34 But when they recognized that he was a Jew, for about two hours they all cried
out with one voice, [l]"Great is Artemis of the Ephesians!"

35 And when the town clerk had quieted the crowd, he said, "Men of Ephesus, who is there
who does not know that the city of the Ephesians is temple keeper of the great Artemis,
and of the sacred stone that fell from [m]the sky?[2] 36 Seeing then that these things cannot be
denied, you ought to be quiet and do nothing rash. 37 For you have brought [n]these men here
who are neither [o]sacrilegious nor blasphemers of our goddess. 38 If therefore Demetrius and
the craftsmen with him have a complaint against anyone, the courts are open, and there
are [p]proconsuls. Let them bring charges against one another. 39 But if you seek anything
further,[3] it shall be settled in the regular assembly. 40 For we really are in danger of being
charged with rioting today, since there is no cause that we can give to justify this commotion." 41 And when he had said these things, he dismissed the assembly.

Paul in Macedonia and Greece

20 After the uproar ceased, Paul sent for the disciples, and after encouraging them,
he said farewell and [q]departed for Macedonia. 2 When he had gone through those
regions and had given them much encouragement, he came to Greece. 3 There he spent

[1] That is, high-ranking officers of the province of Asia [2] The meaning of the Greek is uncertain [3] Some manuscripts *seek about other matters*

28 [g][See ver. 27 above]
29 [h]ch. 20:4; 27:2; Col. 4:10; Philem. 24 [i]2 Cor. 8:19; [ver. 22; ch. 20:34]
32 [j]ch. 21:34
33 [k]See ch. 12:17
34 [l]ver. 28
35 [m][ch. 14:12]
37 [n]ver. 29 [o]Rom. 2:22
38 [p]See ch. 13:7

Chapter 20

1 [q]See ch. 19:21

19:28 Great is Artemis of the Ephesians! Civic and religious pride were the decisive factors provoking the riot.

19:29 The Ephesian **theater** had a capacity of more than 20,000 in Paul's time and was the place of assembly for the regular town business meetings. Apparently **Gaius** and **Aristarchus** were eventually released, since Aristarchus reappears later as Paul's frequent companion (see 20:4; 27:2; Col. 4:10; Philem. 24).

19:30 As the main focus of the riot, Paul was in mortal danger, and his fellow Christians were right to hold him back.

19:31 The **Asiarchs** were the keepers of the imperial Roman cult in Asia; they were of high rank and were concerned about the safety of their fellow citizen Paul. Many inscriptions testify to the use of the title Asiarch during this time (see also Strabo, *Geography* 14.1.42).

19:32 As with most mobs, **confusion** reigned, many not knowing why they had assembled.

19:33–34 The role of the Jew **Alexander** is unclear. Perhaps he wished to dissociate the Jews from the Christians. But the crowd shouted him down, knowing that Jews opposed any foreign gods.

19:35 The **town clerk** was the chief administrative officer of the city, the liaison between the town assembly and the Roman officials. He assured the crowd that their city's reputation was secure. The **sacred stone that fell from the sky** probably refers to a meteorite. Meteorites were associated with Artemis worship.

19:38–40 the courts are open. The legal means for settling disputes were the regular courts conducted by the Roman proconsul and the scheduled meetings of the town assembly. **there are proconsuls.** A "proconsul" (Gk. *anthypatos*) was the head of government in a Roman province (cf. 13:7; 18:12). The plural here may refer to the fact that at that time in Ephesus they were between the reigns of two proconsuls. **in danger.** The crowd in the theater (where regular assemblies were held) had the appearance of an unlawful assembly and risked bringing Roman reprisals. Luke's extensive report of the careful reasoning of the town clerk may have provided an important basis with which Christians in other cities could have defended themselves, since Luke shows here (and elsewhere in Acts; see notes on 18:14; 23:27) that the Christian gospel was not contrary to the Roman rule of law and was not disruptive of public order, and that accusations made to that effect were untrue.

20:1–6 *Paul Completes His Ministry in Greece.* Paul made a final visit to the churches of Macedonia and Achaia, spending the winter in Corinth.

20:1 Paul departed from Ephesus for **Macedonia** (probably going first to Philippi). In the final days of his Ephesian ministry, after writing 1 Corinthians (see note on Acts 19:22), Paul had had considerable conflict with the Corinthian church, making a "painful" visit to them (probably by sea) and writing a "tearful" letter upon his return to Ephesus (2 Cor. 2:1–4), which he at first regretted having sent (2 Cor. 7:8–9). As his time in Ephesus neared its completion Paul wanted to return to Corinth, but feared how he might be received there after having sent the harsh letter. He evidently sent Titus ahead to "test the waters" at Corinth. Upon leaving Ephesus (Acts 20:1), Paul did not head directly to Corinth by sea, but first went north, visiting the Christian communities along the way and hoping to meet up with Titus returning from Corinth. He went to Troas, and then possibly on to other churches in Macedonia (2 Cor. 2:12–13). In Macedonia (perhaps at Philippi, Thessalonica, or Berea) Titus finally joined him and brought the good news that the church had repented of its opposition to Paul's leadership and had become reconciled to him (2 Cor. 7:5–16). Paul then wrote 2 Corinthians.

20:2 Greece (Gk. *Hellas*) is another name for the province of Achaia, where Corinth was located.

20:3 Paul stayed at Corinth for **three months**, likely the winter months (see 1 Cor. 16:6), when sea travel was more dangerous. **Syria**. Paul's goal was to sail to a Syrian port, with Jerusalem as the final destination (Acts 19:21). Paul wrote Romans (c. A.D. 57) during this final Corinthian visit (see Introduction to Romans: The Ancient City of Rome; and note on Rom. 16:1–23). In it he explained that his reason for going to Jerusalem was to take a collection from his Gentile churches to the needy Christians in Jerusalem (Rom. 15:22–29; for other references to this collection, see Acts 24:17; 1 Cor. 16:1–4; 2 Corinthians 8–9). Gathering this collection was one of the purposes behind this final visit to the churches of Macedonia and Achaia. **he decided to return through**

3 [r]ver. 19; [ch. 13:50]; See ch. 9:24
4 [s]ch. 14:6, 21; See ch. 19:29 [t]See ch. 16:1 [u]Eph. 6:21; Col. 4:7; 2 Tim. 4:12; Titus 3:12 [v]ch. 21:29; 2 Tim. 4:20
5 [w]ver. 6-8, 13-15 [x]ch. 16:8-11
6 [y]ch. 12:3; Ex. 12:14, 15; 23:15
7 [z]1 Cor. 16:2; [Mark 16:9; John 20:19; Rev. 1:10] [a]ver. 11; 1 Cor. 10:16; 11:23, 24; See ch. 2:42
8 [b]ch. 1:13; 9:37, 39
9 [c]2 Kgs. 1:2
10 [d][1 Kgs. 17:21; 2 Kgs. 4:34] [e][Matt. 9:23, 24; Mark 5:39]
11 [f]ver. 7
16 [g]ver. 22; ch. 24:11; [ver. 6; ch. 19:21; 1 Cor. 16:8] [h]ch. 2:1
17 [i]See ch. 11:30
18 [j]1 Thess. 1:5; [ver. 31, 34] [k]ch. 18:19; 19:1, 10
19 [l][Rom. 12:11; Col. 3:24] [m][1 Thess. 2:6, 7]; See Eph. 4:2 [n][ver. 31; 2 Cor. 2:4; Phil. 3:18] [o]See ver. 3
20 [p]ver. 27 [q][ver. 31]
21 [r]ver. 24; ch. 18:5 [s]Mark 1:15; Heb. 6:1; See ch. 2:38 [t][Eph. 1:15; Col. 1:4; 1 Tim. 3:13]
22 [u][ch. 17:16]

three months, and when [r]a plot was made against him by the Jews[1] as he was about to set
sail for Syria, he decided to return through Macedonia. 4 Sopater the Berean, son of Pyrrhus,
accompanied him; and of the Thessalonians, [s]Aristarchus and Secundus; and [s]Gaius of Derbe,
and [t]Timothy; and the Asians, [u]Tychicus and [v]Trophimus. 5 These went on ahead and were
waiting for [w]us at [x]Troas, 6 but we sailed away from Philippi after [y]the days of Unleavened
Bread, and in five days we came to them at Troas, where we stayed for seven days.

Eutychus Raised from the Dead

7 [z]On the first day of the week, when we were gathered together [a]to break bread, Paul
talked with them, intending to depart on the next day, and he prolonged his speech until
midnight. 8 There were many lamps in [b]the upper room where we were gathered. 9 And a
young man named Eutychus, sitting at the window, sank into a deep sleep as Paul talked
still longer. And being overcome by sleep, he [c]fell down from the third story and was taken
up dead. 10 But Paul went down and [d]bent over him, and taking him in his arms, said, [e]"Do
not be alarmed, for his life is in him." 11 And when Paul had gone up and [f]had broken bread
and eaten, he conversed with them a long while, until daybreak, and so departed. 12 And
they took the youth away alive, and were not a little comforted.
13 But going ahead to the ship, we set sail for Assos, intending to take Paul aboard there,
for so he had arranged, intending himself to go by land. 14 And when he met us at Assos, we
took him on board and went to Mitylene. 15 And sailing from there we came the following
day opposite Chios; the next day we touched at Samos; and[2] the day after that we went to
Miletus. 16 For Paul had decided to sail past Ephesus, so that he might not have to spend time
in Asia, for he was hastening [g]to be at Jerusalem, if possible, [h]on the day of Pentecost.

Paul Speaks to the Ephesian Elders

17 Now from Miletus he sent to Ephesus and called [i]the elders of the church to come to
him. 18 And when they came to him, he said to them:
[j]"You yourselves know [k]how I lived among you the whole time [j]from the first day that
I set foot in Asia, 19 [l]serving the Lord [m]with all humility and with [n]tears and with trials
that happened to me through [o]the plots of the Jews; 20 how I [p]did not shrink from declaring to you anything that was profitable, and [q]teaching you in public and from house to
house, 21 [r]testifying both to Jews and to Greeks of [s]repentance toward God and of [t]faith
in our Lord Jesus Christ. 22 And now, behold, I am going to Jerusalem, constrained [u]by[3]

[1] Greek *Ioudaioi* probably refers here to Jewish religious leaders, and others under their influence, in that time; also verse 19 [2] Some manuscripts add *after remaining at Trogyllium* [3] Or *bound in*

Macedonia. This would take Paul back once again to the churches of Berea, Thessalonica, and Philippi.

20:4 accompanied him. In discussing the "collection for the saints" in 1 Cor. 16:1–4, Paul noted that it would be accompanied by official representatives from the churches. Their presence would give safety from robbery and also would provide a public guarantee of Paul's integrity in handling the funds. The men listed here (Acts 20:4) as accompanying Paul represent all the areas of his missionary work. **Aristarchus**. See note on 19:29.

20:5 These went on ahead. This group may have included all the representatives or just the two Asians, who perhaps arranged for the final voyage from **Troas** (on this city see note on 16:8).

20:7–16 *Paul Travels to Miletus.* The journey to Jerusalem continued, with an incident at Troas in which Paul restored the life of a youth (vv. 7–12). This is followed by a detailed itinerary of the voyage to Miletus (vv. 13–16).

20:7 On the first day of the week. The first reference in Acts to worship on Sunday.

20:9 The story has a touch of humor and a happy outcome. The etymology of the name **Eutychus** is "lucky, fortunate." The "many lamps" (v. 8) and long sermon likely led "Lucky" to seek air in the window, but he fell asleep anyway and fell three stories. **Taken up dead** (not "as dead") indicates his actual death.

20:13–14 The remains of **Assos** include a monumental temple of Athena atop the acropolis, a market, portions of the city wall, and a Greek theater.

20:15 Chios was the birthplace of Homer, and **Samos** was the birthplace of the mathematician Pythagoras. **Miletus** was a major Aegean harbor, one of the great cities of the province of Asia in Paul's day.

20:16 Having spent three years in Ephesus, Paul knew he would be delayed with too many farewells there, so he chose to **sail past** the city so that he could reach Jerusalem by the feast of Pentecost.

20:17–35 *Paul Addresses the Ephesian Elders at Miletus.* Paul's Miletus address is the sole example in Acts of a major speech to Christians. Of all Paul's speeches in Acts, it has the most in common with his letters, which were addressed to Christians. Paul held out his own ministry as an example for the Ephesian elders (vv. 18–21), spoke of his future prospects (vv. 22–27), warned of coming heresies (vv. 28–31), and encouraged a proper attitude toward material goods (vv. 32–35).

20:17 The four harbors of **Miletus** have long since filled up with sediment from the Meander River. Excavations at Miletus have revealed the substantial theater, an odeion (a small covered theater), an agora, and the Delphinium (dedicated to Apollo). One excavated building at Miletus is considered by some to be a synagogue. The Ephesian church leaders are called **elders** (Gk. *presbyteroi*) and are in v. 28 addressed as "overseers" (Gk. *episkopoi*, sometimes translated "bishops") who are to "care for" (or "shepherd") "the flock" (the role of pastors). This overlap of terminology indicates that "elders," "overseers," and "pastors" likely refer to the same office.

20:20 did not shrink. See note on vv. 26–27.

20:22–23 Constrained (Gk. *deō*, "to bind, tie, constrain") indicates that the Holy Spirit was giving Paul an exceptionally strong sense of compulsion that he had to go quickly and directly to Jerusalem, even though he knew that **imprisonment and afflictions** awaited him there. Paul must have reflected on the similarities between his present journey to Jerusalem and Jesus' final journey to Jerusalem where he was to die (Matt. 16:21; 20:18; Mark 10:32–33; Luke 9:51, 53; 18:31–33), and wondered if he also would

the Spirit, not knowing what will happen to me there, 23 except that [v]the Holy Spirit
testifies to me in every city that [w]imprisonment and [x]afflictions await me. 24 But [y]I do not
account my life of any value nor as precious to myself, if only [z]I may finish my course
and [a]the ministry [b]that I received from the Lord Jesus, [c]to testify to [d]the gospel of [e]the
grace of God. 25 And now, behold, [f]I know that none of you among whom I have gone
about [g]proclaiming the kingdom will see my face again. 26 Therefore [h]I testify to you this
day that [i]I am innocent of the blood of all, 27 for [j]I did not shrink from declaring to you
[k]the whole counsel of God. 28 [l]Pay careful attention to yourselves and to all [m]the flock, in
which [n]the Holy Spirit has made you [o]overseers, [p]to care for [q]the church of God,[1] which
he [r]obtained [s]with his own blood.[2] 29 I [r]know that after my departure [t]fierce wolves will
come in among you, [u]not sparing the flock; 30 and [v]from among your own selves will
arise men speaking twisted things, to draw away the disciples after them. 31 Therefore
[w]be alert, remembering that [x]for three years I did not cease night or day [y]to admonish
every one [z]with tears. 32 And now [a]I commend you to God and to [b]the word of his grace,
which is able to [c]build you up and to give you [d]the inheritance among all those who
are sanctified. 33 [e]I coveted no one's silver or gold or apparel. 34 [f]You yourselves know
that [g]these hands ministered to my necessities and [h]to those who were with me. 35 In
all things [i]I have shown you that [j]by working hard in this way we must [k]help the weak
and [l]remember the words of the Lord Jesus, how he himself said, 'It is more blessed [m]to
give than to receive.'"

36 And when he had said these things, [n]he knelt down and prayed with them all. 37 And
[o]there was much weeping on the part of all; [p]they embraced Paul and [p]kissed him, 38 being
sorrowful most of all because of [q]the word he had spoken, that they would not see his face
again. And [r]they accompanied him to the ship.

[1] Some manuscripts *of the Lord* [2] Or *with the blood of his Own*

23 [v][ch. 21:4, 11]; See ch. 8:29; 9:16 [w]ch. 21:33 [x]ch. 14:22; 1 Thess. 3:3 **24** [y]See ch. 21:13 [z]2 Tim. 4:7 [a]ch. 1:17; 1 Tim. 1:12 [b]Gal. 1:1; 1 Thess. 2:4; [ch. 26:16; Titus 1:3] [c]ver. 21 [d]ch. 15:7 [e][ver. 32; 1 Tim. 1:14]; See ch. 11:23 **25** [f][Phil. 1:25] [g]See ch. 28:31 **26** [h]Deut. 8:19 [i]See ch. 18:6 **27** [j]ver. 20; [Jer. 26:2; Ezek. 33:8] [k]ch. 13:36; Luke 7:30; [ch. 2:23; Eph. 1:11; Heb. 6:17] **28** [l][1 Tim. 4:16] [m]ver. 29; [Eph. 4:11]; See Luke 12:32 [n][ch. 13:2; 1 Cor. 12:8-11] [o]Phil. 1:1; 1 Tim. 3:2; Titus 1:7; [ver. 17] [p]See John 21:16 [q]1 Cor. 1:2; 10:32; 11:16; 15:9 [r][2 Pet. 2:1] [s]Heb. 9:12, 14; [Eph. 1:7; 1 John 1:7]; See 1 Pet. 1:18, 19; Rev. 5:9 **29** [r][See ver. 28 above] [t]See Matt. 7:15 [u]John 10:12; [Col. 2:8] **30** [v][1 Cor. 11:19; 2 Cor. 11:13; 1 Tim. 1:19, 20; 1 John 2:18, 19] **31** [w][Heb. 13:17]; See Matt. 24:42 [x][ch. 19:8, 10; 24:17] [y]Col. 1:28 [z][Heb. 13:17]; See ver. 19 **32** [a]ch. 14:23 [b]ch. 14:3; [ver. 24] [c]See Col. 2:7 [d]ch. 26:18; Eph. 1:14, 18; 5:5; Col. 1:12; 3:24; Heb. 9:15; [1 Pet. 1:4]; See Matt. 25:34; Rom. 8:17 **33** [e]1 Cor. 9:12; 2 Cor. 7:2; 11:9; 12:17; [1 Sam. 12:3; Matt. 10:8; 1 Thess. 2:5] **34** [f][ver. 18] [g]See ch. 18:3 [h]ch. 19:22, 29 **35** [i]2 Thess. 3:7 [j]Eph. 4:28 [k]1 Thess. 5:14; [1 Cor. 12:28] [l]ch. 11:16 [m]Matt. 10:8 **36** [n]See ch. 7:60 **37** [o][2 Tim. 1:4] [p]See Luke 15:20 **38** [q]ver. 25 [r]See ch. 15:3

end his life there (see Acts 20:24). **the Holy Spirit testifies to me in every city**. Such testimony probably came to Paul through both Christian prophets (cf. 21:11) and direct revelation from the Holy Spirit.

20:24 Paul often expressed his willingness to suffer for Christ (2 Cor. 4:7–12; 6:4–10; 12:9–10; Phil. 1:20–21; 2:17; 3:8; Col. 1:24). In 2 Tim. 4:7 he used the same expression of finishing his **course** (or "race," Gk. *dromos*).

20:26–27 For Paul's claim to be **innocent** of their **blood**, see Ezek. 33:1–6 and note on Acts 18:6. Paul is saying that he is not accountable before God for any future doctrinal or moral error that might come to the Ephesian church, **for** (giving the reason why he is not culpable) he **did not shrink from declaring** any part of the teaching of the Word of God. The **whole counsel of God** refers to the entirety of God's redemptive plan unfolded in Scripture. Even though some parts of God's Word were unpopular or difficult, Paul did not omit any of them in his preaching. In refusing to pass over teachings that might have offended some, Paul gave a courageous example that is a model for all who would teach God's Word after him.

20:28 Pay careful attention to yourselves. Spiritual leaders need first of all to guard their own spiritual and moral purity. **the church of God, which he obtained with his own blood**. The last part of this phrase refers to the blood of Christ poured out in his atoning death on the cross (cf. Rom. 3:25; 5:9; Eph. 1:7; etc.). The reference to God in the first part of this phrase ("the church of God") most likely is a reference to Christ as the head of the church and as "God the Son," the second person of the Trinity. Alternatively, if God the Father is in view in the phrase "the church of God," then "his own blood" is a reference to the blood of God's "own," that is, of "God's own Son" (which would be a legitimate alternative reading of the Greek). (See also ESV footnote indicating that some Greek manuscripts read "the church of the Lord" rather than "the church of God.")

20:29–30 Paul showed remarkable insight into the future situation of the Ephesian church (probably through a revelation from the Holy Spirit). The letters of Paul to Timothy, who served Ephesus a decade or so later, attest to the presence of false teachers who were ravaging the church for their own gain and who had indeed come from within the church, in fact, from among the elders themselves (**from among your own selves**). (See 1 Tim. 1:19–20; 4:1–3; 2 Tim. 1:15; 2:17–18; 3:1–9.)

20:31–32 Three years included the "three months" and the "two years" in Ephesus that Luke had mentioned earlier (see 19:8, 10). Paul again challenged the elders to follow the example of his ministry with them (c. A.D. 52–55) and offered a benediction dedicating their service to the power and leadership of God. He particularly emphasized that **the word** of God was to be central in their ministries, for the word **is able to build . . . up** believers; it teaches the gospel of salvation by **grace** so that the final **inheritance** (end-time salvation) is received by those who belong to God. **sanctified**. That is, made holy in heart and life by the Holy Spirit.

20:35 the words of the Lord Jesus. This saying from Jesus is not recorded in the Gospels—a reminder that Jesus did many things that are not recorded in Scripture (see John 21:25). This saying was no doubt passed on to Paul by those who heard Jesus teach. **give**. On Christian generosity, see 2 Cor. 8:9–15.

20:36–21:16 *Paul Journeys to Jerusalem.* Paul traveled to Jerusalem by sea and then by land. Along the way he had sorrowful farewells and ominous warnings from each Christian community about the dangers facing him in Jerusalem. The warnings are reminiscent of the forebodings that accompanied Jesus on his own journey to Jerusalem (see Luke 13:33–35; 18:31–33).

20:38 As Paul prepared to depart, the Ephesian elders were **sorrowful most of all** that they would not see him again (see v. 25). Though Paul was in frequent conflict with hostile unbelievers and with false teachers in the churches, this verse shows that Paul's churches had deep affection for him; no doubt many thought of him primarily as a kind and gentle pastor (cf. 1 Thess. 2:7; 1 Tim. 3:3; 2 Tim. 2:24; Titus 3:2). They probably supplied him with provisions for his voyage.

Chapter 21
1[s]See ch. 16:10 [t]ch. 16:11
4[u]ver. 11; ch. 20:23
5[v]ch. 20:38 [w]ch. 20:36
7[x]See John 21:23
8[y]ch. 6:5; 8:5 [z]Eph. 4:11; 2 Tim. 4:5
9[a]ch. 2:17, 18; Luke 2:36; 1 Cor. 11:5; See ch. 13:1
10[b]ch. 11:28
11[c][1 Sam. 15:27, 28; 1 Kgs. 11:30; Isa. 20:3; Jer. 13:1-11; 27:2] [d]See ch. 20:23 [e][ver. 33]; See ch. 9:16 [f][ver. 31-33; Matt. 20:19]
12[g][Matt. 16:21-23]
13[g][See ver. 12 above] [h]ch. 20:24; Rom. 8:36; 2 Cor. 4:16; 12:10; Phil. 2:17; [ch. 15:26] [i]See ch. 5:41
14[j][Ruth 1:18] [k]See Matt. 6:10
17[l]ver. 7; [ch. 15:4]
18[m]See ch. 12:17 [n]See ch. 11:30

Paul Goes to Jerusalem

21 And when [s]we had parted from them and set sail, we [t]came by a straight course to
Cos, and the next day to Rhodes, and from there to Patara.[1] **2** And having found a
ship crossing to Phoenicia, we went aboard and set sail. **3** When we had come in sight of
Cyprus, leaving it on the left we sailed to Syria and landed at Tyre, for there the ship was
to unload its cargo. **4** And having sought out the disciples, we stayed there for seven days.
And [u]through the Spirit they were telling Paul not to go on to Jerusalem. **5** When our days
there were ended, we departed and went on our journey, and they all, with wives and children, [v]accompanied us until we were outside the city. And [w]kneeling down on the beach,
we prayed **6** and said farewell to one another. Then we went on board the ship, and they
returned home.

7 When we had finished the voyage from Tyre, we arrived at Ptolemais, and we greeted
[x]the brothers[2] and stayed with them for one day. **8** On the next day we departed and came
to Caesarea, and we entered the house of [y]Philip [z]the evangelist, who was one of the seven,
and stayed with him. **9** He had four unmarried daughters, [a]who prophesied. **10** While we
were staying for many days, a prophet named [b]Agabus came down from Judea. **11** And
coming to us, he [c]took Paul's belt and bound his own feet and hands and said, [d]"Thus
says the Holy Spirit, [e]'This is how the Jews[3] at Jerusalem will bind the man who owns
this belt and [f]deliver him into the hands of the Gentiles.'" **12** When we heard this, we and
the people there [g]urged him not to go up to Jerusalem. **13** Then Paul answered, [g]"What are
you doing, weeping and breaking my heart? For [h]I am ready not only to be imprisoned
but even to die in Jerusalem [i]for the name of the Lord Jesus." **14** And since he would not
be persuaded, [j]we ceased and said, [k]"Let the will of the Lord be done."

15 After these days we got ready and went up to Jerusalem. **16** And some of the disciples
from Caesarea went with us, bringing us to the house of Mnason of Cyprus, an early disciple, with whom we should lodge.

Paul Visits James

17 When we had come to Jerusalem, [l]the brothers received us gladly. **18** On the following day Paul went in with us to [m]James, and all [n]the elders were present. **19** After greeting

[1] Some manuscripts add *and Myra* [2] Or *brothers and sisters*; also verse 17 [3] Greek *Ioudaioi* probably refers here to Jewish religious leaders, and others under their influence, in that time

21:1 Paul's ship was probably a "coasting vessel"—one that traveled close to shore. Each of the places mentioned probably represents a day's journey and the stopping place for the night. **Cos** and **Rhodes** are both islands, with port cities of the same name. Paul and his companions boarded a sturdier vessel at **Patara** for the 400-mile (644-km) open-sea voyage to Tyre. Patara was the main port city in Lycia; its immense harbor is now filled up with silt.

21:3 Tyre was in Phoenicia (see note on 11:19).

21:4 through the Spirit they were telling Paul not to go on to Jerusalem. This apparently indicates some prophecies given by the Christians at Tyre. But what these disciples told Paul was wrong, because the narrative clearly shows that Paul was being guided by the Holy Spirit to go to Jerusalem (see 19:21; 20:22–24; 21:14). Interpreters differ over how much of what these disciples told Paul was actually part of their prophesying (or speaking "through the Spirit"): (1) Some hold that this incident shows that there are two potential kinds of problems with early Christian prophecies: first that there could be *mistakes in the prophecies themselves*, and second that there could be *mistakes in the prophet's own interpretation*. This then would be an example of why Paul commands that prophecies must be tested, that is, to guard against both (a) possible *mistakes in the prophecy itself*, and (b) possible *mistakes in the interpretation* of the prophecy (see notes on 1 Cor. 14:29; 1 Thess. 5:20–21). (2) Other interpreters hold that, although such *prophecies themselves are completely accurate* (because they come "through the Spirit"), there still could be *mistakes in the interpretation of the prophecy*. Thus, even though the prophecy is accurate, such prophecies still need to be tested. In the first case, both the prophecy and the interpretation may be wrong; in the second case only the interpretation may be wrong. In either case, all prophecies would need to be tested, as Paul commands.

21:7 Ptolemais is the Roman name of the modern city of Acco.

21:8–9 Caesarea was the closest port to Jerusalem. **four unmarried daughters**. The gift of prophecy was promised to women as well as men in Joel's prophecy (Joel 2:28–29), which was fulfilled at Pentecost (Acts 2:17–18).

21:10–11 Agabus had earlier prophesied a coming famine (11:28). OT prophets often acted out their prophecies (e.g., Isa. 8:1–4; 20:1–4; Jer. 13:1–11; 19:1–13; 27:1–22).

21:13 Paul, as a disciple of Jesus, is willing to follow in Jesus' steps (1 Pet. 2:21) and **to die in Jerusalem** as Jesus did (Luke 9:51; 18:31–33).

21:15 The distance from **Jerusalem** to Caesarea was approximately 62 miles (100 km) by road. Paul probably arrived there in the spring of A.D. 57.

21:17–23:35 *The Arrest in Jerusalem.* While participating in a Nazirite vow at the temple, Paul was attacked by a Jewish mob and rescued by the Romans. After he defended himself before the Jewish crowd and the Sanhedrin, a plot against his life prompted the Roman tribune to send him to the governor in Caesarea.

21:17–26 *Paul Participates in a Nazirite Ceremony.* When Paul arrived in Jerusalem, the Christians rejoiced over the success of his Gentile mission but expressed concern over rumors that he was teaching Jews to abandon their ancestral laws and customs. To disprove the rumors, they asked Paul to participate publicly in a Nazirite vow, as specified in OT law (Num. 6:1–21). (See also note on Acts 21:23.)

21:18 all the elders were present. Apparently leadership of the church at Jerusalem now rested primarily with these "elders." It seems that **James**

them, [o]he related one by one [p]the things that God had done among the Gentiles through
his [q]ministry. 20 And when they heard it, they [r]glorified God. And they said to him, "You
see, brother, how many thousands there are among the Jews of those who have believed.
They are all [s]zealous for the law, 21 and they have been told about you that you teach all
[t]the Jews who are among the Gentiles to forsake Moses, [u]telling them [v]not to circumcise
their children or [w]walk according to [x]our customs. 22 What then is to be done? They will
certainly hear that you have come. 23 Do therefore what we tell you. We have four men
[y]who are under a vow; 24 take these men and [z]purify yourself along with them and pay
their expenses, [y]so that they may shave their heads. Thus all will know that there is nothing in what they have been told about you, but that you yourself also live in observance
of the law. 25 But as for the Gentiles who have believed, [a]we have sent a letter with our
judgment that they should abstain from what has been sacrificed to idols, and from blood,
and from what has been strangled,[1] and from sexual immorality." 26 Then Paul took the
men, and the next day [z]he purified himself along with them and [b]went into the temple,
giving notice when the days of purification would be fulfilled and [c]the offering presented
for each one of them.

Paul Arrested in the Temple

27 When [c]the seven days were almost completed, [d]the Jews from Asia, [e]seeing him in the
temple, stirred up the whole crowd and laid hands on him, 28 crying out, "Men of Israel,
help! This is the man who [f]is teaching everyone everywhere against the people and [g]the
law and [g]this place. Moreover, he even brought Greeks into the temple and [h]has defiled
[g]this holy place." 29 For they had previously seen [i]Trophimus the Ephesian with him in
the city, and they supposed that Paul had brought him into the temple. 30 Then all the city
was stirred up, and the people ran together. They seized Paul and [j]dragged him out of the
temple, and at once the gates were shut. 31 [j]And as they were seeking to kill him, word came
to the tribune of [k]the cohort that all Jerusalem was in confusion. 32 [l]He at once took soldiers

[1] Some manuscripts omit *and from what has been strangled*

19 [o]See ch. 14:27 [p][Rom. 15:18, 19] [q]See ch. 1:17
20 [r]ch. 11:18 [s]ch. 22:3; Rom. 10:2; Gal. 1:14
21 [t][James 1:1] [u]ver. 28 [v][Rom. 2:28, 29; 1 Cor. 7:19] [w][Mark 7:5; Gal. 2:14] [x]ch. 6:14; 15:1
23 [y][ch. 18:18]
24 [z]ver. 26; ch. 24:18; [John 11:55] [y][See ver. 23 above]
25 [a]See ch. 15:19, 20, 29
26 [z][See ver. 24 above] [b][Num. 6:13] [c][Num. 6:9-12]
27 [c][See ver. 26 above] [d]See ch. 13:50 [e]ch. 24:18; 26:21
28 [f]ver. 21 [g]See ch. 6:13 [h]ch. 24:6
29 [i]ch. 20:4
30 [j]ch. 26:21; [2 Kgs. 11:15]
31 [j][See ver. 30 above] [k]See ch. 10:1
32 [l][ch. 23:27]

himself was counted as an apostle (see 15:13–21; 1 Cor. 15:7–9; Gal. 1:19; 2:9), but the text does not say whether other apostles still remained in Jerusalem or if they had departed on other missionary activities (see note on Acts 12:17). In light of 1:8, the latter is likely.

21:21 not to circumcise. Circumcision is singled out because it was considered the badge of God's covenant with the Jews. The rumor was false; Paul did not object to Jewish believers voluntarily following OT ceremonial laws (see 16:3; 1 Cor. 7:18–19).

21:23 under a vow. Those under a Nazirite vow would abstain from wine, strong drink, grape juice, grapes, or raisins; would avoid any contact that would defile them (such as contact with a dead body); and would not cut their hair (cf. Num. 6:1–21). When the time of the vow was over (often 30 days), they would cut their hair and present an offering in the temple (cf. Mishnah, *Nazir* 6.3). If Paul went with them and personally paid for the cost of their offering, it would show that he did not object to Jewish converts following OT customs voluntarily, so long as those same customs were not required of Gentile believers (see note on Acts 18:18).

21:25 as for the Gentiles. The Jerusalem elders reminded Paul of the requirements for Gentile Christians agreed upon in the Jerusalem council (15:28–29). This was to assure Paul that they wanted to avoid giving unnecessary offense to either believers or unbelievers among the Jews. They were not asking Paul's Gentile converts to embrace the Jewish laws beyond those minimal requirements, nor were they requiring Jewish believers to observe OT ceremonial laws (see Gal. 2:11–12; 4:10).

21:26 he purified himself. See note on v. 27. Paul voluntarily went along with the suggestion from James and the elders. There is no basis in the text for the suggestion of some that the Jerusalem leaders were reluctant to accept the gift Paul brought, or that participating in this vow was a "condition" of accepting the gift from the Gentile churches, or anything suggesting reluctance or hostility toward Paul. The text says that the Jerusalem church received Paul and his companions "gladly" (v. 17) and "they glorified God" as a result of all that they heard from Paul (v. 20). Paul's willingness to join with the four men under a Nazirite vow is an example of his willingness to become "all things to all people" (1 Cor. 9:22, cf. vv. 19–23) for the sake of advancing the gospel.

21:27–39 *An Angry Mob Attacks Paul.* Paul was attacked in the temple by a mob incited by the false charge that he had violated the temple. The Romans rescued him and kept him in custody.

21:27 Paul was the one undergoing purification for **seven days** (see v. 26). Nazirites were purified at the *beginning* of their vow, but Jews often underwent formal purification (e.g., Num. 19:11–12) on other occasions, such as when returning from Gentile territory, as in Paul's case. The **Jews from Asia** were probably from Ephesus (cf. Acts 21:29) and knew Paul from his three years in their city.

21:28 defiled this holy place. The Jews from Asia (v. 27) charged Paul with defiling the temple by taking a Gentile ("Trophimus the Ephesian," v. 29) beyond the stone barrier that divided the outer courtyard (Court of the Gentiles) from the inner sanctuary, which was off-limits to Gentiles, under penalty of death. But their accusation was a lie. Paul, knowing of the death penalty, would not have brought a Gentile into the forbidden area.

21:30 The temple grounds were the largest open area of Jerusalem, and crowds often gathered there. The shutting of the **gates** was probably to ward off any further desecration of the sanctuary.

21:31–32 A Roman **tribune** was the commander of a **cohort**, here consisting of up to 1,000 soldiers, under the command of several **centurions** (see note on 10:1). **at once**. The Roman response could have come very quickly. Roman soldiers were quartered in the Herodian fortress known as the Tower of Antonia on the northwest corner of the temple wall (see note on 12:4). Its high tower provided a full view of the temple area, and it had two flights of stairs leading down into the grounds, so that soldiers could run down to the crowd almost immediately. A lookout person on the tower would have observed the mob below.

33 [m]ch. 20:23; [ver. 11] [n]ch. 12:6; [ch. 22:29; 26:29; 28:20; Eph. 6:20; 2 Tim. 1:16]
34 [o]ch. 19:32 [p]ch. 22:24; 23:10
36 [q]ch. 22:22; [Luke 23:18; John 19:15]
38 [r][ch. 5:36] [s]Matt. 24:26
39 [t]ch. 9:11; 22:3
40 [u]See ch. 12:17 [v]ch. 22:2; 26:14

Chapter 22

1 [w]ch. 7:2
2 [x]ch. 21:40
3 [y]ch. 9:11; 21:39; Rom. 11:1; 2 Cor. 11:22; Phil. 3:5 [z]Deut. 33:3; 2 Kgs. 4:38; [Luke 10:39] [a]ch. 5:34 [b]ch. 26:5 [c][John 16:2; Phil. 3:6]; See ch. 21:20 [d]Rom. 10:2
4 [e]ver. 19; See ch. 8:3 [f][ch. 5:20]; See ch. 9:2 [g]ch. 26:10; [ver. 20; ch. 8:1]
5 [h]ch. 9:1 [i]Luke 22:66 (Gk.); 1 Tim. 4:14 (Gk.) [j]ch. 28:21
6 [k]For ver. 6-11, see ch. 9:3-8; 26:12-18
8 [l]ch. 26:9
9 [m][Dan. 10:7]; See ch. 9:7
10 [n]See ch. 16:30
12 [o]ch. 9:10 [p]ch. 24:14 [q]ch. 10:22
13 [r]ch. 9:17 [s]ch. 9:18
14 [t]See ch. 3:13 [u]ch. 9:15; 26:16 [v]ver. 18; ch. 9:17; 26:16; 1 Cor. 9:1; 15:8; [ver. 15] [w]See ch. 3:14 [x][Gal. 1:12]
15 [y]ch. 23:11 [z]ver. 14; ch. 4:20

and centurions and ran down to them. And when they saw the tribune and the soldiers,
they stopped beating Paul.
33 Then the tribune came up and arrested him and ordered him
[m]to be bound [n]with two chains. He inquired who he was and what he had done.
34 [o]Some
in the crowd were shouting one thing, some another. And as he could not learn the facts
because of the uproar, he ordered him to be brought into [p]the barracks.
35 And when he
came to the steps, he was actually carried by the soldiers because of the violence of the
crowd,
36 for the mob of the people followed, crying out, [q]"Away with him!"

Paul Speaks to the People

37 As Paul was about to be brought into the barracks, he said to the tribune, "May I say
something to you?" And he said, "Do you know Greek?
38 Are you not [r]the Egyptian, then,
who recently stirred up a revolt and led the four thousand men of the Assassins out [s]into
the wilderness?"
39 Paul replied, [t]"I am a Jew, from Tarsus in Cilicia, a citizen of no obscure
city. I beg you, permit me to speak to the people."
40 And when he had given him permis-
sion, Paul, standing on the steps, [u]motioned with his hand to the people. And when there
was a great hush, he addressed them in [v]the Hebrew language,[1] saying:

22 [w]"Brothers and fathers, hear the defense that I now make before you."
2 And when they heard that he was addressing them in [x]the Hebrew language,[2]
they became even more quiet. And he said:
3 [y]"I am a Jew, born in Tarsus in Cilicia, but brought up in this city, educated [z]at the feet
of [a]Gamaliel[3] [b]according to the strict manner of the law of our fathers, [c]being zealous
for God [d]as all of you are this day.
4 [e]I persecuted [f]this Way [g]to the death, binding and
delivering to prison both men and women,
5 as [h]the high priest and [i]the whole council of
elders can bear me witness. From them I received letters to [j]the brothers, and I journeyed
toward Damascus to take those also who were there and bring them in bonds to Jerusalem
to be punished.
6 [k]"As I was on my way and drew near to Damascus, about noon a great light from heaven
suddenly shone around me.
7 And I fell to the ground and heard a voice saying to me, 'Saul,
Saul, why are you persecuting me?'
8 And I answered, 'Who are you, Lord?' And he said
to me, 'I am [l]Jesus of Nazareth, whom you are persecuting.'
9 [m]Now those who were with
me saw the light but did not understand[4] the voice of the one who was speaking to me.
10 And I said, [n]'What shall I do, Lord?' And the Lord said to me, 'Rise, and go into Damascus,
and there you will be told all that is appointed for you to do.'
11 And since I could not see
because of the brightness of that light, I was led by the hand by those who were with me,
and came into Damascus.
12 "And [o]one Ananias, a devout man [p]according to the law, [q]well spoken of by all the Jews
who lived there,
13 [r]came to me, and standing by me said to me, 'Brother Saul, receive your
sight.' And [s]at that very hour I received my sight and saw him.
14 And he said, [t]'The God
of our fathers [u]appointed you to know his will, [v]to see [w]the Righteous One and [x]to hear a
voice from his mouth;
15 for [y]you will be a witness for him to everyone of what [z]you have

[1] *Or the Hebrew dialect* (probably Aramaic) [2] *Or the Hebrew dialect* (probably Aramaic) [3] *Or city at the feet of Gamaliel, educated* [4] *Or hear with understanding*

21:33 Bound with two chains probably means bound with a soldier on each side.

21:36 Away with him! This shout echoes the shout of the crowd that had demanded Jesus' crucifixion several years earlier (see Luke 23:18; John 19:15).

21:38 Josephus also mentions the revolt led by an **Egyptian** Jew. It had been put down by the Roman governor Felix, with the Egyptian fleeing and his movement scattered. Josephus also spoke of the **Assassins**, or "dagger men" (Gk. *sikarios*) who terrorized Roman sympathizers by stabbing them under the cover of crowds. The tribune must have thought the Egyptian had returned to stir up another revolt.

21:39 Tarsus in Cilicia. See note on 9:30.

21:40–22:21 *Paul Addresses the Jewish Crowd.* Paul's address to the Jewish crowd sought to establish what he had come to the temple to prove in the first place—his faithfulness to his Jewish heritage. He gave his personal testimony: his former zeal for Judaism (22:3–5), his encounter with the risen Lord (22:6–11), his commission (22:12–16), and his vision in the temple (22:17–21).

22:2 Just as Paul got the tribune's attention with his Greek (21:37), he quieted the Jewish crowd by speaking Aramaic (see ESV footnote on 21:40), the most common language spoken by ordinary Jews in Jerusalem.

22:3 Brought up in this city most likely means that Paul's parents moved to Jerusalem when he was very young and he was reared in the city (cf. 23:16), but some take it to mean only that Paul came to Jerusalem as a young man for his rabbinic training under **Gamaliel**. (On Gamaliel, see note on 5:34.)

22:4 On Paul's persecution of the Christians, see 8:3 and 9:1. **this Way**. See note on 9:1–2.

22:6 The **light from heaven** is the brightness of God's glory (cf. 26:13), as in Ezek. 1:26–28 and Rev. 1:16.

22:12–14 For his Jewish hearers, Paul stressed the piety of **Ananias**: he kept the **law** strictly and was respected **by all the Jews**.

seen and heard. 16 And now why do you wait? [a]Rise and be baptized and [b]wash away your
sins, [c]calling on his name.'
17 [d]"When I had returned to Jerusalem and [e]was praying in the temple, I fell into [f]a trance
18 and saw him saying to me, [g]'Make haste and get out of Jerusalem quickly, because they
will not accept your testimony about me.' 19 And I said, 'Lord, they themselves know that
in one synagogue after another [h]I imprisoned and [i]beat those who believed in you. 20 And
when the blood of Stephen [j]your witness was being shed, [k]I myself was standing by and
[l]approving and [k]watching over the garments of those who killed him.' 21 And he said to
me, 'Go, for I will send you [m]far away to the Gentiles.'"

Paul and the Roman Tribune

22 Up to this word they listened to him. Then they raised their voices and said, [n]"Away
with such a fellow from the earth! For [o]he should not be allowed to live." 23 And as they
were shouting and throwing off their cloaks and flinging dust into the air, 24 the tribune
ordered him to be brought into [p]the barracks, saying that he should be [q]examined by
flogging, to find out why they were shouting against him like this. 25 But when they had
stretched him out for the whips,[1] Paul said to the centurion who was standing by, "Is it
lawful for you to flog [r]a man who is a Roman citizen and uncondemned?" 26 When the
centurion heard this, he went to the tribune and said to him, "What are you about to do?
For this man is a Roman citizen." 27 So the tribune came and said to him, "Tell me, are you
a Roman citizen?" And he said, "Yes." 28 The tribune answered, "I bought this citizenship
for a large sum." Paul said, "But I am a citizen by birth." 29 So those who were about [s]to
examine him withdrew from him immediately, and the tribune also [t]was afraid, [u]for he
realized that Paul was a Roman citizen and that [v]he had bound him.

Paul Before the Council

30 But on the next day, [w]desiring to know the real reason why he was being accused by
the Jews, he unbound him and commanded the chief priests and all the council to meet,
and he brought Paul down and set him before them.

23 And looking intently at the council, Paul said, "Brothers, [x]I have lived my life before
God in all good conscience up to this day." 2 And the high priest [y]Ananias commanded
those who stood by him [z]to strike him on the mouth. 3 Then Paul said to him, "God is going
to strike you, you [a]whitewashed [b]wall! Are you sitting to judge me according to the law,
and yet [c]contrary to the law you [c]order me to be struck?" 4 Those who stood by said, "Would
you revile [d]God's high priest?" 5 And Paul said, [e]"I did not know, brothers, that he was the
high priest, for it is written, [f]'You shall not speak evil of a ruler of your people.'"
6 Now when Paul perceived that one part were [g]Sadducees and the other Pharisees, he
cried out in the council, "Brothers, [h]I am a Pharisee, a son of Pharisees. It is [i]with respect

[1] *Or when they had tied him up with leather strips*

16 [a]ch. 9:18 [b]1 Cor. 6:11; Heb. 10:22; [Ps. 51:2]; See ch. 2:38 [c]See ch. 9:14
17 [d]ch. 9:26; 26:20 [e]ch. 3:1; Luke 18:10 [f]ch. 10:10; 11:5; [2 Cor. 12:1-4]
18 [g][ch. 9:29]
19 [h]ver. 4 [i]ch. 26:11; See Matt. 10:17
20 [j][Rev. 2:13] [k]ch. 7:58 [l]ch. 8:1; [ch. 26:10]; See Rom. 1:32
21 [m]See ch. 2:39; 9:15
22 [n]See ch. 21:36 [o]ch. 25:24
24 [p]ch. 21:34; 23:10 [q]ver. 29
25 [r]ch. 16:37
29 [s]ver. 24 [t]ch. 16:38 [u][ch. 23:27] [v]ch. 21:33
30 [w]ver. 24; ch. 23:28

Chapter 23

1 [x]2 Cor. 1:12; 2 Tim. 1:3; [ch. 24:16; Job 27:5, 6; 1 Cor. 4:4; 2 Cor. 4:2; 5:11; Heb. 13:18]
2 [y]ch. 24:1 [z]1 Kgs. 22:24; Lam. 3:30; Mic. 5:1; 2 Cor. 11:20
3 [a][Matt. 23:27] [b][Isa. 30:13; Ezek. 13:10-14] [c]Deut. 25:1, 2; See John 7:51
4 [d][1 Sam. 2:28; Ps. 106:16]
5 [e][ch. 24:1] [f]Cited from Ex. 22:28
6 [g]See Matt. 22:23 [h]ch. 26:5; Phil. 3:5 [i]ch. 24:15, 21; 26:6-8; 28:20

22:16 Be baptized and wash away your sins does not imply that the physical act of baptism itself cleanses people spiritually from sin, for Ananias gives Paul two distinct commands. Thus baptism should be viewed as an outward symbol of the cleansing from sin that occurs when someone trusts in Jesus (cf. 1 Pet. 3:21). Belief leads to cleansing, but baptism pictures this. Because baptism pictures the reality, the two are often discussed as if they belong to the same act. As Heb. 10:19–22 shows, the believer's sins are "washed away" through faith in "the blood of Jesus," with the result that the believer is "sprinkled clean" and "washed with pure water."

22:17 in the temple, I fell into a trance. This must have taken place upon Paul's visit to Jerusalem after his conversion (9:26). For the Jewish audience, it placed Paul's experience "on holy ground," in the temple, much like Isaiah's call (Isa. 6:1–13).

22:18 him. That is, the Lord Jesus (see v. 19).

22:21 Paul's association with **Gentiles** had stirred up opposition to him in the first place (21:28–29) and now provoked a violent response (see 22:22).

22:22–29 *Paul Reveals His Roman Citizenship.* As the riot against Paul resumed, the tribune took him into the barracks and stretched him on the rack for "examination" by torture. Paul stopped the proceedings by revealing his Roman citizenship.

22:25 Roman law forbade flogging a **Roman citizen** without a hearing or a formal sentence (**uncondemned**). Officers who did this would face serious charges.

22:28 I bought this citizenship. Persons who obtained Roman citizenship other than by birth usually took the name of their sponsor. That the tribune's name was *Claudius* Lysias (23:26) may indicate he purchased his citizenship through the sponsorship of the emperor Claudius. Being a **citizen by birth** was especially prestigious.

22:30–23:11 *Paul Appears before the Sanhedrin.* Unable to get any answers by scourging, the tribune turned to the Jewish court for help.

22:30 unbound him. Since v. 29 implies Paul was already unbound, the tribune's unbinding him in v. 30 may mean he took him out of confinement.

23:3 Paul, like Jesus, used the metaphor of whitewash for hypocrisy (see Matt. 23:27). Ananias was a particularly bad high priest. For the illegality of Ananias's action, see Lev. 19:15.

23:5 It is quite possible that Paul did not know the high priest, since he had been absent from Jerusalem for many years. Other options for understanding this verse include appeals to poor eyesight for Paul, or that he did not realize the act came at the high priest's command.

23:8 The **Pharisees** believed in angels and spirits and in a future resurrection,

6[j][ch. 2:26, 27]; See Col. 1:5
8[k]Luke 20:27; [1 Cor. 15:12]
9[l]ch. 4:5; Mark 2:16; Luke 5:30 [m][ver. 29] [n][ch. 22:7, 17, 18; John 12:29]
10[o]ver. 16, 32; ch. 21:34; 22:24
11[p]ch. 18:9; 27:23 [q]1 Sam. 3:10 [r][2 Tim. 4:17] [s][ch. 19:21] [t]ch. 22:15
12[u]ver. 30 [v]ver. 14, 21
16[w]ver. 10, 32
18[x]See Eph. 3:1
20[y]ver. 14, 15
21[z]ver. 12, 14

to the [j]hope and the resurrection of the dead that I am on trial." 7 And when he had said
this, a dissension arose between the Pharisees and the Sadducees, and the assembly was
divided. 8 For the Sadducees [k]say that there is no resurrection, nor angel, nor spirit, but the
Pharisees acknowledge them all. 9 Then a great clamor arose, and some of [l]the scribes of the
Pharisees' party stood up and contended sharply, [m]"We find nothing wrong in this man.
What [n]if a spirit or an angel spoke to him?" 10 And when the dissension became violent, the
tribune, afraid that Paul would be torn to pieces by them, commanded the soldiers to go
down and take him away from among them by force and bring him into [o]the barracks.
11 [p]The following night [q]the Lord stood by him and said, [r]"Take courage, for [s]as you have
testified to the facts about me in Jerusalem, so you must [t]testify also in Rome."

A Plot to Kill Paul

12 When it was day, [u]the Jews made a plot and [v]bound themselves by an oath neither to eat
nor drink till they had killed Paul. 13 There were more than forty who made this conspiracy.
14 They went to the chief priests and elders and said, "We have strictly bound ourselves
by an oath to taste no food till we have killed Paul. 15 Now therefore you, along with the
council, give notice to the tribune to bring him down to you, as though you were going to
determine his case more exactly. And we are ready to kill him before he comes near."
16 Now the son of Paul's sister heard of their ambush, so he went and entered [w]the barracks and told Paul. 17 Paul called one of the centurions and said, "Take this young man to
the tribune, for he has something to tell him." 18 So he took him and brought him to the
tribune and said, "Paul [x]the prisoner called me and asked me to bring this young man to
you, as he has something to say to you." 19 The tribune took him by the hand, and going
aside asked him privately, "What is it that you have to tell me?" 20 And he said, [y]"The Jews
have agreed to ask you to bring Paul down to the council tomorrow, as though they were
going to inquire somewhat more closely about him. 21 But do not be persuaded by them, for
more than forty of their men are lying in ambush for him, who [z]have bound themselves by
an oath neither to eat nor drink till they have killed him. And now they are ready, waiting
for your consent." 22 So the tribune dismissed the young man, charging him, "Tell no one
that you have informed me of these things."

Paul Sent to Felix the Governor

23 Then he called two of the centurions and said, "Get ready two hundred soldiers, with
seventy horsemen and two hundred spearmen to go as far as Caesarea at the third hour

though they did not accept Jesus' resurrection; the **Sadducees** rejected the very idea of a resurrection as well as belief in angels and spirits. Consistent with this, the Pharisees granted that a spirit or angel might have visited Paul (v. 9), while the Sadducees rejected this possibility altogether. For more on the difference between the Pharisees and Sadducees, see article on Jewish Groups at the Time of the New Testament, pp. 1799–1800.

23:11 Paul's testimony to the Jewish leaders in Jerusalem was an especially significant fulfillment of the prophecy about his life in 9:15.

23:12–22 *Zealous Jews Plot against Paul.* Paul's nephew informed the tribune of a plot by 40 zealous Jews to kill him.

23:14 The chief priests and elders were the dominant force on the Sanhedrin, and the majority of these were Sadducees, who were the ones most opposed to Paul. The conspirators do not seem to have approached the Pharisees.

23:16 the son of Paul's sister. Nothing is known of Paul's family. They possibly moved to Jerusalem when Paul was young (see note on 22:3). **he . . . entered the barracks**. As a Roman citizen Paul was probably given generous visitation privileges.

23:18 The military showed great deference to their Roman prisoner, as evidenced by the quick response of both the centurion and the tribune (Lysias) to Paul and his nephew.

23:21 Since the plot was thwarted, one wonders if the conspirators died of hunger and thirst! Probably not: by rabbinic law, in the event a vow became impossible to fulfill, those under it were released from its terms (see Mishnah, *Nedarim* 3.3).

23:23–35 *Paul Is Delivered to the Governor Felix.* To protect Paul, Lysias the tribune sent him under cover of night and heavy guard to the governor in Caesarea.

23:23–24 The entire Roman force in Jerusalem consisted of a single cohort

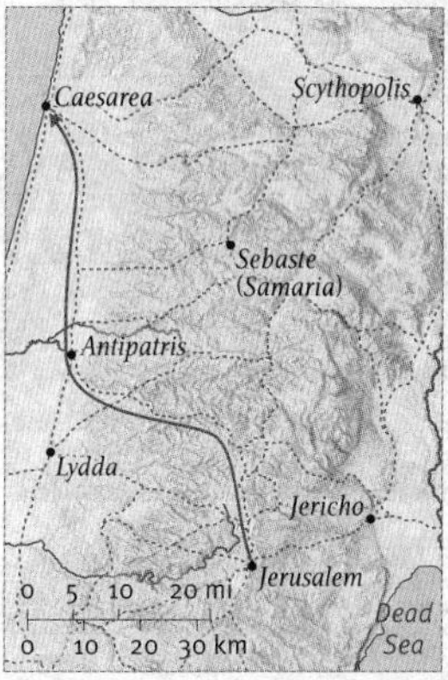

Paul's Arrest and Imprisonment
c. A.D. 58
After Paul's arrest in Jerusalem, the Roman tribune learned of a plot by some Jews to kill Paul. He transferred Paul to the Roman administrative city of Caesarea during the night under heavy guard, going by way of Antipatris.

of the night.[1] 24 Also provide mounts for Paul to ride and bring him safely to [a]Felix [b]the
governor." 25 And he wrote a letter to this effect:
26 "Claudius Lysias, to [c]his Excellency the governor Felix, [d]greetings. 27 [e]This man was
seized by the Jews and [f]was about to be killed by them [f]when I came upon them with the
soldiers and rescued him, [g]having learned that he was a Roman citizen. 28 And [h]desiring to
know the charge for which they were accusing him, I brought him down to their council. 29 I
found that he was being accused [i]about questions of their law, but [j]charged with nothing
deserving death or imprisonment. 30 [k]And when it was disclosed to me [l]that there would
be a plot against the man, I sent him to you at once, [m]ordering his accusers also to state
before you what they have against him."
31 So the soldiers, according to their instructions, took Paul and brought him by night to
Antipatris. 32 And on the next day they returned to [n]the barracks, letting the horsemen go on
with him. 33 When they had come to Caesarea and delivered the letter to the governor, they
presented Paul also before him. 34 On reading the letter, he asked what [o]province he was from.
And when he learned [p]that he was from Cilicia, 35 he said, "I will give you a hearing [q]when
your accusers arrive." And he commanded him to be guarded in Herod's [r]praetorium.

Paul Before Felix at Caesarea

24 And [s]after five days the high priest [t]Ananias came down with some elders and a
spokesman, one Tertullus. They laid before [u]the governor their case against Paul.
2 And when he had been summoned, Tertullus began to accuse him, saying:
"Since through you we enjoy much peace, and since by your foresight, [v]most excellent
Felix, reforms are being made for this nation, 3 in every way and everywhere we accept this
with all gratitude. 4 But, to detain[2] you no further, I beg you in your kindness to hear us
briefly. 5 For we have found this man a plague, [w]one who stirs up riots among all the Jews

[1] That is, 9 P.M. [2] Or *weary*

24 [a]ver. 26; ch. 24:2; 25:14 [b]ver. 33; ch. 24:1, 10; 26:30; See Luke 20:20
26 [c]ch. 24:1 [d]See ch. 15:23
27 [e]ch. 21:27 [f][ch. 21:32, 33] [g][ch. 22:25-29]
28 [h]ch. 22:30
29 [i]ch. 18:15; 25:19 [j]ch. 25:25; 26:31; 28:18; [ver. 9]
30 [k]ver. 20 [l]ver. 12; See ch. 9:24 [m]ver. 35; [ch. 24:19; 25:16]
32 [n]ver. 10, 16
34 [o]ch. 25:1 [p]ch. 21:39
35 [q]ver. 30 [r]See Matt. 27:27

Chapter 24

1 [s][ch. 21:18, 27, with ver. 11] [t]ch. 23:2 [u]ch. 23:24
2 [v]ch. 23:26; Luke 1:3
5 [w]See Luke 23:2

of up to 1,000 soldiers. The importance that Lysias attached to his prisoner is evidenced by his sending approximately half the force to protect him.

23:24 Felix was governor of Judea A.D. 52–59. He was somewhat inept and had his share of weaknesses (see 24:24–27).

23:25–26 Lysias's letter follows standard Greek form: sender (**Lysias**), to recipient (**Felix**), followed by **greetings** (Gk. *chairein*). He gave Felix the deferential title **Excellency** (Gk. *kratistos*).

23:27 Lysias had no charges to list, other than that all complaints against Paul had to do with "their [Jewish] law" (v. 29) and not Roman law. Throughout the rest of Acts, all the Roman officials testify to Paul's innocence of any charges against him.

23:31 Antipatris was 35 of the 62 miles (56 of the 100 km) by road from Jerusalem to Caesarea (v. 33), a difficult but not impossible distance for soldiers to march in the cool of the night. Only the 70 "horsemen" (v. 32) continued to Caesarea. Antipatris (ancient Aphek in Sharon, identified with Tell Ras el-Ain) was rebuilt under Herod the Great in the first century B.C. and renamed for his father Antipater. Herodian-era shops, pavement, Roman coins, and a fortress have been uncovered in excavations at Aphek. On the city of Caesarea, see note on 8:40.

23:34 At this time Judea and **Cilicia** were both a part of the Roman province of Syria. Since Felix administered a portion of that **province** and Paul's home was within it, Felix determined that Paul's case was within his jurisdiction.

23:35 Herod's praetorium was one of his palaces and served as the quarters of the Roman governor.

Paul Collects an Offering for Judea

Activity	Text	Date
The church in Antioch sends Barnabas and Paul to Judea with relief funds.	Acts 11:29–30; 12:25	c. A.D. 44–47
James, Cephas, and John encourage Paul to remember the poor, which he is eager to do.	Gal. 2:10	c. 44–47
Paul raises support for the Christians in Jerusalem while in Ephesus.	1 Cor. 16:1–4 (cf. note on Acts 20:4)	c. 53–55
Paul raises support for the Christians in Jerusalem while in Macedonia.	2 Corinthians 8–9	c. 55–56
Paul raises support for the Christians in Jerusalem while in Achaia.	Rom. 15:25–33 (cf. note on Acts 20:3)	Spring of 57
Paul is arrested when he arrives in Jerusalem to deliver the gift.	Acts 24:17 (cf. Acts 21:17–33)	Pentecost, 57

24:1–26:32 *The Witness in Caesarea.* Imprisoned in Caesarea for more than two years, Paul received formal hearings from the governors Felix and Festus and the Jewish king Agrippa II. When Festus decided to take him to Jerusalem for trial, Paul appealed for trial in Rome before the emperor.

24:1–27 *Paul Appears before Felix.* The closest thing to an actual trial for Paul took place before Felix when the Jewish contingent arrived from Jerusalem bringing their charges against him. Felix was not persuaded, and he dismissed the court but continued to hold Paul in custody, frequently conversing with him privately.

24:1 The **spokesman** (Gk. *rhētōr*) . . . **Tertullus** may have been a Gentile, a professional lawyer.

24:2 Tertullus began with flattering words designed to secure the goodwill of the governor. **we enjoy much peace.** His remarks had little resemblance to reality: Felix had the least peaceful term of any Roman administrator up until his time, was hated by the Jews, and was noted more for his bribe taking than his benevolence.

5[x]ver. 14; ch. 5:17; 15:5; 26:5; 28:22
6[y]ch. 21:27-29
11[z]See ver. 1 [a]ch. 8:27; John 12:20 [b]ch. 20:16
12[c][ch. 25:8]
13[d]ch. 25:7
14[e]ver. 22; See ch. 9:2 [f]ver. 5 [g]2 Tim. 1:3; [ch. 27:23; Luke 1:74; Rom. 1:9; Heb. 9:14; 12:28] [h]See ch. 3:13; 22:3 [i]ch. 26:22; 28:23; [Rom. 3:21]
15[j]See ch. 23:6 [k]Titus 2:13; [Gal. 5:5] [l]Luke 14:14 [m]See Dan. 12:2
16[n][1 Tim. 4:7, 15] [o]1 Cor. 10:32; Phil. 1:10; [Jude 24]; See ch. 23:1
17[p][ch. 20:31] [q]Rom. 15:25-28, 31; 1 Cor. 16:1-3; 2 Cor. 8:1-4; 9:1, 2, 12; [Gal. 2:10] [r]ch. 26:4; 28:19 [s][ver. 11; ch. 20:16]
18[t]ch. 21:26; 26:21 [u]ch. 21:27
19[v]See ch. 23:30
21[w]See ch. 23:6
22[x]ver. 14; See ch. 9:2
23[y][ch. 28:16] [z][ch. 27:3]
24[a]See ch. 20:21 [b]Gal. 2:16; [Rom. 3:24]
25[c][Titus 2:12, 13] [d]ch. 17:32; [2 Tim. 4:2]
26[e][ver. 17]
27[f]ch. 25:1; 26:24 [g]ch. 25:9; [ch. 12:3; Mark 15:15] [h]ch. 25:14; See Luke 21:12

throughout the world and is a ringleader of [x]the sect of the Nazarenes. **6** [y]He even tried to profane the temple, but we seized him.[1] **8** By examining him yourself you will be able to find out from him about everything of which we accuse him."

9 The Jews also joined in the charge, affirming that all these things were so.

10 And when the governor had nodded to him to speak, Paul replied:

"Knowing that for many years you have been a judge over this nation, I cheerfully make my defense. **11** You can verify that [z]it is not more than twelve days since I [a]went up [b]to worship in Jerusalem, **12** and [c]they did not find me disputing with anyone or stirring up a crowd, either in the temple or in the synagogues or in the city. **13** [d]Neither can they prove to you what they now bring up against me. **14** But this I confess to you, that according to [e]the Way, which they call [f]a sect, [g]I worship [h]the God of our fathers, believing everything [i]laid down by the Law and written in the Prophets, **15** [j]having [k]a hope in God, which these men themselves accept, that there will be [l]a resurrection [m]of both the just and the unjust. **16** So I always [n]take pains to have a [o]clear conscience toward both God and man. **17** Now [p]after several years [q]I came to bring alms to [r]my nation and to present [s]offerings. **18** While I was doing this, they found me [t]purified in the temple, without any crowd or tumult. But [u]some Jews from Asia— **19** [v]they ought to be here before you and to make an accusation, should they have anything against me. **20** Or else let these men themselves say what wrongdoing they found when I stood before the council, **21** other than this one thing [w]that I cried out while standing among them: 'It is with respect to the resurrection of the dead that I am on trial before you this day.'"

Paul Kept in Custody

22 But Felix, having a rather accurate knowledge of [x]the Way, put them off, saying, "When Lysias the tribune comes down, I will decide your case." **23** Then he gave orders to the centurion that he [y]should be kept in custody but have some liberty, and that [z]none of his friends should be prevented from attending to his needs.

24 After some days Felix came with his wife Drusilla, who was Jewish, and he sent for Paul and heard him speak about [a]faith [b]in Christ Jesus. **25** And as he reasoned [c]about righteousness and self-control and the coming judgment, Felix was alarmed and said, "Go away for the present. [d]When I get an opportunity I will summon you." **26** At the same time he hoped [e]that money would be given him by Paul. So he sent for him often and conversed with him. **27** When two years had elapsed, Felix was succeeded by Porcius [f]Festus. And [g]desiring to do the Jews a favor, [h]Felix left Paul in prison.

[1] Some manuscripts add *and we would have judged him according to our law. [7]But the chief captain Lysias came and with great violence took him out of our hands, [8]commanding his accusers to come before you.*

24:5 Tertullus accused Paul of three crimes: stirring up **riots**, being a Christian **ringleader**, and profaning "the temple" (v. 6). To a Roman the first charge would have been the most serious, amounting to a charge of sedition, threatening the Roman peace. The second charge Paul readily accepted (v. 14), but the first and third he flatly denied (vv. 12–13).

24:10 Paul's opening words are brief and honest when compared to the flattery of Tertullus (see note on v. 2). Felix's term had begun in A.D. 52, making the **many years** five or six (52–57/58).

24:11–12 Paul denied inciting any riots. **Twelve days** was hardly sufficient time to muster a following.

24:14 Paul proceeded to show how as a Christian he was a faithful Jew, accepting **the Law** and **the Prophets** and sharing the resurrection hope. That the resurrection will include both "the just and the unjust" (v. 15) implies a final judgment (see v. 25).

24:18–19 Paul began to relate the events of his being captured **in the temple** (21:27–36) but cut himself short when he realized his real accusers—the Jews from Asia—were not present. Roman law called for a "face-to-face" confrontation between the accusers and the accused.

24:20–21 when I stood before the council. Ananias and the elders were members of the Sanhedrin and thus could testify to Paul's earlier hearing before them (23:1–10). The key issue both then and here, before Felix, was **the resurrection**—not just the concept but the realization of the resurrection in Jesus.

24:22–23 Felix had an **accurate knowledge of the Way** (see note on 9:1–2), which may have come from his Jewish wife (see 24:24). **but have some liberty.** Paul's "free custody" may have been due to his being a Roman citizen.

24:24 Drusilla was the youngest daughter of Herod Agrippa I (see note on 12:1) and the sister of Agrippa II (who will appear in the next chapter; see 25:13–26:32). Her marriage to Felix was something of a scandal because Felix deceptively precipitated her divorce from her first husband.

24:25 Felix was alarmed. Paul did not flatter this man who had the power of life and death over him, but proclaimed the gospel boldly and clearly.

24:26 money . . . sent for him often. Roman law prohibited officials from taking bribes, but Josephus reports that bribe-taking was rampant.

24:27 Felix seems to have recognized Paul's innocence. Tragically, he was more concerned about currying the favor of his constituents than administering justice. Therefore, he kept Paul in prison for another **two years** (A.D. 57–59). He was removed from office in A.D. 60 for failing to deal properly with a dispute between the Jews and Gentiles in Caesarea.

Paul Appeals to Caesar

25 Now three days after Festus had arrived in [i]the province, he went up to Jerusalem
from Caesarea. 2 And the chief priests and the principal men of the Jews [j]laid
out their case against Paul, and they urged him, 3 asking as a favor against Paul[1] that
he summon him to Jerusalem—because [k]they were planning an ambush to kill him
on the way. 4 Festus replied that Paul was being kept at Caesarea and that he himself
intended to go there shortly. 5 "So," said he, "let the men of authority among you go
down with me, and if there is anything wrong about the man, let them bring charges
against him."
6 After he stayed among them not more than eight or ten days, he went down to Caesarea.
And the next day he took his seat on [l]the tribunal and ordered Paul to be brought. 7 When
he had arrived, the Jews who had come down from Jerusalem stood around him, bringing many and serious charges against him [m]that they could not prove. 8 Paul argued in
his defense, "Neither [n]against [o]the law of the Jews, nor against the temple, nor [p]against
Caesar have I committed any offense." 9 But Festus, [q]wishing to do the Jews a favor, said to
Paul, "Do you wish to go up to Jerusalem and there be tried on these charges before me?"
10 But Paul said, "I am standing before Caesar's [r]tribunal, where I ought to be tried. To the
Jews I have done no wrong, as you yourself know very well. 11 If then I am a wrongdoer
and have committed anything for which I deserve to die, I do not seek to escape death. But
if there is nothing to their charges against me, no one can give me up to them. [s]I appeal
to Caesar." 12 Then Festus, when he had conferred with his council, answered, "To Caesar
you have appealed; to Caesar you shall go."

Paul Before Agrippa and Bernice

13 Now when some days had passed, Agrippa the king and Bernice arrived at Caesarea
and greeted Festus. 14 And as they stayed there many days, Festus laid Paul's case before the
king, saying, [t]"There is a man left prisoner by Felix, 15 and when I was at Jerusalem, the chief
priests and the elders of the Jews laid out their case [u]against him, asking for a sentence of
condemnation against him. 16 [v]I answered them that it was not the custom of the Romans
to give up anyone [w]before the accused met the accusers face to face and had opportunity to
make his defense concerning the charge laid against him. 17 [x]So when they came together
here, I made no delay, but on the next day took my seat on [y]the tribunal and ordered the
man to be brought. 18 When the accusers stood up, they brought no charge in his case of
such evils as I supposed. 19 Rather they [z]had certain points of dispute with him about their
own religion and about [a]a certain Jesus, who was dead, but whom Paul asserted to be alive.
20 Being at a loss how to investigate these questions, I [b]asked whether he wanted to go to
Jerusalem and be tried there regarding them. 21 But [c]when Paul had appealed to be kept in
custody for the decision of [d]the emperor, I ordered him to be held until I could send him to
Caesar." 22 Then [e]Agrippa said to Festus, "I would like to hear the man myself." "Tomorrow,"
said he, "you will hear him."
23 So on the next day [f]Agrippa and Bernice came with great pomp, and they entered the
audience hall with the military tribunes and the prominent men of the city. Then, at the
command of Festus, Paul was brought in. 24 And Festus said, "King Agrippa and all who

[1] Greek *him*

Chapter 25
1 [i]ch. 23:34
2 [j]ver. 15
3 [k]See ch. 9:24
6 [l]ver. 10, 17; See Matt. 27:19
7 [m]ch. 24:13
8 [n][ch. 24:12; 28:17]; See ch. 6:13 [o]John 7:19; 19:7 [p]John 19:12
9 [q]ch. 24:27
10 [r]ver. 6, 17
11 [s]ch. 26:32; 28:19
14 [t]ch. 24:27
15 [u]ver. 2, 3
16 [v]ver. 4, 5 [w][John 7:51]; See ch. 23:30
17 [x]ver. 7, 24 [y]ver. 6, 10
19 [z]ch. 18:15; 23:29 [a][ch. 17:18]
20 [b]ver. 9
21 [c]See ver. 11 [d]ver. 25
22 [e]See ch. 9:15
23 [f]ver. 13; ch. 26:30

25:1–12 *Paul Appeals to Caesar.* The new procurator Festus wanted to win the favor of his constituents. When approached by the Jewish leaders concerning Paul, he at first resisted but later gave in to their desire to try Paul in Jerusalem. To avoid the fate that awaited him there, Paul invoked his citizen's right of appeal for trial before the emperor.

25:2 The chief priests and the principal men probably refers to the Sanhedrin. Previously they had cooperated with the 40 zealots in their plot against Paul (23:12–15); now they themselves plotted against Paul.

25:4 Festus unwittingly protected **Paul** by insisting that any hearing should take place in his headquarters at **Caesarea.**

25:9–11 Felix, "desiring to do the Jews a favor," had kept Paul in prison for two years (24:27). In light of the new plot against Paul (25:2–3), if Festus, **wishing to do the Jews a favor,** had done the same, it could have been deadly for Paul. Festus assured Paul that he—not the Jews—would try him. But Paul was not reassured. He feared Festus would **give** him **up** to the Jews. As a Roman citizen he had the right to appeal his case to **Caesar.** He exercised that right in order to remove the matter from the governor's hands (A.D. 59). "Caesar" was the emperor Nero Caesar, who reigned A.D. 54–68. The first five years of his reign were relatively peaceful; after that his actions became increasingly cruel and irrational.

25:12 In considering difficult or unusual cases, Roman administrators usually had an advisory board or **council** of high-ranking officials for consultation.

25:13–22 *Festus Presents the Case to King Agrippa II.* A visit to Caesarea by the Jewish King Agrippa II afforded Festus an opportunity for a hearing to formulate charges against Paul.

24[g]ver. 2, 7 [h]ch. 22:22
25[i]See ch. 23:29 [j]ver. 11, 12 [k]ver. 21
Chapter 26
1[l]See ch. 9:15

are present with us, you see this man about whom [g]the whole Jewish people petitioned
me, both in Jerusalem and here, [h]shouting that he ought not to live any longer. 25 But I
found that [i]he had done nothing deserving death. And [j]as he himself appealed to [k]the
emperor, I decided to go ahead and send him. 26 But I have nothing definite to write to
my lord about him. Therefore I have brought him before you all, and especially before
you, King Agrippa, so that, after we have examined him, I may have something to write.
27 For it seems to me unreasonable, in sending a prisoner, not to indicate the charges
against him."

Paul's Defense Before Agrippa

26 So [l]Agrippa said to Paul, "You have permission to speak for yourself." Then Paul
stretched out his hand and made his defense:
2 "I consider myself fortunate that it is before you, King Agrippa, I am going to make

25:13 Agrippa the king was Agrippa II, son of Herod Agrippa I (see notes on 12:1; 24:24), and great-grandson of Herod the Great (see note on Matt. 2:1). He ruled over several minor, primarily Gentile territories. The emperor Claudius had conferred on Agrippa II rule over the temple in Jerusalem and the right to appoint the high priest (see Josephus, *Jewish Antiquities* 20.222, 223). **Bernice** was his sister and constant companion.

25:18 Festus's statement that the Jews **brought no charge . . . of such evils as I supposed** indicates his conclusion that Paul had broken no Roman laws. To Festus, this was merely a religious dispute—a judgment Luke as the author of Acts wants the reader to appreciate.

25:23–26:32 *Paul Witnesses to Agrippa II.* Amid considerable pomp (25:23–27), Paul testified before the king (in fulfillment of 9:15). Of the three "defense" speeches (chs. 22, 24, 26), this one before Agrippa gives the most detailed exposition of the gospel.

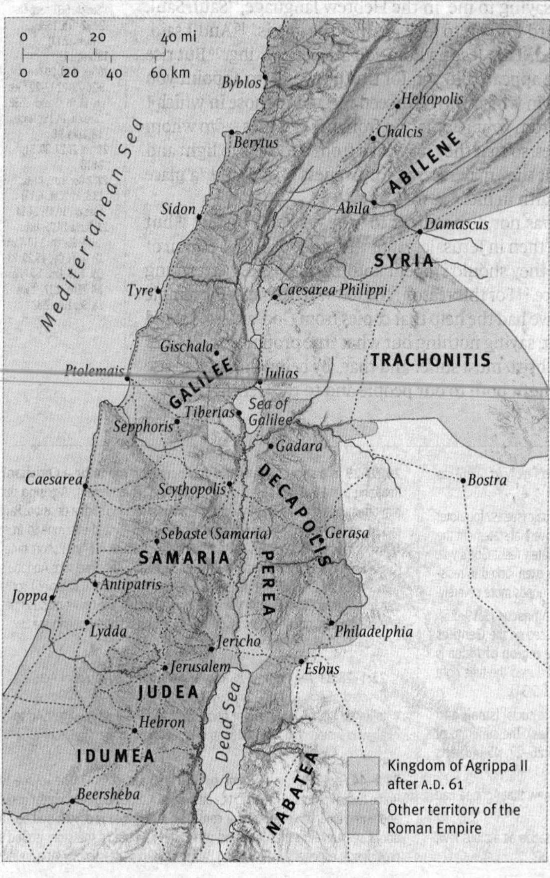

The Kingdom of Herod Agrippa II
c. A.D. 63
Not long after Festus succeeded Felix as procurator over Palestine, Herod Agrippa II came to visit him at Caesarea. Agrippa had come to power after the death of his father, but his territory was greatly reduced by the Romans. Though Agrippa did not hold jurisdiction over Judea or Samaria, Festus, a Roman unfamiliar with Jewish disputes, sought out his advice regarding Paul's case.

my defense today [m]against all the accusations of the Jews, 3 especially because you are
familiar with all the [n]customs and [o]controversies of the Jews. Therefore I beg you to listen
to me patiently.
4 [p]"My manner of life from my youth, spent from the beginning among [q]my own nation
and in Jerusalem, is known by all the Jews. 5 They have known for a long time, if they are
willing to testify, that [r]according to the strictest [s]party of our [t]religion I have lived as [u]a
Pharisee. 6 And now I stand here on trial because of my hope in [v]the promise made by God
to our fathers, 7 [w]to which [x]our twelve tribes hope to [y]attain, as they earnestly worship night
and day. And for this hope [z]I am accused by Jews, O king! 8 Why is it thought [a]incredible
by any of you that God raises the dead?
9 [b]"I myself was convinced that I ought to do many things in opposing the name of
[c]Jesus of Nazareth. 10 [d]And I did so in Jerusalem. I not only locked up many of the saints
in prison after receiving authority [e]from the chief priests, but [f]when they were put to
death I cast my vote against them. 11 And [g]I punished them often in all the synagogues
and tried to make them [h]blaspheme, and [i]in raging fury against them I [j]persecuted them
even to foreign cities.

Paul Tells of His Conversion

12 "In this connection [k]I journeyed to Damascus with the authority and commission of
the chief priests. 13 At midday, O king, I saw on the way a light from heaven, brighter than
the sun, that shone around me and those who journeyed with me. 14 And when we had all
fallen to the ground, I heard a voice saying to me [l]in the Hebrew language,[1] 'Saul, Saul,
why are you persecuting me? It is hard for you to kick against the goads.' 15 And I said,
'Who are you, Lord?' And the Lord said, 'I am Jesus whom you are persecuting. 16 But rise
and [m]stand upon your feet, for I have appeared to you for this purpose, [n]to appoint you
as a servant and witness to the things in which you have seen me and to those in which I
will appear to you, 17 [o]delivering you from your people and from the Gentiles—[p]to whom
I [q]am sending you 18 [r]to open their eyes, so that they may turn from darkness to light and
from [s]the power of Satan to God, that they may receive [t]forgiveness of sins and [u]a place
among those who are sanctified [v]by faith in me.'
19 "Therefore, O King Agrippa, I was not disobedient to [w]the heavenly vision, 20 but
declared first [x]to those in Damascus, [y]then in Jerusalem and throughout all the region of
Judea, and also [z]to the Gentiles, that they should [a]repent and [b]turn to God, performing
deeds [c]in keeping with their repentance. 21 For this reason [d]the Jews seized me in the temple
and tried to kill me. 22 [e]To this day I have had the help that comes from God, and so [f]I stand
here testifying both to small and great, saying nothing but what [g]the prophets and Moses
said would come to pass: 23 [h]that the Christ [i]must suffer and that, [j]by being the first [k]to rise
from the dead, [l]he would proclaim [m]light both to our people and to the Gentiles."

[1] Or *the Hebrew dialect* (probably Aramaic)

2 [m]ch. 25:7, 19; [ver. 7]
3 [n]See ch. 6:14 [o]See ch. 18:15
4 [p][Gal. 1:13] [q]ch. 24:17; 28:19
5 [r]ch. 22:3 [s]See ch. 24:5 [t]James 1:26, 27 [u]ch. 23:6
6 [v]See ch. 13:32
7 [w][ch. 2:33; Heb. 10:36; 11:13, 39] [x]Matt. 19:28; Luke 22:30; James 1:1; Rev. 21:12; [Ezra 6:17] [y]Phil. 3:11 [z]ver. 2
8 [a][ch. 17:3; 1 Cor. 15:12]
9 [b]1 Tim. 1:13; [John 16:2]; See ch. 3:17 [c]ch. 22:8
10 [d]See ch. 8:3 [e]ver. 12; ch. 9:1, 2, 14, 21; 22:4, 5 [f]See ch. 22:20
11 [g]ch. 22:19 [h]See ch. 13:45 [i]ch. 9:1 [j]ch. 22:5
12 [k]For ver. 12-18, see ch. 9:3-8; 22:6-11
14 [l]ch. 21:40; 22:2
16 [m]Ezek. 2:1; Dan. 10:11 [n]See ch. 22:14, 15
17 [o][ch. 12:11; 1 Chr. 16:35; Jer. 1:8, 19; 15:20] [p]See ch. 9:15 [q][Rom. 11:13; 1 Tim. 2:7]
18 [r]Isa. 35:5; 42:7 [s]See Luke 22:53; 1 Cor. 5:5 [t]See ch. 5:31 [u]See ch. 20:32 [v][ch. 15:9; 2 Thess. 2:13]
19 [w]ver. 13
20 [x]ch. 9:19, 20 [y]ch. 9:26-29; 22:17-20 [z]See ch. 13:46 [a]See ch. 2:38 [b]See ch. 14:15 [c]Matt. 3:8; Luke 3:8
21 [d]ch. 21:27, 30, 31; 24:18
22 [e]2 Cor. 1:10; [Heb. 13:5, 6] [f][Eph. 6:13] [g]See ch. 10:43; 24:14
23 [h][Luke 24:26; Heb. 2:10]; See ch. 3:18 [i][John 12:34] [j]1 Cor. 15:20, 23; Col. 1:18; Rev. 1:5 [k]Rom. 1:4 [l][Eph. 2:17] [m]ver. 18; See Luke 2:32

26:13 The **light from heaven** is the brightness of God's glory (cf. 22:6), as in Ezek. 1:26–28 and Rev. 1:16.

26:14 The Hebrew language most likely refers to Aramaic (see ESV footnote; also note on 22:2). **To kick against the goads** is a proverbial statement the Romans probably knew, meaning that one cannot ultimately resist God's will. Goads were sharp sticks used to prod oxen, and if the oxen kicked in resistance, the drivers would keep them in line by using the goads more severely.

26:20 Paul's obedience to his commission began in **Damascus** (9:19–25), continued in **Jerusalem** (9:26–29), and ultimately focused on the **Gentiles** (from 11:26 on). A witness by Paul **throughout all the region of Judea** is not recorded elsewhere in Acts but must have occurred during the time right after his conversion when he was in Jerusalem (9:28; cf. 9:31).

26:22–23 The inclusiveness of Paul's witness was both social (**small and great**) and racial (**our people and . . . the Gentiles**). The suffering of Jesus was the fulfillment of OT **prophets** (see Luke 24:26–27, 45–48; Acts 2:24–36; 3:17–26; 13:32–39; also note on 3:24).

26:26 the king knows about these things. Paul knew that Agrippa had a fairly extensive knowledge of Jewish beliefs.

26:27 I know that you believe. Agrippa had a reputation as a pious Jew, which is why Paul could make this appeal.

26:28–29 In a short time would you persuade me to be a Christian? Realizing that **Paul** was pressing for a "Christian" commitment, **Agrippa** put him off, quipping that it was too "short" a time for making such a decision. Paul picked up on Agrippa's remark: **short or long**, he wanted everyone to trust Christ. The translation of this verse is not easy, because (1) "in a short time" (Gk. *en oligō*) might also mean "with a small effort"; (2) some take Agrippa's words to be a statement rather than a question; (3) "to be" (Gk. *poieō*) could also mean "to act like"; and (4) there is some variation in the Greek manuscripts. However, most commentators favor a sense similar to that given in the ESV.

27:1–28:31 *The Witness in Rome.* The last two chapters of Acts are devoted mainly to Paul's journey to Rome (27:1–28:16). In Rome, he followed his usual pattern of beginning with the Jews then turning to all who would come and listen to his message.

27:1–44 *Paul Journeys to Rome by Sea.* See map, p. 2141. The voyage to Rome (which probably began in the autumn of A.D. 59) is given in great detail and with remarkable exactness, consistent with what is otherwise known about sea travel in that time and place. The keynote of the story is God's providence, especially in preserving Paul for his Roman testimony. At a literary

24[n]ch. 12:15; [ver. 8; ch. 17:32; 2 Kgs. 9:11; Jer. 29:26; Mark 3:21; John 10:20; 1 Cor. 1:23; 2:14; 4:10]
25[o]See ch. 24:2 [p][2 Pet. 1:16] [q][2 Cor. 5:13]
26[r][ver. 3]
28[s]ch. 11:26; 1 Pet. 4:16
29[t][1 Cor. 7:7] [u]See ch. 21:33
30[v]See ch. 23:24
31[w]See ch. 23:29
32[x]ch. 28:18 [y]ch. 25:11; 28:19 [z]See ch. 9:15

Chapter 27

1[a]ch. 25:12, 25 [b]See ch. 16:10 [c]See ch. 10:1

24 And as he was saying these things in his defense, Festus said with a loud voice, "Paul,
[n]you are out of your mind; your great learning is driving you out of your mind." 25 But
Paul said, "I am not out of my mind, [o]most excellent Festus, but I am speaking [p]true and
[q]rational words. 26 For [r]the king knows about these things, and to him I speak boldly. For I
am persuaded that none of these things has escaped his notice, for this has not been done
in a corner. 27 King Agrippa, do you believe the prophets? I know that you believe." 28 And
Agrippa said to Paul, "In a short time would you persuade me to be [s]a Christian?"[1] 29 And
Paul said, "Whether short or long, I would to God that not only you but also all who hear
me this day [t]might become such as I am—except for [u]these chains."

30 Then the king rose, and [v]the governor and Bernice and those who were sitting with
them. 31 And when they had withdrawn, they said to one another, [w]"This man is doing
nothing to deserve death or imprisonment." 32 And Agrippa said to Festus, [x]"This man
could have been set [y]free if he had not appealed [z]to Caesar."

Paul Sails for Rome

27 And when it was decided [a]that [b]we should sail for Italy, they delivered Paul and
some other prisoners to a centurion of the Augustan [c]Cohort named Julius. 2 And
embarking in a ship of Adramyttium, which was about to sail to the ports along the coast

[1] Or *In a short time you would persuade me to act like a Christian!*

level the story is told to indicate how far and difficult the journey to Rome is, as the gospel heads toward the ends of the earth.

27:1 Note the **we**, indicating Luke's presence with Paul all the way to Rome (the last "we" is found at 28:16). For **centurion** and **Cohort**, see note on 10:1.

27:2 The **ship of Adramyttium** was probably a small coasting vessel, not adequate for the open-sea voyage to Rome. Adramyttium was a large port city of Mysia in the province of Asia Minor (opposite the island of Lesbos). **Aristarchus**. See note on 19:29.

Paul's Journey to Rome

c. A.D. 60

Appealing his case to Caesar, Paul was ordered by Festus to be transferred to Rome. Paul's journey was marked by difficult weather, as they had begun their voyage late into the season for sea travel. A bad decision to try to find winter harbor at Phoenix ended with the ship being driven by a storm to the island of Malta, where the ship broke apart. All aboard the ship survived, however, and Paul was soon placed aboard another ship that took him to Puteoli. From there Paul was taken to Rome.

of Asia, we put to sea, accompanied by [d]Aristarchus, a Macedonian from Thessalonica. 3 The
next day we put in at Sidon. And [e]Julius [f]treated Paul kindly and [g]gave him leave to go to
his friends and be cared for. 4 And putting out to sea from there we sailed under the lee of
Cyprus, because the winds were against us. 5 And when we had sailed across the open sea
along the coast of Cilicia and Pamphylia, we came to Myra in Lycia. 6 There the centurion
found [h]a ship of Alexandria sailing for Italy and put us on board. 7 We sailed slowly for a
number of days and arrived with difficulty off Cnidus, and as the wind did not allow us to
go farther, we sailed under the lee of Crete off Salmone. 8 Coasting along it with difficulty,
we came to a place called Fair Havens, near which was the city of Lasea.
9 Since much time had passed, and the voyage was now dangerous because even [i]the
Fast[1] was already over, Paul advised them, 10 saying, "Sirs, I perceive that the voyage will
be with [j]injury and much loss, not only of the cargo and the ship, but also of our lives."
11 But the centurion paid more attention to [k]the pilot and to the owner of the ship than
to what Paul said. 12 And because the harbor was not suitable to spend the winter in, the
majority decided to put out to sea from there, on the chance that somehow they could
reach Phoenix, a harbor of Crete, facing both southwest and northwest, and spend the
winter there.

The Storm at Sea

13 Now when the south wind blew gently, supposing that they had obtained their purpose,
they weighed anchor and sailed along Crete, close to the shore. 14 But soon a tempestuous wind, called the northeaster, [l]struck down from the land. 15 And when the ship was
caught and could not face the wind, we gave way to it and were driven along. 16 Running
under the lee of a small island called Cauda,[2] we managed with difficulty to secure the
ship's boat. 17 After hoisting it up, they used supports to undergird the ship. Then, fearing
that they would [m]run aground on the Syrtis, they lowered the gear,[3] and thus they were
driven along. 18 Since we were violently storm-tossed, they began the next day [n]to jettison
the cargo. 19 And on the third day they threw the ship's tackle overboard with their own
hands. 20 When neither sun nor stars appeared for many days, and no small tempest lay
on us, all hope of our being saved was at last abandoned.
21 Since they had been without food for a long time, Paul stood up among them and
said, "Men, [o]you should have listened to me and not have set sail from Crete and incurred
this [o]injury and loss. 22 Yet now I urge you to [p]take heart, for there will be no loss of life
among you, but only of the ship. 23 For this very night [q]there [r]stood before me [s]an angel of

[1] That is, the Day of Atonement [2] Some manuscripts *Clauda* [3] That is, the sea-anchor (or possibly the mainsail)

2 [d]See ch. 19:29
3 [e]ver. 43 [f]ch. 28:2 [g][ch. 24:23; 28:16, 30]
6 [h]ch. 28:11
9 [i]Lev. 16:29-31; 23:27-29; Num. 29:7
10 [j]ver. 21
11 [k]Rev. 18:17 (Gk.)
14 [l][Mark 4:37]
17 [m]ver. 26, 29
18 [n]Jonah 1:5; [ver. 38]
21 [o]ver. 10
22 [p]ver. 25, 36
23 [q]ch. 18:9; 23:11 [r]2 Tim. 4:17 [s]See ch. 8:26

27:3 The **friends** of Paul were the Christians of **Sidon** (on Sidon, see note on Mark 7:24). Paul's guard **Julius** showed him deference throughout the voyage.

27:4 Under the lee refers to sailing under shelter; they were protected by the island from the contrary winds.

27:5–6 Cilicia, **Pamphylia**, and **Lycia** were districts along the southern coast of what today is Turkey. **Myra** was directly north of **Alexandria** and would have been a good stopping place for a **ship** that was **sailing for Italy**, probably carrying Egyptian grain.

27:7 The normal route from Myra to Rome would have taken them south of Rhodes and north of **Crete** to Sicily. They were already well off course when they reached **Cnidus** (southwestern tip of Asia/Turkey) and even more so when they had to seek shelter on the south side of Crete.

27:8 The location of **Fair Havens** is uncertain, though there is a town on the southern coast of Crete with that name today, probably close to the ancient site.

27:9 The **Fast** refers to the Day of Atonement in the fall, when Mediterranean voyages became too dangerous for sailing vessels. Despite the poor harbor, Paul's advice was that they stay put (v. 10).

27:11 The **pilot** was the ship's captain.

27:12 The majority probably means the majority of the crew. **Phoenix** (Gk. *phoinix*, "palm tree, date-palm") may be the modern Phineka Bay, which is on the southwestern coast of Crete.

27:14 The **wind** is described as **tempestuous** (Gk. *typhōnikos*), and the storm is called in Greek the *eurakylōn* (Gk., based on *euros*, "east wind," and *akylō*, "north wind"—hence, **northeaster**). Such northeasters are extremely dangerous in this region, appearing suddenly with violent, whirling winds caused by a meeting of opposite air currents.

27:16 Cauda is today known as Gozzo. The **ship's boat** (a smaller vessel used to transport people from the ship to land) had probably filled with water and was hard to lift on deck.

27:17 Ancient ships were sometimes secured during storms with cables (**supports**) tied around the ends or across and under the center of the ship. What **gear** was **lowered** is not known—possibly the topsails or a drift anchor to slow the ship's progress. The **Syrtis** was a sandy shoal off the North African coast with a reputation as the graveyard of ships.

27:18–19 The jettisoned **cargo** may have been grain, although they kept some of it (see v. 38). The jettisoned **tackle** may have been the beam that supported the mainsail.

27:20 Before the advent of the compass, sailors depended for their bearings on the **sun** and **stars**, which were not visible in the storm.

27:21 You should have listened to me was probably not a haughty, censorious statement but rather was intended to establish Paul's credibility as he prepared to give the crew some divinely revealed instructions (vv. 22–26).

27:22 At Fair Havens Paul had warned of the danger of loss of life (v. 10), but that was simply his opinion as an experienced traveler who had already

the God [t]to whom I belong and [u]whom I worship, **24** and he said, 'Do not be afraid, Paul;
[v]you must stand before Caesar. And behold, [w]God has granted you all those who sail with
you.' **25** So take heart, men, for I have faith in God that it will be exactly as I have been told.
26 But [x]we must [y]run aground on some island."

27 When the fourteenth night had come, as we were being driven across the Adriatic
Sea, about midnight the sailors suspected that they were nearing land. **28** So they took a
sounding and found twenty fathoms.[1] A little farther on they took a sounding again and
found fifteen fathoms.[2] **29** And fearing that we might [z]run on the rocks, they let down
four anchors from the stern and prayed for day to come. **30** And as the sailors were seeking
to escape from the ship, and had lowered [a]the ship's boat into the sea under pretense of
laying out anchors from the bow, **31** Paul said to the centurion and the soldiers, "Unless
these men stay in the ship, you cannot be saved." **32** Then the soldiers cut away the ropes
of the ship's boat and let it go.

33 As day was about to dawn, Paul urged them all to take some food, saying, "Today is
the fourteenth day that you have continued in suspense and without food, having taken
nothing. **34** Therefore I urge you to take some food. For it will give you strength,[3] for [b]not
a hair is to perish from the head of any of you." **35** And when he had said these things, he
took bread, and [c]giving thanks to God in the presence of all he broke it and began to eat.
36 Then they all [d]were encouraged and ate some food themselves. **37** (We were in all 276[4]
[e]persons in the ship.) **38** And when they had eaten enough, they lightened the ship, [f]throw-
ing out the wheat into the sea.

The Shipwreck

39 Now when it was day, [g]they did not recognize the land, but they noticed a bay with
a beach, on which they planned if possible to run the ship ashore. **40** So they cast off the
anchors and left them in the sea, at the same time loosening the ropes that tied the rudders. Then hoisting the foresail to the wind they made for the beach. **41** But striking a reef,[5]
[h]they ran the vessel aground. The bow stuck and remained immovable, and the stern was
being broken up by the surf. **42** [i]The soldiers' plan was to kill the prisoners, lest any should
swim away and escape. **43** But the centurion, [j]wishing to save Paul, kept them from carrying out their plan. He ordered those who could swim to jump overboard first and make
for the land, **44** and the rest on planks or on pieces of the ship. And so it was that [k]all were
brought safely to land.

23 [t]Ps. 119:94; Dan. 5:23 [u][Dan. 6:16]; See ch. 24:14
24 [v]ch. 23:11 [w][Gen. 18:26; 19:21, 29; Ezek. 14:14]
26 [x]ch. 28:1 [y]ver. 17, 29
29 [z]ver. 17, 26
30 [a]ver. 16
34 [b]1 Sam. 14:45; 2 Sam. 14:11; 1 Kgs. 1:52; Luke 21:18; [Matt. 10:30]
35 [c]See Matt. 15:36
36 [d]ver. 22
37 [e]ch. 2:41; 7:14; Rom. 13:1; 1 Pet. 3:20
38 [f][ver. 18]
39 [g][ch. 28:1]
41 [h][2 Cor. 11:25]
42 [i][ch. 12:19]
43 [j]ver. 3
44 [k]ver. 22

[1] About 120 feet; a fathom (Greek *orguia*) was about 6 feet or 2 meters [2] About 90 feet (see previous note) [3] Or *For it is for your deliverance* [4] Some manuscripts *seventy-six*, or *about seventy-six* [5] Or *sandbank*, or *crosscurrent*; Greek *place between two seas*

---

been shipwrecked three times, reflecting the potential level of risk (see 2 Cor. 11:25). Now, however, he says **there will be no loss of life**. The difference was a revelation from God through an angel (Acts 27:23–24).

27:24 must stand before Caesar. See note on 25:9–11. The ultimate reason for Paul's deliverance was his testimony in Rome (cf. 19:21; 23:11). Therefore, whereas Jonah's presence on the ship threatened to destroy everyone (Jonah 1:12), Paul's presence assured everyone's deliverance.

27:27 Adriatic Sea. In ancient times this designation extended south to Crete and Malta, farther than the modern Adriatic.

27:29 the rocks. The location was probably the rocky promontory on the northeastern coast of Malta, known today as Point Koura. Ancient ships had multiple anchors; the **four anchors from the stern** would keep the ship steady and facing toward land.

27:30 the sailors were seeking to escape. They knew they were nearing land, so they decided to take the ship's only small boat and get themselves safely to shore. But such a selfish action would have left no one on the ship with the skill to handle it, leading to much loss of life. So Paul warned the centurion of the sailors' plan, and he stopped them (vv. 31–32). Paul's action shows the compatibility of divine sovereignty (see vv. 22–24) with human responsibility. God will fulfill his promises, but that doesn't negate the importance of human actions as the means God uses to carry out his promises (cf. note on 18:9–11).

27:33 The rescue was to begin at daybreak, and everyone needed food for maximum strength.

27:34 not a hair is to perish from the head. Cf. 1 Sam. 14:45; 2 Sam. 14:11; 1 Kings 1:52; Matt. 10:30; Luke 12:7; 21:18.

27:35 Paul's giving thanks and breaking bread was not a celebration of the Lord's Supper but a testimony to his faith in the God who was about to deliver them.

27:37 The number of **276** passengers was not too great for large grain ships, which were up to 100 feet (31 m) long.

27:39 Although other locales on Malta have been suggested, the traditional site of Paul's shipwreck is known as St. Paul's Bay; it has a sandy **beach** on its western side.

27:40 The ship's **rudders** would have been pulled out of the water and tied down during the storm but were now placed back in the water to steer the ship. The **foresail** (Gk. *artemōn*) was a small sail in the bow to guide a ship.

27:41 The meaning of **reef** (lit., "a place of two seas") is uncertain; it could also refer to a sandbar. Either way, the **bow** stuck in it and the **stern** was broken to pieces by the pounding **surf**.

27:43 Once again (cf. note on v. 24) Paul's presence assured the deliverance of the others—this time the other prisoners. The soldiers feared the escape of the prisoners (v. 42) because they were accountable for them with their own lives (cf. 12:19).

Paul on Malta

28 After we were brought safely through, [l]we then learned that [m]the island was called
Malta. 2 [n]The native people[1] showed us unusual [o]kindness, for they kindled a fire
and welcomed us all, because it had begun to rain and was cold. 3 When Paul had gathered a bundle of sticks and put them on the fire, a viper came out because of the heat and
fastened on his hand. 4 When [p]the native people saw the creature hanging from his hand,
they said to one another, [q]"No doubt this man is a murderer. Though he has escaped from
the sea, [r]Justice[2] has not allowed him to live." 5 He, however, [s]shook off the creature into
the fire and suffered no harm. 6 They were waiting for him to swell up or suddenly fall
down dead. But when they had waited a long time and saw no misfortune come to him,
[t]they changed their minds and [u]said that he was a god.
7 Now in the neighborhood of that place were lands belonging to the chief man of the
island, named Publius, who received us and entertained us hospitably for three days. 8 It
happened that the father of Publius lay sick with fever and dysentery. And Paul visited him
and [v]prayed, and [w]putting his hands on him healed him. 9 And when this had taken place,
the rest of the people on the island who had diseases also came and were cured. 10 They
also honored us greatly,[3] and when we were about to sail, they put on board whatever
we needed.

Paul Arrives at Rome

11 After three months we set sail in [x]a ship that had wintered in the island, a ship of
Alexandria, with the twin gods[4] as a figurehead. 12 Putting in at Syracuse, we stayed there
for three days. 13 And from there we made a circuit and arrived at Rhegium. And after
one day a south wind sprang up, and on the second day we came to Puteoli. 14 There we
found [y]brothers[5] and were invited to stay with them for seven days. And so we came to
Rome. 15 And [y]the brothers there, when they heard about us, came as far as the Forum
of Appius and Three Taverns to meet us. On seeing them, [z]Paul thanked God and took
courage. 16 And when we came into Rome, [a]Paul was allowed to stay by himself, with the
soldier who guarded him.

[1] Greek *barbaroi* (that is, non-Greek speakers); also verse 4 [2] Or *justice* [3] Greek *honored us with many honors* [4] That is, the Greek gods Castor and Pollux
[5] Or *brothers and sisters*; also verses 15, 21

Chapter 28
1 [l][ch. 27:39] [m]ch. 27:26
2 [n]ver. 4; Rom. 1:14; 1 Cor. 14:11; Col. 3:11 [o]ch. 27:3
4 [p]ver. 2 [q][Job 4:7; Luke 13:2, 4; John 9:2] [r][Num. 32:23; Amos 5:19; 9:3]
5 [s]Mark 16:18; Luke 10:19
6 [t][ch. 14:11, 19] [u][ch. 8:10; 14:11]
8 [v]ch. 9:40; [James 5:14, 15] [w]See Mark 5:23
11 [x]ch. 27:6
14 [y]See John 21:23
15 [y][See ver. 14 above] [z][Rom. 1:9-12]
16 [a][ch. 24:23; 27:3]

28:1–10 *Paul Witnesses on Malta.* The shipwrecked voyagers spent the remainder of the winter on the island. Paul's time there is highlighted by his protection from a viper's bite (vv. 1–6) and his healing of the leading citizen's father (vv. 7–10).

28:1 Malta was on the main route from Myra (27:5) to Rome. God's providence had brought them through the storm and back on course. The most famous archaeological remains on Malta are prehistoric or Phoenician; however, Malta also thrived under the Romans, and residential villas used in the NT period have been excavated.

28:2 In Greek the **native people** are designated "barbarians" (*barbaroi*), a word that did not carry negative connotation but simply referred in a general way to those who did not speak Greek. No doubt the island also had a number of educated people who did speak Greek.

28:4 Greco-Roman lore spoke of fugitives who escaped shipwreck only to be killed by poisonous snakes. Cf. Mark 16:18. **Justice** (Gk. *dikē*) in Greek can refer to justice or to the name of the goddess who dispenses justice.

28:6 When the Lystrans took Paul as a god, he protested vigorously (cf. 14:14–15). The situation differs here, as no attempt to worship him is related. Throughout Acts miracles provide an opportunity for witness, and likely Paul also witnessed to the Maltese.

28:7 Publius is called **chief man** (Gk. *prōtos*) of the island. The term has been found on Maltese inscriptions and was probably a formal title.

28:8 The description of Publius's **father** as having **fever and dysentery** fits the symptoms of an infection caused by goat's milk called "Malta fever." The coming of the whole region with their sick (v. 9) is reminiscent of what happened after Jesus healed Peter's mother-in-law (Luke 4:38–41).

28:10 Travelers on ancient ships had to provide their own meals. The hospitable Maltese people equipped Paul and his shipmates for the remainder of their voyage.

28:11–16 *Paul Arrives in Rome.* These verses relate the final leg of Paul's journey and his arrival in Rome.

28:11 After three months probably indicates March (c. A.D. 60), when, after the winter, it became safe to navigate the Mediterranean. The **ship of Alexandria** was likely a grain ship. Castor and Pollux, the **twin** sons of Zeus and Leda, were viewed as the **gods** who protected seamen.

28:12–13 Syracuse was at the eastern end of Sicily. Its fame as a Hellenistic city rivaled that of Athens, and the extensive archaeological remains at Syracuse include a great theater and the temple of Apollo. **Rhegium** (modern Reggio di Calabria) was at the southern tip of Italy across from Sicily. Inscriptions, literature, and archaeological evidence testify to Rhegium's importance as a port city. **Puteoli** (modern Pozzuoli) was a major port for Roman traffic, some 257 miles (413 km) by road up the western coast of Italy from Rhegium.

28:14 The **brothers** at Puteoli are evidence that Christianity had not only reached Rome by this time (c. A.D. 60) but was widely dispersed in Italy. Luke's comment, **so we came to Rome**, may seem premature (Rome was still 130 miles or 209 km away), but perhaps functions as a summary statement, indicating the process by which Paul reached Rome.

28:15 Paul's party was met by Roman Christians at two points along the way to Rome—the **Forum** (or "marketplace") **of Appius**, some 40 miles (64 km) from Rome, and 12 miles (19 km) farther on at **Three Taverns**. Paul had written his epistle to the Roman church three years earlier, and, though he had not personally visited Rome, his greetings at the end of Romans (Rom. 16:1–16) show that he already had many acquaintances in the church there.

28:16 On the city of **Rome**, see Introduction to Romans: The Ancient City of Rome. Allowing **Paul** to provide his own quarters points to his high status as a prisoner and perhaps to the support of local believers.

28:17–31 *Paul Witnesses to the Jews in Rome.* Unable to visit the synagogues himself, Paul invited the Roman Jews to come to him.

Paul in Rome

17 After three days he called together the local leaders of the Jews, and when they had
gathered, he said to them, "Brothers, [b]though I had done nothing against our people or
[c]the customs of our fathers, yet I was delivered as a prisoner from Jerusalem into the hands
of the Romans. 18 When they had examined me, they [d]wished to set me at liberty, [e]because
there was no reason for the death penalty in my case. 19 But because the Jews objected, I was
compelled [f]to appeal to Caesar—though I had no charge to bring against [g]my nation. 20 For
this reason, therefore, I have asked to see you and speak with you, since it is [h]because of [i]the
hope of Israel that I am wearing [j]this [k]chain." 21 And they said to him, "We have received
no letters from Judea about you, and none of [l]the brothers coming here has reported or
spoken any evil about you. 22 But we desire to hear from you what your views are, for with
regard to this [m]sect we know that everywhere [n]it is spoken against."

23 When they had appointed a day for him, they came to him at his lodging in greater
numbers. From morning till evening [o]he expounded to them, testifying to [p]the kingdom
of God and [q]trying to convince them about Jesus [r]both from the Law of Moses and from
the Prophets. 24 And [s]some were convinced by what he said, but others disbelieved. 25 And
disagreeing among themselves, they departed after Paul had made one statement: [t]"The
Holy Spirit was right in saying to your fathers through Isaiah the prophet:

26 [u]"'Go to this people, and say,
[v]"You will indeed hear but never understand,
and you will indeed see but never perceive."
27 [w]For this people's heart has grown dull,
and with their ears they can barely hear,
and their eyes they have closed;
lest they should see with their eyes
and hear with their ears
and understand with their heart
and [x]turn, and I would heal them.'

28 Therefore let it be known to you that [y]this [z]salvation of God [a]has been sent to the Gentiles;
[b]they will listen."[1]

30 He lived there two whole years at his own expense,[2] and [c]welcomed all who came to
him, 31 [d]proclaiming [e]the kingdom of God and teaching about the Lord Jesus Christ [f]with
all boldness and [g]without hindrance.

[1] Some manuscripts add verse 29: *And when he had said these words, the Jews departed, having much dispute among themselves* [2] Or *in his own hired dwelling*

17 [b][ch. 25:8] [c]ch. 6:14; 15:1; 21:21
18 [d]ch. 26:31, 32 [e]See ch. 23:29
19 [f]ch. 25:11; 26:32 [g]ch. 24:17; 26:4
20 [h]See ch. 23:6 [i][Luke 2:25] [j]ch. 26:29 [k]Eph. 6:20; 2 Tim. 1:16; See ch. 21:33; Phil. 1:7
21 [l]ch. 22:5
22 [m]See ch. 24:5 [n]Luke 2:34; [1 Pet. 2:12; 3:16; 4:14, 16]
23 [o][ch. 17:2, 3] [p]ver. 31 [q][ch. 19:8] [r]ch. 8:35; 24:14; 26:22
24 [s][ch. 14:4; 17:4, 5; 19:9; 23:7]
25 [t]Matt. 15:7
26 [u]Cited from Isa. 6:9, 10 [v]Matt. 13:14, 15; Mark 4:12; [Luke 8:10]
27 [w][John 12:40; Rom. 11:8] [x]See Luke 22:32
28 [y]ch. 13:26 [z]Ps. 67:2; Isa. 40:5; Luke 2:30; 3:6; [Rom. 11:11] [a]See ch. 13:46 [b]John 10:16; [ch. 13:48; Matt. 8:11; 21:43]
30 [c][Phil. 1:13]
31 [d][ch. 8:12; 20:25] [e]ver. 23; See Matt. 12:28; 13:19 [f]See ch. 4:29 [g][Phil. 1:12, 13; 2 Tim. 2:9]

28:17–18 The **local leaders** were probably the elders of the synagogues, of which there were a number in Rome. Paul's main purpose in this meeting was to explain his presence in Rome. He declared his innocence of transgressing any Jewish law. **into the hands of the Romans**. Some interpreters think this refers to Paul's original capture in Jerusalem (21:33–36); others think it refers to his transfer out of Jerusalem into the Roman judicial system to stand trial in Caesarea (23:23–35). **wished to set me at liberty**. See 26:32.

28:19 no charge to bring. Paul was a loyal Jew not only with respect to the Jews' charges against him but also in his refusal to accuse them of any wrongdoing.

28:20 The hope of Israel is the coming of the Messiah as attested by his resurrection (see 23:6; 24:15; 26:8, 23).

28:23 The content of Paul's message was the **kingdom of God** and **Jesus** (see also v. 31). The kingdom represents the fulfillment of God's saving promises to his people (see note on Matt. 12:28 on the kingdom of God). For the OT texts pointing to Jesus, see notes on Luke 24:44; 24:45; Acts 2:31; 3:12–26; 3:24.

28:24 On the Jews' pattern of resistance (cf. 5:33; 7:51; 12:1; 13:45; 25:11), see note on Amos 4:6.

28:26–27 Isaiah 6:9–10 (quoted here) is also quoted by Jesus to explain the failure of the Jews as a body to accept him (see Matt. 13:14–15). They had eyes to **see**, ears to **hear**, but the **heart**—the organ of thinking, willing, and deciding—failed to respond.

28:28 Paul's pattern of turning from the Jews to witness **to the Gentiles** repeated itself in Rome, but there is no reason to think that he gave up on the Jews in Rome at this point (cf. note on 18:7).

28:30–31 For Paul's provision of his own quarters, cf. v. 16. His sharing the gospel with **all** who came to him would have included both Jews and Gentiles (cf. note on v. 28). This situation continued for **two whole years** (A.D. 60–62), at which time Luke's account ends. Information as to what happened beyond that time comes from extrabiblical sources and from hints in the last few of Paul's letters. *First Clement* 5.7 (written A.D. 95, perhaps the earliest known orthodox Christian writing after the NT) speaks of Paul preaching in "the limits of the west," which probably indicates his fulfilling his desire to preach in Spain (see Rom. 15:24). That would point to his release from the first Roman imprisonment. The church historian Eusebius, writing in A.D. 325, cites the tradition that Paul was freed from confinement and carried on a further ministry until he was arrested and placed in a second Roman imprisonment, at which time he was martyred (*Ecclesiastical History* 2.22). In God's sovereignty, Paul's time in prison was not wasted, for it was during his Roman imprisonment that he wrote the letters to the Ephesians, Philippians, Colossians, and Philemon. The time after Paul's release from his first imprisonment (mid-60s) would be when he wrote 1 Timothy and Titus. He probably wrote his last letter, 2 Timothy, during his second imprisonment, as he awaited execution (cf. 2 Tim. 4:6–8).

READING THE EPISTLES

Introduction and Timeline

Knowing how to read the Epistles is very important, since they make up 21 of the 27 books in the NT. Paul wrote 13 of them. Three were written by the apostle John, two by Peter, one each by James and Jude (the brothers of Jesus), and one by the unknown author of Hebrews. Ascertaining the dates of the Epistles, their places of origin, and the recipients is in some instances quite difficult because, unlike modern books, a date is never included, the recipients are not always mentioned, and the place where the letters were written is not stated. In most cases, though, we can be fairly confident of an approximate date, and the recipients are often explicitly named. We suggest for the Epistles the information shown in the chart below (all dates are A.D. and approximate).

Unity

Most of these letters have three parts: (1) the opening; (2) the body; and (3) the closing. The opening of a letter has four different elements: (1) the sender (e.g., Paul); (2) the recipients (e.g., the Corinthians); (3) the salutation (e.g., "grace and peace to you"); and (4) a prayer (usually a thanksgiving). Not all the letters follow this pattern. The sender is not named in Hebrews, nor are the recipients. The author of 1 John never identifies himself, nor does he specifically address the readers. Indeed, there is no salutation or prayer in Hebrews or 1 John; both launch immediately into the content of the letter.

The body of the letter, which is the longest section in all the letters, does not follow any particular pattern. Here we need to trace out the flow of thought in each letter carefully. The Pauline letters and Hebrews are marked by careful logical progression, while 1 John repeatedly circles back to the same themes and James writes in a style that is reminiscent of wisdom literature such as Proverbs, a collection of shorter teachings on many topics but with no clear overall structure.

The closings in letters vary considerably. Paul often includes travel plans, commendation of coworkers, prayer,

Book	Author	Date	Recipients	Place of Writing
James	James	40–45	Jewish Christians in or near Palestine	Jerusalem?
Galatians	Paul	48	South Galatian churches	Syrian Antioch
1 Thessalonians	Paul	49–51	Church in Thessalonica	Corinth
2 Thessalonians	Paul	49–51	Church in Thessalonica	Corinth
1 Corinthians	Paul	53–55	Church in Corinth	Ephesus
2 Corinthians	Paul	55–56	Church in Corinth	Macedonia
Romans	Paul	57	Church in Rome	Corinth
Philippians	Paul	62	Church in Philippi	Rome
Colossians	Paul	62	Church in Colossae	Rome
Philemon	Paul	62	Philemon	Rome
Ephesians	Paul	62	Churches in Asia Minor (circular letter?)	Rome
1 Timothy	Paul	62–64	Timothy	Macedonia?
Titus	Paul	62–64	Titus	Nicopolis
1 Peter	Peter	62–63	Churches in Roman provinces in Asia Minor	Rome
2 Peter	Peter	64–67	Churches in Roman provinces in Asia Minor?	Rome
2 Timothy	Paul	64–67	Timothy	Rome
Jude	Jude	Mid–60s	Jewish Christians in Egypt? Asia Minor? Antioch?	Unknown
Hebrews	Unknown	60–70	Jewish Christians in Rome or in or near Palestine	Unknown
1 John	John	85–95	Churches near Ephesus?	Ephesus
2 John	John	85–95	Church or churches near Ephesus	Ephesus
3 John	John	85–95	Gaius	Ephesus

prayer requests, greetings, final instructions, an autographed greeting, and a grace benediction.

Although critical scholars have often argued that many of the letters are composites, being stitched together from a variety of different letters, scholars now generally affirm the unity of the letters and have noted their careful structure and the artistry of their unified composition. It is helpful, therefore, to compose a detailed outline as we study the letters, so that as readers we are able to trace the flow of the argument. By doing this we gain a greater understanding of each letter as a whole, since we are prone to read small sections without having a clear map of the entire document. Moreover, having a good understanding of the entirety of the letter assists significantly in interpretation. Often one part of the letter (e.g., the closing) casts light on other parts.

Themes

The Epistles are distinguished from the Gospels in that they are not narrative compositions. In terms of redemptive history, they are written on the other side of the cross and resurrection, so that they typically reflect more deeply on the significance of Christ's death and resurrection than the Gospels do. The implications of the fulfillment of God's promises in Jesus Christ are explored and applied to the readers in the Epistles. These same themes are present in the Gospels, of course, but they are not set forth in the same fullness, since the nature of Jesus' messianic mission often perplexed his disciples during his earthly ministry, and they grasped these realities in their fullness (though still not exhaustively!) only after the cross and resurrection and with the outpouring of the Spirit at Pentecost. The Epistles have played a major role in the formation of doctrine and Christian theology throughout church history precisely because they expound on the great themes of God's saving work on the cross. Because they reflect on and explain the fulfillment of God's promises in light of the OT and the Gospels, it is particularly fruitful to study their use of the OT, OT allusions, and citations of and allusions to Jesus' teachings. By doing this we understand more clearly how epistolary writers understood the fulfillment of God's promises in Christ. We also perceive how they related the OT and the gospel traditions to the churches, and such an understanding assists us in applying not only the Epistles but also the OT and the Gospels to today's world.

Among the major themes in the Epistles are the following: (1) Jesus Christ is the fulfillment of God's promises in redemptive history. He is Messiah, Lord, the Son of God, and the true revelation of God. (2) The new life of believers is a gift of God, anchored in the cross and empowered by the Holy Spirit. (3) Christians experience salvation by faith, and faith expresses itself in a transformed life. The Epistles spend considerable space elaborating on believers' newness of life. (4) Believers belong to the restored Israel, the church of Jesus Christ, which must live out her calling as God's people in a sinful world. (5) In this present evil age believers suffer affliction and persecution, but they look forward with joy to the coming of Jesus Christ and the consummation of their salvation. (6) False teachers dangerously subvert the true gospel of Christ.

The Circumstances behind the Letters

The Epistles are not abstract philosophical or theological essays that explain the salvation accomplished by Jesus Christ. In almost every instance, they are addressed to specific situations facing churches. It is clear in reading Galatians, Colossians, 2 Peter, and Jude that the letters were written because false teaching had infiltrated the churches. Upon reading 1–2 Corinthians, we realize that Paul wrote in response to various problems in the Corinthian church. The letters are crafted to speak to readers as they face everyday life. In his first letter, Peter addresses readers who were suffering discrimination and persecution. Colossians responds to some kind of mystical teaching that promises readers fullness of life apart from, or going beyond, Christ. Philippians hints that the church suffered from some type of dissension and lack of unity. In the two Thessalonian letters, the church was confused about eschatology, and some believers were apparently becoming lax and failing to work hard. While many themes in Paul's thought are set forth in Romans, even that letter does not represent a comprehensive exposition of the gospel, for we do not find in the letter a developed Christological exposition (cf. Phil. 2:6–11; Col. 1:15–20), an explanation of Paul's eschatology (cf. 1–2 Thessalonians), or an unfolding of a Pauline doctrine of the church (see Ephesians; 1 Timothy; Titus). Ephesians may be a circular letter sent to a number of churches, in which Paul sets forth a more comprehensive understanding of the church, but even Ephesians lacks a complete exposition of all of Paul's theology. We must mine all of Paul's letters to determine his theology—and God, in his providence, has given us all the letters (and, of course, the whole of Scripture) so that we can understand the "whole counsel of God" (Acts 20:27).

In interpreting the Epistles, then, we should try to understand the specific circumstances that the original readers were facing. Upon reading Galatians, for instance, we see readily enough that Paul is responding to opponents who are subverting the gospel. Our understanding of Paul's purpose in writing Galatians is sharpened if we piece together the clues in the letter to reconstruct the views of Paul's opponents. We see that certain outsiders had infiltrated the church and were arguing that the Galatians must submit to circumcision and keep the OT law in order to be saved (cf. Gal. 1:7; 2:3–5; 3:1–14; 5:2–6, 12; 6:12–13). Paul contends vigorously that no one is saved by works of law but only through faith in Jesus Christ.

As readers of the Epistles today, we face a disadvantage that the first readers did not have, for they knew firsthand the situation that the letter writer addressed. Our knowledge of the circumstances is partial and incomplete. Reading the letters can be like listening to half of a telephone conversation: we hear only the writer's response to the situation in a particular church. Still, we trust that God in his goodness has given us all we need to know in order to interpret the Epistles adequately and to apply them faithfully.

Pseudonymity

Some scholars have argued that the practice of writing a letter in someone else's name ("pseudonymity") was culturally accepted in NT times, and hence they claim that some of the NT letters were not written by the purported authors. For example, it is often claimed that Paul did not write 1–2 Timothy and Titus, or that Peter did not write 2 Peter. But the evidence is lacking that pseudonymity was accepted in letters that were considered to be authoritative and inspired. For instance, in 2 Thessalonians 2:2 Paul specifically criticizes those who claim to write in his name, and he concludes the letter with assurance that the writing is authentically his (3:17). The author of the NT apocryphal book *Acts of Paul and Thecla* was removed from his post as bishop for writing the book as if it were by Paul, even though he claimed that he had written out of love for Paul (Tertullian, *On Baptism* 17). In the same way, the *Gospel of Peter* was rejected as an authoritative book in A.D. 180 by Serapion, the bishop of Antioch, because it was not authentic, even though the author claimed that it had been written by Peter. Serapion said, "For our part, brethren, we both receive Peter and the other apostles as Christ, but the writings which falsely bear their names we reject, as men of experience, knowing that such were not handed down to us" (Eusebius, *Ecclesiastical History* 6.12.1–6).

There is no convincing evidence, then, that pseudonymous writings were accepted as authoritative. Indeed, if Peter did not write 2 Peter, then the author is guilty of deceit and dishonesty because he claims to have been an eyewitness of the transfiguration (2 Pet. 1:16–18) and identifies himself as Peter at the beginning of the letter (2 Pet. 1:1). In the same way, the Pastoral Epistles (1–2 Timothy and Titus) all claim to be by Paul and communicate many details from his life, which would be quite deceptive if Paul did not, in fact, write the letters. Some of the authors may have employed a secretary (*amanuensis*) to assist them in writing, which might account for some of the stylistic differences in the letters. Still, each letter would have been carefully dictated and reviewed by the apostolic author. ◀

INTRODUCTION TO

THE LETTER OF PAUL TO THE

ROMANS

Author and Title

As the opening words of the letter indicate, the apostle Paul wrote the book of Romans. Only a few scholars in history have doubted his authorship, and their doubts have been shown to be groundless. The title of the book indicates that the letter was written to the Christian churches in Rome.

Date

Paul probably wrote Romans from Corinth, on his third missionary journey, in A.D. 57 (Acts 20:2–3). Having completed his work in the eastern part of the Roman Empire, he hoped to travel to Rome and then on to Spain; but first he needed to go to Jerusalem to deliver the money he had collected for the church there (Rom. 15:19–32; see Acts 19:21). Paul commends Phoebe (Rom. 16:1–2), and she was likely the person who brought the letter to Rome. She resided in Cenchreae, which was near Corinth and was one of its port cities. Furthermore, Gaius was Paul's host (16:23), and this is likely the same Gaius who lived in Corinth (1 Cor. 1:14). Finally, two fairly early manuscripts of Romans have subscriptions (brief notes that a copyist added to the end of a document) which say that the letter was written from Corinth.

Theme

The theme of Romans is the revelation of God's judging and saving righteousness in the gospel of Jesus Christ. In the cross of Christ, God judges sin and yet at the same time manifests his saving mercy.

Purpose, Occasion, and Background

Romans provides the fullest expression of Paul's theology, though it is doubtful that he intended it to be a complete summary statement. For example, Romans lacks any detailed treatments of Paul's doctrine of Christ (see Phil. 2:6–11; Col. 1:15–20), of the church (see Ephesians), or of last things (see 1 Thess. 4:13–5:11; 2 Thess. 2:1–12).

It is more likely that Paul wrote the letter to address particular issues of concern to the Roman church. Specifically, he addressed matters of interest for a church that included both Jewish and Gentile Christians: (1) Can one be right with God through obeying the law (Rom. 1:1–3:20)? (2) What can be learned from Abraham, and is he the father of both Jewish and Gentile Christians (4:1–25)? (3) What role does the law play with reference to sin (5:20; 7:1–25)? (4) What does the salvation of Gentiles indicate about the future of Israel as God's people (9:1–11:36)? (5) Should Christians observe OT food laws, and how should they relate to fellow believers on such matters (14:1–15:13)?

The focus on Jew-Gentile issues suggests that tensions existed between Jews and Gentiles in the church in Rome. The Roman church probably began as a Jewish church, though it is not known exactly when it was established. Perhaps Jews from Rome returned from Jerusalem after Pentecost (Acts 2:10) and founded the church, or perhaps the church was established later. Some have suggested that Peter founded the church in Rome, but no significant evidence supports this premise.

As time passed, of course, Gentiles in Rome also became Christians. The Roman historian Suetonius records that the Roman emperor Claudius (reigned A.D. 41–54) expelled Jews from Rome in A.D. 49 because of strife over "Chrestus." Suetonius likely misunderstood the name, so that the dispute probably was about

"Christus" (Latin for Christ). The expulsion of Jews from Rome is confirmed by Acts 18:2. Because of the expulsion, the Gentile churches would have developed for a number of years apart from the Jews. Over the years the Jewish Christians slowly filtered back into Roman churches. It is not difficult to imagine that tensions would develop between law-observing Jewish Christians and Gentile Christians who lived free of the restrictions in the Mosaic law. It seems, however, that the church was made up mainly of Gentile Christians (see Rom. 1:5–6, 13; 11:13; 15:15–16).

Paul's selection of themes (gospel and law; the significance of Abraham; the future of Israel) suggests significant tensions between the Jews and Gentiles in Rome. Paul wrote Romans so that they would be united in the gospel he preached, and so that they would comprehend how the gospel spoke to the issues that divided them.

A closer look at Romans reveals another purpose as well. Paul wanted the Christians in Rome to rally around his gospel so that Rome would become the base of operations by which he could proclaim the gospel in Spain (15:22–24). If Roman Christians did not agree with Paul's gospel message, especially on the issues being debated among Jews and Gentiles, then they would not support his proposed mission to Spain. Paul needed to explain the gospel in some detail so that the Christians in Rome would become the base from which he could proclaim the gospel in new regions.

Of course, the ultimate aim and purpose for the preaching of the gospel is the glory of God. Paul longs for the Gentiles to come to the obedience of faith for the sake of Christ's name (1:5). God has planned all of salvation history to bring glory and praise to his name (11:33–36).

Timeline

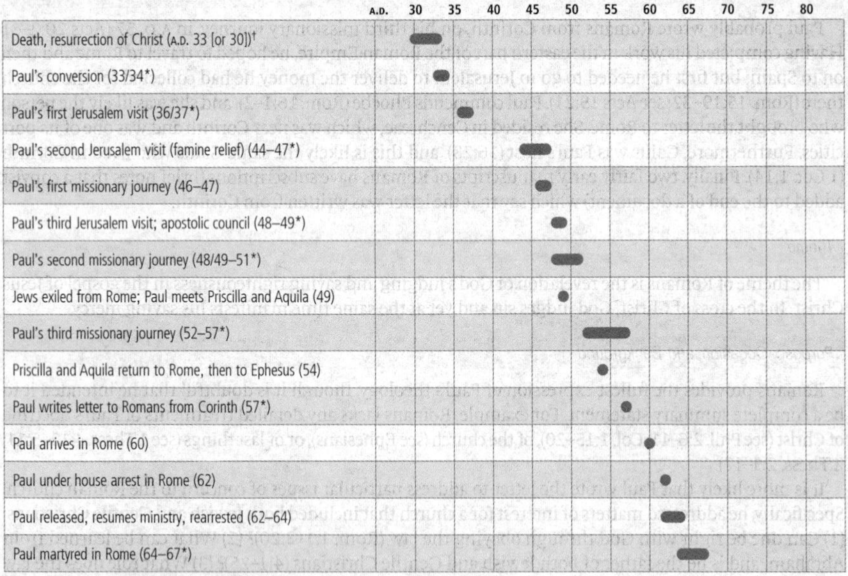

A.D. 30 35 40 45 50 55 60 65 70 75 80
Death, resurrection of Christ (A.D. 33 [or 30])†
Paul's conversion (33/34*)
Paul's first Jerusalem visit (36/37*)
Paul's second Jerusalem visit (famine relief) (44–47*)
Paul's first missionary journey (46–47)
Paul's third Jerusalem visit; apostolic council (48–49*)
Paul's second missionary journey (48/49–51*)
Jews exiled from Rome; Paul meets Priscilla and Aquila (49)
Paul's third missionary journey (52–57*)
Priscilla and Aquila return to Rome, then to Ephesus (54)
Paul writes letter to Romans from Corinth (57*)
Paul arrives in Rome (60)
Paul under house arrest in Rome (62)
Paul released, resumes ministry, rearrested (62–64)
Paul martyred in Rome (64–67*)

** denotes approximate date; / signifies either/or; † see The Date of Jesus' Crucifixion, pp. 1809–1810*

The Ancient City of Rome

The city of Rome was founded upon seven hills on the eastern shore of the Tiber River. Rome grew from a small city to an empire through its conquests of Italy (3rd century B.C.), Carthage in north Africa (3rd century B.C.), Greece and Macedonia (2nd century B.C.), western and northern Europe (2nd century B.C.–2nd century A.D.), and Egypt and much of the Near East (1st century B.C.). By Paul's day, the senatorial rule of the Roman republic had succumbed to a centralized empire under the leadership of Augustus (27 B.C.–A.D. 14), Tiberius (A.D. 14–37), Gaius (37–41), Claudius (41–54), and Nero (54–68).

Archaeological evidence in Rome confirms monumental structures that stood during the time of Paul, such as the Circus Maximus, Tabularium (state archives), theaters (including those of Pompey and of Marcellus), and multiple forums. Later, in the third century A.D., the Umbilicus Romae stood in the center of the city, and this cylindrical monument marked the theoretical "center" of the Roman world (likely this way of thinking about Rome's place in the world stemmed from well before the NT period). The prestige of the early emperors was memorialized during Paul's day in their basilicas, arches, and forums (e.g., the Forums of Caesar and of Augustus), in the Altar of Peace, in the Mausoleum of Augustus, in porticoes and images honoring their extended imperial family, and in imperial cult temples (such as the temple of Julius Caesar from 29 B.C. and the temple of Claudius). Innumerable pagan gods received worship in Rome. Especially impressive temples were dedicated to such ancient gods/goddesses as Mars, Saturn, Castor and Pollux, Vesta, Venus and Roma, Apollo, and Jupiter. Indeed, devotion to all the great Roman gods was offered in the monumental domed Pantheon, which stands in Rome to this day. (An earlier Pantheon—depicted in the illustration—was built in 27 B.C. and destroyed by fire in A.D. 80. The present-day structure was built c. A.D. 120.)

A significant portion of the city was destroyed by fire during Nero's rule in A.D. 64. Nero, who was suspected of having started the blaze, blamed and persecuted Christians for the conflagration. The fire allowed Nero to design and construct his own monumental buildings, including his 200-acre imperial dwelling, the Domus Aurea ("Golden House").

Among the structures that are contemporary with the last books in the NT canon, one should especially note the Arch of Titus and the Colosseum. The Arch of Titus, built in A.D. 81 by the emperor Domitian (reigned 81–96), commemorates the capture and destruction of Jerusalem and its temple in A.D. 70. The two generals who reconquered Palestine received such fame from this war that they both attained imperial

ROME IN THE TIME OF PAUL (C. A.D. 60)

The city plan below shows most of the features of the city of Rome that archaeologists have so far identified as dating from the time of Paul. Sections of the city would have been very impressive in his time, but most of the outstanding buildings visible in Rome today date to after his death.

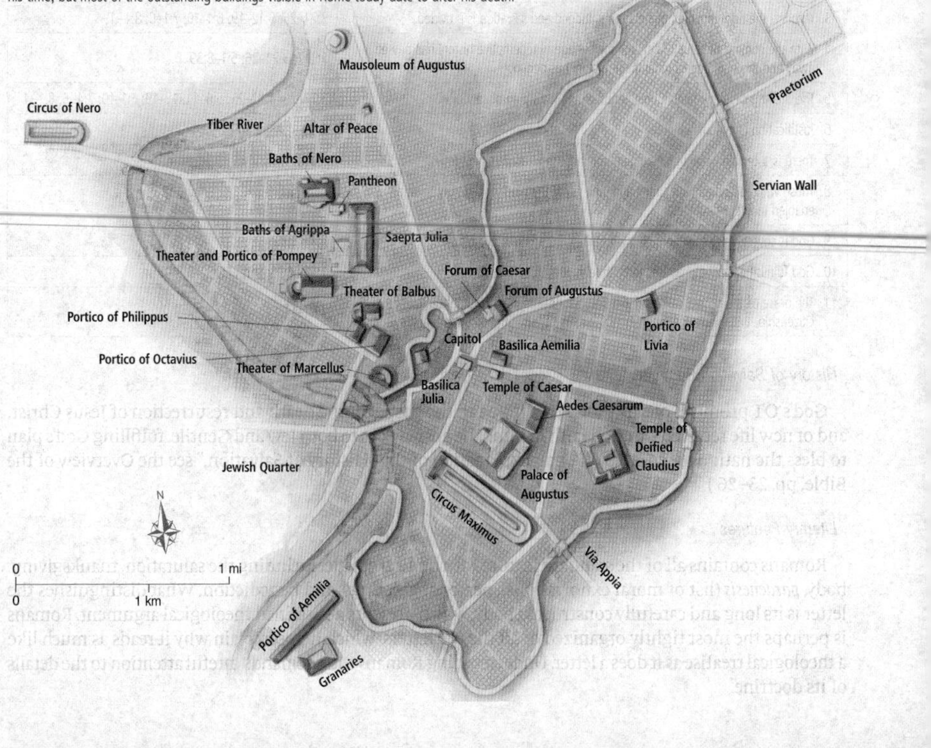

rule, which went first to Vespasian (A.D. 69–79) and then to his son Titus (79–81). The Arch of Titus still manifests a relief portraying the captured temple menorah and other Jewish sacred objects being carried through Rome in processional tribute to Titus. Vespasian and Titus built the Flavian Amphitheater, better known as the Colosseum due to its proximity to a gigantic statue (Gk. *kolossos*) of Nero. The Colosseum is estimated to have seated more than 45,000 for gladiatorial spectacles.

Daily life in Rome could be luxurious for the wealthy but onerous for others. Multiple aqueducts and a huge sewer system provided for the immense water requirements of Rome, including the many bathhouses, fountains, and latrines. Food had to be imported to satisfy the needs of this thriving metropolis, and the emperor often directly oversaw the vital grain supply. Luxury villas in Rome were the privileged possessions of the wealthiest families (often of senatorial or equestrian rank) and especially of the emperors, but most of the housing in ancient Rome consisted of *insulae* (multistory apartment buildings often constructed above first-floor shops). Contemporary authors spoke of a severely overcrowded, loud, and smelly city—a place that provided every virtue and vice known to mankind. The residents of Rome were mostly pagan, although a sizable Jewish population also existed (as evidenced both by 1st-century literature and by later remains of inscriptions). The expulsion of the Jews under the emperor Claudius (A.D. 49) was a limited measure.

Today, churches in Rome built during the fourth- to fifth-century Byzantine period mark the traditional burial places of Paul and of Peter, reflecting the post-NT church tradition which claims that Paul and Peter died as martyrs in Rome during the reign of Nero (c. A.D. 64–65, perhaps after an incarceration in the Mamertine Prison). The Roman catacombs house early Christian burials (from the 2nd century A.D. and after), and these catacombs contain some inscriptions and graffiti testifying to Christian martyrdom prior to the legitimization of Christianity by Licinius and Constantine (by the Edict of Milan in A.D. 313).

Key Themes

1. All people are sinners, therefore all, without exception, need to be saved from their sin.	1:18–3:20; 5:12–19
2. The Mosaic law, though good and holy, cannot counteract the power of sin.	2:12–29; 3:9–20; 5:20; 7:1–25; 9:30–10:8
3. Through the righteousness of God, sin is judged and salvation is provided.	3:21–26; 5:12–19; 6:1–10; 7:1–6; 8:1–4
4. With the coming of Jesus Christ, the former age of redemptive history has passed away and the new age of redemptive history has begun.	1:1–7; 3:21–26; 5:1–8:39
5. The atoning death of Jesus Christ is central to God's plan of salvation.	3:21–26; 4:23–25; 5:6–11, 15–19; 6:1–10; 7:4–6; 8:1–4
6. Justification is by faith alone.	1:16–4:25; 9:30–10:21
7. There is a certain hope of future glory for those who are in Christ Jesus.	5:1–8:39
8. Those who have died with Christ and who enjoy the work of the Holy Spirit are enabled to live a new life.	2:25–29; 6:1–7:6; 8:1–39
9. God is sovereign in salvation; he works all things according to his plan.	9:1–11:36
10. God fulfills his saving promises to both Jews and Gentiles.	1:18–4:25; 9:1–11:36; 15:8–13
11. The grace of the gospel calls Christians to personal holiness, mutual service, good citizenship, and wholehearted neighbor-love in Christ.	12:1–13:14

History of Salvation Summary

God's OT promises of salvation are fulfilled in the gospel of the death and resurrection of Jesus Christ, and of new life received through faith in him. The gospel goes to both Jew and Gentile, fulfilling God's plan to bless the nations (Gen. 12:3). (For an explanation of the "History of Salvation," see the Overview of the Bible, pp. 23–26.)

Literary Features

Romans contains all of the standard features of a biblical epistle, including the salutation, thanksgiving, body, *paraenesis* (list of moral exhortations), personal greetings, and benediction. What distinguishes the letter is its long and carefully constructed body, which presents a sustained theological argument. Romans is perhaps the most tightly organized of all the NT letters, which helps explain why it reads as much like a theological treatise as it does a letter. Understanding Romans thus demands careful attention to the details of its doctrine.

The Setting of Romans
(c. A.D. 57)
Paul probably wrote Romans from Corinth during his third missionary journey (Acts 20:2–3). Rome was the epicenter of the powerful Roman Empire, ruling over many of the great ancient centers of Western civilization. Paul had established the church at Corinth during his second missionary journey (Acts 18:1–11).

As a theological treatise, the book of Romans is a grand edifice. It is filled with lofty theological ideas and vocabulary. The rhetoric is often grand, taking such forms as elaborate sentence construction (syntax) and patterns of verbal repetition. What is often overlooked is that there is a continuous presence of a genre that tends toward the informal and that even lends a colloquial vigor that balances its grandeur. This genre, known as the diatribe, was used extensively by Roman teachers and orators (also known as preachers). The traits of the form included the following: dialogue with hypothetical questioners or opponents; as part of that, question-and-answer constructions, sometimes catechism-like in effect; use of questions or hypothetical objections as a transition to the next topic; rhetorical questions; adducing famous and representative figures from the past as examples; use of analogy as a rhetorical device; and aphoristic style.

The book is unified primarily by the coherence of its central argument, which outlines and explains the eternal plan of God for the salvation of sinners. The book's thesis statement (see 1:16–17) alerts the reader to the central place that the righteousness of God occupies in this plan—the righteousness that God both demands in obedience and offers as a free gift in Christ, received by faith.

Outline

I. The Gospel as the Revelation of the Righteousness of God (1:1–17)
- A. Salutation: the gospel concerning God's Son (1:1–7)
- B. Thanksgiving: prayer for an apostolic visit (1:8–15)
- C. Theme: the gospel of the righteousness of God (1:16–17)

II. God's Righteousness in His Wrath against Sinners (1:18–3:20)
- A. The unrighteousness of the Gentiles (1:18–32)
- B. The unrighteousness of the Jews (2:1–3:8)
- C. The unrighteousness of all people (3:9–20)

III. The Saving Righteousness of God (3:21–4:25)
- A. God's righteousness in the death of Jesus (3:21–26)
- B. Righteousness by faith for Jews and Gentiles (3:27–31)
- C. Abraham as the father of Jews and Gentiles (4:1–25)

IV. Hope as a Result of Righteousness by Faith (5:1–8:39)
- A. Assurance of hope (5:1–11)
- B. Hope in Christ's triumph over Adam's sin (5:12–21)
- C. The triumph of grace over the power of sin (6:1–23)
- D. The triumph of grace over the power of the law (7:1–6)

- E. The law and sin (7:7–25)
- F. Life in the Spirit (8:1–17)
- G. Assurance of hope (8:18–39)

V. God's Righteousness to Israel and to the Gentiles (9:1–11:36)

- A. God's saving promises to Israel (9:1–29)
- B. Israel's rejection of God's saving promises (9:30–11:10)
- C. God's righteousness in his plan for Jews and Gentiles (11:11–32)
- D. Concluding doxology (11:33–36)

VI. God's Righteousness in Everyday Life (12:1–15:13)

- A. Paradigm for exhortations: total dedication to God (12:1–2)
- B. Marks of the Christian community (12:3–13:14)
- C. A call for mutual acceptance between the strong and the weak (14:1–15:13)

VII. The Extension of God's Righteousness through the Pauline Mission (15:14–16:23)

- A. The establishment of churches among the Gentiles (15:14–33)
- B. Appreciation and greetings to coworkers in the gospel (16:1–23)

VIII. Final Summary of the Gospel of the Righteousness of God (16:25–27)

THE LETTER OF PAUL TO THE

ROMANS

Chapter 1
1[a][Gal. 1:10] [b]1 Cor. 1:1; [1 Cor. 9:1; Heb. 5:4]; See 2 Cor. 1:1 [c]See Acts 13:2
2[d]Titus 1:2 [e]ch. 3:21; 16:26; Luke 1:70
3[f]See Matt. 1:1 [g]Gal. 4:4
4[h][Acts 13:33] [i]2 Cor. 13:4; Eph. 1:19, 20; Phil. 3:10; [Acts 10:38; 26:23]
5[j]ch. 12:3; 15:15 [k]See Acts 1:25 [l]ch. 6:16; 16:26; 1 Pet. 1:2; [ch. 15:18; Acts 6:7] [m]See Acts 9:15
6[n]Rev. 17:14; [ch. 8:28, 30]
7[o]1 Cor. 1:3

Greeting

1 Paul, [a]a servant[1] of Christ Jesus, [b]called to be an apostle, [c]set apart for the gospel of
God, 2 which [d]he promised beforehand [e]through his prophets in the holy Scriptures,
3 concerning his Son, [f]who was descended from David[2] [g]according to the flesh 4 and [h]was
declared to be the Son of God [i]in power according to the Spirit of holiness by his resurrection from the dead, Jesus Christ our Lord, 5 through whom [j]we have received grace and
[k]apostleship [l]to bring about the obedience of faith for the sake of his name [m]among all
the nations, 6 including you who are [n]called to belong to Jesus Christ,
7 To all those in Rome who are loved by God and called to be saints:
[o]Grace to you and peace from God our Father and the Lord Jesus Christ.

[1] Or *slave* (for the contextual rendering of the Greek word *doulos*, see Preface) [2] Or *who came from the offspring of David*

1:1–17 *The Gospel as the Revelation of the Righteousness of God.* In this first main section, Paul includes his opening salutation (vv. 1–7), thanksgiving (vv. 8–15), and his statement of the overall theme of Romans (vv. 16–17).

1:1–7 *Salutation: The Gospel Concerning God's Son.* This is the longest introduction of any of Paul's letters. Paul goes into more detail here because he had never been to Rome and he wanted to summarize his gospel for the Roman readers. One remarkable feature of this section is that many of the themes mentioned here also conclude the letter in the final doxology (16:25–27): (1) Paul's apostolic authority; (2) the fulfillment of the OT Scriptures in the gospel; (3) the gospel that centers on Jesus Christ; (4) the obedience of faith; (5) the mission to the Gentiles; and (6) the glory of Jesus Christ and God the Father.

1:1 servant. See note on the first-century institution of "bondservant" (Gk. *doulos*, "servant, slave, bondservant") at 1 Cor. 7:21. This designation indicates that Paul is a slave of Christ, but at the same time the title recalls the honored servants of God in the OT, such as Moses, Joshua, David, and the prophets (Josh. 14:7; 24:29; 2 Kings 17:23; Ps. 89:3). **Apostle** emphasizes that Paul's authority is equal to that of the 12 apostles chosen by Christ. The apostles were specifically called by Christ (Matt. 10:1–7; Acts 1:24–26; Gal. 1:1) and had seen the risen Lord Jesus (Acts 1:22; 1 Cor. 9:1; 15:7–9). They established and governed the whole church, under Jesus Christ, and they had authority to speak and write the words of God, equal in authority to the OT Scriptures (1 Cor. 14:37; 2 Cor. 13:3; Gal. 1:8–9; 1 Thess. 2:13; 4:15; 2 Pet. 3:2, 15–16). Paul was called to be an apostle when Jesus appeared to him on the Damascus road (Acts 9; 22; 26; 1 Cor. 9:1; 15:8–9; Gal. 1:13–17), and the unusual timing of his call led Paul to conclude that no more apostles would be chosen after him (1 Cor. 15:8). **Gospel** (Gk. *euangelion*) means "good news." This included not just a call to initial saving faith but Paul's entire message about Jesus Christ and how Christ's saving activity transforms all of life and all of history.

1:2–3 Jesus fulfilled the OT prophecy that a descendant of **David** would rule forever, and hence he is the Messiah (see 2 Sam. 7:12–16; Psalm 89; 132; Isa. 11:1–5; Jer. 23:5–6; Ezek. 34:23–24). The eternal Son of God assumed humanity to become the messianic King.

1:4 Jesus was **declared** by God the Father to be **the Son of God in power** when he was raised from the dead (see Matt. 28:6) and installed at God's right hand as the messianic King. As the eternal Son of God, he has reigned forever with the Father and the Holy Spirit. But this verse refers to Jesus as the God-man reigning in messianic power ("Son of God" was a Jewish title for the Messiah), and this reign began (i.e., was declared or initiated) at a certain point in salvation history, i.e., when Jesus was raised from the dead through the Holy Spirit. **according to the Spirit of holiness**. Christ's great power is always connected to the holiness of the Holy Spirit as he works in the new covenant age.

1:5 Paul's mission is to all people groups. His goal is **to bring about the obedience of faith** (cf. 16:26). Obedience is required, but it is an obedience that flows from saving faith and is always connected to ongoing faith. Although Paul can speak of people's initial response as obeying the gospel (10:16), it is unlikely that "obedience of faith" here refers only to initial saving faith, because the purpose of Paul's apostleship was not merely to bring people to conversion but also to bring about transformed lives that were consistently obedient to God. Paul's ultimate goal in preaching to the Gentiles is **for the sake of his name**, that is, that Jesus Christ will be glorified. "Name" here means reputation or honor.

1:7 Rome. See Introduction: The Ancient City of Rome. **loved by God and called**. God shows his love by effectually calling his people to himself. **Saints** refers to all Christians; all believers stand before God as his "holy ones." **Grace** means God's unmerited favor. **Peace** is not just the absence of conflict but echoes the OT concept of *shalom*, where a person's life with God and with everything else is in ordered harmony, both physically and spiritually, and "all is well."

Same Themes in Salutation and Doxology of Romans

Salutation	Key Themes	Doxology
1:1	Gospel	16:25
1:3	Son	16:25
1:2	Scriptures	16:26
1:1, 5	Paul/my gospel	16:25
1:5	Obedience of faith among the Gentiles	16:26
1:5	For his name/glory forever	16:27

Longing to Go to Rome

8 First, [p]I thank my God through Jesus Christ for all of you, [q]because your faith is proclaimed in all the world. **9** [r]For God is my witness, [s]whom I serve with my spirit in the
gospel of his Son, [t]that without ceasing I mention you **10** always in my prayers, asking that
somehow [u]by God's will I may now at last succeed in coming to you. **11** For [v]I long to see you,
that I may impart to you some spiritual gift to strengthen you— **12** that is, that we may be
mutually encouraged [w]by each other's faith, both yours and mine. **13** I do not want you to
be unaware, brothers,[1] that [x]I have often intended to come to you (but [y]thus far have been
prevented), in order that I may reap some [z]harvest among you as well as among the rest of
the Gentiles. **14** [a]I am under obligation both to Greeks and to [b]barbarians,[2] both to the wise
and to the foolish. **15** So I am eager to preach the gospel to you also who are in Rome.

The Righteous Shall Live by Faith

16 For [d]I am not ashamed of the gospel, for it is [e]the power of God for salvation to everyone
who believes, to the Jew [f]first and also to [g]the Greek. **17** For in it [h]the righteousness of God
is revealed [i]from faith for faith,[3] [j]as it is written, "The righteous shall live by faith."[4]

God's Wrath on Unrighteousness

18 For [k]the wrath of God [l]is revealed from heaven against all ungodliness and unrighteousness of men, who by their unrighteousness suppress the truth. **19** For what can be

[1] Or *brothers and sisters*. The plural Greek word *adelphoi* (translated "brothers") refers to siblings in a family. In New Testament usage, depending on the context, *adelphoi* may refer either to men or to both men and women who are siblings (brothers and sisters) in God's family, the church [2] That is, non-Greeks [3] Or *beginning and ending in faith* [4] Or *The one who by faith is righteous shall live*

8 [p]1 Cor. 1:4; Eph. 1:15, 16; Phil. 1:3; Col. 1:3, 4; [ch. 6:17; Phil. 4:6; 2 Tim. 1:3] [q]ch. 16:19; [1 Thess. 1:8]
9 [r]Phil. 1:8; 1 Thess. 2:5, 10; [ch. 9:1; 2 Cor. 1:23; 11:10, 31] [s]See Acts 24:14 [t]2 Tim. 1:3
10 [u]ch. 15:32; [1 Thess. 3:10]
11 [v]ch. 15:22, 23; [Acts 19:21]
12 [w]See 2 Pet. 1:1
13 [x]ch. 15:22, 23; [Acts 19:21] [y]ch. 15:22; [1 Thess. 2:18] [z]Phil. 4:17; [John 4:36]
14 [a]1 Cor. 9:16 [b]See Acts 28:2
16 [d][Ps. 40:9, 10]; See Mark 8:38 [e]1 Cor. 1:18, 24 [f]ch. 2:9; See Acts 3:26 [g][Mark 7:26]; See John 7:35
17 [h]ch. 3:21; [2 Cor. 5:21; Phil. 3:9] [i]See ch. 9:30 [j]Gal. 3:11; Heb. 10:38; Cited from Hab. 2:4
18 [k]Eph. 5:6; Col. 3:6; [ch. 5:9] [l][ch. 2:5]

1:8–15 *Thanksgiving: Prayer for an Apostolic Visit.* Paul expresses his desire to come to Rome. Paul had desired to visit Rome for many years because he had a special call as the "apostle to the Gentiles" (11:13) to proclaim the gospel to all peoples.

1:8 thank. Paul typically follows the greeting in his letters with a thanksgiving (cf. 1 Cor. 1:1–9; Phil. 1:1–8; Col. 1:1–8; 1 Thess. 1:2; 2 Thess. 1:3; 2 Tim. 1:3; Philem. 4). He is thankful not for any personal benefit but because he sees here the fulfillment of his goal in life, which was for the kingdom of God to advance throughout **all the world**. Paul likely means that the gospel is no longer confined to the Jews but has also spread to the Gentiles in the Greco-Roman world.

1:9 God is my witness. Paul appeals to God to hold him accountable if he is saying anything false.

1:10 Paul expresses his prayer that he might visit the Romans. The petition in this verse clarifies the request in v. 9.

1:11–12 mutually encouraged. Paul desires as an apostle to encourage the Christians in Rome, but it is also noteworthy that their faith serves to inspire and strengthen him as well.

1:13 harvest. Paul's ministry is like bringing ripened crops as a gift to God. Paul neither "planted" nor "watered" the church at Rome (cf. 1 Cor. 3:6), but its increased maturity and obedience would be a harvest nonetheless.

1:14 Paul was **under obligation** imposed by Jesus Christ, who ordained Paul as the apostle to the Gentiles. **Greeks** refers to those who spoke Greek and adopted Greek culture in the Greco-Roman world. **Barbarians** designates those outside of Greek culture.

1:15 Why would Paul **preach the gospel** to people who were already Christians? For Paul "the gospel" is not just a call to initial saving faith but also a call to continue in a daily walk of faith (6:4; 8:4; 2 Cor. 5:17; Gal. 5:6).

1:16–17 *Theme: The Gospel of the Righteousness of God.* Paul explains why he is so eager to preach the gospel everywhere: the gospel is the saving power of God, in which the righteousness of God is revealed.

1:16 Because of their lack of size, fame, or honor in the Roman corridors of power and influence, Christians might be tempted to be **ashamed** of the Christian message. But Paul says it is nothing to be ashamed of, for it is in fact a message coming with the **power of God** that brings people to salvation. **Jew first** indicates the priority of the Jews in salvation history and their election as God's people. The role of the Jews is a major issue in Romans, as seen especially in the discussion in chs. 9–11. **Greek** is not limited here to people from Greece but refers to all Gentiles.

1:17 the righteousness of God. A crucial phrase that has been the subject of intense debate. It most likely means primarily "righteousness from God," so that it denotes right standing before God (a legal reality) that is given to people by God. A similar expression in Greek clearly has this meaning in Phil. 3:9. Romans 10:5 is parallel to Phil. 3:9 and bears the same meaning. It is likely that the phrase bears this meaning as well in Rom. 3:21–22 and 2 Cor. 5:21 (see notes on these verses). However, the expression in Greek (*dikaiosynē theou*, "the righteousness of God") likely also carries an additional, fuller meaning, which refers directly to God's right moral character, particularly manifested in his holiness and justice, and in the way that his method of saving sinners through Christ's death meets the just demand of his holy nature. Although today's Western world often regards using words that carry a double sense as confusing and ambiguous, in NT times such wording was commonly used to add weight and enrichment. (See, e.g., John 12:32, where "lifted up" refers to Christ being "exalted" by being crucified.) **From faith for faith** probably means that right standing with God is by faith from start to finish. **shall live by faith**. The life of faith is all-encompassing: it is by faith that one initially receives the gift of salvation (eternal life), but it is also by faith that one lives each day. Cf. Hab. 2:4; Gal. 3:11; Heb. 10:38.

1:18–3:20 *God's Righteousness in His Wrath against Sinners*. This next main section shows that God's wrath is being righteously revealed against all people, both Gentiles and Jews, since all have sinned and fall short of God's glory (3:23).

1:18–32 *The Unrighteousness of the Gentiles*. God's wrath is righteously revealed because people suppress the truth about the one true God and turn to idolatry (vv. 18–23). The consequence of idolatry is the moral disintegration of human society (vv. 24–32).

1:18 The **wrath of God** refers to his personal anger against sin. God's anger is not selfish or arbitrary but represents his holy and loving response to human wickedness. Some have understood God's wrath in impersonal cause-effect terms, but that would be a deistic worldview rather than a biblical one.

1:19–20 God's wrath is expressed for good reason since his **power and divine nature** are clearly revealed through the world he has made, and yet he is rejected by all people. These verses show that salvation does not come through "general revelation" (what is known about God through the natural world) since Paul emphasizes the universality of sin and concludes that "no one seeks for God" (3:11). **things that have been made**. The entire natural world bears witness to God through its beauty, complexity, design, and usefulness. **without excuse**. No one should complain that God has left

[m]known about God is plain to them, because God has shown it to them. 20 For his invisible
attributes, namely, his eternal power and divine nature, [n]have been clearly perceived, ever
since the creation of the world,[1] in the things that have been made. So they are without
excuse. 21 For although they knew God, they did not honor him as God or give thanks to
him, but they [o]became futile in their thinking, and their foolish hearts were darkened.
22 [p]Claiming to be wise, they became fools, 23 and [q]exchanged the glory of [r]the immortal
God for images resembling mortal man and birds and animals and creeping things.
24 Therefore [s]God gave them up in the lusts of their hearts to impurity, to [t]the dishonoring of their bodies among themselves, 25 because they exchanged the truth about God
for [u]a lie and worshiped and served the creature rather than the Creator, [v]who is blessed
forever! Amen.

26 For this reason [w]God gave them up to [x]dishonorable passions. For their women
exchanged natural relations for those that are contrary to nature; 27 and the men likewise
gave up natural relations with women and were consumed with passion for one another,
[y]men committing shameless acts with men and receiving in themselves the due penalty
for their error.

28 And since they did not see fit to acknowledge God, [z]God gave them up to [a]a debased
mind to do [b]what ought not to be done. 29 They were filled with all manner of unrighteousness, evil, covetousness, malice. They are full of envy, murder, strife, deceit, maliciousness.
They are gossips, 30 slanderers, haters of God, insolent, haughty, boastful, inventors of
evil, disobedient to parents, 31 foolish, faithless, heartless, ruthless. 32 Though they know
[c]God's righteous decree that those who practice such things [d]deserve to die, they not only
do them but [e]give approval to those who practice them.

God's Righteous Judgment

2 Therefore you have [f]no excuse, O man, every one of you who judges. For [g]in passing
judgment on another you condemn yourself, because you, the judge, practice the very
same things. 2 We know that the judgment of God rightly falls on those who practice such
things. 3 Do you suppose, O man—you who judge those who practice such things and

[1] *Or clearly perceived from the creation of the world*

19 [m]ch. 2:14, 15; Acts 14:17; 17:24-27
20 [n][Ps. 19:1-6; Jer. 5:21, 22]
21 [o]2 Kgs. 17:15; Jer. 2:5; Eph. 4:17, 18
22 [p]Jer. 10:14; 1 Cor. 1:20
23 [q]Ps. 106:20; Jer. 2:11; [Deut. 4:16-18; Acts 17:29] [r]1 Tim. 1:17
24 [s]ver. 26, 28; [Eph. 4:19] [t][1 Thess. 4:4]
25 [u]Isa. 28:15; 44:19, 20; Jer. 10:14; Amos 2:4; [2 Thess. 2:11] [v]ch. 9:5
26 [w]ver. 24, 28 [x][Col. 3:5; 1 Thess. 4:5]
27 [y]Lev. 18:22; 20:13
28 [z]ver. 24, 26 [a][Jer. 6:30] [b][Eph. 5:4]
32 [c]ch. 2:26; 8:4 [d]ch. 6:21 [e]Luke 11:48; Acts 8:1; 22:20; [1 Cor. 13:6; 2 Thess. 2:12]

Chapter 2

1 [f]ch. 1:20 [g]2 Sam. 12:5-7; [John 8:7]; See Matt. 7:2

insufficient evidence of his existence and character; the fault is with those who reject the evidence.

1:21 The root sin is the failure to value God above all things, so that he is not honored and praised as he should be. Human beings are foolish, not in the sense that they are intellectually deficient but in their rejection of God's lordship over their lives. **They knew God** not in a saving sense, but they knew of his existence and his attributes.

1:22 Even brilliant people who do not honor God miss the whole purpose of life and are therefore **fools** (cf. Prov. 1:7, 22; 10:1; 12:15; 14:7; 17:25; 20:3).

1:23 Idolatry is the fundamental sin. **images**. In addition to the images housed in great temples, Roman families commonly kept representations of individual "house gods" in their homes (examples found at Pompeii are particularly striking). Mediterranean and Near Eastern pagan religion worshiped idols in the form of beasts, or in the likeness of mixed beast/human deities such as the ancient gods of Egypt. Modern "idols" don't look like ancient ones; images served today are often mental rather than metal. But people still devote their lives to, and trust in, many things other than God.

1:24 Three times Paul says **God gave them up** (vv. 24, 26, 28). In every instance the giving up to sin is a result of idolatry, the refusal to make God the center and circumference of all existence, so that in practice the creature is exalted over the Creator. Hence, all individual sins are a consequence of the failure to prize and praise God as the giver of every good thing.

1:25 exchanged the truth about God for a lie. Paul implies that all other religions are based on false ideas about the one true God; they are not just "different paths to one God," as some claim.

1:26–27 Not only homosexual acts but also such **passions** or desires are said to be **dishonorable** before God. Just as idolatry is unnatural (contrary to what God intended when he made human beings), so too homosexuality is **contrary to nature** in that it does not represent what God intended when he made men and women with physical bodies that have a "natural" way of interacting with each other and "natural" desires for each other. Paul follows the OT and Jewish tradition in seeing all homosexual relationships as sinful. The creation account in Genesis 1–2 reveals the divine paradigm for human beings, indicating that God's will is for man and woman to be joined in marriage. **Consumed** (or "inflamed") gives a strong image of a powerful but destructive inward desire. The sin in view is not pederasty (homosexual conduct of men with boys) but **men** engaging in sin **with men**. There is no justification here for the view that Paul condemns only abusive homosexual relationships. **Due penalty** could refer to the sin of homosexuality itself as the penalty for idolatry. Or, the "and" in **and receiving** may indicate some additional negative consequences received **in themselves**, that is, some form of spiritual, emotional, or physical blight. The "due" penalty refers to a penalty that is appropriate to the wrong committed.

1:28–31 Human sin is not confined to sexual sins, and Paul now lists a whole catalog of the evils common among human beings as a result of turning from God.

1:32 People do not generally sin in innocent ignorance, for they **know God's righteous decree** (at least in an instinctive way) that their evil deserves condemnation. Indeed, the evil goes further when people **give approval** and applaud others for their sin, probably because having others join in their sin makes them feel better about the evil course they have chosen.

2:1–3:8 *The Unrighteousness of the Jews.* The Jews are not exempt from God's judgment.

2:1–29 Most interpreters argue that Paul focuses on the sin of the Jews throughout this chapter. Another view is that the sin of the moralist, whether Jewish or Gentile, is condemned in vv. 1–16, with the Jews coming into special prominence in vv. 17–29.

2:1 God does not condemn them merely because they judged others but because they practiced the same sins they condemned in others (**the very same things**, esp. those mentioned in 1:29–31). All people are without excuse because all, without exception, have sinned against God.

yet do them yourself—that you will escape the judgment of God? 4 Or do you presume
on [h]the riches of his kindness and [i]forbearance and [j]patience, [k]not knowing that God's
kindness is meant to lead you to repentance? 5 But because of your hard and impenitent
heart you are [l]storing up [m]wrath for yourself on the day of wrath when God's righteous
judgment will be revealed.
6 [n]He will render to each one according to his works: 7 to those who [o]by patience in well-
doing seek for glory and honor and immortality, he will give eternal life; 8 but for those
who are self-seeking[1] and [p]do not obey the truth, but obey unrighteousness, there will be
wrath and fury. 9 There will be tribulation and distress [q]for every human being who does
evil, the Jew [r]first and also the Greek, 10 but glory and honor and [s]peace for everyone who
does good, [t]the Jew first and also the Greek. 11 For [u]God shows no partiality.

God's Judgment and the Law

12 For all who have sinned [v]without the law will also perish without the law, and all who
have sinned under the law will be judged by the law. 13 For [w]it is not the hearers of the law
who are righteous before God, but the doers of the law who will be justified. 14 For when
Gentiles, who do not have the law, [x]by nature do what the law requires, they are a law to
themselves, even though they do not have the law. 15 They show that the work of the law
is [y]written on their hearts, while their conscience also bears witness, and their conflicting
thoughts accuse or even excuse them 16 [z]on that day when, [a]according to my gospel, God
judges [b]the secrets of men [c]by Christ Jesus.
17 But if you call yourself a Jew and [d]rely on the law and boast in God 18 and know his
will and approve what is excellent, because you are instructed from the law; 19 and if you
are sure that you yourself are [e]a guide to the blind, a light to those who are in darkness,
20 an instructor of the foolish, a teacher of children, having in the law [f]the embodiment
of [g]knowledge and truth— 21 [h]you then who teach others, do you not teach yourself?
While you preach against stealing, do you steal? 22 You who say that one must not commit

[1] *Or contentious*

4 [h]ch. 9:23; 10:12 [i]ch. 3:25 [j]ch. 9:22; [Ex. 34:6] [k]Isa. 30:18; 2 Pet. 3:9, 15; Rev. 2:21
5 [l][Deut. 32:34]; See James 5:3 [m]Ps. 110:5
6 [n]Job 34:11; Ps. 62:12; Prov. 24:12; Jer. 17:10; 32:19; See Matt. 16:27
7 [o]See Luke 8:15
8 [p]2 Thess. 2:12
9 [q]Ezek. 18:20 [r]See 1 Pet. 4:17
10 [s]Isa. 57:19 [t]See ch. 1:16
11 [u]See Acts 10:34
12 [v]1 Cor. 9:21
13 [w]See James 1:22, 23
14 [x]See ch. 1:19
15 [y]Jer. 31:33
16 [z][ch. 3:6; 14:10; 1 Cor. 4:5]; See Acts 10:42; 17:31 [a]ch. 16:25; 2 Tim. 2:8; [Gal. 1:11; 1 Tim. 1:11] [b]Eccles. 12:14 [c]ch. 16:25; [1 Tim. 1:11; 2 Tim. 2:8]
17 [d]ver. 23; Mic. 3:11; [ch. 9:4; John 5:45]
19 [e][Job 29:15; Matt. 15:14; 23:16; John 9:39-41]
20 [f]2 Tim. 3:5; [Gal. 4:19; 2 Tim. 1:13] [g]Luke 11:52
21 [h]Matt. 23:3-28; [Ps. 50:16-21; Matt. 15:1-9]

2:4 Do you presume is probably directed against Jews who thought that their covenant relationship with God would shield them from final judgment. After all, they had often experienced **his kindness and forbearance and patience**. They thought such blessings showed that they were right with God and had no need to trust in Christ, but Paul says the opposite is true: God's blessings should have led them to repent of their sins.

2:5 A soft and repentant heart is needed to avert God's wrath on the **day of wrath**, the final judgment. Such repentance would express itself in trust in Jesus Christ for the forgiveness of sins. Paul disagrees with much of the Jewish teaching of his day, according to which the Jews were not **storing up wrath** but were in good standing with God through their covenant relationship, not needing to meet God's standard of perfect obedience but needing only an intention to obey God.

2:6–11 Paul establishes the principle that judgment is **according to . . . works**. The structure of the passage is clear. Verse 6 enunciates the principle. Verses 7–10 work it out more specifically with an ABBA pattern (a chiasm). Verse 11 then explains why God judges according to works (because he is impartial). When Paul speaks of those who are rewarded for doing good works (vv. 7, 10), is he speaking hypothetically or of real obedience? The hypothetical view fits with the theme of the section as a whole (1:18–3:20), where all are condemned for sin, and righteousness does not come by works of law. It seems more likely, however, that Paul is speaking here of real obedience that is rewarded on the last day—such obedience being the result of the regenerating work of the Holy Spirit, as Paul explains at the conclusion of the chapter (2:26–29). Impartiality in judgment (v. 11) is a regular requirement in the OT (see Deut. 1:17; 16:18–20), reflecting the righteousness of God's judgment (Deut. 10:17).

2:12 All will be judged according to the standard they had. The Gentiles will **perish** (i.e., face final judgment) because of their sin (cf. vv. 14–15) even though they are **without the law** (they don't have the written laws of the OT). The Jews are not spared judgment simply because they possess the law (of the OT), for those who transgress the law will be **judged** for their transgressions.

2:13 Paul reaffirms the principle enunciated in vv. 6–11, that the **doers of the law** are the ones **who are righteous before God**, and that their justification **will be** pronounced on the last day.

2:14–16 Some have suggested that these verses speak of Gentile obedience that leads to salvation (cf. vv. 7, 10). It is clear, however, that Paul explains here why Gentiles **who do not have the law** will face judgment apart from the law (see v. 12). The reason it is fair for God to judge them for their evil is that God's law is **written on their hearts**, so that their consciences attest to what is right and what is wrong in their behavior. Paul does not imply that the testimony of human conscience is always a perfect moral guide (for people have **conflicting thoughts** about their moral behavior, sometimes excusing themselves from wrongdoing), but the very existence of this testimony is sufficient to render people accountable to God. (Elsewhere Paul indicates that people's consciences can be distorted by sin; see 1 Cor. 8:7, 10; 10:29; 1 Tim. 4:2; Titus 1:15.)

2:16 my gospel. Not Paul's alone, but the gospel that he preaches.

2:17–24 The Jews are indicted for failing to practice what they preach.

2:17–20 Paul details the privileges of the Jews as the elect people of God. Their advantages are genuine, for God has given them his law and hence they are able to instruct the Gentiles with the truths God revealed to them.

2:21–24 Paul zeros in on the main problem with the Jews. They fail to practice the law they proclaim, and hence they will face judgment. Their boast in God is nullified by their failure to obey him. Obviously, Paul is not accusing *all* Jews of stealing, committing adultery, and robbing temples. It is possible that Paul's critique of the Jews is similar to what Jesus taught in the Sermon on the Mount (Matt. 5:21–48), so that the Jews are criticized for not observing the true intent of the law. But it is more likely that Paul is speaking literally of Jewish disobedience, citing glaring examples to illustrate the principle that the Jews transgress the very law they treasure and teach.

2:22 rob temples. Robbing temples was a common crime in the ancient world because temples housed expensive articles that could be sold for profit. Since the law taught that temples were idolatrous and Jews should not be in them or treasuring things from them (see Deut. 7:25–26), the Jewish plun-

adultery, do you commit adultery? You who abhor idols, do you [i]rob temples? 23 You who [j]boast in the law [k]dishonor God by breaking the law. 24 For, [l]as it is written, "The name of God is blasphemed [m]among the Gentiles because of you."

25 For circumcision indeed is of value [n]if you obey the law, but if you break the law, your circumcision becomes uncircumcision. 26 So, if [o]a man who is uncircumcised keeps [p]the precepts of the law, will not his uncircumcision be regarded[1] as circumcision? 27 Then he who is physically[2] uncircumcised but keeps the law [q]will condemn you who have [r]the written code[3] and circumcision but break the law. 28 For [s]no one is a Jew [t]who is merely one outwardly, nor is circumcision outward and physical. 29 But a Jew is one [u]inwardly, and [v]circumcision is a matter of the heart, by the Spirit, not by the letter. [w]His praise is not from man but from God.

God's Righteousness Upheld

3 Then what advantage has the Jew? Or what is the value of circumcision? 2 Much in every way. To begin with, [x]the Jews were entrusted with [y]the oracles of God. 3 [z]What if some were unfaithful? [a]Does their faithlessness nullify the faithfulness of God? 4 By no means! [b]Let God be true though [c]every one were a liar, as it is written,

> [d]"That you may be justified in your words,
> and prevail when you [e]are judged."

5 But if our unrighteousness serves to show the righteousness of God, what shall we say? That God is unrighteous to inflict [f]wrath on us? ([g]I speak in a human way.) 6 By no means! For then how could [h]God judge the world? 7 But if through my lie God's truth abounds to his glory, [i]why am I still being condemned as a sinner? 8 And why not [j]do evil that good may come?—as some people slanderously charge us with saying. Their condemnation is just.

[1] *Or counted* [2] *Or is by nature* [3] *Or the letter*

22 [i]Acts 19:37; [Mal. 3:8]
23 [j]See ver. 17; ch. 3:27 [k][Mal. 1:6]
24 [l]Cited from Isa. 52:5 [m][2 Sam. 12:14; Ezek. 36:20, 23; 2 Pet. 2:2]
25 [n]Gal. 5:3
26 [o]Eph. 2:11; [ch. 3:30] [p]ch. 1:32; 8:4
27 [q]See Matt. 12:41 [r]ver. 29; ch. 7:6; 2 Cor. 3:6
28 [s]ch. 9:6-8; [Gal. 6:15] [t][ver. 17]
29 [u]See 1 Pet. 3:4 [v][Deut. 10:16; 30:6; Jer. 4:4; Acts 7:51; Phil. 3:3; Col. 2:11] [w]2 Cor. 10:18; 1 Thess. 2:4; [Gal. 1:10]

Chapter 3

2 [x]Deut. 4:8; Ps. 147:19, 20; See John 4:22 [y]See Acts 7:38
3 [z]ch. 10:16; Heb. 4:2 [a][ch. 9:6; 2 Tim. 2:13]
4 [b]See John 8:26 [c]Ps. 62:9; 116:11; [ver. 7] [d]Cited from Ps. 51:4 (Gk.) [e][Job 9:32]
5 [f][ch. 2:5] [g]ch. 6:19; 1 Cor. 9:8; Gal. 3:15; [1 Cor. 15:32]
6 [h][Gen. 18:25; Job 8:3]; See ch. 2:16
7 [i][ch. 9:19]
8 [j][ch. 6:1, 15]

dering of pagan temples would involve not just stealing but self-defilement as well.

2:24 Because they violated the law, the Jews were exiled by God and were therefore reviled by the Gentiles (Paul adapts phrases from the Septuagint translation of Isa. 52:5; cf. Ezek. 36:20–23). This dishonored God because they were known as his people. In Paul's time their sins did not lead to exile but still led Gentiles to dishonor the God whom the sinful Jews claimed to follow.

2:25 The Jews were inclined to believe that they would be spared at the last judgment by virtue of their circumcision. **Circumcision** was required of all Jewish males for entrance into the covenant (Gen. 17:9–14; Lev. 12:3), and hence it was likely viewed as a form of covenant protection. **uncircumcision**. Paul argues, however, that those who violate the law are counted before God as uncircumcised. In other words, they are outside the covenant and therefore destined for judgment. Circumcision would be of **value** (Gk, *ōpheleō*) for salvation if the circumcised would **obey the law** perfectly, but no one can do that. Paul takes up the issue of circumcision again in Rom. 4:9–16; Gal. 2:3–5; 5:2–12; 6:12–15.

2:26 On the other hand, an **uncircumcised** person who keeps the moral norms of the law will be counted as circumcised, i.e., a member of the covenant people.

2:27 And those (**uncircumcised**) Gentiles who keep the law will stand at the judgment and **condemn** (either literally or by the testimony of their good deeds) the Jews who had the covenantal advantages of the law (**the written code**) and circumcision.

2:28 Verses 28–29 function as the ground (**For**) of vv. 26–27. In striking contrast to the Jewish beliefs of his day, Paul claims that true Jewishness and genuine circumcision are not ethnic or physical matters.

2:29 True Jewishness and true circumcision are matters **of the heart**. They are the work of the Holy Spirit. The letter/Spirit contrast occurs three times in Paul (see also 7:6; 2 Cor. 3:6) and always compares the old era of redemptive history with the new age inaugurated by Jesus Christ. The law is described as **letter** because it cannot and does not transform anyone. The reference to the work of the **Spirit** demonstrates that the obedience described in Rom. 2:26–27 and in vv. 7, 10 is the result of the Spirit's work. Therefore, it is not the obedience of the unregenerate that is in view here but rather the obedience of those who, by the convicting work of the Holy Spirit, have repented of their hard hearts (v. 5), who have received the Holy Spirit, and who are being enabled by the Spirit to live a new life characterized by obedience to God.

3:1 After arguing that the Spirit's work in Gentiles renders them true Jews and the true circumcision, Paul raises the logical question of whether there is any **advantage** or **value** in being an ethnic Jew and physically circumcised. He probably means "value for salvation" since he uses a Greek noun (*ōpheleia*) that corresponds to the verb *ōpheleō* ("to give value, benefit") in 2:25.

3:2 One might expect Paul to answer that no advantage or "value" results from being Jews. Instead, he claims that the Jews have great advantages, consisting chiefly in possessing **the oracles of God**, which refers to the OT Scriptures and may focus (given what Paul says in the verses following) on God's promises to save Israel. On the **Jews** being **entrusted** with the oracles of God, see Deut. 4:8; 5:22–27; Ps. 147:20.

3:3–4 Even though the Jews were **unfaithful** and refused to trust and obey God, he remains faithful to them and therefore will fulfill his covenant promises, particularly his promise to save them. (Paul is speaking generally and does not mean that every single Jew will be saved; he further develops God's faithfulness to the Jews in chs. 9–11.) Since every person is a **liar** and a sinner, God is **justified**, i.e., vindicated in the justice of his judgment, especially (in this context) his judgment of unbelieving Jews.

3:5 Paul considers a false implication that could be drawn from his argument. If the Jews could repent only by God's grace, then it would be **unrighteous**, according to Paul's Jewish opponents, for God to pour out his wrath on those who did not repent, since as sinners they were unable to respond to him.

3:6 Paul does not provide a full answer to the objection here (for that, see chs. 9–11). He shows that the Jewish objector's position is untenable, for then God could not **judge the** (Gentile) **world** either, and no evil behavior would be punished.

3:7–8 Indeed, some of Paul's Jewish opponents insisted that he taught a doctrine of "cheap grace," i.e., that God receives more glory when Christians **do evil** and then are forgiven. Paul emphatically rejects such a view (as "slander") but waits until ch. 6 to examine this charge in more detail.

No One Is Righteous

[9]What then? Are we Jews[1] any better off?[2] No, not at all. For we have already charged
that all, both [k]Jews and [l]Greeks, are [m]under sin, [10]as it is written:

[n]"None is righteous, no, not one;
11 no one understands;
no one seeks for God.
12 All have turned aside; together they have become worthless;
no one does good,
not even one."
13 [o]"Their throat is [p]an open grave;
they use their tongues to deceive."
[q]"The venom of asps is under their lips."
14 [r]"Their mouth is full of curses and bitterness."
15 [s]"Their feet are swift to shed blood;
16 in their paths are ruin and misery,
17 and [t]the way of peace they have not known."
18 [u]"There is no fear of God before their eyes."

[19]Now we know that whatever [v]the law says it speaks to those who are under the law, [w]so
that every mouth may be stopped, and [x]the whole world may be held accountable to God.

[1] Greek *Are we* [2] Or *at any disadvantage?*

9[k]ch. 2:1-29 [l]ch. 1:18-32 [m]Gal. 3:22; [ver. 19, 23; ch. 11:32; Prov. 20:9] **10**[n]ver. 10-12, cited from Ps. 14:1-3; 53:1-3 **13**[o]Cited from Ps. 5:9 [p]Jer. 5:16 [q]Cited from Ps. 140:3 **14**[r]Cited from Ps. 10:7 (Gk.) **15**[s]Cited from Prov. 1:16; ver. 15-17, cited from Isa. 59:7, 8 **17**[t]Luke 1:79 **18**[u]Cited from Ps. 36:1 **19**[v]John 10:34; 15:25 [w]Job 5:16; Ps. 63:11; 107:42; Ezek. 16:63; [ch. 1:20; 2:1] [x]See ver. 9

3:9–20 *The Unrighteousness of All People.* The argument of the entire section, 1:18–3:20, is concluded here. Paul cites the OT to charge all with sin, both Jews and Gentiles, preparing the way for the claim that right standing with God is available only for those who trust in the atoning death of Christ.

OT Testimony that All Are under Sin (3:9)

Romans 3	OT Reference
Sinful Condition	
v. 10, none is righteous	Ps. 14:3/53:3; Eccles. 7:20
v. 11a, no one understands	Ps. 14:2/53:2
v. 11b, no one seeks for God	Ps. 14:2/53:2
v. 12, all have turned aside; together they have become worthless; no one does good, not even one	Ps. 14:3/53:3
Sinful Speech (note progression from throat to tongue to lips)	
v. 13a, b, their throat is an open grave; they use their tongues to deceive	Ps. 5:10 LXX (English, 5:9)
v. 13c, the venom of asps is under their lips	Ps. 140:3
v. 14, their mouth is full of curses and bitterness	Ps. 10:7
Sinful Action	
v. 15, their feet are swift to shed blood	Prov. 1:16/Isa. 59:7
v. 16, in their paths are ruin and misery	Isa. 59:7
v. 17, and the way of peace they have not known	Isa. 59:8
Summary Statement	
v. 18, there is no fear of God before their eyes	Ps. 36:1

3:9 Even though God has promised to fulfill his saving promises to the Jewish people (vv. 1–4), they do not possess any inherent advantages, for they too are **under** the power of **sin**. **Greeks** here refers to the entire Gentile world in contrast to the Jews.

3:10–12 Paul focuses on the sinfulness of every human being, citing Ps. 14:1–3 and perhaps echoing Eccles. 7:20. When Paul says **none is righteous, no one seeks for God**, and **no one does good**, he means that no human being on his own seeks for God or does any good that merits salvation. Paul does not deny that human beings perform some actions that conform externally to goodness, but these actions, prior to salvation, are still stained by evil, since they are not done for God's glory (Rom. 1:21) and do not come from faith (14:23).

3:13–14 Paul zeros in on sins of the tongue, quoting from Ps. 5:9 and 10:7. The reference to the **grave** highlights either the corruption of the heart or the deadly effects of sin. Human beings deceive through flattery or lying, and **the venom of asps** points to the poisonous effect of one's speech. Nor is evil speech merely occasional, for people's mouths are **full** of evil, so that cursing and malice characterize their lives before salvation.

3:15–17 Next Paul considers the impact of evil in terms of actions and in society, modifying and abridging Isa. 59:7–8. Human history is littered with murder and warfare. Sinners leave in their wake devastation, **ruin**, and **misery**. Instead of knowing peace (see note on Rom. 1:7) they have sown disorder and confusion into the world.

3:18 This citation from Ps. 36:1 identifies the root cause of sin as the failure to fear and honor God. Any society that commonly assumes that God will not discipline sin in this life or judge it in the next will have **no fear of God** and will therefore give itself increasingly to evil.

3:19–20 These verses represent the culmination and conclusion of vv. 9–18 and all of 1:18–3:20, showing that all, without exception, are sinners.

3:19 The **law** here, as is typically the case in Romans, refers to the Mosaic law. Those **under the law** are the Jews. But why is **every mouth** left without excuse and condemned before God if the law is addressed only to the Jews? Paul's logic is that if the Jews, who are God's special covenant people, cannot keep the law, then it follows that Gentiles, who are taught much of the law by their consciences, will not avoid God's condemnation either.

20 For [y]by works of the law no human being[1] will be justified in his sight, since [z]through
the law comes knowledge of sin.

The Righteousness of God Through Faith

21 But now [a]the righteousness of God [b]has been manifested apart from the law, although
[c]the Law and the Prophets bear witness to it— 22 the righteousness of God [d]through faith
in Jesus Christ for all who believe. [e]For there is no distinction: 23 for [f]all have sinned and fall
short of the glory of God, 24 [g]and are justified [h]by his grace as a gift, [i]through the redemption that is in Christ Jesus, 25 whom God [j]put forward as [k]a propitiation [l]by his blood, to be
received by faith. This was to show God's righteousness, because in [m]his divine forbearance
he had passed over [n]former sins. 26 It was to show his righteousness at the present time, so
that he might be just and the justifier of the one who has faith in Jesus.

27 [o]Then what becomes of our boasting? It is excluded. By what kind of law? By a law
of works? No, but by the law of faith. 28 For we hold that one is justified by faith [p]apart
from works of the law. 29 Or [q]is God the God of Jews only? Is he not the God of Gentiles
also? Yes, of Gentiles also, 30 since [r]God is one—who will justify the circumcised by faith
and [s]the uncircumcised through faith. 31 Do we then overthrow the law by this faith? By
no means! On the contrary, we uphold the law.

[1] Greek *flesh*

20 [y]Gal. 2:16; [Ps. 143:2; Acts 13:39] [z]ch. 7:7; [ch. 4:15; 5:13, 20]
21 [a]See ch. 1:17 [b]ch. 16:26; 2 Tim. 1:10 [c]Acts 10:43; [ch. 1:2; John 5:46]
22 [d]ch. 4:5; [2 Tim. 3:15] [e]ch. 10:12; [Gal. 3:28; Col. 3:11]
23 [f]See ver. 9
24 [g]Titus 3:7 [h]ch. 4:4, 5, 16; See Acts 15:11 [i]Eph. 1:7; Col. 1:14; Heb. 9:15; [1 Cor. 1:30]
25 [j]Eph. 1:9 [k]See 1 John 2:2 [l]ch. 5:9; Eph. 2:13 [m]ch. 2:4 [n][Acts 17:30]
27 [o]ch. 2:17, 23; 4:2; 1 Cor. 1:29-31; Eph. 2:9; 2 Tim. 1:9; See Acts 13:39
28 [p]See James 2:18
29 [q]ch. 9:24; 10:12; 15:9
30 [r]Gal. 3:20; [ch. 10:12] [s]Gal. 3:8; [ch. 4:9]; See ch. 2:26

3:20 Works of the law is understood by some to refer only to the ceremonial law, i.e., those laws that separate Jews from Gentiles (such as circumcision, food laws, and Sabbath). But the context gives no indication of such a restriction, and therefore the phrase should be taken to refer to all the works or deeds required by the law. The law required perfect obedience to God's will. All people sin and fall short of this standard, therefore no one is justified by the law. **Justified** is a legal term and indicates that no one will be declared to be righteous by God, who is the divine judge by virtue of his own goodness, since all violate and none fulfill God's requirements (see note on Gal. 2:16).

3:21–4:25 *The Saving Righteousness of God.* Since no one can be righteous before God by keeping the law, Paul now explains that right standing with God comes through faith in the atoning work of Jesus on the cross.

3:21–26 *God's Righteousness in the Death of Jesus.* God's saving righteousness has been manifested now in the death of Jesus Christ, so that God's justice and love are reconciled in the cross.

3:21 The righteousness of God has been manifested **now**, i.e., in the period of salvation history inaugurated through the death and resurrection of Jesus Christ. On the **righteousness of God**, see note on 1:17. Here in ch. 3 it refers to the morally right character of God that is clearly shown in his saving action by which human beings may stand in the right before God as the divine judge. This righteousness has been revealed **apart from the law**, which means that it is not based on human obedience to the works of the law. Paul may also intend to say it is not based on the Sinai covenant. Even though God's saving righteousness is apart from the law, **the Law and the Prophets bear witness to it**. In other words, the OT Scriptures prophesied this very way of salvation (see 1:2).

3:22 This right standing with God is available to **all who believe**, whether Jew or Gentile. On **the righteousness of God**, see note on 1:17.

3:23 No one can stake a claim to this righteousness based on his or her own obedience, for all people have sinned and fall short of what God demands (see 1:21).

3:24 Therefore, all are **justified** (declared not guilty but righteous by the divine Judge) only by God's **grace** (unmerited favor). The word **redemption** reaches back to the OT exodus and the blood of the Passover lamb (see Exodus 12–15), by which the Lord liberated Israel from Egypt; the exodus likewise points forward to the greater redemption Jesus won for his people through his blood by forgiving them their sins through his death on the cross (cf. Eph. 1:7; Col. 1:14). On justification, see note on Gal. 2:16.

3:25 Jesus' **blood** "propitiated" or satisfied God's wrath (1:18), so that his holiness was not compromised in forgiving sinners. Some scholars have argued that the word **propitiation** should be translated *expiation* (the wiping away of sin), but the word cannot be restricted to the wiping away of sins as it also refers to the satisfaction or appeasement of God's wrath, turning it to favor (cf. note on John 18:11). God's righteous anger needed to be appeased before sin could be forgiven, and God in his love sent his Son (who offered himself willingly) to satisfy God's holy anger against sin. In this way God demonstrated his **righteousness**, which here refers particularly to his holiness and justice. God's justice was called into question because in his patience he had overlooked **former** sins. In other words, how could God as the utterly Holy One tolerate human sin without inflicting full punishment on human beings immediately? Paul's answer is that God looked forward to the cross of Christ where the full payment for the guilt of sin would be made, where Christ would die in the place of sinners. In the OT, propitiation (or the complete satisfaction of the wrath of God) is symbolically foreshadowed in several incidents: e.g., Ex. 32:11–14; Num. 25:8, 11; Josh. 7:25–26.

3:26 Paul repeats again, because of its supreme importance, that God has demonstrated his **righteousness**, i.e., his holiness and justice, **at the present time** in salvation history. In the cross of Christ, God has shown himself to be **just** (utterly holy, so that the penalty demanded by the law is not removed but paid for by Christ) but also **the justifier** (the one who provides the means of justification and who declares people to be in right standing with himself) and the Savior of all those who trust in Jesus. Here is the heart of the Christian faith, for at the cross God's justice and love meet.

3:27–31 *Righteousness by Faith for Jews and Gentiles.* Both Jews and Gentiles obtain a right standing with God by faith alone.

3:27 Since salvation is accomplished through Christ's atoning death, all human **boasting . . . is excluded**. The word **law** in this verse probably means principle, though some think that a reference to the OT law is intended. If righteousness came through works, then human beings could brag about what they have done. But since salvation is through faith, no one can boast before God.

3:28 apart from. Justification is **by faith** alone and does not depend at all on doing any works of the law.

3:29–30 Since **God** is the Lord of all, whether **Jews** or **Gentiles**, there can only be one way of justification—by **faith**.

3:31 overthrow . . . uphold. Justification by faith does not nullify the law but establishes it. That is, the law itself points to the fact that human obedience to the law cannot save and that righteousness can be achieved only through faith in Christ; Christ has achieved this righteousness on behalf of all who believe in him, through his perfect fulfillment of the law and his atoning death on the cross for the salvation of all who believe. When Paul says, "we uphold the law," he also affirms the abiding moral norms of the law and thus anticipates the charge of antinomianism, to which he responds more fully in chs. 6 and 7.

Abraham Justified by Faith

4 What then shall we say was gained by[1] Abraham, [t]our forefather according to the flesh?
2 For if Abraham was justified by works, he has something to boast about, but [u]not
before God. 3 For what does the Scripture say? [v]"Abraham believed God, and it was counted
to him as righteousness." 4 Now [w]to the one who works, his wages are not counted as a gift
but as his due. 5 And to the one who does not work but [x]believes in[2] him who justifies the
ungodly, his faith is counted as righteousness, 6 just as David also speaks of the blessing
of the one to whom God counts righteousness apart from works:

7 [y]"Blessed are those whose lawless deeds are forgiven,
and whose sins are covered;
8 blessed is the man against whom the Lord will not [z]count his sin."

9 Is this blessing then only for [a]the circumcised, or also for the uncircumcised? [b]For we
say that faith was counted to Abraham as righteousness. 10 How then was it counted to
him? Was it before or after he had been circumcised? It was not after, but before he was
circumcised. 11 [c]He received the sign of circumcision as a seal of the righteousness that he
had by faith while he was still uncircumcised. The purpose was [d]to make him the father
of all who believe without being circumcised, so that righteousness would be counted
to them as well, 12 and to make him the father of the circumcised who are not merely
circumcised but who also walk in the footsteps of the faith that our father Abraham had
before he was circumcised.

The Promise Realized Through Faith

13 For [e]the promise to Abraham and his offspring [f]that he would be heir of the world
did not come through the law but through the righteousness of faith. 14 [g]For if it is the
adherents of the law who are to be the heirs, faith is null and the promise is void. 15 For
[h]the law brings wrath, but [i]where there is no law [j]there is no transgression.
16 That is why it depends on faith, [k]in order that the promise may rest on grace and [l]be
guaranteed to all his offspring—not only to the adherent of the law but also to the one
who shares the faith of Abraham, [m]who is the father of us all, 17 as it is written, [n]"I have

[1] Some manuscripts *say about* [2] Or *but trusts*; compare verse 24

Chapter 4
1 [t]ver. 16
2 [u][1 Cor. 1:31]
3 [v]ver. 9, 22; Gal. 3:6; James 2:23; Cited from Gen. 15:6 (Gk.); [Titus 3:8]
4 [w][ch. 11:6; Deut. 9:4, 5]
5 [x]ch. 3:22; See John 6:29
7 [y]Cited from Ps. 32:1, 2
8 [z]2 Cor. 5:19
9 [a]ch. 3:30 [b]ver. 3
11 [c]Gen. 17:10, 11 [d]ver. 12, 16; [ch. 3:22]; See Luke 19:9
13 [e]Gal. 3:16; Heb. 6:15, 17; 7:6; 11:9, 17; [ch. 9:8]; See Acts 13:32 [f]Gen. 17:4-6
14 [g]Gal. 3:17, 18
15 [h]ch. 7:7, 10-25; 2 Cor. 3:7, 9; Gal. 3:10 [i][ch. 3:20] [j]Gal. 3:19
16 [k]See ch. 3:24 [l]Gal. 3:22; [ch. 15:8] [m][ch. 9:8]
17 [n]Cited from Gen. 17:5; [ver. 18]

4:1–25 *Abraham as the Father of Jews and Gentiles.* Abraham is considered here as a test case for the view that justification is by faith alone. Abraham was the progenitor of the Jewish people, and hence his example is crucial for Paul's argument.

4:2 If Abraham stood in the right before God on the basis of his good works, then he could truly **boast**, since his obedience would function as the basis of his relationship with God. But Paul insists that Abraham could **not** boast **before God**.

4:3 The point of the previous verse is not that Abraham could boast before men. Instead, there was no basis for boasting at all, for Abraham stood in the right before God by believing, not by doing, as Gen. 15:6 proves.

4:4 Paul uses an example from everyday life. If salvation were based on **works**, then God, in granting a person salvation, would merely be repaying what he owed that person, just as an employer gives a worker **wages** for his work.

4:5 Under the gospel, however, works come under a completely different equation. **Righteousness** does not come to those who work for God, since all, like Abraham (Josh. 24:2), are by God's absolute standards **ungodly**. Rather, right-standing righteousness comes, as it did for Abraham, by believing in place of working.

4:6–8 Paul introduces **David** as a second example of righteousness by faith, citing Ps. 32:1–2 to demonstrate that David's **righteousness** (**"whose lawless deeds are forgiven, and whose sins are covered"**) was not based on his **works**.

4:9–10 Abraham was righteous before God (Gen. 15:6) before he was circumcised (Genesis 17), and therefore circumcision is unnecessary in order to belong to God.

4:11 Circumcision was the **sign** and **seal** of Abraham's righteousness that belonged to him by faith. In other words, circumcision documented and ratified the righteousness by faith that Abraham enjoyed before his circumcision.

4:13 The promise given to Abraham embraces not only the land of Canaan but also the whole **world**. The final reward (the inheritance, which is another term for final salvation) that will be given to Abraham and all believers is the world to come (cf. Heb. 11:10–16; Revelation 21–22).

4:14 If the inheritance is gained by observing the **law**, then righteousness is no longer by **faith** but by works. Faith and works are fundamentally opposed, for faith means trusting in or relying on a promise of God's work and not depending in any way on human performance.

4:15 Paul explains why one cannot be an heir through the law: human beings cannot keep the law, and they therefore face God's **wrath**. Paul uses the word **transgression** technically, so that it is distinguished from sin. Transgression is defined as the violation of a revealed command, which means that the Jews, who had the written law, had even greater responsibility for their sin and as great a need to be saved from God's wrath and justified by faith. (Paul elsewhere argues that sin also exists where no written law specifies the malfeasance; see 2:12, and note on 5:13).

4:16 That is why points to the special relationship between **faith** and **grace**: Faith means trusting in another, not in one's own efforts. Faith therefore corresponds exactly to grace, which involves trusting God's gift of unmerited favor. **The adherent of the law** refers to the Jewish believer in Christ.

4:17 many nations. Abraham's universal fatherhood is confirmed by Gen. 17:5. **Calls into existence the things that do not exist** underscores the doctrine of creation *ex nihilo* or "out of nothing." Before God created the universe (Gen. 1:1), only God existed, nothing else. Paul uses this general truth to affirm the great power of the God whom Abraham trusted: Abraham believed in a God who could raise the dead and summon into existence what did not exist (e.g., new life in Sarah's womb).

made you the father of many nations"—in the presence of the God in whom he believed,
[o]who gives life to the dead and calls into existence [p]the things that do not exist. 18 In hope
he believed against hope, that he should become the father of many nations, as he had
been told, [q]"So shall your offspring be." 19 He did not weaken in faith when he considered
his own body, which was [r]as good as dead ([s]since he was about a hundred years old), or
when he considered [t]the barrenness[1] of Sarah's womb. 20 No unbelief made him waver
concerning the promise of God, but he grew strong in his faith as he gave glory to God,
21 fully convinced that [u]God was able to do what he had promised. 22 That is why his faith
was "counted to him as righteousness." 23 But [v]the words "it was counted to him" were not
written for his sake alone, 24 but for ours also. It will be counted to us [w]who believe in [x]him
who raised from the dead Jesus our Lord, 25 [y]who was delivered up for our trespasses and
raised [z]for our justification.

Peace with God Through Faith

5 [a]Therefore, since we have been justified by faith, [b]we[2] have peace with God through
our Lord Jesus Christ. 2 Through him we have also [c]obtained access by faith[3] into this
grace [d]in which we stand, and [e]we[4] rejoice[5] in hope of the glory of God. 3 Not only that, but
we [f]rejoice in our sufferings, knowing that suffering [g]produces endurance, 4 and endurance produces character, and character produces hope, 5 and [h]hope does not put us to
shame, because God's love [i]has been poured into our hearts through the Holy Spirit who
has been given to us.

6 For [j]while we were still weak, at the right time [k]Christ died for the ungodly. 7 For one
will scarcely die for a righteous person—though perhaps for a good person one would
dare even to die— 8 but [l]God shows his love for us in that [m]while we were still sinners,
Christ died for us. 9 Since, therefore, [n]we have now been justified by his blood, much more
shall we be saved by him from [o]the wrath of God. 10 For if [p]while we were enemies [q]we

[1] Greek *deadness* [2] Some manuscripts *let us* [3] Some manuscripts omit *by faith* [4] Or *let us*; also verse 3 [5] Or *boast*; also verses 3, 11

17 [o][Heb. 11:19]; See John 5:21 [p]1 Cor. 1:28; [Heb. 11:3]
18 [q]Cited from Gen. 15:5
19 [r]Heb. 11:12 [s]Gen. 17:17 [t]Gen. 18:11
21 [u]Gen. 18:14; [Heb. 11:19]
23 [v]ch. 15:4; 1 Cor. 9:9, 10; 10:6, 11; 2 Tim. 3:16, 17; [Ps. 102:18]
24 [w]ch. 10:9; 1 Pet. 1:21 [x]See Acts 2:24
25 [y]ch. 5:6, 8; 8:32; Isa. 53:5, 6; Matt. 20:28; Gal. 1:4 [z]ch. 5:18; [1 Cor. 15:17]

Chapter 5

1 [a]ch. 3:28 [b][ch. 15:13; Heb. 12:28]
2 [c]Eph. 2:18; 3:12; [Heb. 10:19, 20; 1 Pet. 3:18] [d]1 Cor. 15:1 [e]ver. 11; Heb. 3:6; [ch. 12:12]
3 [f]See Matt. 5:12 [g]See Luke 21:19; James 1:3
5 [h]Ps. 119:116; Phil. 1:20 [i]Acts 2:17, 18, 33; Titus 3:6; [Gal. 4:6]
6 [j]ver. 8, 10; [Hos. 13:9; Eph. 2:5] [k]See ch. 4:25
8 [l]See John 3:16 [m]ver. 6, 10
9 [n]See ch. 3:25 [o]1 Thess. 1:10; 2:16; See ch. 1:18
10 [p]ver. 6, 8; Col. 1:21; [ch. 8:32] [q]2 Cor. 5:18-20; Eph. 2:16; Col. 1:20, 21

4:19 Abraham squarely faced the fact that he and Sarah were too old to have children.

4:20–21 Abraham's faith actually increased as the time of waiting went on: **he grew strong in his faith as he gave glory to God**. He continued trusting that God could be relied on to do what he had promised, and as Abraham trusted God, he honored and glorified him.

4:23–24 Paul applies Gen. 15:6 to his readers. **but for ours also**. Paul sees that, in God's plan, Scriptures as far back as Genesis were written also for the benefit of Christians in the new covenant age.

4:25 Both the death and resurrection of Jesus Christ are necessary for forgiveness of sins and justification. **raised for our justification**. When God the Father raised Christ from the dead, it was a demonstration that he accepted Christ's suffering and death as full payment for sin, and that the Father's favor, no longer his wrath against sin, was directed toward Christ, and through Christ toward those who believe. Since Paul sees Christians as united with Christ in his death and resurrection (6:6, 8–11; Eph. 2:6; Col. 2:12; 3:1), God's approval of Christ at the resurrection results in God's approval also of all who are united to Christ, and in this way results in their "justification."

5:1–8:39 *Hope as a Result of Righteousness by Faith.* The central theme of chs. 5–8 is that believers in Christ, who are righteous in God's sight, have a certain hope of future glory and life eternal.

5:1–11 *Assurance of Hope.* Those who are justified by faith have an unshakable hope, knowing they will be saved from God's wrath on the day of judgment by virtue of Christ's substitutionary death on their behalf.

5:1 Therefore, since we have been justified. Chapter 5 begins with a ringing affirmation of the objective legal standing of the Christian—that the Christian, through faith in Christ, *has been* justified and declared righteous by God, once for all. The result of this is that the Christian no longer lives under the fear of judgment and the wrath of God but has **peace with God**, which is not merely a subjective feeling but an objective reality. See also note on John 14:27.

5:2 The **grace in which we stand** refers to the secure position of the believer's standing (as a blessing of justification), and the **hope of the glory of God** refers to the promise that Christians will be glorified and perfected at the last day—a hope that results in joy.

5:3–4 The people of God rejoice not only in future glory but in present trials and **sufferings**, not because trials are pleasant but because they produce a step-by-step transformation that makes believers more like Christ.

5:5 Followers of Christ have no reason to fear humiliation on the judgment day, for they now belong to God. Indeed, they know that they have received **God's love** because the Holy Spirit **poured** his love into their hearts at conversion.

5:6 In this and the following verses, Paul grounds the subjective experience of God's love (v. 5) in the objective work of Christ on the cross. **Weak** here denotes lack of moral strength and is parallel to **ungodly**.

5:7–8 On rare occasions, even a human being will die for a **righteous** (morally upright) **person** or for a **good person** (one who has done much good). God's love, however, belongs in an entirely different category from human love, for Christ did not die for righteous people or those who have done good for others but for **sinners**, that is, for ungodly, unrighteous people living in willful rebellion against God. It is not just Christ's love that was shown in his death but also **God** the Father's **love**. While God's righteousness and justice led to his plan of salvation through the death of Christ (see 3:25–26), it was his love that motivated this plan.

5:9 Christians are now **justified** (declared to be in the right before God) by virtue of Christ's **blood**, that is, his blood poured out in his death on the cross. Therefore, they can be sure that they will be saved on the day of judgment from God's **wrath**.

5:10 As in v. 9, Paul argues from the greater to the lesser, though here he speaks in terms of reconciliation (the language of friendship) rather than justification (a legal term). Since Christians are now **reconciled** to God through Christ's death, they can be assured that they will be **saved** on the day to come (here "saved," Gk. *sōzō*, includes not only justification at the start of the Christian life but also completed sanctification, glorification, freedom from final condemnation, and future rewards). But here the salvation is based on **his life**. The reference is to Christ's resurrection, showing that both the death and resurrection of Christ are necessary for salvation (see 4:25). Chapter 6 will develop the theme of union with Christ in his resurrection life.

were reconciled to God by the death of his Son, much more, now that we are reconciled,
shall we be saved by [r]his life. 11 More than that, we also rejoice in God through our Lord
Jesus Christ, through whom we have now received [s]reconciliation.

Death in Adam, Life in Christ

12 Therefore, just as [t]sin came into the world through one man, and [u]death through sin,
and [v]so death spread to all men[1] because [w]all sinned— 13 for sin indeed was in the world
before the law was given, but [x]sin is not counted where there is no law. 14 Yet death reigned
from Adam to Moses, even over those whose sinning was not [y]like the transgression of
Adam, [z]who was a type of [a]the one who was to come.

15 But the free gift is not like the trespass. For if many died through one man's trespass,
much more have the grace of God and the free gift by the grace of that one man Jesus
Christ abounded for [b]many. 16 And the free gift is not like the result of that one man's sin.
For [c]the judgment following one trespass brought condemnation, but the free gift following many trespasses brought [d]justification. 17 For if, because of one man's trespass, death
reigned through that one man, much more will those who receive the abundance of grace
and the free gift of righteousness [e]reign in life through the one man Jesus Christ.

18 Therefore, as one trespass[2] led to condemnation for all men, so one act of righteousness[3] leads to justification and life for [f]all men. 19 For as by the one man's [g]disobedience
the many were made sinners, so by the one man's [h]obedience the many will be made

[1] The Greek word *anthropoi* refers here to both men and women; also twice in verse 18 [2] Or *the trespass of one* [3] Or *the act of righteousness of one*

10 [r]2 Cor. 4:10, 11
11 [s]ch. 11:15; 2 Cor. 5:18, 19
12 [t]Gen. 2:17; 3:6; 1 Cor. 15:21, 22; [ver. 15-17; ch. 6:9; Ps. 51:5] [u]ch. 6:23; James 1:15 [v][ver. 14, 21; 1 Cor. 15:22] [w]Eph. 2:3
13 [x]See ch. 3:20
14 [y]Hos. 6:7 [z]1 Cor. 15:45 [a][Matt. 11:3]
15 [b]ver. 19; Isa. 53:11
16 [c]1 Cor. 11:32 [d]ver. 18
17 [e]Rev. 22:5
18 [f]See John 12:32
19 [g][2 Cor. 10:6] [h]Heb. 5:8; [Phil. 2:8]

5:11 Christians go beyond avoiding God's wrath and actually **rejoice** in the same God who would pour out wrath on them (v. 9) were it not for Christ.

5:12–21 *Hope in Christ's Triumph over Adam's Sin.* The main theme of this section continues to be the future hope of those who have trusted in Christ. Adam brought sin and death into the world, but those who have believed in Christ are full of hope, for Christ has reversed the consequences of Adam's sin and has given his own life and righteousness to secure their eternal glory. The extended parallel between the one man Adam's sin and the one man Christ's obedience shows that Paul considered Adam a historical person, not a fictional or mythological character; it also shows the importance of insisting on the historicity of Adam today (cf. 1 Cor. 15:22, 45–49). These verses also show that Adam had a leadership role with respect to the human race that Eve did not have, for even though Eve sinned by eating the forbidden fruit before Adam did so (Gen. 3:6), it was "one man's trespass," that is, Adam's sin, through which "sin came into the world" (Rom. 5:12) and through which "many died" (v. 15), "death reigned" (v. 17), and "many were made sinners" (v. 19).

5:12 Sin came into the world through one man, namely, Adam (v. 14; cf. Gen. 3:17–19; 1 Cor. 15:21–22; also note on Gen. 5:3–5). **And death through sin** is contrary to secular thought that regards death as a "natural" part of human life. In the biblical sense, death is never natural but is "the last enemy" (1 Cor. 15:26; cf. 15:54) that will be conquered finally and forever at the return of Christ (Rev. 21:4). **Death** in these verses most likely denotes both physical death and spiritual death together (Paul often connects the two). Most evangelical interpreters think that **and so** means "and in this way," and the phrase **all sinned** means that all sinned in Adam's sin because he represented all who would descend from him (just as Christ's obedience would count for all his followers, whom he represented, Rom. 5:15–19). Another interpretation is that all sinned personally because they were born into the world spiritually dead. The word translated **men** is the Greek word *anthrōpos*, which in the plural can mean either "people" of both sexes or "men," depending on the context (see ESV footnote). It is translated "men" here (and in v. 18) to show the connection with "man" (*anthrōpos*, singular), referring to Christ.

5:13 Sin **was in the world** before the Mosaic law was instituted, but it was not technically reckoned as sin before the time of the law. Paul does not mean that people were guiltless without the law, for he has already said in 2:12 that those without the written law are still judged by God (e.g., those who perished in the flood [Genesis 6–9] and those who were judged at the tower of Babel [Gen. 11:1–9]). Since people still died, this shows that they were guilty—as a consequence of Adam's sin but possibly also as a consequence of having transgressed the universal moral law in their consciences before the written Mosaic law was given.

5:14 Those who did not live under the law were still judged for their sin, since death held sway over them. Still, their **sinning was not like the transgression of Adam**, since Adam violated a commandment specifically revealed to him by God. Adam is a **type** (model, pattern; Gk. *typos*) of Christ, for both Adam and Christ are covenantal heads of the human race, so that all people are either "in Adam" or "in Christ" (cf. 1 Cor. 15:22). All are in Adam by physical birth, while only those with the new birth are in Christ.

5:15 Paul contrasts the consequences of the work of Adam and of Christ five times in the next five verses, showing their decisive roles as covenantal heads of the people they represent. Paul clearly teaches "original sin," the fact that all people inherit a sinful nature because of Adam's sin. Paul probably is also teaching that all people are in fact guilty before God because of Adam's sin. **Many** (i.e., all human beings excluding Christ) **died** through Adam's one sin. Death begins with spiritual separation from God and culminates in physical death. By contrast Paul emphasizes the lavishness of Christ's grace bestowed on the many that belong to him.

5:16 Again the astonishing depth of God's grace in Christ is featured. The **one trespass** of Adam resulted in the **condemnation** of all, but Christ overcame the flood of sin that overwhelmed the world, so that all who belong to him enjoy **justification**.

5:17 Death ruled the human race by virtue of the one sin of Adam, whereas Christians now stand as rulers because of the work of Christ.

5:18 The **one trespass** of Adam, as the covenantal head of the human race, brought condemnation and guilt to all people. In a similar way, Christ's **one act of righteousness** (either his death as such or his whole life of perfect obedience, including his death) grants righteousness and life to all who belong to him. **for all men**. Some interpreters have advocated universalism (the view that all will be saved) based on these verses. But Paul makes it plain in this context that only those who "receive" (v. 17) God's gift belong to Christ (see also 1:16–5:11, which indicates that only those who have faith will be justified). The wording **"as . . . so"** shows that Paul's focus is not on the number in each group but on the *method* of either sin or righteousness being passed from the representative leader to the whole group: the first "all men" refers to all who are in Adam (every human being), while the second "all men" refers to all believers, to all who are "in Christ." On the translation "men," see note on 5:12.

5:19 Because of Adam's disobedience, all people **were made** (Gk. *kathistēmi*, "cause[d] to be") **sinners**. Thus, when Adam as mankind's representative sinned, God *regarded* the whole human race as guilty sinners, thereby imputing Adam's guilt to everyone. In other words, God regarded Adam's guilt as belonging to the whole human race, while also *declaring* that Adam's guilt does in fact belong to all. All are therefore sinners, and are born with a sinful nature that is set in the mold of Adam's transgression.

20[i]Gal. 3:19; See ch. 3:20 [j]1 Tim. 1:14
21[k][ver. 12, 14] [l]See John 1:17

Chapter 6
1[m]ver. 15; [ch. 3:8]
2[n]ver. 11; ch. 7:4, 6; Gal. 2:19; Col. 2:20; 3:3; 1 Pet. 2:24
3[o]Gal. 3:27 [p]See Matt. 28:19
4[q]Col. 2:12 [r]ver. 9; ch. 8:11; See Acts 2:24 [s][John 11:40; 2 Cor. 13:4] [t]2 Cor. 5:17; Gal. 6:15; Eph. 4:23, 24; Col. 3:10; [ch. 7:6]
5[u][2 Cor. 4:10] [v]Phil. 3:10, 11; [Col. 2:12; 3:1]
6[w]Eph. 4:22; Col. 3:9 [x]Gal. 2:20; 5:24; 6:14 [y][ch. 7:24]
7[z]1 Pet. 4:1 [a][ver. 18]
8[b]2 Tim. 2:11; [2 Cor. 4:10; 13:4]
9[c]Acts 13:34; Rev. 1:18 [d][ch. 5:14, 17]
10[e]See Heb. 7:27
11[f]See ver. 2
12[g]ver. 14; Ps. 19:13; 119:133; Mic. 7:19; [2 Cor. 5:17]
13[h]ch. 7:5; Col. 3:5 [i]ch. 12:1; 1 Pet. 2:24; 4:2
14[j][ch. 8:2, 12] [k]See ver. 12
15[l]ver. 1 [m][1 Cor. 9:21]
16[n][ver. 20; Matt. 6:24]; See John 8:34

righteous. **20** Now [i]the law came in to increase the trespass, but where sin increased, [j]grace
abounded all the more, **21** so that, [k]as sin reigned in death, [l]grace also might reign through
righteousness leading to eternal life through Jesus Christ our Lord.

Dead to Sin, Alive to God

6 What shall we say then? [m]Are we to continue in sin that grace may abound? **2** By no
means! How can [n]we who died to sin still live in it? **3** Do you not know that all of us
[o]who have been baptized [p]into Christ Jesus were baptized into his death? **4** We were [q]buried
therefore with him by baptism into death, in order that, just as [r]Christ was raised from
the dead by [s]the glory of the Father, we too might walk in [t]newness of life.
5 For [u]if we have been united with him in [v]a death like his, we shall certainly be united
with him in a resurrection like his. **6** We know that [w]our old self[1] [x]was crucified with him
in order that [y]the body of sin might be brought to nothing, so that we would no longer
be enslaved to sin. **7** For [z]one who has died [a]has been set free[2] from sin. **8** Now [b]if we have
died with Christ, we believe that we will also live with him. **9** We know that [c]Christ, being
raised from the dead, will never die again; [d]death no longer has dominion over him. **10** For
the death he died he died to sin, [e]once for all, but the life he lives he lives to God. **11** So you
also must consider yourselves [f]dead to sin and alive to God in Christ Jesus.
12 Let not [g]sin therefore reign in your mortal body, to make you obey its passions. **13** [h]Do
not present your members to sin as instruments for unrighteousness, but [i]present yourselves to God as those who have been brought from death to life, and your members to
God as instruments for righteousness. **14** For [j]sin [k]will have no dominion over you, since
you are not under law but under grace.

Slaves to Righteousness

15 What then? [l]Are we to sin [m]because we are not under law but under grace? By no
means! **16** Do you not know that if you present yourselves [n]to anyone as obedient slaves,[3]

[1] Greek *man* [2] Greek *has been justified* [3] For the contextual rendering of the Greek word *doulos*, see Preface (twice in this verse and verse 19; also once in verses 17, 20

5:20 The typical Jewish view in Paul's day was that God gave the law to counteract the sinful human impulse. In Judaism there was the proverb, "The more Torah the more life" (Mishnah, *Aboth* 2.7). But Paul points out that the law came in **to increase the trespass**, probably in the sense that once people had written laws from God, they committed not just "sins" against God's law in their conscience, but, even more seriously, willful "trespasses" (Gk. *paraptōma*), like Adam's first "trespass" against a clear spoken command directly from God (cf. note on Rom. 4:15). Hence, the surpassing excellence of Christ's salvation is shown in that **grace abounded** even **more** than these increasing sins.

6:1–23 *The Triumph of Grace over the Power of Sin.* The law does not and cannot conquer sin, but the grace given to followers of Christ triumphs over sin and death.

6:1 Paul is likely responding to a question posed regularly by his Jewish opponents. They did not raise this question so that they would have an excuse to sin, though in every age some have wrongly interpreted and applied Paul's gospel of grace to rationalize sin. Instead, Paul's opponents argued that his gospel must be mistaken since, in their view, it led people to **continue in sin**. Paul will now show why their interpretation of his gospel is mistaken.

6:2 Paul's gospel does not lead to more sin, since those who belong to Christ have **died to sin** (as explained in the following verses).

6:3 Christians died to sin when they were **baptized into Christ**. Paul is not arguing that baptism magically destroys the power of sin. Baptism is an outward, physical symbol of the inward, spiritual conversion of Christians.

6:4 In the early church, baptism was probably by immersion, at least as a general rule, though Christians dispute whether such a practice must always be followed literally today. Therefore, baptism pictures a person being **buried** with Christ (submersion under water) and being **raised** to new life with Christ (emergence from water). This symbolizes the person's union with, and incorporation into, Christ by the action of the Holy Spirit. Hence, they now have the power to live in **newness** of life.

6:6 The power of sin has been broken in those who believe, for their **old self** (lit., "old man," meaning who they were in Adam) **was crucified** and put to death with Christ. They were born into the world as sinners, with the result that their bodies were ruled by sin. **Body of sin** refers to the rule of sin, but without excluding the involvement of the personal self that lives through the body. Sin's rule, however, was broken when Christians died with Christ, and therefore they are no longer **enslaved to sin**. Paul does not argue that Christians do not sin at all (a view called sinless perfection); instead, the tyranny, domination, and rule of sin have been defeated for them. This means that the normal pattern of life for Christians should be progressive growth in sanctification, resulting in ever greater maturity and conformity to God's moral law in thought and action.

6:7 One who has died means one who has died with Christ.

6:10 died to sin. Jesus died because he took sin upon himself, but his resurrection demonstrates that he has defeated both sin and death.

6:11 Dead to sin means dead to the pervasive love for and ruling power of sin. Christians must realize that the mastery of sin has been broken in their lives (see note on v. 6).

6:12–13 The tension surfaces here between what God has already accomplished and the responsibility of his people to obey. They are still tempted by desires to sin and must not let those desires gain control. Each day they must give themselves afresh to God.

6:14 sin will have no dominion over you. This is not a command but a promise that sin will not triumph in the lives of Christians. Because they live in the new era of fulfillment, they are no longer under the old era of redemptive history; that is, they are no longer **under law**, where the Mosaic law and sin ruled over God's people. By contrast, **under grace** means living under the new covenant in Christ, in an era characterized by grace (cf. 3:24; 4:16; 5:2, 15–21).

6:15–23 The question posed in v. 1 is now explored from another angle, that is, shall a Christian continue to sin because sin's power over him is broken (v. 11) and thus there is little danger in sinning?

6:15 Paul emphatically rejects the idea that freedom from the old covenant era of being **under law** implies freedom to sin.

6:16 Moral decisions still matter for Christians. Giving in to sin results in

you are slaves of the one whom you obey, either of sin, which leads to death, or of obedience, which leads to righteousness? 17 But [o]thanks be to God, that you who were once
slaves of sin have become obedient from the heart to the [p]standard of teaching to which
you were committed, 18 and, [q]having been set free from sin, [r]have become slaves of righteousness. 19 [s]I am speaking in human terms, because of your natural limitations. For [t]just
as you once presented your members as slaves to impurity and to lawlessness leading
to more lawlessness, so now present your members [u]as slaves to righteousness leading
to sanctification.

20 [v]For when you were slaves of sin, you were free in regard to righteousness. 21 [w]But
what fruit were you getting at that time from the things [x]of which you are now ashamed?
[y]For the end of those things is death. 22 But now that you [z]have been set free from sin and
[a]have become slaves of God, [b]the fruit you get leads to sanctification and [c]its end, eternal
life. 23 [d]For the wages of sin is death, but the free gift of God is eternal life in Christ Jesus
our Lord.

Released from the Law

7 Or do you not know, brothers[1]—for I am speaking to those who know the law—that
the law is binding on a person only as long as he lives? 2 For [e]a married woman is bound
by law to her husband while he lives, but if her husband dies she is released from the law
of marriage.[2] 3 Accordingly, [f]she will be called an adulteress if she lives with another man
while her husband is alive. But if her husband dies, she is free from that law, and if she
marries another man she is not an adulteress.

4 Likewise, my brothers, [g]you also have died [h]to the law [i]through the body of Christ,
so that you may belong to another, to him who has been raised from the dead, [j]in order
that we may bear fruit for God. 5 For while we were living in the flesh, our sinful passions,
aroused by the law, were at work [k]in our members [l]to bear fruit for death. 6 But now we
are released from the law, having died to that which held us captive, so that we serve in
the [m]new way of [n]the Spirit and not in the old way of the written code.[3]

The Law and Sin

7 What then shall we say? That the law is sin? By no means! Yet if it had not been for
the law, [o]I would not have known sin. For I would not have known what it is to covet if

[1] Or *brothers and sisters*; also verse 4 [2] Greek *law concerning the husband* [3] Greek *of the letter*

17 [o]See ch. 1:8 [p][2 Tim. 1:13]
18 [q]ver. 22; ch. 8:2; [ver. 7]; See John 8:32 [r][ver. 22]
19 [s]See ch. 3:5 [t]See ver. 13 [u][1 Cor. 9:27]
20 [v]See ver. 16
21 [w]ch. 7:5; [Jer. 12:13] [x][2 Cor. 4:2] [y]ch. 1:32; 8:6, 13; Prov. 14:12; Gal. 6:8
22 [z]See ver. 18 [a]1 Cor. 7:22; 1 Pet. 2:16 [b]ch. 7:4 [c]1 Pet. 1:9
23 [d][ch. 2:7]; See ch. 5:12

Chapter 7

2 [e]1 Cor. 7:39
3 [f]Matt. 5:32
4 [g]ver. 6; See ch. 6:2 [h]ch. 8:2; Gal. 2:19; 5:18; Eph. 2:15; Col. 2:14 [i][Eph. 2:16; Col. 1:22] [j]ch. 6:22; Gal. 5:22; Eph. 5:9
5 [k]ch. 6:13 [l]See ch. 6:21, 23
6 [m]See ch. 6:4 [n]ch. 2:27, 29; 2 Cor. 3:6
7 [o]See ch. 3:20

people increasingly becoming **obedient slaves** to sin. (For a brief description of ancient slavery, see note on 1 Cor. 7:21.) This kind of activity eventually **leads to death**, not implying that genuine believers can actually lose their salvation but that sinning leads them in that direction, away from full enjoyment of life with Christ (cf. note on Gal. 5:4). Those who give themselves utterly to sin will die (face eternal punishment).

6:17–18 True Christians, however, will never live as slaves to sin, for God has transformed their hearts at conversion, so that they will now grow in their love of righteousness and in living according to God's Word.

6:19 Although Paul acknowledges that the illustration from slavery is imperfect, it nonetheless stresses the importance of giving oneself wholly to God rather than to sin.

6:20–21 When the readers were unbelievers, they were totally captivated by sin, and the end result of such sin is death (physical and spiritual death are probably both in view here). Sin always brings destructive results in people's lives.

6:22 Christians have a new status and a new destiny.

6:23 Those who give themselves to sin will die both physically and eternally, whereas Christians are assured of eternal life. **Wages** implies that the punishment for sin is what one has earned and what one deserves. **Free gift** is the opposite of something one deserves, which fits Paul's earlier emphasis on justification by grace alone (God's unmerited favor; see note on 4:16), through faith alone (trusting in Christ for justification; see 1:17; 3:21–4:25).

7:1–6 *The Triumph of Grace over the Power of the Law.* The law does not and cannot bring victory over sin and death since sin is defined and even promoted through the law. But those who have died with Christ are set free from sin and the law.

7:1–3 As in this entire chapter, **law** refers to the Mosaic law given at Mount Sinai. **Those who know the law** includes both Jews and Gentiles who are familiar with the OT. Verse 1 introduces the principle, worked out in the following verses, that the law is in force only while a person is alive. In vv. 2–3, Paul applies the principle to marriage. A married woman who lives with another man is subject to the law regarding adultery only if her husband is still living.

7:4 The principle and illustration from vv. 1–3 are applied to the readers in vv. 4–6. Whereas the *husband* dies in the illustration of vv. 2–3, here *believers* die to the law through the death of *Christ*; the analogy does not match perfectly, but the application is clear.

7:5 Flesh here stands for the old "Adam"—the unregenerate former life of those who now believe. The law, contrary to the view of contemporary Judaism (cf. note on 5:20), did not bring life. Instead it stimulated sin and led to death. Although sin leads to **death** (cf. 6:23), in Christ there is life (John 14:6; 1 John 5:12; cf. Prov. 1:19).

7:6 But now represents the new era of redemptive history. Christians are free from the Mosaic law and now enjoy new life in the Spirit.

7:7–25 *The Law and Sin.* The claim that the Mosaic law produced sin and death raises the question, Is the law itself sinful? In this section Paul explains that the law itself is good and that the fault lies with sin. Interpreters differ as to whether the "I" in these verses is describing (1) unregenerate people who try to keep the law, or (2) believers who, despite being regenerated, find themselves still beset by sinful desires. The second view is more widely held (cf. note on 7:13–25).

7:7 The law defines sin and also provokes sin. Confronted by the law, sin takes on the character of rebellion, so that people enjoy transgressing commands in

[p]the law had not said, "You shall not covet." **8** But sin, [q]seizing an opportunity through
the commandment, produced in me all kinds of covetousness. [r]For apart from the law,
sin lies dead. **9** I was once alive apart from the law, but when the commandment came, sin
came alive and I died. **10** The very commandment [s]that promised life proved to be death
to me. **11** For sin, [t]seizing an opportunity through the commandment, [u]deceived me and
through it killed me. **12** So [v]the law is holy, and the commandment is holy and righteous
and good.

13 Did that which is good, then, bring death to me? By no means! It was sin, producing death in me through what is good, in order that sin might be shown to be sin, and
through the commandment might become sinful beyond measure. **14** For we know that
the law is spiritual, but I am of the flesh, [w]sold under sin. **15** For I do not understand my
own actions. For [x]I do not do what I want, but I do the very thing I hate. **16** Now if I do
what I do not want, I agree with [y]the law, that it is good. **17** So now [z]it is no longer I who
do it, but sin that dwells within me. **18** For I know that nothing good dwells [a]in me,
that is, in my flesh. For I have the desire to do what is right, but not the ability to carry
it out. **19** [b]For I do not do the good I want, but the evil I do not want is what I keep on
doing. **20** Now if I do what I do not want, [c]it is no longer I who do it, but sin that dwells
within me.

21 So I find it to be a law that when I want to do right, evil lies close at hand. **22** For [d]I
delight in the law of God, [e]in my inner being, **23** but I see in my members [f]another law
waging war against the law of my mind and making me captive to the law of sin that
dwells in my members. **24** Wretched man that I am! Who will deliver me from [g]this body
of death? **25** Thanks be to God through Jesus Christ our Lord! So then, I myself serve the
law of God with my mind, but with my flesh I serve the law of sin.

7 [p]ch. 13:9; Ex. 20:17; Deut. 5:21
8 [q]ver. 11; [Gal. 5:13] [r]1 Cor. 15:56
10 [s]See ch. 10:5
11 [t]ver. 8 [u][Gen. 3:13; Heb. 3:13]
12 [v]Ps. 19:8, 9; 119:137; 2 Pet. 2:21; [ver. 16]
14 [w]1 Kgs. 21:20, 25; 2 Kgs. 17:17; Isa. 50:1; 52:3
15 [x]ver. 18, 19; [Gal. 5:17]
16 [y]1 Tim. 1:8; [ver. 12]
17 [z]ver. 20
18 [a]Gen. 6:5; 8:21; Job 14:4; 15:14; Ps. 51:5
19 [b]ver. 15
20 [c]ver. 17
22 [d]Ps. 1:2; 112:1; 119:35 [e]2 Cor. 4:16; Eph. 3:16; [1 Pet. 3:4]
23 [f]Gal. 5:17; [James 4:1]
24 [g][ch. 6:6; 8:23]

order to demonstrate their independence. This principle is illustrated from the tenth commandment, which prohibits coveting (Ex. 20:17).

7:8 The prohibition against coveting exacerbated the desire for what was forbidden. **Sin lies dead** means that sin was latent rather than nonexistent.

7:9 If the verse relates to Paul, he is speaking of his subjective experience. If it relates to Adam, it refers to his relationship with God before he sinned. The prohibition against coveting stimulated the desire to sin, and sin in turn led to death.

7:10–11 God's commands promise eternal **life** if one keeps them; and yet they lead to **death**, since everyone violates what God ordains. This happens when sin deceives a person and uses the law as its instrument.

7:12 In light of vv. 7–11, Paul affirms the holiness of the law and the goodness of God's commands.

7:13–25 If the law is not sin, is it the case that the good law is responsible for death? Paul argues that the fault lies with sin, not with the law. Through the law, sin is revealed in all its hideousness, and the law is vindicated as good. The section can be subdivided into vv. 14–17, 18–20, and 21–25. A long-standing debate centers on whether Paul is describing believers or unbelievers. Although good arguments are given by both sides, the most widely held view—beginning especially with Augustine and reaffirmed in the Reformation—is that Paul's primary reference is to *believers*. In support of this position: (1) the shift to the present tense; (2) unbelievers do not desire so intensely to keep God's law (v. 21); (3) the distinction between the "I" and the "flesh" (v. 18); (4) the delight in God's law (v. 22); (5) deliverance from the sinful body is future (v. 24; 8:10, 11, 23); (6) the tension between good and evil in the concluding statement in 7:25; and (7) the fact that Christians are already righteous in Christ but are not yet perfected until the day of redemption. A second position, not as widely held but supported by a number of evangelical scholars, is that Paul is referring to *unbelievers*. In support of this position: (1) the structure of the passage (vv. 7–25 matches the life of the unregenerate previewed in v. 5, whereas 8:1–17 fits with the life of believers identified in 7:6); (2) the Holy Spirit is not mentioned in vv. 13–25 but is referred to 19 times in ch. 8; (3) to say that Christians are "sold under sin" (7:14) and "captive to the law of sin" (v. 23) stands in tension with chs. 6 and 8, which trumpet the freedom of believers from slavery to sin; (4) the suggestion that the present tense does not denote present time but the spiritual state of Paul when unconverted; (5) the desire to keep God's law reflects the mind-set of the pious Jew who wanted to live a moral life (as the verses emphasize, such people do not and cannot keep the law); and (6) the section's opening verse (v. 13) explains how the law brought death to Paul as an unbeliever. Advocates of both positions agree that (1) Christians still struggle with sin through their whole lives (see Gal. 5:17; 1 John 1:8–9); and (2) Christians can and should grow in sanctification throughout their lives by the power of the Holy Spirit dwelling within them (Rom. 8:2, 4, 9, 13–14). Those who hold to the first position usually see this passage as describing both Paul's own experience and the experience of Christians generally. Although Christians are free from the condemnation of the law, sin nonetheless continues to dwell within, and all genuine Christians (along with Paul) should be profoundly aware of how far they fall short of God's absolute standard of righteousness. Thus Paul cries out, "Wretched man that I am! Who will deliver me from this body of death?" (7:24). The answer follows immediately: the one who *has* delivered Christians once for all (see 4:2–25; 5:2, 9) and the one who *will* deliver them day by day is "Jesus Christ our Lord!" (7:25). As in many other places in Paul's letters, this reflects his emphasis on both the "already" aspect of salvation (that believers *have been* saved) and the "not yet" aspect (that believers *will be* saved ultimately and for all eternity at the return of Christ), and that they live in the tension between the already and the not yet. In the section that immediately follows (8:1–11), Paul shows that the means by which Christians are delivered daily from the indwelling power of sin is: (1) by walking "not according to the flesh but according to the Spirit" (8:4); (2) by not "set[ting] their minds on the things of the flesh, but . . . on the things of the Spirit" (8:5); and (3) by the indwelling presence of "the Spirit of God [who] dwells in you" (8:9, 11).

7:16 Paul's reference to the goodness of the law reflects the main point of these verses.

7:17 Paul is not absolving himself of personal responsibility but emphasizing the power of sin.

7:21–23 The meaning of the word "law" in these verses is the subject of debate. Some think that every use of the word refers to the Mosaic law, but most argue that in vv. 21 and 23 the term means "principle." All agree that the Mosaic law is in view in v. 22. The Greek word *nomos* can take either meaning.

7:24–25 Who will deliver me? The living presence of Jesus Christ is the answer to the problem of sin in one's life.

Life in the Spirit

8 There is therefore now no condemnation for those who are in Christ Jesus.[1] 2 For the
law of [h]the Spirit of life [i]has set you[2] free in Christ Jesus from the law of sin and death.
3 For [j]God has done what the law, [k]weakened by the flesh, [l]could not do. [m]By sending his
own Son [n]in the likeness of sinful flesh and [o]for sin,[3] he condemned sin in the flesh, 4 in
order that [p]the righteous requirement of the law might be fulfilled in us, [q]who walk not
according to the flesh but according to the Spirit. 5 For [r]those who live according to the
flesh set their minds on [s]the things of the flesh, but those who live according to the Spirit
set their minds on [t]the things of the Spirit. 6 For to set [u]the mind on the flesh is death,
but to set the mind on the Spirit is life and peace. 7 For the mind that is set on the flesh is
[v]hostile to God, for it does not submit to God's law; [w]indeed, it cannot. 8 Those who are in
the flesh cannot please God.
9 You, however, are not in the flesh but in the Spirit, if in fact [x]the Spirit of God dwells
in you. [y]Anyone who does not have [z]the Spirit of Christ does not belong to him. 10 But
if Christ is in you, although the body is dead because of sin, the Spirit is life because of
righteousness. 11 If the Spirit of [a]him who raised Jesus from the dead dwells in you, he
who raised Christ Jesus[4] from the dead will also give life to your mortal bodies [b]through
his Spirit who dwells in you.

Heirs with Christ

12 So then, brothers,[5] we are debtors, [c]not to the flesh, to live according to the flesh.
13 For if you live according to the flesh you will die, but if by the Spirit you [d]put to death
the deeds of the body, you will live. 14 For all who are [e]led by the Spirit of God are [f]sons[6]
of God. 15 For [g]you did not receive [h]the spirit of slavery to fall back into fear, but you have

[1] Some manuscripts add *who walk not according to the flesh (but according to the Spirit)* [2] Some manuscripts *me* [3] Or *and as a sin offering* [4] Some manuscripts lack *Jesus* [5] Or *brothers and sisters*; also verse 29 [6] See discussion on "sons" in the Preface

Chapter 8
2 [h]1 Cor. 15:45; 2 Cor. 3:6 [i]ver. 12; See ch. 6:14, 18; 7:4
3 [j]Heb. 10:1, 2, 10, 14; See Acts 13:39 [k]Gal. 4:9; Heb. 7:18 [l]Heb. 10:6, 8 [m]2 Cor. 5:21 [n]Phil. 2:7; See John 1:14 [o]Lev. 16:5; Heb. 10:6, 8; 13:11
4 [p]ch. 1:32; 2:26 [q]Gal. 5:16, 25
5 [r][Gal. 6:8] [s]Gal. 5:19-21 [t]Gal. 5:22, 23, 25
6 [u]ver. 13; [Col. 2:18]; See ch. 6:21
7 [v]James 4:4 [w]1 Cor. 2:14
9 [x]ver. 11; 1 Cor. 3:16; 6:19; 2 Cor. 6:16; 2 Tim. 1:14 [y]Jude 19; [John 14:17] [z]See Acts 16:7
11 [a]See Acts 2:24 [b][2 Cor. 3:6]
12 [c]See ver. 2
13 [d]Col. 3:5
14 [e]Gal. 5:18 [f]ver. 16, 19; ch. 9:8, 26; Deut. 14:1; Hos. 1:10; John 1:12
15 [g]1 Cor. 2:12 [h]2 Tim. 1:7; [Gal. 2:4; Heb. 2:15; 1 John 4:18]

8:1–17 *Life in the Spirit.* Paul celebrates the new life of the Spirit that Christians enjoy as a result of Christ's saving work.

8:1 Therefore indicates that Paul is stating an important summary and conclusion related to his preceding argument. The "therefore" is based first on the exclamation of victory that comes "through Jesus Christ our Lord" (7:23–25), which in turn is linked back to 7:6, where the idea of the "new life of the Spirit" is first mentioned. But more broadly Paul seems to be recalling his whole argument about salvation in Christ from 3:21–5:21. The **now** in 8:1 matches the "now" in 7:6, showing that the new era of redemptive history has "now" been inaugurated by Christ Jesus for those who are "now" in right standing before God because they are united with Christ. But the summary relates further to the whole argument presented in chs. 3, 4, and 5. **No condemnation** echoes the conclusion stated in 5:1 ("Therefore . . . we have peace with God") and underscores the stunning implications of the gospel first introduced in 1:16–17. As Paul immediately goes on to explain, there is "no condemnation" for the Christian because God has condemned sin in the flesh by sending his own Son (8:3) to pay the penalty for sin through his death on the cross. The following verses then show that indwelling sin is overcome through the power of the indwelling Spirit, with ten references to the Spirit in vv. 4–11.

8:2 The evidence that believers are in Christ is that the power of sin has been broken in their lives by the work of the Holy Spirit. **Law** in both instances means principle.

8:3 The law (in this instance, the Mosaic law) could not solve humanity's problem because sin employs the law for its own purposes, as ch. 7 explained. God sent his Son as a sacrifice **for sin** (an idiomatic phrase designating a sin offering) and paid the full penalty for sin in his sacrifice (**condemned sin**). **In the flesh** refers to Christ's body, and **in the likeness of sinful flesh** means that Jesus became fully human, even though he was sinless.

8:4 righteous requirement of the law . . . fulfilled. This could mean the requirement is fulfilled in the new life that Christians live on the basis of Christ's work, or it may refer to the full penalty of the law being met at the cross.

8:6 To set the mind on the flesh means to think continually about and constantly desire the things characteristic of fallen, sinful human nature, that is, to think just the way the unbelieving world thinks, emphasizing what it thinks important, pursuing what it pursues, in disregard of God's will.

8:7 Those who are in the flesh behave as sons and daughters of sinful Adam and are **hostile to God**. They do not keep God's law, and indeed they are unable to keep it because they are slaves to sin (6:6, 17, 19–20).

8:8 Because unbelievers (**those who are in the flesh**) are in bondage to sin and unable to do what God commands, they fail to please God.

8:9 By definition, Christians are not **in the flesh**, for all who believe in Christ are indwelt by the Holy Spirit. Paul alternates between **the Spirit of God** and **the Spirit of Christ** here, showing that Christ and God share the same status.

8:10 The previous verse speaks of the Spirit's indwelling, but here Paul describes Christ's dwelling in Christians. This does not mean that there is no difference between Christ and the Spirit (which is the ancient heresy of modalism), but it does suggest that Christ and the Spirit are both fully God, and work cooperatively. Since the bodies of Christians are not yet redeemed, they still die, even though they are freed from the condemnation of sin. Yet the presence of the Spirit within believers testifies to the new life they enjoy because of the righteousness of Christ that is now theirs.

8:12 A conclusion is drawn from the previous verses. Since Christians live in the Spirit, they are no longer captive to the flesh and should no longer live **according to the flesh**.

8:13 Those who give their lives over to the flesh will face eternal death, but those who slay the desires of the flesh through the power of the Spirit will enjoy eternal life. God and believers each have a role in sanctification: it must be **by the Spirit** and his power, but **you put to death** shows that one must take an active role in battling sinful habits.

8:14 Those **who are led by the Spirit of God** (i.e., those who yield to the Spirit; see notes on Gal. 5:16; 5:17; 5:18) are those who are God's sons, i.e., they truly belong to his family.

8:15 Christians are no longer slaves to sin but are adopted as sons into God's family, as evidenced by the Spirit that cries out within them that God is their father. **sons**. See note on Gal. 3:26. **Abba** is the Aramaic word for Father. Paul's use of the term likely stems from Jesus' addressing God as Abba (Mark 14:36).

8:16 The **witness** of the **Spirit** gives the Christian's **spirit** assurance that he or she is God's child.

received the Spirit of [i]adoption as sons, by whom we cry, [j]"Abba! Father!" 16 [k]The Spirit
himself bears witness with our spirit that we are children of God, 17 and if children, then
[l]heirs—heirs of God and fellow heirs with Christ, [m]provided we suffer with him in order
that we may also be glorified with him.

Future Glory

18 For I consider that the sufferings of this present time [n]are not worth comparing with
the glory that is to be revealed to us. 19 For the creation waits with eager longing for [o]the
revealing of the sons of God. 20 For the creation [p]was subjected to futility, not willingly, but
[q]because of him who subjected it, in hope 21 that [r]the creation itself will be set free from its
bondage to corruption and obtain the freedom of the glory of the children of God. 22 For we
know that [s]the whole creation [t]has been groaning together in the pains of childbirth until
now. 23 And not only the creation, but we ourselves, who have [u]the firstfruits of the Spirit,
[v]groan inwardly as [w]we wait eagerly for adoption as sons, [x]the redemption of our bodies.
24 For [y]in this hope we were saved. Now [z]hope that is seen is not hope. For who hopes for
what he sees? 25 But if we hope for what we do not see, we [a]wait for it with patience.

26 Likewise the Spirit helps us in our weakness. For [b]we do not know what to pray for
as we ought, but [c]the Spirit himself intercedes for us with groanings too deep for words.
27 And [d]he who searches hearts knows what is [e]the mind of the Spirit, because[1] the Spirit
[f]intercedes for the saints [g]according to the will of God. 28 And we know that for those who
love God all things work together [h]for good,[2] for [i]those who are called according to his
purpose. 29 For those whom he [j]foreknew he also [k]predestined [l]to be conformed to the

[1] Or *that* [2] Some manuscripts *God works all things together for good*, or *God works in all things for the good*

29 [j]ch. 11:2; 1 Pet. 1:2 [k]1 Cor. 2:7; Eph. 1:5, 11; [ch. 9:23] [l]Phil. 3:21; [1 Cor. 15:49; Col. 3:10]; See 1 John 3:2

15 [i]ver. 23; Gal. 4:5; [ch. 9:4; Isa. 56:5; Jer. 31:9] [j]Gal. 4:6; [Mark 14:36]
16 [k]2 Cor. 1:22; 5:5; Eph. 1:13, 14; 1 John 3:24
17 [l]Gal. 3:29; 4:7; Titus 3:7 [m]2 Cor. 1:7; 2 Tim. 2:12; See Acts 14:22
18 [n]2 Cor. 4:17; [1 Pet. 1:5, 6]
19 [o]1 Pet. 4:13; 5:1; 1 John 3:2; [ch. 2:7]
20 [p]Gen. 3:18, 19; Eccles. 1:2 [q]Gen. 3:17
21 [r][Acts 3:21]
22 [s]Mark 16:15 [t]Jer. 12:4, 11
23 [u][2 Cor. 5:5; James 1:18] [v]2 Cor. 5:2, 4 [w]ver. 19, 25; Isa. 25:9; Gal. 5:5 [x]See ch. 7:24; Luke 21:28
24 [y][1 Thess. 1:3; 5:8] [z]2 Cor. 4:18; Heb. 11:1
25 [a][1 Thess. 1:3; 5:8]
26 [b][Matt. 20:22; James 4:3] [c]Zech. 12:10; Eph. 6:18; See John 14:16
27 [d]1 Sam. 16:7; 1 Chr. 28:9; Prov. 15:11; 17:3; Jer. 11:20; 17:10; Luke 16:15; 1 Thess. 2:4 [e]See ver. 6 [f][ver. 34] [g][1 John 5:14]
28 [h]Ezra 8:22; [Eccles. 8:12] [i]ch. 9:24; 1 Cor. 1:9; 7:15, 17; Gal. 1:15; 5:8; Eph. 4:1, 4; 2 Tim. 1:9

8:17 All who are God's **children** are also **heirs** of his promises, but a willingness to follow Christ in suffering is another sign of being God's children.

8:18–39 *Assurance of Hope.* Paul began this major section of the letter (5:1–8:39) by emphasizing the final hope of believers (5:1–11), and now he concludes with the same emphasis.

8:18 The ultimate glory that Christians will receive is so stupendous that the **sufferings of this present time** are insignificant in comparison (cf. 2 Cor. 4:17). They look forward both to the resurrection of the body (1 Thess. 4:13–18) and to the new heaven and new earth (Rev. 21:1–22:5; see Isa. 65:17).

8:19 Creation is personified in this verse and the following verses in order to emphasize the wonder of the future glory of God's **sons** (i.e., believers who have the rights of inheritance of all that God has in store for them; on "sons," see ESV Preface: Translation Style).

8:20–21 When Adam sinned, the created world was also **subjected to futility**. One thinks of the thorns and thistles that were to accompany work in Gen. 3:17–19, the pain in childbirth for the woman (Gen. 3:16), and the repeated refrain that all is vanity in Ecclesiastes (where the Septuagint uses the same Greek word here used for "futility"). The original **creation** (Genesis 1–2) did not have these things, and on the last day it also will be transformed and freed from the effects of sin and will instantly become far more beautiful, productive, and easy to live in than one can ever imagine.

8:22 Again **creation** is personified, showing that it also longs for the day when the salvation that has already begun in God's children will be completed.

8:23 God's people also **groan** and long for the completion of his saving work. The tension is seen here between the already and not yet in Paul's theology. Christians already have **the firstfruits of the Spirit**, but they still await the day of their final adoption when their bodies are fully redeemed and they are raised from the dead. Their **adoption** has already occurred in a legal sense (v. 15), and they already enjoy many of its privileges, but here Paul uses "adoption" to refer to the yet greater privilege of receiving perfect resurrection bodies.

8:26 Although Christians do not always know God's will in prayer, the **Spirit himself intercedes** for them in and through their unspeakable groans (cf. v. 23). This does not refer to speaking in tongues, since what Paul says here applies to all Christians and, according to 1 Cor. 12:30, only some Christians speak in tongues.

8:27 God always answers the requests of the Spirit in the affirmative, since the Spirit always prays in accord with God's will.

8:28 God weaves everything **together for good** for his children. The "good" in this context does not refer to earthly comfort but conformity to Christ (v. 29), closer fellowship with God, bearing good fruit for the kingdom, and final glorification (v. 30).

8:29 Verses 29–30 explain why those who believe in Christ can be assured that all things work together for good: God has always been doing good for them, starting before creation (the distant past), continuing in their conversion (the recent past), and then on to the day of Christ's return (the future). **Foreknew** reaches back to the OT, where the word "know" emphasizes God's special choice of, or covenantal affection for, his people (e.g., Gen. 18:19; Jer.

The Trinity in Romans 8

This chart focuses on statements that have Father, Son, or Spirit as the subject. For additional references to Father, Son, or Spirit in Romans 8, see vv. 1–2, 4–7, 13, 15, 17–23, 28.

Father	Son	Spirit
sent his Son (v. 3)		
condemned sin (v. 3)		
gives life to mortal bodies of believers by his Spirit in them (v. 11)	in believers (v. 10)	indwells believers (v. 9)
foreknew, predestined, called, justified, glorified (vv. 29–30)	died, raised, interceding at the right hand of the Father for believers (v. 34)	leads believers (v. 14)
is for us (v. 31)		bears witness with the spirit of believers (v. 16)
gave his Son (v. 32)		helps in weakness and intercedes for believers (vv. 26–27)
justifies (v. 33)		
loves (v. 39)	loves (vv. 35, 39)	

image of his Son, in order that he might be [m]the firstborn among many brothers. 30 And
those whom he predestined he also called, and those whom he called he also [n]justified,
and those whom he justified he also [o]glorified.

God's Everlasting Love

31 What then shall we say to these things? [p]If God is for us, who can be[1] against us? 32 [q]He
who did not spare his own Son but [r]gave him up for us all, how will he not also with him
graciously give us all things? 33 Who shall bring any charge against God's elect? [s]It is God
who justifies. 34 [t]Who is to condemn? Christ Jesus is the one who died—more than that,
who was raised—[u]who is at the right hand of God, [v]who indeed is interceding for us.[2]
35 Who shall separate us from the love of Christ? Shall tribulation, or distress, or persecution, or famine, or nakedness, or danger, or sword? 36 As it is written,

> [w]"For your sake [x]we are being killed all the day long;
> we are regarded as sheep to be slaughtered."

37 No, in all these things we are more than [y]conquerors through [z]him who loved us. 38 For
I am sure that neither death nor life, nor angels nor rulers, nor things present nor things
to come, nor powers, 39 nor height nor depth, nor anything else in all creation, will be able
to separate us from the love of God in Christ Jesus our Lord.

God's Sovereign Choice

9 [a]I am speaking the truth in Christ—I am not lying; my conscience bears me witness
in the Holy Spirit— 2 that I have great sorrow and unceasing anguish in my heart.
3 For [b]I could wish that I myself were [c]accursed and cut off from Christ for the sake of my
brothers,[3] my kinsmen [d]according to the flesh. 4 They are [e]Israelites, and to them belong
[f]the adoption, [g]the glory, [h]the covenants, [i]the giving of the law, [j]the worship, and [k]the

[1] *Or who is* [2] *Or Is it Christ Jesus who died . . . for us?* [3] *Or brothers and sisters*

29 [m]Col. 1:15, 18; Heb. 1:6; Rev. 1:5
30 [n]1 Cor. 6:11 [o]John 17:22; [Heb. 2:10]
31 [p]Num. 14:9; 2 Kgs. 6:16; Ps. 118:6; 1 John 4:4
32 [q]John 3:16 [r]See ch. 4:25
33 [s]Isa. 50:8, 9; [Rev. 12:10, 11]
34 [t]ver. 1 [u]See Mark 16:19 [v]Heb. 7:25; 1 John 2:1; [ver. 27]
36 [w]Cited from Ps. 44:22 [x]1 Cor. 4:9; 15:30, 31; 2 Cor. 4:10, 11; See Acts 20:24
37 [y]1 Cor. 15:57; See John 16:33 [z]Gal. 2:20; Eph. 5:2; Rev. 1:5; 3:9

Chapter 9

1 [a]2 Cor. 11:10; 1 Tim. 2:7; [2 Cor. 12:19; Gal. 1:20]; See ch. 1:9
3 [b][Ex. 32:32] [c]1 Cor. 12:3; 16:22; Gal. 1:8, 9 [d][ch. 11:14]
4 [e][ver. 6; ch. 2:28, 29; Gal. 6:16] [f][Ex. 4:22]; See ch. 8:15 [g]Ex. 40:34; 1 Sam. 4:21; 1 Kgs. 8:11 [h]Gen. 17:2; Deut. 29:14; Gal. 4:24; Eph. 2:12 [i]Deut. 4:14; [Ps. 147:19] [j]Heb. 9:1 (Gk.); [ch. 12:1] [k][Eph. 2:12]; See John 4:22; Acts 13:32

1:5; Amos 3:2). See Rom. 11:2, where "foreknew" functions as the contrast to "rejected," showing that it emphasizes God's choosing his people (see also 1 Pet. 1:2, 20). God also **predestined** (i.e., predetermined) that those whom he chose beforehand would become like Christ.

8:30 The chain that begins with the word "foreknew" in v. 29 cannot be broken. Those who are **predestined** by God are also **called** effectively to faith through the gospel (see 2 Thess. 2:14). And all those who are called are also **justified** (declared to be right in God's sight). Because not all who are invited to believe are actually justified, the "calling" here cannot refer to merely a general invitation but must refer to an effective call that creates the faith necessary for justification (Rom. 5:1). All those who are justified will also be **glorified** (receive resurrection bodies) on the last day. Paul speaks of glorification as if it were already completed, since God will certainly finish the good work he started (cf. Phil. 1:6).

8:31–39 A joyous conclusion to the argument that Paul has carefully unfolded throughout the preceding chapters. The opposition of unbelievers and Satan will never succeed, since **God is for us** (v. 31).

8:33 Satan, their enemies, or even their own consciences may bring charges against **God's elect**, but those who have come to faith in Christ will never be found guilty, for God declares them to be right before all the world at the divine tribunal.

8:34 Who is to condemn? The question posed in v. 33 is repeated. Christians may rejoice with the certainty that they will never be condemned, for (1) Christ died for them and paid the full penalty for their sin; (2) he was raised, showing that his death was effective; (3) he now is seated triumphantly at God's right hand (Ps. 110:1); and (4) he intercedes for his people on the basis of his shed blood. **Interceding** signifies effective intervention.

8:36 As it is written. The quotation from Ps. 44:22 shows that the difficulties listed in Rom. 8:35 do strike Christians. They are not exempted from suffering or even from **being killed**.

8:37 Christians are **more than conquerors**, because God turns everything—even suffering and death—into good.

8:38–39 For I am sure. Paul answers the question he raised in v. 35 with absolute certainty that nothing can ever sever God's people from his **love . . . in Christ**. **Rulers** and **powers** here likely refer to angelic and demonic authorities.

9:1–11:36 *God's Righteousness to Israel and to the Gentiles.* Paul has made it clear that God's saving promises have been fulfilled for the Gentiles. Indeed, the church of Jesus Christ now enjoys the spiritual blessings promised to Israel: the gift of the Spirit (8:9); adoption as God's children (8:14–17); future glory (8:17, 30); election (8:33); and the promise of never being severed from God's love (8:35–39). Paul now asks in chs. 9–11 whether the promises God made to ethnic Israel will be fulfilled. If his promises to the Jews remain unfulfilled, how can Gentile Christians be sure that he will fulfill the great promises that conclude ch. 8? Paul answers that God is faithful to his saving promises to Israel (9:6) and that he will ultimately save his people (11:26).

9:1–29 *God's Saving Promises to Israel.* God's saving promises to Israel are irrevocable since they depend upon his word of promise and his electing grace.

9:1–3 Paul suffers from great **anguish** because his Jewish kinsmen are unsaved (see also 10:1). Indeed, if it were possible, Paul might almost choose to be **accursed** (to suffer God's punishment in hell) so that his fellow Jews would be saved (cf. Moses in Ex. 32:30–32). But he knows this would achieve nothing, for none but Christ could be any person's substitute to bear God's wrath.

9:4 In vv. 4–5 the great privileges of Israel are listed. The six blessings here can be divided into two parallel lists of three:

Adoption	Law
Glory	Worship
Covenants	Promises

The **Israelites** became God's adopted people when God saved them from Egypt. **Glory** here probably refers to the glory of God in the tabernacle and temple. Israel received the **covenants** in which the Lord promised to save them. God gave his people his **law** at Mount Sinai, prescribed their **worship** in the Mosaic law, and gave them his saving **promises**.

promises. 5 To them belong [l]the patriarchs, and from their race, according to the flesh, is
the Christ, [m]who is God over all, [n]blessed forever. Amen.
6 But it is not as though the word of God has failed. For not all who are descended from
Israel belong to Israel, 7 and not all are children of Abraham [o]because they are his offspring,
but [p]"Through Isaac shall your offspring be named." 8 This means that it is not the children
of the flesh who are the children of God, but [q]the children of the promise are counted as
offspring. 9 For this is what the promise said: [r]"About this time next year I will return,
and Sarah shall have a son." 10 And not only so, but [s]also when Rebekah had conceived
children by one man, our forefather Isaac, 11 though they were not yet born and had done
nothing either good or bad—in order that God's purpose of election might continue, not
because of works but because of [t]him who calls— 12 she was told, [u]"The older will serve
the younger." 13 As it is written, [v]"Jacob I loved, but Esau I hated."
14 What shall we say then? [w]Is there injustice on God's part? By no means! 15 For he says
to Moses, [x]"I will have mercy on whom I have mercy, and I will have compassion on whom
I have compassion." 16 So then it depends not on human will or exertion,[1] but on God,
who has mercy. 17 For the Scripture says to Pharaoh, [y]"For this very purpose I have raised
you up, that I might show my power in you, and that my name might be proclaimed in
all the earth." 18 So then he has mercy on whomever he wills, and he hardens whomever
he wills.
19 You will say to me then, "Why does he still find fault? For [z]who can resist his will?"
20 But who are you, O man, [a]to answer back to God? [b]Will what is molded say to its molder,
"Why have you made me like this?" 21 [c]Has the potter no right over the clay, to make out of
the same lump [d]one vessel for honorable use and another for dishonorable use? 22 What if
God, desiring to show his wrath and to make known his power, has endured with much
patience [e]vessels of wrath [f]prepared for destruction, 23 in order to make known [g]the riches
of his glory for vessels of mercy, which he [h]has prepared beforehand for glory— 24 even

[1] Greek *not of him who wills or runs*

5 [l]ch. 11:28 [m][Eph. 4:6; Col. 1:16-19] [n]ch. 1:25; John 1:1; 2 Cor. 11:31; Heb. 1:8
7 [o][Gal. 4:23]; See John 8:33 [p]Heb. 11:18; Cited from Gen. 21:12; [Gal. 3:29]
8 [q]Gal. 4:23, 28
9 [r]Cited from Gen. 18:10, 14; [Gen. 17:21]
10 [s]Gen. 25:21
11 [t][ch. 4:17]; See ch. 8:28
12 [u]Cited from Gen. 25:23
13 [v]Cited from Mal. 1:2, 3
14 [w]Deut. 32:4; 2 Chr. 19:7; Job 8:3; 34:10; Ps. 92:15
15 [x]Cited from Ex. 33:19
17 [y]Cited from Ex. 9:16
19 [z]2 Chr. 20:6; Job 9:12; Dan. 4:35
20 [a]Job 33:13 [b]Isa. 29:16; 45:9
21 [c]Isa. 64:8; Jer. 18:6 [d]2 Tim. 2:20
22 [e][ver. 21, 23; Acts 9:15] [f][Prov. 16:4; 1 Pet. 2:8]
23 [g]Eph. 3:16; See ch. 2:4 [h][ch. 8:29]

9:5 The **patriarchs** (Abraham, Isaac, and Jacob) also come from Israel. Most important, Jesus the Christ is also from the Jewish people, and he is not merely a human being but is also fully **God**. Therefore, the fact that so many Jews have rejected Christ brings acute pain to Paul (v. 2).

9:6–7 Even though many Jews have failed to believe, God's promise to them has not failed, for there was never a promise that every Jewish person would be saved. It was never the case that all the physical **children of Abraham** were truly part of the people of God, for Gen. 21:12 teaches that the line of promise is traced **through Isaac**, not Ishmael.

9:8 The words **children of God** show that Paul is thinking of salvation (see 8:16), and hence he is not thinking merely of physical blessings given to Israel.

9:9–10 The promise (Gen. 18:10, 14) was not given to Hagar (Genesis 16) but was specifically given to Sarah and her offspring. The birth of Esau and Jacob is further evidence that God did not promise that every person of Jewish descent would be saved, for they had the same father and mother and were even twins, and yet God chose Jacob and not Esau.

9:11 God did not choose Jacob on the basis of anything in Jacob or Esau's life but to achieve the fulfillment of **God's purpose of election**. Christians can be assured, therefore, that God's promise will be fulfilled because it depends solely upon his will. The contrast between **works** and calling shows that salvation is in view, not merely the historical destiny of Israel as a nation. For the OT background on "election," see Gen. 18:10; Ex. 33:19; Mal. 1:2. See also Eph. 1:3–6.

9:12 The promise given to Rebekah (Gen. 25:23) was that God had chosen the **younger** Jacob over the **older** Esau. One of the themes in Romans 9–11 is that God works in surprising ways, so that no one can ever presume upon his grace.

9:13 The citation of Mal. 1:2–3 also shows that God set his saving love on Jacob and rejected (**hated**) Esau. "Hated" is startling, but as a sinner Esau did not deserve to be chosen by God, who remains just in not choosing everyone. The salvation of anyone at all comes only from God's mercy.

9:14–15 Since God chose Jacob instead of Esau before they were born, without regard to how good or bad either of them would be, the question naturally arises: Is God just in choosing one over the other? God is just because no one deserves to be saved (cf. 3:23), and the salvation of anyone at all is due to God's **mercy** alone, as the citation of Ex. 33:19 affirms.

9:16 Salvation, then, is not ultimately based on **human** free **will** or effort but depends entirely on God's merciful will.

9:17 For this very purpose. Paul quotes Ex. 9:16 to show that God is sovereign over evil as well. Even the wrath of man praises God (Ps. 76:10), for God installed **Pharaoh** as ruler and hardened his heart so that his own saving power and glorious name would be spread throughout the whole world.

9:19 who can resist his will? If salvation ultimately depends upon God, and he has mercy and hardens whomever he pleases, then how can he find anyone guilty? How can he charge anyone with guilt since his will is irresistible?

9:20–21 Some of Paul's readers might expect him to appeal to human free will to resolve the problem posed in v. 19. Instead, he insists that finite human beings may not rebelliously question God's ways, that God as a **potter** (cf. Jer. 18:1–6) has the right to do what he wishes with his creation. The **honorable** and **dishonorable** vessels in this context represent those who are saved and unsaved. Paul affirms that humans are guilty for their sin, and he offers no philosophical resolution as to how this fits with divine sovereignty. He does insist that God ordains all that happens (cf. Eph. 1:11), even though God himself does not sin and is not morally responsible for sin.

9:22–23 God created a world in which both his **wrath** and his **mercy** would be displayed. Indeed, his mercy shines against the backdrop of his just wrath, showing thereby that the salvation of any person is due to the marvelous grace and love of God. If this is difficult to understand, it is because people mistakenly think God owes them salvation!

9:24 In his grace and mercy God **has called** people to himself from both **the Jews** and **the Gentiles**.

us whom he [i]has called, [j]not from the Jews only but also from the Gentiles? 25 As indeed
he says in Hosea,

[k]"Those who were not my people I will call 'my people,'
and her who was not beloved I will call 'beloved.'"
26 [l]"And in the very place where it was said to them, 'You are not my people,'
there they will be called [m]'sons of the living God.'"

27 And Isaiah cries out concerning Israel: [n]"Though the number of the sons of Israel[1] be
as the sand of the sea, [o]only a remnant of them will be saved, 28 for the Lord will carry out
his sentence upon the earth fully and without delay." 29 And as Isaiah predicted,

[p,q]"If the Lord of hosts had not left us offspring,
[r]we would have been like Sodom
and become like Gomorrah."

Israel's Unbelief

30 What shall we say, then? [s]That Gentiles who did not pursue righteousness have attained
it, that is, [t]a righteousness that is by faith; 31 but that Israel [u]who pursued a law that would
lead to righteousness[2] [v]did not succeed in reaching that law. 32 Why? Because they did not
pursue it by faith, but as if it were based on works. They have stumbled over the [w]stumbling
stone, 33 as it is written,

[x]"Behold, I am laying in Zion [y]a stone of stumbling, and a rock of offense;
[z]and whoever believes in him will not be [a]put to shame."

10 Brothers,[3] my heart's desire and prayer to God for them is that they may be saved.
2 For I bear them witness that [b]they have a zeal for God, [c]but not according to
knowledge. 3 For, being ignorant of [d]the righteousness of God, and seeking to establish
their own, they did not submit to God's righteousness. 4 For [e]Christ is the end of the law
for righteousness to everyone who believes.[4]

The Message of Salvation to All

5 For [f]Moses writes about the righteousness that is based on the law, that [g]the person
who does the commandments shall live by them. 6 But [h]the righteousness based on faith
says, [i]"Do not say in your heart, 'Who will ascend into heaven?'" (that is, to bring Christ
down) 7 "or 'Who will descend into the [j]abyss?'" (that is, [k]to bring Christ up from the dead).

[1] *Or children of Israel* [2] *Greek a law of righteousness* [3] *Or Brothers and sisters* [4] *Or end of the law, that everyone who believes may be justified*

24 [i]See ch. 8:28 [j]See ch. 3:29
25 [k]Cited from Hos. 2:23; [1 Pet. 2:10]
26 [l]Cited from Hos. 1:10 [m]See ch. 8:14; Matt. 16:16
27 [n]Cited from Isa. 10:22, 23; [Hos. 1:10] [o]ch. 11:5
29 [p]Cited from Isa. 1:9 [q]James 5:4 [r]Deut. 29:23; Isa. 13:19; Jer. 49:18; 50:40; Amos 4:11
30 [s][ch. 10:20] [t]ch. 1:17; 3:21, 22; 10:6; Gal. 2:16; 3:24; Phil. 3:9; Heb. 11:7
31 [u][ch. 10:2, 3; 11:7] [v][Gal. 5:4]
32 [w]See 1 Pet. 2:8
33 [x]1 Pet. 2:6, 7; Cited from Isa. 28:16; [Ps. 118:22] [y]Isa. 8:14 [z]ch. 10:11 [a]Isa. 49:23; Joel 2:26, 27

Chapter 10

2 [b]See Acts 21:20 [c][ch. 9:31]
3 [d]See ch. 1:17
4 [e][Matt. 5:17; Gal. 3:24]
5 [f]Cited from Lev. 18:5 [g]Neh. 9:29; Ezek. 20:11, 13, 21; Matt. 19:17; Luke 10:28; Gal. 3:12; [ch. 7:10]
6 [h]See ch. 9:30 [i][Deut. 30:12, 13]
7 [j]See Rev. 9:1 [k]Heb. 13:20

9:25–26 Paul quotes Hos. 2:23 and 1:10 to illustrate the stunning grace of God—that those who **are not my people . . . will be called "sons of the living God."** In calling the Gentiles to salvation, God calls a sinful people to himself, just as in saving Israel he showed mercy to the undeserving. No one can presume on God's grace. In calling anyone to salvation, he shows undeserved mercy to those who were not his people.

9:27–29 The fact that only some of Israel would be saved was prophesied in Isa. 10:22–23. Most of **Israel** was judged, and only **a remnant** experienced salvation. Indeed, as Isa. 1:9 says, Israel deserved to be wiped out like Sodom and Gomorrah, but God had mercy and spared some.

9:30–11:10 *Israel's Rejection of God's Saving Promises.* God's sovereignty is compatible with human responsibility. Israel should have believed the gospel and trusted in Christ, but the majority refused to do so. Still, God's saving promises will be fulfilled.

9:30–31 Paul assesses the situation: **Gentiles**, who were not God's chosen people and did not seek right standing with God, now enjoy that right standing **by faith**. **Israel** pursued right standing with God through the **law** but failed to achieve it.

9:32 Why did Israel fail to achieve right standing with God through the law? They did not pursue obedience to the law in humble trust, but tried to make it a means of establishing their own righteousness. Such a use of the law led them to stumble over the **stone** (which was Christ confronting them), for those attempting to establish their own righteousness see no need to believe in Christ.

9:33 The **stumbling** over Christ was prophesied in Isa. 28:16. Those who trust in Christ will not experience end-time **shame**.

10:1 Salvation is the issue throughout chs. 9–11.

10:2 The Jews' **zeal** and sincerity does not lead them to salvation. The broader principle is that many sincere, "religious" people are wrong in their beliefs.

10:3 Many Jews did not believe in Christ because they failed to submit to **God's righteousness** and instead attempted to be righteous before God on the basis of their own works. On the contrast of the two ways to **righteousness**, see Gal. 3:7–14.

10:4 End probably includes the idea of both goal and termination. The Mosaic law has reached its goal in Christ (it looked forward to and anticipated him), and the law is no longer binding upon Christians (the old covenant has ended). Since Christ is the goal and end of the law, righteousness belongs to all who trust in Christ.

10:5 Paul quotes Lev. 18:5 regarding **the righteousness that is based on the law**, to show that those who keep the law will attain life. But as Paul has already shown, life will not come in this way since all violate the law (Rom. 1:18–3:20).

10:6–8 In vv. 6–8 Paul quotes Deut. 30:12–14 to show the contrast between the **righteousness based on faith** and the righteousness that comes from the law. The righteousness based on faith reinterprets these OT statements and sees them now fulfilled in Christ (see note on Deut. 30:12–14). There is no need to travel to **heaven** to **bring Christ** to earth, for God has already sent him into the world. Nor should anyone think they must **bring Christ up from**

8 [l]Cited from Deut. 30:14
9 [m]Matt. 10:32; Luke 12:8; [1 Cor. 12:3; Phil. 2:11] [n]See Acts 16:31 [o][1 Pet. 1:21]; See Acts 2:24
11 [p]See ch. 9:33
12 [q]See ch. 3:22, 29 [r]Acts 10:36 [s]See ch. 2:4
13 [t]Acts 2:21; Cited from Joel 2:32
14 [u]Eph. 4:21; [John 9:36; 17:20] [v][Acts 8:31; Titus 1:3]
15 [w]Cited from Isa. 52:7; [Nah. 1:15; Eph. 6:15]
16 [x]ch. 3:3; Heb. 4:2 [y]John 12:38; Cited from Isa. 53:1
17 [z]Gal. 3:2, 5
18 [a]Cited from Ps. 19:4; [1 Thess. 1:8] [b][Mark 16:15]; See Matt. 24:14
19 [c]Cited from Deut. 32:21 [d]ch. 11:11, 14 [e][Titus 3:3]
20 [f]Cited from Isa. 65:1; [ch. 9:30]
21 [g]Cited from Isa. 65:2

8 But what does it say? [l]"The word is near you, in your mouth and in your heart" (that is,
the word of faith that we proclaim); 9 because, if [m]you confess with your mouth that Jesus
is Lord and [n]believe in your heart [o]that God raised him from the dead, you will be saved.
10 For with the heart one believes and is justified, and with the mouth one confesses and is
saved. 11 For the Scripture says, [p]"Everyone who believes in him will not be put to shame."
12 [q]For there is no distinction between Jew and Greek; [r]for the same Lord is Lord of all,
[s]bestowing his riches on all who call on him. 13 For [t]"everyone who calls on the name of
the Lord will be saved."

14 How then will they call on him in whom they have not believed? And how are they
to believe in him [u]of whom they have never heard?[1] And how are they to hear [v]without
someone preaching? 15 And how are they to preach unless they are sent? As it is written,
[w]"How beautiful are the feet of those who preach the good news!" 16 But [x]they have not all
obeyed the gospel. For Isaiah says, [y]"Lord, who has believed what he has heard from us?"
17 So [z]faith comes from hearing, and hearing through the word of Christ.

18 But I ask, have they not heard? Indeed they have, for

> [a]"Their voice has gone out [b]to all the earth,
> and their words to the ends of the world."

19 But I ask, did Israel not understand? First Moses says,

> [c]"I will [d]make you jealous of those who are not a nation;
> with a [e]foolish nation I will make you angry."

20 Then Isaiah is so bold as to say,

> [f]"I have been found by those who did not seek me;
> I have shown myself to those who did not ask for me."

21 But of Israel he says, [g]"All day long I have held out my hands to a disobedient and contrary people."

[1] Or *him whom they have never heard*

the realm of **the dead**, for God has raised Christ from the dead. What God requires is not superhuman works but faith in the gospel Paul preaches.

10:9–10 If you confess with your mouth does not mean that a spoken affirmation of one's faith is a "work" that merits justification, but such confession does give outward evidence of inward faith, and often confirms that faith to the speaker himself. **that God raised him from the dead**. Paul does not mean that people need to believe only this individual event with no understanding of Christ's death, but rather they need to believe in the resurrection along with the whole complex of truth connected with it, particularly Jesus' sin-bearing death in mankind's place, followed by his resurrection that showed God the Father's approval of Christ's work (see note on 4:25). **with the heart one believes**. Saving faith is not mere intellectual agreement but deep inward trust in Christ at the core of one's being.

10:11 Paul again cites Isa. 28:16 (cf. Rom. 9:33) to emphasize that trusting in Christ (not works-righteousness) is the pathway to salvation. **Shame** here refers to the end-time humiliation that those judged on the last day will experience when they are sent to hell.

10:12–13 God bestows his saving riches on all, both Jews and Gentiles, **who call on him**—for (as Paul quotes from Joel 2:32) **"everyone who calls on the name of the Lord will be saved."**

10:14–15 How then . . . ? With a series of rhetorical questions, Paul considers the chain of events necessary for a person to be saved. Verse 14 is linked to v. 13 with the word **call**. The logic of these verses is clear: (1) People will call on Jesus to save them only if they believe he can do so; (2) belief in Christ cannot exist without knowledge about him; (3) one hears about Christ only when someone proclaims the saving message; and (4) the message about Christ will not be proclaimed unless someone is sent by God to do so. That is why Paul was so urgent about spreading the gospel to the ends of the earth, for he believed that the only way to be saved was to hear and believe in the gospel (see note on 1:19–20). (Paul is not talking here about OT believers who looked forward to Christ, such as Abraham and David in ch. 4, nor is he talking about infants who die in infancy; see note on 2 Sam. 12:23). Since salvation comes only from hearing the gospel, the **feet** of those who bring the message about Christ are **beautiful** (Isa. 52:7), probably because the feet carry the messengers to their destinations.

10:16 Hearing the gospel is necessary for salvation, but hearing is not enough: people must also respond with personal trust. **Isaiah** (Isa. 53:1) prophesies that not all will believe. In the context of Romans 9–11, Paul is thinking especially of the Jews who did not believe.

10:17 Paul now sums up the argument thus far. One can come to **faith** only through **hearing** the gospel, and the specific message that must be heard is the **word of Christ**, that is, the good news about Jesus Christ as the crucified and risen Savior.

10:18–19 They who have heard the message probably refers to the Jewish people (see vv. 1, 19–20). Paul quotes Ps. 19:4, which in its original context refers to general revelation, but Paul applies it to special revelation (the proclamation of the gospel) to emphasize that the Jews have heard the good news because the gospel has gone even **to the ends of the world** (i.e., to the Gentiles). Israel should have understood from the prophecy of Deut. 32:21 that the Gentiles would believe.

10:20–21 The prophecy of Isa. 65:1 has been fulfilled in that the Gentiles **who did not seek** after God have now experienced God's saving promises. Israel, on the other hand, has fulfilled the words of Isa. 65:2. They have rebelled against and disobeyed the gospel message. Still, God extends his **hands** to them, inviting them to be saved. On the one hand, God predestines some to be saved. On the other hand, God still longs for all to be saved (see note on 1 Tim. 2:4; also Ezek. 33:11). Though it may seem impossible to understand how both of these statements are true, the Bible teaches both, and one should not use either truth to deny the other. On election, see also notes on Eph. 1:4; 1:5; 1:6; 1:11.

The Remnant of Israel

11 I ask, then, [h]has God rejected his people? By no means! For [i]I myself am an Israelite, a
descendant of Abraham,[1] a member of the tribe of Benjamin. 2 [j]God has not rejected
his people whom he [k]foreknew. Do you not know what the Scripture says of Elijah, how he
appeals to God against Israel? 3 [l]"Lord, they have killed your prophets, they have demolished
your altars, and I alone am left, and they seek my life." 4 But what is God's reply to him?
[m]"I have kept for myself seven thousand men who have not bowed the knee to Baal." 5 So
too at the present time there is [n]a remnant, chosen by grace. 6 [o]But if it is by grace, it is no
longer on the basis of works; otherwise grace would no longer be grace.
7 What then? [p]Israel failed to obtain what it was seeking. The elect obtained it, but the
rest [q]were hardened, 8 as it is written,

> [r]"God gave them a spirit of stupor,
> [s]eyes that would not see
> and ears that would not hear,
> down to this very day."

9 And David says,

> [t]"Let their table become a snare and a trap,
> a stumbling block and a retribution for them;
> 10 let their eyes be darkened so that they cannot see,
> and bend their backs forever."

Gentiles Grafted In

11 So I ask, did they stumble in order that they might fall? By no means! Rather through
their trespass [u]salvation has come to the Gentiles, so as to make Israel jealous. 12 Now if
their trespass means riches for the world, and if their failure means riches for the Gentiles,
how much more will their full inclusion[2] mean!
13 Now I am speaking to you Gentiles. Inasmuch then as [v]I am an apostle to the Gentiles,
I magnify my ministry 14 in order somehow to make my fellow Jews jealous, and [w]thus
save some of them. 15 For if their rejection means [x]the reconciliation of the world, what
will their acceptance mean but life from the dead? 16 [y]If the dough offered as firstfruits is
holy, so is the whole lump, and if the root is holy, so are the branches.
17 But if [z]some of the branches were broken off, and you, [a]although a wild olive shoot,

[1] *Or one of the offspring of Abraham* [2] *Greek their fullness*

Chapter 11
1 [h]1 Sam. 12:22; Jer. 31:37; 33:24 [i]2 Cor. 11:22; Phil. 3:5
2 [j]Ps. 94:14 [k]ch. 8:29
3 [l]Cited from 1 Kgs. 19:10, 14
4 [m]Cited from 1 Kgs. 19:18
5 [n]ch. 9:27; [Jer. 3:14; Zech. 13:8]
6 [o][ch. 4:4; Deut. 9:4, 5]
7 [p]See ch. 9:31 [q][ver. 25]
8 [r]Isa. 29:10 [s]Deut. 29:4; [Isa. 43:8; Jer. 5:21; Ezek. 12:2; Eph. 4:18]; See Matt. 13:14
9 [t]Cited from Ps. 69:22, 23
11 [u][Acts 28:28]
13 [v]ch. 15:16; [Acts 26:17]; See Acts 9:15
14 [w]1 Cor. 7:16; 9:22; 1 Tim. 4:16; James 5:20
15 [x]ch. 5:11
16 [y]Num. 15:18-21; Neh. 10:37; Ezek. 44:30
17 [z]Jer. 11:16; [Ps. 52:8; John 15:2] [a][Eph. 2:12]

11:1 The majority of Israel failed to believe. Does this mean that God has **rejected his people**? Paul presents himself as an example of the remnant that has been preserved, a remnant that indicates that God is not finished with Israel and that he will fulfill the promises made to his people.

11:2 God **foreknew**. See note on 8:29.

11:3–5 Elijah in his despair thought Israel would be extinguished. But God assured Elijah that he had preserved a **remnant**, which gave Elijah hope that God would fulfill his saving promises in the future. In Paul's day, as in Elijah's day (v. 4) and today, a remnant of Jews believe in Christ because of God's electing grace (cf. 9:27–29).

11:6 Election and **grace** are inseparable, for both show that salvation is God's work alone, and that it has nothing to do with **works**. On grace, see also 4:4–5; Acts 15:11; Eph. 2:8–9.

11:7–10 The composite citation from Isa. 29:10 and Deut. 29:4 clarifies that God has **hardened** Israel so that they would not see or hear. Paul then prays for judgment (Ps. 69:22–23) over the Jews of his day who have rejected Christ.

11:11–32 ***God's Righteousness in His Plan for Jews and Gentiles.*** God's saving righteousness is featured in the salvation of Israel at the end of history, and in his saving plan for both Jews and Gentiles.

11:11 Israel's hardening is not the final word. God planned salvation history so that Israel's **trespass** would open salvation for the Gentiles, and the Jews in turn would be provoked to jealousy when they see Gentiles being saved and enjoying a relationship with God.

11:12 The term **world** is another word for **Gentiles** here. **Full inclusion** looks forward to the fulfillment of God's saving promises to ethnic Israel. Paul argues from the lesser to the greater: if Israel's sin brought salvation to the Gentiles, then the blessing will be even greater when all Israel is saved (see v. 15).

11:13–14 As **an apostle**, Paul had a special calling and commission to preach the good news **to the Gentiles**. But he uses his ministry to the Gentiles also to benefit the Jews, for he hopes that the more Gentiles come to salvation, the more this will provoke the Jews to jealousy, so that many will be saved.

11:15 If the **rejection** of the majority of Israel has meant that many Gentiles (**the world**) are now reconciled to God through Christ, then the **acceptance** of the Jews (their future coming to Christ in large numbers) will bring about the final resurrection (**life from the dead**) and the end of history, so that from that point on people will praise God forever and ever (see v. 12). Others think "life from the dead" is a figurative expression for great spiritual revival.

11:16 Two illustrations are used that teach the same truth. The **firstfruits** and the **root** probably refer to the patriarchs (Abraham, Isaac, and Jacob) and the saving promises given to them. If the firstfruits and root are consecrated to God, so too are the **whole lump** (of **dough**) and **the branches** (i.e., the Jewish people as a whole); see Num. 15:17–21 for OT origin of the imagery. As Paul has already explained in Romans 9–10, it does not follow from this that every Jewish person will be saved, but it does indicate that God will be faithful to his promises (9:6) and seems to imply that in the future many more Jews will be saved.

11:17 The illustration of the root and its **branches** is elaborated upon in vv. 17–24. The people of God are portrayed here as an **olive tree** (cf. Jer. 11:16–19; Hos. 14:6–7). When Paul says **some** branches were removed, he probably has in mind the majority of the Jews of his day. Gentiles as wild shoots were grafted into the olive tree and now share in the **root** (the promises made to the patriarchs).

20[b]1 Cor. 10:12; 2 Cor. 1:24 [c]ch. 12:3, 16; 1 Tim. 6:17 [d]Prov. 28:14; Isa. 66:2, 5; Jer. 44:10; Phil. 2:12
22[e]1 Cor. 15:2; Heb. 3:6, 14 [f][John 15:2]
23[g]2 Cor. 3:16
25[h]ch. 12:16 [i]2 Cor. 3:14; [ver. 7] [j][Rev. 7:9]; See Luke 21:24
26[k]Cited from Isa. 59:20, 21; [John 4:22; Heb. 8:8-12] [l]Ps. 14:7; 53:6
27[m]See ch. 9:4 [n]Isa. 27:9; [Heb. 8:12]
28[o]ch. 9:5; Deut. 7:8; 10:15
29[p]See ch. 8:28
30[q]Eph. 2:2, 3, 11, 13; Col. 1:21; 3:7; Titus 3:3

were grafted in among the others and now share in the nourishing root[1] of the olive tree,
18 do not be arrogant toward the branches. If you are, remember it is not you who support
the root, but the root that supports you. **19** Then you will say, "Branches were broken off so
that I might be grafted in." **20** That is true. They were broken off because of their unbelief,
but you [b]stand fast through faith. So [c]do not become proud, but [d]fear. **21** For if God did
not spare the natural branches, neither will he spare you. **22** Note then the kindness and
the severity of God: severity toward those who have fallen, but God's kindness to you,
[e]provided you continue in his kindness. Otherwise [f]you too will be cut off. **23** And [g]even
they, if they do not continue in their unbelief, will be grafted in, for God has the power
to graft them in again. **24** For if you were cut from what is by nature a wild olive tree, and
grafted, contrary to nature, into a cultivated olive tree, how much more will these, the
natural branches, be grafted back into their own olive tree.

The Mystery of Israel's Salvation

25 [h]Lest you be wise in your own sight, I do not want you to be unaware of this mystery,
brothers:[2] [i]a partial hardening has come upon Israel, [j]until the fullness of the Gentiles has
come in. **26** And in this way all Israel will be saved, as it is written,

> [k]"The Deliverer will come [l]from Zion,
> he will banish ungodliness from Jacob";
> **27** "and this will be my [m]covenant with them
> [n]when I take away their sins."

28 As regards the gospel, they are enemies for your sake. But as regards election, they are
[o]beloved for the sake of their forefathers. **29** For the gifts and [p]the calling of God are irrevocable. **30** For just as [q]you were at one time disobedient to God but now have received mercy
because of their disobedience, **31** so they too have now been disobedient in order that by

[1] Greek *root of richness; some manuscripts richness* [2] Or *brothers and sisters*

11:18–20 Gentile believers are warned against arrogance, for it is God's saving promises (**the root**), not their own goodness, that saved them. Thus Gentiles might be tempted with pride because God removed the Jewish **branches** from the olive tree and grafted them in instead. But this should provoke **fear** and awe (Gk. *phobeō*, "to be afraid, have profound respect and reverence, have fear of offending"), for the Jews were removed because they failed to believe and the Gentiles remain only because of their continued trust.

11:21 Fear is the appropriate response, for God will not **spare** anyone who does not continue to believe, whether they are Jews or Gentiles. Fear here does not refer to a paralyzing fear. Rather, it is the kind of humble fear that does not take God or salvation for granted, or think lightly of his displeasure.

11:22–24 The Gentile readers must contemplate God's **kindness** and **severity**. His severity has been the portion of Jews who have not believed, but his kindness has been poured out on the Gentiles. Still, they must persevere in faith. Otherwise, they too will be judged as unbelievers. Furthermore, God will **graft** back onto the olive tree any Jews who put their faith in Christ. Paul argues from the lesser to the greater. If God **grafted** onto the olive tree Gentiles, who are the wild branches, then surely he can and will graft back onto the olive tree Jews, who are the original branches from the tree.

11:25 Paul discloses a **mystery** to the Gentiles to prevent them from being proud. The word "mystery" does not necessarily refer to something puzzling or difficult to grasp, but to something that was previously hidden and is now revealed. The mystery here has three elements: (1) at this time in salvation history the majority of Israel has been hardened; (2) during this same time the full number of Gentiles is being saved; and (3) God will do a new work in the future in which he will save all "Israel" (v. 26).

11:26 in this way all Israel will be saved. Various interpreters have claimed that Paul is speaking of: (1) the salvation of the church of Jesus Christ, both Jews and Gentiles, throughout history; or (2) the saving of a remnant of Jews throughout history; or (3) the salvation of the end-time generation of the Jewish people in the future. The first view is unlikely since throughout chs. 9–11 Israel and Gentiles are distinct ethnic entities. Furthermore, in 11:25 Israel refers to ethnic Israel, and it is difficult to see how the referent could suddenly change in v. 26. Finally, v. 28 indicates that ethnic Israel is still distinguished from Gentiles, for "they" in v. 28 clearly refers to ethnic Israel. The third view, that Paul refers to the salvation of Israel at the end of history, seems most likely because: (1) it fits with the promises of God's future work in vv. 12 and 15; (2) it is difficult to see how the salvation of a remnant of Jews all through history would qualify as a mystery; (3) the future salvation of ethnic Israel at the end of history accords with the climactic character of this passage; and (4) it demonstrates finally and fully how God is faithful to fulfill his saving promises to his people (9:6). "All Israel" does not necessarily refer to every single Jewish person but to a very large number, at least the majority of Jews. **The Deliverer** coming from Zion probably refers to Christ (cf. 1 Thess. 1:10), suggesting that the Jews will be saved near or at the second coming.

11:27 when I take away their sins. The salvation of Israel fits with God's covenantal promise to save his people and to forgive their sins.

11:28 for your sake. The unbelief of Israel has benefited the Gentiles, i.e., this is the period of history in which Gentiles are being saved, while most of Israel remains in unbelief. But God's electing promise given to **their forefathers** Abraham, Isaac, and Jacob will be fulfilled in the future.

11:29 Israel will be saved because God never revokes his saving promises. **Gifts** (Gk. *charisma*) means things freely given by God, and the word can be used to refer to different kinds of gifts. Sometimes the word refers to spiritual gifts for ministry (as in 1:11; 12:6; 1 Cor. 12:4) and sometimes to the gift of salvation (Rom. 5:15–16; 6:23), but the context here favors yet a third kind of "gifts," namely, the unique blessings given to Israel which Paul mentioned at the beginning of this long section (9:4–5). **calling** (Gk. *klēsis*, using the same root as Gk. *eklogē*, "election," in 11:28; also in 9:11; 11:7) refers here to calling to salvation (cf. 8:30; 9:11, 24).

11:30–31 Salvation history is structured to feature God's great **mercy**. God saved the Gentiles when one would expect only the Jews to be saved, but in the future he will amaze all by his grace again by saving the Jews, so that it will be clear that everyone's salvation is by **mercy** alone. The final **now** in the text does not mean the promise to the Jews is now fulfilled but that the promise of Jewish salvation could be fulfilled at any time.

the mercy shown to you they also may now[1] receive mercy. 32 For God [r]has consigned all
to disobedience, that he may have mercy on all.
33 Oh, the depth of the riches and [s]wisdom and knowledge of God! [t]How unsearchable
are his judgments and how inscrutable his ways!

34 "For [u]who has known the mind of the Lord,
or [v]who has been his counselor?"
35 "Or [w]who has given a gift to him
that he might be repaid?"

36 For [x]from him and through him and to him are all things. [y]To him be glory forever.
Amen.

A Living Sacrifice

12 [z]I appeal to you therefore, brothers,[2] by the mercies of God, [a]to present your bodies [b]as
a living sacrifice, holy and acceptable to God, which is your spiritual worship.[3] 2 [c]Do
not be conformed to this world,[4] but be transformed by [d]the renewal of your mind, that by
testing you may [e]discern what is the will of God, what is good and acceptable and perfect.[5]

Gifts of Grace

3 For [f]by the grace given to me I say to everyone among you [g]not to think of himself more
highly than he ought to think, but to think with sober judgment, [h]each according to [i]the

[1] Some manuscripts omit *now* [2] *Or brothers and sisters* [3] *Or your rational service* [4] Greek *age* [5] *Or what is the good and acceptable and perfect will of God*

32 [r]See ch. 3:9
33 [s]Col. 2:3; [Ps. 139:6; Eph. 3:10] [t]Deut. 29:29
34 [u]Isa. 40:13; 1 Cor. 2:16; [Job 15:8] [v]Job 36:22, 23
35 [w]Job 35:7; 41:11
36 [x]1 Cor. 8:6; 11:12; Col. 1:16; [Heb. 2:10] [y]ch. 16:27; Eph. 3:21; Phil. 4:20; 1 Tim. 1:17; 1 Pet. 4:11; 2 Pet. 3:18; Jude 25; Rev. 1:6; 5:13

Chapter 12

1 [z]1 Cor. 1:10; 2 Cor. 10:1; Eph. 4:1 [a]ch. 6:13, 16, 19; [Ps. 50:13, 14; 1 Cor. 6:20]; See 1 Pet. 2:5 [b]Heb. 10:20
2 [c]1 Pet. 1:14; [1 John 2:15] [d]Titus 3:5; [Ps. 51:10; 2 Cor. 4:16; Eph. 4:23; Col. 3:10] [e]Eph. 5:10; 1 Thess. 4:3
3 [f]See ch. 1:5 [g]ver. 16; ch. 11:20 [h]1 Cor. 7:17 [i]Eph. 4:7

Spiritual Gifts in Paul's Letters

Romans 12:6–8	1 Corinthians 12:7–10	1 Corinthians 12:28	Ephesians 4:11
Having gifts that differ according to the grace given to us	*To each is given the manifestation of the Spirit for the common good*	*God has appointed in the church*	*And he gave*
		apostles	the apostles
prophecy	prophecy	prophets	the prophets
			the evangelists
	ability to distinguish between spirits		
	utterance of wisdom		
teaching	utterance of knowledge	teachers	the shepherds and teachers
exhorting			
	working of miracles	miracles	
	gifts of healing	gifts of healing	
service		helping	
leading		administrating	
	various kinds of tongues	various kinds of tongues	
	interpretation of tongues		
giving			
	faith		
mercy			

11:32 The word **all** here refers to Jews and Gentiles (all without *distinction*, not all without *exception*). The sin and **disobedience** of both Jews and Gentiles is highlighted, to emphasize God's mercy in saving some among both Jews and Gentiles.

11:33–36 *Concluding Doxology.* As he concludes his setting forth of God's great plan in the history of salvation (chs. 1–11), Paul breaks forth into praise. God's wisdom and ways are far beyond the understanding of human beings, and hence he deserves all the glory.

11:34–35 The words of Isa. 40:13 teach that no human being knows **the mind of the Lord** apart from revelation, and no one can serve as God's adviser. Likewise the majestic words of Job 41:11 are a reminder that no one ultimately gives anything to God. Instead, everything humans have is a gift from God (1 Cor. 4:7).

11:36 Since **all things** are from God, and through God, and for God, it follows that he deserves all the **glory forever**. God's saving plan brings him great honor, praise, and glory forever and ever.

12:1–15:13 *God's Righteousness in Everyday Life.* The gift of God's saving righteousness leads to a new life. In this section Paul works out some of the practical implications of God's saving mercy.

12:1–2 *Paradigm for Exhortations: Total Dedication to God.* These verses summarize the response to God's grace and serve as the introduction for all of 12:1–15:13. They encapsulate what it means to live in a way that pleases God.

12:1 Therefore points back to the entire argument from 1:18–11:36. **mercies of God**. Christians are to give themselves entirely to God because of his saving grace, as shown in 3:21–11:36. Sacrificial language from the OT is used to denote the new life of Christians, and this means that the word **bodies** here refers to Christians as whole persons, for both body and soul belong to God. They are a **living sacrifice**, meaning that they are alive from the dead since they enjoy new life with Christ (6:4). "Living" also means that they will not be put to death as OT animal sacrifices were (see notes on sacrifices in Leviticus 1–7), for Christ has fulfilled what was predicted by those sacrifices. Whereas OT worship focused on offering animal sacrifices in the temple, Paul says that **spiritual worship** in a broad sense now includes offering one's whole life to God (cf. Heb. 13:15–16). Elsewhere, however, the NT can also use the word "worship" in a narrower sense, to speak of specific acts of adoration and praise (Matt. 2:2; John 4:20; Acts 13:2; 1 Cor. 14:25; Heb. 12:28; Rev. 11:1).

12:2 The present evil age still threatens those who belong to Christ, so they must resist its pressure. Their lives are changed as their minds are made new (contrast 1:28), so that they are able to "discern" God's will. **By testing you**

measure of faith that God has assigned. **4** For [j]as in one body we have many members,[1] and
the members do not all have the same function, **5** so we, [k]though many, [l]are one body in
Christ, and individually [m]members one of another. **6** [n]Having gifts that differ according to
the grace given to us, let us use them: if [o]prophecy, [p]in proportion to our faith; **7** if [q]service,
in our serving; the one who teaches, in his teaching; **8** the one who exhorts, in his exhortation; the one who contributes, in generosity; [r]the one who leads,[2] with zeal; the one who
does acts of mercy, with [s]cheerfulness.

Marks of the True Christian

9 [t]Let love be genuine. [u]Abhor what is evil; hold fast to what is good. **10** [v]Love one another
with brotherly affection. [w]Outdo one another in showing honor. **11** Do not be slothful in zeal,
[x]be fervent in spirit,[3] [y]serve the Lord. **12** [z]Rejoice in hope, [a]be patient in tribulation, [b]be constant in prayer. **13** [c]Contribute to the needs of the saints and [d]seek to show hospitality.
14 [e]Bless those who persecute you; bless and do not curse them. **15** [f]Rejoice with those
who rejoice, weep with those who weep. **16** [g]Live in harmony with one another. [h]Do not
be haughty, but associate with the lowly.[4] [i]Never be wise in your own sight. **17** [j]Repay no
one evil for evil, but [k]give thought to do what is honorable in the sight of all. **18** If possible,
so far as it depends on you, [l]live peaceably with all. **19** Beloved, [m]never avenge yourselves,
but leave it[5] to the wrath of God, for it is written, [n]"Vengeance is mine, I will repay, says
the Lord." **20** To the contrary, [o]"if your enemy is hungry, feed him; if he is thirsty, give him
something to drink; for by so doing you will heap burning coals on his head." **21** Do not
be overcome by evil, but overcome evil with good.

Submission to the Authorities

13 Let every person [p]be subject to the governing authorities. For [q]there is no authority except from God, and those that exist have been instituted by God. **2** Therefore
whoever resists the authorities resists what God has appointed, and those who resist will

[1] Greek *parts*; also verse 5 [2] Or *gives aid* [3] Or *fervent in the Spirit* [4] Or *give yourselves to humble tasks* [5] Greek *give place*

4 [j]1 Cor. 12:12-14; Eph. 4:4, 16
5 [k]1 Cor. 10:17, 33 [l]1 Cor. 12:20; Eph. 4:13; See John 17:11 [m]Eph. 4:25; [1 Cor. 6:15; 12:27]
6 [n]1 Cor. 12:4; 1 Pet. 4:10, 11; [1 Cor. 7:7; 12:7-11] [o]1 Cor. 12:10; See Acts 13:1 [p][2 Tim. 2:15]
7 [q]See Acts 6:1
8 [r]1 Tim. 5:17; [1 Cor. 12:28] [s]2 Cor. 9:7
9 [t]2 Cor. 6:6; 1 Tim. 1:5; 1 Pet. 1:22 [u]Ps. 97:10; 101:3; Amos 5:15; [1 Thess. 5:21, 22]
10 [v]See Heb. 13:1 [w]ch. 13:7; Phil. 2:3; 1 Pet. 2:17
11 [x]Acts 18:25 [y]Acts 20:19
12 [z]See ch. 5:2 [a]See Heb. 10:36 [b]See Acts 1:14
13 [c]ch. 15:25; 1 Cor. 16:1, 15; 2 Cor. 9:1, 12; Heb. 6:10; 13:16; [1 Tim. 6:18] [d]See Matt. 25:35
14 [e]See Matt. 5:44; 1 Pet. 3:9
15 [f]1 Cor. 12:26; [Job 30:25; Heb. 13:3]
16 [g]ch. 15:5; 2 Cor. 13:11; Phil. 2:2; 4:2; 1 Pet. 3:8 [h]ver. 3; Ps. 131:1; Jer. 45:5 [i]ch. 11:25; Prov. 3:7
17 [j]Prov. 20:22; Matt. 5:39; [ch. 14:19] [k]2 Cor. 8:21; [ch. 14:16]
18 [l]See Mark 9:50
19 [m]Prov. 20:22; Matt. 5:39; [ch. 14:19] [n]Heb. 10:30; Cited from Deut. 32:35; [Ps. 94:1; 1 Thess. 4:6]
20 [o]Cited from Prov. 25:21, 22; [Ex. 23:4, 5; 2 Kgs. 6:22; Luke 6:27] **Chapter 13** **1** [p]Titus 3:1; 1 Pet. 2:13 [q][John 19:11]; See Dan. 2:21

may discern translates Greek *dokimazō*, which often has the sense of finding out the worth of something by putting it to use or testing it in actual practice (cf. Luke 14:19; 1 Cor. 3:13; 2 Cor. 8:22; 1 Tim. 3:10).

12:3–13:14 *Marks of the Christian Community.* The new life of believers is described in this section.

12:3 God has granted a differing **measure of faith** to each of his children, and Paul calls upon each to assess himself or herself realistically.

12:4–5 The diversity and unity of the church is illustrated by comparison to the human body. Just as the human body is one with many **members** (lit., body parts, limbs), so the church is united though it is composed of many members. On the theme of the church as the **body** of **Christ**, see also 1 Corinthians 12 and Eph. 4:4, 12–16.

12:6 The variety of the body is evident from the various **gifts** God has given the church (see chart, p. 2178). On the gift of **prophecy**, see notes on Acts 21:4; 21:10–11; 1 Cor. 12:10; Eph. 2:20; 1 Thess. 5:20–21; and other notes on 1 Corinthians 12–14. **in proportion to our faith**. Paul instructs prophets to speak only when they have faith or confidence that the Holy Spirit is truly revealing something to them, and not to exceed the faith that God has given them by trying to impress others.

12:7–8 Christians should concentrate upon and give their energies to the gifts God has given them, whether in **serving** others, **teaching** God's Word patiently, or in **exhortation** and encouragement in the things of God. Thus Paul spotlights three attitudes necessary in exercising particular gifts: (1) those who have a special gift of helping others financially should never give grudgingly but always generously; (2) those who lead often have no one to whom they are accountable, and hence they must beware of laziness; (3) those who show mercy to the hurting must not grow weary but continue to minister with gladness.

12:9 The remainder of the chapter is a description of the life that is pleasing to God. Not surprisingly, **love** heads the list, for all that Paul says is embraced by the call to love (see note on John 13:34–35). **genuine**. Love cannot be reduced to sentimentalism. **abhor**. Christians are to hate evil.

12:13 Hospitality was very important for early Christians, for most of them could not afford hotels (lodging houses) when traveling but depended on the provision of fellow believers.

12:14 Bless . . . do not curse. These words reflect the teaching of Jesus (Matt. 5:44).

12:17 Repay no one evil. Again, an allusion to Jesus' teaching (Matt. 5:39).

12:18 If possible. Paul recognizes it is not always possible to be at peace with everyone, even when one makes the effort.

12:19 Vengeance is mine. Another allusion to Jesus' teaching (Matt. 5:39). Feelings of revenge can be overcome by realizing that God will make all things right, and that he will visit his wrath on those who deserve it.

12:20–21 Burning coals is quoted from Prov. 25:21–22. Most interpreters think Paul is teaching that the Christian is to do good to people so that they will feel ashamed and repent, and that sense is possible. But in the OT "burning coals" always represent punishment (2 Sam. 22:13; Ps. 11:6; 18:8, 12–13; 140:10), so another interpretation is that Paul is repeating the thought of Rom. 12:19: Christians are to do good to wrongdoers, recognizing that God will punish them on the last day if they refuse to repent. Overcoming **evil with good** will ordinarily include acts of kindness toward evildoers, but it may sometimes also include the "good" (13:4) of the civil government stopping evil through the use of superior force (military or police), as Paul explains in 13:3–4. See note on Prov. 25:21–22.

13:1–7 This passage addresses the responsibility of Christians to governing authorities. They are to "be subject to" (which generally means to obey, cf. 1 Pet. 3:5–6) the government because it has been ordained by God. Paul is speaking here of the general principle of submission to government. Several other passages show that God approves of Christians disobeying government, but only when obedience to government would mean disobeying God (see Ex. 1:17, 21; 1 Kings 18:4–16; Est. 4:16; Dan. 3:12–18; 6:10; Matt. 2:12; Acts 5:29; Heb. 11:23). There were even times when God raised up leaders to rebel against the government and deliver his people from evil rulers (Exodus 1–14; Judg. 2:16; Heb. 11:32–34).

13:1 It is true that **those** governing authorities **that exist have been instituted by God**, but sometimes God gives good authorities as a blessing, and

incur judgment. 3 For rulers are not a terror to good conduct, but to bad. Would you have
no fear of the one who is in authority? Then do what is good, and you [r]will receive his
approval, 4 for [s]he is God's servant for your good. But if you do wrong, be afraid, for he
does not bear the sword in vain. For he is the servant of God, [t]an avenger who carries out
God's wrath on the wrongdoer. 5 Therefore one must be in subjection, not only to avoid
God's wrath but also [u]for the sake of conscience. 6 For because of this you also pay taxes,
for the authorities are ministers of God, attending to this very thing. 7 [v]Pay to all what is
owed to them: taxes to whom taxes are owed, revenue to whom revenue is owed, respect
to whom respect is owed, honor to whom honor is owed.

Fulfilling the Law Through Love

8 [w]Owe no one anything, except to love each other, for [x]the one who loves another has
fulfilled the law. 9 For the commandments, [y]"You shall not commit adultery, You shall
not murder, You shall not steal, You shall not covet," and any other commandment, are
summed up in this word: [z]"You shall love your neighbor as yourself." 10 Love does no wrong
to a neighbor; therefore [a]love is the fulfilling of the law.

11 Besides this you know the time, that the hour has come for you [b]to wake from sleep.
[c]For salvation is nearer to us now than when we first believed. 12 [d]The night is far gone;
the day is at hand. So then let us [e]cast off [f]the works of darkness and [g]put on the armor
of light. 13 [h]Let us walk properly as in the daytime, [i]not in orgies and drunkenness, not in
sexual immorality and sensuality, [j]not in quarreling and jealousy. 14 But [k]put on the Lord
Jesus Christ, and make no provision for the flesh, [l]to gratify its desires.

Do Not Pass Judgment on One Another

14 As for [m]the one who is weak in faith, welcome him, but not to quarrel over opinions. 2 [n]One person believes he may eat anything, while the weak person eats only
vegetables. 3 Let not the one who eats despise the one who abstains, and [o]let not the one
who abstains pass judgment on the one who eats, for God has welcomed him. 4 [p]Who are

3 [r]1 Pet. 2:14
4 [s]2 Chr. 19:6 [t]1 Thess. 4:6
5 [u]1 Pet. 2:19; [Eccles. 8:2]
7 [v]Matt. 17:25; 22:21; Mark 12:17
8 [w][Lev. 19:13; Prov. 3:27, 28] [x]ver. 10; [Matt. 22:40; Col. 3:14]; See John 13:34
9 [y]Matt. 19:18; Cited from Ex. 20:13-17; Deut. 5:17-21 [z]Cited from Lev. 19:18
10 [a][John 14:15]; See ver. 8
11 [b]1 Cor. 15:34; Eph. 5:14; 1 Thess. 5:6 [c][Isa. 56:1; Luke 21:28]
12 [d][John 9:4] [e]Col. 3:8 [f]Eph. 5:11; [John 3:20] [g]2 Cor. 6:7; Eph. 6:11, 13; 1 Thess. 5:8
13 [h]1 Thess. 4:12 [i]Luke 21:34; Gal. 5:21; 1 Pet. 4:3 [j]James 3:14, 16
14 [k]Gal. 3:27; [Job 29:14; Ps. 132:9; Luke 24:49; Eph. 4:24; Col. 3:10] [l]Gal. 5:16; 1 Pet. 2:11

Chapter 14

1 [m]ch. 15:1; 1 Cor. 8:9-11; 9:22
2 [n]ver. 14
3 [o]Col. 2:16
4 [p]James 4:12

sometimes he institutes evil rulers as a means of trial or judgment (2 Chron. 25:20; 32:24–25). On God's rule over earthly **authorities**, see Ps. 75:7 and Dan. 2:21. These earthly "authorities" will ultimately be superseded by the rule of Christ (Dan. 2:44; Rev. 22:1–5).

13:3 Rulers are not a terror to good conduct, but to bad means that civil government in general is a great blessing from God for which we should be thankful. Without civil government there would be anarchy, a horrible alternative in which evil runs rampant.

13:4 Governing authorities are God's servants and carry out his **wrath** on evildoers, and they do so **for your good**. Even though Christians must not take personal revenge (12:17–20), it is right for them to turn punishment over to the civil authorities, who have the responsibility to punish evil. The reference to the **sword** most likely refers to the penalty of capital punishment (cf. Gen. 9:6).

13:5 Christians should obey the civil authorities not only to avoid **God's wrath** (coming through those authorities, v. 4) but also because their **conscience** tells them that submitting to the government is right (see note on vv. 1–7).

13:6–7 Christians must not refuse to **pay taxes** simply because they think some of the money is used unjustly, for the Roman Empire surely did not use all of its money for godly purposes! So, too, believers are to **honor** their leaders, even if they are not fully admirable.

13:8 Verses 8–10 focus on the Christian's relationship to the Mosaic law. **Owe no one anything** links back to v. 7, and thus the command does not prohibit all borrowing but means that one should always "pay what is owed" (see v. 7), fulfilling whatever repayment agreements have been made. The debt one never ceases paying is the call to **love** one another. Indeed, love fulfills what the Mosaic law demands.

13:9 Paul cites several OT **commandments** regarding responsibility to others, all of which are summed up in the call from Lev. 19:18 to **love your neighbor as yourself**.

13:11–12 In this section (12:3–13:14) the final verses call Christians to action, given the shortness of the time before Jesus returns. **Sleep** here is a metaphor for a life of moral carelessness and laxity. **Salvation** is viewed as a future reality here, and it draws nearer every day. **the day is at hand**. The nearness of the end summons Christians to put off all evil works and to live in the light.

13:13 Things not fitting for those who belong to the light include (1) sins of addiction in drinking and partying; (2) sexual sins; and (3) social sins.

13:14 Paul's exhortations can be summed up in the call to **put on . . . Christ**. The metaphor of putting on clothing implies not just imitating Christ's character but also living in close personal fellowship with him. Even though believers have new life, they still must constantly renounce the **flesh** and refuse to **gratify its desires**.

14:1–15:13 *A Call for Mutual Acceptance between the Strong and the Weak.* Paul addresses a specific dispute, probably over whether Christians need to abide by Jewish food laws. Paul clearly sides theologically with the "strong" (who did not feel compelled to follow those laws), but he encourages them not to despise or scandalize the "weak."

14:1 As for the one who is weak. The exhortation here is directed to the strong, for they are tempted to enter into quarrels with those who have a weaker faith.

14:2 The strong are operating in their belief that all foods are permitted. Notice that Paul does not say that the weak are exhibiting faith by their abstaining. The weak eat only **vegetables**, probably so that they avoid the risk of eating unclean foods (cf. Dan. 1:8, 10, 12, 16).

14:3 The strong are liable to ridicule and mock the weak with their delicate conscience. Conversely, the weak are prone to **pass judgment** on those who feel the liberty to eat anything. The weak must not stand in judgment, for God has accepted the strong believer.

14:4 This verse is likely directed to the weak. It is not their place as fellow servants **to pass judgment** on the strong. The strong stand or fall before God, and they will stand righteous before God on the last day because God will give them grace to keep them from falling away.

you to pass judgment on the servant of another? It is before his own master[1] that he stands
or falls. And he will be upheld, for the Lord is able to make him stand.
5 [q]One person esteems one day as better than another, while another esteems all days
alike. [r]Each one should be fully convinced in his own mind. 6 The one who observes the
day, observes it in honor of the Lord. The one who eats, eats in honor of the Lord, since
[s]he gives thanks to God, while the one who abstains, abstains in honor of the Lord and
gives thanks to God. 7 For [t]none of us lives to himself, and none of us dies to himself. 8 For
if we live, we live to the Lord, and if we die, we die to the Lord. So then, [u]whether we live
or whether we die, we are the Lord's. 9 For to this end Christ [v]died and lived again, that he
might be Lord both [w]of the dead and of the living.
10 Why do you pass judgment on your brother? Or you, why do you despise your brother?
For [w]we will all stand before [x]the judgment seat of God; 11 for it is written,

> [y]"As I live, says the Lord, every knee shall bow to me,
> and every tongue shall confess[2] to God."

12 So then [z]each of us will give an account of himself to God.

Do Not Cause Another to Stumble

13 [a]Therefore let us not pass judgment on one another any longer, but rather decide
[b]never to put a stumbling block or hindrance in the way of a brother. 14 I know and am
persuaded in the Lord Jesus [c]that nothing is unclean in itself, [d]but it is unclean for anyone
who thinks it unclean. 15 For if your brother is grieved by what you eat, [e]you are no longer
walking in love. [f]By what you eat, do not destroy the one for whom Christ died. 16 [g]So do
not let what you regard as good be spoken of as evil. 17 [h]For the kingdom of God is not a
matter of eating and drinking but [i]of righteousness and [j]peace and joy in the Holy Spirit.
18 Whoever thus serves Christ is [k]acceptable to God and approved by men. 19 So then let us
[l]pursue what makes for peace and for [m]mutual upbuilding.
20 [n]Do not, for the sake of food, destroy the work of God. [o]Everything is indeed clean,
but [p]it is wrong for anyone to make another stumble by what he eats. 21 [q]It is good not to
eat meat or drink wine or do anything that causes your brother to stumble.[3] 22 The faith
that you have, keep between yourself and God. [r]Blessed is the one who has no reason to
pass judgment on himself for what he approves. 23 But whoever has doubts is condemned

5 [q]Gal. 4:10; [Zech. 7:5, 6] [r]ver. 23
6 [s]1 Cor. 10:30, 31; 1 Tim. 4:3, 4; See Matt. 15:36
7 [t]2 Cor. 5:15; Gal. 2:20; 1 Pet. 4:2; [1 Cor. 6:19; 1 Thess. 5:10]
8 [u]Phil. 1:20
9 [v]Rev. 1:18; 2:8 [w]See Acts 10:42; Rev. 20:12
10 [w][See ver. 9 above] [x]2 Cor. 5:10
11 [y]Phil. 2:10, 11; Cited from Isa. 45:23
12 [z]Matt. 12:36; 16:27; 1 Pet. 4:5; [Gal. 6:5]
13 [a]See Matt. 7:1 [b][1 Cor. 8:13]
14 [c]ver. 2, 20; See Acts 10:15 [d][1 Cor. 8:7, 10]
15 [e]Eph. 5:2 [f]1 Cor. 8:11; [ver. 20]
16 [g][ch. 12:17; 1 Cor. 10:29, 30]
17 [h]1 Cor. 8:8 [i][1 Cor. 6:9] [j]Gal. 5:22; [ch. 15:13]
18 [k][2 Cor. 8:21]
19 [l]Ps. 34:14; 1 Cor. 7:15; 2 Tim. 2:22 [m]ch. 15:2; 1 Cor. 14:12
20 [n]ver. 15 [o]Titus 1:15; See ver. 14 [p]1 Cor. 8:9-12
21 [q]1 Cor. 8:13
22 [r]1 John 3:21

[1] Or *lord* [2] Or *shall give praise* [3] Some manuscripts add *or be hindered or be weakened*

14:5 The weak thought some days were more important than others. Given the Jewish background here (see v. 14), the **day** that is supremely in view is certainly the Sabbath. The strong think every day is the same. Both views are permissible. Each person must follow his own conscience. What is remarkable is that the Sabbath is no longer a binding commitment for Paul but a matter of one's personal conviction. Unlike the other nine commandments in Ex. 20:1–17, the Sabbath commandment seems to have been part of the "ceremonial laws" of the Mosaic covenant, like the dietary laws and the laws about sacrifices, all of which are no longer binding on new covenant believers (see also Gal. 4:10; Col. 2:16–17). However, it is still wise to take regular times of rest from work, and regular times of worship are commanded for Christians (Heb. 10:24–25; cf. Acts 20:7).

14:6 Whether one observes a special day, or eats all foods, or abstains from some foods, the important thing is the **honor of the Lord** and to give **thanks to God**.

14:7–8 Fundamental to the whole discussion is the reality that the Christian's life is not his own. Both in life and in death, Christians belong **to the Lord**, and he alone is their judge.

14:10–12 The strong should not despise the weak, and the weak should not judge the strong, for everyone will stand before God, who will judge all on the last day. The future day of **judgment** is prophesied in Isa. 45:23. Every person will give **an account** of his life to God at the judgment. Though justification is by faith alone, what Christians do will affect God's evaluation of their service to him and the rewards they will receive (cf. 1 Cor. 3:10–17; 2 Cor. 5:10).

14:14 Christians are no longer under the old covenant, hence Paul no longer accepts the view that some foods are **unclean** (cf. Leviticus 11; Deuteronomy 14). Still, if anyone thinks certain foods are unclean, then they are unclean for that person.

14:15–17 The strong should not cause sorrow to the weak by what they eat but rather should refrain for the sake of the weak. They must beware lest they **destroy** the faith of a brother or sister. If the strong do not act in love, the goodness of the gospel may be wrongly identified as evil, for their lack of love for the weak contradicts Christ's love. God's kingdom centers on the gifts of **righteousness**, **peace**, and **joy** granted by the Holy Spirit, so that bodily appetites become secondary.

14:18–19 Those who show such love for the weak please God and stand out before others as selfless servants of Christ. All Christians are summoned to edify others and to strive for **peace**.

14:20–21 Paul urges the strong not to **destroy** God's **work** in the weak by eating **food** that will scandalize the weak. He assures the strong that all food is **clean** (another indication that Jewish food laws are in view), but even the strong who have no convictions against eating such food fall into sin when others stumble and fall away from Christ upon observing how the strong behave.

14:22 The strong are likely addressed here. **The faith that you have** means their faith that they may eat anything (cf. vv. 1–2, 23). They are not asked to surrender their convictions, but they should not behave in a way that injures the faith of others and thereby brings judgment on themselves.

14:23 No one should eat unclean food if he has **doubts** about the rightness of the activity. Indeed, anything believers do apart from **faith** is sin, for faith glorifies God by trusting him (4:20), and lack of faith dishonors him.

if he eats, because the eating is not from faith. For whatever does not proceed from faith
is sin.[1]

The Example of Christ

15 [s]We who are strong [t]have an obligation to bear with the failings of the weak, and
not to please ourselves. 2 [u]Let each of us please his neighbor for his good, to build
him up. 3 For [v]Christ did not please himself, but as it is written, [w]"The reproaches of those
who reproached you fell on me." 4 For [x]whatever was written in former days was written
for our [y]instruction, that through endurance and through [z]the encouragement of the
Scriptures we might have hope. 5 May the God of endurance and encouragement grant
you [a]to live in such harmony with one another, in accord with Christ Jesus, 6 that together
you may with one voice glorify [b]the God and Father of our Lord Jesus Christ. 7 Therefore
welcome one another as Christ has welcomed you, for the glory of God.

Christ the Hope of Jews and Gentiles

8 For I tell you that Christ [c]became a servant to the circumcised to show God's truthfulness, in order [d]to confirm the promises given to the patriarchs, 9 and in order [e]that the
Gentiles might glorify God for his mercy. As it is written,

> [f]"Therefore I will praise you among the Gentiles,
> and sing to your name."

10 And again it is said,

> [g]"Rejoice, O Gentiles, with his people."

11 And again,

> [h]"Praise the Lord, all you Gentiles,
> and let all the peoples extol him."

12 And again Isaiah says,

> [i, j]"The root of Jesse will come,
> even he who arises to rule the Gentiles;
> [k]in him will the Gentiles hope."

13 May the God of hope fill you with all [l]joy and peace in believing, so that by the power
of the Holy Spirit you may abound in hope.

Paul the Minister to the Gentiles

14 [m]I myself am satisfied about you, my brothers,[2] that you yourselves are full of goodness, filled with [n]all knowledge and able to instruct one another. 15 But on some points

Chapter 15
1 [s][Gal. 6:1] [t]1 Thess. 5:14; See ch. 14:1
2 [u]1 Cor. 10:33; [1 Cor. 9:19, 22; 10:24; Phil. 2:4]
3 [v]Phil. 2:5, 8; [John 5:30; 6:38] [w]Cited from Ps. 69:9
4 [x]ch. 4:23 [y]2 Tim. 3:16 [z]Ps. 119:50
5 [a]See ch. 12:16
6 [b]2 Cor. 1:3; Eph. 1:3; 1 Pet. 1:3; [John 20:17; Eph. 1:17; Rev. 1:6]
8 [c]Matt. 15:24; John 1:11; [Heb. 3:1]; See Acts 3:26 [d][ch. 4:16; 2 Cor. 1:20]
9 [e]See ch. 3:29 [f]Cited from 2 Sam. 22:50; Ps. 18:49
10 [g]Cited from Deut. 32:43
11 [h]Cited from Ps. 117:1
12 [i]Cited from Isa. 11:10 [j]Isa. 11:1; [Rev. 5:5; 22:16] [k]Matt. 12:21
13 [l][ch. 5:1, 2; 14:17]
14 [m][2 Pet. 1:12; 3:1; 1 John 2:21] [n]1 Cor. 1:5; 13:2; [1 Cor. 8:1, 7, 10; 12:8]

[1] Some manuscripts insert here 16:25–27 [2] Or *brothers and sisters*; also verse 30

15:1–3 The **strong** have a responsibility to tolerate and support the **weak** instead of living selfishly to satisfy their own desires. The Christian life centers on strengthening others. **Christ** is the supreme example of living for the glory of God, as is shown in the citation of Ps. 69:9.

15:4 Whatever was written in former days includes the whole of the OT **Scriptures**. Paul expresses confidence that all of the OT was written down for the **instruction** and **encouragement** of God's people, thus indirectly implying that all the words of the OT are words of God, words that he wisely directed to be written not only for his purposes at the time they were written but also for later centuries.

15:7 Therefore, in conclusion, both the strong and the weak are exhorted to accept one another, for they have been accepted by Christ even though they are sinners. Such mutual acceptance will bring great **glory** to **God**.

15:8 The **circumcised** refers to the Jews here. In fulfilling God's saving promises to the Jews, the Lord's **truthfulness** and faithfulness to his word are demonstrated.

15:9–12 Paul cites verses from 2 Sam. 22:50 or Ps. 18:49; Deut. 32:43; Ps. 117:1; and Isa. 11:10, which emphasize the inclusion of the **Gentiles** into the people of God along with the Jews. If the first reference is from 2 Sam. 22:50, citations are provided from the historical books, the law, the writings, and the prophets. The one people of God, both Jews and Gentiles, will praise God forever for his great mercy extended to them in Christ Jesus, showing that the worship of God is his ultimate aim in salvation history.

15:9 The whole of Romans emphasizes the inclusion of the **Gentiles** as well in God's saving plan. They will also **praise** God for his mercy to them.

15:13 Hope is the link word from v. 12 (see also v. 4). **Joy and peace** come from trust in God, but such trust is finally the gift of God, for believers **abound in hope** only by his grace.

15:14–16:23 *The Extension of God's Righteousness through the Pauline Mission.* Paul focuses on his calling as the apostle to the Gentiles, adding some greetings and final instructions.

15:14–33 *The Establishment of Churches among the Gentiles.* Paul explains his unique ministry to the Gentiles and exhorts the Roman church to be a sending base for his mission to Spain.

15:14 The church in one sense did not need to hear what Paul wrote since they already knew the truths in the letter. **Instruct** translates Greek *noutheteō*, "instruct, admonish, warn, counsel," which is often used of warning against wrong conduct (Acts 20:31; 1 Cor. 4:14; Col. 1:28; 1 Thess. 5:12, 14; 2 Thess. 3:15). Paul encourages ordinary Christians (no doubt esp. those who have

I have written to you very boldly by way of reminder, [o]because of the grace given me by
God **16** to be [p]a minister of Christ Jesus to the Gentiles [q]in the priestly service of the gospel of God, so that [r]the offering of the Gentiles may be acceptable, sanctified by the Holy
Spirit. **17** In Christ Jesus, then, I have [s]reason to be proud of [t]my work for God. **18** For I will
not venture to speak of anything except [u]what Christ has accomplished through me [v]to
bring the Gentiles to obedience—by word and deed, **19** [w]by the power of signs and wonders, by the power of the Spirit of God—so that [x]from Jerusalem and all the way around
[y]to Illyricum I have fulfilled the ministry of the gospel of Christ; **20** and thus I make it my
ambition to preach the gospel, not where Christ has already been named, [z]lest I build on
someone else's foundation, **21** but as it is written,

> [a]"Those who have never been told of him will see,
> and those who have never heard will understand."

Paul's Plan to Visit Rome

22 This is the reason why [b]I have so often been hindered from coming to you. **23** But
now, since I no longer have any room for work in these regions, and [c]since I have longed
for many years to come to you, **24** I hope to see you in passing as I go [d]to Spain, and [e]to be
helped on my journey there by you, once I have enjoyed your company for a while. **25** At
present, however, [f]I am going to Jerusalem bringing aid to the saints. **26** For [g]Macedonia
and Achaia have been pleased to make some contribution for the poor among the saints
at Jerusalem. **27** For they were pleased to do it, and indeed [h]they owe it to them. For if the
Gentiles have come to share in their spiritual blessings, they ought also to be of service to
them in material blessings. **28** When therefore I have completed this and have delivered to
them what has been collected,[1] I will leave [i]for Spain by way of you. **29** I know that when I
come to you I will come in the fullness of the blessing[2] of Christ.

30 I appeal to you, brothers, by our Lord Jesus Christ and by [j]the love of the Spirit, [k]to
strive together with me in your prayers to God on my behalf, **31** [l]that I may be delivered

15 [o]See ch. 1:5
16 [p]See ch. 11:13 [q][Mal. 1:11] [r]Isa. 66:20; [Phil. 2:17]
17 [s]Phil. 3:3 [t]Heb. 2:17; 5:1
18 [u]Acts 15:12; 21:19; Gal. 2:8 [v]See ch. 1:5
19 [w]2 Cor. 12:12; [Acts 19:11] [x]Acts 22:17-21 [y][Acts 20:1, 2]
20 [z][2 Cor. 10:13, 15, 16]
21 [a]Cited from Isa. 52:15
22 [b]ch. 1:13; [1 Thess. 2:18]
23 [c]ver. 29, 32; ch. 1:10, 11; Acts 19:21
24 [d]ver. 28 [e]See Acts 15:3
25 [f]Acts 19:21; 20:22; 21:15; 24:17; [ver. 31]
26 [g]1 Cor. 16:1-4; 2 Cor. 8:1; 9:2, 13
27 [h]1 Cor. 9:11; [Gal. 6:6]
28 [i]ver. 24
30 [j][Phil. 2:1; Col. 1:8] [k]Col. 4:12; [2 Cor. 1:11; Col. 2:1, 2; Heb. 13:18]
31 [l]2 Thess. 3:2; [2 Tim. 3:11; 4:17]

[1] Greek *sealed to them this fruit* [2] Some manuscripts insert *of the gospel*

greater maturity and wisdom) to give one another practical, real-life wisdom and counsel.

15:16 Paul functions, so to speak, as priest relative to **the gospel**, and **the offering** he presents to God is Gentile converts. This offering is pleasing to God since it is set apart into the realm of the holy (**sanctified**) by the Holy Spirit.

15:17–18 Paul in a certain sense actually boasts of his ministry, for in doing so he glorifies not himself but Christ, who has worked through him in his ministry to the Gentiles.

15:18 Paul summarizes his entire ministry up to this point by saying that Christ accomplished his work through him **by word and deed**, that is, both by Paul's preaching about Christ and by Paul's actions (lifestyle, with mighty works) that accompanied those words.

15:19 By the power of signs and wonders refers to the miracles that accompanied Paul's gospel proclamation throughout his entire ministry. Such miracles gave a "sign" of (or pointed to) the power of God, the divine origin and truth of the gospel, and God's mercy and love for people. They were "wonders" in that people were amazed by them (cf. Acts 4:30; 5:12; 14:3; 15:12; 2 Cor. 12:12; Heb. 2:4). Paul has fulfilled his mandate to preach the gospel among the Gentiles from **Jerusalem** to **Illyricum** (roughly comprising what is now Albania and also what was formerly Yugoslavia). How can Paul say that his work has been complete when many still have not heard the gospel in this area? It can be seen from the following verses that churches have been planted in key centers, and from there Paul's coworkers will bring the gospel to outlying areas (e.g., Epaphras in Colossae, Col. 1:7).

15:20–21 Paul's aim was **to preach the gospel** in areas where no churches existed. His calling was not to plant churches where they already existed. Thereby he was fulfilling the prophecy of Isa. 52:15.

15:22 Paul had been prevented from coming to Rome because his work of planting churches in unreached areas in the eastern part of the Roman Empire (key cities from which the gospel radiated outward) had not been completed.

15:23–24 Paul now feels that his work in the east has come to an end. So he hopes to see the Roman church, and desires that they would function as his base of support for his mission to **Spain**. By the first century A.D. Spain was firmly a part of the Roman Empire. Spain provided significant crops to the empire, and it was the fatherland of several important Roman authors (and a few later emperors); thus it would have been a strategic location for Paul to evangelize. No visit of Paul to Spain is recorded in the NT, but it is possible that he went there after his release from prison in Rome (after Acts 28:30–31). There is some historical evidence after the NT suggesting that Paul did preach in Spain, but it falls short of clear proof.

15:25 The trip to Rome cannot be carried out immediately. Paul's next task is to travel to **Jerusalem** to bring the money he had collected for the poor saints there (cf. 1 Cor. 16:1–4; 2 Corinthians 8–9).

15:26 Christians from the Roman provinces of **Macedonia** and **Achaia** had gladly contributed to the collection. These provinces are roughly equivalent to northern and southern Greece today. This collection would include gifts from such cities as Philippi, Thessalonica, and Corinth.

15:27 they were pleased. The gladness of the Gentiles in providing for the needs of Jewish Christians is fitting. They stand in debt to the Jews, for they enjoy the **spiritual blessings** of the Jewish people and hence should happily assist them financially. Paul assumes that financial aid for needy Christians is a normal part of the Christian life.

15:28 After the collection has been delivered in Jerusalem, Paul plans to travel to Rome and then on to Spain. Paul was imprisoned, however, after he arrived in Jerusalem. Paul's plan to come to Rome was realized (Acts 22–28), but not in the way he intended, since he arrived in Rome as a prisoner.

15:31 Two prayer requests are found here: (1) that Paul would be **delivered from the unbelievers** in Judea, and (2) that his offering would be **acceptable to the saints** in Jerusalem. Some think the first request was not answered since Paul was arrested in Judea at the impulse of the Jews. But it seems his prayer was answered, for the Jews desired to put him to death (Acts 22–28), and this desire was frustrated, so that Paul *did* go to Rome, even if not in the way he anticipated. Further, Acts suggests that the offering was accepted in Jerusalem (Acts 24:17).

from the unbelievers in Judea, and that [m]my service for Jerusalem may be acceptable to
the saints, 32 so that by God's will I may come to you with joy and [n]be refreshed in your
company. 33 May [o]the God of peace be with you all. Amen.

Personal Greetings

16 I commend to you our sister Phoebe, a servant[1] of the church at [p]Cenchreae, 2 that you
[q]may welcome her in the Lord in a way worthy of the saints, and help her in whatever
she may need from you, for she has been a patron of many and of myself as well.
3 Greet [r]Prisca and Aquila, my fellow workers in Christ Jesus, 4 who risked their necks for
my life, to whom not only I give thanks but all the churches of the Gentiles give thanks
as well. 5 Greet also [s]the church in their house. Greet my beloved Epaenetus, who was
[t]the first convert[2] to Christ in Asia. 6 Greet Mary, who has worked hard for you. 7 Greet
Andronicus and Junia,[3] my kinsmen and my [u]fellow prisoners. They are well known to the
apostles,[4] and they were in Christ before me. 8 Greet Ampliatus, my beloved in the Lord.
9 Greet Urbanus, our fellow worker in Christ, and my beloved Stachys. 10 Greet Apelles,
who is approved in Christ. Greet those [v]who belong to the family of Aristobulus. 11 Greet
my kinsman Herodion. Greet those in the Lord who belong to the family of Narcissus.
12 Greet those workers in the Lord, Tryphaena and Tryphosa. Greet the beloved Persis,
who has worked hard in the Lord. 13 Greet Rufus, chosen in the Lord; also his mother, who
has been a mother to me as well. 14 Greet Asyncritus, Phlegon, Hermes, Patrobas, Hermas,
and the brothers[5] who are with them. 15 Greet Philologus, Julia, Nereus and his sister, and
Olympas, and all the saints who are with them. 16 [w]Greet one another with a holy kiss. All
the churches of Christ greet you.

[1] Or *deaconess* [2] Greek *firstfruit* [3] Or *Junias* [4] Or *messengers* [5] Or *brothers and sisters;* also verse 17

31 [m]2 Cor. 8:4
32 [n][1 Cor. 16:18; 2 Cor. 7:13; Philem. 7, 20]
33 [o]ch. 16:20; 2 Cor. 13:11; Phil. 4:9; 1 Thess. 5:23; Heb. 13:20; [1 Cor. 14:33; 2 Thess. 3:16]

Chapter 16

1 [p]Acts 18:18
2 [q]Phil. 2:29
3 [r]See Acts 18:2
5 [s]1 Cor. 16:19; [Col. 4:15; Philem. 2] [t][1 Cor. 16:15]
7 [u]Col. 4:10; Philem. 23
10 [v]1 Cor. 1:11
16 [w]1 Cor. 16:20; 2 Cor. 13:12; 1 Thess. 5:26; [1 Pet. 5:14]

15:32 Paul arrived in Rome in an unexpected way (as a prisoner), but he did come with the joy of Christ and as an encouragement for fellow Christians (cf. Acts 28:15–16).

16:1–23 *Appreciation and Greetings to Coworkers in the Gospel.* Paul warmly greets those he knows in Rome who are involved in ministry, showing the love that existed among Christians. These greetings also function to support the authenticity of the Pauline gospel, for they show that respected coworkers in Rome are co-laborers in the same gospel that Paul proclaims. It is not surprising he would know so many who are now in Rome, for travel was more common than modern people might think. Further, Paul may not have known every person he greeted. Perhaps he knew of some by virtue of their reputation. Note that Paul says something specific about virtually every person greeted.

16:1 Phoebe probably brought this epistle to the Romans. Scholars debate whether Phoebe is a **servant** in a general sense, or whether she served as a deacon, since the Greek word *diakonos* can mean either "servant" (13:4; 15:8; 1 Cor. 3:5; 1 Tim. 4:6) or "deacon" (referring to a church office; Phil. 1:1; 1 Tim. 3:8, 12). **Cenchreae** was a port town just 6.5 miles (10.5 km) east of Corinth (see note on Acts 18:18).

16:2 Paul calls upon the church to assist Phoebe since she has helped so many. Phoebe served as a **patron**, probably with financial assistance and hospitality.

16:3 Prisca and Aquila are well-known from elsewhere in the NT (cf. 1 Cor. 16:19; 2 Tim. 4:19). Prisca is given the diminutive name Priscilla in Acts (Acts 18:2–3, 18, 26). Scholars have suggested many reasons why Prisca is named first (was it her prominence, or social standing, or that she was converted first, or was it out of courtesy, or a mere stylistic variation?) though there is insufficient evidence to know the answer. Paul also names her first in 2 Tim. 4:19, but second in 1 Cor. 16:19.

16:4 Perhaps Prisca and Aquila **risked** their lives when Paul was in danger in Ephesus (Acts 19:23–41; 1 Cor. 15:32; 2 Cor. 1:8–11).

16:5 the church in their house. See note on 1 Cor. 16:19. Apparently a house church met in the house of Prisca and Aquila. **Asia** here refers to a province in what is modern-day Turkey.

16:6 A number of women, like Mary, are commended in ch. 16 for their hard work, but such work does not mean that these women served as pastors, elders, or overseers (see 1 Tim. 2:12).

16:7 Andronicus and Junia were probably a husband-and-wife ministry team. Most scholars now think that Junia was a woman, though some have argued that a man named Junias is in view (the spelling would be the same in Greek, and both male and female forms are rare in Greek; however, the female equivalent of "Junia" is much more common in Latin, and Paul could have been referring to a woman with a Latin name). Some have said that this verse proves that Junia was an apostle, and thus women can fill any church office. The verse seems to be saying, however, that Andronicus and Junia were **well known to the apostles**, not that Junia was herself an apostle. (Other examples of this construction, Gk. *episēmos* plus *en* plus dative, have been found with the meaning "well known to [someone]": see *Psalms of Solomon* 2.6; Euripides, *Hippolytus* 103; Lucianus, *Harmonides* 1.17.) Some translations render the passage as stating that Andronicus and Junia were "well known *among* the apostles," but "apostle" (Gk. *apostolos*) would probably then mean "messengers" of churches (as it does in 2 Cor. 8:23; Phil. 2:25; also John 13:16) rather than "apostles" in the technical sense of Peter and Paul. In this case, the term would refer to Andronicus and Junia as itinerant missionaries, and (given both biblical patterns of leadership and ancient cultural expectations) Junia probably labored especially among women. This passage also reveals that the couple was Jewish, had been imprisoned, and had become Christians before Paul.

16:8–10 The people greeted in these verses are not mentioned elsewhere in the NT. The **family of Aristobulus** probably refers to the servants in Aristobulus's household. Some think Aristobulus is the grandson of Herod the Great (c. 73–4 B.C.) and the brother of Herod Agrippa I (10 B.C.–A.D. 44), though this remains uncertain.

16:11 The family of Narcissus refers to the servants in Narcissus's household. Some scholars think Narcissus was the wealthy freedman who served the emperor Claudius (A.D. 41–54) and who was compelled by Nero's mother, Agrippina, to kill himself when Nero became emperor (A.D. 54).

16:12 Three women are greeted here who **worked hard in the Lord** (see note on v. 6).

16:13 It is not certain that this is the same **Rufus** as is mentioned in Mark 15:21, but it is possible that he is the son of Simon of Cyrene. Apparently Rufus's mother ministered significantly to Paul.

16:14–15 There is no further information on the saints greeted here.

16:16 Christians greeted one another with a **holy kiss** to signify their warm affection for one another (see note on 1 Cor. 16:20; also 2 Cor. 13:12; 1 Thess. 5:26; 1 Pet. 5:14).

17[x]1 Tim. 1:3; 6:3 [y]See 2 John 10
18[z]Phil. 3:19; [2 Tim. 3:4; Titus 1:12] [a]Col. 2:4; 2 Pet. 2:3
19[b]ch. 1:8 [c][Jer. 4:22]; See Matt. 10:16
20[d]See ch. 15:33 [e]Gen. 3:15; [Luke 10:17-19; Rev. 12:11] [f]1 Cor. 16:23
21[g]See Acts 16:1
22[h]See 1 Cor. 16:21
23[i]1 Cor. 1:14; [Acts 19:29; 20:4; 3 John 1]
25[j]Eph. 3:20; Jude 24 [k]See ch. 2:16 [l]1 Cor. 2:1; 4:1; Eph. 1:9; 3:3-5; 5:32; 6:19 [m][1 Cor. 2:7] [n]2 Tim. 1:9; Titus 1:2
26[o]Col. 1:26; 2 Tim. 1:10; Titus 1:3 [p][Col. 1:6]; See ch. 1:5
27[q]1 Tim. 1:17; 6:16 [r]See ch. 11:36

Final Instructions and Greetings

17 I appeal to you, brothers, to watch out for those who cause divisions and create obstacles
[x]contrary to the doctrine that you have been taught; [y]avoid them. **18** For such persons do
not serve our Lord Christ, but [z]their own appetites,[1] and [a]by smooth talk and flattery they
deceive the hearts of the naive. **19** For [b]your obedience is known to all, so that I rejoice over
you, but I want you [c]to be wise as to what is good and innocent as to what is evil. **20** [d]The
God of peace [e]will soon crush Satan under your feet. [f]The grace of our Lord Jesus Christ
be with you.

21 [g]Timothy, my fellow worker, greets you; so do Lucius and Jason and Sosipater, my
kinsmen.

22 I Tertius, [h]who wrote this letter, greet you in the Lord.

23 [i]Gaius, who is host to me and to the whole church, greets you. Erastus, the city treasurer, and our brother Quartus, greet you.[2]

Doxology

25 [j]Now to him who is able to strengthen you [k]according to my gospel and the preaching of
Jesus Christ, [l]according to the revelation of the mystery [m]that was kept secret for [n]long ages
26 but [o]has now been disclosed and through the prophetic writings has been made known
to all nations, according to the command of the eternal God, [p]to bring about the obedience
of faith— **27** to [q]the only wise God [r]be glory forevermore through Jesus Christ! Amen.

[1] Greek *their own belly* [2] Some manuscripts insert verse 24: *The grace of our Lord Jesus Christ be with you all. Amen.*

16:17–18 On the theme of false teaching, cf., e.g., Jer. 14:14; Matt. 7:15. Christians must be alert, for these false teachers and divisive people are attractive in speech but are motivated by selfish desires.

16:20 With an allusion to Gen. 3:15, the readers are assured that **Satan** will soon be destroyed.

16:21 In vv. 21–23 those who are with Paul greet the Romans. **Timothy** is Paul's most famous coworker (see 1 Timothy) and was probably his most beloved colleague in ministry. **Lucius** is likely not Lucius of Cyrene mentioned in Acts 13:1, nor is he Luke, the author of the Gospel of Luke and Acts. **Jason** is likely the same person named in Acts 17:5–7, 9. And **Sosipater** is probably the same person as Sopater from Berea (Acts 20:4).

16:22 Tertius functioned as Paul's scribe or secretary for the letter. It was common for those writing letters in the first century to dictate to a secretary, but the content of the letter is clearly Paul's.

16:23 Gaius here is not the Gaius of Derbe (Acts 19:29; 20:4) but the Gaius of 1 Cor. 1:14, supporting the idea that the letter was written from Corinth. He was a man of some wealth, for he provided a place for the entire church to meet. It is difficult to know if **Erastus** is the same person mentioned in Acts 19:22 and 2 Tim. 4:20. **the city treasurer**. A large Latin inscription in the limestone pavement near the Corinthian theater reads, "Erastus in return for his aedileship laid [the pavement] at his own expense." An *aedile* was a man elected to oversee aspects of city finances. Often prominent elected officials would fulfill campaign pledges by providing some public structure to the city. Although there is some debate over whether the Greek word for "city treasurer" (*oikonomos*) was the equivalent in the Corinthian Roman colony to the Latin *aedile*, the mid-first-century dating of the pavement and the rarity of the name Erastus in first-century Corinth hold out the distinct possibility that this pavement was laid by Paul's fellow churchman.

16:25–27 *Final Summary of the Gospel of the Righteousness of God.* As stated in the note on 1:1–7, many of the themes in the introduction reappear in the conclusion, showing that the letter was written carefully.

16:25 The gospel is a **mystery** (see note on 11:25) that has been kept secret but is now revealed. The gospel centers on Jesus Christ.

16:26 The prophetic writings are the OT Scriptures (see 1:2). The gospel is not only a mystery that has been revealed but also a prophecy that has been fulfilled. **obedience of faith**. It is God's will that this gospel go to all nations, so that all who are obedient because of their faith will be saved.

16:27 Paul now comes to the main point of the doxology. The God who has planned salvation history in this way is all **wise**, and he deserves **glory forevermore**. Romans could not end in a more fitting way, as God's glory is to be the theme of Christians' lives and the joy of their hearts.

[illegible]

17 I appeal to you, brothers, to watch out for those who cause divisions and create obstacles
contrary to the doctrine that you have been taught; avoid them. 18 For such persons do not
serve our Lord Christ, but their own appetites, and by smooth talk and flattery they
deceive the hearts of the naive. 19 For your obedience is known to all, so that I rejoice over
you, but I want you to be wise as to what is good and innocent as to what is evil. 20 The
God of peace will soon crush Satan under your feet. The grace of our Lord Jesus Christ
be with you.

21 Timothy, my fellow worker, greets you; so do Lucius and Jason and Sosipater, my
kinsmen.

22 I Tertius, who wrote this letter, greet you in the Lord.

23 Gaius, who is host to me and to the whole church, greets you. Erastus, the city treasurer, and our brother Quartus, greet you.

Doxology

25 Now to him who is able to strengthen you according to my gospel and the preaching of
Jesus Christ, according to the revelation of the mystery that was kept secret for long ages
26 but has now been disclosed and through the prophetic writings has been made known to
all nations, according to the command of the eternal God, to bring about the obedience
of faith— 27 to the only wise God be glory forevermore through Jesus Christ! Amen.

[illegible]

INTRODUCTION TO

THE FIRST LETTER OF PAUL TO THE CORINTHIANS

1 CORINTHIANS

Author and Title

The first word of 1 Corinthians states that Paul is its author. There is no good reason to doubt this. The theological concerns of the letter, the energy of its style, its vocabulary, and its historical connections with the other Pauline letters and Acts mark it as Pauline. The traditional title of the letter means that it is the first of two *canonical* letters by Paul to the Corinthians, not that it was Paul's first letter to them (see 5:9).

Date

Paul wrote 1 Corinthians from the city of Ephesus in the Roman province of Asia (16:8, 19) sometime before the final day of Pentecost (16:8; cf. Lev. 23:11, 15), and therefore in the spring. It is unclear whether this was the spring of A.D. 53, 54, or 55. He wrote, in any case, near the end of his three-year ministry in Ephesus (1 Cor. 16:5–9; cf. Acts 19:21–22).

Theme

First Corinthians covers a number of topics (see "Key Themes"). One theme emerges from these discussions, however, as Paul's dominant concern. Paul wants this church, divided because of the arrogance of its more powerful members, to work together for the advancement of the gospel. He wants them to drop their divisive one-upmanship, build up the faith of those who are weak, and witness effectively to unbelievers.

Purpose, Occasion, and Background

Corinth sat on the isthmus connecting the Greek mainland with the Peloponnesian peninsula. This location made it a flourishing crossroads for sea traffic between the Aegean region and the western Mediterranean. It was a place where many cultures and religions mingled. Since it was a Roman colony, Roman law and customs were important, particularly among the upper classes, but "many 'gods' and many 'lords'" found a home in Corinth (8:5). The worship of these gods was fully integrated into governmental affairs, civic festivals, trade guilds, and social clubs, and everyday life in general. Corinth was also a destination for traveling professional orators who charged a fee for attendance at their entertaining rhetorical displays and advised people on how to advance socially.

Into this milieu Paul brought the gospel of Jesus Christ, and soon a church was established. He was aided in his work by two new-found friends from Rome, Priscilla and Aquila, who, like Paul, were displaced Jews and tentmakers by trade (Acts 18:1–4, 18–19, 24–28; Rom. 16:3; 2 Tim. 4:19). Paul, Priscilla, and Aquila spent 18 months in Corinth in the early 50s and then, after a brief trip to Judea and Syria, Paul traveled to Ephesus. Priscilla and Aquila were already there (Acts 18:19; 1 Cor. 16:19) and, by the time Paul arrived, they had already met the skillful Christian apologist Apollos, who had also been in Corinth (Acts 18:24–19:1; 1 Cor. 1:12; 3:4–6, 22; 4:6; 16:12).

Paul settled in Ephesus for three years (Acts 20:31) and at some point wrote to the Corinthians the otherwise unknown letter that he mentions in 1 Corinthians 5:9. It is not known what prompted the letter but it dealt with sexual immorality, a persistent problem for the Corinthian church (5:1–13; 6:12–20). Sometime later, Paul received an oral report indicating that the Corinthians had not only misunderstood his first letter (5:10) but were plagued with serious problems of division, sexual immorality, and social snobbery (1:10;

5:1; 11:18). Around the same time, a letter arrived from the Corinthians that displayed considerable theological confusion about marriage, divorce, participation in pagan religions, order within corporate worship, and the bodily resurrection of Christians (7:1; 8:1; 12:1; 15:12, 35).

In response to these troubling developments, Paul felt compelled to write a substantial letter to Corinth, making the case that much of their conduct was out of step with the gospel. At the root of their disunity lay an arrogance (3:21; 4:6, 8, 18–19; 5:2, 6) that was incompatible with God's free gifts to them in Christ: wisdom, righteousness, sanctification, and redemption (1:30; 4:7). In addition, a self-centered insistence on their own rights (6:12; 8:9; 9:12; 10:23) at the expense of the weak (8:10; 11:22) and marginalized (14:16, 23) revealed that their own social advancement rather than the gospel's advancement was their top priority.

At the root of much of the immorality and idolatry in Corinth, moreover, lay a lack of appreciation for the holiness that God requires of his people. Though the particulars of the Mosaic law were no longer to define the boundaries for God's people (7:19), the law's underlying theme that God's people were to be "set apart"—a people marked off from their culture—remained in place (5:1–2, 13; 7:19; 10:1–5). In addition, the dwelling of God's Spirit within each believer (6:19) and the new unity that believers have with the resurrected, living Christ (6:14–17; 15:30–34) implied that the Corinthians needed to make a clean break from the moral impurity of their culture.

Despite the often stern tone of the letter (4:18–21; 5:2; 11:17, 22; 15:36), Paul was thankful to God for the Corinthians (1:8) and felt a deep personal affection for them (16:24). Because of this love, and for the purpose of God's glory (10:31), Paul wanted the Corinthians to become a well-constructed dwelling place for God's Spirit (3:12, 16) and to be "guiltless in the day of our Lord Jesus Christ" (1:8).

Timeline

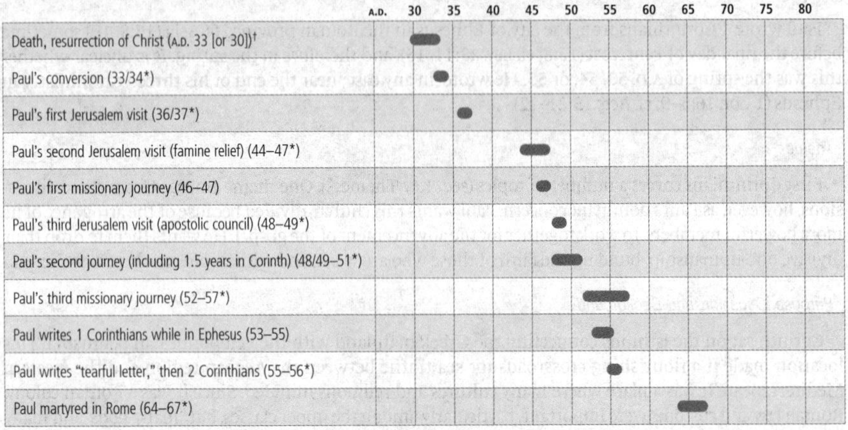

** denotes approximate date; / signifies either/or; † see The Date of Jesus' Crucifixion, pp. 1809–1810*

The Ancient City of Corinth

The Acrocorinth is a small but steep mountain 1,886 feet (575 m) high on the Peloponnesian peninsula in southern Greece. Ancient Corinth was built at the mountain's foot, benefiting also from the natural spring that provided water for the town. In Paul's day Corinth, though a couple of miles inland, oversaw the territory connecting the Adriatic port of Lechaion on the west with the Aegean port of Cenchreae to the east (see Acts 18:18). Ships were often portaged between these seaports across this narrow stretch of the Peloponnesian isthmus, approximately 3.7 miles (6 km) wide at its narrowest. Several rulers in the first century A.D. foolishly attempted to construct a canal across the isthmus, but this was not successfully accomplished until the nineteenth century.

The famed Greek city of Corinth, renowned for its artistry in bronze, its wealth, and its wanton sexuality, was destroyed in 146 B.C. during a war with Rome. The city was re-founded as a Roman colony in 44 B.C. by Roman freedmen, and the distinct archaeological strata in the city center testify to this gap in its history.

Inscriptions from the first hundred years of the new colony were mostly in Latin, although strong marks of Greek culture were also evident in the art and life of the city.

First-century Corinth followed a Roman city plan based on a rectangular grid. Typical urban structures were built (or reconstructed), such as shops, stoas, basilicas, a bouleuterion (for the city council meetings), a gymnasium, baths, latrines, and a theater. A few large houses from this period have also been excavated. The center of town boasted the refashioned Peirene Fountain as a pleasant place from which to draw spring water. To this day a raised speaker's platform stands in the main forum, and a nearby inscription refers to this platform as the *rostra* (equivalent to a *bēma* or tribunal); this is probably the very location where Gallio judged Paul to be innocent (Acts 18:12–17). Some other significant archaeological remains date from post-NT times, such as the odeion (a small covered theater).

In Paul's day the great Doric-style temple (to Athena or Apollo) from the sixth century B.C. remained a central feature in Corinth, and multiple temples to other deities dotted the city. Indeed, when the author Pausanias wrote about Corinth in the mid-second century A.D., his description of the city read like a tour guide of pagan monumental sacred sites. Corinth boasted an important sanctuary of Asklepios (the god of healing), where people would come to offer sacrifices to the god and to seek medical care. Marks of the imperial cult were evident, especially if some are correct in identifying the substantial Temple E as being dedicated to Augustus's sister Octavia (though it may have been for Jupiter). The famous Hellenistic-era temple of Aphrodite atop the Acrocorinth had been rebuilt as a rather small structure during the first-century A.D. Scholars debate whether Strabo's first-century A.D. account of 1,000 temple prostitutes refers to the earlier Hellenistic temple of Aphrodite or to the Roman one of Paul's day; the former seems more probable (Strabo, *Geography* 8.6.20c; see also Athenaeus, *Deipnosophistae* 13.573c–574c). In any case, in Roman times wanton sexuality would have been common at such a port city.

For other important archaeological features see notes on 9:24–27 (Isthmian games), 8:1–11:1 (the meat market), Acts 18:4 (synagogue and Judaism), and Romans 16:23 (Erastus inscription).

CORINTH IN THE TIME OF PAUL (C. A.D. 60)

The city plan below shows those features of the city of Corinth that archaeologists have so far identified as dating from the time of Paul. Others remain to be discovered by future archaeological excavations.

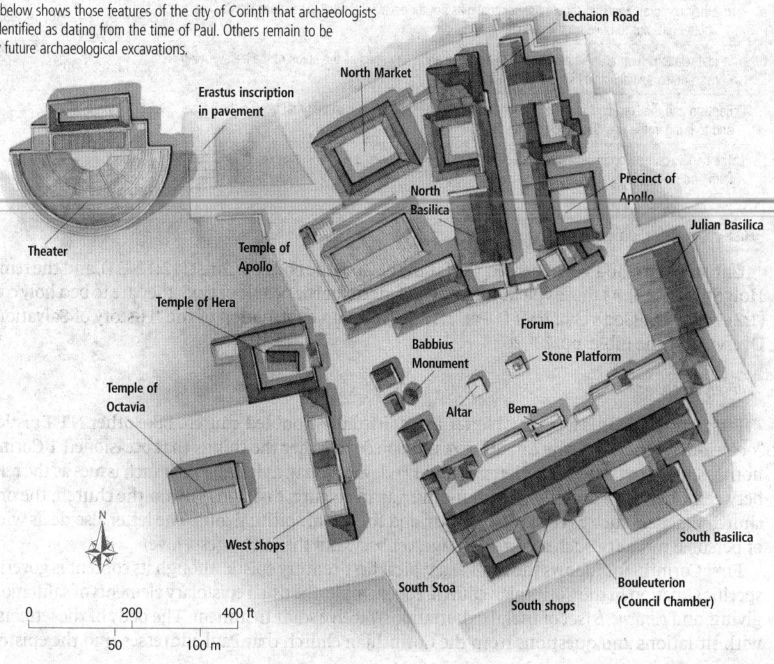

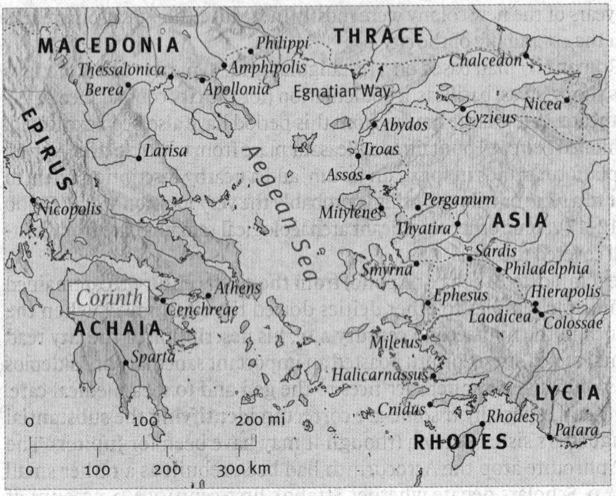

The Setting of 1 Corinthians
c. A.D. 53–55
Paul wrote 1 Corinthians during his third missionary journey, near the end of his three-year ministry in Ephesus (Acts 19:21–22). Both Corinth and Ephesus were wealthy port cities steeped in pagan idolatry and philosophy. Corinth benefited both militarily and economically from its strategic location at one end of the isthmus that connected the southern Greek peninsula to the mainland.

Key Themes

1. Since the church is the dwelling place of God's Spirit, the people who make up the church should work for unity by building each other up.	1:10–4:21 (esp. 3:10–16; 14:12)
2. Christians should build up the church in four practical ways:	
a. they should be sensitive to those of fragile faith.	8:1–9:18; 10:28, 33
b. they should win unbelievers through culturally sensitive evangelism.	9:19–23; 10:27, 32–33
c. they should conduct worship services in such a way that unbelievers present might come to faith.	14:16, 23–25
d. their corporate worship should use spiritual gifts not for personal display, or evaluating who has a better gift, but to build up the church.	11:2–16; 12:12–30; 14:1–35
3. Sexual relations form a union between man and woman as profound as the union of the believer with Christ, and so sexual activity should be confined to marriage.	5:1–13; 6:12–20; 7:5, 9, 36
4. Baptism and the Lord's Supper are important, but both are subordinate to personal trust in the gospel and to living in the way that God commands.	1:14–17; 10:1–5; 11:17–34; 15:29–34
5. The bodily resurrection of Jesus (and of his followers) from the dead is a critical component of Christian faith and practice.	6:14; 15:1–58

History of Salvation Summary

Christians are God's own people, the family of God, the body of Christ (12:12–31), and the temple of the Holy Spirit (3:16). As those who fulfill the OT pattern for the people of God, they are to be a holy community (1:2), reflecting God's character (1 Pet. 1:15–16). (For an explanation of the "History of Salvation," see the Overview of the Bible, pp. 23–26.)

Literary Features

First Corinthians is a pastoral letter to a spiritually troubled church. Like other NT Epistles, it is an "occasional" letter, and one can quite readily piece together the things that occasioned 1 Corinthians by noting signals in the text. The letter is highly relevant today, as it deals with such issues as the relationship between Christians and their surrounding pagan culture, divisions within the church, the ordering of church practices such as the Lord's Supper, and the use of spiritual gifts. The letter also deals with matters of personal morality, such as sex, marriage, celibacy, and the virtues (esp. love).

First Corinthians follows the form of a typical first-century epistle, though its content is governed by the specific situation in the Corinthian church. For example, the usual epistolary elements of salutation, thanksgiving, and *paraenesis* (set of moral exhortations) receive scant treatment. The body of the letter is taken up with situations and questions from the Corinthian church that Paul addresses, and the epistolary close (ch. 16) is extensive because of business Paul has with the church. The rhetorical modes of exhortation and instruction dominate the letter. Chapter 13 is an encomium (a written tribute) in praise of love.

The book makes extensive use of rhetorical techniques such as contrast, repetition, and analogy. It draws sharp contrasts between truth and error, and between moral good and evil. Because Paul regards the Corinthian Christians as being out of line in a number of areas, the letter exhibits a strong corrective tone.

Outline

I. Epistolary Introduction to the Letter's Main Themes (1:1–9)
  A. Greeting: apostleship, sanctity, and unity (1:1–3)
  B. Thanksgiving: speech, knowledge, and spiritual gifts (1:4–9)

II. Divisions over Christian Preachers (1:10–4:21)
  A. The problem reported (1:10–17a)
  B. God's wisdom answers the problem (1:17b–4:21)
    1. The nature of God's wisdom (1:17b–2:16)
    2. God's wisdom applied to Apollos, Paul, and the Corinthians (3:1–4:21)

III. A Report of Sexual Immorality and Legal Wrangling (5:1–6:20)
  A. Incest, arrogance, and the need for discipline (5:1–13)
  B. Trivial cases before unrighteous judges (6:1–11)
  C. Sexual immorality and the body's resurrection (6:12–20)

IV. Three Issues from a Corinthian Letter (7:1–11:1)
  A. Marriage, divorce, and unchangeable circumstances (7:1–24)
  B. The betrothed and widows (7:25–40)
  C. Food offered to idols (8:1–11:1)

V. Divisions over Corporate Worship (11:2–14:40)
  A. Head coverings and worship (11:2–16)
  B. Social snobbery at the Lord's Table (11:17–34)
  C. Elevating one spiritual gift above others (12:1–14:40)

VI. The Futility of Faith If the Dead Are Not Raised (15:1–58)
  A. The truthfulness of the traditions about Christ's resurrection (15:1–11)
  B. Christ's resurrection and the resurrection of believers (15:12–34)
  C. The nature of the resurrection body (15:35–58)

VII. The Collection for the Saints and Travel Plans (16:1–12)

VIII. Closing Admonitions and Greetings (16:13–24)

THE FIRST LETTER OF PAUL TO THE CORINTHIANS

1 CORINTHIANS

Greeting

1 Paul, [a]called [b]by the will of God to be an apostle of Christ Jesus, and our brother
Sosthenes,
2 To the church of God that is in Corinth, to those [c]sanctified in Christ Jesus, [d]called to
be saints together with all those who in every place [e]call upon the name of our Lord Jesus
Christ, both their Lord and ours:
3 [d]Grace to you and peace from God our Father and the Lord Jesus Christ.

Thanksgiving

4 I [f]give thanks to my God always for you because of the grace of God that was given you
in Christ Jesus, 5 that in every way [g]you were enriched in him in all [h]speech and all knowledge— 6 even as [i]the testimony about Christ was confirmed among you— 7 so that you are
not lacking in any gift, as you [j]wait for the revealing of our Lord Jesus Christ, 8 [k]who will
sustain you to the end, [l]guiltless [m]in the day of our Lord Jesus Christ. 9 [n]God is faithful, by
whom you were called into the [o]fellowship of his Son, Jesus Christ our Lord.

Divisions in the Church

10 I appeal to you, brothers,[1] by the name of our Lord Jesus Christ, that all of you agree,

Chapter 1

1 [a]See Rom. 1:1 [b]2 Cor. 1:1; Eph. 1:1; Col. 1:1; 2 Tim. 1:1
2 [c]ch. 6:11; [ver. 30]; See John 17:19 [d]See Rom. 1:7 [e]See Acts 9:14
3 [d][See ver. 2 above]
4 [f]See Rom. 1:8
5 [g]2 Cor. 9:11; [2 Cor. 6:10] [h]2 Cor. 8:7; [ch. 12:8]; See Rom. 15:14; 1 John 2:20
6 [i]2 Tim. 1:8; [2 Thess. 1:10; 1 Tim. 2:6; Rev. 1:2]
7 [j]Rom. 8:19; Phil. 3:20; Heb. 9:28; See Luke 17:30; 2 Pet. 3:12
8 [k][Phil. 1:6; 1 Thess. 3:13] [l]Col. 1:22 [m]ch. 5:5; 2 Cor. 1:14; Phil. 2:16; [Luke 17:24]
9 [n]ch. 10:13; Deut. 7:9; Isa. 49:7; 2 Cor. 1:18 [o]1 John 1:3

[1] Or *brothers and sisters*. The plural Greek word *adelphoi* (translated "brothers") refers to siblings in a family. In New Testament usage, depending on the context, *adelphoi* may refer either to men or to both men and women who are siblings (brothers and sisters) in God's family, the church; also verses 11, 26

1:1–9 *Epistolary Introduction to the Letter's Main Themes.* The opening verses can be divided into an initial greeting (vv. 1–3) and a report to the letter's recipients on how Paul prays for them (vv. 4–9). Both parts use language that anticipates some of the letter's key themes.

1:1–3 *Greeting: Apostleship, Sanctity, and Unity.* Paul's apostleship and the Corinthians' sanctity and unity are among the letter's most important themes.

1:1 On the meaning and background of **apostle**, see notes on Matt. 10:2; Rom. 1:1. The word occurs 10 times in 1 Corinthians, more often than in any other Pauline letter (1 Cor. 1:1; 4:9; 9:1, 2, 5; 12:28, 29; 15:7, 9 [twice]).

1:2 On **Corinth**, see Introduction: The Ancient City of Corinth. **sanctified . . . saints**. These two words are closely related in Greek, one a verb (*hagiazō*) meaning "make holy" and the other an adjective (*hagios*) meaning "holy." Here the adjective is used as a noun and means "holy people." See note on 7:14. Something "holy" is set apart from evil and dedicated to God's service. In the OT, God set Israel apart from all other nations (Ex. 19:5–6). He also gave Israel his law so that they would reveal the holiness of the God who chose them by the way they lived (Lev. 11:44–45). Paul reminds the Corinthians that because they are **in Christ Jesus** God has set them apart as his holy people (see 1 Cor. 1:30; 6:11; 2 Cor. 6:14–7:1), and because they are God's people they should reflect his holiness (Ex. 19:6; Lev. 19:2). Because the Corinthians have a tendency toward self-centeredness and disunity, Paul reminds them that in Christ they are spiritually united to **all** Christians **in every place** (see also 1 Cor. 4:17; 7:17; 11:16; 14:33, 36).

1:3 Grace . . . and peace. See note on Rom. 1:7.

1:4–9 *Thanksgiving: Speech, Knowledge, and Spiritual Gifts.* Paul is thankful that God has richly blessed the Corinthians with speech, knowledge, and spiritual gifts. Despite some problems with these blessings (8:1–3, 10; 12:12–31; 14:1–40), he considers them gifts from God.

1:4 thanks. See note on Rom. 1:8.

1:5 enriched in him. In 4:8 Paul will say that the Corinthians' spiritual riches have led to an inappropriate pride. Paul's thankfulness here shows that the problem lay not with the gifts God had given them but with the way the Corinthians used those gifts. The cure is found in a healthy dose of gratitude (4:7). The Corinthians valued especially the gifts of **speech** and **knowledge** (see 8:1–3, 10; 12:8; 13:2; 14:1–40), but because they had used these gifts in wrong and improper ways, the exercise of the gifts led to disunity (8:1–3; 12:29–30; 14:4).

1:7 When Paul tells them, "you were enriched" in Christ "in all speech and all knowledge" (v. 5) **so that you are not lacking in any gift**, he implies that many spiritual gifts are "enrichments" of speaking abilities, knowledge, or skills that people had before they became Christians. **As you wait for the revealing of our Lord Jesus Christ** implies that spiritual gifts are given as temporary provisions until Christ returns (see 13:10).

1:8–9 guiltless. There is no condemnation on the final day for those who, like the Corinthians, are in Christ Jesus (Rom. 8:1). They already have been justified and, in a sense, even sanctified (1 Cor. 6:11; cf. Rom. 5:1), so no one will be able to bring a charge against them at the judgment (Rom. 8:33). The Corinthians have a long way to go before their behavior matches their status before God (1 Cor. 3:2–3a), but Paul is confident that God, who is **faithful**, will make them what they should be.

1:10–4:21 *Divisions over Christian Preachers.* Paul now states one of the letter's primary concerns: the Corinthians' pride has led them to value outward appearance and eloquence over the genuine work of the Spirit.

1:10–17a *The Problem Reported.* Paul begins with a description of the problem of division as "Chloe's people" have reported it to him. The Corinthians are exhibiting a haughty devotion to one or another of three itinerant Christian preachers.

and that there be no [p]divisions among you, but that you be united [q]in the same mind
and the same judgment. 11 For it has been reported to me by Chloe's people that there is
[r]quarreling among you, my brothers. 12 What I mean is that [s]each one of you says, "I follow
Paul," or "I follow [t]Apollos," or "I follow [u]Cephas," or "I follow Christ." 13 [v]Is Christ divided?
Was Paul crucified for you? Or were you [w]baptized in the name of Paul? 14 I thank God that
I baptized none of you except [x]Crispus and [y]Gaius, 15 so that no one may say that you were
baptized in my name. 16 (I did baptize also [z]the household of Stephanas. Beyond that, I do
not know whether I baptized anyone else.) 17 For Christ did not send me to baptize but
to preach the gospel, and [a]not with words of eloquent wisdom, lest the cross of Christ be
emptied of its power.

Christ the Wisdom and Power of God

18 For the word of the cross is [b]folly to [c]those who are perishing, but to us [d]who are being
saved it is [e]the power of God. 19 For it is written,

> [f]"I will destroy the wisdom of the wise,
> and the discernment of the discerning I will thwart."

20 [g]Where is the one who is wise? Where is the scribe? Where is the debater of this age?
[h]Has not God made foolish the wisdom of the world? 21 For since, in the wisdom of God,
the world did not know God through wisdom, it pleased God through the folly of what
we preach[1] to save those who believe. 22 For [i]Jews demand signs and Greeks seek wisdom,
23 but we preach Christ [j]crucified, a stumbling block to Jews and folly to Gentiles, 24 but to
those who are called, both Jews and Greeks, Christ [k]the power of God and [l]the wisdom of
God. 25 For the foolishness of God is wiser than men, and the weakness of God is stronger
than men.

26 For consider your calling, brothers: [m]not many of you were wise according to worldly
standards,[2] not many were powerful, not many were of noble birth. 27 But [n]God chose what
is foolish in the world to shame the wise; [o]God chose what is weak in the world to shame
the strong; 28 God chose what is low and despised in the world, even [p]things that are not,

[1] *Or the folly of preaching* [2] Greek *according to the flesh*

10 [p]ch. 11:18 [q][Phil. 1:27]
11 [r]ch. 3:3
12 [s]ch. 3:4; [Matt. 23:9, 10] [t]See Acts 18:24 [u]See John 1:42
13 [v][ch. 12:5; 2 Cor. 11:4; Eph. 4:5] [w]See Acts 8:16
14 [x]Acts 18:8 [y]See Rom. 16:23
16 [z]ch. 16:15, 17
17 [a]ch. 2:1, 4, 13; [2 Cor. 10:10; 11:6; 2 Pet. 1:16]
18 [b]ver. 21, 23, 25; ch. 2:14 [c]2 Cor. 2:15; 4:3; 2 Thess. 2:10 [d]ch. 15:2; [Acts 2:47] [e]Rom. 1:16; [ver. 24]
19 [f]Cited from Isa. 29:14; [Job 5:12, 13; Jer. 8:9; Matt. 11:25]
20 [g]Isa. 19:12 [h]ch. 2:6; 3:19; Isa. 44:25; Rom. 1:22; [ver. 26]
22 [i]See Matt. 12:38
23 [j]Gal. 5:11; See 1 Pet. 2:8
24 [k][ver. 18] [l]ver. 30; Col. 2:3; [Luke 11:49]
26 [m]ch. 2:8; John 7:48; [ver. 20]; See Matt. 11:25
27 [n]James 2:5 [o]Ps. 8:2
28 [p]Rom. 4:17

1:11 Reported (Gk. *dēloō*) means to "show," "make clear," or "reveal" something. **Chloe's people** (Gk. *tōn Chloēs*, lit., "the ones of Chloe") may have done this by an oral report (5:1; 11:18). Chloe's identity and her location (Ephesus? Corinth?) are unknown, as well as whether these "people" are friends, business associates, family, or from her household.

1:12 Apparently the Corinthian Christians were divided into factions on the basis of who had baptized them (vv. 14–17). Paul knew **Apollos** well (16:12). His rhetorical skills were impressive, and the Corinthian Christians had received him gladly after Paul's departure (Acts 18:24–19:1). **Cephas** is the Aramaic equivalent of the name Peter (Gal. 2:7–14), and both names refer to Peter the apostle (1 Cor. 15:5; Gal. 1:18; 2:7–14). Unlike Paul (1 Cor. 7:8), Cephas was married and had traveled to Corinth with his wife (9:5). Apparently one faction in Corinth, claiming to be above it all, took the slogan "I follow Christ."

1:17a not . . . to baptize. While Paul considers baptism important (Rom. 6:3; Col. 2:12), it is subordinate to the proclamation of **the gospel**. Hearing and believing the gospel, unlike baptism, is essential to salvation (Rom. 10:17; 1 Cor. 1:21; Eph. 1:13). The Corinthians need to center their lives on the gospel, not on the various preachers in whom they can take pride.

1:17b–4:21 *God's Wisdom Answers the Problem.* The divisions in Corinth can be healed if the Corinthians see the distinction between the world's wisdom and God's wisdom.

1:17b–2:16 *The Nature of God's Wisdom.* God's wisdom is displayed in the message of the cross, the calling of the Corinthians, the preaching of Paul, and the wisdom from the Spirit.

1:17b words of eloquent wisdom. The art of rhetorical persuasion was highly valued in the Greco-Roman world, and professional orators frequented large cities like Corinth, giving impressive displays of their ability to entertain and instruct. Paul's proclamation of the gospel failed to measure up to these standards. This failure, however, served to place the spotlight on the **power** of the message itself (see also 2:1–5), for the Holy Spirit so empowered Paul's words that they awakened faith in Christ (cf. James 1:18; 1 Pet. 1:23–25) and changed people's very hearts and lives.

1:18 cross. See note on the crucifixion at Matt. 27:35. **folly**. Paul's preaching in Corinth focused on the saving fact of Christ's crucifixion, a method of execution considered so crude it was not even mentioned in polite company. The Corinthians' fascination with the rhetorical ability of the ministers rather than their message demonstrated that they were living contrary to the power of the cross.

1:22–25 Jesus' hostile opponents had kept demanding more miraculous **signs** to prove his claims (Matt. 16:1–4; Mark 8:11–12; Luke 11:16; John 2:18–20; 4:48), but they were doing this just to manipulate him, for the signs he had already given were sufficient to leave them without excuse for their unbelief (John 3:2; 12:9–11, 37; 14:11). **Greeks** were viewed in antiquity, in contrast to barbarians, as a cultured people and therefore interested in **wisdom** (Acts 17:21; Rom. 1:14). A crucified Messiah was offensive to an unbelieving Jew (Matt. 16:22; Gal. 3:13; 5:11), and nonsensical to an unbelieving Greek. God's power to call forth his people, however, works through a deeper wisdom than human beings can recognize (unless God grants them faith). Paul writes that the gospel is preached to all (1 Cor. 1:23), but God calls some effectively to salvation from among both Jews and Greeks (v. 24). On Christ as a **stumbling block** (v. 23), see notes on Isa. 8:11–15; 28:16.

1:26–31 Just as the message and its messenger (Paul) were **foolish** by the world's standards, so most of those in Corinth who believed the message were foolish by those same standards. God's transformation of them into his people (by choosing them to be saved) in spite of their humanly unimpressive pedigree excludes all boasting in ancestry, accomplishment, or affiliation with one preacher or another (see also 3:21–22).

1:27 God chose what is weak . . . to shame the strong. The themes of the lifting up of the downtrodden and the reversal of human status are prophesied in the OT (e.g., 1 Sam. 2:1–8; Isa. 61:1; cf. Luke 1:52; John 9:39).

to [q]bring to nothing things that are, **29** so [r]that no human being[1] might boast in the presence of God. **30** And because of him[2] you are in Christ Jesus, who became to us [s]wisdom
from God, [t]righteousness and [u]sanctification and [v]redemption, **31** so that, as it is written,
[w]"Let the one who boasts, boast in the Lord."

Proclaiming Christ Crucified

2 And I, when I came to you, brothers,[3] [x]did not come proclaiming to you [y]the testimony[4]
of God with lofty speech or wisdom. **2** For I decided to know nothing among you except
[z]Jesus Christ and him crucified. **3** And [a]I was with you [b]in weakness and in fear and much
trembling, **4** and my speech and my message were not in plausible words of wisdom, but
in demonstration of [c]the Spirit and of power, **5** so that your faith might not rest in the
wisdom of men[5] but [d]in the power of God.

Wisdom from the Spirit

6 Yet among [e]the mature we do impart wisdom, although it is not [f]a wisdom of this
age or of the rulers of this age, [g]who are doomed to pass away. **7** But we impart a secret
and hidden wisdom of God, [h]which God decreed before the ages for our glory. **8** None of
[i]the rulers of this age understood this, for [j]if they had, they would not have crucified [k]the
Lord of glory. **9** But, as it is written,

> [l]"What no eye has seen, nor ear heard,
> nor the heart of man imagined,
> what God has [m]prepared [n]for those who love him"—

10 these things [o]God has revealed to us through the Spirit. For the Spirit searches everything,
even [p]the depths of God. **11** For who knows a person's thoughts [q]except the spirit of that
person, which is in him? So also no one comprehends the thoughts of God except the Spirit
of God. **12** Now [r]we have received not [s]the spirit of the world, but the Spirit who is from
God, that we might understand the things freely given us by God. **13** And we impart this
[t]in words not taught by human wisdom but taught by the Spirit, [u]interpreting spiritual
truths to those who are spiritual.[6]

14 The natural person does not accept the things of the Spirit of God, for they are [v]folly to
him, and [w]he is not able to understand them because they are spiritually discerned. **15** The
[x]spiritual person judges all things, but is himself to be judged by no one. **16** [y]"For who has
understood the mind of the Lord so as to instruct him?" But [z]we have the mind of Christ.

Divisions in the Church

3 But I, brothers,[7] could not address you as [a]spiritual people, but as [b]people of the flesh,
as [c]infants in Christ. **2** [d]I fed you with milk, not solid food, for [e]you were not ready
for it. And even now you are not yet ready, **3** for you are still of the flesh. For while there

[1] Greek *no flesh* [2] Greek *And from him* [3] Or *brothers and sisters* [4] Some manuscripts *mystery* (or *secret*) [5] The Greek word *anthropoi* can refer to both men and women [6] Or *interpreting spiritual truths in spiritual language, or comparing spiritual things with spiritual* [7] Or *brothers and sisters*

28 [q]ch. 2:6; [Job 34:19, 24]
29 [r]Eph. 2:9; [Judg. 7:2]
30 [s][ver. 24] [t]Jer. 23:5, 6; 33:16; 2 Cor. 5:21; Phil. 3:9 [u][ver. 2] [v]Eph. 1:7; Col. 1:14; [Rom. 3:24]
31 [w]2 Cor. 10:17; [Jer. 9:23, 24]

Chapter 2

1 [x]ver. 4, 13; [2 Cor. 1:12]; See ch. 1:17 [y]See Rom. 16:25
2 [z]Gal. 6:14
3 [a]Acts 18:1, 6, 12 [b]2 Cor. 11:30; 12:5, 9; 13:4, 9; Gal. 4:13
4 [c]ch. 4:20; Rom. 15:13, 19; 1 Thess. 1:5; 2 Pet. 1:16
5 [d]2 Cor. 4:7; 6:7; [Zech. 4:6; 2 Cor. 10:4; 12:9]
6 [e]Phil. 3:15; [ch. 3:1] [f][James 3:15] [g]ch. 1:28
7 [h]Rom. 16:25, 26; Eph. 3:5, 9; Col. 1:26; 2 Tim. 1:9
8 [i]Acts 13:27; See Luke 24:20 [j]See Acts 3:17 [k]James 2:1; [Ps. 24:7-10; Acts 7:2]
9 [l][Isa. 64:4] [m]See Matt. 25:34 [n]James 1:12
10 [o]Matt. 16:17; Gal. 1:12, 16; Eph. 3:3, 5; See John 14:26 [p][Rev. 2:24]
11 [q]Prov. 20:27
12 [r]Rom. 8:15 [s][1 John 4:4]
13 [t]ver. 1, 4; See ch. 1:17 [u]2 Cor. 10:12
14 [v]ch. 1:18 [w]Rom. 8:7
15 [x]ch. 3:1; 14:37; Gal. 6:1; [Prov. 28:5]
16 [y]Cited from Isa. 40:13; See Rom. 11:34 [z][John 15:15]

Chapter 3

1 [a]ch. 2:15; Rom. 7:14 [b][ch. 2:14] [c]Heb. 5:13; [ch. 2:6]
2 [d]Heb. 5:12, 13; 1 Pet. 2:2 [e]John 16:12

2:1–5 not . . . with lofty speech or wisdom. Paul avoided Greek rhetoric and focused on the message of the cross, so that the Corinthians would put their faith in Christ who was crucified rather than in the ability of human messengers.

2:5 that your faith might not rest in the wisdom of men. Mere intellectual persuasion does not save people. Saving faith is produced by the heart-changing power of the Holy Spirit as the gospel is proclaimed.

2:6–10 The rulers who executed Jesus did not understand what they were doing (cf. Luke 23:34). Paul and the Corinthians would also have failed to understand Christ's death apart from the Spirit's revelation to them about its meaning. In Rom. 8:27 the Spirit searches (Gk. *eraunaō*) the human heart, but here **the Spirit searches** (*eraunaō*) the depths of God. God's Spirit bridges the chasm between the deep things of God and the human heart, graciously enabling human beings to understand the message of the cross, which would otherwise be incomprehensible. See also 1 Cor. 2:4.

2:6 rulers of this age. Probably a reference to such earthly rulers as the Jewish chief priests and the Roman procurator Pilate who sentenced Jesus to die (see v. 8), but by analogy it also includes all rulers who do not believe in Jesus.

2:7 secret and hidden wisdom of God. This "wisdom of God" is centered in Christ and includes all of God's plans for the history of salvation from **before the ages** ("before the foundation of the world," Eph. 1:4) to the unending future of eternity (1 Cor. 2:9; Rev. 11:15; 22:5). It includes everything Paul preaches, "the whole counsel of God" (Acts 20:27).

2:11 comprehends. Understands fully.

2:12 the Spirit who is from God. Both the substance and the verbal expression of the apostles' witness to Christ are from God.

2:13 those who are spiritual. Although the adjective "spiritual" (Gk. *pneumatikos*) could refer to things or words rather than to people (see ESV footnote), Paul seems to be turning now to the subject of spiritual people (see v. 15; 3:1). As Paul has just made clear, only the Spirit can render the message of the cross truly comprehensible to someone, so every Christian is a "spiritual" (led and empowered by the Holy Spirit) person; see also Rom. 8:9; 2 Cor. 3:6, 8, 16–18; Eph. 1:13. Unbelievers, on the other hand, do not have the spiritual capacity to understand the things of God (1 Cor. 2:14).

3:1–4:21 *God's Wisdom Applied to Apollos, Paul, and the Corinthians.* Paul now shows the Corinthians how God's choice to work through weakness for his own glory applies to their divided church. Just as Paul

is [f]jealousy and strife among you, are you not of the flesh and behaving only in a human
way? 4 For [g]when one says, "I follow Paul," and another, "I follow Apollos," [h]are you not
being merely human?
5 What then is Apollos? What is Paul? [i]Servants through whom you believed, [j]as the Lord
assigned to each. 6 [k]I planted, [l]Apollos watered, [m]but God gave the growth. 7 So [n]neither he
who plants nor he who waters is anything, but only God who gives the growth. 8 He who
plants and he who waters are one, and each [o]will receive his wages according to his labor.
9 For we are [p]God's fellow workers. You are God's field, [q]God's building.
10 [r]According to the grace of God given to me, like a skilled master builder I laid a [s]founda-
tion, and [t]someone else is building upon it. Let each one take care how he builds upon it.
11 For no one can lay a [u]foundation other [v]than that which is laid, [w]which is Jesus Christ.
12 Now if anyone builds on the foundation with gold, silver, precious stones, wood, hay,
straw— 13 [x]each one's work will become manifest, for the Day will disclose it, because it
will be revealed [y]by fire, and [z]the fire will test what sort of work each one has done. 14 If
the work that anyone has built on the foundation survives, [a]he will receive a reward. 15 If
anyone's work is burned up, he will suffer loss, though he himself will be saved, [b]but only
as through fire.
16 [c]Do you not know that you[1] are God's temple and that God's Spirit dwells in you?
17 If anyone destroys God's temple, God will destroy him. For [d]God's temple is holy, and
you are that temple.
18 [e]Let no one deceive himself. [f]If anyone among you thinks that he is wise in this age, let
him become a fool that he may become wise. 19 For [g]the wisdom of this world is folly with
God. For it is written, [h]"He catches the wise in their craftiness," 20 and again, [i]"The Lord
knows the thoughts of the wise, that they are futile." 21 So [j]let no one boast in men. For [k]all
things are yours, 22 whether Paul or Apollos or Cephas or the world or life or death or the
present or the future—all are yours, 23 and [l]you are Christ's, and [m]Christ is God's.

The Ministry of Apostles

4 This is how one should regard us, as servants of Christ and [n]stewards of the mysteries
of God. 2 Moreover, it is required of stewards that they be found faithful. 3 But with
me it is a very small thing that I should be judged by you or by any human court. In fact,

[1] The Greek for *you* is plural in verses 16 and 17

3 [f]Gal. 5:19, 20; [ch. 1:11; 11:18; Rom. 13:13]
4 [g]See ch. 1:12 [h][ver. 3]
5 [i]2 Cor. 6:4; Eph. 3:7; Col. 1:25; [2 Cor. 3:3] [j]See Rom. 12:6
6 [k]ch. 4:15; 9:1; 15:1; Acts 18:4-11; 2 Cor. 10:14, 15 [l]Acts 18:27 [m][ch. 15:10; Col. 1:18]
7 [n]2 Cor. 12:11; Gal. 6:3; [Gal. 2:6]
8 [o]ver. 14; ch. 15:58; 2 John 8; [ch. 4:5; Gal. 6:4, 5]; See Matt. 16:27; Rom. 2:6
9 [p]Mark 16:20; 2 Cor. 6:1 [q]Eph. 2:20-22; Col. 2:7; [ver. 16; Ps. 127:1]
10 [r][2 Pet. 3:15]; See Rom. 12:3 [s]ver. 11, 12; Rom. 15:20; [Rev. 21:14] [t][ch. 4:15]
11 [u]Isa. 28:16 [v][2 Cor. 11:4; Gal. 1:6, 7] [w][Eph. 2:20]
13 [x]ch. 4:5 [y]ver. 15; 2 Thess. 1:8 [z]1 Pet. 1:7
14 [a]See ver. 8
15 [b][Ps. 66:12; Isa. 43:2; Jude 23]
16 [c]ch. 6:19; 2 Cor. 6:16; Eph. 2:21
17 [d][2 Cor. 7:1]
18 [e][Isa. 5:21; Gal. 6:3] [f][ch. 8:2; Jer. 8:8, 9]
19 [g]See ch. 1:20 [h]Cited from Job 5:13
20 [i]Cited from Ps. 94:11
21 [j]ver. 4-6; ch. 1:12; 4:6 [k]Rom. 8:28
23 [l]2 Cor. 10:7; Gal. 3:29 [m][ch. 11:3]

Chapter 4

1 [n][ch. 9:17]; See 1 Pet. 4:10

and Apollos work together for the advancement of the gospel, so the Corinthians should stop boasting about their favorite Christian leader and build a united church.

3:1–3 of the flesh. The first instance of this phrase (v. 1) represents a Greek word (*sarkinos*) that means "characterized by the flesh" (cf. Rom. 7:14). The second instance (1 Cor. 3:3) represents a slightly different word (*sarkikos*) that means "made of flesh, fleshly" (2 Cor. 10:4; cf. 1:17). Paul uses both terms here in the same way to express his disappointment in the Corinthians' behavior. "Flesh" takes different meanings in Scripture, but in Paul's letters it often refers to "unredeemed human nature" with all of its desires and characteristic behavior. Although the Corinthians are Christians indwelt by the Spirit, their divisive behavior shows that they are acting like the unbelieving world around them.

3:2 not ready. Paul thinks it is unhelpful and dangerous to give advanced teaching to Christians who were morally and spiritually immature and proud.

3:8 wages according to his labor. See note on vv. 14–15. God's blessing and reward in the lives of Christians varies according to their faithfulness to the tasks he entrusts to them.

3:12 gold, silver, precious stones. Materials used in the construction of Solomon's temple (1 Chron. 29:2), and here an image for what will survive the judgment, in contrast to **wood**, **hay**, and **straw**. Work that Christians do in Christlike faith and obedience (1 Cor. 3:10–11) will survive and be rewarded; work done in the power of the "flesh" (v. 1) or in disobedience to Scripture (4:6) will not.

3:14–15 reward . . . loss . . . saved . . . as through fire. See also v. 8 and 4:4–5. Although those who have believed in Jesus have already been justified by faith (Rom. 5:1) and will not face condemnation on the final day (John 5:24; Rom. 8:1, 33), God will still judge their works (Rom. 14:10–12; 2 Cor. 5:10) and reward them accordingly (Matt. 6:1–6, 16, 18; 10:41–42). Paul's point applies not just to church leaders but to **anyone** who contributes in any way to building up the church (1 Cor. 12:7, 12–31; 14:12).

3:16 On the **temple** and God's dwelling, see note on Ex. 25:8.

3:17 God will destroy him. The one who destroys God's temple (in this context, the church) is not part of God's people and so faces eternal destruction on the final day, just as God eventually destroyed the Babylonians who had destroyed Solomon's temple.

3:21–23 let no one boast in men. Arrogance is at the root of the divisiveness in Corinth (4:6, 18). The Corinthians need to learn that they ultimately belong to God, not to the leader who baptized them (1:13–17), who was himself only fulfilling God's purposes (3:7, 11; 4:1). They should, therefore, boast only in God (1:29, 31).

3:21 All things are yours means that they are given by God for the benefit of his people.

4:1 mysteries. Since Paul uses the plural here (see also 13:2; 14:2), he probably has in mind not only the gospel itself (see also Eph. 6:19) but also other truths that God has revealed. See, e.g., Rom. 11:25; 1 Cor. 15:51; Eph. 3:4, 6; 5:32; Col. 2:2. A "mystery" (Gk. *mystērion*) in Paul's letters is something that people, in their human weakness, could not understand unless God graciously revealed it to them (Dan. 2:18–19, 28; Eph. 1:7–9), but now Paul does explain these mysteries.

4:3 judged by you. Some of the Corinthians, perhaps followers of Apollos or Cephas, probably spoke disparagingly of Paul, especially of his speaking ability (1:17; 2:3–4; 4:18–21; 2 Cor. 10:9), thinking they were able to judge his spiritual effectiveness.

I do not even judge myself. 4 [o]For I am not aware of anything against myself, [p]but I am not
thereby acquitted. It is the Lord who judges me. 5 Therefore [q]do not pronounce judgment
before the time, [r]before the Lord comes, [s]who will bring to light the things now hidden
in darkness and will disclose the purposes of the heart. [t]Then each one will receive his
commendation from God.
6 I have applied all these things to myself and Apollos for your benefit, brothers,[1] that
you may learn by us not to go beyond what is written, that none of you may [u]be puffed
up in favor of one against another. 7 For who sees anything different in you? [v]What do
you have that you did not receive? If then you received it, why do you boast as if you did
not receive it?
8 Already you have all you want! Already you have become rich! Without us you have
become kings! And would that you did reign, so that we might share the rule with you!
9 For I think that God has exhibited us apostles as last of all, [w]like men sentenced to death,
because we [x]have become a spectacle to the world, to angels, and to men. 10 [y]We are fools for
Christ's sake, but [z]you are wise in Christ. [a]We are weak, but you are strong. You are held
in honor, but we in disrepute. 11 To the present hour [b]we hunger and thirst, we are poorly
dressed and [c]buffeted and [d]homeless, 12 and we [e]labor, working with our own hands. [f]When
reviled, we bless; [g]when persecuted, we endure; 13 when slandered, we entreat. [h]We have
become, and are still, like the scum of the world, [i]the refuse of all things.
14 I do not write these things [j]to make you ashamed, but to admonish you [k]as my beloved
children. 15 For [l]though you have countless[2] guides in Christ, you do not have many fathers.
For [m]I became your father in Christ Jesus through the gospel. 16 I urge you, then, [n]be imitators of me. 17 That is why [o]I sent[3] you Timothy, [p]my beloved and faithful child in the Lord,
to remind you of my ways in Christ,[4] [q]as I teach them everywhere in every church. 18 Some
are [r]arrogant, [s]as though I were not coming to you. 19 But [t]I will come to you soon, if the
Lord wills, and I will find out not the talk of these arrogant people but their power. 20 For
[u]the kingdom of God does not consist in talk but in power. 21 What do you wish? [v]Shall I
come to you with a rod, or with love in a spirit of gentleness?

[1] Or *brothers and sisters* [2] Greek *you have ten thousand* [3] Or *am sending* [4] Some manuscripts add *Jesus*

21 [v]2 Cor. 1:23; 2:1, 3; 12:20; 13:2, 10

4 [o]See Acts 23:1 [p]Job 9:2, 15; Ps. 130:3; 143:2; [1 John 3:21]
5 [q]Matt. 7:1; Rom. 2:1; [Matt. 13:29] [r]See John 21:22; Rom. 2:16 [s]ch. 3:13 [t]2 Cor. 10:18; See ch. 3:8
6 [u]ver. 18, 19; ch. 5:2; 13:4
7 [v]John 3:27; [1 Chr. 29:14; James 1:17; 1 Pet. 4:10]
9 [w]See Rom. 8:36 [x]Heb. 10:33 (Gk.); [Isa. 20:3]
10 [y][Acts 17:18]; See ch. 1:18; Acts 26:24 [z]2 Cor. 11:19 [a]ch. 2:3; 2 Cor. 13:9
11 [b]Rom. 8:35; 2 Cor. 11:27; Phil. 4:12 [c]2 Cor. 11:20, 23 [d][Matt. 8:20]
12 [e]See Acts 18:3 [f]See 1 Pet. 3:9 [g]See John 15:20
13 [h][Isa. 30:22; 64:6] [i]Lam. 3:45
14 [j][ch. 6:5; 15:34] [k]2 Cor. 6:13; 1 Thess. 2:11; 3 John 4
15 [l][ch. 3:10] [m]Philem. 10; [Gal. 4:19]
16 [n]ch. 11:1; Phil. 3:17; 1 Thess. 1:6; [Phil. 4:9; 2 Thess. 3:9]
17 [o]ch. 16:10 [p]1 Tim. 1:2; 2 Tim. 1:2 [q]ch. 7:17
18 [r]See ver. 6 [s]ver. 21; [2 Cor. 10:2]
19 [t]ch. 11:34; 16:5, 6; Acts 19:21; 20:2; 2 Cor. 1:15, 16
20 [u]See ch. 2:4

4:6 Paul emphasizes the importance of not going **beyond what is written** in Scripture, as exemplified by his five quotations up to this point: Isa. 29:14 (1 Cor. 1:19); Jer. 9:22–23 (1 Cor. 1:31); Isa. 64:4 (1 Cor. 2:9); Job 5:13 (1 Cor. 3:19); and Ps. 94:11 (1 Cor. 3:20).

4:7 This set of rhetorical questions expresses in a nutshell the central theological truth that the Corinthians, in their divisiveness, seem to have forgotten: all their abilities, opportunities, and blessings are from God, so they should not boast. **What do you have that you did not receive?** If Christians repeatedly ask this of themselves, it will produce deep humility and thanksgiving. See also 1:4, 30–31; 3:6–7, 21–23.

Imitating Paul as Paul Imitates Christ

1 Cor. 4:15–17	I became your father in Christ Jesus . . . *be imitators of me*. That is why I sent you Timothy, my beloved and faithful child in the Lord, to remind you of my ways in Christ.
1 Cor. 10:32–11:1	Give no offense . . . just as I try to please everyone in everything . . . *Be imitators of me, as I am of Christ*.
Phil. 3:17	Brothers, *join in imitating me*, and keep your eyes on those who walk according to the example you have in us.
Phil. 4:9	What you have learned and received and heard and seen in me—*practice these things*.
2 Thess. 3:7–9	You yourselves know how *you ought to imitate us* . . . but to give you in ourselves an example to imitate.
2 Tim. 3:10–11	*You . . . have followed my teaching*, my conduct, my aim in life, my faith, my patience, my love, my steadfastness, my persecutions and sufferings.

4:8 you have become kings. Paul is speaking colorfully and ironically of the Corinthians' haughtiness.

4:9 exhibited . . . like men sentenced to death. Paul is probably thinking of the Roman triumphal procession in which captured enemy soldiers were paraded through the streets before being publicly executed. Or he may be thinking of gladiators condemned to die in an arena. See also 2 Cor. 2:14 and, for the image used in a different way, Col. 2:15.

4:10–13 We are fools for Christ's sake. Measured by the "royal" standards of the Corinthians (v. 8), Paul's apostolic calling has involved foolishness, weakness, and suffering. See 2 Cor. 2:14–17; 4:7–12, 16–18; 11:22–33; 12:9; 13:4; Phil. 1:12–18. **when slandered, we entreat**. Paul answers false accusations (cf. Acts 16:37) lest falsehood be established as truth in the public mind and the reputation of the gospel be damaged.

4:15 countless guides. Apollos and Cephas, among others. **father**. See v. 17; Gal. 4:19; Phil. 2:22; 1 Thess. 2:7, 11; 1 Tim. 1:2; 2 Tim. 1:2; Philem. 10.

4:16 be imitators of me. God has designed the Christian life so that much of one's progress comes through imitating other Christians, imperfect though they be (cf. 11:1; Phil. 3:17; 2 Thess. 3:7; 1 Tim. 4:12; Titus 2:7; 1 Pet. 5:3).

4:19 I will find out . . . their power. Apparently Paul expected a confrontation in which the power of the Holy Spirit would manifest some kind of disciplinary force against those who were harming the church (see Acts 5:1–11; 13:9–11; 2 Cor. 10:3–4).

4:20 On the **kingdom of God**, see note on Matt. 3:2.

4:21 rod. A thin stick used for discipline. Paul is speaking metaphorically of the kind of church discipline he is about to describe in 5:3–5.

Sexual Immorality Defiles the Church

5 It is actually reported that there is [w]sexual immorality among you, and of a kind that
is not tolerated even among pagans, [x]for a man has his father's wife. **2** And [y]you are
arrogant! Ought you [z]not rather to mourn? Let him who has done this be removed from
among you.
3 For though [a]absent in body, I am present in spirit; and as if present, I have already
pronounced judgment on the one who did such a thing. **4** When you are assembled [b]in the
name of the Lord Jesus and my spirit is present, with the power of our Lord Jesus, **5** you
are [c]to deliver this man to Satan for the destruction of the flesh, so [d]that his spirit may be
saved [e]in the day of the Lord.[1]
6 [f]Your boasting is not good. Do you not know that [g]a little leaven leavens the whole
lump? **7** Cleanse out the old leaven that you may be a new lump, as you really are unleavened. For Christ, our Passover lamb, has been sacrificed. **8** Let us therefore celebrate the
festival, [h]not with the old leaven, [i]the leaven of malice and evil, but with the unleavened
bread of sincerity and truth.
9 I wrote to you in my letter [j]not to associate with sexually immoral people— **10** [k]not at
all meaning [l]the sexually immoral of this world, or the greedy and swindlers, or idolaters,
[m]since then you would need to go out of the world. **11** But now I am writing to you not to
associate with anyone [n]who bears the name of brother if he is guilty of sexual immorality
or greed, or is an idolater, reviler, drunkard, or swindler—not even to eat with such a one.
12 For what have I to do with judging [o]outsiders? [p]Is it not those inside the church[2] whom you
are to judge? **13** God judges[3] those outside. [q]"Purge the evil person from among you."

[1] Some manuscripts add *Jesus* [2] Greek *those inside* [3] Or *will judge*

Chapter 5
1 [w]2 Cor. 12:21 [x]Lev. 18:8; Deut. 22:30; 27:20
2 [y]See ch. 4:6 [z][2 Cor. 7:7-10]
3 [a]Col. 2:5; [1 Thess. 2:17]
4 [b]2 Thess. 3:6; [Matt. 16:19; 18:18; John 20:23; 2 Cor. 13:3, 10; 1 Tim. 5:20]
5 [c]1 Tim. 1:20; [Job 2:6; Acts 26:18] [d][Prov. 23:14] [e]See ch. 1:8
6 [f]James 4:16; [ver. 2] [g]Gal. 5:9; [ch. 15:33]
8 [h]Ex. 12:15; Deut. 16:3 [i][Matt. 16:6, 12; Mark 8:15; Luke 12:1]
9 [j][2 Cor. 6:14; Eph. 5:11; 2 Thess. 3:6, 14]
10 [k][ch. 10:27] [l]Eph. 5:5; Col. 3:5; [ch. 6:9] [m][John 17:15]
11 [n]2 Thess. 3:6
12 [o]See Mark 4:11 [p][ch. 6:1-4]
13 [q][Deut. 13:5; 17:7, 12; 21:21; 22:21, 22, 24; Judg. 20:13]

5:1–6:20 *A Report of Sexual Immorality and Legal Wrangling.* Paul has heard not only of disunity in the Corinthian church but also of a bizarre case of sexual misconduct (5:1–13), of believers taking other believers before pagan courts (6:1–11), and of sexual immorality with prostitutes (6:12–20). In answer to these problems, Paul instructs the Corinthians on the meaning of Christian holiness and the significance of the final day.

5:1–13 *Incest, Arrogance, and the Need for Discipline.* Paul first tells the Corinthians that God has set certain boundaries to mark out his people as his own. The Corinthians need to maintain these boundaries by disciplining a man in their church involved in incest.

5:1 has his father's wife. Not his biological mother but his stepmother; otherwise Paul would have explicitly said so. Leviticus 18:8 specifically forbids sexual relations between a man and his "father's wife." God's people are to be distinguished from surrounding nations by following God's law rather than the customs of those nations (Lev. 18:1–5). Ironically, the Corinthian Christians were more tolerant of flagrant sin than were the **pagans** among whom they lived.

5:2 arrogant. See v. 6. The arrogance may arise from the Corinthians' mistaken "knowledge" that they are somehow free of normal moral constraints (6:12; 8:1; 10:23). If so, they may have thought of this freedom as an implication of grace (Rom. 3:8; 6:1, 15; Jude 4). It is also possible that Paul simply thinks of their characteristic arrogance (1 Cor. 3:21; 4:6, 8, 18–19) as doubly inappropriate in light of the shocking sin in their midst.

5:3–4 my spirit is present. A difficult phrase that probably means that the disciplinary power of the Holy Spirit, which Paul knew to be present in his own ministry (see note on 4:19), would also be manifested in their meeting, because of the Corinthian church's connection with Paul.

5:5 Deliver this man to Satan probably refers to removing him from the church, since those outside of the church are in Satan's realm (Luke 4:5–6; Eph. 2:2; 1 John 5:19). **destruction of the flesh**. Although it is certainly not always the case (cf. John 9:1–3), personal sin sometimes has grave physical consequences (Acts 5:1–11; 1 Cor. 11:29–30). **spirit may be saved**. The purpose of the discipline was not to punish the man for punishment's sake but to effect his restoration to the church and eventual salvation (see 1 Tim. 1:20).

5:6–7 leaven. Not yeast (which was uncommon in the ancient world) but fermented dough, a little of which would be left from the previous week to be added to a new lump of dough. By analogy, when publicly known sin in the church is not subjected to church discipline, it will silently spread its destructive consequences throughout the whole fellowship.

5:9 my letter. An otherwise unknown letter to the Corinthians, written prior to 1 Corinthians.

5:11 not to associate. See 2 Thess. 3:6, 14. One purpose here, as in 2 Thessalonians, is redemptive with respect to the person committing the sin (1 Cor. 5:5; 2 Thess. 3:14–15). But another purpose is to avoid giving the appearance of approving sinful conduct, lest reproach be brought on the church and the gospel.

5:13 "Purge . . . from among you." As the newly constituted people of God (10:32), the Corinthians are to follow God's instructions to Israel for preserving its holiness when flagrant, unrepented-of sin is in its midst (Deut. 13:5; 17:7, 12; 19:19; 21:21; 22:21–22, 24; 24:7). In this case, they are to do so by excommunicating the man committing incest.

Church Leaders Should Likewise Lead Lives That Are Examples to Imitate

Phil. 3:17	Brothers, join in imitating me, and keep your eyes on those who walk according to *the example* you have in us.
1 Tim. 4:12	Let no one despise you for your youth, but set the believers *an example* in speech, in conduct, in love, in faith, in purity.
Titus 2:7–8	Show yourself in all respects to be *a model of good works*, and in your teaching show integrity, dignity, and sound speech.
Heb. 13:7	Remember your leaders, those who spoke to you the word of God. Consider the outcome of their way of life, and *imitate their faith*.
1 Pet. 5:2–3	Shepherd the flock of God . . . not domineering over those in your charge, but *being examples* to the flock.

Lawsuits Against Believers

6 When one of you has a grievance against another, does he dare go to law before the
unrighteous [r]instead of the saints? 2 Or do you not know that [s]the saints will judge the
world? And if the world is to be judged by you, are you incompetent to try trivial cases?
3 Do you not know that we are to judge angels? How much more, then, matters pertaining to this life! 4 So if you have such cases, [t]why do you lay them before those who have no
standing in the church? 5 [u]I say this to your shame. Can it be that there is no one among
you wise enough to settle a dispute between the brothers, 6 but brother goes to law against
brother, and that before unbelievers? 7 To have lawsuits at all with one another is already
a defeat for you. [v]Why not rather suffer wrong? Why not rather be defrauded? 8 But you
yourselves wrong and defraud—even [w]your own brothers![1]
9 Or do you not know that the unrighteous[2] will not inherit the kingdom of God? Do
not be deceived: [x]neither the sexually immoral, nor idolaters, nor adulterers, nor men
who practice homosexuality,[3] 10 nor thieves, nor the greedy, nor drunkards, nor revilers,
nor swindlers will inherit the kingdom of God. 11 And [y]such were some of you. But [z]you
were washed, [a]you were sanctified, [b]you were justified in the name of the Lord Jesus Christ
and by the Spirit of our God.

Flee Sexual Immorality

12 [c]"All things are lawful for me," but not all things are helpful. "All things are lawful for
me," but I will not be dominated by anything. 13 [d]"Food is meant for the stomach and the

[1] *Or brothers and sisters* [2] *Or wrongdoers* [3] The two Greek terms translated by this phrase refer to the passive and active partners in consensual homosexual acts

Chapter 6
1 [r][Matt. 18:17]
2 [s]Dan. 7:22; [Matt. 19:28; Rev. 20:4]
4 [t][ch. 5:12]
5 [u]ch. 15:34; [ch. 4:14]
7 [v][Matt. 5:39, 40]
8 [w]1 Thess. 4:6
9 [x]ch. 15:50; Gal. 5:21; Eph. 5:5; 1 Tim. 1:9; Heb. 12:14; 13:4; Rev. 21:8; 22:15
11 [y]ch. 12:2; Eph. 2:2, 3; 4:22; 5:8; Col. 3:7; Titus 3:3 [z]Acts 22:16; Heb. 10:22; [Titus 3:5] [a]See ch. 1:2 [b]Rom. 8:30
12 [c]ch. 10:23
13 [d][Matt. 15:17]

6:1–11 *Trivial Cases before Unrighteous Judges.* Some of the Corinthians have wronged each other in various ways, including fraud. Instead of addressing these problems within the church, however, they have taken each other before the local magistrates. The wrongs themselves, and this way of handling them, are both shameful for Christians.

6:1 a grievance against another. Although some have argued that Paul is prohibiting Christians from ever going to court against another Christian, Paul seems in these verses only to be addressing disputes related to property or money (cf. "Why not rather be defrauded?" v. 7), rather than criminal cases, which fall under the jurisdiction of the state. (See Rom. 13:1–5 where Paul shows that God has established civil government for the protection and good of all people.) It is doubtful, therefore, that Paul's intention is that this specific example should be applied in every situation, since not every situation today matches the circumstances of this specific case in Corinth, where the two parties are in the same local church ("among you," 1 Cor. 6:5), and where the dispute is specifically related to property or money ("Why not be defrauded?" v. 7). Whatever the circumstances, it is clear from Scripture that disputes between believers need to be handled with the utmost care (vv. 1–8): in a wise and godly manner before the watching world; wherever possible under the disciplinary authority of the church; and with the counsel of spiritually mature Christians who have no stake in the matter and who can give objective, biblical advice. (See further Matt. 18:15–20 regarding the steps that Christians need to take when one believer sins against another believer, and the authoritative role of the church in such cases.) **the unrighteous**. Paul probably is referring to magistrates who are both unbelievers (1 Cor. 6:4, 6) and who are at times unjust in their judgments.

6:2–3 saints will judge the world . . . angels. See Dan. 7:22; Matt. 19:28; Luke 22:30; Rev. 3:21. The people of God will participate with Christ in the final day of judgment.

6:5 shame. Plagued by arrogance (3:21; 4:6, 8, 18–19), the Corinthians should have been ashamed of their behavior (15:34; see also 14:35; Ps. 35:26; Phil. 3:19), for they were not even **wise enough to settle a dispute between** those in their own congregation. Although they thought themselves to be wise (1 Cor. 3:18; 4:10; 2 Cor. 11:19), their actions belied this self-estimation, resulting in their shame (cf. 1 Cor. 1:27).

6:7–8 suffer wrong . . . wrong. These terms translate the Greek verb *adikeō*. Paul used the adjectival form of this verb, *adikos*, in v. 1 to describe the "unrighteous" magistrates that the Corinthians are using to adjudicate their cases. This implies that the Corinthians are acting like unbelievers rather than like the "saints" (the "sanctified" or "holy" people) that God has called them to be (1:2, 30; 3:17). See also notes on 3:1–3 and 5:1. **defraud**. This word (Gk. *apostereō*) would be particularly appropriate for unethical business practices among wealthy people. See James 5:4, where it is used this way. Although not many of the Corinthians were "powerful" or of "noble birth" (1 Cor. 1:26), some were wealthy enough to "humiliate those who have nothing" at the Lord's Supper (11:22).

6:9–10 Paul's use of the word **unrighteous** (Gk. *adikos* again; see note on vv. 7–8) implies that those whose behavior is indistinguishable from the unbelieving world may not be among the "saints" (v. 1) at all. See also 2 Cor. 13:5. **men who practice homosexuality**. The Greek words *malakos* and *arsenokoitēs* refer specifically to male homosexuals (see ESV footnote), but in Rom. 1:26–27 Paul also refers to female homosexuals, and to homosexual desires or "passions." Both passages (as well as Lev. 18:22; 20:13; and 1 Tim. 1:10) refer to homosexuality in general.

6:11 washed. This refers to the spiritual cleansing from the guilt and dominating power of sin that occurs at regeneration (see Titus 3:5) and that is symbolized in the "washing" of baptism (Acts 22:16). **sanctified**. This is a similar concept, in this instance meaning that an initial break with the love of sin, and with the power and practice of sin, occurs at regeneration (see Acts 20:32; Rom. 6:11; 2 Cor. 5:17). However, in another sense "sanctification" is also an ongoing process in the Christian life (Rom. 6:19; Phil. 3:13–14; Heb. 12:1, 14; see also note on 1 Cor. 1:2). **justified**. The Greek term is *dikaioō* and is the positive counterpart to the terms "unrighteous," "suffer wrong," and "wrong" in 6:1, 7–8, and 9 (see notes on those verses). Here Paul uses *dikaioō* not in its ethical sense ("be seen to be righteous") but in its judicial sense ("declare righteous"). God has already declared the Corinthian Christians to be "righteous" (see Rom. 5:1; 8:1, 33). God was able to do this because the "righteousness" that belongs to Christ, due to his perfect life, has become "our . . . righteousness" (1 Cor. 1:30; see also 2 Cor. 5:21). Paul's point in 1 Cor. 6:1–11 is that the Corinthians need to live in a way that is consistent with this verdict and status.

6:12–20 *Sexual Immorality and the Body's Resurrection.* Some of the Corinthian Christians were using prostitutes, theorizing that bodily appetites were matters of indifference for Christians just as they apparently were for everyone else. Paul reminds them that the bodies of Christians are one with the resurrected Christ and, in risen form, the Christian's body will be eternal. What they do with them now, therefore, is important.

6:12–13 "All things are lawful." The quotation marks around this phrase, both here and in 10:23, have been supplied to indicate that it is probably a commonly used slogan among the Corinthians. **"Food . . . for the stomach."** Probably another Corinthian slogan. The Corinthians have adopted from the culture around them the idea that the body is permitted to have everything

stomach for food"—and God will destroy both one [e]and the other. The body is not meant
for sexual immorality, but [f]for the Lord, and [g]the Lord for the body. **14** And [h]God raised
the Lord and [i]will also raise us up [j]by his power. **15** Do you not know that [k]your bodies are
members of Christ? Shall I then take the members of Christ and make them members of
a prostitute? Never! **16** Or do you not know that he who is joined[1] to a prostitute becomes
one body with her? For, as it is written, [l]"The two will become one flesh." **17** But he who is
joined to the Lord [m]becomes one spirit with him. **18** [n]Flee from sexual immorality. Every
other sin[2] a person commits is outside the body, but the sexually immoral person [o]sins
against his own body. **19** Or [p]do you not know that your body is a temple of the Holy Spirit
within you, whom you have from God? [q]You are not your own, **20** [r]for you were bought
with a price. [s]So glorify God in your body.

Principles for Marriage

7 Now concerning the matters about which you wrote: [t]"It is good for a man not to have
sexual relations with a woman." **2** But because of the temptation to sexual immorality,
each man should have his own wife and each woman her own husband. **3** [u]The husband
should give to his wife her conjugal rights, and likewise the wife to her husband. **4** For
the wife does not have authority over her own body, but the husband does. Likewise the
husband does not have authority over his own body, but the wife does. **5** [v]Do not deprive
one another, except perhaps by agreement for a limited time, that you may devote yourselves to prayer; but then come together again, [w]so that Satan may not tempt you because
of your lack of self-control.

6 Now as a concession, [x]not a command, I say this.[3] **7** [y]I wish that all were [z]as I myself am.
But [a]each has his own gift from God, [b]one of one kind and one of another.

[1] *Or who holds fast* (compare Genesis 2:24 and Deuteronomy 10:20); also verse 17 [2] *Or Every sin* [3] *Or I say this:*

13 [e]Col. 2:22 [f]ver. 15, 19 [g][Eph. 5:23]
14 [h]See Acts 2:24 [i]ch. 15:22, 23; [John 6:39, 40] [j]Matt. 22:29; [Eph. 1:19, 20]
15 [k]ver. 13; Eph. 5:30; [ch. 12:27; Rom. 12:5]
16 [l]Matt. 19:5; Mark 10:8; Eph. 5:31; Cited from Gen. 2:24
17 [m]Eph. 4:4; [John 17:21-23]
18 [n]2 Cor. 12:21; Eph. 5:3 [o][Prov. 5:11]
19 [p][John 2:21]; See ch. 3:16 [q]See Rom. 14:7
20 [r]ch. 7:23; [Acts 20:28; Heb. 9:12, 14]; See 2 Pet. 2:1 [s][Phil. 1:20]

Chapter 7

1 [t]ver. 8, 26
3 [u]Ex. 21:10
5 [v][Ex. 19:15; 1 Sam. 21:4; Eccles. 3:5; Zech. 12:12-14] [w]1 Thess. 3:5
6 [x]ver. 12, 25; 2 Cor. 8:8; [ver. 10, 40]
7 [y][Acts 26:29] [z]ver. 8; [ch. 9:5] [a]ch. 12:4, 11; 1 Pet. 4:10; [Rom. 12:6] [b]Matt. 19:11, 12

that it craves. Paul knows that human desires are tainted with sin, which uses these desires to master the person for its own evil purposes (Rom. 6:6, 12, 16–22; 7:7–25).

6:14 Jesus' resurrection was only the first step in the general resurrection of God's people that will occur on the last day (15:20). Jesus' body and the believer's body, therefore, are eternal (15:42–49), for God **will also raise us up**; the eternal nature of the believer's body should affect his or her present behavior. See 15:30–34.

6:15 bodies . . . members of Christ. Already in 1:13 Paul has hinted that the church is Christ's body and that divisions in the church are incompatible with this truth. See also 12:12, 27; Eph. 1:22–23; 4:13–16; 5:23; Col. 1:18.

6:16–18 Unity with Christ is incompatible with all sin (Rom. 6:6) but particularly with sexual sin. Because sexual union has a spiritual component, sexual activity outside marriage is a unique sin both against Christ (1 Cor. 6:15) and one's own body (v. 18; see Prov. 6:26, 32). Within marriage, sexual union is not only allowed but has positive spiritual significance (Gen. 2:24; Eph. 5:22–33). **Flee**. Paul also tells the Corinthians to "flee from idolatry" in 1 Cor. 10:14. Idolatry and sexual immorality were closely connected in Israel's history (Ex. 32:6; Num. 25:1–2) as well as in Paul's thinking about the problems in Corinth (1 Cor. 10:7–8).

6:19 temple of the Holy Spirit within you. The Spirit of the Lord lives within individual Christians (v. 17), making each Christian's body a temple just as the church, corporately conceived, is also a temple where God's Spirit dwells (3:16). **You are not your own**. As with other gifts from God (4:2, 7), Christians are to exercise responsible stewardship over their bodies.

6:20 bought with a price. The image is borrowed from the slave market (7:23; see also Rom. 6:17–18), Christ's blood being the purchase price (Eph. 1:7; see also 1 Pet. 1:19; Rev. 5:9).

7:1–11:1 *Three Issues from a Corinthian Letter.* Paul now turns to a series of problems raised in a letter from the Corinthians written to him (7:1). He signals a move from one topic to another with the phrase "now concerning" (7:1 [see note], 25; 8:1; the phrase also occurs later at 12:1; 16:1, 12). He first addresses issues related to marriage, divorce, and one's lot in life (7:1–24). He then turns to whether the betrothed and widowed should marry in light of the urgency of the times (7:25–40). Finally, he discusses food sacrificed to idols (8:1–11:1).

7:1–24 *Marriage, Divorce, and Unchangeable Circumstances.* The Corinthians are commanded to be faithful in their marriages, to avoid divorce, and to be content in their calling.

7:1 Now concerning. Paul uses this phrase for the first time here to signal a switch from matters raised in the oral report from Chloe's people (1:10–11) to issues raised in a letter from Corinth. This same phrase is repeated in a number of places throughout the rest of 1 Corinthians (see 7:25; 8:1; 12:1; 16:1, 12) where it introduces additional topics from the Corinthians' letter. **"It is good . . ."** Some Corinthian Christians appear to have adopted the view that sexual relations of any kind, even within marriage, should be avoided. Paul seeks to carefully refute this view throughout this chapter (see 7:2, 5, 9, 10, 28, 36).

7:2–5 the husband . . . the wife. God designed marriage as the place for the expression of human sexuality. Sex within marriage has both relational and spiritual benefits (Gen. 2:24; Eph. 5:31; see also 1 Cor. 6:17). It also has the practical benefit of reducing the temptation to engage in sexual sin (see 7:9).

7:2 Have probably refers to sexual intercourse (cf. 5:1). **Each man . . . his own wife and each woman her own husband** affirms the goodness of monogamous marriage and excludes polygamy, for a "shared" husband would not be "her own" husband.

7:4 The emphasis here is on mutuality in the marriage relationship within the overall framework described in Eph. 5:22–23 and Col. 3:18–19.

7:5 Do not deprive. Abstention from sexual relations in marriage should be limited to short periods of time and only by mutual consent of the husband and wife.

7:6–7 The **concession** refers to permission to refrain from sexual relations for short periods of time (see v. 5). Paul does not demand such periods of abstinence, though he does permit it. **each has his own gift**. Both marriage and celibacy have their own benefits, and both should be considered "gifts." Paul is happy that God has given him the gift of being content with remaining unmarried, since this permits single-minded devotion to the Lord's work (vv. 32–33, 40). Paul recognizes, however, that his situation is not the

8 To the unmarried and the widows I say that [c]it is good for them to remain single [d]as I
am. 9 But if they cannot exercise self-control, [e]they should marry. For it is better to marry
than to burn with passion.
10 To the married [f]I give this charge (not I, but the Lord): [g]the wife should not separate
from her husband 11 (but if she does, [h]she should remain unmarried or else be reconciled
to her husband), and [g]the husband should not divorce his wife.
12 To the rest I say (I, not the Lord) that if any brother has a wife who is an unbeliever, and
she consents to live with him, he should not divorce her. 13 If any woman has a husband
who is an unbeliever, and he consents to live with her, she should not divorce him. 14 For
the unbelieving husband is made holy because of his wife, and the unbelieving wife is
made holy because of her husband. [i]Otherwise your children would be unclean, but as it
is, they are holy. 15 But if the unbelieving partner separates, let it be so. In such cases the
brother or sister is not enslaved. God has called you[1] [j]to peace. 16 For how do you know,
wife, [k]whether you will save your husband? Or how do you know, husband, whether you
will save your wife?

Live as You Are Called

17 Only let each person lead the life[2] [l]that the Lord has assigned to him, and to which
God has called him. [m]This is my rule in [n]all the churches. 18 Was anyone at the time of his

[1] Some manuscripts *us* [2] Or *each person walk in the way*

8 [c]ver. 1, 26 [d]ver. 7
9 [e][1 Tim. 5:14]
10 [f]See ver. 6 [g]Mal. 2:16; See Matt. 5:32
11 [h]Mark 10:12 [g][See ver. 10 above]
14 [i]Ezra 9:2; Mal. 2:15
15 [j]Col. 3:15; See Rom. 14:19
16 [k]1 Pet. 3:1; See Rom. 11:14
17 [l]See Rom. 12:3 [m]ch. 4:17 [n]2 Cor. 8:18; 11:28

norm. Remaining unmarried is a gift that many others do not have. See vv. 28, 36; Matt. 19:12.

7:10–11 Paul now turns to divorce and urges believers to obey the command of **the Lord** (Matt. 5:32; 19:9; Mark 10:11–12; Luke 16:18) that the wife should not **separate from** (Gk. *chōrizō*; the same word is used in Matt. 19:6) a believing husband and that the husband should not **divorce** (Gk. *aphiēmi*, lit., "send away," a term commonly used for divorce) a believing wife. Roman law permitted either a husband or a wife to initiate a divorce with no stated cause required.

7:12–13 I, not the Lord. Paul knows the oral tradition of Jesus' sayings on divorce that were later written down in the Gospels (see note on vv. 10–11), but he is not aware that Jesus ever spoke specifically to a situation in which one spouse becomes a Christian and the other remains unconverted. He carefully distinguishes, therefore, between the written words of Jesus as recorded in the Gospels and Paul's own understanding of how Jesus' teaching would apply to this new situation. Paul views his admonition here as authoritative and inspired, not merely as human wisdom (v. 40; cf. 14:37–38). **a wife . . . a husband who is an unbeliever**. Is the believing partner defiled by being married to and having sexual relations with an unbeliever? Should they divorce? Clearly the believing partner is not defiled, for Paul says that if the believing partner has any say in the matter, they should not divorce.

7:14 made holy . . . are holy. These are the same terms (Gk. *hagiazō*, *hagios*) used earlier for God's separation of Corinthian Christians from their pagan environment as his special people (1:2; 3:17; 6:1, 2, 11). The unbelieving spouse and children in a family with a believing spouse are not saved by this association (7:16), but they do come under the believing spouse's Christian influence and so, Paul notes, they are much more likely to be saved

Divorce and Remarriage in 1 Corinthians 7

vv. 10–11	Don't separate, but if you do, seek reconciliation.
vv. 12–13	If the unbelieving spouse consents to stay, do not seek divorce.
v. 15	If the unbelieving spouse separates (i.e., leaves the marriage), the believer is not bound (i.e., is free to remarry).
v. 39	If a spouse dies, the one who lives is free to remarry, but only to marry another believer (cf. Rom. 7:1–4).

in due course through their own faith. Thus they are in a real sense "set apart" (the basic meaning of *hagiazō* and *hagios*) from other unbelievers and from the evil of the world. Thus the positive spiritual and moral influence of the believing parent outweighs the negative influence of the unbelieving parent.

7:15 let it be so. Paul advises the Christian spouse not to create strife by trying to manipulate reconciliation with an unbelieving spouse who has left the marriage. **not enslaved**. This at least means that the believing spouse is not obligated to seek reconciliation to the unbelieving spouse who abandoned him or her (see v. 11); but the majority of interpreters now think that the phrase also implies the freedom to obtain a legal divorce (if that has not already happened) and the freedom to marry someone else. Jesus' teaching on divorce also appears to allow remarriage when sexual immorality has prompted the divorce (see notes on Matt. 5:31–32; 19:9). **Peace** in the widest sense is meant, in the OT sense that "all is well" in one's life and circumstances, which is the OT concept of *shalom* (see note on John 14:27). Most interpreters hold that God releases the believing spouse from the twin unending distresses of (a) a lifelong vain hope of reconciling with an unbeliever who has abandoned the believing spouse, and (b) a lifelong prohibition against enjoying the blessings of marriage again. Other interpreters, emphasizing 1 Cor. 7:39, hold that remarriage is never allowed after divorce.

7:16 how do you know. Paul probably intends a negative answer to these rhetorical questions—i.e., that there is no assurance that an unbelieving spouse will be saved, and so the believer should feel free not to pursue the spouse who has left.

7:17 God calls people to himself who are in various situations regarding economics (slavery/freedom), family (divorce/marriage), and religious background (circumcision/uncircumcision), and often God has a purpose for the new believer in that very situation (see vv. 20, 24). It is the place **to which God has called him** (Gk. *kaleō*; the idea of life vocation as a "calling" comes from this verse). Paul couples this word with **assigned** (Gk. *merizō*), which can also be translated "deal out" or "apportion."

7:18 circumcised. Although Jews were not the only Semitic people who practiced male circumcision, Greeks, Romans, and the Jews themselves considered the practice a distinguishing characteristic of the Jews. See note on Gen. 17:10. **remove the marks of circumcision**. This verb (Gk. *epispaō*) describes "epispasm," a procedure that reversed the physical appearance of circumcision.

7:19 God's command that his people should practice male circumcision as a sign of his covenant with them (Gen. 17:1–14) had passed away, like the Mosaic law's dietary restrictions (Matt. 15:11; Mark 7:19; Acts 10:13; 11:7). See also Gal. 6:15. However, God still had **commandments** for his people to keep (1 Cor. 9:21; Gal. 6:2).

18[o]Acts 15:1, 5, 19, 24, 28; Gal. 5:2
19[p]Gal. 3:28; 5:6; 6:15; Col. 3:11 [q]See 1 John 2:3
20[r]ver. 24
22[s][Col. 3:24; Philem. 16]; See John 8:36 [t][ch. 9:21; 1 Pet. 2:16]
23[u]See ch. 6:20 [v]Lev. 25:42, 55
24[w]ver. 20
25[x]See ver. 6 [y]2 Cor. 4:1; 1 Tim. 1:13, 16 [z]ch. 4:2
26[a]ver. 1, 8
29[b]See Rom. 13:11
30[c]2 Cor. 6:10
31[d]Ps. 39:6; James 1:10; 1 Pet. 1:24; 4:7; 1 John 2:17
32[e]See Matt. 6:25; Luke 10:41 [f][1 Tim. 5:5]
35[g][Prov. 22:25]

call already circumcised? Let him not seek to remove the marks of circumcision. Was anyone at the time of his call uncircumcised? [o]Let him not seek circumcision. **19** [p]For neither
circumcision counts for anything nor uncircumcision, but [q]keeping the commandments
of God. **20** [r]Each one should remain in the condition in which he was called. **21** Were you a
bondservant[1] when called? Do not be concerned about it. (But if you can gain your freedom,
avail yourself of the opportunity.) **22** For he who was called in the Lord as a bondservant is
[s]a freedman of the Lord. Likewise he who was free when called is [t]a bondservant of Christ.
23 [u]You were bought with a price; [v]do not become bondservants[2] of men. **24** So, brothers,[3]
[w]in whatever condition each was called, there let him remain with God.

The Unmarried and the Widowed

25 Now concerning[4] the betrothed,[5] [x]I have no command from the Lord, but I give
my judgment as [y]one who by the Lord's mercy is [z]trustworthy. **26** I think that in view
of the present[6] distress [a]it is good for a person to remain as he is. **27** Are you bound to
a wife? Do not seek to be free. Are you free from a wife? Do not seek a wife. **28** But if
you do marry, you have not sinned, and if a betrothed woman[7] marries, she has not
sinned. Yet those who marry will have worldly troubles, and I would spare you that.
29 This is what I mean, brothers: [b]the appointed time has grown very short. From now
on, let those who have wives live as though they had none, **30** and those who mourn
as though they were not mourning, and those who rejoice as though they were not
rejoicing, and those who buy [c]as though they had no goods, **31** and those who deal
with the world as though they had no dealings with it. For [d]the present form of this
world is passing away.

32 I want you to be [e]free from anxieties. [f]The unmarried man is anxious about the things
of the Lord, how to please the Lord. **33** But the married man is anxious about worldly things,
how to please his wife, **34** and his interests are divided. And the unmarried or betrothed
woman is anxious about the things of the Lord, how to be holy in body and spirit. But
the married woman is anxious about worldly things, how to please her husband. **35** I say
this for your own benefit, [g]not to lay any restraint upon you, but to promote good order
and to secure your undivided devotion to the Lord.

36 If anyone thinks that he is not behaving properly toward his betrothed,[8] if his[9] passions

[1] Or *slave;* also twice in verse 22 (for the contextual rendering of the Greek word *doulos*, see Preface) [2] Or *slaves* (for the contextual rendering of the Greek word *doulos*, see Preface) [3] Or *brothers and sisters;* also verse 29 [4] The expression *Now concerning* introduces a reply to a question in the Corinthians' letter; see 7:1 [5] Greek *virgins* [6] Or *impending* [7] Greek *virgin;* also verse 34 [8] Greek *virgin;* also verses 37, 38 [9] Or *her*

7:21 a bondservant when called. The Roman institution of being a "bondservant" or "slave" (Gk. *doulos*; see ESV footnote and Preface, p. 21) was different from the institution of slavery in North America during the seventeenth through the nineteenth centuries. Slaves (bondservants, servants) generally were permitted to work for pay and to save enough to buy their freedom (see Matt. 25:15 where the "servants" [again Gk. *doulos*] were entrusted with immense amounts of money and responsibility). The NT assumes that trafficking in human beings is a sin (1 Tim. 1:10; Rev. 18:11–13), and Paul urges Christian bondservants who **can gain . . . freedom** to do so. The released bondservant was officially designated a "freedman" and frequently continued to work for his former master. Many extant inscriptions from freedmen indicate the tendency to adopt the family name of their former master (now their "patron") and to continue honoring them.

7:25–40 *The Betrothed and Widows.* Paul now turns to those eligible for marriage and discusses the advisability of marriage in times of distress.

7:25 the betrothed. This translates the Greek term for "virgins" (plural of *parthenos*). Although the term could apply to either men or women, it most often applied to women of marriageable age who had never married. Paul's use of the term in v. 28 is clearly feminine, so he probably has women in mind here as well. In light of what he says later in vv. 36–38, it seems clear that his comments in vv. 25–26 are directed to any man who has promised to marry a "virgin."

7:26 present distress. This may refer to the urgency of living in the last days (see note on vv. 29–31), or to some difficulty, such as famine, that may have been afflicting Corinth.

7:28 On deciding whether to **marry**, see note on vv. 6–7.

7:29–31 See 10:11. Paul is not saying, as some scholars have claimed, that Christ will definitely come within the Corinthians' lifetimes. The purpose of 1 Corinthians, in large part, is to encourage Christians to attend to the kinds of daily affairs that would be unimportant if Christ were returning within weeks or months. Thus Paul provides practical teaching concerning marriage (7:1–16, 25–40); what type of food to eat at a dinner party (10:23–11:1); collecting money for the needy (16:1–4); and future travel plans (16:5–11). Like other NT writers, Paul considers all of time from the cross forward to be the "last days" (Acts 2:17; Heb. 1:2; James 5:3) and counsels Christians always to live in the light of Christ's certain return at an unforeseen moment (1 Cor. 3:13; 15:52; see also Matt. 24:44; 25:13; Mark 13:32–37; Luke 21:34–36; Rom. 13:11–14; 1 Thess. 5:1–9). Paul's point here is simply that the **form of this world**, or its day-to-day affairs, is not eternal. Christians should prioritize their human relationships, material possessions, and worldly dealings accordingly. See also Matt. 24:37–39; Luke 17:26–30; Rom. 12:2; 1 John 2:16–17.

7:32–35 On living as a single person, see note on vv. 6–7.

7:36 If his passions are strong translates a difficult word (Gk. *hyperakmos*) that can also mean "past one's prime" when used in reference to a woman. The ESV translation is preferable, however, because it is consistent with Paul's reasoning in vv. 2–3 and 9, and it would be strange for Paul to give permission to marry only when women are "past their prime." **And it has to be** probably refers to a sense of both moral and physical necessity to get married. Paul's comment is not intended as a disapproval of marriage (cf. vv. 28, 38; Eph. 5:22–33; 1 Tim. 4:1–4).

are strong, and it has to be, let him do as he wishes: let them marry—it is no sin. 37 But
whoever is firmly established in his heart, being under no necessity but having his desire
under control, and has determined this in his heart, to keep her as his betrothed, he will
do well. 38 So then he who marries his betrothed [h]does well, and he who refrains from
marriage will do even better.
39 [i]A wife is bound to her husband as long as he lives. But if her husband dies, she is free
to be married to whom she wishes, only [j]in the Lord. 40 Yet [k]in my judgment she is happier
if she remains as she is. And I think [l]that I too have the Spirit of God.

Food Offered to Idols

8 Now concerning[1] [m]food offered to idols: we know that [n]"all of us possess knowledge."
This "knowledge" [o]puffs up, [p]but love builds up. 2 [q]If anyone imagines that he knows
something, [r]he does not yet know as he ought to know. 3 But if anyone loves God, [s]he is
known by God.[2]
4 Therefore, as to the eating of food offered to idols, we know that [t]"an idol has no real
existence," and that [u]"there is no God but one." 5 For although there may be [v]so-called
gods in heaven or on earth—as indeed there are many "gods" and many "lords"—
6 yet [w]for us there is one God, the Father, [x]from whom are all things and for whom we
exist, and [y]one Lord, Jesus Christ, through whom are all things and [z]through whom
we exist.
7 However, not all possess this knowledge. But some, [a]through former association with
idols, eat food as really offered to an idol, and [b]their conscience, being weak, is defiled. 8 [c]Food
will not commend us to God. We are no worse off if we do not eat, and no better off if we
do. 9 But take care [d]that this right of yours does not somehow become a stumbling block
[e]to the weak. 10 For if anyone sees you who have knowledge eating[3] in an idol's temple,

[1] The expression *Now concerning* introduces a reply to a question in the Corinthians' letter; see 7:1 [2] Greek *him* [3] Greek *reclining at table*

38 [h]Heb. 13:4
39 [i]Rom. 7:2 [j][2 Cor. 6:14]
40 [k]See ver. 6 [l][Acts 15:28]

Chapter 8

1 [m]ver. 4, 7, 10; See Acts 15:29 [n]See Rom. 15:14 [o]Rom. 14:3 [p]ch. 13:4-13
2 [q]Gal. 6:3; [ch. 3:18] [r][ch. 13:8, 9, 12; 1 Tim. 6:3, 4]
3 [s]Gal. 4:9; [Ex. 33:12, 17; Jer. 1:5; Nah. 1:7; 2 Tim. 2:19]
4 [t]ch. 10:19; Isa. 41:24; [Acts 14:15] [u]ver. 6; See Deut. 4:35, 39
5 [v]2 Thess. 2:4
6 [w]ver. 4; Mal. 2:10; Eph. 4:6 [x]See Rom. 11:36 [y]Eph. 4:5; [ch. 1:2; 1 Tim. 2:5]; See John 13:13 [z]John 1:3; Col. 1:16
7 [a][Rom. 14:14, 22, 23] [b]ch. 10:25, 28, 29
8 [c]Rom. 14:17
9 [d][ch. 10:23; Rom. 14:21; Gal. 5:13] [e]Rom. 14:1, 2

7:37–38 keep her as his betrothed. Paul now turns to the person who has the gift of celibacy and is able to refrain from marrying. **Does well** and **even better** illustrate the general principle that among choices that are morally good and not sinful, God can still give different opportunities for service, which will have different consequences.

7:39 her husband dies. The widow, like any other person of marriageable age (v. 25), is free to marry. Presumably all that Paul has just said of the betrothed applies to the widow as well (vv. 8–9, 40a), and his admonition that she marry **only in the Lord** (that is, she should marry only a fellow Christian) would likewise apply to the betrothed. **To whom she wishes** injects a wonderful note of practical wisdom—that people should marry someone they "wish" (Gk. *thelō*, "desire" or "want") to marry.

8:1–11:1 *Food Offered to Idols.* Because pagan temples offered parts of animals in sacrifice to the gods, they also often functioned as butcher shops and banqueting halls. Sometimes meals for trade guilds, clubs, and private dinner parties were held in a temple dining room. Often meat from a temple was sold to the public in the marketplace. This section of 1 Corinthians gives clear guidance about the use of such food. Paul first urges the Corinthians not to eat in pagan temples (8:10) because it might lead to the destruction of a weaker brother or sister (ch. 8). He then offers himself as an example of giving up something one is convinced is a right for the spiritual edification of others (ch. 9). He urges the Corinthians not to eat in pagan temples because doing so is idolatry (10:1–22). Finally, he says that eating meat purchased in the marketplace (which may have come from a pagan temple) is not wrong unless it hinders the advancement of the gospel (10:23–11:1).

8:1 food offered to idols. In Greek, this phrase is one word (*eidōlothytos*, lit., "something offered to an idol"). Paul is talking about food, however, because he uses the word for "food" (Gk. *brōsis*) in v. 4. Since only part of an animal was used in sacrifices to pagan gods, much of the animal could still be eaten. Paul speaks later in this chapter of eating such food in a banqueting hall attached to a temple and therefore in an explicitly religious setting (v. 10). Pre-Pauline evidence of such temple banquets at Corinth is found at the Sanctuary of Asklepios and at the Sanctuary of Demeter and Kore, and such feasting likely continued during Paul's day. **"all of us possess knowledge."** Quotation marks have been supplied to indicate that this statement probably originated with the Corinthians and that Paul is responding to it (cf. 1:12; 3:4; 6:12, 13; 7:1; 8:4; 10:23). What the Corinthians "know" is explained in 8:4. **puffs up.** Once again, Corinthian arrogance is seen as a problem (see also 3:21; 4:6, 8, 18–19).

8:3 known by God. God knows those who belong to him (13:12; John 10:14; Gal. 4:9; 2 Tim. 2:19), and there is a close bond between belonging to God and sharing love for God and neighbor (1 John 3:16; 4:20).

8:4–6 Paul agrees with what the Corinthians **know**, that idols do not represent real **"gods"** and **"lords."** There is only **one God**, and since he is the creator of the animals that pagan priests offer to nonexistent gods, no problem should be attached to the consumption of the meat itself (see also 10:19–20, 25–26). Paul will later distinguish between eating at a temple dinner (which, as a religious event, is idolatry) and eating meat bought in the marketplace. So far in this passage he is concerned only with the food itself, not the setting in which it is eaten.

8:7 The pagans of Paul's day feared what the gods might do to those who neglected to worship them. Some of the Christians in Corinth probably found it a constant struggle to place their trust solely in Christ instead of trying to placate the gods they used to worship.

8:8 Those who had the supposedly superior "knowledge" (vv. 1, 4) that permitted them to participate in dinners held at pagan temples may have thought that this knowledge gave them special standing with God.

8:9 this right of yours. Paul is speaking from the Corinthians' perspective. He will later deny that anyone in the Corinthian church has the right to eat meals in pagan temples. To do this is to practice idolatry and so to open oneself to the influence of demons (10:7, 14, 20–22). Even if they had the right to eat in temples they should refrain from using this right out of concern for the spiritual well-being of the person whose conscience is weak (8:7). **stumbling block.** See Rom. 14:13, 20.

8:10–11 eating in an idol's temple. See notes on 8:1–11:1; 8:1. Paul elsewhere uses **destroyed** (Gk. *apollymi*) to mean eternal destruction (Rom. 2:12; 1 Cor. 1:18; 15:18; 2 Cor. 2:15; 4:3; 2 Thess. 2:10), and some interpreters take Paul's use of the term here in the same sense. Others see this as a reference to the moral harm done to the weaker brother (his conscience "is defiled," 1 Cor. 8:7).

11 [f]Rom. 14:15, 20
12 [g][Zech. 2:8; Matt. 18:6] [h][Matt. 25:45]
13 [i]Rom. 14:13, 21; [2 Cor. 6:3; 11:29]
Chapter 9
1 [j]ver. 19 [k]Acts 14:14; 2 Cor. 12:12; 1 Thess. 2:6; [2 Cor. 10:7; Rev. 2:2] [l]ch. 15:8; Acts 9:3, 17; 18:9; 22:14, 18; 23:11 [m]See ch. 3:6
2 [n][2 Cor. 3:2]
4 [o]ver. 14; 1 Thess. 2:6, 9; 2 Thess. 3:8, 9
5 [p][ch. 7:7] [q]See Matt. 12:46 [r]Matt. 8:14; See John 1:42
7 [s]2 Cor. 10:4; 1 Tim. 1:18; 2 Tim. 2:3, 4 [t][ch. 3:6-8; Deut. 20:6; Prov. 27:18; Song 8:12]
9 [u]1 Tim. 5:18; Cited from Deut. 25:4
10 [v]See Rom. 4:24 [w]2 Tim. 2:6
11 [x][Rom. 15:27; Gal. 6:6]
12 [y]ver. 15, 18; See Acts 20:33 [z][2 Cor. 6:3; 11:12]
13 [a]Lev. 6:16, 26; 7:6; Num. 5:9, 10; 18:8-20; Deut. 18:1
14 [b]ver. 4; Matt. 10:10
15 [c]See Acts 18:3 [d]2 Cor. 11:10
16 [e][Acts 4:20; 9:6; Rom. 1:14]
17 [f]ch. 4:1; Gal. 2:7; [Phil. 1:16]

will he not be encouraged,[1] if his conscience is weak, to eat food offered to idols? **11** And
so by your knowledge this weak person is [f]destroyed, the brother for whom Christ died.
12 Thus, sinning against your brothers[2] and [g]wounding their conscience when it is weak,
[h]you sin against Christ. **13** Therefore, [i]if food makes my brother stumble, I will never eat
meat, lest I make my brother stumble.

Paul Surrenders His Rights

9 [j]Am I not free? [k]Am I not an apostle? [l]Have I not seen Jesus our Lord? [m]Are not you my
workmanship in the Lord? **2** If to others I am not an apostle, at least I am to you, for
you are [n]the seal of my apostleship in the Lord.
3 This is my defense to those who would examine me. **4** [o]Do we not have the right to
eat and drink? **5** [p]Do we not have the right to take along a believing wife,[3] as do the other
apostles and [q]the brothers of the Lord and [r]Cephas? **6** Or is it only Barnabas and I who
have no right to refrain from working for a living? **7** [s]Who serves as a soldier at his own
expense? [t]Who plants a vineyard without eating any of its fruit? Or who tends a flock
without getting some of the milk?
8 Do I say these things on human authority? Does not the Law say the same? **9** For it is
written in the Law of Moses, [u]"You shall not muzzle an ox when it treads out the grain."
Is it for oxen that God is concerned? **10** Does he not certainly speak for our sake? It was
written [v]for our sake, because [w]the plowman should plow in hope and the thresher thresh
in hope of sharing in the crop. **11** [x]If we have sown spiritual things among you, is it too
much if we reap material things from you? **12** If others share this rightful claim on you,
do not we even more?
Nevertheless, [y]we have not made use of this right, but we endure anything [z]rather than
put an obstacle in the way of the gospel of Christ. **13** Do you not know that [a]those who are
employed in the temple service get their food from the temple, and those who serve at
the altar share in the sacrificial offerings? **14** In the same way, the Lord commanded that
[b]those who proclaim the gospel should get their living by the gospel.
15 But [c]I have made no use of any of these rights, nor am I writing these things to secure
any such provision. For I would rather die than have anyone [d]deprive me of my ground for
boasting. **16** For if I preach the gospel, that gives me no ground for boasting. For [e]necessity
is laid upon me. Woe to me if I do not preach the gospel! **17** For if I do this of my own will, I
have a reward, but if not of my own will, I am still entrusted with [f]a stewardship. **18** What

[1] *Or fortified; Greek built up* [2] *Or brothers and sisters* [3] *Greek a sister as wife*

9:1 Am I not free? Paul offers his own willingness to give up his rights for the spiritual benefit of the Corinthians as an example that those with superior "knowledge" (8:1–2) should follow (see 10:23–11:1).

9:2 seal. Seals in the ancient Near East were used to guarantee the quality and authenticity of a document (such as a letter) or product (such as wine); see note on John 6:27. The change that Paul's preaching of the gospel effected in the hearts of the Corinthians shows that his apostleship is genuine. See also 2 Cor. 1:21–22; 3:3.

9:4–5 right. Paul used the same word (Gk. *exousia*) in 8:8 for the supposed "right" of Corinthians with superior "knowledge" to eat meals in pagan temples. As an apostle whose primary vocation was proclaiming the gospel and establishing churches, Paul had the right to receive material support from those churches (see Matt. 10:9–10; Luke 10:7; 1 Thess. 2:6–7; 2 Thess. 3:9; 1 Tim. 5:17–18) and to travel with a wife (if he were married). **to take along a believing wife.** Paul was not married but he had a high regard for marriage among ministers of the gospel (see 1 Tim. 3:2; 4:3; Titus 1:6). None of **the brothers of the Lord** followed him prior to his resurrection (John 7:5). The risen Lord appeared, however, to his brother James (1 Cor. 15:7; cf. Matt. 13:55; Mark 6:3; Gal. 1:19), who later became the leading figure in the Jerusalem church (Acts 12:17; 15:13; 21:18; Gal. 2:9, 12). Jesus also had a brother named "Judas" (Matt. 13:55; Mark 6:3), and this is probably the same person who authored the Letter of Jude (or Judas) and calls himself "the brother of James" (Jude 1).

9:6 Barnabas was a Jewish Christian from the priestly tribe of Levi, a native of the island of Cyprus, and an early member of the Jerusalem church (Acts 4:36). He and Paul joined forces on Paul's first missionary journey (Acts 13:1–14:28).

9:7 With three examples from everyday life, Paul observes the commonsense principle that those who work hard should benefit from their labor.

9:8–9 The gospel has brought important changes in the application of the Mosaic **Law** to the lives of God's people (7:19; see also the articles on Biblical Ethics, pp. 2535–2560), but it remains God's Word and therefore continues to instruct Christians about God's character and scale of values.

9:12a others. Probably a reference to those listed in v. 5 who had traveled through Corinth and received material support from the Corinthians while ministering there.

9:15 I have made no use. Paul occasionally did receive material support from churches for his proclamation of the gospel (2 Cor. 11:8; Phil. 2:25; 4:14–18), but he appears never to have received such support from the Christians in the immediate geographical location in which he was working at any given time (2 Cor. 11:7–8). **boasting.** Paul uses this word not in its usual sense of pride that steals glory from God (see 1 Cor. 1:29) but rather as expressing a rightful sense of joy and fulfillment in what God has done through him (e.g., see Acts 14:27; Rom. 15:17–19; 2 Cor. 1:14; 10:7–8; Gal. 6:4; Phil. 2:16; 2 Tim. 4:7–8).

9:17 stewardship. This term (Gk. *oikonomia*) refers to the responsibility of managing a household. Paul uses it metaphorically to say that God has entrusted him with a responsibility to which he must be faithful, whether he benefits from it materially or not. That responsibility is to proclaim the gospel and share its blessings (v. 23). (See also Eph. 3:2, 9.)

9:18 free of charge. Paul preached the gospel in urban centers where

then is my reward? That in my preaching [g]I may present the gospel free of charge, so as
not to make full use of my right in the gospel.
19 For [h]though I am free from all, [i]I have made myself a servant to all, that I might [j]win
more of them. 20 [k]To the Jews I became as a Jew, in order to win Jews. To those under the
law I became as one under the law (though not being myself under the law) that I might
win those under the law. 21 To [l]those outside the law I became [m]as one outside the law (not
being outside the law of God but [n]under the law of Christ) that I might win those outside
the law. 22 [o]To the weak I became weak, that I might win the weak. [p]I have become all things
to all people, that [q]by all means I might save some. 23 I do it all for the sake of the gospel,
[r]that I may share with them in its blessings.
24 Do you not know that in a race all the runners run, but only one receives [s]the prize?
So [t]run that you may obtain it. 25 Every [u]athlete exercises self-control in all things. They
do it to receive a perishable wreath, but we [v]an imperishable. 26 So I do not run aimlessly; I
[w]do not box as one [x]beating the air. 27 But I discipline my body and [y]keep it under control,[1]
lest after preaching to others [z]I myself should be [a]disqualified.

Warning Against Idolatry

10 For I do not want you to be unaware, brothers,[2] that our fathers were all under
[b]the cloud, and all [c]passed through the sea, 2 and all were baptized into Moses in
the cloud and in the sea, 3 and [d]all ate the same [e]spiritual food, 4 and [f]all drank the same

[1] Greek *I pummel my body and make it a slave* [2] Or *brothers and sisters*

18 [g]2 Cor. 11:7; 12:13
19 [h]ver. 1; [ch. 10:29] [i][Gal. 5:13] [j]Matt. 18:15; 1 Pet. 3:1
20 [k]Acts 16:3; 21:23-26
21 [l]Rom. 2:12, 14 [m][Gal. 2:3; 3:2] [n]See ch. 7:22
22 [o]2 Cor. 11:29 [p]ch. 10:33 [q]ch. 7:16; Rom. 11:14
23 [r][ch. 10:24]
24 [s]Phil. 3:14; Col. 2:18 [t]Gal. 2:2; 5:7; Phil. 2:16; Heb. 12:1; [2 Tim. 4:7]
25 [u]1 Tim. 6:12; 2 Tim. 2:5; 4:7; [Jude 3] [v]See James 1:12
26 [w][Heb. 12:4] [x][ch. 14:9]
27 [y][Rom. 6:19] [z][Song 1:6] [a][Jer. 6:30; Rom. 1:28; Heb. 6:8]

Chapter 10

1 [b]See Ex. 13:21 [c]See Ex. 14:22
3 [d]Ex. 16:15, 35; Deut. 8:3; Neh. 9:15, 20; Ps. 78:24 [e]Ps. 78:25; 105:40; John 6:31
4 [f]See Ex. 17:6

itinerant orators were a common sight. Some of them openly used their rhetorical skills to seek fame and fortune. Other more philosophically inclined teachers proclaimed self-discipline and verbally despised the world but sometimes actually pocketed large sums from their followers as they moved from town to town. Paul seeks to distinguish himself from such preachers (cf. 1 Thess. 2:3–5, 9–10). It is recorded elsewhere that Paul used his manual labor to set an example of hard work for new Christians, some of whom had a tendency to take advantage of the charitable impulses of the larger group (1 Thess. 4:11; 5:14; 2 Thess. 3:6–9).

9:20 I became as a Jew. Paul was a Jew (2 Cor. 11:22; Gal. 1:13; Phil. 3:5) and valued his Jewish heritage (Rom. 9:3–5), but the Jewish Messiah himself had nullified the distinctively Jewish parts of the Mosaic law (Matt. 15:11; Mark 7:19; Rom. 14:14; 1 Cor. 7:19; Gal. 2:11–14; 6:2; Eph. 2:14–15). In Christ, God had created a newly defined people where there was no distinction between Jew and Gentile (Acts 15:9; Rom. 3:22; 10:12; 1 Cor. 10:32). **became as one under the law.** Paul was willing to adopt the Jewish way of life temporarily to gain a hearing among Jews (Acts 16:3; 21:17–26), but his ethnicity no longer defined his existence (Phil. 3:3).

9:21 those outside the law. Outside the Mosaic law, which defined the Jewish way of life. **not . . . outside the law of God . . . the law of Christ.** Paul seems to distinguish between the Jewish law and something he calls alternately "the commandments of God" (cf. 7:19) and "the law of Christ," which is of continuing validity for Christians, whatever their ethnicity. This second law appears to include the ethical teaching of Jesus as well as absorbing both the theological structure and many of the moral precepts of the Mosaic law. (See, e.g., Rom. 7:7, 12, 22; 13:8–10; Gal. 5:14; 6:2; Eph. 6:2; see also the articles on Biblical Ethics, pp. 2535–2560.) This "law of Christ" today would also include the moral commands of the NT epistles, since in them the apostles interpreted and applied Christ's life and teachings to the NT churches.

9:22 To the weak I became weak. This is the attitude that Paul wants those in Corinth with superior "knowledge" to adopt toward the "weak" in their midst (cf. 8:9–13).

9:24–27 Paul frequently uses athletic metaphors to describe the rigors and single-minded focus of his apostolic work to pursue the advancement of the gospel (see also Phil. 3:12–14; 2 Tim. 4:7–8). The extended metaphor is particularly apt in a letter to Corinth, which was the location of the biennial Isthmian games, at that time second in fame only to the Olympic games. Paul's stay in Corinth during his second missionary journey (Acts 18) may have overlapped with the games in either A.D. 49 or 51. The **perishable wreath** was a crown (Gk. *stephanos*) of foliage (and therefore quick to wither) which was given to the victor in a public athletic contest. Paul thinks of his congregations as the victor's crown that he will wear on the final day (Phil. 4:1; 1 Thess. 2:19).

9:26 Like an athlete, Paul has a single-minded goal: to bring as many people as possible, from whatever station in life, to faith in the gospel (vv. 19–23).

9:27 This verse has a long history of misinterpretation in terms of punishing one's own body as a means of spiritual discipline. Paul's language, however, is governed both by the athletic metaphor of the previous two verses and by the physical demands of his apostolic work (4:9, 11–13; 2 Cor. 4:8–12; 6:3–10; 11:23–12:10; 1 Thess. 2:1–2, 9; 3:7–8). Just as an athlete goes through physical training that is sometimes uncomfortable in order to attain the goal of victory, so Paul endures physical and emotional hardship, and gives up his right to material support, for the gospel's advancement. (See 1 Cor. 9:12 and 2 Cor. 6:1–10.) **Disqualified** (Gk. *adokimos*, "not approved, not standing the test") in this context means "disqualified from receiving rewards" (see 1 Cor. 9:24–26).

10:1 For connects vv. 1–22 to what Paul has been saying about giving up personal rights for the sake of the gospel (chs. 8–9). The example of Israel's experience in the wilderness should warn the Corinthians of what can happen to people who hear God's words and see his works but do not come to true faith. **our fathers.** Most of the Corinthians were Gentiles, but Paul assumes continuity between them and OT Israel. **The cloud . . . the sea** refers to the generation of Israelites that God delivered from slavery in Egypt and led through the wilderness (Ex. 13:17–14:31).

10:2 baptized into Moses. God provided a cloud to lead Israel out of Egypt (Ex. 13:17–22). He also used Moses to part the Red Sea and enable Israel to escape the pursuing Egyptians, who then drowned in the water when God (through Moses) closed it over them (Ex. 14:1–31). Paul interprets these events as analogous to being "baptized into Christ" (Rom. 6:3; Gal. 3:27).

10:3–4 spiritual food . . . drink. Paul is referring to God providing Israel with bread from heaven ("manna," Exodus 16) and water from a rock. This rock appears both at the beginning of their wanderings in the desert (Ex. 17:1–7) and near the end (Num. 20:2–13). Rabbinic exegesis from after Paul's time surmised that the rock followed the Israelites throughout their wanderings. This understanding of the rock may have been current in Paul's time. If so, Paul's claim that the **Rock** following them was both **spiritual** and **Christ** shows that he did not believe that a physical rock traveled with the Israelites, but that Christ (in spiritual form) was ever-present with them: he was there to supply their need for water, and there to judge those who tested him (1 Cor. 10:9). "Rock" is a common OT name for God (e.g., Deut. 32:4, 15, 18, 30–31), and this probably facilitated Paul's identification of the rock with Christ.

spiritual drink. For they drank from the spiritual Rock that followed them, and the Rock
was Christ. 5 Nevertheless, with most of them God was not pleased, for [g]they were overthrown[1] in the wilderness.
6 Now these things took place as examples for us, that we might not desire evil as [h]they
did. 7 [i]Do not be idolaters [j]as some of them were; as it is written, [k]"The people sat down to
eat and drink and rose up to play." 8 [l]We must not indulge in sexual immorality [m]as some
of them did, and [n]twenty-three thousand fell in a single day. 9 We must not put Christ[2] to
the test, [o]as some of them did and [p]were destroyed by serpents, 10 nor grumble, [q]as some
of them did and [r]were destroyed by [s]the Destroyer. 11 Now these things happened to them
as an example, but [t]they were written down for our instruction, [u]on whom the end of the
ages has come. 12 Therefore [v]let anyone who thinks that he stands take heed lest he fall.
13 No temptation has overtaken you that is not common to man. [w]God is faithful, and
[x]he will not let you be tempted beyond your ability, but with the temptation he will also
provide the way of escape, that you may be able to endure it.
14 Therefore, my beloved, [y]flee from idolatry. 15 I speak [z]as to sensible people; judge for
yourselves what I say. 16 [a]The cup of blessing that we bless, is it not a participation in the
blood of Christ? [b]The bread that we break, is it not a participation in the body of Christ?
17 Because there is one bread, we who are many are [c]one body, for we all partake of the one
bread. 18 Consider [d]the people of Israel:[3] [e]are not those who eat the sacrifices participants
in the altar? 19 What do I imply then? That food offered to idols is anything, or that [f]an
idol is anything? 20 No, I imply that what pagans sacrifice [g]they offer to demons and not to
God. I do not want you to be participants with demons. 21 [h]You cannot drink the cup of the

[1] Or *were laid low* [2] Some manuscripts *the Lord* [3] Greek *Consider Israel according to the flesh*

5 [g]Num. 14:29, 37; 26:64, 65; Ps. 106:26; Heb. 3:17; Jude 5
6 [h]Num. 11:4, 33, 34; Ps. 78:18; 106:14
7 [i]ver. 14 [j]Ex. 32:4 [k]Cited from Ex. 32:6
8 [l]See ch. 6:18; Acts 15:20 [m]Num. 25:1 [n][Num. 25:9; Ps. 106:29]
9 [o]Num. 21:5; [Ex. 17:2, 7]; See Ps. 78:18 [p]See Num. 21:6
10 [q]See Num. 14:2 [r]Num. 14:29-37 [s]Ex. 12:23; 2 Sam. 24:16; 1 Chr. 21:15; Ps. 78:49
11 [t]See Rom. 4:23 [u]See Rom. 13:11
12 [v]Rom. 11:20; [2 Pet. 3:17]
13 [w]See ch. 1:9 [x][Dan. 3:17]; See 2 Pet. 2:9
14 [y]ver. 7
15 [z][ch. 8:1]
16 [a]ch. 11:25; Matt. 26:27, 28 [b]ch. 11:23, 24; Matt. 26:26; See Acts 2:42; 20:7
17 [c]ch. 12:12, 13, 20; Rom. 12:5; Eph. 4:4, 16; Col. 3:15
18 [d]Rom. 1:3; 4:1; 9:5; 2 Cor. 11:18 [e]Lev. 3:3; 7:15; [Heb. 13:10]
19 [f]See ch. 8:4
20 [g]Deut. 32:17
21 [h][2 Cor. 6:15, 16] [i][Deut. 32:38] [j][Isa. 65:11]

10:5 overthrown. Because of their disobedience and grumbling against God, the Israelite generation that experienced God's miraculous deliverance from Egypt and his provision of bread and water did not see the Promised Land. (See Num. 14:22–23, 29, 37; 26:64–65.) Though they had seen many of God's miracles, only a few had genuine faith (see Heb. 3:16–19; 4:2).

10:6 as examples for us. See v. 11; 9:10; Rom. 15:4.

10:7 idolaters. Paul begins to make the case that eating in the temple of a pagan god is not actually the "right" that the Corinthians imagined (8:9–10) but is participation in "the table of demons" (10:21) and idolatry. For a Christian to eat meals in such temples is to follow the unhappy example of the Israelites. They benefited from God's redemptive work but still fell into worship of the local gods (Ex. 32:1–6).

10:8 sexual immorality. Glancing back to his discussion of sexual immorality in 5:1–13 and 6:12–20, Paul reminds the Corinthians that God punished the wilderness generation of Israelites for the same sin. See Num. 25:1–9. **twenty-three thousand**. Numbers 25:9 says "twenty-four thousand." Both are fair approximations, rather than an exact number, of the people who died, which probably was all that either writer intended.

10:9 Christ. Paul sees Christ as spiritually present with God's people in OT times (see note on vv. 3–4; cf. Jude 5). The Israelites tested Christ ("God" in Num. 21:5) by becoming "impatient" with his provision of water and food.

10:10 grumble. See the grumbling and divine judgment in Num. 11:1; 14:1–38; 16:11–35. **The Destroyer** is not mentioned in Numbers, although Paul apparently views the angel who executed God's judgment during the exodus as the destroying agent in these instances also (Ex. 12:23; Heb. 11:28).

10:11 See v. 6; 9:10; Rom. 15:4. In saying that **these things happened**, Paul affirms even minor details of the OT, thus indicating his complete confidence in the truthfulness of every detail of the OT Scriptures. Paul's confidence thus supports the doctrine of biblical inerrancy. The OT Scriptures point toward **the end of the ages**, the age in which the Corinthian Christians are living. Cf. Heb. 11:39–40; 1 Pet. 1:10–12. **example**. On the examples ("types") in the OT, see Overview of the Bible, pp. 23–26.

10:12 thinks that he stands. Perhaps a reference to the Corinthians' mistaken "knowledge" that they have the right to eat in an idol's temple (8:9–10).

10:13 will not let you be tempted beyond your ability . . . will also provide the way of escape. Even when Christians face morally confusing situations, they should never think that they have no options other than sinful ones. There will always be a morally right solution that does not require disobedience to any of God's moral laws.

10:14 Therefore, . . . flee from idolatry. This is the point toward which Paul has been moving throughout ch. 10. The Corinthians cannot participate in idolatry and then think that they will receive eternal life on the last day (see notes on 6:16–18; 10:7; 10:8).

10:16 cup of blessing . . . we bless. (See 11:23–26 and notes.) Paul refers to the cup in the Lord's Supper. Jesus gave thanks for the cup (Matt. 26:27; Mark 14:23; Luke 22:17); the earliest Christian observance of the Lord's Supper imitated this custom. **Participation** (Gk. *koinōnia*) sometimes refers to fellowship with Jesus Christ (1 Cor. 1:9) or the Holy Spirit (2 Cor. 13:14; Phil. 2:1); sometimes it means aligning oneself with someone else's plight or cause (Rom. 15:26; 2 Cor. 8:4; 9:13; Gal. 2:9; Phil. 1:5; 3:10). Since this context emphasizes the incompatibility of participating in meals in pagan temples and participating in the Lord's Supper (1 Cor. 10:21), Paul probably means that those who eat the Lord's Supper align themselves with Jesus, share his sufferings (see Phil. 3:10), and benefit from his death. (See also note on 1 Cor. 10:18.)

10:17 one bread . . . one body. After Jesus gave thanks for and broke the bread, he said, "This is my body which is for you" (11:24). The church is also Christ's body (see also 12:12, 27; Eph. 1:22–23; 4:15–16; 5:23, 29–30). The Lord's Supper, therefore, is an occasion when members of the church declare their unity with each other because of their common unity with Christ.

10:18 participants. Greek *koinōnoi*, a term closely related to *koinōnia* (see note on v. 16). The altar in the OT was a table on which food was sacrificed to God, and the priests ate from the offerings (see, e.g., Lev. 6:17–18; 7:32–35). The altar, therefore, provided an apt analogy to "the table of the Lord" (1 Cor. 10:21) since in both instances the benefits of the table belonged to the priests, inasmuch as believers in Christ are priests to God (1 Pet. 2:9; Rev. 1:6).

10:19–20 Paul knows that **demons** delight in the worship of any "god" but the one true God and therefore take a special interest in idolatry. In Deut. 32:17–18 sacrifice to false gods, called "demons" there, is contrasted with worship of God, who is called "the Rock" (cf. 1 Cor. 10:4). False religions are not merely the result of human imagination and human energy but generally have demonic power behind them. Not everything that seems "supernatural" is from God.

Lord and [l]the cup of demons. You cannot partake of the table of the Lord and [l]the table of
demons. 22 [k]Shall we provoke the Lord to jealousy? [l]Are we stronger than he?

Do All to the Glory of God

23 [m]"All things are lawful," but not all things are helpful. "All things are lawful," but not
all things build up. 24 [n]Let no one seek his own good, but the good of his neighbor. 25 [o]Eat
whatever is sold in the meat market without raising any question on the ground of conscience. 26 For [p]"the earth is the Lord's, and the fullness thereof." 27 If one of the unbelievers
invites you to dinner and you are disposed to go, [q]eat whatever is set before you without
raising any question on the ground of conscience. 28 But if someone says to you, "This has
been offered in sacrifice," then do not eat it, for the sake of the one who informed you, and
for the sake of conscience— 29 I do not mean [r]your conscience, but his. For [s]why should
my liberty be determined by someone else's conscience? 30 If I partake with thankfulness,
why am I denounced because of that [t]for which I give thanks?
31 So, whether you eat or drink, or [u]whatever you do, do all to the glory of God. 32 [v]Give
no offense to Jews or to Greeks or to [w]the church of God, 33 just as [x]I try to please everyone
in everything I do, [y]not seeking my own advantage, but that of many, that they may be
saved.

11 [z]Be imitators of me, as I am of Christ.

Head Coverings

2 Now I commend you [a]because you remember me in everything and [b]maintain the
traditions [c]even as I delivered them to you. 3 But I want you to understand that [d]the head
of every man is Christ, [e]the head of a wife[1] is her husband, and [f]the head of Christ is God.
4 Every man who prays or prophesies with his head covered dishonors his head, 5 but every
wife[2] who prays or [g]prophesies [h]with her head uncovered dishonors her head, since it

[1] Greek *gunē*. This term may refer to a *woman* or a *wife*, depending on the context [2] In verses 5–13, the Greek word *gunē* is translated *wife* in verses that deal with wearing a veil, a sign of being married in first-century culture

22 [k]Deut. 32:21 [l]Eccles. 6:10; Ezek. 22:14
23 [m]ch. 6:12; See ch. 8:9
24 [n]ver. 33; ch. 13:5; Phil. 2:21; [ch. 9:23; 2 Cor. 12:14]; See Rom. 15:1
25 [o]ch. 8:7
26 [p]Cited from Ps. 24:1; [Ex. 9:29; 19:5; Deut. 10:14; Job 41:11; Ps. 50:12]
27 [q]Luke 10:8
29 [r][ch. 8:9-12] [s][ch. 9:19; Rom. 14:16]
30 [t]Rom. 14:6; 1 Tim. 4:3, 4
31 [u]Col. 3:17; 1 Pet. 4:11
32 [v]ch. 8:13; Rom. 14:13; 2 Cor. 6:3 [w][ch. 11:16]; See Acts 20:28
33 [x]ch. 9:22; [Gal. 1:10] [y]See ver. 24

Chapter 11

1 [z]See ch. 4:16
2 [a][ch. 4:17; 1 Thess. 3:6] [b]2 Thess. 2:15; 3:6 [c][1 Thess. 4:1, 2]
3 [d]Eph. 1:22; 4:15; 5:23; Col. 1:18 [e]See Gen. 3:16 [f][ch. 3:23]
5 [g]Luke 2:36; Acts 21:9; [ch. 14:34] [h][Num. 5:18]

10:22 God's **jealousy** is not the sinful emotion of envy that characterizes human jealousy. It is God's righteous concern to protect the truth that he is the Creator of the universe and that he alone, not "gods" of human invention, deserves human praise. Those who worship idols provoke God's jealousy and receive his wrath, as Israel had experienced in the wilderness. (See Ex. 20:4–5; Deut. 4:23–24; 5:8–9; 6:14–15; 29:18–20; 32:16, 21.)

10:23–11:1 Paul now begins to address a different issue entirely from the problem that has consumed his attention in ch. 8 and 10:1–22. Those sections dealt with eating meals in pagan temples, but this section deals with meat previously sacrificed to idols being eaten in private homes, especially the home of an unbeliever (10:27–30). The principles Paul has developed in ch. 9, however, still apply. Paul wants the Corinthians to act toward others in a way that will not inhibit the advance of the gospel.

10:23 "All things are lawful." See note on 6:12–13. **build up**. See note on 8:10–11.

10:27 without raising any question. The Christian is not to question the host about whether the food being served had ever been involved in pagan rituals. Such questions are theologically unnecessary (vv. 25–26), and because they could be perceived as rude, they violate the principle of vv. 23–24 and 9:19–23.

10:28 someone says. This person may be: (1) an unbeliever who erroneously thinks that Christians must abstain from such food and is confronting a believer with a test of faith; (2) an unbeliever who thinks Christians abstain from such food and, in good faith, wants the Christian to know where it came from; or (3) a "weak" believer whose conscience erroneously dictates that Christians should avoid such food (8:10; see also Rom. 14:14, 20–21). Since the person's **conscience** motivated the comment, and the weak believer's conscience was an important concern in 1 Cor. 8:7–13, this last option is most likely.

10:31 do all to the glory of God. Every aspect of every Christian's life has the potential to honor God.

11:1 imitators of me. See note on 4:16; see also Phil. 3:17; 4:9; 2 Thess. 3:7–9; 2 Tim. 3:10–12.

11:2–14:40 *Divisions over Corporate Worship.* Paul addresses three issues that have come to his attention, either through the Corinthians' letter to him (7:1; 12:1) or through an oral report (11:18). All three issues relate to the conduct of the Corinthians when they gather for worship.

11:2–16 *Head Coverings and Worship.* Paul first comments on whether certain women, probably wives, may continue to pray and prophesy in corporate worship with their heads uncovered (see v. 13). By uncovering their heads in public worship, Paul says, they bring shame instead of glory to their husbands, and this is not proper.

11:3 But shows that Paul has quickly moved from commendation (in v. 2) to correction. **wife**. See ESV footnote. Since a woman's head covering in first-century Roman society was a sign of marriage, Paul's practical concern in this passage is not with the relationship between women and men generally but with the relationship between husband and wife. **head**. It is sometimes said that this term (Gk. *kephalē*) means "source," but in over 50 examples of the expression "person A is the head of person(s) B" found in ancient Greek literature, person A has authority over person(s) B in every case. Therefore it is best to understand "head" (*kephalē*) here as referring metaphorically to "authority" (see also Eph. 1:22; 5:23; Col. 2:10). As with the authority of Christ over the church, this is not the self-centered exercise of power but leadership that takes care to serve the spiritual, emotional, and physical needs of the wife. See Mark 10:44–45; Eph. 5:23, 25–30. **The head of Christ is God** indicates that within the Trinity the Father has a role of authority or leadership with respect to the Son, though they are equal in deity and attributes (see notes on John 5:19; 14:28; 1 Cor. 15:28). Paul applies this truth about the Trinity to the relationship of husband and wife. In marriage, as in the Trinity, there is equality in being and value but difference in roles (see Eph. 5:22–33).

11:4 head covered. The Greek phrase (*kata kephalēs*) literally means "down from the head" and may refer either to long hair that hangs loose (vv. 14–15), or to a veil that covers the face, or to a piece of cloth pulled over the head (like a modern shawl or scarf) that leaves the face revealed. As background

5[l]Deut. 21:12
7[j]See Gen. 1:26 [k][Prov. 12:4]
8[l]Gen. 2:21-23; [1 Tim. 2:13]
9[m]Gen. 2:18
11[n]Gal. 3:28
12[o]See Rom. 11:36
16[p]1 Tim. 6:3, 4 [q]2 Thess. 1:4; [1 Thess. 2:14]; See ch. 7:17; 10:32
18[r]ch. 1:10-12; [ch. 3:3]
19[s][Matt. 18:7; Luke 17:1; Acts 20:30; 1 Tim. 4:1; 2 Pet. 2:1] [t]1 John 2:19; [Deut. 13:3]
21[u][2 Pet. 2:13; Jude 12]

is the same [l]as if her head were shaven. 6 For if a wife will not cover her head, then she
should cut her hair short. But since it is disgraceful for a wife to cut off her hair or shave
her head, let her cover her head. 7 For a man ought not to cover his head, since [j]he is the
image and glory of God, but [k]woman is the glory of man. 8 For [l]man was not made from
woman, but woman from man. 9 Neither was man created for woman, but [m]woman for
man. 10 That is why a wife ought to have a symbol of authority on her head, because of
the angels.[1] 11 Nevertheless, [n]in the Lord woman is not independent of man nor man of
woman; 12 for as woman was made from man, so man is now born of woman. And [o]all
things are from God. 13 Judge for yourselves: is it proper for a wife to pray to God with
her head uncovered? 14 Does not nature itself teach you that if a man wears long hair it
is a disgrace for him, 15 but if a woman has long hair, it is her glory? For her hair is given
to her for a covering. 16 [p]If anyone is inclined to be contentious, we have no such practice,
nor do [q]the churches of God.

The Lord's Supper

17 But in the following instructions I do not commend you, because when you come
together it is not for the better but for the worse. 18 For, in the first place, when you come
together as a church, [r]I hear that there are divisions among you. And I believe it in part,[2]
19 for [s]there must be factions among you in order [t]that those who are genuine among
you may be recognized. 20 When you come together, it is not the Lord's supper that you
eat. 21 For in eating, each one goes ahead with his own meal. One goes hungry, [u]another

[1] Or *messengers*, that is, people sent to observe and report [2] Or *I believe a certain report*

for understanding Paul's point in this verse, Roman men sometimes practiced the custom of pulling the loose folds of their toga over their head as an act of piety in the worship of pagan gods. Paul thus draws on the example of this pagan custom (which everyone in the Corinthian church would have thought absurd) to make the point that men should not dishonor Christ by praying according to pagan custom (8:4). He then uses the idea to prepare the way for his argument that it is equally absurd for wives to pray or prophesy in public with their heads uncovered (11:5, 11).

11:5–6 head uncovered. A married woman who uncovered her head in public would have brought shame to her husband. The action may have connoted sexual availability or may simply have been a sign of being unmarried. In cultures where women's head coverings are not a sign of being married, wives do not need to cover their heads in worship, but they could obey this command by wearing some other physical symbol of being married (such as a wedding ring). While a shaven head or short hair was considered shameful for a woman in first-century Corinth, long hair was considered to be a woman's "glory" (see v. 15).

11:7–9 See Gen. 1:26–27; 5:1; 9:6. **Woman is the glory of man** probably uses "glory" in the sense of "one who shows the excellence of." Paul argues that a woman, by the excellence of her being, also shows how excellent man is, since she was taken out of man at the beginning (1 Cor. 11:8) and also was created as a helper for man at the beginning (v. 9; see also Gen. 2:20–24). Paul does not deny that the **woman** was also made in God's image, something that Gen. 1:27 explicitly affirms, nor does he deny that the woman reflects God's glory. Paul probably continues to think primarily of husband and wife here since the first man and woman were also the first married couple (Gen. 2:24; Eph. 5:31). Paul's appeal to the order of creation (cf. also 1 Cor. 11:3, 11–12) shows that his words are not merely directed to the cultural situation of his day. The principle of male headship in marriage continues through all generations, though some cultural expressions of that principle (e.g., that women should wear head coverings) may vary.

11:10 wife ought to have a symbol of authority on her head. More literally, a "wife ought to have authority [Gk. *exousia*] over her head," where the word "authority" refers to a head covering, which was a symbol of authority. This probably means, in the context of the Corinthian church, that the wife should wear a covering over her head as a sign that she is under her husband's authority. Others, however, suggest that a head covering is a sign of the woman's authority to prophesy in church, or to participate generally in the church assembly. **because of the angels**. This probably refers to the invisible heavenly beings (6:3; Heb. 1:7) who are present with the Corinthians when they worship (cf. Ps. 138:1) and whose presence makes propriety in worship that much more important. The NT elsewhere uses the fact that angels are watching as one motive for obeying God's commands (see 1 Tim. 5:21; Heb. 13:2; 1 Pet. 1:12).

11:11–12 nevertheless. Paul does not want what he has just said to be misinterpreted as a diminution of the importance of women. Women and men are both God's creation and are mutually interdependent at a basic level.

11:14 Here the word **nature** probably means "your natural sense of what is appropriate for men and women": it would be a **disgrace** for a man to look like a woman because of his hair style. Although the norms of appropriate hair style (and dress) may vary from culture to culture, Paul's point is that men should look like men in that culture, and women should look like women in that culture, rather than seeking to deny or disparage the God-given differences between the sexes.

11:16 See 1:2; 4:17; 7:17; 14:33, 36 for Paul's appeal to the practice of other churches. **no such practice**. That is, "no such practice" as that of those who disagree with Paul (therefore some translations render this "no other practice," giving about the same sense). Paul's objective is to bring the Corinthians into conformity with generally accepted Christian behavior.

11:17–34 *Social Snobbery at the Lord's Table.* The Corinthians were using their gatherings around the Lord's Table as occasions to make social distinctions between rich and poor. Paul is profoundly troubled by this development and argues strongly against it.

11:17–18 hear. Paul now departs from addressing issues raised in the Corinthians' letter to him (7:1) and goes back to commenting on what he has heard by word of mouth (1:11; 5:1).

11:19 there must be factions among you. In God's providential direction of the life of the church, he allowed controversy (see evidence of factions in 1:11–12; 3:4; 4:6–7) in order that the genuine spiritual quality of individual believers would be known. **Those who are genuine . . . may be recognized** thus refers to those who receive God's approval for how they act in the midst of controversy (Gk. *dokimos*, "genuine" in the sense of "tested and approved," is used several times to refer to approval by God; cf. Rom. 16:10; 2 Cor. 10:18; 2 Tim. 2:15; James 1:2). An alternative interpretation is that Paul is using "genuine" to refer to those who are true believers.

11:20 not the Lord's supper. Because of their selfish elitism, when the Corinthians observe the Lord's Supper they are not rightly representing the sacrificial death of Christ (vv. 24, 26) and the true character of the Lord.

11:21–22 Goes ahead reflects the Corinthians' self-centered disregard of others. The few who are wealthy in Corinth (1:26) have no regard for those

gets drunk. 22 What! Do you not have houses to eat and drink in? Or do you despise [v]the
church of God and [w]humiliate those who have nothing? What shall I say to you? Shall I
commend you in this? No, I will not.
23 For [x]I received from the Lord what I also delivered to you, that [y]the Lord Jesus on
the night when he was betrayed took bread, 24 and when he had given thanks, he broke
it, and said, "This is my body which is for[1] you. Do this in remembrance of me."[2] 25 In the
same way also he took the cup, after supper, saying, "This cup is the new covenant in my
blood. Do this, as often as you drink it, in remembrance of me." 26 For as often as you eat
this bread and drink the cup, you proclaim the Lord's death [z]until he comes.
27 [a]Whoever, therefore, eats the bread or drinks the cup of the Lord [b]in an unworthy
manner will be guilty concerning [c]the body and blood of the Lord. 28 [d]Let a person examine
himself, then, and so eat of the bread and drink of the cup. 29 For anyone who eats and
drinks without discerning the body eats and drinks judgment on himself. 30 That is why
many of you are weak and ill, and some [e]have died.[3] 31 [f]But if we judged[4] ourselves truly,
we would not be judged. 32 But when we are judged by the Lord, [g]we are disciplined[5] so
that we may not be [h]condemned along with the world.
33 So then, my brothers,[6] when you come together to eat, wait for[7] one another— 34 [i]if
anyone is hungry, [j]let him eat at home—so that when you come together it will not be for
judgment. About the other things [k]I will give directions [l]when I come.

[1] Some manuscripts *broken for* [2] Or *as my memorial*; also verse 25 [3] Greek *have fallen asleep* (as in 15:6, 20) [4] Or *discerned* [5] Or *when we are judged we are being disciplined by the Lord* [6] Or *brothers and sisters* [7] Or *share with*

22 [v]See Acts 20:28 [w][Prov. 17:5; James 2:6]
23 [x]ch. 15:3; Gal. 1:12 [y]For ver. 23-25, see Matt. 26:26-28; Mark 14:22-24; Luke 22:19, 20
26 [z]See John 21:22
27 [a][Num. 9:10, 13] [b][John 13:27] [c]John 6:51, 53-56
28 [d][2 Cor. 13:5; Gal. 6:4]
30 [e]See Matt. 27:52
31 [f]See 1 John 1:9
32 [g]See Prov. 3:11 [h]Rom. 5:16
34 [i]ver. 21 [j]ver. 22 [k]ch. 7:17; Titus 1:5 [l]See ch. 4:19

who are **hungry** or who **have nothing**, while others have too much and some even get **drunk**.

11:23 received from the Lord. The traditions about Jesus that Paul delivered to the Corinthians (see also 7:10; 15:3) ultimately went back to Jesus himself, but Paul probably learned them from early followers of Christ such as Peter (Gal. 1:18). (See the other records of the Lord's Supper in Matt. 26:26–28; Mark 14:22–24; Luke 22:17–20.) Another possibility is that Paul received this information directly from Christ himself (see 2 Cor. 12:1–4; Gal. 1:12, 17).

11:24 The expression **This is my body** has been subject to widely varying interpretations throughout the history of the church. Roman Catholics understand it literally, and claim that the bread and wine actually become the body and blood of Christ. Lutherans hold that the literal body and blood of Christ are present "in, with, and under" the bread and wine (something like the way water is present in a sponge). Some Anglicans refer to the "real presence" of Christ in the bread and wine. Most other Protestants have argued that the body and blood of Christ are not literally, physically, or "really" present, but that Christ is present "symbolically"; most would also add that Christ is present spiritually, with and in the believing recipients of the bread and wine, strengthening their faith and fellowship in him, and thereby feeding their souls. Christ's spiritual presence can be supported from Matt. 18:20; 28:20. **Do this in remembrance of me**. Remembering the significance of Jesus' death is an important component of observing the Lord's Supper and of obedience ("do this") to Christ's command. Evangelical Protestant Christians have consistently been united on the importance of limiting participation in the Lord's Supper to those who have made a personal commitment to follow Jesus. Jesus' emphasis on remembering the significance of his death when observing the Lord's Supper, and his warnings to those who partake of the bread and the cup in an unworthy manner, both reveal the wisdom of this limitation (cf. notes on 1 Cor. 11:27; 11:28; 11:29).

11:25 The Mosaic covenant, made with Israel and constantly broken because of Israel's sin, was replaced with **the new covenant**, which provided complete atonement for all the sins of God's people, past, present, and future (Rom. 3:25–26; 2 Cor. 3:1–4:6; Heb. 8:6–13).

11:27 Unworthy manner probably refers to the incompatibility of the Corinthians' divisive arrogance as compared to the sacrificial, others-oriented nature of Jesus' death. A broader application of this principle would encourage believers to examine their own lives (see v. 28) and to repent and ask forgiveness for any unconfessed sin before partaking in the Lord's Supper. **guilty concerning the body and blood**. Jesus' body was broken and his blood shed for others. Thus the selfish behavior of the Corinthians is a sin against others, but it also represents a profaning disrespect for Jesus himself.

11:28 Whoever partakes of the Lord's Supper must **examine himself** to see whether he has properly understood the unselfish, atoning nature of Jesus' death "for" others, and how that should be imitated in his own life (cf. note on v. 27).

11:29 Without discerning the body is usually understood in one of two ways. Some hold that it means "not understanding that the bread represents the body of Christ that was sacrificed for us," with the result that such people do not act in a Christlike, self-sacrificial way. Others note that Paul does not mention the blood, and because of this they conclude that Paul has moved beyond the meaning of the bread to the idea of the church as a gathering of the body of Christ (see 12:12–27; cf. 10:16–17). According to this second view, "without discerning the body" would mean "not understanding that Christians, since they are the body of Christ, should act like Christ when they assemble." On either view, these people do not recognize the spiritual reality of what is happening at the Lord's Supper, and therefore they are acting in a way that dishonors Christ. **Eats and drinks judgment on himself** is a sober warning that the Lord will discipline those who dishonor the Lord's Supper (see 11:30), and therefore it should not be entered into lightly.

11:30 weak . . . ill . . . died. The discipline of the Lord sometimes has consequences in real life. See also 5:5 and note there.

11:31 if we judged ourselves truly, we would not be judged. When Christians rightly discern their sins and turn from them and seek forgiveness, then (as a general principle) they will not experience God's disciplinary judgment. In specific application of this principle to the Corinthian situation, God would cease his discipline of the Corinthians if they would cease their misconduct regarding the Lord's Supper. This verse thus teaches Christians not to think that God will somehow punish them for their whole lives for sins committed long ago, if they have sincerely asked forgiveness and made right what they can with those whom they have wronged.

11:32 disciplined. When suffering alerts a Christian to the presence of sin and leads to repentance, it functions as an act of both disciplinary judgment and mercy. (See also 5:5; 2 Chron. 33:12–13; 1 Pet. 4:17.)

Spiritual Gifts

12 Now [m]concerning[1] spiritual gifts,[2] brothers,[3] I do not want you to be uninformed.
[2]You know that [n]when you were pagans [o]you were led astray to [p]mute idols, however you were led. [3]Therefore I want you to understand that [q]no one speaking in the
Spirit of God ever says "Jesus is [r]accursed!" and [s]no one can say "Jesus is Lord" except in
the Holy Spirit.
[4]Now [t]there are varieties of gifts, but [u]the same Spirit; [5]and [v]there are varieties of service, but [u]the same Lord; [6]and there are varieties of activities, but it is [u]the same God who
empowers them all in everyone. [7][w]To each is given the manifestation of the Spirit for the
common good. [8]For to one is given through the Spirit the utterance of [x]wisdom, and to
another the utterance of [y]knowledge according to the same Spirit, [9]to another [z]faith by
the same Spirit, to another [a]gifts of healing by the one Spirit, [10]to another [b]the working

[1] The expression *Now concerning* introduces a reply to a question in the Corinthians' letter; see 7:1 [2] Or *spiritual persons* [3] Or *brothers and sisters*

Chapter 12
1 [m]ch. 14:1
2 [n]Eph. 2:11, 12; [1 Pet. 4:3]; See ch. 6:11 [o]1 Thess. 1:9 [p]Hab. 2:18, 19; [Ps. 115:5; Isa. 46:7; Jer. 10:5]
3 [q]1 John 4:2, 3 [r]See Rom. 9:3 [s]John 15:26; [Matt. 16:17]; See Rom. 10:9
4 [t][Heb. 2:4]; See Rom. 12:6 [u]Eph. 4:4-6
5 [v]Rom. 12:7; [Eph. 4:11] [u][See ver. 4 above]
6 [u][See ver. 4 above]
7 [w]Eph. 4:7; [ch. 14:26; Rom. 12:3]
8 [x]ch. 2:6, 7 [y]See ch. 1:5
9 [z]ch. 13:2; 2 Cor. 4:13 [a]ver. 28, 30
10 [b]ver. 28, 29; [Gal. 3:5]

12:1–14:40 *Elevating One Spiritual Gift above Others.* Some Corinthian Christians seem to have been creating divisions over spiritual gifts. Paul's use of the body analogy in 12:12–27 implies that they have placed so much emphasis on one gift that those without that gift feel that they are not part of the body (12:16–17). Considering its prominence in the discussion, that one gift is probably speaking in tongues.

12:1 Now concerning. Paul now returns to the issues raised in the Corinthians' letter to him (see 7:1, 25; 8:1). **spiritual gifts**. The Greek has only the plural adjective "spiritual" (*pneumatikōn*), and this could refer either to "spiritual people" (2:13, 15) or to "spiritual gifts." In 14:1 the same word clearly refers to gifts, which would indicate that is what it means here.

12:2 pagans. Literally, "Gentiles" (Gk. *ethnē*) or non-Jews. The implication is that the Corinthians, although not Jews in the ordinary sense, are nevertheless now part of the people of God, standing in continuity with OT Israel. See v. 13; 10:1, 32.

12:3 Because of their background in pagan worship services (v. 2), some Corinthians may have had concerns about speech gifts empowered by the Holy Spirit in the church. Paul first assures them that **no one speaking in the Spirit of God ever says "Jesus is accursed!"** (and therefore they should not worry that Christians who speak in tongues might be uttering blasphemous things), and also that **no one can say** in genuine faith that **"Jesus is Lord" except in the Holy Spirit** (and therefore all who genuinely profess faith in Christ have the Holy Spirit within them, and none should be excluded, for they all have valuable gifts for the benefit of the church).

12:4–6 Spirit . . . Lord . . . God. A Trinitarian reference to the Holy Spirit, the Lord Jesus, and God the Father (cf. 2 Cor. 13:14). The most common pattern in the NT Epistles is to refer to God the Father with the word "God" (Gk. *Theos*, which is the normal Septuagint translation for the OT Hb. *'Elohim*, "God") and to refer to God the Son with the word "Lord" (Gk. *Kyrios*, which is used in the Septuagint over 6,000 times to translate the OT Hb. name *YHWH*, "Yahweh" or "LORD"). Therefore both names are evidence of deity. The diversity of divine persons within the unity of the Trinity should be reflected in the diversity of gifts within the unity of the body of Christ in Corinth. (See also Eph. 4:3–16.) Therefore Paul wants the Corinthian church to understand how their unity can be enhanced by appreciating the variety of gifts God has given to them.

12:8 utterance of wisdom . . . utterance of knowledge. Some understand these to be miraculous gifts ("word of wisdom" and "word of knowledge") by which a speaker is given supernatural "wisdom" or "knowledge" from God to impart to a situation. Others take these to be more "natural" gifts: the ability to speak wisely or with knowledge into a situation. The Greek expressions (*logos sōphias* and *logos gnōseōs*) occur nowhere else in the Bible, and Paul does not give any further explanation, so it is difficult to be certain. But since Paul already has a different, broader term that he uses to refer to speech based on something that God suddenly brings to mind ("prophecy"; see note on v. 10), the second view seems preferable.

12:9 faith. This is not the faith that all Christians have in Christ, since Paul implies that some Christians have it and others do not. It is probably a special endowment of faith for accomplishing some task (see 13:2; cf. Acts 14:9; James 5:15). **gifts of healing**. Both terms are plural (lit., "gifts of healings"), suggesting that different people may be gifted regarding different kinds of healing.

12:10 miracles. Probably the ability to work various kinds of miracles, including but not limited to healing (see Acts 8:13; 14:8–10; 19:11–12; Rom. 15:19; Gal. 3:5; Heb. 2:4). **prophecy**. The word "prophecy" (Gk. *prophēteia*) as used by Paul in 1 Corinthians refers generally to speech that reports something that God spontaneously brings to mind or "reveals" to the speaker but which is spoken in merely human words, not words of God. Therefore it can have mistakes and must be tested or evaluated (see 1 Cor. 14:29; 1 Thess. 5:19–21). An alternative view of this gift, held by some, is that it involves speaking the very words of God, with authority equal to the OT prophets and equal to the word of Scripture. A third view is that it is very similar to the gifts of preaching or teaching. This gift is widely indicated throughout the NT churches (see 1 Cor. 11:2–5; 12:28–29; 13:2, 8–9; 14:1–40; Acts 2:17–18; 11:27–28; 19:6; 21:9–11; Rom. 12:6; 1 Thess. 5:19–21; 1 Tim. 1:18; 4:14; 1 John 4:1). Prophecy is used to build up, encourage, and comfort the gathered community (1 Cor. 14:3). Prophecy is also used evangelistically to disclose the secrets of the hearts of unbelievers and lead them to worship God (14:24–25). Because God used this gift to build up the Christian community, Paul urged the Corinthians to value it highly (14:4–5, 39). **distinguish between spirits**. A special ability to distinguish between the influence of the Holy Spirit and the influence of demonic spirits in a person's life. Those who claim to speak under the Spirit's prompting could be mistaken, and so God also gives gifts of discernment to the Christian community (14:29; 1 Thess. 5:20–21; 1 John 4:1–3). **tongues**. Speech in a language the speaker does not know, and that sometimes does not follow the patterns of any known human language (1 Cor. 13:1). Paul sees this gift as a means of expressing prayer or praise to God (14:2, 14–17, 28; cf. Acts 10:46) in which the speaker's human spirit is praying even though the speaker does not understand the meaning (see 1 Cor. 14:2, 11, 13–19, 23). The normally unintelligible nature of **tongues** makes their **interpretation** necessary if the gathered community is to be edified by them (14:1–25). Paul probably placed the last two gifts at the end of the list because an overemphasis on tongues in Corinth had led to the neglect of those with other gifts (12:14–26). See also vv. 28 and 30. Bible-believing Christians disagree as to whether the gift of tongues ceased after the apostolic

Paul's Answers to Questions from the Corinthians

Verse	Introduction to topic
7:1	Now concerning the matters about which you wrote (marriage and sexuality)
7:25	Now concerning the betrothed
8:1	Now concerning food offered to idols
12:1	Now concerning spiritual gifts
16:1	Now concerning the collection for the saints
16:12	Now concerning our brother Apollos

of miracles, to another [c]prophecy, to another [d]the ability to distinguish between spirits,
to another [e]various kinds of tongues, to another [f]the interpretation of tongues. **11** All these
are empowered by one and the same Spirit, [g]who apportions to each one individually
[h]as he wills.

One Body with Many Members

12 For just as [i]the body is one and has many members, and all the members of the body,
though many, are one body, [j]so it is with Christ. **13** For [k]in one Spirit we were all baptized into
one body—[l]Jews or Greeks, slaves[1] or free—and [m]all were made to drink of one Spirit.
14 For the body does not consist of one member but of many. **15** If the foot should say,
"Because I am not a hand, I do not belong to the body," that would not make it any less a
part of the body. **16** And if the ear should say, "Because I am not an eye, I do not belong to
the body," that would not make it any less a part of the body. **17** If the whole body were an
eye, where would be the sense of hearing? If the whole body were an ear, where would
be the sense of smell? **18** But as it is, [n]God arranged the members in the body, each one of
them, [o]as he chose. **19** If all were a single member, where would the body be? **20** As it is, there
are many parts,[2] yet one body.
21 The eye cannot say to the hand, "I have no need of you," nor again the head to the feet,
"I have no need of you." **22** On the contrary, the parts of the body that seem to be weaker are
indispensable, **23** and on those parts of the body that we think less honorable we bestow
the greater honor, and our unpresentable parts are treated with greater modesty, **24** which
our more presentable parts do not require. But God has so composed the body, giving
greater honor to the part that lacked it, **25** that there may be no division in the body, but
that the members may have the same care for one another. **26** If one member suffers, all
suffer together; if one member is honored, [p]all rejoice together.
27 Now [q]you are the body of Christ and individually [r]members of it. **28** And [s]God has
appointed in the church first [t]apostles, second [u]prophets, third teachers, then [v]miracles, then
[w]gifts of healing, [x]helping, [y]administrating, and [v]various kinds of tongues. **29** Are all apostles?
Are all prophets? Are all teachers? Do all work miracles? **30** Do all possess gifts of healing?
Do all speak with tongues? Do all interpret? **31** But [z]earnestly desire the higher gifts.

And I will show you a still more excellent way.

[1] Or *servants*; Greek *bondservants* [2] Or *members*; also verse 22

10[c]ch. 13:2, 8; 14:1 [d][ch. 14:29; 1 John 4:1] [e]See Mark 16:17 [f]ver. 30; ch. 14:26
11[g][2 Cor. 10:13] [h]Heb. 2:4
12[i]See ch. 10:17 [j]ver. 27
13[k][Rom. 6:5; Eph. 2:18] [l]Gal. 3:28; Col. 3:11; [Eph. 2:13-17] [m][John 7:37-39]
18[n]ver. 28 [o]ver. 11; [ch. 3:5; Rom. 12:3]
26[p]Rom. 12:15
27[q][Eph. 1:23; 4:12; 5:30; Col. 1:24] [r]See Rom. 12:5
28[s]ver. 18 [t]Eph. 4:11 [u]Eph. 2:20; 3:5 [v]ver. 10 [w]ver. 9 [x][Acts 20:35] [y][Rom. 12:8; 1 Tim. 5:17; Heb. 13:7, 17, 24]
31[z]ch. 14:1, 39

age of the early church, or whether tongues is a spiritual gift that should continue to be practiced today. In either case, there is no indication that speaking in tongues is a normative requirement that all Christians must experience.

12:12 Paul assumes the Corinthians know that the church is Christ's body (see also v. 27; 6:15; 10:16; Rom. 12:4–8; Eph. 1:22–23; 4:4, 12–16; 5:23; Col. 1:18, 24).

12:13 Since the Spirit is one, he unites peoples across lines of ethnicity and social class that would otherwise divide them. (See Rom. 10:12; Gal. 3:27–28; Col. 3:11.) **in one Spirit we were all baptized**. The same Greek construction (the verb *baptizō* plus *en* ["in"] plus the dative of *pneuma*, "Spirit") is used here as in the other six "baptism in the Holy Spirit" passages in the NT (Matt. 3:11; Mark 1:8; Luke 3:16; John 1:33; Acts 1:5; 11:16), and here it seems clearly to refer to the cleansing and empowering work that the Holy Spirit does in a new convert at the point of conversion. Baptism is used metaphorically here to refer to the Spirit's work within the believer to unite him or her to the body of Christ, which is also the corporate body of believers. Water baptism is an outward symbol of this reality (cf. Rom. 6:4; Gal. 3:27). **made to drink**. Probably not a reference to the cup of the Lord's Supper but to the outpouring of God's Spirit on his people (cf. John 7:37–39; Rom. 5:5).

12:14 body . . . member. See Rom. 12:4–5; Eph. 1:22–23; 4:11–16.

12:17 whole body . . . an eye . . . an ear. See also v. 19. One problem Paul seeks to address throughout 12:1–14:40 is the elevation of one gift (probably speaking in tongues) above all others. The general principle applies to an unbalanced emphasis on any particular spiritual gift at any time or place in the church.

12:18 God arranged. The Corinthians' thinking will be corrected when they consider God's sovereignty in assigning gifts (cf. also vv. 3, 11, 28).

12:20 many parts, yet one body. One of the key themes in these chapters is unity in the midst of diversity.

12:21 This probably reflects Paul's assessment of how those Corinthians with the gift of tongues (and perhaps other more spectacular or "showy" gifts) were treating those with other gifts.

12:25–26 The purpose of the gifts is to build one another up and to care for one another, not to flaunt one's own spirituality.

12:28 On **apostles**, see notes on Matt. 10:2; Rom. 1:1. **prophets**. See note on 1 Cor. 12:10. **First . . . second . . . third . . . then** seems to be a ranking of importance or benefit to the church, with apostles being primary and then prophecy and teaching also contributing greatly to building others up. **Teachers, helping**, and **administrating** do not appear in the list in vv. 8–10, and helping and administrating do not show up in the rhetorical questions in vv. 29–30, indicating that the different lists are representative rather than exhaustive.

12:29–30 Are all apostles? The answer is obviously no, setting up the reader to answer no to all of the following questions (the Greek particle *mē* before each question also shows that Paul expects a negative answer to each one). Therefore, **Do all speak with tongues?** implies that the Holy Spirit does not give the gift of tongues to everybody, but just those to whom "he wills" (v. 11) to give it, as he does with the other gifts.

12:31 Earnestly desire implies that Christians can and should desire additional spiritual gifts (cf. 14:1, 13; James 1:5). **The higher gifts** means those that do more to build up the church (see 1 Cor. 14:5, 12, 17, 26). "Higher" here and "greater" in 14:5 translate the same Greek word (*meizōn*, comparative form of *megas*). **A still more excellent way** than merely seeking the higher gifts is to use the gifts in love (ch. 13) so that others are built up (ch. 14).

12:31b–13:13 Spiritual gifts without love are worthless, and love is supreme because it lasts forever.

The Way of Love

13 If I speak in the tongues of men and of angels, but have not love, I am a noisy gong
or a clanging cymbal. 2 And if I have [a]prophetic powers, and understand all mysteries and all knowledge, and if I have all faith, [b]so as to remove mountains, but have not
love, I am nothing. 3 [c]If I give away all I have, and [d]if I deliver up my body to be burned,[1]
but have not love, I gain nothing.
4 [e]Love is patient and [f]kind; love [g]does not envy or boast; it [h]is not arrogant 5 or rude.
It [i]does not insist on its own way; it [j]is not irritable or resentful;[2] 6 it [k]does not rejoice at
wrongdoing, but [l]rejoices with the truth. 7 [m]Love bears all things, believes all things, hopes
all things, [e]endures all things.
8 Love never ends. As for prophecies, they will pass away; as for tongues, they will cease;
as for knowledge, it will pass away. 9 For [n]we know in part and we prophesy in part, 10 but
[o]when the perfect comes, the partial will pass away. 11 When I was a child, I spoke like a
child, I thought like a child, I reasoned like a child. When I became a man, I gave up childish ways. 12 For [p]now we see in a mirror dimly, but [q]then face to face. Now I know in part;
then I shall know fully, even as [r]I have been fully known.
13 So now faith, hope, and love abide, these three; but the greatest of these is love.

Prophecy and Tongues

14 [s]Pursue love, and [t]earnestly desire the [u]spiritual gifts, especially that you may
[v]prophesy. 2 For [w]one who speaks in a tongue speaks not to men but to God; for no
one understands him, but he utters mysteries in the Spirit. 3 On the other hand, the one
who prophesies speaks to people for their upbuilding and encouragement and consolation.
4 The one who speaks in a tongue builds up himself, but the one who prophesies builds up
the church. 5 Now I want you all to speak in tongues, but [x]even more to prophesy. The one
who prophesies is greater than the one who speaks in tongues, unless someone interprets,
so that the church may be built up.
6 Now, brothers,[3] if I come to you speaking in tongues, how will I benefit you unless

Chapter 13
2 [a][ch. 14:1, 39; Matt. 7:22]; See Acts 2:18 [b]Matt. 17:20; Mark 11:23; [Luke 17:6]
3 [c][Matt. 6:2] [d]Dan. 3:28
4 [e][Prov. 10:12; 17:9; 1 Thess. 5:14; 2 Tim. 2:10; 1 Pet. 4:8] [f][2 Cor. 6:6; Gal. 5:22; Eph. 4:32; Col. 3:12] [g]Acts 7:9 [h]See ch. 4:6
5 [i]See ch. 10:24 [j][Rom. 4:6; 2 Cor. 5:19]
6 [k][Rom. 1:32; 2 Thess. 2:12] [l][2 John 4; 3 John 3, 4]
7 [m]ch. 9:12 [e][See ver. 4 above]
9 [n][ch. 8:2]
10 [o][John 15:15]
12 [p]James 1:23; [Num. 12:8; Job 36:26; 2 Cor. 3:18; 5:7] [q]1 John 3:2; See Matt. 5:8 [r]See ch. 8:3
Chapter 14
1 [s]ch. 16:14 [t]ch. 12:31 [u]ch. 12:1 [v]See ch. 11:4; 13:2
2 [w]ver. 18-23, 27, 28
5 [x][Num. 11:29]

[1] Some manuscripts *deliver up my body* [to death] *that I may boast* [2] Greek *irritable and does not count up wrongdoing* [3] Or *brothers and sisters*; also verses 20, 26, 39

13:1 tongues . . . angels. See note on 12:10. Tongues is probably the first gift mentioned because the Corinthians have used and emphasized it without love (12:21). On **love**, see note on John 13:34–35.

13:3 deliver up my body to be burned. As Shadrach, Meshach, and Abednego did (Dan. 3:19–23; Heb. 11:34). Love cannot be measured by actions alone; motives must be assessed to determine what is loving (see 1 Cor. 4:4–5).

13:7 The terms **believes** and **hopes** are sandwiched between **bears** and **endures** and, like them, probably refer to relationships between people rather than to faith and hope in God. Love believes the best of others and hopes the best for them.

13:8 Interpreters differ over the time when Paul expects **prophecies** to **pass away** and **tongues** to **cease** (along with other gifts represented by these examples). The "cessationist" view is that miraculous gifts such as prophecy, healing, tongues, interpretation, and miracles were given to authenticate the apostles and their writings in the early years of the church, but those gifts "ceased" once the entire NT was written and the apostles died (c. A.D. 100). Others hold that Paul expected these gifts to continue until Christ returns, which will be the time when "the perfect" (v. 10) ways of speaking and knowing in the age to come replace the "in part" (v. 9) gifts of this age. Support for the second position is found in v. 12, which indicates that "then" (the time when these gifts will cease) is the time of Christ's return.

13:12 mirror dimly. Ancient mirrors were made from polished metal (such as bronze), and thus one's reflection was even more "dim" than in modern mirrors. **Face to face** suggests a reference to Christ's second coming (the OT uses this phrase to refer to seeing God personally; cf. Gen. 32:30; Ex. 33:11; Deut. 5:4; 34:10; Judg. 6:22; Ezek. 20:35). Then, the spiritual gifts of this present age will no longer be needed.

13:13 faith, hope, and love. The relationship of these three Christian qualities is a frequent theme in Paul's letters. See Rom. 5:1–5; Gal. 5:5–6; Eph. 4:2–5; Col. 1:4–5; 1 Thess. 1:3; 5:8.

14:1 earnestly desire. Even in the midst of some misuse of spiritual gifts, Paul does not say to discontinue their use but to seek after them all the more, reflecting his conviction that these are given by God for the good of the church (cf. v. 12; 12:31). **that you may prophesy**. See note on 12:10.

14:2 Speaks not to men but to God indicates that Paul views tongues as a form of prayer and praise, but in a language that the speaker does not understand. **No one understands him** implies that Paul expected tongues in Corinth in most cases to be unknown languages, unlike the evangelistic situation in Acts 2:1–13. On tongues and prophecy, see note on 1 Cor. 12:10.

14:4 The one who speaks in a tongue builds up himself because his spirit is praying to God even though he does not understand what is being said (see vv. 2, 14, 28).

14:5 I want you all to speak in tongues. Paul's desire to set boundaries on speaking in tongues does not mean that he thinks the Corinthians should abandon this gift. It builds up the individual who has it (v. 4), and, if interpreted, builds up the church. (See also vv. 13, 18, 27, 39.) Still, prophecy is **greater** because, as intelligible speech that needs no interpretation, it is more directly useful to the church. **Unless someone interprets** implies that if there is an interpreter, then prophecy and tongues have equal value, since then they would both be understandable. But equal value does not imply that the gifts have the same function, for prophecy is based on something that God suddenly brings to the mind of the speaker, and thus is communication from God to man (vv. 25, 30; cf. Acts 11:28; 21:4, 10–11), while tongues is ordinarily prayer or praise from man to God (1 Cor. 14:2, 14–17, 28; cf. Acts 10:46).

14:6–19 Paul uses a variety of illustrations to teach that speaking in tongues

I bring you some [y]revelation or knowledge or prophecy or [z]teaching? **7** If even lifeless
instruments, such as the flute or the harp, do not give distinct notes, how will anyone
know what is played? **8** And [a]if the bugle gives an indistinct sound, who will get ready for
battle? **9** So with yourselves, if with your tongue you utter speech that is not intelligible,
how will anyone know what is said? For you will be [b]speaking into the air. **10** There are
doubtless many different languages in the world, and none is without meaning, **11** but if
I do not know the meaning of the language, I will be [c]a foreigner to the speaker and the
speaker a foreigner to me. **12** So with yourselves, since you are eager for manifestations of
the Spirit, strive to excel in building up the church.

13 Therefore, one who speaks in a tongue should pray that he may interpret. **14** For if I
pray in a tongue, my spirit prays but my mind is unfruitful. **15** What am I to do? I will pray
with my spirit, but I will pray with my mind also; [d]I will sing praise with my spirit, but
I will [e]sing with my mind also. **16** Otherwise, if you give thanks with your spirit, how can
anyone in the position of an outsider[1] say [f]"Amen" to [g]your thanksgiving when he does
not know what you are saying? **17** For you may be giving thanks well enough, but the
other person is not being built up. **18** I thank God that I speak in tongues more than all of
you. **19** Nevertheless, in church I would rather speak five words with my mind in order to
instruct others, than ten thousand words in a tongue.

20 Brothers, [h]do not be children in your thinking. [i]Be infants in evil, but in your thinking be [j]mature. **21** [k]In the Law it is written, [l]"By people of strange tongues and by the lips
of foreigners will I speak to this people, and even then they will not listen to me, says the
Lord." **22** Thus tongues are a sign not for believers but for unbelievers, while prophecy is a
sign[2] not for unbelievers but for believers. **23** If, therefore, the whole church comes together
and all speak in tongues, and outsiders or unbelievers enter, [m]will they not say that you
are out of your minds? **24** But if all prophesy, and an unbeliever or outsider enters, he is
convicted by all, he is called to account by all, **25** [n]the secrets of his heart are disclosed, and
so, [o]falling on his face, he will worship God and [p]declare that God is really among you.

Orderly Worship

26 What then, brothers? When you come together, each one has [q]a hymn, [r]a lesson, [r]a
revelation, [s]a tongue, or [t]an interpretation. [u]Let all things be done for building up. **27** If
any speak in [s]a tongue, let there be only two or at most three, and each in turn, and let
someone interpret. **28** But if there is no one to interpret, let each of them keep silent in
church and speak to himself and to God. **29** Let two or three prophets speak, and let the

[1] Or *of him that is without gifts* [2] Greek lacks *a sign*

6 [y]ver. 26; Eph. 1:17 [z]ver. 26; Acts 2:42; Rom. 6:17
8 [a][Num. 10:9; Isa. 58:1; Jer. 4:19; Ezek. 33:3-6; Joel 2:1]
9 [b][ch. 9:26]
11 [c]See Acts 28:2
15 [d][Eph. 5:19; Col. 3:16; James 5:13] [e]Ps. 47:7
16 [f]1 Chr. 16:36; Neh. 5:13; 8:6; Ps. 106:48; Jer. 11:5; 28:6; Rev. 5:14; 7:12; 19:4; [2 Cor. 1:20] [g]ch. 11:24
20 [h]Eph. 4:14; Heb. 5:12, 13 [i][Ps. 131:2; Isa. 28:9; Rom. 16:19]; See Matt. 18:3 [j]ch. 2:6
21 [k]See John 10:34 [l]Cited from Isa. 28:11, 12; [Deut. 28:49]
23 [m][Acts 2:13]
25 [n][Heb. 4:12] [o]Luke 17:16 [p]Isa. 45:14; Zech. 8:23
26 [q]Eph. 5:19 [r]See ver. 6 [s]ver. 18 [t]ver. 5, 13, 27, 28; ch. 12:10, 30 [u]2 Cor. 12:19; 13:10; [ch. 12:7]
27 [s][See ver. 26 above]

without an interpretation does not edify others, indicating that edification comes through understanding.

14:14 The comparison between **my spirit** and **my mind** shows that Paul is not speaking of the Holy Spirit but of his own human spirit. When Paul uses the term "spirit" of human beings, he means an inner, invisible faculty that can be especially attuned to the things of God (see 2:10–15; 5:3–5; Rom. 1:9; 8:16). "Mind" refers to the human faculty connected with intellectual understanding (1 Cor. 14:19; 1:10).

14:16–17 with your spirit. That is, with your spirit only (in tongues) but not understanding with your mind (see note on v. 2). **outsider**. An interested inquirer into Christianity (see vv. 23–24). Uninterpreted tongues in the assembly do nothing to build this person up and therefore nothing to move him or her toward a full commitment to Christ.

14:18 tongues. See note on 12:10.

14:20 See 3:1–3. Paul is going to tell them not to speak in tongues in church without interpretation, for that is acting like **children** and not caring for the needs of others.

14:21 Paul alludes to Isa. 28:11, where God's word of judgment against Israel is spoken in a foreign, unintelligible language by the invading Assyrian army.

14:22–25 Thus tongues are a sign . . . for unbelievers. Not a positive sign, to lead people to faith (as in John 2:11; 20:30–31), but as in 1 Cor. 14:21 a negative sign that facilitates God's judgment on the unbelieving. Uninterpreted tongues function as a sign of judgment for the outsider and unbeliever because they may conclude from hearing them that Christians are **out of** their **minds** and so leave the church, never to return. **prophecy is a sign . . . for believers**. Although the purpose of prophecy is primarily for the benefit of believers, prophecy (unlike tongues) also has the secondary benefit of convicting the unbeliever, exposing **the secrets of his heart** and causing him to **worship God**. When believers see this happen, prophecy encourages them that God is at work, and thus it serves as a positive "sign" of God's blessing on the congregation (a "sign" in Scripture can be either positive or negative; cf. Ex. 8:23; 10:12; Luke 21:11; Rom. 15:19).

14:26 When you come together. This verse gives a fascinating glimpse into the kinds of activities that took place when the early church gathered as the body of Christ to worship the Lord. The worship included **a hymn, a lesson, a revelation, a tongue, or an interpretation**. In order to prevent discord and confusion (cf. vv. 23, 33), Paul concludes his description of early church worship by emphasizing that all of these activities must be "done decently and in order" (v. 40). The goal of **building up** is analogous to the building of the temple (see 3:16; cf. Ex. 25:8).

14:27 Each in turn implies that speaking in tongues was not "ecstatic speech," for the speakers were aware of what was happening in the meeting and could control themselves and take turns. **And let someone interpret** could include either the person speaking in tongues (see v. 13) or someone else.

14:28 And speak to himself and to God means the speaker would use the gift of tongues privately in prayer, but not in public, since there was no interpreter.

14:29 let the others weigh what is said. "The others" means the whole church, not just those with gifts of prophecy or discernment, for there is no

others [v]weigh what is said. 30 If a revelation is made to another sitting there, [w]let the first be
silent. 31 For you can all prophesy one by one, so that all may learn and all be encouraged,
32 and the spirits of prophets are subject to prophets. 33 For God is not a God of [x]confusion
but of peace.
As in [y]all the churches of the saints, 34 [z]the women should keep silent in the churches.
For they are not permitted to speak, but [a]should be in submission, as [b]the Law also says.
35 If there is anything they desire to learn, let them ask their husbands at home. For it is
shameful for a woman to speak in church.
36 Or was it from you that the word of God came? Or are you the only ones it has reached?
37 [c]If anyone thinks that he is a prophet, or spiritual, he should acknowledge that the things
I am writing to you are a command of the Lord. 38 If anyone does not recognize this, he is
not recognized. 39 So, my brothers, [d]earnestly desire to prophesy, and do not forbid speaking in tongues. 40 [e]But all things should be done decently and [f]in order.

The Resurrection of Christ

15 Now I would remind you, brothers,[1] of the gospel [g]I preached to you, which you
received, [h]in which you stand, 2 and by which [i]you are being saved, if you [j]hold fast
to the word I preached to you—[k]unless you believed in vain.
3 For [l]I delivered to you as of first importance what I also received: that Christ died [m]for
our sins [n]in accordance with the Scriptures, 4 that he was buried, that he was raised [o]on the
third day [p]in accordance with the Scriptures, 5 and that [q]he appeared to Cephas, then [r]to
the twelve. 6 Then he appeared to more than five hundred brothers at one time, most of
whom are still alive, though some have fallen asleep. 7 Then he appeared to [s]James, then

[1] Or *brothers and sisters*; also verses 6, 31, 50, 58

29 [v][ch. 12:10; Job 12:11; 1 John 4:1]
30 [w][1 Thess. 5:19, 20]
33 [x][ver. 40] [y]See ch. 7:17
34 [z][1 Tim. 2:11, 12] [a]See 1 Pet. 3:1 [b][ver. 21]
37 [c][2 Cor. 10:7; 1 John 4:6]
39 [d]ch. 12:31
40 [e][ver. 31, 33] [f]Col. 2:5

Chapter 15

1 [g][2 Tim. 2:8]; See ch. 3:6 [h]Rom. 5:2; [2 Cor. 1:24; 1 Pet. 5:12]
2 [i]ch. 1:18 [j]ch. 11:2; [Heb. 3:6, 14] [k]Gal. 3:4
3 [l]ch. 11:23; Gal. 1:12 [m]John 1:29; Gal. 1:4; Heb. 5:1, 3; 1 Pet. 2:24 [n]Isa. 53; Dan. 9:26; Zech. 13:7; [1 Pet. 1:11]
4 [o][Hos. 6:2; Matt. 12:40; John 2:22] [p]Ps. 16:10; Isa. 53:10; [Acts 2:25-32; 13:33-35; 26:22, 23]
5 [q]Luke 24:34 [r]Mark 16:14; Luke 24:36; John 20:19, 26; Acts 10:41
7 [s]See Acts 12:17

reason to think that those with the gift of prophecy would have better judgment than all the other Christians (cf. 1 Thess. 5:20–21 and 1 John 4:1–3, where the whole church is similarly told to evaluate prophecies). Those who claimed to speak under the Spirit's prompting could be mistaken, so it was important for the assembly to discern whether the prophecies were really from the Lord. Some understand this to imply that Paul did not think the prophecies at Corinth could include absolutely authoritative "words of the Lord" in the manner of OT prophets, although others disagree.

14:32 The spirits of prophets seems to refer to the various workings of the Holy Spirit within the prophets (cf. Rev. 3:1; 4:5 for similar usage). The Holy Spirit will not force people to prophesy against their will.

14:33b As suggested by the punctuation in the ESV, **as in all the churches of the saints** is better taken as the beginning of the sentence in v. 34 (on how the Corinthians should act) than as the end of the sentence in v. 33 (on the character of God). Paul elsewhere tells the Corinthians to follow the patterns of behavior that "all the churches" follow (see 4:17; 7:17; 11:16; 16:1), and the mention of "churches" in 14:34 means that Paul's statement is not limited to one local church situation. (There were no verse numbers in Paul's letters; they were first added by an editor of a Greek NT in 1551.)

14:34–35 the women should keep silent in the churches. Since Paul seems to permit wives to pray and prophesy (11:5, 13) as long as they do not dishonor their husbands by the way they dress (11:5), it is difficult to see this as an absolute prohibition (cf. Acts 2:17; 21:8–9). Paul is likely forbidding women to speak up and judge prophecies (this is the activity in the immediate context; cf. 1 Cor. 14:29), since such an activity would subvert male headship. **Law also says.** Paul is probably thinking of the woman's creation "from" and "for" the man (see 11:8–9; Gen. 2:20–24), as well as a general pattern of male leadership among the people of Israel in the OT.

14:37 a command of the Lord. A very strong affirmation of the absolute divine authority of Paul's writings. Paul seems to have been aware that when he wrote to the churches with his apostolic authority, his words had authority equal to the OT Scriptures (cf. also 1 Tim. 5:18; 2 Pet. 3:15–16).

14:39 As he commonly does in this letter, Paul sums up a complex discussion by clearly stating his main point (cf. 7:39–40; 10:31–11:1; 11:33–34).

15:1–58 *The Futility of Faith If the Dead Are Not Raised.* Many people in the ancient Greco-Roman world believed that death extinguished life completely or led to a permanent but shadowy and insubstantial existence in the underworld. The concept of a physical, embodied existence after death was known mainly from popular fables and was thought laughable by the educated. Paul deals with the Corinthians' denial of (v. 12) and confusion about (v. 35) the future, bodily resurrection of Christians. These issues were probably raised in their letter to him (7:1).

15:1–11 *The Truthfulness of the Traditions about Christ's Resurrection.* Paul first establishes the historical reliability of Jesus' resurrection in order to lay a firm foundation for his argument that it was only the first step in the resurrection of all deceased Christians.

15:1–4 you received . . . I delivered. Paul is using commonly recognized language for handing on, intact, a body of information that one has received from others (see 11:2, 23; Mark 7:13; Luke 1:2; Acts 6:14; Phil. 4:9; Jude 3). **in accordance with the Scriptures**. See also Luke 24:27; John 2:19, 22; Acts 17:2–3; Rom. 1:2–4. Paul may be thinking especially of Isa. 53:3–12, which describes the substitutionary death and the vindication, after death, of God's servant, but he may also be thinking of other OT passages. For the resurrection, see also Hos. 6:2 and Jonah 1:17; 2:1 (Matt. 12:40), and for the OT in general pointing to **Christ**, see Luke 24:25–27 and the article, Overview of the Bible, pp. 23–26.

15:5 Cephas is the Aramaic name for the apostle Peter (Gal. 2:8–9). He and John were the first of the men who followed Jesus to know that his tomb was empty (Luke 24:12; John 20:5–6; cf. Mark 16:7). **The twelve** includes Judas's replacement, Matthias (see Acts 1:21–23, 26).

15:6 These witnesses were **still alive** and therefore able to give firsthand testimony to the truth of this tradition. **though some have fallen asleep**. Paul is careful not to exaggerate (cf. 7:10, 12, where he carefully distinguishes between his own words and Jesus' words), evidence of the great care that early Christians took in their preservation of the historically accurate details about Jesus.

15:7 James was the brother of the Lord (Gal. 1:19) and leader of the Jerusalem church (Acts 12:17; 15:13; 21:18; Gal. 2:9, 12). See note on 1 Cor. 9:4–5. **all the apostles**. The group of apostles is larger than "the Twelve," including, among others, James and Paul (1 Cor. 15:8). One of the qualifications for apostleship was seeing the risen Lord (9:1).

[t]to all the apostles. 8 Last of all, as to one untimely born, [u]he appeared also to me. 9 For [v]I
am the least of the apostles, unworthy to be called an apostle, because [w]I persecuted the
church of God. 10 But by the grace of God I am what I am, and his grace toward me was
not in vain. On the contrary, [x]I worked harder than any of them, [y]though it was not I,
but the grace of God that is with me. 11 Whether then it was I or they, so we preach and
so you believed.

The Resurrection of the Dead

12 Now if Christ is proclaimed as raised from the dead, [z]how can some of you say that
there is no resurrection of the dead? 13 But if there is no resurrection of the dead, [a]then not
even Christ has been raised. 14 And if Christ has not been raised, then our preaching is in
vain and your faith is in vain. 15 We are even found to be misrepresenting God, because we
testified about God that [b]he raised Christ, whom he did not raise if it is true that the dead
are not raised. 16 For if the dead are not raised, not even Christ has been raised. 17 And if
Christ has not been raised, your faith is futile and [c]you are still in your sins. 18 Then those
also who [d]have fallen asleep in Christ have perished. 19 If in Christ we have hope[1] in this
life only, [e]we are of all people most to be pitied.

20 But in fact [f]Christ has been raised from the dead, [g]the firstfruits of those who have
fallen asleep. 21 For as [h]by a man came death, [i]by a man has come also the resurrection of
the dead. 22 For [j]as in Adam all die, so also in Christ shall all be made alive. 23 But each in his
own order: Christ the firstfruits, then [k]at his coming [l]those who belong to Christ. 24 Then
comes the end, when he delivers [m]the kingdom to God the Father after destroying [n]every
rule and every authority and power. 25 For he must reign [o]until he has put all his enemies
under his feet. 26 The last enemy to be [p]destroyed is death. 27 For [q]"God[2] has put all things
in subjection under his feet." But when it says, "all things are put in subjection," it is plain
that he is excepted who put all things in subjection under him. 28 When [r]all things are
subjected to him, then the Son himself will also be subjected to him who put all things
in subjection under him, that [s]God may be all in all.

[1] Or *we have hoped* [2] Greek *he*

7 [t]Luke 24:50; Acts 1:3, 4
8 [u]See ch. 9:1
9 [v]2 Cor. 12:11; Eph. 3:7, 8; 1 Tim. 1:13-16 [w]See Acts 8:3
10 [x]2 Cor. 11:23; 12:11; Col. 1:29 [y][ch. 3:6; 2 Cor. 3:5; Phil. 2:13]; See Matt. 10:20
12 [z][Acts 23:8; 2 Tim. 2:18]
13 [a]1 Thess. 4:14
15 [b]See Acts 2:24
17 [c]See Rom. 4:25
18 [d]1 Thess. 4:16; Rev. 14:13
19 [e][ch. 4:9; 2 Tim. 3:12]
20 [f]2 Tim. 2:8; 1 Pet. 1:3 [g]ver. 23; See Acts 26:23
21 [h]See Rom. 5:12 [i]John 11:25; Rom. 6:23
22 [j][Rom. 5:14-18]
23 [k]See 1 Thess. 2:19 [l]ver. 52; 1 Thess. 4:16; See Luke 14:14
24 [m][Dan. 7:14, 27] [n]Eph. 1:21
25 [o]See Ps. 110:1
26 [p]2 Tim. 1:10; [Rev. 20:14; 21:4]
27 [q]Eph. 1:22; Cited from Ps. 8:6; See Matt. 11:27; 28:18
28 [r]Phil. 3:21 [s][ch. 3:23; 11:3]

15:8 Last of all. Sandwiched between vv. 7 and 9, this suggests that Paul thought there would be no more apostles chosen after him. **appeared also to me**. Making Paul an apostle (see note on 1:1).

15:9 On Paul as persecutor of the church, see Acts 7:58; 8:1–3; 9:1–2; Gal. 1:13; Phil. 3:6; 1 Tim. 1:13.

15:10 grace of God. Paul considered his conversion from "persecutor" to "apostle to the Gentiles" to be a free and wholly undeserved gift of God (Rom. 15:15–16; Gal. 1:15; 2:9; Eph. 3:7–8; Phil. 1:9; 1 Tim. 1:14). God's grace did not lead to passivity, however, for it prompted hard work on Paul's part.

15:11 I or they. Cf. 3:6; Phil. 1:18. Paul does not care who gets the credit for the gospel's advancement, only that it advances.

15:12–34 *Christ's Resurrection and the Resurrection of Believers.* Paul next argues that there is a seamless connection between the resurrection of Christ in the recent past and the future resurrection of believers on the final day.

15:12 raised from the dead. Some of the Corinthians were denying not that Jesus rose from the dead (they "believed" this, v. 11) but that his followers generally would be raised. Paul emphasizes four times in vv. 12–19 that those who deny the physical and bodily resurrection of believers also deny the bodily resurrection of Christ, even if they claim the latter is true.

15:17 still in your sins. The proof that Christ's death was an effective substitutionary sacrifice for sins (v. 3; 11:24–25) lies in Jesus' resurrection from the dead. (See also Rom. 4:25.) If in fact Christ has not been raised, then his death did not pay for sin, and there is no hope for life with God in heaven (see 1 Cor. 15:18–19).

15:18–19 Although Paul believed that those who died went to be with the Lord immediately after their death and prior to their resurrection (2 Cor. 5:8; Phil. 1:21, 23), he also conceived of the believer's eternal existence as an embodied existence. If there is no such existence, then there is no eternal life.

15:20 Christ's resurrection, grounded in the truth of eyewitness testimony (vv. 4–8), changes everything. If God raised Christ from the dead, then Christ truly was the **firstfruits** (Ex. 23:19; Lev. 23:10; Deut. 18:4; Neh. 10:35) or the first of many others who would also be raised from the dead. (See also Rom. 8:29; 1 Cor. 15:23; Col. 1:18.) The term "firstfruits" (Gk. *aparchē*) refers to a first sample of an agricultural crop that indicates the nature and quality of the rest of the crop; therefore, Christ's resurrection body gives a foretaste of what those of believers will be like.

15:22 in Adam all die. See Rom. 5:12, 14–15, 17; Eph. 2:1, 5. **in Christ shall all be made alive**. See Rom. 5:17, 21; 6:4; Eph. 2:5–6. By divine appointment, Adam represented the whole human race that would follow him, and his sin therefore affected all human beings. Similarly, Christ represented all who would belong to him, and his obedience therefore affected all believers (see note on 1 Cor. 15:23).

15:23 at his coming. When Christ returns, all his people from all time will receive resurrection bodies, never again subject to weakness, illness, aging, or death. Until that time, those who have died exist in heaven as spirits without bodies (see 2 Cor. 5:8; Heb. 12:23; Rev. 6:9). **Those who belong to Christ** demonstrates that the "all" in relation to Christ in 1 Cor. 15:22 does not imply universalism.

15:24–27 On the **reign** of Christ and the subjection of all things **under his feet**, see Ps. 8:6; 110:1; Eph. 1:20–21; Col. 2:15; Heb. 2:5–9; 12:2; 1 Pet. 3:18–22. **death**. When believers are finally resurrected from the dead, the destruction of death will be complete. (See 1 Cor. 15:54–55; Heb. 2:14–15; Rev. 20:13–14; 21:4.)

15:28 the Son . . . will also be subjected. Jesus is one with God the Father and equal to the Father in deity (8:6; John 10:30; 14:9; Heb. 1:8) yet functionally subordinate to him (Mark 14:36; John 5:19, 26–27, 30; 17:4), and this verse shows that his subjection to the Father will continue for all eternity. **God** will be **all in all**, not in the sense that God will be everything and everything will be God, as some Eastern religions imagine, but in the sense that God's supreme authority over everything will be eternally established, never to be threatened again.

29 Otherwise, what do people mean by being baptized on behalf of the dead? If the dead
are not raised at all, why are people baptized on their behalf? 30 Why are we [t]in danger
every hour? 31 I protest, brothers, by [u]my pride in you, which I have in Christ Jesus our
Lord, [v]I die every day! 32 What do I gain if, humanly speaking, [w]I fought with beasts at
Ephesus? If the dead are not raised, [x]"Let us eat and drink, for tomorrow we die." 33 [y]Do
not be deceived: [z]"Bad company ruins good morals."[1] 34 [a]Wake up from your drunken
stupor, as is right, and do not go on sinning. For [b]some have no knowledge of God. [c]I say
this to your shame.

The Resurrection Body

35 But someone will ask, [d]"How are the dead raised? With what kind of body do they
come?" 36 You foolish person! [e]What you sow does not come to life unless it dies. 37 And
what you sow is not the body that is to be, but a bare kernel, perhaps of wheat or of some
other grain. 38 But God gives it a body as he has chosen, and to each kind of seed its own
body. 39 For not all flesh is the same, but there is one kind for humans, another for animals,
another for birds, and another for fish. 40 There are heavenly bodies and earthly bodies, but
the glory of the heavenly is of one kind, and the glory of the earthly is of another. 41 There
is one glory of the sun, and another glory of the moon, and another glory of the stars; for
star differs from star in glory.
42 [f]So is it with the resurrection of the dead. What is sown is perishable; what is raised
is imperishable. 43 It is sown in dishonor; [g]it is raised in glory. It is sown in weakness; it is
raised in power. 44 It is sown a natural body; it is raised a spiritual body. If there is a natural
body, there is also a spiritual body. 45 Thus it is written, [h]"The first man Adam became a
living being";[2] [i]the last Adam became a [j]life-giving spirit. 46 But it is not the spiritual that
is first but the natural, and then the spiritual. 47 [k]The first man was from the earth, [l]a man
of dust; [m]the second man is from heaven. 48 As was the man of dust, so also are those who
are of the dust, and as is the man of heaven, [n]so also are those who are of heaven. 49 Just
[o]as we have borne the image of the man of dust, [p]we shall[3] also bear the image of the
man of heaven.

Mystery and Victory

50 I tell you this, brothers: [q]flesh and blood [r]cannot inherit the kingdom of God, nor
does the perishable inherit the imperishable. 51 Behold! I tell you a mystery. [s]We shall not
all sleep, [t]but we shall all be changed, 52 in a moment, in the twinkling of an eye, at the
last trumpet. For [u]the trumpet will sound, and [v]the dead will be raised imperishable, and

[1] Probably from Menander's comedy *Thais* [2] Greek *a living soul* [3] Some manuscripts *let us*

30 [t]2 Cor. 11:26
31 [u]1 Thess. 2:19 [v]Luke 9:23; See Rom. 8:36
32 [w][2 Cor. 1:8] [x]Cited from Isa. 22:13; [Isa. 56:12; Luke 12:19]
33 [y]James 1:16 [z][ch. 5:6]
34 [a]See Rom. 13:11 [b]1 Thess. 4:5 [c]ch. 6:5; [ch. 4:14]
35 [d][Ezek. 37:3]
36 [e]John 12:24
42 [f]Dan. 12:3; [Matt. 13:43]
43 [g]Phil. 3:21; Col. 3:4
45 [h]Cited from Gen. 2:7 [i]Rom. 5:14 [j]John 5:21; [John 6:33, 39, 40, 54, 57; Rom. 8:2, 10]
47 [k]John 3:31 [l][Gen. 2:7; 3:19] [m]John 3:13, 31
48 [n][Phil. 3:20]
49 [o]Gen. 5:3 [p]See Rom. 8:29
50 [q]See Matt. 16:17 [r][John 3:3, 5]
51 [s]1 Thess. 4:15, 17 [t]Phil. 3:21
52 [u]Matt. 24:31; 1 Thess. 4:16; [Isa. 27:13; Zech. 9:14] [v]John 5:25, 28; [Luke 20:36]

15:29 baptized on behalf of the dead. Some interpreters through the centuries have thought this referred to vicarious baptism on behalf of deceased people, probably those who had believed in Christ but had not been baptized before they died (cf. Luke 23:43). But the interpretation is uncertain, and whatever the practice is, Paul reports it without necessarily approving it, and is clearly not commanding it. Baptism for the dead is an important part of Mormonism, but the Bible gives no support to the idea that anyone can be saved apart from personal faith in Christ (see notes on John 3:18; 14:6). Other interpreters argue that by "the dead" Paul means the bodies of living Christians, which are subject to death and decay: they are baptized "on behalf of their dying bodies," showing hope that their bodies will rise again (see Rom. 8:23; 1 Cor. 15:42–44, 47–49, 53–54). On this view, Paul argues here that the baptism of perishing bodies is useless if the dead are not raised.

15:30–34 Risk-taking activities for the sake of the gospel are done in vain if there is no resurrection. **No knowledge of God** (v. 34) manifests itself in denial of the bodily resurrection of believers.

15:35–58 *The Nature of the Resurrection Body.* Apparently the Corinthians did not understand how material bodies, subject as they were to sickness, death, and eventual decay, could live eternally. In this section, Paul explains that God will change the bodies of believers to make them immortal.

15:35–43 How are the dead raised? Using illustrations from various realms of the natural world, Paul explains that God will change the bodies of the deceased to make them appropriate for their new, imperishable existence. Verses 42–43 emphasize the discontinuity between present corruptible bodies and future immortal bodies.

15:42 imperishable. No longer subject to physical decay or aging.

15:43 dishonor . . . glory. These terms have to do with outward physical appearance: the Christian's resurrection body will be physically attractive beyond anything imaginable.

15:44–47 natural. The Greek term is *psychikos*, the adjectival form of the noun *psychē*, which is translated **being** in v. 45 and can also be rendered "life" or "animated existence." Paul's contrast between "natural" and "spiritual" is a contrast between that which is temporally alive and that which has an eternal existence with God (cf. 2:14–3:3). Starting from Gen. 2:7, Paul explains that God created Adam from the **dust** and animated him with breath. Christ, however, is the **last Adam**, and his resurrection gave him a **spiritual** and therefore imperishable body (cf. Phil. 3:21). By **spiritual body** Paul does not mean an immaterial body but a body animated and empowered by the Holy Spirit.

15:50 Corruptible bodies (**flesh and blood**) **cannot** inherit the kingdom. Hence, the need for resurrection.

15:51–53 mystery. See note on 4:1. Christians who are alive at the time of the resurrection will be transformed so that their bodies become spiritual and immortal like the bodies of those who are resurrected from the dead. (See 1 Thess. 4:13–18.)

we shall be changed. 53 For this perishable body must put on the imperishable, and [w]this
mortal body must put on immortality. 54 When the perishable puts on the imperishable,
and the mortal puts on immortality, then shall come to pass the saying that is written:

[x]"Death is swallowed up in victory."
55 [y]"O death, where is your victory?
O death, where is your sting?"

56 The sting of death is sin, and [z]the power of sin is the law. 57 But thanks be to God, [a]who
gives us the victory through our Lord Jesus Christ.
58 [b]Therefore, my beloved brothers, be steadfast, immovable, always abounding in [c]the
work of the Lord, knowing that in the Lord [d]your labor is not in vain.

The Collection for the Saints

16 Now concerning[1] [e]the collection for the saints: as I directed the churches of Galatia,
so you also are to do. 2 On [f]the first day of every week, each of you is to put something
aside and store it up, [g]as he may prosper, [h]so that there will be no collecting when I come.
3 And when I arrive, I will send [i]those whom you accredit by letter to carry your gift to
Jerusalem. 4 If it seems advisable that I should go also, they will accompany me.

Plans for Travel

5 [j]I will visit you after passing through [k]Macedonia, for [l]I intend to pass through Macedonia,
6 and perhaps I will stay with you or even spend the winter, so that you may [m]help me on my
journey, wherever I go. 7 For I do not want to see you now [n]just in passing. I hope to spend
some time with you, [o]if the Lord permits. 8 But I will stay in Ephesus until [p]Pentecost, 9 for
[q]a wide door for effective work has opened to me, and [r]there are many adversaries.
10 [s]When Timothy comes, see that you put him at ease among you, for [t]he is doing [u]the
work of the Lord, as I am. 11 So [v]let no one despise him. [w]Help him on his way [x]in peace,
that he may return to me, for I am expecting him with the brothers.

[1] The expression *Now concerning* introduces a reply to a question in the Corinthians' letter; see 7:1; also verse 12

53 [w][2 Cor. 5:2-4]
54 [x]Cited from Isa. 25:8; [Heb. 2:14, 15; Rev. 20:14; 21:4]
55 [y]Hos. 13:14
56 [z]Rom. 4:15; 5:13; 7:5, 8, 13
57 [a][Rom. 8:37; 1 John 5:4]
58 [b]2 Pet. 3:14 [c]ch. 16:10; Jer. 48:10; John 6:28 [d][Gal. 6:9]; See ch. 3:8

Chapter 16

1 [e]See Acts 24:17
2 [f]Acts 20:7; [Rev. 1:10] [g]2 Cor. 8:3, 11 [h]2 Cor. 9:3
3 [i][2 Cor. 8:18, 19]
5 [j]See ch. 4:19 [k]See Acts 16:9 [l]Acts 19:21
6 [m]ver. 11; See Acts 15:3
7 [n][2 Cor. 1:15, 16] [o]ch. 4:19; Acts 18:21; James 4:15
8 [p]See Acts 2:1
9 [q]See Acts 14:27 [r]Acts 19:9
10 [s]ch. 4:17; [2 Cor. 1:1] [t]Rom. 16:21; 1 Thess. 3:2; [Phil. 2:20, 22] [u]See ch. 15:58
11 [v]1 Tim. 4:12; [Titus 2:15] [w]ver. 6 [x]Acts 15:33

15:54–55 Death is swallowed up. See v. 26.

15:56 power of sin is the law. See Rom. 5:20–21; 7:5–25; 8:1–3.

15:58 Therefore implies a practical application for the doctrine of the resurrection: the **work** (such as evangelism) that Christians do for the kingdom of God will bring results that last forever. On fruitfulness **in the Lord**, see John 15:1–5 and Phil. 2:12–13.

16:1–12 *The Collection for the Saints and Travel Plans.* As Paul draws the letter to a close, his attention turns to the details of his future ministry as it involves the Corinthians.

16:1 Now concerning. Paul turns again to an issue raised in their letter to him. See note on 7:1. **collection**. This is Paul's collection of money for needy Jewish Christians in Jerusalem. (See Acts 24:17; Rom. 15:25–28, 31; 2 Corinthians 8–9.) Paul brought relief aid to the church in Judea more than once. (See Acts 11:27–30, to which Gal. 2:10 may refer.) On generosity among Christians, cf. 2 Cor. 8:9–15.

Earthly Bodies and Resurrection Bodies (1 Corinthians 15)

Verse	Earthly Bodies	Resurrection Bodies
v. 42	perishable	imperishable
v. 43a	exist in dishonor	raised in glory
v. 43b	exist in weakness	raised in power
v. 44	natural	spiritual
vv. 45, 47	first Adam a living being, from the earth	last Adam (Christ) a life-giving spirit, from heaven
vv. 48–49	those who are of earth bear the image of the man of dust	those who are of heaven shall bear the image of the man of heaven
vv. 53–54	mortal	immortal

16:2 first day of every week. A Jewish expression for Sunday, and similar to the phrase used in the Gospels to describe the day of the week on which Jesus rose from the dead (Matt. 28:1; Mark 16:2; Luke 24:1; John 20:1). This shows that Christians gathered for worship on Sunday, not Saturday (cf. Acts 20:7; Rev. 1:10), in order to acknowledge the crucial importance of Christ's resurrection.

16:3 Paul would **send** the money with several representatives chosen by the Corinthian church, showing that he took care to prevent even an appearance of misuse of funds.

16:5 Corinth was located in the Roman province of Achaia, also called Greece, and just south of the Roman province of **Macedonia**. Paul describes a route that would take him from his present location in Ephesus (v. 8), north, probably to Troas, across the Aegean Sea to Macedonia, and south, through Achaia, to Corinth. (See Acts 19:21; 20:1–3.)

16:8 Pentecost. The "Feast of Weeks," described in Lev. 23:15–22, was a grain harvest celebration that culminated and concluded 50 days after Passover. Paul was probably writing, then, in the spring between Passover and this final day of Pentecost.

16:10 When Timothy comes. Timothy is apparently already on his way to Corinth. (See 4:17 and Acts 19:22.)

16:12 Paul would not have urged **Apollos** to visit Corinth if he disagreed with his theology (see 1:12; 3:4; 4:6).

12[y]See Acts 18:24
13[z]See Matt. 24:42 [a]Gal. 5:1; Phil. 1:27; 4:1; 1 Thess. 3:8; 2 Thess. 2:15; See ch. 15:1 [b]1 Sam. 4:9; 2 Sam. 10:12; Isa. 46:8 [c]Eph. 3:16; [Eph. 6:10; Col. 1:11]
14[d]ch. 14:1
15[e]ch. 1:16 [f][Rom. 16:5] [g]See Rom. 15:31
16[h]1 Thess. 5:12; Heb. 13:17
17[i]Phil. 2:30; [2 Cor. 11:9; Philem. 13]
18[j]2 Cor. 7:13; [Rom. 15:32; Philem. 7, 20] [k]Phil. 2:29; 1 Thess. 5:12
19[l]See Acts 18:2 [m]See Rom. 16:5
20[n]See Rom. 16:16
21[o]Col. 4:18; 2 Thess. 3:17; [Rom. 16:22; Gal. 6:11; Philem. 19]
22[p]See Rom. 9:3
23[q]Rom. 16:20

Final Instructions

12 Now concerning [y]our brother Apollos, I strongly urged him to visit you with the
other brothers, but it was not at all his will[1] to come now. He will come when he has
opportunity.
13 [z]Be watchful, [a]stand firm in the faith, [b]act like men, [c]be strong. 14 [d]Let all that you
do be done in love.
15 Now I urge you, brothers[2]—you know that [e]the household[3] of Stephanas were [f]the first
converts in Achaia, and that they have devoted themselves [g]to the service of the saints— 16 [h]be
subject to such as these, and to every fellow worker and laborer. 17 I rejoice at the coming
of Stephanas and Fortunatus and Achaicus, because they have made up for [i]your absence,
18 for they [j]refreshed my spirit as well as yours. [k]Give recognition to such people.

Greetings

19 The churches of Asia send you greetings. [l]Aquila and Prisca, together with [m]the church
in their house, send you hearty greetings in the Lord. 20 All the brothers send you greetings.
[n]Greet one another with a holy kiss.
21 I, Paul, write [o]this greeting with my own hand. 22 If anyone has no love for the Lord,
let him be [p]accursed. Our Lord, come![4] 23 [q]The grace of the Lord Jesus be with you. 24 My
love be with you all in Christ Jesus. Amen.

[1] Or *God's will for him* [2] Or *brothers and sisters*; also verse 20 [3] Greek *house* [4] Greek *Maranatha* (a transliteration of Aramaic)

16:13–24 *Closing Admonitions and Greetings.* Paul admonishes the Corinthians to persevere, love, and submit to good leaders. He then gives greetings from the Christians in Asia.

16:13 Act like men (Gk. *andrizomai*) is a frequent command in the Septuagint and is used in contexts encouraging people (esp. soldiers) to act with courage and strength in obedience to the Lord and with confidence in his power (see Deut. 31:6–7, 23; Josh. 1:6–7, 9; 10:25; 1 Chron. 28:20; Ps. 27:14).

16:16 be subject to such as these. This probably implies that some members of the household of Stephanas were elders at Corinth. (*First Clement* 42.4, written in A.D. 95, mentions that the apostles in Corinth appointed the "first converts" [Gk. *aparchē*, the same word Paul used in 1 Cor. 16:15] "to be bishops and deacons.") **Fellow worker** is a participle of *synergeō*, "to work together with," and apparently refers to those who "work with" these leaders in their governing tasks.

16:17 Stephanas and Fortunatus and Achaicus. Perhaps the bearers of the Corinthians' letter to Paul (7:1).

16:19 the church in their house. See also Rom. 16:3–5. Early Christian churches, since they were small and since Christianity was not recognized as a legitimate (or legal) religion, met in homes (cf. Acts 18:7; Col. 4:15; Philem. 2). There is extensive archaeological evidence from many different cities showing that some homes were structurally modified to hold such churches.

16:20 holy kiss (cf. Rom. 16:16; 2 Cor. 13:12; 1 Thess. 5:26; 1 Pet. 5:14). Like some other practices with symbolic meanings that change from culture to culture (such as footwashing, or head covering for wives; see note on 1 Cor. 11:5–6), a "holy kiss" would not convey the same meaning today that it did in the first century, and in most cultures it would be seriously misunderstood. Such commands are best obeyed by substituting an action (such as a handshake or hug or bow, varying by culture) that would convey the same meaning in a modern culture.

16:21 I, Paul. Paul typically used secretaries to write down his letters as he dictated them (Rom. 16:22). Sometimes Paul picked up the pen himself, either to sign and so authenticate a letter (2 Thess. 3:17), simply to give a personal good-bye (Col. 4:18), or to make a point with special emphasis (Gal. 6:11; Philem. 19). In light of 1 Cor. 16:22, Paul's personal signature here probably falls into the third category.

16:22 Anyone who might say "Jesus is accursed" (12:3) is himself **accursed**. The phrase **Our Lord, come!** (*marana tha*) is Aramaic rather than Greek, probably representing an early Jewish Christian prayer for the return of Jesus (cf. Rev. 22:20). It is additional evidence that at an early date followers of Jesus gave him a title that they used of God. This also reminds us that Christians should always be praying for Christ to return soon.

INTRODUCTION TO

THE SECOND LETTER OF PAUL TO THE CORINTHIANS

2 CORINTHIANS

Author and Title

The apostle Paul is the undisputed author of 2 Corinthians. Although some scholars have questioned whether Paul wrote 6:14–7:1, due to its unique vocabulary and subject matter, these differences are more likely due to the fact that in this passage Paul is quoting a collage of Scripture. Second Corinthians is actually the fourth letter that Paul sent to the church he founded in Corinth (Acts 18:1–17), together with the house churches "in the whole [province] of Achaia," of which Corinth was the capital (2 Cor. 1:1; 11:10; cf. Rom. 16:5, 23; 1 Cor. 16:15, 19). The four letters are (1) the previous letter mentioned in 1 Corinthians 5:9; (2) our 1 Corinthians; (3) the tearful, severe letter mentioned in 2 Corinthians 2:3–4; and (4) our 2 Corinthians.

Date

Paul wrote 2 Corinthians from Macedonia around A.D. 55/56, a year or so after writing 1 Corinthians and a year before he wrote his letter to the Romans from Corinth (Acts 20:2–3).

Theme

The central theme of 2 Corinthians is *the relationship between suffering and the power of the Spirit in Paul's apostolic life, ministry, and message*. In addition to calling into question Paul's motives in organizing a collection for believers in Judea (8:20–21; cf. 2:17; 12:14–18) and questioning his personal courage (10:10–11; 11:21), Paul's opponents had argued that Paul *suffered too much* to be a Spirit-filled apostle of the risen Christ. Paul argues that his weakness as an apostle is the very means by which believers are comforted (1:3–11) and God in Christ is made known in the world (2:14–17; 4:7–12; 6:3–10; 11:23b–33). Paul's sufferings embody the cross of Christ, while his endurance amid adversity, with thanksgiving and contentment, manifests the resurrection power of the Spirit (12:7–10). Paul's suffering as an apostle is thus the very means God uses to reveal his glory (1:3–4, 11, 20; 4:15; 9:11–15; 10:17–18).

Paul therefore sees a close tie between the Corinthians' acceptance of his apostleship and the genuineness of their faith. To reject Paul and his proclamation is to reject Christ himself, since Paul's message, ministry, and manner of life are one. This explains why 2 Corinthians is the most personal of all of Paul's letters, filled with deep emotion.

Purpose, Occasion, and Background

Second Corinthians is a response to a complicated history between Paul and the Corinthian church, which must be reconstructed from the evidence available today (see note on Acts 20:1). Originally, Paul had planned to travel from Ephesus through Macedonia to Corinth (see map, p. 2221) on his way back to Jerusalem to deliver the money he had collected for the believers in Judea (1 Cor. 16:5–9). In the meantime, he sent Timothy to visit the Corinthians on his behalf (Acts 19:22; 1 Cor. 16:10–11). When Timothy arrived in Corinth, he found that the church was in turmoil, most likely in response to the arrival of Paul's opponents from the east. When Paul learned of this he decided to proceed immediately to Corinth to resolve the issues first, then travel on to Macedonia before returning to Corinth for a second visit on his way to Jerusalem (the proposed "second experience of grace" of 2 Cor. 1:15).

Paul's visit, however, turned out to be very "painful" as a result of the church's open rebellion against him

(2:1, 5–8; 7:8–13; 11:4). At that time, Paul decided it was best to suffer humiliation and leave, without retaliating, in order to extend mercy to the Corinthians (1:23–24). Once back in Ephesus, Paul sent Titus back to Corinth with a tearful and severe letter (now lost), warning the church of God's judgment if they did not repent (2:3–4; 7:8–16).

To Paul's great joy, the majority of the Corinthians did repent, which Paul discovered when he met Titus in Macedonia (7:5–16). But there was still a rebellious minority who, under the influence of Paul's opponents (11:12–21), continued to reject Paul and his gospel. In response, and as yet another act of mercy, Paul wrote 2 Corinthians from Macedonia in anticipation of his third, impending visit to Corinth before going on to Jerusalem (12:14; 13:1).

The mixed nature of the church in Corinth, not to mention the opponents whom Paul addresses indirectly throughout the letter, explains the complex nature of 2 Corinthians and its sometimes sudden shifts in focus and tone. This has led some scholars to suggest that it is a compilation of as many as six fragments. There is no evidence, however, that 2 Corinthians ever contained less than or more than its present content, or that it was arranged in a different order.

Paul's letter is an extended defense of the legitimacy of his apostolic ministry and its implications. It is intended to accomplish three overlapping purposes: (1) to strengthen the faithful majority and the purity of the church (primarily chs. 1–7); (2) to complete the collection as the expression of their repentance (primarily chs. 8–9); and (3) to offer the rebellious minority one more chance to repent before Paul returns to judge those still rejecting him and his message (primarily chs. 10–13). Thus, chapters 1–7 focus primarily on the past track record of Paul's ministry, chapters 8–9 on the present responsibility of the repentant, and chapters 10–13 on the future judgment of those still in rebellion against the gospel.

Timeline

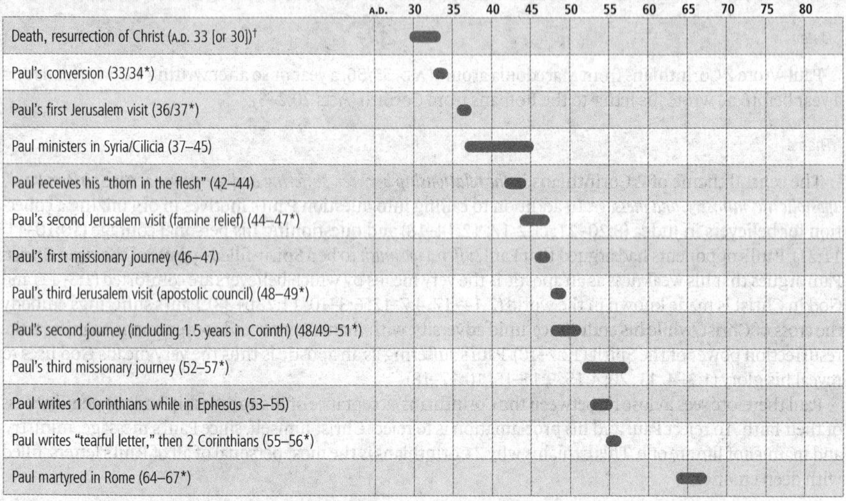

A.D. 30 35 40 45 50 55 60 65 70 75 80
Death, resurrection of Christ (A.D. 33 [or 30])†
Paul's conversion (33/34*)
Paul's first Jerusalem visit (36/37*)
Paul ministers in Syria/Cilicia (37–45)
Paul receives his "thorn in the flesh" (42–44)
Paul's second Jerusalem visit (famine relief) (44–47*)
Paul's first missionary journey (46–47)
Paul's third Jerusalem visit (apostolic council) (48–49*)
Paul's second journey (including 1.5 years in Corinth) (48/49–51*)
Paul's third missionary journey (52–57*)
Paul writes 1 Corinthians while in Ephesus (53–55)
Paul writes "tearful letter," then 2 Corinthians (55–56*)
Paul martyred in Rome (64–67*)

** denotes approximate date; / signifies either/or; † see The Date of Jesus' Crucifixion, pp. 1809–1810*

Literary Features

Second Corinthians is an informal occasional epistle, with a disjointed organization and numerous "asides" that are introduced without smooth tie-ins to the preceding material. The letter is also a missionary manual, based on the author's real-life missionary experiences. The usual conventions of the epistle appear early and late with the epistolary salutation, thanksgiving, and closing. The conventional *paraenesis* (list of moral exhortations) is absent. Occupying prominent places in the body of the letter are an extended defense of the author's life and ministry and a formal boast in a spiritualized version of it. The letter is heavily occa-

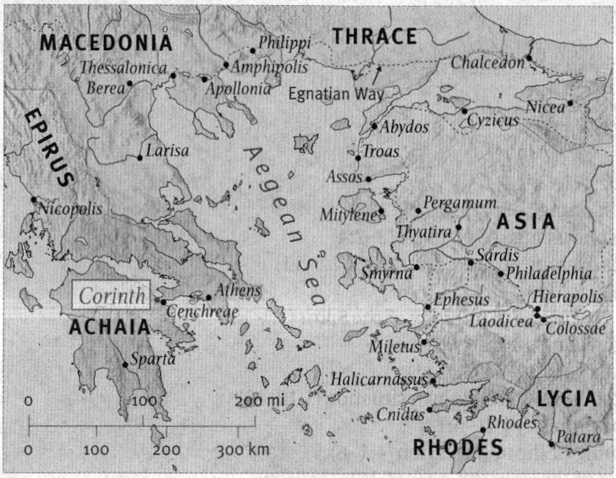

The Setting of 2 Corinthians
c. A.D. 55–56
Paul wrote 2 Corinthians from Macedonia a year or so after writing 1 Corinthians, during his third missionary journey. He had just finished his three-year ministry in Ephesus and was visiting the churches in Macedonia as he made his way to Corinth. In Macedonia he met Titus, who had returned from Corinth with news about the church there.

sional, meaning that it is filled with references to specific events in Paul's life and ministry. In the background can be seen the familiar genre of autobiography. Second Corinthians is also a missionary appeal letter that requests spiritual and financial support.

Second Corinthians mingles a number of stylistic features or ingredients, including self-portraiture, lyric outbursts of emotion, denunciation of opponents, sarcasm, threats, and expressions of personal affection. Further, the style is very personal and autobiographical, filled with references to Paul's own life. Exalted style frequently surfaces, with impressive vocabulary, catalogs or lists, parallel constructions, and rhetorical embellishments such as contrast and paradox.

The inferred literary intentions of the letter are as follows: to provide a vindication of the author's life in the standard literary genre known as *apologia pro vita sua*; to paint a portrait of the author and his life in such a way that the reader in his imagination becomes the author's traveling companion; to inspire the reader with the literary and rhetorical flourishes that appear in abundance; to win the reader with its aphoristic flair; and to persuade readers to support faithful and genuine ministry of the gospel.

Key Themes

1. The cross of Christ, embodied in the suffering of his apostle, unmasks the erroneous teaching of "false apostles" and "servants of Satan."	11:13–15
2. In fulfillment of Jer. 31:31–34 and Ezek. 36:26–27, Paul is a servant of the new covenant (2 Cor. 3:6), whose ministry and message of the cross mediates the Spirit of the living God and God's righteousness to believers.	3:3, 6–9; 5:14–15, 21
3. Endurance amid adversity and Christlike behavior, both made possible by the grace of God and modeled by Paul himself, are the greatest display of God's presence, power, and glory in this fallen world.	1:12–14; 6:1, 14–7:1; 9:13–15; 12:7–10; 13:4
4. The presence and power of the Spirit transforms believers into the image of God seen in Christ, which is the dawning of the new creation characterized by the righteousness of God. Believers therefore embody the new creation of the new covenant by living for the sake of others. This is made possible by the reconciliation with God brought about by the cross.	3:18; 4:4, 6; 5:15, 17–21
5. Repentance expresses itself in holiness, which is defined as a purity-producing love for God and his church and a unity-creating love for one's neighbor.	6:14–7:1; chs. 8–9
6. Christ, as Savior, is also the universal Judge, who will one day pass judgment on all people according to their deeds. In anticipation of this day, the Spirit transforms those in whom he dwells as a guarantee of the "eternal weight of glory" to come for believers at the resurrection.	1:14, 22; 3:6, 8–9, 18; 5:5, 9–11

History of Salvation Summary

God brought about salvation through the weakness of Christ's crucifixion, in fulfillment of Psalm 22 and Isaiah 53. Christians in turn are to find strength in Christ and not in themselves. (For an explanation of the "History of Salvation," see the Overview of the Bible, pp. 23–26.)

Outline

I. Paul's Defense of His Legitimacy as an Apostle (1:1–7:16)
  A. Salutation (1:1–2)
  B. Introduction to the letter (1:3–11)
  C. Paul's boast (1:12–2:17)
    1. The content of Paul's boast (1:12–14)
    2. The reason for Paul's first change of plans (1:15–22)
    3. The reason for Paul's second change of plans (1:23–2:4)
    4. The application of Paul's example to the Corinthians (2:5–11)
    5. Paul's visit to Troas and Macedonia (2:12–17)
  D. Paul's ministry of the new covenant as a ministry of the Spirit (3:1–18)
    1. The reality of the Spirit in Paul's ministry (3:1–6)
    2. Paul's interpretation of Exodus 32–34 (3:7–11)
    3. Paul's application of Exodus 32–34 to his own situation (3:12–18)
  E. Paul's encouragement in his ministry (4:1–6:13)
    1. The new covenant dawning of the new creation (4:1–6)
    2. The new covenant power of the resurrection (4:7–18)
    3. The new covenant motivation for the life of faith (5:1–10)
    4. The new covenant ministry of reconciliation (5:11–6:2)
    5. The new covenant support for the legitimacy of Paul's ministry (6:3–13)
  F. Paul's call for church discipline as an expression of repentance (6:14–7:1)
  G. Paul's joy over the repentant Corinthians (7:2–16)

II. Paul's Appeal to the Repentant Church in Corinth Regarding the Collection (8:1–9:15)
  A. The collection as the grace of God (8:1–15)
  B. The commendation of Titus and the brothers (8:16–9:5)
  C. Generosity, joy, and the glory of God (9:6–15)

III. Paul's Appeal to the Rebellious Minority in Corinth (10:1–13:10)
  A. Paul's defense of his humility as an apostle (10:1–11)
  B. Paul's defense of his authority as an apostle (10:12–18)
  C. Paul's defense of his boasting like a fool (11:1–21a)
  D. Paul's boast in his service and suffering (11:21b–33)
  E. Paul's boast in his heavenly vision and subsequent weakness (12:1–13)
  F. Paul's final defense and appeal to the rebellious (12:14–13:10)

IV. Closing Greetings (13:11–14)

THE SECOND LETTER OF PAUL TO THE CORINTHIANS

2 CORINTHIANS

Chapter 1

1 [a]Eph. 1:1; Col. 1:1; 1 Tim. 1:1; 2 Tim. 1:1; Titus 1:1; [Rom. 1:1; Gal. 1:1] [b]See 1 Cor. 1:1 [c]See 1 Thess. 3:2 [d]Phil. 1:1; Col. 1:2
2 [e]See Rom. 1:7
3 [f]Eph. 1:3; 1 Pet. 1:3 [g]See Rom. 15:6 [h]Rom. 15:5
4 [i][Isa. 51:12; 66:13]
5 [j][ch. 4:10; Phil. 3:10; Col. 1:24]
6 [k]2 Tim. 2:10; [ch. 4:15; 12:15; Eph. 3:13]
7 [l]See Rom. 8:17
8 [m]Acts 19:23; 1 Cor. 15:32

Greeting

1 Paul, [a]an apostle of Christ Jesus [b]by the will of God, and [c]Timothy our brother,
To the church of God that is at Corinth, [d]with all the saints who are in the whole of
Achaia:
2 [e]Grace to you and peace from God our Father and the Lord Jesus Christ.

God of All Comfort

3 [f]Blessed be the [g]God and Father of our Lord Jesus Christ, the Father of mercies and [h]God
of all comfort, 4 [i]who comforts us in all our affliction, so that we may be able to comfort
those who are in any affliction, with the comfort with which we ourselves are comforted
by God. 5 For as we share abundantly in [j]Christ's sufferings, so through Christ we share
abundantly in comfort too.[1] 6 [k]If we are afflicted, it is for your comfort and salvation; and if
we are comforted, it is for your comfort, which you experience when you patiently endure
the same sufferings that we suffer. 7 Our hope for you is unshaken, for we know that as
you [l]share in our sufferings, you will also share in our comfort.
8 For we do not want you to be unaware, brothers,[2] of [m]the affliction we experienced
in Asia. For we were so utterly burdened beyond our strength that we despaired of life
itself. 9 Indeed, we felt that we had received the sentence of death. But that was to make

[1] Or *For as the sufferings of Christ abound for us, so also our comfort abounds through Christ* [2] Or *brothers and sisters*. The plural Greek word *adelphoi* (translated "brothers") refers to siblings in a family. In New Testament usage, depending on the context, *adelphoi* may refer either to men or to both men and women who are siblings (brothers and sisters) in God's family, the church

1:1–7:16 *Paul's Defense of His Legitimacy as an Apostle.* Paul's new covenant ministry reflects the work of the Holy Spirit.

1:1–2 *Salutation.* Paul's opening greetings expand the conventional greetings found in ancient letters.

1:1 apostle of Christ Jesus. See note on Rom. 1:1. The Greek word for "apostle" is *apostolos* ("apostle," i.e., "one who is sent") and is derived from the verb *apostellō* ("to send out"), which was used in the Greek OT to designate those commissioned as authoritative representatives to act in the name of the one who sent them (Ex. 3:10; Judg. 6:8; Jer. 1:7; Ezek. 2:3; etc.). **saints**. Literally, "holy" or "dedicated ones" (Gk. *hagioi*), referring to the identity and way of life of all who belong to God (see 1 Cor. 3:16–17; 5:1–6:20; 2 Cor. 6:14–7:1). **Corinth**. For information on the city see Introduction to 1 Corinthians: The Ancient City of Corinth.

1:2 Grace. A wordplay on the normal Greek greeting. Whereas the Greeks said, "Hello" (Gk. *charein*), the Christians said, "Grace" (Gk. *charis*). **peace**. Not untroubled circumstances but the profound well-being that comes from resting in God's sovereignty and mercy, a concept first expressed by the Hebrew *shalom* (see note on John 14:27).

1:3–11 *Introduction to the Letter.* Paul's prayers not only extol God but also introduce the main themes to follow. He praises God for the very suffering that his opponents use to call his apostleship into question. To support his praise for God as expressed in vv. 3–7, Paul relates in vv. 8–11 how God used his experience in Asia to teach him the same lessons he hopes the Corinthians will learn from him.

1:3 Blessed be. This is a standard Jewish praise formula that introduces the tone and themes to come. Paul begins by identifying the one whom he extols as the **God and Father of our Lord Jesus Christ**. These titles describe Yahweh's relationship to Jesus and Jesus' relationship to his people ("Lord" designates his absolute rule over his people). **Comfort** is the overall disposition that comes from resting in God's sovereign and loving rule as manifested in Christ's lordship (cf. Isa. 40:1).

1:4 so that we may be able to comfort. One of God's purposes in the suffering of Christians is that they would experience direct, personal comfort from God, and then from that experience be able to minister God's comfort to others. **us . . . our**. Most of the plural first-person pronouns in 2 Corinthians ("we," "us," "our") seem to refer to Paul himself (see v. 8; 7:5–7), but these plurals at times (depending on the context) may also include Timothy (who is named as a "co-sender" of the letter in 1:1), other ministry partners (1:19, 21), or Christians generally (5:1–10). In this verse, Paul probably uses the plural to indicate that he views himself as representing both the apostolic office and believers generally. **Affliction** can refer to both outward circumstances (4:17; 6:4; 8:2) and inward states of mind (2:4; 7:4–5).

1:5 Christ's sufferings refers not to Jesus' atonement for sin, which was unique to Christ (Rom. 5:8–10; 6:10), but to Paul's sufferings in imitation of Christ, which Paul endured because of his faithfulness to God and for the sake of God's people.

1:6–7 it is for your comfort. The opponents maintained that Paul's sufferings disqualified him as an apostle, but Paul maintains that his sufferings are the means God uses to strengthen other believers.

1:8 Asia. May refer back to Paul's suffering in Ephesus (1 Cor. 15:32) but the precise location and nature of the affliction are not certain. That Paul was **burdened** (Gk. *bareō*, "weighted down") and **despaired** in Asia points forward to 2 Cor. 4:8, 17 (see note on 4:17–18).

1:9 sentence of death. Paul's suffering was so severe that it seemed to Paul as if a death sentence had been decreed against him by a ruler or a judge.

us [n]rely not on ourselves [o]but on God [p]who raises the dead. 10 [q]He delivered us from such
a deadly peril, and he will deliver us. [r]On him we have set our hope that he will deliver
us again. 11 [s]You also must help us by prayer, so that many will give thanks on our behalf
[t]for the blessing granted us through the prayers of many.

Paul's Change of Plans

12 For our boast is this, [u]the testimony of our conscience, that we behaved in the world
with simplicity[1] and [v]godly sincerity, [w]not by earthly wisdom but by the grace of God, and
supremely so toward you. 13 For we are not writing to you anything other than what you
read and understand and I hope you will fully understand— 14 just as you did [x]partially
understand us—that [y]on the day of our Lord Jesus [z]you will boast of us as [a]we will boast
of you.

15 Because I was sure of this, [b]I wanted to come to you first, so that you might have [c]a
second [d]experience of grace. 16 I wanted to visit you [e]on my way to Macedonia, and to come
back to you from Macedonia and have you send me on my way to Judea. 17 Was I vacillating
when I wanted to do this? Do I make my plans [f]according to the flesh, ready to say "Yes,
yes" and "No, no" at the same time? 18 As surely as [g]God is faithful, [h]our word to you has
not been Yes and No. 19 For [i]the Son of God, Jesus Christ, whom we proclaimed among
you, [j]Silvanus and Timothy and I, was not Yes and No, but [k]in him it is always Yes. 20 For
[l]all the promises of God find their Yes in him. That is why it is through him that we utter
our [m]Amen to God for his glory. 21 And it is God who establishes us with you in Christ,
and [n]has anointed us, 22 and who has also [o]put his seal on us and [p]given us his Spirit in
our hearts as a guarantee.[2]

23 But [q]I call God to witness against me—it was [r]to spare you that I refrained from com-

[1] Some manuscripts *holiness* [2] Or *down payment*

9 [n]Luke 18:9 [o]Ps. 2:12; 25:2; 26:1 [p]ch. 4:14
10 [q]See Rom. 15:31 [r]1 Tim. 4:10
11 [s][Acts 12:5; Rom. 15:30; Phil. 1:19; Philem. 22] [t][ch. 4:15; 9:11, 12]
12 [u][1 Thess. 2:10]; See Acts 23:1 [v]ch. 2:17; 4:2 [w]1 Cor. 2:4, 13
14 [x]ch. 2:5 [y]See 1 Cor. 1:8 [z][ch. 5:12; 9:3] [a]1 Cor. 9:15; Phil. 2:16; 4:1; 1 Thess. 2:19, 20
15 [b]See 1 Cor. 4:19 [c][Acts 18:1-18] [d][Rom. 1:11]
16 [e]Acts 19:21; [1 Cor. 16:5-7]
17 [f]ch. 10:2, 3
18 [g]See 1 Cor. 1:9 [h][ch. 2:17]
19 [i]See Matt. 14:33 [j]Acts 15:22 [k][Heb. 13:8]
20 [l][Rom. 15:8; Heb. 10:23] [m][Rev. 3:14]; See 1 Cor. 14:16
21 [n][1 John 2:20, 27]
22 [o]Eph. 1:13; 4:30 [p]ch. 5:5; Eph. 1:14; See Rom. 8:16
23 [q][Gal. 1:20]; See Rom. 1:9 [r]ch. 2:1, 3; See 1 Cor. 4:21

1:10 Biblical **hope**, as the consequence and expression of faith, is not wishful thinking but an absolute confidence in God's promises for the future (v. 10) based on his faithfulness in the past (v. 9).

1:12–2:17 *Paul's Boast.* Paul begins the body of his letter with a detailed defense of why he had changed his mind more than once regarding his earlier plans to return to Corinth: (1) an initial plan to visit Macedonia first, then Corinth (1 Cor. 16:5); (2) a plan to visit Corinth first, then Macedonia (2 Cor. 1:15); (3) and finally, a decision not to make "another painful visit" to Corinth, so that he went, by way of Troas, to Macedonia first (1:23; 2:1).

1:12–14 *The Content of Paul's Boast.* Paul defends his conduct and integrity in his relationship with the Corinthians.

1:12 To **boast** is by no means a bad thing if the object of one's boasting is not oneself (1 Cor. 1:29; 4:7; Eph. 2:9) but God (Rom. 5:2; 15:17; 1 Cor. 1:31; 2 Cor. 10:17–18). Paul boasts because he acted **with simplicity** (open uprightness; see 4:1–2), which, given human sinfulness, can be true only if God has changed one's life. So, too, Paul's **godly sincerity** explicitly refers to God as its source (see 2:17; 1 Cor. 5:8). Thus, Paul boasts in his conduct because it came about **not by earthly** (lit., fleshly) **wisdom but by the grace of God**—a contrast between living according to the thinking and values of a fallen world that is in rebellion against its Creator and the believer living in accordance with the death of Christ (2 Cor. 5:14–17) and the transforming presence of the Spirit (3:18).

1:14 The day of our Lord Jesus assigns to Jesus the role of judge attributed to Yahweh on "the day of the LORD" (e.g., Isa. 13:9; Joel 1–3; Zechariah 12–14; Mal. 4:5; cf. 1 Cor. 5:5; 1 Thess. 5:2; 2 Pet. 3:10). Jesus' role as judge is a clear affirmation of his messianic identity and divine status.

1:15–22 *The Reason for Paul's First Change of Plans.* Paul explains that his initial decision not to come directly to Corinth as originally planned (see 1 Cor. 16:5) was actually determined by his desire to bring more blessing to them and thus to be like Christ, in whom God's promises are fulfilled (2 Cor. 1:20).

1:15–16 first . . . on my way to Macedonia, and to come back to you from Macedonia . . . on my way to Judea. See Introduction: Purpose, Occasion, and Background. **a second experience of grace** (Gk. *deuteran charin*, lit., "second grace" or "second benefit"). Some think this refers to a second opportunity to contribute to the collection for the believers in Jerusalem (see chs. 8–9). On this interpretation, contributing to the needs of others is called "grace" because it is made possible by God's grace in the lives of those who give (8:1, 4, 6–7, 19; 9:14): the Corinthians are set free to meet the needs of others because God has met their needs in Christ (8:9; 9:6–11). Others see this as a reference to the added experience of various blessings from God that would come from another visit by Paul.

1:17 "Yes, yes" and "No, no." Because of his change in plans (vv. 15–16), Paul's opponents accused him of **vacillating** and being indecisive.

1:18–19 Paul can affirm that his **word . . . was not Yes and No, but in him** (Christ) **it is always Yes** because his change of plan was in accord with God's will.

1:20 God's **promises** find their fulfillment in Christ, indicating that the OT Scriptures should be read as pointing to Christ (see the Overview of the Bible, pp. 23–26). Paul expresses his agreement—i.e., his **Amen** (the Gk. form of the Hb. word meaning "to confirm")—thus confirming what God has done through Christ (**through him**) not only by preaching Christ (v. 19) but also by acting like Christ toward the Corinthians, including changing his plans in order to minister to them.

1:21–22 To be **anointed** is to be set apart and gifted by God for his calling, symbolized in the OT by the pouring of olive oil as a sign of God's rich provision. It is also a play on the word "Christ," which means "anointed one"; Christ's messengers (**us**) are also anointed. **seal**. A mark of ownership, often used by ancient kings to signify ownership. See note on John 6:27. **guarantee**. A financial term (Gk. *arrabōn*, "down payment, deposit, guarantee") referring to the first installment paid as a pledge of faithfulness to complete the purchase. The **Spirit** comes as God's pledge to complete ("pay in full") the final redemption of his people at the end of the age, and the Spirit's presence in Christians' lives now is a reliable "sample" or foretaste of this future fullness (cf. John 5:24 and note; Rom. 8:11).

1:23–2:4 *The Reason for Paul's Second Change of Plans.* See Introduction: Purpose, Occasion, and Background; and note on 1:12–2:17. Paul makes clear that just as his first change of plans was a Christlike act in accordance with the promises of God (see note on 1:15–22), so too his decision not to come but to send them a "tearful letter" was an expression of God's love to them in Christ (2:3–4).

1:23 to spare you. Just as Christ came first to save his people rather than to judge the world, so too Paul did not return immediately to Corinth, in order to spare them a taste of God's wrath. Like Christ, Paul is willing to

ing again to Corinth. 24 Not that we [s]lord it over your faith, but we work with you for your
joy, for you stand firm [t]in your faith.

2 For I made up my mind [u]not to make another painful visit to you. 2 For [v]if I cause you
pain, who is there to make me glad but the one whom I have pained? 3 And I wrote as
I did, so that when I came I might not suffer pain from those who should have made me
rejoice, [w]for I felt sure of all of you, that my joy would be the joy of you all. 4 For [x]I wrote
to you out of much affliction and anguish of heart and with many tears, not to cause you
pain but to let you know the abundant love that I have for you.

Forgive the Sinner

5 Now [y]if anyone has caused pain, [z]he has caused it not to me, but [a]in some measure—not
to put it too severely—to all of you. 6 For such a one, [b]this punishment by the majority is
enough, 7 so [c]you should rather turn to forgive and comfort him, or he may be overwhelmed
by excessive sorrow. 8 So I beg you to reaffirm your love for him. 9 For this is why I wrote,
that I might [d]test you and know [e]whether you are obedient in everything. 10 Anyone whom
you forgive, I also forgive. Indeed, what I have forgiven, if I have forgiven anything, has
been for your sake in the presence of Christ, 11 so that we would not be outwitted by Satan;
for [f]we are not ignorant of his designs.

Triumph in Christ

12 When [g]I came to Troas to preach the gospel of Christ, even though [h]a door was opened
for me in the Lord, 13 my spirit [i]was not at rest because I did not find my brother Titus
there. So I took leave of them and went on to Macedonia.
14 But [j]thanks be to God, who in Christ always [k]leads us in triumphal procession, and

24 [s]1 Pet. 5:3; [ch. 4:5; Matt. 23:8-10] [t]Rom. 11:20; See 1 Cor. 15:1

Chapter 2

1 [u]ch. 1:23; [ch. 12:20, 21; 13:10]
2 [v][ch. 7:8]
3 [w]ch. 8:22; Gal. 5:10; 2 Thess. 3:4; [ch. 7:16]
4 [x]ch. 7:8, 12; See Acts 20:19
5 [y][1 Cor. 5:1, 2] [z][Gal. 4:12] [a]ch. 1:14
6 [b]1 Cor. 5:4, 5; [ch. 7:11]
7 [c]Gal. 6:1; [Eph. 4:32]
9 [d]Phil. 2:22 [e]ch. 7:15; 10:6
11 [f]See 1 Pet. 5:8
12 [g]Acts 16:8; 20:6 [h]See Acts 14:27
13 [i]ch. 7:5
14 [j]ch. 8:16; [ch. 9:15]; See Rom. 6:17 [k]Col. 2:15 (Gk.)

judge those in Corinth who will not repent (see 13:1–10); but before judgment comes mercy.

2:1–2 painful visit. See Introduction: Purpose, Occasion, and Background.

2:4 Paul wrote them a severe letter **with many tears**. As an expression of his **love**, it called the Corinthians to repentance in no uncertain terms (see 7:8–9). See Introduction: Theme.

2:5–11 *The Application of Paul's Example to the Corinthians.* The majority in Corinth had expressed their repentance by punishing the leader of the rebellion against Paul. Paul now calls them to follow his own Christlike example toward them by extending mercy to the offender, lest Satan have his way once again in the church.

The Believer's Apparent (Temporal) Defeat	The Believer's Actual (Spiritual) Victory
For we were so utterly burdened beyond our strength that we despaired of life itself. Indeed, we felt that we had received the sentence of death (1:8–9).	He delivered us from such a deadly peril, and he will deliver us. On him we have set our hope that he will deliver us again (1:10).
When I came to Troas to preach the gospel of Christ . . . my spirit was not at rest . . . (2:12–13).	But thanks be to God, who in Christ always leads us in triumphal procession . . . (2:14).
We are afflicted in every way, but not crushed; perplexed, but not driven to despair; persecuted, but not forsaken; struck down, but not destroyed; always carrying in the body the death of Jesus, so that the life of Jesus may also be manifested in our bodies (4:8–10).	Though our outer self is wasting away, our inner self is being renewed day by day. For this light momentary affliction is preparing for us an eternal weight of glory beyond all comparison, as we look not to the things that are seen but to the things that are unseen (4:16–18).
A thorn was given me in the flesh, a messenger of Satan to harass me, to keep me from becoming conceited (12:7).	But [the Lord] said to me, "My grace is sufficient for you, for my power is made perfect in weakness" (12:9).

2:6 punishment. Most likely excommunication from the fellowship of the church, just as in 1 Cor. 5:2, 5, 13. The person in view is probably the Corinthian leader of the opposition against Paul, not the offender from 1 Cor. 5:1–5, as is often suggested, since the content of the sin was different.

2:10 forgive. Christians are to forgive because they have been forgiven (Matt. 6:14–15; 18:35; Col. 3:13).

2:11 Satan's **designs** are to destroy the mutual forgiveness, love, and unity that is to characterize God's people as those who have been reconciled to God through Christ (see 5:16–6:2). In this way, Satan aims to dishonor God's own glory revealed in Jesus as the Son of God (1:19–20).

2:12–17 *Paul's Visit to Troas and Macedonia.* These paragraphs mark a turning point in Paul's argument as he shifts his attention from the past to the present. They explain some of Paul's actions behind writing 2 Corinthians (vv. 12–13; see also 7:5–16) and reintroduce the main theme of the letter (2:14–17).

2:12–13 Paul **came to Troas** (see note on Acts 16:8) after he left Ephesus for Macedonia in anticipation of meeting up sooner with his coworker **Titus**, whom he had sent to Corinth to present his "tearful letter" (2 Cor. 2:3–4; see ch. 7; and Introduction: Purpose, Occasion, and Background). Despite the receptivity for the gospel in Troas (**a door was opened for me in the Lord**), when Titus failed to show up, Paul's **spirit was not at rest**, a reference to his inward anxiety over the welfare of Titus and the church in Corinth (see 7:5–7). This is yet another example of the suffering Paul endured as an apostle (see 11:28). The NT elsewhere mentions various feelings or perceptions experienced by a person's "spirit"—the nonmaterial part of a person, in effect the conscious self (see Luke 1:47; Acts 17:16; Rom. 8:16; 1 Cor. 7:34; 2 Cor. 7:1, 13; also Mark 2:8; John 13:21).

2:14 thanks be to God. A characteristic thanksgiving formula that, like 1:3, sets the tone and introduces the themes to come (see 1 Cor. 15:57;

The Sufficiency of God in 2 Corinthians

2:16	Who is sufficient for these things?
3:5	Not that we are sufficient in ourselves . . .
3:5	but our sufficiency is from God
12:9	"My grace is sufficient for you . . ."

through us spreads [l]the fragrance of the knowledge of him everywhere. 15 For we are the
aroma of Christ to God among [m]those who are being saved and among [n]those who are perishing, 16 [o]to one a fragrance from death to death, [o]to the other a fragrance from life to life.
[p]Who is sufficient for these things? 17 For we are not, like so many, peddlers of God's word,
but as men of sincerity, as commissioned by God, in the sight of God we speak in Christ.

Ministers of the New Covenant

3 [q]Are we beginning to commend ourselves again? Or do we need, [r]as some do, [s]letters
of recommendation to you, or from you? 2 [t]You yourselves are our letter of recommendation, written on our[1] hearts, to be known and read by all. 3 And you show that you
are a letter from Christ delivered by us, written not with ink but with the Spirit of [u]the
living God, not on [v]tablets of stone but on [w]tablets of [x]human hearts.[2]
4 [y]Such is the confidence that we have through Christ toward God. 5 [z]Not that we are
sufficient in ourselves to claim anything as coming from us, but [a]our sufficiency is from
God, 6 who has made us sufficient to be [b]ministers of [c]a new covenant, not of [d]the letter
but of the Spirit. For the letter kills, but [e]the Spirit gives life.
7 Now if [f]the ministry of death, carved in letters on stone, came with such glory [g]that the

[1] Some manuscripts *your* [2] Greek *fleshly hearts*

7 [f]ver. 9; See Rom. 4:15 [g]ver. 13; Ex. 34:29-35

14 [l]Eph. 5:2; Phil. 4:18; [Song 1:3]
15 [m]See 1 Cor. 1:18 [n]ch. 4:3
16 [o][Luke 2:34; John 9:39; 1 Pet. 2:7, 8] [p]ch. 3:5, 6

Chapter 3

1 [q]ch. 5:12; 10:12; 12:11 [r][ch. 11:4] [s][Acts 18:27; 1 Cor. 16:3]
2 [t][1 Cor. 9:2]
3 [u]See Matt. 16:16 [v]Ex. 24:12 [w]Prov. 3:3; 7:3; Jer. 17:1 [x]Ezek. 11:19; 36:26; [Jer. 31:33; Heb. 8:10]
4 [y]Eph. 3:12
5 [z][Eph. 2:8] [a]See 1 Cor. 15:10
6 [b]Eph. 3:7; Col. 1:23, 25; [ch. 4:1; 5:18; 1 Tim. 1:12] [c]Jer. 31:31; Luke 22:20; 1 Cor. 11:25; Heb. 8:8, 13; [ver. 14; Heb. 9:15] [d]See Rom. 2:27 [e][John 6:63; Rom. 8:2]

2 Cor. 8:16). **leads us in triumphal procession.** Most interpreters see this as a reference to the lavish victory parades celebrated in Rome after great battles. God is depicted as the sovereign victor, with Christ as the general, leading the victory procession, and Paul as "captured" by Christ but now joyfully following him. Images of such parades are still visible in some ancient works of art, such as in the reliefs on the late-first-century Arch of Titus in Rome commemorating the emperor's victory over Jerusalem. The picture here reflects a recurring theme throughout 2 Corinthians, namely, the contrast between the believer's apparent (temporal) defeat and the believer's actual (spiritual) victory (see chart, p. 2225). Another view is that the "triumphal procession" is an expression of Paul's praise to God for leading him (like a prisoner in a Roman triumphal procession) into situations of suffering such as he experienced in Troas (2:12, 13). Thus through Paul's suffering God spreads **the fragrance of the knowledge of him everywhere** (see v. 15).

2:15–16a aroma . . . fragrance. Taken by some as a reference to the incense spread along the streets during the triumphal procession (see note on v. 14). However, the terms used here (Gk. *euōdia*, "fragrance, aroma"; and *osmē*, "aroma, odor") are used often in the Greek OT to refer to the aroma of a sacrifice pleasing to God (e.g., Gen. 8:21; Ex. 29:25; Lev. 1:13; Num. 15:3). With Christ pictured as the primary sacrifice, Paul's offering of his entire life to God (cf. Rom. 12:1; Heb. 13:15–16), including his suffering for the sake of Christ, can then be seen as an extension of Christ's death in the world (see 2 Cor. 1:5), as the aroma **of Christ to God**, **from death to death . . . from life to life.** Some encounter Paul's life and message and dislike it, leading to their own condemnation. Others are attracted by the Christlike beauty seen in Paul and his message, and they accept it, leading to their own eternal life.

2:16b–17 Who is sufficient for these things? The implied answer clearly is "No one." The work of the gospel (and the Christian life as a whole) can never be carried out on the basis of human ability or by human means. As Paul goes on to explain, our "sufficiency" comes only from God by means of his grace ("sufficient" translates Gk. *hikanos*, "sufficient, competent, qualified"; the same term and its related noun occur three times in 3:5–6). (See further the example of Moses in Ex. 4:10–12, where God promises to equip Moses to accomplish the work that God has called him to do.) In contrast to his **many** opponents, some of whom at least demanded payment for their ministries as if they were retail **peddlers of God's word** (see 2 Cor. 11:7–15; 12:13–16), Paul's commitment to support himself brought with it many hardships (see 1 Cor. 4:11–13; 9:18; 15:10; 2 Cor. 6:5; 11:23); as such it is yet another example of his willing, Christlike suffering on behalf of his churches.

3:1–18 *Paul's Ministry of the New Covenant as a Ministry of the Spirit.* In 1:3–2:17, Paul defended his legitimacy as an apostle on the basis of his suffering as the means by which Christians are comforted (1:3–11) and God is made known in the world (2:14–17). Now he does so based on the reality of the life-transforming Spirit being mediated through his apostolic ministry of the new covenant.

3:1–6 *The Reality of the Spirit in Paul's Ministry.* Paul begins this section by making it clear that, as an apostle, he was called to mediate the Spirit in fulfillment of the new covenant.

3:1 Paul expects a negative answer to his two rhetorical questions since his claim to be an apostle is not an empty boast (he does not **commend** himself) but is supported by the Spirit and by his ministry of suffering. For the theme of "commendation" in 2 Corinthians, see notes on 4:2; 5:12; 6:4; 10:12; 10:17–18; 12:11.

3:2–3 The changed lives of the Corinthians give a clear message from Christ (they are a **letter from Christ**) testifying to Paul's true apostleship as the one who brought the gospel to them (**delivered by us**). In fulfillment of Ezek. 11:19 and 36:26, Paul contrasts the old covenant, in which God wrote **on tablets of stone** (see Ex. 24:12; 31:18; 32:15; 34:1; Deut. 9:10), with the apostolic ministry of writing **on tablets of human hearts**. Paul "writes" on hearts **not with ink but with the Spirit of the living God**. The Spirit's work of changing the Corinthians' hearts as a result of Paul's ministry confirms that the new covenant is being established through his ministry.

3:5 Paul's **sufficiency is from God**, not from himself, just as it was for Moses (see note on 2:16b–17; also Ex. 3:1–4:17; see chart, p. 2225). Paul's sufficiency as an apostle recalls the pattern exhibited in the call of the OT prophets: the prophet is not sufficient in himself but is made sufficient by God's grace (see Judg. 6:11–24; Isa. 6:1–8; Jer. 1:4–10; Ezek. 1:1–3:11).

3:6 Paul was **made . . . sufficient** to be a minister of the **new covenant** (Jer. 31:31–34) as a result of his call on the road to Damascus, just as Moses was called to be a minister of the old covenant at the burning bush (see note on 2 Cor. 2:16b–17). Whereas "apostle" refers to Paul's authoritative *office*, "minister" (or "servant," Gk. *diakonos*) refers to his *function* of mediating God's presence and word, a role he can share with non-apostles (e.g., 4:1; 5:18; 1 Cor. 3:5). Here it refers to Paul's role of mediating the Spirit as promised in the new covenant, by which God will create a people who will keep his covenant (Ezek. 36:26–27); in other words, God will write his law on their hearts (Jer. 31:33) and forgive their sins (Jer. 31:34; Ezek. 36:25). The new covenant and its ministry therefore consists **not of the letter but of the Spirit**, because **the letter kills, but the Spirit gives life.** On the letter/Spirit contrast, see Rom. 2:29 and 7:6, the other two NT occurrences of this contrast. The letter kills since it announces God's will without granting the power to keep it, thereby bringing people under God's judgment as covenant breakers. The Spirit alone gives life because only the Spirit can change the heart, thereby enabling God's people to keep his commands.

3:7–11 *Paul's Interpretation of Exodus 32–34.* To support the contrast between the ministries of the old and new covenants in vv. 3, 6, Paul points his readers back to the events of the golden calf and the second giving of the law.

3:7–9 Moses' ministry is described as a **ministry of death** not because there

9 [h]ver. 7; [Heb. 12:18-21] [i]ch. 11:15
12 [j]ch. 7:4; Eph. 6:19
13 [k]ver. 7
14 [l][ch. 4:4; Rom. 11:25] [m]See Mark 6:52 [n]Acts 13:15; 15:21 [o][ver. 6]
16 [p]Rom. 11:23; [Ex. 34:34] [q][Isa. 25:7]
17 [r]Isa. 61:1, 2; [Gal. 4:6] [s]Gal. 5:1, 13; See John 8:32
18 [t]See 1 Cor. 13:12 [u]ch. 4:4, 6; 1 Tim. 1:11; See John 17:24

Israelites could not gaze at Moses' face because of its glory, which was being brought to an
end, **8** will not the ministry of the Spirit have even more glory? **9** For if there was glory in
[h]the ministry of condemnation, [i]the ministry of righteousness must far exceed it in glory.
10 Indeed, in this case, what once had glory has come to have no glory at all, because of the
glory that surpasses it. **11** For if what was being brought to an end came with glory, much
more will what is permanent have glory.
12 Since we have such a hope, [j]we are very bold, **13** not like Moses, [k]who would put a
veil over his face so that the Israelites might not gaze at the outcome of what was being
brought to an end. **14** But [l]their minds were [m]hardened. For to this day, [n]when they read
[o]the old covenant, that same veil remains unlifted, because only through Christ is it taken
away. **15** Yes, to this day whenever Moses is read a veil lies over their hearts. **16** But when
[p]one[1] turns to the Lord, [q]the veil is removed. **17** Now the Lord[2] is the Spirit, and where [r]the
Spirit of the Lord is, there is [s]freedom. **18** And we all, with unveiled face, [t]beholding [u]the

[1] Greek *he* [2] Or *this Lord*

was something wrong with the law; in fact the permanent value of the law is evidenced by the fact that God himself **carved** the Ten Commandments **in letters on stone** (see v. 3 and Ex. 31:18; 32:16; Deut. 5:22). But because Israel remained "stiff-necked" under the old covenant (see Ex. 32:9; 34:9), and because the commandments themselves could not give people the power to obey them, the effect of the commandments was **condemnation** (2 Cor. 3:9). The giving of the law was accompanied by so much glory that **the Israelites could not gaze** (look intently or directly) **at Moses' face because of its glory**. The light of God's glory shone so brightly from Moses' face (see Ex. 34:29–35) that the people were afraid (Ex. 34:30) to look at Moses; possibly the glory also shined so brightly that it was painful to their eyes. Paul's argument seems to be that even this old covenant, which was temporary and ineffective in changing hearts, still had much glory, and therefore the new covenant **ministry of the Spirit** has **even more glory**. Indeed, the new covenant **must far exceed** (the old covenant) **in glory**, for the new covenant ministry brings **righteousness** (right standing with God) rather than "condemnation" (2 Cor. 3:9), as well as the glorious presence of God's power, which transforms believers "from one degree of glory to another" (v. 18).

3:10–11 The old covenant was the focus and realm of God's self-displayed presence (**glory**) in the past. But now that the new covenant has come, the old covenant **has come to have no glory at all**, since God is no longer revealing himself through it. Thus God has even **brought to an end** (Gk. *katargeō*) the glory of the old covenant. The glory of the new covenant also **surpasses** that of the old, in that the new covenant is a **permanent**, everlasting covenant, stretching into the age to come.

3:12–18 *Paul's Application of Exodus 32–34 to His Own Situation.* If Paul's ministry of the Spirit under the new covenant is bringing forth life, not death, then why are the majority of the Jews of Paul's day still rejecting it? Does Israel's rejection of Paul's message call the gospel itself into question? Paul answers these questions in this next section.

3:12 Paul's confident expectation (his **hope**) is that in this more glorious new covenant ministry God is pouring out the Spirit to change people's hearts. For this reason, he can be **very bold**, since he is ministering a much better covenant, in contrast to Moses, who as a minister of the old covenant had veiled his face.

3:13 Veil is the key concept in vv. 13–18, which Paul now develops as an elaborate and complex image (see notes on vv. 14–18). Regarding "gaze," see note on vv. 7–9. **so that the Israelites might not gaze at the outcome of what was being brought to an end**. This gives the reason why Moses veiled his face (Ex. 34:33, 35). Though commentators differ as to what this means, the most likely interpretation is that Moses put a veil over his face so that the Israelites would not see that the glory was gradually fading, signifying the temporary nature of the old covenant (the "outcome" was that it "was being brought to an end," or fading away; 2 Cor. 3:7, 13).

3:14–15 Despite Paul's boldness, Israel's **minds**, which **were hardened** in Moses' day (Ex. 32:9; 33:3, 5; 34:9), remain so **to this day**. Paul's description agrees with Deut. 29:4 and Isa. 29:10, which explain why the majority of Israel continued to reject the law and the prophets throughout their history (see Neh. 9:16–31; Ps. 106:6–39; Ezek. 20:8–36; Rom. 11:7–8; etc.). This is evidenced by the fact that **that same veil remains unlifted** in Paul's day **whenever Moses is read**. Here Paul uses Moses' veil as a symbol for the people's hardened condition that prompted its use under the old covenant and that now keeps most of Israel from recognizing that the law of Moses itself points to Jesus as the Messiah.

3:16 Just as Moses was able to enter into God's presence without a veil (Ex. 34:34), so too when **one turns to the Lord** in faith, the **veil** of separation from God and incomprehension of him brought about by a hardened heart **is removed**.

3:17 the Lord is the Spirit. Different explanations have been offered for this difficult and compressed statement: Paul may be saying that Christ and the Spirit function together in the Christian's experience—i.e., that the Lord (Christ) comes to us through the ministry of the Spirit (though they are still two distinct persons). Another view (based on the reference in v. 16 to Ex. 34:34, "Moses went in before the LORD to speak with him") is that the "Lord" here refers to Yahweh ("the LORD") in the OT (that is, God in his whole being without specifying Father, Son, or Spirit). In this case, Paul is saying that Yahweh in the OT is not just Father and Son, he is also Spirit. In either case, Paul's primary point seems to be that the Christian's experience of the ministry of the Spirit under the new covenant (2 Cor. 3:3–8) is parallel to Moses' experience of the Lord under the old covenant—i.e., that the Spirit (under the new covenant) sets one free from the veil of hard-heartedness (vv. 12–15). Paul regularly distinguishes Christ from the Holy Spirit in his writings, and that is surely the case even here, since later in this verse he speaks of **the Spirit of the Lord**. Moreover, it should not be supposed that Paul is teaching that any of the members of the Trinity (the Father, the Son, or the Spirit) are the same person, which would be the heresy of modalism; instead Paul is stressing the gracious unity of purpose among the three persons of the Trinity. **There is freedom**, though unspecified in the context, most likely refers to the many kinds of freedom that come with salvation in Christ and with the presence of the Holy Spirit: that is, freedom from condemnation, guilt, sin, death, the old covenant, and blindness to the gospel, as well as freedom that gives access to the loving presence of God.

3:18 with unveiled face, beholding the glory of the Lord. The word translated "beholding" (Gk. *katoptrizō*) can mean "behold" or "reflect" or "look at in a mirror," and commentators support all three views. In this context, however, the connection with a mirror does not seem to be necessary to the word, and the meaning "behold" seems more consistent with the idea of having the veil removed and therefore being able to see God's glory, in contrast to the unbelieving Jews who still have a veil blocking their vision (see note on vv. 14–15). Paul continues his comparison of all Christians (**we all**) with Moses by using Moses' experience in Ex. 34:34 as the key to understanding the experience of the Christian. As a result of beholding the Lord through the ministry of the **Spirit**, the believer is **being transformed** (a process of sanctification over time, not an instantaneous change) **into the same image** of God that was distorted at the fall (see Gen. 1:26–27; 2 Cor. 4:4; 5:17; also 1 John 3:2). The "image" of God includes every way in which humans are like God, such as their moral character, their true knowledge, their many God-given abilities, and their dominion over creation (cf. Gen. 1:26–28), to be exercised with dependence on God as the Creator and giver of all things (see 1 Cor. 4:7).

glory of the Lord,[1] [v]are being transformed into the same image [w]from one degree of glory
to another. For this comes from the Lord who is the Spirit.

The Light of the Gospel

4 Therefore, having [x]this ministry [y]by the mercy of God,[2] we do not lose heart. 2 But
we have renounced [z]disgraceful, underhanded ways. We refuse to practice[3] cunning
or [a]to tamper with God's word, but [b]by the open statement of the truth [c]we would commend ourselves to everyone's conscience in the sight of God. 3 And even [d]if our gospel is
veiled, [e]it is veiled to [f]those who are perishing. 4 In their case [g]the god of this world [d]has
blinded the minds of the unbelievers, to keep them from seeing [h]the light of [i]the gospel
of the glory of Christ, [j]who is the image of God. 5 For what [k]we proclaim is not ourselves,
but Jesus Christ as Lord, with [l]ourselves as your servants[4] for Jesus' sake. 6 For God, who
said, [m]"Let light shine out of darkness," [n]has shone in our hearts to give [o]the light of the
knowledge of the glory of God in the face of Jesus Christ.

Treasure in Jars of Clay

7 But we have this treasure in [p]jars of clay, [q]to show that the surpassing power belongs
to God and not to us. 8 We are [r]afflicted in every way, but not crushed; perplexed, but not
driven to despair; 9 persecuted, but [s]not forsaken; [t]struck down, but not destroyed; 10 [u]always
carrying in the body the death of Jesus, [v]so that the life of Jesus may also be manifested
in our bodies. 11 For we who live are always being given over to death for Jesus' sake, so
that the life of Jesus also may be manifested in our mortal flesh. 12 So [w]death is at work in
us, but life in you.
13 Since we have [x]the same spirit of faith according to what has been written, [y]"I believed,
and so I spoke," we also believe, and so we also speak, 14 knowing that [z]he who raised the
Lord Jesus [a]will raise us also with Jesus and [b]bring us with you into his presence. 15 For

[1] *Or reflecting the glory of the Lord* [2] Greek *as we have received mercy* [3] Greek *to walk in* [4] Greek *bondservants*

18 [v]Rom. 8:29; 1 Cor. 15:49 [w][Ps. 84:7]

Chapter 4

1 [x]See ch. 3:6 [y]1 Cor. 7:25; 1 Tim. 1:13
2 [z]See Rom. 6:21 [a]ch. 2:17 [b]ch. 6:7; 7:14 [c]ch. 5:11, 12
3 [d][ch. 3:14] [e][Matt. 13:15] [f]ch. 2:15; 1 Cor. 1:18; 2 Thess. 2:10
4 [g]See John 12:31 [d][See ver. 3 above] [h]ver. 6; See Acts 26:18 [i]See ch. 3:18 [j]Col. 1:15; [Phil. 2:6; Heb. 1:3]
5 [k][1 Thess. 2:6] [l]1 Cor. 9:19; See ch. 1:24
6 [m]Gen. 1:3 [n]2 Pet. 1:19 [o]ver. 4
7 [p]2 Tim. 2:20; [ch. 5:1; Job 10:9; 13:12; Lam. 4:2; 1 Thess. 4:4; 1 Pet. 3:7] [q]1 Cor. 2:5; [Judg. 7:2]
8 [r]ch. 7:5; [Ps. 129:2]
9 [s]Heb. 13:5; [Deut. 4:31] [t]Ps. 37:24; Prov. 24:16; Mic. 7:8
10 [u]ch. 6:9; 1 Cor. 4:9; 15:31; [ch. 1:5, 9; Rom. 6:5; 8:36] [v]2 Tim. 2:11; [Rom. 5:10; 6:8]
12 [w][ch. 13:9]
13 [x]1 Cor. 12:9; 2 Pet. 1:1 [y]Cited from Ps. 116:10
14 [z]1 Thess. 4:14; See Acts 2:24 [a]ch. 1:9 [b][Jude 24]

4:1–6:13 *Paul's Encouragement in His Ministry.* Paul explains why, despite his life of affliction as an apostle of Christ, he does not lose heart in his ministry (4:1, 16; 5:6). He then goes on to define further (5:11–6:2) and support (6:3–13) the message and character of the new covenant ministry itself.

4:1–6 *The New Covenant Dawning of the New Creation.* In spite of those who reject his gospel, Paul does not lose heart in his ministry because through it God is bringing about the beginning of the new creation amid this fallen world.

4:2 Because Paul is not motivated in his ministry by money (2:17), and because he does not crave human approval (Gal. 1:10), Paul refused to **tamper** (a word also used of wine merchants diluting their wares) **with God's word** by watering it down or changing it to suit what people want to hear (cf. 2 Tim. 4:3). Rather, Paul's **open statement of the truth** commends him to **everyone's conscience in the sight of God** as judge (cf. 2 Cor. 2:17; 7:12; 12:19) and shows that he does not proclaim a "secret" or hidden gospel only to a select inner group. Three times in this letter Paul refuses to commend himself by external evidence (see 3:1; 5:12; 10:18), while three times he does commend himself by pointing to his own conduct, although each time he attributes it to the mercy of God (4:2; 6:4; 12:11).

4:3–5 If our gospel is veiled refers to the hardened heart that causes one to be separated from God's presence and makes it impossible to recognize Jesus as the Messiah (see 3:12–15). **The god of this world** refers to Satan. **the light of the gospel of the glory of Christ, who is the image of God**. The gospel illumines how Christ's death on the cross makes it possible for God's people to be in his presence, having been transformed by God's presence and not destroyed by it (see 3:18). This gospel is both proclaimed and embodied by Paul (see 1 Cor. 2:1–5). Thus Paul *preaches* the crucified Christ as **Lord** (the gospel), and Paul himself *lives out* the gospel in the service of his hearers—that is, as an embodiment of the gospel in his own Christlike "slavery" to the needs of his people. See further the contrast between Paul's attitudes and actions and those of his opponents (2 Cor. 11:4).

4:6 Paul uses the provision of **light** in Gen. 1:3 to picture conversion as the dawning of the new creation amid this fallen world. **the glory of God in the face of Jesus Christ**. To know the glory of Christ (2 Cor. 4:4) is to encounter the life-transforming glory of God.

4:7–18 *The New Covenant Power of the Resurrection.* In spite of his suffering as an apostle, Paul does not lose heart (v. 16) because the same power that raised Jesus from the dead enables him to endure adversity (vv. 7–12), reveals the power of God (vv. 7, 11–12), and provides a sure sign that he will experience the resurrection at the end of the age (vv. 16–18).

4:7 treasure. A reference to the "knowledge of the glory of God in the face of Christ" (v. 6) as the content of the gospel (v. 4). **jars of clay**. A common metaphor in the ancient world for human weakness (see Ps. 31:12; Isa. 30:14). This verse thus restates the central thesis of 2 Corinthians as seen in 1:3–11 and 2:14–17: God triumphs amid human weakness, embodying the principle of Christ's crucifixion (cf. 1 Cor. 1:27; 2 Cor. 10:3; 11:30; 12:5, 9; 13:4, 9).

4:8–10 afflicted . . . but not crushed. These verses show the paradox of living as a believer in the present evil age.

4:11–12 Paul is **always being given over** by God **to death for Jesus' sake** so that the power of the resurrection **life of Jesus** (experienced in Paul's ability to endure adversity and in the powerful spread of the gospel in spite of opposition) might be made known in the weakness of his **mortal flesh** (see v. 7). Paul's suffering and endurance are intended to bring about this same resurrection **life** among the Corinthians as they too learn to trust God amid adversity (see 1:6–7).

4:13 we have. These words signal that Paul is summarizing what he has just said (cf. "we have" and "having" in 3:4, 12; 4:1, 7). **the same spirit of faith**. Most interpreters have understood this not as a reference to the Holy Spirit but as a reference to the same kind of attitude of trust in God that David had, in spite of his affliction (see Ps. 116:10). Some hold, however, that this is a reference to the Holy Spirit, since the Holy Spirit is the one who creates faith, who conforms one to Christ, and who secures the promises of God (see 2 Cor. 1:22; 3:6–8, 18; 5:5). In this case, Paul's quotation of Ps. 116:10 would suggest that he views his experience of suffering (as reported in 2 Cor. 4:7–15) as a continuation of the experience of suffering as a righteous person that David expressed in Psalm 116.

15[c][ch. 1:6]; See Rom. 8:28 [d][ch. 1:11; 9:11, 12] [e]ch. 8:19
16[f]See Acts 20:24 [g]See Rom. 7:22 [h][Isa. 40:30, 31]; See Rom. 12:2
17[i]Rom. 8:18; 1 Pet. 1:6; 5:10; [Ps. 30:5; Isa. 54:7]
18[j]ch. 5:7; Rom. 8:24; Heb. 11:1, 13
Chapter 5
1[k]2 Pet. 1:13, 14 [l]See ch. 4:7 [m]Mark 14:58
2[n]Rom. 8:23 [o][1 Cor. 15:53, 54]
4[p]1 Cor. 15:54
5[q][Rom. 8:23]; See ch. 1:22
6[r][Heb. 11:13, 14]
7[s][John 20:29]; See ch. 4:18 [t]1 Cor. 13:12
8[u][Phil. 1:23]
9[v][Col. 1:10; 1 Thess. 4:1]
10[w]Matt. 25:31, 32; [Rom. 14:10]; See Acts 10:42

[c]it is all for your sake, so that as [d]grace extends to more and more people it may increase
thanksgiving, [e]to the glory of God.
16 So we do not lose heart. [f]Though our outer self[1] is wasting away, [g]our inner self [h]is
being renewed day by day. 17 For [i]this light momentary affliction is preparing for us an
eternal weight of glory beyond all comparison, 18 [j]as we look not to the things that are
seen but to the things that are unseen. For the things that are seen are transient, but the
things that are unseen are eternal.

Our Heavenly Dwelling

5 For we know that if [k]the tent that is [l]our earthly home is destroyed, we have a building from God, [m]a house not made with hands, eternal in the heavens. 2 For in this tent
[n]we groan, longing to [o]put on our heavenly dwelling, 3 if indeed by putting it on[2] we may
not be found naked. 4 For while we are still in this tent, we groan, being burdened—not
that we would be unclothed, but that we would be further clothed, so that what is mortal
[p]may be swallowed up by life. 5 He who has prepared us for this very thing is God, [q]who
has given us the Spirit as a guarantee.
6 So we are always of good courage. We know that [r]while we are at home in the body we
are away from the Lord, 7 for [s]we walk by faith, not [t]by sight. 8 Yes, we are of good courage,
and we [u]would rather be away from the body and at home with the Lord. 9 So whether we
are at home or away, we make it our aim to [v]please him. 10 For [w]we must all appear before

[1] Greek *man* [2] Some manuscripts *putting it off*

4:16 outer self . . . inner self. This refers to the weakening of the physical body in contrast with the strengthening of the spirit, and also assumes a contrast between Paul's life of suffering in this present evil age (his outer self) and the moral and spiritual transformation of his life into the image of God as seen in Christ (his inner self; see 3:18). For the inner/outer contrast in reference to the believer's moral transformation amid worldly evil, see Rom. 6:5–6; Eph. 3:16; 4:20–24; Col. 3:5–14.

4:17–18 Earlier Paul's suffering was a burden too heavy to carry (Gk. *bareō*, 1:8), but now it is a **light momentary affliction** in view of the **eternal weight** (Gk. *baros*) **of glory beyond all comparison** (see Rom. 8:18). Far from harming him permanently, the affliction **is preparing** him to receive great eternal reward. Affliction does not by itself bring this benefit, however, but only as it is seen in the light of God's eternal perspective, **as we look not to the things that are seen** (i.e., Paul's suffering and all the shortcomings of this present age) but to **the things that are unseen** (the full restoration of all things at the resurrection to come, and the sure fulfillment of God's purposes for history). **transient . . . eternal**. This contrast shows that "eternal" (lit., belonging to or characterized by the "age" [Gk. *aiōnios*] to come) refers not to timelessness but to that which lasts forever.

5:1–10 *The New Covenant Motivation for the Life of Faith.* In spite of the fact that Paul longs to be "at home" with the Lord, he does not lose heart while he is away from the Lord (vv. 6, 8). His confidence in the future resurrection and in the reality of the judgment to come keeps him faithful in the present as he pursues his goal of pleasing Christ.

5:1 The tent that is our earthly home refers to present human bodies that will die. **Have** refers to the future resurrection, and the **building from God . . . eternal in the heavens** refers to the resurrection body believers will receive on the last day (cf. 1 Thess. 4:13–18; Rev. 21:1–22:5). The tent analogy was quite apt since Paul made tents while living in Corinth (Acts 18:3), and the Corinthians likely sold tents to sailors or used them for housing visitors attending the Isthmian Games.

5:2–4 Paul groans for the resurrection (i.e., being **further clothed**; cf. v. 1) in order to **not be found naked** or **unclothed**, which likely refers to the intermediate state in which believers' spirits are with God but they do not yet enjoy their resurrected bodies.

5:5 the Spirit as a guarantee. The presence of the Spirit in Christians' lives now is the down payment or guarantee that they will receive resurrection bodies when Jesus returns.

5:6 at home . . . away. See note on v. 8.

5:7 by faith, not by sight. This is not a reference to believing the unbelievable but to living all of one's life based on confident trust in God's promises for the future, even when one cannot yet see the fullness of the coming glory (4:18–5:1).

5:8 Away from the body and at home with the Lord refers to the "intermediate state" between a Christian's death and the resurrection of all believers' bodies on the day Christ returns. Paul means that when he dies, though his physical body will be buried here on earth, he expects that he (as a "spirit" or "soul" without a body) will go immediately into the presence of Christ, and will be present with Christ in that condition until the day of resurrection (cf. Luke 23:43; Phil. 1:23; Heb. 12:23).

5:9 we make it our aim to please him. Paul lives his entire life in light of a hope that his actions will bring delight to God day by day. It is possible for Christians to please or displease God in their daily actions (cf. Eph. 5:10; Phil. 4:18; Col. 3:20; Heb. 13:21; by contrast, Paul fears displeasing God; see 2 Cor. 5:11; also Eph. 4:30).

5:10 the judgment seat of Christ. The "judgment seat" (Gk. *bēma*) was the tribunal bench in the Roman courtroom, where the governor sat while rendering judicial verdicts. Remains of such a *bēma* exist in the Corinthian forum today (see Acts 18:12–17 and Introduction to 1 Corinthians: The Ancient City of Corinth). In the coming age, Christ will judge as God the Father's representative, ruling the kingdom the Father has given him (see Rom. 14:10–12; etc.). **so that each one may receive what is due for what he has done . . . whether good or evil**. This underscores the principle that present-day actions have eternal consequences. All Christians will appear before the eternal judgment seat of Christ, to receive "what is due" to them for the deeds that they have done in their earthly life. It is debated, however, (1) whether the aim of this judgment is to determine the measure of reward that the Christian will receive in the age to come; or (2) whether the aim is to provide demonstrative evidence regarding who is lost and who is saved. Because the context of Paul's statement refers back to both the believer's hope for the resurrection (see 2 Cor. 5:1, 4) and to the reward of "glory beyond all comparison" (see 4:16–18), it would seem that both aims are in view. Thus, with regard to the first case, many interpreters hold that the believer's deeds will provide public evidence to indicate the measure of rewards that the believer will receive, corresponding to the believer's "obedience of faith" (acts of service, love, and righteousness; cf. Rom. 1:5; 16:26). In the second case, some interpreters hold that the believer's deeds will also provide public evidence brought forth before the judgment seat of Christ to demonstrate that one's faith is real—that is, public evidence, not as the *basis* for salvation, but as a *demonstration* of the genuineness of one's faith. Paul therefore makes it his aim to "please" Christ (2 Cor. 5:5–9), because the extent to which one does this corresponds to the measure of rewards that one will receive (see Matt. 6:20; Luke 19:17, 19; 1 Cor. 3:12–15; 1 Tim. 6:19; Rev. 22:12), likewise giving evidence for the genuineness of one's faith. Paul is confident that

the judgment seat of Christ, [x]so that each one may receive what is due for what he has
done in the body, whether good or evil.

The Ministry of Reconciliation

11 Therefore, knowing [y]the fear of the Lord, we persuade others. But [z]what we are is
known to God, and I hope it is known also to your conscience. 12 [a]We are not commending
ourselves to you again but [b]giving you cause to boast about us, so that you may be able
to answer those who boast about outward appearance and not about what is in the heart.
13 For if we [c]are beside ourselves, it is for God; if we are in our right mind, it is for you.
14 For the love of Christ [d]controls us, because we have concluded this: that [e]one has died
for all, therefore all have died; 15 and he died for all, [f]that those who live might no longer
live for themselves but [g]for him who for their sake died and was raised.
16 From now on, therefore, [h]we regard no one according to the flesh. Even though we
once regarded Christ according to the flesh, we regard him thus no longer. 17 Therefore,
if anyone is [i]in Christ, he is [j]a new creation.[1] [k]The old has passed away; behold, the new
has come. 18 All this is from God, [l]who through Christ reconciled us to himself and gave
us [m]the ministry of reconciliation; 19 that is, in Christ God was reconciling[2] the world to
himself, [n]not counting their trespasses against them, and entrusting to us [m]the message
of reconciliation. 20 Therefore, [o]we are ambassadors for Christ, [p]God making his appeal
through us. We implore you on behalf of Christ, be reconciled to God. 21 [q]For our sake he

[1] Or *creature* [2] Or *God was in Christ, reconciling*

10 [x]See Ps. 62:12
11 [y][Job 31:23; Acts 9:31; Heb. 10:31; Jude 23] [z]ch. 4:2
12 [a]See ch. 3:1 [b][ch. 1:14]
13 [c]ch. 11:1, 16, 17; 12:6, 11
14 [d]Acts 18:5 [e]Rom. 5:15
15 [f][Rom. 6:11, 12]; See Rom. 14:7 [g][ch. 12:10]
16 [h][Gal. 2:6; Phil. 3:7, 8; Col. 2:11; 1 Tim. 5:21]
17 [i]ch. 12:2; Rom. 16:7; Gal. 1:22 [j][John 3:3]; See Rom. 6:4 [k]Isa. 43:18, 19; Rev. 21:5; [Isa. 65:17; Eph. 2:15; 4:24; Heb. 8:13]
18 [l]Col. 1:20; See Rom. 5:10; 1 John 2:2 [m]Rom. 5:11
19 [n]Ps. 32:2; Rom. 4:8 [m][See ver. 18 above]
20 [o]Eph. 6:20; [Mal. 2:7; Gal. 4:14] [p]ch. 6:1
21 [q]Rom. 8:3; Gal. 3:13; See Rom. 4:25

genuine believers will pass Christ's judgment, since the new covenant ministry of reconciliation has brought them under the life-transforming power of the Spirit—based on the forgiveness of their sins through faith in Christ alone, all of which is the result of God's grace alone (see 2 Cor. 1:12, 22; 3:6, 8–9, 18; 4:4–6, 15; 5:5, 14–15, 16–21; 8:19; 9:8, 14; etc.).

5:11–6:2 *The New Covenant Ministry of Reconciliation.* Paul offers one of his most extensive descriptions of the motivation (5:11–15), content (5:16–19), and call of the new covenant ministry.

5:11 the fear of the Lord. Cf. 7:1; see note on Acts 9:31.

5:12 On Paul's **commending** himself, see note on 4:2. Paul writes so that the Corinthians will be able to respond to false teachers who do not operate on the basis of a new covenant ministry.

5:13 if we are beside ourselves . . . if we are in our right mind. This possibly responds to Corinthian mockery of Paul as crazy; certainly it draws a contrast between Paul's own, private experiences in worship and prayer (see 12:1–4) and his being sober (Gk. *sōphroneō*, "being in a right mind") while also being passionate in his ministry. Since Paul's motivation is to please Christ (5:9), his priority in public is to persuade others (v. 11b), not to seek or urge others to seek exotic religious experiences.

5:14–15 one has died for all, therefore all have died. By Christ's death, the death penalty for sin (see Gen. 2:17) has been paid for all those who trust in him (see Rom. 3:21–26; 5:6–8; 1 Cor. 15:3; Gal. 3:13), and God counts their old life as ended, thus freeing them from any future penal claims. **he died for all, that those who live might no longer live for themselves but for him**. As a consequence of Christ's death, the power of sin in one's life (see Gen. 3:1–7) has also been broken for all those who trust in Christ (cf. Rom. 6:1–14). Christ's cross therefore frees the believer for a new way of life, exemplified by Paul himself as one that **the love of Christ controls** (see Titus 2:11–14).

5:16 Regard no one according to the flesh, that is, according to worldly standards and values that derive from living as if one's present physical life is all that matters. Before Paul's conversion, he **once regarded Christ according to the flesh**, i.e., Paul considered Christ to be a false messiah (according to Jewish standards), viewing his suffering and death as the curse of God (see Deut. 21:23; Gal. 3:13).

5:17 new creation. The redemption of a people who now live for Christ by living for others, effected by the power of the Spirit (3:3, 6, 18) and the death of Christ (5:14–15), is the beginning of the new creation that was destined to come amid this evil age (see Isa. 43:18–19; 65:17–23; 66:22–23). This new creation is also the beginning of Israel's final restoration from God's judgment in the exile (see the context of Isa. 43:1–21; 65:17–25).

5:18–20 reconciliation. An expression of the significance of God's saving activity in Christ that is unique to Paul (see Rom. 5:10–11; 11:15; Eph. 2:16; Col. 1:20, 22). These verses outline (1) the *basis* of Paul's apostolic ministry of the new covenant (Paul's own reconciliation to God through Christ); (2) its *consequence* (his ministry and message of reconciliation to the world for Christ); (3) its essential *content* (the forgiveness of sins by virtue of Christ's death); and (4) its *call* (**on behalf of Christ, be reconciled to God**). **ambassadors for Christ**. Paul is sent as God's prophetic minister of the new covenant (2 Cor. 3:4–6) to announce God's "peace treaty" (cf. Isa. 53:5) with those who will trust in Christ to free them from the penalty and power of sin (2 Cor. 5:14–15; see Isa. 52:6–10; Rom. 10:15). "Be reconciled to God" is a summary of the gospel message Paul proclaims to unbelievers; it is a call to receive the reconciliation that God has wrought (Rom. 5:11).

5:21 This verse is one of the most important in all of Scripture for understanding the meaning of the atonement and justification. Here we see that the one **who knew no sin** is Jesus Christ (v. 20) and that **he** (God) **made him** (Christ) **to be sin** (Gk. *hamartia*, "sin"). This means that God the Father made Christ to be *regarded and treated* as "sin" even though Christ himself never sinned (Heb. 4:15; cf. Gal. 3:13). Further, we see that God did this **for our sake**—that is, God regarded and treated "our" sin (the sin of all who would believe in Christ) as if our sin belonged not to us but to Christ himself. Thus Christ "died for all" (2 Cor. 5:14) and, as Peter wrote, "He himself bore our sins in his body on the tree" (1 Pet. 2:24). In becoming sin "for our sake," Christ became our substitute—that is, Christ took our sin upon himself and, as our substitute, thereby bore the wrath of God (the punishment that we deserve) in our place ("for our sake"). Thus the technical term for this foundational doctrine of the Christian faith is the *substitutionary atonement*—that Christ has provided the atoning sacrifice as "our" substitute, for the sins of all who believe (cf. Rom. 3:23–25). The background for this is Isaiah 53 from the Greek (Septuagint) translation of the Hebrew OT, which includes the most lengthy and detailed OT prophecy of Christ's death and which contains numerous parallels to 2 Cor. 5:21. Isaiah's prophecy specifically uses the Greek word for "sin" (Gk. *hamartia*) five times (as indicated below in italics) with reference to the coming Savior (the suffering servant) in just a few verses—e.g., "surely he has born our *griefs*" (Isa. 53:4); "He was crushed for our *iniquities*" (Isa. 53:5); "the LORD has laid on him the *iniquity* of us all" (Isa. 53:6); "he shall bear their *iniquities*" (Isa. 53:11); "he bore the *sin* of many" (Isa. 53:12). In a precise fulfillment of this prophecy, Christ became "sin" for those who believe in him, **so that in him we might become the righteousness of God**. This means that just as God imputed our sin and guilt to Christ ("he made him to be sin") so God also imputes the righteousness of Christ—a righteousness that is not our own—to all who believe in Christ. Because Christ bore the sins of those who believe, God *regards and treats* believers as having the legal status of "righteousness"

made him to be sin [r]who knew no sin, so that in him we might become [s]the righteousness of God.

6 [t]Working together with him, then, [u]we appeal to you [v]not to receive the grace of God
in vain. **2** For he says,

> [w]"In a favorable time I listened to you,
> and in a day of salvation I have helped you."

Behold, [x]now is the [y]favorable time; behold, now is the day of salvation. **3** We [z]put no
obstacle in anyone's way, so that no fault may be found with our ministry, **4** but [a]as servants
of God we commend ourselves in every way: [b]by great endurance, [c]in afflictions, [d]hardships,
calamities, **5** [e]beatings, imprisonments, [f]riots, labors, sleepless nights, hunger; **6** [g]by purity,
[h]knowledge, patience, kindness, [i]the Holy Spirit, [j]genuine love; **7** by [k]truthful speech, and
[l]the power of God; with [m]the weapons of righteousness for the right hand and for the left;
8 through honor and dishonor, [n]through slander and praise. We are treated as impostors,
and yet are true; **9** as unknown, and [o]yet well known; [p]as dying, and behold, we live; [q]as
punished, and yet not killed; **10** [r]as sorrowful, yet always rejoicing; [s]as poor, yet making
many rich; [t]as having nothing, [u]yet possessing everything.
11 We have spoken freely to you,[1] Corinthians; [v]our heart is wide open. **12** You are not
restricted by us, but [w]you are restricted in your own affections. **13** [x]In return (I speak [y]as to
children) widen your hearts also.

The Temple of the Living God

14 [z]Do not be unequally yoked with unbelievers. For [a]what partnership has righteousness
with lawlessness? Or [b]what fellowship has light with darkness? **15** [c]What accord has Christ

[1] Greek *Our mouth is open to you*

21 [r]See 1 Pet. 2:22 [s]See Rom. 1:17; 1 Cor. 1:30

Chapter 6

1 [t]Mark 16:20; 1 Cor. 3:9; [Acts 15:4] [u]ch. 5:20 [v][Heb. 12:15]
2 [w]Cited from Isa. 49:8 [x][Ps. 32:6; 69:13; Isa. 55:6; Heb. 3:13] [y][Luke 4:19]
3 [z]See 1 Cor. 8:13; 9:12
4 [a][1 Thess. 3:2; 2 Tim. 2:24, 25]; See ch. 3:6 [b]ch. 12:12; 2 Tim. 3:10 [c]Acts 9:16 [d]ch. 12:10
5 [e]ch. 11:23-27; Acts 16:23 [f]Acts 17:5
6 [g]1 Thess. 2:10 [h]ch. 11:6 [i]Rom. 15:19; 1 Thess. 1:5 [j]Rom. 12:9; [James 3:17]
7 [k]Eph. 1:13; Col. 1:5 [l]See 1 Cor. 2:5 [m]ch. 10:4; Eph. 6:11-17
8 [n]Rom. 3:8
9 [o][ch. 11:6] [p]See ch. 4:10 [q]Ps. 118:18
10 [r]John 16:22; [ch. 7:4] [s][ch. 8:9; Prov. 13:7; 1 Cor. 1:5] [t]Acts 3:6 [u]1 Cor. 7:30
11 [v]ch. 7:3; [ch. 11:11; 12:15; Ps. 119:32]
12 [w]ch. 7:2
13 [x][Gal. 4:12] [y]1 Cor. 4:14
14 [z]Deut. 7:3; Josh. 23:12; Ezra 9:2; Neh. 13:25; [1 Cor. 7:39] [a]Eph. 5:7, 11; 1 John 1:6 [b]See Acts 26:18
15 [c][1 Cor. 10:21]

(Gk. *dikaiosynē*). This righteousness belongs to believers because they are "in him," that is, "in Christ" (e.g., Rom. 3:22; 5:18; 1 Cor. 1:30; 2 Cor. 5:17, 19; Phil. 3:9). Therefore "the righteousness of God" (which is imputed to believers) is also the righteousness of Christ—that is, the righteousness and the legal status that belongs to Christ as a result of Christ having lived as one who "knew no sin." This then is the heart of the doctrine of *justification*: God *regards* (or *counts*) believers as forgiven and God *declares* and *treats* them as forgiven, because God the Father has imputed the believer's sin to Christ and because God the Father likewise imputes Christ's righteousness to the believer. (See further notes on Rom. 4:6–8; 5:18; 10:3; 10:6–8; see also Isa. 53:11: "the righteous one, my servant, [shall] make many to be accounted righteous").

6:1 The **grace of God** comes about solely through the death of Christ (5:14–19). Those who turn back from Christ show that their initial, apparent reception of God's grace was not real but **in vain**.

6:2 By quoting Isa. 49:8 to summarize his own appeal to the Corinthians, Paul identifies his apostolic ministry with Isaiah's prophetic role of calling Israel to repentance and perseverance in view of the coming **day** of redemption and judgment (**salvation**). **Behold, now**. Paul declares that this time of salvation has already arrived in Christ! Amazingly, God is already pouring out many of the blessings of the age to come.

6:3–13 *The New Covenant Support for the Legitimacy of Paul's Ministry.* For the Corinthians, being reconciled to God involves affirming Paul's ministry as God's coworker (5:18–6:2) and submitting to what Paul tells them (6:13). As he did in 1:3–11; 2:14–17; and 4:7–12 (see also 11:23–33; 12:7–10), Paul defends his ministry as an apostle by once again calling attention to his faithfulness amid the changing circumstances of his apostolic life. Paul's ministry reflects God's power in spite of human weakness.

6:4 we commend ourselves in every way. Not only through victories and triumphs but also by the way he endures hardship, Paul gives testimony to the truthfulness of his apostolic ministry. The glory of the gospel shines forth from a Christian's life in the way he responds to suffering and opposition. See note on 4:2. **by great endurance**. Paul's divinely enabled endurance is his general testimony to the power of the Spirit in his life and ministry (3:3–8; see 12:12), which is then illustrated by the specific examples that follow (6:4b–10). **servants of God**. As a minister (Gk. *diakonos*) of the new covenant (3:6), Paul is a servant (Gk. *diakonos*) of God.

6:7 Weapons of righteousness for the right hand and for the left is best seen as a reference to the spiritual weapons God provides (see Eph. 6:11), perhaps meaning one for offense, usually a sword (on the right; see Eph. 6:17), and one for defense, usually a shield (on the left; see Eph. 6:16). Others understand Paul's phrase not as limited to two weapons but as a way of saying that he is fully equipped with spiritual power for any situation.

6:13 Paul calls those Corinthians still in rebellion against him, as his spiritual **children** (see 1 Cor. 4:14–15; 2 Cor. 12:14–15), to respond to him in the way he has responded to them.

6:14–7:1 *Paul's Call for Church Discipline as an Expression of Repentance.* This section brings Paul's argument in 2:14–7:1 to its culmination by giving the second, concrete application of what it will mean for the Corinthians to "widen [their] hearts" toward Paul (6:13) amid the current controversy in Corinth.

6:14 Do not be unequally yoked with unbelievers. This command, which is Paul's main point in 6:14–7:1, will be restated in different words at the end of the section (7:1). To be "unequally yoked" is to be "hitched up" or even crossbred with another animal who is not the same (Gk. *heterozygeō*; the related adjective is found in Lev. 19:19; see also Deut. 22:10, though the word does not occur there). It is thus an image for being allied or identified wrongly with unbelievers. In context, it refers especially to those who are still rebelling against Paul within the church, whom Paul now shockingly labels unbelievers (he clearly thinks it possible that some are [2 Cor. 13:5], though he hopes not), but the principle has wider application to other situations where (as with animals yoked together) one person's conduct and direction of life strongly influences or controls the other's.

6:15 Belial (Gk. *Beliar*, also spelled *Belial*, from a Hb. term meaning "worthlessness" or possibly "destruction"). This name for Satan is not found elsewhere in the OT or NT but was used in the Judaism of Paul's day. Derived from one of Satan's characteristics (i.e., that he is "worthless" or "treacherous"; see the same word in Deut. 13:13; 15:9; Judg. 19:22; 1 Kings 21:13; etc.), it was often used in contexts that stress Satan's activity as an opponent of God, which fits Paul's concern with his opponents.

with Belial?[1] Or what portion does a believer share with an unbeliever? 16 What agreement
has the temple of God with idols? For [d]we are the temple of the living God; as God said,

[e]"I will make my dwelling among them and [f]walk among them,
and [g]I will be their God,
and they shall be my people.
17 Therefore [h]go out from their midst,
and be separate from them, says the Lord,
and touch no unclean thing;
then I will welcome you,
18 [i]and I will be a father to you,
and you shall be sons and daughters to me,
says the Lord Almighty."

7 Since we have these promises, beloved, [j]let us cleanse ourselves from every defilement
of body[2] and spirit, bringing holiness to completion in the fear of God.

Paul's Joy

2 [k]Make room in your hearts[3] for us. [l]We have wronged no one, we have corrupted no
one, we have taken advantage of no one. 3 I do not say this to condemn you, for I said
before that [m]you are in our hearts, to die together and to live together. 4 I am acting with
[n]great boldness toward you; [o]I have great pride in you; [p]I am filled with comfort. In all
our affliction, I am overflowing with joy.
5 For even [q]when we came into Macedonia, our bodies had no rest, but we were afflicted
at every turn—[r]fighting without and fear within. 6 But [s]God, who comforts the downcast,
[t]comforted us by the coming of Titus, 7 and not only by his coming but also by the comfort
with which he was comforted by you, as he told us of your longing, your mourning, your
zeal for me, so that I rejoiced still more. 8 For [u]even if I made you grieve with my letter, I
do not regret it—though [v]I did regret it, for I see that that letter grieved you, though only
for a while. 9 As it is, I rejoice, not because you were grieved, but [w]because you were grieved
into repenting. For you felt a godly grief, so that you suffered no loss through us.
10 For [x]godly grief produces a repentance that leads to salvation without regret, whereas
[y]worldly grief produces death. 11 For see what earnestness this godly grief has produced in

[1] Greek *Beliar* [2] Greek *flesh* [3] Greek lacks *in your hearts*

16 [d][Eph. 2:22]; See 1 Cor. 3:16 [e]Cited from Lev. 26:12; See Ex. 29:45 [f][Rev. 2:1; 21:3] [g]Ex. 6:7; Jer. 31:33; Ezek. 11:20
17 [h]Cited from Isa. 52:11; [ch. 7:1; Ezek. 20:34, 41; Zeph. 3:20; Rev. 18:4]
18 [i][Ex. 4:22; 2 Sam. 7:8, 14; Isa. 43:6; Jer. 31:9; Hos. 1:10; Rev. 21:7]

Chapter 7

1 [j]1 Pet. 2:11; 1 John 3:3
2 [k]ch. 6:12, 13 [l]Acts 20:33; [ch. 11:20]
3 [m][ch. 6:11-13]
4 [n]ch. 3:12 [o]ch. 1:12; 8:24; 9:2 [p]ch. 1:4; Phil. 2:17; Col. 1:24; [ch. 6:10]
5 [q]ch. 2:13 [r][Deut. 32:25; Lam. 1:20]
6 [s]ch. 1:4 [t]ver. 13; [1 Thess. 3:6, 7]
8 [u][ch. 2:2] [v]ch. 2:4
9 [w]Ps. 38:18; [1 Cor. 5:2]
10 [x][2 Sam. 12:13; Acts 11:18] [y][Prov. 17:22]

6:16 idols. See note on Rom. 1:23. **we are the temple of the living God.** The word for temple (Gk. *naos*) refers to the Most Holy Place, where God's presence was manifested over the ark of the covenant, not to the more general temple complex or building (the *hieron*). Since Israel is never identified with the temple, this equation of believers with the Most Holy Place (see also 1 Cor. 3:16) reflects the amazing reality of the new covenant, in which God dwells directly and immediately in the midst of his people, a reality inaugurated by his Spirit (see 2 Cor. 3:3). **as God said.** This one phrase introduces the entire chain of six OT quotations in 6:16c–18, which closes with the parallel expression, "says the Lord Almighty" (v. 18). Taken together, these OT texts support the commands of v. 14 and 7:1. The first quotation is the covenant formula from Lev. 26:11–12, here adapted to the Corinthians by combining it with the new covenant promise of Ezek. 37:27 (thereby changing the original "among you" to **among them**). This adaptation affirms that the Corinthian church is experiencing the fulfillment of the covenant promises first given to Israel.

6:17–18 Therefore. Paul draws out the implications of being the new covenant people of God with three commands from Isa. 52:11 (**go out . . . be separate . . . touch no unclean thing**) and three promises from Ezek. 20:34; 2 Sam. 7:14; and Isa. 43:6 (**I will welcome you . . . I will be a father to you . . . you shall be sons and daughters to me**). Paul's application to the Corinthians of promises originally given to Israel reflects his conviction that the church is the fulfillment of God's covenant people, being restored under the new covenant. The combination of 2 Sam. 7:14 ("I will be a father to you") with Isa. 43:6 ("sons and daughters") indicates that God's promise to become the "father" of David's "son," the Messiah, is expanded to include all of God's people who are adopted into his new covenant "family" (see Mark 3:33–34; cf. 2 Sam. 7:24; Jer. 31:1, 9).

7:1 cleanse ourselves from every defilement of body and spirit, bringing holiness to completion. Holiness involves purification of all aspects of life, including how believers treat and use their physical bodies as well as purity in the realm of their spirits, affecting their inward thoughts and desires. **The fear of God**, i.e., reverent obedience, is the only way of wisdom (Ps. 2:11; Prov. 1:7, 29; 8:13; etc.) for the believer in light of the fatherly discipline of God in this life (Heb. 12:5–11) and the coming judgment (2 Cor. 5:10).

7:2–16 *Paul's Joy over the Repentant Corinthians.* Paul's account of his experience of waiting for Titus (2:12–13) introduced the defense of his apostolic ministry (2:14–7:1), which the resolution of the story in 7:2–16 now concludes.

7:2–4 Paul resumes the exhortation from 6:11–13. The Corinthians are to side with Paul and renounce the false teachers (cf. 6:14–7:1).

7:5 Paul picks up the narrative from 2:13. The intervening section has explained his new covenant ministry.

7:6–9 Paul was comforted by Titus's coming because Titus reported that the Corinthians had fully repented and had turned back to Paul, and therefore back to the gospel. Hence, the grief Paul had inflicted on them was worth it, for it produced repentance.

7:10 godly grief. Grief that comes from God is characterized by **repentance**, i.e., remorse caused by having lost God's approval and the consequent resolve to reverse one's conduct and live for God (5:6–10, 15). **worldly grief.** Grief that comes from the world, i.e., a remorse brought about by losing the world's approval, leads to a resolve to regain that approval, and this **produces death**, or divine judgment.

7:11–12 The Corinthians' response to the letter Paul **wrote to** them demonstrated that they truly belonged to God. **in the sight of God.** All of the

11[z][ch. 2:6]
12[a][1 Cor. 5:1, 2]
13[b]ver. 6 [c]See Rom. 15:32
14[d]ch. 8:24; 9:2; 10:8; [2 Thess. 1:4] [e]ch. 4:2; 6:7
15[f]ch. 2:9; 10:6
16[g]See ch. 2:3
Chapter 8
1[h]ver. 5
2[i][Mark 12:44]
3[j]ver. 11; 1 Cor. 16:2
4[k]ch. 9:2; Rom. 15:25, 26; See Acts 24:17 [l]See Rom. 15:31
5[m]ver. 1
6[n]ver. 17; ch. 12:18 [o]ver. 19; [ver. 4]
7[p]See 1 Cor. 1:5 [q]ch. 9:8
8[r]1 Cor. 7:6
9[s]Phil. 2:6, 7; [ch. 6:10; Matt. 20:28]
10[t]1 Cor. 7:25 [u]Deut. 15:7, 8; Prov. 19:17; 28:27; 1 Tim. 6:18, 19; Heb. 13:16 [v]ch. 9:2
12[w][ch. 9:7; Mark 12:43, 44; Luke 21:3]

you, but also what eagerness to clear yourselves, what indignation, what fear, what longing,
[z]what zeal, what punishment! At every point you have proved yourselves innocent in the
matter. **12** So although I wrote to you, it was not for the sake of the one [a]who did the wrong,
nor for the sake of the one who suffered the wrong, but in order that your earnestness for
us might be revealed to you in the sight of God. **13** Therefore [b]we are comforted.
And besides our own comfort, we rejoiced still more at the joy of Titus, because his spirit
[c]has been refreshed by you all. **14** For [d]whatever boasts I made to him about you, I was not
put to shame. But just as everything we said to you [e]was true, so also our boasting before
Titus has proved true. **15** And his affection for you is even greater, as he remembers [f]the
obedience of you all, how you received him with fear and trembling. **16** I rejoice, because
I have complete [g]confidence in you.

Encouragement to Give Generously

8 We want you to know, brothers,[1] about the grace of God that has been [h]given among
the churches of Macedonia, **2** for in a severe test of affliction, their abundance of joy and
[i]their extreme poverty have overflowed in a wealth of generosity on their part. **3** For they
gave [j]according to their means, as I can testify, and beyond their means, of their own accord,
4 begging us earnestly [k]for the favor[2] of taking part in [l]the relief of the saints— **5** and this,
not as we expected, but they [m]gave themselves first to the Lord and then by the will of God
to us. **6** Accordingly, [n]we urged Titus that as he had started, so he should complete among
you [o]this act of grace. **7** But as [p]you excel in everything—in faith, in speech, in knowledge,
in all earnestness, and in our love for you[3]—[q]see that you excel in this act of grace also.
8 [r]I say this not as a command, but to prove by the earnestness of others that your love also
is genuine. **9** For you know the grace of our Lord Jesus Christ, that [s]though he was rich, yet
for your sake he became poor, so that you by his poverty might become rich. **10** And in this
matter [t]I give my judgment: [u]this benefits you, who [v]a year ago started not only to do this
work but also to desire to do it. **11** So now finish doing it as well, so that your readiness in
desiring it may be matched by your completing it out of what you have. **12** For if the readiness
is there, it is acceptable [w]according to what a person has, not according to what he does not
have. **13** For I do not mean that others should be eased and you burdened, but that as a matter

[1] *Or brothers and sisters* [2] The Greek word *charis* can mean *favor* or *grace* or *thanks*, depending on the context [3] Some manuscripts *in your love for us*

Corinthians' actions are done before an all-seeing God, before whom Paul also carries out his ministry (2:17; 4:2; 12:19).

7:13–14 Paul had boasted to Titus that the Corinthians were truly a work of the Spirit, and their response showed that he was correct.

7:15 with fear and trembling. Paul's description of the Corinthians' response to God's call to obedience (cf. 1 Cor. 2:3; Eph. 6:5; Phil. 2:12).

7:16 The first section of the letter ends with Paul's affirmation of **confidence** that the Corinthians as a body are truly believers, as evidenced by their "repentance that leads to salvation" (v. 10) and their "obedience" (v. 15). Paul's expression of confidence in the Corinthians also includes confidence that they will do what Paul asks, and thus serves as a transition to the topic of chs. 8–9 regarding the collection of a generous gift (9:11) from the church to help the impoverished Christians in Jerusalem. Paul's "complete confidence" in the Corinthians is further supported by the "great confidence" (8:22) of Titus, Paul's "partner and fellow worker" (8:23).

8:1–9:15 *Paul's Appeal to the Repentant Church in Corinth Regarding the Collection.* In view of 7:2–16, Paul calls the repentant (that is, the whole church apart from those who still opposed Paul), under Titus's leadership to complete the collection that they had begun earlier for the suffering believers in Jerusalem (see Rom. 15:25–32; 1 Cor. 16:1–4; Gal. 2:9–10).

8:1–15 *The Collection as the Grace of God.* Paul begins his discussion of the collection by demonstrating how the Corinthians' generosity to the believers in Jerusalem manifests the grace of God in their lives, to the glory of God in the world. The Macedonians are an example to the Corinthians in their generous giving.

8:1 the grace of God . . . given among the churches of Macedonia. A reference to the generosity of the churches in the region of Philippi, Thessalonica, and Berea (see Acts 16:9–17:15; 18:5; 19:21–22, 29; 20:1–4; 27:2). Here and throughout 2 Corinthians 8–9 Paul calls the collection an act of "grace" because contributing to the needs of others is made possible by God's undeserved gifts in their lives (8:1, 4, 6–7, 19; 9:14–15; see also 8:9; 9:8).

8:2–5 God's grace was manifested in that the Macedonians gave even though they were poor. **not as we expected**. What surprised Paul was that the Macedonians also gave **themselves first to the Lord** (a recommitment of their lives) **and then . . . to us**; they offered not only money but also any other personal help they could give to Paul.

8:7 you excel in everything. Though beset by several problems (see 1 Corinthians), the Corinthian church also had strengths (see 2 Cor. 7:4, 16). **faith . . . speech . . . knowledge**. A reference especially to the Corinthians' spiritual gifts (see 1 Cor. 1:5, 7–8; 8:1–7; 12:8–10, 28; 14:6, 9, 19, 39). They showed **earnestness** for Paul and the work of the gospel (cf. 2 Cor. 7:7, 11–12). **you excel** (Gk. *perisseuete*). A reference to following the example of the Macedonians in 8:2, whose "abundance" (Gk. *perisseia*) of joy "overflowed" (Gk. *eperisseusen*) in a wealth of giving.

8:8–10 not as a command. Giving to the Lord's work must be voluntary, not compelled. And when it is voluntary it brings much blessing (cf. 9:5–8). **was rich . . . became poor**. A reference to Christ's preexistent status as the eternal Son of God in heaven (John 1:1–3; Gal. 4:4; Phil. 2:6) and the humility of his incarnation, including his death (Rom. 15:3; Phil. 2:7–8), so that the believer **might become rich** (salvation and all the benefits that flow from it). **this work**. What Christ has done for the Corinthians is to be reflected in what they do for others.

8:12 according to what a person has. Paul did not pressure people to give what they did not have or could not afford to give.

8:13–14 Fairness . . . fairness is in both cases Greek *isotēs*, which can also mean "equality," but in Paul's only other use of the term it means

of fairness 14 your abundance at the present time should supply [x]their need, so that their
abundance may supply your need, that there may be fairness. 15 As it is written, [y]"Whoever
gathered much had nothing left over, and whoever gathered little had no lack."

Commendation of Titus

16 But [z]thanks be to God, [a]who put into the heart of Titus the same earnest care I have
for you. 17 For [b]he not only accepted our appeal, but being himself very earnest he is going[1]
to you of his own accord. 18 With him we are sending[2] [c]the brother who is famous among
[d]all the churches for his preaching of the gospel. 19 And not only that, but he has been
[e]appointed by the churches to travel with us as we carry out this act of [f]grace that is being
ministered by us, [g]for the glory of the Lord himself and to show our good will. 20 We
take this course so that no one should blame us about this generous gift that is being
administered by us, 21 for [h]we aim at what is honorable [i]not only in the Lord's sight but
also in the sight of man. 22 And with them we are sending our brother whom we have
often tested and found earnest in many matters, but who is now more earnest than ever
because of his great confidence in you. 23 As for Titus, he is [j]my partner and fellow worker
for your benefit. And as for our brothers, they are messengers[3] of the churches, the glory
of Christ. 24 So give proof before the churches of your love and of [k]our boasting about
you to these men.

The Collection for Christians in Jerusalem

9 Now [l]it is superfluous for me to write to you about [m]the ministry for the saints, 2 for I
know your readiness, [n]of which I boast about you to the people of Macedonia, saying
that Achaia has been ready [o]since last year. And your zeal has stirred up most of them. 3 But
[p]I am sending[4] the brothers so that our boasting about you may not prove empty in this
matter, so that you may be ready, [q]as I said you would be. 4 Otherwise, if some Macedonians
[r]come with me and find that you are not ready, we would be humiliated—to say nothing
of you—for being so confident. 5 So I thought it necessary to urge the brothers to go on
ahead to you and arrange in advance for the [s]gift[5] you have promised, so that it may be
ready [t]as a willing gift, [u]not as an exaction.[6]

The Cheerful Giver

6 The point is this: [v]whoever sows sparingly will also reap sparingly, and whoever sows
bountifully[7] will also reap bountifully. 7 Each one must give as he has decided in his heart,

[1] Or *he went* [2] Or *we sent;* also verse 22 [3] Greek *apostles* [4] Or *I have sent* [5] Greek *blessing;* twice in this verse [6] Or *a gift expecting something in return;* Greek *greed* [7] Greek *with blessings;* twice in this verse

14 [x]ch. 9:12; [Acts 4:34]
15 [y]Cited from Ex. 16:18
16 [z]See ch. 2:14 [a]Rev. 17:17
17 [b]ver. 6
18 [c]ch. 12:18 [d]See 1 Cor. 7:17
19 [e][1 Cor. 16:3, 4] [f]ver. 6 [g]ch. 4:15
21 [h]See Rom. 12:17 [i][Rom. 14:18; Phil. 4:8; 1 Pet. 2:12]
23 [j][Philem. 17]
24 [k]ch. 7:4, 14; 9:2, 3

Chapter 9

1 [l][1 Thess. 4:9] [m]See Rom. 15:25
2 [n]ch. 8:24 [o]ch. 8:10
3 [p]ch. 8:6, 17, 18, 22 [q]1 Cor. 16:2
4 [r][Acts 20:4]
5 [s]Gen. 33:11; Judg. 1:15; 1 Sam. 25:27 [t][Phil. 4:17] [u][ch. 12:17, 18]
6 [v]Prov. 11:24, 25; 22:9; Gal. 6:7, 9; [Mal. 3:10; Luke 6:38]

"with fairness" (Col. 4:1). Paul was not asking all Christians to share their possessions equally, for he did not ask these wealthy Corinthians to send money to the poorer Macedonians (see 2 Cor. 8:2); he simply asked that Corinth do its fair share in meeting the extreme needs of the Christians in Jerusalem. **At the present time** in redemptive history (see 6:2; Rom. 3:26; 8:18; 11:5; Gal. 1:4) the Gentile believers can contribute financially, while the Jewish believers can contribute spiritually with leadership and the ministry of the gospel (cf. Rom. 11:11–12, 25–26, 30–32).

8:15 Like God's provision of manna at the first exodus (Ex. 16:18), the provision at the "second exodus" in Christ has also been equally sufficient between Jews and Gentiles so that each may be able to provide for the other.

8:16–9:5 *The Commendation of Titus and the Brothers.* Paul's coworkers assist him in collecting the gift for Jerusalem.

8:16 Once again, Paul's **thanks . . . to God** begins a new section (cf. 1:3; 2:14), just as his thanksgiving concludes it (9:15; see 1:11).

8:18 The identity of the **famous . . . brother** is unknown.

8:19–22 ministered by us . . . administered by us. This is the same phrase used in 3:3 to describe Paul's new covenant ministry of the Spirit ("delivered by us"), showing that the collection of money for the needy in Jerusalem was an essential part of the apostolic ministry of the gospel. **so that no one should blame us.** As Paul delivers the gift to Jerusalem, he will be accompanied by a team of men well known for their integrity. Their presence will guarantee a public accounting for the gifts and also provide protection from robbers. See chart, p. 2136.

8:23 the glory of Christ. The delegates are equated with the glory of Christ since their love reflects Christ's love for his people (v. 9) and results from their having encountered the glory of God in the face of Christ (3:18; 4:4–6).

9:3 Prove empty (Gk. *kenoō*) belongs to the same stem as the adverb used in 6:1, which there refers to the danger of apparently receiving God's grace in a less than genuine way. Here the danger is that the Corinthians may fail to give generously as Paul had boasted they would (9:2). The implication may be that their failure to give generously would be evidence that their faith was less than genuine, but they would also be missing out on the blessing that is in store for everyone who "sows bountifully" (v. 6).

9:5 be ready as a willing gift, not as an exaction. The word translated "[willing] gift" can also mean "blessing" (Gk. *eulogia*); the collection is to be a response to God's grace in their lives (8:6–9), not something coerced by the fear of judgment.

9:6–15 *Generosity, Joy, and the Glory of God.* The Corinthians' gift will maximize their joy, help fellow believers, and bring honor and praise to God.

9:6 sows bountifully. Paul expands a well-known proverb: "You reap what you sow" (e.g., Job 4:8; Ps. 126:5; Prov. 22:8; Jer. 12:13; Matt. 6:26; John 4:36–37; Gal. 6:7). God does not command Christians to give a certain amount, but he provides opportunities to give generously. Those who sow generously will also **reap bountifully** in terms of bearing fruit for God's kingdom and in other ways as well (2 Cor. 9:11).

9:7–8 God loves (in the sense of "approves of") **a cheerful giver**, an allusion to Prov. 22:9 in the Septuagint (cf. Deut. 15:10; Rom. 12:8). God loves such joy-motivated giving to others because it expresses contentment in

[w]not reluctantly or under compulsion, for [x]God loves a cheerful giver. **8** And [y]God is able
to make all grace abound to you, so that having all sufficiency[1] in all things at all times,
you may abound in every good work. **9** As it is written,

[z]"He has distributed freely, he has given to the poor;
his righteousness endures forever."

10 He who supplies [a]seed to the sower and bread for food will supply and multiply your
seed for sowing and [b]increase the harvest of your righteousness. **11** [c]You will be enriched
in every way to be generous in every way, which [d]through us will produce thanksgiving
to God. **12** For the ministry of this service is not only supplying [e]the needs of the saints
but is also overflowing in many thanksgivings to God. **13** By their approval of this service,
[f]they[2] will glorify God because of your submission that comes from your [g]confession of
the gospel of Christ, and the generosity of your contribution for them and for all others,
14 while they long for you and pray for you, because of the surpassing grace of God upon
you. **15** [h]Thanks be to God for his inexpressible gift!

Paul Defends His Ministry

10 [i]I, Paul, myself entreat you, by the [j]meekness and gentleness of Christ—I who am
humble when face to face with you, but bold toward you when I am away!— **2** I beg
of you [k]that when I am present I may not have to show [l]boldness with such confidence as
I count on showing against some who suspect us of walking according to the flesh. **3** For
though we walk in the flesh, we are not waging war according to the flesh. **4** For the [m]weapons
of [n]our warfare are not of the flesh but have [o]divine power [p]to destroy strongholds. **5** We
destroy arguments and [q]every lofty opinion raised against the knowledge of God, and
take every thought captive to [r]obey Christ, **6** [s]being ready to punish every disobedience,
[t]when your obedience is complete.
7 [u]Look at what is before your eyes. [v]If anyone is confident that he is Christ's, let him
remind himself that just as [w]he is Christ's, [x]so also are we. **8** For even if I boast a little too
much of [y]our authority, which the Lord gave for building you up and not for destroying
you, I will not be ashamed. **9** I do not want to appear to be frightening you with my letters.

7 [w]Deut. 15:10; See ch. 8:12 [x]See Ex. 25:2
8 [y]Phil. 4:19; [Eph. 3:2]
9 [z]Cited from Ps. 112:9
10 [a]Isa. 55:10 [b][Hos. 10:12]
11 [c]1 Cor. 1:5 [d][ch. 1:11]
12 [e]ch. 8:14
13 [f]See Matt. 5:16; 1 Pet. 2:12 [g]1 Tim. 6:12, 13; Heb. 3:1; 4:14; 10:23
15 [h][John 3:16; Eph. 2:8]; See ch. 2:14

Chapter 10

1 [i]See Rom. 12:1 [j]Zech. 9:9; Matt. 11:29; Phil. 2:7, 8
2 [k]ch. 13:2, 10; 1 Cor. 4:18, 21 [l]ver. 6
4 [m]ch. 6:7; [Eph. 6:11; 1 Thess. 5:8] [n]See 1 Cor. 9:7 [o]ch. 13:3, 4; See 1 Cor. 2:5 [p]Jer. 1:10
5 [q][Isa. 2:11, 12] [r]ch. 9:13; [Rom. 5:19]
6 [s]See ver. 2 [t]ch. 2:9; 7:15
7 [u][ch. 5:12; John 7:24] [v][1 Cor. 1:12; 14:37; 1 John 4:6] [w]1 Cor. 3:23 [x][ch. 11:23; 1 Cor. 9:1; Gal. 1:12]
8 [y]ch. 13:10

[1] *Or all contentment* [2] *Or you*

God's gracious giving to the believer (see 2 Cor. 9:14) that makes **every good work** possible and results in thanksgiving and glory to God (see vv. 11–13).

9:9 distributed freely . . . given to the poor. The good work of God's people (v. 8; see 1 Cor. 15:58) corresponds to the description of the man in Ps. 112:9, whose righteousness is manifest in his providing for the poor. **endures forever**. Such righteousness remains beyond the day of judgment because it originates from and is sustained by the Lord's righteousness, expressed in giving to his people, which also "endures forever" (Ps. 111:3).

9:10 The promise that God will **increase the harvest** should not be understood in material terms but in terms of increasing **your righteousness**. Thus the quoted OT texts (Isa. 55:10; Hos. 10:12) refer specifically to the provision of God's word for the redemption of his people. God's promise is that he will use his people and their resources as instruments of his grace for the salvation of others.

9:11 You will be enriched in every way to be generous in every way. God will provide for the Corinthians' needs so that they can continue generously meeting others' needs and giving resources to advance the gospel.

9:12–14 the ministry (Gk. *diakonia*) **of this service** (Gk. *leitourgia*). The collection is an integral part of the ministry of the gospel (cf. 3:7–9; 4:1; 5:18; 6:3) and an act of public worship (cf. also Luke 1:23; Rom. 15:27; Phil. 2:17, 30; Heb. 9:21), which causes others to offer **thanksgivings to God** as they see the work of God's **grace** in the lives of the Corinthians.

9:15 The gift of the Corinthians reflects the **inexpressible gift** God has given to believers in Christ (cf. 8:9; Rom. 8:32).

10:1–13:10 *Paul's Appeal to the Rebellious Minority in Corinth.* In the third major section of his letter, Paul directly appeals to those who are still rejecting his gospel and apostolic authority. For in his third visit, Paul will be forced to judge those who have not repented (10:6; 12:20–21; 13:1–10).

10:1–11 *Paul's Defense of His Humility as an Apostle.* Paul directly responds to those who are criticizing his humble appearance in Corinth (vv. 1–6) and his refusal to employ the professional rhetoric of his day in order to impress others (vv. 7–11; see 1 Cor. 2:1–5).

10:1 the meekness and gentleness of Christ. A reference to Christ's slowness to anger and patience in order to allow time for repentance before he returns to judge (see 2 Pet. 3:8–10), which Paul imitates in his dealings with the Corinthians (1 Cor. 5:1–5; 2 Cor. 1:23–2:4; 7:5–16). **I who am humble when . . . with you, but bold toward you when I am away**. Paul is probably quoting some accusations made by his opponents (see 10:10). Paul is trying to avoid the kind of "consistency" his opponents call for, since it would mean judgment for the Corinthians (see vv. 6, 11).

10:3–4 Paul is not **waging** a fleshly battle but a spiritual one. **The weapons of** his **warfare are not** physical but spiritual, such as prayer, the Word of God, faith, and the power of the Holy Spirit. By the Spirit Paul tears down the **strongholds** of wrong thinking and behavior that are reflected in the lives of those who resist his authority.

10:8 Since Paul's ministry is a fulfillment of Jeremiah's promise of a new covenant (see 3:6), the primary purpose of Paul's authority is **for building you up and not for destroying you**, whereas Jeremiah's primary purpose under the old covenant was just the opposite (see Jer. 1:10; 24:6; 31:27–28; 42:10; 45:4). "Building up" the church is a common Pauline description of new covenant ministry (see Rom. 14:19; 15:2, 20; 1 Cor. 3:9–14; 14:3–5; 1 Thess. 5:11). Paul frames the last section of 2 Corinthians with this theme; cf. 2 Cor. 10:8 with 13:10 (see 12:19).

10:9–11 absent . . . present. See note on v. 1.

10 For they say, "His letters are weighty and strong, but [z]his bodily presence is weak, and
[a]his speech of no account." **11** Let such a person understand that what we say by letter when
absent, we do when present. **12** Not that we dare to classify or [b]compare ourselves with some
of those who [c]are commending themselves. But when they measure themselves by one
another and compare themselves with one another, they are [d]without understanding.
13 But we will not boast [e]beyond limits, but will [f]boast only with regard to the area
of influence God assigned to us, [g]to reach even to you. **14** For we are not overextending
ourselves, as though we did not reach you. [h]For we were the first to come all the way to
you with the gospel of Christ. **15** We do not boast beyond limit in the labors of others. But
our hope is that [i]as your faith increases, our area of influence among you may be [j]greatly
enlarged, **16** so that we may preach the gospel in lands beyond you, without boasting of
work already done in another's area of influence. **17** "Let [k]the one who boasts, boast in
the Lord." **18** For it is [l]not the one who commends himself who is approved, but the one
[m]whom the Lord commends.

Paul and the False Apostles

11 I wish you would bear with me in a little foolishness. Do bear with me! **2** For I feel
a divine jealousy for you, since [n]I betrothed you to one husband, [o]to present you
[p]as a pure virgin to Christ. **3** But I am afraid that [q]as the serpent deceived Eve by his cunning, your thoughts [r]will be led astray from a [s]sincere and [t]pure devotion to Christ. **4** For if
someone comes and [u]proclaims another Jesus than the one we proclaimed, or if you receive
a different spirit from the one you received, or if you accept [v]a different gospel from the
one you accepted, you put up with it readily enough. **5** Indeed, I consider that [w]I am not in
the least inferior to these super-apostles. **6** [x]Even if I am unskilled in speaking, [y]I am not so
in knowledge; indeed, in every way [z]we have made this plain to you in all things.
7 Or [a]did I commit a sin in humbling myself so that you might be exalted, because [b]I
preached God's gospel to you free of charge? **8** I robbed other churches by accepting sup-

10 [z]ch. 11:21; [ch. 12:7] [a]See 1 Cor. 1:17
12 [b]1 Cor. 2:13 [c]ver. 18; ch. 3:1; 12:6; [Prov. 27:2] [d][Prov. 26:12]
13 [e]ver. 15 [f]See Rom. 12:3 [g][Rom. 15:20]
14 [h]1 Cor. 3:5; 4:15; 9:1
15 [i]2 Thess. 1:3 [j][Acts 5:13]
17 [k]1 Cor. 1:31; [Jer. 9:23, 24]
18 [l]See ver. 12 [m]Rom. 2:29; 1 Cor. 4:5

Chapter 11

2 [n][Hos. 2:19, 20] [o]Col. 1:22, 28 [p]Eph. 5:27; Rev. 14:4
3 [q]Gen. 3:4; 1 Tim. 2:14; [John 8:44; 1 Thess. 3:5] [r]Col. 2:4, 8 [s][Eph. 6:5] [t]ch. 6:6
4 [u][1 Cor. 3:11] [v]Gal. 1:6
5 [w]ch. 12:11; Gal. 2:6
6 [x]See 1 Cor. 1:17 [y][Eph. 3:4] [z]ch. 4:2; 5:11; 12:12
7 [a][ch. 12:13] [b]See Acts 18:3

10:12–18 *Paul's Defense of His Authority as an Apostle.* Paul now turns to reestablishing his authority in Corinth by (1) defining the proper criterion for apostolic authority and (2) demonstrating that his ministry, not that of his opponents, actually meets that criterion. Paul does so by comparing his opponents' practice of commending themselves (v. 12) with the basis for his own boasting (vv. 13–18).

10:12 Paul is speaking ironically: though his opponents say he is "bold" and "strong" in his letters (vv. 1–2, 10), Paul does not **dare** to join them in their kind of self-recommendation; they are **without understanding** because their criterion for boasting (**one another**) is wrong. The opponents recommend each other by comparing their abilities, spiritual gifts, and experiences, all of which are irrelevant for establishing apostolic authority in a church.

10:13–14 In contrast to his opponents, Paul does **not boast beyond limits** (i.e., beyond the sphere of his apostolic authority, which God himself has established) because his apostolic authority in Corinth (**the area of influence God assigned to us**) was based on the fact that God had sent Paul to establish the church in Corinth (**to reach . . . you**). See 1 Cor. 4:15; 2 Cor. 3:1–3.

10:15–16 boast . . . in the labors of others. Paul's opponents boast, but they are intruders who create problems in churches he planted. **lands beyond**. Paul's aim is to plant churches in areas where Christ has never been preached (see Rom. 10:14–17), but these false teachers try to pervert the gospel in places where it has already been established (**another's area**).

10:17–18 boast in the Lord. Paul supports his boast as an apostle (vv. 12–16) with his citation of Jer. 9:23–24 (cf. 1 Cor. 1:31). Since all human abilities and attainments are gifts from God, the only true basis for boasting is to "boast in the Lord," i.e., in what the Lord provides, not in one's own presumed accomplishments (on boasting, see note on 2 Cor. 1:12). The **Lord commends** his people by working in and through their lives (see 3:1; 4:2; 5:12; 6:4; 12:11).

11:1–21a *Paul's Defense of His Boasting Like a Fool.* Paul gives his reasons why he feels compelled to act like a fool by boasting of his Jewish pedigree (vv. 21b–23a) and visions (12:1–4), rather than only in the Lord (10:17–18): desperate situations demand desperate measures.

11:2 As their "father" in the faith (see 1 Cor. 4:15; 2 Cor. 6:13; 12:14), Paul feels the same **divine** (i.e., godlike; Ex. 20:5; 34:14; Deut. 4:24; 5:9; 6:15) **jealousy** that a father experiences toward his daughter. In Jewish culture it was the father's responsibility to commit at his daughter's betrothal that he would present her as a **pure virgin** at her wedding (Deut. 22:13–24; see 2 Cor. 6:14–7:1). Here the "betrothal" was the Corinthians' conversion through Paul's ministry, the **husband** is Christ, and the "wedding day" is the day of Christ's return (see 1:14; John 14:3; Eph. 5:27; Col. 1:22; Rev. 19:6–9). Paul's picture of the church as engaged to Christ (cf. Eph. 5:25–27; Rev. 19:7–8) carries on the OT view of Israel as betrothed to God.

11:3 As at the time of Eve's fall in the garden (Gen. 3:1–13), the serpent's (i.e., Satan's; see 2 Cor. 4:4; 6:15; 11:14–15) **cunning**, now represented by Paul's opponents, consists in calling into question the sufficiency of God's provisions and the truth of his word, which is now focused in Christ (see 1:20).

11:4 The instrument of Satan's deception is the opponents' preaching of **another Jesus** (instead of the Jesus proclaimed by Paul), a **different spirit** (not the Holy Spirit but some false or demonic spirit), and a **different gospel** (rather than the gospel of salvation by faith in Christ alone). The "gospel" of Paul's opponents may have promised everyone health and wealth but no suffering, contrary to Paul's message and experiences noted in 4:5; 5:14–15, 18–19; etc.

11:5–6 super-apostles. Paul was probably using a sarcastic title to describe the false apostles who were troubling the Corinthian church, by preaching "another Jesus" and "a different gospel" (see vv. 4, 13–15; see also 12:11). Although Paul may have been **unskilled in speaking** (lacking formal training in rhetoric), his **knowledge** of the gospel greatly surpassed that of his opponents.

11:7 Paul's practice of self-support in Corinth, so that he **preached God's gospel . . . free of charge** for the sake of the Corinthians (which **exalted** them), was a **humbling** experience for Paul because it entailed not only *physical suffering* as a result of his hard work and insufficient earnings as an itinerant craftsman, but also the *cultural disdain* that the upper classes had for manual laborers (see 1 Cor. 4:11–13; 9:4–18; 15:10; 2 Cor. 6:5; 11:23).

11:8–9a I robbed other churches is an example of hyperbole. Paul received financial help from the Macedonian churches to preach the gospel in Corinth.

port from them in order to serve you. 9 And when I was with you and was [c]in need, [d]I did
not burden anyone, for the brothers who came from Macedonia [e]supplied my need. So
I refrained and will refrain [f]from burdening you in any way. 10 [g]As the truth of Christ is
in me, this boasting of mine [h]will not be silenced in the regions of Achaia. 11 And why?
[i]Because I do not love you? [j]God knows I do!

12 And what I am doing I will continue to do, [k]in order to undermine the claim of those
who would like to claim that in their boasted mission they work on the same terms as
we do. 13 For such men are [l]false apostles, [m]deceitful workmen, [n]disguising themselves as
apostles of Christ. 14 And no wonder, for even Satan disguises himself as [o]an angel of light.
15 So it is no surprise if his servants, also, disguise themselves as [p]servants of righteousness.
[q]Their end will correspond to their deeds.

Paul's Sufferings as an Apostle

16 I repeat, [r]let no one think me foolish. But even if you do, accept me as a fool, so that I
too may boast a little. 17 What I am saying [s]with this boastful confidence, [t]I say not as the
Lord would[1] but as a fool. 18 Since [u]many boast according to the flesh, I too will boast. 19 For
you gladly bear with fools, [v]being wise yourselves! 20 For you bear it if someone [w]makes
slaves of you, or [x]devours you, or takes advantage of you, or puts on airs, or [y]strikes you
in the face. 21 To my shame, I must say, [z]we were too weak for that!

But whatever anyone else dares to boast of—I am speaking as a fool—I also dare to boast
of that. 22 Are they Hebrews? [a]So am I. Are they Israelites? So am I. Are they offspring of
Abraham? So am I. 23 Are they [b]servants of Christ? [c]I am a better one—I am talking like a
madman—with far greater labors, [d]far more imprisonments, [e]with countless beatings,
and [f]often near death. 24 Five times I received at the hands of the Jews the [g]forty lashes
less one. 25 Three times I was [h]beaten with rods. [i]Once I was stoned. Three times I [j]was
shipwrecked; a night and a day I was adrift at sea; 26 on frequent journeys, in danger from
rivers, danger from robbers, [k]danger from my own people, [l]danger from Gentiles, [m]danger
in the city, danger in the wilderness, danger at sea, danger from false brothers; 27 [n]in toil
and hardship, through many a sleepless night, [o]in hunger and thirst, often without food,[2]

[1] Greek *not according to the Lord* [2] Or *often in fasting*

9 [c]Phil. 4:12 [d]ch. 12:13, 14 [e][1 Cor. 16:17; Phil. 4:15, 16] [f]ch. 12:16; 1 Thess. 2:6
10 [g]See Rom. 1:9; 9:1 [h]1 Cor. 9:15
11 [i]See ch. 6:11 [j]ver. 31; ch. 12:2, 3
12 [k][1 Cor. 9:12]
13 [l]Rev. 2:2; [Gal. 1:7; 2:4; 6:12; Phil. 1:15; 3:18; Titus 1:10, 12; 2 Pet. 2:1; 1 John 4:1] [m][Phil. 3:2] [n]ver. 14, 15
14 [o]Gal. 1:8
15 [p]ch. 3:9 [q]Phil. 3:19
16 [r]ch. 12:6
17 [s]ch. 9:4 [t][1 Cor. 7:12]
18 [u]Phil. 3:3, 4
19 [v]1 Cor. 4:10
20 [w]Gal. 2:4; [Gal. 4:3, 9; 5:1] [x][ch. 7:2] [y]1 Cor. 4:11
21 [z]ch. 10:10
22 [a]Rom. 11:1; Phil. 3:5
23 [b]See ch. 3:6; 10:7 [c]See 1 Cor. 15:10 [d]ch. 6:5 [e]Acts 16:23 [f]ch. 1:9, 10; 4:11; 6:9; Rom. 8:36; 1 Cor. 15:30-32
24 [g]Deut. 25:3
25 [h]Acts 16:22 [i]Acts 14:19 [j][Acts 27:41]
26 [k]Acts 9:23; 13:50; 14:5; 17:5; 1 Thess. 2:15; [Acts 18:12; 20:3, 19; 21:27; 23:10, 12; 25:3] [l]Acts 14:5; [Acts 19:23; 27:42] [m]Acts 21:31
27 [n]1 Thess. 2:9; 2 Thess. 3:8 [o]1 Cor. 4:11; Phil. 4:12

11:9–10 Macedonia. Northern Greece, where Philippi, Thessalonica, and Berea were located. **Achaia**. Southern Greece, where Corinth was located.

11:9b–14 Paul refused to accept money from the Corinthians because it was imperative that he distinguish his ministry from that of the false apostles who labored in Corinth out of greed (cf. 2:17). They claimed to be messengers of **light** (i.e., truth and salvation), but they were masquerading their true origin (from **Satan**) and destiny (hell).

11:13 false apostles. Cf. 2 Pet. 2:1–3 and notes.

11:15 disguise themselves as servants of righteousness. Paul's opponents, in claiming to be apostles, must also claim to be what Paul truly is, a servant (Gk. *diakonos*) of the new covenant, with its ministry (Gk. *diakonia*) of righteousness (3:6, 9; 5:21). On judgment that will **correspond to** one's deeds, see 5:10; Rom. 2:6; 3:8; 1 Cor. 3:17; Gal. 6:7–9; Eph. 6:8; Phil. 3:18–19; Col. 3:23–24; 2 Tim. 4:14.

11:16–18 In his arrogance the **fool** boasts in himself, not in the Lord (see 10:17–18), for which he is condemned (see, e.g., Ps. 14:1; 53:1–2; Prov. 9:13–18). Almost like a fool, Paul is about to **boast a little** in his own identity to make his point (see 2 Cor. 11:21b–23). Paul recognizes that he does so **not as the Lord would** (lit., not "according to the Lord," i.e., not following out a direct command from the Lord; see note on 1 Cor. 7:12–13) but as a result of the severe situation in Corinth in which **many boast according to the flesh**, i.e., according to a life lived devoid of the Spirit. But Paul's "boasting" is in what the Lord has done (2 Cor. 11:21b–12:21).

11:20–21a strikes you in the face. A reference to the Jewish opponents insulting the Gentile Corinthians, probably by literally striking them (cf. John 18:22; Acts 23:2). All five actions listed in 2 Cor. 11:20 are signs of an arrogant, domineering attitude on the part of these false leaders. In another statement of irony or sarcasm, Paul says that he was too **"weak"** to act like his opponents.

11:21b–33 *Paul's Boast in His Service and Suffering.* Although forced to boast by his opponents, and after a long justification of his doing so (vv. 1–21a), Paul finally and reluctantly boasts in his identity. In stark contrast to his opponents, however, Paul boasts at great length in his weakness as the appropriate way to glorify God's grace and power in one's life (v. 30; see 2:14–16a; 4:7–12; 6:3–10; 12:5–10).

11:21b–23a Hebrews. A reference to Jewish ethnicity. **Israelites**. A reference to being God's chosen people under the old covenant. **offspring of Abraham**. A reference to being part of the new covenant people of God as well as being a true descendant of Abraham (see Rom. 9:6–9; 11:1–6; Gal. 3:8, 16, 29). Measured by his zeal for his heritage, Paul even claims to be a **better** servant of Christ than his opponents (see Gal. 1:14; Phil. 3:4–6). Because he is reluctant to speak of himself in this way, Paul downplays his qualifications, saying that he is **speaking as a fool** (2 Cor. 11:21b) and **talking like a madman** (v. 23a). In spite of his reluctance, however, Paul goes on to give a summary of what he has experienced, not for his own praise but for the "upbuilding" of the Corinthians (12:19), "for the sake of the gospel" (1 Cor. 9:23), and "for the glory of God" (1 Cor. 10:31).

11:24 forty lashes less one. The Jewish punishment of 39 lashes was given by the synagogue for false teaching, blasphemy, and serious lawbreaking, all of which could have been applied to Paul's preaching of the gospel, especially to Gentiles (Acts 9:20; 13:5, 14–43; 17:1–3, 10–21; etc.; see note on Acts 5:40). It was the most severe beating allowed by Scripture (Deut. 25:1–3).

11:25–26 beaten with rods. This was the Gentile punishment for disturbing the peace (Acts 16:22–23, 35–38; 22:25–29; 1 Thess. 2:2). **Once**, in Lystra, Paul **was stoned** (Acts 14:5–19), the most common form of execution in the Bible. **three times I was shipwrecked**. Of course, this would not include the shipwreck described in Acts 27, which occurred after Paul wrote this. Paul's description of shipwrecks and other dangerous aspects of his journeys aligns well with other ancient travel narratives, even if Paul's experiences were especially intense. Nautical archaeologists have identified many ancient shipwrecked boats around the Mediterranean.

in cold and exposure. 28 And, apart from other things, there is the daily pressure on me
of my anxiety for [p]all the churches. 29 [q]Who is weak, and I am not weak? Who is made to
fall, and I am not indignant?
30 [r]If I must boast, I will boast of the things that show my weakness. 31 [s]The God and Father
of the Lord Jesus, [t]he who is blessed forever, [u]knows that I am not lying. 32 At Damascus,
the governor under King Aretas [v]was guarding the city of Damascus in order to seize me,
33 [w]but I was let down in a basket through a window in the wall and escaped his hands.

Paul's Visions and His Thorn

12 I must go on boasting. Though there is nothing to be gained by it, I will go on to
visions and [x]revelations of the Lord. 2 I know a man [y]in Christ who fourteen years
ago was [z]caught up to [a]the third heaven—whether in the body or out of the body I do not
know, [b]God knows. 3 And I know that this man was caught up into [c]paradise—whether
in the body or out of the body I do not know, [b]God knows— 4 and he heard things that
cannot be told, which man may not utter. 5 On behalf of this man I will boast, but on my
own behalf I will not boast, [d]except of my weaknesses— 6 though if I should wish to
boast, [e]I would not be a fool, for I would be speaking the truth; but I refrain from it, so
that no one may think more of me than he sees in me or hears from me. 7 So [f]to keep me
from becoming conceited because of the surpassing greatness of the revelations,[1] [g]a thorn
was given me in the flesh, [h]a messenger of Satan to harass me, to keep me from becoming
conceited. 8 [i]Three times I pleaded with the Lord about this, that it should leave me. 9 But

[1] *Or hears from me, even because of the surpassing greatness of the revelations. So to keep me from becoming conceited*

28 [p]See 1 Cor. 7:17
29 [q]See 1 Cor. 8:13; 9:22
30 [r]ch. 10:10; 12:5, 9; See 1 Cor. 2:3
31 [s]See Rom. 15:6 [t]See Rom. 9:5 [u]ver. 11
32 [v]Acts 9:24
33 [w]Acts 9:25

Chapter 12
1 [x]Gal. 1:12; 2:2; Eph. 3:3
2 [y]See ch. 5:17 [z]ver. 3; 1 Thess. 4:17; Rev. 12:5; [Ezek. 8:3; Acts 8:39] [a]See Ps. 148:4 [b]ch. 11:11
3 [c]Luke 23:43; Rev. 2:7; [Gen. 2:8] [b][See ver. 2 above]
5 [d]See 1 Cor. 2:3
6 [e]ch. 5:13; 11:16, 17; [ver. 11]
7 [f][ch. 10:10] [g][Num. 33:55; Ezek. 28:24] [h][Luke 13:16]; See 1 Cor. 5:5
8 [i][Matt. 26:44]

11:28 And, apart from other things summarizes the other physical sufferings Paul could have listed. **anxiety for all the churches**. See 2:12–13.

11:30 God triumphs amid human **weakness**, embodying the principle of Christ's crucifixion (1 Cor. 1:27; 2 Cor. 10:3; 12:5, 9; 13:4, 9).

11:32–33 Paul's experience in **Damascus** shortly after encountering the risen Christ (Acts 9:8–25) took place under the Nabatean **governor** there during the reign of the Nabatean king **Aretas** IV (9 B.C.–A.D. 40). Having to flee **in a basket** was a striking example of Paul's "weakness" (2 Cor. 11:30) as a result of being called to suffer for Christ's name (see Acts 9:16).

12:1–13 *Paul's Boast in His Heavenly Vision and Subsequent Weakness.* Because his opponents boast in their spiritual experiences as well as in their ethnic identity, Paul is also forced to boast, however foolishly, in his own visions and revelations (see 11:1, 16; 12:11). But then in vv. 7–10 he returns one last time to boasting in his weakness, revealing the presence of a "thorn in the flesh" as the appropriate means for glorifying God's grace and power in his life and ministry. In vv. 9–10 he clearly states the principle behind this aspect of his self-commendation (1:3–11; 2:14–17; 4:7–12; 6:3–10; 11:23–33): Paul's earthly weaknesses, not his revelations, are to be the platform for demonstrating the Lord's power and grace.

12:2–3 I know a man . . . this man. Paul's hesitancy to boast of his visions is reflected in his use of the third person (as if it had happened to someone else). **the third heaven** (i.e., the highest; see 1 Kings 8:27; 2 Chron. 2:6; Neh. 9:6; Ps. 148:4). This phrase does not imply belief in a simplistic "three-story universe" but reflects a commonsense distinction between (1) the atmosphere where birds can be seen to fly, (2) the higher area where the sun, moon, and stars can be seen, and (3) the unseen realm where God dwells. This third area is equated with **paradise** (Gk. *paradeisos*, a Persian loan-word used in the Septuagint to refer to the garden of Eden [see Gen. 2:8–10; 13:10; Isa. 51:3; Ezek. 28:13; 31:8–9] but in the NT to refer to a place of blessedness where God dwells [Luke 23:43; Rev. 2:7]). Both terms would be recognized by Jewish readers as references to the realm of God's direct presence. **fourteen years ago**. Sometime between A.D. 42–44, around Tarsus or Antioch, prior to his first missionary journey (Acts 9:29–30; 11:25–26; see note on Acts 11:27–30 for ancient calculation of years). There is no other known record of this vision.

12:7 a thorn was given me (by God, who is sovereign over all things) **in the flesh, a messenger of Satan**. The nature of this "thorn" or "messenger" is much disputed. The most frequently proposed possibilities include: (1) Paul's inner psychological struggles (such as grief over his earlier persecution of the church, or sorrow over Israel's unbelief, or continuing temptations); (2) Paul's opponents, who continued to persecute him (cf. Num. 33:55 and Ezek. 28:24, where thorns refer to Israel's enemies); (3) some kind of physical affliction (possibly poor eyesight, malaria fever, or severe migraine headaches); or (4) some kind of demonic harassment ("a messenger of Satan"). Most commentators cautiously prefer some form of the third view, since "thorn in the flesh" would seem to suggest a physical condition.

12:8 Three times indicates that Paul has now finished praying for the thorn's removal, having received his answer from Christ (v. 9; cf. Jesus' threefold prayer in Mark 14:32–41).

12:9–10 My grace is sufficient. Paul says that God's grace "is sufficient" (in the present tense), underscoring the ever-present availability and sufficiency of God's grace, for Paul and for every believer, regardless of how critical one's circumstances may be (cf. Rom. 8:31–39). **my power is made perfect in weakness**. Paul was not allowed to speak about his heavenly revelations (2 Cor. 12:4, 6) but he quotes Christ's declaration ("My grace is sufficient") to underscore that his earthly weaknesses (not his revelations) would be the platform for perfecting and demonstrating the Lord's power (see chart below). This is the main point of vv. 1–13 and the foundation of Paul's self-defense throughout 2 Corinthians.

Weakness and Power (or Strength) in 1–2 Corinthians

Verse	Weakness	Power (or Strength)
1 Cor. 1:25	the weakness of God	is stronger than men
1 Cor. 1:27	God chose what is weak	to shame the strong
1 Cor. 2:3, 5	in weakness and in fear	but in the power of God
1 Cor. 15:43	sown in weakness	raised in power
2 Cor. 12:9	I will boast . . . of my weaknesses	so that the power of Christ may rest upon me
2 Cor. 13:3	not weak in dealing with you	but . . . powerful among you
2 Cor. 13:4	he was crucified in weakness	but lives by the power of God
2 Cor. 13:4	we also are weak in him	but . . . live with him by the power of God
2 Cor. 13:9	we are glad when we are weak	and you are strong

he said to me, [j]"My grace is sufficient for you, for [k]my power is made perfect in weakness."
Therefore I will boast all the more gladly of my weaknesses, so that [l]the power of Christ
may rest upon me. 10 [m]For the sake of Christ, then, [n]I am content with weaknesses, insults,
hardships, persecutions, and calamities. For [o]when I am weak, then I am strong.

Concern for the Corinthian Church

11 [p]I have been a fool! You forced me to it, for I ought to have been commended by you.
For I was [q]not at all inferior to these super-apostles, [r]even though I am nothing. 12 [s]The
signs of a true apostle were performed among you [t]with utmost patience, with signs and
wonders and mighty works. 13 For in what were you less favored than the rest of the churches,
except that [u]I myself did not burden you? Forgive me this wrong!
14 Here [v]for the third time I am ready to come to you. And I will not be a burden, for [w]I
seek not what is yours but you. For [x]children are not obligated to save up for their parents,
but [y]parents for their children. 15 [z]I will most gladly spend and be spent for your souls. If
[a]I love you more, am I to be loved less? 16 But granting that [b]I myself did not burden you,
I was crafty, you say, and got the better of you by deceit. 17 Did I take advantage of you
[c]through any of those whom I sent to you? 18 [d]I urged Titus to go, and sent [e]the brother
with him. Did Titus take advantage of you? Did we not act in the same spirit? Did we not
take the same steps?
19 Have you been thinking all along that we have been defending ourselves to you? It is [f]in
the sight of God that we have been speaking in Christ, and [g]all for your upbuilding, beloved.
20 For I fear that perhaps [h]when I come I may find you not as I wish, and that you may find
me not as you wish—that perhaps there may be quarreling, jealousy, anger, hostility, slander, gossip, conceit, and disorder. 21 I fear that when I come again my God may humble me
before you, and I may have to mourn over many of those [i]who sinned earlier and have not
repented of the impurity, [j]sexual immorality, and sensuality that they have practiced.

Final Warnings

13 [k]This is the third time I am coming to you. Every charge must be established [l]by
the evidence of two or three witnesses. 2 [m]I warned [n]those who sinned before and
all the others, and I warn them now while absent, as I did when present on my second
visit, that [o]if I come again I will not spare them— 3 since you seek proof that Christ [p]is

9 [j]Isa. 43:2 [k]Isa. 40:29-31; [Phil. 4:13] [l]See 1 Cor. 2:5
10 [m][ch. 5:15]; See Matt. 5:11, 12 [n]Rom. 5:3 [o][ch. 13:4]
11 [p][ver. 6] [q]See ch. 11:5; 1 Cor. 15:10 [r]See 1 Cor. 3:7; 15:9
12 [s]See Rom. 15:19; 1 Cor. 9:1 [t]ch. 6:4
13 [u]1 Cor. 9:12; See Acts 20:33
14 [v]ch. 13:1; [ch. 1:15; 13:2] [w]1 Cor. 10:24, 33 [x]1 Cor. 4:14, 15 [y][Prov. 19:14; Ezek. 34:2]
15 [z][ch. 1:6; Phil. 2:17; Col. 1:24; 1 Thess. 2:8; 2 Tim. 2:10] [a]See ch. 6:11
16 [b]ch. 11:9
17 [c][ch. 9:5]
18 [d]ch. 8:6 [e]ch. 8:18
19 [f]See Rom. 1:9; 9:1 [g]See 1 Cor. 14:26
20 [h][ch. 2:1-4]; See 1 Cor. 4:21
21 [i]ch. 13:2; [Rev. 2:21] [j]1 Cor. 5:1; See 1 Cor. 6:18

Chapter 13

1 [k]See ch. 12:14 [l]Cited from Deut. 19:15; See Num. 35:30
2 [m]ch. 10:2 [n]ch. 12:21 [o]ver. 10; See 1 Cor. 4:21
3 [p]See Matt. 10:20; 1 Cor. 5:4

12:11 super-apostles. See note on 11:5–6. **even though I am nothing**. Paul was the "least of the apostles," having persecuted the church (1 Cor. 15:8–9), and he owes everything to the grace and call of God in his life (1 Cor. 15:10; 2 Cor. 3:4–6).

12:12 the signs of a true apostle . . . among you with utmost patience. A reference to the work of the Spirit through Paul's ministry as seen in the conversion and gifting of the Corinthians (3:1–3), and seen too in Paul's Christlike behavior, characterized by his endurance in adversity by the power of God (6:4; 10:1–12:10). **with signs and wonders and mighty works**. A threefold description of miraculous acts that accompanied and accredited the ministry of an apostle (see Rom. 15:18–19; Gal. 3:1–5). This triad ties God's saving work under the new covenant to the signs and wonders at the exodus, thus showing the continuity within redemptive history (e.g., Ex. 3:20; 7:3; 10:1–2; Num. 14:22; Deut. 4:34; Josh. 24:17; Ps. 105:27–36; Acts 7:36; see the Overview of the Bible, pp. 23–26).

12:13 With a kind of playful irony, Paul says that the only wrong he did the Corinthians was not asking them for money (see 11:9b–14 for the reason).

12:14–13:10 *Paul's Final Defense and Appeal to the Rebellious.* In final preparation for his third visit (12:14; 13:1), Paul commends his apostleship one last time (12:14–21) and calls the rebellious to test the genuineness of their professed faith (13:1–10).

12:14–15 for the third time I am ready to come to you. On his first visit Paul had planted the church at Corinth (Acts 18:1–18). His second visit was the "painful visit" (2 Cor. 2:1; see Introduction: Purpose, Occasion, and Background). Paul mentions one last time his refusal to **burden** the Corinthians financially (11:7–12; 12:13; see 1 Cor. 9:18) as the loving act of a spiritual parent for his children (1 Cor. 4:14–15; 2 Cor. 6:11–13; 11:11), since acting this way embodies his message and life as an apostle (2:17) and calls into question the claims of Paul's opponents (11:12, 20).

12:16–18 crafty . . . deceit . . . take advantage. Paul emphatically rejects the idea that he used the collection to craftily take money from the Corinthians, since there is no evidence for such a charge. All of those who worked with Paul, including **Titus**, were men of unimpeachable integrity.

12:19 Paul's self-defense is fundamentally for the Corinthians' sake, not his own (see note on 10:8), and is pleasing to God, for he has been speaking **in the sight of God**.

12:20 find you not as I wish. That is, still unrepentant, rebellious, and anchored in their sinful lifestyles, all of which will indicate that they are not, in fact, genuine believers (see 13:5). **find me not as you wish**. If the Corinthians are not repentant, Paul will be called upon to exercise God's judgment rather than continuing to wait patiently for their repentance as in the past (see 1:23–2:4).

12:21 God may humble Paul **before** the Corinthians by using Paul as an instrument of their excommunication, which will mean Paul **may have to mourn** over the rebellious. There is no joy in judgment for an apostle, who under the new covenant is called primarily to build up the church (see 10:8; 12:19; 13:10).

13:1 the third time. See note on 12:14–15. **evidence of two or three witnesses**. According to Deut. 19:15, this was the legal requirement for accepting evidence at a trial (see Matt. 18:16–17; 1 Tim. 5:19).

13:2 Paul spoke of the discipline that would come if the rebellious minority did not repent. **not spare**. He did not specify what form the discipline would take, and perhaps he himself did not know exactly, but it certainly would not be pleasant (cf. Acts 5:1–11; 13:8–11; 1 Cor. 5:4–5).

13:3–4 Following the pattern of Christ's own **weakness** (1:5; 8:9; Phil. 2:7–8), Paul too has been **weak** for the sake of God's people, making evident to them God's Spirit and glory in Christ through his own sufferings (2 Cor. 1:3–11; 2:14–16a; 4:7–15; 6:3–10; 11:23–33; 12:7–10). But also like Christ,

speaking in me. He is not weak in dealing with you, but [q]is powerful among you. 4 For [r]he
was crucified in weakness, but [s]lives by the power of God. For [t]we also are weak in him,
but in dealing with you [u]we will live with him by the power of God.
5 Examine yourselves, to see whether you are in the faith. [v]Test yourselves. Or do you not
realize this about yourselves, that [w]Jesus Christ is in you?—unless indeed you fail to meet
the test! 6 I hope you will find out that we have not failed the test. 7 But we pray to God that
you may not do wrong—not that we may appear to have met the test, but that you may
do what is right, though we may seem to have failed. 8 For we cannot do anything against
the truth, but only for the truth. 9 For we are glad when [x]we are weak and you are strong.
Your [y]restoration is what we pray for. 10 For this reason I write these things while I am away
from you, that when I come [z]I may not have to be [a]severe in my use of [b]the authority that
the Lord has given me for building up and not for tearing down.

Final Greetings

11 Finally, brothers,[1] rejoice. [c]Aim for restoration, comfort one another,[2] [d]agree with one
another, [e]live in peace; and the God of love and [f]peace will be with you. 12 [g]Greet one another
with a holy kiss. 13 [h]All the saints greet you.
14 [i]The grace of the Lord Jesus Christ and [j]the love of God and [k]the fellowship of the
Holy Spirit be with you all.

[1] Or *brothers and sisters* [2] Or *listen to my appeal*

3 [q]ch. 10:4
4 [r][Phil. 2:7, 8; 1 Pet. 3:18] [s]See Rom. 1:4; 6:4 [t][ch. 12:10] [u]See Rom. 6:8
5 [v][1 Cor. 11:28; Gal. 6:4] [w]Rom. 8:10; Gal. 4:19
9 [x]1 Cor. 4:10; [ch. 4:12; 12:5, 9, 10] [y]Eph. 4:12; 1 Thess. 3:10; [ver. 11]
10 [z][ch. 2:3] [a]Titus 1:13 [b]ch. 10:8
11 [c]See Luke 6:40 [d]See Rom. 12:16 [e]See Mark 9:50 [f]See Rom. 15:33
12 [g]See Rom. 16:16
13 [h]Phil. 4:22
14 [i]Rom. 16:20 [j]Jude 21 [k]Phil. 2:1

Paul will manifest the **power of God** in judging the Corinthians' behavior and beliefs (see 1 Cor. 5:12–13; 6:1–3).

13:5 The **test** to **see** if **Christ is in** the Corinthians will be their response to Paul and his call to repent, since God's message and the messenger are one (5:18–6:2).

13:7–9 Paul desires the Corinthians' **restoration** even if at this late hour. Paul **may seem to have failed** again by announcing a plan (this time the threatened return in judgment) that did not come to pass (cf. 1:12–2:4). This apparent failure, like the judgment itself, would once again establish the **truth** of the gospel, whose primary purpose is not tearing down but building up the church (13:10).

13:10 On **building up**, see note on 10:8.

13:11–14 *Closing Greetings.* As he did with the letter's opening, Paul expands the common conventions of ancient letter closings in order to highlight the important themes he has covered.

13:11 Brothers (Gk. *adelphoi*) is used here as a generic reference to both men and women. As believers, the men and women of the Corinthian church are members of God's family and thus "brothers and sisters" in Christ (see further ESV Preface: Translation Principles and Style, p. 20). Paul also speaks of the Corinthians as "brothers" in the first two sections of the letter, where he was primarily addressing those who were repentant (cf. 1:8 and 8:1); however, in chs. 10–13, Paul does not address those who are rebellious as "brothers." Now, in closing the letter, Paul again uses this loving familial expression to address the entire church, which is an indication, no doubt, of his hope that they truly will be "brothers and sisters" in Christ as a result of their right response to his letter (13:6–10). As in the case of 1 Corinthians (see 1 Cor. 16:13–14), Paul also summarizes the central conclusions of this letter with five commands—with the first three commands focusing on the Corinthians' relationship with Paul as their apostle, the last two focusing on their life together as brothers and sisters in Christ, and as a family of believers reconciled to each other and to God their Father.

13:12–13 Greet . . . All the saints greet. These two greetings stress the unity of the church, local and universal. **with a holy kiss**. Usually reserved for special reunions among family members or formal greetings, extending such a public kiss to an entire group was a practice unique to the early church that signified their mutual acceptance as a family. See Rom. 16:16; 1 Thess. 5:26; 1 Pet. 5:14; and note on 1 Cor. 16:20.

13:14 The only Trinitarian benediction in Paul's letters, stressing that **grace**, **love**, and **fellowship** with one another come from God in Christ through the Spirit. Paul's final reference to the **Spirit** recalls that he is writing and praying as a minister of the new covenant (see 1:22; 3:3–18; 4:13–18; 5:5). **you all**. A final stress on the unity of the reconciled church, brought about by God himself, the furthering of which was one of the main goals of Paul's letter (1:7; 2:5–11; 5:18–6:2; 6:11–13; 7:2–4; 9:13–14; 12:19; 13:5–10).

INTRODUCTION TO

THE LETTER OF PAUL TO THE

GALATIANS

Author and Title

The first word of the letter to the Galatians is "Paul," and there has been widespread agreement by scholars down through the ages that Paul is indeed the author. The title in most Greek editions of the NT is "To the Galatians," and the main body of the letter mentions the addressees as "the churches of Galatia" (1:2) and "foolish Galatians!" (3:1). The only debate is, which Galatians? (See Purpose, Occasion, and Background.)

Date

Although the question of the date of Galatians is related to this question of "which Galatians," some clues can probably be found in the letter itself. The main indicator is the lack of reference to the Jerusalem council (Acts 15). Although this is an argument from silence, many commentators have regarded this as a "deafening silence." It would have been enormously helpful to Paul's argument if he could have mentioned the decision of the council that Gentiles should not be circumcised: this, after all, appears to be a major point of contention between Paul and the false teachers influencing the Galatians. Since the council took place in A.D. 48/49, and Paul evangelized South Galatia in A.D. 47/48, some time around A.D. 48 is a plausible date for the composition of Galatians. However, determining dates in Paul's life is always somewhat uncertain, and so one cannot place too much weight on the date in the interpretation of the letter.

Theme

Christ's death has brought in the age of the new covenant (3:23–26; 4:4–5, 24), in which believers do not have to become Jews or follow the outward ceremonies of the Mosaic law (2:3, 11–12, 14; 4:10). To require these things is to deny the heart of the gospel, which is justification by faith alone, not by obedience to the law (2:16; cf. 1:6–7). In this new age, Christians are to live in the guidance and power of the Spirit (chs. 5–6).

Purpose, Occasion, and Background

A crisis has hit the church in Galatia. The church came into being as a result of God's Spirit at work in Paul's proclamation of the gospel (3:1–5; 4:13–15). But within the short space of time since Paul left (1:6), the church has been visited or infiltrated by false teachers whom Paul calls those "who trouble you" (1:7) or "those who unsettle you" (5:12). These teachers have convinced the Galatians of a false gospel which requires them to be circumcised. Paul sees that these pseudo-Christians merely want to win converts for their own prestige: they want to win approval from the Jewish authorities by showing how effective they are in converting Gentiles to a form of Judaism (6:12). Since the Jewish establishment approves of the fact that they are making Gentiles Jewish, the false teachers have the best of both worlds: they have created a sect of which they are the leaders, and they also escape any Jewish persecution. One further effect of this on the Galatians appears to have been the division within their church, presumably over these issues of circumcision and law that the false teachers have raised (5:15).

Although the Galatians appear to have come under the spell of these teachers and have become convinced of their teaching (1:6), Paul does not regard the situation as hopeless (3:4). Nevertheless, Paul is more critical of his audience here than in any other letter, and he chastises the Galatians for being foolish (3:1) and provides numerous reasons why they should return to the truth.

The less important question, which makes little difference to how one interprets the letter, is, which Galatians? There was a *people group* of Galatians who lived in the northern part of what is now Turkey, but there was a *Roman province* called Galatia that extended into southern Turkey. The Galatians in the letter are probably those in the Roman province, especially the southern part, because Paul did much less in the way of missionary activity in the north, and he usually refers to places by their Roman imperial names.

Timeline

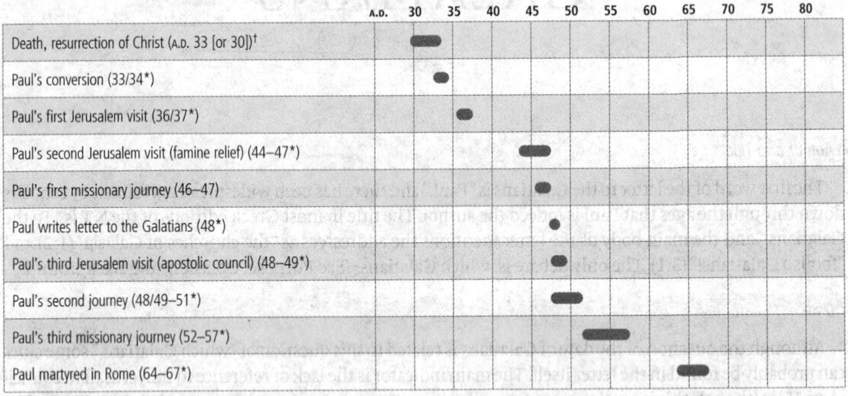

A.D. 30 35 40 45 50 55 60 65 70 75 80
Death, resurrection of Christ (A.D. 33 [or 30])†
Paul's conversion (33/34*)
Paul's first Jerusalem visit (36/37*)
Paul's second Jerusalem visit (famine relief) (44–47*)
Paul's first missionary journey (46–47)
Paul writes letter to the Galatians (48*)
Paul's third Jerusalem visit (apostolic council) (48–49*)
Paul's second journey (48/49–51*)
Paul's third missionary journey (52–57*)
Paul martyred in Rome (64–67*)

* *denotes approximate date; / signifies either/or; † see The Date of Jesus' Crucifixion, pp. 1809–1810*

Key Themes

1. In his sin-bearing death, Christ is a substitute for all Christians, whom he brings into a new realm of freedom and life.	1:4; 2:20; 3:13
2. This gospel of Christ is *for* humanity, but there is no sense in which it has its origin *in* humanity: it comes only from God. Paul is himself an illustration of this: his conversion to Christ and his apostleship were not through human consultation but through the direct revelation of Christ.	1:1, 11–12, 15–20
3. The gospel is appropriated not by works of law but by *faith*, which is the route to justification.	2:16
4. To require circumcision and other Mosaic ceremonies such as dietary laws and Jewish holidays as a supplement to faith is to fall back from the realm of grace, faith, and freedom, and to come under the whole law and its curse, since comprehensive observance of the law is impossible.	2:12–14, 16; 3:10; 4:10; 5:3
5. OT Scripture itself testifies to the truth of justification by faith, both in the life of Abraham and in the prophecy of Habakkuk.	Gen. 15:6; Hab. 2:4
6. The Christian life has its source in the believer having died with Christ to sin, and thereby having renounced the flesh.	5:24; 6:14
7. The Spirit is the source of power and guidance in the Christian life, and the work of the Spirit produces love and faith.	5:6, 16, 18, 25
8. The Christian life consists not in pleasing people but in pleasing Christ our master and being willing to suffer persecution for the sake of his cross.	1:10; 6:12, 14

History of Salvation Summary

Through Jesus Christ, salvation and justification come to both Jew and Gentile, fulfilling the promise to Abraham of blessing to the nations (3:8; Gen. 12:3). (For an explanation of the "History of Salvation," see the Overview of the Bible, pp. 23–26.)

Literary Features

Like the rest of the Pauline letters, Galatians follows the conventions of letter writing in NT times. There is a salutation, a body, a *paraenesis* (set of moral exhortations), greetings, and a benediction. There is no initial thanksgiving, however, which indicates Paul's agitation and alarm over the theological situation in Galatia.

Paul gets right to the point, which is that the Galatians are in danger of turning to a different gospel, thereby risking the everlasting ruin of their souls. The main argument of the epistle is advanced by the use of autobiography, example, allegory, satiric rebuke, and exhortation.

The doctrinal thrust of Galatians gives it a strong internal unity. In one way or another, everything in the epistle is related to Paul's defense of justification by faith alone. The letter is also unified by the apostle's intensity of tone, which comes through as strongly here as it does in any of his writings—especially in his intolerance of false doctrine and his indignation with people who promote it. Stylistically, Galatians finds literary coherence in its thematic contrasts: the true gospel vs. a false gospel, faith vs. works, law vs. grace, liberty vs. legalism, sonship vs. slavery, and the fruit of the Spirit vs. the desires of the flesh.

Ancient Galatia

"Galatia" was originally a Celtic region in north central Asia Minor (modern Turkey). It became a client kingdom of Rome under Pompey (mid-1st century B.C.). With the death of the client king Amyntas (d. 25 B.C.) an expanded Galatia came under a Roman governor. In Paul's day the province of Galatia included parts of Pontus and Paphlagonia to the east and north and encompassed portions of Phrygia, Pisidia, Isauria, Lycaonia, and Cilicia to the south. Thus many of the cities of Paul's first missionary journey (Acts 13–14) were considered part of the province of Galatia (or at least near its sphere of influence). Starting with territorial alterations under the emperor Vespasian (end of the 1st century A.D.), the province changed shape; thus the other ethnic territories were gradually drawn off, back to their earlier affiliations, and the province of Galatia returned to its more ethnically defined northern boundaries. Some contend that these subsequent reductions to the province of Galatia influenced the later church fathers to assume that Paul wrote his epistle to residents of northern Galatia. Archaeological evidence indicates a combination of Hellenistic, Celtic, and Roman influences in the province of Paul's time.

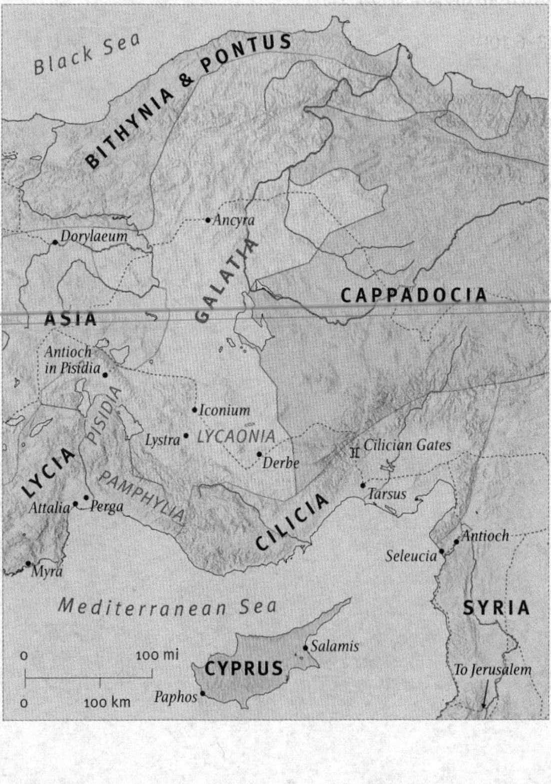

The Setting of Galatians
(c. A.D. 48)
Paul's letter to the Galatians was likely written to the churches he had established during his first missionary journey (Acts 13:1–14:28). He probably wrote the letter from his home church in Antioch in Syria, sometime before the Jerusalem council (Acts 15:1–31).

Outline

It is difficult to divide Galatians into neat sections, since Paul returns to the same themes on numerous occasions and often moves gradually into different topics rather than breaking off sharply to address a new theme. The following can serve as a rough guide.

I. Opening (1:1–9)
   A. Greeting (1:1–5)
   B. Initial rebuke (1:6–9)

II. Indirect Appeal: Paul's Career with the Gospel (1:10–2:21)
   A. Paul's defense of himself and the gospel (1:10–24)
   B. Paul's gospel recognized by the Jerusalem apostles (2:1–10)
   C. Paul's opposition to Peter, to preserve the truth of the gospel (2:11–21)

III. Direct Appeals to the Galatians (3:1–5:12)
   A. The Galatians' experience of conversion (3:1–5)
   B. The gospel in the OT (1): Abraham (3:6–9)
   C. The gospel in the OT (2): Leviticus, Deuteronomy, and Habakkuk (3:10–14)
   D. An illustration from human law (3:15–18)
   E. Passing from slavery to sonship (3:19–4:7)
   F. Passing from idolatry to the true God (4:8–11)
   G. Appeal to the Galatians' knowledge of Paul (4:12–20)
   H. The gospel in the OT (3): Abraham's sons (4:21–31)
   I. Judgment for those who turn from the gospel (5:1–12)

IV. Life in the Spirit and Love (5:13–6:10)
   A. The law of love (5:13–15)
   B. The desires of the flesh vs. the fruit of the Spirit (5:16–26)
   C. A Christian life of concrete love (6:1–10)

V. Final Warning (6:11–18)

THE LETTER OF PAUL TO THE

GALATIANS

Chapter 1

1[a]See 2 Cor. 1:1 [b]ver. 11, 12 [c]Acts 9:6; 20:24; 22:10, 15, 21; 26:16; [1 Tim. 1:1; Titus 1:3] [d]See Acts 2:24
2[e]Phil. 4:21 [f]Acts 16:6; 1 Cor. 16:1
3[g]Rom. 1:7; 1 Cor. 1:3 [h]1 Tim. 1:2
4[i]See Matt. 20:28; Rom. 4:25; 1 Cor. 15:3 [j][Eph. 2:2; 1 John 5:19]; See John 15:19 [k]Phil. 4:20; 1 Thess. 1:3; 3:11, 13
6[l][ch. 4:13; Acts 16:6; 18:23] [m]ch. 5:8 [n]2 Cor. 11:4; [1 Tim. 1:3]
7[o][Acts 4:12; 1 Cor. 3:11] [p]ch. 5:10; Acts 15:24; See 2 Cor. 11:13
8[q]2 Cor. 11:14 [r]See Rom. 9:3
9[r][See ver. 8 above]

Greeting

1 Paul, an [a]apostle—[b]not from men nor through man, but [c]through Jesus Christ and
God the Father, [d]who raised him from the dead— **2** and all [e]the brothers[1] who are
with me,
To [f]the churches of Galatia:
3 [g]Grace to you and peace [h]from God our Father and the Lord Jesus Christ, **4** [i]who gave
himself for our sins to deliver us from the present [j]evil age, according to the will of [k]our
God and Father, **5** to whom be the glory forever and ever. Amen.

No Other Gospel

6 I am astonished that you are [l]so quickly deserting [m]him who called you in the grace of
Christ and are turning to [n]a different gospel— **7** [o]not that there is another one, but [p]there
are some who trouble you and want to distort the gospel of Christ. **8** But even if we or [q]an
angel from heaven should preach to you a gospel contrary to the one we preached to you,
[r]let him be accursed. **9** As we have said before, so now I say again: If anyone is preaching
to you a gospel contrary to the one you received, [r]let him be accursed.

[1] Or *brothers and sisters*. The plural Greek word *adelphoi* (translated "brothers") refers to siblings in a family. In New Testament usage, depending on the context, *adelphoi* may refer either to men or to both men and women who are siblings (brothers and sisters) in God's family, the church; also verse 11

1:1–9 *Opening.* Paul's brief opening includes a greeting (vv. 1–5), after which he addresses the crisis in the Galatian church (vv. 6–9).

1:1–5 *Greeting.* Many of the familiar elements of Paul's greetings are present here (e.g., "grace and peace"), but this is probably the most muted of all of Paul's greetings to churches: there is no thanksgiving or reference to the Galatians' faith, hope, or love.

1:1 apostle. This indicates Paul's authority as one commissioned by God ("apostle," lit., "one who is sent") and entrusted with the sacred deposit of the gospel. On apostleship, see notes on Matt. 10:2; Acts 1:20; Rom. 1:1. Paul's apostleship is especially important in Galatians because the false teachers have evidently raised questions about whether he should really be called an apostle (Gal. 2:7–9). **not from men nor through man**. Paul stresses both here and in 1:11–12, 16–17, 19 that he received the gospel directly from the Lord, not secondhand.

1:2 all the brothers . . . with me. Those with Paul agree with the gospel he proclaims, and hence the Galatians are mistaken if they accept the false gospel that demands circumcision for salvation. **the churches of Galatia**. This probably refers to the churches of Pisidian Antioch, Iconium, Lystra, and Derbe. (See Introduction: Purpose, Occasion, and Background, and the map, p. 2243.)

1:3 Paul, as he often does in his letters, wishes his audience **grace** (God's unmerited favor) **and peace** (God's positive blessing of well-being). See notes on John 14:27 and Rom. 1:7.

1:4 gave himself for our sins. The saving work of Christ on the cross is in the forefront of Paul's mind and therefore shows up here at the very beginning of the letter. Jesus not only saves Christians from their sins but also sets them free from being slaves of this world. Paul will later explain that in wanting to be under the law, the Galatians are effectively wanting to stay anchored in this **present evil age** (3:22–26; 4:1–11), which is the state of the world apart from Christ until his return.

1:5 to whom be the glory. This is not just a formulaic expression but reveals Paul's concern to defend and preserve this central truth of Scripture: that God chose Israel and the church for his own name's sake, redeemed his people in Christ for his praise and glory, and calls believers to declare his majesty in the world. Those who have led the Galatians astray are doing so to "make a good showing in the flesh" (6:12), whereas Paul will conclude the letter by stating that his sole desire is to give all the glory to Christ (6:14).

1:6–9 *Initial Rebuke.* Paul addresses the problem of the Galatians abandoning the true gospel and coming under the sway of the false teachers.

1:6 so quickly. It was a remarkably short time between Paul's first proclamation to the Galatians and their present disarray (see Introduction: Date). The phrases **deserting him** and **different gospel** show that these are not issues over which Christians might legitimately disagree. The Galatians are questioning the very gospel itself, and Paul is a model of forthright frankness when central gospel issues are at stake.

1:7 there are some who trouble you. Visiting preachers who have tried to persuade the Galatians that they should require circumcision and obedience to the whole law as a means of justification before God (see also 4:17; 6:12–13).

1:8–9 a gospel contrary. The gospel is unchanging. Thus Paul pronounces a curse of final judgment on those who proclaim or receive a different gospel. Even if he himself, or **an angel from heaven**, were to preach such a gospel, the Galatians should reject it. Mormonism is an example of a religion that is based on revelation supposedly given by an angel and that teaches a gospel different from justification by faith alone in the substitutionary death of Christ.

10 For am I now seeking the approval of man, or of God? Or am I trying [s]to please man?
If I were still trying to please man, I would not be a [t]servant[1] of Christ.

Paul Called by God

11 For [u]I would have you know, brothers, that [v]the gospel that was preached by me is
not man's gospel.[2] 12 [w]For I did not receive it from any man, nor was I taught it, but I
received it [x]through a revelation of Jesus Christ. 13 For you have heard of [y]my former life
in Judaism, how [z]I persecuted the church of God violently and tried to destroy it. 14 And I
was advancing in Judaism beyond many of my own age among my people, so extremely
[a]zealous was I for [b]the traditions of my fathers. 15 But when he [c]who had set me apart
[d]before I was born,[3] and who [e]called me by his grace, 16 was pleased to reveal his Son to[4]
me, in order [f]that I might preach him among the Gentiles, I did not immediately consult
with anyone;[5] 17 nor did I go up to Jerusalem to those who were apostles before me, but I
went away into Arabia, and returned again to Damascus.

18 Then [g]after three years I went up to Jerusalem to visit Cephas and remained with
him fifteen days. 19 But I saw none of the other apostles except James [h]the Lord's brother.
20 (In what I am writing to you, [i]before God, I do not lie!) 21 [j]Then I went into the regions
of Syria and Cilicia. 22 And I was still unknown in person to [k]the churches of Judea that are
in Christ. 23 They only were hearing it said, "He who used to persecute us is now preaching
the faith he once tried to destroy." 24 And they glorified God because of me.

Paul Accepted by the Apostles

2 Then after fourteen years I went up again to Jerusalem with Barnabas, taking Titus
along with me. 2 I went up because of a revelation and set before them (though privately
before those [l]who seemed influential) the gospel that [m]I proclaim among the Gentiles,

[1] Or *slave*; Greek *bondservant* [2] Greek *not according to man* [3] Greek *set me apart from my mother's womb* [4] Greek *in* [5] Greek *with flesh and blood*

10 [s]1 Thess. 2:4; [Rom. 2:29; 1 Cor. 10:33; Eph. 6:6; Col. 3:22] [t][Rom. 1:1]
11 [u]1 Cor. 15:1 [v]See Rom. 2:16
12 [w]ver. 1; 1 Cor. 11:23; 15:3; [Acts 22:14] [x]ver. 16; See 1 Cor. 2:10; 2 Cor. 12:1
13 [y][Acts 26:4] [z]See Acts 8:3
14 [a]Phil. 3:6; See Acts 21:20 [b][Jer. 9:14; 2 Tim. 1:3]; See Matt. 15:2
15 [c]Acts 13:2; Rom. 1:1 [d]Isa. 49:1, 5; Jer. 1:5; Luke 1:15 [e]ver. 6
16 [f]ch. 2:9; See Acts 9:15
18 [g][Acts 9:22, 23]
19 [h]See Matt. 12:46; Acts 12:17
20 [i]See Rom. 1:9; 9:1
21 [j][Acts 9:30; 11:25, 26; 13:1]
22 [k]1 Thess. 2:14

Chapter 2

2 [l]ver. 6, 9 [m]1 Tim. 3:16

1:10–2:21 *Indirect Appeal: Paul's Career with the Gospel.* Paul received the gospel directly from Jesus Christ on the Damascus road. His gospel was not derived from Peter or any other human authorities. His gospel was validated by the "pillar" apostles (2:9) in Jerusalem. The authority of Paul's gospel is evident in his rebuke of Peter when he failed to live in accord with the gospel (2:11–21).

1:10–24 *Paul's Defense of Himself and the Gospel.* Paul apparently is responding to criticism that he is peddling a gospel received from man, not from God, and that he is doing so simply to please man rather than God. Paul does not simply defend himself out of resentment or wounded pride but shows a pastoral concern: to reassure the Galatians that the gospel they received was the authentic one, not a false message delivered by an untrustworthy messenger (e.g., 2:5).

1:10 Paul poses two absolutely incompatible goals: pleasing man, or pleasing God. There is no possibility of combining the two.

1:12 Paul received the gospel **through a revelation of Jesus Christ** on the Damascus road (see Acts 9:1–19a; 22:3–21; 26:12–23).

1:13–14 Paul distances himself from his **former life in Judaism**, although he does not in any sense renounce his status as an Israelite (cf. Rom. 11:1). Rather, he has broken with the life of seeking righteousness through the Law of Moses. He underlines the shame of this former life by noting his persecution of the church (cf. 1 Cor. 15:9; 1 Tim. 1:13). **the traditions of my fathers.** This rabbinic teaching was the foundation of Jewish life in the first century A.D., particularly for the Pharisees (cf. Mark 7:3–5).

1:15 set me apart before I was born. The emphasis is again on God's initiative: Paul was not called because of anything he himself accomplished.

1:16 to reveal his Son to me, in order that I might preach him among the Gentiles. Paul was converted in order to preach primarily to non-Jews (cf. Acts 9:15). This was revolutionary because God's dealings in the OT had been focused on Israel as his chosen nation. Now, with the coming of Christ, there was no distinction (Gal. 3:28): all must come to faith in Christ.

1:17 The journey to Arabia and back to Damascus takes place in the gap between Acts 9:25 and 9:26. On the city of **Damascus**, see note on Acts 9:3. Roman **Arabia** included much of what is modern Saudi Arabia, Jordan, and southern Syria. Therefore, while Paul may not have traveled far from Damascus here, he can also speak of distant Mount Sinai as being in Arabia (Gal. 4:25).

1:18 after three years. If Paul's conversion was in A.D. 33 (an approximate date), then this places the first Jerusalem visit c. A.D. 36. It probably corresponds to the stay in Jerusalem in Acts 9:26–29. **Cephas** here is Peter.

1:19–20 None of the other apostles except James almost certainly implies that James is counted among "the apostles," even though he was not one of the original 12 (see note on 1 Cor. 9:4–5). Acts 9:27 refers to Barnabas introducing Paul to "the apostles" in Jerusalem. Paul's statement here means that "the apostles" in Acts 9:27 refers to Peter and James.

1:21 Syria is to the north of Judea and Galilee, and **Cilicia** is to the north and west (cf. Acts 9:30).

1:22 Paul is presumably unknown to them because of the short and narrowly focused stay referred to in vv. 18–19. Furthermore, he refers to the province of Judea as a whole, not just Jerusalem.

1:23 The faith is the Christian faith, the message of the gospel.

2:1–10 *Paul's Gospel Recognized by the Jerusalem Apostles.* Paul is not simply telling a story from his past. All this is highly relevant to the Galatians, who are being influenced by ideas that go against the consensus of the apostles.

2:1 after fourteen years. There is debate as to whether this visit took place an *additional* 14 years after the three years mentioned in 1:18 or whether the 14 years starts from Paul's conversion and includes those three. The latter seems slightly more probable, placing this visit c. A.D. 47. It probably corresponds to Acts 11:29–30 rather than to the Jerusalem council visit in Acts 15. (See note on Acts 11:27–30.) **taking Titus along.** Titus was a Gentile, so some have seen this as Paul issuing a challenge to the Jerusalem leaders. This interpretation is unnecessary, but Titus was certainly a "test case," as Gal. 2:3 shows.

2:2 Those who seemed influential probably includes James, Peter, and John (see v. 9). **in vain.** Paul is not seriously imagining that he has actually been preaching a false gospel, but he would regard his work as in vain if it were to result in a divided church—a Gentile half and a Jewish half.

2[n]ch. 4:11; 1 Thess. 3:5 [o]Phil. 2:16
3[p][Acts 16:3]
4[q]Acts 15:24; 2 Cor. 11:26; [ch. 5:12] [r][2 Pet. 2:1; Jude 4] [s]See ch. 5:1 [t]ch. 4:3, 9, 24, 25; 2 Cor. 11:20; [Rom. 8:15]
5[u]ver. 14; [ch. 4:16; 5:7; Titus 1:14; 2 John 1]
6[v]ver. 2, 9; [ch. 6:3; Acts 5:36]; See 1 Cor. 3:7 [w]See Deut. 10:17 [x][2 Cor. 11:5; 12:11]
7[y]1 Thess. 2:4; 1 Tim. 1:11; See 1 Cor. 9:17 [z]ch. 1:16; See Acts 9:15
9[v][See ver. 6 above] [a]Jer. 1:18; Rev. 3:12 [b]See Rom. 1:5 [c][2 Pet. 3:15]
10[d]See Acts 24:17
11[e][Acts 15:1, 35] [f]Job 21:31
12[g]Acts 11:3; [ver. 14; Acts 10:28]; See Luke 15:2 [h]See Acts 11:2

[n]in order to make sure I was not running or had not [o]run in vain. **3**But even Titus, who
was with me, [p]was not forced to be circumcised, though he was a Greek. **4**[q]Yet because of
false brothers secretly brought in—who [r]slipped in to spy out [s]our freedom that we have
in Christ Jesus, [t]so that they might bring us into slavery— **5**to them we did not yield in
submission even for a moment, so that [u]the truth of the gospel might be preserved for
you. **6**And from those [v]who seemed to be influential (what they were makes no difference
to me; [w]God shows no partiality)—those, I say, who seemed influential [x]added nothing
to me. **7**On the contrary, when they saw that I had been [y]entrusted with [z]the gospel to the
uncircumcised, just as Peter had been entrusted with the gospel to the circumcised **8**(for
he who worked through Peter for his apostolic ministry to the circumcised worked also
through me for mine to the Gentiles), **9**and when James and Cephas and John, [v]who seemed
to be [a]pillars, perceived the [b]grace that was given to me, they [c]gave the right hand of fellowship to Barnabas and me, that we should go to the Gentiles and they to the circumcised.
10Only, they asked us to remember the poor, [d]the very thing I was eager to do.

Paul Opposes Peter

11But [e]when Cephas came to Antioch, I opposed him [f]to his face, because he stood
condemned. **12**For before certain men came from James, [g]he was eating with the Gentiles;
but when they came he drew back and separated himself, fearing [h]the circumcision party.[1]
13And the rest of the Jews acted hypocritically along with him, so that even Barnabas was

[1] *Or fearing those of the circumcision*

2:3–4 There is agreement: Titus—and so by implication all Gentiles—does not need to be circumcised. Or at least Paul, James, Peter, and John agree on this. There is, however, a group of **false brothers** who continue to disagree. Paul regards the imposition of circumcision on Gentile Christians as a **slavery** producing betrayal of the **freedom** Christ has given. (On circumcision, see Acts 15:1–35; Rom. 2:25–29; 4:9–16; Gal. 5:2–12; 6:12–15.) The presence of these "false brothers" within the church in Jerusalem shows that churches will sometimes have unbelievers in their midst who seek to harm the church.

2:5 Paul's response to the false brothers was of huge importance, because if he had yielded, Gentiles such as the Galatians would not have been brought the true gospel.

2:6 influential. See note on v. 2.

2:7–8 As an apostle, Paul was in no way inferior to Peter. It was merely a division of labor, with Paul assigned to evangelize **the uncircumcised** (Gentiles) while Peter was sent to **the circumcised** (Jews). What Paul wants to establish for the Galatians, however, is that his own apostleship is just as genuine as Peter's, and therefore the Galatians should not view themselves as inferior to any other group of believers.

2:9 If the church is God's temple (e.g., Eph. 2:21), some had apparently made Peter, James, and John the **pillars**. Significantly, these "pillars" had given **the right hand of fellowship** to Barnabas and Paul, signifying that they approved the message of the gospel as preached by Paul as well as his ministry to the Gentiles. Thus they validated Paul's apostleship by putting him on an equal footing with these other apostles in Jerusalem. This is significant, because it shows that neither Paul nor the Jerusalem apostles had to change their gospel message, but they were fully in agreement, and this "right hand of fellowship" gave clear expression to that agreement.

2:10 Verses 7–9 mark out the division of labor between Peter (to the Jews) and Paul (to the Gentiles). But there was one area of overlap: Paul was to organize collections for **the poor**, probably referring mainly to poor Christians in Jerusalem, who were Jewish. It is recorded elsewhere that Paul did, in fact, undertake a major relief effort on their behalf (see Rom. 15:25–26; 1 Cor. 16:1–3; 2 Corinthians 8–9). Paul's concern for the poor as evidenced here is in accord with the broader principle demonstrated throughout Scripture that genuine preaching of the gospel in every age must be accompanied by the meeting of physical needs as well, just as Jesus healed the sick and cast out demons along with his preaching ministry.

2:11–21 *Paul's Opposition to Peter, to Preserve the Truth of the Gospel.* Paul had said that he was not a people-pleaser (1:10), and his confrontation with Peter as reported here bears that out. It is unclear when Paul's speech to Peter stops and his direct address to the Galatians begins again, but 2:15–16 ("We ourselves are Jews by birth") was surely addressed to Peter.

2:11–12 The setting of Paul's confrontation with Peter was **Antioch**, Paul's missionary base for a number of years. Peter had been participating in meals where Jewish and Gentile Christians ate together, but then he **drew back and separated himself**, eating only with Jewish Christians. Interpreters differ in their explanations of this situation in this passage. One view is that the men who came **from James** (probably sent from the Jerusalem church by the apostle James) encouraged Jewish Christians to eat separately and follow kosher dietary laws. Peter decided to go along with this, perhaps not realizing that his example would make the Gentile Christians feel like second-class citizens in the church unless they followed Jewish ceremonial laws (such as dietary laws [vv. 12–14], circumcision [v. 3; 5:2–12; 6:12–15], and holidays and festivals [4:10]). Paul saw that Peter's behavior threatened the gospel of justification by faith alone because it implied that all Christians had to "live like Jews" (2:14) in order to be justified before God.

2:12 Eating with the Gentiles would mean not eating according to Jewish dietary restrictions. **The circumcision party** advocated following the ceremonies of the Mosaic covenant law at least regarding circumcision, food, and special days (see note on vv. 11–12).

2:13 Not only was Peter guilty of **hypocrisy**; as an influential leader, he also led astray **the rest of the** Jewish Christians, **even Barnabas**.

Paul's Visits to Jerusalem in Galatians and Acts

Galatians	Event	Acts	Event
1:15–17	Paul's conversion	9:1–25	Paul's conversion
1:18	three years after conversion, first visit to Jerusalem	9:26–30	with Barnabas in Jerusalem
2:1–10	14 years after conversion (or after first trip?), Paul meets with "pillars" of the church	11:29–30	famine relief visit to Jerusalem
2:11–14	dispute in Antioch	15:1–2	dispute in Antioch
	Paul writes Galatians		
		15:2–29	council in Jerusalem

led astray by their hypocrisy. 14 But when I saw that their [i]conduct was not in step with
[j]the truth of the gospel, I said to Cephas [k]before them all, "If you, though a Jew, [l]live like
a Gentile and not like a Jew, how can you force the Gentiles to live like Jews?"

Justified by Faith

15 We ourselves are Jews by birth and not [m]Gentile sinners; 16 yet we know that [n]a person
is not justified[1] by works of the law [o]but through faith in Jesus Christ, so we also have
believed in Christ Jesus, in order to be justified by faith in Christ and not by works of the
law, [p]because by works of the law no one will be justified.

[1] Or *counted righteous* (three times in verse 16); also verse 17

14 [i]Heb. 12:13 [j]See ver. 5 [k]1 Tim. 5:20 [l]See ver. 12
15 [m]ver. 17; [Eph. 2:3, 12]
16 [n]ch. 3:11; See Acts 13:39 [o]See Rom. 9:30 [p]Rom. 3:20; [Ps. 143:2]

2:14 force the Gentiles to live like Jews. Peter was guilty of hypocrisy (v. 13) because, though he had been happily living like a Gentile (i.e., not observing food laws), he was now requiring Gentile Christians to observe Jewish table regulations if they wanted to eat with him. Such a requirement, however, would undermine the gospel itself by making justification depend on "works of the law" rather than "faith in Jesus Christ" (see v. 16). **before them all**. Because Peter's sin was a public sin that was setting a bad example for the church, Paul confronted him publicly (compare the different procedure that Jesus commands regarding a private sin against an individual person, which hopefully can be corrected privately; cf. Matt. 18:15–20; James 5:19–20).

2:15 Gentile sinners, that is, Gentiles who do not even attempt to follow the OT laws and therefore clearly do not live up to them.

2:16 "Justified" means "counted righteous" or "declared righteous" by God (see ESV footnote). If people were sinless and perfectly obeyed all of God's perfect moral standards, they could be justified or "declared righteous" on the basis of their own merits. But Paul says that this is impossible for any Gentile or even for any Jew to do (cf. Romans 1–2). **we know that a person is not justified by works of the law**. Paul saw that Christ had taught justification by faith, and so he called God the one "who justifies the ungodly" (Rom. 4:5). Paul will soon show that this view was taught even in the OT (see Gal. 3:6–18), though it was not the view of most of first-century Judaism. (For example, a 1st-century-B.C. Jewish writing states, "The one who does righteousness stores up life for himself with the Lord, and the one who does wickedness is the cause of the destruction of his own soul" [*Psalms of Solomon* 9.5]). In Gal. 2:16, "works of the law" means not only circumcision, food laws, and Sabbath, but any human effort to be justified by God by obeying a moral law. **faith in Jesus Christ**. Some contend that the Greek means the "faithfulness of Jesus Christ." But "faith in Jesus Christ" seems much more likely since "faith in Jesus Christ" is synonymous with the next phrase, "we also have believed in Christ Jesus." "But through faith in Jesus Christ" is the opposite of depending on one's own good deeds for justification, since justification comes through faith in Christ alone. **We also have believed in Christ Jesus, in order to be justified by faith in Christ** implies that justification is the result of saving faith. The contrast **and not by works of the law** shows clearly that no human effort or merit can be added to faith as a basis for justification. (This verse was frequently appealed to in the Reformation by Protestants who insisted on "justification by faith alone" as opposed to the Roman Catholic doctrine of justification by faith plus merit gained through the "means of grace" administered by means of the Roman Catholic sacraments such as penance and the Mass.) Paul concludes decisively: **by works of the law no one will be justified** (cf. 3:10–14; Acts 13:39; Heb. 10:1–14). On justification, see also notes on Rom. 4:25; Phil. 3:9; James 2:21.

2:17 found to be sinners. Paul has just discussed how Gentiles are known among Jews as "sinners" (v. 15). When Jewish Christians associate with them, they are liable to the charge from traditionalist Jews of becoming "sinners" themselves. Paul firmly dismisses any such charge.

2:18 I would **prove myself to be a transgressor**. Ironically, the one who is most clearly seen to be a sinner is not the one outside of the law (i.e., the Gentile), but the one who is under it. So, if Paul were to reintroduce the edifice of the law, he would merely prove that he stands condemned.

2:19 through the law. Paul is not talking about a conscious experience of being dissatisfied with the law, but about how he was unknowingly caught up in God's plan in which the law actually pronounced the sentence of death on Paul's old way of life. Paul has **died to the law**, probably meaning that he no longer lives in the realm of trying to gain justification by obeying the law and that therefore the law can place no demands on him. Paul died to the law,

Spectrum of Early Beliefs about How Christians Should Relate to the Law of Moses

Identity	Beliefs	Examples
Gentile (professing) Christians	The law has absolutely no claim on their lives. (Presupposed in Rom. 6:1, 16.)	
Jewish and Gentile Christians	Christians are not under the law covenant even though they are certainly not free from God's demands. Kosher food laws could be observed and circumcision practiced as pastoral wisdom dictated. (Cf. 1 Cor. 9:19–23.)	Paul
Jewish Christians	They understood and accepted Paul's position, but their personal "comfort zone" was to be observant Jews, at least most of the time. Circumcision and kosher food laws are not necessary for salvation or maturity, and they shouldn't be imposed on Gentile believers.	
Jewish Christians	Jewish Christians should observe the traditions of the Mosaic code, even if it was acceptable for Gentile believers not to see themselves as under its stipulations.	Certain men from James? (Gal. 2:12a)
Jewish Christians	Jewish Christians should observe the Mosaic code, and Gentile believers can come to Christ through faith alone. However, the *really* spiritual should *want* to obey the Mosaic law code (even if it wasn't strictly necessary for salvation).	
Jewish (professing) Christians	The new covenant was a renewal of the old covenant; Jesus is the Messiah, but his life, death, and resurrection restored God's people to faithfulness to the Mosaic covenant. Therefore, if Gentiles want to come to the Messiah, they must first become Jews (and be circumcised, observe kosher and Sabbath laws, etc.). (Cf. Acts 15:1–35; Titus 1:10.)	"Judaizers"
Devout, non-Christian Jews	Christians are mistaken about the identity of Jesus, and the Jewish boundaries should not be opened to the Gentiles. (Cf. Acts 21:27–23:11.)	The circumcised (Rom. 4:12a)

17 But if, in our endeavor to be justified in Christ, we too were found [q]to be sinners, is
Christ then a servant of sin? Certainly not! **18** For if I rebuild what I tore down, I prove
myself to be a transgressor. **19** For through the law I [r]died to the law, so that I might [s]live
to God. **20** I have been [t]crucified with Christ. It is no longer I who live, but Christ who lives
[u]in me. And the life I now live in the flesh I live by faith in the Son of God, [v]who loved me
and [w]gave himself for me. **21** I do not nullify the grace of God, for [x]if righteousness[1] were
through the law, [y]then Christ died for no purpose.

By Faith, or by Works of the Law?

3 O foolish Galatians! Who has bewitched you? [z]It was before your eyes that Jesus Christ
was publicly [a]portrayed as crucified. **2** Let me ask you only this: [b]Did you receive the
Spirit by works of the law or by [c]hearing with faith? **3** Are you so foolish? [d]Having begun
by the Spirit, are you now being perfected by[2] the flesh? **4** [e]Did you suffer[3] so many things
in vain—if indeed it was in vain? **5** Does he who supplies the Spirit to you and [f]works
miracles among you do so [g]by works of the law, or by hearing with faith— **6** just as [h]Abra-
ham "believed God, and it was counted to him as righteousness"?
7 Know then that it is [i]those of faith who are [j]the sons of Abraham. **8** And the Scripture,
foreseeing that [k]God would justify[4] the Gentiles by faith, preached the gospel beforehand
to Abraham, saying, [l]"In you shall all the nations be blessed." **9** So then, those who are of
faith are blessed along with Abraham, the man of faith.

The Righteous Shall Live by Faith

10 For all who rely on works of the law are [m]under a curse; for it is written, [n]"Cursed be
everyone who does not [o]abide by all things written in the Book of the Law, and do them."

[1] *Or justification* [2] *Or now ending with* [3] *Or experience* [4] *Or count righteous; also verses 11, 24*

17 [q]ver. 15
19 [r]See Rom. 6:2; 7:4 [s]Luke 20:38; Rom. 6:11; 14:7, 8; 2 Cor. 5:15; 1 Thess. 5:10; Heb. 9:14; 1 Pet. 4:2
20 [t]ch. 5:24; 6:14; Rom. 6:6 [u]See John 17:23 [v]See Rom. 8:37 [w]See ch. 1:4
21 [x][ch. 3:21; Heb. 7:11] [y][ch. 5:4]
Chapter 3
1 [z][Num. 21:9] [a][1 Cor. 1:23]
2 [b]ver. 14; Eph. 1:13; Heb. 6:4; See Acts 15:8 [c]Rom. 10:17
3 [d]Phil. 1:6; [ch. 4:9]
4 [e]1 Cor. 15:2; [Heb. 10:35; 2 John 8]
5 [f][1 Cor. 12:10] [g]ver. 2
6 [h]Cited from Gen. 15:6; [Rom. 4:9, 21, 22]; See Rom. 4:3
7 [i]ver. 9 [j]See Luke 19:9
8 [k]See Rom. 3:30 [l]Cited from Gen. 12:3
10 [m][ch. 5:4]; See Rom. 4:15 [n]Cited from Deut. 27:26; [Jer. 11:3; Ezek. 18:4] [o][Matt. 5:19]

he says, **so that I might live to God**. That is, since he no longer is under the impossible burden of trying to earn acceptance with God through his own efforts, he has gained God's approval through the justification that is in Christ, and in this new relationship with God he has found an amazing new freedom to live a life devoted to God. Thus Paul is always seeking to live in a way that pleases God, yet not at all depending on his own actions for justification.

2:20 I have been crucified with Christ. Paul's former "self," the person Paul was before he trusted Christ, with all of his sinful goals and proud, self-exalting desires, came to a decisive end—he "died." **It is no longer I who live** does not mean that Paul has no personality of his own (all his writings show that he does) but that his own personal interests and goals no longer direct his life; rather, **Christ who lives in me** now directs and empowers all that he does. How then does he, as a "crucified man," gain any strength to go on living? **the life I now live in the flesh I live by faith in the Son of God**. Paul seems to be saying that, as he trusts Christ moment by moment, Christ then works in and through Paul to give spiritual effectiveness to all that he does. **who loved me and gave himself for me**. The fact that on the cross Jesus bore believers' sins as their personal, individual substitute ("he . . . for me") shows that the crucifixion was not an impersonal, mechanical transaction, but a personal expression of Christ's love for people as individuals.

2:21 Paul returns to the hypothetical situation raised in v. 18 of imagining that the law was back in force again as a means by which he was trying to earn justification. In that case, **if righteousness were through the law**, then Christ's death would have been pointless, for people could earn their own justification by their obedience. But in fact, this is something they can never do. This highlights the depth of the human problem: it cannot be remedied by the God-given law. Sin is so serious that only the substitutionary, atoning death of God's Son can deal with the problem. God's **grace** in the gospel must therefore be humbly and thankfully accepted as the only way of salvation.

3:1–5:12 *Direct Appeals to the Galatians.* Paul offers a variety of reasons why the Galatians should resist the seductive teaching of the people troubling them.

3:1–5 *The Galatians' Experience of Conversion.* Paul interrogates the Galatians, with five questions in as many verses. He despairs that they have come under the spell of the false teachers, and so he returns to their experience of how they first came to know Christ.

3:1 Who has bewitched you. Paul uses the language of pagan magic to characterize the pernicious activity of the false teachers and the perilous situation of the Galatians. **publicly portrayed**. Paul believes that his proclamation of the gospel was so vivid in the Galatians' presence that it was as if they had been eyewitnesses of the crucifixion.

3:2 Let me ask. Using rhetorical questions, Paul shows how illogical it is for the Galatians to seek a fuller Christian life through observance of the law. Did God give them the Spirit and work miracles in their midst (v. 5) because they observed the law? No, it was the result of their **hearing** the gospel and believing it. **Receive the Spirit** refers to the new covenant work of the Holy Spirit that comes after saving faith, at the beginning of the Christian life, to sanctify and to empower the believer in life and various kinds of ministry. Paul knew this experience was so real for the Galatians that they would remember it.

3:5 supplies the Spirit . . . works miracles. In v. 2 Paul mentioned the Holy Spirit's work at the beginning of the Galatians' Christian lives; here he mentions an ongoing, day-by-day work of the Spirit. Though Paul had left these churches, and there were no other apostles present, the Holy Spirit was still present and was still working miracles in their midst. **By hearing with faith** is not only the way to start the Christian life but is also the way to continue it day by day.

3:6–9 *The Gospel in the OT (1): Abraham.* Paul issues a second direct appeal to the Galatians: it is not just their own experience of receiving the gospel by faith that should teach them that salvation is not by the law but by grace. Rather, the OT example of Abraham also teaches that it is through genuine faith, not the law, that one is counted righteous (see Gen. 15:6).

3:7–8 Abraham is the father of God's people not because he is the biological ancestor of the Jews but because he has a family of spiritual children who follow in his footsteps by believing as he did. God promised Abraham that he would bring life from his dead body (see Romans 4). Thus Abraham is a living OT prophecy of the gospel: he was not an Israelite but a pagan, and God justified him **by faith**.

3:10–14 *The Gospel in the OT (2): Leviticus, Deuteronomy, and Habakkuk.* Any attempt to be justified by the law leads to a curse, for righteousness comes only by faith in the atoning work of Jesus Christ. All those indwelt by the Holy Spirit enjoy the blessing of Abraham.

3:10 Paul has just spoken in v. 7 about "those of faith"; now he moves to those **who rely on works of the law**. They are in the situation that

11 Now it is evident that [p]no one is justified before God by the law, for [q]"The righteous
shall live by faith."[1] 12 But the law is not of faith, rather [r]"The one who does them shall
live by them." 13 Christ [s]redeemed us from the curse of the law by becoming a curse for
us—for it is written, [t]"Cursed is everyone who is hanged [u]on a tree"— 14 so that in Christ
Jesus the blessing of Abraham might [v]come to the Gentiles, so that [w]we might receive [x]the
promised Spirit[2] through faith.

The Law and the Promise

15 [y]To give a human example, brothers:[3] [z]even with a man-made covenant, no one annuls
it or adds to it once it has been ratified. 16 Now [a]the promises were made [b]to Abraham and
to his offspring. It does not say, "And to offsprings," referring to many, but referring to one,
[c]"And to your offspring," who is Christ. 17 This is what I mean: the law, which came [d]430
years afterward, does not annul a covenant previously ratified by God, so as [e]to make the
promise void. 18 For if the inheritance comes by the law, it no longer comes by promise;
but [f]God gave it to Abraham by a promise.
19 Why then the law? [g]It was added because of transgressions, [h]until the offspring should

[1] Or *The one who by faith is righteous will live* [2] Greek *receive the promise of the Spirit* [3] Or *brothers and sisters*

11 [p]See ch. 2:16 [q]Rom. 1:17; Heb. 10:38; Cited from Hab. 2:4
12 [r]Cited from Lev. 18:5; See Rom. 10:5
13 [s]ch. 4:5; [Rev. 22:3]; See 2 Pet. 2:1
13 [t]Cited from Deut. 21:23 [u]See Acts 5:30
14 [v]Rom. 4:9, 16; [ver. 28] [w]ver. 2 [x]Acts 2:33; [Isa. 32:15; 44:3; Joel 2:28; John 7:39; Eph. 1:13]
15 [y]See Rom. 3:5 [z][Heb. 9:17]
16 [a]Rom. 4:13, 16; See Luke 1:55 [b]Gen. 12:7; Acts 13:32 [c]Acts 3:25
17 [d]Ex. 12:40, 41; [Gen. 15:13; Acts 7:6] [e]Rom. 4:14
18 [f][Heb. 6:13, 14]
19 [g][Rom. 4:15] [h]ver. 16

Paul talked about in 2:18. Had Paul rebuilt the house of "law," its demands and condemnation would have confronted and confounded him. Those still attached to law-observance are in exactly this position. They have failed to obey the law, and so they stand under the **curse** on unfaithful Israel. They stand in contrast to Abraham and all believers, who are blessed (3:8–9). The history of Israel and human experience demonstrates that all fall short of what God demands (cf. Rom. 1:18–3:20; 3:23) and that all are therefore under the "curse," because no one is able to keep everything commanded in "the law."

3:11 The OT itself points out that righteousness cannot be achieved through the law, as Hab. 2:4 illustrates.

3:12 Paul uses Lev. 18:5 to show that **the law is not of faith**. It is likely that Paul means the same thing here that he meant in Rom. 10:5, where Lev. 18:5 is equated with "the righteousness that is based on the *law*" (cf. Phil. 3:9) in contrast to the "righteousness based on *faith*" (Rom. 10:6). Some interpreters argue that **the one who does them shall live by them** (cf. Lev. 18:5) in its original context had to do with the temporal blessing and fullness of life that would come to the one who "does" the law. But it also seems to be a conditional promise within the law indicating that obedience would lead to righteousness (cf. Deut. 6:25); this promise, however, remains unfulfilled because it relies on the fulfilling of a condition that could never happen: i.e., it relies on a human "doing of the law" in a complete and sufficient way. Others argue the original context of Lev. 18:5 (see note) mainly concerns the means of enjoying life under God's pleasure by keeping God's statutes and rules. Because some think the meaning of Lev. 18:5 in the original context is incompatible with the negative way in which Paul is using the verse here, they believe Paul is citing it as a misused slogan of the Judaizers. It seems better, however, to understand Paul as reading Lev. 18:5 typologically—that is, as seeing life in the land of Israel as a typological reference to eternal life. In the Mosaic covenant, salvation was through faith in God's promise and his atonement, culminating in the Messiah. But now that the new covenant has come, those who insist on the entrance requirements of the old covenant do not have the benefit of sacrifices, so they must "do" all that the Mosaic law requires in order to "live" eternally (cf. Gal. 5:3).

3:13 The divine **curse** is the result of disobedience (v. 10). But the burden of the curse has been lifted by Christ's work on the cross. Paul talked in 2:20 of Christ's death for him personally; now he focuses on Christ's substitutionary work for others.

3:14 Christ hanging on a tree (v. 13) not only brought blessing to Israel but took place **so that . . . the blessing of Abraham might come to the Gentiles**. The coming of the Spirit in new power is one of the central benefits of the new age brought in by Christ (see Isa. 44:3). Believers not only have forgiveness of sins, but also the living presence of God with them. Paul explains more of what it means to have the gift of the Spirit in Galatians 5 and 6.

3:15–18 *An Illustration from Human Law.* The Sinai covenant was an interim covenant that did not contradict the promises of the Abrahamic covenant.

3:15–17 Paul uses an everyday example to explain the place of **the law** in God's scheme. A covenant or a will cannot be changed, and neither can the promises made **to Abraham and to his offspring** be changed just because a law has come into the picture.

3:16 God spoke **promises** to **Abraham** on several occasions, but probably Gen. 13:15 and 17:8 are particularly in view. **And to your offspring**. Paul knows that the singular (Hb. *zera'*) can be used as a collective singular that has a plural sense (he interprets it in a plural sense in Rom. 4:18). But it also can have a singular meaning, and here Paul, knowing that only in **Christ** would the promised blessings come to the Gentiles, sees that the most true and ultimate fulfillment of these OT promises comes to **one** "offspring," namely, Christ. Paul's willingness to make an argument using a singular noun in distinction from its plural form (which occurs in other OT verses) indicates a high level of confidence in the trustworthiness of the small details of the OT text.

3:17 came 430 years afterward. Paul is apparently referring to the Septuagint translation of Ex. 12:40, "The dwelling of the children of Israel . . . in Egypt and in Canaan was 430 years," which would mean 430 years from Abraham to the exodus (the Hb. text does not include "and in Canaan"). Another explanation is that Paul is not counting the time from the first statement of the promise to Abraham but from the last affirmation of that promise to Jacob before he went to Egypt in Gen. 46:3–4. This method would then count the entire time in Egypt as the time from the "promise" to the "law." If this is so, then Paul is relying on the Hebrew text of Ex. 12:40 to affirm a 430-year stay in Egypt.

3:18 In 2:21 Paul said that if righteousness comes through the law, Christ died for nothing. Here he says similarly, **if the inheritance comes by the law**, the **promise** is not the basis for it.

3:19–4:7 *Passing from Slavery to Sonship.* The law was never intended to be in force forever, and now that the promised Messiah has come, those who believe in him are sons of God.

3:19 Why then the law? The question then arises: If the law has no impact on God's plan rooted in his promise, why was the law ever given? **Because of transgressions** might mean (1) "to provide a sacrificial system to deal temporarily with transgressions," (2) "to teach people more clearly what God requires and thereby to restrain transgressions," (3) "to show that transgressions violated an explicit written law," or (4) "to reveal people's sinfulness and need for a savior" (cf. Rom. 3:20: "through the law comes knowledge of sin"). All four senses are theologically true, but the last is probably uppermost in Paul's mind. **put in place through angels by an intermediary**. Deuteronomy 33:2 talks about God coming from Sinai, where he gave the law, "from the ten thousands of holy ones," so the angels were present with God on that occasion (cf. Acts 7:53; Heb. 2:2). Moses was God's "intermediary" in the gift of the law to Israel (Lev. 26:46; John 1:17). The Mosaic law was part of a temporary covenant never intended to last forever. Now that Jesus has come as the true offspring of Abraham, the Mosaic law is no longer

come to whom the promise had been made, and it was [i]put in place through angels [j]by an
intermediary. **20** Now [k]an intermediary implies more than one, but [l]God is one.

21 Is the law then contrary to the promises of God? Certainly not! For [m]if a law had
been given that could give life, then righteousness would indeed be by the law. **22** But the
Scripture [n]imprisoned everything under sin, so that [o]the promise by faith in Jesus Christ
might be given [p]to those who believe.

23 Now before faith came, we were held captive under the law, [q]imprisoned until the coming
faith would be revealed. **24** So then, [r]the law was our [s]guardian until Christ came, [t]in order
that we might be justified by faith. **25** But now that faith has come, we are no longer under a
guardian, **26** for in Christ Jesus [u]you are all sons of God, through faith. **27** For as many of you
as [v]were baptized [w]into Christ have [x]put on Christ. **28** [y]There is neither Jew nor Greek, there
is neither slave[1] nor free, [z]there is no male and female, for you are all one in Christ Jesus.
29 And [a]if you are Christ's, then you are Abraham's offspring, [b]heirs according to promise.

Sons and Heirs

4 I mean that the heir, as long as he is a child, is no different from a slave,[2] though he
is the owner of everything, **2** but he is under guardians and managers until the date
set by his father. **3** In the same way we also, when we were children, [c]were enslaved to the
elementary principles[3] of the world. **4** But [d]when the fullness of time had come, God sent
forth his Son, [e]born [f]of woman, born [g]under the law, **5** [h]to redeem those who were under

[1] Greek *bondservant* [2] Greek *bondservant*; also verse 7 [3] Or *elemental spirits*; also verse 9

19 [i]Acts 7:53; Heb. 2:2 [j]Ex. 20:19, 21, 22; Deut. 5:5, 22, 23, 27, 31; Acts 7:38
20 [k]1 Tim. 2:5; Heb. 8:6; 9:15; 12:24; [Heb. 6:17] [l]Rom. 3:30
21 [m]See ch. 2:21
22 [n]Rom. 11:32; See Rom. 3:9 [o]Rom. 4:16 [p]See Acts 10:43
23 [q][1 Pet. 1:5]
24 [r][Matt. 5:17; Rom. 10:4; Col. 2:17; Heb. 9:9, 10] [s]1 Cor. 4:15 (Gk.) [t]ver. 11; See ch. 2:16
26 [u]ch. 4:5, 6; [John 1:12]; See Rom. 8:14-16
27 [v]Rom. 6:3 [w]See Acts 8:16 [x]See Rom. 13:14
28 [y][ver. 14; ch. 5:6; 6:15]; See Rom. 3:30; 1 Cor. 12:13 [z]1 Cor. 11:11
29 [a]See Rom. 9:7; 1 Cor. 3:23 [b]ch. 4:1, 7; Rom. 8:17; Eph. 3:6; [ch. 4:28; 2 Tim. 1:1; Titus 1:2; Heb. 9:15]

Chapter 4

3 [c]See ch. 2:4
4 [d][1 Tim. 2:6]; See Mark 1:15 [e]Phil. 2:7; See John 1:14 [f][1 Tim. 2:15]; See Gen. 3:15 [g][Luke 2:21, 22, 27]
5 [h]See ch. 3:13

in force. Therefore, circumcision is no longer required, since it is part of the Mosaic covenant.

3:20 There was **more than one** party involved in the presentation of the law to Israel, which involved an **intermediary**, Moses. Because **God is one**, his ultimate revelation comes not through an intermediary but from him alone (this assumes that whatever comes from Christ comes from the one true God, for Christ is fully God). This lies behind Paul's protest in ch. 1 about the gospel coming to him not *from* or *through* a human being but directly from God the Father and his Son Jesus Christ (1:1).

3:21 The law is certainly not **contrary** to **the promises of God**: Paul regards the law as "holy and righteous and good" (Rom. 7:12). But because of human sinfulness, the law was never able to **give life** (see Rom. 8:3).

3:22 The law (**the Scripture**), instead of giving "life" (v. 21) with God, **imprisoned everything under sin** (cf. Rom. 3:9–20). So rather than enabling all Israelites to have access to what was promised, the law was given so that the single "offspring," Christ, would receive the blessing. The blessing is obtained **by faith**, not by their own obedience. God was certainly not surprised by the fact that the Israelites were unable to obey the law. In fact, at the end of the giving of the law, Moses foretold that the Israelites would not obey it (Deut. 31:24–29). Thus the law confirmed the promise to Abraham, that justification would come only by faith (Gal. 3:6–9, 14, 18).

3:23 before faith came. By "faith" Paul means new covenant faith in Christ (cf. v. 22). Thus he is saying, "before Christ came and along with him new covenant faith in him." Since Paul is using Abraham as an example of justification by faith (vv. 6–9, 14, 18), he cannot mean that there was no saving faith before Christ came (cf. note on John 3:18) but only that there was no new covenant faith resting on the knowledge of Christ's finished work.

3:24 The **law**, as **guardian**, had the positive functions of highlighting and restraining transgressions and also of foretelling the coming of Christ.

3:25 faith has come. See note on v. 23.

3:26 you are all sons of God. This is the crucial difference between old covenant and new covenant believers: life under the law was slavery; life in Christ is marked by the freedom that comes from being God's "sons." Both men and women are here characterized as having the rights of "sons," because with sonship comes the right of inheritance. The Greek word *huioi* ("sons") is a legal term used in the adoption and inheritance laws of first-century Rome. As used by Paul here and elsewhere in his letters (cf. 4:5–7; Rom. 8:14–16, 23), this term refers to the status of all Christians, both men and women, who, having been adopted into God's family, now enjoy all the privileges, obligations, and inheritance rights of God's children.

3:27 In addition to sonship (v. 26), Paul adds two more pictures of what is involved in this new age. Being **baptized**, believers have gone down into death, dying to the old era of law, sin, and death (Rom. 6:3–4; Gal. 2:19; 6:14) and have come up out of the water as participants in the new creation (2 Cor. 5:17). **put on Christ**. The language of "putting on," as used of clothing, suggests taking on a new life and purpose through being spiritually united to Christ.

3:28 neither Jew nor Greek. The fact that the Mosaic law has been left behind in the old age means that, in the new creation, the distinction between Jew and Gentile is broken down (see Eph. 2:11–22). Certainly these Galatians do not have to become Jews in order to be Christians (cf. Gal. 3:14). **There is neither slave nor free, there is no male and female** does not imply that there are no distinctions in how these groups should act, for Paul elsewhere commands slaves ("bondservants," ESV footnote) and masters differently (Eph. 6:5–9), and husbands and wives differently (Eph. 5:22–33). Paul clearly is not advocating the elimination of all distinctions nor the acceptability of same-sex marriage or homosexual relations (see Rom. 1:26–27). Rather, he teaches that old divisions and wrongful attitudes of superiority and inferiority are abolished, **for you are all one in Christ Jesus**. He does not take away the distinction between men and women but says they are "united," joined together in "one" body, the church. The verse teaches unity within diversity but not sameness.

3:29 Abraham's offspring. Paul states the main point of his argument: those who belong to Christ are part of Abraham's family, and hence they do not need to be circumcised to become part of God's people.

4:1–3 When a son is a minor and too young to receive his inheritance, he might as well be a **slave**. (On Roman slaves, see note on 1 Cor. 7:21.) This was the situation of Paul and his fellow Israelites under the old covenant.

4:3 elementary principles. Both here and in v. 9 the expression refers to the elementary principles the Galatians previously followed, which for Jews would be the Mosaic law and for Gentiles the basic concepts of their pagan religions. But the additional overtones of demonic bondage in this phrase should not be ignored; they were, in terms of their mind-set and life situation, under a legalistic system and **enslaved**, and Paul explains in v. 8 that this enslavement was "to those that by nature are not gods." Legalistic superstition and demonic domination are closely linked.

4:4 when the fullness of time had come. God sent his Son at the right moment in human history, when God's providential oversight of the events of the world had directed and prepared peoples and nations for the incarnation and ministry of Christ, and for the proclamation of the gospel.

4:5 Paul's **adoption** imagery probably picks up the OT concept of God calling

the law, so that we might receive [i]adoption as sons. 6 And because you are sons, God has
sent [j]the Spirit of his Son into our hearts, crying, "Abba! Father!" 7 So you are no longer a
slave, but a son, and if a son, then [k]an heir through God.

Paul's Concern for the Galatians

8 Formerly, when you [l]did not know God, you [m]were enslaved to those that by nature
[n]are not gods. 9 But now that you have come to know God, or rather [o]to be known by
God, [p]how can you turn back again to [q]the weak and worthless elementary principles of
the world, whose slaves you want to be once more? 10 [r]You observe days and months and
seasons and years! 11 I am afraid [s]I may have labored over you in vain.

12 Brothers,[1] [t]I entreat you, become as I am, for I also have become as you are. [u]You did
me no wrong. 13 You know it was [v]because of a bodily ailment that I preached the gospel
to you [w]at first, 14 and though my condition was a trial to you, you did not scorn or despise
me, but received me [x]as an angel of God, [y]as Christ Jesus. 15 What then has become of
your blessedness? For I testify to you that, if possible, you would have gouged out your
eyes and given them to me. 16 Have I then become your enemy by [z]telling you the truth?[2]
17 They make much of you, but for no good purpose. They want to shut you out, that you
may make much of them. 18 It is always good to be made much of for a good purpose, and
[a]not only when I am present with you, 19 [b]my little children, [c]for whom I am again in the
anguish of childbirth until Christ [d]is formed in you! 20 I wish I could be present with you
now and change my tone, for I am perplexed about you.

[1] Or *Brothers and sisters*; also verses 28, 31 [2] Or *by dealing truthfully with you*

5 [i]ch. 3:26; See Rom. 8:15
6 [j][Rom. 5:5; 2 Cor. 3:17]; See Acts 16:7
7 [k]See ch. 3:29
8 [l]1 Cor. 1:21; 1 Thess. 4:5; 2 Thess. 1:8; 1 John 4:8 [m][Eph. 2:11, 12; 1 Thess. 1:9] [n]2 Chr. 13:9; Isa. 37:19; Jer. 2:11; 5:7; 16:20; [1 Cor. 8:4]
9 [o]See 1 Cor. 8:3 [p][ch. 3:3] [q]Rom. 8:3; Heb. 7:18
10 [r]Rom. 14:5; Col. 2:16
11 [s]ch. 2:2; 5:2, 4; 1 Thess. 3:5
12 [t][2 Cor. 6:13] [u][2 Cor. 2:5]
13 [v]See 1 Cor. 2:3 [w][ch. 1:6]
14 [x]1 Sam. 29:9; [Mal. 2:7 (Gk.); 2 Cor. 5:20] [y]See Matt. 10:40
16 [z]See ch. 2:5
18 [a][ver. 13]
19 [b][1 Cor. 4:15; Philem. 10] [c][James 1:18] [d]Rom. 8:10

Israel his "son" and combines this with the Roman notion of adopting a son (usually already a grown man) in order to designate him as the heir to all the family wealth (see also note on 3:26).

4:6–7 because you are sons. Because Christians are now sons and "of age," they are in a position to receive the inheritance, beginning with the promised **Spirit of his Son**. **Abba** is the Aramaic word for "father" (cf. Rom. 8:14–17).

4:8–11 *Passing from Idolatry to the True God.* The slavery that the Galatians are in danger of embracing again is not just a matter of forfeiting sonship but of abandoning the true God. They would be returning to false gods (v. 8), to worldly principles and structures (vv. 9–10). It would be as if they had never even heard the gospel from Paul (v. 11). For these Gentile Galatian Christians, turning to the Jewish law would be like returning to their paganism.

4:8 Those that by nature are not gods refers to the demonic spirits that controlled the Galatians' former religious practice (cf. 1 Cor. 10:20).

4:9 To know God . . . to be known by God implies a personal relationship with God. **elementary principles**. See note on v. 3.

4:10 Days and months and seasons and years were all part of the ceremonial laws of the Mosaic covenant (cf. Lev. 23:5, 16, 28; 25:4). To require Christians to follow such OT laws is to forfeit the gospel of justification by faith alone, in Christ alone. This also clearly implies that Christians are no longer under the Mosaic covenant. Some see "days" in this verse as evidence that the Jewish seventh-day Sabbath commandment was also part of the ceremonial law that Christians, under the new covenant, no longer need to follow (cf. Acts 20:7; 1 Cor. 16:2; Col. 2:16–17). Others believe that the weekly Sabbath command is not temporary but goes back to God's pattern in creation (Ex. 20:8–11) and that this verse relates only to other days of rest in the Jewish festal calendar.

4:12–20 *Appeal to the Galatians' Knowledge of Paul.* As in 3:1–5, Paul reminds the Galatians of what happened when they heard the gospel and he contrasts his own ministry with that of the false teachers.

4:12 as I am. Paul is free from following Mosaic ceremonial regulations, and living by faith in Christ. **as you are**. Paul had become like the Gentiles in that he did not live under the Jewish law when ministering to them.

4:13 because of a bodily ailment . . . I preached the gospel to you. The exact nature of this illness is not known. "Because" apparently means that Paul was detained in Galatia by this illness and therefore took the opportunity to preach to them.

4:15 Your blessedness probably refers to the sense of joy and divine approval the Galatians had when they believed Paul's gospel preaching and received the Holy Spirit (cf. 3:2).

4:17 The false teachers have been flattering the Galatians, but only to receive flattery back. **to shut you out**. They want to form an exclusive club of people who observe Jewish ceremonial laws, keeping out any who will not give in to their demands.

4:18 Paul's tribute to the Thessalonians (1 Thess. 1:2–9) is an example of what he means by **to be made much of for a good purpose**.

4:19–20 Though Paul chastises the Galatians for being "foolish" (3:1, 3), he nonetheless has deep emotional feelings of anguish for them—because they, like **little children**, have not been growing but need almost to be delivered again, and Paul's feelings about them are as agonizing as birth pangs.

4:21–31 *The Gospel in the OT (3): Abraham's Sons.* Paul continues to emphasize the chasm between being a free child of God and being a slave to the law, sin, and false gods. The background to this passage is Genesis 16–17 and 21. Abraham's son Ishmael—technically the firstborn—represents the slave sons of Abraham and hence the enslaving Sinai covenant, because he was Abraham's son through the slave woman Hagar. Isaac, on the other hand, represents the free sons of Abraham (see Gal. 3:7, 29).

4:21 law . . . law. Paul plays on the different senses of "law": it can mean the commandments given by God to Moses during the wilderness wanderings

Contrasts in Paul's Allegory (4:21–31)

slave woman	free woman
Ishmael	Isaac
according to flesh	through promise
Hagar	Sarah
slavery	freedom
present Jerusalem	Jerusalem above
persecuting	persecuted

Example of Hagar and Sarah

21 Tell me, you who desire to be under the law, do you not listen to the law? 22 For it is
written that Abraham had two sons, [e]one by a slave woman and [f]one by a free woman.
23 But [g]the son of the slave was born according to the flesh, while [h]the son of the free
woman was born through promise. 24 Now this may be interpreted allegorically: these
women are two [i]covenants. [j]One is from Mount Sinai, bearing children for slavery; she is
Hagar. 25 Now Hagar is Mount Sinai in Arabia;[1] she corresponds to the present Jerusalem,
for she is in slavery with her children. 26 But [k]the Jerusalem above is free, and she is our
mother. 27 For it is written,

> [l]"Rejoice, O barren one who does not bear;
> break forth and cry aloud, you who are not in labor!
> For the children of the desolate one will be more
> than those of the one who has a husband."

28 Now you,[2] brothers, [m]like Isaac, [n]are children of promise. 29 But just as at that time he
who was born according to the flesh [o]persecuted him who was born according to the Spirit,
[p]so also it is now. 30 But what does the Scripture say? [q]"Cast out the slave woman and her
son, for the son of the slave woman shall not inherit with the son of the free woman." 31 So,
brothers, we are not children of the slave but [r]of the free woman.

Christ Has Set Us Free

5 For [s]freedom Christ has [t]set us free; [u]stand firm therefore, and do not submit again
to [v]a yoke of [w]slavery.
2 Look: I, Paul, say to you that [x]if you accept circumcision, [y]Christ will be of no advantage
to you. 3 I testify again to every man who accepts circumcision that [z]he is obligated to keep
the whole law. 4 You are [a]severed from Christ, [b]you who would be justified[3] by the law; [c]you
have fallen away from grace. 5 For through the Spirit, by faith, we ourselves eagerly [d]wait

22 [e]Gen. 16:5 [f]Gen. 21:2
23 [g]ver. 29; [Rom. 9:7] [h]ver. 28; Gen. 17:16-19; 18:10, 14; 21:1, 2; Heb. 11:11
24 [i]See Rom. 9:4 [j]Deut. 33:2
26 [k][Heb. 12:22; Rev. 3:12; 21:2, 10]
27 [l]Cited from Isa. 54:1
28 [m]See ver. 23 [n]Rom. 9:8; See ch. 3:29
29 [o]Gen. 21:9 [p]See ch. 5:11
30 [q]Cited from Gen. 21:10; [John 8:35]
31 [r][1 Pet. 3:6]

Chapter 5

1 [s]ver. 13; ch. 2:4; See James 1:25 [t]See John 8:32 [u]See 1 Cor. 16:13 [v]Acts 15:10 [w]See ch. 2:4
2 [x]ver. 3, 11; Acts 15:1; 1 Cor. 7:18 [y]See ch. 4:11
3 [z]Rom. 2:25
4 [a]Rom. 7:6 (Gk.) [b][ch. 2:21; 3:10; Rom. 9:31, 32] [c][Heb. 12:15; 2 Pet. 3:17]
5 [d]See Rom. 8:23, 25

[1] Some manuscripts *For Sinai is a mountain in Arabia* [2] Some manuscripts *we* [3] Or *counted righteous*

(which the Galatians misguidedly want to obey in their totality), but it can also mean the first five books of the Bible as a whole.

4:23 Flesh represents human desires, principles, and the sin that contaminates them: Ishmael was the son born when Abraham and Sarah took matters into their own hands by trying to perpetuate their family line through Hagar. The **promise** is the absolute opposite of flesh, since it is a word *from God* that will be fulfilled *by God* (see Rom. 4:18–21), just as Isaac was born by God's miraculous work.

4:24 allegorically. As an illustration that depicts a general principle (see chart, p. 2252).

4:25 Arabia. See note on 1:17. **in slavery**. The city of **Jerusalem** ought to be the capital city of the "Israel of God" (6:16), but instead it remains a stronghold of Israel according to the flesh, i.e., Jews who have not turned to Jesus. As a result, the city is just as it was when occupied in Isaiah's day—enslaved.

4:26–27 All those who believe in Christ belong to the heavenly **Jerusalem** and are the true Israel. As Isaiah prophesied (Isa. 54:1), the exile did not spell the end for the people of God. God will again work supernaturally to bring about the (new) birth of **children** where there are none, even among the Gentiles.

4:28 like Isaac. In a way analogous to Isaac's miraculous birth, the Galatians have become God's children by an act of God's gracious and miraculous power, not by human effort.

4:29 so also it is now. Just as Ishmael persecuted Isaac (not explicitly mentioned in the OT, but suggested by Gen. 21:9), so now the Jews who seek justification by human effort are persecuting Christians who trust God's promise of justification by faith. In Gen. 16:4, when Hagar conceived, "she looked with contempt on her mistress." This too is mirrored in the fact that now non-Christian and pseudo-Christian Jews are persecuting Christians like Paul (as seen in Gal. 6:17). History is repeating itself.

4:30 Cast out the slave woman and her son, and, by implication, all those represented by them in this allegory, i.e., those who seek justification through their own efforts. This implies that those who teach the false gospel of justification by works should not be allowed to remain and teach in a church that follows Christ.

5:1–12 *Judgment for Those Who Turn from the Gospel.* Those who turn to the law for salvation will cut themselves off from salvation. Hence Paul warns and encourages his readers not to defect.

5:1 Christ has set us free from Jewish ceremonial laws and regulations (see note on 2:11–12) but not from obedience to God's moral standards (5:14–6:1).

5:2 The Galatians may have thought that requiring circumcision would not make much difference, but Paul knows that if they require obedience to any one part of the Mosaic law for justification, then they are committed to obeying all of it perfectly for their justification (v. 3), something none of them can do (cf. 3:10–11, 21). Therefore he says, **if you accept circumcision, Christ will be of no advantage to you.**

5:4 severed from Christ . . . fallen away from grace. Paul is not discussing here the question of whether a genuine believer can lose his or her salvation. He is only saying that people who may once have made a profession of faith, if they now are truly seeking to be **justified by the law**, must not really have a relationship with Christ and have fallen away from the grace that was offered and available to them.

5:5 We . . . wait for the hope of righteousness means that Christians do not attempt to produce perfect righteousness in their lives by their own efforts (as Paul's opponents were futilely trying to do), for their hope is not in themselves; instead, they wait for God to complete righteousness in them—either when they die and are with the Lord (Heb. 12:23) or at Christ's return (1 Cor. 15:49; cf. Rev. 21:27). An alternative explanation is that "the hope of righteousness" refers to the believer's hope and expectation that God will declare that the believer is in fact going to be judged righteous at the final judgment.

for the hope of righteousness. 6 For in Christ Jesus [e]neither circumcision nor uncircumcision counts for anything, but [f]only faith working through love.
7 [g]You were running well. Who hindered you from obeying [h]the truth? 8 This persuasion
is not from [i]him who calls you. 9 [j]A little leaven leavens the whole lump. 10 [k]I have confidence
in the Lord that you will [l]take no other view, and [m]the one who is troubling you will bear
the penalty, whoever he is. 11 But if I, brothers,[1] still preach[2] circumcision, [n]why am I still
being persecuted? In that case [o]the offense of the cross has been removed. 12 I wish [p]those
who unsettle you would emasculate themselves!
13 For you were called to freedom, brothers. [q]Only do not use your freedom as an opportunity for the flesh, but through love [r]serve one another. 14 For [s]the whole law is fulfilled
in one word: [t]"You shall love your neighbor as yourself." 15 But if you [u]bite and devour one
another, watch out that you are not consumed by one another.

Keep in Step with the Spirit

16 But I say, [v]walk by the Spirit, and you will not gratify [w]the desires of the flesh. 17 For [x]the
desires of the flesh are against the Spirit, and the desires of the Spirit are against the flesh, for
these are opposed to each other, [y]to keep you from doing the things you want to do. 18 But
if you are [z]led by the Spirit, [a]you are not under the law. 19 Now [b]the works of the flesh are
evident: sexual immorality, impurity, sensuality, 20 idolatry, sorcery, enmity, strife, jealousy,
fits of anger, rivalries, dissensions, [c]divisions, 21 envy,[3] drunkenness, orgies, and things like
these. I warn you, as I warned you before, that [d]those who do such things will not inherit

[1] Or *brothers and sisters;* also verse 13 [2] Greek *proclaim* [3] Some manuscripts add *murder*

6 [e]ch. 6:15; 1 Cor. 7:19; Col. 3:11; See ch. 3:28 [f][Eph. 6:23; 1 Thess. 1:3; James 2:18, 20, 22]
7 [g]See 1 Cor. 9:24 [h]See ch. 2:5
8 [i]ch. 1:6
9 [j]1 Cor. 5:6; [1 Cor. 15:33; Heb. 12:15]
10 [k]See 2 Cor. 2:3 [l][Phil. 3:15] [m]ch. 1:7; [ver. 12]
11 [n]ch. 4:29; 6:12 [o]1 Cor. 1:23; See 1 Pet. 2:8
12 [p][ver. 10]; See ch. 2:4
13 [q]1 Pet. 2:16; Jude 4; [1 Cor. 8:9; 2 Pet. 2:19]
13 [r]1 Cor. 9:19
14 [s][Matt. 7:12; 22:40] [t]Cited from Lev. 19:18; [ver. 22; ch. 6:2]; See Matt. 19:19; John 13:34
15 [u][Phil. 3:2]
16 [v]ver. 24, 25; Rom. 8:4; See Rom. 13:14 [w]Eph. 2:3
17 [x]Rom. 7:23; 8:5-7 [y]Rom. 7:15, 18, 19
18 [z]Rom. 8:14 [a]See Rom. 7:4
19 [b]1 Cor. 3:3; Eph. 5:3; Col. 3:5; James 3:14, 15; [Matt. 15:18-20]
20 [c]1 Cor. 11:19
21 [d][Col. 3:6]; See 1 Cor. 6:9

5:6 Paul is not opposed to **circumcision** in and of itself but only if it is required for salvation. True **faith** is a living and active thing and produces love.

5:11 If Paul was still preaching that people had to be circumcised, then **the offense of the cross** would be **removed** because human pride in human effort would return. In other words, there would be no "offense" to humble us by declaring that no work of ours can make us righteous before God.

5:13–6:10 *Life in the Spirit and Love.* Freedom from the law does not lead to libertinism, for believers by the power of the Spirit live a new life characterized by love.

5:13–15 *The Law of Love.* Serving one another in love fulfills the law.

5:13–14 Far from the Christian life being enslaving, it is the only way to resist the various slaveries offered by the world. But this does not mean that Christians can do whatever they feel like doing (which itself is just another form of slavery). Rather, serving and loving others is the route to escaping bondage and fulfilling the ultimate content of the law.

5:13 freedom. From Mosaic laws, as represented by circumcision. **Opportunity for the flesh** means "opportunity to follow your fallen, sinful desires and act contrary to God's moral laws."

5:14 When Paul says **the whole law is fulfilled** in the commandment to "love your neighbor as yourself," and when he uses that command as the reason why the Galatians are to "serve one another" (v. 13), he implies that Christians still have a moral obligation to follow the moral standards found in God's "law" in Scripture. Obedience is not a means of justification, but it is a crucial component of the Christian life.

5:16–26 *The Desires of the Flesh vs. the Fruit of the Spirit.* Life under the law expresses itself in the works of the flesh, but those who live by the Spirit bear fruit pleasing to God.

5:16 Having contrasted the flesh with love (vv. 13–14), Paul now sets it against the Spirit. The only way to conquer the flesh is to yield to the Spirit. **Walk by the Spirit** implies both direction and empowerment; that is, making decisions and choices according to the Holy Spirit's guidance, and acting with the spiritual power that the Spirit supplies. To "walk" in Scripture regularly represents the pattern of conduct of all of one's life. **The desires of the flesh** would mean not just bodily cravings but all of the ordinary desires of fallen human nature (see examples in vv. 19–21).

5:17 to keep you from doing the things you want to do. Paul acknowledges that the Christian life is a struggle—a war between the flesh and the Spirit (see also Eph. 6:10–18).

5:18 led by the Spirit. The verb (Gk. *agō*) implies an active, personal involvement by the Holy Spirit in guiding Christians, and the present tense ("if you are being led . . .") indicates his ongoing activity. **you are not under the law**. The Spirit's active presence in believers' lives shows that they are no longer under the pre-Christian system (cf. 3:2, 5, 14; 4:6).

5:19 Works of the flesh means actions flowing out of fallen human nature and its desires. Apart from the transforming work of the Holy Spirit, these are the actions toward which sinful humans instinctively gravitate.

5:20 idolatry, sorcery. These are evidences of a desire to be in touch with the spiritual realm through humanly invented means: they supposedly have God as their ultimate object, but they reject the revealed way in which he should be worshiped. Because Christ is "the way, and the truth, and the life" (John 14:6), all other ways to God are false. **enmity, strife**, etc. When people reject God, they turn in on themselves, and so relationships between human beings are destroyed as well.

5:21 Envy comes about when people are not content with what God has given them, longing instead for what he has given others. **Drunkenness** and **orgies** are examples of how people misuse God's good gifts in destructive and sinful ways, in rebellion against God as the gracious giver of all good things. In the OT, wine was associated with joy and celebration (e.g., Neh. 8:10; Ps. 104:15; see note on John 2:3) but when abused was seen as being highly destructive (Prov. 20:1; 21:17; 23:29–35), and drunkenness is consistently condemned throughout Scripture (e.g., Eph. 5:18). Sex is a precious gift for husband and wife, but when abused it also has highly destructive consequences for all involved (1 Cor. 6:18). **those who do such things**. The present participle (Gk. *prassontes*, translated here as "do") refers to those who "make a practice of doing" such things, as a pattern of life. Their outward conduct indicates their inward spiritual status: that they are not born of God, do not have the Holy Spirit within, and are not God's true children.

5:22–23 The Spirit fights against sin not merely in defense but also in attack by producing in Christians the positive attributes of godly character, all of which are evident in Jesus in the Gospels. **Love** appears first because it is the greatest quality (1 Cor. 13:1–13; 2 Pet. 1:5–7) in that it most clearly reflects the character of God. **Joy** comes in at a close second, for in rejoicing in God's salvation Christians show that their affections are rightly placed in God's will and his purpose (see John 15:11; 16:24; Rom. 15:13; 1 Pet. 1:8; Jude 24; etc.). **Peace** is the product of God having reconciled sinners to himself, so that they are no longer his enemies, which should result in confi-

the kingdom of God. 22 But [e]the fruit of the Spirit is [f]love, joy, peace, patience, [g]kindness,
goodness, faithfulness, 23 [h]gentleness, [i]self-control; [j]against such things there is no law. 24 And
those who belong to Christ Jesus [k]have crucified the flesh with its [l]passions and desires.
25 If we live by the Spirit, [m]let us also keep in step with the Spirit. 26 [n]Let us not become
conceited, provoking one another, envying one another.

Bear One Another's Burdens

6 Brothers,[1] [o]if anyone is caught in any transgression, [p]you who are spiritual should
restore him in [q]a spirit of gentleness. Keep watch on yourself, lest you too be tempted.
2 [r]Bear one another's burdens, and [s]so fulfill [t]the law of Christ. 3 For [u]if anyone thinks he
is something, [v]when he is nothing, he deceives himself. 4 But let each one [w]test his own
work, and then his reason to boast will be in himself alone and not in his neighbor. 5 For
[x]each will have to bear his own load.
6 [y]Let the one who is taught the word share all good things with the one who teaches. 7 [z]Do
not be deceived: God is not mocked, for [a]whatever one sows, that will he also reap. 8 For [b]the
one who sows to his own flesh [c]will from the flesh reap corruption, but [d]the one who sows
to the Spirit will from the Spirit reap eternal life. 9 And [e]let us not grow weary of doing good,
for in due season we will reap, [f]if we do not give up. 10 So then, [g]as we have opportunity, let
us [h]do good to everyone, and especially to those who are [i]of the household of faith.

Final Warning and Benediction

11 See with what large letters I am writing to you [j]with my own hand. 12 [k]It is those
who want to make a good showing in the flesh [l]who would force you to be circumcised,

[1] Or *Brothers and sisters*; also verse 18

11 [j]See 1 Cor. 16:21 12 [k]See 2 Cor. 11:13 [l]ch. 2:3

22 [e][Rom. 7:4; 8:5; Eph. 5:9] [f]See Rom. 5:1-5; Col. 3:12-17 [g]2 Cor. 6:6
23 [h]Eph. 4:2 [i]Acts 24:25 [j]1 Tim. 1:9
24 [k][ver. 16]; See Rom. 6:6 [l]Rom. 7:5
25 [m][ver. 16]
26 [n]Phil. 2:3

Chapter 6

1 [o][Ps. 141:5; 2 Cor. 2:7; Heb. 12:13; James 5:19] [p][Rom. 15:1; 1 Cor. 10:15]; See 1 Cor. 2:15 [q]1 Cor. 4:21; [2 Tim. 2:25]
2 [r]Rom. 15:1; 1 Thess. 5:14 [s][ch. 5:14] [t]1 John 4:21; See John 13:34
3 [u][ch. 2:6]; See 1 Cor. 3:7, 18 [v]2 Cor. 12:11
4 [w][1 Cor. 11:28; 2 Cor. 13:5]
5 [x][Rom. 14:12]
6 [y][Rom. 15:27; 1 Cor. 9:11]
7 [z]1 Cor. 6:9; 15:33; James 1:16 [a]See 2 Cor. 9:6
8 [b][Hos. 8:7]; See Job 4:8 [c]See Rom. 6:21 [d]See James 3:18
9 [e]2 Thess. 3:13; [1 Cor. 15:58] [f]Heb. 12:3, 5; [Heb. 10:36]; See Matt. 10:22
10 [g]Prov. 3:27; John 9:4; 12:35 [h]Eph. 4:28; 1 Tim. 6:18; [1 Thess. 5:15] [i][Eph. 2:19; 1 Tim. 5:8; Heb. 3:6]

dence and freedom in approaching God (Rom. 5:1–2; Heb. 4:16). **Patience** shows that Christians are following God's plan and timetable rather than their own and that they have abandoned their own ideas about how the world should work. **Kindness** means showing goodness, generosity, and sympathy toward others, which likewise is an attribute of God (Rom. 2:4). **Goodness** means working for the benefit of others, not oneself; Paul mentions it again in Gal. 6:10. **Faithfulness** is another divine characteristic; it means consistently doing what one says one will do. **Gentleness** is a quality Jesus attributes to himself in Matt. 11:29; it enables people to find rest in him and to encourage and strengthen others. **Self-control** is the discipline given by the Holy Spirit that allows Christians to resist the power of the flesh (cf. Gal. 5:17). **Against such things there is no law**, and therefore those who manifest them are fulfilling the law—more than those who insist on Jewish ceremonies, and likewise more than those who follow the works of the flesh surveyed in vv. 19–21.

5:24 Again, **Christ** and the Spirit (v. 25) come together as the source of the believer's life. Christians have **crucified the flesh**, or died with Christ to sin (see 6:14; Rom. 6:4–6). Now that the old order of things has passed away for believers, their old sinful selves that belonged to that order have crumbled as well—so they should pay no attention to them. "Flesh" here should not be understood to mean physical bodies but rather fallen, sinful human nature with all its desires.

5:25 keep in step with the Spirit. A different verb than in v. 16, meaning "walk in line behind a leader" (Gk. *stoicheō*).

5:26 Paul is probably referring specifically to attitudes that seem to have become a problem in the Galatian churches (see v. 15). But these sinful attitudes and actions obviously extend beyond one Roman province: Paul has just mentioned enmity, strife, jealousy, and envy as "works of the flesh" in general (vv. 19–21).

6:1–10 *A Christian Life of Concrete Love.* Paul illustrates what he means by the life of love in the Spirit, which he described in more general terms in the previous section.

6:1 you who are spiritual. This does not refer to an elite class of Christians but rather to those who have more maturity and experience in the Christian life and who are therefore in a position to help their beleaguered brother or sister. The adjective "spiritual" means "living and walking according to the Holy Spirit" (see note on 5:16; also 1 Cor. 2:15; 3:1; 14:37) and includes, but is not limited to, the qualities listed in Gal. 5:22–23.

6:2 To **bear one another's burdens** is the supreme imitation of Jesus, the ultimate burden-bearer (see Rom. 15:1–3). He has even gone to the length of taking mankind's sins (Gal. 1:4) and the curse of the law (3:13) upon himself. **and so fulfill the law of Christ**. Though Paul insists that the Galatians are free from obeying Jewish ceremonial laws (see note on 2:11–12), this does not mean they are free from all of God's moral requirements. The "law of Christ" in a broad sense means the entire body of ethical teaching that Jesus gave and endorsed (see note on 1 Cor. 9:21), but in a specific sense here it probably refers to the command to love one's neighbor as oneself (Matt. 22:39; John 13:34), which, if followed fully, will result in obeying the rest of God's moral law (Rom. 13:8–10).

6:6 Paul instructs the church to support its teachers materially—with food, money, and whatever **good things** are appropriate.

6:7–8 whatever one sows, that will he also reap. In this context, Paul's reference to "reaping" is a reference to the blessings of **eternal life** (rather than to temporal blessings) that the believer will "reap" as the result of "sowing" his life **to the Spirit**. As Paul argues elsewhere (2 Cor. 4:17), the believer's expectation and experience in this life will be persecution and affliction, but "this light momentary affliction is preparing for us an eternal weight of glory beyond all comparison." (Cf. Jesus' words in John 15:18–21; 16:33.)

6:10 While believers await their rewards (vv. 7–9) they should **do good**. The primary focus should be on serving those in the church, but never to the exclusion of people in the wider world. As Jesus made clear (e.g., Matt. 6:33), the Christian's primary allegiance is to the kingdom of God, with God as our heavenly Father (Matt. 6:9, 32; 12:50; cf. Matt. 8:21–22), rather than to friends, the workplace, school, sports, or to anything else, even earthly families.

6:11–18 *Final Warning.* Paul summarizes the main themes of the letter and challenges the reader to stay true to the gospel. To require circumcision is to deny the cross and the dawning of the new creation. Those who belong to the new creation comprise the true Israel.

6:11 Paul probably has been dictating the letter to a scribe (see also Rom.

and only [m]in order that they may not be persecuted for the cross of Christ. 13 For even
those who are circumcised do not themselves keep the law, but they desire to have you
circumcised that they may boast in your flesh. 14 But far be it from me to boast [n]except in
the cross of our Lord Jesus Christ, by which[1] the world [o]has been crucified to me, and I
to the world. 15 For [p]neither circumcision counts for anything, nor uncircumcision, but
[q]a new creation. 16 And as for all who walk by this rule, [r]peace and mercy be upon them,
and upon [s]the Israel of God.

17 From now on let no one cause me trouble, for I bear on my body the marks of Jesus.
18 [t]The grace of our Lord Jesus Christ be [u]with your spirit, brothers. Amen.

12[m]ch. 5:11
14[n]1 Cor. 2:2; [Phil. 3:3, 7, 8] [o]See Rom. 6:6
15[p][Rom. 2:28]; See ch. 5:6 [q][John 3:5, 7]; See Rom. 6:4
16[r]Ps. 125:5; 128:6 [s]ch. 3:7, 9, 29; Rom. 2:29; 4:12; 9:6-8; Phil. 3:3
18[t]Philem. 25; See Rom. 16:20 [u]2 Tim. 4:22

[1] *Or through whom*

16:22). Now, however, he adds his "signature" to the letter (see 2 Thess. 3:17)—a postscript in his own handwriting, which entailed **large letters**!

6:14 the world has been crucified to me. Paul is saying that the entire world system in all its glory, but in opposition to God, is dead or destroyed in its power to attract him; it has no influence or power over Paul, no appeal to him. **and I to the world**. Paul is (similarly) dead to the desires and attractions of the world, for he serves Christ as his new master.

6:15 On Christians as **a new creation**, see 2 Cor. 5:17.

6:16 and upon. "And" (Gk. *kai*) can also mean "even," in which case Paul would be equating the church with "the Israel of God." Which sense is best here must be decided with reference to the larger context of Paul's thought both in Galatians and in his other epistles. **Israel of God**. That is, in contrast to the children of the "present Jerusalem" (4:25), the true people of God are the *believing* children of Abraham (3:7, 29), who belong to "Jerusalem above" (4:26–27).

6:17 The false teachers, perhaps followed by some of the Galatian Christians themselves, have obviously been slandering Paul to some degree. But Paul insists on the respect that is due to his ministry. He is a genuine minister of Christ and has the scars to prove it—what he calls **the marks of Jesus** that resulted from his being persecuted (see 2 Cor. 11:23–27).

6:18 Paul's final prayerful blessing shows that he has not given up on the Galatians. He still refers to them as **brothers** and calls on Christ and the Spirit to give them grace.

INTRODUCTION TO

THE LETTER OF PAUL TO THE

EPHESIANS

Author and Title

Pauline authorship of Ephesians was universally accepted until modern times. Today a number of scholars claim that it was written in Paul's name by an unknown follower or imitator of Paul, and they give two main reasons: (1) the letter's style and thought does not strike everyone as characteristically Pauline; and (2) the author of Ephesians does not seem to be familiar with the letter's recipients (see 1:15; 3:2; 4:21), which seems odd given Paul's extended stay at Ephesus (Acts 19:10).

However, there are sound reasons to affirm that Paul wrote Ephesians. First, the letter explicitly claims to be Paul's (1:1; 3:1), which should weigh heavily in the debate unless there is overwhelming evidence to the contrary. The early church—which rejected other spurious letters—unanimously accepted this letter to Ephesus as being written by Paul, and this was a city with a reputation for discernment regarding false apostolic claims (Rev. 2:2). Furthermore, letters in antiquity were usually transmitted through a person known by both author and recipient(s) who would have guaranteed the original copy's genuineness and elaborated on its details—see note on Ephesians 6:21–22 regarding Tychicus.

Second, analyses of an author's style are often subjectively based on incomplete evidence. With the aid of more sophisticated computer analysis, further careful study has shown that Ephesians has more similarities to Paul's accepted style than was earlier recognized. In addition, recent research suggests that the role of secretaries in the composition of ancient letters should be given greater consideration than it has been given in the past. Ephesians does indeed demonstrate close similarity with Paul's forms of expression and thought. Critics have used this evidence to ascribe authorship to someone Paul had influenced, but it is more likely that these marks of Pauline thought and writing style confirm that he himself wrote the book.

The question of Paul's apparent unfamiliarity with his readers can easily be explained. Ancient archaeological evidence has shown that Ephesus controlled a large network of outlying villages and rural areas up to 30 miles (48 km) from the city. Also, Acts 19:10 reveals that reports of Paul's preaching during his stay at Ephesus had radiated out to "all the residents of Asia." Hence, Paul would not have been personally acquainted with newer pockets of believers in the Ephesian villages and rural farms that had sprung up since his stay in the city a few years before the writing of this letter.

Moreover, many have suggested that Ephesians in its present form stems from the Ephesus copy of a circular letter to several Asian churches that Tychicus was delivering in the course of his journey to Colossae, along with the letter to the Colossians (Col. 4:7–9). Therefore, the absence of personal greetings is no cause for surprise.

Finally, it would be extraordinarily odd for someone to write so forcefully that his readers should "speak the truth" and "put away falsehood" (4:15, 25) in a letter he was deceptively forging! Consequently, it can be affirmed with good confidence that Paul wrote Ephesians.

The title "to the Ephesians" is found in many early manuscripts (see note on 1:1). It indicates that the letter was written to the churches in Ephesus and the surrounding dependent region.

Date

Because Paul mentions his imprisonment (3:1; 4:1; 6:20), this letter should be dated to c. A.D. 62 when Paul was held in Rome (Acts 28). Critics who date Ephesians later in the first century do so from doubts about Paul's authorship rather than from strong evidence against the earlier date.

Theme

There are two main themes of Ephesians: (1) Christ has reconciled all creation to himself and to God, and (2) Christ has united people from all nations to himself and to one another in his church. These great deeds were accomplished through the powerful, sovereign, and free working of the triune God—Father, Son, and Holy Spirit—and are recognized and received by faith alone through his grace. In light of these great truths, Christians are to lead lives that are a fitting tribute of gratitude to their great Lord.

Purpose, Occasion, and Background

There was no specific occasion or problem that inspired this letter, though Paul does mention that he desired the Ephesians to know how he was faring in confinement (6:21–22). Ephesians articulates general instruction in the truths of the cosmic redemptive work of God in Christ; the unity of the church among diverse peoples; and proper conduct in the church, the home, and the world. Unity and love in the bond of peace mark the work of the Savior as well as Christians' grateful response to his free grace in their lives.

Ancient Ephesus forms an appropriate background to the book of Ephesians because of this city's fascination with magic and the occult (see Acts 19:19, and below). This helps explain Paul's emphasis on the power of God over all heavenly authorities and on Christ's triumphant ascension as head over the church and over all things in this age and the next. The Ephesians needed to be reminded of these things in order to remain resolute in their allegiance to Christ as the supreme power in the world and in their lives.

Timeline

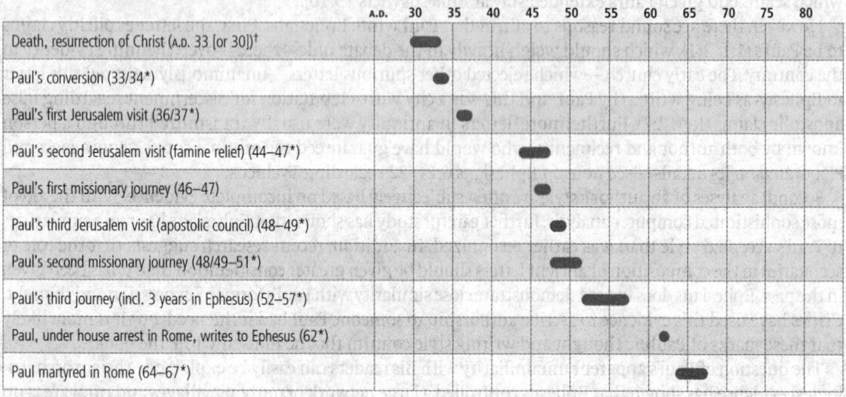

A.D. 30 35 40 45 50 55 60 65 70 75 80
Death, resurrection of Christ (A.D. 33 [or 30])†
Paul's conversion (33/34*)
Paul's first Jerusalem visit (36/37*)
Paul's second Jerusalem visit (famine relief) (44–47*)
Paul's first missionary journey (46–47)
Paul's third Jerusalem visit (apostolic council) (48–49*)
Paul's second missionary journey (48/49–51*)
Paul's third journey (incl. 3 years in Ephesus) (52–57*)
Paul, under house arrest in Rome, writes to Ephesus (62*)
Paul martyred in Rome (64–67*)

** denotes approximate date; / signifies either/or; † see The Date of Jesus' Crucifixion, pp. 1809–1810*

The Ancient City of Ephesus

An important port city on the west coast of Asia, Ephesus boasted the temple of Artemis (one of the Seven Wonders of the ancient world). Just a few decades before Paul, Strabo called Ephesus the greatest emporium in the province of Asia Minor (*Geography* 12.8.15; cf. 14.1.20–26). However, the silting up of the harbor and the ravages of earthquakes caused the abandonment of the harbor city several centuries later. Today, among the vast archaeological remains, some key structures date from the actual time of the NT.

The grandiose theater, where citizens chanted "great is Artemis of the Ephesians" (Acts 19:29–40), had been enlarged under Claudius near the time when Paul was in the city. It held an estimated 20,000 or more spectators. The theater looked west toward the port. From the theater a processional way led north toward the temple of Artemis. In the fourth century B.C. the Ephesians proudly rebuilt this huge temple with their own funds after a fire, even refusing aid from Alexander the Great. The temple surroundings were deemed an official "refuge" for those fearing vengeance, and they played a central part in the economic prosperity of the city, even acting at times like a bank. A eunuch priest served the goddess Artemis, assisted by virgin women. Today very little remains of that once great temple beyond its foundations and a sizable altar, although the nearby museum displays two large statues of Artemis discovered elsewhere in Ephesus.

Other archaeologically extant religious structures include a post-NT temple of Serapis and several important imperial cult temples. Before Paul's day, Ephesus had proudly obtained the right to host the Temple of the Divine Julius [Caesar] and the goddess Roma. The city later housed memorials to the emperors Trajan (A.D. 98–117) and Hadrian (A.D. 117–138); and it possessed a huge temple of Domitian (A.D. 81–96), which may have been constructed during the time the apostle John was in western Asia. Luke testifies to Jewish presence in Ephesus (Acts 18:19, 24; 19:1–10, 13–17), and this is confirmed by inscriptions and by literary sources (e.g., Josephus, *Against Apion* 2.39; *Jewish Antiquities* 14.262–264).

Civic structures during the time of Paul included the state agora (marketplace) with its stoa, basilica, and town hall. This spilled out onto Curetes Street, which contained several monuments to important citizens such as Pollio and Memmius. Curetes Street led to the commercial agora neighboring the theater; this large market square could be entered through the Mazaeus and Mithradates Gate (erected in honor of their patrons Caesar Augustus and Marcus Agrippa). Shops lined this agora and part of Curetes Street. A building across the street from the agora has frequently been called a brothel, although some have questioned this. On the way to the Artemis temple from the theater, one would have passed the huge stadium renovated or built under Nero (A.D. 54–68).

The wealth of some residents of Ephesus is apparent in the lavish terrace houses just off Curetes Street. Later inscriptions mention a guild of silversmiths and even give the names of specific silversmiths (cf. Demetrius the silversmith, mentioned in Acts 19:24). However, as in most Roman cities, many people would have been in the servant class, and others would not have claimed much wealth. By the end of the second century (after the NT period) many other monumental structures were added, including some important gymnasia and the famous Library of Celsus. Remains of the giant Byzantine Church of Mary remind one that this former pagan town later hosted an important church council (the Council of Ephesus, A.D. 431).

History of Salvation Summary

Christians have experienced in Christ the salvation and blessings that God promised through the ages, and look forward to the consummation of God's purposes in Christ. (For an explanation of the "History of Salvation," see the Overview of the Bible, pp. 23–26.)

EPHESUS IN THE TIME OF PAUL (C. A.D. 60)

The city plan below shows those features of the city of Ephesus that archaeologists have so far identified as dating from the time of Paul. Many of the notable buildings uncovered in the excavation at Ephesus date from later periods.

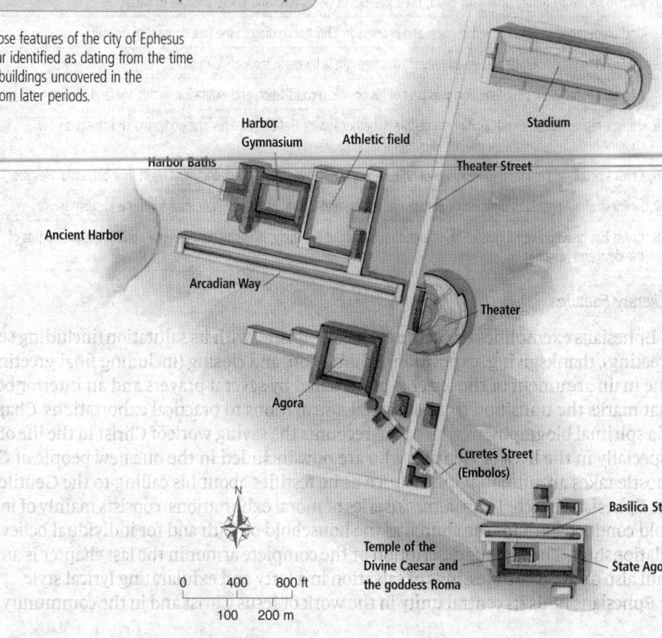

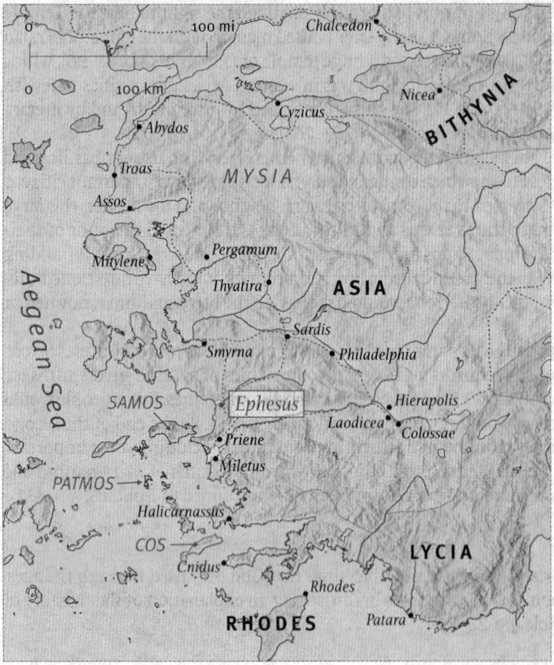

The Setting of Ephesians
(c. A.D. 62)
Ephesus was a wealthy port city in the Roman province of Asia. It was a center of learning and was positioned near several key land routes in western Asia Minor. Paul probably wrote his letter to the Ephesians while under house arrest in Rome (Acts 28).

Key Themes

1. All people are by nature spiritually dead, transgressors of God's law, and under the rule of Satan.	1:7; 2:1–3, 5, 11–12
2. God predestined his elect to redemption and holiness in Christ according to the free counsel of his will.	1:3–14; 2:4, 8–9
3. God's rich mercy in Christ has saved sinners; this free gift is by grace through faith alone.	1:7–8; 2:4–14
4. Christ's earthly work of redemption was part of his cosmic reconciliation and exaltation in this age and the next.	1:15–23; 3:1–13
5. Christ's reconciliation entails uniting all people, whether Jew or Gentile, into his one body, the church, as a new creation.	1:23; 2:10–22; 3:1–21; 4:1–6
6. Christ's people are renewed to new lives of holiness in thought, word, and deed, and must reject their old, sinful lifestyles.	4:1–3, 17–32; 5:1–20
7. Holiness of life entails submission to proper authorities, and loving and considerate care for those in submission.	5:21–6:9
8. Christ has given powerful gifts to his church to bring about her unity, maturity, and defense against the onslaughts of the devil and his allies.	4:7–16; 6:10–19

Literary Features

Ephesians exemplifies the genre of the NT epistle, with its salutation (including sender, recipients, and greeting), thanksgiving, exposition, exhortation, and closing (including final greetings and benediction). The main argument of the letter is punctuated by several prayers and an interior benediction (3:20–21) that marks the transition from doctrinal affirmations to practical exhortations. Chapter 2 takes the form of a spiritual biography, in which Paul recounts the saving work of Christ in the life of every Christian, and especially in the lives of Gentiles who are now included in the one new people of God. In chapter 3 the apostle takes an autobiographical turn as he testifies about his calling to the Gentiles and his prayers for the Ephesian church. The *paraenesis* (series of moral exhortations) consists mainly of instructions for household conduct, both for the church as the household of faith and for individual believers in their domestic relationships. The famous description of the complete armor in the last chapter is an extended metaphor. Paul also catalogs the blessings of salvation in a lofty and exhilarating lyrical style.

Ephesians finds its central unity in the work of Jesus Christ and in the community of people (both Jews and Gentiles) who are corporately united in him. The strong opening statement of praise and the absence of any theological polemics make Ephesians pervasively positive in tone. The clear division of the epistle into two halves of nearly equal length (namely, the doctrinal section in chs. 1–3 and the practical section in chs. 4–6) also provides a strong sense of structural unity.

Outline

I. Introduction (1:1–14)
   A. Greetings (1:1–2)
   B. Spiritual blessings in Christ (1:3–14)

II. Paul's Prayer of Thanksgiving (1:15–23)

III. Salvation by Grace through Faith (2:1–10)
   A. Hopelessness and helplessness without Christ (2:1–3)
   B. Hope in Christ (2:4–10)

IV. Unity and the Peace of Christ (2:11–22)
   A. Unity of Christ's people (2:11–15)
   B. Peace with God (2:16–18)
   C. Implications of Christ's peace (2:19–22)

V. Revelation of the Gospel Mystery (3:1–13)
   A. Paul's apostolic ministry (3:1–7)
   B. The mystery and wisdom (3:8–13)

VI. Paul's Prayer for Strength and Insight (3:14–21)

VII. Unity of the Body of Christ (4:1–16)
   A. Exhortation to unity (4:1–6)
   B. The different gifts (4:7–10)
   C. The gifts for edification of the church (4:11–16)

VIII. Paul's Testimony (4:17–24)

IX. Exhortation to an Edifying Lifestyle (4:25–32)

X. New Life in Love (5:1–20)
   A. Exhortation to self-sacrificial love (5:1–2)
   B. Instruction in holy living (5:3–20)

XI. Submission to One Another (5:21–6:9)
   A. Submission in general (5:21)
   B. Wives and husbands (5:22–33)
   C. Children and parents (6:1–4)
   D. Slaves, bondservants, and masters (6:5–9)

XII. The Whole Armor of God (6:10–20)
   A. The Lord's strength (6:10–13)
   B. Standing firm (6:14–17)
   C. Being constant in prayer (6:18–20)

XIII. Conclusion (6:21–24)

THE LETTER OF PAUL TO THE

EPHESIANS

Greeting

1 Paul, [a]an apostle of Christ Jesus [b]by the will of God,
To the saints who are in Ephesus, and [c]are faithful[1] in Christ Jesus:
2 [d]Grace to you and peace from God our Father and the Lord Jesus Christ.

Spiritual Blessings in Christ

3 [e]Blessed be [f]the God and Father of our Lord Jesus Christ, who has blessed us in Christ
with every spiritual blessing [g]in the heavenly places, 4 [h]even as he [i]chose us in him [j]before
the foundation of the world, that we should be [k]holy and blameless before him. In love 5 [l]he
predestined us[2] for [m]adoption as sons through Jesus Christ, [n]according to the purpose of
his will, 6 [o]to the praise of his glorious grace, with which he has blessed us in [p]the Beloved.
7 [q]In him we have [r]redemption [s]through his blood, [t]the forgiveness of our trespasses,

[1] Some manuscripts *saints who are also faithful* (omitting *in Ephesus*) [2] Or *before him in love, having predestined us*

Chapter 1
1 [a]See 2 Cor. 1:1 [b]See 1 Cor. 1:1 [c]Col. 1:2
2 [d]See Rom. 1:7
3 [e]2 Cor. 1:3; 1 Pet. 1:3 [f]See Rom. 15:6 [g]ver. 20; ch. 2:6; 3:10; 6:12
4 [h][ch. 2:10; 2 Thess. 2:13; 1 Pet. 1:2] [i]James 2:5; [Deut. 7:6; 26:18] [j][2 Tim. 1:9]; See Matt. 13:35 [k]ch. 5:27; Col. 1:22; 1 Thess. 4:7
5 [l]ver. 11; Rom. 8:29, 30 [m]See Rom. 8:15 [n]ver. 9; [Luke 2:14; Heb. 2:4]; See Luke 12:32
6 [o]ver. 12, 14 [p][John 3:35; 10:17; Col. 1:13]; See Matt. 3:17
7 [q]Col. 1:14 [r]Rom. 3:24; 1 Cor. 1:30; [ch. 4:30] [s]See Acts 20:28 [t]See Acts 2:38

1:1–14 *Introduction.* Paul opens his letter with greetings (vv. 1–2) and a lengthy blessing of God (vv. 3–14) where he expresses the two main themes of the letter: Christ has reconciled all of creation and has united the church in himself.

1:1–2 *Greetings.* This salutation is briefer than many in Paul's letters. Paul saves his richest introductory remarks for the long blessing of God in vv. 3–14.

1:1 apostle. See note on Rom. 1:1. Paul expresses his authority simply but powerfully: he is an apostle **of Christ Jesus. saints**. The saints ("holy ones" or "consecrated people") are the faithful members of God's people. In Ephesians, Paul clearly uses the term for all members of the church (Eph. 1:15, 18; 2:19; 3:8; 4:12; 6:18), who are directly called to be holy (1:4; 5:3) and are **faithful in Christ Jesus. in Ephesus**. It is best to read these words as original even though they are missing in several early manuscripts. The ESV alternative footnote reading, "saints who are also faithful," is less likely because it is clumsy in Greek and because the phrase "saints who are" normally expects a place name like "in Ephesus," rather than "also faithful." Some scholars who believe Ephesians is a circular letter suggest that the words "in Ephesus" were deleted in the copies that were sent to places outside of Ephesus. On Ephesus, see Introduction: The Ancient City of Ephesus.

1:3–14 *Spiritual Blessings in Christ.* In the original Greek, this section is one long, elegant sentence. Paul shows that the triune God initiated and accomplished cosmic reconciliation and redemption for the praise of his glory.

1:3 Blessed be. The blessing that opens Paul's prayer is similar to those that began first-century Jewish prayers that were commonly recited throughout the day (cf. 2 Cor. 1:3; 1 Pet. 1:3). **in Christ**. Paul's praise emphasizes the mediation of Christ for all God's blessings by repeating that these good things are ours "in Christ" (Eph. 1:3, 9), "in the Beloved" (v. 6), or "in him" (vv. 4, 7, 11, 13). **Spiritual** (Gk. *pneumatikos*) here communicates that the saving gifts of God are conveyed by the Holy Spirit (Gk. *Pneuma*), whose personal presence throughout this age is the guarantee of future heavenly blessings (see "spiritual songs" in 5:19; Col. 3:16). Hence, these blessings are in **heavenly places**, since that is the Christian's future abode in imperishable glory when he is resurrected in a spiritual body through the "last Adam," the "life-giving spirit" (1 Cor. 15:40, 44–50).

1:4 He chose us in him means that the Father chose Christians in the Son (Christ), and this took place in eternity past, **before the foundation of the world**. This indicates that for all eternity the Father has had the role of leading and directing among the persons of the Trinity, even though Father, Son, and Holy Spirit are equal in deity and attributes. God's initiative in redeeming the believer from sin and death was not an arbitrary or whimsical decision but something God had planned all along "in Christ." Since God chose his people in his love, they can take no credit for their salvation. God was determined to have them as his own (see note on 2:8). **holy**. God chose them with the goal that they be holy and **blameless before him**. This goal is not optional for Christians—it is the purpose of election. Holiness here expresses moral purity, while blamelessness expresses freedom from the guilt of trespasses and sins in which the Christian formerly walked (1:7; 2:1, 5). **In love**, at the end of 1:4, properly belongs to v. 5, describing predestination, though the ESV footnote indicates that "in love" can also be taken with the preceding phrase ("that we should be holy and blameless before him in love"). Versification was introduced into Bibles in the sixteenth century A.D. for convenience and is not part of the original inspired text.

1:5 predestined. Previously ordained or appointed to some position. God's election of Christians (v. 4) entails his predestining them *to* something—in this case to **adoption as sons** (see also v. 11; Rom. 8:29–30). Hence, election and predestination in this context refer to God's decision to save someone. All Christians, male and female, are "sons" in the sense of being heirs who will inherit blessings from their Father in heaven. Paul qualifies and stresses God's plan and initiation of redemption with the phrase **according to the purpose of his will** here and elsewhere in the passage (Eph. 1:9, 11). God cannot be constrained by any outside force, and his inexorable will for believers is to pour out his grace and goodness on them in Christ Jesus.

1:6 God's ultimate purpose is not redemption as such but the **praise** of his glorious name through redemption. This theme is repeated at key junctures in the argument (see vv. 12, 14).

1:7 Redemption denotes ransoming someone from captivity or from slavery. The supreme OT example was the exodus, where God redeemed Israel from slavery in Egypt (see Ex. 15:13; Deut. 7:8; 2 Sam. 7:23; Mic. 6:4). **Forgiveness of our trespasses** explains the nature of redemption: Christians are freed from slavery to sin and guilt. This was effected by Christ's **blood**, which means his death as an atoning sacrifice (see also Rom. 3:24; Eph. 1:14; 2:13; 4:30; Heb. 9:15).

[u]according to the riches of his grace, 8 which he lavished upon us, in all wisdom and insight
9 [v]making known[1] to us the mystery of his will, [n]according to his purpose, which he [w]set
forth in Christ 10 as a plan for [x]the fullness of time, [y]to unite all things in him, things in
heaven and things on earth.
11 In him we have obtained [z]an inheritance, [a]having been predestined [b]according to
the purpose of him who works all things according to [c]the counsel of his will, 12 so that
we who were the first to hope in Christ might be [d]to the praise of his glory. 13 In him you
also, when you heard [e]the word of truth, the gospel of your salvation, and believed in him,
[f]were sealed with the [g]promised Holy Spirit, 14 who is [h]the guarantee[2] of our [i]inheritance
until [j]we acquire [k]possession of it,[3] [l]to the praise of his glory.

Thanksgiving and Prayer

15 For this reason, [m]because I have heard of your faith in the Lord Jesus and your love[4]
toward all the saints, 16 I [n]do not cease to give thanks for you, [o]remembering you in my
prayers, 17 that [p]the God of our Lord Jesus Christ, the Father of glory, [q]may give you the
Spirit of wisdom and of revelation in the knowledge of him, 18 [r]having the eyes of your
hearts enlightened, that you may know what is [s]the hope to which he has called you, what
are [t]the riches of his glorious inheritance in the saints, 19 and what is the immeasurable
greatness of his power toward us who believe, [u]according to the working of [v]his great
might 20 that he worked in Christ [w]when he raised him from the dead and [x]seated him at
his right hand [y]in the heavenly places, 21 [z]far above [a]all rule and authority and power and
dominion, and above [b]every name that is named, not only in [c]this age but also in the one

[1] Or *he lavished upon us in all wisdom and insight, making known . . .* [2] Or *down payment* [3] Or *until God redeems his possession* [4] Some manuscripts omit *your love*

9 [u][ch. 3:8, 16; Col. 1:27]; See Rom. 2:4 [v]See Rom. 16:25 [n][See ver. 5 above] [w][ver. 11; Rom. 8:28; 9:11]
10 [x]See Mark 1:15 [y]Col. 1:16, 20; [ch. 3:15; Phil. 2:9, 10]
11 [z]Deut. 4:20; 32:9; See ver. 14 [a]ver. 5 [b]ch. 3:11; [Rev. 4:11]; See Rom. 8:28 [c][Acts 20:27]
12 [d]ver. 6, 14; [Phil. 1:11]
13 [e]2 Cor. 6:7; Col. 1:5; 2 Tim. 2:15; [Acts 13:26; 15:7] [f]ch. 4:30 [g]See Acts 1:4
14 [h]2 Cor. 1:22 [i]Acts 20:32; [ver. 18] [j]Titus 2:14; See ver. 7 [k]See 1 Pet. 2:9 [l]ver. 6, 12
15 [m]Col. 1:4; Philem. 5; See Rom. 1:8
16 [n]Col. 1:9 [o]Rom. 1:9; 2 Tim. 1:3
17 [p]See Rom. 15:6 [q][Col. 1:9]
18 [r][Heb. 6:4; 10:32; Rev. 3:17, 18]; See Acts 26:18 [s]ch. 4:4; [ch. 2:12] [t]ch. 3:8, 16; Col. 1:27; See ver. 7
19 [u]ch. 3:7; Phil. 3:21; Col. 1:29; 2:12 [v]ch. 6:10; [Dan. 4:30]
20 [w]See Acts 2:24 [x]See Mark 16:19; Acts 2:33; 1 Pet. 3:22 [y]See ver. 3
21 [z]ch. 4:10; Col. 2:10; See John 3:31 [a]1 Cor. 15:24 [b]ch. 3:15; Phil. 2:9; [Heb. 1:4] [c][Matt. 12:32]

1:9 Mystery as used in Scripture (Gk. *mystērion*) refers to the revelation of something that was previously hidden or known only vaguely but now is more fully made known (see note on Col. 1:26–27). The mystery of God's will, now revealed **in Christ**, is "to unite all things in him" (Eph. 1:10; see also 3:3–11).

1:10 fullness of time. "When the time was ripe," i.e., the time for the fulfillment of God's plan. **unite**. This is the central theme of the passage: God has effected cosmic reconciliation in Christ. The work of Christ on the cross is the central axis for the history of creation, whether **in heaven** or **on earth** (see also Col. 1:15–20), since he has redeemed his people and silenced all hostile powers (see Eph. 3:10).

1:11 Obtained an inheritance seems the best rendering of the Greek verb that normally means "to allot [a portion]." Some believe the meaning is that God has claimed his own portion, the believing Jews (see v. 14). **predestined**. Making those who believe in him heirs with Christ was not an ad hoc event; God had planned it from all eternity. By definition God is sovereign, directing all things freely according to his royal counsel. This is in sharp contrast with the pagan gods of the time, who were understood to be often fickle or bound by an inscrutable and arbitrary fate. God's predestination gives his people tremendous comfort, for they know that all who come to Christ do so through God's enabling grace and appointment (see 2:8–10). **Who works all things according to the counsel of his will** is best understood to mean that every single event that occurs is in some sense predestined by God. At the same time, Paul emphasizes the importance of human responsibility, as is evident in all of the moral commands later in Ephesians (chs. 4–6) and in all of Paul's letters. As Paul demonstrated in all of his remarkable efforts in spreading the gospel (Acts 13–28; cf. 2 Cor. 11:23–28), he believed that doing personal evangelism and making conscious choices to obey God are also absolutely essential in fulfilling God's plan. God uses human means to fulfill what he has ordained. With regard to tragedies and evil, Paul and the other biblical writers never blame God for them (cf. Rom. 5:12; 2 Tim. 4:14; also Job 1:21–22). Rather, they see the doctrine of God's sovereignty as a means of comfort and assurance (cf. Rom. 8:28–30), confident that evil will not triumph, and that God's good plans for his people will be fulfilled. How God's sovereignty and human responsibility work together in the world is a mystery no one can fully understand.

1:12 praise. See note on v. 6.

1:13 Sealed can mean either that the Holy Spirit protects and preserves Christians until they reach their inheritance (see 4:30; 2 Cor. 1:22; 1 Pet. 1:5; Rev. 7:2–3) or that he "certifies" the authenticity of their acceptance by God as being genuine—they bear the "royal seal" (see John 3:33; Acts 10:44, 47). The first interpretation seems best here, though both ideas are biblically true.

1:14 God pours out his Holy Spirit on all of his children to **guarantee** (or to provide a "down payment" on [ESV footnote]) their share in his eternal kingdom because he applies to them all God's powerful working in redemption. **until we acquire possession of it**. This phrase can also be rendered "until God redeems his possession" (ESV footnote). In that case it means that, like the Levites in the OT, believers are the Lord's specially treasured possession (see Num. 3:12, 45; 8:14; Josh. 14:3–4; 18:7).

1:15–23 *Paul's Prayer of Thanksgiving.* This section, like vv. 3–14, is a single sentence in the original Greek. Paul prays that the church will gain deep insight into the Lord's powerful working and rich gifts in Christ.

1:15 because I have heard. See Introduction: Author and Title.

1:16 do not cease . . . in my prayers. See note on 6:18.

1:17 To name **the Father of glory** as **the God of our Lord Jesus Christ** is not to deny Christ's deity but to affirm his true incarnate humanity. Further, it expresses that Christians know God through the Lord Jesus as their mediator. **The Spirit of wisdom** refers to the Holy Spirit's secret working in Christians to give them insights into God's Word and the saving knowledge of him (1 Cor. 2:6–12).

1:18–19 Paul prays that believers will comprehend the blessings that are theirs in Christ: (1) their future **hope**; (2) God's **inheritance in the saints**; and (3) their **power** in Christ. The "inheritance" here is not the Christian's inheritance but **his** (God's). This indicates how precious his people are to God. They are, so to speak, what he looks forward to enjoying forever. Paul piles up "power words" to express the **immeasurable greatness** of God's power, **working**, and **great might** toward believers. Power over supernatural forces through magic and the occult was a great concern in ancient Ephesus (Acts 19:19), but the power of the living God in Christ trumps all competing authorities (Acts 19:20).

to come. 22 And [d]he put all things under his feet and gave him as [e]head over all things to
the church, 23 [f]which is his body, [g]the fullness of him [h]who fills [i]all in all.

By Grace Through Faith

2 [j]And you were [k]dead in the trespasses and sins 2 [l]in which you once walked, following
the course of this world, following [m]the prince of the power of the air, the spirit that is
now at work in [n]the sons of disobedience— 3 among whom we all once lived in [o]the passions of our flesh, carrying out the desires of the body[1] and the mind, and [p]were by nature
[q]children of wrath, like the rest of mankind.[2] 4 But[3] God, being [r]rich in mercy, [s]because
of the great love with which he loved us, 5 even [t]when we were dead in our trespasses,
[u]made us alive together with Christ—[v]by grace you have been saved— 6 and raised us up

[1] Greek *flesh* [2] Greek *like the rest* [3] Or *And*

22 [d]Cited from Ps. 8:6; See 1 Cor. 15:27 [e]ch. 4:15; 5:23; Col. 1:18; 2:19; [1 Cor. 11:3; Col. 2:10] **23** [f]ch. 4:12, 16; 5:30; Col. 1:18, 24; [ch. 5:23; 1 Cor. 12:27] [g]ch. 3:19; See John 1:16 [h]ch. 4:10 [i][Jer. 23:24; Col. 3:11]

Chapter 2

1 [j]Col. 2:13; [Col. 1:21] [k]ver. 5; [ch. 4:18]; See Luke 15:24 **2** [l]ch. 4:17, 22; 5:8; Col. 3:7; See Rom. 11:30; 1 Cor. 6:11 [m][ch. 6:12; Rev. 9:11]; See John 12:31 [n]ch. 5:6; [1 Pet. 1:14] **3** [o]Gal. 5:16 [p]See Ps. 51:5; Rom. 5:12 [q][2 Pet. 2:14] **4** [r]ver. 7; Titus 3:5; See Rom. 2:4 [s]See John 3:16 **5** [t]ver. 1; [Rom. 5:6, 8, 10] [u]Col. 2:12, 13; [John 14:19; Rev. 20:4] [v]ver. 8; See Acts 15:11

1:22 put all things. Paul quotes Ps. 8:6 as being fulfilled by Christ's exaltation over all creation and as head over the church. **head**. Like a present-day "head of government," this term points to Christ's preeminence as Lord (see note on 1 Cor. 11:3).

1:23 body. Christ has so identified himself with his church that it is said to be his very body, much as Adam described Eve as "bone of my bones and flesh of my flesh" (Gen. 2:23) and as God declared man and wife to be "one flesh" (see note on Eph. 5:28–30). **fullness**. The church, filled by Christ, fills all creation as representatives of Christ.

2:1–10 *Salvation by Grace through Faith.* This section, like 1:3–14 and 1:15–23, is a single sentence in the original Greek. The overarching theme is that God lavishes his grace on Christians through his saving initiative. There are two subsections: 2:1–3 and 2:4–10.

2:1–3 *Hopelessness and Helplessness without Christ.* "God helps those who help themselves" is not from the Bible but from the ancient Greeks. As Paul emphasizes in this section, the truth is the exact opposite: God helps the helpless! Even more, he helps his enemies who have transgressed his holy law.

2:1 you were dead. Human beings as sons and daughters of Adam enter the world spiritually dead. They have no inclination or responsiveness toward God and no ability to please God. Paul begins with this phrase then breaks off with other thoughts until he returns to it again in v. 5. **trespasses**. Violations of divine commandments. **sins**. Offenses against God in thought, word, or deed.

2:2 prince . . . spirit. This refers to Satan as he dominates his human subjects, here called **sons of disobedience**, a Hebrew-inspired phrase like "sons of this world" in contrast to "sons of light" (Luke 16:8). They belong to the family of those who rebel against the holy and true God.

2:3 by nature. To be sons and daughters of Adam is to be born into a fallen state (Ps. 51:5) and subject to God's condemnation as **children of wrath**. To escape this hopeless imprisonment requires nothing short of a new birth or a new creation (Eph. 2:10).

2:4–10 *Hope in Christ.* In contrast to the hopeless state of the nonbeliever, Christians exult in hope because of God's incredible grace and free salvation. Paul accents this grace in contrast to the pre-Christ hopelessness analyzed in vv. 1–3.

2:4 But God. No hopeless fate looks any grimmer than that which awaits the forlorn company of mankind marching behind the "prince of the power of the air" (v. 2) to their destruction under divine wrath. Just when things look the most desolate, Paul utters the greatest short phrase in the history of human speech: "But God!" **rich in mercy**. God's mercy on his helpless enemies flows from his own loving heart, not from anything they have done to deserve it.

2:5 when we were dead. Paul resumes his original thought, which began with "you were dead" in v. 1. **made us alive**. That is, God gave us regeneration (new spiritual life within). This and the two verbs in v. 6 ("raised up" and "seated with") make up the main verbs of the long sentence in vv. 1–10. Since Christians were dead, they first had to be made alive before they could believe (and God did that **together with Christ**). This is why salvation is **by grace** alone (see notes on v. 8; vv. 9–10).

2:6–7 Raised us up with him means that, because of Christ's resurrection, those who believe in him are given new life spiritually in this age (regeneration). They will also be given renewed physical bodies when Christ returns (future resurrection). **seated us with him in the heavenly places**. God has allowed his people even now to share in a measure of the authority that Christ has, seated at the right hand of God (cf. 1:20–22; 6:10–18; James 4:7; 1 John 4:4), a truth that would be especially important in Ephesus with all of its occult practices (see Introduction: Purpose, Occasion, and Background; also note on Eph. 1:18–19). Verse 7 of ch. 2 answers the question of why God lavished such love upon his people: so that they will marvel for all of eternity over the incredible kindness and love of God. It will take all of eternity to fathom God's love, and those who are saved will never plumb the depths of it.

Trinitarian Formulas and Expressions in Ephesians

Reference	Father	Son	Spirit
1:3	Blessed be the God and Father	of our Lord Jesus Christ	every spiritual blessing
1:11–13	him who works all things according to . . . his will	to hope in Christ	sealed with the promised Holy Spirit
1:17	God . . . the Father of glory	our Lord Jesus Christ	a spirit of wisdom and of revelation
2:18	access . . . to the Father	through him	in one Spirit
2:22	a dwelling place for God	In him	by the Spirit
3:2–5	the stewardship of God's grace	the mystery of Christ	revealed . . . by the Spirit
3:14–17	the Father . . . the riches of his glory	so that Christ may dwell in your hearts	through his Spirit
4:4–6	one God and Father	one Lord	one Spirit
5:18–20	giving thanks . . . to God the Father	in the name of our Lord Jesus Christ	be filled with the Spirit

with him and [w]seated us with him in the heavenly places in Christ Jesus, 7 so that in the
coming ages he might show the immeasurable [x]riches of his grace in [y]kindness toward us
in Christ Jesus. 8 For [z]by grace you have been saved [a]through faith. And this is [b]not your
own doing; [c]it is the gift of God, 9 [d]not a result of works, [e]so that no one may boast. 10 For
[f]we are his workmanship, [g]created in Christ Jesus [h]for good works, [i]which God prepared
beforehand, [j]that we should walk in them.

One in Christ

11 Therefore remember that at one time you Gentiles in the flesh, called "the uncircumcision" by what is called [k]the circumcision, which is made in the flesh by hands— 12 remember
[l]that you were at that time separated from Christ, [m]alienated from the commonwealth of
Israel and strangers to [n]the covenants of promise, [o]having no hope and without God in the
world. 13 But now in Christ Jesus you who once were [p]far off have been brought near [q]by the
blood of Christ. 14 For [r]he himself is our peace, [s]who has made us both one and has broken
down [t]in his flesh the dividing wall of hostility 15 by abolishing the law of commandments
expressed in [u]ordinances, that he might create in himself one [v]new man in place of the
two, so making peace, 16 and might [w]reconcile us both to God in one body through the
cross, thereby killing the hostility. 17 And he came and [x]preached peace to you who were
[y]far off and peace to those who were [z]near. 18 For [a]through him we both have [b]access in [c]one
Spirit to the Father. 19 So then you are no longer [d]strangers and aliens,[1] but you are [e]fellow

[1] Or *sojourners*

6 [w]See ch. 1:20
7 [x]ver. 4 [y]Titus 3:4
8 [z]ver. 5 [a]1 Pet. 1:5; [Rom. 4:16] [b][2 Cor. 3:5] [c][John 4:10; Heb. 6:4]
9 [d]2 Tim. 1:9; Titus 3:5; See Rom. 3:20, 28 [e]1 Cor. 1:29; [Judg. 7:2]
10 [f]Deut. 32:6, 15; Ps. 100:3 [g][ch. 3:9; 4:24; Col. 3:10] [h]ch. 4:24 [i][ch. 1:4] [j]Col. 1:10
11 [k]Rom. 2:26, 28; [Col. 2:11, 13]
12 [l]1 Cor. 12:2; [ch. 5:8; Col. 3:7] [m]ch. 4:18; Col. 1:21; [Ezek. 14:5; Gal. 2:15; 4:8] [n]See Rom. 9:4 [o]1 Thess. 4:13; See ch. 1:18
13 [p]ver. 17; Acts 2:39 [q][Col. 1:20]; See Rom. 3:25
14 [r]Ps. 72:7; Mic. 5:5; Zech. 9:10; [Col. 3:15]; See Luke 2:14 [s]See Gal. 3:28 [t]Col. 1:21, 22; [Rom. 7:4]
15 [u]Col. 2:14, 20 [v]See Rom. 6:4
16 [w]Col. 1:20-22; [1 Cor. 12:13]
17 [x]Isa. 57:19 [y]ver. 13 [z]Deut. 4:7; Ps. 148:14
18 [a][John 14:6] [b]ch. 3:12; [John 10:7, 9]; See Rom. 5:2 [c]ch. 4:4; 1 Cor. 12:13; [John 4:23] 19 [d]ver. 12; [Heb. 11:13; 13:14] [e]Phil. 3:20; [Heb. 12:22, 23]

2:8 By grace refers to God's favor upon those who have transgressed his law and sinned against him. But grace may also be understood as a "power" in these verses. God's grace not only offers salvation but also secures it. **Saved** refers to deliverance from God's wrath at the final judgment (Rom. 5:9); "by grace you have been saved" is repeated from Eph. 2:5 for emphasis. The verb form for "have been saved" (Gk. *sesōsmenoi*, perfect tense) communicates that the Christian's salvation is fully secured. **through faith**. Faith is a confident trust and reliance upon Christ Jesus and is the only means by which one can obtain salvation. **this**. The Greek pronoun is neuter, while "grace" and "faith" are feminine. Accordingly, "this" points to the whole process of "salvation by grace through faith" as being **the gift of God** and not something that we can accomplish ourselves. This use of the neuter pronoun to take in the whole of a complex idea is quite common in Greek (e.g., 6:1); its use here makes it clear that faith, no less than grace, is a gift of God. Salvation, therefore, in every respect, is **not your own doing**.

2:9–10 Salvation is not by **works**. If it were, then those who are saved would get the glory. **created . . . for good works**. Salvation is not based on works, but the good works Christians do are the result and consequence of God's new creation work.

2:11–22 *Unity and the Peace of Christ.* Paul continues the theme of the new creation which he introduced in v. 10. In the previous sections God had been the main subject of the action, but now the focus falls on Christ Jesus and his redemption. There are three subsections: vv. 11–15, 16–18, and 19–22.

2:11–15 *Unity of Christ's People.* Christ makes peace between Jew and Gentile to unify both in the church. There is only one unified people of God.

2:11 the circumcision. That is, the Jews. To be called "uncircumcised" was a Jewish term of derision (see 1 Sam. 17:26 and note on Acts 15:1) and signified that one was a Gentile, outside the covenant people of God.

2:12 separated. To be separated from OT Israel was to be separated from Christ, because "salvation is from the Jews" (John 4:22; Rom. 9:4–5). **commonwealth**. For "citizenship" and **strangers**, see note on Eph. 2:19. **covenants of promise**. God administered his OT redemption and promises by his oath-bound covenants (Luke 1:72–73), the chief of which were the Abrahamic, Mosaic, and Davidic covenants. The new covenant fulfills all the divine promises (2 Cor. 1:20; Heb. 7:20–22; 8:6; 9:15). Note that Paul believed that all Gentiles apart from Christ were unsaved and **without God**.

2:13 in Christ Jesus. The old division of all people into two classifications, Jews or Gentiles (Acts 14:5; Rom. 3:29; 9:24; 1 Cor. 1:23), or Jews and Greeks (John 7:35; Acts 14:1; 18:4; Rom. 3:9; 1 Cor. 1:22, 24; etc.), has been transcended by a new entity in Christ: "the church of God" (1 Cor. 10:32). **near**. To be brought near means to have access to God (see Eph. 2:18). **blood**. Christ's substitutionary death. He died not only for the Jews but for all his sheep (John 10:16), even those who are **far off** (cf. Acts 2:39).

2:14 peace. This refers to the state of harmonious friendship with God and with one another in the church. **made us both one**. That is, Jews and Gentiles. The opposite of peace is the **hostility** that Christ has quenched. Christ created a unified new people from the old hostile camps (Col. 3:15; cf. John 17:20–21). **in his flesh**. This refers to Christ's bodily death on the cross (see Eph. 2:16). **dividing wall**. There was an inscription on the wall of the outer courtyard of the Jerusalem temple warning Gentiles that they would only have themselves to blame for their death if they passed beyond it into the inner courts. Paul may or may not be alluding to this wall, but it well illustrates Christ's reconciliation of all people into a new humanity (see v. 15).

2:15 law. The additional mention of **commandments** and **ordinances** identifies this as the Mosaic law, which included many commandments that served to separate Israel from the other nations. Thus the law was a "dividing wall" (v. 14) which Christ has abolished or rendered powerless both by fulfilling it and by removing believers from the law's condemnation (see Matt. 5:17; Rom. 8:1; Heb. 9:11–14; 10:1–10). The result is a **new man**, denoting a new human race under the second Adam (Christ), in whose image the Christian is re-created (1 Cor. 15:45, 49; see also Eph. 4:24).

2:16–18 *Peace with God.* On the cross, Christ put to death the hostility between Israel and the other nations. In this section the focus shifts to the new, unified group being brought near to God.

2:16–17 reconcile. To bring two parties into peaceful relations, in this case, to satisfy God's wrath against his enemies (see Rom. 5:1–11). They are now friends (John 15:13–15) **in one body**, the church (see Eph. 4:4–5). Paul describes Christ's reconciliation very vividly as **killing the hostility** that stood in the way of peace with God. **preached peace**. Paul refers to Christ's messianic ministry to the whole world both **far** and **near**, alluding to Isa. 57:19.

2:18 access. To draw near to God and to enjoy him forever in a new creation is both mankind's greatest good and the ultimate accomplishment of Christ's earthly work of redemption. **one Spirit**. See note on 4:4.

2:19–22 *Implications of Christ's Peace.* Paul indicates with "So then" that he is drawing out key implications of what he has taught in vv. 11–18. The Christian's assurance is based on these facts.

2:19 So then. Christians have to know and be thoroughly convinced of who they are as **saints and members of the household of God** if they are to live accordingly. **strangers**. As in v. 12 ("commonwealth"), Paul employs a

citizens with the saints and [f]members of the household of God, **20** [g]built on the foundation
of the [h]apostles and prophets, [i]Christ Jesus himself being [j]the cornerstone, **21** [k]in whom
the whole structure, being joined together, grows into [l]a holy temple in the Lord. **22** In him
[m]you also are being built together [n]into a dwelling place for God by[1] the Spirit.

The Mystery of the Gospel Revealed

3 For this reason I, Paul, [o]a prisoner for Christ Jesus [p]on behalf of you Gentiles— **2** assuming that you have heard of [q]the stewardship of [r]God's grace that was given to me for you,
3 [s]how the mystery was made known to me [t]by revelation, [u]as I have written briefly. **4** [v]When
you read this, you can perceive my insight into [w]the mystery of Christ, **5** which was not made
known to the sons of men in other generations as it has now been revealed to his holy apostles
and prophets by the Spirit. **6** This mystery is[2] that the Gentiles are [x]fellow heirs, [y]members
of the same body, and [z]partakers of the promise in Christ Jesus through the gospel.

7 [a]Of this gospel I was made [b]a minister according to the gift of [c]God's grace, which
was given me [d]by the working of his power. **8** To me, [e]though I am the very least of all the
saints, this grace was given, [f]to preach to the Gentiles the [g]unsearchable [h]riches of Christ,
9 and [i]to bring to light for everyone what is the plan of the mystery [j]hidden for ages in[3]
God [k]who created all things, **10** so that through the church the manifold [l]wisdom of God
[m]might now be made known to [n]the rulers and authorities [o]in the heavenly places. **11** This

[1] Or *in* [2] The words *This mystery is* are inferred from verse 4 [3] Or *by*

19 [f]See Gal. 6:10
20 [g][Jer. 12:16]; See 1 Cor. 3:9 [h]Matt. 16:18; Rev. 21:14 [i][1 Cor. 3:11] [j]Ps. 118:22; Isa. 28:16
21 [k]ch. 4:15, 16 [l]See 1 Cor. 3:16, 17
22 [m]1 Pet. 2:5 [n][ch. 3:17; 2 Cor. 6:16; 1 Tim. 3:15]

Chapter 3

1 [o]ch. 4:1; Acts 23:18; Phil. 1:7; [ch. 6:20] [p]ver. 13; Col. 1:24
2 [q]ch. 1:10; Col. 1:25; 1 Tim. 1:4 [r]ver. 7; ch. 4:7; See Acts 11:23; Rom. 1:5
3 [s]Acts 22:17, 21; 26:16-18 [t][Dan. 2:29]; See Rom. 16:25; 2 Cor. 12:1 [u][ch. 1:9, 10]
4 [v][2 Cor. 11:6] [w]Col. 4:3
6 [x]See Gal. 3:29 [y]ch. 2:16 [z]ch. 5:7
7 [a]Col. 1:23, 25 [b]See 2 Cor. 3:6 [c]See ver. 2 [d][ver. 20]; See ch. 1:19
8 [e]See 1 Cor. 15:9 [f]See Acts 9:15 [g][Job 5:9; Rom. 11:33] [h]See ch. 1:18; Rom. 2:4
9 [i]See ver. 2, 3 [j]Col. 1:26 [k]Rev. 4:11; [ch. 2:10]
10 [l]Rom. 11:33 [m][1 Pet. 1:12] [n]ch. 1:21; [ch. 6:12] [o]See ch. 1:3

term that was common to political life in ancient cities like Ephesus. Strangers (also v. 12) were complete foreigners with no rights or privileges (see Acts 16:20–23); **aliens** were non-citizens who dwelt in the city and were accorded customary privileges as neighbors. Only **citizens** had full protections and rights in the city (see Acts 21:39).

2:20 built on the foundation of the apostles and prophets. There are several views about the apostles and prophets referred to here: (1) Some think that they were "foundational" because they proclaimed the very words of God, and some of their words became the books of the NT. Since a "foundation" is laid only once (i.e., at the beginning of the church) there are no more apostles or prophets today, but their function of speaking the words of God has been replaced by the written Bible, which is the foundation today. (2) Others argue that these "prophets" are very closely tied to apostles in the phrase "the apostles and prophets," and that these prophets do not represent all who had a gift of prophecy in the early church (see note on 1 Cor. 12:10); they were a small group closely associated with the apostles (or else identical to the apostles) to whom God had revealed the mystery of the Gentile inclusion in the church (see Eph. 3:5, where the same phrase, "the apostles and prophets," occurs). In this case ordinary Christians who had the gift of prophecy in Ephesus (4:11) and other churches (cf. Acts 11:27; 19:6; 21:9–10; Rom. 12:6; 1 Cor. 12:10; 1 Thess. 5:19–21; 1 Tim. 1:18; 4:14) were not part of the "foundation" but were part of the rest of the building that was being built (that is, the church) and would continue so throughout the church age. (3) Finally, some think the "prophets" here could be the OT prophets, though the same words in Eph. 3:5 point to prophets of the NT era. **cornerstone**. The critical stone in the corner of the foundation that ensures that a stone building is square and stable.

2:21 joined together. Christians are the temple of God corporately; belonging to the visible church is not optional for followers of Christ. **holy temple**. Where God meets with his people in joyful worship and fellowship. Believers do not have to worship in Jerusalem today because they themselves have become the new temple of God (see John 4:21).

3:1–13 *Revelation of the Gospel Mystery.* Paul explains his calling and ministry as an apostle to the Gentiles. This was to assure his Gentile readers that their share in the inheritance is authentic because of its divine origin.

3:1–7 *Paul's Apostolic Ministry.* Paul elaborates on his call to apostleship. He was sent as a gracious gift to the Gentiles.

3:1 For this reason. Paul breaks off his thought here only to resume it in v. 14, where the opening phrase is repeated (cf. the similar break in 2:1, 5). **prisoner for Christ**. Paul suffered imprisonment or confinement several times in the service of Christ (4:1; Acts 16:23; 24:23; Col. 4:10; 2 Tim. 1:8; Philem. 1). **on behalf of you Gentiles**. Paul was the apostle, teacher, and preacher to the Gentiles (1 Tim. 2:7; 2 Tim. 1:11), so the sufferings he experienced during his ministry were on their behalf (2 Cor. 6:5; 11:23).

3:2 assuming that you have heard. Cf. 4:21. Paul may not have known the recent Ephesian converts, especially in the outlying villages (see Introduction: Author and Title), though he had spent three years in Ephesus (Acts 20:31).

3:3 mystery. See note on Col. 1:26–27. This mystery is now revealed: Christ has come to unify Jew and Gentile in one body through the gospel, about which Paul had just **written briefly** (see the parallels with Eph. 1:9, 17). Christ revealed this mystery to Paul **by revelation** on the road to Damascus (Acts 9:1–7) and more fully at other times (cf. Acts 22:17–21; 2 Cor. 12:1–7; Gal. 1:12; 2:2).

3:5 not made known. While Moses and the prophets had written of Christ and his salvation to the ends of the earth (John 5:46; 1 Pet. 1:10–12), and while God had even promised to Abraham that all the nations of the earth would be blessed through him (Gen. 12:3), the full realization of who Christ was and the extent of the salvation that would come to the Gentiles was not clear until after the giving of **the Spirit** (1 Cor. 2:8–10). **apostles and prophets**. See note on Eph. 2:20.

3:6 the Gentiles are fellow heirs. Paul explains the content of the "mystery" mentioned in vv. 3–4: Gentile and Jewish Christians are now united in God's new family as equal heirs with one another and with Christ (Rom. 8:17; Gal. 3:28–29).

3:7 minister. A servant or official charged with an area of responsibility. Paul was duty bound to proclaim the gospel (1 Cor. 9:16), yet he regards this burden as a **gift of God's grace** because he served out of gratitude for the grace that he himself had received.

3:8–13 *The Mystery and Wisdom.* God's wisdom is revealed in Christ. Before being revealed, it was a mystery.

3:8 very least of. This is not false humility on Paul's part, since he is acutely aware that he had once been a persecutor of Christ and his church (Acts 9:4; Phil. 3:6; 1 Tim. 1:13). **saints**. See note on Eph. 1:1.

3:10 manifold. Taking various forms, or of many different kinds. God's **wisdom** has many facets and aspects, like an intricately cut diamond (see 1 Cor. 1:26–29). **now**. In this age, in contrast to the time before Christ's first coming. **Rulers and authorities in the heavenly places** refers to angelic beings. God's redemptive purposes are of interest to angels (1 Pet. 1:12) and the whole host of heaven, who are better able to glorify God when they behold in wonder what God has done and does in creating **the church** (Psalm 148; Rev. 7:11; 19:1–8). See note on Eph. 6:12.

3:11 eternal purpose. God's redemption in Christ originated in the fathomless sea of eternity with God's "manifold wisdom" (v. 10). See the emphasis on

11[p]See ch. 1:11
12[q]Heb. 4:16; 10:19 [r]See ch. 2:18 [s]2 Cor. 3:4 [t]Mark 11:22; Phil. 3:9
13[u]ver. 1 [v][2 Cor. 1:6]
15[w]See ch. 1:10, 21
16[x]See ver. 8 [y]1 Cor. 16:13; [ch. 6:10; Phil. 4:13; Col. 1:11] [z]See Rom. 7:22
17[a][ch. 2:22] [b]Col. 2:7 [c]Col. 1:23
18[d][John 1:5] [e]Rom. 8:39; [Job 11:8, 9]
19[f][Phil. 4:7] [g]Col. 2:10 [h]ch. 1:23
20[i]Rom. 16:25; Jude 24 [j][2 Cor. 9:8] [k][ver. 7]
21[l]See Rom. 11:36

Chapter 4

1[m]See ch. 3:1 [n]Col. 1:10; 2:6; 1 Thess. 2:12; [Phil. 1:27] [o]See Rom. 8:28
2[p]Acts 20:19; Phil. 2:3; Col. 3:12; 1 Pet. 3:8; 5:5; [Col. 2:18, 23] [q]Gal. 5:23 [r]Col. 1:11 [s]Col. 3:13
3[t]Col. 3:14; [Acts 8:23]

was [p]according to the eternal purpose that he has realized in Christ Jesus our Lord, **12** in
whom we have [q]boldness and [r]access with [s]confidence through our [t]faith in him. **13** So I
ask you not to lose heart over what I am suffering [u]for you, [v]which is your glory.

Prayer for Spiritual Strength

14 For this reason I bow my knees before t … hom [w]every family[1] in
heaven and on earth is named, **16** that accordi … his glory [y]he may grant
you to be strengthened with power through … inner being, **17** [a]so that
Christ may dwell in your hearts through fait … [b]rooted and [c]grounded
in love, **18** may have strength to [d]comprehend … what is the breadth and
length and [e]height and depth, **19** and to know t … at surpasses knowledge,
that [g]you may be filled with all [h]the fullness o …
20 [i]Now to [j]him who is able to do far more … ll that we ask or think,
[k]according to the power at work within us, **21** [l]t … the church and in Christ
Jesus throughout all generations, forever and …

Unity in the Body of Christ

4 I therefore, [m]a prisoner for the Lord, urge yo … anner worthy of [o]the calling to which you have been called, **2** with all … entleness, with [r]patience,
[s]bearing with one another in love, **3** eager to m … of the Spirit in [t]the bond

[1] Or *fatherhood*; the Greek word *patria* is closely related to the word for *Father* in v …

God's plan and purpose in 1:3–14. **realized in Christ Jesus**. God's plan of salvation to the ends of the earth had to be put into effect in human history, which God did through the earthly work of his incarnate Son.

3:14–21 *Paul's Prayer for Strength and Insight.* Paul resumes his thought broken off in v. 1 and reports his prayer for the readers' strength and understanding of God's power (vv. 14–19). He concludes by blessing God (vv. 20–21).

3:14–15 For this reason. Paul had broken off his thought in v. 1, so he repeats this phrase to indicate that he is returning to that original thought. **bow**. When Paul considers the majesty of God's worldwide work of redemption in Christ, he responds in the only appropriate way: humble adoration of God **the Father**, the Great King. To be **named** in biblical usage refers to the definition of one's identity. God the Father, the creator of all things (v. 9), is also the one who "names" (i.e., defines the identity of) all creatures, even to the extent of "naming" **every family in heaven and on earth**. God's present action in the naming of "every family" is a further affirmation of his sovereignty over all creation.

3:16 Spirit. The Holy Spirit applies to believers the personal presence and power of God. **inner being**. Or "inner man," referring to one's inner self as a human being.

3:17–18 Christ already dwells in Christians, but Paul prays here for his indwelling with power. In v. 16 Paul speaks of the indwelling "Spirit" and here of the indwelling **Christ**, suggesting the deity of the Spirit as well as the Son. **rooted and grounded in love**. Love is the natural and necessary outcome of a living faith that is the fruit of Christ's work in the Christian. **comprehend**. Godliness leads to greater understanding of God and his works (see Ps. 119:100). **Breadth . . . length . . . height . . . depth** expresses the immeasurable dimensions of God's riches in Christ. On **saints**, see note on Eph. 1:1.

3:19 surpasses knowledge. To *know* what surpasses *knowledge* is the sublime privilege of the Christian. The purpose ultimately is to be filled with God's **fullness**.

3:21 church. Paul conceives of the church as a unified whole, not as isolated entities (see 4:4–6).

4:1–16 *Unity of the Body of Christ.* Paul now turns to exhortation (with three subsections in vv. 1–6, 7–10, and 11–16) based upon the truths he has been teaching—a common format for his letters, in which doctrinal truths are stated first (here, chs. 1–3), then application to life is built on that doctri … ations of Scripture become empty moralism w … tion.

4:1–6 *Exhort* … orts the church to unity based on the truths of the c … k of salvation.

4:1 prisoner. … the sake of the gospel is **for the Lord** (see 3:1). His e … ower, since he himself has taken these matters seriou … nement in the Lord's service. Christians are to live **in a manner worthy** of the adoption, holiness, and unity to which they were **called** (see 1:4–5; 4:4).

4:2 Humility was regarded as distasteful by the pagan world of Paul's day. Pride was more highly prized. All of the virtues mentioned—humility, **gentleness, patience**, and most of all, **love**—were displayed in Christ's own character and are to be evident in the daily walk of every Christian.

4:3 Peace is a state of reconciliation and love and therefore acts as a **bond** to unite believers in Christ. Believers do not create **unity** but are to preserve the unity already established.

Christ and the Church

The relationship between Christ and the church is described by Paul as a profound mystery (5:32)—a hidden plan of God now revealed and fulfilled in Christ Jesus.

Christ is the head of the church	1:22–23; 4:15; 5:23
Christ is the cornerstone of the church	2:20
Christ is the Savior and sanctifier of the church	5:23, 26–27
Christ gives the church ministry workers	4:11–16
Christ loved and sacrificed himself for the church	5:25
Christ nourishes and cherishes the church	5:29
the church and her members dwell and grow in Christ	2:21–22; 4:15
the church is a means through which God manifests his manifold wisdom	3:10
the church submits to Christ	5:24
the church is Christ's body, and individual believers are members of his body	1:22–23; 3:6; 4:4, 16; 5:23, 30

of peace. 4 There is [u]one body and [v]one Spirit—just as you were called to the one [w]hope
that belongs to your call— 5 [x]one Lord, [y]one faith, [z]one baptism, 6 [a]one God and Father
of all, [b]who is over all and through all and in all. 7 But [c]grace was given [d]to each one of us
[e]according to the measure of Christ's gift. 8 Therefore it says,

> [f]"When he ascended on high [g]he led a host of captives,
> and he gave gifts to men."[1]

9 ([h]In saying, "He ascended," what does it mean but that he had also descended into [i]the
lower regions, the earth?[2] 10 He who descended is the one who also [j]ascended [k]far above all
the heavens, that he might [l]fill all things.) 11 And [m]he gave the [n]apostles, the prophets, the
[o]evangelists, the [p]shepherds[3] and teachers,[4] 12 [q]to equip the saints for the work of ministry,
for [r]building up [s]the body of Christ, 13 until we all attain to [t]the unity of the faith and of
the knowledge of the Son of God, [u]to mature manhood,[5] to the measure of the stature of
[v]the fullness of Christ, 14 so that we may no longer be children, [w]tossed to and fro by the
waves and carried about by every wind of doctrine, by human cunning, by craftiness in

[1] The Greek word *anthropoi* can refer to both men and women [2] Or *the lower parts of the earth?* [3] Or *pastors* [4] Or *the shepherd-teachers* [5] Greek *to a full-grown man*

4 [u]ch. 2:16 [v]See ch. 2:18 [w]ch. 1:18
5 [x]Zech. 14:9; See 1 Cor. 1:13; 8:6 [y][ver. 13; Jude 3] [z]See Gal. 3:27, 28
6 [a]1 Cor. 12:5, 6 [b]Rom. 9:5
7 [c]See ch. 3:2 [d][Matt. 25:15; 1 Cor. 12:7] [e]Rom. 12:3; [ver. 16]
8 [f]Cited from Ps. 68:18 [g]Judg. 5:12; [Col. 2:15]
9 [h]See John 3:13 [i]Ps. 63:9; Isa. 44:23
10 [j]See Mark 16:19 [k]Heb. 4:14; 7:26; 9:24 [l]ch. 1:23
11 [m][1 Cor. 12:5, 6] [n]See 1 Cor. 12:28 [o]Acts 21:8; 2 Tim. 4:5 [p]Jer. 3:15; [Acts 20:28]
12 [q]See 2 Cor. 13:9 [r]ver. 16, 29 [s]See 1 Cor. 12:27
13 [t][ver. 5] [u]Heb. 5:14 [v]ch. 1:23
14 [w][Matt. 11:7; Heb. 13:9; James 1:6; Jude 12]

4:4 Spirit. Just as a human body has one spirit that animates it, so Christ's body, the church, is enlivened by one Holy Spirit who enlivens Christians to eternal life. **one hope**. Christians do not have separate "hopes" but are together called to eternal life and to enjoy God forever in resurrection glory. They are also called to express that unity this side of eternity. On the church as a **body**, see Rom. 12:4–8; 1 Cor. 12:12–31.

4:5 One Lord refers to Jesus Christ. **One faith** refers to the doctrinal truths Christians commonly confess. "One Spirit" (v. 4), "one Lord [Christ]" (v. 5), and "one God and Father" (v. 6) constitute a Trinitarian formula. **one baptism**. Christians have disagreed about the proper mode of baptism beginning in the early history of the church. "One baptism" here, however, may refer to the baptism of all believers into one body (as described in 1 Cor. 12:13), which is the result of the regenerating work of the Holy Spirit when one becomes a genuine believer in Christ. If this view is correct, water baptism would be an outward sign of the inward reality of the believer being in Christ as the result of the regenerating work of the Holy Spirit (cf. John 3:5, 8; Titus 3:5). There is therefore a profound spiritual unity of all genuine believers who are "in Christ" (see John 17:21, 23), founded on "one faith" in "one Lord," irrespective of denominational differences. Others hold that the reference here is to water baptism, but would disagree concerning the proper mode.

4:6 over all . . . through all . . . in all. God is omnipresent (see Ps. 139:7–12; Isa. 66:1). Thus the Christian church is "one body" (Eph. 4:4), wherever its separate congregations may be found throughout the world (see Rom. 3:30).

4:7–10 *The Different Gifts*. Paul describes diverse gifts in the church. These come from the ascended Christ.

4:7 Grace . . . according to the measure of Christ's gift does not refer to different levels of *saving* grace but of grace given to serve Christ's church. To hold an office in Christ's church (see 3:2; 4:11–16) requires a special calling from Christ himself, who rules his body as its head (see 1:22; 4:15; 5:23).

4:8 it says. Paul cites Ps. 68:18, where the one who ascends is the triumphant Lord God. Paul sees this as referring to Christ Jesus in his resurrection as head of the church. **gifts**. In Ps. 68:18, the divine victor is seen "receiving gifts among men," but Paul adapts the passage to his purposes (as NT authors sometimes do in citing the OT) to show that Christ **gave** gifts to his people from his spoils of victory (interestingly, ancient Syriac and Aramaic translations of Ps. 68:18 also have "gave"). The "gifts" given by Christ turn out to be the church leaders described in Eph. 4:11. The **captives** over whom Christ triumphed are most likely demons (cf. this theme of victory over demonic forces in 1:19–22).

4:9 lower regions, the earth. In the incarnation, Christ descended from the highest heavens to the lowest regions (i.e., to the earth), where he suffered, died, and was buried, but where he also defeated death and rose again. He then **ascended** (Acts 1:9) 40 days later to be seated in the highest heavens at the right hand of the Father (Acts 2:33).

4:10 far above. Christ is the supreme head of the church who fills **all things** (see 1:23) with his glory, power, and sovereign prerogative to dispense gifts to his people (see 4:11–16).

4:11–16 *The Gifts for Edification of the Church*. The list in v. 11 is not complete since deacons are omitted. The focus here is gifted people who articulate the gospel.

4:11 Christ gives specific spiritual gifts to people in the church whose primary mission is to minister the Word of God (v. 12). For **apostles**, see note on 1:1. Regarding **prophets**, different views on the nature of the gift of prophecy in the NT affect one's understanding of this verse (see notes on 2:20; 1 Cor. 12:10). Since the Greek construction here is different from Eph. 2:20 and 3:5, some see this verse as a broader reference to the gift of prophecy generally in the NT church, rather than a reference to the "foundational" prophets mentioned in 2:20 and 3:5. From the Greek word for the "gospel" (*euangelion*), **evangelists** denotes people like Philip and Timothy who proclaimed the gospel (Acts 21:8; 2 Tim. 4:5). **shepherds** (or "pastors" [ESV footnote]). In the OT these are kings and judges (2 Sam. 5:2; 7:7). In the NT, elders "shepherd" by watching over and nurturing the church (Acts 20:28; 1 Pet. 5:1–2). There is some uncertainty as to whether "shepherds and **teachers**" refers here to two different ministry roles or functions, or whether the reference is to a single "shepherd-teacher" ministry role (cf. ESV footnote), since Paul uses a different Greek conjunction at the end of the list, joining the two nouns more closely together than the other nouns in the list. If "teachers" are a separate group, they can be understood as a special branch of shepherds (overseers, elders) responsible for instruction in God's Word (cf. 1 Tim. 5:17).

4:12 Those church leaders with various gifts (v. 11) are to **equip the saints** (all Christians) so that they can do **the work of ministry**. All Christians have spiritual gifts that should be used in ministering to one another (1 Cor. 12:7, 11; 1 Pet. 4:10).

4:13 The diversity of gifts serves to bring about the **unity** of Christ's people. **Mature manhood** extends the body metaphor used earlier for the church and contrasts with "children" in the next verse (see Heb. 5:11–14). Some people think that the learning of doctrine is inherently divisive, but it is *people* who divide the church, whereas the **knowledge of the Son of God** (both knowing Christ personally and understanding all that he did and taught) is edifying and brings about "mature manhood" when set forth in love (Phil. 3:10). The work of the gifted ministers (Eph. 4:11) was to proclaim and teach the word centered on Christ rather than on speculative or eccentric teachings of their own (cf. 1 Cor. 2:2). **measure**. Christ Jesus is the standard of the maturity to which the church must aspire. Christ's **fullness** is the full expression of his divine and human perfection (see Eph. 1:23; 3:19; Col. 1:19; 2:9).

4:14 children. Immaturity in the truths of Christian doctrine makes the church like gullible children tossed helplessly by the **waves** and **wind** of **cunning** and **deceitful schemes** of false teachers (1 Pet. 2:1; 1 John 4:1–3; Jude 4; Rev. 2:2).

[x]deceitful schemes. 15 Rather, [y]speaking the truth in love, we are to [z]grow up in every way
into him who is [a]the head, into Christ, 16 [b]from whom the whole body, joined and held
together by every joint with which it is equipped, [c]when each part is working properly,
makes the body grow so that it builds itself up in love.

The New Life

17 Now this I say and [d]testify in the Lord, [e]that you must no longer walk as the Gentiles
do, [f]in the futility of their minds. 18 They [g]are darkened in their understanding, [h]alienated
from the life of God because of the ignorance that is in them, due to [i]their hardness of
heart. 19 They [j]have become callous and [k]have given themselves up to sensuality, greedy to
practice every kind of impurity. 20 But that is not the way you [l]learned Christ!— 21 assuming
that [m]you have heard about him and [n]were taught in him, as the truth is in Jesus, 22 to [o]put
off [p]your old self,[1] which belongs to your former manner of life and is corrupt through
[q]deceitful desires, 23 and [r]to be renewed in the spirit of your minds, 24 and to put on [s]the
new self, [t]created after the likeness of God in true righteousness and holiness.

25 Therefore, having put away falsehood, let each one of you [u]speak the truth with his
neighbor, for [v]we are members one of another. 26 [w]Be angry and do not sin; do not let the
sun go down on your anger, 27 and [x]give no opportunity to the devil. 28 Let the thief no
longer steal, but rather [y]let him labor, [z]doing honest work with his own hands, so [a]that
he may have something to share with anyone in need. 29 [b]Let no corrupting talk come out
of your mouths, but only such as is good for building up, as fits the occasion, that it may
give [c]grace to those who hear. 30 And [d]do not grieve the Holy Spirit of God, [e]by whom
you were sealed for the day of [f]redemption. 31 [g]Let all bitterness and wrath and anger and

[1] Greek *man;* also verse 24

14 [x]ch. 6:11
15 [y]1 John 3:18; [ver. 25] [z]ch. 2:21 [a]See ch. 1:22
16 [b]Col. 2:19 [c][ver. 7]
17 [d]1 Thess. 2:12 [e]ver. 22; ch. 2:1-3; Col. 3:7; 1 Pet. 4:3 [f]Rom. 1:21; 1 Pet. 1:18; [Col. 2:18; 2 Pet. 2:18]
18 [g][Rom. 11:10] [h]See ch. 2:12 [i]See Mark 3:5
19 [j][Prov. 23:35]; 1 Tim. 4:2 [k][1 Kgs. 21:25; Rom. 1:24, 26, 28]
20 [l]See Matt. 11:29
21 [m]ch. 1:13 [n]Col. 2:7
22 [o]Col. 3:8; Heb. 12:1; James 1:21; 1 Pet. 2:1 [p]Rom. 6:6; Col. 3:9 [q][Heb. 3:13]
23 [r]See Rom. 12:2
24 [s]See Rom. 6:4 [t]See ch. 2:10
25 [u]Zech. 8:16; Col. 3:9; [ver. 15] [v]Rom. 12:5
26 [w][Ps. 37:8]
27 [x]See James 4:7
28 [y]Acts 20:35; Gal. 6:10 [z]1 Thess. 4:11; 2 Thess. 3:8, 11, 12 [a][Prov. 21:26]
29 [b]ch. 5:4; Col. 3:8; [Matt. 12:34] [c]Col. 4:6; [Eccles. 10:12]
30 [d]Isa. 63:10; [1 Thess. 5:19] [e]ch. 1:13 [f]See ch. 1:7
31 [g]Col. 3:8, 19

4:15 The **truth** must not be used as a club to bludgeon people into acceptance and obedience but must always be presented **in love**. The truth leads the Christian to maturity, which is defined here as growing up **into Christ**. As **head**, Christ leads, directs, and guides the body (see 5:23; 1 Cor. 11:3).

4:16 joint. Paul continues the body metaphor to describe the church's maturity. Every member (i.e., every believer, viewed as a limb, or unit, in Christ's body) plays a crucial role in this growth. **in love**. There is no Christian maturity or true Christian ministry without love (1 Corinthians 13), and every act of love in the name of Christ is valued and remembered by him, as **each part is working properly** (illustrated in Eph. 4:25–32; cf. Matt. 25:31–43; 26:6–13).

4:17–24 *Paul's Testimony.* Paul testifies to the new life in Christ experienced by the Gentile Christians of Ephesus.

4:17–18 Paul affirms most solemnly **in the Lord** that his Gentile readers, as part of the new creation, should no longer live **as the Gentiles do** (vv. 22–24; Col. 3:9–10). **futility of their minds . . . darkened**. Both in antiquity and today, people who reject the knowledge of God think of themselves as "enlightened" (cf. Heb. 10:32). Their **ignorance** here is not lack of general education; some are brilliant in their own way, but such brilliance is all wasted and futile in the end when combined with **hardness of heart** toward the truth of the gospel in Christ (cf. Matt. 13:14–15; John 12:40; Acts 28:26–27; Rom. 11:8).

4:22 put off your old self. As Christians seek to do this, God makes it a reality, as seen in Col. 3:9–10. Even Paul's Gentile readers can be part of the new creation in Christ. (As the ESV footnote indicates, "self" is the generic Gk. for "man" or "human"—perhaps an allusion to Adamic man apart from Christ.) Ephesians 4:22 describes the negative side of regeneration, while vv. 23–24 point to the positive side. **corrupt**. People need inner transformation because their hearts are "deceitful above all things, and desperately sick" (Jer. 17:9).

4:23 renewed. Paul expressed the negative side of the new creation in v. 22 as putting off the "old self," while vv. 23–24 express the positive side as an entire transformation of believers' inner selves, focusing here on their **minds** (see also John 3:3–6; Col. 3:9–10). Christians sometimes distinguish between knowledge of head and of heart, but the Bible shows that they should love and serve the Lord with all that is in them, including their minds, at all times (Deut. 6:5; 10:12; 13:3; Matt. 22:37; Mark 12:30; Luke 10:27). The "renewal" or "transformation" of the mind (Rom. 12:2) is a process in which believers begin to think in new and right ways as they meditate on the truths of God's Word.

4:24 put on the new self (lit., "man"; see note on v. 22). Paul focuses on the individual aspect of the corporate "new man" as described in 2:15. Believers are **created** anew in Christ (see also 2:10). Created **after the likeness of God** further shows the connection with the original creation in Genesis, where "God created man in his own image" (Gen. 1:27; cf. 1 Cor. 15:49).

4:25–32 *Exhortation to an Edifying Lifestyle.* Paul gives practical examples of how church members build up Christ's body (cf. vv. 13–16), based on what is true of them as Christians.

4:25 Therefore. In vv. 25–32 Paul will show how Christians are to put into practice the truths explored in vv. 17–24.

4:26–27 Be angry. Not all anger is **sin**, but the believer should not be consumed by anger, nor should one's anger even be carried over into the next day, as this will only **give** an **opportunity to the devil**.

4:28 Paul uses the **thief** to illustrate how repentance impacts one's lifestyle. Repentance involves both stopping (negative) and starting (positive). The thief must stop stealing and start doing **honest work**. Stealing arises out of laziness and greed, so the repentant thief must display the opposite: diligence at **labor** and willingness to **share**.

4:29 corrupting talk. As with the "stopping" and "starting" noted in v. 28, Christians are to stop evil speech, substituting talk that is **good for building up** and giving **grace**. "Corrupting" (Gk. *sapros*) also applies to "bad" (rotten) fruit (Luke 6:43) or "bad" (putrid) fish (Matt. 13:48). To "give grace" in speaking means to benefit others rather than corrupt them through what is said.

4:30 grieve. Grieving the Holy Spirit means to cause him sorrow by one's sin. **sealed**. See note on 1:13. The **day of redemption** is the day of Christ's return (see Luke 21:28; Rom. 8:23).

4:31 All bitterness means "every kind of bitterness." "All" also modifies

clamor and slander be put away from you, along with all malice. **32** [h]Be kind to one another,
tenderhearted, [i]forgiving one another, as God in Christ forgave you.

Walk in Love

5 [j]Therefore be imitators of God, as beloved children. **2** And [k]walk in love, [l]as Christ loved
us and [m]gave himself up for us, a [n]fragrant [o]offering and sacrifice to God.
3 But [p]sexual immorality and all impurity or covetousness [q]must not even be named
among you, as is proper among saints. **4** Let there be [r]no filthiness nor foolish talk nor crude
joking, [s]which are out of place, but instead [t]let there be thanksgiving. **5** For you may be
sure of this, that [u]everyone who is sexually immoral or impure, or who is covetous ([v]that
is, an idolater), has no inheritance in the kingdom of Christ and God. **6** [w]Let no one [x]deceive
you with empty words, for because of these things [y]the wrath of God comes upon [z]the
sons of disobedience. **7** Therefore [a]do not become partners with them; **8** for [b]at one time
you were [c]darkness, but now you are light in the Lord. [d]Walk as children of light **9** (for [e]the
fruit of light is found in all that is good and right and true), **10** and [f]try to discern what is
pleasing to the Lord. **11** [g]Take no part in the [h]unfruitful [i]works of darkness, but instead
[j]expose them. **12** For [k]it is shameful even to speak of the things that they do in secret. **13** But
when [l]anything is exposed by the light, it becomes visible, **14** for anything that becomes
visible is light. Therefore it says,

32 [h]Col. 3:12, 13; 1 Pet. 3:8 [i][2 Cor. 2:7, 10]; See Matt. 6:14

Chapter 5

1 [j][ch. 4:32; Matt. 5:7, 48; Luke 6:36]
2 [k]Rom. 14:15; [Col. 3:14]; See John 13:34 [l]See Rom. 8:37 [m]See Rom. 4:25 [n]See Gen. 8:21 [o]Heb. 7:27; 9:14; 10:10, 12
3 [p]1 Cor. 6:18; See Gal. 5:19 [q][ver. 12; Ps. 16:4]
4 [r]ch. 4:29; [Eccles. 10:13] [s][Rom. 1:28] [t]ver. 20
5 [u]See 1 Cor. 6:9 [v]Col. 3:5
6 [w]See Matt. 24:4 [x]Col. 2:8 [y]Rom. 1:18; Col. 3:6 [z]ch. 2:2; [1 Pet. 1:14]
7 [a]ch. 3:6
8 [b]See ch. 2:1, 2 [c]See Acts 26:18 [d]Isa. 2:5; See Luke 16:8; John 12:35, 36
9 [e][Gal. 5:22]; See Rom. 7:4
10 [f]1 Thess. 2:4; 5:21
11 [g]See 1 Cor. 5:9 [h]Rom. 6:21 [i]Rom. 13:12 [j]Lev. 19:17; 1 Tim. 5:20
12 [k][ver. 3] **13** [l]John 3:20, 21; [ver. 9]

the other items in the list, telling readers to put away all **wrath**, **anger**, **clamor**, **slander**, and **malice**. "Bitterness" may head the list because it so often leads to the other sins that Paul names. Bitterness comes from a heart that is not right before God (Acts 8:21–23); it is a primary characteristic of an unregenerate person (Rom. 3:10–14); and it causes destruction and defilement (Heb. 12:15). Bitterness and resentment are thus incompatible with Christian character and must be **put away**. People often are very careless with their speech ("slander"), even though the tongue can ignite a forest fire of harm to others (James 3:5–6).

4:32 Being **kind**, **tenderhearted**, and **forgiving** flows from constantly remembering that God first **forgave** us and that we need his forgiveness daily, as the Lord's Prayer reminds us: "forgive us our debts, as we also have forgiven our debtors" (Matt. 6:12; cf. Luke 11:4).

5:1–20 *New Life in Love.* After a two-verse transitional section, Paul gives general instructions for holy living. He focuses on purity of life—both by avoiding evil deeds and associations and by adopting holy practices. Verse 21 connects vv. 1–20 with vv. 22–6:9.

5:1–2 *Exhortation to Self-Sacrificial Love.* Paul's discussion of love serves also as an introduction to further instructions on holy living (vv. 3–20). **imitators**. Believers are to imitate God's holiness in all of their conduct. They are to be like him, not as slaves trying to earn a wage but as **children**—and **beloved** children at that! **loved**. The past tense does not suggest that Christ has *stopped* loving us but only that, when he **gave himself up for us**, it was the supreme act of his love (see John 15:13).

5:3–20 *Instruction in Holy Living.* Paul gives general instructions on how Christians are to lead holy lives. He centers on wisdom in speech, sexual purity, associations, and other similar aspects of a thankful life.

5:3 sexual immorality. This general term (Gk. *porneia*) covers all sexual sins, including adultery, fornication, homosexuality, etc. **Covetousness** is a jealous longing for what others possess (Ex. 20:17), and it amounts to idolatry (Eph. 5:5; Col. 3:5). **named**. Christians must be careful to guard their integrity and public reputation because public sins dishonor God, who has chosen them to be holy (see note on Eph. 1:4). **saints**. See note on 1:1.

5:4 Thanksgiving, in contrast to **crude joking** and **foolish talk**, is the positive way to speak, and it also counteracts covetousness (see v. 3). The way to avoid coveting others' possessions is to concentrate with thanks upon the good things the Lord has given (see vv. 19–20).

5:5 idolater. Covetousness places one's ultimate allegiance in the acquisition of the possessions of others, which often leads to other grave sins (e.g., 1 Kings 21:1–19). Paul says this is tantamount to idolatry (see also Col. 3:5). **inheritance**. See Eph. 1:13–14; 4:30. **kingdom**. Paul speaks of Christ ruling now from the right hand of God (see 1:20–22; cf. Rom. 8:34; 1 Cor. 15:24–27; Col. 3:1; etc.). Believers have already been brought into his redemptive kingdom (see Eph. 2:6; Col. 1:13–14), although it will be consummated only at his second coming (1 Cor. 15:20–24; 2 Tim. 4:1). For Paul the kingdom of God in its fullness is the eternal realm that believers will finally and fully enter through resurrection immortality (1 Cor. 15:50; 1 Thess. 2:12), but it should also be experienced in some measure now in this age, through the indwelling presence of the Holy Spirit (Rom. 14:17).

5:6 deceive you . . . because of these things. A common deception throughout church history has been the notion that professing Christians can lead unrepentant, sinful lives after conversion to Christ (see 2 Tim. 3:1–9; 2 Pet. 2:1–3; Rev. 2:14, 20) and not suffer the consequences. But these practices lead to **the wrath of God** in judgment (e.g., Rev. 2:21–23). **sons of disobedience**. This Hebrew-inspired phrase describes people who habitually live in disobedient sin without repentance and thereby prove themselves to be children of the devil (see note on Eph. 2:2; also John 8:44; 1 John 3:10), like Judas, "the son of destruction" (John 17:12).

5:7 become partners. Paul is not telling Christians to avoid all contact with nonbelievers but to avoid joining with them in their sin.

5:8 Walk as children of light. See 1 John 1:5–7. Cf. also Ps. 27:1; Isa. 9:2; 42:6; 49:6; John 9:5; Acts 13:47; 26:18.

5:9 Fruit of light is similar to fruit of the Spirit (cf. Gal. 5:22–23).

5:10 The Bible gives general principles for life, but followers of Christ must use wisdom to **discern** how to apply those principles to the concrete issues of their lives. The book of Proverbs is of great help in this regard. Such wisdom may be defined as "the skill of godly living," which one must thoughtfully discern, apply, and practice in order to live in a way that **is pleasing to the Lord**.

5:11 Expose means either to reprove or to convince through argument and discussion (also v. 13), at the same time taking great care not to gossip or to slander others. Instead, Christians should show by their lives and their wise interactions that the **works of darkness** are not to be ignored among God's holy people.

5:14 it says. The quotation is not of any one OT passage but is probably a combined reference to several places, especially in Isaiah: "Arise, shine, for your light has come, and the glory of the LORD has risen upon you" (Isa. 60:1; see 9:2; 26:19).

14[m][Isa. 51:17; 52:1; 60:1; Mal. 4:2]; See Rom. 13:11 [n]Isa. 26:19 [o]Luke 1:78, 79
15[p]Col. 4:5; [Prov. 15:21]
16[p][See ver. 15 above] [q]ch. 6:13; Eccles. 12:1; Amos 5:13; Gal. 1:4
17[r]Rom. 12:2; 1 Thess. 4:3; 5:18
18[s]Prov. 20:1; 23:20, 31; 1 Cor. 5:11 [t]Titus 1:6; 1 Pet. 4:4 [u][Luke 1:15]
19[v]Acts 16:25; 1 Cor. 14:26; Col. 3:16; James 5:13
20[w]Col. 3:17; 1 Thess. 1:2; 2 Thess. 1:3 [x]Heb. 13:15; [John 14:13]
21[y][Phil. 2:3]
22[z]For ch. 5:22–6:9, see Col. 3:18–4:1 [a]See Gen. 3:16 [b][ch. 6:5]
23[c]1 Cor. 11:3 [d]See ch. 1:22, 23 [e][1 Cor. 6:13]

[m]"Awake, O sleeper,
and [n]arise from the dead,
and [o]Christ will shine on you."

15 [p]Look carefully then how you walk, not as unwise but as wise, 16 [p]making the best use
of the time, because [q]the days are evil. 17 Therefore do not be foolish, but understand what
[r]the will of the Lord is. 18 And [s]do not get drunk with wine, for that is [t]debauchery, but [u]be
filled with the Spirit, 19 addressing one another in [v]psalms and hymns and spiritual songs,
singing and making melody to the Lord with your heart, 20 [w]giving thanks always and for
everything to God the Father [x]in the name of our Lord Jesus Christ, 21 [y]submitting to one
another out of reverence for Christ.

Wives and Husbands

22 [z]Wives, [a]submit to your own husbands, [b]as to the Lord. 23 For [c]the husband is the
head of the wife even as [d]Christ is the head of the church, his body, and is [e]himself its
Savior. 24 Now as the church submits to Christ, so also wives should submit [f]in everything
to their husbands.

24[f][Col. 3:20, 22; Titus 2:9]

5:16 making the best use of. This phrase translates the Greek *exagorazō*, which can also mean "redeem" or "purchase." Christians must actively take advantage of the opportunity to do good (cf. Ps. 90:12). Wisdom is especially needed in an **evil** age where the pathway of holiness is not always immediately clear until one reflects upon God's Word and discerns his holy will.

5:17 understand . . . the will of the Lord. This does not mean that a person tries to discern God's secret counsel (his "hidden will") but that he applies God's general guidelines for life as found in the Bible (his "revealed will"; cf. Deut. 29:29 and note on Eph. 5:10).

5:18 Wine was the staple drink of the ancient Mediterranean world and was fermented in order to preserve it from turning into vinegar. **be filled with the Spirit.** As earlier (see note on 4:28), Paul expresses a negative exhortation (what the saints are to stop doing) along with a positive command (what the saints are to start doing). Whereas wine can control the mind and ruin one's judgment and sense of propriety, leading to **debauchery**, in contrast with this, being "filled with the Spirit" leads to self-control along with the other fruits of "love, joy, peace, patience, kindness, goodness, faithfulness, [and] gentleness" (Gal. 5:22–23). The command in Greek (*plērousthe*) is a present imperative and does not describe a onetime "filling" but a regular pattern of life.

5:19 Being filled with the Spirit results in joyful praise through **singing** and **making melody**. This may refer to different kinds of **psalms and hymns and spiritual songs** found in the OT Psalter. It seems more likely, however, that Paul is referring both to the canonical psalms and to contemporary compositions of praise (see also Col. 3:16). "Spiritual" communicates the influence of the Holy Spirit's filling (Eph. 5:18) in the believer's acts of praise.

5:20 To pray **in the name of** Jesus means to pray in faith, trusting in him as our mediator with God the Father on "the throne of grace" (John 14:6; Heb. 4:16; 10:20; see also note on John 14:13).

5:21–6:9 *Submission to One Another.* Verse 21 is transitional, connecting with the previous section and leading to what follows. Submission is illustrated in various family relations in 5:22–33 (wives/husbands), 6:1–4 (children/parents), and 6:5–9 (servants/masters). See also Col. 3:18–25.

5:21 *Submission in General.* Grammatically, "submitting" is a participle in Greek and is dependent on the verb in v. 15. It explains further how to walk in wisdom (vv. 15–21 are one long sentence in Gk.). It also states a general principle of submission, which is illustrated in 5:22–6:9. Absolute "mutual submission" is popular today, particularly where egalitarian philosophies are the rule. But what Paul meant by submitting "to one another" is explained through the particular examples of family relations (5:22–6:4), so it is likely that **submitting to one another** means "submitting to others according to the authority and order established by God," as reflected in the examples that Paul gives in the following verses.

5:22–33 *Wives and Husbands.* The first example of general submission (v. 21) is illustrated as Paul exhorts wives to submit to their husbands (vv. 22–24, 33). Husbands, on the other hand, are not told to submit to their wives but to love them (vv. 25–33).

5:22 submit. Paul's first example of general submission from v. 21 is the right ordering of the marriage relationship (see also Col. 3:18; 1 Pet. 3:1–7). The submission of wives is not like the obedience children owe parents, nor does this text command all women to submit to all men (**to your own husbands**, not to all husbands!). Both genders are equally created in God's image (Gen. 1:26–28) and heirs together of eternal life (Gal. 3:28–29). This submission is in deference to the ultimate leadership of the husband for the health and harmonious working of the marriage relationship.

5:23–24 the husband is the head of the wife. This is the grounds of the wife's submission to her husband and is modeled on Christ's headship over the church. Just as Christ's position as **head of the church** and **its Savior** does not vary from one culture to another, neither does the headship of a husband in relation to his wife and her duty to submit to her husband **in everything**. "Head" (Gk. *kephalē*) here clearly refers to a husband's authority over his wife and cannot mean "source," as some have argued. In fact, there is no sense in which husbands are the source of their wives either physically or spiritually. In addition, in over 50 examples of *kephalē* in ancient Greek

Principles of Marriage	Scripture Reference
Marriage is part of the "mystery" of God's will	Eph. 1:9; 3:3; 5:32
Paul's instructions are directed to Spirit-filled believers	Eph. 5:18
Wives are called to submit, men are called to love	Eph. 5:21–33
Headship entails authority	Eph. 5:23–24 (cf. Eph. 1:22; 4:15)
Submission is still required of Christian wives	Eph. 5:22; Col. 3:18 (cf. Gen. 2:18; 1 Cor. 11:3)
Marriage involves spiritual warfare, which requires husbands and wives to put on the full armor of God	Eph. 6:10–18

25 [g]Husbands, love your wives, as Christ loved the church and [h]gave himself up for her,
26 that he might sanctify her, having cleansed her by [i]the washing of water [j]with the word,
27 so [k]that he might present the church to himself in splendor, [l]without spot or wrinkle or
any such thing, that she might be holy and without blemish.[1] 28 In the same way [m]husbands
should love their wives as their own bodies. He who loves his wife loves himself. 29 For no
one ever hated his own flesh, but nourishes and cherishes it, just as Christ does the church,
30 because [n]we are members of his body. 31 [o]"Therefore a man shall leave his father and
mother and hold fast to his wife, and [p]the two shall become one flesh." 32 This mystery is
profound, and I am saying that it refers to Christ and the church. 33 However, [q]let each one
of you love his wife as himself, and let the wife see that she [r]respects her husband.

Children and Parents

6 [s]Children, obey your parents in the Lord, for this is right. 2 [t]"Honor your father and
mother" (this is the first commandment with a promise), 3 "that it may go well with
you and that you may live long in the land." 4 Fathers, do not provoke your children to
anger, [u]but bring them up in the discipline and instruction of the Lord.

Bondservants and Masters

5 [v]Bondservants,[2] obey your earthly masters[3] with fear and trembling, [w]with a sincere

[1] Or *holy and blameless* [2] Or *slaves*; also verse 6 (for the contextual rendering of the Greek word *doulos*, see Preface) [3] Or *your masters according to the flesh*

25 [g]ver. 28, 33; [1 Pet. 3:7] [h]ver. 2
26 [i]Titus 3:5; [Rev. 7:14] [j]ch. 6:17; Heb. 6:5; See John 15:3
27 [k]2 Cor. 11:2; See ch. 1:4 [l]Song 4:7
28 [m]ver. 25, 33
30 [n][Gen. 2:23]; See 1 Cor. 6:15
31 [o]Matt. 19:5; Mark 10:7, 8; Cited from Gen. 2:24 [p]1 Cor. 6:16
33 [q]ver. 25, 28 [r]1 Pet. 3:2, 6

Chapter 6

1 [s]Prov. 1:8; 6:20; 23:22
2 [t]Cited from Ex. 20:12
4 [u]Gen. 18:19; Deut. 4:9; 6:7; 11:19; Ps. 78:4; Prov. 19:18; 22:6; 29:17; [2 Tim. 3:15]
5 [v]See 1 Pet. 2:18 [w][2 Cor. 11:3]

literature, with the idea "person A is the head of person(s) B," person A has authority over person(s) B in every case (see also 1:22; Col. 2:10; see note on 1 Cor. 11:3).

5:25 love. Paul now turns to the duty of husbands. He does not command the husband to submit to his wife but instead tells the husband that he must give **himself up for her**. Thus, husbands are to love their wives in a self-sacrificial manner, following the example of Christ, who "gave himself up for" the church in loving self-sacrifice. Clearly the biblical picture of a husband laying down his life for his wife is directly opposed to any kind of male tyranny or oppression. The husband is bound by love to ensure that his wife finds their marriage a source of rich fulfillment and joyful service to the Lord. Notably, Paul devotes three times more space to the husband's duty (nine verses) than to the wife's (three verses).

5:26–27 The focus in these verses is on Christ, for husbands do not "sanctify" their wives or "wash" them of their sins, though they are to do all in their power to promote their wives' holiness. **Sanctify** here means to consecrate into the Lord's service through cleansing. **washing of water**. This might be a reference to baptism, since it is common in the Bible to speak of invisible, spiritual things (in this case, spiritual cleansing) by pointing to an outward physical sign of them (see Rom. 6:3–4; and note on John 4:15). There may also be a link here to Ezek. 16:1–13, where the Lord washes infant Israel, raises her, and eventually elevates her to royalty and marries her, which would correspond to presenting **the church to himself in splendor** at his marriage supper (see also Ezek. 36:25; Rev. 19:7–9; 21:2, 9–11). **without blemish**. The church's utter holiness and moral perfection will be consummated in resurrection glory, but is derived from the consecrating sacrifice of Christ on the cross.

5:28–30 Paul reiterates a husband's calling to self-sacrificial **love** for his wife by comparing this love to regard for one's own body (**their own bodies**), **himself**, and **his own flesh** (vv. 28–29; see also v. 33) and then to Christ's love for his body. As vv. 29–30 make explicit, the "body" for which Christ sacrificed himself was not his own person but the "body" which is the church.

5:31 one flesh. The command for a husband to love his wife as he loves "his own flesh" (v. 29) originates in the creation reality that God joins husbands and wives together to "become one flesh." Paul's quotation is from Gen. 2:24, speaking of marriage before there was any sin in the world; see also Matt. 19:5; Mark 10:8; 1 Cor. 6:16.

5:32 By **mystery** Paul means the hidden plan of God that has come to fulfillment in Christ Jesus (see 1:9; 3:3–4, 9; and 6:19), thus his quotation about marriage from Genesis 2 (in Eph. 5:31) ties in to the relationship between Christ and his church. Paul's meaning is **profound**: he interprets the original creation of the husband-and-wife union as itself modeled on Christ's forthcoming union with the church as his "body" (see v. 23). Therefore, marriage from the beginning of creation (Genesis 1) was created by God to be a reflection of and patterned after Christ's relation to the church. Thus Paul's commands regarding the roles of husbands and wives do not merely reflect the culture of his day but present God's ideal for all marriages at all times, as exemplified by the relationship between the bride of Christ (the church) and Christ himself, the Son of God.

6:1–4 *Children and Parents.* The submission of 5:21 is further explained as meaning that children should submit to their parents. This submission takes the form of obedience to them. Parents are to nurture their children in the Lord.

6:1 Children. The second family relationship illustrating submission to proper authority (5:21) is that of children and parents. The Mosaic law prescribed death for the child who struck or cursed a parent (Ex. 21:15, 17; Lev. 20:9), and Paul lists such disobedience as one of many grave sins (Rom. 1:30; 2 Tim. 3:2). However, Paul urges in Eph. 6:1–3 the positive duty of children to **obey** their **parents**. Obedience is due to both parents; the mother's submission to her husband does not remove her parental dignity but rather increases it. **In the Lord** modifies the verb "obey." **right**. What makes such obedience "right" or "just" is that it conforms to God's holy commandment, quoted in vv. 2–3.

6:2–3 Honor. Children obeying their parents (v. 1) is in part how they honor them; see also Prov. 31:28, which describes children rising to bless a wise and godly mother. **promise**. There were earlier commands of God with promises (e.g., Gen. 17:1–2), but this is the first and only of the Ten Commandments to contain a promise (see also Ex. 20:12). In the new covenant the promise of **the land** is not physical land on earth but eternal life, which begins when one is regenerated here and now and comes to full reality in the age to come. Paul is not teaching salvation on the basis of works. The obedience of children is evidence that they know God, and it results in receiving blessings from God.

6:4 Fathers. As earlier, Paul begins his admonition with a negative action to avoid, followed by a positive action to develop (see note on 4:28). Paul addresses the responsibility of fathers in particular, though this does not diminish the contribution of mothers in these areas (see Proverbs 31). **provoke . . . to anger**. Obedient children are particularly vulnerable, so a domineering and thoughtless father's actions would be discouraging to them (Col. 3:21). **bring them up**. Parents play a crucial, God-ordained role in the discipleship of their children "in the Lord" (Eph. 6:1); see Deut. 6:1–9. Parental discipleship **in the discipline and instruction of the Lord** should center on the kinds of practices already outlined in Ephesians 4–5.

6:5–9 *Slaves, Bondservants, and Masters.* The submission of 5:21 is further illustrated with slaves (or bondservants; see ESV Preface, p. 21) and masters. The duty of both is based on their both being fellow heirs of eternal life.

6:5 Bondservants. See note on 1 Cor. 7:21. It is estimated that slaves

heart, [x]as you would Christ, 6 not by the way of eye-service, as [y]people-pleasers, but as
bondservants of Christ, doing the will of God from the heart, 7 rendering service with a
good will as to the Lord and not to man, 8 [z]knowing that whatever good anyone does, this
he will receive back from the Lord, [a]whether he is a bondservant[1] or is free. 9 Masters, do
the same to them, [b]and stop your threatening, knowing that [c]he who is both their Master[2]
and yours is in heaven, and that [d]there is no partiality with him.

The Whole Armor of God

10 Finally, [e]be strong in the Lord and in [f]the strength of his might. 11 [g]Put on [h]the whole
armor of God, that you may be able to stand against [i]the schemes of the devil. 12 For [j]we do
not wrestle against flesh and blood, but against [k]the rulers, against the authorities, against
[l]the cosmic powers over [m]this present darkness, against [n]the spiritual forces of evil [o]in the
heavenly places. 13 Therefore [p]take up the whole armor of God, that you may be able to
withstand in [q]the evil day, and having done all, to stand firm. 14 Stand therefore, [r]having
fastened on the belt of truth, and [s]having put on the breastplate of righteousness, 15 and,
[t]as shoes for your feet, having put on the readiness given by the gospel of peace. 16 In all
circumstances take up [u]the shield of faith, with which you can extinguish all [v]the flaming
darts of [w]the evil one; 17 and take [s]the helmet of salvation, and [x]the sword of the Spirit,

[1] Or *slave* (for the contextual rendering of the Greek word *doulos*, see Preface) [2] Greek *Lord*

5 [x][ch. 5:22]
6 [y]See Gal. 1:10
8 [z]See Ps. 62:12 [a]Gal. 3:28; Col. 3:11
9 [b]Lev. 25:43 [c]John 13:13; [Job 31:13-15] [d]See Deut. 10:17
10 [e]Rom. 4:20 (Gk.); 2 Tim. 2:1; [1 John 2:14]; See ch. 3:16 [f]ch. 1:19
11 [g]ver. 14; Job 29:14; See Rom. 13:12 [h]ver. 13; [2 Cor. 10:4] [i]ch. 4:14
12 [j]See 1 Cor. 9:25 [k]ch. 1:21 [l]See ch. 2:2 [m]Luke 22:53; Col. 1:13 [n][ch. 3:10] [o]See ch. 1:3
13 [p][1 Pet. 4:1] [q]ch. 5:16
14 [r]1 Pet. 1:13; [Isa. 11:5]; See Luke 12:35 [s]Isa. 59:17; 1 Thess. 5:8; [Isa. 61:10; 2 Cor. 6:7]
15 [t]Isa. 52:7; Rom. 10:15; [Ex. 12:11]
16 [u][1 John 5:4] [v][Ps. 120:4] [w]See Matt. 13:19
17 [s][See ver. 14 above] [x]Heb. 4:12; [Isa. 49:2; Hos. 6:5; 2 Cor. 6:7]

(or bondservants) composed about one-third of the population of a city like Ephesus. They were considered an integral part of a family, so Paul's instructions for bondservants were a natural part of his dealing with family relationships. In both Greek and Roman culture, bondservants had limited rights and were subject to exploitation and abuse. Paul does not condone the existing system of servitude but instead provides instructions to believing masters and bondservants regarding their relationship to each other in the Lord, and how this should be lived out within the bounds of their social and legal culture. The result, as is often observed, is that this kind of servitude slowly died out in antiquity through the influence of Christianity (see Introduction to Philemon: Purpose, Occasion, and Background). The principles in this passage apply today in terms of submission to any lawfully constituted authority, the only exception being if such a lawfully constituted authority were to require a believer to disobey God's Word or to fundamentally compromise one's commitment to Christ (as in the case of Acts 4:19, 20). **Christ**. It would be natural for Christian bondservants to despise their **earthly masters** in the name of their heavenly one; however, fulfilling one's earthly obligations is, in fact, service to the Lord (cf. Eph. 6:6–7).

6:8 whatever good anyone does . . . he will receive back from the Lord. Selfless service is not ignored or forgotten by God. There is no discrimination with the Lord, for he will reward every faithful servant equally, **whether he is a bondservant or is free**.

6:9 Masters in antiquity had the power of life and death over their slaves and bondservants (see ESV Preface, p. 21). Beatings, imprisonment, or sale into harsher servitude were other punishments masters meted out. The duty of masters and all in authority is to do good to those in submission and not to take advantage of their authority by **threatening** them. There is no **partiality** with the Lord (see 1 Sam. 16:7; 2 Chron. 19:7; Rom. 2:11): he will judge fairly both masters and servants.

6:10–20 *The Whole Armor of God.* Paul concludes his exhortations with instructions for all Christians. His imagery is a sustained portrayal of the Christian life as spiritual warfare using the Lord's resources. There are three subsections: vv. 10–13, 14–17, and 18–20.

6:10–13 *The Lord's Strength.* Paul introduces the armor of God by focusing on the strength it gives.

6:10 be strong. Because Christians cannot stand on their own against superhuman powers, they must rely upon the **strength** of the Lord's own **might** (see 1:19), which he supplies chiefly through prayer (6:18).

6:11 The Greek word for **whole armor** (*panoplia*) refers to the complete equipment of a fully armed soldier, consisting of both shields and weapons like those described in vv. 14, 16–17. Paul's description here draws primarily on OT allusions, yet the terms used also overlap well with Roman weaponry (esp. the terms for the large, door-shaped shield and the short stabbing sword). Visible portrayals of such weaponry can be found on the numerous military reliefs (esp. on sarcophagi) throughout the Roman Empire. **schemes**. Here the diabolical origin is exposed, regarding the "deceitful schemes" of those teaching false doctrine (4:14; see also 1 John 2:18, 22; 4:3; 2 John 7).

6:12 This list of spiritual **rulers**, **authorities**, and **cosmic powers** (see 3:10) gives a sobering glimpse into the devil's allies, the **spiritual forces of evil** who are exceedingly powerful in their exercise of cosmic powers **over this present darkness**. And yet Scripture makes clear that the enemy host is no match for the Lord, who has "disarmed the rulers and authorities and put them to open shame, by triumphing over them in him" (Col. 2:15; see also Eph. 1:19–21).

6:13 Therefore. Because the Christian's enemies are superhuman spiritual forces, he cannot rely upon mere human resources but must **take up the whole armor of God** (see note on v. 11). The divine armor and "sword of the Spirit"—which belong to the Lord himself and to his Messiah in Isa. 11:4–5 and 59:17—are made available for believers. **withstand**. Along with "stand" in Eph. 6:11 and **stand firm** later in v. 13, Paul portrays Christians as soldiers in the battle line holding fast against the enemy's charge. **evil day**. In 5:16 Paul identifies this whole age as "evil days," yet the outbreak of the Satanic onslaught against Christ's people ebbs and flows throughout this era until the final day when the Lord of Hosts will return in power and great glory (Luke 21:27) to rend the heavens and rescue his people forever.

6:14–17 *Standing Firm.* Paul reiterates the charge to stand in the face of dreaded spiritual enemies because the Lord has not left his people defenseless. They have the complete armor of God from head to foot, which consists of the belt, breastplate, shoes, shield, helmet, and sword. These are metaphors for the spiritual resources given to them in Christ, namely, the truth, righteousness (v. 14), gospel (v. 15), faith (v. 16), salvation, and the Word of God (v. 17). As mentioned in the note on v. 13, these are aspects of God's and the Messiah's own character and work (as depicted in Isaiah) with which Christians are now equipped. For example, the Lord saw no one to deliver his oppressed people, so he put on his own "breastplate [of righteousness]" and "helmet of salvation" (Isa. 59:17; cf. Eph. 6:14, 17) before coming in wrath against his enemies.

6:14 With the simple, rousing order, **stand**, Paul urges the Ephesians to withstand the enemy (cf. vv. 11, 13), and not give in to fear.

6:15 Believers must always be ready to proclaim the gospel.

6:16–17 flaming darts. Burning arrows were designed to destroy wooden shields and other defenses, but the **shield of faith** is able to extinguish the devil's attacks. **the sword of the Spirit, which is the word of God**. The spiritual nature of the church's resources is nowhere more plain than in its reliance upon God's Word, which is the only offensive weapon mentioned in this

which is the word of God, 18 praying [y]at all times [z]in the Spirit, [a]with all prayer and supplication. To that end [b]keep alert with all perseverance, making [c]supplication for all the
saints, 19 and [d]also for me, that words may be given to me in opening my mouth [e]boldly
to proclaim [f]the mystery of the gospel, 20 for which I [g]am an ambassador [h]in chains, that
I may declare it boldly, as I ought to speak.

Final Greetings

21 [i]So that you also may know how I am and what I am doing, [j]Tychicus the beloved
brother and faithful minister in the Lord will tell you everything. 22 I have sent him to
you for this very purpose, that you may know how we are, and that he may [k]encourage
your hearts.
23 [l]Peace be to the brothers,[1] and [m]love with faith, from God the Father and the Lord
Jesus Christ. 24 Grace be with all who [n]love our Lord Jesus Christ with love incorruptible.

[1] *Or brothers and sisters*

18 [y]Luke 18:1 [z]Jude 20; See Rom. 8:26 [a]Col. 4:2-4 [b]See Mark 13:33 [c]1 Tim. 2:1
19 [d]Col. 4:3; 1 Thess. 5:25; 2 Thess. 3:1; [Isa. 50:4] [e]See Acts 4:29 [f]ch. 3:3
20 [g]See 2 Cor. 5:20 [h]See Acts 28:20
21 [i]Col. 4:7-9 [j]Acts 20:4; 2 Tim. 4:12; Titus 3:12
22 [k]Col. 2:2
23 [l]Gal. 6:16; 2 Thess. 3:16; 1 Pet. 5:14 [m][Gal. 5:6; 1 Thess. 5:8]
24 [n][1 Cor. 16:22]

list of spiritual armor. The Word of God is to be wielded like a sharp two-edged sword, in the mighty power of his Holy Spirit (see Heb. 4:12).

6:18–20 *Being Constant in Prayer.* This section offers instruction on prayer (the main weapon of spiritual warfare) and explains when, how, and for whom to pray.

6:18 praying. The weapons for warfare are spiritual because they are rooted in prayer, which is the Christian's most powerful resource. Prayer is to permeate believers' lives as a universal practice, as seen by the use of "all" four times in this verse: **at all times . . . with all prayer . . . with all perseverance . . . for all the saints**. Prayer **in the Spirit** is a form of worship (John 4:23–24) enabled by the Spirit of God, who intercedes on behalf of the person who prays (Rom. 8:26–27).

6:21–24 *Conclusion.* Paul concludes his letter with closing remarks (vv. 21–22) and a final benediction (vv. 23–24). The remarks concern his introduction of Tychicus.

6:21–22 Tychicus the beloved brother had served Paul faithfully for some time (see Acts 20:4; Col. 4:7; 2 Tim. 4:12; Titus 3:12) and probably carried the original letter to Ephesus.

6:23–24 Paul concludes his letter with a benediction of **peace, love, faith,** and **grace** upon the church, as he had done in the opening (1:2). He mentions "love" three times, which is fitting for a letter where the love of God, the love of Christ, and Christian love have been prominent themes.

INTRODUCTION TO

THE LETTER OF PAUL TO THE

PHILIPPIANS

Author and Title

Paul is the stated author of Philippians, and few have questioned his authorship. It was written to the Christians in the Roman colony of Philippi.

Date

Scholars have debated Paul's location when he wrote Philippians. Caesarea, Ephesus, and Rome have been the three most commonly proposed locations. Paul was in fact imprisoned in the "praetorium" of Herod the Great in Caesarea (Acts 23:35; cf. ESV footnote on Phil. 1:13) around A.D. 60. But his statements to the Philippians about his possibly imminent death (e.g., 1:20) would be puzzling if coming from Caesarea, since he would have been able to request a trial in Rome, as in fact he did. Ephesus was close enough to Philippi for Paul to receive regular news from there, but there is no mention of his ever being imprisoned in Ephesus. On balance, it seems most likely that the letter was written from Rome, c. A.D. 62. This also fits most naturally with the mention of the praetorium and "Caesar's household" (1:13 and 4:22).

Theme

The chief theme of Philippians is encouragement: Paul wants to encourage the Philippians to live out their lives as citizens of a heavenly colony, as evidenced by a growing commitment to service to God and to one another. The way of life that Paul encourages was manifested uniquely in Jesus Christ; it was also evident in the lives of Paul, Timothy, and Epaphroditus.

Purpose, Occasion, and Background

The church at Philippi had a special significance for Paul, since it was the first church he founded in Europe (see Acts 16:6–40). The first convert was Lydia, a seller of purple goods, and women continued to have a prominent role in the Philippian church (e.g., Phil. 4:2). Paul and Silas were imprisoned there for exorcising a demon from a fortune-telling slave girl, but God miraculously delivered them, and they proclaimed the gospel to the Philippian jailer. Paul likely visited the Philippians a few times after his initial departure, and they maintained active support for his ministry (4:15–16).

Paul wrote to the Philippians from prison (see above), prompted in part by his reception of their latest gift, sent with Epaphroditus (himself a member of the Philippian congregation). But the letter is far more than an extended thank-you note. Paul wanted to pass along the important news that Epaphroditus had recovered from a serious illness (2:25–30), and that he was sending him along to them with the hope that soon he might also send Timothy for a visit (2:19). Timothy and Epaphroditus were also mentioned because they exemplified the Christ-centered, gospel-focused life Paul wanted the Philippians to live.

Paul himself also wanted to encourage the Philippians in their faith, and his imprisonment meant he could do that only through a letter. Even a house imprisonment (assuming Paul was in Rome, Acts 28:16) could have been a source of great anguish, particularly with the possibility of execution looming, and so Paul wanted to assure the church that he was still in good spirits through his faith in Christ (Phil. 1:12–18). He was also eager to thank them for their continued support: imprisonment carried with it a social stigma, and it would have been easy for the Philippians to turn their back on Paul at this point. But they had remained faithful to him.

Yet Paul's purpose in writing goes even further. He is above all concerned that the Philippians continue to make progress in their faith (1:25). While there were no doubt conflicts within the congregation (notably that of Euodia and Syntyche, 4:2), the Philippians appear to be a healthy congregation, in contrast to the troubled groups in Corinth and Galatia. Can they then relax and rest? Paul's answer is an emphatic no. The world is too perilous, and the gospel too glorious, for them to be content with past achievements (3:12–16). They must follow Paul's example and "press on toward the goal for the prize of the upward call of God in Christ Jesus" (3:14).

Paul explains what spiritual progress will look like. Christian maturity does not come through special mystical insights available to only a few, but rather through the patient practice of the familiar virtues of love and service to others. Paul presents himself as one model for such a lifestyle (1:12–18; 3:17; 4:9), and he commends Timothy and Epaphroditus in similar terms (2:19–30). But the supreme model for progress in faith is Jesus himself, and the centerpiece of Philippians is the magnificent "hymn of Christ" in 2:5–11. Jesus willingly let go of the privileges of divine glory to take up the form of a servant, and even embraced the ultimate humiliation of the cross, in order to liberate the world from sin. He is thus accorded the highest glory, receiving universal worship as God's Messiah.

Those who follow Christ's example have the hope that God will also vindicate them on the day of Christ, and thus they can rejoice (1:18; 3:1; 4:4). They can also be confident that God will not leave them alone to make their way through the world as best they can. Spiritual progress involves effort: they are encouraged to "work out [their] own salvation with fear and trembling" (2:12). But they can do so knowing that "it is God who works in [them], both to will and to work for his good pleasure" (2:13).

Timeline

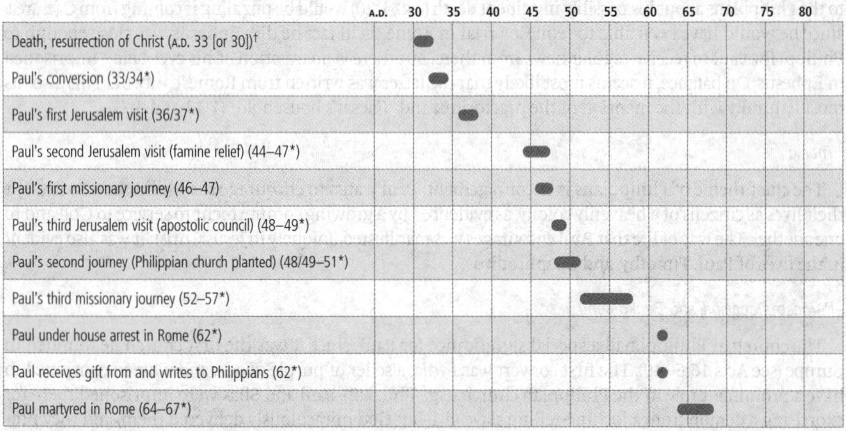

A.D. 30 35 40 45 50 55 60 65 70 75 80
Death, resurrection of Christ (A.D. 33 [or 30])†
Paul's conversion (33/34*)
Paul's first Jerusalem visit (36/37*)
Paul's second Jerusalem visit (famine relief) (44–47*)
Paul's first missionary journey (46–47)
Paul's third Jerusalem visit (apostolic council) (48–49*)
Paul's second journey (Philippian church planted) (48/49–51*)
Paul's third missionary journey (52–57*)
Paul under house arrest in Rome (62*)
Paul receives gift from and writes to Philippians (62*)
Paul martyred in Rome (64–67*)

** denotes approximate date; / signifies either/or; † see The Date of Jesus' Crucifixion, pp. 1809–1810*

The Ancient City of Philippi

After their victory at the Battle of Philippi in 42 B.C., Antony and (later) Augustus re-founded this Macedonian city with army veterans. Its special status as an Augustan colony exempted the city from significant forms of taxation and gave it additional privileges of land ownership. The city encompassed good agricultural land, and it was on the Egnatian Way, an important Roman commercial road (built mid-2nd century B.C.). The Roman ethos of the colony is evident in Philippi's Latin civic inscriptions and in the worship of Roman gods. Extant archaeological remains from Paul's day testify to the presence of a theater, a large forum (beneath the later 2nd-century-A.D. forum), shops, and two city gates (designated Krenides to the west and Neapolis to the east). There is a speaker's platform (Gk. *bēma*) in the existing second-century forum between a pair of large fountains. One small stone crypt (built over a cistern) near the forum was designated in later church tradition as the prison site of Paul and Silas (Acts 16:23–34). Other structures

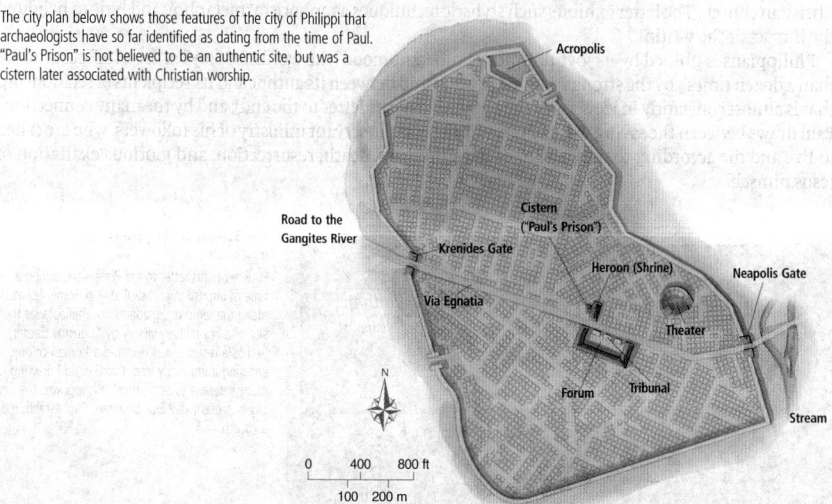

PHILIPPI IN THE TIME OF PAUL (C. A.D. 60)

The city plan below shows those features of the city of Philippi that archaeologists have so far identified as dating from the time of Paul. "Paul's Prison" is not believed to be an authentic site, but was a cistern later associated with Christian worship.

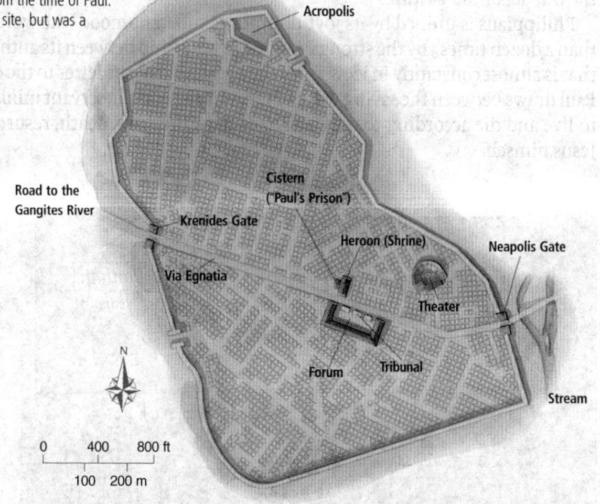

dating from NT times and the early centuries of the church (e.g., a sports facility, pagan temples, octagonal and basilica style churches) can still be seen in Philippi.

Key Themes

1. Christians need to keep making progress in their lives.	1:12, 25; 3:12–16
2. A proper spiritual outlook is critical for progress in the faith.	1:5–11; 2:1–11; 3:7, 15; 4:7–9
3. Christ is the supreme example of loving and faithful service to God, and mature Christians can also serve as role models in this regard.	1:12–26; 2:5–11, 19–30; 3:3–17; 4:9
4. Suffering will come, but through faith it can be met with joy.	1:12–26; 2:14–15; 4:4, 11–13, 19
5. Prayer is crucial for maintaining a joyful Christian life.	1:3–11; 4:5–7
6. The gospel is not individualistic: Christians are to share in rich fellowship with one another, and to be united together in service to promote the gospel.	1:4, 7, 24–27; 2:1–4, 19–30; 4:2–4, 14
7. The old covenant and observance of the law cannot provide the necessary right standing with God. Believers can be saved only through faith in Jesus Christ.	3:2–10
8. Jesus is fully God and fully man. Because of his suffering on the cross, he is now exalted as Lord and Christ.	2:5–11

History of Salvation Summary

God works in the Philippians in accordance with the achievements of Christ, who has fulfilled the promises of the OT (cf. 2 Cor. 1:20). (For an explanation of the "History of Salvation," see the Overview of the Bible, pp. 23–26.)

Literary Features

Philippians follows many of the same conventions as the other Pauline epistles. The salutation, thanksgiving, prayer, body, *paraenesis* (series of moral exhortations), greeting, and benediction are all readily identifiable. Today Philippians would be called a missionary support letter. Paul is writing to people who help provide the prayer support and financial assistance necessary for his ministry as an apostle to the Gentiles. To fulfill his end of the partnership, Paul assures the Philippians of his prayers, updates them on his personal circumstances, reports on the effectiveness of gospel ministry in his area, offers spiritual encouragement, and expresses heartfelt gratitude for the many ways they support his ministry. With its highly patterned lines of praise to Christ, 2:5–11 is usually identified as one of the earliest hymns or confessions of the Christian church. The letter exhibits such stylistic techniques as aphorism, metaphor, and lyric to heighten the impact of the writing.

Philippians is unified by its joyful, almost exuberant mood (the words for "joy" or "rejoice" occur more than a dozen times); by the strong personal relationship between its author and its recipients (a relationship that is almost constantly in view, from the beginning of the letter to the end); and by the many connections Paul draws between the saving work of Jesus Christ and the servant ministry of his followers, who are called to live and die according to the pattern of the sufferings, death, resurrection, and glorious exaltation of Jesus himself.

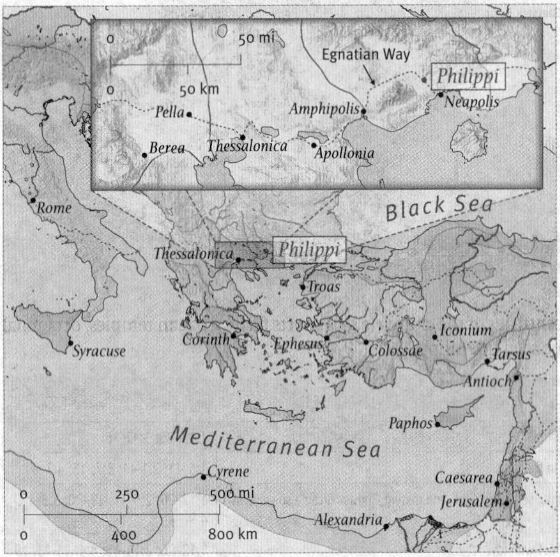

The Setting of Philippians
(c. A.D. 62)
Paul wrote his letter to the Philippians during a time of imprisonment, probably in Rome. Located along the famous Egnatian Way, Philippi was the site of a key military victory by Augustus Caesar, and as a result it was declared a Roman colony, ensuring it immunity from taxation and drawing many veterans to settle there. Philippi was the first city in present-day Europe where Paul established a church.

Outline

I. Greeting and Prayer (1:1–11)
  A. Salutation from Paul and Timothy (1:1–2)
  B. Paul's thanksgiving and prayer for the Philippians (1:3–11)

II. Paul's Reflections on His Imprisonment (1:12–30)
  A. Paul's imprisonment has meant progress for the gospel (1:12–18)
  B. To live is Christ (1:19–26)
  C. Encouragement to walk worthy of the gospel (1:27–30)

III. Exhortation to Humble Service (2:1–30)
  A. Encouragement to unity in the faith and service to one another (2:1–4)
  B. Christ's example of humble service (2:5–11)
  C. Living as lights in the world (2:12–18)
  D. Timothy as an example of a service-centered life (2:19–24)
  E. Epaphroditus as another example of service (2:25–30)

IV. Opponents of the Gospel: Where Does Righteousness Come From? (3:1–21)
   A. Initial call to rejoice in the Lord (3:1)
   B. Contrast between the opponents of the gospel and the true people of God (3:2–3)
   C. Paul's renunciation of spiritual and ethnic privileges for the sake of knowing Christ (3:4–11)
   D. Paul's progress in the gospel: through Christ, not the law (3:12–16)
   E. A call to follow Paul's example of commitment to Jesus as Lord (3:17–21)

V. Concluding Exhortations and Thanksgiving (4:1–23)
   A. Standing together for the gospel (4:1–3)
   B. Rejoicing in faith (4:4–9)
   C. Thanksgiving for the Philippians' gift; Paul's contentment in God (4:10–20)
   D. Greetings (4:21–22)
   E. Benediction (4:23)

THE LETTER OF PAUL TO THE

PHILIPPIANS

Greeting

1 Paul and Timothy, servants[1] of Christ Jesus,
To all the [a]saints in Christ Jesus who are at Philippi, with the [b]overseers[2] and
[c]deacons:[3]
2 [d]Grace to you and peace from God our Father and the Lord Jesus Christ.

Thanksgiving and Prayer

3 [e]I thank my God [f]in all my remembrance of you, 4 always in every prayer of mine for
you all making my prayer with joy, 5 [g]because of your partnership in the gospel from the
first day until now. 6 And I am sure of this, that he who began [h]a good work in you [i]will
bring it to completion at [j]the day of Jesus Christ. 7 It is right for me to feel this way about
you all, because I hold you [k]in my heart, for you are all [l]partakers with me of grace,[4] both
[m]in my imprisonment and in [n]the defense and confirmation of the gospel. 8 For [o]God is
my witness, [p]how I yearn for you all with the affection of Christ Jesus. 9 And it is my prayer

[1] Or *slaves* (for the contextual rendering of the Greek word *doulos*, see Preface) [2] Or *bishops;* Greek *episkopoi* [3] Or *servants, or ministers;* Greek *diakonoi* [4] Or *you all have fellowship with me in grace*

Chapter 1
1 [a]2 Cor. 1:1; Col. 1:2 [b]See Acts 20:28 [c]1 Tim. 3:8, 12
2 [d]Rom. 1:7; 1 Cor. 1:3
3 [e]See Rom. 1:8 [f]Rom. 1:9; Eph. 1:16; 2 Tim. 1:3
5 [g][ch. 2:12; 4:15; Acts 16:12-40]
6 [h][1 Thess. 1:3] [i]Ps. 57:2 (Heb.); 138:8; [1 Thess. 5:24] [j]See 1 Cor. 1:8
7 [k]2 Cor. 7:3 [l][ch. 4:14] [m]Acts 20:23; 26:29; Col. 4:18; 2 Tim. 2:9; Philem. 10, 13; See Eph. 3:1 [n]ver. 16
8 [o]See Rom. 1:9; 9:1 [p][ch. 4:1; Rom. 1:11; 15:23; 1 Thess. 3:6; 2 Tim. 1:4]

1:1–11 *Greeting and Prayer.* Paul greets his readers, expressing his gratitude (vv. 3–6) and affection (vv. 7–8) for them, followed by a prayer that their love would abound and their holiness increase (vv. 9–11).

1:1–2 *Salutation from Paul and Timothy.* Paul, along with Timothy, gives the standard early Christian greeting of **grace** and **peace**. Paul does not identify himself as an apostle but designates Timothy and himself as **servants**. The emphasis on service anticipates the rest of the letter, and this emphasis is seen especially in what is said of the humiliation of Christ Jesus (2:5–11). It is uncertain what level of formal church governance is implied by **overseers and deacons**. The former are presumably elders, who would be charged with spiritual oversight of the congregation (cf. Acts 14:23 [with note]; 20:17, 28; 1 Tim. 3:1–7; Titus 1:5–9; James 5:14; 1 Pet. 5:1–4), while the latter would be entrusted with matters of practical service (cf. Acts 6:1–7; 1 Tim. 3:8–13).

Joy and Rejoicing in Philippians

Reference	Paul . . .
1:4	prays with joy
1:18	rejoices that Christ is proclaimed
1:25	will remain living on earth, for the Philippians' joy in the faith
2:2	asks the Philippians to complete his joy
2:17–18	is glad and rejoices with the Philippians
2:28	sends Epaphroditus, that the Philippians might rejoice
2:29	tells the Philippians to receive Epaphroditus with joy
3:1	tells the Philippians to rejoice in the Lord
4:1	tells the Philippians they are his joy
4:4	tells the Philippians twice to rejoice in the Lord
4:10	rejoiced in the Lord at the Philippians' concern for him

1:3–11 *Paul's Thanksgiving and Prayer for the Philippians.* Paul's letters frequently begin with thanksgiving and prayer. The prayer here helps establish the major themes of the letter.

1:3–5 Paul prays for the Philippians with **joy**, a word that will become a keynote theme in ch. 4. This joy springs from their **partnership in the gospel**, which involves not only their financial support of the apostle (4:15–16) but also their deep personal concern for his well-being.

1:6 Paul is **sure** about God's commitment to the Philippians. The foundation for spiritual growth is recognizing that it is God who **began a good work in you** and **will bring it to completion**. Genuine spiritual progress is rooted in what God has done, is doing, and will do. His faithfulness ensures that he will be with believers until Jesus returns (**the day of Jesus Christ**; cf. 2:16; 1 Thess. 5:2–11; 2 Pet. 3:10–13; Rev. 20:11–21:8). They can have confidence that the God who has saved them will never let them go, and that they will inherit their eternal reward.

1:7–8 Again Paul expresses his warm thoughts about the Philippians and the fellowship they enjoy in God's grace. Paul's **imprisonment** would have been a source of great shame in the ancient world, but the Philippians have nonetheless stood in solidarity with him. This was no doubt an encouragement as he shared the good news with his captors and judges.

1:9–11 The first petition in Paul's prayer is that God would cause the cardinal Christian virtue of **love** to **abound more and more**, and that it would be accompanied by **knowledge** and **all discernment**, so that the Philippians' love would find expression in wise actions that would truly benefit others and glorify God. As Christians grow in their understanding of what it means to follow Jesus, they will increasingly be able to affirm and practice **what is excellent**. Such joyful obedience to God will give them the confidence of being found **pure and blameless** when Jesus returns. This does not imply instantaneous spiritual perfection but rather an increasing likeness to Christ. But **fruit of righteousness** is not produced in the believer's own power. Because that fruit comes **through Jesus Christ**, it will result in the **glory and praise of God**.

9[q]1 Thess. 3:12; 2 Thess. 1:3 [r]Col. 1:9; 3:10; Philem. 6
10[s]Acts 24:16; 1 Thess. 3:13; 5:23 [t]ver. 6
11[u][Col. 1:6, 10]; See James 3:18 [v][John 15:4, 5] [w]See Eph. 1:12, 14
12[x]ver. 25; 1 Tim. 4:15
13[y][Acts 28:30, 31; 2 Tim. 2:9] [z][Luke 21:13]; See ver. 7
14[a][Acts 4:31]
15[b]See 2 Cor. 11:13
16[c][1 Cor. 9:17] [d]ver. 7
17[e]ch. 2:3; See James 3:14
19[f]See 2 Cor. 1:11 [g]Gal. 3:5 [h]See Acts 16:7
20[i]Rom. 5:5; [Joel 2:27; 2 Tim. 2:15] [j]See Acts 4:13 [k][1 Cor. 6:20] [l]Rom. 14:8
21[m][Gal. 2:20]

that [q]your love may abound more and more, [r]with knowledge and all discernment, **10** so
that you may approve what is excellent, [s]and so be pure and blameless [t]for the day of
Christ, **11** filled [u]with the fruit of righteousness that comes [v]through Jesus Christ, [w]to the
glory and praise of God.

The Advance of the Gospel

12 I want you to know, brothers,[1] that what has happened to me has really [x]served to
advance the gospel, **13** so that it has become known throughout the whole imperial guard[2]
and [y]to all the rest that [z]my imprisonment is for Christ. **14** And most of the brothers, having become confident in the Lord by my imprisonment, are much more bold [a]to speak
the word[3] without fear.

15 [b]Some indeed preach Christ from envy and rivalry, but others from good will. **16** The
latter do it out of love, [c]knowing that I am put here for [d]the defense of the gospel. **17** The
former proclaim Christ [e]out of selfish ambition, not sincerely but thinking to afflict me in
my imprisonment. **18** What then? Only that in every way, whether in pretense or in truth,
Christ is proclaimed, and in that I rejoice.

To Live Is Christ

Yes, and I will rejoice, **19** for I know that [f]through your prayers and [g]the help of [h]the
Spirit of Jesus Christ this will turn out for my deliverance, **20** as it is my eager expectation
and hope [i]that I will not be at all ashamed, but that with full [j]courage now as always Christ
[k]will be honored in my body, [l]whether by life or by death. **21** For to me [m]to live is Christ,
and to die is gain. **22** If I am to live in the flesh, that means fruitful labor for me. Yet which

[1] Or *brothers and sisters.* The plural Greek word *adelphoi* (translated "brothers") refers to siblings in a family. In New Testament usage, depending on the context, *adelphoi* may refer either to men or to both men and women who are siblings (brothers and sisters) in God's family, the church; also verse 14
[2] Greek *in the whole praetorium* [3] Some manuscripts add *of God*

1:12–30 *Paul's Reflections on His Imprisonment.* Paul assures the Philippians that, though he is imprisoned, the gospel is still advancing (vv. 12–18). He is joyfully confident that no matter what happens, he will be delivered and Christ will be honored, because to live is Christ and to die is gain (vv. 19–26). Paul then encourages his readers to walk worthy of the gospel, even amid suffering (vv. 27–30).

1:12–18 *Paul's Imprisonment Has Meant Progress for the Gospel.* Paul realizes that the Philippians are grieved over his imprisonment, so he encourages them by pointing out that his circumstances are furthering the proclamation of the gospel. His joy in difficult circumstances is meant to be an example to the Philippians to likewise rejoice even in difficult times. Further, Paul's charitable attitude toward fellow believers who make life hard for him is also to function as a model for the Philippians, since it is evident that there is some disunity in the congregation (4:2–3).

1:12 The word Paul uses for the **advance** of the gospel (Gk. *prokopēn*) is the same word he will use in v. 25 for the Philippians' "progress" in faith. He thus underscores the need to push God's kingdom forward rather than dwelling on past or present problems.

1:13 The gospel has advanced because Paul has let the **whole imperial guard** (Gk. *praitōrion*) know that he is imprisoned only because of his testimony that Jesus is Lord. The Latin word *praetorium* could refer to a governor's residence and by extension those living in the residence. Those who believe that Paul wrote from Caesarea would understand the word in that sense here (see Acts 23:35). However, the word could also refer to the special guard of the emperor in Rome, as the translation above suggests. (See Introduction: Date.)

1:14 When the Christians in Rome, where Paul was imprisoned, saw his boldness even as his life was in danger, his example inspired them to be more courageous as well, so that they were **much more bold** in proclaiming the good news of Jesus Christ.

1:15–18 The identity of those here who **preach Christ from envy and rivalry** is difficult to determine. They are clearly antagonistic to Paul, and thus one could imagine they are the same "Judaizing" people mentioned in ch. 3. But it is hard to see how Paul could **rejoice** in the proclamation of something (namely, a return to the old covenant) which he saw as a betrayal of the good news (see esp. the letter to the Galatians). It seems more likely that these were other Christians who preached a generally sound gospel but were personally at odds with Paul. They may have dismissed him because of his poor speaking abilities (see 1 Corinthians 1–2) or his constant suffering and weakness (see 2 Corinthians); whatever their rationale, they were not motivated by **love** but only by a desire to harm Paul in some way. But Paul, like Jesus, is not concerned for his own interests (cf. Phil. 2:4), and he will "rejoice" as long as the gospel is progressing.

1:19–26 *To Live Is Christ.* Paul expresses the grounds of his confidence that he will be released from prison (see note on vv. 12–30). He assures the Philippians that he believes he will remain alive to minister to them.

1:19 Paul, who has prayed for the Philippians, now solicits their **prayers** for **deliverance** (Gk. *sōtēria*), a term that could mean deliverance from prison (as some commentators understand it) or that could mean deliverance in the ultimate sense of eternal salvation (as others understand it). It seems likely that Paul intentionally left some ambiguity here, in light of the mention of his imprisonment in the preceding verses (see vv. 12–14) and in light of the eternal focus in the verses that follow (e.g., Paul's desire "to depart and be with Christ, which is far better"; v. 23). The tension between temporal deliverance and eternal salvation is, in fact, evident throughout this passage (vv. 19–26), as evidenced by Paul's words: "whether by life or by death" (in v. 20) and "I am hard pressed between the two" (in v. 23). Although Paul seems to have alluded to his temporal deliverance, clearly his longing for eternal salvation is "far better" (v. 23). In this regard, Paul alludes to Job 13:13–18 in this passage, where Job clearly speaks of his final destiny; and Paul speaks of his hope of not being ashamed, which is elsewhere related to the final judgment (cf. Rom. 5:4–5). Either way, Paul wants the Philippians to know that even if his expected deliverance from prison fails to materialize, and he is executed, he will still be "saved" to eternal life by God.

1:20 The crucial thing for Paul is not **life** or death. It is maintaining his faithful witness to Christ. **Or by death** indicates that Paul hopes to honor Christ even in the way he eventually dies.

1:21 Paul's life is not a matter of seeking his own comfort or advancement. It is all about seeking the advancement of Christ's kingdom: **to live** is tantamount to serving **Christ**. In fact, **to die** should be seen as **gain**, because it would mean that Paul would be freed from his trouble-filled life on earth to rejoice in Christ's presence.

1:22–26 In light of v. 21, Paul is **hard pressed** as to which outcome he should desire. Being with Christ now would be more attractive for him, while

I shall choose I cannot tell. **23** [n]I am hard pressed between the two. My desire is [o]to depart
and [p]be with Christ, for that is far better. **24** But to remain in the flesh is more necessary
on your account. **25** [q]Convinced of this, [r]I know that I will remain and continue with you
all, for your [s]progress and [t]joy in the faith, **26** so that in me [u]you may have ample cause to
glory in Christ Jesus, because of my coming to you again.
27 Only [v]let your manner of life be [w]worthy[1] of the gospel of Christ, so that whether I
come and see you or am absent, I may hear of you [x]that you are standing firm in one spirit,
with [y]one mind [z]striving side by side for the faith of the gospel, **28** and not frightened in
anything by your opponents. This is [a]a clear sign to them of their destruction, but [b]of
your salvation, and that from God. **29** For [c]it has been granted to you that for the sake of
Christ you should not only believe in him but also [b]suffer for his sake, **30** engaged in the
same [d]conflict that [e]you saw I had and now hear that I still have.

Christ's Example of Humility

2 So if there is any encouragement in Christ, any comfort from [f]love, any [g]participation
in the Spirit, any [h]affection and sympathy, **2** [i]complete my joy by being [j]of the same
mind, having the same love, being in full accord and of one mind. **3** Do nothing from [k]selfish
ambition or [l]conceit, but in [m]humility count others more significant than yourselves. **4** Let
each of you [n]look not only to his own interests, but also to the interests of others. **5** [o]Have

[1] Greek *Only behave as citizens worthy*

23 [n][2 Cor. 5:8] [o]2 Tim. 4:6 [p]See John 12:26
25 [q][ch. 2:24] [r][Acts 20:25] [s]ver. 12 [t]Rom. 15:13
26 [u]See 2 Cor. 1:14
27 [v][ch. 3:20] [w]See Eph. 4:1 [x]See 1 Cor. 16:13 [y][ch. 2:2; 1 Cor. 1:10] [z]Jude 3
28 [a][2 Thess. 1:5] [b]See Acts 14:22
29 [c]See Matt. 5:12 [b][See ver. 28 above]
30 [d]Col. 1:29; 2:1; 1 Tim. 6:12; 2 Tim. 4:7; [Heb. 10:32] [e]Acts 16:19-40; 1 Thess. 2:2

Chapter 2

1 [f][Rom. 15:30; 2 Thess. 2:16] [g]2 Cor. 13:14 [h]Col. 3:12
2 [i]John 3:29; 15:11 [j]See Rom. 12:16
3 [k]ch. 1:17 [l]Gal. 5:26 [m][Eph. 5:21]; See Rom. 12:10; Eph. 4:2
4 [n]See Rom. 15:2
5 [o]Rom. 15:3; See Matt. 11:29

remaining alive (**in the flesh**) would enable him to help the Philippians further on their own spiritual journey. Since Paul knows that the way of Jesus is the way of service (cf. 2:5–11), he is **convinced** that his own preferences will be put aside so that he can **remain and continue** with the Philippians for their **progress and joy in the faith**. Paul is not merely musing on his own crisis; he is giving the Philippians a model of the service-driven life.

1:23 My desire is to depart and be with Christ indicates that when Christians die they are immediately with Christ, long before their bodies are raised from the dead (see note on 1 Cor. 15:23).

1:27–30 *Encouragement to Walk Worthy of the Gospel.* Paul's sacrifice will be futile, however, if the Philippians do not continue to live in a way that is "worthy of the gospel of Christ."

1:27 As the ESV footnote indicates, the Greek for **Only let your manner of life be worthy of the gospel** can also be translated "only behave as citizens [Gk. *politeuesthe*] worthy [of the gospel]," a phrasing that nicely captures Paul's play on words here and in 3:20, "our citizenship [Gk. *politeuma*] is in heaven." Philippi prided itself on being a Roman colony, offering the honor and privilege of Roman citizenship. Paul reminds the congregation that they should look to Christ, not Caesar, for their model of behavior, since their primary allegiance is to God and his kingdom. They need to stand together with one another and with Paul in **striving** for the gospel. Paul's emphasis on unity may suggest some division within the Philippian congregation (cf. 4:2–3). Perhaps the disunity is one reason he mentions the "overseers and deacons" at the outset of the letter (1:1), for they are required to minister in a way that promotes unity.

1:28 As the Philippians maintain courage in the face of their **opponents**, these opponents will realize that such remarkable strength could come only from God, and thus anyone who continues to oppose God's people will be marked for **destruction**. "Destruction" (Gk. *apōleia*) here means eternal destruction, hence these are different opponents from those who antagonized Paul in vv. 15–18, who seem to have been Christians. A different city is in view as well, for here Paul speaks about what is happening in Philippi, while in vv. 15–18 his opposition is (presumably) in Rome. But God's sustaining grace amid trouble will assure the believers of their own final **salvation**. Paul follows the teaching of Jesus here (Matt. 5:10–12), reminding them that persecution is a sign that they belong to Christ.

1:29–30 Troubles will come, because the reality is that believers in Christ will **suffer for his sake**. Paul teaches that both suffering and faith are gifts of God; for both, Paul says, have **been granted to you**. Suffering for the sake of Jesus is a great privilege (see Matt. 5:10–12; Acts 5:41). Paul again holds himself out as an example of one who has maintained his joy while experiencing the **same conflict** (i.e., opposition from hostile unbelievers).

2:1–30 *Exhortation to Humble Service.* Paul calls the Philippians to unite in love and humility (vv. 1–4), as exemplified by Christ's humble service (vv. 5–11). They are to live as lights in the world (vv. 12–18), just like Christ's faithful servants Timothy (vv. 19–24) and Epaphroditus (vv. 25–30).

2:1–4 *Encouragement to Unity in the Faith and Service of One Another.* The Philippians are encouraged to live out their life in Christ and in the Spirit by living in unity.

2:1–2 Paul is not *doubting* that **encouragement**, **participation in the Spirit**, **affection**, and **sympathy** are realities **in Christ** and are present in the congregation at Philippi. He uses a conditional sentence (**if**) to provoke the Philippians so that they will reflect on whether these qualities are evident in their lives. The Philippian believers must make sure they continue to progress in the absolutely critical area of love for one another. As Paul emphasizes, they must be **of the same mind**. This does not imply a drab intellectual uniformity; rather, the Philippians are to use their diverse gifts (cf. 1 Corinthians 12) in an agreeable, cooperative spirit, with a focus on the glory of God.

2:3–4 There is always a temptation to be like Paul's opponents in 1:17 and operate in a spirit of **selfish ambition**, looking to advance one's own agenda. Such **conceit** (lit., "vainglory") is countered by counting others **more significant than yourselves**. Paul realizes that everyone naturally looks out for his or her **own interests**. The key is to take that same level of concern and apply it **also** to the **interests of others**. Such radical love is rare, so Paul proceeds to show its supreme reality in the life of Christ (2:5–11).

2:5–11 *Christ's Example of Humble Service.* This passage is often referred to as the "hymn of Christ." Paul depicts Christ's example of service in a stirring poem that traces his preexistence, incarnation, death, resurrection, and ascension to the right hand of God. Paul wrote this magnificent theology to encourage the Philippians to consider other people's interests first (see v. 4). Jesus is the paradigm of genuine spiritual progress: not a self-aggrandizing struggle for supremacy, but a deep love for God and neighbor shown in deeds of service. Verses 6–11 have some clear indications of poetic structure, leading some to believe that this is a pre-Pauline hymn adapted by Paul. It is just as likely, however, that Paul composed the hymn for this setting. In view of the myriad theological questions that arise in these verses, it is critical to keep two things in mind: (1) these verses were written not to spur Christians to theological debate but to encourage greater humility and love; and (2) the summary of Christ's life and ministry found here is not unique: the same themes are evident throughout the NT.

2:5 The believer's **mind** needs to reflect on the proper model, if life is

this mind among yourselves, which is yours in Christ Jesus,[1] 6 [p]who, though he was in
[q]the form of God, did not count equality with God [r]a thing to be grasped, 7 but [s]emptied
himself, by taking the form of a [t]servant,[2] [u]being born in the likeness of men. 8 And being
found in human form, he humbled himself by [v]becoming obedient to the point of death,
[w]even death on a cross. 9 [x]Therefore [y]God has [z]highly exalted him and bestowed on him
[a]the name that is above every name, 10 so that at the name of Jesus [b]every knee should
bow, [c]in heaven and on earth and under the earth, 11 and [d]every tongue confess that Jesus
Christ is [e]Lord, to the glory of God the Father.

[1] Or *which was also in Christ Jesus* [2] Greek *bondservant*

6 [p]See John 1:1 [q]See 2 Cor. 4:4 [r]John 5:18; 10:33; [John 14:28]
7 [s]2 Cor. 8:9; 13:4; See Mark 9:12 [t]See Isa. 42:1; Matt. 20:28 [u]Rom. 8:3; Gal. 4:4; See John 1:14
8 [v]Heb. 5:8; [Matt. 26:39; John 10:18; Rom. 5:19] [w]Heb. 12:2
9 [x]John 10:17; [Isa. 52:13; 53:12; Heb. 2:9] [y]See Matt. 28:18 [z]Acts 2:33 [a]Eph. 1:21; Heb. 1:4; [Acts 5:41]
10 [b]Isa. 45:23; Rom. 14:11 [c][Rev. 5:3, 13]; See Eph. 1:10
11 [d][Rom. 10:9; 1 Cor. 12:3] [e][Rom. 14:9]; See John 13:13

to be lived for God. There is some debate as to whether this mind-set is something Christians receive by virtue of being *united to Christ* (**which is yours in Christ Jesus**), or whether it is to be based on *the model of Christ* (ESV footnote: "which was also in Christ Jesus"). (The Gk. has no verb; either "is" or "was" has to be supplied.) In light of the consistent theme of behavior modeling in this letter (Jesus, Paul, Timothy, and Epaphroditus are all held out as examples), many interpreters have adopted the latter meaning. Both ideas are theologically true. In either case, the central theme of vv. 1–5 is the same—that the Philippian church would be of one mind (v. 2), united by love (v. 2) and humility (v. 3), and looking out for the interests of others (v. 4).

2:6 Prior to the incarnation, Christ was in the **form of God** (Gk. *morphē theou*). Despite the assertions of some scholars to the contrary, this most naturally refers to the "preexistence" of Christ—he, the eternal Son, was there with the Father (John 1:1; 17:5, 24) before he was born in Bethlehem. "Form" here means the true and exact nature of something, possessing all the characteristics and qualities of something. Therefore having the "form of God" is roughly equivalent to having **equality with God** (Gk. *isa theō*), and it is directly contrasted with having the "form of a servant" (Phil. 2:7). The Son of God is and always has been God. "Form" could also be a reference to Christ being the ultimate image of God, "the exact imprint of his nature" (Heb. 1:3). It might also refer to the fact that he is the visible expression of God's invisible glory (Col. 1:15). Remarkably, Christ did not imagine that having "equality with God" (which he already possessed) should lead him to hold onto his privileges at all costs. It was not something to be **grasped**, to be kept and exploited for his own benefit or advantage. Instead, he had a mind-set of service. "Christ did not please himself" (Rom. 15:3). In humility, he counted the interests of others as more significant than his own (Phil. 2:3–4).

2:7 Emptied himself has occasioned much controversy. Greek *kenoō* can mean "empty, pour out" or also (metaphorically) "give up status and privilege." Does this mean that Christ temporarily relinquished his divine attributes during his earthly ministry? This theory of Christ's *kenosis* or "self-emptying" is not in accord with the context of Philippians or with early Christian theology (see the article on The Person of Christ, pp. 2515–2519). Paul is not saying that Christ became less than God or "gave up" some divine attributes; he is not even commenting directly on the question of whether Jesus was fully omnipotent or omniscient during his time on earth. Nor is he saying that Christ ever gave up being "in the form of God." Rather, Paul is stressing that Christ, who had all the privileges that were rightly his as king of the universe, gave them up to become an ordinary Jewish baby bound for the cross. Christ "emptied himself" **by taking the form of a servant, being born in the likeness of men** (roughly equivalent phrases). While he had every right to stay comfortably where he was, in a position of power, his love drove him to a position of weakness for the sake of sinful mankind (cf. 2 Cor. 8:9, "though he was rich, yet for your sake he became poor, so that you by his poverty might become rich"). The "emptying" consisted of his becoming human, not of his giving up any part of his true deity.

2:8 It is remarkable enough that God the Son would take on **human form** (Gk. *schēma*, "outward appearance, form, shape," a different term from *morphē*, used in vv. 6–7 for "form of God" and "form of a servant") and thus enter into all the vicissitudes of a broken world. But Jesus went much farther, **becoming obedient** (cf. Rom. 5:19) **to the point of death, even death on a cross**. Crucifixion was not simply a convenient way of executing prisoners. It was the ultimate indignity, a public statement by Rome that the crucified one was beyond contempt. The excruciating physical pain was magnified by the degradation and humiliation. No other form of death, no matter how prolonged or physically agonizing, could match crucifixion as an absolute destruction of the person (see note on Matt. 27:35). It was the ultimate counterpoint to the divine majesty of the preexistent Christ, and thus was the ultimate expression of Christ's obedience to the Father.

2:9 Therefore. It was precisely Jesus' humiliation that became the grounds for his exaltation. By humbling himself on the cross out of love, he demonstrated that he truly shared the divine nature of God, who is love (1 John 4:8). *For this reason* ("therefore") God raised him to life and **highly exalted him**, entrusting him with the rule of the cosmos and giving him **the name that is above every name**. This name is not specified here, but many think it refers to the name Yahweh (Hb. *YHWH*), God's personal name, which in the Septuagint is regularly translated as Greek *Kyrios*, "Lord," the name specified in Phil. 2:11. In any case, Paul means that the eternal Son of God received a status and authority (cf. Matt. 28:18 and note on Acts 2:33) that had not been his before he became incarnate as both God and man. Jesus' being given this name is a sign that he exercises his messianic authority in the name of Yahweh.

2:10–11 While Christ now bears the divine name Yahweh ("Lord"), he is still worshiped with his human name, **Jesus**, since it was in the flesh that he most clearly displayed his divine glory to the world. This astounding union of Jesus' divine and human natures is reinforced by the allusion to Isa. 45:23 in the words **every knee should bow . . . and every tongue confess**, which in Isaiah refer exclusively to Yahweh (cf. Isa. 45:24: "Only in the LORD . . . are righteousness and strength"). The fact that these words can now be applied to God's messianic agent—**Jesus Christ is Lord**—shows that Jesus is fully divine. But the worship of Jesus as Lord is not the final word of the hymn. Jesus' exaltation also results in **the glory of God the Father**. This identical pattern is found in 1 Cor. 15:23–28: God gives Jesus messianic dominion over all creation, and everyone will one day rightly give praise to him as their Lord. But when his kingdom reaches its fullness, Jesus does not keep the glory for himself. Instead, "the Son himself will also be subjected to him who put all things in subjection under him, that God may be all in all" (1 Cor. 15:28). Even in his exaltation, Jesus remains the model of loving service to God.

Partnering with Paul in the Gospel in Many Ways

1:5	"partnership in the gospel"
1:7	"partakers with me of grace"
1:14–19	"through your prayers"
1:27	"striving side by side for the faith"
2:22	"served with me in the gospel"
2:25	"my brother, and fellow worker, and fellow soldier"
3:17	"join in imitating me"
4:3	"labored side by side with me"
4:15	"partnership with me in giving and receiving"

Lights in the World

[12]Therefore, my beloved, [f]as you have always [g]obeyed, so now, not only as in my presence
but much more in my absence, work out your own salvation with fear and trembling, [13]for
[h]it is God who works in you, both to will and to work for [i]his good pleasure.
[14]Do all things [j]without grumbling or [k]disputing, [15]that you may be blameless and
innocent, [l]children of God [m]without blemish [n]in the midst of [o]a crooked and twisted
generation, among whom you shine [p]as lights in the world, [16]holding fast to [q]the word
of life, so that in [r]the day of Christ [s]I may be proud that [t]I did not run in vain or labor
in vain. [17]Even if I am to be [u]poured out as a drink offering upon [v]the sacrificial offering
of your faith, I am glad and rejoice with you all. [18]Likewise you also should be glad and
rejoice with me.

Timothy and Epaphroditus

[19]I hope in the Lord Jesus [w]to send Timothy to you soon, so that I too may be cheered
by news of you. [20]For I have no one [x]like him, who will be genuinely concerned for your
welfare. [21]For they all [y]seek their own interests, not those of Jesus Christ. [22]But you know
Timothy's[1] [z]proven worth, how [a]as a son[2] with a father [b]he has served with me in the
gospel. [23]I hope therefore to send him just as soon as I see how it will go with me, [24]and
[c]I trust in the Lord that shortly I myself will come also.
[25]I have thought it necessary to send to you [d]Epaphroditus my brother and fellow worker
and [e]fellow soldier, and your messenger and [f]minister to my need, [26]for he has been longing for you all and has been distressed because you heard that he was ill. [27]Indeed he was
ill, near to death. But God had mercy on him, and not only on him but on me also, lest I
should have sorrow upon sorrow. [28]I am the more eager to send him, therefore, that you
may rejoice at seeing him again, and that I may be less anxious. [29]So [g]receive him in the
Lord with all joy, and [h]honor such men, [30]for he nearly died [i]for the work of Christ, risking
his life [j]to complete what was lacking in your service to me.

[1] Greek *his* [2] Greek *child*

12 [f][ch. 1:5; 4:15] [g]Heb. 5:9; [2 Cor. 10:5; 1 Pet. 1:2]
13 [h]1 Cor. 12:6; [Heb. 13:21]; See 1 Cor. 15:10 [i][1 Tim. 2:4]
14 [j]1 Pet. 4:9 [k]1 Tim. 2:8
15 [l][Matt. 5:45; Eph. 5:1] [m]Jude 24 [n]1 Pet. 2:12 [o]See Deut. 32:5 [p]Matt. 5:14, 16; [Titus 2:10]
16 [q][Acts 5:20] [r]See 1 Cor. 1:8 [s]See 2 Cor. 1:14 [t]Gal. 2:2; 1 Thess. 3:5; [Gal. 4:11]
17 [u][1 John 3:16]; See 2 Cor. 12:15 [v][Rom. 15:16]
19 [w][1 Cor. 4:17; 1 Thess. 3:2]
20 [x][1 Cor. 16:10]
21 [y][2 Tim. 3:2]; See 1 Cor. 10:24
22 [z]2 Cor. 2:9 [a]1 Cor. 4:17; 1 Tim. 1:2; 2 Tim. 1:2 [b][2 Tim. 3:10]
24 [c][ch. 1:25; Philem. 22]
25 [d]ch. 4:18 [e]Philem. 2 [f][ch. 4:18]
29 [g]Rom. 16:2 [h]1 Cor. 16:18; 1 Thess. 5:12, 13; 1 Tim. 5:17
30 [i][Acts 20:24] [j][ch. 4:10]; See 1 Cor. 16:17

2:12–18 *Living as Lights in the World.* With the breathtaking portrayal of Christ before them (vv. 5–11), Paul exhorts the Philippians to demonstrate the same faith and obedience in their everyday lives.

2:12–13 The Philippians have **obeyed** (cf. Christ's obedience, v. 8) in the past and should continue to do so as they **work out** their **salvation with fear and trembling**. They cannot be content with past glories but need to demonstrate their faith day by day as they nurture their relationship with God. But while God's justice is a cause for sober living ("fear and trembling"), it is not as though Paul wants the Philippians to be anxious that they can never be good enough to merit God's favor. Rather, it is God's love and enabling grace that will see them through: **it is God who works in you**. They can rejoice in God's empowering presence even as they work hard at living responsible Christian lives. While v. 12 may seem to suggest salvation by works, it is clear that Paul rejects any such teaching (cf. 3:2–11). In 2:12 Paul means "salvation" in terms of progressively coming to experience all of the aspects and blessings of salvation. The Philippians' continued obedience is an inherent part of "working out" their salvation in this sense. But as v. 13 demonstrates, these works are *the result* of God's work within his people. **both to will and to work for his good pleasure**. Even the desire ("to will") to do what is good comes from God; but he also works in the believer to generate actual choices of the good, so that the desires result in actions. (On fear of God, see notes on Acts 5:5; 9:31.)

2:14–15 Paul continues the theme of "working out" one's salvation (vv. 12–13). The Philippians should **shine as lights** amid a **crooked and twisted generation**. Paul's choice of words recalls the wilderness generation of Israel, who in Deut. 32:5 are described by these very words ("crooked and twisted generation") and whose spiritual progress was thwarted by **grumbling** and **disputing** (cf. 1 Cor. 10:1–12). Shining "as lights" probably alludes to Dan. 12:2–3. Those who express their faith by living in this way will be raised to eternal life (see Dan. 12:2), to Paul's great joy.

2:16 The Philippians' obedience to the **word of life** is not merely a matter of private concern. As an apostle and fellow sharer in the gospel, Paul's own **labor** would be **in vain** if they failed to hold fast until **the day of Christ** (cf. 1:6; 1 Thess. 5:2–11; 2 Pet. 3:10–13; Rev. 20:11–21:8) and thus proved not to be genuine believers. **Holding fast** means both believing God's Word and following it. Since the Greek *epechō* can mean either "hold fast" or "hold out to, offer," some think that Paul may have in mind "holding forth," i.e., proclaiming, the word of life.

2:17 Paul compares himself to a **drink offering** (cf. 2 Tim. 4:6). This type of offering, familiar in both the OT and Greco-Roman culture, involved pouring out wine, either onto the ground or, as here, on an altar along with an animal or grain sacrifice (see Num. 28:7). It was a vivid illustration of a life "poured out" for God's service. The Philippians, too, are a **sacrificial offering**; they are to emulate Paul's joyful service to God.

2:19–24 *Timothy as an Example of a Service-centered Life.* Paul's desire to send his protégé **Timothy** highlights the very personal nature of early church life. Timothy emulates Christ in that he is **concerned for** the Philippians' **welfare**; he does not look out for his own **interests**, but for those of **Christ**.

2:25–30 *Epaphroditus as Another Example of Service.* Epaphroditus, who is himself from Philippi, is another example of genuine Christian love. He has been longing for the Philippians just as Paul longs for them (1:8; 4:1), and has been eager to let them know that God has spared him from his severe illness.

2:27 To die and be with Christ is far better (1:21), and yet God shows **mercy** to Epaphroditus in sparing his life. Christians can be assured that a fellow Christian truly is in Christ's presence upon his or her death (see note on 1:23); even so, it is proper on such occasions to feel **sorrow upon sorrow**.

2:30 The Christlikeness of Epaphroditus is highlighted by Paul's careful use of words. Having said that Christ was obedient "to the point of death" (v. 8, Gk. *mechri thanatou*), Paul now says that Epaphroditus was "near to death" (v. 27) and that **he nearly died** (v. 30, also with Gk. *mechri thanatou*). Epaphroditus had faced this peril on behalf of the Philippians, who had desired to send gifts to support Paul but had not been able to do so (**what was lacking in your service to me**) until Epaphroditus made it possible (see 4:10, 18).

Chapter 3
1 [k]ch. 4:4; 1 Thess. 5:16 [l][2 Pet. 1:12]
2 [m]Ps. 22:16, 20; Isa. 56:10, 11; Rev. 22:15; [Gal. 5:15] [n][2 Cor. 11:13]
3 [o]See Rom. 2:29 [p][John 4:23] [q][Gal. 5:25; Jude 20] [r]Rom. 15:17; [Gal. 6:14]
4 [s]2 Cor. 11:18
5 [t]See Gen. 17:12 [u]2 Cor. 11:22 [v]Rom. 11:1 [w]Acts 23:6; 26:5
6 [x]Acts 22:3, 4; Gal. 1:13, 14 [y]See Acts 8:3 [z][ver. 9]
7 [a][Luke 14:33] [b][Heb. 11:26]
8 [c][2 Cor. 5:15] [d]Isa. 53:11; Jer. 9:23, 24; John 17:3; 2 Pet. 1:3 [e]Luke 9:25 (Gk.)
9 [f]Rom. 10:5; [ver. 6] [g]See Rom. 9:30; 1 Cor. 1:30
10 [h][Eph. 4:13]

Righteousness Through Faith in Christ

3 Finally, my brothers,[1] [k]rejoice in the Lord. [l]To write the same things to you is no trouble
to me and is safe for you.
2 Look out for [m]the dogs, look out for [n]the evildoers, look out for those who mutilate
the flesh. 3 For [o]we are the circumcision, [p]who worship [q]by the Spirit of God[2] and [r]glory in
Christ Jesus and put no confidence in the flesh— 4 [s]though I myself have reason for confidence in the flesh also. If anyone else thinks he has reason for confidence in the flesh, I have
more: 5 [t]circumcised on the eighth day, [u]of the people of Israel, [v]of the tribe of Benjamin, [u]a
Hebrew of Hebrews; as to the law, [w]a Pharisee; 6 [x]as to zeal, [y]a persecutor of the church; [z]as
to righteousness under the law,[3] blameless. 7 But [a]whatever gain I had, [b]I counted as loss
for the sake of Christ. 8 Indeed, I count everything as loss because of [c]the surpassing worth
of [d]knowing Christ Jesus my Lord. For his sake I [e]have suffered the loss of all things and
count them as rubbish, in order that I may gain Christ 9 and be found in him, not having
[f]a righteousness of my own that comes from the law, but [g]that which comes through faith
in Christ, the righteousness from God that depends on faith— 10 [h]that I may know him

[1] *Or brothers and sisters; also verses 13, 17* [2] Some manuscripts *God in spirit* [3] Greek *in the law*

3:1–21 *Opponents of the Gospel: Where Does Righteousness Come From?* Paul begins this section by calling the Philippians to rejoice in the Lord (v. 1) but then warns them about the Judaizing opponents of the gospel (vv. 2–3). In contrast, Paul has renounced his spiritual and ethnic privileges for the sake of knowing Christ (vv. 4–11); his righteousness comes through Christ, not the law (vv. 12–16). He then calls the Philippians to follow his example of commitment to Jesus as Lord (vv. 17–21). Some interpreters suppose that the abrupt transition after v. 1 indicates that ch. 3 is a later interpolation into the letter. But there is no need for such a theory. The vocabulary of ch. 3 is reflected in the rest of the letter, and its themes of "progress" and "example" are central to Paul's overarching purposes. While the Judaizers (people who insisted that Christians had to obey all the OT ceremonial laws) hold out a promise of spiritual progress through adherence to the rules of the old covenant, Paul holds himself out as an example of someone who knows that real progress consists only in being increasingly conformed to the image of Christ's death and resurrection. Paul's conflicts with the Judaizers can be seen in greater detail in Acts and Galatians (e.g., Acts 15:1–19; Gal. 2:15–21; 3:6–4:31), as well as in the rest of his letters. Their teaching that Gentiles must first become Jews and obey all the OT laws in order to be saved was abhorrent to Paul. Not only did it show a lack of welcome (in complete contrast to God's own attitude) but it also sought in effect to divert Gentiles away from Christ into a covenant that could never save them. While the law might be "holy and righteous and good" (Rom. 7:12), the old covenant pertained to the age before the giving of the Spirit, and thus inevitably brought curse rather than blessing since human beings were unable to keep it. The "righteousness" it offered could only be an incomplete, superficial righteousness, in contrast to the perfect righteousness given as a gift to believers by virtue of the life and death of Christ. The fury of Paul's response in these verses was fueled by his thankfulness for his own deliverance from this system.

3:1 *Initial Call to Rejoice in the Lord.* Paul will pick up the theme of joy again in ch. 4, but first he must deal with the Judaizers.

3:2–3 *Contrast between the Opponents of the Gospel and the True People of God.* Paul critiques the Judaizers and explains the contrasting characteristics of the true church.

3:2 Dogs was not only a general term of derision in the ancient world, it was particularly a word used by some Jews in reference to Gentiles, who were considered ritually unclean. With biting irony, Paul says that the Judaizers, not the Gentiles, deserve that label. Paul's irony continues as he labels those who extol good works of the law as **evildoers** and **those who mutilate the flesh**. This last phrase (Gk. *tēn katatomēn*) is a play on words with circumcision (Gk. *peritomē*). The Judaizers' supposed badge of pride turns out to be the sign of their destruction. On Jewish views of circumcision, see note on Acts 15:1.

3:3 In contrast to those promoting physical circumcision (v. 2), the true people of God (**the circumcision**) are those who **worship by the Spirit of God** (cf. John 4:23–24). They **glory in Christ Jesus** (cf. Phil. 1:26) and **put no confidence in the flesh** (that is, as Calvin put it, in "everything that is outside of Christ"). This verse mentions all three members of the Trinity: "God" (the Father), "Christ Jesus" (the Son), and "the Spirit of God" (the Holy Spirit).

3:4–11 *Paul's Renunciation of Spiritual and Ethnic Privileges for the Sake of Knowing Christ.* Paul regards his prior privileges and achievements as spiritual rubbish in comparison to the surpassing worth of knowing Christ, and being justified (v. 9), sanctified (v. 10), and glorified (v. 11) in him.

3:4–6 Paul's opposition to the Judaizers was not because he himself in any way lacked a Jewish "pedigree." When it came to the things of the **flesh**—the whole system of life that held sway before the coming of Christ and the giving of the Spirit—Paul had perfect credentials. He was **circumcised on the eighth day** in accord with OT law (Lev. 12:3). He was an ethnic Israelite and knew the tribe from which he came. **Hebrew of Hebrews** probably indicates his descent from Jewish ancestors, and many think it also means that he spoke Aramaic (the national language of Israel in his day), even though he came from Greek-speaking Tarsus. He was from the strictest religious sect—the Pharisees (Acts 26:5). His **zeal** was such that he had even been a **persecutor of the church**. He probably had thought of himself as following in the footsteps of Phinehas (Num. 25:11) and Elijah (1 Kings 19:10, 14) in his zeal. If anyone could be said to be **blameless** in following the law, it was Paul. But before God it was no righteousness at all, for though Paul thought he was pleasing God, in persecuting the church he had shown himself to be the "foremost" of sinners (1 Tim. 1:15).

3:7–8 gain . . . loss. Paul's accounting, however, has now changed completely: what formerly went into the *gain* column—his power, prestige, and "obedience"—now goes into the *loss* column. Likewise, the crucified Messiah, whom he had assumed must be a "loss," is now seen as the ultimate "gain." The language of loss and gain probably alludes to Jesus' teaching (see Matt. 16:25–26).

3:9 Found in him means being spiritually united to Christ and therefore found not guilty before God as divine judge. Paul had trusted in **a righteousness of my own** based on obedience to the law rather than the right standing before God that **comes through faith in Christ**. God "imputes" Christ's lifelong record of perfect obedience to the person who trusts in him for salvation; that is, he thinks of Christ's obedience as belonging to that person, and therefore that person stands before God not as "guilty" but as "righteous." This is the basis on which justification by faith alone is considered "fair" in God's sight. As explained in Rom. 10:1–8, righteousness cannot come by the law because all human beings sin, and therefore right standing before God as the divine judge is possible only through faith in Jesus Christ, who *is* the believer's righteousness before God. See note on Gal. 2:16.

3:10–11 The goal of trusting in Christ is to **know him**, that is, to know Christ in a personal relationship, and also to know **the power of his resurrection**—namely, the power Christ exerts now from the right hand of God. But this power is made known as the believer shares the same kind of **sufferings** Jesus faced—the sufferings that attend faithful witness in a fallen world. The good news is that those who suffer with and for Christ will **attain the resurrection from the dead**, even as he did.

and [i]the power of his resurrection, and [j]may share his sufferings, becoming like him in his
death, 11 that by any means possible I may [k]attain the resurrection from the dead.

Straining Toward the Goal

12 Not that I have already [l]obtained this or [m]am already perfect, but I press on to make
it my own, because Christ Jesus has made me his own. 13 Brothers, I do not consider that
I have made it my own. But one thing I do: [n]forgetting what lies behind and straining
forward to what lies ahead, 14 I press on toward the goal for [o]the prize of the upward [p]call
of God in Christ Jesus. 15 Let those of us who are [q]mature think this way, and if in anything
[r]you think otherwise, [s]God will reveal that also to you. 16 Only [t]let us hold true to what
we have attained.

17 Brothers, [u]join in imitating me, and keep your eyes on those who walk [v]according to
the example you have in us. 18 For [w]many, of whom I have often told you and now tell you
[x]even with tears, walk as enemies of the cross of Christ. 19 [y]Their end is destruction, [z]their
god is their belly, and [a]they glory in their shame, with [b]minds set on earthly things. 20 But
[c]our citizenship is in heaven, and [d]from it we [e]await a Savior, the Lord Jesus Christ, 21 who
will transform [f]our lowly body [g]to be like his glorious body, [h]by the power that enables
him even [i]to subject all things to himself.

4 Therefore, my brothers,[1] whom I love and [j]long for, [k]my joy and [l]crown, [m]stand firm
thus in the Lord, my beloved.

Exhortation, Encouragement, and Prayer

2 I entreat Euodia and I entreat Syntyche to [n]agree in the Lord. 3 Yes, I ask you also, true
companion,[2] help these women, who have labored side by side with me in the gospel together
with Clement and the rest of my fellow workers, [o]whose names are in the book of life.

4 [p]Rejoice in the Lord always; again I will say, rejoice. 5 Let your reasonableness be known

[1] *Or brothers and sisters; also verses 8, 21* [2] *Or loyal Syzygus; Greek true yokefellow*

10 [i][Rom. 1:4; 6:5] [j]1 Pet. 4:13; See 2 Cor. 1:5
11 [k]Acts 26:7
12 [l][1 Tim. 6:12, 19] [m]Heb. 11:40; 12:23; [Heb. 5:9]
13 [n][Ps. 45:10; Luke 9:62; Heb. 6:1]
14 [o]1 Cor. 9:24 [p][Heb. 3:1; 1 Pet. 5:10]; See Rom. 8:28
15 [q]1 Cor. 2:6; See Matt. 5:48 [r][Gal. 5:10] [s][John 7:17]
16 [t]Gal. 6:16
17 [u][ch. 4:9]; See 1 Cor. 4:16 [v]1 Pet. 5:3
18 [w]See 2 Cor. 11:13 [x][Acts 20:31]
19 [y]2 Cor. 11:15; [2 Thess. 1:9; 2 Pet. 2:1, 3] [z]See Rom. 16:18 [a][Hos. 4:7; 2 Cor. 11:12; Gal. 6:13; Jude 13] [b]Rom. 8:5; Col. 3:2
20 [c]See Eph. 2:19 [d]Acts 1:11 [e]See 1 Cor. 1:7
21 [f][1 Cor. 15:43-53] [g][ver. 10; Col. 3:4]; See Rom. 8:29 [h]See Eph. 1:19 [i]1 Cor. 15:28

Chapter 4

1 [j]See ch. 1:8 [k]ch. 1:4; 2:16; See 2 Cor. 1:14 [l]Prov. 16:31; 17:6 [m]ch. 1:27
2 [n]ch. 2:2
3 [o]See Luke 10:20
4 [p]ch. 3:1

3:12–16 *Paul's Progress in the Gospel: Through Christ, Not the Law.* Paul emphasizes the need for progress in Christian living, presenting himself as one who continually reaches ahead to see God's kingdom expanded.

3:12 Paul stresses that he is not **already perfect**—he is still involved in the struggles of life in a fallen world and hence he still sins; the full glory of the resurrection remains in the future. **I press on to make it my own, because Christ Jesus has made me his own.** There is a balance of faith and works, of God's call and the believer's response.

3:14 Goal (Gk. *skopos*) could also refer to the finish line in a race or an archery target. Paul's life is purposeful, for he constantly aims toward a heavenly goal. **The prize** is the fullness of blessings and rewards in the age to come, most especially being in perfect fellowship with Christ forever.

3:15 are mature. "Mature" (Gk. *teleios*) is the same adjective translated "perfect" in v. 12 ("not . . . perfect"). Thus, Paul is saying, in effect, "If you are really perfect/mature, you will realize you are not yet perfect/mature!"

3:17–21 *A Call to Follow Paul's Example of Commitment to Jesus as Lord.* Paul calls the Philippians to imitate him, a common theme in his letters (cf. 1 Cor. 4:16; 11:1; 2 Thess. 3:7–9). Paul's intent is not for the Philippians to focus on him per se but rather for them to join him in humble, radical dependence on Christ.

3:17 While Paul is not yet perfected, he is confident enough in his Christian walk to ask the Philippians to **join in imitating me** and other mature Christians. Much Christian growth comes through imitation of other Christians (4:9; 1 Cor. 11:1; 2 Thess. 3:8–9; 1 Tim. 4:12, 15–16; 2 Tim. 3:10–11; Heb. 13:7; 1 Pet. 5:3).

3:18–19 The **enemies of the cross** could be the Judaizers of v. 2 or "worldly" people in general. Their destiny is final judgment (**destruction**), they worship themselves (**their belly**), and they are consumed with **earthly things**.

3:20 citizenship. See note on 1:27.

3:21 Transform our lowly body to be like his glorious body echoes 2:5–11. Those who follow Christ's example of service will share in his vindication and glory as well. Perfection will come only at the resurrection (cf. 3:11–12; 1 Cor. 15:12–28). **To subject all things to himself** is messianic language drawn from the OT (e.g., Ps. 8:6; 110:1).

4:1–23 *Concluding Exhortations and Thanksgiving.* Paul encourages the Philippians, calling for reconciliation, joyful faith, and disciplined thinking (vv. 2–9).

4:1–3 *Standing Together for the Gospel.* Paul entreats the Philippians to stand unified in the Lord for the sake of the gospel.

4:1 Therefore. This transitional verse can be read as either the conclusion to the previous section or the introduction to ch. 4. **my joy and crown**. The Philippians' spiritual success would be Paul's "crowning achievement" (cf. 1 Thess. 2:19–20), and their perseverance and final salvation will bring him great joy (cf. Phil. 2:17).

4:2 Paul does not reveal the source of tension between **Euodia** and **Syntyche**. He exhorts them to apply the principle stated in 2:2; **agree** (4:2) and "being of the same mind" (2:2) are the same Greek phrase (*to auto phronein/phronēte*).

4:3 Reconciliation often requires third-party intervention, in this case a **true companion**. This person is unnamed in the ESV, although the word (Gk. *syzygos*, "true yokefellow," see ESV footnote) could be read as a proper name. Paul is especially eager to see Euodia and Syntyche reconciled because they have **labored side by side** with him **in the gospel**. Cf. 1:27, where Paul also encourages unity among those who are "striving side by side" (Gk. *synathleō*, the same verb used here) for the gospel. Paul did not isolate himself and minister alone; he deliberately worked with many others. In view of first-century culture, Euodia and Syntyche probably ministered mainly among women (cf. notes on Acts 18:26; Rom. 16:7; 1 Tim. 2:12). The **book of life** has OT roots (e.g., Ex. 32:33; Ps. 69:28; cf. Rev. 3:5; 13:8; 17:8; 20:12, 15; 21:27) and refers to God's record of those who belong to him.

4:4–9 *Rejoicing in Faith.* Paul calls the Philippians to attitudes of joy and reason, so that they replace anxiety with expectant, grateful prayer. He also calls them to think upon and practice Christian virtues.

4:4 Rejoice. The joy that Paul calls for is not a happiness that depends on circumstances but a deep contentment that is **in the Lord**, based on trust in the sovereign, living God, and that therefore is available **always**, even in difficult times.

4:5 Reasonableness is crucial for maintaining community; it is the disposi-

to everyone. [q]The Lord is at hand; **6** [r]do not be anxious about anything, [s]but in everything
by prayer and supplication [t]with thanksgiving let your requests be made known to God.
7 And [u]the peace of God, [v]which surpasses all understanding, will guard your hearts and
your minds in Christ Jesus.
8 Finally, brothers, whatever is true, whatever is honorable, whatever is just, whatever is
pure, whatever is lovely, whatever is commendable, if there is any excellence, if there is anything worthy of praise, think about these things. **9** What you have learned and [w]received and
heard and seen [x]in me—practice these things, and [y]the God of peace will be with you.

God's Provision

10 I rejoiced in the Lord greatly that now at length [z]you have revived your concern for me.
You were indeed concerned for me, but you had no opportunity. **11** Not that I am speaking
of being in need, for I have learned in whatever situation I am to be [a]content. **12** I know
how to be brought low, and I know how to abound. In any and every circumstance, I have
learned the secret of facing plenty and [b]hunger, abundance and [c]need. **13** I can do all things
[d]through him who strengthens me.
14 Yet it was kind of you [e]to share[1] my trouble. **15** And you Philippians yourselves know that
[f]in the beginning of the gospel, when I left Macedonia, [g]no church entered into partnership
with me in giving and receiving, except you only. **16** Even in Thessalonica you sent me help
for my needs once and again. **17** [h]Not that I seek the gift, but I seek [i]the fruit that increases to
your credit.[2] **18** I have received full payment, and more. I am well supplied, [j]having received
from Epaphroditus the gifts you sent, [k]a fragrant offering, [l]a sacrifice acceptable and pleasing to God. **19** And my God [m]will supply every need of yours [n]according to his riches in glory
in Christ Jesus. **20** To [o]our God and Father be [p]glory forever and ever. Amen.

Final Greetings

21 Greet every saint in Christ Jesus. [q]The brothers who are with me greet you. **22** [r]All the
saints greet you, especially those of Caesar's household.
23 [s]The grace of the Lord Jesus Christ be with your spirit.

[1] *Or have fellowship in* [2] *Or I seek the profit that accrues to your account*

5 [q]See James 5:8
6 [r]See Matt. 6:25 [s][Prov. 16:3] [t]See Rom. 1:8
7 [u][ver. 9; Isa. 26:3; Col. 3:15]; See John 14:27 [v][Eph. 3:19]
9 [w]1 Thess. 4:1 [x][ch. 3:17] [y][ver. 7]; See Rom. 15:33
10 [z][2 Cor. 11:9; ch. 2:30]
11 [a]1 Tim. 6:6, 8; [2 Cor. 9:8; Heb. 13:5]
12 [b]1 Cor. 4:11; 2 Cor. 11:27 [c]2 Cor. 11:9
13 [d][2 Cor. 12:9]; See Eph. 3:16; 1 Tim. 1:12
14 [e][ch. 1:7; Rev. 1:9]
15 [f]ch. 1:5 [g]2 Cor. 11:8, 9
17 [h][2 Cor. 9:5] [i]Rom. 1:13; [Titus 3:14]
18 [j]ch. 2:25 [k]See Gen. 8:21 [l]Heb. 13:16
19 [m]Ps. 23:1; 2 Cor. 9:8 [n]See Rom. 2:4
20 [o]Gal. 1:4; 1 Thess. 1:3; 3:11, 13 [p]Gal. 1:5; See Rom. 11:36
21 [q]Gal. 1:2
22 [r]2 Cor. 13:13
23 [s]See Rom. 16:20

tion that seeks what is best for everyone and not just for oneself. **The Lord is at hand** emphasizes the fact that Jesus will surely return as judge and will hold people responsible for their deeds (cf. James 5:9). Paul does not specify when this will happen (cf. Matt. 24:36–44; 2 Pet. 3:1–13).

4:6–7 Paul echoes Jesus' teaching in the Sermon on the Mount (see Matt. 6:25–34) that believers are not to **be anxious** but are to entrust themselves into the hands of their loving heavenly Father, whose **peace** will **guard** them **in Christ Jesus.** Paul's use of "guard" may reflect his own imprisonment or the status of Philippi as a Roman colony with a military garrison. In either case, it is not Roman soldiers who guard believers—it is the peace of God Almighty. Because God is sovereign and in control, Christians can entrust all their difficulties to him, who rules over all creation and who is wise and loving in all his ways (Rom. 8:31–39). An attitude of **thanksgiving** contributes directly to this inward peace.

4:8 think about these things. The Philippians are to fill their minds with things that will inspire worship of God and service to others.

4:9 Beyond having a proper spiritual outlook (v. 8), the Philippians are to **practice** what they have seen Paul doing. As they make progress in this way, they will find that it is not simply the peace of God but **the God of peace** *himself* who **will be with** them.

4:10–20 *Thanksgiving for the Philippians' Gift; Paul's Contentment in God.* Paul thanks the Philippians for their gift to him and assures them that God will in turn supply all of their needs.

4:10–11 Paul is grateful for the Philippians' support, but he wants them to know that even in difficult circumstances he has **learned . . . to be content**.

4:12–13 The **secret** of living amid life's difficulties is simple: trusting God in such a way that one can say, **I can do all things through him who strengthens me.** This does not mean God will bless whatever a person does; it must be read within the context of the letter, with its emphasis on obedience to God and service to God and others.

4:14–16 The Philippians **share** in Paul's ministry, not just at the spiritual level but at the practical level of financial support (cf. note on 1:3–5). They contributed to his work after he had **left Macedonia** (4:15) as well as when he was just down the road in **Thessalonica**, which was also in Macedonia (v. 16; cf. Acts 17:1).

4:17 Lest they imagine he has moved away from the service-centered perspective of the earlier chapters, Paul reminds the Philippians that even his reception of their gifts is ultimately for *their* benefit. Likely using a business metaphor, he is seeking **the fruit that increases to your credit** (cf. ESV footnote: "the profit that accrues to your account"). God sees their sacrifice and is pleased.

4:18 Paul is **well supplied** by the Philippians' gift, and because it has been offered to him for the service of the gospel, he can return to images drawn from Israel's worship. The gift is a **fragrant offering** (the Gk. *osmēn euōdias* occurs often in the Septuagint in connection with the "pleasing aroma" of sacrifices to God; see Gen. 8:21; Ex. 29:18; Lev. 4:31) and a **sacrifice acceptable** to God. While the literal offerings of the OT system have been done away with in Christ, the principle behind them of costly devotion to God remains.

4:19 Those who are generous toward God will find that he is generous toward them and **will supply** their **every need . . . in Christ Jesus**.

4:20 Just as the "hymn of Christ" (2:5–11) ended with "to the glory of God the Father," so Paul concludes the body of his letter with a doxology: **To our God and Father be glory forever and ever. Amen**.

4:21–22 *Greetings.* The exhortation to **greet every saint** reinforces the personal nature of Paul's communication and shows that the truths of the letter were to be lived out by real people in the real world. **Caesar's household** could refer not only to the "royal family" but to anyone connected with the emperor's service, including soldiers, slaves, or freedmen. It is likely that some of the latter group had responded positively to Paul's message; there is no evidence that the emperor's actual family were believers at this point. The fact that some within Caesar's circles had believed would have had particular resonance in Roman Philippi.

4:23 *Benediction.* Paul ends his letter with a reminder that true progress in life is a gift of God through **the grace of the Lord Jesus Christ**.

INTRODUCTION TO

THE LETTER OF PAUL TO THE

COLOSSIANS

Author and Title

Paul and Timothy are explicitly named as the authors of Colossians (1:1). Timothy probably served as Paul's secretary (amanuensis) since the first person singular ("I") is used throughout the letter (e.g., 1:24). The title indicates that Paul wrote the letter to Christians living in the small city of Colossae.

Some scholars have doubted Paul's authorship based on (1) *a style of writing* that they deem inconsistent with his uncontested letters, and (2) *a set of theological statements* that they regard as more developed than what he wrote in previous letters. The latter objection is readily answered by the unique situation reflected in the letter, leading Paul to address these particular concerns with the most relevant theological emphases. There is nothing in the theology that is inconsistent with what he wrote elsewhere, and many of his statements are simply logical developments of previous thoughts. The argument about style is much weaker since there is, in fact, strong continuity of style between this letter and his other letters. It is also quite precarious to make a judgment about authorship based on such a small sampling of letters. It is inappropriate to expect an author to demonstrate stylistic uniformity throughout all his works.

Date

The letter was probably written c. A.D. 62. Paul wrote it at roughly the same time that he wrote Philemon and Ephesians. All three letters were sent with Tychicus (see Eph. 6:21) and Onesimus. This date assumes that the imprisonment Paul speaks of is his Roman imprisonment that followed his harrowing voyage to Rome (Acts 27–28).

Theme

Christ is Lord over all of creation, including the invisible realm. He has secured redemption for his people, enabling them to participate with him in his death, resurrection, and fullness.

Purpose, Occasion, and Background

The church at Colossae apparently got its start during Paul's three-year ministry in Ephesus (A.D. 52–55). During this time, a Colossian named Epaphras probably traveled to Ephesus and responded to Paul's proclamation of the gospel (see Acts 19:10). This new believer returned to his hometown and began sharing the good news of Christ, which resulted in the birth of the Colossian church (Col. 1:7). At the time of this writing, Epaphras is with Paul in Rome and has likely shared the bad news that there was a dangerous teaching threatening the church at Colossae (4:12). Paul writes this letter to respond to this situation and to encourage these believers in their growth toward Christian maturity.

Scholars have long been puzzled over the precise nature of the destructive teaching facing the Colossians. This uncertainty does not, however, hinder accurate interpretation of the letter's rich theological teaching. A previous generation of scholars thought that the problem at Colossae was Gnosticism, an early heresy that taught that the world was created by an inferior god, that the material world is evil, and (in some cases) that asceticism should be practiced. But an improved understanding of Gnosticism, aided in part by the discovery of Gnostic documents in Egypt, has led most scholars to discount this interpretation. Missing from Colossians is any polemic against the Gnostic view that there is an unknown god who is distinct from the creator God. There is also no discussion of the Gnostic conviction that matter and material existence are inherently evil.

The fact that there are many distinctively Jewish elements to the false teaching (such as Sabbath observance, Jewish festivals, and an interest in angels; see 2:16–18) has led a number of scholars to contend that the competing teaching had something to do with Judaism. Some have suggested that a form of Jewish mysticism had influenced the church, resulting in Colossian Christians engaging in ascetic practices (such as fasting) in preparation for a visionary ascent to heaven where they would join the angels in worshiping God at his heavenly throne (see 2:18). This is a possibility, but it does not provide the most convincing explanation of the "worship of angels" and some of the other elements of the false teaching (2:18).

Others advocate a similar view, contending that the principal problem at Colossae was not a dangerous teaching from within the church but one coming from outside. They suggest that the local Jewish synagogue was mounting a campaign to discredit and denounce the Christian assembly, especially because this group of predominately Gentile believers was now claiming a Jewish heritage in the OT. One of the problems with this view, however, is that the role of the Jewish law is never mentioned in Colossians. It also does not adequately take into account the role of other syncretistic elements from other local religions.

The best explanation for this dangerous teaching is that it comes from the context of the local Jewish and pagan folk belief. A central feature of the local folk belief was a tendency to call on angels for help and protection from evil spirits. This characteristic is well attested in many inscriptions and ancient documents. For instance, a magical stone amulet designed to be worn around the neck for protection from evil spirits reads, "Michael, Gabriel, Ouriel, Raphael, protect the one who wears this.... Flee, O hated one, Solomon pursues you."

What likely happened at Colossae is that a shaman-like figure within the church had attracted a following and was presenting himself as something of a Christian spiritual guide (cf. "his sensuous mind," 2:18). This person probably claimed to have superior insight into the spiritual realm and was advising the Colossian Christians to practice certain rites, taboos, and rituals as a means of protection from evil spirits and for deliverance from afflictions. When Paul hears of the spreading influence of this teaching that devalues Christ and fails to appreciate the new identity of believers "in Christ," he writes this letter of warning and encouragement. He does not minimize the threat presented by the demonic powers but emphasizes the supremacy of Christ over all powers. He asserts the unity of Christians with the exalted Christ, which entails their sharing in his power and authority.

Paul also takes the opportunity to encourage these believers to press on to maturity in Christ by continuing in their battle against sin, pursuing holiness in Christ, and learning to live as distinctively Christian households.

Key Themes

1. Jesus Christ is preeminent over all creation, Lord over all human rulers and cosmic powers.	1:15–20; 2:9–10; 3:1
2. God has worked through Christ to secure redemption and reconciliation for all who put their faith in him.	1:13–14, 20–22
3. Believers are in Christ and thus participate in a relationship of solidarity with Christ in his death on the cross, his resurrection from the dead, his new life, and his fullness.	2:9–14; 3:1–4
4. Christ has defeated the powers of darkness on the cross, and Christians share in his power and authority over that realm.	2:10, 15; see also 2:8, 20
5. Jesus is the fulfillment of Jewish expectation, and Christians now share in the heritage of the old covenant people of God through their union with him.	1:12, 21–22, 27
6. Believers are called to grow in maturity in Christ by getting rid of sinful practices and cultivating Christian virtues.	1:10–12, 28; 3:1–4:6

History of Salvation Summary

Christians are to hold fast to the one way of salvation in Christ, in contrast to false teaching. (For an explanation of the "History of Salvation," see the Overview of the Bible, pp. 23–26.)

Literary Features

Colossians closely follows the epistolary conventions of Paul's other letters to congregations in the early church. The letter opens with the customary greetings, including thanksgiving and prayer. The main body of the letter is divided fairly equally between theological exposition and practical application (including household instructions), followed by personal greetings that reinforce the relationship between the writer and his correspondents. Because of its polemical (persuasive and argumentative) thrust, Colossians also takes the form of a disputation in which the apostle argues the gospel side of a debate between the all-sufficiency of Christ and the spurious claims of man-made religion. The lines of praise given to Christ in 1:15–20 have the form of a hymn or creed celebrating him.

As one of the most thoroughly Christ-centered books in the Bible, Colossians finds its essential unity in the divine and exalted person of the preeminent Christ. The letter presents variations on this central theme, with Christ celebrated as the object of the believer's faith, the image of the invisible God, the creator of all dominions, the head of the church, the firstborn from the dead, the unifier and reconciler of all things, the Savior through his sufferings on the cross, the treasury of all wisdom and knowledge, the triumphant victor over sin and Satan, the exalted Lord of life and glory, and the true pattern for the life of Christian faith. The letter is also unified by Paul's pastoral concern to dissuade the Colossians from getting caught up in useless religious regulations and to awaken exaltation of Christ and exultation in him. Paul writes with stylistic flair and aphoristic brilliance.

Timeline

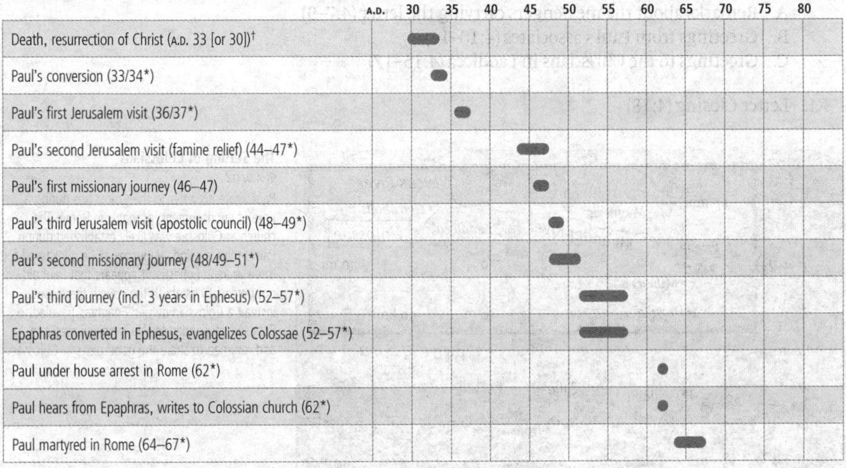

A.D. 30 35 40 45 50 55 60 65 70 75 80
Death, resurrection of Christ (A.D. 33 [or 30])†
Paul's conversion (33/34*)
Paul's first Jerusalem visit (36/37*)
Paul's second Jerusalem visit (famine relief) (44–47*)
Paul's first missionary journey (46–47)
Paul's third Jerusalem visit (apostolic council) (48–49*)
Paul's second missionary journey (48/49–51*)
Paul's third journey (incl. 3 years in Ephesus) (52–57*)
Epaphras converted in Ephesus, evangelizes Colossae (52–57*)
Paul under house arrest in Rome (62*)
Paul hears from Epaphras, writes to Colossian church (62*)
Paul martyred in Rome (64–67*)

** denotes approximate date; / signifies either/or; † see The Date of Jesus' Crucifixion, pp. 1809–1810*

Outline

I. Greeting (1:1–2)

II. Thanksgiving (1:3–8)

III. Prayer (1:9–14)

IV. Praise to Christ (1:15–20)
   A. Christ is Lord of creation (1:15–17)
   B. Christ is Lord of redemption (1:18–20)

V. Reconciliation of the Colossians to God (1:21–23)

VI. The Apostle Paul's Labor for the Gospel (1:24–2:3)
   A. Paul's suffering and stewardship of the mystery (1:24–28)
   B. Paul's labor for the Colossians (1:29–2:3)

VII. The Dangerous Teaching at Colossae (2:4–23)
   A. Warning about a deceptive teaching (2:4–8)
   B. Help for the danger: resources in Christ (2:9–15)
   C. Additional warnings about the teaching (2:16–23)

VIII. The Proper Focus: Christ and the Life Above (3:1–4)

IX. Instructions on Living the Christian Life (3:5–4:6)
   A. Dealing with the sins of the past (3:5–11)
   B. Putting on the virtues of Christ (3:12–17)
   C. Living in the Christian household (3:18–4:1)
   D. Persistence in prayer (4:2–4)
   E. Good behavior toward those outside the community (4:5–6)

X. Personal Greetings and Instructions (4:7–17)
   A. Remarks about the messengers carrying the letter (4:7–9)
   B. Greetings from Paul's associates (4:10–14)
   C. Greetings to the Christians in Laodicea (4:15–17)

XI. Letter Closing (4:18)

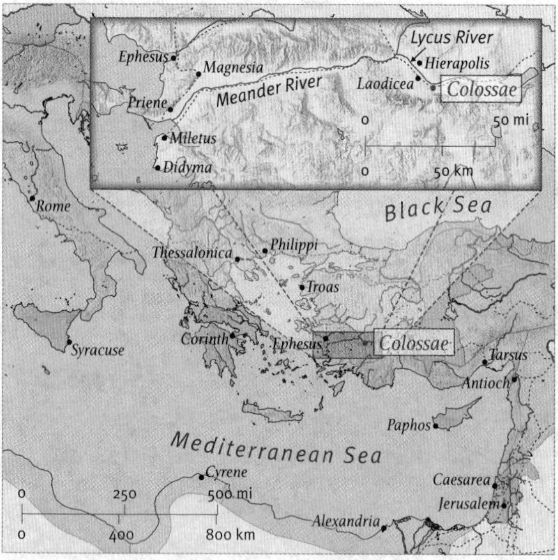

The Setting of Colossians
c. A.D. 62
Paul wrote his letter to the Colossians during a time of imprisonment, probably in Rome. The church at Colossae was likely established during Paul's third missionary journey as he ministered for three years in Ephesus. It appears that Paul did not personally establish the church there, but instead a Colossian named Epaphras traveled to Ephesus, responded to Paul's gospel message, and returned to share the good news in Colossae.

THE LETTER OF PAUL TO THE

COLOSSIANS

Chapter 1
1[a]See 2 Cor. 1:1 [b]See 1 Cor. 1:1 [c]See 1 Thess. 3:2
2[d]Eph. 1:1; See Phil. 1:1 [e]Rom. 1:7
3[f]Eph. 1:15, 16; Philem. 4
4[g]See 1 Thess. 1:3
5[h]ver. 23; See Acts 23:6; Titus 1:2; Heb. 3:6 [i]2 Tim. 4:8; 1 Pet. 1:4 [j]See Eph. 1:13
6[k][ver. 23; Ps. 98:3]; See Matt. 24:14 [l]John 15:5, 16; [Phil. 1:11] [m][Rom. 16:26; Eph. 4:21] [n]See Acts 11:23
7[o]ch. 4:12; Philem. 23 [p]ch. 4:7
8[q][Rom. 15:30]
9[r]ver. 4 [s]2 Thess. 1:11 [t][Eph. 1:17]

Greeting

1 Paul, [a]an apostle of Christ Jesus [b]by the will of God, and Timothy [c]our brother,
2 To the [d]saints and faithful brothers[1] in Christ at Colossae:
[e]Grace to you and peace from God our Father.

Thanksgiving and Prayer

3 [f]We always thank God, the Father of our Lord Jesus Christ, when we pray for you,
4 since we heard of [g]your faith in Christ Jesus and of [g]the love that you have for all the
saints, **5** because of [h]the hope [i]laid up for you in heaven. Of this you have heard before in
[j]the word of the truth, the gospel, **6** which has come to you, as indeed [k]in the whole world
it is [l]bearing fruit and increasing—as it also does among you, since the day you [m]heard
it and understood [n]the grace of God in truth, **7** just as you learned it from [o]Epaphras our
beloved [p]fellow servant.[2] He is [p]a faithful minister of Christ on your[3] behalf **8** and has made
known to us your [q]love in the Spirit.
9 And so, [r]from the day we heard, [s]we have not ceased to pray for you, asking that [t]you

[1] Or *brothers and sisters*. The plural Greek word *adelphoi* (translated "brothers") refers to siblings in a family. In New Testament usage, depending on the context, *adelphoi* may refer either to men or to both men and women who are siblings (brothers and sisters) in God's family, the church [2] Greek *fellow bondservant* [3] Some manuscripts *our*

1:1–2 *Greeting.* Paul begins the letter in his typical fashion by calling on God to pour out his grace and peace upon the Colossians.

1:1 Paul, an apostle. Although Paul has likely never been to Colossae, he nevertheless feels a pastoral responsibility for this church. He writes to the Colossians with the authority of an apostle to assist the church in dealing with the problem of the dangerous teaching threatening its health (cf. 2 Cor. 1:1; Gal. 1:1). **Timothy**. See Introduction to 1 Timothy: Purpose, Occasion, and Background.

1:2 Colossae. A city in Phrygia, in the Roman province of Asia, Colossae was located on the Lycus River just over 100 miles (161 km) east of Ephesus. A significant earthquake occurred in the Lycus Valley during the reign of Nero (c. A.D. 60). Surface surveys of the site of Colossae have discovered inscriptions, a theater, a cemetery, and other structures. Coins point to official worship of the main Roman deities, plus the presence of mystery cults. Jewish presence in the Lycus Valley was likely strong, given the extant inscriptions and the literary references to Jews in Phrygia during the second and first centuries B.C. (Josephus, *Jewish Antiquities* 12.147–153; Cicero, *For Flaccus* 68).

1:3–8 *Thanksgiving.* Paul thanks God for the Colossians and their tangible expressions of faith, hope, and love.

1:3 God, the Father of our Lord Jesus Christ. Paul will place a significant emphasis on the lordship of Jesus Christ in this letter. He is careful to affirm, however, that Jesus is not a separate God, yet he has a close relationship with the Father, for he is the Son and agent of God.

1:4–5 faith . . . love . . . hope. Paul spoke frequently of the importance of these three Christian virtues (see Rom. 5:1–5; 1 Cor. 13:13; Gal. 5:5–6; Eph. 4:2–5; 1 Thess. 1:3; 5:8), which were seen as foundational to the Christian life (see also Heb. 6:10–12; 1 Pet. 1:3–8, 21–22). In this passage, faith and love are based on hope, which is presented not as the action of hoping but as something objective—in the sense of "the thing hoped for"—that Christians can anticipate with confidence (see Col. 3:4). Because it is **laid up for you in heaven**, no earthly ruler or demonic power can rob believers of the reality of this hope.

1:5 the word of the truth. This contrasts with the false teaching Paul later describes as "empty deceit" (2:8).

1:6 in the whole world. It has now been roughly 30 years since Christ's death and resurrection and Pentecost (see Introduction: Timeline). The gospel has indeed spread from Jerusalem into Syria, Asia Minor, Greece, Italy, and likely into Egypt, North Africa, and Persia as well.

1:7 You learned it from Epaphras makes it clear that Paul did not plant the church at Colossae. The people heard the gospel from Epaphras (a shortened form of "Epaphroditus"), who is a fellow Colossian (4:12). The term for "learned" (Gk. *manthanō*) is closely related to the term "disciple" (Gk. *mathētēs*). More than merely listening to a simple gospel presentation, Paul makes it clear that the gospel involves systematic instruction in the faith and in how to live as a Christian. **on your behalf**. The ESV footnote indicates that some manuscripts read "on *our* behalf" (rather than "on *your* behalf"). If this is the original reading (as several scholars suggest), this would mean that Epaphras has been a faithful ambassador in place of (or on behalf of) Paul among the Colossians. The name T. Asinius Epaphroditus occurs in an inscription found at Colossae, showing that the name "Epaphroditus" (Epaphras) was in use in the region.

1:9–14 *Prayer.* Paul reports in summary fashion how he regularly prays for the Colossians. He prays that they will know God's will and that God will give them the power to live it out. The prayer concludes with an expression of thanksgiving for God's mighty act of deliverance and redemption.

1:9 Knowledge and wisdom were offered by the false teachers in Colossae (cf. 2:4, 8, 16–23). Paul prays that the Colossians will have the wisdom and understanding that comes only from God. **Spiritual** means given by the Holy Spirit.

may be filled with the knowledge of his will in all [u]spiritual wisdom and understanding,
10 so as [v]to walk in a manner worthy of the Lord, [w]fully pleasing to him, [x]bearing fruit in
every good work and increasing in the knowledge of God. 11 [y]May you be strengthened
with all power, according to his glorious might, for [z]all endurance and patience [a]with joy,
12 [b]giving thanks[1] to the Father, who has qualified you[2] to share in [c]the inheritance of the
saints in light. 13 He [d]has delivered us from [e]the domain of darkness and transferred us to [f]the
kingdom of [g]his beloved Son, 14 [h]in whom we have redemption, the forgiveness of sins.

The Preeminence of Christ

15 [i]He is the image of [j]the invisible God, [k]the firstborn of all creation. 16 For by[3] him all
things were created, [l]in heaven and on earth, visible and invisible, whether [m]thrones or
[n]dominions or rulers or authorities—all things were created [o]through him and for him.
17 And [p]he is before all things, and in him all things [q]hold together. 18 And [r]he is the head of
the body, the church. He is [s]the beginning, [t]the firstborn from the dead, that in everything
he might be preeminent. 19 For [u]in him all the [v]fullness of God was pleased to dwell, 20 and

[1] *Or patience, with joy giving thanks* [2] Some manuscripts *us* [3] That is, by means of; *or in*

19 [u]ch. 2:9 [v]See John 1:16

9 [u]ch. 4:5; Eph. 1:8; [1 Cor. 12:8]
10 [v][Ps. 1:1, 3]; See Eph. 4:1 [w][2 Cor. 5:9; Eph. 5:10; 1 Thess. 4:1] [x]ver. 6
11 [y]See Eph. 3:16 [z]Eph. 4:2 [a]See Matt. 5:12
12 [b]ch. 3:15; Eph. 5:20 [c]See Acts 26:18
13 [d]1 Thess. 1:10 [e]Luke 22:53; Eph. 6:12 [f]2 Pet. 1:11 [g][Eph. 1:6]
14 [h]See Eph. 1:7
15 [i]See 2 Cor. 4:4 [j]See 1 Tim. 1:17 [k][Ps. 89:27]; See Rom. 8:29
16 [l]Eph. 1:10 [m][Ezek. 10:1] [n]Eph. 1:21 [o]Rom. 11:36; 1 Cor. 8:6
17 [p][John 8:58]; See John 1:1 [q][Heb. 1:3]
18 [r]See Eph. 1:22, 23 [s]Rev. 3:14 [t]Acts 26:23; 1 Cor. 15:20; Rev. 1:5

1:10 so as. The "wisdom and understanding" (v. 9) would then lead to changed lives, for it would enable these Christians **to walk in a manner worthy of the Lord**. "To walk" is a Jewish metaphor for conducting or behaving oneself. It corresponds to the Hebrew term *halak*. The rabbis had an entire oral tradition, later written down (especially in the Mishnah and the Talmuds), called *Halakah*, that guided them in their behavior. As a former rabbi, Paul calls believers "to walk" not according to the oral traditions of Judaism but in a way that is **fully pleasing to** the Lord Jesus Christ. Although Christians are completely justified from the moment of initial saving faith, they are not fully sanctified, and they can do things that either please or displease God each day. **Every good work** is here viewed as the fruit of salvation in the life of a Christian, not as the prerequisite for entering a relationship with Christ. Paul's reference to **bearing fruit . . . and increasing** brings to mind the parable of the sower (Mark 4:1–9, 13–20). The seed sown on the good soil bore fruit thirtyfold, sixtyfold, and a hundredfold.

1:11 be strengthened with all power. Spiritual power was a key issue in the Greco-Roman world. People sought power through connection with various gods and pagan rituals in order to protect them from evil spirits and to help them acquire wealth or influence. Paul wants the Colossians to know that he prays regularly that God would impart his power to them, not for selfish aims but so that they can live for God in a worthy manner. **for all endurance and patience with joy**. The purpose (as indicated by the word "for") of this God-given power is to provide the divine strength needed for the believer to attain Christian virtues, to persevere in the faith, to resist temptation and deceitful teachers, and so to know the joy of the Lord.

1:12 who has qualified you to share in the inheritance. Paul has taken language normally reserved for the Jewish people under the old covenant (see Gen. 13:14–17; Num. 26:52–56; Josh. 19:9) and applied it to Gentiles under the new covenant. Gentiles now have equal access to the Father and are heirs to the inheritance he has promised his people. This is based on the fact that God has made Gentiles **saints** ("holy ones" or "consecrated people") through the redemption he has procured through his Son.

1:13 He has delivered us. Just as God rescued his people from slavery in Egypt under the old covenant (Ex. 6:6; 14:30), he has delivered them now **from the domain of darkness**, that is, from the realm of Satan and the powers of evil (see Acts 26:18). **the kingdom of his beloved Son**. This kingdom is the same as the "kingdom of God" (or "kingdom of heaven") that Jesus spoke of (e.g., Matt. 3:2; Mark 1:15; etc.), which was central to Jesus' teaching throughout the four Gospels. Jesus is the agent of God who will presently reign (1 Cor. 15:24) until he hands his kingdom over to the Father, when the kingdom of God comes into its full manifestation at the end of the present age. The emphasis here is on the present lordship of Christ.

1:14 Redemption means deliverance or liberation, emphasizing here that believers have been delivered and have received **forgiveness of** their **sins**.

1:15–20 *Praise to Christ.* In a strongly moving and poetic way, which some scholars think is a quotation from an early Christian hymn, Paul praises the lordship of Christ in relation to both creation and redemption.

1:15–17 *Christ Is Lord of Creation.* Jesus is the Lord, the maker and upholder of all things in the universe.

1:15 the image of the invisible God. Paul depicts Christ in terms similar to the presentation of "wisdom" in Proverbs 8 ("When he established the heavens, I [wisdom] was there . . . I was beside him, like a master workman" [Prov. 8:27, 30]). In later Jewish wisdom literature, personified divine wisdom is described as the image of God. **firstborn of all creation**. It would be wrong to think in physical terms here, as if Paul were asserting that the Son had a physical origin or was somehow created (the classic Arian heresy) rather than existing eternally as the Son, with the Father and the Holy Spirit, in the Godhead. (See the article on The Trinity, pp. 2513–2515.) What Paul had in mind was the rights and privileges of a firstborn son, especially the son of a monarch who would inherit ruling sovereignty. This is how the expression is used of David: "I will make him the firstborn, the highest of the kings of the earth" (Ps. 89:27).

1:16 by him all things were created. Jesus did not come into existence when he was born of the virgin Mary. He was the agent of creation through whom God made heaven and earth (John 1:3 and note; 1 Cor. 8:6). Jesus cannot be the first thing created (as the ancient Arian heresy claimed) since "all things" without exception were created by him. **thrones or dominions or rulers or authorities**. Paul is using the current Jewish terms for various rankings of angels (although he doesn't explain their relative ranks). His emphasis here may be on the evil angels, since they play a significant part in this letter (Col. 2:8, 10, 15, 20). This would not mean, however, that Jesus created evil angels; all spiritual powers were **created** by Jesus, but some later chose to rebel against God and so to become evil. Jesus is not only the agent of creation but is also the *goal* of creation, for everything was created by him and **for him**, that is, for his honor and praise. Since Jesus is in this sense the goal of creation, he must be fully God (see notes on John 1:1; 8:58).

1:17 in him all things hold together. Christ continually sustains his creation, preventing it from falling into chaos or disintegrating (cf. Heb. 1:3).

1:18–20 *Christ Is Lord of Redemption.* Christ is Head of the church and has accomplished reconciliation at the cross.

1:18 he is the head of the body. Paul spoke elsewhere of the church as the body of Christ (1 Cor. 12:27), but he takes the image a step further here and envisions Christ as the head of the body (see also Eph. 1:22–23; 5:25). This metaphor conveys Christ's leadership over the body and may also suggest his role in providing sustenance for it (see notes on 1 Cor. 11:3; Col. 2:10; 2:19).

1:19 For in him all the fullness of God was pleased to dwell. The "fullness" language here and throughout the letter is reminiscent of its use in the OT, where it was said that God "filled" the temple with his presence. For instance, the prophet Ezekiel exclaims, "I looked, and behold, the glory of the LORD filled the temple" (Ezek. 44:4). Jesus not only bears God's glory, but all that God *is* also dwells in him. He possesses the wisdom, power, Spirit, and

[w]through him to reconcile to himself all things, whether on earth or in heaven, [x]making
peace [y]by the blood of his cross.
21 [z]And you, who once were alienated and hostile in mind, [a]doing evil deeds, **22** he has now
reconciled [b]in his body of flesh by his death, [c]in order to present you holy and blameless
and [d]above reproach before him, **23** [e]if indeed you continue in the faith, [f]stable and steadfast,
not shifting from [g]the hope of the gospel that you heard, which has been proclaimed [h]in
all creation[1] under heaven, [i]and of which I, Paul, became a minister.

Paul's Ministry to the Church

24 Now [j]I rejoice in my sufferings for your sake, and in my flesh [k]I am filling up [l]what
is lacking in Christ's afflictions [m]for the sake of his body, that is, the church, **25** [n]of which I
became a minister according to [o]the stewardship from God that was given to me for you,
to make the word of God fully known, **26** [p]the mystery hidden for ages and generations
but now revealed to his saints. **27** [q]To them God chose to make known how great among
the Gentiles are [r]the riches of the glory of [p]this mystery, which is Christ in you, [s]the hope
of glory. **28** Him we proclaim, warning everyone and teaching everyone with all wisdom,
that [t]we may present everyone [u]mature in Christ. **29** For this [v]I toil, [w]struggling [x]with all
his energy that he powerfully works within me.

[1] *Or to every creature*

20 [w]See 2 Cor. 5:18; Eph. 1:10 [x]See Eph. 2:14 [y][Eph. 2:13]
21 [z]See Eph. 2:1, 2, 12 [a][Titus 1:16]
22 [b][Rom. 7:4] [c]Jude 24; See Eph. 1:4; 5:27 [d]1 Cor. 1:8
23 [e]See John 15:4 [f]ch. 2:7; Eph. 3:17 [g]ver. 5, 6 [h]Mark 16:15; [Acts 2:5] [i]See 2 Cor. 3:6
24 [j]See 2 Cor. 7:4 [k][2 Tim. 1:8; 2:10] [l]See 2 Cor. 1:5 [m][Eph. 4:12]
25 [n]ver. 23 [o]See Eph. 3:2
26 [p]Eph. 3:9; See Rom. 16:25, 26
27 [q][ch. 2:2] [r]Eph. 1:18; 3:16 [p][See ver. 26 above] [s]1 Tim. 1:1
28 [t]See ver. 22, 23 [u]See Matt. 5:48
29 [v]1 Cor. 15:10; 1 Tim. 4:10 [w]ch. 4:12; [ch. 2:1] [x]See Eph. 1:19

glory of God. To say that all this divine fullness dwells in Jesus is to say that he is fully God (see also Col. 2:9).

1:20 to reconcile to himself all things. As the "Prince of Peace" (Isa. 9:6), Jesus will ultimately quell all rebellion against God and his purposes. For believers, this means present reconciliation to God as his friends. As for nonbelievers and the demonic powers, Christ's universal reign of peace will be enforced on them, for their rebellion will be decisively defeated by Christ as conquering king (cf. 1 Cor. 15:24–28; Rev. 19:11–21; 20:7–10) so that they can no longer do any harm in the universe. The basis for Christ's reign of **peace** is **the blood of his cross**. The cross truly is the pivotal point in human and cosmic history. On crucifixion, see note on Matt. 27:35. See also note on Phil. 2:8.

1:21–23 *Reconciliation of the Colossians to God.* This next section explains the meaning of reconciliation (see note on v. 20) for the church.

1:21–22 once . . . now. Paul presents a strong contrast between the Colossians' pre-Christian status and their favorable situation now as Christians. **alienated**. Sin has resulted in estrangement from God (Eph. 2:12; 4:18) and thus creates the need for reconciliation. This is due, in part, to the fact that nonbelievers are **hostile in mind** to God (Rom. 1:21). The result of reconciliation is that Christ is now working in all the believers **to present you holy and blameless** before God. This is the same language used in the OT to describe the unblemished animals that the Levitical priest would bring for a sacrifice to God. When Christ brings his followers to the Father for inspection, they will be found to be **above reproach**.

1:23 if indeed you continue in the faith. The form of this phrase in Greek (using the Gk. particle *ei* and the indicative mood of the verb *epimenō*) indicates that Paul fully expects that the Colossian believers will continue in the faith; no doubt is expressed. Nevertheless, the statement shows that faithfulness to the end is essential in the Christian life (cf. Matt. 10:22). **not shifting**. The idea here is very similar to Jesus' story contrasting the person who built his house on the sand with the one who built his house on the rock (Matt. 7:24–27). Paul wanted the Colossians to build their house on the solid foundation of truth and not on the shifting sands of false teaching. **In all creation** is a general statement meaning that the gospel has gone widely throughout the Greco-Roman world, to both Jews and Gentiles (cf. Col. 1:6).

1:24–2:3 *The Apostle Paul's Labor for the Gospel.* Paul shifts the focus to describe his own work for the gospel generally and then more specifically for the Colossians.

1:24–28 *Paul's Suffering and Stewardship of the Mystery.* Paul's sufferings are the means God uses to extend the message of the gospel to others.

1:24 I am filling up (Gk. *antanaplēroō*) **what is lacking** (Gk. *hysterēma*) **in Christ's afflictions** does not imply that there is a deficiency in Christ's atoning death and suffering on the cross, which would contradict the central message of this letter and all the rest of Scripture as well (cf. Heb. 9:12, 24–26; 10:14). Christ's sufferings are in fact sufficient, and nothing of one's own can be added to secure salvation. What was "lacking" in Christ's afflictions was the future suffering of all who (like Paul) will experience great affliction for the sake of the gospel, as Paul described, e.g., in 2 Cor. 1:8–10. (Cf. Phil. 2:30, where Paul tells the Philippians that Epaphroditus risked his life "to complete [Gk. *anaplēroō*] what was lacking [Gk. *hysterēma*] in your service to me".)

1:25 according to the stewardship from God. Paul views himself as a divinely commissioned "steward" or "administrator" (Gk. *oikonomos*), a word used widely in the Roman world for the administrator of a large household or estate. Paul's responsibility was to **make the word of God fully known**. The "filling up" (Gk. *antanaplēroō*, v. 24) of Christ's afflictions takes place as the proclamation of the word is made "fully known" (Gk. *plēroō*, v. 25). Paul suffers as he proclaims the gospel, and he declares that the basis of forgiveness of sins is Christ's once-for-all suffering and sacrifice.

1:26–27 The mystery does not refer to something mysterious or to a secret ritual. Rather, Paul is speaking of God's unfolding plan for the world and, above all, his plan of redemption through the Messiah (cf. 2:2; 4:3; Eph. 1:9; 3:3–4, 9; 5:32; 6:19). Although elements of God's design were already known through the prophets, key aspects of it were **hidden for ages and generations** and thus were a mystery, which could only be known and understood when they were **revealed** by God. This language occurs often in the book of Daniel. After God reveals to Daniel that Nebuchadnezzar's dream foretold four successive kingdoms culminating in the kingdom of God, Daniel tells the king, "there is a God in heaven who reveals mysteries, and he has made known to King Nebuchadnezzar what will be in the latter days" (Dan. 2:28). At the heart of the mystery that God is now revealing through Paul is the amazing hallmark of the new covenant, **Christ in you, the hope of glory**. God himself, in the person of Christ, will be directly and personally present in the lives of his people, and his presence assures them of a future life with him when he returns. Moreover, Christ does not reside only in believing Jews but also in believing Gentiles, so that there is one unified people of God (cf. Eph. 2:11–22; 3:2–6).

1:28 that we may present everyone mature (Gk. *teleios*) **in Christ**. It was not enough for Paul to see people make a profession of faith in Christ, as important as this is. *Teleios* could be translated as "perfect," but full perfection will be attained only when Christ returns and believers are fully transformed. Until that time, the maturity Christians are to seek stands in contrast with the immaturity of infancy (cf. Eph. 4:14).

1:29–2:3 *Paul's Labor for the Colossians.* Paul ministers so that every person will be complete in Christ and will see that all wisdom and knowledge are in him.

1:29 Paul is **struggling with all his** [that is, Christ's] **energy** to help them grow and mature in Christ.

2 For I want you to know [y]how great a [w]struggle I have for you and for those at Laodicea
and for all who have not seen me face to face, 2 that [z]their hearts may be encouraged,
being [a]knit together in love, to reach all the riches of full assurance of understanding and
the knowledge of [b]God's mystery, which is Christ, 3 [c]in whom are hidden all the treasures
of wisdom and knowledge. 4 I say this in order [d]that no one may delude you with plausible
arguments. 5 For [e]though I am absent in body, yet I am with you in spirit, rejoicing to see
your [f]good order and [g]the firmness of your faith in Christ.

Alive in Christ

6 [h]Therefore, as you received Christ Jesus the Lord, so walk in him, 7 [i]rooted and [j]built up in
him and [k]established in the faith, just [l]as you were taught, abounding [m]in thanksgiving.
8 See to it that no one takes you captive by [n]philosophy and [o]empty deceit, according to
[p]human tradition, according to the [q]elemental spirits[1] of the world, and not according to
Christ. 9 For [r]in him the whole fullness of deity dwells [s]bodily, 10 and [t]you have been filled

[1] *Or elementary principles; also verse 20*

Chapter 2

1 [y]Phil. 1:30 [w][See ch. 1:29 above]
2 [z]ch. 4:8; Eph. 6:22 [a][ch. 3:14] [b]See ch. 1:27
3 [c]Isa. 11:2; 45:3; 1 Cor. 1:24, 30; 2:6, 7; [Luke 11:49; Eph. 1:8]
4 [d]Rom. 16:18; [Eph. 5:6; 2 Pet. 2:3]
5 [e]1 Cor. 5:3 [f]1 Cor. 14:40 [g]1 Pet. 5:9
6 [h]ch. 1:10; 1 Thess. 4:1
7 [i]Eph. 3:17 [j]Acts 20:32; Eph. 2:20; See 1 Cor. 3:9 [k]Heb. 13:9 [l]Eph. 4:21 [m]ch. 4:2; Eph. 5:20
8 [n][1 Tim. 6:20] [o]Eph. 5:6 [p]See Matt. 15:2 [q]ver. 20
9 [r]ch. 1:19; John 1:14 [s][ver. 17]
10 [t]Eph. 3:19

2:1 for those at Laodicea. Laodicea (cf. Rev. 3:14–22) was the nearest city to Colossae, only 9 miles (14.5 km) away (see note on Rev. 3:14–22). There was a close relationship between these churches as well as with the church at Hierapolis (see Col. 4:13).

2:2 The false teachers presumably claimed access to the mysteries of God's truth, but Paul insists that **Christ** is **God's mystery**, and all understanding is to be found in him.

2:3 in whom are hidden all the treasures of wisdom and knowledge. Anticipating what he will soon say about false sources of knowledge (vv. 4–23), Paul emphasizes that Christ is the ultimate storehouse of divine wisdom and spiritual knowledge. His language parallels what the OT says about wisdom (Prov. 2:3–6).

2:4–23 *The Dangerous Teaching at Colossae.* Paul delivers a series of warnings about the teaching that is threatening the Colossian church. In doing so, he also provides important teaching on the Christians' new identity in Christ that will help them resist the arguments of the false teachers and live worthily of the Lord.

2:4–8 *Warning about a Deceptive Teaching.* Even though the Colossians are doing well spiritually, they must be on guard against false teaching.

"In Christ": A Central Theme in Colossians

1:14	*in whom* we have redemption
1:16	*in him* all things were created
1:19	*in him* all the fullness of God was pleased to dwell
1:22	reconciled *in his body* of flesh
2:3	*in whom* are hidden all the treasures of wisdom and knowledge
2:6	walk *in him*
2:7	rooted and built up *in him*
2:9	*in him* all the fullness of deity dwells bodily
2:10	you have been filled *in him*
2:11	you were circumcised *in him*
2:12	*in him* you were raised up
2:15	triumphing over them *in him*
3:20	pleasing *in the Lord*
4:7	fellow servant *in the Lord*
4:17	the ministry that you have received *in the Lord*

2:4 that no one may delude you with plausible arguments. Paul warns the Colossians about the direct and dangerous threat in their midst. It is important to see that the threat comes from within the church and that what the teacher(s) are saying sounds reasonable and even persuasive.

2:5 I am with you in spirit. Because both the Colossians and Paul live "in Christ" and possess the Spirit of God, there is a sense in which Paul is, in fact, present with them (see also 1 Cor. 5:3–5). To express the stability that Paul wants to see continue in the Colossian church, he employs two military metaphors—**good order** and **firmness**. The Colossians should be like troops drawn up in battle formation, standing firm like soldiers resisting the enemy.

2:6–7 you received Christ Jesus the Lord. Paul calls the Colossians back to the foundational teaching passed on to them by Epaphras when they first became Christians. At the heart of this is the confession that Jesus Christ is Lord (1 Cor. 12:3). Paul uses the images of a tree (**rooted**) and a building (**built up**) to remind them of their firm foundation in what they have already been taught. The implication is, why should they now give a hearing to any rival teaching?

2:8 See to it that no one takes you captive (Gk. *sylagōgeō*, commonly used of the plundering of cargo from a ship). The false teacher(s) in Colossae pose a very real threat to the church. **philosophy**. The Greek for this word includes the article (*tēs philosophias*), suggesting that the ringleaders of the faction called their teaching "the philosophy." When Paul speaks of "filling" and "fullness" in this letter (see v. 10), he is clearly echoing the jargon of the erring teachers, and he may be doing the same here. The term "philosophy" was used much more broadly in the ancient world than it is today. Josephus, for instance, could call the teachings of the Pharisees and Sadducees "philosophies." Even a magician could be called a philosopher. Paul is not making a blanket condemnation of the traditional Greek philosophical schools (e.g., Platonism, Stoicism, Aristotelianism, etc.). His remarks are focused on the particular factional teaching being disseminated at Colossae. He makes the incisive claim that this teaching is not only **empty deceit** but that it has been inspired by **the elemental spirits** (Gk. *stoicheia*) **of the world**. *Stoicheia* is sometimes translated "the basic principles" of the world and then interpreted to be something like the fundamental principles of pagan religion. In the ancient world, however, the term *stoicheia* was widely used for spirits in Persian religious texts, magical papyri, astrological documents, and some Jewish texts. Paul is likely using it here to refer to demonic spirits; it is the equivalent of "rulers and authorities" (vv. 10, 15). Although the false teaching is handed down as **human tradition**, it can ultimately be traced to the influence of demonic forces. The fundamental problem with this philosophy is that it is not in accord with Jesus Christ and the gospel proclaimed by him and the apostle Paul.

2:9–15 *Help for the Danger: Resources in Christ.* The Colossians have everything they need in Jesus Christ. Since they are forgiven of their sins by virtue of the cross of Christ and are already living a new life in him, they should not turn to anything or anyone else to "complete" their spiritual well-being.

2:9 in him the whole fullness of deity dwells bodily. Christ is the visible expression of God. In his incarnation and now in his glorification, Jesus is God in the flesh (cf. 1:15–20).

2:10 you have been filled in him. In this remarkable statement, Paul affirms that believers share in Christ's power and authority over every **rule**

in him, who is [u]the head of all rule and authority. 11 In him also [v]you were circumcised
with a circumcision made without hands, by [w]putting off the body of the flesh, by the
circumcision of Christ, 12 [x]having been buried with him in baptism, in which [y]you were
also raised with him through faith in [z]the powerful working of God, [z]who raised him
from the dead. 13 [a]And you, who were dead in your trespasses and the uncircumcision of
your flesh, God [b]made alive together with him, having forgiven us all our trespasses, 14 by
[c]canceling [d]the record of debt that stood against us with its legal demands. This he set
aside, nailing it to the cross. 15 [w]He disarmed the rulers and authorities[1] and [e]put them to
open shame, by [f]triumphing over them in him.[2]

Let No One Disqualify You

16 Therefore let no one [g]pass judgment on you [h]in questions of food and drink, or with
regard to [i]a festival or [j]a new moon or a Sabbath. 17 [k]These are a shadow of the things to
come, but [l]the substance belongs to Christ. 18 Let no one [m]disqualify you, [n]insisting on
asceticism and worship of angels, [o]going on in detail about visions,[3] [p]puffed up without
reason by [q]his sensuous mind, 19 and [r]not [s]holding fast to the Head, from whom the whole
body, nourished and knit together through its joints and ligaments, grows with a growth
that is from God.

20 If with Christ [t]you died to the [u]elemental spirits of the world, [v]why, as if you were still

[1] Probably demonic rulers and authorities [2] Or *in it* (that is, the cross) [3] Or *about the things he has seen*

10 [u]See Eph. 1:21, 22
11 [v][Eph. 2:11]; See Rom. 2:29 [w]ver. 15; ch. 3:9
12 [x]Rom. 6:4 [y]ch. 3:1; [Rom. 6:5] [z][1 Cor. 6:14]; See Acts 2:24; Eph. 1:19
13 [a]See Eph. 2:1 [b]See Eph. 2:5
14 [c]See Acts 3:19 [d]See Rom. 7:4
15 [w][See ver. 11 above] [e][Gen. 3:15; Ps. 68:18; Isa. 53:12; Matt. 12:29; Luke 10:18; John 12:31; 16:11; Eph. 4:8; Heb. 2:14] [f]Eph. 2:16
16 [g]Rom. 14:3, 10, 13 [h]Rom. 14:17; Heb. 9:10; See Lev. 11:2 [i]Lev. 23:2; Rom. 14:5 [j][Mark 2:28]; See Num. 28:11
17 [k]Heb. 8:5; 10:1 [l][ver. 2]
18 [m]1 Cor. 9:24 [n]ver. 23 [o][Ezek. 13:7; 1 Tim. 1:7] [p][Eph. 4:17] [q][Rom. 8:7]
19 [r]See Eph. 4:15, 16 [s]Rev. 2:13; 3:11
20 [t]See Rom. 6:2 [u]ver. 8 [v][Gal. 4:9]

and authority by virtue of their union with him. Here is the main theme of Colossians. The divine "fullness" is in Christ (v. 9), and believers are "filled in him." Hence, they have everything they need in Christ. They do not need any other teaching to become like God. The term **head** is clearly used here with the sense of "authority over" (see note on 1 Cor. 11:3). This would have been an encouraging and helpful teaching for the Colossians, who clearly continued to live in fear of the demonic realm.

2:11 In him also you were circumcised. Paul here uses circumcision metaphorically for a spiritual (**made without hands**) action, which he describes as **putting off the body of the flesh**. Believers no longer live in the sphere of the flesh and its influence (Gal. 5:24) but have been transferred to the kingdom of Christ and live through and in him, under his lordship (Col. 1:13). In this "circumcision" performed by Christ, Christians have been removed from their solidarity with Adam and his sin (see Rom. 6:6) and are now in solidarity with Christ and his righteousness and can live for him, as they before could not.

2:12–13 buried with him in baptism . . . also raised with him . . . made alive together with him. In a second metaphor drawn from Christ's work on the cross, Paul says that the Christian rite of baptism represents an identification with Christ in his death (cf. Rom. 6:4–6) along with an identification with Christ in his resurrection (cf. Eph. 2:6). Dying and rising with Christ signifies death to the power of sin and Satan plus empowerment to live the new life that Jesus calls believers to live in imitation of him (see Rom. 6:3–11).

2:14 the record of debt that stood against us. In the Greco-Roman world, the "record of debt" (Gk. *cheirographon*) was a written note of indebtedness. Paul uses this as a word picture to characterize each person's indebtedness to God because of sin. God himself has mercifully resolved this problem for all who put their faith in Jesus by taking this note and **nailing it to the cross**, where Jesus paid the debt. The image comes from the notice fastened to a cross by the Roman authorities, declaring the crime for which the criminal was being executed (see John 19:19–22).

2:15 He disarmed the rulers and authorities. The cross of Christ marks the decisive defeat of the demonic powers. On the cross, they were stripped of their power to accuse Christians before God. (Gk. *diabolos*, "devil," means "accuser, slanderer.") Nevertheless, these demons continue to exist and to exercise power to incite evil, so Christians must continue to struggle with them (see Eph. 6:12, 16). **put them to open shame**. This is the same term (Gk. *deigmatizō*) used in Matt. 1:19 to refer to Joseph's unwillingness to expose Mary's pregnancy and bring public shame on her. The cross publicly reveals the failure of the demonic powers to thwart God's plan of salvation through Christ (see 1 Cor. 2:6–8). **triumphing over them**. The image is of a triumphal Roman military procession. The defeated king with all of his surviving warriors and the spoils of war were paraded through the streets of Rome, as a public spectacle for all to see.

2:16–23 *Additional Warnings about the Teaching.* Apparently the false teachers advocated asceticism for spiritual growth. The true path to spiritual maturity is holding fast to Christ as the head, not following these misguided human rules.

2:16 food and drink . . . a festival or a new moon or a Sabbath. The false teacher(s) were advocating a number of Jewish observances, arguing that they were essential for spiritual advancement. On "new moon," see note on Num. 28:11–15.

2:17 a shadow of the things to come. The old covenant observances pointed to a future reality that was fulfilled in the Lord Jesus Christ (cf. Heb. 10:1). Hence, Christians are no longer under the Mosaic covenant (cf. Rom. 6:14–15; 7:1–6; 2 Cor. 3:4–18; Gal. 3:15–4:7). Christians are no longer obligated to observe OT dietary laws ("food and drink") or festivals, holidays, and special days ("a festival . . . new moon . . . Sabbath," Col. 2:16), for what these things foreshadowed has been fulfilled in Christ. It is debated whether the Sabbaths in question included the regular seventh-day rest of the fourth commandment, or were only the special Sabbaths of the Jewish festal calendar.

2:18 Paul lists a variety of ways the false teachers had tried to **disqualify** the genuine believers in Colossae. **Asceticism** translates the Greek word for "humility" (*tapeinophrosynē*). Paul probably had in mind fasting and perhaps also the taboos mentioned in v. 21. **Worship of angels** involves invoking angels for help and protection from evil spirits (see Introduction: Purpose, Occasion, and Background). The verb translated **going on in detail** (Gk. *embateuō*) is rare in Greek literature and difficult to interpret. The use of this word on a series of inscriptions found near Ephesus, however, has clarified its meaning here. It denoted the higher stage of mystery cult initiation that involved "entering" the innermost sanctuary of the pagan temple. The term suggests that the leader of the Colossian faction may be basing part of his teaching on spiritual experiences he gained in a pagan ritual initiation, thus showing the syncretistic nature of his false teaching. **about visions**. Some form of visionary experience and, thus, mystical insight was offered as part of the false teaching.

2:19 not holding fast to the Head. The fundamental problem with the competing teacher at Colossae is that he has not maintained contact with Christ and has thus become influenced by evil spirits (see v. 8). As the head of the body, Christ not only provides leadership but is also a source of provision for every member of the body (**its joints and ligaments**) so that it grows and matures (see note on 1 Cor. 11:3). On the church as a body, see Rom. 12:5–8; 1 Corinthians 12; Eph. 4:4, 12–16.

2:20 the elemental spirits. See note on v. 8.

alive in the world, do you submit to regulations— 21 [w]"Do not handle, Do not taste, Do
not touch" 22 ([x]referring to things that all perish as they are used)—according to [y]human
precepts and teachings? 23 These have indeed an appearance of wisdom in [z]promoting
self-made religion and asceticism and severity to the body, but they are [a]of no value in
stopping the indulgence of the flesh.

Put On the New Self

3 [b]If then you have been raised with Christ, seek [c]the things that are above, where Christ
is, [d]seated at the right hand of God. 2 [e]Set your minds on things that are above, not on
things that are on earth. 3 For [f]you have died, and your life is hidden with Christ in God.
4 When Christ [g]who is your[1] life [h]appears, then you also will appear with him [i]in glory.
5 [j]Put to death therefore [k]what is earthly in you:[2] [l]sexual immorality, impurity, [m]pas-
sion, evil desire, and covetousness, [n]which is idolatry. 6 [o]On account of these the wrath of
God is coming.[3] 7 [p]In these you too once walked, when you were living in them. 8 But now
[q]you must put them all away: [r]anger, wrath, malice, [s]slander, and obscene talk from your
mouth. 9 [t]Do not lie to one another, seeing that [u]you have put off [v]the old self[4] with its
practices 10 and [w]have put on [x]the new self, [y]which is being renewed in knowledge [z]after the
image of [a]its creator. 11 [b]Here there is not Greek and Jew, circumcised and uncircumcised,
barbarian, Scythian, slave,[5] free; but Christ is [c]all, and in all.
12 [d]Put on then, as [e]God's chosen ones, holy and beloved, [f]compassionate hearts, [g]kindness,
[h]humility, meekness, and patience, 13 [h]bearing with one another and, [i]if one has a complaint

[1] Some manuscripts *our* [2] Greek *therefore your members that are on the earth* [3] Some manuscripts add *upon the sons of disobedience* [4] Greek *man*; also as supplied in verse 10 [5] Greek *bondservant*

21 [w]ver. 16; 1 Tim. 4:3
22 [x]1 Cor. 6:13 [y]Isa. 29:13; Matt. 15:9; [Titus 1:14]
23 [z]ver. 18 [a][1 Tim. 4:8]

Chapter 3

1 [b]ch. 2:12 [c][Phil. 3:14] [d]See Eph. 1:20
2 [e]See Matt. 16:23
3 [f]ch. 2:20; See Rom. 6:2
4 [g]See John 11:25 [h][Phil. 3:21; 1 Pet. 1:1, 7, 13; 1 John 2:28; 3:2] [i]1 Cor. 15:43
5 [j]Rom. 8:13; [Gal. 5:24] [k]Rom. 6:13 [l]See Eph. 5:3, 5 [m]Rom. 1:26 [n][Job 31:25, 26]
6 [o]See Eph. 5:6
7 [p]See Eph. 2:2, 11
8 [q]See Eph. 4:22 [r]Eph. 4:31 [s]See Eph. 4:29
9 [t]Lev. 19:11; See Eph. 4:25 [u]ch. 2:11 [v]Rom. 6:6; Eph. 4:22
10 [w]Eph. 4:24 [x]See Rom. 6:4 [y]See Rom. 12:2 [z]See Rom. 8:29 [a][Eph. 2:10]
11 [b][Rom. 10:12]; See 1 Cor. 12:13; Gal. 5:6 [c]Eph. 1:23
12 [d]ver. 10 [e]Rom. 8:33 [f]Phil. 2:1 [g]Eph. 4:32 [h]See Eph. 4:2
13 [h][See ver. 12 above] [i]Mark 11:25

2:21 "Do not handle, Do not taste, Do not touch." Quotation marks are used here to indicate that these are specific taboos, which the teacher of the false philosophy is insisting the Colossians must obey. These rules are not divine but human, for the food a person eats is not crucial in his or her spiritual life (cf. Mark 7:18–19).

2:23 an appearance of wisdom. The ringleader of the faction in Colossae was advocating an esoteric wisdom for daily life that would allegedly help the Colossians deal with evil spirits and cope with life's circumstances. **self-made religion.** The Greek word (*ethelothrēskia*) could also be translated "voluntary worship," which may allude to the fact that the false teacher was stressing the Colossians' freedom to choose this syncretistic path contrary to apostolic tradition. **severity to the body.** This refers to the fasting and taboos that were part of the ascetic behavior advocated by "the philosophy." It may have gone beyond this, however, to include forms of self-mutilation similar to what was practiced in some of the local cults. Such asceticism may appear to be spiritual, but it actually promotes nothing more than confidence in self rather than in Christ.

3:1–4 *The Proper Focus: Christ and the Life Above.* This pivotal section marks an end to Paul's polemic against the false teacher and is a bridge to his appeals for the Colossians to live in a manner pleasing to the Lord.

3:1–2 raised with Christ. See 2:13–14. **Set your minds on things that are above** contrasts with the **things that are on earth** and refers to pursuing a deeper knowledge of Christ himself (Phil. 3:10) and all that belongs to living with and for him. This would include seeking first his kingdom (Matt. 6:33) and living a life worthy of his name (Col. 1:10; 2:6). Christ is presently **seated at the right hand of God** (Ps. 110:1; Eph. 1:20) in a position of authority where he can make intercession with the Father. The false teacher may have claimed to have heavenly secrets, but Paul dismisses his theology as earthly.

3:3 your life is hidden with Christ in God. Paul uses the language of Isaiah and the Psalms to express the security of the people of God as they trust in him (Isa. 49:2; Ps. 27:5–6; 31:19–20).

3:4 The centrality of Christ in Colossians blazes into view again. Believers know that **Christ** is their **life**. Perfection in glory will be theirs when Christ returns (when they **appear with him in glory**).

3:5–4:6 *Instructions on Living the Christian Life.* Based on their death and resurrection with Christ and the hope of a future life with him, Paul encourages the Colossians to continue eliminating sinful behaviors from their lives and cultivating Christian virtues.

3:5–11 *Dealing with the Sins of the Past.* Paul calls the Colossians to make a decisive break with the sinful tendencies they have carried with them into their Christian lives.

3:5 Put to death. Because believers have died with Christ (2:20; 3:3), they can get rid of sinful practices (Rom. 6:11; 8:13). The language of putting to death indicates that Christians have to take severe measures to conquer sin. Watchfulness and prayerfulness against it will be the first steps (see Matt. 26:41), with self-discipline following (Matt. 5:29–30). **Sexual immorality** (Gk. *porneia*) refers to every kind of sexual activity outside of marriage. Five of the items that Paul lists have to do with sexual purity, stressing the importance of bringing this area of life under the control and lordship of Christ. **which is idolatry.** Greed, sexual sin, and other vices can intrude into one's relationship with God, taking his place as a focus of devotion.

3:6 the wrath of God is coming. In line with the OT prophets, who spoke of the day of the Lord as a time of coming wrath (e.g., Zeph. 1:14–15), Paul reminds the Colossians that God will suddenly intervene in human history and will hold everyone accountable. Those who live evil lives will face final judgment.

3:8 put them all away. Paul lists five more vices (cf. v. 5) that Christians need to get rid of. These five all have a bearing on social relationships among believers.

3:9–10 seeing that you have put off the old self . . . and have put on the new self. (On "self" as a rendering of "man" [ESV footnote], see note on Eph. 4:22.) Paul picks up here what he has said earlier about Christ circumcising Christians by removing "the body of the flesh" (see Col. 2:11). Here he employs the metaphor of "taking off" and "putting on" clothing. The aorist tense of the two participles suggests that it is an event that has already taken place. A qualitative change of identity has already occurred in the lives of believers. It now only remains for them to bring their behavior into line with their new identity (see also Rom. 6:6; Eph. 4:24). **Being renewed** (present tense) indicates that the transformation of Christians is an ongoing process.

3:11 Here there is not Greek and Jew. There are no status distinctions among the new covenant people of God (cf. Gal. 3:28). No one has a special claim on God or is treated with less dignity than any other. **Scythian.** This was a people group located along the northern coast of the Black Sea. To the Greeks, the Scythians were a violent, uneducated, uncivilized, and altogether inferior people. In contrast to such discrimination and prejudice against other

against another, [g]forgiving each other; [g]as the Lord has forgiven you, so you also must forgive.
14 And above all these put on [j]love, which [k]binds everything together in [l]perfect harmony.
15 And let [m]the peace of Christ rule in your hearts, to which indeed you were called [n]in one
body. And [o]be thankful. 16 Let [p]the word of Christ dwell in you richly, teaching and admonishing one another in all wisdom, [q]singing psalms and hymns and spiritual songs, [r]with
thankfulness in your hearts to God. 17 And [s]whatever you do, in word or deed, do everything
in the name of the Lord Jesus, [t]giving thanks to God the Father through him.

Rules for Christian Households

18 [u]Wives, submit to your husbands, as [v]is fitting in the Lord. 19 Husbands, love your wives,
and [w]do not be harsh with them. 20 Children, obey your parents [x]in everything, for this
pleases the Lord. 21 Fathers, do not provoke your children, lest they become discouraged.
22 Bondservants,[1] obey [x]in everything those who are your earthly masters,[2] not by way of
eye-service, as people-pleasers, but with sincerity of heart, fearing the Lord. 23 [y]Whatever
you do, work heartily, [z]as for the Lord and not for men, 24 knowing that from the Lord
[a]you will receive the inheritance as your reward. [b]You are serving the Lord Christ. 25 For
the wrongdoer will be paid back for the wrong he has done, and there is no partiality.

4 Masters, treat your bondservants justly and fairly, knowing that you also have a Master
in heaven.

Further Instructions

2 [c]Continue steadfastly in prayer, being watchful in it [d]with thanksgiving. 3 At the same
time, pray also for us, that God may [e]open to us a door for the word, [f]to declare the mystery

[1] Or *Slaves*; also 4:1 (for the contextual rendering of the Greek word *doulos*, see Preface) [2] Or *your masters according to the flesh*

13 [g][See ver. 12 above]
14 [j][1 Thess. 5:8]; See Eph. 5:2 [k]Eph. 4:3 [l]Heb. 6:1; [John 17:23]
15 [m]See Phil. 4:7 [n]Eph. 2:16 [o]ver. 17
16 [p]John 15:3 [q]See Eph. 5:19 [r]ch. 4:6
17 [s]ver. 23; 1 Cor. 10:31 [t]ch. 1:12; 4:2; See Eph. 5:20
18 [u]For ch. 3:18–4:1, see Eph. 5:22–6:9 [v]Eph. 5:4; Philem. 8
19 [w]Eph. 4:31
20 [x][Eph. 5:24; Titus 2:9]
22 [x][See ver. 20 above]
23 [y]ver. 17 [z][Philem. 16]
24 [a][Eph. 6:8]
24 [b][1 Cor. 7:22]

Chapter 4

2 [c]For ver. 2-4, see Eph. 6:18-20 [d]ch. 2:7
3 [e]See Acts 14:27 [f]See Rom. 16:25

races and cultures, Paul shows that Jesus, who **is all, and in all**, binds all Christians together in equality, irrespective of such differences.

3:12–17 *Putting on the Virtues of Christ.* Paul calls the Colossians to a holy lifestyle, consistent with their new identity. Believers have been chosen by God and stand before him as his beloved holy ones. They are to live up to what they are in Christ.

3:13 bearing with one another. Tolerance is a virtue within the Christian community, although Paul clearly does not want the Colossians to tolerate the false teaching. **forgiving each other . . . as the Lord has forgiven you**. When wronged and betrayed, Christians are called to forgive others, even as they have been forgiven for their betrayal of Christ. See Matt. 6:12, 14–15; 18:21–22.

3:14 Above all else, Christians are called on to **love** one another (see 1 Corinthians 13). **Binds . . . together** may suggest that love unites all the virtues.

3:16 The word of Christ probably refers to the teaching about Christ as well as the words of Christ himself, which were part of the oral traditions passed on to believers in the early years after Christ ascended to heaven, before the Gospels had been written. **Psalms and hymns and spiritual songs** (see note on Eph. 5:19) is one means of **teaching and admonishing**. Corporate worship has a teaching function through the lyrics of its songs. This was particularly important in the oral culture of Paul's day.

3:17 in the name of the Lord Jesus, giving thanks to God the Father. The centrality of Christ does not diminish the Father but brings him glory.

3:18–4:1 *Living in the Christian Household.* Paul gives instructions for the various members of a Christian household. He addresses wives and husbands, children and fathers, and slaves (or bondservants) and masters. Significantly, he addresses the women, children, and slaves (or bondservants) directly as equal members of the Christian household, and he addresses each of them first in their respective sections. Cf. Eph. 5:22–6:9. On the Gk. word *doulos*, see the ESV Preface, p. 21.

3:18 Wives, submit to your husbands. Instead of telling wives to "obey" (Gk. *hypakouō*), as was typical in Roman households, Paul appeals to them to "submit" (Gk. *hypotassō*), based on his conviction that men have a God-given leadership role in the family. The term suggests an ordering of society in which wives should align themselves with and respect the leadership of their husbands (see Eph. 5:22–33). Paul is not enjoining the wives to follow the prevailing cultural patterns of the day but to live **as is fitting in the Lord**. Seven times in these nine verses (Col. 3:18–4:1) Paul roots his instructions in "the Lord" or an equivalent term, thus stressing the importance of evaluating everything in light of Christ and his teaching.

3:19 do not be harsh with them. There was a tendency in the Roman world for men to rage bitterly against their wives and mistreat them. Because of their greater strength and louder voices, men in their sinful natures are prone to use harsh words, threats, unkindness, and even physical violence to intimidate their wives. There is no room for even a hint of this in a Christian home; instead, men are called to **love** their wives as Christ loved the church (Eph. 5:25).

3:20 Paul's words to children reflect the fifth commandment (Ex. 20:12).

3:21 do not provoke your children. Men are urged to restrain their anger and any other attitudes that can embitter their children (cf. Eph. 6:4), lest they despair of pleasing their parents.

3:22–25 Bondservants, obey in everything those who are your earthly masters. The relationships between husbands and wives and parents and children are ordained by God from creation. Hence, Paul's instructions on marriage represent the perfect will of God. On the other hand, the kind of servitude practiced in the first century was seldom in keeping with God's will; the Scriptures regulate the institution without commending it (see notes on 1 Cor. 7:21; Eph. 6:5; 1 Tim. 1:10), and the evil of trafficking in human beings is condemned in the NT (1 Tim. 1:10; cf. Rev. 18:11–13). As in any other city or village in the Roman world, there would have been many slaves (or bondservants) at Colossae; Paul treats them with dignity and appeals to them directly to honor Christ in their hearts, work, and behavior. Philemon (see the book of Philemon) was a wealthy Colossian who benefited from the labors of his bondservant, Onesimus. Slaves (or bondservants) should **work heartily**, not primarily to please their earthly masters but as if they were working **for the Lord**. The principles of Col. 3:22–4:1 apply to employers and employees today.

4:1 treat your bondservants justly and fairly. Paul does not condone the Roman system of servitude but instead provides instructions to believing masters and slaves (or bondservants) regarding their relationship to each other in the Lord. Such instruction clearly sows the seeds for the eventual dismantling of this unjust socioeconomic structure (see note on Eph. 6:5). On the Gk. word *doulos*, see the ESV Preface, p. 21.

4:2–4 *Persistence in Prayer.* Paul calls all Christians to a lifestyle of constant prayer.

4:2 being watchful in it. Jesus likewise admonished his disciples to "watch and pray" (Mark 14:38) so that they would not fall into temptation. **Thanksgiving** leavens prayer, so that it does not become merely a selfish pleading to have one's desires fulfilled (cf. James 4:1–3).

4:3–4 that God may open to us a door for the word. In spite of his imprisonment and difficult circumstances, Paul asks the Colossians to pray

of Christ, [g]on account of which I am in prison— 4 that I may make it clear, which is how
I ought to speak.
5 [h]Walk in wisdom toward [i]outsiders, making the best use of the time. 6 Let your speech
always [j]be gracious, [k]seasoned with salt, [l]so that you may know how you ought to answer
each person.

Final Greetings

7 Tychicus will tell you [m]all about my activities. He is a beloved brother and faithful
minister and fellow servant[1] in the Lord. 8 I have sent him to you for this very purpose,
that you may know how we are and that he may encourage your hearts, 9 and with him
[n]Onesimus, our faithful and [o]beloved brother, who is one of you. They will tell you of
everything that has taken place here.
10 [p]Aristarchus my fellow prisoner greets you, and Mark [q]the cousin of Barnabas (concerning whom you have received instructions—[r]if he comes to you, welcome him), 11 and
Jesus who is called [s]Justus. [t]These are the only men of the circumcision among my fellow
workers for the kingdom of God, and [u]they have been a comfort to me. 12 [v]Epaphras, who
is one of you, a servant of Christ Jesus, greets you, always [w]struggling on your behalf in his
prayers, that you may stand [x]mature and fully assured in all the will of God. 13 For I bear
him witness that he has worked hard for you and for those in Laodicea and in Hierapolis.
14 [y]Luke the beloved physician greets you, as does [z]Demas. 15 Give my greetings to the
brothers[2] at Laodicea, and to Nympha and [a]the church in her house. 16 And when [b]this
letter has been read among you, have it also read in the church of the Laodiceans; and see
that you also read the letter from Laodicea. 17 And say to [c]Archippus, "See that you fulfill
[d]the ministry that you have received in the Lord."
18 I, Paul, [e]write this greeting with my own hand. [f]Remember [g]my chains. [h]Grace be
with you.

[1] Greek *fellow bondservant;* also verse 12 [2] Or *brothers and sisters*

3 [g]ver. 18; Eph. 6:20; See Phil. 1:7
5 [h]See Eph. 5:15-17 [i]See Mark 4:11
6 [j]ch. 3:16 [k]See Mark 9:50 [l]1 Pet. 3:15
7 [m]For ver. 7-9, see Eph. 6:21, 22
9 [n]Philem. 10 [o]Philem. 16
10 [p]Acts 19:29; 20:4; 27:2; Philem. 24; [Rom. 16:7] [q]See Acts 15:37, 39 [r][2 Tim. 4:11]
11 [s][Acts 1:23; 18:7] [t]See Acts 11:2 [u][Philem. 7]
12 [v]ch. 1:7; Philem. 23 [w]See Rom. 15:30 [x]See Matt. 5:48
14 [y]2 Tim. 4:11; See Acts 16:10 [z]2 Tim. 4:10; Philem. 24
15 [a]See Rom. 16:5
16 [b]1 Thess. 5:27
17 [c]Philem. 2 [d]2 Tim. 4:5
18 [e]See 1 Cor. 16:21 [f][Heb. 13:3] [g]ver. 3; See Phil. 1:7 [h]1 Tim. 6:21; 2 Tim. 4:22; [Titus 3:15]

that he will have opportunities to share the good news of Jesus Christ (Eph. 6:18–20; 2 Thess. 3:1). Christians should pray for missionaries and church leaders around the world. **to declare the mystery**. See note on Col. 1:26–27.

4:5–6 *Good Behavior toward Those Outside the Community.* Paul encourages the Colossians to manifest a powerful and attractive testimony to non-Christians. **seasoned with salt**. This statement echoes the teaching of Jesus when he called his disciples to be "the salt of the earth" (Matt. 5:13). When applied to conversation, the metaphor suggests speaking in an interesting, stimulating, and wise way. Paul's comments assume that the Colossian believers are vitally involved in the local community and have ample opportunities to interact with **outsiders** in a way that would commend the gospel to them.

4:7–17 *Personal Greetings and Instructions.* After commending the "letter carriers" to the Colossians, Paul extends greetings to this church from the ministry associates who are with him during his imprisonment.

4:7–9 *Remarks about the Messengers Carrying the Letter.*

4:7–8 Tychicus was a native of Asia Minor who became a Christian and a member of Paul's ministry team (Acts 20:4). He will carry this letter (as well as Ephesians and Philemon; see Eph. 6:21–22; and Introduction to Philemon: Date) and bring them news about Paul and his situation.

4:9 Onesimus. This was Philemon's converted bondservant (see notes on Philemon).

4:10–14 *Greetings from Paul's Associates.*

4:10–11 Mark the cousin of Barnabas. This is the same person as "John Mark," who accompanied Paul on his first missionary journey and suddenly departed (Acts 13:13) and over whom Paul and Barnabas had a sharp disagreement (Acts 15:39). Paul's perspective on Mark has decidedly changed (probably corresponding to a change in Mark himself). Now Mark has been reconciled to Paul and is ministering to him and on his behalf. The five people mentioned here are the same five that Paul mentions in Philemon, with the exception of **Jesus who is called Justus**, about whom nothing else is known. The last three are identified as **men of the circumcision**, indicating that they are Jewish Christians.

4:12–13 Epaphras. See note on 1:7. Epaphras's love and prayer for the Colossians and Christians in nearby cities is an example for all believers.

4:13 in Laodicea and in Hierapolis. These were neighboring towns to Colossae in the Lycus Valley (on Laodicea, see 2:1; Rev. 3:14). Hierapolis (modern Pamukkale) boasts a large mineral spring, famous also in Paul's day. However, much of what visitors see today dates from the rebuilding and expansion that occurred under Domitian (A.D. 81–96) and later. Hierapolis was known for the worship of Apollo, Leto, and Pluto; yet inscriptions in the ancient cemetery also point to a Jewish presence.

4:14 Luke the beloved physician is the same Luke who authored Luke's Gospel and Acts (see also 2 Tim. 4:11; Philem. 24). He accompanied Paul on some of his journeys (see Introduction to Acts: Author and Title) and was apparently with Paul throughout his two-year imprisonment in Caesarea and then in his two-year Roman imprisonment. Since Luke is not identified among "the only men of the circumcision" (Col. 4:9–11), he was probably a Gentile. Lamentably, **Demas** later followed worldly pursuits and deserted Paul (2 Tim. 4:10).

4:15–17 *Greetings to the Christians in Laodicea.*

4:15 Nympha and the church in her house. On house churches, see note on 1 Cor. 16:19.

4:16 when this letter has been read among you. Public reading in the churches points to the authority of Paul's letters and also assumes that they were written to be understood by ordinary believers. **the letter from Laodicea**. Although some have thought this might be a reference to Ephesians (understood to be a circular letter, with Laodicea as one of its destinations) or a letter from the Laodiceans to Paul, it is probably best to take it as a reference to a letter Paul wrote to Laodicea that is now lost.

4:17 Archippus may have been the son of Philemon and Apphia (see Philem. 2).

4:18 *Letter Closing.* Paul ends his letter by asking the Colossian Christians to remember him before the Lord. **I, Paul, write this greeting with my own hand**. If Timothy has so far been functioning as Paul's secretary to whom he dictates the letter (see 1:1), Paul now takes the stylus and signs the letter personally (cf. 1 Cor. 16:21; 2 Thess. 3:17).

INTRODUCTION TO

THE FIRST LETTER OF PAUL TO THE THESSALONIANS

1 THESSALONIANS

Author and Title

Paul is widely regarded as the author of 1 Thessalonians, as evidenced by how compatible the vocabulary, style, and theology are with his other letters. The mention of Silas ("Silvanus") and Timothy as co-senders (1:1) may indicate Paul's care to present the missionaries as a united band in order to offset any Thessalonian disappointment that Paul had not come to visit them again but had sent Timothy instead (see 2:17–18; 3:1–2, 6, 11).

Date

Most scholars today date 1 Thessalonians to A.D. 49–51, early in Paul's 18-month stay in Corinth during his second missionary journey (Acts 18:1–18). Only a small minority of scholars, who do not regard Acts as historically dependable, place it in the early 40s A.D. The Delphi Inscription—a letter from the emperor Claudius to the city of Delphi—dates Gallio's proconsulship of Achaia to A.D. 51–52, and Acts 18:12–17 mentions Gallio, toward the end of Paul's Corinthian stay.

Theme

The most prominent theme in 1 Thessalonians is the second coming of Jesus. It is mentioned in every chapter of the book (1:10; 2:19–20; 3:13; 4:13–18; 5:1–11, 23–24). At Jesus' future coming, the dead in Christ will rise and will be caught up along with the living to meet the Lord in the air (4:15–17). Unbelievers will be subject to his wrath, but Christians will be delivered from this, inheriting salvation instead (1:10; 5:2–4, 9–10). Those who are destined to participate as saints (lit., "holy ones") in the second coming must be holy and blameless (3:11–4:8; 5:23), and God, who is faithful, will produce holiness in the lives of those whom he calls (5:24).

Purpose, Occasion, and Background

Thessalonica was the proud capital of the Roman province of Macedonia and had a population of over 100,000. Its natural harbor and placement on the busy east-west Egnatian Way as well as key north-south trade routes meant that it was a flourishing center of trade and philosophy. It was a free city and was governed by local officials called "politarchs" (cf. Acts 17:6, 8). Religiously, the city was committed to the Greco-Roman pantheon and the imperial cult; Egyptian cults were also prominent. There was a sizable population of Jews in Thessalonica (Acts 17:5).

Paul, Timothy, and Silas preached in the Thessalonian synagogue over three Sabbaths, and a number of Jews and God-fearing Gentiles believed (Acts 17:4). First Thessalonians 1:9–10 suggests that Paul subsequently spent some weeks ministering fruitfully to pagan Gentiles. However, rioters instigated by Jewish opponents dragged Jason (Paul's host) and some other Christians before the politarchs and charged them with sedition against Caesar (Acts 17:5–8), forcing the missionaries to leave Thessalonica prematurely (Acts 17:9–10). Paul was concerned for the new Christians, and therefore a few months later he sent Timothy back to Thessalonica (1 Thess. 3:1–2, 5; see note on Acts 17:15). Catching up with Paul in Corinth (Acts 18:5), Timothy updated him on the Thessalonian church (1 Thess. 3:6).

Timothy reported that generally the church community was doing well. However, not everything at Thessalonica was rosy. Some members of the church had died (4:13), and because they were not fully informed about what would happen to deceased Christians at Christ's return (3:10; 4:13), some apparently thought that those who had died would miss out on the second coming, and they had plunged into hopeless grieving for them (4:13).

In addition, Timothy related to Paul a Thessalonian question about *the timing of the day of the Lord* (5:1–2). A number of scholars believe that the query reflected restless impatience or a false sense of security, but this view is countered by Paul's repeated assurances in 5:4–5, 9, along with the lack of threat or warning in 5:1–11. Paul reassures the Thessalonians that they are destined not for wrath but for salvation on the day of the Lord. Some think that the Thessalonians were concerned that they would be unprepared for Jesus' return, but 4:3–8 suggests that they were not concerned *enough* about holy living. Perhaps the simplest explanation is that these new Christians were questioning their own final salvation in view of the recent unexpected deaths (4:13). They may even have wondered whether the deaths were an expression of divine disapproval.

Whatever the specifics, clearly the Thessalonians needed reassurance about those who had died (4:13–18) and about their own destiny at the second coming (5:1–11).

The Thessalonians seem to have been vulnerable in other ways too. They had not expected the initial persecution to continue unabated for so long (3:3–4; cf. 2 Thess. 1:5–7). Moreover, they missed Paul, apparently disappointed that he himself had not yet returned to see them (1 Thess. 3:6–10).

Yet another problem in Thessalonica demanded Paul's attention: some Christians were bringing the church into disrepute by depending on wealthier Christians to provide for them rather than earning their own living (4:10b–12; 5:14; cf. 2 Thess. 3:6–15). It is possible that this problem was a result of the Thessalonians' erroneous thinking about the future. However, it may simply be that some church members were selfishly and lazily exploiting the charity of wealthier members to avoid having to work.

When Paul heard Timothy's generally positive report, he was filled with joyful relief and was eager to encourage the embattled and discouraged Christians and to answer their questions. So he immediately began composing 1 Thessalonians (1 Thess. 3:6–8). Paul's main purpose was to repair the hope of the Thessalonian Christians in the wake of the unexpected deaths of people in their congregation and to reassure them that both the dead and the living were destined to be saved at the second coming (4:13–5:11). Related to this was his desire to reassure the Thessalonians that they were among those elected by God for salvation (1:4; 5:24).

Paul also wished to underline the missionaries' authenticity as preachers of the gospel of God (1:5; 2:1–12; 2:17–3:10) in the face of real or potential questions relating to his lengthy absence (2:17–3:10), the unrelenting persecution (3:3–4), and the unexpected deaths (4:13). Paul also sought to encourage the Thessalonians by explaining that persecution is normal for the Christian (3:3–4). In addition, Paul is calling the recently converted, predominantly pagan community to sexual holiness (4:3–8) and the idle members of the community to gainful employment (4:9–12).

It also seems that Paul is seeking to undo their heavy dependence on him by urging the church to respect and defer to its own ministers (5:12–13). This can be seen in his forbidding the despising of prophesying

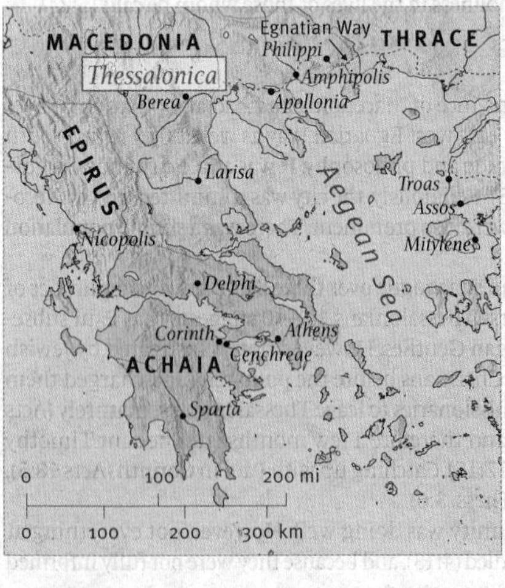

The Setting of 1 Thessalonians

c. A.D. 49–51

Paul wrote 1 Thessalonians from Corinth near the end of his second missionary journey. Paul and his companions had established the church in Thessalonica but were forced to leave by opponents of the gospel. Later, Paul sent Timothy back to Thessalonica to check on the church there, and Timothy's report led Paul to write this letter. Thessalonica enjoyed privileged status as the capital of Macedonia and was located on a natural harbor along the busy east-west Egnatian Way.

(5:19–22), his emphasizing Timothy's credentials (3:2), and his presenting the missionaries as a team (hence the use of the first person plural through much of the letter).

History of Salvation Summary

Christians should look back on the accomplished salvation of Christ, which fulfills OT promises, and look forward to the second coming, which consummates the promises. (For an explanation of the "History of Salvation," see the Overview of the Bible, pp. 23–26.)

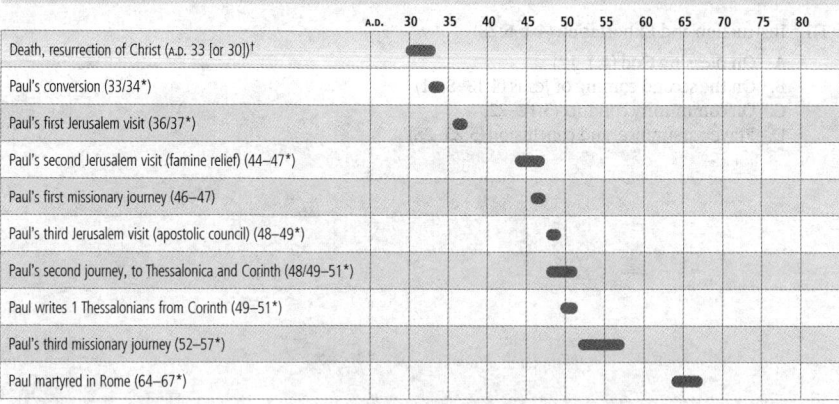

Timeline

Event (A.D. 30–80)
Death, resurrection of Christ (A.D. 33 [or 30])†
Paul's conversion (33/34*)
Paul's first Jerusalem visit (36/37*)
Paul's second Jerusalem visit (famine relief) (44–47*)
Paul's first missionary journey (46–47)
Paul's third Jerusalem visit (apostolic council) (48–49*)
Paul's second journey, to Thessalonica and Corinth (48/49–51*)
Paul writes 1 Thessalonians from Corinth (49–51*)
Paul's third missionary journey (52–57*)
Paul martyred in Rome (64–67*)

** denotes approximate date; / signifies either/or; † see The Date of Jesus' Crucifixion, pp. 1809–1810*

Key Themes

1. The wrath of God comes on those who reject the gospel.	2:16; 5:3
2. Jesus' death and resurrection are the basis for the Christian's hope.	4:14; 5:10
3. Christians are destined not for wrath but for salvation at Jesus' coming.	1:10; 5:4, 9
4. Christians who die will participate fully in the second coming.	4:14–17; 5:10
5. Those who respond to the gospel have been elected by God in prehistory and called by God, and they continue to be called by God throughout their earthly lives.	1:4; 2:12; 4:7; 5:9, 24
6. Christians should live lives of comprehensive holiness.	3:13; 4:3–8; 5:23
7. Christians must never shirk their responsibility to work.	4:9–12; 5:14
8. The authenticity of the gospel is confirmed by the integrity of its preachers.	1:5; 2:1–12
9. Joy, especially in suffering, is a mark of the Christian.	1:6; 5:16
10. Christians experience the realities of the prophesied new covenant.	4:8–9
11. Faith, hope, and love are essential and universal traits of the Christian.	1:2–3; 5:8

Literary Features

First Thessalonians is an informal epistle that contains all of the usual ingredients of NT epistles. It is a public letter in the sense of being addressed to a whole group, but at many points it reads more like a personal letter to an individual, as it highlights the relationship between author and recipients. The purpose of letters is usually to inform, and this letter informs the Thessalonian church about Paul's feelings toward them, events in his own life, and Christian doctrine and practice.

Distinguishing literary features include: a strong apologetic and autobiographical element; exuberant expressions of thanksgiving for people who are living the Christian life correctly; repeated direct addresses to the recipients of the letter; extended teaching on the second coming of Christ, so that even some of the moral exhortations are related to that doctrine; and the conclusion of each chapter with a reference to Christ's second coming.

Outline

I. Opening (1:1)

II. Thanksgiving and Encouragement (1:2–3:13)
   A. Thanksgiving for the Thessalonians' faith, love, and hope (1:2–3)
   B. Paul's confidence in the election of the Thessalonians (1:4–2:16)
   C. Paul's defense of the missionaries during their absence (2:17–3:10)
   D. A pastoral prayer for the Thessalonians (3:11–13)

III. Instruction and Exhortation (4:1–5:28)
   A. On pleasing God (4:1–12)
   B. On the second coming of Jesus (4:13–5:11)
   C. On community conduct (5:12–22)
   D. Prayer, assurance, and conclusion (5:23–28)

THE FIRST LETTER OF PAUL TO THE THESSALONIANS

1 THESSALONIANS

Chapter 1

1 [a]Acts 15:22; 2 Cor. 1:19; 2 Thess. 1:1; 1 Pet. 5:12 [b]See Acts 17:1 [c]Rom. 1:7
2 [d]ch. 2:13; See Rom. 1:8; Eph. 5:20 [e]Rom. 1:9; 2 Tim. 1:3
3 [f]See Gal. 1:4 [g]2 Thess. 1:11; [John 6:29; Gal. 5:6; Heb. 6:10; James 2:22] [h]2 Thess. 1:3, 4; [Col. 1:4; 1 Tim. 1:14; Rev. 2:19] [i]Rom. 8:25; 15:4
4 [j]2 Thess. 2:13 [k]2 Pet. 1:10
5 [l]2 Thess. 2:14 [m]2 Cor. 6:6; See 1 Cor. 2:4 [n]Col. 2:2; [Heb. 2:3] [o][ch. 2:10; Acts 20:18; 2 Thess. 3:7]
6 [p][ch. 2:14; 2 Thess. 3:7, 9]; See 1 Cor. 4:16 [q]1 Cor. 11:1 [r]Acts 17:5-10 [s]See Matt. 5:12 [t]Acts 13:52; Gal. 5:22

Greeting

1 Paul, [a]Silvanus, and Timothy,
To the church of the [b]Thessalonians in God the Father and the Lord Jesus Christ:
[c]Grace to you and peace.

The Thessalonians' Faith and Example

2 [d]We give thanks to God always for all of you, constantly[1] [e]mentioning you in our
prayers, 3 remembering before [f]our God and Father [g]your work of faith and labor of [h]love
and [i]steadfastness of hope in our Lord Jesus Christ. 4 For we know, [j]brothers[2] loved by God,
[k]that he has chosen you, 5 because [l]our gospel came to you not only in word, but also in
power and [m]in the Holy Spirit and with full [n]conviction. You know [o]what kind of men we
proved to be among you for your sake. 6 And [p]you became imitators of us [q]and of the Lord,
for [r]you received the word in much affliction, [s]with the [t]joy of the Holy Spirit, 7 so that
you became an example to all the believers in Macedonia and in Achaia. 8 For not only has
the word of the Lord [u]sounded forth from you in Macedonia and Achaia, but your faith in

[1] Or *without ceasing* [2] Or *brothers and sisters*. The plural Greek word *adelphoi* (translated "brothers") refers to siblings in a family. In New Testament usage, depending on the context, *adelphoi* may refer either to men or to both men and women who are siblings (brothers and sisters) in God's family, the church

8 [u][Rom. 10:18; 2 Thess. 3:1]

1:1 *Opening.* **Paul** makes no mention of his apostolic status, perhaps because there are no false teachers challenging it within the Thessalonian church. **Silvanus** and **Timothy** were coworkers with Paul during his second missionary journey. Silvanus, or Silas, was a Judean Christian (Acts 15:22) who joined Paul after he separated from Barnabas (Acts 15:39–40). Timothy, of Lystra in south Galatia, was a son of a Jewish mother and Greek father and became partners with Paul when Paul passed through his hometown early on his second journey (see Acts 16:1–4; Introduction to 1 Timothy). Timothy had just returned from a visit to the Thessalonian church (1 Thess. 3:6), and his report is Paul's major source of information as he writes. While Silas and Timothy are included as co-senders, Paul was clearly the main author (see 2:18; 3:5; 5:27). **in God the Father and the Lord Jesus Christ**. Believers enjoy a mysterious union with both the Father and the Son and hence are supremely secure and safe from spiritual harm. **Grace . . . and peace**. See note on Rom. 1:7.

1:2–3:13 *Thanksgiving and Encouragement.* It is typical for Paul to include a thanksgiving near the beginning of his letters (Galatians is a striking exception).

1:2–3 *Thanksgiving for the Thessalonians' Faith, Love, and Hope.* Paul thanks God that the Thessalonians are evidencing the essential marks of the Christian life—faith, love, and hope.

1:3 remembering. Paul may be recalling the events of his mission to Thessalonica, or this may just be standard prayer language. **faith . . . love . . . hope**. A common Pauline triad (cf. 5:8; Rom. 5:2–5; 1 Cor. 13:13; Gal. 5:5–6; Eph. 4:2–5). The prominent final position here belongs to hope, which seems fitting in a letter so concerned with the end times (1 Thess. 1:10; 2:12, 19–20; 3:13; 4:13–18; 5:1–11, 23–24). **work . . . labor . . . steadfastness**. These are the practical outworking of the Thessalonians' conversion. The "work" the Thessalonians do is a result or consequence of their "faith." So, too, their "labor" flows from "love," and their endurance or "steadfastness" comes from "hope."

1:4–2:16 *Paul's Confidence in the Election of the Thessalonians.* Paul is confident that the Thessalonians are elect because of God's blessing on the missionaries during the mission and the authenticity of the Thessalonians' reception of the gospel and subsequent obedience.

1:4 The ultimate reason for Paul's certainty regarding the Thessalonians' election is that they are **brothers loved by God**. God's love undergirds election (Eph. 1:4–5; cf. Rom. 1:7; 9:13) and is demonstrated by it (Rom. 8:35–39; 11:28). **Chosen** (lit., "elected," using Gk. *eklogē*, "choice, selection, election") refers to God's antecedent sovereign act of appointing people for eternal life (see notes on Rom. 10:20–21; Eph. 1:4; 1:5; 1:11). Paul infers from the events of the mission that the Thessalonians were elect and therefore he can reassure them that they are forever secure.

1:5–10 because. Paul grounds his confidence that the Thessalonians are elect in two things: the undeniable authenticity and authority of those preaching the gospel to them (v. 5) and the exemplary nature of the Thessalonians' response to the gospel (vv. 6–10). First, he appeals to the fact that the missionaries' preaching (**our gospel**) was characterized by **power** (miraculous power, or power in preaching, or both), **the Holy Spirit** (manifestations of the Spirit's approving presence), and **full conviction** (transparent sincerity and integrity, bringing certainty to the hearers' minds). **You know what kind of men we proved to be among you for your sake**. The genuineness of the gospel was reinforced, as it always should be, by the evident integrity of its preachers.

1:6 imitators of us. The Thessalonians followed Paul's example even as Paul followed Christ's example. **for you received the word in much affliction**. See Acts 17:5–9; 1 Thess. 2:14. Suffering affliction is normal for those destined to be saved at the end (see Rom. 8:17–18; 1 Pet. 4:12–14). **with the joy of the Holy Spirit**. The remarkable joy in suffering that characterized the Thessalonian Christians was patterned after the joy of Jesus and Paul.

1:7 Macedonia and **Achaia** were the two Greek provinces of the Roman Empire.

1:8 not only has the word of the Lord sounded forth. This may refer to evangelistic activities or, more likely, news of the Thessalonians'

God has gone forth [v]everywhere, so that we need not say anything. 9 For they themselves
report concerning us the kind of [w]reception we had among you, and how [x]you turned to
God [y]from idols to serve the living and [z]true God, 10 and [a]to wait for his Son [b]from heaven,
[c]whom he raised from the dead, Jesus [d]who delivers us from [e]the wrath to come.

Paul's Ministry to the Thessalonians

2 For you yourselves know, brothers,[1] that our [f]coming to you [g]was not in vain. 2 But
though we had already suffered and been shamefully treated [h]at Philippi, as you know,
[i]we had boldness in our God [j]to declare to you the gospel of God in the midst of much
[k]conflict. 3 For [l]our appeal does not spring from [m]error or [n]impurity or [o]any attempt to
deceive, 4 but just as we have been approved by God [p]to be entrusted with the gospel, so
we speak, not [q]to please man, but to please God [r]who tests our hearts. 5 [s]For we never came
with words of flattery,[2] as you know, nor with a pretext for greed—[t]God is witness. 6 [u]Nor
did we seek glory from people, whether from you or from others, [v]though we could have
made [w]demands as [x]apostles of Christ. 7 But we were [y]gentle[3] among you, [z]like a nursing
mother taking care of her own children. 8 So, being affectionately desirous of you, we were
ready to share with you not only the gospel of God [a]but also our own selves, because you
had become very dear to us.
9 For you remember, brothers, [b]our labor and toil: we [c]worked night and day, that we

[1] *Or brothers and sisters; also verses 9, 14, 17* [2] *Or with a flattering speech* [3] Some manuscripts *infants*

9 [b]2 Thess. 3:8; [Phil. 4:16] [c]See Acts 18:3

8 [v][Rom. 1:8; 16:19; 2 Thess. 1:4]
9 [w]ch. 2:1 [x]See Acts 14:15 [y]1 Cor. 12:2; [Gal. 4:8] [z]See John 17:3
10 [a]See 1 Cor. 1:7 [b]ch. 4:16; [2 Thess. 1:10]; See Acts 1:11 [c]See Acts 2:24 [d]Col. 1:13 [e]ch. 2:16; 5:9; Matt. 3:7; Rom. 5:9

Chapter 2

1 [f]ch. 1:9 [g][2 Thess. 1:10]
2 [h]Acts 16:22-24 [i]See Acts 4:13 [j]Acts 17:2-9 [k]Phil. 1:30
3 [l][2 Cor. 2:17] [m]2 Thess. 2:11 [n]ch. 4:7 [o]2 Cor. 4:2
4 [p]See Gal. 2:7 [q]See Gal. 1:10 [r]Ps. 17:3; See Rom. 8:27
5 [s]See Acts 20:33 [t]ver. 10; See Rom. 1:9
6 [u][2 Cor. 4:5]; See John 5:41 [v]1 Cor. 9:4; 2 Thess. 3:9; [Philem. 8, 9] [w][ver. 9; 2 Cor. 11:9] [x]See 1 Cor. 9:1
7 [y]2 Tim. 2:24; [1 Cor. 14:20] [z][ver. 11; Isa. 49:23; 60:16]
8 [a]See 2 Cor. 12:15

newfound faith. Either way, what transpired in Thessalonica resulted in the gospel being proclaimed far and wide, no doubt aided by the fact that Thessalonica was strategically located (see Introduction: Purpose, Occasion, and Background).

1:9–10 The Greeks from other areas **report** that the Thessalonians had repented of their idolatrous past, had committed themselves to serve God, and were waiting for Jesus' second coming—the key traits of genuine Christian conversion. **living and true God**. In contrast to idols, God is the only real Deity. **wait for his Son**. This is the first of many references to the second coming in this letter (cf. 2:12, 19–20; 3:13; 4:13–18; 5:1–11, 23–24). **whom he raised from the dead**. This may anticipate 4:13–18, where Paul affirms the Thessalonians' hope for the deceased on the foundation of Jesus' resurrection from the dead (4:14). **delivers us from the wrath to come**. This may anticipate 5:1–11, where Paul emphasizes that the Thessalonians are not destined for wrath at the final judgment.

2:1–12 Paul expands upon what he had said in summary form in 1:5: the missionaries in Thessalonica displayed all the traits of authentic ministers of the gospel. Some suggest that Paul is giving a model for imitation, and this is probably part of what Paul is emphasizing here. However, the appeals to witnesses (2:5, 10) and the references to the Thessalonians' knowledge (vv. 1, 2, 5, 11) suggest that Paul in vv. 1–12 is primarily defending the missionaries' integrity with respect to the mission, just as in 2:17–3:10 he will offer a defense of his subsequent absence from Thessalonica. Paul may be responding to real accusations, or merely anticipating concerns in the wake of the Thessalonians' crisis regarding the day of the Lord (see 5:1–11). Paul distinguishes the missionaries from charlatans, perhaps especially Cynic philosophers and/or Jewish false prophets.

2:1 in vain (Gk. *kenos*, "empty, without content, without result"). Empty of results or empty of substance and character.

2:2 shamefully treated at Philippi. See Acts 16:19–39. **boldness**. Despite experiencing fierce persecution in Philippi, Paul did not shrink from proclaiming the gospel in Thessalonica, even when it entailed further suffering. **conflict**. Persecution.

2:3–4 Paul states his thesis in general terms before demonstrating it with specific regard to the Thessalonian mission in vv. 5–12. Negatively, Paul insists that the missionaries were not characterized by a faulty message, impure motives, or dubious methods (v. 3). Positively, he states that they preached the gospel as those **approved by God** and as those committed to speaking in order not to please their human audience but to **please God** (v. 4). **who tests our hearts**. Not only did God sanction the missionaries to proclaim his gospel; he continues to approve of their inner motives and integrity.

2:5–9 Negatively, Paul asserts that he and his fellow missionaries had not spoken as charlatans or false prophets in order to gratify their own vanity, line their own pockets, or gain (even legitimate) honor (vv. 5–6). Positively, he stresses the missionaries' sincerity and selfless and profound devotion toward the Thessalonian believers, extending beyond the call of duty (vv. 7–9).

2:5 words of flattery. If the missionaries had employed flattery, there might have been legitimate doubt as to whether their message was trustworthy. **pretext for greed**. Paul did not minister for financial gain; this is made abundantly clear by his insistence on working at a trade rather than depending on his converts for his keep (v. 9; 2 Thess. 3:8). **God is witness**. Only God can attest to the inner motives of a human heart.

2:6 Nor did we seek glory. Paul's ministry in Thessalonica was not a quest for personal glory or fame. **made demands as apostles of Christ**. As apostles, they had unique authority to request support (cf. Rom. 15:24; 1 Cor. 9:3–14).

2:7–8 gentle. Paul is highlighting the fact that he and his fellow missionaries did not exploit their rights and privileges but acted in an unassuming manner toward the converts. **like a nursing mother**. Paul and his fellow missionaries were without guile, loving, and selfless in their devotion to the converts.

2:9 Paul's love was shown by the fact that he had undertaken long hours of manual **labor** in order to avoid burdening the Thessalonians financially.

The Second Coming in 1 Thessalonians

1:3	"hope in our Lord Jesus Christ"
1:10	"to wait for his Son from heaven"
2:19	"before our Lord Jesus at his coming"
3:13	"at the coming of our Lord Jesus with all his saints"
4:15	"the coming of the Lord"
4:16	"the Lord himself will descend from heaven"
5:2	"the day of the Lord will come like a thief in the night"
5:3	"as labor pains come upon a pregnant woman"
5:23	"at the coming of our Lord Jesus Christ"

might not be a burden to any of you, while we proclaimed to you the gospel of God. 10 You
are witnesses, and [d]God also, [e]how holy and righteous and blameless was our conduct
toward you believers. 11 For you know how, [f]like a father with his children, 12 we exhorted
each one of you and encouraged you and [g]charged [h]you to walk in a manner worthy of
God, [i]who calls you into his own kingdom and glory.

13 And [j]we also thank God constantly[1] for this, that when you received [k]the word of God,
which you heard from us, you accepted it [l]not as the word of men[2] but as what it really is,
the word of God, [m]which is at work in you believers. 14 For you, brothers, [n]became imitators
of [o]the churches of God in Christ Jesus that are in Judea. For [p]you suffered the same things
from your own countrymen [q]as they did from the Jews,[3] 15 [r]who killed both the Lord Jesus
and [s]the prophets, and drove us out, and displease God and [t]oppose all mankind 16 [u]by
hindering us from speaking to the Gentiles that they might be saved—so as always [v]to
fill up the measure of their sins. But [w]wrath has come upon them at last![4]

Paul's Longing to See Them Again

17 But since we were torn away from you, brothers, for a short time, [x]in person not in heart,
we endeavored the more eagerly and with great desire [y]to see you face to face, 18 because
we wanted to come to you—I, Paul, again and again—but Satan [z]hindered us. 19 For what
is our hope or [a]joy or crown of boasting [b]before our Lord Jesus at his [c]coming? Is it not
you? 20 For you are our glory and joy.

3 Therefore when we could bear it no longer, we were willing [d]to be left behind at Athens
alone, 2 and we [e]sent Timothy, [f]our brother and God's coworker[5] in the gospel of Christ,
to establish and exhort you in your faith, 3 that no one be moved by these afflictions. For
you yourselves know that [g]we are destined for this. 4 For when we were with you, we kept

[1] Or *without ceasing* [2] The Greek word *anthropoi* can refer to both men and women [3] The Greek word *Ioudaioi* can refer to Jewish religious leaders and others under their influence, who opposed the Christian faith in that time [4] Or *completely*, or *forever* [5] Some manuscripts *servant*

10 [d]ver. 5 [e]See ch. 1:5
11 [f][ver. 7]; See 1 Cor. 4:14
12 [g]Eph. 4:17 [h]See Eph. 4:1 [i]ch. 5:24; 2 Thess. 2:14; 1 Pet. 5:10; See Rom. 8:28
13 [j]See ch. 1:2, 3 [k][Rom. 10:17] [l][Gal. 4:14]; See Matt. 10:20 [m]Heb. 4:12
14 [n]See ch. 1:6 [o]See 1 Cor. 7:17 [p]ch. 3:4; Acts 17:5; 2 Thess. 1:4, 5 [q][Heb. 10:33, 34]
15 [r]See Luke 24:20 [s]Jer. 2:30; Matt. 23:29-34; See Matt. 5:12 [t][Esth. 3:8]
16 [u]Acts 13:45, 50; 14:2, 19; 17:5, 13; 18:12; 22:21, 22 [v]See Gen. 15:16 [w]See ch. 1:10
17 [x]1 Cor. 5:3; Col. 2:5 [y]ch. 3:10
18 [z]Rom. 15:22; [Rom. 1:13]
19 [a]See Phil. 4:1 [b]1 Cor. 15:31; [2 Thess. 1:4]; See 2 Cor. 1:14 [c]ch. 3:13; 4:15; 5:23; Matt. 24:3; 1 Cor. 15:23; 2 Thess. 2:1, 8; James 5:7, 8; 2 Pet. 1:16; 3:4, 12; 1 John 2:28

Chapter 3

1 [d]Acts 17:15, 16
2 [e]See Phil. 2:19 [f]2 Cor. 1:1; Col. 1:1; Philem. 1; Heb. 13:23
3 [g]See Acts 9:16; 14:22

2:10–12 Paul forcefully insists that the missionaries had been **holy, righteous,** and **blameless** in everything they did while among the new converts. Note the strong familial language in vv. 7, 11–12 (also v. 17). Paul stresses again that the manner and content of the missionaries' proclamation demonstrated their authenticity and authority (v. 12). **kingdom and glory**. At Jesus' second coming, Christians will enjoy the full blessings of the kingdom and will participate in God's glory.

2:13–16 Paul continues to underscore his certainty regarding the Thessalonians' election (1:4). They put their trust in the Word of God (2:13), and they suffered persecution just as the mother churches in Judea had (v. 14). Paul then denounces apostate Jews who had opposed the prophets and Jesus, and who had more recently driven Paul out of Thessalonica (vv. 15–16).

2:13 not as the word of men but as . . . the word of God. Paul clearly claims an absolute divine authority for his words as an apostle, and contrasts his words with ordinary human words. His apostolic teaching **really is** the "word of God," and should be received as from God himself. **which is at work in you**. The word of God is still active in the Thessalonian community (see 1 Cor. 1:18; Heb. 4:12).

2:14 Genuine offspring bear the traits of their parents. The Judean churches were the first, indisputably authentic churches, and the mother churches of all those planted by Paul. They established a standard by which all other churches might measure themselves. Like them, the Thessalonian Christians suffered persecution for Jesus. **your own countrymen**. The Thessalonians' Gentile compatriots were stirred up against them by Jewish opponents of the gospel (Acts 17:5–10). **Jews**. Paul so loved his fellow Jews that he would almost be willing to be eternally damned if it would mean that they would come to faith (Rom. 9:1–3), but here he points out that in their hard-heartedness they consistently reject God's Word (see Matt. 23:29–35).

2:15 drove us out. See Acts 17:5–10. Paul sees what happened to the missionaries in Thessalonica as the latest in a long series of examples of Jewish hostility to the word of God. **oppose all mankind**. It is in all humanity's interest to hear the gospel that offers salvation; to stand in the way of the gospel is therefore to oppose all mankind.

2:16 wrath has come upon them at last. It is possible that Paul has in mind here (1) the Judean famine in A.D. 44–47, (2) the riot and massacre in Jerusalem in 48–49, or (3) the expulsion of Jews from Rome in 49—although each seems too local and insignificant to warrant such a dramatic description here. Alternatively, a future event may be in view, spoken of here as having come (Gk. aorist tense) because it is so certain (e.g., Mark 11:24; John 13:31; Rom. 8:30) or because it has already begun to be fulfilled.

2:17–3:10 *Paul's Defense of the Missionaries during Their Absence.* Just as 2:1–12 is a defense of the missionaries during the mission in Thessalonica, 2:17–3:10 is a defense of the missionaries' absence. Thus Paul expresses his concern that the missionaries' premature departure from Thessalonica, the length of the absence, and his own failure to return should not be misinterpreted as evidence of a lack of pastoral concern.

2:17 The missionaries left Thessalonica against their will in the face of persecution. **Torn away** (Gk. *aporphanizō*, "orphaned") suggests deep distress at involuntary separation. **for a short time**. Timothy's recent visit ended the brief absence. **in person not in heart**. Physical absence did not reflect a lack of concern. **we endeavored . . . to see you**. Contrary to what the Thessalonians might think, the missionaries had repeatedly tried to get back to Thessalonica.

2:18 I, Paul. This reveals that Paul is the author of this letter and that he feels the need to defend himself with respect to the period of absence. **Satan hindered us**. It is not known what means Satan used to prevent a reunion.

2:19–20 Presenting his converts to Jesus at the second coming is an integral part of Paul's Christian hope. **crown**. Crowns or wreaths were given to winning athletes.

3:1 The sending of Timothy was due to Paul's inability to endure any longer his separation from the Thessalonians, and not knowing how they were doing. Moreover, it was a sacrificial act, reflecting deep pastoral love, since Paul was **left behind at Athens alone** (see note on Acts 17:15).

3:2 God's coworker. A remarkably lofty title (see 1 Cor. 3:9). Paul seems to be highlighting Timothy's credentials to offset any negative sentiment on the part of the Thessalonians at Paul's sending his junior associate to them instead of coming himself.

3:3–4 Paul's motive for sending Timothy was to strengthen the persecuted Thessalonians (cf. 2 Thess. 1:5–7). **we are destined for this**. Christians are destined to suffer tribulation for their faith (Rom. 8:17–18; 2 Tim. 3:12; also Mark 10:30; 1 Pet. 4:12–13). Apparently the Thessalonians had been taken aback by the unrelenting persecution.

telling you beforehand that we were to suffer affliction, [h]just as it has come to pass, and
just as you know. 5 For this reason, [i]when I could bear it no longer, [i]I sent to learn about
your faith, [j]for fear that somehow [k]the tempter had tempted you and [l]our labor would
be in vain.

Timothy's Encouraging Report

6 But [m]now that Timothy has come to us from you, and has brought us the good news of
[n]your faith and love and reported [o]that you always remember us kindly and [p]long to see
us, as we long to see you— 7 for this reason, brothers,[1] in all our distress and affliction [q]we
have been comforted about you through your faith. 8 For now we live, if you [r]are standing
fast in the Lord. 9 For [s]what thanksgiving can we return to God for you, for all the joy that
we feel for your sake before our God, 10 as we pray most earnestly [t]night and day [u]that we
may see you face to face and [v]supply what is lacking in your faith?
11 Now may [w]our God and Father himself, and our Lord Jesus, [x]direct our way to you,
12 and may the Lord [y]make you increase and abound in love [z]for one another and for all,
as we do for you, 13 so that he may [a]establish your hearts blameless in holiness before [w]our
God and Father, at [b]the coming of our Lord Jesus [c]with all his saints.

A Life Pleasing to God

4 Finally, then, brothers,[2] we ask and urge you in the Lord Jesus, that as you [d]received
from us [e]how you ought to walk and [f]to please God, just as you are doing, that you [g]do
so more and more. 2 For [h]you know what instructions we gave you through the Lord Jesus.
3 For this is the will of God, [i]your sanctification:[3] [j]that you abstain from sexual immorality;
4 that each one of you know how to control his own [k]body[4] in holiness and [l]honor, 5 not in
[m]the passion of lust [n]like the Gentiles [o]who do not know God; 6 that no one transgress and

[1] *Or brothers and sisters* [2] *Or brothers and sisters; also verses 10, 13* [3] *Or your holiness* [4] *Or how to take a wife for himself; Greek how to possess his own vessel*

4 [h]See ch. 2:14
5 [i]ver. 1, 2 [j][1 Cor. 7:5; 2 Cor. 11:3] [k]Matt. 4:3 [l]See Phil. 2:16
6 [m]Acts 18:5; [2 Cor. 7:6, 9] [n]See ch. 1:3 [o][1 Cor. 11:2] [p]See Phil. 1:8
7 [q]2 Cor. 1:4
8 [r]See 1 Cor. 16:13
9 [s][ch. 1:2]
10 [t]2 Tim. 1:3 [u]ch. 2:17; [Rom. 1:10] [v]See 2 Cor. 13:9
11 [w]See Gal. 1:4 [x]2 Thess. 3:5
12 [y]ch. 4:1, 10; Phil. 1:9; 2 Thess. 1:3 [z]ch. 4:9; 5:15
13 [a]James 5:8 [w][See ver. 11 above] [b]See ch. 2:19 [c]Zech. 14:5; Jude 14

Chapter 4

1 [d]Phil. 4:9; Col. 2:6 [e]See Eph. 4:1 [f]See Col. 1:10 [g]See ch. 3:12
2 [h][1 Cor. 11:2]
3 [i]Rom. 6:19, 22; 1 Cor. 1:30; 2 Thess. 2:13; 1 Tim. 2:15; Heb. 12:14; 1 Pet. 1:2 [j]See 1 Cor. 6:18
4 [k]1 Pet. 3:7; [2 Cor. 4:7] [l][Rom. 1:24]
5 [m]See Rom. 1:26 [n]Eph. 4:17 [o]Ps. 79:6; Jer. 9:3; 10:25; See Gal. 4:8

3:5 tempter. Satan tempted Jesus (Matt. 4:1–11) and tempts Christians (1 Cor. 7:5). **our labor would be in vain**. If Satan had succeeded in tempting the Thessalonians to abandon their newfound faith, Paul's missionary work would have been fruitless.

3:6–10 Paul outlines his **distress** as he waited for Timothy's report, his relief and thanksgiving upon learning the good news about the Thessalonian Christians, and his longing to see them again.

3:6 As soon as Timothy returns from Thessalonica, Paul composes his letter to the Thessalonians. Timothy has reported **good news** concerning the Thessalonians' **faith and love** (strikingly, there is no mention here of hope; see 4:13) and that the Thessalonians **long to see** Paul. Paul reassuringly reiterates that he also longs to see them.

3:7 in all our distress and affliction. The missionaries, like the Thessalonians, are suffering for Christ (see vv. 3–4).

3:9–10 Paul gives thanks for Timothy's great news (v. 9) and then highlights by means of a prayer report his eagerness for a return visit to Thessalonica (v. 10). **what is lacking in your faith**. Due to their premature departure from Thessalonica, the missionaries had been unable to complete their usual instruction of Christians in the fundamentals of the faith. One particular lack in their instruction related to the second coming and the final resurrection (4:13–18).

3:11–13 *A Pastoral Prayer for the Thessalonians.* Paul concludes his thanksgiving and encouragement (1:3–3:13) with a pastoral prayer for his converts. He prays that he may be able to revisit the community (3:11) and that the Thessalonians will abound in love (v. 12), with the result that they will be blamelessly holy at Jesus' second coming (v. 13). The fact that holiness will characterize those who participate in the second coming lends urgency to Paul's teaching on sexual holiness in 4:3–8. In 5:23–24 Paul assures the Thessalonians that God will produce the necessary holiness in them.

3:13 with all his saints. Angels, Christians, or (most likely) both (Gk. *hagios* is plural here and means "holy ones"). There may well be an allusion to Zech. 14:5 in this verse. On the second coming of Christ, see 1 Thess. 5:1–11; 1 Pet. 4:7; 2 Pet. 3:2–18.

4:1–5:28 *Instruction and Exhortation.* In the main body of the letter Paul gives instructions on pleasing God (4:1–12), the second coming (4:13–5:11), community conduct (5:12–22), and prayer and assurance (5:23–24).

4:1–12 *On Pleasing God.* Paul calls on the Thessalonians to please God (vv. 1–2) by living in holiness (vv. 3–8) and love (vv. 9–12).

4:1 Finally (Gk. *loipon*). Paul is either indicating that he is approaching the end of his letter or simply that he is beginning a new section (cf. Phil. 3:1); clearly, there is much still to come. **To walk and to please God** is to live a life that is pleasing to God (see note on Col. 1:10). **do so more and more**. Their process of growth in sanctification and in their ability to "please God" has not yet been completed.

4:2 instructions (Gk. *parangelia*). Originally a military word, it usually denotes authoritative commands.

4:3–8 Paul commands the Thessalonians to live in sexual holiness. Some converts may have found it a struggle to adjust to Christianity's demanding ethical code.

4:3 that you abstain from sexual immorality. For former pagans, the lure of sexual sins was strong (see 1 Corinthians 5–6). By using the Greek term *porneia* (which referred to adultery, fornication, or other sexual immorality), Paul forbids any sexual activity outside the bounds of heterosexual marriage (see Eph. 5:3; 1 Pet. 1:15–22).

4:4 control his own body. The Greek could be rendered "take a wife for himself" (see ESV footnote). However, in view of vv. 4–5 and 1 Corinthians 7, sexual self-control is more likely the intended meaning. **in holiness and honor**. Behavior suitable before God and humans respectively.

4:5 in the passion of lust like the Gentiles. See Rom. 1:24–27. Paul is concerned that some of the Thessalonian Christians may fall back into their former ways.

4:6 wrong (Gk. *pleonekteō*, "to defraud, exploit, cheat"). Defrauding a fellow Christian through sexual sin. **the Lord is an avenger**. Those who ignore the Christian sexual ethic will face the wrath of Jesus when he returns, and perhaps even before.

6 [p]1 Cor. 6:8 [q]Rom. 13:4; [Rom. 12:19; Heb. 13:4]
7 [r]ver. 3; See 1 Pet. 1:15 [s]ch. 2:3
8 [t][ch. 2:13]; See Luke 10:16 [u]1 John 3:24; 4:13
9 [v]See Heb. 13:1 [w]ch. 5:1 [x]John 6:45; [1 John 2:27] [y]See John 13:34
10 [z]ch. 1:7 [a]See ch. 3:12
11 [b]Prov. 17:14; 20:3; 25:8; 2 Thess. 3:12 [c]2 Thess. 3:11; 1 Pet. 4:15 [d][Acts 18:3]; See Eph. 4:28
12 [e]Rom. 13:13; [Col. 4:5] [f]See Mark 4:11
13 [g][Lev. 19:28; Deut. 14:1; 2 Sam. 12:20-23; Mark 5:39] [h]Eph. 2:12
14 [i]1 Cor. 15:13; [2 Cor. 4:14; Rev. 1:18] [j]1 Cor. 15:18
15 [k]See 1 Kgs. 13:17 [l]1 Cor. 15:51 [m]See ch. 2:19
16 [n]See Matt. 16:27 [o]2 Thess. 1:7 [p][Joel 2:11]

[p]wrong his brother in this matter, because the Lord is [q]an avenger in all these things, as we
told you beforehand and solemnly warned you. **7** For [r]God has not called us for [s]impurity,
but in holiness. **8** Therefore [t]whoever disregards this, disregards not man but God, [u]who
gives his Holy Spirit to you.
9 Now concerning [v]brotherly love [w]you have no need for anyone to write to you, for you
yourselves have been [x]taught by God [y]to love one another, **10** for that indeed is what [z]you
are doing to all the brothers throughout Macedonia. But we urge you, brothers, to [a]do
this more and more, **11** and to aspire [b]to live quietly, and [c]to mind your own affairs, and
[d]to work with your hands, as we instructed you, **12** so that you may [e]walk properly before
[f]outsiders and be dependent on no one.

The Coming of the Lord

13 But we do not want you to be uninformed, brothers, about those who are asleep, [g]that
you may not grieve as others do [h]who have no hope. **14** For [i]since we believe that Jesus died
and rose again, even so, through Jesus, God will bring with him [j]those who have fallen
asleep. **15** For this we declare to you [k]by a word from the Lord,[1] that [l]we who are alive, who
are left until [m]the coming of the Lord, will not precede those who have fallen asleep. **16** For
[n]the Lord himself will descend [o]from heaven [p]with a cry of command, with the voice of

[1] *Or by the word of the Lord*

4:7 called. When the Thessalonians embraced Paul's gospel, they were responding to God's effectual call (see note on Rom. 8:30; cf. note on 1 Thess. 1:4). That call did not have as its goal **impurity** but rather a life of **holiness**.

4:8 Therefore. In view of v. 7, to reject Paul's teaching on sex is to reject not merely Paul but God, who is the source of Paul's sexual ethic. **who gives his Holy Spirit to you.** In the OT (e.g., Ezek. 36:26–27) God promised that he would establish a new covenant in which the Holy Spirit would write the law on people's hearts and cause them to obey. This new covenant reality, which has been inaugurated by Christ, makes sexual sin inexcusable. To reject the giver of the Holy Spirit is to cut oneself off from the sanctifying power that enables the Christian to be "blameless in holiness" at the second coming (1 Thess. 3:13).

4:9–12 Paul urges the Thessalonians to continue showing **brotherly love** and to be financially self-supporting. Some in the church have abandoned gainful employment and are living off the charity of wealthier Christians (see 2 Thess. 3:6–15). It is unclear whether or not this problem was related to the Thessalonians' confusion about the end times.

4:9 taught by God to love one another. Jeremiah 31:33–34 prophesied that God would write his law on the hearts of his people and directly teach them as part of the new covenant. Christians already know this reality (1 John 2:27): by love they fulfill the law (Rom. 13:8–10; cf. Lev. 19:18; John 13:34).

4:11 live quietly. Live peaceably with others (see 2 Thess. 3:11–12), instead of meddling in others' affairs. **work with your hands.** Paul calls on Thessalonian believers to earn their own living rather than to depend on wealthier Christians, as Paul had **instructed** them when he was at Thessalonica.

4:12 walk properly before outsiders. For some Christians to be shamelessly exploiting the charity of wealthier Christians would have been disgraceful in a first-century Greco-Roman environment.

4:13–5:11 *On the Second Coming of Jesus.* Paul first deals with the issue of whether and how deceased Christians will participate in the second coming (4:13–18) and then reassures the Thessalonians that they are destined for salvation rather than wrath (5:1–11).

4:13–18 Paul responds to the main problem facing the young church. They lacked detailed knowledge about what happens to Christians who die, because Paul did not have the opportunity to complete his teaching there (3:10) on account of being forced to leave (2:15, 17; Acts 17:5–10). Consequently, the Thessalonians did not have the understanding to cope with the recent deaths of some community members, and so they responded with bewildered hopelessness.

4:13 we do not want you to be uninformed. The Thessalonians are unaware of the things Paul will explain in vv. 14–17. **those who are asleep.** Paul refers to Christians who have died as being "asleep" (cf. vv. 14, 15; 5:10; also 1 Cor. 15:6, 18, 20, 51), which reinforces his main point that they will awake from the grave at the second coming. The metaphor is not intended to deny that the dead are in conscious fellowship with God in the intermediate state. Referring to death with the metaphor of sleep is simply suggested by the physical condition of those who sleep. It gains appropriateness from the fact that all who have died will rise at Christ's return. **grieve as others do who have no hope.** Grieving per se is not wrong (cf. Acts 8:2), but it is wrong to grieve in a hopeless manner like unbelievers. The Thessalonians apparently did not understand that deceased Christians would rise from the dead and thus would not miss out on the blessings brought by the second coming. Epitaphs from the first century indicate that most first-century Greeks had a strongly pessimistic view of death.

4:14 rose again. The resurrection of Christ is the center of God's plan for history and is the basis for hope in the future resurrection of the body (1 Cor. 15:42–57; Rev. 21:4). **through Jesus, God will bring.** Jesus is shown to be God's mediator of salvation who will "bring" deceased Christians with him (**those who have fallen asleep**), that is, the souls of those who have been in heaven with Christ up to this point. The direction of movement (whether upward or downward) is debated, although the allusion to Zech. 14:5 suggests a picture of Christ coming down from heaven, bringing with him the souls of those who have already died. Paul's point is that all the Christians who have died ("fallen asleep") will be with Christ in his second coming, as Christ descends to earth. Paul then explains in more detail (in 1 Thess. 4:16–17) how the dead are able to be present with Christ—that is, because their bodies will, at that moment, be resurrected and reunited with their souls, as they are "caught up to meet the Lord in the air" (v. 17).

4:15 Word from the Lord probably refers to something the Lord revealed personally to Paul, which he then states in vv. 15b–17. **We who are alive** does not imply that Paul was convinced that he himself would be alive at the second coming, but rather that all Christians should be prepared for Christ to return during their lifetime. **who are left.** Left behind, that is, by all Christians who have already departed this life. **will not precede those who have fallen asleep.** It is unclear whether the Thessalonians were assuming that the dead would rise only after the second coming, or whether they thought that the dead had no hope of salvation at all.

4:16–17 cry of command . . . voice of an archangel . . . trumpet of God. The three noises summon the dead to wake from their slumber. The only "archangel" identified in the Bible is Michael (Jude 9). Trumpets in the OT proclaimed the Lord's presence (Ex. 19:16; 1 Chron. 16:6; Ps. 47:5; Joel 2:1; Zech. 9:14); in Jewish tradition, the "trumpet" was associated with battle, the day of the Lord, and the resurrection (cf. 1 Cor. 15:52). **first . . . Then.** Dead Christians rise from their graves to the realm of the living, and then the living and the dead together are **caught up** from the earth into the air to

[q]an archangel, and [r]with the sound of the trumpet of God. And [s]the dead in Christ will
rise first. 17 Then we who are alive, who are left, will be [t]caught up together with them [u]in
the clouds to meet the Lord in the air, and so [v]we will always be with the Lord. 18 Therefore
encourage one another with these words.

The Day of the Lord

5 Now concerning [w]the times and the seasons, brothers,[1] [x]you have no need to have anything written to you. 2 For you yourselves are fully aware that [y]the day of the Lord will
come like a thief in the night. 3 While people are saying, "There is peace and security," then
[z]sudden destruction will come upon them [a]as labor pains come upon a pregnant woman,
and they will not escape. 4 But you [b]are not in darkness, brothers, for that day to surprise
you like a thief. 5 For you are all [c]children[2] of light, children of the day. We are not of the
night or of the darkness. 6 So then [d]let us not sleep, as others do, but let us [e]keep awake
and [f]be sober. 7 For those who sleep, sleep at night, and those who get drunk, [g]are drunk
at night. 8 But since we belong to the day, let us be sober, [h]having put on the breastplate
of [i]faith and love, and for a helmet the hope of salvation. 9 For God has not destined us
for [j]wrath, but [k]to obtain salvation through our Lord Jesus Christ, 10 [l]who died for us so
that whether we are awake or asleep we might live with him. 11 Therefore encourage one
another and build one another up, just as you are doing.

[1] Or *brothers and sisters*; also verses 4, 12, 14, 25, 26, 27 [2] Or *sons*; twice in this verse

16 [q]Jude 9 [r]Matt. 24:31; 1 Cor. 15:52 [s]1 Cor. 15:23; [2 Thess. 2:1; Rev. 14:13]
17 [t]See 2 Cor. 12:2 [u][Dan. 7:13; Acts 1:9; Rev. 11:12] [v]See John 12:26

Chapter 5

1 [w]Dan. 2:21; Acts 1:7 [x]ch. 4:9
2 [y][2 Thess. 2:2]; See Matt. 24:43; Luke 17:24
3 [z]Luke 21:34; [Ps. 35:8; Luke 17:26-30; 2 Thess. 1:9] [a]See Isa. 13:8
4 [b]1 John 2:8
5 [c]See Luke 16:8
6 [d][Mark 13:36]; See Rom. 13:11-13 [e]See Matt. 24:42 [f]See 1 Pet. 1:13
7 [g][Acts 2:15; 2 Pet. 2:13]
8 [h]Isa. 59:17; Eph. 6:14, 17 [i][Eph. 6:23]
9 [j]See ch. 1:10 [k]2 Thess. 2:13, 14; [Heb. 10:39]
10 [l]Rom. 14:9; [2 Tim. 2:11]

meet Christ. The Greek for "caught up" (*harpazō*, "to grab or seize suddenly, to snatch, take away") gives a sense of being forcibly and suddenly lifted upward (see John 6:15; Acts 8:39). **together with**. The dead Christians would suffer no disadvantage (cf. "we who are alive . . . will not precede," 1 Thess. 4:15). **clouds**. Probably not earthly rain clouds but the clouds of glory that surround the presence of God (cf. Ex. 13:21; 33:9–10; 40:38; Num. 12:5; 1 Kings 8:10–11; Ps. 97:2; Dan. 7:13; Matt. 17:5; Mark 13:26; Acts 1:9; Rev. 14:14). **to meet**. The Greek term *apantēsis* is often used of an important dignitary's reception by the inhabitants of a city, who come out to greet and welcome their honored guest with fanfare and celebration, then accompany him into the city (cf. Matt. 25:6; Acts 28:15; a related term *hypantēsis* is used in Matt. 25:1; John 12:13). It may indicate that the subsequent movement of the saints after meeting Christ "in the air" conforms to Christ's direction, thus in a downward motion toward the earth. However, some interpreters caution that the vivid symbolism of apocalyptic language must be kept in mind to avoid over-interpretation of the apocalyptic details. **in the air**. The sky.

4:18 Clear teaching about the Lord's return should result in comfort and encouragement (Paul's goal), rather than fear and divisiveness. **These words** refers to vv. 13–17.

5:1–11 These verses are closely linked to 4:13–18: both offer reassurance concerning the fate of Christians at the second coming, and 5:9–10 alludes back to 4:13–18. It seems that the Thessalonians either were worried that they might not be prepared for the day of the Lord or were insecure about their status on that day in view of the recent unexpected deaths.

5:1 Now concerning. Paul may be responding to a question from the Thessalonians communicated by Timothy. **the times and the seasons**. That is, when the day of the Lord will occur (cf. Acts 1:7). The Thessalonians' question likely arose more from anxiety than idle curiosity, since Paul's answer reassures rather than rebukes them and seems concerned with both the "how" and the "when" of the day of the Lord. **you have no need to have anything written to you**. In spite of what the Thessalonians apparently think, there is no real need for Paul to write them on this matter.

5:2–3 The phrase **day of the Lord** is common in the OT Prophets (see note on Amos 5:18–20). It refers to the great and terrible day when Yahweh will intervene to punish the disobedient (e.g., Isa. 13:6–16; Joel 1:13–15; 2:1–11; Obad. 15–20; Mal. 4:5) and to save the faithful (e.g., Isa. 27:2–13; Jer. 30:8–9; Joel 2:31–32; Obad. 21). In Paul's letters it is equated with the second coming. **like a thief in the night**. Throughout the NT, the thief simile suggests unexpectedness and unwelcomeness (Matt. 24:43–44; Luke 12:39–40; 2 Pet. 3:10; Rev. 3:3; 16:15). The negative aspect is clearly present in 1 Thess. 5:4, and there is no reason to think that it is absent here. However, although some have wondered whether Paul is threatening the Thessalonians with the prospect of final judgment, it seems more likely, in view of vv. 4 and 9, that he is actually reassuring believers who are insecure, perhaps as a result of the recent deaths in their midst. **people**. That is, unbelievers. **peace and security**. Possibly an allusion to imperial Roman propaganda or (perhaps more likely) to Jer. 6:14 (or Jer. 8:11), where similar language is used of a delusional sense of immunity from divine wrath. **labor pains**. An analogy referring to the judgment and destruction on the day of the Lord. Cf. Isa. 13:8; Jer. 6:24.

5:4 But you. The Thessalonian Christians are not among the people who say "peace and security" and upon whom sudden destruction will come (v. 3). **in darkness**. The realm of sin, evil, unenlightenment, and estrangement from God. **surprise you like a thief**. The **day** of the Lord will not be a "thief-like," unwelcome surprise for the Thessalonian Christians, as it will be for unbelievers (see v. 2).

5:5 For. Paul grounds his assurance of v. 4 in the Thessalonians' status and destiny. **children of light**. This phrase is used in Jewish literature and in the NT (e.g., Luke 16:8; John 12:36) of those who belong to the realm of God and his salvation (Col. 1:13). **children of the day**. This phrase, which is unique to Paul, seems to link the concepts of "light" and "day" together. Thus, because Jesus is "the light of the world" (John 8:12; 9:5), Christians are "children of the light"; but Christians are also those who are called to live a godly life as people who "belong to the day" (1 Thess. 5:8) and who are destined to inherit salvation on "the day of the Lord," when Christ (the light of the world) will return in power and great glory (cf. Matt. 24:30; Mark 13:26; Luke 21:27). **We**. Paul shifts to the first person plural to reinforce his confirmation and perhaps to prepare for and soften the exhortation of 1 Thess. 5:6–8. **night . . . darkness**. The dominion of evil and enmity with God.

5:6 So then. Paul gives general exhortations based on the reassurances of v. 5. To **sleep** is to be morally and spiritually disengaged, and/or living without a consciousness of the coming day.

5:8 breastplate . . . helmet. Paul is drawing on Isa. 59:17, where the Lord is portrayed as a warrior wearing armor. Here Christians, as those destined to stand alongside the Lord on the last day, are called to put on his armor (see Eph. 6:10–20). **faith and love . . . hope**. The triad of essential Christian traits (see 1 Cor. 13:13; 1 Thess. 1:3).

5:9 For connects this verse with either vv. 6–8 in general or the specific exhortation in v. 8 to put on the helmet of hope. Paul restates what he said in v. 4: the Thessalonians have nothing to worry about, because they are destined not for **wrath** but for **salvation** at the second coming.

5:10 awake or asleep. Alive or dead. "Awake" alludes to the concern of the living Christians regarding their destiny on the day of the Lord (vv. 1–11), while "asleep" alludes to the destiny of deceased Christians (4:13–18). **live**. At the second coming, Christians will experience a new quality of life in the company of Christ.

5:11 just as you are doing. As elsewhere (e.g., 4:1), Paul seeks to avoid

12[m]1 Cor. 16:18; Phil. 2:29 [n]1 Cor. 16:16; Heb. 13:17
13[o]See Mark 9:50
14[p]2 Thess. 3:6, 7, 11 [q]Isa. 35:4; [Heb. 12:12] [r]Acts 20:35; See Rom. 15:1 [s]See 1 Cor. 13:4
15[t]1 Pet. 3:9; See Rom. 12:17 [u][Rom. 12:9]; See Gal. 6:10
16[v]Phil. 4:4
17[w]See Luke 18:1
18[x]See Eph. 5:20
19[y][1 Cor. 14:30; Eph. 4:30; 1 Tim. 4:14; 2 Tim. 1:6]
20[z]See 1 Cor. 11:4
21[a]1 John 4:1; [Job 34:4]; See Eph. 5:10
23[b]See Rom. 15:33 [c]Ex. 31:13; John 17:17 [d]2 Pet. 3:14; Jude 1 [e]Luke 1:46, 47; Heb. 4:12; [1 Cor. 14:14] [f]See ch. 2:19
24[g]See 1 Cor. 1:9 [h][Phil. 1:6]
25[i]2 Thess. 3:1; Heb. 13:18
26[j]See Rom. 16:16
27[k]Col. 4:16

Final Instructions and Benediction

12 We ask you, brothers, [m]to respect those who labor among you and [n]are over you in the
Lord and admonish you, 13 and to esteem them very highly in love because of their work. [o]Be
at peace among yourselves. 14 And we urge you, brothers, admonish [p]the idle,[1] [q]encourage
the fainthearted, [r]help the weak, [s]be patient with them all. 15 See that [t]no one repays anyone
evil for evil, but always [u]seek to do good to one another and to everyone. 16 [v]Rejoice always,
17 [w]pray without ceasing, 18 [x]give thanks in all circumstances; for this is the will of God in
Christ Jesus for you. 19 [y]Do not quench the Spirit. 20 Do not despise [z]prophecies, 21 but [a]test
everything; hold fast what is good. 22 Abstain from every form of evil.
23 Now may [b]the God of peace himself [c]sanctify you completely, and may your [d]whole
[e]spirit and soul and body be kept blameless at [f]the coming of our Lord Jesus Christ. 24 [g]He
who calls you is faithful; [h]he will surely do it.
25 [i]Brothers, pray for us.
26 [j]Greet all the brothers with a holy kiss.
27 I put you under oath before the Lord to have [k]this letter read to all the brothers.
28 [l]The grace of our Lord Jesus Christ be with you.

[1] Or *disorderly, or undisciplined*

28[l]See Rom. 16:20

looking as if he is criticizing the Thessalonians. As in 4:18, his purpose is encouragement.

5:12–22 *On Community Conduct.* Paul gives exhortations on community life and relationships.

5:12–13 respect those who labor . . . admonish you. The young Thessalonian community was not adequately appreciating and respecting its leaders. **are over you**. The Greek term *proistēmi* here means "rule, direct, be at the head of," and would refer to the elders in the church (see notes on Acts 14:23; Titus 1:5). **Be at peace among yourselves** may suggest (though not necessarily) that there were tensions within the community.

5:14 idle (Gk. *ataktos*, "undisciplined, insubordinate"). Some Thessalonians were shirking their responsibility to work in accord with the creation mandate (Gen. 2:15). See 1 Thess. 4:9–12; also 2 Thess. 3:6–15. **fainthearted**. Due to persecution (1 Thess. 3:3–4) or the unexpected deaths (4:13–5:11). **weak**. Either those with weak consciences (see 1 Corinthians 8–9), those rattled by the ongoing persecution, or those anxious about the day of the Lord (1 Thess. 5:1–11).

5:16 Rejoice always. Joy in Paul's letters is a basic mark of the Christian (Rom. 14:17) and a fruit of the Spirit (Gal. 5:22). It is often associated with the firm hope of the Christian (e.g., Rom. 5:2–5; 12:12).

5:17 Pray without ceasing suggests a mental attitude of prayerfulness, continual personal fellowship with God, and consciousness of being in his presence throughout each day.

5:18 give thanks. Christians are to be marked by thanksgiving (Eph. 5:4, 20; Col. 2:7; 3:15, 17; 4:2). **This** probably refers to all of 1 Thess. 5:16–18.

5:19 Do not quench the Spirit. The manner in which the Thessalonians were extinguishing the Holy Spirit's fire is specified in the next verse.

5:20–21 Do not despise prophecies. Believers are to be open to the disclosure of God's will through fellow Christians exercising the gift of prophecy (see note on 1 Cor. 14:22–25). The Thessalonians apparently despised manifestations of prophecy and hence were cutting off a valuable source of encouragement and extinguishing the Spirit's fire. **test everything**. Rather than rejecting prophecies outright on the basis of inferior prophetic words, the Thessalonians need to weigh prophecies to distinguish the true from the false. Tests presumably include the prophecy's conformity with authoritative revelation, its value for edification, and its evaluation by those with spiritual discernment. See 1 Cor. 14:29–33 and the note on 1 Cor. 12:10 regarding the operation of prophecy in the church. **what is good**. In context, this most likely refers to prophecies that pass the test.

5:22 Abstain from. Paul now moves on to stress, more generally, the importance of rejecting **every form of evil**.

5:23–28 *Prayer, Assurance, and Conclusion.* Just as the first half of the letter ended with a pastoral prayer that the Thessalonians be marked by holiness at the second coming of Christ (3:11–13), this half does too. However, here Paul adds reassurance (5:24). **God of peace**. God initiated the reconciliation of Christians with himself and is now at peace with them. **Spirit, soul,** and **body** represent the entirety of human nature. It seems unlikely that this is a tripartite division of human nature into body, soul, and spirit, where "spirit" and "soul" would refer to different parts; more likely Paul is simply using several terms for emphasis. For similar ways of expressing the totality of human nature see Matt. 10:28; Mark 12:30; 1 Cor. 7:34. There is no need for the Thessalonians to worry about whether they will be sufficiently holy and **blameless at the coming** of the Lord. God is faithful, and he will **surely** make it happen.

5:26 holy kiss. A symbol of Christian fellowship and holiness (see note on 1 Cor. 16:20; also cf. Acts 20:37; Rom. 16:16; 2 Cor. 13:12; 1 Pet. 5:14).

5:27 I. As usual, having dictated his letter to a secretary, Paul wrote the final greeting in his own handwriting as an authenticating mark (cf. 2 Thess. 3:17). **have this letter read to all**. The letter was to be read aloud to all community members, including the fainthearted and idle. See note on Col. 4:16.

INTRODUCTION TO

THE SECOND LETTER OF PAUL TO THE THESSALONIANS

2 THESSALONIANS

See Introduction to 1 Thessalonians, pp. 2301–2304.

Author and Title

Although some scholars today have questioned Pauline authorship of 2 Thessalonians, the unanimous testimony of the early church fathers supports Pauline authorship. The main reasons given by those who question Pauline authorship include: (1) The eschatology of 2 Thessalonians is regarded as different from that of 1 Thessalonians. Specifically, the sudden/imminent expectation of Christ's return in 1 Thessalonians 4:13–5:11 is said to be inconsistent with the requirement in 2 Thessalonians 2:1–12 that specific signs must first take place. (2) The many commonalities between 1 and 2 Thessalonians are alleged to reflect literary dependence, which is regarded as inconsistent with Paul's authorship of both. (3) Second Thessalonians supposedly has a colder tone than 1 Thessalonians. (4) Second Thessalonians 2:2 and 3:17 are thought to make best sense if written by a pseudonymous author.

A careful evaluation of these objections, however, supports the conclusion that Paul was in fact the writer of 2 Thessalonians. The duplicity entailed in the forgery hypothesis (see 3:17) is hardly credible. In addition, the above objections can be readily refuted: (1) Both letters portray the second coming as an unwelcome and sudden surprise for unbelievers (1 Thess. 5:2–3; 2 Thess. 2:8–12) but an anticipated and welcome event for those who are in Christ (1 Thess. 5:4–8; 2 Thess. 1:6–10; 2:13–17). Moreover, certain events precede the Lord's return in 1 Thessalonians 5:3 as well as 2 Thessalonians 2:3–4, 9–10, and imminence can be seen both in 1 Thessalonians 4:15–17 and in 2 Thessalonians 1:7, 10; 2:1. A sudden and imminent eschaton was regarded as compatible with signs in Jewish and early Christian writings (e.g., Matthew 24–25). (2) Paul probably wrote 2 Thessalonians shortly after 1 Thessalonians, and may have referred to a copy of it. (3) The idea of a colder tone in 2 Thessalonians is exaggerated (see "Literary Features" below). (4) Second Thessalonians 2:2 and 3:17 probably reflect Paul's concern that a forged letter may once have existed.

Date

Second Thessalonians was probably penned from Corinth in A.D. 49–51, shortly after 1 Thessalonians.

Relationship to 1 Thessalonians

Some have proposed that 2 Thessalonians preceded 1 Thessalonians, but 2 Thessalonians 2:15 rules this out. Others have postulated that Paul wrote 2 Thessalonians for a Jewish group within the church or even to the Philippians, but such hypotheses are in tension with 2 Thessalonians 1:1. Probably Paul wrote 2 Thessalonians soon after dispatching 1 Thessalonians, because he had received a report (2 Thess. 3:11) that the situation at Thessalonica had taken a surprising turn.

Theme

The theme of the second coming of Jesus dominates 2 Thessalonians just as it dominated 1 Thessalonians. Jesus' coming will be preceded by an "apostasy" (or rebellion) and by the revelation of the man of lawlessness, the Antichrist (2 Thess. 2:3). When Jesus comes, he will defeat this rebellious world ruler (2:8) and bring justice to oppressed Christians, and wrath to their persecutors and to unbelievers in general (1:5–10; 2:9–15).

Purpose, Occasion, and Background

The Thessalonian church had accepted the strange claim that "the day of the Lord has come" (2:1–2). How could they have thought this? Some think they spiritualized the concept of the day of the Lord, but Paul's argumentation seems inconsistent with this. Others postulate that they thought that tribulation was part of the day of the Lord and that it had begun, and consequently the second coming was imminent. However, Paul assumes that they knew the second coming occurred at the same time as the coming of the day of the Lord. As strange as it may seem, the Thessalonians may simply have fallen victim to the bizarre notion that the day of the Lord, understood in its normal sense, had come. As a result they were shaken and frightened (2:2). The Thessalonians were also undergoing persecution (1:4), which may have exacerbated their confusion about the end. Furthermore, the community had a problem with idlers refusing to work (3:6–15). They may have stopped working to await and preach the second coming, but evidence for connecting the problems in this way is lacking. Lazy Christians may simply have been exploiting wealthier Christians' generosity in order to avoid work.

Paul wrote 2 Thessalonians (1) to reassure those terrified by the thought that the day of the Lord had come (2:1–3:5), (2) to strengthen the Thessalonians in the face of unremitting persecution (1:3–12), and (3) to deal with the problem of some of the church members refusing to earn their own living (3:6–15).

Timeline

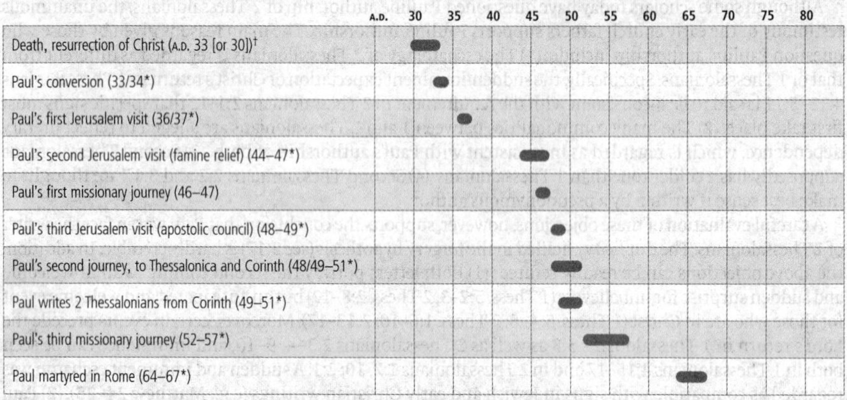

A.D. 30 35 40 45 50 55 60 65 70 75 80
Death, resurrection of Christ (A.D. 33 [or 30])†
Paul's conversion (33/34*)
Paul's first Jerusalem visit (36/37*)
Paul's second Jerusalem visit (famine relief) (44–47*)
Paul's first missionary journey (46–47)
Paul's third Jerusalem visit (apostolic council) (48–49*)
Paul's second journey, to Thessalonica and Corinth (48/49–51*)
Paul writes 2 Thessalonians from Corinth (49–51*)
Paul's third missionary journey (52–57*)
Paul martyred in Rome (64–67*)

** denotes approximate date; / signifies either/or; † see The Date of Jesus' Crucifixion, pp. 1809–1810*

History of Salvation Summary

Christians are to wait expectantly for the second coming of their Savior, Jesus Christ. (For an explanation of the "History of Salvation," see the Overview of the Bible, pp. 23–26.)

Literary Features

Second Thessalonians follows the customary order of a NT letter. It begins with a salutation and ends with a prayer and benediction. Between these bookends is found the type of informal letter that meanders through a series of topics in the way that present-day informal letters often do. There is the usual mixture of personalia (references to the letter writer's relationship with his recipients) and public information, and Christian doctrine and practical application.

In contrast to the warm and effusive tone of 1 Thessalonians, 2 Thessalonians includes some blunt commands as Paul addresses bad behavior and bad thinking. Further, this letter is noteworthy for the author's tough-mindedness in predicting judgment on the ungodly and rebuking church members who behave and think incorrectly. Still, there is a regular swing back and forth between reproof and warm encouragement.

Key Themes

1. God's righteous judgment will be fully manifest when Jesus returns. At that time unbelievers will be condemned and believers will be saved.	1:5–10; 2:9–14
2. Christians will share Christ's glory.	1:10, 12; 2:14
3. The lawless one's revelation and humanity's final rebellion are prerequisites for Jesus' second coming.	2:3–4, 9–12
4. The lawless one will deceive all those who have rejected the gospel, guaranteeing their condemnation when Jesus returns.	2:3, 6–12
5. Christians must not exploit the charity of fellow Christians.	3:6–15

Outline

I. Opening (1:1–2)

II. Thanksgiving and Comfort for the Persecuted Thessalonians (1:3–12)
- A. Thanksgiving proper (1:3–4)
- B. Justice guaranteed when Jesus returns (1:5–10)
- C. Prayer report (1:11–12)

III. Refuting the False Claim about the Day of the Lord (2:1–17)
- A. The false claim (2:1–2)
- B. The false claim refuted (2:3–12)
- C. Reassurance (2:13–14)
- D. Exhortation (2:15)
- E. Prayer (2:16–17)

IV. Transition (3:1–5)
- A. Request for prayer (3:1–2)
- B. Reassurance (3:3–4)
- C. Prayer (3:5)

V. The Problem of the Idlers (3:6–15)
- A. The command to the community (3:6)
- B. The tradition (3:7–10)
- C. The problem (3:11)
- D. The command to the idlers (3:12)
- E. Instructions to the community (3:13–15)

VI. Conclusion (3:16–18)

THE SECOND LETTER OF PAUL TO THE THESSALONIANS

2 THESSALONIANS

Greeting

1 [a]Paul, Silvanus, and Timothy,
To the church of the Thessalonians in God our Father and the Lord Jesus Christ:
2 Grace to you and peace from God our Father and the Lord Jesus Christ.

Thanksgiving

3 [b]We ought always to give thanks to God for you, brothers,[1] as is right, because your
faith is growing abundantly, and the love of every one of you for one another is increasing.
4 Therefore [c]we ourselves boast about you [d]in the churches of God for your steadfastness
and faith [e]in all your persecutions and in the afflictions that you are enduring.

The Judgment at Christ's Coming

5 This is [f]evidence of the righteous judgment of God, that you may be [g]considered worthy
of the kingdom of God, for which you are also suffering— 6 since indeed God considers
it [h]just [i]to repay with affliction those who afflict you, 7 and to grant [j]relief to you who are
afflicted as well as to us, when [k]the Lord Jesus is revealed from heaven [l]with his mighty
angels 8 [m]in flaming fire, inflicting vengeance on those [n]who do not know God and on
those who [o]do not obey the gospel of our Lord Jesus. 9 They will suffer the punishment
of [p]eternal destruction, [q]away from[2] the presence of the Lord and from the glory of his

[1] Or *brothers and sisters*. The plural Greek word *adelphoi* (translated "brothers") refers to siblings in a family. In New Testament usage, depending on the context, *adelphoi* may refer either to men or to both men and women who are siblings (brothers and sisters) in God's family, the church [2] Or *destruction that comes from*

Chapter 1
1 [a]For ver. 1, 2, see 1 Thess. 1:1
3 [b]ch. 2:13; See Eph. 5:20; 1 Thess. 1:2, 3
4 [c][2 Cor. 7:14]; See 1 Thess. 2:19 [d][1 Thess. 1:8]; See 1 Cor. 7:17 [e][Mark 10:30]; See 1 Thess. 2:14
5 [f][Phil. 1:28] [g][Acts 14:22]; See Luke 20:35
6 [h][Rev. 6:10] [i][Ex. 23:22; Joel 3:4, 7]
7 [j][Rev. 6:11; 11:18; 14:13] [k]See Luke 17:30 [l]See Jude 14
8 [m]Isa. 66:15, 16; Matt. 25:41; 1 Cor. 3:13; Heb. 10:27; 12:29; 2 Pet. 3:7; [Mal. 4:1] [n]See Gal. 4:8 [o]Rom. 2:8
9 [p][Phil. 3:19; 1 Thess. 5:3] [q]Isa. 2:10, 19, 21; [ch. 2:8]

1:1–2 *Opening.* Paul's opening here is very similar to 1 Thess. 1:1 (see note). On authorship, see Introduction: Author and Title. The fact that all three missionaries are still together suggests that 2 Thessalonians was written shortly after 1 Thessalonians.

1:3–12 *Thanksgiving and Comfort for the Persecuted Thessalonians.* In Greek, vv. 3–10 are one long, unwieldy sentence containing Paul's gratitude and encouragement.

1:3–4 *Thanksgiving Proper.* Paul gives thanks for the faith and love of the Thessalonians, even while they are suffering persecution.

1:3 ought . . . as is right. Paul is reassuring the Thessalonians that his giving **thanks to God** for them is both legitimate and necessary in the face of their concern caused by misunderstanding the Lord's return (2:1–2). Specifically he gives thanks for their increasing **faith** and **love** (cf. 1 Thess. 3:6). "Hope" is not mentioned here (cf. 1 Cor. 13:13; 1 Thess. 1:3; 5:8), which may suggest that the Thessalonians were in need of it. The fact that their love **for one another is increasing** is an answer to Paul's prayer in 1 Thess. 3:12.

1:4 The Thessalonians are so highly thought of that Paul and his coworkers **boast** about them to other **churches of God** concerning their **steadfastness and faith** in the context of unrelenting and severe **persecutions** and **afflictions**.

1:5–10 *Justice Guaranteed When Jesus Returns.* The wicked will be punished and the righteous vindicated.

1:5 The Thessalonians' endurance and faith under persecution constitute **evidence of the righteous judgment of God**. Since God is granting them the grace to endure, he is clearly on their side and is working to make them **worthy** for entrance into the **kingdom of God**. Cf. Phil. 1:28, where the Philippian Christians' fearless perseverance in persecution is a proof (Gk. *endeixis*, from the same root as *endeigma*) that they will be saved and their enemies destroyed when Jesus returns.

1:6–7a No one can doubt the fairness of God's judgment when he dispenses justice according to *lex talionis* (the principle of an eye for an eye): those now afflicting (Gk. *thlibō*) the Thessalonian Christians will be afflicted (Gk. *thlipsis*, a noun from the same root), and the afflicted believers will get relief at the second coming. **as well as to us**. The Thessalonians are not alone with respect to their suffering for Christ or their destiny when Jesus returns.

1:7b The just judgment of God comes in fullness at the second coming, **when the Lord Jesus is revealed from heaven** (cf. 1 Thess. 4:16–17). Jesus is called "Lord," which identifies him as Yahweh who executes final judgment (see Isaiah 64; 66; cf. Introduction to Mark: Key Themes).

1:8 in flaming fire. Jesus the judge will be awesome and devastating, and he will instill fear in the hearts of unbelievers. See Isa. 66:15–16; Dan. 7:9–10.

1:9 When Jesus comes again, unbelievers **will suffer the punishment of eternal destruction**, a ruinous and unending judgment of separation from Jesus. Against the idea of the final annihilation of unbelievers, see Matt. 25:46; Rev. 14:9–11.

1:10 when he comes. The punishment of unbelievers and the reward of believers both occur on the day of the Lord (**that day**), when Jesus comes to save his people. Confusion regarding the timing of the day of the Lord is a major problem in Thessalonica (2:2). Paul's description of the day in 1:7b–10 would have helped to alleviate the crisis. Jesus will at that time be **glorified** in his saints, that is, his glory will be seen in them (see Rom. 8:17–18, 30).

might, **10** [r]when he comes on [s]that day [t]to be glorified in his saints, and to be marveled
at among all who have believed, because our [u]testimony to you [v]was believed. **11** To this
end we [w]always pray for you, that our God may [x]make you worthy of his calling and may
fulfill every resolve for good and every [y]work of faith by his power, **12** so that the name of
our Lord Jesus [z]may be glorified in you, and you in him, according to the grace of our God
and the Lord Jesus Christ.

The Man of Lawlessness

2 Now concerning [a]the coming of our Lord Jesus Christ and our [b]being gathered together
to him, we ask you, brothers,[1] **2** not to be quickly shaken in mind or [c]alarmed, either
[d]by a spirit or a [e]spoken word, or [e]a letter seeming to be from us, to the effect that [f]the
day of the Lord has come. **3** [g]Let no one deceive you in any way. For that day will not come,
[h]unless the rebellion comes first, and [i]the man of lawlessness[2] is revealed, [j]the son of

[1] Or *brothers and sisters;* also verses 13, 15 [2] Some manuscripts *sin*

10 [r]See 1 Thess. 1:10 [s]See 1 Cor. 3:13 [t]Ps. 89:7 (Gk.); Isa. 49:3; John 17:10 [u][1 Cor. 1:6] [v][1 Thess. 2:1, 13; 1 Tim. 3:16]
11 [w]Col. 1:9 [x][ver. 5] [y]1 Thess. 1:3
12 [z][Isa. 66:5; Acts 13:48]

Chapter 2

1 [a]See 1 Thess. 2:19 [b][Matt. 24:31; 1 Thess. 4:15-17]
2 [c]Matt. 24:6; Mark 13:7 [d][1 John 4:1] [e]ver. 15; [1 Thess. 5:2] [f]See 1 Cor. 1:8
3 [g]Eph. 5:6 [h]1 Tim. 4:1 [i][ver. 8; Dan. 7:25; 8:25; 11:36; Rev. 13:5, 6] [j]John 17:12; [Matt. 23:15]

saints. Lit., "holy ones" (plural of Gk. *hagios*). Believers will be fully and finally transformed so that they are holy and blameless at the second coming (see 1 Thess. 3:13; 5:23–24). In addition, Jesus will be **marveled at among all who have believed**. Paul assumes that the Thessalonian Christians are included in this group, so he writes **because our testimony to you was believed**. To proclaim the gospel is to bear "testimony" to the saving act of God in Christ.

1:11–12 *Prayer Report.* Paul's prayer for the Thessalonians is that God will make them worthy of their calling, so that Jesus may be glorified in them.

1:11 To this end. That is, in view of vv. 5–10. **our God**. Paul unites himself with the Thessalonians with respect to God. **make you worthy**. Having declared that the Thessalonian Christians will be considered worthy (Gk. *kataxioō*) of the kingdom when Jesus the judge comes (v. 5), Paul's prayer for them is that they may even now be made worthy (Gk. *axioō*) of this **calling** (see 1 Thess. 2:12). **resolve for good**. A God-imparted resolution to do good. **work of faith**. Work inspired by faith.

1:12 according to the grace of our God and the Lord Jesus Christ. The glorification of Christ's name in the Thessalonians occurs when they exalt him as Lord in their daily lives.

2:1–17 *Refuting the False Claim about the Day of the Lord.* Paul reassures the Thessalonians that the day of the Lord has not come. In 1 Thess. 5:1–11 Paul responded to a question from the community relating to the timing of the day of the Lord. He has now heard that they have succumbed to the false notion that the day of the Lord has already arrived (2 Thess. 2:1–2). Paul first points out that, before that day, a final rebellion and the revelation of the "man of lawlessness" must occur (vv. 3–12). Then he reassures the Thessalonians that they are destined for glory (vv. 13–14), and calls on them to hold firmly to the traditions he passed on to them (v. 15). He concludes with prayer (vv. 16–17).

2:1–2 *The False Claim.* The Thessalonians were alarmed by a false claim concerning the day of the Lord.

2:1 Paul discusses Christ's **coming** (Gk. *parousia*), his return in glory at the end of the age to save the elect and punish the wicked, and **our being gathered together** (Gk. *episynagōgē*) **to him** (see Matt. 24:31 with the related verb *episynagō*; cf. also 1 Thess. 4:16–17). The idea that the day of the Lord had already come (2 Thess. 2:2) may have made the Thessalonians fear that Jesus' coming and the gathering of his people to him were no longer legitimate or realistic expectations.

2:2 The Thessalonians were **shaken** into mindless panic and were **alarmed** or frightened by the false claim that the day of the Lord had already come. Though the source of the confusion was unknown to Paul, he suggests a number of possibilities: **a spirit**. An alleged prophetic word. **a spoken word**. A word of teaching or a sermon. **a letter seeming to be from us**. Paul seems to have suspected that a letter forged in his name was circulating (3:17). **the day of the Lord**. See notes on Amos 5:18–20; 1 Thess. 5:2–3. Although some believe that the Thessalonians were thinking in terms of a complex of events that would lead to the second coming, Paul seems to assume here, as elsewhere (1 Cor. 1:8; Phil. 1:10; 1 Thess. 5:1–4; 2 Thess. 1:7–10), that the arrival of the day of the Lord and the second coming occur at the same time, as aspects of a single event. **has come**. The Thessalonians have fallen victim to the implausible notion that the day of the Lord has come, presumably because some source they regard as authoritative has claimed this. There is no reason to think that the idea was part of a developed heresy.

2:3–12 *The False Claim Refuted.* Paul insists that the Thessalonians can know that the day of the Lord has not come.

2:3 The day of the Lord will be preceded by two events, neither of which has been fulfilled. The **first** prerequisite is **the rebellion**. Although some have suggested that this refers to a Christian or Jewish apostasy, in view of vv. 9–12 a rebellion of humanity as a whole against God is probably in view. Just as humanity in Adam has rejected God and has been plunged into ever greater depths of sin as a result (Rom. 1:18–32), so it will move into all-out rebellion against God when the Antichrist appears (2 Thess. 2:4). **the man of lawlessness is revealed**. This second prerequisite, elsewhere called the "antichrist" (see 1 John 2:18, 22; 4:3; 2 John 7), will personify hostility to God and his revelation. He will disclose who he is, the rebel par excellence. He is **the son of destruction**, the one whose destiny is to be defeated and destroyed when Jesus returns (2 Thess. 2:8).

The Authentication of Paul's Letters

In 2 Thess. 2:2 Paul warns against letters that claim to come from him but do not. Thus in 11 places in his letters Paul either identifies himself or gives his signature. These features support the conclusion that all the NT letters attributed to Paul are in fact authentic (rather than having been written by someone else "pseudonymously" in Paul's name).

1 Cor. 16:21	I, Paul, write this greeting with my own hand
2 Cor. 10:1	I, Paul, myself entreat you
Gal. 5:2	Look: I, Paul, say to you
Gal. 6:11	See with what large letters I am writing to you with my own hand
Eph. 3:1	I, Paul, a prisoner for Christ Jesus
Col. 1:23	of which I, Paul, became a minister
Col. 4:18	I, Paul, write this greeting with my own hand
1 Thess. 2:18	we wanted to come to you—I, Paul, again and again
2 Thess. 2:2	not to be . . . alarmed . . . by . . . a letter seeming to be from us
2 Thess. 3:17	I, Paul, write this greeting with my own hand. This is the sign of genuineness in every letter of mine; it is the way I write
Philem. 19	I, Paul, write this with my own hand

destruction,[1] 4 who opposes and exalts himself against every so-called god or object of
worship, so that he takes his seat in the temple of God, [k]proclaiming himself to be God.
5 Do you not remember that when I was still with you I told you these things? 6 And you
know what is restraining him now so that he may be revealed in his time. 7 For [l]the mystery
of lawlessness [m]is already at work. Only he who now restrains it will do so until he is out
of the way. 8 And then [n]the lawless one will be revealed, whom the Lord Jesus [o]will kill
with [p]the breath of his mouth and bring to nothing by [q]the appearance of his coming.
9 The coming of the lawless one is by the activity of Satan [r]with all power and false signs
and wonders, 10 and with all wicked deception for [s]those who are perishing, because they
refused to love the truth and so be saved. 11 Therefore [t]God sends them a strong delusion,
so that they may believe [u]what is false, 12 in order that all may be condemned [v]who did
not believe the truth but [w]had pleasure in unrighteousness.

Stand Firm

13 But [x]we ought always to give thanks to God for you, [y]brothers beloved by the Lord,
because God chose you [z]as the firstfruits[2] [a]to be saved, [b]through sanctification by the Spirit
and belief in the truth. 14 To this he called you through [c]our gospel, [a]so that you may obtain
the glory of our Lord Jesus Christ. 15 So then, brothers, [d]stand firm and hold to [e]the traditions that you were taught by us, either [f]by our spoken word or by [f]our letter.
16 Now may our Lord Jesus Christ himself, and God our Father, [g]who loved us and gave
us eternal comfort and good [h]hope through grace, 17 comfort your hearts and [i]establish
them in every good work and word.

[1] Greek *the son of perdition* (a Hebrew idiom) [2] Some manuscripts *chose you from the beginning*

4[k][Isa. 14:14; Ezek. 28:2]
7[l]Rev. 17:5, 7 [m]1 John 2:18; 4:3
8[n]See ver. 3 [o][Dan. 7:10, 11] [p]Isa. 11:4 [q][1 Tim. 6:14; 2 Tim. 1:10; 4:1, 8; Titus 2:13]
9[r][Rev. 13:14]; See Matt. 24:24
10[s]See 1 Cor. 1:18
11[t][1 Kgs. 22:22; Ezek. 14:9; Rev. 17:17] [u][1 Thess. 2:3; 1 Tim. 4:2]; See Rom. 1:25
12[v]Rom. 2:8 [w]See Rom. 1:32
13[x]ch. 1:3 [y]1 Thess. 1:4; [Deut. 33:12] [z]Eph. 1:4 [a]1 Thess. 5:9; [2 Tim. 1:9] [b]See 1 Thess. 4:3
14[c]1 Thess. 1:5 [a][See ver. 13 above]
15[d]See 1 Cor. 16:13 [e]ch. 3:6; 1 Cor. 11:2 [f]ver. 2
16[g]John 3:16; 1 John 4:10; Rev. 1:5 [h]1 Pet. 1:3
17[i]ch. 3:3; 1 Thess. 3:13

2:4 Paul draws on Dan. 11:36–37 when he says that the lawless one **opposes and exalts himself against every so-called god or object of worship**. The Antichrist will not countenance any rivals but will insist that he alone is God. The **temple of God** has been variously interpreted as the church, the heavenly temple, the Jerusalem temple, and a metaphor for supreme blasphemous arrogance modeled on the activities of Antiochus IV Epiphanes (see notes on Dan. 11:31–35). Whatever the meaning, the context seems to indicate a concrete and observable act of defiance against God.

2:5–7 Paul is apparently surprised that his own teaching on the end times had not stopped the Thessalonians from believing the false claim (v. 5; cf. v. 2), so he rehearses that teaching (vv. 6–7). The man of lawlessness cannot be unveiled while **what is restraining** (Gk. *to katechon*, neuter participle of *katechō*, "to prevent, hinder, restrain") **him now** is at work. In v. 7 Paul refers to **he who now restrains** (Gk. *ho katechōn*, masculine participle of the same word). Scholarly theories on the identity of this restrainer include the Roman Empire/emperor, the Holy Spirit, and the archangel Michael. According to Dan. 10:13, 20–21, Michael restrains satanic principalities (cf. Rev. 12:7), and in rabbinical traditions and the Septuagint of Dan. 12:1, Michael is said to "pass away" when the Antichrist pitches his tents in Judea (Dan. 11:45) just before the great tribulation begins (Dan. 12:1). The restrainer functions to make sure that the man of lawlessness is **revealed** (see 2 Thess. 2:3) **in his time** and not before. Prior to the revelation of lawlessness personified, it operates as an impersonal **mystery**, stirring up hostility to Christ and his people. Lawlessness remains in mystery form until the restrainer is taken **out of the way**.

2:8 And then the lawless one will be revealed. As soon as the restrainer is removed, lawlessness is free to manifest itself in unrestrained fashion in the Antichrist. In God's providence, Jesus' second coming overthrows the rule of the Antichrist. **the breath of his mouth** (cf. Isa. 11:4). The Lord will destroy the Antichrist with overwhelming ease when he comes again.

2:9–10 The coming of the lawless one. The Antichrist has a "coming" (Gk. *parousia*) which is a poor substitute for Jesus' coming (Gk. *parousia*, v. 8). Satan is the power behind the Antichrist, working with unrestricted **power** on his behalf through **signs and wonders**—which (though they are **false**) lead people to believe that the Antichrist is God. Unbelievers are **those who are perishing** because they have failed to embrace the gospel, God's only way of salvation.

2:11–12 Because unbelievers have rejected God's offer of salvation in the gospel, **God sends them a strong delusion**. As part of his righteous judgment, God is instrumental in causing these unbelievers to embrace the Antichrist (**believe what is false**) so that they advance to a whole new level of rebellion and are thus **condemned** as allies of the Antichrist at the second coming.

2:13–14 *Reassurance.* Paul reassures the Thessalonians that, in contrast to unbelievers (vv. 10–12), they have accepted God's call and so have demonstrated that they were elected by God to be saved when Jesus returns.

2:13 ought. See 1:3. **give thanks**. This is technically the second thanksgiving in the letter (see 1:3; cf. 1 Thess. 1:2; 2:13). **beloved by the Lord . . . God chose you**. See note on 1 Thess. 1:4. This may echo Deut. 26:18, where the reference is to God's choice of Israel. **as the firstfruits**. This indicates that the Thessalonians, as early Christians, are the firstfruits of the new humanity, or of Thessalonica. (On firstfruits offerings, see Ex. 23:19; 34:26.) However, as the ESV footnote indicates, some manuscripts read "from the beginning" (Gk. *ap' archēs*) rather than "as firstfruits" (Gk. *aparchēn*; see note on 1 Cor. 15:20). In that case, Paul's point is that God's choice was in eternity past. Either way, Christians were divinely elected **to be saved**, and this was to be the ultimate end of a journey marked by **sanctification by the Spirit and belief in the truth**, in contrast to the way of unbelievers, who are marked by unrighteousness and will believe the Antichrist's lie (2 Thess. 2:10–12). Note the involvement of each person of the Trinity: the Father elects, the Son loves, and the Holy Spirit makes holy.

2:14 To this (i.e., salvation) **he called you through our gospel**. The divine call was effectual and was actualized in history through Paul's preaching. **obtain the glory**. See 1:10; 1 Thess. 5:9.

2:15 *Exhortation.* Paul exhorts the Thessalonians to hold on to the true traditions that were passed on from him to them. This verse contrasts with v. 2, where Paul warns them not to be shaken by a false prophecy or teaching or by a forged letter attributed to the missionaries. Rather, they are to **stand firm and hold to the traditions** that were communicated directly to them **by our spoken word** during his ministry among them and later by 1 Thessalonians (**our letter**).

2:16–17 *Prayer.* Paul prays that the Thessalonians will be divinely comforted and established **in every good work and word**.

Pray for Us

3 Finally, brothers,[1] [j]pray for us, that [k]the word of the Lord may speed ahead and be
honored,[2] as happened among you, 2 and [l]that we may be delivered from wicked and
evil men. For [m]not all have faith. 3 But [n]the Lord is faithful. He will establish you and [o]guard
you against [p]the evil one.[3] 4 And [q]we have confidence in the Lord about you, that you are
doing and will do the things that we command. 5 May the Lord [r]direct your hearts to the
love of God and to the steadfastness of Christ.

Warning Against Idleness

6 Now we command you, brothers, [s]in the name of our Lord Jesus Christ, [t]that you
keep away from any [u]brother [v]who is walking in idleness and not in accord with the tradition that you received from us. 7 For you yourselves know [w]how you ought to imitate
us, because [x]we were not idle when we were with you, 8 nor did we eat anyone's bread
without paying for it, but [y]with toil and labor we worked night and day, that we might
not be a burden to any of you. 9 It was [z]not because we do not have that right, but to give
you in ourselves [a]an example to imitate. 10 For even when we were with you, we would
give you this command: [b]If anyone is not willing to work, let him not eat. 11 For we hear
that some among you [c]walk in idleness, not busy at work, but [d]busybodies. 12 Now such
persons we command and encourage in the Lord Jesus Christ to do their work quietly
and to earn their own living.[4]
13 As for you, brothers, [e]do not grow weary in doing good. 14 If anyone does not obey what

[1] Or *brothers and sisters;* also verses 6, 13 [2] Or *glorified* [3] Or *evil* [4] Greek *to eat their own bread*

Chapter 3
1 [j]See 1 Thess. 5:25 [k]Ps. 147:15; [1 Thess. 1:8]
2 [l]Rom. 15:31 [m][Deut. 32:20]
3 [n]See 1 Cor. 1:9 [o]Matt. 6:13; John 17:15 [p]See Matt. 13:19
4 [q]See 2 Cor. 2:3
5 [r]1 Thess. 3:11
6 [s]1 Cor. 5:4 [t]ver. 14; [Matt. 18:17; 2 Tim. 3:5]; See 1 Cor. 5:9; 2 John 10 [u]1 Cor. 5:11 [v]ver. 11; 1 Thess. 5:14
7 [w][Acts 20:35]; See 1 Thess. 1:6 [x]1 Thess. 1:5
8 [y]See 1 Thess. 2:9
9 [z]1 Cor. 9:4; 1 Thess. 2:6 [a]ver. 7; 1 Pet. 5:3
10 [b][Gen. 3:19]; See 1 Thess. 4:11
11 [c]ver. 6 [d]1 Tim. 5:13; 1 Pet. 4:15
13 [e]Gal. 6:9; [1 Cor. 15:58]

3:1–5 *Transition.* Paul requests prayer for his work, reassures the Thessalonians regarding God's faithfulness, and closes by praying for the Thessalonians.

3:1–2 *Request for Prayer.* Paul requests prayer for the gospel's advance through his ministry and for deliverance from wicked opponents. He prays that **the word of the Lord** (the gospel) would **speed ahead** (enjoy unhindered progress) and **be honored** (by people acknowledging its truth and embracing God's offer of salvation). **For not all have faith.** The gospel is not always embraced with faith; indeed, it frequently provokes violent hostility.

3:3–4 *Reassurance.* Paul gives some final words of comfort to the Thessalonians in the wake of the false claim about Christ's return (2:2). In Greek, the last word of 3:2 is "faith" (Gk. *pistis*) and the first word of v. 3 is **faithful** (Gk. *pistos*)—the unbelievers' lack of faith contrasts with God's faithfulness. **guard you against the evil one.** Satan has been seeking to destroy the Thessalonians' young faith. But God's faithfulness assures Paul that the Evil One will not succeed: the Thessalonians will overcome him by responding appropriately to Paul's two letters. He has confidence that they already **are doing** and, when they get this letter, **will do the things that we command.** Paul may have in mind his instruction to discipline those within their community who are idle (vv. 6–15) and/or his command to hold to the traditions about the day of the Lord (2:15).

3:5 *Prayer.* Paul prays that the Thessalonians will be directed toward **the love of God** and **the steadfastness of Christ,** by which he means either Christ's endurance as a model for Christians or the perseverance imparted by Christ.

3:6–15 *The Problem of the Idlers.* Paul instructs the Thessalonian community to exercise church discipline on those refusing to work. Although there is nothing in 1 or 2 Thessalonians that explicitly links the idleness with the confusion about the end times, many think that the Thessalonians stopped working to await and proclaim the Lord's coming. Others believe that the problem was merely one of lazy Christians exploiting the charity of wealthier Christians, and using their free time to meddle in others' affairs. Whatever the cause of the idleness, Paul's patience has evidently now run out (cf. 1 Thess. 4:9–12).

3:6 *The Command to the Community.* Paul strongly commands (Gk. *parangellō*) the community as a whole to discipline by disassociation those who are not working but are depending on others for a living. The community is to **keep away from** these idlers, which probably means excommunicating them. Paul takes the sin of these people seriously, but at this point he still regards them as "brothers" (v. 15). **In idleness** (Gk. *ataktōs*) means "in an undisciplined, irresponsible, or disorderly manner." These people are shirking their obligation to work (see Gen. 2:15). This behavior was **not in accord with the tradition** passed on by the missionaries regarding the necessity of working for one's keep.

3:7–10 *The Tradition.* The missionaries had passed on the tradition about the need to work for a living both by example (vv. 7–9) and through oral instruction (v. 10).

3:8–9 eat anyone's bread without paying for it. Paul refused to depend on others for his living. Indeed he took on a heavy workload of manual labor in addition to his ministry commitments in order to avoid being a financial **burden** to any Thessalonian Christian, even though (in contrast to the idle Thessalonians) it was his God-given **right** to be supported (see 1 Cor. 9:3–15; 2 Cor. 11:7–9; 1 Thess. 2:9). He wanted to provide his converts with **an example to imitate.**

3:11 *The Problem.* **not busy at work, but busybodies.** There is a wordplay here in Greek: not *ergazomenous* ("working") but *periergazomenous* ("being a busybody, meddling"). Those who refused to work were exploiting their free time to meddle in others' affairs. Cf. 1 Tim. 5:13, where irreligious prying flows from idleness.

3:12 *The Command to the Idlers.* Paul forcefully commands the idle to get back to work, so that they may be financially independent. **work quietly.** The opposite of being nuisances or "busybodies" (v. 11).

3:13–15 *Instructions to the Community.* The community is to keep doing good (v. 13) and to discipline any unrepentant idlers (vv. 14–15).

3:13 The community as a whole, particularly wealthier members exploited by the idle, might **grow weary in doing good,** but Paul calls on them to continue being charitable, albeit only to those who are deserving.

3:14 Paul believes it is very possible that some will ignore his warning and continue in their idle ways, so he instructs the community as a whole to **take note of** such people and **have nothing to do with** them (cf. v. 6). The purpose of this disassociation is so that the stubbornly insubordinate brothers will **be ashamed,** repent, and be restored to the community. Church discipline must always aim at renewing discipleship.

we say in this letter, take note of that person, and [f]have nothing to do with him, that he
may be ashamed. 15 [g]Do not regard him as an enemy, but [h]warn him as a brother.

Benediction

16 Now may [i]the Lord of peace himself [j]give you peace at all times in every way. [k]The
Lord be with you all.

17 I, Paul, write [l]this greeting with my own hand. This is the sign of genuineness in every
letter of mine; it is the way I write. 18 [m]The grace of our Lord Jesus Christ be with you all.

14 [f]See ver. 6
15 [g]See Lev. 19:17; Matt. 18:15 [h]1 Thess. 5:12, 14; [Titus 3:10]
16 [i]See Rom. 15:33; Eph. 6:23 [j]Num. 6:26 [k]Ruth 2:4
17 [l]See 1 Cor. 16:21
18 [m]See Rom. 16:20

3:15 Disciplining a fellow Christian can easily degenerate into the community treating him **as an enemy**, so Paul says **warn him as a brother**.

3:16–18 *Conclusion.* The letter concludes with a benediction, a final greeting, and a prayer for grace.

3:16 Paul offers a benediction. **Lord of peace**. Jesus has reconciled the Thessalonian Christians to God and is at peace with them, able to replace their disturbed fear (2:2) with an experience of inner peace. **in every way**. Especially peace as opposed to consternation regarding the end times (2:1–3:5) and peace amid ongoing persecution (1:5–10).

3:17 Paul makes explicit what would have been clear to readers of the original letter: the bulk of the letter was dictated to a secretary, and the final **greeting** was written in Paul's own unique handwriting, which served as a mark of authenticity, much like signatures at the end of modern letters. Paul's highlighting of this fact may reflect a suspicion that a forgery in his name was in existence, which may have been the source of the idea that the day of the Lord had already come (see 2:2). This affirmation of genuineness also shows that writing in another person's name was condemned among early Christians.

INTRODUCTION TO

THE FIRST LETTER OF PAUL TO TIMOTHY

1 TIMOTHY

Author and Title

The first verse of 1 Timothy clearly states that Paul is the author, and this was universally affirmed until the nineteenth century. In the last 200 years a significant shift has occurred in biblical scholarship so that many today deny that Paul actually wrote 1 Timothy, 2 Timothy, or Titus. Critics point to ways in which these three letters (the "Pastoral Epistles") differ from Paul's other letters in style, vocabulary, theology, church order, and the way in which Paul is portrayed. However, the differences in theology and church order, for example, are typically overstated based on a particular reading of Paul's earlier letters, and based on the effect of reading these three letters as a unit rather than individually (as the rest of Paul's letters are read). For example, some claim that the Pastoral Epistles picture a much more structured church with an emphasis on church officers (esp. elders and deacons) rather than the dynamic, Spirit-directed church in Paul's other letters. This overstates the evidence of both groups of letters in opposite directions. Elders are mentioned as early as Paul's first missionary journey (Acts 14:21–23), and Philippians is addressed to the "overseers and deacons" of the church in Philippi (Phil. 1:1). Furthermore, difference in style and vocabulary is not unusual for a creative mind, especially considering that these letters differ from the other letters in purpose, subject matter, and audience, these being the only ones written to coworkers.

Additionally, it is problematic to argue that these works were written under a false name since the early church clearly excluded from the apostolic canon any works they thought to be pseudonymous. While critics point to the common practice of pseudonymous writing in the ancient world, they usually fail to point out that this practice, though common in the culture, was not common in personal letters, and was categorically rejected by the early church (cf. 2 Thess. 2:2; 3:17; also *Muratorian Canon* 64–67; Eusebius, *Ecclesiastical History* 6.12.3). Tertullian (c. A.D. 160–225) wrote that when it was discovered that a church elder had composed a pseudonymous work, *The Acts of Paul* (which included a purported Pauline letter, *3 Corinthians*), the offending elder "was removed from his office" (*On Baptism* 17). Accepting as Scripture letters that lie about their origin is also a significant ethical problem. Thus, there is a good basis for affirming the straightforward claim of these letters as authentically written by Paul.

The title indicates that this letter was sent to Timothy (1:2), and its contents confirm that, chronologically, it precedes 2 Timothy.

Date

Some critics have suggested that 1 Timothy does not seem to fit into the narrative of Acts. Others have responded that it could fit into the events in Acts 20. However, the traditional position has been that Paul was released from his first Roman imprisonment (the one mentioned at the close of Acts; see Acts 28:16, 30–31), did further mission work, and was then imprisoned a second time, leading to his execution. This reconstruction is supported by statements from *1 Clement* 5.7 and Eusebius, *Ecclesiastical History* 2.22.2–8. First Timothy then would fit well during Paul's work between the two imprisonments. If Paul's arrival in Rome, as narrated in Acts, is dated about A.D. 59–61, then, allowing a couple of years for the imprisonment, he would have been released in about 62. If Paul was executed under Nero (d. A.D. 68), 1 Timothy would have been written somewhere in the mid-60s (cf. note on Acts 28:30–31).

Theme

The theme of 1 Timothy is that the gospel leads to practical, visible change in the lives of those who believe it. It is often thought that the theme is church order, but the discussion of church offices is simply a piece of the larger argument that the true gospel, in contrast to false teaching, will always lead to godliness in its adherents.

Purpose, Occasion, and Background

Paul wrote 1 Timothy in order to advise his young coworker Timothy concerning issues that were arising at the church in Ephesus. When Paul left Timothy in Ephesus, he had specifically charged him to deal with some false teachers in the church (1:3). Since Paul was then separated from Timothy and the church, he wrote back to him with further instructions. He hoped to return for a visit but wrote in the meantime to address the way in which Christians should behave (3:14–15). Throughout the letter Paul grounds Christian behavior in the gospel.

The false teachers are the primary occasion for the letter. The letter as a whole is bracketed by discussion of the false teaching (see Outline), and the positive instruction is crafted in direct contrast to the false teachers. The exact nature of the false teaching is unclear. It apparently involved speculation about the law (1:7–11) and asceticism (4:1–5). Paul's real concern is with the results of the false teaching—for example, promoting speculations (1:4; 6:4), arrogance (6:4), and greed (6:5–10). Paul addresses the content of the false teaching only in passing but focuses on the fact that true Christianity is evidenced by lifestyles shaped by the gospel. Those whose lives are not shaped by the gospel show that they have turned away from the faith (1:6, 19–20; 4:1; 5:6, 8, 11–12, 15; 6:9–10).

First Timothy is a clear call for the church to live out in tangible ways the ethical implications of the gospel.

Key Themes

1. The gospel produces holiness in the lives of believers, and there is no legitimate separation between belief and behavior. Thus, those who profess faith but do not demonstrate any progress in godliness should question their spiritual state.	1:5; 2:8–15; 3:1–16; 4:6–16; 5:4–6, 8; 6:3–5, 11–14, 18–19
2. Worldwide evangelization is essential and is rooted in God's own evangelistic desire.	1:15; 2:1–7; 3:16; 4:10
3. One key evidence of reception of the gospel is proper behavior in corporate worship (evangelistic prayer, unity, modesty, and submission).	2:1–15
4. Church leaders should be people whose lives are shaped by the gospel.	3:1–13; 4:6–16
5. Appropriate honor is a key element in how Christians should relate to one another in the church.	5:1–6:2
6. The created order (e.g., wealth) is good and is to be appreciated, though not worshiped.	4:4–5; 6:17–19
7. It is important to labor for the purity and preservation of the gospel.	1:3–7, 18–20; 4:6–16; 6:2b–3, 12, 20–21

History of Salvation Summary

God's plan brings the blessings of Christ's salvation to people partly by means of the church and its ministries. (For an explanation of the "History of Salvation," see the Overview of the Bible, pp. 23–26.)

Literary Features

The general form of 1 Timothy is that of a NT *epistle*, and 1 Timothy, 2 Timothy, and Titus have been called more specifically "Pastoral Epistles" because each one is a letter written to someone who has pastoral leadership responsibilities. The letter gives advice on the issues of church life on which the recipient needs guidance and encouragement—though Timothy was not actually one of the pastors of a church but was Paul's liaison who implemented Paul's instructions to the churches. The resulting letter is occasional, meaning that the author of the letter addresses the specific situations in the recipient's church that need attention. The Pastoral Epistles are not theological treatises in which Paul systematically explores topics of his choice. Paul takes up the topics in this letter because they are the topics that have been raised. Finally, near the end of the opening chapter, Paul labels his remarks up to that point as "this charge" that he has committed to Timothy. It is helpful to regard the entire letter as a formal, authoritative charge—a list of duties that Paul is challenging and directing Timothy to perform.

The stance of the author is that of a friend and father in the faith expressing personal concern over the well-being of a younger church leader and the church in which he ministers. The overarching concern of the letter is to combat false teaching and false teachers. Accordingly, there are detailed contrasts between good and bad spiritual leadership in the church.

Additionally, this letter provides the most complete summary in the Bible of a pastor's ministry and spirituality. There are also lists of spiritual qualifications for officers in the church, as well as advice about caring for people with special needs, such as widows and servants. Three times Paul says that a statement he makes is "trustworthy" (1:15; 3:1; 4:9).

Timeline

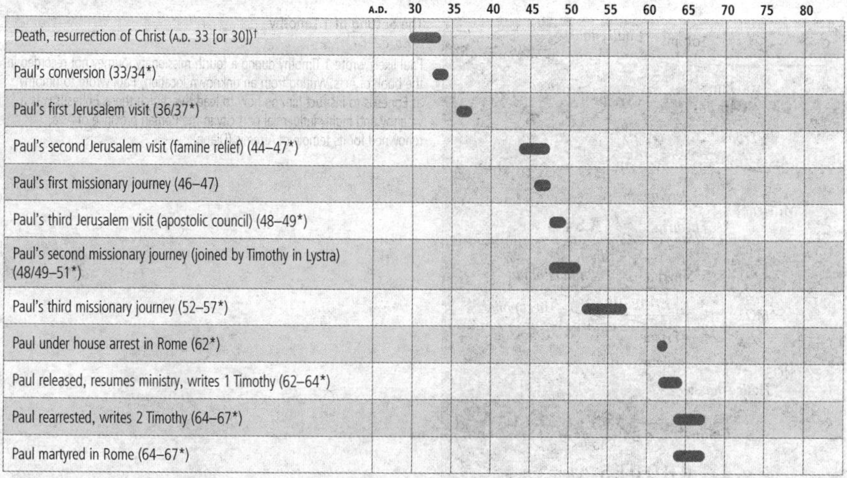

A.D. 30 35 40 45 50 55 60 65 70 75 80
Death, resurrection of Christ (A.D. 33 [or 30])†
Paul's conversion (33/34*)
Paul's first Jerusalem visit (36/37*)
Paul's second Jerusalem visit (famine relief) (44–47*)
Paul's first missionary journey (46–47)
Paul's third Jerusalem visit (apostolic council) (48–49*)
Paul's second missionary journey (joined by Timothy in Lystra) (48/49–51*)
Paul's third missionary journey (52–57*)
Paul under house arrest in Rome (62*)
Paul released, resumes ministry, writes 1 Timothy (62–64*)
Paul rearrested, writes 2 Timothy (64–67*)
Paul martyred in Rome (64–67*)

** denotes approximate date; / signifies either/or; † see The Date of Jesus' Crucifixion, pp. 1809–1810*

Outline

I. Salutation (1:1–2)

II. Confronting the False Teaching (1:3–20)
   A. The charge to deal with false teachers (1:3–7)
   B. Proper use of the law (1:8–11)
   C. Paul: an example of the effect of the true gospel (1:12–17)
   D. Restatement of the charge to deal with false teachers (1:18–20)

III. Descriptions of Gospel-Shaped Living (2:1–3:13)
   A. Corporate prayer and issues arising from it (2:1–15)
   B. Qualifications for overseers (3:1–7)
   C. Qualifications for deacons (3:8–13)

IV. Purpose of Writing: Behavior in the Church (3:14–16)

V. Identifying the False Teaching (4:1–5)

VI. How Timothy Should Be Shaped by the Gospel (4:6–16)

VII. How Specific Groups in the Church Should Be Shaped by the Gospel (5:1–6:2a)
   A. Respectful dealing with church members by age and gender (5:1–2)
   B. Honoring widows (5:3–16)

C. Honoring elders (5:17–25)
D. Honoring masters (6:1–2a)

VIII. Confronting the False Teaching Again (6:2b–21)
A. False teachers and greed (6:2b–10)
B. Timothy's behavior in contrast (6:11–16)
C. Charge to the rich (6:17–19)
D. Closing exhortation to Timothy (6:20–21)

The Setting of 1 Timothy
c. A.D. 62–64
Paul likely wrote 1 Timothy during a fourth missionary journey not recorded in the book of Acts. Writing from an unknown location, Paul wrote to Timothy at Ephesus to instruct him on how to lead the church there. Ephesus was a wealthy and highly influential port city in the Roman province of Asia, renowned for its temple of Artemis (Diana).

THE FIRST LETTER OF PAUL TO TIMOTHY

1 TIMOTHY

Greeting

1 Paul, [a]an apostle of Christ Jesus [b]by command of [c]God our Savior and of Christ Jesus
[d]our hope,
2 To Timothy, [e]my true child in the faith:
[f]Grace, mercy, and peace from God the Father and Christ Jesus our Lord.

Warning Against False Teachers

3 [g]As I urged you when I was going to Macedonia, remain at Ephesus so that you may charge
certain persons not [h]to teach any different doctrine, 4 nor [i]to devote themselves to myths and
endless [j]genealogies, which promote [k]speculations rather than the stewardship[1] from God
that is by faith. 5 The aim of our charge is love [l]that issues from a pure heart and [m]a good

[1] Or *good order*

Chapter 1
1 [a]See 2 Cor. 1:1 [b]Titus 1:3; [Rom. 16:26] [c]See Luke 1:47 [d]Col. 1:27
2 [e]Titus 1:4 [f]2 Tim. 1:2; 2 John 3; [Jude 2]
3 [g][Titus 1:5] [h]ch. 6:3; [Gal. 1:6, 7]
4 [i]ch. 4:7; 2 Tim. 4:4; Titus 1:14; 2 Pet. 1:16 [j]Titus 3:9 [k]ch. 6:4
5 [l]2 Tim. 2:22 [m]1 Pet. 3:16, 21

1:1–2 *Salutation.* This letter clearly claims to be written by Paul. A denial of its Pauline authorship raises significant issues regarding the reliability of Scripture. See Introduction: Author and Title.

1:1 Paul reinforces his apostolic authority by stating that his apostleship came **by command of God**. On the basis of this command, he charges Timothy with his task (v. 3) and provides a general charge to Christians (v. 5). On "God **our Savior**," cf. note on 2 Tim. 1:8–10.

1:2 Paul's normal greeting in his letters is simply **grace . . . and peace**. Some wonder at the addition of **mercy** here (cf. 2 Tim. 1:2), but Paul often introduced things in the opening of his letters that he would deal with later in the letter (cf. 1 Tim. 1:13, 16).

1:3–20 *Confronting the False Teaching.* Paul charges Timothy to deal with the false teachers (vv. 3–7), briefly corrects their understanding of the law (vv. 8–11), presents himself as an example of the intended effect of the gospel (vv. 12–17), and restates his basic charge with some specific examples of false teachers (vv. 18–20).

1:3–7 *The Charge to Deal with False Teachers.* At least one of Timothy's purposes in Ephesus was to deal with false teaching that was troubling the church. Not enough information is given to determine exactly what the false teaching was. The concern here is not so much the *identity* of the false teachers but their *effect*, which was in direct contrast to the goal of apostolic instruction. The results of false teaching were "speculations" (v. 4) and "vain discussion" (v. 6) while the result of true teaching is "love" coming from "a pure heart and a good conscience and a sincere faith" (v. 5). The focus of false teaching led to "swerving" and wandering (v. 6) while the focus of true teaching was a steadfast "aim" (v. 5). And regarding the law, the advocates of false teaching were "without understanding" (v. 7) while the advocates of true teaching had correct knowledge (vv. 8–11).

1:4 Myths (Gk. *mythos*) in the NT is a negative term characterizing beliefs as fanciful, untrue, and even deceptive (cf. 2 Tim. 4:4; Titus 1:14). Such myths were often used to excuse immoral behavior. With the later reference to the misuse of the law (1 Tim. 1:7–10), **genealogies** here seems to refer to speculative use of OT accounts of biblical characters or family trees. **Stewardship from God** translates a phrase (Gk. *oikonomian theou*) that is difficult to capture in translation (Gk. *oikonomia* can mean "orderly plan" or "household management, stewardship"). In this context it either refers to God's orderly outworking of his plan of salvation in all human history, or to human responsibility ("stewardship") in advancing that plan. In either case, the false teachers produce speculation rather than the advance of the kingdom by faith in Christ.

1:5 The aim of our charge, that is, the goal of apostolic instruction, **is love**—a clear indication of the intended result of Paul's teaching in 1 Timothy. Whereas false teaching results in meaningless speculation, proper apostolic teaching results in practical good behavior rooted in love. And that love must come from internal, Spirit-worked changes that have produced **a pure heart** (rather than one filled with sinful desires), **a good conscience** (rather than one laden with guilt), and **a sincere faith** (rather than pretense and hypocrisy). This verse is central for the whole letter.

False Teaching and Teachers

1:3	teaching a different doctrine
1:6	swerving from a pure heart, good conscience, and sincere faith
1:6	wandering away into vain discussions
1:7	lacking understanding
1:10	practicing something contrary to sound doctrine
1:19	making shipwreck of their faith
1:20	blaspheming
4:1	departing from the faith
4:1	devoting themselves to deceitful spirits and teachings of demons
4:2	insincere, lying, having a seared conscience
4:7	perpetuating irreverent, silly myths
5:15	straying after Satan
5:20	persisting in sin
6:10	wandering away from the faith
6:20	irreverent babble and contradictions
6:21	swerving from the faith

conscience and [n]a sincere faith. 6 Certain persons, by [o]swerving from these, have wandered
away into [p]vain discussion, 7 desiring to be teachers of the law, [q]without understanding
either what they are saying or the things about which they make confident assertions.
8 Now we know that [r]the law is good, if one uses it lawfully, 9 understanding this, that
the [s]law is not laid down for the just but for the lawless and disobedient, for the ungodly
and sinners, for the unholy and profane, for those who strike their fathers and mothers,
for murderers, 10 the sexually immoral, men who practice homosexuality, enslavers,[1] liars,
perjurers, and whatever else is contrary to [t]sound[2] doctrine, 11 in accordance with [u]the
gospel of the glory of [v]the blessed God [w]with which I have been entrusted.

Christ Jesus Came to Save Sinners

12 I thank him [x]who has given me strength, Christ Jesus our Lord, because he judged me
faithful, [y]appointing me to his service, 13 though formerly I was a blasphemer, [z]persecutor,
and insolent opponent. But [a]I received mercy [b]because I had acted ignorantly in unbelief,
14 and [c]the grace of our Lord overflowed for me with the [d]faith and love that are in Christ
Jesus. 15 The saying is [e]trustworthy and deserving of full acceptance, that Christ Jesus [f]came
into the world to save sinners, [g]of whom I am the foremost. 16 But I received mercy for this
reason, that in me, as the foremost, Jesus Christ might display his perfect patience as an

[1] That is, those who take someone captive in order to sell him into slavery [2] Or *healthy*

5 [n]Rom. 12:9; 2 Tim. 1:5
6 [o]ch. 6:21 [p]Titus 1:10
7 [q][ch. 6:4; Col. 2:18]
8 [r]Rom. 7:16
9 [s]Gal. 5:23
10 [t]2 Tim. 4:3; [ch. 6:3; 2 Tim. 1:13; Titus 1:13; 2:2]
11 [u][2 Cor. 4:4] [v]ch. 6:15 [w]Titus 1:3; See Rom. 2:16; Gal. 2:7
12 [x]Acts 9:22; Phil. 4:13 [y]See 2 Cor. 3:6
13 [z]See Acts 8:3 [a]1 Cor. 7:25; 2 Cor. 4:1 [b]See Acts 3:17
14 [c]Rom. 5:20 [d][Luke 7:47, 50]; See 1 Thess. 1:3
15 [e]ch. 3:1; 4:9; 2 Tim. 2:11; Titus 3:8; [Rev. 22:6] [f]Matt. 9:13; See John 3:17; Rom. 4:25 [g][1 Cor. 15:9]

1:8–11 *Proper Use of the Law.* The false teachers do not know what they are talking about (v. 7), but Paul and his coworkers ("we," v. 8) know the truth about the law (v. 9).

1:8 the law is good. Many Christians today think of the Mosaic law negatively, but Paul clearly states that it is good. Some have certainly misused the law (e.g., the false teachers in this letter), but the law itself was a gracious gift of God to Israel (see Psalm 119).

1:9–11 the law is not laid down for the just. People who are "just" do not need the law to restrain them, but those who are **lawless and disobedient** need such restraint. Paul is not denying that the law has a use in teaching Christians how to live, for he has said it is "good" (v. 8) and in vv. 9–10 he echoes several of the Ten Commandments (Ex. 20:1–17), in their OT order. Exactly how the law applies to the NT believer is a matter of some debate. Some argue that the Mosaic law has been entirely superseded, and what remains is the "Law of Christ" (see note on 1 Cor. 9:21). Others argue for an abiding authority of certain aspects of the Mosaic code. Paul elsewhere affirms that Christians are no longer under the Mosaic law (see Rom. 7:6; Gal. 2:16; 3:19–26), and that fits well with what he writes here. As in those other passages, these verses indicate that one purpose of the law is to expose sin. In addition, though believers are no longer under the Law of Moses, they are, as noted, under the Law of Christ and are governed by the Spirit (Rom. 7:6). All interpreters agree that the Mosaic laws, rightly understood, still give Christians wisdom about the kind of conduct that pleases or displeases God. See notes on 1 Cor. 9:21; Gal. 4:10; 5:14; 6:2.

1:9 Those who strike their fathers and mothers violate Ex. 20:12. **Murderers** violate Ex. 20:13.

1:10 The sexually immoral violate Ex. 20:14, but the term includes more than just adultery; Greek *pornos* refers to one who practices any sexual conduct contrary to God's moral law. **men who practice homosexuality.** The Greek noun *arsenokoitēs* refers to males who engage in homosexual acts and echoes the Septuagint wording of Lev. 18:22; 20:13. Though some have argued that only certain kinds of homosexual conduct are in view (such as homosexual prostitution or pedophilia or unfaithful relationships or conduct by people who do not naturally have homosexual desires), there is no evidence in the words of the text, the context, or in evidence from the ancient world to prove that Paul was referring to anything other than all kinds of homosexual conduct. See notes on Rom. 1:26–27; 1 Cor. 6:9–10. **enslavers.** The Greek *andrapodistēs* (see ESV footnote) shows that Paul considered all kinds of forcible enslavement to be sinful and a violation of Ex. 20:15. **Liars** and **perjurers** violate Ex. 20:16. **sound doctrine.** The participle of the Greek verb *hygiainō* (found also at 1 Tim. 6:3; 2 Tim. 1:13; 4:3; Titus 1:9, 13; 2:1, 2), here translated "sound," includes the idea of "health" (in the sense of "healthy" or "health giving" doctrine), and in 2 Timothy it contributes to an extended metaphor in which false doctrine spreads poison insidiously through the body ("like gangrene," 2 Tim. 2:17) while true doctrine makes the body healthy.

1:11 "Sound doctrine" (v. 10) by definition is that which flows out of the **gospel**.

1:12–17 *Paul: An Example of the Effect of the True Gospel.* The reference to being "entrusted" with the "gospel" (v. 11) leads Paul to give thanks to God for this manifestation of grace to him. This is not, however, merely a personal aside for Paul. The discussion of Paul's conversion and commission also illustrates the transforming effect of the gospel (see v. 5) in contrast to the uselessness of the false teaching.

1:12 Paul gives thanks because Christ was willing to appoint him to service in spite of his past sins. Paul marvels that God graciously considered him worthy of trust (Gk. *pistos*, translated here as **faithful**) in spite of the fact that he had been unbelieving (Gk. *apistia*, v. 13).

1:13 Paul **received mercy because** he **acted ignorantly.** The point is that his salvation was undeserved; his ignorance did not excuse his sin or warrant God's mercy. Most likely Paul is contrasting himself with the false teachers. When Paul so opposed Christ, he had not yet professed faith. These men profess to follow Christ and still live in an evil manner. In so doing, they are coming dangerously close to being cut off from the possibility of God's mercy (cf. Matt. 12:31–32; Mark 3:28–30; Luke 12:10; 1 John 5:16).

1:15–16 Earlier statements in this section (vv. 12–17) may seem to suggest that Paul viewed his salvation as resulting from his own faithfulness or even his ignorance (but see also note on v. 13). These two verses make it clear that Paul is marveling at his conversion specifically because he knew himself to be so bad, for in his religious endeavors he had persecuted God's people.

1:15 Calling attention to certain sayings as **trustworthy** is a particular distinctive of the Pastoral Epistles (cf. 3:1; 4:9; 2 Tim. 2:11; Titus 3:8). **Christ Jesus came . . . to save sinners, of whom I am the foremost** (cf. Luke 19:10). Paul cannot mean that he *now* sins more than anyone in the world, for he elsewhere says that he has lived before God with a clear conscience (Acts 23:1; 24:16), and he asks other believers to follow his example (see note on Phil. 3:17). Apparently he means that his previous persecution of the church (1 Tim. 1:13; cf. 1 Cor. 15:9–10) made him the foremost sinner, for it did the most to hinder others from coming to faith (cf. 1 Thess. 2:15–16). Yet it also allowed God to save Paul as an "example" of grace (1 Tim. 1:16). Another interpretation is that, in light of the Holy Spirit's powerful conviction in his heart, and his nearness to God, Paul could not imagine anyone being a "worse" sinner than he. Godly people with some self-knowledge are prone to think of themselves in this way.

1:16 Paul is an **example** of the effect of true Christian instruction. He was the sort of person for whom the law was intended (see note on vv. 9–11), and the result of the gospel in his life was not mere idle speculation but transformation.

example to those who were to believe in him for eternal life. **17** To [h]the King of the ages,
[i]immortal, [j]invisible, [k]the only God, [l]be honor and glory forever and ever.[1] Amen.
18 This charge [m]I entrust to you, Timothy, my child, in accordance with [n]the prophecies
previously made about you, that by them you may [o]wage the good warfare, **19** [p]holding
faith and a good conscience. By rejecting this, some have [q]made shipwreck of their faith,
20 among whom are [r]Hymenaeus and [s]Alexander, whom I [t]have handed over to Satan that
they may learn not to [u]blaspheme.

Pray for All People

2 First of all, then, I urge that supplications, prayers, intercessions, and thanksgivings
be made for all people, **2** [v]for kings and all who are in high positions, that we may lead
a peaceful and quiet life, godly and [w]dignified in every way. **3** This is good, and [x]it is pleasing in the sight of [y]God our Savior, **4** who desires [z]all people to be saved and [a]to come to
[b]the knowledge of the truth. **5** For [c]there is one God, and there is one mediator between
God and men, the man[2] Christ Jesus, **6** [d]who gave himself as a ransom for all, which is [e]the
testimony given [f]at the proper time. **7** [g]For this I was appointed a preacher and an apostle
([h]I am telling the truth, I am not lying), [i]a teacher of the Gentiles in faith and truth.

[1] Greek *to the ages of ages* [2] *men* and *man* render the same Greek word that is translated *people* in verses 1 and 4

17 [h][Ps. 10:16; Rev. 4:9, 10] [i]ch. 6:15, 16; Rom. 1:23 [j]John 1:18; Col. 1:15; Heb. 11:27; 1 John 4:12 [k]Jude 25 [l]1 Chr. 29:11
18 [m]2 Tim. 2:2 [n]ch. 4:14 [o]1 Cor. 9:7; 2 Cor. 10:4; 2 Tim. 2:3, 4; [ch. 6:12]
19 [p][ch. 3:9] [q][ch. 6:9]
20 [r]2 Tim. 2:17 [s]2 Tim. 4:14 [t]See 1 Cor. 5:5 [u]Acts 13:45

Chapter 2

2 [v]Ezra 6:10 [w]ch. 3:4
3 [x]ch. 5:4 [y]ch. 1:1
4 [z]ch. 4:10; Ezek. 18:23, 32 [a]2 Tim. 3:7 [b]2 Tim. 2:25; Titus 1:1; Heb. 10:26
5 [c]See Gal. 3:20
6 [d]See Matt. 20:28 [e]See 1 Cor. 1:6 [f]ch. 6:15; Titus 1:3; [Gal. 4:4]
7 [g]ch. 1:11; Eph. 3:7, 8; 2 Tim. 1:11 [h]See Rom. 9:1 [i]See Acts 9:15

1:17 Paul gives glory to God as the transcendent King who is eternal, **immortal**, and **invisible**, and yet who intervenes personally in this world to save his people.

1:18–20 *Restatement of the Charge to Deal with False Teachers.* These verses, together with vv. 3–7, form bookends around this section (vv. 3–20). Paul restates his "charge" (v. 18; see vv. 3, 5) and calls for specific action against the false teachers.

1:18 prophecies. God had spoken clearly through others to set Timothy aside for his ministry (see note on 1 Cor. 12:10). This assurance of a specific divine calling is to strengthen Timothy for the work. See note on 1 Tim. 4:14.

1:19 This represents a singular pronoun in Greek and refers to **a good conscience**. The false teachers, **rejecting** their consciences, plowed ahead in their sin. **shipwreck of their faith**. This most likely refers to the false teachers who claimed to be believers but had fallen away from the faith they initially professed, thereby showing they were never truly converted (cf. 1 John 2:19).

1:20 Hymenaeus. A false teacher also mentioned in 2 Tim. 2:17. **handed over to Satan**. Refers to being put out of the church (i.e., excommunication). See note on 1 Cor. 5:5. This language highlights the importance and protection of church membership, since being put out of the church leaves one more exposed to Satan. **may learn not to blaspheme**. If the false teachers repent, they may still be saved; church discipline is motivated by love, with the hope that the one disciplined will turn back to the Lord. There is no explicit indication that the false teachers directly uttered evil statements about God ("blasphemed"). However, to misrepresent God's truth is to speak ill of him.

2:1–3:13 *Descriptions of Gospel-Shaped Living.* Having denounced the idle speculations of the false teachers, Paul turns to expounding in specific terms what true gospel living (1:5) should look like. He calls for prayer and he addresses hindrances to prayer (2:1–15), qualifications for overseers (3:1–7), and qualifications for deacons (3:8–13).

2:1–15 *Corporate Prayer and Issues Arising from It.* In describing life that properly emerges from the gospel, Paul first mentions prayer for the salvation of all people. This also leads to a discussion of godly living and appropriate behavior in corporate worship, particularly unity, modesty, and proper submission.

2:1 supplications, prayers, intercessions, and thanksgivings. Paul's point is not to list all the ways to pray but to pile up various terms in reference to prayer for their cumulative impact. This is a call for all sorts of prayer for all sorts of people.

2:2 Kings and other authorities are mentioned as examples of the "all people" for whom Christians are to pray. The lifestyle encouraged here (**peaceful, quiet, godly, dignified**) corresponds to the goal of apostolic teaching in 1:5 and contrasts with the behavior of the false teachers. This sort of living commends the gospel, a theme that will recur throughout this letter (2:11; 3:7; 5:7, 14; 6:1) as well as in 2 Timothy and Titus.

2:4 Evangelistic prayer for all people is rooted in the fact that God **desires all people to be saved**. It appears that Paul is countering an exclusivist tendency in the false teachers or at least their downplaying of the importance of evangelizing the Gentiles (along with their emphasis on the Jewish law). This statement figures prominently in theological disagreements over the extent of the atonement. It cannot be read as suggesting that everyone will be saved (universalism) because the rest of the letter makes it clear that some will not be saved (4:1; 5:24; 6:10; cf. Matt. 25:30, 41, 46; Rev. 14:9–11). Does that mean God desires something (all people being saved) that he cannot fulfill? Both Arminian and Calvinist theologians respond that God "desires" something more than universal salvation. Arminians hold that God's greater desire is to preserve genuine human freedom (which is necessary for genuine love) and therefore he must allow that some may choose to reject his offer of salvation. Calvinists hold that God's greater desire is to display the full range of his glory (Rom. 9:22–23), which results in election depending upon the freedom of his mercy and not upon human choice (Rom. 9:15–18). However one understands the extent of the atonement, this passage clearly teaches the free and universal offer of the gospel to every single human being; "desires" shows that this offer is a bona fide expression of God's good will. **Come to the knowledge of the truth** highlights the cognitive aspect of conversion, i.e., individuals must come to understand key truths in order to be converted. "The truth" occurs often in the Pastorals as a synonym for the gospel (cf. 1 Tim. 3:15; 4:3; 2 Tim. 2:15, 18, 25; 3:7, 8; 4:4; Titus 1:1, 14).

2:5 For. Verses 5–6 provide the theological basis for the preceding statement that God wants people to be saved. **There is** only **one God**, therefore this God seeks "all people" (v. 4; cf. Rom. 3:29–30; Gal. 3:20). Various people groups do not each have their own gods, though they may imagine they do; all must come to the one true God for salvation. This means that Jesus, God's incarnate Son, Israel's Messiah, is the one and only mediator, the only way to salvation (cf. Acts 4:12). Furthermore, this verse allows no place for intermediaries between people and Jesus, such as saints or human priests. See Overview of the Bible, pp. 23–26.

2:6 Ransom (Gk. *antilytron*) refers to purchasing someone's release and describes a common Pauline and NT understanding of Christ's work as *redemptive* (cf. Gal. 1:4; 2:20; Eph. 5:2; and related NT concepts of "redemption" [Luke 1:68; 2:38; 24:21; Titus 2:14; Heb. 9:12; 1 Pet. 1:18] and "ransom" [Matt. 20:28 par.; cf. Rev. 5:9]). This language also reflects Jesus' words, "the Son of Man came . . . to give his life as a ransom [Gk. *lytron*] for many" (Mark 10:45). Since Jesus **gave himself** as this "ransom," the idea of substitution (dying on behalf of sinners) is also included.

2:7 Paul defends his mission to the Gentiles on the basis of God's desire that all be saved (cf. v. 4).

8 I desire then that [j]in every place the men should pray, [k]lifting [l]holy hands without
anger or quarreling; 9 likewise also [m]that women should adorn themselves in respectable
apparel, with modesty and self-control, not with braided hair and gold or pearls or costly
attire, 10 [n]but with what is proper for women who profess godliness—with good works.
11 Let a woman learn quietly [o]with all submissiveness. 12 [p]I do not permit a woman to teach
or to exercise authority over a man; rather, she is to remain quiet. 13 [q]For Adam was formed
first, [r]then Eve; 14 and Adam was not deceived, but [s]the woman was deceived and became
a transgressor. 15 Yet she will be saved through [t]childbearing—if they continue in [u]faith
and love and holiness, with self-control.

8 [j][John 4:21] [k]Ps. 63:4; 119:48; [Isa. 1:15] [l]Job 17:9; Ps. 24:4
9 [m]1 Pet. 3:3; [Isa. 3:18-23]
10 [n][1 Pet. 3:4]
11 [o]Titus 2:5
12 [p][1 Cor. 14:34]
13 [q]Gen. 1:27; 2:8 [r]Gen. 2:18, 22
14 [s]Gen. 3:6, 13
15 [t][Gal. 4:4] [u]ch. 1:14

2:8–10 the men should . . . likewise also that women. Paul addresses particular concerns in regard to each gender. The issue for men is **anger** and for women it is **modesty** and proper submission. **not with . . . gold or pearls or costly attire.** Paul is not prohibiting the wearing of jewelry (see note on 1 Pet. 3:3–4); the principle is that women should not dress ostentatiously or seductively, but in a way that is **proper**. True doctrine produces **good works** (see note on 1 Tim. 1:5).

2:8 Then (or "therefore," Gk. *oun*) resumes the call to prayer from v. 1. **Lifting . . . hands** is a typical posture for prayer in the Bible: see Ex. 9:29; 1 Kings 8:22; Ps. 28:2; 63:4; Isa. 1:15; Luke 24:50 (Jesus). By taking up the issues of 1 Tim. 2:8–15 immediately following vv. 1–7, Paul suggests that the way the church conducts itself in corporate worship (unity, modesty, proper submission) bears significantly on its effectiveness in world evangelization.

2:10 With good works continues the stress on the proper result of true doctrine. See note on 1:5.

2:11 Women are not to teach men in the church but are to submit and defer to male leadership (see notes on vv. 12, 13, 14).

2:12 I do not permit. Paul self-consciously writes with the authority of an apostle (e.g., 1 Thess. 4:1; 2 Thess. 3:6), rather than simply offering an opinion. This statement is given in the context of Paul's apostolic instructions to the church for the ordering of church practice when the church is assembled together. In that context, two things are prohibited: (1) Women are not permitted to publicly **teach** Scripture and/or Christian doctrine to men in church (the context implies these topics), and (2) women are not permitted to **exercise authority** over men in church. (The reference for both "teaching" and "exercise authority" here is within the context of the assembled church.) Women teaching other women, and women teaching children, are not in view here, and both are encouraged elsewhere (on women teaching women, cf. Titus 2:4; on women teaching children, cf. 2 Tim. 1:5). Nor does this passage have in view the role of women in leadership situations outside the church (e.g., business or government). The presence of the word **or** (Gk. *oude*) between "to teach" and "to exercise authority" indicates that two different activities are in view, not a single activity of "authoritative teaching." "Exercise authority" represents Greek *authenteō*, found only here in the NT. Over 80 examples of this word exist outside the NT, however, clearly establishing that the meaning is "exercise authority" (not "usurp authority" or "abuse authority," etc., as sometimes has been argued). Since the role of pastor/elder/overseer is rooted in the task of teaching and exercising authority over the church, this verse would also exclude women from serving in this office (cf. 1 Tim. 3:2). Thus when Paul calls for the women to be **quiet**, he means "quiet" with respect to the teaching responsibility that is limited in the assembled church. Paul elsewhere indicates that women do speak in other ways in the church assembly (see 1 Cor. 11:5). See also note on 1 Cor. 14:34–35.

2:13 For introduces the biblical basis for the prohibition of v. 12. Paul indicates that the prohibition is based on two grounds, the first being the order of creation (**Adam was formed first**), and the second being the deception of Eve (v. 14). "Formed" (Gk. *plassō*) is the same term that the Septuagint uses in Gen. 2:7, 8, which evidently refers to creation (cf. 1 Cor. 11:8–9). Paul's argument indicates that gender roles in the church are not simply the result of the fall but are rooted in creation and therefore apply to all cultures at all times. The meaning of this passage, however, is widely contested today. Some interpreters argue that the prohibition of 1 Tim. 2:12 does not apply today because: (1) the reason for Paul's command was that women were teaching false doctrine in Ephesus; or (2) Paul said this because women in that culture were not educated enough to teach; or (3) this was a temporary command for that culture only. But Paul's appeal to the creation of Adam and Eve argues against those explanations. In addition, the only false teachers named in connection with Ephesus are men (1:19–20; 2 Tim. 2:17–18; cf. Acts 20:30), and no historical evidence exists of women teaching false doctrine in first-century Ephesus. Moreover, ancient inscriptions and literature speak of a number of well-educated women in that area of Asia Minor at that time (cf. also Luke 8:1–3; 10:38–41; John 11:21–27; Acts 18:2–3, 11, 18–19, 26; 2 Tim. 4:19). Finally, some have claimed that this passage only prohibits a "wife" from teaching or exercising authority over her "husband," since the Greek words *gynē* and *anēr* (translated "woman" and "man" in 1 Tim. 2:12) can also mean "wife" and "husband" in certain contexts. Given the immediate context of vv. 8–9, however, the most likely meaning of the Greek words *gynē* and *anēr* here in vv. 11–14 would seem to be "woman" and "man" (rather than "wife" and "husband").

2:14 Adam was not deceived, but the woman was. Paul's second reason (cf. v. 13). Though Eve sinned first as a result of being deceived, Adam's sin was conscious and willful, with devastating consequences for the whole human race (see Rom. 5:12).

2:15 This is a notoriously difficult-to-understand verse. Paul clearly does not believe people can **be saved** in the sense of earning justification through **childbearing** or any other means (e.g., Eph. 2:8–9). But the NT can also use the term "saved" (Gk. *sōzō*) in the sense of progressively coming to experience all the aspects of salvation. In that sense, "salvation" is ongoing (see note on Phil. 2:12–13). A similar view is that "saved" can be understood as referring especially to the endurance and perseverance in faith that is necessary for eternal salvation (cf. Matt. 10:22; 24:13; etc.). People are saved as they persevere (**continue**) in the faith to carry out the Lord's calling in their life, one example being the unique role of women in childbearing. (The change from singular **she** to plural **they** is a literal rendering of the Gk. text.)

3:1–7 *Qualifications for Overseers.* After dealing with issues that arise from corporate worship, including the barring of women from the role of teaching and authority over the assembled congregation, Paul now discusses who should exercise these roles. Paul does not give a job description of the pastor but instead describes the character of one who would serve in this office. The list of qualities is not intended to be exhaustive but pictures a person of mature Christian character, one whose faith has had tangible impact on his behavior (unlike Paul's opponents).

3:1 The terms **overseer**, "elder," and "pastor" (or "shepherd") are all used in

Godliness

2:2	"a quiet and peaceful life, godly and dignified in every way"
2:9–10	dress in a way that is appropriate for "women who profess godliness"
3:16	"Great . . . is the mystery of godliness"
4:7	"train yourself for godliness"
4:8	"godliness is of value in every way"
5:4	"to show godliness to their own household"
6:3	"the teaching that accords with godliness"
6:5	"imagining that godliness is a means of gain"
6:6	"great gain in godliness with contentment"
6:11	"Pursue righteousness, godliness, faith, love, steadfastness, gentleness"

Chapter 3
1[v]See ch. 1:15 [w]See Acts 20:28
2[x]Titus 1:6-9 [y][ch. 5:9] [z]ver. 11; Titus 2:2 [a]1 Pet. 4:9 [b]2 Tim. 2:24
3[c]Titus 3:2 [d]Heb. 13:5; [ch. 6:10]
4[e][ver. 12]
5[w][See ver. 1 above]
6[f]ch. 6:4; 2 Tim. 3:4

Qualifications for Overseers

3 The saying is [v]trustworthy: If anyone aspires to [w]the office of overseer, he desires a
noble task. **2**Therefore [x]an overseer[1] must be above reproach, [y]the husband of one wife,[2]
[z]sober-minded, self-controlled, respectable, [a]hospitable, [b]able to teach, **3**not a drunkard,
not violent but [c]gentle, not quarrelsome, [d]not a lover of money. **4**He must manage his own
household well, with all dignity [e]keeping his children submissive, **5**for if someone does
not know how to manage his own household, how will he care for [w]God's church? **6**He
must not be a recent convert, or he may [f]become puffed up with conceit and fall into the

[1] Or *bishop;* Greek *episkopos;* a similar term occurs in verse 1 [2] Or *a man of one woman;* also verse 12

the NT to refer to the same office. In Titus 1:5–9 "elder" and "overseer" are used interchangeably. In Acts 20:28 Paul tells the Ephesian elders (Gk. *presbyteros*, Acts 20:17) that "the Holy Spirit has made you overseers [Gk. *episkopos*], to care for [Gk. *poimainō*, "to pastor, serve as shepherd of"] the church of God." Peter also writes, "I exhort the elders [Gk. *presbyteros*] among you, as a fellow elder . . . : shepherd [Gk. *poimainō*, "to pastor"] the flock of God that is among you, exercising oversight" (1 Pet. 5:1–2). Paul commends the role of serving the church in this way as a **noble task**. "Overseer" stresses the role of watching over the congregation (see Heb. 13:17).

3:2–3 Above reproach heads the list as the key qualification for an **overseer**; it is then expounded by the words and phrases that follow in these verses (see note on Titus 1:6). The meaning of **husband of one wife** (Gk. *mias gynaikos andra*) is widely debated. The Greek phrase is not common, and there are few other instances for comparison. The phrase literally states, "of one woman [wife] man [husband]." (1) Many commentators understand the phrase to mean "having the character of a one-woman man," that is, "faithful to his wife." In support of this view is the fact that a similar phrase is used in 1 Tim. 5:9 as a qualification for widows (Gk. *henos andros gynē*; "one-man woman," i.e., "wife of one husband"), and in that verse it seems to refer to the trait of faithfulness, for a prohibition of remarriage after the death of a spouse would be in contradiction to Paul's advice to young widows in 5:14. Interpreters who hold this first view conclude that the wording of 3:2 is too specific to be simply a requirement of marriage and not specific enough to be simply a reference to divorce or remarriage after divorce. In the context of this passage, the phrase therefore prohibits any kind of marital unfaithfulness. (2) Another view is that "husband of one wife" means polygamists cannot be elders. Interpreters who hold this view note that there is evidence of polygamy being practiced in some Jewish circles at the time. On this view, the phrase means "*at the present time* the husband of one wife," in line with other qualifications which refer to present character. On either of these views, Paul is not prohibiting all second marriages; that is, he is not prohibiting from the eldership a man whose wife has died and who has remarried, or a man who has been divorced and who has remarried (these cases should be evaluated on an individual basis). (3) A third view is that Paul is absolutely requiring that an elder be someone who has never had more than one wife. But that does not fit the context as well, with its emphasis on present character. On any of these views, Paul is speaking of the ordinary cases and is not absolutely requiring marriage or children (cf. v. 4) but is giving a picture of the typical approved overseer as a faithful husband and father. **able to teach**. This is the one requirement in this list that is not necessarily required of all believers. It is also not required of deacons. Thus, it is a distinguishing skill required of the pastor/elder. It yields the only reference in this list to his actual duties (see note on Titus 1:9).

3:4–5 The management of one's **own household** is highlighted as a qualification for eldership by the greater amount of discussion given to it. The home is the proving ground of Christian character and therefore the preparation field for ministry. This makes further sense in light of the picture of the church as "the household of God" (v. 15).

3:6 not be a recent convert, or he may become puffed up with conceit. No matter the level of giftedness, time is needed to demonstrate maturity and character.

Qualifications for Elders in 1 Timothy and Titus

	1 Timothy		Titus
3:2	above reproach	1:6, 7	above reproach
3:2	husband of one wife	1:6	husband of one wife
3:2	sober-minded	1:8	disciplined
3:2	self-controlled	1:8	self-controlled
3:2	respectable		—
3:2	hospitable	1:8	hospitable
3:2	able to teach	1:9	able to give instruction
3:3	not a drunkard	1:7	not . . . a drunkard
3:3	not violent but gentle	1:7	not . . . violent
3:3	not quarrelsome	1:7	not be arrogant or quick-tempered
3:3	not a lover of money	1:7	not . . . greedy for gain
3:4–5	manage his own household well, care for God's church	1:7	God's steward
3:4	keeping his children submissive	1:6	children are believers (or "faithful"), not insubordinate
3:6	not a recent convert		—
3:7	well thought of by outsiders		—
	—	1:8	a lover of good; upright, holy

condemnation of the devil. **7** Moreover, he must be well thought of by [g]outsiders, so that
he may not fall into disgrace, into [h]a snare of the devil.

Qualifications for Deacons

8 [i]Deacons likewise must be dignified, not double-tongued,[1] [j]not addicted to much wine,
[k]not greedy for dishonest gain. **9** They must [l]hold the mystery of the faith with [m]a clear
conscience. **10** And [n]let them also be tested first; then let them serve as deacons if they prove
themselves blameless. **11** [o]Their wives likewise must[2] be dignified, not slanderers, but sober-
minded, [p]faithful in all things. **12** Let deacons each be [q]the husband of one wife, [q]managing
their children and their own households well. **13** For [r]those who serve well as deacons gain a
good standing for themselves and also great confidence in the faith that is in Christ Jesus.

The Mystery of Godliness

14 I hope to come to you soon, but I am writing these things to you so that, **15** if I delay,
you may know how one ought to behave in the household of God, which is the church
of the living God, a pillar and buttress of the truth. **16** Great indeed, we confess, is the
mystery of godliness:

[1] *Or devious in speech* [2] *Or Wives, likewise, must, or Women, likewise, must*

7 [g]See Mark 4:11 [h]2 Tim. 2:26; [ch. 6:9]
8 [i]Phil. 1:1 [j][ch. 5:23; Titus 2:3] [k]Titus 1:7; 1 Pet. 5:2
9 [l][ch. 1:19] [m]See Acts 23:1
10 [n][ch. 5:22]
11 [o]Titus 2:3 [p][Titus 2:10]
12 [q]ver. 2, 4
13 [r]See Matt. 25:21

3:7 The concern for the opinion of **outsiders** emerges again. There is a concern throughout this letter for how the church (and therefore the gospel) is portrayed to the watching world (cf. 2:2, 10; 5:7, 14; 6:1).

3:8–13 *Qualifications for Deacons.* Along with elders (vv. 1–7), deacons are officers of the NT church (cf. Phil. 1:1). "Likewise" (1 Tim. 3:8) suggests a link between the lists of qualifications, and indeed there are striking similarities. Deacons, like overseers, are to exhibit lives shaped by the gospel. One key distinction is that deacons are not required to be able to teach. This list, like the one for the overseers, focuses on character rather than duties. The NT contains little explicit discussion of the role of deacons (unless Acts 6 is understood to refer to the installation of the first deacons; see note on Acts 6:6), but the Greek word *diakonos* means "servant," so the office probably involved being responsible for various areas of service in the church.

3:9 Mystery (Gk. *mystērion*) is a common Pauline word and refers here to the entire revealed content of God's plan to bring salvation through Christ (see 1 Cor. 2:7; 4:1; 15:51; Eph. 3:4–13; Col. 1:26–27; 2:2; 4:3). **with a clear conscience**. While deacons are not required to be able to teach, they are required to have a good grasp of the gospel, and their behavior is to be consistent with the gospel.

3:10 Deacons should be **tested**, presumably under the leadership of the overseers.

3:11 As the ESV footnote indicates, the Greek word for "wives" (*gynē*, here plural) can mean either "women" or "wives." This ambiguity results in at least three interpretations. The text could refer to (1) the wives of deacons (**their wives**), (2) women deacons, or (3) women who assist the deacons (in some denominations called "deaconesses") but who are distinct from the deacons. (The word "their" is not explicit in the Greek text but, according to the first interpretation, it represents the sense of the verse in the context of vv. 8–13.) These women appear abruptly in the flow of the text. A reference to the wives of deacons would make good sense, leading into the discussion of the deacon's family in v. 12. However, the term **likewise** in similar cases often introduces a new group (e.g., 2:9; 3:8; Titus 2:3, 6). Also, the discussion of overseers lacked any reference to their wives. This would support understanding these women as deacons or assistants. Romans 16:1 refers to Phoebe as a "servant" or "deacon" or "deaconess" (Gk. *diakonos*; see ESV footnote); see note on Rom. 16:1. If the office of deacon is understood as involving church-wide teaching or governing authority, then 1 Tim. 2:11–15 would not permit women to carry out these functions. The fact that teaching is not mentioned as a responsibility of the deacons would seem to indicate that this was not a role that Paul intended for deacons.

Qualifications for Deacons

3:8	dignified
3:8	not double-tongued
3:8	not addicted to much wine
3:8	not greedy for dishonest gain
3:9	clear conscience
3:10	tested
3:10	blameless
3:12	husband of one wife
3:12	managing children and household well

3:12 husband of one wife. See notes on vv. 2–3, 4–5.

3:13 Paul highlights the value and importance of deacons by stating two results of good service in this role: (1) **good standing** refers to respect and appreciation from the church to one who serves in this way; and (2) **great confidence** probably refers to the increase in confidence that comes from seeing the power of the gospel regularly proven in ministry.

3:14–16 *Purpose of Writing: Behavior in the Church.* Paul pauses to state the purpose of his letter and in so doing reveals its central focus. "How one ought to behave" in the church appropriately summarizes the instructions to groups in the church (2:1–3:13; 5:1–6:2), the instructions to Timothy, and the warnings against false teachers (1:3–20; 4:1–16; 6:3–20). True doctrine leads to right living.

3:15 In this very significant verse, Paul states his reason for writing 1 Timothy, providing one of the key NT descriptions of the church's identity and mission. The use of **household** (Gk. *oikos*) and related words to describe the church and its ministry is common in Paul (cf. 1 Cor. 4:1; Gal. 6:10; Eph. 2:19; as well as 1 Tim. 3:4–5, 12, 15; 5:4, 8, 14; cf. 1 Pet. 4:17). It describes the church as God's family, especially with reference to authority and responsibility within the church and the home. The stress is on God's authority over the church and the behavior of people in the church. **Church of the living God** highlights the church as *the* gathering (Gk. *ekklēsia*, "assembly") where God most clearly manifests his presence. Thus, references to God as the "living God" in Scripture often refer to his reality and presence in the community of believers (cf. Num. 14:28; Josh. 3:10; Matt. 16:16; 2 Cor. 6:16; Heb. 3:12; 9:14; 10:31). Identifying the church as a **pillar and buttress of the truth** is a way of saying that God has entrusted to the church the task of promoting and protecting the gospel (i.e., "the truth"; see note on 1 Tim. 2:4). The architectural imagery presents the church's responsibility of "holding up" the gospel before a watching world, probably with a view to repelling the attack of false teaching. This picture of the church is striking. The role of advancing the gospel is divinely given to the church, not (at least not in the same way) to any other body. Parachurch organizations have value, but they must support and not supplant the church.

3:16 The **mystery of godliness** refers to the entire content of God's revealed plan of salvation (cf. note on v. 9). Next comes a poetic exposition of that great gospel message. **great indeed, we confess.** This introduction may implicitly

[s]He[1] was manifested in the flesh,
vindicated[2] by the Spirit,[3]
[t]seen by angels,
[u]proclaimed among the nations,
[v]believed on in the world,
[w]taken up in glory.

Some Will Depart from the Faith

4 Now [x]the Spirit expressly says that [y]in later times some will depart from the faith by
devoting themselves to [z]deceitful spirits and teachings of demons, **2** through the insincerity of [a]liars whose consciences are seared, **3** [b]who forbid marriage and [c]require abstinence
from foods [d]that God created [e]to be received with thanksgiving by those who believe and
know the truth. **4** For [f]everything created by God is good, and [g]nothing is to be rejected if
it is [e]received with thanksgiving, **5** for it is made holy [h]by the word of God and prayer.

A Good Servant of Christ Jesus

6 [i]If you put these things before the brothers,[4] you will be a good servant of Christ Jesus,
being trained in the words of the faith and of the good doctrine that you have [j]followed.
7 Have nothing to do with irreverent, [k]silly myths. Rather [l]train yourself for godliness; **8** for
while [m]bodily training is of some value, godliness [n]is of value in every way, as [o]it holds
promise for the present life and also for the life to come. **9** The saying is [p]trustworthy and
deserving of full acceptance. **10** For to this end we toil and strive,[5] because we have our hope
set on the living God, [q]who is the Savior of all people, especially of those who believe.

[1] Greek *Who;* some manuscripts *God;* others *Which* [2] Or *justified* [3] Or *vindicated in spirit* [4] Or *brothers and sisters.* The plural Greek word *adelphoi* (translated "brothers") refers to siblings in a family. In New Testament usage, depending on the context, *adelphoi* may refer either to men or to both men and women who are siblings (brothers and sisters) in God's family, the church [5] Some manuscripts *and suffer reproach*

16 [s]John 1:14; 1 Pet. 1:20 [t]Luke 2:13; 24:4 [u]Gal. 2:2 [v]2 Thess. 1:10 [w]See Acts 1:2

Chapter 4

1 [x]See John 14:17 [y][2 Thess. 2:3-9; 2 Tim. 3:1]; See 1 Cor. 11:19 [z]1 John 4:6 (Gk.); See Matt. 7:15
2 [a][1 Thess. 2:3; 2 Thess. 2:11]
3 [b][Dan. 11:37; Heb. 13:4] [c]See Col. 2:16 [d]Gen. 1:29; 9:3 [e]See Rom. 14:6
4 [f]Gen. 1:31 [g]See Acts 10:15 [e][See ver. 3 above]
5 [h]Gen. 1:25, 31
6 [i][2 Tim. 3:14, 15] [j]2 Tim. 3:10
7 [k]See ch. 1:4 [l]Heb. 5:14
8 [m][Col. 2:23] [n][ch. 6:6] [o]Ps. 37:4, 9, 11; 84:11; 112:2; 145:19; Prov. 19:23; 22:4; Matt. 6:33; Mark 10:30; 1 Pet. 3:9
9 [p]See ch. 1:15
10 [q]See ch. 2:4; John 4:42

call upon the Ephesian church to affirm this confession and therefore the ethical and doctrinal implications drawn from it throughout the letter. The exact structure of this "hymn" is debated, but the basic idea is clear. God the Son has been revealed in human flesh (resulting in the crucifixion, line 1), but he was **vindicated** by the resurrection (line 2) and afterward was displayed in victory before heavenly beings (line 3; cf. Eph. 1:20–21; Phil. 2:9–11; Heb. 1:3–4; 1 Pet. 3:21–22; Rev. 5:6–14). While the ESV footnote says that "vindicated" could be translated "justified," the sense here clearly is vindication, which is a common use of the Greek verb *dikaioō*. Line 4 continues with the result of Christ's life and ministry. The message of Christ has been (and continues to be) **proclaimed among the nations** (Gk. *ethnos*), that is, it has been preached specifically to the Gentiles. This preaching has been effective (**believed on,** line 5). Then **taken up** (Gk. *analambanō*) in line 6 would naturally be understood as a reference to the ascension (the same verb is used in Mark 16:19; Luke 24:51; Acts 1:2, 11, 22). A difficulty with this view is that line 6 does not fit chronologically. One possible explanation is that the ascension is presented as a foretaste of the ultimate exaltation of Christ.

4:1–5 *Identifying the False Teaching.* After his triumphant celebration of the advance of the gospel (3:16), Paul returns to the current challenge of false teaching (cf. ch. 1).

4:1 The means by which the **Spirit . . . says** is not made clear. It may have been something the Holy Spirit revealed directly to Paul (cf. Acts 20:29–30) or a prophecy that came through others. **expressly**. Explicitly, clearly. The **later times** (Gk. *hysterois kairois*) in view here clearly include Timothy's day (see the similar phrase in 2 Tim. 3:1). As is typical in the NT, "later times" refers to the time that began with the outpouring of the Spirit after the work of Christ. Those who hold to the false teaching **depart from the faith**, which shows that this teaching is outside the bounds of true Christianity. Furthermore, the source of the error is demonic, for these teachers follow **deceitful spirits**. The false teaching and resultant apostasy are no surprise. God said this would happen, so his church should not panic but should carry on in faithfulness (see 2 Tim. 2:17–19).

4:2 The **consciences** of the false teachers have been **seared** (that is, desensitized and rendered ineffective) by their rebellion against the gospel. Cf. "good conscience," 1:5.

4:3–5 Paul reveals some of the content of the false teaching, though he does not explain the overall view that led to these prohibitions. Questions of propriety in regard to **foods** and **marriage** were significant issues elsewhere in Paul's letters (see Romans 14; 1 Cor. 7:25–35; 8:1–10:33; Col. 2:16–23). The false teaching seems to gauge holiness by what is denied or given up. In response, Paul affirms the goodness of **everything created by God** and the propriety of enjoying it as a gift from him (cf. Eccles. 9:7–9). **Made holy** translates Greek *hagiazō* ("sanctify, make holy, consecrate"). Ordinary food should be considered "made holy" by God, and Christians have the privilege of eating such "holy" food every day. **The word of God** is probably a reference to Gen. 1:12, 21, 25, 31 ("God saw that it was good").

4:6–16 *How Timothy Should Be Shaped by the Gospel.* Both paragraphs in this section (vv. 6–10 and 11–16) open with a call for Timothy to speak certain truths to the congregation. The focus is on how Timothy, by his teaching and lifestyle, can help the church persevere in the face of the false teaching.

4:6 The referent of **these things**, here and in v. 11, is debated. It refers each time at least to the preceding paragraph, and it may refer more broadly to the entire letter. See also 3:14; 4:15; 5:7; 6:2b.

4:9 The saying probably refers specifically to the "value" of "godliness" (v. 8).

4:10 to this end. The goal of Paul's labors is that people attain "godliness" (v. 8) and its eternal "value." **Toil and strive** is typical of Paul's description of gospel ministry (cf. 5:17; Rom. 16:6, 12; 1 Cor. 15:10; 16:16; Gal. 4:11; Eph. 4:28). The statement that God is the **Savior of all people, especially of those who believe** could seem to teach universalism, that every person will eventually go to heaven. However, the rest of Scripture clearly denies this idea (see note on 1 Tim. 2:4). There are several other possible explanations for this phrase: (1) It means that Christ *died for* all people, but only those who believe in him are saved. (2) It means he is *offered to* all people, though not all receive him. (3) It means "the Savior of all people, *namely*, those who believe" (a different translation of Gk. *malista*, based on extrabiblical examples). (4) It means "the helper of all people," taking Greek *Sōtēr*, "Savior," to refer not to forgiveness of sins but to God's common grace by which God helps and protects people in need. (5) It means "the Savior of all kinds of people, not Jews only but both Jews and Greeks." In any case, the emphasis is on God's care for the unsaved world, and in the flow of the letter Paul is stressing once more (cf. 2:3–5) that God's will that people would be saved is the basis of the universal mission (cf. Matt. 28:19–20). On God as "Savior," see note on 2 Tim. 1:8–10.

11 Command and teach [r]these things. 12 [s]Let no one despise you for your youth, but set
the believers [t]an example in speech, in conduct, in love, in faith, in purity. 13 Until I come,
devote yourself to the public reading of Scripture, to exhortation, to teaching. 14 [u]Do not
neglect the gift you have, which was given you [v]by prophecy when the council of elders
[w]laid their hands on you. 15 Practice these things, immerse yourself in them,[1] so that [x]all
may see your progress. 16 [y]Keep a close watch on yourself and on the teaching. Persist in
this, for by so doing you will save [z]both yourself and [a]your hearers.

Instructions for the Church

5 [b]Do not rebuke an older man but encourage him as you would a father, [c]younger men
as brothers, 2 older women as mothers, younger women as sisters, in all purity.
3 Honor widows [d]who are truly widows. 4 But if a widow has children or grandchildren,
let them first learn [e]to show godliness to their own household and to make some return
to their parents, for [f]this is pleasing in the sight of God. 5 She [g]who is truly a widow, left
all alone, has set her hope on God and [h]continues in supplications and prayers night and
day, 6 but [i]she who is self-indulgent is [j]dead even while she lives. 7 [k]Command these things
as well, so that they may be without reproach. 8 But if anyone does not provide for his
relatives, and especially for [l]members of his household, he has [m]denied the faith and is
worse than an unbeliever.
9 Let a widow be enrolled if she is not less than sixty years of age, having been [n]the wife
of one husband,[2] 10 and having a reputation for good works: if she has brought up children,
has [n]shown hospitality, [o]has washed the feet of the saints, has [p]cared for the afflicted, and has
[q]devoted herself to every good work. 11 But refuse to enroll younger widows, for when [r]their
passions draw them away from Christ, they desire to marry 12 and so incur condemnation
for having abandoned their former faith. 13 Besides that, they learn to be idlers, going about
from house to house, and not only idlers, but also [s]gossips and [t]busybodies, saying what
they should not. 14 So I would have [u]younger widows marry, bear children, [v]manage their

[1] Greek *be in them* [2] Or *a woman of one man*

11 [r]ch. 5:7; 6:2
12 [s]1 Cor. 16:11; [2 Tim. 2:22; Titus 2:15] [t]Titus 2:7; 1 Pet. 5:3
14 [u]See 1 Thess. 5:19 [v]ch. 1:18 [w]See Acts 6:6
15 [x]Phil. 1:12
16 [y][Acts 20:28] [z]Ezek. 33:9 [a]See Rom. 11:14

Chapter 5

1 [b][Lev. 19:32] [c]Titus 2:6
3 [d]ver. 5, 16
4 [e]Matt. 15:4-6; Mark 7:10-13; Eph. 6:1, 2; [Gen. 45:9-11] [f]ch. 2:3
5 [g]ver. 3, 16 [h][Luke 2:37; 18:1-5]
6 [i]James 5:5; [Ezek. 16:49] [j]Rev. 3:1
7 [k]ch. 4:11; 6:2
8 [l]See Gal. 6:10 [m]Rev. 2:13; [2 Tim. 3:5; Titus 1:16; 2 Pet. 2:1; Rev. 3:8]
9 [n][ch. 3:2]
10 [n][See ver. 9 above] [o]See Gen. 18:4 [p]ver. 16 [q][ch. 6:18]
11 [r][Rev. 18:3, 7, 9]
13 [s]3 John 10 (Gk.) [t]2 Thess. 3:11; 1 Pet. 4:15
14 [u][1 Cor. 7:9] [v][Titus 2:5]

4:11 these things. See note on v. 6.

4:12 your youth. From an analysis of other uses of this word (Gk. *neotēs*) and the chronology of Timothy's life to this point (starting in Acts 16:1), commentators estimate Timothy's age to be somewhere from his late 20s to mid-30s, with most favoring the mid-30s.

4:13 public reading. See Acts 13:15; 2 Cor. 3:14; and note on Col. 4:16.

4:14 Gift probably refers to something related to Timothy's calling to and gifting for ministry, as indicated by God (**by prophecy**) and recognized by the church **when the council of elders laid their hands on you**, though the exact gift that Timothy received is not specified. Cf. note on 2 Tim. 1:6.

4:15 These things that Timothy is to **practice** and **immerse** himself **in** are the things commanded in vv. 12–13, encompassing his behavior and teaching (cf. "yourself and . . . the teaching," v. 16).

4:16 Timothy's perseverance in sound doctrine and practice will **save** him, i.e., it will lead him to persevere in the faith, confirming his salvation. This type of ministry will be effective in preserving his **hearers** as well.

5:1–6:2a *How Specific Groups in the Church Should Be Shaped by the Gospel.* Earlier Paul had addressed specific groups in the church (2:1–3:13), and this section returns to doing so, though the groups are different. "Honor" (5:3, 17; 6:1) serves as the connecting point for the three groups mentioned (widows, elders, masters). There is a progression in the thought, with the call increasing from "honor" (5:3) to "double honor" (5:17) to "all honor" (6:1). Each paragraph explains what "gospel living" looks like in relation to that group.

5:1–2 *Respectful Dealing with Church Members by Age and Gender.* The church is conceived of as family (see 3:4–5, 15). Though the term "honor" does not appear in 5:1–2, it applies here as surely as it does in vv. 3, 17; 6:1. Verse 1 of ch. 5 does not prohibit the correcting of an **older man** but speaks to the manner (respectfully) in which this should be done.

5:3–16 *Honoring Widows.* Providing for widows was an important role for the church from its earliest days (see Acts 6). The primary concern in this passage is to identify which widows should be provided for by the church. There are two key indicators: not having other family (1 Tim. 5:4–8, 16); and godliness (vv. 5, 9–15). Along the way, the duty of caring for one's family and the propriety of younger widows remarrying are emphasized. Some have suggested that an order of widows as an office in the church is in view here, but this is unlikely since the stated issue is provision for those in need.

5:4 Make some return indicates financial support.

5:8 worse than an unbeliever. Provision for one's own family is a spiritual issue of utmost importance. Failure to live out the gospel in this way is tantamount to a denial of **the faith**.

5:9–10 Paul begins to explain what qualifications a widow must meet in order to warrant financial support from the church. **Having been the wife of one husband** (Gk. *henos andros gynē*) is the feminine form of a phrase in the requirements for overseers and deacons (see note on 3:2–3). Some interpreters think the point here, as in ch. 3, is marital faithfulness. Others think that, while Paul is not discouraging a second marriage after the death of one's husband (cf. 5:14; 1 Cor. 7:39), simply as a practical matter he wants to focus the church's help on widows who have the fewest relatives to support them. **good works**. The list of qualifications provides a picture of a godly older woman, something for younger women to aspire to.

5:11–12 desire to marry . . . incur condemnation. These verses may at first appear to condemn remarriage; however, v. 14 encourages it (cf. 1 Cor. 7:39b), so another, more specific concern must be in view here. The issue is either that these widows who are being supported by the church have pledged to remain unmarried (so that to remarry would be to renounce this pledge) or that these younger widows might be tempted by their desires to marry unbelievers, thus turning away from the **faith**. Since these concerns are in some way prompted by the fact that "some have already strayed after Satan" (1 Tim. 5:15), a grave issue must be in view. With remarriage to an unbeliever, the concern was that the wife would take the religion of her husband (as was usual in that culture).

5:14 No occasion for slander continues the theme of concern about the impact of believers' actions on the perceptions of unbelievers (2:2; 3:7; 5:7, 14; 6:1; see also Titus 3:1–2).

5:16 relatives. The church is to render assistance only if the family is unable to do so.

14[w]ch. 6:1; Titus 2:5, 8
15[x][ch. 1:20]
16[y]ver. 3, 5
17[z]Rom. 12:8; 1 Thess. 5:12; [1 Cor. 12:28] [a]Deut. 21:17
18[b]1 Cor. 9:9; Cited from Deut. 25:4 [c]Matt. 10:10; Luke 10:7; [Lev. 19:13; Deut. 24:15; 1 Cor. 9:4, 7-14]
19[d]See Deut. 19:15
20[e]Titus 1:13; 2:15 [f]Deut. 13:11
21[g]ch. 6:13; 2 Tim. 2:14; 4:1 [h]See 2 Cor. 5:16
22[i][ch. 3:10] [j]See Acts 6:6 [k][2 John 11]
23[l][ch. 3:8] [m]Ps. 104:15
25[n][Ps. 37:6; Prov. 10:9]

Chapter 6

1[o]See 1 Pet. 2:18 [p]Isa. 52:5; Rom. 2:24; Titus 2:5
2[q]See Philem. 16 [r]ch. 4:11, 13; 5:7
3[s]ch. 1:3 [t]See ch. 1:10 [u]Titus 1:1
4[v]ch. 3:6; 2 Tim. 3:4 [w]1 Cor. 8:2; [ch. 1:7]

households, and [w]give the adversary no occasion for slander. 15 [x]For some have already strayed
after Satan. 16 If any believing woman has relatives who are widows, let her care for them.
Let the church not be burdened, so that it may care for those [y]who are truly widows.
17 Let the elders [z]who rule well be considered worthy of [a]double honor, especially those
who labor in preaching and teaching. 18 For the Scripture says, [b]"You shall not muzzle an
ox when it treads out the grain," and, [c]"The laborer deserves his wages." 19 Do not admit
a charge against an elder except [d]on the evidence of two or three witnesses. 20 As for those
who persist in sin, [e]rebuke them in the presence of all, [f]so that the rest may stand in fear.
21 In the presence of God and of Christ Jesus and of the elect angels [g]I charge you to keep
these rules without prejudging, [h]doing nothing from partiality. 22 [i]Do not be hasty in the
[j]laying on of hands, nor [k]take part in the sins of others; keep yourself pure. 23 (No longer
drink only water, but [l]use a little wine [m]for the sake of your stomach and your frequent
ailments.) 24 The sins of some people are conspicuous, going before them to judgment,
but the sins of others appear later. 25 So also good works are conspicuous, and [n]even those
that are not cannot remain hidden.

6 [o]Let all who are under a yoke as bondservants[1] regard their own masters as worthy of
all honor, [p]so that the name of God and the teaching may not be reviled. 2 Those who
have believing masters must not be disrespectful on the ground that they are [q]brothers;
rather they must serve all the better since those who benefit by their good service are
believers and beloved.

False Teachers and True Contentment

[r]Teach and urge these things. 3 If anyone [s]teaches a different doctrine and does not
agree with [t]the sound[2] words of our Lord Jesus Christ and the teaching [u]that accords with
godliness, 4 [v]he is puffed up with conceit and [w]understands nothing. He has an unhealthy

[1] Or *slaves* (for the contextual rendering of the Greek word *doulos*, see Preface) [2] Or *healthy*

5:17–25 *Honoring Elders.* Honoring elders includes providing for them financially and being careful in handling accusations against them.

5:17 rule. The role of elder (pastor) involves authority, particularly in **preaching and teaching. Labor** (Gk. *kopiaō*), translated "toil" in 4:10, implies hard work that makes a person tired. Such exertion in "preaching and teaching" calls for **double honor**, which could include financial remuneration (5:18). "Double" could imply ample provision, or financial provision in addition to proper respect. **worthy**. Paul does not actually require that pastors be paid a double amount, but Paul clearly indicates that pastors should receive generous remuneration.

5:18 The command not to **muzzle an ox** is a quotation from Deut. 25:4, which requires an owner to allow an ox to eat of the grain he is grinding. One who works for something should be able to benefit from it. **The laborer deserves his wages** is a direct quotation from Luke 10:7 (cf. Matt. 10:10). Thus, it seems that Paul is already referring to the written records of the statements of Jesus (the Gospels) as **Scripture**. See 2 Tim. 3:16.

5:19 two or three witnesses. Accusations against leaders must not be based on unsubstantiated charges (cf. Deut. 19:15).

5:20 The ones to be rebuked **in the presence of all** are elders who **persist in sin**, or who sin in a way that betrays the trust that the church has placed in them as spiritual leaders. Such public rebuke goes beyond the discipline procedures that apply to other church members (cf. Matt. 18:15–20), and it reassures the congregation that disqualifying sin on the part of an elder will not be covered up. As a result of this public rebuke, **the rest** will **stand in fear** (of sinning). This refers specifically to "the rest of the elders," but it probably also implies "the rest of the congregation," since the rebuking was done "in the presence of all" (see further Deut. 19:15–21, which also supports this).

5:21 In the presence of God and of Christ Jesus and of the elect angels. Paul presents this charge (v. 20) as being delivered in view of the heavenly court, thus adding a strong note of solemnity. On Paul's inclusion of angels, cf. their involvement at the final judgment (e.g., Matt. 25:31; Rev. 14:10; cf. note on 1 Cor. 11:10; also 1 Pet. 1:12).

5:22 laying on of hands. Setting aside for service, ordination. See 4:14. **hasty**. If, out of negligence, people appoint unqualified men as elders, they are implicated in the future sin of those elders. Cf. note on 5:24.

5:23 How this verse connects to the rest of the paragraph is not entirely clear. Drinking **only water** was often indicative of asceticism. In light of the asceticism of the false teachers (4:1–5), Paul may be providing a qualification to the call for purity in 5:22, clarifying that there would be nothing wrong with Timothy using **a little wine**, emphasizing here its usefulness for the sake of his health (cf. note on John 2:3).

5:24 After the aside of v. 23, Paul returns to the issue of carefulness in the appointing of elders (v. 22). Because some **sins . . . appear later**, it is important to be patient in assessing potential elders, to let the quality of their lives become evident.

6:1–2a *Honoring Masters.* Paul addresses Christian bondservants (see ESV footnote and note on 1 Cor. 7:21) who are under either unbelieving or believing masters. This issue shows up often in early Christian literature (e.g., Eph. 6:5–8; Col. 3:22–25; 1 Pet. 2:18–25). On the Gk. word *doulos*, see the ESV Preface, p. 21.

6:1 worthy of all honor. See note on 5:1–6:2a. **may not be reviled**. The motive for bondservants honoring their masters is similar to the motive mentioned previously in the letter: giving a good impression of the faith to unbelievers (2:2; 3:7; 5:7, 14; cf. note on Titus 2:5, 8, 10).

6:2b–21 *Confronting the False Teaching Again.* This concluding section of the letter bears strong similarity to the opening section (1:3–20). Both sections are bracketed by discussion of false teachers (1:3–7, 18–20; 6:2b–10, 20–21). Both contain exhortations to Timothy in light of this false teaching, specifically calling him to fight the good fight of faith against it (1:18; 6:12); and both contain a doxology (1:17; 6:15–16).

6:2b–10 *False Teachers and Greed.* The concern with false teachers here centers on their greed and their apparent exploiting of the faith for material gain. A number of the problems listed here are answered in vv. 17–19.

6:2b Teach and urge these things. This summary statement connects strongly with what precedes and what follows. "These things" most likely refers to the preceding section of instructions (5:1–6:2a), though some take it to refer to all that Paul has taught up to this point in the letter. This sound teaching then provides a contrast to the false teachers (6:3–10).

6:3 Sound words of our Lord Jesus Christ does not refer to specific statements of Jesus but affirms that Paul's gospel and its ethical implications flow out of the teaching and work of Jesus. **teaching that accords with godliness**. True (apostolic) teaching is that which fits with or leads to

craving for [x]controversy and for [y]quarrels about words, which produce envy, dissension,
slander, evil suspicions, 5 and constant friction among people [z]who are depraved in mind
and deprived of the truth, [a]imagining that godliness is a means of gain. 6 But [b]godliness
[c]with contentment is great gain, 7 for [d]we brought nothing into the world, and[1] we cannot
take anything out of the world. 8 But [e]if we have food and clothing, with these we will be
content. 9 But [f]those who desire to be rich fall into temptation, [g]into a snare, into many
senseless and harmful desires that [h]plunge people into ruin and destruction. 10 For the love
of money is a root of [i]all kinds of evils. It is through this craving that some have wandered
away from the faith and pierced themselves with many pangs.

Fight the Good Fight of Faith

11 But as for you, [j]O man of God, [k]flee these things. [l]Pursue righteousness, godliness,
faith, love, steadfastness, gentleness. 12 [m]Fight the good fight of the faith. [n]Take hold of
the eternal life [o]to which you were called and about which you made [p]the good confession
in the presence of many witnesses. 13 [q]I charge you in the presence of God, who gives life
to all things, and of Christ Jesus, [r]who in his testimony before[2] Pontius Pilate made [p]the
good confession, 14 to keep the commandment unstained and free from reproach until [s]the
appearing of our Lord Jesus Christ, 15 which he will display [t]at the proper time—he who
is [u]the blessed and only Sovereign, [v]the King of kings and Lord of lords, 16 [w]who alone has
immortality, [x]who dwells in [y]unapproachable light, [z]whom no one has ever seen or can
see. To him be honor and eternal dominion. Amen.

17 As for the rich in [a]this present age, charge them [b]not to be haughty, nor [c]to set their
hopes on [d]the uncertainty of riches, but on God, [e]who richly provides us with everything
to enjoy. 18 They are to do good, [f]to be rich in good works, to be generous and [g]ready to
share, 19 thus [h]storing up treasure for themselves as a good foundation for the future, so
that they may [i]take hold of [j]that which is truly life.

20 O Timothy, guard the deposit entrusted to you. [k]Avoid the [l]irreverent babble and contradictions of what is falsely called "knowledge," 21 for by professing it some have swerved
from the faith.

[m]Grace be with you.[3]

[1] Greek *for;* some manuscripts insert [it is] *certain* [that] [2] Or *in the time of* [3] The Greek for *you* is plural

4 [x]ch. 1:4; 2 Tim. 2:23; Titus 3:9 [y]2 Tim. 2:14; [Acts 18:15]
5 [z]2 Tim. 3:8; [Eph. 4:22; Titus 1:15] [a]Titus 1:11; 2 Pet. 2:3
6 [b][ch. 4:8] [c]Ps. 37:16; Prov. 15:16; 16:8; Phil. 4:11; Heb. 13:5
7 [d]Job 1:21; Ps. 49:17; Eccles. 5:15
8 [e]Gen. 28:20; Prov. 30:8
9 [f]Prov. 15:27; 23:4; 28:20; Matt. 13:22 [g][ch. 3:7] [h][ch. 1:19]
10 [i][Ex. 23:8; Deut. 16:19]
11 [j]2 Tim. 3:17 [k]2 Tim. 2:22 [l]See Prov. 15:9
12 [m][ch. 1:18]; See 1 Cor. 9:25 [n][Phil. 3:12] [o]1 Pet. 5:10 [p]See 2 Cor. 9:13
13 [q]See ch. 5:21 [r][Matt. 27:11; John 18:37; Rev. 1:5; 3:14] [p][See ver. 12 above]
14 [s]See 2 Thess. 2:8
15 [t]See ch. 2:6 [u]ch. 1:11 [v]See Rev. 17:14
16 [w]See ch. 1:17 [x][Ps. 104:2] [y]Job 37:23 [z]See John 1:18
17 [a]2 Tim. 4:10; Titus 2:12 [b]Rom. 11:20; 12:3, 16 [c]See Mark 10:24 [d]Prov. 23:5; [Matt. 13:22] [e]See Acts 14:17
18 [f]Luke 12:21; Titus 3:8, 14 [g]See Rom. 12:13
19 [h]See Matt. 6:19, 20 [i]ver. 12 [j][2 Tim. 1:1]
20 [k]2 Tim. 3:5; [Col. 2:8; 2 Tim. 4:4; Titus 1:14] [l]2 Tim. 2:16
21 [m]See Col. 4:18

godliness, as opposed to the negative effects of the false teaching (1:4, 6–7; 4:6; 6:4–5; see 2 Tim. 2:14, 16–18, 23). True doctrine is often recognizable by the impact it has on everyday living.

6:5 depraved in mind. The false teachers are often referred to in the Pastorals as having faulty reasoning (v. 4; 1:7; 2 Tim. 3:8). Since the gospel is the truth, to deny it is to think in a faulty manner. **imagining that godliness is a means of gain.** People who wrongly preach that God will give material health and wealth if only one has enough faith fall under the condemnation of this passage.

6:6–8 An eternal perspective (v. 7) helps believers to avoid the allure of greed, with the result that they are **content** with what God has given them, even if it consists of only **food and clothing**.

6:9–10 What is condemned here is the **desire to be rich**, not material things per se when rightly used for the glory of God. The desire to be rich leads one to **fall into temptation**. This in turn results in **the love of money**, which Paul identifies as **a root of all kinds of evils** (v. 10). The connection between false teaching and the desire to be rich has been a problem from the church's very beginning. **wandered away from the faith.** The warning is not simply that "love of money" is harmful but that this has led some to deny the faith, showing themselves to be unbelievers (cf. 1:19).

6:11–16 *Timothy's Behavior in Contrast.* Paul draws a direct and intentional contrast ("But as for you") between Timothy and the false teachers. True ministry is not motivated by greed but by the reality of eternal life and an awareness of accountability to God.

6:11–12 The reference to Timothy as a **man of God** affirms his authority and stands in contrast with the false teachers, who are *not* men of God. "Man of God" is used often in the OT of a prophet (e.g., Deut. 33:1; 1 Sam. 9:6; Ps. 90:1). The call to **fight the good fight of the faith** and to **take hold of the eternal life** involves both fleeing from sin and vigorously pursuing virtue (cf. note on 2 Tim. 2:22).

6:13–14 Another solemn **charge** (see 5:21 and note). Jesus' **good confession** before **Pontius Pilate** (see, e.g., Matt. 27:11; John 18:37) is the example for the believer's "good confession" (1 Tim. 6:12, 14).

6:15–16 While there are some who currently oppose his work in Ephesus, Timothy is to labor on in view of one day standing before God, **who dwells in unapproachable light** (v. 16). Paul focuses on the glory of God in order that the corresponding smallness of Timothy's opponents might be seen.

6:17–19 *Charge to the Rich.* The charge directly to rich believers may seem unexpected in this place. However, it provides a corrective to the wrong view of wealth seen in the false teachers (see notes on vv. 2b–10). Furthermore, the downplaying of riches by stressing that they are merely for "this present age" appropriately follows the moving description of appearing before God on the final day (vv. 15–16). The call for the wealthy to use their wealth to prepare for the future either means that how they use their wealth demonstrates whether they are saved, or that they should seek for greater reward in heaven, or both.

6:18 rich in good works. The rich, who may not need to work any longer to earn a living, have many opportunities to spend their workdays doing "good works" for others and building up the church.

6:20–21 *Closing Exhortation to Timothy.* In this brief closing Paul reiterates Timothy's commission (1:3–5, 18–20).

6:20 the deposit entrusted to you. The gospel. **what is falsely called "knowledge."** The false teaching addressed elsewhere in the letter. Some have thought this to be evidence that the false teaching was a form of Gnosticism. However, there is very slim evidence for this. More likely this is another instance of Paul critiquing the false teachers' "thinking" (see 1:7; 6:4–5). The false teachers may flatter themselves by labeling their teaching "knowledge," but since they reject "the truth" (i.e., the gospel; see note on 2:4), their teaching cannot be true knowledge.

INTRODUCTION TO

THE SECOND LETTER OF PAUL TO TIMOTHY

2 TIMOTHY

Author and Title

The first two verses of 2 Timothy clearly present the author as Paul and the recipient as Timothy. As with 1 Timothy and Titus (the other two "Pastoral Epistles"), the authorship of 2 Timothy has been challenged in the past 200 years. The challenges to Pauline authorship are the same as those leveled against 1 Timothy (see Introduction to 1 Timothy: Author and Title). However, a number of the scholars who deny Pauline authorship of 1 Timothy and Titus still affirm Pauline authorship of 2 Timothy. The arguments for the authenticity of 1 Timothy apply to 2 Timothy as well, providing a good basis for affirming the straightforward claims of 2 Timothy (and of 1 Timothy and Titus) to be authentic letters written by Paul.

Date

The letter pictures Paul in prison in Rome, awaiting death. Most likely, then, this letter was written during Paul's second Roman imprisonment (later than the imprisonment recorded in Acts 28). Therefore this letter would have been written after 1 Timothy and Titus. Eusebius (*Ecclesiastical History* 2.25; 3.1) claims that Paul was martyred sometime during Nero's reign (which ended in A.D. 68, but intense persecution began in 64). Since Paul wrote 2 Timothy shortly before his death, it was probably written in A.D. 64–65, though some would place it as late as 67.

Theme

Second Timothy is a bold, clear call for perseverance in the gospel in spite of suffering. Paul calls on his young coworker to continue the fight of faith, even as Paul approaches the end of his own life.

Purpose, Occasion, and Background

Paul wrote this letter while in prison in Rome. He mentions that several have abandoned him in this difficult time, and several others are away on duties (1:15; 4:9–12). In such a time Paul's recollection of the sincerity and devotion of Timothy is especially poignant (1:3–5). Paul anticipates death soon (4:6–8). Therefore he writes a final exhortation to Timothy to urge him to stand firm and to ask him to come for one final visit before Paul is executed.

Though death is imminent, the timing is uncertain, so Paul also asks Timothy to bring his books and parchments with him. Presumably Paul intends to keep studying and writing until the end.

Second Timothy is very personal, as would be expected in a final letter to a close friend and coworker. Paul exhorts Timothy to continue in faithfulness and points to his own life as an example for Timothy to follow. What he calls on Timothy to do, he himself has done already.

History of Salvation Summary

Christians must live on the basis of Christ's salvation, looking forward to his second coming. (For an explanation of the "History of Salvation," see the Overview of the Bible, pp. 23–26.)

Literary Features

The genre of 2 Timothy is at least similar to the farewell discourse, and many would classify it as such. There are famous farewell discourses in the Bible—e.g., by Moses (the book of Deuteronomy), Joshua (Joshua 23–24), David (1 Chronicles 28–29), and Jesus (the Upper Room Discourse, John 14–16). Conventional motifs include the speaker's announcement of his imminent departure, directives to keep God's commandments, predictions of what will happen after the speaker's departure, words of comfort and instruction for the benefit of those who will survive the speaker, and appeals to the addressees to remember what the speaker has taught. If 2 Timothy, Paul's last letter, is read with these features in mind, the book will fall neatly into place. Paul's charges to Timothy in this letter are not limited to a specific situation (as 1 Timothy was) but are what Paul most wants Timothy to heed for the rest of his life and ministry—the last word from a spiritual father. The reader is led to share Paul's reflective mood as he looks back over past experiences.

Timeline

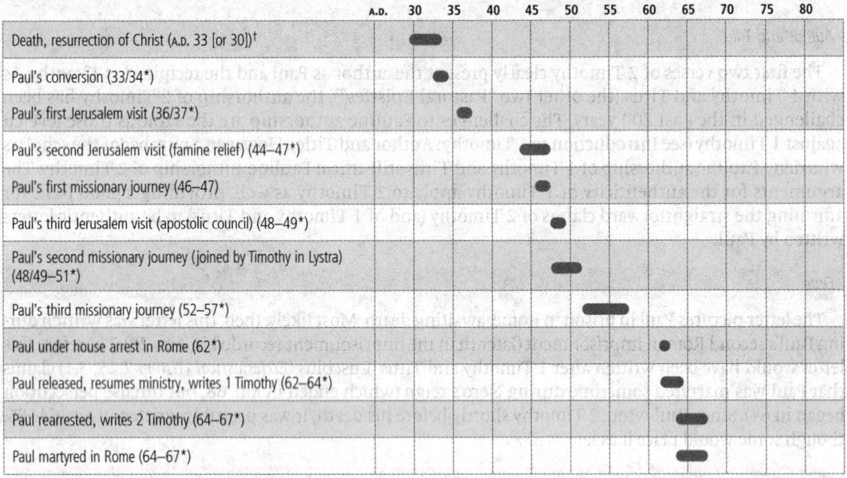

A.D. 30 35 40 45 50 55 60 65 70 75 80
Death, resurrection of Christ (A.D. 33 [or 30])†
Paul's conversion (33/34*)
Paul's first Jerusalem visit (36/37*)
Paul's second Jerusalem visit (famine relief) (44–47*)
Paul's first missionary journey (46–47)
Paul's third Jerusalem visit (apostolic council) (48–49*)
Paul's second missionary journey (joined by Timothy in Lystra) (48/49–51*)
Paul's third missionary journey (52–57*)
Paul under house arrest in Rome (62*)
Paul released, resumes ministry, writes 1 Timothy (62–64*)
Paul rearrested, writes 2 Timothy (64–67*)
Paul martyred in Rome (64–67*)

** denotes approximate date; / signifies either/or; † see The Date of Jesus' Crucifixion, pp. 1809–1810*

Outline

I. Opening (1:1–2)

II. Exhortation to Endurance for the Gospel (1:3–2:13)
- A. Thanksgiving for Timothy's sincere faith (1:3–5)
- B. A call to bold endurance in ministry, part 1 (1:6–14)
- C. Examples, positive and negative (1:15–18)
- D. A call to bold endurance in ministry, part 2 (2:1–13)

III. Dealing with False Teachers (2:14–3:9)
- A. Timothy in contrast to the false teachers (2:14–26)
- B. Description of the false teachers (3:1–9)

IV. Exhortation to Timothy in Contrast to False Teachers (3:10–4:8)
- A. Call to hold fast to Scripture and Paul's example (3:10–17)
- B. The ultimate charge (4:1–8)

V. Conclusion (4:9–22)

Key Themes

1. Suffering is a standard part of Christian experience.	1:8, 12; 2:3, 9; 3:11–12; 4:5, 14–18
2. The Christian response to suffering is faithful perseverance by God's power.	1:8; 2:1, 11–13; 4:1–8
3. The gospel is the ground for the Christian's endurance.	1:9–11; 2:8–10
4. The Scriptures have power to save and preserve.	2:15; 3:15–17; 4:1–2
5. True believers will persevere; failure to persevere proves one is not converted.	2:11–13, 19; 3:14; 4:7, 10
6. False teaching is deadly and must be dealt with firmly.	2:16–18, 23–26; 3:1–9; 4:3–5

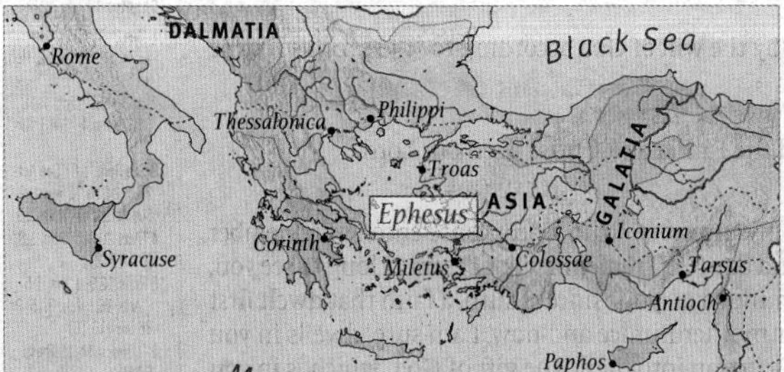

The Setting of 2 Timothy

c. A.D. *64–67*

Paul likely wrote 2 Timothy during a second imprisonment in Rome following a fourth missionary journey which is not recorded in the book of Acts. Expecting that death would come soon, Paul wrote this "farewell" letter to Timothy, who was at Ephesus, urging him to stand firm and asking him to come for one final visit.

THE SECOND LETTER OF PAUL TO TIMOTHY

2 TIMOTHY

Greeting

1 Paul, [a]an apostle of Christ Jesus [b]by the will of God according to [c]the promise of the
life that is in Christ Jesus,
2 To Timothy, [d]my beloved child:
[e]Grace, mercy, and peace from God the Father and Christ Jesus our Lord.

Guard the Deposit Entrusted to You

3 [f]I thank God [g]whom I serve, as did my ancestors, [h]with a clear conscience, as I remember
you [i]constantly in my prayers night and day. 4 [j]As I remember your tears, [k]I long to see you,
that I may be filled with joy. 5 I am reminded of [l]your sincere faith, a faith that dwelt first
in your grandmother Lois and [m]your mother Eunice and now, I am sure, dwells in you
as well. 6 For this reason I remind you [n]to fan into flame the gift of God, which is in you
through the laying on of my hands, 7 for God gave us [o]a spirit not of fear but [p]of power
and love and self-control.
8 Therefore [q]do not be ashamed of [r]the testimony about our Lord, nor of [s]me his prisoner,
but [t]share in suffering for the gospel by the power of God, 9 [u]who saved us and [v]called us
to[1] a holy calling, [w]not because of our works but because of [v]his own purpose and grace,
which he gave us in Christ Jesus [x]before the ages began,[2] 10 and which now has [y]been
manifested through [z]the appearing of our Savior Christ Jesus, [a]who abolished death and
[b]brought life and [c]immortality to light through the gospel, 11 [d]for which I was appointed
a preacher and apostle and teacher, 12 [e]which is why I suffer as I do. But [f]I am not ashamed,

[1] Or *with* [2] Greek *before times eternal*

11[d]See 1 Tim. 2:7 **12**[e]ch. 2:9 [f]ver. 8

Chapter 1
1[a]See 2 Cor. 1:1 [b]See 1 Cor. 1:1 [c]Titus 1:2; Heb. 9:15
2[d]1 Cor. 4:17; [ch. 2:1]; See 3 John 4 [e]See 1 Tim. 1:2
3[f]See Rom. 1:8 [g]See Acts 22:3; 24:14 [h]1 Tim. 3:9; See Acts 23:1 [i]Rom. 1:9
4[j][Acts 20:37] [k]Phil. 1:8; [ch. 4:9, 21]
5[l]Rom. 12:9; 1 Tim. 1:5 [m]Acts 16:1; [ch. 3:15; Ps. 86:16; 116:16]
6[n]1 Tim. 4:14; [1 Thess. 5:19]
7[o]Rom. 8:15; [John 14:27; Rev. 21:8] [p]Luke 24:49; Acts 1:8
8[q]See Mark 8:38 [r]See 1 Cor. 1:6 [s][ver. 16]; See Eph. 3:1 [t]ch. 2:3, 9; 4:5
9[u]1 Tim. 1:1; Titus 3:4 [v][Heb. 3:1]; See Rom. 8:28 [w]Titus 3:5; See Rom. 3:27 [x]Titus 1:2; [Rom. 16:25]; See Eph. 1:4
10[y]See Rom. 16:26 [z]See 2 Thess. 2:8 [a]1 Cor. 15:26; [1 Cor. 15:54, 55; Heb. 2:14, 15] [b][Job 33:30] [c]Rom. 2:7

1:1–2 *Opening.* Paul opens this letter in the standard way. But as he awaits death, he reminds Timothy that the purpose of his apostleship has been to proclaim the gospel, **the promise of the life that is in Christ Jesus**.

1:3–2:13 *Exhortation to Endurance for the Gospel.* Paul's thanksgiving (1:3–5) leads directly into strong exhortations to Timothy (1:6–14; 2:1–13) with an intervening paragraph that provides positive and negative examples of his exhortation (1:15–18). In light of his imminent death, Paul urges Timothy to continue in faithfulness for the sake of the gospel in spite of hardship.

1:3–5 *Thanksgiving for Timothy's Sincere Faith.* In typical Pauline fashion, this letter opens with thanksgiving to God for the recipient. Paul notes that both he ("my ancestors") and Timothy ("your grandmother . . . your mother") have a heritage of faith.

1:3 constantly in my prayers night and day. Timothy is on Paul's mind and in his prayers throughout the day, every day (see 1 Thess. 5:17 and note).

1:6–14 *A Call to Bold Endurance in Ministry, Part 1.* Verse 6 marks a shift from the opening thanksgiving to Paul's first exhortation to Timothy, a passionate challenge to continue following in Paul's footsteps (cf. 3:10–11). There is a clear connection between the call for Timothy to "not be ashamed . . . but share in suffering for the gospel" (1:8) and Paul's statement that for the gospel "I suffer. . . . But I am not ashamed" (v. 12). The call for Timothy to follow Paul's example is central in this letter (see 3:10–11).

1:6 fan into flame the gift of God. Paul does not explain what this gift is (see note on 1 Tim. 4:14), which allows the principle here to be seen as applicable to all kinds of spiritual gifts. Such gifts tend to fade in strength when they are not used and encouraged. The **laying on of my hands** may refer to Timothy's ordination. This passage focuses on Paul's part in that event, whereas 1 Tim. 4:14 mentions the involvement of "the council of elders."

1:7 spirit. Probably the Holy Spirit. **fear**. The Greek (*deilia*) in extrabiblical literature refers to one who flees from battle, and has a strong pejorative sense referring to cowardice. Boldness, not cowardice, is a mark of the Spirit (see Prov. 28:1; Acts 4:31).

1:8–10 These verses summarize the **gospel** for which God's servants suffer. They are a reminder of the **power** of God on whom Christians rely. Paul's exalted language suggests he is also arguing that such a glorious message is worthy of their suffering. Paul contrasts **works**, which do not save, with God's **purpose and grace**, which brings life. **God, who saved us . . . our Savior Christ Jesus**. In the Pastoral Epistles, Paul often describes both God the Father and God the Son as Saviors of their people (cf. 1 Tim. 1:1; 2:3; 4:10; Titus 1:3–4; 2:10; 2:13 [and note]; 3:4, 6).

1:12 Paul suffers (**as I do**) because of his current imprisonment and impending death. **Guard . . . what has been entrusted to me** (Gk. *tēn parathēkēn mou*, "my deposit") means either that God will guard the gospel, which has been entrusted to Paul, or that God will guard Paul's life ("what I have entrusted to him," see ESV footnote). Either way, it is this confidence in God

for [g]I know whom I have believed, and I am convinced that he is able to guard until [h]that
Day [i]what has been entrusted to me.[1] **13** [j]Follow [k]the pattern of [l]the sound[2] words [m]that
you have heard from me, in [n]the faith and love that are in Christ Jesus. **14** By the Holy Spirit
[o]who dwells within us, guard [i]the good deposit entrusted to you.

15 You are aware that [p]all who are in Asia turned away from me, among whom are
Phygelus and Hermogenes. **16** May the Lord grant mercy to [q]the household of Onesiphorus,
for he often [r]refreshed me and was not ashamed of [s]my chains, **17** but when he arrived in
Rome [t]he searched for me earnestly and found me— **18** may the Lord grant him to find
mercy from the Lord on [u]that Day!—and you well know all the service he [v]rendered
at Ephesus.

A Good Soldier of Christ Jesus

2 You then, [w]my child, [x]be strengthened by the grace that is in Christ Jesus, **2** and [y]what
you have heard from me in the presence of many witnesses [z]entrust to faithful men[3]
[a]who will be able to teach others also. **3** [b]Share in suffering as [c]a good soldier of Christ
Jesus. **4** No soldier [d]gets entangled in civilian pursuits, since his aim is to please the one
who enlisted him. **5** [e]An athlete is not [f]crowned unless he competes according to the rules.
6 It is [g]the hard-working farmer who ought to have the first share of the crops. **7** Think over
what I say, for the Lord will give you understanding in everything.

8 Remember Jesus Christ, [h]risen from the dead, the [i]offspring of David, [j]as preached in
my gospel, **9** [k]for which I am suffering, [l]bound with chains as a criminal. But [m]the word
of God is not bound! **10** Therefore [n]I endure everything for the sake of the elect, that they
also may obtain [o]the salvation that is in Christ Jesus with [p]eternal glory. **11** The saying is
[q]trustworthy, for:

[1] Or *what I have entrusted to him;* Greek *my deposit* [2] Or *healthy* [3] The Greek word *anthropoi* can refer to both men and women, depending on the context

12 [g][Ps. 10:14; 1 Pet. 4:19] [h]ver. 18; ch. 4:8; See 1 Cor. 3:13 [i]1 Tim. 6:20
13 [j][ch. 3:14; Titus 1:9; Rev. 3:3] [k][Rom. 2:20; 6:17] [l]See 1 Tim. 1:10 [m]ch. 2:2 [n]1 Tim. 1:14
14 [o]See Rom. 8:9 [i][See ver. 12 above]
15 [p]Acts 19:10; [ch. 4:10, 11, 16]
16 [q]ch. 4:19 [r]Philem. 7, 20 [s][ver. 8]; See Acts 28:20
17 [t]Matt. 25:36-40
18 [u]ver. 12 [v]Heb. 6:10

Chapter 2

1 [w]See ch. 1:2 [x]See Eph. 6:10
2 [y]ch. 1:13 [z]1 Tim. 1:18 [a][Titus 1:5]
3 [b]ch. 1:8; 4:5 [c]1 Tim. 1:18
4 [d]2 Pet. 2:20
5 [e]See 1 Cor. 9:25 [f][ch. 4:8]
6 [g]1 Cor. 9:10; [Heb. 6:7]
8 [h]1 Cor. 15:20 [i]See Matt. 1:1 [j]See Rom. 2:16
9 [k]ch. 1:8, 12 [l]See Phil. 1:7 [m][ch. 4:17]; See Phil. 1:13
10 [n]Eph. 3:13; Col. 1:24; [1 Cor. 13:7] [o]2 Cor. 1:6 [p]1 Pet. 5:10
11 [q]See 1 Tim. 1:15

that prevents Paul from being **ashamed**. Cf. note on v. 14. His boldness arises not from self-confidence but from God-confidence (cf. 2 Cor. 3:5). **until that Day**. See 1 Cor. 3:13; 2 Tim. 1:18; 4:8; Heb. 10:25; and notes on Amos 5:18–20; 1 Thess. 5:2–3.

1:13 sound words. See note on 1 Tim. 6:3.

1:14 the good deposit entrusted to you. The gospel in the fullest sense, the entire content of the Christian faith. Cf. note on v. 12.

1:15–18 *Examples, Positive and Negative.* Paul supports his exhortation of vv. 6–14 with concrete examples of some who have endured well and others who have not—a common technique in both ancient and modern exhortation.

1:15 Asia was the Roman province in which Ephesus, Timothy's current place of service, was located. **all . . . turned away from me**. Key people who could have supported Paul, perhaps in his arrest and imprisonment, failed to do so, and so it appeared as if "all" had deserted him (cf. 4:16, a reference to a more specific event). There is no further information about **Phygelus and Hermogenes**. These details highlight the low situation in which Paul found himself and probably help explain why Timothy, the faithful one, was such a source of joy for Paul (see 1:3–5).

1:16–18 Onesiphorus is an example of faithfulness, in contrast to those who abandoned Paul. Paul prays, therefore, that the Lord will **grant mercy** to **the household of** Onesiphorus, and that Onesiphorus himself will **find mercy** on **that Day** (see note on v. 12).

2:1–13 *A Call to Bold Endurance in Ministry, Part 2.* This section resumes the call to Spirit-empowered boldness. As in 1:6–14, Timothy's call to "share in suffering" (2:3) is paralleled by Paul's own suffering (v. 9), and the endurance to which Timothy is called (v. 1) is mirrored by Paul's endurance (v. 10). Furthermore, both sections open with a call to stay strong in Christ (1:6–7; 2:1–2), and the exhortations are each time rooted in the saving work of Christ (1:9–10; 2:8–10).

2:2 what you have heard from me. Throughout this letter, Paul emphasizes the message Timothy has received from him (see 1:13; 2:8). As Paul faces death, he encourages Timothy to pass the gospel on to **faithful men** who will in turn **teach others**, so that the gospel is preserved for coming generations.

2:4–6 Using three analogies, Paul sets forth the call to service and suffering. Verse 4 calls for single-minded desire to please God. Verse 5 reiterates that one must obey God's rules in order to succeed. Verse 6 is the least clear but seems to encourage hard work by holding out the promise of blessing.

2:4 This verse has at times been misinterpreted as a call away from "secular," **civilian pursuits**. The Bible, however, does not allow Christians to separate life into distinct realms, "spiritual" and "secular." All of life is to be lived spiritually, in obedience to the Spirit according to the Word of God. Paul does not see secular activities as being out of bounds but is warning Timothy not to allow anything (even perhaps things that could be considered "spiritual") to distract him from his task.

2:7 Paul exhorts Timothy to make the effort to **think** and meditate on what Paul has written; as he does so, God will give him **understanding in everything** about which Paul has instructed him. The believer's efforts and God's empowering work together.

2:8 Paul continues the thought of vv. 1–7 by rooting his exhortation in the realities of the gospel (cf. 1:9–11). **Remember Jesus Christ**. Paul certainly doesn't think that Timothy is in danger of forgetting Jesus! Rather, this is a call to remain mindful of the truths of the **gospel**, which is centered on Jesus, the **risen** Messiah (**offspring of David**).

2:10 endure . . . for the sake of the elect. While there is disagreement among Christians on the doctrine of election, a biblical understanding of the doctrine does not undercut mission work but enables it. Paul endures precisely because of a certainty that, through his ministry, God will save some. See notes on Rom. 8:29; 8:30; Eph. 1:11.

2:11–13 The **trustworthy** statement moves from comfort to challenge and back to comfort: v. 11b is a reminder of life even in the face of death; v. 12 calls for perseverance; v. 13 is a reminder of God's preserving power and faithfulness. In this context, to **deny him** must entail a more serious offense than being **faithless**. Denying Christ envisions final apostasy, in contrast with a temporary lapse in trusting Christ ("if we are faithless"). Those who deny Jesus will be judged forever; but all believers sin, and God is faithful and will pardon, restore, and keep those who are truly his.

[r]If we have died with him, we will also [s]live with him;
12 [t]if we endure, we will also reign with him;
[u]if we deny him, he also will deny us;
13 [v]if we are faithless, [w]he remains faithful—
for [x]he cannot deny himself.

A Worker Approved by God

14 Remind them of these things, and [y]charge them before God[1] [z]not to quarrel about
words, [a]which does no good, but only ruins the hearers. 15 Do your best to present yourself
to God as one approved,[2] a worker [b]who has no need to be ashamed, rightly handling the
word of truth. 16 But [c]avoid [d]irreverent babble, for it will lead people into more and more
ungodliness, 17 and their talk will spread like gangrene. Among them are [e]Hymenaeus and
Philetus, 18 who have swerved from the truth, [f]saying that the resurrection has already happened. They are upsetting the faith of some. 19 But God's firm foundation stands, bearing
this seal: [g]"The Lord knows those who are his," and, "Let everyone [h]who names the name
of the Lord depart from iniquity."
20 Now in [i]a great house there are not only vessels of gold and silver but also of wood
and clay, [j]some for honorable use, some for dishonorable. 21 Therefore, [k]if anyone cleanses
himself from what is dishonorable,[3] he will be a vessel for honorable use, set apart as holy,
useful to the master of the house, [l]ready for every good work.
22 So [m]flee [n]youthful passions and pursue righteousness, faith, love, and peace, along
with [o]those who call on the Lord [p]from a pure heart. 23 Have nothing to do with foolish,
ignorant [q]controversies; you know that they breed quarrels. 24 And [r]the Lord's servant[4]
must not be quarrelsome but [s]kind to everyone, [t]able to teach, patiently enduring evil,
25 correcting his opponents [u]with gentleness. God [v]may perhaps grant them repentance

[1] Some manuscripts *the Lord* [2] That is, one approved after being tested [3] Greek *from these things* [4] Greek *bondservant*

11 [r][1 Thess. 5:10]; See Rom. 6:8 [s]Rev. 20:4
12 [t][2 Thess. 1:4, 5]; See Rom. 8:17; Heb. 10:36; Rev. 20:4 [u]See Matt. 10:33
13 [v]See Rom. 3:3 [w]See 1 Cor. 1:9 [x]Num. 23:19; Titus 1:2
14 [y]1 Tim. 5:21; 6:13 [z]1 Tim. 6:4; [ver. 23] [a]Titus 3:9
15 [b][Phil. 1:20]
16 [c]Titus 3:9 [d]1 Tim. 6:20
17 [e]1 Tim. 1:20
18 [f][1 Cor. 15:12]
19 [g]Num. 16:5; Nah. 1:7; John 10:14, 27; [Luke 13:27]; See 1 Cor. 8:3 [h]Isa. 26:13
20 [i]See 1 Tim. 3:15 [j]Rom. 9:21
21 [k][Prov. 25:4; Isa. 52:11] [l]ch. 3:17; Titus 3:1; [1 Tim. 5:10]
22 [m]1 Tim. 6:11 [n][1 Tim. 4:12] [o]Acts 7:59; 9:14 [p]1 Tim. 1:5
23 [q]See 1 Tim. 6:4
24 [r][1 Tim. 3:3] [s]1 Thess. 2:7 [t]1 Tim. 3:2
25 [u]Gal. 6:1; Titus 3:2; [1 Tim. 6:11; 1 Pet. 3:15] [v]Dan. 4:27; Acts 8:22; See Acts 5:31

2:14–3:9 *Dealing with False Teachers.* These verses divide into two sections. In 2:14–26 Paul introduces the false teaching (v. 16) and explains how Timothy should respond to it and be different from the false teachers. In 3:1–9 he describes the false teachers more extensively. Having exhorted Timothy to steadfast endurance, Paul now begins to address the problem directly.

2:14–26 *Timothy in Contrast to the False Teachers.* Paul contrasts Timothy and the false teachers: vv. 14–19 contrast Timothy's faithful ministry with the worthless ministry of the opponents; vv. 20–21 provide an illustration; in vv. 22–26 Paul exhorts Timothy not to be drawn into sinful desire and needless controversy, and counsels him on how to handle his opponents.

2:14 Remind them. Thus far in the letter Timothy has been the primary object of the exhortations and the one who is to "remember" (v. 8). Here Paul shifts to Timothy's role in reminding the congregation. **not to quarrel about words.** Paul is clearly willing to argue when the gospel is at stake—he opposed Peter to his face (Gal. 2:11). What is prohibited here is meaningless argument. **does no good.** The concern here, as in 1 Timothy, is a teaching that has no positive, practical impact on its adherents (see 2 Tim. 2:16–17).

2:15 Do your best, i.e., "Be zealous" (Gk. *spoudazō*). The believer must zealously pursue God's approval. One way to do this is to make sure one is **rightly handling** Scripture, which contrasts with the meaningless disputes of the false teachers.

2:17 spread like gangrene. This Greek idiom stresses the repulsiveness of the false view as well as the danger of its spreading. Medical imagery is used to describe the bad effects of the false teaching in contrast to the "healthy" or "sound" teaching of Paul (see note on 1 Tim. 1:10; also 2 Tim. 4:3; Titus 1:9; 2:1). **Hymenaeus** was mentioned as a false teacher in 1 Tim. 1:20, but **Philetus** is not mentioned elsewhere.

2:18 The idea that the **resurrection has already happened** seems similar to some errors Paul counters in 1 Corinthians 15 (see esp. 1 Cor. 15:12–20). Apparently some taught that believers had already entered the glorified post-resurrection state; although nothing more is known about the content of this heresy.

2:19 But. In spite of the work of evildoers and evil teachers, **God's firm foundation** (probably meaning the elect members of the church; see v. 10) still **stands** firm. **bearing this seal.** The twofold inscription that follows emphasizes (1) divine sovereignty (preserving) and (2) human responsibility (persevering). While some believers may have apostatized (v. 18), Paul finds assurance in the fact that God **knows those who are his.** At the same time, those who claim to be the Lord's must demonstrate this as they **depart from iniquity.**

2:20–21 Paul uses an illustration to support his call to "depart from iniquity" (v. 19). **What is dishonorable** includes doctrinal and moral error, since both are in view in the letter. Those who depart from such errors and avoid impurity in their lives prepare themselves to be **useful to the master** and **ready for every good work.** This is a promise of blessing in the pursuit of holiness.

2:22 youthful passions. "Passions" (Gk. *epithymia*) in this context refers to sinful desires in general (not only sexual desire), especially those that tend to be characteristic of youth. Paul may hint in vv. 23–25 that one of these would be a tendency to quarrel or be hotheaded. The command to **flee** what is wrong is combined with the command to **pursue** what is right (cf. note on 1 Tim. 6:11–12). The pursuit of right is not to be done alone but **along with** other believers. Connection with the community of faith is essential for both progress in sanctification and perseverance in the faith.

2:23 False teaching produces **quarrels** rather than godliness. See note on v. 14.

2:24 Servant is the common word for "slave" or "bondservant" (Gk. *doulos*), but Paul uses it also to refer to those who preach the gospel, e.g., himself (Rom. 1:1; Gal. 1:10; Titus 1:1) and Epaphras (Col. 4:12). This section (2 Tim. 2:24–26) is a key passage concerning a pastor's handling of troublesome people in the church.

2:25 Most interpreters see these **opponents** as unbelievers who do not have a **knowledge of the truth** (i.e., salvation; cf. note on 1 Tim. 2:4). Paul emphasizes the importance of not dealing with such "quarrelsome" people in a "quarrelsome" manner (2 Tim. 2:24) but rather **correcting** the opponents in a spirit of **gentleness** (2 Cor. 10:1; Gal. 6:1; Eph. 4:2; 1 Pet. 3:15; cf. gentleness as a fruit of the spirit; Gal. 5:23). This verse further emphasizes the sovereignty of God in granting **repentance.**

25[w]See 1 Tim. 2:4
26[x]1 Tim. 3:7

Chapter 3

1[y]See 1 Tim. 4:1
2[z][Phil. 2:21] [a]Luke 16:14; [1 Tim. 6:10] [b]Rom. 1:30
3[c]Rom. 1:31 [d][Titus 1:8]
4[e]1 Tim. 3:6; 6:4 [f]Phil. 3:19
5[g]See 1 Tim. 5:8 [h]1 Tim. 6:20; [Titus 1:14]
6[i][Titus 1:11]
7[j]1 Tim. 2:4
8[k]Ex. 7:11 [l][Acts 13:8] [m]See 1 Tim. 6:5 [n]Titus 1:16
9[o]Ex. 7:12; 8:18; 9:11
10[p][Phil. 2:22]
11[q]Acts 13:14, 45, 50 [r]Acts 14:1, 2, 5 [s]Acts 14:6, 19 [t]Ps. 34:19 [u]ch. 4:17; [2 Cor. 1:10]
12[v]Titus 2:12 [w]See Acts 14:22
13[x][Rev. 22:11]

[w]leading to a knowledge of the truth, 26 and [illegible] may come to their senses and escape from
[x]the snare of the devil, after being captured by him [illegible] his will.

Godlessness in the Last Days

3 But understand this, that [y]in the last days there will come times of difficu[illegible]. 2 For people
will be [z]lovers of self, [a]lovers of money, [b]proud, [b]arrogant, abusive, [b]disobedient to their
parents, ungrateful, unholy, 3 [c]heartless, unappeasable, slanderous, without self-control, brutal, [d]not loving good, 4 treacherous, reckless, [e]swollen with conceit, [f]lovers of pleasure rather
than lovers of God, 5 having the appearance of godliness, but [g]denying its power. [h]Avoid such
people. 6 For among them are [i]those who creep into households and capture weak women,
burdened with sins and led astray by various passions, 7 always learning and never able to
[j]arrive at a knowledge of the truth. 8 Just as [k]Jannes and Jambres [l]opposed Moses, so these men
also oppose the truth, [m]men corrupted in mind and [n]disqualified regarding the faith. 9 But
they will not get very far, for their folly will be plain to all, [o]as was that of those two men.

All Scripture Is Breathed Out by God

10 [p]You, however, have followed my teaching, my conduct, my aim in life, my faith, my
patience, my love, my steadfastness, 11 my persecutions and sufferings that happened to
me [q]at Antioch, [r]at Iconium, and [s]at Lystra—which persecutions I endured; yet [t]from
them all [u]the Lord rescued me. 12 Indeed, all who desire to [v]live a godly life in Christ Jesus
[w]will be persecuted, 13 while [x]evil people and impostors will go on from bad to worse,

2:26 come to their senses. Although the fall (Genesis 3) brought about a destructive effect on human reason (see notes on Rom. 1:21; 1:22), salvation brings the ability to begin to see reality. Paul's regular reference to the false teachers' lack of knowledge and understanding (e.g., 2 Tim. 2:16, 23; 3:8) points to the fact that they fail to grasp what is really true. **the snare of the devil**. Paul often describes humanity as enslaved by the devil and in need of rescue (see 2 Cor. 4:4).

3:1–9 *Description of the False Teachers.* This paragraph opens by signaling a contrast from the previous paragraph ("**but**"). Although Paul hopes that some false teachers will repent, he does not want to give an unrealistic picture of the situation. While God may grant repentance to some, it is also clear that opposition will continue.

3:1 Paul's reference to the **last days** (Gk. *eschatais hēmerais*) puts the present evil situation in solemn eschatological (or "end times") perspective. As Acts 2:17 indicates, "the last days" began with the coming of the Spirit at Pentecost (see also note on 1 Tim. 4:1). Thus Paul's prediction of **times of difficulty** that will occur in "the last days" is already beginning to be fulfilled, even in the present situation.

3:2–5 This "list of vices" vividly describes the negative impact of those who were opposing Paul and Timothy. The list begins and ends with references to misplaced love—i.e., people who are **lovers of self**, **lovers of money** (v. 2), and **lovers of pleasure rather than lovers of God** (v. 4).

3:5 Paul uses a common technique, emphasizing an item in a list (vv. 2–5) by placing it either first or last and expanding upon it more than the other items in the list: while Paul and Timothy's opponents have the external **appearance of godliness**, they do not have its real essence. **Power** means the present, effective working of God in and through believers' lives (see note on Acts 1:8). "Godliness" (Gk. *eusebeia*) means genuine piety, including holiness, reverence, faith, and love and devotion to God. In 2 Tim. 1:7, Paul linked "power" to the presence of the Holy Spirit, and this power enabled perseverance through suffering (1:8; see 2:1) and faithful defense of the gospel (1:14). The people referenced in 3:1–9 claim to know God, but their lives are devoid of the work of the Spirit, which would have resulted in holiness, perseverance, and effectiveness in advancing God's kingdom. **Avoid such people**. This is the only command in vv. 1–9. This avoidance most likely involves excommunication. Although there may appear to be a contradiction between this and the exhortation in 2:24–26, the point in 2:24–26 is to seek the repentance of such people. In 3:5, however, Paul envisions those who remain obstinate and states clearly that there comes a time when such people must be excluded from Christian fellowship.

3:6 women, burdened with sins. Due to their guilt from their past, these women are particularly susceptible to both the asceticism (promoting artificial self-denial; see 1 Tim. 4:3) and the antinomianism (teaching that all sorts of sins are really acceptable; see 2 Tim. 3:2–4) set forth by the false teachers.

3:8 Jannes and Jambres are the names given in early extrabiblical Jewish writings to the Egyptian magicians who **opposed Moses** in Ex. 7:8–13. In these writings, these men became key symbols of opposition to God's truth. Though their names do not appear in the OT itself, they would be familiar to Timothy and other Jews; identifying the opponents with these archetypal enemies of God's truth would have significant rhetorical power. **corrupted in mind**. Again false teaching is cast in terms of deficient thinking (see note on 2 Tim. 2:26). This is why divine aid is necessary for coming to the "knowledge of the truth" (2:7, 25–26). **disqualified regarding the faith**. In spite of their claims, these people do not have saving faith, since they oppose the gospel both in their teaching and in their living (see Titus 1:16).

3:9 Another note of encouragement similar to 2:19. In spite of the current success of the false teachers, they will ultimately fail.

3:10–4:8 *Exhortation to Timothy in Contrast to False Teachers.* Having focused almost exclusively on the false teachers in 3:1–9, Paul addresses Timothy directly on how he must resist the opponents and remain faithful to the gospel.

3:10–17 *Call to Hold Fast to Scripture and Paul's Example.* This paragraph opens with a clear, strong contrast: "You, however." The false teachers live and teach one way (vv. 1–9), but Paul provides a totally different model for Timothy. The repetition of "my" in vv. 10–11 places clear emphasis on Paul as the model for faithful living and ministry, in contrast to that proposed by the opponents. See note on Phil. 3:17.

3:11 Antioch, **Iconium**, and **Lystra** are cities Paul visited on his first missionary journey (Acts 13–14), prior to Timothy joining him during his second journey (Acts 16:1). Since Lystra was Timothy's hometown (Acts 16:1–2), he was probably aware of what happened to Paul on this first journey. Thus Timothy would have known from his earliest awareness of Paul that suffering had been a central part of Paul's work. **From them all the Lord rescued me** does not mean that God kept Paul from experiencing any harm in these instances, for in Lystra he was stoned and left for dead (Acts 14:19–20), and it is possible that Timothy even witnessed this. Instead, Paul is probably referring both to the fact that the Lord preserved him from death so that he could continue preaching, and to the Lord's work in Paul's heart to keep him faithful even in suffering. See 2 Tim. 4:18.

3:12 will be persecuted. Suffering is an expected element in Christian living (see 2:3; see also John 15:18–21; 16:33). The actual "persecution" may be less when there has been more Christian influence on the laws and cultural values of a society, but the unbelieving world will always remain deeply hostile to the gospel.

3:13 The false teachers will "progress" **from bad to worse** (see 2:16). Those doing the **deceiving** are themselves **deceived**.

deceiving and [y]being deceived. 14 Bu[illegible] you, [z]continue in what you have learned and
have firmly believed, knowin[illegible] whom[1] you learned it 15 and how [a]from childhood
you have been acquain[illegible] with [b]the sacred writings, [c]which are able to make you wise for
salvation thr[illegible] faith in Christ Jesus. 16 [d]All Scripture is breathed out by God and profitable f[illegible] teaching, for reproof, for correction, and for training in righteousness, 17 that [e]the
man of God[2] may be complete, [f]equipped [g]for every good work.

Preach the Word

4 [h]I charge you in the presence of God and of Christ Jesus, [i]who is to judge the living and
the dead, and by [j]his appearing and his kingdom: 2 preach the word; be ready in season
and out of season; [k]reprove, rebuke, and [l]exhort, with complete patience and teaching.
3 [m]For the time is coming when people will not endure [n]sound[3] teaching, but having itching ears they will accumulate for themselves teachers to suit their own passions, 4 and [o]will
turn away from listening to the truth and [p]wander off into myths. 5 As for you, [q]always be
sober-minded, [r]endure suffering, do the work of [s]an evangelist, [t]fulfill your ministry.
6 For [u]I am already being poured out as a drink offering, and the time of my [v]departure
has come. 7 [w]I have fought the good fight, [x]I have finished the race, I have kept the faith.

[1] The Greek for *whom* is plural [2] That is, a messenger of God (the phrase echoes a common Old Testament expression) [3] Or *healthy*

13 [y]Titus 3:3
14 [z][1 Tim. 4:6]
15 [a][Eph. 6:4]; See ch. 1:5 [b][John 5:39] [c]Ps. 119:99
16 [d]Rom. 15:4; 2 Pet. 1:20, 21
17 [e]See 1 Tim. 6:11 [f][Luke 6:40] [g]See ch. 2:21

Chapter 4

1 [h]ch. 2:14; 1 Tim. 5:21; 6:13 [i]See Acts 10:42 [j]ver. 8; See 2 Thess. 2:8
2 [k]1 Tim. 5:20; Titus 1:13; 2:15 [l]1 Tim. 4:13
3 [m]ch. 3:1 [n]See 1 Tim. 1:10
4 [o]See 1 Tim. 6:20 [p]See 1 Tim. 1; 4, 6
5 [q]1 Pet. 1:13 [r]ch. 1:8; 2:3, 9 [s]Acts 21:8; Eph. 4:11 [t]Col. 4:17
6 [u]Phil. 2:17 [v]Phil. 1:23; [2 Pet. 1:14]
7 [w]See 1 Tim. 6:12 [x]Acts 20:24

3:14 from whom you learned. This could refer to Paul but may also refer back to Timothy's mother and grandmother (1:5), especially since 3:15 mentions the teaching he received in childhood (see ESV footnote on v. 14).

3:15 to make you wise for salvation. Scripture can lead to the "knowledge of the truth" (2:25; 1 Tim. 2:4). It has the power to bring its readers to faith (cf. James 1:18; 1 Pet. 1:23). This is in direct contrast to the false teaching which, as stated throughout the letter, leads only to useless disputes and ungodliness.

3:16 All Scripture would refer first to the OT but by implication also to at least some NT writings, which by this time were already being considered as Scripture (see 1 Tim. 5:18 and note; 2 Pet. 3:15–16 and note). **Breathed out by God** translates a Greek word (*theopneustos*) that does not occur in any other Greek text (biblical or otherwise) prior to this letter. Some therefore suggest that Paul coined this term from words meaning "God" and "breathed," which is certainly possible. The term stresses the divine origin and thus the authority of Scripture. Paul does not point to the human authors of Scripture as inspired people but says that the writings themselves ("Scripture," Gk. *graphē*, "writing," which in the NT always refers to biblical writings) are the words spoken ("breathed out") by God. Whereas it seems that Paul and Timothy's opponents stressed certain aspects or portions of Scripture (e.g., genealogies, 1 Tim. 1:4; cf. Titus 3:9), Paul stresses the authoritativeness of all of Scripture. The divine origin of Scripture is the reason for its power to convert (2 Tim. 3:15) and its usefulness in training (v. 17). Because Scripture comes from God himself, "all" of it is profitable in a range of ways, ultimately leading to **righteousness**.

3:17 That (in the sense of "in order that") refers back to the preceding verse (v. 16), indicating the purpose of Scripture for the believer. **man of God**. Both the OT background of this phrase (see ESV footnote and note on 1 Tim. 6:11–12) and the context show that Paul is thinking specifically of Timothy as his delegate and a leader over the church (see 1 Tim. 1:3–4; 6:11). While this verse applies generally to all believers, Paul's specific focus here is the preparation of Timothy to continue in his task when Paul is no longer present. **equipped for every good work**. In a broad sense this includes everything that God calls a believer to do. But, in a specific sense, this also supports the doctrine of the "sufficiency of Scripture," that is, the idea that the truth contained in Scripture is sufficient in all matters pertaining to doctrine and moral behavior. Although there are no commands outside the Bible that apply to all of God's people, this does not exclude individual guidance by the Holy Spirit on how to apply the universal commands of Scripture in particular situations (cf. notes on Gal. 5:16; 5:18).

4:1–8 ***The Ultimate Charge.*** Having just reminded Timothy of his early training in Scripture and of the power and divine origin of Scripture (3:15–17), Paul exhorts him to preach this word (4:2ff.). Chapter 3 ends with a reference to being competent and equipped, and 4:1–8 then describes the specific "good work" of leadership that Timothy is now to show himself competent to do: vv. 1–2 present the charge, followed by the reason why this is necessary (vv. 3–4); v. 5 returns to the charge in contrast to the evil of the current situation; and in vv. 6–8 Paul provides another example, heightening the seriousness of his charge with a reminder that his death is imminent.

4:1 Paul places his **charge** to Timothy in solemn eschatological perspective by reminding him that he conducts himself under the gaze of God and Christ, that Christ (not those around him, whether opponents or faithful believers) is the one who will **judge** him, and that Christ will certainly return (**his appearing**). Christ's **kingdom** is then the ultimate reality with which Timothy should be concerned.

4:2 The charge itself is spelled out in five imperative verbs (with four more in v. 5). **Preach the word** refers back to "Scripture" (see 3:16) and thus includes proclaiming the "good news" of the gospel in a broad, biblically anchored sense. "Gospel" for Paul is not only an evangelistic presentation; the gospel is the core message (found in the whole of Scripture; cf. 3:16) which can be applied to unbelievers (a call to faith) or to believers (a call to continue to believe in and live out the implications of this message). Thus, the way to preach the gospel is by expounding the Scriptures. **be ready in season and out of season**. When it is convenient and when it is inconvenient. **Reprove, rebuke, and exhort** means the communicating of all that Scripture includes—doctrine, instruction, correction, and encouragement. **Patience** in such teaching is again encouraged (see 2:24–26).

4:3 the time is coming. Since Paul exhorts Timothy on how to respond when these things occur, it is apparent that he is not referring merely to some time in the distant future but to a situation he expects Timothy to face (or to be already facing; see 3:1; 1 Tim. 4:1–3). **Itching ears** indicates a yearning for novelty that results in a pursuit of teachers who will tell people what they want to hear (**to suit their own passions**) instead of orthodox teachers like Timothy.

4:4 Driven by their own desires, people will readily accept fanciful **myths** (see note on 1 Tim. 1:4) rather than the **truth**.

4:5 the work of an evangelist. The full scope of "evangelist" is not made explicit here or elsewhere in Scripture. Paul instructs Timothy in terms of the "gospel" (cf. 1 Tim. 1:11; 2 Tim. 1:8, 10; 2:8), which certainly includes proclamation to the unconverted, i.e., the continuation of Paul's mission to the Gentiles. However, Paul does not typically distinguish between "evangelism" and "discipleship" (see note on 2 Tim. 4:2).

4:6 a drink offering. Paul describes his impending death in OT sacrificial language (cf. Gen. 35:14; Ex. 29:40–41; Lev. 23:13; Num. 15:5–10; 28:7–8), suggesting he sees himself as laying down his life for the sake of the gospel. However, the use of the passive voice (**I am . . . being poured out**) stresses that it is God who is acting here. The fact that Paul's death is close at hand underlies the urgency of the entire letter.

4:7 I have fought the good fight. Using athletic imagery (as is typical of Paul; cf. 1 Cor. 9:24–27; Phil. 3:14), he affirms at the close of his life that he has engaged himself in the one event truly worth one's life (i.e., the gospel mission). Some have objected that Paul's statement sounds prideful. But there is no claim of personal glory here. Paul is simply saying that he has finally completed the course God ordained for him (see Acts 20:24). He has done, clearly by God's grace (1 Cor. 15:10), what he is exhorting Timothy to do (2 Tim. 4:5). See note on 1 Cor. 4:16.

8 [y]Col. 1:5; 1 Pet. 1:4 [z]See James 1:12 [a]Ps. 7:11 [b]ch. 1:12 [c][Rev. 22:20]
9 [d]ch. 1:4
10 [e]Col. 4:14; Philem. 24 [f]See 1 John 2:15 [g]1 Tim. 6:17; Titus 2:12 [h][ch. 1:15] [i][Titus 3:12]
11 [h][See ver. 10 above] [j]See Acts 12:12
12 [k]Acts 20:4; Eph. 6:21; Col. 4:7; Titus 3:12
14 [l]See 1 Tim. 1:20 [m]Ps. 62:12; Prov. 24:12; [Neh. 6:14; 13:29; Ps. 28:4; Rev. 18:6]
16 [n][Acts 7:60]
17 [o]Acts 23:11; 27:23; [Matt. 10:19] [p]See 1 Tim. 1:12 [q]See Acts 9:15 [r]ch. 3:11 [s]Ps. 22:21; [1 Sam. 17:37]
18 [t]See Rom. 11:36
19 [u]See Acts 18:2 [v]ch. 1:16
20 [w]Acts 20:4; 21:29
21 [x]ver. 9
22 [y]Gal. 6:18; Philem. 25 [z]See Col. 4:18

8 Henceforth there is [y]laid up for me [z]the cr… of righteousness, … the Lord, [a]the
righteous judge, will award to me on [b]that Day, and … only to me but also … all [c]who
have loved his appearing.

Personal Instructions

9 [d]Do your best to come to me soon. 10 For [e]Demas, [f]in love with [g]this present world, [h]has
deserted me and gone to Thessalonica. Crescens has gone to Galatia,[1] [i]Titus to Dalmatia.
11 [h]Luke alone is with me. Get [j]Mark and bring him with you, for he is very useful to me
for ministry. 12 [k]Tychicus I have sent to Ephesus. 13 When you come, bring the cloak that I
left with Carpus at Troas, also the books, and above all the parchments. 14 [l]Alexander the
coppersmith did me great harm; [m]the Lord will repay him according to his deeds. 15 Beware
of him yourself, for he strongly opposed our message. 16 At my first defense no one came
to stand by me, but all deserted me. [n]May it not be charged against them! 17 But [o]the Lord
stood by me and [p]strengthened me, so that through me the message might be fully proclaimed and [q]all the Gentiles might hear it. So [r]I was rescued [s]from the lion's mouth. 18 The
Lord will rescue me from every evil deed and bring me safely into his heavenly kingdom.
[t]To him be the glory forever and ever. Amen.

Final Greetings

19 Greet [u]Prisca and Aquila, and [v]the household of Onesiphorus. 20 Erastus remained at
Corinth, and I left [w]Trophimus, who was ill, at Miletus. 21 [x]Do your best to come before
winter. Eubulus sends greetings to you, as do Pudens and Linus and Claudia and all the
brothers.[2]
22 The Lord be [y]with your spirit. [z]Grace be with you.[3]

[1] Some manuscripts *Gaul* [2] Or *brothers and sisters*. The plural Greek word *adelphoi* (translated "brothers") refers to siblings in a family. In New Testament usage, depending on the context, *adelphoi* may refer either to men or to both men and women who are siblings (brothers and sisters) in God's family, the church [3] The Greek for *you* is plural

4:8 crown of righteousness. One interpretation holds that this means "the crown that consists of righteousness," referring to the final righteous state of believers. Another interpretation is "the crown that is the reward for righteousness," that is, a victory crown (this is the meaning of Gk. *stephanos*, "crown," and fits with v. 7). If this crown is understood as a reward for Paul's perseverance, this would be in accord with a common theme in Paul's epistles (e.g., 1 Cor. 3:14; Col. 3:24) and in the NT more generally (e.g., Matt. 5:12, 46; 6:1–6, 16–18; 10:41–42; Heb. 10:35; 11:26; 2 John 8). It is clear, though, that the rewarded behavior is possible only because of grace (Phil. 2:13). On either interpretation, Christ will give a crown not only to Paul but to **all who have loved his appearing**, meaning all true believers who set their heart on the return of Christ. Hoping for Christ's return is an essential element of perseverance (contrast Demas, 2 Tim. 4:10; cf. Titus 2:13).

4:9–22 *Conclusion.* Paul, in typical fashion for first-century letters, closes with some final particular notes concerning travel and greetings. The key themes of the letter continue to resonate even here.

4:10 In contrast to Paul, who is persevering in spite of suffering (1:11–12; 2:8–13) because he has an eternal perspective (4:6–8), **Demas** (cf. Col. 4:14; Philem. 24) abandoned Paul because he loved **this present world**.

4:11 Despite his earlier disapproval of Mark (Acts 15:36–40), Paul now desires Mark's presence and considers him **useful . . . for ministry**. Clearly, Mark has by now demonstrated his effectiveness and commitment as a missionary pioneer.

4:13 cloak. A heavy coat that would be especially important in the winter (see v. 21). **Books** refers to scrolls made of papyrus, while **parchments** would be vellum sheets made of animal skins. The papyrus scrolls may have included writing materials, official documents, or Paul's personal correspondence. It seems most likely that the parchments would have been books of some kind. In any case, although Paul is expecting to die soon, he is still concerned about getting his "books [and] parchments," so that he can continue to work for the sake of the gospel.

4:14 The **Alexander** mentioned here cannot be identified with certainty. He may or may not be the same Alexander that Paul mentions in 1 Tim. 1:20 as one who has been excommunicated. If he is the same person, he may still have been in Ephesus causing trouble. However, since he is identified as a **coppersmith** and there is evidence of a guild of coppersmiths in Troas, this may be a different man living in Troas. This would explain his mention here after Paul has asked Timothy to collect his cloak in Troas (2 Tim. 4:13).

4:16 first defense. Paul's preliminary hearing before Caesar during his second imprisonment. **May it not be charged against them!** In his extension of forgiveness to those who abandoned him, Paul is following the teaching and model of Jesus (Luke 23:34); the practice of Stephen, whom Paul saw die (Acts 7:60); and his own teaching (1 Cor. 13:5).

4:17 But the Lord stood by me recalls the Lord's promise that he will never "leave or forsake" his children (Deut. 31:6, 8; Josh. 1:5; 1 Chron. 28:20; Heb. 13:5). **And strengthened me** recalls Paul's confidence in the sufficiency of God's power and strength, which is "made perfect in weakness" (2 Cor. 12:8, 9). The result of God strengthening Paul is that the **message** of the gospel would be **fully proclaimed** through Paul, so that **all the Gentiles might hear it**, signifying that Paul has "finished the race" (2 Tim. 4:7) and completed the mission and calling that God had entrusted to him. Deliverance from the **lion's mouth** was a common biblical metaphor for rescue from great danger (cf. Ps. 22:21; Dan. 6:22; Heb. 11:33), and here it probably means Paul was not put to death immediately after his trial (2 Tim. 4:16).

4:18 will rescue me. An assurance of ultimate well-being, not an assurance of release from his present danger. Paul entirely expects execution, but even through death God will bring him **safely into his heavenly kingdom** (cf. Luke 21:16–19).

4:19 Prisca (a variant of Priscilla) and **Aquila** are often mentioned in connection with Paul (e.g., Acts 18:2, 18, 26).

4:20 Trophimus, who was ill. Even Paul, with his apostolic gifts (cf. Acts 19:11–12; 2 Cor. 12:12), was not always empowered to heal. Christians today should pray earnestly for physical healing, but God is still sovereign in whether he grants healing in each specific case.

4:21 Travel in the Mediterranean was basically suspended during **winter** due to dangerous conditions by both land and sea. If his trip to Rome was not completed **before** then, Timothy would not be able to come "soon" (v. 9).

4:22 be with your spirit. Paul uses this language also in his closing in Gal. 6:18; Phil. 4:23; and Philem. 25. Cf. "be with you" in other letters (e.g., Rom. 16:20; 1 Cor. 16:23; 2 Cor. 13:14; 1 Thess. 5:28).

8 [y]Col. 1:5; 1 Pet. 1:4 [z]See James 1:12 [a]Ps. 7:11 [b]ch. 1:12 [c][Rev. 22:20]
9 [d]ch. 1:4
10 [e]Col. 4:14; Philem. 24 [f]See 1 John 2:15 [g]1 Tim. 6:17; Titus 2:12 [h][ch. 1:15] [i][Titus 3:12]
11 [h][See ver. 10 above] [j]See Acts 12:12
12 [k]Acts 20:4; Eph. 6:21; Col. 4:7; Titus 3:12
14 [l]See 1 Tim. 1:20 [m]Ps. 62:12; Prov. 24:12; [Neh. 6:14; 13:29; Ps. 28:4; Rev. 18:6]
16 [n][Acts 7:60]
17 [o]Acts 23:11; 27:23; [Matt. 10:19] [p]See 1 Tim. 1:12 [q]See Acts 9:15 [r]ch. 3:11 [s]Ps. 22:21; [1 Sam. 17:37]
18 [t]See Rom. 11:36
19 [u]See Acts 18:2 [v]ch. 1:16
20 [w]Acts 20:4; 21:29
21 [x]ver. 9
22 [y]Gal. 6:18; Philem. 25 [z]See Col. 4:18

8 Henceforth there is [y]laid up for me [z]the crown of righteousness, which the Lord, [a]the
righteous judge, will award to me on [b]that Day, and not only to me but also to all [c]who
have loved his appearing.

Personal Instructions

9 [d]Do your best to come to me soon. **10** For [e]Demas, [f]in love with [g]this present world, [h]has
deserted me and gone to Thessalonica. Crescens has gone to Galatia,[1] [i]Titus to Dalmatia.
11 [h]Luke alone is with me. Get [j]Mark and bring him with you, for he is very useful to me
for ministry. **12** [k]Tychicus I have sent to Ephesus. **13** When you come, bring the cloak that I
left with Carpus at Troas, also the books, and above all the parchments. **14** [l]Alexander the
coppersmith did me great harm; [m]the Lord will repay him according to his deeds. **15** Beware
of him yourself, for he strongly opposed our message. **16** At my first defense no one came
to stand by me, but all deserted me. [n]May it not be charged against them! **17** But [o]the Lord
stood by me and [p]strengthened me, so that through me the message might be fully proclaimed and [q]all the Gentiles might hear it. So [r]I was rescued [s]from the lion's mouth. **18** The
Lord will rescue me from every evil deed and bring me safely into his heavenly kingdom.
[t]To him be the glory forever and ever. Amen.

Final Greetings

19 Greet [u]Prisca and Aquila, and [v]the household of Onesiphorus. **20** Erastus remained at
Corinth, and I left [w]Trophimus, who was ill, at Miletus. **21** [x]Do your best to come before
winter. Eubulus sends greetings to you, as do Pudens and Linus and Claudia and all the
brothers.[2]

22 The Lord be [y]with your spirit. [z]Grace be with you.[3]

[1] Some manuscripts *Gaul* [2] Or *brothers and sisters*. The plural Greek word *adelphoi* (translated "brothers") refers to siblings in a family. In New Testament usage, depending on the context, *adelphoi* may refer either to men or to both men and women who are siblings (brothers and sisters) in God's family, the church [3] The Greek for *you* is plural

4:8 crown of righteousness. One interpretation holds that this means "the crown that consists of righteousness," referring to the final righteous state of believers. Another interpretation is "the crown that is the reward for righteousness," that is, a victory crown (this is the meaning of Gk. *stephanos*, "crown," and fits with v. 7). If this crown is understood as a reward for Paul's perseverance, this would be in accord with a common theme in Paul's epistles (e.g., 1 Cor. 3:14; Col. 3:24) and in the NT more generally (e.g., Matt. 5:12, 46; 6:1–6, 16–18; 10:41–42; Heb. 10:35; 11:26; 2 John 8). It is clear, though, that the rewarded behavior is possible only because of grace (Phil. 2:13). On either interpretation, Christ will give a crown not only to Paul but to **all who have loved his appearing**, meaning all true believers who set their heart on the return of Christ. Hoping for Christ's return is an essential element of perseverance (contrast Demas, 2 Tim. 4:10; cf. Titus 2:13).

4:9–22 *Conclusion.* Paul, in typical fashion for first-century letters, closes with some final particular notes concerning travel and greetings. The key themes of the letter continue to resonate even here.

4:10 In contrast to Paul, who is persevering in spite of suffering (1:11–12; 2:8–13) because he has an eternal perspective (4:6–8), **Demas** (cf. Col. 4:14; Philem. 24) abandoned Paul because he loved **this present world**.

4:11 Despite his earlier disapproval of Mark (Acts 15:36–40), Paul now desires Mark's presence and considers him **useful . . . for ministry**. Clearly, Mark has by now demonstrated his effectiveness and commitment as a missionary pioneer.

4:13 cloak. A heavy coat that would be especially important in the winter (see v. 21). **Books** refers to scrolls made of papyrus, while **parchments** would be vellum sheets made of animal skins. The papyrus scrolls may have included writing materials, official documents, or Paul's personal correspondence. It seems most likely that the parchments would have been books of some kind. In any case, although Paul is expecting to die soon, he is still concerned about getting his "books [and] parchments," so that he can continue to work for the sake of the gospel.

4:14 The **Alexander** mentioned here cannot be identified with certainty. He may or may not be the same Alexander that Paul mentions in 1 Tim. 1:20 as one who has been excommunicated. If he is the same person, he may still have been in Ephesus causing trouble. However, since he is identified as a **coppersmith** and there is evidence of a guild of coppersmiths in Troas, this may be a different man living in Troas. This would explain his mention here after Paul has asked Timothy to collect his cloak in Troas (2 Tim. 4:13).

4:16 first defense. Paul's preliminary hearing before Caesar during his second imprisonment. **May it not be charged against them!** In his extension of forgiveness to those who abandoned him, Paul is following the teaching and model of Jesus (Luke 23:34); the practice of Stephen, whom Paul saw die (Acts 7:60); and his own teaching (1 Cor. 13:5).

4:17 But the Lord stood by me recalls the Lord's promise that he will never "leave or forsake" his children (Deut. 31:6, 8; Josh. 1:5; 1 Chron. 28:20; Heb. 13:5). **And strengthened me** recalls Paul's confidence in the sufficiency of God's power and strength, which is "made perfect in weakness" (2 Cor. 12:8, 9). The result of God strengthening Paul is that the **message** of the gospel would be **fully proclaimed** through Paul, so that **all the Gentiles might hear it**, signifying that Paul has "finished the race" (2 Tim. 4:7) and completed the mission and calling that God had entrusted to him. Deliverance from the **lion's mouth** was a common biblical metaphor for rescue from great danger (cf. Ps. 22:21; Dan. 6:22; Heb. 11:33), and here it probably means Paul was not put to death immediately after his trial (2 Tim. 4:16).

4:18 will rescue me. An assurance of ultimate well-being, not an assurance of release from his present danger. Paul entirely expects execution, but even through death God will bring him **safely into his heavenly kingdom** (cf. Luke 21:16–19).

4:19 Prisca (a variant of Priscilla) and **Aquila** are often mentioned in connection with Paul (e.g., Acts 18:2, 18, 26).

4:20 Trophimus, who was ill. Even Paul, with his apostolic gifts (cf. Acts 19:11–12; 2 Cor. 12:12), was not always empowered to heal. Christians today should pray earnestly for physical healing, but God is still sovereign in whether he grants healing in each specific case.

4:21 Travel in the Mediterranean was basically suspended during **winter** due to dangerous conditions by both land and sea. If his trip to Rome was not completed **before** then, Timothy would not be able to come "soon" (v. 9).

4:22 be with your spirit. Paul uses this language also in his closing in Gal. 6:18; Phil. 4:23; and Philem. 25. Cf. "be with you" in other letters (e.g., Rom. 16:20; 1 Cor. 16:23; 2 Cor. 13:14; 1 Thess. 5:28).

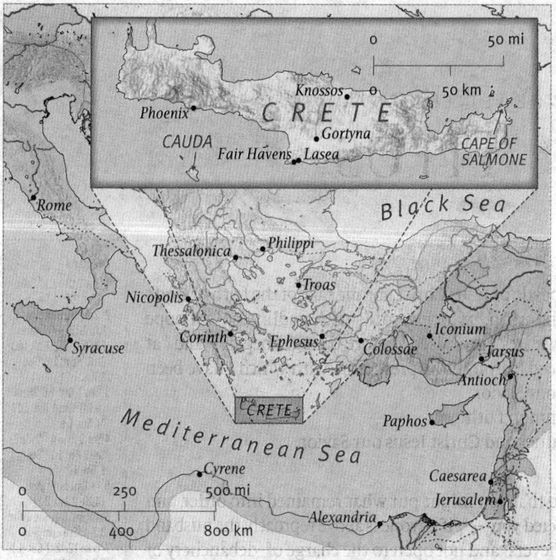

The Setting of Titus
c. A.D. 62–64
Paul likely wrote Titus during a fourth missionary journey not recorded in the book of Acts. Writing from an unknown location, he instructed Titus in how to lead the churches on the island of Crete. The churches there had apparently been founded by Paul.

Outline

I. Opening (1:1–4)

II. The Occasion: The Need for Proper Leadership (1:5–9)

III. The Problem: False Teachers (1:10–16)

IV. Christian Living in Contrast to the False Teachers (2:1–3:8)

- A. Proper living by age and gender groups (2:1–10)
- B. Gospel basis (2:11–14)
- C. Summary command (2:15)
- D. Proper living, particularly with respect to outsiders (3:1–2)
- E. Gospel basis (3:3–7)
- F. Summary command (3:8)

V. The Problem Restated: False Teachers (3:9–11)

VI. Closing Exhortation (3:12–15)

THE LETTER OF PAUL TO

TITUS

Greeting

1 Paul, a servant[1] of God and [a]an apostle of Jesus Christ, for the sake of the faith of God's
elect and [b]their knowledge of the truth, [c]which accords with godliness, 2 [d]in hope
of eternal life, which God, [e]who never lies, [f]promised [g]before the ages began[2] 3 and [h]at
the proper time manifested in his word [i]through the preaching [j]with which I have been
entrusted [k]by the command of God our Savior;
4 To Titus, [l]my true child in [m]a common faith:
[n]Grace and peace from God the Father and Christ Jesus our Savior.

Qualifications for Elders

5 [o]This is why I left you in Crete, so that you might put what remained into order, and
[p]appoint elders in every town as I directed you— 6 [q]if anyone is above reproach, the husband
of one wife,[3] and his children are believers[4] and not open to the charge of [r]debauchery or
insubordination. 7 For an overseer,[5] [s]as God's steward, must be above reproach. He must not

[1] Or *slave* (for the contextual rendering of the Greek word *doulos*, see Preface) [2] Greek *before times eternal* [3] Or *a man of one woman* [4] Or *are faithful* [5] Or *bishop;* Greek *episkopos*

Chapter 1

1 [a]See 2 Cor. 1:1 [b]See 1 Tim. 2:4 [c]1 Tim. 6:3
2 [d]2 Tim. 1:1; Heb. 9:15; [ch. 2:13; 3:7] [e]Num. 23:19; 2 Tim. 2:13; Heb. 6:18 [f]Rom. 1:2 [g]See 2 Tim. 1:9
3 [h]See 1 Tim. 2:6 [i][Rom. 10:14] [j]See 1 Tim. 1:11 [k]1 Tim. 1:1
4 [l]See 3 John 4 [m]Jude 3; See 2 Pet. 1:1 [n]See 1 Tim. 1:2
5 [o][1 Tim. 1:3] [p][Acts 14:23; 2 Tim. 2:2]
6 [q]For ver. 6-8, see 1 Tim. 3:2-4 [r]See Eph. 5:18
7 [s]Luke 12:42; 1 Cor. 4:1; 1 Pet. 4:10

1:1–4 *Opening.* Among the Pauline letters, only Romans and Galatians have longer openings. The theological emphases in this section are picked up again in the two other doctrinal sections of the letter (2:11–14; 3:3–7).

1:1 servant of God. Paul often uses "servant" (or "slave," Gk. *doulos*; see ESV Preface, p. 21) as a designation for himself (Rom. 1:1; Gal. 1:10; Phil. 1:1) and other Christians (1 Cor. 7:22; Eph. 6:6; Col. 4:12; see also 2 Pet. 1:1, Jude 1; Rev. 2:20). Typically, though, Paul refers to himself as "servant of Christ," and this is the only place he uses "servant of God." While the meaning is not greatly different, this wording would suggest a direct connection to Moses, David, and others in the OT who were described as servants of God (e.g., Moses, Ps. 105:26; David, 2 Sam. 7:4, 8; and the prophets, Jer. 7:25; 25:4; Amos 3:7; Hag. 2:23). The effect is to place Paul in the long line of those who have been God's spokesmen from the beginning. Furthermore, a servant in the first century did not act on his own authority but on the authority of his master. This concept of received authority is furthered by the phrase **apostle of Jesus Christ** (see note on Rom. 1:1). At the outset of the letter the divine source of Paul's authority is made very clear. **For the sake of** points to the purpose or goal of Paul's apostleship. He labors to see people saved, coming to **faith** and the **knowledge of the truth** (see 1 Tim. 2:4; 2 Tim. 2:25; 3:7), i.e., the entire gospel proclamation (see note on 2 Tim. 4:2), including in a broad sense all of Paul's apostolic teaching. **accords with godliness**. The true gospel always produces "godliness" in its adherents, "godliness" being the hallmark of the true gospel. This sets up the primary problem with the false teachers that Paul will discuss in the letter.

1:2–3 Paul's mission is rooted in the certainty of God's promise of **eternal life**. **Hope** is not wishful thinking but certainty. Furthermore, God has **promised** eternal life, and God **never lies**. It is contrary to God's character and thus impossible for God to lie (cf. Heb. 6:18). God's truthfulness is a common biblical assertion, but it would be particularly meaningful in the Cretan context (see Titus 1:12–13 and note). This promise has been fulfilled specifically in Paul's ministry, a ministry that he did not choose for himself but received **by the command of God our Savior**. On God as "Savior," see note on 2 Tim. 1:8–10.

1:5–9 *The Occasion: The Need for Proper Leadership.* Paul begins the body of the letter with a reminder to Titus of the directions for ministry that he had left with him. Unlike most of Paul's letters, there is no thanksgiving section. While this is unusual for Paul, it is not unique (cf. Galatians) and it is not unusual in first-century letters. A "virtue list" provides the portrait of the sort of leadership needed for the new churches in Crete. The emphasis is on good behavior (seen esp. in the home) and the ability to teach. Thus these leaders embody the fact that the gospel ("the truth"; see note on 1 Tim. 2:4) results in "godliness" (Titus 1:1).

1:5 The fact that the churches in Crete do not yet have **elders** and that there are things that need to be **put . . . into order** suggests that these churches are still fairly young. Titus is there as Paul's delegate to get these churches properly established. **In every town** is the consistent pattern of government in all NT churches: elders govern the churches (cf. notes on Acts 1:26; 14:23; 20:17). As is typical in the NT, "elders" is plural. Here it is used interchangeably with "overseer" (Titus 1:7). The rest of the NT shows that these two terms, as well as "pastor" (cf. Eph. 4:11, ESV footnote), refer to the same office (see note on 1 Tim. 3:1).

1:6 Above reproach (repeated in v. 7) summarizes the main point, which the rest of the list (vv. 6–9) fills out: there should be no legitimate accusation that could be brought against the elder that would bring disrepute on the gospel or the church; his life should be seen as worthy of imitation. **husband of one wife**. See note on 1 Tim. 3:2–3. **His children are believers** can also be rendered "his children are *faithful*" (Gk. *pistos*). The primary argument for rendering it as "believers" is that in the letters to Timothy and Titus, this word almost always refers to saving faith. Those who think it should be rendered "faithful" would argue that no father can guarantee the conversion of his own children, but he can ordinarily ensure that they act in a "faithful" way. Also, the parallel passage in 1 Timothy 3 says only that the children must be well-behaved, not that their conversion is a requirement for their father to be an overseer. The concern in the passage is that the children behave appropriately and are **not open to the charge of debauchery or insubordination**. The word "children" (plural of Gk. *teknon*) would apply only to children living at home and still under their father's authority.

7 [t]2 Pet. 2:10 [u]1 Tim. 3:8; 1 Pet. 5:2
8 [v][1 Cor. 9:25]
9 [w][2 Thess. 2:13, 15]; See 1 Tim. 1:15; 2 Tim. 1:13 [x]See 1 Tim. 1:10
10 [y]1 Tim. 1:6 [z]See Acts 11:2
11 [a][2 Tim. 3:6] [b]1 Tim. 6:5; 2 Pet. 2:3
12 [c][Acts 17:28]
13 [d]ch. 2:15; 1 Tim. 5:20 [e]2 Cor. 13:10 [f]ch. 2:1, 2
14 [g]See 1 Tim. 1:4 [h]See Col. 2:22 [i]See 1 Tim. 6:20
15 [j][Luke 11:41; 1 Tim. 4:3]; See Acts 10:15 [k][Rom. 14:23] [l]See 1 Tim. 6:5
16 [m][1 John 2:4] [n]See 1 Tim. 5:8 [o]2 Tim. 3:8

Chapter 2

1 [p]See 1 Tim. 1:10
2 [p][See ver. 1 above]
3 [q][1 Tim. 2:9] [r]1 Tim. 3:11 [s][1 Tim. 3:8; 5:23]

[t]be arrogant or quick-tempered or a drunkard or violent [u]or greedy for gain, **8** but hospitable, a lover of good, self-controlled, upright, holy, [v]and disciplined. **9** He must [w]hold firm
to the trustworthy word as taught, so that he may be able to give instruction in [x]sound[1]
doctrine and also to rebuke those who contradict it.
10 For there are many who are insubordinate, [y]empty talkers and deceivers, especially
those of [z]the circumcision party.[2] **11** They must be silenced, since [a]they are upsetting whole
families by teaching [b]for shameful gain what they ought not to teach. **12** [c]One of the Cretans,[3]
a prophet of their own, said, "Cretans are always liars, evil beasts, lazy gluttons."[4] **13** This
testimony is true. Therefore [d]rebuke them [e]sharply, that they [f]may be sound in the faith,
14 [g]not devoting themselves to Jewish myths and [h]the commands of people [i]who turn away
from the truth. **15** [j]To the pure, all things are pure, but to the defiled and [k]unbelieving,
nothing is pure; but both [l]their minds and their consciences are defiled. **16** [m]They profess
to know God, but they [n]deny him by their works. They are detestable, disobedient, [o]unfit
for any good work.

Teach Sound Doctrine

2 But as for you, teach what accords with [p]sound[5] doctrine. **2** Older men are to be sober-
minded, dignified, self-controlled, [p]sound in faith, in love, and in steadfastness. **3** [q]Older
women likewise are to be reverent in behavior, [r]not slanderers [s]or slaves to much wine.

[1] Or *healthy*; also verse 13 [2] Or *especially those of the circumcision* [3] Greek *One of them* [4] Probably from Epimenides of Crete [5] Or *healthy*; also verses 2, 8

1:9 able to give instruction. It was common in the ancient world to emphasize one item in a list by placing it at the beginning or end and giving it more attention than the other items. The ability to teach is the distinguishing mark of a pastor or elder. This includes both teaching what is right and refuting error. The reason for this emphasis is clear from what follows (vv. 10–16). **sound doctrine**. See note on 1 Tim. 1:10.

1:10–16 *The Problem: False Teachers.* The description of the false teachers contrasts directly (and probably intentionally) with the descriptions of what the elders should be (vv. 5–9). Whereas the elders are to live out and teach the truth, these false teachers belie their profession of faith by their conduct (v. 16). Christian standards must be established at the outset for the new churches.

1:10 especially those of the circumcision party. The false teachers emerged particularly from among Jewish Christians. "Especially" (Gk. *malista*) could also be translated "that is" (see note on 1 Tim. 4:10).

1:11 They must be silenced. One responsibility of church leaders is to prevent false teaching from having a platform in the church. **upsetting whole families**. The faith of some has already been overturned by these false teachers. **shameful gain**. These teachers are motivated by greed (cf. 1 Tim. 6:5, 9–10).

1:12–13 Cretans are always liars, evil beasts, lazy gluttons. Crete was proverbial in the ancient world for its moral decadence. The ancient historian Polybius wrote that it was "almost impossible to find . . . personal conduct more treacherous or public policy more unjust than in Crete" (*Histories* 6.47). Cicero also stated, "Moral principles are so divergent that the Cretans . . . consider highway robbery honorable" (*Republic* 3.9.15). **a prophet of their own**. Wisely, Paul does not criticize the decadence of Cretan society directly but quotes a Cretan author instead and then quickly agrees with him (**this testimony is true**). Of course Paul means this as a generalization, not necessarily true of every single inhabitant of Crete. The quotation seems to be from Epimenides of Crete, though some have questioned this since his writings are known only through other authors' quotations of him (see note on Acts 17:28).

1:14 Jewish myths. On "myths," see note on 1 Tim. 1:4. The specific content of these myths is unknown, but the false teaching in Titus is more explicitly tied to a Jewish background (see Titus 1:10) than was the false teaching in 1 and 2 Timothy.

1:15 To the pure, all things are pure echoes Jesus' teaching (Luke 11:41) and Paul's earlier writing (Rom. 14:20). In light of the Jewishness of the false teaching and the contexts of the earlier similar teaching by Jesus and Paul, the issue here seems to concern Jewish food laws. The false teachers seem in some way to be concerned with this ritual purity, although they are themselves **defiled** by their unbelief and sin.

1:16 The **works** of the false teachers prove that they are unbelievers, despite their claim to **know God**. Paul is not the least bit hesitant to make such a judgment.

2:1–3:8 *Christian Living in Contrast to the False Teachers.* Paul describes proper Christian living rooted in the gospel, which is in direct contrast to the behavior of the false teachers (1:10–16) but in conformity to what is required of true church leaders (1:5–9). This is the primary concern of the letter: right doctrine leads to right behavior. This section is composed of two parallel units (2:1–15 and 3:1–8) that describe right behavior, root this behavior in the gospel, and close with a charge to Titus to teach these things with authority.

2:1–10 *Proper Living by Age and Gender Groups.* Paul describes "what accords with sound doctrine" (v. 1), i.e., the type of living that corresponds with the gospel. Some argue that the behavior commanded here is not universally required but is culturally bound to the first century. They argue that the ground for this behavior is to avoid offense (see note on 2:5, 8, 10). However, v. 1 roots this behavior not in cultural ideas but in "sound doctrine" itself. Paul addresses the behavior of the church according to typical groups within the family structure (older men, older women, younger women, younger men, bondservants), with special attention to age and gender. While there are similarities in what is expected of each group, there are also distinctives.

2:1 But as for you indicates the sharp contrast that must exist between people, on one hand, whose deeds disprove their claim to know God (1:16), and Titus, on the other hand, who must teach the people to live in a way that **accords with sound doctrine**, i.e., that will affirm rather than deny their claim to know God.

2:2 The overall picture of **older men** is of Christian dignity and vibrant faith.

2:3–5 The instruction to **older women** and **young women** is intertwined because part of the role of a Christian older woman is to **train** (Gk. *sōphronizō*, "to give instruction in wise behavior and good judgment") the younger women. The topics comprising the teaching of the older women in vv. 4–5 are very practical and focused on the domestic sphere. **Working at home** does not prohibit working outside the home (cf. Prov. 31:16, 18, 24) but it does indicate that Paul expects wives to carry the primary responsibility for the day-to-day care of their homes and children. Yet this is to be done while being **submissive to their own husbands**, supporting their husbands' leadership role in the family. See notes on Eph. 5:22; 5:23–24. While other instructions could be included, the focus here is on older women helping younger women learn about being godly wives and mothers.

They are to teach what is good, 4 and so train the young women to love their husbands and
children, 5 to be self-controlled, [t]pure, [u]working at home, kind, and [v]submissive to their
own husbands, [w]that the word of God may not be reviled. 6 Likewise, urge [x]the younger
men to be self-controlled. 7 Show yourself in all respects to be [y]a model of good works,
and in your teaching [z]show integrity, [a]dignity, 8 and [b]sound speech that cannot be condemned, [c]so that an opponent may be put to shame, having nothing evil to say about us.
9 [d]Bondservants[1] are to be submissive to their own masters [e]in everything; they are to be
well-pleasing, not argumentative, 10 not pilfering, [f]but showing all good faith, [g]so that in
everything they may adorn the doctrine of God our Savior.
11 For [h]the grace of God [i]has appeared, bringing salvation [j]for all people, 12 training us
to renounce ungodliness and [k]worldly passions, and [l]to live self-controlled, upright, and
godly lives in [m]the present age, 13 [n]waiting for our blessed [o]hope, the [p]appearing of the
glory of our great [q]God and Savior Jesus Christ, 14 [r]who gave himself for us to [s]redeem us
from all lawlessness and [t]to purify for himself [t]a people for his own possession who are
[u]zealous for good works.
15 Declare these things; exhort and [v]rebuke with all authority. [w]Let no one disregard
you.

Be Ready for Every Good Work

3 Remind them [x]to be submissive to rulers and authorities, [y]to be obedient, to be ready
for every good work, 2 [z]to speak evil of no one, [a]to avoid quarreling, to be gentle, and
[b]to show perfect courtesy toward all people. 3 For [c]we ourselves were once foolish, disobedient, led astray, slaves to various passions and pleasures, passing our days in malice

[1] Or *Slaves* (for the contextual rendering of the Greek word *doulos*, see Preface)

5 [t]1 Pet. 3:2 [u][1 Tim. 5:14] [v]See Gen. 3:16 [w]See 1 Tim. 6:1
6 [x]1 Tim. 5:1
7 [y]1 Tim. 4:12; 1 Pet. 5:3 [z][2 Cor. 11:3] [a]1 Tim. 2:2
8 [b][1 Tim. 6:3] [c]Neh. 5:9; 1 Tim. 5:14; 1 Pet. 2:12; 3:16
9 [d]See 1 Pet. 2:18 [e][Col. 3:22]
10 [f][1 Tim. 3:11] [g]Matt. 5:16; Phil. 2:15
11 [h]ch. 3:7; See Acts 11:23 [i]ch. 3:4 [j][Ps. 67:2]; See 1 Tim. 2:4
12 [k]1 Pet. 4:2; 1 John 2:16 [l]2 Tim. 3:12; [Acts 24:25] [m]1 Tim. 6:17; 2 Tim. 4:10
13 [n]See 1 Cor. 1:7; 2 Pet. 3:12 [o]See ch. 1:2 [p]See 2 Thess. 2:8 [q]2 Pet. 1:1
14 [r]See Matt. 20:28 [s]Ps. 130:8; See 1 Pet. 1:18 [t]Ezek. 37:23; See Ex. 19:5 [u]ch. 3:8; Eph. 2:10
15 [v]ch. 1:13; 1 Tim. 5:20 [w]See 1 Tim. 4:12

Chapter 3

1 [x]Rom. 13:1; 1 Pet. 2:13 [y]See 2 Tim. 2:21
2 [z]Eph. 4:31 [a]1 Tim. 3:3 [b]See 2 Tim. 2:25
3 [c]See 1 Cor. 6:11

2:5, 8, 10 In each of these verses, important statements are made concerning the desired result of "gospel living." Such living keeps Christians from providing any legitimate grounds for the gospel (**the word of God**) to be **reviled** (v. 5; cf. v. 8). More positively, such living highlights the attractiveness of the gospel ("adorn," v. 10). In keeping with the overall thrust of the letter, this kind of living "proves" the gospel. **Doctrine of God our Savior** (v. 10) sets up the description of this doctrine in vv. 11–14. On God as "Savior," see note on 2 Tim. 1:8–10; chart below.

2:11–14 *Gospel Basis.* Paul gives the theological basis for the lifestyles he has described in vv. 1–10. Christians should live this way because ("for") the grace of God that saves also instructs its recipients to live in a new way. One cannot truly claim to be a recipient of saving grace without also being a pupil of "training grace." This change in lifestyle is rooted in the atonement (v. 14) and the expectation of Christ's return (v. 13).

2:11 Bringing salvation for all people is sometimes misunderstood as meaning that all people will be saved. However, such a reading is not necessary here and flatly contradicts other Scripture (see note on 1 Tim. 2:4). It means, rather, that salvation has been offered to all people (including all ethnic groups), not just to some.

2:12 Saving grace teaches its recipients to say no to sin and yes to godliness. **In the present age** stresses that this godliness is to be lived out in the here and now. It also sets up the reference to the future return of Christ (v. 13). Certainty about the future enables constancy in the present.

2:13 The Greek for **waiting** (*prosdechomai*) often carries a connotation of eagerness. Eagerly expecting the return of Christ is the way grace trains

God and Christ as "Our Savior" in Titus

"the preaching with which I have been entrusted by the command of *God our Savior*" (1:3)	"Grace and peace from God the Father and *Christ Jesus our Savior*" (1:4)
"so that in everything they may adorn the doctrine of *God our Savior*" (2:10)	"the glory of *our great God and Savior Jesus Christ*" (2:13)
"when the goodness and loving kindness of *God our Savior*" (3:4)	"he poured out on us richly through *Jesus Christ our Savior*" (3:6)

Christians to renounce sin and live in a godly way (see vv. 11–12). Setting one's mind on the truth of Christ's return impels a person to holiness (see 1 John 3:2–3). **Our blessed hope** means Christ's second coming, which Paul calls the **appearing of . . . our great God and Savior Jesus Christ**. It may seem unclear whether Paul refers here to two persons of the Godhead (God the Father and Jesus Christ) or whether he describes Jesus *as* God and Savior. The Greek grammar, however, is well reflected in this translation and indicates that Jesus is being identified as "our great God and Savior" (cf. John 1:1; 20:28; etc.).

2:14 Paul anchors his call for godliness in the fact that one purpose of Jesus' death was to make his people holy. To forsake godliness is to despise the sacrifice of Christ. Paul roots this in the OT with the phrase **to redeem us from all lawlessness**, which in Greek closely resembles the Septuagint of Ps. 130:8. **A people for his own possession** translates an unusual phrase (Gk. *laon periousion*) with intentional echoes from the OT (see esp. Ex. 19:5; Mal. 3:17). It has the sense of "prized, treasured possession." These people are to be **zealous for good works**, so again redemption is tied specifically to living in a godly manner. There is no room for claiming to be redeemed while providing no evidence of practical transformation (see James 2:14–26).

2:15 *Summary Command.* After describing the gospel, Paul returns to commanding Titus (as in vv. 1–10). The reference to **all authority**, and not allowing anyone to **disregard** Titus, shows that Paul expects this instruction to be given clearly and with certainty.

3:1–2 *Proper Living, Particularly with Respect to Outsiders.* Paul returns to describing "gospel living," this time with reference to interaction with outsiders. In general the qualities encouraged here (vv. 1–2) are in contrast to the description of the false teachers in 1:10–16.

3:1 ready for every good work. Whereas the false teachers are "unfit for any good work" (1:16), one of the purposes of the cross is to create a people "zealous for good works" (2:14).

3:2 The list closes with a call to take the initiative **to show** all manner of good to **all** sorts of **people**. **Perfect courtesy** (Gk. *prautēta*) is a good translation of an often misunderstood word literally meaning "meekness/gentleness."

3:3–7 *Gospel Basis.* As in 2:11–14, Paul explains how his exhortations to godly living (3:1–2) are based on the gospel. This gospel statement is presented in a traditional "conversion" formula—"formerly . . . but now"—highlighting the ethical and practical change effected by grace.

and envy, hated by others and hating one another. 4 But when [d]the goodness and loving
kindness of God our Savior appeared, 5 he saved us, [e]not because of works done by us
in righteousness, but [f]according to his own mercy, by [g]the washing of regeneration and
[h]renewal of the Holy Spirit, 6 whom he [i]poured out on us richly through Jesus Christ our
Savior, 7 so that [j]being justified by his grace we might become [k]heirs [l]according to the
hope of eternal life. 8 The saying is [m]trustworthy, and I want you to insist on these things,
so that those who have believed in God may be careful [n]to devote themselves to good
works. These things are excellent and profitable for people. 9 But [o]avoid foolish [p]contro-
versies, [q]genealogies, dissensions, and quarrels about the law, for [r]they are unprofitable
and worthless. 10 As for a person who stirs up division, [s]after warning him once and then
twice, [t]have nothing more to do with him, 11 knowing that such a person is warped and
sinful; he is self-condemned.

Final Instructions and Greetings

12 When I send Artemas or [u]Tychicus to you, do your best to come to me [v]at Nicopolis,
for I have decided to spend the winter there. 13 Do your best to speed Zenas the lawyer and
[w]Apollos on their way; see that they lack nothing. 14 And let our people learn [x]to devote
themselves to good works, so as to help cases of urgent need, and not [y]be unfruitful.
15 All who are with me send greetings to you. Greet those who love us in the faith.
[z]Grace be with you all.

4 [d]See Rom. 2:4
5 [e]See Rom. 3:27 [f]Eph. 2:4; 1 Pet. 1:3 [g]See John 3:5; 1 Cor. 6:11; 1 Pet. 3:21 [h]See Rom. 12:2
6 [i]Joel 2:28; Acts 2:33; 10:45; Rom. 5:5
7 [j]ch. 2:11 [k]Rom. 8:17 [l]See ch. 1:2
8 [m]See 1 Tim. 1:15 [n]ver. 14; ch. 2:14
9 [o]2 Tim. 2:16 [p]See 1 Tim. 6:4 [q]1 Tim. 1:4 [r]2 Tim. 2:14
10 [s]See Matt. 18:15 [t]See 2 John 10
12 [u]See 2 Tim. 4:12 [v][2 Tim. 4:10]
13 [w]See Acts 18:24
14 [x]ver. 8 [y]2 Pet. 1:8; [Phil. 1:11; 4:17; Col. 1:10]
15 [z]See Col. 4:18

3:4 Goodness and loving kindness stand in stark contrast to the description of lost humanity in v. 3. The difference is due to the appearance of **God our Savior** (see note on 2 Tim. 1:8–10).

3:5 The transformation described in vv. 3–7 (formerly . . . but now) is not based on human effort. "We . . . were once enslaved" (v. 3) but **he saved us**. God must act before salvation occurs. Salvation comes **not because of works** but **by the washing of regeneration and renewal of the Holy Spirit**. Some have understood this as saying that baptism ("the washing") causes salvation. However, in this context human deeds are clearly downplayed ("not because of works") and the emphasis is on divine action and initiative ("he saved us"). The "washing" described here is the spiritual cleansing, which is outwardly symbolized in baptism.

3:8 *Summary Command.* The command to **insist on these things** is similar to 2:15, both statements carrying a significant tone of authority. Again note the emphasis on **good works** as a mark of believers (see 1:16; 2:14; 3:1).

3:9–11 *The Problem Restated: False Teachers.* Paul returns to the problem of false teachers. Thus, the discussion of gospel living (2:1–3:8) is flanked by discussion of those who claim to believe this gospel but fail to live it out.

3:9 But. The reference to the usefulness of correct doctrine in v. 8 sets up the contrast with the **worthless** nature of the false teaching. As elsewhere in the letters to Timothy and Titus, the exact content of the false teaching is not clear. The point is that it is **foolish, unprofitable**, and worthless.

3:10–11 Have nothing more to do with him describes the final stage of church discipline (see also 1 Corinthians 5). A divisive person who refuses to repent and change after being confronted (see Matt. 18:15–20) shows himself to be twisted by sin (**warped**); thus, he is **self-condemned**. The NT is clear about seeking the repentance of such people, but it is equally clear that refusal to receive rebuke eventually shows that one is not in Christ and must be excluded from the Christian community.

3:12–15 *Closing Exhortation.* In typical fashion for first-century letters, Paul closes with reference to travel plans and greetings. As is also typical of Paul, even these items echo the main thrust of the letter.

3:12 do your best to come to me. Although Paul had left Titus in Crete in order to get the churches there properly established, he was not expected to stay there indefinitely. **Artemas** is not mentioned elsewhere in the NT. **Tychicus** is mentioned as an Asian who accompanied Paul on his third journey (Acts 20:4). In Eph. 6:21 and Col. 4:7 he is referred to as a "beloved brother and faithful minister" (see also 2 Tim. 4:12). **Nicopolis** was a port city in Epirus, on the west coast of the Greek peninsula and about 200 miles (322 km) northwest of Athens.

3:13–14 Speed . . . on their way; see that they lack nothing shows Paul's concern for the support of fellow missionaries and thus speaks to the church's role in supporting missions—and addressing cases of **urgent need**—today. **Zenas** is not mentioned elsewhere in the NT. **Apollos** is undoubtedly the popular speaker mentioned in Acts and 1 Corinthians (Acts 18:24; 19:1; 1 Cor. 3:6; etc.).

3:14 Having stressed **good works** throughout the letter, and having just called for assistance of fellow laborers (v. 13), Paul addresses this theme once more. This opportunity to assist Zenas and Apollos is one more example of how Christians can be involved in good works, relieving needs and furthering the gospel.

3:15 Grace be with you all. Paul's letter, though written primarily to Titus, will be read to the entire congregation.

INTRODUCTION TO

THE LETTER OF PAUL TO

PHILEMON

Author and Title

Paul and Timothy are explicitly named as the authors in verse 1. It becomes apparent, however, that the apostle Paul is the principal author when the first person singular ("I") is used from verse 4 throughout the rest of the letter. The title indicates that it is a personal letter to a man named Philemon. Nevertheless, Paul intends it to be read to the entire church that meets in Philemon's home (v. 2).

Date

The letter was probably written c. A.D. 62. Paul may have written it at roughly the same time that he wrote Colossians and Ephesians. All three letters were sent with Tychicus and Onesimus. This date assumes that the imprisonment Paul refers to (see vv. 1, 9, 10, 13, 23) is his imprisonment in Rome (Acts 27–28).

Theme

The theme of Philemon is the power of the gospel to transform lives ("formerly he was useless" but "now he is indeed useful," v. 11) and to impact human relationships (receive him "no longer as a bondservant [or slave] but more than a bondservant, as a beloved brother," v. 16). On the Gk. word *doulos*, see the ESV Preface, p. 21.

Purpose, Occasion, and Background

Philemon was a wealthy Christian who lived in the city of Colossae, about 100 miles (161 km) inland from Ephesus (see map, p. 2292). Apparently during Paul's three-year ministry in Ephesus (A.D. 52–55), Philemon heard the gospel and was saved. He began serving the cause of Christ in the Colossian community, opening his home for a group of Christians to meet there regularly.

At some point, Onesimus, one of Philemon's bondservants, fled to Rome. Possibly having stolen money (or property) from Philemon and now a fugitive, Onesimus was living in the most populated city of the Roman Empire, hoping to escape detection. In a rather remarkable set of circumstances—not recounted in the letter but certainly reflective of God's sovereignty—Onesimus somehow came into contact with the apostle Paul and became a Christian. As he grew in Christ, he spent much time and effort helping Paul, who was severely constrained by his imprisonment.

As much as Paul would like to have retained the services of Onesimus, Paul knew that Onesimus's fugitive status, severed relationship, and wrongdoing against his master needed to be addressed. Paul thus wrote this letter as an appeal to Philemon to appreciate the transformation that has occurred in Onesimus's life and to receive him back not merely as a bondservant but as a "beloved brother" (v. 16).

It is difficult to know if Paul was seeking Onesimus's full emancipation and freedom (see notes on vv. 16 and 21). It is clear, however, that he was seeking a transformed relationship between bondservant and master—a new relationship that would defy all of the ingrained status distinctions of the surrounding Greek and Roman culture. There is no doubt that it would have been difficult for this kind of servitude to survive in the atmosphere of love created by the letter, and in fact the elements of Paul's appeal found in this letter helped lay the foundation for the abolition of such servitude.

Timeline

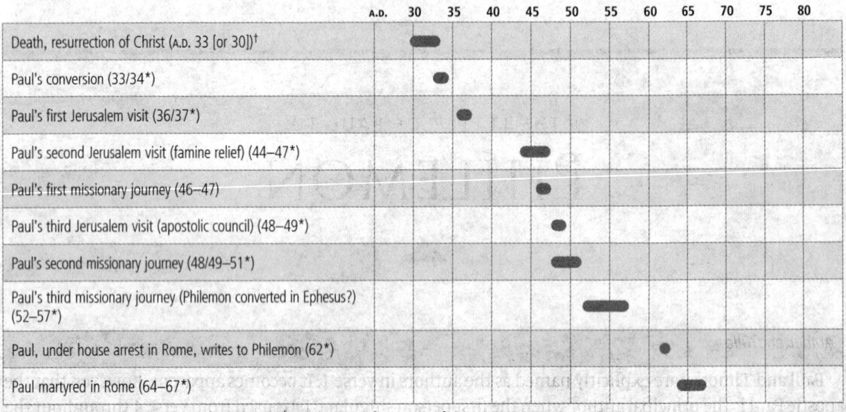

A.D.
30
35
40
45
50
55
60
65
70
75
80
Death, resurrection of Christ (A.D. 33 [or 30])†
Paul's conversion (33/34*)
Paul's first Jerusalem visit (36/37*)
Paul's second Jerusalem visit (famine relief) (44–47*)
Paul's first missionary journey (46–47)
Paul's third Jerusalem visit (apostolic council) (48–49*)
Paul's second missionary journey (48/49–51*)
Paul's third missionary journey (Philemon converted in Ephesus?) (52–57*)
Paul, under house arrest in Rome, writes to Philemon (62*)
Paul martyred in Rome (64–67*)

** denotes approximate date; / signifies either/or; † see The Date of Jesus' Crucifixion, pp. 1809–1810*

History of Salvation Summary

Christians' treatment of one another in Christ is to be transformed in the light of his grace toward them. (For an explanation of the "History of Salvation," see the Overview of the Bible, pp. 23–26.)

Literary Features

This simplified letter approximates the letters that people ordinarily write, in contrast to the more stylized and literary five-part format that characterizes most NT epistles. The letter is a masterpiece of persuasion and can be analyzed in terms of how Paul seeks a favorable reception for the returning bondservant, where the normal response of the master would be vindictive. Paul's strategy follows that prescribed by Greek and Roman rhetoricians of the day: begin by building rapport and goodwill with an audience (vv. 4–10), then lay out the facts in a way that will convince the mind or intellect (vv. 11–19), and finally appeal to the emotions of the audience (vv. 20–21).

Key Themes

1. At the heart of this letter is the theme of reconciliation. Onesimus is reconciled to God, and now he is in the process of being reconciled to a fellow believer.
2. The basis for Paul's appeal to Philemon is the supreme Christian virtue of love (not Roman social convention). Paul commends Philemon for the love he has shown not only to him but also to all of the believers in that area.

Outline

I. Greetings (vv. 1–3)

II. Thanksgiving and Prayer (vv. 4–7)

III. Paul's Appeal to Philemon for Onesimus (vv. 8–20)

IV. Personal Remarks and Greetings (vv. 21–25)

THE LETTER OF PAUL TO

PHILEMON

1[a]ver. 9; See Eph. 3:1 [b]See 1 Thess. 3:2
2[c]Col. 4:17 [d]Phil. 2:25 [e]See Rom. 16:5
3[f]See Rom. 1:7
4[g]See Rom. 1:8, 9
5[h]Col. 1:4 [i]Eph. 1:15
6[j]Phil. 1:9; Col. 1:9
7[k][2 Cor. 7:4, 13; Col. 4:11] [l]ver. 20; 2 Tim. 1:16; [Rom. 15:32; 2 Cor. 7:13]
8[m][1 Thess. 2:6] [n]Eph. 5:4
9[o]ver. 1
10[p]See 3 John 4 [q]Col. 4:9 [r]ver. 13; 1 Cor. 4:15; [Gal. 4:19]

Greeting

1 Paul, [a]a prisoner for Christ Jesus, and [b]Timothy our brother,
To Philemon our beloved fellow worker 2 and Apphia our sister and [c]Archippus our
[d]fellow soldier, and [e]the church in your house:
3 [f]Grace to you and peace from God our Father and the Lord Jesus Christ.

Philemon's Love and Faith

4 [g]I thank my God always when I remember you in my prayers, 5 because I [h]hear of your
love and [i]of the faith that you have toward the Lord Jesus and for all the saints, 6 and I
pray that the sharing of your faith may become effective for the full [j]knowledge of every
good thing that is in us for the sake of Christ.[1] 7 For I have derived much joy and [k]comfort
from your love, my brother, because the hearts of the saints [l]have been refreshed through
you.

Paul's Plea for Onesimus

8 Accordingly, [m]though I am bold enough in Christ to command you to do [n]what is
required, 9 yet for love's sake I prefer to appeal to you—I, Paul, an old man and now [o]a
prisoner also for Christ Jesus— 10 I appeal to you for [p]my child, [q]Onesimus,[2] [r]whose father I
became in my imprisonment. 11 (Formerly he was useless to you, but now he is indeed useful

[1] *Or for Christ's service* [2] *Onesimus means useful* (see verse 11) *or beneficial* (see verse 20)

1–3 *Greetings.* The beginning of this letter follows Paul's typical style, but it is addressed to a person rather than an entire community of believers.

1 On **Timothy**, see Introduction to 1 Timothy.

2 Apphia may have been Philemon's wife; **Archippus** may have been Philemon's son and may have had a significant ministry in Colossae (see Col. 4:17). **the church in your house**. Because of the political status of Christianity, there were no buildings dedicated to church services. The early Christians met in private homes. Philemon opened his home in Colossae, and someone named Nympha hosted the church in Laodicea (Col. 4:15; see note on 1 Cor. 16:19).

4–7 *Thanksgiving and Prayer.* Before Paul makes his appeal, he graciously and tactfully expresses his thanksgiving for Philemon (vv. 4–5) and describes how he prays for him (vv. 6–7).

6 Sharing (Gk. *koinōnia*) as used here would seem to carry a wide range of meaning, including the ideas of generosity, partnership, and fellowship that result from the common faith and common life that believers have in Christ. This usage of *koinōnia* is similar to the way Paul commends the Philippians for their tangible generosity ("partnership," see note on v. 17) in supporting the cause of the gospel (Phil. 1:5). Paul is laying the groundwork for his appeal to Philemon on behalf of Onesimus. Philemon's sharing will result in his own deeper **knowledge of every good thing** in Christ, that is, a deeper awareness and experience of the blessings that Christ has for him.

7 the hearts of the saints have been refreshed through you. Philemon was well known for his **love** for his fellow believers, which brought Paul great **joy**. He had been actively involved in ministering to other Christians in a way that had profoundly encouraged them. On "hearts" (Gk. *splagchna*), see note on v. 12.

8–20 *Paul's Appeal to Philemon for Onesimus.* Paul makes his appeal by first describing the remarkable change that has happened to Onesimus (vv. 8–12) and then suggesting how helpful Onesimus would be to him in his imprisonment (vv. 13–14). Paul then wonders if God has been sovereignly involved in this situation so that Philemon may receive Onesimus back now as a fellow Christian (vv. 15–16) who will therefore be all the more useful to Philemon. He concludes with a direct appeal that Philemon take Onesimus back as he would receive Paul himself (vv. 17–20).

8–9 to command you. Paul chooses not to demand anything of Philemon but to appeal to him on the basis of love. **Bold** (Gk. *parrēsia*) suggests "frankness" or "openness" to speak freely about difficult matters. **an old man**. Paul may have been 60 years old, or older; he was a "young man" 30 years earlier when, as Saul of Tarsus, he supported the persecution of Stephen and the other Christians (Acts 7:58).

10 The name **Onesimus** means "useful" or "profitable" and was frequently given to bondservants. He is also mentioned in Col. 4:9 as accompanying Tychicus with the letter to the Colossians. **Whose father I became** (lit., "I gave birth to him"; cf. 1 Cor. 4:15 and Gal. 4:19, where Paul employs the image of labor pains) describes the "spiritual birthing" of Onesimus.

11 useless . . . useful (Gk. *achrēstos . . . euchrēstos*). The play on words describes the before and after of Onesimus's conversion. By stealing from Philemon and running away, Onesimus had become "useless," but having repented and become obedient to Christ, Onesimus had now become "useful" both to Paul and to Philemon. This change particularly highlights the transforming power of the gospel.

to you and to me.) 12 I am sending him back to you, sending my very heart. 13 I would have
been glad to keep him with me, in order that he might serve me [s]on your behalf [t]during
my imprisonment for the gospel, 14 but I preferred to do nothing without your consent in
order that your goodness might not be [u]by compulsion but of your own accord. 15 For this
perhaps is why [v]he was parted from you for a while, that you might have him back forever,
16 [w]no longer as a bondservant[1] but more than a bondservant, as [x]a beloved brother—
especially to me, but how much more to you, [y]both in the flesh and in the Lord.
17 So if you consider me [z]your partner, receive him as you would receive me. 18 If he has
wronged you at all, or owes you anything, charge that to my account. 19 [a]I, Paul, write this
with my own hand: I will repay it—to say nothing of your owing me even your own self.
20 Yes, brother, I want some benefit from you in the Lord. [b]Refresh my heart in Christ.
21 [c]Confident of your obedience, I write to you, knowing that you will do even more than
I say. 22 At the same time, prepare a guest room for me, for [d]I am hoping that [e]through
your prayers [f]I will be graciously given to you.

Final Greetings

23 [g]Epaphras, my [h]fellow prisoner in Christ Jesus, sends greetings to you, 24 and so do
[i]Mark, [i]Aristarchus, [j]Demas, and [j]Luke, my fellow workers.
25 [k]The grace of the Lord Jesus Christ be with your spirit.

[1] Or *slave*; twice in this verse (for the contextual rendering of the Greek word *doulos*, see Preface)

13 [s]See 1 Cor. 16:17 [t]ver. 10; See Phil. 1:7
14 [u][2 Cor. 9:7; 1 Pet. 5:2]
15 [v][Gen. 45:5, 8]
16 [w]See 1 Cor. 7:22 [x]Matt. 23:8; Col. 4:9; 1 Tim. 6:2 [y]Col. 3:22, 23; [Eph. 6:5]
17 [z]2 Cor. 8:23
19 [a]See 1 Cor. 16:21
20 [b]See ver. 7
21 [c]See 2 Cor. 2:3
22 [d]Phil. 1:25; 2:24 [e]See 2 Cor. 1:11 [f][Heb. 13:19]
23 [g]See Col. 1:7 [h]Rom. 16:7
24 [i]See Col. 4:10 [j]See Col. 4:14; 2 Tim. 4:10, 11
25 [k]See Gal. 6:18

12 my very heart. Not the common word for heart (Gk. *kardia*) but *splagchna*, literally "internal organs" (esp. the stomach and intestines). It connotes affection, intimacy, and a deep love (cf. vv. 7, 20; Phil. 2:1; Col. 3:12). Paul is not handling this situation as a detached arbitrator but as one who has developed a fond affection for Onesimus.

13–14 not . . . by compulsion. Paul does not want to compel Philemon but to persuade him, so that his love is authentic and not coerced.

15 why he was parted from you. The Greek verb is passive, without indicating any agent of the action explicitly expressed. It is best seen as a "divine passive," where God is understood to be sovereignly behind the events. It is thus reminiscent of Joseph's betrayal by his brothers, which resulted in his long sojourn in Egypt. After Joseph reveals himself to his brothers, he remarks, "it was not you who sent me here, but God" (Gen. 45:8).

16 no longer as a bondservant. Paul could have said more explicitly, "no longer a bondservant," which would make it clear that he expected Onesimus's emancipation. On the Gk. word *doulos*, see the ESV Preface, p. 21. The particle "as" (Gk. *hōs*) allowed more freedom for Philemon to ponder and then choose to do what was right, rather than having Paul command him directly. Clearly, however, Paul expected an entirely transformed relationship between the two of them based on the fact that Onesimus was now Philemon's **beloved brother**.

17 Partner (Gk. *koinōnos*) is from the same root as "sharing" (Gk. *koinōnia*) in v. 6. The good that is in Philemon should now be expressed in his new relationship with Onesimus. As God has received his people for the sake of Christ, they are to receive one another (see Rom. 5:6–11; 2 Cor. 5:16–21; note on 2 Cor. 2:10).

18–19 If he has wronged you suggests that Onesimus not only ran away from Philemon but probably took money from him as well. This would have provided him the means to purchase passage to Rome and to live there for a time. Roman society expected brutal punishment of fugitive slaves and bondservants, at times resulting in death. Thus Paul is asking Philemon to do something quite extraordinary by forgiving Onesimus's debt. (Regarding servitude in Roman society, see notes on 1 Cor. 7:21 and Eph. 6:5; and ESV Preface, p. 21.) **I, Paul, write this with my own hand**. Although Paul was probably dictating the letter to Timothy (see Philem. 1), Paul takes the stylus at this juncture and signs his own name. This action underlines his personal guarantee that he **will repay** any loss Philemon has incurred—a remarkable offer considering the fact that Paul, an impoverished prisoner, is accepting full financial liability for anything that Onesimus might owe to Philemon, a person of considerable wealth. **owing me even your own self**. A reference to the fact that Philemon was converted through Paul's ministry, so that Philemon "owed" Paul something far greater, namely, his eternal life. The debt that Onesimus owed to Philemon, therefore, is insignificant by comparison.

20 In v. 7 Paul had rejoiced because "the hearts of the saints have been refreshed through [Philemon]", and in v. 12 he said, "I am . . . sending my very heart." Now in v. 20 Paul picks up this language again, using the Greek *splagchna* ("heart") for the third time, and commands Philemon to **refresh my heart in Christ**. What the Lord has already worked into Philemon's life is now to become a reality in his relationship with Onesimus.

21–25 *Personal Remarks and Greetings.* Paul concludes the letter by indicating that he plans to travel to Colossae (vv. 21–22) and by extending greetings from various coworkers in Rome (vv. 23–25).

21 Some think that **even more** could suggest freeing Onesimus. Others think Paul was hinting that Philemon should send Onesimus back to minister to Paul (cf. vv. 13–14). Paul may have deliberately not given specific instructions to Philemon, giving him the freedom to decide which course of action would be best.

22 prepare a guest room for me. Paul expects to be released from prison and come to Colossae for a visit. It is uncertain if this indicates that Paul has abandoned (or at least delayed) his previous plans to go further west to Spain.

23 Epaphras is one of Philemon's fellow Colossians, whom God had used to plant the church in that city (Col. 1:7; 4:12). He is now in Rome as Paul's **fellow prisoner in Christ Jesus**. The circumstances of his arrest are unknown.

24 Mark, Aristarchus, Demas, and Luke are also named in Col. 4:10, 14. For Mark, see Acts 12:12. For Aristarchus, see Acts 19:29. Luke is almost certainly the one who authored the Gospel of Luke as well as Acts (see also Col. 4:14; 2 Tim. 4:11). Luke was apparently with Paul throughout his two-year imprisonment in Caesarea and then in his two-year Roman imprisonment. Lamentably, Demas later followed worldly pursuits and deserted Paul (2 Tim. 4:10).

INTRODUCTION TO

THE LETTER TO THE

HEBREWS

Author, Audience, and Title

The author of Hebrews neither names himself nor clearly designates his audience. The traditional title "to the Hebrews" reflects the ancient assumption that the original recipients were Jewish Christians.

The author's identity has been a matter of significant conjecture throughout church history. In antiquity, authorship was attributed to figures such as Barnabas or especially Paul. However, several of the most astute church fathers recognized considerable differences in style and method of argument between this book and Paul's named writings. Scholars have suggested other possible authors, such as Clement, Luke, or Apollos. However, most today concede that this author remains anonymous. It seems that the judgment expressed by Origen (d. c. A.D. 254) remains correct: "Who actually wrote the epistle, only God knows" (cited in Eusebius, *Ecclesiastical History* 6.25.14).

The author clearly knew his recipients and longed to be reunited with them (Heb. 13:19). They had a mutual friend in Timothy (13:23), and probably this was the same Timothy who ministered alongside Paul. The author was presumably male, since he refers to himself using a masculine participle (see 11:32: "would fail me to tell"). Since "us" included the author in 2:3 (the salvation "attested to us by those who heard"; also 2:1), it appears that he was not an eyewitness of Jesus. The author passed on the greetings of those "from Italy" (13:24). Scholars debate whether he was in Italy writing to the church elsewhere or was outside Italy (though accompanied by Italians) and writing back to an audience in Italy (possibly at Rome).

The audience's social situation can be inferred from commands to "remember those who are in prison" and who are "mistreated" (13:3). Timothy himself had just been set free (13:23). Indeed, the author of Hebrews commended his audience for their former endurance of persecution, for their compassion on those in prison, and for having "joyfully accepted the plundering of your property" (10:32–34).

The author warned against "strange teachings" in the church (13:9), and these teachings may have been related to the use of ritual foods (13:9–10). Moreover, he repeatedly called his audience to persevere in the faith and cautioned them about the danger of leaving the Christian communion, as he sought to show the superiority of Christ to Mosaic sacrifices and rituals (chs. 3–10). Hence the early church was likely correct to assert that Jewish Christians (as well as Gentiles who had previously been drawn to the Jewish religion) were the intended audience for this book (see "our fathers," 1:1). Furthermore, such an audience would have well understood the book's many citations and allusions to the OT (and would have shared in the writer's frequent use of the Septuagint, the Greek translation of the OT).

Date

Hebrews was almost certainly written in the first century and probably before A.D. 70. Reasons for asserting a first-century date include the mention of Timothy (13:23), who was known to be active in the first century, and the influence of Hebrews (and its way of thinking) on *1 Clement* (written c. A.D. 96).

The crucial issue in dating the book concerns whether the destruction of the Jerusalem temple (A.D. 70) had already occurred. Hebrews speaks of the Jewish sacrificial system as if it were a still-present reality (Heb. 7:27–28; 8:3–5; 9:7–8, 25; 10:1–3; 13:10–11), which does not seem likely after the cessation of the Jerusalem temple sacrifices in A.D. 70. Admittedly, Hebrews focuses on the Mosaic tabernacle rather than the Solomonic (or the Herodian) temple. Nonetheless, if the writer was attempting to convince his readers of the inferiority of the Mosaic system (and possibly dissuade church members from returning to Jewish practices), an obvious argument would have been to mention the cessation of the temple sacrifices, if they were in fact no longer taking place.

Theme

Christ is greater than any angel, priest, or old covenant institution; thus each reader, rather than leaving such a great salvation, is summoned to hold on by faith to the true rest found in Christ and to encourage others in the church to persevere.

Purpose, Occasion, and Background

The genre of Hebrews is unusual. The book is without an introduction or other early indications that it is a letter. Yet the final verses do pass on greetings and blessings (13:23–25), and the author speaks of having "written to you" (13:22). However, the author also identifies his work as a "word of exhortation" (13:22). The careful rhetorical progression of the book, along with its frequent practical exhortations, has led many to consider it a single sermon. Perhaps Hebrews is best understood as a sermonic letter.

Hebrews frequently encourages the audience to endure and warns against leaving Christ (2:1–4; 3:7–4:13; 5:11–6:12; 10:19–39; 12:1–29). These warning passages are interspersed throughout the book (see chart, p. 2366) and have noticeable structural similarities (esp. in terms of exhortation and threatened consequence). Around these passages the argument of the book progresses carefully. Moreover, these specific exhortations themselves flow out of the surrounding material. Thus the book is unified in both structure and intent.

The warning passages exhort church participants to remain faithful. The more expository sections of the epistle show the superiority of Christ and his new covenant work to angels, Moses, the tabernacle priesthood, and the sacrificial system. The implication is that these are so inferior to Christ that it is futile to return to them (or to go anywhere else). Thus the book encourages the church to hold fast to its faith, because that faith is grounded in the most superior revelation.

The background of such exhortations must have been the audience's need to continue enduring through persecution and the trials of life (e.g., ch. 12). They appear to have grown less attentive to Christian instruction (5:11–14); and some apparently have ceased regular attendance at their meetings (10:25). Nonetheless, the author reminds them of their past faithfulness and communal love in the midst of persecution (10:32–34). He encourages their faithfulness by careful exposition of the OT in light of the revelation in Jesus Christ.

The soteriology (salvation teaching) of Hebrews is rooted in its Christology—the Son of God became the heavenly high priest, who offered himself as a sacrifice once for all. Christ obtained salvation for all who approach in faith (6:1; 11:6; cf. 4:2), and such faith perseveres until it receives the promised eternal reward (6:12; 10:22, 38–39).

Key Themes

1. Jesus is fully God and fully man.	1:1–14; 2:5–18
2. Jesus as Son of God reveals God the Father, is the agent of creation, and sustains all creation.	1:1–14
3. Jesus serves as the eternal high priest, who as a man sympathizes with human weaknesses, and yet who offered himself as the perfect sacrifice for sin.	1:3; 2:10–18; 4:15–16; 9:11–10:19
4. Jesus is superior to angels, to Moses and the Mosaic covenant, and to the earthly tabernacle and its priesthood.	1:4–2:18; 3:1–6; 5:1–10; 7:1–10:18
5. All humanity faces eternal judgment for sin.	4:12–13; 9:27–28; 10:26–31
6. Faith is necessary to please God and to participate in his eternal salvation promises. Faith requires conviction about the unseen realities of God and his promises. Such faith produces perseverance.	4:2–3; 6:1, 12; 10:22, 38–39; 11:1–40
7. Perseverance is necessary in the Christian life, and thus church participants are warned against a lack of endurance.	2:1–4; 3:7–4:13; 5:11–6:12; 10:19–39; 12:1–29
8. God's promises are trustworthy, including his promise of eternal salvation.	6:13–20
9. With the advent of Jesus Christ, the last days have begun, though they await consummation at his return.	1:2; 2:5; 4:9–11; 9:9–28; 12:22–29

History of Salvation Summary

Christ has accomplished final salvation, has brought the final word of God, and has become the final priest and the one atoning sacrifice to which the OT pointed. (For an explanation of the "History of Salvation," see the Overview of the Bible, pp. 23–26.)

Timeline

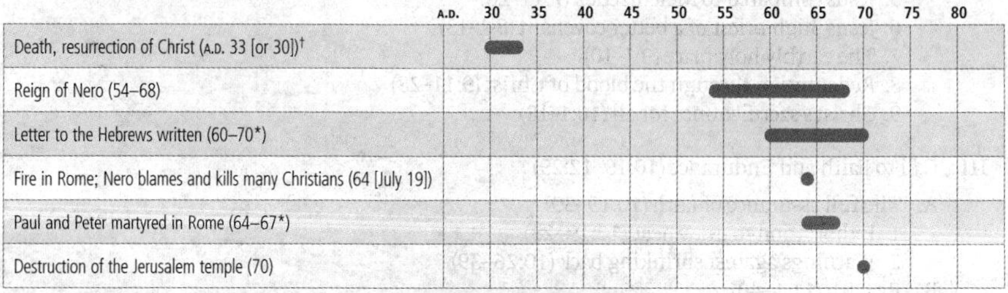

** denotes approximate date; / signifies either/or; † see The Date of Jesus' Crucifixion, pp. 1809–1810*

Literary Features

As noted above (see Purpose, Occasion, and Background), the book of Hebrews has affinities with the genres of both the epistle and the sermon. The first 12 chapters conduct a sustained theological argument about the superiority of Christ over a number of rivals and about the need to persevere in following this vastly superior Messiah. While following many ancient customs of rhetorical argumentation, these chapters can remind the modern reader of an essay with a thesis, a series of subordinate generalizations, and supporting proof consisting of data and commentary on that data.

The book of Hebrews is one of the most stylistically polished books in the NT. The writer is a master of imagery and metaphor, allusions to the OT, comparison and analogy, contrast, and long, flowing sentences that build to a climax and often use parallel construction of clauses.

The rhetoric of the book is partly argumentative, as the author conducts a sustained theological exposition such as modern readers might expect in a debate or in a theology book. The persuasive strategy adheres to one of the classical ways of arguing a thesis, which is to repeat the main idea often and from a variety of angles. In addition to the rhetoric of argument and debate, readers will find in the book of Hebrews a persuasive rhetoric of exhortation in which the writer appeals to his readers not to abandon their faith.

The central motif of the book is the formula "better," with the cluster of words "better," "more," and "greater" appearing a combined total of 25 times. The comparative motif, in which one thing is declared superior to another thing, is the main rhetorical strategy of the book. A common rhetorical form by which the comparison is conducted is analogy, with something in the OT being declared similar to the person and work of Christ. But the analogies are not between two equal things; rather, the author argues from the lesser to the greater.

Outline

I. Jesus Is Superior to Angelic Beings (1:1–2:18)
   A. The supremacy of God's Son (1:1–14)
      1. Introduction: summary of the Son's person and work (1:1–4)
      2. Evidence of his status as Son (1:5–14)
   B. Warning against neglecting salvation (2:1–4)
   C. The founder of salvation (2:5–18)

II. Jesus Is Superior to the Mosaic Law (3:1–10:18)
   A. Jesus is greater than Moses (3:1–6)
   B. Warning: a rest for the people of God (3:7–4:13)
      1. The failure of the exodus generation (3:7–19)
      2. Entering God's rest (4:1–13)
   C. The high priesthood of Jesus (4:14–10:18)
      1. Jesus the great high priest (4:14–5:10)
      2. Pause in the argument: warning against apostasy (5:11–6:12)
      3. The certainty of God's promise (6:13–20)

4. Return to main argument: the priestly order of Melchizedek (7:1–10)
5. Jesus compared to Melchizedek (7:11–28)
6. Jesus, high priest of a better covenant (8:1–13)
7. The earthly holy place (9:1–10)
8. Redemption through the blood of Christ (9:11–28)
9. Christ's sacrifice once for all (10:1–18)

III. Call to Faith and Endurance (10:19–12:29)

A. The full assurance of faith (10:19–39)
1. Exhortation to draw near (10:19–25)
2. Warnings against shrinking back (10:26–39)
B. By faith (11:1–40)
C. Endurance until the kingdom fully comes (12:1–29)
1. Jesus, founder and perfecter of faith (12:1–2)
2. Do not grow weary (12:3–17)
3. A kingdom that cannot be shaken (12:18–29)

IV. Concluding Exhortations and Remarks (13:1–25)

A. Sacrifices pleasing to God (13:1–19)
B. Benediction (13:20–21)
C. Final greetings (13:22–25)

THE LETTER TO THE

HEBREWS

The Supremacy of God's Son

1 Long ago, at many times and [a]in many ways, God spoke to our fathers by the prophets,
2 but [b]in these last days [c]he has spoken to us by [d]his Son, whom he appointed [e]the heir
of all things, [f]through whom also he created [g]the world. 3 He is the radiance of the glory of
God and [h]the exact imprint of his nature, and he upholds the universe by the word of his
power. [i]After making purification for sins, [j]he sat down [k]at the right hand of the Majesty
on high, 4 having become as much superior to angels as the name [l]he has inherited is more
excellent than theirs.
5 For to which of the angels did God ever say,

> [m]"You are my Son,
> today I have begotten you"?

Chapter 1
1 [a][Num. 12:6, 8; Joel 2:28]
2 [b]1 Pet. 1:20; [ch. 9:26; Acts 2:17] [c]ch. 2:3 [d]See Matt. 14:33 [e]Ps. 2:8; Matt. 21:38; See Matt. 28:18 [f][ch. 3:3]; See John 1:3 [g]ch. 11:3
3 [h]See 2 Cor. 4:4 [i]See ch. 9:14 [j]See Mark 16:19 [k][Luke 22:69]
4 [l]Eph. 1:21; Phil. 2:9
5 [m]ch. 5:5; Acts 13:33; Cited from Ps. 2:7

1:1–2:18 *Jesus Is Superior to Angelic Beings.* A summary of who Jesus is (1:1–4) culminates in the announcement of his superiority to angels. This superiority is proven first in his unique quality as Son of God (1:5–14), and second in his humanity as Son of Man, which permits him to serve as the perfect founder of salvation (2:5–18). Amid this comes the first warning/exhortation (2:1–4).

1:1–14 *The Supremacy of God's Son.* Jesus is God's final and definitive revelation (surpassing the OT, vv. 1–2), for he is the Son of God (v. 2), the agent of creation (v. 2), the very glory of God (v. 3), and the one who purifies from sin (v. 3). In all this he is superior even to angelic beings, especially in his unique sonship (vv. 4–14). This leads to a warning to attend to the words of salvation, since they are from and about the Son (2:1–4).

1:1–4 *Introduction: Summary of the Son's Person and Work.* Many themes of Hebrews are announced in this opening (a single Gk. sentence). These include the contrasting periods of revelation (1:1–2; cf. 2:2–4; 3:1–6; 4:14–5:10; 6:13–10:18), Jesus' unique status as Son of God (1:2–3; cf. vv. 5–14; 3:1–6; 5:5–10; 7:26–28), his purifying work (1:3; cf. 9:11–10:18), and his supremacy (in this case to angels in 1:4; cf. 1:5–2:18). To the extent that this brief description of the Son parallels the understanding of "wisdom" in some extra-biblical Jewish literature (esp. *Wisdom of Solomon* 7:22–30), the author may also allude to the Son's partaking of, and superiority to, wisdom.

1:1 Long ago contrasts here with "these last days" in v. 2. Two similar Greek words (*polymerōs* and *polytropōs*) emphasize the **many times** and **many ways** in which God has spoken. This speaking was through **prophets**, which in Jewish thought included the authors of both the prophetic and the historical books of the OT (even Moses and David; cf. Deut. 18:15; Acts 1:16; 3:22; 4:25; 7:37; 26:22). **Our fathers** are the OT patriarchs (cf. Heb. 3:9; 8:9), whom the author considers his audience's spiritual forebears.

1:2 Four points of contrast occur between vv. 1 and 2: time of revelation ("long ago" vs. **these last days**); agent of revelation ("prophets" vs. **Son**); recipients of revelation ("fathers" vs. **us**); and, implicitly, the unity of the final revelation in the Son (cf. the "many times and in many ways" in v. 1, implying, by contrast, that this last revelation came at one time, in one way, in and through God's Son). Since God has spoken finally and fully in the Son, and since the NT fully reports and interprets this supreme revelation once the NT is written, the canon of Scripture is complete. No new books are needed to explain what God has done through his Son. Now believers await his second coming (9:28) and the city to come (13:14). Jesus is **heir of all things** (i.e., what he "inherits" from his Father is all creation) by virtue of his dignity as Son (1:4). The preexistence, authority, power, and full deity of the Son are evident in his role in creating **the world**; cf. John 1:3, 10; Col. 1:16.

1:3 The greatness of the Son is further exhibited. **Glory** is often viewed metaphorically as light (e.g., Isa. 60:1, 19; 2 Cor. 4:4–6; Rev. 21:23), and here the Son is that glorious light of God. Jesus is the full and definitive representation, the **exact imprint** (Gk. *charaktēr*), of God's real being (his **nature**, Gk. *hypostasis*). Thus the Son is identical in substance to God, being himself fully God. In all attributes and abilities, the Son is exactly like the Father. The Son, who created the **universe** (Heb. 1:2), **upholds** it by his own powerful **word** (cf. Col. 1:17). Jesus deals with the human need of **purification for sins** (see Heb. 9:11–10:18). Jesus ascends to the place of supreme authority (the **right hand** of God); see 1:13; 8:1; 10:12; 12:2; also e.g., Mark 14:62; Acts 2:33; Rom. 8:34; Eph. 1:20; 1 Pet. 3:22. The fact that he has **sat down** there indicates that his work of salvation had been completed. **Majesty** also describes God in Heb. 8:1 (cf. Deut. 32:3; Ps. 145:3, 6; 150:2; Jude 25).

1:4 The main theme of chs. 1 and 2 is announced: Jesus is **superior to angels**. Angels were objects of much speculation in first-century Judaism. Certainly they were known to appear in human form, to minister before the very throne of God, to guide and protect humans, and to have revealed the Mosaic law (see 1:7; 2:2; 12:22; 13:2). Yet Jesus is deemed superior to them, in part because his **name** (i.e., his essence) is "Son" (1:5), which points to a more intimate relationship and which speaks of a better family inheritance (all that belongs to the Father belongs to his unique Son).

1:5–14 *Evidence of His Status as Son.* A chain of OT citations supports the claim that Jesus is superior to angels (v. 4) since Jesus has the position, nature, and authority of God's Son.

1:5 You are my Son. This citation from Ps. 2:7 invokes the whole Psalm: the Messiah is the Anointed One (Ps. 2:2), is king over all (Ps. 2:6–8), and especially is God's Son (Ps. 2:7). **today I have begotten you**. A poetic expression reflecting the unique relationship of the Son to God Almighty (see further Heb. 1:6); this speaks of entering into a new phase of that Father-Son relationship and should not be pressed to suggest that the Son once did not exist (he has begotten the *already living* Son "today"). Similar words of divine sonship are spoken at Jesus' baptism (Mark 1:11; Luke 3:22; cf. Matt. 3:17) and his transfiguration (Matt. 17:5; Mark 9:7; Luke 9:35); see also Acts 13:33; Heb. 5:5. **he shall be to me a son**. This proclamation (2 Sam. 7:14; also 1 Chron. 17:13) is declared to King David concerning his covenant heir, whom

Or again,

[n]"I will be to him a father,
and he shall be to me a son"?

6 And again, when he brings [o]the firstborn into the world, he says,

[p]"Let all God's angels worship him."

7 Of the angels he says,

[q]"He makes his angels winds,
and his ministers a flame of fire."

8 But of the Son he says,

[r]"Your throne, O God, is forever and ever,
the scepter of uprightness is the scepter of your kingdom.
9 You have loved righteousness and hated wickedness;
therefore God, your God, [s]has anointed you
with [t]the oil of gladness beyond your companions."

10 And,

[u]"You, Lord, laid the foundation of the earth in the beginning,
and the heavens are the work of your hands;
11 they will perish, but you remain;
they will all wear out like a garment,
12 like a robe you will roll them up,
like a garment they will be changed.[1]
But you are [v]the same,
and your years will have no end."

13 And to which of the angels has he ever said,

[w]"Sit at my right hand
[x]until I make your enemies a footstool for your feet"?

14 Are they not all ministering spirits [y]sent out to serve for the sake of those who are to
[z]inherit salvation?

[1] Some manuscripts omit *like a garment*

5 [n]Cited from 2 Sam. 7:14; [Ps. 89:26, 27]
6 [o]See Rom. 8:29 [p]Cited from Deut. 32:43 (Gk.); [Ps. 97:7]
7 [q]Cited from Ps. 104:4
8 [r]Cited from Ps. 45:6, 7
9 [s]Isa. 61:1 [t]Isa. 61:3
10 [u]Cited from Ps. 102:25-27
12 [v]ch. 13:8
13 [w]Cited from Ps. 110:1 [x]ch. 10:13
14 [y]Gen. 19:16; 28:12; 32:1, 2; Judg. 6:11; 13:3; Ps. 34:7; 91:11; 103:20, 21; Dan. 3:28; 6:22; 10:11; Matt. 18:10 [z]See Matt. 25:34

God will designate God's own "Son." In the context of Samuel, the reader might assume this refers to David's son Solomon, but Solomon failed to follow the law and was not "established forever" (2 Sam. 7:16); hence, the promise can only be fulfilled by the Davidic Messiah. Psalm 2 and 2 Samuel 7 are linked by the special designation "Son," and by their messianic theology (a link also assumed in NT-era Judaism, e.g., 4QFlorilegium in the Dead Sea Scrolls).

1:6 Firstborn is a title (see Rom. 8:29; Col. 1:15, 18; Rev. 1:5; cf. 2 Sam. 7:12–14; Ps. 89:27) that conveys preeminence in family lineage and rights of inheritance (see Gen. 43:33; Ex. 4:22; Heb. 1:4–5). It does not mean that Jesus was created (see note on Col. 1:15). **Let all God's angels worship him** may be an interpretative citation of either Ps. 97:7 or Deut. 32:43 (LXX)—or possibly both. In both cases angels are considered "sons of God," but without the rights of the unique Son of God. The job of angels is to worship God, and hence to worship his Son (the "exact imprint of his nature," Heb. 1:3). Since only God is worthy of worship (Ex. 20:3–5; Isa. 42:8; Matt. 4:10; Rev. 19:10; 22:9), this is further evidence of the Son's full deity.

1:7 The splendor of **angels** is acknowledged here, proving that the Son, who is superior to all the angels, is all the more glorious. The OT context of the quotation from Psalm 104 points to the Lord God as creator and sustainer of all things, including angels (Ps. 104:1–30; v. 4 is quoted). Since the Son is designated creator and sustainer (Heb. 1:2–3; 10:1–12:29), it is implicit that the splendor of the angels also stems from his creative hand.

1:8–9 The quotation (Ps. 45:6–7) is from a psalm extolling the Davidic king. Only Jesus, as the Davidic Messiah (the **anointed** One), truly meets this description, since by reigning at God's right hand (Heb. 1:3, 13) he possesses an eternal kingdom (**forever and ever**) and reigns in true **righteousness** (4:15; 7:26–28). **Your throne, O God**. The messianic Son is rightfully also called God, in this case by God the Father. (For other verses where Jesus is called "God," see John 1:1, 18; 20:28; Rom. 9:5; Titus 2:13; 2 Pet. 1:1; see also note on 1 Cor. 12:4–6.)

1:10–12 In light of the clear designation of deity in vv. 8–9 and the consequent eternality of the Son (v. 8, "forever and ever"), the author connects God's Son with Ps. 102:25–27. This emphasizes the role of the Son in creation (Heb. 1:10; cf. vv. 2–3) and his eternality (vv. 11–12).

1:13 Cited from Ps. 110:1. This psalm of David is quite significant in Hebrews (see Heb. 5:6; 7:17, 21) and elsewhere (e.g., Matt. 22:44; Acts 2:34; cf. 1 Cor. 15:25). It applies to "great David's greater son," the Messiah. In the Gospels (see Matt. 22:44 par.) Jesus applied this verse to himself, arguing that when David says, "The LORD said to my Lord," David must be prophetically ascribing deity both to God himself and to David's messianic "Lord." This context of messianic deity is likely also implied here (given Heb. 1:2–3, 8–12); however, here the author emphasizes the exaltation of the Son to the **right hand** of God—the position of privilege and power (see v. 3).

1:14 ministering spirits. Angels are called "ministers" in v. 7. Their particular role is to **serve** those **who are to inherit salvation**, that is, Christian believers (on inheritance see 6:12, 17; 9:15). Salvation (see 2:3; 6:9) is possible only through Jesus' work (2:10; 5:9; 9:28). The angels' important role still pales in comparison to Jesus' authority as Son of God exalted at the "right hand of the Majesty" (1:3, 13).

Warning Against Neglecting Salvation

2 Therefore we must pay much closer attention to what we have heard, lest we drift away
from it. 2 For since [a]the message declared by angels proved to be reliable, and [b]every
transgression or disobedience received a just [c]retribution, 3 [d]how shall we escape if we
[e]neglect such a great salvation? It was [f]declared at first by the Lord, and it was [g]attested to
us [h]by those who heard, 4 [g]while God also bore witness [i]by signs and wonders and various
miracles and by [j]gifts of the Holy Spirit [k]distributed according to his will.

The Founder of Salvation

5 For it was not to angels that God subjected the world [l]to come, of which we are speaking. 6 It has been testified somewhere,

> [m]"What is man, that you are mindful of him,
> or the son of man, that you care for him?
> 7 You made him for a little while lower than the angels;
> you have crowned him with glory and honor,[1]
> 8 putting everything in subjection under his feet."

Now in putting everything in subjection to him, he left nothing outside his control. At
present, [n]we do not yet see everything in subjection to him. 9 But we see him [o]who for a

[1] Some manuscripts insert *and set him over the works of your hands*

Chapter 2
2 [a]See Acts 7:53 [b][ch. 10:28; Num. 15:30, 31; Deut. 4:3; 17:2, 5, 12; 27:26] [c]ch. 10:35; 11:26
3 [d][ch. 10:28, 29; 12:25] [e]Matt. 22:5 (Gk.) [f]ch. 1:2 [g]Mark 16:20; [Acts 5:32] [h][Luke 1:2]
4 [g][See ver. 3 above] [i]Acts 2:22, 43 [j][1 Cor. 12:4, 11] [k][Eph. 1:5]
5 [l]ch. 6:5
6 [m]Cited from Ps. 8:4-6
8 [n][1 Cor. 15:25]
9 [o]ver. 7

2:1–4 *Warning against Neglecting Salvation.* This warning calls the reader to pay heed to the greater salvation which was declared by the Lord himself, attested by human eyewitnesses, and authenticated by God's power. Following standard Jewish argumentation (see 9:14; 10:28–29), the argument proceeds from the lesser (retributions under the Mosaic law; 2:2) to the greater (the danger of neglecting the greater salvation; 2:3–4).

2:1 Therefore. Since Jesus is superior to the angels, **we must pay much closer attention to what we have heard** because this message of the Son of God is also superior to prior revelation, which came through angels (cf. v. 2). To **drift away** results in dangerous "neglect" of the message (v. 3).

2:2 The **message declared by angels** is the Mosaic law, which was given by angels (deduced in Jewish tradition from Deut. 33:2; see Acts 7:53; Gal. 3:19). **reliable**. Even though the revelation in Christ is superior (Heb. 1:2; 2:3–4), the author does not diminish the importance of the Mosaic law, which was "reliable" and which bears **just retribution** (Gk. *misthapodosia*, "reward, recompense"; here conveying legal sanctions). **every transgression or disobedience**. Two words here express both a refusal to follow (Gk. *parabasis*) and a refusal to heed (Gk. *parakoē*) the law. Every act of disobedience merits retribution—all sin merits punishment.

2:3 how shall we escape? If the Mosaic law came with retribution for failure to follow and obey it (v. 2), then surely the greater salvation announced by the Lord comes with more dangerous retribution for those who **neglect** it (cf. "showed no concern," 8:9; see also 10:28–29; 12:25). **salvation**. See note on 1:14. **declared**. Jesus himself (the **Lord**; cf. 1:10; 13:20) first announced this salvation, and his superiority proves the superiority of this revelation. **attested**. The Greek verb (*bebaioō*) also conveys a sense of assurance and confirmation. **by those who heard**. Eyewitnesses to Jesus' life and teaching. Apparently the audience (and probably the author) of Hebrews were not eyewitnesses of Jesus, but received the testimony from others.

2:4 God also bore witness. God's witness came through miracles performed alongside the gospel's proclamation, confirming it. The three terms **signs**, **wonders**, and **miracles** overlap in meaning and thus should not be finely distinguished (they appear together in Acts 2:22; 2 Cor. 12:12; cf. 2 Thess. 2:9; and elsewhere "signs and wonders" are often connected). **gifts**. "Apportionings," "distributions" (Gk. *merismos*) from the Holy Spirit. **distributed according to his will**. This probably refers not just to the distribution of spiritual gifts (see, however, 1 Cor. 12:4–11, esp. v. 11) but also to all the works of God in Heb. 2:4; these are works done according to God's will, not of human volition (cf. Gal. 3:5).

2:5–18 *The Founder of Salvation.* Jesus is shown to be further superior to angels since as Son of Man the world is subjected to him, though this has yet to be fully revealed (vv. 5–9). Jesus' glorious sacrificial suffering and death required him to partake of humanity (vv. 10–18).

2:5 For continues the argument from 1:5–14 (and 2:2–4). The superior son of man (v. 6) has responsibilities of worldwide rule not accorded to angels. **the world to come**. A common Jewish expression for the future age in which all of God's purposes in salvation will be fulfilled. The author is **speaking** of a future salvation (see note on 9:27–28), though the "last days" have already been inaugurated (1:2).

2:6 What is man, that you are mindful of him, or the son of man, that you care for him? This quotation from Ps. 8:4–6 (cf. Heb. 4:4) displays God's exalted care for the human race generally in his creation, but "son of man" also hints at a special focus on the Messiah as the truest representative of mankind (cf. 2:9; Dan. 7:13). The author of Hebrews turned to this "son of man" passage with full awareness of Jesus' frequent application of the "son of man" title to himself (see notes on Matt. 8:20; John 1:51), and now the author is about to show how Ps. 8:4–6 is fulfilled in Jesus.

2:7 You made him. Some interpreters think the author of Hebrews, quoting Psalm 8, is talking only about man in general, the human race. Others think he is already talking about Jesus, the true Son of Man (see note on Heb. 2:6). **for a little while lower**. If this refers to mankind in general, then it means that during this earthly life believers are lower in status and authority than angels. But that situation is temporary, lasting for this life only. If, however, the writer is already referring to Jesus, it means that in his earthly suffering Jesus' glorious divine nature was temporarily obscured (cf. Phil. 2:6–8).

2:8 Putting everything in subjection to him echoes Gen. 1:28, where God put everything under the stewardship of Adam and Eve (Gen. 1:26–28). But if Jesus, the true representative of humanity, is specifically in view, then it means that the "world to come" (Heb. 2:5) is subjected to Jesus, indicating his superiority to angels in his authority to rule the world. This also implies that he rules the angels themselves, since **nothing** is **outside his control**. However, **at present** believers do not see the entire world subject either to human beings or to Christ. This raises the question, What has happened to God's plan to put everything in subjection under man (or under Christ)?

2:9 But we see him, that is, Jesus. At this point all interpreters agree that the focus of the passage is Jesus (cf. notes on vv. 7, 8). The phrase **little while** and the sequence of events in vv. 7–8 (cf. Ps. 8:5–6) demonstrate that, after first being **made lower than the angels**, Jesus was subsequently **crowned** and exalted. While Jesus' sufferings indicated his humiliation and subjection, his **suffering of death** was also the reason for his being crowned with **glory and honor**. Jesus tasted **death** as a work of God's grace done on behalf of **everyone** (i.e., all who follow him; Heb. 9:15, 28; 10:39). **Jesus**. This is

little while was made lower than the angels, namely Jesus, [p]crowned with glory and honor
[q]because of the suffering of death, so that by the grace of God he might [r]taste death [s]for
everyone.
10 For it [t]was fitting that he, [u]for whom and by whom all things exist, in bringing many
sons [v]to glory, should make the [w]founder of their salvation [x]perfect through suffering.
11 For [y]he who sanctifies and [z]those who are sanctified [a]all have one source.[1] That is why
he is not ashamed to call them [b]brothers,[2] 12 saying,

> [c]"I will tell of your name to my brothers;
> in the midst of the [d]congregation I will sing your praise."

13 And again,

> [e]"I will put my trust in him."

And again,

> [f]"Behold, I and the children [g]God has given me."

14 Since therefore the children share in flesh and blood, he himself likewise [h]partook
of the same things, that [i]through death he might [j]destroy [k]the one who has the power of
death, that is, the devil, 15 and deliver all those who [l]through fear of death were subject to
lifelong slavery. 16 For surely it is not angels that he helps, but he [m]helps the offspring of
Abraham. 17 Therefore he had [n]to be made like his brothers in every respect, [o]so that he
might become a merciful and faithful high priest [p]in the service of God, to make propitiation for the sins of the people. 18 For because he himself has suffered [q]when tempted, he
is able to help those who are being tempted.

[1] Greek *all are of one* [2] Or *brothers and sisters.* The plural Greek word *adelphoi* (translated "brothers") refers to siblings in a family. In New Testament usage, depending on the context, *adelphoi* may refer either to men or to both men and women who are siblings (brothers and sisters) in God's family, the church; also verse 12

9 [p]Acts 3:13; 1 Pet. 1:21; See Acts 2:33 [q]Phil. 2:7-9; See John 10:17 [r]Matt. 16:28; John 8:52 [s]See John 12:32
10 [t][Luke 24:26] [u]Rom. 11:36 [v][ch. 3:1; Rom. 8:30] [w][ch. 5:9] [x]ch. 5:9; 7:28; Luke 13:32; [Phil. 3:12]
11 [y]ch. 13:12 [z]ch. 10:10, 14, 29 [a]Acts 17:28 [b]Matt. 25:40
12 [c]Cited from Ps. 22:22 [d]ch. 12:23
13 [e][Ps. 18:2; Isa. 8:17; 12:2] [f]Cited from Isa. 8:18 [g]See John 17:2
14 [h]See John 1:14 [i]See 1 Cor. 15:54-56 [j][Col. 2:15; 2 Tim. 1:10] [k]1 John 3:8; [John 16:11]
15 [l]See Rom. 8:15
16 [m]Isa. 41:8, 9; [ch. 8:9]
17 [n]Phil. 2:7 [o]ch. 4:15, 16; [ch. 5:2, 7, 8] [p]ch. 5:1; Rom. 15:17
18 [q]ch. 4:15; Luke 22:28

the first mention of Jesus' name in Hebrews (see 3:1; 4:14; etc.; "Christ" first appears in 3:6). "Crowned with glory and honor" echoes the same phrase used in 2:7. Though the human race generally did not fulfill God's plan to put everything on earth under man's feet (vv. 6–8), there is one man who is fulfilling God's great plan for human beings, and that is Jesus.

2:10 he, for whom and by whom all things exist. This is God the Father, who acts to "make perfect" the "founder of their salvation" (Jesus). **many sons**. The followers of the one unique Son of God are now also called "sons," for they are adopted into the glory of the newly redeemed human family (see "brothers," vv. 11–12; and "children," v. 13; also 12:5–8). **founder**. The Greek can designate either an originator or a leader (see 12:2). **salvation**. See 1:14 and 2:3. **suffering**. Especially Jesus' suffering of death (v. 9, see vv. 14–18). The concept of making **perfect** is applied elsewhere in Hebrews both to Jesus himself (5:9; 7:28) and to his work in sanctifying his followers (10:14; 12:23). In saying that Jesus was made perfect, the author is not suggesting that Jesus was sinful (cf. 4:15; 7:26) but that as he lived his life, his maturity and experience deepened, yet always with full obedience to the Father. As a human being, he needed to live his life and obey God (which he did perfectly) to become the perfect sacrifice for sins.

2:11 he who sanctifies. Jesus makes his people holy through his blood (13:12). **those who are sanctified**. Jesus' true followers, who are made holy by his sacrifice (10:10, 14; 13:12). Some commentators think **one source** is a reference to the common humanity shared by Jesus and those being saved (see 2:12–18), or to their common descent from Abraham. Others think that the "one source" is God the Father. **That is why he is not ashamed to call them brothers**. Since they share a common descent (or, since God is their common Father), they are members of the same family, and therefore brothers.

2:12 Psalm 22, from which this verse quotes, is associated with Jesus' death (e.g., Ps. 22:1, 16–18) and resurrection (Ps. 22:19–24). The resurrected Messiah, his suffering completed, calls his **brothers** to join with him in worship. Both this verse and Matt. 26:30 speak of Jesus singing, but here the **congregation** in view is the assembly of all the redeemed in heaven.

2:13 The second citation in this verse clearly comes from Isa. 8:18, and thus the first likely derives from Isa. 8:17 (following the Septuagint). The prophet links himself with the **children** who will follow God. Jesus as the Messiah/prophet similarly associates himself with believers, who are the Father's human "children."

2:14–15 A human Savior was necessary, because human beings (**children**) are in need of a propitiatory sacrifice (see note on v. 17) and a sympathetic high priest (vv. 17–18). **share in flesh and blood**. Jesus was fully human, as the "children" are and as the high priest had to be (see 5:1–2). Jesus' **death**, by cleansing his followers of sin, destroys the death grip of the **devil** (cf. 1 John 3:8) and gives hope and deliverance to those who were in **slavery** to the **fear of death**. **the one who has the power of death**. Satan's power is not absolute, but is under the control of God, who ultimately rules over life and death (Deut. 32:39; Job 2:6; Ps. 90:3; 139:16; Rev. 1:18). Nevertheless, Satan "was a murderer from the beginning" (John 8:44), and he does have power to harm people to some extent (cf. Mark 5:2–5; Luke 13:16). The verse at least means Satan has power to work in the realm of death, and to incite people into sin that leads to death (cf. Rom. 6:16, 23). However, the emphasis of the verse is not on Satan's power but on Christ's triumph over Satan and over death.

2:16 Angels recalls the superiority of the Son to angels (see notes on 1:1–2:18; 1:6) and the need for him to partake of human nature. **Offspring of Abraham** connects to the OT story, referring not merely to Jewish Israel but also to the more expansive promises to Abraham (Gen. 12:1–3; 17:4–21; see Heb. 6:13–7:10; 11:8–19).

2:17 had to be. Unless Jesus became fully human in **every respect** (except for sin), he could not represent believers as their high priest. **like his brothers**. Cf. vv. 11–12, emphasizing Jesus' human nature. **high priest**. See also 3:1–2; 4:14–5:10; 6:19–20; 7:11–10:18; 13:8–13. Jesus must be human in order to serve as high priest on behalf of humanity. **Propitiation** (Gk. *hilaskomai*) conveys the sense of an atoning sacrifice that puts away sin and satisfies God's wrath (cf. Deut. 21:8; Ps. 25:11; 65:3; 78:38; 79:9; Luke 18:13; see note on Rom. 3:25).

2:18 suffered. Jesus' sufferings as a human, especially his death (vv. 9–10). **tempted**. Jesus, as high priest, was tempted in every way and yet did not sin (4:15; also 7:26). **help**. Jesus is a sympathetic and merciful high priest who knows human spiritual infirmities since he experienced the full range of temptations, and he has atoned for transgressions.

Chapter 3
1[r]Eph. 4:1; Phil. 3:14 [s][John 20:21; Rom. 15:8]
2[t]ver. 5
4[u]Eph. 2:10; 3:9
5[v]ver. 2; Cited from Num. 12:7 [w]Ex. 14:31; Deut. 34:5; Josh. 1:2; 8:31; Ps. 105:26; Rev. 15:3 [x]Deut. 18:15, 18, 19
6[y]See ch. 1:2 [z]1 Cor. 3:16; 6:19; 2 Cor. 6:16; Eph. 2:21; 1 Tim. 3:15; 1 Pet. 2:5 [a]ver. 14; ch. 6:11; Ps. 119:33, 112; Matt. 10:22; Rev. 2:26
7[b]ver. 15; ch. 4:7; Cited from Ps. 95:7-11
9[c]See Acts 7:36
11[d]ch. 4:3, 5
12[e]See Matt. 16:16
13[f][ch. 10:24, 25] [g][Isa. 44:20; Rom. 7:11; Eph. 4:22]

Jesus Greater Than Moses

3 Therefore, holy brothers,[1] you who share in [r]a heavenly calling, consider Jesus, [s]the
apostle and high priest of our confession, 2 who was faithful to him who appointed
him, [t]just as Moses also was faithful in all God's[2] house. 3 For Jesus has been counted worthy
of more glory than Moses—as much more glory as the builder of a house has more honor
than the house itself. 4 (For every house is built by someone, but [u]the builder of all things
is God.) 5 [v]Now Moses was faithful in all God's house [w]as a servant, [x]to testify to the things
that were to be spoken later, 6 but Christ is faithful over God's house as [y]a son. And [z]we are
his house if indeed we [a]hold fast our confidence and our boasting in our hope.[3]

A Rest for the People of God

7 Therefore, as the Holy Spirit says,

> [b]"Today, if you hear his voice,
> 8 do not harden your hearts as in the rebellion,
> on the day of testing in the wilderness,
> 9 where your fathers put me to the test
> and saw my works for [c]forty years.
> 10 Therefore I was provoked with that generation,
> and said, 'They always go astray in their heart;
> they have not known my ways.'
> 11 [d]As I swore in my wrath,
> 'They shall not enter my rest.'"

12 Take care, brothers, lest there be in any of you an evil, unbelieving heart, leading you
to fall away from [e]the living God. 13 But [f]exhort one another every day, as long as it is
called "today," that none of you may be hardened by [g]the deceitfulness of sin. 14 For we

[1] Or *brothers and sisters*; also verse 12 [2] Greek *his*; also verses 5, 6 [3] Some manuscripts insert *firm to the end*

3:1–10:18 *Jesus Is Superior to the Mosaic Law.* Having concluded that Jesus is superior to the mediators of the Mosaic law (i.e., angels, 2:2), the author now establishes the superiority of Jesus to Moses himself (3:1–6), of Jesus to the Aaronic high priesthood (4:14–7:28), of the new covenant in Jesus' blood to the former covenant (8:1–13), and of Jesus' death to the Mosaic sacrifices (9:1–10:18). This exposition also leads to three prolonged exhortations to Christian perseverance (3:7–4:13; 5:11–6:12; 10:19–39).

3:1–6 *Jesus Is Greater than Moses.* While Moses was one of God's most faithful servants (vv. 2, 5), Jesus is the faithful high priest and Son of God. Thus Jesus is worthy of more glory (vv. 1–2, 6). This leads to exhortations and warnings (3:6–4:13).

3:1 Therefore. That is, in light of Jesus' high priesthood (2:17). **holy brothers.** Members of the family of God (3:12; 10:19; 13:22); also called "saints" or sanctified ones (13:24). **heavenly calling.** "Heavenly" elsewhere describes God's perfect order (8:5; 9:23) and the future life with God (11:16; 12:22); for "calling," see 2:11 and 9:15. Jesus is an **apostle** in the most basic sense of that term ("one who is sent," cf. "messenger," John 13:16; and references to Jesus as one who is "sent": Luke 4:18; 9:48; 10:16; John 3:17; 6:57). **our confession.** The gospel, possibly already codified in an oral creed (see Heb. 4:14; 10:23; cf. 2 Cor. 9:13; 1 Tim. 6:12).

3:2 faithful. Jesus and **Moses** fulfilled their God-appointed roles (2:17; 3:5; cf. Num. 12:7; 1 Chron. 17:14 LXX). Although Jesus is superior to Moses, Moses still receives significant respect (cf. Num. 12:7–8), which elevates Jesus all the more.

3:3–6 more glory. Despite Moses' great faithfulness in following God's redemptive plan in the exodus and in recording the law, Jesus is superior (on Jesus' glory, see 1:3; 2:9; 13:21). The **house** analogy shows that Jesus as the Son of God (who was also actively involved in creation; see 1:2–3) has a privileged place in the household of God (1 Chron. 17:14), while Moses remains a servant in that household (Num. 12:7).

3:6 Christ. First mentioned here in Hebrews (cf. v. 14; 5:5; etc.), this title is the Greek equivalent of "Messiah," meaning "anointed one" (see 1:9). (The name "Jesus" first appears in Hebrews in 2:9.) **we are his house.** Like other NT building metaphors for the church (see ESV cross-references), this speaks to the corporate identity of the church as God's own abode. **If indeed we hold fast** introduces a series of exhortations and warnings. Given this confident message of hope, the Christian life involves endurance. See note on 3:14.

3:7–4:13 *Warning: A Rest for the People of God.* The contrasting of Jesus and Moses (3:1–6) transitions to a comparison of their followers' responses. The followers of Moses failed to enter God's promised rest due to their disobedience and unbelief. So the author exhorts the followers of the superior Son of God to be careful not to repeat this pattern by failing to enter even now, as a foretaste, into God's future, end-time rest.

3:7–19 *The Failure of the Exodus Generation.* The author describes the failure of the exodus generation to respond faithfully to God's redemptive work. Their failure then becomes the negative example for the exhortations of vv. 12–14 and 4:1–13.

3:7–11 Therefore. In contrast to Moses' faithfulness (vv. 1–6), the author refers to the people of Moses' day, citing Ps. 95:7–11. Hebrews attributes this psalm to the work of the **Holy Spirit**, thus emphasizing the authority of the words (cf. Mark 12:36; Acts 1:16; 4:25).

3:12–13 Drawing on several key words in Psalm 95, Hebrews warns against allowing the unbelief of a **hardened**, sinful **heart** to cause one to **fall away** (Gk. *apostēnai*, "turn away from, forsake, apostatize from"; cf. Luke 8:13; 1 Tim. 4:1). His counter to this danger is both to encourage personal commitment (**take care**) and to call on the church to walk together in mutual encouragement (**exhort one another**). **as long as it is called "today."** From the perspective of God's saving plans for world history, the church lives in a special moment in which the Lord has come, spoken, and gone, and believers await his return—faith is called for in this hour, and mutual exhortation sustains and strengthens faith.

3:14 For we have come to share in Christ. The evidence of the Christian truly partaking of Christ's salvation involves endurance **to the end**. The condition (**if indeed**) has been understood in various ways. Some have argued that the condition ("if") indicates that true Christians can lose their salvation. Scripture is clear, however, that true believers cannot lose their salvation, as evidenced, e.g., by John 10:27–29 ("no one is able to snatch them out of

have come to share in Christ, [h]if indeed we hold our original confidence firm to the end.
15 As it is said,

> [b]"Today, if you hear his voice,
> do not harden your hearts as in the rebellion."

16 For [i]who were those who heard and yet rebelled? Was it not [j]all those who left Egypt
led by Moses? 17 And with whom was he provoked for forty years? Was it not with those
who sinned, [k]whose bodies fell in the wilderness? 18 And to whom did he swear that [l]they
would not enter his rest, but to those who were disobedient? 19 So we see that [m]they were
unable to enter because of unbelief.

4 Therefore, while the promise of entering his rest still stands, let us fear lest any of you
should seem [n]to have failed to reach it. 2 For good news came to us just as to them, but
the message they heard did not benefit them, because [o]they were not united by faith with
those who listened.[1] 3 For we who have believed enter that rest, as he has said,

> [p]"As I swore in my wrath,
> 'They shall not enter my rest,'"

although his works were finished from the foundation of the world. 4 For he has somewhere
spoken of the seventh day in this way: [q]"And God rested on the seventh day from all his
works." 5 And again in this passage he said,

> [r]"They shall not enter my rest."

[1] Some manuscripts *it did not meet with faith in the hearers*

14 [h]ver. 6; ch. 10:23; 1 Cor. 15:2
15 [b][See ver. 7 above]
16 [i]Num. 14:2; Deut. 1:34, 35 [j][Num. 14:24, 30; Deut. 1:36, 38]
17 [k]Num. 14:29; See Jude 5
18 [l]Deut. 1:34, 35; [ch. 4:2]
19 [m]ch. 4:6; Ps. 78:22; 106:24

Chapter 4

1 [n]ch. 12:15
2 [o]Rom. 3:3
3 [p]ch. 3:11; Cited from Ps. 95:11
4 [q]Cited from Gen. 2:2; [Ex. 20:11; 31:17]
5 [r]ver. 3

the Father's hand"), Eph. 1:4 ("he chose us in him before the foundation of the world"), and many other Scripture passages (e.g., John 6:39–40; Rom. 8:35, 38–39; Phil. 1:6; 1 Pet. 1:3–5). Hebrews 3:14 should be understood in connection with v. 13, as is indicated by the linking word "for" (Gk. *gar*). That is, v. 14 is linked to the exhortation not to become hardened (in unbelief and sin). Thus the logic of the argument is that those who are hardened or who become hardened (v. 13) give outward *evidence* that they are not (and never have been) genuine believers who "share in Christ," because genuine believers do not become hardened; instead they *persevere*—that is, they **hold** on to their **original confidence** firm to the end. Of course, Scripture also encourages believers to pray for and seek to bring back any who have fallen away (James 5:20; 1 John 5:16), in the hope that they will turn back. Still, this passage should be viewed as a sober warning—intended as a *means* that God uses to keep Christians resolved in faith and obedient until the end. The ongoing experience of perseverance results in "confidence" and assurance that one does in fact "share in Christ." This verse then provides a grave warning to everyone who claims to be saved—that is, to examine oneself carefully to be sure that one is in fact a genuine believer, because if there is no evidence of perseverance in faith and obedience, then there is real reason to doubt that such a person has ever been saved.

3:15–19 Quoting Ps. 95:7–8 again for emphasis, the author draws several points from the failure of the exodus generation (see esp. Ex. 17:1–7; Num. 14:20–38). They had witnessed God's salvation in the exodus; in fact, they had **left Egypt led by Moses**, which means that they had personally witnessed many of God's mighty miracles. Yet in spite of this, they had responded in disobedience and **unbelief**. The result was their death and consequent inability to enter into the rest of the Promised Land. The parallel structure in Heb. 3:18–19 stresses that disobedience flows from unbelief.

Warning Passages in Hebrews

2:1–4	how shall we escape if we neglect such a great salvation? (v. 3).
3:7–18	do not harden your hearts. . . . Take care, brothers, lest there be in any of you an evil, unbelieving heart, leading you to fall away from the living God (vv. 8–13).
6:4–8	For it is impossible, in the case of those who have once been enlightened . . . and then have fallen away, to restore them again to repentance (vv. 4–6).
10:26–31	For if we go on sinning deliberately . . . there no longer remains a sacrifice for sins. . . . How much worse punishment . . . will be deserved . . . ? (vv. 26, 29).
12:25–29	See that you do not refuse him who is speaking. For if they did not escape . . . much less will we (v. 25).

4:1–13 *Entering God's Rest.* Continuing with his exposition of Psalm 95, the author focuses on the word "rest." Although some believe he has in view either an entirely present or an entirely future rest, the following section makes most sense if the rest is understood as already inaugurated but awaiting consummation. He looks primarily to the future, as indicated by the need to continue striving to enter this rest (Heb. 4:1, 11, 14) and by the promise of a cessation from the struggles of this life (vv. 9–10). Yet there remains a sense in which that future rest touches the experience of this life (hence "today," v. 7).

4:1 Therefore. Verses 1–13 connect closely to the preceding argument (cf. 3:7–11, 16–19 with 4:2–10) and to the previous exhortation (cf. 3:12–14 with 4:1–2, 11–13). **promise**. Promises are important in Hebrews, especially those made and secured by God himself (see 6:12–20; 8:6; 9:15; 10:23, 36; cf. 11:13). There remains a future, end-time Sabbath **rest** from God that can be entered in some measure even in this life (4:3–10), and care must be taken to enter that rest. **fear** (Gk. *phobeomai*). Reverent fear before God, here concerning a person's spiritual state (e.g., Acts 10:35; Rom. 11:20; 1 Pet. 2:17; Rev. 19:5; cf. notes on Prov. 1:7; Acts 5:5; 9:31; Rom. 3:18; Phil. 2:12–13; 1 Pet. 1:17; 1 John 4:18). **should seem to have failed to reach it**. The author holds out the possibility that some in his audience lacked acquaintance with this spiritual "rest" since they did not possess true faith (see note on Heb. 4:2).

4:2 Comparisons between the exodus generation and the church continue. Both received the divine proclamation of deliverance (**good news**) and both were called to respond in **faith**. However, the exodus generation did not receive the promised benefit since they failed to respond in faith. Their failure serves to caution the Christian community against unbelief. The "good news" of the exodus included God's promised deliverance from Egypt, the covenant he established with his people, and the hope of entering the Promised Land (e.g., Ex. 6:1–9). The good news for the church includes the revelation and deliverance found in the Lord Jesus, the new covenant he established through his high priestly sacrifice, and the hope of eternity with him (e.g., Heb. 1:1–4; 2:14–18).

4:3–5 we who have believed. Faith in God's good news is necessary to **enter** God's **rest** (cf. 3:12, 19; 4:2; and more positively, see 6:12; 10:22, 37–39; 11:1–39; 13:7). The "rest" of God in Ps. 95:11 (**they shall not enter**

6[s]See ch. 3:19
7[t]See ch. 3:7, 8
10[u][Rev. 14:13]
11[v][ch. 3:12]
12[w]1 Pet. 1:23 [x][Jer. 23:29; 1 Thess. 2:13] [y]Isa. 49:2; Eph. 6:17 [z]Prov. 5:4; Rev. 1:16; 2:12 [a][1 Cor. 14:24, 25]
13[b]2 Chr. 16:9; Job 34:21; Ps. 33:13-15 [c]Job 26:6
14[d]ch. 2:17, 18; [ch. 10:21] [e]Eph. 4:10 [f]ch. 10:23
15[g][ch. 5:2; Isa. 53:3] [d][See ver. 14 above] [h]ch. 9:28; 1 Pet. 2:22; 1 John 3:5; [ch. 7:26; John 8:46; 14:30]
16[i]ch. 10:19; Eph. 3:12; [ch. 7:19, 25]

6 Since therefore it remains for some to enter it, and those who formerly received the good
news [s]failed to enter because of disobedience, **7** again he appoints a certain day, "Today,"
saying through David so long afterward, in the words already quoted,

> [t]"Today, if you hear his voice,
> do not harden your hearts."

8 For if Joshua had given them rest, God[1] would not have spoken of another day later on.
9 So then, there remains a Sabbath rest for the people of God, **10** for whoever has entered
God's rest has also [u]rested from his works as God did from his.

11 Let us therefore strive to enter that rest, so [v]that no one may fall by the same sort of
disobedience. **12** For [w]the word of God is living and [x]active, [y]sharper than any [z]two-edged
sword, piercing to the division of soul and of spirit, of joints and of marrow, and [a]discern-
ing the thoughts and intentions of the heart. **13** And [b]no creature is hidden from his sight,
but all are [c]naked and exposed to the eyes of him to whom we must give account.

Jesus the Great High Priest

14 Since then we have [d]a great high priest [e]who has passed through the heavens, Jesus,
the Son of God, [f]let us hold fast our confession. **15** For we do not have a high priest [g]who is
unable to sympathize with our weaknesses, but one who in every respect has been [d]tempted
as we are, [h]yet without sin. **16** [i]Let us then with confidence draw near to the throne of grace,
that we may receive mercy and find grace to help in time of need.

[1] Greek *he*

my rest) is connected with God's resting **on the seventh day** after the six days of creation (quoted from Gen. 2:2). The fact that the exodus generation was not allowed to enter that rest proves that God's Sabbath rest (begun in Genesis 2) was still open. Even "today," at the time of the writing of Hebrews, this rest could still be entered. The implication is that until Christ returns people throughout the entire age can similarly enter into this rest.

4:6–7 Verse 6 restates the conclusions of vv. 2–5 (cf. 3:15–19). **good news**. See 4:2. Verse 7 advances the argument by suggesting that the **today** of Ps. 95:7–8 holds out to the worshiper the possibility of entering even now in a partial way into the end-time "rest" and blessing that the exodus generation missed. God's rest centered upon recognizing that his work of creation was now completed; Christians enter into his rest through recognizing that Christ's work of redeeming them from sin has also been completed.

4:8–10 For if Joshua had given them rest. One could conceivably argue that the "rest" that the exodus generation sought was their entrance into the Promised Land. However, that entrance occurred in the days of Joshua, and Psalm 95 (with its promise of "today" entering into God's rest) is subsequent to Joshua's day (referred to as "so long afterward" in Heb. 4:7). Therefore, the **Sabbath rest** remains possible for God's people to enter even now, in this life (v. 9). The promise of entering now into this rest means ceasing from the spiritual strivings that reflect uncertainty about one's final destiny; it means enjoyment of being established in the presence of God, to share in the everlasting joy that God entered when he rested on the seventh day (v. 10).

4:11 therefore (in light of the conclusion from vv. 9–10) **strive to enter that rest**. This again emphasizes the need for perseverance (cf. 2:1; 3:14; 4:14). It should be remembered, however, that salvation is based not on good works but on Jesus' high priestly sacrifice (e.g., vv. 14–16; 5:9; 10:10–14), and anything believers can do to please God comes from his working in them (13:20–21). The opposite of perseverance is **disobedience**, the sin of the faithless exodus generation (3:18; 4:6).

4:12–13 The warning continues: faithless disobedience will not go unnoticed. **word of God**. Usually this phrase in Hebrews refers to the message of salvation (13:7; cf. 4:2), but here the "word" is pictured as God's personal utterance, **living, active**, sharp, **piercing**, and **discerning** (v. 12), with **eyes** that expose (v. 13). The Word of God then acts as God himself, so that one's innermost **thoughts and intentions** are **exposed**. This happens constantly in Christians' lives.

4:14–10:18 *The High Priesthood of Jesus.* Jesus' high priestly call is superior to the Mosaic priesthood due to (1) Jesus' ability to sympathize with human need, (2) his perfect holiness, (3) his eternal call to the priestly order of Melchizedek (combined with his eternal sonship), (4) his initiating a new and better covenant, (5) his ministering in the true heavenly tabernacle, and (6) his presenting himself as a once-for-all sacrifice for the salvation and perfection of all his followers. The writer pauses in the middle of this section to warn once more against the danger of apostasy (5:11–6:12) and to express confidence in God's promises (6:13–20).

4:14–5:10 *Jesus, the Great High Priest.* Using themes announced in 2:17–3:12, the author calls for Christian faithfulness based on Jesus' role as the holy and sympathetic high priest, appointed by God his Father to suffer so that others would receive the gift of eternal salvation.

4:14 high priest. Jesus' role as high priest is announced in 2:17 (see note), expounded here (4:14–5:10), and further explained in 7:1ff. **passed through the heavens**. A reminder that Jesus is seated at the right hand of God the Father (see note on 1:3). **Son of God**. Jesus' role as a human high priest (2:5–18) is united with his position as God's unique Son (5:5–6; see 1:1–14; 3:5–6). **Let us hold fast** continues the theme of perseverance (2:1; 3:6, 12–14; 4:11). **confession**. See 3:1; 10:23.

4:15 sympathize. Jesus is able to identify with his people (cf. 10:34) because of his human experience and the sufferings he endured while being tempted (2:10–18, esp. vv. 17–18). **tempted**. The Greek (*peirazō*) can refer either to temptation intended to bring one down or to testing designed to build one up; both connotations probably apply here (cf. Matt. 4:1–11; Luke 22:28). **without sin**. Though Jesus was tempted in **every respect**, that is, in every area of personal life, he (unlike every other human) remained sinless, and thus he is truly the holy high priest (Heb. 7:26–28; cf. 5:2–3). In their temptations, Christians can be comforted with the truth that nothing that entices them is foreign to their Lord. He too has felt the tug of sin, and yet he never gave in to such temptations.

4:16 Draw near (Gk. *proserchomai*, "approach, go to, draw near to") is used consistently in Hebrews to represent a person approaching God (7:25; 10:1, 22; 11:6; 12:18, 22; cf. Ex. 16:9; 34:32; Lev. 9:5; Deut. 4:11), which is possible only when one's sins are forgiven through the sacrificial and intercessory ministry of a high priest (Heb. 7:25; 10:22). The encouragement to "draw near" to God's throne implies that Christians have the privilege of a personal relationship with God. **Confidence** translates Greek *parrēsia* ("boldness," "confidence," "courage," esp. with reference to speaking before someone of great rank or power; cf. 3:6; 10:19, 35). It indicates that Christians may come before God and speak plainly and honestly (yet still with appropriate reverence), without fear that they will incur shame or punishment by doing so. **throne of grace**. God the Father, with Jesus at his right hand (8:1; 12:2;

5 For every high priest chosen from among men [j]is appointed to act on behalf of
men [k]in relation to God, [l]to offer gifts and sacrifices for sins. 2 [m]He can deal gently
with the ignorant and wayward, since he himself [n]is beset with weakness. 3 Because of
this he is obligated to offer sacrifice for his own sins [o]just as he does for those of the
people. 4 And [p]no one takes this honor for himself, but only when called by God, [q]just
as Aaron was.
5 So also Christ [r]did not exalt himself to be made a high priest, but was appointed by
him who said to him,

> [s]"You are my Son,
> today I have begotten you";

6 as he says also in another place,

> [t]"You are a priest forever,
> after the order of Melchizedek."

7 In the days of his flesh, [u]Jesus[1] offered up prayers and supplications, [v]with loud cries
and tears, to him [w]who was able to save him from death, and [x]he was heard because of
his reverence. 8 Although [y]he was a son, [z]he learned obedience through what he suffered.
9 And [a]being made perfect, he became the source of eternal salvation to all who obey him,
10 being designated by God a high priest [b]after the order of Melchizedek.

Warning Against Apostasy

11 About this we have much to say, and it is [c]hard to explain, since you have become
dull of hearing. 12 For though by this time you ought to be teachers, you need someone to
teach you again [d]the basic principles of the oracles of God. You need [e]milk, not solid food,
13 for everyone who lives on milk is unskilled in the word of righteousness, since he is [f]a

[1] Greek *he*

Chapter 5
1 [j]ch. 8:3 [k]ch. 2:17 [l]ch. 8:3, 4; 9:9; 10:11; 11:4
2 [m]ch. 2:18; 4:15 [n][ch. 7:28]
3 [o]ch. 7:27; 9:7; Lev. 4:3; 9:7; 16:6
4 [p]Num. 16:5, 40; 18:7; 2 Chr. 26:18 [q]Ex. 28:1; 1 Chr. 23:13
5 [r]John 8:54 [s]See ch. 1:5
6 [t]ch. 7:17, 21; Cited from Ps. 110:4
7 [u]Matt. 26:39, 44; Mark 14:36, 39; Luke 22:41, 44 [v]Ps. 22:1, 2; [Matt. 27:46, 50; Mark 15:34, 37; Luke 23:46] [w]Mark 14:36 [x]Ps. 22:24
8 [y]See ch. 1:2 [z]Phil. 2:8
9 [a]See ch. 2:10
10 [b]ver. 6; ch. 6:20
11 [c][2 Pet. 3:16]
12 [d]ch. 6:1 [e]1 Cor. 3:2
13 [f]1 Cor. 3:1; [1 Pet. 2:2]

cf. 1:8), graciously dispenses **help** from heaven to those who **need** forgiveness and strength in temptation (see 2:18).

5:1–4 He can deal gently (v. 2). High priests are human and understand human weakness (vv. 1–2); they present **sacrifices for sins** for others and for themselves (vv. 1, 3); and they are appointed by God (v. 4; as were **Aaron** and his lineage, see e.g., Ex. 28:1; 29:1–46; cf. Heb. 7:11). Jesus fulfills these high priestly criteria (5:5–10), except that he is the perfect high priest since he is without sin (4:15) and therefore does not need to present a sacrifice for himself (7:26–28).

5:5–6 God the Father **appointed** Jesus to be **high priest** (cf. vv. 1, 4), as is shown in the Psalms. Psalm 2:7 is quoted again (cf. Heb. 1:5), followed by Ps. 110:4. Jesus combines the role of high priest with his status as **Son** of God (see Heb. 4:14; 5:8–10). In Psalm 110 David speaks of his "Lord," who sits at the right hand of God and is a priest **after the order of Melchizedek** (see Heb. 7:1–28 and note on 1:13).

5:7 In the days of his flesh. That is, during his entire life on earth (cf. 2:14–15). **offered up prayers**. The Gospels record many prayers of Jesus (esp. at Gethsemane; see Luke 22:39–46). **supplications** (Gk. *hiketēria*). A rare word in the NT and Septuagint, it indicates a submissive request (esp. in prayer). **with loud cries and tears**. Readers would first recall Jesus' agonizing prayer in Gethsemane (Luke 22:44), but the broad time reference, "in the days of his flesh," suggests that Jesus' earthly prayers were constantly heartfelt, earnest, and accompanied by tears. **able to save him from death**. The author, clearly aware of the reality of Jesus' death (cf. Heb. 9:11–14), speaks of Jesus' resurrection as his being saved from or "out of" (Gk. *ek*) death (13:20). **he was heard**. Even as Son of God, it was appropriate that, having been made human, Jesus submitted to the Father and waited on the Father's answer (Luke 22:42, etc.). **Because of his reverence** (Gk. *eulabeia*) describes a reverential regard or fear in the presence of God (see Prov. 28:14 LXX; Heb. 12:28). Jesus' piety formed the basis for his prayers being answered; and now he stands to intercede for, and help, every Christian (4:16; cf. Rom. 8:34).

5:8 Although he was a son. See 1:1–14 and 5:5. Jesus, though fully divine, was also fully human. **he learned obedience through what he suffered**. Though always without sin (4:15; 7:26) and thus always obedient, Jesus nevertheless acquired knowledge and experience by living as a human being (cf. Luke 2:40, 52), and he especially came to know firsthand what it cost to maintain obedience in the midst of suffering (see notes on Heb. 2:9; 2:10; 2:18; 4:15). As Jesus "increased in wisdom and stature" (Luke 2:52), successive temptations were no doubt more difficult to deal with (cf. Luke 4:12), and as he obeyed his Father in the face of each temptation, he "learned obedience," so that his human moral ability was strengthened.

5:9–10 being made perfect. During his childhood, Jesus was not lacking in any godly character quality, but he was lacking in the full experience of having lived a perfect human life, obeying the Father in everything, without sin. The lifelong perfect obedience of Jesus (v. 8; 7:26–28) provides the basis for **eternal salvation** (2:10; 9:23–28) and for the ultimate "perfection" of those who respond in faith and obedience (10:14; 11:40; 12:23; cf. 7:19; 9:9; 10:1). **order of Melchizedek**. See 5:6 and ch. 7.

5:11–6:12 *Pause in the Argument: Warning against Apostasy*. The author interrupts his exposition of Jesus' role as high priest (4:14–5:10; chs. 7–10) in order to challenge his readers to mature further in their faith. He rebukes them for their lack of maturity (5:11–14), lists the basics that they should already know (6:1–3), and warns them about the danger of falling away from the faith (6:4–8). Nevertheless, he states his confidence in them (6:9–10) while once again encouraging their perseverance (6:11–12).

5:11 Though he often encourages his readers (e.g., 6:9–10; 10:32–34), here the author scolds them. **hard to explain**. Nevertheless, he will later (ch. 7) "explain" the reference to Melchizedek (5:10). Earlier, the author had urged his readers to "pay much closer attention to what we have heard" (2:1). Now, he calls them **dull of hearing**. "Sluggish" (6:12) is the same word as "dull."

5:12–14 Hebrews rebukes the readers, since by now they should have matured enough in the faith to instruct others. **basic principles of the oracles of God**. The most fundamental truths of God (see partial list in 6:1–2; on "oracles" [Gk. *logia*], cf. Acts 7:38 and Rom. 3:2, with reference to the law). **Milk** versus **solid food** shows the readers' immaturity in the faith; they are like infants, whereas they should be **mature** adults, well-learned (Heb. 5:12, 14) and well-practiced (v. 14) in the faith.

14[g]Eph. 4:13 [h]Gen. 3:22; 1 Kgs. 3:9; Isa. 7:15

Chapter 6

1[i][Phil. 3:12-14] [j]ch. 5:12 [k]ch. 9:14
2[l]Acts 19:4, 5 [m]Acts 8:17; 19:6 [n]Acts 17:31, 32 [o]See Acts 10:42
3[p]See 1 Cor. 16:7
4[q]ch. 10:32 [r][John 4:10; Eph. 2:8] [s]ch. 2:4, 5; Gal. 3:2, 5
5[t]Ps. 34:8
6[u][Matt. 19:26]; See 1 John 5:16 [v][ch. 10:29]
7[w]Ps. 65:10
8[x]Isa. 5:1-7; [Gen. 3:17, 18; Deut. 29:22, 23; Jer. 44:22; Luke 13:6-9] [y][Mal. 4:1; John 15:6]

child. **14** But solid food is for [g]the mature, for those who have their powers [h]of discernment
trained by constant practice to distinguish good from evil.

6 Therefore [i]let us leave [j]the elementary doctrine of Christ and go on to maturity, not
laying again a foundation of repentance [k]from dead works and of faith toward God,
2 and of [l]instruction about washings,[1] [m]the laying on of hands, [n]the resurrection of the
dead, and [o]eternal judgment. **3** And this we will do [p]if God permits. **4** For it is impossible,
in the case of those [q]who have once been enlightened, who have tasted [r]the heavenly gift,
and [s]have shared in the Holy Spirit, **5** and [t]have tasted the goodness of the word of God
and the powers of the age to come, **6** and [u]then have fallen away, to restore them again
to repentance, since [v]they are crucifying once again the Son of God to their own harm
and holding him up to contempt. **7** For [w]land that has drunk the rain that often falls on
it, and produces a crop useful to those for whose sake it is cultivated, receives a blessing
from God. **8** But [x]if it bears thorns and thistles, it is worthless and near to being cursed,
[y]and its end is to be burned.

9 Though we speak in this way, yet in your case, beloved, we feel sure of better things—

[1] Or *baptisms* (that is, cleansing rites)

6:1–2 elementary doctrine of Christ. Cf. "basic principles" (5:12). Three paired examples of doctrine are given: (1) Christian conversion through **repentance** (i.e., turning away) from works that cannot save and through **faith** in God (on faith, see 6:12; 10:22, 38–39; 12:2; 13:7; and ch. 11; on **dead** works, see 9:14); (2) **washings** (plural of Gk. *baptismos*), where the plural may refer to teaching about the differences between Jewish purification rites and Christian baptism, and **laying on of hands**, which could refer to an initiatory rite at the time of baptism (cf. Acts 8:14–17; 9:12, 17–19; 19:5–6) or to other hand-laying practices during prayers for healing and during commissioning of individuals for ministry (see notes on Luke 4:40; Acts 6:6; 9:17; 13:3); and (3) the believers' future hope of **resurrection** and the **eternal judgment** upon all people (see Heb. 9:27; 10:27; 11:19, 35).

6:4–8 This passage has been subject to substantially different interpretations. The central debate concerns whether the descriptions of vv. 4–5 (e.g., "enlightened," "tasted the heavenly gift," "shared in the Holy Spirit," "tasted of the goodness of the word of God") depict people who were once true Christians. (1) Some argue these phrases do describe true Christians, implying that Christians can "fall away" and lose their salvation (cf. note on 3:14, however, indicating a fundamental difficulty with this view). Nonetheless, most who advocate this view hold that some who backslide can still return to Christian faith, thus limiting 6:4–6 to hardened cases of apostasy in which it is "impossible . . . to restore them again to repentance" (vv. 4, 6). (2) Most argue, however, that although these people may have participated fully in the Christian covenantal community (where they experienced enlightened instruction in the Word of God, where they saw public repentance occur, and where the Holy Spirit was at work in powerful ways), when such people do "fall away" it is clear that they are not true Christians because they have not made a true, saving response to the gospel, resulting in genuine faith, love, and perseverance (vv. 9–12). Significantly, they are like land that received much rain but bore no good fruit, only "thorns and thistles" (v. 8). They may have participated outwardly in the Christian community and they even may have shared in the blessings of Christian fellowship; but, like the seed that fell on rocky ground in the parable of the sower, "they have no root" (Mark 4:17) and they "fall away" when faced with persecution. (3) Another view is that the warnings are addressed to true believers, and though they will never completely fall away, the warnings are still the *means* that God uses to challenge them to persevere in their faith and so to preserve those whom the Lord has chosen. (4) A fourth view is that the "falling away" described in Heb. 6:6 has to do with loss of heavenly rewards. In any case, though the author recognizes that there may be a few in the congregation who fit the description of vv. 4–8, in general he does not think it to be true as a whole of the congregation to which he is writing, for he says, "yet in your case, beloved, we feel sure of better things—things that belong to salvation" (v. 9).

6:4 For explains "if God permits" (v. 3); in some cases it is fruitless to expound the deeper truths of the faith (or even lay again a foundation of elementary doctrines, v. 1), since it is **impossible** to restore some people again to repentance (cf. 12:15–17). This likely refers to persons who in the past may have participated in acts of public repentance, which were common in early Christian worship. Here, however, they have apparently "fallen away" in such a decisive and irrevocable manner that "they are crucifying once again the Son of God . . . and holding him up to contempt" (6:6). Having committed such deliberate apostasy, it is impossible (at least from a human perspective) "to restore" such a person "again to repentance." While Christians understand these verses differently, it is wise pastoral advice to encourage a person who worries that he may have committed such a deep sin, that the very desire to repent and to be restored in fellowship with the Christian community is evidence that he has not "fallen away" in the permanent, irrevocable way described in this verse (cf. note on "blasphemy against the Holy Spirit" at Matt. 12:31–32). **enlightened**. Being listed first, this likely describes the initial entrance into Christian community through explanation of the Christian faith (cf. Heb. 10:32). Some have suggested that this may also have included baptism. **Tasted the heavenly gift** probably refers either (or both) to the Lord's Supper or the general blessing that one encounters in the fellowship of the Christian community. **have shared in** (lit., "have become a partaker of") **the Holy Spirit**. Some understand this as a reference to a person who has experienced the laying on of hands in the Christian community; others link it to the communal experience of the Spirit active in their midst producing fellowship and powerful wonders.

6:5 tasted the goodness of the word of God. These people (see note on v. 4) have heard the truth explained and thus have also learned of God's creative word (1:3; 11:3). This word will be fully exhibited in **powers** that bring about the world's renewal in the age to come (2:5; 13:14), yet, through the present ministry of the Spirit, these powers are partially experienced now in the Christian community (cf. 2:4).

6:6 Fallen away involves a sustained, committed rejection of Christ and a departure from the Christian community. **To restore them again to repentance** means to bring them once again to repent of their sins. This wording alone does not specify whether the earlier repentance was merely outward (cf. Luke 17:4), or whether it was a genuine, heartfelt repentance that accompanied true saving faith (see note on Heb. 6:4–8). The author is speaking in terms of what can be known from observing a person's behavior. **Crucifying once again** graphically portrays rejection of Jesus. **Holding . . . up to contempt** (Gk. *paradeigmatizō*) conveys the idea of a public, shameful display. The warning of vv. 4–8 is substantial: such a falling away treats God's own Son with such serious rejection that it is as if the person wanted again to put Christ on a cross; after such a departure there can be no return (though see note on v. 4).

6:7–8 land that has drunk the rain. Drawing on a common agricultural metaphor used in the OT and NT alike (see ESV cross-references on v. 7; also Matt. 13:24–30, 36–43; Luke 3:17), the author warns that those who fall away are like land that does not bear a **crop** that is **useful**, but only **bears thorns and thistles**. In a picture of impending final judgment and condemnation, the author says that such land is **near to being cursed** and **its end is to be burned**.

6:9 Following the dire warning of vv. 4–8, the author expresses confidence in

things that belong to salvation. **10** For [z]God is not unjust so as to overlook [a]your work and
the love that you have shown for his name in [b]serving the saints, as you still do. **11** And we
desire each one of you to show the same earnestness to have the full assurance [c]of hope
until the end, **12** so that you may not be sluggish, but [d]imitators of those who through
faith and patience inherit the promises.

The Certainty of God's Promise

13 For when God made a promise to Abraham, since he had no one greater by whom to
swear, [e]he swore by himself, **14** saying, [f]"Surely I will bless you and multiply you." **15** And
thus Abraham,[1] [g]having patiently waited, obtained the promise. **16** For people swear by
something greater than themselves, and in all their disputes [h]an oath is final for confirmation. **17** So when God desired to show more convincingly to [i]the heirs of the promise [j]the
unchangeable character of his purpose, [k]he guaranteed it with an oath, **18** so that by two
unchangeable things, in which [l]it is impossible for God to lie, we who have fled for refuge
might have strong encouragement to hold fast to the hope [m]set before us. **19** We have this
as a sure and steadfast anchor of the soul, a hope that enters into [n]the inner place behind
the curtain, **20** where Jesus has gone [o]as a forerunner on our behalf, [p]having become a high
priest forever after the order of Melchizedek.

The Priestly Order of Melchizedek

7 For this [q]Melchizedek, king of [r]Salem, priest of [s]the Most High God, met Abraham
returning from the slaughter of the kings and blessed him, **2** and to him Abraham
apportioned a tenth part of everything. He is first, by translation of his name, king of
righteousness, and then he is also king of Salem, that is, king of peace. **3** He is without father

[1] Greek *he*

10 [z]Prov. 19:17; Matt. 10:42; 25:40; Mark 9:41 [a]1 Thess. 1:3 [b]Rom. 15:31; 2 Cor. 8:4; 9:1, 12; 2 Tim. 1:18; Rev. 2:19
11 [c]Rom. 5:2-5
12 [d]ch. 13:7; [ch. 10:36]
13 [e]Gen. 22:16
14 [f]Cited from Gen. 22:17
15 [g]ver. 12, 17; [ch. 7:6]; See Rom. 4:13
16 [h]Ex. 22:11
17 [i]ch. 11:9 [j]ver. 18; [Ps. 110:4; Prov. 19:21] [k][Gal. 3:20]
18 [l]See Titus 1:2 [m]ch. 12:1, 2
19 [n]ch. 9:7; Lev. 16:15
20 [o]ch. 4:14; 8:1; 9:24 [p]ch. 3:1; 5:6, 10; 7:17, 21

Chapter 7

1 [q]Gen. 14:18-20 [r]Ps. 76:2 [s]Num. 24:16; Deut. 32:8

the salvation of his **beloved** audience (cf. 10:32–34, 39). Though he warns that some may fall away (6:4–8), he thinks that, generally speaking, his readers will not do this, for they have **better things** than those described in vv. 4–6; in fact, their lives give evidence of genuine spiritual renewal, for they have **things that belong to salvation**.

6:10 Evidence is given for the author's confidence in the salvation of his readers (v. 9; cf. 10:32–34), including the good fruit of their service (**work**) and the **love** of the **saints** (see 3:1; 13:24).

6:11–12 The purpose of the warning (vv. 4–8), indeed of the whole letter, is to encourage earnest perseverance **until the end**. This demands **hope**, which is closely allied with **faith** (see 11:1; cf. 10:22), and enduring **patience** (cf. 6:15). For **sluggish**, see note on 5:11. **imitators of those who . . . inherit the promises**. Abraham is the immediate example in 6:13–15; other examples are found in ch. 11 (OT saints) and in 13:7 (church leaders).

6:13–20 *The Certainty of God's Promise.* Abraham is shown to be an example of one who, through patience and faith, "inherited the promises" (vv. 13–15; cf. vv. 11–12). God's promises are guaranteed by God's own perfectly trustworthy character (vv. 16–18). Therefore the promise of salvation through Jesus' high priesthood is a secure and trustworthy hope (vv. 19–20).

6:13–14 promise to Abraham. God's promises to Abraham include those found in Gen. 12:1–3; 17:1–22; 22:16–18. Here the author focuses on the blessing God promised to Abraham and his offspring in Gen. 22:16–17 (partially quoted in Heb. 6:14), concerning which God—since there is **no one greater** who could assure his promises—pledged by oath upon his own character (see Gen. 22:16; Heb. 6:16–18).

6:15 having patiently waited. Abraham waited 25 years for the birth of Isaac (cf. Gen. 12:4 with Gen. 21:5), and he did not witness the fulfilled promise of innumerable offspring in his lifetime (see note on Heb. 11:13). His patience in faithful waiting is to be imitated (6:12; cf. 11:8–19). In his lifetime, Abraham **obtained the promise** through seeing Isaac born, and through the ram offered on Isaac's behalf (Genesis 22). But now there is even greater fulfillment for Abraham, through the fact that Abraham's descendants are indeed too many to count.

6:16 Oaths were common legal devices in ancient times as in the modern world (**disputes** implies a legal context). Oaths usually required appeal to some greater authority (often a deity; see v. 13).

6:17–18 The **two unchangeable things** are God's **promise/purpose** and his **oath**. The character of God is holy, and he does not **lie**. Thus his announcement of his promise is sure, and doubly sure when combined with his oath. This encourages one to **hold fast** (see 4:14) **to the hope** (3:6; 6:11; 7:19; 10:23) of God's promises.

6:19–20 The Christian **hope** is in the person and saving work of Christ (pictured here as the high priest). **Anchor** was a common ancient metaphor for stability; hope provides security and stability for the soul. Clearly, even though the author warns the readers concerning apostasy (vv. 4–8), he believes they can have assurance of their salvation. The **curtain** (Gk. *katapetasma*) is the veil in the tabernacle or temple separating the **inner place** (i.e., "Most Holy Place," 9:3) from the rest of the tabernacle/temple. On this veil, see Ex. 26:31; Num. 18:7; Matt. 27:51; Heb. 9:3; 10:20. **forerunner**. Jesus, who went beforehand and opened the veil, now permits others to draw near (9:3, 6–14; esp. cf. 9:8; 10:19–20). **high priest**. The author now returns to the subject of 5:5–10 (see 5:11).

7:1–10 *Return to Main Argument: The Priestly Order of Melchizedek.* This section discusses Melchizedek, drawing out points later applied to Jesus in vv. 11–28.

7:1–2 The author summarizes the brief account of Melchizedek found in Gen. 14:18–20, highlighting important interpretative points. Elsewhere in the OT, Melchizedek is mentioned only in Ps. 110:4; however, Judaism around the time of Christ did speculate about him (e.g., in the Qumran scroll 11QMelchizedek). **translation of his name**. In the OT (and in later Judaism) the meaning of a name could indicate a person's relationship to God (e.g., Gen. 17:5; 25:25–26; 32:28). **Melchizedek**. The Hebrew name means "king of righteousness" (Hb. *melek*, "king"; *tsedeq*, "righteousness"). **Salem** is Melchizedek's city (Hb. *shalem*, Gen. 14:18), and is from the same root as the Hebrew for "peace" (*shalom*).

7:3 Some have suggested that Melchizedek was a preincarnate, temporary appearance of the eternal Son of God. As this passage indicates, however, Melchizedek was not in fact the Son of God but someone **resembling the Son of God** (lit., "having been made like the Son of God"); he was an ordinary human being who was "king of Salem" (v. 1). **He is without father or mother or genealogy** probably means simply that this information is not given anywhere *in Scripture* (in contrast to the Levitical priests, whose genealogies are recorded). The next phrase should probably be understood in the same way—that is, Melchizedek had **neither beginning of days**

or mother [t]or genealogy, having neither beginning of days nor end of life, but resembling
the Son of God he continues a priest forever.
[4]See how great this man was to whom Abraham [u]the patriarch gave a tenth of the spoils!
[5]And [v]those descendants of Levi who receive the priestly office have a commandment in
the law to take tithes from the people, that is, from their brothers,[1] though these also are
descended from Abraham. [6]But this man [w]who does not have his descent from them received
tithes from Abraham and blessed [x]him who had the promises. [7]It is beyond dispute that
the inferior is blessed by the superior. [8]In the one case tithes are received by mortal men,
but in the other case, by one [y]of whom it is testified that [z]he lives. [9]One might even say
that Levi himself, who receives tithes, paid tithes through Abraham, [10]for he was still in
the loins of his ancestor when Melchizedek met him.

Jesus Compared to Melchizedek

[11][a]Now if perfection had been attainable through the Levitical priesthood (for under it
the people received the law), what further need would there have been for another priest
to arise after the order of Melchizedek, rather than one named after the order of Aaron?
[12]For when there is a change in the priesthood, there is necessarily a change in the law as
well. [13]For the one of whom these things are spoken belonged to another tribe, from which
no one has ever served at the altar. [14]For it is evident that our Lord was descended [b]from
Judah, and in connection with that tribe Moses said nothing about priests.
[15]This becomes even more evident when another priest arises in the likeness of
Melchizedek, [16]who has become a priest, not on the basis of a legal requirement concerning
bodily descent, but by the power of an indestructible life. [17]For it is witnessed of him,

> [c]"You are a priest forever,
> after the order of Melchizedek."

[18]For on the one hand, a former commandment is set aside [d]because of its weakness and
uselessness [19](for [e]the law made nothing perfect); but on the other hand, [f]a better hope is
introduced, through which [g]we draw near to God.

3 [t][ver. 6]
4 [u][Acts 2:29; 7:8, 9]
5 [v]Num. 18:21, 26; 2 Chr. 31:4, 5
6 [w][ver. 3] [x]See Rom. 4:13
8 [y][ch. 5:6; 6:20] [z][John 6:57; Rev. 1:17, 18]
11 [a]ver. 18, 19; ch. 8:7; [Gal. 2:21]
14 [b]Isa. 11:1; Mic. 5:2; Matt. 1:3; Luke 3:33; Rev. 5:5
17 [c]ver. 21; ch. 5:6; 6:20; Cited from Ps. 110:4
18 [d]Rom. 8:3; Gal. 4:9
19 [e]ch. 9:9; 10:1; Lev. 16:16; See Acts 13:39 [f]ch. 6:18 [g][ver. 25; Lev. 10:3]; See ch. 4:16

[1] *Or brothers and sisters*

nor end of life *recorded in Scripture*; he suddenly appeared in Genesis 14 and then disappeared. As far as the OT narrative is concerned, it shows no end to his priesthood, so in that sense he **continues a priest forever**. Thus Hebrews seems to view Melchizedek as an ordinary man, who was a "type" or foreshadowing of Christ (see note on Rom. 5:14). In this way, Melchizedek is comparable to the eternal high priesthood of the righteous Son of God, who is truly the king of righteousness and who brings true peace.

7:4 tenth of the spoils. Abraham tithed to Melchizedek (Gen. 14:20). **Patriarch** here means "father of a nation or people." This is a reminder that all Israel traces its lineage through Abraham (see Heb. 7:9–10).

7:5–6 In the Mosaic law, God commanded the Israelites to tithe to the Levitical priesthood (e.g., Num. 18:21–24), who are themselves fellow descendants of Jacob/Israel and of Abraham. Abraham **had the promises** (see Heb. 6:13–15)—these promises also encompass the offspring of Abraham (see note on 7:9–10).

7:7 The **superior** person (Melchizedek) **blessed** the **inferior** (Abraham), thus the Melchizedek priesthood is superior to Abraham and all his descendants (implicitly including the Levitical priesthood).

7:8 he lives. Melchizedek is a "priest forever" (Ps. 110:4; cf. Heb. 7:3), hence the Melchizedek priesthood, being eternal, is superior to the mortal Levitical priesthood (vv. 23–25). The author is probably not arguing that Melchizedek never died, but that he is a type of Christ in that nothing is stated in the biblical text about his death (see note on v. 3), and so the figure of Melchizedek forecasts the risen Jesus.

7:9–10 Levi himself . . . paid tithes (to Melchizedek) **through Abraham**. The author's reasoning is that the offspring of Abraham (esp. Levi), who share in Abraham's promises (see note on vv. 5–6), also share in Abraham's tithe to Melchizedek, and therefore the Levitical priesthood is inferior to the Melchizedekian priesthood.

7:11–28 *Jesus Compared to Melchizedek.* The Mosaic law was unable to make men perfect, since it was administered by a succession of sinful, mortal priests. Jesus, however, is by God's oath established forever as the holy priest/Son, permitting his followers to draw near to God on the basis of his person and work.

7:11–12 In Hebrews, several reasons are presented for why the Mosaic law could not bring people to **perfection** (vv. 18–19; 9:9; 10:1; cf. the work of Jesus in 10:14; 11:40; 12:23). Here, the fact that there existed a priestly order of Melchizedek (Ps. 110:4) shows that the **Levitical priesthood** (and its high priesthood reserved for the Aaronic line; see Ex. 28:1; 29:1–46) was insufficient to the task. **change in the law**. The establishment of a better priesthood (Christ's) shows Christians that there also has been a change from the Mosaic law, since that law required a succession of priests, all descended from Levi (Heb. 7:18–19). Thus, Jesus' role as a non-Levitical high priest is strong evidence that the Mosaic covenant (the "old covenant") is no longer in effect.

7:13–14 Jesus was from the tribe of **Judah** rather than the priestly tribe of Levi. Yet he qualifies as the eternal high priest because he is the Davidic Messiah, called both Lord and a priest after the messianic priestly order of Melchizedek (Ps. 110:1, 4).

7:15–17 the power of an indestructible life. Jesus' resurrection from the dead indicates his eternal priesthood (Ps. 110:4; see Heb. 5:6). Death could not conquer Jesus; therefore, his priesthood lasts **forever** (see 7:23–24).

7:18–19 former commandment. The institution of the Levitical priesthood is **set aside** and thus so is the Mosaic law (see v. 12), since it was not able to accomplish God's saving purpose (hence its **weakness and uselessness**). In other words, only Jesus' work on the cross brought people to perfection (see v. 11; also 9:9; 10:1). **better hope**. That is, the hope of salvation and perfection through Jesus' high priesthood (7:25–28; on hope, see 3:6; 6:11, 18; 10:23). **draw near to God**. Jesus' work permits true interpersonal fellowship with God (see note on 4:16; also 7:25; 10:22; 11:6).

20 And it was not without an oath. For those who formerly became priests were made
such without an oath, **21** but this one was made a priest with an oath by the one who said
to him:

> [h]"The Lord has sworn
> and will not change his mind,
> 'You are a priest forever.'"

22 This makes Jesus the guarantor of [i]a better covenant.
23 The former priests were many in number, because they were prevented by death from
continuing in office, **24** but he holds his priesthood permanently, because he continues
[j]forever. **25** Consequently, he is able to save to the uttermost[1] [k]those who draw near to God
[l]through him, since he always lives [m]to make intercession for them.
26 For it was indeed fitting that we should have such a high priest, [n]holy, innocent,
unstained, [o]separated from sinners, and [p]exalted above the heavens. **27** He has no need,
like those high priests, to offer sacrifices daily, [q]first for his own sins and then for those of
the people, since he did this [r]once for all when he offered up himself. **28** For the law appoints
men [s]in their weakness as high priests, but the word of the oath, which came later than
the law, appoints a Son who has been made [t]perfect forever.

Jesus, High Priest of a Better Covenant

8 Now the point in what we are saying is this: we have such a high priest, [u]one who is
seated at the right hand of the throne of the Majesty in heaven, **2** a minister in the holy
places, in [v]the true tent[2] that the Lord [w]set up, not man. **3** For [x]every high priest is appointed
to offer gifts and sacrifices; thus [y]it is necessary for this priest also to have something to

[1] That is, completely; or *at all times* [2] Or *tabernacle*; also verse 5

21 [h]See ver. 17
22 [i]ch. 8:6
24 [j]ver. 21, 28
25 [k][ver. 19] [l][John 14:6] [m]ch. 9:24; See Rom. 8:34
26 [n]Ps. 16:10; Rev. 15:4; 16:5; [Mark 1:24] [o]See ch. 4:15 [p][ch. 8:1]; See ch. 4:14
27 [q]See ch. 5:3 [r]ch. 9:12; 10:10; [ch. 9:28]
28 [s][ch. 5:2] [t]ch. 2:10; 5:9

Chapter 8

1 [u]See Mark 16:19
2 [v]ch. 9:24; [ch. 9:11] [w]Ex. 33:7
3 [x]See ch. 5:1 [y]ch. 9:12-14; 10:9-12; Eph. 5:2

7:20–21 Although God instituted the Levitical priesthood, he did not promise its eternal validity. The priesthood of Jesus rests securely on God's promise/oath (cf. 6:13–20) in Ps. 110:4.

7:22 The new, **better covenant** based on Jesus' eternal high priesthood comes with God's oath and with Jesus as the **guarantor**, and thus it is superior to the Mosaic covenant (see further 8:6–13; 9:15; 10:15–18; 12:24; 13:20).

7:23–25 The mortality of the **many** Levitical **priests** is again contrasted with the eternality of Jesus as high priest (see v. 8). **To the uttermost** does not specify whether completeness in time ("forever") or completeness in extent ("completely") is intended; the Greek *eis to panteles* can mean both. Since a "complete" salvation would endure for all time, and since a salvation "for all time" would eventually include every aspect of life, perhaps the author intends readers to hear both senses. On **draw near to God**, see note on 4:16. Jesus Christ **always lives to make intercession** (that is, to bring the requests of believers to the Father; cf. Rom. 8:34) for those who approach God **through him**. Since the ever-living Christ intercedes for believers, they can have great confidence that they will never perish. In fact, they can know that "all things" in their lives will "work together for good" (Rom. 8:28), for God the Father will answer the prayers of his Son.

Levitical High Priests	Reference	Jesus the High Priest
many in number	7:23–24	one
temporary	7:23–24	permanent and eternal
sinners who had to offer sacrifices for their "own sins"	7:26–27	holy, innocent; offers sacrifice only for others
had to sacrifice "daily"	7:27	sacrificed "once for all"
offered sacrificial animals	7:27; 9:11–14	"offered up himself"
entered the holy places through a man-made tent and by means of the blood of goats and calves	9:11–12	entered the holy place of the presence of God and by means of his own blood

7:26 fitting that we should have. Jesus' high priesthood is appropriate and is for the benefit of believers. Several words emphasize Jesus' excellence in terms of his sinlessness (**holy, innocent, unstained, separated from sinners**; see 4:15; also 9:14 and Jer. 11:19) and his heavenly position (**exalted**).

7:27 Multiple points of contrast are made between the Levitical high priests and Jesus as the one eternal high priest (see chart to the left).

7:28 The law in its weakness (vv. 18–19) appoints sinful mortal **men in their weakness** to be a continuous succession of **high priests** (vv. 23–24). God, however, made an **oath** (Ps. 110:4), promising an eternal high priest (Heb. 7:20–22). This oath through David came after the Mosaic law and sets aside the previous Mosaic priesthood by appointing the messianic **Son** of God (1:1–14; 5:5–10) as eternal high priest. **made perfect**. See 5:9 and note on 5:9–10.

8:1–13 *Jesus, High Priest of a Better Covenant*. Jesus is shown to be the eternal high priest, ministering from heaven in the true tabernacle and enacting the better promises of the new covenant.

8:1–2 The author reminds readers of the main **point** of the letter: Christians have a **high priest** who has brought full forgiveness of sins, and this is evident by his being **seated** at God's **right hand**. See 1:3, 13; 10:12; 12:2. **Majesty**. An indirect Semitic term for God himself (see 1:3). The Greek translated **holy places** will refer later to the "Holy Place" (9:2) and the "Most Holy Place" (lit., "Holy of Holies," 9:3) in the earthly tabernacle constructed at the time of Moses (Ex. 26:33–34) as well as in the Jerusalem temple. But here the author is speaking of something even better, the actual heavenly "holy places," that is, the area before the very throne of God himself. This is where Christ is now a **minister**. The **true tent** (Gk. *skēnē*) refers to heaven, God's very presence; the earthly tabernacle functions as a picture of entering into God's presence in heaven. Human beings made the earthly tabernacle; the heavenly tabernacle (Heb. 8:5; 9:11, 23–24) was **set up** by **the Lord** himself—probably a reference to God the Father (see 8:8–11; also 7:14; 12:5–6), though possibly to Jesus (1:10; 2:3; 7:14; 13:20).

8:3 High priests offered **gifts** of thanksgiving and **sacrifices** for sin; Jesus as high priest must **offer** a sacrifice, which he does in the true heavenly tabernacle (v. 2; see 9:11–14, 23–28; 10:12–14).

5[z]ch. 9:23 [a]ch. 10:1; Col. 2:17 [b]Cited from Ex. 25:40
6[c]ch. 1:4; 2 Cor. 3:6-11 [d]ch. 7:22 [e]ch. 9:15; 12:24; [Gal. 3:19]
7[f]See ch. 7:11
8[g]Cited from Jer. 31:31-34
10[h]ch. 10:16; Rom. 11:27 [i][2 Cor. 3:3]
11[j]Isa. 54:13; John 6:45; 1 John 2:27
12[k]ch. 10:17; Rom. 11:27
13[l][2 Cor. 5:17]

Chapter 9

1[m]Ex. 25:8
2[n]Ex. 26:1 [o]Ex. 25:31-39; 26:35; 40:4 [p]Ex. 25:23-29 [q]Ex. 25:30; Lev. 24:5-8
3[r]Ex. 26:31-33; 40:3, 21

offer. **4** Now if he were on earth, he would not be a priest at all, since there are priests who
offer gifts according to the law. **5** They serve [z]a copy and [a]shadow of the heavenly things.
For when Moses was about to erect the tent, he was instructed by God, saying, [b]"See that
you make everything according to the pattern that was shown you on the mountain." **6** But
as it is, Christ[1] has obtained a ministry that is [c]as much more excellent than the old as [d]the
covenant [e]he mediates is better, since it is enacted on better promises. **7** [f]For if that first
covenant had been faultless, there would have been no occasion to look for a second.

8 For he finds fault with them when he says:[2]

> [g]"Behold, the days are coming, declares the Lord,
> when I will establish a new covenant with the house of Israel
> and with the house of Judah,
> **9** not like the covenant that I made with their fathers
> on the day when I took them by the hand to bring them out of the land of Egypt.
> For they did not continue in my covenant,
> and so I showed no concern for them, declares the Lord.
> **10** [h]For this is the covenant that I will make with the house of Israel
> after those days, declares the Lord:
> I will put my laws into their minds,
> and [i]write them on their hearts,
> and I will be their God,
> and they shall be my people.
> **11** And they shall not teach, each one his neighbor
> and each one his brother, saying, 'Know the Lord,'
> for they shall [j]all know me,
> from the least of them to the greatest.
> **12** For I will be merciful toward their iniquities,
> [k]and I will remember their sins no more."

13 In speaking of a new covenant, he makes the first one obsolete. And [l]what is becoming obsolete and growing old is ready to vanish away.

The Earthly Holy Place

9 Now even the first covenant had regulations for worship and [m]an earthly place of
holiness. **2** For [n]a tent[3] was prepared, the first section, in which were [o]the lampstand
and [p]the table and [q]the bread of the Presence.[4] It is called the Holy Place. **3** Behind [r]the

[1] Greek *he* [2] Some manuscripts *For finding fault with it he says to them* [3] Or *tabernacle*; also verses 11, 21 [4] Greek *the presentation of the loaves*

8:4 Jesus could not serve in the earthly tabernacle, since the law requires Levitical/Aaronic lineage (7:11–19).

8:5 The earthly tabernacle (**tent**), in which the Levitical priesthood served, was only a lesser **copy** of the heavenly **pattern** shown to Moses (Ex. 25:40).

8:6 The words **than the old** are not in the Greek but are supplied from the context for clarity (see vv. 7–13). Evidence for Jesus' superior ministry is found in the new **covenant** (vv. 8, 13), of which he is the mediator (see 9:15; 12:24; cf. 2:2) and which is legally ordained (**enacted**) on **better promises**. On "promises," see 4:1 and 6:12–20. The better promises of the new covenant are cited in 8:8–12.

8:7 if that first covenant had been faultless. The Mosaic covenant was not wrong; rather, it was weak and ineffective (7:18–19) since it could not bring people to perfection. God's purposes in the old covenant (among others) were to inform his people of the moral law, to convict them of sin (10:3), and (prominently featured in the book of Hebrews) to establish the pattern of sacrifice, priesthood, and promise of salvation that is fulfilled in Christ. Yet the inability of sinful humanity to achieve perfection under the old covenant required the promise of a **second** covenant, proving the ineffectiveness (i.e., the shortcomings) of the first.

8:8–12 he finds fault with them. God blames sinful humanity for the failure of the first covenant. Jeremiah 31:31–34, quoted here, supports several arguments in Hebrews: (1) this "second" covenant (Heb. 8:7) comes after the Mosaic covenant (**the days are coming**, v. 8); (2) it is established by the Lord (vv. 8, 13); (3) it is a **new covenant** (vv. 8, 13); (4) it is unlike the former covenant of the exodus (vv. 9, 13); (5) the former covenant failed because of the fault of Israel (**for they did not continue in my covenant**, v. 9; see v. 8); (6) this new covenant involves a transformation of the inner life of its recipients by writing God's laws into their **minds** and **hearts** so that all **know** him (vv. 10–11; see 10:14–17; cf. 9:9); and (7) it brings true, final forgiveness of sins (8:12; see 9:15; 10:12–18).

8:13 The **new covenant** makes **the first one** old (Gk. *palaioō*, here translated **obsolete**)—so old that it is becoming like a person of extreme age (Gk. *gēraskō*, here translated **growing old**) and thus is near to disappearing (**ready to vanish away**).

9:1–10 *The Earthly Holy Place.* This section describes the OT tabernacle, its furnishings, and its worship practices. This depiction of the "first covenant" lays the groundwork for the discussion of the new covenant in the next section.

9:1 The Mosaic **covenant** came with legislation governing how to **worship** God and where to approach God in **holiness**.

9:2–5 The tabernacle (an elaborate "tent" for worship, see 8:2, 5; 13:10; also Ex. 25:9; 26:1–37; see The Tabernacle Tent, p. 186) is divided into two portions—the Holy Place and the **Most Holy Place**, literally the "Holy of Holies" (indicating "most holy"). The items within each of these sections are mentioned in accordance with the OT (e.g., Exodus 25; 30; 37).

second curtain was a second section[1] called the Most Holy Place, **4** having the golden [s]altar
of incense and [t]the ark of the covenant covered on all sides with gold, in which was [u]a
golden urn holding the manna, and [v]Aaron's staff that budded, and [w]the tablets of the
covenant. **5** Above it were [x]the cherubim of glory overshadowing [y]the mercy seat. Of these
things we cannot now speak in detail.
6 These preparations having thus been made, [z]the priests go regularly into the first section, performing their ritual duties, **7** but into the second only [a]the high priest goes, and
he but [a]once a year, and not without taking blood, [b]which he offers for himself and for the
unintentional sins of the people. **8** By this the Holy Spirit indicates that [c]the way into the
holy places is not yet opened as long as the first section is still standing **9** (which is symbolic
for the present age).[2] According to this arrangement, gifts and sacrifices are offered [d]that
cannot perfect the conscience of the worshiper, **10** but deal only with [e]food and drink and
[f]various washings, regulations for the body imposed until the time of reformation.

Redemption Through the Blood of Christ

11 But when Christ appeared as a high priest [g]of the good things that have come,[3] then
through [h]the greater and more perfect tent ([i]not made with hands, that is, not of this creation) **12** he [j]entered [k]once for all into the holy places, not by means of [l]the blood of goats
and calves but [m]by means of his own blood, [n]thus securing an eternal redemption. **13** For

[1] Greek *tent;* also verses 6, 8 [2] Or *which is symbolic for the age then present* [3] Some manuscripts *good things to come*

4 [s]Lev. 16:12, 13 [t]Ex. 25:10; 26:33; 40:3, 21; Rev. 11:19 [u]Ex. 16:33, 34 [v]Num. 17:10 [w]Ex. 25:16; 40:20; Deut. 10:2, 5; 1 Kgs. 8:9, 21; 2 Chr. 5:10
5 [x]Ex. 25:18-22; [1 Kgs. 8:6, 7] [y]Lev. 16:2
6 [z][Num. 28:3]
7 [a]Lev. 16:15, 34; [ch. 10:3; Ex. 30:10] [b]See ch. 5:3
8 [c]ch. 10:20; [John 14:6]
9 [d]See ch. 7:19
10 [e]See Lev. 11:2 [f]Mark 7:4, 8; See Lev. 11:25
11 [g]ch. 10:1 [h][ver. 24; ch. 8:2] [i]See Mark 14:58
12 [j]ver. 24 [k]ch. 7:27; 10:10 [l]ch. 10:4 [m]See Acts 20:28 [n]Job 33:24; [Dan. 9:24; 1 Cor. 6:20]

9:4 The text describes the Most Holy Place as **having the golden altar of incense**. The altar of incense, however, was not in the Most Holy Place but in the Holy Place, just "in front of the veil" (Ex. 30:6) that separated it from the Most Holy Place; and it was tended daily by the priests (Ex. 30:7–8; cf. Luke 1:9–11), not just once a year (see note on Heb. 9:7). It is unlikely that the author of Hebrews, familiar with the OT tabernacle and its sacrifices, would mistakenly think this altar was inside the Most Holy Place. A better solution is to understand "having" (participle of Gk. *echō*) to mean that this altar of incense was closely tied in its function to the Most Holy Place, so that it "belonged to" the Most Holy Place, for as its incense burned, the smoke drifted into the Most Holy Place (1 Kings 6:22 speaks of this altar in a similar way; cf. also 2 Chron. 2:4; Ps. 141:2; Rev. 5:8; 8:3–4). The text also says that a **golden urn holding the manna, and Aaron's staff that budded** were in the **ark of the covenant**. However, the OT says the urn and the staff were placed in front of the ark (Ex. 16:32–34; Num. 17:10–11), not in it, and speaks only of the two tablets of stone as being within the ark (Ex. 25:16, 21; Deut. 10:1–2). But it would not be unlikely for the urn and the rod to have subsequently been stored in the ark, and the author of Hebrews may be depending on other information that is no longer available. By the time of Solomon's temple, it was noted that there was nothing in the ark except the two tablets of stone (1 Kings 8:9; 2 Chron. 5:10), but that may suggest that other items had previously been in the ark (see note on 2 Chron. 5:10). The **tablets of the covenant** are the two tablets containing the Ten Commandments (Ex. 34:1, 4, 28–29; Deut. 9:11; 10:5).

9:6 Having described the tabernacle (**These preparations having thus been made**), the writer describes the worship that took place therein. **priests go regularly into the first section**. Only the Levitical priests were permitted access. They went into the Holy Place (i.e., the "first section" or first "tent"; see note on vv. 2–5) to perform their regular **duties** (changing the lamp oil, the bread of the presence, and the incense fire; see Ex. 25:30; 30:7–8; Lev. 24:4) and to offer daily offerings (e.g., Num. 28:7).

9:7 Once a year, on the Day of Atonement, the **high priest** entered **into the second** section, that is, the Most Holy Place (Lev. 16:2–3, 11–17); after the incense cloud had shielded him from the mercy seat, he sprinkled it with the **blood** of a bull and a goat as sin offerings (Lev. 16:6, 9, 11, 15). Atonement for sins was required for the high priest **himself** and for all **the people** (e.g., Lev. 16:6, 11, 17; see Heb. 7:27–28). The law distinguishes **unintentional sins** (e.g., Leviticus 4) from deliberate sins, and early Judaism debated which kinds of sins the Day of Atonement covered.

9:8 By this. That is, by the system that restricted to the Levitical priests the right of access into the presence of God in the Holy Place and especially the Most Holy Place. **the Holy Spirit indicates**. The Mosaic covenant was the command of God, through the Holy Spirit, and by the Mosaic law God revealed both the spiritual separation of man from God due to sin and the pattern for Jesus' high priestly ministry. **way into the holy places**. Only the priests can enter the Holy Place, and only the high priest goes behind the veil, into the Most Holy Place; thus, while the veil and the Holy Place were **still standing**, the rest of God's people could not directly draw near to God's throne of mercy (the Most Holy Place), since the way was **not yet opened**.

9:9–10 Two ages (both Gk. *kairos*, "time") are here contrasted: the **present age** (either the old covenant era or simply the "present circumstances of the church"; see ESV footnote), and the **time of reformation**. The latter age has been inaugurated by Christ (vv. 11–12, 26). The "present age" is described as a time of impure consciences and of separation from access to God. Through Christ's work, this present age is passing away and the new time of reformation, which has already been inaugurated, will later be fully consummated (see note on vv. 25–26, where Christ has appeared at "the end of the ages").

9:9 cannot perfect the conscience. The Mosaic sacrificial system brought neither sanctification of the soul nor the fullness of God's peace into the inner life of the worshiper (7:18–19; 10:1–2). This is in contrast with the new covenant (8:10–12; 9:14; 10:22; also 10:14; 11:40; 12:23).

9:10 food and drink and various washings. The OT teachings (later expanded in early Judaism) about clean and unclean foods, sacrificial food and drink offerings, and ritual purification washings. This may indirectly critique those holding "diverse and strange teachings" about "foods" (13:9). **Regulations for the body** implies their ineffectiveness at reaching the conscience (9:9).

9:11–28 *Redemption through the Blood of Christ.* When compared to Mosaic tabernacle worship (vv. 1–10), the new covenant high priesthood of Jesus provides a single superior sacrifice in a superior heavenly tabernacle (which stands for God's very presence); and thus it brings complete forgiveness of sins, eternal salvation, purified consciences, and direct access to God.

9:11 The **greater and more perfect tent** is the area that immediately surrounds God's very presence in heaven, and is not a literal tabernacle at all (cf. 8:2, 5; 13:10). This tabernacle is superior to the Mosaic tabernacle since it is not made by mortal **hands** and is **not of this creation**—i.e., it is not earthly (9:1) but heavenly (8:5; 9:23).

9:12 entered once for all. This sacrifice does not need to be repeated (vv. 25, 28; cf. 7:27–28); and now Christ continues in the Most Holy Place, at the throne of God (8:1; 12:2). **blood of goats and calves**. See 9:19 ("calves" can refer to oxen or bulls in the Septuagint; see Ex. 20:24; 29:1–14; Lev. 16:6–19). **by means of his own blood**. Jesus' sacrificial death (see, e.g., Heb. 9:14, 26–28; 10:1–21) is the basis of **eternal redemption**, the paid release from the oppression of sin (see Luke 1:68; 2:38; cf. Mark 10:45; Titus 2:14; 1 Pet. 1:18).

9:13 sprinkling of defiled persons. Through OT sacrifices and purification rites. **blood of goats and bulls**. See vv. 12, 19 (and note on v. 12).

13[o]Lev. 16:14-16 [p]Num. 19:2, 17, 18
14[q]ver. 12; 1 John 1:7; Rev. 7:14 [r]ch. 7:27; 8:3 [s]ch. 1:3; 10:22 [t]ch. 6:1 [u]Rom. 6:13; 1 Pet. 4:2
15[v]ch. 8:6; 12:24 [w][ch. 3:1]; See Rom. 8:28 [x][ch. 10:36; Ex. 32:13] [y]Rom. 3:24, 25; 5:6
17[z][Gal. 3:15]
18[a]Ex. 24:6, 8

if [o]the blood of goats and bulls, and the sprinkling of defiled persons with [p]the ashes of
a heifer, sanctify[1] for the purification of the flesh, **14** how much more will [q]the blood of
Christ, who through the eternal Spirit [r]offered himself without blemish to God, [s]purify
our[2] conscience [t]from dead works [u]to serve the living God.
15 Therefore he is [v]the mediator of a new covenant, so that [w]those who are called may
[x]receive the promised eternal inheritance, [y]since a death has occurred that redeems them
from the transgressions committed under the first covenant.[3] **16** For where a will is involved,
the death of the one who made it must be established. **17** For [z]a will takes effect only at
death, since it is not in force as long as the one who made it is alive. **18** Therefore not even
the first covenant was inaugurated [a]without blood. **19** For when every commandment of

[1] Or *For if the sprinkling of defiled persons with the blood of goats and bulls and with the ashes of a heifer sanctifies* [2] Some manuscripts *your* [3] The Greek word means both *covenant* and *will*; also verses 16, 17

ashes of a heifer. In Num. 19:1–22 (esp. vv. 9, 17–19) these ashes are reserved outside the camp, mixed in water, and sprinkled upon people to remove impurity due to proximity to a corpse. **of the flesh**. As opposed to the inner conscience in Heb. 9:14.

9:14 how much more. An argument from the lesser to the greater (see notes on 2:1–4; 10:28–29). **blood of Christ**. See 9:11; here contrasted with "blood of goats and calves" (vv. 12–13). **through the eternal Spirit offered himself**. Jesus was both the high priest (for "offered," see 5:1, 3; 8:3; 9:7; esp. 10:11–12) and the sacrifice itself (offered "himself"; cf. 9:25–26), but this verse specifies that the Holy Spirit in some way aided or empowered Christ in making this offering. OT sacrifices had to be **without blemish**; Jesus is "holy, innocent, unstained" (see 7:26). **purify our conscience**. Mosaic sacrifices did not affect the conscience (9:9; cf. 10:2), but Christ's sacrifice purifies the innermost being (10:22). **from dead works**. Deeds that cannot save due to human sinfulness (see 6:1). **to serve the living God**. Salvation brings people into God's service (see 12:28). God is called "living" elsewhere (3:12; 10:31; 12:22; cf. e.g., Matt. 16:16; Acts 14:15; Rom. 9:26; Rev. 7:2), indicating his eternality; here there is also a contrast with the "dead works."

9:15 mediator. See 8:6; 12:24; cf. 1 Tim. 2:5. **new covenant**. See Heb. 8:6–13. Christ mediates the covenant first by revealing it (1:2; cf. 2:2) and then by serving as its priest who offers himself in sacrifice (9:11–14, hence **therefore**). **those who are called**. A reference to God's electing call to salvation (cf. Rom. 8:30; 1 Thess. 5:24; 2 Tim. 1:9; 1 Pet. 5:10; 2 Pet. 1:10). **promised eternal inheritance**. On promises, see notes on Heb. 4:1 and 6:13–20. Followers of Christ inherit everlasting salvation (1:14; 5:9; 9:12). **redeems them from the transgressions**. The payment of sin's penalty (cf. v. 12) requires a death (see vv. 16–28). **first covenant**. The Mosaic covenant (see v. 1).

9:16–17 will. The Greek (*diathēkē*) either designates a "will," the legally binding final directions of the deceased (cf. "inheritance" in v. 15), or it signifies an ancient Near Eastern "covenant," which required a sacrificial animal in order to be enacted. In either case, a *diathēkē* (elsewhere translated "covenant" in Hebrews) comes into force only after a **death**. This implies that the institution of the new covenant actually took place at the time of Christ's death.

9:18–21 Therefore. Since a **covenant** cannot begin until a death occurs (see note on vv. 16–17), the Mosaic covenant also began with **blood**. The Mosaic covenant-initiation ceremony (Ex. 24:3–8) is recalled in Heb. 9:19–20. The author adds some specific details, such as **scarlet wool and hyssop**, and the sprinkling of **the book itself**, which are not mentioned in Ex. 24:3–8. While the source of the author's information is unknown, these details are not improbable, since these elements were used in other such purifying ceremonies (see ESV cross-references; also Ex. 12:22). The purification of the tabernacle and its vessels is summarized in Heb. 9:21, recalling the events of Exodus 40 (also Exodus 29; Leviticus 8–9) and providing details from other rituals of atonement (e.g., Leviticus 16; see also Josephus, *Jewish Antiquities* 3.206).

Redemptive History in the Book of Hebrews

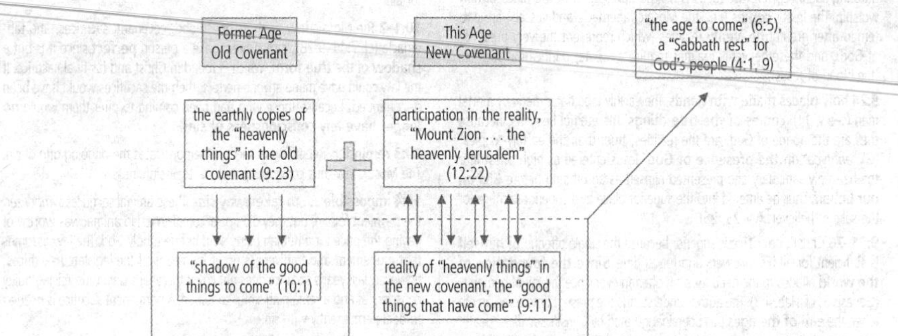

Hebrews teaches a contrast between the realities of the old covenant and the new covenant. In the old covenant, the law and its ceremonies were a shadow of the good things to come. They only *reflected* the reality of the "heavenly things" (depicted by arrows intruding into the old covenant). The inauguration of the new covenant is described as a change in priesthood and law that brings about a change in reality because of the cross. After the work of Christ in the new covenant, the heavenly reality (Mount Zion, the heavenly Jerusalem) not only intrudes into history but Christians actually participate in this new reality (arrows now go both ways) because the good things have come through Christ in his death, resurrection, and ascension. Christians live in a semi-heavenly (or semi-eschatological) age, whereas in the old covenant with its laws, rules, and regulations, people could not fully participate in the "heavenly things." Although they participate in the heavenly reality now, in the age to come God's people will fully realize their Sabbath rest.

the law had been declared by Moses to all the people, he took [b]the blood of calves and
goats, [c]with water and scarlet wool and hyssop, and sprinkled both the book itself and all
the people, 20 saying, [d]"This is the blood of the covenant that God commanded for you."
21 And in the same way he sprinkled with the blood both [e]the tent and all the vessels used
in worship. 22 Indeed, under the law almost everything is purified with blood, and [f]without
the shedding of blood there is no forgiveness of sins.
23 Thus it was necessary for [g]the copies of the heavenly things to be purified with these
rites, but the heavenly things themselves with better sacrifices than these. 24 For Christ has
entered, not into holy places [h]made with hands, which are copies of the true things, but
into heaven itself, now to appear in the presence of God [i]on our behalf. 25 Nor was it to offer
himself repeatedly, as [j]the high priest enters [k]the holy places every year with blood not his
own, 26 for then he would have had to suffer repeatedly since the foundation of the world.
But as it is, [l]he has appeared [m]once for all [n]at the end of the ages to put away sin by the
sacrifice of himself. 27 And just as [o]it is appointed for man to die once, and [p]after that comes
judgment, 28 so Christ, having been offered once [q]to bear the sins of [r]many, will appear [s]a
second time, [t]not to deal with sin but to save those who are eagerly [u]waiting for him.

Christ's Sacrifice Once for All

10 For since the law has but [v]a shadow [w]of the good things to come instead of the
true form of these realities, [x]it can never, by the same sacrifices that are continually
offered every year, make perfect those who draw near. 2 Otherwise, would they not have
ceased to be offered, since the worshipers, having once been cleansed, would no longer
have any consciousness of sins? 3 But [y]in these sacrifices [z]there is a reminder of sins every
year. 4 For [a]it is impossible for the blood of bulls and goats to take away sins.
5 Consequently, [b]when Christ[1] came into the world, he said,

[c]"Sacrifices and offerings you have not desired,
but a body have you prepared for me;

[1] Greek *he*

19 [b]ver. 12 [c][Lev. 14:4, 7; Num. 19:6, 17]
20 [d]Cited from Ex. 24:8; [Matt. 26:28]
21 [e][Ex. 29:12, 36; Lev. 8:15, 19; 16:14, 16; 2 Chr. 29:22]
22 [f]Lev. 17:11
23 [g]ch. 8:5
24 [h]ch. 8:2; [ver. 11] [i]ch. 7:25; See Rom. 8:34
25 [j]See ver. 7 [k]ch. 10:19
26 [l]1 John 3:5 [m]ver. 12; ch. 7:27; 10:10; 1 Pet. 3:18 [n][ch. 1:2; 1 Cor. 10:11]
27 [o]See Gen. 3:19 [p]See Matt. 16:27
28 [q]Isa. 53:12; 1 Pet. 2:24; 3:18 [r]Matt. 20:28; 26:28; Mark 10:45; Rev. 5:9 [s]Acts 1:11 [t]See ch. 4:15 [u]Titus 2:13; [Isa. 25:9]

Chapter 10

1 [v]ch. 8:5; Col. 2:17 [w]ch. 9:11 [x][ch. 9:9]
3 [y]See ch. 9:7 [z]Lev. 16:21
4 [a]ver. 11
5 [b][ch. 1:6] [c]Cited from Ps. 40:6-8

9:22 purified with blood. In the Mosaic law, the initial purification of the people of God and of his sanctuary required sacrificial blood (vv. 18–21), and such sacrifices continued to be required in the law on behalf of God's people (e.g., v. 7; 10:1–4). This is because sin necessitates an atoning blood sacrifice (Lev. 17:11). The OT sacrifices were given by God as types of Christ's greater, perfect sacrifice to come.

9:23 Covenantal structure, and the need of purification, requires an inaugurating sacrifice. Here the focus is on the purification of the place of holy worship. The lesser **copies** (i.e., the Mosaic tabernacle and vessels) are patterned after greater **heavenly** realities (which represent the very presence of God), and these heavenly realities require a greater purification sacrifice (the blood of Jesus).

9:24 holy places made with hands. The earthly tabernacle made by mortal men (see v. 11). **copies of the true things**. The eternal heavens, because they are the abode of God, are the realities, truer than the earthly "copies" (Gk. *antitypa*). **in the presence of God**. Jesus entered as high priest into the heavenly sanctuary and presented himself as an offering before God **on our behalf**. Thus he entered into the superior place by a superior sacrifice for the sake of believers (vv. 23, 25).

9:25–26 Christ's **sacrifice** is superior because the single offering **of himself** is sufficient for all his followers and for all time. **Since the foundation of the world** alludes to the need for a sin offering ever since the fall of humanity (Genesis 3; cf. Heb. 4:3). The author understands the present time to be an era when the **end of the ages** has been inaugurated by Christ's sacrificial death, even though it still awaits its consummation at Christ's return (see 9:28).

9:27–28 appointed . . . to die once. Every person has but a single life before eternal **judgment**. This repudiates reincarnation and any idea that there will be a second chance to believe after death, since immediately after the reference to the fact of death comes the phrase "and after that comes judgment," with no hint of any intervening opportunity for change of status. The final judgment will take place when Christ comes again—he died **once** as an offering for the **sins of many**, and he will appear a second time in judgment, when he will **save** his followers. **those who are eagerly waiting for him**. This clear anticipation of Christ's return (see 10:25; cf. Rom. 8:19, 23, 25; 1 Cor. 1:7; Gal. 5:5; Phil. 3:20) calls all who hope for salvation to expectant perseverance.

10:1–18 *Christ's Sacrifice Once for All*. In contrast to the repeated Mosaic animal sacrifices, Jesus came into the world according to God's will in order to eternally sanctify a people through offering himself as a sacrifice once for all.

10:1–2 The Mosaic **law**, with its priesthood, covenant, sacrifices, and tabernacle (cf. 7:11–9:28), **can never** make a person **perfect** since it is but a **shadow** of the **true form**, which is found in Christ and his final sacrifice. If the law could have made anyone perfect, then the sacrifices would have been discontinued, because those who had been coming to offer them would **no longer have any consciousness of sins**.

10:3 reminder. Repetition in sacrifice demonstrates the ongoing grip of sin. The Mosaic law thus convinces people of their sinfulness.

10:4 impossible . . . to take away sins. These animal sacrifices *symbolized* the payment for sin, but they did not accomplish it. No animal was worthy of paying the price for a human being's sin before a holy God. The law assumes that atonement and forgiveness occur by means of the legislated sacrifices; however, last year's sacrifice does not cover this year's sins, thus leaving guilty consciences and a remaining sinful condition. A permanent sacrifice is needed to deal permanently with sin.

10:5–7 The quotation is from Ps. 40:6–8, a Davidic psalm applied here to the Davidic Messiah. This shows David's awareness, as seen elsewhere in the OT, that God desired faithful hearts and lives more than mere performance of sacrificial rituals (cf. Hos. 6:6). It also prophesies the coming of one who will do God's **will**, and God's preparation of a body for that person. **a body have you prepared for me**. The ESV translates the corresponding phrase in Ps. 40:6 as, "you have given me an open ear." Literally, the Masoretic (Hb.) text reads, "ears you have dug for me" (Ps. 40:7–9 MT). The Hebrew metaphor

8 [c][See ver. 5 above]
9 [d]ver. 7
10 [e]ch. 2:11; 13:12 [f]Matt. 26:26; Mark 14:22; Luke 22:19; 1 Cor. 11:24; [ver. 5] [g]ch. 7:27; 9:12
11 [h][Num. 28:3] [i]See ch. 5:1 [j]ver. 1, 4; [ch. 9:9]
12 [k]ch. 1:3; See Mark 16:19
13 [l]ch. 1:13; [1 Cor. 15:25-28]
14 [m]ver. 1
16 [n]ch. 8:10; Rom. 11:27; Cited from Jer. 31:33

6 in burnt offerings and sin offerings
you have taken no pleasure.
7 Then I said, 'Behold, I have come to do your will, O God,
as it is written of me in the scroll of the book.'"

8 When he said above, "You have neither desired nor taken pleasure in [c]sacrifices and offerings and burnt offerings and sin offerings" (these are offered according to the law), 9 then
he added, [d]"Behold, I have come to do your will." He does away with the first in order to
establish the second. 10 And by that will [e]we have been sanctified through the offering of
[f]the body of Jesus Christ [g]once for all.

11 And every priest stands [h]daily at his service, [i]offering repeatedly the same sacrifices,
[j]which can never take away sins. 12 But when Christ[1] had offered for all time a single sacrifice
for sins, he [k]sat down at the right hand of God, 13 waiting from that time [l]until his enemies
should be made a footstool for his feet. 14 For by a single offering [m]he has perfected for all
time those who are being sanctified.

15 And the Holy Spirit also bears witness to us; for after saying,

16 [n]"This is the covenant that I will make with them
after those days, declares the Lord:
I will put my laws on their hearts,
and write them on their minds,"

[1] Greek *this one*

has been understood by the Septuagint translators (Ps. 39:7–9 LXX) and by the writer of Hebrews to indicate the physical creation of a person's body. (NT quotations of OT texts are not always precise; NT authors often reword them or adapt them to suit their own purposes, yet always in a way that is compatible with their original meaning.)

10:8–9 The OT sacrifices were not **desired** (lit., "willed") by God because of any intrinsic value they possessed. However, it *was* God's will for the messianic speaker of Ps. 40:6–8 to **come to do your will**. God did ordain the OT **sacrifices and offerings** for the time when the Mosaic covenant was in force, but not for the future time anticipated in this messianic psalm. **He does away with the first** refers to the "sacrifices and offerings" (Heb. 10:8) of the old covenant. Christians no longer have to offer animal sacrifices and keep other ceremonial parts of the OT laws, for these have been "abolished." **In order to establish the second** means "in order to establish obedience to God's 'will'" (v. 9). The sacrifices had to be abolished in order for God's moral and spiritual will for his people to be done.

10:10 God's **will** (see vv. 8–9) thus provides sanctification (the state of being made holy) through a different, onetime **offering**, namely, **the body of Jesus Christ**, i.e., his physical death.

10:11–13 Previous arguments are summarized, focusing on the efficacy of the **single sacrifice** offered by Christ. The priest **stands**, showing that his work of offering sacrifices never ends. **which can never take away sins**. See notes on vv. 1–4. Christ's sacrificial work has ended, and now he sits **at the right hand of God** (see esp. Ps. 110:1, cited in Heb. 1:13; see chart to the right), showing that the securing of full and final forgiveness of sins has been accomplished.

10:14 Perfected for all time does not mean that believers are now already sinless, but that Christ has fully earned their perfection, which will certainly be applied to Christians in God's good time. The eternal perfection (see 11:40; 12:23) of the saints stems from the once-for-all-nature of Jesus' sacrifice. Hence, believers look to Christ and not to themselves for a cleansed conscience, full forgiveness of sins, and total flawlessness in the future. **those who are being sanctified** (i.e., those who are made holy; 2:11; 10:10; 13:12). The Greek present participle allows for the idea of progressive sanctification in this life and/or present positional sanctification of the believer as one who from the start is deemed perfectly holy (see 10:10; and "saints" in 6:10; 13:24).

10:15–18 The new covenant passage from Jeremiah 31 (see Heb. 8:8–12), cited as the utterance of the **Holy Spirit**, supports the preceding argument (esp. 10:14). The internalization of God's **laws** (v. 16) means that God's people now do his will (not yet perfectly, but in intention and endeavor) by the power of the Holy Spirit. **I will remember their sins . . . no more** indicates that Christ's single new covenant offering was eternal, and such forgiveness means **there is no longer any** (other) **offering for sin**. The

Psalm 110 in Hebrews

Psalm 110	Hebrews
"The LORD says to my Lord: 'Sit at my right hand, until I make your enemies your footstool'" (v. 1).	Jesus "sat down at the right hand of the Majesty on high" (1:3).
	God says to Jesus: "Sit at my right hand until I make your enemies a footstool for your feet" (1:13).
	Jesus is "seated at the right hand of the throne of the Majesty in heaven" (8:1).
	Jesus "sat down at the right hand of God, waiting . . . until his enemies should be made a footstool for his feet" (10:12–13).
	Jesus is "seated at the right hand of the throne of God" (12:2).
"The LORD has sworn and will not change his mind, 'You are a priest forever after the order of Melchizedek'" (v. 4).	Jesus is "a priest forever, after the order of Melchizedek" (5:6).
	Jesus is "designated by God a high priest after the order of Melchizedek" (5:10).
	Jesus has "become a high priest forever after the order of Melchizedek" (6:20).
	Jesus is a "priest . . . after the order of Melchizedek" (7:11).
	Jesus is a "priest [who] arises in the likeness of Melchizedek" (7:15).
	Jesus is "a priest forever, after the order of Melchizedek" (7:17).
	Jesus was made a priest by this oath: "The Lord has sworn and will not change his mind, 'You are a priest forever'" (7:21).

17 then he adds,

[o]"I will remember their sins and their lawless deeds no more."

18 Where there is forgiveness of these, there is no longer any offering for sin.

The Full Assurance of Faith

19 [p]Therefore, brothers,[1] since we have confidence to enter [q]the holy places by the blood
of Jesus, 20 by [r]the new and living way that he opened for us through [s]the curtain, that
is, through his flesh, 21 and since we have [t]a great priest over the house of God, 22 let us
draw near with a true heart in full assurance of faith, with our hearts [u]sprinkled clean
[v]from an evil conscience and our bodies [w]washed with pure water. 23 [x]Let us hold fast the
confession of our hope without wavering, for [y]he who promised is faithful. 24 And [z]let us
consider how to stir up one another to love and good works, 25 [a]not neglecting to meet
together, as is the habit of some, but encouraging one another, and [b]all the more as you
see [c]the Day drawing near.

26 For [d]if we go on sinning deliberately [e]after receiving the knowledge of the truth,
[f]there no longer remains a sacrifice for sins, 27 [g]but a fearful expectation of judgment, and
[h]a fury of fire that will consume the adversaries. 28 [i]Anyone who has set aside the law of

[1] *Or brothers and sisters*

17 [o]ch. 8:12; Cited from Jer. 31:34
19 [p]See ch. 4:16 [q]ch. 9:25
20 [r]ch. 9:8; [John 10:9; 14:6] [s]ch. 9:3
21 [t]Zech. 6:11-13; [ch. 4:14]; See ch. 2:17
22 [u]Ezek. 36:25; [ch. 12:24; 2 Cor. 7:1; 1 Pet. 1:2] [v]ch. 9:14 [w][1 Cor. 6:11]
23 [x]ch. 4:14 [y]ch. 11:11; See 1 Cor. 1:9
24 [z][ch. 3:13]
25 [a][Acts 2:42] [b]Rom. 13:11-13 [c]See 1 Cor. 3:13
26 [d]Num. 15:30; Deut. 17:12 [e]ch. 6:4; 2 Pet. 2:20, 21 [f][ch. 6:6; 1 John 5:16]
27 [g]ch. 2:3; 12:25 [h]Ps. 79:5; Isa. 26:11; Zeph. 1:18; 3:8; [Ezek. 36:5; Zech. 8:2]; See 2 Thess. 1:8
28 [i]Deut. 17:2-6

new covenant's superiority to the old is shown most clearly in the full and final forgiveness of sins.

10:19–12:29 *Call to Faith and Endurance.* The exposition of the superiority of Christ and his salvation culminates in exhortations to faith and perseverance (10:19–39; 12:1–29) and in an extended series of examples of how faith endures through hope in God (11:1–40).

10:19–39 *The Full Assurance of Faith.* The truth of Christ's person and work leads to encouragement to draw near to God (vv. 19–25) and to exhortations against shrinking back from faith (vv. 26–39).

10:19–25 *Exhortation to Draw Near.* Since the priestly work of Christ has established the privilege of access to God, the author exhorts his readers to approach God faithfully, to firmly maintain their confession, and to find ways to encourage others.

10:19 Therefore . . . since. Verses 19–21 draw upon Christological arguments made earlier in the book. **confidence to enter**. The readers have the privilege of following the Messiah into the heavenly **holy places** (see 9:12, 24). "Confidence" in access to God is based upon Christ's saving work (3:6; 4:16; 10:35). **by the blood of Jesus**. See 9:11–14.

10:20 by the new and living way. This entrance (v. 19) has been newly inaugurated by Christ's consecrating work, and it is "living" just as God himself is "living" (3:12; 9:14; 10:31; 12:22), as the word of God lives (4:12), and as those who follow Christ truly "live" (12:9). **through the curtain**. The veil of the heavenly tabernacle (cf. 9:3) lies open due to the sanctifying work of Christ (6:19–20; 9:11–12, 24). **that is, through his flesh**. Although some suggest that Jesus' "flesh" is itself the "way," the word order (and the neuter gender of the Greek *tout' estin*, rendered "that is") makes it much more likely that Jesus' flesh is identified with the tabernacle "curtain" or veil, which was torn open just as Jesus' own flesh was metaphorically torn at his death (cf. Matt. 27:51).

10:21 great priest. Jesus is the superior high priest (e.g., 5:5–10; 7:11–8:7). **house of God**. See 3:1–6.

10:22 let us draw near. In the first of three exhortations in vv. 22–25, Christians are called to act faithfully upon their confidence to enter by the blood of Christ (v. 19) into God's presence (see 4:16; 7:25; 11:6; cf. 10:1). **true heart**. In context this is a cleansed ("sprinkled") and believing (**in full assurance of faith**) heart that is submissive to God (v. 26; also 13:9; cf. 3:8, 10, 12; 4:12). **hearts sprinkled clean**. Jesus' atoning work purifies the inner person (see notes on 9:14; 10:15–18). **bodies washed**. Likely a reference to baptism (see 6:2; Acts 22:16; 1 Cor. 6:11; cf. Heb. 9:10), which employs ritually **pure water** (cf. Lev. 11:36; Num. 5:17; Ezek. 36:25).

10:23 Let us hold fast. The second exhortation of vv. 22–25 calls forth a faithful, unwavering embrace (see 3:6, 14) of the **confession of our hope**, i.e., the church's assent to the teachings concerning Christ and his work (see 3:1; 4:14; cf. 2 Cor. 9:13; 1 Tim. 6:12), teachings that produce hope (Heb. 6:18–20; 7:19). **for he who promised is faithful**. Confident hope in God's promises (see 6:12–20) stems from God's trustworthy character (also 11:11).

10:24–25 let us consider. The third and final exhortation in vv. 22–25 calls for serious thinking about other Christians with a purpose to **stir up** (or "provoke") them in their **love** and service (**good works**). Christian perseverance is thus also a community endeavor. **meet together**. Community encouragement toward perseverance requires being together. That some were **neglecting** this duty may have been among the motives for the author's warnings throughout this book. **encouraging**. Voicing exhortation with the goal of strengthening another's faith (see 3:13; cf. 13:22). **the Day drawing near**. The coming day of Christ's return and judgment (9:28; 10:37; see notes on Amos 5:18–20; 2 Tim. 1:12).

10:26–39 *Warnings against Shrinking Back.* The author warns of the impending judgment upon those who willfully reject the faith. Yet his purpose is to exhort the readers in their faith, a faith that he affirms based on their past perseverance.

10:26–27 sinning deliberately. Willfully sinning and refusing to repent. **after receiving**. The author refers especially to people within the Christian community, who have thus heard the **truth**. The fact that they "go on sinning deliberately even after receiving **knowledge** of the truth" indicates that the people in view are not (and never were) genuine believers; that is, these are people who have never genuinely embraced the gospel in a way that has resulted in a life of faith, obedience, and the bearing of fruit. **no longer remains a sacrifice for sins**. This could refer to the inability of willful, unrepentant sinners to be restored (see 6:4–6), or more likely to the fact that there is no place for them to turn for forgiveness outside of Christ's sacrifice—which they have rejected. **judgment**. All people face judgment (see 9:27–28), and apart from Christ's sacrifice his **adversaries** receive eternal damnation. These verses, then, function as a *means* used by God to call genuine Christians to faith, obedience, and perseverance; and, if there is no evidence of fruit in one's life, to challenge such people to give fearful consideration as to whether they are in fact genuine believers.

10:28–29 These verses argue from the lesser to the greater (cf. 2:1–4; 9:14). In the Mosaic law, the death penalty comes upon those who blaspheme God or who worship other deities (e.g., Lev. 24:13–16; Deut. 17:2–7), so in the superior new covenant the expectation of judgment would be even stronger. **How much worse punishment . . . will be deserved by the one who . . . ?** The description that follows is of a person who has deliberately, consciously, and persistently deserted "the living God" (cf. Heb. 3:12; 10:31; 12:22), renouncing Christ and the community of faith (6:4–8). It is a description of outright apostasy, involving a person who has done three specific things: (1) **trampled underfoot the Son of God**, (2) **profaned the blood of the covenant**, and (3) **outraged the Spirit of grace**. Such rejection of

Moses dies without mercy [j]on the evidence of two or three witnesses. **29** How much worse
punishment, do you think, will be deserved by the one [k]who has trampled underfoot the
Son of God, and has profaned [l]the blood of the covenant [m]by which he was sanctified, and
has [n]outraged the Spirit of grace? **30** For we know him who said, [o]"Vengeance is mine; I
will repay." And again, [p]"The Lord will judge his people." **31** [q]It is a fearful thing to fall into
the hands of the living God.

32 But recall the former days when, after [r]you were enlightened, you endured [s]a hard
struggle with sufferings, **33** sometimes being [t]publicly exposed to reproach and affliction,
and sometimes being partners with those so treated. **34** For [u]you had compassion on those
in prison, and [v]you joyfully accepted the plundering of your property, since you knew that
you yourselves had [w]a better possession and an abiding one. **35** Therefore do not throw away
your confidence, which has [x]a great reward. **36** For [y]you have need of endurance, so that
[z]when you have done the will of God you may [a]receive what is promised. **37** For,

> [b]"Yet a little while,
> and [c]the coming one will come and will not delay;
> **38** [d]but my righteous one shall live by faith,
> and if he shrinks back,
> my soul has no pleasure in him."

39 But we are not of those who shrink back and are destroyed, but of those who have faith
and preserve their souls.

By Faith

11 Now faith is the assurance of things hoped for, the conviction of [e]things not seen.
2 For by it the people of old received their commendation. **3** By faith we understand
that the universe was created by [f]the word of God, so that what is seen was not made out
of [g]things that are visible.

28 [j]See Num. 35:30
29 [k][ch. 6:6] [l]ch. 13:20; Zech. 9:11 [m]ch. 9:13, 14 [n][Matt. 12:31, 32; Eph. 4:30]
30 [o]Rom. 12:19; Cited from Deut. 32:35 [p]Ps. 50:4; 135:14; Cited from Deut. 32:36
31 [q]Isa. 33:14; Luke 12:5
32 [r]ch. 6:4 [s]See Phil. 1:30
33 [t]1 Cor. 4:9 (Gk.)
34 [u][ch. 13:3; Matt. 25:36; 2 Tim. 1:16] [v]See Matt. 5:12 [w]1 Pet. 1:4
35 [x]ch. 2:2; 11:26
36 [y]ch. 12:1-7; Luke 21:19; Rom. 2:7; 12:12; See Matt. 10:22 [z]ch. 13:21; [1 John 2:17] [a]ch. 11:39
37 [b]Isa. 26:20; Hag. 2:6; Luke 18:8 [c]Cited from Hab. 2:3, 4
38 [d]Rom. 1:17; Gal. 3:11

Chapter 11

1 [e]Rom. 8:24; 2 Cor. 4:18; 5:7; 1 Pet. 1:8
3 [f]See Gen. 1:1 [g][Rom. 4:17]

the knowledge of the truth (10:26) through willful disobedience is tantamount to trampling upon God's Son, reckoning his blood to be defiled, and insulting the Spirit who has offered such grace; the one who does this deserves eternal judgment (v. 27). Some have argued that the statement **by which he was sanctified** (Gk. *hagiazō*, "set apart," "sanctify") indicates that the person in view here was a true believer (see note on 3:14, however, indicating a fundamental difficulty with this view). Given the immediate context, it seems most likely that "he was sanctified" should be understood in the sense of someone who had been "set apart" or identified as an active participant in the Christian community of believers, but who has subsequently committed apostasy by renouncing his identification with other believers, by denying the "knowledge of the truth" that he had heard, and by repudiating the work and the person of Christ himself. Such a person's apostasy is thus *evidence* that his identification with the Christian community was only superficial and that he was not a genuine believer. Another view is that the author is confident that the grave warning in these verses will be the *means* by which those who are truly elect will be braced to persevere in faith and obedience, and so to be saved (see note on 6:4–8).

10:30–31 The **living God** (cf. 3:12; 9:14; 12:22) is here portrayed through two citations from Deut. 32:35–36 as the heavenly **judge**, who will judge even his own people.

10:32–34 recall the former days. Having severely warned his audience, the author reminds them of the previous evidence of their faith in persevering amid suffering (see 6:9–12). **enlightened**. See note on 6:4. The **sufferings** he lists include public **reproach** (cf. 11:26; 13:13), imprisonments, associating with **those in prison** (cf. 13:3), and the **plundering** of their possessions. Officially sanctioned persecution seems likely here, especially regarding imprisonments. The author lauds their endurance, their **compassion**, and their confidence in their future, eternal **better possession**.

10:35–36 Given his readers' previous perseverance through persecution (vv. 32–34), the author encourages continuing **confidence** (3:6; 4:16; 10:19). They are to exercise **endurance** (see 12:1), by practicing God's **will** (13:21), with the goal of inheriting the **promised** salvation (4:1; 6:12; 8:6; 9:15).

10:37–38 The quote from Hab. 2:3–4 encourages perseverance; it announces that the wait for the end will be short, that **faith** is required from the **righteous**, and that "shrinking back" invites God's displeasure; and this displeasure, as the next verse clarifies, means final judgment.

10:39 The author reasserts his confidence in the readers, associating himself with them (**we**). To **shrink back** invites divine displeasure (see v. 38) unto destruction (cf. vv. 26–27), but **faith** results in salvation, i.e., preservation of the soul ("life").

11:1–40 *By Faith.* Faith consists of persistent hope in the promises of God, and it is such faith, as 10:39 indicates, that obtains salvation on the last day. Here faith is illustrated from OT examples.

11:1 assurance. Greek *hypostasis*, also translated "confidence" (3:14). **hoped for**. On hope, see 3:6; 6:11, 18; 7:19; 10:23. **conviction of things not seen**. By defining faith (Gk. *pistis*) as "assurance" and "conviction," the author indicates that biblical faith is not a vague hope grounded in imaginary, wishful thinking. Instead, faith is a settled confidence that something in the future—something that is not yet seen but has been promised by God—will actually come to pass because God will bring it about. Thus biblical faith is not blind trust in the face of contrary evidence, not an unknowable "leap in the dark"; rather, biblical faith is a confident trust in the eternal God who is all-powerful, infinitely wise, eternally trustworthy—the God who has revealed himself in his word and in the person of Jesus Christ, whose promises have proven true from generation to generation, and who will "never leave nor forsake" his own (13:5). Such faith in the unseen realities of God is emphasized throughout ch. 11 (e.g., 11:7, 8; cf. v. 3) and has provided confidence and assurance to all who receive Christ as their Lord and Savior.

11:2 The **people of old** (Gk. *presbyteroi*, "elders"), especially those listed as examples of faith throughout the chapter, received **commendation** in the form of a good testimony from God. The author does not focus on their failings (e.g., Gen. 9:20–27; 12:10–20; 17:17–21; 18:11–15), since his goal is to positively illustrate what faith looks like and to connect the current people of God with this "cloud of witnesses" (Heb. 12:1).

11:3 God's creation of the **universe** was accomplished by his **word** (Gk. *rhēma*). **So that what is seen was not made out of things that are visible** is consistent with the doctrine of creation *ex nihilo* (Latin, "from nothing"), but is not itself a full statement about this reality. It does, however, seem to correct Greco-Roman notions about eternally existing matter. The

4 By faith [h]Abel offered to God [i]a more acceptable sacrifice than Cain, through which he
was commended as righteous, God commending him by accepting his gifts. And [j]through
his faith, though he died, he [k]still speaks. **5** By faith [l]Enoch was taken up so that he should
not see death, and he was not found, because God had taken him. Now before he was
taken he was commended as having pleased God. **6** And without faith it is impossible to
please him, for whoever would draw near to God [m]must believe that he exists and [m]that he
rewards those who seek him. **7** By faith [n]Noah, being warned by God concerning [o]events as
yet unseen, in reverent fear constructed an ark for the saving of his household. By this he
condemned the world and became an heir of [p]the righteousness that comes by faith.

8 By faith [q]Abraham obeyed when he was called to go out to a place [r]that he was to receive as
an inheritance. And he went out, not knowing where he was going. **9** By faith he went to live
in [s]the land of promise, as in a foreign land, [t]living in tents [u]with Isaac and Jacob, heirs with
him of the same promise. **10** For he was looking forward to [v]the city that has [w]foundations,
[x]whose designer and builder is God. **11** By faith [y]Sarah herself received power to conceive,
even when she was past the age, since she considered [z]him faithful who had promised.
12 Therefore from one man, and [a]him as good as dead, were born descendants [b]as many as
the stars of heaven and as many as the innumerable grains of sand by the seashore.

13 These all died in faith, [c]not having received the things promised, but [d]having seen
them and greeted them from afar, and [e]having acknowledged that they were [f]strangers
and exiles on the earth. **14** For people who speak thus make it clear that they are seeking a
homeland. **15** If they had been thinking of that land from which they had gone out, [g]they
would have had opportunity to return. **16** But as it is, they desire a better country, that is, a
heavenly one. Therefore God is not ashamed [h]to be called their God, for [i]he has prepared
for them a city.

4 [h]Gen. 4:4-8; 1 John 3:12 [i]Prov. 15:8 [j]Gen. 4:10 [k]ch. 12:24
5 [l]Gen. 5:22-24; [2 Kgs. 2:11]
6 [m]1 Chr. 28:9; Jer. 29:12-14; [John 4:24]
7 [n]Gen. 6:13-22; Luke 17:26; 1 Pet. 3:20 [o]ver. 1 [p]Rom. 4:13; [Gen. 6:9; Ezek. 14:14, 20]
8 [q]Gen. 12:1-4; Acts 7:2-4 [r]Gen. 12:7
9 [s]Acts 7:5 [t]Gen. 12:8; 13:3, 18; 18:1, 9 [u]Gen. 35:27
10 [v]ch. 12:22; [ch. 13:14] [w]Ps. 87:1; Rev. 21:14 [x]Rev. 21:2, 10
11 [y]Gen. 17:19; 18:11-14; 21:2 [z]ch. 10:23
12 [a]Rom. 4:19 [b]Gen. 22:17; 32:12; See Gen. 15:5
13 [c]ver. 39 [d]ver. 27; John 8:56; [Matt. 13:17] [e]Gen. 23:4; 47:9; [1 Chr. 29:15; Ps. 39:12] [f]Eph. 2:19
15 [g][Gen. 24:6-8]
16 [h]Gen. 26:24; 28:13; Ex. 3:6; 4:5; [ch. 2:11] [i][ver. 10; Matt. 25:34; John 14:2]

idea that God created the visible universe out of some other kind of invisible ("not . . . visible") matter is not in the author's mind; rather, he is saying that God did not make the universe out of any preexisting matter as humans know it, which is close to saying that he made it "out of nothing." Further support for this idea is found in Gen. 1:1; Ps. 33:6, 9; 90:2; John 1:3; Acts 14:15; Rom. 4:17.

11:4 Abel's **sacrifice** was **acceptable** to God (Gen. 4:4, 7) while Cain's was not (cf. Matt. 23:35; 1 John 3:12). **commended as righteous**. The acceptance of the offering was evidence of God's acceptance of the person (see Gen. 4:7). **still speaks**. The story of Abel's faith, as recorded in the Bible, still speaks to generation after generation. This mention of Abel's faith indicates that, from the very outset of human history, some OT figures were saved by means of faith (though Heb. 10:4 reminds readers that the faith of those OT saints was effective only because of the future sacrifice of Christ, which animal sacrifices foreshadowed).

11:5 Enoch was taken up. Genesis 5:21–24 indicates that Enoch did not die but that God "took" him. **having pleased God**. Genesis also states (twice) that Enoch "walked with God" (Gen. 5:22, 24), and this phrase is interpreted in the Septuagint as Enoch having "pleased God."

11:6 to please him. The Septuagint of Genesis states that certain patriarchs "pleased God" (using Gk. *euaresteō* to translate the Hb. for "walked with God"): Enoch (Gen. 5:22, 24), Noah (Gen. 6:9), Abraham (Gen. 17:1; 24:40; 48:15), and Isaac (Gen. 48:15; cf. Joseph in Gen. 39:4). Each is discussed in Hebrews 11. **Faith** includes belief in God's existence (possibly a reference to v. 3) and especially in God's trustworthiness to keep his promise to reward his followers (see 10:35; 11:26; cf. 10:23 and note on 11:1). **draw near**. See note on 4:16.

11:7 Noah. Cf. Gen. 6:9–9:29. **events as yet unseen**. See Heb. 11:1. **reverent fear**. Cf. 5:7 and 12:28, where such an attitude is also commended. **saving of his household**. A visible example of God's salvation. **Condemned the world** means that Noah's righteous obedience to God showed, by contrast, how sinful the world was to reject Noah's message (cf. 2 Pet. 2:5) and God's moral standards. "World" in Hebrews generally signifies creation (Heb. 4:3; 9:26; 10:5), though here it especially pictures sinful humanity (see 11:38; cf. John 15:18–19; James 4:4; 1 John 2:15). **heir of the righteousness that comes by faith**. Noah is called "righteous" in Gen. 7:1, after his faithful response in building the ark (Gen. 6:22).

11:8–9 God called **Abraham** to leave Haran and go to Canaan (Gen. 12:1–4). **obeyed**. Faith leads to obedience to God's promise and calling. **inheritance**. Also used of Christian salvation (Heb. 9:15). **not knowing where he was going**. See 11:1. **land of promise**. See Gen. 15:18–21. On God's promises, see Heb. 6:12–15. **foreign land**. See 11:13–16.

11:10 Abraham is portrayed as yearning for the heavenly **city** (developed further in vv. 13–16; 12:22–24; 13:13–14).

11:11–12 Sarah. See Gen. 21:1–7. That Sarah laughed, apparently in unbelief (Gen. 18:9–15), is potentially problematic for her role as an example of faith; however: (1) the author is happy to speak of the true faith of Sarah despite her failings, and (2) Sarah apparently later had a change of heart, as her laughter became a genuine expression of joy at the birth of Isaac (Gen. 21:6), whose name means "laughter." **received power to conceive** (lit., "power for the foundation of seed"). Although some translations give Abraham as the subject, it is best to take "Sarah" as the subject here (as the ESV does), because (1) both Sarah's name and "herself" (Gk. *autē*) are in the nominative case (indicating the subject of the sentence), and because (2) making Abraham the subject requires either an unusual grammatical understanding of the words for "Sarah herself" or an assumption that an early copyist made an error in transcribing those two words. **considered him faithful**. See Heb. 10:23. **stars . . . sand**. An allusion to Gen. 22:17.

11:13 died in faith. They were faithful even unto death. **not having received**. Abraham and Sarah especially exemplify this: called to a Promised Land and promised innumerable offspring, they merely embraced these promises while living nomadically in a land not wholly theirs, where they had just one son together. **strangers and exiles on the earth**. See especially Gen. 23:4; also Ex. 2:22; Lev. 25:23. This physical reality for the descendants of Abraham was applied spiritually in the Psalms; see Ps. 39:12; 119:19 (also 1 Chron. 29:15; cf. 1 Pet. 1:1; 2:11).

11:14–16 The author says that the people he has mentioned in vv. 1–13 were seeking a **better (heavenly) country**, which would be their true **homeland**. First, if Abraham (for example) were looking for an earthly "homeland" (Gk. *patris* refers to a place of one's fathers), he could have returned to Haran; but he persisted in following God's leading and focusing on his promise (v. 15). Second, the Psalms' spiritual application of exile terminology to this whole mortal life indicates the expectation of a life to come (Ps. 39:12; 119:19; cf. Heb. 11:13–14). **prepared for them a city**. See v. 10; 12:22–24; 13:13–14.

17 By faith [j]Abraham, when he was tested, offered up Isaac, and he who had received the
promises was in the act of offering up his only son, 18 of whom it was said, [k]"Through Isaac
shall your offspring be named." 19 [l]He considered that God was able even to raise him from
the dead, from which, figuratively speaking, he did receive him back. 20 By faith [m]Isaac
invoked future blessings on Jacob and Esau. 21 By faith [n]Jacob, when dying, blessed each
of the sons of Joseph, [o]bowing in worship over the head of his staff. 22 By faith [p]Joseph,
at the end of his life, made mention of the exodus of the Israelites and gave directions
concerning his bones.

23 By faith [q]Moses, when he was born, was hidden for three months by his parents,
because they saw that the child was beautiful, and they were not afraid of [r]the king's
edict. 24 By faith Moses, when he was grown up, [s]refused to be called the son of Pharaoh's
daughter, 25 [t]choosing rather to be mistreated with the people of God than to enjoy [u]the
fleeting pleasures of sin. 26 [v]He considered the reproach of Christ greater wealth than the
treasures of Egypt, for he was looking to [w]the reward. 27 By faith he [x]left Egypt, [y]not being
afraid of the anger of the king, for he endured [z]as seeing him who is invisible. 28 By faith
[a]he kept the Passover and sprinkled the blood, so that the Destroyer of the firstborn might
not touch them.

29 By faith [b]the people crossed the Red Sea as on dry land, but the Egyptians, when they
attempted to do the same, were drowned. 30 By faith [c]the walls of Jericho fell down after
they had been encircled for seven days. 31 By faith [d]Rahab the prostitute did not perish with
those who were disobedient, because she [e]had given a friendly welcome to the spies.

32 And what more shall I say? For time would fail me to tell of [f]Gideon, [g]Barak, [h]Samson,
[i]Jephthah, of [j]David and [k]Samuel and the prophets— 33 who through faith conquered kingdoms, enforced justice, obtained promises, [l]stopped the mouths of lions, 34 [m]quenched the

17 [j]Gen. 22:1-10; James 2:21
18 [k]Rom. 9:7; Cited from Gen. 21:12
19 [l]Rom. 4:17-21
20 [m]Gen. 27:27-29, 39, 40
21 [n]Gen. 48:16, 20 [o][Gen. 47:31]
22 [p]Gen. 50:24, 25; Ex. 13:19
23 [q]Ex. 2:2, 3; Acts 7:20 [r]Ex. 1:16, 22
24 [s]Ex. 2:10, 11
25 [t][Job 36:21; Ps. 84:10] [u]1 John 2:17
26 [v]ch. 13:13; [Ps. 89:50, 51; Phil. 3:7, 8; 1 Pet. 4:14] [w]ch. 2:2; 10:35
27 [x]Ex. 12:37; 13:17, 18 [y]Ex. 10:28, 29 [z]ver. 13; See 1 Tim. 1:17
28 [a]Ex. 12:21-30
29 [b]Ex. 14:21-30
30 [c]Josh. 6:15, 16, 20
31 [d]Josh. 6:25; James 2:25 [e]Josh. 2:1, 8-13
32 [f]Judg. 6:11 [g]Judg. 4:6 [h]Judg. 13:24 [i]Judg. 11:1 [j]1 Sam. 16:1, 13 [k]1 Sam. 1:20
33 [l]Judg. 14:6; 1 Sam. 17:35; Dan. 6:22
34 [m]Dan. 3:25

11:17–19 Abraham, when he was tested (see Gen. 22:1–19). The Greek for "tested" (*peirazō*) appears also in Gen. 22:1 (LXX). The word occurs elsewhere in Hebrews, though with a focus on temptation to sin; see Heb. 2:18; 4:15 (cf. James 1:2–4, 12–15; 1 Pet. 1:6–7; 4:12–14). **only son**. Greek *monogenēs*; cf. Gen. 22:2, 12 (where it reads "your only son" in Hb., but "your beloved son" in the LXX). Although Abraham also had Ishmael (Gen. 16:4, 11–16) and other children (Gen. 25:1–2), this word designates Isaac as Abraham's unique son, the son who is "one of a kind," his only heir and the only recipient of covenant promises (Gen. 21:12; 22:15–18; 25:5). **raise him from the dead**. Abraham expressed confidence that he would return with Isaac (Gen. 22:5; cf. v. 8). Hebrews makes a figurative analogy between resurrection and Isaac being saved from the sacrificial knife. Some interpreters perceive here an Isaac-Christ typology such as was common in the post-apostolic church fathers: as Isaac, Abraham's only son, was offered in sacrifice and "raised," so Jesus, God's only Son, is sacrificed and raised. Others doubt that such typology is intended here (see note on Gen. 22:16–17).

11:20 Isaac. See Gen. 27:1–45. These predictive **future blessings** (esp. Gen. 27:28–29, 39–40) demonstrate Isaac's hope for the future.

11:21 Jacob. See Gen. 48:8–22. Similar to Isaac, Jacob's future hope (predicated on God's promises; see Gen. 48:3–6) is evident in his blessing of his sons (Gen. 49:1–27) and especially in his blessing of the **sons of Joseph** (Ephraim and Manasseh, Gen. 48:8–22).

11:22 Joseph. Joseph's future hope is his confidence that God will redeem his people through the exodus and lead them to the Promised Land, thus allowing Joseph's own **bones** to be moved to that land (Gen. 50:24–25).

11:23 The parents of **Moses** preserved his life in hope. **beautiful**. Cf. Ex. 2:2; Acts 7:20.

11:24–26 Moses refused the sinful privileges of Egypt, including those of being **the son of Pharaoh's daughter** (Ex. 2:10). Instead he identified with God's people (Ex. 2:11–12) and thus sought God's reward (Heb. 10:35; 11:6). **fleeting pleasures of sin**. Contrasted with eternal reward (cf. Ps. 16:11). **reproach of Christ**. As Christ (the true Israel, e.g., Matt. 2:15) truly suffered on behalf of the people of God, so too Moses, who similarly suffered on behalf of the people, is said to bear Christ's reproach. Hence Moses serves as a model for Christians to endure such reproach (Heb. 10:33; 13:13).

11:27 By faith he left Egypt could refer to the exodus (though it would then not be in chronological order with v. 28), which would explain the reference to Moses' **seeing him who is invisible** (i.e., in the burning bush, Ex. 3:1–4:17). Or it could refer to Moses' earlier escape from Pharaoh (Ex. 2:14–15).

11:28 By faith he kept the Passover. Moses celebrated Passover before seeing the deliverance it would bring (Ex. 12:1–32).

11:29 It took faith to walk through the **Red Sea**, with walls of water on each side (Ex. 14:10–31), relying only on God's promise (Ex. 14:1–4, 15–18).

11:30 As at **Jericho**, faith repeatedly caused the Israelites to follow God's commandment before seeing his promised victory (Josh. 6:1–21).

11:31 Before the destruction of Jericho (v. 30; cf. Josh. 2:1–21; 6:17, 22–23), **Rahab** said, "I know that the LORD has given you the land . . . . for the LORD your God, he is God in the heavens above and on the earth beneath" (Josh. 2:9–11). As a Gentile and a sinner (**prostitute**), her faith was particularly remarkable.

11:32–40 This summary invokes great names and faithful deeds of OT saints (see ESV cross-references for likely identifications).

11:32 time would fail me to tell. For OT references to the people listed in vv. 32–38, see chart, p. 2382. For a discussion of the reason why the author of Hebrews included **Gideon**, **Barak**, **Samson**, and **Jephthah** as examples of faith (even though their mistakes and sins are presented so clearly in the OT), see Introduction to Judges: Assessment of the Judges. **The prophets** refers to OT prophets who either wrote the OT Prophetic Books or appear in OT historical narratives (e.g., Elijah, Elisha, Isaiah, Jeremiah, etc., some of whom are clearly alluded to in Heb. 11:33–38).

11:33 through faith. The focus remains more on the faith of these OT people than on their deeds alone. **Who . . . conquered kingdoms** includes the conquests God accomplished through those specifically named in v. 32 (even the prophet Samuel; see 1 Sam. 7:3–14). **enforced justice**. Or "worked righteousness," which was especially important in the roles of the judge (e.g., Samuel in 1 Sam. 7:15–17) and the king (see David in 2 Sam. 8:15; cf. Jer. 23:5–6). **obtained promises**. God fulfilled many promises to the leaders of Israel (e.g., Judg. 4:6–7, 14; 6:12–16; 7:7; 13:5), especially to David and his messianic heir (2 Sam. 7:11–14; Heb. 1:5). **stopped the mouths of lions**. Likely a reference to Daniel (Dan. 6:16–28), though Samson and David also combated lions (Judg. 14:5–6; 1 Sam. 17:34–37; cf. Ps. 22:21).

11:34 quenched the power of fire. In light of the reference to lions (v. 33; see Dan. 6:16–28), this likely refers to Shadrach, Meshach, and Abednego

power of fire, escaped the edge of the sword, were made strong out of weakness, [n]became
mighty in war, [n]put foreign armies to flight. **35** [o]Women received back their dead by resurrection. Some were tortured, refusing to accept release, so that they might rise again to a
better life. **36** Others suffered mocking and flogging, and even [p]chains and imprisonment.
37 [q]They were stoned, they were sawn in two,[1] [r]they were killed with the sword. [s]They
went about in skins of sheep and goats, destitute, afflicted, mistreated— **38** of whom the
world was not worthy—[t]wandering about in deserts and mountains, and in dens and
caves of the earth.
39 And all these, [u]though commended through their faith, [u]did not receive what was
promised, **40** since God had provided something better for us, [v]that apart from us they
should not be made perfect.

Jesus, Founder and Perfecter of Our Faith

12 Therefore, since we are surrounded by so great a cloud of witnesses, let us also lay
aside every weight, and [w]sin which clings so closely, and [x]let us run [y]with endurance the race that is [z]set before us, **2** looking to Jesus, the founder and perfecter of our faith,

[1] Some manuscripts add *they were tempted*

34 [n]Judg. 7:21; 1 Sam. 17:51; 2 Sam. 12:29
35 [o]1 Kgs. 17:22; 2 Kgs. 4:35
36 [p]Gen. 39:20; Jer. 20:2; 37:15
37 [q]1 Kgs. 21:13; 2 Chr. 24:21 [r]1 Kgs. 19:10; Jer. 26:23 [s]2 Kgs. 1:8
38 [t]1 Sam. 22:1; 1 Kgs. 18:4; 19:9
39 [u]ver. 2, 13; [1 Pet. 1:12]
40 [v][Rev. 6:11]

Chapter 12

1 [w]See Eph. 4:22 [x]See 1 Cor. 9:24 [y]See ch. 10:36 [z]ch. 6:18

(Dan. 2:49–3:30). The other descriptions in this verse apply to many OT leaders and prophets; e.g., for **escaped the edge of the sword** see 1 Kings 19:2; 2 Kings 6:31–33; Jer. 36:26; and contrast Heb. 11:37. **made strong out of weakness**. Perhaps serving thereby as an example to the audience, who have "weaknesses" (4:15).

11:35 Women received back their dead by resurrection. Elijah raised the son of the widow of Zarephath (1 Kings 17:17–24), and Elisha raised the son of a Shunammite woman (2 Kings 4:18–37). **tortured**. Probably in the form of beating (some commentators compare this to the intertestamental story of Eleazar in *2 Macc.* 6:18–31). **rise again to a better life**. Literally, "obtain a better resurrection," which means better than the OT "resurrections" just mentioned (which were really just resuscitations back to mortal life, and did not impart a perfect resurrection body).

The Hall of Faith in Hebrews 11

OT person of faith	Reference in Hebrews 11	Reference in OT
Abel	11:4	Genesis 4
Enoch	11:5	Gen. 5:18–24
Noah	11:7	Gen. 5:29–10:32
Abraham	11:8–19	Genesis 12–25; etc.
Sarah	11:11	Genesis 12–23; Isa. 51:2
Isaac	11:17–20	Genesis 17–35; etc.
Jacob	11:21	Genesis 25–50; etc.
Joseph	11:21–22	Genesis 37–50; etc.
Moses	11:23–28	Ex. 2:10 and throughout the Pentateuch; etc.
Rahab	11:31	Josh. 2:1, 3; 6:17–25
Gideon	11:32	Judges 6–8
Barak	11:32	Judges 4–5
Samson	11:32	Judges 13–16
Jephthah	11:32	Judges 11–12; 1 Sam. 12:11
David	11:32	Ruth 4; 1–2 Samuel; etc.
Samuel	11:32	1 Samuel; 1 Chronicles 6; 9; 11; 26; 2 Chron. 35:18

11:36 mocking . . . imprisonment. Much like some of the readers of Hebrews (10:32–34; 13:3). This verse is especially reminiscent of the treatment of Jeremiah (see Jer. 20:2; 37:4, 15–21), though others were similarly abused (e.g., 2 Chron. 36:15–16; also 1 Kings 22:26–27; 2 Chron. 16:7–10).

11:37 stoned . . . sawn in two. These likely represent the traditional accounts of the deaths of Jeremiah and Isaiah in early Jewish and Christian extrabiblical literature, though other prophets were also stoned (2 Chron. 24:21; Matt. 23:37; cf. Luke 11:49–51; 13:33–34; see also Introduction to Isaiah: Author and Title). **killed with the sword**. While some through faith escape the sword (Heb. 11:34), others do not (e.g., 1 Kings 19:10, 14; Jer. 2:30; 26:20–23). **skins of sheep and goats**. The clothing of prophets, such as Elijah (2 Kings 1:8) and others (Zech. 13:4; Matt. 7:15).

11:38 world was not worthy. See v. 7. Their presence in the world was itself evidence of God's grace, for their proclamation of the word of God to sinful people was a greater privilege than people deserved. **dens and caves**. Especially associated with prophets in hiding (1 Kings 18:4, 13; 19:9).

11:39–40 commended through their faith. Cf. vv. 2, 4–5. **did not receive what was promised**. Most of those mentioned in this chapter saw only preliminary glimpses of what was specifically promised (see v. 13), and all were anticipating a greater future hope (v. 16). In light of chs. 1–10, **something better for us** refers to the new covenant realities of the superior Son of God, with his superior priesthood, and the consequent eternal perfection of the faithful. **made perfect**. The perfection of believers is elsewhere the goal (10:14; 12:23; cf. 7:19; 9:9; 10:1), accomplished through the work of the perfect Son of God (2:10; 5:9; 7:28). **apart from us**. The saints of the OT, along with those of this era, will partake together of the same end-times perfection: sinless selves in deathless resurrection bodies.

12:1–29 *Endurance until the Kingdom Fully Comes.* Given past examples of faith (ch. 11) and of Jesus' own endurance of the cross (12:1–2), Christians are to run with endurance the race of faith, knowing that God disciplines his children for their good (vv. 3–11). The readers are thus also cautioned against rejecting God's grace (vv. 12–17, 25), since (in comparison with lesser yet still awesome events at Mount Sinai) the overwhelming final judgment will surely come, when God will fully establish his rule and when all the saints will join the great heavenly celebration.

12:1–2 *Jesus, Founder and Perfecter of Faith.* In light of the previous examples of faith (ch. 11), and especially in light of Jesus' own model of endurance, believers are called to endure as runners in a race.

12:1 cloud of witnesses. These are the OT "heroes of the faith" in ch. 11, as is indicated by the **therefore** in 12:1 and by the Greek wordplay between "witnesses" (*martys*, v. 1) and "commended" (*martyreō*, 11:39). "Witnesses" may have a double meaning: (1) These OT heroes witnessed to their faith by their words and their faithful lives. (2) Like spectators watching an athletic contest in an arena, they may now be watching or "witnessing" believers' lives. The first sense is a common meaning for the word, but in this verse the

2[a] Luke 24:26; Phil. 2:8; [Isa. 53:11] [b] Ps. 22:6, 7; 69:19; Isa. 53:3 [c] ch. 1:3
3[d] [Matt. 10:24; Rev. 2:3] [e] Gal. 6:9
5[f] Cited from Prov. 3:11, 12 [g] Job 5:17
6[h] Ps. 94:12; 119:67, 75; Rev. 3:19
7[i] Deut. 8:5; 2 Sam. 7:14; [Prov. 13:24; 19:18; 23:13]
8[j] [1 Pet. 5:9]
9[k] See Num. 16:22 [l] [Isa. 38:16]
10[m] [2 Pet. 1:4]; See Lev. 11:44
11[n] [1 Pet. 1:6] [o] James 3:17, 18
12[p] Cited from Isa. 35:3; [Job 4:3, 4]
13[q] Prov. 4:26, 27 [r] James 5:16; [Gal. 6:1]
14[s] See Rom. 14:19 [t] 1 Thess. 4:7 [u] Matt. 5:8; [2 Cor. 7:1; Eph. 5:5; Rev. 21:27; 22:4]
15[v] ch. 4:1; [2 Cor. 6:1; Gal. 5:4] [w] Deut. 29:18

[a]who for the joy that was set before him endured the cross, despising [b]the shame, and [c]is
seated at the right hand of the throne of God.

Do Not Grow Weary

3 [d]Consider him who endured from sinners such hostility against himself, so that you may
not grow weary or [e]fainthearted. **4** In your struggle against sin you have not yet resisted to
the point of shedding your blood. **5** And have you forgotten the exhortation that addresses
you as sons?

> [f]"My son, [g]do not regard lightly the discipline of the Lord,
> nor be weary when reproved by him.
> **6** For [h]the Lord disciplines the one he loves,
> and chastises every son whom he receives."

7 It is for discipline that you have to endure. [i]God is treating you as sons. For what son is
there whom his father does not discipline? **8** If you are left without discipline, [j]in which all
have participated, then you are illegitimate children and not sons. **9** Besides this, we have
had earthly fathers who disciplined us and we respected them. Shall we not much more
be subject to [k]the Father of spirits [l]and live? **10** For they disciplined us for a short time as it
seemed best to them, but he disciplines us for our good, [m]that we may share his holiness.
11 [n]For the moment all discipline seems painful rather than pleasant, but later it yields
[o]the peaceful fruit of righteousness to those who have been trained by it.

12 Therefore [p]lift your drooping hands and strengthen your weak knees, **13** and [q]make
straight paths for your feet, so that what is lame may not be put out of joint [r]but rather
be healed. **14** [s]Strive for peace with everyone, and for the [t]holiness [u]without which no one
will see the Lord. **15** See to it that no one [v]fails to obtain the grace of God; that no [w]"root of
bitterness" springs up and causes trouble, and by it many become defiled; **16** that no one

imagery of being **surrounded** by these witnesses gives the sense that they are eagerly watching from heaven, and the image of running **the race that is set before us** might lead one to think of an athletic race in a sports arena, with all these heroes of the faith from ch. 11 watching as present-day believers take their turn in the same race that they once ran. However, nowhere else does the NT envisage saints in heaven watching saints on earth, nor does it encourage Christians ever to pray to these believers in heaven or to ask for their prayers. Christ prays for his people (Rom. 8:34; Heb. 7:25) and is the only mediator between them and God (1 Tim. 2:5). The Holy Spirit helps their prayers (Rom. 8:26–27), and all Christians are priests with the right of direct access to God (Heb. 4:16; 10:22; 1 Pet. 2:5, 9). **lay aside**. This first exhortation pictures **sin** as a **weight** (or "impediment") to be discarded, since otherwise it ensnares or obstructs the athlete. **let us run**. A metaphor also found in Paul (1 Cor. 9:24–27; 2 Tim. 4:7–8), with a focus on **endurance** in the faith (see Heb. 12:2–3; cf. 10:32, 36).

12:2 founder. See note on 2:10. **perfecter**. Through his atoning work, Christ's perfection leads to the perfection of his people (which will be realized fully on the last day; see note on 11:39–40). **for the joy that was set before him endured**. The **cross** of Christ represents the greatest suffering in history, for Jesus not only suffered physically but also experienced God's just wrath in taking upon himself the sin of the world. Still, the promise of future reward and joy gave Jesus strength to suffer. **despising the shame**. Crucifixion, performed naked and in public, and inflicting prolonged pain on the victim, was intended to cause shame as well as death (cf. 6:6; see note on Matt. 27:35). **at the right hand**. See Heb. 1:3, 13; 8:1; 10:12.

12:3–17 *Do Not Grow Weary.* Earthly trials actually testify to the fatherly discipline of God. Such trials call for a response of endurance, and the author cautions against rejection of this character training.

12:3 Consider him. Jesus (v. 2). **endured**. Again emphasizing perseverance (as in vv. 1–2). Many of the readers could identify with the **hostility** shown to Jesus (see 10:32–34; 13:3), though on a lesser scale (12:4). **weary or fainthearted**. See v. 5.

12:4 struggle against sin. Although they are suffering persecution, the readers were not suffering martyrdom, and hence their main test is fighting their own sinful nature. **Not yet resisted to the point of shedding your blood** contrasts with Jesus' endurance of the cross (v. 2; cf. 11:37).

12:5–8 Verses 5–6 cite Prov. 3:11–12. **exhortation that addresses you as sons**. God is viewed as speaking through the proverb; God's discipline proves that he considers believers to be his sons (on sonship, see Heb. 2:10), since God **chastises every son whom he receives** (12:6; see vv. 7–8). **Discipline** (Gk. *paideia*) was a common term for childrearing through instruction, training, and correction; however, here Hebrews focuses on the call for perseverance (**endure** in v. 7) in the painful tests of life (v. 11). These tests are to their benefit, prove their sonship, and require a response of perseverance. The readers, then, should not be discouraged.

12:9–10 This lesser-to-greater analogy from the readers' own childhood training shows that it is appropriate for the heavenly Father to discipline, and it calls for a response of respect and submission; as a loving Father, the Lord always disciplines his children **for** their **good**.

12:12–13 In poetic OT language (perhaps intentionally drawn from Isaiah and Proverbs) the author exhorts his readers to endurance in the race set before them.

12:14 peace with everyone. Cf. Mark 9:50; Rom. 12:18–21; 14:19; 2 Cor. 13:11. **Holiness** is clearly expected of all Christians (**without which no one will see the Lord**). This is not salvation by works, however, for Christians are sanctified once for all by the death of Christ (Heb. 10:14); holy living is a part of the perseverance encouraged throughout Hebrews.

12:15 See to it that. As they pursue peace and holiness (v. 14), Christians should watch out for each other (cf. 3:13; 10:24–25) in order that no one falls short of the gift of eternal salvation (i.e., **fails to obtain the grace of God**; cf. 4:16; 10:29). **root of bitterness**. The author warns against "bitterness" by alluding to Deut. 29:18, which describes one who turns away from God and pursues other gods. A bitter and resentful person is like a contagious poison, spreading his resentment to others.

12:16–17 Esau is deemed **unholy** (likely due to his treating his birthright as profane; Gen. 25:33–34); **sexually immoral** probably also applies to him (there is no direct OT evidence of this, but cf. Gen. 26:34–35; 28:6–8). Clearly the author calls his readers to be holy and sexually responsible (see

is [x]sexually immoral or unholy like Esau, who sold his birthright for a single meal.
17 For you know that [y]afterward, when he desired to inherit the blessing, he was rejected, for he found no chance to repent, though he sought it with tears.

A Kingdom That Cannot Be Shaken

18 For you have not come to [z]what may be touched, a blazing fire and darkness and gloom and a tempest
19 and [a]the sound of a trumpet and a voice whose words [b]made the hearers beg that no further messages be spoken to them.
20 For they could not endure the order that was given, [c]"If even a beast touches the mountain, it shall be stoned."
21 Indeed, [d]so terrifying was the sight that Moses said, "I tremble with fear."
22 But you have come to [e]Mount Zion and to the city of the living God, [f]the heavenly Jerusalem, and to [g]innumerable angels in festal gathering,
23 and to [h]the assembly[1] of the firstborn who are [i]enrolled in heaven, and to [j]God, the judge of all, and to the spirits of the righteous made perfect,
24 and to Jesus, [k]the mediator of a new covenant, and to [l]the sprinkled blood [m]that speaks a better word than the blood of Abel.

25 See that you do not refuse him who is speaking. For [n]if they did not escape when they refused him who warned them on earth, much less will we escape if we reject him who warns from heaven.
26 At that time [o]his voice shook the earth, but now he has promised, [p]"Yet once more I will shake not only the earth but also the heavens."
27 This phrase, "Yet once more," indicates [q]the removal of things that are shaken—that is, things that have been made—in order that the things that cannot be shaken may remain.
28 Therefore let us be grateful for receiving [r]a kingdom that cannot be shaken, and thus [s]let us offer to God acceptable worship, with reverence and awe,
29 for our [t]God is a consuming fire.

[1] Or *church*

16 [x]ch. 13:4; Gen. 25:33
17 [y]Gen. 27:34, 36, 38
18 [z]Ex. 19:18; 20:18; Deut. 4:11; 5:22; [2 Cor. 3:9]
19 [a]Ex. 19:16, 19 [b]Ex. 20:19; Deut. 5:5; 18:16
20 [c]Cited from Ex. 19:12, 13
21 [d][Ex. 19:16; Deut. 9:19]
22 [e]Rev. 14:1 [f]See Gal. 4:26 [g]Jude 14
23 [h][Ex. 4:22] [i]Luke 10:20 [j]Gen. 18:25
24 [k]ch. 8:6; 9:15 [l]See ch. 10:22 [m]ch. 11:4; Gen. 4:10
25 [n]See ch. 2:3
26 [o]Ex. 19:18 [p]Cited from Hag. 2:6; [Hag. 2:21]
27 [q]See Ps. 102:26
28 [r]Dan. 2:44 [s]ch. 13:15
29 [t]Cited from Deut. 4:24; See 2 Thess. 1:8

Heb. 12:10, 14; 13:4). **afterward, when he desired to inherit the blessing, he was rejected**. Esau's failure to win back the inheritance he had rejected (Gen. 25:33–34; 27:34–40) also serves to caution the Christian community against rejecting the inheritance offered to believers (Heb. 6:4–6; 10:26–31; 12:25; on inheritance, see 1:14; 6:12; 9:15). **no chance to repent**. The author is not saying that Esau longed to repent but God refused to forgive him, for it can be seen from Peter's denials and subsequent forgiveness that those who repent are always forgiven. **though he sought it with tears**. "It" probably refers to the blessing rather than repentance. Esau still wanted the blessing. If one understands "it" to refer to repentance, then the verse likely means that Esau desired the good consequences of repentance but was not truly sorry for his sins.

12:18–29 *A Kingdom that Cannot Be Shaken.* The new covenant is far superior to the covenant at Sinai. Therefore, one must respond in faithful worship, since God will ultimately judge all people.

12:18–21 The experience of Israel at Mount Sinai (esp. Ex. 19:12–25; 20:18–21; Deut. 18:16) shows how great and fearful was the Mosaic covenant. **Moses said, "I tremble with fear."** This quote is from Deut. 9:19, where on Mount Sinai Moses feared that God might destroy Israel after their worship of the golden calf. The author may intend this allusion to warn against similar idolatry (cf. Heb. 12:15, 25–29).

12:22–24 The greatness of the new covenant exceeds the old covenant revelation at Sinai, so it is all the more important to accept the new (v. 25; cf. 10:28–31).

12:22 you have come to Mount Zion. This draws on extensive OT imagery of a new heavenly Zion/Jerusalem (e.g., Ps. 2:6; 110:2; Isa. 62:6–12; see "city" in Heb. 11:10, 16; 13:14; also, e.g., Rev. 21:1–22:5) to say that Christian believers have access, in the invisible, spiritual realm, into **the heavenly Jerusalem**, and therefore participate in worship with **innumerable angels** (cf. Heb. 1:7; also Deut. 33:2; Dan. 7:10) and the great "assembly" (Heb. 12:23) of those who have died in faith and are already in God's presence. **living God**. See note on 9:14.

12:23 assembly of the firstborn. "Firstborn" is plural in Greek and modified by "who are enrolled." Jesus was previously called *the* firstborn Son (1:6); here his followers are also granted an inheritance as if they too were firstborn sons (1:14; 2:10; 9:15; 12:5–8). **Enrolled** alludes to the book of life (e.g., Dan. 7:10; Phil. 4:3; Rev. 20:12–15), listing the true followers of Jesus. The title **judge of all** recalls previous warnings (e.g., Heb. 10:30–31). **Spirits of the righteous** refers to the saints of the old and new covenants, here portrayed as holy ("righteous") and as personally **made perfect**, which was the goal of Christ's work (10:14; 11:40), though with their reembodiment still to come at the final resurrection.

12:24 This picture of a present spiritual realm (vv. 22–24) culminates with **Jesus**. **mediator**. See notes on 8:6 and 9:15. **sprinkled blood**. See 9:11–14, 24–28; 10:19, 22, 29; 13:12, 20. The **blood of Abel** cries out a curse for vengeance (Gen. 4:10–11; cf. Heb. 11:4), but Jesus' blood brings forgiveness and atonement.

12:25 Given the superior nature of the new covenant, and the reign of Christ **who warns from heaven**, the author calls for a response of faith. **They did not escape** applies especially to the exodus generation (vv. 18–21, 26), who rejected the voice of the one who spoke (3:7–19; also cf. 4:2; 10:28–30). **much less will we escape**. A similar lesser-to-greater argument is made in 10:28–30. Most commentators believe that this refers to the danger of eternal judgment upon those who "reject him who warns from heaven." Some have argued that such rejection of God can be committed by true believers, since "we" (in the phrase "much less will we escape") includes the believing author; see the note on 3:14, however, indicating a fundamental difficulty with this view. It seems most likely to understand the "we" as a reference to the current church participants, some of whom may not have possessed true faith (see notes on 10:26–27; 10:28–29). Another view is that the warnings are addressed to true believers and that the warnings are the *means* that God uses to keep his own from committing apostasy and to challenge believers to persevere in their faith (see note on 6:4–8).

12:26–27 At that time. At Mount Sinai (v. 19). **Yet once more**, both **earth** and **the heavens** will be judged in order to establish the future reality, which is eternal (**the things that cannot be shaken**).

12:28–29 Gratitude and worship are due in light of salvation. **Acceptable worship** takes into account (in **reverence and awe**) God's holiness and his position as a judge to whom alone worship is due (see the context of Deut. 4:24, quoted here). Some say that this "acceptable worship" is depicted in the conduct described in Heb. 13:1–19 (cf. Rom. 12:1–2).

Chapter 13
1 [u]Rom. 12:10; 1 Thess. 4:9; 1 Pet. 1:22; 2 Pet. 1:7; [1 Pet. 2:17; 3:8; 1 John 3:10; 4:7, 20, 21]
2 [v]See Matt. 25:35; 1 Pet. 4:9 [w]Gen. 18:3; 19:2
3 [x]ch. 10:34; Matt. 25:36
4 [y]1 Cor. 7:38; [1 Tim. 4:3] [z]See 1 Cor. 6:9
5 [a]1 Tim. 3:3 [b]1 Tim. 6:7, 8; [Phil. 4:11]; See Matt. 6:25 [c]Cited from Josh. 1:5; [Ps. 37:25; 2 Cor. 4:9]
6 [d]Cited from Ps. 118:6; [Ps. 27:1] [e]Ps. 56:4, 11
7 [f]ver. 17, 24 [g][ch. 6:12]
8 [h]ch. 1:12; John 8:58; Rev. 1:4, 8; [2 Cor. 1:19]
9 [i]Jude 12; See Eph. 4:14 [j]See Col. 2:16
10 [k][1 Cor. 9:13; 10:18]
11 [l]See Ex. 29:14 [m]ver. 13
12 [n]ch. 9:12 [o]Matt. 21:39; 27:32; John 19:17, 20; [Acts 7:58] [p][Rev. 14:20]
13 [q]ch. 11:26; 1 Pet. 4:14
14 [r][ch. 11:10, 16; 12:28; Mic. 2:10]; See Eph. 2:19
15 [s]Eph. 5:20

Sacrifices Pleasing to God

13 Let [u]brotherly love continue. 2 [v]Do not neglect to show hospitality to strangers,
for thereby [w]some have entertained angels unawares. 3 [x]Remember those who are
in prison, as though in prison with them, and those who are mistreated, since you also
are in the body. 4 [y]Let marriage be held in honor among all, and let the marriage bed be
undefiled, for God will judge [z]the sexually immoral and adulterous. 5 Keep your life [a]free
from love of money, and [b]be content with what you have, for he has said, [c]"I will never
leave you nor forsake you." 6 So we can confidently say,

> [d]"The Lord is my helper;
> [e]I will not fear;
> what can man do to me?"

7 Remember [f]your leaders, those who spoke to you the word of God. Consider the outcome
of their way of life, and [g]imitate their faith. 8 Jesus Christ is [h]the same yesterday and today
and forever. 9 Do not be [i]led away by diverse and strange teachings, for it is good for the
heart to be strengthened by grace, [j]not by foods, which have not benefited those devoted
to them. 10 We have an altar [k]from which those who serve the tent have no right to eat.
11 For [l]the bodies of those animals whose blood is brought into the holy places by the high
priest as a sacrifice for sin are burned [m]outside the camp. 12 So Jesus also [n]suffered [o]outside
the gate in order to sanctify the people [p]through his own blood. 13 Therefore let us go to
him outside the camp and bear [q]the reproach he endured. 14 For [r]here we have no lasting
city, but we seek the city that is to come. 15 [s]Through him then let us continually offer up

13:1–25 *Concluding Exhortations and Remarks.* As he finishes his letter, the author states some specific points of application for the community (vv. 1–19), invokes a word of blessing (vv. 20–21), and greets the community (vv. 22–25).

13:1–19 *Sacrifices Pleasing to God.* As is common in other NT epistles (e.g., Romans 12–15), the author concludes the letter with a series of specific moral exhortations.

13:1 brotherly love. Relationships in the church, marked by love (6:10; 10:24), are the fruit of faith (10:32–34; ch. 11).

13:2 hospitality. The virtue of hosting and caring for visitors was especially valued in antiquity since travel was difficult and inns could be dangerous (e.g., Rom. 12:13; 1 Tim. 3:2; Titus 1:8; 1 Pet. 4:9). **entertained angels**. Cf. Gen. 18:1–15; also Judg. 6:11–24; 13:3–24.

13:3 Remember those . . . in prison. See 10:32–34; examples of believers being imprisoned include Acts 28:14–15; this command is also combined with hospitality in Matt. 25:35–36. Rather than avoiding them out of shame or fear, the church is to care for the persecuted. "Remembering" implies active response to needs. **In the body** here probably means "in the real world of everyday life" (it could also mean "in the church," though this is less likely); Christians should not separate themselves from the needs all around them.

13:4 Marriage is to be **held in honor**, and chastity in marriage is called for, with the warning that **God will judge** anyone who is **sexually immoral** (Gk. *pornos*, a general term referring to anyone who engages in sexual conduct outside of marriage between a man and a woman) or **adulterous** (Gk. *moichos*, referring to anyone who is unfaithful to a spouse). This warning is addressed to members of the church, and if they are genuine Christian believers, this judgment of God would not mean final condemnation to hell (cf. Rom. 8:1) but would bring disciplinary judgment in this life (cf. Heb. 12:5–11) or loss of reward at the last day, or both. However, in light of the earlier warning passages (3:12–14; 6:4–8; 10:26–31; 12:14–17), it is possible that such sexual immorality will be an indication that the person committing it is in fact not a true believer and not born again.

13:5–6 The antidote to **love of money** is contentment, which comes from trusting in God's promised provision (see Deut. 31:6, 8; also Josh. 1:5). The citation from Ps. 118:6 applies the idea of trusting in God for more than just financial needs (esp. in light of persecution, Heb. 13:3).

13:7 leaders. See also v. 17; the repetition may indicate some disharmony in the church. Those who **spoke** the **word of God** (likely referring to doctrinal instruction; see 6:2) are especially significant in their positive model of **faith**. The primary role of leaders is to preach and teach God's Word, and their lives should reflect the Word that is taught.

13:8 Jesus the Messiah (**Christ**) is eternally trustworthy in his position as high priest and as Son of God—**yesterday** active in creation (e.g., 1:2–4), **today** offering salvation (e.g., 4:7–10), and **forever** reigning in heaven (e.g., 10:12). This verse may be a transition from 13:7 (their leaders trusted in this Christ, and Jesus remains trustworthy) to v. 9 (strange teachings are departures from the Jesus who is always the same).

13:9–11 led away. The author warns of heresy. The central concern appears to be doctrines about **foods** (9:10; Rom. 14:17; Col. 2:16–17; 1 Tim. 4:3; cf. 1 Cor. 8:13). The author argues against such doctrines by: (1) juxtaposing them with **grace** (which truly nourishes the **heart**); (2) noting that special foods are of no spiritual benefit (cf. 1 Cor. 8:8); and (3) observing that the Christian **altar** is better than the food of the tabernacle. This may indicate that some Jewish notions (perhaps in a syncretistic mix) are being combated. Unlike most OT offerings, the tabernacle priests could not eat the sin offering from the Day of Atonement, since it was **burned outside the camp** (Lev. 16:27). However, all Christians partake of the Christian altar (i.e., Jesus' sacrifice). Some see a reference to the Lord's Supper here, while others view this as a broader reference to the saving results of the shedding of Jesus' blood.

13:12 outside the gate. Jesus went to the place of sacrificial animals (v. 11), referring to Calvary, outside the gate of Jerusalem. Jesus' sufferings and death render his people holy (**sanctify**; see 2:11; 10:10, 14), since his **blood** provides forgiveness and atonement (9:11–14).

13:13–14 Go to him outside the camp speaks metaphorically of leaving behind the love of this world and desire for its approval, and embracing the **reproach** of Christ, emulating Jesus' response to his shameful sufferings (see 12:2–3). Moreover, such Christian endurance is founded on a realization that this world is a mere temporary dwelling (**no lasting city**) en route to an eternal abode (cf. 11:14–16; 12:22–24).

13:15–16 Sacrifice of praise is a concept found repeatedly in the Psalms (Ps. 50:14, 23; 107:22; 116:17). Here it is not an offering of a sacrificial animal but the verbal praise of God's name (see also Heb. 12:28–29). **To do good and to share what you have** are also called **sacrifices** that are **pleasing to God**. When Christians realize that such things actually bring joy to God (they are "pleasing" to him), they are all the more motivated to do them, and they too find joy in the process.

[t]a sacrifice of praise to God, that is, [u]the fruit of lips that acknowledge his name. **16** Do not
neglect to do good and [v]to share what you have, for such [w]sacrifices are pleasing to God.
17 Obey [x]your leaders and submit to them, [y]for they are keeping watch over your souls, as
those who will have to [z]give an account. [a]Let them do this with joy and not with groaning,
for that would be of no advantage to you.
18 [b]Pray for us, for we are sure that we have a clear conscience, desiring to act honorably
in all things. **19** I urge you the more earnestly to do this in order [c]that I may be restored
to you the sooner.

Benediction

20 Now [d]may the God of peace [e]who brought again from the dead our Lord Jesus, [f]the
great shepherd of the sheep, by [g]the blood of the eternal covenant, **21** [h]equip you with
everything good that you may do his will, [i]working in us[1] that which is pleasing in his
sight, through Jesus Christ, [j]to whom be glory forever and ever. Amen.

Final Greetings

22 I appeal to you, brothers,[2] bear with my word of exhortation, for [k]I have written to
you briefly. **23** You should know that [l]our brother Timothy has been released, with whom
I shall see you if he comes soon. **24** Greet all [m]your leaders and all the saints. Those who
come from Italy send you greetings. **25** [n]Grace be with all of you.

[1] Some manuscripts *you* [2] Or *brothers and sisters*

15 [t]Lev. 7:12; Ps. 107:22; 116:17 [u]Isa. 57:19; Hos. 14:2; [Ps. 119:108]
16 [v]See Rom. 12:13 [w]Mic. 6:7, 8; Phil. 4:18
17 [x]ver. 7, 24 [y]See Ezek. 3:17 [z]Jer. 13:20; Ezek. 34:10 [a][Acts 20:24, 31]
18 [b]1 Thess. 5:25; 2 Thess. 3:1
19 [c][Philem. 22]
20 [d]See Rom. 15:33 [e]See Acts 2:24 [f]Isa. 63:11; See John 10:11 [g]ch. 10:29; Zech. 9:11; [Isa. 54:10]
21 [h]2 Thess. 2:17; 1 Pet. 5:10 [i]ch. 10:36; [Phil. 2:13] [j]See Rom. 11:36
22 [k][1 Pet. 5:12]
23 [l]See 1 Thess. 3:2
24 [m]ver. 7, 17
25 [n]See Col. 4:18

13:17 Obey, submit. These statements are stronger than the related comments about leaders in v. 7, for here submission to leaders is directly commanded. Such obedience will benefit those who submit, since their **souls** will be cared for and there will be harmony and **joy** in their mutual responsibilities. The leaders are also reminded that they will **give an account** to God.

13:18–19 The author, who has a **clear conscience** regarding his Christian service (cf. Acts 24:16; 2 Cor. 1:12; 2 Tim. 1:3), requests prayer, especially that he might be **restored** to those to whom he is writing. Clearly the author knew them previously, no doubt in a pastoral relationship.

13:20–21 *Benediction.* Following a common practice in NT letters (drawing on OT examples), the author invokes God's blessing on his readers. **God of peace**. Cf. Rom. 15:33; 16:20; Phil. 4:9; 1 Thess. 5:23. **from the dead**. See Heb. 5:7; 7:16. **shepherd**. Cf. John 10:1–18; 1 Pet. 2:25; 5:4. **blood**. See note on Heb. 12:24. **eternal covenant**. The new covenant (see note on 7:22) has been established forever. **equip**. The purpose of this equipping is that God's will might be done (cf. 10:36).

13:22–25 *Final Greetings.* The author concludes with a final appeal, some brief news, and closing greetings.

13:22 word of exhortation. Elsewhere the author calls for Christians to exhort/encourage one another (3:13; 10:25). He has modeled such encouragement in the extended discourse/sermon of this letter.

13:23 Timothy. Likely Paul's fellow worker (to whom Paul addressed two epistles). The author and audience had a mutual friend in Timothy, and thus both were in contact with Pauline thought (see Introduction: Author, Audience, and Title). **released**. Presumably from prison (cf. 10:32–34; 13:3).

13:24 Greet. NT letters often end with a series of greetings. **your leaders**. Perhaps driving home the submission to leaders earlier enjoined upon the church (vv. 7, 17). **saints**. A common NT expression for believers (6:10; cf. 3:1). **Those who come from Italy**. Literally, "those from Italy"; this may indicate that the author is writing from Italy, or more likely that he is elsewhere and is passing on the greeting of Italians living at his current location. This last option has led to the suggestion that the recipients were also Italians, perhaps from the churches around Rome.

13:25 Cf. Titus 3:15; also Eph. 6:24; Col. 4:18; 1 Tim. 6:21; 2 Tim. 4:22.

INTRODUCTION TO

THE LETTER OF

JAMES

Author and Title

The title of this book derives from the name of its author, James the Just (as he was called), the brother of Jesus (Matt. 13:55) and leader of the Jerusalem church (Acts 15). There is general consensus regarding his authorship, though some have challenged this on the grounds that: (1) the Greek is too polished and the rhetoric too Hellenistic for someone who never left Palestine; (2) the author never calls himself Jesus' brother; and (3) the author seems to be interacting with Pauline issues on faith and works, justification, and liberty and so had to write much later than James could have written, since he was executed in A.D. 62.

There is no good reason, however, to deny that James the Just is the author. As scholars now recognize, there was substantial contact between Jews and Gentiles, especially in Galilee where James grew up. Moreover, James is not reacting to Pauline issues but rather addressing similar themes in his own church; it is possible he is addressing a misunderstanding of Paul's teaching, but that could have been quite early since Paul wrote Galatians in A.D. 48. It is also possible that James is writing so early that he has no knowledge of any of Paul's letters.

The historicity of James the Just is well confirmed in historical literature (e.g., Josephus, *Jewish Antiquities* 20.200–201; Eusebius, *Ecclesiastical History* 2.23).

Date

Since James died in A.D. 62, the letter had to precede that date. Further, if this had been written after the apostolic council in Jerusalem (A.D. 48–49), it surely would have mentioned the issues from that momentous occasion. Thus the letter was most likely written in the early to mid-40s.

Theme

James's primary theme is living out one's faith, being a doer and not just a hearer of the word. This theme is developed in view of the social conflict between rich and poor and the spiritual conflict between factions in the church. James rebukes his readers for their worldliness and challenges them to seek divine wisdom in working out these problems and getting right with God.

Purpose, Occasion, and Background

The audience for James's letter is almost certainly Jewish Christians, as evidenced by the designations "the twelve tribes in the Dispersion" (1:1) and "assembly" (Gk. *synagōgē*, 2:2), the Jewish reasoning throughout, and James's frequent reflection on the Torah (Mosaic law). If "Dispersion" is literal as well as metaphorical (see note on 1:1; cf. Acts 2:9–11), then these are a group of Jewish Christian house churches outside Palestine, which fits the situation of persecution and poverty in the letter. More than that cannot be said, but the social situation can be gleaned from the letter. As a result of the troubles, conflict has entered the churches, and they have splintered into fighting factions. Moreover, some have fallen into a worldly lifestyle (James 1:27; 4:4) and have failed to put their faith into practice (1:19–26), with the result that they have become "double-minded," wavering between God and the world (1:8; 4:8).

The Setting of James

c. A.D. 40–45

The epistle of James was likely written to predominantly Jewish Christian house churches outside of Palestine, based on its mention of the "twelve tribes in the Dispersion" (1:1), its distinctly Jewish content, and its focus on persecution and poverty. This would mean it was sent throughout most of the ancient Mediterranean world. The author has traditionally been believed to be James the Just, the half-brother of Jesus and an early leader of the church in Jerusalem.

Key Themes

1. God is seen as a gracious giver, the unchanging Creator, merciful and compassionate, a Judge, the one and only God, a jealous God, a gracious God, and a healing God.	1:5, 17–18; 2:5, 13, 19; 4:5–6; 5:1–3, 9, 15
2. Wisdom comes "from above" and enables one both to withstand trials and to bring peace rather than discord.	1:5; 3:13, 17
3. God allows tests and trials (1:2–4), but temptation comes not from God but from self and Satan. The required response is patient endurance.	1:3, 13–14; 4:7; 5:7–8
4. The primary trial is poverty and oppression from the rich. The poor are the special focus of God's care and must be cared for by his people and not shown prejudice or ignored. The wealthy are condemned for presumptuous pride and for stealing from the poor.	1:9, 27; 2:1–5, 15–16; 4:13–17; 5:1–6
5. Apocalyptic themes are prevalent in terms of both future judgment and reward.	1:12; 2:5, 12–13; 3:1; 4:12; 5:1–7, 9, 20
6. The power of the tongue to destroy or to bring peace dominates the middle section.	3:1–4:12
7. The ethical mandate to go beyond hearing the word to living it out in daily conduct is made explicit early on and is implicit throughout the letter.	1:19–27; 2:14–26
8. Prayer is the proper response to trials, but it must not be self-seeking. It is to be central in life not only when afflicted or sick but also when cheerful. God has great power to heal, both physically and spiritually.	1:5–7; 4:2–3; 5:13–18
9. Faith, in its relationship to both works and justification, does not contradict but supplements Paul's teaching. James and Paul are united in teaching that justification comes only by the grace of God through faith but will of necessity result in works. If there are no resultant works, there was no justification in the first place.	2:14–26

History of Salvation Summary

Christians are to live with the wisdom (Prov. 1:2, 7) that befits followers of Christ. (For an explanation of the "History of Salvation," see the Overview of the Bible, pp. 23–26.)

Literary Features

Even though James begins with an epistolary salutation, the rest of the book does not have the format of an epistle but rather is a collection of wisdom sayings, much like the genre of wisdom literature as seen in the OT. The generic format of that wisdom literature is the collection of proverbs. Additionally, the book of James belongs to an ancient Greek form of satire known as the diatribe, the traits of which include: imaginary dialogues (including question and answer constructions); apostrophe (direct address to absent people or things as though they are present and can hear); metaphors taken from nature and everyday life; allusions to famous people from the past (stock instances, or well-known representations of the qualities that are under discussion); harsh addresses to readers; and heightened contrasts.

The most pervasive technique in the book of James is the proverb or aphorism, in the mode of ancient wisdom teachers. Next in frequency is the rhetorical device of direct command, expressed in the imperative mood of the verb (e.g., "be doers of the word, and not hearers only," 1:22). In fact, there are over 50 imperatives in the book's 108 verses. This abundance of commands is a signal that the writer has a practical bent and is interested in action rather than mere belief as the distinguishing characteristic of Christians. There is also a strongly persuasive stance as the author seeks to move his readers to action. The tone is continuously energetic, and satire is never far from the surface, sometimes couched in a somewhat scolding manner.

Timeline

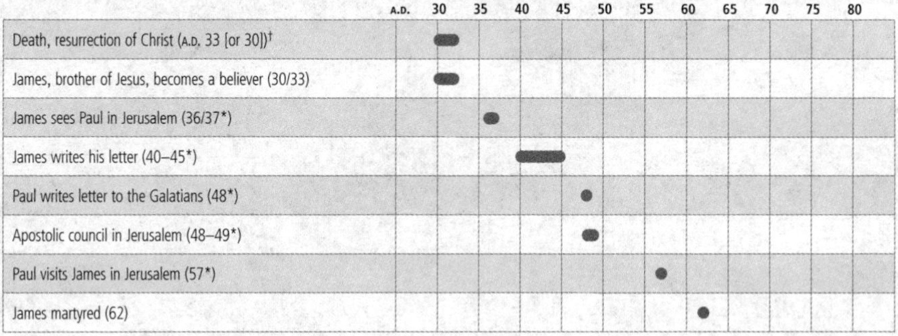

A.D. 30 35 40 45 50 55 60 65 70 75 80
Death, resurrection of Christ (A.D. 33 [or 30])†
James, brother of Jesus, becomes a believer (30/33)
James sees Paul in Jerusalem (36/37*)
James writes his letter (40–45*)
Paul writes letter to the Galatians (48*)
Apostolic council in Jerusalem (48–49*)
Paul visits James in Jerusalem (57*)
James martyred (62)

** denotes approximate date; / signifies either/or; † see The Date of Jesus' Crucifixion, pp. 1809–1810*

Outline

I. Greeting (1:1)

II. The Testing of Faith (1:2–18)
   A. Joy in trials (1:2–4)
   B. Wisdom from God for trials (1:5–8)
   C. The place of rich and poor before God (1:9–11)
   D. Reward for those who endure (1:12)
   E. The process of temptation (1:13–18)

III. Hearing and Doing the Word (1:19–27)
   A. Hearers of the word (1:19–21)
   B. Doers of the word (1:22–25)
   C. True, practical religion (1:26–27)

IV. The Sin of Partiality (2:1–13)
   A. Preferring the wealthy over the poor in the assembly (2:1–7)
   B. The royal law of love (2:8–11)
   C. Acting in light of judgment (2:12–13)

V. Faith without Works Is Dead (2:14–26)
   A. Faith without works (2:14–17)
   B. Response of a critic (2:18–20)
   C. Examples of Abraham and Rahab (2:21–26)

VI. The Sin of Dissension in the Community (3:1–4:12)
   A. Taming the tongue (3:1–12)
   B. The solution: wisdom from above (3:13–18)
   C. Warning against worldliness (4:1–12)

VII. The Sins of the Wealthy (4:13–5:12)
   A. Boasting about tomorrow (4:13–17)
   B. Warning to the rich (5:1–6)
   C. Patience in suffering (5:7–12)

VIII. The Prayer of Faith (5:13–18)

IX. Concluding Admonition (5:19–20)

THE LETTER OF

JAMES

Greeting

1 [a]James, a servant[1] of God and [b]of the Lord Jesus Christ,
To [c]the twelve tribes in [d]the Dispersion:
Greetings.

Testing of Your Faith

2 [e]Count it all joy, my brothers,[2] when you meet trials [f]of various kinds, **3** for you know
that [g]the testing of your faith [h]produces steadfastness. **4** And let steadfastness have its full
effect, that you may be [i]perfect and complete, lacking in nothing.
5 [j]If any of you lacks wisdom, [k]let him ask God, [l]who gives generously to all without
reproach, and it will be given him. **6** But [m]let him ask in faith, [n]with no doubting, for the
one who doubts is like [o]a wave of the sea that is driven and tossed by the wind. **7** For that
person must not suppose that he will receive anything from the Lord; **8** [p]he is a double-
minded man, [q]unstable in all his ways.
9 Let the lowly brother boast in his exaltation, **10** and [r]the rich in his humiliation, because
[s]like a flower of the grass[3] he will pass away. **11** For the sun rises with its scorching heat and
[t]withers the grass; its flower falls, and its beauty perishes. So also will the rich man fade
away in the midst of his pursuits.

[1] Or *slave* (for the contextual rendering of the Greek word *doulos*, see Preface) [2] Or *brothers and sisters*. The plural Greek word *adelphoi* (translated "brothers") refers to siblings in a family. In New Testament usage, depending on the context, *adelphoi* may refer either to men or to both men and women who are siblings (brothers and sisters) in God's family, the church; also verses 16, 19 [3] Or *a wild flower*

Chapter 1
1 [a]See Acts 12:17 [b]Rom. 1:1; 2 Pet. 1:1; Jude 1 [c]Luke 22:30; Acts 26:7 [d]1 Pet. 1:1; [Acts 2:9-11]; See John 7:35
2 [e]See Matt. 5:12 [f]1 Pet. 1:6
3 [g]1 Pet. 1:7 [h]Rom. 5:3; [ch. 5:11; Heb. 10:36; 2 Pet. 1:6]
4 [i]1 Thess. 5:23; See Matt. 5:48
5 [j]1 Kgs. 3:9-12; Prov. 2:3-6 [k]See Matt. 7:7 [l]Prov. 28:5
6 [m]Mark 11:24 [n]Matt. 21:21 [o][Isa. 57:20; Eph. 4:14]
8 [p]ch. 4:8 [q][2 Pet. 2:14; 3:16]
10 [r]Jer. 9:23 [s][Ps. 102:4, 11; 1 Cor. 7:31; 1 Pet. 1:24]
11 [t]Isa. 40:7

1:1 *Greeting.* Jesus chose 12 disciples to signify the **twelve tribes** and thus to identify the church as the new Israel (see note on Matt. 10:1). James reminds these Jewish Christians of their spiritual heritage as the people of God, gathered by Jesus the Messiah. **in the Dispersion**. The tribes of Israel were scattered throughout the world by the Assyrians and Babylonians. They looked forward to being regathered as a people (Jer. 31:7–14; Ezek. 37:15–28). James implies that the true Israel is now also dispersed (away from its heavenly homeland) and oppressed, but assured of their final gathering to the Lord.

1:2–18 *The Testing of Faith.* Trials test faith in order to make spiritual pilgrimages complete. They are part of the "good gifts" (v. 17) God gives his people in order to make them whole.

1:2–4 *Joy in Trials.* Trials are designed to produce spiritual maturity and should therefore be counted as joy.

1:2 Trials are "tests" that challenge faith (vv. 2–5). When trials occur, one should **count it all joy**—not meaning mere worldly, temporal happiness, but rather spiritual, enduring, "complete joy" in the Lord who is sovereign over all things, including trials.

1:3 Testing of your faith defines the meaning of a trial for the Christian: as Jesus was "tested" in the wilderness (Matt. 4:1–13), so believers are tested. The Greek *dokimion* ("testing") denotes a positive test intended to make one's faith "genuine" (cf. 1 Pet. 1:7). The result is **steadfastness**, a life of faithful endurance amid troubles and afflictions.

1:4 Steadfastness leads ultimately to perfection. Believers grow in holiness but are not yet perfected in it; such perfection will be realized only when Jesus returns.

1:5–8 *Wisdom from God for Trials.* Believers are to have an undivided faith, asking for wisdom from their ever-wise and all-generous God.

1:5 James addresses the believer who **lacks wisdom** in handling trials. Wisdom, as in the OT, is a God-given and God-centered discernment regarding the practical issues in life. Wisdom comes from prayer for God's help. God **gives generously** (with "single-minded" liberality) and **without reproach** (he does not want anyone to hesitate to come to him).

1:6 faith. A settled trust and confidence in God, based on his character and promises as revealed in Scripture (cf. Heb. 11:1). **doubting**. Vacillating between trusting God and trusting the world or one's own natural abilities. This makes a person **like a wave of the sea**, a picture of instability and uncertainty.

1:7–8 A person who doubts God's goodness dishonors him. Such a person **must not suppose that he will receive anything from the Lord**, since he is unsure whether God is good or will do good. He is a **double-minded man**, that is, in "two minds," torn between God and the world, and is therefore **unstable in all his ways** (cf. v. 6).

1:9–11 *The Place of Rich and Poor before God.* Both poverty and riches bring enormous pressure on a person to focus on the world rather than on Christ. Thus James exhorts the poor to **boast** (or glory) in their high status in Christ. The **lowly brother** will be exalted or vindicated by God. In contrast, James exhorts the **rich** to boast in their **humiliation**, (1) by realizing that their wealth is temporary and that it brings them no advantage before God, and (2) by identifying with the poor in their affliction. The church is to be a "countercultural" community, which reverses the values of the world (cf. 2:2–4). Given the context, James seems to be saying that the challenges of poverty and wealth may be one of the greatest "trials" for Christians, as would be suggested by his immediate emphasis (see 1:12) on the "blessed" status of those who remain "steadfast under trial." James also echoes Jesus' warning that "You cannot serve God and money" (Matt. 6:24).

12 [u]Blessed is the man who remains steadfast under trial, for when he has stood the test
he will receive [v]the crown of life, [w]which God has promised to those who love him. 13 Let
no one say when he is tempted, "I am being tempted by God," for God cannot be tempted
with evil, and he himself tempts no one. 14 But each person is tempted when he is lured
and enticed by his own desire. 15 Then desire [x]when it has conceived gives birth to sin, and
[y]sin when it is fully grown brings forth death.
16 Do not be deceived, my beloved brothers. 17 [z]Every good gift and every perfect gift is
from above, coming down from [a]the Father of lights [b]with whom there is no variation
or shadow due to change.[1] 18 [c]Of his own will he [d]brought us forth by the word of truth,
[e]that we should be a kind of [f]firstfruits of his creatures.

Hearing and Doing the Word

19 [g]Know this, my beloved brothers: let every person [h]be quick to hear, [i]slow to speak, [j]slow
to anger; 20 for the anger of man does not produce the righteousness of God. 21 Therefore
[k]put away all filthiness and rampant wickedness and receive with [l]meekness the implanted
word, [m]which is able to save your souls.
22 But be [n]doers of the word, and not hearers only, deceiving yourselves. 23 For if anyone
is a hearer of the word and not a doer, he is like a man who looks intently at his natural

[1] Some manuscripts *variation due to a shadow of turning*

12 [u]ch. 5:11; Matt. 10:22; 1 Pet. 3:14; [Dan. 12:12] [v]Rev. 2:10; 3:11; [1 Cor. 9:25; 2 Tim. 4:8; 1 Pet. 5:4] [w]ch. 2:5
15 [x]Job 15:35; Ps. 7:14; Isa. 59:4 [y]Rom. 5:12; 6:23
17 [z]Ps. 85:12; John 3:27; 1 Cor. 4:7 [a]1 John 1:5 [b]Mal. 3:6
18 [c]John 1:13 [d][Gal. 4:19; 1 Pet. 1:3, 23] [e][Eph. 1:12] [f]Jer. 2:3; Rev. 14:4; [Rom. 8:19-23]
19 [g]1 John 2:21 [h][Eccles. 5:1, 2] [i]Prov. 10:19; 17:27 [j]See Prov. 14:29
21 [k]Col. 3:8 [l]ch. 3:13 [m]1 Cor. 15:2; Eph. 1:13
22 [n]Rom. 2:13; [ch. 2:14-20; Matt. 7:21, 24-27; Luke 8:21; John 13:17]

1:12 *Reward for Those Who Endure.* James returns to the theme introduced in v. 2. **Crown of life** alludes not to the jewel encrusted ruler's crown but to the laurel wreath given to winners in athletic games (1 Cor. 9:25) and victorious emperors. The reward for faithful perseverance is eternal life, with all its abundant blessings (cf. Rev. 2:10).

1:13–18 *The Process of Temptation.* James turns to the other side of trials, namely, when testing becomes temptation (see note on v. 2).

1:13 God *tests* his people (e.g., Abraham, Genesis 22; Israel, Ex. 16:4; Hezekiah, 2 Chron. 32:31) so that their character is strengthened, but he never *tempts* (i.e., lures people into sin). Since **God cannot be tempted with evil**, and he is unreservedly good, he would never entice human beings to sin or seek to harm their faith. **Tempted** (Gk. *peirazō*) is the verb form of the noun translated "trial" (Gk. *peirasmos*) in James 1:12, but the context shows that different senses of the word are intended. God brings trials in order to strengthen the Christian's faith. He never tempts, however, because he never desires his people to sin. Christians should never blame God when they do wrong.

1:14 lured and enticed. A fishing metaphor for drawing prey away from shelter in order to trap them with a deadly hook. Here it is the person's evil **desire** that ensnares; in 1 Pet. 5:8–9 it is Satan who "seeks to devour." Sin is never God's fault.

1:15 The picture changes to a birth/rebirth metaphor, as full-grown **desire** bears its own child, **sin**, which itself grows into maturity and bears the grandchild, **death**. This dramatic depiction shows the terrible result when one gives in to temptation.

1:17 James moves from evil temptations (which God never gives) to the observation that **every good gift and every perfect gift** comes from God (cf. Matt. 7:11). As in James 1:5, James reminds the readers of God's goodness. In their trials, God is not tempting them to sin, but the difficulties in life are intended to strengthen and perfect them and make them more like God. God's intentions for them are always for good (cf. Rom. 8:28). There is nothing in this world that is truly good that has any other origin than **from above**, namely heaven, descending from the **Father of lights**, which refers to God as creator of the heavenly "lights" (Ps. 74:16; 136:7–9)—a prime example of his good gifts. God is unchanging in his character and therefore in his giving of good, unlike the **variation** of the night changing to day or the shifting **shadow** caused by the sun or moon.

1:18 Brought us forth by the word of truth speaks of spiritual salvation, with "us" meaning believers, the "word of truth" being the gospel, and "brought . . . forth" (that is, from the womb) being a metaphor for the new birth. The **firstfruits** of the harvest (cf. Ex. 23:16–19; Lev. 23:9–14) are pioneer believers, who are a prelude to further conversions yet to come (cf. Rom. 16:5; 1 Cor. 16:15).

1:19–27 *Hearing and Doing the Word.* The central theme of this section is practical Christianity mandated by "the word of truth," which is the gospel (v. 18), and characterized by both truly "hearing" and then resolutely "doing" the truth. Obedience is the hallmark of the true child of God.

1:19–21 *Hearers of the Word.* James encourages the church to pursue hearing the word, and to avoid hasty speech and unrighteous anger.

1:19 James echoes Jewish Wisdom tradition on the misuse of the tongue and the anger that can result (cf. Prov. 10:19; 11:12; 15:1; 17:28). **quick to hear**. Lack of listening, combined with lack of restraint in speech, leads to ill-tempered action. **Slow to anger** does not mean that all human anger is sinful (cf. Eph. 4:26), but the quick-tempered, selfish anger of the world ("the anger of man," James 1:20) betrays lack of trust in God and lack of love for others.

1:20 The self-reliant **anger of man**, even when directed against some wrongdoing, fails to recognize that mere human reproach cannot change another person's heart, and thus it **does not produce the righteousness of God**; nor indeed is such anger fully righteous itself. God is holy and righteous, requiring that his people emulate his righteous character (e.g., Lev. 19:2; Matt. 5:48; 1 Pet. 1:16). "Righteousness" here is not Pauline legal or forensic righteousness proclaimed in God's court of law (e.g., see notes on Rom. 3:20; 5:10) but is closer to the usage of the OT (Isa. 61:3) and Jesus (Matt. 3:15; 5:6, 10, 20; 6:1, 33; 21:32), in the sense of conducting one's life by the will of God, according to his standards.

1:21 Put away all filthiness pictures the stripping off of dirty clothes (cf. Rom. 13:12; Eph. 4:22; Col. 3:8) based on a desire to have nothing to do with the dirt (here, moral evil) ever again. In place of filthy behavior, the **implanted word** must take root in God's people. This idea of God planting his revealed truth reflects Deut. 30:14 ("the word is very near you. It is in your mouth and in your heart") and especially the new covenant of Jer. 31:33 ("I will put my law within them, and I will write it on their hearts"). **Save your souls** refers here to progressive sanctification and ultimately the completion of God's saving work on the last day.

1:22–25 *Doers of the Word.* Hearing the word without action is self-deceptive, while hearing that results in doing the word is a blessing.

1:22 Being **doers of the word, and not hearers only** is the only proper response to the Word of God (not only the gospel but the entirety of Scripture), allowing it to take root in one's life (cf. v. 21).

1:23–24 Looking **intently at his natural face in a mirror** and then forgetting **what he was like** demonstrates the folly of examining oneself in God's "mirror" of the "implanted word" (v. 21) and then doing nothing about it (v. 22). When one sees imperfections (as when looking in a mirror), common sense says something should be done about it.

face in a mirror. **24** For he looks at himself and goes away and at once forgets what he was like. **25** But the one who looks into the perfect law, [o]the law of liberty, and perseveres, being no hearer who forgets but a doer who acts, [p]he will be blessed in his doing.

26 If anyone thinks he is religious [q]and does not bridle his tongue but deceives his heart, this person's [r]religion is worthless. **27** Religion that is pure and undefiled before God, the Father, is this: [s]to visit [t]orphans and widows in their affliction, and [u]to keep oneself [v]unstained from the world.

The Sin of Partiality

2 My brothers,[1] [w]show no partiality as you hold the faith in our Lord Jesus Christ, [x]the Lord of glory. **2** For if a man wearing a gold ring and fine clothing comes into your assembly, and a poor man in shabby clothing also comes in, **3** and if you pay attention to the one who wears the fine clothing and say, "You sit here in a good place," [y]while you say to the poor man, "You stand over there," or, "Sit down at my feet," **4** have you not then made distinctions among yourselves and become [z]judges with evil thoughts? **5** Listen, my beloved brothers, [a]has not God chosen those who are poor in the world to be [b]rich in faith and heirs of [c]the kingdom, [d]which he has promised to those who love him? **6** But you [e]have dishonored the poor man. Are not the rich the ones who oppress you, and the ones who [f]drag you [g]into court? **7** Are they not the ones who blaspheme the honorable [h]name by which you were called?

8 If you really fulfill the royal law according to the Scripture, [i]"You shall love your neighbor as yourself," you are doing well. **9** But if you [j]show partiality, you are committing sin and are convicted by the law as transgressors. **10** For whoever keeps the whole law but fails in one point [k]has become accountable for all of it. **11** For he who said, [l]"Do not commit

[1] *Or brothers and sisters; also verses 5, 14*

25 [o]ch. 2:12; [Gal. 2:4; 5:1, 13; 1 Pet. 2:16; 2 Pet. 2:19]; See John 8:32 [p]Ps. 1:1, 2; Luke 11:28
26 [q]ch. 3:2, 3; Ps. 39:1; [ch. 3:6; Ps. 34:13; 141:3] [r]Acts 26:5
27 [s]Matt. 25:36 [t]Job 31:17, 18; Isa. 1:17, 23 [u]1 Tim. 5:22; 1 John 5:18 [v]2 Pet. 3:14

Chapter 2

1 [w]ver. 9; Lev. 19:15; Deut. 1:17; 16:19; Prov. 24:23; Rom. 2:11; Eph. 6:9 [x]1 Cor. 2:8; [Acts 7:2]
3 [y][Prov. 18:23]
4 [z]John 7:24
5 [a]1 Cor. 1:27, 28; [Job 34:19] [b]2 Cor. 8:9; Rev. 2:9; See Luke 12:21 [c]Matt. 5:3; Luke 6:20; 12:32 [d]See ch. 1:12
6 [e][1 Cor. 11:22] [f]Acts 16:19 [g]Acts 8:3; 17:6; 18:12; [ch. 5:6]
7 [h][Isa. 63:19; 65:1; Amos 9:12; Acts 15:17]
8 [i]Cited from Lev. 19:18
9 [j]ver. 1
10 [k]Matt. 5:19; Gal. 3:10
11 [l]Cited from Ex. 20:14, 13

1:25 the law of liberty (cf. 2:12). In James, the "law" and the "word" are two different ways of describing the same reality. Earlier, the "word of truth" (1:18) is the gospel of Christ, and the "law" here refers to the OT law as it has been interpreted and fulfilled in Christ. Though the OT law was "holy and righteous and good" (Rom. 7:12), it had no power by itself to enable sinful people to conform to it. Thus, the OT law did not liberate God's people but enslaved them, as Paul taught (Gal. 3:10–4:7; cf. Rom. 2:1–3:20; 5:20; 6:14–15; 7:1–25). But the law is one of "liberty" when it comes along with the word of the gospel and the power of the Holy Spirit to change hearts. See also note on James 2:12.

1:26–27 *True, Practical Religion.* This section on obedience (vv. 19–27) concludes with three characteristics of the one whose **religion** is **pure and undefiled**, that is, one who "does" the word. First, he refuses self-deception and bridles **his tongue**, which means he keeps a tight rein on his speech like a bridle controlling a horse. Second, he shows mercy and love to the oppressed. **Orphans** and **widows** were frequent OT examples of this (see Deut. 10:18; Isa. 1:17; Jer. 7:5–7) because of their particularly helpless state (on widows in NT times, see note on 1 Tim. 5:3–16). Third, he remains **unstained from the world**; James uses the sacrificial language of "the lamb without blemish" (Ex. 12:5; 1 Pet. 1:19) to describe the pure religious person.

2:1–13 *The Sin of Partiality.* The problem of the poor and the rich, already emphasized in 1:9–11, 27, now comes to center stage with this warning about discriminating against the poor in favor of the wealthy in the Christian assembly.

2:1–7 *Preferring the Wealthy over the Poor in the Assembly.* James shows the fundamental incompatibility of holding faith in Christ and showing partiality among people.

2:1 partiality as you hold the faith. There is no place for prejudice in the life of faith. "Partiality" combines a group of terms signifying "to accept/judge according to face" and refers to favoritism shown on the basis of status in society. **Jesus**, according to James, is the exalted and glorious **Lord** and **Christ**, and is always to be thought of as such.

2:2–4 Assembly probably refers to a Christian house church. Here two types of people arrive: one with a **gold ring and fine clothing**, and another with **shabby clothing**. The wealthy person is told to **sit here in a good place**, a place of honor, perhaps in the front, while the poor person is shown contempt and told either to **stand** (probably in the back) or **sit down at my feet** like a servant. Those who make such **distinctions** show themselves to be **judges with evil thoughts**. Christians are not to "judge" each other (Matt. 7:1–5; Rom. 14:4; 1 Cor. 5:12), and to do so can only mean one's mind is consumed with evil "thoughts" (Gk. *dialogismos*, which can mean "opinions," "reasoning," or "conclusions").

2:5 chosen . . . to be rich in faith. Using the language of election, James declares that the poor have a special place in God's economy of salvation. They are rich in an eternal sense because they are **heirs of the kingdom** (cf. "poor in spirit, . . . theirs is the kingdom of heaven," Matt. 5:3).

2:6–7 oppress you. This oppression, or exploitation, reflects a situation of radical social polarization in the first century, with merchants and landowners taking land and possessions from the poor (cf. 5:1–6). James challenges his Christian readers as to why they would honor the rich in the assembly when it is the **rich** unbelievers of the world who **blaspheme** the **name** of Christ. **drag you into court**. As frequently recorded in the OT (e.g., Amos 4:1; Hab. 1:4; Mal. 3:5), the wealthy often used the court system to steal from the poor. This situation was the primary reason for the revolts in Galilee that led to the war of A.D. 66–70.

2:8–11 *The Royal Law of Love.* Favoritism and discrimination are violations of the kingdom law of love.

2:8 Royal law (Gk. *basilikos*), i.e., "law belonging to the king," with reference here to God's law in Lev. 19:18 ("love your neighbor"; cf. Matt. 22:34–40) as the apex of kingdom rules for ethical conduct. Cf. Rom 13:8–10.

2:9 Partiality is the antithesis of the love command (see v. 8). Favoritism toward the rich breaks the OT commands to treat the poor equitably (Lev. 19:15; Deut. 16:19; Job 34:19) and is a serious transgression of God's **law**.

2:10–11 accountable for all of it. The law was considered an interdependent whole, and any infraction constituted a breaking of the law as a whole. Jesus said, "not an iota, not a dot, will pass from the Law until all is accomplished" (Matt. 5:18). Thus favoritism (James 2:9) makes one "accountable" (Gk. *enochos*, a legal term for "liable" or "guilty" before God's court) for the **whole law**.

adultery," also said, [l]"Do not murder." If you do not commit adultery but do murder, you
have become a transgressor of the law. 12 So speak and so act as those who are to be judged
under [m]the law of liberty. 13 For [n]judgment is without mercy to one who has shown no
mercy. Mercy triumphs over judgment.

Faith Without Works Is Dead

14 What good is it, my brothers, if someone says he has faith [o]but does not have works?
Can that faith save him? 15 [p]If a brother or sister is poorly clothed and lacking in daily
food, 16 [q]and one of you says to them, "Go in peace, be warmed and filled," without giving
them the things needed for the body, what good[1] is that? 17 So also faith by itself, if it does
not have works, is dead.

18 But someone will say, "You have faith and I have works." Show me your faith [r]apart
from your works, and I will show you my faith [s]by my works. 19 [t]You believe that God is
one; you do well. Even [u]the demons believe—and shudder! 20 Do you want to be shown,
you foolish person, that faith apart from works is useless? 21 [v]Was not Abraham our
father justified by works when he offered up his son Isaac on the altar? 22 You see that
[w]faith was active along with his works, and faith was completed [x]by his works; 23 and
the Scripture was fulfilled that says, [y]"Abraham believed God, and it was counted to

[1] *Or benefit*

11 [l]Cited from Ex. 20:14, 13
12 [m]See ch. 1:25
13 [n]Job 22:6-11; Ps. 18:25, 26; Prov. 21:13; Ezek. 25:11-14; Matt. 6:15; 18:32-35; Luke 6:38
14 [o][ch. 1:22]
15 [p][Job 31:19, 20]; See Luke 3:11
16 [q]1 John 3:17, 18
18 [r][Rom. 3:28; 4:6; Heb. 11:33] [s]Matt. 7:16, 17; Gal. 5:6
19 [t]Deut. 6:4; [Rom. 2:17-25] [u]Matt. 8:29; Mark 1:24; 5:7; Luke 4:33, 34; Acts 16:17; 19:15
21 [v]Gen. 22:9, 12, 16-18
22 [w]Heb. 11:17 [x]See 1 Thess. 1:3
23 [y]Rom. 4:3; Gal. 3:6; Cited from Gen. 15:6

2:12–13 *Acting in Light of Judgment.* Believers must speak and act in accordance with the law of liberty and with a view to the coming judgment.

2:12 the law of liberty. True freedom is freedom to obey God and do what pleases him. The law of Christ provides freedom from sin through the gospel. In the context of James's discussion of rich and poor (vv. 1–7), he may also be suggesting that God's law will set the poor free from prejudice, oppression, and exploitation. Every Christian will be **judged** by God (1 Cor. 3:12–15; 2 Cor. 5:10; 1 Pet. 1:17).

2:13 For judgment is without mercy to one who has shown no mercy. This proverbial saying sums up the implications of vv. 1–12 and leads into the "faith without works" discussion in vv. 14–26. It was the core of Roman law (*lex talionis*, "the law of retribution"), but more importantly it is central to God's law: what you do to others will be done to you in the judgment (i.e., rewarded for good and punished for evil). **Mercy triumphs over judgment** does not, in this context, mean that God's mercy is extended to believers at the judgment. Rather, believers' acts of mercy (e.g., caring for the poor and hurting) will mean that they are vindicated at the judgment (cf. Matt. 25:34–40). Mercy was an essential OT requirement for dealing with the poor (Mic. 6:8; Zech. 7:9–10). Mercy is likewise a requirement of believers in the NT (e.g., Matt. 5:7; 6:15; 18:32–35), or they will experience God's judgment rather than his mercy.

2:14–26 *Faith without Works Is Dead.* James continues the theme that hearing/faith must lead to doing/works. Although it may seem as if James is contradicting Paul's "by grace you have been saved through faith . . . not a result of works" (Eph. 2:8–9), in reality there is no dichotomy between faith and works, for Paul and James would agree that the basis of salvation is grace alone through faith, with works not the *basis* but the necessary *result* thereof (Eph. 2:10).

2:14–17 *Faith without Works.* Faith that is not accompanied by action is useless and dead, unable to save.

2:14 What good . . . ? The form of the question indicates that a negative answer (i.e., "no good") is expected. The Greek particle *mē* at the beginning of the next question (**Can that faith save him?**) shows that James again expects a negative answer. If someone **says he has faith** but lacks the resulting evidential works, one must doubt that he has been saved. James is not implying that even genuine faith is the basis of salvation; rather, it is the means and instrument by which one is saved (see Eph. 2:8–9).

2:15–16 An illustration of what faith without works looks like in everyday life. In itself the phrase **Go in peace, be warmed and filled** is a pious wish and prayer for the welfare of the poor, but in reality it is a cop-out, masking a refusal to help the person in need. There is no **good** (Gk. *ophelos*, "profit, honor") in such a prayer. "What good is it?" frames vv. 14–16.

2:17 dead. Useless, without any life at all. It brings no results, and cannot lead to salvation (v. 14). There can be no true faith that fails to produce **works** (here seen as care for the poor, but including good works of all kinds).

2:18–20 *Response of a Critic.* An objector argues that faith and works are indeed separable, and James responds that faith can be shown only through righteous deeds.

2:18 But someone will say. As was common in Hellenistic rhetoric, James introduces a hypothetical respondent into his discussion of faith and works, continuing his argument against those who think that faith can save without works.

2:19 God is one. This affirmation of monotheism stems from the core Jewish creed called the *Shema* (Deut. 6:4; see Mark 12:29; Rom. 3:30). But James stresses its inadequacy, since **even the demons believe** this, and they **shudder**. Mere mental assent to the Christian faith does not save anyone. The faith that saves, as both Paul and James affirm, embraces the truth of the gospel and acts accordingly.

2:21–26 *Examples of Abraham and Rahab.* James continues his rebuttal by citing the examples of Abraham and Rahab, who were both shown by their deeds to be righteous.

2:21 Abraham . . . justified by works. On the surface James may seem to contradict Paul. I.e., Paul denies that Abraham was "justified by works" (Rom. 4:2), arguing from Gen. 15:6 that Abraham's *faith* "was counted to him as righteousness" (Rom. 4:3). However, James's assertion in this verse (that "Abraham [was] . . . justified by works") is based not on Gen. 15:6 but on Gen. 22:9–10, where (many years later) Abraham began to offer Isaac as a sacrifice. Thus James apparently has a different sense of the word "justify" in view here, as evidenced by the different Scripture passages, and the different events in Abraham's life, to which James and Paul refer. The primary way in which Paul uses the word "justify" (Gk. *dikaioō*) emphasizes the sense of being *declared righteous by God through faith*, on the basis of Jesus' atoning sacrifice (Rom. 3:24–26), whereas the primary way that James uses the word "justify" (Gk. *dikaioō*) here in James 2:21 seems to emphasize the way in which *works demonstrate that someone has been justified*, as evidenced by the good works that the person does (cf. Matt. 12:33–37). Some others hold a similar view, which understands "justify" (Gk. *dikaioō*) here to mean *to declare someone to be righteous* because, at the final judgment, the person's works give evidence of true saving faith. See note on Gal. 2:16.

2:22 faith was completed by his works. James does not disagree that faith alone saves (Rom. 3:28). "Completed" (Gk. *eteleiōthē*) often means

23[z]2 Chr. 20:7; Isa. 41:8
25[a]Heb. 11:31 [b]Josh. 2:1-22; 6:23
Chapter 3
1[c]Matt. 23:8; [Rom. 2:20, 21; 1 Tim. 1:7]
2[d]1 Kgs. 8:46; Prov. 20:9; Eccles. 7:20; 1 John 1:8 [e][Matt. 12:37] [f]See ch. 1:26
3[g]Ps. 32:9
5[h][Ps. 12:3, 4; 73:8, 9]
6[i]Ps. 120:2-4; Prov. 16:27 [j]Matt. 15:18
8[k]Ps. 140:3; Eccles. 10:11; Rom. 3:13
9[l]See Gen. 1:26

him as righteousness"—and he was called a [z]friend of God. 24 You see that a person is
justified by works and not by faith alone. 25 And in the same way was not also [a]Rahab
the prostitute justified by works [b]when she received the messengers and sent them out
by another way? 26 For as the body apart from the spirit is dead, so also faith apart from
works is dead.

Taming the Tongue

3 [c]Not many of you should become teachers, my brothers, for you know that we who
teach will be judged with greater strictness. 2 For [d]we all stumble in many ways. And
if anyone does not stumble in what he says, [e]he is a perfect man, [f]able also to bridle his
whole body. 3 If we put [g]bits into the mouths of horses so that they obey us, we guide their
whole bodies as well. 4 Look at the ships also: though they are so large and are driven by
strong winds, they are guided by a very small rudder wherever the will of the pilot directs.
5 So also the tongue is a small member, yet [h]it boasts of great things.

How great a forest is set ablaze by such a small fire! 6 And [i]the tongue is a fire, a world
of unrighteousness. The tongue is set among our members, [j]staining the whole body,
setting on fire the entire course of life,[1] and set on fire by hell.[2] 7 For every kind of beast
and bird, of reptile and sea creature, can be tamed and has been tamed by mankind, 8 but
no human being can tame the tongue. It is a restless evil, [k]full of deadly poison. 9 With it
we bless our Lord and Father, and with it we curse people [l]who are made in the likeness
of God. 10 From the same mouth come blessing and cursing. My brothers,[3] these things
ought not to be so. 11 Does a spring pour forth from the same opening both fresh and salt
water? 12 Can a fig tree, my brothers, bear olives, or a grapevine produce figs? Neither can
a salt pond yield fresh water.

[1] *Or wheel of birth* [2] Greek *Gehenna* [3] *Or brothers and sisters; also verse 12*

"bring to maturity." Full-grown and genuine faith is seen in the good deeds it produces.

2:23 James uses Gen. 15:6 in a way that complements rather than contradicts Paul (Rom. 4:1–9; Gal. 3:6), for he sees it as having been **fulfilled** (see James 2:22) in Abraham's offering of Isaac (Genesis 22). James centers on Abraham's act of obedience while Paul centers on God's declaration of Abraham's righteousness. Abraham **was called a friend of God**, in contrast to those who have no acts of obedience to prove their claims to faith and are therefore seen to be friends of this world (James 4:4).

2:24 not by faith alone. James again seems at first to contradict Paul's teaching that one is justified by faith alone (Rom. 3:28), but the two are compatible. For James, "faith alone" means a bogus kind of faith, mere intellectual agreement without a genuine personal trust in Christ that bears fruit in one's life. On **justified**, see note on James 2:21. James, in agreement with Paul, argues that true faith is never alone, that it always produces works (cf. Eph. 2:10).

2:25 Rahab the prostitute believed the stories of God's saving work for the Hebrews (Josh. 2:8–11). So, at some personal risk, she hid the Jewish spies from her own people, then lowered them on a rope so they could escape (Josh. 2:15). Thus she became a model of faith completed in works.

3:1–4:12 *The Sin of Dissension in the Community.* This section, the lengthiest of the letter, has an ABA pattern: A, danger of the tongue (3:1–12); B, the solution, "wisdom from above" (3:13–18); A, danger of the tongue (4:1–12). The main issue is the problem of dissension (4:1) and slander (3:9; 4:11), perhaps beginning with the leaders/teachers (3:1) but also involving the whole "body" of the church (3:6).

3:1–12 *Taming the Tongue.* James establishes the general principle that small things can cause great results (vv. 1–5a) then more specifically applies this to the power of the tongue to destroy (vv. 5b–12).

3:1 Teachers were important in the early church (Acts 2:42; Rom. 12:7; 1 Cor. 12:28; Eph. 4:11), and those who were ambitious sought teacher status for the wrong reasons. However, with greater responsibility comes greater expectations by God (Luke 12:48; Heb. 13:17), and teachers **will be judged with greater strictness** (lit., "greater judgment"), since they are accountable for more.

3:2 in what he says. A person's words reflect his character and thus are a key to his whole being. James emphasizes the importance of good works but also acknowledges that all Christians **stumble** (a metaphor for sinning; Gk. *ptaiō*, translated "fails" in 2:10) **in many ways**. James's call for good works, therefore, must not be seen as expecting perfection. When James says that a person who can control his mouth is a **perfect man**, he probably has absolute perfection in view. It is a perfection, however, that will be attainable only in heaven. Still, believers should always seek to grow in holiness.

3:3–4 Bits in a horse's mouth and the **small rudder** on a ship are examples of very small things that control large objects. The tongue, one of the smaller organs of the body, has a similar control over everything a person is and does.

3:5–6 boasts of great things. Pride (cf. "bitter jealousy," "boast," v. 14) is a major cause of the misuse of the tongue. In a progressive series framed by the imagery of fire, the tongue is presented in all its terrible potential. The **small fire** is the proud "boast" or other careless use of the tongue, and the great forest fire is the resulting conflagration. **a world of unrighteousness**. The tongue represents and puts into expression all the wickedness of the world. **The entire course of life** (lit., "the cycle of existence") likely means the "ups and downs" of life. The tongue turns upside down every aspect of life in the community as well as in the individual. **set on fire by hell**. Evil speech destroys because it comes from Satan himself.

3:9 It is both hypocrisy and folly to **bless** God during a worship service and then, after the service, to **curse** someone made in God's image (see Gen. 1:26–27). If the "curse" implies the common practice of invoking the name of God against the person, then this is doubly heinous.

3:11–12 In three illustrations of ridiculous natural contrasts, James drives home the point that blessing God while cursing his people cannot be countenanced. **spring**. Springs were the key to survival in dry Palestine, and the placement of villages and towns tended to depend on their presence. **olives . . . figs**. Just as no tree would produce two kinds of fruit, so also a true believer would not produce both blessings of God and curses toward others.

Wisdom from Above

13 Who is wise and understanding among you? [m]By his good conduct let him show his
works [n]in the meekness of wisdom. **14** But if you have bitter [o]jealousy and selfish ambition in your hearts, do not boast and be false to the truth. **15** This is not [p]the wisdom that
comes down from above, but is earthly, unspiritual, [q]demonic. **16** For where jealousy and
selfish ambition exist, there will be disorder and every vile practice. **17** But [r]the wisdom
from above is first pure, then [s]peaceable, gentle, open to reason, [t]full of mercy and good
fruits, [u]impartial and [v]sincere. **18** And [w]a harvest of righteousness [x]is sown in peace by
those who make peace.

Warning Against Worldliness

4 What causes quarrels and what causes fights among you? Is it not this, that your passions[1] are [y]at war within you?[2] **2** You desire and do not have, so you murder. You covet
and cannot obtain, so you fight and quarrel. You do not have, because you do not ask.
3 You ask and do not receive, because you ask [z]wrongly, to spend it on your passions. **4** [a]You
adulterous people![3] Do you not know that friendship with the world is enmity with God?
[b]Therefore whoever wishes to be a friend of the world makes himself an enemy of God.
5 Or do you suppose it is to no purpose that the Scripture says, "He yearns jealously over
the spirit [c]that he has made to dwell in us"? **6** But [d]he gives more grace. Therefore it says,

[1] Greek *pleasures;* also verse 3 [2] Greek *in your members* [3] Greek *You adulteresses!*

13 [m]ch. 2:18 [n]ch. 1:21
14 [o]ver. 16; Acts 5:17; Rom. 2:8; 2 Cor. 12:20; Gal. 5:20; Phil. 1:17; 2:3; [Rom. 13:13]
15 [p]ch. 1:17 [q][1 Kgs. 22:22; 2 Thess. 2:9, 10; 1 Tim. 4:1; Rev. 2:24]
17 [r][1 Cor. 2:6, 7] [s]Heb. 12:11 [t][Luke 6:36] [u]ch. 2:4 (Gk.) [v]Rom. 12:9
18 [w]Prov. 11:18; Isa. 32:17; Hos. 10:12; Amos 6:12; Phil. 1:11 [x]Matt. 5:9; Gal. 6:7, 8

Chapter 4

1 [y]Rom. 7:23; 1 Pet. 2:11
3 [z][1 John 5:14]
4 [a]Isa. 54:5; Jer. 2:2 [b]John 15:19; 1 John 2:15; [Matt. 6:24]
5 [c]1 Cor. 6:19; 2 Cor. 6:16
6 [d]Isa. 54:7, 8; See Matt. 13:12

3:13–18 *The Solution: Wisdom from Above.* These verses could be called "the tale of two cities"—the realm of wisdom (framing the passage in vv. 13, 17) contrasted with that of selfish ambition. The one "from above" leads to "peace," while the "earthly" one leads to "disorder."

3:13 wise and understanding . . . conduct. Wisdom for James is not merely intellectual but also behavioral. **meekness of wisdom**. Meekness (Gk. *prautēs*, translated "gentleness" in Gal. 5:23) was considered weakness by the Greeks, but Jesus elevated it to a primary Christian virtue (Matt. 5:5; 11:29). Meekness comes not from cowardice or passivity but rather from trusting God and therefore being set free from anxious self-promotion.

3:14 Bitter jealousy and selfish ambition are the antithesis of true wisdom as characterized by "meekness" (v. 13). They are also far different from the righteous character of a "jealous God" (Ex. 20:5; 34:14; Deut. 4:24; see James 4:5), who appropriately yearns for his own honor and the loyal devotion of his people, while the envious yearn for what does not belong to them. "Selfish ambition" is a divisive willingness to split the group in order to achieve personal power and prestige (it is translated "rivalry" in Gal. 5:20; Phil. 1:17; 2:3).

3:15 earthly, unspiritual, demonic. James describes worldly behavior in terms that "progress" from bad to worse, recalling the list in vv. 5b–6. Such behavior is ultimately earthbound, absolutely sensual as opposed to spiritual, and its origin is in the cosmic powers of darkness.

3:16 The final result of such Satan-driven conflict can only be **disorder and every vile practice**. "Disorder" (Gk. *akatastasia*) connotes a chaotic frenzy of fighting (cf. 4:1) in the church. The related adjective (Gk. *akatastatos*) means "unstable" (1:8) and "restless" (3:8).

3:17 The answer to the "disorder" of v. 16 is to seek **wisdom from above**, which produces character qualities beginning with purity and concluding with peace (cf. Gal. 5:22–23, where godly qualities are the fruit of the Spirit). **first pure, then**. Purity (blamelessness) is the primary virtue, with the rest providing aspects of this moral purity. **Peaceable** is the polar opposite of "selfish ambition" and the discord it produces. Peace, further emphasized in James 3:18, is one of the critical attributes of the pure believer (Matt. 5:9; Gal. 5:22; Heb. 12:11).

3:18 The legacy of those who bring **peace** rather than conflict is a **harvest of righteousness**. The "fruit" that comes from peacemaking in the Christian community will be the righteous conduct that God will bless (but this is not produced by "the anger of man"; see note on 1:20).

4:1–12 *Warning against Worldliness.* This is written in the rhetorical form of a diatribe against those who fracture the community due to "selfish ambition" (3:14). Such people are God's enemies (4:4) and the devil's allies (v. 7), and they must repent (vv. 8–10). Finally, this all returns to the tongue, i.e., "speaking evil" against others in the community (vv. 11–12).

4:1 In contrast to those who make peace, **quarrels** and **fights** are caused by the **passions** or self-centered desires ("hedonism" comes from Gk. *hēdonē*, "passions") that are causing these people to make **war** against each other in the church. This is extremely violent language for dissension, and some even think it should be taken literally of people killing each other (v. 2), though it is best to view this as a metaphor for the devastating effect of unrestrained hostility.

4:2 This verse consists of several short statements; there was no punctuation in ancient Greek, and various translations connect the statements in different ways. The ESV punctuation works well when comparing this verse to 3:13–18: people **desire** and **covet** (Gk. *zēloō*, cf. *zēlos*, "jealousy," 3:14), which leads to the terrible wars and infighting in the church. **You do not have, because you do not ask** is a reminder that believers should ask God for what they seek rather than fighting each other. Prayerlessness results in failure to receive many of God's blessings. James does not imply that God wills to grant sinful, selfish desires (4:3), but bringing requests before God can have a purifying influence on one's desires.

4:3 you ask wrongly. Not all prayers are pleasing to God, only those consistent with his will as revealed in Scripture (cf. 1 John 5:14–15 and notes). Rather than seeking to honor God and advance his kingdom purposes, such prayers seek only to gratify self-centered **passions** (Gk. *hēdonē*, see note on v. 1) or desires. James is not saying all pleasure is wrong (cf. Gen. 1:31; Ps. 16:11; 84:1–4, 10–12; 1 Tim. 6:17), only pleasure that does not have the glory of God as the goal (1 Cor. 10:31).

4:4 Adulterous people recalls OT prophets who used this language to describe Israel's unfaithfulness to God (e.g., Jer. 2:20; 3:6–10; Hos. 1:2). Such people have chosen **friendship with the world** by imitating worldly ways of thinking and worldly activities, making them enemies **of God**. It will always be impossible to satisfy the expectations of unbelievers, whose hearts are set on this world (1 John 2:15–16; 5:19), and at the same time please God (Gal. 1:10; 2 Tim. 3:12; 1 John 3:13). Cf. also Matt. 6:24; James often alludes to the teaching of Jesus (see chart, p. 2397), which is not surprising if he was Jesus' earthly brother.

4:5 He yearns jealously over the spirit that he has made to dwell in us. God created mankind with a "spirit," and he deeply desires that our spirits worship him (cf. John 4:23–24). Some interpreters believe the verse speaks of human jealousy ("The spirit that he has made to live in us envies intensely"). But the idea of divine jealousy fits the context best, since the surrounding verses (James 4:4, 6, 7, 8) deal with man's relationship with God. **Scripture says**. See further the note on 3:14 regarding references to a "jealous God."

4:6 God's **grace** will be extended to those who are **humble** before him; cf. Prov. 3:34 (cf. also James 4:10; 1 Pet. 5:5). **God opposes** means he resists and sends judgment, for the **proud** have chosen the praise and the methods of the world and are acting as God's enemies (James 4:4).

6[e]1 Pet. 5:5; Cited from Prov. 3:34 (Gk.)
7[f]1 Pet. 5:8, 9; [Eph. 4:27; 6:11]
8[g]2 Chr. 15:2; Lam. 3:57; Zech. 1:3; Mal. 3:7; [Luke 15:20] [h]Isa. 1:16 [i]Jer. 4:14 [j]ch. 1:8
9[k][Matt. 5:4]
10[l]ver. 6; Isa. 57:15; [Luke 1:52]; See Matt. 23:12
11[m]2 Cor. 12:20; 1 Pet. 2:1; [ch. 5:9] [n]See Matt. 7:1
12[o]Isa. 33:22 [p]ch. 5:9 [q]Matt. 10:28 [r]Rom. 14:4
13[s]Prov. 27:1; Luke 12:18-20
14[t]Ps. 102:3; [Job 7:7]
15[u]See Acts 18:21
16[v][1 Cor. 5:6]
17[w][Luke 12:47, 48; 2 Pet. 2:21]; See John 9:41

[e]"God opposes the proud, but [d]gives grace to the humble." 7 Submit yourselves therefore
to God. [f]Resist the devil, and he will flee from you. 8 [g]Draw near to God, and he will draw
near to you. [h]Cleanse your hands, you sinners, and [i]purify your hearts, [j]you double-minded.
9 [k]Be wretched and mourn and weep. Let your laughter be turned to mourning and your
joy to gloom. 10 [l]Humble yourselves before the Lord, and he will exalt you.
11 [m]Do not speak evil against one another, brothers.[1] The one who speaks against a brother
or [n]judges his brother, speaks evil against the law and judges the law. But if you judge the
law, you are not a doer of the law but a judge. 12 There is only [o]one lawgiver and [p]judge, he
who is able to save and [q]to destroy. But [r]who are you to judge your neighbor?

Boasting About Tomorrow

13 Come now, you who say, [s]"Today or tomorrow we will go into such and such a town
and spend a year there and trade and make a profit"— 14 yet you do not know what tomorrow will bring. What is your life? For [t]you are a mist that appears for a little time and then
vanishes. 15 Instead you ought to say, [u]"If the Lord wills, we will live and do this or that."
16 As it is, you boast in your arrogance. [v]All such boasting is evil. 17 [w]So whoever knows the
right thing to do and fails to do it, for him it is sin.

[1] *Or brothers and sisters*

4:7–8a The only way to **resist the devil** is by also submitting and drawing near to God (cf. 1 Cor. 10:13). Satan will be defeated and will have to **flee**, as indeed he did from Christ (Luke 4:13).

4:8b–9 Cleanse and **purify** are OT terms for ritual purity (e.g., the priests at the bronze basin, Ex. 30:18) and ethical purity. **Laughter** shows how casually James's readers were treating their sin. The only proper reaction to God's impending judgment is to **be wretched and mourn and weep**, as is seen often in the OT (e.g., Isa. 15:2; 22:4; Jer. 6:26).

4:10 Returning to the theme emphasized in v. 6, it is the **humble** whom God will **exalt** (cf. Matt. 23:12 par.; Luke 1:52; 14:11; 18:14; 1 Pet. 5:6). But as long as people exalt themselves, God will not exalt them.

4:11 James restates the basic problem behind the issues discussed in 3:1–4:10: the misuse of the tongue to **speak evil** or to slander others. Speaking ill of others is the result of all the arrogant boasting (3:5), jealousy (vv. 14, 16), self-centered desires (4:1, 3), and pride (v. 6) that James is warning against. Such slanderous conduct is decried in both the OT (Lev. 19:16; Ps. 50:20; Jer. 6:28) and NT (Rom. 1:30; 2 Cor. 12:20; 1 Pet. 2:1). **judges the law**. The "law" likely refers to these OT laws against slander, particularly Lev. 19:16, which leads to 19:18, "You shall love your neighbor as yourself," which James calls "the royal law" (James 2:8). Yet it also includes in a broader sense Jesus' kingdom laws regarding love for neighbor (Matt. 22:39) and for one another (John 13:34–35; 15:12, 17). Those who inappropriately judge others (Matt. 7:1–5; Rom. 2:1; 1 Cor. 4:5) break God's law and show contempt for God.

4:12 When a person begins to "judge the law," he is usurping the place of the **one lawgiver and judge**. God alone gave the law, and he alone is judge of all (Ps. 9:19; Isa. 2:4; Joel 3:12). **to save and to destroy**. Possibly an implicit message to the divisive boasters, warning them of future judgment.

4:13–5:12 *The Sins of the Wealthy.* James condemns the sins of the wealthy (arrogant presumption, 4:13–17; and robbing the poor, 5:1–6), then issues a call for patience in suffering (5:7–11).

4:13–17 *Boasting about Tomorrow.* James addresses merchants, showing that the sovereignty of God precludes presumption and arrogance in making one's plans.

4:13 trade and make a profit. On the surface this sounds like good business sense, but it masks a secular worldview that ignores God. These people are probably Christians belonging to the wealthy merchant class, whereas the rich people mentioned in 5:1–6 are probably not believers (cf. 2:6–7).

4:14 you. These business people think they control events but fail to recognize God's providential control and the temporary nature of **life**, which is like a **mist** that can fade away at any moment. Planning and investing are not wrong, but arrogant self-confidence and boasting are.

4:15 The key to vv. 13–17 is **if the Lord wills**, with "Lord" referring to Yahweh as the Creator who sustains the universe and whose will controls all that happens. Every business decision must be based on submission to God's will.

4:17 Fails to do it describes what are commonly called "sins of omission." It is not only what people do that matters; the good that they fail to do is equally important to God.

Echoes of Jesus' Sermon on the Mount in James

James	Teaching	Matthew
1:2	joy amid trials	5:10–12
1:4	exhortation to be perfect	5:48
1:5	asking God for good things	7:7–11
1:17	God the giver of good	7:11
1:20	against anger	5:22
1:22	hearers and doers of the word	7:24–27
2:5	poor inherit the kingdom	5:3, 5
2:10	keeping the whole law	5:19
2:13	merciful receive mercy	5:7
3:12	know them by their fruits	7:16
3:18	blessings of peacemakers	5:9
4:2–3	ask and you will receive	7:7–8
4:4	serving God vs. friendship with the world	6:24
4:9–10	consolation for mourners	5:4
4:11–12	against judging others	7:1–5
4:13–14	living for today	6:34
5:2–5	moth and rust spoiling earthly treasures	6:19
5:10	prophets as examples and patterns	5:12
5:12	against oaths	5:33–37

Warning to the Rich

5 Come now, [x]you rich, weep and howl for the [y]miseries that are coming upon you.
2 [z]Your riches have rotted and [z]your garments are moth-eaten. 3 Your gold and silver
have corroded, and their corrosion will be evidence against you and will eat your flesh like
fire. [a]You have laid up treasure [b]in the last days. 4 Behold, [c]the wages of the laborers who
mowed your fields, which you kept back by fraud, are crying out against you, and [d]the cries
of the harvesters have reached the ears of [e]the Lord of hosts. 5 [f]You have lived on the earth
in luxury and [g]in self-indulgence. You have fattened your hearts in [h]a day of slaughter.
6 You have condemned and [i]murdered [j]the righteous person. He does not resist you.

Patience in Suffering

7 Be patient, therefore, brothers,[1] until the coming of the Lord. See how the farmer waits
for the precious fruit of the earth, being patient about it, until it receives [k]the early and
the late rains. 8 You also, be patient. [l]Establish your hearts, for the coming of the Lord [m]is
at hand. 9 Do not grumble against one another, brothers, [n]so that you may not be judged;
behold, [o]the Judge is standing [p]at the door. 10 As an example of suffering and patience,
brothers, take [q]the prophets who spoke in the name of the Lord. 11 Behold, we consider
those blessed who remained steadfast. You have heard of [r]the steadfastness of Job, and you
have seen [s]the purpose of the Lord, how [t]the Lord is compassionate and merciful.
12 But above all, my brothers, [u]do not swear, either by heaven or by earth or by any

[1] Or *brothers and sisters*; also verses 9, 10, 12, 19

Chapter 5

1 [x]Luke 6:24; [Prov. 11:28; Amos 6:1; 1 Tim. 6:9] [y]Rom. 3:16
2 [z]Job 13:28; Isa. 50:9; Matt. 6:19, 20
3 [a]Matt. 6:19; Luke 12:21; Rom. 2:5 [b][ver. 8, 9]
4 [c]Job 24:10; See Lev. 19:13 [d]Deut. 24:15 [e]Rom. 9:29
5 [f][Job 21:13; Luke 16:19; 2 Pet. 2:13] [g]1 Tim. 5:6 [h]Jer. 12:3
6 [i]ch. 4:2 [j][Acts 3:14]
7 [k]See Deut. 11:14
8 [l]1 Thess. 3:13 [m]1 Pet. 4:7; [Rom. 13:11, 12; Phil. 4:5; Heb. 10:25, 37]
9 [n]Matt. 7:1 [o][1 Pet. 4:5; Rev. 22:12] [p]Matt. 24:33; Mark 13:29; [1 Cor. 4:5]
10 [q]Matt. 5:12; 23:34; Acts 7:52; Heb. 11:32-38
11 [r]Job 1:21, 22; 2:10 [s]Job 42:10, 12 [t]See Ex. 34:6
12 [u]Matt. 5:34

5:1–6 *Warning to the Rich.* James turns his attention from businesspeople (4:13–17) to wealthy landowners (5:4) who controlled much of Galilee, and indeed much of the Roman Empire. He denounces them for their materialistic accumulation of wealth, for defrauding their workers, and for their self-indulgent actions that have led to the deaths of innocent, righteous people.

5:1 weep and howl. Prophetic language for those under indictment by God when the day of the Lord arrives (e.g., Isa. 13:6; 15:3; Hos. 7:14; Amos 8:3). **miseries that are coming**. Referring to final judgment, rather than the miseries of this life.

5:2–3 Riches, garments, and **gold** sum up the sumptuous, materialistic lifestyle of these landowners. These things will not only be lost forever but will be **evidence** at their final trial before God and will feed the very flames of the lake of **fire**, where they will spend eternity (Rev. 20:11–15).

5:4 the cries of the harvesters. These landowners have cheated their field workers and harvesters to support their own lavish lifestyle, and now the cries of the defrauded have **reached the ears** of the final Judge, who will soon act in response. **The Lord of hosts**, or "Lord of heaven's armies," pictures God as a warrior going into battle against his enemies (1 Sam. 17:45; Rev. 17:14; 19:14).

5:5 fattened your hearts in a day of slaughter. Like the cattle in their fields, the rich gorge themselves on luxuries and fail to realize that they are headed for the final slaughter (see Isa. 30:25; Jer. 12:3; Rev. 19:17–21).

5:6 Righteous (Gk. *dikaios*) **person** may have a double meaning: both "one of God's forgiven people" and "a person who is innocent" of the death sentence that the wealthy have handed him. **He does not resist**. The righteous person does not avenge himself (Matt. 5:38–42).

5:7–12 *Patience in Suffering.* The attention turns from rich to poor, from the evil oppressors to the righteous oppressed, from presumption to patience. Rather than fighting back, they are called to patient endurance and to trust in God to vindicate them.

5:7 The righteous are to wait **until the coming of the Lord** (see 1 Thess. 4:15), when he will right all wrongs. **The early and the late rains** describe the Palestinian climate, in which the autumn rains occur just after sowing and the spring rains just before harvest (Jer. 5:24; Joel 2:23). Even though three-fourths of Palestine's rain fell from December to February, these two rains were the most critical.

5:9 Do not grumble sums up the divisive complaining behind 3:1–4:12. It can be particularly painful in times of suffering when people explode in frustration and turn upon each other.

5:10 The **example** of the **prophets** centers on the many who suffered and died (see Heb. 11:32–38) for speaking **in the name of the Lord**.

5:11 The theme of enduring trials recalls 1:2–4, 12.

5:12 It is not entirely clear how **do not swear** is connected to vv. 7–11. **Above all** may indicate that this begins a three-part conclusion to the letter (vv. 12, 13–18, 19–20). Yet it could also refer back to the sins of the tongue and hence the grumbling of v. 9. Oaths were allowed in Israel, but the person was required to fulfill them, especially because they so often involved invoking the name of God (see Lev. 19:12; Jer. 5:2). James's prohibition of oaths builds on Jesus' prohibition in Matt. 5:33–37, and the point in both cases is that one's word should be enough. Still, this does not mean all oaths (e.g., official oaths) are prohibited (cf. Rom. 1:9; 2 Cor. 1:23; Phil. 1:8). (See Jesus' prohibition of oaths in Matt. 23:16–22.)

Leviticus 19 in James

Leviticus 19		**James**	
v. 12	"You shall not swear"	5:12	"do not swear"
v. 13	"The wages of a hired servant shall not remain with you all night"	5:4	"Behold, the wages of the laborers . . . which you kept back by fraud"
v. 15	"You shall not be partial"	2:1, 9	"My brothers, show no partiality"
v. 16	"You shall not go around as a slanderer"	4:11	"Do not speak evil against one another"
v. 18a	"You shall not take vengeance or bear a grudge"	5:9	"Do not grumble against one another"
v. 18b	"you shall love your neighbor as yourself"	2:8	"You shall love your neighbor as yourself"

other oath, but let your "yes" be yes and your "no" be no, so that you may not fall under
condemnation.

The Prayer of Faith

13 Is anyone among you suffering? Let him pray. Is anyone cheerful? Let him [v]sing praise.
14 Is anyone among you sick? Let him call for the elders of the church, and let them pray
over him, [w]anointing him with oil in the name of the Lord. 15 And the prayer of faith
will save the one who is sick, and the Lord will raise him up. And [x]if he has committed
sins, he will be forgiven. 16 Therefore, [y]confess your sins to one another and pray for one
another, [z]that you may be healed. [a]The prayer of a righteous person has great power as it
is working.[1] 17 Elijah was a man [b]with a nature like ours, and [c]he prayed fervently that it
might not rain, and for [d]three years and six months it did not rain on the earth. 18 [e]Then
he prayed again, and heaven gave rain, and the earth bore its fruit.

19 My brothers, [f]if anyone among you wanders from the truth and someone [g]brings him
back, 20 let him know that whoever brings back a sinner from his wandering [h]will save his
soul from death and [i]will cover a multitude of sins.

[1] Or *The effective prayer of a righteous person has great power*

13 [v][Col. 3:16]
14 [w]Mark 6:13; [Mark 16:18]
15 [x]Isa. 33:24; Matt. 9:2; Mark 2:5; Luke 5:20
16 [y]Acts 19:18 [z]Heb. 12:13 [a]Gen. 18:23-32; 20:17; Num. 11:2; 1 Kgs. 13:6; 17:22; 2 Kgs. 4:33; 19:15-20; 20:2-5; Job 42:8; Prov. 15:29
17 [b]Acts 14:15 [c]1 Kgs. 17:1; 18:1 [d]Luke 4:25
18 [e]1 Kgs. 18:42, 45
19 [f][Matt. 18:15; Gal. 6:1] [g]Ps. 51:13; Dan. 12:3; Mal. 2:6; [Luke 1:16]
20 [h]See Rom. 11:14 [i]1 Pet. 4:8; [Neh. 4:5; Ps. 32:1; 85:2; Prov. 10:12]

5:13–18 *The Prayer of Faith.* Speaking mainly of prayer, James restates some of the letter's key themes, including trials (cf. 1:2–4) and misuse of the tongue. The ultimate way to "tame" one's tongue (cf. 3:8) is to "pray for one another" (5:16).

5:13–14 There is another ABA pattern in these verses (cf. note on 3:1–4:12). James begins with those **suffering** (A), then addresses the **cheerful** (B), and concludes with those who are **sick** (A). He alludes back to 1:2, where the one under trial was to "count it all joy." Though "sick" (Gk. *astheneō*) can also mean "to be weak" (even spiritually weak, as in Rom. 14:1), when used (as it is here) without any qualifiers, it usually refers to physical sickness. **Elders** were pastors and overseers (cf. Acts 20:17, 28; Titus 1:5, 7; 1 Pet. 5:1–2), known for wisdom and maturity, who functioned as leaders in the churches. This provides evidence for a plurality of elders in all the churches to which James was writing, for he simply assumes a sick person could call for "the elders of the church." Some think that **anointing . . . with oil** was medicinal or sacramental (as in Roman Catholic extreme unction at death), but it is best seen as a symbol representing the healing power of the Holy Spirit to come upon the sick person (cf. the use of "anointing" for symbolic consecration to God's use and service, both in the OT [Ex. 28:41] and in the NT [Luke 4:18; Acts 4:27; 10:38; 2 Cor. 1:21; Heb. 1:9]). **In the name of the Lord** means it is God, not the oil, that heals.

5:15 the prayer of faith. Not the faith of the sick person but the faith of those praying. In this instance, James mentions no requirement for the sick person to exercise faith, only that he call for the elders. Christians who are ill often find personal prayer difficult. **Will save** perhaps carries a double meaning here: (1) the sick person will be physically healed (one meaning of Gk. *sōzō*), and/or (2) the sick person may also experience spiritual salvation (another meaning of Gk. *sōzō*), or growth in the blessings of salvation (**sins . . . forgiven**). As seen throughout the Gospels, Jesus healed both physically and spiritually, and the same double connotation may be present here as well. James is not teaching that all illnesses will be healed if people would simply call on the elders, or try to make themselves have enough faith, or pray with enough conviction. Healing, when it does come, is always a gift from God, who is sovereign over all circumstances, including sickness and health. It does not follow, therefore, that lack of faith on the part of the sick person is the reason that the sick person may not be healed. (On the gifts of faith and of healing, see note on 1 Cor. 12:9.) Some interpreters suggest that James is referring to the promise of the resurrection rather than physical healing. **If**, in the phrase "if he has committed sins," implies that not all sickness is connected to specific sins, though James seems to expect that some sickness is (cf. 1 Cor. 11:30).

5:16 confess your sins to one another. Sometimes confession in the community is needed before healing can take place, since sin may be the cause of the illness (cf. 1 Cor. 11:29–30). **Pray for one another** is directed to all the readers of James's letter and indicates that he did not expect prayer for healing to be limited to the elders (James 5:14). The **righteous** will have **great power** in prayer, as God grants their requests.

5:17–18 Elijah illustrates how a **man with a nature like ours** could have the powerful prayer life of "a righteous person." The drought recorded in 1 Kings 17–18 was punishment on King Ahab and Israel for idolatry, and the **three years and six months** is probably derived from "in the third year" (1 Kings 18:1) as symbolic of judgment (half of seven; see Dan. 7:25; 12:7; Rev. 11:2; 12:6, 14; 13:5).

5:19–20 *Concluding Admonition.* The style of James is abrupt, and there is no concluding greeting as in most NT letters. Instead, James calls the community to action in helping those who have fallen into the ethical sins dealt with in the book. Therefore, this closing section acts as a summary of various sins and their solutions.

5:19 The righteous saints must be vigilant in spotting anyone who **wanders from the truth**, namely, by not living in accord with the word of truth (1:18) as enunciated in this letter. Right belief is exhibited in right living (1:19–27).

5:20 save his soul from death. Not physical death (cf. 1 Cor. 11:30) but spiritual death (cf. 1 John 5:16–17). Timely intervention (see Gal. 6:1; Heb. 3:13) will "save his soul" and bring forgiveness from God. The person who saves the sinner in this case is the person who restores the one who has fallen. Ultimately, of course, only the Lord saves a person. The one who restores the person will **cover** the many **sins** of the one who had strayed, for the one who returns from the way of error receives forgiveness. Again, only God can cover sin, but Christians can be agents of God's forgiveness.

INTRODUCTION TO

THE FIRST LETTER OF PETER

1 PETER

Author and Title

That this letter was written by the apostle Peter is explicitly affirmed by 1:1 and by the author's claim to be an "eyewitness of the sufferings of Christ" (5:1). The title of the letter, The First Letter of Peter, functions as early external evidence for the view that the letter was written by Peter. Indeed, in the early church there was no dispute over the authenticity of the letter, for it was regularly ascribed to Peter by the early church fathers.

Some recent scholars maintain that the letter is pseudonymous (falsely ascribed to Peter). Thus some have argued that: (1) the cultivated Greek of the letter could not have been written by a Galilean fisherman like Peter; (2) the theology is too much like Paul's to be ascribed to Peter; (3) the OT citations come from the Greek OT (Septuagint), but the genuine Peter would have cited the Hebrew OT; (4) the background of the letter reflects the reign of the Roman emperors Domitian (A.D. 81–96) or Trajan (98–117), both of whom reigned after Peter's death; and (5) the genuine Peter would have referred more to the historical Jesus.

None of these objections are compelling, and there are persuasive reasons for continuing to support Petrine authorship: (1) Peter was a middle-class fisherman who very likely knew Greek from his youth. There is significant evidence that Greek was spoken quite commonly in Galilee. Furthermore, Peter may have used a secretary, namely Silvanus (cf. note on 1 Pet. 5:12), to assist him in composing the letter. (2) Although the common elements in the theology of Peter and Paul should not be exaggerated (for there are distinctive themes in Peter; e.g., the particular emphasis on suffering), it should not be surprising that Peter and Paul shared the same theology. (3) It is hardly unexpected that Peter would cite the Greek OT in writing to Greek readers. (4) There is no clear evidence that the letter was written under the reign of Domitian or Trajan (see Purpose, Occasion, and Background). (5) The reader must be careful of saying what an author "must do"; i.e., although one cannot demand that Peter refer to the historical Jesus in a short letter written for a specific purpose, there is significant evidence that Peter alludes to some of the sayings of Jesus (e.g., Luke 12:35 in 1 Pet. 1:13; Matt. 5:16 in 1 Pet. 2:12; Matt. 5:10 in 1 Pet. 3:14). (6) Finally, there is no historical evidence in early church history that pseudonymous books, especially letters, were accepted as authoritative and inspired. Indeed, writing in someone else's name was considered deceptive (cf. 2 Thess. 2:2; 3:17). On balance, there are compelling reasons to conclude that the apostle Peter is in fact the author of 1 Peter.

Date

The date of 1 Peter is linked with the issue of authorship. Those who reject Peter as the author typically date the letter in the reign of Domitian (A.D. 81–96) or Trajan (98–117). Since there are good grounds for holding to Petrine authorship, the letter probably should be dated during the reign of Nero (A.D. 54–68). The reference to Babylon in 5:13 is almost certainly a reference to Rome, leading one to conclude that Peter wrote the letter from Rome. He probably wrote before the Neronian persecution in Rome, and thus the date of composition is likely A.D. 62–63.

Theme

Those who persevere in faith while suffering persecution should be full of hope, for they will certainly enjoy end-time salvation since they are already enjoying God's saving promises here and now through the death and resurrection of Christ.

The Setting of 1 Peter
c. A.D. 62–63
Peter, probably writing from Rome (called "Babylon" in 5:13), addressed 1 Peter to believers in Pontus, Galatia, Cappadocia, Asia, and Bithynia. These names all referred to Roman provinces in Asia Minor, north of the Taurus Mountains.

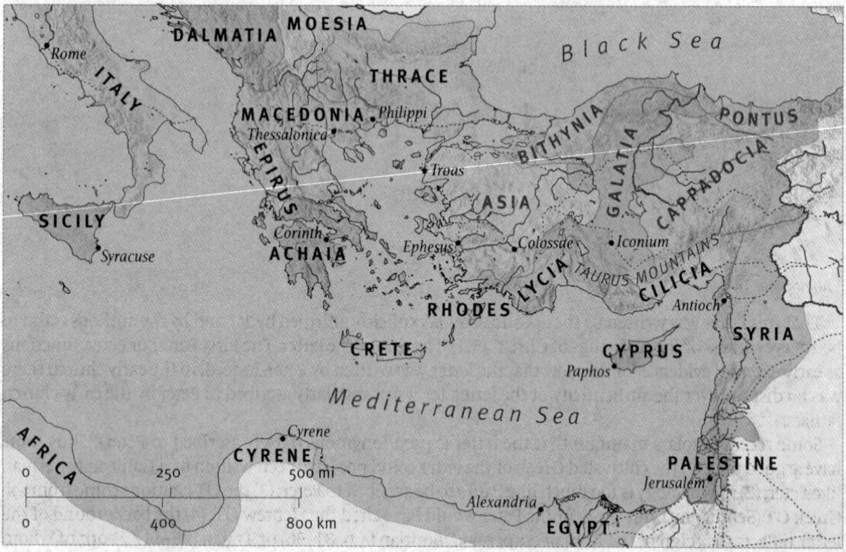

Purpose, Occasion, and Background

Peter encourages his readers to endure suffering and persecution (1:6–7; 2:18–20; 3:9, 13–17; 4:1–4, 12–19; 5:9) by giving themselves entirely to God (4:19). They are to remain faithful in times of distress, knowing that God will vindicate them and that they will certainly enjoy the salvation that the Lord has promised. The death and resurrection of Christ stand as the paradigm for the lives of believers. Just as Christ suffered and then entered into glory, so too his followers will suffer before being exalted.

The letter is addressed to Christians dispersed in "Pontus, Galatia, Cappadocia, Asia, and Bithynia" (1:1), an area north of the Taurus Mountains in Asia Minor (modern-day Turkey); see map above. These provinces were ethnically (and at times linguistically) diverse, yet all these territories had been impacted by Greco-Roman culture and were firmly under Roman control from the mid-first century B.C. The order in which the areas are listed probably designates the order in which the courier (Silvanus, see 5:12) would carry the letter to its intended readership.

Most scholars are convinced that the recipients of 1 Peter were primarily Gentiles. The reference to their "former ignorance" (1:14) and "the futile ways inherited from your forefathers" (1:18) suggests a pagan past that would not fit with Jewish readers. Further, the former lifestyle of the readers (4:3–4) fits with Gentiles rather than Jews. But undoubtedly there were also some Jewish Christians in these churches, for Jewish residents of "Cappadocia, Pontus and Asia" were present at Pentecost and heard the gospel at that early date (Acts 2:9; see note on Acts 9:19b–20). Though the recipients may have been literally "exiles" (1 Pet. 1:1, 17; 2:11), it is more likely that Peter speaks figuratively here: they are spiritual exiles awaiting their heavenly inheritance.

In the past, many scholars detected an empire-wide persecution of Christians in 1 Peter, whether under Nero (A.D. 54–68), Domitian (81–96), or Trajan (98–117), and even used this argument to deny that Peter wrote the letter by specifically placing 1 Peter in the reign of either Domitian or Trajan. However, the evidence is lacking for an official government policy against Christians in the reign of all these emperors. Instead, there were spasmodic and general outbursts against Christians during the first century. Nero's persecution of Christians after the great fire in Rome (A.D. 64) did not launch official empire-wide persecution of all Christians; nor does 1 Peter reflect an official policy against Christians. Also, an empire-wide decree against Christians is not necessitated by Peter's writing about the need to respond when asked about one's faith (3:15), the charges brought against Christians (4:14–16), or the reference to believers suffering worldwide (5:9). The questions and charges brought against Christians that Peter mentions in 3:15 and 4:14–16 were typical of the everyday questions believers would encounter because of their faith. In some instances, Roman authorities punished Christians, but even in these cases it was a local and restricted response. The reference to believers suffering throughout the world (5:9) does not signal that the Roman Empire had passed a decree against the Christian faith. This verse simply reveals that the Christian faith was under threat in the entire Greco-Roman world. Indeed, 1 Peter says nothing about Christians suffering physically for their faith. The focus is on the verbal abuse and discrimination they receive because of their Christian commitment (4:3–4). Of course, verbal abuse easily leads to physical mistreatment, and it is possible that some of the believers to whom Peter wrote were suffering physical abuse for their faith as well (cf. 2:18–20).

Key Themes

1. Those who suffer as Christians will be exalted.	1:6–9; 2:18–25; 3:13–22; 4:12–19
2. The church of Jesus Christ is the new temple, the new Israel, the new people of God.	1:1–2; 2:4–10
3. Believers should set their hope on their end-time inheritance.	1:3–9, 13–16
4. Christ died as a substitute for sinners, and his death is the basis for their new life.	1:17–21; 2:24; 3:13–22
5. Christ's suffering is an example to his disciples.	2:21–23
6. At his resurrection, Christ triumphed over his enemies.	3:18–22
7. Christians should live righteously in their homes and in society.	2:11–3:7
8. New life in Christ is the basis for a life of love and holiness.	1:3; 1:13–2:3

History of Salvation Summary

Christians are to endure suffering for the sake of Christ, looking back on Christ's sufferings and forward to the consummation of salvation in his second coming. (For an explanation of the "History of Salvation," see Overview of the Bible, pp. 23–26.)

Literary Features

First Peter follows the usual contours of the NT epistles. Along with the standard ingredients of salutation-thanksgiving-body-*paraenesis* (moral exhortations)-closing, there is a pattern of back-and-forth movement between theological assertions and either practical application or lyric celebration. The book moves in a fluid manner between two poles: the *riches* that believers have in Christ and the *duties* they need to shoulder, within the implied situation of their living in a hostile surrounding culture.

First Peter is exuberant in tone and exalted in language. Virtually every paragraph contains vivid imagery and a skillful use of figurative language. The tone of the book is urgent and intense, as signaled by the presence of more than 30 imperative verbs (an average of one command in every three verses). The content and style are thus elevated and elevating.

Outline

I. Opening (1:1–2)

II. Called to Salvation as Exiles (1:3–2:10)
- A. Praise for salvation (1:3–12)
- B. The future inheritance as an incentive to holiness (1:13–21)
- C. Living as the new people of God (1:22–2:10)

III. Living as Aliens to Bring Glory to God in a Hostile World (2:11–4:11)
- A. The Christian life as a battle and a witness (2:11–12)
- B. Testifying to the gospel in the social order (2:13–3:12)
- C. Responding to suffering in a godly way (3:13–4:11)

IV. Persevering in Suffering (4:12–5:11)

V. Concluding Words (5:12–14)

Timeline

Event (A.D. 30–80)
Peter becomes a disciple of Jesus (A.D. 28/30)
Just before the crucifixion, Peter denies Jesus (30/33)
Death, resurrection of Jesus (33 [or 30])[†]
Peter witnesses resurrection, preaches at Pentecost (30/33)
Peter becomes key church leader (30/33)
Peter witnesses to Cornelius (38*)
Peter imprisoned by Agrippa, rescued (41–44*)
Peter leaves Jerusalem (44)
Peter goes to Rome (50–54*)
Nero's reign (54–68)
Peter writes first letter, from Rome (62–63*)
Fire in Rome; Nero blames, kills many Christians (64 [July 19])
Peter, after writing second letter, is martyred in Rome (64–67*)

** denotes approximate date; / signifies either/or; † see The Date of Jesus' Crucifixion, pp. 1809–1810*

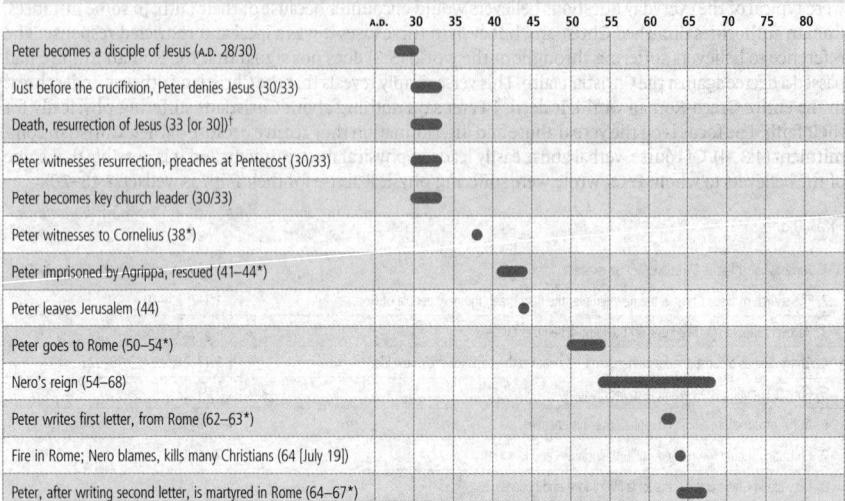

THE FIRST LETTER OF PETER

1 PETER

Greeting

1 Peter, an apostle of Jesus Christ,
To those who are elect exiles of [a]the Dispersion in Pontus, Galatia, Cappadocia, Asia,
and Bithynia, 2 according to [b]the foreknowledge of God the Father, [c]in the sanctification
of the Spirit, for obedience to Jesus Christ and [d]for sprinkling with his blood:
May [e]grace and [f]peace be multiplied to you.

Born Again to a Living Hope

3 [g]Blessed be the God and Father of our Lord Jesus Christ! [h]According to his great mercy,
[i]he has caused us to be born again to a living hope [j]through the resurrection of Jesus Christ
from the dead, 4 to [k]an inheritance that is imperishable, undefiled, and [l]unfading, [m]kept
in heaven for you, 5 who by God's power are being guarded [n]through faith for a salvation
[o]ready to be revealed in the last time. 6 In this you rejoice, though now for a little while,

Chapter 1

1 [a]See James 1:1
2 [b]Acts 2:23; [Rom. 8:29; 11:2] [c]See 1 Thess. 4:3 [d]Heb. 10:22; 12:24 [e]2 Pet. 1:2 [f]Dan. 4:1; Jude 2
3 [g]2 Cor. 1:3; Eph. 1:3 [h]Titus 3:5 [i]ver. 23 [j]ch. 3:21; [1 Cor. 15:20]
4 [k]Rom. 8:17 [l][ch. 5:4] [m][Col. 1:5; 2 Tim. 4:8]
5 [n]Eph. 2:8 [o][ch. 5:10; Rom. 8:18; 2 Cor. 4:17; Heb. 12:11]

1:1–2 *Opening.* Peter identifies himself as the author. The geographical location of the recipients is indicated (see Introduction: Purpose, Occasion, and Background), and they are greeted with "grace" and "peace." The introduction is theologically weighty, for the readers are identified as "elect exiles" and the salvation accomplished is attributed to the work of the Father, Spirit, and Son.

1:1 Peter designates himself as an **apostle**, an authoritative messenger of Jesus Christ (see note on Rom. 1:1). The people receiving his letter are **elect exiles of the dispersion**. Peter is not speaking of a literal exile (cf. 1 Pet. 1:17; 2:11). Believers long for their true home in the new world that is coming and for their end-time inheritance, for they do not conform to the values and worldviews of this present evil age. Believers are not only exiles but God's "elect exiles." They are his chosen people, just as Israel is designated as God's chosen people in the OT (Deut. 4:37; 7:6–8; Ps. 106:5; Isa. 43:20; 45:4). Since the recipients of his letter were primarily Gentiles, Peter explicitly teaches that the church of Jesus Christ is the new Israel—God's new chosen people. "Dispersion" (Gk. *diaspora*) points to the same truth. It is typically used to describe the scattering of the Jews throughout the world (Deut. 28:25; 30:4; Neh. 1:9; Ps. 147:2; Isa. 49:6; Jer. 15:7; 41:17; cf. also John 7:35; James 1:1; note on Acts 2:9–11), but Peter sees a parallel in the church being dispersed throughout the world. (Another view is that these verses show that the church is *like* Israel but that the ultimate fulfillment of these OT prophecies pertains mainly to future ethnic Israel rather than to the church; this also applies to the notes on 1 Pet. 1:22–2:10; 2:9; 2:10.)

1:2 Peter celebrates the work of the triune God in saving his people; the descriptive phrases in v. 2 modify "elect exiles" in v. 1 (the Gk. has no verb in v. 1; the ESV supplies "are" to make the sense more clear). They are God's people because of his **foreknowledge**. This does not merely refer to God's foreknowing that they would belong to him but also means that he set his covenantal affection upon them in advance, foreordaining that they would belong to him (cf. Rom. 8:29). **In the sanctification of the Spirit** may refer here either to conversion or to gradual progress in the Christian life, or possibly to both. The Spirit sets apart God's people into the sphere of the holy, so that believers are now holy and righteous in their standing before God, and they grow in actual holiness in their lives. **For obedience to Jesus Christ** may also refer either to conversion, when Christians confessed Jesus as Lord (Rom. 10:9; cf. 1 Pet. 1:22), or to God's purpose for their lives, that they obey Christ. **For sprinkling with his blood** refers to Christ's atoning work on the cross, where all the believers' sins were washed away, just as the old covenant was inaugurated with the shedding of blood (cf. Ex. 24:3–8). Peter sees believers "sprinkled" with the blood of Christ, referring either to their initial entrance into a covenant with God (similar to Ex. 24:3–8) or to their subsequent cleansings by the blood of Christ (i.e., growth in holiness) or possibly to both (similar to Lev. 14:6–7; cf. Ps. 51:7; 1 John 1:7).

1:3–2:10 *Called to Salvation as Exiles.* Those who have trusted in Christ are to praise God for his promised salvation and live out that salvation in their daily lives.

1:3–12 *Praise for Salvation.* Peter begins the body of the letter by blessing God because he has given believers new life and guaranteed their future glory (vv. 3–5). Believers rejoice in their sufferings because they are designed for their purity (vv. 6–9). Christians are wonderfully blessed, for they know the fulfillment of OT prophecies, all of which point to Christ (vv. 10–12).

1:3 Salvation is due to God's mercy, grace, and sovereignty, for he miraculously gave sinners new life (**caused us to be born again**, cf. v. 23). Peter may be connecting "born again" to **through the resurrection of Jesus Christ**, meaning that the new birth was made possible because God thought of those who believe in Christ as being united to him in his resurrection (cf. Rom. 6:4; Eph. 1:19–20; 2:5–6; Col. 3:1). Or he may be linking the resurrection to the **living hope** of believers, since that hope immediately follows the resurrection. In the latter case, the hope of Christians is their future resurrection. Believers have an unshakable hope for the future, for Christ's resurrection is a pledge of their own future resurrection.

1:4 The "hope" of v. 3 is now described as an **inheritance**, which in the OT typically describes the Promised Land and Israel's place in it (Num. 32:19; Deut. 2:12; 12:9; 25:19; 26:1; Josh. 11:23; Ps. 105:11). But the OT inheritance points ahead to an even greater inheritance, reserved **in heaven** for the people of the new covenant. **imperishable.** Nothing can tarnish or extinguish that secure inheritance.

1:5 Salvation in this context is a further description of the inheritance of v. 4 and the hope of v. 3. Peter lifts his readers' minds to what will **be revealed in the last time**. They will certainly receive this future salvation, for God will protect them through his **power** by sustaining their **faith** to the end.

1:6–7 Peter realizes that joy is mingled with grief as Christians in Asia Minor suffer **various trials**. **Little while** denotes the whole of their earthly life before they inherit future salvation. **if necessary**. These sufferings are God's will for his people, so that their **faith** might be purified and shown to be genuine. Such

if necessary, you have been grieved by [p]various trials, **7** so that [q]the tested genuineness of
your faith—more precious than gold that perishes [r]though it is tested by [s]fire—may be
found to result in [t]praise and glory and honor at the revelation of Jesus Christ. **8** [u]Though
you have not seen him, you love him. [v]Though you do not now see him, you believe in him
and rejoice with joy that is inexpressible and filled with glory, **9** obtaining [w]the outcome
of your faith, the salvation of your souls.

10 Concerning this salvation, [x]the prophets who prophesied about the grace that was to be
yours searched and inquired carefully, **11** inquiring [y]what person or time [z]the Spirit of Christ
in them was indicating [a]when he predicted [b]the sufferings of Christ and the subsequent
glories. **12** [c]It was revealed to them that [d]they were serving not themselves but you, in the
things that have now been announced to you through those who preached the good news
to you [e]by the Holy Spirit sent from heaven, [f]things into which angels long to look.

Called to Be Holy

13 Therefore, [g]preparing your minds for action,[1] and [h]being sober-minded, set your hope
fully on the grace that will be brought to you at the revelation of Jesus Christ. **14** As obedient children, [i]do not be conformed to the passions [j]of your former ignorance, **15** but [k]as
he who called you is holy, you also be holy [l]in all your conduct, **16** since it is written, [m]"You
shall be holy, for I am holy." **17** And if you [n]call on him as Father who [o]judges [p]impartially
according to each one's deeds, conduct yourselves [q]with fear throughout the time of your
exile, **18** knowing that you [r]were ransomed from [s]the futile ways inherited from your forefathers, not with perishable things such as silver or gold, **19** but [t]with the precious blood
of Christ, like that of [u]a lamb [v]without blemish or spot. **20** He was foreknown before the
foundation of the world but [w]was made manifest [x]in the last times for the sake of you
21 [y]who through him are believers in God, [z]who raised him from the dead and [a]gave him
glory, so that your faith and hope are in God.

[1] Greek *girding up the loins of your mind*

[x]Heb. 1:2 **21** [y]John 12:44 [z][Rom. 10:9]; See Acts 2:24 [a]Acts 3:13; Heb. 2:9; [ch. 3:22]; See John 7:39

6 [p]James 1:2; [ch. 4:12]
7 [q]James 1:3 [r]Job 23:10; Ps. 66:10; Prov. 17:3; Isa. 48:10 [s]1 Cor. 3:13 [t]Rom. 2:7, 10; 1 Cor. 4:5; [2 Thess. 1:7-12]
8 [u][1 John 4:20] [v][Heb. 11:27]; See John 20:29
9 [w]Rom. 6:22
10 [x]2 Pet. 1:19; [Dan. 8:15; Matt. 13:17; Luke 10:24]
11 [y]Dan. 9:24-26 [z]Rom. 8:9; [2 Pet. 1:21]; See Acts 16:7 [a]See Matt. 26:24 [b]Isa. 52:13–53:12; Luke 24:26; Acts 3:18
12 [c]Dan. 12:4, 9, 13 [d][Matt. 13:17; Heb. 11:39, 40] [e]Acts 2:2-4 [f][Dan. 8:13; 12:5-7; Eph. 3:10]
13 [g]See Luke 12:35 [h]ch. 4:7; 5:8; 1 Thess. 5:6, 8; 2 Tim. 4:5
14 [i]ch. 4:2, 3; Rom. 12:2; Titus 3:3 [j]Acts 17:30
15 [k]1 John 3:3; [2 Cor. 7:1; 1 Thess. 4:7; Heb. 12:14] [l]James 3:13
16 [m]Cited from Lev. 11:44
17 [n]Jer. 3:19; Mal. 1:6; 2 Cor. 6:18; [Matt. 6:9] [o]See Ps. 62:12 [p]See James 2:1 [q]ch. 3:15; 2 Cor. 7:1; [Rom. 11:20]
18 [r][Ps. 49:8; 130:8; 1 Cor. 6:20; Titus 2:14; 2 Pet. 2:1] [s]See Eph. 4:17
19 [t]See Acts 20:28 [u]See John 1:29 [v]Heb. 9:14; [Ex. 12:5]
20 [w]See Rom. 16:26

faith has a great reward, for at the **revelation** (that is, the return) **of Jesus Christ**, **honor** and **praise** will belong both to Christians and to Christ.

1:8–9 Joy is not reserved only for the future when Jesus will be clearly seen at his revelation (v. 7). Even now, his followers **love him**, **believe in him**, and **rejoice** with an **inexpressible** joy. The end result is eternal **salvation**—the completion of God's saving work.

1:10–11 Even though the OT **prophets** did not see clearly when their prophecies would be realized, they did foretell that Christ would suffer and then be glorified. See Overview of the Bible, pp. 23–26. **The Spirit of Christ** is the Holy Spirit, who was speaking through the prophets.

1:12 Christians have received astounding blessings, for the OT prophets **were serving not themselves but you**, that is, NT believers, and **angels long** to understand fully what has been accomplished. Christians have heard this **good news** in the gospel proclaimed to them.

1:13–21 *The Future Inheritance as an Incentive to Holiness.* The inheritance promised to followers of Christ should motivate them to set their hope entirely on their future reward (vv. 13–16) and to live in fear of the God who redeemed them at the cost of his own Son (vv. 17–21).

1:13 set your hope fully. The fullness of **grace** and its complete work will come only when Jesus returns, and believers are to long for that day. They do so by thinking rightly about reality and by living **sober-minded** and sensible lives in this present evil age.

1:14–15 While living on this earth, Christians have to fight the desires of sin, so they are called to be **obedient children**, separated from evil in all that they do. They are to **be holy** (cf. Lev. 18:2–4), for that accords with the character of God who **is holy** and has **called** believers to himself.

1:17 Father who judges impartially may refer only to the final judgment, when believers will be judged according to their **deeds** (cf. Rom. 2:6, 16; 2 Cor. 5:10). More likely, Peter has in mind both this present life and the last day as well. God is not only the Father of his people but also their judge. **Fear** is not a paralyzing terror but a fear of God's discipline and fatherly displeasure; it is a reverence and awe that should characterize the lives of believers during their **exile** (cf. 1 Pet. 1:1) on this earth.

1:18–19 The reason for the call to fear (v. 17) is given in vv. 18–19. Believers were ransomed by Christ's **precious blood**. "Ransom" recalls Israel's deliverance from Egypt (Deut. 7:8; 9:26; 15:15; 24:18), which in turn points to the greater deliverance accomplished by Jesus Christ. Believers are delivered from a life of futility and meaninglessness to one of great significance. **you were ransomed from the futile ways inherited from your forefathers**. Christ's sacrifice breaks the inevitability and power of "generational sin," the idea that the sins of parents and grandparents are often repeated in later generations (cf. Ex. 20:5–6). Christ's sacrifice is compared to a **lamb without blemish or spot**. The references to "lamb" and "blood" point to the OT sacrifices and especially to Christ as the Passover Lamb (Exodus 12) and the servant of the Lord (cf. "lamb," Isa. 53:7). As the perfect sacrifice, Christ atoned for the sins of the unrighteous (cf. John 1:29; 1 Pet. 3:18).

1:20–21 Christians should live in holy fear (v. 17) because they are deeply loved and should not despise that love. God planned (Christ was **foreknown**, cf. v. 2) from eternity past when he would send Christ, and he chose to reveal him at the time in history when these believers lived (**for the sake of you**) so that they would enjoy the inexpressible privilege of living in the days of fulfillment (cf. vv. 10–12). They should be full of **hope** (hope functions as an *inclusio*—a literary envelope—beginning and ending this section; vv. 13, 21), for Christ's being **raised** reminds them of their future reward.

1:22–2:10 *Living as the New People of God.* Since Christians have been given new life by the Word of God, they are to love one another fervently (1:22–25). They are to long for God's Word so that they will continue to grow in faith (2:1–3). They are like living stones which together build up a spiritual house, with Jesus as the cornerstone (2:4–8). Believers are chosen by God to be his people (2:9–10).

1:22 Peter's call for his readers to **love one another** is grounded in their conversion, which occurred when they were obedient to the **truth** (i.e., the gospel) and therefore were **purified** and cleansed (see note on v. 2 for "obedience" and "sprinkling").

1:23 Believers were born anew through the **living and abiding word of**

22 Having purified your souls by your obedience to the truth for [b]a sincere brotherly
love, [c]love one another earnestly from a pure heart, 23 [d]since you have been born again,
[e]not of perishable seed but of imperishable, through [f]the living and abiding word of
God; 24 for

> [g]"All flesh is like grass
> and all its glory like the flower of grass.
> The grass withers,
> and the flower falls,
> 25 [h]but the word of the Lord remains forever."

And this word [i]is the good news that was preached to you.

A Living Stone and a Holy People

2 [j]So put away all malice and all deceit and hypocrisy and envy and all slander. 2 [k]Like
newborn infants, long for the pure spiritual [l]milk, that by it you may grow up into
salvation— 3 if indeed you have [m]tasted that the Lord is good.
4 As you come to him, a living stone [n]rejected by men but in the sight of God chosen and
precious, 5 [o]you yourselves like living stones are being built up as [p]a spiritual house, to be
[q]a holy priesthood, [r]to offer spiritual sacrifices [s]acceptable to God through Jesus Christ.
6 For it stands in Scripture:

> [t]"Behold, I am laying in Zion a stone,
> a cornerstone chosen and precious,
> [u]and whoever believes in him will not be put to shame."

7 So the honor is for you who [v]believe, but for those who [v]do not believe,

22 [b]Rom. 12:9; See Heb. 13:1 [c]1 Tim. 1:5
23 [d]ver. 3; [John 3:3; James 1:18] [e]John 1:13 [f]Heb. 4:12
24 [g]James 1:10, 11; Cited from Isa. 40:6, 8
25 [h][Matt. 24:35] [i]Isa. 40:9

Chapter 2

1 [j]Eph. 4:22, 25, 31; Col. 3:8
2 [k]See Matt. 18:3 [l]1 Cor. 3:2; Heb. 5:12, 13
3 [m]Ps. 34:8; Heb. 6:5
4 [n]ver. 6, 7
5 [o]Eph. 2:20-22; [1 Cor. 3:9] [p]Heb. 3:4, 6 [q]ver. 9 [r]Isa. 56:7; Mal. 1:11; Rom. 12:1; Heb. 13:15 [s]Rom. 15:16; Phil. 4:18
6 [t]Cited from Isa. 28:16 [u]Rom. 9:33; 10:11
7 [v][2 Cor. 2:16]

God, meaning the whole of written Scripture (cf. v. 25) but especially the saving message of the gospel. The exhortation to love (v. 22) flows from their new life as members of God's family.

1:24–25 Peter cites Isa. 40:6, 8 to contrast the weakness of human flesh with the power of **the word of the Lord** that has granted new life to believers.

2:1–2 In comparing believers to **newborn infants**, Peter is not saying that they are immature in their faith but that all Christians are to be like infants in their longing for **pure spiritual milk**, which likely refers to God's Word (cf. 1:23–25). "Spiritual" comes from Greek *logikos*, which echoes "word" (*logos*) of 1:23.

2:3 Christians will continue to long for the Word **if** they **have tasted that the Lord is good**, which they did in conversion. Cf. Ps. 34:8; in writing this letter, Peter likely meditated at length upon this psalm, which is about how the Lord delivers the righteous in their sufferings (cf. 1 Pet. 3:10–12 and Ps. 34:12–13).

2:4 As you come to him indicates a daily personal relationship with Christ, beginning at but not limited to the time of conversion. As believers continue in fellowship with Christ, they "are being built up as a spiritual house" (v. 5). Just as his followers suffer persecution, Jesus also was **rejected by men**. Still, he is risen from the dead and hence is the **living stone**—the foundation of God's new temple. He is God's elect (**chosen**) one, and as the exalted Lord he is honored above all.

2:5 Believers are **living stones** in God's new temple (i.e., **spiritual house**). Since the components that make up the house are "living," the house itself is also growing: **you yourselves . . . are being built up**. Peter sees that the OT temple anticipated the new temple where God dwells (i.e., in his people). But believers are not only God's temple but are also a **holy priesthood**, which offers **spiritual sacrifices** (cf. Rom. 12:1; Phil. 4:18; Heb. 13:15–16) by the power of the Holy Spirit.

2:6 In support of the idea that Jesus is the **cornerstone** (see note on Eph. 2:20) of God's temple, Peter cites Isa. 28:16 (cf. Rom. 9:33; 10:11). Jesus is the elect Messiah whom God has honored by raising him from the dead. Those who put their trust **in him** will enjoy vindication on the last day.

2:7 Eschatological (i.e., end-time) **honor** belongs to believers, but unbelievers will find the prophecy from Ps. 118:22 fulfilled. The **stone** the **builders** repudiated is the foundation of God's temple, his new people.

Regeneration in the New Testament

John 1:13	"born . . . of God"
John 3:3	"born again"
John 3:5	"born of water and the Spirit"
John 3:6	"born of the Spirit"
John 3:7	"born again"
John 3:8	"born of the Spirit"
Eph. 2:4–5	"God . . . even when we were dead . . . made us alive together with Christ"
Col. 2:13	"you, who were dead . . . God made alive together with him"
Titus 3:5	"he saved us . . . by the washing of regeneration and renewal of the Holy Spirit"
James 1:18	"he brought us forth by the word of truth"
1 Pet. 1:3	"he has caused us to be born again"
1 Pet. 1:23	"you have been born again"
1 John 2:29	"everyone who practices righteousness has been born of him"
1 John 3:9	"No one born of God makes a practice of sinning"
1 John 4:7	"whoever loves has been born of God"
1 John 5:1	"Everyone who believes that Jesus is the Christ has been born of God"
1 John 5:4	"everyone who has been born of God overcomes the world"
1 John 5:18	"everyone who has been born of God does not keep on sinning"

[w]"The stone that the builders rejected
has become the cornerstone,"[1]
8 and
[x]"A stone of stumbling,
and a rock of offense."
They stumble because they disobey the word, [y]as they were destined to do.
9 But you are [z]a chosen race, [a]a royal [b]priesthood, [c]a holy nation, [d]a people for his own
possession, that you may proclaim the excellencies of him who called you [e]out of darkness
into [f]his marvelous light. 10 [g]Once you were not a people, but now you are God's people;
once you had not received mercy, but now you have received mercy.
11 Beloved, I urge you [h]as sojourners and exiles [i]to abstain from the passions of the flesh,
[j]which wage war against your soul. 12 [k]Keep your conduct among the Gentiles honorable, so
that when they speak against you as evildoers, [l]they may see your good deeds and glorify
God on [m]the day of visitation.

Submission to Authority

13 [n]Be subject for the Lord's sake to every human institution,[2] whether it be to the emperor[3]
as supreme, 14 or to governors as sent by him [o]to punish those who do evil and [p]to praise
those who do good. 15 For this is the will of God, [q]that by doing good you should put to
silence the ignorance of foolish people. 16 [r]Live as people who are free, not using your
freedom as a cover-up for evil, but [s]living as servants[4] of God. 17 [t]Honor everyone. [u]Love
the brotherhood. [v]Fear God. Honor the emperor.
18 [w]Servants, be subject to your masters with all respect, not only to the good and gentle
but also to the unjust. 19 For this is a gracious thing, when, [x]mindful of God, one endures

[1] Greek *the head of the corner* [2] Or *every institution ordained for people* [3] Or *king*; also verse 17 [4] Greek *bondservants*

7 [w]Cited from Ps. 118:22
8 [x]Rom. 9:33; Cited from Isa. 8:14 [y][Rom. 9:22; Jude 4]
9 [z]Deut. 10:15; Isa. 43:20 [a]Ex. 19:6; Rev. 1:6; 5:10 [b]Isa. 61:6; 66:21 [c]Deut. 7:6 [d]Ex. 19:5; Deut. 7:6; Isa. 43:21; Mal. 3:17 [e][Isa. 42:16]; See Acts 26:18 [f]Ps. 36:9
10 [g]Hos. 1:6, 9, 10; 2:23; Rom. 9:25, 26; 10:19
11 [h]See Lev. 25:23 [i]Rom. 13:14; Gal. 5:24 [j]James 4:1
12 [k][ch. 3:16; 2 Cor. 8:21; Phil. 2:15; Titus 2:8] [l]Matt. 5:16; 2 Cor. 9:13; Gal. 1:24 [m]Isa. 10:3; Luke 19:44
13 [n]Rom. 13:1; Titus 3:1
14 [o]Rom. 13:4 [p]Rom. 13:3
15 [q]ver. 12
16 [r]See James 1:25 [s]1 Cor. 7:22; [Rom. 6:22]
17 [t]Rom. 12:10; 13:7 [u]See Heb. 13:1 [v]Prov. 24:21
18 [w]Eph. 6:5; Col. 3:22; 1 Tim. 6:1; Titus 2:9
19 [x]ch. 3:14, 17; [ch. 4:16]

2:8 In **stumbling**, unbelievers fulfill the prophecy in Isa. 8:14, where the **stone** God has established becomes the means of their falling. Their stumbling, however, is their own fault, for they are tripped up because of their refusal to obey the "word" of the gospel. **They stumble because they disobey the word, as they were destined to do**. Some understand this to teach that God has predestined not *who* will disobey but only what the *result* of disobedience will be for those who disobey (i.e., that those who disobey will stumble). It is more likely that Peter teaches that God appoints all that will occur (cf. note on Eph. 1:11). In teaching this, Peter does not deny human responsibility, for he emphasizes that people are guilty if they fail to believe (they "stumble because they disobey").

2:9 a chosen race. God's grace rather than human choice is the ultimate explanation for why some people come to faith and others do not. God has elected ("chosen") some to be his people, therefore no one can boast of being included. Peter views the church as a new Israel, for he picks up what is said of Israel in Ex. 19:5–6 and applies it to the church. The church is a **royal priesthood** and God's **holy nation**. As God's chosen ones, Christians are to **proclaim the excellencies** of the one who summoned them from **darkness** and ushered them **into his marvelous light** (cf. Isa. 43:20b–21).

2:10 Peter alludes to texts in Hosea that refer to Israel (Hos. 1:6, 9, 10; 2:23) and sees them fulfilled in the church.

2:11–4:11 *Living as Aliens to Bring Glory to God in a Hostile World.* Peter explains how believers should live as exiles amid a world that rejects their message. They bear witness to the gospel when they live in a way that pleases God.

2:11–12 *The Christian Life as a Battle and a Witness.* These verses introduce 2:11–4:11, emphasizing that those who have trusted in Christ bear witness to the gospel by their conduct.

2:11 Beloved signals a major new section in the letter (cf. 4:12). Believers are **sojourners and exiles** (cf. 1:1, 17), awaiting their end-time inheritance. The pleasures of the world are tempting and enticing nonetheless, hence there is a great struggle and warfare against such desires. Believers are to **abstain** from sinful **passions**, for they **wage war against your soul**: holding on to sinful desires brings spiritual harm.

2:12 Peter refers to unbelievers as **Gentiles**, which is in keeping with his understanding of believers being a new Israel (see note on 1:1). Believers are to live godly lives even though they will often be criticized by unbelievers. When believers do **good deeds**, some unbelievers will repent and believe and thus **glorify God**. Peter clearly alludes to Matt. 5:16 here ("let your light shine before others, so that they may see your good works and give glory to your Father who is in heaven"). **On the day of visitation** may refer to the initial conversion of the believer through the regenerating work ("visitation") of the Holy Spirit, or it may refer to the way in which those who become believers will glorify God on the last day, the day of judgment. To "glorify God" should probably be understood in the broad sense that the believer will glorify God in many ways—e.g., by believing (cf. Acts 13:48; Rom. 15:7, 9), through the doing of "good deeds" (cf. Matt. 5:16), and at the end of the age (cf. Rev. 14:7; 19:7).

2:13–3:12 *Testifying to the Gospel in the Social Order.* Peter exhorts Christians to goodness as citizens (2:13–17), slaves (2:18–25), wives (3:1–6), and husbands (3:7). The section is summed up in 3:8–12: those who imitate Christ and pursue goodness will receive an eternal reward.

2:13–14 Christians are to **be subject** to every civil authority (cf. Rom. 13:1–7). **To punish** (Gk. *ekdikēsis*, "justice, punishment, retribution") includes not just deterring evil but carrying out retribution against **those who do evil** (see note on Rom. 13:4). By contrast, governments are to **praise** or reward **those who do good**, thus encouraging more good behavior.

2:15 The godly lives of believers will **put to silence** any false charges raised against them.

2:16 Freedom in Scripture is not a license to sin but expresses itself in devotion to what is good (cf. Gal. 5:13–14).

2:17 everyone. All people deserve the same honor and respect as the **emperor**. Only **God** is to be feared. Believers should have a tender **love** for each other as members of the same family.

2:18 On slavery in the Greco-Roman world, see note on 1 Cor. 7:21. **Masters** had extensive authority over slaves, and slaves were often mistreated by their masters. Still, Peter calls on slaves to **be subject** even to evil masters, **with all respect**.

2:19–20 Gracious thing comes from "grace" (Gk. *charis*) and in this context

sorrows while suffering unjustly. 20 For what credit is it if, when you sin and are beaten for
it, you endure? But [y]if when you do good and suffer for it you endure, this is a gracious
thing in the sight of God. 21 For [z]to this you have been called, [y]because Christ also suffered
for you, [a]leaving you an example, so that you might follow in his steps. 22 [b]He committed
no sin, neither was deceit found in his mouth. 23 [c]When he was reviled, he did not revile in
return; when he suffered, he did not threaten, [d]but continued entrusting himself to him
who judges justly. 24 [e]He himself bore our sins in his body on the tree, that we [f]might die
to sin and [g]live to righteousness. [h]By his wounds you have been healed. 25 For [i]you were
straying like sheep, but have now returned to [j]the Shepherd and Overseer of your souls.

Wives and Husbands

3 Likewise, wives, [k]be subject to your own husbands, so that [l]even if some do not obey
the word, [m]they may be won without a word by the conduct of their wives, 2 when
they see your [n]respectful and pure conduct. 3 [o]Do not let your adorning be external—the
braiding of hair and the putting on of gold jewelry, or the clothing you wear— 4 but let
your adorning be [p]the hidden person of the heart with the imperishable beauty of a gentle
and quiet spirit, which in God's sight is very precious. 5 For this is how the holy women
who hoped in God used to adorn themselves, by submitting to their own husbands, 6 as
Sarah obeyed Abraham, [q]calling him lord. And you are her children, if you do good and
[r]do not fear anything that is frightening.
7 Likewise, [s]husbands, live with your wives in an understanding way, showing honor

20 [y]ch. 3:17, 18; 4:13, 16
21 [z]ch. 3:9; See Acts 14:22 [y][See ver. 20 above] [a]See Matt. 11:29
22 [b]Isa. 53:9; [2 Cor. 5:21; Heb. 4:15; 1 John 3:5]
23 [c]ch. 3:9; Isa. 53:7; Heb. 12:3 [d]Luke 23:46
24 [e]Isa. 53:4, 11; Matt. 8:17; Heb. 9:28 [f]Rom. 6:2, 11; 7:4, 6; Col. 2:20; 3:3 [g]Rom. 6:13 [h]Isa. 53:5
25 [i]Isa. 53:6; [Ps. 119:176; Ezek. 34:6; Luke 15:4] [j]See John 10:11

Chapter 3

1 [k]See Gen. 3:16 [l]1 Cor. 7:16 [m]Matt. 18:15; 1 Cor. 9:19-22
2 [n]Titus 2:5
3 [o]1 Tim. 2:9; [Isa. 3:18-23]
4 [p]Rom. 2:29; [Rom. 7:22; 2 Cor. 4:16; Eph. 3:16]
6 [q]Gen. 18:12 [r]Prov. 3:25
7 [s]Eph. 5:25; Col. 3:19

seems to be synonymous with **credit**. Both words indicate that God's people will receive a reward from him if they endure suffering righteously. Cf. Luke 6:34–35, where *charis* is translated "credit" and is parallel with "reward" (Gk. *misthos*). "Gracious thing" could also mean that patient endurance of suffering is evidence of God's grace at work. The two interpretations are compatible, for along with God's enabling grace come his favor and blessing.

2:21 Christ's substitutionary sacrifice in which he gave his life for sinners is unique, and yet those he has saved may follow Christ's **example** when they suffer unjustly, even though their sufferings do not atone for sin.

2:22 This crucial verse underscores the sinlessness of Christ (**committed no sin**) and his substitutionary death for sinners (cf. 3:18). Jesus' freedom from **deceit** alludes to Isa. 53:9. Isaiah 52:13–53:12 especially emphasizes that the servant of the Lord died as a substitute to remove the sins of his people.

2:23 when he suffered, he did not threaten. It is common to long for retaliation in the face of unjust criticism or suffering, but Jesus behaved like the meek lamb of Isa. 53:7. He could do so because he **continued entrusting** both himself and those who mistreated him entirely to God, knowing that God is just and will make all things right in the end. Likewise believers, knowing that God **judges justly**, are able to forgive others and to entrust all judgment and vengeance to God (cf. Rom. 12:19). Every wrong deed in the universe will be either covered by the blood of Christ or repaid justly by God at the final judgment.

2:24 Tree was often used as a synonym for "cross" in first-century Judaism, possibly due to association with Deut. 21:22–23 (cf. Gal. 3:13; also Acts 5:30; 10:39; 13:29; and see note on crucifixion at Matt. 27:35). The unique, substitutionary, sin-bearing death of Jesus is described here, with allusions to Isa. 53:4, 5, 11. **healed**. The healing in the atonement does not refer to physical healing in this context (though cf. Matt. 8:17) but to the forgiveness of sins. Jesus' death should lead to a profound change in the lives of believers, so that they now sever all ties with evil (**die to sin**) and devote themselves to living in a holy manner (**live to righteousness**).

3:1–2 Husbands are to be the leaders in their homes (cf. Eph. 5:22–33; Col. 3:18–19), and wives are to **be subject to** (cf. 1 Pet. 3:5–6) and follow their leadership. If a wife has an unbelieving husband who is disobedient to the **word** (i.e., the gospel), she should not try to pressure him into converting. Instead, her godly **conduct** will testify **without a word** to the truth of the gospel. **your own husbands**. Scripture never says that women in general are to be subject to men in general, but it does affirm male headship in the home (see also Titus 2:5) and in the church (see notes on 1 Tim. 2:11–15; 3:2–3). Scripture also affirms the equality of man and woman as being made in the image of God (Gen. 1:27; cf. 1 Pet. 3:7).

3:1 For a Christian wife to have a different religion than her husband was quite astonishing for that culture. For example, the Greek historian Plutarch (c. A.D. 46–127) said, "A wife should not acquire her own friends, but should make her husband's friends her own. The gods are the first and most significant friends. For this reason, it is proper for a wife to recognize only those gods whom her husband worships" (*Advice to Bride and Groom* 19, *Moralia* 140D). Even though Peter calls on wives to submit to their husbands, it was a different submission than was common in that culture, for the wives' devotion was first and foremost to Christ.

3:3–4 Do not let your adorning be external. Peter's instructions here were common in his day (see Seneca, *Epistles*, *To Helvia* 16.3–4; Dio Chrysostom, *Orations* 7.117; Juvenal, *Satire* 6.457–463; 490–511; Plutarch, *Advice to Bride and Groom*, *Moralia* 141E; Epictetus, *Handbook* 40). Such "external . . . adorning" can be witnessed in portraits and sculptures from the first century, where the elaborate **braiding of** women's **hair** and the wearing of ostentatious **jewelry** was common in upper-class Roman society. In contrast to this, the Christian woman should focus on inner (**hidden**) beauty **of the heart**. What matters to God is the godly character of the wife, characterized by a **gentle and quiet spirit**. It is clear that Peter is not literally prohibiting all braiding of hair or all wearing of gold jewelry, because if this were the case the same prohibition would apply also to wearing clothing! Instead, Peter warns against both an inordinate preoccupation with personal appearance and material excess in such matters.

3:5 Hope **in God** is expressed in a wife honoring her husband **by submitting** to him, as the venerable women in the OT did.

3:6 Sarah obeyed Abraham. Peter describes Sarah's submission in terms of obedience. Such obedience does not mean the relationship between husbands and wives is like that of parents and children, but it does show that a wife is to follow her husband's direction and leadership. In the culture of her day, Sarah expressed her submission by respectfully referring to Abraham as **lord** (see Gen. 18:12). **do not fear**. Peter calls on wives to model themselves after such godly women, not fearing that harm will come to them, but trusting God as Sarah did.

3:7 Peter's advice to **husbands** is compressed, perhaps because he addresses at more length those under authority who are more likely to be mistreated (slaves and wives). The word **likewise** is merely a transition (cf. v. 1; 5:5); it does not mean husbands should submit to their **wives**, since Scripture never teaches this (see Eph. 5:21–33). To **live . . . in an understanding way** probably focuses on living in accord with God's will, which includes understanding the needs of a wife. Interpreters differ over whether **weaker vessel** means weaker in terms of delegated authority, emotions, or physical strength. Peter is probably thinking of the general truth that men are physically stronger than women and may be tempted to threaten their wives through physical or verbal abuse. Women and men share an equal destiny as **heirs . . . of the grace**

to the woman as the weaker [t]vessel, since they are heirs with you[1] of the grace of life, so
that your prayers may not be hindered.

Suffering for Righteousness' Sake

8 Finally, all of you, [u]have unity of mind, sympathy, [v]brotherly love, [w]a tender heart, and
[x]a humble mind. **9** [y]Do not repay evil for evil or reviling for reviling, but on the contrary,
[z]bless, for [a]to this you were called, that you may obtain a blessing. **10** For

> [b]"Whoever desires to love life
> and see good days,
> let him keep his tongue from evil
> and his lips from speaking deceit;
> **11** let him turn away from evil and do good;
> let him seek peace and pursue it.
> **12** For the eyes of the Lord are on the righteous,
> and his ears are open to their prayer.
> But the face of the Lord is against those who do evil."

13 Now [c]who is there to harm you if you are zealous for what is good? **14** [d]But even if you
should suffer for righteousness' sake, you will be blessed. [e]Have no fear of them, [f]nor be
troubled, **15** but [g]in your hearts honor Christ the Lord as holy, [h]always being prepared to
make a defense to anyone who asks you for a reason for the hope that is in you; yet do it
with gentleness and [i]respect, **16** [j]having a good conscience, so that, [k]when you are slandered,
those who revile your good behavior in Christ may be put to shame. **17** For [l]it is better to
suffer for doing good, if that should be God's will, than for doing evil.
18 For Christ also [m]suffered[2] [n]once for sins, the righteous for the unrighteous, [o]that he
might bring us to God, being put to death [p]in the flesh but made alive [q]in the spirit, **19** in

[1] Some manuscripts *since you are joint heirs* [2] Some manuscripts *died*

7 [t]See 1 Thess. 4:4
8 [u]See Rom. 12:16 [v]See Heb. 13:1 [w]Eph. 4:32 [x]See Eph. 4:2
9 [y]ch. 2:23; See Rom. 12:17 [z]Luke 6:28; Rom. 12:14; 1 Cor. 4:12 [a]ch. 2:21
10 [b]Cited from Ps. 34:12-16
13 [c][Prov. 16:7]
14 [d]ch. 2:19, 20; 4:14, 16; Matt. 5:10 [e]Isa. 8:12, 13; [ver. 6; Matt. 10:28] [f]John 14:1, 27
15 [g][Isa. 29:23; Matt. 6:9] [h]Col. 4:6; [2 Tim. 2:25] [i]See ch. 1:17
16 [j]Heb. 13:18 [k]ch. 2:12
17 [l]ch. 2:20; [ch. 4:15, 16]
18 [m]ch. 2:21; 4:1; See Rom. 4:25 [n]Heb. 9:26, 28 [o]Rom. 5:2 [p]ch. 4:1; Col. 1:22; [2 Cor. 13:4] [q]ch. 4:6

of life. Peter does not think women are inferior to men, for both are equally made in God's image (cf. Gal. 3:28). If husbands do not treat their wives in a godly way, the Lord will pay no heed to their **prayers**.

3:8–9 Finally, all of you provides a transition from the preceding specific instructions to a list of godly virtues that all believers are called to exemplify at all times. Those who **bless** others will receive a **blessing** from God, which Peter explains in the following verses.

3:10–12 Peter draws on Ps. 34:12–16 (see note on 1 Pet. 2:3). To **love life** and **see good days** is the result of the "blessing" (3:9) of God in one's life. Peter says this will come to the person who will **keep his tongue from evil** and who will **turn away from evil and do good**. Obedience to God in daily life is the path to experiencing God's blessing (cf. Ps. 34:4–10), and by implication disobedience will lead to God's discipline (cf. Ps. 34:16, 21; Heb. 12:4–11). Peter continues his quotation of Psalm 34: **For the eyes of the Lord are on the righteous** (to observe and care for them) and **his ears are open to their prayer** (for various needs and cares). This does not mean that God keeps obedient believers from suffering (cf. 1 Pet. 2:19–23; 3:14, 17; 4:12–19) but that God will provide his grace "to strengthen and establish" believers in the midst of suffering (5:10) and in times of great need (cf. 2 Cor. 12:9; Heb. 4:16).

3:13–4:11 *Responding to Suffering in a Godly Way.* Believers are to endure hardship, knowing that they will receive a final reward (3:13–17). Christ suffered at his death but was raised from the dead, and thus has triumphed over all demonic powers (3:18–22). Christians are urged to give themselves wholly to God, being willing to suffer and do what is right (4:1–6). Expectation of the end times should motivate believers to live in a way that pleases God and to exercise their spiritual gifts (4:7–11).

3:13–14 even if. Peter is writing to Christians already suffering for their faith, therefore he is not saying that such suffering is improbable. His point is that no one will ultimately or finally **harm** Christians, "even if" they suffer now, for God will reward them (cf. Rom. 8:31). Indeed, they **will be blessed** by God in their sufferings (cf. Matt. 5:10).

3:15–17 Believers should always be ready to provide a rationale for their faith, but they should do so winsomely and righteously. And if they keep a **good conscience**, any accusations against them will prove groundless, and their accusers will be **put to shame**. It is sometimes **God's will** that Christians **suffer for doing good**.

3:18 A key statement on the substitutionary atonement of Christ. He suffered and died as the **righteous** one in place of the **unrighteous**, in order to **bring us to God**. One interpretation of **being put to death in the flesh but made alive in the spirit** is that "in the flesh" means in the visible, physical realm in which Jesus was crucified and "in the spirit" (as in 4:6) means in the invisible, spiritual realm where Christ now lives. Another view is that Jesus died physically but was raised from the dead by the Holy Spirit.

3:19 spirits in prison. There is much debate about the identity of these spirits. The Greek term *pneuma* ("spirit"), in either singular or plural, can mean either human spirits or angels, depending on the context (cf. Num. 16:22; 27:16; Acts 7:59; Heb. 12:23; etc.). Among the three most common interpretations, the first two fit best with the rest of Scripture and with historic orthodox Christian doctrine. These are:

(1) The first interpretation understands "spirits" (Gk. *pneumasin*, plural) as referring to the unsaved (human spirits) of Noah's day. Christ, "in the spirit" (1 Pet. 3:18), proclaimed the gospel "in the days of Noah" (v. 20) through Noah. The unbelievers who heard Christ's preaching "did not obey . . . in the days of Noah" (v. 20) and are now suffering judgment (they are "spirits in prison," v. 19). Several reasons support this view: (a) Peter calls Noah a "herald of righteousness" (2 Pet. 2:5), where "herald" represents Greek *kēryx*, "preacher," which corresponds to the noun *kēryssō*, "proclaim," in 1 Pet. 3:19. (b) Peter says the "Spirit of Christ" was speaking through the OT prophets (1:11); thus Christ could have been speaking through Noah as an OT prophet. (c) The context indicates that Christ was preaching through Noah, who was in a persecuted minority, and God saved Noah, which is similar to the situation in Peter's time: Christ is now preaching the gospel through Peter and his readers (v. 15) to a persecuted minority, and God will save them.

(2) In the second interpretation, the spirits are the fallen angels who were cast into hell to await the final judgment. Reasons supporting this view include: (a) Some interpreters say that the "sons of God" in Gen. 6:2–4 are angels (see note on Gen. 6:1–2) who sinned by cohabiting with human women "when God's patience waited in the days of Noah" (1 Pet. 3:20). (b) Almost without exception in the NT, "spirits" (plural) refers to supernatural beings rather than people (e.g., Matt. 8:16; 10:1; Mark 1:27; 5:13; 6:7; Luke 4:36; 6:18; 7:21;

19[q][See ver. 18 above]
20[r]Gen. 6:3, 5, 13, 14 [s]Heb. 11:7 [t]Gen. 7:1, 7, 23; 8:18; 2 Pet. 2:5
21[u]Mark 16:16; Acts 16:33; Rom. 6:3-6; Titus 3:5 [v][Rom. 10:10] [w]ch. 1:3
22[x]Acts 2:33, 34; Rom. 8:34; Eph. 1:20; Col. 3:1; Heb. 1:3 [y]Rom. 8:38; 1 Cor. 15:24; Eph. 1:21

Chapter 4
1[z]ch. 3:18 [a][Eph. 6:13] [b]Rom. 6:2, 7; Gal. 5:24; Col. 3:3, 5 [c][2 Pet. 2:14]
2[d]Rom. 6:14; 14:7; 2 Cor. 5:15 [e]ch. 1:14 [f]Titus 2:12; 1 John 2:16 [g]Rom. 6:11
3[h]Ezek. 44:6; 45:9; Acts 17:30 [i]Eph. 4:17-19; 1 Thess. 4:5; [1 Cor. 12:2]
4[j]See Eph. 5:18 [k]ch. 2:12; 3:16
5[l][James 5:9]; See Acts 10:42
6[m]ch. 3:19
7[n]See James 5:8 [o]See ch. 1:13 [p]Matt. 26:41; Luke 21:36
8[q][1 Cor. 13:5, 6]; See James 5:20

which[1] he went and [q]proclaimed[2] to the spirits in prison, **20** because[3] they formerly did not
obey, [r]when God's patience waited in the days of Noah, [s]while the ark was being prepared,
in which a few, that is, [t]eight persons, were brought safely through water. **21** Baptism, which
corresponds to this, [u]now saves you, not as a removal of dirt from the body but [v]as an
appeal to God for a good conscience, [w]through the resurrection of Jesus Christ, **22** who has
gone into heaven and [x]is at the right hand of God, [y]with angels, authorities, and powers
having been subjected to him.

Stewards of God's Grace

4 Since therefore [z]Christ suffered in the flesh,[4] [a]arm yourselves with the same way of
thinking, for [b]whoever has suffered in the flesh [c]has ceased from sin, **2** [d]so as to live for
[e]the rest of the time in the flesh [f]no longer for human passions but [g]for the will of God. **3** For
the time that is past [h]suffices [i]for doing what the Gentiles want to do, living in sensuality,
passions, drunkenness, orgies, drinking parties, and lawless idolatry. **4** With respect to this
they are surprised when you do not join them in the same flood of [j]debauchery, and [k]they
malign you; **5** but they will give account to him who is ready [l]to judge the living and the
dead. **6** For this is why [m]the gospel was preached even to those who are dead, that though
judged in the flesh the way people are, they might live in the spirit the way God does.
7 [n]The end of all things is at hand; therefore [o]be self-controlled and sober-minded [p]for
the sake of your prayers. **8** Above all, keep loving one another earnestly, since [q]love covers

[1] Or *the Spirit, in whom* [2] Or *preached* [3] Or *when* [4] Some manuscripts add *for us*; some *for you*

8:2; 10:20; 11:26; Acts 5:16; 8:7; 19:12, 13; 1 Tim. 4:1; 1 John 4:1; Rev. 16:13–14; cf. Heb. 1:7). (c) The word "prison" is not used elsewhere in Scripture as a place of punishment *after death* for human beings, while it is used for Satan (Rev. 20:7) and other fallen angels (2 Pet. 2:4; Jude 6). In this case the message that Christ **proclaimed** is almost certainly one of triumph, after having been "put to death in the flesh but made alive in the spirit" (1 Pet. 3:18).

(3) In a third view, some have advocated the idea that Christ offered a second chance of salvation to those in hell. This interpretation, however, is in direct contradiction with other Scripture (cf. Luke 16:26; Heb. 9:27) and with the rest of 1 Peter and therefore must be rejected on biblical and theological grounds, leaving either of the first two views as the most likely interpretation.

3:21 A comparison is drawn between salvation in the ark and **baptism**. In both instances, believers are saved through the waters of judgment, since baptism portrays salvation through judgment. The mere mechanical act of baptism does not save, for Peter explicitly says, "**not as a removal of dirt from the body**," meaning that the passing of water over the body does not cleanse anyone. Baptism **saves you** because it represents inward faith, as evidenced by one's **appeal to God** for the forgiveness of one's sins (**for a good conscience**). Furthermore, baptism "saves" only insofar as it is grounded in the death and **resurrection of Jesus Christ**. Baptism is a visual representation of the fact that Christians are clothed with Christ (cf. Gal. 3:27), and in union with Christ they share his victory over sin. Though Christians have disagreed about the proper mode of water baptism beginning in the early history of the church, Christians have generally agreed (irrespective of denominational differences) that water baptism is an outward sign of the inward reality of regeneration, which is the result of the work of the Holy Spirit (cf. John 3:5, 8; Titus 3:5), and which may be received only by grace through faith (see Eph. 2:8).

3:22 The central truth of vv. 18–22 is that Christ has triumphed over his enemies. He is now ascended to **the right hand of God**, and all **angels** and demonic **powers** are **subjected to him** since he is Lord and Christ. Christians can therefore rejoice in their sufferings, knowing that Christ has triumphed.

4:1–2 Since therefore Christ suffered. The suffering of Christ again functions as a model and inspiration for the readers. Concerning the phrase **whoever has suffered in the flesh has ceased from sin**, three different interpretations have been suggested: (1) Some suggest that this could refer to the suffering of Christ ("the one who has suffered")—who, though he was not himself a sinner, took sin upon himself and then triumphed over it forever through his suffering and death. This interpretation seems unlikely, however, because "whoever" seems too broad and imprecise to be a clear reference to Christ. (2) Others have suggested that this is a reference to the believer being dead to the power of sin, as a result of having died with Christ (similar to Paul's concept in Rom. 6:1–11). (3) More likely, Peter's point is that when believers are willing to suffer, the nerve center of sin is severed in their lives. Although believers will never be totally free from sin in this life (cf. James 3:2; 1 John 1:8), when believers endure suffering for the sake of Christ they show that their purpose in life is not to live for their own pleasures but according to **the will of God** and for his glory.

4:3–4 living in sensuality . . . drinking parties, and lawless idolatry. The lives of unbelievers have not fundamentally changed from the first century to the twenty-first; believers should have nothing to do with such behavior, even when their nonparticipation means that others will **malign** them.

4:5 Unbelievers do not have the last word; **they will give account** and face God's judgment.

4:6 the gospel was preached even to those who are dead. Although some maintain that Peter offers a second chance after death for those who rejected Christ, this view is untenable since it contradicts both the clear teaching of Scripture throughout the rest of the Bible (e.g., Luke 16:26; Heb. 9:27; see note on 1 Pet. 3:19) and the immediate context, concerning the importance of perseverance of believers (4:1–6) and the coming judgment of "the living and the dead" (v. 5). Given the immediate context, "those who are dead" refers to Christians to whom "the gospel was preached" when they were alive but who have since died. This fits with the meaning of "dead" in v. 5. Even though believers will experience physical death (i.e., they are **judged in the flesh the way people are**), believers who have died **live in the spirit the way God does** (that is, they live in heaven now, and they will live as well at the resurrection when Christ returns).

4:7 The end of all things is at hand does not mean Peter was expecting Christ to return in a few weeks or months. It means, rather, that all the major events in God's great salvation plan—culminating in the death, resurrection, and ascension of Christ and the outpouring of the Spirit at Pentecost—had already occurred. Therefore Christ's return could happen at any time: it was "at hand" in Peter's day, and it still is today. But the imminent arrival of the end is not a call simply to look into heaven and wait for Jesus' return. Instead, believers are to be **self-controlled** and **sober-minded**, so that they may be devoted to prayer and maximize their usefulness in God's kingdom.

4:8–9 Enduring love for others testifies that a person is living in light of the future. True **love covers a multitude of** other people's **sins** (Prov. 10:12). Where love abounds, offenses are frequently overlooked and quickly forgotten. **Hospitality**, much admired in both Greco-Roman and Jewish sources (cf. 1 Tim. 3:2; Titus 1:8), was much needed in an era when inns could be dangerous and unpleasant.

a multitude of sins. 9 [r]Show hospitality to one another without grumbling. 10 [s]As each has
received a gift, use it to serve one another, [t]as good stewards of God's varied grace: 11 whoever speaks, as one who speaks [u]oracles of God; whoever serves, as one who serves [v]by the
strength that God supplies—in order that in everything [w]God may be glorified through
Jesus Christ. [x]To him belong glory and [y]dominion forever and ever. Amen.

Suffering as a Christian

12 Beloved, do not be surprised at [z]the fiery trial when it comes upon you to test you, as
though something strange were happening to you. 13 But rejoice [a]insofar as you share Christ's
sufferings, that you may also rejoice and be glad [b]when his glory is revealed. 14 [c]If you are
insulted [d]for the name of Christ, you are blessed, because the Spirit of glory[1] and of God rests
upon you. 15 But [e]let none of you suffer as a murderer or a thief or an evildoer or [f]as a meddler.
16 Yet [e]if anyone suffers as a [g]Christian, let him not be ashamed, but let him glorify God [d]in
that name. 17 For it is time for judgment [h]to begin at the household of God; and [i]if it begins
with us, what will be the outcome for those who [j]do not obey the gospel of God? 18 And

> [k]"If the righteous is scarcely saved,
> what will become of the ungodly and the sinner?"[2]

19 Therefore let those who suffer according to God's will [l]entrust their souls to a faithful
Creator while doing good.

Shepherd the Flock of God

5 So I exhort the elders among you, [m]as a fellow elder and [n]a witness of the sufferings
of Christ, as well as a partaker in the glory that is going to be revealed: 2 [o]shepherd the
flock of God that is among you, exercising oversight,[3] [p]not under compulsion, but will-

[1] Some manuscripts insert *and of power* [2] Greek *where will the ungodly and sinner appear?* [3] Some manuscripts omit *exercising oversight*

9 [r]Heb. 13:2; [1 Tim. 3:2; Titus 1:8]
10 [s]Rom. 12:6, 7; 1 Cor. 4:7; [Matt. 25:15] [t]Luke 12:42; 1 Cor. 4:1, 2; Titus 1:7
11 [u]Acts 7:38; Rom. 3:2; Heb. 5:12 [v]Rom. 12:3 [w]1 Cor. 10:31 [x]See Rom. 11:36 [y]ch. 5:11; Jude 25; Rev. 1:6; 5:13
12 [z]ch. 1:7
13 [a]Phil. 3:10, 11; See Acts 5:41 [b][ch. 1:5-7; 5:1; Rom. 8:17, 18; Jude 24]
14 [c]Ps. 89:51; Matt. 5:11 [d]John 15:21; [Heb. 11:26]
15 [e]ch. 2:19, 20; 3:14, 17 [f]1 Thess. 4:11; 2 Thess. 3:11; 1 Tim. 5:13
16 [e][See ver. 15 above] [g]See Acts 26:28 [d][See ver. 14 above]
17 [h]Jer. 25:29; Ezek. 9:6; Amos 3:2; Rom. 2:9 [i][Luke 23:31] [j][2 Thess. 1:8]
18 [k]Prov. 11:31
19 [l]Ps. 31:5; Luke 23:46; [Ps. 10:14; 2 Tim. 1:12]

Chapter 5

1 [m][2 John 1; 3 John 1] [n]See Luke 24:48
2 [o][Jude 12]; See John 21:16 [p][Philem. 14]

4:10 All believers have **received** at least one spiritual **gift** from God, and they are not to hoard these gifts but use them faithfully as **stewards** of God's **grace** (cf. 1 Corinthians 12–14).

4:11 whoever speaks . . . whoever serves. Peter divides spiritual gifts generally into speaking and serving gifts (for more detailed lists, see Rom. 12:6–8; 1 Cor. 12:8–10, 28–30; and Eph. 4:11). Those who speak must not propound their own ideas but faithfully declare God's words (**oracles**). Similarly, those who serve must not depend on their own strength but draw their strength from God, so that God alone **may be glorified through Jesus Christ**.

4:12–5:11 *Persevering in Suffering.* As the letter draws to a close, Peter reminds his readers that they should not be astonished when they suffer. God is using the suffering to purify the church; therefore they should unreservedly give themselves to God in their sufferings (4:12–19). Peter concludes his letter with exhortations for the leaders and the congregation as a whole to continue in the faith, knowing that their final reward is certain (5:1–11).

4:12–13 Beloved marks the beginning of a new section of the letter (cf. 2:11). Suffering is the norm for Christians, not a surprising exception. To suffer as a Christian is a call to **rejoice** as a disciple of Christ, and such joy is the prelude to the joy that is to come at the return of Christ (**when his glory is revealed**).

4:14 To be **insulted** because one belongs to Christ is to be **blessed** by God, **because** in such times the **Spirit of glory**, the Holy Spirit, **rests upon** believers in an especially powerful way. Further, it is the same Spirit that rested on Jesus (Isa. 11:2; cf. Matt. 3:16) who now rests upon the believer.

4:16 The term **Christian** in the NT is always (except in this case) used by opponents of believers. The term was coined in Antioch (Acts 11:26), and Agrippa used it in his conversation with Paul (Acts 26:28). The term means "follower of Christ." Christians are to suffer in such a way that they bring honor to God instead of disrepute.

4:17–18 In the OT, **household of God** (lit., "house of God") refers to the temple but now God's people are his temple (see 2:4–10). "**Judgment** beginning with God's house" alludes to Ezek. 9:1–6 and Mal. 3:1–4, where the Lord purifies his people. Judgment here is not punitive, however, but purifying and cleansing. The suffering of God's people refines them (1 Pet. 1:6–7). **what will be the outcome . . . ?** If the people of God need purifying, then surely the judgment of **those who do not obey the gospel** will be much more severe (cf. vv. 3–5). Peter reinforces this point by quoting Prov. 11:31 from the Septuagint (Greek OT). **Scarcely saved** does not mean that the **righteous** just barely receive salvation. "Scarcely" (Gk. *molis*, "with difficulty") means that the righteous are saved in the midst of suffering; their salvation is not easy and simple.

4:19 This verse encapsulates the message of 1 Peter: Believers **suffer** in accord with the **will** of God, for he rules over everything that happens to them. As the sovereign **Creator**, God is also loving and **faithful**, therefore they should **entrust** their lives entirely to him, just as Jesus did when he suffered (2:23). Such trust manifests itself in **doing** what is **good**.

5:1 The most common NT term for church leaders is **elders** (see notes on Acts 14:23; 1 Tim. 3:1). Apparently elders served as leaders in all the churches, including those in the northern part of Asia Minor, showing that this was the typical form of leadership in NT churches. Peter, who is an apostle (1 Pet. 1:1), also serves as a fellow **elder** and an authoritative **witness** of Christ's ministry, especially his **sufferings**. Peter often reminds those to whom he writes that suffering precedes **glory** (cf. 1:6–7, 11, 21; 2:4, 7, 19–20; 3:13–14, 18; 4:6, 13; 5:4, 6, 10).

5:2–3 Elders (v. 1) are entrusted with the responsibility to **shepherd the flock** (Gk. *poimainō*, "to tend sheep; to act as a shepherd"; cf. John 21:16; Acts 20:28; Eph. 4:11), from which the English verb and noun "pastor" is derived (Latin *pastor* means "shepherd"). Elders are also entrusted with **exercising oversight** (translating Gk. *episkopeō*), which is the verb form of the noun "overseer" (Gk. *episkopos*), which is another title for those who serve as elders (cf. Acts 20:28). The terms "shepherd" and "exercising oversight" emphasize the *function* of elders (i.e., they are to feed and watch over "the flock"), while the title "elder" focuses on the *office*. Peter now gives three exhortations to elders as to how they are to carry out the responsibilities entrusted to them: (1) elders are to "shepherd" the church gladly or **willingly**, in accord with God's will, instead of doing it out of a sense of **compulsion**; (2) they are to do the work **eagerly** and not out of greed or for **shameful gain** (Gk. *aischrokerdōs*, "in fondness for dishonest gain, greedily"); (3) they are to serve as **examples** to the congregation, and not use their place of leadership as a means to be **domineering**.

2 [q]1 Tim. 3:8; Titus 1:7
3 [r]Ezek. 34:4; Matt. 20:25; Mark 10:42; 2 Cor. 1:24 [s]Phil. 3:17; 2 Thess. 3:9; 1 Tim. 4:12; Titus 2:7
4 [t]Heb. 13:20 [u][ch. 1:4] [v]1 Cor. 9:25; See James 1:12
5 [w][Matt. 20:26, 27; John 13:4, 5, 14] [x]See James 4:6, 10
6 [x][See ver. 5 above]
7 [y][Ps. 37:5; 55:22]; See Matt. 6:25 [z]Ps. 40:17
8 [a]See ch. 1:13 [b]See Matt. 24:42 [c]Eph. 4:27; 6:11; Rev. 12:9, 12; [Job 1:9-12; Luke 22:31; 2 Cor. 2:11] [d]Job 1:7; 2:2 [e][Ps. 22:21]
9 [f]James 4:7 [g]Col. 2:5 [h]Acts 14:22; 1 Thess. 3:3; 2 Tim. 3:12
10 [i]ch. 1:6 [j]1 Cor. 1:9; 1 Thess. 2:12; 1 Tim. 6:12 [k]2 Tim. 2:10 [l]Heb. 13:21 [m]Luke 22:32; Rom. 16:25
11 [n]See ch. 4:11
12 [o]Acts 15:22; 2 Cor. 1:19; 1 Thess. 1:1; 2 Thess. 1:1 [p][Heb. 13:22] [q]See Acts 11:23 [r]See 1 Cor. 15:1
13 [s]See Acts 12:12
14 [t]See Rom. 16:16

ingly, as God would have you;[1] [q]not for shameful gain, but eagerly; **3** not [r]domineering over
those in your charge, but [s]being examples to the flock. **4** And when [t]the chief Shepherd
appears, you will receive the [u]unfading [v]crown of glory. **5** Likewise, you who are younger,
be subject to the elders. [w]Clothe yourselves, all of you, with humility toward one another,
for [x]"God opposes the proud but gives grace to the humble."

6 [x]Humble yourselves, therefore, under the mighty hand of God so that at the proper
time he may exalt you, **7** [y]casting all your anxieties on him, because [z]he cares for you. **8** [a]Be
sober-minded; [b]be watchful. Your [c]adversary the devil [d]prowls around [e]like a roaring lion,
seeking someone to devour. **9** [f]Resist him, [g]firm in your faith, knowing that [h]the same kinds
of suffering are being experienced by your brotherhood throughout the world. **10** And [i]after
you have suffered a little while, the God of all grace, [j]who has called you to his [k]eternal
glory in Christ, will himself [l]restore, [m]confirm, strengthen, and establish you. **11** [n]To him
be the dominion forever and ever. Amen.

Final Greetings

12 By [o]Silvanus, a faithful brother as I regard him, [p]I have written briefly to you, exhorting and declaring that this is [q]the true grace of God. [r]Stand firm in it. **13** She who is at
Babylon, who is likewise chosen, sends you greetings, and so does [s]Mark, my son. **14** [t]Greet
one another with the kiss of love.

[u]Peace to all of you who are in Christ.

[1] Some manuscripts omit *as God would have you*

[u]Eph. 6:23

5:4 The **chief Shepherd** is Jesus Christ, and when he comes again he will reward with **glory** every pastor who has served faithfully.

5:5 You who are younger probably means younger members of the congregation, who are more likely to be headstrong and resistant to leadership. They are to **subject** themselves to **the elders. all of you**. Christians, as well as nonbelievers, are self-oriented by nature and therefore need to relate **with humility toward one another**. Peter cites Prov. 3:34 (cf. James 4:6) to remind his readers that God is against the **proud** but will lavish his favor upon those who are **humble**.

5:6 Humble yourselves. In their suffering, God's people are to give themselves entirely to him, submitting to his wise ordering of their lives. **Mighty hand of God** brings to mind the exodus, where the Lord delivered Israel from Egypt "by a mighty hand" (e.g., Ex. 3:19; 32:11; Deut. 4:34; 5:15; Dan. 9:15). Those who suffer can likewise be confident that the day of humiliation will not last forever. Whether later in this earthly life or on the last day, God will **exalt** his people **at the proper time**.

5:7 casting all your anxieties on him. The participle "casting" modifies the main verbal phrase "humble yourselves" from v. 6. Worry is a form of pride because it involves taking concerns upon oneself instead of entrusting them to God. Believers can trust God because, as their Father, **he cares** for them.

5:8 Be sober-minded; be watchful. Christians need to be spiritually vigilant, watching for attacks from **the devil**, their great enemy and opponent. Peter uses the graphic image of a **lion** to describe Satan's destructive threat: he **prowls around . . . seeking someone to devour**, hoping that believers will be terrified in their hardship and persecutions, or that they will be deceived and fall into sin. Though the devil may threaten to "devour" Christians, they nonetheless have assurance that they will be guarded by God's power (1:5).

5:9 Resist him. Christians need not fear the devil, for the Lord has given them power to stand against him by being **firm in your faith** (cf. Eph. 6:12–18). Trusting in God's promises, believers know that suffering is not the final word and that ultimately they will be exalted (cf. James 4:7). The suffering experienced by the believers in northern Asia Minor is not unique to them, for it is the portion of believers everywhere (**your brotherhood throughout the world**). Hence, they can take courage that they are not alone. Though "throughout the world" does not indicate an empire-wide decree against Christians in Peter's day (see Introduction: Purpose, Occasion, and Background), Christians who suffer in any age can be assured that they are not alone in their distress.

5:10 a little while (cf. 1:6). This includes the period of time beginning with Christ's ascension (cf. Acts 1:6–11) until Christ comes again at the end of the age. From God's perspective, one's time in this world is notably brief (cf. James 4:14; 2 Pet. 3:8). Thus, no matter how long or intense one's suffering may be, it will be short compared to the joys of eternity. Four verbs (**restore, confirm, strengthen, establish**) remind believers that God will eventually restore whatever they have lost for the sake of Christ. Though suffering will come first, it will be followed by **eternal glory**. The God who effectually **called** believers by his **grace** will fortify them with his strength, so that they are able to endure to the end.

5:11 Because God is sovereign and rules over all, believers have nothing to fear.

5:12–14 *Concluding Words.* The letter concludes with greetings and a final exhortation to stand firm.

5:12 Some scholars have suggested that **by Silvanus . . . I have written** designates Silvanus as the secretary who helped compose the letter, but the Greek construction here (*dia* plus genitive of a person's name) would indicate instead that Silvanus delivered the letter (see, e.g., Acts 15:23, where the same construction occurs with this meaning). Silvanus is elsewhere called "Silas" (e.g., Acts 15:22; 16:19; 17:4; 2 Cor. 1:19; 1 Thess. 1:1). Peter sums up his letter by emphasizing that **this is the true grace of God**, urging his readers, in the midst of persecution and suffering, not to forsake the faith and to **stand firm** in that grace.

5:13 She who is at Babylon, who is . . . chosen almost certainly refers to the church in Rome, not a literal woman (cf. "elect lady," 2 John 1, 13). Although the Babylon of the OT was in ruins, the reference resonates with the OT, where "Babylon" represents a center of earthly power opposed to God (cf. Isaiah 13–14; Jeremiah 50–51; see also Revelation 17–18), and in Peter's day that city would be Rome. The language of "Babylon" and "chosen" forms an *inclusio* (a literary envelope) with the first verse of the book: the OT background to "Babylon" reminds believers that though they are exiles, they are "elect exiles" (1 Pet. 1:1) who will receive the promised inheritance. **Mark** is the same John Mark who traveled with Paul and Barnabas on their first missionary journey (cf. Acts 12:25; 13:5, 13; 15:36–39). Though he left Paul and Barnabas, he was later restored to his former usefulness (Col. 4:10; 2 Tim. 4:11; Philem. 24). Peter would have known Mark from the earliest days, because the church met in his mother's home (Acts 12:12). In addition, this verse shows a close relationship between Peter and Mark (**my son**) and is one indication of the validity of the early church tradition that Mark wrote his Gospel at Peter's direction (see Introduction to Mark: Author and Title).

5:14 kiss of love. See note on 1 Cor. 16:20; cf. also Rom. 16:16; 1 Cor. 16:20; 2 Cor. 13:12; 1 Thess. 5:26. Peter closes his letter with a final prayer that his readers will know **peace**, which will be their portion because they are **in Christ** (cf. 1 Pet. 1:2 and note on John 14:27).

INTRODUCTION TO

THE SECOND LETTER OF PETER

2 PETER

Author and Title

Within 2 Peter itself there is strong evidence for authorship by the apostle Peter. In 1:1 the author claims to be "Simeon Peter . . . apostle of Jesus Christ." Moreover, he claims to have been an eyewitness of the transfiguration (1:16–18; cf. Matt. 17:1–8), an event where Peter is featured prominently in the Gospel accounts. If someone other than Peter wrote the letter under his name, as some scholars have claimed, it would be a case of deliberate deception, especially given the author's claims to have witnessed the transfiguration. But there is no historical evidence in support of such a theory. Furthermore, writing in another person's name was condemned among early Christians (cf. 2 Thess. 2:2; 3:17; see Introduction to 1 Timothy: Author and Title).

Some have suggested that the literary style of 2 Peter, which differs from that of 1 Peter, indicates an author other than Peter. But Peter may have used a secretary to help write this second letter, which would not affect the genuineness of his authorship if he ultimately approved what was written.

Scholars have also questioned Petrine authorship of 2 Peter because of the similarities between chapter 2 of this letter and the book of Jude. But this is not a problem for apostolic authorship, since Peter may have included in his letter elements from Jude that he thought would be helpful for his readers. It also could have worked the other way, with Jude using Peter's letter as *his* source. The parallels are close but almost never exact, so it is difficult to sort out the relationship between 2 Peter and Jude with any degree of certainty.

It is reasonable in light of all the evidence, and clearly supported by the claims of the letter itself, to conclude that the apostle Peter wrote 2 Peter.

Date

Peter probably wrote this letter from Rome not too long before his martyrdom, sometime during A.D. 64–67. Elements within the letter lead many scholars to conclude that Peter wrote during a time of persecution by Rome (perhaps during the persecution by Nero, who died in A.D. 68), while Peter himself was in a Roman prison awaiting imminent execution (cf. 1:12–15). The dating of the letter, then, depends largely on the dating of Peter's death.

Theme

Second Peter teaches that the grace of God in Christ truly transforms and empowers Christians to live righteously, even in the face of opposition. This grace, introduced in 1:2–4, serves as the foundation for the remainder of the exhortations. The indwelling Holy Spirit (cf. 1:4, which characterizes Christians as "partakers of the divine nature") produces virtuous "qualities" in followers of Christ (1:8–12), which in turn results in fruitful lives.

Purpose, Occasion, and Background

Peter writes this brief, final reminder to the churches so that his readers will by God's grace live a life that is pleasing to God. In doing so, Peter must also combat the false teachers who were apparently exerting pressure on the churches to depart from the true knowledge of Christ (see esp. ch. 2). The false teaching is not only a theological challenge but also a moral one, holding forth some form of sexual permissiveness as a legitimate Christian lifestyle. While the false teaching can be described based on what Peter writes, it is historically impossible to identify who the false teachers were. For example, there is no clear historical evidence that these teachers were Gnostic or proto-Gnostic.

It is also impossible to identify with certainty the churches Peter is addressing. The leading historical candidates are the churches of Asia Minor, for Peter wrote his first letter to these churches (1 Pet. 1:1–2), and in this letter Peter mentions that this is his second letter to these same people (2 Pet. 3:1).

Key Themes

1. God, through his grace in Jesus Christ, has granted to Christians the privilege of partaking of the divine nature.	1:2–4
2. God's grace results in godliness.	1:5–15
3. The revelation of truth in Christ (and in Scripture, 1:19) is sure because it is from God and not from man-made myths.	1:16–21
4. False teachers are bound over for destruction at the hand of God.	2:1–10
5. False teachers are ethically bankrupt.	2:11–22
6. Believers must endure in the face of opposition, knowing that they live in the last days.	3:1–13
7. The Lord is patient with his creation, but will surely return in judgment like a thief in the night.	3:8–10
8. God rescues the righteous.	2:7–9; 3:13–18

History of Salvation Summary

Christians are to hold fast to the truth in Christ while patiently awaiting the second coming. (For an explanation of the "History of Salvation," see the Overview of the Bible, pp. 23–26.)

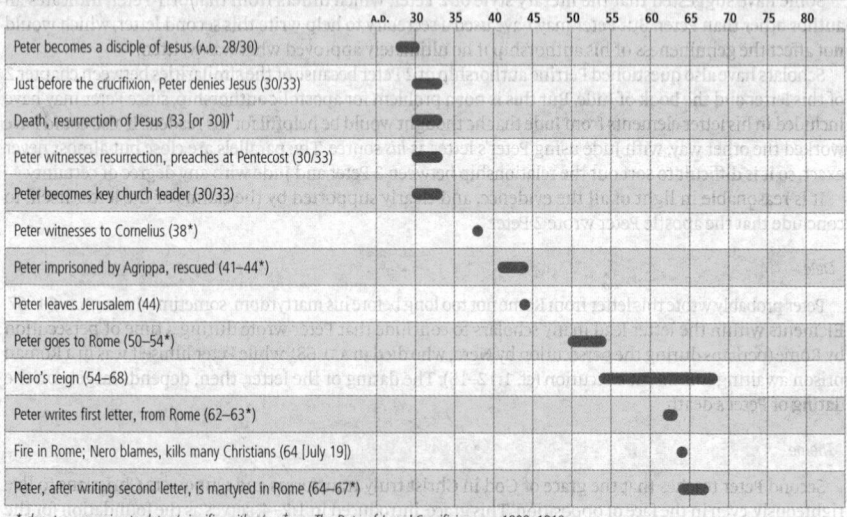

Timeline

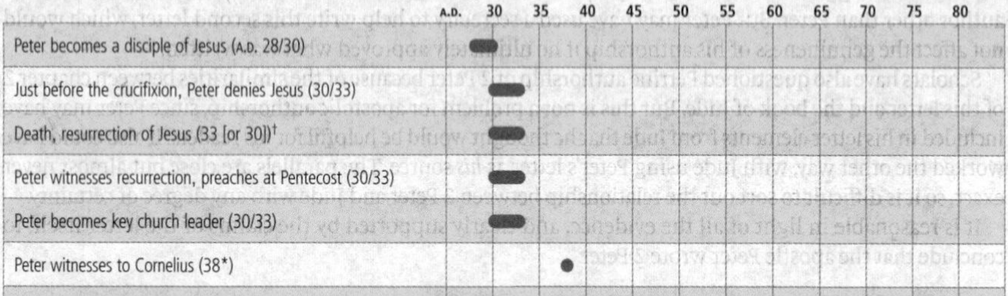

A.D. 30 35 40 45 50 55 60 65 70 75 80
Peter becomes a disciple of Jesus (A.D. 28/30)
Just before the crucifixion, Peter denies Jesus (30/33)
Death, resurrection of Jesus (33 [or 30])†
Peter witnesses resurrection, preaches at Pentecost (30/33)
Peter becomes key church leader (30/33)
Peter witnesses to Cornelius (38*)
Peter imprisoned by Agrippa, rescued (41–44*)
Peter leaves Jerusalem (44)
Peter goes to Rome (50–54*)
Nero's reign (54–68)
Peter writes first letter, from Rome (62–63*)
Fire in Rome; Nero blames, kills many Christians (64 [July 19])
Peter, after writing second letter, is martyred in Rome (64–67*)

** denotes approximate date; / signifies either/or; † see The Date of Jesus' Crucifixion, pp. 1809–1810*

Literary Features

The primary form is the epistle, with its usual elements. Partly on the basis of 1:13–14, where Peter asserts that he will soon depart this life, it is customary to view 2 Peter as adhering to some of the conventions of the farewell discourse. Motifs that belong to that genre include the author's (a) announcing that he is near the end of his earthly life, (b) reminding his followers of what he has taught them, (c) commanding his followers how to live, and (d) predicting what will happen in the future. In a farewell discourse, a leader has his last chance to influence his followers in the right direction for the sake of the movement in which he has been a guiding light. Second Peter is also filled with famous proverbs and aphoristic statements, vivid poetry and imagery, and an eschatological (end-time) discourse (ch. 3).

Much of the letter falls into place if one grasps that Peter's horror at false teaching (see esp. ch. 2) is set over against the reliability of God's prophetic word (1:19–21; 3:1–2). These two motifs converge in the vision of the last chapter, where biblical prophecy about the return of Christ is aggressively offered as a rebuttal of scoffers (false teachers) who denigrate biblical prophecy. In 2 Peter, true and false teaching engage in a combat of huge proportions.

Outline

I. Initial Greeting (1:1–2)

II. God's Grace in Christ Is the Source of Godly Living (1:3–11)
   A. God's power exercised on our behalf (1:3–4)
   B. Making every effort to live a godly life (1:5–7)
   C. Living an effective life for Christ (1:8–11)

III. Peter's Reminder to the Churches (1:12–21)
   A. Stirring up Christians to holiness (1:12–15)
   B. Peter's preaching results from his own eyewitness experience (1:16–18)
   C. Truth about Jesus Christ anchored in the prophetic word of Scripture (1:19–21)

IV. Evaluation of False Teachers (2:1–22)
   A. Influence of false teachers (2:1–3)
   B. Judgment of false teachers (2:4–10a)
   C. Character of false teachers (2:10b–16)
   D. Influence of false teachers revisited (2:17–22)

V. The Day of the Lord Will Surely Come (3:1–13)
   A. Scoffers challenge the truth of Scripture concerning the coming of the Lord (3:1–7)
   B. The Lord's patience determines the timing of his return (3:8–10)
   C. Living effectively in view of the Lord's return (3:11–13)

VI. Concluding Exhortations (3:14–18)
   A. Concerning diligence (3:14)
   B. Concerning the distortion of Paul's teaching (3:15–16)
   C. Concerning the proper response to Paul's teaching (3:17–18)

THE SECOND LETTER OF PETER

2 PETER

Greeting

1 Simeon[1] Peter, a servant[2] and apostle of Jesus Christ,
To those who have obtained [a]a faith of equal standing with ours [b]by the righteousness
of our [c]God and Savior Jesus Christ:
2 [d]May grace and peace be multiplied to you [e]in the knowledge of God and of Jesus
our Lord.

Confirm Your Calling and Election

3 His divine power has granted to us all things that pertain to life and godliness, through
the knowledge of him [f]who called us to[3] his own glory and excellence,[4] 4 by which he
has granted to us his precious and very great promises, so that through them you may
become [g]partakers of the divine nature, [h]having escaped from the corruption that is in
the world because of sinful desire. 5 For this very reason, make every effort to supplement
your faith [i]with virtue,[5] and virtue [j]with knowledge, 6 and knowledge with self-control,
and self-control [k]with steadfastness, and steadfastness with godliness, 7 and godliness [l]with
brotherly affection, and brotherly affection [m]with love. 8 For if these qualities[6] are yours

[1] Some manuscripts *Simon* [2] Or *slave* (for the contextual rendering of the Greek word *doulos*, see Preface) [3] Or *by* [4] Or *virtue* [5] Or *excellence*; twice in this verse [6] Greek *these things*; also verses 9, 10, 12

Chapter 1

1 [a]Rom. 1:12; 2 Cor. 4:13; Titus 1:4 [b]Rom. 3:21-26 [c]Titus 2:13
2 [d]1 Pet. 1:2; Jude 2 [e]ver. 3, 8; ch. 2:20; [John 17:3; Phil. 3:8]
3 [f][1 Thess. 2:12; 2 Thess. 2:14; 2 Tim. 1:9; 1 Pet. 5:10]
4 [g][Eph. 4:24; Heb. 12:10; 1 John 3:2] [h]ch. 2:18, 20
5 [i]Phil. 4:8 [j]1 Pet. 3:7
6 [k]See Heb. 10:36; James 1:3
7 [l]See Heb. 13:1 [m]1 Cor. 13; 1 John 4:16

1:1–2 *Initial Greeting.* Peter's greeting is concise and to the point, identifying the author and the audience, and expressing a blessing.

1:1 Simeon. A Hebrew spelling of Simon (cf. Acts 15:14). **Peter**, as an **apostle of Jesus Christ**, is writing to those who have a faith of **equal standing**, showing that all believers share equal privileges before God. This standing was accomplished **by the righteousness of our God and Savior Jesus Christ**. "Righteousness" refers here to God's saving righteousness, showing that faith is a gift from Jesus. Jesus is called "God and Savior," making this one of the clearest NT declarations of the divinity of Christ.

1:2 In his initial blessing of those to whom he writes, Peter mentions a recurring idea in the letter: true **knowledge of God and of Jesus**. Verse 2, like v. 1, points to the deity of Christ (cf. note on v. 1), for both God and Christ are the object of this knowledge.

1:3–11 *God's Grace in Christ Is the Source of Godly Living.* In this first main section of his letter, Peter emphasizes that God's grace results in godliness.

1:3–4 *God's Power Exercised on Our Behalf.* God has provided blessing for the Christian in all things pertaining to life.

1:3 divine power. God himself has acted in his infinite power to accomplish salvation, something only he could accomplish and what human ability could not accomplish. He has **called us to his own glory and excellence**. Believers are called to live in harmony with God's own moral character. On God's "glory," see notes on John 1:14; Acts 6:15; cf. Rev. 21:23. The word "excellence" (Gk. *aretē*, "virtue, excellence") was used by Greek writers to describe the sum of all desirable character qualities.

1:4 God has granted believers his **precious** and **great promises**. It is through these promises that they become **partakers** (Gk. *koinōnos*, "sharer, partaker") **of the divine nature**. They never become part of God, but amazingly they share in his nature as they become increasingly like him. The "great promises" include the promises Peter identifies in his Pentecost sermon in Acts 2:14–41, especially the outpouring of the Holy Spirit in new power. But they also include other promises such as likeness to God (2 Pet. 1:4; cf. 1 John 3:2), Christ's return (2 Pet. 3:4), eternal life in heaven (1 Pet. 1:4), and more broadly, all the promises of Scripture that relate to the gift of new life. "Divine nature" uses terms familiar to Peter's Hellenistic readership to help them understand the idea of transformation into the image of Christ. Peter emphasizes the moral focus of the believer's transformed life. At conversion, Christians are delivered from the **corruption** of this world, which is rooted in **sinful desire**.

1:5–7 *Making Every Effort to Live a Godly Life.* Peter lists "qualities" (v. 8) that characterize a life partaking of the divine nature. These verses contain a straightforward catalog of biblical virtues (cf. Gal. 5:22–23; Heb. 12:10–11). This list does not reflect a legalistic code but rather the desires and features of a transformed heart (cf. "for this very reason," 2 Pet. 1:5). The exhortations to live a new life are grounded in the divine power and promises that were granted to believers when they came to know Jesus Christ as Savior and Lord.

1:5 supplement your faith. Peter exhorts Christians not merely to confess faith in Christ but actually to live as he taught. He is not saying that works are a prerequisite for salvation but rather is arguing that faith must take concrete form in life. All the virtues listed in vv. 5–7 are results of faith, so faith is listed first, while love (the ultimate result of faith) is listed last (v. 7; cf. 1 Tim. 1:5). **Virtue** translates Greek *aretē*; see note on 2 Pet. 1:3.

1:6 Godliness translates Greek *eusebeia*, "devoutness, piety, devotion to God" (also in vv. 3, 7; 3:11; see 2 Tim. 3:5).

1:8–11 *Living an Effective Life for Christ.* Peter explains the necessary relationship between regeneration and a life that reflects the virtues inherent in the knowledge of Christ.

1:8 if these qualities are yours and are increasing. A lifelong pattern of growth in Christlike character is expected of Christians and is the key to fruitful ministry. By contrast, **knowledge** (Gk. *epignōsis*) **of . . . Christ** is **ineffective** and **unfruitful** unless accompanied by a life that increasingly exhibits the qualities of vv. 5–7.

and are increasing, they keep you from being ineffective or [n]unfruitful in the knowledge of
our Lord Jesus Christ. 9 For whoever lacks these qualities is so nearsighted that he [o]is blind,
having forgotten that he was [p]cleansed from his former sins. 10 Therefore, brothers,[1] be all
the more diligent to confirm your calling and [q]election, for if you practice these qualities
[r]you will never fall. 11 For in this way there will be richly provided for you [s]an entrance
into the eternal kingdom of our Lord and Savior Jesus Christ.

12 Therefore I intend [t]always to remind you of these qualities, though you know them
and are established in [u]the truth that you have. 13 I think it right, as long as I am in this
[v]body,[2] [w]to stir you up by way of reminder, 14 [x]since I know that the putting off of my body
will be soon, [y]as our Lord Jesus Christ made clear to me. 15 And I will make every effort so
that after my departure you may be able at any time to recall these things.

Christ's Glory and the Prophetic Word

16 For we did not follow [z]cleverly devised [a]myths when we made known to you [b]the power
and [c]coming of our Lord Jesus Christ, but [d]we were eyewitnesses of his majesty. 17 For when
he received honor and glory from God the Father, and the voice was borne to him by the
Majestic Glory, [e]"This is my beloved Son,[3] with whom I am well pleased," 18 we ourselves
heard this very voice borne from heaven, for we were with him on [f]the holy mountain.
19 And [g]we have the prophetic word more fully confirmed, to which you will do well to pay

[1] Or *brothers and sisters*. The plural Greek word *adelphoi* (translated "brothers") refers to siblings in a family. In New Testament usage, depending on the context, *adelphoi* may refer either to men or to both men and women who are siblings (brothers and sisters) in God's family, the church [2] Greek *tent*; also verse 14 [3] Or *my Son, my* (or *the*) *Beloved*

8 [n]See John 15:2; Titus 3:14
9 [o]Job 5:14; 12:25; Isa. 59:10; Zeph. 1:17; [1 John 2:9-11] [p]Eph. 5:26; Titus 2:14; Heb. 9:14; 1 John 1:7; Rev. 7:14
10 [q]1 Thess. 1:4 [r][ch. 3:17; 1 John 2:10]
11 [s]Col. 1:13; [Acts 14:22]
12 [t]Jude 5; [Rom. 15:14, 15; Phil. 3:1; 1 John 2:21] [u]2 John 2
13 [v]2 Cor. 5:1, 4 [w]ch. 3:1
14 [x][Deut. 4:21, 22; 31:14; 2 Tim. 4:6] [y]John 21:18, 19
16 [z]See 1 Cor. 1:17 [a]See 1 Tim. 1:4 [b]1 Cor. 2:4 [c]See 1 Thess. 2:19 [d]Matt. 17:1, 2, 6; Mark 9:2; Luke 9:28, 29; John 1:14
17 [e]Matt. 17:5; Mark 9:7; Luke 9:35; [Matt. 3:17]
18 [f][Ex. 3:5; Josh. 5:15]
19 [g]See 1 Pet. 1:10

1:9 The one who **lacks these qualities** (cf. vv. 5–7) **is** spiritually **blind** and has **forgotten that he was cleansed** (cf. Titus 3:5–7) from his **sins**. This lack of fruit could exist because a person's "cleansing" was merely an external reformation that did not come from a truly changed heart. But it could also describe a genuine Christian who has fallen into serious error regarding the Christian life. Only God knows the person's true status (cf. 2 Tim. 2:19).

1:10 Christians should be **diligent to confirm** their **calling and election** (Gk. *eklogē*). God calls believers to faith through the gospel (2 Thess. 2:14), but he has also chosen (elected) them "before the foundation of the world" (Eph. 1:4). But God's grace in salvation should not be taken for granted. Growing in the Christlike virtues mentioned in 2 Pet. 1:5–7 will give believers increasing confidence that God really did call them and really did elect them to salvation before the foundation of the world. Thus their election becomes "sure," as a sure foundation. Those who **practice these qualities . . . will never fall**, probably meaning apostasy (falling away from the faith). Good works are evidence of and give assurance of salvation, though they are never the basis for it. Peter's wording does not imply that true followers of Christ can ever apostatize; those who do so were never really "called," "elected," or born again (cf. notes on John 6:39; 6:40; 10:26–29; 1 Thess. 1:4; Heb. 6:4–8).

1:11 in this way. That is, by doing the things Peter mentions in vv. 5–10. This way of life is the path into the **eternal kingdom** of Christ. Those who practice these qualities will be **richly provided** with the reward of eternal life. Some interpreters think "richly" indicates degrees of blessing and reward both in this life and in heaven. Others think that eternal life is itself the reward in view, in contrast to the prospect facing the false teachers.

1:12–21 *Peter's Reminder to the Churches.* Peter contrasts the truth about Christ as revealed by God with the falsehood of man-made myths. In light of this certain truth, the church should be focused on living faithfully.

1:12–15 *Stirring Up Christians to Holiness.* Thinking of his impending death, Peter urgently reminds the churches to continue living in a godly way.

1:12 The readers of this letter already **know** these godly **qualities** (cf. vv. 5–10) and are already **established in the truth** concerning life in Christ. Peter's intent is simply to keep biblical morality in the forefront of the Christian's daily pursuits.

1:14 Peter expects that his execution by Rome is imminent, **as our Lord Jesus Christ made clear to me**. The nearness of his death seems to have been recently revealed to Peter, but he may also be reflecting on his conversation with Jesus in John 21:18–19.

1:16–18 *Peter's Preaching Results from His Own Eyewitness Experience.* Peter recounts his personal experience with Jesus during the transfiguration (Matt. 17:1–8; Mark 9:2–8; Luke 9:28–36a). He contrasts this truth with man-made myths. The content of Peter's preaching is not of human origin but is based on direct revelation from God.

1:16 cleverly devised myths. "Myth" translates Greek *mythos*, "a story without basis in fact, a legend." The gospel of Christ was no myth, because the apostles **were eyewitnesses of his majesty**. Peter had observed the "majesty" of Christ firsthand at the transfiguration. He knew that Christ had come in **power**; he was no mere literary character invented for a mythological narrative. But Jesus' transfiguration also functions as a prelude and anticipation of his coming in glory. Readers learn from 3:3–4 that the false teachers believed that the second coming was also a myth, but Peter refutes this, underscoring the certainty of Christ's return.

1:17 Majestic Glory. A name for God the Father emphasizing the transcendence of his glorious presence (see Ex. 33:12–23; 34:29–35; 2 Cor. 3:12–18). At the transfiguration, God displayed the **honor and glory** of his **beloved Son**, a declaration by the Father of Jesus' divine sonship (cf. Ps. 2:7; Isa. 42:1; Matt. 3:17; Mark 1:11; Luke 3:22).

1:18 we ourselves heard. Peter emphasizes his own eyewitness status, and that of the other apostles, with regard to the transfiguration (Matt. 17:1–8); he personally heard the voice of the Father declare Jesus to be his Son. If someone else had written this letter in Peter's name (see Introduction: Author and Title), that person's claim of eyewitness status would have been a lie.

1:19–21 *Truth about Jesus Christ Anchored in the Prophetic Word of Scripture.* The truth about Christ is based on the prophecies of Scripture, something even more certain than (or just as sure as; see note on v. 19) eyewitness testimony.

1:19 more fully confirmed. Some have understood that Peter's experience of the Transfiguration provides confirmation of OT prophecy, making the already-sure prophecy of the OT even more sure as confirmed by the experience of the Transfiguration. Others have understood "more fully confirmed" as an affirmation that the prophetic writings of the OT are even more sure than Peter's spectacular personal experience at the Transfiguration, thereby underscoring the complete reliability of written Scripture. In either case, believers are admonished to **pay attention** to the certainty of the **prophetic word**. In the contrast between "**we have**" and "**you will do well**," Peter is apparently emphasizing that the interpretation of the apostles ("we") is to be regarded as authoritative for the church ("you"). **Day dawns** and **morning star** both refer to the second coming. The day of the Lord is the day of final judgment and salvation, as the OT often teaches (Isa. 13:6, 9; Ezek. 13:5; Joel 1:15; Amos 5:18, 20). Jesus' second coming will

attention [h]as to a lamp shining in a dark place, until [i]the day [j]dawns and the morning star
rises in your hearts, 20 knowing this first of all, that no prophecy of Scripture comes from
someone's own interpretation. 21 For [k]no prophecy was ever produced by the will of man,
but men spoke from God [l]as they were carried along by the Holy Spirit.

False Prophets and Teachers

2 But [m]false prophets also arose among the people, [n]just as there will be false teachers
among you, who will [o]secretly bring in destructive heresies, even denying the Master
[p]who bought them, bringing upon themselves swift destruction. 2 And many will follow
their sensuality, and because of them the way of truth [q]will be blasphemed. 3 And [r]in their
greed they will exploit you [s]with false words. [t]Their condemnation from long ago is not
idle, and their destruction is not asleep.
4 For if God did not spare [u]angels when they sinned, but [v]cast them into hell[1] and committed them to chains[2] of gloomy darkness [w]to be kept until the judgment; 5 if he did
not spare the ancient world, but [x]preserved Noah, a herald of righteousness, with seven
others, when he brought [y]a flood upon the world of the ungodly; 6 if by [z]turning the cities
of Sodom and Gomorrah to ashes he condemned them to extinction, [a]making them an
example of [b]what is going to happen to the ungodly;[3] 7 and [c]if he rescued righteous Lot,

[1] Greek *Tartarus* [2] Some manuscripts *pits* [3] Some manuscripts *an example to those who were to be ungodly*

19 [h]Ps. 119:105; John 5:35 [i]Rev. 2:28; 22:16; [Mal. 4:2] [j]2 Cor. 4:6
21 [k]2 Tim. 3:16 [l]1 Pet. 1:11; [2 Sam. 23:2; Luke 1:70; Acts 1:16; 3:18]

Chapter 2

1 [m]Deut. 13:1; See Matt. 7:15 [n]Acts 20:30; 2 Cor. 11:13; 1 Tim. 4:1; [Matt. 24:11] [o]Jude 4; [Matt. 10:33; Gal. 2:4] [p]1 Cor. 6:20; 7:23; Gal. 3:13; 4:5; Rev. 5:9; [Ex. 15:16; 1 Pet. 1:18; Rev. 14:3, 4]
2 [q]Rom. 2:24
3 [r][2 Cor. 12:17, 18; 1 Tim. 6:5; Titus 1:11] [s]Rom. 16:18; Col. 2:4 [t][Deut. 32:35; Phil. 3:19]
4 [u]Jude 6 [v][Rev. 20:2, 3, 10] [w]Matt. 25:41
5 [x]See 1 Pet. 3:20 [y]ch. 3:6; Job 22:16
6 [z]See Gen. 19:24 [a][Num. 26:10] [b]Jude 15
7 [c]Gen. 19:16

not only be an objective event in history, it will also rise **in your hearts** as the full light of Christ's presence transforms the hearts of his church to perfect purity.

1:20 Two main views of this verse have been proposed: (1) The first view, the one most in harmony with the ESV rendering, understands the verse to explain the origin of the prophecies of OT Scripture, namely, that **no prophecy of Scripture comes from** (i.e., originates out of) **someone's own interpretation** (i.e., from someone's individual understanding of events, visions, or other things), but rather, that "all prophecy of Scripture" came about from the Holy Spirit's leading (see v. 21). (This takes the Gk. word *ginomai* in its most common sense, as meaning "come into existence".) According to this first view, then, Peter is assuring his readers that all the OT Scriptures that pointed to Christ were inspired by the Holy Spirit, and that the readers should pay close attention to them (v. 19), perhaps in contrast to false teachers who were denigrating Scripture. (2) The second view understands the verse to be speaking of *how* OT prophecies are to be interpreted, therefore some translations render this verse, "no prophecy of Scripture is a matter of [or "for"] one's own interpretation." According to this second view, Peter is saying that one must interpret the OT Scriptures as they are interpreted by the apostles, and hence the interpretations of the OT by the false teachers should be rejected. Although this second view is possible, the first seems more likely, in light of the immediate context and Peter's overall emphasis on the authority of Scripture.

1:21 No biblical **prophecy** was ever **produced** merely because a man wanted to prophesy (**by the will of man**). The prophecy in Scripture was given only by God through men, who "spoke" as they **were carried along by the Holy Spirit**. The Holy Spirit was the active, revelatory agent working within the OT prophets and through their lives and circumstances as they prophesied. This is a key verse for the doctrine of Scripture, indicating that Scripture is inspired by the Holy Spirit, but at the same time **men spoke** God's words, using their own personalities, knowledge, background, vocabulary, and style. "They were carried along" implies that the inspiration of Scripture was invisibly directed by the Holy Spirit, though without overriding the personalities of the human authors. Thus Scripture is fully the Word of God, even though it is recorded in the words of human beings. The exact way in which this was accomplished remains a divine mystery. What is true of OT prophecy is true of "all Scripture" (see 2 Tim. 3:16 and note).

2:1–22 *Evaluation of False Teachers.* In this third main section of his letter, Peter engages in a polemic against the false teachers, using biblical analogies to do so.

2:1–3 *Influence of False Teachers.* Just as there arose false prophets alongside the true prophets of God in OT times, so also there will arise false teachers who will try to mislead the church.

2:1 Peter describes the false teachers. **secretly**. They will subvert the truth by surreptitiously bringing **destructive heresies** into the church. These heresies will be contrary to what Christ and the apostles laid down as foundational doctrines (cf. Eph. 2:20–22), resulting in spiritual ruin rather than life. The false teachers will even deny the truth about the **Master** (Jesus Christ) **who bought them**. Peter apparently uses the language of redemption ("bought them") here in the same way that he describes the counterfeit "salvation" of the false teachers at the end of ch. 2: that is, they claimed to be "redeemed" and "saved" because they were part of the church, but their apostasy showed that they were not truly believers. Another interpretation is that Christ's death paid the penalty for their sins ("bought them") but God did not apply this payment to them because they rejected Christ.

2:2 The heresy will be characterized in part by **sensuality** (Gk. *aselgeia*, "lack of self-constraint, abandonment to immoral behavior"), which most often refers to sexual sin.

2:3 Greed drives the false teachers as well. They **exploit** believers with their **false words** for the sake of material gain. False teachers throughout history have been marked by sexual sin, a lust for money, and dishonesty. All such teachers face **condemnation** and **destruction**.

2:4–10a *Judgment of False Teachers.* Peter turns to a detailed argument proving God's certain judgment on the false teachers. He uses a rabbinic form of proof that moves from minor premise to major premise (if A is true, how much more is B also true), and his analogies in vv. 4–8 amount to minor premises leading to the major premise of vv. 9–10a.

2:4 First minor premise: **if God did not spare angels**. If (A) God has eternally condemned the sinful angels, then (B) how much more certainly will he condemn the false teachers and their followers (major premise, vv. 9b–10a). (See note on Jude 6.)

2:5 Second minor premise: **if** (A) **he did not spare the ancient world, but preserved Noah . . . with seven others**, then (B) will he not even more certainly judge the false teachers (major premise, vv. 9b–10a) while at the same time preserving the godly (major premise, v. 9a). Christians may be a small minority, but God will protect them.

2:6 Third minor premise: Peter sees the judgment of **Sodom and Gomorrah** as a "type" (a divine foreshadowing) of judgment by fire on the last day (3:10–12), an event that will be denied by false teachers (2:4). If (A) God condemned Sodom and Gomorrah, then (B) how much more certain it is that the same thing will **happen to the ungodly** who reject the gospel.

2:7–8 Fourth minor premise: if (A) God **rescued righteous Lot**, who was **greatly distressed** and even tormented by the **conduct of the wicked**

greatly distressed by the sensual conduct of the wicked **8**(for as that righteous man lived
among them day after day, [d]he was tormenting his righteous soul over their lawless deeds
that he saw and heard); **9** then [e]the Lord knows how to rescue the godly from trials,[1] and
to keep the unrighteous under punishment until the day of judgment, **10** and especially
[f]those who indulge[2] in the lust of defiling passion and [g]despise authority.

Bold and willful, they do not tremble [g]as they blaspheme the glorious ones, **11** [h]whereas
angels, though greater in might and power, do not pronounce a blasphemous judgment
against them before the Lord. **12** [i]But these, like irrational animals, [j]creatures of instinct,
born to be caught and destroyed, blaspheming about matters of which they are ignorant, will also be destroyed in their destruction, **13** suffering wrong as [k]the wage for their
wrongdoing. They count it pleasure [l]to revel in the daytime. They are blots and blemishes,
reveling in their deceptions,[3] while [m]they feast with you. **14** They have eyes full of adultery,
[n]insatiable for sin. They entice unsteady souls. They have hearts [o]trained in greed. [p]Accursed
children! **15** Forsaking the right way, [q]they have gone astray. They have followed [r]the way
of Balaam, the son of Beor, who loved [s]gain from wrongdoing, **16** but was rebuked for
his own transgression; [t]a speechless donkey spoke with human voice and restrained the
prophet's madness.

17 [u]These are waterless springs and mists driven by a storm. [v]For them the gloom of utter
darkness has been reserved. **18** For, [w]speaking loud boasts of folly, they entice by sensual
passions of the flesh those who are barely [x]escaping from those who live in error. **19** They
promise them [y]freedom, [z]but they themselves are slaves[4] of corruption. For whatever overcomes a person, to that he is enslaved. **20** For if, [a]after they have escaped the defilements

[1] Or *temptations* [2] Greek *who go after the flesh* [3] Some manuscripts *love feasts* [4] Greek *bondservants*

8 [d]Ps. 119:136, 158; [Ezek. 9:4]
9 [e]1 Cor. 10:13; Rev. 3:10
10 [f]Jude 16, 18 [g]Jude 8; [Ex. 22:28]
11 [h]Jude 9
12 [i]Jude 10 [j][Jer. 12:3; Phil. 3:19]
13 [k]ver. 15 [l][Rom. 13:13; 1 Thess. 5:7]; See James 5:5 [m][1 Cor. 11:21]
14 [n][1 Pet. 4:1] [o]ver. 3; [1 Tim. 4:7] [p][Eph. 2:3]
15 [q]Ezek. 14:11 [r]Num. 22:5, 7; Deut. 23:4; Neh. 13:2; Jude 11; Rev. 2:14 [s]ver. 13
16 [t]Num. 22:21, 23, 28
17 [u]Jude 12 [v]Jude 13
18 [w]Jude 16 [x]ver. 20; ch. 1:4
19 [y]Gal. 5:13; See James 1:25 [z]John 8:34; Rom. 6:16
20 [a]ver. 18

in Sodom (v. 6), then (B) how much more will he "rescue the godly" (major premise, v. 9a). Some have questioned whether Lot was truly **righteous**, given the serious sins he committed (Genesis 19). But the righteous are never considered to be perfect. Moreover, Scripture distinguishes Lot from the citizens of Sodom in that he received the angelic visitors and attempted to protect them from harm—a crucial and courageous action in his lawless and morally depraved environment.

2:9–10a Having stated his minor premises, Peter moves now to his major premise (see note on vv. 4–10a): "If" vv. 4–8 are true, **then** how much more true are vv. 9–10a. God indeed knows how to **rescue the godly from trials**. In the case of Peter's audience, this would have evoked hope of divine deliverance from the false teachers and their influence. God also will certainly **keep the unrighteous under punishment until the day of judgment**. He will punish them in a partial, preliminary way before the final day of judgment (cf. Luke 16:23–24; Heb. 9:27). This applies **especially** to those who engage in **defiling passion** and who **despise authority**—probably a reference to false teachers (cf. 2 Pet. 2:12, 18; 3:3; Jude 8, 16, 18).

2:10b–16 *Character of False Teachers.* Peter gives a lengthy description of the debased character of the false teachers.

2:10b–11 The false teachers are **bold** (in a reckless, foolhardy way) **and willful** (stubborn and arrogant), behaving in ways that even the **angels** avoid. They **blaspheme the glorious ones**, probably evil angels (cf. v. 11; Jude 8–9). In so doing, they recklessly dismiss any thought that these demonic forces have power or that their willful sins will open them to demonic attack. But good angels, like wise humans, do not take these evil powers lightly.

2:12–13 The false teachers operate in **irrational** ways. They act **like . . . animals**, following neither reason nor truth but **instinct**, ignoring even the most basic of human values. Yet they behave like this while posturing as Christians, even to the point that **they feast with you**, probably a reference to the Lord's Supper. They are guilty of profound blasphemy and live licentiously.

2:14 Their **eyes** desire **adultery** with virtually every woman they meet. **insatiable for sin**. Their appetite for sin is never satisfied. Even worse, they **entice** (Gk. *deleazō*, "lure with bait") **unsteady** people to join them in their debauchery. Sexual sin and greed characterize these false teachers (cf. v. 3 and note). **Accursed children!** Peter assures his readers that the heretics will face God's curse.

2:15–16 They have followed the way of Balaam (Numbers 22–24), which is a life spent gaining things at other people's expense by means of wrongdoing. Balaam was particularly condemned for his greed. He was supposedly a man of spiritual insight, but God can use even a **donkey** to restrain someone who is following the way of **madness** rather than living as a rational, responsible human being.

2:17–22 *Influence of False Teachers Revisited.* False teachers lead astray weaker people, enticing them back into lives of sin.

2:17 The false teachers are **waterless springs** (they promise refreshment and bring none) and **mists driven** by the wind (they sow confusion wherever they go), devoid of any inherent value. The **gloom of utter darkness has been reserved** (Gk. *tēreō*, "keep, guard, hold, preserve") for them, as for the evil angels ("kept," v. 4) and the unrighteous ("keep," v. 9).

2:18 The false teachers **entice by sensual passions . . . those who are barely escaping** from the clutches of sin. They prey on newly professed Christians, teaching that they can do whatever they wish sexually and no harm will come of it.

2:19 The false teachers operate under the guise of **freedom**, but in actuality they entice others to become as they are, **slaves of corruption**, once again overcome by evil.

2:20–22 It would have been better for these false teachers never to have **escaped** the world in the first place, than to follow in the path of the **knowledge of . . . Christ** only to abandon that path and return to a life of sin and darkness. One reason it is better not to have known about the **holy commandment** is that those who turn away after falsely confessing the Christian faith will not be inclined to consider Christ again. Another reason is that their knowledge and experience of the Christian life makes them more accountable before God (cf. Luke 12:47–48). Some understand these verses to teach that true believers can lose their salvation. It is more likely that Peter refers to those who *appeared* to be Christians but then showed by their apostasy and their behavior that they never truly belonged to Christ (see notes on John 6:66; 15:2; Gal. 2:3–4; 1 John 2:19). God promises that those who truly know him will never fall away because he will keep them by his grace (cf. John 10:27–29; Rom. 8:28–39; Phil. 1:6). Those who do **turn back** show that their true character is like that of a **dog** (cf. Prov. 26:11) or a **sow**. They appeared to have been saved, but by returning to the vomit and mire of the world, they demonstrated that they were never truly regenerated.

of the world [b]through the knowledge of our Lord and Savior Jesus Christ, they are again
entangled in them and overcome, [c]the last state has become worse for them than the first.
21 For [d]it would have been better for them never to have known the way of righteousness
than after knowing it to turn back from [e]the holy commandment delivered to them. **22** What
the true proverb says has happened to them: "The [f]dog returns to its own vomit, and the
sow, after washing herself, returns to wallow in the mire."

The Day of the Lord Will Come

3 This is now the second letter that I am writing to you, beloved. In both of them [g]I am
stirring up your sincere mind by way of reminder, **2** [h]that you should remember the
predictions of [i]the holy prophets and the commandment of the Lord and Savior through
your apostles, **3** knowing this first of all, that scoffers will come [j]in the last days with scoffing,
[k]following their own sinful desires. **4** [l]They will say, "Where is the promise of [m]his coming? For ever since the fathers fell asleep, all things are continuing as they were from the
beginning of creation." **5** For they deliberately overlook this fact, that the heavens existed
long ago, and the earth [n]was formed out of water and through water [o]by the word of God,
6 and that by means of these the world that then existed [p]was deluged with water and
[q]perished. **7** But by the same word [r]the heavens and earth that now exist are stored up for
fire, being kept until the day of judgment and [s]destruction of the ungodly.
8 But do not overlook this one fact, beloved, that with the Lord one day is as a thousand
years, and [t]a thousand years as one day. **9** [u]The Lord is not slow to fulfill his promise [v]as
some count slowness, but [w]is patient toward you,[1] [x]not wishing that any should perish,
but [y]that all should reach repentance. **10** But [z]the day of the Lord will come like a thief, and

[1] Some manuscripts *on your account*

20 [b]See ch. 1:2 [c]Matt. 12:45
21 [d][Ezek. 18:24; Luke 12:47; Heb. 6:4-6; 10:26, 27; James 4:17] [e]Rom. 7:12
22 [f]Prov. 26:11

Chapter 3
1 [g]ch. 1:13
2 [h]Jude 17 [i]Luke 1:70; Acts 3:21
3 [j]Jude 18 [k]ch. 2:10
4 [l]Isa. 5:19; Jer. 17:15; Ezek. 11:3; 12:22, 27; Mal. 2:17 [m]See 1 Thess. 2:19
5 [n]Ps. 24:2; 136:6 [o]Gen. 1:6, 9; Ps. 33:6; [Heb. 11:3]
6 [p]ch. 2:5 [q]Gen. 7:11, 21
7 [r]ver. 10, 12 [s][2 Thess. 1:9]
8 [t]Ps. 90:4
9 [u]Hab. 2:3; Heb. 10:37 [v][Eccles. 8:11; Rev. 2:21] [w]Isa. 30:18; Luke 18:7 [x]Ezek. 18:23, 32; 33:11 [y]1 Tim. 2:4
10 [z]See Matt. 24:43

3:1–13 *The Day of the Lord Will Surely Come.* Peter turns his attention to explaining the Lord's promised return, and specifically to an apparent debate concerning the timing of the return.

3:1–7 *Scoffers Challenge the Truth of Scripture Concerning the Coming of the Lord.* Peter offers a biblical perspective on the skeptics who attempt to create doubt concerning the Lord's return.

3:1 Peter mentions that this is the **second letter** he has written to this particular audience. It is all but certain that 1 Peter was the earlier letter in view here. Peter calls his readers **beloved** (Gk. *agapētos*), demonstrating his deep concern for them as he reminds them of the Lord's return. On the importance of reminders, see 1:12–15.

3:2 remember. Peter wants the church to remember what the **holy prophets** predicted, and what the **apostles** handed down as the commandment of the Lord. The prediction Peter especially has in mind is the second coming.

3:3 The **last days** will feature **scoffers** who mock according to **their own sinful desires**. Their desire to live in sin with impunity drives them to deride biblical truth and those who believe it. Peter understands, as do the rest of the NT authors, that the "last days" have already arrived (see note on Acts 2:17).

3:4–6 Scoffers (v. 3) will call into question the biblical **promise** of the Lord's **coming** (Gk. *parousia*). They scoff at the promise of the Lord's return, arguing that because everything has remained the same since creation, God will not intervene in the world (cf. 2:10b–11). **Fathers** (plural of Gk. *patēr*) is a reference to the OT patriarchs, since this term is never used in the NT to refer to first-generation Christians. But these scoffers **deliberately overlook** (consciously, willfully ignore) the **fact** that God did intervene when he created the **heavens** and the **earth** with the **word** of his mouth (Gen. 1:3–31; Ps. 33:6; Heb. 11:3), and also when he judged the earth with water and it **perished** (Genesis 6–9). God in fact intervenes in his creation whenever he desires, as is evidenced numerous times in both the OT and NT. Peter cites two obvious occasions of God's intervention, namely, when God acted at creation to form the earth (**out of water and through water**, see Gen. 1:6–10), and also when he acted decisively in history, destroying the earth by means of the flood in the days of Noah (see Gen. 7:17–24).

3:7 By the same word, the powerful word of God that creates and sends judgment, the present heavens and earth **are stored up for fire**, when the ungodly will also be judged. The day of reckoning is coming for scoffers, and their place is reserved for them. History will not go on forever; the end is coming.

3:8–10 *The Lord's Patience Determines the Timing of His Return.* The Lord's perspective on time is different from that of humans. It is not that God is slow in fulfilling his promise, but rather that he is patient.

3:8–9 Beloved (cf. note on v. 1) introduces a new paragraph. Peter explains that the delay of the second coming is not a long time from God's perspective. He then explains further that the delay is also because God is **patient**, and he has not quickly brought the present period of history to an end because he does not wish that **any should perish** (see note on 1 Tim. 2:4; cf. also Rom. 2:4). Though Christians long for Christ's return and the defeat of all evil, as long as the present period of history lasts, an opportunity remains for people to turn to God in faith.

3:10 the day of the Lord. God's judgment will not be delayed forever (see note on vv. 8–9). When Christ returns it will be sudden, without warning, like the strike of a **thief**. **The heavens** (the sky) will **pass away** (cf. Ps. 102:25–26; Heb. 1:10–12; Rev. 6:14) and **the heavenly bodies** (stars, etc.) will be **burned up and dissolved**. There will be no place to hide (cf. Rev. 6:15–16), for **the earth** and every person's **works** on the earth **will be exposed** (Gk. *heurethēsetai*, lit., "will be found," a divine passive meaning "found by God") to God's judgment. Some translations read "will be burned up" (Gk. *katakaēsetai*) because some Greek manuscripts have this wording (instead of Gk. *heurethēsetai*). But the earliest and most reliable manuscripts have "will be found" (Gk. *heurethēsetai*), indicating with this reading that the annihilation of the earth is not taught in this passage. Scholars have debated whether the NT speaks of an annihilation of the present cosmos and the creation of a new universe, or whether it indicates the transformation of the present cosmos, including the earth. The latter seems more likely in light of: (1) the preferred reading of this passage (see above); (2) Rom. 8:18–25; (3) many OT

The Deity of Jesus Christ in 2 Peter

1:1	our God and Savior Jesus Christ
1:11	our Lord and Savior Jesus Christ
2:20	our Lord and Savior Jesus Christ
3:18	our Lord and Savior Jesus Christ

then [a]the heavens will pass away with a roar, and [b]the heavenly bodies[1] will be burned up
and dissolved, and the earth and the works that are done on it will be exposed.[2]
11 Since all these things are thus to be dissolved, [c]what sort of people ought you to be in
lives of holiness and godliness, **12** [d]waiting for and hastening the coming of the day of God,
because of which the heavens will be set on fire and dissolved, and [e]the heavenly bodies
will melt as they burn! **13** But according to his promise we are waiting for [f]new heavens
and a new earth [g]in which righteousness dwells.

Final Words

14 [h]Therefore, beloved, since you are waiting for these, be diligent to be found by him
[i]without spot or [j]blemish, and [k]at peace. **15** And count [l]the patience of our Lord as salvation,
just as [m]our beloved brother Paul also wrote to you [n]according to the wisdom given him,
16 as he does in all his letters when he speaks in them of these matters. [o]There are some
things in them that are hard to understand, which the ignorant and unstable twist to their
own destruction, [p]as they do the other Scriptures. **17** You therefore, beloved, [q]knowing this
beforehand, [r]take care that you are not carried away with the error of lawless people and
lose your own stability. **18** But [s]grow in the grace and knowledge of our Lord and Savior
Jesus Christ. [t]To him be the glory both now and to the day of [u]eternity. Amen.

[1] Or *elements;* also verse 12 [2] Greek *found;* some manuscripts *will be burned up*

10 [a][Rev. 6:14; 20:11; 21:1]; See Matt. 24:35 [b]Isa. 34:4; [Isa. 24:19; Mic. 1:4; Nah. 1:5]
11 [c]1 Pet. 1:15
12 [d][Luke 12:36; 1 Cor. 1:7; 1 Thess. 1:10; Titus 2:13; Jude 21] [e]See ver. 10
13 [f]Isa. 65:17; 66:22; Rev. 21:1 [g]Isa. 60:21; Rev. 21:27
14 [h]1 Cor. 15:58 [i]James 1:27 [j]Phil. 2:15; [Phil. 1:10; 1 Thess. 3:13] [k][1 Thess. 5:23]
15 [l]See ver. 9 [m][Acts 15:25] [n]1 Cor. 3:10
16 [o][Heb. 5:11] [p][Isa. 28:13]
17 [q]ch. 1:12; [Mark 13:23] [r]ch. 1:10; 1 Cor. 10:12
18 [s]ch. 1:5; Eph. 4:15; Col. 1:10; 2:19; 1 Pet. 2:2 [t]See Rom. 11:36 [u][ver. 8]

prophecies about the renewal of the earth; (4) Christ's resurrection body being in continuity with his earthly body; and (5) the fact that Christ's resurrection body is a pattern for the resurrection bodies of Christians (1 Cor. 15:12–58). God seems always to renew, not destroy and recreate, parts of his creation that are marred by sin. See note on Rev. 21:1–8.

3:11–13 *Living Effectively in View of the Lord's Return.* Peter concludes his treatment of the Lord's return by turning the discussion once again to Christian lifestyle. The second coming should be a motivation to live a holy life.

3:11 The people of God ought to live in **holiness** and **godliness**, to avoid the punishment coming to the ungodly and to devote themselves to things that will last beyond the judgment.

3:12 Hastening (Gk. *speudō*, "hurry [by extra effort]") **the coming of the day of God** suggests that, by living holy lives, Christians can actually affect the time of the Lord's return. That does not mean, of course, that the Lord has not foreknown and foreordained when Jesus will return (cf. Matt. 24:36; Acts 17:31). But when God set that day, he also ordained that it would happen *after* all of his purposes for saving believers and building his kingdom in this present age had been accomplished, and those purposes are accomplished when he works through his human agents to bring them about. Therefore, from a human perspective, when Christians share the gospel with others, and pray (cf. Matt. 6:10), and advance the kingdom of God in other ways, they do "hasten" the fulfillment of God's purposes, including Christ's return.

3:13 The hope of Christians ultimately depends, though, not on their works (cf. note on v. 12) but on God's **promise**. Their hope is not in the destruction of the wicked and their works, even though that is a necessary part of God's final judgment. Their hope is in the promise that God will bring about a **new heavens and a new earth** (see Isa. 65:17; 66:22; Rev. 21:1–22:5), which will be the eternal abode of the righteous. "New" could mean "newly created" but probably means "renewed, made new" (see notes on Rom. 8:20–21; 2 Pet. 3:10).

3:14–18 *Concluding Exhortations.* To obtain the final reward, believers must live a godly life and resist the sexual permissiveness of false teachers (cf. 1:5–11).

3:14 *Concerning Diligence.* Peter calls his readers **beloved** for the third of four times in this chapter (cf. vv. 1, 8, 17). In light of the Lord's return, Christians are to **be diligent** to be found **without spot or blemish** (doctrinally and morally pure), thereby receiving the full reward of eternal life. This is in stark contrast to the spiritual condition of the wicked (2:10b–22, esp. v. 22).

3:15–16 *Concerning the Distortion of Paul's Teaching.* The delay of Christ's return should be reckoned as his **patience** leading people to **salvation** (cf. v. 9; Rom. 2:4). The apostle Paul **also wrote to** these same readers at some point prior to the composition of 2 Peter, and apparently the false teachers of ch. 2 used a twisted version of Paul's gospel of freedom (see 2:19; also Rom. 8:1–5; 2 Cor. 3:1–18; Gal. 5:1–6) to entice some of them into sin.

3:16 In all his letters shows awareness of some kind of collection of Paul's letters, with the number unspecified here. **Some things . . . hard to understand** does not say that everything in Paul's letters is hard to understand, nor does it say that anything is "impossible to understand," but it does imply that correctly interpreting some hard passages of Scripture requires much effort and God-given wisdom. **The ignorant and unstable twist** Paul's teachings **as they do the other Scriptures**, implying that Paul's writings were also considered Scripture in NT times, on the same level of divine authority as the OT Scripture. Greek *graphē*, here translated "Scriptures," occurs 51 times in the NT, and every time it refers to the canonical OT Scripture, and not to any other writings, except that twice (here and 1 Tim. 5:18) some NT writings are also included. This indicates that NT books written or authorized by Christ's apostles were recognized, at a very early date, to be God's Word.

3:17–18 *Concerning the Proper Response to Paul's Teaching.* The fourth use of **beloved** in ch. 3 (cf. vv. 1, 8, 14). **knowing this beforehand**. The readers now know, if they did not know previously, that the false teachers are distorting Paul's teaching. Paul advocates neither sin nor lawlessness, so they should take care not to be carried away by the false teaching, even if it appeals to Paul as the authority. They should not lose their own **stability** by following after a false interpretation of Paul; rather, they should cultivate stability through Christian growth, especially growing in Christ's **grace** (Gk. *charis*, "favor, esp. unmerited favor") and **knowledge** (Gk. *gnōsis*).

INTRODUCTION TO

THE FIRST LETTER OF JOHN

1 JOHN

Author and Title

Manuscript evidence is unanimous that someone named "John" wrote this little treatise, which is consistently labeled the "first" of his extant letters in titles found in ancient copies. But who is this "John"? For a number of reasons, John the son of Zebedee, author of the Fourth Gospel, is the most likely candidate (see Introduction to John: Author and Title).

First, the style and vocabulary of John's Gospel and 1 John are so similar that a common author is extremely likely. This is particularly evident in the opening verses of the respective writings, but the language of the Gospel echoes across the whole epistle. For example, only verbal forms of "believe" occur (about a hundred times) in John's Gospel; the noun "faith" never appears. First John follows suit, with nine occurrences of a verbal form of "believe" and just one use of the word "faith" (5:4). Second, major themes and emphases of the writings overlap. These include Christ's simultaneous full humanity and divinity, the close relationship between believing (faith, doctrine) and obeying God's commandments (ethics), and the primacy of love as marking authentic knowledge of the true God through trust in his Son.

While John is not mentioned by name in the Fourth Gospel, he is likely to have been "the beloved disciple" who reclined next to Jesus at the Last Supper (John 13:23; arguments that he was Lazarus, an "elder" John, or a fictional creation are unconvincing). He stood at the foot of the cross when Jesus was crucified; Jesus entrusted his mother Mary to John's care (John 19:26–27). Along with Peter he witnessed the empty tomb on the first Easter morning (John 20:2–10). He also saw, spoke with, and ate breakfast at a lakeside fire kindled by the resurrected Jesus (John 21:7, 20). He was therefore highly qualified to write of what he and others had heard, seen, gazed upon, and touched (1 John 1:1). As Jesus' "beloved disciple," he was also well suited to plumb the depths of the meaning of Jesus' coming (1:2; 4:9), life (2:6; 4:14), death (1:7), resurrection (5:11; "eternal life . . . in his Son" implies his death was not final), intercessory ministry at the Father's right hand (2:1), and eventual return (2:28)—all matters playing a role in the witness, instruction, and admonition of this rich and highly concentrated letter.

Date

Early post-apostolic figures like Polycarp and Papias (c. A.D. 100) presuppose or cite 1 John in their writings. This suggests a date of composition no later than the 90s A.D. This dovetails with the testimony of church fathers that, shortly before A.D. 67, John joined other Christians in departing from Jerusalem prior to the destruction of the city by Rome. John reportedly resumed his apostolic ministry in the vicinity of the great but highly idolatrous city of Ephesus (in modern western Turkey). He likely wrote 1 John as an elder statesman of the faith in the last third of the first century, perhaps to churches in the surrounding region. This might have included towns like those mentioned alongside Ephesus in the opening chapters of Revelation: Smyrna, Pergamum, Thyatira, Sardis, Philadelphia, and Laodicea (Rev. 2:8–3:22).

Genre

First John lacks certain earmarks of a typical Hellenistic letter. For example, the writer does not name himself at the outset (as Paul always does), and the book is somewhat sermonic in tone. Yet on several counts it is highly letter-like, as seen from the expressed motive of shared joy (1:4), the repeated mentions of the act and purpose of writing to his recipients (13 uses of the Gk. verb "I write"), and the many instances of direct address to the readers. First John was judged to be in the form of a letter by ancient writers such as Irenaeus, Dionysius of Alexandria, and Eusebius, who would have understood the prevailing conventions of letter writing.

Style and Substance

The rhetoric of 1 John is challenging. John rarely sustains a clear line of argument for more than a few lines or verses. He wanders from subject to subject, unencumbered by any discernible outline. Yet if he has no plan, he does follow a pattern: after leaving a subject he often returns to it. His style of thought has been termed circular rather than linear. It has also been termed symphonic, in that he states themes, moves away from them, and then revisits them with variations (see chart, p. 2427).

While the rhetoric of 1 John poses difficulties, his content is rich in doctrinal substance, ethical challenge, and devotional fervor. John is insistent that no one has ever seen God the Father in his unmediated glory (4:12; see John 1:18), yet just as insistent that to know Jesus is to know "the true God and eternal life" (1 John 5:20). The mystery of this dialectic suffuses the letter from start to finish and moves John to write with insight, consistency, intensity, and depth. Yet his language is for the most part simple and his vocabulary modest. Line for line there are few biblical writings that surpass 1 John in the imposing demands made on the reader along with the rich rewards that studied interpretation will yield.

Theme

In 1 John the author calls readers back to the three basics of Christian life: true doctrine, obedient living, and fervent devotion. Because "God is light" (1:5), Christ's followers overcome evildoers who seek to subvert them. The one who lives in and among them—God's Son—is greater than the spirit of "the antichrist" now in the world (4:3–4). To believe in the name of the Son of God is to know the assurance of eternal life (5:13).

Purpose, Occasion, and Background

It is customary to understand 1 John as a response to the rise of an early form of Gnosticism. This was a religious mysticism that pirated Christian motifs to propagate an understanding of salvation based on esoteric "knowledge" (Gk. *gnōsis*). According to this view, redemption is through affirming the divine light already in the human soul, not through repentance of sin and faith in Christ's death to bring about spiritual rebirth. Writings widely publicized in recent years, like the Gospel of Thomas and Gospel of Judas, for example, were products of Gnostic writers. But the heyday of Gnostic thought was the second through fifth centuries, well after the time the NT books were written. It can neither be proven nor ruled out that John had this movement in mind as he wrote.

The study notes for this book will focus on what seems definite in 1 John rather than what can be imagined. John wrote to Christians who had witnessed an exodus from their ranks (2:19). This does not mean that all John wrote should be interpreted as a response to schism—John is neither anti-Gnostic nor anti-schismatic. John's focus is positive, not polemical. His aim is redemptive, not reactionary. He urges readers to refine their theological understanding, sharpen their ethical rigor, and heighten their devotional intensity. That is, they must grow in faith, obedience, and love. Yet the letter is not a list of dos and don'ts. It is rather a manifesto of "Done!"—Jesus' words "It is finished" (John 19:30) come to mind. First John highlights what God the Father has "done" in sending Christ the Son, offering him up as a sacrifice for sins, and sending forth "the word of life" (1 John 1:1) that is causing this world's darkness to pass away and the true light of the coming age to shine (2:8).

God's action becomes the mandate of those who believe in his Son. "Whoever does the will of God abides forever" (2:17). God's will is for readers to receive the saving message of Christ's coming, rejoice in the commands of Christ's teaching, and revel in the love of the Father as it continually translates into Christian love for one another and ministry to the world. This is "not love in word or talk but in deed and in truth" (3:18).

Key Themes

1. The one eternal God became incarnate in his Son, Jesus the Christ, who is "the true God and eternal life."	1:1–3; 4:2; 5:20
2. All humans are sinful, but Christians have joyful fellowship with the Father, with the Son, and with each other through repentance and faith in Christ.	1:3–10
3. Christ is our advocate with the Father and the propitiation for our sins.	2:1–2; 4:10
4. Those who know Christ forsake sin and keep God's commandments—in particular the love commandment.	2:3–11; 3:4–24; 4:7–21
5. Denial of Jesus Christ as God's Son in the flesh is denial of God the Father.	2:22–23; 4:2–3; 5:10–12
6. Faith in Christ results in forgiveness of sins, eternal life, confidence in prayer, protection from the evil one, and understanding and knowing the true God.	5:12–21

Theological Themes of 1 John

As noted in Style and Substance, the letter's themes are presented, moved away from, then resumed. Though a linear progression is not presented in 1 John, many of the themes that are repeated may be set forth as follows.

God is light and love. Those who are now Christians have passed out of death into life. Christians did not do this on their own ability; God loved them and sent Jesus to be the propitiation for their sins. God then caused those who were dead to be born again, giving them life. With life, God gave the Spirit and spiritual understanding, with the result that believers are no longer "of the world" or "of the devil" but are "from/of God" and "of the truth." God now abides in his people, his Word abides in them, and they abide in God; thus they abide in the light, for God is light. Another way of describing this relationship is to say that Christians know and love God. Being made alive, receiving the Spirit, and knowing God naturally results in transformed behavior, which John describes in terms of loving God, obeying God, and loving one another.

God is light (1:5; 2:8)	God is love (4:8, 16, 19)
Christians were spiritually dead: they have "passed out of death into life" (3:14)	
God loved his people and sent Jesus to die for them (3:16; 4:10, 14, 19; 5:11)	
Christians have been born of God (2:29; 3:9; 4:7; 5:1, 4, 18)	
God gave them life (3:14; 4:9; 5:11, 16)	
God gave Christians the Spirit (2:20, 27; 3:24; 4:13) along with understanding (5:20)	
Christians are of/from God/the truth (3:10, 19; 4:4, 6; 5:19)	
God abides in Christians, and his Word abides in them (2:14, 24, 27; 3:9, 24; 4:12, 13, 15, 16)	Christians abide in God, and thus abide in the light (2:5, 6, 27, 28; 3:6, 24; 4:13, 16)
Christians know God (2:13, 14; 4:6, 7), they know the Father (2:13; 5:20), they know Jesus (1:3; 2:3), and they know the Spirit (4:2, 6)	Christians love God (2:5; 4:21; 5:2, 3)
Being born again, having received the Spirit, abiding in God and God abiding in them, and knowing and loving God, Christians bear observable fruit: • Practice truth/righteousness (1:6; 2:29; 3:7, 10) • Walk in the light/as he walked (1:7; 2:6) • Confess sins and have forgiveness (1:9; 2:12) • Keep/obey his commandments/Word (2:3, 5; 3:22, 24; 5:2, 3) • Love one another/the brothers (2:10; 3:10, 11, 14, 16, 18, 23; 4:7, 11, 21) • Overcome the evil one/them/the world (2:13, 14; 4:4; 5:4) • Do the will of God/cannot keep on sinning (2:17; 3:9, 22) • Confess the Son/believe in Jesus (2:23; 3:23; 4:2, 15; 5:1, 4, 13)	

History of Salvation Summary

Christians are to live in love, as Christ loved us (see note on John 13:34–35). (For an explanation of the "History of Salvation," see the Overview of the Bible, pp. 23–26.)

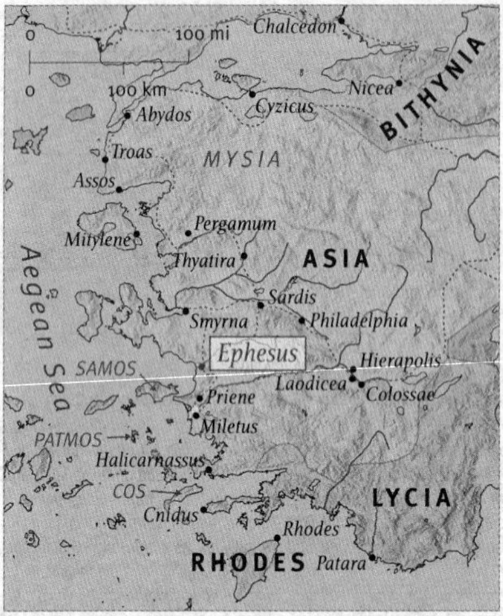

The Setting of 1 John

c. A.D. 85

John likely wrote 1 John from Ephesus, where apparently he had relocated near the time of the fall of Jerusalem to the Romans in A.D. 70. The letter was probably intended to be read by the church in Ephesus and perhaps also by other churches in the surrounding cities. Ephesus was a wealthy and highly influential port city in the Roman province of Asia, and it was renowned for its temple of Artemis (Diana).

Literary Features

First John is ostensibly an epistle, but its content is more fluid than what is found in most NT epistles. There is no epistolary salutation, nor is there a conventional epistolary conclusion. A more accurate designation is to call this book a treatise or pamphlet. Alternately, it can be read as an address or loosely structured sermon. The topic changes with virtually every paragraph, so the best advice for reading the book is to "think paragraphs."

Nonetheless, even though the structure of 1 John is not strictly linear, the author keeps coming back to topics that have been introduced earlier, so that readers can profitably think of the book as being arranged like a musical symphony. The main theme is *tests by which we can know if we are in Christ*—beliefs and attitudes that authenticate one's claims to be a Christian. Under that umbrella, subordinate themes appear: Christology (doctrine about the person and work of Christ); walking in the light; love; and the need to reject fallen, worldly culture. These topics weave in and out of the book. The book is structured on an implied dialectical principle in which John continuously seeks to oppose viewpoints that are contrary to his assertions. For example, John's assertions that Christ has come in the flesh (1:1–3 and 4:2) are an implied refutation of those who deny the incarnation. Finally, there is an incipient poetry and mysticism about John's writing, so that, for example, a lot of what John asserts about the Christian life is embodied in great symbols like light and darkness, or walking and abiding in Christ.

Timeline

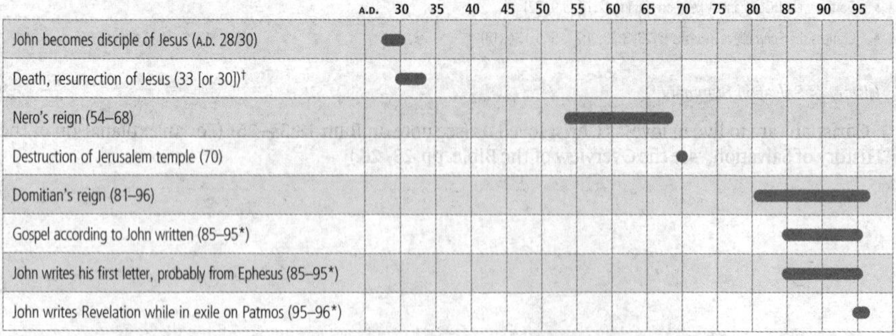

A.D. 30 35 40 45 50 55 60 65 70 75 80 85 90 95
John becomes disciple of Jesus (A.D. 28/30)
Death, resurrection of Jesus (33 [or 30])†
Nero's reign (54–68)
Destruction of Jerusalem temple (70)
Domitian's reign (81–96)
Gospel according to John written (85–95*)
John writes his first letter, probably from Ephesus (85–95*)
John writes Revelation while in exile on Patmos (95–96*)

** denotes approximate date; / signifies either/or; † see The Date of Jesus' Crucifixion, pp. 1809–1810*

Outline

I. God Is Light and Christ Is the Way (1:1–2:6)
   A. Prologue (1:1–4)
   B. God's nature and human sin (1:5–10)
   C. Jesus Christ in everyday life (2:1–6)

II. The Abiding Commandment in a Transient World (2:7–17)
   A. The primacy of love (2:7–11)
   B. The confidence of God's people (2:12–14)
   C. The lure of this fleeting age (2:15–17)

III. Overcoming Antichrist by Confession of the Son (2:18–3:10)
   A. Warning and assurance (2:18–27)
   B. Christians as children of God (2:28–3:3)
   C. Children of God and the forsaking of sin (3:4–10)

IV. Overcoming Evil by Listening to the Apostle (3:11–4:6)
   A. Overcoming Cain's malice (3:11–24)
   B. Overcoming the Antichrist's deception (4:1–6)

V. The Assurance of God through the Love of God (4:7–21)
   A. The perfecting of God's love (4:7–12)
   B. The assurance of God's Spirit (4:13–21)

VI. Faith in the Son as the Way to Life (5:1–12)
   A. Faith keeps the commandments of God (5:1–5)
   B. Faith receives the testimony of God (5:6–12)

VII. Final Call to Faith and Understanding (5:13–21)
   A. The confidence that faith furnishes (5:13)
   B. The prayer that faith enables (5:14–17)
   C. The understanding that faith grants (5:18–21)

THE FIRST LETTER OF JOHN

1 JOHN

The Word of Life

1 [a]That which was [b]from the beginning, [c]which we have heard, [d]which we have seen
with our eyes, [e]which we looked upon and [f]have touched with our hands, concerning
the word of life— 2 [g]the life [h]was made manifest, and we have seen it, and [i]testify to it and
proclaim to you the eternal life, [a]which was with the Father and [h]was made manifest to
us— 3 [c]that which we have seen and heard we proclaim also to you, so that you too may
have fellowship with us; and indeed [j]our fellowship is with the Father and with his Son
Jesus Christ. 4 And we are writing these things so [k]that our[1] joy may be complete.

Walking in the Light

5 [l]This is the message we have heard from him and proclaim to you, that [m]God is light,
and in him is no darkness at all. 6 [n]If we say we have fellowship with him while we walk
in darkness, we lie and [o]do not practice the truth. 7 But [p]if we walk in the light, [q]as he is
in the light, we have fellowship with one another, and [r]the blood of Jesus his Son cleanses
us from all sin. 8 [s]If we say we have no sin, we deceive ourselves, and [t]the truth is not in
us. 9 [u]If we confess our sins, he is [v]faithful and just to forgive us our sins and [r]to cleanse us

[1] Some manuscripts *your*

Rom. 3:26] [r][See ver. 7 above]

Chapter 1

1 [a]See John 1:1 [b][ch. 2:13, 14] [c]Acts 4:20 [d]John 19:35 [e]ch. 4:14; John 1:14; 2 Pet. 1:16 [f]Luke 24:39; John 20:27
2 [g]John 1:4; 11:25; 14:6 [h]ch. 3:5, 8; Rom. 16:26; 1 Tim. 3:16 [i]See John 15:27 [a][See ver. 1 above]
3 [c][See ver. 1 above] [j]John 17:21; 1 Cor. 1:9; [ch. 2:24]
4 [k]John 15:11; 16:24
5 [l]ch. 3:11 [m]James 1:17; [ch. 4:8; John 4:24]
6 [n]ch. 2:11; John 12:35; 2 Cor. 6:14 [o]John 3:21
7 [p][Isa. 2:5] [q][Ps. 104:2; 1 Tim. 6:16] [r]Eph. 1:7; Heb. 9:14; 1 Pet. 1:19; Rev. 5:9; 7:14; 12:11
8 [s][Job 15:14; Jer. 2:35]; See James 3:2 [t]ch. 2:4
9 [u]Ps. 32:5; 51:3; Prov. 28:13 [v][Ps. 143:1;

1:1–2:6 *God Is Light and Christ Is the Way.* John begins his letter by directing attention to Christ's divinity, incarnation, saving death, and intercessory ministry. He also stresses God's ineffable brilliance ("light," 1:5) and the ubiquity of human sin.

1:1–4 *Prologue.* A dozen or so first-person plural references ("we," "our," "us") highlight the eyewitness testimony of John and other early Christians, particularly the apostles. They know "fellowship with the Father and with his Son" (v. 3) and yearn to see it extend to readers.

1:1 From the beginning could refer to the time of Jesus' birth or the beginning of his ministry. But it more likely refers to the predawn of time (see John 1:1), just as the Septuagint uses the same expression (Gk. *ap' archēs*) to say that the Lord existed "from the beginning" (Hab. 1:12 LXX) and that the origins of the Promised One would be "from the beginning" (Mic. 5:1 LXX). In other words, John is pointing to Christ's preexistence. **seen . . . looked upon . . . touched**. John was an eyewitness to the physical and historical reality of Jesus' life on earth. His message is not based on an ecstatic vision, grand idea, or mere human religious conviction.

1:2 The repetition of **made manifest** (publicly seen and known) stresses the revelatory nature of Christ's coming: he was sent from and revealed by God. **Life . . . eternal life** refers to the nature and quality of life in fellowship with God (cf. John 5:24), as revealed primarily in the life of Christ and then experienced secondarily by Christians. Such fellowship grows out of the vital and dynamic existence enjoyed by the Son **with the Father**.

1:3 John is moved to **proclaim** what he has witnessed in keeping with the commission he and other apostles received (Matt. 28:19–20; Acts 1:8). The purpose of this proclamation is not just forgiveness of people's sins (as a simplified view of evangelism would have it) but is far richer, for the gospel message binds together those who receive it: **so that you too may have fellowship with us**. Yet the purpose is still richer than mere human fellowship, for believers' fellowship **is with the Father and with his Son**. Such "fellowship" is personal communion with the Father made possible by the mediation of the Son.

1:4 writing . . . so that. One of 1 John's several stated purposes is to promote **joy**. Jesus promoted joy as well (John 15:11; 16:24). It is difficult to decide between "our joy" (ESV text) and "your joy" (ESV footnote), for several very early and reliable manuscripts have one reading, and several have the other (the only difference is one letter in Greek). "Our" probably includes the readers (with the sense "all of our," cf. 1 John 1:3).

1:5–10 *God's Nature and Human Sin.* "God is light" (v. 5) reflects an OT background where "light" symbolizes both knowledge and purity (see notes on John 1:4–5; 8:12). All of John's writing flows from the reality of God in his spiritual perfection, moral excellence, and utter transcendence—his light (see 1 Tim. 6:16). This will contrast sharply with errant humans protesting their innocence (1 John 1:6, 8, 10).

1:6 If we say. John may be paraphrasing what some were falsely claiming. If God is light (v. 5), then those who **walk in darkness** are not walking with God, no matter what they say.

1:7 Walk in the light means to reflect God's perfection (see v. 5) in the human sphere and includes both correct doctrine (truth) and moral purity (holiness). The symbolism of light as knowledge (see note on vv. 5–10) also implies that when Christians "walk in the light" their lives will be known, and will not contain hidden sins, falsehoods, or deception. Such walking "in the light" results in deep divine and human **fellowship** (see v. 3) and progressive cleansing **from all sin**.

1:8 have no sin. See note on 3:9–10. **we deceive ourselves**. The devil (3:8) or the world (2:15) may contribute to human straying, but in the end each individual bears responsibility for his or her own sin. Some sin remains in every Christian's life ("have," present tense), even that of the elderly apostle John ("we").

1:9 Christians must **confess** (their) **sins**, initially to receive salvation and then to maintain fellowship with God and with one another (v. 3). **faithful and just to forgive**. God is "slow to anger and abounding in steadfast love, forgiving iniquity and transgression" (Num. 14:18). Yet John also makes

from all unrighteousness. 10 If we say we have not sinned, [w]we make him a liar, and [x]his
word is not in us.

Christ Our Advocate

2 My little children, I am writing these things to you so that you may not sin. But if
anyone does sin, [y]we have an advocate with the Father, Jesus Christ the righteous.
2 [z]He is the propitiation for our sins, and not for ours only but [a]also for the sins of the
whole world. 3 And by this we know that we have come to know him, if we [b]keep his
commandments. 4 Whoever says "I know him" but does not keep his commandments [c]is
a liar, and [c]the truth is not in him, 5 but whoever [d]keeps his word, in him truly [e]the love
of God is perfected. [f]By this we may know that we are in him: 6 whoever says he [g]abides
in him [h]ought to walk in the same way in which he walked.

The New Commandment

7 Beloved, I am writing you [i]no new commandment, but [j]an old commandment [k]that
you had from the beginning. The old commandment is the word that you have heard. 8 At
the same time, it is [l]a new commandment that I am writing to you, which is true in him
and in you, because[1] [m]the darkness is passing away and [n]the true light is already shining.
9 Whoever says he is in the light and [o]hates his brother is still in darkness. 10 Whoever loves
his brother abides in the light, and in him[2] there is no [p]cause for stumbling. 11 But whoever
hates his brother is in the darkness and [q]walks in the darkness, and does not know where
he is going, because the darkness has blinded his eyes.

12 I am writing to you, little children,
because [r]your sins are forgiven for his name's sake.
13 I am writing to you, fathers,
because you know [s]him who is from the beginning.

[1] Or *that* [2] Or *it*

10 [w]ch. 5:10 [x]John 5:38; 8:37
Chapter 2
1 [y]Rom. 8:34; 1 Tim. 2:5; Heb. 7:25
2 [z]ch. 4:10; Rom. 3:25; [2 Cor. 5:18, 19; Col. 1:20] [a]ch. 4:14; John 1:29; 4:42; 11:51, 52; 12:32
3 [b]John 14:15; 15:10
4 [c]ch. 1:8; John 8:44
5 [d]ch. 5:3; John 14:23 [e]ch. 4:12 [f]ch. 3:24; 4:13; 5:2
6 [g]John 15:4, 5, 7 [h]See Matt. 11:29
7 [i]2 John 5 [j]Lev. 19:18 [k][ver. 24; ch. 3:11; 2 John 5, 6]
8 [l]See John 13:34 [m]Rom. 13:12; Eph. 5:8; 1 Thess. 5:4, 5 [n]John 1:9; 8:12
9 [o]ch. 4:20; [ch. 3:14, 15; Titus 3:3]
10 [p]John 11:10; [Prov. 4:19; 2 Pet. 1:10]
11 [q]See ch. 1:6
12 [r]Luke 24:47; Acts 10:43; 13:38
13 [s][ch. 1:1]

it clear (1 John 3:6, 9) that persistent unrepented sin is not the mark of a Christian—God "will by no means clear the guilty" (Num. 14:18).

1:10 have not sinned. See note on 3:9–10. **his word is not in us**. A person may have heard and assented to the gospel message, but until it brings him to acknowledge his sin, it has not taken root.

2:1–6 *Jesus Christ in Everyday Life.* The light (1:5) that God sheds on daily living comes through his Son.

2:1 My little children. John's way of addressing his readers (cf. vv. 12, 28; 3:7, 18; 4:4; 5:21) exemplifies the love to which he summons readers. **may not sin**. See note on 3:9–10. Jesus is an **advocate**, taking up the cause of believers in the presence of God the Father. Otherwise their sin would bring judgment upon them. Paul speaks of Christ as mediator (1 Tim. 2:5), and Heb. 8:1 refers to him as high priest.

2:2 Propitiation (Gk. *hilasmos*) here means "a sacrifice that bears God's wrath and turns it to favor," and that is also the meaning of the English word "propitiation." (See note on Rom. 3:25.) As the perfect sacrifice for sin, Jesus turns away God's wrath (see also 1 John 4:10). **For the sins of the whole world** does not mean that every person will be saved, for John is clear that forgiveness of sins comes only to those who repent and believe the gospel (see 2:4, 23; 3:10; 5:12; cf. John 3:18; 5:24). But Jesus' sacrifice is offered and made available to everyone in "the whole world," not just to John and his current readers.

2:3 by this we know. Assurance of salvation is possible (see note on 2 Pet. 1:10). First John gives numerous means of self-diagnosis (cf. 1 John 1:7; 2:5; 3:14; 4:13; 5:2). Here the test is ethical: do professing Christians have a changed life and **keep** the Lord's **commandments**? Obedience to God does not bring about justification (which comes by faith alone), but obedience as a pattern of life does give evidence that one has been born again. To **know him** involves a personal relationship that transforms practical behavior.

2:5 love of God is perfected. This love is not only a feeling but also an ethical response (**keeps his word**). **may know**. See note on v. 3.

2:6 walk in the same way. The way that led to the cross. Believers need not and cannot repeat Christ's unique saving death, but they can mirror his faith, love, piety, obedience, and self-sacrifice, and this pattern of life will give greater assurance "that we are in him" (v. 5).

2:7–17 *The Abiding Commandment in a Transient World.* John's focus shifts to the love commandment and the challenge of living out the Christian message in a world where "darkness" (vv. 8, 9, 11) and "the evil one" (vv. 13, 14) seem to dominate.

2:7–11 *The Primacy of Love.* It is easy to lose touch with the basics of knowing the God who is love (4:8).

2:7 The **old commandment** is love for God and love for others, both of which are commanded in the OT (Lev. 19:18; Deut. 6:5). Jesus confirmed (Matt. 22:34–40) but also renewed these teachings, so they also constitute a **new commandment** (John 13:34). It is what the apostles were given **from the beginning** (cf. 1 John 3:11).

2:8 the darkness is passing away. The age to come has not yet fully arrived (see 3:2), but it is progressively advancing in this world, for **the true light is already shining**. God's people can reflect his light by embracing the **new commandment** to love.

2:9–11 hates his brother. John often writes in black-and-white terms for emphasis (e.g., light vs. darkness, truth vs. lies). **darkness has blinded his eyes**. In contrast to "light" (see note on 1:5–10), "darkness" and "blindness" in Scripture often represent rejecting God's truth and persisting in sin (see John 3:19; 12:39–40; 2 Cor. 4:4). On the central role of love in the Christian life, see note on John 13:34–35.

2:12–14 *The Confidence of God's People.* John knows his message is greater than the sinister realities against which he warns. **I am writing to you . . . I write to you**. The emphatic, repeated direct address points to John's strong feeling and determination to bring assurance to his readers. He expresses his confidence in the role of **the Father** and **the word of God** in their lives. Some view (**little**) **children**, **fathers**, and **young men** as symbolizing the stages of spiritual maturity in a Christian's life. Others think "little children" refers to all of John's readers (cf. note on v. 1), while "fathers" refers to older believers and "young men" to those newer in the faith.

I am writing to you, young men,
because [t]you have overcome the evil one.
I write to you, children,
because [u]you know the Father.
14 I write to you, fathers,
because you know [s]him who is from the beginning.
I write to you, young men,
because [t]you are strong,
and the word of God abides in you,
and you have overcome the evil one.

Do Not Love the World

15 [v]Do not love the world or the things in the world. [w]If anyone loves the world, the love
of the Father is not in him. 16 For all that is in the world—[x]the desires of the flesh and
[y]the desires of the eyes and pride of life[1]—is not from the Father but is from the world.
17 And [z]the world is passing away along with its desires, but whoever does the will of God
abides forever.

Warning Concerning Antichrists

18 Children, [a]it is the last hour, and as you have heard that [b]antichrist is coming, so
now [c]many antichrists have come. [d]Therefore we know that it is the last hour. 19 [e]They
went out from us, but they were not of us; for [f]if they had been of us, they would have
continued with us. But they went out, [g]that it might become plain that they all are not
of us. 20 But you have been [h]anointed by [i]the Holy One, and [j]you all have knowledge.[2] 21 I
write to you, not because you do not know the truth, but because you know it, and because
no lie is of the truth. 22 Who is the liar but [k]he who denies that Jesus is the Christ? This is
[b]the antichrist, he who denies the Father and the Son. 23 [l]No one who denies the Son has

[1] Or *pride in possessions* [2] Some manuscripts *you know everything*

13 [t]Eph. 6:10; [ch. 5:4, 5] [u]John 14:7
14 [s][See ver. 13 above] [t][See ver. 13 above]
15 [v][Rom. 12:2; 2 Tim. 4:10] [w]See James 4:4
16 [x]Rom. 13:14; Eph. 2:3; 1 Pet. 4:2; 2 Pet. 2:18 [y]Eccles. 4:8; 5:11
17 [z]See 1 Cor. 7:31
18 [a][2 Tim. 3:1; James 5:3; 2 Pet. 3:3; Jude 18] [b]ver. 22; ch. 4:3; 2 John 7; [Matt. 24:5, 24] [c][ch. 4:1; Matt. 24:5] [d]1 Tim. 4:1
19 [e]Deut. 13:13; Acts 20:30 [f]See John 17:12 [g]1 Cor. 11:19
20 [h]ver. 27; [2 Cor. 1:21] [i]See Mark 1:24 [j]ver. 27; See John 14:26
22 [k]ch. 4:3; 2 John 7 [b][See ver. 18 above]
23 [l]ch. 4:15; 5:1; 2 John 9

2:15–17 *The Lure of This Fleeting Age.* The love of the Father implants a desire to break with idolization of the world.

2:15 Do not love the world should not be read as an utter rejection of the world, for "God . . . loved the world" (John 3:16). Rather, John warns against devotion to a world system that is opposed to God (cf. John 12:31; James 4:4; 1 John 5:19). **Love of the Father** probably carries a double meaning, referring both to the love God has for his people and the love they have for him. The former generates the latter (4:7, 9–10).

2:16 In warning against **all that is in the world**, John does not demonize the whole created order (cf. Gen. 1:31). Rather, he gives examples (**desires of the flesh**, etc.) of what the believer should guard against. Human desires are part of God's creation and therefore not inherently evil, but they become twisted when not directed by and toward God.

2:17 the world is passing away. Its appearance of permanence is deceptive. History is not an endless cycle but is speeding toward a conclusion willed by God (cf. v. 8). **abides forever**. Augustine in a sermon on this text wrote, "Hold fast to Christ. For you he became temporal, so that you might partake of eternity" (*Homilies on the First Epistle of John* 2.10).

Equivalent Expressions for the "Last Days"

The "last days" (the day of salvation, 2 Cor. 6:2) have already come but the "last day" (the day of salvation and wrath, 1 Thess. 5:1–11) has not yet arrived. The following are equivalent expressions for the "last days" (the period of time between Jesus' death and resurrection and the final judgment).

"the last days"	Acts 2:17; 2 Tim. 3:1; Heb. 1:2; James 5:3
"the last hour"	1 John 2:18
"the last time"	Jude 18
"the last times"	1 Pet. 1:20

2:18–3:10 *Overcoming Antichrist by Confession of the Son.* John sketches details of the challenges Christians face and how these may be surmounted.

2:18–27 *Warning and Assurance.* The existence of "antichrist" (v. 18) and those trying to deceive (v. 26) Christians is alarming. But John is confident that they can find the resources to abide in Christ (v. 29).

2:18 The **last hour** began with the death and resurrection of Jesus Christ (cf. Heb. 1:2); his second coming could occur at any time (cf. notes on Acts 2:17; 1 Cor. 7:29–31; 2 Tim. 3:1; see chart to the left). **Antichrist** is mentioned with this name in the NT only here and in 1 John 2:22; 4:3; 2 John 7 (but cf. the "man of lawlessness," 2 Thess. 2:1–10; see note on 2 Thess. 2:3). Broadly, an "antichrist" is anyone "who denies that Jesus is the Christ" (1 John 2:22). More specifically, John understands such a person to be a human representative of the "evil one" of whom Jesus spoke (John 17:15). **many antichrists**. Persons doing the devil's bidding and not God's will.

2:19 John's readers had recently seen people leave the church (**out from us**). Though they outwardly belonged to the church, their departure revealed that they were not truly **of us**; that is, they did not have genuine faith. **If they had been of us**, that is, if they had been genuine Christians, **they would have continued with us**. This implies that those who are truly saved will never abandon Christ, for they will be kept by his grace (cf. Jude 24). **That it might become plain** shows divine purpose behind the departure of this group.

2:20 Anointed by the Holy One probably means being regenerated by the Holy Spirit. In the OT, physical anointing with oil (cf. Ex. 28:41; 1 Sam. 16:13) was an outward sign of the inward transforming and empowering work of the Holy Spirit (cf. Isa. 61:1; 2 Cor. 1:21).

2:22 John clearly describes **the antichrist** as **he who denies that Jesus is the Christ** and who **denies the Father and the Son** (see note on v. 18).

2:23 Whoever confesses the Son has the Father also (cf. 5:13; John 14:6; Acts 4:12; note on John 3:18). The world's religions do not constitute

24 [m]ch. 3:11; 2 John 6 [n][John 14:23]; See ch. 1:3
25 [o]John 17:2
26 [p]ch. 3:7; 2 John 7
27 [q]ver. 20 [r]Jer. 31:34; Heb. 8:11 [s]John 14:17
28 [t]ch. 3:2; [Col. 3:4] [u]ch. 3:21; 4:17; 5:14 [v]See 1 Thess. 2:19
29 [w]ch. 3:7 [x]ch. 3:9; 4:7; 5:1, 4, 18; 3 John 11
Chapter 3
1 [y]ch. 4:10; John 3:16 [z]John 1:12 [a][ch. 4:17] [b]John 16:3; 17:25
2 [z][See ver. 1 above] [c]Rom. 8:15; Gal. 3:26; Eph. 1:5 [d][Rom. 8:18; 2 Cor. 4:17] [e]ch. 2:28 [f]Rom. 8:29; 2 Cor. 3:18; 4:11; Phil. 3:21; 2 Pet. 1:4 [g]John 17:24; 1 Cor. 13:12; Rev. 22:4
3 [h]Rom. 15:12 [i]2 Cor. 7:1
4 [j]ch. 5:17; Rom. 4:15]
5 [k]Heb. 9:26; See ch. 1:2 [l][Isa. 53:11, 12] [m]See 1 Pet. 2:22
6 [n]ch. 2:4; 4:8; 3 John 11
7 [o]ch. 2:26 [p]ch. 2:29
8 [q]Matt. 13:38; John 8:44 [r]Heb. 2:14; [Gen. 3:15; Luke 10:18; John 16:11]
9 [s]ch. 5:18
10 [t]ch. 4:8 [u]ch. 4:20, 21

the Father. Whoever confesses the Son has the Father also. 24 Let [m]what you heard from
the beginning abide in you. If what you heard from the beginning abides in you, then
[n]you too will abide in the Son and in the Father. 25 And this is the promise that he made
to us[1]—[o]eternal life.
26 I write these things to you about [p]those who are trying to deceive you. 27 But [q]the
anointing that you received from him abides in you, and [r]you have no need that anyone
should teach you. But as his anointing teaches you about everything, and [s]is true, and is
no lie—just as it has taught you, abide in him.

Children of God

28 And now, little children, abide in him, so that [t]when he appears [u]we may have confidence
and not shrink from him in shame at his [v]coming. 29 If you know that [w]he is righteous, you
may be sure that [x]everyone who practices righteousness has been born of him.
3 See [y]what kind of love the Father has given to us, that we should be called [z]children of
God; and so we are. The reason why [a]the world does not know us is that [b]it did not know
him. 2 Beloved, we are [z]God's children [c]now, and what we will be [d]has not yet appeared;
but we know that [e]when he appears[2] [f]we shall be like him, because [g]we shall see him as
he is. 3 And everyone who [h]thus hopes in him [i]purifies himself as he is pure.
4 Everyone who makes a practice of sinning also practices lawlessness; [j]sin is lawlessness.
5 You know that [k]he appeared in order to [l]take away sins, and [m]in him there is no sin. 6 No
one who abides in him keeps on sinning; [n]no one who keeps on sinning has either seen
him or known him. 7 Little children, [o]let no one deceive you. [p]Whoever practices righteousness is righteous, as he is righteous. 8 [q]Whoever makes a practice of sinning is of the devil,
for the devil has been sinning from the beginning. The reason the Son of God appeared
was [r]to destroy the works of the devil. 9 [s]No one born of God makes a practice of sinning,
for God's[3] seed abides in him, and he cannot keep on sinning because he has been born of
God. 10 By this it is evident who are the children of God, and who are the children of the
devil: whoever does not practice righteousness is not of God, [t]nor is the one who [u]does
not love his brother.

[1] Some manuscripts *you* [2] Or *when it appears* [3] Greek *his*

"many paths to the one God," for all except the Christian faith refuse to confess that Jesus is God's Son (cf. notes on 1 John 4:3; 4:15).

2:24 what you heard from the beginning. The original and authentic saving message of Christ's death for sin and his conquest of death.

2:27 anointing. See note on v. 20. That this anointing **abides** implies that Christians have the resources to discern doctrinal error. **no need that anyone should teach you.** Yet by writing this letter, John is obviously teaching them. He means, rather, that they have no need for any instruction that diverges from the gospel message.

2:28–3:3 *Christians as Children of God.* Having reaffirmed his readers' commitment to the true Son of God, not the Antichrist (vv. 18–27), John urges them to strive for the ethical integrity and sense of urgency appropriate to their spiritual identity.

2:28 abide in him. See notes on John 8:31; 15:4. **so that.** Maintaining one's personal relationship with Christ will prevent straying into doctrine or conduct of which one will be ashamed **at his coming. When he appears,** many will lack **confidence** and will **shrink from him,** because he will come in judgment.

2:29 To **know that he is righteous** is to have placed one's faith in Christ, not in one's own moral uprightness.

3:1 the world does not know us. There is built-in friction between those who know and serve Christ and those who do not.

3:2 What we will be means having glorified bodies that will never be sick or grow old or die, and being completely without sin. No one like that has yet **appeared** on earth (except Christ himself after his resurrection). **we shall be like him.** In eternity, Christians will be morally without sin, intellectually without falsehood or error, physically without weakness or imperfections, and filled continually with the Holy Spirit. But "like" does not mean "identical to," and believers will never be (e.g.) omniscient or omnipotent as Christ is, since he is both man and God.

3:4–10 *Children of God and the Forsaking of Sin.* To confess the Son and to have the Father (2:23) profoundly alters daily living.

3:4 Lawlessness (Gk. *anomia*) is activity bereft of God's guidance and in violation of his law. **sin is lawlessness.** Even Christians sin (1:9; 2:1), so it may seem like a trivial matter. But to disregard sin's grave implications is disastrous.

3:5 Jesus **appeared in order to take away sins,** not only so that sin might be forgiven (1:9) but also so that it might cease to exercise its tyrannical bondage. **in him there is no sin.** A reminder that "God is light" (1:5), and his Son embodies his sinlessness.

3:6–7 No one who abides . . . keeps on sinning. True followers of Christ do not recklessly and habitually violate what their anointing (2:20, 27) has planted within them (see note on 3:9–10). Those who do habitually sin have neither **seen him** nor **known him.** They are not genuine Christians. On "abides," see also notes on John 8:31; 15:4.

3:8 The reason the Son of God appeared restates v. 5 but here specifies the connection of sin to the devil. Knowing Christ means becoming involved in an all-out war against **the works of the devil,** that is, the **practice of sinning.**

3:9–10 born of God. See John 3:3–8. **God's seed.** Some take this to be the Word of God that brings about the new birth (cf. James 1:18, 22; 1 Pet. 1:23, 25). Others see it as a way of speaking of the Holy Spirit in his regenerating and transforming presence within the believer. Since the Holy Spirit works through the Word in regeneration, both of these ideas are likely intended here. In other words, because the Word is present in the believer's heart through the work of the Spirit, the believer **cannot keep on sinning.** Thus the hearts of genuine Christians (those who are truly **children of God**) have been so transformed that they cannot live in a pattern of continual sin—though this does not mean that Christians are ever completely free from sin in this life (see 1 John 1:8–10). **By this it is evident.** Or, as Jesus said of false prophets, "You will recognize them by their fruits" (Matt. 7:16). **does not love his**

Love One Another

11 For [v]this is the message that you have heard from the beginning, [w]that we should
love one another. 12 We should not be like [x]Cain, who was of the evil one and murdered his
brother. And why did he murder him? [y]Because his own deeds were evil and his brother's
righteous. 13 Do not be surprised, brothers,[1] [z]that the world hates you. 14 We know that [a]we
have passed out of death into life, because we love the brothers. Whoever does not love
abides in death. 15 [b]Everyone who hates his brother is a murderer, and you know that [c]no
murderer has eternal life abiding in him.
16 By this we know love, that [d]he laid down his life for us, and [e]we ought to lay down our
lives for the brothers. 17 But [f]if anyone has the world's goods and sees his brother in need,
yet [g]closes his heart against him, [h]how does God's love abide in him? 18 Little children, let
us not [i]love in word or talk but in deed and [j]in truth.
19 By this we shall know that we are of the truth and reassure our heart before him; 20 for
whenever our heart condemns us, God is greater than our heart, and he knows everything. 21 Beloved, [k]if our heart does not condemn us, [l]we have confidence before God;
22 and [m]whatever we ask we receive from him, because we keep his commandments and
[n]do what pleases him. 23 And this is his commandment, [o]that we believe in the name of
his Son Jesus Christ and [p]love one another, [q]just as he has commanded us. 24 [r]Whoever
keeps his commandments abides in God,[2] and God[3] in him. And [s]by this we know that
he abides in us, by the Spirit whom he has given us.

Test the Spirits

4 Beloved, [t]do not believe every spirit, but [u]test the spirits to see whether they are from
God, for [v]many [w]false prophets [x]have gone out into the world. 2 By this you know
the Spirit of God: [y]every spirit that confesses that [z]Jesus Christ has come in the flesh is
from God, 3 and every spirit [a]that does not confess Jesus is not from God. This is the spirit

[1] Or *brothers and sisters*. The plural Greek word *adelphoi* (translated "brothers") refers to siblings in a family. In New Testament usage, depending on the context, *adelphoi* may refer either to men or to both men and women who are siblings (brothers and sisters) in God's family, the church; also verses 14, 16
[2] Greek *him* [3] Greek *he*

11 [v]ch. 1:5; 2:24 [w]See John 13:34
12 [x]Gen. 4:4, 8; Heb. 11:4; Jude 11 [y]Ps. 38:20; Prov. 29:10
13 [z]John 15:18; 17:14
14 [a]John 5:24
15 [b]Matt. 5:21, 22 [c]Gal. 5:21; Rev. 21:8
16 [d]See John 15:13 [e][Phil. 2:17]
17 [f]James 2:15, 16 [g]Deut. 15:7 [h][ch. 4:20]
18 [i]Ezek. 33:31; Eph. 4:15 [j]2 John 1; 3 John 1
21 [k][1 Cor. 4:4] [l]ch. 5:14; [Job 11:15; 22:26; Rom. 14:22]
22 [m]See Matt. 7:7 [n]John 8:29
23 [o]John 6:29; [Acts 18:8] [p]ver. 11 [q][ch. 2:8]
24 [r][John 6:56; 14:20; 15:4, 5; 17:21] [s]ch. 4:13; Rom. 8:9

Chapter 4

1 [t]Jer. 29:8 [u]1 Thess. 5:21; [1 Cor. 12:10; 14:29; Rev. 2:2] [v]See ch. 2:18 [w]2 Pet. 2:1 [x]2 John 7
2 [y][1 Cor. 12:3] [z]2 John 7
3 [a]ch. 2:22; 2 John 7

brother. John returns to the ethical dimension, the true barometer of what people really believe, whatever they may say.

3:11–4:6 *Overcoming Evil by Listening to the Apostle.* The beginning of this section (3:11, "this is the message") and its summary (4:6, "Whoever knows God listens to us") mark these verses as describing how to avoid the "practice of sinning" and "lawlessness" (3:4).

3:11–24 *Overcoming Cain's Malice.* In John 8:44 Jesus points to the devil as the arch liar and murderer. Here John uses Cain (Gen. 4:1–16) to introduce discussion of what Christians must both avoid and pursue.

3:13 Do not be surprised. Abel did the right thing and was bitterly opposed (v. 12). John knows this dynamic is at work in every age (see John 16:2–3, 33).

3:14 We know . . . because we love. An assurance of salvation is the inner drive that leads one to care for fellow believers (see note on 2:3).

3:15 is a murderer. John agrees with the teaching of Jesus (Matt. 5:22, 28) that outward conformity to God's command ("You shall not murder," Ex. 20:13) is not enough, for even a heartfelt desire to break the command violates it (note the command about inward desires in Ex. 20:17).

3:16 By this we know love, that he laid down his life for us. Jesus' path to the cross marks the selfless, self-giving way of life to which his followers are called.

3:20 whenever our heart condemns us. Whenever one has an inward conviction of sin. It is vital in such times to have a living faith; the proposition that **God is greater than our heart** grants us assurance that he has forgiven us through the atoning work of Christ.

3:21 A clear conscience before God leads to boldness and **confidence before God** in prayer.

3:22 whatever we ask we receive. Cf. note on 5:15. **Because we keep his commandments** implies a direct connection between obeying God and receiving answers to prayer. **Do what pleases him** implies it is possible to do things each day that actually "please" God.

3:23 his commandment, that we believe. Personal trust in Christ is just as important as the ethical behavior stressed in vv. 11–22.

3:24 the Spirit. This is the letter's first explicit mention of the third person of the Trinity (see also 4:2, 6, 13; 5:6, 8). But as author of the Fourth Gospel, John would have presupposed from the start of this letter the existence and importance of the "Helper," "the Spirit of truth," whom Jesus promised to send (see John 14:16–18, 26; 15:26; 16:7–14; 20:22).

4:1–6 *Overcoming the Antichrist's Deception.* It is not only Cain's bad precedent of lack of love that John fears for his readers; it is also the forces of spiritual deception. John furnishes a litmus test to detect them.

4:1 do not believe every spirit. Christian faith is not spiritual gullibility. **test the spirits**. The unseen spiritual influences that guide people's speech and actions can be "tested" by observing their doctrine and conduct as well as by the gift of spiritual discernment (cf. 1 Cor. 12:10; 14:29). **False prophets** are people who claim to speak for God but are actually speaking by demonic influence (1 John 4:3–4). In today's age of "tolerance," discriminating discernment can be viewed as being judgmental (cf. "Judge not," Matt. 7:1). Yet Jesus also taught, "Do not judge by appearances, but judge with right judgment" (John 7:24).

4:2 By this you know. John establishes a doctrinal standard, specifically a Christological one, for testing spirits (see v. 1). If a **spirit** (or a person moved to speak by such a spirit) does not confess that **Jesus Christ has come in the flesh**, that spirit or person is misleading God's people. Apparently many false teachers were saying that Jesus only "appeared" to be human. This was probably based on a false idea that the material creation was inherently evil and therefore physical bodies were evil.

4:3 every spirit that does not confess Jesus. That is, whoever refuses to acknowledge that Jesus is God the Son, "who has come in the flesh" (v. 2). Anyone can talk about Jesus and even believe that he lived on earth, as other religions, cults, and philosophies often affirm. But unless such people affirm both the full deity and the full humanity of Jesus, they are not truly "confessing

of the antichrist, which you heard was coming and [b]now is in the world already. 4 Little
children, you are from God and have overcome them, for [c]he who is in you is greater
than [d]he who is in the world. 5 [e]They are from the world; therefore they speak from the
world, and [f]the world listens to them. 6 We are from God. [g]Whoever knows God listens
to us; whoever is not from God does not listen to us. By this we know [h]the Spirit of truth
and [i]the spirit of error.

God Is Love

7 Beloved, [j]let us love one another, for love is from God, and [k]whoever loves has been
born of God and knows God. 8 [l]Anyone who does not love does not know God, because
[m]God is love. 9 In this the love of God was made manifest among us, that [n]God sent his
only Son into the world, so that we might live through him. 10 In this is love, [o]not that we
have loved God [n]but that he loved us and sent his Son to be [p]the propitiation for our sins.
11 Beloved, if God so loved us, we also ought to love one another. 12 [q]No one has ever seen
God; if we love one another, God abides in us and [r]his love is perfected in us.

13 [s]By this we know that we abide in him and he in us, because he has given us of his
Spirit. 14 And [t]we have seen and testify that [u]the Father has sent his Son to be the Savior
of [v]the world. 15 [w]Whoever confesses that Jesus is the Son of God, God abides in him, and
he in God. 16 So [x]we have come to know and to believe the love that God has for us. [y]God
is love, and [z]whoever abides in love abides in God, and God abides in him. 17 By this [a]is
love perfected with us, so that [b]we may have confidence for the day of judgment, because
[c]as he is so also are we in this world. 18 There is no fear in love, but [d]perfect love casts out
fear. For fear has to do with punishment, and whoever fears has not [a]been perfected in

3 [b]ch. 2:18; [2 Thess. 2:3-7]
4 [c]See Rom. 8:31 [d][1 Cor. 2:12]; See John 12:31
5 [e]John 3:31; 8:23 [f]John 15:19
6 [g][John 8:47; 10:16; 18:37; 1 Cor. 14:37] [h]John 14:17; 15:26; 16:13 [i][1 Cor. 2:12; 1 Tim. 4:1]
7 [j]ch. 3:11 [k]ch. 2:29
8 [l]ch. 3:10 [m]ver. 16; 2 Cor. 13:11; [ch. 1:5; John 4:24]
9 [n]See John 3:16
10 [o]Rom. 5:8, 10 [n][See ver. 9 above] [p]See ch. 2:2
12 [q]ver. 20; John 1:18; 1 Tim. 6:16 [r]ch. 2:5
13 [s]ch. 3:24
14 [t]ch. 1:1, 2 [u]See John 3:17 [v]See ch. 2:2
15 [w]ch. 5:5; [Rom. 10:9]; See Matt. 14:33
16 [x]John 6:69 [y]See ver. 8 [z]ver. 12; ch. 3:24
17 [a][ch. 2:5] [b]ch. 2:28; 3:21 [c][ch. 3:1]
18 [d][John 3:18; Rom. 8:15] [a][See ver. 17 above]

Jesus," but, as John states in unequivocal terms, they are under the influence of **the spirit of the antichrist**.

4:4 he who is in you. The Holy Spirit (see vv. 2, 6). **he who is in the world**. Satan and, by implication, his demons (cf. v. 3; 5:19).

4:5 They are from the world . . . the world listens to them. Jesus himself did not convince most leaders of his time (John 7:48; Acts 4:26), and even the common people who followed him were often fickle (John 6:66). **they speak from the world**. Their speech originates from and is empowered by the world's viewpoint and values.

4:6 does not listen to us. People who are not true believers resist sound doctrine. It does not make sense to them and does not fit their man-centered, materialistic system of thought (cf. 1 Cor. 2:14).

4:7–21 *The Assurance of God through the Love of God.* John's teaching in these verses bears comparison with the apostle Paul's "love chapter," 1 Corinthians 13.

4:7–12 *The Perfecting of God's Love.* The closing words of this section, "his love is perfected in us" (v. 12), capture the direction of John's claims and exhortation.

4:7 whoever loves has been born of God and knows God. This does not rule out the need for faithful confession of Christ (2:23; 4:2) and ethical integrity (3:16). But love completes the picture of a life in fellowship with God. Love is presented here as a consequence of, not a precondition for, being born of God. Unbelievers can love others to some degree, but not in the way that God's indwelling presence enables Christians to love (cf. 4:8–11).

4:8 does not know God, because God is love. The person who lacks love shows himself to be unchanged at the core of his being by the gospel message. John is not saying that God is *only* love (he has numerous other attributes), nor that love is God (a statement for which there is no scriptural support). "God is love" means that God continually gives of himself to others and seeks their benefit. There was eternal love between the persons of the Trinity even before the world was created (John 17:24), and God's love is the ultimate source of any love that Christians are able to display (1 John 4:11, 12, 19).

4:9 God's love is not an abstract principle or sentiment but was **made manifest** in the sending of **his only Son into the world, so that** sinful humanity **might live**, i.e., receive eternal life.

4:10 not that we have loved God. God's love sets the standard for the love Christians are called to embody. **propitiation**. See note on 2:2. Sin brings divine wrath. On the cross, Jesus bore that wrath **for our sins** (see 2 Cor. 5:21).

4:11 Here and in v. 7 John uses a strong term of endearment, **beloved** (Gk. *agapētoi*), evidence that he himself has been mastered by the love he calls for. He uses the same word also at 2:7; 3:2, 21; 4:1. See also note on 2:1, "my little children."

4:12 No one has ever seen God. See note on John 1:18.

4:13–21 *The Assurance of God's Spirit.* God's Spirit (v. 13) gives impetus for and assurance in the high calling of mutual love.

4:13 The presence and activity of the Holy **Spirit** within Christians are evidence that they are abiding in God (see notes on John 8:31; 15:4).

4:14 we have seen and testify. This was particularly and uniquely true for apostles like John, who were Jesus' hand-picked witnesses. By extension and through faith, all subsequent believers testify to the same truths. **Savior** occurs in John's writings only here and in John 4:42.

4:15 Jesus is the Son of God, not in the derived sense that all Christians as God's children are his adopted "sons" and heirs (Rom. 8:14; Gal. 3:26) but in a unique sense (*the* Son of God) in which Jesus is acknowledged as personally divine and as sharing fully every attribute of God (see note on John 1:14). In 1 John 4:2 it was required that true teachers affirm Christ's full humanity; here it is required that they affirm his full deity.

4:16 we have come to know and to believe. Assurance of salvation, while never an arrogant presumption, can become a settled state of mind and heart (see notes on 2:3; 5:13).

4:17 By this refers to the previous verse, where John speaks of believers abiding in God and God abiding in them. **confidence for the day of judgment**. Either eternal life or eternal punishment awaits all humanity (see John 3:36), and God's love furnishes a sure hope for those who have trusted in him. **as he is so also are we in this world**. Just as the Son was and is present in the world in a loving fashion that in no way attracted divine displeasure, so are the Son's followers. The love that Christ embodied and lived out among believers is their confidence in the day of judgment.

4:18 No fear in love does not rule out the presence and constructive effect of "the fear of the Lord" that is "the beginning of knowledge" (Prov. 1:7). Here John speaks of fear of final judgment (cf. 1 John 4:17). God's **perfect love** for believers **casts out** the **fear** of wrath and eternal punishment.

love. 19 [e]We love because he first loved us. 20 [f]If anyone says, "I love God," and [g]hates his
brother, he is a liar; for he who does not love his brother whom he has seen cannot[1] love
God [h]whom he has not seen. 21 And [i]this commandment we have from him: [j]whoever
loves God must also love his brother.

Overcoming the World

5 [k]Everyone who believes that [l]Jesus is the Christ has been born of God, and [m]everyone
who loves the Father loves whoever has been born of him. 2 [n]By this we know that
we love the children of God, when we love God and obey his commandments. 3 For [o]this
is the love of God, that we [p]keep his commandments. And [q]his commandments are not
burdensome. 4 For [r]everyone who has been born of God overcomes the world. And this is
the victory that has overcome the world—[s]our faith. 5 Who is it that overcomes the world
except the one who believes [t]that Jesus is the Son of God?

Testimony Concerning the Son of God

6 This is he who came [u]by water and blood—Jesus Christ; not by the water only but
by the water and the blood. And [v]the Spirit is the one who testifies, because [w]the Spirit is
the truth. 7 For there are three that testify: 8 the Spirit and the water and the blood; and
these three agree. 9 [x]If we receive the testimony of men, the testimony of God is greater,
for this is the testimony of God [y]that he has borne concerning his Son. 10 Whoever believes
in the Son of God [z]has the testimony in himself. Whoever does not believe God [a]has made
him a liar, [b]because he has not believed in the testimony that God has borne concerning
his Son. 11 And this is the testimony, that God gave us [c]eternal life, and [d]this life is in his
Son. 12 [e]Whoever has the Son has life; whoever does not have the Son of God does not
have life.

[1] Some manuscripts *how can he*

19 [e]ver. 10
20 [f]ch. 2:4; 3:17 [g]ch. 2:9, 11 [h]ver. 12; [1 Pet. 1:8]
21 [i]Gal. 6:2 [j]ver. 7; ch. 3:11

Chapter 5

1 [k]John 1:12 [l]ch. 2:22 [m]John 8:42
2 [n]ch. 2:5; 3:24; 4:13
3 [o]2 John 6; See John 14:15 [p]See ch. 2:3 [q]Matt. 11:30
4 [r]ch. 3:9; 4:4; John 16:33 [s][1 Cor. 15:57; Eph. 6:16]
5 [t]ch. 4:15
6 [u][ver. 8] [v]John 15:26; [Acts 5:32] [w]John 14:17; 15:26; 16:13
9 [x]John 5:34, 36, 37; 8:17, 18 [y]See Matt. 3:17
10 [z][Rom. 8:16; Gal. 4:6; Rev. 12:17; 19:10] [a]ch. 1:10; [John 3:33] [b][John 5:38]
11 [c]ch. 2:25; [ch. 4:9] [d]See John 1:4
12 [e][John 3:15, 36; 5:24; 6:40, 47]

4:19 We love because. Christian love is a gift from God, demonstrated supremely in the cross (see Rom. 5:8). God's love always takes the initiative, and the love of Christians is a response to that love. Likewise, all morally good human actions are good not because they conform to some arbitrary human standard of good but because they are rooted in imitation of the morally perfect character of God and conform to God's commands.

5:1–12 *Faith in the Son as the Way to Life.* So far, John has spoken much of love and obedience but not so much of faith. The emphasis now shifts to believing in the Son. Of 1 John's 10 references to believing, seven are in ch. 5.

5:1–5 *Faith Keeps the Commandments of God.* The road to love—such a great concern of John's—is paved with faith in Christ.

5:1 Everyone who believes that. The word "that" underscores that saving faith has a particular content. It is not a vague religious commitment but a wholehearted trust in the saving work of Christ. Everyone who believes **has been born of God**. Regeneration precedes faith (cf. 2:29; 3:9; 4:7; note on Eph. 2:5).

5:2 Obeying God's **commandments** in Scripture is the way to **love the children of God** because God's commandments show believers the true way to do good for others (cf. Rom. 13:9; Gal. 5:14). Love and law are complementary.

5:3 not burdensome. God's love in his people gives them the desire to love and please him. So with eagerness they keep **his commandments**. Rightly understood and followed, God's commandments bring believers great joy and freedom, not a sense of oppression (cf. Matt. 11:28–30).

5:4 overcomes the world. Genuine Christians are not defeated by the world's hostility or compelled by it to turn from Christ.

5:6–12 *Faith Receives the Testimony of God.* Having taught and urged so many things in his letter, John underscores the basis for his authority: the testimony of God (v. 9) in the coming of Jesus, which John personally witnessed.

5:6 Water most likely refers to Jesus' baptism by John the Baptist. **Blood** signifies Christ's atoning death on the cross. **the Spirit is the one who testifies**. The structure of the verse emphasizes that it is the characteristic work of the Holy Spirit to bear witness to the fact that Christ **came** (see v. 6a). It is the inward work of the Spirit in the heart of the believers to convict of sin and to open their eyes to see the truth of who Christ is and to understand the meaning of his atoning death for their sins (cf. 5:10). Likewise, the indwelling presence of the Spirit is given to abide in believers and to teach them the truth of God's Word (2:27; 4:13).

5:7–8 three that testify. The gospel is not based on merely human testimony. John indicates that there are in fact "three that testify," namely, the witness of the **Spirit** (cf. note on v. 6), the **water** baptism of Jesus (including the "Spirit descending on him like a dove" and the voice of the Father from heaven; Mark 1:10–11; cf. John 1:32–34), and the **blood** (which "cleanses us from all unrighteousness"; 1 John 1:7). **These three agree**, thereby providing persuasive confirmation for believing in Jesus as the "Son of God" (5:10). The OT taught that every charge must be confirmed by "two or three witnesses" (Deut. 17:6; 19:15), a principle continued in the NT (Matt. 18:16; 2 Cor. 13:1).

5:9 the testimony of God. In the strongest possible terms, John claims divine authority for his teaching. It is not merely his **testimony**; it is God's.

5:10 has the testimony in himself. This is the "inward testimony of the Spirit," the internal realization that Christians have of the Holy Spirit's presence and work within them. **has made him a liar**. People who reject the Son of God as Savior, or are indifferent to the Son, are provoking God to his face.

5:11 The **testimony** supporting faith in Christ is not a vague spiritual inkling but has definite substance. It is the message of Jesus' incarnation, death, and resurrection, through which **eternal life** has been made available through faith **in his Son**.

5:12 Has the Son implies a faith that is evident in love for others and devotion to God. Whoever **does not have life** is subject to eternal punishment (John 3:36). On Jesus as the one and only way to God, see notes on John 14:6; 1 John 2:23.

That You May Know

13 I write [f]these things to you who [g]believe in the name of the Son of God that you may
know that you have eternal life. 14 And this is [h]the confidence that we have toward him,
that [i]if we ask anything according to his will he hears us. 15 And if we know that he hears
us in whatever we ask, we know that we have the requests that we have asked of him.
16 If anyone sees his brother committing a sin not leading to death, he shall ask, and
[j]God[1] will give him life—to those who commit sins that do not lead to death. [k]There is
sin that leads to death; [l]I do not say that one should pray for that. 17 [m]All wrongdoing is
sin, but there is sin that does not lead to death.
18 We know that [n]everyone who has been born of God does not keep on sinning, but [o]he
who was born of God [p]protects him, and the evil one does not touch him.
19 We know that we are from God, and [q]the whole world lies in the power of the evil
one.
20 And we know that the Son of God has come and [r]has given us understanding, so that
we may know [s]him who is true; and we are in him who is true, in his Son Jesus Christ. He
is the true God and [t]eternal life. 21 Little children, [u]keep yourselves from idols.

[1] Greek *he*

13 [f]John 20:31 [g]John 1:12
14 [h]ch. 2:28; 3:21; 4:17 [i]ch. 3:22; [Prov. 10:24]
16 [j][Job 42:8; James 5:15] [k]Matt. 12:31, 32; Mark 3:29; Luke 12:10; Heb. 6:4-6; 10:26 [l][Jer. 7:16; 14:11]
17 [m][ch. 3:4]
18 [n]ch. 3:9 [o]John 1:18 [p]John 17:12
19 [q][Luke 4:6; Gal. 1:4]
20 [r][Luke 24:45] [s]See John 17:3; Rev. 3:7 [t]ver. 11-13
21 [u]1 Cor. 10:7, 14

5:13–21 *Final Call to Faith and Understanding.* John summarizes and extends many things already discussed. "Know" occurs seven times in these verses, indicating his focus on the assurance and even certainty of Christian faith and salvation.

5:13 *The Confidence that Faith Furnishes.* Belief can be shaky, and John writes to believers who have seen their congregation split (cf. 2:19). **That you may know** implies that it is possible for Christians to have assurance of salvation (cf. 2:3; 3:14; note on 2 Pet. 1:10).

5:14–17 *The Prayer that Faith Enables.* Prayer is central to a living faith. By refining his readers' understanding of prayer, John promotes healthy and growing faith.

5:14 To **ask** God **according to his will** does not mean that, before Christians can pray effectively, they need somehow to discover God's secret plans for the future (sometimes called his "hidden will" or "will of decree"; cf. Deut. 29:29). Rather, it means they should ask according to what the Bible teaches about God's will for his people (sometimes called God's "revealed will" or "will of precept"). If Christians are praying in accordance with what pleases God as found in the teaching of Scripture, then they are praying according to his will (cf. Matt. 6:10; Eph. 5:17).

5:15 To **know that he hears us in whatever we ask** is enough, because communion with God is the goal of prayer. **we have the requests**. Human experience testifies that Christians do not always receive all the things they ask from God, even things that seemingly accord with his revealed will (see note on v. 14). This verse must be understood in light of other passages of Scripture which show that praying according to God's will includes the need to pray in faith (Matt. 21:22; James 1:6), with patience (Luke 18:1–8), in obedience (Ps. 66:18; 1 Pet. 3:12), and in submission to God's greater wisdom (Luke 22:42; Rom. 8:28; 1 Pet. 4:19).

5:16 Sin not leading to death is sin for which forgiveness is possible because (1) forgiveness is sought and (2) God is willing to grant it. **Death** and eternal **life** are present spiritual states as well as ultimate actual destinies (hell, heaven). **Sin that leads to death** is probably sin that is (1) unrepented of and (2) of the kind or nature that John has warned about throughout the letter: resolute rejection of the true doctrine about Christ, chronic disobedience to God's commandments, persistent lack of love for fellow believers—all indications of a lack of saving faith—which will not be forgiven. **I do not say**. John leaves open whether to **pray for that** situation if it arises. It would be better in such cases to pray for repentance.

5:17 All wrongdoing is a matter of grave concern given God's utter perfection and zealous love. However, not all sin leads **to death**, so Christians should be proactive in praying for their own and others' forgiveness.

5:18–21 *The Understanding that Faith Grants.* The letter concludes on a note of high confidence and deep spiritual insight.

5:18 does not keep on sinning. See notes on 3:6–7; 3:9–10. **He who was born of God** is a reference to Jesus Christ, who in his physical birth was "born of God" in that he was sent from God the Father and was conceived by the Holy Spirit (Luke 1:35) and in his resurrection from the dead was "born of God" in that he was brought back to life (Col. 1:18). The **evil one does not touch** believers in the sense of causing permanent spiritual loss. See 1 John 4:4.

5:19 we are from God. Christians have been spiritually reborn and are in that sense children of God. **the whole world**. See note on 2:15.

5:20 Has come points to the incarnation. **given . . . understanding**. Christians receive grace in order to grasp biblical teaching and receive the will to put it into practice. **so that we may know him**. True knowledge of God is a gracious act and gift of God (John 1:13).

5:21 Most NT letters contain final words of warning in their closing lines. **Keep yourselves from idols** means keep yourselves from trusting, obeying, revering, and following—that is, in effect, worshiping—anyone or anything other than God himself, and his Son Jesus Christ.

INTRODUCTION TO

THE SECOND LETTER OF JOHN

2 JOHN

Author and Title

Ancient manuscripts uniformly identify this as a second letter by "John." Due to the writing style, position in the Canon, and theological outlook, it is best viewed as written by the apostle John (see Introduction to 1 John: Author and Title). The document itself identifies its author as "the elder" (v. 1). Theories that this was some "elder John" different from the apostle are interesting but lack compelling support. "Elder" was a common term for pastoral leaders of local congregations in the early church. In calling himself "the elder," John is simply affirming his pastoral role, as Peter also does ("fellow elder," 1 Pet. 5:1), not somehow disqualifying himself from being identified as Jesus' disciple and ultimately an apostle. (See also Introduction to 3 John: Author and Title.)

Date

Like 1 John, 2 John probably was written in the vicinity of Ephesus near the end of the first century A.D. Ancient sources suggest John spent the closing decades of his life in this area, ministering to churches like those listed in Revelation 2–3.

Recipients

John writes to "the elect lady." This more likely refers to a congregation than to an individual, because much of 2 John is written in the second-person plural. It is also questionable whether John would write to a female Christian that he and she should "love one another" (v. 5); the phrase makes better sense if addressed to a church. There are three additional reasons why "elect lady" may refer to a whole congregation. First, the word "church" in Greek is feminine in gender, and "lady" would go along with that. Second, the church is depicted as "bride" elsewhere in John's writings (Rev. 21:2, 9; 22:17). Third, the Greek word *kyria* ("lady") referred to a social subunit in the Greek city-state. John may use this word for a local congregation instead of the more common feminine word *ekklēsia*.

Verse 13 of 2 John suggests that John writes to one congregation from another, which he terms "your elect sister."

Theme

The focus of 2 John is living in the love of God in accordance with the truth of Jesus Christ. This love extends not only to God but to other people. It is also discerning; it does not "go on ahead" of biblical revelation (v. 9), and it does not lend aid to enemies of the gospel message (vv. 10–11). Instead, Christ's followers "walk according to his commandments" (v. 6) and through faith "win a full reward" (v. 8).

Purpose, Occasion, and Background

John writes to urge readers to love each other (v. 5) and beware of deceivers (vv. 7–8). He offers practical counsel on showing hospitality to traveling missionaries (vv. 10–11) and seeks to prepare "the elect lady" for his anticipated visit in the near future (v. 12).

Timeline

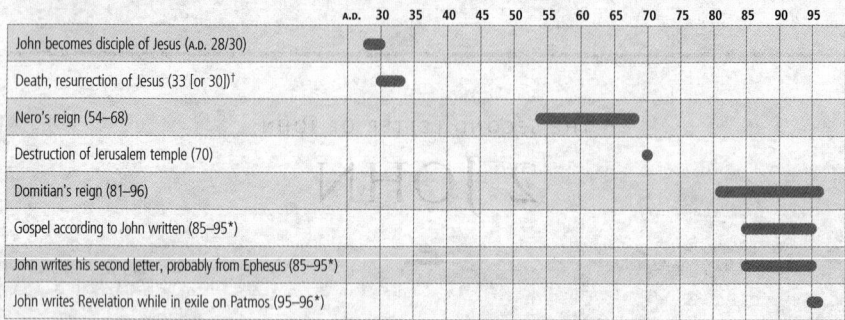

	A.D. 30	35	40	45	50	55	60	65	70	75	80	85	90	95
John becomes disciple of Jesus (A.D. 28/30)														
Death, resurrection of Jesus (33 [or 30])†														
Nero's reign (54–68)														
Destruction of Jerusalem temple (70)														
Domitian's reign (81–96)														
Gospel according to John written (85–95*)														
John writes his second letter, probably from Ephesus (85–95*)														
John writes Revelation while in exile on Patmos (95–96*)														

** denotes approximate date; / signifies either/or; † see The Date of Jesus' Crucifixion, pp. 1809–1810*

Key Themes

1. The truth of Jesus Christ is eternal.	2
2. Christian love and compliance with God's commandments are inseparable.	6
3. False teaching about Christ abounds.	7
4. Purveyors of false teaching have to be identified and left to their own devices, not welcomed and supported by upholders of authentic Christian teaching.	9–11

History of Salvation Summary

Now that Christ has accomplished salvation, believers are to follow him and his teaching. (For an explanation of the "History of Salvation," see the Overview of the Bible, pp. 23–26.)

Literary Features

In format, this brief book is a conventional NT epistle, consisting of a salutation, a body, and a conclusion. As in most epistles, the body of the letter consists of mingled instruction and commands, and although readers do not find the concentrated list of commands that comprise the familiar *paraenesis* (set of ethical commands) of NT letters, verses 8–11 have affinities with that conventional motif.

Outline

I. Greeting: The Elder's Love (vv. 1–3)

II. The Elder's Joy and Request (vv. 4–6)

III. The Elder's Concern (vv. 7–8)

IV. The Elder's Warning (vv. 9–11)

V. Closing: The Elder's Farewell (vv. 12–13)

THE SECOND LETTER OF JOHN

2 JOHN

Greeting

1 [a]The elder to the elect lady and her children, [b]whom I love in truth, and not only I,
but also all who [c]know [d]the truth, **2** [e]because of the truth that abides in us and will be
with us forever:

3 [f]Grace, mercy, and peace will be with us, from God the Father and from Jesus Christ
the Father's Son, in truth and love.

Walking in Truth and Love

4 [g]I rejoiced greatly to find some of your children walking in the truth, just as we were
commanded by the Father. **5** And now I ask you, dear lady—[h]not as though I were writing
you a new commandment, but the one we have had from the beginning—[i]that we love
one another. **6** And [j]this is love, that we walk according to his commandments; this is the
commandment, just [k]as you have heard from the beginning, so that you should walk in
it. **7** For [l]many deceivers [m]have gone out into the world, [n]those who do not confess the
coming of Jesus Christ in the flesh. Such a one is the deceiver and the antichrist. **8** Watch
yourselves, [o]so that you may not lose what we[1] have worked for, but [p]may win a full reward.
9 Everyone who goes on ahead and does not abide in the teaching of Christ, [q]does not have
God. Whoever abides in the teaching [q]has both the Father and the Son. **10** If anyone comes

1 [a]3 John 1; [1 Pet. 5:1] [b]1 John 3:18; 3 John 1 [c]John 8:32; [1 Tim. 2:4; Heb. 10:26] [d]John 1:17; 14:6; See Gal. 2:5
2 [e][1 Cor. 13:6]
3 [f]1 Tim. 1:2; 2 Tim. 1:2; [Jude 2]
4 [g]3 John 3, 4
5 [h]1 John 2:7 [i]See 1 John 3:11
6 [j]1 John 5:3; [1 John 2:5]; See John 14:15 [k]1 John 2:24
7 [l]See 1 John 2:18, 26 [m]1 John 4:1 [n]1 John 2:22; 4:2, 3
8 [o][Gal. 3:4; Heb. 10:35] [p]See 1 Cor. 3:8
9 [q]See 1 John 2:23

[1] Some manuscripts *you*

1–3 *Greeting: The Elder's Love.* Love frames the opening section, appearing in vv. 1 and 3.

1 The elect lady and her children probably refers to a local congregation and its members (see Introduction: Recipients). The word **truth** is prominent in John's greeting, perhaps because early Christians saw themselves as being in close communion with Jesus, who called himself "the truth" (see note on John 14:6) and whom they acknowledged as such, and perhaps because John knows he will shortly write about the untruth of spiritual deceivers (2 John 7–11).

2 abides in us. The gospel that unites John and his readers is personally present. "In us" could be translated "among us." Christian faith is shared and is not just a personal conviction.

4–6 *The Elder's Joy and Request.* "Walk," prominent in this section, refers to everyday ethical conduct. John's concern is with his readers' practical lives as Christians.

4 Apparently John had encountered members of the congregation who were **walking in the truth**, i.e., living in a manner pleasing to God. Perhaps it was from them that he determined he needed to pen this letter to their church.

5 Love one another may suggest there was dissent and discord among the readers. On the central role of love in Scripture, see note on John 13:34–35.

6 Love has a strong ethical dimension. The **commandments** that the readers have **heard from the beginning** must constantly steer their lives. **Commandment** (singular) probably refers to the love commandment introduced by Jesus (John 13:34–35).

7–8 *The Elder's Concern.* Doctrinal confusion was a threat to the congregation's integrity.

7 the coming of . . . Christ in the flesh. See 1 John 4:2–3 and notes. **antichrist**. See 1 John 2:18, 22 and notes. **many deceivers**. On false teaching, see note on Matt. 7:15–20.

8 Watch yourselves. Jesus used similar language in warning about end-time perils (Mark 13:5, 9, 23, 33). **win a full reward**. The hope of transformation and greater eternal reward in Christ's very presence (cf. 1 John 3:2–3).

9–11 *The Elder's Warning.* The congregation must withstand pressure from persons or forces who do not "abide in the teaching of Christ" (v. 9).

9 Goes on ahead probably refers to "new" teaching that amounted to rejection of the apostolic faith. **Does not have God**, i.e., does not have eternal life in fellowship with God. Threats to church purity come not only from the outside but often from within. Paul wrote that some at Corinth had "no knowledge of God" (1 Cor. 15:34).

10 The context of **if anyone comes** makes clear that this refers to traveling teachers or preachers working against true Christian teaching. **do not receive him into your house**. Such a welcome would give the appearance of endorsing the false teaching (early churches were house churches). This is not a prohibition about showing the hospitality to sinners for which Jesus himself was well known (and criticized; see Matt. 9:10–13; 11:19); Paul also warned against overzealous separation from non-Christians (1 Cor. 5:9–10). It is rather *false Christians* that require caution and perhaps rejection (see 1 Cor. 5:11–13). The significance of John's call to reject the false teacher was heightened in a society that considered hospitality a great virtue (see note on 1 Pet. 4:8–9).

to you and does not bring this teaching, [r]do not receive him into your house or give him
any greeting, 11 for whoever greets him [s]takes part in his wicked works.

Final Greetings

12 [t]Though I have much to write to you, I would rather not use paper and ink. [u]Instead
I hope to come to you and talk face to face, [v]so that our joy may be complete.
13 The children of your elect sister greet you.

10[r][Rom. 16:17; Gal. 1:8, 9; 2 Thess. 3:6, 14; Titus 3:10]
11[s][1 Tim. 5:22]
12[t]3 John 13 [u]3 John 14 [v]John 15:11; 17:13

11 Greets means to extend approval, assistance, and full fellowship. **takes part in his wicked works.** To support someone who is working against the true Christian message is to incur that person's guilt.

12–13 *Closing: The Elder's Farewell.* John makes it clear that his letter is only a prelude to a pastoral visit that he hopes to accomplish soon.

12 so that our joy may be complete. See 1 John 1:4 and note. Doctrinal deviation threatens the joy of the church because it destroys unity and imperils the approving presence of Christ in personal lives and the corporate assembly.

13 Children of your elect sister are the believers in the congregation from which John writes.

INTRODUCTION TO

THE THIRD LETTER OF JOHN

3 JOHN

Author and Title

See Introductions to 1 and 2 John. Like 2 John, 3 John claims to have been written by "the elder," most likely the apostle John. In NT times and into the post-apostolic era, "elders" (Gk. *presbyteroi*) could refer to the pastoral leaders of local congregations. They appear by this title first in Acts 11:30, which speaks of church leaders (pastors) in Jerusalem in the mid-40s A.D. Paul and Barnabas appointed "elders" to be ministers in the churches they planted (Acts 14:23). "Elders" presided at the Jerusalem council (c. A.D. 49) alongside the apostles (Acts 15:2, 4, 6, 22, 23; 16:4). Nearly a decade later Paul addressed the "elders," apparently the pastors of churches at and probably around Ephesus (Acts 20:17). "Elders" at Jerusalem were alongside head elder James when Paul reported back to the church at the end of his third missionary journey (Acts 21:18). This shows that the title "elder" for pastoral leaders at Ephesus had been in use 20 to 40 years by the time 2 and 3 John were written. It was widely employed in the early church, particularly around Jerusalem but also in distant areas like Ephesus. The fact that Peter understood himself to be a "fellow elder" of church leaders across a wide geographical area (1 Pet. 5:1) makes it plausible for John to have referred to himself in the same manner.

Date

See Introduction to 2 John. John probably writes from around Ephesus in the last quarter of the first century.

Theme

The theme of 3 John is steadfastness in the face of opposition. The recipient of the letter, Gaius, faces a troublemaker named Diotrephes. By "walking in the truth" (vv. 3, 4), Christians can embrace and live out the apostolic message that John conveys in all his letters.

Purpose, Occasion, and Background

It has been suggested that 2 and 3 John were originally preserved because they were part of a single packet containing all three Johannine letters. On this view, 3 John was a personal letter to Gaius commending the courier of the shipment, Demetrius (v. 12); 2 John was to be read aloud to Gaius's church; and 1 John was a sermon for general distribution and not a letter in the strict sense. This scenario cannot be verified but is a useful hypothesis in envisioning how John's letters could have arisen and been preserved in early Christianity. Unfortunately, no other information about Gaius has survived.

Key Themes

Third John is so brief, personal, and situation-specific that its "themes" are really just emphases:

1. The support of traveling Christian workers is noble and needful.	5–8
2. Church discipline can be necessary for healthy ministry to flourish.	9–10
3. The integrity of faith is proven by actions.	11

Timeline

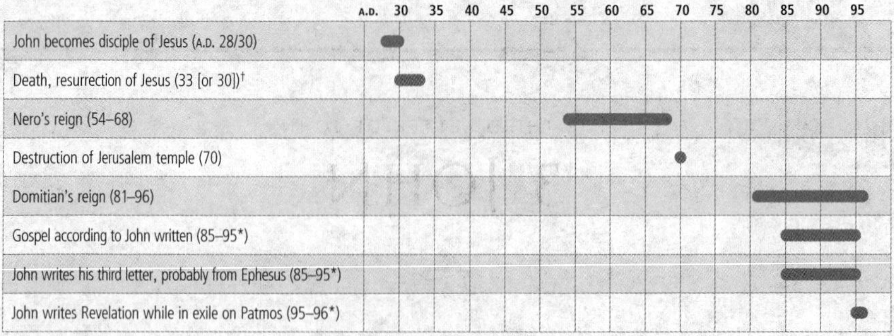

A.D. 30 35 40 45 50 55 60 65 70 75 80 85 90 95
John becomes disciple of Jesus (A.D. 28/30)
Death, resurrection of Jesus (33 [or 30])†
Nero's reign (54–68)
Destruction of Jerusalem temple (70)
Domitian's reign (81–96)
Gospel according to John written (85–95*)
John writes his third letter, probably from Ephesus (85–95*)
John writes Revelation while in exile on Patmos (95–96*)

** denotes approximate date; / signifies either/or; † see The Date of Jesus' Crucifixion, pp. 1809–1810*

History of Salvation Summary

Since Christ has accomplished salvation, believers are to continue in his truth. (For an explanation of the "History of Salvation," see the Overview of the Bible, pp. 23–26.)

Literary Features

Third John is a personal epistle, addressed to a friend of the author. The customary epistolary conventions are evident: an opening salutation, a body of instruction, and concluding greetings. Reinforcing the identity of this book as a personal letter is the way in which it is built around references to specific acquaintances from start to finish. Whereas 2 John was written to an unidentified church, this letter is filled with references to specific people and situations. It speaks of hospitality to traveling Christians. The main motif is "a home away from home," and accompanying that, the pattern of arrival and welcoming of guests.

Outline

I. Greeting: The Elder's Joy at Gaius's Faithfulness (vv. 1–4)

II. Praise for Gaius's Support for Itinerant Christian Workers (vv. 5–8)

III. Concern about Diotrephes (vv. 9–10)

IV. Advice and Commendation of Demetrius (vv. 11–12)

V. Closing with Promise to Visit (vv. 13–15)

THE THIRD LETTER OF JOHN

3 JOHN

1[a]2 John 1 [b]1 John 3:18; 2 John 1
3[c]2 John 4
4[d][1 Cor. 4:14, 15; Gal. 4:19; 1 Tim. 1:2; 2 Tim. 1:2; Titus 1:4; Philem. 10]
5[e][Gal. 6:10; Heb. 13:1] [f]See Matt. 25:35
6[g]1 Thess. 2:12; [Col. 1:10]
7[h]See Acts 5:41 [i]1 Cor. 9:12, 15
11[j][Ps. 34:14; 37:27; Isa. 1:16, 17] [k]1 John 2:29

Greeting

1 [a]The elder to the beloved Gaius, [b]whom I love in truth.
2 Beloved, I pray that all may go well with you and that you may be in good health, as
it goes well with your soul. 3 For [c]I rejoiced greatly when the brothers[1] came and testified
to your truth, as indeed you are walking in the truth. 4 I have no greater joy than to hear
that [d]my children are walking in the truth.

Support and Opposition

5 Beloved, it is a faithful thing you do in all your efforts for [e]these brothers, [f]strangers
as they are, 6 who testified to your love before the church. You will do well to send them
on their journey in a manner [g]worthy of God. 7 For they have gone out for the sake of [h]the
name, [i]accepting nothing from the Gentiles. 8 Therefore we ought to support people like
these, that we may be fellow workers for the truth.
9 I have written something to the church, but Diotrephes, who likes to put himself first,
does not acknowledge our authority. 10 So if I come, I will bring up what he is doing, talking
wicked nonsense against us. And not content with that, he refuses to welcome the brothers,
and also stops those who want to and puts them out of the church.
11 Beloved, [j]do not imitate evil but imitate good. [k]Whoever does good is from God;

[1] Or *brothers and sisters.* The plural Greek word *adelphoi* (translated "brothers") refers to siblings in a family. In New Testament usage, depending on the context, *adelphoi* may refer either to men or to both men and women who are siblings (brothers and sisters) in God's family, the church; also verses 5, 10

1–4 *Greeting: The Elder's Joy at Gaius's Faithfulness.* John's opening tone is affectionate and positive.

1 Beloved (cf. vv. 5, 11) conveys the truth that Christians are linked by the love God has shown them in Christ (cf. 1 John 4:9–10). **Love in truth** could mean simply "truly love" as a Christian brother, or it could refer to the "truth" of the gospel, in the service of which the lives of John and Gaius are intertwined.

2 Wishes for **good health** were standard in the openings of ancient Greek letters, but John prays for Gaius's health and also expresses care for his **soul**. Though spiritual growth can come through sickness and affliction (cf. Ps. 119:67, 71), it is right to pray for good health, as Jesus' earthly healing ministry also demonstrated.

3 the brothers came. Apparently John had been visited by Christians from Gaius's church, who told John of Gaius's faithful Christian life. **Truth** is fidelity to Christ and his commands. (See also note on John 14:6.)

4 joy. See 1 John 1:4 and note. **my children**. His readers are first of all "children of God" (a signature Johannine expression; John 1:12; 11:52; 1 John 3:1, 2, 10; 5:2). But John as their spiritual overseer could view them as his own children too (see note on 1 John 2:1). Paul's usage was similar (1 Tim. 1:2, 18; Titus 1:4; Philem. 10).

5–8 *Praise for Gaius's Support for Itinerant Christian Workers.* Whereas 2 John 10 warns against supporting the wrong people, John affirms Gaius's work on the behalf of faithful laborers, even though they are "strangers" (3 John 5).

5 these brothers. Traveling Christian workers. The early church was centered on missionary outreach, otherwise it would not have survived and spread (see Heb. 13:2).

6 Send . . . on their journey (Gk. *propempō*, "to send forth") in contexts like this carries the sense of sending with necessary material (e.g., financial) support. The word with this sense is found also in Rom. 15:24; 1 Cor. 16:6, 11; 2 Cor. 1:16; Titus 3:13. **worthy of God**. Those laboring at large for the gospel work not for themselves but for the One who sends them.

7 the name. The very person of God himself, though John may refer here to Christ, signifying his deity. Cf. Acts 5:41 and Phil. 2:9. The workers accepted **nothing from the Gentiles**, that is, the non-Christian populace. Just as Paul normally did not accept aid from those among whom he labored (1 Cor. 9:14–15, 18; 2 Cor. 11:8; 1 Thess. 2:9), the workers did not want to be accused of hawking their message for personal gain.

8 we ought to support. Not everyone is called to go and minister elsewhere. But all Christ's followers are called to play their part in this enterprise (Matt. 28:19–20). **the truth**. The gospel message (see Col. 1:5).

9–10 *Concern about Diotrephes.* Just as Jesus and Paul had their detractors, John and Gaius encountered people who worked against the progress of God's kingdom.

10 talking . . . against us. The problem of "Christians" who reject things taught by the apostles persists today. **not content with that**. Sinful personal ambition is never satisfied but seeks to expand. **refuses to welcome the brothers**. Stands in the way of the support of traveling Christian workers.

11–12 *Advice and Commendation of Demetrius.* As John prepares to end his letter, he issues terse remarks of guidance.

11 do not imitate evil. Probably encouragement not to give in to Diotrephes or to descend to his level of "dirty politics."

[l]whoever does evil has not seen God. 12 Demetrius [m]has received a good testimony from
everyone, and from the truth itself. We also add our testimony, and [n]you know that our
testimony is true.

Final Greetings

13 [o]I had much to write to you, but I would rather not write with pen and ink. 14 I hope
to see you soon, and we will talk face to face.
15 Peace be to you. The friends greet you. Greet the friends, [p]each by name.

11 [l]See 1 John 3:6
12 [m][1 Tim. 3:7] [n]John 21:24
13 [o]2 John 12
15 [p]John 10:3

12 Normal postal service could not be entrusted with Christian correspondence like this letter (and possibly other letters from John as well; see Introduction: Purpose, Occasion, and Background). So someone like **Demetrius** served as courier. Phoebe probably served this function in delivering Romans (Rom. 16:1–2), and Tychicus likely hand-carried Ephesians (Eph. 6:21–22) and Colossians (Col. 4:7–8).

13–15 *Closing with Promise to Visit.* John echoes the words of 2 John 12. Sometimes pastoral oversight requires physical presence for successful execution.

13 had much to write. Third John is a bare outline of many more things that John wants to communicate.

15 friends. An unusual term for fellow believers; but see John 15:15. **each by name**. John's pastoral care is not remote and bureaucratic but personal, as Jesus commended and modeled (John 10:3, 14).

INTRODUCTION TO

THE LETTER OF

JUDE

Author and Title

As its title implies, the book was written by Jude, brother of James and Jesus (cf. Matt. 13:55; Mark 6:3, where Gk. "Judas" is the same as "Jude" in Jude 1). There is little debate regarding the authenticity of the letter because of the strength of internal evidence (e.g., v. 1). Some have claimed that an anonymous author wrote this using Jude's name, but it is unlikely that any imposter would choose the name of such an insignificant figure for his writing. Also, such a pseudonymous work would have been rejected by the church (see Introduction to 1 Timothy: Author and Title), and Jude has been accepted as canonical from earliest times.

Date

Since Jude addresses a situation similar to that addressed by 2 Peter and exhibits a literary relationship (probably as a source) to 2 Peter, the two letters are commonly dated in fairly close proximity. (See Introduction to 2 Peter: Author and Title.) Therefore, while external evidence is sparse, Jude is best dated in the mid-60s A.D.

Theme

The church must contend for the one true faith once for all delivered to the saints (v. 3), and people of faith must persevere to the end by resisting the false teachers and following the truth.

Purpose, Occasion, and Background

Jude warns against following those who have surreptitiously gained entry to the church and are perverting the one true faith with false teaching. Indeed, the letter warns against allowing the false teachers to continue to have influence. Jude calls the church to defend the truth aggressively against this infiltration. While the false teachers of Jude were profoundly libertine (morally unrestrained), it would be anachronistic to argue that they were Gnostic (an early heretical sect, or group of sects, influential from the 2nd century A.D. onward).

Jude accomplishes his purpose by interpreting the OT analogically, using the same principles of interpretation found in 2 Peter (and elsewhere in the NT). He also draws on Jewish apocalyptic traditions (he refers to *1 Enoch* and the *Testament of Moses*) in building his case. Thus, as literature, Jude has a distinctively Jewish flavor.

Given the apparent Jewish perspective of the letter itself, the audience of Jude is frequently identified as Jewish, or as a mixture of Jewish and Gentile readers where the Gentiles are familiar with Jewish traditions. However, any identification of the audience is largely conjecture.

History of Salvation Summary

Since Christ has accomplished salvation, believers are to hold fast to him and reject false ways. (For an explanation of the "History of Salvation," see the Overview of the Bible, pp. 23–26.)

Literary Features

The format is that of the NT epistle, with its loose divisions of salutation, body, and closing. But the central unit of the letter (vv. 5–16) falls decisively into the genre of a judgment oracle: it has an object of attack, a many-sided vehicle in which the attack is embodied, a discernible harsh tone, and an implied standard by which the attack is being conducted ("the faith that was once for all delivered to the saints," v. 3). The description of the apostates (vv. 8–16) uses the portrait technique in which, as one learns more and more about the apostates, one finally has a picture of their character and actions. The concentrated use of images and allusions (e.g., to Sodom and Gomorrah and the archangel Michael) lends a poetic quality to the letter.

The writer displays horror over the spectacle of apostasy and the false teachers who induce it. The only NT passage that surpasses Jude in these traits is Jesus' denunciation of the religious leaders in Matthew 23. But the letter begins with the usual soothing notes of NT epistles, and in the last two verses it modulates into one of the most moving benedictions in the NT.

Timeline

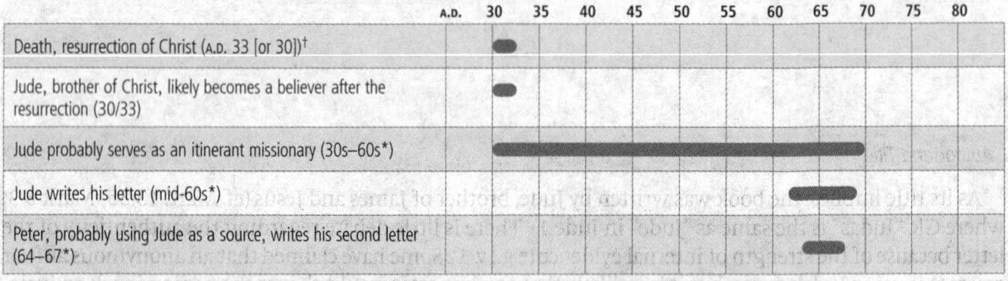

A.D. 30 35 40 45 50 55 60 65 70 75 80
Death, resurrection of Christ (A.D. 33 [or 30])†
Jude, brother of Christ, likely becomes a believer after the resurrection (30/33)
Jude probably serves as an itinerant missionary (30s–60s*)
Jude writes his letter (mid-60s*)
Peter, probably using Jude as a source, writes his second letter (64–67*)

* denotes approximate date; / signifies either/or; † see The Date of Jesus' Crucifixion, pp. 1809–1810

Key Themes

1. Christians need to defend the doctrines of the faith.	3
2. False teachers may be identified by their immoral character.	4, 8, 10, 12–13, 16, 18–19
3. God will judge false teachers.	4, 5–7, 11, 14–15
4. Saints must persevere to be saved.	17–23
5. As God grants mercy to those who are called, they must show mercy to others.	2, 21–23
6. God grants grace that ensures that his own will persevere.	1–2, 24–25

Outline

I. Initial Greeting (vv. 1–2)

II. Jude's Appeal: Contend for the Faith (vv. 3–4)
- A. The urgency of the defense (v. 3)
- B. Description of the false teachers and their teaching (v. 4)

III. Immoral Character and Consequent Judgment of the False Teachers (vv. 5–16)
- A. Judgment reserved for the false teachers (vv. 5–7)
  - 1. The analogy of Egypt (v. 5)
  - 2. The analogy of the rebellious angels (v. 6)
  - 3. The analogy of Sodom and Gomorrah (v. 7)
- B. Nature of the false teachers (vv. 8–13)
  - 1. The false teachers are blasphemers (vv. 8–10)
  - 2. The false teachers are motivated by greed (v. 11)
  - 3. The false teachers exemplify depravity with impunity (vv. 12–13)
- C. Judgment on the false teachers revisited (vv. 14–16)
  - 1. Description of the judgment (vv. 14–15)
  - 2. Further reasons for judgment (v. 16)

IV. Concluding Exhortations (vv. 17–25)
- A. On the apostolic warnings (vv. 17–19)
- B. On the antidote to the false teachers (vv. 20–21)
- C. On showing mercy (vv. 22–23)
- D. Doxology of great joy (vv. 24–25)

THE LETTER OF

JUDE

1[a]Rom. 1:7; 1 Cor. 1:24 [b]1 Thess. 1:4; 2 Thess. 2:13 [c]John 17:11, 15; 1 Thess. 5:23
2[d][2 John 3] [e]1 Pet. 1:2; 2 Pet. 1:2
3[f]Titus 1:4 [g]1 Tim. 6:12; 2 Tim. 4:7; [Luke 13:24; 1 Cor. 9:25; Phil. 1:27]
4[h]2 Pet. 2:1 [i][Gal. 2:4] [j]1 Pet. 2:8 [k]See Acts 11:23 [l]Titus 1:16; 2 Pet. 2:1; 1 John 2:22
5[m]2 Pet. 1:12; 3:17 [n][1 Cor. 10:4, 5, 9]

Greeting

1 Jude, a servant[1] of Jesus Christ and brother of James,
[a]To those who are called, [b]beloved in God the Father and [c]kept for[2] Jesus Christ:
2 May [d]mercy, [e]peace, and love be multiplied to you.

Judgment on False Teachers

3 Beloved, although I was very eager to write to you about our [f]common salvation, I
found it necessary to write appealing to you [g]to contend for the faith that was once for all
delivered to the saints. **4** For [h]certain people [i]have crept in unnoticed [j]who long ago were
designated for this condemnation, ungodly people, who pervert [k]the grace of our God
into sensuality and [l]deny our only Master and Lord, Jesus Christ.
5 Now I want [m]to remind you, although you once fully knew it, that [n]Jesus, who saved[3]

[1] Or *slave* (for the contextual rendering of the Greek word *doulos,* see Preface) [2] Or *by* [3] Some manuscripts *although you fully knew it, that the Lord who once saved*

1–2 *Initial Greeting.* Although he is the brother of Jesus, Jude identifies himself as his **servant** (Gk. *doulos*), acknowledging Jesus as Lord. He is also the **brother of James**, who plays a major role in the NT (Matt. 13:55; Acts 12:17; 15:13; 21:18; 1 Cor. 15:7; Gal. 1:19; 2:9, 12; by this time, the only "James" who could be identified by name only without further description was James the Lord's brother—see note on Acts 12:17). **called**. See note on Rom. 8:30. **Beloved** (Gk. participle of *agapaō*) shows the intimate relationship between **God the Father** and the readers. It also shows that God has set his special love on them for salvation. At the outset of his letter to Christians who are threatened by false teachers, Jude reminds them that they will be **kept** and preserved by God's power from falling away. The introduction thus anticipates the confident and joyful conclusion in Jude 24–25.

3–4 *Jude's Appeal: Contend for the Faith.* Jude strongly urges his readers to contend for the faith against the subversive false teachers.

3 *The Urgency of the Defense.* **Beloved** (Gk. *agapētos*). Jude, like Peter, writes in this way to emphasize his strong personal concern (cf. vv. 17, 20; 1 Pet. 2:11; 4:12; 2 Pet. 3:1, 8, 14, 17). Though Jude had wanted to write about **our common salvation**, the urgent need to **contend for the faith** took precedence over even the exalted theme of salvation. "The faith" (i.e., the known and received body of truth about Jesus and salvation through him) had been **once for all delivered to the saints** (i.e., Christians). In other words, by the time that Jude wrote his letter, "the faith" had already been fixed and established in the apostolic teaching of the early church, and therefore could not be changed, but was under attack and in need of defense. Although the NT documents had not yet been collected into a complete canon of Scripture, by this time the foundational NT teachings were circulating in oral form through the apostolic circles. In addition, some NT documents had already begun to circulate among the churches (cf. Col. 4:16; also The Canon of the New Testament, pp. 2579–2581). A further implication of this verse is that, after the writings authorized by the apostles were included in the NT canon, nothing more could ever be added to Scripture, since the content of the faith had been delivered "once for all." This is at odds with the teachings of other religions such as Mormonism and Islam, which hold that the NT writings existing today contain corrupted teachings, and that additional authoritative teachings came from God later (e.g., the Book of Mormon or the Qur'an, both of which contradict the NT at many points). This conclusion also differs from the Roman Catholic view that official church tradition (in addition to Scripture) also has absolute divine authority. Since the letter of Jude was included in the NT canon, his letter must also have received early apostolic endorsement for inclusion, and everything in Jude's letter is in complete accord with apostolic teaching and writings of the early church and with "the faith once for all delivered to the saints."

4 *Description of the False Teachers and Their Teaching.* **crept in unnoticed**. Jude begins his account of the false teachers by describing the devious way they have slipped into the church. They began by acting like Christians and operating subversively. **Designated** translates Greek *prographō*, "to write about or identify beforehand." The false teachers did not take God by surprise, for he predicted their coming and their **condemnation** long before they even existed. They **pervert** (that is, twist and distort) God's **grace** (esp. his free forgiveness of sin) into a license for **sensuality** (see note on 2 Pet. 2:2), and they **deny** the **Lord, Jesus Christ**, apparently using the gospel teaching about grace as an excuse for ungodly living (cf. Rom. 3:8; 6:1, 15; 2 Pet. 3:15–16).

5–16 *Immoral Character and Consequent Judgment of the False Teachers.* Jude employs biblical and traditional analogies to document the certainty of judgment for the false teachers. He also describes the debased morality that characterizes this group, for which they have already been eternally condemned (see v. 13).

5–7 *Judgment Reserved for the False Teachers.* Jude applies examples of judgment from the whole of biblical history in his polemic against the heretics.

5 *The Analogy of Egypt.* Jude reminds his readers that they **once fully knew** about God's judgment, but apparently their sense of its certainty has waned. He refers them to the Exodus account as a reminder. **Jesus . . . saved a people out of the land of Egypt** (cf. Exodus 1–15). This may seem puzzling, because the name "Jesus" is not applied to the Son of God in the OT. It is a prime example of the apostolic understanding of the OT, according to which the Son of God, in his eternal divine nature, was active in the world from the beginning of creation, long before his incarnation (cf. Luke 24:27; John 1:3; 8:56–58; 12:41; 1 Cor. 10:4, 9; Col. 1:16; Heb. 1:8–12; 11:26). Jesus, then, judged and **destroyed** those in Israel who escaped from Egypt but failed to keep

a people out of the land of Egypt, [o]afterward destroyed those who did not believe. 6 And
[p]the angels who did not stay within their own position of authority, but left their proper
dwelling, he has kept in eternal chains under gloomy darkness until the judgment of the
great day— 7 just as [q]Sodom and Gomorrah and [r]the surrounding cities, which likewise
indulged in sexual immorality and [s]pursued unnatural desire,[1] serve as an example by
undergoing a punishment of eternal fire.

8 Yet in like manner these people also, relying on their dreams, defile the flesh, reject
authority, and [t]blaspheme the glorious ones. 9 But when [u]the archangel [v]Michael, contending with the devil, was disputing [w]about the body of Moses, he did not presume
to pronounce a blasphemous judgment, but said, [x]"The Lord rebuke you." 10 [y]But these
people blaspheme all that they do not understand, and they are destroyed by all that they,
like unreasoning animals, understand instinctively. 11 Woe to them! For they walked in
[z]the way of Cain and abandoned themselves for the sake of gain [a]to Balaam's error and
[b]perished in Korah's rebellion. 12 These are hidden reefs[2] [c]at your love feasts, as they feast
with you without fear, [d]shepherds feeding themselves; [e]waterless clouds, [f]swept along

5 [o]Num. 14:29, 37; 26:64, 65; Ps. 106:26; Heb. 3:17-19
6 [p]2 Pet. 2:4; [Rev. 20:2]
7 [q]See Gen. 19:24 [r]Deut. 29:23; Hos. 11:8 [s]2 Pet. 2:10
8 [t]2 Pet. 2:10
9 [u]1 Thess. 4:16; [2 Pet. 2:11] [v]Dan. 10:13; 12:1; Rev. 12:7 [w][Deut. 34:6] [x]Zech. 3:2
10 [y]2 Pet. 2:12
11 [z]See Gen. 4:5-8 [a]See 2 Pet. 2:15 [b]Num. 16:1-3, 31-35
12 [c]2 Pet. 2:13 [d]Ezek. 34:2, 8, 10 [e]Prov. 25:14; 2 Pet. 2:17 [f]Heb. 13:9

[1] Greek *other flesh* [2] Or *are blemishes*

trusting in God, and therefore they did not reach the Promised Land (cf. 1 Cor. 10:5; Heb. 3:16–19). Instead of the name "Jesus," some Greek manuscripts have *ho Kyrios*, "the Lord," and some English translations follow that reading. Most of the oldest and most reliable manuscripts have *Iēsous* ("Jesus").

6 *The Analogy of the Rebellious Angels.* The heart of Jude's next comparison is the **angels who did not stay within their own position of authority** but apparently rebelled against God's authority and sought to be equal to him. God has **kept** these beings **in eternal chains** ever since. Some scholars think this refers to the original fall of angels from heaven. Others think Jude is referring to the sin of angels in Gen. 6:1–4 (see note on 1 Pet. 3:19). This view is strengthened by Jude's citation of *1 Enoch* 1.9 (Jude 14–15), which contains much discussion on the fall of these angels.

7 *The Analogy of Sodom and Gomorrah.* As with the unfaithful Israelites and the rebellious angels (vv. 5–6), so also the people of **Sodom and Gomorrah** (Genesis 19) received the judgment of **eternal fire**. Smoke was still rising from the site of Sodom and Gomorrah in the first century A.D. (see Philo, *On Abraham* 141; Philo, *Life of Moses* 2.56; *Wisdom of Solomon* 10:7), and this was taken as a physical symbol of eternal divine judgment. **Pursued unnatural desire** refers to the homosexual activity of Sodom (Gen. 19:5; cf. Josephus, *Jewish Antiquities* 1.200–201; Philo, *On Abraham* 134–136; *Testament of Naphtali* 3.4). The Greek is literally "went after other flesh," meaning "other" or "different" than the **sexual immorality** with women that Jude had just mentioned (cf. Rom. 1:26–27). The judgment of Sodom and Gomorrah in history functions as a "type" (a foreshadowing planned by God, cf. Rom. 5:14) of eternal judgment to come.

Jude's Application of Prophecies and Events

Jude often refers to prophecies or events and then applies them to the false teachers with the word "these," thereby showing how these past events and prophecies are to be understood.

Reference	Past event	Application to false teachers	Reference
vv. 5–7	Judgment on Israel, angels, and Sodom and Gomorrah	"these people also"	v. 8
v. 9	Michael did not rebuke the devil	"But these people"	v. 10
v. 11	Cain, Balaam, Korah	"These"	v. 12
vv. 14–15	Enoch's proclamation of judgment	"These"	v. 16
vv. 17–18	Predictions of apostles	"It is these"	v. 19

8–13 *Nature of the False Teachers.* Jude turns his attention to the immoral character of the opponents of Christ, carrying forward the analogies of vv. 5–7.

8–10 *The False Teachers Are Blasphemers.* **These people also** refers to the false teachers (see chart to the left). They are led astray by **relying on their dreams**, thus mistakenly following subjective experiences that they claim are from God but that lead them to disobey God's written Word (cf. "following . . . ungodly passions," v. 18). Following their "dreams," they are sexually immoral (**defile the flesh**), **reject authority**, and **blaspheme the glorious ones** (probably evil angels; see note on 2 Pet. 2:10b–11). Even **the archangel Michael** did not speak to the devil flippantly, or blaspheme him, when he disputed with him over **the body of Moses**. This event is not in the OT (but cf. Deut. 34:5–6; Zech. 3:1–5), and whatever story Jude is referring to has been lost to history. In any case, Michael, understanding his own place in God's design, did not pronounce a sentence of condemnation on the devil but left that to God's authority, simply telling the devil, **"The Lord rebuke you."** This demonstrates the exclusive power and authority of Jesus Christ, something the false teachers deny (see Jude 4). The point of vv. 8–10 is the false teachers' refusal to submit to rightful authority, and it should not be understood as denying that Christ gives believers authority over demons (see note on Acts 16:18). Jude's use of a story from nonbiblical literature (perhaps a lost section of a work called *Testament of Moses*) does not indicate that Jude thought the book was inspired. Elsewhere in the NT, writers quote uninspired sources to make a point (see notes on Acts 17:28; Titus 1:12–13). Michael is the only archangel identified by name in Scripture (cf. 1 Thess. 4:16).

10 All that they do not understand includes true biblical doctrine about God, angels and demons, and human sin and forgiveness through Christ. What they **understand instinctively**, like **animals**, is how to follow their bodily instincts and feelings, flouting God's moral standards. Following subjective feelings and desires, for someone whose conscience is not trained and governed by God's Word, will lead that person ultimately to be **destroyed** by his own sinful compulsions.

11 *The False Teachers Are Motivated by Greed.* **Cain** (Gen. 4:5–8), **Balaam** (Num. 22:5–7; 2 Pet. 2:15), and **Korah** (Num. 16:1–3, 31–35) were all characterized by their dissatisfaction with the place they occupied, and so they engaged in rebellion against God, greedily seeking selfish **gain** at any cost.

12–13 *The False Teachers Exemplify Depravity with Impunity.* Jude compares the false teachers to **hidden reefs** that will suddenly destroy ships that come too near. These opponents of the gospel constitute concealed dangers because they participate in the **love feasts** (including the Lord's Supper), thus acting as if they were Christians. They do not shepherd and care for others but only look after **themselves**. They are like **waterless clouds**, promising rain that never falls. They promise fruit but are like **fruitless trees**. They are like **wandering stars** (probably meaning planets) that give misleading guidance to travelers. **casting up the foam of their own shame**.

12 [g]Matt. 15:13
13 [h]Isa. 57:20 [i][2 Cor. 4:2; Phil. 3:19] [j][Isa. 14:12] [k]2 Pet. 2:17
14 [l]Gen. 5:18 [m]See Deut. 33:2; [Dan. 7:10; Mark 8:38; 1 Thess. 3:13; 2 Thess. 1:7]
15 [n][2 Pet. 2:5] [o]2 Pet. 2:6 [p]1 Sam. 2:3; Ps. 94:4; John 6:60
16 [q]2 Pet. 2:10 [r]2 Pet. 2:18 [s]Lev. 19:15; Deut. 10:17
17 [t]2 Pet. 3:2
18 [u]2 Pet. 3:3
19 [v][Rom. 8:9; Phil. 3:3]
20 [w]See Col. 2:7 [x]Eph. 6:18; [Rom. 8:26]
21 [y]2 Cor. 13:14; [Acts 13:43] [z]Titus 2:13; 2 Pet. 3:12
23 [a]Amos 4:11; Zech. 3:2 [b]See 1 Cor. 3:15 [c][2 Cor. 5:11] [d]Rev. 3:4; [Zech. 3:4]

by winds; fruitless trees in late autumn, twice dead, [g]uprooted; **13** [h]wild waves of the sea,
casting up the foam of [i]their own shame; [j]wandering stars, [k]for whom the gloom of utter
darkness has been reserved forever.
14 It was also about these that Enoch, [l]the seventh from Adam, prophesied, saying,
[m]"Behold, the Lord comes with ten thousands of his holy ones, **15** [n]to execute judgment
on all and to convict all the ungodly of all their deeds of ungodliness that they have [o]com-
mitted in such an ungodly way, and of all [p]the harsh things that ungodly sinners have
spoken against him." **16** These are grumblers, malcontents, [q]following their own sinful
desires; [r]they are loud-mouthed boasters, [s]showing favoritism to gain advantage.

A Call to Persevere

17 But you must [t]remember, beloved, the predictions of the apostles of our Lord Jesus
Christ. **18** They[1] said to you, [u]"In the last time there will be scoffers, following their own
ungodly passions." **19** It is these who cause divisions, worldly people, [v]devoid of the Spirit.
20 But you, beloved, [w]building yourselves up in your most holy faith and [x]praying in the
Holy Spirit, **21** [y]keep yourselves in the love of God, [z]waiting for the mercy of our Lord Jesus
Christ that leads to eternal life. **22** And have mercy on those who doubt; **23** save others by
[a]snatching them out of [b]the fire; to others show mercy [c]with fear, hating even [d]the garment[2] stained by the flesh.

[1] Or *Christ, because they* [2] Greek *chiton*, a long garment worn under the cloak next to the skin

The heretics' sexual permissiveness shows that they are in spiritual darkness. Their eternal condemnation in **the gloom of utter darkness has been reserved forever**.

14–16 *Judgment on the False Teachers Revisited.* Jude turns his primary focus back to judgment, using an extrabiblical Jewish work, *1 Enoch* (2nd or 1st century B.C.), to make his point. The use of extrabiblical literature does not mean that any of these literary works are authoritative words of God in the same category as Scripture (see note on vv. 8–10). Jude is simply drawing from *1 Enoch* another example of judgment, which means that, in at least this specific instance, *1 Enoch* 1.9 contains truth.

14–15 *Description of the Judgment.* **Enoch, the seventh from Adam** does not necessarily imply that Enoch was literally the seventh generation descended from Adam; it may mean simply that he is the seventh one listed in the line of Adam in the Genesis narrative (Gen. 5:18–24; cf. 1 Chron. 1:3). Jude describes the coming of the Lord as Enoch **prophesied**, and he quotes from *1 Enoch* 1.9. Again, with regard to this particular statement, Jude is citing the content of *1 Enoch* as true and prophetic of the return of the Lord (see note on Jude 14–16). The Lord will return with hosts of angels to **execute judgment** on all the ungodly. Enoch (and thus also Jude) focuses on blasphemy against God (e.g., in vv. 3–4, the opponents' denial of Jesus Christ). **to convict**. For punishment, not for repentance (as in John 16:8). Jude places great emphasis on the **ungodliness** of those judged ("ungodliness," Gk. *asebeia*, vs. "godliness," Gk. *eusebeia*; see note on 2 Pet. 1:6).

16 *Further Reasons for Judgment.* Jude applies the citation from *1 Enoch* (see vv. 14–15) to the false teachers, probably using this vice list to focus on some of their more pronounced and obvious misbehaviors. **Grumblers** calls to mind the wilderness generation (Ex. 16:7–12; Num. 14:27; 16:41; 17:5). **To gain advantage** probably refers to financial gain, and ties in with an earlier mention of greed (Jude 11).

17–25 *Concluding Exhortations.* The conclusion of Jude's letter continues to highlight the false teachers, only now with a view toward the proper response of believers to them. It also contains one of the most elegant doxologies in the entire Bible.

17–19 *On the Apostolic Warnings.* Jude redirects the readers' attention to their own knowledge of apostolic predictions concerning the last days.

17–18 Beloved emphasizes Jude's personal concern for the readers and God's love for them (see notes on vv. 1–2 and 3). Jude reminds them of **the predictions of the apostles** concerning the emergence of ungodly **scoffers** within the church during the last days. These apostolic warnings were probably oral, but such warnings were part of the common stock of early Christian preaching (e.g., Acts 20:29–30; 1 Tim. 4:1–5; 2 Tim. 3:1–5). These critics come from within, having become part of the church by clandestine means and acting as if they were true Christians (see Jude 3–4, 19). But they are led astray by **following** their subjective feelings and **ungodly passions** that are contrary to the Word of God (cf. v. 8).

19 It is these indicates that the "scoffers" described in v. 18 are the very false teachers that Jude is warning against (see chart, p. 2450). These **worldly people** (Gk. *psychikos*, "natural, unspiritual, worldly, of this world") **cause divisions** within the church over many things, but especially over issues of morality and doctrine (cf. notes on vv. 10, 17–18). They are unbelievers like the "natural" (also Gk. *psychikos*) person of 1 Cor. 2:14. **Devoid of** (Gk. *mē echontes*, "not having") **the Spirit** is another indication that these opponents are unbelievers (cf. Rom. 8:9). This fits with the repeated statements affirming their designated condemnation "from long ago" (see note on Jude 4).

20–21 *On the Antidote to the False Teachers.* The way to minimize the influence of the scoffers is to live proactively as a follower of Christ (cf. "contend for the faith," v. 3).

20 praying in the Holy Spirit. That is, in the sense of praying in harmony with the leading of the Holy Spirit, rather than according to one's own agenda (cf. Rom. 8:26–27; Eph. 6:18). The context here suggests the idea of praying in the Spirit in a general sense, rather than the specific sense of speaking in tongues described in 1 Cor. 14:14–19.

21 Keep (or guard) **yourselves in the love of God** is the main clause in vv. 20–21 and is modified by the two participles ("building," "praying") in v. 20 and the participle (**waiting**) in v. 21. Christians keep themselves in God's love by growing strong doctrinally, persevering in prayer, and "waiting" for the Lord's coming. Christians are to keep themselves in God's love, and vv. 1–2 and vv. 24–25 teach that God keeps them as well. Ultimately, God promises to keep and preserve the faith of his own people, so that no true believer will ever lose his or her salvation (cf. notes on Heb. 6:4–8; 2 Pet. 1:10).

22–23 *On Showing Mercy.* The church is called to show mercy to everyone, even its opponents.

23 To **save** (Gk. *sōzō*) some people (i.e., to lead them to faith in Christ) involves **snatching them out of the fire**, meaning they were close to the fire of God's judgment. **Others** who are caught up in immorality should also be shown **mercy**, but **with fear**, lest the faithful Christian be influenced for evil by the person he is trying to restore. **Hating even the garment stained by the flesh** (cf. Zech. 3:3–5) implies hating the sin and everything connected with it; but the sinner himself should be treated with mercy rather than hatred.

Doxology

[24] [e]Now to him who is able [f]to keep you from stumbling and [g]to present you [h]blame-
less before the presence of his glory with great joy, [25] to [i]the only God, our Savior, through
Jesus Christ our Lord, [j]be glory, majesty, dominion, and authority, before all time and
now and forever. Amen.

24[e]Rom. 16:25; Eph. 3:20 [f]John 17:12 [g]Col. 1:22; [1 Pet. 4:13] [h]Eph. 1:4; 5:27; Phil. 2:15; Rev. 14:5
25[i]John 5:44; 1 Tim. 1:17 [j]See Rom. 11:36

24–25 *Doxology of Great Joy.* As Jude ascribes all glory, majesty, dominion, and authority to God, he reminds believers of what God is doing for them as they await Christ's return.

24 Just as the false teachers are "kept" by God for judgment (see 2 Pet. 2:9; cf. 2 Pet. 2:4; 3:7; Jude 6), so also he has infinite power **to keep** from **stumbling** those who have put their faith in him. By "stumbling" Jude means falling into sin or error (Gk. *aptaistos*, "without stumbling"; cf. *ptaiō*, "stumble," in Rom. 11:11; James 2:10; 3:2; 2 Pet. 1:10). If such stumbling is left unchecked it will eventually lead to falling away from the faith. Yet Jude says God will never let his own fall away but will "keep" them by his grace (cf. note on Jude 21). He will **present** the Christian **blameless** (with no stain or sin) **before the presence of his glory**, the brightness that surrounds the presence of God and visibly manifests his holy character. This can only be effected by God's power, through Jesus Christ the Lord. The only possible response to the work of God on behalf of believers is **great joy** (Gk. *agalliasis*, "great joy, exultation"), which suggests an exclamation of joy and praise.

25 the only God. There is only one God, who has acted redemptively (**our Savior**), once for all, in his one and only Son, the Lord Jesus Christ. (On God as "Savior," see note on 2 Tim. 1:8–10.) **through Jesus Christ our Lord**. Jesus is the mediator through whom the person who trusts in him is able to give praise and thanksgiving to God. The church praises God through Christ, saying, to God **be glory** (here in the sense of great honor), **majesty** (Gk. *megalōsynē*; he is greater than all), **dominion** (Gk. *kratos*; his sovereign reign has no boundaries), **and authority** (Gk. *exousia*; he rules over all creation); in other words, may the praiseworthiness of God, who is as gracious as he is great, be fully acknowledged in his people's adoration of him. **Before all time** means before the beginning of creation (Gen. 1:1) and suggests that time began when God created the material universe (cf. 2 Tim. 1:9; Titus 1:2). **And now and forever** shifts the focus into the present and then into the infinite future. **Amen**. I.e., "let it be so."

INTRODUCTION TO

THE REVELATION TO JOHN

Author and Title

Revelation 1:1 announces both the book's title (it is a "revelation") and its divine author ("Jesus Christ"). The book is an "unveiling" of unseen spiritual forces operating behind the scenes in history and controlling its events and outcome. This disclosure is conveyed in a series of symbolic visions that exhibit the influence of OT prophecies, especially those received by Daniel, Ezekiel, and Zechariah. The book is also "prophecy" (Rev. 1:3; 22:7), not only as divine prediction of future events but also as divine diagnosis of the present state of affairs.

The divine author identified in the opening verse, Jesus the Messiah, has authority from God to describe coming events to his servant John (see also 1:4, 9; 22:8) for communication to the church.

Without denying his own role in the composition of the book, John presents himself more as a recipient and recorder of visions than as the author of Revelation's message. Although John does not call himself an apostle and he numbers himself among the prophets (22:9), early church fathers—notably Justin Martyr (writing c. A.D. 135–150), Melito of Sardis (mid-2nd century), and Irenaeus of Lyons (writing c. 185)—consistently identified him as John the son of Zebedee, the beloved disciple who authored the Fourth Gospel and three NT epistles. Because Revelation's Greek style differs markedly from other Johannine literature and its theological emphases are distinctive, a number of contemporary scholars think it was written by another John, called "John the elder," someone otherwise unknown (who also wrote 2 and 3 John). These scholars give weight to another early tradition (beginning with Dionysius of Alexandria in the 3rd century) that attributes Revelation to "John the elder." Nevertheless, both thematic links (e.g., Jesus as Lamb and Word of God [John 1:1, 14, 29; Rev. 5:6; 19:13]) and the earliest church tradition favor the traditional attribution of Revelation to John, the "beloved disciple," who with Peter and James belonged to Jesus' inner circle (John 21:20, 24).

Date

Irenaeus reports, on the basis of earlier sources, that "John received the Revelation almost in our own time, toward the end of the reign of Domitian" (*Against Heresies* 5.30.3). Since Domitian's reign ended in A.D. 96, most scholars date Revelation in the mid-90s. Some, however, have argued for a date during Nero's reign (A.D. 54–68) and before the fall of Jerusalem in 70, basing their conclusion in part on the belief that Revelation 11:1–2 is a predictive prophecy of the Roman siege and destruction of the earthly Jerusalem during the Jewish War. However, the conditions in the churches of chapters 2–3 and their cities favor a date around A.D. 95–96, and in Revelation "the holy city" does not seem to refer to the earthly Jerusalem (see note on 11:1–2). Assuming this later date, events relating to Nero's reign and Jerusalem's destruction, both of which would now have been in the past, are woven into John's visions as portents and prototypes of present pressures and coming traumas in the world's assault on Christ's church.

Genre

The book of Revelation identifies itself both as "apocalypse" (or "revelation," 1:1) and as prophecy (1:3; 22:7, 10, 18, 19; see also 10:11; 22:9).

"Apocalypse" is derived from the Greek noun *apokalypsis*, meaning "revelation, disclosure, unveiling"—that is, the disclosure of unseen heavenly or future realities. Jewish apocalyptic literature flourished in the centuries following the completion of the OT canon, perhaps in part to help the oppressed people of God find purpose in their sufferings and hope for their future in the absence of genuine prophetic words from God. Apocalyptic literature inherited and magnified features appearing in such OT books as Ezekiel, Daniel, and Zechariah. These features include visions that dramatize the prophet's admission to God's heavenly council and that convey meaning through symbolism, promising an end-time intervention of God to reverse present injustices.

Yet Jewish apocalyptic literature of the period between the OT and NT differs from OT prophecy in important respects. Apocalyptic authors remained anonymous and attributed their works to prominent figures of the distant past (e.g., Enoch, Abraham, Moses, Baruch, Ezra), using this literary device ("pseudepigraphy") to invest their message with the weight of antiquity and to suggest that those ancients foretold events in the readers' past and present. Whereas OT prophecy was primarily preached orally and only secondarily preserved in writing, apocalyptic works were crafted literary pieces from their inception. Old Testament prophecy not only comforted a righteous remnant but also called faithless Israel to repent and anticipated the gracious ingathering of Gentiles. Apocalyptic literature, on the other hand, divided humanity into two immutable camps: (1) the holy minority who await God's deliverance, and (2) their persecutors, destined for wrath and beyond the reach of redemption. Finally, although OT prophets pointed ahead to the Lord's future coming, they also emphasized his present involvement with his people in their sins and trials; but apocalyptic literature saw the present as so pervaded by corruption that no saving work of God could be expected before his cataclysmic intervention at the end.

Like Jewish apocalyptic literature and some OT prophecy, the Revelation to John is imparted in symbolic visions and conveyed not in oral preaching but in literary form. Unlike extrabiblical apocalyptic authors, however, John writes in his own name, not that of an ancient saint, and he brings a balanced message of comfort, warning, and rebuke. Because Christ's death has already won the decisive victory over evil, Revelation does not share the pessimism of Jewish apocalyptic literature regarding the present age (transient and sin-infected though it is). Rather, Revelation sees believers as conquerors even now through endurance under suffering and fidelity to the testimony of Jesus, through which even their persecutors are called to salvation through repentance and faith.

Revelation therefore stands in the apocalyptic "wing" of authentic, divinely inspired prophecy (emphasizing visionary experience, symbolism, and literary art), along with such NT texts as Jesus' Olivet Discourse (Mark 13) and Paul's discussion of the man of lawlessness (2 Thessalonians 2).

Theme

Revelation unveils the unseen spiritual war in which the church is engaged: the cosmic conflict between God and his Christ on the one hand, and Satan and his evil allies (both demonic and human) on the other. In this conflict, Jesus the Lamb has already won the decisive victory through his sacrificial death, but his church continues to be assaulted by the dragon, in its death-throes, through persecution, false teaching, and the allure of material affluence and cultural approval. By revealing the spiritual realities lying behind the church's trials and temptations during the time between Christ's first and second comings, and by dramatically affirming the certainty of Christ's triumph in the new heaven and earth, the visions granted to John both warn the church and fortify it to endure suffering and to stay pure from the defiling enticements of the present world order.

Purpose, Occasion, and Background

Revelation is addressed to first-century churches in seven cities of the Roman province of Asia (now western Turkey, see map, p. 2461) (1:4, 11) as representative of all Christ's churches (cf. "all the churches," 2:23; and "to the churches," 2:7, etc.). These churches were threatened by false teaching (such as that of the Nicolaitans, 2:6, 15), by persecution (2:10, 13), by compromise with surrounding paganism through idolatry and immorality (2:14, 20–21), and by spiritual complacency (3:1–3, 15–17). Jesus sent his revelation to John to fortify his churches to resist the wiles of the devil, whether in the form of intimidating violence (the beast), deceptive heresy (the false prophet), or beguiling affluence (the prostitute).

History of Salvation Summary

Christians are called to be faithful to Christ amid spiritual war against Satan and sin (see note on Matt. 12:28) as they await Christ's second coming. (For an explanation of the "History of Salvation," see the Overview of the Bible, pp. 23–26.)

Timeline

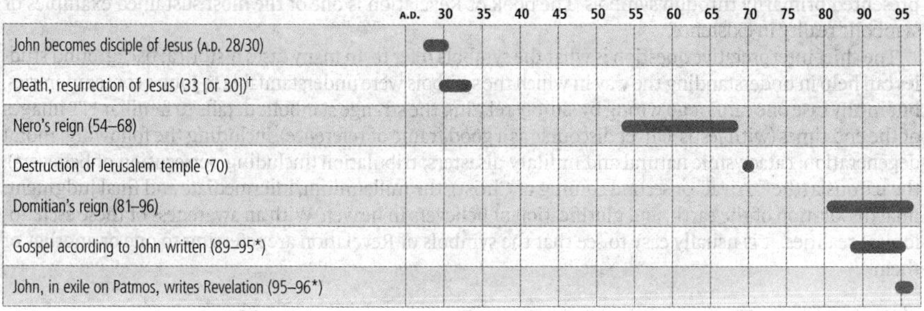

A.D. 30 35 40 45 50 55 60 65 70 75 80 90 95
John becomes disciple of Jesus (A.D. 28/30)
Death, resurrection of Jesus (33 [or 30])†
Nero's reign (54–68)
Destruction of Jerusalem temple (70)
Domitian's reign (81–96)
Gospel according to John written (89–95*)
John, in exile on Patmos, writes Revelation (95–96*)

** denotes approximate date; / signifies either/or; † see* The Date of Jesus' Crucifixion, *pp. 1809–1810*

Key Themes

1. Through his sacrificial death, Jesus Christ has conquered Satan, the accuser, and has ransomed people from every nation to become a kingdom of priests, gladly serving in God's presence.	1:5, 18; 5:5–10; 12:1–11
2. Jesus Christ is present among his churches on earth through his Holy Spirit, and he knows their trials, triumphs, and failures.	1:12–3:22
3. World history, including its woes and disasters, is firmly in the control of Jesus, the victorious Lamb.	5:1–8:1
4. God is presently restraining his own wrath and his enemies' efforts to destroy the church as he patiently gathers his redeemed people through the testimony that his suffering people proclaim about Jesus.	6:5–11; 7:1–3; 8:6–12; 9:4–6, 18; 11:3–7; 12:6, 13–17
5. Present disasters (war, drought, famine, epidemic disease), though limited in scope by God's restraint, are foreshadows and warnings of escalating judgments to come.	6:3–17; 8:6–13; 11:13; 16:1–21; 20:11–15
6. By maintaining their faithful testimony to the death, believers in Jesus will conquer both the dragon and the beast. The martyrs' victory, now hidden, will be manifest in their vindication at Christ's return.	2:10–11, 26–29; 3:11–13; 6:9–11; 7:9–17; 11:7–12, 17–18; 12:10–11; 14:1–5; 15:2–4; 20:4–6
7. Satan attacks the church's perseverance and purity through violent persecution, through deceptive teaching, and through affluence and sensual pleasure.	2:1–3:22; 13:1–18; 17:1–18:24
8. At the end of the age, the church's opponents will intensify persecution, but Jesus, the triumphant Word of God, will defeat and destroy all his enemies; the old heaven and earth, stained by sin and suffering, will be replaced by the new heaven and earth; and the church will be presented as a bride in luminous purity to her husband, the Lamb.	16:12–16; 19:11–21; 20:7–22:5

Literary Features

Numerous literary genres converge in the book of Revelation, one of the most complex books in the Bible. The overall genre is prophecy (22:19). Like biblical prophecy generally, the actual medium is visionary writing; the book unfolds as a pageant of visions, much like modern cinematic effects. Furthermore, the way in which real persons and events are actually portrayed is the way of imagination, with unlifelike details. The title of the book indicates further that it belongs to the genre of apocalyptic writing. Additionally, at every turn the author uses the resources of poetry—imagery, metaphor, simile, and allusion. The book begins and ends with the standard features of NT epistles. The overall shape of the book, following the introductory letters from Christ to the churches, is narrative or story, with the usual ingredients of setting, characters, and plot (including plot conflict, progression, and resolution). Greek drama was also an influence, seen in the attention John gives to the staging of events, positioning of characters in settings, crowd scenes, and costuming of characters.

The most important thing to know about the literary form of the book of Revelation is that it uses the technique of symbolism from start to finish. Instead of portraying characters and events directly, much of the time the author portrays them indirectly by means of symbols. For example, Jesus is portrayed as a lamb, churches are portrayed as lamps on lampstands, and Satan is portrayed as a dragon with seven heads and 10 horns. The symbols are sometimes familiar, and sometimes original and strange. Whenever a work of literature presents a preponderance of symbols instead of realistic details, readers should recognize the technique of symbolic reality, meaning that as they enter the work in their imaginations, information is presented primarily through symbols. The book of Revelation is one of the most sustained examples of symbolic reality in existence.

The chief interpretative question is what the symbols refer to. In many cases historical background studies can help in understanding the way in which the symbols were understandable to John's contemporaries, but in any case one cannot go wrong by simply relating the strange symbolic details to familiar NT images of the end times (with Jesus' Olivet discourse as a good frame of reference), including the following: moral degeneration; cataclysmic natural and military disasters; tribulation (including persecution of believers); the parousia (the "arrival" or second coming of Christ); the millennium; intermediate and final judgment; final dissolution of the earth; and glorification of believers in heaven. With an awareness of these eschatological realities, it is usually easy to see that the symbols of Revelation are referring to one or another of them.

Schools of Interpretation

Four approaches for interpreting Revelation have been distinguished by their understanding of the relationship of the visions to one another and the relationship of the visions to the events of history:

1. *Historicism* understands the literary order of the visions, especially in 4:1–20:6, to symbolize the chronological order of successive historical events that span the entire era from the apostolic church to the return of Christ and the new heaven and earth.

Historicist School

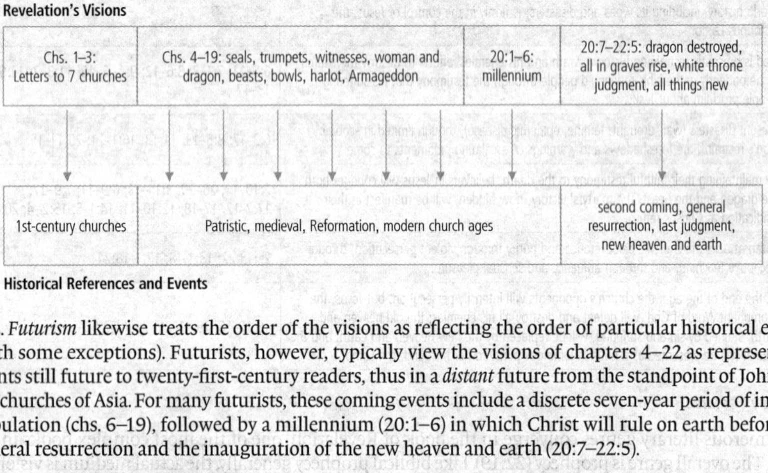

2. *Futurism* likewise treats the order of the visions as reflecting the order of particular historical events (with some exceptions). Futurists, however, typically view the visions of chapters 4–22 as representing events still future to twenty-first-century readers, thus in a *distant* future from the standpoint of John and the churches of Asia. For many futurists, these coming events include a discrete seven-year period of intense tribulation (chs. 6–19), followed by a millennium (20:1–6) in which Christ will rule on earth before the general resurrection and the inauguration of the new heaven and earth (20:7–22:5).

Futurist (Historical Premillennialism)

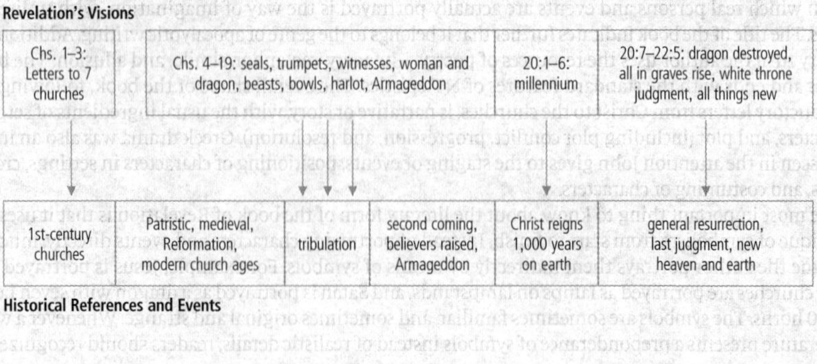

Futurist (Dispensational Premillennialism)

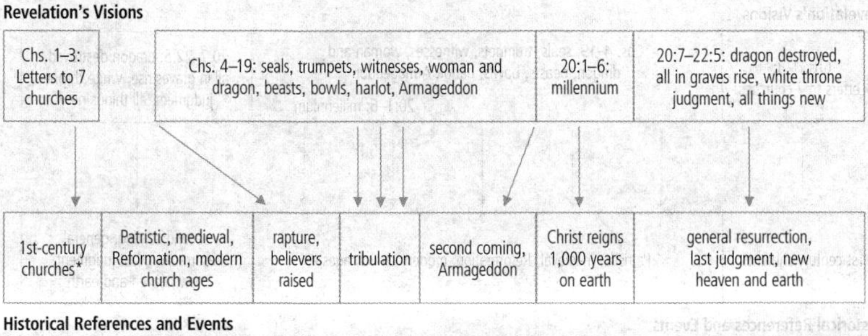

* Some dispensational interpreters think the churches addressed in chs. 2–3 predict different periods in church history.

3. *Preterism* (from Latin *praeteritum*, "the thing that is past") thinks that the fulfillment of most of Revelation's visions already occurred in the distant past, during the early years of the Christian church. Preterists think these events—either the destruction of Jerusalem or the decline and fall of the Roman Empire, or both—would "soon take place" only from the standpoint of John and the churches of Asia. Some preterists interpret the order of the visions as reflecting the chronological succession of the events they signify, but others recognize the presence of recapitulation (that is, that distinct, successive visions sometimes symbolize the same historical events or forces from complementary perspectives; see Structure and Outline). Full preterism—which insists that *every* prophecy and promise in the NT was fulfilled by A.D. 70—is not a legitimate evangelical option, for it denies Jesus' future bodily return, denies the physical resurrection of believers at the end of history, and denies the physical renewal/re-creation of the present heavens and earth (or their replacement by a "new heaven and earth"). However, preterists who (rightly) insist that these events are still future are called "partial preterists."

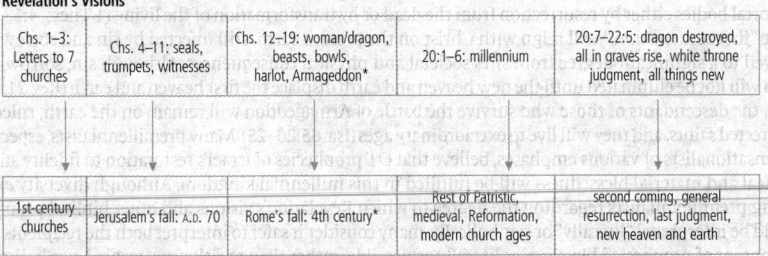

Partial Preterist School(s)

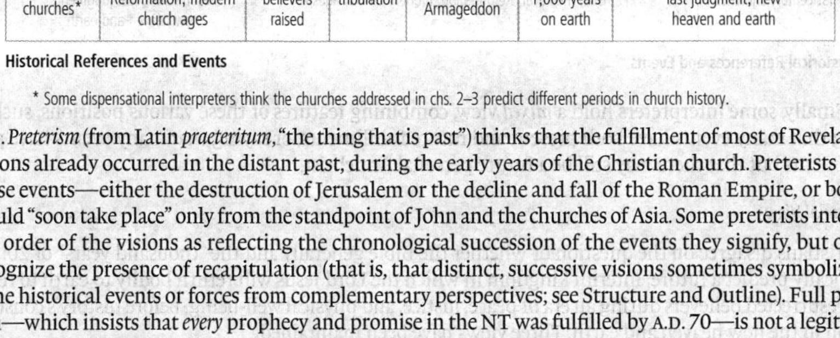

* Partial preterists differ on what would (from the original recipients' viewpoint) precipitate the millennium. This chart represents the view that sees ancient Rome as the church's main enemy. Others would understand Second Temple Judaism as the church's main enemy.

4. *Idealism* agrees with historicism that Revelation's visions symbolize the conflict between Christ and his church on the one hand, and Satan and his evil conspirators on the other, from the apostolic age to Christ's second coming. Yet idealist interpreters believe that the presence of recapitulation (see Structure and Outline) means that the visions' literary order need not reflect the temporal order of particular historical events. The forces and conflicts symbolized in Revelation's vision cycles manifest themselves in events that were to occur "soon" from the perspective of the first-century churches (as preterists maintain), but they also find expression in the church's ongoing struggle of persevering faith in the present and foretell a still-future escalation of persecution and divine wrath leading to the return of Christ and the new heaven and earth.

Idealist School

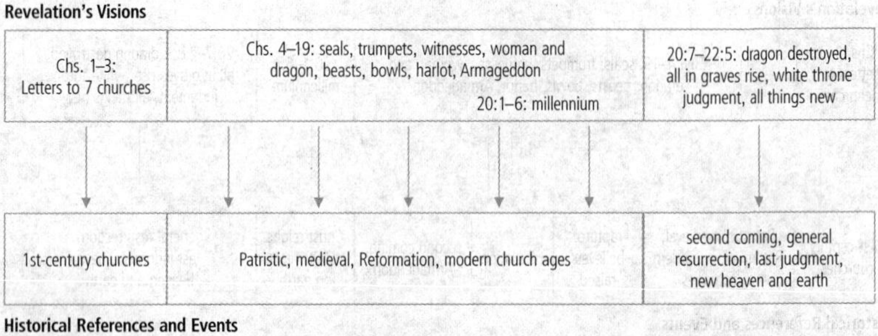

5. Finally, some interpreters hold a *mixed* view, combining features of these various positions, such as saying that many events have both present and future fulfillments, or saying that many events have past fulfillments but that there may still be a future personal Antichrist.

Millennial Views

Christians disagree on the question of whether the Bible generally and the "thousand years" of 20:1–6 specifically predict a future, interim kingdom in which the Lord Jesus will return bodily to earth to reign with resurrected believers during an era of peace, justice, and physical well-being, before history's consummation in the new heaven and earth. Three views have been maintained.

1. *Premillennialism*, usually associated with a *futurist* reading of Revelation (see Schools of Interpretation), teaches that Christ will return bodily in power and glory *before* (pre-) the "thousand years" (millennium) to defeat and destroy the beast and false prophet in the battle on the "great day of God the Almighty" at Armageddon (16:14–16; 19:11–21). This battle will issue in the binding (but not the destruction) of the devil, preventing him from deceiving the nations for a thousand years (interpreted literally by many premillennialists, but symbolically by others) (20:1–3). During that time Christ's saints, having received their immortal bodies either by resurrection from the dead or by transformation of the living (1 Thess. 4:13–18) in the "first resurrection," will reign with Christ on the present earth, still infected by sin and sorrow but relieved to a significant degree from sin's societal and physical consequences. Although sin, sorrow, and death will not be eliminated until the new heaven and earth displace the first heaven and earth (Rev. 21:1–4; 22:3), the descendants of those who survive the battle of Armageddon will remain on the earth, ruled by resurrected saints, and they will live to extraordinary ages (Isa. 65:20–25). Many premillennialists, especially dispensationalists of various emphases, believe that OT prophecies of Israel's restoration to fidelity and to political and material blessedness will be fulfilled in this millennial kingdom. Although diversity exists among premillennialists regarding the degree to which Revelation's visions and other biblical prophecy should be interpreted "literally" or symbolically, many consider it safer to interpret both the recipients and the content of prophesied blessings as literally as possible, rather than to risk unwarranted symbolism.

At the end of this idyllic foretaste of "paradise restored," a second worldwide rebellion against Jesus' reign will provoke another war, in which the dragon itself will be defeated and finally destroyed. At that point the wicked will be raised bodily to face God's last judgment and eternal wrath in the lake of fire, the "second death" (20:6, 11–14). God will replace the old, curse-infected heaven and earth with the new heaven and earth, where there will be no curse, sin, suffering, sorrow, or death—the eternal home of those whose names are written in the Lamb's book of life (chs. 21–22).

Classical premillennialism expects a future thousand-year reign of Christ on earth (the millennium), with both believers and unbelievers present, prior to the final judgment. Therefore it expects that Christ will come back before (pre-) the millennium. It also expects that believers will go through a time of "great tribulation" before Christ returns.

Pretribulational premillennialism also expects a future thousand-year reign of Christ on earth, but it expects that Christ will first come secretly to take believers from the earth before a "great tribulation" of seven years occurs. After the tribulation, it expects that Christ will come back publicly to reign on the earth, and that he will bring believers back with him at that time.

Classical Premillennialism
(Christ comes before the millennium but *after* the tribulation; the chair, in this and following illustrations, represents the judgment seat of Christ)

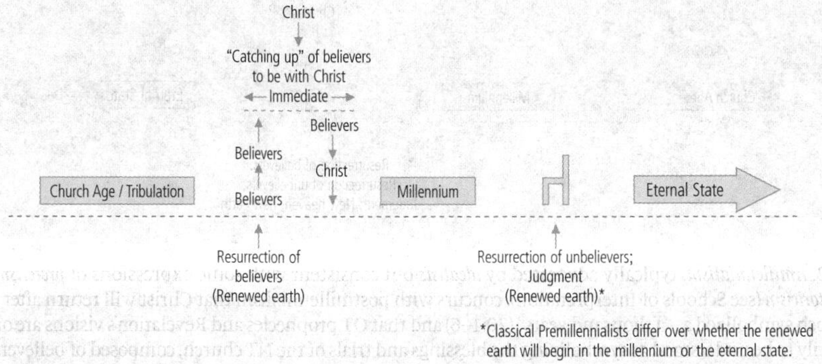

Pretribulational Premillennialism
(Christ comes before the millennium and *before* the tribulation)

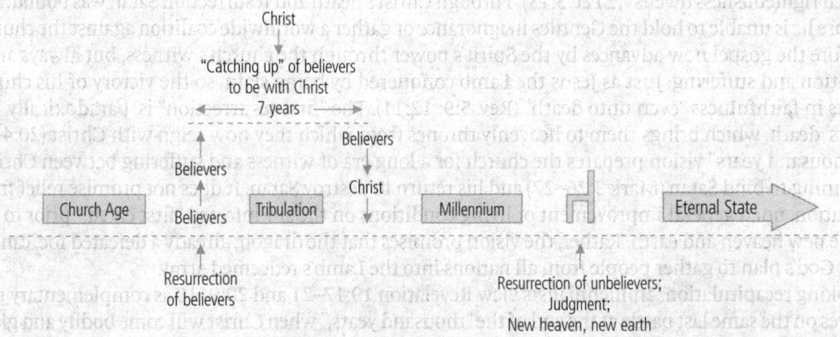

2. *Postmillennialism*, often associated today with *preterism* but also compatible with *historicism* (see Schools of Interpretation), teaches that Christ will return *after* (post-) the "thousand years" in which the dragon is bound. Classical postmillennialism holds that the "thousand years" is still a future time, a wonderful coming age in which the gospel will triumph so greatly as to thoroughly transform the world's societies and cultures. However, a few postmillennialists think the "thousand years" symbolically portray the historical epoch that began with Christ's ascension and that conditions in this long period will continually improve until they conclude with his glorious second coming. In the postmillennial view, during the millennium Christ is in heaven, not on earth; but he exercises his reign through his Spirit and the church's preaching of the gospel. The "first resurrection" is believers' spiritual transition from death to life through union with the risen Christ (Eph. 2:4–6). Because Satan cannot "deceive the nations any longer" (Rev. 20:3), the church's mission will result in the conversion of all nations and peoples, until the earth is "filled with the knowledge of the glory of the LORD as the waters cover the sea" (Hab. 2:14). This fruit of Jesus' victory will be plain for all to see, as political and legal systems are conformed to God's righteousness, cultural pursuits such as labor and the arts are redeemed, and increasing quality and length of life are displayed as God's blessing.

After this "millennium," however, for a brief interval before Jesus' return, God will release his restraint on Satan and wicked humanity will converge in a defiant assault on Christ's church. But Jesus will return bodily from heaven in power and glory to defeat and destroy his enemies, to administer the last judgment, and to introduce the new heaven and earth, untainted by sin and its toxic byproducts, in the eternal state.

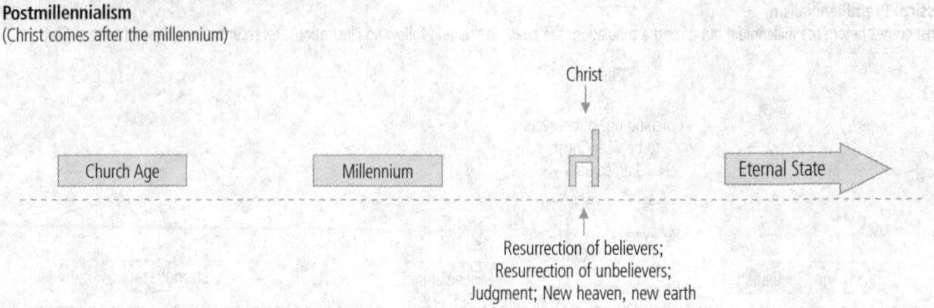

3. *Amillennialism,* typically advocated by *idealists* but consistent with some expressions of *preterism* or *historicism* (see Schools of Interpretation), concurs with postmillennialism that Christ will return after the epoch symbolized as "a thousand years" (20:1–6) and that OT prophecies and Revelation's visions are ordinarily to be understood as symbolizing the blessings and trials of the NT church, composed of believers in Christ from every nation. However, amillennialists believe that the biblical evidence indicates that there is and will be *no* (a-) millennium in the sense anticipated by premillennialism or postmillennialism before the consummation of history, when sin and curse are utterly banished in the "new heavens and a new earth in which righteousness dwells" (2 Pet. 3:13). Through Christ's death and resurrection Satan was bound, and therefore he is unable to hold the Gentiles in ignorance or gather a worldwide coalition against the church. Therefore the gospel now advances by the Spirit's power through the church's witness, but always amid opposition and suffering. Just as Jesus the Lamb conquered by being slain, so the victory of his church consists in faithfulness "even unto death" (Rev. 5:9; 12:11). The "first resurrection" is, paradoxically, the martyrs' death, which brings them to heavenly thrones from which they now reign with Christ (20:4–5). The "thousand years" vision prepares the church for a long era of witness and suffering between Christ's first coming to bind Satan (Mark 3:26–27) and his return to destroy Satan. It does not promise relief from persecution, nor a general improvement of living conditions on the sin-infected "first earth," prior to the pristine new heaven and earth. Rather, the vision promises that the dragon, already a defeated foe, cannot thwart God's plan to gather people from all nations into the Lamb's redeemed army.

Invoking recapitulation, amillennialists view Revelation 19:17–21 and 20:9–10 as complementary perspectives on the same last battle at the end of the "thousand years," when Christ will come bodily and gloriously to rescue his suffering church and destroy its enemies: beasts, dragon, their deceived and defiant followers, and—in the general resurrection of the just and the unjust—death itself (20:14; see 1 Cor. 15:26, 54–55). The "appearing of the glory of our great God and Savior Jesus Christ" is the "blessed hope" for which believers wait (Titus 2:13).

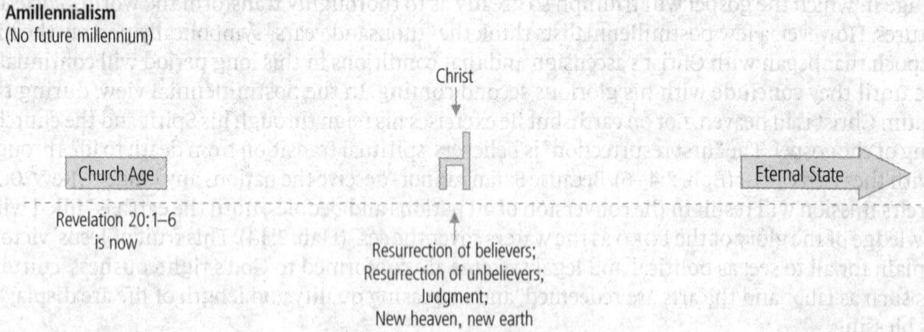

Each of these three primary millennial views falls within the framework of historic Christian orthodoxy. Though they differ in significant ways with regard to the interpretation of the book of Revelation and other passages related to eschatology, each view is well represented among Bible-believing, orthodox Christians.

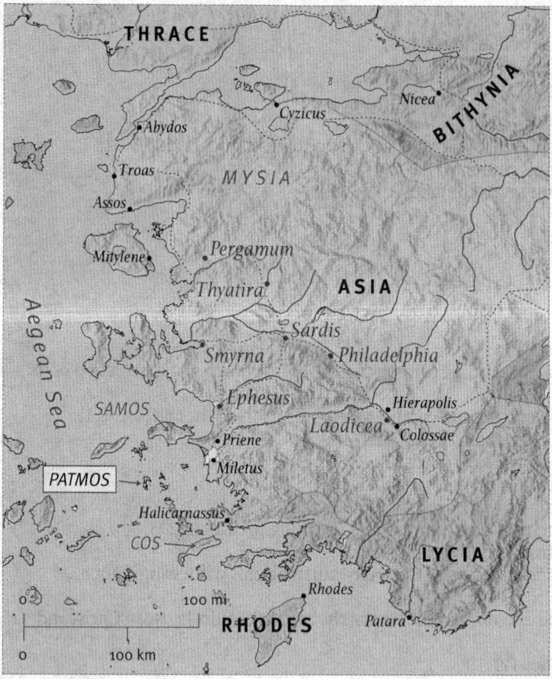

The Setting of Revelation
c. A.D. 95
John addressed the book of Revelation "to the seven churches that are in Asia," namely Ephesus, Smyrna, Pergamum, Thyatira, Sardis, Philadelphia, and Laodicea, although there were undoubtedly other churches elsewhere in the province of Asia (e.g., Miletus and Colossae, see Acts 20:17; Col. 1:2). John had apparently been exiled from Ephesus to the island of Patmos, southwest of Ephesus, and it was there that he recorded his visions.

Structure and Outline

Revelation is composed of a prologue (1:1–8), a body (1:9–22:5), and an epilogue (22:6–21). The prologue and epilogue are linked by repeated themes: an angel sent to show God's servants what must soon take place (1:1; 22:6, 16), blessings on those who keep the prophecy (1:3; 22:7, 9), John's self-identification (1:1, 4; 22:8), and the designation of God as Alpha and Omega (1:8; 22:13). The body contains four enumerated series of seven messages or visions: letters to churches (chs. 2–3), seals on a scroll (4:1–8:1), trumpets (8:2–11:19), and bowls of wrath (chs. 15–16). See chart, p. 2477.

The general movement of the book is from "the things that are"—the first-century churches' present situation (chs. 2–3)—to "the things that are to take place after this," climaxing with the destruction of the enemies of God and his church and the presentation of the church as the Lamb's bride in a new heaven and earth (1:19; 4:1). Within this general temporal movement, however, visions "double back" to present distinct, complementary perspectives on the same event or phase of the cosmic conflict between Christ and Satan. For instance, 12:1–6 portrays the defeat of the dragon in its desire to destroy the child of the heavenly woman (vv. 1–5), followed by her flight for safety into the wilderness (v. 6); then 12:7–17 again portrays the defeat of the dragon, now in its desire to accuse believers (vv. 7–12), followed by the heavenly woman's flight for safety into the wilderness (vv. 13–17). Earlier visions sometimes portray later events, and later visions portray earlier conditions. For example, 6:12–17 shows the shaking of earth and sky, so that the stars are cast to earth as by a great wind; then 7:1–8 shows angels restraining the winds of woe until God's people are sealed; and still later, John sees sun, moon, and stars still in the sky and only partially darkened (8:12). This principle of repetition or *recapitulation* to elaborate God's purposes and confirm their certainty is seen in earlier Scripture (see Gen. 1:1–2:25; 37:5–11; 41:1–32; Dan. 2:1–45 [with Dan. 7:1–28]; Acts 10:10–16). In Revelation, recapitulation means that the order in which John received visions does not necessarily indicate the order of the events they symbolize. These observations regarding the structure intrinsic to Revelation are reflected in this outline:

- I. Prologue (1:1–8)
  - A. Title, transmission, promise of blessing (1:1–3)
  - B. Epistolary opening (1:4–6)
  - C. Announcement of the coming King (1:7–8)
- II. Body (1:9–22:5)
  - A. "Things that are": Christ's presence with and knowledge of his churches (1:9–3:22)
    - 1. The Son of Man among his churches (1:9–20)
    - 2. Christ's edict-letters to his seven churches (2:1–3:22)
      - a. To Ephesus (2:1–7)
      - b. To Smyrna (2:8–11)
      - c. To Pergamum (2:12–17)
      - d. To Thyatira (2:18–29)
      - e. To Sardis (3:1–6)
      - f. To Philadelphia (3:7–13)
      - g. To Laodicea (3:14–22)
  - B. "Things that shall take place after this": Christ's defense of his church and destruction of its enemies (4:1–22:5)
    - 1. The Lamb and the scroll: current and coming woes, precursors of the end (4:1–8:1)
      - a. Heaven opened: the Lamb receives the scroll (4:1–5:14)
      - b. The Lamb opens the scroll's seven seals (6:1–8:1)
        (*Interlude*: the sealing of God's international Israel, 7:1–17)
    - 2. The angels and the trumpets: warnings of coming wrath (8:2–11:18)
      - a. Heaven's incense altar: the saints' prayers, and fire flung to earth (8:2–5)
      - b. Angels sound seven trumpets (8:6–11:18)
        (*Interlude*: the safety and suffering of God's city-sanctuary, his witnessing church, 10:1–11:14)
    - 3. The woman, her son, the dragon, and the beasts: the cosmic conflict between Christ and Satan (11:19–14:20)
      - a. Heaven's temple opened (11:19)
      - b. The woman's son defeats the dragon (12:1–6)
      - c. Michael and heaven's armies defeat the dragon (12:7–17)
      - d. The beast from the sea (13:1–10)
      - e. The false prophet from the land (13:11–18)
      - f. The Lamb and his sealed victors (14:1–5)
      - g. Angelic announcements of judgment (14:6–13)
      - h. Harvests of earth and vine (14:14–20)
    - 4. The bowls of God's final wrath (15:1–16:21)
      - a. Heaven's sanctuary filled with glory (15:1–8)
      - b. Angels pour out seven bowls (16:1–21)
    - 5. Babylon the prostitute (17:1–19:10)
      - a. Babylon's power and luxury (17:1–15)
      - b. Babylon's fall lamented and celebrated (17:16–19:10)
    - 6. The defeat and destruction of the beasts, the dragon, and death (19:11–20:15)
      - a. Christ defeats and destroys the beast, the false prophet, and their gathered armies (19:11–21)
        (*Interlude*: the thousand years of the dragon's binding and the martyrs' reign, 20:1–6)
      - b. God defeats and destroys the dragon and its gathered armies (20:7–10)
      - c. The last judgment and the destruction of death, the last enemy (20:11–15)
    - 7. "All things new" (21:1–22:5)
      - a. The new heaven and earth, home of the Lamb's bride (21:1–8)
      - b. The new Jerusalem, the Lamb's pure bride (21:9–22:5)
- III. Epilogue (22:6–21)
  - A. Transmission and trustworthiness of the Revelation, promise that Jesus is coming soon, promise of blessing (22:6–9)
  - B. Prohibition of sealing the book, promise that Jesus is coming soon, promise of blessing (22:10–15)
  - C. Transmission of the Revelation (22:16–17)
  - D. Prohibition of altering the book, promise that Jesus is coming soon, and final pronouncement of blessing (22:18–21)

THE

REVELATION

TO JOHN

Prologue

1 The revelation of Jesus Christ, which God [a]gave him [b]to show to his servants[1] the things
that must soon take place. [c]He made it known by sending his angel to his servant[2] John,
2 [d]who bore witness to the word of God and to [e]the testimony of Jesus Christ, even [f]to all
that he saw. 3 [g]Blessed is the one who reads aloud the words of this prophecy, and blessed
are those who hear, and who keep what is written in it, [h]for the time is near.

Greeting to the Seven Churches

4 John to the seven churches that are in Asia:
Grace to you and peace from [i]him [j]who is and [k]who was and who is to come, and from
[l]the seven spirits who are before his throne, 5 and from Jesus Christ [m]the faithful witness,
[n]the firstborn of the dead, and [o]the ruler of kings on earth.
To [p]him who loves us and [q]has freed us from our sins by his blood 6 and made us [r]a
kingdom, [r]priests to [s]his God and Father, to him be [t]glory and [u]dominion forever and ever.
Amen. 7 Behold, [v]he is coming with the clouds, and [w]every eye will see him, even those who
pierced him, and all tribes of the earth will wail[3] on account of him. Even so. Amen.
8 [x]"I am the Alpha and the Omega," says the Lord God, [y]"who is and who was and who
is to come, the Almighty."

[1] Greek *bondservants* [2] Greek *bondservant* [3] Or *mourn*

Chapter 1
1 [a]John 17:7, 8; [John 8:26; 14:10] [b]ch. 22:6 [c]ch. 22:16
2 [d]John 19:35 [e]ch. 6:9; 12:17; 19:10; See 1 Cor. 1:6 [f]ver. 11, 19
3 [g]ch. 22:7; [Luke 11:28; John 8:51; 1 John 2:3] [h]ch. 22:10; [1 John 2:18]; See Rom. 13:11
4 [i]ver. 8; ch. 4:8; Heb. 13:8 [j]Ex. 3:14 (Gk.) [k]John 1:1 [l]ch. 3:1; 4:5; 5:6
5 [m]ch. 3:14; John 18:37; 1 Tim. 6:13; [ch. 2:13; Ps. 89:37; Isa. 55:4] [n]Col. 1:18; [Ps. 89:27; Acts 26:23; 1 Cor. 15:20] [o]ch. 17:14; 19:16; [Ps. 89:27] [p]John 13:34; 15:9 [q]1 Pet. 1:18, 19
6 [r]ch. 5:10; 20:6; 1 Pet. 2:9 [s]See Rom. 15:6 [t]See Rom. 11:36 [u]1 Pet. 4:11
7 [v]Dan. 7:13; See Matt. 16:27 [w]Zech. 12:10; John 19:37
8 [x]ch. 21:6; 22:13; [Isa. 41:4; 43:10; 44:6] [y]ver. 4

1:1–8 *Prologue.* John signals how to read the book and receive its promised blessings. The terms "revelation," "show," "made it known" (a Gk. verb related to "sign," 12:1, 3; 15:1), and "he saw" prepare the reader and hearers for symbolic visions, which make history's hidden realities visible.

1:1–3 *Title, Transmission, Promise of Blessing.* The opening paragraph identifies this book's genre ("revelation" or apocalypse, a disclosure of unseen realities), its divine author ("Jesus Christ"), and the process by which he is conveying it through the human author ("his servant John") to believers ("his servants"). It then pronounces the first of seven benedictions on those who rightly receive the book's message.

1:1 revelation of Jesus Christ. Jesus is both the One revealed (referred to variously as Son of Man, Lion of Judah, Lamb, Word of God) and the Revealer. God transmits the unveiled truth to Jesus (5:7), and his **angel** conveys it to **John** (10:9) for God's **servants** in the churches. The prophecy **must . . . take place** because it is secured by God's sovereign purpose and power. It will take place **soon**, because "the time is near" (1:3). In the epilogue, John, unlike Daniel, is told *not* to seal his prophecy (22:10; cf. Dan. 12:4). John's visions are important for his first-century readers as well as for later generations of believers.

1:3 Blessed. The first of seven blessings is given to **those who hear** and **keep** God's Word. Later blessings (14:13; 16:15; 19:9; 20:6; 22:7, 14) commend purity and perseverance, even to the death. In the early church **one** would read **aloud** while others listened. Revelation's message and its blessing can be received even by hearing it read, but only if that hearing is accompanied by obeying as well. **the time is near**. See notes on 1 Thess. 5:2–3; 5:4.

1:4–6 *Epistolary Opening.* This greeting identifies author and recipients, then pronounces blessing upon the recipients. **the seven churches that are in Asia**. Since churches existed in other cities of Roman Asia (e.g., Colossae, Troas), Christ's selection of "seven," symbolizing completeness, implies that he addresses the whole church through them. **him who is and who was and who is to come**. God is eternal, and in Christ he will come at the end of history to judge and save. **the seven spirits**. Revelation presents the Holy Spirit as one person (3:6, 13; cf. Eph. 4:4), but he also appears as "seven spirits" (cf. Rev. 3:1; 4:5; etc.), representing perfection, and as "seven torches of fire" (4:5) and "seven eyes" (5:6) to express his omnipresence and omniscience. **from** him who is . . . **from** the seven spirits . . . **and from Jesus Christ**. John's greeting comes "from" all three persons of the Trinity. **the faithful witness**. Witness (cf. "testimony," 1:2) is central to the church's calling amid suffering. As Jesus was the faithful witness even to death (1 Tim. 6:13), so must his followers be (Rev. 2:13; 12:11; 20:4). Christians are called to be faithful witnesses, but Jesus is "the" faithful witness par excellence. John comforts his persecuted readers with the truth that Jesus has triumphed over death (**the firstborn of the dead**) and that he is sovereign over all earthly powers, even Caesar, since he is **the ruler of kings on earth** (cf. 19:16). **made us a kingdom, priests**. Israel's roles now belong to those of all nations who are freed from sins by Jesus' blood (5:10; Ex. 19:6). From the outset, Jesus' death is central to the message of Revelation.

1:7–8 *Announcement of the Coming King.* **coming with the clouds**. See note on 1 Thess. 4:16–17. Jesus will come as the Son of Man with universal dominion (cf. Dan. 7:13–14), though his subjects **pierced** him (Zech. 12:10). **wail**. Most scholars think the wailing is a reaction to judgment instead of the kind of grief that leads to salvation. The coming one is **the Lord God**, **Alpha** and **Omega** (first and last letters of the Gk. alphabet) (see Rev. 1:17; 22:13). Jesus is the beginning of all history (the Creator) and also the goal for whom all things are made (all history is moving toward glorifying him).

Vision of the Son of Man

9 I, John, your brother and [z]partner in [a]the tribulation and [b]the kingdom and [c]the patient
endurance that are in Jesus, was on the island called Patmos [d]on account of the word of
God and the testimony of Jesus. 10 [e]I was in the Spirit [f]on the Lord's day, and I heard behind
me a loud voice [g]like a trumpet 11 saying, [h]"Write what you see in a book and send it to
the seven churches, to Ephesus and to Smyrna and to Pergamum and to Thyatira and to
Sardis and to Philadelphia and to Laodicea."
12 Then I turned to see the voice that was speaking to me, and on turning I saw [i]seven
golden lampstands, 13 and in the midst of the lampstands [j]one like [k]a son of man, [l]clothed
with a long robe and [m]with a golden sash around his chest. 14 [n]The hairs of his head were
white, like white wool, like snow. [o]His eyes were like a flame of fire, 15 [p]his feet were like
burnished bronze, refined in a furnace, and [q]his voice was like the roar of many waters.
16 [r]In his right hand he held seven stars, [s]from his mouth came a sharp two-edged sword,
and [t]his face was like the sun shining [u]in full strength.
17 [v]When I saw him, I fell at his feet as though dead. But [v]he laid his right hand on me,
[w]saying, "Fear not, [x]I am the first and the last, 18 and the living one. [y]I died, and behold I
am alive forevermore, and [z]I have the keys of Death and Hades. 19 [a]Write therefore [b]the
things that you have seen, those that are and those that are to take place after this. 20 As
for the mystery of the seven stars that you saw in my right hand, and [c]the seven golden
lampstands, the seven stars are the angels of the seven churches, and [d]the seven lampstands
are the seven churches.

To the Church in Ephesus

2 "To the angel of the church in Ephesus write: 'The words of [e]him who holds the seven
stars in his right hand, [f]who walks among the seven golden lampstands.
2 [g]"'I know your works, your toil and your patient endurance, and how you cannot bear

9 [z][Phil. 4:14] [a]John 16:33 [b]2 Tim. 2:12 [c]ch. 3:10 [d]See ver. 2
10 [e]ch. 4:2; [ch. 17:3; 21:10; 1 Kgs. 18:12; Ezek. 3:12; Matt. 22:43; 2 Cor. 12:2] [f]Acts 20:7; 1 Cor. 16:2 [g]ch. 4:1
11 [h]ver. 2, 19
12 [i]ver. 20; ch. 2:1; Ex. 25:37; 2 Chr. 4:20; Zech. 4:2; [ch. 11:4]
13 [j]Dan. 7:13 [k]ch. 14:14; Dan. 10:16 [l]Dan. 10:5 [m]ch. 15:6
14 [n]Dan. 7:9 [o]ch. 2:18; 19:12; [Dan. 10:6]
15 [p]Ezek. 1:7; Dan. 10:6 [q]ch. 14:2; 19:6; Ezek. 43:2
16 [r]ver. 20; ch. 2:1; 3:1 [s]ch. 19:15; [ch. 2:12, 16; Isa. 49:2; Eph. 6:17; Heb. 4:12] [t]Matt. 17:2 [u]Judg. 5:31
17 [v]Dan. 8:17, 18; 10:9, 10, 15; [Luke 24:37; John 21:12] [w]Matt. 17:7 [x]ch. 2:8; 22:13; Isa. 41:4; 44:6; 48:12
18 [y]Rom. 6:9; 14:9 [z][ch. 9:1; 20:1]
19 [a]ver. 2, 11 [b]ver. 12-16
20 [c]See ver. 12 [d][Matt. 5:14, 15]

Chapter 2

1 [e]ch. 1:16, 20 [f]ch. 1:13
2 [g]ver. 19; ch. 3:1, 8, 15

1:9–22:5 *Body.* John begins the body of his letter with a vision of "one like a son of man," who addresses edicts of commendation and critique to his seven churches.

1:9–3:22 *"Things That Are": Christ's Presence with and Knowledge of His Churches.* John's first vision, of the glorious Son of Man who is spiritually present with his struggling churches on earth, initiates a cycle of seven letters or edicts in which Jesus omnisciently diagnoses each church's condition and sovereignly commands appropriate responses of repentance and persevering faithfulness.

1:9–20 *The Son of Man among His Churches.* Jesus Christ appears in resplendent and overpowering glory to reassure his churches that by his death and resurrection he has control of the danger and death that threaten them. Although he is exalted in heaven, he is also present with his churches on earth and knows their needs better than they themselves do.

1:9 John's confinement on **Patmos**, an Aegean island to which Rome exiled political criminals, shows that he is a **partner** with the churches' **tribulation** and **patient endurance**. Patmos is an arid island approximately 24 square miles (62 sq. km) in area and roughly 40 miles (64 km) from the mainland of Asia Minor. Since antiquity, it has possessed a working protected harbor near its center (modern Skala) and other places for small boats to anchor. Inscriptions and archaeological remains indicate the existence of a fortress before John's arrival, and the clear presence of the Artemis cult afterward. The limited population of the island during John's day was probably largely pagan. Assuming (with church tradition) that John had been officially banished to Patmos, he may have been granted some freedom of movement on the island (even if, as claimed in later tradition, he lived in a cave) and may not actually have been in a prison, though he would have been barred from leaving Patmos.

1:10 in the Spirit. John was conscious of being surrounded by the manifest presence of the Holy Spirit. Such strong influence of the Holy Spirit leads to prophetic visions (4:2; 17:3; 21:10; cf. Ezek. 3:12). **The Lord's day** is Sunday, the first day of the week, the day on which Christ rose.

1:11 The order in which the churches are listed traces the route along which a courier from Patmos would have carried the scroll.

1:13 son of man (see note on John 1:51). Jesus' preferred self-designation in the Synoptic Gospels, derived primarily from the book of Daniel. In contrast to four beasts, symbolizing evil kingdoms, the son of man receives from the Ancient of Days universal and eternal dominion as the saints' representative (Dan. 7:1–14). Revelation 1:12–20 displays Christ's divine glory both visually and audibly, setting the scene for his royal edicts to the seven churches (chs. 2–3).

1:14 Hairs . . . like white wool show infinite, divine wisdom (Dan. 7:9; cf. Lev. 19:32; Prov. 16:31; 20:29). As he stands among the lampstands, Jesus' eyes **like a flame of fire** see through facades. He can say to each church, "I know," infallibly diagnosing its condition (e.g., Rev. 2:18–19).

1:15 Christ's feet, **like burnished bronze** (cf. 2:18), will crush any opponents. **roar of many waters**. Cf. Ezek. 1:24, "like the sound of many waters, like the sound of the Almighty."

1:16 two-edged sword. God's Word, which searches hearts and judges rebels (cf. Isa. 49:2; Eph. 6:17; Heb. 4:12; Rev. 19:15).

1:17 the first and the last. The Son of Man affirms his divine eternity, echoing the Lord's boast over idols (Isa. 41:4; 44:6).

1:18 I died . . . I am alive forevermore. Paradoxically, this ever-living One died to redeem believers and now lives forever as "the firstborn of the dead" (v. 5). Because Jesus died and rose again, John must "fear not" (v. 17), and the churches should not fear death, because Jesus has conquered it forever. On Christ's resurrection, see 1 Cor. 15:42–57.

1:19 Jesus' command to **write** forecasts the book's main divisions: The letters (royal edicts) to the churches (chs. 2–3) address the things **that are**. Thereafter John's visions turn primarily to **those that are to take place after this** (see 4:1).

1:20 Angels of the seven churches might be human messengers, human pastors, or literal angels sent as messengers, but they are probably personifications of each church's identity. Jesus will address his encouragement and/or rebuke for each church to that church's angel. Cf. Dan. 10:13–14.

2:1–3:22 *Christ's Edict-letters to His Seven Churches.* Revelation's first sevenfold series (followed by seals, trumpets, and bowls) consists of seven "letters" or royal edicts, each of which follows a pattern: (1) The royal author describes himself in terms from ch. 1. (2) "I know" introduces his diagnosis

2 [h]See 1 John 4:1 [i]See 2 Cor. 11:13
3 [j]John 15:21 [k][Heb. 12:3, 5]
4 [l]Jer. 2:2
5 [m]ver. 2; [Heb. 10:32] [n]ch. 3:3, 19
6 [o]ver. 15
7 [p]ver. 11, 17, 29; ch. 3:6, 13, 22; 13:9

with those who are evil, but [h]have tested those [i]who call themselves apostles and are not,
and found them to be false. 3 I know you are enduring patiently and bearing up [j]for my
name's sake, and you [k]have not grown weary. 4 But I have this against you, that you have
abandoned [l]the love you had at first. 5 Remember therefore from where you have fallen;
repent, and do [m]the works you did at first. If not, [n]I will come to you and remove your
lampstand from its place, unless you repent. 6 Yet this you have: you hate the works of
[o]the Nicolaitans, which I also hate. 7 [p]He who has an ear, let him hear what the Spirit says

of the church's condition, both positive (except for Sardis and Laodicea) and negative (except for Smyrna and Philadelphia). (3) Comfort and commands flow from the diagnosis. (4) All of the churches are commanded to hear and heed all of the letters ("what the Spirit says to the churches," 2:7, etc.). (5) A blessing is promised to "the one who conquers," foreshadowing the final visions in chs. 21–22.

2:1–7 *To Ephesus.* The church in Ephesus was commended for doctrinal vigilance and endurance but was rebuked for its loss of love. The city's landmark was the temple of Artemis, and one of its symbols was the date palm tree (contrast "tree of life," v. 7). See Introduction to Ephesians: The Ancient City of Ephesus.

2:1 The words of reflects the expression "thus says," which in the OT could introduce either a word from God (e.g., Amos 1:6, 9, 11) or a royal edict (e.g., 2 Chron. 36:23).

2:4–5 the love you had at first. One interpretation is that Ephesus had lost its early love for Christ. Another interpretation is that Ephesian believers had lost love for one another and needed to revive the compassionate **works you did at first**. Many interpreters think both are in view, since love for Christ and love for one another are related (cf. Mark 12:29–31; 1 John 4:20). **Remove your lampstand** means that both in the near future and when Christ returns, they would lose their status as a church and Christ would treat them like apostate Israel.

2:6 Nicolaitans. Obviously a heretical Christian sect, but not identifiable with certainty from NT or extrabiblical evidence. Like the prophet Balaam, they seduced God's people to participate in idolatry and sexual immorality (vv. 14–15), perhaps disguising antinomian license as freedom in Christ (see 1 Cor. 6:12–20; 8:1–11:1).

2:7 the one who conquers. Victory is the objective in a Christian's spiritual warfare. The Lion of Judah conquered as a slain Lamb, redeeming people for God from every nation (5:5, 9). Believers who hold to their testimony conquer the dragon (12:11) and the beast (15:2). **tree of life**. Access to this tree in Eden, and the eternal life it promised to the pure, was banned after humanity's fall (Gen. 3:22–24). It reappears in the new Jerusalem, its roots watered by living water from God's throne, its fruit a constant source of nourishment, and its leaves bringing healing to the city's inhabitants, whose names appear in the Lamb's book of life (Rev. 22:1–2).

Christ's Edict-letters to His Seven Churches

Church	Reference	Description of Christ	Commendation	Rebuke	Solution	Consequence of Disobedience	Promise for Conquerors
Ephesus	2:1–7	holds the seven stars in his right hand; walks among the seven golden lampstands	doctrinal vigilance and endurance	loss of first love	remember, repent, and do the works done at first	removal of their lampstand	will be given the tree of life in paradise to eat
Smyrna	2:8–11	the first and the last, who died and came to life	spiritually rich, enduring persecution	—	be faithful unto death	—	will be given the crown of life and will not be hurt by the second death
Pergamum	2:12–17	has the sharp two-edged sword	holding fast Christ's name, not denying their faith	false teaching	repent	war against them with the sword of Christ's mouth	will be given hidden manna and a white stone with a new name on it
Thyatira	2:18–29	has eyes like a flame of fire, feet like burnished bronze	growing love, evidenced in deeds of service	lack of discernment; toleration of heresy	hold fast and keep Christ's works till the end	each given as their works deserve	will be given the morning star and authority over the nations
Sardis	3:1–6	has the seven spirits of God and the seven stars	a few remain pure and loyal	dead works	keep the Word and repent	Christ will come like a thief	will be clothed in white garments; name never blotted out of the book of life; name confessed before God and angels
Philadelphia	3:7–13	the holy one, the true one, who has the keys of David	patiently enduring, keeping God's word and not denying his name	—	hold fast what you have	—	will be made a pillar in the temple of God, inscribed with the names of God, the new Jerusalem, and Christ
Laodicea	3:14–22	the Amen, the faithful and true witness, the beginning of God's creation		spiritually blind, bankrupt, naked, lukewarm	buy gold, white garments, and salve from Christ; be zealous and repent	will be spit out of Christ's mouth	will dine with Christ; will be granted to sit with Christ on his throne

to the churches. [q]To the one who conquers I will grant to eat of [r]the tree of life, which is
in [s]the paradise of God.'

To the Church in Smyrna

8 "And to the angel of the church in Smyrna write: 'The words of [t]the first and the last,
[u]who died and came to life.
9 " 'I know your tribulation and [v]your poverty ([v]but you are rich) and the slander[1] of [w]those
who say that they are Jews and are not, but are a synagogue of Satan. 10 Do not fear what
you are about to suffer. Behold, the devil is about to throw some of you into prison, [w]that
you may be tested, and for [x]ten days [y]you will have tribulation. [z]Be faithful [a]unto death,
and I will give you [b]the crown of life. 11 [c]He who has an ear, let him hear what the Spirit
says to the churches. [c]The one who conquers will not be hurt by [d]the second death.'

To the Church in Pergamum

12 "And to the angel of the church in Pergamum write: 'The words of him who has [e]the
sharp two-edged sword.
13 " 'I know where you dwell, [f]where Satan's throne is. Yet you hold fast my name, and
you did not [g]deny my faith[2] even in the days of Antipas [h]my faithful witness, who was
killed among you, where Satan dwells. 14 But I have a few things against you: you have
some there who hold the teaching of [i]Balaam, who taught Balak to put a stumbling block
before the sons of Israel, so that they might [j]eat food sacrificed to idols and [k]practice
sexual immorality. 15 So also you have some who hold the teaching of [l]the Nicolaitans.
16 Therefore repent. If not, [m]I will come to you soon and [n]war against them with [e]the sword
of my mouth. 17 [c]He who has an ear, let him hear what the Spirit says to the churches.
[c]To the one who conquers I will give some of [o]the hidden manna, and I will give him a
white stone, with [p]a new name written on the stone [q]that no one knows except the one
who receives it.'

[1] Greek *blasphemy* [2] Or *your faith in me*

7 [q]ch. 3:5; 21:7 [r]See Gen. 2:9 [s]Ezek. 28:13; 31:8 (Gk.)
8 [t]See ch. 1:17 [u]ch. 1:18
9 [v]James 2:5; [1 Tim. 6:18; Heb. 10:34; 11:26] [w]ch. 3:9, 10
10 [w][See ver. 9 above] [x][Gen. 24:55; Dan. 1:12, 14] [y]Matt. 24:9 [z]See Matt. 10:22; Heb. 3:6 [a]ch. 12:11 [b]See James 1:12
11 [c]See ver. 7 [d]ch. 20:6, 14; 21:8
12 [e]ver. 16; ch. 1:16
13 [f]ver. 9 [g]See 1 Tim. 5:8 [h]Acts 22:20
14 [i]See 2 Pet. 2:15 [j]ver. 20; Acts 15:29; 1 Cor. 8:10; 10:19 [k]Num. 25:1; 31:16; 1 Cor. 10:8
15 [l]ver. 6
16 [m][ch. 22:7] [n]See 2 Thess. 2:8 [e][See ver. 12 above]
17 [c][See ver. 11 above] [o][John 6:48-50] [p]ch. 3:12; Isa. 62:2; 65:15 [q]ch. 19:12; [ch. 14:3]

2:8–11 *To Smyrna.* Churches in Smyrna and Philadelphia (3:7–13) receive no rebuke from King Jesus, who encourages them as they endure persecution. Roman Smyrna (modern Izmir) was a harbor city renowned for its temple to the Mother Goddess and for its provincial imperial cult temples to Tiberius (1st century A.D.) and Hadrian (2nd century). Strabo in his *Geography* (14.1.37) reported early-first-century Smyrna to be a beautiful city possessing paved streets, a library, a gymnasium, and a shrine to Homer, who may have been born there. A few inscriptions point to a Jewish presence in the city. Jewish opposition to Christians in Smyrna was alleged in the martyrdom accounts of Polycarp and of Pionius (2nd and 3rd centuries, respectively; cf. 2:9).

2:8 the first and the last, who died and came to life. To a church already suffering "slander" (v. 9) and soon to face persecution "unto death" (v. 10), Jesus identifies himself as Israel's eternal Redeemer who prepared the way through death to resurrection life (1:17–18).

2:9 your poverty (but you are rich). Physically poor, the Smyrnan believers were spiritually rich (cf. James 2:5), whereas the Laodiceans thought themselves affluent but in Jesus' eyes were bankrupt (Rev. 3:17). The church's opponents may **say that they are Jews**, but they have no legitimate claim to that name (John 8:39–44; Rom. 2:12–29). Quite to the contrary, they belong to the **synagogue of Satan**. The NT defines God's people in relation to Jesus, not their genealogy.

2:10–11 ten days . . . unto death. The tribulation for Smyrnan Christians will be brief (cf. Dan. 1:12–16), yet it may end not in discharge from **prison** but in martyrdom, an even better release (Rev. 7:14–17). The **crown of life** (i.e., eternal life) is the laurel wreath of victory that God promises to those who love him (1 Cor. 9:25; 2 Tim. 4:6–8; James 1:12). **The one who conquers** by faithfulness in the face of death is immune from the **second death** (see Rev. 20:4–6).

2:12–17 *To Pergamum.* The church at Ephesus resisted false teaching, and Smyrna endured persecution. Believers at Pergamum faced both assaults, withstanding persecution well but wrongly condoning dangerous deception. Pergamum was built on terraces leading up the only accessible slope of its acropolis. It was an important center for pagan and imperial religion, but there are also indications of Jewish religion (e.g., Cicero, *For Flaccus* 28; Josephus, *Jewish Antiquities* 14.247–255).

2:12 Christ's reference to **the sharp two-edged sword** proceeding from his mouth (cf. 1:16) forewarns that the church's failure to discipline false teachers will prompt him to intervene directly (2:16).

2:13 Pergamum hosted temples dedicated to "the divine Augustus and the goddess Roma" and to Asklepios (the god of healing, symbolized by serpents), and a large altar dedicated to Zeus. The worship of the emperor as a god was also strongly emphasized, even required, in the province of Asia, and it was a major problem for Christians at the time. All of this qualifies Pergamum to be called the site of **Satan's throne**. Amid oppressive paganism, a believer named **Antipas** had sealed his testimony with his life, and Jesus shares with Antipas his own title, **faithful witness** (cf. 1:5).

2:14–16 As the Israelites migrated through the wilderness, the prophet **Balaam**, prevented from cursing them, advised Moab's king to seduce them into both sexual and spiritual adultery (Num. 25:1–2; 31:16). Likewise the **Nicolaitans**, though opposed in Ephesus, were spreading sexual and spiritual infidelity at Pergamum (see Rev. 2:6).

2:16 If not, I will come to you soon. Jesus' threat to come soon refers not to the second coming but to his intervention through providence, as at Corinth (1 Cor. 11:30–32).

2:17 As God fed Israel in the wilderness, Christ supplies **hidden manna** to **the one who conquers**, who endures persecution and stays pure from defilement (12:6, 14–17). Historically, a **white stone** was given to victors at games for entrance to banquets (cf. the messianic banquet); such a stone was also used by jurors at trials to vote for acquittal. The **new name**, given to the one who holds fast to Jesus' name (2:13), may refer to the Holy Spirit's work of conforming believers to the holiness of Christ (Rom. 8:29). The manna and the white stone suggest differing types of eternal blessings and rewards, as appropriate in each situation.

2:18–29 *To Thyatira.* Thyatira was a politically and culturally marginalized city, finding its identity economically, with guilds dealing in metals and fabric (Acts 16:14). Guilds celebrated their patron deities in periodic festivities, so

To the Church in Thyatira

18 "And to the angel of the church in Thyatira write: 'The words of the Son of God, [r]who
has eyes like a flame of fire, and whose feet are like burnished bronze.
19 [s]"'I know your works, your love and faith and service and patient endurance, and that
your latter works exceed the first. 20 But I have this against you, that you tolerate that woman
[t]Jezebel, who calls herself a prophetess and is teaching and seducing my servants[1] [u]to practice sexual immorality and [u]to eat food sacrificed to idols. 21 I gave her time to repent, but
[v]she refuses to repent of her sexual immorality. 22 Behold, I will throw her onto a sickbed,
and those who commit adultery with her I will throw into great tribulation, unless they
repent of her works, 23 and I will strike her children dead. And all the churches will know
that I am he [w]who searches mind and heart, and [x]I will give to each of you according to
your works. 24 But to the rest of you in Thyatira, who do not hold this teaching, who have
not learned what some call [y]the deep things of Satan, to you I say, I [z]do not lay on you any
other burden. 25 Only hold fast [a]what you have until I come. 26 [b]The one who conquers and
who keeps my works [c]until the end, [d]to him I will give authority over the nations, 27 and
[e]he will [f]rule them with a rod of iron, [g]as when earthen pots are broken in pieces, even as
I myself have received authority from my Father. 28 And I will give him [h]the morning star.
29 [p]He who has an ear, let him hear what the Spirit says to the churches.'

To the Church in Sardis

3 "And to the angel of the church in Sardis write: 'The words of him [i]who has the seven
spirits of God and the seven stars.
"'I know your works. You have the reputation [j]of being alive, [k]but you are dead. 2 Wake
up, and strengthen what remains and is about to die, for I have not found your works
[l]complete in the sight of my God. 3 [m]Remember, then, what you received and heard. Keep
it, and repent. If you will not wake up, [n]I will come [o]like a thief, and you will not know at
what hour I will come against you. 4 Yet you have still a few names in Sardis, people who

[1] Greek *bondservants*

18 [r]ch. 1:14, 15
19 [s]ver. 2
20 [t]1 Kgs. 16:31; 21:25; 2 Kgs. 9:7 [u]See ver. 14
21 [v][ch. 9:20, 21; 16:9, 11]; See Rom. 2:4
23 [w]Ps. 7:9; 26:2; Jer. 20:12; See Rom. 8:27 [x]See Matt. 16:27
24 [y][1 Cor. 2:10] [z][Acts 15:28]
25 [a]ch. 3:11
26 [b]See ver. 7 [c]See Heb. 3:6 [d]Ps. 2:8; [ch. 3:21; 20:4]
27 [e]Ps. 2:9 [f]ch. 12:5; 19:15 [g]Isa. 30:14; Jer. 19:11
28 [h][2 Pet. 1:19]; See ch. 22:16
29 [p][See ver. 7 above]

Chapter 3

1 [i]See ch. 1:4, 16 [j]1 Tim. 5:6 [k]See Luke 15:24
2 [l]Acts 14:26
3 [m][2 Tim. 1:13] [n]ch. 2:5 [o]ch. 16:15; Matt. 24:43; 1 Thess. 5:2, 4; 2 Pet. 3:10

Christians may have been tempted toward the message of a "prophetess" who advocated participation in illicit sex and food sacrificed to idols, both staples of the social scene. Archaeological soundings at modern Ak-Hissar have yielded evidence of a few ancient architectural elements from Thyatira. Coins point to the ongoing NT-era worship of Apollo, who had been assimilated with the Lydian sun-god Tyrimnos.

2:18 Christ's **eyes like a flame of fire** and **feet . . . like burnished bronze** (cf. 1:14–15) evoke images familiar to Thyatiran metalworkers, as well as echoing OT visions of God's glory (Ezek. 1:27). With fiery eyes, Jesus "searches mind and heart" (Rev. 2:23), and his feet will crush his enemies.

2:19–20 Thyatira's strengths and weaknesses are the inverse of those at Ephesus. This church is strong in **love** evidenced in **works**; but it lacks discernment and tolerates heresy. The self-proclaimed **prophetess** who endorses idolatry and immorality resembles **Jezebel** of Tyre, who married Israel's King Ahab and violently imposed Baal-worship on the northern kingdom (1 Kings 16:30–33; 19:1–2). Many scholars think "Jezebel" represented an actual woman "prophetess" who was leading people astray in the church of Thyatira. In any case, she symbolizes the prostitute Babylon, who seduces through pleasure and luxury as well as ruthless violence (Revelation 17).

2:21–23 The Lord has given the "prophetess" (v. 20) **time to repent**, or the church time to bring her to discipline. Neither has occurred, and she proliferates lovers and **children**—spiritual offspring who exhibit her influence and will share in her **great tribulation, unless they repent**.

2:24–25 Jesus' eyes distinguish sincere believers from those who abandon God's Word to search elsewhere for **the deep things of Satan**, deceptive promises of secret spiritual knowledge through false religions. Those content with the gospel have nothing to fear and no **other burden**, as long as they **hold fast**.

2:26–28 The "Son of God" (v. 18) will share with **the one who conquers** his own authority to rule the **nations** (Ps. 2:7–9). **The morning star** is Christ himself (cf. Rev. 22:16), Israel's ruler and rescuer, who was foreseen by Balaam, the unwilling seer (Num. 24:17). Premillennialists see here a reference to reigning with Christ in the millennium (cf. note on Rev. 20:4–5).

3:1–6 *To Sardis.* Sardis's capture twice in its history while watchmen neglected their duty became a cautionary tale of misguided complacency and lack of vigilance (see note on vv. 2–3). Although Jesus' rebuke identifies no specific source of attack, this congregation was similarly asleep, at death's door. Most of the impressive Roman-era remains now visible at Sardis were constructed after the tragic earthquake of A.D. 17. The emperor Tiberius helped sponsor reconstruction efforts, earning greater local renown for himself. In John's day the civic structures included a theater, a stadium, a central marble road, and multiple temples (esp. the monumental temple of Artemis). Many Jewish inscriptions also exist in Sardis, confirming the multiple references in Josephus to Sardis's Jewish population (*Jewish Antiquities* 14.235, 259–261; 16.171).

3:1 the seven spirits of God (cf. note on 1:4–6). A figurative description of the one Holy Spirit, who issues an edict to each of the seven churches (2:7, 11, 17; etc.). He will also appear as the Lamb's seven eyes, sent throughout the earth (5:6). Jesus knows this church's reality (**dead**), not just its **reputation** (**alive**); he holds **the seven stars** that signify the churches' true identities.

3:2–3 The church in Sardis is in a deep spiritual coma, approaching death but not beyond Christ's summons to **wake up**, to **strengthen** what is **about to die**, to **remember** and **keep** the message of grace that the church had **received and heard**, and to pursue the holiness that flows from grace. **like a thief**. A frequent NT simile (Luke 12:39–40; 1 Thess. 5:2–4; 2 Pet. 3:10; Rev. 16:15); humans cannot predict the timing of Christ's return. The command to "wake up" is a reminder that twice in its history Sardis had been sacked (in 547/546 B.C. by Cyrus II, and in 214 B.C. by Antiochus III) when the watchmen on the walls failed to detect an enemy army sneaking up its supposedly impregnable cliffs and walls.

3:4–5 Hope for revival is in the fact that **a few names**—alert and unstained disciples—can still be found in this church. Their unsoiled **garments** symbolize consistent obedience and courageous faith. Christ promises them the conqueror's reward: communion with himself (**walk with me**) and the **white**

have not [p]soiled their garments, and they will walk with me [q]in white, for they are [r]worthy.
5 [s]The one who conquers will be clothed thus in white garments, and I will never [t]blot his
name out of [u]the book of life. [v]I will confess his name before my Father and before his
angels. 6 [p]He who has an ear, let him hear what the Spirit says to the churches.'

To the Church in Philadelphia

7 "And to the angel of the church in Philadelphia write: 'The words of [w]the holy one,
[x]the true one, [y]who has the key of David, [z]who opens and no one will shut, who shuts
and no one opens.
8 " 'I know your works. Behold, I have set before you [a]an open door, which no one is able
to shut. I know that you have but little power, and yet you have kept my word and have
not denied my name. 9 Behold, I will make those of [b]the synagogue of Satan who say that
they are Jews and are not, but lie—behold, [c]I will make them come and bow down before
your feet, and they will learn that [d]I have loved you. 10 [e]Because you have kept my word
about patient endurance, I will keep you from the hour of trial that is coming on the whole
world, to try [f]those who dwell on the earth. 11 [g]I am coming soon. [h]Hold fast what you have,
so that no one may seize [i]your crown. 12 [j]The one who conquers, I will make him [k]a pillar
in the temple of my God. Never shall he go out of it, and I will write on him [l]the name of
my God, and [m]the name of the city of my God, [m]the new Jerusalem, [n]which comes down
from my God out of heaven, and my own [o]new name. 13 [p]He who has an ear, let him hear
what the Spirit says to the churches.'

To the Church in Laodicea

14 "And to the angel of the church in Laodicea write: 'The words of the [p]Amen, [q]the
faithful and true witness, [r]the beginning of God's creation.

4 [p]Jude 23 [q]ch. 6:11; 7:9; [Eccles. 9:8] [r][Luke 20:35]
5 [s]See ch. 2:7 [t]See Ex. 32:32 [u]ch. 13:8; 17:8; 20:12, 15; 21:27; Phil. 4:3 [v]Matt. 10:32; Luke 12:8
6 [p][See ch. 2:7 above]
7 [w]ch. 6:10 [x]ver. 14; ch. 19:11; 1 John 5:20 [y]Isa. 22:22; [Luke 1:32] [z]Job 12:14; [Matt. 16:19]
8 [a]Acts 14:27; 1 Cor. 16:9; 2 Cor. 2:12; Col. 4:3
9 [b]ch. 2:9 [c][Isa. 45:14; 49:23; 60:14] [d]Isa. 43:4
10 [e]ch. 1:9; 2 Pet. 2:9 [f]ch. 6:10; 8:13; 11:10; 13:8, 14; 17:8
11 [g]ch. 22:7, 12, 20 [h]ch. 2:25 [i]ch. 2:10
12 [j]See ch. 2:7 [k]1 Kgs. 7:21; 2 Chr. 3:17; Jer. 1:18; Gal. 2:9; [Ps. 23:6; 27:4] [l]ch. 14:1; 22:4 [m]ch. 21:2; Ezek. 48:35; [Gal. 4:26; Heb. 12:22] [n]ch. 21:10 [o]ch. 2:17
13 [p][See ch. 2:7 above]
14 [p]2 Cor. 1:20 [q]ver. 7; ch. 1:5; 19:11; 22:6 [r]Col. 1:15, 18; [ch. 21:6; 22:13; Prov. 8:22]

raiment of victory (cf. note on 2:17; also 7:14). Their **name** is secure in his **book of life** (20:15), and he will confess their **name** before the Father, since they have confessed Jesus in hostile circumstances (Matt. 10:32).

3:7–13 *To Philadelphia.* In appreciation for imperial reconstruction aid after an earthquake (A.D. 17), Philadelphia was briefly renamed Neocaesarea ("Caesar's New City"), but Jesus promises his suffering church an infinitely greater name, "the city of my God, the new Jerusalem" (v. 12). Philadelphia lies near a fertile valley, especially suited for growing wine grapes. Inscriptions from Philadelphia mention worship of Zeus and Hestia, and the Roman imperial cult was already present by the first century A.D. An inscription from a nearby town mentions a synagogue in that town. Christians in Philadelphia later received a letter from the early church father Ignatius (c. A.D. 110), and they suffered during the martyrdom of Polycarp (c. 155).

Promises to Overcomers

The following images depict ways in which God will be God to those who conquer (cf. Rev. 21:7).

Promise	What Will Happen	Fulfillment
2:7	will eat from the tree of life	22:2
2:11	will not be hurt by the second death	20:6; 21:7–8
2:17	will be given a white stone	21:11, 18–21
2:26–27; 3:21	will reign with Christ on his throne	20:4
2:28	will be given the morning star	21:23; 22:5, 16
3:5	will be clothed in bright garments	19:7–8; 21:2, 9–10
3:5	name will be in the book of life	21:27
3:12	will be made a pillar in God's temple	21:22–23
3:12	will participate in the new Jerusalem	21:10
3:12	will have God's name written on them	22:4

3:7 Jesus holds the **key of David**, meaning that his authority to admit to or exclude from God's kingdom cannot be reversed (cf. Isa. 22:22; Matt. 16:19).

3:8 an open door. For Paul, open doors were opportunities for ministry (1 Cor. 16:9; 2 Cor. 2:12; Col. 4:3). That sense is possible here; but since these Christians, excluded by the synagogue, would become pillars in God's temple (Rev. 3:12), probably Jesus sets before them the "door standing open" into God's heavenly sanctuary (4:1). **little power**. As Christians in Smyrna were physically poor yet spiritually rich, so those in Philadelphia were weak yet holding fast to Jesus' word (3:10–11).

3:9 Members of **the synagogue of Satan** (cf. 2:9) **say that they are Jews** but instead are serving God's enemy as they persecute Christians. Christ will compel these persecutors to **bow down** at the **feet** of his followers and acknowledge that he has **loved** them, just as Isaiah foresaw Gentiles bowing before Israelites (Isa. 45:14; 49:23).

3:10 To those who **have kept** his word, Christ promises, **"I will keep you"** from the coming **hour of trial**, which will put **those who dwell on the earth** to the test. Because this trial is **coming on the whole world**, it seems that before the final consummation, Revelation envisions a brief future period of intensified persecution for the church (see 19:19; 20:7–9) and of escalating manifestations of God's wrath against "those who dwell on the earth," a phrase designating rebellious humanity (6:10; 8:13; 11:10; 13:8, 12, 14; 17:2, 8). Jesus does not promise to spare believers from suffering or martyrdom but to shield them from his wrath and to transform martyrdom into triumph (6:10–11; 12:11). Many who hold a "pretribulation rapture" position believe that this verse means Christ will take them out of the world before a literal "great tribulation" period begins. Other interpreters, however, see this as God's promise to safeguard and remain faithful to believers who endure patiently in the midst of "the hour of trial that is coming," though it does not imply that he will take believers out of the world at that time (cf. a similar but not identical Gk. expression in James 1:27, where it does not imply removal from the world).

3:12 As a pillar in God's temple, inscribed with the **name** of **God**, the **one who conquers** can never be excluded from God's presence, for he will dwell in God's **new Jerusalem** (21:2) as David's royal heir (3:7).

3:14–22 *To Laodicea.* Damaged by an earthquake in A.D. 60, self-sufficient Laodicea, a commercial center and site of thriving medical and textile industries, declined imperial disaster relief. The city did not see itself as "poor, blind, and naked" (v. 17), nor did the complacent church within it. In this last church

15[s][2 Pet. 2:21]
17[t]Hos. 12:8; Zech. 11:5; 1 Cor. 4:8 [u]John 9:39-41; Eph. 1:18
18[v]Isa. 55:1; Matt. 13:44; 25:9; [Prov. 8:19] [w][ch. 19:8]; See ver. 4 [x]ch. 16:15 [u][See ver. 17 above]
19[y]See Heb. 12:6
20[z][Song 5:2] [a]Luke 12:36 [b]John 14:23; [Luke 24:29, 30]
21[c]See ch. 2:7 [d]ch. 20:4; [ch. 2:26; John 12:26; 2 Tim. 2:12]; See Matt. 19:28 [e]ch. 5:5; 6:2; 17:14; John 16:33
22[p][See ch. 2:7 above]
Chapter 4
1[f]ch. 1:10; [Ex. 19:19, 20] [g]ch. 11:12 [h]ch. 1:1, 19; 22:6
2[i]See ch. 1:10 [j]Ps. 11:4; 103:19; Isa. 66:1; Matt. 5:34; 23:22; See 1 Kgs. 22:19
3[k]ch. 21:11 [l]Ezek. 1:28; [ch. 10:1; Gen. 9:13-17]
4[m]ch. 11:16 [n]See ch. 3:4 [o]ver. 10; See James 1:12
5[p]ch. 8:5; 11:19; 16:18; [Ex. 19:16]

15 " 'I know your works: you are neither cold nor hot. [s]Would that you were either cold
or hot! **16** So, because you are lukewarm, and neither hot nor cold, I will spit you out of
my mouth. **17** [t]For you say, I am rich, I have prospered, and I need nothing, not realizing
that you are wretched, pitiable, poor, [u]blind, and naked. **18** I counsel you [v]to buy from
me gold refined by fire, so that you may be rich, and [w]white garments so that you may
clothe yourself and [x]the shame of your nakedness may not be seen, and salve to anoint
your eyes, [u]so that you may see. **19** [y]Those whom I love, I reprove and discipline, so be
zealous and repent. **20** Behold, I stand at the door and [z]knock. [a]If anyone hears my voice
and opens the door, [b]I will come in to him and eat with him, and he with me. **21** [c]The one
who conquers, [d]I will grant him to sit with me on my throne, as [e]I also conquered and sat
down with my Father on his throne. **22** [p]He who has an ear, let him hear what the Spirit
says to the churches.' "

The Throne in Heaven

4 After this I looked, and behold, a door standing open in heaven! And the first voice, which
I had heard speaking to me [f]like a trumpet, said, [g]"Come up here, and [h]I will show you
what must take place after this." **2** At once [i]I was in the Spirit, and behold, [j]a throne stood
in heaven, with one seated on the throne. **3** And he who sat there had the appearance of
[k]jasper and carnelian, and around the throne was [l]a rainbow that had the appearance of an
emerald. **4** Around the throne were [m]twenty-four thrones, and seated on the thrones were
twenty-four elders, [n]clothed in white garments, with [o]golden crowns on their heads. **5** From
the throne came [p]flashes of lightning, and rumblings[1] and peals of thunder, and before the

[1] Or *voices, or sounds*

alone Jesus finds nothing to commend. Laodicea was famous for its worship of Zeus, who appears on some of the city's coinage. Today one can still view unexcavated remnants of the city wall, two theaters, a stadium from the time of Vespasian (c. A.D. 79), and a second-century bath and/or gymnasium with adjacent water tower. An aqueduct came from the south toward Laodicea, bringing water rich in minerals. There is evidence of Jewish presence in Laodicea. Twenty pounds of gold were confiscated in the first century B.C. from Jews who intended to send it as a temple tax to Jerusalem (Cicero, *For Flaccus* 28). Paul was in contact with the church there (Col. 2:1; 4:13–16).

3:14 As the **faithful and true witness** (cf. 1:5), Jesus brings accusing testimony that contradicts the church's boast, "I am rich, I have prospered, and I need nothing" (3:17). Jesus' self-designation as **the beginning of God's creation** does not mean that he is God's first creation (cf. notes on Col. 1:15–17) but that he is the one who began God's creation (cf. note on John 1:3). In Revelation, "the beginning" with its complement "the end" is an expression for God's eternity (cf. Rev. 21:6; 22:13), and here it signifies Christ's sovereign rule over the created order.

3:15–16 The waters of the nearby Lycus River were muddy and undrinkable, and the waters flowing by aqueduct from hot springs 5 miles (8 km) away were **lukewarm** when they reached Laodicea. Likewise, Jesus found his church's tepid indifference repugnant. **Cold** and **hot** water represent something positive, for cold water refreshes in the heat, and hot water is a tonic when one is chilly.

3:17–18 The spiritually blind, bankrupt, naked Laodiceans obviously had no resources to **buy** from Jesus **gold** or **garments** or **salve** for their eyes. They could "purchase" these necessities only by his grace, as the Lord had once invited thirsty spiritual paupers to "buy wine and milk without money" (Isa. 55:1–4).

3:19–20 Like a loving father, Christ will **reprove** those whom he loves (cf. Prov. 3:12), calling them to repent before he intervenes in judgment. **I stand at the door and knock**, not as a homeless transient seeking shelter but as the master of the house, expecting alert servants to respond immediately to his signal and welcome his entrance (Luke 12:35–36; James 5:9). To the one who **opens the door**, Christ will **come in** and will **eat with him**, a picture of close personal fellowship.

3:21 I will grant him to sit with me on my throne implies that Christ will delegate some of his ruling authority to his people (cf. 20:4; 22:6; Luke 19:17; 1 Cor. 6:3; 2 Tim. 2:12). Premillennialists also see this as a promise of reigning with Christ in the millennium (see notes on Rev. 2:26–28; 20:1–6).

4:1–22:5 *"Things That Shall Take Place after This": Christ's Defense of His Church and Destruction of Its Enemies.* Having identified the strengths and weaknesses of the seven Asian churches (2:7, 11, 17, 29; 3:6, 13, 22), which represent "all the churches" (2:23), Jesus speaks again. He summons John "in the Spirit" to heaven, to receive visions that portray the future working out of his victory on the cross until its consummation in the new heaven and earth at the end of history.

4:1–8:1 *The Lamb and the Scroll: Current and Coming Woes, Precursors of the End.* John receives a heavenly vision of God on his throne and of the slain Lamb, whose triumph qualifies him to open a scroll and execute God's future purposes for history, the destruction of all his foes, and the vindication of those who trust in him. As the Lamb opens the scroll's seals, John sees images of God's instruments of judgment and of the saints who will receive salvation.

4:1–5:14 *Heaven Opened: The Lamb Receives the Scroll.* These visions, portraying events to take place after the first-century churches' struggles, begin with a door standing open in heaven, leading to a vision of God on his throne receiving ceaseless worship, and of the Lamb, who receives from him a mysterious sealed scroll.

4:1–2 the first voice . . . like a trumpet (cf. 1:10). The Son of Man summons John through the door into heaven, and **in the Spirit** (see note on 1:10) the prophet sees a **throne, with one seated** on it, "the Lord God Almighty" (4:8), adored by his heavenly attendants as "our Lord and God" (v. 11; cf. Isa. 6:1–5; Ezek. 1:26–28).

4:3 Imitating Isaiah's and Ezekiel's reserve in describing visions of God's glory (cf. Isa. 6:1–6; Ezek. 1:26–28), John suggests luminous colors—**jasper, carnelian, rainbow, emerald**—but avoids precise description of the Almighty's visible features, perhaps because he knew no language to describe what he saw. The jewels of this book (cf. Rev. 21:19–20) are not meant to be interpreted individually but together signify the splendor and majesty of God.

4:4 On **twenty-four thrones** sat **twenty-four elders**. Their number may reflect the orders of priests serving in the OT temple (cf. 1 Chron. 24:7–19) but more likely they symbolize the unity of God's people, encompassing OT Israel (led by the heads of the 12 tribes) and the NT church (led by the 12 apostles), like the new Jerusalem's 12 gates and 12 foundations (Rev. 21:12, 14). Their thrones resemble those of God's heavenly court in Dan. 7:9–10 (cf. Rev. 20:4). Some interpreters believe that these elders are angels, and that therefore they do not include themselves among the redeemed in 5:8–10.

4:5 Lightning, rumblings, and **thunder** display the terrifying splendor of God's glory, as at Mount Sinai (Ex. 19:16).

throne were burning [q]seven torches of fire, [r]which are the seven spirits of God, 6 and before
the throne there was [s]as it were a sea of glass, like crystal.
And around the throne, on each side of the throne, are [t]four living creatures, [u]full of eyes
in front and behind: 7 [v]the first living creature like a lion, the second living creature like an
ox, the third living creature with the face of a man, and the fourth living creature like
an eagle in flight. 8 And the four living creatures, [w]each of them with six wings, are [x]full
of eyes all around and within, and [y]day and night they never cease to say,

> [z]"Holy, holy, holy, is the Lord God Almighty,
> [a]who was and is and is to come!"

9 And whenever the living creatures give glory and honor and thanks to him who is seated
on the throne, [b]who lives forever and ever, 10 the twenty-four elders [c]fall down before him
who is seated on the throne and worship him who lives forever and ever. They cast [d]their
crowns before the throne, saying,

> 11 [e]"Worthy are you, our Lord and God,
> to receive glory and honor and power,
> for [f]you created all things,
> and [g]by your will they existed and were created."

The Scroll and the Lamb

5 Then I saw in the right hand of him who was seated on the throne [h]a scroll written
within and on the back, [i]sealed with seven seals. 2 And [j]I saw a mighty angel proclaiming
with a loud voice, "Who is worthy to open the scroll and break its seals?" 3 And no one in
heaven or on earth or under the earth was able to open the scroll or to look into it, 4 and I
began to weep loudly because no one was found worthy to open the scroll or to look into it.
5 And one of the elders said to me, "Weep no more; behold, [k]the Lion [l]of the tribe of Judah,
[m]the Root of David, has conquered, so that he can open the scroll and its seven seals."
6 And between the throne and the four living creatures and among the elders I saw [n]a
Lamb standing, as though it had been slain, with seven horns and with [o]seven eyes, which
are [p]the seven spirits of God sent out into all the earth. 7 And he went and took the scroll

5 [q][Zech. 4:2] [r]See ch. 1:4
6 [s]ch. 15:2; [ch. 21:18, 21; Ps. 77:19] [t]Ezek. 1:5 [u]Ezek. 10:12
7 [v][Ezek. 1:10; 10:14]
8 [w]Isa. 6:2 [x]ver. 6 [y]ch. 14:11 [z]Isa. 6:3 [a]See ch. 1:4
9 [b]ch. 1:18; 5:13; 15:7; Dan. 4:34; 12:7
10 [c]ch. 5:8, 14; 7:11; 11:16; 19:4 [d]ver. 4
11 [e]ch. 5:12 [f]ch. 10:6; 14:7; Gen. 1:1; Acts 14:15 [g]Ps. 33:9-11; [Eph. 1:11]

Chapter 5

1 [h]Ezek. 2:9, 10 [i]Isa. 29:11; Dan. 12:4
2 [j][ch. 10:1; 18:21]
5 [k]Gen. 49:9 [l]Heb. 7:14 [m]ch. 22:16; Isa. 11:1, 10; Rom. 15:12
6 [n]ver. 9, 12; ch. 13:8; Isa. 53:7; John 1:29, 36; 1 Pet. 1:19 [o]Zech. 3:9; 4:10 [p]See ch. 1:4

4:6–8 The **sea of glass** appears in prophetic visions of God's throne room (Ex. 24:10; Ezek. 1:22, 26; Rev. 15:2). It is the "floor" of heaven and the "ceiling" of the created universe, and its transparent tranquility shows heaven's peace in contrast to earthly turmoil. Four living creatures exhibit features of cherubim (**full of eyes**; **lion**; **ox**; **man**; **eagle**) and seraphim (**six wings**; **"Holy, holy, holy"**) glimpsed by previous prophets (Isa. 6:2–3; Ezek. 1:10, 18). Variation and blending of such features is a reminder that in prophetic visions, images symbolize mysterious unseen realities. These close attendants represent and yet transcend the whole of the created order on earth and in heaven as they ceaselessly praise God for his intrinsic attributes: infinite holiness and power, and eternal life (in the repeated description, "who lives forever and ever," in Rev. 4:9–10). When the Lamb breaks the scroll's seals, these living creatures will summon four horsemen to bring judgment (6:1–8).

4:9–11 The chorus of four living creatures swells as the **twenty-four elders fall down** and **cast their crowns before the throne**, offering worship and expressing submission to God's authority. The elders extol God as **worthy** of threefold tribute (**glory**, **honor**, **power**) because he exerts his sovereign **will** in creating and sustaining all things. God receives "power," not in the sense that an omnipotent being can become stronger, but in the sense that the strength of his creatures is used to honor him. These praises of God for his eternal perfection and creative achievement are the prelude to a "new song," which will laud God and the Lamb for redemption, the climactic display of their divine worthiness (5:9–10).

5:1–4 The theme of worthiness continues as John sees in God's hand a sealed scroll so sacred that it seems no one in the universe is **worthy** to open it.

5:1 A scroll written within and on the back is like the scroll given to Ezekiel (Ezek. 2:9–3:3) but is atypical of most ancient manuscripts, since the irregular texture of the reverse side of either vellum (leather) or papyrus made them hard to inscribe. However, such a doubly inscribed scroll would resemble a Roman will or contract deed, with the contents written in detail inside and summarized briefly outside, then **sealed with seven seals**. The scroll John sees could symbolize a will that is to be opened and its contents executed; or it could symbolize God's covenant with mankind, with the covenant curses that will be poured out due to mankind's breaking of the contract. In a broader sense, the scroll contains God's purposes for history, but its seven seals prevent the full disclosure and enactment of its contents.

5:2–4 The scroll awaited one **worthy to open the scroll and break its seals**, and no servant of God introduced so far—neither elders nor living creatures nor anyone else in **heaven**, on **earth**, or **under the earth**—had sufficient authority to unveil and implement God's secret agenda. Sensing that the church's hope stood in jeopardy, John **began to weep loudly**.

5:5–14 The apparent absence of one worthy to open the scroll was a dramatic interlude calculated to impress on John and his hearers the unique dignity of the scroll's recipient—the Lamb—who is now introduced.

5:5 The Lion of the tribe of Judah echoes Jacob's blessing on Judah, conferring leadership over his brothers (Gen. 49:8–12). In the OT, the Messiah was the branch to spring from Jesse's root to restore David's dynasty (Isa. 11:1, 10). But now he is also called the **Root of David**, because Jesus is not only the royal descendant (Rev. 22:16) but also the source of David's rule (Mark 12:35–37; cf. "root of Jesse," Rom. 15:12). The Lion is worthy to **open the scroll** because he **has conquered**. The OT promise of a conquering Lion is fulfilled in the NT reality of one who is also the slain Lamb (Rev. 5:9).

5:6–7 The conquering Lion now appears as a **Lamb standing, as . . . slain**—as "the living one" who died and rose again, "alive forevermore" (1:18). The Lord's servant was led like a lamb to slaughter, bearing the iniquity of others and achieving their healing (Isa. 53:4–7; John 1:29; 1 Pet. 1:19). The Lamb's **seven horns** symbolize great power (Ps. 18:2; Dan. 7:24; Zech. 1:18–21). His **seven eyes**, identified with God's "seven spirits" (cf. note on Rev. 1:4–6; also Zech. 4:10), show that the Lamb's knowledge extends through **all the earth**.

5:8–10 When the Lamb receives the scroll, **the four living creatures and the twenty-four elders**, who had praised God for his perfection and his creation, now sing a **new song** that celebrates the Lamb's redemption. As they had previously fallen before God's throne (4:10), now they prostrate

from the right hand of him who was seated on the throne. 8 And when he had taken the
scroll, the four living creatures and the twenty-four elders [q]fell down before the Lamb,
[r]each holding a harp, and [s]golden bowls full of incense, [t]which are the prayers of the saints.
9 And they sang [u]a new song, saying,

"Worthy are you to take the scroll
  and to open its seals,
for [v]you were slain, and by your blood [w]you ransomed people for God
  from [x]every tribe and language and people and nation,
10 and you have made them [y]a kingdom and priests to our God,
  and they shall reign on the earth."

11 Then I looked, and I heard around the throne and the living creatures and the elders
the voice of many angels, numbering [z]myriads of myriads and thousands of thousands,
12 saying with a loud voice,

[a]"Worthy is the Lamb who was slain,
  to receive power and wealth and wisdom and might
  and honor and glory and blessing!"

13 And I heard [b]every creature in heaven and on earth and under the earth and in the sea,
and all that is in them, saying,

"To him who sits on the throne and to the Lamb
  be blessing and honor and glory and might forever and ever!"

14 And the four living creatures [c]said, "Amen!" and the elders [d]fell down and worshiped.

The Seven Seals

6 Now I watched when the Lamb opened one of [e]the seven seals, and I heard [f]one of
the four living creatures say [g]with a voice like thunder, [h]"Come!" 2 And I looked, and
behold, [i]a white horse! And [j]its rider had a bow, and [k]a crown was given to him, and he
came out [l]conquering, and to conquer.

8 [q]See ch. 4:10 [r]ch. 14:2; 15:2 [s][ch. 15:7] [t]ch. 8:3, 4; Ps. 141:2
9 [u]ch. 14:3; See Ps. 33:3 [v]ver. 6 [w]ch. 14:3, 4; See 2 Pet. 2:1 [x]ch. 7:9; 11:9; 14:6; See Dan. 3:4
10 [y]See ch. 1:6
11 [z]Dan. 7:10; [Heb. 12:22]
12 [a]ch. 4:11
13 [b]Ps. 145:21; 150:6
14 [c]ch. 7:12; 19:4 [d]ver. 8; See ch. 4:10

Chapter 6

1 [e]ch. 5:1, 5-7 [f]ch. 4:7 [g]ch. 14:2; 19:6 [h]ch. 22:20
2 [i]Zech. 6:3; [ch. 19:11, 19, 21] [j][Ps. 45:4, 5; Hab. 3:8, 9; Zech. 9:13, 14] [k]ch. 14:14; [Zech. 6:11] [l]See ch. 3:21

themselves in worship before the Lamb, an affirmation of his deity. **Incense** symbolizes **the prayers of the saints** and shows that their pleas for relief are heard and will be answered in God's providential judgments (8:3–5).

5:9 Paradoxically, the Lion's victory is his being **slain** as the Lamb, ransoming a multiethnic multitude (7:9) by his **blood** (1:5–6). Likewise, his martyrs' faithfulness even to death is their victory (12:11).

5:10 kingdom and priests. See 1:6; Ex. 19:6; 1 Pet. 2:9. **reign on the earth**. The earth will not always be tyrannized by Satan and destroyed by his followers (Rev. 11:18; 12:12; 13:8). The first heaven and earth, stained by the curse through human sin, will be replaced by a new (or fully renewed) heaven and earth (21:1, 4) in which Christ's saints will reign in righteousness (2 Pet. 3:13).

5:11–12 The choir expands to include **myriads of myriads** (hundreds of millions) and **thousands of thousands** of angels, who acclaim the Lamb worthy of sevenfold tribute (**power**, **wealth**, **wisdom**, **might**, **honor**, **glory**, **blessing**). The worship of the Lamb in this chapter testifies to his deity.

5:13–14 Finally, **every creature in heaven and on earth and under the earth and in the sea** (Ps. 146:6) offers a fourfold doxology (**blessing**, **honor**, **glory**, **might**) to God and to the Lamb. Eventually, every knee "in heaven, on earth, and under the earth" will bow and "every tongue confess that Jesus Christ is Lord, to the glory of God the Father" (Phil. 2:11).

6:1–8:1 *The Lamb Opens the Scroll's Seven Seals.* As the vision of the Son of Man introduced edicts to seven churches (chs. 2–3), so the vision of the Lamb's receiving the scroll (4:1–5:14) introduces a series of seven visions as the scroll's seals are broken. These visions introduce instruments employed by the Lamb to bring his enemies to justice (seals 1–4), the rationale for his righteous wrath (seals 5 and 7), and the climax of judgment at history's end (seal 6). Many who take a futurist view of Revelation (see Introduction: Schools of Interpretation) hold that the "great tribulation" (see 7:14) begins with the opening of the first seal (6:1). Other futurists think the great tribulation begins in ch. 11 with the "1,260 days" (11:3).

6:1–8 As the Lamb opens each of the first four seals, one of the living creatures shouts, **"Come!"** and a horse with its rider (or riders) responds to the summons. The horses' colors generally reflect those of the horses in Zech. 1:8–10 and 6:1–8, symbolizing emissaries sent by God to patrol the earth. Only by the Lamb's permission and under his direction can the forces symbolized by these horses and their riders inflict death through sword, famine, pestilence, and wild beasts. The seal, trumpet, and bowl judgments all have a format of four (judgments on the earth) plus three (cosmic judgments).

6:1–2 the Lamb opened one of the seven seals. Many futurists understand this to mark the beginning of the great tribulation. The rider on the **white horse**, armed with a **bow** and given a **crown**, rode forth **to conquer**. Some

Doxologies to God and the Lamb

Ascription	To God/One on the Throne	To the Lamb
Dominion		1:6
Thanksgiving	4:9; 7:12	
Honor	4:9, 11; 5:13; 7:12	5:12, 13
Glory	4:9, 11; 5:13; 7:12; 19:1b	1:6; 5:12, 13
Worth	4:11	5:9, 12
Power	4:11; 7:12; 19:1b	5:12
Blessing/Praise	5:13; 7:12	5:12, 13
Salvation	7:10; 19:1b	7:10
Might	7:12	5:12
Wealth		5:12
Wisdom	7:12	5:12

3 When he opened the second seal, I heard [m]the second living creature say, "Come!" 4 And
out came another horse, [n]bright red. Its rider was permitted [o]to take peace from the earth,
so that people should slay one another, and he was given a great sword.
5 When he opened the third seal, I heard the [m]third living creature say, "Come!" And I looked,
and behold, [p]a black horse! And its rider had a pair of scales in his hand. 6 And I heard what
seemed to be a voice in the midst of the four living creatures, saying, [q]"A quart[1] of wheat for
a denarius,[2] and three quarts of barley for a denarius, and [r]do not harm the oil and wine!"
7 When he opened the fourth seal, I heard the voice of [m]the fourth living creature say,
"Come!" 8 And I looked, and behold, [s]a pale horse! And its rider's name was Death, and
Hades followed him. And they were given authority over a fourth of the earth, to kill [t]with
sword and with famine and with pestilence and [u]by wild beasts of the earth.
9 When he opened the fifth seal, I saw under [v]the altar [w]the souls of those who had been
slain [x]for the word of God and for [y]the witness they had borne. 10 They cried out with a loud
voice, "O Sovereign Lord, [z]holy and true, [a]how long [b]before you will judge and [c]avenge our
blood on [d]those who dwell on the earth?" 11 Then they were each given [e]a white robe and
[f]told to rest a little longer, [g]until the number of their fellow servants[3] and their brothers[4]
[h]should be complete, who were to be killed as they themselves had been.
12 When he opened the sixth seal, I looked, and behold, [i]there was a great earthquake,
and [j]the sun became black as [k]sackcloth, the full moon became like blood, 13 and [l]the
stars of the sky fell to the earth [m]as the fig tree sheds its winter fruit when shaken by
a gale. 14 [n]The sky vanished [m]like a scroll that is being rolled up, and [o]every mountain

3 [m]ch. 4:7
4 [n]Zech. 1:8; 6:2 [o][Matt. 10:34; 24:6, 7]
5 [m][See ver. 3 above] [p]Zech. 6:2
6 [q][Ezek. 4:10, 11; 5:10, 16] [r]ch. 7:3; 9:4
7 [m][See ver. 3 above]
8 [s][Zech. 6:3] [t]Ezek. 14:21 [u]Lev. 26:22; Deut. 32:24
9 [v]ch. 14:18; 16:7 [w]ch. 20:4 [x]ch. 1:9 [y]See ch. 1:2
10 [z]ch. 3:7 [a][Ps. 94:3; Zech. 1:12] [b]ch. 11:18; 19:2 [c]Ps. 79:10; 119:84; Luke 18:7, 8 [d]See ch. 3:10
11 [e]ch. 3:4; 7:9 [f]ch. 14:13 [g][Heb. 11:40] [h][Gen. 15:16]
12 [i]ch. 11:13; 16:18; [Heb. 12:26] [j]See Matt. 24:29 [k]Isa. 50:3
13 [l][ch. 8:10; 9:1] [m]Isa. 34:4
14 [n][ch. 20:11; 21:1] [m][See ver. 13 above] [o]ch. 16:20; [Isa. 54:10; Jer. 4:24; Ezek. 38:20; Nah. 1:5]

[1] Greek *choinix*, a dry measure equal to about a quart [2] A *denarius* was a day's wage for a laborer [3] Greek *fellow bondservants* [4] Or *brothers and sisters*. The plural Greek word *adelphoi* (translated "brothers") refers to siblings in a family. In New Testament usage, depending on the context, *adelphoi* may refer either to men or to both men and women who are siblings (brothers and sisters) in God's family, the church

think this rider represents Christ, the sword-wielding "Word of God" who rides a white horse in 19:11–16. However, this rider, armed with a bow (like the Parthians, a frequent enemy on the Roman Empire's eastern border), probably symbolizes political and military leaders' destabilizing quest to expand their realms, leading to war (red horse), famine (black horse), and epidemic disease (pale horse). Others think this rider on the white horse represents the Antichrist.

6:3–4 The next horse was **red**, the color of blood. Its rider was **given a great sword**, symbolizing permission to **take peace from the earth**, with the result that warring armies slay each other. The pursuit of conquest brings bloodshed. Futurists see this as representing the spread of war over the earth in the middle of the great tribulation.

6:5–6 The rider on the **black horse** carries **scales** for measuring grains and their prices. A heavenly voice comments on the scales' significance, citing inflated grain prices (8 to 10 times normal). Siege and disruption of commercial routes will produce scarcity, driving prices up (see Deut. 28:49–57; 2 Kings 6:24–25; 7:1–2). Local crops such as **oil and wine** are unaffected, however, showing that the scarcity is limited, not comprehensive. Some think the command not to **harm** the oil and wine may have a social significance, since the rich were the primary consumers of oil and wine. It could also be a prediction of events like that of A.D. 92, when the emperor Domitian during a grain shortage ordered the vineyards cut down to make room for more wheat fields. This caused such a backlash that he rescinded the order. In other words, extreme measures would have to be taken due to the progressive pouring out of judgment. (See chart below.)

6:7–8 Death and **Hades** ride the **pale** horse (Gk. *chlōros*, "pale green"; either yellowish green or grayish green, the color of corpses). Their authority to kill is limited to **a fourth of the earth**: God's providence restrains both his own wrath and humanity's violence. **Sword**, **famine**, and **pestilence** (Gk. *thanatos*, lit., "death," but here meaning epidemic disease, such as

Progressively Increasing Destruction

6:8	Seals	Death and Hades given authority over one *fourth* of the earth
8:7–12	Trumpets	one *third* of all affected
16:3	Bowls	*every* living creature

bubonic plague) sum up the disasters symbolized by the red, black, and pale horses. They also echo covenant curses inflicted on Jerusalem in the exile (Ezek. 14:12–21). The death of "a fourth of the earth" would be a "great tribulation, such as has not been from the beginning of the world until now" (Matt. 24:21), which futurists take as support for viewing Revelation 6–19 as representing the great tribulation.

6:9–11 The **fifth seal** reveals the Lamb's rationale for releasing combatants to devastate the earth. Under the altar in heaven, where sacrificial blood would pool (Ex. 29:12), John sees the **souls** of believers who were **slain** (thus they are pictured as sacrifices) for bearing witness about Jesus (cf. Rev. 20:4). Their lament, **how long . . . ?** echoes that of the psalmists (Ps. 13:1; 89:46). The surprising answer is that the Lamb will restrain his wrath against his witnesses' assailants until the last martyr has been slain. Until then, the souls of deceased saints will **rest a little longer** (Rev. 14:13) in the **white robe** of victory and purity (cf. note on 2:17; also 3:4–5; 7:9, 14). The rest of the book progressively shows how the Lord answers their prayers to avenge their deaths, beginning in 6:15–17 with the very ones who had put them to death.

6:12–17 The **sixth seal** shows a preview of the coming destruction of the first heaven and earth (20:11; 21:1) at the full display of **the wrath of the Lamb**. An **earthquake** previously announced the terrifying arrival of the Lord in his glory (Ex. 19:18; Ps. 97:5; Ezek. 38:19–20), but his final coming will shake both earth and heaven (Hag. 2:6; Heb. 12:26–27). Most of the seven cities mentioned in Revelation 2–3 had experienced devastating earthquakes during the century before the book of Revelation. Christians in these cities could graphically imagine earthquakes preceding the Lord's terrifying arrival. John sees the **sun** blackened, the **moon** turned blood red, the **stars** cast like figs in the wind, the **sky** rolled up like a scroll, and **every mountain and island** displaced (Isa. 34:4). The luminaries that have marked earth's times since creation (Gen. 1:14) will be removed. All of this communicates the truth that the end has arrived. Rebellious humanity—from **kings** and **the rich and the powerful** to **everyone, slave and free**—will seek cover from God and the Lamb, begging mountains and rocks, **Fall on us and hide us** (cf. Isa. 2:20–21; Hos. 10:8). Their desperate question, **"Who can stand** in the face of God and the Lamb?" (Nah. 1:5–6; Mal. 3:2), assumes that none can. Yet John is about to see those who stand by grace (Rev. 7:1–17).

6:13 the stars of the sky fell to the earth. Those who do not view the sixth seal (vv. 12–17) as predicting the destruction of the first heaven and earth

15[p]Isa. 2:19, 21
16[q]Hos. 10:8; Luke 23:30
[r]ch. 4:2
17[s]Jer. 30:7; Joel 2:11, 31
[t]Ezra 9:15; Ps. 76:7; Mal. 3:2; Luke 21:36
Chapter 7
1[u]Jer. 49:36; Dan. 7:2
[v][ver. 3]
2[w]ch. 16:12 [x]ch. 9:4
3[y]ch. 6:6; 9:4 [z]ch. 14:1; 22:4; Ezek. 9:4; [ch. 13:16; Ezek. 3:8, 9]
4[a]ch. 9:16
9[b][Rom. 11:25] [c]ch. 5:9

and island was removed from its place. 15 Then the kings of the earth and the great
ones and the generals and the rich and the powerful, and everyone, slave[1] and free,
[p]hid themselves in the caves and among the rocks of the mountains, 16 [q]calling to the
mountains and rocks, "Fall on us and hide us from the face of [r]him who is seated on the
throne, and from the wrath of the Lamb, 17 for [s]the great day of their wrath has come,
and [t]who can stand?"

The 144,000 of Israel Sealed

7 After this I saw four angels standing at the four corners of the earth, holding back
[u]the four winds of the earth, [v]that no wind might blow on earth or sea or against any
tree. 2 Then I saw another angel ascending [w]from the rising of the sun, with [x]the seal of the
living God, and he called with a loud voice to the four angels who had been given power
to harm earth and sea, 3 saying, [y]"Do not harm the earth or the sea or the trees, until we
have sealed the servants[2] of our God [z]on their foreheads." 4 And [a]I heard the number of
the sealed, 144,000, sealed from every tribe of the sons of Israel:

5 12,000 from the tribe of Judah were sealed,
12,000 from the tribe of Reuben,
12,000 from the tribe of Gad,
6 12,000 from the tribe of Asher,
12,000 from the tribe of Naphtali,
12,000 from the tribe of Manasseh,
7 12,000 from the tribe of Simeon,
12,000 from the tribe of Levi,
12,000 from the tribe of Issachar,
8 12,000 from the tribe of Zebulun,
12,000 from the tribe of Joseph,
12,000 from the tribe of Benjamin were sealed.

A Great Multitude from Every Nation

9 After this I looked, and behold, [b]a great multitude that no one could number, [c]from
every nation, from all tribes and peoples and languages, standing before the throne and

[1] *Or servant; Greek bondservant* [2] *Greek bondservants*

(in light of the presence of stars in the sky in 8:12) believe that this may refer to a massive meteor shower.

7:1–17 *Interlude: The Sealing of God's International Israel.* There are three interludes (vv. 1–17; 10:1–11:14; 20:1–6) explaining the place of the saints in the events of Revelation. (As with the Egyptian plagues, the seals, trumpets, and bowls relate only to sinners.) Literal and symbolic approaches differ sharply in interpreting the vision of the "144,000, sealed from every tribe of the sons of Israel" (7:4) and its relation to the next vision of an innumerable multitude "from every nation" (v. 9). Many understand this to be a reference to ethnic (or biological) Israel, and they would view the 144,000 as a symbolic or actual number of Jewish believers brought to faith immediately after Jesus returns and removes the church from the earth before (or during) a seven-year tribulation (this is a "pretribulation rapture" view). However, another common approach understands "Israel" as a reference to the church, the new covenant people of God, and in this view the visions of the 144,000 and of the international multitude are complementary perspectives on the church, believers from every nation including ethnic Israel. They are protected from the Lamb's wrath as his own flock (v. 17) but are exposed to persecution by evil enemies. The 144,000 reappear in 14:1–4, and their description there has a bearing on the interpretation here.

7:1–3 The sixth seal (6:12–17) showed an earthquake and a wind that shook the stars from the sky. God's cringing enemies asked, "Who can stand?" (6:17). The answer is, those "sealed" (7:4) with **the seal of the living God** (cf. Ezek. 9:4–6). Therefore John sees **four angels** charged to hold back those winds of judgment until all of God's servants have received his seal. "The seal of the living God" evokes a picture of a royal signet ring by which kings authenticated documents or marked ownership of an item (see note on John 6:27). This seal is the name of the Lamb and of God (Rev. 14:1), a gift promised to all who conquer by faith (3:12). It is antithetical to the mark of the beast (13:16) and symbolizes God's ownership and protection of his people. Circumcision functioned as such a seal under the old covenant (Rom. 4:11), and God's Holy Spirit seals God's people as his property under the new (Eph. 1:13–14). **foreheads**. Cf. Ezek. 9:4–6 for a similar instance of sealing God's people against outpoured judgment.

7:4–8 The selection and order of the 12 tribes suggest that the **144,000, sealed from every tribe of the sons of Israel** have symbolic significance, representing the church (however, see note on vv. 1–17 for an alternative view). These are not Jacob's sons, for Dan is omitted and Manasseh included. They are not the tribes that inherited land in Canaan, for Dan is omitted, Levi (the priestly tribe) is included, and Joseph is listed instead of his son Ephraim. Judah, the tribe of the Messiah (5:5), appears first rather than Reuben, the firstborn. When 7:5–8 is compared with the list of Jacob's sons in Gen. 35:22–26, the promotion of tribes descended from concubines Bilhah and Zilpah (Gad, Asher, Naphtali) over the sons of Leah and Rachel suggests that those once excluded from privilege are now included. The number **12,000** reappears in the dimensions of the new Jerusalem (Rev. 21:16). Indeed, the number 144,000 (12 x 12 x 1,000) suggests symbolism here, but that does not necessarily decide the question of whether "Israel" is also a symbol for the church, or is intended to refer to literal, ethnic Israel.

7:9 As in 5:4–5, where John first *heard* an OT title (the Lion of Judah) and then *saw* its NT fulfillment (the Lamb slain), so here John hears (7:4) the names of the sealed sons of Israel and then sees the NT fulfillment: a countless multitude **from every nation, from all tribes and peoples and languages** (cf. 5:9), whom God has rescued from wrath through the blood of the Lamb (7:14). They stand **before the throne and before the Lamb** in heaven, worshiping their Savior. They wear the **white robes** of victorious martyrs (6:11; see note on 2:17). Many who hold to a pretribulation "rapture" of

before the Lamb, [d]clothed in white robes, with [e]palm branches in their hands, 10 and crying
out with a loud voice, [f]"Salvation belongs to our God who sits on the throne, and to the
Lamb!" 11 And all the angels were standing around the throne and around the elders and
[g]the four living creatures, and they [h]fell on their faces before the throne and worshiped
God, 12 [i]saying, "Amen! Blessing and glory and wisdom and thanksgiving and honor and
power and might be to our God forever and ever! Amen."

13 Then one of the elders addressed me, saying, "Who are these, [d]clothed in white robes,
and from where have they come?" 14 I said to him, "Sir, you know." And he said to me,
"These are the ones coming out of [j]the great tribulation. [k]They have washed their robes
and [l]made them white [m]in the blood of the Lamb.

15 "Therefore they are before the throne of God,
and [n]serve him day and night in his temple;
and he who sits on the throne [o]will shelter them with his presence.
16 [p]They shall hunger no more, neither thirst anymore;
[q]the sun shall not strike them,
nor any scorching heat.
17 For the Lamb in the midst of the throne [r]will be their shepherd,
and he will guide them to springs of [s]living water,
and [t]God will wipe away every tear from their eyes."

The Seventh Seal and the Golden Censer

8 When the Lamb opened [u]the seventh seal, there was silence in heaven for about half an
hour. 2 Then I saw the seven angels [v]who stand before God, and seven trumpets were
given to them. 3 And another angel came and stood [w]at the altar with a golden censer, and
he was given much incense to offer with [x]the prayers of all the saints on [y]the golden altar
before the throne, 4 and [z]the smoke of the incense, with the prayers of the saints, rose before
God from the hand of the angel. 5 Then the angel took the censer and [a]filled it with fire

9 [d]ver. 14; See ch. 3:4 [e][Lev. 23:40; John 12:13]
10 [f]ch. 12:10; 19:1; See Ps. 3:8
11 [g]ch. 4:6 [h]See ch. 4:10
12 [i]ch. 5:14; 19:4; [1 Chr. 29:10, 11]
13 [d][See ver. 9 above]
14 [j]See Matt. 24:21 [k]ch. 22:14; [Isa. 1:18; Zech. 3:3-5] [l][Dan. 12:10; 1 John 1:7] [m]ch. 1:5
15 [n]ch. 22:3 [o]ch. 21:3; [Isa. 4:5, 6]
16 [p]Isa. 49:10 [q]Ps. 121:6
17 [r]Ps. 23:1, 2; [Matt. 2:6]; See John 10:11 [s]ch. 22:1; [Ps. 36:8, 9; John 4:14] [t]ch. 21:4; Isa. 25:8

Chapter 8

1 [u]ch. 5:1; 6:1
2 [v]Luke 1:19
3 [w]Amos 9:1 [x]ch. 5:8 [y]ch. 9:13; Ex. 30:1, 3
4 [z][Ps. 141:2]
5 [a]Lev. 16:12

the church think that the two groups of 7:1–8 and 7:9–17 are different (converted Jewish people still suffering on earth in vv. 1–8, but the raptured church rejoicing in heaven in vv. 9–17). Others think these are Gentiles converted during the tribulation through the witness of the 144,000 Jewish believers who remain on earth (v. 4). Those who do not hold to a pretribulation rapture usually see vv. 1–8 and vv. 9–17 as the same group, with their suffering in vv. 1–8 turned to joy and reward in vv. 9–17.

7:10–12 When the multitude extols God and the Lamb for **salvation**, angels and living creatures fall down and break out in a sevenfold doxology, almost replicating the sevenfold praise of the Lamb (5:12).

7:13–14 An elder identifies the multitude as the **ones coming out of the great tribulation**. Some understand the definite article (Gk. *hē*, "the") to refer to one great final period of suffering, but others take this to represent the sufferings of the church throughout all history. The source of their robes' whiteness is **the blood of the Lamb** (cf. Ps. 51:7). John will later hear that "our brothers" have conquered their accuser by the blood of the Lamb and their testimony (Rev. 12:11).

7:15–17 The sufferings on earth of those mentioned in vv. 13–14 are left behind, showing that John now reflects on the future heavenly inheritance. They **hunger no more, neither thirst anymore**. As priests, they serve God in his temple, in which he will **shelter** them from **sun** and **scorching heat** (cf. Isa. 49:10), spreading his tent over them and "dwelling" with them (cf. Ezek. 37:27; John 1:14). Under the protective care of **the Lamb**, **their shepherd**, they find refreshment in **springs of living water** (Ps. 23:1–2), tasting the promised joys of the new Jerusalem even before its final descent from heaven (Rev. 22:1), their **every tear** dried by God himself (Isa. 25:8; Rev. 21:4). Such comfort gives martyrs and other deceased believers rest as they await their resurrection and their persecutors' destruction (6:11; 14:13).

8:1 An interlude promising the sealing and safety of God's servants (7:1–17) has delayed the opening of the final seal. The **silence in heaven** that ensues when the Lamb breaks the seventh seal further sustains the suspense. Yet God's patience in delaying judgment should not be mistaken for indifferent slowness (cf. Luke 18:1–8; 2 Pet. 3:4–13). The brief period of silence—**about half an hour**—displaces ceaseless praises by living creatures (Rev. 4:8), elders (5:9), angels (5:11–12), and the church triumphant (7:9–10). Silence is appropriate in anticipation of the Lord's coming judgment (Zeph. 1:7–10; Zech. 2:13).

8:2–11:18 *The Angels and the Trumpets: Warnings of Coming Wrath.* A brief vision of God's heavenly temple, focusing on a golden incense altar, opens a new cycle of seven visions, each of which is introduced by an angelic trumpet blast. Fiery devastation descends from God's altar in response to his people's pleas. It despoils the entire environment inhabited by rebellious humanity: land and sea, rivers and springs, lights in the sky overhead—yet divine restraint and forbearance delay the final cataclysm, prolonging the opportunity for repentance. Visions of woe initiated by the last three trumpets disclose intensified demonic activity and global violence as the consummation approaches, at which time "the kingdom of the world" will have "become the kingdom of our Lord and of his Christ" (11:15), and every rebel against his reign will endure eternal condemnation and punishment.

8:2–5 *Heaven's Incense Altar: The Saints' Prayers, and Fire Flung to Earth.* Like the just-completed cycle of visions associated with the Lamb's breaking the scroll's seven seals, a sevenfold vision series begins with a glimpse into God's heavenly sanctuary. As seven angels stand ready to sound warning trumpets, the incense altar from which smoke rises (symbolizing the prayers of the suffering church) is the source of a succession of fiery judgments cast from heaven to the earth—devastating, but still restrained, foretastes of final judgment to come.

8:2 Seven angels stand ready to sound **seven trumpets**, initiating limited judgments that warn of coming destruction (cf. Ezek. 33:1–6; Joel 2:1) and summon rebels to repent (Rev. 9:21).

8:3–5 The earthly OT sanctuary had two altars, one for bloody sacrifice in the courtyard and the other for smoky incense inside, adjacent to the veil

5[b][Ps. 18:7, 8] [c]See ch. 4:5
7[d]Ex. 9:23, 24; Ps. 18:13; Ezek. 38:22 [e]Joel 2:30 [f]ver. 8-12; ch. 9:15, 18; 12:4; [Zech. 13:8, 9] [g]ch. 9:4; Isa. 2:13
8[h]Jer. 51:25; [Mark 11:23] [i]ch. 11:6; [Ex. 7:17, 19]
9[j]Isa. 2:16
10[k]ch. 9:1; [Isa. 14:12] [l]ch. 14:7; 16:4
11[m]Deut. 29:18; Jer. 9:15; 23:15 [n][Ex. 15:23]
12[o][Ex. 10:21-23; Isa. 13:10; 30:26]
13[p][ch. 9:12; 11:14]

from the altar and threw it on the earth, and [b]there were peals of [c]thunder, rumblings,[1]
flashes of lightning, and an earthquake.

The Seven Trumpets

6 Now the seven angels who had the seven trumpets prepared to blow them.
7 The first angel blew his trumpet, and there followed [d]hail and [e]fire, mixed with blood,
and these were thrown upon the earth. And a [f]third of the earth was burned up, and a
third of [g]the trees were burned up, and all green grass was burned up.
8 The second angel blew his trumpet, and something like [h]a great mountain, burning
with fire, was thrown into the sea, and a third of the sea [i]became blood. 9 A third of the
living creatures in the sea died, and a third of [j]the ships were destroyed.
10 The third angel blew his trumpet, and [k]a great star fell from heaven, blazing like a
torch, and it fell on a third of the rivers and on [l]the springs of water. 11 The name of the
star is Wormwood.[2] A third of the waters [m]became wormwood, and many people died
from the water, [n]because it had been made bitter.
12 The fourth angel blew his trumpet, and a third of [o]the sun was struck, and a third of
the moon, and a third of the stars, so that a third of their light might be darkened, and a
third of the day might be kept from shining, and likewise a third of the night.
13 Then I looked, and I heard an eagle crying with a loud voice as it flew directly overhead,
[p]"Woe, woe, woe to those who dwell on the earth, at the blasts of the other trumpets that
the three angels are about to blow!"

[1] Or *voices*, or *sounds* [2] *Wormwood* is the name of a plant and of the bitter-tasting extract derived from it

into the Most Holy Place (Ex. 27:1–8; 30:1–10). John sees only one **altar** in heaven, fulfilling both functions (Rev. 6:9; 8:3). As incense was associated with the **prayers of the saints** in the earthly sanctuary (see Ps. 141:2; Luke 1:9–11), so it is in John's visions (see Rev. 5:8). Not only martyrs under the heavenly altar (6:9–10) but also suffering saints on earth cry out for justice. Therefore **fire from the altar**, from which the saints' prayers rise, will be flung to earth in judgment, indicating that the judgments to follow answer the prayers of the saints.

8:6–11:18 *Angels Sound Seven Trumpets.* Revelation's third sevenfold series (with a second interlude in 10:1–11:14) portrays judgments sent from heaven in response to the saints' prayers. Judgments revealed by the first four trumpets harm the same spheres that will be destroyed when the first four bowls are poured out (16:1–9): earth, sea, rivers and springs, and sky. The damage done with the trumpets is limited to "a third": God restrains his wrath, while giving foretastes of total devastation to come if rebels ignore his warnings. "Woes" introduced by the last three trumpets are increasingly severe (8:13; 9:12; 11:14). Futurists (see Introduction: Schools of Interpretation) generally see these trumpets and plagues as signifying actual calamities to be suffered by unrepentant unbelievers during the great tribulation. They may be either supernatural judgments or symbols for events caused by man (such as nuclear, biological, or chemical warfare). See note on 6:1–8 for the "four-plus-three" format of the judgments.

8:6–7 At the **first** trumpet blast **hail and fire, mixed with blood**, are **thrown** from the heavenly altar to **earth**, consuming **a third of the earth** and its **trees**, and **all green grass**. This reproduces the seventh plague on Egypt (Ex. 9:24). The first four seals (Rev. 6:1–8) signified the Lamb's power to use human aggressors to punish persecutors of his people. Here God's providential rule makes use of human combatants' military strategy of ruthless defoliation (cf. Deut. 20:19–20) to call rebellious nations to repentance.

8:8–9 The **second** trumpet reveals **a great mountain, burning with fire, thrown into the sea**, turning **a third** of it to **blood** and destroying a third of its **creatures** and **ships**. Volcanic eruptions such as Vesuvius and bloody battles on the Mediterranean show the Lamb's sovereignty over another sphere of human life. The first plague on Egypt turned the Nile to blood (Ex. 7:20–21). The imagery echoes Jer. 51:25, 42, where God announced that he would make Babylon, Zion's destroyer, a "burnt mountain" and cover it with the sea.

8:10–11 At the **third** trumpet, fire falls from heaven as a blazing **star** named **Wormwood** (see note on Amos 5:7), which embitters and poisons **a third** of the **rivers** and **springs** (sources of drinking water) just as the Nile's bloodied waters became undrinkable (Ex. 7:24). Besieged cities could be driven to surrender by sheer thirst (see 2 Kings 20:20; 2 Chron. 32:30; Ps. 46:4). If Rev. 8:10 is understood literally, it may represent a great meteorite falling to earth.

8:12 The darkening (at the **fourth** trumpet) of **a third of the sun, moon,** and **stars**, obscuring their **light** for **a third of the day** and **the night**, resembles the ninth plague on Egypt (Ex. 10:21–23). Since stars are still in the sky, this judgment apparently precedes the shaking of heaven and earth portrayed with the sixth seal (Rev. 6:12–14; but see note on 6:13 for another view). The means causing this darkness may be billowing smoke from burning cities, but the ultimate source is the Lamb's reign.

8:13 Woe, woe, woe. The last three trumpets signify escalating judgments on rebellious humanity as the end approaches.

The Seven Trumpets of 8:7–11:19

Restrained judgments from heaven are sent in response to the saints' prayers.

Trumpet	Reference	Result
Trumpet 1	8:7	hail, fire, and blood cast on land—one-third burned
Trumpet 2	8:8–9	burning mountain cast into sea—one-third bloodied
Trumpet 3	8:10–11	burning stars fall on rivers and springs—one-third embittered
Trumpet 4	8:12	sun, moon, and stars—one-third darkened
Trumpet 5 (1st Woe)	9:1–11	demons from the Abyss
Trumpet 6 (2nd Woe)	9:13–21	invasion from the east—one-third of mankind killed
Trumpet 7 (3rd Woe)	11:15–19	kingdom of world becomes kingdom of God

9 And the fifth angel blew his trumpet, and [q]I saw a star fallen from heaven to earth,
and he was given [r]the key to the shaft of [s]the bottomless pit.[1] 2 He opened the shaft of
the bottomless pit, and from the shaft [t]rose smoke like the smoke of a great furnace, and
[u]the sun and the air were darkened with the smoke from the shaft. 3 Then from the smoke
came [v]locusts on the earth, and they were given power like the power of scorpions of the
earth. 4 They were told [w]not to harm [x]the grass of the earth or any green plant or any tree,
but only those people who do not have [y]the seal of God on their foreheads. 5 They were
allowed to torment them [z]for five months, but not to kill them, and their torment was like
the torment of a scorpion when it stings someone. 6 And in those days [a]people will seek
death and will not find it. They will long to die, but death will flee from them.
7 [b]In appearance the locusts were like horses prepared for battle: [c]on their heads were
what looked like crowns of gold; their faces were [d]like human faces, 8 their hair like women's
hair, and [e]their teeth like lions' teeth; 9 they had breastplates like breastplates of iron, and
the noise of their wings was [f]like the noise of many chariots with [g]horses rushing into
battle. 10 They have tails and stings like scorpions, and their power to hurt people [h]for five
months is in their tails. 11 They have [i]as king over them the angel of the bottomless pit.
His name in Hebrew is [j]Abaddon, and in Greek he is called Apollyon.[2]
12 [k]The first woe has passed; behold, two woes are still to come.
13 Then the sixth angel blew his trumpet, and I heard a voice from [l]the four horns of
the golden altar before God, 14 saying to the sixth angel who had the trumpet, "Release
[m]the four angels who are bound at [n]the great river Euphrates." 15 So the four angels, who
had been prepared for the hour, the day, the month, and the year, were released [o]to kill
a third of mankind. 16 The number of [p]mounted troops was [q]twice ten thousand times
ten thousand; [r]I heard their number. 17 And this is how I saw the horses in my vision and

[1] Greek *the abyss*; also verses 2, 11 [2] *Abaddon* means *destruction*; *Apollyon* means *destroyer*

Chapter 9

1 [q]ch. 8:10; [ch. 12:9; Luke 10:18] [r]See ch. 1:18 [s]ver. 2, 11; ch. 11:7; 17:8; 20:1, 3; Luke 8:31; Rom. 10:7
2 [t][Gen. 19:28; Isa. 34:10] [u][Joel 2:10]
3 [v]See Ex. 10:4
4 [w]ch. 6:6; 7:3 [x]ch. 8:7 [y]See ch. 7:2, 3
5 [z]ver. 10
6 [a]Job 3:21; 7:15, 16; Jer. 8:3
7 [b]Joel 2:4 [c][Nah. 3:17] [d]Dan. 7:8
8 [e]Joel 1:6
9 [f]Joel 2:5 [g]Jer. 8:6; [Job 39:21-25]
10 [h]ver. 5
11 [i][Job 18:14; Prov. 30:27; Eph. 2:2] [j]See Job 26:6
12 [k][ch. 8:13; 11:14]
13 [l]Ex. 30:3
14 [m][ch. 7:1] [n]ch. 16:12
15 [o]See ch. 8:7
16 [p]Ezek. 38:4 [q][Ps. 68:17; Dan. 7:10] [r]ch. 7:4

9:1–12 Whereas the star that fell at the third trumpet symbolized the polluting effects of ancient and modern warfare on rivers and springs, the **star fallen from heaven to earth** (v. 1) when the **fifth** trumpet sounds is Satan, **the angel of the bottomless pit**, whose names mean "Destroyer" (see note on v. 11). This vision shows the increase of demonic activity, plunging rebellious humans into desperation, as the era of God's patient restraint draws to a close.

9:1 The **star fallen from heaven to earth** is Satan, whom Jesus saw fall like lightning as a result of his disciples' ministry (Luke 10:18). Three chapters later in Revelation, John will see the "dragon," whom he identifies as Satan, cast down from heaven to earth (Rev. 12:9). The fact that the **key to the shaft** of the Abyss **was given** to him shows that Satan can do nothing apart from God's permission (cf. "were told," 9:4). However, many scholars think that this "star" represents a good angel, and that this verse in connection with 20:1 marks the beginning and the end of the middle section of the book.

9:2–3 When the fallen star unlocked the bottomless pit, **locusts** emerged in billowing **smoke** that darkened the sky. An echo of the eighth plague on Egypt (Ex. 10:14–15), this infestation of locusts also recalls the swarm summoned by trumpet to strip the land bare on the "awesome day of the LORD" (Joel 2:31).

9:4–6 What John sees as locusts are no threat to earth's vegetation (**grass**, **green plant**, or **tree**), nor can they harm those who bear God's seal (cf. 3:12; 7:3; 14:1). And their strange composite appearance (9:7–9) gives the impression of symbolism. Therefore, it seems that these invaders are not literal insects but demonic spirits (with Satan as their leader, v. 11), released to torment their own worshipers (v. 20), who serve their king, the "Destroyer" (see note on v. 11). Thus their **scorpion**-like **stings** cannot inflict death, which would bring relief to their victims. Others think these locusts represent military forces, and still others consider them to be actual locusts but with their destructive power described in figurative imagery. **Five months** signifies the divinely imposed brevity of their power to torture even those who oppose the Lamb.

9:7–11 The locusts' visible similarities to **horses**, **human faces**, lions, and **scorpions** caution against reading John's visions as physical descriptions. Rather, these images show demons to be powerful, swift, intelligent, fierce, and capable of inflicting intense mental and spiritual torment.

9:11 Abaddon, Apollyon. In **Hebrew** and **Greek**, respectively, these words refer to "destruction" and the "one who destroys." Satan's demonic hordes wage war against his own human subjects. Later the enemy will be called the "accuser," as his Hebrew and Greek names, Satan and Devil, signify (12:9–10).

9:13–21 The cavalry revealed with the **sixth** trumpet resembles the demon swarm of the fifth, like **horses** and lions, with **breastplates** and venomous power in their **tails**. Yet these warriors are authorized to take human life on a massive scale (cf. "but not to kill," v. 5), showing that Satan is waging war against his own followers. These warriors, with their origin beyond the Euphrates, suggest that John now sees the carnage wrought by military aggression and warfare. Yet, devastating as the bloodshed is, God still imposes limits: **a third of mankind was killed** (vv. 15, 18). This is the last limited judgment and warning blast, for when the seventh, last trumpet sounds, "the mystery of God will be fulfilled" (10:7; cf. 1 Cor. 15:52; 1 Thess. 4:16), and the opportunity to **repent** will be past (Rev. 9:20–21).

9:13–14 the golden altar before God. These woes come in answer to the saints' prayers, offered as incense on that altar (8:4–5). Ancient Israel's captors, Assyria and Babylon, had come from **the great river Euphrates**. In John's day it also marked the eastern boundary of Rome's influence, beyond which barbarian powers such as Parthia threatened the empire's peace. This river represents that which keeps civil chaos and wanton violence at bay. The release of its four destructive **angels** here, like the drying of its waters in 16:12–16, unleashes unprecedented bloodshed and suffering.

9:16–19 twice ten thousand times ten thousand. Two hundred million is an incredibly large army but not as great as the countless multitude that worships the Lamb (7:9). This cavalry, like the locusts from the Abyss (9:1–12), consists of demons. Their horses have heads **like lions' heads** and tails **like serpents**. But God's faithful servant can trample both of these deadly enemies underfoot (cf. Ps. 91:13). (Satan is the "ancient serpent" [Rev. 12:9; see Gen. 3:15].) Red **fire**, blue **smoke** (like **sapphire**), and yellow, rancid **sulfur** spewing from the horses' **mouths** reflect the colors of their riders' **breastplates**. What proceeds from the mouth represents the power of words, either to judge justly or to deceive and destroy, as when the Euphrates reappears in Rev. 16:12–14. The demonic horsemen kill by deluding human armies into war. Some think these 200 million troops represent a very large actual human army.

those who rode them: they wore breastplates the color of fire and of sapphire[1] and of
sulfur, and the heads of the horses were [s]like lions' heads, and fire and smoke and sulfur
came out of their mouths. 18 By these three plagues a third of mankind was killed, by the
fire and smoke and sulfur coming out of their mouths. 19 For the power of the horses is in
their mouths and in their tails, for their tails are like serpents with heads, and by means
of them they wound.

20 The rest of mankind, who were not killed by these plagues, [t]did not repent of [u]the
works of their hands nor give up worshiping [v]demons [w]and idols of gold and silver and
bronze and stone and wood, which cannot see or hear or walk, 21 nor did they repent of
their murders or their [x]sorceries or their sexual immorality or their thefts.

The Angel and the Little Scroll

10 Then I saw another mighty angel coming down from heaven, wrapped in a cloud,
with [y]a rainbow over his head, and [z]his face was like the sun, and [a]his legs like pillars of fire. 2 [b]He had a little scroll open in his hand. And he set his right foot on the sea,
and his left foot on the land, 3 and called out with a loud voice, [c]like a lion roaring. When
he called out, the seven thunders sounded. 4 And when the seven thunders had sounded,
I was about to write, but I heard a voice from heaven saying, [d]"Seal up what the seven
thunders have said, and do not write it down." 5 And the angel whom I saw standing on
the sea and on the land [e]raised his right hand to heaven 6 and swore by [f]him who lives
forever and ever, [g]who created heaven and what is in it, the earth and what is in it, and
the sea and what is in it, that there would be no more delay, 7 but that [h]in the days of the
trumpet call to be sounded by the seventh angel, the mystery of God would be fulfilled,
[i]just as he announced to his servants[2] the prophets.

8 Then the voice that I had heard from heaven spoke to me again, saying, "Go, take the
scroll that is open in the hand of the angel who is standing on the sea and on the land."

[1] Greek *hyacinth* [2] Greek *bondservants*

17 [s][1 Chr. 12:8; Isa. 5:28, 29]
20 [t]See ch. 2:21 [u]Deut. 31:29; Jer. 1:16; 25:14 [v]See 1 Cor. 10:20 [w]Ps. 115:4-7; 135:15-17; Dan. 5:23
21 [x]ch. 21:8; 22:15; Gal. 5:20

Chapter 10

1 [y]Ezek. 1:28 [z]ch. 1:16; Matt. 17:2 [a]ch. 1:15
2 [b]ver. 8-10
3 [c]Joel 3:16; Amos 1:2
4 [d]Dan. 8:26; 12:4, 9; [ch. 22:10]
5 [e]See Gen. 14:22
6 [f]See ch. 4:9 [g]See ch. 4:11
7 [h]ch. 11:15 [i][Amos 3:7]

9:20–21 did not repent. Although those rebelling against God have been tortured by the very demons they worshiped, the survivors will take no warning from these final trumpet blasts. This shows the total depravity of the sinners (also 16:9, 11, 21; 20:7–10). Every time Christ offers them repentance, they reject his offer and prefer to follow Satan. **idols . . . cannot see or hear or walk.** Senseless and impotent, images of metal, stone, or wood cannot protect or rescue, as Daniel told King Belshazzar on the night that his life was taken and his kingdom seized (Dan. 5:23; cf. Ps. 115:4–8; 135:15–18; Isa. 44:12–20).

10:1–11:14 *Interlude: The Safety and Suffering of God's City-Sanctuary, His Witnessing Church.* Between the sixth trumpet (9:13–21) and the seventh (11:15–18), another interlude is inserted. Like the visions that separated the sixth from the seventh seals (7:1–17), this interlude dramatizes God's patient delay in inflicting his full and final wrath, and it assures believers that God will protect his own through the coming traumas. The vision of the angel with the scroll (10:1–11) reveals John's authority to prophesy and God's perfect timing in consummating history.

10:1–3 another mighty angel. Like God on his throne, he is surrounded by a **rainbow** (cf. 4:3). Like the Son of Man, he comes with a **cloud**, and his **face** shines **like the sun** (cf. 1:7, 16). **His legs like pillars of fire** reflect the glory of God's presence in the wilderness (Ex. 13:21–22; 14:24). His voice **like a lion roaring** could belong to the Lion of Judah (Rev. 5:5; see Amos 3:7–8). Therefore some interpreters think this is Jesus himself. However, since Rev. 1:1 describes an angel sent by Christ to deliver God's revelation to John, many see this as simply "another" great angel.

10:2 The **scroll** is **open** because the Lamb has broken its seals. The scroll is **little** compared to the great size of the angel, whose stride spans **sea** and **land.** It will be given to John to eat and to proclaim (vv. 10–11), completing the process of transmission (from God to Christ to angel to John to the churches) initiated in 5:7.

10:3–4 John must **seal up**—keep secret by not writing—the messages of **the seven thunders.** This prohibition may serve a similar purpose to the angel's announcement that "there would be no more delay" (v. 6), since reporting these seven messages would have further delayed the seventh trumpet's blast. Christ's church must live by faith amid the unrevealed mysteries of God's purposes.

10:5–7 The angel's stance—one foot on **sea**, one on **land**, and **right hand** raised to **heaven**—unites three spheres of the created order (see 5:13; Gen. 1:6–10) as their divine Creator is invoked to witness the angel's oath (cf. Dan. 12:7; also Gen. 14:22; Deut. 32:40). The angel swears that the era of God's longsuffering, which entailed **delay** of his martyrs' vindication (Rev. 6:10), will end when the last trumpet sounds. The **mystery of God** to **be fulfilled** when the seventh trumpet sounds is his plan to unite all things in heaven and earth under Christ's headship (Eph. 1:10), making visible to all the sovereignty by which the Son now orchestrates every event for his church's welfare (Eph. 1:20–22). This "mystery" includes the unrestrained expression of God's wrath, signified in the bowl judgments, toward all who resist his reign (cf. Rev. 15:1, where "finished" translates the same verb [Gk. *teleō*] rendered "fulfilled" in 10:7).

10:8–11 As Ezekiel ate a scroll and found it **sweet as honey** in his **mouth**, so John must do the same, receiving God's words in his heart before he speaks them (cf. Ezek. 3:1–3, 10). The sweet word made his **stomach . . . bitter.** Although some "from every tribe and language and people and nation" will be redeemed by the Lamb (Rev. 5:9; 7:9–17), at this particular time John will see **peoples and nations and languages** resisting Christ and his witnesses (11:9; 13:7; 17:15). **Kings** in particular will ally themselves with evil (6:15; 16:12–14; 17:2, 18; 19:18–19).

Four Series of Seven Messages or Visions

Seven Letters to Churches	chs. 2–3
Seven Seals on a Scroll	5:1–8:1
Seven Trumpets	8:2–11:19
Seven Bowls of Wrath	chs. 15–16

9 So I went to the angel and told him to give me the little scroll. And he said to me, [j]"Take
and [k]eat it; it will make your stomach bitter, but in your mouth it will be sweet as honey."
10 And I took the little scroll from the hand of the angel and ate it. It was sweet as honey in
my mouth, but when I had eaten it my stomach was made bitter. 11 And I was told, [l]"You
must again prophesy about many peoples and nations and languages and kings."

The Two Witnesses

11 Then I was given [m]a measuring rod like a staff, and I was told, "Rise and measure
the temple of God and the altar and those who worship there, 2 but do not measure
[n]the court outside the temple; leave that out, for [o]it is given over to the nations, and they
will trample the holy city for [p]forty-two months. 3 And I will grant authority to my two
witnesses, and they will prophesy for [p]1,260 days, [q]clothed in sackcloth."
4 These are [r]the two olive trees and the two lampstands that stand before the Lord of
the earth. 5 And if anyone would harm them, [s]fire pours from their mouth and consumes
their foes. If anyone would harm them, [t]this is how he is doomed to be killed. 6 They have
the power [u]to shut the sky, that no rain may fall during the days of their prophesying, and
they have power over the waters to turn them into blood and [v]to strike the earth with every
kind of plague, as often as they desire. 7 And when they have finished their testimony, [w]the
beast that rises from [x]the bottomless pit[1] [y]will make war on them and conquer them and kill
them, 8 and their dead bodies will lie in the street of the great city that symbolically[2] is called
[z]Sodom and [a]Egypt, where their Lord was crucified. 9 For three and a half days some from
the peoples and tribes and languages and nations will gaze at their dead bodies and [b]refuse
to let them be placed in a tomb, 10 and [c]those who dwell on the earth will rejoice over them
and make merry and [d]exchange presents, because these two prophets [e]had been a torment to

[1] *Or the abyss* [2] *Greek spiritually*

9 [j]Ezek. 2:8; 3:1-3 [k][Jer. 15:16]
11 [l][Ezek. 37:4]

Chapter 11

1 [m]ch. 21:15, 16; Ezek. 40:3; Zech. 2:1
2 [n]Ezek. 40:17, 20 [o]See Luke 21:24 [p]ch. 12:6; 13:5
3 [p][See ver. 2 above] [q]Isa. 20:2
4 [r]Zech. 4:3, 11, 14; [Ps. 52:8; Jer. 11:16]
5 [s][2 Kgs. 1:10, 12; Jer. 5:14] [t][Num. 16:29, 35]
6 [u][1 Kgs. 17:1; Luke 4:25; James 5:17] [v][Ex. 7–10; 1 Sam. 4:8]
7 [w]ch. 17:8; [ch. 13:1] [x]See ch. 9:1 [y]Dan. 7:21
8 [z]Isa. 1:10; 3:9 [a][Ezek. 23:3, 8, 19, 27]
9 [b]Ps. 79:2, 3
10 [c][John 16:20]; See ch. 3:10 [d]Neh. 8:10, 12; Esth. 9:19, 22 [e][1 Kgs. 18:17]

11:1–14 The complementary visions of the temple and the witnesses, like those of the 144,000 and the international multitude between seals 6 and 7 (ch. 7), provide reassurance of God's protection. Here, however, consistent with the bittersweet message committed to John (10:10–11), the motif of spiritual protection is interwoven with the darker thread of physical suffering.

11:1–2 John was **given a measuring rod** and instructed to **measure the temple of God**. Many dispensationalists understand this to imply that during the great tribulation the Jewish temple will be rebuilt in Jerusalem, and Jewish worship will be reinstituted there, and that it is here that, in the middle of the tribulation, the Antichrist will take "his seat in the temple of God, proclaiming himself to be God" (2 Thess. 2:4). They understand the reference to **the holy city** to mean literal, earthly Jerusalem. Others see the "temple" in Revelation 11 as a symbol for believers. In the OT, Ezekiel in his vision watched an angel measure the temple (Ezek. 40:2–3), but John must measure not only the sanctuary and its **altar** but also **those who worship there**. This "measuring" of persons shows both God's protection and his ownership and suggests that the temple itself symbolizes the saints, as the NT elsewhere affirms (1 Cor. 3:16–17; Eph. 2:20–22; 1 Pet. 2:4–10; see Rev. 3:12; 21:22). John must **not measure the court outside**, because "the holy city" will be **given over to the nations** for trampling. Because this language echoes Jesus' prediction of Jerusalem's destruction (Luke 21:24; cf. Dan. 8:13), some believe that Revelation was written before A.D. 70 and predicted that disaster. Again, however, others do not think that "the holy city" (cf. Rev. 21:2; 22:19) refers to earthly Jerusalem. Instead, they understand it as a reference to the true church. They argue that 11:8 implies that the earthly Jerusalem that rejected its Messiah now belongs to "the great city," along with Sodom and Egypt (see 17:18). **Forty-two months** (see also 13:5) is equivalent to "1,260 days" (counting 30 days to a month; cf. 11:3; 12:6) and "a time, times, and half a time" (three and a half years; 12:14), which is one-half of a sabbatical-year cycle, symbolizing the brevity of the church's suffering, which lasts until Christ comes. These calculations of time echo Dan. 7:25; 12:7 and are thought by premillennialists to refer to a final "great tribulation" period (Rev. 7:14) during which the Antichrist will "make war" against the saints (13:7).

11:3–14 Scripture requires **two witnesses** to confirm testimony (Deut. 19:15; Matt. 18:16). The two witnesses here may symbolize the saints, as the parallel between Rev. 11:7 and 13:7 suggests. Wearing the **sackcloth** of repentance (cf. Isa. 37:1–2; Jonah 3:5; Matt. 11:21) to symbolize their message, they **prophesy** while the holy city suffers trampling (Rev. 11:2), the Messiah's mother is nourished in the wilderness (12:6, 14), and the beast wields its authority (13:5). Some scholars believe that these are two actual individuals who will appear at the end of history.

11:4 These are the two olive trees. In Zechariah's vision, the "two olive trees" symbolized "two anointed ones" (Zech. 4:11, 14): a royal leader to rebuild God's temple (Zech. 4:6–10) and a high priest to lead worship in it (Zech. 3:1–5). Thus the witnesses of Rev. 11:3 aptly represent all whom the Lamb has redeemed to serve as *priests* and rule as *kings* (1:6; 5:10).

11:5–6 The witnesses especially fulfill the church's *prophetic* role, pouring God's word as fiery judgment **from their mouth** (cf. 2 Kings 1:10–12), announcing drought like Elijah (1 Kings 17:1), and turning **waters . . . into blood** like Moses (Ex. 7:14–25).

11:7–10 Although the witnesses are invincible until **they have finished their testimony**, when their mission is accomplished the **beast** from the bottomless pit (13:1) will **conquer them**, not through spiritual seduction (God will soon vindicate them) but through martyrdom (11:7; cf. 13:7). The **great city** that **symbolically is called Sodom and Egypt** is identified as the site of the martyrs' death and their Lord's crucifixion. See also references to "the great city" in 16:19; 17:18; and five times in 18:10–21, where in these instances "the great city" is symbolically identified as "Babylon," a euphemism for Rome. In this verse (11:8), however, the symbol is apparently to be understood in a broader sense to include Jerusalem, where the two martyrs are killed and the "Lord was crucified." It is likely that John has merged Rome and Jerusalem here into one combined symbol, which would be fitting because Jerusalem was under the domination of Roman rule and because Jerusalem is identified as the capital of the new "unholy Roman Empire," where the Antichrist himself will establish his rule (cf. Matt. 24:15; 2 Thess. 2:3). "The great city" is further identified symbolically (or "spiritually"; see ESV footnote) as "Sodom" (known for its depravity and rebellion against God) and as "Egypt" (known for its persecution of God's people), both of which again correspond to the city of Jerusalem, both in its persecution and martyrdom of the prophets and its rejection and crucifixion of the Messiah. Thus the symbol of "the great city" had broad significance in John's day, but it also stands as a representative symbol for every empire that grasps after divine glory and afflicts Christ's church even in this present day. **three and a half days**. The celebration of the rebellious over the church's apparent demise through persecution will be short-lived.

11:11–14 they stood up on their feet . . . they went up to heaven in a cloud. If the two witnesses (v. 3) symbolize the church, then these verses

11 [f]Gen. 2:7; Ezek. 37:5, 9, 10, 14
12 [g]ch. 4:1 [h][ch. 12:5; 2 Kgs. 2:11] [i][Acts 1:9]
13 [j]ch. 6:12 [k][ch. 16:19] [l]ch. 14:7; 16:9; 19:7; Josh. 7:19 [m]2 Chr. 36:23
14 [n][ch. 8:13; 9:12]
15 [o]ch. 10:7 [p]ch. 16:17; 19:1; [Isa. 27:13] [q]ch. 12:10 [r]Ps. 2:2 (Gk.); Luke 9:20 [s]See Luke 1:33
16 [t]ch. 4:4 [u]See ch. 4:10
17 [v]ch. 16:5; [ch. 1:4, 8; 4:8] [w]ch. 19:6; Ps. 97:1
18 [x]Ps. 2:5; 110:5 [y]ch. 6:10; 20:12; [Dan. 7:10; 2 Thess. 1:6, 7] [z]ch. 19:5 [a][ch. 13:10]
19 [b]ch. 15:5 [c]See Heb. 9:4 [d]ch. 16:21

Chapter 12

1 [e][Ps. 104:2] [f][Song 6:10]
2 [g][Isa. 66:7-10; Mic. 4:10]

those who dwell on the earth. **11** But after the three and a half days [f]a breath of life from God
entered them, and they stood up on their feet, and great fear fell on those who saw them.
12 Then they heard a loud voice from heaven saying to them, [g]"Come up here!" And [h]they
went up to heaven [i]in a cloud, and their enemies watched them. **13** And at that hour there
was [j]a great earthquake, and [k]a tenth of the city fell. Seven thousand people were killed in
the earthquake, and the rest were terrified and [l]gave glory to [m]the God of heaven.
14 [n]The second woe has passed; behold, the third woe is soon to come.

The Seventh Trumpet

15 Then [o]the seventh angel blew his trumpet, and [p]there were loud voices in heaven,
saying, [q]"The kingdom of the world has become the kingdom of our Lord and of [r]his
Christ, and [s]he shall reign forever and ever." **16** And the twenty-four elders [t]who sit on their
thrones before God [u]fell on their faces and worshiped God, **17** saying,

"We give thanks to you, Lord God Almighty,
  [v]who is and who was,
for you have taken your great power
  and [w]begun to reign.
18 The nations raged,
  but [x]your wrath came,
  and [y]the time for the dead to be judged,
and for rewarding your servants,[1] the prophets and saints,
  and [z]those who fear your name,
  both small and great,
and [a]for destroying the destroyers of the earth."

19 Then [b]God's temple in heaven was opened, and [c]the ark of his covenant was seen within
his temple. There were flashes of lightning, rumblings,[2] peals of thunder, an earthquake,
and [d]heavy hail.

The Woman and the Dragon

12 And a great sign appeared in heaven: a woman [e]clothed with [f]the sun, with [f]the
moon under her feet, and on her head a crown of twelve stars. **2** She was pregnant and
[g]was crying out in birth pains and the agony of giving birth. **3** And another sign appeared

[1] Greek *bondservants* [2] Or *voices, or sounds*

predict the vindication of God's witnessing church in resurrection (cf. Ezek. 37:10) and enthronement in heaven (see Dan. 7:13; Acts 1:9). If they are two actual individuals, then they are miraculously resurrected at this point (cf. Rev. 11:7). Even if they are taken as literal people, their resurrection could still symbolize the resurrection of the saints either in the middle or at the end of the "great tribulation" period (7:14). As in 1:7, Acts 1:9, and several OT passages, the "cloud" symbolizes the mysterious active presence of God. This event will coincide with **a great earthquake** (Rev. 11:13; cf. 6:12; 16:18) that strikes terror in the hearts of survivors. The **third woe is soon to come**: the seventh and last trumpet (10:7; 11:15–18).

11:15–18 the seventh angel blew his trumpet. Nearly all futurists and many idealists (see Introduction: Schools of Interpretation) see this trumpet as heralding the second coming of Christ. As with the seventh seal (8:1–6), the scene now shifts from woes on earth to worship **in heaven**. Songs from the future consummation speak back through time to the suffering church, announcing the day when the world's kingdom **has become the kingdom of our Lord and of his Christ**, reversing the present when the **nations** and their rulers still "rage . . . against the LORD and against his Anointed" (Ps. 2:1–2). God's redemptive kingdom was inaugurated in Christ's first coming, death, and exaltation (Mark 1:15; 9:1; Acts 2:30–36). Here the elders celebrate a day still future, when God and his Christ have **begun** their unchallenged **reign** by judging **the dead** (foreshadowing Rev. 20:11–13), **rewarding** their **servants** (cf. 21:1–7; 22:1–5), and **destroying the destroyers of the earth** (cf. 20:14–15). Many futurists think that 11:18 skips forward beyond the millennium to the final judgment.

11:19–14:20 *The Woman, Her Son, the Dragon, and the Beasts: The Cosmic Conflict between Christ and Satan.* At the center point of the book, John records the vision that reveals the deepest dimension of the conflict in which the church is engaged: through his sacrificial blood Christ (the seed of the woman) has defeated Satan (the accuser of his people). In light of the cross, believers' sufferings, though intensely painful and inflicted by powerful opponents, are merely symptoms of the dragon's desperation, since "he knows that his time is short" (12:12).

11:19 *Heaven's Temple Opened.* A deeper opening of **God's temple in heaven** brings **the ark of his covenant** into view as John peers into the Most Holy Place itself, prepared to receive visions that expose the deepest perspective on the church's spiritual conflict.

12:1–17 Two signs in heaven—a **woman** who gives **birth**, and a **dragon** intent on destroying her offspring—dominate the two visions in this chapter. Twice John sees the dragon decisively defeated, and both descriptions of the battle's aftermath describe the woman's protection in the wilderness (vv. 6, 13–17). The first vision (vv. 1–6) portrays a decisive battle at the turning point of history when Christ's incarnation, obedience, sacrifice, and exaltation forever disqualified Satan as the accuser of believers (see v. 10). Some interpreters think the second vision (vv. 7–17) also represents the same series of events, while others think it portrays events at the beginning of the great tribulation.

12:1–6 *The Woman's Son Defeats the Dragon.* Christ, the promised son of Israel and of Eve, though apparently a defenseless newborn before the mighty dragon, has been caught up to reign with God.

12:1–2 The woman's description as a **great sign** in **heaven** and her clothing with **sun**, **moon**, and **twelve stars** show that she symbolizes Israel (cf. Joseph's dream, Gen. 37:9).

12:3 The **great red dragon** is "that ancient serpent, the devil and Satan" (v. 9; cf. 20:2; Gen. 3:1–15; Isa. 27:1). Its **seven heads** with **seven diadems**

in heaven: behold, a great [h]red dragon, [i]with seven heads and [j]ten horns, and on his heads
[k]seven diadems. 4 His tail swept down [l]a third of the stars of heaven and [m]cast them to
the earth. And the dragon stood before the woman who was about to give birth, so that
when she bore her child [n]he might devour it. 5 She gave birth to a male child, [o]one who is
to rule all the nations with a rod of iron, but her child was [p]caught up to God and to his
throne, 6 and the woman fled into the wilderness, where she has a place prepared by God,
in which she is to be nourished for [q]1,260 days.

Satan Thrown Down to Earth

7 Now war arose in heaven, [r]Michael and [s]his angels fighting against the dragon. And
the dragon and his angels fought back, 8 but he was defeated, and there was no longer any
place for them in heaven. 9 And [t]the great dragon was thrown down, [u]that ancient serpent,
who is called the devil and Satan, [v]the deceiver of the whole world—[w]he was thrown down
to the earth, and his angels were thrown down with him. 10 And I heard a loud voice in
heaven, saying, "Now [x]the salvation and the power and the kingdom of our God and the
authority of his Christ have come, for the accuser of our brothers[1] has been thrown down,
[y]who accuses them day and night before our God. 11 And [z]they have conquered him by
the blood of the Lamb and by the word of their testimony, for [a]they loved not their lives
[b]even unto death. 12 Therefore, [c]rejoice, O heavens and you who dwell in them! But [d]woe
to you, O earth and sea, for the devil has come down to you in great wrath, because [e]he
knows that his time is short!"

13 And when the dragon saw that he had been thrown down to the earth, he pursued
[f]the woman who had given birth to the male child. 14 But the woman was given the two
[g]wings of the great eagle so that she might fly from the serpent [h]into the wilderness, to
the place where she is to be nourished [i]for a time, and times, and half a time. 15 The serpent
poured water [j]like a river out of his mouth after the woman, to sweep her away with a
flood. 16 But the earth came to the help of the woman, and the earth opened its mouth

[1] *Or brothers and sisters*

3 [h][ch. 17:3; Isa. 27:1] [i]ch. 13:1; 17:9, 12 [j]Dan. 7:7 [k][ch. 19:12]
4 [l]See ch. 8:7 [m]Dan. 8:10 [n][Matt. 2:16]
5 [o]Matt. 2:6; See ch. 2:27 [p]See 2 Cor. 12:2
6 [q]ch. 11:2; 13:5
7 [r]See Jude 9 [s]See Matt. 25:41
9 [t]Luke 10:18; John 12:31 [u]ch. 20:2; Gen. 3:1 [v]ch. 20:3, 10; [ch. 13:14; John 8:44] [w]See ch. 9:1
10 [x]ch. 7:10; 19:1 [y]Job 1:9; 2:5; Zech. 3:1
11 [z]ch. 15:2; [Rom. 16:20]; See John 16:33 [a]Luke 14:26; John 12:25 [b]ch. 2:10
12 [c]ch. 18:20; Ps. 96:11; Isa. 44:23; 49:13 [d]ch. 8:13 [e][Matt. 8:29]; See ch. 10:6
13 [f]ver. 5
14 [g]See Ex. 19:4 [h]ver. 6 [i]Dan. 7:25; 12:7; See ver. 6
15 [j][Isa. 59:19]

and **ten horns** symbolize great power (cf. Dan. 7:6–7). Cf. the description of the beast (Rev. 13:1).

12:4 His tail swept down a third of the stars of heaven. Evil spirits (demons) in league with Satan share his defeat and downfall before the forces of God (cf. vv. 7–9). Some interpreters think this refers to the original fall of Satan, taking one-third of the angels with him (cf. 2 Pet. 2:4; Jude 6; perhaps Isa. 14:12–15). The dragon's intent to **devour** the woman's child at birth recalls Gen. 3:15, which predicts that the woman's offspring will bruise the serpent's head as the serpent bruises his heel.

12:5 This **male child**, the promised Messiah who is born to **rule all the nations with a rod of iron** (cf. Ps. 2:9), is not destroyed by the dragon but is exalted to God's **throne** (cf. Acts 2:33–36; Rev. 3:21). Yet the second vision (12:7–17) will reveal that the Messiah's suffering was integral to his victory (v. 11; cf. 5:9–10). The "rod of iron" (also 2:27; 19:15) is not a royal scepter (as in some translations) but the shepherd's club, here used to shatter the nations like pottery (cf. Ps. 2:9).

12:6 The child's mother **fled into the wilderness**, a setting in which God's people are utterly dependent on him but are protected from the dragon's rage (vv. 13–14). There, she was **nourished** by God's provision, as were Israel (Ex. 16:13–18) and Elijah (1 Kings 17:6; 19:5–8). Some scholars think the time period symbolized as **1,260 days** (or "a time, and times, and half a time," Rev. 12:14; cf. 11:2–3) began with Christ's ascension and will end when God withdraws his restraint on the dragon's power to deceive the nations and gather them against the church (20:7–10). Others understand the "1,260 days" (three and a half years) to represent the second half of the great tribulation, and to be the same period as the second half of Daniel's seventieth week (Dan. 9:27). On this view, the woman's fleeing into the wilderness indicates that during the great tribulation Jewish believers will be persecuted by the Antichrist and will flee into the wilderness (see note on Rev. 11:1–2).

12:7–17 *Michael and Heaven's Armies Defeat the Dragon.* The second of the two visions of vv. 1–17 reveals more detail about Christ's victory and the dragon's ongoing attempt to destroy the people of God.

12:7 In Daniel, **Michael** is the spiritual prince and guardian of God's people (Dan. 10:13, 21; 12:1). Jude 9 identifies Michael as the archangel, attributing to him words that echo the angel of the Lord's answer to Satan the accuser (Zech. 3:2). Many futurists think Michael's battle with the **dragon** marks the beginning of the "time of trouble" (Dan. 12:1), which is also the great tribulation.

12:8–9 The victory of Michael and the holy angels over the **dragon** and its coconspirators may symbolize the triumphant power of Jesus' cross (cf. Col. 2:15), or a subsequent defeat of demonic forces flowing from Christ's victory at the cross, or the original casting of Satan and his demons out of heaven (see note on Rev. 12:4). **The devil** (Gk.) and **Satan** (Hb.) describe a legal opponent, an accuser at law (see note on vv. 10–11). Many futurists think **he was thrown down to the earth** indicates intensified demonic activity on earth during the great tribulation.

12:10–11 The dragon's expulsion from heaven shows that Satan cannot press charges as **the accuser of our brothers** because **the Lamb** shed his **blood** for them and they maintain **their testimony** of trust **even unto death**. Although "conquered" by the beast physically in death (11:7; 13:7), in fact the martyrs have conquered both the beast (15:2) and the dragon that empowers it. **They have conquered him** is set in ironic and beautiful contrast to 13:7.

12:12 his time is short. Jesus' death and exaltation inaugurated "the kingdom of our God" (v. 10) and guaranteed the certain and approaching demise of Satan's tyranny. All the demonic activity here and in the Gospels is connected to Satan's frustrated anger.

12:14 two wings of the great eagle. A metaphor of the exodus (see Ex. 19:4) becomes an image of God's care for his church, exposed in the wilderness yet guarded and nourished in its pilgrimage. **a time, and times, and half a time**. This half-sabbatical period, derived from Dan. 7:25, signifies the brevity of the saints' suffering and of their persecutors' power (see note on Rev. 11:1–2; also 12:6; 13:7).

12:15 water like a river. The serpent tries to destroy the people of God by lies and false teaching from its mouth, as it had deceived Eve (Gen. 3:13).

17[k]ch. 11:7; 13:7 [l]Gen. 3:15 [m]ch. 14:12; See 1 John 2:3 [n]ch. 1:2; 6:9; 19:10

Chapter 13

1[o]Dan. 7:3; See ch. 12:3 [p]ch. 17:3
2[q]Dan. 7:6 [r]Dan. 7:5 [s]Dan. 7:4 [t]ver. 4, 11; [Luke 4:6] [u]ch. 16:10
3[v][ch. 17:8]
4[w][ch. 18:18]
5[x]Dan. 7:8, 11, 20; 11:36; [2 Thess. 2:4] [y]ch. 11:2; 12:6
7[z]ch. 11:7; 12:17; Dan. 7:21
8[a]See ch. 3:10 [b]See ch. 3:5 [c]See ch. 5:6 [d][Acts 2:23; 1 Pet. 1:19, 20]
9[e]See ch. 2:7

and swallowed the river that the dragon had poured from his mouth. 17 Then the dragon
became furious with the woman and went off [k]to make war on the rest of [l]her offspring,
[m]on those who keep the commandments of God and hold to [n]the testimony of Jesus. And
he stood[1] on the sand of the sea.

The First Beast

13 And I saw a beast rising out of the sea, [o]with ten horns and seven heads, with ten
diadems on its horns and [p]blasphemous names on its heads. 2 And the beast that I
saw was [q]like a leopard; its feet were like [r]a bear's, and its mouth was like [s]a lion's mouth.
And to it [t]the dragon gave his power and [u]his throne and great authority. 3 One of its heads
seemed to have a mortal wound, but its mortal wound was healed, and [v]the whole earth
marveled as they followed the beast. 4 And they worshiped the dragon, for he had given
his authority to the beast, and they worshiped the beast, saying, [w]"Who is like the beast,
and who can fight against it?"

5 And the beast was given [x]a mouth uttering haughty and blasphemous words, and it
was allowed to exercise authority for [y]forty-two months. 6 It opened its mouth to utter
blasphemies against God, blaspheming his name and his dwelling,[2] that is, those who
dwell in heaven. 7 Also it was allowed [z]to make war on the saints and to conquer them.[3]
And authority was given it over every tribe and people and language and nation, 8 and all
[a]who dwell on earth will worship it, everyone whose name has not been written before
the foundation of the world in [b]the book of life of [c]the Lamb [d]who was slain. 9 [e]If anyone
has an ear, let him hear:

[1] Some manuscripts *And I stood*, connecting the sentence with 13:1 [2] Or *tabernacle* [3] Some manuscripts omit this sentence

12:17 Having failed to destroy the Messiah (cf. 12:4–5) and his mother (i.e., Israel; see note on 12:1–2), the frustrated dragon makes war on **the rest of her offspring**—that is, war on either the church on earth down through the ages (including the last three and a half years), or, as some hold, war on believing Israel (or the remnant in ch. 7). These include all who **hold to the testimony of Jesus**—that is, all who persevere in faithfulness and obedience to the gospel while under the persistent attack of Satan. The dragon's weapon is the "beast" that emerges from the sea to wage war on the saints (13:2, 7).

13:1–10 *The Beast from the Sea.* As the dragon stands on the seashore (12:17), a beast emerges from the sea. This beast is sometimes identified with the Antichrist (see 1 John 2:18, 22; 4:3; 2 John 7) or the man of lawlessness (2 Thess. 2:3–12). Its blasphemous words and demand for worship reinforce the connections between these predictions of a final, future opponent to Christ's reign. Yet the imagery of Daniel 7 that appears in the description of the beast shows that it represents not only a future individual but also present world powers that wage Satan's war against the Lamb and his church. Most dispensationalists, and many other futurists, think the first beast (Rev. 13:1–10) is a political world leader and the second beast (vv. 11–18) is his religious counterpart, who enforces worship of the first beast.

13:1–2 The **beast** looks **like a leopard** but has feet **like a bear's**, a mouth **like a lion's mouth**, and **ten horns**, and it wages "war on the saints" (v. 7). Thus it resembles all four beasts that Daniel saw emerge from the sea before the Son of Man appeared (Dan. 7:1–8, 21). As those beasts symbolized kingdoms (Dan. 7:17, 23), so this beast, a composite of them all, represents every human empire—Egypt, Assyria, Babylon, Persia, Greece, Rome, and their successors—that demands absolute allegiance and trust, enforcing its demand with coercion. Its 10 horns and **seven heads** mirror those of the dragon (Rev. 12:3), who gives the beast its **great authority**.

13:3 seemed to have a mortal wound. Lit., "as slain to death." The beast falsely imitates the Lamb, "standing, as though it had been slain" (5:6; cf. chart to the right). Rome, the manifestation of the beast in John's day, seemed to have been mortally wounded by Nero's suicide (A.D. 68) and the civil chaos that followed, but experienced a "resurrection" in the reigns of Vespasian and his sons Titus and Domitian. Then in Domitian's reign (A.D. 81–96), Nero's beastly persecution of the church also revived. Many interpreters think this verse also predicts a future remarkable recovery of the Antichrist from a deadly wound, a deceptive attempt to parallel Christ's resurrection.

13:4 Who is like the beast . . . ? The worshipers' question copies Israel's praise of the Lord after the exodus (Ex. 15:11), reinforcing the beast's arrogant claim to divine honors. It also mirrors the acclamation often given to Caesar as he entered cities.

13:5 was given . . . was allowed. See note on 9:1. The beast uttered **haughty and blasphemous words**, like the horn (king) on the fourth beast in Daniel's vision (Dan. 7:20, 25). **forty-two months**. See note on Rev. 11:1–2; also 12:6, 14. Many futurists think this is the second half of the great tribulation.

13:6 The identification of God's **dwelling** as **those who dwell in heaven** confirms that the measured sanctuary (11:1) symbolized the worshipers in it. Likewise, the "holy city" is the Lamb's church-bride (21:2, 9–27; see Eph. 2:22).

13:7 to make war on the saints and to conquer them. The martyrdom of believers seems to be their defeat, but their death-defying faithfulness conquers the dragon and the beast (12:11; 15:2).

13:8 written before the foundation of the world in the book of life of the Lamb who was slain. Before creation and by grace alone, God chose individuals to be redeemed by Christ's death (see Eph. 1:4–14; and note on Eph. 1:11). God's registry of life appears in Ex. 32:32–33; Dan. 12:1; Luke 10:20; Rev. 3:5; 17:8; 20:15. Those not enrolled in the Lamb's book blindly worship the beast and will be cast with it into the lake of fire. The parallel expression in 17:8 shows that "before the foundation of the world" is best taken to modify "written" rather than "slain" as in some translations.

13:9–10 Because **captivity** and **sword** are God's ordained route to victory

Satanic Imitations of God's Reality

God's Reality		Satanic Imitation	
the real Trinity (Father, Son [Lamb], Spirit)	1:4–5	the false trinity (dragon, beast, false prophet)	16:13; 20:10
Lamb standing, as though it had been slain	5:6	many-headed beast with mortal wound healed	13:3
sealing of the saints	7:2–3	mark of the beast	13:16–18
Bride in white	19:7–8	prostitute in purple and scarlet	17:1–6

10 [f]If anyone is to be taken captive,
to captivity he goes;
[g]if anyone is to be slain with the sword,
with the sword must he be slain.

[h]Here is a call for the endurance and faith of the saints.

The Second Beast

11 Then [i]I saw another beast rising out of the earth. It had two horns like a lamb and it
spoke like a dragon. 12 It exercises all the authority of the first beast in its presence,[1] and
makes the earth and its inhabitants worship the first beast, [j]whose mortal wound was
healed. 13 [k]It performs great signs, even [l]making fire come down from heaven to earth
in front of people, 14 and by the signs that it is allowed to work in the presence of[2] the
beast [m]it deceives those who dwell on earth, telling them to make an image for the beast
[n]that was wounded by the sword and yet lived. 15 And it was allowed to give breath to
the image of the beast, so that the image of the beast might even speak and might cause
those who would not [o]worship the image of the beast [p]to be slain. 16 Also it causes all,
both small and great, both rich and poor, both free and slave,[3] [q]to be marked on the right
hand or the forehead, 17 so that no one can buy or sell unless he has the mark, that is, [r]the
name of the beast or [s]the number of its name. 18 [t]This calls for wisdom: let the one who
has understanding calculate the number of the beast, for it is the number [u]of a man, and
his number is 666.[4]

The Lamb and the 144,000

14 Then I looked, and behold, on [v]Mount Zion [w]stood the Lamb, and with him [x]144,000
who [y]had his name and his Father's name written [z]on their foreheads. 2 And I heard
a voice from heaven [a]like the roar of many waters and [b]like the sound of loud thunder.
The voice I heard was like the sound of [c]harpists playing on their harps, 3 and they were

[1] *Or on its behalf* [2] *Or on behalf of* [3] *Greek bondservant* [4] *Some manuscripts 616*

10 [f][Isa. 33:1; Jer. 15:2; 43:11] [g]See Gen. 9:6 [h]ch. 14:12
11 [i][ver. 1, 14; ch. 16:13]
12 [j]ver. 3
13 [k]ch. 16:14; 19:20; Deut. 13:1-3; Matt. 24:24; 2 Thess. 2:9-11 [l]ch. 20:9; 1 Kgs. 18:38; 2 Kgs. 1:10, 12; Luke 9:54
14 [m][ch. 12:9] [n]ver. 3, 12
15 [o]ch. 14:9, 11; 16:2; 19:20; 20:4 [p][ch. 16:6]
16 [q][ch. 7:3]; See Gal. 6:17
17 [r]ch. 14:11 [s]ch. 15:2
18 [t][ch. 17:9] [u][ch. 21:17]

Chapter 14

1 [v]Ps. 2:6; Heb. 12:22 [w]See ch. 5:6 [x]ch. 7:4 [y]ch. 3:12 [z]ch. 7:3
2 [a]See ch. 1:15 [b]ch. 6:1; 19:6 [c]ch. 5:8; 15:2

for his saints, they must practice **endurance**. Perseverance is a major theme in Revelation (12:17; 14:12; 16:15; 17:14; 21:7–8; 22:7, 10, 12, 14; see also "overcoming" in the seven letters, chs. 2–3, and chart, p. 2468).

13:11–18 *The False Prophet from the Land.* A second beast rose out of the earth to enlist worshipers for the first beast through lying words and miracles. Later called the "false prophet" (16:13; 19:20), this beast wields power through deceptive words. In John's day the imperial cult in Asia fostered "worship" of the empire and the emperor as divine savior and lawgiver. The abuse of religious devotion to manipulate thoughtless allegiance to the state is an ageless phenomenon.

13:11 The second beast resembles the Lamb, but its lying words expose its real nature; it is **like a dragon** (cf. 12:15; 16:13–14; 19:20).

13:13 making fire come down from heaven. The false prophet (the second beast) counterfeits God's judgments to bolster the specious claim that the first beast is divine (cf. 1 Kings 18:38; 2 Kings 1:10; Rev. 8:7; 11:5).

13:14–15 Since idols "have mouths but cannot speak" (Ps. 115:5), the impression that the first beast's image has **breath** and **might even speak** may simply be another hoax, one with which it deceives those who dwell on the earth. But it is more likely that this describes some kind of miracle worked by demonic power yet still subject to God's sovereign control (**it is allowed**, Rev. 13:14; cf. 19:20; Deut. 13:1–4; 2 Thess. 2:9). Those who refuse to worship the symbol of the state, whether bowing to Nebuchadnezzar's statue (Daniel 3) or burning incense to the Roman emperor, will be **slain**.

13:16–17 marked on the right hand or the forehead. The Israelites bore God's law on their hands and foreheads to signify his authority over their deeds and thoughts (Deut. 6:8). Neither the beast's mark nor the seal of God on believers' foreheads (cf. Rev. 7:3; 14:1; cf. also Ex. 28:36–38; Ezek. 9:4) have to be understood as physical features, though they may be that. Both symbolize the spiritual control of heart allegiance and behavior, either by the beast or by the Lamb; but God's seal secures safety.

13:18 The **number of the beast**, which is **666**, may symbolize creaturely deficiency as **the number of a man** in contrast to divine completeness (symbolized by seven). The invitation to one with understanding to **calculate** this number, however, suggests the use of gematria, an ancient code using the numerical values of letters. Both "beast" and "Nero Caesar," written in Hebrew characters, add up to 666, but many interpreters expect a future, greater fulfillment in a world ruler who is violently opposed to God and his people.

14:1–15:8 The vision sequence leading to the seven last plagues (which will be described as "bowls" of God's wrath, 16:1–21) opens and closes with scenes of a heavenly choir singing praise to God (14:1–5; 15:2–4). Between these anthems John sees three angels who announce impending judgment (14:6–13) and three who order and execute harvests (14:15–20). At the center, between the three announcing angels and the three harvesting angels, John sees a seventh figure, **one like a son of man**, gathering his grain from the earth (14:14). Despite the beast's cruel persecution (ch. 13), these visions (like those in chs. 7 and 10–11) provide reassurance that God and the Lamb rule, and that martyrs already celebrate victory.

14:1–5 *The Lamb and His Sealed Victors.* John's second vision of the 144,000 (cf. 7:1–8) interprets the seal they had received and the protection it provided.

14:1 Mount Zion. Fulfilling Ps. 2:6, the Lamb stands in glory on God's holy hill in heaven (cf. Heb. 12:22), accompanied by his army. The sound of their harps and voices descends from heaven like a waterfall's thundering cascades as they sing "before the throne, the four living creatures," and "the elders" (Rev. 4:2–8; 7:9–12). The seal on their **foreheads** (see note on 13:16–17) is the **name** of the Lamb and of his Father—a token of possession and protection by God, promised to every conqueror in the spiritual war (3:12). Most dispensationalists see these **144,000** as the same group mentioned in 7:4: Jewish believers who have trusted in Christ as their Messiah during the great tribulation.

14:2 The singers with their **harps** will reappear beside the sea of glass (15:2–4; see 4:6); their song indicates that they are redeemed.

14:3 The **new song** celebrates God's triumph over sin through the Lamb (5:9; 15:3), just as the Lord's prior victories were celebrated in new songs (Ps. 96:1; 98:1; 144:9). Their song belongs only to those who have experienced the Lamb's redemption (Ps. 107:1–3), into whose salvation angels "long to look" (1 Pet. 1:12). This is another indication that **144,000** should not be taken as a literal number; they represent those who have been redeemed (see notes on Rev. 7:1–17; 7:4–8).

singing [d]a new song before the throne and before the four living creatures and before
the elders. [e]No one could learn that song except the 144,000 who had been redeemed
from the earth. 4 It is these who have not defiled themselves with women, for [f]they are
virgins. It is these [g]who follow the Lamb wherever he goes. These have been redeemed
from mankind as [h]firstfruits for God and the Lamb, 5 and [i]in their mouth no lie was found,
for they are [j]blameless.

The Messages of the Three Angels

6 Then I saw another angel [k]flying directly overhead, with an eternal gospel to proclaim
to [l]those who dwell on earth, to every nation and tribe and language and people. 7 And
he said with a loud voice, [m]"Fear God and [n]give him glory, because the hour of his judgment has come, and [o]worship him who made heaven and earth, the sea and the [p]springs
of water."

8 Another angel, a second, followed, saying, [q]"Fallen, fallen is [r]Babylon the great, [s]she
who made all nations drink [t]the wine of the passion[1] of her sexual immorality."

9 And another angel, a third, followed them, saying with a loud voice, "If anyone [u]wor-
ships the beast and its image and receives [v]a mark on his forehead or on his hand, 10 he
also will drink [w]the wine of God's wrath, [x]poured full strength into the cup of his anger,
and [y]he will be tormented with fire and sulfur in the presence of the holy angels and in
the presence of the Lamb. 11 And [z]the smoke of their torment goes up forever and ever,
and [a]they have no rest, day or night, these [u]worshipers of the beast and its image, and
whoever receives the mark of its name."

12 [b]Here is a call for the endurance of the saints, those who [c]keep the commandments
of God and their faith in Jesus.[2]

13 And I heard a voice from heaven saying, "Write this: [d]Blessed are the dead [e]who die
in the Lord from now on." "Blessed indeed," says the Spirit, [f]"that they may rest from their
labors, for their deeds follow them!"

The Harvest of the Earth

14 Then I looked, and behold, a white cloud, and seated on the cloud one [g]like a son of
man, [h]with a golden crown on his head, and a sharp sickle in his hand. 15 And another
angel [i]came out of the temple, calling with a loud voice to him who sat on the cloud,
[j]"Put in your sickle, and reap, for the hour to reap has come, for [k]the harvest of the earth
is fully ripe." 16 So he who sat on the cloud swung his sickle across the earth, and the earth
was reaped.

[1] *Or* wrath [2] *Greek* and the faith of Jesus

3 [d]ch. 5:9 [e][ch. 2:17; 19:12]
4 [f]2 Cor. 11:2 [g][ch. 3:4; 17:14] [h]James 1:18
5 [i]Zeph. 3:13; [Ps. 32:2; Isa. 63:8; John 1:47] [j]See Jude 24
6 [k]ch. 8:13 [l][ch. 3:10]
7 [m]ch. 15:4 [n]See ch. 11:13 [o]Neh. 9:6; See ch. 4:11 [p]ch. 8:10; 16:4
8 [q]ch. 18:2; Isa. 21:9; Jer. 51:8 [r]ch. 16:19; 17:5; 18:10; [Dan. 4:30] [s]Jer. 51:7 [t]ch. 18:3
9 [u]See ch. 13:15 [v]ch. 13:16
10 [w]ch. 16:19; See Job 21:20 [x][ch. 18:6; Isa. 1:22] [y]ch. 20:10
11 [z]Isa. 34:10; [ch. 18:18; 19:3; Gen. 19:28] [a]ch. 4:8 [u][See ver. 9 above]
12 [b]ch. 13:10 [c]ch. 12:17
13 [d]ch. 20:6; [Eccles. 4:2] [e]1 Cor. 15:18; 1 Thess. 4:16 [f]ch. 6:11
14 [g]See ch. 1:13 [h]ch. 6:2
15 [i][ch. 15:6; 16:17] [j]ver. 18; Joel 3:13; Mark 4:29; [Matt. 13:39] [k]Jer. 51:33

14:4–5 have not defiled themselves with women, for they are virgins. The spiritual purity of those who bear the Lamb's name is symbolized by the sexual self-denial that consecrated Israel for the wars that God commanded (cf. Deut. 23:9–11; 1 Sam. 21:5). Although portrayed as celibate males, the 144,000 (Rev. 14:3) signify believers of both sexes who, dying in faith, are gathered as **firstfruits for God**, foreshadowing a greater harvest. **in their mouth no lie was found**. They resemble Jesus, the **blameless** servant of the Lord (cf. Isa. 53:9).

14:6–13 *Angelic Announcements of Judgment.* Three angels announce the hour of God's judgment, the fall of Babylon, and the eternal punishment of the beast's worshipers.

14:6–7 The flying angel proclaims **an eternal gospel**. Its command that **every nation** is to **fear, give . . . glory** to, and **worship** God the Creator means that the long-awaited reign of God and his Christ is about to be consummated (cf. 11:15–18).

14:8 Another angel announces that **Babylon** is **fallen** (echoing Isa. 21:9) before Babylon even appears in the narrative (Rev. 16:19; 17:1–18). As ancient Babylon had carried Judah into captivity, so in John's day Rome was the pagan power with "dominion over the kings of the earth" (17:18) that oppressed Christ's people (17:6). Yet Revelation's "Babylon" transcends Rome, since its fall awaits the end of history (15:1; 16:17–19). **the passion of her sexual immorality**. Babylon the prostitute represents society's allure of material prosperity and pleasure, seducing the unwary into adultery against the Lord.

14:9–11 A **third** angel announces that the beast's worshipers (like the prostitute Babylon, 16:19) will **drink the wine of God's wrath** and endure constant torment in eternal restlessness. **The smoke of their torment goes up forever and ever** shows that hell is eternal, and that the wicked are not annihilated and put out of existence at death.

14:12–13 Blessed. Revelation's second of seven benedictions (see chart, p. 2484). Saints who heed God's call to **endurance**, keeping God's **commandments** and **their faith in Jesus**, are **blessed** at death with **rest from their labors**.

14:14–20 *Harvests of Earth and Vine.* Two reapers appear in heaven, sharp sickles in hand. Angels emerge from the temple with God's directive, "Put in your sickle, and reap." First "one like a son of man" gathers the grain of the earth, then an angel gathers grapes from the earth's vine, to be crushed in the "winepress of the wrath of God." Although both harvests could signify either God's judgment on the wicked or Christ's gathering of his saints, probably the grain harvest shows the Son of Man's gathering of believers (cf. Matt. 13:30) and the grape harvest envisions the bloody destruction of the wicked. Cf. the Lord's gathering of nations in the valley of judgment because the harvest is ready for reaping (Joel 3:12–13).

14:14 One like a son of man, seated on the cloud and wearing **a golden crown** (cf. Dan. 7:13–14; Rev. 1:7, 13) is Jesus, the Lord of the harvest. He came first as gospel sower (Matt. 13:37) but will return as just reaper.

14:15–16 The **harvest of the earth** refers to wheat or barley, for **ripe** (Gk.

17 Then another angel came out of the temple in heaven, and he too had a sharp sickle.
18 And another angel came out from the altar, [l]the angel who has authority over the fire,
and he called with a loud voice to the one who had the sharp sickle, "Put in your sickle and
gather the clusters from the vine of the earth, [m]for its grapes are ripe." 19 So the angel swung
his sickle across the earth and gathered the grape harvest of the earth and threw it into the
great [n]winepress of the wrath of God. 20 And [o]the winepress was trodden [p]outside the city,
and blood flowed from the winepress, as high as [q]a horse's bridle, for 1,600 stadia.[1]

The Seven Angels with Seven Plagues

15 Then [r]I saw another sign in heaven, great and amazing, [s]seven angels with seven
plagues, which are the last, for with them the wrath of God is finished.
2 And I saw [t]what appeared to be a sea of glass mingled with fire—and also those [u]who
had conquered the beast and its image and [v]the number of its name, standing beside the
sea of glass [w]with harps of God in their hands. 3 And they sing [x]the song of Moses, [y]the
servant[2] of God, and the song of the Lamb, saying,

[z]"Great and amazing are your deeds,
O Lord God the Almighty!
[a]Just and true are your ways,
O King of the nations![3]
4 [b]Who will not fear, O Lord,
and glorify your name?
For you alone are [c]holy.
[d]All nations will come
and worship you,
for your righteous acts have been revealed."

5 After this I looked, and [e]the sanctuary of [f]the tent[4] of witness in heaven was opened,
6 and out of the sanctuary came [g]the seven angels with the seven plagues, clothed in pure,
bright [i]linen, [j]with golden sashes around their chests. 7 And one of [k]the four living creatures

[1] About 184 miles; a *stadion* was about 607 feet or 185 meters [2] Greek *bondservant* [3] Some manuscripts *the ages* [4] Or *tabernacle*

18 [l][ch. 16:8] [m]Joel 3:13
19 [n]ch. 19:15
20 [o]Isa. 63:3; Lam. 1:15 [p][Heb. 13:12] [q][ch. 19:14]

Chapter 15

1 [r][ch. 12:1, 3] [s]ch. 16:1; 17:1; 21:9
2 [t]ch. 4:6; 21:18, 21 [u]ch. 12:11 [v]ch. 13:17 [w]ch. 5:8; 14:2
3 [x]Ex. 15:1; Deut. 31:30 [y]See Heb. 3:5 [z]Deut. 32:3, 4; [Job 37:5; Ps. 111:2; 139:14; 145:17] [a]ch. 16:7; Hos. 14:9
4 [b]ch. 14:7; Mal. 2:2 [c]ch. 16:5; Heb. 7:26 [d]See Ps. 86:9
5 [e]ch. 11:19 [f]Ex. 38:21; Num. 1:50; Acts 7:44
6 [g]See ver. 1 [i]ch. 19:8 [j]ch. 1:13
7 [k]ch. 4:6

xēraino, "to dry up, be ripe"; a different word from that used of "ripe" grapes in v. 18) describes dried heads of grain. Christ's harvest, of which the martyrs were firstfruits (v. 4), is gathered safely into his barns (Matt. 3:12).

14:17–20 The second harvest involves not only cutting grape clusters from the vine but also crushing them in God's winepress. **Trodden** translates Greek *pateō*, rendered "trample" in 11:2. The Lord will trample nations that have trampled God's holy city, as Isaiah foretold (Isa. 63:1–6). Their blood is shed **outside the city** (probably Jerusalem), where all defiled things belong (cf. Rev. 21:27).

15:1–16:21 *The Bowls of God's Final Wrath.* Another view of the victors' choir prepares for the seven "last" plagues, envisioned as "bowls full of the wrath of God" poured out on earth's inhabitants. Futurists see these bowls as representing future global judgments unlike anything seen before in history. They occur at the end of the great tribulation period and culminate in the battle of Armageddon (16:14–16), just prior to Christ's return to establish his millennial kingdom.

15:1–8 *Heaven's Sanctuary Filled with Glory.* Just as earlier vision cycles began with an opening of God's heavenly sanctuary (4:1; 8:1; 11:19), so the cycle of bowls containing the last plagues, in which God's wrath on rebels is completed, is preceded by a scene of celebratory worship offered by believers who share the Lamb's victory.

15:1 another sign in heaven. Like the woman and the dragon (12:1, 3), these **angels** signify another turning point in the war between Christ and Satan: the completion of God's triumph in the destruction of his enemies.

15:2–4 The **harps of God** and the **song of the Lamb** suggest to some that this choir is the same as the 144,000 (the redeemed people of God) who appeared with the Lamb before God's throne (7:9–12; 14:1–3). Others see them as those converted and perhaps martyred during the great tribulation. They **conquered the beast** by holding fast to their faith even when threatened with death (12:11). The **sea of glass** is the transparent pavement surrounding God's throne (cf. 4:6; Ex. 24:10; Ezek. 1:22).

15:3–4 The song of Moses, celebrating Israel's exodus from Egypt (Ex. 15:1–18), is fulfilled in **the song of the Lamb**, which tells of a greater redemption of a new kingdom of priests (Rev. 5:9–10). A later song of Moses extolled the Lord whose **ways** are **just** (Deut. 32:1–43; esp. v. 4). In keeping with the angel's eternal gospel (Rev. 14:7), the **King of the nations** will be feared, glorified, and worshiped by **all nations** (Ps. 86:9; Jer. 10:7) for his **righteous acts** of judgment (Ps. 98:2).

15:5–8 Seven angels emerge from the **opened . . . sanctuary** (cf. 11:19), the inner chamber, of **the tent of witness in heaven** (cf. Heb. 8:2–5; 9:11–12) to execute God's final sequence of judgments upon a defiant world.

15:6 pure, bright linen. A preview of the bride's holy beauty (19:7–8). The angels' **golden sashes** resemble that of the Son of Man (1:13; see Dan. 10:5).

The Seven Benedictions

Blessed is the one who reads aloud, hears, and keeps the words of this prophecy	1:3
Blessed are the dead who die in the Lord	14:13
Blessed is the one who stays awake, keeping his garments on	16:15
Blessed are those who are invited to the marriage supper of the Lamb	19:9
Blessed and holy is the one who shares in the first resurrection	20:6
Blessed is the one who keeps the words of the prophecy of this book	22:7
Blessed are those who wash their robes	22:14

7 [l]ch. 5:8] [m]ch. 1:18; 4:9; 5:13
8 [n]Ex. 40:34; Isa. 6:4; Hag. 2:7; [1 Kgs. 8:10, 11; 2 Chr. 5:13, 14] [o]Ex. 40:35; 1 Kgs. 8:11
Chapter 16
1 [p]See ch. 15:1 [q]Ps. 79:6; Jer. 10:25; Zeph. 3:8 [r]ch. 15:7
2 [s]ver. 11; Ex. 9:9-11 [t]ch. 13:16
3 [u]ch. 8:8 [v]ch. 8:9
4 [w]ch. 8:10 [x]Ex. 7:17-20
5 [y]Jer. 12:1; John 17:25 [z]ch. 15:4 [a]ch. 11:17; [ch. 1:4, 8; 4:8]
6 [b]ch. 18:24; [ch. 13:15] [c]ch. 11:18 [d][Isa. 49:26; Luke 11:49, 50]
7 [e]ch. 6:9 [f]ch. 15:3; 19:2; [Ps. 119:137]
8 [g]ch. 9:17; [ch. 14:18]
9 [h]ver. 11, 21 [i][Dan. 5:22]; See ch. 2:21 [j][Dan. 5:23]; See ch. 11:13
10 [k]ch. 13:2 [l]ch. 9:2; Ex. 10:21
11 [m]ch. 11:13 [n]ver. 2 [o]See ch. 2:21

gave to the seven angels seven [l]golden bowls full of the wrath of God [m]who lives forever
and ever, 8 and [n]the sanctuary was filled with smoke from the glory of God and from his
power, and [o]no one could enter the sanctuary until the seven plagues of the seven angels
were finished.

The Seven Bowls of God's Wrath

16 Then I heard a loud voice from the temple telling [p]the seven angels, "Go and [q]pour
out on the earth [r]the seven bowls of the wrath of God."
2 So the first angel went and poured out his bowl on the earth, and harmful and painful
[s]sores came upon the people who bore [t]the mark of the beast and worshiped its image.
3 The second angel poured out his bowl into the sea, and [u]it became like the blood of a
corpse, and [v]every living thing died that was in the sea.
4 The third angel poured out his bowl into [w]the rivers and the springs of water, and
[x]they became blood. 5 And I heard the angel in charge of the waters[1] say,

[y]"Just are you, [z]O Holy One, [a]who is and who was,
for you brought these judgments.
6 For [b]they have shed the blood of [c]saints and prophets,
and [d]you have given them blood to drink.
It is what they deserve!"

7 And I heard [e]the altar saying,

"Yes, Lord God the Almighty,
[f]true and just are your judgments!"

8 The fourth angel poured out his bowl on the sun, and it was allowed to scorch people
[g]with fire. 9 They were scorched by the fierce heat, and [h]they cursed[2] the name of God who
had power over these plagues. [i]They did not repent [j]and give him glory.
10 The fifth angel poured out his bowl on [k]the throne of the beast, and [l]its kingdom was
plunged into darkness. People gnawed their tongues in anguish 11 and cursed [m]the God
of heaven for their pain and [n]sores. [o]They did not repent of their deeds.

[1] Greek *angel of the waters* [2] Greek *blasphemed*; also verses 11, 21

15:8 As when the tabernacle (Ex. 40:34–35) and temple (1 Kings 8:10–11) were consecrated, God's holy **glory** is so intense that **no one could enter the sanctuary**. In this case, they couldn't enter **until the seven plagues . . . were finished** (cf. "finished," Rev. 15:1). The seven bowls (16:1–21) complete God's judgment and mark the end of history, as confirmed by the severity of the judgments.

16:1–21 *Angels Pour Out Seven Bowls.* The bowls present varying perspectives on the final destruction of the first heaven and earth. The first four bowls inflict plagues on the same spheres as the first four trumpets (8:7–12): earth, sea, rivers and springs, and sun. The trumpet judgments were limited to one-third of each sphere (see also 9:4–5, 18), but the destruction poured out from the bowls is total. Unlike the seal and trumpet sequences, no interlude (7:1–17; 10:1–11:14) injects delay between the sixth and seventh bowls. The end has come. See note on 6:1–8 for the "four-plus-three" format of the judgments.

16:2 When the **first** bowl is **poured** out **on the earth**, it will afflict not the land itself (contrast the first trumpet, 8:7) but earth's inhabitants, who bear the beast's **mark**, with **painful sores**, like the sixth plague on Egypt (Ex. 9:8–12; Deut. 28:27, 35).

16:3 The **second** bowl will turn the waters of **the sea** into **blood**, and all sea life will die. The first plague on Egypt (Ex. 7:21) is magnified to universal dimensions.

16:4–7 With the **third** bowl, **rivers** and **springs** (sources of drinking water) will be turned to **blood**. **"It is what they deserve,"** declares **the angel . . . of the waters**, referring to those who shed the **blood of saints and prophets** (see 17:6). Isaiah 49:26 promises that Israel's bloodthirsty oppressors will be forced to drink their own blood. The heavenly **altar**, under which the martyrs' souls pooled like sacrificial blood (Rev. 6:9), agrees with the angel's judgment, echoing the song just sung by the victors (16:7; cf. 15:3). People will receive from God exactly what they deserve (see notes on 20:12; 20:13).

16:8–9 Instead of darkening the **sun** (see 8:12), the **fourth** bowl will intensify its **heat** to inflict a terrible foretaste of the coming lake of fire (20:15) on those who defiantly refuse to **repent** and **give** God the **glory** (cf. 9:20–21; 14:7).

16:10–11 The **fifth** bowl shows that the very **throne of the beast** is not immune to God's just wrath. **Darkness** was the ninth plague on Egypt, the last before the slaughter of the firstborn compelled a heart-hardened Pharaoh to release Israel (Ex. 10:21–29). It is appropriate that a regime founded on deceit (Rev. 13:5, 13–14) should be plunged into darkness. Although reaping the **anguish** they have sown in rebellion, hardened people will react by cursing their just Judge rather than forsaking their self-destroying deeds. The refusal to **repent** (cf. 9:20–21; 16:9, 21) shows the total depravity of those who dwell in the earth, and it shows the justice of eternal punishment (20:3–15).

The Seven Bowls of Wrath (16:2–21)

The Unrestrained, Comprehensive Expression of God's Wrath

Bowl	Area Affected	Reference	Result
Bowl 1	earth	16:2	sores on the beast's worshipers
Bowl 2	sea	16:3	blood and death
Bowl 3	rivers and springs	16:4–7	blood to drink
Bowl 4	sun	16:8–9	burning heat
Bowl 5	beast's throne	16:10–11	palpable darkness
Bowl 6	Euphrates River	16:12–16	gathering for the battle
Bowl 7	air	16:17–21	earthquake shattering the great city

12 The sixth angel poured out his bowl on [p]the great river Euphrates, and [q]its water
was dried up, [r]to prepare the way for the kings [s]from the east. 13 And I saw, coming out
of the mouth of [t]the dragon and out of the mouth of [u]the beast and out of the mouth
of [v]the false prophet, three [w]unclean spirits like [x]frogs. 14 For they are [y]demonic spirits,
[z]performing signs, who go abroad to the kings of the whole world, [a]to assemble them
for battle on [b]the great day of God the Almighty. 15 ("Behold, [c]I am coming like a thief!
[d]Blessed is the one who stays awake, keeping his garments on, [e]that he may not go about
naked and be seen exposed!") 16 And [f]they assembled them at the place that in Hebrew is
called [g]Armageddon.

The Seventh Bowl

17 The seventh angel poured out his bowl into [h]the air, and a loud voice came out of
the temple, from the throne, saying, [i]"It is done!" 18 And there were [j]flashes of lightning,
rumblings,[1] peals of thunder, and [k]a great earthquake [l]such as there had never been since
man was on the earth, so great was that earthquake. 19 [m]The great city [n]was split into
three parts, and the cities of the nations fell, and God [o]remembered [p]Babylon the great,
[q]to make her drain the cup of the wine of the fury of his wrath. 20 And [r]every island fled
away, and no mountains were to be found. 21 And [s]great hailstones, about one hundred
pounds[2] each, fell from heaven on people; and [t]they cursed God for [u]the plague of the
hail, because the plague was so severe.

The Great Prostitute and the Beast

17 Then [v]one of the seven angels who had [w]the seven bowls came and said to me,
"Come, I will show you the judgment of [x]the great prostitute [y]who is seated on
many waters, 2 [z]with whom the kings of the earth have committed sexual immorality, and
[a]with the wine of whose sexual immorality [b]the dwellers on earth have become drunk."
3 And [c]he carried me away in the Spirit [d]into a wilderness, and I saw a woman sitting on [e]a

[1] *Or voices, or sounds* [2] *Greek a talent in weight*

12 [p]ch. 9:14 [q]Isa. 11:15; 44:27; Jer. 50:38; 51:32, 36 [r][Isa. 41:2, 25; 46:11] [s]ch. 7:2
13 [t]ch. 12:3, 9 [u]ch. 13:1 [v]ch. 19:20; 20:10; [ch. 13:11, 14] [w]ch. 18:2 [x][Ex. 8:6]
14 [y][1 Tim. 4:1] [z]See ch. 13:13 [a]ch. 20:8; [ch. 17:14; 19:19; 1 Kgs. 22:20] [b]See ch. 6:17
15 [c]See ch. 3:3 [d]ch. 3:2, 3; See Matt. 24:42 [e]ch. 3:18
16 [f]ch. 19:19 [g]Zech. 12:11; See Judg. 5:19
17 [h][Eph. 2:2] [i]See ch. 10:6
18 [j]ch. 4:5; 8:5; 11:19 [k]ch. 6:12; 11:13 [l]Dan. 12:1; Joel 2:2; Matt. 24:21
19 [m]ch. 11:8 [n][ch. 11:13] [o]ch. 18:5; [Ps. 74:18] [p]See ch. 14:8 [q]See ch. 14:10
20 [r]See ch. 6:14
21 [s]ch. 11:19 [t]ver. 9, 11 [u]Ex. 9:23-25

Chapter 17

1 [v]ch. 21:9 [w]ch. 15:7 [x]ch. 19:2; Nah. 3:4; [Isa. 1:21; Jer. 2:20] [y]ver. 15; [Jer. 51:13]
2 [z]ch. 18:3, 9; [Isa. 23:17] [a]ch. 14:8; Jer. 51:7 [b]See ch. 3:10
3 [c]ch. 21:10 [d]ch. 12:6, 14 [e][ch. 12:3]

16:12–14 The **sixth** bowl prepares for the **battle on the great day of God the Almighty**. The drying up of **the great river Euphrates**, on which ancient Babylon foolishly relied for defense (Isa. 44:27–28; Jer. 50:38; 51:36), symbolizes God's removal of restraint on Satan's capacity to assemble a global conspiracy against the church (see Rev. 20:7–9). The Euphrates was also the eastern boundary of the Roman Empire, and it kept the Parthians out (see note on 6:1–2). **Unclean spirits** emerge as **frogs** (cf. Ex. 8:2–11) from the mouths of the dragon, the beast, and the false prophet in order to deceive world rulers with delusions of victory over "the LORD and . . . his Anointed" (Ps. 2:1–2) and to **assemble** them for their final defeat and destruction.

16:15 Blessed. This is Revelation's third of seven benedictions (see chart, p. 2484). Jesus interjects a summons to spiritual vigilance, echoing his rebukes to the complacent churches of Sardis and Laodicea. Because he is **coming like a thief** at an unexpected moment (cf. 3:3), his soldiers must stay **awake** and dressed lest they be caught **naked**, to their shame (cf. 3:18).

16:16 Armageddon means "Mount Megiddo" in **Hebrew**. In ancient Israel, Megiddo was a plain, not a mountain; but it was also the site of some key battles (Judg. 5:19; 2 Kings 23:29), so in the symbolic geography of John's visions it aptly represents the global combat zone (see Rev. 20:9) in which the final conflict between Christ and Satan will be fought.

16:17–21 The **seventh** bowl evokes a pronouncement from God's throne: **"It is done!"** This declaration, repeated in 21:6, affirms that God's plan has reached completion (10:7), his wrath against evil is finished (15:1, 8), and his kingdom is fully come (11:15). **A great earthquake** of unprecedented severity will shatter **the great city**, the site of Jesus' crucifixion and the murder of his martyrs (11:7–10). It is **Babylon the great**, which rules the "kings of the earth" (17:18). Human civilization will disintegrate when the Lord comes with **lightning, rumblings**, and **peals of thunder** (11:19). This is the earthquake foreseen in the sixth seal (6:12–17), which darkens sun and moon, shakes stars from their places, rolls up the sky like a scroll, and displaces the **mountains** and **every island** (cf. 6:14 with 16:20). This is the flight of the first heaven and earth before God's terrible presence, giving way to a new heaven and earth, unstained by human sin (20:11; 21:1; 22:3).

17:1–19:10 *Babylon the Prostitute.* An extended vision elaborates on the fall of Babylon, previously announced by an angel (14:8) and portrayed in the seventh bowl (16:18–19). The city appears as a woman, a prostitute (17:1–6); then an angel explains the meaning of the woman and the beast on which she sits (17:7–18). Finally, a series of voices comment on her fall—from the perspective of heaven (18:1–8), through earthly laments (18:9–19), and again from heaven's viewpoint (18:20–19:10). The "great prostitute" and "Babylon the great" (chs. 17 and 18) are synonymous, both depicting the empire of the beast. Many futurists think that Babylon represents a great religious entity (not identified more specifically) that will follow and support the Antichrist in the end times. Historically, many Protestants identified Babylon with the Roman Catholic Church, but that view is not widely held today. Others foresee an actual restoration of ancient Babylon, while still others think this represents some kind of revived Roman Empire or similar political entity (see note on 17:9–11).

17:1–15 *Babylon's Power and Luxury.* Babylon's sumptuous clothing and jewelry signify the allure of prosperity. Her name, "mother of prostitutes and of earth's abominations" (v. 5), represents the lust of godless societies for sensual pleasure and their rejection of all restraints. Her becoming drunk on the blood of the saints, and the beast on which she sits, reveals that, in cultures that defy God, an insidious conspiracy unites the relentless pursuit of wealth and pleasure and the ruthless exercise of political and coercive power.

17:1 Many waters symbolizes the many peoples and nations over which Babylon rules (vv. 15, 18). The contrast between the prostitute and the Lamb's bride is emphasized by similarities in the way they are introduced. In both cases, one of the angels with the seven bowls tells John, "Come, I will show you," and then carries him away in the Spirit (cf. 21:9–10).

17:2 Sexual immorality and spiritual infidelity are interlinked; in Scripture the former often symbolizes the latter (2:20–23; Ezek. 16:15–43). Babylon's wanton beauty seduces and intoxicates both heart and body.

17:3 carried me away in the Spirit. John was transported by the Holy Spirit in a prophetic vision, as was Ezekiel (Ezek. 3:12; 11:24; cf. 2 Pet. 1:21; Rev. 19:10). **wilderness.** A place of spiritual protection (cf. 12:6, 14) but also physical deprivation, where John could see through Babylon's surface beauty to her underlying ugliness. The beast of ch. 13 is now **a scarlet beast**

scarlet beast that was full of [f]blasphemous names, and [g]it had seven heads and ten horns.
4 The woman [h]was arrayed in purple and scarlet, and adorned [i]with gold and jewels and
pearls, holding in her hand [j]a golden cup full of abominations and the impurities of her
sexual immorality. 5 And on her forehead was written a name of [k]mystery: [l]"Babylon the
great, mother of prostitutes and of earth's abominations." 6 And I saw the woman, drunk
[m]with the blood of the saints, the blood of [n]the martyrs of Jesus.[1]

When I saw her, I marveled greatly. 7 But the angel said to me, "Why do you marvel? I
will tell you [o]the mystery of the woman, and of the beast with seven heads and ten horns
that carries her. 8 The beast that you saw [p]was, and is not, and [q]is about to rise from [r]the
bottomless pit[2] and [s]go to destruction. And [t]the dwellers on earth whose names have not
been written in [u]the book of life from the foundation of the world will marvel to see the
beast, because [p]it was and is not and is to come. 9 [v]This calls for a mind with wisdom: the
seven heads are seven mountains on which the woman is seated; 10 they are also seven kings,
five of whom have fallen, one is, the other has not yet come, and when he does come he
must remain only a little while. 11 As for the beast [w]that was and is not, it is an eighth but
it belongs to the seven, and it goes to destruction. 12 And [x]the ten horns that you saw are
ten kings who have not yet received royal power, but they are to receive authority as kings
[y]for one hour, together with the beast. 13 These are of one mind, and they hand over their
power and authority to the beast. 14 They [z]will make war on the Lamb, and [a]the Lamb will
conquer them, for he is [b]Lord of lords and [b]King of kings, and those with him are [c]called
and chosen and faithful."

15 And the angel[3] said to me, [d]"The waters that you saw, where the prostitute is seated,
are peoples and multitudes and nations and languages. 16 And [e]the ten horns that you saw,
they and the beast [f]will hate the prostitute. They will make her [g]desolate and [h]naked, and
[i]devour her flesh and [j]burn her up with fire, 17 for [k]God has put it into their hearts to carry

[1] Greek *the witnesses to Jesus* [2] Greek *the abyss* [3] Greek *he*

3 [f]ch. 13:1 [g]ver. 7, 9, 12
4 [h]ch. 18:16 [i]Dan. 11:38 [j]Jer. 51:7; [ch. 18:6]
5 [k]ver. 7; 2 Thess. 2:7 [l]See ch. 14:8
6 [m]ch. 16:6; [ch. 13:15] [n]ch. 2:13
7 [o]ver. 5
8 [p]ver. 11; [ch. 1:4; 13:3] [q]ch. 11:7 [r]See ch. 9:1 [s]ch. 13:10 [t]See ch. 3:10 [u]See ch. 3:5
9 [v][ch. 13:18]
11 [w]ver. 8; [ch. 11:17]
12 [x]ver. 16; Dan. 7:24; [ch. 13:1; Zech. 1:18-21] [y][ch. 18:10, 17, 19]
14 [z]See ch. 16:14 [a]See ch. 3:21 [b]ch. 19:16; Deut. 10:17; Ps. 136:3; Dan. 2:47; 1 Tim. 6:15; [ch. 1:5; Matt. 28:18; Acts 10:36] [c]See ch. 2:10; Luke 18:7 (Gk.); Rom. 1:6
15 [d]ver. 1; [Isa. 8:7]
16 [e]See ver. 12 [f][Jer. 50:41, 42] [g]ch. 18:17, 19 [h]Ezek. 16:37, 39 [i][ch. 19:18] [j]ch. 18:8; [Lev. 21:9]
17 [k]2 Cor. 8:16

on which the woman sits. Some understand this to be the Antichrist, who supports Babylon.

17:4 Both prostitute and bride are adorned in **gold**, **jewels**, **pearls**, and fine linen (cf. 18:16; 19:8; 21:18–21). Babylon's apparel is opulent **purple and scarlet**, while the bride's is bright, pure white. As the beast portrays the state's power to coerce religious conformity through violence, so the prostitute symbolizes the seductive appeal of a worldly economic system driven by the quest of affluence and pleasure (18:11–19). The disgusting brew that brims from her **golden cup** drives her lovers insane (cf. Jer. 51:7).

17:6 drunk with the blood of the . . . martyrs of Jesus. Pleasure-addicted society conspires with the power-addicted state to silence the testimony of Jesus' witnesses by putting them to death (13:15–17).

17:7 In vv. 7–18, the angel interprets the mystery portrayed in the prostitute and the beast.

17:8 The **beast . . . was and is not and is to come**; it had received a mortal wound yet came back to life (13:12–14). The prediction that the beast was **about to rise from the bottomless pit** (11:7) and **go to destruction** means that its present power to persecute Christians is inhibited, and that its future appearance in unprecedented violence will be short-lived (see 19:19–21; 20:7–10).

17:9–11 Rome, which then had "dominion over the kings of the earth" (v. 18), rests on **seven mountains** (or seven hills; cf. Introduction to Romans: The Ancient City of Rome). In prophetic imagery, mountains symbolize the seat of power (Jer. 51:24–25; Dan. 2:35, 44–45). The beast's **seven heads**, symbolizing both mountains and **kings**, show its power over earth-dwellers whose names are not in the book of life. Efforts to identify in history the **five . . . fallen** kings (or kingdoms), the sixth (current) king, a seventh (future) king who would reign briefly, and the **eighth** that **belongs to the seven** have yielded conflicting conclusions (proposals include several Roman emperors, several world empires, or simply numerical symbols standing for all worldly kingdoms that culminate in the **beast**). Even if they cannot be identified specifically, these details send the message that, although the dragon and beast's final assault has not yet begun, their "time is short" (Rev. 12:12), for the beast **goes to destruction**.

17:12–14 The beast's **ten horns** symbolize **ten kings** not yet in power and destined to reign merely **for one hour**, under the beast's control. These 10 probably represent all of the earth's kings (not just 10 specific kings or nations), deceived and gathered by the dragon and the beast for a momentary, final, futile insurrection against the Lamb and an assault on his **called and chosen and faithful** followers (see 16:14; 19:19–21; 20:7–10). John will see the Lamb as the Word of God, **Lord of lords and King of kings**, riding into triumph over the beast and its coconspirators (19:11–21). Some dispensationalists identify these 10 horns with political entities represented by the 10 toes of the image in Nebuchadnezzar's dream (Dan. 2:41–42) and the "ten horns" on the fourth beast that Daniel saw rising from the sea (Dan. 7:7, 20, 24).

17:16–19:10 *Babylon's Fall Lamented and Celebrated.* The depraved militant powers that now sustain Babylon's pursuit of pleasure will dismantle and destroy its affluence and social order, to the distress of those who idolized and profited from its wealth—and to the delight of believers, who have suffered its violent attacks.

17:16–17 The satanic alliance of prostitute and beast will disintegrate, and military power will ravage the economic system it once supported. When the beast and its allies strip the prostitute **naked**, and **devour her flesh and burn her up with fire**, they will imitate the judgment pronounced by God on Israel, his unfaithful bride (Ezek. 16:39–41). God sovereignly uses even his enemies **to carry out his purpose** and fulfill his words, both for the salvation of his own people (Acts 2:23; 4:24–28) and for the destruction of the enemies themselves.

Enemies of the Church (Revelation 13–19)

Enemy	Method of Attack
The beast	intimidating violence
The false prophet	deceptive heresy
The prostitute	beguiling affluence

out his purpose by being of one mind and [l]handing over their royal power to the beast,
until the words of God are fulfilled. 18 And the woman that you saw is [m]the great city that
has dominion over the kings of the earth."

The Fall of Babylon

18 After this I saw [n]another angel coming down from heaven, having great authority, and
[o]the earth was made bright with his glory. 2 And he called out with a mighty voice,

[p]"Fallen, fallen is Babylon the great!
She has become [q]a dwelling place for demons,
a haunt [r]for every unclean spirit,
a haunt [s]for every unclean bird,
a haunt for every unclean and detestable beast.
3 For all nations have drunk[1]
[t]the wine of the passion of her sexual immorality,
and [u]the kings of the earth have committed immorality with her,
and [v]the merchants of the earth have grown rich from the power of
her luxurious living."

4 Then I heard another voice from heaven saying,

[w]"Come out of her, my people,
lest you take part in her sins,
lest you share in her plagues;
5 for [x]her sins are heaped high as heaven,
and [y]God has remembered her iniquities.
6 [z]Pay her back as she herself has paid back others,
and repay her [a]double for her deeds;
mix a double portion for her [b]in the cup she mixed.
7 [c]As she glorified herself and lived in luxury,
so give her a like measure of torment and mourning,
since in her heart she says,
[d]'I sit as a queen,
I am no widow,
and mourning I shall never see.'
8 For this reason her plagues will come [e]in a single day,
death and mourning and famine,
and [f]she will be burned up with fire;
for [g]mighty is the Lord God who has judged her."

9 And [h]the kings of the earth, who committed sexual immorality and lived in luxury
with her, [i]will weep and wail over her [j]when they see the smoke of her burning. 10 [k]They
will stand far off, in fear of her torment, and say,

[1] Some manuscripts *fallen by*

17[l][2 Thess. 2:11]
18[m]ch. 16:19

Chapter 18

1[n]ch. 17:1, 7 [o]Ezek. 43:2
2[p]See ch. 14:8 [q]Isa. 13:21; 34:14; Jer. 50:39; 51:37; [Zeph. 2:14, 15] [r]ch. 16:13 [s]Isa. 14:23; 34:11
3[t]ch. 14:8 [u]ver. 9; ch. 17:2 [v]ver. 11, 15; Ezek. 27:33
4[w][2 Cor. 6:17]; See Isa. 48:20
5[x]Jer. 51:9; [Gen. 18:20, 21; Ezra 9:6; Jonah 1:2] [y]ch. 16:19
6[z]Ps. 137:8; Jer. 50:15, 29; 51:24, 49 [a]Jer. 16:18 [b][ch. 14:10; 16:19; 17:4]
7[c][Ezek. 28:2-8] [d]Isa. 47:7, 8; Zeph. 2:15; [ch. 3:17]
8[e]Isa. 47:9; [ver. 10] [f]ch. 17:16 [g]Jer. 50:34
9[h]ver. 3; ch. 17:2; [Ezek. 26:16, 17] [i][Jer. 50:46] [j]ver. 18; ch. 19:3
10[k]ver. 15, 17

17:18 The **great city** is identified with Rome, which had **dominion over the kings of the earth**.

18:1–19:10 As the ancient Greek chorus interpreted actions in a drama, so a succession of speakers explains the significance of the prostitute's desolation as she is deserted by the beast that once supported her and the kings who once adored her.

18:1–3 Another **angel** with **authority** and **glory** reaffirms the verdict pronounced in 14:8: **Fallen, fallen** (echoing Isa. 21:9). It is fitting that John views Babylon from a wilderness (see note on Rev. 17:3), for its fall will turn the great city into wilderness, inhabited by **every unclean spirit**, **bird**, and **beast**, full of defilement and danger (see Isa. 13:21–22). Laments for the destruction of the city with its **power** and **luxurious living** will soon be heard from earth's **kings** (Rev. 18:9–10) and **merchants** (vv. 11–17). This next section (vv. 4–24) adds economic sins to the other kinds of sins specified in the rest of the book.

18:4–8 Another voice from heaven first warns the church against aligning itself with Babylon and then asserts the equity of God's justice in repaying Babylon's arrogance and cruelty.

18:4 The prophets' appeals for the OT Israelites to **come out of** the cultures in which they sojourned as exiles (Isa. 52:11; Jer. 51:6–9, 45) are equally relevant to the NT church in the apostles' day and today (2 Cor. 6:14–18; see 1 Pet. 2:11–12). Churches in Thyatira, Laodicea, and elsewhere failed to keep their distance from Babylon's power-driven, pleasure-crazed value system.

18:6 In perfect equity, God will **pay** (Babylon) **back as she herself has paid back** (see Ex. 21:23–25). The **double portion** (see Isa. 40:2; Jer. 16:18) from her own cup is the just retribution that duplicates the violence she inflicted on the saints, whose blood she wantonly shed (Rev. 19:2).

18:7–8 Babylon's boast, **I sit as a queen, I am no widow**, mimics her OT namesake and will be silenced **in a single day** (cf. Isa. 47:7–9). Her delusion of affluent security also finds a chilling parallel in the blind self-reliance of the Laodicean church (Rev. 3:17).

18:9–10 Laments from **kings**, merchants, and mariners who profited from Babylon's power and prosperity provide earthly commentary on the great city's fall. When her fall comes, her lovers will **stand far off, in fear** and horror; but it will be too late to distance themselves from her fate. Kings will mourn

10[l]See ch. 14:8 [m]ver. 17, 19; [ver. 8]
11[n]ver. 3, 15; [Ezek. 27:36]
15[o]ver. 3, 11 [p]ver. 10
16[q]ch. 17:4
17[r]ver. 10, 19 [s]ch. 17:16 [t]Ezek. 27:28, 29
18[u]Ezek. 27:30 [v]ver. 9 [w]Ezek. 27:32; [ch. 13:4]
19[x]See Josh. 7:6; Job 2:12 [y]ver. 3, 15 [z]ver. 10, 17
20[a]Deut. 32:43; Jer. 51:48; See ch. 12:12 [b]Luke 11:49, 50 [c]ch. 19:2
21[d]ch. 5:2; 10:1 [e][Jer. 51:63, 64] [f]ver. 10

"Alas! Alas! [l]You great city,
you mighty city, Babylon!
For [m]in a single hour your judgment has come."

11 And [n]the merchants of the earth weep and mourn for her, since no one buys their cargo
anymore, **12** cargo of gold, silver, jewels, pearls, fine linen, purple cloth, silk, scarlet cloth,
all kinds of scented wood, all kinds of articles of ivory, all kinds of articles of costly wood,
bronze, iron and marble, **13** cinnamon, spice, incense, myrrh, frankincense, wine, oil, fine
flour, wheat, cattle and sheep, horses and chariots, and slaves, that is, human souls.[1]

14 "The fruit for which your soul longed
has gone from you,
and all your delicacies and your splendors
are lost to you,
never to be found again!"

15 [o]The merchants of these wares, who gained wealth from her, [p]will stand far off, in fear
of her torment, weeping and mourning aloud,

16 "Alas, alas, for the great city
[q]that was clothed in fine linen,
in purple and scarlet,
adorned with gold,
with jewels, and with pearls!
17 For [r]in a single hour all this wealth [s]has been laid waste."

And [t]all shipmasters and seafaring men, sailors and all whose trade is on the sea, stood
far off **18** and [u]cried out [v]as they saw the smoke of her burning,

[w]"What city was like the great city?"

19 And they threw [x]dust on their heads as they wept and mourned, crying out,

"Alas, alas, for the great city
[y]where all who had ships at sea
grew rich by her wealth!
For [z]in a single hour she has been laid waste.
20 [a]Rejoice over her, O heaven,
and you saints and [b]apostles and prophets,
for [c]God has given judgment for you against her!"

21 Then [d]a mighty angel [e]took up a stone like a great millstone and threw it into the
sea, saying,

"So will Babylon [f]the great city be thrown down with violence,
and will be found no more;

[1] *Or and slaves, and human lives*

Babylon as the **mighty city** that God judged **in a single hour** (see vv. 17, 19), suddenly and swiftly, when his patience had reached its limit.

18:11–17 The **merchants, who gained wealth from** the great prostitute (v. 15) issue a lengthy lament, since the great prostitute especially represents the lust for materialistic acquisition and luxury.

18:12–13 The list of **cargo** for which no market will remain after Babylon's fall resembles the goods transported by the Phoenician merchants of ancient Tyre, which arrogantly boasted of its beauty (Ezekiel 27). As Revelation's beast incorporates every expression of corrupt government (see note on Rev. 13:1–2), so its prostitute includes every corrupt economic system. Even **human souls** are reduced to cargo, traded as **slaves** to drive the engines of production and prosperity.

18:16–19 The merchants' lament echoes that of the kings (v. 10) but focuses on the prostitute's costly apparel and accessories—**fine linen, purple, scarlet, gold, jewels, pearls** (cf. 17:4). They grieve that such **wealth** is **laid waste** (cf. "desolate," 17:16) **in a single hour**. God quickly destroys all human wealth that is not used in obedience and devotion to him. Finally, **shipmasters** and other seamen, who **grew rich** by transporting the treasures of the world to feed Babylon's voracious appetite for luxury, will add their lament to that of kings and merchants. Their cry, **"What city was like the great city?"** no longer ascribes incomparable excellence (13:4) but mourns incomparable destruction (Ezek. 27:32).

18:20 When all in **heaven**, including its **saints and apostles and prophets**, are invited to **rejoice** in God's **judgment** of Babylon (cf. 12:12), a transition is made from earthly lament to the heavenly celebration.

18:21 As Jeremiah cast a stone and scroll into the Euphrates to show that ancient Babylon would "sink, to rise no more" (Jer. 51:63–64), so **a mighty**

22 and [g]the sound of harpists and musicians, of flute players and
trumpeters,
will be heard in you no more,
and a craftsman of any craft
will be found in you no more,
and [h]the sound of the mill
will be heard in you no more,
23 and the light of a lamp
will shine in you no more,
and [i]the voice of bridegroom and bride
will be heard in you no more,
for [j]your merchants were the great ones of the earth,
and all nations were deceived [k]by your sorcery.
24 And [l]in her was found the blood of prophets and of saints,
and of [m]all who have been slain on earth."

Rejoicing in Heaven

19 After this I heard [n]what seemed to be the loud voice of a great multitude in heaven,
crying out,

"Hallelujah!
[o]Salvation and glory and power belong to our God,
2 for [p]his judgments are true and just;
for he has judged [q]the great prostitute
who corrupted the earth with her immorality,
and [r]has avenged on her the blood of his servants."[1]

3 Once more they cried out,

"Hallelujah!
[s]The smoke from her goes up forever and ever."

4 And [t]the twenty-four elders and the four living creatures fell down and worshiped God
who was seated on the throne, saying, "Amen. Hallelujah!" 5 And from the throne came
a voice saying,

[u]"Praise our God,
all you his servants,
[v]you who fear him,
small and great."

[1] Greek *bondservants*; also verse 5

22 [g]Isa. 14:11; 24:8; Ezek. 26:13 [h]Eccles. 12:4; Jer. 25:10
23 [i]Jer. 7:34; 16:9; 33:11 [j]Isa. 23:8 [k]Nah. 3:4
24 [l]ch. 17:6; [Matt. 23:35, 36] [m][Jer. 51:49]

Chapter 19

1 [n]See ch. 11:15 [o]ch. 4:11; 7:10; 12:10
2 [p]ch. 15:3; 16:7 [q]See ch. 17:1 [r]Deut. 32:43; 2 Kgs. 9:7; [ch. 16:6]; See ch. 6:10
3 [s]ch. 18:9, 18; Isa. 34:10; [ch. 14:11]
4 [t]ch. 4:4, 6, 10; 5:14
5 [u]Ps. 22:23; 113:1; 134:1; 135:1 [v]ch. 11:18

angel threw a **great millstone** into the sea to illustrate Babylon's fall, to **be found no more** (see also Ezek. 26:21).

18:22–23 The pleasant sights and sounds of everyday life—music, labor, food preparation, lamplight, marital love—will be seen and heard **no more** in Babylon (cf. Jer. 7:34; 25:10). Ordinary cultural activities and artifacts, though proper in themselves, become unsustainable when human civilization, having defied the Creator, receives his judgment. Babylon's **sorcery** (Rev. 21:8) has **deceived . . . all nations**, as the false prophet's signs tricked earth dwellers, small and great, into worshiping the beast (13:13–16; 17:8).

18:24 In Babylon's fall and the beast's impending defeat, God will at last avenge the **blood** of his martyrs—i.e., of **prophets** and **saints** (6:10; 11:8; 17:6)—and of all who have suffered undeserved violence **on earth** (11:18).

19:1–2 John had seen **a great multitude**, representing every nation, standing before God's throne **in heaven** and extolling his **salvation** (see 7:9–10). Now that countless choir, redeemed by the Lamb (7:14), praises God also for his just vengeance on the prostitute who murdered the saints. **Hallelujah**, which occurs only here in the NT (19:1, 3, 4, 6), comes from a Hebrew term for "praise Yahweh," seen often in the Psalms (esp. Psalms 113–118). **true and just**. God's judgments will expose every lie and right every wrong (Rev. 15:3; 16:7). As in 18:23–24, **the great prostitute** is condemned for twin crimes: she **corrupted the earth** (11:18) through beguiling pleasure, and she shed the **blood** of God's **servants** (17:6), which he has finally avenged (6:10).

19:3 Babylon's **smoke . . . goes up forever and ever**, symbolizing irreversible judgment (like the millstone in the sea, 18:21). The heavenly praise of God (**Hallelujah!**) for this judgment can be understood only in light of the pervasive evil of "the great prostitute" (19:2) and the infinite worthiness of the God whom she repeatedly blasphemed.

19:4 The worship offered by the **elders** and **living creatures** links this consummation celebration with the earlier vision of God and the Lamb (5:8–10). **Amen** (the English transliteration of the Gk. word *amēn*, which was itself taken from a word with the same sound in Hebrew, *'amen*) expresses confident certainty (John 10:7) or strong agreement (1 Cor. 14:16).

19:5 A voice **from the throne** transposes the Hebrew expression "Hallelujah" (see note on vv. 1–2) into the Greek language of John's hearers, with the

The Marriage Supper of the Lamb

6 Then I heard what seemed to be [w]the voice of a great multitude, like [x]the roar of many
waters and [y]like the sound of mighty peals of thunder, crying out,

"Hallelujah!
For the Lord our God
the Almighty [z]reigns.
7 Let us rejoice and exult
and give him the glory,
for [a]the marriage of the Lamb has come,
and [b]his Bride has made herself ready;
8 [c]it was granted her to clothe herself
with fine linen, bright and pure"—

for the fine linen is [d]the righteous deeds of the saints.
9 And the angel said[1] to me, "Write this: [e]Blessed are those who are invited to the marriage supper of the Lamb." And he said to me, [f]"These are the true words of God." 10 Then
[g]I fell down at his feet to worship him, [h]but he said to me, "You must not do that! I am a
fellow servant[2] with you and your brothers who hold to [i]the testimony of Jesus. Worship
God." For the testimony of Jesus is the spirit of prophecy.

The Rider on a White Horse

11 Then I saw [j]heaven opened, and behold, [k]a white horse! The one sitting on it is called
[l]Faithful and True, and [m]in righteousness he judges and makes war. 12 [n]His eyes are like a
flame of fire, and on his head are [o]many diadems, and he has [p]a name written that no one
knows but himself. 13 He is clothed in [q]a robe dipped in[3] blood, and the name by which
he is called is [r]The Word of God. 14 And the armies of heaven, [s]arrayed in fine linen, white
and pure, [t]were following him on white horses. 15 [u]From his mouth comes a sharp sword
[v]with which to strike down the nations, and [w]he will rule them with a rod of iron. [x]He
will tread the winepress of the fury of the wrath of God the Almighty. 16 On his robe and
on his thigh [y]he has a name written, [z]King of kings and Lord of lords.
17 Then I saw an angel standing in the sun, and with a loud voice he called to [a]all the

[1] Greek *he said* [2] Greek *fellow bondservant* [3] Some manuscripts *sprinkled with*

6 [w]Dan. 10:6; [ver. 1] [x]See ch. 1:15 [y]ch. 6:1; 14:2 [z]ch. 11:15, 17; Ps. 97:1
7 [a]Matt. 22:2; 25:10; Luke 12:36; 14:8; John 2:1; [Eph. 5:22-32] [b]ch. 21:2, 9; [Isa. 54:5; Hos. 2:19, 20]
8 [c][Ps. 45:13-15; Ezek. 16:10] [d][Ps. 132:9; Isa. 61:10]
9 [e]Luke 14:15; See ver. 7 [f][ch. 21:5; 22:6]
10 [g]ch. 22:8 [h]ch. 22:9; See Acts 10:26 [i]ch. 1:2; 6:9; 12:17
11 [j]See Ezek. 1:1 [k]See ch. 6:2 [l]See ch. 3:7, 14 [m][Ps. 96:13; Isa. 11:4]
12 [n]ch. 1:14; 2:18 [o][ch. 12:3] [p]ver. 16; ch. 2:17; [Prov. 30:4]
13 [q]Isa. 63:2, 3 [r]See John 1:1
14 [s]ch. 3:4; 7:9 [t][ch. 14:20]
15 [u]ver. 21; See ch. 1:16 [v][Isa. 11:4; 2 Thess. 2:8] [w]ch. 2:27; 12:5 [x]ch. 14:20; Isa. 63:3
16 [y]ver. 12 [z]See ch. 17:14
17 [a]ver. 21

command, **"Praise our God."** As God's **servants** include both **small and great**, so also, sadly, does the army that follows the beast (v. 18).

19:6 The next voice is like that of a **great multitude, many waters,** and **mighty peals of thunder**, and it comes from a great worshiping multitude in heaven (cf. 14:2). **The Almighty reigns** throughout history, but here (as in 11:15–17) he is praised for establishing his reign without rival or resistance at Christ's return (see 1 Cor. 15:24).

19:7–8 With the prostitute destroyed, the Lamb's pure **Bride** is announced, arrayed in purity. **it was granted**. Her gown of righteous deeds is her groom's gift of grace (cf. Isa. 61:10; Rev. 6:11; 7:14). On the church as bride of Christ, see 21:2, 9; 22:17; 2 Cor. 11:2; Eph. 5:25–27.

19:9–10 Blessed. Revelation's fourth of seven benedictions (see note on 1:3). Those **invited to the marriage supper of the Lamb** are believers who belong to his beloved bride, the church, who have been called through the gospel of grace (Isa. 25:6–9; Luke 14:15–24). This "marriage supper of the Lamb" was anticipated in the predictions of a messianic banquet in Isa. 25:6–8; Matt. 22:1–14; 25:10; 26:29. John is twice reprimanded (**"You must not do that!"**) for attempting to worship the angel (cf. Rev. 22:8–9). Instead, John is commanded to **worship God** alone, in dramatic confirmation of the deity of Jesus, the Lamb who is rightly worshiped (cf. 5:8–14).

19:11–20:15 ***The Defeat and Destruction of the Beasts, the Dragon, and Death.*** An opening of heaven (cf. 4:1; 11:19; 15:5) introduces a vision sequence that signifies the last battle between Christ and the forces of evil, resulting in their defeat and destruction. This passage shows the fulfillment of the single greatest promise of history: the return of Christ to reign on earth.

19:11–21 ***Christ Defeats and Destroys the Beast, the False Prophet, and Their Gathered Armies.*** The climactic battle for which the dragon, the beast, and the false prophet gathered the earth's kings (16:13–16) is introduced with a description of Christ the victor (19:11–16), then with a grim "dinner invitation" forecasting the battle's outcome (vv. 17–18). Finally, the conflict occurs (vv. 19–21).

19:11 The rider of the **white horse** is already victorious, and white is the color of victory (see note on 2:17). The rider's titles, **Faithful and True**, identify him as Jesus, the faithful and true witness (1:5; 3:14).

19:12–16 The horse's rider (v. 11) is the Son of Man, with **eyes . . . like a flame of fire** and a **sharp sword**, whom John saw on the Lord's Day (see notes on 1:14; 1:16). His **many diadems** (crowns signifying royalty) show his supremacy as **King of kings and Lord of lords**. Although he is named **the Word of God** as the greatest revelation of the Father (John 1:1, 14; Heb. 1:1–2), he also has a **name written that no one knows but himself**, since the infinite being of the Son of God can never be fully known (on "name," see note on John 1:12–13). Divine mystery veils part of the nature of the Son in whom God speaks most fully (Luke 10:22).

19:14 Fine linen, white and pure, identifies **the armies of heaven** as the bride of the Lamb (v. 8; 6:11; 7:14). They ride **white horses**, sharing his victory (see note on 2:17; also 12:11; 15:2).

19:15 Jesus is the Messiah who will **rule** the nations **with a rod of iron** (see note on 12:5; also Ps. 2:9), judging justly and striking down the wicked. As the Divine Warrior who treads the **winepress** of God's **wrath**, his robe is dipped in his foes' blood (cf. Isa. 63:1–6).

19:17–18 The angel's invitation for **birds** to pick corpses clean at **the great supper of God** reflects an OT covenant curse (Deut. 28:26) and echoes God's prophetic word against Gog and Magog, who oppressed his people (Ezek. 39:17–20; see Rev. 20:8). The beast's army, to be consumed as carrion, includes not only kings (16:14) and warriors, but also **all** who serve the beast, **both free and slave, both small and great** (13:16).

birds that fly directly overhead, [b]"Come, gather for [c]the great supper of God, **18** [d]to eat the
flesh of kings, the flesh of captains, the flesh of mighty men, the flesh of horses and their
riders, and the flesh of all men, both free and slave,[1] both small and great." **19** And I saw
[e]the beast and the kings of the earth with their armies [f]gathered to make war against him
who was sitting on the horse and against his army. **20** And the beast was captured, and with
it [g]the false prophet [h]who in its presence[2] had done the signs by which he deceived those
who had received the mark of the beast and those who [i]worshiped its image. These two
were [j]thrown alive into the lake of [k]fire that burns with sulfur. **21** And the rest were slain
by the sword [l]that came from the mouth of him who was sitting on the horse, and [m]all
the birds were gorged with their flesh.

The Thousand Years

20 Then I saw an angel coming down from heaven, [n]holding in his hand the key to
[o]the bottomless pit[3] and a great chain. **2** And he seized [p]the dragon, that ancient
serpent, who is the devil and Satan, and [q]bound him for a thousand years, **3** and threw
him into [o]the pit, and shut it and [r]sealed it over him, so that [s]he might not deceive the
nations any longer, until the thousand years were ended. After that he must be released
for a little while.

4 Then I saw [t]thrones, and [u]seated on them were those to whom the authority to judge
was committed. Also I saw [v]the souls of those who had been beheaded for the testimony
of Jesus and for the word of God, and those [w]who had not worshiped the beast or its
image and had not received its mark on their foreheads or their hands. [x]They came to

[1] Greek *bondservant* [2] Or *on its behalf* [3] Greek *the abyss*; also verse 3

17 [b]Jer. 12:9; Ezek. 39:17 [c][Isa. 34:6; Jer. 46:10; Ezek. 39:19]
18 [d]Ezek. 39:18, 20
19 [e]ch. 11:7; 13:1 [f]ch. 16:16
20 [g]ch. 16:13; 20:10 [h]ch. 13:11-14 [i]See ch. 13:15 [j]ch. 20:10, 14, 15; [Dan. 7:11] [k]ch. 14:10; 21:8; See 2 Thess. 1:8
21 [l]ver. 15 [m]ver. 17

Chapter 20

1 [n]See ch. 1:18 [o]See ch. 9:1
2 [p]See ch. 12:9 [q][2 Pet. 2:4; Jude 6]
3 [o][See ver. 1 above] [r]Dan. 6:17; [Matt. 27:66] [s]ver. 8, 10
4 [t]Dan. 7:9; Matt. 19:28 [u]ch. 3:21; Dan. 7:22 [v]ch. 6:9 [w]ch. 13:12, 14-16 [x][John 14:19; 2 Tim. 2:11]

19:19 gathered to make war. Literally, to make "the battle" (Gk. *ton polemon*), probably referring back to the "battle on the great day of God the Almighty" (16:14). "Assembled" (16:14) and "gathered" here translate Greek *synagō*.

19:20 As in 12:5–8, the forces of evil cannot resist Christ's power. The beast and false prophet are **thrown alive into the lake of fire**, whereas their followers suffer physical death (19:21). The beast and the false prophet, like the great prostitute, represent not merely individuals but corrupt human institutions.

19:21 The rest are "the kings of the earth and their armies" (v. 19), including all categories of people (v. 18). Only the Lamb and his army will survive this battle.

20:1–6 *Interlude: The Thousand Years of the Dragon's Binding and the Martyrs' Reign.* These verses are among the most controversial in Revelation. Responsible scholars disagree regarding the meaning of the "thousand years" in vv. 2–7 (see Introduction: Millennial Views). The three main views are represented by: (1) *Premillennialists* (those who believe Christ will return "pre" [before] the millennium) think that this thousand years (Latin, *millennium*) is a future time of great peace and justice, which is usually thought to be a literal 1,000-year period that will begin when Christ returns to reign on earth as a physically present King, and which will include resurrected believers reigning with him. (2) *Postmillennialists* (those who believe that Christ will return "post" [after] the millennial period) think that before Christ returns to earth the gospel will spread and triumph so powerfully that societies will be transformed and peace and justice will reign on earth for a thousand years (or for a long period of time), after which Christ will return for the final judgment. (3) *Amillennialists* (those who hold an "a" [non-literal] millennial view) think this thousand years is the same period as this present church age, and that there will be no future "millennium" before Christ returns for the final judgment. Related to this is the question of whether the thousand years are to be interpreted literally (most premillennialists hold this view) or symbolically (most postmillennialists and amillennialists and some premillennialists hold this view). Those holding each view read John's millennial vision in terms of their understanding of other biblical texts and their approach to prophetic literature as a whole. Likewise, each of these views falls within the framework of historic Christian orthodoxy.

20:1–3 The **dragon** is identified as the **ancient serpent . . . the devil and Satan**, as in 12:9–17, which portrayed its expulsion from God's heavenly court and the thwarting of its efforts to destroy the church. The dragon's being **bound** with a **great chain** and thrown into the **bottomless pit**, which is **shut** and **sealed**, symbolizes God's restriction of Satan's ability to inflict harm for a long but limited era. God's purpose is that Satan **might not deceive the nations any longer, until the thousand years were ended**. The nature of this binding of Satan is important to the three millennial views. *Premillennialists* read this as predicting a complete removal of Satan from the earth during a future golden age (a "millennium") of social righteousness, international peace, and physical well-being, with Christ reigning on earth. They argue that the phrases "shut it" and "sealed it over him" picture a removal of Satan from the earth too complete to represent the current age. *Postmillennialists* also think this will be a future golden age, but that Christ will not return until the end of that time. *Amillennialists* note that the NT affirms that Jesus' first coming has already bound Satan (Matt. 12:29) and brought God's light to the nations (Matt. 4:14–16; Luke 2:32; Acts 14:15–17; 17:30–31). Therefore they argue that this binding of Satan for "a thousand years" refers to the gospel's spread among all nations during the present age, and to the present restraint of the church's persecutors until an outbreak of rebellion before Christ's return (see 2 Thess. 2:3–8).

20:4–5 I saw thrones, and seated on them were those to whom the authority to judge was committed. *Premillennialists* argue that "coming down from heaven" (v. 1) and the reference to "the nations" (v. 3) show that these "thrones" are on earth (during Christ's millennial reign). *Amillennialists* argue that the echoes in these verses from Daniel's vision (cf. Dan. 7:9, 22) signal that the thrones are in heaven. Whatever view one takes of the millennium, **the souls of those who had been beheaded** probably represents just a few of all the people represented by the words **and those who had not worshiped the beast** ("and those" represents Gk. *kai hoitines*, "and whoever, and everyone who"). These faithful believers **came to life**. *Premillennialists* think this means that deceased believers will experience bodily resurrection at the beginning of the millennium, and that is what is meant by **this is the first resurrection** (they say this is the clear meaning of the aorist indicative of *zaō*, "live, come to life"). *Amillennialists* think "they came to life" and "the first resurrection" means their souls entered into the presence of God in heaven after they died, and their deaths were in fact their victory over the dragon and beast (Rev. 12:11; 15:2), imparting to them a foretaste of the final resurrection (20:12–15). Some *postmillennialists* agree with the amillennial view of "the first resurrection," while other postmillennialists think it refers to the future victory of Christianity in the world after its earlier persecution. **and**

life and [y]reigned with Christ for a thousand years. **5** The rest of the dead did not come
to life until the thousand years were ended. This is the first resurrection. **6** [z]Blessed and
holy is the one who shares in the first resurrection! Over such [a]the second death has no
power, but they will be [b]priests of God and of Christ, and they [c]will reign with him for
a thousand years.

The Defeat of Satan

7 And when the thousand years are ended, [d]Satan will be released from his prison
8 and will come out [e]to deceive the nations that are at the four corners of the earth, [f]Gog
and Magog, [g]to gather them for battle; their number is like the sand of the sea. **9** And
[h]they marched up over the broad plain of the earth and surrounded [i]the camp of the
saints and [j]the beloved city, but [k]fire came down from heaven[1] and consumed them,
10 and the devil [l]who had deceived them was [m]thrown into the lake of fire and sulfur
where [n]the beast and the false prophet were, and they will be tormented day and night
forever and ever.

Judgment Before the Great White Throne

11 Then I saw a great white throne and him who was seated on it. From his presence
[o]earth and sky fled away, and [p]no place was found for them. **12** And I saw the dead, great
and small, standing before the throne, and [q]books were opened. Then another book was
opened, which is [r]the book of life. And [s]the dead were judged by what was written in the
books, [t]according to what they had done. **13** And the sea gave up the dead who were in it,
[u]Death and Hades gave up the dead who were in them, and they were judged, each one
of them, [t]according to what they had done. **14** Then [u]Death and Hades [v]were thrown into
the lake of fire. This is [w]the second death, the lake of fire. **15** And if anyone's name was not
found written in the book of life, [x]he was thrown into the lake of fire.

[1] Some manuscripts *from God, out of heaven,* or *out of heaven from God*

4 [y]ver. 6; ch. 5:10; 22:5; Dan. 7:18; Matt. 20:21, 27; 2 Tim. 2:12; [Ps. 45:16]
6 [z]ch. 14:13 [a]ver. 14; ch. 2:11; 21:8 [b]See ch. 1:6 [c]ver. 4
7 [d]ver. 2
8 [e]ver. 3, 10 [f]Ezek. 38:2; 39:1 [g]See ch. 16:14
9 [h][Isa. 8:8; Ezek. 38:9, 16; Hab. 1:6] [i]Heb. 13:11, 13 [j][Ps. 132:13] [k]See ch. 13:13
10 [l]ver. 3, 8 [m]See ch. 19:20 [n]See ch. 16:13
11 [o]See Ps. 102:26 [p]ch. 12:8; Dan. 2:35
12 [q]Dan. 7:10 [r]See ch. 3:5 [s]Rom. 14:10; 2 Cor. 5:10; See ch. 11:18 [t]See Matt. 16:27
13 [u]ch. 6:8 [t][See ver. 12 above]
14 [u][See ver. 13 above] [v][ch. 21:4; Luke 20:36; 1 Cor. 15:26] [w]ver. 6
15 [x]Matt. 13:42, 50

reigned with Christ for a thousand years. *Premillennialists* think this means that these resurrected believers will assist with Christ's thousand-year reign as righteous King over the whole earth. *Amillennialists* think this means deceased believers now (and during the entire "thousand years," which means the time from Pentecost to the second coming) are "reigning" with Christ from heaven. *Postmillennialists* see it as a future triumph of Christianity in the world.

20:6 Blessed. Revelation's fifth of seven benedictions (see chart, p. 2484). **second death.** When the wicked are returned to bodily existence and condemned for evil deeds, they will be cast eternally into the lake of fire (vv. 12–15). The victors, who maintain their testimony of Jesus and resist the beast, worship as **priests** and **reign** as kings with Christ throughout the era of Satan's binding.

20:7–10 *God Defeats and Destroys the Dragon and Its Gathered Armies.* Satan's release after the thousand years will free him to **deceive the nations** and to **gather them** for the last **battle**. *Amillennialists* see this as the same battle as the one described in 16:13–16 and 19:17–21. *Premillennialists* see this as a separate, later battle. The gathered armies are called **Gog and Magog**, titles of Israel's pagan oppressors, who would be destroyed by **fire . . . from heaven** (Ezek. 38:22; 39:6) and consumed as carrion (Ezek. 39:1–6, 17–20; Rev. 19:17–18, 21). Although the **saints** are exposed as a **camp** and, as inhabitants of God's **beloved city** (11:2; 21:2), are besieged by foes as countless as **the sand of the sea** (see 12:17), their enemies will be consumed by God's fiery judgment. The deceiver will be **thrown into the lake of fire and sulfur**.

20:11–15 *The Last Judgment and the Destruction of Death, the Last Enemy.* All the dead will be raised from the grave and the sea, to be judged either by their *deeds* recorded in "the books" (v. 12) or by God's gracious registration of their *names* in the Lamb's "book of life" (v. 12; see note on v. 13). This judgment was announced in 11:18.

20:11 The **great white throne** reflects the purity and wisdom of the Ancient of Days (cf. Dan. 7:9). **earth and sky fled away.** This removal of the first heaven and earth (foretold in Hag. 2:6; Heb. 12:26–28; and previewed in Rev. 6:12–14; 16:18–21) prepares for the new heaven and earth (21:1, 4–5; Isa. 65:17; 66:22; 2 Pet. 3:10–13).

20:12 The dead, great and small, include both God's saints (11:18; 19:5) and the beast's worshipers (13:16; 19:18). **Books** recording their deeds will be opened (Dan. 7:10), providing the grounds on which each is judged (Rom. 2:6–11). God keeps an accurate record of every human deed, and will reward and punish with perfect justice. **another book, the book of life.** See note on Rev. 20:13; cf. 3:5; 13:8; 17:8; 20:15; 21:27.

20:13 The **sea, Death,** and **Hades** (the realm of the dead, cf. 6:8) will give up their dead as all people return to bodily existence to be judged (2 Cor. 5:10) by Jesus (Matt. 16:27; John 5:28–29; Acts 17:31). **they were judged . . . according to what they had done.** Unbelievers will be rightly condemned for their sins (cf. Rom. 3:23; Rev. 20:15). Believers, whose names are in the "book of life" (vv. 12, 15), will enter into "a new heaven and a new earth" (21:1) because the names in that book are of those who have been redeemed by "the Lamb who was slain" (13:8; cf. 21:27) for their sins (1:5). Their recorded deeds attest to their trust in Christ and are also the basis for determining their rewards (cf. notes on 1 Cor. 3:14–15; 2 Cor. 5:10; Rev. 22:12–16).

20:14 Death, the last enemy, will be destroyed when Christ returns and raises believers (1 Cor. 15:23–26). Therefore **Death and Hades** will be the last to be thrown into **the lake of fire, the second death,** where they will join the beast and the false prophet (Rev. 19:20) and the devil (20:10).

20:15 All whose *names* are **not found written in the book of life** will be condemned for the record of their *deeds* (cf. note on 20:11–15) and **thrown into the lake of fire.** Those enrolled in the Lamb's book of life enter the new Jerusalem (21:27).

God and Jesus Are Alpha and Omega

God is the Alpha and the Omega (1:8; 21:6)	God is the beginning and the end (21:6)
Jesus is the Alpha and the Omega (22:13; cf. 2:8; 22:13)	Jesus is the beginning and the end (22:13; cf. 2:8; 22:13)

The New Heaven and the New Earth

21 Then I saw [y]a new heaven and a new earth, for [z]the first heaven and the first earth
had passed away, and the sea was no more. 2 And I saw [a]the holy city, [b]new Jerusalem,
[c]coming down out of heaven from God, [d]prepared [e]as a bride adorned for her husband.
3 And I heard a loud voice from the throne saying, "Behold, [f]the dwelling place[1] of God is
with man. He will [g]dwell with them, and they will be his people,[2] and God himself will
be with them as their God.[3] 4 [h]He will wipe away every tear from their eyes, and [i]death
shall be no more, [j]neither shall there be mourning, nor crying, nor pain anymore, for the
former things have passed away."
5 And [k]he who was seated on the throne said, "Behold, I [l]am making all things new."
Also he said, "Write this down, for [m]these words are trustworthy and true." 6 And he said
to me, [n]"It is done! [o]I am the Alpha and the Omega, the beginning and the end. [p]To the
thirsty I will give from the spring of the water of life without payment. 7 [q]The one who
conquers will have this heritage, and [r]I will be his God and [s]he will be my son. 8 [t]But as
for the cowardly, the faithless, the detestable, as for murderers, the sexually immoral,
sorcerers, idolaters, and all liars, [u]their portion will be in [v]the lake that burns with fire and
sulfur, which is [w]the second death."

The New Jerusalem

9 Then came [x]one of the seven angels who had the seven bowls full of [y]the seven last
plagues and spoke to me, saying, "Come, I will show you [z]the Bride, the wife of the Lamb."

[1] Or *tabernacle* [2] Some manuscripts *peoples* [3] Some manuscripts omit *as their God*

Chapter 21
1 [y]Isa. 65:17; 66:22; 2 Pet. 3:13 [z]ch. 20:11
2 [a]ch. 11:2; 22:19; Isa. 52:1 [b]See ch. 3:12 [c][Heb. 11:10] [d]ch. 19:7; [John 14:3] [e]Isa. 61:10
3 [f]See Lev. 26:11, 12 [g][ch. 7:15]
4 [h]See ch. 7:17 [i][ch. 20:14; 1 Cor. 15:26] [j]Isa. 35:10; 51:11; 65:19
5 [k]ch. 4:2, 9; 5:1; 20:11 [l]See 2 Cor. 5:17 [m]ch. 22:6; [ch. 3:14; 19:11; 1 Tim. 1:15]
6 [n]See ch. 10:6 [o]ch. 1:8; 22:13 [p]ch. 22:17; See John 4:10; 7:37
7 [q]ch. 2:7 [r]ver. 3 [s]See 2 Cor. 6:18
8 [t]ch. 22:15; 1 Cor. 6:9, 10; Gal. 5:19-21; Eph. 5:5; 1 Tim. 1:9; Heb. 12:14 [u]Luke 12:46 [v]ch. 19:20 [w]ch. 2:11; 20:6, 14
9 [x]ch. 17:1 [y]ch. 15:1 [z]ver. 2

21:1–22:5 *"All Things New."* The destruction of the last enemy, death, and the last judgment will finally lead to the renewal of the entire created order, heaven and earth, to be the perfect home in which the Lamb will live forever with his bride, the people whom he has redeemed out of all the nations through his atoning death.

21:1–8 *The New Heaven and Earth, Home of the Lamb's Bride.* Having seen Christ's enemies destroyed, John finally sees "a new heaven and a new earth," the eternal home of the Lamb with his bride. After the new cosmos is described, the bride herself is introduced (21:9–22:5). Scholars differ as to whether this "new earth" is entirely new (newly created) or is the old earth transformed in a way analogous to the transformation of believers' resurrection bodies (1 Cor. 15:35–49; Phil. 3:21; see note on 2 Pet. 3:10).

21:1 Then I saw a new heaven and a new earth. The removal of the **first heaven** and **earth** eliminates the fatal infection of evil in the cosmic order and gives way to God's creation of a new cosmic order where sin and suffering and death are forever banished. The old order was in "bondage to decay" (Rom. 8:21) and "groaning . . . in pains of childbirth until now" (Rom. 8:22), awaiting the day when "the heavens . . . will be dissolved" and "new heavens and a new earth in which righteousness will dwell" will be established to forever replace the old (2 Pet. 3:12–13). This represents the specific fulfillment of the prophecy given to Isaiah: "Thus says the Lord GOD . . . 'I create new heavens and a new earth . . .'" (Isa. 65:13, 17; cf. 66:22). Scholars differ, however, as to the extent and way in which the "first heaven and the first earth" will pass **away** and be transformed into something new—especially as to whether this represents an entirely new creation, or whether (and to what extent) this represents a "renewed" creation that retains some degree of continuity with the old order. As seen in the example of 1 Cor. 15:35–44, it is clear, with respect to the believer's resurrection body, that although there is some kind of continuity between the old and the new order, the new reality will also be qualitatively different—for example, as different as a kernel or a seed is from a full-grown wheat plant (1 Cor. 15:35–39). Thus "new" (Gk. *kainos*) is best understood here in terms of something that has been qualitatively transformed in a fundamental way, rather than as an outright new creation *ex nihilo* (Latin, "out of nothing"), as in the case of God's original creation in Genesis 1. By comparison to the old order that is coming to an end, the new cosmic order is radically different—a place where "righteousness will dwell" (2 Pet. 3:13), where God "will wipe away every tear from their eyes" (Rev. 21:4; cf. Isa. 25:8 and Rev. 7:17), where "death shall be no more" (Rev. 21:4; cf. Isa. 25:8 and 1 Cor. 15:26), where "the creation itself will be set free from its bondage to decay" (Rom. 8:21), and where all that is "perishable" will be raised and transformed into a glorious new "imperishable" reality (1 Cor. 15:42–43), where the redeemed will rejoice in the eternal presence of "God and the Lamb" (Rev. 14:4; cf. 22:1–5). **The sea was no more** does not mean there will be no bodies of water in the new earth (cf. 21:6; 22:1–2) but refers to the source of earthly rebellion, chaos, and danger—the sea from which the beast emerged (13:1; Dan. 7:3). This symbolic (or literal) source of rebellion will no longer threaten creation's perfection.

21:2 The holy city, new Jerusalem (cf. Gal. 4:26; Heb. 12:22–24), the church redeemed by Jesus Christ, will no longer be trampled by nations (Rev. 11:2) but rather, will be **adorned** as **a bride**.

21:3 He will dwell with them. The greatest blessing of heaven will be unhindered fellowship with God himself. The goal of God's covenant, "God with us" (Isa. 7:14, ESV footnote; Matt. 1:23), foreshadowed in the OT tabernacle and temple, will be achieved. **his people . . . their God.** See Lev. 26:11–12; Ezek. 37:27.

21:4 By wiping away **every tear** and eliminating **death, mourning,** and **pain** (Isa. 25:8; 65:19–20), God will reverse the curse that entered the world through human sin.

21:6 It is done! The destruction of God's enemies (16:17) and the salvation of his saints are both completed. **the Alpha and the Omega.** First and last letters of the Greek alphabet (cf. 1:8; 22:13). The Lord stands beyond the universe's **beginning** and its **end** as Sovereign Creator and Consummator, the first and the last (Isa. 41:4; 44:6; 48:12). The **spring of the water of life** is the throne of God and the Lamb (Rev. 22:1), a throne of grace (Heb. 4:16) because here the thirsty drink **without payment**, by God's free gift (Isa. 55:1).

21:7 The one who conquers. The promises to conquerors (2:7, 11, 17; etc.) are summed up in this assurance that the new heaven and earth are their **heritage** as God's children. **he will be my son.** This promise to David's descendants (2 Sam. 7:14), fulfilled preeminently in Jesus (Heb. 1:5), also includes those who belong to him (Gal. 3:26). On "son," see note on Gal. 3:26.

21:8 The conqueror's blessedness contrasts with the **second death** awaiting those who renounced faith because of cowardice or compromise with idolatry and sensuality. **Sorcerers** is also used of Egyptian and Babylonian magicians in the OT (e.g., Ex. 7:11; Dan. 2:2); on ancient magic, see note on Acts 13:6.

21:9–22:5 *The New Jerusalem, the Lamb's Pure Bride.* As in the disclosure of the prostitute Babylon (17:1–3), an angel with one of the seven bowls helps John see the bride, the wife of the Lamb. She is the holy city Jerusalem. Some take this as a literal description of this new city; others understand it as a complex symbol for the life in heaven of the Lamb's redeemed people.

10[a]ch. 17:3; [Ezek. 43:5] [b]Ps. 87:1; Ezek. 40:2
11[c]ver. 23; [ch. 22:5; Ps. 84:11; Ezek. 43:2, 4] [d][Matt. 5:14; Phil. 2:15] [e]ch. 4:3, 6
12[f]Ezek. 48:31-34
14[g]Heb. 11:10; [1 Cor. 3:11] [h]Matt. 16:18; Eph. 2:20
15[i]See ch. 11:1
17[j]Deut. 3:11; [ch. 13:18] [k]ver. 9
18[l]ver. 11

10 And [a]he carried me away in the Spirit to [b]a great, high mountain, and showed me the
holy city Jerusalem coming down out of heaven from God, 11 [c]having the glory of God, [d]its
radiance [e]like a most rare jewel, like a jasper, clear as crystal. 12 It had a great, high wall, [f]with
twelve gates, and at the gates twelve angels, and on the gates the names of the twelve tribes
of the sons of Israel were inscribed— 13 on the east three gates, on the north three gates,
on the south three gates, and on the west three gates. 14 And the wall of the city had twelve
[g]foundations, and [h]on them were the twelve names of the twelve apostles of the Lamb.
15 And the one who spoke with me [i]had a measuring rod of gold to measure the city
and its gates and walls. 16 The city lies foursquare, its length the same as its width. And
he measured the city with his rod, 12,000 stadia.[1] Its length and width and height are
equal. 17 He also measured its wall, 144 cubits[2] by [j]human measurement, which is also [k]an
angel's measurement. 18 The wall was built of [l]jasper, while the city was pure gold, like

[1] About 1,380 miles; a *stadion* was about 607 feet or 185 meters [2] A *cubit* was about 18 inches or 45 centimeters

21:10 a great, high mountain. After Gog and Magog's destruction (Ezekiel 38–39), Ezekiel was transported to "a very high mountain" (Ezek. 40:2–3) to view God's future temple. Although believers are exposed to suffering on earth (Rev. 11:2), their true life in the **holy city** has been secured in **heaven**, from which it will suddenly be revealed (Col. 3:3–4).

21:11 The glory of God, resembling **jasper** (cf. 4:3), radiates from the transparent city, which is **clear as crystal** and "glass" (21:18).

21:12–14 The city's **high wall** and **twelve gates** guarded by angels (see Gen. 3:24) signify invulnerability to attack. The gates bear the names of Israel's **twelve tribes**, and the Lamb's **twelve apostles** are named on the wall's **foundations** (Eph. 2:20), signifying the unity of OT and NT believers.

21:15–17 The **measuring rod of gold** is more glorious than the reed in Ezekiel's vision (Ezek. 40:3). The city's **length and width and height are equal**, having a cubic shape like the Most Holy Place in the OT sanctuary (1 Kings 6:20; Ezek. 41:4). Since the entire city is the Most Holy Place (the place of God's presence), John saw no temple in it (Rev. 21:22). The length, width, and height of the city (**12,000 stadia**, or 1,380 miles [2,221 km]) and the width (**144 cubits**) of the city wall are multiples of 12. This may indicate the literal dimensions of the city or may symbolize the perfect life of the people of God (see 7:4–8).

21:18 Pure gold may be literal gold that is appropriate to the bride's priceless value and transparent purity, or the expression may simply be symbolic of those things.

The "Bookends" of Biblical Theology

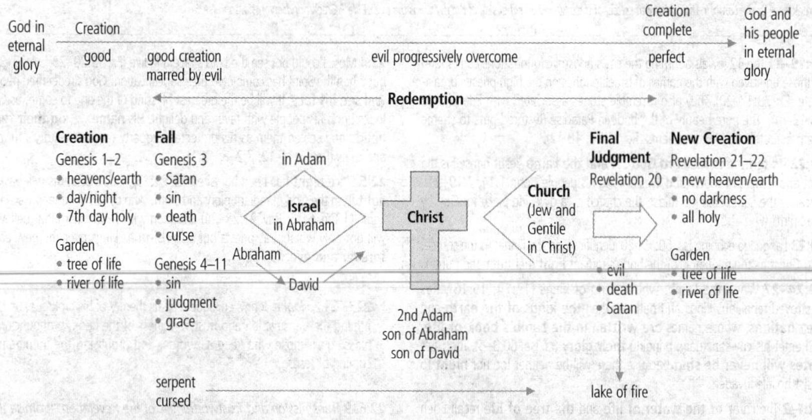

God's ultimate purpose in redemptive history is to create a people to dwell in his presence, glorifying him through numerous varied activities and enjoying him forever. The story begins with God in eternal glory, and it ends with God and his people in eternal glory. At the center stands the cross, where God revealed his glory through his Son.

The biblical story of redemption must be understood within the larger story of creation. First Adam, and later Israel, was placed in God's sanctuary (the garden and the Promised Land, respectively), but both Adam and Israel failed to be a faithful, obedient steward, and both were expelled from the sanctuary God had created for them. But Jesus Christ—the second Adam, the son of Abraham, the son of David—was faithful and obedient to God. Though the world killed him, God raised him to life, which meant that death was defeated. Through his Spirit, God pours into sinners the resurrection life of his Son, creating a new humanity "in Christ." Those who are "in Christ" move through death into new life and exaltation in God's sanctuary, there to enjoy his presence forever.

The "bookends" concept of biblical theology illustrates that in the third-to-last chapter of the Bible (Revelation 20) God removes his enemies—Satan, death, and evil—that entered the story line in the third chapter of the Bible (Genesis 3), thus completing the story of redemption. The last two chapters (Revelation 21–22) don't simply restore the first two chapters (Genesis 1–2); they go beyond them to a world that is fully ordered and holy, in which God is fully present with his people, completing the story of creation. (Chapter divisions in the Bible are, of course, human contributions, not divinely inspired.)

[l]clear glass. **19** [m]The foundations of the wall of the city were adorned with every kind of
jewel. The first was jasper, the second sapphire, the third agate, the fourth emerald, **20** the
fifth onyx, the sixth carnelian, the seventh chrysolite, the eighth beryl, the ninth topaz,
the tenth chrysoprase, the eleventh jacinth, the twelfth amethyst. **21** And the twelve gates
were twelve pearls, each of the gates made of a single pearl, and [n]the street of the city was
pure gold, like transparent glass.
22 And [o]I saw no temple in the city, for its temple is the Lord God the Almighty and the
Lamb. **23** And the city [p]has no need of sun or moon to shine on it, for [q]the glory of God gives
it light, and its lamp is the Lamb. **24** By its light [r]will the nations walk, and the kings of the
earth [s]will bring their glory into it, **25** and [t]its gates will never be shut by day—and [u]there
will be no night there. **26** They will bring into it the glory and the honor of the nations.
27 But [v]nothing unclean will ever enter it, nor anyone who does what is detestable or false,
but only those who are written in the Lamb's [w]book of life.

The River of Life

22 Then the angel[1] showed me [x]the river of [y]the water of life, bright as crystal, flowing
from the throne of God and of the Lamb **2** through the middle of [z]the street of the
city; [a]also, on either side of the river, [b]the tree of life[2] with its twelve kinds of fruit, yielding its fruit each month. The leaves of the tree were [c]for the healing of the nations. **3** [d]No
longer will there be anything accursed, but [e]the throne of God and of the Lamb will be in
it, and [f]his servants[3] will worship him. **4** [g]They will see his face, and [h]his name will be on
their foreheads. **5** And [i]night will be no more. They will need no light of lamp [j]or sun, for
[k]the Lord God will be their light, and [l]they will reign forever and ever.

Jesus Is Coming

6 And he said to me, [m]"These words are trustworthy and true. And the Lord, the God
of [n]the spirits of the prophets, [o]has sent his angel to show his servants what must soon
take place."

[1] Greek *he* [2] *Or the Lamb. In the midst of the street of the city, and on either side of the river, was the tree of life* [3] *Greek bondservants;* also verse 6

18 [l]ver. 11
19 [m][Isa. 54:11, 12]
21 [n]ch. 22:2
22 [o][John 4:23]
23 [p]ch. 22:5; Isa. 60:19, 20; [ver. 25] [q]ver. 11
24 [r]Isa. 60:3; [ch. 22:2] [s]ver. 26; [Isa. 60:5, 16]
25 [t]Isa. 60:11 [u]See ver. 23
27 [v][ch. 22:14, 15; Isa. 35:8; 52:1; Ezek. 44:9; Joel 3:17; Zech. 14:21] [w]See ch. 3:5

Chapter 22

1 [x]Ezek. 47:1; Zech. 14:8; [Ps. 46:4] [y]See ch. 21:6
2 [z]ch. 21:21 [a]Ezek. 47:12 [b]ver. 14, 19; ch. 2:7; Gen. 2:9 [c][ch. 21:24]
3 [d]Zech. 14:11; [Gen. 3:17] [e]ch. 21:3, 23; Ezek. 48:35 [f]ch. 7:15
4 [g]Matt. 5:8; 1 Cor. 13:12; 1 John 3:2 [h]ch. 3:12; 7:3; 14:1
5 [i]ch. 21:25 [j]See ch. 21:23 [k]Ps. 36:9; See ch. 21:11 [l]Dan. 7:18, 27; Rom. 5:17; 2 Tim. 2:12; See ch. 20:4
6 [m]See ch. 21:5 [n]1 Cor. 14:32 [o]ch. 1:1

21:19–21 The 12 jewels adorning the city's apostolic foundations correspond to those engraved with the names of Israelite tribes on the high priest's breastplate (Ex. 28:17–20). They also resemble stones associated with Eden (Ezek. 28:13–14). The pure beauty of the bride in Paradise Restored puts to shame the prostitute's tawdry ornaments (Rev. 17:4; 18:12).

21:22 its temple is the Lord God . . . and the Lamb. Jesus himself is the tent and temple in which God lives among his people (John 1:14; 2:19–21). Because the Lamb is in her midst, the church is "a dwelling place for God by the Spirit" (Eph. 2:22).

21:23 Language echoing Isa. 60:19–20 identifies God the Father as the source, and Christ as the mediator, of the bride's radiant **light** (her truth and purity).

21:24–27 When the Lamb, who is King of kings (17:14; 19:16), has destroyed rebellious kings and nations, then **the kings of the earth** and their **nations**, whose names **are written in the Lamb's book of life**, will enter his city-sanctuary, bringing **their glory** (cf. Isa. 60:3–5). The city's **gates will never be shut** because there will be neither foe nor **night** to assist hostile invaders.

22:1–2 The **river of the water of life** and **the tree of life** recall Eden before the fall into sin (Gen. 2:8–10) and Ezekiel's vision of a future glorious temple (Ezek. 47:1–12; see Zech. 14:8). Refreshment and life flow from **the throne of God and of the Lamb**, carried by the Holy Spirit, as Jesus promised (John 4:10–14; 7:38–39; see also Isa. 44:3; Ezek. 36:25–27). Living believers and martyrs taste this life-giving water even now in this present age (Rev. 7:17; 22:17), but its fullness awaits the new heaven and earth. This ever-flowing river gives a picture of an unending stream of abundant blessings and joy. The tree of life, once banned to guilty humanity (Gen. 3:22–24), will satisfy the city's residents year-round (Rev. 2:7). The **healing of the nations** will have been completed in the destruction of death (20:14; see Ezek. 47:12).

22:3 anything accursed. Earth was cursed for Adam's sin (Gen. 3:17). Guilt, strife, struggle for survival, sickness, sorrow, and death resulted. In the consummated new creation no such woes will remain (Rev. 21:4). God's **throne** will make the entire city a temple (21:22) in which **his servants will worship him** as his priests.

22:4 Moses could not see the Lord's face and live (Ex. 33:20–23; 34:29–35), but when the Spirit has completed their sanctification, God's redeemed people **will see his face**. It will be the greatest blessing of the age to come, as God looks upon his people with favor and delight. His **name . . . on their foreheads** had sealed them as his protected property through history's turmoil and trials (Rev. 3:11–12; 7:2–8; 14:1).

22:5 Since **night** has been banished (cf. 21:25), God's servants will bask in **light** from the God of radiant glory and truth, who dwells in "unapproachable light" (1 Tim. 6:16; Rev. 21:23–24). In union with Jesus their king, believers will not only worship as priests but also **reign** as kings over the new earth **forever and ever** (5:10).

22:6–21 *Epilogue.* John's epilogue repeats themes of his prologue, reaffirming the transmission and trustworthiness of the book, pronouncing blessing on those who keep its words, and promising the imminent coming of Jesus.

22:6–9 *Transmission and Trustworthiness of the Revelation, Promise that Jesus Is Coming Soon, Promise of Blessing.* As at the end of the vision of the prostitute (19:9–10), in concluding the revelation of the bride, the angel affirms that God's words are trustworthy, pronounces one of Revelation's seven benedictions (see chart, p. 2484), and rebukes John for starting to worship a creature rather than God alone. This exchange also echoes the prologue: God sent his angel to show his servants what must soon take place (cf. 1:1); the one who keeps the words of the prophecy is "blessed"; and Jesus affirms, "I am coming soon" (cf. 1:7).

22:6–7 These words are trustworthy and true. The unique truth and trustworthiness of the revealed word (and words) of God are underscored seven times in the last two chapters of Revelation, as indicated first in 21:5, as repeated in 22:6, 7, 9, 10, and then in the solemn warning in vv. 18 and 19 to anyone who "takes away from the words of this book." The centrality, authority, sufficiency, and eternality of the word (and words) of God are foundational to all of Scripture, from the first words of Genesis to the last words

7 “And behold, [p]I am coming soon. [q]Blessed is the one who keeps the words of the prophecy of this book.”
8 I, [r]John, am the one who heard and saw these things. And when I heard and saw them,
[s]I fell down to worship at the feet of the angel who showed them to me, 9 [s]but he said to
me, “You must not do that! I am a fellow servant[1] with you and your brothers the prophets,
and with those [m]who keep the words of this book. Worship God.”
10 And he said to me, [t]“Do not seal up the words of the prophecy of this book, for the
time is near. 11 [u]Let the evildoer still do evil, and the filthy still be filthy, and the righteous
still do right, and the holy still be holy.”
12 “Behold, [v]I am coming soon, [w]bringing my recompense with me, [x]to repay each one
for what he has done. 13 [y]I am the Alpha and the Omega, [z]the first and the last, [a]the beginning and the end.”
14 Blessed are those who [b]wash their robes,[2] so that they may have the right to [c]the tree
of life and that [d]they may enter the city by the gates. 15 [e]Outside are [f]the dogs [g]and sorcerers and the sexually immoral and murderers and idolaters, and everyone who loves and
practices falsehood.
16 [h]“I, Jesus, have sent my angel to testify to you about these things [i]for the churches. I
am [j]the root and [k]the descendant of David, [l]the bright morning star.”
17 The Spirit and [m]the Bride say, “Come.” And let the one who hears say, “Come.” And [n]let
the one who is thirsty come; let the one who desires take the [o]water of life without price.
18 I warn everyone who hears the words of the prophecy of this book: [p]if anyone adds to
them, God will add to him the plagues described in this book, 19 and if anyone takes away
from the words of the book of this prophecy, God will take away his share in [q]the tree of
life and in [r]the holy city, which are described in this book.
20 He who testifies to these things says, “Surely [s]I am coming soon.” Amen. [t]Come, Lord
Jesus!
21 The grace of the Lord Jesus be with all.[3] Amen.

[1] Greek *fellow bondservant* [2] Some manuscripts *do his commandments* [3] Some manuscripts *all the saints*

7 [p]ver. 12, 20; ch. 3:11 [q]ch. 1:3
8 [r]ch. 1:1, 4, 9 [s]ch. 19:10
9 [s][See ver. 8 above] [m][See ver. 6 above]
10 [t][ch. 10:4]
11 [u]Ezek. 3:27; [Dan. 12:10; 2 Tim. 3:13]
12 [v]ver. 7, 20 [w]Isa. 40:10; 62:11 [x]See Matt. 16:27
13 [y]See ch. 1:8 [z]See ch. 1:17 [a]ch. 21:6
14 [b]See ch. 7:14 [c]ver. 2, 19 [d]Ps. 118:20; See ch. 21:27
15 [e][Gal. 5:19-21]; See Matt. 8:12 [f]See Phil. 3:2 [g]See ch. 21:8
16 [h]ch. 1:1 [i]ch. 1:4 [j]See ch. 5:5 [k]See Matt. 1:1 [l][ch. 2:28; Num. 24:17; Isa. 60:3; Matt. 2:2]
17 [m]ch. 21:2, 9 [n]ch. 21:6; Isa. 55:1; John 7:37 [o]See ch. 21:6
18 [p]Deut. 4:2; 12:32; [Prov. 30:6]
19 [q]ver. 2, 14 [r]See ch. 21:2
20 [s]ver. 7, 12 [t][2 Tim. 4:8]

of Revelation, as seen, e.g., in: Gen. 1:3 (“And God said”); Ex. 20:1 (“God spoke all these words”); Deut. 6:6 (“these words . . . shall be on your heart”); Deut. 32:47 (“by this word you shall live”); Psalm 12:6 (“The words of the LORD are pure words”); Isa. 40:8 (“the word of our God will stand forever”); Matt. 4:4 (“Man shall not live by bread alone, but by every word”); Matt. 24:35 (“Heaven and earth will pass away, but my words will not pass away”); Luke 24:44 (“These are my words”); John 1:1 (“In the beginning was the Word”); John 6:68 (“You have the words of eternal life”); and 1 Pet. 1:25 (“the word of the Lord remains forever”). **Blessed is the one who keeps the words of . . . this book**. A timeless promise for believers in every age. “Blessed” here in Rev. 22:7 echoes the first “blessed” (see 1:3 and note) and is the sixth of seven benedictions throughout the book of Revelation.

22:8–9 Human beings must not worship even the angels who inflict the last plagues (15:1; 21:9), for they are fellow servants. **God** alone must be worshiped. Since the Lamb is rightly worshiped (5:8–14), he is God.

22:10–15 *Prohibition of Sealing the Book, Promise that Jesus Is Coming Soon, Promise of Blessing.* John must not “seal” his prophecy as Daniel did his, because the fulfillment of John’s visions was temporally “near” to his first-century readers, as it is to believers 20 centuries later. The assurance that, when Jesus comes “soon,” he will bring blessing to believers and judgment to rebels, should motivate believers to perseverance and purity.

22:10 Do not seal up the words of the prophecy. John must not imitate Daniel, whose visions concerned events in a remote future (Dan. 12:4, 9). **The time is near** (cf. notes on 1 Thess. 5:2–3; 5:4) for the fulfillment of John’s visions because the dragon was already defeated at Christ’s cross. The end will consummate the spiritual conflict in which the first-century churches were engaged, as is the church today (see Mark 1:15; 1 Cor. 10:11).

22:11 Let the evildoer still do evil . . . and the righteous still do right. Patterns of behavior, whether controlled by unbelief or by faith, will eventually be irreversible (cf. Dan. 12:10).

22:12–16 Jesus speaks (v. 16), promising to come soon (see vv. 7, 20), affirming his divine eternity (v. 13) and messianic authority (v. 16), and pronouncing the book’s final of seven benedictions (v. 14; see note on 1:3). **bringing my recompense**. As the Divine Warrior of Isa. 62:10–63:6, Christ will come to **repay each one for what he has done**, rewarding faithful servants and punishing every evildoer. “Recompense” (Gk. *misthos*, “wages, reward”) indicates degrees of reward for believers and punishment for unbelievers (cf. Luke 12:47–48; and 1 Cor. 3:14–15 with note).

22:13 the Alpha and the Omega, the first and the last. See note on 21:6. Eternal life and lordship characterize God (1:8) and his Christ, who is coming soon (1:17; 2:8).

22:14–15 Blessed. The final of the seven benedictions of Revelation (see chart, p. 2484) is for **those who wash their robes** in the conscience-cleansing blood of the Lamb (7:14; Heb. 9:14). They have access to **the tree of life** within God’s **city**. **Outside** the gates in eternal torment will be everyone who **loves** Satanic **falsehood**, sensuality, and murder (cf. Rev. 21:8, 27).

22:16–17 *Transmission of the Revelation.* As promised in 1:1, Jesus has conveyed his revelation through his angel and through John to his churches, for their comfort and warning.

22:16 the root and the descendant of David. Jesus is both David’s “son” and his Lord, the source of his royalty (5:5; Isa. 11:1, 10; Mark 12:35–37). **bright morning star**. This is the ruler whom Balaam foresaw arising from Israel to conquer the nations (Num. 24:17).

22:17 In v. 20, “Come” is a prayer addressed to Jesus, who promises to come soon. Here it is an invitation to the spiritually thirsty, to **take the water of life without price**, for it is freely provided by God’s grace (21:6; Isa. 55:1).

22:18–21 *Prohibition of Altering the Book, Promise that Jesus Is Coming Soon, and Final Pronouncement of Blessing.* **I warn** is the same verb as **testifies** in v. 20. Jesus bears witness that no mere human may **add to** or **take away** from God’s words without incurring **the plagues described in this book** and forfeiting its blessings. Moses had warned against adding to or subtracting from the Lord’s commands (Deut. 4:2; 12:32). A prophet who spoke without God’s authorization deserved death (Deut. 18:20–22). When Jesus testifies once more, **Surely I am coming soon**, his church responds, **Come, Lord Jesus!** echoing the early prayer of the Aramaic-speaking church, *marana tha* (“Our Lord, come!”; cf. 1 Cor. 16:22).

Articles and Resources

God's Plan of Salvation

A troubled jailer in the first century once asked two Christian leaders, "what must I do to be saved?" (Acts 16:30). This in fact is the most important question that anyone can ask. We are troubled not only by the evils of our world but also by our own faults. We often feel guilty for those words and deeds that our own consciences tell us are wrong. We probably sense that we deserve God's judgment, not his favor. What can be done—or what has been done—to rescue us from our helpless situation? We begin our answer by offering an overview of God's plan and his work to bring salvation, followed by a more detailed unpacking of these truths.

An Overview

Creation

God made this world and all that is in it: "In the beginning God created the heavens and the earth.... God created man in his own image, in the image of God he created him; male and female he created them" (Gen. 1:1, 27). He created human beings to be like him and to have unhindered fellowship with him, and when his work of creation was finished he saw that it was "very good" (Gen. 1:31).

Rebellion

Although the first people God created, Adam and Eve, had complete freedom to live in friendship and trust with him, they chose to rebel (Gen. 3:1–7). Because God designed that Adam would represent the entire human race, his sin was catastrophic not only for him but for us: "one trespass led to condemnation for all men" (Rom. 5:18). Our fellowship with God was broken. Instead of enjoying his holy pleasure, we instead face his righteous wrath. Through this sin, we all died spiritually (see Rom. 3:1–20; Eph. 2:1–10) and the entire world was affected. God also cursed the world over which humanity had been set to reign as his lieutenants (see Gen. 3:17–19). "The creation was subjected to futility, not willingly, but because of him who subjected it" (Rom. 8:20). And we all individually sin against God in our own lives: "for all have sinned and fall short of the glory of God" (Rom. 3:23).

Redemption

God would have been perfectly just to leave matters there, with all human beings under his holy judgment, but he didn't. God instead set in motion his plan to save his people from sin and judgment and set free the entire creation from its subjugation to sin and the curse. How? By sending his Son as a true man who would bear the penalty for our sin and die in our place: "Christ died for our sins in accordance with the Scriptures" (1 Cor. 15:3).

The best-known verse in the Bible summarizes the required response to this good news: "For God so loved the world, that he gave his only Son, that *whoever believes in him* should not perish but have eternal life" (John 3:16). To "believe in" Jesus includes both a wholehearted trust in him for forgiveness of sins and a decision to forsake one's sin or to "repent": All who truly "repent [or turn from their sins] and believe [in Jesus for the forgiveness of their sins]" will be redeemed (Mark 1:15) and restored to a right relationship with God. To "believe in" Jesus also requires relating to, and putting trust in, Jesus as he truly is—not just a man in ancient history but also a living Savior today who knows our hearts and hears our prayers.

Consummation

God not only rescues lost sinners but he restores all of creation. We read in Romans 8:21: "the creation itself will be set free from its bondage to corruption and obtain the freedom of the glory of the children of God." The heavens and the earth will "pass away" and be radically transformed (2 Pet. 3:7–13; Rev. 21:1). We read of the glorious culmination of this in the book of Revelation, where God's people, the redeemed, are brought into the presence of God to live forever (Rev. 21:1–22:6). This is life as it should be, literally as it was meant to be.

Filling in the Details

Let's now stop and review this more carefully and specifically, addressing the questions of God, man, Christ, the response, and the result.

God

The God of the Bible is the one and only true God. He is the greatest of all beings. He depends on no other being for his existence. He exists eternally as one God in three persons—Father, Son, and Holy Spirit—a mystery beyond our understanding, but not a contradiction. He plans and acts according to his own good pleasure. He "works all things according to the counsel of his will" (Eph. 1:11). God created the world and acts in it today in accordance with his own perfect, holy, good, and loving plan.

In the same way that this perfectly good God created everything according to his own purposes, so he has acted to save people who have rebelled against him. This action, too, is not because of anything external compelling him, but it is "according to his great mercy" that "he has caused us to be born again to a living hope through the resurrection of Jesus Christ from the dead" (1 Pet. 1:3).

Man

People are made *in the image of God* (Gen. 1:27–28). What does that mean? In part it means that we are privileged to act as God's representatives, as sub-rulers over God's creation, subduing the creatures of the earth, reflecting God's good rule over us. Our authority is derived from God's (Eph. 3:14–15) and is meant to reflect his own. But beyond function, being in God's image also means that we are *like God* in many ways. Like God, we are spiritual and rational beings. Like God, we communicate and establish relationships. Like God, our souls endure eternally.

However, the Bible also teaches that there has been an enduring effect of the sin of Adam and Eve recorded in Genesis 3. Because of that sin, we are born morally *fallen*. We are naturally turned away from God and toward sin in every area of life. We are not as bad as we possibly could be, but we are at no point as good as we ought to be. We are now all sinners, and we sin in all areas of life (Rom. 3:23). We are corrupted and make the wrong choices. We are not holy, and are in fact inclined to evil; we do not love God, and therefore we are under just condemnation to eternal ruin, without defense or excuse. We are guilty of sinning against God, fallen from his favor, and under the curse of Genesis 3, and the promise of his right and just judgment of us in the future and forever is guaranteed to us ("the wages of sin is death," Rom. 6:23). This is the state from which we need to be saved.

Jesus Christ

It was, then, when all human beings were desperate and helpless, that God "loved us and sent his Son to be the propitiation for our sins" (1 John 4:10).

Fully God. The Son of God, who has eternally existed with the Father and the Holy Spirit, and who has eternally possessed all the attributes of God, became a man. He was born as Jesus, son of the virgin Mary. The Son entered this world with a purpose: he came "to give his life as a ransom for many" (Mark 10:45), which means he came to redeem us from sin and guilt. He was not an unwitting or unwilling sacrifice. He, following his Father, chose to love the world in this way. Though now fully human, he was also fully God throughout the time of his life on earth (and remains fully God to this day). Jesus himself clearly taught his deity in the way he fulfilled prophecy, which was associated with the coming of God himself (Mark 14:61–62). Jesus forgave sins (Mark 2:5), he accepted worship (John 20:28; Revelation 5), and he taught, "I and the Father are one" (John 10:30).

Fully man. Jesus Christ was also fully man. He was not a deity pretending to be human when he was not. Jesus was fully human (and remains fully human to this day). He was born and lived in submission to his earthly parents. He had a fully human body. He "grew and became strong, filled with wisdom" (Luke 2:40). He learned the carpentry trade (Mark 6:3). He experienced hunger, felt thirst and tiredness, faced temptation, and eventually suffered even death itself. Jesus Christ was, and is, fully God and fully man. The eternal Son of God became a man in order to save sinners.

Perfect life. Jesus Christ lived a perfect life. Indeed, all his actions were as they should be. His words were perfect. He said only what the Father commanded. "What I say, therefore, I say as the Father has told me" (John 12:50). He did only what the Father willed (John 5:19; e.g., Luke 22:42). So, the writer to the Hebrews concludes, "we do not have a high priest who is unable to sympathize with our weaknesses, but one who in every respect has been tempted as we are, yet without sin" (Heb. 4:15). Jesus lived the life of consistent, wholehearted love to the Father that Adam and Eve and Israel—and all of us—should have lived. He deserved no punishment from God because he was never disobedient.

Teaching. Jesus came to teach God's truth, especially about himself (Mark 1:38; 10:45; Luke 20:42; 24:44). He taught the truth about God, about his relationship with God the Father (John 14), about our sin, about what he had come to do, and about what we must do in response. He explained that the Scriptures of the OT were about him (Luke 24:44).

Crucifixion. But God sent his Son especially to die for us (Mark 10:45; John 3:16–18). This is how God has shown his love for us (Rom. 5:8; 1 John 4:9–10). Christ gave his life as a ransom for us (Mark 10:45; 1 Tim. 2:6). By his death he paid the penalty for our sin. Jesus Christ's crucifixion was a horrible act of violence by the people who rejected, sentenced, mocked, tortured, and crucified him. And yet it was also a display of the self-giving love of God, as the Son of God bore the penalty of God's wrath against us for our sin (Deut. 21:23; Isa. 53:5; Rom. 3:25–26; 4:25; 5:19; 8:3; 2 Cor. 5:21; Phil. 2:8; Heb. 9:28).

Resurrection, ascension, return. On the third day after his crucifixion, Jesus was raised from the dead by God. This demonstrated an acceptance of Christ's service in his ministry and specifically showed God's acceptance of his sacrifice for all those who would repent and believe (Rom. 1:4; 4:25). He ascended to heaven and "will come in the same way as you saw him go into heaven" (Acts 1:11). Christ's return will bring God's plan of salvation to completion.

Response

So if God has done this in Christ, what are we to do to be saved? We must turn to God in Christ, which entails turning back from sin. If we *repent* of (decide to forsake and turn from) our sin (as best we understand it) and *trust* in Christ as a living person, we will be saved from God's righteous wrath against our sins. This response of repentance and faith (or trust) can be explained in more detail as follows:

Turn to God. In the OT, God commands people to turn or return to him, and so be saved (e.g., Isa. 6:10; Jer. 18:8). In the NT, Christ preached that people should turn to God, and Paul summarized his account of his preaching with that phrase: "that they [everyone] should repent and turn to God, performing deeds in keeping with their repentance" (Acts 26:20; cf. Acts 26:18). Thus, as Paul said earlier, he preached "testifying both to Jews and to Greeks of repentance toward God and of faith in our Lord Jesus Christ" (Acts 20:21). To repent means to turn. And the turning that we are called to do in order to be saved is fundamentally a turning to God. James could refer to the Gentiles who "turn to God" (Acts 15:19). To "turn to," in this sense in the Bible, is to orient your life toward someone. As God's people—those who are being saved—we are to play the part of the Prodigal Son who, though conscious of sin, guilt, and folly, flees to the Father (Luke 15:20). Paul at Lystra calls the people to turn to the living God (Acts 14:15). Paul refers to the Galatian Christians as those who had come to "know God" (Gal. 4:9); this is what we do in repentance: we repent *to*, we turn *to* God, and henceforth know him as the God who forgives our sins and accepts us for Christ's sake.

Turn away from sin. Turning to God necessarily implies our turning away from sin. The whole Bible—OT and NT—clearly teaches that to repent is to "acknowledge [God's] name and turn from [our] sins" (1 Kings 8:35; cf. 2 Chron. 7:14; Jer. 36:3; Ezek. 14:6; 18:30; Acts 3:19; 8:22; 26:18; Rev. 2:21–22; 9:20–21; 16:11). We cannot start to pursue God and sin at the same time. First John makes it clear that our basic way of life will either be oriented toward God and his light, or toward the darkness of sin. Christians in this life still sin, but against our deepest desires and better judgment; our lives are not guided and directed by sin as before. We are no longer enslaved to sin. Though we still struggle with it (Gal. 5:17), God has given us the gift of repentance (Acts 11:18), and we have been freed from sin's dominating power.

Believe and trust. Put another way, our response is to believe and trust God's promises in Christ, and to commit ourselves to Christ, the living Lord, as his disciples. Among Jesus' first words in Mark's Gospel are "repent and believe in the gospel" (Mark 1:15). The obedience that typifies God's people, beginning with repentance, is to result from the faith and trust we have in him and his word (e.g., Josh. 22:16; Acts 27:25). Thus sins are sometimes called "breaking faith with God" (e.g., Ezra 10:2, 10). Having faith in Christ, which seals our union with him through the Holy Spirit, is the means by which God accounts Christ's righteousness as our own (Rom. 3:21–26; 5:17–21; Gal. 2:16; Eph. 2:8–9; Phil. 3:9). Paul could refer to "salvation through faith in Christ" (2 Tim. 3:15). Frequently this initial repentance and faith can be simply expressed to God himself in prayer.

Grow in godliness and battle for holiness. Such saving faith is something that we exercise, but even so it is a gift from God. Paul writes, "For by grace you have been saved through faith. And this is not your own doing; it is the gift of God, not a result of works, so that no one may boast" (Eph. 2:8–9). At the same time, Paul explained that Christians know an internal battle: "For the desires of the flesh are against the Spirit, and the desires of the Spirit are against the flesh, for these are opposed to each other, to keep you from doing the things you want to do" (Gal. 5:17). God's *gift* of salvation has been given to Christians, but the evidence of that salvation is *lived out* in the continual work of God's Spirit. We can deceive ourselves, and so Paul encourages his readers to "Examine yourselves, to see whether you are in the faith. Test yourselves" (2 Cor. 13:5). Peter encourages Christians to grow in godliness and so become more confident of their election (2 Peter 1). We don't create our own salvation by our actions, but we reflect and express it and so grow in our certainty of it. Because we Christians are liable to deceive ourselves, we should give ourselves to the study of God's Word to be instructed and encouraged in our salvation, and to learn what is inconsistent with it. Jesus' descriptions of his followers (see Matthew 5–7), or Paul's list of the fruit of the Spirit's work in us (see Gal. 5:22–23), act as spiritual maps that help us locate ourselves to see if we are on the path of salvation.

Result

God's plan is to save his people from their sins—and to bring his people fully and finally to himself (Matt. 1:21; 2 Tim. 2:10). Christians experience salvation in this life in both a past and present sense, and we anticipate salvation in a future sense. Christians have been saved from the *penalty* of our sins; we are currently being saved from the *power* of sin; and one day, when God's plan of salvation is completed and we are with Christ, we shall be like him, and we shall be saved even from the very *presence* of sin. This is God's plan of salvation. ◂

Biblical Doctrine: An Overview

True Theology: Knowing and Loving God

The study of theology is considered by many to be dry, boring, irrelevant, and complicated. But for those who want to know God, the study of theology is indispensable. The word "theology" comes from two Greek words, *theos* ("God") and *logos* ("word"). The study of theology is an effort to make definitive statements about God and his implications in an accurate, coherent, relevant way, based on God's self-revelations. Doctrine equips people to fulfill their primary purpose, which is to glorify and delight in God through a deep personal knowledge of him. Meaningful relationship with God is dependent on correct knowledge of him.

Any theological system that distinguishes between "rational propositions about God" and "a personal relationship with God" fails to see this necessary connection between love and knowledge. The capacity to love, enjoy, and tell others about a person is increased by greater knowledge of that person. Love and knowledge go hand in hand. Good lovers are students of the beloved. Knowledge of God is the goal of theology.

Knowledge without devotion is cold, dead orthodoxy. Devotion without knowledge is irrational instability. But true knowledge of God includes understanding everything from his perspective. Theology is learning to think God's thoughts after him. It is to learn what God loves and hates, and to see, hear, think, and act the way he does. Knowing how God thinks is the first step in becoming godly.

Many would like to think that just being a "good" person and "loving" God, without an emphasis on doctrine, is preferable. But being a good person can mean radically different things depending on what someone thinks "good" is, or what constitutes a "person." Loving God will look very different depending on one's conception of "God" or "love." The fundamental connections between belief and behavior, and between love and knowledge, demand a rigorous pursuit of truth for those wanting to love God and to be godly. Hebrews 5:11–6:3 teaches that deepening theological understanding equips one to be able to differentiate good from evil, and it exhorts believers to mature in their knowledge of God and his ways:

> For though by this time you ought to be teachers, you need someone to teach you again the basic principles of the oracles of God. You need milk, not solid food, for everyone who lives on milk is unskilled in the word of righteousness, since he is a child. But solid food is for the mature, for those who have their powers of discernment trained by constant practice to distinguish good from evil. Therefore let us leave the elementary doctrine of Christ and go on to maturity (Heb. 5:12–6:1).

Good theology is based in the belief that God exists, is personal, can be known, and has revealed himself. These presuppositions motivate theologians to devote themselves to a passionate pursuit of knowledge from God's Word. Unfortunately, the word "theologian" is used almost exclusively for vocational theologians rather than for anyone earnestly devoted to knowing God. On one level everyone who thinks about God is a theologian. But a believer whose life is consumed with knowing his Lord is most certainly a theologian, and theologians are committed to truth.

Loving God means loving truth. God is a God of truth; he *is* truth. In Scripture, all three persons of the Trinity are vitally related to truth (see chart below).

In light of this relationship between God and truth, it should be no surprise that the Great Commandment includes loving God with one's mind: "And you shall love the Lord your God with all your heart and with all your soul and with all your mind and with all your strength" (Mark 12:30, quoting Deut. 30:6). Fully loving God and obeying the Great Commandment requires actively engaging the mind in the pursuit of truth.

The second half of the Great Commandment—love your neighbor as yourself (Mark 12:31)—also requires a

All Three Persons of the Trinity Vitally Related to Truth

Father	"What if some were unfaithful? Does their faithlessness nullify the faithfulness of God? By no means! Let God be true though every one were a liar, as it is written, 'That you may be justified in your words, and prevail when you are judged'" (Rom. 3:3–4).
	"For I tell you that Christ became a servant to the circumcised to show God's truthfulness, in order to confirm the promises given to the patriarchs" (Rom. 15:8).
Son	"Jesus said to him, 'I am the way, and the truth, and the life. No one comes to the Father except through me'" (John 14:6).
	"But that is not the way you learned Christ!—assuming that you have heard about him and were taught in him, as the truth is in Jesus" (Eph. 4:20–21).
Spirit	"But when the Helper comes, whom I will send to you from the Father, the Spirit of truth, who proceeds from the Father, he will bear witness about me" (John 15:26).
	"When the Spirit of truth comes, he will guide you into all the truth, for he will not speak on his own authority, but whatever he hears he will speak, and he will declare to you the things that are to come" (John 16:13).

great commitment to truth. Love, kindness, and compassion must include profound concern that people understand the truth, since their lives depend on it. God meets man's greatest need of relationship with him through an understanding of truth: "Of his own will [God] brought us forth *by the word of truth*, that we should be a kind of firstfruits of his creatures" (James 1:18; cf. 1 Pet. 1:23). Sanctification also happens by means of the truth: "Sanctify them in the truth; your word is truth" (John 17:17; cf. Rom. 12:2). Authentic discipleship is marked by knowing and obeying truth: "If you abide in my word, you are truly my disciples, and you will know the truth, and the truth will set you free" (John 8:31–32). Therefore, loving others involves having a deep desire that they understand truth. This is the reason the Great Commission has a vital teaching element. Making disciples of Christ involves teaching them to observe all he has commanded (Matt. 28:20). Jesus wants people to understand and obey truth and thereby find life in him. Failure to care whether or not loved ones understand the truth is failure to care about their abundant and eternal lives. People are judged and go to hell because they fail to love and obey God's truth (2 Thess. 2:11–13; cf. Rom. 1:18, 21, 25; James 1:18; 1 Pet. 1:23).

Theological Method

Systematic theology seeks to summarize biblical teaching on particular topics in order to draw definitive conclusions that intersect with life. God has revealed himself to his people in human history, which is why he can be known personally. He has not only revealed himself in facts and statements, but what is objectively true of him has also been revealed in the subjective experience of historical events. The experiences God's people had with him in the Bible become the basis for all believers experiencing him now.

God's revelation in history is rich, personal, and wedded to real life. It can also be more difficult to understand than mere facts and propositions because the historical context of the revelation is often foreign to modern people. Because revelation of God is personal and historical, the biblical understanding of God is progressive and cumulative. The theologian then must consider the historical context and progressive nature of revelation at every stage. The theological process must include careful exegesis of passages that are relevant to the question being answered. Furthermore, exegesis should be done with great sensitivity to the historical context of the passages being studied. This theological method has produced several focused areas of study.

The Theological Process

The theological process can be categorized under several aspects and disciplines, as shown on the chart, above right. In particular, systematic theology (the focus of these articles) builds on the conclusions of exegesis and biblical theology. It attempts to summarize the teaching of Scripture in a brief, understandable, and carefully formulated statement. It involves appropriately *collecting*, *synthesizing*, and *understanding* all the relevant passages in the Bible on various topics, and then *summarizing* their teachings clearly so that God's people know what to believe and how to live in relation to theological questions.

Reference to this sort of whole-Bible theology can be seen in Paul's insistence that he did not shrink back from declaring "the whole counsel of God" (Acts 20:27) and in Jesus' Great Commission that the church should "make disciples of all nations" by "teaching them to observe all that I have commanded you" (Matt. 28:19–20).

The Theological Process

Exegesis	The process of seeking to determine the correct meaning out of a particular passage of Scripture.
Biblical theology	The study of scriptural revelation based on the historical framework presented in the Bible.
Systematic theology	A study that answers the question, "What does the whole Bible teach us today about a given topic?"
Historical theology	The study of how believers in different eras of the history of the church have understood various theological topics.
Philosophical theology	The study of theological topics primarily through the use of the tools and methods of philosophical reasoning and information gained from nature and reason ("general revelation") apart from the Bible.
Practical theology	The study of how to best apply theological truths to the life of the church and the world (including preaching, Christian education, counseling, evangelism, missions, church administration, worship, etc.).
Apologetics	The study of theology for the purpose of defending Christian teaching against criticism and distortion, and giving evidences of its credibility.

Major Categories of Study in Systematic Theology

The major topics covered in the study of systematic theology can be seen in the chart below.

Studies in Systematic Theology

Area of Study	Technical Title
Method and foundation	Prolegomena
The Bible	Bibliology
God	Theology proper
Humanity (or man)	Anthropology
Sin	Hamartiology
Christ	Christology
Holy Spirit	Pneumatology
Salvation	Soteriology
Church	Ecclesiology
Last things	Eschatology

Essential vs. Peripheral Doctrine

The ability to discern the relative importance of theological beliefs is vital for effective Christian life and ministry. Both the purity and unity of the church are at stake in this matter. The relative importance of theological issues can fall within four categories: (1) *absolutes* define the core beliefs of the Christian faith; (2) *convictions*, while not core beliefs, may have significant impact on the health and effectiveness of the church; (3) *opinions* are less-clear issues that generally are not worth dividing over; and

(4) *questions* are currently unsettled issues. These categories can be best visualized as concentric circles, similar to those on a dart board, with the absolutes as the "bull's-eye" (see diagram).

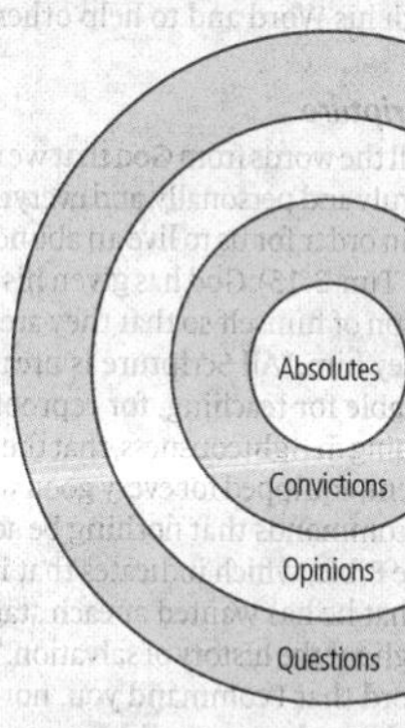

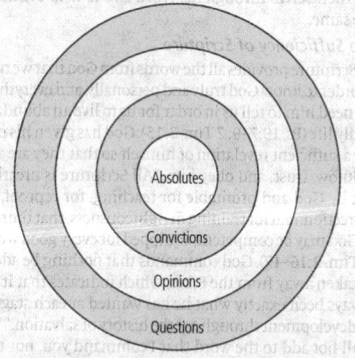

Where an issue falls within these categories should be determined by weighing the cumulative force of at least seven considerations: (1) biblical clarity; (2) relevance to the character of God; (3) relevance to the essence of the gospel; (4) biblical frequency and significance (how often in Scripture it is taught, and what weight Scripture places upon it); (5) effect on other doctrines; (6) consensus among Christians (past and present); and (7) effect on personal and church life. These criteria for determining the importance of particular beliefs must be considered in light of their cumulative weight regarding the doctrine being considered. For instance, just the fact that a doctrine may go against the general consensus among believers (see item 6) does not necessarily mean it is wrong, although that might add some weight to the argument against it. All the categories should be considered collectively in determining how important an issue is to the Christian faith. The ability to rightly discern the difference between core doctrines and legitimately disputable matters will keep the church from either compromising important truth or needlessly dividing over peripheral issues. ◂

The Bible and Revelation

Knowing God is the most important thing in life. God created people fundamentally for relationship with himself. This relationship depends on knowing who he is as he has revealed himself. God is personal, which means he has a mind, will, emotions, relational ability, and self-consciousness. Because he is personal, and not merely an impersonal object, God must personally reveal himself to us. He has done this in general revelation (the world) and special revelation (the Word of God).

General Revelation

General revelation is revelation of God given to all people at all times. This revelation is found both in the external creation (Ps. 19:1, "the heavens declare the glory of God") and in internal human experience (Rom. 1:19–20, "what can be known about God is plain to them, because God has shown it to them. For his invisible attributes, namely, his eternal power and divine nature, have been clearly perceived, ever since the creation of the world, in the things that have been made. So they are without excuse"). General revelation shows attributes of God—such as his existence, power, creativity, and wisdom; in addition, the testimony of human conscience also provides some evidence of God's moral standards to all human beings (Rom. 2:14–15). This means that from general revelation all people have *some* knowledge that God exists, *some* knowledge of his character, and *some* knowledge of his moral standards. This results in an awareness of guilt before God as people instinctively know that they have not lived up to his moral requirements. Thus in the many false religions that have been invented people attempt to assuage their sense of guilt.

But general revelation does not provide knowledge of the only true solution to man's guilt before God: the forgiveness of sins that comes through Jesus Christ. This means that general revelation does not provide personal knowledge of God as a loving Father who redeems his people and establishes covenants with them. For this, one needs *special revelation*, which God has provided in his historical supernatural activities, in the Bible, and definitively in Jesus Christ.

Special Revelation

The Bible is God's written revelation of who he is and what he has done in redemptive history. Humans need this divine, transcendent perspective in order to break out of their subjective, culturally bound, fallen limitations. Through God's written Word, his people may overcome error, grow in sanctification, minister effectively to others, and live abundant lives as God intends.

The Inspiration of Scripture

The Bible is "God-breathed" (cf. 2 Tim. 3:16) and gets its true, authoritative, powerful, holy character from God himself, who inspired human authors to write exactly what he wanted them to write. Instead of merely dictating words to them, God worked through their unique personalities and circumstances. Scripture is therefore both fully human and fully divine. It is both the testimony of men to God's revelation, and divine revelation itself. "No prophecy of Scripture comes from someone's own interpretation. For no prophecy was ever produced by the will of man, but men spoke from God as they were carried along by the Holy Spirit" (2 Pet. 1:20–21). Because the Bible is God's Word in human words, it can be trusted as the definitive revelation from the mouth of God himself.

The Inerrancy of Scripture

The doctrine of inerrancy means that the Bible is entirely truthful and reliable in all that it affirms in its original manuscripts. Another way of saying this is that the Bible does not affirm anything that is contrary to fact. Because God is the ultimate author of the Bible, and because God is always perfectly truthful, it follows that his Word is completely truthful as well: He is the "God who never lies"

(Titus 1:2). It would be contrary to his character to affirm anything false. God is all-knowing, always truthful and good, and all-powerful, so he always knows and tells the truth and is able to communicate and preserve his Word. "O Lord GOD, you are God, and *your words are true*, and you have promised this good thing to your servant" (2 Sam. 7:28). "Every word of God proves true" (Prov. 30:5; cf. Ps. 12:6; 119:42; John 17:17).

Inerrancy does not require twenty-first-century precision or scientifically technical language. The following quotation from the Chicago Statement on Biblical Inerrancy summarizes what inerrancy does *not* mean:

> We affirm the propriety of using inerrancy as a theological term with reference to the complete truthfulness of Scripture. We deny that it is proper to evaluate Scripture according to standards of truth and error that are alien to its usage or purpose. We further deny that inerrancy is negated by Biblical phenomena such as a lack of modern technical precision, irregularities of grammar or spelling, observational descriptions of nature, the reporting of falsehoods, the use of hyperbole and round numbers, the topical arrangement of material, variant selections of material in parallel accounts, or the use of free citations (*Chicago Statement on Biblical Inerrancy*, Art. XIII).

The inerrancy of Scripture gives the believer great confidence in the Bible as his sure foundation for understanding all God wants him to know and all that he needs for godliness and eternal life.

The Clarity of Scripture

The Bible itself acknowledges that some passages of Scripture are "hard to understand" (2 Pet. 3:16, referring to some aspects of Paul's letters). In general, however, with the illumination of the Spirit (2 Tim. 2:7), the teaching of the Bible is clear to all who seek understanding with the goal of knowing and obeying God. OT believers were instructed to teach God's commands continually to their children with the expectation that they would understand it: "These words that I command you today shall be on your heart. You shall teach them diligently to your children, and shall talk of them when you sit in your house, and when you walk by the way, and when you lie down, and when you rise" (Deut. 6:6–7). God's Word is said to "make wise the simple" (Ps. 19:7; 119:30). Jesus based his teaching squarely on the OT Scriptures: he assumed its teaching was clear and would often ask, "Have you not read . . . ?" (cf. Matt. 12:3, 5; 19:14; 21:42; 22:31).

Because of the basic clarity of the Bible, when Christians disagree over the meaning of a passage they can assume that the problem is not with the Bible but rather with themselves as interpreters. Misunderstandings may be due to various factors such as human sin, ignorance of enough of the relevant data, faulty assumptions, or perhaps trying to reach a definite conclusion about a topic where the Bible has not given enough information to decide the question. Yet the emphasis of the Bible is not on difficulties in understanding but on the fact that ordinary believers are capable of comprehending Scripture for themselves. In addition, God provides teachers of his Word to further help his people's understanding (1 Cor. 12:28; Eph. 4:11). Believers have the responsibility to read, interpret, and understand the Bible because it is basically clear. This was an assumption of the Protestant Reformers who sought to translate the Bible into the language of the common people. They believed that all true Christians are priests who are able to know God for themselves through his Word and to help others do the same.

The Sufficiency of Scripture

Scripture provides all the words from God that we need in order to know God truly and personally, and everything we need him to tell us in order for us to live an abundant, godly life (Ps. 19:7–9; 2 Tim. 3:15). God has given his people a sufficient revelation of himself so that they are able to know, trust, and obey him. "All Scripture is breathed out by God and profitable for teaching, for reproof, for correction, and for training in righteousness, that the man of God may be competent, equipped for every good work" (2 Tim. 3:16–17). God commands that nothing be added or taken away from the Bible, which indicates that it has always been exactly what he has wanted at each stage in its development throughout the history of salvation. "You shall not add to the word that I command you, nor take from it, that you may keep the commandments of the LORD your God that I command you" (Deut. 4:2; cf. Deut. 12:32; Prov. 30:5–6). The powerful admonition against tampering that stands at the conclusion of the entire Bible (Rev. 22:18–19) applies primarily, of course, to the book of Revelation, but in a secondary sense what it says may be applied to the Bible as a whole: "I warn everyone who hears the words of the prophecy of this book: if anyone adds to them, God will add to him the plagues described in this book, and if anyone takes away from the words of the book of this prophecy, God will take away his share in the tree of life and in the holy city, which are described in this book" (Rev. 22:18–19).

Believers should find freedom and encouragement in the knowledge that God has provided all of the absolutely authoritative instruction that they need in order to know him and live as he intends. God's people should never fear that he has withheld something they might need him to say in order for them to know how to please him, or that he will have to somehow supplement his Word with new instructions for some new situation that arises in the modern age. (The NT allows for the activity of the Holy Spirit in leading and guiding individuals, as in Rom. 8:14; Gal. 5:16, 18, 25; but this guidance is always in line with Scripture, never in opposition to scriptural commands.) Therefore believers should be satisfied with what Scripture teaches and what it leaves unsaid. "The secret things belong to the LORD our God, but the things that are revealed belong to us and to our children forever, that we may do all the words of this law" (Deut. 29:29).

Jesus' View of Scripture

The most convincing reason to believe that the Bible is inspired, inerrant, clear, and sufficient is because this is what Jesus believed. His teaching assumed that the OT was the authoritative Word of his Father: "Do not think that I have come to abolish the Law or the Prophets; I have not come to abolish them but to fulfill them. For truly, I say to you, until heaven and earth pass away, not an iota, not a dot, will pass from the Law until all is accomplished" (Matt. 5:17–18). Jesus referred to dozens of OT persons and events and always treated OT history as historically accurate. He quoted from Genesis as his Father's Word when he said,

"Have you not read that he who created them from the beginning made them male and female, and said, 'Therefore a man shall leave his father and his mother and hold fast to his wife, and the two shall become one flesh'? So they are no longer two but one flesh. What therefore God has joined together, let not man separate" (Matt. 19:4–6). Jesus not only assumed that the creation story was true, he also freely quoted words from the OT narrator as words that God himself "said." It is not uncommon for Jesus' theological arguments to depend on the truthfulness of the OT account (Matt. 5:12; 11:23–24; 12:41–42; 24:37–39; Luke 4:25–27; 11:50–51; John 8:56–58). Jesus' view of the OT as the Word of God aligns with the way the OT regularly speaks of itself.

Jesus saw his entire life as a fulfillment of Scripture (Matt. 26:54; Mark 8:31). Throughout his life, Jesus used Scripture to resist temptation (Matt. 4:1–11) and to settle disputes (Matt. 19:1–12; 22:39; 27:46; Mark 7:1–13; Luke 10:25–26). At the end of his life, Jesus died quoting Scripture (cf. Matt. 27:46 with Ps. 22:1). On his resurrection day he explained Scripture at length on the Emmaus road and to his disciples in Jerusalem (Luke 24:13–17, 44–47).

Conscious of his identity as God the Son, Jesus saw his teaching as no less divinely inspired than the OT. Jesus taught with an authority that distinguished him from other teachers of the law. He interpreted the law on his own authority rather than depending on rabbinic sources (Matt. 5:21–48). He described his teaching and the law as sharing the same permanence: "heaven and earth will pass away, but my words will not pass away" (Matt. 24:35, cf. Matt. 5:17–18; John 14:10, 24). Jesus viewed both the OT and his own teaching as the Word of God. The NT apostolic witness was a result of Jesus giving his disciples authority and power through the Holy Spirit to impart spiritual truths in writing no less than by word of mouth (Mark 3:13–19; John 16:12–14; Acts 26:16–18; 1 Cor. 2:12–13).

Jesus took Scripture to be the authoritative Word of God upon which he based his entire life. Those who follow Christ are called to treat Scripture (OT and NT together) in the same way. For Christians, the Bible is a source of great delight and joy. God is to be diligently sought in his Word (1 Pet. 2:2). The Word of God is a precious treasure that deserves to be studied, meditated upon, and obeyed:

> My son, if you receive my words and treasure up my commandments with you, making your ear attentive to wisdom and inclining your heart to understanding; yes, if you call out for insight and raise your voice for understanding, if you seek it like silver and search for it as for hidden treasures, then you will understand the fear of the LORD and find the knowledge of God (Prov. 2:1–5). ◂

What It Means to Know God

In the quest to know God, it is vital to understand just what it means to really know him. Methods, expectations, and attitudes in studying theology are determined by one's definition of "knowing God." Central to understanding this is the fact that God is both incomprehensible and knowable.

The Incomprehensibility of God

Scripture teaches that we can have a true and personal knowledge of God, but this does not mean we will ever understand him exhaustively. The Bible is clear that God is ultimately *incomprehensible to us*; that is, we can never fully comprehend his whole being. The following passages show this:

> Great is the LORD, and greatly to be praised, and his greatness is unsearchable (Ps. 145:3).
>
> "Behold, these are but the outskirts of his ways, and how small a whisper do we hear of him! But the thunder of his power who can understand?" (Job 26:14).
>
> "For my thoughts are not your thoughts, neither are your ways my ways, declares the LORD. For as the heavens are higher than the earth, so are my ways higher than your ways and my thoughts than your thoughts" (Isa. 55:8–9).
>
> Oh, the depth of the riches and wisdom and knowledge of God! How unsearchable are his judgments and how inscrutable his ways! "For who has known the mind of the Lord, or who has been his counselor?" (Rom. 11:33–34; cf. Job 42:1–6; Ps. 139:6, 17–18; 147:5; Isa. 57:15; 1 Cor. 2:10–11; 1 Tim. 6:13–16).

These verses teach that not only is God's whole being incomprehensible but each of his attributes—his greatness, power, thoughts, ways, wisdom, and judgments—are well beyond human ability to fathom fully. Not only can we never know everything there is to know about God, we can never know everything there is to know about even one aspect of God's character or work.

Why God Is Incomprehensible

The main reasons for God's incomprehensibility are: (1) *God is infinite and his creatures are finite*. By definition, creatures depend on their Creator for their very existence and are limited in all aspects. Yet God is without limitations in every quality he possesses. This Creator/creature, infinite/finite gap will always exist. (2) *The perfect unity of God's attributes* is far beyond the realm of human experience. God's love, wrath, grace, justice, holiness, patience, and jealousy are continually functioning in a perfectly integrated yet infinitely complex way. (3) *The effects of sin* on the minds of fallen humans also greatly inhibit the ability to know God. The tendency of fallen creatures is to distort, pervert, and confuse truth and to use, or rather abuse, it for selfish ends rather than for God's glory (Rom. 1:18–26). (4) A final reason God can never be fully known is that in his sovereign wisdom *God has chosen not to reveal some things*: "The secret things belong to the LORD our God, but the things that are revealed belong to us and to our children forever, that we may do all the words of this law" (Deut. 29:29). Many would label it unloving for God to decide to withhold some information from his people. They wrongly believe God should reveal everything they may want to know. Yet, as with all good fathers, God's wisdom leads him to refrain from answering all the questions his children ask him, and this contributes to his incomprehensibility.

In heaven, God's incomprehensibility will no doubt be lessened when the effects of sin no longer ravage minds and when he will most likely share some of his secrets. However, God will always be infinite and humans will always be finite, so he will always be beyond human ability to know exhaustively.

Implications of God's Incomprehensibility

Because God can never be fully known, those who seek to know God should be deeply humbled in the process, realizing that they will always have more to learn. The appropriate response to God is a heart of wonder and awe in light of his incomprehensible greatness. God's incomprehensibility also means that beliefs can be held with firm conviction even though they may be filled with inexplicable mystery. The Trinity, the divine and human natures of Christ, divine sovereignty and human responsibility, and many other core teachings of the Christian faith are profoundly mysterious; believing them requires a robust affirmation of the incomprehensibility of God.

The Knowability of God

The incomprehensibility of God could lead to despair or apathy in the quest to know God, but the Bible also teaches that God is knowable. While God can never be exhaustively understood, he can be known truly, personally, and sufficiently. God is personal, has definite characteristics, and has personally revealed himself so that he can be truly known. The multiplication of grace and peace in our lives is dependent on knowing God (2 Pet. 1:2–3), and this knowledge provides sufficient resources for life and for becoming the people God wants us to be.

Knowledge of God in Christ should be our greatest delight (Jer. 9:23–24; 1 Cor. 2:2; Gal. 6:14). It is the basis of attaining eternal life (John 17:3); it is at the heart of life in the new covenant (Heb. 8:11–12); it was Paul's primary goal (Phil. 3:10); and it leads to godly love (1 John 4:7–8). God will never be known absolutely, but we can know things about him that are absolutely true, so much so that we can be willing to live and die for those beliefs. God has provided knowledge of himself that is personal, relational, and sufficient for fruitful, faithful, godly living. No one will ever be able to say he lacked the necessary revelation to know God and to start living as God intends.

Implications of the Knowability of God

God's personal and sufficient revelation of himself should foster solid conviction among believers. We need not live in ambiguity and uncertainty about who God is and what he demands of his creatures. The increasing influence of Eastern religions on the West, certain postmodern views of truth, and religious pluralism all emphasize God's incomprehensibility so much that he is eventually made to seem unknowable. It then becomes impossible to say anything definitively true or false about him, and people then think that the only heresy is claiming that there is any heresy at all! On the contrary, because of his gracious revelation and illumination, God can indeed be known. God's knowability should lead to eager, diligent, devoted study of God's Word so that we can understand him as he has revealed himself and avoid any false view of God that will dishonor him. We should never grow apathetic in seeking to know God because we are in fact able and equipped to know him and to please him with our lives. ◀

The Character of God

"Without faith it is impossible to please [God]" (Heb. 11:6)—but it is also impossible to have *faith in God* without knowing the *character of God*. Faith is belief in God's promises, which in turn are grounded in his character.

Ways in Which God Reveals Himself

God has revealed himself primarily in four overlapping ways: (1) actions; (2) names; (3) images; and (4) attributes, as seen in the chart below. God reveals himself through actions, names, and images because they carry vivid, experiential, creative, and situational power. However, it is God's attributes that are the fundamental descriptions of who he is.

Means of Revelation	Examples
actions	creating, judging, redeeming
names	"Lord" (Hb. *YHWH*, or *Yahweh*)
	"God Almighty" (Hb. *el Shaddai*)
	"Master, Lord" (Hb. *'Adon*)
images	Father, Rock, Husband, Shepherd
attributes	holiness, goodness, love, grace, wrath

Actions of God

God shows who he is in what he does. In creating the world, God shows his power, wisdom, beauty, goodness, and prodigious creativity. After the creation of humanity God talks to, walks with, and seeks out humans, even when they lapse into rebellion against him, showing that he is relational, personal, engaged, and caring. God demonstrates his holiness, wrath, and justice when he curses human rebellion in the garden and judges the unrighteous through the flood in Noah's day. He shows his grace and mercy in establishing a covenant with Noah and Abraham. In sending his Son to live and die for humanity, he shows amazing love and compassion. Whenever God acts, we see his character displayed.

Names of God

God offers his name as a personal introduction and as a window into his character. This is why David says, "Those who know your name put their trust in you" (Ps. 9:10). To know his name is to know he is trustworthy. God's act of naming himself is a profoundly gracious act of accommodation and engagement.

Among the many names for God in the Bible, there is none more important than *Yahweh* (translated "Lord"), a name that was revealed to Moses at the burning bush (Ex. 3:15). Linguistically related to the verb "I am," *Yahweh* is packed with theological import. It most likely communicates God's self-existence, independence, self-sufficiency, eternality, and unchanging character. These transcendent qualities are powerfully complemented when God also tells Moses to refer to him as "the God of your fathers" (Ex. 3:15). God is both majestic and intimate, the great, eternal "I AM," the God who knows his children by name and keeps his covenant promises. Christian worship, discipleship, and preaching must maintain both healthy fear of the Lord *and* freedom and confidence in his presence.

Another striking and revealing name for God is "Jealous" (Hb. *'El qana'*). God tells Moses that he is so jealous for his glory expressed in the faithfulness of his people that "Jealous" is an appropriate name for himself. The reason God gives for his commandment against idolatry is grounded in his character as a jealous God: "For you shall worship no other god, for the LORD, whose name is Jealous, is a jealous God" (Ex. 34:14). God deserves and demands absolute, exclusive loyalty and hates spiritual adultery. In his jealous love he refuses to allow his people to be supremely devoted to anything but himself. Because he is absolutely worthy of worship, allowing his people to love anything more than him would compromise his justice and love.

Images of God

Images of God are analogies from daily life that serve to illustrate his attributes. Among many other images, God is: Father, King, Consuming Fire, Judge, Husband, Shepherd, Potter, Farmer, Refiner, Landowner, Lion, Bear, Light, Water, Tower, and Lamb! These amazingly diverse descriptions from a multitude of human experiences offer pictures of God that reach minds and hearts in ways that abstract definitions do not. Images, like attributes and names, must be considered in relation to one another. If certain images are emphasized at the expense of others, God's character will be misunderstood. The varied images in the Bible are all complementary to each other, and each is vital for understanding God. For example, God as the Rock points out his strength, stability, and justice, while God as Husband gives insight into his loving, faithful, committed heart for his covenant people.

The image of God as a Rock is used in both OT and NT. Deuteronomy 32 especially highlights God as Rock in light of Israel's unfaithfulness: "You were unmindful of *the Rock* that bore you, and you forgot the God who gave you birth" (Deut. 32:18; cf. Deut. 32:4, 13, 15, 30, 31, 37). Paul uses this image as a title of strength and applies it to Christ in 1 Corinthians 10:4: "and all drank the same spiritual drink. For they drank from the spiritual Rock that followed them, and the Rock was Christ." Although the Rock (Hb. *tsur*) of Deuteronomy 32 is *Yahweh*, Paul applies the same title to Jesus. The Rock that followed and provided for the Israelites in the wilderness in the old covenant was the Christ who provides for the Corinthian believers in the new covenant. The Rock in the wilderness shares the same attributes as the Rock of the table, cup, and bread.

The strength and stability of the rock imagery is beautifully complemented by the tender, compassionate image of God as the Husband of his people. "For your Maker is your husband, the LORD of hosts is his name; and the Holy One of Israel is your Redeemer, the God of the whole earth he is called" (Isa. 54:5; cf. Jer. 2:2; Hosea 1–3). God's relational in-

vo[illegible]ement with his people is so intimate and personal that
he is [illegible]lous when his people are unfaithful. God speaks
with the [illegible]lous voice of a husband who has been betrayed
by an adul[illegible] "Surely, as a treacherous wife leaves
her husband, so [illegible]ve [illegible] treacherous to me, O house
of Israel, declares the LORD [illegible] 3:20). The idea of God as
a rock could lead to impers[illegible] cold conceptions,
were it not for the intensely lov[illegible]ed husband imagery. The marriage metaphor co[illegible]
weak, vulnerable, and pathetic if not [illegible]
(and a king, warrior, fire, etc.). Images of God to being
tributes from being mere abstractions in[illegible] a rock
because they are based on our experiences of [illegible] at-

Attributes of God

The attributes of God are the normative descriptions that images, names, and actions illuminate from different perspectives. His attributes are his essential characteristics that make him who he is. God's attributes are typically classified as either incommunicable or communicable. Incommunicable attributes are not shared by humans as are communicable attributes. The attributes can be organized using the classifications shown in the two charts below.

Incommunicable Attributes
Independence (self-existence, self-sufficiency, aseity)
Unchangeableness (immutability)
Eternity
Omnipresence
Unity (simplicity)

Communicable Attributes
Attributes Describing God's Being Spirituality Indivisibility
Mental Attributes Knowledge (omniscience) Wisdom Truthfulness (faithfulness)
Moral Attributes Goodness Love Mercy (grace, patience) Holiness Peace (or order) Righteousness or Justice Jealousy Wrath
Attributes of Purpose Will Freedom Omnipotence (sovereignty)
Summary Attributes Perfection Blessedness Beauty Glory

Practical Implications of the Incommunicable Attributes of God

Attribute	Scripture	Implication
Independence: God does not need us or the rest of creation for anything, yet we and the rest of creation can glorify him and bring him joy.	"Th[illegible] who made the world and everything in it, being Lord of [illegible] and earth, does not live in temples made by man, nor is served by human hands, as though he needed anything, since he himself gives to all mankind life and breath and everything" (Acts 17:24–25; cf. Ex. 3:14; Job 41:11; Ps. 50:9–12; 90:2).	God never experiences need, so serving God should never be motivated by the thought that he needs us. He is the provider in everything.
Immutab[illegible] [illegible] in his [illegible] un[illegible]d [illegible], pu[illegible]cts in response [illegible] although he feels emotions. [illegible]erent situa[illegible]	"For I the Lord do not change; therefore you, O children of Jacob, are not consumed" (Mal. 3:6; for "being," cf. Ps. 102:25–27; Mal. 3:6; James 1:17; for "purposes," cf. Ps. 33:11; Isa. 46:9–11; for "promises," cf. Num. 23:19; Rom. 11:29).	God can always be trusted because he always keeps his word, and is never capricious or moody.
Eternity: G[illegible] has no beginning or end and is in [illegible]way bound by time, althou[illegible] he sees events and acts in his wo[illegible]in time, which is in fact one dimension of the created order.	"Before the mountains were brought forth, or ever you had formed the earth and the world, from everlasting to everlasting you are God" (Ps. 90:2; cf. Ex. 3:14; Job 36:26; Ps. 90:4; Isa. 46:9–10; John 8:58; 1 Tim. 6:16; 2 Pet. 3:8; Jude 24–25; Rev. 1:8; 4:8).	Those who trust the God of eternity can know peace, rest, and comfort in the busyness of life and in spite of impending death, for God keeps them in safety and joy forever.
Omnipresence: God does not have spatial dimensions and is present everywhere with his whole being, though he acts differently in different situations.	"Am I a God at hand, declares the Lord, and not a God far away? Can a man hide himself in secret places so that I cannot see him? declares the Lord. Do I not fill heaven and earth?" (Jer. 23:23–24; cf. 1 Kings 8:27; Ps. 139:7–10; Isa. 66:1–2; Acts 7:48–50).	God can be sought anywhere regardless of place. Believers should never feel lonely, and the wicked should never feel safe.

Practical Implications of the Communicable Attributes of God

Attribute	Scripture	Implication
Holiness: God is absolutely and uniquely excellent above all creation (majesty) and without sin (purity).	"And the four living creatures, each of them with six wings, are full of eyes all around and within, and day and night they never cease to say, 'Holy, holy, holy, is the Lord God Almighty, who was and is and is to come!'" (Rev. 4:8; for "majestic holiness," cf. Ex. 15:11; 1 Chron. 16:27–29; Isa. 57:15; for "moral holiness," cf. Isa. 5:16; 6:1–8; Acts 3:14; Heb. 7:26).	God should be feared and obeyed, and his people should earnestly pursue moral purity.
Omnipotence: God is able to do all his holy will.	"Remember the former things of old; for I am God, and there is no other; I am God, and there is none like me, declaring the end from the beginning and from ancient times things not yet done, saying, 'My counsel shall stand, and I will accomplish all my purpose'" (Isa. 46:9–10; cf. Ex. 6:3; Job 37:23; 40:2; 42:1–6; Ps. 24:6; 33:10–11; 91:1; Dan. 4:34–35; Matt. 28:18).	God's ultimate will is never frustrated by evil, so there is peace and confidence in the face of suffering for those who trust God.
Sovereignty: God has absolute rule over creation as King and total control and determination over all that happens.	"His dominion is an everlasting dominion, and his kingdom endures from generation to generation; all the inhabitants of the earth are accounted as nothing, and he does according to his will among the host of heaven and among the inhabitants of the earth; and none can stay his hand or say to him, 'What have you done?'" (Dan. 4:34–35; cf. 1 Chron. 29:11–13; Ps. 22:28; 24:1; 47:7–9; 103:19; Prov. 16:19, 21, 33; Dan. 4:25; 7:1–28; 12:1–13; Matt. 6:13; 10:29; Acts 17:26; Eph. 1:11; 1 Tim. 6:15; James 1:13–15).	Mankind should obey and submit to God as humble subjects of his kingdom.
Omniscience: God fully knows himself and all things actual and possible—past, present, and future.	"Whenever our heart condemns us, God is greater than our heart, and he knows everything" (1 John 3:20; cf. Job 28:24; 37:16; Ps. 139:1–3; 147:5; Isa. 55:8–9; Matt. 10:29–30; Rom. 11:33–34; 1 Cor. 2:10–11; Heb. 4:13).	All God's thoughts and actions are perfectly informed by perfect knowledge, so he is perfectly trustworthy.
Wisdom: God always knows and chooses the best goals and the best means to those goals. Wisdom is a moral as well as an intellectual quality.	"Blessed be the name of God forever and ever, to whom belong wisdom and might" (Dan. 2:20; cf. Job 9:4; 12:13; Ps. 104:24; Rom. 11:33; 16:27; 1 Cor. 1:21–29; Eph. 3:10–11).	God's wisdom is not always clear to us, but it is great, deep, valuable, and should be highly desired and sought, and we should not doubt its reality even in circumstances that upset us.
Love: God freely and eternally gives of himself. The ultimate historical demonstration of God's love is seen in the cross of Christ.	"Anyone who does not love does not know God, because God is love. In this the love of God was made manifest among us, that God sent his only Son into the world, so that we might live through him. In this is love, not that we have loved God but that he loved us and sent his Son to be the propitiation for our sins" (1 John 4:8–10; cf. John 3:16; 15:13; 17:24; Rom. 5:8; 8:31–39; Gal. 2:20; 1 John 3:16; 4:16).	God is eager to extravagantly give of himself to meet the needs of lost sinners, so they should flee to him with confidence (cf. Rom. 8:32).
Wrath: God intensely hates and responds with anger to all sin and rebellion. God hates every threat to what he loves.	"Then the kings of the earth and the great ones and the generals and the rich and the powerful, and everyone, slave and free, hid themselves in the caves and among the rocks of the mountains, calling to the mountains and rocks, 'Fall on us and hide us from the face of him who is seated on the throne, and from the wrath of the Lamb'" (Rev. 6:15–16; cf. Ex. 34:7; Rom. 1:18; 2:4; 2 Cor. 5:10; 2 Thess. 1:5; 2 Pet. 3:9).	God should be greatly feared. Unbelievers should fear his judgment and turn to Christ for salvation. Believers should fear God's fatherly discipline. The God who loves us is also the holy God who hates sin (1 Pet. 1:17).

The Unity of God

This list of classified attributes of God can be helpful in developing an organized perspective on God's character. However, his character cannot be reduced to a quantifiable list of properties. Maintaining the unity of God's attributes is essential in the study of his character. His unity means that although we experience certain attributes more clearly at certain times, nevertheless, his attributes are not divided into parts and must always be understood interdependently. His attributes are not petals on a flower to be plucked off and viewed in isolation from the rest. The unity of God requires finite creatures to pursue a holistic understanding of him. When God expresses judgment and wrath, he does not cease to be merciful, patient, or kind in that moment. He never expresses certain attributes at the expense of others. Fallen humans tend to emphasize attributes that affirm our personal inclinations, experience, and contemporary sensibilities. Considering God's attributes independently of each other leads to unbalanced idolatrous conceptions of God. A biblically integrated understanding of God involves, along with a list of attributes, the work of the Spirit, the whole counsel of God's Word accurately interpreted, the input of church history, and the input of believers from diverse cultures.

Examples of Application to Life

The two charts to the left labeled "Practical Implications" offer a brief survey of some of God's attributes. Each section of the charts provides a basic definition of an attribute (based on Wayne Grudem's *Systematic Theology*), a key passage of supporting Scripture, and one basic implication for daily life.

God's Attributes Are Seen Most Clearly in Christ

Jesus Christ is the most definitive revelation of all of these attributes. To see God's character we look ultimately to God incarnate: "For God, who said, 'Let light shine out of darkness,' has shone in our hearts to give the light of the knowledge of the glory of God in the face of Jesus Christ" (2 Cor. 4:6). In the cross of Christ all God's major attributes are displayed in condensed lucidity. His wrath, grace, justice, mercy, sovereignty, goodness, love, holiness, compassion, wisdom, and power meet there for the world to see. When discussions of God's attributes become esoteric and sterile, it is the face and cross of Christ that restores radical clarity, reality, and compelling beauty. ◂

The Trinity

The biblical teaching on the Trinity embodies four essential affirmations:

1. There is one and only one true and living God.
2. This one God eternally exists in three persons—God the Father, God the Son, and God the Holy Spirit.
3. These three persons are completely equal in attributes, each with the same divine nature.
4. While each person is *fully* and *completely* God, the persons are not identical.

The differences among Father, Son, and Holy Spirit are found in the way they relate to one another and the role each plays in accomplishing their unified purpose.

The unity of nature and distinction of persons of the Trinity is helpfully illustrated in the diagram below.

God Is One God: Monotheism

There is nothing more fundamental to biblical theology than monotheism (the biblical belief that there is one and only one God): "Hear, O Israel: the LORD our God, the LORD is one" (Deut. 6:4). This verse, known as the *Shema* in Hebrew (from the opening verb of the verse, meaning "hear" or "listen"), is one of the most familiar and foundational verses in the OT. God rejects polytheism (belief in many gods) and demands exclusive devotion: "I am the LORD, and there is no other, besides me there is no God" (Isa. 45:5; cf. Deut. 4:35, 39; 1 Kings 8:60; Isa. 40:18; 46:9). The NT affirms the deity of the Father, Son, and Holy Spirit, as we shall see, but does not waver from OT monotheism (John 17:3; 1 Cor. 8:4–6; 1 Tim. 2:5; James 2:19). Jesus quotes the *Shema* in a debate with the Jewish leaders (Mark 12:29), and Paul continues to teach that there is one God while recognizing Jesus as the divine-human Mediator between God and man (1 Tim. 2:5).

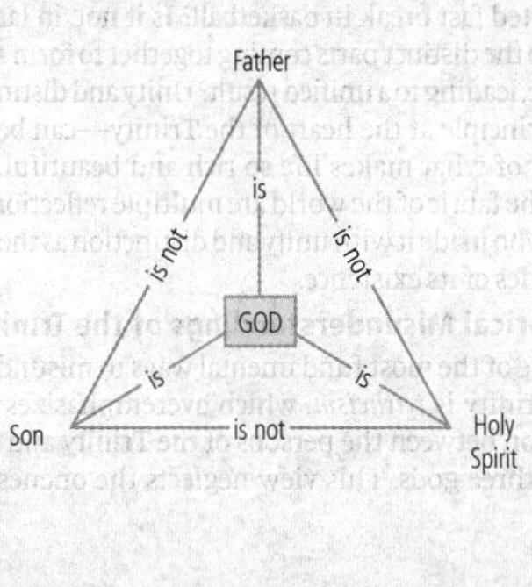

Implications of Monotheism

Because there is only one God, idolatry of any kind is evil, foolish, wrong, and harmful. Worship of other "gods" robs the true God of the devotion and glory he alone deserves. Idolatry can take many forms. Idols are not only man-made objects but are *anything* allowed to compete with God for ultimate loyalty. According to Jesus, money can become an idol: "You cannot serve God and money" (Matt. 6:24). Greed, lust, and impurity can also become indicators of idolatry (Eph. 5:5; Col. 3:5). Idolatry is foolish, deceptive, and dangerous—and may even involve demonic activity (1 Cor. 10:19–20).

Because there is only one God, he alone should be the ultimate object of the believer's affections. He alone deserves absolute allegiance and obedience. The Great Commandment that follows the *Shema* is the obvious implication of monotheism: "You shall love the LORD your God with all your heart and with all your soul and with all your might" (Deut. 6:5). The one true God deserves all we are and have. He deserves wholehearted love because nothing compares with him.

God Is Three Persons: The Tri-unity of God

As the nature of God is progressively revealed in Scripture, the one God is seen to exist eternally in three persons. These three persons share the same divine nature yet are different in role and relationship. The basic principle at the heart of God's triune being is *unity* and *distinction*, both coexisting without either being compromised. Anything that is necessarily true of God is true of Father, Son, and Spirit. They are equal in essence yet distinct in function.

The doctrine of the Trinity is most fully realized in the NT where the divine Father, Son, and Spirit are seen accomplishing redemption. But while the NT gives the clearest picture of the Trinity, there are hints within the OT of what is yet to come. In the beginning of the Bible, the Spirit of God is "hovering over the face of the waters" at creation (Gen. 1:2) and is elsewhere described as a personal being, possessing the attributes of God and yet distinct from Yahweh (Isa. 48:16; 61:1; 63:10). Some interpreters think that the plurality within God is seen in the Hebrew word for God, *'Elohim*, which is plural in form (though others disagree that this is significant; the word is used with singular verbs and all agree that it has a singular meaning in the OT). In addition, the use of plural pronouns when God refers to himself hints at a plurality of persons: "Then God said, 'Let *us* make man in *our* image'" (Gen. 1:27; cf. Gen. 3:22; 11:7; Isa. 6:8). The plurality of God also seems to be indicated when the Angel of the Lord appears in the OT as one who represents Yahweh, while yet at times this angel seems to be no different in attributes or actions from God himself (cf. Gen. 16:7, 10–11, 13; 18:1–33; Ex. 3:1–4:31; 32:20–22; Num. 22:35, 38; Judg. 2:1–2; 6:11–18). There are also passages in the OT that call two persons God or Lord: "Your throne, O God, is forever and ever. The scepter of your kingdom is a scepter of uprightness; you have loved righteousness and hated wickedness. Therefore God, your God, has anointed you with the oil of gladness above your companions" (Ps. 45:6–7). David says, "The LORD says to my Lord: 'Sit at my right hand, until I make your enemies your footstool'" (Ps. 110:1). The God who is set above his companions (Ps. 45:6) and the Lord of Psalm 110:1 are recognized as Christ in the NT (Heb. 1:8, 13). Christ himself applies Psalm 110:1 to himself (Matt. 22:41–46). Other passages give divine status to a messianic figure distinct from Yahweh (Prov. 8:22–31; 30:4; Dan. 7:13–14).

The OT glimpses of God's plurality blossom into the full picture of the Trinity in the NT, where the deity and distinct personalities of Father, Son, and Spirit function together in perfect unity and equality (on the deity of Christ and the Holy Spirit, see pp. 2515–2522). Perhaps the clearest picture of this distinction and unity is Jesus' baptism, where the Son is anointed for his public ministry by the Spirit, descending as a dove, with the Father declaring from heaven, "This is my beloved Son, with whom I am well pleased" (Matt. 3:13–17). All three persons of the Trinity are present, and each one is doing something different.

The NT authors employ a Trinitarian cadence as they write about the work of God. Prayers of blessing and descriptions of gifts within the body of Christ are Trinitarian in nature: "The grace of the Lord Jesus Christ and the love of God and the fellowship of the Holy Spirit be with you all" (2 Cor. 13:14); "Now there are varieties of gifts, but the same Spirit; and there are varieties of service, but the same Lord; and there are varieties of activities, but it is the same God who empowers them all in everyone" (1 Cor. 12:4–6). The persons of the Trinity are also linked in the baptismal formula of Matthew 28:19–20, "baptizing them in [or into] the name of the Father and of the Son and of the Holy Spirit." There are many other passages that reveal the Trinitarian, or at least the plural, nature of God (e.g., John 14:16, 26; 16:13–15; 20:21–22; Rom. 8:9; 15:16, 30; 2 Cor. 1:21–22; Gal. 4:4–6; Eph. 2:18; 4:4–6; 1 Pet. 1:1–2; 1 John 4:2, 13–14; Jude 20–21).

Differences in roles also appear consistently in biblical testimonies concerning the relationships between the Father, Son, and Holy Spirit. The uniform pattern of Scripture is that the Father plans, directs, and sends; the Son is sent by the Father and is subject to the Father's authority and obedient to the Father's will; and both Father and Son direct and send the Spirit, who carries out the will of both. Yet this is somehow consistent with equality in being and in attributes. The Father created through the Son (John 1:3; 1 Cor. 8:6; Col. 1:16; Heb. 1:2), and the Father planned redemption and sent the Son into the world (John 3:16; Rom. 8:29; Gal. 4:4; Eph. 1:3–5). The Son obeyed the Father and accomplished redemption for us (John 4:34; 5:19; 6:38; Heb. 10:5–7; cf. Matt. 26:64; Acts 2:33; 1 Cor. 15:28; Heb. 1:3). The Father did not come to die for our sins, nor did the Holy Spirit, but that was the role of the Son. The Father and Son both send the Holy Spirit in a new way after Pentecost (John 14:26; 15:26; 16:7). These relationships existed eternally (Rom. 8:29; Eph. 1:4; Rev. 13:8), and they provide the basis for simultaneous equality and differences in various human relationships.

Within God there is both unity and diversity: unity without uniformity, and diversity without division. The early church saw this Trinitarian balance clearly. For example, the Athanasian Creed (c. A.D. 500) says:

> We worship one God in the Trinity and the Trinity in unity; we distinguish among the persons, but we do not divide the substance.... The entire three persons are co-eternal and co-equal with one another, so that... we worship complete unity in Trinity and Trinity in Unity.

This unity and diversity is at the heart of the great mystery of the Trinity. Unity without uniformity is baffling to finite minds, but the world shows different types of reflections of this principle of oneness and distinction at every turn. What is the source of the transcendent beauty in a symphony, the human body, marriage, ecosystems, the church, the human race, a delicious meal, or a perfectly executed fast break in basketball? Is it not, in large part, due to the distinct parts coming together to form a unified whole, leading to a unified result? Unity and distinction—the principle at the heart of the Trinity—can be seen in much of what makes life so rich and beautiful. Woven into the fabric of the world are multiple reflections of the One who made it with unity and distinction as the parallel qualities of its existence.

Historical Misunderstandings of the Trinity

One of the most fundamental ways to misunderstand the Trinity is *tritheism*, which overemphasizes the distinction between the persons of the Trinity and ends up with three gods. This view neglects the oneness of the natures of Father, Son, and Holy Spirit. At the other end of the spectrum is the heresy of *modalism* (also known as Sabellianism, named after its earliest proponent, Sabellius, 3rd century), which loses the distinctions between the persons and claims that God is only one person. In this view, the appearance of the three persons is merely three *modes* of existence of the one God. For instance, God reveals himself as Father when he is creating and giving the law, as Son in redemption, and as Spirit in the church age. A contemporary version of modalism is found in the teaching of Oneness Pentecostalism. Both tritheism and modalism fail to maintain the biblical balance between the one reality of God and his eternal existence in three persons. A third error is to deny the full deity of the Son and of the Holy Spirit, and to say that they were at some time created. This is the heresy of *Arianism* (after a teacher named Arius, c. A.D. 256–336), and it is held today by Jehovah's Witnesses.

Practical Implications of the Trinity

What are some of the practical implications of the doctrine of the Trinity?

1. The doctrine of the Trinity makes definitive revelation of God possible as he is known in Christ: "No one has ever seen God; the only God, who is at the Father's side, he has made him known" (John 1:18). No man can see God and live (Ex. 33:20; 1 Tim. 6:16), but God the Son provided an actual manifestation of God in the flesh.

2. The Trinity makes the atonement possible. Redemption of sinful man is accomplished through the distinct and unified activity of each person of the Godhead: "how much more will the blood of *Christ*, who through the eternal *Spirit* offered himself without blemish to *God*, purify our conscience from dead works to serve the living God" (Heb. 9:14).

3. Because God is triune, he has eternally been personal and relational in his own being, in full independence from his creation. God has never had any unmet needs, "nor is he served by human hands, as though he needed anything, since he himself gives to all mankind life and breath and everything" (Acts 17:25). Personhood becomes real only within realized relationships, and the reality of relationship can only exist where one has something or someone that is not oneself to relate to; if, then, God had not been plural in himself he could not have been a personal, relational God till he had begun creating, and thus would have been dependent on creation for his own personhood, which is a notion as nonsensical as it is unscriptural. Between the persons of the Trinity, there has always existed total relational harmony and expression; God is, from this standpoint, a perfect society in himself. Apart from the plurality in the Trinity, either God's eternal independence of the created order or his eternally relational personal existence would have to be denied.

4. The Trinity provides the ultimate model for relationships within the body of Christ and marriage (1 Cor. 11:3; 12:4–6; Eph. 4:4–7).

The doctrine of the Trinity is well beyond human ability to ever fully comprehend. However, it is central to understanding the nature of God and the central events in the history of salvation, in which God is seen acting as, in effect, a tripersonal team. Biblical Christianity stands or falls with the doctrine of the Trinity. ◀

The Person of Christ

Four statements must be understood and affirmed in order to attain a complete biblical picture of the person of Jesus Christ:

1. Jesus Christ is fully and completely *divine*.
2. Jesus Christ is fully and completely *human*.
3. The divine and human natures of Christ are *distinct*.
4. The divine and human natures of Christ are completely *united* in one person.

The Deity of Christ

Many passages of Scripture demonstrate that Jesus is fully and completely God:

> In the beginning was the Word, and the Word was with God, and *the Word was God*. . . . And the Word became flesh and dwelt among us, and we have seen his glory, glory as of the only Son from the Father, full of grace and truth (John 1:1, 14).

> No one has ever seen God; the only God, who is at the Father's side, he has made him known (John 1:18).

> Thomas answered him, "My Lord and my God!" (John 20:28).

> To them belong the patriarchs, and from their race, according to the flesh, is the *Christ who is God over all*, blessed forever. Amen (Rom. 9:5).

> Have this mind among yourselves, which is yours in Christ Jesus, who, though he was *in the form of God*, did not count *equality with God* a thing to be grasped, but emptied himself, by taking the form of a servant, being born in the likeness of men (Phil. 2:5–7).

> . . . waiting for our blessed hope, the appearing of the glory of *our great God* and Savior Jesus Christ (Titus 2:13).

> He is the radiance of the glory of God and the exact imprint of his nature, and he upholds the universe by the word of his power (Heb. 1:3).

> But of the Son he says, "Your throne, O God, is forever and ever." . . . And, "You, Lord, laid the foundation of the earth in the beginning, and the heavens are the work of your hands" (Heb. 1:8, 10).

> Simeon Peter, a servant and apostle of Jesus Christ, To those who have obtained a faith of equal standing with ours by the righteousness of *our God and Savior Jesus Christ* (2 Pet. 1:1).

Jesus' Understanding of His Own Deity

Even though the passages cited above clearly teach the deity of Christ, this truth is often challenged. Some say that Jesus never claimed to be God and that these verses were written by his disciples who deified him because of the impact he had on their lives. Jesus, it is claimed, only saw himself as a great moral teacher on a par with other religious leaders. However, Jesus' understanding of his own deity in the Gospels does not support this perspective. He clearly saw himself as God. This can be seen primarily in six ways.

1. Jesus taught with *divine authority*. At the end of the Sermon on the Mount, "the crowds were astonished at his teaching, for he was *teaching them as one who had authority*, and not as their scribes" (Matt. 7:28–29). The teachers of the law in Jesus' day had no authority of their own. Their authority came from their use of earlier authorities. Even Moses and the other OT prophets and authors did not speak in their own authority, but would say, "This is what the Lord says." Jesus, on the other hand, interprets the law by saying, "You have heard that it was said. . . . But *I say to you*" (see Matt. 5:22, 28, 32, 34, 39, 44). This divine authority is shown with staggering clarity when he speaks of himself as the Lord who will judge the whole earth and will say to the wicked, "I never knew you; depart from me, you workers of lawlessness" (Matt. 7:23). No wonder the crowd was amazed at the authority with which Jesus spoke. Jesus recognized that his words carried divine weight. He acknowledged the permanent authority of the law (Matt. 5:18) and put his words on an equal plane with it: "For truly, I say to you, until heaven and earth pass away, not an iota, not a dot, will pass from *the Law* until all is accomplished" (Matt. 5:18); "Heaven and earth will pass away, but *my words* will not pass away" (Matt. 24:35).

2. Jesus had a *unique relationship with God the Father*. When he was a young boy, Jesus sat with the religious leaders in the temple, amazing people with the answers he gave. When his distraught parents finally found their "lost" adolescent, he replied by saying, "Why were you looking for me? Did you not know that I must be in *my Father's* house?" (Luke 2:49). Jesus' reference to God as "my Father" is a radical statement of a unique, intimate relationship with God, of which he was already fully conscious. Such a reference by an individual was unprecedented in Jewish literature. Jesus took this unique personal address to another level by referring to God the Father using the affectionate Aramaic expression *'Abba'*.

3. Jesus' favorite self-designation was the title *Son of Man*. The phrase "a son of man" could mean merely "a human being." But Jesus refers to himself as *the* Son of Man (implying the unique, well-known Son of Man), which indicates that he sees himself as the Messianic Son of Man in Daniel 7 who is to rule over the whole world for all eternity:

> I saw in the night visions, and behold, with the clouds of heaven there came *one like a son of man*, and he came to the Ancient of Days and was presented before him. And to him was given *dominion and glory* and a kingdom, that *all peoples, nations, and languages should serve him*; his dominion is an *everlasting dominion*, which shall not pass away, and his kingdom one that shall not be destroyed (Dan. 7:13–14).

Jesus establishes his divine authority as the glorious Messianic Son of Man by declaring that he has the power to forgive sin and is lord of the Sabbath: "'But that you may know that the *Son of Man* has authority on earth *to forgive sins*'—he said to the paralytic—'I say to you, rise, pick up your bed, and go home'" (Mark 2:10–11); "And he said to them, 'The Sabbath was made for man, not man for the Sabbath. So *the Son of Man is lord even of the Sabbath*'" (Mark 2:27–28).

4. Jesus' teaching emphasized *his own identity*. Jesus came teaching the kingdom of God, and in it he was the King. His teaching dealt with many topics but was centrally about himself. His question to his disciples, "But who do you say that I am?" (Matt. 16:15), is the ultimate question of his ministry.

5. Jesus *received worship*. Perhaps the most radical demonstration of Jesus' belief that he was God is the fact that when he was worshiped, as he sometimes was, he accepted that worship (Matt. 14:33; 28:9, 17; John 9:38; 20:28). If Jesus did not believe he was God, he should have vehemently rejected being worshiped, as Paul and Barnabas did in Lystra (Acts 14:14–15). That a monotheistic Jew like Jesus accepted worship from other monotheistic Jews shows that Jesus realized that he possessed a divine identity.

6. Jesus *equated himself with the Father*, and as a result the Jewish leaders accused him of blasphemy:

> But Jesus answered them, "My Father is working until now, and I am working." This was why the Jews were seeking all the more to kill him, because not only was he breaking the Sabbath, but he was even calling God his own Father, making himself equal with God (John 5:17–18).

> Jesus said to them, "Truly, truly, I say to you, before Abraham was, *I am*" [a clear allusion to the sacred divine name of Yahweh; cf. Ex. 3:14]. So they picked up stones to throw at him (John 8:58–59).

> "I and the Father are one." The Jews picked up stones again to stone him. . . . The Jews answered him, "It is not for a good work that we are going to stone you but for blasphemy, because you, being a man, *make yourself God*" (John 10:30–33).

> Again the high priest asked him, "Are you the Christ, the Son of the Blessed?" And Jesus said, "I am, and you will see the *Son of Man* seated at the right hand of Power, and coming with the clouds of heaven" [a reference to Daniel 7; see point 3]. And the high priest tore his garments and said, "What further witnesses do we need? You have heard his *blasphemy*. What is your decision?" And they all condemned him as deserving death (Mark 14:61–64).

Implications of Christ's Deity

Because Jesus is God, the following things are true:

1. God can be known definitively and personally in Christ: "No one has ever seen God; the only God, who is at the Father's side, he has made him known" (John 1:18); "Whoever has seen me has seen the Father" (John 14:9).

2. Redemption is possible and has been accomplished in Christ: "For there is one God, and there is one mediator between God and men, the man Christ Jesus" (1 Tim. 2:5).

3. In Christ risen, ascended, and enthroned we have a sympathetic high priest who has omnipotent power to meet our needs: "For we do not have a high priest who is unable to sympathize with our weaknesses, but one who in every respect has been tempted as we are, yet without

sin. Let us then with confidence draw near to the throne of grace, that we may receive mercy and find grace to help in time of need" (Heb. 4:15).

4. Worship of and obedience to Christ is appropriate and necessary.

Historical Misunderstandings of Christ's Deity

The earliest and most radical denial of the deity of Christ is called *Ebionism* or *Adoptionism*, which was taught by a small Jewish-Christian sect in the first century. They believed that the power of God came on a man named Jesus to enable him to fulfill the Messianic role, but that Christ was not God. A later and more influential Christological heresy was *Arianism* (early 4th century), which denied the eternal, fully divine nature of Christ. Arius (c. 256–336) believed Jesus was the "first and greatest of created beings." Arius's denial of Jesus' full deity was rejected at the Council of Nicea in 325. At this council, Athanasius showed that according to Scripture Jesus is fully God, being of the *same essence* as the Father.

The Humanity of Christ

From the moment of Mary's virginal conception of Jesus, his divine nature became permanently united to his human nature in one and the same person, the now incarnate Son of God. The biblical evidence for Jesus' humanity is strong, showing that he had a human body, and a human mind, and experienced human temptation.

Jesus had a *human birth* and a *human genealogy*: "But when the fullness of time had come, God sent forth his Son, born of woman, born under the law, to redeem those who were under the law, so that we might receive adoption as sons" (Gal. 4:4–5).

Jesus had a *human body* that experienced growth (Luke 2:40, 52) as well as physical susceptibilities like hunger (Matt. 4:2), thirst (John 19:28), tiredness (John 4:6), and death (Luke 23:46).

As an old man, the apostle John was still in awe of the fact that he had been able to experience God the Son in the flesh. Like an excited child, he keeps repeating himself as he describes the incarnation:

> That which was from the beginning, which we have *heard*, which we have *seen with our eyes*, which we *looked upon* and have *touched with our hands*, concerning the word of life—the life was *made manifest*, and we have *seen it*, and testify to it and proclaim to you the eternal life, which was with the Father and was made manifest to us—that which *we have seen* and *heard* we proclaim also to you, so that you too may have fellowship with us; and indeed our fellowship is with the Father and with his Son Jesus Christ (1 John 1:1–3).

John has known about the incarnation for over 50 years when he writes this letter, yet he still writes with wide-eyed wonder as he reflects on walking the shores of Galilee, fishing, eating, and laughing with, and having his feet washed by, a carpenter who was God in flesh!

Jesus continues to have a physical body in his resurrected state, and he went to great lengths to make sure his disciples realized this: "See my hands and my feet, that it is I myself. Touch me, and see. For a spirit does not have flesh and bones as you see that I have" (Luke 24:39; cf. Luke 24:42–43; John 20:17, 25–27). After his resurrection, Jesus returned to the Father by ascending in his divinely reanimated body before his disciples' wondering eyes, thus affirming his ongoing full physical humanity (Luke 24:50–51; Acts 1:9–11). The ascension has been included in every important creed of the church because it teaches the enduring complete humanity of Jesus as the only mediator between God and man.

Jesus had a *human mind* that, according to the will of the Father, had limitations in knowledge: "But concerning that day or that hour, no one knows, not even the angels in heaven, nor the Son, but only the Father" (Mark 13:32). His human mind grew and increased in wisdom (Luke 2:52), and he even "learned obedience" (Heb. 5:8–9). To say Jesus "learned obedience" does not mean he moved from disobedience to obedience, but that he grew in his capacity to obey as he endured suffering.

Jesus experienced *human temptation*: "For we do not have a high priest who is unable to sympathize with our weaknesses, but one who in every respect has been tempted as we are, yet without sin" (Heb. 4:15; cf. Luke 4:1–2). While Jesus experienced every kind of human temptation, he never succumbed to sin (John 8:29, 46; 15:10; 2 Cor. 5:21; Heb. 7:26; 1 Pet. 2:22; 1 John 3:5).

Jesus practiced spiritual disciplines. He regularly prayed with passion (Mark 14:36; Luke 10:21; Heb. 5:7), worshiped at services in the synagogue (Luke 4:16), read and memorized Scripture (Matt. 4:4–10), practiced the discipline of solitude (Mark 1:35; 6:46), observed the Sabbath (Luke 4:16), obeyed OT ceremonial laws (John 8:29, 46; 15:10; 2 Cor. 5:21; Heb. 4:15), and received the fullness of the Spirit (Luke 3:22; 4:1). These religious activities were done earnestly (Heb. 5:7) and habitually (Luke 4:16) as the means of a truly human spiritual growth process.

Given Jesus' divine nature, the normality of most of his earthly life is staggering. It seems that Jesus spent the first 30 years of his life in relative obscurity, doing manual labor, taking care of his family, and being faithful to whatever his Father called him to do. In his public ministry Jesus performed miraculous signs and delivered authoritative teaching that could only come from God, and this was shockingly offensive for the people of his hometown, who saw Jesus' simplicity and humility as incompatible with messianic wisdom and power:

> Coming to his hometown he taught them in their synagogue, so that they were astonished, and said, "Where did this man get this wisdom and these mighty works? Is not this the carpenter's son? Is not his mother called Mary? And are not his brothers James and Joseph and Simon and Judas? And are not all his sisters with us? Where then did this man get all these things?" And they took offense at him. But Jesus said to them, "A prophet is not without honor except in his hometown and in his own household" (Matt. 13:54–57).

Jesus did not cease to be fully human after the resurrection. He will be a man forever as he represents redeemed humanity for all of eternity (Acts 1:11; 9:5; 1 Cor. 9:1; 15:8; 1 Tim. 2:5; Heb. 7:25; Rev. 1:13).

Implications of the Humanity of Christ

Humans have obviously been sinful ever since the fall. Therefore, it is easy to assume that being sinful is an essential, necessary part of being a "human being." But this is not true. Jesus was human and yet did not sin. The fact that he became man *reveals the nature of true humanity*. His humanity gives a glimpse of what our humanity would be, were it not tainted with sin. He shows that the problem with humanity is not that we are humans, but rather that we are *fallen*. Jesus' human nature shows the potential of humanity as God intended. This display of sinless humanity reaffirms God's declaration that creation in all its original dimensions (material and spiritual), including humanity, is by divine definition *very* good (Gen. 1:31).

Jesus' humanity enables *his representative obedience* for us. "Therefore, as one trespass led to condemnation for all men, so one act of righteousness leads to justification and life for all men. For as by the one man's disobedience the many were made sinners, so by the one man's obedience the many will be made righteous" (Rom. 5:18–19). Because Jesus is truly human, his perfect life of obedience and overcoming all temptations—culminating in his perfect substitutionary death—can take the place of human rebellion and failure.

Because of Jesus' humanity, he can truly be a *substitutionary sacrifice* for mankind. "Therefore he had to be made like his brothers in every respect, so that he might become a merciful and faithful high priest in the service of God, to make propitiation for the sins of the people" (Heb. 2:17). A man died on the cross when Jesus died, and his death truly atones for the sin of human beings, whose nature he shared.

Jesus' humanity makes him the only *effective mediator* between God and man: "For there is one God, and there is one mediator between God and men, the man Christ Jesus" (1 Tim. 2:5). Jesus' divine and human natures enable him to stand in the gap between fallen humans and a holy God.

Jesus' humanity enabled him to become a *sympathetic high priest* who experientially understands the difficult plight of humanity in a fallen world: "For we do not have a high priest who is unable to sympathize with our weaknesses, but one who in every respect has been tempted as we are, yet without sin. Let us then with confidence draw near to the throne of grace, that we may receive mercy and find grace to help in time of need" (Heb. 4:15–16; cf. Heb. 2:18).

Jesus' humanity means he is a *true example* and pattern for human character and conduct. "For to this you have been called, because Christ also suffered for you, leaving you an example, so that you might follow in his steps" (1 Pet. 2:21; cf. 1 John 2:6).

Historical Misunderstandings of the Humanity of Christ

A second-century heresy called *Docetism* denied the true humanity of Christ. Docetism (from the Gk. verb *dokeō*, "to seem, to appear to be") was based on the presuppositions of Gnosticism, which held to a radical dichotomy between the physical and spiritual realms, and a very negative view of the physical order as worthless. These beliefs led to denying any real physical substance to Jesus' humanity. Docetic Christology taught that Jesus' physical humanity was just an illusion; one of their statements was that "when Jesus walked on the beach, he left no footprints." Docetism has devastating effects on the correct view of Christ, salvation, revelation, and creation. In this view, Christ does not represent humanity in his atoning work, nor does he show us God in human form. It also erodes a biblically positive view of creation which leads to either a negative or an indifferent perspective on life in the body. The NT refutes the seeds of what later became Gnosticism, with its Docetic view of Christ. John strongly condemns any view that denies Christ's full, physical humanity: "By this you know the Spirit of God: every spirit that confesses that *Jesus Christ has come in the flesh* is from God, and every spirit that does not confess Jesus is not from God. This is the spirit of the antichrist, which you heard was coming and now is in the world already" (1 John 4:2).

Apollinarianism was another early heresy that denied Christ's full humanity. Apollinarius (4th century A.D.) believed humans had bodies, animal souls, and rational spirits. He thought the divine *logos* in Christ took the place of the rational spirit of a human. This view was successfully opposed in the fourth century by Gregory of Nazianzen and Athanasius, and rejected at the Council of Constantinople in A.D. 381. The council showed that if Jesus is only, as it were, two-thirds human, full redemption of fully human people is lost. Gregory's famous quotation was "that which He has not assumed He has not healed; but that which is united to His Godhead is also saved." Jesus had to assume every element in a human nature in order to fully redeem humanity.

These two heresies teach believers to appreciate the importance of the humanity of Christ as well as provide a lesson on theological method. Both of these views bring presuppositions about humanity to the Bible and conform biblical teaching to them, rather than allowing Scripture to dictate everything, including the presuppositions. Evangelical theological method must always allow the teaching of Scripture to shape theological conclusions rather than transform its teaching on the basis of alien assumptions. Countless theological errors have occurred by imposing human ideas on the Bible.

The Distinction and Unity of Christ's Two Natures

Along with Jesus' full deity and humanity, the third and fourth necessary affirmations of biblical Christology are that in the incarnation, the divine and human natures remain *distinct*, and the natures are completely *united* in one person. The best evidence of these two realities are passages of Scripture where Jesus' divine glory and human humility are brought together:

> For to us a *child is born*, to us a *son is given*; and the government shall be upon his shoulder, and his name shall be called Wonderful Counselor, *Mighty God*, Everlasting Father, Prince of Peace (Isa. 9:6).

> "For unto you is *born* this day in the city of David a Savior, who is Christ the *Lord*" (Luke 2:11).

> And the Word became *flesh* and dwelt among us, and we have seen his *glory*, glory as of the only Son from the Father, full of grace and truth (John 1:14).

> . . . concerning his Son, who was *descended from David according to the flesh* and was declared to be the *Son of God* in power *according to the Spirit of holiness* by his resurrection from the dead, Jesus Christ our Lord (Rom. 1:3–4).

> None of the rulers of this age understood this, for if they had, they would not have *crucified* the *Lord of glory* (1 Cor. 2:8).

> But when the fullness of time had come, *God sent forth his Son, born of woman*, born under the law, to redeem those who were under the law, so that we might receive adoption as sons (Gal. 4:4–5).

These verses present the profound mystery of the eternal, infinite Son of God stepping into time and space and taking on a human nature. There is no greater thought that could ever be pondered than this.

Implications of the Two Natures of Christ

The belief that Jesus is one person with both divine and human natures has great significance for the possibility of fallen people entering into a relationship with God. Christ must *be* both God and man if he is to mediate *between* God and man, make atonement for sin, and be a sympathetic high priest:

> For in him *all the fullness of God* was pleased to dwell, and through him *to reconcile* to himself all things, whether on earth or in heaven, *making peace by the blood of his cross* (Col. 1:19–20).
>
> For there is one God, and there is *one mediator between God and men*, the man Christ Jesus (1 Tim. 2:5).
>
> Therefore he *had to be made like his brothers in every respect*, so that he might become a merciful and faithful high priest in the service of God, to *make propitiation* for the sins of the people (Heb. 2:17).

In his seminal work *Why God Became Man*, Anselm of Canterbury (c. A.D. 1033–1109) summarized the importance of the two natures of Christ for his atoning work by saying, "It is necessary that the self-same Person who is to make this satisfaction [for humanity's sins] be perfect God and perfect man, since He *cannot* make it unless He be really God, and He *ought not* to make it unless He be really man" (Book II, ch. 7).

Historical Misunderstandings of the Unity of Christ's Natures

There are six historical heresies related to the person of Christ listed in the chart below. The first four heresies are explained above. *Nestorianism* emphasized the distinction between the natures of Christ so much that Christ was made to appear as two persons in one body. *Eutychianism* stressed the unity of the natures to the point where any distinction between them was lost, and Christ was thought to be some new entity, with only one nature, greater than mere man while being fully God in a novel way.

Heresies Concerning the Person of Christ

Ebionism	denies the deity of Christ
Arianism	denies the fullness of the deity of Christ
Docetism	denies the humanity of Christ
Apollinarianism	denies the fullness of the humanity of Christ
Nestorianism	denies the unity of the natures in one person
Eutychianism	denies the distinction of the natures

In A.D. 451, leaders of the church assembled at Chalcedon (outside of ancient Constantinople) and wrote a creed affirming both Jesus' full humanity and his full deity, with his two natures united in one person. Hereby all six Christological heresies were rejected. This creed, formulated at Chalcedon, became the church's foundational statement on Christ. The Chalcedonian Creed reads as follows:

> We, then, following the holy Fathers, all with one consent, teach men to confess one and the same Son, our Lord Jesus Christ, the same perfect in Godhead and also perfect in manhood; truly God and truly man, of a reasonable soul and body; consubstantial with the Father according to the Godhead, and consubstantial with us according to the Manhood; in all things like unto us, without sin; begotten before all ages of the Father according to the Godhead, and in these latter days, for us and for our salvation, born of the Virgin Mary, the Mother of God, according to the Manhood; one and the same Christ, Son, Lord, Only-begotten, *to be acknowledged in two natures, inconfusedly, unchangeably, indivisibly, inseparably; the distinction of natures being by no means taken away by the union, but rather the property of each nature being preserved, and concurring in one Person and one Subsistence*, not parted or divided into two persons, but one and the same Son, and only begotten, God the Word, the Lord Jesus Christ, as the prophets from the beginning have declared concerning him, and the Lord Jesus Christ himself has taught us, and the Creed of the holy Fathers has handed down to us (emphasis added).

Implications of Chalcedonian Christology

The Chalcedonian Creed teaches the church how to talk about the two natures of Christ without falling into error. In particular, Chalcedon teaches the church to affirm that:

1. One nature of Christ is sometimes seen doing things in which his other nature does not share.
2. Anything that either nature does, the person of Christ does. He, God incarnate, is the active agent every time.
3. The incarnation is a matter of Christ's *gaining* human attributes, not of his *giving up* divine attributes. He gave up the glory of divine life (2 Cor. 8:9; Phil. 2:6), but not the possession of divine powers.
4. We must look first to the Gospel accounts of Jesus Christ's ministry in order to see the incarnation actualized, rather than follow fanciful speculations shaped by erroneous human assumptions.
5. The initiative for the incarnation came from God, not from man.

While this creed does not solve all questions about the mystery of the incarnation, it has been accepted by Roman Catholic, Orthodox, and Protestant churches throughout history, and it has never needed any major alteration because it effectively articulates the biblical tension of Christ's two natures, completely united in one person. ◀

The Holy Spirit

The Holy Spirit is a fully and completely divine person who possesses all of the divine attributes. God the Spirit applies the work of God the Son. The Spirit's distinct role is to accomplish the unified will of the Father and the Son and to be in personal relationship with both of them.

The Personality of the Holy Spirit

The Holy Spirit is a distinct personal being with definite characteristics. He is not merely an impersonal force or an emanation of the power of God. (See the article on the Trinity and the discussion of modalism, pp. 2513–2515.)

The baptismal formula of Matthew 28:19–20, "baptizing them in [or into] the name [singular; not, names] of the Father and of the Son and of the Holy Spirit," puts the Spirit on an equal plane with the Father and the Son in his deity and personhood (cf. also Matt. 3:13–17; Rom. 8:9; 1 Cor. 12:4–6; 2 Cor. 13:14; Eph. 4:4–6; 1 Pet. 1:2; Rev. 1:4–5).

The personal nature of the Holy Spirit is evident in his title "Comforter" or "Helper" (Gk. *Paraklētos*) found in John 12:26; 14:16, 26; 15:26; 16:7. Jesus says he will send the Comforter, who will take his place as his disciples' helper: "Nevertheless, I tell you the truth: it is to your advantage that I go away, for if I do not go away, the Helper will not come to you. But if I go, I will send him to you" (John 16:7). An impersonal force could never provide as good a comfort as Jesus. The Holy Spirit must be personal in order to fulfill this most personal ministry.

Scripture speaks of several activities of the Spirit (see chart below) that can only be performed if he is a personal agent. All of these activities of the Holy Spirit are profoundly personal and interrelate with the Father and Son in a way that could only be through the Spirit's distinct personal nature.

The Deity of the Holy Spirit

The Holy Spirit possesses all the divine attributes, as shown in the chart (next column). When the Holy Spirit works, it is God who is working. Jesus taught that regeneration is the work of God: "Truly, truly, I say to you, unless one is born of water and the Spirit, he cannot enter the kingdom of God" (John 3:5). The divine agent that brings this rebirth is the Spirit: "The wind blows where it wishes, and you hear its sound, but you do not know where it comes from or where it goes. So it is with everyone who is born of the Spirit" (John 3:8). God's speaking through the prophets is accomplished through the work of the Spirit. As Paul says in Acts 28:25–26, "The Holy Spirit was right in saying to your fathers through Isaiah the prophet: 'Go to this people, and say, You will indeed hear but never understand, and you will indeed see but never perceive.'" This is a quotation from Isaiah 6:9–10, which is an address from Yahweh to Isaiah. Here in Acts 28:25–26, Paul attributes the words to the Holy Spirit.

Furthermore, the Bible equates a believer's relationship to the Spirit and his relationship with God. To lie to the Spirit is to lie to God: "But Peter said, 'Ananias, why has Satan filled your heart to *lie to the Holy Spirit* and to keep back for yourself part of the proceeds of the land? While it remained unsold, did it not remain your own? And after it was sold, was it not at your disposal? Why is it that you have contrived this deed in your heart? *You have not lied to man but to God*'" (Acts 5:3–4). The Holy Spirit is the one who guarantees God's redeeming work in the lives of believers, and he is the one directly grieved by their sin: "Do not grieve the Holy Spirit of God, by whom you were sealed for the day of redemption" (Eph. 4:30).

Personal Actions of the Holy Spirit

The Spirit comforts	John 12:26; 14:16, 26; 15:26; 16:7
The Spirit teaches	John 14:26; 1 Cor. 2:13
The Spirit speaks	Acts 8:29; 13:2
The Spirit makes decisions	Acts 15:28
The Spirit grieves over sin	Eph. 4:30
The Spirit overrules human actions	Acts 16:6–7
The Spirit searches the deep things of God and knows the thoughts of God	1 Cor. 2:10–11
The Spirit determines the distribution of spiritual gifts	1 Cor. 12:11
The Spirit interprets and brings human prayer before the throne of the Father	Rom. 8:26–27
The Spirit assures believers of their adoption	Rom. 8:16
The Spirit bears witness to and glorifies Christ	John 15:26; 16:14

Divine Attributes of the Holy Spirit

The Holy Spirit is eternal	Heb. 9:14
The Holy Spirit is omnipresent	Ps. 139:7–10
The Holy Spirit is omniscient	1 Cor. 2:10–11
The Holy Spirit is omnipotent	Luke 1:35–37
The Holy Spirit is holy	Rom. 1:4

The Work of the Holy Spirit

The Father, Son, and Holy Spirit are equal in nature but distinct in role and relationship. The distinct roles typically have the Father willing, the Son accomplishing, and the Spirit applying the work of the Son. The Spirit is clearly at work in the key events throughout the history of salvation, including the creation, Christ's incarnation, Christ's resurrection, human regeneration, the inspiration and illumination of Scripture, and the believer's sanctification.

The Spirit's Role in the Ministry of Jesus

The Spirit's role in the human life of the incarnate Christ is often underappreciated. The Spirit brings about the incarnation (Luke 1:35), anoints Jesus for his public ministry at his baptism (Matt. 3:16; Mark 1:10; Luke 3:21–22), fills Jesus (Luke 4:1), leads and empowers Jesus throughout his earthly life (Luke 4:14, 18), and raises Jesus from the dead (Rom. 8:11). The atoning work of Christ is also a Trinitarian accomplishment, with the Spirit playing a prominent role, as seen in Hebrews 9:14: "how much more will the blood of Christ, who *through the eternal Spirit* offered himself without blemish to God, purify our conscience from dead works to serve the living God."

The Spirit's Work in God's People

The reality of God's presence is brought to God's people by God's Spirit. His work is central in the promises of new covenant realities. "And it shall come to pass afterward, that I will pour out my Spirit on all flesh; your sons and your daughters shall prophesy, your old men shall dream dreams, and your young men shall see visions" (Joel 2:28); "And I will not hide my face anymore from them, when I pour out my Spirit upon the house of Israel, declares the Lord GOD" (Ezek. 39:29). These promises are inaugurated at Pentecost when the Spirit's power is poured out on all nations.

The Spirit is the primary person of the Trinity at work in applying the finished work of Christ in the lives of God's people. The acts of the Holy Spirit—rather than the acts of the apostles—are the focal point of the book of Acts. He is the one who enables the apostles to accomplish all their kingdom-advancing work. The power of the Spirit is the catalyst of spiritual transformation. Prayer, church attendance, moral living, coming from a Christian family, and knowing all the right religious words are not a sufficient basis for assurance of one's salvation. But one clear guarantee that someone has passed from death into life is the Spirit's work transforming that person's manner of living. He marks the life and character of believers in a definitive way, as seen in Ephesians 1:13: "In him you also, when you heard the word of truth, the gospel of your salvation, and believed in him, were sealed with the promised Holy Spirit" (cf. 2 Cor. 1:21–22).

In the book of Acts, the Spirit's work was often immediately manifested in miraculous gifts such as speaking in tongues and prophesying. While the Spirit may still choose to work in these ways, it is the fruit of the Spirit that is the normative and necessary evidence of God's work in someone's life: "But the fruit of the Spirit is love, joy, peace, patience, kindness, goodness, faithfulness, gentleness, self-control; against such things there is no law" (Gal. 5:22–23). After the inward renewal that makes someone who has trusted Christ a new creation, the Spirit also brings spiritual understanding, convicts of sin, reveals the truth of the Word, brings assurance of salvation, empowers for holy living, teaches, and comforts.

Although the Holy Spirit's work is evident in the life of someone who is truly born again, even believers can operate "in the flesh" (i.e., by their own self and natural ability apart from God), rather than by Spirit-empowered transformation. God is pleased when his people walk in the Spirit and thus show evidence of his work. God-honoring, unified Christian community is possible only when believers walk in the Spirit. This is why Christians are reminded to "walk in a manner worthy of the calling to which you have been called, with all humility and gentleness, with patience, bearing with one another in love, eager to maintain *the unity of the Spirit* in the bond of peace" (Eph. 4:1–3).

The Holy Spirit Glorifies Christ

The Holy Spirit's work can easily be neglected. Perhaps the reason for this is that one of his primary roles is to glorify Christ by testifying to his kingdom and his saving work, past, present, and future: "When the Spirit of truth comes, he will guide you into all the truth, for he will not speak on his own authority, but whatever he hears he will speak, and he will declare to you the things that are to come. *He will glorify me*, for he will take what is mine and declare it to you" (John 16:13–14). Because the Holy Spirit's purpose is to glorify Christ, he is honored when this objective is accomplished. The Spirit's deepest longing is that the Son be honored. Jesus is the focus of the Spirit's ministry, and believers honor the Spirit by depending on his help in order to honor Christ. The Holy Spirit works to advance the work of Christ to the glory of the Father, and he empowers and anoints the people of God to do the same.

As seen in the chart below, the Holy Spirit glorifies Christ in four fundamental ways. The Spirit continually points to the beauty and wonder of the Son so that people will be drawn to him, become like him, and point others to him as well: "And we all, with unveiled face, beholding the glory of the Lord, are being transformed into the same image from one degree of glory to another. For this comes from the Lord who is the Spirit" (2 Cor. 3:18).

How the Holy Spirit Glorifies Christ

The Spirit illumines the Bible (the centrality of Christ)	Luke 24:27, 44–48
The Spirit empowers gospel preaching (proclamation of Christ)	Acts 1:8
The Spirit brings regeneration (new life in Christ)	John 3:5–8
The Spirit sanctifies the believer (transformation into the image of Christ)	Rom. 8:29; 1 John 3:2

Humans become like what they adore. The Spirit works to foster adoration of Christ so that people will become like him. Thus, sanctification flows from adoration, and both are accomplished by the Spirit in the believer's life.

Implications of the Spirit's Work

The ultimate goal of all of life is to know and love God, make him known, and thereby glorify him. This goal is accomplished primarily through the work of the Holy Spirit. Reading the Bible, going to church, Christian fellowship, spiritual disciplines, service, and worship are merely playing at religion if all of these activities are not empowered, guided, and filled by the Spirit. If he is not present, even these good things are fleshly, empty, and repugnant to God: "For if you live according to the flesh you will die, but if by the Spirit you put to death the deeds of the body, you will live" (Rom. 8:13). A life pleasing to God involves daily dependence on the precious Holy Spirit. He is to be known, sought, and loved. His awakening and empowering have always been the essential ingredients of true and lasting works of God in the lives of his people. His work in the transformed lives of believers is the key to a Christian life that experiences God's blessing and becomes an effective witness to a cynical, skeptical world. Because of the Spirit's presence, true Christians are no longer slaves to sin: "You, however, are not in the flesh but in the Spirit, if in fact the Spirit of God dwells in you. Anyone who does not have the Spirit of Christ does not belong to him" (Rom. 8:9).

It is often too quickly assumed that Jesus' holiness and power in ministry were because of his divine nature rather than the work of the Holy Spirit in his human life. As a result, believers may discount Jesus as their true example. In his holy living and powerful ministry, Jesus often drew on the same resources as are available to all believers, especially the leading and empowering of the Holy Spirit.

The three persons of the Trinity have now been fully revealed in redemptive history, and the Holy Spirit is bringing their work to a magnificent consummation. Many believers expect a world revival in the last days that will include all peoples. Even if such a revival does not come in the generation that is now alive, God's people should be giving glimpses of that coming revival in the character of their lives even today. Such glimpses contribute to fulfilling the Great Commission. Jesus sent his followers even as the Father sent him (John 20:21), and living under and in that authority they are able to say with Jesus, "The Spirit of the Lord is upon me, because he has anointed me to preach good news to the poor. He has sent me to proclaim liberty to the captives" (Luke 4:18). When the Spirit works, the gospel will be boldly proclaimed and God's kingdom will advance. ◀

The Work of Christ

The doctrine of the work of Christ is traditionally organized by the *offices* he fulfilled and the *stages* of his work.

The Offices of Christ

Christ perfectly fulfilled the OT offices of *prophet*, *priest*, and *king*. These offices or roles in the OT reveal aspects of God's word, presence, and power. The anointing and empowering of the Holy Spirit and favor of God was essential if these offices were to truly represent God. OT prophets, priests, and kings foreshadowed the Messiah who would one day ultimately and definitively be manifest as God's Son and Word, bringing access to God's presence and inaugurating the kingdom of God.

The Prophetic Work of Christ

A true prophet of God proclaims God's word to people. God promised Moses that he would raise up a messianic prophet who would authoritatively speak for him: "I will raise up for them a prophet like you from among their brothers. And I will put my words in his mouth, and he shall speak to them all that I command him. And whoever will not listen to my words that he shall speak in my name, I myself will require it of him" (Deut. 18:18–19). Those in Jesus' day expected the Messiah to fulfill the prophetic role the OT foretold. As the author of Hebrews tells us, Jesus' prophetic ministry brought all that previous prophets of God had proclaimed to a definitive culmination: "Long ago, at many times and in many ways, God spoke to our fathers by the prophets, but *in these last days* he has spoken to us by his Son, whom he appointed the heir of all things, through whom also he created the world" (Heb. 1:1–2). Jesus equated his own words with the authoritative words of the Hebrew Scriptures, showing that he knew his words were the very words of God. He recognized the unchanging authority of the Mosaic law (Matt. 5:18) and gave his teaching the same weight: "Heaven and earth will pass away, but *my words* will not pass away" (Matt. 24:35). Because Jesus' words are the very words of God, they are divinely authoritative, eternal, and unchangeable.

Jesus' prophetic authority is vastly superior to that of any other prophet because he speaks God's words *as* God. The divine authority of his words is based on his identity as God incarnate. He proclaimed God's truth as the One who is the Truth (John 14:6). His word is the ultimate Word.

IMPLICATIONS OF THE PROPHETIC OFFICE OF CHRIST

Since Jesus Christ is the true and perfect prophet, he is the ultimate source of truth about God, ourselves, the meaning of life, the future, right and wrong, salvation, and heaven and hell. The voice of Jesus in the Word of God should be eagerly sought and obeyed without reservation or delay. Even though Jesus perfectly fulfills the office of prophet, God's plan is for the church to represent him with its own ongoing prophetic voice, proclaiming truth into the world. Paul certainly saw his own ministry as speaking for God: "Therefore, we are ambassadors for Christ, God making his appeal through us. We implore you on behalf of Christ, be reconciled to God" (2 Cor. 5:20).

The Priestly Work of Christ

While a prophet speaks God's words to the people, a priest represents the people before God and represents God before the people. He is a man who stands in the presence of God as a mediator (Heb. 5:1). The priestly work of Christ involves both *atonement* and *intercession*.

THE ATONEMENT OF CHRIST

The atonement is central to God's work in the history of salvation (1 Cor. 15:4). Atonement is the making of enemies into friends by averting the punishment that their sin would otherwise incur. Sinners in rebellion against God need a representative to offer sacrifice on their behalf if they are to be reconciled to God. Jesus' righteous life and atoning death on behalf of sinners is the only way for fallen man to be restored into right relationship with a holy God.

Even with the extensive requirements for the priesthood in the OT, there was nevertheless a realization that these human priests were unable to make lasting atonement (Ps. 110:1, 4; cf. Heb. 10:1–4). Jesus alone was able to make an offering sufficient for the eternal forgiveness of sins. Because Jesus was without sin, he was uniquely able to offer sacrifice without needing atonement for himself. In offering himself as the perfect, spotless Lamb of God, he could actually pay for sins in a way that OT sacrifices could not. Jesus' atoning offering was thus eternal, complete, and once-for-all. No other sacrifice will ever be needed to pay the price for human sin.

THE NECESSITY OF THE ATONEMENT

Jesus died because of human sin, but also in accordance with God's plan. The reality of human sin is vividly seen in the envy of the Jewish leaders (Matt. 27:18), Judas's greed (Matt. 26:14–16), and Pilate's cowardice (Matt. 27:26).

However, Jesus gave his life of his own initiative and courageous love: "I am the good shepherd. The good shepherd lays down his life for the sheep. . . . For this reason the Father loves me, because I lay down my life that I may take it up again. No one takes it from me, but I lay it down of my own accord. I have authority to lay it down, and I have authority to take it up again. This charge I have received from my Father" (John 10:11, 17–18; cf. Gal. 2:20).

The Father's divine initiative also led to Jesus' atoning work: "He who did not spare his own Son but gave him up for us all, how will he not also with him graciously give us all things?" (Rom. 8:32; cf. Isa. 53:6, 10; John 3:16). As in all events of human history, God's sovereign determination works in a way compatible with human decisions and actions. Even human sin is woven into God's divine purposes, as is seen in verses that say Jesus was "delivered up according to the definite plan and foreknowledge of God" (Acts 2:23), and that "Herod and Pontius Pilate, along with the Gentiles and the peoples of Israel" were gathered together to do "whatever [God's] hand and [God's] plan had predestined to take place" (Acts 4:27–28).

Christ came to save sinners in order to accomplish God's will. Christ died in accordance with God's sovereign, free, gracious choice—not because he was in any way compelled to offer salvation to mankind because of something inherent in us. God did not save fallen angels (2 Pet. 2:4), and he would have been entirely justified in condemning all of fallen humanity to hell; only by reason of his amazing mercy and grace can anyone be saved.

Atonement in the Bible is explained with numerous metaphors and images. The chart below shows the varied images the Bible uses to describe the achievement that is at the heart of the gospel.

Throughout church history, various aspects of the atonement have garnered particular attention. For instance, at different times theologians have stressed the *ransom* imagery, the selfless *example* of Christ, and the *victory* of Christ over evil. These aspects of the atonement, rightly understood, contain true and important insights, but the crux of the atonement is Christ taking the place of sinners and enduring the wrath of God as their substitute sacrifice. This is evident in passages like 2 Corinthians 5:21 ("For our sake he made him to be sin who knew no sin, so that in him we might become the righteousness of God") and Isaiah 53:4–5 ("Surely he has borne our griefs and carried our sorrows; yet we esteemed him stricken, smitten by God, and afflicted. But he was pierced for our transgressions; he was crushed for our iniquities; upon him was the chastisement that brought us peace, and with his wounds we are healed"; cf. Rom. 3:25; Heb. 2:17; 1 John 2:2; 4:10). The fundamental problem of human sin has been solved in Christ's dying for sinners who deserved eternal judgment. Any attempt to diminish the importance of the penal substitution of Christ for us (i.e., the truth that Christ died to pay the *penalty* for our sins) will diminish God's holiness and wrath, as well as the heinous depth of human sin.

Christ's physical suffering on the cross was outweighed by the emotional, psychological, and spiritual anguish of bearing the sin of mankind and having the wrath of the Father poured out on him. The abandonment and bearing of God's wrath that Jesus experienced on the cross is beyond our comprehension. On account of this merciful, substitutionary sacrifice he will be worshiped for all eternity by those who are his (Rev. 5:11–12). While Jesus' death for sinners was the basis of his atoning work, his life of perfect righteousness in their place was also necessary to win their forgiveness. He not only *died* for rebels, he also *lived* for them (Rom. 5:19; Phil. 3:9).

THE INTERCESSION OF CHRIST

Jesus' priestly work on the cross atoned for sin once for all. Grounded in that atoning work, his priestly work of intercession continues now and forevermore on behalf of his people: "Who is to condemn? Christ Jesus is the one who died—more than that, who was raised—who is at the right hand of God, *who indeed is interceding for us*" (Rom. 8:34); Christ "is able to save to the uttermost those who draw near to God through him, *since he always lives to make intercession for them*" (Heb. 7:25). Jesus is alive and always at work representing and bringing requests for believers before the throne of God, intervening in heaven for them. He is the God-man who mediates and represents fallen people based on his fully sufficient work on the cross, and his intervention never fails. Jesus, the sinner's divine lawyer, never loses a case: "My little children, I am writing these things to you so that you may not sin. But if anyone does sin, we have an advocate with the Father, Jesus Christ the righteous" (1 John 2:1).

As the people who constitute the church are intended to have a prophetic voice as Christ's ambassadors, God also intends to use the church in a priestly role to usher people into his presence. Because of Christ's work, all of God's people are viewed as priests with priestly access into his presence and with the privilege of representing people before God (1 Pet. 2:9; Rev. 5:9–10). Prayer, preaching, gospel proclamation, and taking initiative in personal, spiritual ministry are all ways in which God's people can encourage

Biblical Descriptions of the Atonement

Type of Language	Biblical Words	Human Need	The Result
Language of OT sacrifices	Blood, lamb, sacrifice	We are guilty	We are forgiven
Language of personal relationships	Reconciliation	We are alienated from God	We are brought back into intimate fellowship with God
Language of righteous anger at wrongdoing	Propitiation	We are under God's holy wrath	God's wrath is satisfied/quenched
Language of the marketplace	Redemption, ransom	We are enslaved	We are set free
Language of the law court	Justification	We are condemned	We are pardoned and counted as righteous
Language of the battlefield	Victory, deliverance, rescue	We are facing dreadful enemies	We are delivered and are triumphant in Christ

others to seek and know God and can thereby fulfill their call to represent Christ as a kingdom of priests.

The Kingly Work of Christ

Christ is not only the ultimate prophet and priest, he is also the divine king. Unlike the kings of Israel who were intended to foreshadow the Messiah, Jesus' reign as messianic King is in no way limited. He rules over all creation and for all time (Luke 1:31–33; Col. 1:17). This rule most directly touches believers at present, but one day all peoples will bow to his royal authority (Phil. 2:9–10). In addition to his comprehensive rule, Christ the King also defends, protects, and shepherds his people and will one day judge all the world's inhabitants—past, present, and future.

God's people represent their King when they work to see kingdom realities spread in the world. When they seek social justice—fighting to relieve the plight of the poor, disenfranchised, or unborn—they are working to spread the values of their King. When they work hard and live as good citizens, they are salt and light in a dark world, ultimately serving the interest of their King. One day, when Christ makes all things new, those who are in him will reign with their King: "The saying is trustworthy, for: If we have died with him, we will also live with him; if we endure, we will also reign with him" (2 Tim. 2:11–12a; cf. Rev. 5:9–10).

The Stages of Christ's Work

There is perhaps no more comprehensive yet concise statement on the work of Christ than Philippians 2:5–11:

> Have this mind among yourselves, which is yours in Christ Jesus, who, though he was in the form of God, did not count equality with God a thing to be grasped, but emptied himself, by taking the form of a servant, being born in the likeness of men. And being found in human form, he humbled himself by becoming obedient to the point of death, even death on a cross. Therefore God has highly exalted him and bestowed on him the name that is above every name, so that at the name of Jesus every knee should bow, in heaven and on earth and under the earth, and every tongue confess that Jesus Christ is Lord, to the glory of God the Father.

These verses teach the profound humility and eventual exaltation of Christ in the history of salvation. The key sequence set out here has been described as the 10 stages of Christ's work, divided into a humiliation phase and an exaltation phase. The stages are: (1) preincarnate glory; (2) incarnation; (3) earthly life; (4) crucifixion; (5) resurrection; (6) ascension; (7) sitting at God's right hand; (8) second coming; (9) future reign (some think this will be a millennial reign; see Introduction to Revelation); (10) eternal glory.

The 10 stages and two phases can be visualized as shown in the diagram, p. 2525.

Preincarnate Glory

To truly understand the humility of Christ in becoming a man, one must ponder what he gave up in order to make this possible. While we know very little about the experience of God before this world's creation, we do know that he has always existed as one being, the three persons within his being perfectly relating in mutual love and glorification as Father, Son, and Holy Spirit (John 1:1; 17:5, 24). Along with this intra-Trinitarian glorification, angelic beings (creatures themselves) unceasingly worship the infinite worth of the triune God. Jesus consented to surrender this perfect heavenly state so he could represent humanity in his incarnation. When he took the role of a servant and assumed a human nature in addition to his divine nature (Phil. 2:5–11), his divinity was veiled in his humanity. He willingly surrendered the continuous heavenly display and acknowledgment of his glorious divine nature. This amazing humility is taught in 2 Corinthians 8:9: "For you know the grace of our Lord Jesus Christ, that though he was rich, yet for your sake he became poor, so that you by his poverty might become rich." Only when the glories of heaven are finally revealed will what Jesus temporarily gave up in coming to earth as a man be most fully understood. What amazing, loving condescension!

The Humiliation of Christ

INCARNATION

In the incarnation (lit., "in flesh") Christ took on a full, complete human nature, including a physical body, so that he could truly represent humanity (Phil. 2:6; Heb. 2:17). God the Son chose to come to earth in the most humble way, defying all expectation. His contemporaries saw him as the son of a poor couple, born in a small, obscure village, and with nothing in his appearance to attract them to himself (cf. Isa. 53:2). In the incarnation, God shows in striking manner that he does not value what the world so often values.

EARTHLY LIFE

Christ's earthly life was one of continual humiliation. He subtly and selectively revealed his divine glory, even keeping it a secret at times (Matt. 9:30; Mark 1:44; 5:43). He radically altered the prevalent conception of the Messiah, combining the suffering servant of Isaiah 53 with the glorious Conquering King of Daniel 7. Throughout his life Jesus was poor and at times homeless: "Foxes have holes and birds of the air have nests, but the Son of Man has nowhere to lay his head" (Matt. 8:20). His life was one of great and consistent service for the good of others. The last grand gesture of his life before going to the cross was washing his disciples' feet (John 13:1–17). Although multitudes followed him during his public ministry, he also faced frequent persecution and rejection, at times even in his hometown (Luke 4:28–29). The creatures' rejection of their Creator epitomizes human rebellion. John 1:10–11 describes this tragedy: "He was in the world, and the world was made through him, yet the world did not know him. He came to his own, and his own people did not receive him."

Jesus' earthly life ended with some of his closest friends betraying him (Judas), denying him (Peter), and deserting him (all the disciples, Matt. 26:56). His life was filled with rejection, loneliness, poverty, persecution, hunger, temptation, suffering, and finally death.

CRUCIFIXION

Christ's humiliation reached its greatest depth when he gave his life on a criminal's cross for sinful humanity. The cross stands at the center of human history as God's supreme act of love (1 John 4:10, 17) and the only source of redemption for lost and fallen humanity (Rom. 14:9).

The Humiliation and Exaltation of Christ

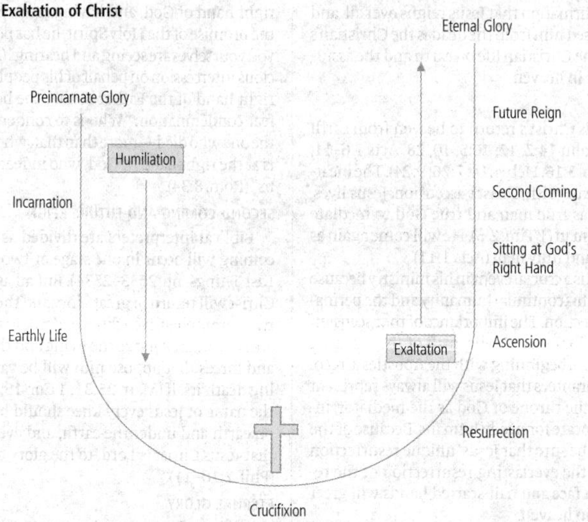

The Humiliation of Christ

Incarnation	"And the Word became flesh and dwelt among us, and we have seen his glory, glory as of the only Son from the Father, full of grace and truth" (John 1:14).
Earthly Life	"For even the Son of Man came not to be served but to serve, and to give his life as a ransom for many" (Mark 10:45).
Crucifixion	"And being found in human form, he humbled himself by becoming obedient to the point of death, even death on a cross" (Phil. 2:8).

The Exaltation of Christ

Resurrection	"Jesus said to her, 'I am the resurrection and the life. Whoever believes in me, though he die, yet shall he live, and everyone who lives and believes in me shall never die. Do you believe this?'" (John 11:25–26).
Ascension	"Men of Galilee, why do you stand looking into heaven? This Jesus, who was taken up from you into heaven, will come in the same way as you saw him go into heaven" (Acts 1:11).
Heavenly Session	"Who is to condemn? Christ Jesus is the one who died—more than that, who was raised—who is at the right hand of God, who indeed is interceding for us" (Rom. 8:34).
Second Coming	"For the Lord himself will descend from heaven with a cry of command, with the voice of an archangel, and with the sound of the trumpet of God. And the dead in Christ will rise first" (1 Thess. 4:16).
Eternal Glory	"And I heard every creature in heaven and on earth and under the earth and in the sea, and all that is in them, saying, 'To him who sits on the throne and to the Lamb be blessing and honor and glory and might forever and ever!'" (Rev. 5:13).

The Exaltation of Christ

RESURRECTION

While Jesus' life of humiliation represented the life of human beings living in a fallen world, his victorious exaltation represents a pattern that will someday be reproduced (and is partially reproduced already) in those who believe in him. The exaltation of Christ began when he left his grave clothes in an empty tomb. Sin, Satan, and death were decisively defeated when Jesus rose from the dead. Jesus foretold his resurrection (e.g., Mark 8:31; 9:31; 10:34) and then actually did rise from the dead (as is shown by convincing historical evidence, such as the empty tomb, numerous eyewitness accounts, the radical change in the disciples' lives, etc.). In addition to defeating sin and death, the resurrection was the Father's validation of the Son's ministry (Rom. 1:3) and demonstrates the complete effectiveness of Christ's atoning work (Rom. 4:25).

First Corinthians 15 provides the most comprehensive treatment of the benefits of the resurrection. By explaining what would be lost if Jesus had not risen from the dead, Paul provides abundant reason for hope in the truth of the resurrection because "in fact Christ has been raised from the dead, the firstfruits of those who have fallen asleep" (v. 20). Because Christ rose from the dead, the sins of those who rely on him are forgiven (v. 17), the apostolic preaching is true (v. 15), faith in Christ is true and he can be fully trusted (v. 14), those who follow Christ are to be emulated and their preaching is of great value (v. 19), and those who die in Christ will be raised (v. 18). Because of the resurrection, the Christian has great hope that generates confidence in all circumstances. The resurrection is not merely a doctrine to be affirmed intellectually; it is the resounding affirmation that Jesus reigns over all, and the power that raised him from the dead is the Christian's power for living the Christian life on earth and the assurance of eternal life in heaven.

ASCENSION

The ascension is Christ's return to heaven from earth (Luke 24:50–51; John 14:2, 12; 16:5, 10, 28; Acts 1:6–11; Eph. 4:8–10; 1 Tim. 3:16; Heb. 4:14; 7:26; 9:24). The incarnation does not cease with Christ's ascension. Jesus lives, now and forever, as true man and true God to mediate between God and man (1 Tim. 2:5). He will come again as he left, fully God and fully man (Acts 1:11).

Jesus' ascension is a crucial event in his ministry because it explicitly shows his continual humanity and the permanence of his resurrection. The importance of the ascension is seen in the fact that it is taught in all of the essential creeds of the church, beginning with the Apostles' Creed. The ascension guarantees that Jesus will always represent humanity before the throne of God as the mediator, intercessor, and advocate for needy humans. Because of the ascension, we can be sure that Jesus' unique resurrection leads the way for the everlasting resurrection of the redeemed. A human face and nail-scarred hands will greet believers one day in heaven.

Jesus also ascended to prepare a place for his people (John 14:2–3) and to enable the Holy Spirit to come (John 16:7), which he said was more advantageous for the church than if he had stayed on earth (John 14:12, 17).

SITTING AT GOD'S RIGHT HAND

The current state of Christ's work is called his "heavenly session," meaning that he is seated at the right hand of the Father, actively interceding and reigning over his kingdom, awaiting his second coming (Acts 2:3–36; Rom. 8:34; Eph. 1:20–22; Col. 3:1; Heb. 1:3, 13; 8:1; 10:12; 12:2; 1 Pet. 3:22; Rev. 3:21; 22:1). The OT foretold this phase of the Messiah's work: "The LORD says to my Lord: 'Sit at my right hand, until I make your enemies your footstool'" (Ps. 110:1). Jesus told of the heavenly session which would precede his return when he referred to the messianic imagery of Daniel 7: "from now on you will see the Son of Man seated at the right hand of Power and coming on the clouds of heaven" (Matt. 26:64). The right hand of God is the symbolic place of power, honor, distinction, and prestige. Jesus "sits" to portray the sufficiency of his saving work on earth; he continues a vital, active ministry as he reigns over all creation.

Jesus' current ministry is a great source of comfort, authority, and encouragement for the believer because it ensures that his ministry as Prophet, Priest, and King continues and will one day be acknowledged by all creation. From his current exalted position Jesus pours out his Spirit on his people: "Being therefore exalted at the right hand of God, and having received from the Father the promise of the Holy Spirit, he has poured out this that you yourselves are seeing and hearing" (Acts 2:33). His precious intercession on behalf of his people takes place at the right hand of the Father so that the believer need never fear condemnation: "Who is to condemn? Christ Jesus is the one who died—more than that, who was raised—who is at the right hand of God, who indeed is interceding for us" (Rom. 8:34).

SECOND COMING AND FUTURE REIGN

Biblical interpreters are divided as to whether Jesus' coming will occur in one stage or two (see the article on Last Things, pp. 2533–2534). But all agree that someday Christ will return in great glory and there will be a definitive, comprehensive acknowledgment that he is Lord over all. He will then judge the living and the dead. All people and forces that oppose him will be vanquished, including death itself (Matt. 25:31; 1 Cor. 15:24–28), "so that at the name of Jesus every knee should bow, in heaven and on earth and under the earth, and every tongue confess that Jesus Christ is Lord, to the glory of God the Father" (Phil. 2:10–11).

ETERNAL GLORY

Prior to the incarnation Jesus was glorious. But by displaying his holy character through his incarnate life, death, and resurrection, he received even greater glory. Jesus' preincarnate glory was taken to a new level when he entered into his eternal glory not only as God but now as God-Man. Jesus displayed his divine character through the human actions of his incarnate life, death, and resurrection. His majesty, mercy, love, holiness, wisdom, and power have been manifested sinlessly in a true man, and for this Jesus will be praised for all eternity. Therefore, the worship of heaven focuses on the work of Christ as the worthy Lamb who was slain:

> And they sang a new song, saying, "Worthy are you to take the scroll and to open its seals, for you were slain, and by your blood you ransomed people for God from every tribe and language and people and nation, and you have made them a kingdom and priests to our God, and they shall reign on the earth. . . . Worthy is the Lamb who was slain, to receive power and wealth and wisdom and might and honor and glory and blessing!" (Rev. 5:9–10, 12)

Christ's eternal glory, which he shares with the Father and the Holy Spirit, is the supreme goal of all that he did. In redeeming a people for himself, he displayed his many perfections in such a way that he will now receive the glory he deserves. That glory will be displayed and acknowledged around his throne, in the songs of heaven forever! ◀

Mankind

God as Creator

God created human beings and everything else that has ever existed in distinction from himself. From the first verse of the Bible (which declares that God created the heavens and the earth) to the last chapters of the Bible (where God brings about a new heaven and earth), God is seen as the praiseworthy source of all that is. Worship is the right response to God's creative and sustaining power. Often in the Bible the praise of God's people arises out of the recognition that God made the heavens and the earth:

> "You are the LORD, you alone. You have made heaven, the heaven of heavens, with all their host, the earth

and all that is on it, the seas and all that is in them; and you preserve all of them; and the host of heaven worships you" (Neh. 9:6).

Oh come, let us worship and bow down; let us kneel before the LORD, our Maker! (Ps. 95:6; cf. Acts 14:15).

God's personal, wise power is clearly seen in creation, especially in humanity:

For you formed my inward parts; you knitted me together in my mother's womb. I praise you, for I am fearfully and wonderfully made. Wonderful are your works; my soul knows it very well. My frame was not hidden from you, when I was being made in secret, intricately woven in the depths of the earth (Ps. 139:13–15).

The key passage for understanding the nature of mankind is Genesis 1:26–28:

Then God said, "Let us make man in our image, after our likeness. And let them have dominion over the fish of the sea and over the birds of the heavens and over the livestock and over all the earth and over every creeping thing that creeps on the earth." So God created man in his own image, in the image of God he created him; male and female he created them. And God blessed them. And God said to them, "Be fruitful and multiply and fill the earth and subdue it and have dominion over the fish of the sea and over the birds of the heavens and over every living thing that moves on the earth" (Cf. Gen. 2:7; 5:1–2; 9:6; Matt. 19:4; Acts 17:24–25).

Both men and women are made in God's image (Gen. 1:27), and therefore they are more like God than anything else in all creation. Human beings are intended to live as God's created analogy for his own glory. God did not create humans because of any need within himself (Job 41:11; Ps. 50:9–12; Acts 17:24–25) but primarily so that he would be glorified in them as they delight in him and reflect his character. We were created primarily to be in relationship with our Creator and find our greatest joy in him. When people are supremely satisfied in him, God is rightly honored and delights in his creation. God describes his people as "everyone who is called by my name, *whom I created for my glory*, whom I formed and made" (Isa. 43:7; cf. Eph. 1:11–12).

Although God has no unmet needs, humans bring delight to his heart as they trust and obey him.

You shall be a crown of beauty in the hand of the LORD, and a royal diadem in the hand of your God.... As the bridegroom rejoices over the bride, so shall your God rejoice over you (Isa. 62:3–5).

The LORD your God is in your midst...he will rejoice over you with gladness...he will exult over you with loud singing (Zeph. 3:17).

God's delight in the Spirit-empowered faithfulness of his people is the believer's greatest motive for holy living in the Christian life. Unbiblical motives for obeying God's commands include pragmatism, legalism, utilitarianism, and man-centeredness. But biblical ethics insists that our deepest desire should be to find our greatest joy in bringing joy to the heart of our Creator.

Implications of Being Created in God's Image for His Glory

1. Humility, Purpose, and Accountability

When God is recognized as the Creator of everything, he takes his rightful place as the one upon whom we are utterly dependent for all we are and have. Nothing exists apart from the creative and sustaining power of God, and all things owe honor and submission to him. This dependence should lead to deep humility and accountability before the God who made us (Rom. 9:20–21). God's personal creation of all humans (Ps. 139:13–16) is the basis for human purpose and meaning. The doctrine of creation ensures that we recognize God as majestic and great, and recognize that we are very small before him. When people truly understand God as Creator, they recognize that he is eternal, powerful, wise, good, the owner of all things, and the judge of all. Because God is Creator, all people must answer to him; he, however, need not answer to anyone: "But who are you, O man, to answer back to God? Will what is molded say to its molder, 'Why have you made me like this?' Has the potter no right over the clay, to make out of the same lump one vessel for honorable use and another for dishonorable use?" (Rom. 9:20–21).

2. Seeing the Gifts and Glory of God in Creation

At the culmination of God's creation he declared it to be "very good" (Gen. 1:31), but it was later marred and distorted by the fall and God's curse (Genesis 3; Rom. 8:20–23). Nevertheless, the heavens continue to declare the glory of God (Ps. 19:1–14), God continues to give bountiful gifts to be gratefully enjoyed (1 Tim. 6:17), and God's image-bearers are encouraged to see and glorify him in all things (1 Cor. 10:31).

3. Hope Due to God's Creative Work and Power

The NT compares God's work of redemption with his work in creation: "For God, who said, 'Let light shine out of darkness,' has shone in our hearts to give the light of the knowledge of the glory of God in the face of Jesus Christ" (2 Cor. 4:6). When God redeems someone, he is re-creating with the same power with which he spoke the world into existence (2 Cor. 5:17; Eph. 2:10). God is the powerful, wise, good God who made everything; knowing this provides great hope for personal and cosmic transformation. There is never room for a believer to despair over his or her own level of sanctification, nor is it legitimate to doubt God's ability to change someone we are ministering to, because God's power as Creator is more than able to change rebellious hearts into worshipful ones. We can also be sure that this fallen and cursed world will one day be made new by the One who created it in the first place.

4. Philosophy of Ministry

Because God created everything with his glory as the ultimate goal, bringing honor to his name is the appropriate, explicit, overarching objective of all life and ministry: "So, whether you eat or drink, or whatever you do, do all to the glory of God" (1 Cor. 10:31). When planning a worship service or church program, thinking through a business plan, raising a family, creating art, or running a farm, the fundamental question must always be, "Will God be glorified?"

Man Made in the Image of God

Man is made in the image of God, which means that he is like God and represents God on the earth:

> Then God said, "Let us make man *in our image, after our likeness*. And let them have dominion over the fish of the sea and over the birds of the heavens and over the livestock and over all the earth and over every creeping thing that creeps on the earth." So God created man *in his own image, in the image of God* he created him; male and female he created them (Gen. 1:26–27).

While everything in creation to some degree reflects something of who God is (Ps. 19:1–6), humans stand alone as made in the image and likeness of God. People are intended to live as God's created analogies, showing his character more clearly than anything else can show it. Being made in the image of God distinguishes mankind from all other living things.

While humans are the pinnacle of creation, to say we are *like* God also means that we are not and will never *be* God. We have great dignity because we are made in God's image, but our worth is not autonomous. God is the source of all human value.

The fall and curse of humanity distorts the image of God in man but does not remove it from him. After the fall, the image of God remains the basis for human dignity and biblical ethics (Gen. 9:6; James 3:8–9).

The image of God is evident in our unique spiritual, moral, mental, relational, and physical capacities. Humans reflect the image of God in varying degrees and ways, but no one is made in *more* of God's image or *less* of God's image. The foundation of Christian ethics is the assumption that *all* humans are made in God's image regardless of the presence or absence of certain abilities. From conception to death all human beings are God's image-bearers, and all are creatures of profound dignity and value, equally worthy of protection and respect. The value of human life is not affected or determined by age, disability, race, intellectual ability, emotional or mental state, relational powers, or gender.

The Great Commandment—to love God with all our heart, soul, mind, and strength—obviously entails the second greatest commandment: to love our neighbor as ourselves (Matt. 22:37–40). Love for God *must* be expressed in love for people, even one's enemies (Luke 6:27). "If anyone says, 'I love God,' and hates his brother, he is a liar; for he who does not love his brother whom he has seen cannot love God whom he has not seen. And this commandment we have from him: *whoever loves God must also love his brother*" (1 John 4:20–21). Christians are called to see beyond mankind's fallen condition to the image of God in the people they interact with every day, and to love them based on what God says is true of them. This means they no longer regard anyone from a worldly point of view but rather see them with God's eyes: "From now on, therefore, we regard no one *according to the flesh*. Even though we once regarded Christ *according to the flesh*, we regard him thus no longer" (2 Cor. 5:16). As Augustine wrote, "Yet men go out and gaze in astonishment at high mountains, the huge waves of the sea, the broad reaches of rivers, the ocean that encircles the world, or the stars in their courses. But they pay no attention to themselves" (*Confessions* 10.8).

Jesus, who in his divinity is already the image of the invisible God (2 Cor. 4:4; Col. 1:15), perfectly reflects the divine image in his true humanity and holy life on earth. Jesus shows perfect humanness in his perfect fellowship with and obedience to the Father, which leads to his selfless love for others. These characteristics of Christ's life are foundational to all other God-glorifying manifestations of the image of God in humanity. Therefore, to experience true humanity, God's people should pattern their lives after Jesus' exemplary relationship to God the Father. In this way, they will be conformed more and more to the image of Christ (Rom. 8:29; cf. 1 John 3:2).

The Constitutional Makeup of Human Beings

Biblically, there are at least two distinct aspects of a human being—spiritual (spirit/soul) and physical (body). Some interpreters hold that the "soul" and "spirit" are distinct parts of a human being, and therefore that we are composed of three parts: body, soul, and spirit. This view is called "trichotomy." However, the vast majority of evangelical scholars today hold that "spirit" and "soul" are basically synonymous and are two different ways of talking about the immaterial aspect of our being, "soul" pointing to our personal selves as responsible individuals and "spirit" pointing to those same selves as created by and dependent on God. This view is called "dichotomy" (see note on 1 Thess. 5:23–28). It is important to see that there is a fundamental unity between the physical and spiritual within humans. While a distinction is made in the Bible between the material and immaterial parts of the human being, the emphasis is on the necessary connection between body and soul. Regeneration and sanctification for the Christian is a spiritual experience intended to be expressed in the physical body in and through which we have been made to live. The separation of body and soul caused at death is an unnatural tragedy, which will be remedied when the body is resurrected, allowing humans to exist as they were intended to do.

Humanity as Male and Female

God made man (Hb. *'adam*) as male and female from the beginning, completely equal in their value and in their full humanity (Gen. 1:26–27; 9:6), and yet distinct in the way they relate and function. The distinct roles of men and women are grounded in the nature of God (1 Cor. 11:3) and were part of God's very good creation before the fall (1 Cor. 11:8–10; 1 Tim. 2:13). These role distinctions in no way minimize the worth of men or women. Both are equally made in God's image, equally fallen (Genesis 3; Rom. 3:23), equally redeemable (Gal. 3:28; 1 Pet. 3:7), and are equally to be resurrected and glorified (1 John 3:2). This equality is expressed, however, with the husband serving in his God-ordained role as authority and servant leader (Gen. 2:23) and with the wife fulfilling her vital role as supporter and helper (Gen. 2:18; 1 Pet. 3:1–6) in the family and the church. Male authority is to be exercised with love, humility, and respect, under the authority of Christ (Eph. 5:25–33; Col. 3:19; 1 Pet. 3:7). Female submission is not servile weakness but rather a display of strength and trust in God as the woman uses all her God-given abilities while refusing to usurp the male authority in her life (Eph. 5:22–25; Col. 3:18; 1 Tim. 2:12; 3:2; Titus 2:4–5; 1 Pet. 3:1–6). The fall greatly distorted the harmonious yet distinct way men and women were intended to function together (Gen. 3:16), and God's people are called to show the world how men and women are meant to relate in mutually beneficial ways for the glory of God. When men and women function in this complementary way, they display something profoundly and mysteriously like the relationship between Jesus and his Bride, the church. After quoting a verse from Genesis 2:24 that refers to the marriage between Adam and Eve as God originally created it, Paul gives a theological explanation that shows God's purpose for all marriages, namely, to be a picture of Christ and his church (Eph. 5:32). ◂

God's Relationship with Creation

Transcendence and Immanence

God is both transcendent (majestic and holy, far greater than his creatures) and immanent (near and present, fully involved with his creatures). To understand the God of the Bible, this vital biblical tension must be appreciated. God is distinct from and far above all he has made: "The LORD is high above all nations, and his glory above the heavens! Who is like the LORD our God, who is seated on high, who looks far down on the heavens and the earth?" (Ps. 113:4). Yet he is also always actively, personally engaged with his creation: "Yet he is actually not far from each one of us, for 'In him we live and move and have our being'; as even some of your own poets have said, 'For we are indeed his offspring'" (Acts 17:27–28). Those most humbled by God's majesty and holiness most experience personal closeness with him: "For thus says the One who is high and lifted up, who inhabits eternity, whose name is Holy: 'I dwell in the high and holy place [transcendence], and also with him who is of a contrite and lowly spirit, to revive the spirit of the lowly, and to revive the heart of the contrite [immanence]'" (Isa. 57:15).

Non-Christian religions tend to one extreme or the other; either to a god who is so "other than" creation that nothing meaningful can be said about him (e.g., Eastern and New Age religions) or who is so "identified with" creation that his majestic holiness is lost (e.g., Greco-Roman and much current Western religion). An accurate understanding of God deeply appreciates both his awesome otherness and his intimate nearness. Christians relate to a God who is both the great "I AM" and the "God of our Fathers" (Ex. 3:14–15). He is the eternal, infinite God who has stepped not only into time and space but also into covenant relationship with his people through the incarnation of Christ. The biblical balance between God's transcendence and his immanence is hard to maintain, but the best worship, prayer, and daily relating to God is that which has in it a deep recognition of both God's majestic holiness and his personal engagement with the creatures he has made.

The Providence of God

God is always personally involved with his creation in sustaining and preserving it, and acting within it to bring about his own perfect goals. Everything that takes place is under God's control. He "works all things according to the purpose of his will" (Eph. 1:11). His providential dominion is over all things (Prov. 16:9; 19:21; James 4:13–15)—like weather (Job 38:22–30), food (Ps. 145:15), and sparrows (Matt. 10:29), as well as kings (Prov. 21:1), kingdoms (Dan. 4:25), and the exact times and places in which people live (Acts 17:26). Salvation is a work of God's governing power: "For by grace you have been saved through faith. And this is not your own doing; it is the gift of God, not a result of works, so that no one may boast" (Eph. 2:8–9; cf. Ezek. 36:24; John 6:37–40; Acts 13:48; 16:14; Rom. 9:16; Phil. 1:29; 2 Pet. 1:1). God's providential power also brings about sanctification (Phil. 2:12–13) and fruitfulness in ministry (Col. 1:28–29).

God is able to work out his sovereign will within the distinctive characteristics of what he has created. He moves a rock as a rock, and moves a human heart as a human heart. He does not turn a person into a thing when he brings about his sovereign intentions in a person's life. Paul describes sanctification as the result of both human effort and ultimate divine enabling when he commands believers to "work out your own salvation with fear and trembling, for it is God who works in you, both to will and to work for his good pleasure" (Phil. 2:12). He sees no conflict between divine and human activity. Rather, God is uniquely able to bring about his purposes within human beings so that they are fully engaged as persons and responsible for their own decisions, attitudes, and actions.

God's Relationship to Evil

God controls and uses evil but is never morally blameworthy for it (Ex. 4:11; Deut. 32:39; Isa. 45:7; Amos 3:6). However God's relationship to evil is understood, both his complete sovereignty and his complete holiness must be maintained. In his great suffering, Job says, "the LORD gave, and the LORD has taken away; blessed be the name of the LORD" (Job 1:21). We are told that Job's assessment of God's providence over evil is correct in that "in all this Job did not sin or charge God with wrong" (Job 1:22). Joseph expresses a similar attitude of the God-ordained evil actions of his brothers toward him when he says, "as for you, *you meant evil* against me, but *God meant it for good*, to bring it about that many people should be kept alive, as they are today" (Gen. 50:20). The greatest evil ever done, the crucifixion of Christ, happened because of unspeakable human sin, but all within God's perfect plan. "This Jesus, delivered up *according to the definite plan and foreknowledge of God*, you crucified and *killed by the hands of lawless men*" (Acts 2:23; cf. Acts 4:27–28). Even human rebellion unintentionally ends up serving the perfectly wise purposes of God. Nothing—not even sin and great evil—can ever ultimately frustrate God's sovereignty. Christians can be sure that God will one day defeat all sin, evil, and suffering. Until then, God can be trusted because he is wise, holy, sovereign, and powerful and is always working out his plan to perfection (Rom. 8:28)—even when in the short term it may not seem to be so from our earthly, human perspective. ◂

Sin

Biblical Terms for Sin

The Bible explains human rebellion against God from several perspectives and with various images:

"doing . . . evil" (Judg. 2:11)
"disobedience" (Rom. 5:19)
"transgression" (Ex. 23:21; 1 Tim. 2:14)
"iniquity" (Lev. 26:40)
"lawlessness" (Titus 2:14, 1 John 3:4)
"trespass" (Eph. 2:1)
"ungodliness" (1 Pet. 4:18)
"unrighteousness" (1 John 1:9)
"unholy" (1 Tim. 1:9)
"wickedness" (Prov. 11:31)

The Definition of Sin

Sin is anything (whether in thoughts, actions, or attitudes) that does not express or conform to the holy character of God as expressed in his moral law.

Elements of the Definition of Sin

1. *Sin is moral evil* (e.g., murder) as opposed to natural evil (e.g., cancer). Moral evil is personal rebellion against God, and it is what brought natural evil into the world.

2. *Sin is always and ultimately related to God.* While sin has devastating societal, relational, and physical ramifications, the central problem of sin is that it offends and incurs the wrath of God. David demonstrates this understanding in his confession of adultery and murder: "Against you, you only, have I sinned and done what is evil in your sight, so that you may be justified in your words and blameless in your judgment" (Ps. 51:4). This is not to minimize his sin against Bathsheba, her husband Uriah, or the people of Israel, but rather to recognize that, relatively speaking, it is God he has ultimately offended, and it is to God alone that he must finally answer. Sin is a personal attack on the character and ordinances of God.

3. *Sin is breaking God's law*, which can take several forms. There are sins of omission (not doing what we should) as well as sins of commission (doing what we should not do). Breaking one of God's commandments is rebellion against the entire character of God, and in that sense it is equivalent to breaking all of the commandments: "For whoever keeps the whole law but fails in one point has become accountable for all of it" (James 2:10; cf. Gal. 3:10). God's unified law is a reflection of his personal nature and claims, which means that rejecting one of his laws amounts to rejecting him.

Although breaking one commandment makes one guilty of breaking God's entire law, God recognizes that there are gradations of sin. These gradations are based on differences in *knowledge* (Ezek. 8:6, 13; Matt. 10:15; Luke 12:47–48; John 19:11), *intent* (Num. 15:30–31), *kind*, and *effect*. Nevertheless, even sin done in ignorance is still sin, and everyone still equally needs Jesus to pay the penalty for their sin. While God recognizes degrees of sin on a human, ethical level, it remains the case that all people are equally guilty before God and equally in need of Christ's atoning work.

4. *Sin is rooted deep in our very nature*, and sinful actions reveal the condition of a depraved heart within: "Out of the heart come evil thoughts, murder, adultery, sexual immorality, theft, false witness, slander" (Matt. 15:19; cf. Matt. 7:15–19). Internal attitudes are frequently identified as sinful or righteous in the Bible, and God demands not only correct outward actions but also that the heart be right (Ex. 20:17; Heb. 13:5).

5. Sin has brought about a *guilty standing before God* and a *corrupted condition* in all humans. The pronouncement of guilt is God's legal determination that people are in an unrighteous state before him, and the condition of corruption is our polluted state which inclines us toward ungodly behavior. By the grace of God, both this inherited guilt and this inherited moral pollution are atoned for by Christ: "If we confess our sins, he is faithful and just to forgive us our sins and to cleanse us from all unrighteousness" (1 John 1:9).

The Origin of Sin

Sin entered the human race in the Garden of Eden through an attack of Satan, who led Adam and Eve to doubt God's word and trust their own ability to discern good and evil (Genesis 3). Sometime prior to this, Satan (a fallen angel) must himself have rebelled against God and become evil, though Scripture does not say much about that event (cf. notes on 2 Pet. 2:4; Jude 6). Satan's strategy was to bring disorder to the created order by approaching Eve and getting her to lead her husband away from God. Adam, so it appears, allowed his wife to be deceived by failing to take up his God-ordained responsibility to lead and protect her. Satan then questioned God's goodness, wisdom, and care for Adam and Eve by suggesting that God was a miserly legalist in his prohibition of the fruit of the tree of the knowledge of good and evil. Satan then simply lied, saying, "you will not surely die" (Gen. 3:4). Such deception and rebellion against God stem from a failure to trust him and be satisfied with him and his commands and arrangements. Satan and our first parents demanded autonomy and rejected God's authority, and this has been the source and shape of human sin ever since. Unbelief (Rom. 14:23; Heb. 11:6), pride, and selfishness lead us to think we know better than God and to try to put ourselves in his place. All people, in their fallen condition, are indeed "lovers of self . . . rather than lovers of God" (2 Tim. 3:2, 4).

The Consequences and Condition of the Fall

God rightly judged the rebellion of Adam and Eve and brought a curse on them and all their offspring. The curse brought physical and spiritual death, separation from God, and alienation from him and others. All people are now conceived, born, and live in this fallen, depraved condition: "None is righteous, no, not one; no one understands; no one seeks for God. All have turned aside; together they have become worthless; no one does good, not even one" (Rom. 3:10–12); "All we like sheep have gone astray; we have turned every one to his own way; and the LORD has laid on him the iniquity of us all" (Isa. 53:6).

Inherited guilt and corruption leave every person completely unable to save himself or to please God. There are at least six ways this pervasive inability affects everyone. Until God intervenes with his sovereign, gracious, saving power, mankind is totally unable to:

- repent or trust Christ (John 6:44; cf. John 3:3; 6:65)
- see or enter the kingdom of God (John 3:3)
- obey God and thereby glorify him (Rom. 8:6–8)
- attain spiritual understanding (1 Cor. 2:14)
- live lives pleasing to God (Rom. 14:23; Heb. 11:6)
- receive eternal or spiritual life (Eph. 2:1–3)

Because of God's common grace (that is, his kindly providence whereby sin's energies within us are partly restrained), total depravity does not mean that every person apart from Christ is as bad as possible. It does mean, however, that none by nature can fulfill man's primary purpose of glorifying God in relationship with him. ◀

Salvation

When the Bible speaks of "salvation" (Gk. *sōtēria*) in a spiritual sense, the thought can embrace the whole broad range of God's activity in rescuing people from sin and restoring them to a right relationship with himself. Because of this broad sense, we find that the noun "salvation," and the verb "save," are used in the Bible with past, present, and future reference.

Thus, salvation may signify any or all of the blessings outlined in the chart below. While the *subjective experience* of being saved may have degrees and look very different from person to person, the *objective state* of being saved is categorical and absolute. From God's perspective there is a definite point in time when those who have trusted in Christ pass from death into life (1 John 3:14). This, however, is not where salvation starts. From God's vantage point salvation begins with his *election* of individuals, which is his determination beforehand that his saving purpose will be accomplished in them (John 6:37–39, 44, 64–66; 8:47; 10:26; 15:16; Acts 13:48; 16:14; Romans 9; 1 John 4:19; 5:1). God then in due course *brings* people to himself by *calling* them to faith in Christ (Rom. 8:30; 1 Cor. 1:9; 2 Tim. 1:9; 1 Pet. 2:9).

God's calling produces *regeneration*, which is the miraculous work of the Holy Spirit in which a spiritually dead person is made alive in Christ (Ezek. 11:19–20; Matt. 19:28; John 3:3, 5, 7; Titus 3:5). The revived heart *repents* and trusts Christ in *saving faith* as the only source of *justification*. To be a Christian means one has traded in his "polluted garment" of self-righteousness for the perfect righteousness of Christ (Phil. 3:8–9; cf. Isa. 64:6). He has ceased striving and now rests in the finished work of Christ—no longer depending on personal accomplishments, religious pedigree, or good works for God's approval, but only on what Christ has accomplished on his behalf (Phil. 2:8–9). A Christian understands with Paul that "it is no longer I who live, but Christ who lives in me. And the life I now live in the flesh I live by faith in the Son of God, who loved me and gave himself for me" (Gal. 2:20). As regards Jesus paying the penalty for our sins, the Christian believes that when Jesus said, "it is finished" (John 19:30), it really was. Because of this, "there is therefore now no condemnation for those who are in Christ Jesus" (Rom. 8:1), and they have been "saved to the uttermost" (Heb. 7:25). A miraculous transformation has taken place in which the believer has "passed from death to life" (John 5:24). The Holy Spirit empowers the transformation from rebellious sinner to humble worshiper, leading to "confidence for the day of judgment" (1 John 4:17).

The Blessings of Salvation

Justification	has been saved	from the guilt of sin	Eph. 2:8
Sanctification	is being saved	from the power of sin	1 Cor. 1:18
Glorification	will be saved	from the presence of sin	Acts 15:11

Much of Protestantism in the last two centuries has been influenced by revivalism, which puts a great emphasis on "making a decision for Christ" in a public and definitive way. These "moments of decision" often come to be treated as the crucial evidence that one is truly saved. Other Protestant traditions, less influenced by revivalism, are often content to leave the conversion experience less clearly identified, and put the focus rather on Christian experience, identification with the church, or reliance upon the sacraments. Both of these traditions have benefits and strengths, as well as potential problems. The "decision" approach rightly emphasizes the need for personal commitment to Christ Jesus and the idea that regeneration takes place at a specific time. The potential downside is that this view can lead to a simplistic, human-centered understanding of being saved where one depends too heavily on the initial, specific act of trusting Christ as the primary evidence of conversion. As a result, one can doubt that the "decision" was real, leading to numerous journeys down the aisle (just in case), or else to total dependence on the onetime walk down the aisle, even in the absence of the necessary fruit of salvation. Other traditions appreciate the sovereignty of God and role of the church in the salvation process but can leave conversion so vague that the need for personal trust in Christ and the resulting evidence of a changed life can be neglected.

God uses vastly different circumstances and experiences to bring people to himself. As C. H. Spurgeon said, "God's Spirit calls men to Jesus in diverse ways. Some are drawn so gently that they scarce know when the drawing began, and others are so suddenly affected that their conversion stands out with noonday clearness." The best evidence of true salvation is not having raised a hand or prayed a prayer, *or* having been baptized or christened. Instead, the true test of an authentic work of God in one's life is *sanctification* as God continues the moral transformation he began in regeneration. This transformation will continue until the redeemed person is *resurrected* and made completely holy in heaven (*glorification*; cf. Rom. 8:28–30; Phil. 1:6; 1 John 3:2).

God's sanctifying work is seen in growing Christlike character, increasing love for God and people, and the fruit of the Spirit (John 14:2; 15:1–16:33; Gal. 5:22–25; James 2:18). Of course, a memorable conversion experience may serve as an important reference point for a saving work of God in one's life, but it is only the obvious, ongoing work of the Holy Spirit in making one more and more like Jesus that gives sufficiently clear indication that a person has been made a new creation in Christ. While a

Christian should never be satisfied with his current state of holiness, he should be confident that through God's sovereign, sanctifying grace he will one day have totally won the victory over sin once and for all. This will be the moment of entering by death into a larger life in which our sinful heart is finally purified. Meanwhile, living with this hope as one battles sin daily is true Christian *perseverance* (1 Cor. 1:8–9; Eph. 1:13–14; 1 Thess. 5:23–24; 1 Pet. 1:4–5; 1 John 2:19; Jude 1, 24–25), which is itself a sign that one has been born again. ◀

The Church

The church is the community of God's redeemed people—all who have truly trusted Christ alone for their salvation. It is created by the Holy Spirit to exalt Jesus Christ as Lord of all. Christ is the Head, Savior, Lord, and King of the church. The relationship between its members results from their common identity as brothers and sisters adopted into God's family. The identity of this family is grounded in Christ's person and work and therefore transcends any earthly distinctions of race, class, culture, gender, or nationality. True Christian fellowship is divinely brought about by God, for the purpose of displaying and advancing God's kingdom on earth. As Christians love one another and submit to the lordship of Christ, they show glimpses of heavenly realities that are to come.

There is ultimately only one church, the global community of believers on earth plus those already in glory. In this world, however, the one church takes the form of countless local churches, each of which must be viewed as a microcosm, outcropping, and sample of the larger whole. Jesus Christ's headship of the church that is his body is a relationship that applies both to the universal church and to each local church. Denominational identities are secondary to these primary and fundamental realities.

The Visible Church and the Invisible Church

Theologians sometimes distinguish between the "visible church" (the church as Christians on earth see it) and the "invisible church" (the church as God in heaven sees it). This distinction emphasizes two truths. First, only God, who reads hearts, knows the ultimate makeup of the "invisible church"—those whom he has called ("The Lord knows those who are his," 2 Tim. 2:19). Second, there are some within the "visible church" who are not genuine believers, though they may look as if they are (cf. Matt. 7:15–16; Acts 20:29–30; 1 John 2:19).

Images of the Church

The Bible explains the profound mystery of the church (Eph. 5:32) using varied images and illustrations. Among the most important are the church as the building, body, bride, and family of Christ.

The Building of Christ

Jesus Christ is building his church, and even the gates of hell will not defeat it (Matt. 16:18). He is the foundational cornerstone providing unyielding stability (Matt. 21:42 par.; Acts 4:11; Eph. 2:20; 1 Pet. 2:6–7), and he promises that he will complete the building he is making (Eph. 2:21–22). Therefore, even when the church appears weak, corrupt, and lost, there is always reason for deep confidence in its continued growth and enduring strength. God's people are "living stones" (1 Pet. 2:5) who have received their life from the Cornerstone, who is the giver of life. The building image is grounded in the temple imagery of the OT, as the place where God's presence and glory were most often seen. The church is now the place on earth where God primarily dwells and makes himself known. This temple is not made with human hands but exists in the corporate life of those who have been transformed through faith in Christ. The presence and work of God in worship, the ministry of the Word, service to others, discipline, baptism, the Lord's Supper, and gospel proclamation are now the primary source of the presence and glory of God in the world: "Do you not know that you are God's temple and that God's Spirit dwells in you? If anyone destroys God's temple, God will destroy him. For God's temple is holy, and you are that temple" (1 Cor. 3:16–17; cf. 2 Cor. 6:16; 1 Pet. 2:4–10). The church will last even beyond the time of Christ's return, and any predictions that warn of the demise of the church of Jesus Christ are greatly mistaken.

The Body of Christ

Christ is the head of the church, which is his body (Eph. 1:22–23; 4:15; 5:23). He has authority over his people and determines their direction and destiny. Each member of Christ's body serves an important and distinct role, and none have life, power, or ability of any kind apart from Christ (1 Corinthians 12).

The Bride of Christ

Christ saves and sanctifies his people through his sacrifice on the cross, which serves as the model of the relationship between a husband and wife (Eph. 5:25). Christ's self-sacrificial love for his bride continues as he feeds and cares for her; she who will one day be presented to him in spotless perfection (Eph. 5:29; Heb. 12:23). As the bride of Christ, the church should strive for undiluted devotion to Christ, who is her jealous husband (2 Cor. 11:2–4). God's people should be motivated by and longing for the great wedding banquet as they await the return of their Bridegroom (Rev. 19:7–9; 21:1–4).

The Family of God

God's adoption of lost and unworthy children of wrath into his family is a key aspect of his redeeming work (1 John 3:1–2). This adoption through new birth leads to astounding privileges that come with being fellow heirs with Christ. Those in God's family become full beneficiaries of all his promises to his children! As adopted children of God, believers are bound by a family relationship as brothers and sisters that is greater and more enduring than biological family ties (Mark 3:31–35; cf. Matt. 19:29 par.). Earnest brotherly love should characterize relationships within the church (Rom. 12:10; 1 Tim. 5:1–2; Heb. 13:1; 1 Pet. 1:22). Such love is one of the primary ways Christians know they have truly been saved by God: "We know that we have passed out of death into life, because we love the brothers" (1 John 3:14). All earthly obstacles to brotherly affection (e.g., differences in culture, race, income, personality, and nationality) are done away with when God adopts his people into his family (Gal. 3:28).

To love Christ means to love his church and seek to build it by word and deed. The sin and apathy often seen in the church may at times require strong criticism and be a cause for grief. But Christ shed his own blood to create the church (Acts 20:28), and the church is God's primary conduit of his grace and glory to the world. There should be no doubt that by the grace of God his community of unworthy redeemed sinners will be triumphant and beautiful one day. Meaningful local church involvement is not an optional spiritual discipline; it is the essential context within which believers are intended to find Christ and grow in him. ◂

Last Things

The Return of Christ

The return of Jesus Christ is the central hope of the NT. His second coming will be sudden (Matt. 24:44; 2 Pet. 3:10), personal, bodily (John 14:3; Acts 1:11; 1 Thess. 4:16), and visible to the whole world (Rev. 1:7). He will come again to reign in power as the King of kings for all eternity (Phil. 2:9–11). While he has given signs that will indicate that the end times are near (Matt. 24:14, 23–29; Mark 13:10, 19–26; 2 Thess. 2:1–10), God has not revealed the time of Christ's return (Matt. 24:44; Mark 13:32–33; Luke 12:40). Therefore, the setting of dates is fruitless and unbiblical speculation. The warnings that Christ will come unexpectedly and suddenly are intended to motivate believers to live in eager expectation and preparedness, which involves holy living and an eternal perspective. Followers of Christ are to "renounce ungodliness and worldly passions, and to live self-controlled, upright, and godly lives in the present age, waiting for our blessed hope, the appearing of the glory of our great God and Savior Jesus Christ" (Titus 2:12–13). As good as life in this world may be at times, it can never compare to the ultimate liberation from sin and the unhindered fellowship with Christ that his return will bring (1 John 3:2). This does not preclude Christians from deeply investing in and appreciating this world; it only means that believers should realize that the best is yet to come and they should ultimately live for the day when Christ returns. Their greatest hope and the definitive solution to present suffering is to be found in the hope of Christ's return. On that day "the Lord himself will descend from heaven with a cry of command, with the voice of an archangel, and with the sound of the trumpet of God. And the dead in Christ will rise first. Then we who are alive, who are left, will be caught up together with them in the clouds to meet the Lord in the air, and so we will always be with the Lord" (1 Thess. 4:16–18). Christians are commanded to "encourage one another with these words" (1 Thess. 4:18), which are words of great hope.

The Millennial Reign of Christ

Revelation speaks of Christ reigning for "a thousand years" when Satan is bound and some of God's people come to life to reign with him (Rev. 20:1–10). Christians have interpreted this millennium in one of three ways: amillennialism, premillennialism, and postmillennialism (for details, see Introduction to Revelation: Millennial Views, pp. 2458–2460). (1) *Amillennialists* believe that the thousand years in Revelation 20 is figurative language, showing that the reign of Christ from heaven is *presently* being fulfilled in the church age and will continue until the return of Christ. In this view, all the end-time events, such as Christ's return and the final judgment, happen at once. (2) *Premillennialists* believe that, long before the final judgment, Christ will first return and establish his millennial kingdom—that is, his reign as King over all the earth for 1,000 years. Within this view there are various views of the timing of the great tribulation (whether Christians will go through it or will escape it by being suddenly removed from the earth before the tribulation begins), and of whether the 1,000 years is a literal or a symbolic number. (3) *Postmillennialists* believe the millennial reign of Christ will be ushered in after remarkable gospel progress establishes Christ's reign on earth, not with Christ physically present but with the majority of the world obedient to him, and that at the end of that "millennium," Christ will return in bodily form to reign over the new heavens and new earth forever.

While there has been much debate over the nature and timing of the millennial events, what is certainly clear in Scripture is that Christ will return and establish his kingdom and that all mankind will finally acknowledge his lordship over all creation. Once and for all, creation will undeniably submit to Christ the King, and he will reign on earth as already he does in heaven (Matt. 6:10; Phil. 2:10).

The Final Judgment and Hell

God expresses both personal (Rom. 1:18–32) and national judgment (Isaiah 13–23), and his judgments have taken place throughout history and in the heavenly realm (2 Pet. 2:4). But after the millennium (or, according to amillennialists, after the present age) Christ will judge the whole world once and for all (Matt. 25:31–33; 2 Tim. 4:1; Rev. 20:11–15). At this time the righteous wrath of a holy God will be unleashed on a rebellious world (Rom. 2:5; 3:19). Jesus often warned that he would usher in the day of wrath (Matt. 10:15; 11:22, 24; 12:36; 25:31–46), and other NT writers repeated this idea (1 Cor. 4:5; Heb. 6:2; 2 Pet. 2:4; Jude 6). Unbelievers will be judged, and the result will be punishment for even careless words that were spoken (Matt. 12:36). Those who refuse God's gracious offer of forgiveness in Christ will suffer eternal conscious punishment in hell, a condition of torment cut off from the presence of God (Matt. 25:30, 41, 46; Mark 9:43, 48; Rev. 14:9–11). Christian believers, who understand the holiness and justice of God and the depth of human sin, should be able to relate to the martyrs in heaven who long for the day of judgment (Rev. 6:10). However, in this age, the church is primarily called to warn people everywhere to repent and flee the wrath that will come when Christ returns as Judge: "The times of ignorance God overlooked, but now he commands all people everywhere to repent, because he has fixed a day on which he will judge the world in righteousness by a man whom he has appointed; and of this he has given assurance to all by raising him from the dead" (Acts 17:30–31).

Believers, as well as unbelievers, will be judged by Christ. As the apostle Paul writes to the Christians at Corinth, "we must all appear before the judgment seat of Christ, so that each one may receive what is due for what he has done in the body, whether good or evil" (2 Cor. 5:10; cf. Rom. 2:6–11; 14:10–12; Rev. 20:12, 15). The judgment of believers will test the worth of the way they lived. It will reveal some tragic lack of true good works in the sanctification process and will show that some were saved "but only as through fire" (1 Cor. 3:15). Here the testing ("fire") of God's judgment at the return of Christ will reveal the quality of a believer's works, and some will have little to show for their salvation. On the other hand, what was done to glorify God will be rewarded (1 Cor. 4:5; Col. 3:23–24). Although God seeks to motivate his people to holy living by the rewards they will receive, ultimately, believers can stand before God only because of Christ's finished work on their behalf. The basis for justification is only the perfect righteousness imputed to believers and the diverting of sin's penalty from them to Christ, and never the false security of self-righteousness (2 Cor. 5:21; Phil. 3:8–9). There is no fear of the final judgment for those who have trusted Christ for salvation because there is "no condemnation for those who are in Christ Jesus" (Rom. 8:1), which means they "have confidence for the day of judgment" (1 John 4:17).

The New Heavens and New Earth

God's creation of the new heavens and earth is the final phase of his redeeming work. The restored creation will be freed from the tragic effects of sin and the curse, and perfect fellowship with God will be restored. The OT promised this wonderful reality as the culmination of the new covenant: "For behold, I create new heavens and a new earth, and the former things shall not be remembered or come into mind" (Isa. 65:17). The NT writers still long for God to finish his work in this way, as Peter says, "but according to his promise we are waiting for new heavens and a new earth in which righteousness dwells" (2 Pet. 3:13). John's Revelation gives a powerful glimpse of the end of all things: "Then I saw a new heaven and a new earth, for the first heaven and the first earth had passed away, and the sea was no more. And I saw the holy city, new Jerusalem, coming down out of heaven from God, prepared as a bride adorned for her husband" (Rev. 21:1–2). The entire world that was subjected to futility and decay in the fall will be freed from this bondage "far as the curse is found" when God recreates everything anew (Rom. 8:19–23; 2 Pet. 3:13; Rev. 21:1). There will be a joining together of heaven and the renewed earth (Rev. 21:1–3), and in company with Jesus Christ their Lord God's people will work, play, eat, learn, and worship in their resurrected, glorified bodies (Luke 22:18; Rev. 19:9; 22:1–2) in the place that the church down through the ages has always called heaven, but which the Bible calls "a new heaven and a new earth" (Rev. 21:1). The very goodness of the original creation (Gen. 1:31) will here be restored and redeemed to perfection.

The knowledge of God's future restoration of all creation should deepen one's appreciation of the created order now. The created physical realm, although marred by the fall, maintains a goodness that is redeemable and is intended to be enjoyed now as God's abundant blessing: "For everything created by God is good, and nothing is to be rejected if it is received with thanksgiving, for it is made holy by the word of God and prayer" (1 Tim. 4:4–5). However, hope for the world to come motivates the believer to live ultimately for that world rather than this one. As Jesus said, "Do not lay up for yourselves treasures on earth, where moth and rust destroy and where thieves break in and steal, but lay up for yourselves treasures in heaven, where neither moth nor rust destroys and where thieves do not break in and steal. For where your treasure is, there your heart will be also" (Matt. 6:19–21). The tremendous blessing of a restored heaven and earth will be cause for extravagant praise, but the greatest blessing will be the glorious presence of God himself, and of Jesus our Lord and Savior. Fellowship with Jesus, it has been said, is what makes heaven to be heaven, and that is something that Christian people will be proving true for all eternity. ◀

Biblical Ethics: An Overview

Biblical Ethics: An Introduction

From the beginning of the Bible to the end, God gives people specific instructions about how he wants them to conduct their lives. The study of these instructions and their wise application to life is known as the discipline of biblical ethics. These instructions from God about ethical living involve many commands, laws, moral standards, ideals, prohibitions, and principles of wisdom relating to moral judgment. They also concern matters of moral accountability, including rewards and punishments that provide incentives for pleasing God and avoiding what he abhors. From start to finish, ethical understanding in the Bible is about applying the holiness of God to human life on earth (Lev. 11:44–45; 19:2; 20:7; 1 Pet. 1:14–16). This article offers an overview of such biblical ethics as based on the totality of moral revelation in the Word of God, and several articles that follow it show the application of Christian ethics to specific moral issues.

An Overview of Ethical Instruction and Example in the Bible

The first example of ethical instruction in the Bible is seen when God gave Adam and Eve commands, both positively, "Be fruitful and multiply and fill the earth and subdue it" (Gen. 1:28), and negatively, "of the tree of the knowledge of good and evil you shall not eat" (Gen. 2:17). Later in the Bible God gave his people the foundational guidelines set forth in the Ten Commandments (Ex. 20:1–17; cf. Deut. 5:6–21), and then he added the numerous, even more detailed laws that are found in large portions of Exodus, Leviticus, Numbers, and Deuteronomy. These laws not only prescribed and prohibited certain actions but also taught people about right attitudes of heart: "You shall love the LORD your God with all your heart" (Deut. 6:5; cf. Lev. 19:18; Ps. 40:8; 119:16). In addition to direct commands, the Bible also teaches about moral living through narrative literature (revealing what pleases or displeases God), wisdom literature (revealing characteristics of good judgment), and prophetic words (revealing how people and nations are accountable to God), all of which indicate the kinds of conduct, character, and goals that God either approves or disapproves.

When Jesus came, he lived a life of perfect obedience to God, for he said, "I always do the things that are pleasing to him" (John 8:29), and many passages affirm that Jesus' life was completely free of sin: He was "one who in every respect has been tempted as we are, yet without sin" (Heb. 4:15), and he was "obedient to the point of death, even death on a cross" (Phil. 2:8; cf. John 15:10; Acts 3:14; 2 Cor. 5:21; Heb. 7:26; 1 Pet. 1:19; 1 John 2:1; 3:5). Jesus employed three characteristic motifs in his ethical teaching. First, he often described moral living in terms of *God reigning as a king and his people's duty as citizens to obey the rules of his kingdom* (cf. esp. Matt. 5:3, 10, 19–20; 6:10, 33; 13:37–43, 47–50; 18:23–35; 21:31–32, 43). Second, he frequently described moral living in terms of *the obligations, loyalties, and privileges of children in a family headed by God as a loving Father* (cf. esp. Matt. 5:9, 16, 43–48; 6:1–4, 14–15; 12:50; 23:9; Mark 3:35; John 12:36). Third, Jesus taught in terms of *disciples following, imitating, and obeying him as a beloved teacher, mentor, and role model* (cf. esp. Matt. 10:24–25; 16:24; Mark 10:43–45; Luke 6:40; John 13:15–17; 14:15, 21, 23–24; 15:10, 12). And at the end of his ministry he commissioned his followers to teach other disciples from all nations "to observe all that I have commanded you" (Matt. 28:20). In addition to his teaching, Jesus' life is also a pattern for believers to imitate, for "whoever says he abides in him ought to walk in the same way in which he walked" (1 John 2:6).

The Bible ends with a picture of the new Jerusalem, a city in which the only residents are those who obey God's moral standards, for "nothing unclean will ever enter it, nor anyone who does what is detestable or false" (Rev. 21:27), and those who are kept "outside" are "sorcerers and the sexually immoral and murderers and idolaters, and everyone who loves and practices falsehood" (Rev. 22:15). Obedience to God's ethical standards brings him glory (Matt. 5:16; 1 Cor. 6:20) and is also best for his people (Ps. 1:1; John 14:21; Rom. 12:2; Heb. 12:10).

Justification by Faith and the Importance of Moral Obedience

The NT clearly teaches that justification, that is, pardon and acceptance with God, comes to people only through faith in Christ alone, who is offered to sinful humanity as Savior by God's grace alone: "by grace you have been saved through faith" and "this is not your own doing; it is the gift of God, not a result of works" (Eph. 2:8–9). But then Paul immediately says that God wants Christians to live in obedience to him: "For we are his workmanship, created in Christ Jesus *for good works*, which God prepared beforehand, that we should walk in them" (Eph. 2:10). It is impossible to read the NT epistles, or to listen to the teachings of Jesus in the Gospels, without hearing dozens upon dozens of moral commands, standards, warnings, and promises telling Christians how they should live in order to please God in their daily conduct. Therefore it must be seen as a matter of great importance to God that his people, who have been justified by faith alone, live every day of their lives walking in obedience to God's moral standards (Heb. 12:14). In fact, in John 14, Jesus four times stresses the essential connection between loving him and obeying what he commands

(John 14:15, 21, 23, 24). Empowered by the Holy Spirit, daily obedience expressing faith, loyalty, and love toward Christ will have a transforming effect. The conscience will be clear (1 Tim. 3:9; cf. 1:5); the heart will know great peace (Phil. 4:9); joy will abound (Rom. 14:17); assurance will be strong (2 Pet. 1:5–10); and distressing experiences will be taken in stride (1 Pet. 2:18–24).

God's Holy Character as the Source of His Moral Standards

God's moral standards are never arbitrary or capricious, but are all consistent with and derived from his own moral character. This is why Paul can say, "be *imitators of God*, as beloved children" (Eph. 5:1). This theme of imitating God's moral character is found throughout the Bible: "we love because he first loved us" (1 John 4:19). "Be merciful, even as your Father is merciful" (Luke 6:36). "You shall be holy, for I am holy" (1 Pet. 1:15, quoting Lev. 11:44). The commands not to lie but to speak truthfully are grounded in the imperative that believers should increasingly live out the image of their Creator, who does not lie (Col. 3:9–10).

Other commands also reflect the pattern of imitation of God. "Honor your father and your mother" (Ex. 20:12) is a reflection of the Son honoring the Father and being obedient to the Father's will within the counsels of the Trinity (cf. John 4:34; 5:30; 6:38). The command not to murder (Ex. 20:13) is grounded in the fact that God is the Creator and sustainer of life and places immense value on the lives of human beings created in his image (Gen. 9:6). The command "You shall not commit adultery" (Ex. 20:14) is a command to be faithful in marriage relationships, based on imitating God's faithfulness in all his covenant commitments. The command not to steal (Ex. 20:15) is grounded in a respect for the fact that a sovereign God has entrusted stewardship of possessions to various individuals, and people should respect that stewardship. The command not to covet (Ex. 20:17) is based on imitation of the fact that God himself delights in the excellence of his holy character and his providential arranging of things; therefore, we too should delight in his arrangements and never be discontented with them.

But if all God's moral standards are grounded in his unchanging moral character, it follows that he could not have given commands that were substantially different from these. He could not have commanded people, e.g., to be unfaithful, or to lie, or to murder others. Why? Because such commands would be contrary to the moral character of God himself, or would suggest that God's moral character changes so that he is sometimes actually unfaithful, or tells lies, or unjustly hates and destroys human lives. Anything contrary to the holiness of God is abhorrent and dishonoring to God because it violates his moral character (cf. Prov. 30:9). God cannot issue, and could never have issued, moral standards in contradiction to those he gave, not because God's sovereignty is limited by anything or anyone other than himself, but only because God can never be other than he is. He can never cease to be God. And he can never be untrue to his unchanging moral character.

If one understands the ethical system found in the Bible to be grounded in the moral character of God, this also provides an answer to the age-old philosophical question, "How can one ever reason from *what is* (a description of reality) to *what ought to be* (a prescription of right and wrong)?" If *what is* (that is, what exists in the universe) begins with God himself and his moral character, then *God's very being* determines the nature of the things that are right and wrong, and thus God's being determines, in an ultimate sense, *what ought to be*.

This understanding of the Bible's ethical system also implies that God's moral standards (when rightly understood and applied) are for all people and all cultures throughout all history, because they are the moral standards of the eternal Creator of the universe.

How Can People Discover God's Moral Standards?

It may at first seem overwhelming when someone is told, "Just obey the entire Bible as it applies to your situation in life." The Bible is a large and diverse book and contains some stipulations (esp. in the OT) that hardly seem to apply today. Must all biblical commands be treated the same, or does the Bible itself provide reasons for classifying various commands in different categories? To address this, most Christian interpreters have agreed to some broad principles for determining how various biblical commands apply today. These principles of interpretation include the following:

1. *The NT is written directly for followers of Christ living under the new covenant.* Though "all Scripture" (including all of the OT) is "profitable" for the Christian (2 Tim. 3:16), immediate application to life is clearer when reading the NT, for these books were written to Christian believers who were in the same situation as Christians are today with respect to God's overall plan for the history of salvation; they were living in the new covenant age, and so are God's people today. Searching the NT is a good "first step" in resolving an ethical question.

2. *Many details of the Mosaic law are either no longer binding or were never meant for everyone.* While some aspects of God's law delivered to Moses reflected God's standards of moral holiness for all time, many other aspects did not deal directly with morality but with procedures for conducting the Levitical worship system under the old covenant, or with ceremonies and rituals that showed Israel to be a distinct nation, or with administrating the civil government of Israel upon entering the Promised Land. Most interpreters agree, therefore, that what God ordered for the civil government of Israel (though wise) was never meant for other nations and other governments, and that the ceremonial requirements of the old covenant are not applicable today. Thus, e.g., laws concerning circumcision, sacrifices, unclean foods, and clothing are part of the "ceremonial" regulations that set Israel apart from other nations but are no longer binding today, in the NT (or new covenant) age (cf. Heb. 9:1–10:18). Similarly, many of the laws and penalties in the Mosaic law code were intended only for the civil government of the nation of Israel at that period of time (such as laws in Israel that applied the death penalty to the serving of other gods, witchcraft, persistently disobedient children, adultery, and homosexual behavior). But many other sections of the OT (e.g., Proverbs, but also other parts of the OT including many Mosaic laws) contain teaching that conveys God's wisdom regarding human conduct in general. (A detailed solution to the question of which, and in what way, OT laws apply to NT believers is beyond the scope of this article.)

3. *Some general principles must be applied with wisdom from the rest of the Bible.* There are some passages, especially in Jesus' earthly teaching, that are difficult to understand in terms of how broadly they should be taken and to whom

they should apply. Passages like "Do not refuse the one who would borrow from you" (Matt. 5:42) are generalizations that powerfully address attitudes of the heart. But like every command, applying them to specific situations requires interpreting them in light of the whole of Scripture, including passages that command wisdom and good stewardship. Similarly, "Judge not, that you be not judged" (Matt. 7:1) must be interpreted in light of Jesus' other command to "judge with right judgment" (John 7:24).

4. *Where it is necessary to apply a command under far different cultural circumstances, there is usually enough similarity between the biblical context and present circumstances for Christian readers to make an appropriate connection.* For example, it is not difficult to move from "the wages of the *laborers who mowed your fields*, which you kept back by fraud" (James 5:4) to "the wages of the *employees who work in your factory*, which you kept back by fraud." It is not difficult to move from "honor the *emperor*" (1 Pet. 2:17) to "honor *government officials*." And it is not difficult to move from "You shall not covet your neighbor's . . . *ox*" (Ex. 20:17) to "You shall not covet you neighbor's *car* or *boat*."

Similarly adjusted application seems to be required in the case of certain NT commands dealing with physical actions that carried symbolic meaning, when the meaning of the same action would be different today. In such cases, Christians should not apply the commands as first expressed unless situated in a similar cultural circumstance where the physical action would have the same meaning. Such physical actions with culturally-variable symbolic meaning include at least these: (1) Greeting one another with a holy kiss (Rom. 16:16; 1 Cor. 16:20; 2 Cor. 13:12; 1 Thess. 5:26; 1 Pet. 5:14) simply conveyed the idea of a welcoming greeting, and other actions (such as shaking hands, or bowing, or hugging) symbolize the same thing in different cultures. (2) Washing one another's feet (John 13:14) symbolized taking a servant-like attitude that can be expressed in other ways in settings where it is not customary for people to take off their shoes and wash their feet on coming in from the outside. (3) Women or wives wearing head coverings in worship (1 Cor. 11:4–16) apparently symbolized that a woman was married (see notes on 1 Corinthians 11), which is similar to what a wedding band symbolizes in many cultures today. But while a few such physical actions, by their symbolic nature, are culturally relative, readers should understand that the number of commands in this category is really quite small, and that it would be a mistake to exaggerate their significance and begin to wonder if vast sections of the ethical teachings of the Bible are culturally relative. The vast majority of NT ethical teachings, together with those OT teachings that apply to NT believers, require the direct obedience of Christians today just as in the first century.

Developing a Framework for Ethical Decision Making

The overall goal for making ethical decisions should be to understand and then obey the teaching of the entire Bible with regard to any particular situation. Here are some steps readers should follow when having to make important ethical decisions: (1) *Pray*. All decisions should rely on praying for God's wisdom at the beginning and throughout the process (James 1:5). (2) *Study the Bible*. Search for and seek understanding of all biblical passages and their principles that have relevance for the situation under consideration. (3) *Study the situation*. Understand the situation by gathering and assessing relevant information (it is often impossible to make a wise decision until the facts become more clear). (4) *Study the people involved*. Try to understand the character, motives, and values of the people involved or affected by the decision to be made, including any relevant background, personal habits and characteristics, motivations, and relationships, as well as special interests that may be influencing the reactions of each relevant party. (5) *The goal*. Understand that the glory of God and the good of others are ever the twin purposes of moral action, and that the merely good or permissible must never be allowed to obstruct the quest for the best.

Wisdom is the skill of combining these factors so as to rightly apply the teachings of the Bible to real people in real-life situations, in such a way that one is truly thinking God's thoughts after him. Such wisdom is a skill that can be improved over time through repeated practice and nearness to God (Heb. 5:14; James 1:5–8). Mature Christians who have grown through testing (James 1:2–4; 2 Pet. 1:5–9), pastors, and pastoral counselors are often especially skilled in doing this.

A good answer to an ethical question will not limit itself to a discussion of right and wrong actions, for good moral conduct in any situation will involve (1) *good ends* (that is, the results sought or achieved), (2) *good motives* (the desires and attitudes that people have in the situation), and (3) *good means* (the actions that are taken to achieve the ends). The Bible itself requires people to consider all three of these factors, for good ends are mentioned (see 1 Cor. 10:31; 14:26), good motives are required (see Ex. 20:17 and Matt. 5:28), and good means or actions are commanded while bad ones are prohibited (Ex. 20:12–15). A life fully pleasing to God will conform to each of these three standards set by Scripture. ◀

The Beginning of Life and Abortion

The Image of God

The ethics of abortion, embryonic stem cell research, fetal tissue transplantation, and other issues at the beginning of life will not be fully and rightly understood apart from God's revelation about the origin and sanctity of human life. At the zenith of God's creative activity, he made man (as male and female) in his own image and likeness (Gen. 1:26–27). From the "dust from the ground" God made a "living creature," Adam (Gen. 2:7), whose material body was absolutely earthly (cf. Ps. 90:3 and 103:14) but whose source of life was decidedly divine. Therefore, any view of origins that does not affirm that humanity began through a special creative act of God is sub-biblical.

Since God is the Creator of human life, all human beings belong to God. As the apostle Paul would later declare before the philosophers in Athens, "In [God] we live and move and have our being; as even some of your own poets have said, 'For we are indeed his offspring'" (Acts 17:28).

Thus, being created by God both *elevates* human beings in that they are not accidents of history and *humbles* them because God is gracious and sovereign over them.

Although God's words when he first created human beings were, "Let us make man in our *image*, after our *likeness*" (Gen. 1:26), the Bible nowhere explains precisely what constitutes the image of God (Latin, *imago Dei*). Interpreters have suggested that it includes: (1) humankind's upright bodily form, (2) human dominion over nature, (3) human reason, (4) human pre-fallen righteousness, (5) human capacities, (6) the juxtaposition between man and woman, (7) responsible creaturehood and moral conformity to God, (8) personhood, and (9) various composites of the above views. Because the Hebrew words for "image" (*tselem*) and "likeness" (*demut*) are used for things that are similar to, and representative of, something else, a combination of the above views is best: the image of God means that human beings are like God (in several ways) and represent God on the earth. The image of God is a rich relational and functional status that human beings enjoy by virtue of being God's creation.

It is clear from Scripture that *only* human beings are said to bear the image of God. Humans are unique. In fact, the covenant with Noah specifies that while humans may kill animals for food, "Whoever sheds the blood of man, by man shall his blood be shed, *for God made man in his own image*" (Gen. 9:6). Animals may be killed for human sustenance, but human beings may not murder other human beings. Thus the entire human race is morally distinguishable from other living species. Even before homicide was forbidden by a direct command not to murder (Ex. 20:13), unjustifiable killing was a violation of the special dignity vested in human beings by God himself (cf. Gen. 4:8–16). This is the foundation of the doctrine of the sanctity, or sacredness, of every human life.

When the second person of the Trinity, God the Son, took on human flesh through the incarnation, God sanctified humanity. In Jesus we see both perfect God and real humanity, and in his incarnation and resurrection we see the importance of the physical aspect of human nature. The affirmation of the Apostles' Creed that Jesus was "born of the Virgin Mary" entails that, like every other member of the human race, Jesus was once a human embryo. The creedal affirmations of "the resurrection of the body; and the life everlasting" mean that the body is a constituent aspect of humanity from the beginning of life throughout eternity. Thus every human life—from conception to natural death—is to be received as a gift from the sovereign Creator, is to be treated with reverence and respect, and is not to be harmed without biblical justification.

OT Texts

God's people were warned not to imitate their neighbors who committed infanticide through child sacrifice. The law strictly instructed them to "not give any of your children to offer them to Molech" (Lev. 18:21), prescribing the death penalty for violating this command (Lev. 20:2–5). Child sacrifice was also known during Solomon's reign (1 Kings 11:7). The brutal practice spread to Moab (2 Kings 3:27), Judah (2 Kings 16:3), and the northern kingdom of Israel (2 Kings 17:17). But Isaiah, Jeremiah, and Ezekiel condemned the practice, calling on God's people to repent of it (Isa. 57:5; Jer. 7:31; Ezek. 16:20–21).

It is in this context that the ethics of abortion should be determined. Like infanticide, abortion was not unknown in the ancient world. The most common means were mechanical methods and drugs delivered through pessaries (devices placed in the vagina).

OT Judaism always forbade abortion. Only one biblical text has been used to argue to the contrary (Ex. 21:22–25), and its interpretation is disputed. The text says, "When men strive together and hit a pregnant woman, so that her children come out, but there is no harm, the one who hit her shall surely be fined" (Ex. 21:22). Some interpret "that her children come out" as a miscarriage ("so that there is a miscarriage, but there is no further harm"). According to this interpretation, unborn human life does not have the same value as someone already born, because the normal penalty for causing death is a capital sentence (a life for a life), and yet, in this passage, the one causing the injury is merely fined.

There are good textual reasons, however, for another interpretation, namely, that the Bible is describing a premature live birth ("so that she gives birth prematurely, but there is no injury"). First, the Hebrew word *yeled* is used for what comes from the womb in this case. This word is never used for anything other than for a child who can live outside the womb. Another Hebrew word, *golem*, means "fetus" and is used only one time in the OT (Ps. 139:16, "unformed substance"). Furthermore, *yatsa'*, the verb that refers to what happened to the child, ordinarily refers to live births (Gen. 25:26; 38:28–30; Job 3:11; 10:18; Jer. 1:5; 20:18). The word normally used for miscarriage, *shakal*, is *not* used here (cf. Gen. 31:38; Ex. 23:26; Job 21:10; Hos. 9:14). Finally, even *if* the text were referring to a miscarriage, it would not indicate that an unborn child is valued less than one who is already born, for this hypothetical situation refers to an *accidental* occurrence. Most societies, including ancient Israel, recognized that unintentional manslaughter should be distinguished from premeditated killing. In the latter case, the death penalty was imposed. In the former, cities of refuge were established (cf. Num. 35:6). Thus, more literal translations render Exodus 21:22, "When men strive together and hit a pregnant woman, so that *her children come out*, but there is no harm, the one who hit her shall surely be fined" (ESV). This text then places great protection on the unborn child, for "if there is harm, then you shall pay life for life" (Ex. 21:23). The death of the baby is at least judged according to the same principles that apply to the taking of other human life (e.g., the death of the mother); see note on Exodus 21:22–25.

Psalm 139 speaks powerfully to the nature of unborn human life. David exults in God's omniscience and his omnipresence (Ps. 139:1–12). In verse 13 he celebrates God's intricate involvement in his own fetal development: "For you formed my inward parts; you knitted me together in my mother's womb." The word *kilyah* is used to refer to the "inward parts" (lit., kidneys). In Hebrew poetry the inward parts were typically the seat of the affections, the hidden part of a person where grief may be experienced (Job 16:13), where the conscience exists (Ps. 16:7), and where deep spiritual distress can be felt (Ps. 73:21). God formed David's deepest being. He wove him, or colorfully embroidered him, in his mother's womb, so that he was "fearfully and wonderfully made" (Ps. 139:14). In verse 16 the psalmist refers to his "unformed substance" being observed by God. David suggests that God's knowledge of him reached even to his earliest development *in utero* (in the uterus). No wonder the Hebrews found abortion and infanticide morally blameworthy. In addition, David's confession that he was a sinner from conception (Ps. 51:5) further testifies to his belief in personhood from conception, since only persons can be considered sinners.

God's judgment fell on those who killed the unborn. Elisha wept when he foresaw the crimes of the king of Syria, who would "kill their young men with the sword and dash in pieces their little ones and rip open their pregnant women" (2 Kings 8:12). Amos prophesied against the Ammonites because they "have ripped open pregnant women in Gilead, that they might enlarge their border" (Amos 1:13).

Extrabiblical Jewish Literature

The noncanonical Jewish wisdom literature further clarifies first-century Judaism's view of abortion. For example, the *Sentences of Pseudo-Phocylides* 184–186 (c. 50 B.C.–A.D. 50) says that "a woman should not destroy the unborn in her belly, nor after its birth throw it before the dogs and vultures as a prey." Included among those who do evil in the apocalyptic *Sibylline Oracles* were women who "aborted what they carried in the womb" (2.281–282). Similarly, the apocryphal book *1 Enoch* (2nd or 1st century B.C.) declares that an evil angel taught humans how to "smash the embryo in the womb" (69.12). Finally, the first-century Jewish historian Josephus wrote that "*the law* orders all the offspring to be brought up, and forbids women either to cause abortion or to make away with the fetus" (*Against Apion* 2.202).

Contrast these injunctions with the barbarism of Roman culture. Cicero (106–43 B.C.) records that according to the Twelve Tables of Roman Law, "deformed infants shall be killed" (*De Legibus* 3.8). Plutarch (c. A.D. 46–120) spoke of those who he said "offered up their own children, and those who had no children would buy little ones from poor people and cut their throats as if they were so many lambs or young birds; meanwhile the mother stood by without a tear or moan" (*Moralia* 2.171D).

Early Christian Literature

Against the bleak backdrop of Roman culture, the Hebrew "sanctity of human life" ethic provided the moral framework for early Christian condemnation of abortion and infanticide. For instance, the *Didache* 2.2 (c. A.D. 85–110) commands, "thou shalt not murder a child by abortion nor kill them when born." Another noncanonical early Christian text, the *Letter of Barnabas* 19.5 (c. A.D. 130), said: "You shall not abort a child nor, again, commit infanticide." There are numerous other examples of Christian condemnation of both infanticide and abortion. In fact, some biblical scholars have argued that the silence of the NT on abortion per se is due to the fact that it was simply assumed to be beyond the pale of early Christian practice. Nevertheless, Luke (a physician) points to fetal personhood when he observes that the unborn John the Baptist "leaped for joy" in his mother's womb when Elizabeth came into the presence of Mary, who was pregnant with Jesus at the time (Luke 1:44).

More than merely condemning abortion and infanticide, however, early Christians provided alternatives by rescuing and adopting children who were abandoned. For instance, Callistus (d. c. A.D. 223) provided refuge to abandoned children by placing them in Christian homes, and Benignus of Dijon (3rd century) offered nourishment and protection to abandoned children, including some with disabilities caused by unsuccessful abortions.

Ethical Conclusions

Based on the consistent testimony of Scripture, the early Jewish and Christian tradition, and what can be known of God's moral law through natural revelation (Rom. 2:15), the unborn child should be protected as a person from the moment of conception. A strong argument can in fact be made for this even apart from biblical revelation, for the only differences between babies *in utero* and babies that are born are: (1) their location; (2) their size; (3) their level of dependence; and (4) their level of development—but these are not morally relevant factors that would allow death for one set of babies (the preborn) and life for the other (those who have been born).

What then of the "hard cases" concerning pregnancy resulting from rape or incest? Christians should give compassionate care to those affected by such sins—including both the mother and the unborn child. But if it is wrong to put such a child to death after it is born (and surely this is wrong), then surely it is wrong to put that same child to death before it is born. The preborn baby should be treated as a person in the image of God.

For this reason, embryonic stem cell research, which involves the creation of human embryos in order to harvest their stem cells for medical uses, should be viewed as the intentional creation and destruction of distinct, individual, tiny human lives. Other sources of stem cells should be used instead, where the removal of the cells does not harm a human being.

What if abortion is necessary to save the life of the mother? Here it is necessary to recognize that removing the unborn child (e.g., from the fallopian tube) is done with the direct intention of saving the life of the mother, not with the direct intention of taking the child's life (which, if the medical technology exists, should also be preserved). Nevertheless, in such a rare and tragic case the choice would be between the loss of one life (the baby's) and the loss of two lives (both the baby's and the mother's). This is the only type of situation in which abortion would be morally justified, as making the best of an extremely difficult situation.

The witness of Scripture, as confirmed by the testimony of the early church, is that every human being, from conception through natural death, is to be respected as a person created in the image of God, whose life has special dignity by virtue of his or her relationship to the Creator. Like the early church, Christians should be known as a people who protect, nurture, and cherish children as gifts from the Lord (Ps. 127:3). ◀

Bioethics

Bioethics is a relatively new term that literally means "life ethics." The umbrella category of bioethics generally includes the ethics of human medicine, the biosciences, and biotechnology.

The Ethics of Western Medicine and the Hippocratic Oath

Medicine has a long and laudable history. Western scientific medicine began with the Greeks, who developed much of the early knowledge of anatomy, physiology, and even modern symbols of medicine. From the start, both Jews and Christians have had a positive view of medicine. The healing ministry of Jesus, the Great Physician (Matt. 4:23; 9:35; Luke 9:6), did much to provide the warrant for medicine among Christians.

The ethics of Western medicine reaches back to the Greek physician Hippocrates (460–370 B.C.). The son of a physician himself, Hippocrates practiced as an itinerant doctor in Thrace, Thessaly, and Macedonia. The philosopher Plato referred to Hippocrates as "a professional trainer of students" (*Phaedrus* 270C–D). The medical oath that bears his name was probably formulated by the Hippocratic school after his death. Jewish and Christian versions of the oath were produced after that time.

Over against the charlatans of the day, a Hippocratic physician could be counted on as someone who had mastered a particular set of skills and whose ethical standards were reflected in the oath he swore. Those who took the Hippocratic Oath promised to use their skills to help the sick and pledged not to euthanize a patient, perform abortions, prescribe abortifacient drugs, or have a sexual relationship with a patient, among other things. They also promised to teach their skills to worthy apprentices. The so-called Hippocratic consensus dominated medicine for nearly 2,500 years. Jews and Christians rejected the polytheism of the Hippocratic school but affirmed its ethical and professional ideals. Medical historian Albert Jonsen writes in *The Birth of Bioethics*: "The Judeo-Christian religious tradition, with its strong emphasis on divine commands that enforce respect for the sanctity of life, enhanced the prohibitions of abortion and euthanasia that are obscurely expressed in the Oath and prescribed caring compassion for the poor and even enemies. The literature of medical duty is profoundly marked by these moral traditions" (p. 7).

Only a very few medical schools still require that graduating physicians affirm the original oath. In a recent survey of the schools that used some form of the oath, only 8 percent of the oaths forbade abortion and only 14 percent prohibited euthanasia. Thus, Christians today have the opportunity to revive life-affirming ethics amid a very pluralistic medical and scientific culture in which affirmation of life is frequently downplayed.

Contemporary Medical Ethics

Current discussions of medical ethics have arisen in large part from the Nuremberg Trials in post-World War II Germany (1945–1949), which focused on the way human subjects were abused in medical research, and from debates in the 1960s over the allocation of scarce medical resources, like kidney dialysis. Early ethics committees serving medical treatment centers were disparaged in the media as "God squads" because they determined who did and did not receive life-sustaining treatment. Today, hospital ethics committees meet regularly to consult on difficult moral questions that arise in patient care and to help fashion hospital policies that enhance overall medical care.

Increasingly, emerging biotechnologies are coming under the scrutiny of the bioethics community. Genetic engineering, human stem cell research, human and animal cloning, artificial intelligence, cybernetics, nanotechnology, robotics, and an ever-expanding array of technologies require wise ethical reflection and careful policy recommendations.

Theologian Nigel Cameron has helpfully categorized the issues in bioethics under the rubric of "taking life," "making life," and "remaking life."

Taking Life

While Christians differ on the issues of euthanasia, assisted suicide, and abortion, which have long been within the realm of bioethics, it is accurate to say that in general Christians are life-affirming. In fact, as the article on The End of Life (pp. 2542–2543) argues in more detail, the vast majority of Christians agree, for various reasons, that euthanasia and assisted suicide are not consistent with the biblical witness concerning the sanctity of human life (cf. Ex. 20:13) and the role of others in providing compassionate care. Likewise, most Christians believe that inducing abortion is wrong, except to save a mother's life (see The Beginning of Life and Abortion, pp. 2537–2539).

Christians are often at the forefront of alternatives to medicalized forms of killing. The early church, e.g., rescued children from infanticide by providing homes and building orphanages. Many contemporary Christians support pregnancy care centers that provide alternatives to abortion by offering pregnant mothers education, resources, and shelter as they await the delivery of their children. The hospice and palliative care movement was begun by a Christian nurse and physician, Dame Cicely Saunders (1918–2005), as a means of caring compassionately for the terminally ill.

Making Life

The range of ethical issues surrounding procreation and contraception fall under the category of "making life." Contraception has been debated since ancient times. Christians generally divide into two camps. Those who affirm so-called natural family planning believe that every act of sexual union should be open to the possibility of procreation. From this viewpoint, no method of birth control is allowed that either presents a barrier to fertilization or introduces hormones that make the uterus inhospitable to a maturing embryo. Other Christians believe that contraception may be used to limit the number of children born to a family as long as the method is not abortifacient (i.e., something that causes an abortion).

Assisted reproductive technologies (ARTs) pose significant moral questions for Bible believers. Louise Brown, the world's first "test tube" baby, was born in 1978. Since then, in vitro fertilization (IVF, the fertilization of egg cells by sperm outside the woman's womb) has been quite controversial. Typically, IVF involves the fertilization of about a dozen ova in a medical laboratory. Only two or three ova are transferred to a woman's uterus, leaving the others to be cryopreserved (frozen) for later use. Given that the embryo is a human person with a right to life, many Christians have repudiated the practice due to the fact that 25 percent of these human embryos often die in the thawing process and many are likely to be discarded or used for research purposes. (However, it is possible that newer technology will allow the fertilization of only one or two ova that will actually be implanted in the woman's womb.)

Additional reproductive arrangements—like surrogate motherhood, artificial insemination using donor sperm, and sperm or egg donation—introduce third parties or their gametes into the reproductive relationship. The biblical ideal, however, is for procreation to take place within the context of a one-man, one-woman union (see Marriage and Sexual Morality, pp. 2543–2545). Intentionally causing conception outside of that framework and introducing third parties into the procreative relationship raises significant ethical, legal, social, psychological, and familial concerns. The intrusion of the sperm of a man other than a woman's husband into the intimate process of pregnancy and birth, e.g., can introduce significant difficulties into a marriage relationship. The relationship of Abraham, Sarah, and Hagar in the OT illustrates the tensions that may be present in even "low-tech" reproductive relationships (Genesis 16).

Even more ethical objections arise when a human embryo is conceived and allowed to develop for a short time solely for the purpose of harvesting its stem cells for the purpose of scientific research. In such cases, a new human life is created (see The Beginning of Life and Abortion, pp. 2537–2539) solely so that it would be destroyed for research purposes. This is inconsistent with the Bible's view of the sanctity of human life (cf. Ex. 20:13). Other sources of stem cells (such as those taken from adults or from umbilical cord blood) can be used in medical research without destroying a human life.

Adoption has always been commended as an ethical option for Christian couples facing infertility, and is a practical way to care for orphans (cf. James 1:27) and to provide a living parable of the Christian's spiritual adoption by God. A particular form of adoption seems morally commendable for Christians, in which a husband and wife decide to adopt a so-called "snowflake baby" (a previously frozen embryo that would otherwise have been discarded). The embryo is implanted in the adopting wife's womb, develops as a normal baby, and is born as a normal, healthy child. In this case, conception of the baby had already occurred as a result of the decision of others, and the couple who adopts such a baby is actually saving a life. (However, the potential "third-party" difficulties mentioned in the previous paragraph should be fully taken into account.)

Remaking Life

Researchers are increasing exploration into new ways to either repeat or reconstruct God's fundamental design for human life. These new scientific technologies are laudable when used for healing purposes. Thus, e.g., Christians should affirm the use of implantable computer chips to assist the blind to see, and the development of high-tech prostheses to replace limbs lost in accidents or war. But using these technologies for reasons beyond healing to allegedly "enhance" human capacities is problematic.

Using pharmaceuticals (such as steroids) or genetic engineering to create higher-than-normal IQs or faster-than-normal athletes not only raises profound ethical questions about justice in academics or sports respectively but also challenges the understanding of what it means to be human and who has the authority to alter the human species.

Some suggest that life-prolonging technologies might enable people to live forever, either in their physical bodies or in some other way. Again, while few question the morality of using technology for therapeutic purposes, many worry that enhancement technologies entail a sort of hubris, sometimes described as "playing God." The Bible warns against the sin of questioning the Creator. "Will what is molded say to its molder, 'Why have you made me like this?'" (Rom. 9:20). After all, Christians know that they are already guaranteed immortality through the resurrection of Jesus Christ (1 Cor. 15:12–20) and that physical death will be followed by a resurrection to a renewed, eternally healthy physical body freed from the ravages of disease and death. This hope does not totally nullify health-enhancing and life-prolonging technologies, but it does mean that they should never be the believer's ultimate hope (1 Cor. 15:51–54; Rev. 21:4). The wise use or nonuse of new technologies—medical or otherwise—must be seen as part of Christian discipleship.

Science and Ethics within a Christian Worldview

Christians have often been at the cutting edge of science, medicine, and compassionate care. Because they believe that all truth is God's truth, there is no arena excluded from the lordship of Christ, including the biological sciences. At the same time, Christians are "people of the Book" and bring a Christian world- and life-view—including ethical perspectives—into their thinking about science. The world cannot afford the development of science without ethical reflection. Ethical reflection must be developed in the context of accurate information. Therefore, Christians should see it as an expression of their discipleship to celebrate biological sciences that enable them to better understand just how fearfully and wonderfully made humans are (Ps. 139:14). Christians should seek to be good stewards over the opportunities that these developments offer (Gen. 1:28; 1 Cor. 4:2; 1 Pet. 4:10). At the same time, Christians should affirm that science is to serve the glory of God and the good of his creatures (1 Chron. 16:24; Ps. 96:3; Isa. 6:3), not to provide yet another opportunity for the self-aggrandizement that constitutes idolatry. Finally, Christians must continue to demonstrate love for God and neighbor that extends itself in compassionate care of those who are suffering (Luke 10:33–37). ◀

The End of Life

The Origin of Death

God did not originally create human beings to be subject to death, but "sin came into the world through one man, and *death through sin*, and so death spread to all men because all sinned" (Rom. 5:12). This refers to the sin of Adam recorded in Genesis 3.

God had previously instructed Adam, "of the tree of the knowledge of good and evil you shall not eat, for in the day that you eat of it you shall surely die" (Gen. 2:17). Therefore when Adam and Eve sinned, they immediately experienced *spiritual "death,"* that is, a separation from God. In addition, the just sentence of *physical death* began to be gradually imposed on them in that they experienced aging, leading eventually to death. God told Adam, "By the sweat of your face you shall eat bread, till you return to the ground, for out of it you were taken; for you are dust, and to dust you shall return" (Gen. 3:19). Since the time of Adam, all human beings have been subject to aging and inevitable physical death (except Enoch in Gen. 5:24; cf. Heb. 11:5; and Elijah in 2 Kings 2:11–12).

Why Do Christians Die?

Although Christians have been forgiven of their sins and are no longer under sentence to suffer the penalty of death for those sins (Rom. 6:23; 8:1; 1 Cor. 15:3), they are still subject to physical death because God has not yet applied to their lives all of the benefits that were earned by Christ for his people. In fact, Paul says that death will be the "last enemy to be destroyed" (1 Cor. 15:26). For this reason, believers today, living in a fallen world, are still subject to aging and death.

Yet death does not come to believers because God is punishing them, for, "There is therefore now no condemnation for those who are in Christ Jesus" (Rom. 8:1). Rather, death is the final outcome of living in a fallen world. Just as Christians are not kept from all sicknesses, floods, and earthquakes, etc., and just as the agricultural fields of Christians still grow as many weeds as the fields of non-Christians, so Christians will experience death as well.

However, Christians should have confidence that God will use even the experience of final illness and death as one of those events that "work together for good" for those who "love God and are called according to his purpose" (Rom. 8:28). Jesus Christ, who himself experienced physical death as a human being, often seems particularly near to Christians as they die, for they "suffer with him" (Rom. 8:17; cf. Phil. 3:10; 1 Pet. 4:13). Paul hoped to honor Christ in his death as he had in his life: "it is my eager expectation and hope that with full courage now as always Christ will be honored in my body, whether by life or by death" (Phil. 1:20). The risen Lord Jesus encouraged Christians in Smyrna, "Be faithful unto death, and I will give you the crown of life" (Rev. 2:10; cf. Heb. 11:35; Rev. 12:11).

What Happens When People Die?

When Christians die, their physical bodies are buried in the earth, but their spirits (or souls) go immediately into the Lord's presence in heaven. Paul said, "My desire is to depart *and be with Christ*" (Phil. 1:23), and "we would rather be away from the body and at home with the Lord" (2 Cor. 5:8). When Stephen was dying, he cried out, "Lord Jesus, receive my spirit" (Acts 7:59; cf. Gen. 35:18; Eccles. 12:7; Luke 23:43; Heb. 12:23; Rev. 6:9). Then at Christ's second coming, when he returns to the earth, believers' bodies will be raised from the dead, made perfect, and reunited with their spirits (1 Cor. 15:23, 51–52; 1 Thess. 4:16–17).

When unbelievers die, their bodies also are buried in the earth, but their spirits go immediately to experience separation from God and punishment for their sins. "It is appointed for man to die once, and after that comes judgment" (Heb. 9:27; cf. Luke 16:24–26; see also notes on 1 Pet. 3:18; 4:6).

Funerals and Burial

It is not wrong for Christians to grieve deeply over the loss of fellowship with those who have died, even if the deceased were believers and there is great confidence that they are with the Lord in heaven. Grief at loss of any sort is natural. Although the apostles themselves were present in the early church in Jerusalem, and the believers in Jerusalem were sure that Stephen was in heaven with Christ (cf. Acts 7:59), they still expressed profound grief: "Devout men buried Stephen *and made great lamentation over him*" (Acts 8:2). Although Jesus knew he would raise Lazarus from the dead, when he came to the tomb of Lazarus, "Jesus wept" (John 11:35). These examples indicate that it is right and proper to grieve at the death of a Christian loved one. But Christians should not "grieve as others do who have no hope" (1 Thess. 4:13), that is, their grief should not be the grief of despair, but grief mixed with joy and hope for future reunion (see 1 Cor. 15:55–57; Rev. 14:13).

When unbelievers die, if there has been no indication of saving faith in the person's life, it would not be right to give the person's loved ones assurance that the one who has died is in heaven. But it is still right to recall and speak of pleasant memories, and to remember the good things that the person did in his or her lifetime, much as David did after hearing that Saul had died (see 2 Sam. 1:19–25).

The Bible does not give any direct commands about how to treat the body of a person who has died, but there are recurring instances in Scripture of treating a person's body with dignity and respect, up to and including the time of burial (cf. 1 Sam. 31:11–12; 1 Kings 13:29–30; Mark 6:29; Luke 23:56; John 19:38–42). This can be done in a variety of ways according to what is understood in each culture as signifying respect and honor to the memory of the person who has died.

Regarding cremation, Christians have held differing views. Some object that cremation (which entails destroying the physical body) undermines the expectation of a future resurrection of the body when Christ returns. (When Jesus rose from the dead, it was his same body that was raised and made perfect, and so it will be with Christian believers; see 1 Cor. 15:35–45.) Others, however, think cremation is sometimes the wisest choice, perhaps for economic reasons, because burial land is scarce, or for other reasons. The body is eventually going to die and disintegrate in any case, and God will raise it from the dead and re-create it in its more perfect condition (i.e., in its glorified prime), no matter how scattered it is. If cremation is chosen for a Christian who has died, care should be taken to make clear that the family still should expect a future resurrection of the very same body that has died and now returns "to dust" (Gen. 3:19). But many Christians still prefer a simple and dignified burial of the person's body in the ground, in part because this gives a clear picture of awaiting the resurrection on the day Christ returns.

Euthanasia

The sixth commandment, "You shall not murder" (Ex. 20:13), prohibits any act that would intentionally, or through carelessness, take the life of another human being (see note on Deut. 5:17; the exceptions of capital punishment, killing in war, and self-defense are not in view here, nor are they implied by the meaning of the Hebrew terminology in the passage). The expression most frequently used for violating the sixth commandment is "shedding innocent blood" (cf. Ex. 23:7; Deut. 19:10, 13; Ps. 10:8; Prov. 6:17).

This prohibition against murder applies to all human beings, including: the elderly, those who are terminally ill, and those who wish to die. Intentionally taking the life of any of these people would break the commandment, "You shall not murder" (cf. also 2 Sam. 1:10, 14–15). Nations that have allowed for physician-assisted suicide find that a society can quickly move from merely *allowing* "the right to die" to the belief that there is "an *obligation* to die" on the part of the elderly and the very ill people who are "draining resources" from the society. In such situations it becomes likely that a number of elderly people will be put to death against their will.

It is important, however, to maintain a clear distinction between *killing a person* and *letting someone die*. Killing in the wrongful sense of murder, as prohibited in Exodus 20:13, means actively doing something to a patient that hastens or causes his or her death. But "letting someone die" means allowing someone to die without interfering with the process that is already taking place. In cases where it is clearly known to be the patient's wish to be allowed to die, and when there is no reasonable human hope of recovery, and where death seems imminent—then it does not seem wrong to allow such a person to die, rather than either to initiate an artificial life support system or to prolong the natural dying process by artificial means. For such situations, nothing in Scripture would prohibit a dying person from praying for God to take his life. On the other hand, where there is a reasonable human hope of recovery, and where there is a realistic, practical ability to help, the obligation to "love your neighbor as yourself" (Matt. 22:39) implies that active measures should be taken to save the person's life. In the parable of the good Samaritan, Jesus indicated that the priest and the Levite were both wrong for neglecting to do what could be done to save a badly injured man, who with care was able to recover (Luke 10:30–37).

The hardest end-of-life decisions are often related to removing a dying patient from artificial life support, which can involve various measures from an artificial lung to simply providing artificial hydration and nutrition. Christians hold different positions over exactly when in such cases the moral line is crossed from *letting someone die* to *killing*. When considering the proper course of action, Christians should remember that while death is an enemy to resist (1 Cor. 15:26), natural mortality is still part of living in a fallen world (cf. Gen. 2:17; Rom. 5:12; Heb. 9:27). There is therefore nothing wrong with accepting natural mortality by removing a dying patient from artificial means that are only slowing the natural death process.

There are more complex cases where medication given to alleviate a patient's pain may also have a secondary effect of hastening a person's death. In such cases, some Christian ethicists say that the two most important considerations are: (1) the primary purpose for giving the medication and (2) the patient's own wishes regarding the alleviation of pain. Other Christian ethicists claim that, in such cases, the moral value of improving life quality is always less than the moral value of honoring the sanctity of human life, and, while doing what they can to alleviate pain, Christians should never give higher priority to improving the quality of life (reducing pain) over honoring the sanctity of life (not killing a person).

Wherever possible, it is both wise and loving for people who are still in good health to complete the appropriate legal and medical forms to make known their wishes regarding medical care at the end of life. These decisions should also be verbally communicated to those who will likely have to make end-of-life decisions about each person.

Suicide

Suicide is murder of oneself, and it is prohibited by the command, "You shall not murder" (Ex. 20:13). It is a serious sin against God and brings immense, lifelong grief to loved ones who are left, but the Bible nowhere teaches that suicide is a unique and unforgiveable sin that prevents a person who has lived by faith in Christ from being saved.

Christ's Victory over Death

Finally, Christians need have no fear of death: "O death, where is your victory? O death, where is your sting?" The verse continues, "The sting of death is sin, and the power of sin is the law. But thanks be to God, who gives us the victory through our Lord Jesus Christ" (1 Cor. 15:55–57). ◂

Marriage and Sexual Morality

What Is Marriage?

Marriage is the fundamental institution of all human society. It was established by God at creation, when God created the first human beings as "male and female" (Gen. 1:27) and then said to them, "Be fruitful and multiply and fill the earth" (Gen. 1:28).

Marriage begins with a commitment before God and other people to be husband and wife for life. In Malachi 2:14, marriage is viewed as a "covenant" commitment in which God stands as a "witness." And Jesus says that a married couple constitutes a unity that "God has joined together" (Matt. 19:6). Therefore when a marriage occurs, a man and woman have a new status before God: he now considers them to be husband and wife together.

Some kind of public commitment is also necessary to a marriage, for a society must know to treat a couple as married and not as single. Sexual intercourse alone does not constitute a marriage, as was evident from the conversation between Jesus and the woman at the well in Samaria, where he said to her, "For you have had five husbands, and the one you now have is not your husband" (John 4:18). She was living with a man but that did not mean she was married to him, for there had been no public commitment recognized by God or by the community (cf. also Ex. 22:16–17).

Both Genesis 2:24 and Matthew 19:5 view the "one flesh" unity that occurs as an essential part of the marriage. That is why sexual intercourse after a marriage ceremony is often said to "consummate" the marriage, and (except in cases where it is physically impossible, because of disability, injury, or advanced age) it is thought that a marriage has not fully begun until sexual intercourse has occurred.

Marriage is a picture of the covenantal relationship between Christ and the church, with the husband representing the former and the wife representing the latter: "This mystery is profound, and I am saying that it refers to Christ and the church" (Eph. 5:32).

Some Will Not Be Married

The Bible also recognizes that not everyone will be married, and even among those who are married some will be widowed or divorced and therefore will become single again. In 1 Corinthians 7:7–40, Paul sees advantages to both being single and being married. Jesus himself was never married, and Paul was not married at the time of his ministry (see 1 Cor. 7:7; 9:5; it is impossible to know whether he was previously married or not). Jesus and Paul are examples of godly singleness coupled with wonderful effectiveness in ministry. But Paul says, "Each has his own gift from God, one of one kind and one of another" (1 Cor. 7:7), and therefore both remaining single and becoming married are morally permissible choices depending on the kind of life that God has called each person to live (see 1 Cor. 7:17, 27–28, 36–38).

Polygamy

Why did God allow polygamy in the OT? Nowhere in the Bible did God ever command polygamy or tell anyone to marry more than one wife. Rather, God temporarily allowed polygamy to occur (he did not give any general prohibition against it) without giving it any explicit moral approval. Nevertheless, in the OT narratives, whenever a man has two or more wives, it seems to lead to trouble (see Genesis 16; 29–31; 1 Samuel 1; 1 Kings 11; note the prohibition in Deut. 17:17). In addition, polygamy is horribly dehumanizing for women, for it does not treat them as equal in value to their husbands, and therefore it does not recognize that they share fully in the high status of being created "in the image of God" (Gen. 1:27) and of being worthy of honor as "heirs with you of the grace of life" (1 Pet. 3:7). The requirement that an elder be "husband of one wife" (1 Tim. 3:2) would exclude polygamists from being elders (evidence for polygamy among Jews in the 1st century is found in Josephus, *Jewish Antiquities* 17.14; Mishnah, *Yebamoth* 4.11; *Ketuboth* 10.1, 4, 5; *Sanhedrin* 2.4; *Kerithoth* 3.7; *Kiddushin* 2.7; *Bechoroth* 8.4; and Justin Martyr, *Dialogue* 134; for polygamy among non-Jews, see *2 Macc.* 4:30; Josephus, *Jewish Antiquities* 17.19; Tertullian, *Apology* 46). This has practical application today in missionary contexts in cultures where polygamy is still practiced: the Bible would not encourage a husband to divorce any of his multiple wives when this would leave them without support and protection. But it would not allow a man with multiple wives to be an elder. This restriction would provide a pattern that would generally lead to the abolition of polygamy in a church in a generation or two.

Sexual Intimacy and Moral Standards for Marriage

The Bible views sexual intimacy in marriage as a blessing from God. God said to Adam and Eve, "Be fruitful and multiply and fill the earth" (Gen. 1:28), which implies that God created them so that they would have sexual intercourse together and thereby bear children (cf. Gen. 1:31). Sex is seen within the context of marriage ("his wife," Gen. 2:24) from the very beginning of creation. After the fall, sexual intimacy in marriage is still viewed positively (see Prov. 5:15–19; Song of Solomon; 1 Cor. 7:2–5).

Why is adultery wrong? (1) Because God says it is wrong: "You shall not commit adultery" (Ex. 20:14). (2) Adultery pictures unfaithfulness in the relationship between Christ and the church, giving a picture of Christ being unfaithful to his people and abandoning them, and not keeping his covenant with them, or else picturing the church as worshiping other gods and being unfaithful to Christ (cf. Mal. 2:14; Eph. 5:31–32). (3) Adultery intrudes another person into the "one flesh" relationship of marriage (cf. Gen. 2:24; Eph. 5:31). (4) Adultery destroys trust within a marriage because it is the most serious kind of violation of a marriage vow. (5) Adultery often leads to children being born without two parents to raise them or else leads to abortion to end an unwanted pregnancy, both of which consequences contradict God's ideal. (6) Adultery is thus frequently and understandably pictured in Scripture as destroying a person's life: "He does not know that it will cost him his life" (Prov. 7:23; cf. 5:3–14; 6:27–29, 32–33; 7:21–23).

Sexual intercourse between unmarried persons is also consistently viewed as morally wrong throughout Scripture, from the laws of Moses (Ex. 22:16–17; Deut. 22:13–21) to the teachings of Jesus, who implicitly rebuked the woman at the well for living with someone to whom she was not married (John 4:16–18; cf. also Gen. 38:24; Matt. 15:19 [*porneia* or "sexual immorality" is distinguished from adultery, and the 1st-century understanding of the word would certainly include any sexual intercourse outside of marriage]; John 8:41; Acts 15:20; 1 Cor. 6:18; 7:2, 9; 1 Thess. 4:3; note the imagery in 2 Cor. 11:2).

God requires not only right conduct but also purity of heart: "You shall not covet . . . your neighbor's wife" (Ex. 20:17; cf. Prov. 6:25; Matt. 5:27). The opposite of desiring to commit adultery is having a deep love for one's wife or husband and a strong desire for a positive sexual relationship within one's own marriage, as well as a sense of revulsion at the thought of embracing anyone else in the same way. This purity of heart, like other inward virtues, needs prayerful cultivation if it is to be sustained.

Looking at pornography is a direct violation of Jesus' command against gazing at a woman "with lustful intent" (Matt. 5:28; cf. Job 31:1–2). Pornography attracts a man's affections and desires away from his marriage and away from his wife. It inevitably brings moral uncleanness in the heart, long-lasting harmful memories, and destructive consequences to one's marriage relationship (the same is true for the future marriage of those who are single). It ultimately leads in many cases to other sins, such as prostitution, rape, and other kinds of violence against women, because it dehumanizes them and fails to recognize and respect them as persons made in God's image and valuable in his sight.

Differing Roles in Marriage

The Bible clearly affirms that both men and women are created in God's image and have equal value and dignity in God's sight and for the work of his kingdom on earth (Gen. 1:27, 31; Acts 2:17–18; 8:12; Gal. 3:28; 1 Pet. 3:7). At the same time, the Bible indicates that husband and wife are called to different roles in marriage. God gives to the husband a responsibility for loving, humble headship (or leadership) in the marriage. Husbands are to love their wives "as Christ loved the church" (Eph. 5:25), and "the husband is the head of the wife even as Christ is the head of the church" (Eph. 5:23). God has given to the wife a responsibility for joyful, intelligent submission to her husband's headship and support of her husband's leadership role (though never to comply if her husband tells her to sin against God). The NT says, "Wives, submit to your own husbands, as to the Lord" (Eph. 5:22). These distinct roles are affirmed in a number of NT passages (cf. 1 Cor. 11:3; Col. 3:18–19; Titus 2:5; 1 Pet. 3:1–7). Since these responsibilities are patterned on the relationship between Christ and the church, they are not due to particular circumstances in individual cultures or societies but are applicable for all marriages, for all cultures and all time. They are a part of the "very good" creation that God established from the beginning. In addition, such "equality in value" but "difference in roles" between husbands and wives reflects the equality in deity but differences in roles between the Father and the Son in the Trinity (see note on 1 Cor. 11:3).

Are there other distinctive roles for men and women in marriage? Husbands and wives will often share in responsibilities and help each other as partners in establishing a household and raising a family. Yet a number of passages suggest that the primary responsibility for providing for the family and protecting the family belongs to the husband, while the primary responsibility for caring for the home and children belongs to the wife. See, e.g., Genesis 3:14–19 (note that pain is introduced into Eve's responsibility of childbearing and Adam's responsibility of tilling the ground to raise food); Isaiah 4:1 (a reversal of the normal order in a time of God's judgment); 1 Timothy 5:3–16 (widows, not widowers, are to be supported by the church); and Titus 2:5. There is a pattern of men having responsibility to protect women and children in Numbers 1:2–3; Deuteronomy 3:18–19; 20:7–8; 24:5; Joshua 1:14; 23:10; Judges 4:8–10; 9:54; 1 Samuel 4:9; Nehemiah 4:13–14; Jeremiah 50:37; Nahum 3:13. Yet these passages (concerning men providing for and protecting their loved ones, and women caring for children) present narrative patterns rather than direct commands (as with headship and submission), so it seems that Scripture gives somewhat more freedom for individual differences in these areas. ◂

Divorce and Remarriage

God's Original Plan

God's original plan for the human race, as indicated in his creation of Adam and Eve as husband and wife, is lifelong, monogamous marriage. Jesus affirmed this in responding to a question about divorce:

> And Pharisees came up to him and tested him by asking, "Is it lawful to divorce one's wife for any cause?" He answered, "Have you not read that he who created them from the beginning made them male and female [from Gen. 1:27], and said, 'Therefore a man shall leave his father and his mother and hold fast to his wife, and the two shall become one flesh' [from Gen. 2:24]? So they are no longer two but one flesh. What therefore God has joined together, let not man separate" (Matt. 19:3–6).

In this reply Jesus rebukes and corrects a first-century practice of easy divorce for trivial reasons. For example, the Mishnah said, "The school of Shammai say: A man may not divorce his wife unless he has found unchastity in her.... And the school of Hillel say [he may divorce her] even if she spoiled a dish for him.... Rabbi Akiba says, [he may divorce her] even if he found another fairer than she" (Mishnah, *Gittin* 9.10). Rather than entering into this debate among rabbis, Jesus first affirms God's original plan for marriage and shows that it remains God's ideal for all marriages.

Malachi views marriage as a "covenant" between a husband and wife, a covenant to which God was a witness and to which therefore God will hold people accountable: "the LORD was witness between you and the wife of your youth, to whom you have been faithless, though she is your companion and your wife by covenant" (Mal. 2:14). Therefore marriage is an especially serious commitment (1) between husband and wife, (2) to the society in which they live, and (3) before God himself (whether or not he is explicitly acknowledged in the marriage ceremony).

But What If One Spouse Is Unfaithful?

In marriage, a man and a woman commit to live with each other as husband and wife for life. In order for them to keep this commitment, both parties have to remain in the marriage. But when one party decides to leave the marriage for another partner, it becomes impossible for the remaining spouse to faithfully fulfill his or her commitment (a husband, e.g., cannot live with and act as a husband to a wife who is living with another man). Because of such cases, it seems that in both the OT and the NT God allowed divorce, in order to give some relief to the one spouse when the other has deserted the marriage or desecrated it by adultery.

Although divorces took place in OT times (assumed by Lev. 21:7, 14; Num. 30:9; Deut. 24:1–4), the only OT law concerning divorce is found in Deuteronomy 24:1–4 (see note). It envisions a situation in which a man divorces and sends away his wife, she subsequently remarries, and then becomes divorced or widowed. In such a case the law forbids the first husband to marry her again.

Jesus' Teachings on Divorce

Many of the first-century rabbis expanded on Deuteronomy 24:1–4, using it to justify divorce for many reasons, even trivial ones (see above). This fact lies behind the remainder of the exchange between the Pharisees and Jesus in Matthew 19:

> They said to him, "Why then did Moses command one to give a certificate of divorce and to send her away?" He said to them, "Because of your hardness of heart Moses allowed you to divorce your wives, but from the beginning it was not so. And I say to you: whoever divorces his wife, except for sexual immorality, and marries another, commits adultery" (vv. 7–9).

Jesus' statement, "Because of your hardness of heart," should not be understood to imply that only "hard-hearted" individuals initiate divorce but rather, "because your hard-hearted rebellion against God led to serious defilement of marriages." The presence of sin in the community meant that some marriages would be deeply harmed, and God therefore provided divorce as a solution in those cases.

When Jesus says that anyone who divorces his wife "*except for sexual immorality*, and marries another, commits adultery" (Matt. 19:9), he implies the converse: divorce and remarriage on the ground of one's spouse's sexual immorality are *not* prohibited and do *not* constitute adultery. It is the one exception Jesus makes to the requirement that marriage be lifelong, for sexual immorality seriously defiles, indeed disrupts, the "one flesh" union (Matt. 19:5). When Jesus says, "and marries another," he implies that both divorce and remarriage are allowed in the case of sexual immorality and that someone who divorces because his spouse has committed adultery may marry someone else without committing sin (see notes on Matt. 19:3–9). Therefore, if "sexual immorality" (Gk. *porneia*, which included any sexual intercourse contrary to the moral commands of Scripture) occurs, then divorce is allowed but not required. In fact, forgiveness and reconciliation, restoring the marriage, should always be the first option.

Where divorce was allowed—in Greek, Roman, and Jewish culture—the right to remarry (another person) was always assumed in the first century. For example, the Mishnah says, "The essential formula in the bill of divorce is, 'lo, thou art free to marry any man'" (Mishnah, *Gittin* 9.3).

But in Matthew 19:1–9 where Jesus allows divorce on the grounds of *porneia*, Jesus was simultaneously prohibiting divorce on the numerous other grounds that were being invoked in the first century. If divorce is secured for other reasons (but see a further exception below), then God does not count the divorce as valid (for such divorcers would be committing adultery should they marry someone else; see Matt. 19:9).

In Matthew 5:32, Jesus affirms essentially the same teaching:

> But I say to you that everyone who divorces his wife, except on the ground of sexual immorality, makes her commit adultery, and whoever marries a divorced woman commits adultery.

Jesus says that the husband who wrongfully divorces his wife "makes her commit adultery" because in that society, it was assumed that a divorced woman would usually need to marry someone else for financial support and protection, and yet Jesus still says this new relationship is, at least initially, "adultery" because there was not a proper reason for the divorce. But Jesus places most of the blame on the husband who wrongly divorced her, saying that he thereby "makes her commit adultery." In the last sentence of the passage, "whoever marries a divorced woman" should be taken in context with the preceding sentences, and so it means, "and whoever marries such a wrongly divorced woman as I have just spoken about . . ." (see note on Matt. 5:31–32).

In the parallel statements about divorce in Mark 10:11–12 and Luke 16:18, Jesus does not include the exception clause, "except for sexual immorality." The most likely reason is that there was no dispute or disagreement among Jews, or in Greek or Roman culture, that adultery was a legitimate ground for divorce, and Jesus is not addressing that issue (see notes on Mark 10:10–11 and Luke 16:18). This does not invalidate the more extensive teaching given in Matthew, because Jesus' acceptance of the exception for adultery, though not stated explicitly by Mark and Luke, was assumed as being beyond question. (Other interpreters think that Mark 10:11–12 and Luke 16:18 prohibit all divorces and they then understand Matt. 5:32 and 19:9 to refer to special circumstances of some kind, not divorce in general.)

Does Paul Add a Second Reason for Divorce?

Many interpreters hold that Paul adds a second legitimate reason for divorce in 1 Corinthians 7:12–15. Paul is facing a new situation that was not addressed by Jesus—the situation of a Christian and non-Christian married to one another. (In the context to which Jesus was speaking, Jewish people only married other Jews, and both husband and wife therefore were part of the Jewish religious community.) When a believer has an unbelieving spouse, Paul says that they should remain married if the unbeliever is willing to do so (1 Cor. 7:12–14). "But if the unbelieving partner separates, let it be so. In such cases the brother or sister is not enslaved. God has called you to peace" (1 Cor. 7:15). Most interpreters think this implies the freedom to obtain a legal divorce and the freedom to marry someone else. When an unbelieving spouse has deserted the marriage, God releases the believing spouse from the twin unending stresses of (1) a lifelong vain hope of reconciling with an unbeliever who has left, and (2) a lifelong prohibition against enjoying the good blessings of marriage again. (But some interpreters hold that remarriage is never allowed after divorce. On that view, Paul is saying only that the believing spouse is not bound to continue to seek reconciliation.)

Would this passage apply to desertion by someone who professes to be a Christian? In such cases, a question arises as to whether the person is genuinely a believer or is making a false profession of faith. Each situation will be different, and a Christian involved in such a difficult circumstance should seek wise counsel from the leaders of his or her church. Where possible, the steps of church discipline outlined in Matthew 18:15–17 should be followed in an attempt to bring reconciliation to the marriage. If that process results in the final step of excommunication from the church, then it would seem appropriate to treat the deserting spouse as an unbeliever ("let him be to you as a Gentile and a tax collector"; Matt. 18:17). But it must be emphasized that, if reconciliation of the marriage can at all be brought about, that should always be the first goal.

Are There Other Grounds for Divorce?

In addition to the two grounds of sexual immorality or desertion by an unbelieving spouse, are there any other legitimate, biblical grounds for divorce? Some interpreters have argued that repeated instances of physical abuse should be seen as an additional legitimate ground for divorce. Others would respond that many other means should be used to bring the abuse to an immediate halt, including separation (for the eventual purpose of bringing restoration along with the complete cessation of the abuse), church discipline, confrontation and counseling, police action, a court order, and other kinds of intervention by church members, family, and friends. But these would stop short of adding a reason for divorce that neither Jesus nor Paul specified.

Some have argued that a prominent school of rabbinic interpretation in the time of Jesus allowed divorce in cases where a husband did not provide enough material or emotional support to his wife. This was based on their interpretation of a law concerning a slave woman in Exodus 21:10–11. Since Jesus did not explicitly correct this view, they argue that he must have allowed the legitimacy of some other kinds of divorces, such as divorce for prolonged, unrepented physical or emotional abuse. But an argument from what Jesus did *not* say is of dubious validity, especially since Jesus' words "whoever divorces his wife" (Matt. 19:9) are so extensive in scope and seem to rule out additional exceptions not specified in the Bible itself.

What should be done if someone has been divorced for other reasons than those given in the Bible and then has married someone else? Jesus says that in such a case the person has committed "adultery" (Matt. 19:9), so the marriage began with adultery. But when Jesus says, "and marries another" in that same verse, he implies that the second marriage is in fact a true marriage. Jesus does not say, "and *lives outside of marriage* with another" (which was possible, see John 4:18), but "and *marries* another." Therefore, once a second marriage has occurred, it would be further sin to break it up, for it would be destroying another marriage. The second marriage should not be thought of as continually living in adultery, for the man and woman are married to each other, not to anyone else. The responsibility of the husband and wife in such a case is to ask God for his forgiveness for previous sin, and then for his blessing on the current marriage, and to strive to make the current marriage a good and lasting one.

With respect to the phrase "husband of one wife" in 1 Timothy 3:2 and Titus 1:6, some argue that this means that a person has never been married more than once, and therefore that it excludes from the office of elder all men who have been divorced for whatever reason and also all whose wives have died and who have subsequently married someone else. But a better understanding of this passage is that it refers to the *present status* of a man, either to his character of being faithful to his wife, or else to the fact that he does not have more than one wife (see note on 1 Tim. 3:2–3). In either of these better interpretations, the verse does not prohibit all divorced men from being elders, but each case should be evaluated on an individual basis.

Since marriage is not an institution only for Jews and Christians but is an institution established by God at creation, it is for all people, believers and unbelievers alike, and is in fact universal in the human community. The standards expressed here for divorce and remarriage are therefore applicable to all people. The church, where it has opportunity, should encourage non-Christians as well as Christians to abide by God's high moral standards regarding divorce and remarriage. However, in cultures where rampant divorce for all sorts of reasons is common and has been occurring for decades, individual Christians as well as churches should seek to support and minister to the many women and men and children who have been hurt by divorces in the past, as well as the casualties of divorces in the present.

The principles expressed in this article represent the most commonly held view among Protestants since the time of the Reformation (e.g., see the 17th-century *Westminster Confession of Faith*, 24.5, 6). Other views are also held by some evangelicals, however. Some hold that the exception clauses in Matthew 5:32 and 19:9 apply only to sexual immorality committed during the betrothal period (when a couple was legally pledged to be married), and do not apply to marriage proper, and therefore there are no legitimate grounds for divorce. Others argue that, where a divorce has occurred, for whatever reason, remarriage is never allowed. And others have argued that there should be some additional, but limited, grounds for divorce. But these views have not gained majority support among evangelical interpreters of the Bible. ◀

Homosexuality

God's Original Design

In God's original design, human sexual conduct was to occur within the context of marriage between one man and one woman. The first chapter of the Bible says, "God created man in his own image, in the image of God he created him; male and female he created them" (Gen. 1:27). Differentiation of the human race into two complementary sexes ("male and female") is the first fact mentioned in connection with being "in the image of God." In Genesis 2, which describes in more detail the process summarized in 1:27, God said, "It is not good that the man should be alone; I will make him a helper fit for him" (Gen. 2:18). Genesis then applies the example of Adam and Eve to all marriages: "Therefore a man shall leave his father and his mother and hold fast to his wife, and they shall become one flesh" (Gen. 2:24). This "one flesh" sexual union was thus established as the pattern for marriage generally, and Jesus cites Genesis 1:27 and 2:24 as the normative pattern that God expects all marriages to follow (see Matt. 19:4–6). Furthermore Paul, as a good disciple of Jesus, likewise strongly echoes Genesis 1:27 and 2:24 in his two primary texts on homosexual practice, Romans 1:23–27 and 1 Corinthians 6:9. Jesus and Paul both assume the logic of sexual intercourse implied in Genesis: a sexual bond between a man and a woman requires two (and only two) different sexual halves ("a man" and "his wife") being brought together into a sexual whole ("one flesh").

This is further emphasized in the story of the creation of Eve from Adam's side:

> And the rib that the LORD God had taken from the man he made into a woman and brought her to the man. Then the man said, "This at last is bone of my bones and flesh of my flesh; she shall be called Woman, because she was taken out of Man." Therefore a man shall leave his father and his mother and hold fast to his wife, and they shall become one flesh (Gen. 2:22–24).

The word "therefore" connects the making of Eve from a part of Adam's body with the "one flesh" sexual union between a man and a woman in marriage: it is the reunion of the two constituent parts of a sexual whole. It is not another man who is the missing part or sexual complement of a man, but rather a woman. (Jesus emphasizes this connection between the two different sexes, "male and female," in Matt. 19:4–6 and Mark 10:6–8.)

Prohibited Sexual Relations

Consistent with the pattern in Genesis 1–2, sexual intercourse outside of the marriage relationship between one man and one woman is prohibited. For example, "You shall not commit adultery" (Ex. 20:14; reaffirmed by Jesus in Matt. 19:18; cf. Rom. 13:9; James 2:11). In addition, other specific kinds of sexual intercourse outside of marriage are also prohibited, such as prostitution (1 Cor. 6:15–18), incest (Lev. 20:11–21; 1 Cor. 5:1–2), and bestiality (Lev. 18:23; 20:15–16).

Homosexual conduct is also viewed as a sin (something contrary to God's will) in several passages of the Bible. Leviticus 18:22 says, "You shall not lie with a male as with a woman; it is an abomination [Hb. *to'ebah*, actions that are extremely displeasing to God]." Similarly, "If a man lies with a male as with a woman, both of them have committed an abomination" (Lev. 20:13; cf. Genesis 19; also Jude 7). These absolute Levitical prohibitions are grouped with other relevant sex proscriptions (incest, adultery, bestiality) and are considered first-tier sexual offenses that are grouped together in Leviticus 20:10–16.

In the NT, Paul speaks of homosexual conduct:

> For this reason God gave them up to dishonorable passions. For their women exchanged natural relations for those that are contrary to nature; and the men likewise gave up natural relations with women and were consumed with passion for one another, men committing shameless acts with men and receiving in themselves the due penalty for their error (Rom. 1:26–27).

The phrase "contrary to nature" means that homosexual conduct does not represent what God intended when he made men and women with physical bodies that have a "natural" way of interacting with each other and "natural" desires for each other. (See note on Rom. 1:26–27; cf. also Rom. 1:19–20, that the truth about God and his moral law is visible and apparent in the material creation.) Homosexual desires are "dishonorable" both because they are contrary to God's purpose and because they treat a person's biological sex as only half of what it is. While the logic of a heterosexual bond is that of bringing together the two (and only two) different and complementary sexual halves into a sexual whole, the logic of a homosexual bond is that another person of the *same* sex complements, and fills what is lacking in, that same sex, implying that each participant is only half of his or her own sex: two half males making a full male or two half females making a full female. In other words, the logic of sexual intercourse requires a sexual complement, and thus a same-sex bond is a self-devaluing of one's own gender inasmuch as one sees the need to complement structurally one's own sex with someone of the same sex.

In a long list of sins, Paul also includes "men who practice homosexuality" (1 Cor. 6:9). This phrase translates two different Greek terms: *malakos* means "soft" or "effeminate" and was commonly used in the Greco-Roman world to refer to the "passive" partner in homosexual acts, while *arsenokoitēs* is a combination of Gk. *arsēn* (meaning "man") and *koitē* (here meaning "sexual intercourse"). The term *arsenokoitēs* was apparently coined by Paul from the Septuagint (Greek translation) of Leviticus 20:13, and means (in plural) "men who have intercourse with men." In 1 Timothy 1:10 Paul uses the same word *arsenokoitēs* in the midst of vices derived from "the law" (here, the second half of the Ten Commandments), which means that this verse also should be interpreted as an absolute prohibition of male-with-male intercourse, in keeping with Leviticus 18:22; 20:13. Early Jewish interpretation of Leviticus 18:22 and 20:13, and early Christian interpretation of 1 Corinthians 6:9 and 1 Timothy 1:10, also show that these verses were understood as absolute prohibitions against all types of homosexual conduct.

Does the Bible address the question of homosexual attitudes and desires? It must be remembered that God ultimately requires moral perfection, not only in human actions but also in attitudes of the heart. Therefore the Bible prohibits not only adultery but also a desire for adultery (Ex. 20:17; cf. Matt. 5:28), not only theft but also coveting (Ex. 20:17). This is because "the LORD sees not as man sees: man looks on the outward appearance, but the LORD looks on the heart" (1 Sam. 16:7). Therefore Scripture teaches that any desire to break God's commandments is also viewed as wrong in God's sight. "Blessed are the pure in heart, for they shall see God" (Matt. 5:8). While an impulse to do what God expressly forbids is (by definition) an impulse contrary to God's will, the Bible recognizes that Christians will be "tempted" by their "own desire" (James 1:14) and encourages Christians in such circumstances to "remain steadfast" (James 1:12) and to "be doers of the word" (James 1:22). This implies not actively entertaining the wrongful impulse (cf. Matt. 5:28), and not dwelling on it so that it "gives birth to sin" (James 1:15).

It is not surprising, therefore, that not only homosexual conduct but also homosexual desires are viewed as contrary to God's will. Homosexual desires are viewed as "dishonorable passions" (Rom. 1:26), and Paul also says that homosexual partners are "consumed with passion for one another" (Rom. 1:27), giving a strong image of a powerful but destructive inward craving.

This is not to say that homosexual *desire* is as harmful as homosexual *conduct*. Though all sin is wrong and brings legal guilt before God (cf. James 2:10–11), a distinction between wrongful desires and wrongful actions can be made with regard to many areas of life. Hatred of another person is wrong in God's sight, but murdering the person is far more harmful. Coveting a neighbor's farm animals is wrong, but actually stealing them is much more harmful. And lustful desires for adultery are wrong, but actually committing adultery is far more harmful. Similarly, homosexual desires are wrong in God's sight, but actually committing homosexual acts is far more harmful.

The Bible's Solution regarding Homosexuality

As with every other sin, the Bible's solution to homosexuality is trusting in Christ for the forgiveness of sin, the imputation of righteousness, and the power to change. After talking about the "sexually immoral" and "adulterers" and "men who practice homosexuality" and "thieves" and "drunkards" (1 Cor. 6:9–10), Paul tells the Corinthian Christians, "And such were some of you" (1 Cor. 6:11). Then he tells them, "But you were washed, you were sanctified, you were justified in the name of the Lord Jesus Christ and by the Spirit of our God" (1 Cor. 6:11; cf. Rom. 6:23; Phil. 2:13; 1 John 1:9). This implies that some former homosexuals in the church at Corinth had left their previous homosexual lifestyle and, by the power of the Holy Spirit, were seeking to live lives of sexual purity, whether in celibacy or in faithful, heterosexual marriages.

It is important that the Christian community always show love and compassion toward those engaged in homosexual conduct, and also extend friendship toward them where opportunities arise, though not in a way that signals approval of homosexual practice. It is also important to extend hope for change, since many homosexuals will say that they long to establish a different pattern of life. However, a number of studies have concluded that long-term change from a homosexual lifestyle seldom occurs without a program of help and encouragement from others.

Objections

Numerous objections have been presented against the view that homosexuality is morally wrong. One objection is that some people are "born gay," that is, that many homosexuals do not choose their homosexual orientation but it is part of their genetic makeup from birth, and so homosexuals can never change, and for them homosexual behavior cannot be wrong. But, as noted above, Paul, in talking about "men who practice homosexuality" (1 Cor. 6:9), says to the Corinthian church, "And such were some of you" (1 Cor. 6:11), indicating that homosexuals can change and become former homosexuals. This does not mean that homosexual desires will automatically or necessarily be eradicated for those who come to Christ. Becoming a Christian does not mean that people will no longer experience intense sinful urges (sexual or otherwise). But genuine faith does produce the fruit of obedience and real, substantive change, and Paul indicates that this is precisely what happened with some who had practiced homosexuality in Corinth.

Some argue that science supports the argument that homosexuality is determined by one's biological makeup from before the time of birth. Studies have in fact shown some indirect, congenital influences on homosexual development that may increase the *likelihood* of homosexual development. But there are certain hereditary factors that give people a greater likelihood of developing all sorts of different sinful behavior patterns (such as frequent wrongful anger, violence, adultery, alcoholism, and so forth), and it would not be surprising to find that some people, from certain hereditary backgrounds, have a greater likelihood of developing homosexual desires and conduct. But this is far different from proving congenital *determinism* of homosexuality, that is, that some people are genetically incapable of making any other choice than to entertain homosexual desires and engage in homosexual conduct. Especially significant are studies of identical twins, where one has become a homosexual and the other has not, even though they have identical genetic makeup.

The moral teachings of God's Word, not people's inward desires, must be the final standard of right and wrong. It is important to recognize that (1) virtually all behavior is, at some level, biologically influenced, and that (2) no command of God is predicated for its validity on humans first losing all desire to violate the command in question.

As for environmental factors that have been shown to increase the likelihood of homosexual behavior, two of the most significant, particularly for male homosexuals, are the physical or emotional absence of a caring father during childhood years, and sexual abuse sometime during childhood or adolescence.

Another objection is to say that the biblical passages concerning homosexuality only prohibit certain kinds of homosexual conduct, such as homosexual prostitution or pedophilia, or unfaithful homosexual relationships. (This is sometimes called the "exploitation argument": the Bible only prohibits exploitative forms of homosexuality.) But there is no legitimate evidence in the words of any of these verses, or their contexts, or in evidence from the ancient world, to prove that the verses were referring to anything less than all kinds of homosexual conduct by all kinds of people. Two biblical counterarguments against the "exploitation argument" may be briefly mentioned: (1) In Romans 1:23–27 Paul clearly echoes Genesis 1:27, indicating that Paul viewed any sexual relationship that did not conform to the creation paradigm of "male and female" to be a violation of God's will, irrespective of whether the relationship is loving. (2) Paul's absolute indictment against all forms of homosexuality is underscored by his mention of lesbian intercourse in Romans 1:26, since this form of intercourse in the ancient world was not typically characterized by sex with adolescents, slaves, or prostitutes.

Some have suggested that the Sodom and Gomorrah episode does not point to judgment on homosexual practice, but relates only to coercive homosexual practice. But Genesis 19:4–5 indicates that homosexual conduct was characteristic of the entire city and was a primary reason for God's judgment (cf. the note on Jude 7).

Some object that the phrase "contrary to nature" in Romans 1:26–27 shows that Paul is only talking about people who "naturally" feel desires toward a person of the opposite sex but who then practice homosexuality. Paul says, "For their women exchanged natural relations for those that are contrary to nature; and the men likewise gave up natural relations with women and were consumed with passion for one another" (Rom. 1:26–27). According to this view, Paul is not saying anything about people who "naturally" feel desires for a person of the same sex, for such desires would not be "contrary to *that person's* nature." However, this is reading into the text a restriction that has no basis in the actual words that Paul wrote. He does not say "contrary to *their* nature," but "contrary to nature" (Gk. *para physin*), a phrase that is used several times in literature outside the Bible to speak of all kinds of homosexual conduct as something contrary to the natural order of the world. In other words, Paul is not saying in Romans 1:24–27 that some people switched their innate heterosexual urges for contrived homosexual urges, but rather that people exchanged or left behind sexual relations with a true sexual complement (someone of the other sex) to gratify their inward urges for sex with members of the same sex. Paul sees such people as choosing to follow their desires over God-ordained creation structures.

Finally, there is an objection from experience: some homosexual "couples" have faithful, fulfilling relationships, so why should these be thought immoral? But experience should not be used as a higher standard for moral right and wrong than the teaching of the Bible. In addition, many studies indicate that, particularly among male homosexuals, long-term one-partner relationships are uncommon, and the widespread pattern is many sexual partners, often numbering many hundreds over the years. An additional harmful result of homosexual conduct is often immense damage to the family structures of a society and also to physical health (e.g., various studies have shown a significant reduction in life expectancy for homosexual males compared to the general population).

Same-sex Marriage?

Proposals for governments to recognize "same-sex marriage" should be evaluated in light of the Bible's teaching that one role of civil government is to "praise those who do good" (1 Pet. 2:14). Government recognition of a relationship as a "marriage" carries with it the *endorsement* and *encouragement* of that relationship by a society. Married couples enjoy many protections and benefits (legal, financial, and interpersonal) that society has granted in order to encourage marriage and signal that the institution of marriage brings benefits to society as a whole. So the question is really whether a society, through its laws, should give approval and encouragement to homosexual relationships that both the Bible and most cultures throughout history have considered to be morally wrong rather than "good," and that also bring significant harmful consequences. Governmental recognition of "same-sex marriage" would imply a requirement to allow homosexual couples to adopt and raise children, and this would rob many children of the opportunity to be raised in a home with both a father and a mother, which is by far the best environment for them. In addition, government recognition would likely soon carry with it governmental prohibitions against criticizing homosexual conduct.

Conclusion

Homosexual conduct of all kinds is consistently viewed as sin in the Bible, and recent reinterpretations of the Bible that have been raised as objections to that view do not give a satisfactory explanation of the words or the context of the relevant verses. Sexual intimacy is to be confined to marriage, and marriage is to be only between one man and one woman, following the pattern established by God in creation. The church should always act with love and compassion toward homosexuals, yet never affirm homosexual conduct as morally right. The gospel of Jesus Christ offers the "good news" of forgiveness of sins and real hope for a transformed life to homosexuals as well as to all sinners. ◂

Civil Government

God Established Civil Government

God has established civil government for the good of all people: "Let every person be subject to the governing authorities. For there is no authority except from God, and those that exist have been instituted by God. . . . [T]he one who is in authority . . . is God's servant for your good" (Rom. 13:1, 3, 4). This indicates that God has established an order of authority regarding civil government: those who are in authority have responsibility to judge right from wrong and to distinguish good from evil by rewarding good behavior and punishing wrongdoing. This means that those in authority should not use power in ways that are arbitrary or that merely serve their own personal advantage. Those who are not in authority are to "be subject" to those who are in authority.

Paul also indicates that God is sovereign over both evil governments and good ones. God not only raises nations up, he also brings them down: "He makes nations great, and he destroys them; he enlarges nations, and leads them away" (Job 12:23; cf. Ps. 75:7). In fact, he will sometimes use one nation to judge another (cf. Jer. 25:7–14). Isaiah 10:5–11 says that God raised up Assyria, which he used to judge all of the surrounding nations. But then he judged Assyria as well, at the appropriate time, using another nation. When God allows evil governments to persist, sometimes believers suffer greatly, but in such situations they also glorify God through their courage and faithfulness (cf. Dan. 3:16–23; Matt. 14:10–11; Acts 5:29, 40–42; 12:2; Heb. 11:35–38; Rev. 2:10; 12:11).

All citizens should obey the laws of the state (for exceptions, see below): Romans 13:2 says, "Whoever resists the authorities resists what God has appointed, and those who resist will incur judgment." In other words, those who reject the authority of a civil government reject God's authority as well. Romans 13:3–4 says,

> For rulers are not a terror to good conduct, but to bad. Would you have no fear of the one who is in authority? Then do what is good, and you will receive his approval, for he is God's servant for your good. But if you do wrong, be afraid, for he does not bear the sword in vain. For he is the servant of God, an avenger who carries out God's wrath on the wrongdoer.

This passage also indicates the purpose of government: it is established by God in order to restrain evil, punish wrongdoers, and promote the order and well-being of society.

First Peter 2:13–17 articulates similar truths: "Be subject for the Lord's sake to every human institution" (v. 13), which includes persons in authority like "the emperor," or "governors," or, by implication, other officials who are sent "to punish those who do evil and to praise those who do good" (v. 14). The reason Christians must obey in this way is because "this is the will of God" (v. 15), and, further, "that by doing good you should put to silence the ignorance of foolish people" (v. 15). This also means that Christians should honor those in authority, show them proper respect, and pray for them (cf. 1 Tim. 2:1–3).

Christian Influence on Governments

Since the moral standards of the Bible come from the God of all creation, who holds all people in all societies accountable to him, Christians should act upon opportunities given them to influence government to make laws consistent with the Bible's moral standards (cf. Dan. 4:27; Luke 3:18–19; Acts 24:24–25; also the prophetic warnings to pagan nations in Isaiah 13–23; Ezekiel 25–32; Amos 1–2; Obadiah; Jonah; Nahum; Habakkuk 2; Zephaniah 2). Influencing a government to make good laws is one way of obeying Jesus' command, "You shall love your neighbor as yourself" (Matt. 22:39), for good laws bring many benefits to people. However, civil governments should not make laws enforcing allegiance to, or prohibiting the practice of, any particular religion, for Jesus divided the realms of responsibilities between the things that "are Caesar's" and the things that "are God's," thus establishing two distinct areas or spheres of authority (Matt. 22:21; cf. also Luke 9:52–55; 12:13–14; John 18:36).

When Obedience to Government Is Wrong

Christians should *not* obey the government, however, when obedience would mean disobeying a command of God. This is indicated by several passages showing approval of disobedience to governments. For example, when commanded not to preach the gospel, Peter says, "We must obey God rather than men" (Acts 5:29). Another example is found in Daniel 3:13–27, where Nebuchadnezzar commanded Shadrach, Meshach, and Abednego to worship the golden statue; they stood firm against the king: "we will not serve your gods or worship the golden image that you have set up" (Dan. 3:18). God rescued them from the fiery furnace, thus confirming his approval of their stand (Dan. 3:19–30). Other examples of obeying God through disobedience to civil governments include the Egyptian midwives (Ex. 1:17, 21), Esther (Est. 4:16); Daniel (Dan. 6:10); and the wise men (Matt. 2:8, 12).

Is Revolution or a War of Independence Ever Right?

Christians have differed over the question of whether God's people should ever support revolutions against evil governments or wars to gain independence from evil governments. Some Christians argue that Romans 13:1–5 prohibits this, especially where Paul says, "whoever resists the authorities resists what God has appointed." Others have argued that Paul has in mind here only the conduct of private individuals, but that lower officials who are under a wicked higher official are in a different situation. They argue that lower officials may in fact be obeying God by leading a revolution or fighting a civil war against wicked rulers, in order to protect those whom God has given into their charge, and that thus, in protecting their people, they are fulfilling their responsibility before God to be "not a terror to good conduct, but to bad" (Rom. 13:3). Biblical examples would be Moses against Pharaoh (Exodus 1–14), and some of the judges (Judg. 2:14–16; cf. Heb. 11:33).

Methods of Selecting Leaders for Government

Because the Bible speaks so frequently about kings, for many centuries it was assumed that only a monarchy fit the biblical pattern for civil government. People believed in the "divine right of kings," by which kings were thought to rule by God's ordination (an idea that some supported from Rom. 13:1–2), and the people were thought to be subject to their almost unlimited power. The common method of succession was hereditary monarchy, in which the king's oldest son would succeed him on the throne.

But over the course of centuries more careful examination of the Bible has brought a widespread recognition among Christians that the Bible does not endorse hereditary monarchy as the only proper form of government. When read in their overall context, the tragic narratives of the hereditary monarchies that followed after David, beginning with Solomon and then continuing in both the northern kingdom of Israel and the southern kingdom of Judah (see 1–2 Kings), show a progressive turning of these kingdoms away from God and a decline in their circumstances until both Israel and Judah were carried away into exile in disgrace. Though there were a few good kings, most of the kings of Israel and Judah fulfilled Samuel's dire warnings about the ways in which kings would abuse their powers and eventually enslave the people (1 Sam. 8:10–18). And many of the pagan kings who opposed God's people were quite uniformly evil. The overall portrait of monarchies in the Bible is not a positive one (except for the future rule of Jesus, who will one day reign over a renewed world as "King of kings and Lord of lords," Rev. 19:16).

But what is the alternative to a hereditary monarchy? Several strands of biblical teaching combine to show the benefits of some sort of system by which (1) government gains legitimacy by the consent of the governed, (2) rulers are selected by the consent of those who are governed, and are accountable to them, and (3) the power of government is divided among several persons and groups in order to provide a check against the tendency of all sinful human beings to abuse power, especially great power. The arguments in favor of such a form of government are these:

1. All human beings share equally the status of being made "in the image of God" (see notes on Gen. 1:26; 1:27). This is a powerful concept that leads to the conclusion that no family should think it has by heredity a "right" to rule over other families and people, or to govern others without their consent.

2. If the government is to be "God's servant for your good" (Rom. 13:4), government should exist for the benefit of the people, not for the special benefit of the king and his family (cf. the negative example in 1 Sam. 8:10–18 in contrast with the good examples in 1 Sam. 12:3–5; Num. 16:15). But who can best judge what is best for the people of a nation? A good argument can be made that, over the long run, the people themselves are the best judge of what is good for them. To be sure, the people may err, but they are not likely to err as grievously as a non-accountable paternalist ruler, making decisions on their behalf, might be expected to do.

3. Scripture contains several positive examples of rulers seeking the consent of those whom they govern (cf. Ex. 4:29–31; 1 Sam. 7:5–6; 10:24; 2 Sam. 2:4; 1 Kings 1:39–40; 12:1; and, in the early church, cf. Acts 6:3).

4. The fact that "there is no authority except from God, and those that exist have been instituted by God" (Rom. 13:1) does not require a monarchy, for God can institute governments through a process by which the people are able to select their own leaders and keep a check on their powers. ◀

Capital Punishment

The Bible places much importance on the sanctity of human life; therefore any theological argument for capital punishment—the legal execution of someone guilty of a heinous crime—must meet high standards of biblical support and practical justice. Since human beings are made in God's image and likeness, only God has the ultimate authority to specify if, and under what conditions, it is morally justified to take a human life.

The Covenant with Noah

After the flood, God commanded Noah and his children to be fruitful, to multiply, and to have dominion and stewardship over the earth and all of its creatures. Permission was given to kill animals for food (Gen. 9:3); but murdering a human being meant forfeiting one's own life, for God said, "Whoever sheds the blood of man, by man shall his blood be shed, for God made man in his own image" (Gen. 9:5–6). In this verse, "shedding blood" refers to the violent, unjustified taking of human life (cf. Gen. 37:22; Num. 35:33; 1 Kings 2:31; Ezek. 22:4).

This part of God's covenant with Noah (Gen. 9:1–17) is a crucial text related to capital punishment for two reasons: (1) the provisions of this covenant were not limited to one specific nation for one specific period of time, as the Mosaic laws were, but were given at the time of a new beginning for all of human society following the flood; and (2) the reason for the command regarding murder is one that remains perpetually valid: "for God made man in his own image" (Gen. 9:6). The previous verse indicates that this command shows how God will execute justice on a murderer, namely, by requiring that other human beings, as God's representatives, put the murderer to death: "From his fellow man I will require a reckoning for the life of man" (Gen. 9:5).

This passage in Genesis explains what is wrong with murdering a human being and why the punishment for intentional murder should be execution: because human beings are made in the image of God. The severity of the crime dictates the severity of the punishment. This is consistent with an overarching principle known as *lex talionis* (i.e., the law of retribution). Exodus 21:22–25 (see note) is one example: "if there is harm, then you shall pay life for life, eye for eye, tooth for tooth, hand for hand, foot for foot, burn for burn, wound for wound, stripe for stripe." In contrast to the malicious practices of the nations surrounding God's people, the *lex talionis* was a civilizing influence in three ways (cf. Gen. 4:23–24). First, it prevented private vengeance, since the context of such laws showed that this was a principle reserved for judges. Second, it prevented excessive punishment by insuring that *only* an eye could be taken for damaging an eye. (For example, one could not *kill* another in return for blinding him.) Third, it prevented insufficient punishment by ensuring that social prejudice did not lead to treating some lives as less valuable than others. One could not require an eye for damaging an eye in one case but not another.

In biblical moral understanding, equally shared reflection of the divine image is what demands taking the life of the one who has wrongly taken the life of another. But the Bible never requires more than the life of the murderer; e.g., it never allows killing a whole village to avenge the murder of one person. According to the Bible, the value of human life does not come from anything that human beings control. It comes from reflecting something (or someone) other than themselves; it is something that all possess and that they can never lose.

Some interpreters disagree with this view. They argue that Genesis 9:6 does not *prescribe* capital punishment but merely *describes* what often results from living a life of violence. They claim that the statement "Whoever sheds the blood of man, by man shall his blood be shed" is only a prediction equivalent to the saying "all who take the sword will perish by the sword" (Matt. 26:52). Against this interpretation is (1) the fact that Genesis 9:5 says *God himself* will require this "reckoning" for the taking of human life; (2) the reason given for taking human life is not to satisfy a subjective feeling but is rather to hold perpetrators accountable for destroying God's "own image"; and (3) subsequent laws show that God in fact commanded that human beings carry out the death penalty for various crimes (cf. Num. 35:16–21).

Many who oppose the death penalty subscribe to the so-called "seamless garment" argument. For them, the sanctity of human life means that killing another human being is never permissible, whether in abortion, euthanasia, capital punishment, or war. Those who support the death penalty respond that specific teachings of the Bible, not an abstract theory (such as "never take a human life"), should determine the Christian position. And specific teachings of the Bible do give support to the principle of capital punishment. One of the strongest biblical refutations of the "seamless garment" theory is in Ezekiel 13:19 where God not only condemns "putting to death souls who should not die" but also "keeping alive souls who should not live." Someone who is "pro-life" on abortion and euthanasia can, therefore, at the same time consistently favor capital punishment. The principle remains the same in both cases: justice for and protection of the innocent, and punishment for the guilty in proportion to what they have done.

The Sixth Commandment

The sixth of the Ten Commandments forbids the unjustified taking of a person's life: "You shall not murder" (Ex. 20:13). The ESV footnote to this verse explains that the Hebrew term used (*ratsakh*) is somewhat broader than the contemporary English word "murder" when it says, "The Hebrew word also covers causing human death through carelessness or negligence." The commandment does not, however, prohibit all killing. The verb *ratsakh* is never used, e.g., for killing in war. Another reason the sixth commandment cannot prohibit capital punishment is that God himself said in the very next chapter of Exodus that "if a man willfully attacks another to kill him by cunning, you shall take him from my altar, that he may die" (Ex. 21:14). (However, cities of refuge were established for those guilty of accidental [unintentional] manslaughter [Ex. 21:13; cf. Joshua 20].)

In the OT it was God who prescribed the death penalty. Therefore capital punishment cannot be contrary to God's character or inconsistent with God's command to "love your neighbor as yourself" (Lev. 19:18). God's laws are always consistent with his moral character, and his moral character never changes (Ps. 102:27; Mal. 3:6; Heb. 13:8; James 1:17).

The laws God gave Moses at Sinai for governing Israel in the Promised Land included death penalties for several other crimes besides the intentional shedding of innocent human blood, which had already been prohibited under the Noahic covenant (Gen. 9:5–6). But these additional death penalties were *only* given to govern the theocracy of Israel and were never universally applied even in the OT. While the death penalty for murder is universally commanded based on an enduring theological principle (i.e., man being made in the image of God; Gen. 9:5–6), the other death penalties later included in the Mosaic law are not. Therefore these laws were specific to the particular history of Israel at that time, and they should not be treated as necessary patterns for civil governments today. (For many of these cases regarding worship of other gods, the NT parallel would be excommunication from the fellowship of the church.)

Methods of execution in the OT included stoning (Lev. 20:2, 27; 24:14; Deut. 21:21), hanging (Deut. 21:22–23; Josh. 8:29), burning (Lev. 20:14; 21:9), and the sword (Ex. 32:27–28). OT law also ensured that capital punishment could only be carried out based on the testimony of at least two witnesses (Num. 35:30; Deut. 17:6, 19). In some cases, the punishment was to be executed by the witnesses themselves (Deut. 13:6–10; 17:7), while in others it was to be inflicted by the congregation (Num. 15:32–36), the nearest of kin, or the avenger of blood (Deut. 19:11–12).

The NT on Capital Punishment

The most definitive NT text on capital punishment is Romans 13, where the apostle Paul discusses the nature of punishment and the role of civil magistrates. He writes, "Let every person be subject to the governing authorities. For there is no authority except from God, and those that exist have been instituted by God. . . . Would you have no fear of the one who is in authority? Then do what is good, and you will receive his approval, for he is God's servant for your good. But if you do wrong, be afraid, for he does not bear the sword in vain. For he is the servant of God, an avenger who carries out God's wrath on the wrongdoer" (Rom. 13:1–4). It is important to recall, however, that just three verses earlier Paul forbids personal revenge: "Beloved, never avenge yourselves, but leave it to the wrath of God, for it is written, 'Vengeance is mine, I will repay, says the Lord'" (Rom. 12:19). Then in Romans 13, with no sense of inconsistency, Paul moves right on to explain that leaving punishment "to the wrath of God" means allowing punishment to come through the civil government, which is "the servant of God, an avenger who carries out God's wrath on the wrongdoer" (13:4). So, while personal retaliation is forbidden, civil authorities are to punish evildoers justly and dispassionately.

Both proponents and opponents of capital punishment point to "the sword" (Gk. *machaira*) in Romans 13:4 to support their view. Opponents note that "the sword" is sometimes used as a symbol or metaphor (i.e., the "sword of the Spirit," Eph. 6:17; the word of God is "sharper than any two-edged sword," Heb. 4:12). They understand "the sword" in Romans 13:4 to be only a symbol of governing authorities. Against this, proponents of capital punishment maintain that the image of "the sword" stands for governmental authority to use even lethal force if necessary. They note that even where "the sword" symbolizes authority, that symbol has no meaning without the reality backing it up. The NT also uses the same word for sword (Gk. *machaira*) on several occasions that clearly refer to the real use of lethal force, e.g., when Herod "killed James the brother of John with the sword" (Acts 12:2), and when it refers to martyrs who were "killed with the sword" (Heb. 11:37; cf. also Matt. 26:52; Acts 16:27; Rom. 8:35; Rev. 13:10).

The apostle Paul, who used the word "sword" in this text, showed that he knew that some crimes are worthy of death, saying, "If . . . I . . . have committed anything for which I deserve to die, I do not seek to escape death" (Acts 25:11). It is unlikely that Paul would have said this if he thought capital punishment was never justifiable. Even so, except for crimes of murder, neither God's command to Noah in Genesis 9:6 nor any NT statement makes it necessary to treat any other specific crime as so horrible that all societies everywhere must always apply capital punishment when someone commits it. Apparently that question is left for each society or government to seek to decide wisely and justly.

The two sides on the issue of capital punishment also differ over Jesus' command to turn the other cheek (Matt. 5:38–39). Proponents of capital punishment think that Jesus only addressed personal conduct, not how governments carry out assigned duties, while opponents claim that Jesus addressed government duties as well. The story of the woman caught in the act of adultery (John 7:53–8:11) is not thought to be as relevant by either side, both because there is doubt about whether the text itself was originally part of John's Gospel (see note) and because Jesus' words in the story ("Let him who is without sin . . . be the first to throw a stone at her") do not pertain to the crime of murder.

Justice and the Role of Government

At the heart of the moral debate over capital punishment are often different views of justice and the role that is assigned to government in relation to it. Those favoring capital punishment usually stress the retributive view of justice (i.e., wrongdoing calls for proportional punishment). They argue that the Bible reveals that God has ordained human government to act as his agent in applying retributive justice to wrongdoers. Human government is "an *avenger* who carries out God's wrath on the wrongdoer" (Rom. 13:4; cf. 1 Pet. 2:14). Thus capital punishment is seen as (1) an outpouring of divine justice in this present life, (2) a deterrent from personal vengeance (Rom. 12:19), and (3) a deterrent from further crimes (see Eccles. 8:11; Rom. 13:3–4). Those opposing capital punishment either define justice differently (e.g., as distributing benefits or restoring damages), or hold that government should be less concerned with retribution (treating people as they deserve) than with mercy (*not* treating people as badly as they deserve).

Finally, Christians who believe that capital punishment has biblical justification also hold that it must be carried out in a just manner. So, among other things, this means that holding people accountable for wrongdoing should be done in a way that requires: (1) clear evidence of guilt established by eyewitnesses or irrefutable forensic evidence (cf. Num. 35:30; Deut. 17:6, 19); (2) granting the accused due process without discrimination based on social status, beliefs, race, or economic class; (3) rendering judgment based on adequate proof of moral culpability; and (4) making sure that any punishment assigned is proportional to the crime. ◂

War

Definition of War

War is a large-scale armed conflict between countries or between groups within a country aiming at changing or dividing established government. Throughout history, wars have frequently been started by rulers seeking to expand their territory and power, but wars can be started for a variety of economic, political, religious, or ethnic reasons.

Biblical Justifications for Some Wars

No recognized Christian group or Christian leader today argues that any government should engage in war to compel people to support the Christian religion. This is because of the recognition that Christian faith, by its nature, must be voluntary if it is to be genuine (note the invitations in various parts of the Bible that appeal to people's freedom to choose whether or not they will follow God: Ezek. 33:11; Matt. 11:28–30; Rev. 22:17). Jesus distinguished between "the things that are Caesar's" and "the things that are God's" (Matt. 22:21), thus establishing that the civil government ("Caesar") and the church ("the things that are God's") have different responsibilities and different tasks, and that the government should not use its power to attempt to control people's religious faith. Jesus himself refused to use deadly force to advance his kingdom or compel allegiance to him (see Matt. 26:52–55; John 18:36).

However, God does give civil government the responsibility and the authority to use superior force, even deadly force, to protect its citizens from evil. This is because, until Jesus returns (Dan. 9:26; Matt. 24:6), there are some people so deeply committed to doing evil that they can be restrained, not by reason and persuasion, but only by superior force. Therefore, in the OT God says that rulers must "give justice to the weak" and must "deliver them from the hand of the wicked" (Ps. 82:3–4). The NT maintains that the civil government has been established by God with responsibility for maintaining justice. This is why the government has a rightful duty to "bear the sword" (Rom. 13:4), to be "a terror" to bad conduct, and thus to be "God's servant" to do "good" for its citizens (Rom. 13:3–4). Part of this responsibility is acting as a "servant of God ... who carries out God's wrath on the wrongdoer" (Rom. 13:4). Peter likewise affirms that civil government is sent "to punish those who do evil and to praise those who do good" (1 Pet. 2:14). Therefore one of the primary duties of government is to protect its citizens, even through the use of force ("the sword") if that is necessary in order to restrain evil. This is the justification for police forces that protect citizens from any harm that would come from others within a nation. And this responsibility from God also provides justification for nations to engage in armed conflict ("to bear the sword") in order to protect their citizens from evildoers who would attack them from outside the nation, including a defense against armies sent by other nations when those armies and nations are "those who do evil" (1 Pet. 2:14) in the pursuit of such a war.

Several wars in the OT fall under this category of a war of defense against evil aggression (such as Abraham's war to rescue Lot in Gen. 14:1–16; Saul's war against the Ammonites in 1 Sam. 11:1–11; and Gideon's war to defend Israel against the Midianites in Judges 6–7). Therefore it should not be thought inconsistent in the OT for God to command people to go to war (see Deuteronomy 20, for example) and *also* to command his people, "You shall not murder" (Ex. 20:13; Deut. 5:17). The Hebrew word translated "murder" (*ratsakh*) in the sixth commandment is used 49 times in the OT but is never used to refer to killing in war (for which other Hebrew words are used; see note on Deut. 5:17).

Over the ages, Christians have adopted three different views on the ethics of war: crusade, just war, and pacifism.

Crusade

The crusade ethic treats war as the most effective means for destroying all resistance to establishing some idealistic vision of social order: it does so by religious authority; it is led by a religious figure such as a prophet, pope, or imam; it accepts no compromise; it spares no prisoners; it sets no limits on force; it sends soldiers into battle with zeal; it ignores all odds; it demonizes opponents; it distinguishes only between friend or foe (not between combatants and noncombatants); it never surrenders; and it never ceases so long as opposition exists. But while God does order wars of crusade in the OT (such as Moses' war of vengeance against the Midianites in Numbers 31, and Joshua's conquest of Canaan in the book of Joshua; see The Destruction of the Canaanites, pp. 390–391), and while Jesus is pictured as leading a war of crusade when he returns to rule the earth on all levels (Rev. 19:11–21), the Bible never gives *human* rulers a choice of electing to fight wars of crusade on their own initiative.

Biblically approved use of the crusade ethic occurs only at God's initiative (see Num. 31:1–2), is led only by God himself (see Josh. 5:13–15), and occurs only in such a way that those called to participate can readily verify that this is done at the direct command of God (see Rev. 19:11–16). When Pope Urban II launched wars of crusade during the Middle Ages, he violated biblical moral boundaries in a way that has shamed the cause of Christ and the reputation of the church ever since.

Just War

The just war ethic argues that warfare is sometimes necessary in order to resist or reverse specific unjust actions taken by one government or nation against another, but it also insists that war is always regrettable, is always something to avoid if possible, and is never to be used to establish some new vision of a social order.

The just war ethical tradition arises from both biblical and classical sources. In the Bible, just war principles can be found in rules revealed for engaging enemies outside the territory of the Promised Land (Deut. 20:1–20), in God's judgment of war actions taken by the Gentile nations around Israel (Amos 1), and in the regard Jesus had for moral wisdom relating to the way kings go to war (Luke 14:31).

The NT church included many soldiers serving on active duty and saw nothing morally inconsistent with Christians serving as military professionals. The conversion of Cornelius, a Roman centurion, was confirmed by the Holy Spirit with no question of his profession compromising his faith (Acts 10). John the Baptist responded to soldiers in a way that implied they were serving in a morally legitimate profession (Luke 3:14). And when Paul was imprisoned in Rome, many in the Praetorian guard became Christians (cf. Phil. 1:13). As a result, Christians soon came to fill the Roman "fortresses," military "camps," and army "companies" (see evidence provided by Tertullian in *Apology* 37; c. A.D. 200), and the first persecutions of the church arose because of the high number of Christians serving in the Roman army. While some early Christians opposed military service (cf. Tertullian and Origen), the majority tradition of the church has never considered military service to be inconsistent with biblical standards.

Over time, the just war ethic has developed a common set of criteria that can be used to decide if going to war in a specific situation is right. These include the following: (1) *just cause* (is the reason for going to war a morally right cause, such as defense of a nation? cf. Rev. 19:11); (2) *competent authority* (has the war been declared not simply by a renegade band within a nation but by a recognized, competent authority within the nation? cf. Rom. 13:1); (3) *comparative justice* (it should be clear that the actions of the enemy are morally wrong, and the motives and actions of one's own nation in going to war are, in comparison, morally right; cf. Rom. 13:3); (4) *right intention* (is the purpose of going to war to protect justice and righteousness rather than simply to rob and pillage and destroy another nation? cf. Prov. 21:2); (5) *last resort* (have all other reasonable means of resolving the conflict been exhausted? cf. Matt. 5:9; Rom. 12:18); (6) *probability of success* (is there a reasonable expectation that the war can be won? cf. Luke 14:31); (7) *proportionality of projected results* (will the good results that come from a victory in a war be significantly greater than the harm and loss that will inevitably come with pursuing the war? cf. Rom. 12:21 with 13:4); and (8) *right spirit* (is the war undertaken with great reluctance and sorrow at the harm that will come rather than simply with a "delight in war," as in Ps. 68:30?).

In addition to these criteria for deciding whether a specific war is "just," advocates of just war theory have also developed some moral restrictions on how a just war should be fought. These include the following: (1) *proportionality in the use of force* (no greater destruction should be caused than is needed to win the war; cf. Deut. 20:10–12); (2) *discrimination between combatants and noncombatants* (insofar as it is feasible in the successful pursuit of a war, is adequate care being taken to prevent harm to noncombatants? cf. Deut. 20:13–14, 19–20); (3) *avoidance of evil means* (will captured or defeated enemies be treated with justice and compassion, and are one's own soldiers being treated justly in captivity? cf. Ps. 34:14); and (4) *good faith* (is there a genuine desire for restoration of peace and eventually living in harmony with the attacking nation? cf. Matt. 5:43–44; Rom. 12:18).

If a war is just, it should not be viewed as morally wrong but still necessary, nor as morally neutral, but as something that is morally right, carried out (with sorrow and regret) in obedience to responsibilities given by God (Rom. 13:4). Those who serve in a just war should understand that such service is not sinful in God's sight but that they do this as "God's servant for your good" (Rom. 13:4; cf. Luke 3:14; John 15:13; also Num. 32:6, 20–23; Ps. 144:1).

Most nations throughout history, and most Christians in every age, have held that fighting in combat is a responsibility that should fall only to men, and that it is contrary to the very idea of womanhood, and shameful for a nation, to have women risk their lives as combatants in a war. The assumption that only men and not women will fight in battle is also a frequent pattern in the historical narratives and is affirmed by leaders and prophets in the OT (see Num. 1:2–3; Deut. 3:18–19; 20:7–8; 24:5; Josh. 1:14; 23:10; Judg. 4:8–10; 9:54; 1 Sam. 4:9; Neh. 4:13–14; Jer. 50:37; Nah. 3:13).

Pacifism

Since the time of Tertullian and Origen (2nd–3rd centuries A.D.), some Christians have advocated pacifism, the idea that participating in war is always wrong, or is always wrong at least for Christians. Arguments used to support pacifism are: (1) Jesus taught us to turn the other cheek (Matt. 5:39); (2) Jesus taught us that "You shall love your neighbor as yourself" (Matt. 22:39); (3) Jesus refused to use the power of the sword to advance his kingdom (Matt. 26:52–53); (4) the use of military force shows lack of trust in God; and (5) violence always begets more violence and does not really solve the underlying problems.

Those who differ with pacifism respond to each of those arguments as follows: (1) Jesus' teaching on turning the other cheek was intended as a guide for individual conduct, not for the conduct of governments or soldiers or police in the service of governments (see note on Matt. 5:39). (2) The command to love one's neighbor is consistent with going to war to protect one's neighbor from an aggressor, as is evident from the fact that the OT commanded love for one's neighbor (Lev. 19:18) as well as directions for the conduct of war (Deuteronomy 20). It is also evident from the example of David, who loved his son Absalom but sent the army against him when Absalom sought to usurp the throne (2 Sam. 18:1–33). (3) It is never right to use military force to advance the gospel message, or compel adherence to Christianity, but that is different from the responsibility of government to protect its citizens. (4) The believer's trust in God must be defined by what Scripture says, including its teachings on God's appointment of civil government to use force to protect its citizens. Therefore one should trust God to work through the power of the sword exercised by government. (5) It is simply not true that wars never solve problems: war was necessary to defeat slavery in the nineteenth century in the United States and to defeat Hitler in World War II, as well as to defeat other tyrants throughout history. In addition, non-pacifist Christians also note (6) that although Jesus stopped Peter from using a sword to resist arrest on his way to the cross (Matt. 26:52), he did not consider it inconsistent with directions given hours earlier that same evening when he instructed his disciples to carry weapons for self-defense (Luke 22:35–36; see note); and if using deadly force is justified as required under individual circumstances, there can be no objection to using deadly force as required under civil community circumstances. ◂

Lying and Telling the Truth

The God of the Bible is the God of truth, beauty, and goodness. As seen in the Ten Commandments ("You shall not bear false witness against your neighbor," Ex. 20:16), God expects his people to adhere to his standard of truth. But is it ever permissible to tell a lie?

Telling the truth and the permissibility of lying have been perennial issues of concern for both Christian ethicists and for the individual Christian facing an ethical dilemma. For instance, if a killer inquires about the whereabouts of his next potential victim, is a Christian permitted to lie in order to protect the innocent? Is it acceptable to lie in order to achieve great good? May a Christian falsify documents in order to smuggle Bibles into a "closed" country?

The Sanctity of Truth and the Condemnation of Lying

The Bible clearly emphasizes the sanctity of truth. God "never lies" (Titus 1:2) and his people are to imitate him by being people "of the truth" (John 18:37). Jesus described himself as "the way, and the truth, and the life" (John 14:6). Moreover, Jesus promises that "the truth will set you free" from the bondage of sin (John 8:32). Finally, one of the evidences of human depravity is that people "exchanged the truth about God for a lie" (Rom. 1:25).

By contrast, lying is condemned in Scripture: "Lying lips are an abomination to the LORD" (Prov. 12:22). The devil "is a liar and the father of lies" (John 8:44). Paul tells Christians, "Do not lie to one another" (Col. 3:9). He also commands, "Therefore, having put away falsehood, let each one of you speak the truth with his neighbor" (Eph. 4:25) and says that believers should be "speaking the truth in love" (Eph. 4:15). At the final judgment, those who are thrown in the lake of fire include "all liars" (Rev. 21:8). Telling the truth, therefore, is to characterize followers of Christ.

Does Scripture Sometimes Approve of Lying?

At the same time, however, Scripture records incidents that seem to approve certain examples of telling a lie. For instance, in Exodus 1, the midwives disobeyed the pharaoh's command to kill the male Hebrew children ("the midwives feared God and did not do as the king of Egypt commanded them, but let the male children live," v. 17). When asked why they did not kill the male babies, they said to Pharaoh, "Because the Hebrew women are not like the Egyptian women, for they are vigorous and give birth before the midwife comes to them" (v. 20). In other words, the midwives claimed that the births happened so quickly that they could not get to the mothers in time to make it appear that there had been a stillbirth. This was at best a half-truth (applying in only some cases), and the explanation that they "let the male children live" (v. 17) suggests that they were lying to the king. But at the beginning and end of the narrative, it says that "the midwives feared God" (vv. 17, 21).

Another example is the case of Rahab the prostitute, who hid two Hebrew spies (Joshua 2). When Joshua sent two men to evaluate the situation in Jericho, Rahab took them to her rooftop, where she hid them under stalks of flax (v. 6). When a messenger from the king insisted that Rahab turn the men over to the authorities, she replied, "True, the men came to me, but I do not know where they were from. And when the gate was about to be closed at dark, the men went out. I do not know where the men went" (vv. 4–5). Despite her lies, Rahab is commended in the so-called "hall of faith" in Hebrews 11:31 "because she had given a friendly welcome to the spies."

On the other hand, some interpreters argue that in neither case were the lies to be considered morally praiseworthy. Their lifesaving acts had a good motivation (to save lives) and good results, but those should be distinguished from the wrongful means that they chose to employ (i.e., telling a lie). In addition, some would argue that since Rahab was a Canaanite prostitute (Josh. 2:1), there is no indication that she had any knowledge of God's moral instructions to Israel. This makes it doubtful that every aspect of her conduct is intended to be read as an example for believers to imitate.

Is Lying Ever Permissible?

Several notable Christian theologians, including Augustine (A.D. 354–430), John Wesley (1703–1791), and John Murray (1898–1975), have taught that deliberate lying is never permissible. For instance, Augustine argued in his essay *On Lying* that telling a lie had the effect of eroding confidence in the truth and therefore weakened the Christian faith. Like every good theologian, he first defined his terms. A joke, even if involving factual falsehoods, is not a lie because everyone knows from the tone of the voice or the mood of the person telling it that it is meant to be taken not literally but humorously. Lying, strictly speaking, is seriously affirming as true something that one knows to be false. Augustine stated explicitly that one should never lie, even to prevent rape or to save a life. Lying, he argued, would ultimately undermine the gospel by destroying all certainty that one is telling the truth. If one cannot be trusted to speak truthfully about some things, how could one be believed when it comes to matters as important as the resurrection of Christ? Besides, Augustine observed, lying is a web that entangles a person. One lie requires another lie to cover it up, which requires yet another lie, and so on.

Others, such as Martin Luther (1483–1546) and Dietrich Bonhoeffer (1906–1945), have argued that, while Christians should be known for their commitment to the sanctity of truth, there are exceptions to the rule against lying. Present-day ethicists who identify themselves as hierarchialists maintain that Scripture teaches that some moral principles take precedence over others. Lying may be appropriate in cases where telling the truth conflicts with obeying a higher commandment of God. For instance, one may lie in order to save a life. This hierarchialist view does not represent a cavalier attitude toward lying but holds that one is sometimes faced with conflicting moral absolutes, and it takes this situation seriously and tries to find the solution that more fully expresses God's ideals and priorities. Thus, someone who tries to smuggle Bibles into another country probably believes that the Great Commission takes precedence over atheistic law (as in Acts 5:29, where the apostles said, "We must obey God rather than men").

While some hierarchialists hold that breaking a lower moral command to obey a higher one is what God requires, and is therefore not sinful, others hold that breaking any of God's commands is always sinful even though sometimes it is morally necessary. Against this position, it is argued that such a view cannot be reconciled with the life of Christ. If one is ever tempted with a situation in which all of his choices require him to disobey something in God's Word, and so commit sin, then Jesus must have been faced with a situation like that too, because he is the "one who in every respect has been tempted as we are" (Heb. 4:15). However, that would mean that Jesus actually disobeyed a moral command of God, and if disobeying any of God's moral laws is sin, then that contradicts the final phrase of verse 15 that says Jesus "in every respect has been tempted as we are, *yet without sin*." Therefore the life of Christ encourages believers to think that they will never face a situation in which they are forced to disobey one of God's commands in order to obey another one.

German theologian Helmut Thielicke (1908–1986) maintained that an individual or group may forfeit its right to be told the truth. In those cases, some would argue, truth telling is not obligatory. An example would be the deception and concealment involved in military contexts. In war, the "tacit agreement" of truthfulness has been made null and void. No one expects the enemy to speak truthfully about military strategy, prowess, or power. As a result, says Thielicke, the situation involves "mutual mistrust." These are the rules of the game, as it were. Lying is not wrong in these cases because the parties involved are not committed to mutual trust. Another example might be when someone intends to use truth as a weapon against an innocent individual. If, e.g., someone is holding innocent people hostage at gunpoint, some would argue that the police are not obligated to tell the truth when negotiating with the hostage-taker. By harming others, the criminal has forfeited his claim to the truth.

In response, those who hold that it is always wrong to lie would say that there will always be another solution, often involving various ways of hiding facts but not lying (cf. 1 Cor. 10:13). They would argue that the obligation to speak truthfully is not annulled by the debased moral condition of those to whom one speaks, but is based on an obligation to always reflect the character of God (cf. Matt. 5:48; Eph. 5:1; Col. 3:9–10). And God himself "never lies" (Titus 1:2; cf. Heb. 6:18), not even to sinful unbelievers. Therefore God's people should not do so either.

Is It Permissible to Conceal Truth in Order to Mislead?

What about *actions* intended to conceal truth or to mislead others? While such actions are related to the issue of lying, they are still a distinct issue, and individual examples are more complex because the meaning of an action is often ambiguous. In addition, an examination of particular cases in the Bible reveals some instances where misleading actions are wrong (cf. 1 Sam. 14:2–6; 28:8; 1 Kings 22:30; Prov. 13:7b; 2 Cor. 11:15) and other situations where they seem to be right (cf. Josh. 8:1–21; 1 Sam. 16:1–3: 19:11–13; 21:13–15; Ps. 34:1; Prov. 13:7a; Matt. 6:17–18). In any case, careful thought about lying requires treating such actions as a distinct category.

Finally, whether or not one believes that God ever approves of false statements, there are surely conditions under which it is appropriate to tell someone less than one knows or believes. For example, candor—being totally frank, or saying exactly what is on one's mind—must be used judiciously. Charity should temper how one responds to another person. To say to the pastor bluntly, "Your sermon was terrible," would not be edifying, but destructive. Speaking the truth in love requires discernment and restraint. Tact is a Christian virtue. In any case, the obligation never to speak a falsehood does not imply that one has an obligation to tell everything that one knows. There are many times when silence is appropriate (cf. Matt. 26:63).

Charitable Truthfulness

In sum, followers of Christ are to live lives characterized by charitable truthfulness. Failure to speak the truth in love to, or about, one's neighbor should be resisted. Lying is a sin of which one should repent. Even those ethicists who argue that there may be rare occasions when it is appropriate to lie agree that the temptation to lie to protect one's ego or status is so great, that few in practice are able to limit their lying to appropriate cases. In an age in which "everyone utters lies to his neighbor; with flattering lips and a double heart they speak" (Ps. 12:2), Christians should, by contrast, be known as those who speak the truth and whose words can always be trusted. ◀

Racial Discrimination

The Unity of the Human Race: Evidence from Scripture

Racial discrimination has a long and sad history, but the Bible consistently views it as contrary to God's moral will. The entire human race has descended from Adam and Eve (Gen. 1:26–28), and Eve is "the mother of all living" (Gen. 3:20), that is, of all living human beings. This means that all human beings share equally in the exalted status of being made "in the image of God" (Gen. 1:27). Furthermore, Paul says in Acts 17:26 that God "made from one man every nation of mankind to live on all the face of the earth, having determined allotted periods and the boundaries of their dwelling place." The biblical record clearly indicates there is only one fundamental race of human beings, all descended from a single set of parents.

The Unity of the Human Race: Evidence from Genetic Science

Recent genetic studies from the Human Genome Project give interesting confirmation to the very large degree of genetic similarity shared by all human beings and the extremely small degree of genetic dissimilarity distinguishing one people group from another. The best of contemporary science shows that the human genome sequence is almost exactly the same (99.9%) in all people. In fact,

> DNA studies do not indicate that separate classifiable subspecies (races) exist within modern humans. While different genes for physical traits such as skin and hair color can be identified between individuals, no consistent patterns of genes across the

human genome exist to distinguish one race from another. There also is no genetic basis for divisions of human ethnicity. People who have lived in the same geographic region for many generations may have some alleles [possible forms in which a gene for a specific trait can occur] in common, but no allele will be found in all members of one population and in no members of any other.

Why then do people with different racial characteristics originate from different regions of the world? The human race, starting with Adam and Eve, has always included not only genetic variations of eye color, height, and facial appearance, but also of skin and hair color now associated with different racial groups. At some early point when people began migrating to various parts of the earth, some variations within the one human gene pool became geographically isolated from other variations, so that people living in what is now northern Europe came to look more like each other and different from people living in what is now Africa, or Asia, or North America.

Another interesting implication of this has to do with genetic inheritance of skin color. Modern genetic studies show that when a lighter-skin person has a child with a darker-skin person, none of their children will have skin darker than that of the darkest parent. This means that if the hereditary transfer of skin color has operated in the same way from the beginning of human history, then the genetic variety in skin color (which is a very tiny difference from the standpoint of human genetics) must have existed from the very beginning. This suggests that Adam and Eve's children (see Gen. 5:4) would have likely had different skin colors, and that Adam and Eve would have likely had different skin colors as well.

Interracial Marriage in the Bible

Given the biblical evidence regarding the unity of the human race, it is not surprising to find that the Bible includes examples of marriages between different ethnicities or "races" that are treated as perfectly normal and good. For instance, Joseph (who was of Semitic origin, a descendant of Abraham) married Asenath (Gen. 41:50), the daughter of an Egyptian priest (who was African). From this marriage came Ephraim and Manasseh, two of the largest of the 12 tribes of Israel (Gen. 41:51–52). In addition, Moses married a "Cushite" woman, also an African woman from the region of modern Ethiopia and Sudan (Num. 12:1). Indeed, God punished Miriam and Aaron for criticizing this marriage (Num. 12:4–9). In addition, there are non-Jewish ancestors in the line of Jesus the Messiah. Matthew's genealogy mentions that Jesus' ancestry included Rahab, who was a Canaanite (Matt. 1:5), and Ruth, who was a Moabite (Ruth 1:4, 22; 2:2, 6, 21; 4:5, 10; Matt. 1:5).

There was some prohibition of marrying foreigners in the OT (see Deut. 7:3; Ezra 10:11), but as the verses in the previous paragraph show, this did not necessarily prohibit marrying people of a different ethnic group but only prohibited marrying outside of faith in the one true God (see Deut. 7:1–2; Ezra 9:1–2, 11, 14). The NT counterpart to this OT law has nothing to do with race or ethnic identity, but only teaches that believers should not marry unbelievers (cf. 1 Cor. 7:39; 2 Cor. 6:14–18).

The Curse of Canaan

Sometimes in the history of the church an invalid and indeed shameful argument has been used to justify racial discrimination. The argument is based on a false interpretation of the curse uttered against Noah's grandson, Canaan: "Cursed be Canaan; a servant of servants shall he be to his brothers" (Gen. 9:25). It is simply not possible to connect this curse of Canaan's descendants with people of dark skin, or with the members of any contemporary portion of the human race. Genesis 10:15–19 shows that the descendants of Canaan actually moved to the region of modern Palestine, where they lived in Sodom and Gomorrah as well as other nearby cities. Therefore, Noah's curse on the descendants of Canaan was fulfilled initially when God, in the day of Abraham, destroyed the cities of the Jordan plain (Gen. 19:24), and then later when Israel, led by Joshua, conquered the land of Canaan and in the process destroyed what remained of the sinful Canaanite tribes (see Deut. 7:1–2). These groups were not connected to the people of Africa.

NT Teaching

Several NT teachings are relevant to the issue of racial prejudice and discrimination. The parable of the good Samaritan (Luke 10:25–27) was in part designed to expose the wrong of the ethnic prejudice that existed between Jews and Samaritans (the Samaritans were a mixed race of people—half Jewish, half Gentile). In Matthew 28:19 (cf. Acts 1:8), Jesus told his followers that they should "make disciples of all nations" (i.e., all ethnic groups), and Paul condemned racial discrimination in the church when he said, "There is neither Jew nor Greek . . . for you are all one in Christ Jesus" (Gal. 3:28). Paul also taught that the wonderful "mystery" revealed in God's plan for the church is that "the Gentiles are fellow heirs [with the Jews], members of the same body, and partakers of the promise in Christ Jesus through the gospel" (Eph. 3:6). He taught that unity among multiple ethnic and racial groups in the church demonstrates in an amazing way "the manifold [Gk. *polypoikilos*, "having many facets, diversified, very many-sided"] wisdom of God" so that it is "made known to the rulers and authorities in the heavenly places" (Eph. 3:10). In other words, when the gospel brings Jews and Gentiles, and by implication people of every ethnic background, together in one church, it gives testimony, even to the angels and demons in the spiritual realm, of how wonderful God's plan is to unite all different kinds of human beings in one body, the church of Jesus Christ.

It is therefore a terrible tragedy when Christians of any particular racial background exclude people of other racial or ethnic backgrounds from participating in certain local churches. Such thinking is completely contrary to what God intends. In the book of Revelation John's heavenly vision of the glorified church is described as:

> a great multitude that no one could number, from every nation, from all tribes and peoples and languages, standing before the throne and before the Lamb, clothed in white robes, with palm branches in their hands, and crying out with a loud voice, "Salvation belongs to our God who sits on the throne, and to the Lamb!" (Rev. 7:9–10).

If this is God's great plan from the beginning of time until the end, then surely the Christian church of today should be a living example of racial harmony, characterized by full inclusion of people from all racial and ethnic backgrounds united in serving Christ and his universal kingdom on earth. ◂

Stewardship

The Concept of Stewardship

The entire earth belongs to God, for he created it: "The earth is the LORD's and the fullness thereof, the world and those who dwell therein" (Ps. 24:1; cf. Gen. 1:1; Lev. 25:23; Ps. 50:10–12; Hag. 2:8). But while God made animals simply to dwell on the earth and eat the food they found on it (Gen. 1:30), he made man (as male and female) to rule over all the earth and develop its resources in wise and useful ways: "Be fruitful and multiply and fill the earth and *subdue it* and *have dominion* over the fish of the sea and over the birds of the heavens and over every living thing that moves on the earth" (Gen. 1:28). To "subdue" the earth meant to exercise wise control over it in such a way that it will produce useful goods for the people who "subdued" it. This command therefore implied an expectation that Adam and Eve, and their descendants, as God's image-bearers, would investigate, understand, develop, and enjoy the resources of the earth, with thanksgiving to God who had entrusted such a responsibility to them. This implied not merely harvesting food from the vines and fruit trees in the garden of Eden but also domesticating animals (cf. note on Gen. 2:20), developing the mineral resources of the earth (cf. Gen. 2:11–12), and eventually developing dwelling places and means of transportation, learning artistry and craftsmanship, and so forth. The ability to develop and enjoy the resources of the earth in this way is an ability unique to human beings, one that is shared neither by animals nor by angels. Therefore the innate human desire to develop the resources of the earth and produce useful goods for human beings should not be immediately dismissed as sinful or greedy, but is an essential aspect of how God created human beings to function on the earth.

Stewardship and the Environment

The responsibility to be stewards of God's creation does not mean that humans have a right to *abuse or destroy* his material creation, for wisdom dictates that they should take appropriate steps to protect this gift of God from unwarranted defilement and inappropriate use. Nor does stewardship mean that people are to *ignore* God's material creation, either through passive neglect or through a philosophical decision to leave nature in its "natural state." After the fall, "the creation was subjected to futility" (Rom. 8:20; cf. Gen. 3:17–18) in such a way that nature now includes floods, forest fires, hurricanes, weeds, insects that can destroy crops, etc. Wise stewardship involves active steps to "subdue" and "have dominion" over such factors, with thoughtful development of the world's resources, in gratitude to God and in accord with his moral laws.

Stewardship in All of Life

Whatever a person "owns," he or she is to manage as a steward who is responsible to God. Stewardship responsibilities extend not only to the creation, material possessions, and natural resources, but also to other things such as talents or skills that have been given by God (1 Cor. 4:7), time and opportunities (Eph. 5:15–16), the wonderful responsibility of bearing and raising children (Eph. 6:4), and spiritual gifts and ministries (1 Cor. 4:1–2; Eph. 3:2; 1 Pet. 4:10).

Stewardship and Ownership of Property

The idea of private stewardship or ownership of property is implicit in the Ten Commandments, for when God says, "You shall not *steal*" (Ex. 20:15), it implies that one should not steal his neighbor's ox or donkey because it belongs to the neighbor. It is, in a sense, "private property." This becomes more explicit when the tenth commandment focuses on the desires of one's heart: "You shall not *covet* your neighbor's house . . . or his ox, or his donkey, or anything that is your neighbor's" (Ex. 20:17). The neighbor's ownership of his house and his donkey gives him control over those things and also provides the basis on which God will hold him responsible for faithfully discharging his stewardship responsibilities. Therefore the Bible does not view the ownership of property as something that is wrong or evil in itself, but rather as a solemn responsibility that God entrusts to human beings created in his image. (Regarding the statement in Acts 2:44 that believers in the early church "had all things in common," see notes on Acts 2:44; 4:34; and 5:4.)

Stewardship and Various Uses of Possessions

The concept of responsible stewardship before God requires that believers use all their property and possessions in ways that are pleasing to God and faithful to his teachings in Scripture.

1. Some resources should be used to support oneself and one's family. Paul instructed the Thessalonians "to work with your hands . . . so that you may walk properly . . . and be dependent on no one" (1 Thess. 4:11–12), and to tell those "walking in idleness" "to do their work quietly and to earn their own living" (2 Thess. 3:6, 12; cf. 1 Tim. 5:8). The NT does not command Christians to follow rigid asceticism (see 1 Tim. 4:1–5) but encourages believers to enjoy the resources of the earth "with thanksgiving" (1 Tim. 4:4) to God, "who richly provides us with everything to enjoy" (1 Tim. 6:17; cf. Eccles. 6:1–2). Yet there are also strong warnings against the love of money, the temptations of wealth, and spending that is wasteful, selfish, or self-indulgent: "Keep your life free from love of money, and be content with what you have" (Heb. 13:5). "If riches increase, set not your heart on them" (Ps. 62:10; cf. Eccles. 5:10; Matt. 6:19–21; Luke 12:15–21; 15:11–13; James 5:5; 1 John 2:16; 3:17). Jesus gave a number of warnings about wealth: "You cannot serve God and money" (Matt. 6:24). "The deceitfulness of riches and the desires for other things enter in and choke the word, and it proves unfruitful" (Mark 4:19). "Woe to you who are rich, for you have received your consolation" (Luke 6:24).

2. Another morally good use of some resources is to save for future needs. Because "you do not know what tomorrow will bring" (James 4:14), it is wise, for those who are able to do so, to save some of what they have for a time when they will not be able to work (due to age, weakness, sickness, or loss of employment). A person who assumes that he will need no savings to depend on in the future is very likely deciding to impose a later financial burden on his children or relatives. However, accumulating savings also provides significant temptations to sin: Jesus says, "Do not lay up for yourselves treasures on earth . . . but lay up for yourselves treasures in heaven. . . . For where your treasure is, there your heart will be also" (Matt. 6:19–21; cf. Ps. 62:10; Matt. 6:24; Luke 12:15–21; Heb. 13:5). And Christians should continually realize that whatever amount they save, that amount is not being given to the needs of others or to the building up of the church or to the spread of the gospel throughout the world.

3. A third use of resources, one repeatedly emphasized in Scripture, is giving money to those in need, or to the Lord's work in the church and in missions. In the OT, God required his people to give a "tithe" (that is, 10 percent) of their grain (see Lev. 27:30) and of their "herds and flocks, every tenth animal" (Lev. 27:32; see also Gen. 14:20; 28:22; Num. 18:21, 26; Deut. 12:17; 14:22; 26:12–13). But while Jesus spoke about the tithing of the scribes and Pharisees (Matt. 23:23) during his earthly ministry, after his resurrection and the establishment of the NT church at Pentecost (Acts 2) the requirement to give a "tithe" or a tenth of one's income is never explicitly imposed on Christians. Rather than stipulating a fixed amount, the NT places emphasis on generous, abundant, cheerful giving: "God loves a cheerful giver" who "sows bountifully" (2 Cor. 9:6–7), and promises that "you will be enriched in every way to be generous in every way" (2 Cor. 9:11). So, while Christians are not obligated to give a fixed amount, it is hard to imagine that God expects people of the new covenant to give any *less* than the 10-percent tithe in the old covenant.

The NT specifically encourages giving to assist others in need: "If anyone has the world's goods and sees his brother in need, yet closes his heart against him, how does God's love abide in him?" (1 John 3:17; cf. James 2:14–17). Jesus even encourages active imitation of God in doing good for "the ungrateful and the evil" (Luke 6:32–36). Paul devoted a significant portion of his third missionary journey to collecting funds for the needs of poor Christians in Jerusalem (see Acts 21:17; 24:17; Rom. 15:25–28, 31; 1 Cor. 16:1–4; 2 Cor. 8:1–4; 9:1–5; cf. chart, p. 2136). Though it is right to give to the material needs of all people, both believers and unbelievers, the NT prioritizes giving to the needs of Christian brothers and sisters: "So then, as we have opportunity, let us do good to everyone, and especially to those who are of the household of faith" (Gal. 6:10; cf. "brother" in 1 John 3:17).

The NT also encourages Christians to support the needs of the church and of those who do the work of evangelism. Paul received financial support from the church at Philippi (cf. Phil. 4:15–19), and he told churches to support their elders, "especially those who labor in preaching and teaching," for "the laborer deserves his wages" (1 Tim. 5:17–18; cf. 1 Cor. 9:6–14; Gal. 6:6). This would require that those who are part of a church should regularly give to support the ministry of the church.

Stewardship and the Poor

The Bible clearly and repeatedly emphasizes the need for Christians to care for the poor as one of the fundamental requirements of the gospel message. Jesus himself was born to poor parents (cf. Luke 2:24 and note) and had few possessions during his public ministry (Matt. 8:20). Jesus says that as his followers do, or do not do, to "the least of these" (i.e., those who are hungry, thirsty, strangers, naked), so they either do it, or do not do it, to him (Matt. 25:35–45; cf. the teaching in Proverbs that connects one's attitude to the poor with his or her relationship to God: Prov. 14:31; 19:17; 21:13). Paul and the early church took Jesus' teaching seriously and were "eager" "to remember the poor" (Gal. 2:10). In fact, Paul anchored his appeal to care for the poor in Jerusalem in the cross, that is, in Jesus' own atoning self-sacrifice: "though he was rich, yet for your sake he became poor" (2 Cor. 8:9). The generosity of the church both within and outside the family of faith eventually led the anti-Christian Roman emperor, Julian the Apostate (4th century A.D.), to complain, "Nothing has contributed to the progress of the superstition of the Christians as their charity to strangers. . . . The impious Galileans provide not only for their own poor, but for ours as well" (Julian, *Epistles* 84). Such care for the poor often takes the form of meeting immediate needs for food, clothing, and other essentials (cf. Luke 10:25–36; James 2:15–17; 1 John 3:17–18).

Meeting the needs of the poor will also mean seeking to bring about long-term solutions. These solutions, which can often require greater time and energy to implement, enable those who are poor to obtain jobs by which they can support themselves and be able to "earn their own living" (2 Thess. 3:12), as Paul commands. Useful in this regard are programs that provide job training, related educational programs, microloans to begin small businesses, and changes in any governmental policies or cultural traditions that hinder long-term economic growth.

While nearly all Christian ethicists believe that civil government should take *some* role in assuring that everyone has access to the most basic human needs, they differ over the degree to which civil government (as distinguished from nongovernment entities such as relatives, neighbors, churches, and charitable organizations) should assume responsibility or authority for meeting those needs. Points of difference often arise with regard to government programs to rehabilitate and train individuals, create new jobs, change social and economic structures, and/or redistribute wealth. Questions raised by these differences do not fall into categories of clearly defined biblical right or wrong, but tend rather to entail philosophical differences in economic or social theory. ◂

NT Guidelines for Giving

Giving Should Be	References
willing and cheerful	"Each one must give as he has decided in his heart, not reluctantly or under compulsion, for God loves a cheerful giver" (2 Cor. 9:7; cf. 8:2–3).
a regular pattern of life	"On the first day of every week, each of you is to put something aside and store it up" (1 Cor. 16:2).
proportionate to one's ability	"Each of you is to put something aside and store it up, as he may prosper" (1 Cor. 16:2).
generous	"In a severe test of affliction, [the Macedonians'] abundance of joy and their extreme poverty have overflowed in a wealth of generosity on their part. For they gave . . . beyond their means" (2 Cor. 8:2–3; cf. Prov. 14:21, 31; 19:17; 2 Cor. 9:6; 1 Tim. 6:18).
sacrificial	The poor widow with "two small copper coins" is commended by Jesus for putting into the offering "everything she had, all she had to live on" (Mark 12:42–44; cf. Acts 4:32–33; 2 Cor. 8:3).

INTERPRETING THE BIBLE

Interpreting the Bible: An Introduction

The Bible contains 66 books, written in three languages over 1,500 years by dozens of authors writing in numerous genres for diverse audiences. Scripture is clear enough that anyone can grasp the essentials of the faith. At the same time, extensive reading leads to riddles: Why does Moses apparently condone polygamy and slavery? What is a denarius? Who is Apollyon? Why do the apostles care about meat that is offered to idols?

The Requirements for Interpretation

Skill in interpretation is needed to gain the most from the Bible. When Scriptures are read in the church, leaders can answer questions and orient listeners to its great themes. Still, people rightly desire to read and understand the Bible for themselves (Jer. 31:31–34; 1 John 2:27).

Interpretation of the Bible requires technical skill and spiritual receptivity. Though all God's people have a significant ability to read and understand the great teachings of the Bible in their own language (see Deut. 6:6–7; Ps. 1:1–2; 19:7; 119:130; 1 Cor. 1:2; Eph. 3:4; Col. 4:16), there also remain more detailed and precise questions about meaning that sometimes require technical knowledge of Greek and Hebrew, as well as of Scripture's historical, cultural, and intellectual backgrounds. Here interpretation resembles the reading of dense poetry or constitutional documents. Interpretation is also an art, mastered not by rigid adherence to procedures but by long practice conducted under tutors. Interpretation is also a spiritual task. To read the Bible is not to dissect a lifeless text that only contains marks on a page. As people read Scripture, Scripture reads them, questions them, reveals their thoughts (Heb. 4:12)—and it leads to a Person, not just truths. All Scripture points to Jesus' death and resurrection, to forgiveness, and to personal knowledge of God through him.

To profit from Scripture, one must take the right posture. At one extreme, the skeptic questions and judges whatever he or she reads. At the other, the overconfident believer, convinced that he has mastered biblical or systematic theology, ignores or explains away whatever fails to support his system. Interpreters should come to Scripture humbly, expecting to learn and be corrected, willing to observe Scripture closely and accept whatever they find. All Scripture is breathed out by God (2 Tim. 3:16), so every word counts. If a biblical narrator mentions something as seemingly insignificant as a character's hair, this detail will probably be important—as the hair of Esau, Samson, and Absalom shows!

Interpreters also need skills. The remainder of this article explains the skills necessary to read the Bible in context, to find the main point of a passage, to develop a theme, and to apply Scripture.

Knowing the Context

It is a truism that one must read the Bible in context, but the truism hides a distinction. "Context" can refer to the historical or the literary context. The *literary context* includes the words, sentences, and paragraphs preceding and following a passage. The literary context locates a passage within the larger purposes of a book. Readers should ask why a particular passage is *here* and not elsewhere, how it builds upon prior passages, and how it prepares for the next. The disciples once said to Jesus, "Increase our faith" (Luke 17:5). Absent a context, it seems like a godly request (which it may be in some contexts). But here the disciples say it after they hear a difficult command and before Jesus tells them they merely need the faith of a mustard seed. Considering this context, some interpreters have seen "Increase our faith" as an excuse, not a godly request.

One should also locate a passage in *the context of its entire book*. Paul's statement "I appeal to you therefore, brothers, by the mercies of God, to present your bodies as a living sacrifice, holy and acceptable to God . . ." (Rom. 12:1) stands at a hinge in Romans. Paul had just finished recounting God's mercies in Romans 3–11. His "therefore" summons readers to see that God's abundant mercies lead them into heartfelt service.

The *historical context* includes knowledge of the culture, economy, geography, climate, agriculture, architecture, family life, morals, and social structure of the Bible's actors, authors, and readers. Over the centuries, climate and topography hardly vary, but other factors shift more. For example, Israel was poor and weak under Samuel and Saul, strong and rich under David and Solomon.

Historical contexts help readers make sense of passages like Deuteronomy 22:8, which says a builder "shall make a parapet" around the roof of a new home, lest someone fall from it and "bring the guilt of blood" upon the house. A parapet is a retaining wall around the edge of a flat roof. Since Israelites worked, ate, and slept on their roofs, parapets kept reckless boys and restless sleepers from tumbling off. The law taught Israel how to preserve life and to love neighbors.

Again, in Luke 11:27–28 a woman called out to Jesus, "Blessed is the womb that bore you and the breasts at which you nursed." The woman's mind-set explains her odd-sounding speech. In antiquity, women gained honor by marrying a great man or bearing great children. The woman praised Jesus by praising his mother—only a great woman could bear such a great son. Jesus nudges her in another direction: "Blessed rather are those who hear the word of God and obey it." In other words, a woman finds greatness in discipleship more than in matrimony or maternity.

Interpreters must read carefully to recognize both obvious and hidden riddles. Some matters are less clear than they seem. Do contemporary readers know precisely what judges, elders, and talents are? Study resources include a study Bible, and also, in increasing depth, a Bible dictionary, an encyclopedia, and scholarly commentaries. The quality of sources, not the quantity, is paramount.

Background studies permit more accurate study of a text's line of thought. The genre of the passage must be noted, since narrative, law, prophecy, visions, wisdom literature, and epistles all have distinct modes of operation, with subtypes within each genre. To simplify, however, the most basic distinction in terms of genre is between *narrative* and *discourse*.

Interpreting Narratives

Narratives can be long or short, complex or simple. They can be distinguished as speech stories, reports, and dramatic narratives. A speech story sets up a significant teaching, usually delivered near the end. Consider Jesus' encounters with a centurion (Matt. 8:5–13) and with Zacchaeus (Luke 19:1–10). Reports briefly describe battles, travels, or minor kings. They lack drama and reveal their secrets through patterns. For example, taken together, the reports of Solomon's reign show gold slowly becoming more prominent, and more highly valued, than wisdom. Solomon spent more on his palace than on the temple, and his adherence to the law steadily declined (1 Kings 4–11). Readers can draw conclusions as they read the reports in canonical perspective.

Many narratives feature complex characters and dramatic tension. To interpret narrative, one must note the story's time and place, its characters, and their interests. Soon conflict develops, leading to a crisis, then resolution. The reader should enter the story as if he or she were there, especially at the dramatic climax—when Abraham's knife is poised, when David strides toward Goliath. The resolution follows—the angel calls out, the stone finds its mark. Narratives convey moral, spiritual, and theological truths (1 Cor. 10:11), but one must first look for God's action. He is the prime character in biblical narratives. Readers should ask therefore how God reveals himself, and how he fulfills his covenant promises, in this or that particular story.

The main point of a narrative typically appears in the climax-resolution nexus. The narrator or a character in the story will often reveal that central truth. Dialogue discloses character and motivation (e.g., Luke 15:28–32). In the Abraham-Isaac account, both Abraham and the narrator say that the Lord will provide, and he does (Gen. 22:8, 14). In the David-Goliath narrative, David says, "The battle is the LORD's, and he will give you into our hand," and he does (1 Sam. 17:45–49). The main point in these narratives is not "Abraham obeyed a hard command and believers should, too," or "David was brave and Christians should be, too." The lessons are that "the Lord provides" and "the battle is the Lord's" (and then, also, that he is certainly worthy of trust!). The stories' characters go on quests, face choices, and respond to God faithfully or unfaithfully—but the Lord is the main agent, and believers, unbelievers, and bystanders are always responding to him. In the process they show how people tend to respond, for good or ill, and Bible readers should imitate their good responses and avoid their mistakes.

Interpreting Discourse

In discourse, which is the other main type of text in the Bible, the search for the main point (not necessarily the point that most interests the reader) remains central as well. This is true whether the text is poetry, prophecy, or an epistle. The point commonly appears first or last in a passage. (Whole books also have themes that are stated first or last; see Matt. 28:18–20 and Rom. 1:16–17.) Many Psalms reveal their theme at once: "Bless the LORD, O my soul" (103:1; cf. 42:1; 107:1). Passages in the Epistles sometimes start with the main point and then elaborate on it. James, for instance, says straight off that not many should aspire to be teachers (3:1a) because they face stricter judgment (3:1b) and because the tongue is beyond control (3:2–8). Other passages build to a climax, as in Jesus' teaching on the law, "You therefore must be perfect as your heavenly father is perfect" (Matt. 5:48). On numerous occasions, writers repeat the main point. The author of Judges says twice that "Everyone did what was right in his own eyes" (17:6; 21:25). Paul tells the Corinthians three times to be content in their assigned calling (1 Cor. 7:17, 20, 24). Careful students of Scripture will reread a passage, both to find the main point and to observe the way the biblical authors think. Illustrations, elaborations, and answers to foes are best understood by seeing how they serve the principal lesson.

This is not to say that the main point should be considered the only point or the only important point. For example, though Romans 1:16–17 is the overall theme of Romans, literally hundreds of other theological and ethical truths are taught throughout the pages of this letter. The individual parts are best understood in light of how they contribute to the whole.

Tracing Specific Themes throughout the Bible

Interpreters also need to learn how to search through Scripture to collect its comprehensive teaching on various specific themes. Students can start topical studies by reading passages listed in their Bibles' cross-references. Concordances are valuable, but they can mislead if readers simply limit their scope to verses that use a particular word. Students of the Bible must locate concepts, not just words, to develop a theme. For example, a concordance search on "pray/prayer/praying" would turn up only one verse in John's Gospel (John 17:9), but several other verses tell how to "ask" God for various things, and those verses also teach a number of particular lessons about prayer. Ideas also unfold progressively within the OT, into the NT, and sometimes even within a single book. Wise interpreters still locate every verse in its context and ask how the original audience understood it. For great topics such as work, marriage, or the love of God, it helps to note what the Bible says within the frame of each of the four great epochs: creation, fall, redemption, and restoration.

Applying God's Word

Biblical application chiefly requires careful prayer and meditation, but one must realize that application is more than following commands. Applying Scripture means accepting and fulfilling God-given duties, seeking a godly character, pursuing goals that the Lord blesses, and seeing the world his way. This produces four questions readers can ask themselves that often lead to helpful application: What should I do? Who should I be (or who should I realize that I am, in Christ)? Where should I go? How can I see?

People also apply the Bible when they let it lead them to Christ. After the fall, the Lord promised a redeemer. Every good prophet, priest, king, and judge points to one who would perfectly fulfill their roles, and every false leader causes the reader to cry out for one who would be true. (For further development of this idea throughout the OT, see The History of Salvation in the Old Testament: Preparing the Way for Christ, pp. 2635–2661.) From the start of the Gospels, Jesus is portrayed as Son of God and Son of Man. Each phase in the Gospel accounts leads toward the climax in the crucifixion and its resolution in the resurrection. Each epistle interprets that great event until Scripture ends in Revelation's songs of praise to the Lamb and the Lion, the King of kings and Lord of lords, contemplated, trusted, and adored. Thus interpretative skills must lead beyond conceptual knowledge to a Person, and a vital relationship with him. ◀

Interpreting the Bible: A Historical Overview

Is there any benefit to reading the Bible as it was understood by previous generations of Christians? Yes, certainly, because the Bible was written for them as well as us. God spoke to them through the Bible as he does to us today, and the spiritual gift of teaching was given to individuals then as it is now. Therefore when we read the biblical interpretations of previous generations, going all the way back to the earliest days of the church, we can often gain insight and perspectives that we might otherwise overlook because of the cultural biases of our own time.

However, before we seek to benefit from the interpretations of previous generations, it is helpful to have a broad overview of the dominant methods of biblical interpretation from various periods in church history.

The earliest followers of Christ interpreted the Hebrew Scriptures (the OT) as Jesus taught them—as a book of anticipations pointing to Christ himself. He was the long-promised Messiah, the Redeemer who would reverse the effects of the primal fall and restore the world to pristine holiness. Jesus taught that the OT spoke of him. To his critics he said, "You search the Scriptures because you think that in them you have eternal life; and it is they that bear witness about me" (John 5:39). The Gospel accounts suggest that Jesus understood the OT from a Christocentric, typological perspective; he is repeatedly cast as the fulfillment of the Scriptures. In the Sermon on the Mount, Jesus made it clear that his views did not contradict Moses, but he had come to invest the Law and the Prophets with their proper and full meaning (Matt. 5:17). Two themes run through Jesus' teaching: (1) the Law was the perfect revelation of God to humanity, and (2) Jesus came to fulfill the Law by meeting its exacting demands for a righteous standing before God.

This approach to the OT is how the earliest writers of the Christian Scriptures (the NT) approached their own writings. They spoke of the OT in the same way that Jesus had: as a book not merely telling the pre-Christian history of Israel but telling that history in a way that had present and future significance for Christians. The OT was the original sacred book of the church, giving assurance that Jesus was the promised and anointed one predicted by the prophets.

Marcion

Not everyone in the early church grasped the concept of continuity between the two Testaments, as evidenced by Marcion, who taught in Rome between A.D. 140 and 160. He argued that the OT was vastly inferior to the writings of the apostles, most notably Paul. He adopted a literal approach to interpretation, but his dualistic grid discounted the OT, which he believed set forth a different God from the Father of the Lord Jesus Christ, and was not to be read in the churches. His approach pitted law against grace, and the OT God against a God of love. The wider church, however, soon recognized Marcion's innovations as a mistake.

Justin Martyr and Irenaeus

In reaction to Marcion, other Christian teachers formulated a more orthodox way of approaching the sacred writings. Justin Martyr (c. A.D. 100–165), an early defender of Christianity, argued that the difference between the OT and NT is only a matter of degree. The OT anticipated and foretold events, and was superseded by the NT writings because they represented the fulfillment of earlier anticipations. Thus, Justin Martyr, particularly in his *Dialogue*, stressed a messianic continuity and utilized a literal-historical approach to interpretation.

However, it was Irenaeus (c. A.D. 130–200) who gathered the threads of interpretation more systematically. Though his approach to the OT was more literal than that of his predecessors, he also saw a typological meaning in the text. In Irenaeus's view the Scriptures are like "treasure hidden in a field" (Matt. 13:44) in that the literal was also the typological: the Bible is full of prefigurements, especially of the Messiah. Irenaeus also championed ideas that are still generally accepted by modern interpreters: (1) exegesis should pay careful attention to context; (2) unclear or obscure texts should be interpreted by clearer ones; and (3) a nonliteral reading of some passages may be warranted. Irenaeus held that the true meaning of the Scriptures is the interpretation of the apostles as presented in the NT and is embodied in the Rule of Faith (that is, the established and widely accepted understanding of the main doctrines of Scripture) as preserved through the teachings of the church.

Clement and Origen

Christian teachers in Alexandria, such as Clement (c. A.D. 150–215) and Origen (c. 185–254), were profoundly influenced by the work of Philo (a Jewish philosopher who wrote, and thought, in Greek; d. 50) and Plato's philosophy of Idealism. Clement and Origen read the Bible as having multiple levels of meaning. The surface meaning was literal, but it often hid a deeper, spiritual meaning. They held the Bible to be verbally accurate, and in this manner the integrity of the text was preserved; but where the literal meaning was obscure, this was thought to suggest a more profound, allegorical meaning. To Origen, who systematized this newer approach, the literal or simple meaning of the text was for those who could not grasp the intricate nature of languages (i.e., figures of speech, mysterious sayings), while the deeper meaning was for the learned or more spiritual. Using the body-soul-spirit analogy, he argued that the Bible should be interpreted literally, morally, and mystically. As a result, the historical meaning of Scripture was devalued. The deep meaning of the text could be separated from the literal meaning, resulting in theological speculation. This approach, therefore, was marked by subjectivity, depending more upon the insight of the interpreter rather than seeking consistency with other established doctrines of Scripture. Though Origen never contradicted the Rule of Faith, he did in fact speculate beyond it.

Theodore, Jerome, and Augustine

Later teachers such as Theodore of Mopsuestia (c. A.D. 350–428), Jerome (c. 342–420), and Augustine (354–430) criticized the allegorical method of the Alexandrians as being arbitrary and nonrational. These teachers argued that the Scriptures are to be interpreted in both a literal and a Christocentric sense. They insisted that their method was not the same as the allegorical approach, because it was rooted in the text of Scripture itself. They refused to disconnect the literal, historical meaning of the text from its spiritual meaning. Jerome, though initially a proponent of allegorization, later embraced the literal-historical approach to Scripture without abandoning the deeper spiritual meaning of the text that had been championed by Theodore and others. Jerome insisted that scriptural texts should be read in a historical context, something the allegorical approach had de-emphasized.

The greatest theologian of the early church was Augustine. He championed a literal, historical approach to reading the Bible, insisting that a proper understanding must begin with the mind of the writer, which required knowing the biblical languages and paying attention to context. The fourfold approach to Scripture that he put forth (see below) was widely used, and abused, in the Medieval era.

Medieval Churchmen

The Medieval church gradually became enamored of the allegorical method of interpretation, which was used to buttress church dogma that lacked a strong basis in Scripture. Medievalists developed a fourfold approach to interpreting the Bible: the *literal*, showing what God did; the *allegorical*, showing what at surface level God hid; the *moral*, revealing what believers should do; and the *mystical*, or *anagogical*, showing the heavenly life in which, for Christians, things will end. In effect, the method obscured the true meaning of the Bible by imposing arbitrary meanings on it. Theology took precedence over careful literal-historical exegesis.

In the high Middle Ages, the great scholastic Thomas Aquinas (1225–1274) embraced the literal-historical (as opposed to allegorical) approach. In his skillful hands the proper approach to the Bible was an exegetical method that assumed the primacy of the literal meaning of the text. To Aquinas, multiplying levels of meaning in a single text was confusing in that it would blunt the force of any biblical argument; further, he thought that a parabolic sense of Scripture could be part of its proper meaning. He recognized that the intended meaning of a text is contained in words, and words can be used both literally (in a narrow sense, excluding images and metaphors) and figuratively.

The Reformers

The Protestant Reformers of the sixteenth century reacted against the misuse of the Bible in Late Medieval theology. They insisted that authority rested not in the leaders or fathers of the church but in a proper understanding of the text derived from correct methods of literary interpretation. Reformers starting with John Wycliffe (c. 1330–1384) insisted on a grammatical-historical approach to the Bible. The German reformer Martin Luther (1483–1546) broke with the nonliteral, allegorical approach that was dominant in his training and returned to the patristic emphasis on the centrality of Christ in the Scriptures. He was adamant that the Bible be approached not through fanciful allegories or merely to support established dogma but through ordinary language and literal, historical, and grammatical exegesis. A proper understanding of the Bible should be the product of such interpretation of the scriptural texts and should lead to healthy theology and a robust Christian life.

The most prolific expositor of Scripture, as well as the first major systematizer of Protestant theology, was John Calvin (1509–1564). Calvin stressed Scripture over theology and saw theology as the fruit resulting from the proper interpretation of Scripture. He was a skilled linguist who approached the Bible from the viewpoint of its historical veracity, literal interpretation, and contextual analysis. He often interpreted prophetic texts in a typological manner (as looking forward to Christ), yet he strenuously opposed arbitrary allegorization, which he believed undermined the certainty and clarity of Scripture. Some assign to Calvin the designation "the founder of modern grammatical-historical exegesis," which is confirmed by the continued popularity of his commentaries and the way in which modern interpreters still interact with him as a sober, accurate exegete.

The Enlightenment

In the generations following Calvin, the role of tradition in biblical interpretation was increasingly limited by a growing emphasis on the individual interpreter, a trend seen in the rise of the Enlightenment. (The Renaissance led to two great movements: the *Protestant Reformation*, which emancipated the Bible from ecclesiastical imprisonment, and the *Enlightenment*, which carried forward the attack on authority structures to ridicule the authority of the Bible, birthing the Modern era.) The essence of the Enlightenment was a rejection of the biblical doctrine of the utter brokenness of humanity and a belief that the human mind was capable of arriving at truth when unhindered by external authorities such as the church, tradition, or the Bible.

To many Enlightenment thinkers, the Bible became an untrustworthy book created by churchmen to keep minds captive under the threat of punishment. Thus, in the eighteenth and nineteenth centuries, university scholarship embraced the intellectual and philosophical assumptions of the Enlightenment, turning its full force against the veracity of the Scriptures. The Bible became viewed as a parched landscape with an occasional oasis. At best, it merely contained truth; it was not itself truth. The lasting effects of this approach have contributed to the dissolution of the Christian worldview, at least in Western industrialized nations.

The Heirs of the Reformation: Evangelical Protestantism

However, from the Reformation until today, the large central core of the Protestant church worldwide has held to an "evangelical" view of Scripture, rejecting the skepticism of post-Enlightenment Naturalism and Rationalism, and continuing to believe in the complete truthfulness and reliability of the Bible. In answer to the attacks of rationalism, evangelicals have shown that there is no contradiction between full trust in the Bible and intellectual integrity. With respect to proper biblical interpretation, they have appreciated the various understandings of Scripture held by previous generations but have also sought to correct previous misunderstandings by developing more precise standards for right interpretation (see Interpreting the Bible: An Introduction, pp. 2561–2563). This Study Bible is written from within this broad post-Reformation evangelical Protestant tradition.

Conclusion

After centuries of the most rigorous scrutiny, the Bible is still the most widely read book in the world. The God of the Scriptures has preserved his divine Word—recorded in human language and illumined by the Spirit. This Word reveals the Savior of the world to the hungry hearts who affectionately embrace him and walk in his ways. Some may argue that the Bible is not true, yet the Holy Scriptures will remain an eternal testimony to God's truthfulness long after the last critic is silenced. While not perfect, the long history of interpretation by those who read the Bible as God's Word in previous centuries is still a storehouse of great riches for modern readers. Because the Bible uses ordinary language and teaches through concepts and experiences common to all human life, interpreters of previous centuries often were accurate in their understanding of vast parts of Scripture. For those who will read the Bible in the light of this long tradition (yet correcting and supplementing that tradition's inadequacies), it promises to reveal the truth of a divine Redeemer and to instruct us in walking humbly before him in reverence and awe. ◀

Reading the Bible

Reading the Bible Theologically

To read the Bible "theologically" means to read the Bible "with a focus on God": his being, his character, his words and works, his purpose, presence, power, promises, and precepts. The Bible can be read from different standpoints and with different centers of interest, but this article seeks to explain how to read it theologically.

The Bible: The Church's Instruction Book

All 66 books of the Bible constitute the book of the Christian church. And the church, both as a whole and in the life of its members, must always be seen to be the people of the book. This glorifies God, its primary author.

God has chosen to restore his sin-spoiled world through a long and varied historical process, central to which is the creating—by redemptive and sanctifying grace—of what is literally a new human race. This unfinished process has so far extended over four millennia. It began with Abraham; it centers on the first coming of the incarnate Lord, Jesus Christ; and it is not due for completion till he comes again. Viewed as a whole, from the vantage point of God's people within it, the process always was and still is covenantal and educative. *Covenantal* indicates that God says to his gathered community, "I am your God; you shall be my people," and with his call for loyalty he promises them greater future good than any they have yet known. *Educative* indicates that, within the covenant, God works to change each person's flawed and degenerate nature into a new, holy selfhood that expresses in responsive terms God's own moral likeness. The model is Jesus Christ, the only perfect being that the world has ever seen. For God's people to sustain covenantal hopes and personal moral ideals as ages pass and cultures change and decay, they must have constant, accessible, and authoritative instruction from God. And that is what the Bible essentially is.

This is why, as well as equipping everywhere a class of teachers who will give their lives to inculcating Bible truth, the church now seeks to translate the Bible into each person's primary language and to spread universal literacy, so that all may read and understand it.

The Bible Is Canonical

God's plan is that through his teaching embodied in the Bible, plus knowledge and experience of how he rewards obedience and punishes disobedience in a disciplinary way, his people should learn love, worship, and service of God himself, and love, care, and service of others, as exemplified by Jesus Christ. To this end each generation needs a written "textbook" that sets forth for all time God's unchanging standards of truth, right, love and goodness, wisdom and worship, doctrine and devotion. This resource will enable people to see what they should think and do, what ideals they should form, what goals they should set, what limits they should observe, and what life strategies they should follow. These are the functions that are being claimed for the Bible when it is called "canonical." A "canon" is a rule or a standard. The Bible is to be read as a God-given rule of belief and behavior—that is, of faith and life.

The Bible Is Inspired

Basic to the Bible's canonical status is its "inspiration." This word indicates a divinely effected uniqueness comparable to the uniqueness of the person of the incarnate Lord. As Jesus Christ was totally human and totally divine, so is the Bible. All Scripture is witness to God, given by divinely illuminated human writers, and all Scripture is God witnessing to himself in and through their words. The way into the mind of God is through the expressed mind of these human writers, so the reader of the Bible looks for that characteristic first. But the text must be read, or reread, as God's own self-revelatory instruction, given in the form of this human testimony. In this way God tells the reader the truth about himself; his work past, present, and future; and his will for people's lives.

The Bible Is Unified

Basic also to the Bible's canonical status is the demonstrable unity of its contents. Scripture is no ragbag of religious bits and pieces, unrelated to each other; rather, it is a tapestry in which all the complexities of the weave display a single pattern of judgment and mercy, promise and fulfillment. The Bible consists of two separate collections: the OT, written over a period of about 1,000 years, and the NT, written within a generation several centuries after the OT was completed. Within such a composite array one would expect to find some crossed wires or incoherence, but none are found here. While there are parallel narratives, repetitions, and some borrowings from book to book, the Bible as a whole tells a single, straightforward story. God the Creator is at the center throughout; his people, his covenant, his kingdom, and its coming king are the themes unfolded by the historical narratives, while the realities of redemption from sin and of godly living (faith, repentance, obedience, prayer, adoration, hope, joy, and love) become steadily clearer. Jesus Christ, as fulfiller of OT prophecies, hopes, promises, and dreams, links the two Testaments together in an unbreakable bond. Aware that at the deepest level the whole Bible is the product of a single mind, the mind of God, believers reading it theologically always look for the inner links that bind the books together. And they are there to be found.

Theological Reading of the Bible: A Quest for God

Reading Scripture theologically starts from the truths reviewed above: (1) that the Bible is a God-given guide to sinners for their salvation, and for the life of grateful godliness to which salvation calls them; (2) that the Bible is equally the church's handbook for worship and service; (3) that it is a divinely inspired unity of narrative and associated admonition, a kind of running commentary on the progress of God's kingdom plan up to the establishing of a world-embracing, witnessing, suffering church in the decades following Christ's ascension and the Pentecost outpouring of the Spirit; and (4) that the incarnate Son of God himself, Jesus the Christ, crucified, risen, glorified, ministering, and coming again, is the Bible's central focus, while the activities of God's covenant people both before and after Christ's appearing make up its ongoing story. Theological reading follows these leads and is pursued theocentrically, looking and listening for God throughout, with the controlling purpose of discerning him with maximum clarity, through his own testimony to his will, works, and ways. Such reading is pursued prayerfully, according to Martin Luther's observation that the first thing one needs to become a theologian through Bible reading is prayer for the illumination and help of the Holy Spirit. And prayerful theological Bible reading will be pursued in light of three further guiding principles, as follows.

First, *revelation was progressive*. Its progress, in its written form, was not (as has sometimes been thought) from fuzzy and sometimes false (OT) to totally true and clear (NT), but from partial to full and complete. "Long ago, at many times and in many ways, God spoke to our fathers by the prophets, but in these last days [the concluding era of this world's life] he has spoken to us by his Son" (Heb. 1:1–2). In the Gospels, the Epistles, and the books of Acts and Revelation, readers are now faced with God's final word to the world before Christ comes again. Theological Bible reading maintains this perspective, traversing the OT by the light of the NT.

Second, *the Bible's God-language is analogical*. Today's fashion is to call it "metaphorical," which is not wrong, but "analogical" is the term that makes clearest the key point: the difference involved when everyday words—nouns, verbs, adjectives—are used of God. Language is God's gift for personal communication between humans and between God and humans. But when God speaks of himself—or when people speak to him or about him—the definitions, connotations, implications, valuations, and range of meaning in each case must be adjusted in light of the differences between him and his creation. God is infinite and flawless; people are both finite and flawed. So when everyday words are used of God, all thought of finiteness and imperfection must be removed, and the overall notion of unlimited, self-sustaining existence in perfect loving holiness must be added in. For instance, when God calls himself "Father," or his people in response call him their "Father," the thought will be of authoritative, protecting, guiding, and enriching love, free from any lack of wisdom that appears in earthly fathers. And when one speaks of God's "anger" or "wrath" in retribution for sin that he as the world's royal Judge displays, the thought will be as free from the fitful inconsistency, irrationality, bad temper, and loss of self-control that regularly mars human anger.

These mental adjustments underlie the biblical insistence that all God's doings, even those that involve human distress, are glorious and praiseworthy. This doxological, God-glorifying tone and thrust marks even books such as Job and Lamentations, and the many complaint prayers in the Psalter. The Bible writers practice analogical adjustment so smoothly, unobtrusively, and unselfconsciously that it is easy to overlook what they are doing. But the theological reader of the Bible will not miss this point.

Third, *the one God of the Bible is Trinitarian and triune*. God is three persons in an eternal fellowship of love and cooperation within the one divine Being. Each person is involved in all that God does. God is a team no less than he is a complex entity. In the NT this concept is apparent, but in the OT, where the constant emphasis is on the truth that Yahweh is the one and only God, the truth of the Trinity hardly breaks the surface. God's triunity is, however, an eternal fact, though it has been clearly revealed only through Christ's coming. Theological Bible readers are right to read this fact back into the OT, following the example of NT writers in their citing of many OT passages.

Theological Reading of the Bible: The Quest for Godliness

Theology is for doxology, that is, glorifying God by praise and thanks, by obedient holiness, and by laboring to extend God's kingdom, church, and cultural influence. The goal of theological Bible reading is not just to know truth about God (though one's quest for godliness must start there) but to know God personally in a relationship that honors him—which means serving Jesus Christ, the Father's Son, the world's real though unrecognized Lord, who came to earth, died, rose, and ascended for his people, and has given them the Holy Spirit. To have him fill believers' horizons and rule their lives in his Father's name is the authentic form—the foundation, blueprint, scaffolding, and construction—of Christian godliness, to which theological Bible reading is a God-intended means. So, three questions must govern readers of the inspired Word:

First, in the passage being read, *what is shown about God the Father, Son, and Holy Spirit?* What does it say about what the holy Three are doing, have done, and will do in God's world, in his church, and in lives committed to him? What does it reveal about God's attributes, that is, God's power and character, how he exists and how he behaves? One reason, no doubt, for God's panoramic, multigenred layout of the Bible—with history, homily, biography, liturgy, practical philosophy, laws, lists, genealogies, visions, and so on, all rubbing shoulders—is that this variety provides so many angles of illumination on these questions for theological Bible readers' instruction.

Second, in the passage being read, *what is shown about the bewildering, benighted world with all its beautiful and beneficial aspects alongside those that are corrupt and corrupting?* Discerning the world's good and evil for what they are, so as to embrace the world's good and evade its temptations, is integral to the godliness that theological Bible reading should promote.

Third, in the passage being read, *what is shown to guide one's living, this day and every day?* The theological logic of this question, through which the reader must work each time, is this: since God, by his own testimony, said *that* to those people in their situation, what does it follow that he says to readers today in their own situation? The Holy Spirit answers prayer by giving discernment to apply Scripture in this way. Those who seek will indeed find. ◀

Reading the Bible as Literature

Three primary modes of writing converge in the Bible: theological, historical, and literary. Overwhelmingly, theology and history are embodied in literary form.

A crucial principle of interpretation thus needs to be established at the outset: meaning is communicated *through form*, starting with the very words of a text but reaching beyond that to considerations of literary genre and style. We cannot properly speak about the theological or moral content of a story or poem (for example) without first interacting with the story or poem.

Literary form exists prior to content; no content exists apart from the form in which it is embodied. As a result, the first responsibility of a reader or interpreter is to understand the form of a discourse. It is a common misconception to think that the literary dimension of the Bible is *only* the form in which the message is presented. Actually, without some kind of literary form, the content would not even exist. The concept of literary form needs to be construed very broadly here. Anything having to do with *how* a biblical author has expressed his message constitutes literary form. We tend to think (erroneously) that authors tell us *about* characters, actions, and situations, whereas actually they speak *with* or *by means of* these things—*about* God, people, and the world.

The Bible as Literature

The idea of the Bible as literature began with the Bible itself. The writers refer to a whole range of literary genres in which they write: proverb, saying, chronicle, complaint (lament psalm), oracle, apocalypse, parable, song, epistle, and many others. Secondly, some of these forms correspond to the literary forms current in the authors' surrounding cultures. For example, the Ten Commandments are cast in the form of the suzerainty treaties that ancient Near Eastern kings imposed on their subjects, and the NT epistles show many affinities to the structure of Greek and Roman letters of the same era.

Mainly, though, we can look to the Bible itself to see the extent to which it is a literary book. Virtually every page of the Bible is replete with literary technique, and to possess the individual texts fully, we need to read the Bible as literature, just as we need to read it theologically and (in the narrative parts) historically.

Literary Genres

The most customary way to define literature is by the external genres (types or kinds of writing) in which its content is expressed. The two main genres in the Bible are narrative and poetry. Numerous categories cluster under each of these. Narrative subtypes, e.g., include hero story, gospel, epic, tragedy, comedy (a U-shaped plot with a happy ending), and parable. Specific poetic genres keep multiplying as well: lyric, lament psalm, praise psalm, love poem, nature poem, *epithalamion* (wedding poem), and many others.

But those are only the tip of the iceberg. In addition to narrative and poetry, we find prophecy, visionary writing, apocalypse, pastoral, encomium, oratory, drama (the book of Job), satire, and epistle. Then if we add more specific forms like travel story, dramatic monologue, doom song, and Christ hymn, the number of literary genres in the Bible readily exceeds a hundred.

The importance of genre to biblical interpretation is that genres have their own methods of procedure and rules of interpretation. An awareness of genre should alert us to what we can expect to find in a text. Additionally, considerations of genre should govern the terms in which we interact with a text. With narrative, e.g., we are on the right track if we pay attention to plot, setting, and character. If the text before us is a satire, we need to think in terms of object of attack, the satiric vehicle in which the attack is couched, and satiric norm (stated or implied standard by which the criticism is being conducted).

In view of how many literary genres are present in the Bible, it is obvious that the overall literary form of the Bible is the anthology, as even the word Bible (Gk. *biblia*, "books") hints. As an anthology, the Bible possesses the same kinds of unity that other anthologies exhibit: multiple authorship (approximately three dozen authors), diverse genres, a rationale for collecting these particular materials (a unifying religious viewpoint and story of salvation history), comprehensiveness, and an identifiable strategy of organization (a combination of historical chronology and groupings by genre).

Literary Subject Matter

Literature is also identifiable by its subject matter. It is differentiated from expository (informational) writing by the way in which it presents concrete human experience instead of stating abstract propositions, logical arguments, or bare facts. We can profitably think of biblical writing as existing on a continuum, with abstract propositional discourse on one end and concrete presentation of human experience on the other. The more thoroughly a piece of writing falls on the experiential end of the spectrum, the more "literary" it is.

To illustrate, the command "you shall not murder" is an example of expository discourse. The story of Cain and Abel embodies the same truth in the form of characters in concrete settings performing physical and mental actions. Expository writing gives us the precept; literature gives us the example. "God's provision extends to all aspects of our lives" is a thematic summary of Psalm 23; rather than such abstraction, however, the psalm incarnates the truth about providence through the poetic image of a shepherd's daily routine with his sheep.

The subject of literature is human experience rendered as concretely as possible. The result is that it possesses a universal quality. Whereas history and the daily news tell us what *happened*, literature tells us what *happens*—what is true for all people in all places and times. A text can be both informational and literary, but its literary dimension resides in its embodiment of recognizable human experience.

The goal of literature is to prompt a reader vicariously to share or relive an experience. The truth that literature imparts is not simply ideas that are true but *truthfulness to human experience*. The implication for interpreting the Bible as literature is that readers and expositors need to actively recreate experiences in their imaginations, identify the recognizable human experiences in a text (thereby building bridges to life in the modern world), and resist the impulse immediately to reduce every biblical passage to a set of theological ideas.

Archetypes and Motifs

An archetype is a plot motif (such as initiation or quest), character type (such as the villain or trickster), or image (such as light or water) that recurs throughout literature and life. The presence of archetypes signals a text's literary quality. When we read literature, we are continuously aware of such archetypes as the temptation motif, the dangerous valley, and the hero, whereas with other types of writing we are rarely aware of archetypes.

Archetypes are the building blocks of literature. The Bible is the most complete repository of archetypes in the Western world, something that makes the Bible universal, reaching down to bedrock human experience. Awareness of archetypes helps us see the unity of the Bible (since we keep relating one instance of an archetype to other instances), and also the connections between the Bible and other literature.

Stylistics and Rhetoric

Literature also uses distinctive resources of language that set it apart from ordinary expository discourse. The most obvious example is poetry. Poets speak a language all their own, consisting of images and figures of speech. Other important examples include: imagery, metaphor, simile, symbol, allusion, irony, wordplay, hyperbole, apostrophe (direct address to someone or something absent as though present), personification, paradox, and pun. The presence of these elements push a text into the category of literature.

The most concentrated repository of such language in the Bible is the books that are poetic in their basic format—the Prophetic Books, Job, Psalms, Proverbs, Ecclesiastes (a book of prose poems), Song of Solomon, and Revelation. But literary resources of language also appear on virtually every page of the Bible beyond the poetic books—most obviously in the discourses of Jesus and in the Epistles, but less pervasively in the narratives as well.

A related literary phenomenon is rhetoric—arrangement of content in patterns and use of conventional literary techniques or formulas. Parallelism of sentence elements, e.g., is an instance of stylized rhetoric. Patterns of repetition—of words, phrases, or content units—are a distinguishing feature of the Bible. So is aphoristic conciseness that continuously raises the Bible to a literary realm of eloquence far above everyday discourse. A page from a NT epistle might include rhetorical questions, question-and-answer constructions, direct addresses to real or imaginary respondents, or repeated words or phrases.

Artistry

Literature is an art form in which beauty of expression, craftsmanship, and verbal virtuosity are valued as self-rewarding and as an enhancement of effective communication. The writer of Ecclesiastes states his philosophy of composition, portraying himself as a self-conscious stylist and wordsmith who arranged his material "with great care" and who "sought to find words of delight" (Eccles. 12:9–10). Surely other biblical writers did the same.

The standard elements of artistic form include unity, theme-and-variation, pattern, design, progression, contrast, balance, recurrence, coherence, and symmetry. Authors cultivate artistry because it is important to their effect and intention. The Bible is an aesthetic as well as utilitarian book, and we need to experience it as such.

Reading and Interpreting the Bible as Literature

Any piece of writing needs to be interpreted in terms of the kind of writing that it is. The Bible is a literary book in which theology and history are usually embodied in literary forms. Those forms include genres, the incarnation of human experience in concrete form, stylistic and rhetorical techniques, and artistry.

These literary features are not extraneous aspects of the text. Instead, they are the forms *through which* the content is mediated. If the writing of the Bible is the product of divine inspiration—if it represents what the Holy Spirit prompted the authors to write as they were "carried along" (2 Pet. 1:21)—then the literary forms of the Bible have also been inspired by God and need to be granted an importance congruent with that inspiration. ◂

Reading the Bible in Prayer and Communion with God

Communion with God is a staggering thought. God created billions of galaxies and calls every star by name (Isa. 40:26; 42:5). He never had a beginning and will never end (Ps. 90:2). His ways are inscrutable and his judgments unsearchable (Rom. 11:33). His thoughts are as different from ours as the heavens are high above the earth (Isa. 55:8). "The nations are like a drop from a bucket, and are accounted as the dust on the scales" (Isa. 40:15).

If that were not enough to make communion with God unthinkable, consider that all of us are naturally rebellious against him. Therefore, his omnipotent wrath rests on us. We are by nature hostile to God and do not submit to his law (Rom. 8:7). Therefore, the wrath of God is revealed from heaven against us (Rom. 1:18). We are "by nature children of wrath," "sons of disobedience," and "dead in . . . trespasses and sins" (Eph. 2:1–5). How then can there be any thought of communion with God?

For Our Joy

Before we see the Bible's answer, let's clarify what we mean by "communion." Communion refers to God's communication and presentation of himself to us, together with our proper response to him with joy. We say "with joy" because it would not be communion if God revealed himself in total wrath and we were simply terrified. That would be *true* revelation and a *proper* response, but it would not be communion.

Communion assumes that God comes to us in love and that we respond joyfully to the beauty of his perfections and the offer of his fellowship. He may sometimes come with a rod of discipline. But even in our tears, we can rejoice in our Father's loving discipline (Heb. 12:6–11). Communion with God may lay us in ashes or make us leap. But it never destroys our joy. It *is* our joy (Ps. 43:4).

To God's Glory

Communion with God is the end for which we were created. The Bible says that we were created for the glory of God (Isa. 43:7). Yet glorifying God is not something we do *after* communing with him, but *by* communing with him. Many human deeds magnify the glory of God's goodness, but only if they flow from our contentment in communion with him. This is why we pray, "*Satisfy us* in the morning with your steadfast love" (Ps. 90:14). The joy of this communion in the love of God confirms God's worth and shows his glory.

Because of the Gospel

But how is this unthinkable privilege of communion with God possible for sinners like us? The answer of the Bible is that God himself took the initiative to be reconciled to his enemies. He sent his Son, Jesus Christ, to die in our place and bear the curse that we deserved from God. "Christ redeemed us from the curse of the law by becoming a curse for us" (Gal. 3:13). So the wrath of God that we deserved fell on Christ (Isa. 53:4–6, 10).

Because God gave Christ as our substitute, we can be reconciled to God and enjoy peaceful communion with him. "While we were enemies we were reconciled to God by the death of his Son" (Rom. 5:10). "Therefore, since we have been justified by faith, we have peace with God through our Lord Jesus Christ" (Rom. 5:1). This peace leads to the unparalleled joy of communion with God (Rom. 5:11).

The Gospel: The Bible's Central Message

Therefore, the first thing to say about the Bible in relation to communion with God is that the message of how to be reconciled to God for the glory of God is the central message of the Bible. There is no communion with God without salvation from *our* sin and *God's* wrath. The Bible is the only book with final authority that tells us what God did through Christ and how we must respond through faith to be saved and to enjoy communion with God (2 Tim. 3:15).

But the Bible is more. The Bible tells the story of creation, of the fall of humanity into sin, and of the history of God's chosen people Israel leading up to the coming of the Messiah, Jesus. Then it recounts the life of Christ and his teachings, his mighty works, his death, his resurrection, and his ascension. Finally, it tells the story of the early church after Jesus had returned to heaven, and how we are to live until Jesus comes again.

The Bible Reveals God

The God-inspired record of this history (the Bible) is the only infallible and authoritative book communicating and presenting God himself (2 Tim. 3:16–17; 2 Pet. 1:21). To be sure, God is active everywhere in the world today, and we experience his precious power wherever we trust him and do his will. But we will go astray if we make this daily experience of God the basis of our communion with him. We know God for who he is, and meet him as he is, when we meet him through his Word—the Bible. We see this principle at work, for example, in 1 Samuel 3:21: "The LORD revealed *himself* to Samuel at Shiloh by the *word* of the LORD." The Lord *himself* is revealed by his *word*, that is, by what he *says* to us, whether audibly or in written form.

Therefore, when we seek to enjoy communion with the Lord—and not to be led astray by the ambiguities of religious experience—we read the Bible. From Genesis to Revelation, God's words and God's deeds reveal God himself for our knowledge and our enjoyment. Of course, it is possible to read the Bible without enjoying communion with God. We must seek to understand the Bible's meaning, and we must pause to contemplate what we understand and, by the Spirit, to feel and express the appropriate response of the heart.

God communicates with us in many ways through the Bible and seeks the response of our communion with him. If God indicts us (2 Cor. 7:8–10), we respond to him with sorrow and repentance. If he commends us (Ps. 18:19–20), we respond to him with humble gratitude and joy. If he commands us to do something (Matt. 28:19–20), we look to him for strength and resolve to obey with his help. If he makes a promise (Heb. 13:5–6), we marvel at his grace and trust him to do what he says. If he warns us of some danger (Luke 21:34), we take him seriously and watch with a thankful sense of his presence and protection. If he describes something about himself (Isa. 46:9–11), his Son (Mark 1:11), or his Holy Spirit (John 16:13–14), we affirm it and admire it and pray for clearer eyes to see and enjoy his greatness and beauty.

Fellowship with the Triune God

In all these communications, it is God himself that we most want to see. Communion with God is not merely *learning about* God but enjoying *fellowship with* God in the truth he reveals about himself. The apostle John, who enjoyed unusually close communion with Jesus while he was on the earth, said that he wrote his letters so that we might enjoy this fellowship: "That which we have seen and heard we proclaim also to you, so that you too may have fellowship with us; and indeed our fellowship is with the Father and with his Son Jesus Christ" (1 John 1:3). In other words, the Bible records the words and deeds of God so that by means of these we have fellowship—that is, communion—with God.

This fellowship is with each person in the Trinity: with the Father (1 John 1:3), with the Son (1 Cor. 1:9), and with the Holy Spirit (2 Cor. 13:14). This is possible because each person of the Godhead communicates with us in a way that corresponds to his unique role in creation, providence, and salvation. As the great Puritan John Owen wrote in his classic *Communion with God*, the Father communicates himself to us by the way of "original authority," the Son from a "purchased treasury," and the Spirit by an "immediate efficacy." Each person, as Owen says, communicates with us "distinctly" in the sense that we may discern from which person particular realizations of the grace of God come to us. But "distinctly" does not mean "separately": particular fellowship with each person of the Trinity is always one facet of ongoing communion with all three.

Humble, Bold Prayer

Finally, from this Father-initiated, Son-purchased, Spirit-effected communion with God, we *pray* with humble boldness (Heb. 4:16). That is, we speak to God the Father, on the basis of Christ's work, by the help of the Spirit. This speaking is called *prayer*. It includes our confessions of sin (1 John 1:9), our praises of God's perfections (Ps. 96:4), our thanks for God's gifts (Ps. 118:21), and our requests that he would help us (Ps. 38:22) and others (Rom. 15:30–31)—all to the glory of God (Ps. 50:15), for the hallowing of his name, which must ever be our goal.

Prayer is the verbal aspect of our response to God in

communion with him. The Bible does speak of "groanings too deep for words" (Rom. 8:26), but ordinarily prayer is the response of our heart to God in words. It may be in private (Matt. 6:6) or in public (1 Cor. 14:16). It may last all night (Luke 6:12) or be summed up in a moment's cry (Matt. 14:30). It may be desperate (Jonah 2:2) or joyful (Ps. 119:162). It may be full of faith (Mark 11:24) or wavering with uncertainty (Mark 9:24).

But it is not optional. It is commanded—which is good news, because it means that God loves being the giver of omnipotent help (Ps. 50:15). The Bible reminds us that ordinary people can accomplish great things by prayer (James 5:17–18). It tells us about great answers to prayer (Isa. 37:21, 36). It gives us great examples of how to pray (Matt. 6:9–13; Eph. 3:14–19). And it offers amazing encouragements to pray (Matt. 7:7–11).

God Gets the Glory; We Get the Joy

The Bible shows that prayer is near the heart of why God created the world. When we pray for God to do what only he can do, he alone gets the glory while we get the joy. We see this when Jesus says, "Whatever you ask in my name, this I will do, *that the Father may be glorified* in the Son" (John 14:13), and then later says, "Ask, and you will receive, *that your joy may be full*" (John 16:24). In prayer, God gets the *glory* and we get the *joy*. God is the overflowing fountain; we are satisfied with the living water. He is infinitely rich; we are the happy heirs.

Central to all our praying, as we have seen, must be our longing that God's name be hallowed in the world—known and honored and loved (Matt. 6:9). To that end, we pray (1) for his church to be "filled with the fruit of righteousness . . . to the glory and praise of God" (Phil. 1:11); (2) that the gospel would spread and awaken faith in Jesus among all the nations (2 Thess. 3:1); and (3) that many who do not believe would be saved (Rom. 10:1). In this way, the aim of God's Word and the aim of prayer become the same: the glory of God and the salvation of the nations through Jesus Christ. ◂

Reading the Bible for Personal Application

It is a marvel how personally the Bible applies. The words pointedly address the concerns of long-ago people in faraway places, facing specific problems, many of which no longer exist. They had no difficulty seeing the application. Much of what they read *was* personal application to actual situations they were facing. But nothing in the Bible was written directly to you or specifically about what you face. We are reading someone else's mail. Yet the Bible repeatedly affirms that these words are also written for us: "Whatever was written in former days was written for our instruction" (Rom. 15:4; cf. Deut. 29:29; 1 Cor. 10:11; 2 Tim. 3:15–17). Application today discovers ways in which the Spirit reapplies Scripture in a timely fashion.

Furthermore, the Bible is primarily about God, not you. The essential subject matter is the triune Redeemer Lord, culminating in Jesus Christ. When Jesus "opened their minds to understand the Scriptures" (Luke 24:45), he showed how everything written—creation, promises, commands, history, sacrificial system, psalms, proverbs—reveals him. We are reading someone else's biography. Yet that very story demonstrates how he includes us within his story. Jesus *is* the Word of God applied, all-wisdom embodied. As his disciples, we learn to similarly apply the Bible, growing up into his image. Application today experiences how the Spirit "rescripts" our lives by teaching us who God is and what he is doing.

"Personal application" proves wise when you reckon with these marvels. The Bible was written to others—but speaks to you. The Bible is about God—but draws you in. Your challenge is always to *reapply* Scripture afresh, because God's purpose is always to *rescript* your life. How can you expand your wisdom in personal application? The following four ways are suggested.

1. Consolidate What You Have Already Learned

Assuming that you have listened well to some parts of the Bible, consider these personal questions. What chunk of Scripture has made the most difference in your life? What verse or passage have you turned to most frequently? What makes these exact words frequently and immediately relevant? Your answer will likely embody four foundational truths about how to read the Bible for wise application.

First, this passage becomes your own because you listen. You remember what God says. He is saying this to you. You need these words. This promise, revelation, or command *must* be true. You *must* act on this call to faith and love. When you forget, you drift, stray, and flounder. When you remember and put it to work, bright truth rearranges your life. The foundation of application is always attentive listening to what God says.

Second, the passage and your life become fused. It is not simply a passage in the Bible. A specific word from God connects to some pointed struggle inside you and around you. These inner and outer troubles express your experience of the dual evil that plagues every human heart: sin and confusion from within; trouble and beguilement from without (1 Kings 8:37–39; Eccles. 9:3). But something God says invades your darkness with his light. He meets your actual need with his actual mercies. Your life and God's words meet. Application depends on honesty about where you need help. Your kind of trouble is everywhere in the Bible.

Third, your appropriation of this passage reveals how God himself does the applying. He meets you before you meet him. The passage arrested you. God arranged your struggle with sin and suffering so that you would need this exact help. Without God's initiative ("I will write it on their hearts," Jer. 31:33) you would never make the connection. The Spirit chose to rewrite your inner script, pouring God's love into your heart, inviting you to live in a new reality. He awakens your sense of need, gives you ears to hear, and freely gives necessary wisdom. Application is a gift, because wisdom is a gift.

Fourth, the application of beloved passages is usually quite straightforward. God states something in general terms. You insert your relevant particulars. For example:

"Even though I walk through the valley of the shadow of death, I will fear no evil, for you are with me" (Ps. 23:4). What troubles are you facing? Who is with you?

"All we like sheep have gone astray; we have turned—every one—to his own way; and the LORD has laid on him the iniquity of us all" (Isa. 53:6). What is your particular way of straying? How does the Lamb of God connect with your situation?

"Do not be anxious about anything, but in everything by prayer and supplication with thanksgiving let your requests be made known to God" (Phil. 4:6). With what are you obsessed? What promises anchor your plea for help (Phil. 4:5, 7–9)?

Such words speak to common human experiences. A passage becomes personal when your details participate in what is said. The gap across centuries and between cultures seems almost to disappear. Your God is a very present help in trouble—this trouble. Application occurs in specifics.

2. Look for the Directly Applicable Passages

How do you widen your scope of application? Keep your eye out for *straightforward passages*. Typically they generalize or summarize in some manner, inviting personal appropriation. Consider the core promises of God, the joys and sorrows of many psalms, the moral divide in many proverbs, the call of many commands, the summary comment that interprets a story. As examples of the first, Exodus 34:6–7; Numbers 6:24–26; and Deuteronomy 31:6 state foundational promises that are repeatedly and variously applied throughout the rest of Scripture. Pay attention to how subsequent scriptures specifically reapply these statements, and to how the entire Bible illustrates them. Make such promises part of your repertoire of well-pondered truth. They are important for a reason. Get a feel for how these words come to a point in Jesus Christ and can rescript every life, including yours.

Consider how *generalization* occurs. In narratives, details make the story come to life. But psalms and proverbs adopt the opposite strategy. They intentionally flatten out specific references, so anyone can identify. David was troubled when he wrote Psalm 25—his emotions are clearly felt. But he left his own story at the door: "For your name's sake, O LORD, pardon my guilt, for it is great. . . . Consider my affliction and my trouble, and forgive all my sins" (Ps. 25:11, 18). He gives no details. We are given a template flexible enough to embrace any one of us. As you reapply, *your* sins and sufferings make Psalm 25 come to life as it leads you to mercy.

In matters of obedience, the Bible often proclaims a general truth without mentioning any of the multitude of possible applications. When Jesus says, "You cannot serve God and money" (Luke 16:13), he leaves you to puzzle out the forms of money-worship particular to your personality and your culture. In such cases, the Bible speaks in large categories, addressing many different experiences, circumstances, and actions. Sorting out what it specifically means is far from being mechanical and automatic, but the application process follows a rather direct line.

If you have a favorite Bible passage, it is likely one of these parts of Scripture whose application is relatively direct. But our experience of immediate relevance can skew our expectations for how the rest of God's revelation applies to our lives.

3. Recognize the Sorts of Passages where Personal Application Is Less Direct

Here is the core dilemma. Most of the Bible does *not* speak directly and personally to you. How do you "apply" the stories in Genesis? What about genealogies and census data? Leviticus? The life stories of Esther, Job, Samson, or Paul? The distribution of land and villages in Joshua? The history of Israel's decline detailed through 1 and 2 Kings? The prophetic woes scorching Moab, Philistia, Egypt, and Babylon, fulfilled so long ago? The ruminations of Ecclesiastes? The Gospel stories showing Jesus in action? The New Testament's frequent preoccupation with Jew-Gentile relations? The apocalyptic images in the Revelation?

The Bible's stories, histories, and prophecies—even many of the commands, teachings, promises, and prayers—take thoughtful work in order to reapply with current relevance. If you receive them directly—as if they speak directly to you, about you, with your issues in view—you will misunderstand and misapply Scripture. For example, the angel's command to Joseph, "take the child and his mother and flee to Egypt" (Matt. 2:13), is not a command to anyone today to buy a ticket to Egypt! Those who attempt to take the entire Bible as if it directly applies today end up distorting the Bible. It becomes an omni-relevant magic book teeming with private messages and meanings. God does not intend that his words function that way.

These passages *do* apply. But most of the Bible applies differently from the passages tilted toward immediate relevance. What you read applies by extension and analogy, not directly. Less sizzle, but quietly significant. In one sense, such passages apply exactly because they are *not* about you. Understood rightly, such passages give a changed perspective. They locate you on a bigger stage. They teach you to notice God and other people in their own right. They call you to understand yourself within a story—many stories—bigger than your personal history and immediate concerns. They locate you within a community far wider than your immediate network of relationships. And they remind you that you are always in God's presence, under his eye, and part of his program.

4. Tackle the Application of Less-direct Passages

Application is a lifelong process, seeking to expand and deepen wisdom. At the simplest level, simply read through the Bible in its larger chunks. The cumulative acquisition of wisdom is hard to quantify. A sense of what truth means and how truth works is overheard as well as heard. But also wrestle to work out the implications of specific passages.

Consider two examples. The first presents an extreme challenge to personal application: a genealogy or census. These are directly *irrelevant* to your life. Your name is not on the list. The reasons for the list disappeared long ago. You gain nothing by knowing that "Koz fathered Anub, Zobebah, and the clans of Aharhel" (1 Chron. 4:8). But when you learn to listen rightly, such lists intend many good things—and each list has a somewhat different purpose. Among the things taught are these:

- The Lord writes down names in his book of life.
- Families and communities matter to him.

- God is faithful to his promises through long history.
- He enlists his people as troops in the redemptive reconquest of a world gone bad.
- All the promises of God find their "Yes" in Jesus Christ (2 Cor. 1:20).

You "apply" a list of ancient names and numbers by extension, not directly. Your love for God grows surer and more intelligent when you ponder the *kind* of thing this is, rather than getting lost in the blizzard of names or numbers.

The second example presents a mid-level challenge. Psalms are often among the most directly relevant parts of Scripture. But what do you do when Psalm 21:1 says, "O LORD, in your strength the king rejoices"? The psalm is not talking about you, and it is not you talking—not directly. A train of connected truths apply this psalm to you, leading you out of yourself.

First, David lived and wrote these words, but Jesus Christ most fully lived—is now living, and will finally fulfill—this entire psalm. He is the greatest human king singing this song of deliverance; and he is also the divine Lord whose power delivers. We know from the perspective of NT fulfillment that this psalm is overtly by and about Jesus, not about any particular individual.

Second, you participate in the triumph of your King. You are caught up in all that the psalm describes, because you are in this Christ. So pay attention to *his* experience, because he includes you.

Third, your participation arises not as a solo individual but in company with countless brothers and sisters. You most directly apply this psalm by joining with fellow believers in a chorus of heartfelt gladness: "O LORD, *we* will sing and praise your power" (Ps. 21:13). The king's opening joy in God's power has become his people's closing joy.

Finally, figuratively, you are also kingly in Christ. In this sense, Jesus' experience of deliverance (the entire psalm) does apply to your life. Having walked through the psalm as an expression of the exultant triumph of Christ Jesus himself, you may now make it your experience too. You could even adapt Psalm 21 into the first person, inserting "I/me/my" in place of "the king" and "he/him/his." It would be blasphemous to do that at first. It is fully proper and your exceeding joy to do this in the end. This is a song in which all heaven will join. As you grasp that your brothers and sisters share this same goal, you will love them and serve their joy more consistently.

God reveals himself and his purposes throughout Scripture. Wise application always starts there.

Conclusion

You started by identifying one passage that speaks persistently, directly, and relevantly into your life. You have seen how both the direct and the indirect passages intend to change you. Learning to wisely apply the harder, less relevant passages has a surprising benefit. Your whole Bible "applies personally." This Lord is your God; this history is your history; these people are your people; this Savior has brought you in to participate in who he is and what he does. Venture out into the remotest regions of Scripture, seeking to know and love your God better.

Hopefully, you better understand why your most reliable passage so changed your life. Ponder those familiar words once more. You will notice that they also lift you out of self-preoccupation, out of the double evil of sin and misery. God brought his gracious care to you through that passage, and rearranged your life. You love him who first loved you, so you love his other children. And that is how the whole Bible, and each of its parts, applies personally. ◂

Reading the Bible for Preaching and Public Worship

The Bible, as holy Scripture, is the only certain source of God's words in the entire world. Paul's statement that "All Scripture is breathed out by God" (2 Tim. 3:16; see note) means that all the words of the Bible are God's words to us. Therefore if we want to hear our Creator and Lord speaking to us, we must continually give attention to the authoritative words of the Bible. This means that the Bible must be the only true foundation and constant guide for all that we do in the life of the church, and the Bible must be central to all that happens in preaching and public worship.

Moses and Jesus confirm how God's people are to regard his holy Word. On the very day that Moses completed the writing of the Book of the Law, he directed that it be placed beside the ark (Deut. 31:26), sang his final song (the great Song of Moses; Deut. 31:30–32:43), and then declared that "it is no empty word for you, but your very life" (Deut. 32:47). Moses' declaration set the standard for the primacy and sufficiency of God's Word (cf. Psalms 19; 119). A millennium and a half later Jesus, the second Moses, after defeating Satan with three deft quotations from Deuteronomy, declared, "Man shall not live by bread alone, but by every word that comes from the mouth of God" (Matt. 4:4). The Scriptures were life to Moses and food to Jesus; as such they together establish the ideal for God's people and directly inform the Bible's use in preaching and public worship. Jesus' dependence on the sufficiency and potency of God's Word raised the standard high for all apostolic and post-apostolic preaching and worship.

The Bible's Use in Preaching

When the apostle Paul instructs his younger colleague Timothy in the conduct of public worship, he places the Bible at its very center: "Until I come, devote yourself to the public reading of Scripture, to exhortation, to teaching. . . . Practice these things, immerse yourself in them" (1 Tim. 4:13, 15). Paul's direction was: read the Word; preach the Word! (Cf. 2 Tim. 4:2.) The early church sought to follow Paul's exhortation. Justin Martyr, writing c. A.D. 150–155, describes a typical Lord's Day: "On the day called Sunday, all who live in cities or in the country gather together in one place, and the memoirs of the apostles and the writings of the prophets are read, as long as time permits; then, when the reader has finished, the president speaks, instructing and exhorting the people to imitate these good things" (*First Apology* 1.67). In other words, the practice of these earliest churches was that the Scripture was to be read, and then preaching was to be based on that reading of the Word.

From the text. Paul directs Timothy, "Do your best to present yourself to God as one approved, a worker who has no need to be ashamed, rightly handling the word of truth" (2 Tim. 2:15). "Rightly handling" is a compound word in Greek, in which the first part comes from the Greek word *orthos*—"straight." The exact charge to Timothy is to impart the word of truth *without deviation* and *without dilution*—to get it straight and give it straight! The preacher must preach the text, not the idea that brought him to the text. He must stand behind the Bible, not in front of it. He must preach what the passage says, not what he wants it to say.

Good preaching requires prayerfully interpreting the text in its context. This involves using the established rules of interpretation; understanding the text's application both in its historical setting and in the whole of Scripture; discerning how it is a revelation of Jesus Christ and making the appropriate biblical connections; taking the trip from Jerusalem to one's own town and coming to see its present relevance; articulating the theme of the text; using stories and illustrations which truly illuminate the text; and employing language that actually communicates in today's culture.

From the heart. However, the proper use of the Bible in preaching requires more than good hermeneutics and homiletics; it also requires a heart that has been softened and prepared and sanctified by the Word that is to be preached. The Puritan William Ames (1576–1633) expressed it well:

> Next to the evidence of truth, and the will of God drawn out of the Scriptures, nothing makes a sermon more to pierce, than when it comes out of the inward affection of the heart without any affectation. To this purpose it is very profitable, if besides the daily practice of piety we use serious meditation and fervent prayer to work those things upon our own hearts, which we would persuade others of.

Every appropriation of the truth preached will strengthen the preacher for preaching. Every act of repentance occasioned in his soul by the Word he now preaches will give conviction to his voice.

Jonathan Edwards's *Treatise Concerning the Religious Affections* (1746) has provided the best explanation of what must take place within the preacher. By "affections" Edwards meant one's *heart*, one's *inclinations*, and one's *will*. As Edwards said, "true religion *consists in a great measure* in vigorous and lively actings and the inclination and will of the soul, or the fervent exercises of the heart." Edwards demonstrates from a cascade of Scriptures that real Christianity so impacts the affections that it shapes one's fears, hopes, loves, hatreds, desires, joys, sorrows, gratitudes, compassions, and zeals.

This is what should routinely happen to the preacher: the message should work its way through his whole intellectual and moral being as he prepares for and practices the proclamation of God's Word. When the message has affected him deeply, then he is ready to preach. Sermon preparation is twenty hours of prayer. It is humble, holy, critical thinking. It is repeatedly asking the Holy Spirit for insight. It is the word penetrating into the depths of the preacher's own soul. It is ongoing repentance. It is utter dependence. It is a singing heart.

The Bible's Use in Public Worship

God's Word deserves great reverence from his people. Isaiah writes, "But this is the one to whom I will look: he who is humble and contrite in spirit and trembles at my word" (Isa. 66:2). Therefore when Scripture is read aloud in a worship service, the reader and the congregation should take care to convey the reverent attention that Scripture deserves.

From its earliest days the church gave primacy to the reading of Holy Scripture, as seen in the apostle Paul's aforementioned charge to Timothy to devote himself to "the public reading of Scripture," as well as Justin Martyr's account of the apostolic church's practice of reading "the memoirs of the apostles and writings of the prophets . . . as long as time permits." The regular custom soon was to have two extended public readings, one from the OT and one from the NT.

Reading of Scripture. Every Bible-believing church must give preeminence to Scripture in its public services of worship. This means that the Scripture to be expounded should be read aloud, and should be set forth in its full context. After all, the reading of God's Word is the one place where we can be sure that we are hearing God. Responsive readings can be beneficial because they involve the congregation in voicing the sacred text.

There is substantial wisdom in keeping to the apostolic church's custom of reading passages from the OT and NT in pairs, as it were, because this practice weekly reaffirms the continuity of the two Testaments, encourages biblical theology, and counters the tendencies of many today to pit the two Testaments against each other. It also substantially contributes to the service as a service of the Word in its unity and fullness.

Congregational response to the reading with a hearty "Amen!" or the time-honored "Thanks be to God" can further elevate the corporate assent to the centrality and authority of God's Word. Jerome said of the congregational "Amen" in his day that at times it "seemed like a crack of thunder." How glorious and how good for the soul!

Of course, such attention to God's Word can also prove ineffective if the reading itself is left to a last-minute assignment, such that the reader fails to prepare mentally and spiritually for what he or she is required to do. All of us have heard the Scripture abused by a reader who hasn't the faintest idea of the meaning of what he is reading, or by reading too fast, or mispronouncing common words, or by losing his place. This is not to suggest that the Scripture is to be read as dramatically as possible or performed as a reader's theater. But how God-honoring it is to read God's Word well, with a prayerful spirit. Pastors and readers can serve their congregations well by prayerfully reading the text a dozen times with pencil in hand *before* reading it to God's people.

A service of the Word. The Bible's use in preaching and public worship should be in such a way as to result in a Christ-exalting service of the Word. This requires work by the preacher and the leaders of the congregation, so that God's Word is read to his glory, the sermon is derived from the faithful exposition of the text reading, and the reading and preaching of the biblical passage is set in the context of songs and hymns and programs that are redolent with the substance of God's holy Word. ◂

THE CANON OF SCRIPTURE

The Canon of the Old Testament

The word "canon" (Gk. for "a rule") is applied to the Bible in two ways: first, in regard to the Bible as the church's *standard* of faith and practice, and second, in regard to its contents as the *correct collection and list* of inspired books. The word was first applied to the identity of the biblical books in the latter part of the fourth century A.D., reflecting the fact that there had recently been a need to settle some Christians' doubts on the matter. Before this, Christians had referred to the "Old Testament" and "New Testament" as the "Holy Scriptures" and had assumed, rather than made explicit, that they were the *correct* collections and lists.

The Causes of Uncertainty about the OT Canon

The Christian OT corresponded to the Hebrew Bible, which Jesus and the first Christians inherited from the Jews. In the Gentile mission of the church, however, it was necessary to use the Septuagint (a translation of the OT that had been made in pre-Christian times for Greek-speaking Alexandrian Jews; see pp. 2601–2603). Because knowledge of Hebrew was uncommon in the church (esp. outside Syria and Palestine), the first Latin translation of the OT came from the Septuagint and not from the original Hebrew. Where there was no knowledge of Hebrew and little acquaintance with Jewish tradition, it became harder to distinguish between the biblical books and other popular religious reading matter circulating in the Greek or Latin language. These factors led to the uncertainty about the composition of Scripture, which the coiners of the term "canon" sought to settle.

Did the Hebrew Bible Contain the Same Books as Today's OT?

The above analysis assumes that the Hebrew Bible, which the church inherited in the first century, comprised the same books as it does today, and that uncertainty developed only later. Many in modern times have denied this view, but for mistaken reasons.

Are the Sections of Scripture Arbitrary Groups, Canonized in Different Eras?

Until recently, the accepted critical view was that the three sections of the Hebrew Bible—the Law, the Prophets, and the Writings (or Hagiographa)—were arbitrary groupings of books acknowledged as canonical in three different eras: the first section in the time of Ezra and Nehemiah (5th century B.C.); the last section at the synod of Jabneh or Jamnia (as late as A.D. 90); and the middle section sometime in between (perhaps in the 3rd century B.C.). The reasons given for the datings were as follows: (1) Because the Samaritans acknowledged only the Pentateuch (the five books of the Law) as Scripture, therefore the Pentateuch must have constituted the whole Jewish canon when the Samaritan schism took place at the time of Ezra and Nehemiah. (2) Because the synod of Jamnia discussed the canonicity of Ecclesiastes, the Song of Solomon, and presumably the other three books with which some rabbis had problems (Ezekiel, Proverbs, and Esther), these must still have been outside the Canon at the time. (3) Chronicles and Daniel, which are found in the Writings section of the Hebrew Bible, would have belonged more naturally with Kings and the oracular Prophets than with the Hagiographa; from this it was concluded that the Prophets section had been closed too soon to include them.

Recent study, however, has demolished this hypothesis. The five books of the Law are obviously not an arbitrary grouping. They follow a chronological sequence, concentrate on the Law of Moses, and trace history from the creation of the world to Moses' death. Moreover, the Prophets and the Writings, if arranged in the traditional order recorded in the Talmud (see chart, p. 2578), are not arbitrary groupings either. The Prophets begin with four narrative books—Joshua, Judges, Samuel, and Kings—tracing history through a second period, from the entry into the Promised Land to the Babylonian exile. They end with four oracular books—Jeremiah, Ezekiel, Isaiah, and the Book of the Twelve (Minor Prophets)—arranged in descending order of size. The Hagiographa (Writings) begin with six lyrical or wisdom books—Psalms, Job, Proverbs, Ecclesiastes, Song of Solomon, and Lamentations—arranged in descending order of size, and end with four narrative books—Daniel, Esther, Ezra–Nehemiah, and Chronicles—covering a third period of history, the period of the exile and the return. (The remaining book of the Writings, Ruth, is prefixed to Psalms, since it ends with the genealogy of the psalmist David.) The four narrative books in the Hagiographa are this time put second, so that Chronicles can sum up the whole biblical story, from Adam to the return from exile, and for this reason also Ezra–Nehemiah is put before Chronicles, not after it. A small anomaly is that the Song of Solomon is in fact slightly shorter than Lamentations, not longer, but it is put first to keep the three books related to Solomon together. That Daniel is treated as a narrative book may be surprising, but it is undeniable that it begins with six chapters of narrative.

Each of the three sections of the OT canon has a *narrative component*, covering one of three successive periods of history, and a *literary component*, representing one of three different types of religious literature: law, oracles, and lyrics or wisdom. The narrative material is, as far as possible, arranged in chronological order, and the literary material, when not united with the narrative material

The Traditional Order of OT Canonical Books according to the Talmud

The Law
Chronological (from the creation of the world to Moses' death): Genesis, Exodus, Leviticus, Numbers, Deuteronomy
The Prophets
Narrative books (from the entry into the Promised Land to the Babylonian exile): Joshua, Judges, Samuel, Kings
Oracular books (in descending order of size): Jeremiah, Ezekiel, Isaiah, The Book of the Twelve
The Writings
Lyrical/wisdom books (in descending order of size): Psalms (with Ruth prefixed), Job, Proverbs, Ecclesiastes, Song of Songs, Lamentations
Narrative books (from the period of exile to the return): Daniel, Esther, Ezra–Nehemiah, Chronicles

(as in the Pentateuch), is arranged in descending order of size. The shape of the Canon is therefore no accident of history but a work of art, and in its final form must be due to a single thinker, living before c. 130 B.C., when the three sections are first mentioned in the Greek prologue to *Sirach* (in the Apocrypha).

The datings assigned to the recognition of the three sections are also misconceived. First, it is now known that the Samaritans continued to follow Jewish customs long after the time of Ezra and Nehemiah, and that the schism did not become complete until the Jews destroyed the Samaritan temple on Mount Gerizim in about 110 B.C. It seems that the Samaritans only then rejected the Prophets and Writings because of the recognition those books give to the temple at Jerusalem.

Second, the problems that some rabbis had with as many as five biblical books do not mean that those books were outside the Canon, since the rabbinical literature notes similar problems with many other biblical books, including all five books of the Pentateuch. The problems with the five disputed books may have been particularly difficult, but they, too, were eventually solved in the same way as the other problems. There was no "synod of Jamnia" but simply a discussion at its academy that confirmed the canonicity of Ecclesiastes and the Song of Solomon—though that discussion did not end the controversy. Esther, in particular, continued to be discussed long after A.D. 90. Further, the same kinds of questions were raised about Ezekiel, which is found in the Prophets, not in the Writings; if the reasoning of the critical view were sound, then the Prophets also could not have been in the Canon, which would be absurd.

Third, contrary to what the critical view suggested, there would have been no strong incentive to put Chronicles and Daniel in the Prophets, since they were both being treated as narrative books relating to the final period of OT history and therefore belonging in the Hagiographa.

Was There a Distinct Alexandrian Canon?

A further fallacious argument that many critics have used to show that the OT canon was still open at the beginning of the Christian era is the hypothesis of a distinct Alexandrian canon, including at least some of the apocryphal books. For discussion of this argument, see the discussion of "How the Greek and Latin Translations Came to Contain the Apocrypha," in The Apocrypha, pp. 2581–2583.

Did the Qumran Sect Have a Broader OT Canon?

The discovery of the Dead Sea Scrolls at Qumran has turned the attention of critics to the pseudepigrapha—notably *1 Enoch*, *The Testament of Levi*, *Jubilees*, and *The Temple Scroll*. It is today frequently claimed that the men of Qumran (probably Essenes) had a broad canon that included these books. But it should be noted that (1) the pseudonyms used in these works belong to the biblical period, indicating a recognition that prophetic inspiration had now ceased; (2) the inspiration claimed at Qumran was an inspiration to *interpret* the Scriptures, not to add to them; (3) the quotations from authoritative works made in the Qumran writings are almost exclusively from the OT books, and the formulas used for quoting Scripture are not used with the few quotations from elsewhere; and (4) though the Essenes may have added an interpretative appendix to the three standard sections of the OT canon, containing their favored pseudepigrapha, it is significant that they did not try to insert them into the three standard sections, which were now evidently closed (i.e., seen as complete).

The Truth about the OT Canon

So much for fashionable errors regarding the assembling and recognition of the OT canon. The true evidence of the process is comparatively simple. First, it was recognized from ancient times that, if revelation was to be preserved, it needed to be written down (see Ex. 17:14; Deut. 31:24–26; Ps. 102:18; Isa. 30:8). This process of writing the words had been begun by God himself at Mount Sinai, when he gave Moses the two tablets of stone with his own words written on them: "The tablets were the work of God, and the writing was the writing of God, engraved on the tablets" (Ex. 32:16). These tablets were deposited in the ark of the covenant (Deut. 10:5) and were the basis of the covenant relationship between God and his people. Then, later writings were added to "the Book of the Covenant" (see Ex. 24:7; Josh. 24:26; 2 Kings 23:2). A significant object lesson on the importance of preserving God's words in written form was the later discovery of the Book of the Law by Hilkiah, after it had been lost during the reigns of Manasseh and Amon: its teaching came as a great shock because it had been forgotten (2 Kings 22–23; 2 Chronicles 34).

Second, on great national occasions the Book of the Law was read to the people (Ex. 24:7; 2 Kings 23:2; Neh. 8:9, 14–17, etc.). Deuteronomy provides for it to be read regularly every seven years (Deut. 31:10–13). An extension of the same practice was the later reading of the Pentateuch in the synagogue on the Sabbath, supplemented by a reading from the Prophets (Luke 4:16–20; Acts 13:15, 27; 15:21, etc.).

Third, Deuteronomy was to be laid up in the sanctuary (Deut. 31:24–26), and that was where Hilkiah found the Book of the Law (2 Kings 22:8; 2 Chron. 34:15). It is known from Josephus and the earliest rabbinical literature that the practice of laying up the Scriptures in the temple still continued down to the first century A.D. To lay up any book there as Scripture must have been a solemn and carefully deliberated act of national significance.

Fourth, the calendar of the book of *1 Enoch*, followed at Qumran, seems to have been devised in about the third century B.C. so as to avoid having any dated act recorded in the Scriptures occur on the Sabbath. At least 10 (and probably more) of the present OT books are shown to be acknowledged as canonical at this time by this listing.

Fifth, *Sirach* 44–49, written about 180 B.C., provides a catalog of famous men, and these are probably all meant to be biblical figures, since they are all now found in the Bible. The end of *Sirach* 49 sums them up, while chapter 50 moves on to describe Simon the son of Onias, a later worthy figure not found in the Bible. Accounting for these men raises the number of books to at least 16 for which there is specific extrabiblical attestation to canonicity.

Sixth, Josephus relates that the Pharisees, Sadducees, and Essenes first became distinct and rival schools of thought in the time of Jonathan Maccabeus (d. 143 B.C.). To alter the Canon after this time would have been very controversial, and can hardly have occurred. So the Canon must have been acknowledged as closed before 143 B.C.

Seventh, the final touches may have been put to the Canon in 165 B.C. by Judas Maccabeus (making it a listed collection of 24 books in three sections, beginning with Genesis and ending with Chronicles; see chart, p. 2578), when he gathered the scattered Scriptures after Antiochus's persecution (*2 Macc.* 2:14). This is the Bible that, two centuries later, the NT and other first-century writings reflect.

Eighth, in spite of numerous differences between Jesus and the Jewish religious leaders of his time, there is no record of any dispute between them, or any later dispute with Jesus' apostles, over which OT books were canonical. The OT canon accepted by the early church was identical to the canon of books accepted by the Jewish people.

Ninth, Jesus and the NT authors quote the words of the OT approximately 300 times (see Old Testament Passages Cited in the New Testament, pp. 2608–2611; uncertainty about the exact number arises because of a few instances where it is not clear whether it is an OT quotation or only an echoing expression using similar words). They regularly quote it as having divine authority, with phrases such as "it is written," "Scripture says," and "God says," but no other writings are quoted in this way. Occasionally the NT writers will quote some other authors, even pagan Greek authors, but they never quote these other sources as being the words of God (see notes on Acts 17:28; Titus 1:12–13; Jude 8–10, 14–16), as they do the canonical OT books.

Tenth, Josephus (born A.D. 37/38) explained, "From Artaxerxes to our own times a complete history has been written, but has not been deemed worthy of equal credit with the earlier record, because of the failure of the exact succession of the prophets" (*Against Apion* 1.41). Josephus was aware of the writings now considered part of the Apocrypha, but he (and, he implies, mainstream Jewish opinion) considered these other writings "not . . . worthy of equal credit" with what are now known as the OT Scriptures.

Eleventh, additional Jewish tradition after the time of the NT also expresses the conviction that no more prophetic writings had been given after the time of the last OT prophets Haggai, Zechariah, and Malachi (see Babylonian Talmud, *Yoma* 9b; *Sotah* 48b; *Sanhedrin* 11a; and *Midrash Rabbah on Song of Songs* 8.9.3).

Sound historical study shows, therefore, that the Hebrew OT contains the true canon of the OT, shared by Jesus and the apostles with first-century Judaism. No books are left out that should be included, and none are included that should be left out. ◂

The Canon of the New Testament

The foundations for a NT canon lie not, as some would assert, in the needs or the practices of the church in the second, third, and fourth centuries A.D., but in the gracious purpose of a self-revealing God whose word carries his own divine authority. Just as new outpourings of divine word-revelation accompanied and followed each major act of redemption in the ancient history of God's people (the covenant with Adam and Eve, the covenant with Abraham, the redemption from Egypt, the establishment of the monarchy, the exile, and the restoration), so when the promised Messiah came, a new and generous outpouring of divine revelation necessarily ensued (see 2 Tim. 1:8–11; Titus 1:1–3).

The OT Authorization

The prospect of a NT Scripture to stand alongside the OT was anticipated, even authorized, in the OT itself, embedded in the promise of God's ultimate act of redemption through the Messiah, in faithfulness to his covenant (Jer. 31:31–33; cf. Heb. 8:7–13; 10:16–18). Jesus taught his disciples after his resurrection that "the Law of Moses and the Prophets and the Psalms" predicted not only the Messiah's suffering and resurrection but also that "repentance and forgiveness of sins should be proclaimed in his name to all nations, beginning from Jerusalem" (Luke 24:44–48). Prophetic passages such as Isaiah 2:2–3; 49:6; and Psalm 2:8 spoke of a time when the light of God's grace in redemption would be proclaimed to all nations. It naturally follows that this proclamation would eventuate in a new collection of written Scriptures complementing the books of the old covenant—both from the pattern of God's redemptive work in the past (mentioned above) and from the actual writing ministry of some of Jesus' apostles (and their associates) in the accomplishment of their commission.

The Commission of Jesus

God, who spoke in many and various ways in times past, chose to speak in these last days to mankind through his Son (see Heb. 1:1–2, 4). Bringing this saving message to Israel and the nations was a crucial part of the mission of Jesus Christ (Isa. 49:6; Acts 26:23), the Word made flesh (John 1:14). He put this mission into effect through chosen apostles, whom he commissioned to be his authoritative representatives (Matt. 10:40, "whoever receives you receives me"). Their assignment was to "bring to . . . remembrance," through the work of the Spirit, his words and works (John 14:26; 16:13–14) and to bear witness to Jesus "in Jerusalem and in all Judea and Samaria, and to the end of the earth" (Acts 1:8; cf. Matt. 28:19–20; Luke 24:48; John 17:14, 20). In time, the apostolic preaching came to written form in the books of the NT, which now function as "the commandment of the Lord and Savior through your apostles" (2 Pet. 3:2).

Paul and the other apostles wrote just as they preached: conscious of Jesus' mandate. From the beginning, the full authority of the apostles (and prophets) to deliver God's word was recognized, at least by many (Acts 10:22; Eph. 2:20; 1 Thess. 2:13; Jude 17–18). This recognition is accordingly reflected in the earliest non-apostolic writers. For example, Clement of Rome attested that "The apostles received the gospel for us from the Lord Jesus Christ; Jesus the Christ was sent forth from God. So then Christ is from God, and the apostles are from Christ. Both, therefore, came of the will of God in good order" (*1 Clement* 42.1–2 written c. A.D. 95).

The Recognition of New Covenant Scriptures

As God's word to mankind, the "God-breathed" Scripture (2 Tim. 3:16) is self-attesting, and thus the Canon may be said to be self-establishing. Yet history records that for centuries there were variations in local church practice and disagreements among churches and early theologians about several books of the NT. Such variations, however, are not unexpected, given that the process of recognition involved more than two dozen books that came into being over a period of perhaps 50 years, circulating unsystematically to churches as they were springing up in widely diffused parts of the Roman Empire.

In its deliberations about the particular books that make up the canon of Scripture, the church did not sovereignly "determine" or "choose" the books it most preferred—whether for catechetical, polemical, liturgical, or edificatory purposes. Rather, the church saw itself as empowered only to receive and recognize what God had provided in books handed down from the apostles and their immediate companions (e.g., Irenaeus, *Against Heresies* 3.preface; 3.1.1–2). This is why discussions of the so-called "criteria" of canonicity can be misleading. Qualities such as "apostolicity," "antiquity," "orthodoxy," "liturgical use," and "church consensus" are not criteria by which the church autonomously judged which documents it would receive. The first three are qualities the church recognizes in the voice of its Savior, to which voice the church willingly submits itself ("My sheep hear my voice . . . and they follow me," John 10:27).

The Gospels according to Matthew, Mark, Luke, and John (the earliest Gospels known) gained universal acceptance while arousing very little controversy within the church. If the latest of these, the Gospel of John, was published near the end of the first century (as most scholars think), it is remarkable that its words are echoed around A.D. 110 in the writings of Ignatius of Antioch, who also knew Matthew, and perhaps Luke. At about the same time, Papias of Hierapolis in Asia Minor received traditions about the origins of Matthew's and Mark's Gospels, and quite probably Luke's and John's. In the middle of the second century, Justin Martyr in Rome reported that the Gospels (apparently the four)—which he calls "memoirs of the apostles"—were being read and exposited in Christian services of worship.

In 2 Peter 3:16, a collection of at least some of Paul's letters was already known and regarded as Scripture and therefore enjoyed canonical endorsement. Furthermore, a collection (of unknown extent) of Paul's letters was known to Clement of Rome and to the recipients of his letter in Corinth before the end of the first century, then also to Ignatius of Antioch and Polycarp of Smyrna and their readers in the early second century. The Pastoral Letters (1–2 Timothy and Titus), rejected as Paul's by many modern critics, are attested at least from the time of Polycarp.

By the end of the second century a "core" collection of NT books—21 of the 27—was generally recognized: four Gospels, Acts, 13 epistles of Paul, 1 Peter, 1 John, and Revelation. By this time Hebrews (accepted in the East and by Irenaeus and Tertullian in the West, but questioned in Rome due to doubts about authorship), James, 2 Peter, 2 and 3 John, and Jude were only minimally attested in the writings of church leaders. This infrequent citation led to the expression of doubts by later fathers (e.g., Eusebius, *Ecclesiastical History* 2.23.25). Yet, by some time in the third century, codices (precursors of the modern book form, as opposed to scrolls) containing all seven of the "general epistles" were being produced, and Eusebius reports that all seven were "known to most."

An unusual case is the book of Revelation, which seems to have been accepted everywhere at first (in the West by Justin, Irenaeus, the Muratorian Fragment, and Tertullian; in the East by Clement of Alexandria and Origen). But due to its exploitation by Montanists and others, it was criticized by Gaius, a Roman writer in the early third century. Several decades later, Dionysius of Alexandria, while not rejecting the book, argued that it could not have been written by the apostle John. These factors led to enduring doubts in the East and to Revelation's absence from later Eastern canon lists, though its reputation in the West did not suffer.

To complicate matters, many documents were produced in the course of the second century which in some way paralleled or imitated NT books. Many of these made some claim to apostolic authority, and some gained considerable popularity in certain quarters. One or more "Gospels" written in Aramaic attracted interest because of a presumed connection to an original Aramaic Matthew. Other "Gospels" were essentially combinations of the four (i.e., *The Gospel of Peter* and *The Egerton Gospel*), a practice that culminated in Tatian's *Diatessaron*, a harmony of the four (c. A.D. 172), which was the first form of the Gospels translated into Syriac.

There was a profusion of "Acts" literature, usually following, in novel-like fashion, the fictional exploits of a single apostle (Paul, John, Andrew, Peter). Letters forged in the name of Paul (*To the Laodiceans*, *To the Alexandrians*, *3 Corinthians*) sought to attract adherents to an assortment of special causes. Works in various genres written to advance unorthodox interpretations of Christianity often borrowed the names of apostles (*Apocryphon of John*, *Gospel of Thomas*). In addition, a few writings, probably never intended to be regarded as Scripture, were honored as such by some Christians partly because of assumed authorship by companions of apostles (*1* and *2 Clement*, *The Letter of Barnabas*, *The Shepherd of Hermas*).

By the 240s A.D. Origen (residing in Caesarea in Palestine) acknowledged all 27 of the NT books but reported that James, 2 Peter, 2 and 3 John, and Jude were disputed. The situation is virtually the same for Eusebius, writing about 60 years later, who also reports the doubts some had about Hebrews and Revelation. Still, his two categories of "undisputed" and "disputed but known to most" contain only the 27 and no more. He named five other books (*The Acts of Paul, The Shepherd of Hermas, The Apocalypse of Peter, The Letter of Barnabas*, and *The Didache*) which were known to many churches but which, he believed, had to be judged as spurious.

In the year A.D. 367 the Alexandrian bishop Athanasius, in his annual Easter letter, gave a list of the NT books which comprised, with no reservations, all 27, while naming several others as useful for catechizing but not as scriptural. Several other fourth-century lists essentially concurred, though with various individual deviations outside of the most basic core (four Gospels, Acts, 13 epistles of Paul, 1 Peter, 1 John). Three African synods—at Hippo Regius in A.D. 393 and at Carthage in 397 and 419—and the influential African bishop Augustine affirmed the 27-book Canon. It was enshrined in Jerome's Latin translation, the Vulgate, which became the normative Bible for the Western church. In Eastern churches, recognition of Revelation lagged for quite some time. The churches of Syria did not accept Revelation, 2 Peter, 2 and 3 John, or Jude until the fifth (Western Syria) or sixth (Eastern Syria) centuries.

The apostolic word gave birth to the church (Rom. 1:15–17; 10:14–15; James 1:18; 1 Pet. 1:23–25), and the written form of this word remains as the permanent, documentary expression of God's new covenant. It may be said that only the 27 books of the NT manifest themselves as belonging to that original, foundational, apostolic witness. They have demonstrated themselves to be the Word of God to the universal church throughout the generations. Here are the pastures to which Christ's sheep from many folds continually come to hear their Shepherd's voice and to follow him. ◂

The Apocrypha

Larger editions of the English Bible—from the Great Bible of Tyndale and Coverdale (1539) onward—have often included a separate section between the OT and the NT titled "The Apocrypha," consisting of additional books and substantial parts of books. The Latin Vulgate Bible translated by Jerome (begun A.D. 382, completed 405) had placed them in the OT itself—some as separate items and some as attached to or included in the biblical books of Esther, Jeremiah, and Daniel. In Roman Catholic translations of the Bible, such as the Douay Version and the Jerusalem Bible, these items are still placed in their pre-Reformation positions. In Protestant translations, however, the Apocrypha is either omitted altogether or grouped in a separate section.

How Jerome's Vulgate Came to Contain the Apocrypha

In distinguishing the Apocrypha from the OT books, the Protestant translators were not doing something completely novel but were carrying out more thoroughly than ever before the principles on which Jerome (A.D. 345–420) had made his great Latin Vulgate translation of the OT. The Vulgate was translated from the original Hebrew. But a translation prior to the Vulgate, the Old Latin translation, had been made from the Greek OT, the Septuagint (or LXX). At some stage, early or late, additional books and parts of books, which were not in the Hebrew Bible, had found their way into the Greek OT, and from there into the Old Latin version. Jerome retained these in his new translation, the Latin Vulgate, but added prefaces at various points to emphasize that they were not true parts of the Bible, and he called them by the name "apocrypha" (Gk. *apokrypha*, "those having been hidden away"). In accordance with his teaching—and with the understanding of the OT canon held by Jesus, the NT authors, and the first-century Jews (see The Canon of the Old Testament, pp. 2577–2579)—the sixteenth-century Protestant translators did not consider those writings part of the OT but gathered them together in a separate section, to which they gave Jerome's name, "The Apocrypha."

Jerome's reason for choosing this name is not readily apparent. He probably took a hint from Origen, who a century and a half earlier had stated that the Jews applied this name to the most esteemed of their noncanonical books. Origen and Jerome were two of the most distinguished students of Judaism among the Fathers, so it would be natural for them to use the term in a Jewish sense, though applying it to the noncanonical Jewish books that were most esteemed by Christians. Jews would never destroy respected religious books but, if unfit for use, hid them away and left them to decay naturally. So "hidden" came to mean "highly esteemed, though uncanonical."

Jerome did not actually confine his name "apocrypha" to Jewish books but used it also of noncanonical Christian books, such as *The Shepherd of Hermas*, which were likewise popular religious reading among Christians. The modern expression "New Testament Apocrypha," for late works that imitate NT literature, is similar.

How the Greek and Latin Translations Came to Contain the Apocrypha

How the Greek OT, and by consequence the Latin OT, came to contain apocryphal items has been variously understood. Codex Alexandrinus (the great 5th-century A.D. manuscript of the whole Greek Bible) was printed and published in the eighteenth century. Because it contained the Apocrypha, the editors in the eighteenth century assumed that the OT of this Christian manuscript had been copied from Jewish manuscripts equally inclusive, and that consequently the Apocrypha must have been in the LXX translation, and in the canon of the Greek-speaking Jews of Alexandria who produced it from pre-Christian times (though not in the Bible or canon of the Semitic-speaking Jews of Palestine). This hypothesis held the field for a long time, and a further assumption—that most of the apocryphal books had been composed in Greek, outside Palestine—was made to support it.

All the elements of this theory are now known to be false. (1) Leather manuscripts large enough to contain the whole OT did not exist among either Christians or Jews until the latter part of the fourth century. The earlier Christian biblical manuscripts are on papyrus, and extend only to about three of the larger books. (2) The Jews of Alexandria took their lead largely from Palestine, and would have been unlikely to establish their own distinct canon; moreover, their greatest writer, Philo, though frequently quoting from the OT in his voluminous works, never refers to any of the Apocrypha whatsoever. (3) The earliest Christian biblical manuscripts contain the fewest books of the Apocrypha, and up until A.D. 313, only *Wisdom*, *Tobit*, and *Sirach* ever occur in them; other books of the Apocrypha were not added until later. (4) That the Apocrypha was mostly composed in Greek or outside Palestine is no longer widely believed, and *Sirach* (*Ecclesiasticus*) itself states that it was composed in Hebrew (see its prologue; much of its Hebrew text has now been recovered). All the Apocrypha except *Wisdom* and *2 Maccabees* may in fact have been translated from a Hebrew or Aramaic original, written in Palestine.

The way in which Christian writers used the Apocrypha confirms the above analysis. The NT seems to reflect knowledge of one or two of the apocryphal texts, but it never ascribes authority to them as it does to many of the canonical OT books. While the NT quotes various parts of the OT about 300 times (see Old Testament Passages Cited in the New Testament, pp. 2608–2611), it never actually quotes anything from the Apocrypha (Jude 14–16 does not contain a quote from the Apocrypha but from another Jewish writing, *1 Enoch*; see note on Jude 14–16; also notes on Acts 17:28; Titus 1:12–13; Jude 8–10). In the second century, Justin Martyr and Theophilus of Antioch, who frequently referred to the OT, never referred to any of the Apocrypha. By the end of the second century *Wisdom*, *Tobit*, and *Sirach* were sometimes being treated as Scripture, but none of the other apocryphal books were. Their eventual acceptance was a slow development. Much the same is true with Christian lists of the OT books: the oldest of them include the fewest of the Apocrypha; and the oldest of all, that of Melito (c. A.D. 170), includes none.

Acceptance and Rejection of the Apocrypha

The growing willingness of the pre-Reformation church to treat the Apocrypha as not just edifying reading but Scripture itself reflected the fact that Christians—especially those living outside Semitic-speaking countries—were losing contact with Jewish tradition. Within those countries, however, a learned Christian tradition akin to elements of Jewish tradition was maintained, especially by scholars such as Origen, Epiphanius, and Jerome, who cultivated the Hebrew language and Jewish studies. By the late fourth century, Jerome found it necessary to assert the distinction between the Apocrypha and the inspired OT books with great emphasis, and a minority of writers continued to make the same distinction throughout the Middle Ages, until the Protestant Reformers arose and made the distinction an important part of their doctrine of Scripture. At the Council of Trent (1545–1563), however, the church of Rome attempted to obliterate the distinction and to put the Apocrypha (with the exception of *1* and *2 Esdras* and *The Prayer of Manasseh*) on the same level as the inspired OT books. This was a consequence of (1) Rome's exalted doctrine of oral tradition, (2) its view that the church creates Scripture, and (3) its acceptance of certain controversial ideas (esp. the doctrines of purgatory, indulgences, and works-righteousness as contributing to justification) that were derived from passages in the Apocrypha. These teachings gave support to the Roman Catholic responses to Martin Luther and other leaders of the Protestant Reformation, which had begun in 1517.

Because of these controversial passages, some Protestants ceased to use the Apocrypha altogether. But other Protestants (notably Lutherans and Anglicans), while avoiding such passages and the ideas they contain, continued to read the Apocrypha as generally edifying religious literature. The Apocrypha, together with other post-canonical literature (esp. the pseudepigrapha, the Dead Sea Scrolls, the writings of Philo and Josephus, the Targums, and the earliest rabbinical literature) can be helpful in additional ways. They provide the earliest interpretations of the OT literature; they explain what happened in the time between the two Testaments; and they introduce customs, ideas, and expressions that provide a helpful background when reading the NT.

The Contents of the Apocrypha

Individually, the books of the Apocrypha are 15 in number (but some count 14 or 12 by combining some books; see list) and consist of various kinds of literature—narrative, proverbial, prophetic, and liturgical. They probably range in date from the third century B.C. (*Tobit*) to the first century A.D. (*2 Esdras* and perhaps *The Prayer of Manasseh*).

1. *First Esdras* (Gk. for "Ezra"), sometimes called *3 Esdras*, covers the same ground as the book of Ezra, with a little of Chronicles and Nehemiah added. It also relates a debate on "the strongest thing in the world."

2. *Second Esdras*, sometimes called *4 Esdras*, is a pseudonymous apocalypse, preserved in Latin, not Greek, with two Christian chapters added at the beginning and two at the end. Chapter 14 gives the number of the OT books. *First* and *Second Esdras* are not included in the Roman Catholic canon.

3. *Tobit* is a moral tale with a Persian background, dealing with almsgiving, marriage, and the burial of the dead.

4. *Judith* is an exciting story, in a confused historical setting, about a pious and patriotic heroine.

5. *The Additions to Esther* are a collection of passages added to the LXX version of Esther, bringing out its religious character.

6. *Wisdom* is a work inspired by Proverbs and written in the person of Solomon.

7. *Sirach*, also called *Ecclesiasticus*, is a work somewhat similar to *Wisdom*, by a named author (Jeshua ben Sira, or Jesus the son of Sirach). It was written about 180 B.C., and its catalog of famous men bears important witness to the contents of the OT canon at that date. Its translator's prologue, written half a century later, refers repeatedly to the three sections of the Hebrew Bible (see The Canon of the Old Testament, pp. 2577–2579.)

8. *Baruch* is written in the person of Jeremiah's companion, and somewhat in Jeremiah's manner.

9. *The Epistle of Jeremiah* is connected to *Baruch*, and sometimes the two are counted together as one book (as in the KJV, which therefore lists 14 books rather than 15).

The Additions to Daniel consist of three segments (10, 11, and 12 in this list):

10. *Susanna* and

11. *Bel and the Dragon* are stories that tell how wise Daniel exposed unjust judges and deceitful pagan priests.

12. *The Song of the Three Young Men* contains a prayer and hymn put into the mouths of Daniel's three companions when they are in the fiery furnace; the hymn is the one

used in Christian worship as the *Benedicite* (in the Church of England's services).

As stated before, some authorities count these three books (items 10, 11, and 12) as one book, namely, *The Additions to Daniel*, and they also count *Baruch* as one book that includes *The Epistle of Jeremiah*; in that way, they count only 12 books in the Apocrypha.

13. *The Prayer of Manasseh* puts into words Manasseh's prayer for forgiveness in 2 Chronicles 33:12–13. It is not included in the Roman Catholic canon.

14–15. *First* and *Second Maccabees* relate the successful revolt of the Maccabees against the Hellenistic Syrian persecutor Antiochus Epiphanes in the mid-second century B.C. The first book and parts of the second book are the primary historical sources for a knowledge of the Maccabees' heroic faith, though the second book adds legendary material. The LXX also contains a *3* and *4 Maccabees*, but these are of less importance.

The Development of Religious Thought in the Apocrypha

The development of religious thought found in the Apocrypha, going beyond the teaching of the OT, must be assessed by the teaching of the NT. For example, *Wisdom* 4:7–5:16 teaches that all face a personal judgment after this life. This is consistent with later NT teaching (Heb. 9:27).

Other teachings add doctrinal material foreign to NT teaching, such as the following:

1. In *Tobit* 12:15 seven angels are said to stand before God and present the prayers of the saints.
2. In *2 Maccabees* 15:13–14 a departed prophet is said to pray for God's people on earth.
3. In *Wisdom* 8:19–20 and *Sirach* 1:14 the reader is told that the righteous are those who were given good souls at birth.
4. In *Tobit* 12:9 and *Sirach* 3:3 readers are told that their good deeds atone for their evil deeds.
5. In *2 Maccabees* 12:40–45 the reader is told to pray for the sins of the dead to be forgiven.

The first two ideas find no support in the OT or NT, and the second may be thought to give some support to the Roman Catholic idea of prayer to the saints who have died. The last three tenets are clearly at variance with what the NT teaches about regeneration, justification, and the present life as one's only period of probation.

The Apocrypha, consequently, must be read with discretion. Though much in it simply reflects Judaism as practiced at a date somewhat later than the OT, and some parts reflect developments in the direction of the NT, there are also certain misleading passages that have historical interest but, in terms of Christian theology and practice, are to be avoided. ◂

The Reliability of Bible Manuscripts

The Reliability of the Old Testament Manuscripts

Introduction

At the beginning of the twentieth century, textual criticism of the OT was in its infancy, with few extant early Hebrew manuscripts. However, with the discoveries of the Dead Sea Scrolls beginning in A.D. 1947, scholars found themselves in a better position than ever before to evaluate whether the OT texts are reliable.

At present there exist over 3,000 Hebrew manuscripts of the OT, 8,000 manuscripts of the Latin Vulgate, over 1,500 manuscripts of the Septuagint, and over 65 copies of the Syriac Peshitta.

This article examines the reliability of the OT manuscripts in respect to three main areas: (1) transmission of the OT; (2) OT textual criticism; and (3) primary OT sources.

Transmission of the OT

Jewish tradition maintains that Moses wrote the Pentateuch. If so, then portions of the OT were passed down through scribes for more than 3,000 years before becoming part of modern translations. This naturally gives rise to questions like: How did the OT text come about? How were the books copied and by whom? Are the texts available today an accurate reproduction of the originals?

How did the OT text come about? While some divine revelation may originally have been handed down from generation to generation orally, at some point it was committed to writing to ensure its accuracy. Several biblical passages indicate that from an early period parts of Scripture were held in honor and were considered authoritative (e.g., Ex. 17:14–16; 24:3–4, 7). The stone tablets of the Ten Commandments were to be stored in the ark of the covenant (e.g., Ex. 25:16, 21; Heb. 9:4), and the Book of the Law was to be kept in the tabernacle next to the ark (Deut. 31:24–26). Moses commanded the Israelites to teach God's laws and statutes to their children and grandchildren (Deut. 4:9). The Law of Moses was entrusted to the priests, who were to teach it to the people (Deut. 33:10) and read it aloud publicly every seven years to ensure that the Israelites would remember it (Deut. 31:9–11). They were also commanded not to add to or delete from it at all (Deut. 4:2; 12:32). Both the OT (Josh. 23:6; 1 Kings 2:3; 1 Chron. 22:13) and NT (e.g., Mark 10:5; 12:26; Luke 2:22; 16:29, 31) refer to the Law of Moses as a distinct, authoritative source.

OT passages also refer to written forms of prophetic oracles (Isa. 30:8; Jer. 25:13; 29:1; Ezek. 43:11; Dan. 7:1; Hab. 2:2) and histories recorded by prophets (1 Chron. 29:29; 2 Chron. 9:29; 12:15; 13:22; 20:34). However, the first mention of a collection of biblical books is in Daniel 9:2, which suggests that by the time of Daniel, the book of Jeremiah was part of a larger collection of authoritative works that he calls "the books."

Later biblical writers make reference to earlier biblical books (2 Kings 14:6; 2 Chron. 25:4; 35:12; Ezra 3:2; 6:18; Neh. 8:1), and the prophets commonly rebuke the people for not obeying the words of previous prophets (Jer. 7:25; 25:4; Ezek. 38:17; Dan. 9:6, 10; Hos. 6:5; 12:10).

There is good evidence from Jewish tradition and other sources that the Jewish people believed that the prophetic voice ceased following the deaths of Haggai, Zechariah, and Malachi (*Tosefta, Sotah* 13.2; Babylonian Talmud, *Sotah* 48b, *Sanhedrin* 11a, and *Baba Bathra* 12a; *Seder Olam Rabbah* 30; Jerusalem Talmud, *Taanith* 2.1; *1 Macc.* 9:27; *2 Baruch* 85.3). Therefore, it is likely that by about 300 B.C. the canon of the OT was set in all its essentials. (See The Canon of the Old Testament, pp. 2577–2579.) While minor discussions about certain books continued well into the Christian era, they had little effect on the form of the Canon.

Jesus accepted the authority of the Hebrew canon and taught his disciples to reverence it (Matt. 5:17–18). The Christian church, which had its roots in the Jewish nation, maintained the same Hebrew canon (Matt. 23:34–35; Luke 11:50–51) and added the NT works to it.

How were the books copied, and by whom? There are no remaining original manuscripts (commonly called "autographs") of the OT, but there do exist an abundance of copies made by scribes whose only job was to preserve God's revelation. The autographs were probably written on scrolls made from papyrus or leather (see Jeremiah 36) that deteriorated from everyday use. When scrolls showed signs of wear, they were copied and reverently buried (since they contained the sacred name of God). Sometimes worn copies were placed in a *genizah* ("hidden" place) until enough were gathered for a ritual burial ceremony. One of these *genizahs* was found in an old synagogue in Cairo around 1890.

Initially, priests (or a special group of priests) maintained the sacred traditions. Then, from about 500 B.C. to A.D. 100, an influential group of teachers and interpreters of the law arose, called the *soperim* ("scribes"), who meticulously copied and preserved the most accurate form of the Hebrew text that they could determine. The Babylonian Talmud states: "The older men were called *soperim* because they counted [Hb. *soper* may also mean "one who counts"] all the letters in the Torah" (Babylonian Talmud, *Kiddushin* 30a). There has been significant discussion as to what their early text looked like and how closely it corresponded to the modern Masoretic text (MT), the common form of today's Hebrew Bible, but it is not an easy question to answer.

Evidence from about the mid-third century B.C. and following indicates that a variety of OT texts coexisted for several centuries (e.g., proto-MT [an early form of the Hebrew Masoretic text]; Greek Septuagint, a sometimes loose translation; Samaritan Pentateuch). Manuscripts copied before the first century A.D. show two tendencies on the part of the scribes: they preserved the accuracy of the text and, at the same time, they were willing to revise or update the specific words of the text. These tendencies are not contradictory—scribes assigned to the Scriptures a high degree of authority and upheld them with great reverence, but their desire was that readers understand them. Sometimes scribes intentionally changed texts because of things they felt were inappropriate or objectionable. Still, they carefully noted changes out of reverence for the text (e.g., in Judg. 18:30 scribes added the Hebrew letter *nun* above the line so that it read "Manasseh" instead of "Moses" because Jonathan was acting more like a son of wicked Manasseh than of Moses).

A group of scribes called the *tannaim* (repeaters) maintained the sacred traditions from about A.D. 100 to 300 and developed meticulous rules to follow when copying synagogue scrolls (e.g., no word or letter was to be written from memory; if more than three mistakes were made on any page, it was destroyed and redone). While the text was reverenced and carefully maintained, it could be updated within specific, limited parameters: (1) By about 350 B.C., texts had begun to be written in Assyrian (square) script instead of paleo-Hebrew. (2) Even before this, *matres lectionis* (Hebrew consonants added to a word to indicate how it should be pronounced—these were precursors to vowel points) were starting to be added and archaic spellings were modernized. (3) Some corrections were made (see 4QIsa[a]). It was common practice throughout the ancient Near East to update and revise texts.

Following the first century A.D., however, the priority of scribes narrowed to preserving the accuracy of Scripture, which they did with amazing precision. Manuscripts dated to the first and second centuries A.D. (e.g., from Masada, Nahal Hever, Wadi Murabba'at, and Nahal Se'elim) reflect the proto-MT in orthography and content with very little variation. Debate continues over how and why the text became so unified following the first century A.D. Some argue that the group who maintained the proto-MT was the only one to survive the destruction of the second temple. Others suggest there was a purposeful standardization of the text. The latter seems more likely for two reasons: (1) There was a desire to provide a consistent standard for debates between Christians and Jews in the first century A.D. (cf. Justin Martyr, *Dialogue* 68). (2) Hillel the Elder needed a standardized text on which to base his seven rules of biblical hermeneutics (*Aboth of Rabbi Nathan* 37A).

The sheer number of manuscripts, as well as quotations in rabbinic literature, suggest that the proto-MT was the primary text maintained by the authoritative center of Judaism. At the same time, other textual traditions were also circulated (e.g., Septuagint; Samaritan Pentateuch). However, sometime during the first century A.D. the proto-MT apparently became the dominant textual tradition.

Are the texts available today an accurate reflection of the originals? To adequately answer this question requires some understanding of OT textual criticism, which we will now briefly explore.

OT Textual Criticism

Scholars agree that no single witness perfectly reproduces the original Hebrew text (generally called "Urtext") of the entire OT, and therefore textual criticism is necessary. *Textual criticism* is the science and art that seeks to determine the most reliable original wording of a text. It is a science because specific rules govern the evaluation of various types of copyist errors and readings, but it is also an art because these rules cannot be rigidly applied in every situation. The goal of OT textual criticism is to work back as closely as possible to the final form of the text as it was canonized and maintained by the scribes. Since the texts were transmitted over such a long period, one could expect that minor errors might have crept in. Comparison of various forms of the OT text helps determine the most plausible reading of the original texts. Intuition and common sense must guide this process. Informed judgments about a text depend upon one's familiarity with copyist errors, manuscripts, versions, and their authors.

Types of errors. Even given a strong desire to maintain an authoritative, standardized text, common copyist errors can creep in, including: confusion of similar letters, homophony (substitution of similar sounding letters or words), haplography (omission of a letter or word), dittography (doubling a letter or word), metathesis (reversal in the order of two letters or words), fusion (two words being joined as one), and fission (one word separated into two).

The process. Modern critical editions of the MT include the *BHS* (*Biblia Hebraica Stuttgartensia*) and the *BHQ* (*Biblia Hebraica Quinta*), which follow the Codex Leningradensis (A.D. 1008), and the Hebrew University Bible Project, which follows the Aleppo Codex (c. 930). They derive from the longest and, to date, most reliable textual tradition overall. This tradition was maintained by the Masoretes, and when compared to the Qumran manuscripts dated about 1,000 years earlier, was found to be very accurate. These critical editions also provide a summary of pertinent information from other sources in their textual apparatus. The process of OT textual criticism includes examining the external evidence from various Hebrew sources (e.g., Dead Sea Scrolls, Samaritan Pentateuch, medieval manuscripts) and versions (e.g., Septuagint, Latin Vulgate, etc.) to determine which is the most plausible original reading of the text.

When weighing evidence, scholars generally agree that the Hebrew sources take precedence over the versions, though versions sometimes contain what appears as a plausible original reading. Internal evidence is then examined to see if there are any hints to help determine the original reading (e.g., grammatical structures, common spelling). At times, discoveries from other ancient Semitic languages have shed light on previously unintelligible texts. Guidelines to use in determining the most plausible original readings include: (1) Which reading could most likely give rise to the others? (2) Which reading is most appropriate in its context? (3) The weight of the manuscript evidence is then evaluated to determine whether it may contain a secondary reading or gloss. Only a very small percentage of the Hebrew text has any questionable readings, and of these only a small portion make any significant difference in the meaning of the text.

Primary OT Sources

The following are the primary sources for present-day knowledge of the original OT text:

Codex Leningradensis: The oldest complete copy of the MT, dated to A.D. 1008. Both the *BHS* and the *BHQ* follow this text.

Aleppo Codex: The oldest, incomplete copy of the MT, dated to about A.D. 930. About one-quarter of this manuscript was burned by fire, but its text is very similar to the Codex Leningradensis. The Hebrew University Bible Project uses this text as a base.

Dead Sea Scrolls: More than 200 biblical manuscripts dated from about 250 B.C. to A.D. 135 from the area around the Dead Sea. The largest number of these texts agree closely with the readings of the proto-MT (35 percent of manuscripts) and help confirm the accuracy of the MT.

Conclusion

Although some textual puzzles remain, and though scholars still differ among themselves in how they weigh some of the evidence, careful application of these principles allows a high level of confidence that close access to the original texts does indeed exist. Moreover, ordinary English readers should not suppose that there are hundreds of significant textual variants whose existence is known only to specialized scholars, for all the variants that translation teams thought to be significant for interpreting the text have been indicated in the footnotes of the ESV and other modern English translations. Looking through those footnotes will show a reader that the significant variants affect far less than 1 percent of the words of the ESV text, and even among that 1 percent, there are no variants that would change any point of doctrine. Therefore, while some places remain where it is hard to be sure of the original reading (see ESV footnotes and the notes on specific verses in this Study Bible), as a general assessment it is safe to say that the OT text that is the basis of modern English translations is remarkably trustworthy. ◂

The Reliability of the New Testament Manuscripts

Today, any group of Christians gathered together can all read exactly the same words in their Bibles. That luxury is made possible by the invention of the movable-type printing press over five centuries ago. But such a luxury can also breed a false sense of confidence that the precise original wording of the Bible can be known. When it comes to the NT, the original 27 books disappeared long ago, probably within decades of their composition. Handwritten copies, or manuscripts, must be relied on to determine the wording of the original text. Yet no two manuscripts are exactly alike, and even the closest two early manuscripts have at least half a dozen differences per chapter (most of them inconsequential variations, however, as will be seen). The discipline known as NT textual criticism is thus needed because of these two facts: disappearance of the originals, and disagreements among the manuscripts.

But even though the original wording of the NT cannot be known, that fact is not necessarily cause for alarm. It is true that the NT manuscripts contain thousands of wording differences. It is also true that a few favorite passages are of dubious authenticity. But this is not the whole picture. Christians can, in fact, have a very high degree of confidence that what they have in their hands today is the Word of God.

This article's specific task is to (1) compare the number and antiquity of NT manuscripts with those of other ancient literature, (2) note the number and nature of the wording differences in the NT (including a discussion of a few of the more notable places in which the wording is in doubt), and (3) identify what is, and what is not, at stake in this discussion.

The Number and Antiquity of NT Manuscripts Compared with Other Ancient Literature

In comparison with the remaining manuscripts of any other ancient Greek or Latin literature, the NT suffers from an embarrassment of riches. It is almost incomprehensible to think about the disparity. When it comes to quantity of copies, the NT has no peer. More than 5,700 Greek NT manuscripts are still in existence, ranging in date from the early second century to the sixteenth century. To be sure, the earliest ones (i.e., through the 3rd century) are all fragmentary, but they cover a substantial amount of the NT. And Greek manuscripts do not tell the whole story. The NT was translated early on into a variety of languages, including Latin, Coptic, Syriac, Armenian, Georgian, Gothic, and Arabic. All told, there are between 20,000 and 25,000 handwritten copies of the NT in various languages. Yet if all of these were destroyed, the NT text could be reproduced almost in its entirety by quotations of it in sermons, tracts, and commentaries written by ancient teachers of the church (known as church fathers or Patristic writers). To date, over a million quotations from the NT by the church fathers have been cataloged.

How does this compare with the average classical author? The copies of the average ancient Greek or Latin author's writings number fewer than *20* manuscripts! Thus, the NT has well over 1,000 times as many manuscripts as the works of the average classical author.

When it comes to the temporal distance of the earliest copies of the NT from the original, NT textual critics again enjoy an abundance of materials. From 10 to 15 NT manuscripts were written within the first 100 years of the completion of the NT. To be sure, they are all fragmentary, but some of them are fairly sizable fragments, covering large portions of the Gospels or Paul's letters, for example. Within two centuries, the numbers increase to at least four dozen manuscripts. Of manuscripts produced before A.D. 400, an astounding 99 still exist—including the oldest complete NT, Codex Sinaiticus.

The gap, then, between the originals and the early manuscripts is relatively slim. By comparison, the average classical author has no copies for more than half a millennium.

Comparing the NT text to some better-known ancient authors, it still has no equal. The chart below illustrates this by comparing the copies of five Greco-Roman historians' works with the NT. If one is skeptical about what the original NT text said, that skepticism needs to be multiplied many times over when it comes to the writings of all other ancient Greek and Latin authors. Although it is true that there are some doubts about the precise wording of the original in some places, NT textual criticism has an unparalleled abundance of materials to work with, in terms of both quantity and age of manuscripts. Nothing else comes close.

The Number and Nature of the Wording Differences

The Greek NT, as it is known today, has approximately 138,000 words. The best estimate is that there are as many as 400,000 textual variants among the manuscripts. That means that, on average, for every word in the Greek NT there are almost three variants. If this were the only piece of data available, it might discourage anyone from attempting to recover the wording of the original. But the large number of variants is due to the large number of manuscripts. Hundreds of thousands of differences among the Greek manuscripts, ancient translations, and patristic commentaries exist only because tens of thousands of such documents exist. Further, the vast majority of textual alterations are accidental and trivial, and hence easy for textual critics to spot.

These textual differences can be broken down into four categories. The largest group involves *spelling and nonsense errors*. The single most common textual variant involves what is known as a movable "nu." This is an "n" that is placed at the end of certain words when the next word begins with a vowel. The same principle is seen in English: *a* book, *an* apple. Nonsense errors occur when a scribe wrote a word that makes no sense in its context, usually because of fatigue, inattentiveness, or misunderstanding of the text in front of him. Some of these errors are quite comical, such as "we were *horses* among you" (Gk. *hippoi*, "horses," instead of *ēpioi*, "gentle," or *nēpioi*, "little children") in 1 Thessalonians 2:7 in one late manuscript.

The second-largest group of variant readings consists of *minor changes, including synonyms and alterations, that do not affect translation*. A common variation is the use of the definite article with proper names. Greek can say, "*the* Barnabas," while English translations will drop the article. The manuscripts vary in having the article or not. Word-order differences account for many of the variants. But since Greek is a highly inflected language, word order does not affect meaning nearly as much as it does in English. These two phenomena can be illustrated in a sentence such as "Jesus loves John." In Greek, that sentence can be expressed in at least 16 different ways without affecting the basic sense. Factoring in spelling variations and other nontranslatable differences, "Jesus loves John" could, in fact, be a translation of hundreds of different Greek constructions. In this light, the fact that there are only three variants for every word in the NT, when the potential is seemingly infinitely greater, seems almost trivial.

The third-largest category of textual variants involves *meaningful changes that are not "viable."* "Viable" means that a variant has some plausibility of reflecting the wording of the original text. For example, in 1 Thessalonians 2:9, instead of "the gospel of *God*" (the reading of almost all the manuscripts), a late medieval copy has "the gospel of *Christ*." This is meaningful but not viable. There is little chance that one late manuscript could contain the original wording when the textual tradition is uniformly on the side of another reading.

The smallest category of textual changes involves *those that are both meaningful and viable*. These comprise less than one percent of all textual variants. "Meaningful" means that the variant changes the meaning of the text *to some degree*. It may not be terribly significant, but if the variant affects one's understanding of the passage, then it is meaningful. Most of these meaningful and viable differences involve just a word or a phrase. For example, in Romans 5:1, some manuscripts read "we have (Gk. *echomen*) peace," while others have "let us have (Gk. *echōmen*) peace." The difference in Greek is but a single letter, but the meaning is changed. If "we have peace" is authentic, Paul is speaking about believers' status with God; if "let us have peace" is authentic, the apostle is urging Christians to enjoy the experience of this harmony with God in their lives. As important as this textual problem is, neither variant contradicts any of the teachings of Scripture elsewhere, and both readings state something that is theologically sound.

There are two large textual variants in the entire NT, each involving 12 verses: Mark 16:9–20 and John 7:53–8:11. The earliest and best manuscripts lack these verses. In addition, these passages do not fit well with the authors' style. Although much emotional baggage is attached to these two texts for many Christians, no essential truths are lost if these verses are not authentic.

Should the presence of textual variants, then, undermine the confidence of ordinary laypersons as they read the Bible in their own language? No—actually, the op-

Comparison of Extant Historical Documents

Histories	Oldest Manuscripts	Number Surviving
Livy 59 B.C.–A.D. 17	4th century A.D.	27
Tacitus A.D. 56–120	9th century A.D.	3
Suetonius A.D. 69–140	9th century A.D.	200+
Thucydides 460–400 B.C.	1st century A.D.	20
Herodotus 484–425 B.C.	1st century A.D.	75
New Testament	c. 100–150 A.D.	c. 5,700 (counting only Greek manuscripts) plus more than 10,000 in Latin, more than a million quotations from the church fathers, etc.

posite is the case. The abundance of variants is the result of the very large number of remaining NT manuscripts, which itself gives a stronger, not weaker, foundation for knowing what the original manuscripts said.

In addition, modern Bible translation teams have not kept the location of major variants a secret but have indicated the ones they think to be most important in the footnotes of all "essentially literal" modern English translations, so that laypersons who read these footnotes can see where these variants are and what they say. (Textual variants are noted in the ESV with a footnote that begins, "Some manuscripts . . .") The absence of any such footnote (which is the case with far more than 99 percent of the words in the English NT) indicates that these translation teams have a high degree of confidence that the words in their English translation accurately represent the words of the NT as they were originally written.

What Is at Stake?

The most significant textual variants certainly alter the meaning of various verses. And where the meaning of verses is changed, paragraphs and even larger units of thought are also affected to some degree. At times, a particular doctrine may not, after all, be affirmed in a given passage, depending on the textual variant. But this is not the same thing as saying that such a doctrine is denied. Just because a particular verse may not affirm a cherished doctrine does not mean that that doctrine cannot be found in the NT. In the final analysis, no cardinal doctrine, no essential truth, is affected by any viable variant in the surviving NT manuscripts. For example, the deity of Christ, his resurrection, his virginal conception, justification by faith, and the Trinity are not put in jeopardy because of any textual variation. Confidence can therefore be placed in the providence of God in preserving the Scriptures.

In sum, although scholars may not be certain of the NT wording in a number of verses, for the vast majority of the words in the NT the modern English translations accurately represent what the original authors wrote, and therefore these translations can be trusted as reproducing the very words of God. ◂

Archaeology and the Bible

Archaeology and the Reliability of the Old Testament

Definition of Archaeology

Archaeology may be defined as *the systematic study of the material remains of human behavior in the past*. It includes written documents and objects of everyday life that are preserved in a fragile or ruined condition. In reality, as archaeologist Stuart Piggott famously remarked, archaeology is the "science of rubbish." Indeed, archaeologists spend their time and efforts in long-forgotten heaps of ancient refuse: broken pots, shattered buildings, and crumbling documents.

The Purpose and Aim of Archaeology

The aim of archaeology is *to discover, record, observe, and preserve the buried remains of antiquity and to use them to help reconstruct ancient life*. In fact, archaeology is merely one of numerous disciplines that contribute to the understanding of ancient times and ways. Other fields, such as paleography and epigraphy (the study of ancient writing systems and inscriptions), history, linguistics, numismatics (the study of coins), and literature are also utilized to recover antiquity. Archaeology can paint only part of the picture; it is not exhaustive. For example, the site of Megiddo has been heavily excavated since the end of the nineteenth century, and yet only a slice of it has been unearthed. What archaeology provides for the reconstruction of ancient life at Megiddo is piecemeal and fragmentary. One cannot expect a complete picture through archaeology alone.

Archaeology in the lands of the Bible has a checkered past. It began in the mid-nineteenth century with Western pioneers who traveled throughout Palestine on horseback, compass in hand, attempting to identify and mark ancient sites from the time of the Bible. Actual excavation did not begin until the end of that century and, unfortunately, much of the work was no more than treasure-hunting. The object often was to recover as many valuable relics as possible in the shortest time. Early archaeologists would not hesitate to use gunpowder to blast open a pyramid or a burial chamber. Mummy hunters in Egypt literally waded through piles of discarded coffins to reach their prey. Much has changed since those early days. Today excavation is systematic, scientific, and multidisciplinary.

Much of archaeology in the lands of the Bible focuses on sites that have been occupied for hundreds and even thousands of years. The site of Megiddo has occupational remains dating from the Neolithic period (c. 5000 B.C.) to the Persian period (5th–4th centuries B.C.). Such settlements are called "tells" (from the Arabic word; cf. Hb. *tel*, "heap, mound," Josh. 8:28; 11:13; Jer. 30:18; 49:2), which are artificial mounds. The first settlers would come to an area and build there, usually for three reasons: defense, a dependable water source, and a reliable food source. When the first settlement was destroyed by any of a number of causes, succeeding builders normally built a new settlement directly on top of the previous rubble. After each settlement, the mound would grow higher and thus be of greater strategic value. A tell, then, is like a layered cake in which each layer was put down sequentially, the most modern period being on top. The goal of the archaeologist is to disassemble in reverse the layers of the tell, and then to reconstruct the history and culture of the people who lived there; in other words, to dig up the story that is hidden in the mound.

Three primary categories of remains are uncovered through excavation: pottery, architecture, and various other small finds. Of the three, pottery is especially important for archaeology because of its durability and changeability. Pottery is found in every layer of a site because it lasts, and each layer has its own distinctive and typical pottery. By comparing pottery from different sites, archaeologists are able to derive a dating sequence and order for those locations.

The Relationship of Archaeology to the Biblical Disciplines

No greater dilemma exists in archaeology in the land of the Bible than the question of what motivates excavation. What is the relationship of biblical studies to the scientific discipline of archaeology? What is the place of the scientific disciplines in archaeology? Is there a place for "biblical archaeology" today?

Historically, archaeology in Palestine has been uniquely the work of biblical scholars. Many of the archaeology pioneers of the nineteenth century were trained in and motivated by biblical studies. Edward Robinson (1794–1863), often considered the father of scientific topography and archaeology of Palestine, was primarily trained in Hebrew and the OT. The first systematic excavators of Palestine were biblical scholars such as W. F. Albright, N. Glueck, and G. E. Wright. In the second half of the twentieth century, however, there was a loud call from the scientific community for a distinct separation between biblical studies and archaeological research. The argument was that the relationship between the two is largely artificial, and now it was time for archaeology to stand on its own as a scientific discipline. It is only natural, however, that the two disciplines work hand in hand because they are a source of knowledge and discovery for each other.

Today, a proper balance is necessary between archaeology in Palestine and biblical studies. While there have been some attempts to use archaeological finds to deconstruct ancient history and the life-setting of antiquity, the aim should rather be reconstruction: a harmonization in which biblical studies, archaeology, and other disciplines are used to recover and to understand the way people lived in the times and lands of the Bible. A prime purpose of archaeology is to shed light on the historical and material contexts in which the stories of the Bible took place. Thus, archaeology provides a life-setting for biblical texts. In that regard, archaeology can be a confirmatory tool, especially when the textual and archaeological evidence converge.

A good example of how archaeology illumines the Bible is the case of the Egyptian pharaoh Shishak and his invasion of Israel and Judah at the close of the tenth century B.C. This attack is mentioned in 1 Kings 14:25–26: "In the fifth year of King Rehoboam, Shishak king of Egypt came up against Jerusalem. He took away the treasures of the house of the LORD and the treasures of the king's house. He took away everything." Extrabiblical sources confirm that this attack did take place, and they provide a wider understanding of it than what is recorded in the Bible. At the temple of Amun at Karnak, Shoshenk I (Shishak) built the Bubastite Portal, and on it appears a relief of Shishak's invasion of Palestine. The relief contains the names of various sites on the campaign route that were either captured or destroyed.

One conclusion that may be drawn from the Bubastite Portal is that Shishak's invasion of Palestine included more than a campaign against Jerusalem, and was leveled against the kingdoms of both Israel and Judah. Another important point is that Jerusalem is not mentioned on the relief. Why not? It is likely that it does not appear because it was not captured. King Rehoboam of Judah eluded Jerusalem's capture by paying heavy tribute to the Egyptians (as is recorded in 1 Kings 14:25–26). In this case, the biblical evidence illumines archaeological finds.

Archaeology provides even further insight into this invasion. One of the cities listed as either captured or destroyed by Shishak is Megiddo. At the site of Megiddo, excavators uncovered a stele (or inscribed pillar) of Shishak on which is written two common titles for Shishak. Stelae like this one were commonly set up by pharaohs to claim a region as a vassal (or subject) state. In addition, there is a "destruction layer" at Megiddo that can be associated with the campaign of Shishak. Further evidence for this association appears at the site of Ta'anach, where a huge destruction layer covered the site. The pottery sealed beneath the destruction is the same as that of the destruction layer at Megiddo. Ta'anach was also mentioned as a city subdued by Shishak in the relief of the Bubastite Portal. It is indeed compelling to relate the destruction layers at Ta'anach and Megiddo to the Shishak campaign of the late tenth century B.C.

Archaeology complements both the Hebrew and Egyptian written sources as well in regard to the historical event of Shishak's invasion of Israel and Judah. A fuller picture of the event is painted by bringing these separate sources together. And this convergence is not unique: the biblical authors set events like the invasions of Sennacherib and Nebuchadnezzar in their proper chronological framework and setting (cf. 2 Kings 18:13; 19:16; 24:1–10; 1 Chron. 6:15; 2 Chron. 32:1–22). These events are confirmed and filled out by contemporary ancient Near Eastern texts—the prism of Sennacherib for the former campaign, and the Lachish Letters for the latter. Excavation work has also brought to light numerous destruction layers at Judean sites that reflect both of those campaigns.

As for the bearing of archaeological study on the historical reliability of the OT, what has been the result of many decades of archaeological investigation? The answer is simple: archaeology has time and again supported and confirmed the biblical record, and many such examples are mentioned in the notes in this Study Bible. ◂

Archaeology and the Reliability of the New Testament

Christians have often looked to archaeology to provide confirmation of the biblical record, which it indeed can. Yet the main advantage of archaeology lies in its ability to bring twenty-first-century readers into physical contact with the cultures in which Jesus and his apostles lived and ministered.

Archaeological Methodology

Archaeology today stands at the intersection of science and the humanities. Gone are the days when the amateur could take a spade and go hunting for treasures. Modern archaeology requires careful procedures, meticulous recording techniques, and a vast array of scientific technologies. Yet after all the data has been accumulated, the most interesting jobs entail interpreting the evidence.

Excavations at NT cities often uncover large structures such as monuments, tombs, and buildings (whether residential, civic, or commercial). These can be quite interesting, yet the smaller finds are often equally (if not more) illuminating. Such small finds include inscriptions, coins, papyri, figurines, and day-to-day artifacts (e.g., pottery, glass, furniture, and remnants of clothing). Visual art (such as mosaics, frescoes [paintings on moist plaster], friezes [carved reliefs], and statuary) can reveal many aspects of ancient life—from dress to social and religious practices.

Archaeological digs proceed slowly, layer by layer, in well-marked squares in order to understand each square's relative chronology. Written records, drawings, and photographs accompany every square. While sophisticated dating procedures can be employed (such as radiocarbon), the primary techniques of dating archaeological strata typically still rely on pottery finds (both their form and their fabric) or on datable coins and inscriptions. The type of building can be identified by its architectural style, but this may not yield results as precise as those provided by the firmer dates of coins and inscriptions. Most dating methods require some degree of interpretation. It is important to realize that many excavated structures and artifacts from a city may stem from a time before or after the NT; although these can still be pertinent to understanding the cultures of the apostolic period, caution should be employed when correlating them with the NT.

Because the complete excavation of a large site can take many decades, knowledge of most ancient places is limited.

For example, even though the ancient cities of Jerusalem, Rome, Ephesus, and Corinth have each been under excavation for over a century, much remains to be done in all of them. Thus, there should be caution concerning arguments from silence (claiming that because something has not been found, it does not exist). Furthermore, excavations have historically focused on the monumental architecture of those who were rich, while smaller residential structures (often constructed of short-lasting materials) may be underrepresented.

Interpreting Archaeological Finds

When there are varying opinions about a discovery, these usually occur at the level of interpretation. One of the initial interpretative acts of an excavator concerns "site identification"—discovering the ancient name of a known archaeological site. The identification of a particular locale synthesizes modern local traditions, ancient written sources, and the actual finds at that place (esp. inscriptions and coins). Sometimes biblical sites are hard to find, or more than one possibility exists. For example, both Cana (John 2:1) and Bethany across the Jordan (John 1:28) have more than one possible location. Fortunately, most NT towns are fairly well identified.

Particular architectural features within towns also require identification. Structures such as theaters and stadiums are fairly obvious, and baths have special features (such as particular heating systems), but understanding the use of other buildings may be complex. For example, the architecture of temples is often straightforward, but determining which deity was worshiped where can be difficult (e.g., the great temple in Corinth has been variously identified with Apollo or Athena). What was the purpose of a given civic building? Which set of shops in Corinth housed the meat market? In some cases, ancient literary sources may help (such as Pausanias's *Description of Greece*, essentially a 2nd-century A.D. tour guide), but often interpretation involves intricate arguments based on specific features.

Even ancient inscriptions can raise questions. Do any of the extant Sergius Paulus inscriptions relate to the governor of Cyprus in Acts 13:7? How does one interpret the unusual Greek reference to the "place of the Jews who also fear God" in Miletus (see note on Acts 20:17)? At times a name appears, such as the name "Caiaphas" on the side of a richly decorated ossuary (Jewish bone reburial box), and the identification with a NT person seems probable (see John 18:24). On other occasions, some media personalities are too quick to correlate ancient finds with NT figures. Many names mentioned in the NT were common, such as the Jewish names Jesus, Joseph, Mary, James, and Matthew. Thus, when someone claims that the bones of Jesus Christ have actually been found in one of a few extant Jerusalem ossuaries labeled "Jesus son of Joseph," skepticism is warranted, given that hundreds of people would have been so named in antiquity.

Certainly, archaeology involves scientific methods, but archaeological interpretation also requires professional competencies and a good bit of wisdom. Perhaps the best advice for those interested in archaeology would be to encourage them to read reliable sources and not to rely heavily on exciting new finds reported first in the popular media.

Archaeology and the Historicity of the NT

Many historical features of the NT can be supported from the archaeological record, and in fact one overwhelming result of archaeological research into the NT period has been to give strong confirmation to the NT writings' historical accuracy. For example, the Gospel of John evidences an amazingly accurate awareness of the geography of Palestine. John's descriptions of ancient Samaria have been confirmed by archaeology, including Samaritan worship on Mount Gerizim (4:20) and the location of Jacob's well (4:6). Concerning Jerusalem, John's Gospel carefully depicts the pool of Bethesda (5:2) and Solomon's colonnade (10:22–23), which archaeology has been able to authenticate. Also, discoveries in 2005 helped confirm John's portrayal of the pool of Siloam (9:7).

The book of Acts has been shown to well represent the geography of antiquity. Nearly every town in the book has been identified, and many cities have been excavated. The Acts record of Paul's travels to Rome, including his shipwreck, presents one of the most detailed and useful travel accounts from antiquity (Acts 27). Luke, the author of Acts, even knows the correct terms for specific governors—as shown by uncovered inscriptions mentioning the proconsul Gallio (18:12), the asiarchs of Ephesus (19:30–31), and the politarchs of Thessalonica (17:1, 6).

Many other examples could be cited of historical aspects of the NT also found in the archaeological record. Inscriptions mention NT figures such as Pontius Pilate (Luke 23:1) and Herod the Great (Matt. 2:1). The synagogue of Capernaum has been found beneath another structure from late antiquity (Mark 1:21). Crucifixions were performed with nails, as the Gospel of John indicates (John 20:25), and such nails survive. The cities addressed in Revelation 2–3 often have historical features that line up well with aspects of their biblical description.

Furthermore, archaeology occasionally provides the scholar with new discoveries of biblical manuscripts. Archaeologists are partially responsible for the fact that there are now thousands of Greek manuscripts of the NT and even more manuscripts of early NT translations. All these manuscripts, some from a time close to the age of the apostles, have made the NT the best-attested set of writings from antiquity (see the article on The Reliability of the New Testament Manuscripts, pp. 2587–2589).

Archaeology and NT Cultural Contexts

A fuller understanding of the meaning of the NT can be achieved by learning more about the world in which its human authors and recipients lived. Biblical interpretation begins with understanding the original meaning of each passage before applying it to one's contemporary life or situation. The original meaning was targeted toward people in particular cultures; the better those cultures are understood, the more accurately the NT can be interpreted. Archaeology can assist in this cultural understanding. In fact, while archaeological finds occasionally confirm the historicity of the NT, archaeological discoveries regularly provide insights into ancient culture. Moreover, archaeology serves as a reminder that NT events occurred in real time-space history.

If one were to tour with Paul the great Roman-era cities of his day, familiar features would appear at every juncture, and these can be reimagined with the aid of recent excavations. The shops and markets indicate a general prosperity in the cities. The civic structures show the power of Rome yet also suggest how it often worked through local governments. The theaters and odeions (buildings for music and recitations) testify to artistic endeavors, as do the many works of mosaic, fresco, and sculpture. The stadiums and their hero sculptures boast of athletic achievement. Baths, gymnasiums, and latrines evidence both the cultural aspiration to cleanliness and the training of youth. And all these theatrical, artistic, athletic, and civic functions were intricately tied to the cults of the pagan religions. More than anything, the modern reader would probably be shocked at how many pagan religious structures (from small niches to monumental temples) are found at seemingly every turn.

Inscriptions that exhibit Jewish symbols, names, and synagogue references significantly illustrate the great expanse of the Jewish Diaspora (Jews living outside the land of Palestine) throughout the Mesopotamian and Mediterranean world. Many synagogues have been found both inside and outside of Palestine. Jewish cultic objects, inscriptions, and other excavated remains increasingly reveal the complex interplay that existed between Jew and Gentile in Galilee. From Judea, Samaria, and Galilee, the structures of Jesus' day are being unearthed.

Aspects of daily life can be understood by examining everything from the most mundane pot to the huge homes of the elite (whether in Jerusalem, Pompeii, or Ephesus). Christians adapted some homes to serve as churches (1 Cor. 16:19). Clothing and personal aesthetics are displayed in art and are attested in the occasional preserved find (such as 2,000-year-old sandals from the Judean desert). Pottery, glass, furniture, and other artifacts help explain how people lived. Animal bones, ancient seeds, and farm tools reveal agricultural practices. Coins illustrate rulers and the symbols they valued.

Ancient tombs testify to views of death. The Roman world had a range of burial practices—from cremation, to shallow graves, to family cave-tombs, to monumental mausoleums. Some Jewish family tombs clearly employed rolling stones as doors (see Mark 15:46). Jewish people would reuse their burial niches, and around Jerusalem they might rebury the skeletons in ossuaries (reburial boxes). People were often buried alongside cultural objects (perhaps viewed as special to a person or as needed in the life to come)—these tomb remains are frequently some of the best-preserved small objects from any excavation. Modern osteologists analyze excavated skeletons for such matters as age, gender, general health, and cause of death.

Papyri (such as those from Oxyrhynchus or Tebtunis) provide ancient letters and legal documents not otherwise passed down in the literary record. These give a "behind the scenes" view into how people lived. Other excavated writings allow access to previously unknown literature. Especially important have been texts from post-NT Gnosticism (found at Nag Hammadi) and the extensive collection of Jewish manuscripts from Qumran, Masada, Nahal Hever, and Murabbaat.

More could certainly be said about how archaeology has enhanced the knowledge of the cultures in which NT people lived. Yet this article should suffice to show that archaeology, in addition to its significant contribution in supporting the historical reliability of the NT, renders an even greater service by inviting readers into the world of Jesus and his followers. ◀

The Original Languages of the Bible

Hebrew and Aramaic, and How They Work

Introduction

The main language of the OT is Classical Hebrew, but some parts are in Aramaic (Ezra 4:7–6:18; 7:12–26; Jer. 10:11; Dan. 2:4–7:28). Two words of Aramaic also occur in the place name *Jegar-sahadutha* in Genesis 31:47.

The form of Hebrew found in the Bible was probably spoken from as early as 1500 B.C. to some time after 400 B.C. Although Aramaic (the official international language of the Assyrian, Babylonian, and Persian Empires) came increasingly into daily use among Jews, many Jews (at least in the Jerusalem area) continued to use a form of Hebrew (which later developed into "Mishnaic" Hebrew, the language of the Mishnah). Hebrew documents with varying degrees of similarity to Biblical Hebrew have been found at Qumran and in the desert of Judah, with dates from the second century B.C. to the second century A.D. The synagogues in Palestine retained the use of Hebrew as a sacred language. Modern Hebrew, which was developed in the late nineteenth and early twentieth centuries, is based on the earlier forms of Hebrew and is one of the official languages of the modern state of Israel (founded in 1948).

Both Hebrew and Aramaic are part of the wider family of languages that since 1781 have been labeled "Semitic," a name derived from that of Noah's son *Shem*. However, languages from this group were also spoken by some peoples (such as the Amorites, Babylonians, and Canaanites) that Genesis does not record as being descended from Shem.

Semitic Languages

While there are many Semitic languages, they can generally be organized according to the three regions where they were spoken: (1) East Semitic (Mesopotamia), including Old Akkadian, Assyrian, and Babylonian; (2) South-West Semitic (parts of northeastern Africa), including North Arabic (the language of the Qur'an) and Ethiopian; and (3) North-West Semitic (Syro-Palestine), including Amoritic and Ugaritic, along with Hebrew, Phoenician, Moabite (the Canaanite branch), and Aramaic and Syriac (the Aramaic branch). When considered together, the Semitic languages have a longer continuous history of being written than almost any other group.

Alphabet

Hebrew, Aramaic, and some neighboring Semitic languages share an alphabet of 22 consonant letters only (23 if the *sin* and *shin* are counted separately) and are read from right to left. The shape and order of these Hebrew characters had been distilled by the second millennium B.C., before the time of Moses (and the writing of the OT). This alphabet was then passed by way of the Phoenicians to the Greeks, while the Hebrew and Aramaic forms of the script began to diverge. The form of Hebrew script generally used until at least the Babylonian exile, and still found in some Dead Sea Scrolls, is known as the Paleo-Hebrew script. Some of its letters still resemble their equivalents in the Greek alphabet. During the rule of the Persians (539–332 B.C.) the square Aramaic (or Assyrian) script was adopted for writing Hebrew, with the result that the forms of letters originally used for Aramaic are now almost universally associated in people's minds with Hebrew (see chart, p. 2596).

The alphabet itself has had an effect on the form of certain texts in the OT. A number of the Psalms (Psalms 9; 10; 25; 34; 37; 111; 112; 119; 145) are arranged as types of acrostic poems composed around the 22 letters of the Hebrew alphabet, as are the first four chapters of Lamentations (see Introduction to Lamentations: Literary Features).

Matres Lectionis

In order to give further precision to pronunciation of words, and to clarify ambiguities between words that shared the same consonants, three of the consonant letters came to be used to represent vowels. The letter *h* (ה) represented *a* or *e*; *w* (ו) represented *o* or *u*, and *y* (י) represented *e* or *i*. In inscriptions from biblical times, these *matres lectionis* (Latin for "mothers of reading," i.e., "vowel letters") were rare before the exile, and it is therefore often held that preexilic biblical writings that display extensive use of *matres lectionis* had these letters added after the time of composition to help readers understand the words properly. It is still the case, however, that earlier texts, such as the Pentateuch, are more sparing in the use of these than, e.g., postexilic writings such as the books of Chronicles.

Roots

Semitic words are generally based on so-called roots consisting of three consonants. Vowels and a limited range of other consonants are arranged around these roots to produce words. Consider the following Hebrew words:

melek ("king")
malkah ("queen")
mamlakah ("kingdom")
malak ("he reigned")
malkut ("reign")

The constant element in all of these words is the consonant sequence *m-l-k*, which is associated with royal rule. Sometimes a particular word may occur only once in the whole OT, and the question naturally arises as to how its meaning is known. If, however, there are other words from the same root, its meaning can be identified in relation to them (with due consideration given also to its context).

Hebrew name	Square (Assyrian or Aramaic) script	Paleo-Hebrew form	Sound	Traditional transliteration
Aleph	א	𐤀	glottal stop	'
Beth	ב	𐤁	b	b
Gimel	ג	𐤂	g	g
Daleth	ד	𐤃	d	d
He	ה	𐤄	h	h
Waw	ו	𐤅	w	w
Zayin	ז	𐤆	s	z
Heth	ח	𐤇	ch ("loch")	ḥ
Teth	ט	𐤈	t	ṭ
Yod	י	𐤉	y	y
Kaph	כ, ך	𐤊	k	k
Lamedh	ל	𐤋	l	l
Mem	מ, ם	𐤌	m	m
Nun	נ, ן	𐤍	n	n
Samekh	ס	𐤎	s	s
Ayin	ע	𐤏	—	'
Pe	פ, ף	𐤐	p	p
Tsadhe	צ, ץ	𐤑	ts	ṣ
Qoph	ק	𐤒	q	q
Resh	ר	𐤓	r	r
Sin	שׂ	𐤔	s	ś
Shin	שׁ	𐤔	sh	š
Taw	ת	𐤕	t	t

(The transliteration style of Hebrew characters followed in this Study Bible has been somewhat simplified from the more precise traditional transliteration depicted in this chart. See transliteration charts, pp. 2597, 2599.)

Masoretic Pointing

The OT writings were produced using consonants only. Pronunciation was possible by adding vowel sounds to the consonantal words, and thus the particular vocalization and accentuation of Biblical Hebrew was understood aurally, and was therefore taught and memorized and passed down to each successive generation orally through the Jewish schools and synagogues (cf. the anecdote in Babylonian Talmud, *Baba Bathra* 21a–b). However, as Biblical Hebrew was no longer in use as a spoken language among the Jews, and in order to avoid ambiguities in the text by ensuring that the correct pronunciation was not lost, Jewish textual scholars between the fifth and eighth centuries A.D. devised and inserted into the OT text a system of vowel points to guide readers in how the words should be correctly vocalized and accented. These Jewish scribes, known as the Masoretes (from the Hb. *masorah*, "what was handed down," i.e., "tradition"), applied this system of "pointing" by adding marks (dots and strokes) around the consonants without disturbing or changing any of them. The Masoretes thus "pointed" the Hebrew text of the OT with symbols indicating vowel sounds so that the traditional way Scripture had been read and heard in the synagogues would be preserved even though Biblical Hebrew was ceasing to be spoken among the Jewish people. Here is an example of the word "king" in unpointed and pointed form:

Unpointed	מלך	*mlk*
Pointed	מֶלֶךְ	*melek*

In addition to providing guidance as to which vowels occur within a word, the Masoretic pointing also distinguishes between different pronunciations of the same letter. The so-called *begadkephath* letters—*b, g, d, k, p*, and *t*—also had the spirant (or fricative) pronunciations *bh, gh, dh, kh, ph*, and *th*. A single dot (called a *daghesh*) inside the letter (e.g., בּ) would specify the "hard" pronunciation *b* rather than the "soft" pronunciation *bh* (ב), etc. By the position of a point, Masoretic notation also distinguished two different sounds that lay behind the Hebrew letter ש. Hebrew שׂ represented *s* (*sin*) and שׁ represented *sh* (*shin*). Medieval Hebrew manuscripts also contain a further set of marks known as accents or cantillation signs, which indicate division and cohesion in the text and specify the way the text should be sung in the synagogue.

Masoretes actively worked in three areas—Babylon, Palestine, and Tiberias—and eventually it was the tradition from Tiberias (called Tiberian vocalization), particularly the work of the Ben Asher family in Tiberias (c. A.D. 900), which is preserved in the Hebrew Bible today (i.e., the Masoretic text [MT]; thus also the *Biblia Hebraica Stuttgartensia* [BHS]). However, a further guide to the historical pronunciation of words is available in the tradition of pronunciation of the Pentateuch among the Samaritans. On the surface, the Samaritan pronunciation usually seems rather different from the Tiberian vocalization. Yet when historical sound changes are taken into account, it often shows regular correspondence to that of the Masoretes.

Verbal System

Almost all Hebrew verbs are built upon three root or stem consonants (alluded to above), though these will rarely appear in the text without an accompanying affix of some kind. There are seven main stem formations (or *binyanim*) of Hebrew verbs: *Qal, Niphal, Piel, Pual, Hithpael, Hiphil*, and *Hophal*. Each of these seven divisions convey something different about the relationship between the subject and the verbal action (active, passive, reflexive, causative, etc.), and these are apparent by the characteristic changes that the same three-consonant verbal stem undergoes within each division (though most verbs do not occur in all seven stem formations).

The many structural differences between Hebrew and English influence translation. Whereas English has a system of verbal *tenses* (i.e., time of action—past, present, future, etc.), many grammarians prefer to say that Hebrew has two verbal *aspects* (i.e., kind of action—complete, incomplete, etc.) known as the perfect and imperfect. In the simplest terms, these aspects consider actions as either complete or incomplete, respectively. Thus, the Hebrew imperfect is frequently used for referring both to events in the future and to repeated events in the past. A further complication is the relationship that the perfect and the imperfect verb have with the conjunction "and" (Hebrew letter *waw*). When *waw* (ו) attaches as a prefix to a perfect or imperfect verb, it may at times appear to reverse the function of the perfect or imperfect aspect so that the perfect then communicates incomplete action and the imperfect communicates complete action, even if, from a historical perspective, this is not actually what is happening (it actually preserves an old tense form). Such differences between the Hebrew and English verbal systems can make translation difficult at times. However, in most prose texts, the temporal location of the narrative is immediately clear and, consequently, so is the way in which one should render a passage. Poetic texts are more complex, but there is still a surprising agreement between English translations as to which tense to use.

The *Waw* Particle

Closely connected with the verbal system is the ubiquity of *waw* (וְ; "and") in the Hebrew Bible. It is used to begin books with no previous connection with another narrative (e.g., Esther, Ezekiel, Jonah) and is the main particle connecting clauses in prose texts. Although Hebrew has some particles that carry senses such as "but," "therefore," and "because," these words are less commonly used than *waw*, which in connection with various clauses can be rendered by a range of terms. The ESV renders *waw* by the neutral "and" where appropriate, but also uses words such as "now" (Judg. 2:1), "so" (Judg. 2:14), "then" (Judg. 2:16), and "but" (Judg. 2:19) when the context calls for it.

Prepositions

Hebrew also has fewer prepositions than English, with the result that the same Hebrew preposition can be rendered in a variety of ways. For instance, renderings of the preposition *b* (בּ) may include "in," "on," "by," and "with." Hebrew has no word for "of," but the possessive and other relationships expressed by English "of" can be represented in Hebrew by using the "construct state." In the construct state, a noun is placed immediately before another noun in an inseparable (attached) position. Sometimes this involves a change in the form of the first noun as it loses stress. Thus, the underlined word is in the construct state in the following examples: *melek* ("king") + *yisra'el* ("Israel") → <u>*melek*</u> *yisra'el* ("king *of* Israel"); *malkah* ("queen") + *yisra'el* ("Israel") → <u>*malkat*</u> *yisra'el* ("queen *of* Israel").

Articles

Hebrew has a definite article: *h* (הַ) precedes the noun, usually with a short *a*-vowel (ַ) and doubling of the initial consonant of the noun. There is no indefinite article in Biblical Hebrew. Thus *melek* means "king" or "a king," but *hammelek* means "the king." In poetic texts, however, the definite article is used more sparingly, and it is therefore sometimes legitimate to use a definite article in translating

Transliteration of Hebrew Words in the ESV Study Bible

CONSONANTS

Letter	Name of Letter	Transliteration
א	aleph	' (a closing single quotation mark)
ב	beth	b
ג	gimel	g
ד	daleth	d
ה	he	h
ו	waw	w
ז	zayin	z
ח	heth	kh (but h in *hesed*)
ט	teth	t
י	yod	y
כ, ך	kaph, final kaph	k
ל	lamedh	l
מ, ם	mem, final mem	m
נ, ן	nun, final nun	n
ס	samekh	s
ע	ayin	' (an opening single quotation mark)
פ, ף	pe, final pe	p
צ, ץ	tsadhe, final tsadhe	ts
ק	qoph	q
ר	resh	r
שׂ	sin	s
שׁ	shin	sh
ת	taw	t

VOWELS

Symbol	Name of Vowel	Transliteration
ַ	patakh, furtive patakh	a
ָ	qamets	a
הָ	final qamets he	ah
ֶ	segol	e
ֵ	tsere	e
ֵי	tsere yod	e
ִ	hireq	i
ִי	hireq yod	i
ָ	qamets hatuph	o
ֹ	holem	o
וֹ	full holem	o
ֻ	qibbuts	u
וּ	shureq	u
ֳ	hateph qamets	o
ֲ	hateph patakh	a
ֱ	hateph segol	e
ְ	vocal shewa	e
	daghesh or mapiq	if a vowel precedes a daghesh, double the consonant

a Hebrew phrase that lacks one (as in the ESV rendering "in the scroll of the book," in Ps. 40:7).

Gender and Number

Hebrew has two genders (masculine and feminine) and three numbers (singular, dual, and plural). The dual is used only to refer to two items that occur in a pair (e.g., "eyes," "knees," "teeth," "millstones"). Verbs and pronouns also distinguish between a masculine and a feminine form of the second person ("you") in singular and plural forms, and between a masculine and a feminine form of the third-person plural ("they"). The distinction between the genders of the pronouns plays a significant part in the ESV identification of speakers in the Song of Solomon (see, e.g., ESV footnote on Song 1:11).

Diversity

The Hebrew of the OT is not uniform. Certain songs, such as the Song of Deborah (Judges 5) and the Song of Moses (Ex. 15:1–18), display archaic linguistic features. Though there is still a strong underlying linguistic unity to the OT, the language found throughout the 39 books shows that the OT was composed over a considerable period of time. Moreover, the language of the OT also reflects dialectal differences (cf. Judg. 12:6). Occasionally features of certain OT texts are identified by scholars as coming from the northern kingdom (Israel), as opposed to Judah, for example.

Aramaic

The term "Aramaic" comes from the people of Aram (an ancient region of upper Mesopotamia), the Arameans, whom Old Akkadian writings mention as early as the third millennium B.C. During the eighth and seventh centuries B.C., the Assyrian Empire controlled much of the ancient Near East, and Aramaic spread in usage as an international language (cf. 2 Kings 18:26; Isa. 36:11) until the Persian Empire of the sixth century B.C. established it as the official language. The few Aramaic sections of the OT (Gen. 31:47; Ezra 4:8–6:18; 7:12–26; Jer. 10:11; Dan. 2:4–7:28) fit clearly within the category of Imperial Aramaic, the language of Persian administration. Much of the grammatical description of Biblical Hebrew given above could, with minor changes, also apply to Aramaic. Eventually, Aramaic came into daily use with many Jews, especially those in Galilee. Aramaic words appear in the NT on the lips of Jesus (e.g., Mark 5:41; 7:34), and the name Golgotha (Mark 15:22) is Aramaic in form. The term of respectful address, *'abba'*, seems also to be Aramaic, but it became standard in later Hebrew as well. The expression *ephphatha* ("be opened!" Mark 7:34) may be Aramaic, though some think it is the equivalent form in Hebrew. Paul uses the Aramaic expression *marana tha* ("our Lord, come!") in 1 Corinthians 16:22.

Conclusion

While Biblical Hebrew enjoyed over 1,000 years of existence as a spoken language—from the middle of the second millennium B.C. until the close of the B.C. era—it has never truly "died" but continues to thrive today through the perpetual study and translation of the writings of the OT Scriptures. Furthermore, it is still actively spoken and used in Jewish religious life and synagogues around the world. It is taught and passed down in both Christian seminaries and Jewish yeshivas. And because of its use by God as the language of the OT, it will continue to enjoy a detailed preservation and rich textual tradition virtually unparalleled by any other ancient language. ◀

Greek, and How It Works

Background

Starting in May of 334 B.C., Alexander, the 21-year-old king of Macedon, led his victorious army through four pitched battles, two sieges, and innumerable smaller engagements that enabled him to conquer territory that now goes under the names of Turkey, Syria, Lebanon, Israel, Egypt, Iraq, Iran, and Afghanistan. Reaching the banks of the Beas River in Pakistan, he reluctantly turned back as his exhausted troops threatened mutiny. Three years later, in 323 B.C., he died (at age 32) in Babylon, just as he was planning an expedition all the way from Egypt along the North African coast to the Atlantic.

When Alexander died, his empire broke up into separate kingdoms headed by his disgruntled generals. But he had changed the world. In the old, now liberated cities of Asia Minor—Ephesus and Pergamum—as well as in the newly founded cities of the Middle East—Antioch and Alexandria—the culture and language of the colonial aristocracy was Greek. Three centuries after Alexander's death, when the life and teaching of Jesus of Nazareth was written down, the language used was not Jesus' native Aramaic but Greek, which, thanks to Alexander's conquests, had become the common language of the Mediterranean world. The conclusion now universally accepted by philologists is that the Greek of the NT, in all essential respects, is the vernacular Koine of the first century A.D., the language of the Roman imperial period.

Koine Greek

"Koine" means "common" in the sense of pertaining to the public at large. Hence, "Koine Greek" means the language commonly spoken everywhere—the basic means of communication of people throughout the Roman Empire. This dialect was basically the late Attic vernacular, spoken in Athens, with dialectal and provincial influences. In addition to the Greek NT, the Koine has left other literary monuments that are invaluable sources of light on the sacred text, including papyri, inscriptions, the writings of numerous Jewish and early Christian authors, and above all the Septuagint, the ancient version of the OT that became the Bible of the early church and was used extensively by the NT writers.

Koine Greek itself exhibits three important characteristics. The first, *semantic change*, is a natural feature of any language. The meanings of certain words were weakened in the Koine period. For example, the noun *dōma* meant "house" or "room" in Classical Greek, but in the NT it came to mean "roof" of a house (Luke 5:19). In the NT the preposition *eis* can mean "in" as well as "into," though it meant only "into" in Classical Greek. The conjunction *hina* has a much wider meaning in Koine than "in order that," which was the meaning in Classical Greek. For instance, *hina* is often used in content clauses simply to mean "that." The tendency in Koine to use the comparative degree of the adjective for the superlative may also be noted. Second, Koine Greek exhibits *greater simplicity* than Classical Greek. This is seen primarily in the composition of its sentences, which tend toward coordination rather than subordination of clauses. Finally, Koine Greek shows unmistakable traces of a tendency toward *more explicit* (some would say more redundant) *expression*, as seen, for example, in the use of pronouns as subjects of verbs and the use of prepositional phrases to replace simple cases. Adverbs abound, as do parenthetical statements and emphatic expressions such as "each and every" and "the very same."

At the same time, Koine Greek was not entirely uniform. Various literary levels existed, depending on the writer's background, education, or even sources. In the first century A.D., some writers even attempted to turn back the clock by advocating a return to the old classical form of Greek, decrying the Koine as a debased form of the language. The artificial style they produced (called "Atticistic" Greek) contrasted with the dialect of everyday life.

Styles of Greek in the NT

The NT itself reveals several styles of Greek among its authors. The highly literary epistle to the Hebrews, with its careful progression of argument and elevated diction, lies at one extreme. Luke and Acts also reveal good literary style, though the author (Luke) is able to vary his style considerably (cf. the colloquial Greek of Peter's speech in Acts 15:7–11 with the rhetorical nature of Paul's Areopagus speech in Acts 17:22–31, or the Classical introduction in Luke 1:1–4 to the more Septuagintal style of Luke 1:5–2:52). Paul's Greek is more or less colloquial, but that may be partly due to his amanuenses, the secretaries who wrote from his dictation. At the other end of the spectrum lies the grammar of Revelation, which may reflect the work of a Semitic-speaking person who lacks a polished knowledge of Greek (though many of the idioms John uses have direct parallels in colloquial papyri texts).

Greek Linguistics

Greek linguistics has emerged as one of the most fundamental disciplines in biblical studies—as important, e.g., as the study of molecular physics in the natural sciences. Biblical scholars have recently become concerned with the problems of language to a degree equaled only in the early history of modern comparative linguistics, when NT scholars such as Deissmann and Moulton began demolishing the myth of "Holy Ghost" Greek (the belief that God created a special language in which to inscripturate the NT). Today several scholars are specifically interested in what they call the "semantics of biblical language."

It is a central concern of semantics that a clear distinction be maintained between words as linguistic units and the concepts associated with them. All languages have several ways of expressing a concept, and rarely does a concept consist of only one word. This confusion of word and concept is one of the chief faults of Kittel's *Theological Dictionary of the New Testament*. In treating words as if they were concepts, it incorrectly implies that the words themselves contain the various theological meanings assigned to them. But the meanings of words are determined from the way they are used in context. There is now consensus that interpreters must work at the level of the paragraph to discern meaning.

The capacity of a word to have two or more meanings is technically known as *polysemy*—a particular form of a word can belong to different fields of meaning, only one of which need be its semantic contribution to a single sentence or context. The principle of polysemy is frequently ignored in exegesis, leading to what is called the fallacy of "illegitimate totality transfer," which occurs when the various meanings of a word in different contexts are gathered together and then all those meanings are presumed to be present in any single context. For example, it would be illegitimate to presume without further indication that in any single passage the word *ekklēsia* must refer to the church, the body of Christ. In Acts 7:38, e.g., "church" (in the NT sense) would clearly *not* be the author's meaning and would actually be contradictory to the sense of the passage.

Another important linguistic concept is *synonymy*. Synonymy can be considered the opposite of polysemy: in synonymy, two or more words may be associated with the same meaning, whereas in polysemy two or more meanings are associated with the same word. A biblical example of synonymy involves the Greek vocabulary for "love." The relationship between the meanings of *agapaō* and *phileō* is such that the words may be used interchangeably in some contexts. One thereafter need not be surprised that *agapaō* (popularly considered to refer to divine love) can describe Amnon's incestuous relationship with his

Transliteration of Greek Words in the ESV Study Bible

Letter	Name of Letter	Transliteration
α	alpha	a
β	bēta	b
γ	gamma	g
γ	gamma nasal	n (before g, k, x, c)
δ	delta	d
ε	epsilon	e
ζ	zēta	z
η	ēta	ē
θ	thēta	th
ι	iōta	i
κ	kappa	k
λ	lambda	l
μ	mu	m
ν	nu	n
ξ	xi	x
ο	omicron	o
π	pi	p
ρ	rho	r
ῥ	initial rho	rh (or in medial double rho)
σ, ς	sigma, final sigma	s
τ	tau	t
υ	upsilon	y (not in diphthong)
υ	upsilon	u (in diphthongs: au, eu, ēu, ou, ui)
φ	phi	ph
χ	chi	ch
ψ	psi	ps
ω	ōmega	ō
ʽ	rough breathing mark	h (preceding initial vowel)

half sister Tamar (2 Sam. 13:15 LXX) or that *phileō* (popularly taken to refer to a lower form of love) can refer to the Father's love for the Son (John 5:20). Other NT examples of synonymy are *logos/rhēma* ("word"), *horaō/blepō* ("I see"), and *oida/ginōskō* ("I know"). In each case, according to the principle of "semantic neutralization," any of the terms in these pairs may in some contexts be used interchangeably without any significant difference in meaning, depending on the purpose of the biblical author. (Smaller differences in nuance or connotation, however, are often still present among synonyms.)

Greek as an Inflected Language

Greek is a highly inflected language (like its contemporary, Latin). This means that most Greek words undergo changes in keeping with their function in the sentence in which they occur. For example, Greek nouns have five basic cases (or sets of forms): nominative, vocative, genitive, dative, and accusative. (English still bears a faint resemblance to this trait in such words as "dog," "dogs," "dog's," and "dogs'," or in "I" and "he" used as subjects, "me" and "him" used as objects, and "my" and "his" used to show possession.) Because Greek word inflections designate the function of each word in its sentence, Greek allows much more variation in word order than English does, e.g., where a different word order often changes the meaning. In addition, Greek verbs function within an extensive and highly developed system of tenses, voices, moods, gender, and number, giving modern Greek students considerable consternation, but providing flexibility for a very broad range of nuances of meaning. Koine Greek's linguistic stock (the set of words available for use) was incredibly rich, and new words could easily be coined by combining older words or adding a variety of common prefixes. These features all made Koine Greek a wonderfully resourceful language with a remarkable ability to express an author's meaning precisely and understandably.

The Importance of Studying Greek Today

Is this ancient language worth studying today? Yes, indeed! The many tools available can give modern readers the knowledge and understanding to incorporate Greek into their own life and ministry, and into their personal Bible study. A knowledge of Greek will probably not make a reader think that the meaning of a verse is completely different from that indicated in a reliable, essentially literal modern translation, but it will certainly give the reader the ability to understand the meaning more precisely, to decide more accurately among various nuances that might be allowed by the English text, to understand why many popular interpretations are incorrect, and to have deeper confidence in knowing the precise sense of the verse. Meanwhile, those who will never learn Greek can still be thankful for scholars who have studied it extensively and who have prepared modern English translations that make available to the reading public an accurate rendering of what the original says. ◀

The Septuagint

The term *Septuagint* is commonly used today to refer to the Greek translation of the Jewish Scriptures, the books that are called the "Old Testament" in Christian terminology. Scholars who specialize in Septuagint studies point out, however, that in a more technical sense the word *Septuagint* refers only to the Greek translation of the Pentateuch. Uncertainties about the history of the process of translation are responsible for the variation in meaning of the term.

It is generally agreed that the Pentateuch (Genesis–Deuteronomy) was translated in Egypt early during the reign of Ptolemy II Philadelphus (285/282–246 B.C.), possibly around 280 if one can rely on the testimony of the church fathers. The books in the Prophets and Writings were translated later, certainly most of them by 130 B.C. as is indicated by the Prologue to the Greek translation of *Sirach* (*Ecclesiasticus*). Questions arise about the date of translation of each of the books in the collection known as Megilloth (Ruth, Song of Solomon, Ecclesiastes, Lamentations, and Esther). Some of these may have been first translated after 100 B.C.

To complicate matters further, long before all the books had been translated, revisions were already being made of existing translations. The process of making systematic, thoroughgoing revisions (called recensions) continued from possibly 200 B.C. through A.D. 200. The precise line of demarcation between original translations and revisions in this body of texts has not yet been clearly established. Scholars are still working to prepare editions of these translations based on careful study of all available evidence in Greek manuscripts, citations by church fathers, and early daughter translations.

The Motivation for the Translation

What motivated the translation of the Septuagint continues to be debated. Five major hypotheses have been advanced: (1) A generation of Greek-speaking Jews in the Hellenistic period begun by the conquest of Alexander the Great (333–323 B.C.) required Greek Scriptures for their religious life and liturgy and/or (2) for the education of their young. (3) The translation was required as a legal document or (4) as cultural heritage for the royal library being assembled in Alexandria. (5) Aristarchus's new edition of Homer around 150 B.C. employed textual criticism to produce an authoritative text, and this served as an incentive and a model to produce an authoritative text of the Bible for Alexandrian Jews (hence early revisions and *The Letter of Aristeas*).

The Origin of the Septuagint

A document known as *The Letter of Aristeas* purports to relate the story of the origin of the Greek Pentateuch. This document is actually a propaganda piece, written in 150–100 B.C. to authenticate the Greek version in the face of criticisms circulating at that time—criticisms to the effect that the Greek translation did not adequately reflect the Hebrew text current in Palestine.

The name Septuagint comes from *septuaginta*, the Latin word for "70." (The common abbreviation for the Septuagint is LXX, the Roman numeral for 70.) According to *Aristeas*, there were 72 translators. The number 70 is an adaptation of 72 based on models like the 70 Elders at Sinai, the 70 Judges who assisted Moses, the 70 Elders of the Sanhedrin, etc. Likely there were just five translators for the Pentateuch, as rabbinic versions of the story indicate (*Aboth of Rabbi Nathan* 37; *Soferim* 1.7). While church fathers like Justin Martyr (c. A.D. 135) refer to the 70 translators, the earliest use of the term Septuagint as a reference to the translation itself is found in Eusebius's *Ecclesiastical History* (c. A.D. 303).

Different Translation Approaches within the Septuagint

In both ancient and modern times, different approaches to the task of translation have been adopted. Each language employs its words as a code to "cut up" and represent the "pie" of reality. The code of one language may overlap with that of another in multiple ways or perhaps not at all in some aspects. Just as light may be refracted as a continuum of colors on a spectrum, so translations may be characterized as a continuum on a spectrum from highly literal (sometimes called formal equivalence) to functional equivalence (also called dynamic equivalence).

At one end of the spectrum translations can be woodenly literal, simply translating item for item, word for word, even copying the word order of the original language in ways that make the translation sound unnatural. The code of the receptor language is conformed as closely as possible to that of the source language. Then further along the spectrum are "essentially literal" translations that seek to render the meaning of each word in the original but to do so in contextually sensitive ways and to produce a readable, natural-sounding translation. *Functional equivalence*, at the other end of the spectrum, is dynamic, idiomatic, idea for idea or "thought for thought," so to speak. The code of the *receptor* language (even when it differs significantly from the original language) is followed as closely as possible to maximize effective communication and understanding for the audience.

Thus different notions of fidelity in transmitting the Word of God motivate the different ends of the spectrum. When the codes of source and target languages overlap in multiple ways, often more than one correct translation of an expression is possible. For example, if the source language specifies a relationship of possession between the nouns "Mary" and "purse," there are a number of right ways to say this: "Mary's purse," "the purse of Mary," "the purse that belongs to Mary," "the purse that Mary has," etc.

The books in the Greek Pentateuch as well as those in the Prophets and Writings vary widely within this spectrum of types of translation. Some are literal in the extreme; others are more idiomatic and represent various gradations of functional equivalence.

Genesis and Exodus in the Septuagint range from essentially literal to fairly dynamic translations, while Leviticus, Numbers, and Deuteronomy are quite literal. The translator of the book of Job abbreviated many of the long, windy speeches for his Hellenistic readership so that the book is one-sixth shorter in Greek. The translator of Proverbs rearranged the material to enhance the figure of Solomon. Other books, such as Esther and Daniel, have additions to them. The Septuagint version of Jeremiah for some reason differs significantly from the Hebrew text in both arrangement and text. Most of the books, however, reflect the same Hebrew text preserved in the Masoretic text.

The differences between the Septuagint and the later standard Hebrew text (the Masoretic text) are due to a number of factors. In some cases, the translators were using a Hebrew parent text that differs somewhat from the Masoretic text. In most cases, differences are due simply to a different way of reading the same text or understanding the grammar and meaning of words.

The Septuagint quickly became popular among the Jews of the Diaspora for whom Greek was the familiar spoken language. When the Christian church began to spread beyond Jewish borders, they adopted the Septuagint as their ordinary Bible, with minor modifications (while still recognizing that it was a translation). For example, the book of Daniel in the Septuagint was considered so deficient by the Christian church that they rejected it, and in its place used a later Greek translation attributed to Theodotion.

Many of the quotations of the OT in the NT are from the Septuagint, or even early revisions of it, and as a result differ from the Masoretic text. The differences range from superficial to significant. Sometimes the "quotations" are not actually quotations in a modern sense but are the NT author's modification and adaptation of the Septuagint wording to apply to a new circumstance (see, e.g., Acts 4:11, borrowing words from Ps. 118:22; and 2 Cor. 6:18a, borrowing from 2 Sam. 7:14). At other times the NT authors correct the Septuagint reading, bringing it closer to the Hebrew (e.g., 1 Cor. 14:21, using Isa. 28:11–12; Eph. 4:30, using Isa. 63:10).

Differences due to copyist errors in textual transmission and variations in translation do not in any way weaken the strong claim made by Jesus and the apostles concerning the inspiration and accuracy of the Scriptures. They affirmed the divine authority both of the OT itself and of their own writings as they at various times used and adapted both the Masoretic text and some of the readings found in copies of the Septuagint. The differences and variations in the texts were there in Jesus' time just as they are today. No doubt in many cases the NT authors were aware of the differences but were able to use them for their own purposes. This does not imply that they thought the Septuagint always represented the wording of the documents as originally written, but only that they affirmed the truthfulness of the words they quoted or adapted to the new context of their own writing.

Revisions of the Septuagint

Before the end of the first century A.D., Jews were reacting against the use of the Septuagint, partly because it did not reflect current rabbinic teaching and partly because of Christian apologetics based on the Septuagint, not only where it was accurate but even sometimes where it had faulty renderings. Therefore, the Jews produced a number of revisions of the Septuagint to make it conform to the Hebrew text more closely. The most important of these were by Theodotion (50 B.C.–A.D. 50; literal), Aquila (c. A.D. 120; extremely literalistic), and Symmachus (c. 180; dynamic). Almost all later translations of the OT (Old Latin, Syro-Hexapla, Coptic, Armenian, Ethiopic, Arabic, Gothic, Old Georgian, Old Slavic) were made from the Septuagint rather than directly from the Hebrew. (But the Syriac Peshitta version and the Latin Vulgate made extensive use of a Hebrew text, and the Samaritan Pentateuch was itself a Hebrew text.)

Christian codices (plural of "codex," which is an early kind of book consisting of bound sheaves of handwritten pages) of the Bible from the fourth/fifth century A.D. contain additional books beyond the 39 books of the OT and 27 books of the NT. Some of these additional books are translations of Hebrew originals, but most were originally written in Greek. These books represent Jewish literature written between 300 B.C. and A.D. 100 and were called the Apocrypha by Jerome. (See The Apocrypha, pp. 2581–2583.) Some have mistakenly thought that these books were included by Alexandrian Jews in their canon. Yet Judaism in Alexandria was not independent of Palestinian Judaism, as even *Aristeas* reveals.

Not all of the books of the Apocrypha were originally composed in Greek or even in Egypt. Moreover, *1 Maccabees*, one of the books of the Apocrypha, acknowledged that inspiration had ceased (*1 Macc.* 4:46; 9:27; 14:41) before it was written. The prologue to *Sirach* (c. 130 B.C.) does not seem to include the Apocrypha as Scripture, and Philo, who ought to be a key source of information on Alexandria, does not quote the Apocrypha. Nor did he write commentaries on these books, even though he wrote on all the books in the Hebrew canon. Since the extant manuscripts of the Septuagint are of Christian, not Jewish, origin and are copies made 500 years after the original translations, the great uncial codices (early codices written entirely with capital letters called "uncials") cannot be guides as to what was canonical in Alexandria in the third century B.C. The books of the Apocrypha were not considered inspired by either Jews or Christians, but were popular reading among both groups.

The Importance of the Septuagint

The Septuagint is important for many reasons. First, the Septuagint represents an extremely early text of the OT. Our oldest complete manuscripts of the Hebrew OT date to c. A.D. 1000, and even the portions of the OT found in the Dead Sea Scrolls date from around 200 B.C. to A.D. 68. But the Septuagint translation of the Pentateuch was done in the third century B.C. To the extent that we can use it to determine the Hebrew text from which it was translated, we have a much older testimony to the text of the OT. (On the other hand, the Hebrew Masoretic text is the result of an extremely careful process of copying and transmission and often represents a more accurate preservation of the original wording than that found in the Septuagint, although this can be decided only on a case-by-case basis.

At times the Septuagint better preserves the more original wording.) And in spite of some variations, the Septuagint usually shows the same text later preserved in the Masoretic text. Since the Septuagint predates the Dead Sea Scrolls and is complete while they are fragmentary, it is more important than the Dead Sea Scrolls as a textual witness.

Second, the Greek OT, as a translation, gives us an extremely early understanding of difficult points of grammar in the Hebrew text and the meanings of Hebrew words otherwise unknown to us.

Third, since all translation involves interpretation, the Greek OT is, in effect, the earliest commentary on the Hebrew text.

Fourth, since the Greek OT was produced between the end of the OT and the beginning of the NT, it represents a key witness to the thought and worldview of Second Temple Judaism (c. 516 B.C.–A.D. 70).

Fifth, the Greek translation was often used by the apostles when quoting the OT in the NT and was adopted early on as the ordinary Bible of the Christian church. Understanding the language of the Greek OT is key to understanding the Greek of the NT. The Septuagint affected the language of the apostles just as the KJV has influenced the vocabulary of Christians in our time. Such influence is especially evident in the writings of Luke, who contributed more to the NT than Paul in amount of text. For example, in the parable of the good Samaritan (Luke 10) Jesus asks who was a neighbor to the man who fell among thieves. An expert in the Torah answers, "the one who did 'mercy' with him." The expression is as strange in Greek as in English, but comes by way of the Septuagint from the expression in Hebrew for performing acts of kindness that demonstrate and fulfill covenant loyalty and love.

Finally, the history of the Greek Old Testament bears witness to debates over approaches to translation and to the problem of variations in the text of the Bible at the time of Jesus. This can shed some light on debates over similar topics today.

For these reasons, the study of the Greek OT can be of great value to the church today. ◀

How the New Testament Quotes and Interprets the Old Testament

As C. S. Lewis once observed, "one of the rewards of reading the Old Testament regularly" is that "you keep on discovering more and more what a tissue of quotations from it the New Testament is." Conscientious readers of the Bible may well acknowledge this; but there is much disagreement among NT interpreters on just *how* the NT authors saw the OT from which they quoted. Questions include: Did the NT authors respect the original meaning of the OT texts? Did they put new meanings into these OT texts, and if so, how closely tied were these new meanings to the original meaning? Did a citation of an OT passage invoke the whole context of the OT passage, or was the NT writer really only interested in what he could make a particular "verse" do for him? What kind of text did the NT authors use: the original Hebrew, or the Septuagint, or another Greek version—and did the NT authors depend on the Greek, even when its rendering of the Hebrew was inadequate?

This short article cannot supply a complete discussion of all these questions, nor does it suggest that all faithful interpreters (or even all contributors to this Study Bible) see things the same way. Rather, the aim here is to offer a way of looking at these issues that does justice both to the NT and to the OT.

A Variety of Kinds of "Uses"

We begin by observing that there is a variety of ways the NT authors can refer to the OT. They can quote it directly (as Matt. 1:23 cites Isa. 7:14); they can allude to it (as John 1:1–5 alludes to Genesis 1); they can use OT vocabulary with a meaning conditioned by OT usage (e.g., "the righteousness of God"); they can refer to the OT's broad concepts (such as monotheism and creation); and they can refer to the basic overarching story of the OT (e.g., Rom. 1:1–6).

The second observation is that there is no reason to expect a single, one-size-fits-all explanation that covers every instance of the NT using the OT. For example, an author may be intending to specify the one meaning of the OT text, or he may be using the OT text as providing an example or pattern that illuminates something he is writing about. He may draw a moral lesson from some event (e.g., Mark 2:25–26), and he might find an analogy between his audience and the ancient people (e.g., 1 Cor. 10:6–11). He might be making a point about how the Gentile Christians inherit the privileges of Israel (1 Pet. 2:9–10), or he might be explaining why Christians need not keep some provision of the OT (e.g., Mark 7:19; Eph. 2:19). Paul describes his own calling in terms that remind us of the servant of the Lord (Gal. 1:15 evoking Isa. 49:1): since Isaiah's servant is a messianic figure (as Paul knew, cf. Acts 13:47; Rom. 10:16; 15:21), it is best to see Paul as likening his own calling in some way to that of the servant, rather than as claiming that *he* was the servant.

Text Form

This part is the least controversial. As a general rule, NT authors cite the OT in a Greek form that is basically the Septuagint that is available in printed form today (see The Septuagint, pp. 2601–2603). There are places where the NT author's citation differs slightly from that of the Septuagint: either because the author has adjusted the quotation to fit the syntax of his own sentence or otherwise adapted it to his purpose, or because he has quoted the Septuagint from memory, or because the quotation represents a textual variation. There are places where the NT author has apparently corrected the Septuagint in order to be closer to the Hebrew: for example, "grieve" in Ephesians 4:30 is far closer to the Hebrew of Isaiah 63:10 than the Septuagint's "provoke." In John 1:14 "full of grace and truth" may be a free paraphrase of "abounding in steadfast love and faithfulness" (Ex. 34:6).

Many Hebraists view the Septuagint as a translation with some value, but with many obvious deficiencies. The truth is, the translation quality varies with the kind of material being translated (poetry is harder than narrative), the skill of the individual translator, and the purposes of the translation (e.g., it seems that the translators of Proverbs intended to adapt the Hebrew wisdom to their setting in the high Hellenistic culture of Alexandria, at the expense of faithfully conveying the meaning of the Hebrew). More to the point, it is not clear that translational infelicities cloud any particular NT use of the Septuagint—generally the point for which the verse is cited depends on the part where the translation is close enough to the original.

Therefore one cannot say that, in using a Greek version, the NT authors have in any way slighted the original intent of the OT authors.

NT Reflection on the Use of the OT

Several NT texts discuss the general stance by which Christians do, and should, approach the OT. The first is Romans 1:1–6, where Paul describes the "gospel of God" as "promised beforehand through his prophets in the holy Scriptures." The content that follows narrates Jesus' public entry onto his Davidic throne through his resurrection, and Paul's apostleship as the outworking of Jesus' program "to bring about the obedience of faith for the sake of his name among all the nations": Paul is explaining that the events of Jesus' victory, and the witness of the early Christians, are just what the OT had foretold. This is the kind of reading the OT itself invites (see The Theology of the Old Testament, pp. 29–31). Later in the same letter (Rom. 15:4), Paul says, "For whatever was written in former days [i.e., in the OT] was written for our instruction [i.e., as Christians]." He then goes on (in vv. 9–13) to cite several OT texts about the expectation of the coming era when the Gentiles would receive the light and join in worship with the faithful of Israel: the mixed congregations of Jewish and Gentile Christians are the fulfillment of that hope.

In 1 Corinthians 10:1, Paul alludes to OT events, saying "our fathers" experienced them. The church in Corinth, however, had a considerable proportion of converted Gentiles; so this means that Paul is treating the Gentile Christians as having been "grafted in" (Rom. 11:17ff.) to the olive tree (the people of God, cf. Jer. 11:16), and every bit as much heirs of the story as Jewish Christians are. After listing the ways that God judged the unfaithful among the ancient people (1 Cor. 10:6–10), Paul explains that "these things happened to them as an example, but they were written down for our instruction, on whom the end of the ages has come." God expects those who profess to be Christians to be sure their faith is real, just as he did the people in the Pentateuch.

Hebrews 11 is able to parade the OT faithful before its audience (probably mostly Jewish Christians) to show them that they must persevere in faith just as the ancients did.

In Luke 24:25–27, 44–47, Jesus "interpreted to [his disciples] in all the [OT] Scriptures the things concerning himself." Luke does not tell us what that Bible study actually said. Some Christian interpreters have understood this to mean that it is possible to find in every part of the OT a "foreshadowing" of some aspect of the work of Jesus. However, other interpreters think it is enough to recognize both that there are specific texts that predict the messianic work, and that the entire trend of the OT story was heading toward Jesus' victory after his suffering, which would usher in the era in which the Gentiles would receive God's light (Luke 24:47, "to all nations").

Basic Catalog of NT Uses of the OT

When the apostles applied the OT to NT realities, they were following a long line of citing earlier Scripture, using a set of practices that can be found in the OT itself. For example, OT writers could allude to an earlier passage and elaborate on it (e.g., Psalms 8 and 104 use Genesis 1–2); or they could allude to an earlier text and give a more precise nuance to it (as Ps. 72:17 takes the more general Gen. 22:18 and ties it specifically to the house of David). They could recognize a promise (e.g., Dan. 9:2 finding in Jer. 25:12 a promise for the length of Babylonian domination). They could see patterns of God's behavior repeated (e.g., many Psalms allude to Ex. 34:6–7 as God's way of dealing with his people). They could also take texts from earlier generations and apply them to new situations (e.g., Neh. 8:14–17 is often seen as an example of actualizing the laws of Lev. 23:39–42 in concert with Deut. 16:13–15; cf. also the well-known pairing of Jer. 22:24–27 and Hag. 2:23).

The NT writers exhibit these uses due to their conviction that Christians are the heirs of Israel's story; they exhibit other uses as well due to their conviction that the resurrection of Jesus had ushered in a new era, the messianic age—"the last days" foretold by the prophets. These authors saw themselves as God's authorized interpreters for this new era that God had opened in the story of his people.

The early Christian missionaries went to synagogues to prove from the OT Scriptures that Jesus is the Christ (cf. Acts 17:1–3; 18:26–28). This implies that they relied on and used publicly accessible arguments from the text itself, rather than merely private insights—otherwise, they would have been unjust to hold anyone responsible for failing to see something that was not truly there. Luke praises the Berean Jews, who examined the OT to see whether what Paul and Silas told them was so (Acts 17:11): this implies that the NT invites critical interaction over its appeal to the OT, and is not solely dependent on the "insider's" point of view.

In classifying these uses, the basic questions are:

- What is it about the OT text that enables the NT writer to use it the way he does?
- What is the NT writer's stance toward the "original meaning" of the OT text?
- What rhetorical goal is the NT writer trying to achieve by using the OT text as he does?
- In what ways does the NT author resemble and differ from interpretative principles found among other interpreters who come from the same period of time, particularly other Second Temple Jewish authors who were not Christians?

The categories in this catalog are intended to be broad and suggestive; there is no substitute for a case-by-case examination of the various passages.

Promise and fulfillment. In many cases the NT writers understood their OT texts as providing a promise about where the story was headed, and identify a particular event as the fulfillment (or partial fulfillment) of a promise. For example, Matthew 12:17–21 understood the servant of the Lord in Isaiah 42:1–3 as the Messiah, with Jesus being the promised person. Likewise, in Romans 15:12 Paul sees the spread of Christian faith among the Gentiles as fulfilling the expectation of Isaiah 11:1–10.

Pattern and fulfillment. This is often called "typology," and it refers to the way patterns found in the OT enable Christians to understand their own situation in, through, and under Christ. For example, the way that a lamb in the sin or guilt offering serves as an innocent substitute to work atonement explains how Jesus' sacrifice benefits believers (see note on Isa. 53:7, the probable background to John 1:29).

Analogy and application. Sometimes the NT writers find some kind of resemblance between their situation and an earlier one, and derive principles from the OT passage for addressing the new situation. The examples of Mark 2:25–26 and 1 Corinthians 10:6–10 have already been mentioned.

When an author is using an analogy, he is not offering an interpretation of the original intent of the OT text; nevertheless, the analogies respect the original intent. For example, in Matthew 21:42, Jesus uses Psalm 118:22–23 (about "the stone the builders rejected") to describe the way the Jewish leaders rejected him. Though many understand this to be a messianic prediction, the main point Jesus makes is that Jewish leaders who rejected him are (by analogy) just as wrong and wretched (Matt. 21:41) as the great world powers that thought so little of Israel (see note on Ps. 118:22–23).

Understanding the use of analogy in this way will help when encountering some NT texts that are more difficult. In 1 Corinthians 9:9 and 1 Timothy 5:18, Paul cites an OT law (Deut. 25:4) about not muzzling an ox, and he applies it as a justification for paying those in ministry.

The OT text is based on a principle of caring for working animals; Paul's application seems to be based on a "How much more should we care for those who serve us with the word" kind of argument. In Galatians 4:21–31, Paul constructs an "allegory" from Hagar and Sarah in Genesis, in order to convince his readers to reject the false teachers. There is no need to think he is disclosing any kind of additional meaning in Genesis, nor is he disregarding the original intent of the OT passages; he is simply likening those who follow his message to the "children of promise" (supernaturally produced like Isaac), and those who follow the false teachers to him "who was born according to the flesh" (i.e., to Ishmael).

Eschatological continuity. As indicated in The Theology of the Old Testament (pp. 29–31), "eschatology" in the OT is focused on the coming era in which the Messiah will lead his people in bringing the light to the Gentiles; the NT position is that this era began with the resurrection and ascension of Jesus. These are separate chapters in the unfolding story of God's work in the world, but they exhibit continuity because it is the same God at work, who saves people in the same way (cf. Rom. 4:1–8), who grafts believing Gentiles into the olive tree of his people (Rom. 11:17), and who is restoring the image of God in them. Hence Christian believers, both Jew and Gentile, share the privilege of the mission of Israel (e.g., 1 Pet. 2:9–10, looking back to Ex. 19:5–6 and other texts). Thus, the Ten Commandments supply moral guidance to Christians (Rom. 13:8–10). The same "righteousness of God"—God's uprightness and faithfulness in keeping his promises—that the OT celebrates lies behind God's sending Jesus (Rom. 1:17).

Eschatological discontinuity. This category is related to the previous one and reflects the change in redemptive era. For example, God's faithful no longer need to observe the OT food laws, whose purpose was to distinguish Israel from the Gentiles (Lev. 20:24–26; cf. Acts 10:9–23). Other aspects of the Sinai covenant are likewise no longer directly applicable to God's people, such as the sacrificial system and the theocratic government centered in Jerusalem.

Development. Psalm 72:17 does not change the promise of blessing-to-the-nations of Genesis 22:18 but rather develops it by bringing the manner of fulfillment into sharper focus. In the same way, Isaiah 52:13–53:12 certainly describes the career of the Messiah in terms of rejection and humiliation followed by vindication and victory. As the note on Isaiah 53:10 explains, death is clearly not the messianic servant's end; but resurrection is not explicit there (although it now seems to be the natural inference). Thus 1 Corinthians 15:3–4 can say, "Christ died for our sins in accordance with the Scriptures" (probably echoing Isa. 53:10), and "he was raised on the third day in accordance with the Scriptures" (developing, or clarifying, Isa. 53:10). The assumption behind these examples is that the story is moving along, and God can feed new events and insights into the process (in the case of Ps. 72:17, by giving an oracle establishing the Davidic covenant; in the case of 1 Cor. 15:4, by raising Jesus from the dead).

"Fuller sense." Christians have used the Latin term *sensus plenior* ("fuller sense") for cases where the NT seems to find a meaning in the OT that goes much farther beyond the original intent of the earlier passage than simple development. There is every reason to allow for such cases, when one considers that God is both planning events and inspiring the biblical authors as his authentic interpreters. Nevertheless it is wise to be careful: in many cases the suggestion of *sensus plenior* stems from a misapprehension of the earlier text or of the NT usage (see discussion of Matt. 2:15/Hos. 11:1 below; see note on Ps. 16:9–11). There are some instances, however, where this does in fact seem to be what the NT author has done: e.g., in John 1:1–5, John describes "the Word" as a divine Person active in the creation; he is echoing Genesis 1:1–2:3 but seeing something there that Moses did not say. Nevertheless, as the notes on Psalm 33:4–9 explain, this is not out of step with Genesis (see also note on Gen. 1:26 for the Trinity). One can imagine Moses saying, if he had been presented with John's Gospel, "Well, I never thought of it that way, but now that you come to say it like that, I can see where you got it, and I like it": that is, he would not think that his original intent had been violated. It is tenuous, however, to advocate a *sensus plenior* that dispenses with original intent.

Matthew 2:15 is often taken as a case of *sensus plenior* because it says that when the holy family took shelter in Egypt (later to return to Palestine), this was to "fulfill" the words of Hosea 11:1, "Out of Egypt I called my son." Is Matthew finding a "messianic meaning" in Hosea that no one could have seen before? Probably not: it is more likely that Matthew found in Hosea a convenient summary of the exodus that contained the term "son." (Many prophets summarize the exodus as a way of reminding Israel of their obligations to the Lord: cf. Amos 3:1–2.) One of Matthew's themes is that Jesus showed himself the true Messiah (the Davidic representative of Israel) by embodying all that Israel was called to be, and doing so faithfully (in contrast to Israel). On the "son of God" idea, an important theme for Matthew, see note on Psalm 2:7. So Jesus' experience "fulfilled" the pattern of the exodus, which means that this is a case of pattern and fulfillment.

Deity of Christ. NT authors often apply OT texts to Jesus that originally applied to Yahweh, the God of Israel. For example, Hebrews 1:10–12 describes Jesus by using Psalm 102:25–27, which is about God's eternity. This is not because the psalm is directly messianic but because NT authors accept that Jesus is Yahweh incarnate (cf. John 1:1–14). Thus the NT uses these texts consistently with their original intent—they describe the Lord—and recognize that their description applies to Jesus as being no less truly the Lord than is God the Father.

In all of these cases the NT authors view themselves as the proper heirs and faithful interpreters of the OT. ◂

Old Testament Passages Cited in the New Testament

This chart is adapted from the lists in the standard Greek texts, NA27 and UBS4. It may appear to include considerably fewer citations than would be expected, because it focuses only on exact quotations. The NT is filled with allusions to the OT, so the fact that, e.g., there are only five places where the NT gives an exact quotation of a passage from Numbers should not be used as a measure of the influence Numbers had on the biblical authors. Even though exact quotations of the OT may be relatively few, the influence of the OT on the thinking and language of the NT writers is pervasive. Further, it is often a judgment call in distinguishing between a "quotation" and an "allusion," and sometimes the NT author uses only a phrase from the OT text.

Passages marked (LXX) denote those where the Greek translation is cited, and if the versification of the Hebrew OT differs from that of English translations, the abbreviation ET (for English Translation) precedes the English verse number.

Old Testament Passage	New Testament Passage(s)
Genesis	
1:27	Matt. 19:4; Mark 10:6
2:2	Heb. 4:4
2:7	1 Cor. 15:45
2:24	Matt. 19:5; Mark 10:7–8; 1 Cor. 6:16; Eph. 5:31
5:2	Matt. 19:4; Mark 10:6
12:1	Acts 7:3
12:3	Gal. 3:8; Rev. 1:7
14:17–20	Heb. 7:1
14:20	Heb. 7:4
15:5	Rom. 4:18
15:6	Rom. 4:3, 9, 22; Gal. 3:6; James 2:23
15:13–14	Acts 7:6
17:5	Rom. 4:17
18:10	Rom. 9:9
18:14	Rom. 9:9
21:10	Gal. 4:30
21:12	Rom. 9:7; Heb. 11:18
22:17	Heb. 6:14
22:18	Acts 3:25; Gal. 3:8, 16
24:7	Gal. 3:16 (?)
25:23	Rom. 9:12
26:4	Acts 3:25
28:12	John 1:51
28:14	Rev. 1:7 (?)
47:31 (LXX)	Heb. 11:21
48:4	Acts 7:5
Exodus	
1:8	Acts 7:18
2:14 (LXX)	Acts 7:27–28
2:22	Acts 7:6
3:5	Acts 7:33
3:6	Matt. 22:32; Mark 12:26; Luke 20:37; Acts 3:13; 7:32
3:7–10	Acts 7:34
9:16	Rom. 9:17
12:11	Luke 12:35
12:46	John 19:36
13:2, 12, 15	Luke 2:23
16:18	2 Cor. 8:15
19:5–6	1 Pet. 2:9
19:12	Heb. 12:20
20:11	Acts 4:24; 14:15
20:12	Matt. 15:4; Mark 7:10; Eph. 6:2
20:12–16	Matt. 19:18; Mark 10:19; Luke 18:20
20:13	Matt. 5:21; James 2:11
20:13–17	Rom. 13:9
20:14	Matt. 5:27; James 2:11
20:17	Rom. 7:7
21:17	Matt. 15:4; Mark 7:10
21:24	Matt. 5:38
22:27 (ET 28)	Acts 23:5
23:20	Matt. 11:10; Mark 1:2; Luke 7:27
24:8	Heb. 9:20
25:40	Heb. 8:5
32:1	Acts 7:40
32:6	1 Cor. 10:7
32:23	Acts 7:40
33:19	Rom. 9:15
34:34	2 Cor. 3:16
Leviticus	
11:44	1 Pet. 1:16
12:8	Luke 2:24
18:5	Rom. 10:5; Gal. 3:12
19:2	1 Pet. 1:16
19:12	Matt. 5:33
19:18	Matt. 5:43; 19:19; 22:39; Mark 12:31, 33; Luke 10:27; Rom. 12:19; 13:9; Gal. 5:14; James 2:8
20:9	Matt. 15:4; Mark 7:10
23:29	Acts 3:23
24:20	Matt. 5:38
26:12	2 Cor. 6:16
Numbers	
6:3	Luke 1:15
12:7	Heb. 3:2, 5
16:5	2 Tim. 2:19
27:17	Matt. 9:36; Mark 6:34
30:2	Matt. 5:33
Deuteronomy	
4:24	Heb. 12:29
4:35	Mark 12:32
5:16	Matt. 15:4; Mark 7:10; Eph. 6:2
5:16–20	Matt. 19:18; Mark 10:19; Luke 18:20
5:17	Matt. 5:21; James 2:11
5:17–21	Rom. 13:9

5:18	James 2:11
5:21	Rom. 7:7
6:4	Mark 12:29, 32
6:5	Matt. 22:37; Mark 12:30, 33; Luke 10:27
6:13	Matt. 4:10
6:16	Matt. 4:7; Luke 4:12
8:3	Matt. 4:4; Luke 4:4
9:3	Heb. 12:29
9:4	Rom. 10:6
9:19	Heb. 12:21
10:20	Matt. 4:10; Luke 4:8
17:7	1 Cor. 5:13
18:15	Acts 7:37
18:15–20	Acts 3:22
19:15	Matt. 18:16; 2 Cor. 13:1; 1 Tim. 5:19
21:23	Gal. 3:13
24:1	Matt. 5:31; 19:7; Mark 10:14
25:4	1 Cor. 9:9; 1 Tim. 5:18
25:5	Matt. 22:24; Mark 12:19; Luke 20:28
27:26	Gal. 3:10, 13
29:3 (ET 4)	Rom. 11:8
29:17 (ET 18)	Heb. 12:15
30:12	Rom. 10:6
30:14	Rom. 10:8
31:6	Heb. 13:5
32:4	Rev. 15:3
32:21	Rom. 10:19
32:35	Rom. 12:19; Heb. 10:30
32:36	Heb. 10:30
32:43	Rom. 15:10; Heb. 1:6 (citing LXX)
Joshua	
1:5	Heb. 13:5
22:5	Matt. 22:37; Mark 12:30, 33; Luke 10:27
1 Samuel	
12:22	Rom. 11:1–2
2 Samuel	
5:2	Matt. 2:6
7:8	2 Cor. 6:18
7:14	2 Cor. 6:18; Heb. 1:5; Rev. 21:7
22:50	Rom. 15:9
1 Kings	
19:10, 14	Rom. 11:3
19:18	Rom. 11:4
2 Kings	
1:10, 12	Luke 9:54; Rev. 20:9
19:15	Acts 4:24
1 Chronicles	
17:13	Heb. 1:5
2 Chronicles	
2:12	Acts 4:24
18:16	Matt. 9:36

Job	
5:12	1 Cor. 3:19
16:19	Matt. 21:9; Mark 11:10
41:3 (ET 11)	Rom. 11:35
Psalms	
2:1	Acts 4:25
2:7	Acts 13:33; Heb. 1:5; 5:5
2:9	Rev. 2:27; 19:15
4:5 (ET 4)	Eph. 4:26
5:10 (ET 9)	Rom. 3:13
6:4 (ET 3)	John 12:27
6:9 (ET 8)	Matt. 7:23; Luke 13:27
8:3 (ET 2)	Matt. 21:16
8:5–7 (ET 4–6)	Heb. 2:6–8
8:7 (ET 6)	1 Cor. 15:27; Eph. 1:22
10:7	Rom. 3:14
14:1–3	Rom. 3:10–12
16:8–11	Acts 2:25–28
16:10	Acts 13:35
18:50 (ET 49)	Rom. 15:9
19:5 (ET 4)	Rom. 10:18
22:2 (ET 1)	Matt. 27:46; Mark 15:34
22:14 (ET 13)	1 Pet. 5:8
22:19 (ET 18)	Matt. 27:35; Mark 15:24; Luke 23:34; John 19:24
24:1	1 Cor. 10:26
31:6 (ET 5)	Luke 23:46
32:1	Rom. 4:7
34:9 (ET 8)	1 Pet. 2:3
34:13–17 (ET 12–16)	1 Pet. 3:10–12
34:21 (ET 20)	John 19:36
35:19	John 15:25
36:2 (ET 1)	Rom. 3:18
40:7–9 (ET 6–8)	Heb. 10:5–7
40:8 (ET 7)	Heb. 10:9
41:10 (ET 9)	John 13:18
42:6, 12 (ET 5, 11)	Matt. 26:38; Mark 14:34
43:5	Mark 14:34
44:23 (ET 22)	Rom. 8:36
45:7 (ET 6)	Heb. 1:8
51:6 (ET 4)	Rom. 3:4
53:2–4 (ET 1–3)	Rom. 3:10–12
62:13 (ET 12)	Matt. 16:27; Rom. 2:6
68:19 (ET 18)	Eph. 4:8
69:10 (ET 9)	John 2:17; Rom. 15:3
69:23 (ET 22)	Rom. 11:9
69:26 (ET 25)	Acts 1:20
78:2	Matt. 13:35
78:24	John 6:31
82:6	John 10:34
86:9	Rev. 15:4

91:11	Matt. 4:6; Luke 4:10, 11
94:11	1 Cor. 3:20
94:14	Rom. 11:2
95:7–8	Heb. 3:15; 4:7
95:7–11	Heb. 3:7–11
95:11	Heb. 4:3, 5
97:7 (LXX)	Heb. 1:6
102:26–28 (ET 25–27)	Heb. 1:10–12
104:4	Heb. 1:7
104:12	Matt. 13:32; Mark 4:32; Luke 13:19
107:26	Rom. 10:7
109:8	Acts 1:20
110:1	Matt. 22:44; Mark 12:36; Luke 20:42–43; Acts 2:34–35; 1 Cor. 15:25; Heb. 1:13
110:4	Heb. 5:6; 7:17
111:2	Rev. 15:3
112:9	2 Cor. 9:9
116:10	2 Cor. 4:13
117:1	Rom. 15:11
118:6	Heb. 13:6
118:22	Matt. 21:42; Mark 12:10; Luke 20:17; 1 Pet. 2:7
118:23	Matt. 21:42; Mark 12:11
118:26	Matt. 21:9; Mark 11:9; John 12:13; Matt. 23:39; Luke 13:35; 19:38
119:32	2 Cor. 6:11
135:14	Heb. 10:30
139:14	Rev. 15:3
140:4 (ET 3)	Rom. 3:13
145:17	Rev. 15:3
146:6	Acts 4:24; 14:15
148:1	Matt. 21:9; Mark 11:10
Proverbs	
3:11	Heb. 12:5
3:34 (LXX)	James 4:6; 1 Pet. 5:5
10:12	James 5:20; 1 Pet. 4:8
11:31 (LXX)	1 Pet. 4:18
22:8 (LXX)	2 Cor. 9:7
24:12	Matt. 16:27; Rom. 2:6
25:21	Rom. 12:20
Ecclesiastes	
7:20	Rom. 3:10
Isaiah	
1:9	Rom. 9:29
5:9 (LXX)	James 5:4
6:3	Rev. 4:8
6:9 (LXX)	Matt. 13:14; Mark 4:12; Acts 28:26
6:10	John 12:40
7:14	Matt. 1:23
8:10	Matt. 1:23
8:12	1 Pet. 3:14
8:13	1 Pet. 3:15
8:14	Rom. 9:33; 1 Pet. 2:8
8:17 (LXX)	Heb. 2:13
8:18	Heb. 2:13
8:23–9:1 (ET 9:1–2)	Matt. 4:15–16
10:3	1 Pet. 2:12
10:22	Rom. 9:27
11:2	1 Pet. 4:14
11:10	Rom. 15:12
12:2	Heb. 2:13
13:10	Matt. 24:29; Mark 13:24
22:13	1 Cor. 15:32
25:8	1 Cor. 15:54; Rev. 7:17; 21:4
26:13 (LXX)	2 Tim. 2:19
26:19	Matt. 11:5; Luke 7:22
26:20 (LXX)	Heb. 10:37
27:9	Rom. 11:27
28:11	1 Cor. 14:21
28:16	Rom. 9:33; 10:11; 1 Pet. 2:6
29:10	Rom. 11:8
29:13	Matt. 15:8–9; Mark 7:6–7
29:14	1 Cor. 1:19
29:16	Rom. 9:20
29:18	Matt. 11:5; Luke 7:22
34:4	Matt. 24:29; Mark 13:25; Luke 21:26
35:4	John 12:15
35:5	Matt. 11:5; Luke 7:22
37:16	Acts 4:24
40:3	Matt. 3:3; Mark 1:3; John 1:23
40:3–5	Luke 3:4–6
40:6	1 Pet. 1:24
40:8	1 Pet. 1:25
40:13	Rom. 11:34; 1 Cor. 2:16
42:1–4	Matt. 12:18–21
42:12	1 Pet. 2:9 (?)
42:18	Matt. 11:5; Luke 7:22
43:20–21	1 Pet. 2:9 (?)
45:14	1 Cor. 14:25
45:21	Mark 12:32; Acts 15:18
45:23	Rom. 14:11
49:6	Acts 13:47
49:8	2 Cor. 6:2
49:10	Rev. 7:16
49:18	Rom. 14:11
52:4	2 Cor. 6:17
52:5	Rom. 2:24
52:7	Rom. 10:15
52:11	2 Cor. 6:17
52:15	Rom. 15:21
53:1	John 12:38; Rom. 10:16
53:4	Matt. 8:17; 1 Pet. 2:24
53:5	1 Pet. 2:24

53:6	1 Pet. 2:25
53:7–8	Acts 8:32–33
53:9	1 Pet. 2:22; Rev. 14:5
53:12	Luke 22:37; 1 Pet. 2:24
54:1	Gal. 4:27
54:13	John 6:45
55:3	Acts 13:34
55:10	2 Cor. 9:10
56:7	Matt. 21:13; Mark 11:17; Luke 19:46
59:7	Rom. 3:15–17
59:20	Rom. 11:26
61:1–2	Luke 4:18–19
62:11	Matt. 21:5
65:1	Rom. 10:20
65:2	Rom. 10:21
65:17	2 Pet. 3:13
66:1–2	Acts 7:49–50
66:14	John 16:22
66:22	2 Pet. 3:13
66:24	Mark 9:48
Jeremiah	
5:21	Mark 8:18
6:16	Matt. 11:29
7:11	Matt. 21:13; Mark 11:17; Luke 19:46
9:22–23 (ET 23–24)	1 Cor. 1:31; 2 Cor. 10:17
10:7	Rev. 15:3, 4
12:3	James 5:5
12:15	Acts 15:16
22:24	Rom. 14:11
31:15	Matt. 2:18
31:31–34	Heb. 8:8–12
31:33–34	Heb. 10:16–17
31:33	Rom. 11:26 (?)
Ezekiel	
5:11	Rom. 14:11
11:20	Rev. 21:7
37:5	Rev. 11:11
37:10	Rev. 11:11
37:27	2 Cor. 6:16
Daniel	
3:6	Matt. 13:42, 50
7:13	Matt. 24:30; 26:64; Mark 13:26; 14:62; Luke 21:27; Rev. 1:7
9:27	Matt. 24:15
11:31	Matt. 24:15; Mark 13:14
12:11	Mark 13:14
Hosea	
1:6	1 Pet. 2:10
1:9	1 Pet. 2:10
2:1	Rom. 9:26–27
2:25 (ET 23)	Rom. 9:25; 1 Pet. 2:10
6:6	Matt. 9:13; 12:7
10:8	Luke 23:30; Rev. 6:16
11:1	Matt. 2:15
13:14	1 Cor. 15:55
Joel	
3:1–5 (ET 2:28–32)	Acts 2:17–21
3:5 (ET 2:32)	Rom. 10:13
Amos	
3:13	Rev. 4:8; 15:3
5:25–27 (LXX)	Acts 7:42
9:11	Acts 15:16
Jonah	
2:1 (ET 1:17)	Matt. 12:40
Micah	
5:1, 3 (ET 5:2, 4)	Matt. 2:6
7:6	Matt. 10:35–36; Luke 12:53
Nahum	
2:1 (ET 1:15)	Rom. 10:15
Habakkuk	
1:5	Acts 13:41
2:3	Heb. 10:37
2:4	Rom. 1:17; Gal. 3:11; Heb. 10:38
Zephaniah	
3:13	Rev. 14:5
Haggai	
2:6	Heb. 12:26
2:21	Heb. 12:26
Zechariah	
3:2	Jude 9
8:16	Eph. 4:25
9:9	Matt. 21:5; John 12:15
11:13	Matt. 27:9
12:10	John 19:37; Rev. 1:7
13:7	Matt. 26:31; Mark 14:27
Malachi	
1:2	Rom. 9:13
3:1	Matt. 11:10; Mark 1:2; Luke 7:27
3:17	1 Pet. 2:9
3:23 (ET 4:5)	Matt. 17:10; Mark 9:11

The Bible in Christianity

Roman Catholicism

Roman Catholicism and Protestantism have many beliefs in common, both adhering to the truths expressed in the Apostles' Creed and the doctrines crystallized and codified at Nicea and Chalcedon (regarding the Trinity and Christology, respectively). However, they have serious differences in their understanding of doctrines such as Scripture, salvation, purgatory, Mary, and the church.

The Canon of Scripture

Though all the books of the Protestant Bible are found in the Catholic Bible, the Catholic Bible contains additional books (e.g., *Tobit*, *Judith*) not found in the Protestant Bible, and additional sections in certain books (e.g., Esther, Daniel) that it otherwise shares in common with the Protestant Bible. These additional books and sections—called the Apocrypha—are all related to the OT. (See The Apocrypha, pp. 2581–2583.) The Catholic Bible's NT and that of the Protestant Bible are identical in all aspects.

How did this difference come about? It should be recalled that what Christians now call the "Old Testament" was once the entire Bible of the Jews and was originally written in Hebrew. Beginning in the third century B.C., a Greek translation of this Hebrew Bible was undertaken. Called the Septuagint (Gk. "seventy"; often abbreviated LXX; see The Septuagint, pp. 2601–2603), it is more extensive than Hebrew Scripture, and its additions are called the *apocryphal* (or hidden) *writings*, or the Apocrypha for short. Beginning in the second century A.D., a Latin translation of the entire Bible was undertaken. The version of the OT that was originally translated was the Septuagint, not the Hebrew Bible. As the church in the West began to adopt Latin as its primary language, the Latin translation *including the Apocrypha* became its Bible.

In A.D. 382 Jerome embarked on a new Latin translation of Scripture, called the Vulgate. As he commenced his work on the OT, he translated from the Hebrew Bible. He considered only the writings in the Hebrew Bible to be authoritative Scripture, and he knew that the Apocrypha never had a place in the Hebrew Bible. However, Augustine urged Jerome to include translations of the apocryphal writings. As the Vulgate became the church's new Bible, the apocryphal writings were increasingly regarded as part of canonical Scripture. Several church councils around the beginning of the fifth century A.D. ratified the Latin Vulgate. Thus, the OT with the Apocrypha (together with the NT) would be the Bible of the church. This view would go without significant challenge until the Reformation.

In the sixteenth century, one of the major disagreements between the Roman Catholic Church and the new Protestant movement was the canon of Scripture. (See The Canon of the Old Testament, pp. 2577–2579.) Protestants insisted that the church's OT should match the shorter Hebrew Bible, not the Septuagint with its additional apocryphal writings. They argued that the Jewish Bible, which did not include those writings, had been the Scripture used by Jesus and the disciples; therefore, it must be considered the basis for the church's Bible. Also, some of the apocryphal writings included incorrect historical or chronological information, and had been considered unsound by the early church. Thus, the Reformers dismissed the Apocrypha from the canonical OT.

Because of this development, the Protestant Bible was different from the Roman Catholic Bible. The effects of this were far-reaching, as the Protestant churches appealed to canonical Scripture alone as the ultimate, divine authority to establish their beliefs and practices. Because the Apocrypha was considered noncanonical, it could not be used as the basis for church doctrine. This meant, e.g., that belief in purgatory and the practice of praying for the dead (which were supported by *2 Maccabees* 12, a passage in the Apocrypha) were without *biblical* support and were therefore discontinued by Protestant churches.

In summary, the Roman Catholic Bible is different from the Protestant Bible because of the presence of the Apocrypha in the Catholic OT. This divergence was the result of significant disputes about the proper source for the Bible's translation, the range of the Holy Spirit's inspiration of Scripture, and the limits of the Word of God as used by Jesus and his disciples. This continues to be a major difference between Roman Catholicism and Protestantism.

The Interpretation of Scripture

Another important matter separating Roman Catholics and Protestants is over the interpretation of the Bible. The Roman Catholic Church insists that the prerogative to determine the proper and authoritative interpretation of Scripture belongs solely to its magisterium, or teaching office (consisting of the pope and bishops). This was a decision that the Council of Trent made (in 1546) in response to the growing Protestant movement. Trent decreed "that no one relying on his own judgment shall, in matters of faith and morals pertaining to the edification of Christian doctrine, distorting the Holy Scriptures in accordance with his own conceptions, presume to interpret them contrary to that sense which holy mother Church, to whom it belongs to judge of their true sense and interpretation, has held and holds." Thus, the Roman Catholic Church claims that it possesses the sole right to give the correct interpretation of Scripture.

Protestant churches do not have such an authoritative teaching office to decide correct and authoritative interpretations. Rather, they urge all believers to engage in careful and responsible interpretation of the Bible by observing sound interpretative principles, under the guidance of the Holy Spirit and with the help of divinely ordained and gifted elders (1 Tim. 3:2; 5:17; Titus 1:9) or pastor-teachers (Eph. 4:11), also taking account of the way other believers have interpreted texts, especially in published commentaries that have interacted with the history of prior interpretation. Protestantism rejects the Roman Catholic magisterium and insists on personal Bible study because of its conviction that Scripture is clear and is necessary for all Christians, who are also made competent by the Holy Spirit for such an interpretative task. In an encouraging development since Vatican Council II (1962–1965), more and more Roman Catholics are becoming involved in Bible study and familiarizing themselves with Scripture.

The Sufficiency and Authority of Scripture

Another important difference between Roman Catholics and Protestants concerns the sufficiency and authority of Scripture. From its beginning, the early church viewed Scripture as the sole and sufficient source of authoritative revelation from God. This meant that all Christians were to give their attention to the Bible, finding in it the very words of God that are to be believed and obeyed, just as God himself is to be believed and obeyed. Furthermore, it meant that God does not require or prohibit anything of Christians that is not contained in Scripture either explicitly or by implication.

But a change took place in the latter part of the Middle Ages. As the Catholic Church permitted other sources to lay claim to the title of authoritative truth, a multiple-source notion of divine revelation arose. This consisted of written Scripture, church tradition, and the magisterium (see above). This meant that Scripture alone is not sufficient for salvation and becoming Christlike. And Scripture is not the only authority for the church. It must be supplemented by tradition—teachings that Christ passed down orally to the apostles, and from them to their successors, the bishops, in the Catholic Church—and by the Church's teaching office. Against this disturbing trend the Protestant motto *sola Scriptura*—Scripture alone!—was sounded. More than a motto, however, this "formal principle of Protestantism" became a decisive point of division between Protestantism and Catholicism. It meant that Scripture alone is absolutely authoritative for doctrine and practice, and following Scripture alone is sufficient to please God in all things.

The Doctrine of Salvation

Many more differences arise because of these foundational issues of the canon of Scripture, proper biblical interpretation, and the sufficiency and authority of the Bible. Another key area, the Protestant doctrine of salvation, also differs from its Catholic counterpart. According to the Protestant understanding of Romans 3:21–4:8 and 5:15–19, justification is the act of God by which he declares a sinful person to be no longer under judgment for his or her guilt, but forgiven and righteous instead, because the sin-bearing righteousness of Christ is accredited to the person (see also 2 Cor. 5:21; Phil. 3:9). This declarative act is not based on any inherent goodness or any personally achieved righteousness of the sinful person, and it does not render that person morally transformed (other divine acts achieve this). Rather, justification is grounded solely on the grace of God as expressed by the atoning death of Christ. Furthermore, this gracious provision can be appropriated only by faith; salvation cannot be merited by human effort in whole or even in part through moral conduct or religious activity (Eph. 2:8–9).

The Roman Catholic understanding incorrectly extends justification to include other acts of God in salvation: "Justification is not only the remission of sins, but also the sanctification and renewal of the interior man" (Council of Trent, *Decree on Justification* 6). Accordingly, justification remains a work in process which increases or decreases in relation to the degree of inward renewal of the sinful person, rendering any assurance of salvation impossible in this life. In addition, justification is said to be conferred in (infant) baptism and continued and increased through the other Catholic sacraments. Thus, a cooperative effort between God's grace and human effort is established so that a sinful person not only expresses faith in Christ's atoning death but also, moved by love and the Holy Spirit, merits eternal life through participation in the church and good deeds. Protestants have considered this a very serious difference, since this faith-plus-human-effort view of justification is so different from the true gospel message of salvation by grace alone, through faith alone (Rom. 4:4–5, 16; 5:1; Gal. 2:16; Eph. 2:8–9).

The Doctrine of Eschatology

This divergence in the doctrine of salvation leads to a difference in eschatology, or personal future hope. For Protestants, only two eternal destinies await human beings: eternal life for all who are justified by God's grace through faith in Christ alone (John 3:16; Rom. 8:1, 33–34), or eternal condemnation for all who reject this salvation (John 3:18; 2 Thess. 1:5–10). Although Roman Catholics agree with Protestants concerning these two eternal destinies, they add a third destiny: temporal punishment in purgatory for all who are on the way to final bliss. "All who die in God's grace and friendship, but still imperfectly purified, are indeed assured of their eternal salvation; but after death they undergo purification, so as to achieve the holiness necessary to enter the joy of heaven" (*Catechism of the Catholic Church* 1030). Purgatory is this temporal punishment as a means of final purification.

Protestants deny this doctrine. It is based on an apocryphal writing (*2 Macc.* 12:45, which is not canonical Scripture) and on misinterpreted biblical passages (Matt. 12:31; 1 Cor. 3:15). Furthermore, the doctrine is the logical outgrowth of the Roman Catholic misunderstanding of salvation. Purgatory makes sense with a view of justification that combines a declarative act of forgiveness with inward renovation, for if this latter renewal process is not sufficiently advanced, such a sinful person will need further purification in purgatory.

However, in the Protestant view, through justification God declares sinful persons to not be penally liable, now or ever, but righteous. He does so by the forgiveness of their sins through the cross and by the imputing of Christ's righteousness to them in and through their union with him. Therefore there can be no purging punishment in purgatory after death due to being imperfectly purified in this life. At death, with their sanctifying process completed in that moment, Christians go to be with Christ in endless joy. The Protestant doctrine of justification leaves no room for a doctrine of purgatory, because it has no need for it.

The Role of Mary

Whereas Protestantism rivets attention on Jesus Christ, Roman Catholicism adds to this singular focus some attention to Mary, his mother. In terms of her personal history, Catholics believe in Mary's immaculate conception (she was "preserved from all stain of original sin" from the moment of her conception; *Ineffabilis Deus*), her complete sinlessness, her perpetual virginity, and her bodily assumption to heaven immediately after death (she "was taken up body and soul into heavenly glory"; *Munificentissimus Deus*).

Because of this personal history and her inseparable union with her Son, "the Blessed Virgin is invoked in the Church under the titles of Advocate, Helper, Benefactress, and Mediatrix" (*Lumen Gentium* 62; "invoked" means "prayed to"). Catholicism honors her maternal mediation and spiritual motherhood, affirming that Mary cooperates "in the birth and development of divine life in the souls of the redeemed" (*Credo of the People of God*). Furthermore, "the Church's devotion to the Blessed Virgin is intrinsic to Christian worship" (*Marialis Cultus* 56) as seen in the 17 festival days annually dedicated to her and the 50 "Hail Mary" prayers in the set of prayers known as the rosary.

Protestant churches acknowledge the unique role Mary played. While they agree that she is in a true sense *theotokos* ("God-bearer," i.e., the one to whom she gave birth is fully God), admire her faith and obedience (Luke 1:26–38), acknowledge her suffering (Luke 2:35; John 19:25–27), and call her "blessed" (Luke 1:48), they repudiate the above-stated Catholic beliefs about her. Protestants, as did the other early disciples, recognize that Mary struggled to understand the significance of her Son Jesus (Mark 3:20–35; Luke 2:25–35; 11:27–28; John 2:1–11; 19:25–27). She also confessed that she was in need of a "Savior" (Luke 1:47) and bore other children after Jesus (see note on Matt. 13:55–56). Protestants maintain that the claims made by Roman Catholicism about her share in her Son's mediation, and the fitness of praying to her, are either the result of poor interpretation of Scripture or arise from unchastened church tradition.

The Role of the Church

Protestantism and Roman Catholicism also differ on the role of the church as a means of the grace that is necessary for salvation. At the heart of the Catholic doctrine of the church is the idea of the *sacramental economy*: As Redeemer, Jesus Christ accomplished salvation through the Paschal (Easter) mystery—his passion, death, and resurrection—that occurred in history and that gave birth to the sacramental reality of the Church. As High Priest, he continues to accomplish salvation through the Church, working originally through the apostles and now through their successors, the bishops, who teach, govern, and sanctify the Church through the gospel and the seven sacraments. Thus, it is through the Roman Catholic Church alone that the fullness of salvation is extended to a sinful world.

This teaching is held to be particularly true because the Church dispenses the grace of God through its sacraments, which are necessary for salvation: baptism (which regenerates a sinful person who in most cases is an infant); confirmation (by which the empowerment of the Holy Spirit is conferred); the Eucharist (which represents the once-and-for-all sacrifice of Jesus on the cross, a reality that is ever-present in the Catholic Mass, as the bread and the wine are transubstantiated into his body and blood through the power of the Holy Spirit at the request of the priest); penance (or reconciliation for all post-baptismal sins); marriage; holy orders (for men ordained to the priesthood); and the anointing of the sick.

No Protestant denomination or church has a view of the church that even remotely resembles this Roman Catholic idea of the sacramental economy. Furthermore, Protestants have always rejected the notion of seven sacraments, maintaining that only two—baptism and the Lord's Supper—were ordained by Christ (Matt. 26:26–29; 28:19; 1 Cor. 11:17–34), with accompanying tangible signs (water; bread and wine).

Conclusion

Despite the many points of doctrine they hold in common, there remains a vast difference between Roman Catholics and Protestants. Their Bibles are different, their idea of interpretation is different, and their view of Scripture's clarity, authority, sufficiency, and necessity is different. And because of these differences, Protestant and Roman Catholic theologies also diverge on the crucial doctrines of salvation, purgatory, Mary, and the church. ◀

Eastern Orthodoxy

Historical Background of Orthodoxy

Orthodoxy comprises a range of autocephalous and autonomous churches, the Russian and Greek being the most prominent. During the first millennium A.D. the Latin West and the predominantly Greek-speaking East drifted apart linguistically, culturally, and theologically. Rome's claims to universal jurisdiction and its acceptance of the *filioque* clause in the Niceno-Constantinopolitan creed led to severed relations.

In the following years, many countries in the East, overrun by the Muslims, had limited freedom, both politically and ecclesiastically. Constantinople, or Byzantium (modern Istanbul), the capital of the Christian East, was conquered in 1453. In the twentieth century, Orthodoxy in Russia and Eastern Europe lived under Communist rule, suffering intense persecution. Orthodox churches include about 218 million adherents today, compared to 1.1 billion Roman Catholics and about 830 million Protestants.

Orthodoxy's doctrinal basis is the teachings of the seven ecumenical councils (between A.D. 325 and 787), with reference especially to the Trinity and Christology. Evangelicals agree with most of these dogmatic decisions. The division in 1054 was prompted by objections to the pope's endorsement of the addition of the Latin term *filioque* ("and the Son") to the Nicene Creed, so that it said that "the Holy Spirit . . . proceeds from the Father *and the Son*" (a reference to the eternal relations between the Son and the Holy Spirit).

Orthodoxy is highly visual, with icons dominating its churches. Its ancient liturgy, rooted in the fourth century, is central to its theology and life.

Positive Elements of Orthodoxy That Evangelicals Can Learn From

The Trinity

The Orthodox liturgy is full of Trinitarian prayers, hymns, and doxologies; the Trinity is a vital part of belief and worship, whereas in the West it often appears as little more than an arcane mathematical riddle. Paul describes our relationship with God in Trinitarian terms: "through [Christ] we . . . have access in one Spirit to the Father" (Eph. 2:18).

Union with Christ and God

Crucial to Orthodox theology is "deification," in which humans (while remaining humans) are indwelt by the Holy Spirit, transformed by divine grace, and in this sense become "partakers of the divine nature" (2 Pet. 1:4). Though talk of deification sounds alarming to many evangelicals, the difference is largely one of emphasis. Orthodoxy has maintained a focus on the union of the three persons in God, the union of deity and humanity in Christ, the union of Christ and the church (central in the NT, e.g., John 14:18–24; 17:20–23; Eph. 1:3–14), and the union of the Holy Spirit and the saints. In contrast, the West has often emphasized the juridical aspects of doctrine, such as the doctrines of atonement and justification.

Freedom from Concerns Raised by the Enlightenment

Due to its historical avoidance of the Enlightenment in the eighteenth century (with its emphasis on the primacy of reason), Orthodox theology never became preoccupied with unbelieving critical challenges to and revisions of the faith, which in the West have often bred a detached, academic approach to theology divorced from the life of the church. This is evident in Orthodoxy's firm belief in heaven, hell, and the return of Christ—topics that many in the West (esp. among more liberal Protestant groups) have sidelined due to possible embarrassment. There is strong commonality here between evangelicals and the Orthodox.

Unity of Theology and Piety

In Orthodoxy, the knowledge of God is received and cultivated by prayer and meditation aided by the Holy Spirit, in battle against the forces of spiritual darkness. Therefore, asceticism and monasticism have had a contemplative character in Orthodoxy. By contrast, since the Enlightenment, Western theology has centered in academic institutions, many of them unconnected to the church. Orthodoxy has profoundly integrated liturgy, piety, and doctrine.

Agreements between Evangelicalism and Orthodoxy

The ecumenical councils' declarations on the Trinity and Christ show the extensive agreement between Orthodoxy and evangelicalism, despite their disagreement on the *filioque* clause in the Nicene Creed. Although they have different emphases, Orthodoxy and evangelicalism agree on the Bible's authority, on sin, and on the fall (however, the Orthodox do not accept the specific Augustinian doctrine of original sin). They also agree on Christ's death and resurrection (although the Orthodox regard the atonement more as conquest of death than payment for the penalty of sin), the Holy Spirit, the return of Christ, the final judgment, heaven, and hell.

Historically the justification controversy of the Reformation was not an issue in the Eastern church, but there is generally an underlying consensus between the East and several Reformation doctrines in the West. Eastern patristic writers occasionally spoke of salvation as a gift of God's grace, and of faith as a gift of God; the famous Jesus Prayer ("Lord Jesus Christ, Son of God, have mercy on me, a sinner") attests to Orthodoxy's rejection of good works contributing to justification. In a similar way, there are echoes in the West of something like the Orthodox doctrine of "deification"—which is no more incompatible with justification by faith than are the doctrines of sanctification and glorification.

Additionally, the Orthodox doctrine of the church resonates with many evangelical concerns. Orthodox opposition to Rome is underlined by Cyprian's stress on the unity of the church, the parity of bishops, and the equality of all church members—a model of the church close to post-Reformation Anglicanism.

Significant Misunderstandings

Evangelical Misunderstandings of Orthodoxy

Orthodoxy's use of icons (visual representations of Christ and the saints) has bothered evangelicals, who argue that it can easily tend toward idolatry and worship of images of God. However, the Second Council of Nicea (A.D. *787*) emphatically denied that icons are worshiped. Following John of Damascus, it distinguished between honor (Gk. *proskynēsis*) given to saints and icons, and worship (Gk. *latreia*) owed to the indivisible Trinity alone. Icons are regarded as windows to the spiritual realm, betokening in the church's worship on earth the presence of the saints in heaven. Moreover, the idea of image (Gk. *eikon*) is prominent in the Bible. The whole creation reveals the glory of God (Ps. 19:1 ff.; Rom. 1:18–20).

On Scripture and tradition (the teaching of the church), both sides appeal to both sources. There is an overwhelming biblical emphasis in Orthodox liturgy—the Bible has been translated into the local vernacular wherever Orthodox missionaries have gone—while the Reformation did not ignore tradition but had a high view of the teaching of the church. The issue is not the Bible alone vs. tradition; it is which has the decisive voice, the last word over the other? For evangelicalism, the Bible is unequivocally the Word of God (e.g., 2 Tim. 3:16), while all human councils may err, and therefore the Bible must finally judge the tradition that seeks to expound it. For Orthodoxy, however, the decisions of the early church councils and church fathers often function in practice as equal to the Bible in authority.

Orthodox Misunderstandings of Evangelicalism

The Orthodox confuse the Protestant doctrine of predestination with Islamic fatalism. The Bible teaches *both* the absolute sovereignty of God *and* the full responsibility of man, God's decrees contemplating the free actions of secondary causes. As such, the Orthodox idea that the doctrine of predestination is monothelite, short-circuiting the human will, is misplaced.

Many Orthodox polemicists accuse evangelicals of ignoring the church's part in salvation. However, the classic Protestant confessions attest that the church is integral to the process of salvation, the Christian faith being found in the Bible and taught by the church. Orthodoxy at this point confuses classic Protestantism with later individualist views.

Substantive Disagreement

The Eastern Tendency to Downplay the Preaching of God's Word

Largely due to historical events (the depredations of Islam) and despite Orthodoxy's heritage of superlative preaching (Chrysostom, Gregory Nazianzen), worship in the East is more visual than worship in evangelical churches. Sermons are part of the liturgy, but the focus is as much on the icons and the symbolic movements of the clergy. Gregory of Nyssa stressed God's visible revelation in creation, along with the ambiguity and inadequacy of language.

The way Calvin resolved this question was to understand the knowledge of God in auditory terms: God's Word must be heard by us in faith. For Calvin, God reveals himself *in his Word* by the Holy Spirit. In the Word read and proclaimed, God addresses us personally. We cannot see him but we hear him. Moreover, his verbal revelation is true and reliable.

The Relationship between Scripture and Tradition

For Orthodoxy, tradition is a living, dynamic movement, the Bible existing within it and not apart from it. Orthodoxy also believes in biblical authority but as part of a larger whole. Evangelicals believe that the Bible is the ultimate authority.

The Palamite Doctrine of the Trinity

The influential archbishop of Thessalonica, Gregory Palamas (1296–1359), promoted a distinction, later widely accepted in Orthodoxy, between the unknowable essence (being) of God and his "energies." But this view has driven a wedge between God in himself and God as he has revealed himself, threatening our knowledge of God with profound agnosticism, since we have no way of knowing whether God is as he has revealed himself in Jesus Christ. This formulation defies rational discourse, since it tells us that we cannot say anything definitive about who God is, with the result that the Christian life is reduced to non-cognitive mystical contemplation. It introduces into God a division, not a distinction.

The Veneration of Mary and the Saints

Orthodoxy considers it possible, legitimate, and desirable for Christians to ask Mary and other departed saints to intercede with God on their behalf. But neither Jesus nor Paul ever suggest that this is possible.

The point is not that request for prayer is made to saints as such, for all Christians ask *living* saints to intercede with God for them. What evangelicals object to is the belief that *departed* saints can receive our prayers and so intercede on our behalf. The Bible does not encourage us to put our hope in the prayers of departed saints; it directs our hope to Christ, his return, and the resurrection, not to contact with saints departed (1 Thess. 4:13–18; cf. 1 Samuel 28; 1 Chron. 10:13; 1 Tim. 2:5).

Orthodoxy insists that the incarnation mandates icons of Christ, since God has chosen to reveal himself in human form. Evangelicals are equally emphatic that the second commandment prohibits the use of images in worship, and many think that using icons of Christ as aids to worship oversteps acceptable boundaries in that regard. Both sides claim the other is heretical; Orthodoxy considers evangelicals guilty of Manicheeism, entailing a deficient view of matter, while evangelicals argue that icons of Christ imply a Nestorian abstraction of Christ's humanity. (Manicheeism holds that there are two coequal realities, spirit and matter, which are respectively good and evil. Nestorianism is a heresy that separated Christ's divine and human natures.)

Synergism in Salvation

The East has a vigorous doctrine of free will and an implacable opposition to the Reformed teaching on predestination and the sovereignty of God's grace in Christ. In this aspect, Orthodoxy is farther away from the Reformation than is Rome. The difference in respective weighting of grace and the human will is far-reaching. It entails differing understandings of the extent of human sin and the nature of Christ's work.

Compared with Rome, How Far Away from Protestantism Is Orthodoxy?

There are ways in which Orthodoxy is closer to classic Protestantism than is Rome. Both were forced into separation from the Roman Church, and both agree in their opposition to the claims of the papacy. The structure of Orthodox churches is much closer to that of Reformed churches, especially the Anglican church. The Orthodox recognition of the parity of all believers, and the autonomy and autocephalous nature of local churches, is far closer to Reformed polity than is the Roman hierarchy. Hence, Orthodoxy does not have the same accumulation of authoritative dogmas as Rome. Moreover, the Orthodox stress on the Bible opens up a large commonality of approach.

There are, however, ways in which Orthodoxy is further removed from evangelicalism than is Rome. Protestantism shares the Roman Catholic understanding of the Trinity. Orthodoxy's stance on the *filioque* controversy, and its distinction between the essence of God and the divine energies, produce a different form of piety. Western faith is centered in Christ; the East's is more focused on the Holy Spirit. As Orthodox theologian Kallistos Ware put it, Rome and Protestantism share the same questions, but supply different answers; with Orthodoxy, the questions themselves are different. ◀

Liberal Protestantism

Liberal Protestantism can best be understood if one begins with a brief look at the thinkers most influential in its development.

Immanuel Kant

Liberal Protestantism arose out of the Enlightenment of the eighteenth century. To understand liberalism and its view of the Bible, one must grasp something of this Enlightenment influence. The German philosopher Immanuel Kant (1724–1804) produced what he called a "Copernican revolution" in epistemology (the study of how one comes to know what is known). In contrast to the geocentric Ptolemaic worldview (the sun and other planets were understood to orbit around the earth), Copernicus had correctly come to see the solar system heliocentrically (the planets, including the earth, orbit around the sun). Kant's thinking underwent a similar massive paradigm shift. He had believed that *external* objects determine what one sees and claims to know about the world. But Kant came to believe that one's mind contains certain structures called "intuitions" (e.g., space and time) and "categories" (e.g., cause and effect) that provide all the color, shape, relations, location, temporality, and spatiality that one "sees" of the external world. A person may think, e.g., that he is seeing a towering green fir tree out the window, but in fact he simply cannot know what he is seeing. All he can know is that his mind is producing the colors, shapes, relations, and other aspects that give him the impression of what he claims to "see" as a fir tree. Therefore, the towering green fir tree is, in a very real sense, the creation of the person's own mind. Yes, something is "out there," but what is actually seen, in the way that it is actually seen, is the result of the mind "shaping" the external data into what the person perceives.

Kant distinguished, then, between two realms of reality. The *noumenal* realm referred to the actual external world that exists outside of the mind (what Kant called "the thing in itself"). Of this realm nothing can be known except that something external "is" (i.e., exists). Just what it is—e.g., how big or tall, or what color or shape—cannot be known at all. The *phenomenal* realm, however, is "the thing as it appears." Whatever that "thing in itself" is, at least a person can know this: it appears to him as tall and green with broad, sweeping branches, and so it appears to him to be a fir tree. So "the thing in itself" cannot be known, and one can know only "the thing as it appears."

Friederich Schleiermacher

The German theologian almost universally recognized as the father of modern theological liberalism, Friederich Schleiermacher (1768–1834), was heavily influenced by Kant's philosophy. Schleiermacher applied the same "Copernican revolution" to theology that Kant had applied to epistemology. Schleiermacher proposed that the study of God must consider both the noumenal and phenomenal realms of knowledge. Certainly God himself would rightly be located within the "noumenal realm" (the realm of the "thing in itself" that would be beyond human ability to know). As many in the mystical tradition of the church had already affirmed, God is beyond human comprehension or knowledge and exists in a "cloud of unknowing." Schleiermacher adapted this tradition within the Romanticism of his day and combined it with Kant's notion of God existing within the noumenal realm. God "in himself," then, cannot be known. But in the "phenomenal realm" (the realm of God "as he appears" to someone), God can be known. That is, although one cannot know God as he actually is, one can know his own *experience* of God.

Schleiermacher resisted the "cultured despisers of religion" of his day. From the very fact that religious experience is universal and has always been an integral part of the experience of human cultures through time, he argued that it is evident that humans generally have this phenomenal experience of God. In fact, argued Schleiermacher, religion rightly understood should be seen as one's own "feeling of absolute dependence" before some supreme deity. Theology, then, cannot be *the study of God himself* but should rather be understood as *the study of the human experience of God*, in different ways and throughout different cultures. Theology does not attempt to describe God objectively but rather expresses ways in which thoughtful religious people experience their personal "God-consciousness" or "feeling of absolute dependence." The religious liberalism stemming from Schleiermacher, then, was "immanentalistic" (i.e., that God-awareness, not God himself, is the heart of religion) and "anti-authoritarian" (i.e., that subjective experience takes precedence over Scripture, tradition, church declarations, and creedal statements).

The Effect of Liberalism on the Doctrine of Scripture

The implications of this liberal shift from the study of God to the study of humanity's religious experience were enormous. One very important part of this shift was a radically different view of the Bible. Previously, the Bible had been thought of as divine revelation. That is, the God who created humankind and sent his Son to redeem them from their sin had actually revealed truth about himself and his plan of salvation, and this revelation was given in God's own Word, the Bible. But with Schleiermacher's Copernican revolution in theology, the Bible could no longer be "God's word," since God cannot be known and no word from him is possible. What is the Bible, then? For Schleiermacher and the liberal tradition that followed, the Bible was the product of various religious cultures and peoples, who recorded their own experiences with God as they imagined him to be. The Bible, then, contributed more directly to a "sociology of religions" inquiry than it did to a traditional "theology" (i.e., study of God). Since the Bible was merely the product of human cultures, over vast times, and through ancient and primitive understandings of the world, it certainly could not be understood as presenting truth that would be binding on anyone today, even if it did contain certain religious insights helpful for people of all times. Much less should the Bible be seen as divine truth, since God is beyond anyone's tangible grasp, and no book—including the Bible—could be *God's* word to humanity.

The nineteenth century, then, saw this liberal view of the Bible extended as historical-critical approaches to study of the Bible were developed. Two areas that received especially heated criticism were (1) the biblical teachings on the origins of the world and of human and other life on earth, and (2) the biblical teachings regarding Jesus' eternal existence, supernatural origin, miracles, atoning death, and bodily resurrection. A naturalistic understanding of the world had begun to prevail among the educated elites in Europe and America, and the very notion of supernatural intervention through miracles was deemed both unscientific and unnecessary in accounting for the world. The publication by Charles Darwin (1809–1882) of *On the Origin of Species* (1859) signaled for liberals not only the negation of miracles in explaining life but the end of any need for God's supernatural intervention in any form in accounting for life here on earth.

Albrecht Ritschl

Another German theology professor, Albrecht Ritschl (1822–1889), took Schleiermacher's insights and applied them particularly to the question of the meaning of Jesus' life. For Ritschl, Jesus was the supreme embodiment of God-consciousness and God-dependence. While being threatened by hostile forces, Jesus nonetheless trusted absolutely in God's love and power. He is therefore the Archetypal Man, a model for affirming value and worth in dependence on God. For Ritschl, the moral value of Christ and Christianity was central, for this provides the means by which contemporary people, in the community of the church, may overcome hostile pressures by dependence on God. So even though the historical facts of Jesus' life could never be known or verified, the moral value of Jesus' life constitutes the religious significance of Jesus for people today.

Adolf von Harnack

German theologian and historian Adolf von Harnack (1851–1930), raised in the home of an orthodox Christian scholar, was influenced by Ritschlian liberalism. He came to see the orthodox Christian tradition as being wrongly preoccupied with doctrines and standards of belief while missing the primary thrust of Jesus' teachings, namely, the moral responsibility to live out the righteousness of the kingdom. One must separate the essential "kernel" of the gospel (i.e., Christ's kingdom and its victory over evil) from the dispensable "husk" of the gospel (i.e., changing forms of life and thought). When this is done, the fatherhood of God and the brotherhood of man is exposed for every new generation, and the law of love is seen to govern all relationships.

The Effect of Liberalism on Other Doctrines

Given the prominence of Darwinist evolutionary theory and historical criticism (which attacked the historical reliability of the Bible) at the beginning of the twentieth century, liberalism was clearly prevailing over the defenders of orthodoxy. Under attack by liberalism were such cardinal doctrines as the special creation of Adam and Eve, the literal fall of Adam into sin, the virginal conception of Christ, the incarnation of Christ as fully God and fully human, the miracles that Christ and others performed, the substitutionary atoning death of Christ, the bodily resurrection of Christ—and underlying all of these, the full divine inspiration, inerrancy, and authority of Scripture, which teaches these doctrines as historically and theologically real and true. And of course, since conceptions such as sin, wrath, and hell were rejected, the gospel of liberalism was morphed into the so-called social gospel. Saving of souls was replaced with relieving people's present physical and social needs. The "good news" that liberals proclaimed was of a loving God who, through Christ's example of care for the poor and outcast, calls his people to help bring in the kingdom by showing love to others. The growing liberalism of the mainline Christian denominations of the early twentieth century was pervaded by an optimism regarding human nature that casts off human sinfulness and depravity, and an exclusive attention to God's love that turns a deaf ear to notions of God's anger and just judgment. Human reason had replaced revelation as the only reliable source for knowledge, and scientific naturalism had made it clear that the supernaturalist dogmas of orthodoxy simply had to be discarded if Christianity was to survive in this brave new world.

A Blow to the Optimism of Liberalism

The outbreak of the First World War was a blow to the optimistic outlook of liberalism. Many younger liberals became disenchanted with their heritage and followed the lead of Karl Barth (1886–1968) and Emil Brunner (1889–1966) toward a somewhat more conservative movement called "neo-orthodoxy." But liberalism's influence continued, particularly through the mainline denominations and many prestigious institutions of higher education. Gordon Kaufman, for over 30 years professor of theology and divinity at Harvard Divinity School, in 1981 published a book whose title beautifully captures the liberal mind-set—*The Theological Imagination: Constructing the Concept of God.* Since liberalism does not have divine revelation to read and study, and since it regards the Bible as a collection merely of human opinion and experience of God, theological liberals are left with only their own experience, reason, and imagination. Replacing the divine revelation in Scripture on which evangelicals depend is the imagination of their own human minds. Rather than receiving the revelation of God, they construct from their own thoughts the concept of God that they believe is most helpful to an ailing world.

Conclusion

Protestant liberalism continues to have significant influence. It represents the underlying theological position held by most of the leadership and professors in the theological seminaries of several mainline denominations in the United States (such as the Episcopal Church, the Evangelical Lutheran Church in America, the United Methodist Church, the American Baptist Convention, the Presbyterian Church–USA, and the United Church of Christ), though all these denominations still have some conservative evangelical congregations, teachers, and people within them as well. In addition, Protestant liberalism is the most common viewpoint in campus ministry offices in secular universities, and also among the professors who teach the Bible in religion departments of those universities. (Campus parachurch ministries, however, tend to be more in line with evangelical Protestantism.)

But liberalism's disregard for the church's long-standing claim that Scripture is divinely inspired and authoritative has left its adherents with an authority residing only in their own minds, and with understandings of what is acceptable that are mere echoes of secular values. Reason replaces revelation, cultural relativism replaces absolute truth, human optimism replaces divine salvation—and in all this, the gospel and historic orthodox faith is lost. The sad heritage of liberalism is a warning to all Christians to continue firm in the conviction that Scripture alone is God's inspired and authoritative Word from which one learns the truth that alone can set people free. ◀

Evangelical Protestantism

Reformation (16th Century)

Evangelical Protestantism arose out of the Reformation of the sixteenth century. The commitment of Martin Luther (1483–1546) to *sola Scriptura*—i.e., to "Scripture alone" as the only absolute and ultimately authoritative written revelation of God—along with other factors, brought about a separation from the Roman Catholic Church (see pp. 2613–2615). Roman Catholicism had understood other sources of revelation to be equal in authority to Scripture. Catholics understood the Bible to include several apocryphal books in addition to the 66 books accepted by Protestants as canonical Scripture; significantly, they also extended infallibility to church dogma pronounced by the magisterium (the pope and the bishops) and by the pope when speaking *ex cathedra* (lit., "out of his chair"). (This latter point was formally defined only in 1870, but most Catholics had taken it for granted since the Middle Ages.) This Roman Catholic extension of infallibility and authority was the backdrop for *sola Scriptura*, one of the heart-cries of the Reformation. This proclaimed Scripture alone as possessing complete infallibility and exclusive absolute authority for the church. One tangible effect of the Protestant commitment to the exclusive divine authority of Scripture for faith and practice was the diligent and courageous production of numerous translations of the Bible into the native languages of various countries and peoples. Protestants believed then, as now, that the Bible is for all the people of God. Only as people can read and study the Bible for themselves will they be able to learn well the teaching of God's Word and, in the manner of the Bereans of old (Acts 17:11), be able to assess various and divergent views of Scripture being advocated.

Protestantism (17th–18th Centuries)

The seventeenth and eighteenth centuries saw the rise and spread of various Protestant groupings that formed into denominations, some more directly tied to the "magisterial Reformers" Martin Luther and John Calvin (1509–1564) (e.g., Lutheranism, Presbyterianism, Anglicanism), and others that were indebted to that tradition yet differed from both Luther and Calvin, particularly in the doctrines of the church and salvation (e.g., Methodists, Baptists, Mennonites). But what these various Protestant groups had in common was a continued commitment to the Bible as the final written revelation of God, in contrast to the Roman Catholic tradition from which they all had retreated. Especially important during these centuries was the Protestant Scholastic reinforcement of the full divine inspiration, infallibility, inerrancy, and authority of Scripture. Pastors and theologians such as William Ames (1576–1633), John Gerhard (1582–1637), John Owen (1616–1683), John Quenstedt (1617–1688), Francis Turretin (1623–1687), Peter von Maastricht (1630–1706), Jonathan Edwards (1703–1758), and John Wesley (1703–1791) strongly defended the full inspiration and authority of Scripture. While differing, sometimes vigorously, on what Scripture taught on various doctrines, they affirmed the truthfulness and authority of the Bible to which they appealed. The sixteenth-century cry of *sola Scriptura* was echoed with force and vitality in the various seventeenth- and eighteenth-century Protestant traditions stemming from the Reformation.

Protestant Liberalism (19th Century)

The rise of Protestant liberalism (see pp. 2618–2619) in the nineteenth century had a chilling effect on Christian confidence in the Bible as fully divine and authoritative. Following principles made popular in the Enlightenment (an 18th-century intellectual movement in European and American philosophy and culture), liberal scholars and teachers such as Friederich Schleiermacher (1768–1834), Albrecht Ritschl (1822–1889), and Adolf von Harnack (1851–1930) called into question the historicity of the narrative accounts in both the OT and the NT, and they rejected the Bible's many claims to be testifying to God's supernatural activity. As a result, a line of demarcation was established over the divine authorship and full infallibility and authority of the Bible, with liberal Protestants rejecting it and evangelical Protestants accepting it. Add to this the rising liberal biblical scholarship and the developments in evolutionary biology through the publication of *On the Origin of Species* (1859) by Charles Darwin (1809–1882), and one can clearly understand the mounting pressure that evangelicals faced in defending their long-standing conviction that Scripture is God's Word and hence is utterly true.

Fundamentalism (19th–20th Centuries)

The late nineteenth and early twentieth centuries saw the outbreak of what came to be called the Fundamentalist-Modernist controversy. The conservative and evangelical defenders of the truthfulness and authority of Scripture eventually came to be known as "fundamentalists" because they devoted themselves to defending and preserving for the church the most fundamental doctrines of the Christian faith that were being denied and ridiculed by so-called "modernists" (i.e., liberals). Influential scholarly defenders of Christian orthodoxy in the face of mounting liberalism included B. B. Warfield (1851–1921), R. A. Torrey (1856–1928), and J. Gresham Machen (1881–1937). They labored hard to interact with liberal attacks against the fundamentals of the faith through their teaching, preaching, and prodigious efforts in writing.

A massive project was undertaken in 1909 to assemble a formidable collection of essays written by recognized conservative scholars defending the major doctrines being assailed by liberals. *The Fundamentals: A Testimony to the Truth*, published in 12 volumes from 1910 to 1915, was mailed to pastors and missionaries throughout the world. These volumes contained no fewer than 90 chapters defending against liberal higher criticism such doctrinal fundamentals as the historicity and truthfulness of the Bible, the virgin birth and deity of Christ, the personality and deity of the Holy Spirit, the saving death of Christ, and justification by faith, as well as a number of chapters devoted to the errors of liberalism, Darwinism, Roman Catholicism, Mormonism, and other false teachings of the day. Hope was high that liberalism might thus be answered and that a strong orthodoxy would prevail in mainline denominations and churches.

The 1920s saw only increased conflict, however, between fundamentalists and modernists. In religious institutions of higher education and within the mainline denominations, fundamentalist positions and arguments were routinely rejected in favor of more "tolerant" understandings that accorded with modern learning. The most symbolically important defeat to fundamentalism came with the Scopes "Monkey Trial" of 1925. John T. Scopes was tried for his teaching of Darwinist evolution in a Tennessee public school. Defending him was Clarence Darrow, a highly respected Chicago lawyer, and prosecuting the case against him was William Jennings Bryan, well known both as a fundamentalist Presbyterian and for his national political involvements. Although Bryan won the case against Scopes, Darrow publicly ridiculed Bryan's fundamentalist position in ways that were picked up by the national media and published throughout the country. As a result, fundamentalism was decisively rejected by intellectual elites as a repressive and backward set of views, resistant to modern learning and advancement. Along with this rejection of fundamentalism was a rejection of the fundamentalist commitment to the inerrant Bible, the only absolutely authoritative written revelation from God.

The next 20-plus years witnessed a marked departure from the aggressive and culture-confronting approach of the earlier work of Warfield, Torrey, and Machen. Post-1925 fundamentalism came to be characterized more by retreat and separation from the culture than by an effort to engage and transform that broader culture. While fundamentalists continued to hold fast to the authority of Scripture, they knew that their views of the Bible and its teachings were largely rejected by the increasingly secular media and schools of higher education. As a result, they tended to become more isolationist, regularly highlighting the Bible's call to "come out from among them, and be ye separate" (2 Cor. 6:17, KJV). Furthermore, because of liberalism's advocacy of the "social gospel" in place of the traditional Christian gospel of faith in Christ for personal salvation from the wrath of God because of human sin, fundamentalists tended to view most kinds of social involvement with a high degree of suspicion, fearing that the "saving of souls" might be displaced by caring for human physical and social needs. In short, the fundamentalism of the decades immediately following the Scopes trial retreated from any aggressive intellectual engagement on behalf of the Bible's truth with the culture's most educated elites, and also withdrew from any intentional effort to address the physical and social needs of society.

Evangelicalism (20th Century)

Responding to this trend were people such as Harold John Ockenga (1905–1985) and Carl F. H. Henry (1913–2003). Ockenga and Henry were typical of a group of young evangelicals in the 1940s who were fully in agreement with fundamentalist commitments to the inerrancy and authority of Scripture and its attending orthodox beliefs, yet were deeply disturbed by the fundamentalist retreat from culture. Henry wrote what would become a clarion call to fundamentalists to reengage the culture, both intellectually and socially. His first published book, *The Uneasy Conscience of Modern Fundamentalism* (1947), questioned the separatist mind-set of fundamentalism. Henry called for a new and vibrant defense of evangelical faith in the face of the best (or worst) that liberals could produce, and for a recommitment to join social action with gospel witness such that true evangelical love and care for others might be manifest along with sharing the good news of the gospel of Jesus Christ. Also in 1947, Ockenga and Charles E. Fuller (1887–1968) cofounded Fuller Theological Seminary (Pasadena, California) with hopes that a vibrant intellectual evangelical approach to the study of Scripture might take place in full engagement with and in response to liberal scholarship. Charter faculty members were Wilbur M. Smith (1894–1977), Everett F. Harrison (1902–1999), Harold Lindsell (1913–1998), and Carl Henry. In 1956, under the auspices of L. Nelson Bell and Billy Graham, Henry became the first editor-in-chief of *Christianity Today*, a magazine intended to bring evangelical scholarship and editorial commentary into evangelical homes across the country, much as *The Christian Century* had for decades conveyed more liberal viewpoints predominantly to those in mainline denominations.

Much health and vitality was evident in the evangelical movement of the 1940s, 50s, 60s, and 70s. Consider just some of the organizations and institutions that began during these years: Tyndale Fellowship and Tyndale House (1944) in the UK, the International Fellowship of Evangelical Students (1947), the Evangelical Theological Society, World Vision (1950), the Billy Graham Evangelistic Association (1950), Campus Crusade for Christ (1951), Fellowship of Christian Athletes (1954), the National Association of Evangelicals, Bible Study Fellowship (1959), Youth With A Mission (1960), Operation Mobilization (1960), National Black Evangelical Association (1963), Gordon-Conwell Theological Seminary (1969), Food for the Hungry (1971), Prison Fellowship (1976), and Focus on the Family (1977). So strong was the evangelical presence throughout the country that *Newsweek* declared 1976 "The Year of the Evangelical."

Along with this growth and increased influence, however, some of the underpinnings of biblical authority were eroding. On December 1, 1962 (so-called Black Saturday), Fuller Theological Seminary took steps to remove "inerrancy" from its doctrinal statement regarding Scripture, and this was just one notable indication of a divide within various segments of evangelicalism between those who understood divine inspiration to entail biblical inerrancy and those who denied this. So in the 1960s and 1970s, evangelical growth was paralleled by evangelical division over the inerrancy of Scripture.

In 1977 a prominent group of concerned conservative evangelicals met to design a meeting to take place the next year to define the "inerrancy" of Scripture. The International Council on Biblical Inerrancy met in Chicago in October 1978 for the first of what would be three summits. Out of this first summit came "The Chicago Statement on Biblical Inerrancy," the most widely used and definitive statement on its subject for the conservative evangelical movement. At its November 2006 annual meeting, the Evangelical Theological Society adopted the Chicago Statement as its own defining declaration of the inerrancy of Scripture.

Evangelical Protestantism Today

Evangelical Protestantism today consists of hundreds of denominational groups and parachurch organizations, and represents numerous theological streams (such as the Bible-believing segments of Reformed, Arminian,

Baptist, Lutheran, Anglican, dispensational, Restorationist, charismatic, and Pentecostal groups as well as many independent groups with mixtures of these traditions). In spite of the differences among these traditions, evangelicals are united in the belief that the Bible is not a merely human record of people's religious experiences (the position of Protestant liberalism) but is actually the Word of God.

Under the large umbrella of those who believe that the Bible is the Word of God remains a continued division over what the divine inspiration of Scripture entails. Some deny the complete truthfulness of Scripture, and this inevitably leads to rejecting certain biblical teachings that one finds objectionable for one reason or another. Others, usually referred to as conservative evangelicals, continue to uphold, defend, and celebrate the full truthfulness of Scripture, since it is, in part and in whole, the very inspired (lit., "breathed out") Word of God (2 Tim. 3:16). Clearly, the evangelical heritage that stems from the Reformers through the early fundamentalist defenders of the Bible to the fathers of contemporary evangelicalism would call readers to affirm, with them, the complete truthfulness of all that the Bible teaches, for all of the Bible is none other than the full Word of God. ◂

Evangelical Protestantism and Global Christianity

Although often regarded as a Western religion, Christianity (which had its birth in Asia) has always been much broader than its European expression and is today a genuinely global religion. During the first two centuries of the Christian era, the centers of Christianity were in Syria, Egypt, and Mesopotamia. The faith spread rapidly, so that by the second century A.D. the church was in India, and Christians were in major centers of the Persian Empire. Christian communities were in Ethiopia by the fourth century and in China by the seventh century. It was only after about the fourteenth century that Europe, and later North America, became the heartland of Christianity. Even after the rise of Western European Christianity, however, Christian communities continued to exist elsewhere, including in lands conquered by Muslims in Arabia and Persia.

Furthermore, during the last half of the twentieth century Christianity experienced a dramatic shift in demographics, so that by the early twenty-first century roughly two-thirds of all Christians were located—not in Europe and North America—but in Asia, Latin America, and Africa. The Christian church has experienced explosive growth in places such as China, South Korea, Guatemala, El Salvador, Brazil, Nigeria, Kenya, and Ghana. Many factors contributed to this change, including the decline of Christianity in parts of Europe, the modern missionary movements of the eighteenth through twentieth centuries, and the evangelizing efforts of indigenous Christians.

The Bible has been central to the growth of the Christian church worldwide. Early Protestant missionaries such as William Carey, Adoniram Judson, and Hudson Taylor were motivated by the message of the Bible and convinced that all people should have the opportunity to respond to it. Moreover, from early times the Bible has been translated into local languages, and the Protestant missionary movements of the past three centuries have emphasized biblical translation. The translatability of the Bible into local languages (1) is a recognition of the capacity of all people in all cultures to understand and respond to the Word of God in their own language; (2) gives dignity to local linguistic and cultural expressions; and (3) provides resources for social change. Thus, there is remarkable diversity within global Christianity today. In his book *Disciples of All Nations*, historian Lamin Sanneh observes:

> More people pray and worship in more languages and with more differences in styles of worship in Christianity than in any other religion. Well over three thousand of the world's languages are embraced by Christianity through Bible translation, prayer, liturgy, hymns, and literature. More than 90 percent of these languages have a grammar and a dictionary at all only because the Western missionary movement provided them, thus pioneering arguably the largest, most diverse and most vigorous movement of cultural renewal in history (p. *xx*).

While the rapidly growing Christian communities in Latin America, Africa, and Asia are in some ways distinctive, and not simply mirror images of denominations and movements in the West, they also have much in common with Western evangelicalism. Most are theologically conservative and embrace worldviews which acknowledge the reality of the supernatural. Most have not been influenced by Enlightenment rationalism and higher-critical approaches to Scripture; they regularly take the Bible in a straightforward manner, with utmost seriousness.

Protestant Christianity is undergoing massive cultural shifts and realignments worldwide, but there are common commitments and institutions which provide cohesion to those identifying themselves as evangelicals. The Lausanne Movement and the World Evangelical Alliance (WEA) have been significant in shaping evangelical identity worldwide, and both are based upon strong commitments to the full authority of the Bible. The Lausanne Movement, which grew out of the 1974 Lausanne Congress on World Evangelization, produced the Lausanne Covenant, widely recognized and accepted as a statement of evangelical theological commitment unifying Christians across the globe. The Covenant embraces "the divine inspiration, truthfulness and authority" of the Bible as the "written word of God, without error in all that it affirms." The WEA is an international network of churches in over 120 nations and over 100 international organizations which together represent over 400 million evangelical Christians worldwide. The WEA statement of faith affirms belief in the Bible as "divinely inspired, infallible, entirely trustworthy" and "the supreme authority in all matters of faith and conduct."

Although there are significant differences among evangelicals throughout the world, they are united by a common commitment to the Lordship of Jesus Christ in all of life and the authority of the Bible as God's divinely inspired written revelation. ◂

The Bible and World Religions

The Bible and Contemporary Judaism

Early History (c. 2100 B.C.–586 B.C.)

Beginning with Abraham, the founding "rock" of the Jewish people, and continuing to the modern era, Judaism has maintained continuity and passed down a remarkable legacy (cf. Isa. 51:1–2). Judaism has also been a religion of innovation, adaptability, and change. God progressively revealed his will and teachings to Abraham and his descendants (cf. Rom. 4:11–18; Gal. 3:29). The cataclysmic events leading to the exodus, and the revelation at Sinai, gave the nation of Israel its foundational spiritual identity. The religion of Moses, and later that of King David and the prophets, was far more dynamic than static. The understanding of Israel's faith continued to be shaped and reshaped by social expansion, cultural interaction, and critical events such as the destruction of the temple, the exile, and restoration, all of which were recorded and interpreted in the Hebrew Scriptures.

Second Temple Judaism (c. 516 B.C.–A.D. 70)

After the exile to Babylon in 586 B.C., Jews returned to Jerusalem to rebuild their temple. (Five centuries later, Herod the Great [who ruled 37–4 B.C.] lavishly expanded this second temple.) In the mid-fifth century B.C., Ezra, a priest and scribe, was a major force in reforming and reshaping the postexilic Jewish community. Ezra introduced the public reading and explanation of the Torah (that is, the Scriptures; cf. Nehemiah 8), which has remained a focal point of Jewish religious life to this day. The era between the Testaments was a very creative time for Judaism. During this period: the synagogue emerged; the Pharisees, Sadducees, and Essenes all took shape (see Jewish Groups at the Time of the New Testament, pp. 1799–1800); and the oral law became increasingly important—especially for the Pharisees—in defining the boundaries of Jewish religious life. The rapid rise of Hellenism (the adoption of Greek culture) posed other challenges, some of which threatened the stability, purity, and piety of the Jewish community. In response to the surge of Hellenism, Jews in the third and second centuries B.C. produced a translation of their Hebrew Scriptures into Greek, the Septuagint Version (see The Septuagint, pp. 2601–2603). These and other factors contributed to the diversity and complexity of the Jewish movements at the time of Jesus. Christianity is an outgrowth of Second Temple Judaism, i.e., "pre-A.D. 70 Judaism."

Judaism after A.D. 70 (c. A.D. 70–c. 1750)

After the destruction of the temple (A.D. 70), only two Jewish sects survived. One sect, the Pharisees, gave rise to the rabbis of subsequent centuries and eventually developed into modern Judaism. A second major sect that survived, the "Nazarenes," were the Jewish followers of Jesus (cf. Acts 24:5). For the first few years after the death of Jesus, the earliest church was comprised mostly of Jewish believers and was viewed as a movement within Judaism (cf. "temple" in Acts 2:46). Beginning with Peter's ministry to Cornelius (Acts 10) and Paul's initial ministry to the Gentiles (Acts 9:1–43; 11:20–26; 13:1–52), the church expanded rapidly with the inclusion of many non-Jews, and thus the modern Christian church was firmly established (cf. Acts, esp. chs. 2; 15; Eph. 2:11–22).

One cannot draw a straight line from the Bible to every current Jewish belief and practice. After A.D. 70, Judaism continued to undergo significant reformulation and change. For example, the temple sacrifice of Passover lambs was discontinued, and the yearly entry of the high priest into the Most Holy Place was no more. The rabbis replaced these and other rituals of the temple with symbolic reminders, liturgical references, and spiritual exercises such as repentance, prayer, and good deeds. With the destruction of the central sanctuary in Jerusalem and the scattering of Jews from their land, the home became increasingly important as the fountainhead of Jewish religious life.

The most significant source in the development of postbiblical (rabbinic) Judaism is the Talmud (lit., "learning"). This massive compilation of rabbinic teachings and discussions accumulated its material in both oral and written form for several centuries, and attained its final written form about A.D. 500. Centuries later, medieval scholars such as Abraham Ibn Ezra, Maimonides, and Rashi, along with modern scholars, would further shape postbiblical Jewish thought. Contemporary Judaism thus rests on more than the Jewish Scriptures (what Christians call the Old Testament). A significant hallmark of contemporary Judaism is its recognition of an ongoing, living tradition: the commentary of the rabbis and sages, both past and present.

Contemporary Judaism (c. A.D. 1750–present)

Modern Judaism is a development of rabbinic Judaism. Like Second Temple Judaism, it is greatly diverse and sometimes difficult to define. Furthermore, there is often a difference between what a religion formally teaches and what an individual adherent may practice. Judaism today does not see itself as a dead, legalistic religion, whose mission is long over, now replaced by Christianity. Rather, Judaism considers itself a valid and dynamic faith whose followers are in covenant relationship with God. In the Jewish view, the claims of Christ are not valid, so the NT writings are not considered binding, authoritative sources, as are the Tanach (the Hebrew Bible), the Talmud, and other rabbinic writings. Therefore, Jewish interpreters of a passage in the Tanach will often differ from Christian interpreters, since Jews are not reading it through the inspired lens of the NT writers.

Judaism is a religion of laypeople. As such, it reflects the early concept of "freedom of the synagogue," valuing individual expression and thriving on reasoning through dialogue and polarity of thought. With its community-centeredness, today's synagogue maintains its historic threefold function as a house of study, prayer, and assembly. A congregational rabbi, though ordained by the laying on of hands, carries no vested authority over that congregation. The rabbi is primarily a scholar-teacher, a transmitter of Jewish heritage. The rabbi speaks *to* the people, not *for* the people.

Contemporary Branches or Movements

Today, Judaism is comprised of several branches or movements, each with certain distinguishing features. *Orthodox Judaism* is strongly committed to *halakhah*, the legal tradition of the Talmud and other law codes. In Orthodoxy, God is personal. The Torah (Scripture) and its *mitswot*, or "commandments," are divinely revealed. The Torah is unchanging, a focal point for study and living. Orthodox Jews usually hold to a more literal interpretation of Scripture, a distinctive dress code, dietary laws, and strict Sabbath observance.

Reform Judaism, by contrast, does not view *halakhah* as binding. Reform Judaism seeks to adapt to modern times by encouraging innovation, diversity, and egalitarianism. In Reform Judaism, the basis for decision making is not a legal system but individual autonomy, informed by reason and experience. Consistent with that approach, Reform Judaism adopts a modern, higher-critical approach to the Hebrew Scriptures and mainly deems the Scriptures to be a product of human reflection, not a result of divine inspiration (see Liberal Protestantism, pp. 2618–2619, for a similar approach). Reform Jews tend to emphasize human progress, social justice, and the ethical teachings of the prophets more than specific doctrines or ritualistic observances.

Conservative Judaism, a third major branch, falls theologically between Orthodoxy and Reform. Conservative Jews accept tradition but with an openness to change. *Halakhah* is not "frozen" but is a dynamic entity, subject to modification or adjustment in order to make it more relevant in light of current cultural concerns. Consistent with this understanding, Conservative Jews understand the Scriptures to be the words of God but would also see God's revelation as an ongoing process, not confined to the ancient Hebrew Scriptures alone. For Conservative Jews, the decision for change is not based on an individual's right to choose but on the congregation or the community itself, informed by the consensus of current historical scholarship.

Two additional groups—though very dissimilar theologically—are the Hasidic Jews and the Messianic Jews. *Hasidism* is the mystical movement in Judaism. Hasidic Jews are very "Torah-centric," and they are traditional in their lifestyle. God is to be celebrated, for he is present everywhere; he seeks loving, sincere hearts to let him in. Hasidic worship is characterized by dancing, spontaneity, joy, and great intensity. Folk tales abound in the Hasidic movement.

Messianic Jews are culturally Jewish people who believe Jesus is the Messiah. As a means of affirming their Jewish identity, many messianic believers attend messianic Christian congregations. Services are structured along the lines of synagogue worship, in music and liturgy. As a movement, messianic Judaism has struggled to find acceptance within the larger Jewish community. Opponents have often marginalized messianic Judaism both theologically and socially, claiming its adherents really belong to the Christian church, not the Jewish community. The theology of many messianic Jews is closely linked to that of the evangelical Christian community, from which it has generally found support.

Today, numerous Jews do not identify with a synagogue or live religiously observant lives. The religion of Judaism and being culturally Jewish are not synonymous. Jews who do not choose to practice Judaism often define themselves as culturally or ethnically Jewish; others variously identify themselves as humanistic, secular, or agnostic. For many Bible-centered Christians who are unaware of the great diversity in Judaism, such definitions appear incongruous or simply confusing. For these Jews, however, it may in part reflect the influence of modernity, the Age of Reason, and the decimating tragedy of the Holocaust upon their understanding of God and the Jewish experience.

Judaism and Evangelicalism

Evangelical Christianity and traditional Judaism share many biblically-based beliefs and much ethical common ground. Some of these concepts, however, may be nuanced differently. This common heritage is not surprising. Evangelicals and Jews share the Scriptures of the OT and are heirs of the same spiritual ancestry: early Israelite religion through Second Temple Judaism. Areas of basic agreement include belief in one eternal, omniscient God, the Creator of heaven and earth. Further, God revealed his Torah to Moses, and his word to the prophets. In the future, he will send the Messiah, will raise the dead, and will judge (Jews look forward to this as the Messiah's first coming; Christians think of it as his second coming). Other jointly held beliefs include: the necessity to bear witness to one's faith, the imperative to love one's neighbor, and the recognition that all individuals are created in the image of God. Evangelicals and most Jews also agree on the sacredness of life, the integrity of the family, the pursuit of justice and peace, and the recognition that God is providentially and progressively guiding history toward a glorious climax.

While acknowledging that both faiths hold much in common, it must be recognized that major differences exist, especially in the area of theology. Jews do not consider the NT of equal authority to the Tanach. Jews are monotheists, but not Trinitarian monotheists. Jews do not embrace the concept of original sin inherited from Adam. Jews do not accept the divinity of Jesus, his messiahship, and his vicarious atonement. Jews do not teach salvation by faith, apart from works, through Christ alone.

Growing numbers of evangelicals see the importance of becoming involved in Jewish-Christian dialogue. Interfaith encounters give opportunities to build respectful friendships, thoughtful alliances, and a deeper understanding of the Jewish roots of the Christian faith. Dialogue provides an occasion to define oneself spiritually, and an avenue to eliminate misconceptions and stereotypes. Evangelicals have much to learn from Jews, and likewise Jews from evangelicals. While contemporary Judaism and evangelical Christianity are in the end two different faiths, authentic witness to one another—conducted with genuine humility and without theological compromise—allows for the establishment of trust and beneficial spiritual growth.

Evangelicals have been among the strongest non-Jewish supporters of the modern state of Israel. Many evangelicals base their solidarity and support on various prophetic passages which seem to imply a future restoration of Jews to their land prior to God's final act of redemption at the end of the age; others appeal to certain biblical texts emphasizing God's covenant faithfulness to his people and the promise of land (cf. Gen. 17:7–8; Jer. 31:35–36; Amos 9:14–15). However, some evangelicals prefer to support Israel's right to a homeland more on historical, judicial, and moral grounds, rather than on specific scriptural or theological considerations. Still other evangelicals are reluctant to take a position of active support for Israel. Their reasons include: the church is a universal body and has permanently replaced Israel in God's economy; the modern state of Israel is a secular nation and not biblical Israel; justice concerns on the part of Palestinian Arabs will be compromised if active support is given to Israel.

Eschatology should never annul justice. If evangelicals believe Israel has an unconditional "divine right" to the land, it would be unwise to uphold such a claim without first thinking through its implications for justice and compassion toward every inhabitant of the land. For evangelicals to express their "solidarity" with Israel, however, it need not imply evangelical support for any unjust treatment of Palestinian Arabs. God loves all people and he delights when the land is shared with a maximum of justice and a minimum of injustice. The preservation and return of the Jewish people to their ancestral homeland is, at the very least, evidence of God's ongoing faithfulness and love for them (Rom. 11:1, 28–29). Whatever millennial views evangelicals hold, they must not absolutize the land, nor in any way idolize it. God alone is sovereign; he is Lord of life, Lord of history, and Lord of land. ◂

The Bible and Other World Religions

Although the Bible nowhere discusses "other religions" as such, much in it is relevant to the subject. The OT includes repeated references to the deities and religious practices of the Egyptians, Canaanites, Philistines, and Babylonians. The NT world was populated with "many 'gods' and many 'lords'" (1 Cor. 8:5) and characterized by religious syncretism. But the religions of the ancient world have been replaced today by the so-called major world religions. This article will briefly examine Hinduism, Buddhism, Confucianism, and Islam, noting similarities and differences between their teachings and Christian faith.

Hinduism

Hinduism is a family of diverse religious traditions that are the product of some 4,000 years of development in India. There is no single founder of Hinduism; it has no prescribed ecclesiastical structure; nor does it have a carefully defined creed. A Hindu may believe in one god, many gods, or no god. Some Hindus think of the religious "ultimate" as a personal being; others regard it as a nonpersonal reality. Any unity that exists within Hinduism is found in the common acceptance of the authority of the Vedas, composed between 1400 and 400 B.C., as sacred literature; belief in reincarnation of the soul in accordance with *karma*; and, at least until modern times, the importance of caste.

According to the doctrine of reincarnation, persons are continually being reborn as the *atman* (the soul) passes from one life to another. A person's present life is one in an unimaginably long series of past and future lives. Rebirths are regulated by *karma*, a metaphysical principle that determines current and future states on the basis of past actions and dispositions. The repeated cycle of birth, death, and rebirth is *samsara* (lit., "wandering"), and the traditional soteriological goal of Hinduism is *moksha*, or liberation from rebirths through breaking the causal conditions of *karma*.

Traditionally there are three ways to attain *moksha*:

1. The way of right action (*karma marga*) involves living in accordance with one's duty as determined by gender, caste, and stage in life. Classical Hinduism divided society into four major castes, with hundreds of smaller subdivisions. At the top were the *Brahmins* (teachers, priests), followed by the *Kshatriyas* (rulers, warriors). *Vaishyas* (merchants, craftsmen) and *Sudras* (laborers, servants) formed the two lower castes. Menial laborers who perform "unclean" tasks were regarded as "outcastes" or "untouchables," although they are now referred to as *Dalits* ("oppressed ones").

2. The second way to liberation is that of liberating knowledge (*jnana marga*). A central question in the later Vedas concerned the relation between Brahman (the supreme being; see below) and the human self, and in an influential text the self is identified with Brahman: "That thou art" (*Chandogya Upanishad* 6.9–13). What breaks the cycle of rebirths, then, is the existential realization of one's essential identity with Brahman.

3. The way of devotion (*bhakti marga*) is open to members of any caste and is the most popular way of seeking liberation. *Bhakti* means love, reverence, or adoration for a particular deity, and involves *puja*, or ritual worship of deities such as Vishnu, Shiva, or Krishna.

Most Hindus accept the idea of Brahman as the supreme being and sustaining power of the cosmos. But there is disagreement over the nature of Brahman and its relation to the human person. An early text declares, "He is one, [though] wise men call Him by many names" (*Rigveda* I.164.46). The idea that the religious ultimate can be understood and experienced in many different ways is central to Hinduism.

Thus, Hinduism includes both monistic and theistic traditions. The Advaita Vedanta (non-dualism) tradition of Shankara (d. A.D. 820), e.g., claims that the sole reality is Nirguna Brahman, a nonpersonal reality utterly beyond human concepts and categories. The world of ordinary experience is *maya* (appearance), a lower level of reality, and *moksha* comes through an existential awareness of one's essential identity with Brahman.

More theistic forms of Hinduism regard Brahman (or Shiva or Vishnu) as a personal deity and insist that liberation comes not through knowledge alone but through devotion to the deity. The Vishisht Advaita (qualified nondualism) of Ramanuja (d. A.D. 1137) teaches that there is only one reality, Saguna Brahman, or Brahman with personal attributes. Brahman is thus a personal being. The world is real and is the "body" of Brahman.

Theistic Hinduism teaches that Vishnu has taken on human or animal form as ten *avatars* ("descents" or "manifestations"), most famously as Krishna in the *Bhagavad Gita*. Other *avatars* include nonhuman appearances as a fish, a tortoise, a boar, and a man-lion.

Buddhism

The founder of Buddhism, Siddhartha Gautama (traditionally, 563–483 B.C.; also known as "the Buddha"), was born into a wealthy chieftain's family in northern India. Determined to find the cause of suffering and pain, he rejected his luxurious lifestyle and became a wandering ascetic. After much meditation and ascetic discipline, Gautama experienced "enlightenment," and for the next 40 years he traveled throughout India preaching the *dharma* (truth) and attracting a large following.

The heart of the teaching of the Buddha (lit., "awakened one") is the Four Noble Truths. The First Truth states that all existence is characterized by *dukkha* ("suffering," "pain," or "discontent"). The Second Truth holds that the root cause of suffering is *tanha* (lit., "thirst" but often translated "desire"). It is not simply wrong desires but desire itself that results in suffering. The Third Truth says that when desire ceases, then suffering ceases as well. The Fourth Truth introduces the Noble Eightfold Path, which sets out ideals in moral self-discipline, meditation, and wisdom that provide the way to eliminate desire and suffering.

The Buddha held that everything that exists is characterized by *anitya*, or impermanence, and is continually coming into being and passing out of being as a result of certain interrelated causal conditions. A 12-link chain of causation (the "wheel of life") explains how these causal conditions produce people's mistaken perceptions of enduring realities.

The Buddha rejected contemporary Hindu views about the reality of an enduring self (*atman*), an indestructible soul that passes from one life to another. He claimed that belief in a substantial self is mistaken and results in the grasping or desire that produces suffering. What is normally thought of as a person is merely the ever-changing combination of psychophysical forces—the "Five Aggregates" of matter, sensations, perceptions, mental formations, and consciousness. At death, what passes from this life to the next is not a soul but simply the cumulative *karmic* effects of actions, which then produce in the next life the (mistaken) perception of an enduring person.

Only *nirvana* is permanent, unconditioned, and ultimately real. *Nirvana* is not heaven. Rather, it is a state that is realized when the fires of desire and the conditions producing rebirth are eliminated. Since it is the absence of suffering in any form, it is a state of utter bliss.

Buddhism today is divided into two major groups. Theravada Buddhism, found in Sri Lanka, Burma, Thailand, Laos, and Cambodia, accepts only the writings of the Pali canon as authoritative, emphasizes the Four Noble Truths in attaining *nirvana*, and generally avoids metaphysical speculation. Early Buddhists rejected Hindu belief in Brahman, and this atheism is retained in Theravada. Moreover, each person is said to be responsible for attaining his or her own enlightenment ("self-effort"), which is restricted to the few who can master the required disciplines.

Mahayana Buddhism is today found in China, Korea, Vietnam, Japan, and the West and includes a wide variety of schools. It has developed its own sacred texts and metaphysical doctrines. In China, the traditional understanding of *nirvana* as release from the cycle of rebirths was largely replaced by Mahayana, with an emphasis on attaining enlightenment in this life. Whereas Theravada Buddhism emphasized self-effort in attaining *nirvana*, Mahayana opened the way to the masses by acknowledging a vast multitude of spiritual beings, such as the *bodhisattvas*, who assist in the quest for enlightenment. Moreover, the Pure Land schools, the most popular form of Buddhism in Japan today, teach that rebirth in the Pure Land (a kind of Buddhist paradise) is possible, not by one's own efforts but solely by relying on the compassion, merit, and "other power" of the Amida Buddha.

Whereas Theravada Buddhism regards Gautama largely as an extraordinary human being who attained enlightenment, Mahayana developed the doctrine of the Three Bodies of the Buddha (*Trikaya*). The ultimate reality is the *Dharmakaya*, or the Law Body, an all-inclusive Buddha essence sometimes identified with the Void or Emptiness (*sunyata*). The many enlightened *buddhas* and *bodhisattvas* constitute the *Sambhogakaya*, or Body of Bliss. The *Nirmanakaya*, or Transformation Body, refers to the man Gautama as a specific historical manifestation of the universal Buddha nature.

Confucianism

Confucianism is a system of social, ethical, and religious teachings derived from Confucius. It has been influential in Chinese, Korean, and Japanese cultures. Confucius (552–479 B.C.) was born into a poor but respected family in northwestern China. He became educated in the ancient Chinese classical writings and offered instruction in history, poetry, government, music, and moral conduct. Confucius was given various ministerial positions in the government of the Duke of Lu, eventually becoming prime minister. Tradition maintains that his honesty and eagerness to implement changes in government led to his dismissal. After traveling widely, seeking in vain a "wise ruler" who would implement his ideas, Confucius returned to his native area and continued teaching and editing the classics. After his death his disciples compiled the *Lun Yu* or *Analects*, a collection of Confucius's sayings that form the basic understanding of his teachings. The *Analects*, along with the *Da Xue* (*Great Learning*), *Zhong Yong* (*Doctrine of the Mean*), and *Meng Tzu* (*Mencius*) constitute the authoritative Four Books of Confucianism. Mencius (372–289 B.C.) was the most influential Confucian thinker after Confucius.

Sixth-century B.C. China was undergoing severe social and political pressures that eventually resulted in civil war. Confucius called for a return to the practice of ethical and social principles of an earlier era in order to produce order and harmony within the family, society, and the nation at large. During the Han Dynasty (206 B.C.–A.D. 220) Confucianism became the established social and religious philosophy of the state.

Order within the family, society, and nation is patterned after the way of Heaven (*Tian*). Confucius's views on God/gods are unclear, but he did speak often of Heaven. Although Heaven seems to be purposive in directing cosmic affairs, it is perhaps not so much a personal being as a cosmic principle or the ground of the moral order. The universe has a moral character, so that when one practices the moral law in social relationships, one reflects the moral will of Heaven.

Li ("propriety"), a central concept in Confucian thought, refers to a proper and appropriate way of being and doing things, including the proper way of conducting rites and ceremonies, proper interpersonal relationships, and the ideal standards of social and religious conduct. The ideal of *li* is reflected socially in the Five Relationships: father/son; elder brother/younger brother; husband/wife; elder/younger; ruler/subject. Each relationship is hierarchical, with distinctive roles for both superiors and inferiors. Central to harmonious family relationships is filial piety (*xiao*), or respect and reverence for one's parents and ancestors. Filial piety includes participating in proper rites for honoring one's parents when they are dead. While the practice of offering sacrifices to one's ancestors predates Confucius, he encouraged it as a way of solidifying the family and honoring one's elders.

Confucius sought the cultivation of the "superior man" (*jun-zi*), who exemplifies moral virtues such as *ren* ("humaneness," "benevolence," or "love"). *Ren* is what makes humans uniquely human. On one occasion Confucius said that *ren* means "to love men" (*Analects* 12.22). On another he described *ren* by giving his statement of the Golden Rule: "Do not impose on others what you yourself do not desire" (*Analects* 12.2; cf. 15.24). Although Confucius was ambivalent on whether human nature is inherently good or evil, he taught the perfectibility of humankind. Mencius later taught that human nature is inherently good and is corrupted by external factors, and this view eventually became Confucian orthodoxy.

Confucius never regarded himself as anything other than a man. Nevertheless, in time a state religious cult of devotion to Confucius developed, so that by the seventh century A.D. the Tang emperor mandated that every prefecture in China have a state temple to Confucius in which sacrifices to him were offered. The state cult of Confucius languished in the early twentieth century with the demise of the emperor system.

Islam

Islam, the second largest religion in the world after Christianity, is found not only in the Middle East but throughout Asia, Africa, Europe, and North America. (See also The Bible and Islam, pp. 2628–2630.) Although historically discussion of Islam begins with Muhammad (c. A.D. 570–632), Muslims insist that Islam is God's eternal religion for all humankind and that Muhammad was simply the last and greatest in a long line of prophets. Born in Mecca, an important trading center in the Arabian peninsula, Muhammad was an orphan by age six and was reared by his grandfather and uncle. At age 25 Muhammad married a wealthy widow named Khadija, and he became engaged in various business ventures.

The Arabs of Mecca were largely animists and polytheists, although there were Jewish and Christian influences in the area. Living in Mecca, Muhammad was troubled by the polytheism and superstition all around him. Around the year 610 he began to have experiences that he took to be revelations from Allah, the one true God. Convinced that he had been called to be a "Messenger of God," Muhammad continued to receive revelations supposedly dictated by the angel Gabriel over a 20-year period. The revelations were memorized by Muhammad's followers and were eventually written and codified in the Qur'an, which is understood to be the Word of God. Muhammad regarded himself as being in continuity with prophets of the OT and Jesus. He claimed to be restoring the original revelation of God that Jews and Christians had corrupted.

But Muhammad met stiff resistance to his message in Mecca, and in 622 he and his followers moved to Medina (in western Saudi Arabia). Under Muhammad's leadership, Medina was transformed into an Islamic theocracy, and the social and religious patterns of Medina are regarded as an ideal for Islamic societies. In 630 Muhammad returned to Mecca, captured it, and began transforming the city. Then suddenly, in 632, at about 62 years of age, Muhammad died.

Questions about the legitimate successors to Muhammad resulted in the two major divisions within Islam. Sunni Islam, comprising roughly 85 percent of Muslims today, recognized caliphs (Islamic leaders) not necessarily related to Muhammad as his legitimate successors. Shi'a Islam, comprising 10 to 15 percent of Muslims, insisted that legitimate successors must descend directly from Muhammad and that Ali (Muhammad's son-in-law, who was martyred) and his sons were the rightful heirs to leadership.

Both branches of Islam embrace a strict monotheism. Islam calls for acknowledgment of the incomparable greatness of Allah and submission to his sovereign will in all of life. Allah is the eternal creator who sovereignly rules over nature and the affairs of humankind.

The religious, intellectual, and social life of devout Muslims is structured around the "Five Pillars": (1) the *Shahada*, or "witness" of the basic creed of Islam ("I bear witness that there is no god but Allah, and that Muhammad is the prophet of Allah"); (2) prayer; (3) fasting; (4) almsgiving; and (5) the pilgrimage to Mecca.

Islam teaches that the present world will one day be destroyed by Allah and that all humankind, past and present, will then be raised to face divine judgment. Human beings have a weakness of will and a tendency toward sin. Although humans are tempted by Iblis (the devil), it is within their power to resist and remain faithful to the will of Allah. In the judgment, each person's deeds will be impartially weighed in the balance. Salvation is strictly on the basis of submission to Allah and faithful adherence to the teachings of Islam. Some will be admitted to Paradise, others consigned to Hell.

Jesus is mentioned frequently in the Qur'an. He is called the Messiah, Son of Mary, Messenger, Prophet, Servant, Word, and a Spirit from God. Jesus is portrayed as a great miracle worker and one of the greatest of the prophets. The virgin conception of Jesus is affirmed in the Qur'an.

But the Qur'an omits Jesus' teachings as contained in the Gospels and provides no narrative description of his ministry. The Qur'an depicts Jesus as explicitly disclaiming deity (5:109–119) and includes numerous denunciations of what seem to have been views that were common in Muhammad's lifetime regarding the Christian doctrines of the incarnation and the Trinity (cf. 4:171; 5:17; 9:30–31). Although a great prophet of God, Jesus is said to have been in no sense divine. Particularly offensive is the Christian title "Son of God," which is understood by Muslims as referring to physical generation. "Never has Allah begotten a son, nor is there any other god besides Him" (23:93). Muhammad seems to have thought of the Trinity as consisting of the Father, the Virgin Mary, and their child, Jesus.

Traditionally, most Muslims have believed that Jesus was not crucified. Surah 4:155–159 denies that Jesus was in fact killed on the cross. A widely accepted interpretation of this text has been that the Jews tried to kill Jesus but were unable to do so, and that God rescued him and carried him away to a safe place in the heavens. Islam denies the need for a Savior and the substitutionary atonement. The Qur'an states that "no soul shall bear another's burden and that each man shall be judged by his own labors" (53:38). Salvation is by works. "On that day no soul shall suffer the least injustice. You shall be rewarded according only to your deeds" (36:54).

Biblical Themes and Other Religions

Even this cursory survey indicates that there are some similarities between Christian faith and other religions. Islam and Christianity, e.g., both believe in an eternal Creator God and a judgment to come after death. Both Jesus and Confucius taught a version of the Golden Rule, and both Christianity and Confucianism teach respect for one's parents. Such similarities are not surprising and can be understood in light of the biblical teaching that all people, including adherents of other religions, have been created by God in his image (Gen. 1:26–27; 5:1–2) and that God has revealed himself in a general manner to all peoples through the created order (Ps. 19:1–4; Acts 14:15–17; 17:22–31; Rom. 1:18–32; 2:14–15).

But the differences between Christian faith and other religions are greater and more significant than any similarities.

1. *God.* The Bible teaches that there is one eternal Creator God who has created all else that exists (Genesis 1–2). Hinduism has theistic traditions, but it also includes polytheistic, monistic, and atheistic traditions. Confucianism's views on the religious ultimate are unclear, and Buddhism explicitly denies the existence of an eternal Creator.

2. *Death.* Hinduism and Buddhism both accept the idea of multiple rebirths regulated by *karma*. The Bible, by contrast, teaches that there is only one life, after which all persons face judgment before God (Heb. 9:27; Rev. 20:11–15).

3. *Sin.* Many religions, particularly Hinduism and Buddhism, identify the root problem afflicting humankind as ignorance about the true nature of reality. But the Bible teaches that the problem is not ignorance but sin, that is, deliberate rejection of God and his ways (Isa. 59:2; Rom. 3:9–26). Moreover, contrary to Confucianism, the Bible teaches that after the fall of Adam and Eve all humankind has been corrupted by sin infecting their moral nature, so that people are not inherently good but sinful (Genesis 3; Rom. 3:9–20; 5:12–14).

4. *Soul.* Buddhism teaches that there is no enduring, substantial soul that passes from one life to another. But the Bible teaches that there is an immaterial dimension of the person, created by God, which continues to exist after death (Matt. 10:28; Rev. 6:9; 20:4).

5. *Salvation.* Although some forms of *bhakti* Hinduism and Pure Land Buddhism do teach that salvation cannot be attained through one's own efforts but rather is a gift from another being, Islam, along with most other religious traditions, teaches that salvation is based on one's own deeds. But the Bible clearly states that salvation is not something that human beings can earn through their own efforts; it is the gift of God's grace, which is to be accepted by faith (Rom. 3:20, 28; Eph. 2:8–9).

6. *Christ's incarnation.* The Bible teaches that the eternal Creator is a tripersonal Being, and that the second person of this Trinity, while remaining fully God, became a man (John 1:1–14; Rom. 1:3–4; Phil. 2:7–8; Col. 2:9). In a unique onetime event, the Son of God became incarnate as the historical person Jesus of Nazareth. The Hindu notion of *avatar*, by contrast, concerns multiple manifestations of Vishnu as both humans and animals, and involves legendary figures such as Krishna, not actual historical persons. In fact, no other world religions teach that the eternal Son of God became a true man.

7. *Christ's preeminence.* Jesus is not just another great religious teacher. The truth of Jesus' teachings cannot be separated from its grounding in the person of Christ as the incarnate Word of God, the eternal, omnipotent Son of God who shares fully in all the attributes of God. It is because of who he is and what he has done on the cross that Jesus is himself the Way, the Truth, and the Life (John 14:6), the only Savior for all humankind (Acts 4:12).

8. *Christ's substitution.* The Bible teaches that salvation is based on the sinless life (Heb. 4:15) and the substitutionary death of Jesus Christ on the cross, as he took upon himself the punishment for the sins of the world (Rom. 3:25–26; 1 Pet. 3:18; 1 John 2:2). There is nothing like this teaching in Hinduism, Buddhism, or Confucianism, and it is explicitly denied in Islam.

9. *Christ's resurrection.* The Buddha, Confucius, Muhammad, and Jesus all died, but there is no reliable historical record of any—apart from Jesus—being resurrected after death (1 Cor. 15:1–8). It is because of the resurrection of Jesus Christ that we, too, can have victory over sin and death and anticipate our own resurrection to eternal life with God (Rom. 8:11; 1 Cor. 15:20–22, 54–58). ◀

The Bible and Islam

The Revelations of the Qur'an

There is no more widely recognized utterance of the Islamic faith than the declaration known as the *shahadah*: "There is no god but Allah, and Muhammad is the prophet of Allah." Islam is about Allah and his prophet, Muhammad. The Qur'an teaches that Muhammad was an ordinary man (43:31). Yet, according to Muslims, Allah sovereignly chose Muhammad to receive a series of revelations through the intermediary presence of the angel Gabriel. While Muhammad was praying and fasting in the hills outside of

Mecca in A.D. 610, Gabriel appeared to him. Many Muslims believe the first revelation to Muhammad was the command to "Recite in the Name of Thy Lord" (96:1). These revelations continued until Muhammad's death in A.D. 632 (17:82). According to Islamic traditions, approximately 20 years after Muhammad's death his "recitations" were written down and codified into a collection of 114 chapters (called *surahs*) known as the Qur'an. The word "Qur'an" is Arabic for "recitation." The Qur'an, containing 6,346 verses (known as *aya*), is approximately the same size as the NT. The first chapter of the Qur'an is known as "The Opening" and is widely regarded as the greatest summary of the Islamic message. The remaining chapters are arranged by length from the longest to the shortest.

The Qur'an and the OT

The emergence of Islam and the Qur'an can be properly understood only within the larger context of the Bible and the monotheism of Islam's two main predecessors, Judaism and Christianity. The dozens of superficial similarities between the Qur'an and the Bible are striking. For example, in the Qur'an, Allah creates the earth in six days (25:59), culminating in the creation of the first man, Adam. Adam and his wife eat of the forbidden fruit and become aware of their nakedness (20:115–122). Allah sends Moses to confront Pharaoh, inflict the plagues on Egypt, and lead the Israelites out of Egypt through the parting of the Red Sea (26:9–75). Allah gives Moses the Ten Commandments on two stone tablets, which are subsequently broken (7:143–150). Throughout the Qur'an several of the Ten Commandments are repeated, including the commands to "serve no other gods" (24:55), refrain from making idols (4:116), not covet (4:32), not murder (6:151), and honor one's father and mother (6:151). In the Qur'an one can read about such familiar OT stories as Noah building the ark and preaching judgment to his generation (11:25–49; 23:23–32); Joseph being betrayed by his brothers, sold to a caravan of travelers, and brought to Egypt (12:7–21); King David's adultery with Bathsheba (28:21–25); the queen of Sheba's visit to Solomon (27:22–44); and Jonah being swallowed by the great fish (37:139–148). There are times, however, when the Qur'anic version has surprising departures, historically and theologically, from the biblical account. For example, Abraham is asked to sacrifice Ishmael rather than Isaac (cf. 37:100–111), and Jesus Christ is not accorded his full status.

The Qur'an and Christian Theology

Islamic View of God and the Trinity

Islam teaches a doctrine of absolute monotheism known as *tawhid. Absolute* monotheism is distinct from the *Trinitarian* monotheism of Christianity in that the Qur'an permits no distinctions within God. Christianity teaches that there is one God, known in three eternal persons. While Muslims welcome the Christian affirmation of one God, they maintain that belief in the three persons compromises the unity of God and makes Christianity functionally tritheistic (i.e., believing in three gods; see 4:171).

Islamic View of Jesus Christ

The Qur'an has dozens of references to Jesus (*Isa* in Arabic), found in 15 different surahs of the Qur'an. Jesus is often called *ibn Maryam* ("son of Mary"), a phrase that appears only once in the NT (Mark 6:3). The Qur'an also refers to him as "servant of Allah" (19:30), "messiah" (5:75), and "messenger/prophet" (61:6). The Qur'an even gives Jesus several honorific titles, including a "Word from Him" (3:45; 4:171), a "Spirit from God" (4:171), and a "Sign for all peoples" (19:21; 21:91).

Several of these titles appear consistent with Christian claims about Jesus. Indeed, the Qur'an often speaks positively about him: Jesus was born without sin to the Virgin Mary (3:47; 19:19, 20; 21:91; 66:12) and was a miracle worker (2:253; 3:49; 5:110; 43:63; 61:6) whose ministry was foretold by John the Baptist (3:39). Yet, several surahs denounce any view of Christ that would elevate him beyond the status of a human prophet. Indeed, some passages in the Qur'an seem to deliberately contradict the biblical proclamation about Jesus Christ. For example, "Those who say: 'The Lord of Mercy has begotten a son,' preach a monstrous falsehood, at which the very heavens might crack, the earth break asunder, and the mountains crumble to dust . . . that they should ascribe a son to the Merciful, when it does not become Him to beget one!" (19:88–91). In Surah 61, Jesus is pictured as a prophet heralding the way for the coming of Muhammad (61:6). Surah 4 teaches that Jesus was not crucified on the cross (4:155–159). Thus, while respecting Jesus as a prophet of God, the Qur'an does not affirm the deity of Jesus Christ or his death as a substitute payment for sins.

Islamic View of Sin and Humanity

Traditional Islamic teaching does not accept that humans were created in the image of God. Islam has no doctrine of a sin nature and therefore does not believe that humanity is either depraved or fallen. Instead, men and women have the innate capacity to believe and submit to the Islamic revelation. Islam classifies the entire human race into four categories. The first is *jahiliyyah*, meaning those in a "state of ignorance" (5:50) who do not have a monotheistic revelation and have not yet heard Muhammad's message. The second are the *ahl al-kitab*, or "People of the Book." These are monotheistic people who have not received the Qur'an but who have a book of revelation, such as Christians and Jews (see, e.g., 2:105; 3:64–199; 4:123; 5:15; 29:46; 33:26; 57:29; 59:11; 98:1–6). The third category is *Muslim*, an Arabic word meaning "those who submit"; it refers to monotheists who have submitted to Allah and regard the Qur'an as Allah's greatest (some say, eternal) revelation and Muhammad as the final "seal" of the prophets (33:40). The fourth category refers to those peoples who have heard the message of Islam but rejected it, the *kafir* (meaning "unbeliever" or "infidel").

Islamic View of Other Religions

Muslims universally affirm that Islam is the highest and only non-corrupted religion. Christianity and Judaism are accorded some respect as monotheistic religions flowing from the Abrahamic tradition (29:46). All other religions are generally regarded as expressions of human ignorance and an unwillingness to submit to Allah.

Islamic View of Salvation

Since Muslims do not accept the doctrine of the fall or of a subsequent sin nature, there is no need of redemption. Islamic "salvation" is understood almost wholly as future deliverance from final judgment. Many Muslims maintain that whoever believes in the oneness of God (*tawhid*) and the prophethood of Muhammad will be saved from the fire of judgment. Other Muslims insist on submission to Allah through adherence to the five pillars of Islam:

confession of faith (*shahadah*), daily ritual prayer (*salat*), the giving of alms (*zakat*), fasting during Ramadan (*sawm*), and a pilgrimage to Mecca (*Hajj*). Based on revered Islamic traditions known as *Hadith*, some Muslims believe that Allah grants Muhammad the honor of interceding for the entire Islamic community at the final judgment, allowing all Muslims to be saved.

Islamic View of the Bible

Muslims universally regard the Bible as a corrupted text. The doctrine of corruption (*tahrif*) asserts that the transmission of Jewish and Christian texts was unreliable (5:13–14), or Christians and Jews willfully altered the biblical texts because of enmity or jealously (2:109) (see the articles on The Reliability of the Old Testament Manuscripts, pp. 2585–2587; and The Reliability of the New Testament Manuscripts, pp. 2587–2589). On the other hand, the Qur'an does affirm Allah's sending revelation in the Torah and the Gospels (*Injil*) (5:46, 67, 69, 71). Furthermore, the Qur'an says that Jesus' words should be "believed" (4:171; 5:78), and even commands the Muslims to listen to those who had the Torah/*Injil* before the Qur'an, calling it a "Truth come to thee from Thy Lord" (10:94).

Islamic Attitudes toward the Use of Violence

There is no single Islamic attitude toward the use of violence, and scholars of Islam are divided over the extent to which the Qur'an permits or even advocates violence against unbelievers. The Qur'an asserts that there should be "no compulsion in religion" (2:256) and peacefully calls or invites (*dawah*) people to follow Islam (16:125). The Qur'an also permits the use of violence in certain circumstances (8:38, 39; 47:4), and two texts in particular have sometimes been cited as justification for violence against unbelievers (9:5, 29). Historically, the Islamic caliphate extended protected status (*dhimmi*) to other monotheistic religions and prohibited the exercise of violence against them as long as a special tax, known as *jizyah*, was paid.

Islam generally embraces the honor of martyrdom and affirms that integral to Islamic faithfulness is a struggle (*jihad*) against idolatry and unbelief. Some Muslims emphasize the "higher jihad," which is nonviolent and focuses on the internal struggle within the individual to live in purity. However, many Muslims accept the use of violence in certain instances, especially against *kafirs* (or unbelievers). In the last few centuries more radical groups, such as the Wahabis and Salafis, have accepted violence even against other confessing Muslims who behaved in ways they deemed idolatrous. Most recently, the growth of extremist movements such as Islamism, the writings of intellectuals such as Sayyid Qutb (1906–1966), and the emergence of terrorist networks such as al-Qaeda (lit., "the base") have served to make the use of violence more widely acceptable.

Islamic Attitudes toward Civil Government

Historically, Islam has envisioned the unity of civil and religious life under the all-encompassing guidance of Islamic law, known as *Sharia*. Until modern times, the only acceptable form of Islamic government has been the caliphate, which unites civil and religious authority under the rule of a caliph. Sunnis and Shiites differ as to how this caliph is chosen. (For the distinction between Sunnis and Shiites, see the section on Islam in The Bible and Other World Religions, pp. 2625–2628.) Over the centuries, Muslims have lived under a wide range of caliphates including the Rightly Guided Caliphs (7th century), the Umayyads (7th and 8th centuries), the Abbasids (8th to 13th centuries), and the Ottomans (15th to 20th centuries). In 1924 Kemal Ataturk, the president of Turkey, constitutionally abolished the caliphate. Several contemporary Islamic movements have encouraged political pluralism and even acceptance of religious diversity. However, since the 1970s more Islamist movements have emphasized the need to assert Islamic hegemony and to resist the secularization of Islamic governments. ◂

The Bible and Religious Cults

Almost every book in the NT has something to say about false beliefs and those who advocate them. We are warned, e.g., about false prophets (Matt. 7:15–16; 24:11), false christs (Matt. 24:5, 24; Mark 13:22), a different Jesus and a different spirit (2 Cor. 11:4), false apostles (2 Cor. 11:13–15), and "another gospel" (Gal. 1:8). With so many warnings, it is clear God knew that many false teachers would come, and that he did not want his people to be deceived (cf. Eph. 4:14; 2 John 7). In what follows, notable deceptions of prominent cults will be summarized, along with a brief biblical response.

From the viewpoint of those who hold to historic, evangelical Christianity, a "cult" is any religious movement that claims to be derived from the Bible and/or the Christian faith, and that advocates beliefs that differ so significantly with major Christian doctrines that two consequences follow: (1) The movement cannot legitimately be considered a valid "Christian" denomination because of its serious deviation from historic Christian orthodoxy. (2) Believing the doctrines of the movement is incompatible with trusting in the Jesus Christ of the Bible for the salvation that comes by God's grace alone (Eph. 2:8–9). By this traditional understanding of the word "cult," the following groups described are "cults," though this does not imply that they share the extremely oppressive, authoritarian, life-controlling, and often immoral practices that are found in what the secular world calls "cults," using the term in a more extreme sense.

The Church of Jesus Christ of Latter-day Saints (Mormonism)

Apostasy and restoration. Mormons claim that "total" apostasy overcame the church following apostolic times, and that the Mormon Church (founded in 1830) is the "restored church." If the Mormon Church were truly a "restored church," however, one would expect to find first-century historical evidence for Mormon doctrines like the plurality of gods and God the Father having once been a man. Such evidence is completely lacking. Besides, the Bible disallows a *total* apostasy of the church (e.g., Matt. 16:18; 28:20; Eph. 3:21; 4:11–16), warning instead of *partial* apostasy (1 Tim. 4:1).

God. Mormons claim that God the Father was once a man and that he then progressed to godhood (that is, he is a now-exalted, immortal man with a flesh-and-bone body). However, based on the Bible, God is not and has never been a man (Num. 23:19; Hos. 11:9). He is a spirit (John 4:24), and a spirit does not have flesh and bones (Luke 24:39). Furthermore, God is eternal (Ps. 90:2; 102:27; Isa. 57:15; 1 Tim. 1:17) and immutable (or unchangeable in his being and perfections; see Ps. 102:25–27; Mal. 3:6). He did not "progress" toward godhood, but has always been God.

Polytheism. Mormons believe that the Trinity consists not of three persons in one God but rather of three distinct gods. According to Mormonism, there are potentially many thousands of gods besides these. However, trusting in or worshiping more than one god is explicitly condemned throughout the Bible (e.g., Ex. 20:3). There is only one true God (Deut. 4:35, 39; 6:4; Isa. 43:10; 44:6, 8; 45:18; 46:9; 1 Cor. 8:4; James 2:19), who exists eternally in three persons—the Father, the Son, and the Holy Spirit (Matt. 28:19; 2 Cor. 13:14). (See the discussion of the Trinity in the section on Jehovah's Witnesses.)

Exaltation of humans. Mormons believe that humans, like God the Father, can go through a process of exaltation to godhood. But the Bible teaches that the yearning to be godlike led to the fall of mankind (Gen. 3:4ff.). God does not look kindly on humans who pretend to attain to deity (Acts 12:21–23; contrast Acts 14:11–15). God desires humans to humbly recognize that they are his creatures (Gen. 2:7; 5:2; Ps. 95:6–7; 100:3). The state of the redeemed in eternity will be one of glorious immortality, but they will forever remain God's creatures, adopted as his children (Rom. 8:14–30; 1 Cor. 15:42–57; Rev. 21:3–7). Believers will never become gods.

Jesus Christ. Mormons believe that Jesus Christ was the firstborn spirit-child of the heavenly Father and a heavenly Mother. Jesus then *progressed* to deity in the spirit world. He was later physically conceived in Mary's womb, as the literal "only begotten" Son of God the Father in the flesh (though many present-day Mormons remain somewhat vague as to how this occurred). Biblically, however, the description of Jesus as the "only begotten" refers to his being the Father's *unique, one-of-a-kind* Son for all eternity, with the same divine nature as the Father (see note on John 1:14; cf. John 1:18; 3:16, 18; see also John 5:18; 10:30). Moreover, he is eternal deity (John 1:1; 8:58) and is immutable (Heb. 1:10–12; 13:8), meaning he did not *progress* to deity but has *always been* God. And Mary's conception of Jesus in his humanity was through a miracle of the Holy Spirit (Matt. 1:20).

Three kingdoms. Mormons believe that most people will end up in one of three kingdoms of glory, depending on one's level of faithfulness. Belief in Christ, or even in God, is not necessary to obtain immortality in one of these three kingdoms, and therefore only the most spiritually perverse will go to hell. But the Bible teaches that people have just *two* possibilities for their eternal futures: the saved will enjoy eternal life with God in the new heavens and new earth (Phil. 3:20; Rev. 21:1–4; 22:1–5), while the unsaved will spend eternity in hell (Matt. 25:41, 46; Rev. 20:13–15).

Sin and atonement. Mormons believe that Adam's transgression was a noble act that made it possible for humans to become mortal, a necessary step on the path to exaltation to godhood. They think that Christ's atonement secures immortality for virtually all people, whether they repent and believe or not. Biblically, however, there was nothing noble about Adam's sin, which was not a stepping-stone to godhood but rather brought nothing but sin, misery, and death to mankind (Gen. 3:16–19; Rom. 5:12–14). Jesus atoned for the sins of all who would trust him for salvation (Isa. 53:6; John 1:29; 2 Cor. 5:21; 1 Pet. 2:24; 3:18; 1 John 2:2; 4:10).

Salvation. Mormons believe that God gives to (virtually) everyone a general salvation to immortal life in one of the heavenly kingdoms, which is how they understand salvation by grace. Belief in Christ is necessary only to obtain passage to the highest, celestial kingdom—for which not only faith but participation in Mormon temple rituals and obedience to its "laws of the gospel" are also prerequisites. Biblically, however, salvation by grace must be received through faith in Christ (John 3:15–16; 11:25; 12:46; Acts 16:31; Rom. 3:22–24; Eph. 2:8–9), and all true believers are promised eternal life in God's presence (Matt. 5:3–8; John 14:1–3; Rev. 21:3–7). ◂

Jehovah's Witnesses

The divine name. Jehovah's Witnesses believe that God's one true name—the name by which he must be identified—is Jehovah. Biblically, however, God is identified by many names, including: God (Hb. *'elohim*; Gen. 1:1), God Almighty (Hb. *'El Shadday*; Gen. 17:1), Lord (Hb. *'Adonay*; Ps. 8:1), and Lord of hosts (Hb. *yhwh tseba'ot*; 1 Sam. 1:3). In NT times, Jesus referred to God as "Father" (Gk. *Patēr*; Matt. 6:9), as did the apostles (1 Cor. 1:3).

The Trinity. Jehovah's Witnesses believe that the Trinity is unbiblical because the word is not in the Bible and because the Bible emphasizes that there is one God. Biblically, while it is true that there is only one God (Isa. 44:6; 45:18; 46:9; John 5:44; 1 Cor. 8:4; James 2:19), it is also true that three persons are called God in Scripture: the Father (1 Pet. 1:2), Jesus (John 20:28; Heb. 1:8), and the Holy Spirit (Acts 5:3–4). Each of these three possesses the attributes of deity—including omnipresence (Ps. 139:7; Jer. 23:23–24; Matt. 28:20), omniscience (Ps. 147:5; John 16:30; 1 Cor. 2:10–11), omnipotence (Jer. 32:17; John 2:1–11; Rom. 15:19), and eternality (Ps. 90:2; Heb. 9:14; Rev. 22:13). Still further, each of the three is involved in doing the works of deity—such as creating the universe: the Father (Gen. 1:1; Ps. 102:25), the Son (John 1:3; Col. 1:16; Heb. 1:2), and the Holy Spirit (Gen. 1:2; Job 33:4; Ps. 104:30). The Bible indicates that there is three-in-oneness in the godhead (Matt. 28:19; cf. 2 Cor. 13:14). Thus doctrinal support for the Trinity is compellingly strong.

Jesus Christ. Jehovah's Witnesses believe that Jesus was created by Jehovah as the archangel Michael before the physical world existed, and is a lesser, though mighty, god. Biblically, however, Jesus is eternally God (John 1:1; 8:58; cf. Ex. 3:14) and has the exact same divine nature as the Father (John 5:18; 10:30; Heb. 1:3). Indeed, a comparison of the OT and NT equates Jesus with Jehovah (compare Isa. 43:11 with Titus 2:13; Isa. 44:24 with Col. 1:16; Isa. 6:1–5 with John 12:41). Jesus himself created the angels (Col. 1:16; cf. John 1:3; Heb. 1:2, 10) and is worshiped by them (Heb. 1:6).

The incarnation. Jehovah's Witnesses believe that when Jesus was born on earth, he was a mere human and not God in human flesh. This violates the biblical teaching that in the incarnate Jesus, "the whole fullness of deity dwells bodily" (Col. 2:9; cf. Phil. 2:6–7). The word for "fullness" (Gk. *plērōma*) carries the idea of the *sum total*. "Deity" (Gk. *theotēs*) refers to the *nature, being, and attributes of God*. Therefore, the incarnate Jesus was the sum total of the nature, being, and attributes of God in bodily form. Indeed, Jesus was Immanuel, or "God with us" (Matt. 1:23; cf. Isa. 7:14; John 1:1, 14, 18; 10:30; 14:9–10).

Resurrection. Jehovah's Witnesses believe that Jesus was resurrected *spiritually* from the dead, but not physically. Biblically, however, the resurrected Jesus asserted that he was *not* merely a spirit but had a flesh-and-bone body (Luke 24:39; cf. John 2:19–21). He ate food on several occasions, thereby proving that he had a genuine physical body after the resurrection (Luke 24:30, 42–43; John 21:12–13). This was confirmed by his followers who physically touched him (Matt. 28:9; John 20:17).

The second coming. Jehovah's Witnesses believe that the second coming was an invisible, spiritual event that occurred in the year 1914. Biblically, however, the yet-future second coming will be *physical, visible* (Acts 1:9–11; cf. Titus 2:13), and will be accompanied by visible cosmic disturbances (Matt. 24:29–30). Every eye will see him (Rev. 1:7).

The Holy Spirit. Jehovah's Witnesses believe that the Holy Spirit is an impersonal force of God and not a distinct person. Biblically, however, the Holy Spirit has a mind (Rom. 8:27), emotions (Eph. 4:30), and will (1 Cor. 12:11)—the three primary attributes of personality. Moreover, personal pronouns are used of him (Acts 13:2). Also, he does things that only a person can do, including: teaching (John 14:26), testifying (John 15:26), commissioning (Acts 13:4), issuing commands (Acts 8:29), and interceding (Rom. 8:26). The Holy Spirit is the third person of the Trinity (Matt. 28:19).

Salvation. Jehovah's Witnesses believe that salvation requires faith in Christ, association with God's organization (i.e., their religion), and obedience to its rules. Biblically, however, viewing obedience to rules as a requirement for salvation nullifies the gospel (Gal. 2:16–21; Col. 2:20–23). Salvation is based wholly on God's unmerited favor (grace), not on the believer's performance. Good works are the fruit or result, not the basis, of salvation (Eph. 2:8–10; Titus 3:4–8).

Two redeemed peoples. Jehovah's Witnesses believe there are two peoples of God: (1) the Anointed Class (144,000) will live in heaven and rule with Christ; and (2) the "other sheep" (all other believers) will live forever on a paradise earth. Biblically, however, a heavenly destiny awaits *all* who believe in Christ (John 14:1–3; 17:24; 2 Cor. 5:1; Phil. 3:20;

Col. 1:5; 1 Thess. 4:17; Heb. 3:1), and these same people will also dwell on the new earth (2 Pet. 3:13; Rev. 21:1–4).

No immaterial soul. Jehovah's Witnesses do not believe that humans have an immaterial nature. The "soul" is simply the life-force within a person. At death, that life-force leaves the body. Biblically, however, the word "soul" is multifaceted. One key meaning of the term is man's immaterial self that consciously survives death (Gen. 35:18; Rev. 6:9–10). Unbelievers are in conscious woe (Matt. 13:42; 25:41, 46; Luke 16:22–24; Rev. 14:11) while believers are in conscious bliss in heaven (1 Cor. 2:9; 2 Cor. 5:6–8; Phil. 1:21–23; Rev. 7:17; 21:4).

Hell. Jehovah's Witnesses believe hell is not a place of eternal suffering but is rather the common grave of humankind. The wicked are annihilated—snuffed out of conscious existence forever. Biblically, however, hell is a real place of conscious, eternal suffering (Matt. 5:22; 25:41, 46; Jude 7; Rev. 14:11; 20:10, 14). ◀

Christian Science

Sin, sickness, and death. Christian Science teaches that sin, sickness, and death are illusions that can be conquered by correct thinking. The rationale for this unusual idea is that all things in the universe are ultimately God. Since *everything* is God, there can be no sin and no matter. Since matter does not exist, neither can sickness, pain, or death exist.

If *everything* is God, however, one must wonder where this widespread, universal delusion about the material nature of the world emerged. Is delusion a part of God? Further, the Christian Science worldview seems utterly unlivable. Why lock the front door at night if there is no sin? Why go to the dentist if there is no pain? Why buckle seatbelts in the car if there is no death? According to the Bible, God created the material universe (Genesis 1; Ps. 102:25; Isa. 44:24) and pronounced it "very good" (Gen. 1:31). The emergence of sin (Genesis 3), however, brought ruin to the creation (Rom. 8:20; cf. Gen. 3:17) and introduced the realities of sickness and death (Gen. 2:17; 5:5, 8, 11, 14, 17, 20, 27, 31; cf. Rom. 5:12).

God. Christian Science holds to a pantheistic view of God (i.e., God and the universe are the same reality). Biblically, however, God is distinct from his creatures and is a personal loving Father unto whom believers may cry, "Abba" (Rom. 8:15; Gal. 4:6). This personal God is a conscious being who thinks, feels, plans (Jer. 9:23–24; cf. Isa. 46:10), and engages in personal relationships with others (e.g., Gen. 5:22, 24; 6:9). This personal God created all things out of absolute nothingness (Heb. 11:3; cf. Gen. 1:1; Neh. 9:6; Ps. 33:8–9; 148:5). While he is omnipresent (Ps. 139:7–9), he is not "one with" the universe; he remains eternally distinct from the creation that he made and from humankind (Num. 23:19; Eccles. 5:2; Heb. 11:3).

Jesus Christ. Christian Science teaches that Jesus was a mere human who, as an adult, embodied "the Christ" (i.e., a manifestation of divinity), as other humans also can. Biblically, however, Jesus did not become the Christ as an adult, but rather was the one and only Christ from the very beginning (Luke 2:11; cf. 1 John 2:22). The precise NT counterpart of the OT word "Messiah" is "Christ" (John 1:41). The OT presents numerous prophecies regarding the coming of a single Messiah (e.g., Isa. 7:14; 53:3–5; Mic. 5:2; Zech. 12:10). *Jesus alone* fulfilled these prophecies, and hence he alone is the Christ (Luke 9:20). He is also absolute deity (John 1:1; 8:58; 10:30; 20:28).

Humanity. In keeping with its pantheistic views, Christian Science teaches that human beings, too, are God. Biblically, however, human beings are creatures (Gen. 1:26–27; 2:7) who remain eternally distinct from God (Eccles. 5:2) and are intrinsically weak and dependent upon God (Ps. 95:6–7; 100:3; Mic. 6:8; John 15:5; 2 Cor. 3:5; James 4:6). Christian Science proponents would do well to consider: if the essence of human beings is God, and if God is an infinite, *changeless* being, then how is it possible for man (if he is a manifestation of divinity) to go through a *changing* process of enlightenment, by which he discovers his divinity? Biblically, God does not "blossom" or grow to maturity; he has always been in "full bloom" as the perfect and unchanging God (Ps. 90:2).

Salvation. Christian Science teaches that when one ceases believing in sin, sickness, and death, one becomes "saved." Theologically, a weak view of sin blinds one to the need for a savior. Such is the case with Christian Science. A biblical view of sin (e.g., Rom. 5:12), however, points to a dire need for salvation—*especially* dire in view of the hard biblical realities of death (Gen. 2:17; Rom. 6:23) and hell (Rev. 20:14–15) as the wages of sin. Biblical salvation is based wholly on the sacrificial death of Jesus (Rom. 5:8; cf. Isa. 53:6) and is received as a grace-gift (Rom. 5:1–11; Eph. 2:8–9) by faith in him (John 3:15–16; 5:24; 11:25; 12:46; 20:31).

Heaven and hell. Christian Science teaches that people make their own hell by thinking wrongly and their own heaven by thinking rightly. Biblically, however, heaven is the splendor-filled eternal abode of the saved (1 Cor. 2:9; 2 Cor. 12:4; Col. 1:12; 2 Pet. 3:13; Rev. 21:1–2), while hell is the horrific eternal abode of the unsaved (Matt. 13:42; 25:41, 46; 2 Thess. 1:8–9; Rev. 19:20; 20:14–15). ◀

New Age Movement

Unlike the preceding movements, the New Age Movement has no one organizational headquarters or leadership, but consists of hundreds of informally associated small organizations and groups. Nevertheless, it continues to gain followers in the twenty-first century.

Revelation. New Agers believe divine revelation has been expressed not only in Christianity but also in other religions including: Islam, Hinduism, Buddhism, and Zoroastrianism. These religions allegedly teach the same "core truths." Such a claim contradicts the facts. Consider the doctrine of God. The Bible teaches the Trinity, the Qur'an (Islam's scripture) denies the Trinity, the Hindu Vedas teach pantheism and polytheism, Zoroastrianism teaches religious dualism, and Buddhist writings teach that God is essentially irrelevant. Since God is the most fundamental doctrine of any religious system, the claim that these religions teach the same "core truths" is flatly false.

Christianity is exclusivistic at its core. Jesus said he is uniquely and exclusively humanity's *only* means of coming into a relationship with God (John 14:6; cf. Acts 4:12; 1 Tim. 2:5). His exclusivity caused him to warn against false religious leaders who contradict his teachings (Matt. 24:4–5, 23–24).

God. New Agers hold to a pantheistic, impersonal view of God. Biblically, however, God is a personal being who hears (Ex. 2:24), sees (Gen. 1:4), knows (Jer. 29:11; 2 Tim. 2:19), has a will (1 John 2:17), communicates (Ex. 3:13–14), plans (Eph. 1:11), expresses emotion (Gen. 6:6), and demonstrates character (2 Pet. 3:9). He also engages in personal relationships with others (e.g., Gen. 5:22, 24; 6:9).

Jesus Christ. New Agers claim that Jesus was a "human vessel" who, as an adult, embodied "the Christ" (variously defined, but always divine). Jesus is viewed as a prototype for the rest of humanity, since all people can embody the Christ. As noted previously in response to Christian Science, however, Jesus did not become the Christ as an adult but rather was the *one and only* Christ from the very beginning. Jesus even made his identity *as* the Christ the primary issue of faith on at least two different occasions (Matt. 16:13–20; John 11:25–27). When Jesus was acknowledged as the Christ, he did not say to people, "You, too, have the Christ within." Instead he warned that others would come falsely claiming to *be* the Christ (Matt. 24:4–5, 23–24).

Humankind. New Agers hold that human beings are God and therefore have unlimited potential. If this were true, however, one would expect humans to have the same attributes as God. Biblically, though, God is *all-knowing* (Ps. 147:5; Heb. 4:13), while man is limited in knowledge (Job 38:4). God is *all-powerful* (Rev. 19:6), while man is weak (Heb. 4:15). God is *holy* (1 John 1:5), while fallen man's "righteous" deeds are as filthy garments before God (Isa. 64:6). Such scriptural facts illustrate the apostle Paul's affirmation that all humans "fall short of the glory of God" (Rom. 3:23). Humans are mere finite creatures (Gen. 1:26–27; 2:7), now fallen in sin (Rom. 5:12).

Sin and salvation. New Agers say humans do not have a "sin problem" but an "ignorance problem." All they need is enlightenment regarding their divinity. Then, through reincarnation, the human soul can eventually reach a state of perfection and merge back with its source (pantheistic God).

Biblically, Christian morality begins with a *personal* God (see above) who makes moral requirements of his creatures (Ex. 15:26; 20:1–17; Deut. 8:6; John 14:15). While moral terms like "right" and "wrong" may not have any relevance to an impersonal, pantheistic God, they *do* have relevance to the God of the Bible, who calls us to obey his moral commandments (Ex. 19:5; Deut. 12:28; John 14:21). Because humans have failed to do this, they stand guilty before God (Genesis 3; Isa. 53:6; Rom. 3:23).

Jesus did not teach that humans have a mere *ignorance* problem but a grave *sin* problem that is altogether beyond their means to solve (Mark 7:20–23; cf. Ps. 53:2–3; Isa. 53:6; 64:6; Jer. 17:9; Rom. 3:23; 6:23). He also taught that salvation is found *not* by enlightenment but by placing faith in him (John 3:16; Acts 16:31) who is the Light of the world (John 8:12). Trusting in reincarnation will not suffice, for Scripture affirms that each person *lives once, dies once,* and then *faces judgment* (Heb. 9:27; cf. Rev. 20:11–15). There are no second chances following death (cf. 2 Cor. 6:2). ◄

History of Salvation in the Old Testament: Preparing the Way for Christ

(See Overview of the Bible, pp. 23–26, for a fuller explanation of the "History of Salvation." The notes in this feature are identified by single verses only, for easy cross-reference with the main study notes on Bible-text pages. However, many of these notes apply to more than just the one verse by which they are identified. Directions for the reader to "see note on" another verse refer only to notes within this feature, not to the main study notes on Bible-text pages.)

Genesis

After God creates a world of fruitfulness and blessing, Adam's fall disrupts the harmony. God purposes to renew fruitfulness and blessing through the offspring of the woman (3:15). Christ is the ultimate offspring (Gal. 3:16) who brings climactic victory (Heb. 2:14–15). Genesis traces the beginning of a line of godly offspring, through Seth, Enoch, Noah, and then God's choice of Abraham and his offspring (Gen. 12:2–3, 7; 13:14–17; 15:4–5; 17:1–14; 18:18; 22:16–18; 26:2–5; 28:13–15).

1:1 God's act of creation is the foundation for the entire biblical history. A considerable number of passages refer back to creation (e.g., Psalms 8; 104; 148; John 1:1–3; 1 Cor. 8:6; Col. 1:15–17; Heb. 1:2; 11:3; 1 John 1:5–7). All the rest of the Bible depends indirectly on it.

1:3 God speaks, and it is done. The centrality of the word of God in the acts of creation anticipates the deeper truth given in John 1:1, that the second person of the Trinity is the Word.

1:3 God created physical light. The Bible also says that God *is* light in a moral and spiritual sense (1 John 1:5). By God's design, the physical aspects of creation can serve as vehicles for developing themes about God and his salvation. Jesus is "the light of the world" (John 8:12).

1:26 The divine Son is "the image of the invisible God" (Col. 1:15). Man was created in a way that reflects the imaging relation among the persons of the Trinity. The redemption of man from the fall and sin includes re-creation (2 Cor. 5:17), his being "created after the likeness of God in true righteousness and holiness," in the image of Christ (Eph. 4:24).

1:28 God created a permanent *order* of creation. But he also intended a *development* in which man would play a central role. Because Adam failed and fell into sin, Christ came as the last Adam to achieve dominion (see 1 Cor. 15:22, 45–49; Eph. 1:21–22).

1:31 Sin is a later intrusion into an originally good creation. It is not inherent in the world, and so it can be completely removed when God achieves his purposes in the consummation (Rev. 22:3–5).

2:2 God rested from his works of creation. But he continues to work in providence and (after sin enters) in redemption. See John 5:17. As human beings we look forward to entering into God's consummation rest (Heb. 4:4, 9–11).

2:3 Man imitates the pattern of God's work and rest in the sabbath cycle of days (Ex. 20:8–11) and years (Leviticus 25). The sabbath points forward to the rest that Christ achieved with his resurrection and ascension (Heb. 10:12–13), and which will be fully manifested in the consummation (Rev. 22:4–5).

2:7 God has life in himself and imparts life to his creatures. The impartation of physical life anticipates the impartation of spiritual life (John 1:4; see 1 Cor. 15:45). Life is in the Son (John 5:21, 26; 1 John 5:12) and comes to us through the Spirit (John 3:5).

2:8 The garden of Eden and paradise reminds us of what we have lost (Joel 2:3) but also of what will yet be renewed in the world to come (Isa. 51:3; Rev. 22:1–3).

2:9 After the fall, the tree of life was barred to man (3:24). But God promises fruitfulness to those who know him (Ps. 1:3) and to those who obtain wisdom (Prov. 3:18). Eternal life is obtained in Christ (John 5:24), and free access to the tree of life reappears in the consummation (Rev. 22:2).

2:24 Divorce is a deviation from God's design in creation (Matt. 19:4). The marriage relationship anticipates the relation of Christ to the church (Eph. 5:22–33). See Overview of the Bible, pp. 23–26, concerning Christ as the last Adam.

3:1 Later Scripture indicates that Satan worked through the serpent (Isa. 27:1; Rev. 12:9). He was defeated by Christ's work on the cross (Heb. 2:14–15), and will be utterly destroyed in the events leading to the consummation (Rev. 20:7–10).

3:4 Throughout history Satan is engaged in deceiving (2 Thess. 2:9–12; Rev. 12:9) and casting doubt on the word of God. When tempted by Satan, Christ rejected his lies (Matt. 4:1–11). In spite of Satan's attacks, the word of God will stand forever (Ps. 119:89; Matt. 24:35).

3:8 God appears and judges Adam and Eve, anticipating the final day of judgment in Christ (John 5:22). Because of the sacrificial work of Christ, judgment can be tempered with mercy on those who belong to Christ.

3:15 The offspring of the woman who inflicts decisive defeat on the serpent is Christ (Heb. 2:14). But earlier in time, within the OT, there are partial defeats through people who prefigure Christ and foreshadow the final conflict. (See Overview of the Bible, pp. 23–26.)

3:24 When Christ opens the way to eternal life, the barring of the way to life is removed (John 14:6; Heb. 10:19–22; Rev. 22:2).

4:26 The line of Seth appears to be a more godly line, corresponding to the promise of the offspring of the woman (3:15), while Cain and his descendants correspond more to the offspring of the serpent. The line of Seth ultimately leads to Christ (Luke 3:38).

5:5 Death is a repeated, grim occurrence, reminding us of the reality of the curse (2:17; 3:19) and the need for God in mercy to provide a final remedy for death through Christ (John 11:25–26; Rev. 1:18; 21:4).

5:24 Enoch's walk with God makes him an early example of faith (Heb. 11:5–6), and his being taken by God without dying anticipates the eternal resurrection life that Christ gives (Rom. 8:11).

6:9 For Noah's faith, see Heb. 11:7. Noah by his righteousness saved not only himself but his family, prefiguring the righteousness of Christ by which Christ saved his spiritual family.

6:18 God promises in a covenant (see Overview of the Bible, pp. 23–26) to save Noah, prefiguring the new covenant in Christ by which we receive eternal salvation (1 Cor. 11:25; Heb. 10:15–18).

7:23 The flood brought a whole world to an end (2 Pet. 2:5; 3:6). It prefigures the final judgment, which ends the present heavens and earth and brings a new world (Rev. 21:1). God preserves those who belong to Christ, the final Noah.

8:13 The emerging of a new world prefigures the creation of the new heaven and the new earth (Rev. 21:1–4; see 2 Pet. 3:5–7).

9:7 God repeats the command given to man in 1:28. Noah is a new head or representative for humanity, prefiguring Christ, who will be the final head of the new humanity (1 Cor. 15:45–48). All those descending from Noah are privileged for his sake.

9:11 In a covenant God guarantees to all mankind blessings that come through Noah. He shows mercy, based on sacrifice (8:21), pointing forward ultimately to the mercy that comes through the sacrifice of Christ (Heb. 10:12).

10:32 All the nations of the world are encompassed in the plan of God. He chooses Abram alone (12:1–3), but eventually "all the nations of the earth shall be blessed in him" (18:18; see 12:3; Rev. 5:9).

11:4 Babel, and later Babylon (Revelation 17–18), is the quintessential worldly city, where man tries to exalt himself to the position of a god. It contrasts with the holy city of God's people, whose name is made great not through their prideful self-exaltation but by the power of God (Gen. 12:2; Rev. 21:2).

12:1 God will give Abram a great name, in contrast to the self-exalting desire in Babel (11:4). The choice of Abram narrows down the line of the offspring of the woman (3:15) to Abram's offspring. Ultimately, Abraham is great as a progenitor of Christ (Rom. 9:5).

12:2 God's promise is reiterated and expanded as time passes (13:14–17; 15:4–5; 17:1–14; 18:18; 22:16–18; 26:2–5; 28:13–15; 35:10–12).

12:3 The inclusion of all the families of the earth anticipates the spread of the gospel and salvation in Christ to the ends of the earth (Matt. 28:18–20; Acts 1:8; Gal. 3:8).

12:7 God's promise has a short-range fulfillment when the nation of Israel conquers Canaan under Joshua (Josh. 21:43; see 1 Kings 4:21). Ultimately the *offspring* narrows down to Christ (Gal. 3:16), whose dominion extends not only over the land of Canaan but over all the world (Matt. 28:18). The land of Canaan prefigures the eternal inheritance of the world in Christ (Heb. 4:1–11; 11:10, 13–16). In Christ believers are the offspring of Abraham (Gal. 3:7, 29).

13:15 God confirms and expands his promise to Abram (see notes on 12:1; 12:2; and 12:7).

14:18 Melchizedek, a priest and king, prefigures Christ's priesthood (Heb. 7:1–8:6).

15:6 Abram's trust in God is the model for Christians' trust in God's promises in Christ (Gal. 3:6–9). Righteousness is "counted" or reckoned, not on the basis of our achievement, but because in faith we look to God who supplies righteousness in Christ (Rom. 4:5–9; 2 Cor. 5:21; Gal. 3:6).

15:17 The flame, symbolizing God, passes between the pieces, symbolizing that God himself will bear the penalty if the promise is broken. Ultimately, Christ bears the penalty for our disobedience.

16:10 Because of the line of chosen offspring, leading to Christ (Gal. 3:16), some blessings overflow and extend even to collateral descendants like Ishmael.

16:13 Hagar perceives that the Lord has spoken to her, which implies that "the angel of the LORD" is divine. Some think that this is a preincarnate appearance of Christ. Christ is the final, divine messenger of the covenant (Mal. 3:1) who is anticipated in this scene.

17:4 The multiplication of the nation of Israel represents the proximate fulfillment of God's promise (Ex. 1:7). Those who place their trust in Christ, the offspring of Abraham (Gal. 3:16), now become sons of Abraham (Gal. 3:6–9), so that ultimately all the multitude of the saved (Rev. 5:9) have Abraham as father (Rom. 4:17–18).

17:10 Circumcision symbolizes the covenant relation to God, which demands holiness. It is fulfilled in Christ's purification of believers (Col. 2:11).

18:2 Two of the "men" turn out to be angels (19:1), while the third is the Lord (18:22). The appearance of God in human form anticipates the incarnation of the Son (John 1:1–18).

18:10 The miraculous birth of a son according to the power of God's word anticipates later instances where God's word overcomes a "dead" womb and brings new life: 25:21; 30:22; 1 Sam. 1:20; Isa. 54:1. The pattern culminates in the virgin birth of Christ (Luke 1:35), and has relevance for understanding God's sovereignty in election (Rom. 9:8–9).

18:24 Abraham's limited intercession fails to spare Sodom. Christ's perfect intercession always succeeds (Heb. 7:23–25).

19:16 Though Lot is a mixed character who makes compromises, God saves him and his family, prefiguring his mercy in eternal salvation (2 Pet. 2:7–9).

19:24 The destruction of Sodom and Gomorrah prefigures eternal judgment (2 Pet. 2:6, 9–10; Rev. 14:10–11).

20:6 Even though Abraham misuses her, God in mercy preserves Sarah, who embodies the line of holy offspring leading to Christ.

21:2 The miraculous birth of Isaac, the special offspring of promise, prefigures the coming birth of Christ, in accordance with all the promises of God.

21:4 Circumcision represents purification and holiness, anticipating the purity of Christ (Luke 2:21; 3:22; Col. 2:11; see Gen. 17:10).

21:10 The distinction between the miraculous son of promise and the son from human planning prefigures the distinction between the church and natural descendants of Abraham (Gal. 4:30).

22:3 Abraham demonstrates the reality of his faith in action, serving as a model for how our good works demonstrate our faith (James 2:18–24).

22:8 Isaac comes near to being sacrificed, but God provides a substitute. Ultimately God will sacrifice his only Son, who dies in our place (Gal. 3:13, 16). The ram prefigures the sacrifice of Christ.

22:16 Abraham's willingness to sacrifice his son leads to great blessing to his offspring. God's sacrifice of his only Son leads to even greater blessings to Christ's spiritual offspring (Rom. 5:8–11; Heb. 6:13–14).

23:19 Abraham takes care about Sarah's burial, expressing thereby his faith in God's promise that he will possess the land. The fact that the land is not theirs during Sarah's or Abraham's earthly life points forward to the resurrection of the dead (Heb. 11:13–16).

24:4 The marriage of Isaac is important, because he is the offspring of promise through whose offspring the world will be blessed. The special provision of a wife for Isaac prefigures God's offspring of promise, Christ, receiving a bride, the church (Rev. 19:7).

25:23 Jacob the chosen one and Esau the one not chosen prefigure the age-long struggle between the chosen people and their adversaries (Mal. 1:2–3; Rom. 9:10–13). The principle applies in the OT to Israel and in the NT to the church.

26:28 Abimelech's respect for Isaac prefigures the salvation of the nations through Abraham's offspring in Christ (18:18).

27:35 God carries out his sovereign purpose of confirming Jacob as the chosen line of the offspring of Abraham (12:7; 25:23), in spite of Isaac's intent to bless Esau and in spite of the sinfulness in Jacob's deceit.

28:12 The opening of access to heaven anticipates Christ, who opens access permanently (John 1:51; Heb. 10:19–20).

29:25 Even in the midst of trickery God sovereignly works to give Jacob wives, through whom he will fulfill the promise to multiply Abraham's offspring (15:5).

30:1 In the midst of sordid competition between Leah and Rachel, God sovereignly fulfills the first stage of his promise to multiply Abraham's offspring (12:2; 15:5; 17:5; 26:4; 28:14).

31:24 God protects Jacob, fulfilling his earlier promise (28:13–15) and protecting the line of chosen offspring leading to Christ (Gal. 3:16).

32:24 God appears in human form, anticipating the incarnation of Christ.

33:4 God delivers Jacob and his family from a feared attack by Esau, fulfilling his promise to Jacob and his offspring (28:14–15) and protecting the offspring leading to Christ.

34:9 Though Simeon and Levi are later criticized for their deceit and violence (49:5–7), God uses them in preserving the line of holy offspring from intermarriage (see Deut. 7:3), thus protecting the line until the coming of Christ the final offspring (Gal. 3:16).

35:10 God confirms earlier promises to Abraham and his offspring (see note on 12:2).

36:1 The record of collateral, rejected offspring (25:23) is given before continuing with the record of the line leading to Christ (Gal. 3:16).

37:7 Prophetic dreams concerning God's plan for the offspring of promise foreshadow the final prophetic unveiling of God's purposes through Christ.

37:20 Joseph, who is to be the key deliverer of God's people, has a scrape with death, and is finally glorified (41:41), foreshadowing the suffering and glorification of Christ the final deliverer.

38:29 In spite of unrighteous sexual behavior by several males, God brings about his own purpose of continuing the offspring leading to Christ (Matt. 1:3).

39:9 Joseph, in contrast to Adam and Eve, firmly rejected temptation, anticipating Christ's rejection of temptation (Matt. 4:1–11; 16:23).

40:23 The trials of Joseph, testing his faith, anticipate the trials that come to Christ as man (Matt. 4:1–11), and that come to disciples of Christ (Acts 14:22; 1 Thess. 3:4).

41:36 Through prophetic gifts given by God, Joseph is able to save from famine not only Jacob and his family, but Egypt. He foreshadows Christ, whose prophetic teaching and suffering bring eternal salvation both to Jews and to Gentiles. (See 18:18.)

42:9 God works according to his plan, which was already revealed in Joseph's dreams (37:5–9). God cares for the line of offspring leading to Christ (3:15; Gal. 3:16).

43:9 Judah offers himself as a substitute, prefiguring the substitution of Christ the offspring of Judah.

44:33 See note on 43:9.

44:29 Salvation through Joseph includes not only rescue from famine, but a change of heart in the brothers, compared to their earlier envy and violence toward Joseph. The change prefigures the change of heart that Christ works through the Spirit (John 3:3–8).

45:15 Reconciliation springs from forgiveness, prefiguring God's reconciliation and forgiveness in Christ.

46:4 God delivers the entire family from famine and promises permanent care, anticipating both the exodus from Egypt (Exodus 1–14) and the subsequent generations leading to Christ.

47:6 Through Joseph's deliverance abundant blessings come to his family, prefiguring the blessings of deliverance in Christ.

48:5 The transformation of one tribe (Joseph) into two further illustrates the fruitfulness of blessing to the line of offspring that God has chosen and blessed.

49:10 At this early point God already reveals that through Judah will come a line of kings, leading finally to Christ the great, eternal king (Matt. 1:1–16).

50:20 God uses even evil to work out his good purposes, foreshadowing the time when he will bring the supreme good, namely, eternal salvation, out of the wicked actions of the men who condemned and crucified Jesus (Acts 2:23; 4:25–28).

50:24 God's promises stand firm through generations (12:7; 15:13–14). His faithfulness is expressed climactically in Christ (2 Cor. 1:20).

Exodus

Through Moses God redeems his people from slavery in Egypt, prefiguring Christ's eternal redemption of his people from slavery to sin.

1:7 The multiplication of the people fulfills God's promise to multiply Abraham's descendants (Gen. 15:5) and to bless the world through them (Gen. 18:18), specifically through Christ (Gal. 3:8).

1:13 Bitter suffering precedes release, symbolizing that suffering under sin precedes the deliverance from sin in Christ.

2:10 Moses, the special agent for God's deliverance, has his life preserved, anticipating the rescue of baby Jesus from Herod's murders (Matt. 2:13).

2:15 God brings deliverance through *his* power and in *his* way, through the weakness of the cross, not through merely human impulses for justice (1 Cor. 1:25).

3:5 The overwhelming holiness of the presence of God anticipates the presence of God in Christ's incarnation.

3:12 The commissioning of Moses by God's word and God's power prefigures the commissioning of Christ for his work (Matt. 3:17).

3:14 The name "I AM" anticipates the "I am" sayings of Jesus (see John 8:58), which show his deity.

4:13 Moses' reluctance points forward ultimately to the need for a *divine* deliverer, Jesus Christ.

5:2 Pharaoh's refusal to recognize the true God prefigures the resistance of people to Christ's claims, even though miracles supported his claims.

6:8 The mention of the patriarchs (see Gen. 12:7) shows the faithfulness of God and the continuity of his purposes over time. This faithfulness comes to ultimate fruition with the sending of the Son.

7:17 The plagues on Egypt foreshadow the plagues preceding the second coming (Rev. 11:6).

9:16 God uses even those who resist his will, prefiguring his use of Herod and Pilate (Acts 2:23).

10:4 The locusts prefigure the judgments associated with the day of the Lord (Joel 1–2; Rev. 9:1–11).

11:5 The plague of death reminds us that the wages of sin is death (Rom. 6:23). Only through the death of God's Son are we delivered.

12:6 Deliverance through the blood of a lamb prefigures the coming of the Lamb of God to obtain final salvation through his death (John 1:29).

12:46 Because Jesus is the fulfillment of the Passover lamb (1 Cor. 5:7), it is fitting that none of Jesus' bones were broken (John 19:36).

13:3 We now look back to the final Passover in which Christ brought eternal salvation from sin (1 Cor. 5:7), and we remember it in the Lord's Supper (1 Cor. 11:23–26).

14:19 God's special presence in the cloud prefigures his presence in Christ, who is our protection and refuge against all the attacks of Satan.

14:22 The people go down symbolically into death and come up alive, prefiguring the reception of resurrection life through Christ (see Rom. 6:4; 1 Cor. 10:2).

14:30 The death of Egyptians prefigures that final destruction of all God's enemies (Rev. 20:15; 21:8).

15:2 Praise for God's salvation anticipates the songs of praise for Christ's final work of salvation (Rev. 5:9–14; 15:3).

15:17 The conquest of Canaan prefigures the entrance into the final sanctuary of God's presence, mediated by Christ (Heb. 10:19–20; Rev. 21:22).

16:4 Manna prefigures Christ the bread of heaven, who gives eternal life (John 6:31–35).

16:18 The sufficiency of the manna prefigures the sufficiency of Christ to meet every need of his people (Phil. 4:19).

17:6 God providing water after striking the rock prefigures Christ, who is stricken to provide the water of eternal life (John 4:14; 19:34).

18:18 The limitations of Moses prefigure the need for Christ, the *divine* judge, and Christ's appointment of shepherds under him (elders) to carry out his will (1 Pet. 5:1–4).

19:6 The privileges of Israel prefigure the higher privileges of the NT church (1 Pet. 2:9–10), won through Christ's redemption (Heb. 10:10).

19:12 The threat of death illustrates the impossibility of sinful people approaching a holy God. The impossibility is overcome only through the sacrifice and mediation of Christ (Heb. 10:19–20).

20:2 Christians now obey God's commandments because he has brought us out of sin and death (Rom. 13:9; Col. 1:13; Rev. 1:5–6).

20:11 The celebration of the Sabbath looks back to creation (see notes on Gen. 2:2 and 2:3), back to redemption from Egyptian slavery (Deut. 5:15), and forward to final rest through faith in Christ (Heb. 4:1–11).

20:13 The Ten Commandments are deepened through Jesus' teaching (Matt. 5:17–48) and fulfilled in Jesus' perfect righteousness (Heb. 4:15; 5:9).

21:2 The ordinances concerning slavery anticipate our being freed from slavery to sin and becoming slaves to Christ (Rom. 6:20–22; 1 Cor. 7:22).

21:12 The principles of retribution and restitution, though they hedge in sin and give partial remedies, do not bring a perfect kingdom, but look forward to the perfection of the kingdom of Christ (Isa. 9:6–7; Matt. 5:38–48).

23:1 The truthfulness of God, coming to its climax in Christ, is to be reflected in truthfulness displayed to fellow human beings, and the compassion and justice of God is to be reflected in treatment of fellow humans.

24:8 Consecration through blood prefigures consecration through the blood of Christ (Heb. 9:18–26).

24:11 Fellowship with God prefigures our seeing God in the face of Jesus Christ (John 14:9). Christians enjoy fellowship with God in Christ, who is the food of eternal life (John 6:53–58), symbolized in the Lord's Supper and consummated in the final feast (Rev. 19:9; 22:4).

25:8 The making of a dwelling place anticipates Solomon's temple (1 Kings 6) and prefigures God's dwelling with humanity in Christ (Matt. 1:23; John 2:19–21; Rev. 21:22), in the church (1 Cor. 3:16; Eph. 2:19–22), in the individual Christian (1 Cor. 6:19), and in the consummation (Rev. 21:3, 22–27). The actual construction of the tabernacle is described in Exodus 36–39.

25:22 God's meeting with and speaking to his people prefigures his intimacy and communion with believers in Christ (John 15:4).

25:30 Bread expressing fellowship with God prefigures Jesus feeding us as the bread of life (John 6:35, 52–58).

25:37 The provision of light in the presence of God prefigures Jesus as the light of the world (John 1:4–9; 3:19–21; 8:12; 9:5).

25:40 The tabernacle is a shadow or copy of the heavenly, final dwelling of God, as indicated in Heb. 8:5. The symbolism in the tabernacle therefore consistently prefigures Christ and the church (see note on Ex. 25:8).

26:33 The curtain bars access to all except the specially qualified high priest (Leviticus 16), prefiguring that only Christ can open the way to God (Heb. 9:7–14; 10:20).

27:1 Access to God is only through sacrifice on the altar (Lev. 4:10), prefiguring the necessity of the sacrifice of Christ (Heb. 9:12–14).

27:9 The hangings of the court erect one more barrier to approaching God, thereby emphasizing his holiness. See note on 26:33.

28:2 The external holiness and beauty of the priest prefigures the perfect holiness of Christ (Heb. 7:23–8:6).

29:1 The priests, being sinful, need atoning sacrifice for themselves, contrasting with the perfection of Christ's priesthood (Heb. 7:26–28).

30:1 Burning incense represents intercessory prayer (Rev. 5:8), prefiguring Christ's intercession (Heb. 7:25).

30:16 Atonement money prefigures Christ's buying us at the price of his own blood (1 Pet. 1:18–19).

30:20 Washing prefigures cleansing from sin in Christ (Zech. 13:1; 1 Cor. 6:11).

31:3 The giving of the Spirit prefigures Christ's building the church through the Spirit (Matt. 16:18; 1 Cor. 14:12; Eph. 2:20–22). The building of the church is based on Christ's resurrection through the Spirit (John 2:19–21; Rom. 8:11). See note on 1 Kings 7:14.

32:12 Moses' intercession prefigures the intercessory prayers of Christ (Heb. 7:25).

32:32 Moses offers himself as a substitute, prefiguring Christ's substitutionary death (Heb. 10:10).

33:19 God as sovereign works his will in election (Rom. 9:15).

33:22 Moses as sinful must be shielded from the full weight of God's holiness, prefiguring Christ's shielding us from the wrath of God (Rom. 5:9–11).

34:9 God's mercy prefigures the mercy given in Christ (Rom. 4:8).

35:21 The willingness of the people prefigures the willingness of Christ's self-giving sacrifice (John 10:18), and then the willingness that he works in us to be used by God (Rom. 12:1; 2 Cor. 8:9–15; 9:7, 13–15).

36:10 The construction exactly according to God's design (26:1–6; see 39:42) prefigures the construction of the church according to God's design (Eph. 4:11–16) and the construction of the new world (Rev. 21:2).

37:1 The construction matches 25:10–22. See note on 25:22.

37:10 The construction matches 25:23–30. See note on 25:30.

37:17 The construction matches 25:31–39. See note on 25:37.

37:25 The construction matches 30:1–10. See note on 30:1.

38:1 The construction matches 27:1–8. See note on 27:1.

38:8 The construction matches 30:17–21. See note on 30:20.

38:9 The construction matches 27:9–19. See note on 27:9.

39:1 The garments match 28:1–43. See note on 28:2.

40:34 See the parallel in 1 Kings 8:10–11. The filling of the tent with God's glory prefigures the fullness of the Spirit in Christ (Matt. 3:16–17; John 1:14; 3:34–35) and in the church (Acts 2:3–4; 1 Cor. 3:16).

Leviticus

The requirement of holiness points to the holiness of Christ (Heb. 7:26–28). The sacrifices prefigure the sacrifice of Christ (Heb. 10:1–10).

1:9 The offering of the whole sacrifice to God prefigures Christ's giving of his whole self (Heb. 10:5–10). The whole sacrifice ascends in smoke, prefiguring the ascension of Christ (Heb. 9:24).

2:1 The offering of the fruitfulness of the land prefigures the honor given to God through the fruitfulness of Christ (John 13:31–32; 1 Cor. 15:23).

3:1 Most of the peace offering is eaten by the worshiper (7:15–16), signifying fellowship with and blessing from God. It is fulfilled in Christ's reconciliation and giving himself as food (John 6:52–57; Rom. 5:9–11).

4:2 The promise of forgiveness is fulfilled in Christ's giving himself as a sacrifice for sin (Rom. 8:3; Heb. 10:1–10).

4:12 The position outside the camp prefigures Christ's crucifixion outside Jerusalem (Heb. 13:11–14).

5:1 Sins of falsehood and sins against holiness are forgiven in anticipation of Christ's work in holiness (Heb. 9:23–26; 10:11–20).

6:13 The continuation of the altar fire indicates the insufficiency of repeated sacrifices (Heb. 10:1–4), in contrast to the sufficiency of Christ's sacrifice (Heb. 10:10) and intercession (Heb. 7:25).

7:20 Fellowship with God and with the things of God requires holiness, prefiguring the holiness of Christ purifying us (Heb. 10:10; 12:14).

8:1 For the instructions for consecration, see Exodus 29.

8:30 Consecration through oil and blood prefigures purification from sin through the Spirit and the blood of Christ (Heb. 9:19–26; 1 Pet. 1:2).

9:24 God's acceptance of the offering prefigures his acceptance of the sacrifice of Christ (Heb. 9:13–14).

10:2 The rejection of human inventions prefigures the fact that Christ is the only way to God (John 14:6; Acts 4:12).

11:45 Separation from uncleanness symbolizes separation from sin in order to be intimate with God. It prefigures Christ's work bringing holiness (Heb. 7:26; 10:10).

12:7 Human birth is contaminated with sin ever since Adam. The remedy is in new birth (John 3:3–8) through Christ (Rom. 5:15–21).

13:46 Skin disease symbolizes the contagion of sin, which alienates us from God and man. Only Christ can restore the fellowship broken by sin (1 John 1:3).

14:2 Cleansing prefigures Christ's work of cleansing from sin (Luke 5:12–14; Heb. 9:9–14).

15:1 Disorders of the body symbolize the disorder of sin, to be cleansed by Christ (Heb. 9:9–14).

16:16 Symbolical atonement prefigures Christ's final atonement (Heb. 9:7–14).

17:11 The blood symbolizing life prefigures the blood of Christ, whose poured-out life brings atonement for sin (Rom. 3:25; Heb. 9:12–14, 18–26).

17:14 In the superior blessing of the new covenant we partake of the blood of Christ as the source of spiritual life (John 6:53–56).

18:3 Separation from pagan practices is part of holiness with God, prefiguring the holiness of Christ (Heb. 7:26) and his people (2 Cor. 6:14–18).

18:5 Ultimately, the holiness of God requires perfect obedience, which is found in Christ (2 Cor. 5:21). Sinful man cannot keep the law (Rom. 10:5; Gal. 3:12–14).

19:2 Loyalty to God requires a life of holiness (1 Pet. 1:15–22).

19:18 The love commandment finds fulfillment in Christ and in those who are his (Matt. 22:39; Rom. 13:9; Gal. 5:14; James 2:8; 1 John 3:11–18; 4:7–21).

20:2 Sin has consequences in curse and death, prefiguring both the death of Christ as sin-bearer (1 Pet. 2:24) and eternal death in hell (Rev. 20:14–15).

21:1 Holiness requires separation from death, which symbolizes sin. The priests prefigure the priesthood of Christ (Heb. 7:26–28) and of his redeemed people (1 Pet. 2:5, 9; Rev. 1:6; 5:10).

22:3 Sin, symbolized by uncleanness, disqualifies us from heavenly things and must be cleansed by Christ (Heb. 9:8–13).

23:5 See Deut. 16:1–8. The Passover prefigures the Last Supper and Christ's death (Matt. 26:19, 26–28; 1 Cor. 5:7).

23:16 See Deut. 16:9–12. This is the feast of "Pentecost," fulfilled in Acts when the firstfruits from the nations are gathered into the church (Acts 2:1–11).

23:28 The day of atonement, an annual day described in chapter 16, prefigures the once-for-all atonement of Christ (Heb. 9:7–14; 10:3–5).

24:2 Continual light prefigures Jesus as the light of the world (John 1:4–9; 3:19–21; 8:12; 9:5).

24:8 Continual bread prefigures Jesus as the bread of life (John 6:35, 48–51).

25:4 The rest given to the land prefigures the final rest given in the consummation (Heb. 4:9–11; Rev. 21:1–22:5). See notes on Gen. 2:2 and 2:3.

25:10 The year of liberty prefigures the liberty given by Christ (Isa. 61:1–2; Luke 4:18–21).

26:14 Sin leads to a curse, anticipating Christ's sin-bearing (Gal. 3:13–14), and sin ultimately leads to hell (Rev. 20:14–15).

27:10 The permanence of holiness prefigures the permanence of redemption (John 10:28–29) and of the new world (Rev. 22:5).

Numbers

The journey through the wilderness prefigures the Christian journey through this world to the new world (1 Cor. 10:1–11; Heb. 4:3–10).

1:3 Readiness for war prefigures spiritual war (Eph. 6:13).

2:17 The people of God are to be organized with God at the center (Eph. 4:4–6).

3:12 The Levites as a holy substitute prefigure Christ as priest, representative, and substitute (Heb. 7:23–28).

4:15 The penalty of death for approaching God's holiness indicates the need for perfect mediation through Christ (Heb. 9:23–26).

5:20 The need for faithfulness in marriage prefigures the faithfulness of the church to Christ (2 Cor. 11:2–4; Eph. 5:25–27).

6:5 The special holiness of the Nazirite prefigures the holiness of Christ (Heb. 7:26).

7:5 Holy service prefigures the service of Christ (Heb. 7:23–8:2) and his people (Rom. 12:1–2).

8:16 Christ substitutes for us and represents us before God (Heb. 7:23–28).

9:10 Being clean for the Passover prefigures moral purity in the church (1 Cor. 5:7–8).

10:2 Summoning prefigures God's instruction to the church (Eph. 4:1; 1 Thess. 4:1–3).

11:17 The distribution of the Spirit foreshadows the wider distribution at Pentecost (11:29; Joel 2:28; Acts 2:4, 16–18).

12:8 Rejection of Moses prefigures the seriousness of rejecting Christ's unique prophetic ministry (John 3:32–36; 5:23).

13:31 The unbelief of Israel contrasts both with the faithfulness of Christ (Matt. 4:1–10) and the faith of Christians (Heb. 3:7–4:3).

14:35 Death indicates judgment on unbelief (Heb. 3:16–19).

15:30 Cutting off prefigures apostasy from Christ (Heb. 10:26–31).

16:2 Rebellion prefigures false teaching in the church (Jude 10–13).

17:5 The choice of Aaron alone prefigures Christ as the one way (John 14:6).

18:5 The priests turn away wrath, prefiguring Christ's propitiation (Rom. 3:23–25).

19:9 Purification prefigures the purification of Christ's work (Heb. 9:13–14).

20:24 The failures in the priests point to the need for the greater priesthood of Christ (Heb. 7:23–25).

21:9 Looking at the serpent prefigures faith in Christ who is lifted up (John 3:14–16).

22:12 God overrules all plots against his purposes (Acts 2:23; Eph. 1:11–12).

24:17 Partial fulfillments in David's and Solomon's rule anticipate Christ's rule over his enemies (1 Cor. 15:24–27; Eph. 1:20–22).

25:3 Idolatry leads to chastisement and death (1 Cor. 10:20; Rev. 14:9–11).

27:4 Inheritance of the land anticipates eternal inheritance of the new world (Heb. 11:13–16).

28:3 Repeated, scheduled offerings anticipate one final offering by Christ (Heb. 10:1–10).

30:3 The authority of a man anticipates the authority of Christ over the church (Eph. 5:21–24).

31:16 The war prefigures holy war against sin (Eph. 6:11; 1 Pet. 2:11).

32:17 The 2 1/2 tribes receive their inheritance in Josh. 13:8–33. The tribes' commitment to the whole nation prefigures cooperative work in the church (1 Corinthians 12).

33:2 The names of the locations record God's faithfulness to his promise to bring his people to the land (Gen. 12:7; Ex. 6:4), prefiguring his faithfulness to believers in Christ (2 Cor. 1:20).

34:13 The inheritance is distributed in Joshua 14–19. The allotment of this land prefigures allotment to each of Christ's people of an eternal inheritance (Eph. 1:11; Col. 1:12).

35:11 See Joshua 20. Deliverance from death prefigures Christ becoming a refuge from death for his people (John 8:51; Heb. 2:14; 6:18).

36:2 See note on 27:4.

Deuteronomy

The righteousness and wisdom of the law of God prefigure the righteousness of Christ, which is given to his people. The anticipation of entering the Promised Land prefigures Christians' hope for the new heaven and the new earth (Rev. 21:1–22:5).

1:32 The people's unbelief (see Numbers 14) contrasts with faith for entering God's rest (Heb. 3:7–4:11).

2:24 God, not human strength, gives victory (3:22), prefiguring victory in Christ (Heb. 2:14–15).

3:12 Moses recalls Numbers 32; see note on Num. 32:17.

3:26 The insufficiency of Moses contrasts with the sufficiency of Christ, who has entered the eternal inheritance on our behalf (Heb. 9:23–26; 10:19–22).

4:6 Israel by obeying would have been a light to the nations. Christ in his obedience is the light that Israel failed to be (Isa. 42:6; John 1:4–9).

5:2 The covenant at Horeb (Sinai) anticipates the new covenant, where obedience will spring from the heart (Heb. 8:8–13), because of Christ's purification (Heb. 10:14).

6:5 Love for God is the greatest commandment (Matt. 22:37–38). One's relation to God himself is central to life, and true love for God and reconciliation to God are possible only in Christ (John 14:6; Rom. 5:1–10).

6:14 Holiness before God avoids compromise with evil, prefiguring the holiness of Christ (Heb. 7:26) and his people (1 Pet. 1:15–16; 2:11).

8:18 Gratitude rather than pride characterizes the people of God (1 Cor. 1:28–31; 2 Cor. 9:15).

9:19 Moses' intercession prefigures Christ's intercession (Heb. 7:23–25).

10:16 Circumcision of the heart comes from renewal through the Spirit of Christ (Rom. 8:9–13; Col. 2:11; Heb. 8:8–13).

11:9 Obedience is the basis for life, prefiguring Christ's resurrection life as the reward for his obedience (Phil. 2:8–11).

12:5 Access to God at a single location (Jerusalem, 1 Kings 8:16; Ps. 122:4) prefigures access through Christ alone (John 14:6).

13:2 False prophets prefigure the danger of false teachings drawing people away from serving God through Christ (2 Pet. 2:1).

14:2 Refraining from unclean foods symbolizes separation from sin (2 Cor. 6:17).

15:2 Release of debtors anticipates the great release from sin through Christ (Luke 4:18–19).

16:1 The great feasts (see Leviticus 23) prefigure the celebration of Christ's deliverance (1 Cor. 5:7).

17:7 The purging of evil prefigures the purging of evil from the church (1 Cor. 5:13) and from the consummation (Rev. 21:8).

17:15 Kings prefigure the righteousness of Christ the perfect king (Isa. 9:6–7; Matt. 27:37; Rev. 19:16).

18:18 Prophets anticipate Christ, the final prophet (Acts 3:22–26).

19:4 The provision for justice prefigures the justice of Christ's rule (Isa. 9:6–7).

20:4 God fights in anticipation of Christ's fight against evil during his earthly life (Matt. 12:28–29), in his death (Heb. 2:14–15), and in his second coming (Rev. 19:15–21).

21:9 Provisions for purity and justice anticipate final purification and justice in Christ (Heb. 9:23–28).

21:23 The curse anticipates Christ bearing the curse of God on our behalf when he is crucified ("hanged on a tree") (Gal. 3:13).

22:22 Provisions for sexual purity anticipate the purity of the church as Christ's bride (Eph. 5:25–27; Rev. 19:7–8).

23:9 God's presence in the camp for war (20:4) requires holiness, prefiguring holy war in Christ (Rev. 19:14–16).

24:1 Provisions for divorce are due to hardness of heart and are inferior to God's design (Matt. 19:3–9), which is to be fulfilled in Christ (Eph. 5:22–33).

25:4 Provision for the ox is an illustration of a larger principle of provision for labor in the church (1 Cor. 9:9–11; 1 Tim. 5:18).

25:5 Provision for a continuing name and inheritance prefigures God's promise and provision for our name (Rev. 2:17) and our inheritance (Eph. 1:13–14; 1 Pet. 1:4–5). It also prefigures Christ, who as younger "brother" to Adam raises up spiritually alive children (Heb. 2:13).

26:8 Thanksgiving for redemption prefigures Christian thanksgiving for redemption in Christ (Heb. 13:15–16).

27:26 All are subject to the curse, and can escape only through Christ's taking the curse on himself (Gal. 3:10–14).

28:1 Eternal blessings of salvation come in Christ (Gal. 3:14), who removed the curse we deserved (Gal. 3:13).

29:4 Renewal of the heart is to come in Christ (Rom. 11:8; Heb. 8:8–13).

30:12 Christ brings power to obey God from the heart (Rom. 10:6–8).

31:26 God makes provision for the preservation of the law for future generations, including us (Rom. 15:4; 1 Cor. 10:11).

32:5 Israel's rebellion contrasts with the faithfulness that is to characterize God's children (Phil. 2:15).

32:6 God's care for Israel prefigures his care for Christ's people (Rom. 8:15–17).

32:21 The apostasy of Israel anticipates the rejection of the gospel (Rom. 10:19).

34:10 The uniqueness of Moses anticipates the uniqueness of Christ (Acts 3:22–26).

Joshua

The conquest through Joshua prefigures Christ conquering his enemies, both Satan (Heb. 2:14–15) and rebellious human beings. The conquest takes place both through the gospel (Matt. 28:18–20) and in the destruction at the second coming (Rev. 19:11–21).

1:6 Joshua's role prefigures Jesus empowering his disciples (Matt. 28:18–20; Acts 1:8).

2:9 Rahab in her faith anticipates the salvation of Gentiles through faith (Gal. 3:6–9; Heb. 11:31; James 2:25).

3:11 God's presence brings the people through the waters of death into the land, prefiguring Christ leading us to eternal life (John 11:25–26).

4:6 Memorials of God's faithfulness look forward to the message of Christ's salvation.

5:14 The divine commander anticipates Christ, who is the commander in climactic spiritual war (Matt. 28:18; Heb. 2:14–15; Rev. 17:14; 19:11–21).

6:2 The fall of Jericho prefigures the fall of Babylon and the end of the world (Rev. 18:2).

7:11 Israel's suffering because of unholiness prefigures the need for holiness in the church (1 Cor. 5:1–13).

8:32 A permanent record and a recital of the covenant fulfill the instructions given under Moses (Deut. 27:2–8). Intimacy with God through the covenant looks forward to the new covenant in Christ (Heb. 8:8–13).

9:3 Though Israel fails in not consulting the Lord (9:14), the result prefigures the time when through the gospel people from many nations will come to recognize the God of Israel (Luke 24:47; Acts 1:8; Rev. 5:9–10).

10:14 The great display of God's power on behalf of his people prefigures the power of Christ's resurrection and God's commitment to save those who belong to Christ (Eph. 1:19–23).

11:23 The whole conquest takes place according to the plan and promise of God (Deuteronomy 7, etc.), illustrating God's commitment to Israel in love and anticipating his commitment to believers in Christ (Eph. 1:3–14).

12:1 The list of defeated kings prefigures the triumph of Christ over all nations (Eph. 1:22; Rev. 5:9–10; 19:11–21; 20:8–9).

13:8 Inheritance takes place according to plan (Numbers 32), prefiguring God's faithfulness with respect to the eternal inheritance in the new heaven and the new earth (Eph. 1:11, 14; 2:18; 1 Pet. 1:4; 2 Pet. 3:13).

14:2 See Numbers 32–35, especially 32:33; 33:54; 34:17; 35:2. Inheritance takes place according to the plan of God, anticipating eternal inheritance.

14:6 See Num. 14:6–8. Caleb is a special example showing that inheritance comes to those who have faith in God and his promises. He prefigures eternal inheritance by faith (Rom. 4:13–16; Gal. 3:7, 18).

15:1 Detailed specification of boundaries underlines for future generations their participation in the promise. It prefigures the detailed care and provision that God makes for each of us, anticipating the full inheritance in the new heaven and the new earth (1 Pet. 1:4; 2 Pet. 3:13; Rev. 21:1).

16:1 Each of the tribes is provided for (Num. 33:54), and with it each of the members of the tribes, prefiguring God's provision for each follower of Christ (John 10:3, 14; see also John 6:35).

18:4 The situation is reminiscent of the spying of the land in Numbers 13. But this time the result is more favorable, prefiguring the even greater blessings that God has in store through the new covenant (Heb. 8:8–13).

19:1 See note on 15:1.

20:1 The selection of cities of refuge fulfills the instructions through Moses (Num. 35:9–29; Deut. 19:1–13). It makes provision for refuge from death, prefiguring the coming of Christ as final refuge and solution to death (Heb. 2:14–15; Rev. 1:18).

21:2 The distribution of the Levites among the tribes fulfills Gen. 49:7 and Num. 35:1–8, and provides all the tribes with people to teach the law (Lev. 10:11; Mal. 2:4–9). Their teaching prefigures the knowledge of God from the heart in the new covenant (Heb. 8:8–13).

22:26 The altar confirming participation in God's promises prefigures the Holy Spirit sealing participation in Christ (2 Cor. 1:22; Eph. 1:13).

23:6 The call to loyalty to the Mosaic covenant prefigures the call to faith in Christ (Matt. 28:18–20; Heb. 3:12–14).

24:15 God must be served with exclusive loyalty (Deut. 5:7), prefiguring the exclusivity of commitment to Christ as the one way of salvation (Matt. 6:24; 10:34–39; John 14:6; Acts 4:12; 1 Cor. 10:21–22).

Judges

The judges save Israel, thus prefiguring Christ. But the judges have flaws and failures, and Israel repeatedly slips back into idolatry (2:19), spiraling downward to chaos. They need a king (21:25), and not only a king but a perfect king, the Messiah (Isa. 9:6–7).

1:2 The leading role of Judah anticipates the rise of kings from the line of Judah (Gen. 49:10), beginning with King David and culminating in Jesus Christ (Matt. 1:1–16).

2:18 God raises judges to save the people, prefiguring the sending of Christ (Matt. 1:21). But the judges' help is only temporary (Judg. 2:19).

3:20 The surprise prefigures the surprising character of salvation in Christ, which seems to the world to be weakness (1 Cor. 1:25).

4:9 The glory goes ultimately to God, not to human strength or courage, prefiguring the divine glory through human weakness in the cross of Christ (1 Cor. 1:25).

5:4 God's power and glory at Seir (Deut. 33:2) prefigure his present and future triumphs (Rev. 19:6).

6:15 God again chooses to save Israel through a weak and timid person (cf. 4:9), prefiguring the triumph of divine glory through human weakness in Christ (1 Cor. 1:25; 2 Cor. 13:4).

7:3 God reduces the number of troops, prefiguring his work of eternal salvation through a single person, Jesus Christ.

8:16 Those who despise the work of God through a small number prefigure those who despise the work of God in Christ (1 Cor. 1:18–31).

9:56 The horrors due to Abimelech give evidence for the need for a king, thus looking forward to the coming of David and his descendants, above all Jesus Christ, the son of David and final king.

10:6 Disobedience and idolatry further multiply (see 2:19), giving further evidence for the need of permanent salvation through the coming line of King David.

11:2 Jephthah is a flawed judge because of his ancestry, because of his appointment by the elders rather than a direct call from God, and because of his foolish vow. He makes evident the need for permanent salvation through the coming line of King David.

12:4 The fighting among the Israelites shows the need for a king in the coming line of David who will bring unity to the people.

13:5 Samson is to be a Nazirite (see Numbers 6) and especially holy. He shows great promise as a savior of Israel, prefiguring Christ.

13:8 The "man of God," "the angel of the Lord" (v. 15) is God himself (v. 22), anticipating the incarnation of Christ.

14:3 Israel is told not to intermarry with the Canaanites (Deut. 7:3). In Samson's case the Lord uses it for good (Judg. 14:4), but it ultimately becomes Samson's downfall (ch. 16), indicating the need for a perfect savior to deliver people from their spiritual "marriage" to idolatry.

15:14 Samson triumphs after being delivered as a captive over to the enemies, prefiguring Christ's victory after being delivered to his enemies.

16:30 Samson, though sinful, delivers Israel through his death, prefiguring Christ the sinless one delivering his people.

17:2 Sin is compounded, in stealing, making an idol, partly backing down from a vow (v. 4), and making a false priesthood (v. 5). This shows further descent into sinfulness and the need for the coming king in the line of David.

18:19 The multiplication of sin shows the need for salvation through the coming king in the line of David.

19:30 Gibeah has become like Sodom (Genesis 19), showing the depths of sin and the need for salvation.

20:14 Division and war, rather than unity in righteousness, show the need for salvation through the coming king in the line of David.

21:10 The tribe of Benjamin is saved from utter annihilation, but only through further disunity, slaughter, and disorder. The disaster shows the need for permanent salvation through the king.

Ruth

The line of offspring leading to Christ goes through Judah to Boaz to David (4:18–22; Matt. 1:5–6). Boaz the redeemer (Ruth 2:20), prefiguring Christ, enables Naomi's disgrace to be removed and Ruth, a foreigner, to be included in God's people (pre-

figuring the inclusion of the Gentiles, Gal. 3:7–9, 14–18, 29).

1:16 Ruth expresses faith in the God of Israel, as well as love for Naomi, anticipating the role of faith when Christ comes to bring salvation.

1:20 Naomi's transition from bitterness to blessedness prefigures the participation of God's people in Christ's death and resurrection (Phil. 3:10).

2:20 The kindness and protection of Boaz, the kinsman-redeemer, prefigure the work of Christ the redeemer.

3:9 Christ spreads his protection over the church, his bride (2 Cor. 11:2; Eph. 5:25–27).

4:11 The blessing of fruitfulness has a near fulfillment in the birth of Obed (v. 13), but points ultimately to Christ and his fruitfulness (Heb. 2:10).

1 Samuel

David, the king after God's heart (16:7; Acts 13:22), prefigures Christ, in contrast to Saul, who is the kind of king that the people want (1 Sam. 8:5, 19–20). Saul's persecution of David prefigures worldly people's persecution of Christ and of Christ's people.

1:11 By his power to bring life out of barrenness God raises up Samuel as his representative, prefiguring the virgin birth of Christ (Matt. 1:25).

2:7 The raising of the downtrodden that Hannah experiences prefigures the reversal of positions with Christ's coming (Luke 1:48–53).

3:19 Samuel's calling at an early age prefigures the intimacy with God that Christ as the Son enjoys with the Father from all eternity.

4:11 The capture of the ark, which symbolizes God himself, and the death of the priests is a kind of "humiliation" of God's name, prefiguring the humiliation of Christ in his crucifixion. But it all takes place in accordance with God's sovereign purpose (2:34–35; Acts 2:23; 4:25–28).

5:4 God executes judgment on Dagon, prefiguring the judgment in Christ against all idols and idol worship (Rev. 2:20).

6:12 By miraculous power God delivers the ark, the symbol of his name, prefiguring the miraculous deliverance of Christ from death.

7:8 Samuel acts as a faithful judge (v. 15; cf. Judg. 13:5), prophet (1 Sam. 3:19–20), and priest (7:8–9), prefiguring the work of Christ as king, prophet, and priest (Heb. 1:1–3).

8:5 A king like the nations contrasts with God's kingship (v. 7). God intends Israel to have a king (Deut. 17:14–20), but the people's desires and the kings themselves fall short. Saul's failure contrasts with David's success. But eventually David too fails (2 Samuel 11). The failure of merely human kings points to the need for the perfect king, Christ, who will be divine and human (Isa. 9:6–7).

8:7 The people's rejection of God's ways prefigures the rejection of Christ (Acts 3:13–15; 7:51–53).

9:16 God indicates his sovereignty over the appointment of kings, prefiguring the appointment of Christ as king over all (Ps. 2:6; Eph. 1:20–22; Phil. 2:9–11).

10:1 The oil prefigures the coming of the Holy Spirit to empower. Saul's later failures show that he is only a shadow of the greater anointing that comes to David (16:13) and climactically to Christ (Luke 4:18; John 3:34), and then to those who belong to Christ (2 Cor. 1:21–22).

11:15 Saul is initially successful, receiving the benefits of God's favor. This temporary favor contrasts with the lasting favor on David and his offspring, supremely on Christ (Matt. 3:17).

12:14 As the king goes, so go the people. Their failures show the need for the coming of Christ the perfect king, who is able to change the hearts of his people.

13:12 Saul knew that sacrifice was supposed to be offered only by the priests (Num. 18:7). Saul's sins lead to his replacement by David (1 Sam. 13:14; 16:7), prefiguring the need for Christ the perfect king.

14:6 The Lord saved Israel through Jonathan that day (v. 23). Ultimate salvation comes through one man, Christ Jesus (1 Tim. 2:5).

15:22 Sinners replace real obedience with outward tokens (see Mic. 6:6–8). Full obedience from the heart is found in Christ (Heb. 10:5–10).

16:7 The choice of David contrasts with people's looking on outward appearance (10:23–24). The contrast prefigures people's rejection of Christ's humiliation and suffering (Isa. 53:3; 1 Cor. 1:18–31).

17:47 God's working national deliverance through David prefigures international salvation through Christ, who defeats Satan (Heb. 2:14–15).

18:3 Despite Saul's antagonism, Saul's son Jonathan and daughter Michal go over to David's side. David prefigures the spiritual attraction of Jesus Christ, who is the final David (Matt. 4:18–22; 8:9–13).

19:10 Saul's repeated persecution of David in his innocence prefigures the repeated persecution of Christ (John 8:44–47).

20:33 The conflict with Jonathan prefigures the conflict within households over loyalty to Christ (Matt. 10:34–39).

21:5 The exception made for David as God's anointed prefigures the role of Christ, God's anointed, in relation to the law (Matt. 12:3–4, 8).

22:16 As Saul continues to pursue David, Saul's sins multiply, prefiguring the progressive enslavement to sin on the part of those who refuse to come to Christ.

23:2 Directions from God repeatedly help David to choose a path forward, prefiguring the direction from God through Christ to the road to eternal life (Matt. 7:24–27; John 5:24).

24:6 David respects Saul's position as God's anointed king, unlike Pilate, who failed to recognize Jesus' position as God's anointed King (John 19:10).

24:17 David shows mercy to Saul, prefiguring the mercy of Christ even toward those who have opposed him (1 Tim. 1:13–16).

25:24 Abigail offers herself as a guilt-bearer for her worthless husband, prefiguring the gracious guilt-bearing of Christ (1 Pet. 2:23–25).

25:29 Vengeance belongs to the Lord (Rom. 12:19). In recalling this, David prefigures Christ's willingness to leave vengeance in God's hands (1 Pet. 2:23).

26:9 See the note on 24:6.

27:1 Though David loses heart, God continues to protect David in fulfillment of his purpose to make David king (16:1). God's faithfulness even to an imperfect man magnifies his faithfulness in the case of Christ, the perfect king.

28:7 By consulting a medium, Saul makes a further step into wickedness, further contrasting his life with the righteousness of David, and the climactic righteousness of the Messiah.

29:11 God continues faithfulness to David by removing him from involvement in the death of Saul and Jonathan (31:2) and enabling him to return to Ziklag in time to rescue the wives and children (30:1–31). See note on 27:1.

30:6 David through the strength of God acts as deliverer, prefiguring Christ the deliverer of captives (Luke 4:18–19).

31:6 God fulfills his word against Saul (28:19), showing that sin in a ruler brings suffering and death not only on himself but on others under his care. The failure of Saul shows the need for a perfect ruler in the line of David (Isa. 9:6–7).

2 Samuel

David as a model king brings blessing to the nation until he falls into sin with Bathsheba (ch. 11). Though he repents, the remainder of his reign is flawed, pointing to the need for the coming of Christ the perfect messianic king.

1:23 David mentions nothing of Saul's failures and sins, prefiguring the grace and forgiveness of Christ.

2:10 Judah and Israel are eventually united under David and Solomon (5:1–5; 1 Kings 4:20), but division reappears under Rehoboam and his successors (1 Kings 11:11–13; 12:16–24). The strife points to the need for permanent union, which will be achieved only through Christ the king.

3:37 David's graciousness and respect for Abner, in contrast to Joab's vengeance, display the qualities of a godly king, prefiguring the graciousness of Christ.

4:11 David's respect for Ish-bosheth, like his respect for Abner, shows the desire for reconciliation and forgiveness, prefiguring Christ's reconciliation.

5:2 David unites Israel and Judah under one head, fulfilling God's prophetic purpose (1 Sam. 16:1) and prefiguring the greater unity of God's people to be accomplished in Christ (1 Corinthians 12; Eph. 4:1–16).

6:7 Only the Levites were to carry the ark, touching only its poles (Ex. 25:14; Num. 4:15). God in his holiness destroys sinners who approach him unauthorized, but his presence can also bring blessing (2 Sam. 6:12). The tension is resolved only when the way to approach God is opened through Christ's work of purification (Heb. 10:19–22).

7:12 God's covenant with David has a proximate fulfillment with Solomon (1 Kings 1:46; 8:15–21). But Solomon fails (1 Kings 11:1–10). God preserves the line of offspring (1 Kings 11:12, 36; 15:4; 2 Kings 8:19) until Christ the everlasting king comes (Matt. 1:1–16).

7:14 God promises David that he will be a father to Solomon. As God's son, Solomon prefigures Christ the eternal Son (Heb. 1:5).

8:15 David as model king subdues enemies and brings justice, prefiguring the work of Christ the king (Isa. 9:6–7).

9:1 David's graciousness toward the house of Saul fulfills his earlier promise to Saul (1 Sam. 24:21–22) and Jonathan (1 Sam. 20:15–17), and it prefigures the graciousness of Christ the king.

10:2 Willingly or unwillingly Ammon comes to acknowledge David's rule, prefiguring the willing or unwilling submission of all nations to Christ's rule (Psalm 2).

11:4 David later repents (12:13). But David and his house and his rule over the whole nation suffer various consequences for the rest of his life. The devastation from one sin points to the need for Christ the perfect, sinless king (Isa. 42:1–4).

12:13 God is gracious to forgive, ultimately for the sake of Christ (1 John 1:9). But sin still brings consequences (2 Sam. 12:10–12, 14). See note on 11:4.

13:22 The sin of Amnon, in its similarity to David's sin (11:4), begins a series of devastating consequences for David's house (12:10–12), including not only Absalom's actions but David's neglect of discipline and justice toward Amnon and Absalom. See note on 11:4.

14:1 David's love for Absalom prefigures Christ's love for sinners. But David falls short of Christ by neglecting justice: murder deserves death (Num. 35:31–34).

15:1 Absalom's betrayal of his father prefigures Judas's betrayal of Jesus (John 13:18), and more broadly the treachery of all who rebel against God the Father and Christ.

15:30 David's sorrow prefigures the sorrow of Christ as he leaves Jerusalem and prays in Gethsemane (Matt. 26:30, 36–46).

16:12 David leaves vengeance to God, prefiguring the patience of Christ before his enemies (1 Pet. 2:23).

16:22 Absalom's sordid behavior fulfills God's prophecy in 12:11–12, further illustrating the devastation of sin and the need for a perfect redeemer king.

17:5 Through Hushai and other circumstances, God shows mercy to David and answers David's need expressed in 15:31–37. The turning back of the effects of sin, and David's rescue from death, look forward to final redemption in Christ.

18:33 David's grief, though flawed (19:2, 5–7), prefigures the willingness of the Son of God to die in place of sinners (Rom. 5:8).

19:22 Forgiveness under the reestablished kingship prefigures forgiveness for former rebels under Christ's kingship (1 Tim. 1:12–16).

20:1 Divisiveness continues to rear its head after Absalom's death, partly because of David's preference for Judah in 19:11–15, leading to the anger in 19:43. The kingdom continues to suffer indirect consequences from David's sin with Bathsheba, underlining the need for Christ the perfect king. See note on 11:4.

20:10 Though David is reconciled to Amasa (v. 4), Joab kills him, probably because of his role in Absalom's rebellion (17:25). See note on 20:1.

21:3 Atonement and blessing are needed, but David's solution (v. 6) does not give ultimate satisfaction (Deut. 24:16). Full resolution of justice requires Christ the divine king with infinite wisdom, and the coming of resurrection from the dead (Rev. 20:11–15).

22:1 This song is included in the Psalter in Psalm 18, indicating that it is to be sung by the people of God as well as David. See note on 1 Chron. 15:16.

22:50 The spread of praise among the nations anticipates the spread of the gospel (Acts 1:8; Rom. 15:9).

22:51 God's salvation for David prefigures his salvation through Christ the king.

23:8 The list of mighty men prefigures the might in the army of God under Christ the king (Rev. 19:11–14).

24:1 Out of the need for atonement comes the designation of the site for the temple of Solomon (1 Chron. 21:28–22:1), which prefigures Christ as the final temple where atonement is accomplished (John 2:19–21). See note on 1 Chron. 22:1.

24:17 The suffering of the sheep for the sin of their king is reversed when Christ suffers for the sins of the sheep (John 10:15). Christ's suffering answers David's request that God's hand would be against "my father's house," the line leading to Christ.

1 Kings

The reign of Solomon fulfills the first stage of God's promise to David to establish the kingdom of his offspring (2 Sam. 7:12). Solomon in some ways is a model king, prefiguring Christ. But his decline into sin (1 Kings 11), the sins of his offspring, the division and strife between Israel and Judah, and the continual problems with false worship indicate the need for a perfect king and an everlasting kingdom (Isa. 9:6–7) surpassing the entire period of the monarchy. Many passages in 1 Kings have parallels in 2 Chronicles.

1:13 David's purpose prefigures the purpose of God to establish Christ as king, when many prefer alternatives (Psalm 2; Acts 13:33).

2:6 Solomon's wisdom is tested in dealing with unfinished business from the reign of David. Solomon's wisdom prefigures the wisdom of Christ (Matt. 12:42; Col. 2:3). The combination of mercy and justice characterizes David and Solomon in anticipation of Christ.

3:9 See note on 2:6. God promises wisdom in 3:12, and fulfillment is seen in 3:28 and 4:29–34.

4:1 The blessings of order, peace, justice, and prosperity in Solomon's reign prefigure the blessings of Christ's reign.

4:34 The attraction of Solomon's wisdom prefigures all nations hearing the wisdom of Christ (Acts 1:8).

5:5 Solomon's building of the temple fulfills God's promise in 2 Sam. 7:13 (cf. 1 Chron. 17:12) and prefigures the building of an everlasting temple. Christ's resurrection body is an everlasting temple (John 2:19–22), and then Christ builds the church as a temple (Matt. 16:18; 1 Cor. 3:16).

5:8 The aid in building from Hiram, a Gentile, prefigures the inclusion of the Gentiles in the building of the church as a temple (Eph. 2:19–22).

6:2 The temple is like the tabernacle of Moses (Exodus 25–27; see note on Ex. 25:8), but it is larger and more magnificent, symbolizing an expansion and a further stage in God's purpose to dwell with his people. Still further development takes place with Ezekiel's vision of a new temple (Ezekiel 40–43), with the church (Eph. 2:19–22), and with the new Jerusalem in the consummation (Rev. 21:3, 10–22:5).

7:14 See note on 5:8. Hiram's God-given wisdom is like that of Bezalel and Oholiab, who supervised the construction of the tabernacle (Ex. 31:1–6). It prefigures the wisdom of Christ and of his servants in the building of the church (Eph. 2:19–22).

7:23 The sea greatly enlarges the basin for washing that was in the tabernacle (Ex. 30:17–21). See note on Ex. 30:20.

7:27 The stands with their basins (v. 38) represent small, mobile versions of the sea (vv. 23–26), further underlining the abundance of water (see note on v. 23). The multiplication of water, compared with the single basin for washing in Ex. 30:17–21, anticipates the even greater abundance when the water provided by God becomes a river of life (Ezek. 47:1–12; John 4:10–14; 19:34; Rev. 22:1–2).

8:11 See Ex. 40:34–35. The glory of the Lord later departs, because of the apostasy of the people (Ezekiel 10). The coming of God's presence prefigures the fullness of the Spirit in Christ (Matt. 3:16–17; John 3:34–35; 1:14) and within the church (Acts 2:3–4; 1 Cor. 3:16).

8:24 The promise to David is in 2 Sam. 7:13. The temple anticipates the greater fulfillment in the dwelling of God with man through Christ. See notes on 1 Kings 5:5 and 6:2.

8:30 The key role of the temple in prayer prefigures the role of Christ, through whose name we have access to God (John 14:13–14; Heb. 10:19–22).

9:8 The desolation comes to pass in 2 Kings 25:9–11, indicating the need for true obedience and a greater temple that is to come in Christ (John 2:19–21).

10:1 The queen of Sheba's coming to hear wisdom, mentioned also in Matt. 12:42, prefigures the coming of the nations to Christ (Acts 1:8; Col. 2:3).

11:2 Solomon's disobedience leads to disastrous judgment (vv. 9–11), anticipating the judgments on later idolatries among God's people. Solomon's failure indicates the need for Christ the perfect king in the line of David (Matt. 1:1–16).

12:15 God's prophecy in 11:29–39 begins to be fulfilled, and God's people split into two kingdoms. Both Rehoboam's failure and the resulting disunity and strife among God's people show the need for Christ the perfect king as the unifier of his people (1 Corinthians 12; Eph. 4:1–6).

13:2 A striking prophecy, fulfilled in 2 Kings 23:15–17, shows the power of God's word even in the midst of sin, corruption of worship, and chaos. The power of the prophetic word prefigures the power of Christ, the final prophet (Acts 3:22–26; Heb. 1:1–2).

13:34 See the description of Jeroboam's sin in 12:26–33. Judgment for sin is prophesied in 14:9–12, and falls in 14:17–18, 15:29–30. Jeroboam's sin continues with his successors (15:34; 16:2, 7, 19, 26; 22:53; 2 Kings 3:3; 10:29, 31;

13:2, 11; 14:24; 15:9, 18, 24, 28), ultimately leading to the exile of the northern kingdom (2 Kings 17:21–23). The judgments on false worship show the need for true worship, prefiguring Christ as the one way to God (John 14:6).

14:10 See note on 13:34. The power of God's word is seen when the judgment falls in 14:17–18 and 15:29–30.

14:22 Just as in the northern kingdom (v. 9), false worship in the southern kingdom eventually leads to exile (2 Kings 23:26–27; 25:1–21; see note on 1 Kings 13:34).

15:4 In spite of sin God is faithful to the promise to David (2 Sam. 7:5–17), and maintains the line of David (1 Kings 11:12, 32, 34, 36; 2 Kings 8:19; 19:34) down through a list of kings of Judah leading to Christ (Matt. 1:1–16).

15:18 In contrast to the kings of Israel (vv. 26, 34), Asa is a good king (v. 11), prefiguring the righteousness of Christ his descendant. Yet in this case he fails to rely on God (see 2 Chron. 16:7–12), underlining the need for perfect righteousness in the king.

15:29–30 The killing fulfills the prophecy in 14:9–11 (see note on 13:34). The wiping out of the king's line of descent contrasts with God's faithfulness in maintaining the line of David leading to Christ (see note on 15:4).

16:3 See 15:29–30. Judgments on the northern kingdom show the consistency of God's word and his holiness (see note on 13:34).

17:1 The power of the prophetic word prefigures the power of Christ's word (Heb. 1:1–3).

17:14 The miraculous supply of food through the power of God's word prefigures the power of Christ to multiply bread (Matt. 14:13–21; Mark 8:1–9) and to himself be the bread of heaven (John 6:26–51).

17:21 Impartation of life prefigures Christ's resurrection of Jairus's daughter (Matt. 9:18–25), his resurrection of Lazarus (John 11:38–44), his own resurrection (John 10:18), and his role as "the resurrection and the life" (John 11:25–26) who gives spiritual life to us in anticipation of the resurrection of the body (John 5:28–29).

18:39 Miraculous power anticipates the resurrection of Christ, which displays the power of God and draws the nations to acknowledge him (John 12:32).

19:2 Jezebel's opposition undermines Elijah's previous work, seeming to lead to failure (v. 4). But God's purpose through his prophetic word stands (vv. 12, 15–18), prefiguring the victory when Christ fulfills prophecy.

19:16 See v. 19. Elijah is not the end, but one of a succession of prophets leading to Christ, the final prophet (Heb. 1:1–2).

19:18 The 7,000 illustrate the concept of a remnant, to be fulfilled by the Jews who believe in Christ (Rom. 11:3–10; see note on Isa. 6:13).

20:28 God's desire to magnify his glory enables Ahab to defeat Ben-hadad twice (see vv. 19–21). The victory in battle prefigures the final victory of Christ and his army (Rev. 19:11–21).

20:42 Ahab's failure contrasts with the complete elimination of enemies in the final battle led by Christ (Rev. 19:11–21).

21:19 The prophecy is fulfilled in 2 Kings 9:25–26, 36–37; 10:10–11, 17, showing the power of God's word in judgment. This power prefigures the power of Christ's word (Heb. 1:1–2; 4:12–13; Rev. 19:15, 21).

22:19 The superiority of God to all earthly thrones is shown when Micaiah's prophecy (vv. 23, 28) is fulfilled (vv. 34–36). The power of God and of his word anticipates the power shown in the resurrection of Christ (Eph. 1:20–22) and in the spread of the gospel, which confounds worldly authorities (1 Cor. 2:6–9).

2 Kings

Following the history in 1 Kings, Israel and Judah continue to decline through their false worship and disobedience, leading to exile (2 Kings 17; 25). Some good kings (notably Hezekiah and Josiah, chs. 18–20; 22:1–23:30) prefigure the need for Christ the perfect king, while Elisha prefigures the need for Christ the final prophet (Heb. 1:1–3). Many passages in 2 Kings have parallels in 2 Chronicles.

1:4 The prophecy is fulfilled in v. 17. The triumph of God's word over all opposition prefigures the triumph of Christ and of the gospel.

2:11 Elijah's ascent prefigures the triumph of Christ over death and his ascension (Luke 24:51; Acts 1:9).

2:14 The dividing of the waters, reminiscent of Moses at the Red Sea (Ex. 14:21–22), Joshua at the Jordan (Josh. 3:7–17), and Elijah at the Jordan (2 Kings 2:8), confirms that Elisha has received the prophetic succession from Elijah (v. 9). The power over the waters (which are a symbol of death and chaos) prefigures the resurrection of Christ.

3:17 The provision of water, like the provision under Moses (Ex. 17:6; 20:8–11), prefigures Christ as the giver of the water of eternal life (John 4:10, 13–14; Rev. 22:1).

4:34 The giving of life, like the instance with Elijah (1 Kings 17:17–24), prefigures the resurrection of Christ and the life he gives to us through union with him (Rom. 6:4, 8–11; 8:10–11; Col. 3:1–4).

5:14 Cleansing from leprosy (Leviticus 14) prefigures cleansing from sin through the power of Christ (Luke 5:12–14). The inclusion of Naaman, a Syrian, prefigures the inclusion of the Gentiles in God's salvation (Luke 24:47).

6:17 The vision of God's angelic army indicates dimensions of spiritual warfare. It anticipates the spiritual war with the coming of Christ (Matt. 12:28–29; Luke 10:18–19; John 12:31; Rev. 19:11–21).

7:1 The provision of food in spite of unbelief (see Ex. 16:1–21) prefigures Christ giving himself as the bread of heaven (John 6:35, 47–51).

8:15 Hazael's fulfillment of earlier prophetic words (1 Kings 19:15; 2 Kings 8:10) shows the power of God's word in judgment. (See 10:32.) This power anticipates the power of Christ's words (John 12:48; Heb. 1:1–2; 4:12–13; Rev. 1:16).

9:25 This fulfillment of earlier prophecy (1 Kings 19:16–17; 21:19–24) emphasizes the power of God's word in bringing judgment. See notes on 1 Kings 21:19 and 2 Kings 8:15.

10:10 Jehu fulfills God's prophetic words of judgment against Ahab's house and wipes out the worship of Baal introduced by Jezebel (1 Kings 16:31–33), showing God's power in judgment and anticipating the day of judgment (Rev. 20:11–15). See note on 1 Kings 21:19.

11:2 The rescue of Joash prefigures the rescue of Jesus from Herod (Matt. 2:13–15). God preserves the line of David for the sake of his promise (2 Sam. 7:16) and to carry out his purpose of salvation through the work of Christ (Rev. 12:4–5).

12:9 The attention to the temple prefigures the importance of building the church (Matt. 16:18; 1 Cor. 14:12; Eph. 2:20–22).

13:23 God's compassion even toward a sinful people prefigures his compassion in Christ toward sinners (Matt. 9:13; Luke 5:32).

14:10 A single act of pride from Amaziah brings disaster on the people, indicating the need for Christ as the perfect, humble king (Zech. 9:9).

15:9 See note on 1 Kings 13:34. The northern kingdom goes downhill toward eventual exile in 2 Kings 17:6–23. The degeneration points to the need for perfect kingship and redemption from the heart, both of which await the coming of Christ.

16:3 Under Ahaz the southern kingdom also suffers serious spiritual degeneration, pointing to the need for perfect kingship in Christ.

17:7 The exile is God's judgment on sin (see note on 1 Kings 13:34), prefiguring the judgment on sin that Christ bore as a substitute (1 Pet. 2:21–24) and the final judgment at the consummation (Rev. 20:11–15).

18:5 Hezekiah as a faithful king prefigures the faithfulness and righteousness of Christ (Isa. 9:6–7; 42:1–4) and its fruits in the lives of Christ's people. See the parallel passages in 2 Chronicles 32 and Isaiah 36–38.

18:30 Rabshakeh symbolizes the voice of Satan, who deceives and attacks the faith of God's people (Gen. 3:4–5; Matt. 4:1–10; Eph. 6:16; Rev. 12:9).

19:22 God vindicates his name against all slanders, prefiguring the vindication of his name in the resurrection of Christ (John 12:28).

20:5 God mercifully hears prayer, anticipating his mercy in Christ, through whom he hears our prayers (John 14:13–14; 15:16; 16:26–27).

21:8 Manasseh directly affronts God's command and his holiness, which leads to a prophecy of judgment (vv. 12–15) and illustrates the pattern of rebellion leading to exile (24:2–4). By contrast, Manasseh's evil points to the need for Christ as the perfect king.

22:2 Josiah as a righteous king prefigures Christ.

22:13 Words of prophecy, not only from Elijah and Elisha but from Moses (Deut. 11:26–28), show that God judges in accordance with his purpose and his righteousness. This righteousness is supremely manifested in Christ, both when in his innocence he bears sin (2 Cor. 5:21) and when he comes to judge the world (Acts 17:31).

22:20 See 23:30. Because of his righteousness and humility, Josiah receives a blessing. But unlike Christ (Gal. 3:13–14), he is unable to reverse the impending curse and punishment that will come to his people (see 2 Kings 23:26–27).

24:2 See notes on 21:8 and 22:13.

25:9 God's righteous judgment falls because of accumulated sins (23:26–27; 24:2–4). The judgment also destroys God's own house, prefiguring the judgment that will fall on Christ, whose body is the temple (John 2:19–21; Gal. 3:13–14).

25:27 The provision for the king of Judah, in the line of David, indicates that God still remembers his promise to David (2 Sam. 7:16) and anticipates the eventual coming of Jesus the Messiah through the line of Jehoiachin (also called Jeconiah, 1 Chron. 3:16; Matt. 1:11–12).

1 Chronicles

David as the righteous leader and king prefigures Christ the king, not only in his rule over the people of God but in his role in preparing to build the temple. First Chronicles looks back on the faithfulness of God to his people in the entire period from Adam (1:1) to David (3:1) and even beyond (3:10–24; 9:1–34), indicating the steadfastness of God's purpose in preparing for the coming of the Messiah as the offspring of Adam (1:1; Gen. 3:15; Luke 3:38), offspring of Abraham (1 Chron. 1:28; Gal. 3:16), and offspring of David (1 Chron. 3:1; 17:11, 14; Luke 3:23–38; Acts 13:23).

1:1 God promises victory over Satan by the offspring of the woman (Gen. 3:15) and of Abraham (Gen. 17:7; see notes on Gen. 3:15 and 12:1). The line of chosen offspring goes from Adam through Seth and Noah (1 Chron. 1:4) to Abraham (vv. 27–28), Isaac (v. 34), and Israel (v. 34; 2:1), earlier called Jacob (Gen. 32:27–28). It will culminate in Christ (Matt. 1:1–16; Gal. 3:16).

2:1 The line of chosen offspring goes from Israel to David and includes the blessing of multiplication of offspring in the form of the 12 tribes (see Gen. 13:16; 15:5). See note on 1 Chron. 1:1.

3:1 The line of the Messiah comes through King David (2 Sam. 7:16; Matt. 1:1, 6; see note on 1 Chron. 1:1).

3:10 Solomon and his offspring are a stage in the fulfillment of the promise to David for his offspring (2 Sam. 7:16). The offspring ultimately lead to Christ (Matt. 1:1–16; see note on 1 Chron. 1:1).

4:1 After recording the Messianic line of David, which will lead to Christ (see note on 3:10), Chronicles gives the record for Judah, the tribe of David. The recording of individual names and families underlines their inclusion in the promise to Abraham concerning blessing, land, and fellowship with God (Gen. 17:4–8). It prefigures the blessing (Gal. 3:14), land (Rom. 4:13; Heb. 11:16; 12:22; Rev. 21:1), and fellowship with God (Rom. 5:1; Gal. 3:26–29) that come from union with Christ the greater David. God has enrolled our names in his book of life (Rev. 13:8; 17:8; 20:15; see John 10:3, 14; Eph. 1:4).

5:1 The record of Reuben, Gad (v. 11), and Manasseh (v. 23) indicates their continued inclusion among God's people as offspring of Abraham and Israel (2:1–2). It answers doubts that might arise because of the location of their land east of the Jordan (Numbers 32; Josh. 13:8–32; 22:24–29). The reassurance prefigures the guarantee given to Christians (2 Cor. 1:22; Eph. 1:13–14). See note on 1 Chron. 4:1.

6:49 The special list for Aaron the priest and for the tribe of Levi, which indicates some of their priestly privileges before God, prefigures the priestly privileges given to Christians through Christ the final high priest (Heb. 7:23–8:2; 10:19–22).

7:1 Other tribes descending from Israel (2:1–2) are briefly listed. See note on 4:1.

8:33 Special focus is given to Saul, because he was king of Israel (10:14; 1 Sam. 10:1). But he was superseded by David (1 Sam. 16:1, 12; 2 Sam. 7:15; 1 Chron. 10:13–14; 17:13), whose line of kings leads forward to Christ the king (Matt. 1:6–16).

9:2 The enrollment of names of returned exiles indicates God's continued faithfulness to the offspring of Israel. It prefigures God's enrollment and faithfulness to those who belong to Christ the Israelite (Gal. 3:14, 16, 28–29; see note on 1 Chron. 4:1).

10:14 The movement of kingship to David is the beginning of the line of kingly offspring leading to Christ (17:11, 14; Matt. 1:6–16).

11:3 David is established as king in fulfillment of God's purpose (v. 2), prefiguring the establishment of Christ the son of David as the final king (Ps. 2:6–12; Acts 13:33; Eph. 1:20–22).

12:23 The unification of God's people under David, and their strength for war, prefigures the unification and spiritual strength under Christ the king (Eph. 4:1–16; 6:10–20).

13:10 See note on 2 Sam. 6:7. When the Levites take the appropriate role (Ex. 25:14; Num. 4:15; 1 Chron. 15:2, 13–15), the ark is brought up safely (1 Chron. 15:26).

13:12 The supreme holiness of God, and his reaction to the approach of sinners, produces fear. The resolution comes through Christ's propitiation, which permanently answers God's wrath (Rom. 3:20–26; 5:1).

14:15 God fights with David against Israel's enemies, prefiguring Christ defeating Satan and his hosts (Matt. 12:28–29; Luke 10:18–19; John 12:31; Rev. 19:11–21; 20:7–10).

15:2 Unlike Uzzah (13:10), the Levites bring up the ark safely, because they are following God's instructions (Ex. 25:14; Num. 4:15). The importance of following God's way prefigures the one way to God opened through Christ (John 14:6; Heb. 10:19–22).

15:16 David and the singers are involved in writing and singing many of the Psalms (see 1 Chron. 16:8–36 and parallels in the Psalms: Ps. 96:1–13; 105:1–15; 106:47–48). They prefigure the role of Christ in leading his people in singing praise to God for climactic salvation (Heb. 2:12; 13:15; Rev. 19:6–8).

16:4 See note on 15:16.

16:8 See Ps. 105:1–15. Songs of praise are to be sung repeatedly, not only to give praise to God, but to remind people of his excellence and to anticipate the surpassing display of his excellence when Christ comes. See note on 1 Chron. 15:16.

16:23 See Ps. 96:1–13 and note on 1 Chron. 16:8.

16:35 See Ps. 106:47–48 and note on 1 Chron. 16:8.

17:4 To underline the importance of Davidic kingship as leading to Christ, Chronicles records the all-important covenant with David given in 2 Sam. 7:5–16. See note on 2 Sam. 7:12.

17:16 David's marveling over God's grace prefigures the marveling over the grace that has come in Christ (John 1:16; Eph. 2:7–9).

18:6 The subduing of Israel's enemies prefigures Christ winning victory over Satan and his hosts (see note on 14:15).

18:14 The coming of justice prefigures the justice of the Messiah (Isa. 9:6–7; 42:1–4; 2 Cor. 5:10; Rev. 20:11–15).

19:2 See note on 2 Sam. 10:2.

20:1 Chronicles, unlike the parallel in 2 Samuel 11, omits mention of David's sin with Bathsheba, highlighting more effectively ways in which David's kingship points positively forward to the triumphs of Christ as final king.

20:8 David's victory over Goliath in 1 Samuel 17 is one of a series of victories that destroy terrifying enemies of God's people. The victories prefigure the victory of Christ and his people (Matt. 12:28–29; Luke 10:18–19; John 12:31; Rev. 2:7, 11, 17, 26; 12:11; 19:11–21; 20:7–10).

21:7 See note on 2 Sam. 24:1.

21:17 See note on 2 Sam. 24:17.

22:1 The selection of the site for Solomon's temple takes place according to God's word through Gad the prophet (21:18). Once the temple is built, it will be the exclusive place for atonement and approach to God (Deuteronomy 12), prefiguring Christ as the final one who brings atonement and opens the way to God (John 14:6; Heb. 10:19–22).

22:9 Solomon prefigures Christ as prince of peace, who opens the way to peace with God (Rom. 5:1–10).

23:26 See Num. 4:5–15. God inspires David to make a change in the duties of the Levites, corresponding to the change in the house of God. The service of the Levites prefigures the service of Christ as high priest to God (Heb. 7:23–8:6) and subordinately the service of Christians (Rom. 12:1; Eph. 4:1–16; Heb. 13:15).

24:7 The priests are a special group within the tribe of Levi, chosen to minister in the sanctuary (Numbers 18). The priesthood prefigures Christ the great high priest (Heb. 7:23–8:6). The duties rotate to the different divisions (see Luke 1:5, 8), indicating that no one priest is permanent, until the coming of Christ the everlasting priest (Heb. 7:23–24).

25:1 See note on 15:16. The attention to arrangements for singing prefigures the ordering of the church's worship through the power of the Holy Spirit (1 Corinthians 12; Eph. 2:22; 5:18–21).

26:1 The gatekeepers protect access to the presence of God in the temple (Num. 18:7, 22), prefiguring the one way of access to God through Christ (John 10:7; 14:6). Church discipline, exercised under the authority of Christ (1 Cor. 5:4–5), warns the unrepentant of their danger.

26:20 The care for God's gifts prefigures the guarantee of the inheritance of eternal life in Christ (1 Pet. 1:4–5) and the advice to lay up treasure in heaven (Matt. 6:19–34; see 2 Cor. 9:6–15). Money given for the needs of God's people is to be carefully handled (2 Cor. 8:20–21).

27:1 Arrangements for the military prefigure the spiritual war fought under Christ's command (Eph. 6:10–20; see note on 1 Chron. 14:15).

28:6 See the promise to David in 17:11–14, now being fulfilled. See note on 2 Sam. 7:12.

28:19 The temple is built in accordance with God's instructions, just as the tabernacle was (see note on Ex. 36:10).

28:20 The empowering of God is essential, prefiguring the centrality of God's power in building the church, the new temple (1 Cor. 3:16; Eph. 2:20–22).

28:21 The previous arrangements of various divisions of the Levites and the people (chs. 23–27) have all been for the purpose of aiding in the service of the house of God. They prefigure God's planning for the building of the church as temple (1 Cor. 3:16; Eph. 2:20–22) and the new Jerusalem as final temple (Rev. 21:22–27).

29:6 The generous offering is like that for the tabernacle (Ex. 35:4–36:7). It prefigures the generosity of Christ (see note on Ex. 35:21).

29:18 Wholehearted commitment comes ultimately with the perfection of Christ (Heb. 10:7–10) and the change of the heart that he works in us in the new covenant (Heb. 10:16–17).

2 Chronicles

Solomon as a wise king and temple builder prefigures Christ the king and temple builder. After Solomon the line of Davidic kings continues, leading forward to Christ the great descendant of David (Matt. 1:6–16). But many of the later kings go astray from God, and they and the people suffer for it, showing the need for Christ as the perfect king. Hezekiah (2 Chronicles 29–32) and Josiah (chs. 34–35) as righteous kings prefigure Christ. Second Chronicles has parallels in 1–2 Kings but focuses on the southern kingdom (Judah) and the line of David, and it shows focused concern for the temple and its worship, anticipating the fulfillment of temple and worship with the coming of Christ (John 2:19–21; 4:20–26; Eph. 2:20–22; Rev. 21:22–22:5).

1:10 See note on 1 Kings 3:9. Wisdom is needed to build the temple (1 Chron. 29:1; 2 Chron. 2:6, 12).

2:3 See note on 1 Kings 5:8.

2:13 See note on 1 Kings 7:14.

3:1 See note on 1 Kings 6:2. The location for the temple was appointed in 1 Chron. 22:1 (see note on 1 Chron. 22:1).

4:1 The altar is twice as large as the one for the tabernacle (Ex. 27:1–8), indicating the more abundant provision for atonement. See note on Ex. 27:1.

4:7 There are ten lampstands instead of the one in the tabernacle (Ex. 25:31–39), indicating the more abundant provision of light. See notes on Ex. 25:37 and 1 Kings 6:2.

5:14 See note on 1 Kings 8:11.

6:6 The selection of Jerusalem fulfills the plan given through Moses in Deuteronomy 12. It prefigures the appointment of Christ as the one way of salvation (John 14:6; Heb. 5:5–10).

6:15 See note on 1 Kings 8:24.

6:21 See note on 1 Kings 8:30.

7:1 The miraculous approval by God is like what happens with Elijah in 1 Kings 18:39 (see note).

7:2 The glory of the Lord signifies the magnificence of his presence, prefiguring Christ's presence. See 5:14 and note on 1 Kings 8:11.

7:20 See note on 1 Kings 9:8.

8:5 Solomon takes care to provide security against foreign enemies, performing one of the important duties of ancient kings and prefiguring the spiritual security given through Christ the king (John 10:28–29; see Rev. 21:24–27; 22:3).

8:14 David's instructions are found in 1 Chronicles 23–27. See the note on 1 Chron. 28:21.

9:1 See note on 1 Kings 10:1.

9:22 Solomon's riches and wisdom prefigure the riches and wisdom of Christ the king (Eph. 1:18; Col. 2:3; 1 Cor. 1:30).

10:15 See note on 1 Kings 12:15.

11:14 The Levites were distributed among the tribes (Joshua 20–21; see note on Josh. 21:2). But Jeroboam's false worship (see 1 Kings 12:25–13:5) forces them and others who follow God to join Judah. The conflict over worship prefigures the conflict over the exclusive claims of Christ (see note on 1 Kings 13:34).

12:6 Rebellion against the Lord leads to disaster, but repentance brings relief. The pattern anticipates God's final judgment on rebellion (Rev. 20:11–15) and relief through repentance and faith in Christ (John 5:24; Rev. 20:15).

13:9 For Jeroboam's promotion of false worship, see 1 Kings 12:25–33 and note on 1 Kings 13:34. The blessing on true worshipers prefigures the blessing on worship in spirit and truth that Christ brings (John 4:20–24).

14:7 Blessings come from following God's way, prefiguring the blessings through Christ the final way (John 14:6; Eph. 1:3–14).

15:8 Asa continues to work for true worship according to the law (Ex. 27:1–8; Deut. 11:28; 12:1), prefiguring Christ's establishment of true worship (Matt. 21:12–16; John 4:20–24).

16:9 God's judgment takes place within history, as well as at the consummation (Rev. 20:11–15). Judgment comes climactically when Christ as a substitute takes judgment on himself, and then in his resurrection receives the reward for his blamelessness (Phil. 2:10–11). See note on 1 Kings 15:18.

17:5 See note on 14:7.

18:18 See note on 1 Kings 22:19.

19:7 Mosaic instructions for judgeship are in Ex. 23:8; Deut. 16:18–20. Promoting justice is one of the duties of the king, prefiguring the justice of Christ the king (Isa. 9:6–7; 42:1–4).

20:22 God honors those who trust in him, anticipating the giving of honor to Christ in his resurrection (Phil. 2:10–11) and the blessing to Christians who trust in Christ (Galatians 3).

21:7 The line of David is nearly, but not quite, wiped out, prefiguring the attack by Herod (Matt. 2:13–18) and God's faithfulness to Christ the offspring of David. See note on 1 Kings 15:4.

22:11 See note on 2 Kings 11:2.

23:11 The establishment of the true king, in spite of all opposition, prefigures the establishment of Christ as king (Ps. 2:7–12; Acts 13:33).

24:4 See note on 2 Kings 12:9.

24:20 See note on 12:6.

25:16 Prophetic warning gives opportunity for repentance, but Amaziah hardens himself instead. Amaziah's failure points to the need for a perfect king (Matt. 21:5). The call to repentance prefigures the call to repentance and faith in the NT. See note on 2 Chron. 12:6.

25:19 See note on 2 Kings 14:10.

26:16 Uzziah's sin and its consequences point to the need for a perfect king (Matt. 21:5).

27:6 See note on 14:7.

28:3 See note on 2 Kings 16:3.

28:15 The unusual kindness shows God's mercy (v. 9) and anticipates the love that Jesus embodies (Matt. 8:14–17; Luke 7:21–22; 1 John 3:16; 4:7–12), that he teaches (Luke 10:25–37), and that he creates in his followers (John 13:34–35; 1 John 4:17–21).

29:8 Judgments against false worship (predicted in Deut. 11:28) are reversed by Hezekiah, prefiguring Christ the king coming to remove the curse on sin (Gal. 3:13–14).

30:9 The theme of mercy and repentance looks forward to God's mercy in Christ to those who repent and turn to him (Luke 18:13). See notes on 2 Chron. 12:6 and 25:16.

30:19 The desire of the heart is of greater importance than mere external conformity (1 Sam. 15:22; Hos. 6:6; Mic. 6:6–8; Matt. 9:13; 25:25–28), anticipating the centrality of renewal of the heart in Christ's work (Heb. 8:10).

30:26 The contrast between Hezekiah and the past shows the difference that a good leader can make, prefiguring the climactic renewal with the coming of Christ (Heb. 8:8–12).

31:2 Hezekiah restores the temple service as specified by Moses (Numbers 18) and David (1 Chronicles 23–26). His obedience prefigures Christ's obedience and the obedience of those who follow Christ (Eph. 4:1–16). See note on 2 Kings 18:5.

32:8 Trusting the Lord to fight prefigures trust in Christ as the victor against the kingdom of evil (Col. 1:13; 2:15; Heb. 2:14–15).

32:15 See note on 2 Kings 18:30.

32:17 See note on 2 Kings 19:22.

33:7 See note on 2 Kings 21:8.

33:12 See note on 12:6.

34:2 Josiah as a righteous king prefigures Christ.

34:21 See note on 2 Kings 22:13.

35:1 The keeping of the Passover is another high point in serving God (see note on 30:26).

35:4 See note on 31:2.

36:16 God shows his righteous judgment against sin, prefiguring the even greater manifestations of righteousness in the death and resurrection of Christ and in the final judgment (Rev. 20:11–15). See notes on 2 Chron. 12:6; 16:9; and 2 Kings 25:9.

36:21 The judgment confirms God's faithfulness to his word, anticipating his faithfulness in Christ. It also gives the land rest in accordance with Leviticus 25, prefiguring final rest (see note on Lev. 25:4).

36:23 Cyrus's proclamation, prophesied in Isa. 44:28 and recorded in Ezra 1:1–4, shows that

God has not forgotten his people (Rom. 11:1). His continued faithfulness and repeated acts of mercy and salvation look forward to the coming of Christ as the climax of faithfulness and mercy.

Ezra

The restoration and rebuilding after the exile, in fulfillment of prophecy (1:1), prefigure Christ's salvation (Col. 1:13) and the building of the church (Matt. 16:18; Eph. 2:20–22). They also look forward to the consummation of salvation in the new heaven and new earth (Rev. 21:1).

1:1 God's raising of Cyrus prefigures his raising of Christ, who in the gospel sends out the proclamation to build the new people of God (Isa. 44:28–45:1).

1:5 It is God who empowers the restoration in the people as well as in Cyrus, prefiguring the empowering of his people through the Spirit (Acts 1:8; 2:1–4; Rom. 8:10–11).

2:1 The detailed record of people shows God's knowledge of individuals and families, symbolizing his detailed knowledge of those chosen for salvation (Eph. 1:4; Rev. 13:8; 17:8; see note on 1 Chron. 4:1).

3:2 Restoration of true worship of God is central to the restoration as a whole. Sacrificial worship prefigures the sacrifice of Christ (Heb. 10:1–10).

3:10 Temple building, analogous to what Solomon did (2 Chronicles 3), prefigures Christ's body as a temple (John 2:19–21), the church as a temple (Matt. 16:18; 1 Cor. 3:16; Eph. 2:20–22), and the new Jerusalem as a temple (Rev. 21:9–22:5). See Haggai and Zechariah for prophecy relating to the restoration.

3:11 The singing, using the refrain of 1 Chron. 16:34 and Psalm 136, follows the pattern in 1 Chronicles 25 and looks forward to the praise offered by Christ (Heb. 2:12) and his people (Heb. 13:15).

4:1 The adversaries, incited ultimately by Satan, symbolize opposition to God's purposes for his people and prefigure opposition to Christ and his people (Matt. 4:1–11; Rev. 12:3–4, 7–17).

5:1 Directives both from prophets and from Cyrus (1:1–4) have a key role in the restoration, prefiguring the role of God's word in building the church (Eph. 2:20–22; 4:6–16).

6:6 God reverses the plans of the opponents and uses Darius to favor the restoration, prefiguring God's work in blessing the church (Rom. 8:28; Acts 4:29–31; 8:4).

7:27 Through Ezra and Artaxerxes, God shows his providential blessing on the restoration, prefiguring his willingness to supply our needs (2 Cor. 9:6–12).

8:31 God provides protection, prefiguring his protection to those in Christ (John 10:27–29).

9:1 Intermarriage was forbidden in Deut. 7:3–4 because it led to idolatry (see Ezra 9:11–14). Separation prefigures the need for uncompromising allegiance to Christ (Matt. 10:34–39; Luke 14:26–33; 2 Cor. 6:14–7:1).

10:2 See note on 2 Chron. 12:6.

10:3 Families are put away for the sake of holiness, to eliminate compromise with idolatry (Deut. 7:3–4; see note on Ezra 9:1). The superior power of Christ's holiness is such that, in the NT, a Christian may remain in an unbelieving family with the hope that others may come to know Christ (1 Cor. 7:12–16).

Nehemiah

The restoration and rebuilding after the exile prefigure Christ's salvation (Col. 1:13) and the building of the church (Matt. 16:18; Eph. 2:20–22).

1:11 Nehemiah's intercession for the people prefigures Christ's intercession for us before God the Father (Heb. 7:25).

2:18 Rebuilding Jerusalem prefigures building the church (Matt. 16:18; 1 Cor. 14:4–5, 12; Gal. 4:26; Eph. 2:20–22).

3:1 God records the names of the builders, indicating his knowledge of each contribution. The division of labor prefigures the cooperation in the body of Christ (Rom. 12:3–8; 1 Corinthians 12; Eph. 4:1–16).

4:1 Opposition to building prefigures opposition to the church and to Christians (John 15:18–20).

5:7 God's law through Moses forbids exacting interest from a fellow Israelite (Ex. 22:25; Lev. 25:36). The help to the poor anticipates the church's helping the poor (Acts 2:44–45; 4:32–37; 2 Cor. 9:6–15) on the basis of God's generosity in Christ (2 Cor. 8:9; 9:15).

6:2 Opposition includes deceit as well as mocking and threats (see note on 4:1). This deceit manifests the deceitfulness of Satan the great enemy (John 8:44; 2 Thess. 2:9–10; Rev. 12:9; 20:3).

7:6 See note on Ezra 2:1.

8:3 Instruction from God's Word plays a key role in building up the people of God. It prefigures the role of Christ as the Word of God (John 1:1; Rev. 19:13), the role of the gospel (Rom. 1:16–17; 1 Thess. 2:13; 1 Pet. 1:23), and the role of Scripture (1 Tim. 3:13; 2 Tim. 3:16–17; see Psalm 119).

9:8 God's faithfulness is displayed in fulfilling the promise to Abraham (Gen. 12:1–3, 7; 13:14–17; 15:4, 13–21; 17:1–14). His faithfulness to his promises is supremely manifested in Christ (2 Cor. 1:20–22), who has brought everlasting blessings to God's people (Eph. 1:3–14).

9:38 The names indicate the personal commitment of individuals and families, prefiguring personal commitment to Christ (Acts 2:38–41; see note on Ezra 2:1).

10:29 Obedience to the law anticipates the obligation of disciples of Christ to follow him in everything (Matt. 10:37–39; Luke 14:25–33; John 14:15, 23). Christ alone is perfectly obedient to God (Heb. 4:15).

11:1 Jerusalem has a key role as the holy city. In the NT *all* of God's people are citizens in the heavenly Jerusalem (Gal. 4:26–28; Phil. 3:20; Heb. 12:22–24).

11:4 The list of names and numbers indicates God's knowledge of the details of individuals and families. See note on Ezra 2:1.

12:27 The Levites' role in singing was established in 1 Chronicles 25. The celebration anticipates the celebration and praise to God for the resurrection of Christ (Eph. 5:19–20; Heb. 13:15) and for the consummation (Rev. 19:1–8).

13:3 See note on Ezra 9:1.

13:15 The people promised to keep the Sabbath in 10:31. The Sabbath is a sign of the covenant with God (Ex. 20:8–11; 31:12–17), celebrating creation (Ex. 20:11) and redemption (Deut. 5:15). It points forward to Christ, who is Creator (Col. 1:15–16) and Redeemer (Col. 1:18–20), and who has prepared our place of rest (John 14:2–3). See notes on Gen. 2:2 and 2:3.

13:23 See note on Ezra 9:1.

Esther

God providentially brings deliverance to his people through Esther, prefiguring final deliverance through Christ.

1:12 The rejection of Vashti is one step in God's providential acts to deliver the Jews (see note on 2:15). It introduces the key theme of rejection and selection, by which God prepares the way for salvation.

2:15 God causes Esther the Jew to be chosen, which will later play a key role in delivering the Jews. Esther in her beauty prefigures the church as the bride of Christ (2 Cor. 11:2; Eph. 5:26–27; Rev. 19:7–8; see note on Est. 1:12).

2:22 God's hand of providence leads to key action from Mordecai, which will later prove important (6:2). God's providential control illustrates his continual care for his people (John 10:27–29; Rom. 8:28; Eph. 1:22).

3:1 The conflict between Mordecai and Haman is explained 1 Sam. 15:2–3, 32–33. Haman is an Agagite, an Amalekite, an opponent of Israel and a descendant of the people whom Saul should have wiped out.

3:6 Haman exemplifies all who oppose God's people, and especially Satan (see Rev. 12:10–12).

4:16 Esther is willing to sacrifice her own life, prefiguring the willingness of Christ to die for us (Rom. 5:6–11).

5:2 The king's favor toward Esther prefigures the favor resting on Christ as the obedient son of God who redeems us (Matt. 3:17; 2 Pet. 1:17). It is the turning point in the story, prefiguring the resurrection as the turning point in redemption.

5:11 Pride goes before destruction (Prov. 16:18). Haman typifies the false confidence of those belonging to the kingdom of Satan.

6:1 A number of seemingly "chance" events show God's providential control and his power to act secretly on behalf of his people (see note on 2:22).

7:10 Fitting retribution comes as Haman receives what he would have done to Mordecai (Obad. 15). The retribution prefigures the justice of God's final judgment (Rev. 20:11–15) and the elimination of the enemies of God's people (Rev. 20:7–10; 21:8, 27).

8:8 The effects of victory now extend to all the Jews, prefiguring the extending of Christ's victory to those who are his (Rom. 8:10–11; 1 Cor. 15:54–57; Col. 3:1–4).

9:1 The reversal anticipates the reversal of positions with Christ's coming (Luke 1:48–53; 14:11;

18:14) and the justice of God's final judgment (see note on Est. 7:10).

10:3 The blessings to the Jews through Esther and Mordecai prefigure the blessings that come to us through Christ (Eph. 1:3–14; see note on Est. 8:8).

Job

Job's suffering and relief prefigure the suffering and glory of Christ.

1:1 Job, though not sinlessly perfect, is upright, prefiguring the righteousness of Christ (Heb. 4:16).

1:11 Satan is an accuser of God's people (Rev. 12:10). Redemption in Christ includes giving a final answer to Satan's accusations, both by justifying the ungodly (Rom. 4:5) and by making the ungodly into godly people (Rom. 6:4, 15–19; Rev. 19:8; 21:27).

1:21 Job trusts God even though he does not know about Satan's accusation. He exemplifies all who walk by faith and not by sight (2 Cor. 5:7). Christ as man trusted in God perfectly (Heb. 2:13; 5:7–10).

2:6 God uses even the works of Satan for his own glory and for the sanctification of his people. God forbids Satan to take Job's life. But when Christ comes, he is allowed to die at the hands of sinful men (Acts 2:23). It is the supreme act of trust and of vindication of the name of God, as well as victory over Satan (John 12:31).

3:3 Intense suffering negates all the meaning of life, underlining the fact that both suffering and death are horrible effects from the fall (Gen. 3:19). An answer comes only with the meaningful sufferings of Christ (Phil. 3:10) and his resurrection from the dead, which is the beginning of the end to all suffering (Rev. 21:4).

4:7 Eliphaz speaks as if God's protection to the righteous were a universal rule. But the mystery of the death of Christ the innocent one shows the superficiality of his reasoning.

4:15 Eliphaz does not realize that he may have seen an evil spirit who, like Satan, accuses God's people (see note on 1:11).

4:17 Yes, a man can be pure, as is demonstrated by the purity of Christ. Moreover, Christ gives his righteousness to his people through justification (Rom. 5:1; 2 Cor. 5:21).

5:13 God catches the wise with the foolishness of the cross, according to 1 Cor. 3:19. Ironically, Eliphaz, who claims to be wise, is himself caught in his speeches (Job 42:7), because he does not know the wisdom of the cross, and its meaning for the suffering of the innocent.

5:18 The statement parallels Hos. 6:1. Eliphaz correctly describes God's discipline to sinful people. But he does not see that God may discipline the innocent for more mysterious purposes (Job 1:12; 2 Cor. 5:21; see note on Job 4:7).

6:15 Job's misery is increased by his friends. It anticipates Christ's betrayal by Judas (John 13:18) and abandonment by the disciples (Matt. 26:31).

7:17 Note similarities with Ps. 8:4 and Heb. 2:6. God has set his heart on man and brought suffering with a view to redemption in Christ, but Job cannot see the full picture yet.

8:3 God is just, but his justice is deeper than straightforward rewards and punishments in this life. The issue of justice points forward to the achievement of justice in the work of Christ (Rom. 3:23–26) and in the final judgment (Rev. 20:11–15).

9:2 See note on 4:17.

9:14 Job sees the need for an intercessor, anticipating the intercession of Christ (Heb. 7:25).

9:24 The frustration over injustices finds resolution only in the future, with the coming of final salvation (Rev. 20:11–22:5). In the meantime, the righteous may suffer and the wicked prosper, anticipating the human injustice in the crucifixion of Christ.

9:30 Isaiah 1:18 gives hope that God will himself makes us white as snow, which he accomplishes in Christ (Rom. 8:1).

9:33 Christ is both God and man, and will stand in between (1 Tim. 2:5–6; see note on Job 9:14).

10:4 Doubts about whether God sympathizes with man are resolved with Christ's manifestation of sympathy (Heb. 4:15).

10:11 God's creation of Job shows care and intimacy (see Ps. 139:13–16), anticipating the love displayed in the incarnation of Christ (John 1:14).

11:17 The life of the righteous will end in bright day (Prov. 4:18), ultimately the day of consummation (Rev. 21:23–22:5). But Zophar underestimates the complexity. The mysteries of God's providence lead to consummation only through the sufferings of Christ (1 Pet. 2:21–25) and his people (Phil. 2:10–11).

12:3 Job's anguish is increased by what he knows concerning God's wisdom and power, because it seems inconsistent with his sufferings. God's wisdom and power are climactically manifested in the suffering of Christ (1 Cor. 1:18–25).

13:3 See note on 9:14.

13:15 Job's continued hope anticipates Christ's trust even to the point of death (Matt. 26:38–39).

14:14 Job sees that resurrection is needed to solve the mystery of suffering. He thereby anticipates the resurrection of Christ (Rom. 4:25) and of Christ's people (John 5:24–25, 29; 1 Thess. 4:13–18).

14:17 Job anticipates forgiveness, which has now been accomplished in Christ (Rom. 4:7–8; 8:1).

15:9 See note on 12:3.

15:14 See note on 4:17.

16:11 Job's abandonment prefigures the abandonment of Christ (Matt. 20:18–19).

16:17 See the parallel in the sufferings of Christ in Isa. 53:9.

16:19 Job anticipates the intercession of Christ, who pleads our cause (Rom. 8:34).

16:21 See note on 9:14.

17:6 The despising of Job anticipates the despising of Christ (Ps. 69:11; Isa. 50:6; Matt. 27:30).

18:21 God will judge the wicked (Rev. 20:11–15). But justice is delayed for the sake of salvation (Ps. 73:3; 2 Pet. 3:9).

19:7 See the parallel in Hab. 1:2–4. Faith is necessary in waiting for the justice of Christ.

19:19 Job's abandonment by friends anticipates the abandonment of Christ on the cross (Ps. 55:13; John 13:18).

19:25 Job anticipates both the vindication of Christ's justification (Rom. 4:25) and the open manifestation of righteousness at the last judgment (2 Cor. 5:10; Rev. 20:11–15).

19:26 Seeing God takes place through seeing Christ, both now (John 14:9) and in the consummation (Rev. 22:4). See note on Ex. 33:22.

20:29 See note on 18:21.

21:7 A similar struggle is found in Ps. 73:3. See notes on Job 18:21 and 19:7.

22:8 False accusations imitate those of Satan (1:11; 2:5) and anticipate the false accusations against Christ (Matt. 26:59–60; 27:13; Luke 23:10, 14) and against his people (Rev. 12:10).

23:7 Job's desire for God and for acquittal anticipates the justification that is found in Christ (Rom. 4:25–5:1; 8:1).

24:12 See Ps. 50:21 and note on Job 9:24.

25:4 See note on 4:17.

26:13 God's victory over the serpent anticipates the final victory over Satan through Christ (John 12:31; Rev. 20:7–10). Job knows that God's ways are mysterious, but he continues to hope.

27:5 Job's holding fast to the right anticipates Christ's steadfastness toward God and our privilege of holding fast to his righteousness (2 Cor. 5:21).

28:12 Job cannot fathom God's ways, but wisdom is found ultimately in Christ (1 Cor. 1:30; Col. 2:3).

28:27 Wisdom was with God even in creation, as in Prov. 8:22–31. The association of wisdom with creation anticipates the revelation that Christ (the wisdom of God) was with God in the beginning and was mediator of creation (John 1:1–3; Col. 1:15–17).

28:28 See Prov. 1:7.

29:3 Job's time of blessing anticipated the blessings that come through Christ (John 8:12).

30:10 See note on 17:6.

30:20 The unanswered cries anticipate the abandonment of Christ on the cross (Ps. 22:1–2; Matt. 27:46).

31:1 Job's commitment to God anticipates the integrity of Christ (Heb. 4:15).

32:12 God has put in us a desire for wisdom and understanding that will be satisfied only in Christ (1 Cor. 1:30; Col. 2:3; see notes on Job 28:12 and 28:27).

33:23 The desire for a mediator anticipates the exclusive mediation of Christ (1 Tim. 2:5–6; see notes on Job 9:14 and 9:33).

34:11 God's reward or punishment according to justice is a regular theme (e.g., Ps. 62:12; Prov. 24:12; Rev. 2:23; 20:12–13). But final payment awaits the working out of justice and mercy in Christ (see notes on Job 8:3 and 11:17). God's justice does not endorse a superficial conclusion about Job's situation.

35:2 See notes on 34:11 and 8:3.

37:5 The wisdom of God is inaccessible, except through Christ (Col. 2:3; 1 Cor. 1:30; see note on Job 28:12).

37:24 The danger of man-centered wisdom is real (as in Prov. 3:7; Rom. 11:25; 12:16) and holds people back from humbly seeking God and his wisdom in Christ (1 Cor. 1:18–31).

38:4 See note on 28:27.

38:17 Only God has power over death, anticipating the victory of Christ over death (Heb. 2:14–15; Rev. 1:18).

39:9 Both wisdom and power belong to God but not to man (see note on 12:3).

40:8 Man has a God-given sense of justice, but it is inadequate in the face of the depths of God. The depths of God's justice and mercy and wisdom are to be revealed in Christ (1 Cor. 1:30; see notes on Job 12:3 and 28:12).

40:14 Job confronts not only the issue of wisdom and justice, but salvation. Salvation ultimately is worked out in Christ (1 Cor. 1:30).

41:1 God has power even over the most untamable creature, and ultimately even over Satan, who is named Leviathan (Isa. 27:1). Christ's victory over Satan (John 12:31) will ultimately answer all the human frustrations of suffering and injustice (Rev. 21:4).

42:3 Job finds satisfaction in knowing God and his wisdom. Final satisfaction is to be found in Christ (John 16:33; 17:3; Col. 2:3; Rev. 21:4).

42:10 Job's vindication after his sufferings anticipates the vindication of Christ after his sufferings.

Psalms

By expressing the emotional heights and depths in human response to God, the Psalms provide a permanent treasure for God's people to use to express their needs and their praises, both corporately and individually. Christ as representative man experienced our human condition, yet without sin, and so the Psalms become his prayers to God (see esp. Heb. 2:12; cf. Matt. 27:46 with Ps. 22:1). The Psalms are thus to be seen as his words, and through our union with him they become ours.

1:1 God's commitment to bless the righteous is supremely shown when he blesses Christ, the perfectly righteous man, by raising him from the dead and enthroning him (Phil. 2:10–11).

2:1 The rebellion of the peoples anticipates the rebellion against the message of Christ (Acts 4:25–27).

2:6 God uses David and other Israelite kings to protect his people against enemies. These kings prefigure Christ, who is enthroned after his resurrection (Acts 13:33) and now rules on behalf of his people (Eph. 1:20–22).

2:8 Christ rules over all nations (Matt. 28:18; Eph. 1:21).

2:12 Salvation or damnation depends on one's relation to the Son (John 3:36).

3:1 Protection from earthly enemies prefigures protection from the ultimate evils of Satan, sin, and death (Heb. 2:14–15). God the Father delivered Christ from his enemies in his resurrection (Acts 3:13–15), and that is the basis for our deliverance (Rom. 4:25).

3:5 Being preserved through the night anticipates the hope of resurrection after the "sleep" of death (13:3; 1 Thess. 4:13–18).

4:7 The joy of knowing God anticipates the joy and peace that Christ promises (John 15:11; 16:33).

5:4 Sinners cannot stand before God's holiness. Christ's perfection allows us to come into God's presence and for our prayers for deliverance to be heard (Heb. 10:19–22).

5:9 See Rom. 3:13 and note on Ps. 14:1.

5:12 See note on 1:1.

6:2 Sufferings of God's people ultimately turn out to be analogous, on a lesser level, to the sufferings of Christ (Ps. 22:14; Phil. 3:10).

7:8 God's justice gives hope for vindication when we are in the right. But in the matter of eternal salvation, no one is in the right except Christ alone, and in him we take refuge (Rom. 3:23–26).

8:2 Praise from infants anticipates children's praise of Christ (Matt. 21:16).

8:5 God gave Adam a distinguished role (Gen. 1:28–30). But because of the disobedience of Adam and his posterity (Rom. 5:12–21), it is Christ who fulfills the role and receives glory and honor in his resurrection and ascension (Heb. 2:5–9).

8:6 Dominion is finally achieved through Christ's reign (1 Cor. 15:25–28; Eph. 1:22; Heb. 2:5–9).

9:13 Deliverance from death anticipates the resurrection of Christ, and through him the resurrection of his people (1 Cor. 15:42–49; Col. 3:1–4).

10:1 The lack of immediate answers from God frustrates our desire for justice. This frustration finds its climax in the death of Christ, which from a human point of view was supremely unjust (Luke 23:14–16). But God answers in the resurrection (Acts 3:13–16), and therefore we hope for further answers, culminating in the consummation (Rev. 21:4).

10:7 The treachery of man contrasts with the righteousness to be found in Christ alone (Rom. 3:14–26; see note on Ps. 14:1).

11:4 The Lord's holiness and power, which are supremely revealed in Christ, guarantee an answer to the distress of his people.

12:6 In the midst of lies from man, God's word is supremely true, anticipating the truthfulness of Christ (John 14:6), who is able to deliver us from lies (John 8:44–47).

13:1 See note on 10:1.

13:3 See note on 3:1.

13:5 Salvation includes both the deliverance of Christ himself from death in his resurrection (Heb. 5:7) and the deliverance of believers through Christ (Col. 1:13).

14:1 In ultimate terms, none is righteous except Christ, through whom we may be part of the generation of the righteous (Rom. 3:10–12).

15:2 Fellowship with God in his holiness ultimately requires perfection, which we receive through the mediation of Christ the final high priest (Heb. 10:19–22).

16:8 God's mercies to David look forward to the climactic answer when Christ does not remain in the grave but is raised (Acts 2:25–33).

17:2 See note on 7:8.

17:7 Christ above all others waited for God to deliver him from his adversaries (Matt. 26:53; 27:43; 1 Pet. 2:23).

17:15 Awaking may mean awaking from sleep, but it looks forward ultimately to the new life of the resurrection and seeing God face to face (Rev. 22:4; see note on Ps. 3:5).

18:1 David's song from 2 Samuel 22 has been included in the book of Psalms, indicating its relevance to the people of God as a whole.

18:4 See note on 9:13.

18:17 Christ's resurrection is the ultimate case of deliverance from enemies.

18:20 See note on 7:8.

18:34 God gives the king effectiveness in war for the sake of defending his people from their enemies in other nations. OT war prefigures Christ's conquest of all enemies (Matt. 28:18–20; Eph. 1:20–22; Rev. 19:11–21).

18:49 See note on 2 Sam. 22:50.

18:50 Victory to David's offspring ultimately points to the victory of Christ in his resurrection (Rom. 6:8–10).

19:1 Revelation of God through nature leaves man with no excuse (Rom. 1:18–23).

19:7 The close relation between God's instruction through creation (vv. 1–6) and through his law (vv. 7–14) anticipates the role of Christ as mediator in creation and redemption (Col. 1:15–20).

20:6 The key to salvation to all the people is salvation to the anointed king. Christ's deliverance in his resurrection is the foundation for our salvation (1 Cor. 15:17–22).

21:4 The blessing of long life to the king in the line of David anticipates the blessing of eternal resurrection life that Christ possesses as he sits at the right hand of God (John 11:25; Rev. 1:18).

21:8 See note on 18:34.

22:1 The suffering and abandonment of the psalmist prefigure the suffering of Christ (Matt. 27:46).

22:8 The bystanders mock Christ's trust (Matt. 27:43).

22:18 The soldiers around the cross divide Christ's garments (Matt. 27:35 and John 19:23–24).

22:22 Public praise prefigures Christ praising God to his people for the salvation that God has accomplished in him (Heb. 2:12).

22:27 The Abrahamic promise of salvation to all nations (Gen. 12:3) will be fulfilled as the message of Christ's resurrection spreads (Matt. 28:18–20; Luke 24:47; Gal. 3:14).

23:1 Jesus is the good shepherd (John 10:11–18, 27–29) who embodies God's care for his people.

23:4 See note on 9:13.

23:6 Dwelling in the presence of God is fulfilled for Christ personally in his ascension (John 16:10; Acts 1:9–11) and for believers in the consummation (Rev. 22:4).

24:4 See note on 15:2.

24:7 Heaven is opened to receive Christ in his ascension (Luke 24:51; Heb. 9:24).

25:2 See note on 3:1.

25:4 Christ perfectly followed the path of the Lord (John 5:36; 14:31). Through Christ and his instruction and through the teaching of the Spirit of Christ believers learn to be disciples and follow his path (John 14:6; 16:13).

26:1 The ultimate vindication takes place in Christ (1 Tim. 3:16), who perfectly trusted in the Lord without wavering. In him his people find vindication (Rom. 4:25).

26:12 See note on 22:22.

27:1 Christ is the light of the world (John 8:12).

27:4 Enjoyment of fellowship with God in his presence anticipates the joy of knowing God through Christ (John 15:11; 16:24; 17:3; Rev. 22:4). Christ opens the way into the heavenly sanctuary (Heb. 10:19–22).

27:11 See note on 25:4.

28:8 Salvation to God's people and salvation to the anointed king go together. Both are fulfilled in Christ the anointed One (Luke 4:18).

29:3 God's word is powerful to save and to destroy, anticipating the power of Christ the Word (John 1:1) and the power of the gospel (Rom. 1:16; 2 Cor. 2:15–17).

30:2 God's healing from physical sickness anticipates rescue from death (v. 3) and eternal salvation through the resurrection of Christ (John 5:24; 11:25).

31:5 Trust in God for deliverance anticipates Christ's trust as he dies (Luke 23:46).

32:1 Forgiveness of sins anticipates the sacrifice of Christ as the ultimate basis for forgiveness (Rom. 4:7–8).

33:6 God's power and wisdom displayed in creation and in providence encourage praise and encourage hope in his salvation. Instances of temporal salvation look forward to eternal salvation in Christ (see 33:22; Matt. 1:21; Luke 2:30).

34:8 Experiencing God's goodness anticipates the experience of goodness in Christ (1 Pet. 2:3).

34:12 Christians now imitate Christ the Righteous One (Acts 3:14) in walking in the way of righteousness (1 Pet. 3:10–12).

34:20 The OT deliverances of the righteous prefigure the deliverance of Christ (John 19:36).

35:3 Small acts of salvation prefigure the climactic salvation in Christ—that Christ is raised from the dead and that through him we are rescued from sin and Satan (Col. 1:13–14).

35:4 See note on 3:1.

35:18 See note on 22:22.

35:19 Hatred for the righteous prefigures hatred against Christ (John 15:25).

36:1 See Rom. 3:18 and note on Ps. 14:1.

36:8 Joy in God's presence anticipates the joy that Christ gives (John 15:11), which is to be fulfilled in the consummation (Rev. 19:6–9).

36:11 See note on 3:1.

37:9 In the consummation ultimate blessing will come to God's people and ultimate overthrow to his enemies (Rev. 20:11–21:8). The first stage of this goal occurs in Christ's resurrection, where he as our representative inherits the earth (Matt. 28:18) and triumphs over his enemies (Col. 2:15).

38:1 Deliverance from God's wrath comes ultimately through Christ (John 3:36; Rom. 5:1).

38:4 See note on 32:1.

39:4 The threat of death hangs over all human existence and finds relief ultimately only through the resurrection of Christ (1 Cor. 15:12–26, 35–58).

40:7 The psalmist's eagerness to serve God prefigures the perfection of Christ's willingness and the perfection of his sacrifice (Heb. 10:5–10).

40:9 See note on 22:22.

41:9 The treachery against the psalmist prefigures Judas's treachery against Christ (John 13:18).

41:12 The eternal enjoyment of God's presence anticipates the resurrection of Christ (Heb. 9:24).

42:7 The waters of suffering threaten death (see Jonah 2:3). Such suffering according to God's will anticipates the suffering and death of Christ, and the hope for deliverance anticipates his resurrection.

43:1 See note on 26:1.

43:3 Coming into the presence of God prefigures Christ as our representative coming into heaven (Heb. 9:12).

44:22 Victory based on Christ's resurrection sustains God's people in the midst of oppression (Rom. 8:36).

45:6 The kings in the line of David prefigure the reign of God the king through the reign of the divine Son (Heb. 1:8–9).

45:11 The marriage of the Davidic king prefigures the marriage of Christ to the church (Eph. 5:25–27).

46:5 The dwelling of God with his people anticipates his coming to dwell with us in Christ (John 1:14; 2:19–21; Eph. 2:20–22).

47:9 The promise of God's subduing the nations is fulfilled in Christ (Matt. 28:18–20; Luke 24:47; Eph. 1:20–22; Rev. 5:9–10).

48:1 Jerusalem as the holy city prefigures the heavenly Jerusalem (Gal. 4:26; Heb. 12:22–24; Rev. 21:2, 9–10), both as a present reality in Christ and as a future hope.

49:7 Reliance on God is the only solution to death. Such reliance anticipates faith in Christ's resurrection (Rom. 10:9) and the hope for our future resurrection (1 Cor. 15:42–57; 1 Thess. 4:13–18).

50:4 God acts to judge, both in preliminary ways and climactically in the final judgment (Rev. 20:11–15).

50:15 True reliance on God is fulfilled both in Christ's trust in God (see note on 31:5) and in our faith in Christ (Rom. 10:9).

51:1 See note on 32:1.

51:7 Hyssop alludes to cleansing ceremonies (Lev. 14:4; Num. 19:18) that point forward to the final cleansing from sin through the work of Christ (Heb. 9:19–28).

52:5 See note on 3:1.

52:8 Enjoyment of the house of God in the OT prefigures eternal enjoyment of the presence of God in Christ, both in this life (John 15:11–16) and in the consummation (Rev. 22:2–4).

53:1 This psalm is very similar to Psalm 14. See note on 14:1.

54:1 The role of the name of God in salvation anticipates the fact that salvation is in the name of Christ alone (Acts 4:12).

54:4 God's upholding of life prefigures the giving of eternal life in the resurrection of Christ (1 Cor. 15:42–57; Col. 3:1–4).

54:5 See note on 3:1.

55:3 See note on 3:1.

55:13 The treachery of friends anticipates Judas's betrayal of Christ (John 13:18).

56:1 See note on 3:1.

56:3 The psalmist's trust in God anticipates both Christ's trust in the Father during his earthly life (Heb. 2:13; see note on Ps. 31:5) and Christians' trust in Christ (Acts 16:31).

56:13 Deliverance from death anticipates the resurrection (see note on 9:13).

57:2 God's acts of salvation work out his plan and purpose from all eternity (Eph. 1:3–4, 11).

57:9 The spread of the message of salvation among the nations anticipates the spread of the gospel message (Luke 24:47; see note on Ps. 22:27).

58:2 Distress over injustice will be satisfied when God brings righteous judgment (58:11). The longing for justice anticipates the justice accomplished in the resurrection of Christ (Rom. 4:25) and in the last judgment (Rev. 20:11–21:8). See note on Ps. 10:1.

59:1 See note on 3:1.

59:8 As in 2:4, God will triumph over the rebellious nations through his anointed, the Messiah (2:6–7; Acts 13:33).

60:12 Earthly foes prefigure the ultimate foes of sin, death and Satan, which are subdued by Christ (1 Cor. 15:25–28; Eph. 1:20–22; Heb. 2:14–15; see note on Ps. 3:1).

61:7 Blessing to the king is a key to the salvation of God's people as a whole. The king in the line of David anticipates Christ the king (Matt. 1:1–16).

62:1 Salvation comes from God, not man, anticipating the fact that Christ who brings salvation is God incarnate (John 1:14; 10:30).

63:2 True satisfaction is to be found in God alone, anticipating the satisfaction and blessing in Christ (John 15:11; Eph. 1:3–14; Rev. 22:3–5).

63:11 See note on 61:7.

64:2 Wickedness can be all the more dangerous when it is secret and deceitful. The deceit anticipates Satan's deceitfulness (Rev. 12:9). See note on Ps. 3:1.

65:4 Salvation means enjoying the presence of God. It is accomplished through Christ, the unique one whom God chooses to come near as our representative (Luke 9:35; Heb. 10:19–22) and through whom we can come near and be blessed (Eph. 1:3–14).

65:9 The prosperity of the land, which is a blessing to its people, anticipates the prosperity of the consummation (Rev. 22:1–5).

66:6 God's salvation in the exodus produces hope for further acts of salvation, culminating in salvation in Christ (Col. 1:13).

67:2 Salvation is to be made known among the nations, anticipating the spread of the gospel to the nations (Luke 24:47).

68:1 God's arising against his enemies anticipates the resurrection of Christ as a triumph over demonic enemies (Col. 2:15; Heb. 2:14–15).

68:18 God's ascending to reign anticipates Christ's resurrection and ascension, through which his enemies are subdued and his people delivered (Eph. 4:8–16).

68:26 Praise is the appropriate response to God's salvation (Eph. 5:19–20; Heb. 13:15; see note on Ps. 22:22).

69:2 See note on 42:7.

69:9 The zeal of the psalmist prefigures the zeal of Christ for the honor of God's name and God's house (John 2:17; Rom. 15:3).

69:21 The mercilessness of enemies prefigures the action of the enemies of Christ when he is on the cross (Matt. 27:48).

69:22 The desire for judgment on God's enemies finds fulfillment in Rom. 11:9–10.

69:25 Retribution for the wicked has an notable fulfillment in the fate of Judas (Acts 1:20).

70:4 Praise and admiration for God's salvation anticipates the praise for the salvation in Christ (Eph. 1:3–14; 5:19–20).

71:6 The psalmist's trust in God prefigures Christ's trust in the Father (22:8–9) and is also a model for our trust in Christ (see note on 56:3).

71:11 The enemies prefigure Christ's enemies, who imagine that they have won when Christ is on the cross.

71:14 See notes on 22:22 and 68:26.

72:1 The king in the line of David has a key role in bringing justice. Justice is climactically achieved through Christ the king (Matt. 1:1–16; Rom. 3:24–26; 4:25).

72:8 Dominion for the Davidic king is fulfilled in the universal reign of Christ (Isa. 9:6–7; 1 Cor. 15:24–28; Eph. 1:20–21).

72:19 The filling of the earth with God's glory will be fulfilled in the consummation (Rev. 21:22–27).

73:3 See note on 10:1.

73:17 In the presence of God in the sanctuary one finds an answer to frustration. His presence anticipates God's presence in Christ (John 1:14; 2:19–21; 14:9–10).

74:3 The destruction of the sanctuary, the place of God's presence, prefigures the destruction of Christ in death. But God answers and fulfills his promises in Christ's resurrection (2 Cor. 1:20). In union with Christ we participate in his death and resurrection (2 Cor. 4:7–15; Phil. 3:10–11).

74:10 See note on 10:1.

74:13 God's dividing the sea in the exodus symbolizes his power over chaos and his power to deliver his people from death. His victory in the exodus anticipates Christ's victory over death and Satan (Heb. 2:14–15).

75:7 God's providential control of rulers and his preliminary judgments within history give us hope for climactic judgment. And the climactic judgment began when God lifted up Christ from death to the highest position (1 Cor. 15:20–28; Phil. 2:10–11).

75:8 See note on 3:1.

76:3 The establishment of peace in God's dwelling place prefigures the peace that Christ brings (John 16:33), first in reconciling us to God (Rom. 5:1–10), but also in reconciliation with one another (Matt. 18:15–20; 1 Corinthians 12).

76:9 See note on 50:4.

77:11 Remembrance of God's past acts of salvation, like the exodus (v. 19), strengthen the hope for present and future salvation. Now we look back on the climactic salvation in the death and resurrection of Christ (Acts 2:29–41; Rom. 4:25).

78:2 The expounding of the deeper meaning of God's past acts of salvation anticipates the role of Christ in expounding the meaning of God's ways (Matt. 13:34–35).

78:4 See note on 77:11.

78:17 The rebellious hearts in Israel are ultimately overcome only through the renewal in the heart that takes place in the new covenant in Christ (Heb. 8:8–13).

78:72 The rebellion in Israel points to the need for a shepherd-king who will guide them. David is a preliminary fulfillment (v. 70) pointing forward to Christ as the final shepherd (Ezek. 34:23–24; John 10:11, 14).

79:1 See note on 74:3.

79:9 Ultimate salvation and the glorification of God's name come through Christ (John 13:31–32; 17:1–5).

80:1 Christ is the true shepherd (John 10:11, 14).

80:17 The "son of man," the key representative for the people of God, is ultimately Christ (Matt. 26:64; see note on Ps. 61:7).

81:1 Praise is the appropriate response to God's salvation (see note on 68:26).

81:13 See note on 78:17.

82:2 The failure of judges to bring justice points to the need for God's ultimate judgment. He has brought justice in Christ (Rom. 4:25) and will bring ultimate judgment in the consummation (Rev. 20:11–21:8).

82:6 Judges reflecting God's authority (Rom. 13:1) foreshadow Christ, who is the exact image of God (Heb. 1:3) and is God himself (John 10:34–36).

83:1 See note on 10:1.

83:9 The destruction of Israel's enemies prefigures the destruction of the ultimate enemies—sin, death, and Satan (Heb. 2:14–15; Rev. 21:4; see note on Ps. 3:1).

84:1 God's dwelling place in the OT prefigures Christ as the dwelling place of God (John 1:14; 2:19–21), the church as dwelling place through the Spirit (1 Cor. 3:16; Eph. 2:20–22), and the new Jerusalem as final dwelling place (Rev. 21:2–3, 21:22–22:5). See notes on Ps. 23:6 and 27:4.

85:4 The forgiveness of Israel in the OT anticipates the permanent forgiveness in Christ (Col. 1:13–14).

86:2 See note on 35:3.

86:9 The coming of the nations to worship is fulfilled in Christ (Luke 24:47; see note on Ps. 57:9).

86:11 See note on 25:4.

87:4 The incorporation of other nations into the holy city is fulfilled as the nations come to Christ (Luke 24:47; Rev. 5:9–10; 21:24–26).

88:3 The miseries of the psalmist prefigure the sufferings of Christ (Luke 24:26–27; see note on Ps. 22:1).

89:4 The promise concerning offspring is ultimately fulfilled in Christ (Matt. 1:1–16). But victory is preceded by suffering, abandonment, and apparent failure of the promise, all anticipating the sufferings of Christ.

89:48 In the resurrection of Christ is the ultimate answer to death (1 Cor. 15:50–57; Heb. 2:14–15).

90:3 See note on 89:48.

90:17 Despite the reality of death, Christ's resurrection guarantees victory and demonstrates that work has eternal meaning (1 Cor. 15:58).

91:1 God is our ultimate dwelling place and protection, prefiguring Christ as dwelling place and protection (John 1:14; 10:27–30).

92:1 See note on 68:26.

92:13 Fruitfulness is found in the presence of God (see 1:3). Fruitfulness prefigures the fruitfulness of Christ (Isa. 53:10) and of his people (John 15:1–16).

93:1 See note on 11:4.

93:4 The Lord's power is greater than the threat of overwhelming waters. The power over waters threatening death prefigures the power in Christ's resurrection (Eph. 1:19–22; see note on Ps. 42:7).

94:2 See notes on 50:4 and 58:2.

94:3 See note on 10:1.

94:11 The limitations of human thinking contrast with the wisdom of God, which is to be found in Christ (1 Cor. 3:20; Col. 2:3).

94:15 Final justice, accomplished in Christ, will have benefits for all who are his (1 Cor. 15:42–49).

95:1 See note on 68:26.

95:8 Israel's rebellion (Numbers 14; Deut. 32:5) serves as a negative example for all time (Heb. 4:7–12). Faith in God, culminating in faith in Christ, is the proper response to God (Heb. 4:2).

96:1 See note on 68:26.

96:3 The declaration to the nations anticipates the spread of the gospel (Luke 24:47; Acts 1:8; see note on Ps. 22:27).

97:2 See note on 7:8.

97:8 God's people can rejoice in judgment, ultimately because Christ has taken away the negative judgment against their sins and they may receive blessing in him (2 Cor. 5:21).

98:1 See Psalm 96 and note on 68:26.

98:7 Ultimate salvation in Christ includes blessing to all nations (see note on 22:27) and renewal of the world itself (2 Pet. 3:13; Rev. 21:1).

99:3 See note on 11:4.

99:4 The experience of the benefits of justice make us long for ultimate justice, which is to be found in Christ and his justification (Rom. 3:23–26; 4:25–5:1). Justice includes both the vindication of God's people and the removal of enemies. The ultimate enemies are sin, death, and Satan (see note on Ps. 3:1).

100:4 Entering the presence of God has been made possible through Christ who opened the way (John 14:6; Heb. 10:19–22).

101:5 The zeal of the Davidic king to remove wickedness prefigures the power of Christ in triumphing over all evil and making people new (John 13:10; Eph. 4:20–24).

102:3 See note on 6:2.

102:15 See note on 22:27.

102:16 God appears in his glory climactically in Christ (John 1:14; 13:31–32; 17:1–5).

102:26 Through Christ the abiding character of God benefits us (Heb. 1:10–12).

103:4 Earlier redemptions look forward to the climactic redemption in Christ.

104:2 God's people are to praise God for his works of creation and providence, seeing in them displays of God's power and goodness. His power and goodness and blessing are supremely manifested in Christ (John 1:14; Eph. 1:3–14).

105:5 The faithfulness of God in past generations encourages Israel to respond in faithfulness. Christians look back not only on God's acts of salvation in the OT, but on the climactic salvation in Christ, which gives the ultimate basis for our trust.

106:6 The unfaithfulness of Israel in response to God is answered by Christ's obedience, and then by the obedience of God's people who follow Christ (John 14:15; Eph. 2:10).

107:2 God's acts of redemption in the OT prefigure final redemption in Christ (Col. 1:13–14).

108:6 See note on 35:3.

108:7 God is committed to subduing his enemies, and this commitment is fulfilled climactically in Christ, both in his resurrection (Heb. 2:14–15) and in his second coming (Rev. 19:11–21).

109:8 Judas is a chief example of the enemies whom God judges (Acts 1:20; see note on Ps. 69:25).

109:31 Christ, having been himself saved from death in his resurrection, is able to save us from death (John 11:25; Heb. 2:14–15; Rev. 1:18).

110:1 The Messiah is superior even to David and exercises universal rule (Matt. 22:44–45; Acts 2:34–36; 1 Cor. 15:25–28; Eph. 1:22; Heb. 1:13).

110:4 The Messiah has an eternal priesthood superior to Aaron's (Heb. 5:6; 7:21–8:2).

111:1 See note on 22:22.

111:9 Final redemption and final fulfillment of God's covenant is accomplished in Christ (2 Cor. 1:20; Heb. 7:25; 8:6–13).

112:1 Christ is the supremely righteous man (Acts 3:14), and in him we too receive the reward for righteousness (Eph. 1:3–14). See note on Ps. 1:1.

112:9 The principle of generosity continues in the NT (2 Cor. 9:9).

113:7 Attentiveness to the needy is supremely manifested in Christ (Luke 1:48–55; 6:20).

114:3 The crossing of the Red Sea (Exodus 14–15) and of the Jordan River (Joshua 3) are acts of salvation and symbolic triumphs over death that anticipate the triumph of Christ (John 10:18; 11:25; Rev. 1:18; 21:4).

115:1 God is supremely glorified and his faithfulness manifested in Christ's work (John 13:31–32; 17:1–5).

116:3 See notes on 9:13 and 13:5.

116:13 See note on 68:26.

116:15 God continues to care for his saints even after death, hinting at the hope for the resurrection (John 11:25; 1 Thess. 4:13–18).

117:1 All nations will come to [illegible] result of his salvation in Christ (Rom. 15:11), [illegible] ing the promise to Abraham (Gen. 12:3; see note on Ps. 22:27).

118:5 See note on 35:3.

118:6 God has expressed his commitment in Christ, giving us all the more reason to trust him (Heb. 13:6).

118:22 The Lord's exaltation of the one rejected by man is fulfilled in the exaltation of Christ (Matt. 21:42; Luke 20:17; Acts 4:11–12; Eph. 2:20–22; 1 Pet. 2:4–7).

118:26 Israel ought to recognize Jesus as one who brings the salvation of God (Matt. 23:39).

119:1 People with renewed hearts delight to obey God and learn from his word, which guides them. Christ was perfectly obedient to God (Heb. 10:7–10), and through his Spirit we are transformed into his image (Rom. 8:9–17; 2 Cor. 3:18) and become obedient servants of God. Delight in God's word anticipates delight in Christ, who is the Word of God (John 1:1).

119:11 Having God's word in the heart anticipates the new covenant (Heb. 8:10–13; 10:16–18).

120:1 See note on 35:3.

120:2 Deliverance from deceit anticipates the purity of God's word and God's work of deliverance from Satanic deceit through Christ (Rev. 12:9; see note on Ps. 64:2).

121:2 Salvation comes from God alone, anticipating the fact that Christ is the divine Savior.

122:1 Joy in experiencing the presence of God in his house anticipates the joy of the presence of God in Christ (John 1:14; 15:11; see note on Ps. 27:4).

122:6 Jerusalem as the city of God prefigures the heavenly Jerusalem (Gal. 4:26–28; Heb. 12:22–24) of which we are citizens (Phil. 3:20). Christ has given peace to his people (John 16:33; Eph. 4:3; Col. 3:15).

123:2 Mercy is received ultimately through Christ (Eph. 2:4; see note on Ps. 121:2).

124:4 See note on 42:7.

125:1 Trust in the Lord anticipates trust in Christ (Acts 16:31), who has supremely manifested God's faithfulness.

126:1 Relief from misfortune prefigures the great salvation in Christ (John 16:20–22).

127:1 The necessity of the Lord's power for temporal achievements anticipates the necessity for God, and him alone, to accomplish eternal salvation through Christ (John 15:4–5; Acts 4:12).

128:1 See note on 112:1.

128:2 Temporal blessings prefigure the eternal blessings in Christ (Eph. 1:3–14; Rev. 21:1–4).

129:1 See note on 6:2.

129:5 See note on 60:12.

130:4 Forgiveness is ultimately accomplished in Christ (Col. 1:13–14; see note on Ps. 32:1).

131:1 The psalmist's humble trust anticipates the humble trust of Christ in the Father (Matt. 11:29; Heb. 5:7–10) and the trust that Christians are to have in Christ (Acts 16:31).

132:12 The promise to David culminates in Christ the offspring of David (Matt. 1:1–16), who is both king in the line of David and priest in God's heav[illegible]welling (Ps. 110:2, 4; Heb. 8:1–2).

[illegible] Christ and in [illegible] mong God's people is produced in [illegible] Eph. 4:1–6).

134:1 Praise of God looks [illegible] to the praises offered by Christ (Heb. 2:12), the praises [illegible] God's NT people (Eph. 5:19–20; Heb. 13:15), and the praises of the consummation (Rev. 19:1–10).

135:4 God's acts of grace and salvation to his people in the OT anticipate the climactic salvation accomplished in Christ (Luke 2:30–32; Acts 4:12).

136:4 God's works of creation, providence, and merciful deliverance show the steadfast love that has now been climactically revealed through salvation in Christ (John 1:14).

137:6 Devastation to God's holy city makes people long for future blessing and destruction to God's enemies. God's ultimate answer is found in salvation in Christ and in the last judgment (Rev. 20:11–21:8). Jerusalem prefigures the heavenly Jerusalem (Gal. 4:26–27; Heb. 12:22–24).

138:3 See note on 35:3.

138:4 See note on 22:27.

138:6 Mercy to the lowly comes in Christ (Luke 1:48–55).

139:1 Detailed knowledge and care for the psalmist anticipates God's care for us (John 10:14–16).

140:1 Deliverance from enemies prefigures Christ's deliverance from his enemies, both human and demonic (Matt. 26:46; Col. 2:15); it also prefigures our deliverance in Christ from sin, death, and Satan (Heb. 2:14–15).

140:3 See Rom. 3:13 and note on Ps. 14:1.

141:3 The need for wise speech, in prayer as well as in other circumstances, anticipates the purity of Christ's speech (John 8:43–47) and the purity that we receive from Christ (John 17:17–19). Our prayers are heard because of him (John 14:13–14; 1 John 5:14–15).

142:4 See notes on 6:2 and 22:1.

142:6 Deliverance from persecutors anticipates the deliverance of Christ from his persecutors, after he was brought low in his crucifixion and death.

143:2 Perfect righteousness is found only in Christ, who provides righteousness for those who are his (2 Cor. 5:21; see notes on Ps. 7:8 and 14:1).

144:1 See note on 18:34.

144:10 Deliverance for David prefigures final deliverance given to Christ the offspring of David. See notes on 2:6 and 18:50.

145:1 See note on 68:26.

145:8 The Lord's grace and mercy is climactically poured out in the salvation in Christ (Rom. 8:32).

146:3 Mere man cannot save, pointing to the need for Christ to be God as well as man (John 1:14).

147:5 God's greatness and goodness, in both providence and redemption, motivates praise and trust. God's goodness has now been supremely manifested in Christ (Rom. 8:32).

148:3 The created world declares the character of its maker (19:1–6), anticipating the final, even more glorious praise in the consummation (Rev. 21:1–4). The creation reflects the glory of the Son, who is mediator of creation (John 1:[illegible] Col. 1:15–17).

149:4 See note on 68:26.

149:7 At Christ's [illegible] coming rebellious nations will be sub[illegible] (Rev. 19:11–21). In the meantime, [illegible]ous subduing comes through the power of the gospel (Matt. 28:18–20).

150:2 See note on 68:26. Praise, not a cry of distress, has the final position in the Psalms, anticipating the victory of Christ (Eph. 4:8) and the final abolition of suffering (Rev. 21:4).

Proverbs

Wisdom ultimately comes from God and his instruction, which anticipates the fact that Christ is the wisdom of God (1 Cor. 1:30; Col. 2:3) and that in him and his instruction we find the way of life and righteousness (John 14:6, 23–24). Through the Spirit we may walk in the right way (Gal. 5:16–26).

1:1 Solomon's wisdom prefigures the wisdom of his greater descendant, Jesus Christ (1 Cor. 1:30; see note on 1 Kings 2:6).

1:7 Wisdom is to be sought from God, anticipating that we seek wisdom from Christ, the incarnate God (John 1:14; Col. 2:3).

1:8 Listening to parents is one aspect of honoring them, which is an abiding principle (Ex. 20:12; Eph. 6:1–3). Within the church we are now to have specifically Christian instruction of children (Eph. 6:4). The archetype for this obedient listening is found in the relation of the Son of God to the Father (John 8:28–29).

1:18 The principle of just retribution is broad (Obad. 15) and is to be fulfilled ultimately in the consummation (Rev. 20:12–14).

1:19 Sin leads to death (Rom. 6:23), but in Christ there is life (John 14:6; 1 John 5:12).

1:20 The call of wisdom prefigures the call of the gospel, which contains the wisdom of God (1 Cor. 1:18–25; 2:6–10).

2:4 The diligent seeking for wisdom prefigures the need to seek the kingdom of God (Matt. 13:44).

2:13 The path of righteousness is ultimately that of Jesus Christ, the perfectly Righteous One (John 14:6). All other ways lead to destruction (Matt. 7:13–14; Acts 4:12).

2:16 Wisdom involves the avoidance both of literal adultery and of the spiritual adultery of idolatry (Ex. 34:16; Hos. 1:2; 2:1–5; 3:1–3; 2 Cor. 11:3).

2:21 Temporal blessings prefigure the blessings of eternal salvation (Eph. 1:3–14).

3:2 Length of days prefigures eternal life that comes through fellowship with Christ, who is the wisdom of God (1 Cor. 1:30).

3:5 Trust in the Lord anticipates trust in Christ, who is the Lord's salvation (Acts 16:31).

3:11 Christians as sons of God receive the Lord's discipline (Heb. 12:5–6).

3:18 The possession of the tree of life anticipates the final inheritance in the consummation (Rev. 2:7; 22:1–2).

3:34 The call for humility anticipates the role of humility in the NT (Matt. 11:29; James 4:6; 1 Pet. 5:5).

[illegible] instruction for the path of life anticipates the instruction of Christ, who is the way and the truth and the life (John 14:6).

5:3 See note on 2:16.

5:5 Ultimately Christ delivers us from death (John 11:25–26), and as one aspect of deliverance he gives wisdom and integrity of heart (1 Cor. 1:30).

6:6 Diligent work now has as its deepest motivation the hope of final satisfaction in Christ (1 Cor. 15:58).

6:24 See note on 2:16.

7:21 Smooth, deceitful talk is linked ultimately to the deceit of Satan (John 8:44–47; Rev. 12:9).

8:1 See note on 1:20.

8:22 The eternality of wisdom with God anticipates the eternality of the second person of the Trinity, who is the Word of God and who mediated creation (John 1:1–3).

8:35 Life is obtained ultimately from Christ, who is the life (John 14:6) and the wisdom of God (1 Cor. 1:30).

9:2 The invitation to feasting anticipates the spiritual food of Christ (John 6:52–58) and the future marriage supper of the Lamb (Rev. 19:9).

9:18 See note on 1:19.

10:1 On Solomon, see notes on 1:1 and 1 Kings 2:6.

10:2 Blessings on the righteous anticipate the blessings on Christ, the perfectly righteous man, and the blessings that come to those in Christ (Eph. 1:3–14).

10:12 Wisdom transforms relations with others, anticipating the NT transformation through love (John 13:34–35; 1 John 3:16–18; 4:7–21).

10:21 The blessing to others anticipates the blessing of gracious words in the church (Eph. 4:14–16; Col. 3:16; 4:6).

11:2 The value of humility anticipates the humility of Christ (Matt. 11:29) and of his people (Luke 14:11; Eph. 4:2; see note on Prov. 3:34).

11:3 See note on 2:13.

11:4 Temporary avoidance of death prefigures the promise of eternal life, based on the righteousness of Christ (John 5:24; Rom. 4:25; see note on Prov. 2:13).

12:18 The blessing of wise words anticipates the blessings of the words of Christ (John 6:63) and of his followers (Eph. 4:29; Col. 4:6).

13:4 See note on 6:6.

13:14 Christ the supremely wise One has the words of eternal life (John 6:68–69).

13:24 Christians are to train their children in Christ (Eph. 6:1–4; see note on Prov. 1:8).

14:2 True trust in Christ manifests itself in obedience (Gal. 5:13–26; James 2:14–26).

15:1 Gentle words anticipate the gentleness of Christ (Matt. 11:29). Gentleness is also to characterize his people (Gal. 5:23; Eph. 4:2, 25–29).

16:3 Only through union with Christ can we bear fruit (John 15:1–11).

16:12 The duty of kings to bring justice anticipates Christ, who is the great king and the one who brings perfect justice (Rom. 3:26; Rev. 19:11).

17:3 The Lord's discernment is perfect (Heb. 4:12–13), implying the need for purification (Heb. 9:9–14).

18:3 Temporal judgments on wickedness prefigure final judgment (Rev. 20:11–15), underlining the need for repentance.

19:1 We must be discerning about real value and seek first the kingdom of God (Matt. 6:33).

19:5 See note on 18:3.

19:11 Readiness to forgive anticipates the forgiveness of Christ (Col. 1:14) and the practice of forgiving among his people (Col. 3:13; James 1:19).

20:8 Authorities have an obligation to punish evildoing (Deut. 16:18–20; Rom. 13:1–4). In this they anticipate the final judgment of God (Rev. 20:11–15).

20:22 Vengeance belongs to God (Rom. 12:17–21). Christ himself waited patiently for vindication (1 Pet. 2:21–23).

21:3 See 1 Sam. 15:22–23 and Mic. 6:6–8. The requirement for real obedience, and ultimately for perfect obedience, is fulfilled in Christ (Heb. 10:5–10).

22:4 See note on 2:21.

23:4 Counsel against lust for money anticipates Jesus' counsel about true riches (Luke 12:22–40; 16:10–13; Eph. 5:5).

23:13 See note on 13:24.

23:19 The way of righteousness is found ultimately in Christ (John 14:6). See note on Prov. 1:8.

23:30 The warning against drunkenness is repeated in the NT, and it is complemented by a positive command to be filled with the Spirit (Eph. 5:18).

24:3 Human use of wisdom imitates God's use of wisdom (8:22–31) and anticipates Christ, who is the wisdom of God (1 Cor. 1:30) and who builds the church (Matt. 16:18).

24:19 See note on Ps. 10:1.

24:30 See note on 6:6.

25:7 The principle of humility is further developed in Christ's teaching and example (Luke 14:7–11).

25:11 See notes on 12:18 and 15:1.

25:21 The principle of doing good to enemies is further developed in Christ's example and his teaching (Matt. 5:43–48; Rom. 12:20–21).

26:3 The answer to folly and its disasters is found in seeking the wisdom of Christ (1 Cor. 1:30; Col. 2:3).

26:11 It is folly to turn back from following Christ (2 Pet. 2:22).

26:13 See note on 6:6.

26:20 The answer to words of strife is found in Christ's peace and his empowering of his people to be at peace with one another (Col. 3:13–15).

27:3 See note on 26:20.

27:11 See note on 13:24.

28:1 The boldness of the righteous anticipates the boldness of followers of Christ (2 Cor. 3:12; Phil. 1:28–30).

28:2 See note on 16:12.

28:9 God desires righteousness and obedience, which are fulfilled in Christ (2 Cor. 5:21; see note on Prov. 21:3).

29:2 See note on 16:12.

7:11 Israel's hypocrisy anticipates the hypocrisy and corrupt worship that Christ confronts (Matt. 21:13).

7:14 The destruction of the temple anticipates the later destruction of Herod's temple that Christ predicts (Matt. 24:2).

8:3 The remedy for death and for sin that leads to death is the resurrection of Christ (1 Cor. 15:42–57).

8:11 See note on 6:14.

9:1 Apostasy is a deep grief both to Jeremiah and to Christ, the final prophet (Luke 19:41–44).

9:23–24 The principle of boasting in God alone is fulfilled in 1 Cor. 1:29–31 (see 2 Cor. 10:17).

10:5 Only God, not idols, offers salvation. The uniqueness of God and his way anticipates the unique role of Christ as the way to God (John 14:6; Heb. 10:19–22; see note on Isa. 46:1).

11:8 Through Moses God predicts that disasters and exile will result from disobedience (Deuteronomy 28).

11:19 The hostility to Jeremiah prefigures the hostility to Christ as prophet (Isa. 53:7; Matt. 27:1; Luke 6:11).

12:7 God forsakes his house and his people on account of their sin. This anticipates later judgments on sin, including the forsaking of Christ when he is the sin-bearer (Matt. 27:46).

13:9 The pride of God's people contrasts with the need for people who truly serve him. The need is answered in the new covenant (31:31–34) in Christ (Heb. 8:8–13; 10:15–25).

14:3 Drought fulfills the curse in Deut. 28:22 that must come when Israel forsakes the Lord. It contrasts with the blessing of living water in Christ (John 4:14; 6:35).

14:14 The conflict between true and false prophets anticipates the conflict between Jesus and his opponents, and between true and false teaching in the church (2 Pet. 2:1–3).

15:2 Judgments fulfill the prophetic curses in Deut. 28:15–68 (see Rev. 6:8). God's wrath against sin anticipates the final judgment (Rev. 20:11–15; see note on Jer. 1:16).

15:10 Jeremiah as a rejected prophet prefigures the rejection of Christ's prophetic ministry (Luke 11:49–51).

16:15 Restoration, prophesied in Deut. 30:1–5, prefigures final salvation in Christ (Isa. 40:1–11).

17:8 The blessing promised to the righteous man (Ps. 1:3) is fulfilled in Christ the perfectly righteous man (Acts 3:14) and in those who are righteous in him (2 Cor. 5:21).

18:6 God's power as creator can bring salvation even to the wayward (Rom. 9:20–24; Eph. 2:4–10).

18:11 The call to repent anticipates the call to repent from John the Baptist (Matt. 3:2) and in gospel proclamation (Luke 24:47; Acts 2:38).

19:3 See note on 1:16.

19:9 The specific horror of eating human flesh was prophesied in Deut. 28:53–55. Horror upon horror shows the results of the degradation of sin, and prefigures the final judgment (Rev. 20:11–15; see note on Jer. 1:16).

20:2 Opposition to Jeremiah the prophet prefigures opposition to Christ the final prophet (Luke 11:49–51). Those who oppose Christ will experience judgment (Rev. 20:11–15).

21:8 Even in the midst of the greatest disaster God in mercy holds open a way of escape. The escape prefigures the escape from sin, death, and destruction through the salvation in Christ (John 11:25–26; 14:6).

22:3 The demand for justice from the king fails to be answered. The answer finally comes in Christ the king (Isa. 9:6–7; Rev. 19:11).

23:1 The false shepherds contrast with Jesus the true shepherd (John 10:11, 14).

23:5 The "Branch," alluding to Isa. 11:1, is the Messiah in the line of David (see Zech. 6:12; John 15:1–17).

23:8 The restoration, which is parallel to the exodus (Ex. 12:33–38), prefigures rescue from sin and the kingdom of Satan (Col. 1:13–14).

23:16 See note on 14:14.

24:5 The exiles are the remnant to whom God gives favor, illustrating the remnant theme (see notes on 1 Kings 19:18; Isa. 1:9; and 6:13).

24:7 The renewal of the heart, already prophesied in Deut. 30:6, is further explained in the promise of the new covenant (Jer. 31:31–34; Heb. 8:8–13; 10:15–25).

25:11 Daniel relies on the prophecy of 70 years when he prays for restoration (Dan. 9:2). The 70 years are years of sabbath rest for the land (2 Chron. 36:21). The restoration looks forward to final rest in the consummation (Heb. 4:9–10).

25:15 The cup of wrath prefigures the wrath of God in final judgment (Rev. 14:10; 16:1, 19). Christ on the cross drank the cup of wrath as our substitute (Matt. 26:39, 42).

26:6 See note on 7:14.

26:8 The desire for death illustrates a pattern of opposing the prophets, a pattern that culminates in the death of Christ (Matt. 21:33–41; Luke 11:49–51; see note on Jer. 20:2).

27:9 See note on 14:14.

27:11 To those who listen the service to Babylon becomes a judgment tempered with mercy, prefiguring the mercy in Christ (Heb. 12:5–11; see note on Jer. 21:8).

28:9 Peace with God does not come without first dealing with the issue of sin. The answer is to be found in Christ (Col. 1:13–14; see note on Jer. 6:14).

28:15 See note on 14:14.

29:8 See note on 14:14.

29:10 See note on 25:11.

29:13 See notes on 24:7 and 31:31.

29:14 Restoration from exile prefigures the reconciliation with God by which we may be gathered into the presence of God in heaven (Rom. 5:1–10; Gal. 4:26–28; Heb. 10:19–22; 12:22–24; see notes on Jer. 3:17 and 16:15).

30:18 The rebuilding of cities prefigures the heavenly Jerusalem (Gal. 4:26–28; Heb. 12:22–24; Rev. 21:9–14).

31:1 The promise, "I will be . . . God . . . , and they shall be my people," is a repeated refrain in Jeremiah (11:4; 24:7; 30:22; 31:33; 32:38). It builds on the promise to Abraham (Gen. 17:7) and to Israel through Moses (Ex. 19:5–6). It is fulfilled in the new covenant in Christ (Jer. 31:33; Heb. 8:10; see note on Jer. 31:31).

31:15 Past devastations to Israel anticipate the devastation when Herod kills the children (Matt. 2:16–18).

31:31 The new covenant is fulfilled in the covenant that Christ makes at the Last Supper (Matt. 26:28; 1 Cor. 11:25; 2 Cor. 3:6; Heb. 8:8–13; 10:15–25) and includes Gentiles as well as Jews through union with Christ (Gal. 3:9, 14, 27–29).

32:20 A long history of God's demonstrations of faithfulness is linked to his faithfulness in Jeremiah's time and in the climactic salvation in Christ (Rom. 3:3–4).

32:40 See notes on 24:7 and 31:31.

33:8 Forgiveness is foreshadowed in the restoration from exile, but it is fully accomplished in Christ (Col. 1:13–14).

33:15 See note on 23:5.

34:11 The faithlessness of the people concerning the law in Ex. 21:2 and Deut. 15:12 contrasts with the faithfulness of Christ, who brings full and permanent liberty from sin (Luke 4:18–19).

35:10 The obedience of the Rechabites contrasts with the disobedience of Israel and prefigures the obedience of the Christ the Son to his Father (John 8:29).

36:2 The triumph of the word of God over opposition prefigures Christ (John 1:10–11) and his triumph over opposition.

37:18 The innocent suffering of Jeremiah prefigures the innocent suffering of Christ (Matt. 27:24).

37:19 See note on 14:14.

38:6 Jeremiah's brush with death prefigures Christ's being put to death (see notes on 11:19 and 15:10).

38:17 See note on 21:8.

39:1 The prophecies of disaster from Jeremiah and from other prophets (2 Chron. 36:15–16; Jer. 25:4–11) now come to pass, confirming the faithfulness of God in judgment. Judgments in history prefigure the final judgment (see note on 1:16).

39:18 See note on 21:8.

40:4 God shows mercy to Jeremiah and to those who are left, anticipating the mercy he will show in Christ (Rom. 6:23).

41:14 God shows mercy to the captives, anticipating the mercy he will show in Christ (Rom. 6:23; Col. 1:13–14).

42:6 After all of the rebellion in previous times, the people finally resolve to obey the Lord. But then they prefer their own judgment (43:1–7). Their stubbornness shows the need for renewal of the heart that will come in Christ (31:31–34; see notes on 4:4 and 31:31).

44:16 The persistence in rebellion shows the justice of God's judgment but also the need for a radical renewal of heart, promised in the new covenant (see note on 31:31).

45:5 Even the righteous suffer as a result of the sins of the people. The righteous suffering prefig-

46:1 The worthlessness of idols is expressive of the principle that only Christ, the one way of salvation that God has established (John 14:6; Acts 4:12), is worthy of trust.

47:3 The oppressor of God's people will be judged (see note on 14:4).

47:8 See Rev. 18:7 and note on Isa. 14:4.

48:20 Rescue from Babylon prefigures rescue from sin and death (Col. 1:13–14; Rev. 18:4).

49:2 The word of God is like a sharp sword (Eph. 6:17; Heb. 4:12; Rev. 1:16; 2:12, 16; 19:15).

49:6 See Acts 13:47 and 26:23, and note on Isa. 42:6.

49:8 Now, subsequent to Christ's resurrection, is the time of salvation (2 Cor. 6:2).

49:10 Protection and blessing ultimately come through the Lamb (Rev. 7:16–17).

50:6 The Messianic servant undergoes suffering and humiliation for the sake of accomplishing salvation (Matt. 27:26–31).

51:10 God's redemption in the exodus is analogous to his redemption of his people from Babylonian exile, and both look forward to his climactic redemption in Christ.

51:11 See note on 35:10.

51:17 Wrath is followed by exaltation, prefiguring the movement from the wrath of Christ's crucifixion to the exaltation of his resurrection and ascension. On the cup of wrath, see note on Jer. 25:15.

52:7 The gospel is the good news of salvation (Rom. 10:15).

52:10 The inclusion of the nations fulfills the promise to Abraham concerning blessing to all nations (Gen. 12:3; Luke 2:30–31; see note on Isa. 42:6).

52:11 The Israelites' departure from pagan Babylon prefigures the departure of believers from the contamination of the world (2 Cor. 6:14–7:1).

52:13 Exaltation of the servant, the Messiah, follows his suffering (v. 14; 53:3–9; see note on 51:17).

52:15 Many who have not heard of Christ will be awed (v. 14) by his suffering sacrifice. Paul spreads the message to those who have not heard (Rom. 15:14–21).

53:1 The message of salvation in Christ often meets an unbelieving response (John 12:37–43; Rom. 10:16).

53:5 The messianic servant undergoes substitutionary suffering (Rom. 4:25; 2 Cor. 5:21; 1 Pet. 2:24–25).

53:9 Christ was put to death between two robbers (Matt. 27:38) and buried in the tomb of a rich man, Joseph of Arimathea (Matt. 27:57–60).

53:11 Christ's death and resurrection results in our justification (Rom. 3:23–26; 4:25; 5:19).

54:1 The return of Jerusalem's inhabitants from exile prefigures the multiplication of children of the promise (Rom. 9:8) who will return to God through Christ (Gal. 4:27).

54:7 See note on 51:17.

54:10 The new covenant results in permanent peace with God (Rom. 5:1) and is secure forever (Heb. 9:12).

55:2 God's offer of food is fulfilled in Christ, who is the food and drink of eternal life (John 6:52–58).

56:7 The extension of salvation to the nations takes place in Christ (Matt. 21:13; Acts 1:8; Rev. 5:9).

57:3 See notes on 1:4 and 34:2.

57:19 God gives the invitation of salvation to all, anticipating the spread of the gospel (Acts 2:39; Eph. 2:17).

58:1 See note on 1:4.

58:2 Israel's hypocrisy anticipates the hypocrisy and externalism that Christ will confront (Matt. 15:1–10).

59:2 See note on 1:4.

59:7 Paul uses these words (Rom. 3:15–17) to show that Jews and Gentiles alike are guilty of sin. See note on Ps. 14:1.

59:17 God's battle anticipates (1) the coming of righteousness and salvation at Christ's first coming (Rom. 3:23–26), (2) Christians' battle against evil (Eph. 6:10–20; 1 Thess. 5:8), and (3) the war at Christ's second coming (Rev. 19:11–21).

59:20 The Redeemer is Christ, who saves both Jews and Gentiles (Rom. 11:25–32).

60:1 God's glory is seen in Christ (John 1:14).

60:3 Nations come to Christ through the gospel (Luke 24:47; John 1:32; Acts 1:8; Rev. 21:24–25; see notes on Isa. 2:2 and 11:10).

60:6 The wise men, representing the nations, bring gold and frankincense and myrrh (Matt. 2:11).

60:19 God is the sole light in the new Jerusalem (Rev. 21:22–24).

61:1 Christ applies these words to himself and his work of salvation (Luke 4:18).

61:10 The church as Christ's bride is given beautiful clothing (Rev. 19:8; see Eph. 5:25–27).

62:1 Righteousness and salvation come in Christ (see note on 9:7).

62:4 God's restoration of Israel prefigures Christ as husband to the church (2 Cor. 11:2; Eph. 5:25–27; Rev. 19:7–9).

63:3 The execution of punishment anticipates final punishment (Rev. 14:20; 19:15).

63:4 See notes on 13:6 and 13:9.

63:12 Past acts of salvation foreshadow the great future salvation (see note on 51:10).

64:1 God comes from heaven both at the first and second coming of Christ (John 6:33, 38, 50; Rev. 19:11).

64:11 See note on 51:17.

65:1 The resistance and rebellion of Israel fits into the plan of God to extend salvation to all nations (Rom. 10:20–21; 11:11–32).

65:9 See note on 1:9.

65:17 Ultimate blessing to God's people comes in the consummation (2 Pet. 3:13; Rev. 21:1). The new creation has come in its beginnings already in Christ (2 Cor. 5:17).

66:1 The inadequacy of a house of stone indicates by contrast the fact that God's purpose to dwell with man is fulfilled in Christ (Matt. 1:23; John 1:14; 2:19–21; Acts 7:48–50; 17:24).

66:8 The restoration of inhabitants to Jerusalem prefigures the multiplication of children of God in the church, the heavenly Jerusalem (Isa. 54:1; Gal. 4:26–27).

66:18 On the gathering of the nations, see notes on 2:2 and 11:10.

66:24 The picture of unending judgment anticipates the NT teaching about Gehenna, the lake of fire (Mark 9:48; Rev. 20:15; 21:8).

Jeremiah

Jeremiah's prophetic indictment of Israel is largely rejected, prefiguring the rejection of Christ's prophetic message to Israel (Luke 11:49–51). God's judgment on Israel for apostasy prefigures the judgment that Christ bears as substitute for the apostasy of mankind (1 John 2:2). It also prefigures final judgment (Rev. 20:11–15). Restoration from exile prefigures final restoration to God through Christ (Heb. 10:19–22).

1:2 God gives the prophecies during the time covered in 2 Kings 22–25 and 2 Chron. 34:1–36:20.

1:5 God's care from the womb prefigures the Father's relation to the Son in the incarnation (Luke 1:35) and also the calling of the apostle Paul (Gal. 1:15).

1:8 God delivers Paul from plots at Corinth (Acts 18:9–11) and elsewhere.

1:9 The firmness of the prophet amid opposition prefigures the firmness of Christ's teaching amid opposition.

1:16 God's judgment on evil and apostasy (see 2 Chron. 36:15–16) anticipates the final judgment (Rev. 20:11–15). Christ in the crucifixion bears judgment for our apostasy (1 Pet. 2:24; 1 John 2:2).

2:2 In forsaking the Lord, Israel is like an adulteress. Her unfaithfulness contrasts with the faithfulness and purity that will be worked out in the church (2 Cor. 11:2; Eph. 5:25–27; Rev. 19:7–8).

2:11 The folly of apostasy prefigures the folly of rejecting Christ, who opens the way of salvation (John 14:6; Acts 4:12).

2:13 Living water is found in Christ (John 4:10–14).

2:21 See Isa. 5:1–4.

3:1 See note on 2:2 and the connection with Deut. 24:1–4.

3:10 The pretense in Judah illustrates the hypocrisy that can infect religion (Matt. 23:13–36; see note on Isa. 58:2).

3:13 Forgiveness comes to those who acknowledge guilt, but not to those who continue to think they are righteous (Luke 18:9–14).

3:17 The gathering to Jerusalem anticipates the NT gathering to heavenly Jerusalem (Heb. 12:22–24) and the future gathering to the new Jerusalem (Rev. 21:24–26).

4:4 Circumcision of the heart comes in Christ (Col. 2:11; Heb. 8:8–13).

5:1 The lack of a righteous man is finally remedied in Christ (Acts 3:14).

5:9 See note on 1:16.

5:14 See note on 1:9.

6:1 See note on 1:16.

6:14 True peace with God can come only through the definitive overcoming of sin in Christ (John 16:33; Rom. 5:1).

102:15 See note on 22:27.

102:16 God appears in his glory climactically in Christ (John 1:14; 13:31–32; 17:1–5).

102:26 Through Christ the abiding character of God benefits us (Heb. 1:10–12).

103:4 Earlier redemptions look forward to the climactic redemption in Christ.

104:2 God's people are to praise God for his works of creation and providence, seeing in them displays of God's power and goodness. His power and goodness and blessing are supremely manifested in Christ (John 1:14; Eph. 1:3–14).

105:5 The faithfulness of God in past generations encourages Israel to respond in faithfulness. Christians look back not only on God's acts of salvation in the OT, but on the climactic salvation in Christ, which gives the ultimate basis for our trust.

106:6 The unfaithfulness of Israel in response to God is answered by Christ's obedience, and then by the obedience of God's people who follow Christ (John 14:15; Eph. 2:10).

107:2 God's acts of redemption in the OT prefigure final redemption in Christ (Col. 1:13–14).

108:6 See note on 35:3.

108:7 God is committed to subduing his enemies, and this commitment is fulfilled climactically in Christ, both in his resurrection (Heb. 2:14–15) and in his second coming (Rev. 19:11–21).

109:8 Judas is a chief example of the enemies whom God judges (Acts 1:20; see note on Ps. 69:25).

109:31 Christ, having been himself saved from death in his resurrection, is able to save us from death (John 11:25; Heb. 2:14–15; Rev. 1:18).

110:1 The Messiah is superior even to David and exercises universal rule (Matt. 22:44–45; Acts 2:34–36; 1 Cor. 15:25–28; Eph. 1:22; Heb. 1:13).

110:4 The Messiah has an eternal priesthood superior to Aaron's (Heb. 5:6; 7:21–8:2).

111:1 See note on 22:22.

111:9 Final redemption and final fulfillment of God's covenant is accomplished in Christ (2 Cor. 1:20; Heb. 7:25; 8:6–13).

112:1 Christ is the supremely righteous man (Acts 3:14), and in him we too receive the reward for righteousness (Eph. 1:3–14). See note on Ps. 1:1.

112:9 The principle of generosity continues in the NT (2 Cor. 9:9).

113:7 Attentiveness to the needy is supremely manifested in Christ (Luke 1:48–55; 6:20).

114:3 The crossing of the Red Sea (Exodus 14–15) and of the Jordan River (Joshua 3) are acts of salvation and symbolic triumphs over death that anticipate the triumph of Christ (John 10:18; 11:25; Rev. 1:18; 21:4).

115:1 God is supremely glorified and his faithfulness manifested in Christ's work (John 13:31–32; 17:1–5).

116:3 See notes on 9:13 and 13:5.

116:13 See note on 68:26.

116:15 God continues to care for his saints even after death, hinting at the hope for the resurrection (John 11:25; 1 Thess. 4:13–18).

117:1 All nations will come to praise God as a result of his salvation in Christ (Rom. 15:11), fulfilling the promise to Abraham (Gen. 12:3; see note on Ps. 22:27).

118:5 See note on 35:3.

118:6 God has expressed his commitment in Christ, giving us all the more reason to trust him (Heb. 13:6).

118:22 The Lord's exaltation of the one rejected by man is fulfilled in the exaltation of Christ (Matt. 21:42; Luke 20:17; Acts 4:11–12; Eph. 2:20–22; 1 Pet. 2:4–7).

118:26 Israel ought to recognize Jesus as one who brings the salvation of God (Matt. 23:39).

119:1 People with renewed hearts delight to obey God and learn from his word, which guides them. Christ was perfectly obedient to God (Heb. 10:7–10), and through his Spirit we are transformed into his image (Rom. 8:9–17; 2 Cor. 3:18) and become obedient servants of God. Delight in God's word anticipates delight in Christ, who is the Word of God (John 1:1).

119:11 Having God's word in the heart anticipates the new covenant (Heb. 8:10–13; 10:16–18).

120:1 See note on 35:3.

120:2 Deliverance from deceit anticipates the purity of God's word and God's work of deliverance from Satanic deceit through Christ (Rev. 12:9; see note on Ps. 64:2).

121:2 Salvation comes from God alone, anticipating the fact that Christ is the divine Savior.

122:1 Joy in experiencing the presence of God in his house anticipates the joy of the presence of God in Christ (John 1:14; 15:11; see note on Ps. 27:4).

122:6 Jerusalem as the city of God prefigures the heavenly Jerusalem (Gal. 4:26–28; Heb. 12:22–24) of which we are citizens (Phil. 3:20). Christ has given peace to his people (John 16:33; Eph. 4:3; Col. 3:15).

123:2 Mercy is received ultimately through Christ (Eph. 2:4; see note on Ps. 121:2).

124:4 See note on 42:7.

125:1 Trust in the Lord anticipates trust in Christ (Acts 16:31), who has supremely manifested God's faithfulness.

126:1 Relief from misfortune prefigures the great salvation in Christ (John 16:20–22).

127:1 The necessity of the Lord's power for temporal achievements anticipates the necessity for God, and him alone, to accomplish eternal salvation through Christ (John 15:4–5; Acts 4:12).

128:1 See note on 112:1.

128:2 Temporal blessings prefigure the eternal blessings in Christ (Eph. 1:3–14; Rev. 21:1–4).

129:1 See note on 6:2.

129:5 See note on 60:12.

130:4 Forgiveness is ultimately accomplished in Christ (Col. 1:13–14; see note on Ps. 32:1).

131:1 The psalmist's humble trust anticipates the humble trust of Christ in the Father (Matt. 11:29; Heb. 5:7–10) and the trust that Christians are to have in Christ (Acts 16:31).

132:12 The promise to David culminates in Christ the offspring of David (Matt. 1:1–16), who is both king in the line of David and priest in God's heavenly dwelling (Ps. 110:2, 4; Heb. 8:1–2).

133:1 Unity among God's people is produced in Christ and in his Spirit (Eph. 4:1–6).

134:1 Praise of God looks forward to the praises offered by Christ (Heb. 2:12), the praises of God's NT people (Eph. 5:19–20; Heb. 13:15), and the praises of the consummation (Rev. 19:1–10).

135:4 God's acts of grace and salvation to his people in the OT anticipate the climactic salvation accomplished in Christ (Luke 2:30–32; Acts 4:12).

136:4 God's works of creation, providence, and merciful deliverance show the steadfast love that has now been climactically revealed through salvation in Christ (John 1:14).

137:6 Devastation to God's holy city makes people long for future blessing and destruction to God's enemies. God's ultimate answer is found in salvation in Christ and in the last judgment (Rev. 20:11–21:8). Jerusalem prefigures the heavenly Jerusalem (Gal. 4:26–27; Heb. 12:22–24).

138:3 See note on 35:3.

138:4 See note on 22:27.

138:6 Mercy to the lowly comes in Christ (Luke 1:48–55).

139:1 Detailed knowledge and care for the psalmist anticipates God's care for us (John 10:14–16).

140:1 Deliverance from enemies prefigures Christ's deliverance from his enemies, both human and demonic (Matt. 26:46; Col. 2:15); it also prefigures our deliverance in Christ from sin, death, and Satan (Heb. 2:14–15).

140:3 See Rom. 3:13 and note on Ps. 14:1.

141:3 The need for wise speech, in prayer as well as in other circumstances, anticipates the purity of Christ's speech (John 8:43–47) and the purity that we receive from Christ (John 17:17–19). Our prayers are heard because of him (John 14:13–14; 1 John 5:14–15).

142:4 See notes on 6:2 and 22:1.

142:6 Deliverance from persecutors anticipates the deliverance of Christ from his persecutors, after he was brought low in his crucifixion and death.

143:2 Perfect righteousness is found only in Christ, who provides righteousness for those who are his (2 Cor. 5:21; see notes on Ps. 7:8 and 14:1).

144:1 See note on 18:34.

144:10 Deliverance for David prefigures final deliverance given to Christ the offspring of David. See notes on 2:6 and 18:50.

145:1 See note on 68:26.

145:8 The Lord's grace and mercy is climactically poured out in the salvation in Christ (Rom. 8:32).

146:3 Mere man cannot save, pointing to the need for Christ to be God as well as man (John 1:14).

147:5 God's greatness and goodness, in both providence and redemption, motivates praise and trust. God's goodness has now been supremely manifested in Christ (Rom. 8:32).

148:3 The created world declares the character of its maker (19:1–6), anticipating the final, even more glorious praise in the consummation (Rev. 21:1–4). The creation reflects the glory of the Son, who is mediator of creation (John 1:1–3; Col. 1:15–17).

149:4 See note on 68:26.

149:7 At Christ's second coming rebellious nations will be subdued (Rev. 19:11–21). In the meantime, gracious subduing comes through the power of the gospel (Matt. 28:18–20).

150:2 See note on 68:26. Praise, not a cry of distress, has the final position in the Psalms, anticipating the victory of Christ (Eph. 4:8) and the final abolition of suffering (Rev. 21:4).

Proverbs

Wisdom ultimately comes from God and his instruction, which anticipates the fact that Christ is the wisdom of God (1 Cor. 1:30; Col. 2:3) and that in him and his instruction we find the way of life and righteousness (John 14:6, 23–24). Through the Spirit we may walk in the right way (Gal. 5:16–26).

1:1 Solomon's wisdom prefigures the wisdom of his greater descendant, Jesus Christ (1 Cor. 1:30; see note on 1 Kings 2:6).

1:7 Wisdom is to be sought from God, anticipating that we seek wisdom from Christ, the incarnate God (John 1:14; Col. 2:3).

1:8 Listening to parents is one aspect of honoring them, which is an abiding principle (Ex. 20:12; Eph. 6:1–3). Within the church we are now to have specifically Christian instruction of children (Eph. 6:4). The archetype for this obedient listening is found in the relation of the Son of God to the Father (John 8:28–29).

1:18 The principle of just retribution is broad (Obad. 15) and is to be fulfilled ultimately in the consummation (Rev. 20:12–14).

1:19 Sin leads to death (Rom. 6:23), but in Christ there is life (John 14:6; 1 John 5:12).

1:20 The call of wisdom prefigures the call of the gospel, which contains the wisdom of God (1 Cor. 1:18–25; 2:6–10).

2:4 The diligent seeking for wisdom prefigures the need to seek the kingdom of God (Matt. 13:44).

2:13 The path of righteousness is ultimately that of Jesus Christ, the perfectly Righteous One (John 14:6). All other ways lead to destruction (Matt. 7:13–14; Acts 4:12).

2:16 Wisdom involves the avoidance both of literal adultery and of the spiritual adultery of idolatry (Ex. 34:16; Hos. 1:2; 2:1–5; 3:1–3; 2 Cor. 11:3).

2:21 Temporal blessings prefigure the blessings of eternal salvation (Eph. 1:3–14).

3:2 Length of days prefigures eternal life that comes through fellowship with Christ, who is the wisdom of God (1 Cor. 1:30).

3:5 Trust in the Lord anticipates trust in Christ, who is the Lord's salvation (Acts 16:31).

3:11 Christians as sons of God receive the Lord's discipline (Heb. 12:5–6).

3:18 The possession of the tree of life anticipates the final inheritance in the consummation (Rev. 2:7; 22:1–2).

3:34 The call for humility anticipates the role of humility in the NT (Matt. 11:29; James 4:6; 1 Pet. 5:5).

4:13 Instruction for the path of life anticipates the instruction of Christ, who is the way and the truth and the life (John 14:6).

5:3 See note on 2:16.

5:5 Ultimately Christ delivers us from death (John 11:25–26), and as one aspect of deliverance he gives wisdom and integrity of heart (1 Cor. 1:30).

6:6 Diligent work now has as its deepest motivation the hope of final satisfaction in Christ (1 Cor. 15:58).

6:24 See note on 2:16.

7:21 Smooth, deceitful talk is linked ultimately to the deceit of Satan (John 8:44–47; Rev. 12:9).

8:1 See note on 1:20.

8:22 The eternality of wisdom with God anticipates the eternality of the second person of the Trinity, who is the Word of God and who mediated creation (John 1:1–3).

8:35 Life is obtained ultimately from Christ, who is the life (John 14:6) and the wisdom of God (1 Cor. 1:30).

9:2 The invitation to feasting anticipates the spiritual food of Christ (John 6:52–58) and the future marriage supper of the Lamb (Rev. 19:9).

9:18 See note on 1:19.

10:1 On Solomon, see notes on 1:1 and 1 Kings 2:6.

10:2 Blessings on the righteous anticipate the blessings on Christ, the perfectly righteous man, and the blessings that come to those in Christ (Eph. 1:3–14).

10:12 Wisdom transforms relations with others, anticipating the NT transformation through love (John 13:34–35; 1 John 3:16–18; 4:7–21).

10:21 The blessing to others anticipates the blessing of gracious words in the church (Eph. 4:14–16; Col. 3:16; 4:6).

11:2 The value of humility anticipates the humility of Christ (Matt. 11:29) and of his people (Luke 14:11; Eph. 4:2; see note on Prov. 3:34).

11:3 See note on 2:13.

11:4 Temporary avoidance of death prefigures the promise of eternal life, based on the righteousness of Christ (John 5:24; Rom. 4:25; see note on Prov. 2:13).

12:18 The blessing of wise words anticipates the blessings of the words of Christ (John 6:63) and of his followers (Eph. 4:29; Col. 4:6).

13:4 See note on 6:6.

13:14 Christ the supremely wise One has the words of eternal life (John 6:68–69).

13:24 Christians are to train their children in Christ (Eph. 6:1–4; see note on Prov. 1:8).

14:2 True trust in Christ manifests itself in obedience (Gal. 5:13–26; James 2:14–26).

15:1 Gentle words anticipate the gentleness of Christ (Matt. 11:29). Gentleness is also to characterize his people (Gal. 5:23; Eph. 4:2, 25–29).

16:3 Only through union with Christ can we bear fruit (John 15:1–11).

16:12 The duty of kings to bring justice anticipates Christ, who is the great king and the one who brings perfect justice (Rom. 3:26; Rev. 19:11).

17:3 The Lord's discernment is perfect (Heb. 4:12–13), implying the need for purification (Heb. 9:9–14).

18:3 Temporal judgments on wickedness prefigure final judgment (Rev. 20:11–15), underlining the need for repentance.

19:1 We must be discerning about real value and seek first the kingdom of God (Matt. 6:33).

19:5 See note on 18:3.

19:11 Readiness to forgive anticipates the forgiveness of Christ (Col. 1:14) and the practice of forgiving among his people (Col. 3:13; James 1:19).

20:8 Authorities have an obligation to punish evildoing (Deut. 16:18–20; Rom. 13:1–4). In this they anticipate the final judgment of God (Rev. 20:11–15).

20:22 Vengeance belongs to God (Rom. 12:17–21). Christ himself waited patiently for vindication (1 Pet. 2:21–23).

21:3 See 1 Sam. 15:22–23 and Mic. 6:6–8. The requirement for real obedience, and ultimately for perfect obedience, is fulfilled in Christ (Heb. 10:5–10).

22:4 See note on 2:21.

23:4 Counsel against lust for money anticipates Jesus' counsel about true riches (Luke 12:22–40; 16:10–13; Eph. 5:5).

23:13 See note on 13:24.

23:19 The way of righteousness is found ultimately in Christ (John 14:6). See note on Prov. 1:8.

23:30 The warning against drunkenness is repeated in the NT, and it is complemented by a positive command to be filled with the Spirit (Eph. 5:18).

24:3 Human use of wisdom imitates God's use of wisdom (8:22–31) and anticipates Christ, who is the wisdom of God (1 Cor. 1:30) and who builds the church (Matt. 16:18).

24:19 See note on Ps. 10:1.

24:30 See note on 6:6.

25:7 The principle of humility is further developed in Christ's teaching and example (Luke 14:7–11).

25:11 See notes on 12:18 and 15:1.

25:21 The principle of doing good to enemies is further developed in Christ's example and his teaching (Matt. 5:43–48; Rom. 12:20–21).

26:3 The answer to folly and its disasters is found in seeking the wisdom of Christ (1 Cor. 1:30; Col. 2:3).

26:11 It is folly to turn back from following Christ (2 Pet. 2:22).

26:13 See note on 6:6.

26:20 The answer to words of strife is found in Christ's peace and his empowering of his people to be at peace with one another (Col. 3:13–15).

27:3 See note on 26:20.

27:11 See note on 13:24.

28:1 The boldness of the righteous anticipates the boldness of followers of Christ (2 Cor. 3:12; Phil. 1:28–30).

28:2 See note on 16:12.

28:9 God desires righteousness and obedience, which are fulfilled in Christ (2 Cor. 5:21; see note on Prov. 21:3).

29:2 See note on 16:12.

29:25 Trust in the Lord anticipates trust in Christ (see 3:5).

30:4 The inaccessibility of wisdom to man points to the need for Christ, who comes down from heaven (John 3:12–15; 6:33, 50–51).

31:3 See note on 2:16.

31:10 The excellent wife prefigures the excellence of the church, the bride of Christ (Eph. 5:25–27; Rev. 19:7–8).

Ecclesiastes

The meaninglessness, frustrations, and injustices of life "under the sun" call out for a solution from God. Christ through his suffering and resurrection provides the first installment (1 Cor. 15:22–23) of meaning, fulfillment, and new life (John 10:10), to be enjoyed fully in the consummation (Rev. 21:1–4).

1:14 The crumbling of human works makes life pointless, unless there is relief in God. Knocking down false ambitions creates a longing for the relief that will come in Christ (Matt. 11:28–30).

2:10 The fading pleasures in this life contrast with the eternal pleasures in God's presence (Ps. 16:11; John 15:11; Rev. 21:4).

2:14 Wisdom in this world contrasts with the wisdom in Christ that will last forever (1 Cor. 1:30).

2:16 What is needed is a remedy for death, and this remedy comes through Christ (1 Cor. 15:54–58).

3:11 Now in the light of revelation we can know that God's purpose is to unite all things in Christ (1 Cor. 2:9–10; Eph. 1:10).

3:12 Man need not understand everything but can live a life of joy as a servant of Christ (John 15:11), trusting that God's plans are good (Rom. 8:28).

3:17 God will execute final judgment (Rev. 20:11–21:8). But in the meantime we must endure much injustice (John 16:33).

3:20 See note on 2:16.

4:1 See note on 3:17.

4:9 The virtue of cooperation anticipates the mutual help in the body of Christ (1 Corinthians 12).

5:8 See note on 3:17.

5:10 The fleeting character of riches implies that we should invest in God's kingdom (Matt. 6:33; Luke 12:22–34).

7:2 See notes on 2:10 and 2:16.

7:15 See note on 3:17.

7:18 In the midst of much confusion and frustration about outward circumstances, we must hold fast to God. God brings ultimate salvation from vanity in Christ (Rev. 21:1–4).

8:14 See note on 3:17.

8:15 See note on 3:12.

9:5 See note on 2:16.

9:7 See note on 3:12.

9:16 The seeking for wisdom ultimately culminates in Christ, who is the wisdom of God (Matt. 12:42; 1 Cor. 1:30).

10:17 Good rulers make a notable difference in the character of a nation. The final, perfect ruler is Christ himself, who brings the kingdom of God and everlasting righteousness (Matt. 12:28; Rev. 21:1–4).

11:1 Work done for Christ will be rewarded (Col. 3:22–25).

12:1 See note on 1:14.

12:7 Reckoning with death leads to abandoning a focus on selfish achievement and pleasure and seeking God (see note on 2:16).

12:14 Reckoning with the final judgment (Rev. 20:11–21:8) changes the orientation of life. We are to follow Christ who delivers us from condemnation (Rom. 8:1) and death (John 11:25–26) and gives meaning to work in fellowship with him (1 Cor. 15:58).

Song of Solomon

The Song of Solomon depicts marital love. But after the fall merely human love is always short of God's ideal, and so we look for God's remedy in the perfect love of Christ (Eph. 5:22–33; 1 John 3:16; 4:9–10). The connection with Solomon (Song 1:1; 3:7, 9, 11; 8:11) invites us to think especially of the marriage of the king in the line of David (Ps. 45:10–15), and the kings point forward to Christ the great king, who has the church as his bride (Rev. 19:7–9, 21:9).

1:1 The marriage of the Davidic king points forward to Christ (Ps. 45:10–15; cf. Ps. 45:6–7 with Heb. 1:8–9).

1:2 Perfect love has been demonstrated in Christ (1 John 4:9–10).

1:4 Longing for intimacy prefigures the longing for intimacy with the love of Christ (1 John 4:7–21).

1:15 The beauty of the lovers anticipates the beauty of Christ and his bride (Eph. 5:26–27; Rev. 19:7–8).

2:3 Delight in love prefigures the joy in Christ (John 15:11).

2:16 The possession of the loved one prefigures the possession of Christ and the church.

3:1 See note on 1:4.

3:11 The wedding of Solomon prefigures the wedding of the Messiah (Ps. 45:10–15).

4:1 See note on 1:15.

4:13 Edenic abundance in the "garden" anticipates the abundance and satisfaction and fulfillment of the final consummation (Rev. 22:1–5).

5:1 Satisfaction with the loved one contrasts with God's dissatisfaction with the disobedience and disloyalty of Israel (Isa. 5:1–4), who was supposed to be married to the Lord (Ezek. 16:8–15). The remedy is found in Christ's salvation (Eph. 5:25–27).

5:8 See note on 1:4.

5:10 See note on 1:15.

6:9 The focus on the beloved anticipates the uniqueness of God's love for the church.

7:1 See note on 1:15.

7:6 Delight in the loved one prefigures Christ's delight in the church (Eph. 5:26–27; Rev. 19:8).

8:6 The abiding character of commitment in love prefigures the abiding character of the new covenant (John 10:27–29; Phil. 1:6; Heb. 8:8–13).

Isaiah

Isaiah prophesies exile because of Israel's unfaithfulness. But then God will bring Israel back from exile; this restoration prefigures the climactic salvation in Christ. Christ as Messiah and "servant" of the Lord will cleanse his people from sin, fill them with glory, and extend blessing to the nations. Christ fulfills prophecy in both his first coming and his second coming.

1:1 God gives the prophecies during the time covered in 2 Kings 15–20 and 2 Chronicles 26–32.

1:4 The failures of Israel precipitate the exile, and indicate the need for the messianic servant of the Lord, who will faithfully obey the Lord (42:1–4; 49:1–12).

1:9 The Lord preserves a few, a remnant for Israel. The theme of the remnant is fulfilled in Christ, who is the ultimate remnant of one, and then the remnant is expanded to include Christ's people (see Rom. 11:5 and note on Isa. 6:13).

1:18 Ultimate cleansing comes through Christ's sacrifice (Heb. 10:1–10).

2:2 Christ himself is the ultimate "house" or dwelling place of God (John 1:14; 2:19–21). Through him the church becomes a temple (1 Cor. 3:16; Eph. 2:20–22), and through Christ's exaltation the nations are drawn to him (Luke 24:47; John 12:32).

2:6 See note on 1:4.

2:11 The humbling of human pride takes place in Christ (Matt. 20:25–28; Luke 1:48–53; 1 Cor. 1:31).

3:2 The lack of adequate leaders shows the need for the Messiah as the final, perfect leader (9:6–7).

4:4 Cleansing looks forward to the forgiveness and purification in Christ (Col. 1:13–14; Heb. 10:10–14).

5:7 The lack of fruit from Israel contrasts with the fruitfulness of Christ and those in him (John 15:1–6; see also Matt. 21:33–44).

6:1 Isaiah's vision of the glory of God anticipates the glory of God in Christ (John 1:14; 12:41; Rev. 4:2–10).

6:9 The resistance of Israel to Isaiah's message anticipates resistance to the gospel (Matt. 13:11–17; Acts 28:24–28; Rom. 11:7–8).

6:13 The holy seed, the remnant, are those in Israel who remain faithful to God. Ultimately none is completely faithful except Christ, who is the final remnant (11:1; Gal. 3:16; see note on Isa. 1:9).

7:14 The prophecy concerning Immanuel (see also Gen. 3:15) is fulfilled in Jesus Christ (Matt. 1:20–23). It is related to the larger OT theme in which God brings new life and offspring to barren women (see note on Gen. 18:10).

8:13 Treating the Lord as holy culminates in the holiness of Christ (Acts 2:27) and our obligation to holiness (1 Pet. 1:15–16; 3:15).

8:14 The nation of Israel being offended by the Lord Almighty prefigures their rejection of Christ (Matt. 21:43–44; Rom. 9:31–33; 1 Pet. 2:6–8).

9:1 Jesus brings light by preaching in Galilee (Matt. 4:12–17). He is the light of the world (John 1:5, 8–9; 8:12; 9:5).

9:6 The Messiah is both human (from the line of David) and divine (see John 1:14; Col. 2:9).

9:7 The Messiah establishes his rule in justice (Rom. 3:26; Eph. 1:20–22) and peace (John 16:33).

10:22 In NT times, the remnant consists of those who believe in Christ (Rom. 11:1–10; see note on Isa. 1:9).

11:1 The Messiah is from the line of Jesse, the father of David (1 Sam. 16:1). He is filled with the Spirit (Matt. 3:16; Luke 4:18), with wisdom (Col. 2:3), and with justice (Rev. 19:11).

11:10 Christ draws the nations to himself (John 12:32; Rom. 15:12; see note on Isa. 2:2).

12:1 The song of praise for God's salvation anticipates the praise for God's salvation in Christ (Eph. 5:19–20; Heb. 2:12; 13:15; Rev. 19:1–8).

13:6 The day of the Lord is a day of judgment. Judgments within history, such as the judgment of the exile of Israel, anticipate the final judgment (1 Thess. 5:2–11; 2 Pet. 3:10–13; Rev. 20:11–21:8). Because of Christ's salvation, the day is a day for which Christians hope (Titus 2:13).

13:9 All sinners will be swept away in the ultimate judgment. We must take refuge in Christ (2 Cor. 5:21).

13:10 The darkening is a symbol of judgment, prefiguring judgment at the crucifixion (Matt. 27:45) and at the second coming (Matt. 24:29; Rev. 6:12–13; see Rev. 8:12).

14:4 The fall of Babylon to the Medes and Persians (Dan. 5:28) prefigures the final fall of Babylon the Great (Rev. 17:15–19:3) and the defeat of Satan (Luke 10:15; Rev. 12:7–9; 20:10), as well as looking back on the fall of Babel (Gen. 11:1–9).

15:1 Moab, one of the traditional enemies of Israel (Num. 22:1–6), is defeated, prefiguring final judgment on God's enemies (Rev. 20:11–15) and fulfilling Num. 21:29.

16:5 Despite her record of enmity, Moab (like other hostile nations) can find refuge in the Messiah. Christ's mercy extends to all nations (Acts 1:8; Rev. 5:9–10).

17:6 See note on 1:9.

17:7 God the Maker is seen in Christ (John 14:9) and will be seen face to face by the pure in heart (Matt. 5:8; Rev. 22:4).

18:7 The coming of the nations takes place as Christ draws them (Matt. 28:18–20; John 12:32; Acts 1:8; see note on Isa. 2:2).

19:18 Egypt, traditionally an enemy to God's people, will come to submit to God. Christ calls the nations to himself (Acts 2:10; see notes on Isa. 2:2 and 18:7).

20:6 The failure of human hopes highlights the need to hope in God through the way that he has provided in Christ (Ps. 146:3–4; John 14:6).

21:9 The fall of Babylon prefigures the defeat of all evil and the victory of Christ over evil (Col. 2:15; Rev. 14:8; 18:2; see note on Isa. 14:4).

22:11 A basic temptation is to trust in man rather than in God (Acts 4:12; 16:31; see note on Isa. 20:6).

22:13 Abandonment of hope would be appropriate only if God did not provide salvation in Christ (1 Cor. 15:19, 32).

22:22 Kingly authority in the right hands provides security. But even Eliakim (v. 20) is ultimately not up to the task (v. 25). Only the Messiah in the line of David can bear the full weight of responsibility that will bring final salvation (Matt. 1:21; see Rev. 3:7).

23:9 After destroying human pride, the Lord brings about blessing and glory to himself (v. 18). The reversal of human ambitions takes place preeminently in the death and resurrection of Christ (Phil. 2:6–11; see note on Isa. 2:11).

24:6 In fulfillment of the curse from the fall of Adam, all the earth will ultimately be judged (2 Pet. 3:10; Rev. 20:11–15). But through the work of Christ blessing comes to the godly (Isa. 24:15; Rev. 21:3–4).

25:8 God's overwhelming victory, resulting in blessing, will come at the consummation (1 Cor. 15:54; Rev. 7:17; 21:4).

26:4 Trusting in God anticipates trusting in Christ, who has accomplished climactic salvation (Phil. 4:7).

26:5 See notes on 2:11 and 23:9.

26:19 The hope for reversal of death is fulfilled in Christ's resurrection (John 11:25–26; 1 Cor. 15:46–57; Eph. 5:14).

27:1 Satan will be completely defeated (John 12:31; Rev. 20:10).

27:6 Fruitfulness is found ultimately in Christ (John 15:1–17).

28:1 See note on 2:11.

28:11 The foreign tongue is analogous to speaking in tongues in the NT (1 Cor. 14:21).

28:16 Christ is the stone, both providing a foundation to those who trust in him (Eph. 2:20–22; 1 Cor. 3:11; 1 Pet. 2:4) and becoming a cause of stumbling to those who reject him (Matt. 21:42–44; Rom. 9:31–33; 1 Pet. 2:6–8; see Ps. 118:22).

29:10 Spiritual hardness comes to part of Israel in Rom. 11:7–8 (see note on Isa. 6:9).

29:13 The stubbornness and disobedience of God's people comes to a climax with the opposition to and rejection of Jesus (Matt. 15:8–9; see Col. 2:22).

29:14 Human wisdom is confounded by the gospel (1 Cor. 1:18–25).

29:18 Jesus' healing of the blind and the deaf symbolizes the giving of spiritual light (John 9:39–41).

30:2 See note on 22:11.

30:20 Christ is the ultimate teacher who instructs us in the way of the Lord (Matt. 23:10) through the Spirit (John 16:12–15).

31:1 See note on 22:11.

31:5 The protection of Jerusalem prefigures God's protection of his people in Christ (John 10:27–29; see Isa. 40:11).

32:3 See note on 29:18.

32:15 The blessings of salvation in Christ come in two stages, in his first coming (Acts 1:8; Eph. 1:3–14) and his second coming (Rev. 21:1–22:5).

33:6 See note on 32:15.

33:14 Only perfect righteousness will remedy sin. Such righteousness is found in Christ (Rom. 3:21–26; 2 Cor. 5:21; Heb. 10:1–14; see Heb. 12:29).

34:2 God's judgment against sin and evil anticipates the final judgment (Rev. 20:11–15; see notes on Isa. 13:6; 13:9; and 15:1).

34:4 The skies disappear at the second coming (Rev. 6:13–14; 20:11).

35:3 The call for strengthening occurs in responding to God's NT discipline (Heb. 12:12).

35:5 Christ gives sight and hearing, symbolizing the giving of spiritual sight and hearing (Luke 7:20–22; Acts 26:18; see note on Isa. 29:18).

35:10 The return to Palestine in the restoration prefigures the coming to heavenly Jerusalem and the presence of God in heaven (Heb. 10:19–23; 12:22–24; Rev. 21:4).

36:1 The threat from Assyria anticipates the later threat from Babylon (39:6), which in turn illustrates all the attacks of Satan on God's people. God answers with redemption that prefigures redemption in Christ. See the parallels in 2 Kings 18:13–20:19 and 2 Chronicles 32.

36:15 See note on 2 Kings 18:30.

37:1 God is our refuge in time of distress (Ps. 46:1). We now look to Christ for salvation (Acts 4:12).

37:23 See note on 2 Kings 19:22.

38:5 See note on 2 Kings 20:5.

38:10 The ultimate remedy for death is found in the resurrection of Christ (see note on 26:19).

39:6 God's judgment of exile, which comes on account of sin (2 Kings 23:26–27; 2 Chron. 36:15–16), prefigures final judgment (Rev. 20:11–15). But through Christ we may escape condemnation (Rom. 8:1).

40:1 Comfort to Jerusalem prefigures the comfort that is found in Christ (2 Cor. 1:3–7).

40:3 John the Baptist uses these words to announce the coming of the Lord (Matt. 3:3; John 1:23) in the person of Christ (John 10:30; 14:9).

40:5 The glory of the Lord is revealed in Christ (Luke 2:32; John 1:14; 13:31–32; 17:1–5).

40:6 The fading of human life contrasts with eternal salvation in Christ (1 Pet. 1:24–25; see James 1:10–11).

40:11 Jesus is the good shepherd (John 10:11, 14).

41:17 God's mercy to the poor is manifest in Christ (Luke 4:18–19; 7:22).

42:1 The servant, the Messianic king (9:6–7), rules with justice and mercy (Matt. 12:17–21; see Matt. 3:17).

42:6 Christ the light of the world (John 8:12; 9:5) brings light to the nations (John 12:32; Acts 26:18, 23), fulfilling the promise to Abraham of blessing to the nations (see note on Gen. 12:3).

43:25 Forgiveness is found ultimately in Christ (Mark 2:7; Col. 1:14; Heb. 10:1–18).

44:3 See note on 32:15.

44:28 The restoration under Cyrus (Ezra 1) prefigures the eternal salvation in Christ in the heavenly Jerusalem (Heb. 12:22–24).

45:1 Cyrus as anointed by God prefigures the Messiah and his salvation (Luke 4:18–19).

45:23 The submission of the nations is accomplished in Christ (Phil. 2:10–11; Rev. 15:4).

ures the suffering of Christ as the sin-bearer (2 Cor. 5:21; 1 Pet. 2:22–24).

46:2 God as judge of the whole world executes judgment on the nations as well as on his own people, prefiguring final judgment (Rev. 20:11–15; see note on Jer. 1:16).

46:10 See note on Isa. 13:6.

47:1 The destruction of the Philistines, one of the long-time enemies of Israel, prefigures final judgment (Rev. 20:11–15; see note on Jer. 1:16; cf. the note on Isa. 15:1).

48:7 Chemosh, the patron god of Moab, is shown to be worthless. Destruction of false hopes and the punishment for idolatry looks forward both to the final judgment (Rev. 20:11–15) and to the gospel as a call to worship God in truth (John 4:23; 14:6).

48:47 See note on Isa. 16:5.

49:2 Deliverance for God's people includes judgment on their oppressors. Judgments within history look forward to final judgment (Rev. 20:11–15). Sin, Satan, and death, as ultimate oppressors, have already been defeated in Christ (Heb. 2:14–15; see note on Jer. 1:16).

49:9 Some verses about Edom are similar to Obadiah (Obad. 5).

49:12 See note on 25:15.

50:1 See note on Isa. 14:4.

50:8 The command to flee prefigures the command to flee the final Babylon, the city of sin (Rev. 18:4).

50:20 Forgiveness of sins is found ultimately in Christ (Col. 1:14; Heb. 10:1–14). On the remnant, see note on Isa. 6:13.

51:9 Judgment on Babylon prefigures final judgment against God's enemies (Rev. 18:5; see note on Jer. 1:16).

51:11 Judgment through the Medes is predicted also in Isa. 13:17 and comes to pass in Dan. 5:31.

52:1 See the parallel in 2 Kings 24:18–25:21.

52:3 See note on 2 Chron. 36:16.

52:7 Jeremiah's earlier prophecies about destruction (e.g., 7:14; 34:2–4) are here fulfilled, underlining the faithfulness of God and the power of his word. The words of judgment foreshadow Christ's prophecies about the destruction of Jerusalem (Matt. 24:2; Luke 19:43–44) and the prophecies of final judgment (Rev. 20:11–15). See note on 2 Chron. 36:21.

52:13 See note on 2 Kings 25:9.

52:31 See note on 2 Kings 25:27.

Lamentations

The lament over Jerusalem anticipates Christ's lamenting over the future fall of Jerusalem (Luke 19:41–44). In both cases, Jerusalem suffers for her own sins. But suffering for sin finds a remedy when Christ suffers as a substitute for the sins of his people (2 Cor. 5:21; 1 Pet. 2:22–24).

1:5 God shows his justice in judging the sins of Jerusalem. He prefigures the manifestation of justice in the last judgment (Rev. 20:11–15) and in the work of Christ.

2:14 On false prophets, see note on Jer. 14:14.

2:17 God's fulfillment of prophecy underlines his faithfulness and the power of his word. His faithfulness is supremely manifested in the suffering and vindication of Christ (see note on Ps. 105:5).

3:14 The sufferings of the prophet prefigure the sufferings of Christ (Matt. 27:27–31, 39–44).

3:26 Even in the midst of disaster and pain there is final hope for the salvation of the Lord. This hope has come to fruition in the salvation that Christ has accomplished (Matt. 1:21), and we now wait for its consummation (Rom. 8:18–25).

4:11 The pouring out of God's wrath on Jerusalem prefigures the wrath poured out on Christ as sin-bearer (Gal. 3:13), the wrath on Jerusalem in its second destruction (Luke 21:22–24), and the wrath in the final judgment (Rev. 20:11–15).

5:21 Restoration is promised to Jerusalem after 70 years of exile (Jer. 25:11–12; 29:10–14). The restoration prefigures final salvation in Christ (Col. 1:13–14; see note on Jer. 29:14).

Ezekiel

God judges Israel's apostasy through the exile. Israel suffers for her own sin, and in so doing anticipates God's final judgment against sin (Rev. 20:11–15). But the suffering also anticipates the suffering of Christ for the sins of others. The subsequent blessing in restoration prefigures the blessings of eternal salvation in Christ (Eph. 1:3–14).

1:26 God appears in human form, anticipating the incarnation of Christ and his glory (John 1:14; Rev. 1:12–16).

2:3 The resistance to Ezekiel as a prophet prefigures the resistance to Christ as final prophet (Luke 11:49–51; see note on Jer. 1:9).

2:8 The picture of eating, symbolizing an appropriation of the words of God, anticipates Rev. 10:9–11.

3:8 See note on Jer. 1:9.

3:12 The empowering by the Spirit prefigures the role of the Spirit in Christ's prophetic ministry (Luke 4:18), and then his empowering of gospel proclamation (Acts 1:8).

3:17 Ezekiel has a responsibility for faithfulness analogous to the responsibility in gospel proclamation (2 Cor. 2:14–17; 3:5; 4:2).

4:4 Ezekiel's identification with the punishment of the people prefigures Christ's bearing the sins of his people (2 Cor. 5:21; 1 Pet. 2:22–24).

5:1 The prophet's own body becomes a symbol for the sinful people. It prefigures Christ's identification with the sins of his people (2 Cor. 5:21).

5:2 The casting off of much of the hair leaves a remnant, anticipating the remnant in the NT (Rom. 9:27; 11:5; see note on Isa. 6:13).

5:8 Judgment against sin prefigures the final judgment (Rev. 20:11–15).

5:13 Knowing that "I am the LORD"—an important theme in Ezekiel—anticipates the deeper knowledge of God given in Christ (John 14:9; 17:1–5).

6:4 God's judgment makes plain the worthlessness of idols. God destroys false hopes to make plain that Christ is the one, God-ordained way of salvation (John 14:6; Acts 4:12; see notes on Isa. 46:1; Jer. 48:7).

7:2 See note on 5:8.

8:2 See note on 1:26.

8:3 God judges idolatry, making plain that the true God alone is the source of salvation (see note on 6:4).

9:4 Mercy comes to those who follow God's ways, prefiguring the mercy in Christ. The mark prefigures the seal of the Holy Spirit and of the name of God, guaranteeing our salvation (2 Cor. 1:22; Eph. 1:13; Rev. 7:2–8; 14:1–3).

9:8 On the remnant, see notes on Isa. 1:9 and 6:13.

10:18 The departure of God's presence from the temple is one aspect of judgment. It contrasts with the dwelling of God in the temple, which prefigures the coming of God to dwell with us in Christ (Matt. 1:23).

11:13 On the remnant, see notes on Isa. 1:9 and 6:13.

11:19 The promise of a new heart, reiterated in 36:25, is connected to the new covenant that will come in Christ (Jer. 31:31–34; Heb. 8:8–13; 10:16–18; see note on Jer. 31:31).

12:11 On the exile as judgment, see note on Isa. 39:6.

13:2 The false prophets prefigure Christ's opponents and false teachers in the church (2 Pet. 2:1–3; see note on Jer. 14:14).

13:10 The religious leaders opposing Jesus are like whitewashed tombs (Matt. 23:27). On false peace, see note on Jer. 6:14.

14:3 God does not reveal himself to the rebellious. The lack of understanding anticipates the lack of understanding of Jesus' teaching (Matt. 13:10–17).

14:6 On repentance, see note on Jer. 18:11.

14:9 The deception that falls on the rebellious anticipates the deception on those who refuse the truth of the gospel (2 Thess. 2:10–12).

15:2 Israel is a vine without fruit. See note on Isa. 5:7.

16:8 The faithlessness of Israel contrasts with the faithfulness of the bride of Christ (Eph. 5:25–27; Rev. 19:7–8). The church also is tempted to go astray from her covenant with Christ (2 Cor. 11:2–3). See note on Jer. 2:2.

17:13 The penalty for breaking a covenant with a human king shows by analogy the seriousness of breaking the covenant with God (Heb. 10:29–31).

17:22 After destruction comes a new beginning, symbolizing the kingdom of Christ and its growth to fill the nations (see Isa. 11:1).

18:4 God will execute justice. The judgments within history look forward to the final judgment, when perfect justice will come (Rev. 20:11–21:8).

18:9 The granting of life to the righteous in the short run prefigures the granting of eternal life. The gift of eternal life comes only through perfect righteousness, the righteousness of Jesus Christ (Rom. 3:23–26; 6:23).

19:9 On the exile as judgment, see note on Isa. 39:6.

20:3 See note on 14:3.

20:8 The repeated rebellion of Israel calls for judgment. God must also be faithful to his name in rescuing them. Judgment and mercy are finally both achieved in Christ (Rom. 3:25–26).

20:11 See note on Lev. 18:5.

21:31 Fire and wrath anticipate the final judgment (Rev. 20:11–15). The sword (Ezek. 21:28) anticipates the sword of Christ in final judgment (Rev. 19:15; see Heb. 4:12–13).

22:15 On the exile, see note on Isa. 39:6.

22:20 The melting process prefigures the coming of the Messiah as refiner (Mal. 3:3).

22:30 No man is adequate to the task of redemption except Jesus Christ (1 Tim. 2:5–6).

23:3 See note on 16:8.

23:22 Any lover other than the true God will be found to be treacherous, resulting in judgment. The failure of other gods points to the one way of salvation through the true God (John 14:6; Acts 4:12).

23:32 On the cup of wrath, see note on Jer. 25:15.

24:8 The coming of God's wrath prefigures his wrath in the final judgment (Rev. 20:11–15).

24:21 The destruction of the temple destroys false pride and confidence. By contrast it points to confidence in God alone for salvation (John 2:19–21; Acts 4:12).

25:2 God's judgment against Israel's traditional enemies prefigures future judgments against enemies, including the final judgment (Rev. 20:11–15).

26:4 The completeness of destruction indicates God's zeal to remove evil completely. His zeal is manifested both in the death of Christ and in the last judgment (Rev. 20:11–15).

27:9 The fall of Tyre with its riches prefigures the fall of Babylon the prostitute (Rev. 18:19).

28:13 The fall of Tyre is reminiscent of the fall of Adam (Gen. 3:1–19), and some think it is also reminiscent of the fall of Satan. The proud beauty of Tyre also prefigures the beauty of Babylon (Rev. 17:4), in contrast with the true beauty of the new Jerusalem (Rev. 21:18–21).

29:3 Egypt, another traditional enemy of God and God's people, is judged by God, prefiguring the last judgment. By depicting Egypt as a dragon, Ezekiel makes the connection between her and the defeat of Satan the dragon (Rev. 12:3–17).

29:13 God shows mercy to Egypt, in analogy with the mercy shown to Israel in bringing them back from exile. This mercy anticipates the mercy in Christ (Rom. 5:6–11).

30:3 On the day of the Lord, see note on Isa. 13:6.

31:14 Human pride is put down (see note on Isa. 2:11), anticipating the humbling of pride through salvation in Christ (1 Cor. 1:26–31).

32:2 On Egypt as a dragon, see note on 29:3.

32:7 The darkening of light prefigures the darkening at the second coming of Christ (Matt. 24:29–31; Rev. 6:12–13).

32:21 An answer to the powerlessness and humiliation of death is found only in Christ and his resurrection (John 11:25–26; 1 Cor. 15:42–58).

33:2 On the watchman, see note on 3:17.

33:11 The invitation to repent anticipates the gospel invitation (2 Pet. 3:9; Acts 2:38–41).

33:16 See note on 18:9.

33:17 See note on 18:4.

33:31 Hypocrisy among the people anticipates the hypocrisy that Christ confronts (Matt. 23:13–36; see Jer. 7:11).

34:2 The false shepherds in Israel contrast with God, who is the true shepherd through Christ (vv. 11–31; Isa. 40:11; Luke 15:1–7; John 10:11, 14).

34:23 God is shepherd in connection with David, prefiguring the fact that Christ is both God and man, and that as man he is the king in the line of David (Matt. 1:1–16).

35:5 See note on 25:2.

35:6 The principle of retribution manifests God's justice and anticipates the final judgment (Rev. 20:11–15; see note on Prov. 1:18).

36:10 The return from exile prefigures God's climactic redemption from sin through Christ (Col. 1:13–14; see note on Isa. 39:6).

36:22 The Lord vindicates his name in Christ when he shows holiness and justice in punishing sins and mercy in saving the sinner (Rom. 3:23–26).

36:25 Cleansing from sins is accomplished in Christ (Col. 1:14; Heb. 9:23–28).

36:27 The promise of the Holy Spirit is fulfilled at Pentecost (Acts 2:1–21) and in the giving of the Spirit to those who believe in Christ (Rom. 8:9–17).

37:5 The vision of new life through the Spirit has a partial fulfillment in the return from exile (37:12). It prefigures the giving of resurrection life through the Spirit of Christ (John 11:25–26; Rom. 8:9–17; Col. 3:1–4).

37:24 See note on 34:23.

38:2 Gog and Magog attack, pointing to the final war between God and his enemies in Rev. 20:8–10.

38:22 Fire comes from heaven in Rev. 20:9.

39:17 The sacrificial feast is depicted in Rev. 19:17–21.

39:29 On the pouring out of the Spirit, see notes on 36:27 and 37:5.

40:2 The vision of a new temple builds on the earlier passages about the tabernacle of Moses (Exodus 25–40) and the temple of Solomon (1 Kings 5–8). Ezekiel's temple is even more glorious, pointing forward to several realities: (1) the glory in which God dwells with man in Christ (John 1:14); (2) Christ's body that is the temple (John 2:19–21); (3) the church as a temple (1 Cor. 3:16; Eph. 2:20–22; 1 Pet. 2:5); (4) the body of the individual believer (1 Cor. 6:19); and (5) the heavenly Jerusalem (Rev. 21:9–22:5).

40:6 The gateways give access to the presence of God from all four directions. This access prefigures the access to God through Christ, an access extending to all nations (Heb. 10:19–22; Rev. 21:12–13, 24–26).

40:38 The burnt offering, described in Lev. 1:1–17; 6:8–13, prefigures the sacrifice of Christ (Eph. 5:2; Heb. 10:5–10; and note on Lev. 1:9). God gives the vision to Israel (Ezek. 43:10–11) using the symbolism belonging to the Mosaic covenant, but all the symbolism finds its culmination and fulfillment in Christ (Heb. 8:8–13).

40:45 The priesthood descending from Aaron is described in Leviticus 9–10; 21–22; Numbers 3–4; 8; 17–18; and other passages. This priesthood is a shadow and a symbol, to be fulfilled in the eternal priesthood of Christ (Heb. 7:23–8:6).

41:2 The spaciousness prefigures free access to God through Christ (see notes on 40:2 and 40:6).

42:13 The eating of the holy food prefigures spiritual food in Christ (John 6:53–58; see note on Ezek. 40:45).

43:3 The coming of the glory of the Lord, as described in chapter 1, indicates the blessing of his presence, giving a remedy for God's departure in chapter 10. The presence of God comes to the church as a temple through the Holy Spirit (Acts 2:2–4; 1 Cor. 3:16).

43:18 On the burnt offering, see note on 40:38.

44:4 See note on 43:3.

44:15 The holiness required to serve God prefigures the holiness of Christ (Heb. 7:23–8:6; 9:11–28; see note on Ezek. 40:45).

45:1 The expansion of holy area prefigures the holiness of the church, which is an international community (Rev. 5:9–10), and the holiness of the new heaven and the new earth (Rev. 21:1–22:5).

45:4 On the priests, see note on 40:45.

45:7 The princes as leaders of Israel belong to the symbolism of the Mosaic order that God uses in this vision (see notes on 40:2 and 40:38). They point forward to the leaders in the church (Eph. 4:11; 1 Pet. 5:1–5) and in the new heaven and new earth. Christ is the supreme Lord over all (Eph. 1:19–23). Fulfillment in Christ transforms the nature of worship and so displaces the forms of worship belonging to the shadows of the Mosaic order (Heb. 8:1–9:14).

45:18 Permanent purification has now been accomplished through the offering of Jesus Christ once and for all (Heb. 10:1–14).

45:21 Christ is our Passover lamb (1 Cor. 5:7; see notes on Ezek. 40:38 and 40:45).

46:2 On the prince and the priests, see notes on 40:45 and 45:7.

47:1 Refreshing water from the presence of God (see Ps. 46:4) prefigures the living water that Christ offers through the Spirit (John 4:10, 13–14; 6:35; 7:37–39; Rev. 22:1–2).

47:12 The trees prefigure the tree of life as a symbol of abundant blessing from God (Rev. 22:2).

47:13 The inheritance of the land with its boundaries picks up the theme from Numbers 34, Joshua 14–19, and other passages. The land prefigures the new heaven and the new earth (Heb. 11:13–16; Rev. 21:1).

47:22 The inclusion of foreigners prefigures the inclusion of the Gentiles in the blessing of the gospel and the inheritance from Abraham (Gal. 3:9, 14, 26–29; 4:28–31).

48:1 See note on 47:13.

48:21 God dwells consummately in the midst of his people in Rev. 21:1–22:5. See notes on Ezek. 40:2 and 40:38.

48:31 The gates are found in Rev. 21:12–13 (see notes on Ezek. 40:2 and 40:6).

Daniel

Daniel and his friends exemplify the conflict between the kingdom of God and the kingdoms of this world, a conflict that will come to its climax in Christ, in both his first coming and his second coming.

1:5 Daniel and his friends resist the temptation to assimilate to the idolatrous culture in which they are immersed. Christ was in this world but did not yield to temptation (Matt. 4:1–11; Heb. 4:15), and we are called to follow in his steps (John 17:14–19; 1 Pet. 2:21).

1:17 Daniel is like Joseph (Gen. 40:8; 41:39) and prefigures the wisdom of Christ (1 Cor. 1:30; Col. 2:3).

2:11 God by answering Daniel shows that he is the true God, and anticipates the time when God's dwelling will be in the flesh (John 1:14).

2:24 Daniel also saves the lives of others, prefiguring Christ who saves us (Heb. 2:14–15).

2:44 In the days of the fourth kingdom, the Roman Empire, the kingdom of God is established through Christ (Matt. 3:2), especially through his resurrection (Matt. 28:18; Eph. 1:19–23).

3:6 The forcing of false worship anticipates the situation with the beast (Rev. 13:12–15) and the persecution against the church (Acts 8:1–3).

3:18 The willingness to die for the faith anticipates Christ's willingness to die (John 10:17–18) and the willingness of Christians to be martyrs (Acts 7:55–60; Rev. 6:9; 12:11).

3:25 The one like "a son of the gods" is the preincarnate Christ (cf. Rev. 1:12–16). Christ identifies with the persecution of the Jews and in his power protects them.

3:29 The resurrection-like deliverance from death results in the spread of the message about the true God. The message prefigures the message of the gospel announcing the resurrection of Christ.

4:9 Daniel's wisdom and ability to interpret dreams is like that of Joseph (Gen. 41:38). Daniel serves to mediate divine wisdom to Nebuchadnezzar, and so prefigures the unique mediation of Christ, who is the wisdom of God (1 Cor. 1:30; Col. 2:3).

4:30 Nebuchadnezzar is humbled by God's judgment. The putting down of human pride anticipates the putting down of pride when God brings salvation in Christ (1 Cor. 1:26–31; see Dan. 4:37).

5:4 The judgment on idolatry anticipates the last judgment (Rev. 20:11–15) and demonstrates the sovereignty of God.

5:11 See note on 4:9.

5:20 See note on 4:30.

6:7 See note on 3:6.

6:23 The resurrection-like deliverance of Daniel prefigures the resurrection of Christ.

6:26 The message concerning the true God is spread, prefiguring the spread of the gospel, which announces the resurrection of Christ (see note on 3:29).

7:3 The four beasts are four kingdoms (v. 17), corresponding to the four kingdoms of 2:36–40. Features of the four beasts are combined in the beast of Rev. 13:1–8, which represents a final opponent of God's people.

7:9 Features of this appearance of God reappear in Christ (Rev. 1:12–16), who is God in the flesh (John 1:14).

7:13 Jesus is the Son of Man (Matt. 24:30; 26:64).

7:14 The dominion of Christ is associated with his resurrection and ascension (Matt. 28:18; Acts 2:33–35; Eph. 1:20–22) and continues until the consummation (Rev. 22:1).

7:21 The war against the saints is described in Rev. 11:7; 13:7–10.

7:25 The period of "a time, times, and half a time" (also in 12:7) is echoed in the half week in 9:27 and is the time of persecution of the church in Rev. 11:2, 3, 11; 12:6, 14. See also Dan. 8:14 and 12:11, 12 for possible further echoes.

8:10 The little horn, Antiochus Epiphanes, persecuted the faithful Jews and profaned the temple (168 B.C.; see 8:23). He prefigures the man of lawlessness, the final Antichrist, the great opponent of God's people (2 Thess. 2:3–4, 7–12; Rev. 12:4).

9:2 See 2 Chron. 36:21; Jer. 25:11–12; and 29:10.

9:9 Definitive forgiveness comes only in Christ (Rom. 4:6–8; Col. 1:14).

9:24 Atonement comes in Christ (Heb. 7:23–8:6; 10:1–14). Everlasting righteousness comes both with Christ the perfectly Righteous Savior (Acts 3:14) and with the righteousness that he gives to his people in justification (Rom. 3:23–26; 2 Cor. 5:21).

10:6 The glorious appearance, reflecting the glory of God, prefigures the glory of Christ in Rev. 1:12–16.

10:12 Daniel's intercession for Israel prefigures the intercession of Christ the great high priest (Heb. 7:25).

10:13 The angelic war prefigures the spiritual war in Revelation (Rev. 12:7–9).

11:2 Tumults and wars on earth continue until the end (Matt. 24:6–7; Rev. 6:2–4) and remind us of spiritual war, part of which is invisible (Rev. 12:7–9). In the midst of tumult, Christ alone provides true peace (John 16:33; cf. Phil. 4:6–7; 1 Thess. 3:4).

11:31 See note on 8:10.

11:35 The refining process looks forward to God's refining of the church (Rom. 5:3–5; Heb. 12:3–11; 1 Pet. 1:6–7).

11:36 The king is either the man of lawlessness of 2 Thess. 2:3–4 or a foreshadowing of him.

12:1 The book is identified as the book of life of the Lamb that was slain (Eph. 1:4; Rev. 13:8; 17:8), guaranteeing the salvation of those who belong to Christ.

12:2 Life and final judgment are controlled by the power of Christ (John 5:27–29).

12:3 The brightness looks forward to the brightness in the new Jerusalem (Rev. 21:22–27; 22:5).

Hosea

The unfaithfulness of Israel calls for a permanent remedy, which will come in the faithfulness of Christ to the Father and the faithfulness that Christ then works through the Spirit in his people. God's love for Israel foreshadows Christ's love for the church (Eph. 5:25–27).

1:1 God gives the prophecies during the time covered in 2 Kings 15–20 and 2 Chronicles 26–32.

1:2 Israel's spiritual adultery, indicated also in Jeremiah (see note on Jer. 2:2), is a shocking rebellion that must lead to judgment on God's part (Hos. 1:4). Yet God will eventually bring a remedy in Christ (1:10; Rom. 9:26). Christ prepares the church as a faithful bride (Eph. 5:25–27).

1:10 In faithfulness to the promise to Abraham (Gen. 13:16; 22:17) God will remember Israel. The remembrance takes surprising form in that it includes Gentiles (Rom. 9:25–26) as well as Jews (Rom. 11:25–32).

2:3 God in justice brings judgment on unfaithfulness. His justice is climactically manifested in Christ, through whom we escape condemnation (Rom. 3:23–26; 8:1), and is manifested in the final judgment (Rev. 20:11–21:8).

2:14 Punishment and restoration for Israel prefigure the punishment and resurrection of Christ, the true Israel (Rom. 4:25).

2:23 See note on 1:10.

3:1 God's love for the wayward prefigures his love for sinners in Christ (Rom. 5:6–11).

4:5 On false prophets, see note on Jer. 14:14.

4:10 False gods are not able to satisfy. Their failure shows the folly of false worship and points by contrast to the one true God, and ultimately to his way of salvation in Christ (John 14:6).

5:4 The lack of knowledge of God points by contrast to true knowledge, which is to be found ultimately in Christ (John 14:7; 17:3).

5:14 See note on 2:3.

6:2 The invitation to come to the Lord prefigures the invitation of the gospel (Acts 16:31; 17:30–31). The granting of life on the third day prefigures the resurrection of Christ as the source of life to his people (Col. 3:1–4).

6:3 God is known truly in Christ (Matt. 11:27; John 14:6; 17:3).

6:6 Jesus teaches the centrality of steadfast love (Matt. 9:13; 12:7).

7:5 The king and princes participate in sin with the people, pointing to the need for a faithful king. Christ is the faithful king in the line of David (Matt. 1:1–16).

8:13 God in his justice punishes. Since the people have broken his covenant, he reverses the deliverance from Egypt that was an aspect of covenantal redemption. A greater redemption is needed, which is to be found in Christ (Matt. 2:15; Heb. 8:8–13).

9:10 Israel's present apostasy repeats the old apostasy at Baal-peor (Num. 25:1–5), pointing to the need for a permanent remedy and a permanent change of heart, which will come in Christ (Heb. 8:8–13).

10:6 See note on 4:10.

10:8 Fear of God's wrath prefigures the fearful character of the final judgment (Luke 23:30; Rev. 6:16).

10:12 Full righteousness comes in Christ (Rom. 3:23–26; 8:1–4).

11:1 Israel, labeled God's "son" in Ex. 4:22 (see Deut. 8:5), came out of Egypt in the exodus (Exodus 14). The movement of Israel prefigures the movement of Christ (Matt. 2:15), who is the faithful Son (Matt. 3:17), whereas Israel as son repeatedly failed (Hos. 11:2).

11:11 On the restoration from exile, see note on Isa. 35:10.

12:2 God's punishments are the product of his justice, prefiguring the justice of final judgment (Rev. 20:11–15). Such demonstrations of justice make plain the need for pardon through the propitiation of Christ (1 John 2:1–2).

13:14 The threat of death as punishment for sin (Rom. 6:23) is finally answered through the resurrection of Christ (John 11:25–26; 1 Cor. 15:55–57; Heb. 2:14–15).

14:1 The command to repent anticipates the command to repent in the gospel (Acts 2:38).

14:5 The promise of blessing prefigures the blessings of salvation in Christ (Eph. 1:3–14; see note on Isa. 27:6).

Joel

The day of the Lord, the day of God's coming (see note on Isa. 13:6), brings judgment on sin but also may include blessing. Both aspects are fulfilled in both the first coming and the second coming of Christ.

1:4 God sent a locust plague on the Egyptians during the time of Moses (Ex. 10:1–20). But the plague in Joel's day comes on God's own people because of their sins (see Deut. 28:38). It shows the desperate need for forgiveness in Christ and prefigures the locust plague preceding the judgment of the second coming (Rev. 9:1–11).

1:13 See note on 2:12.

1:15 The day of the Lord, the day when God appears, is a day of judgment (see note on Isa. 13:6).

2:12 The call to repent anticipates the gospel call to repent (Acts 2:38).

2:18 Christ welcomes repentant sinners (Luke 5:32; 15:7).

2:28 The climactic blessing is the pouring out of the Spirit, accomplished at Pentecost (Acts 2:16–21).

2:32 NT preaching invites listeners to be saved by the name of Christ (Acts 2:38–41; Rom. 10:13; see Acts 4:12).

3:13 At the second coming God executes judgment (Rev. 14:14–20).

3:15 The light is darkened at the second coming as part of God's judgment (Matt. 24:29–31; Rev. 6:12; see Rev. 8:12). The darkening at the crucifixion also indicates judgment (Matt. 27:45).

3:17 The holiness of Jerusalem is perfected in the consummation (Rev. 21:27).

Amos

God comes to Israel with both judgment for sin and promises of restoration. The judgment and restoration anticipate the crucifixion and resurrection of Christ, as well as the final judgment (Rev. 20:11–15). The demand for righteousness is fulfilled in the righteousness of Christ (Rom. 8:1–4).

1:1 God gives the prophecies during the time covered in 2 Kings 14:23–15:7.

1:2 The power of God's word in judgment anticipates the power of Christ's word, both in his first coming and in his second coming (John 12:48–50; Rev. 19:15, 21).

1:3 Damascus, the capital of Syria, is judged, prefiguring final judgment on God's enemies (Rev. 20:11–15). On the display of God's justice in judgment, see notes on Lam. 1:5 and Ezek. 18:4.

2:4 God does not overlook the sins of his own people, but calls them to account just as he did the other nations (1:3–2:3). He shows his impartiality (Rom. 2:11–16). All are subject to curse for their disobedience, and escape is found only in Christ (Gal. 3:13–14; Rom. 3:9–31).

3:2 Those with greater privileges are liable to greater punishment (Luke 12:48). The principle is shown in the guilt that comes to those Jews who reject Christ (Matt. 11:20–24; John 15:22–25).

3:8 See note on 1:2.

3:10 The demand for righteousness is an integral part of God's law. Righteousness is to be fulfilled in the righteousness of Christ (Rom. 1:17; 2 Cor. 5:21) and in his followers (Rom. 8:1–4).

3:12 On the remnant, see note on Isa. 1:9 and 6:13.

4:6 Stubbornness, like the stubbornness of Pharaoh in the exodus, increases guilt. Stubbornness characterizes Israel's history, and comes to a climax in the rejection of Christ (Acts 7:51–53; see note on Isa. 29:13). The judgments on Israel were prophesied in Deut. 28:15–68.

5:18 People hoped that the day of the Lord would mean judgment against Israel's enemies. But it involves judgment on sinners universally, including Israel. See notes on 2:4; Isa. 13:6; and 13:9.

5:27 The exile of the northern kingdom to lands beyond Damascus and then the southern kingdom to Babylon prefigures final judgment.

6:1 Pride and self-confidence are judged by God, anticipating the judgment against human pride in the gospel (1 Cor. 1:26–31).

7:3 The Lord in mercy does not simply destroy, but refines his people. His mercy anticipates the mercy to be manifested in Christ (Matt. 9:27).

8:9 The darkening is a symbol of judgment, prefiguring the judgment at the crucifixion (Matt. 27:45) and at the second coming (Matt. 24:29–31; Rev. 6:12; see Joel 3:15 and Rev. 8:12).

9:1 The lack of escape prefigures the universality of the last judgment (Rev. 20:11–15).

9:8 On the remnant, see 3:12 and notes on Isa. 1:9 and 6:13.

9:11 The house of David is raised up when Christ is raised.

9:12 When Christ is raised, the nations (Gentiles) become included in God's blessings, in fulfillment of the promise to Abraham (Gen. 12:3).

Obadiah

The judgment against Edom, a traditional enemy of Israel, contributes to the blessing of God's people. The judgment and vindication prefigure the vindication of Christ and the judgments against his enemies, both in his first coming and in his second coming.

3 God judges human pride, anticipating the gospel's judgment on pride (1 Cor. 1:26–31).

10 Those who attack God's people will ultimately be destroyed in the last judgment (Rev. 20:11–15).

15 On the day of the Lord, see note on Isa. 13:6. On the principle of just retribution, see note on Prov. 1:18.

Jonah

Jonah's rescue from death prefigures the resurrection of Christ (Matt. 12:39–40). The repentance of the Ninevites prefigures the repentance of Gentiles who respond to the gospel (Matt. 28:18–20; Luke 24:47).

1:15 The saving of mariners through the sacrifice of Jonah prefigures the salvation of all nations through the death of Christ (1 John 2:2).

1:17 Jonah is under the sea, symbolizing the realm of death. His state prefigures the death of Christ (Matt. 12:40).

2:6 Jonah's rescue from death prefigures the resurrection of Christ from the dead (Matt. 12:40).

3:5 Gentiles repent in response to the preaching of Jonah, who figuratively has been raised from the "death" of the belly of the fish. Gentiles repent in response to the preaching of the resurrection of Christ (Matt. 28:18–20).

3:10 The repentance of Gentiles contrasts with the repeated lack of repentance on the part of Israel (Matt. 12:41; 21:43).

4:11 God's mercy is shown abundantly in the gospel and in the salvation of Gentiles who deserve nothing (Rom. 9:30–31; 11:30).

Micah

God pronounces judgment on Israel, prefiguring final judgment (Rev. 20:11–15) and the judgment that fell on Christ (Gal. 3:13). He promises blessing through the Messiah, anticipating the blessings of salvation in Christ (Eph. 1:3–14).

1:1 God gives the prophecies during the time covered in 2 Kings 16–20 and 2 Chronicles 27–32.

1:5 God in justice cannot overlook the sins of his people. Punishment prefigures the punishment of the last judgment (Rev. 20:11–15) and the substitutionary punishment that Christ bore for his people (1 Pet. 2:24).

2:3 On the judgment of human pride, see notes on Isa. 2:11; Ezek. 31:14; and Amos 6:1.

2:12 On the remnant, see notes on Isa. 1:9 and 6:13.

3:5 On false prophets, see note on Jer. 14:14.

3:12 On the destruction of the holy city, see note on Ps. 74:3.

4:1 The exaltation of the name of God is accomplished in Christ (see note on Isa. 2:2).

5:2 The Messiah is to be born in Bethlehem (Matt. 2:1–6).

5:8 On the remnant, see 2:12 and notes on Isa. 1:9 and 6:13.

6:2 Israel does not escape judgment for her sins. This judgment prefigures the justice and thoroughness of final judgment (Rev. 20:11–15).

6:8 Sacrifices cannot replace the need for justice and kindness. The focus on real righteousness anticipates Jesus' teaching (Matt. 5:23–24; 9:13; 15:10–20) and is fulfilled in Jesus' own righteousness (Acts 3:14; Rom. 8:1–4).

7:6 The family treachery in Israel anticipates the family treachery from resistance to Christ (Matt. 10:35–36).

7:18 Pardon is accomplished in Christ (Rom. 3:23–26; 1 John 2:2). On the remnant, see notes on Isa. 1:9 and 6:13.

Nahum

Judgment on Nineveh, a traditional enemy of God's people, prefigures final judgment and final release from oppression (Rev. 20:11–21:8).

1:15 The good news of deliverance from the oppression of Nineveh prefigures the good news of eternal deliverance from sin and death in the gospel (Isa. 52:7; Mark 1:1; Rom. 1:1).

2:3 The attack and destruction of Nineveh prefigures God's war through Christ against his ultimate enemies (Matt. 12:29; Luke 10:17–19; John 12:31; Rev. 19:11–21; 20:7–10).

3:4 Nineveh's punishment prefigures the punishment for the idolatrous seduction of Babylon the prostitute (Rev. 17:1–6; 18:1–3).

Habakkuk

God's use of a wicked nation to accomplish his righteousness foreshadows the use of wicked opponents to accomplish his purpose in the crucifixion of Christ.

1:4 The perversion of justice in the triumph of the wicked prefigures the temporary triumph of the wicked in the crucifixion of Christ.

1:5 The unbelievability of God's use of a wicked people, the Chaldeans, prefigures the unbelievability of the way in which the injustice of the crucifixion of Christ is used by God for salvation.

1:13 In the crucifixion of Christ the wicked leaders swallowed up Christ the righteous one.

2:4 The righteous person trusts in God; he believes that God's promises are true and that he will bring to pass his righteous purposes. This trust anticipates trust in Christ (Rom. 1:17; Gal. 3:11; Heb. 10:37–38), in whom the promises of God are fulfilled (2 Cor. 1:20).

2:8 On the principle of just retribution, see note on Prov. 1:18.

2:16 On the cup of God's wrath, see note on Jer. 25:15.

3:13 God appears to bring salvation to his people and to the anointed king. Salvation comes when God appears in Christ (John 1:14; 14:9), when Christ the anointed king is saved from death in his resurrection, and when his people are saved through Christ.

Zephaniah

Judgments on evil people anticipate the final judgment (Rev. 20:11–15) and indicate the necessity of Christ's work and sin-bearing in order to save us from judgment (see note on Isa. 13:9).

1:1 God gives the prophecies during the time covered in 2 Kings 22–23 and 2 Chronicles 34–35.

1:2 God in his holiness is zealous to eliminate all evil. His commitment anticipates the final judgment and renewal of the consummation (2 Pet. 3:10–13; Rev. 21:1).

1:7 On the day of the Lord, see note on Isa. 13:6.

2:3 The call for humility prefigures the gospel call to repent and turn to the Lord (Acts 2:38), and the call to avoid the coming wrath (Acts 17:30–31).

2:9 On the remnant, see notes on Isa. 1:9 and 6:13.

2:10 On the punishment of pride, see note on Ezek. 31:14.

3:15 The removal of judgments and curse comes with Christ (Rom. 8:1; Gal. 3:13–14). Christ is the Lord in our midst (Matt. 1:23; John 1:14) and now indwells the church through the Spirit (John 14:20; Rom. 8:9–10).

Haggai

The rebuilding of the temple prefigures the building of NT temples: the church (1 Cor. 3:16; Eph. 2:20–22) and the new Jerusalem (Rev. 21:9–22:5).

1:1 God gives the prophecies during the time covered in Ezra 5–6 (see Ezra 5:1 and 6:14).

1:2 The house of the Lord symbolizes his presence and looks forward to Christ as temple (John 1:14; 2:19–21), the church as temple (1 Cor. 3:16; Eph. 2:20–22), and the dwelling of God in the new Jerusalem (Rev. 21:3; 21:22–22:5).

1:13 The promise to be with the people anticipates God being with his people in Christ (Matt. 1:23, "Immanuel") and through the Spirit of Christ (Rom. 8:9–10; 1 Cor. 3:16).

2:4 Our work is not in vain in the Lord (1 Cor. 15:58; Phil. 2:12–13).

2:6 God shakes the old order, showing that we should put our hope in his unshakable kingdom in Christ (Heb. 12:26–28).

2:7 The ultimate glory of God is found in Jesus Christ (John 1:14; Rev. 21:22–23).

Zechariah

The rebuilding in the time of the restoration from exile prefigures the eternal salvation that comes in Christ.

1:1 God gives the prophecies during the time covered in Ezra 5–6 (see Ezra 5:1 and 6:14).

1:3 The call to return prefigures the gospel call to repent and come to God (Acts 2:38; 17:30–31).

1:16 Mercy on Jerusalem prefigures the mercy on sinners in Christ (Luke 5:32).

2:5 The glory of God is manifest in Jesus Christ (John 1:14; 17:1–5; Rev. 21:22–27).

2:11 On the coming of the nations, see notes on Isa. 2:2; 11:10; and 42:6.

3:4 The removal of iniquity symbolizes justification in Christ (Rom. 3:23–26; 5:1).

3:8 The Branch is the Messiah (based on Isa. 11:1).

4:6 The Spirit of Christ gives a permanent supply of power and light (John 16:13–15; Rom. 8:9–13).

5:3 We can escape the curse for wrongdoing through Christ, who bore the curse for us (Gal. 3:13–14).

6:12 On the Branch, see notes on 3:8 and Isa. 11:1.

6:13 Christ builds the temple, the church (Matt. 16:18; 1 Cor. 3:10–16).

7:9 The central importance of righteousness, rather than sacrifice, appears in 1 Sam. 15:22–23, Amos 5:21–27; Mic. 6:7–8, and Matt. 9:13, and underlines the superiority of the righteousness of Christ over all animal sacrifices (Heb. 10:1–14).

8:3 On God's dwelling, see note on Hag. 1:2.

8:11 On the remnant, see notes on Isa. 1:9 and 6:13.

8:22 On the coming of the nations, see notes on Isa. 2:2 and 11:10.

9:9 Jesus the king comes to Jerusalem on a donkey (Matt. 21:1–9).

10:9 The restoration from exile prefigures final salvation and life in Christ (John 6:35; 14:6).

11:10 Faithlessness leads to annulling the covenant, indicating the need for a new covenant (Heb. 8:8–13).

11:12 Thirty pieces of silver is the payoff connected with repudiating the Lord as true shepherd. It anticipates the payoff for Judas (Matt. 26:15; 27:9–10).

12:10 Repentance involves looking on the crucified Messiah (John 3:14–15; 19:37).

13:1 Cleansing from sin comes in Christ (1 John 2:1–2).

13:7 The disciples are scattered at the time when Christ the shepherd is crucified (Matt. 26:31).

14:8 The living waters are found in Christ (John 4:10; Rev. 22:1; see note on Ezek. 47:1.

14:20 Holiness is found in Christ (Acts 2:27; Heb. 7:26) and in the new Jerusalem that he establishes (Rev. 21:22–22:5).

Malachi

Disobedience and compromise are eliminated with the coming of Christ and his purification.

1:2 God's sovereign love for Jacob prefigures the sovereignty of his love for the elect (Rom. 9:1–29).

1:7 The danger of despising God continues in the church at the Lord's Supper (1 Cor. 10:21).

2:8 The corruption of the covenant shows the need for a new covenant (Heb. 8:8–13) and a perfect priest (Heb. 7:11–8:6).

3:1 John the Baptist is the messenger preparing the way for Christ, who is the Lord, the messenger of the covenant (Matt. 11:10–11).

3:7 On the call to repentance, see note on Jer. 18:11.

4:1 On the day of the Lord, see note on Isa. 13:6.

4:6 John the Baptist prepares hearts for the coming of the Lord in the person of Christ (Luke 1:17).

Charts and Diagrams

Maps

Concordance

As an essentially literal translation, the ESV Bible is ideally suited for use with a concordance, as the ESV seeks to use the same English word, as far as possible and where appropriate to the meaning in each context, to translate important recurring words in the original languages. However, with a total of more than 757,000 words appearing in the ESV Bible, a shorter concordance such as this must be selective in the words it includes.

In choosing which words to list, the guiding principles were importance, familiarity, and breadth of coverage. Since the ESV is within the stream of English Bible translations that began with the King James Version of 1611, there was a special effort to include references to as many familiar Bible passages as possible. As to breadth of coverage, the goal has been to list key references for many different words rather than more lengthy listings for fewer words.

Passages appearing in more than one of the Synoptic Gospels usually have only one reference, most often to the book of Matthew.

Readers will find the functionality of this concordance greatly increased if, after locating a Bible passage, the cross-reference system is then utilized for further research.

Those desiring a more complete concordance for the ESV Bible should consult the *ESV Comprehensive Concordance of the Bible*, which has more than 300,000 verse listings for nearly 14,000 different words. Readers with internet access will find optimal word-search capability with the search engine at the ESV web site, www.esvbible.org.

Abbreviations

Old Testament

Genesis	Gn
Exodus	Ex
Leviticus	Lv
Numbers	Nm
Deuteronomy	Dt
Joshua	Jos
Judges	Jgs
Ruth	Ru
1 Samuel	1 Sm
2 Samuel	2 Sm
1 Kings	1 Kgs
2 Kings	2 Kgs
1 Chronicles	1 Chr
2 Chronicles	2 Chr
Ezra	Ezr
Nehemiah	Neh
Esther	Est
Job	Jb
Psalms	Ps
Proverbs	Prv
Ecclesiastes	Eccl
Song of Solomon	Sg
Isaiah	Is
Jeremiah	Jer
Lamentations	Lam
Ezekiel	Ezk
Daniel	Dn
Hosea	Hos
Joel	Jl
Amos	Am
Obadiah	Ob
Jonah	Jon
Micah	Mi
Nahum	Na
Habakkuk	Hb
Zephaniah	Zep
Haggai	Hg
Zechariah	Zec
Malachi	Mal

New Testament

Matthew	Mt
Mark	Mk
Luke	Lk
John	Jn
Acts	Acts
Romans	Rom
1 Corinthians	1 Cor
2 Corinthians	2 Cor
Galatians	Gal
Ephesians	Eph
Philippians	Phil
Colossians	Col
1 Thessalonians	1 Thes
2 Thessalonians	2 Thes
1 Timothy	1 Tm
2 Timothy	2 Tm
Titus	Ti
Philemon	Phlm
Hebrews	Heb
James	Jas
1 Peter	1 Pt
2 Peter	2 Pt
1 John	1 Jn
2 John	2 Jn
3 John	3 Jn
Jude	Jude
Revelation	Rv

ABANDON
For you will not **a** my soul to . . . . Ps 16:10
he will not **a** his heritage; . . . . Ps 94:14
For you will not **a** my soul to . . . . Acts 2:27

ABANDONED
'Because they **a** the LORD . . . . 1 Kgs 9:9
that you have **a** the love you . . . . Rv 2:4

ABBA
"**A**, Father, all things are. . . . . Mk 14:36
whom we cry, "**A**! Father!" . . . . Rom 8:15
crying, "**A**! Father!" . . . . Gal 4:6

ABHOR
and my soul will **a** you. . . . . Lv 26:30
You shall utterly detest and **a**. . . . . Dt 7:26
I hate and **a** falsehood, but . . . . Ps 119:163

ABIDE
"My Spirit shall not **a** in man . . . . Gn 6:3
of the Most High will **a** . . . . Ps 91:1
A in me, and I in you. As the . . . . Jn 15:4

ABIDES
be moved, but **a** forever. . . . . Ps 125:1
flesh and drinks my blood **a** . . . . Jn 6:56
No one who **a** in him keeps . . . . 1 Jn 3:6

ABIDING
shadow, and there is no **a**. . . . . 1 Chr 29:15
do not have his word **a** in you . . . . Jn 5:38
through the living and **a** word . . . . 1 Pt 1:23

ABILITY
have given to all able men **a**, ... Ex 31:6
to each according to his **a**. . . . . Mt 25:15
tempted beyond your **a**, ... 1 Cor 10:13

ABLE
Moses chose **a** men out of all. . . . . Ex 18:25
man shall give as he is **a**, ... Dt 16:17
silver and gold are not **a** . . . . Ez 7:19
our God whom we serve is **a** . . . . Dn 3:17
Are you **a** to drink the cup . . . . Mt 20:22
will be **a** to separate us from . . . . Rom 8:39

ABODE
strength to your holy **a**. . . . . Ex 15:13
His **a** has been established in . . . . Ps 76:2
From your lofty **a** you water . . . . Ps 104:13

ABOMINABLE
And you shall not bring an **a** . . . . Dt 7:26
doing **a** iniquity; there is none . . . . Ps 53:1

ABOMINATION
as with a woman; it is an **a**. . . . . Lv 18:22
does these things is an **a** . . . . Dt 18:12
seven that are an **a** to him: . . . . Prv 6:16
are both alike an **a**. . . . . Prv 17:15
the scoffer is an **a** to mankind. . . . . Prv 24:9
when they committed **a**? . . . . Jer 6:15
And they shall set up the **a**. . . . . Dn 11:31
is taken away and the **a** . . . . Dn 12:11
"So when you see the **a**. . . . . Mt 24:15

ABOUND
in sin that grace may **a**? . . . . Rom 6:1

ABOUNDING
a in steadfast love and faithfulness. . . . . . Ex 34:6
LORD is slow to anger and **a** . . . . Nm 14:18
slow to anger and **a** in . . . . Ps 86:15
and **a** in steadfast love; and he. . . . . Jl 2:13
slow to anger and **a** in . . . . Jon 4:2
taught, **a** in thanksgiving. . . . . Col 2:7

ABRAHAM
but your name shall be **A**, ... Gn 17:5
"**A** believed God, and it was. . . . . Rom 4:3
By faith **A** obeyed when he. . . . . Heb 11:8

ABUNDANCE
bread from heaven in **a**. . . . . Ps 105:40
contributed out of their **a**, ... Mk 12:44
for out of the **a** of the heart . . . . Lk 6:45

ABUNDANT
according to your **a** mercy blot . . . . Ps 51:1
Lord, and **a** in power; his . . . . Ps 147:5

ABUNDANTLY
God, for he will **a** pardon. . . . . Is 55:7
may have life and have it **a**. . . . . Jn 10:10
your faith is growing **a**, ... 2 Thes 1:3

ABYSS
them to depart into the **a**. . . . . Lk 8:31
into the **a**?" (that is, to bring. . . . . Rom 10:7

ACCEPTANCE
but the upright enjoy **a**. . . . . Prv 14:9
and deserving of full **a**, ... 1 Tm 1:15

ACCEPTED
to be **a** it must be perfect; . . . . Lv 22:21
and the LORD **a** Job's prayer. . . . . Jb 42:9
and their sacrifices will be **a**. . . . . Is 56:7

ACCESS
him we have also obtained **a** . . . . Rom 5:2
him we both have **a**. . . . . Eph 2:18
we have boldness and **a**. . . . . Eph 3:12

ACCOMPLISH
and I will **a** all my purpose,' . . . . Is 46:10
of him who sent me and to **a** . . . . Jn 4:34

ACCOMPLISHED
from the Law until all is **a**. . . . . Mt 5:18
having **a** the work that you . . . . Jn 17:4
except what Christ has **a** . . . . Rom 15:18

ACCORD
the prophets with one **a**. . . . . 1 Kgs 22:13
and serve him with one **a**. . . . . Zep 3:9
I lay it down of my own **a**. . . . . Jn 10:18

ACCOUNT
"You will not call to **a**"? . . . . Ps 10:13
against you falsely on my **a**. . . . . Mt 5:11
On **a** of these the wrath of God . . . . Col 3:6
but they will give **a** to him . . . . 1 Pt 4:5

ACCOUNTABLE
whole world may be held **a** . . . . Rom 3:19

ACCURSED
God ever says "Jesus is **a**!" . . . . 1 Cor 12:3

ACCUSATION
"What **a** do you bring against . . . . Jn 18:29
you and to make an **a**, ... Acts 24:19

ACCUSE
so that they might **a** him. . . . . Mt 12:10
And they began to **a** him, ... Lk 23:2

ACCUSER
appeal for mercy to my **a**. . . . . Jb 9:15
lest your **a** hand you over to. . . . . Mt 5:25
for the **a** of our brothers has . . . . Rv 12:10

ACKNOWLEDGE
In all your ways **a** him, and he . . . . Prv 3:6
Only **a** your guilt, that you . . . . Jer 3:13
the fruit of lips that **a** his name. . . . . . . Heb 13:15

ACQUIRE
Do not toil to **a** wealth; be. . . . . Prv 23:4
our inheritance until we **a** . . . . Eph 1:14

ACQUIT
for I will not **a** the wicked. . . . . Ex 23:7
who **a** the guilty for a bribe, ... Is 5:23

ACQUITTED
and I would be **a** forever by . . . . Jb 23:7
but I am not thereby **a**. . . . . 1 Cor 4:4

ACT
place and forgive and **a** . . . . 1 Kgs 8:39
trust in him, and he will **a**. . . . . Ps 37:5

ACTED
We have **a** very corruptly . . . . Neh 1:7
I know that you **a** in ignorance, ... Acts 3:17

ACTS
of the land of Egypt by great **a**. . . . . Ex 7:4
repays the one who **a** in pride . . . . Ps 31:23

ADAM
Thus all the days that **A** lived . . . . Gn 5:5
For as in **A** all die, so also . . . . 1 Cor 15:22

ADD
You shall not **a** to the word that. . . . . Dt 4:2
Do not **a** to his words, lest he. . . . . Prv 30:6
them, God will **a** to him the . . . . Rv 22:18

ADDED
and all these things will be **a** . . . . Mt 6:33
And the Lord **a** to their. . . . . Acts 2:47
law? It was **a** because of . . . . Gal 3:19

ADMINISTERED
he **a** justice and equity . . . . 1 Chr 18:14
gift that is being **a** by us . . . . 2 Cor 8:20

ADMONISH
while I **a** you! O Israel, if you . . . . Ps 81:8
a the idle, encourage the . . . . 1 Thes 5:14

ADOPTION
received the Spirit of **a**. . . . . Rom 8:15
that we might receive **a** as sons. . . . . Gal 4:5

ADULTERERS
They are all **a**; they are like a . . . . Hos 7:4
a, or even like this tax collector. . . . . Lk 18:11
nor **a**, nor men who practice. . . . . 1 Cor 6:9

ADULTEROUS
me and of my words in this **a**. . . . . Mk 8:38
the sexually immoral and **a**. . . . . Heb 13:4
You **a** people! Do you not know . . . . Jas 4:4

ADULTERY
"You shall not commit **a**. . . . . Ex 20:14
He who commits **a** lacks. . . . . Prv 6:32
already committed **a** with her . . . . Mt 5:28
marries another commits **a**, ... Lk 16:18

ADVANTAGE
and man has no **a** over the . . . . Eccl 3:19
it is to your **a** that I go away, ... Jn 16:7
Christ will be of no **a** to you. . . . . Gal 5:2
for that would be of no **a**. . . . . Heb 13:17
favoritism to gain **a**. . . . . Jude 1:16

ADVERSARY
and give the **a** no occasion. . . . . 1 Tm 5:14
Your **a** the devil prowls. . . . . 1 Pt 5:8

ADVERSITY
and opens their ear by **a**. . . . . Jb 36:15
and a brother is born for **a**. . . . . Prv 17:17
and in the day of **a** consider: . . . . Eccl 7:14

ADVICE
but a wise man listens to **a**. . . . . Prv 12:15
Listen to **a** and accept . . . . Prv 19:20

AFFAIRS
who conducts his **a** with justice. . . . . Ps 112:5
and to mind your own **a**, ... 1 Thes 4:11

AFFECTION
another with brotherly **a**. . . . . Rom 12:10
and brotherly **a** with love. . . . . 2 Pt 1:7

AFFLICT
taskmasters over them to **a** . . . . Ex 1:11
And I will **a** the offspring . . . . 1 Kgs 11:39

AFFLICTED
He delivers the **a** by their . . . . Jb 36:15
your hand; forget not the **a**. . . . . Ps 10:12

AFFLICTION
LORD has listened to your **a**. . . . Gn 16:11
tried you in the furnace of **a**. . . . Is 48:10
momentary **a** is preparing. . . . 2 Cor 4:17

AFFLICTIONS
Many are the **a** of the . . . . Ps 34:19
what is lacking in Christ's **a** . . . . Col 1:24

AFRAID
and I was **a**, because I was. . . . Gn 3:10
Do not be **a** and do not be. . . . 1 Chr 28:20
it is I. Do not be **a**." . . . . Mt 14:27

AGE
and of the end of the **a**?" . . . . Mt 24:3
he is of **a**. He will speak for . . . . Jn 9:21

AGES
O LORD, throughout all **a**. . . . Ps 135:13
God decreed before the **a**. . . . 1 Cor 2:7
for all at the end of the **a**. . . . Heb 9:26

AGONY
pangs and **a** will seize them; . . . . Is 13:8
And being in an **a** he prayed . . . . Lk 22:44

AGREE
their testimony did not **a**. . . . Mk 14:56
a with one another, live . . . . 2 Cor 13:11
the blood; and these three **a**. . . . 1 Jn 5:8

AGREEMENT
except perhaps by **a** for a. . . . 1 Cor 7:5
What **a** has the temple of. . . . 2 Cor 6:16

AIM
who **a** bitter words like arrows, ... Ps 64:3
A for restoration, comfort. . . . 2 Cor 13:11

AIR
prince of the power of the **a**, ... Eph 2:2
to meet the Lord in the **a**, ... 1 Thes 4:17

ALARM
I had said in my **a**, "I am cut . . . . Ps 31:22
Let not your thoughts **a** you. . . . Dn 5:10

ALARMED
See that you are not **a**, for this. . . . Mt 24:6
"Do not be **a**. You seek Jesus . . . . Mk 16:6

ALERT
Therefore be **a**, remembering . . . . Acts 20:31
To that end keep **a** with all. . . . Eph 6:18

ALIEN
or violence to the resident **a**, ... Jer 22:3

ALIVE
is **a**; he was lost, and is found.'" . . . . Lk 15:32
dead to sin and **a**. . . . Rom 6:11
in the flesh but made **a** . . . . 1 Pt 3:18

ALLEGIANCE
of Canaan and swear **a** . . . . Is 19:18
every tongue shall swear **a**.' . . . . Is 45:23

ALLOWED
no evil shall be **a** to befall . . . . Ps 91:10
Also it was **a** to make war on. . . . Rv 13:7

ALMIGHTY
"I am God **A**: be fruitful and . . . . Gn 35:11
contend with the **A**? . . . . Jb 40:2
and who is to come, the **A**." . . . . Rv 1:8
is the Lord God the **A**. . . . Rv 21:22

ALMS
But give as **a** those things . . . . Lk 11:41
the Beautiful Gate to ask **a** . . . . Acts 3:2

ALONE
that the man should be **a**; . . . . Gn 2:18
O LORD, are God **a**." . . . . 2 Kgs 19:19
shall not live by bread **a**.'" . . . . Lk 4:4
can forgive sins but God **a**?" . . . . Lk 5:21
Yet I am not **a**, for the Father . . . . Jn 16:32
by works and not by faith **a**. . . . Jas 2:24

ALPHA
"I am the **A** and the Omega," . . . . Rv 1:8
I am the **A** and the Omega, ... Rv 22:13

ALTAR
Then Noah built an **a** to the . . . . Gn 8:20
So he built there an **a** to the . . . . Gn 12:7
make atonement for the **a** . . . . Ex 29:37
And Saul built an **a** to the . . . . 1 Sm 14:35
David built there an **a** . . . . 2 Sm 24:25
He erected an **a** for Baal . . . . 1 Kgs 16:32
And he repaired the **a** . . . . 1 Kgs 18:30
up his son Isaac on the **a**? . . . . Jas 2:21

ALTARS
You shall tear down their **a** . . . . Dt 12:3
And he built **a** in the house . . . . 2 Kgs 21:4
will break down their **a** . . . . Hos 10:2

ALWAYS
and his commandments **a**. . . . Dt 11:1
For you **a** have the poor with . . . . Mk 14:7

AMAZED
And the disciples were **a** . . . . Mk 10:24
so that Pilate was **a**. . . . Mk 15:5
come with Peter were **a**, ... Acts 10:45

AMBUSH
Lay an **a** against the city, ... Jos 8:2
us **a** the innocent without reason; . . . . Prv 1:11
they were planning an **a**. . . . Acts 25:3

AMEN
shall answer and say, '**A**.' . . . . Dt 27:15
to everlasting! **A** and **A**. . . . Ps 41:13
him that we utter our **A** . . . . 2 Cor 1:20
Lord Jesus be with all. **A**. . . . Rv 22:21

ANCHOR
as a sure and steadfast **a** . . . . Heb 6:19

ANCIENT
and the **A** of Days took . . . . Dn 7:9
until the **A** of Days came, and. . . . Dn 7:22

ANGEL
The **a** of the LORD found her . . . . Gn 16:7
And the **a** of the LORD appeared . . . . Ex 3:2
Now the **a** of the LORD came . . . . Jgs 6:11
The **a** of the LORD encamps. . . . Ps 34:7
My God sent his **a** and shut . . . . Dn 6:22
And the **a** said to them, "Fear . . . . Lk 2:10
Now an **a** of the Lord said to . . . . Acts 8:26
disguises himself as an **a** . . . . 2 Cor 11:14
But even if we or an **a** from . . . . Gal 1:8

ANGELS
The two **a** came to Sodom in . . . . Gn 19:1
the **a** of God were ascending . . . . Gn 28:12
and all the **a** with him, then . . . . Mt 25:31
the **a** were ministering to him. . . . Mk 1:13
some have entertained **a** . . . . Heb 13:2
things into which **a** long to look. . . . 1 Pt 1:12
And the **a** who did not stay . . . . Jude 1:6
Michael and his **a** fighting . . . . Rv 12:7

ANGER
And the **a** of the LORD burned. . . . Jos 7:1
rebuke me not in your **a**, nor . . . . Ps 6:1
slow to **a** and abounding in . . . . Ps 86:15
but a harsh word stirs up **a**. . . . Prv 15:1
Therefore the **a** of the LORD . . . . Is 5:25
Why do you provoke me to **a** . . . . Jer 44:8
He does not retain his **a**. . . . Mi 7:18
provoke your children to **a**, ... Eph 6:4
lifting holy hands without **a** . . . . 1 Tm 2:8
slow to speak, slow to **a**; . . . . Jas 1:19

ANGRY
"Why are you **a**, and why has . . . . Gn 4:6
And the LORD was so **a** with . . . . Dt 9:20
And the LORD was **a** with . . . . 1 Kgs 11:9
Be **a**, and do not sin; ponder in . . . . Ps 4:4
I will not be **a** forever. . . . . Jer 3:12
you that everyone who is **a** . . . . Mt 5:22
Be **a** and do not sin; do not . . . . Eph 4:26

ANGUISH
I will speak in the **a** of my . . . . Jb 7:11
My heart is in **a** within me; the. . . . Ps 55:4
When **a** comes, they will seek. . . . Ez 7:25
for I am in **a** in this flame.' . . . . Lk 16:24

ANOINT
and shall **a** them and ordain. . . . Ex 28:41
You did not **a** my head with. . . . Lk 7:46

ANOINTED
And the priest who is **a** . . . . Lv 16:32
could; she has **a** my body. . . . Mk 14:8
It was Mary who **a** the Lord . . . . Jn 11:2
has **a** you with the oil of . . . . Heb 1:9

ANOINTING
Then you shall take the **a** oil. . . . Ex 40:9
But the **a** that you received . . . . 1 Jn 2:27

ANSWER
A me, O LORD, **a** me, ... 1 Kgs 18:37
A soft **a** turns away wrath, ... Prv 15:1
"And in that day I will **a**, ... Hos 2:21
that you may be able to **a** . . . . 2 Cor 5:12

ANTICHRIST
a is coming, so now many . . . . 1 Jn 2:18
This is the spirit of the **a**, ... 1 Jn 4:3
is the deceiver and the **a**. . . . 2 Jn 1:7

ANXIETIES
you to be free from **a**. . . . 1 Cor 7:32
casting all your **a** on him, ... 1 Pt 5:7

ANXIETY
A in a man's heart weighs . . . . Prv 12:25
bread by weight and with **a**, ... Ez 4:16
pressure on me of my **a** . . . . 2 Cor 11:28

ANXIOUS
Say to those who have an **a** . . . . Is 35:4
do not be **a** beforehand what. . . . Mk 13:11
do not be **a** about your life, ... Lk 12:22
do not be **a** about anything, ... Phil 4:6

APOLLOS
Now a Jew named **A**, a . . . . Acts 18:24
or "I follow **A**," or "I follow . . . . 1 Cor 1:12

APOSTLE
Am I not an **a**? Have I not . . . . 1 Cor 9:1
The signs of a true **a** . . . . 2 Cor 12:12
a and high priest of our confession, ... Heb 3:1

APOSTLES
The names of the twelve **a** . . . . Mt 10:2
with the eleven **a**. . . . Acts 1:26
that God has exhibited us **a** . . . . 1 Cor 4:9
in the church first **a**, ... 1 Cor 12:28
on the foundation of the **a** . . . . Eph 2:20
And he gave the **a**, the prophets, ... Eph 4:11

APOSTLESHIP
have received grace and **a** . . . . Rom 1:5
for you are the seal of my **a** . . . . 1 Cor 9:2

APPEAL
you think that I cannot **a** . . . . Mt 26:53
God making his **a** through . . . . 2 Cor 5:20
from the body but as an **a** . . . . 1 Pt 3:21

APPEAR
and let the dry land **a**." And it . . . . Gn 1:9
When shall I come and **a** . . . . Ps 42:2
Then will **a** in heaven the. . . . Mt 24:30

APPEARANCES
for you are not swayed by **a**. . . . Mt 22:16
Do not judge by **a**, but judge . . . . Jn 7:24

APPEARED
But the glory of the LORD **a** ... Nm 14:10
of King Belshazzar a vision **a** ... Dn 8:1
And a great sign **a** in heaven: ... Rv 12:1

APPEARS
but we know that when he **a** ... 1 Jn 3:2

APPOINT
"You shall **a** judges and ... Dt 16:18
whom we will **a** to this duty ... Acts 6:3

APPOINTED
but I chose you and **a** you ... Jn 15:16
And just as it is **a** for man to ... Heb 9:27

APPROVAL
not only do them but give **a** ... Rom 1:32
For am I now seeking the **a** ... Gal 1:10

APPROVE
yet after them people **a** of ... Ps 49:13
and know his will and **a** ... Rom 2:18

ARCHANGEL
with the voice of an **a**, ... 1 Thes 4:16
But when the **a** Michael, ... Jude 1:9

ARISE
A, walk through the length ... Gn 13:17
"**A**, go to Nineveh, that great ... Jon 1:2
I say to you, **a**." ... Mk 5:41
a." And she opened her eyes, ... Acts 9:40
and **a** from the dead, and ... Eph 5:14

ARK
Make yourself an **a** of gopher ... Gn 6:14
"They shall make an **a** of ... Ex 25:10
"As soon as you see the **a** ... Jos 3:3
and the **a** of his covenant ... Rv 11:19

ARM
you with an outstretched **a** ... Ex 6:6
You with your **a** redeemed ... Ps 77:15

ARMAGEDDON
that in Hebrew is called **A** ... Rv 16:16

ARMOR
strap on your **a** and be shattered ... Is 8:9
Put on the whole **a** of God, ... Eph 6:11

ARMS
are the everlasting **a** ... Dt 33:27
strength and makes her **a** ... Prv 31:17
gather the lambs in his **a**; ... Is 40:11

ARROGANCE
let not **a** come from your ... 1 Sm 2:3
Pride and **a** and the way of ... Prv 8:13
who say in pride and in **a** of heart: ... Is 9:9

ARROGANT
Everyone who is **a** in heart is ... Prv 16:5
do not be **a** toward the ... Rom 11:18
envy or boast; it is not **a** ... 1 Cor 13:4

ASCEND
If I **a** to heaven, you are ... Ps 139:8
For David did not **a** into the ... Acts 2:34
'Who will **a** into heaven?'" ... Rom 10:6

ASCENDED
You **a** on high, leading a host ... Ps 68:18
for I have not yet **a** to the ... Jn 20:17
"When he **a** on high he led a ... Eph 4:8

ASCENDING
the angels of God were **a** ... Gn 28:12
and the angels of God **a** and ... Jn 1:51
were to see the Son of Man **a** ... Jn 6:62

ASCRIBE
LORD; **a** greatness to our God! ... Dt 32:3
knowledge from afar and **a** ... Jb 36:3
A to the LORD, O heavenly ... Ps 29:1
A power to God, whose ... Ps 68:34
A to the LORD, O families of the ... Ps 96:7

ASHAMED
All my enemies shall be **a** ... Ps 6:10
For whoever is **a** of me and of ... Lk 9:26
For I am not **a** of the gospel, ... Rom 1:16

ASHES
I who am but dust and **a** ... Gn 18:27
with sackcloth, and sat in **a** ... Jon 3:6
long ago in sackcloth and **a** ... Mt 11:21

ASIDE
You shall not turn **a** to the ... Dt 5:32
They have all turned **a**; ... Ps 14:3
Let not your heart turn **a** ... Prv 7:25
But you have turned **a** from ... Mal 2:8

ASLEEP
or perhaps he is **a** and ... 1 Kgs 18:27
friend Lazarus has fallen **a**, ... Jn 11:11
about those who are **a**, ... 1 Thes 4:13

ASSEMBLY
day you shall hold a holy **a**, ... Ex 12:16
It is a solemn **a**; you shall ... Lv 23:36
his praise in the **a** of the godly! ... Ps 149:1
a fast; call a solemn **a**; ... Jl 2:15

ASSIGNED
as my Father **a** to me, a kingdom, ... Lk 22:29
as the Lord **a** to each ... 1 Cor 3:5
area of influence God **a** ... 2 Cor 10:13

ASSOCIATE
therefore do not **a** with a ... Prv 20:19
but **a** with the lowly. Never ... Rom 12:16
not to **a** with sexually immoral ... 1 Cor 5:9

ASSURANCE
and of this he has given **a** ... Acts 17:31
with a true heart in full **a** ... Heb 10:22
Now faith is the **a** of things ... Heb 11:1

ASTONISHED
passing by it will be **a** ... 1 Kgs 9:8
the crowds were **a** at his teaching, ... Mt 7:28
they were amazed and **a**, ... Acts 2:7

ASTRAY
they go **a** from birth, speaking lies ... Ps 58:3
and whoever is led **a** by it is ... Prv 20:1
we like sheep have gone **a**; ... Is 53:6
to lead **a**, if possible, the elect ... Mk 13:22

ATE
she took of its fruit and **a**, ... Gn 3:6
and he **a**; and he brought ... Gn 27:25
Then I **a** it, and it was in my ... Ez 3:3
And they all **a** and were satisfied ... Mk 6:42

ATHLETE
Every **a** exercises self-control ... 1 Cor 9:25
An **a** is not crowned unless ... 2 Tm 2:5

ATONE
you will not be able to **a**; ... Is 47:11

ATONED
so that their blood guilt be **a** ... Dt 21:8
and faithfulness iniquity is **a** ... Prv 16:6
away, and your sin **a** for." ... Is 6:7
this iniquity will not be **a** for you ... Is 22:14

ATONEMENT
a bull as a sin offering for **a** ... Ex 29:36
And the priest shall make **a** ... Lv 4:20
month is the Day of **A** ... Lv 23:27
days shall they make **a** ... Ez 43:26

ATTAINED
righteousness have **a** ... Rom 9:30
true to what we have **a** ... Phil 3:16

ATTENTIVE
be open and your ears **a** ... 2 Chr 6:40
Let your ears be **a** to the ... Ps 130:2
be **a** to the words of my mouth ... Prv 7:24

AUTHORITIES
many even of the **a** believed ... Jn 12:42
subject to the governing **a** ... Rom 13:1

AUTHORITY
"All **a** in heaven and on ... Mt 28:18
A new teaching with **a**! He ... Mk 1:27
"Tell us by what **a** you do ... Lk 20:2
to teach or to exercise **a** over ... 1 Tm 2:12
exhort and rebuke with all **a** ... Ti 2:15

AVENGE
and shall I not **a** myself on a ... Jer 5:9
I will **a** their blood, blood ... Jl 3:21
never **a** yourselves, but ... Rom 12:19

AVENGER
to still the enemy and the **a** ... Ps 8:2
an **a** who carries out God's ... Rom 13:4
because the Lord is an **a** ... 1 Thes 4:6

AVOID
But **a** irreverent babble, for ... 2 Tm 2:16
to **a** quarreling, to be gentle, ... Ti 3:2

AWAKE
a and sing for joy! For your ... Is 26:19
Therefore stay **a** — for you ... Mk 13:35
"**A**, O sleeper, and arise from ... Eph 5:14

AWE
the ends of the earth are in **a** ... Ps 65:8
of Jacob and will stand in **a** ... Is 29:23
they were filled with **a** and ... Mt 27:54

AWESOME
the great and **a** God who ... Neh 1:5
"How **a** are your deeds! So ... Ps 66:3
them praise your great and **a** ... Ps 99:3
Holy and **a** is his name! ... Ps 111:9

AXE
his **a** head fell into the ... 2 Kgs 6:5
Even now the **a** is laid to the ... Lk 3:9

BABEL
of his kingdom was **B**, ... Gn 10:10
Therefore its name was called **B**, ... Gn 11:9

BABY
the **b** leaped in her womb ... Lk 1:41
you will find a **b** wrapped in ... Lk 2:12
she has delivered the **b**, ... Jn 16:21

BABYLON
Nebuchadnezzar the king of **B** ... Ezr 2:1
fallen is **B**; and all the carved ... Is 21:9
"I will repay **B** and all the ... Jer 51:24
fallen is **B** the great! She has ... Rv 18:2

BAD
good for **b**, or **b** for good; ... Lv 27:10
nothing either good or **b** ... Rom 9:11

BAG
would be sealed up in a **b**, ... Jb 14:17
he took a **b** of money with ... Prv 7:20

BAKER
cupbearer and the chief **b**, ... Gn 40:2
like a heated oven whose **b** ... Hos 7:4

BALANCE
me be weighed in a just **b**, ... Jb 31:6
A false **b** is an abomination to ... Prv 11:1

BALANCES
You shall have just **b**, just ... Lv 19:36
have been weighed in the **b** ... Dn 5:27

BALDNESS
cut yourselves or make any **b** ... Dt 14:1
and **b** on all their heads ... Ez 7:18

BELT
Righteousness shall be the **b** . . . Is 11:5
of camel's hair and a leather **b** . . . Mt 3:4
having fastened on the **b** . . . Eph 6:14

BENEFITS
and forget not all his **b**, . . . Ps 103:2
A man who is kind **b** . . . Prv 11:17

BEREFT
Why should I be **b** of you . . . Gn 27:45
evil for good; my soul is **b**. . . . Ps 35:12
my soul is **b** of peace; I have . . . Lam 3:17

BESTOW
splendor and majesty you **b** . . . Ps 21:5
less honorable we **b** . . . 1 Cor 12:23

BESTOWED
sight of all Israel and **b** . . . 1 Chr 29:25
many who were blind he **b**. . . . Lk 7:21
highly exalted him and **b** . . . Phil 2:9

BETHLEHEM
O **B** Ephrathah, who are too . . . Mi 5:2
which is called **B**, because he . . . Lk 2:4

BETRAY
many will fall away and **b**. . . . Mt 24:10
sought an opportunity to **b**. . . . Mt 26:16
who is it that is going to **b** you?" . . . Jn 21:20

BETRAYED
Judas Iscariot, who **b** him. . . . Mt 10:4
the night when he was **b** . . . 1 Cor 11:23

BETRAYER
see, my **b** is at hand." . . . Mt 26:46
Now the **b** had given them a . . . Mk 14:44

BETROTHED
is there any man who has **b** . . . Dt 20:7
his mother Mary had been **b** . . . Mt 1:18
since I **b** you to one husband, . . . 2 Cor 11:2

BETTER
your steadfast love is **b** . . . Ps 63:3
A good name is **b** than. . . . Eccl 7:1
For it is **b** that you lose one of . . . Mt 5:29
For it is **b** to marry than to . . . 1 Cor 7:9
Jesus the guarantor of a **b** . . . Heb 7:22
For it is **b** to suffer for doing . . . 1 Pt 3:17

BEWARE
B lest you say in your heart, . . . Dt 8:17
"**B** of false prophets, who come . . . Mt 7:15
B of the leaven of the . . . Mt 16:11

BIND
You shall **b** them as a sign on . . . Dt 6:8
b them around your neck; . . . Prv 3:3
'**B** him hand and foot and . . . Mt 22:13

BIRDS
the **b** of the heavens, and the. . . . Ps 8:8
Look at the **b** of the air: they . . . Mt 6:26

BIRTH
go astray from **b**, speaking lies. . . . Ps 58:3
And she gave **b** to her firstborn . . . Lk 2:7
it has conceived gives **b** . . . Jas 1:15

BIRTHRIGHT
said, "Sell me your **b** now." . . . Gn 25:31
firstborn according to his **b**. . . . Gn 43:33
who sold his **b** for a single meal. . . . Heb 12:16

BITTERLY
She weeps **b** in the night, . . . Lam 1:2
he went out and wept **b**. . . . Mt 26:75

BITTERNESS
The heart knows its own **b**, . . . Prv 14:10
Let all **b** and wrath and . . . Eph 4:31
that no "root of **b**" springs. . . . Heb 12:15

BLACK
and the day shall be **b** over them; . . . Mi 3:6
the sun became **b** as sackcloth, . . . Rv 6:12

BLAMELESS
walk before me, and be **b**, . . . Gn 17:1
May my heart be **b** in your . . . Ps 119:80
to present you holy and **b** . . . Col 1:22

BLAMELESSLY
He who walks **b** and does . . . Ps 15:2
God, walking **b** in all the . . . Lk 1:6

BLASPHEMED
"The name of God is **b**. . . . Rom 2:24
the way of truth will be **b**. . . . 2 Pt 2:2

BLASPHEMES
Whoever **b** the name of the . . . Lv 24:16
but the one who **b** against . . . Lk 12:10

BLEMISH
lamb shall be without **b**, . . . Ex 12:5
offered himself without **b** . . . Heb 9:14
like that of a lamb without **b** . . . 1 Pt 1:19

BLESS
The LORD **b** you and keep you; . . . Nm 6:24
I will **b** the LORD at all times; . . . Ps 34:1
LORD, **b** his name; tell of his . . . Ps 96:2
B the LORD, O my soul, and all . . . Ps 103:1
him, that I might **b** him and . . . Is 51:2
b those who curse you, pray. . . . Lk 6:28
we **b**; when persecuted, we . . . 1 Cor 4:12

BLESSED
For the LORD your God has **b** . . . Dt 2:7
B is the man who walks not in . . . Ps 1:1
B be the LORD forever! Amen . . . Ps 89:52
B is he who comes in the . . . Ps 118:26
And **b** is the one who is not . . . Mt 11:6
more **b** to give than to receive. . . . Acts 20:35
shall all the nations be **b**." . . . Gal 3:8
who has **b** us in Christ with . . . Eph 1:3

BLESSING
so that you will be a **b**. . . . Gn 12:2
turned the curse into a **b**. . . . Neh 13:2
and after **b** it broke it and . . . Mt 26:26

BLIND
LORD opens the eyes of the **b**. . . . Ps 146:8
Then the eyes of the **b** shall be. . . . Is 35:5
the **b** receive their sight and. . . . Mt 11:5
"Can a **b** man lead a **b** man? . . . Lk 6:39

BLOOD
Whoever sheds the **b** of man, . . . Gn 9:6
in the Nile turned into **b**. . . . Ex 7:20
I do not delight in the **b** of. . . . Is 1:11
on my flesh and drinks my **b**. . . . Jn 6:54
as a propitiation by his **b**, . . . Rom 3:25
now been justified by his **b**, . . . Rom 5:9
redemption through his **b**, . . . Eph 1:7
peace by the **b** of his cross. . . . Col 1:20
freed us from our sins by his **b** . . . Rv 1:5

BLOODGUILT
has restrained you from **b** . . . 1 Sm 25:26
so his Lord will leave his **b** . . . Hos 12:14

BLOODSHED
because you did not hate **b**, . . . Ez 35:6
and **b** follows **b**. . . . Hos 4:2

BLOSSOM
and may people **b** in the . . . Ps 72:16
Israel shall **b** and put forth . . . Is 27:6
the fig tree should not **b**, . . . Hb 3:17

BLOT
that I have made I will **b** . . . Gn 7:4

BLOW
And God made a wind **b** over. . . . Gn 8:1
the priests shall **b** the trumpets. . . . Jos 6:4
He caused the east wind to **b**. . . . Ps 78:26

BOAST
Do not **b** about tomorrow, for. . . . Prv 27:1
but let him who boasts **b** . . . Jer 9:24
boasts, **b** in the Lord." . . . 1 Cor 1:31
Therefore I will **b** all the . . . 2 Cor 12:9
works, so that no one may **b**. . . . Eph 2:9

BOASTING
gives me no ground for **b**. . . . 1 Cor 9:16
without **b** of work already . . . 2 Cor 10:16
arrogance. All such **b** is evil. . . . Jas 4:16

BODIES
the dishonoring of their **b**. . . . Rom 1:24
to present your **b** as a living. . . . Rom 12:1
be manifested in our **b**. . . . 2 Cor 4:10

BODILY
Spirit descended on him in **b** . . . Lk 3:22
fullness of deity dwells **b**, . . . Col 2:9
for while **b** training is of. . . . 1 Tm 4:8

BODY
with him in order that the **b**. . . . Rom 6:6
will deliver me from this **b** . . . Rom 7:24
For as in one **b** we have. . . . Rom 12:4
members of the same **b**, and . . . Eph 3:6
There is one **b** and one Spirit . . . Eph 4:4
will transform our lowly **b**. . . . Phil 3:21
has now reconciled in his **b** . . . Col 1:22
the offering of the **b** of Jesus . . . Heb 10:10
bore our sins in his **b** . . . 1 Pt 2:24

BOLD
but the righteous are **b** as a lion. . . . Prv 28:1
a hope, we are very **b**, . . . 2 Cor 3:12

BOLDLY
He began to speak **b** in the . . . Acts 18:26
that I may declare it **b**, as I . . . Eph 6:20

BOND
I will bring you into the **b**. . . . Ez 20:37
unity of the Spirit in the **b** . . . Eph 4:3

BONDAGE
out of the house of **b**, saying, . . . Jer 34:13
will be set free from its **b** . . . Rom 8:21

BONE
"This at last is **b** of my bones. . . . Gn 2:23
"Surely you are my **b** and. . . . Gn 29:14
also that I am your **b** . . . Jgs 9:2

BONES
He keeps all his **b**; not one of. . . . Ps 34:20
dry **b**, hear the word of the LORD. . . . Ez 37:4
Not one of his **b** will be broken. . . . Jn 19:36

BOOK
This **B** of the Law shall not. . . . Jos 1:8
blot his name out of the **b** . . . Rv 3:5

BORN
For to us a child is **b**, to us a son . . . Is 9:6
unless one is **b** again he cannot . . . Jn 3:3
he has caused us to be **b** . . . 1 Pt 1:3
because he has been **b**. . . . 1 Jn 3:9

BORNE
Surely he has **b** our griefs and . . . Is 53:4
And I have seen and have **b** . . . Jn 1:34

BOW
let us worship and **b** down; let . . . Ps 95:6
Jesus every knee should **b**, . . . Phil 2:10

BRANCH
In that day the **b** of the LORD . . . Is 4:2
up for David a righteous **B**, . . . Jer 23:5
and every **b** that does bear. . . . Jn 15:2

For the body does not **c** ... 1 Cor 12:14

CONSUMING
For the LORD your God is a **c**. ... Dt 4:24
us can dwell with the **c** ... Is 33:14
for our God is a **c** fire. ... Heb 12:29

CONTAIN
highest heaven cannot **c**. ... 1 Kgs 8:27
the world itself could not **c**. ... Jn 21:25

CONTEMPT
c comes also, and with ... Prv 18:3
and treated others with **c**: ... Lk 18:9
and holding him up to **c**. ... Heb 6:6

CONTENT
situation I am to be **c**. ... Phil 4:11
and be **c** with what you ... Heb 13:5

CONTINUE
but **c** in the fear of the LORD. ... Prv 23:17
C steadfastly in prayer, being ... Col 4:2
c in what you have learned ... 2 Tm 3:14

CONTRITE
a broken and **c** heart, O God, ... Ps 51:17
also with him who is of a **c** ... Is 57:15
he who is humble and **c** in ... Is 66:2

CONTROL
having his desire under **c**, ... 1 Cor 7:37
body and keep it under **c**, ... 1 Cor 9:27
know how to **c** his own body ... 1 Thes 4:4

CONTROVERSIES
ignorant **c**; you know that ... 2 Tm 2:23
But avoid foolish **c**, genealogies, ... Ti 3:9

CONVICT
he will **c** the world concerning ... Jn 16:8
judgment on all and to **c** ... Jude 1:15

CONVICTION
Holy Spirit and with full **c**. ... 1 Thes 1:5
the **c** of things not seen. ... Heb 11:1

CONVINCED
fully **c** that God was able to ... Rom 4:21
C of this, I know that I will ... Phil 1:25
and I am **c** that he is able ... 2 Tm 1:12

CORNERSTONE
rejected has become the **c**. ... Ps 118:22
rejected has become the **c**; ... Mt 21:42
Jesus himself being the **c**, ... Eph 2:20

CORRUPT
Now the earth was **c** in God's ... Gn 6:11
manner of life and is **c** ... Eph 4:22

COUNSEL
man who walks not in the **c** ... Ps 1:1
Without **c** plans fail, but ... Prv 15:22

COUNT
but in humility **c** others more ... Phil 2:3
I **c** everything as loss because ... Phil 3:8
C it all joy, my brothers, when ... Jas 1:2

COUNTED
he **c** it to him as righteousness. ... Gn 15:6
is why his faith was "**c** ... Rom 4:22
it was **c** to him as righteousness"? ... Gal 3:6

COUNTS
man against whom the LORD **c** ... Ps 32:2
For neither circumcision **c** ... Gal 6:15

COURAGE
and let your heart take **c**, ... Ps 31:24
"Take **c**, for as you have ... Acts 23:11
but that with full **c** now as ... Phil 1:20

COURAGEOUS
Be strong and **c**. Do not fear or ... Dt 31:6
Be strong and **c**, for you shall ... Jos 1:6

COURTS
For a day in your **c** is better ... Ps 84:10
and his **c** with praise! Give ... Ps 100:4

COVENANT
obey my voice and keep my **c**, ... Ex 19:5
with me an everlasting **c**, ... 2 Sm 23:5
The LORD made a **c** with ... 2 Kgs 17:35
Therefore let us make a **c** ... Ezr 10:3
for those who keep his **c** ... Ps 25:10
with you an everlasting **c**, ... Is 55:3
But this is the **c** that I will ... Jer 31:33
and your wife by **c**. ... Mal 2:14
for this is my blood of the **c**, ... Mt 26:28
"This cup is the new **c** ... 1 Cor 11:25
I will establish a new **c** ... Heb 8:8
the blood of the eternal **c**, ... Heb 13:20

COVENANTS
the **c**, the giving of the law, ... Rom 9:4
these women are two **c**. ... Gal 4:24
Israel and strangers to the **c** ... Eph 2:12

COVER
and I did not **c** my iniquity; I ... Ps 32:5
soul from death and will **c** ... Jas 5:20

COVERED
His splendor **c** the heavens, and ... Hb 3:3
and whose sins are **c**; ... Rom 4:7
prophesies with his head **c** ... 1 Cor 11:4

COVERS
but love **c** all offenses. ... Prv 10:12
Whoever **c** an offense seeks ... Prv 17:9

COVET
"You shall not **c** your ... Ex 20:17
You shall not **c**," and any ... Rom 13:9
You **c** and cannot obtain, so ... Jas 4:2

COVETOUSNESS
on your guard against all **c**, ... Lk 12:15
produced in me all kinds of **c**. ... Rom 7:8
and all impurity or **c** ... Eph 5:3

CRAFTY
Now the serpent was more **c** ... Gn 3:1
I was **c**, you say, and got ... 2 Cor 12:16

CREATE
C in me a clean heart, O God, ... Ps 51:10
that he might **c** in himself ... Eph 2:15

CREATED
God **c** the heavens and the earth. ... Gn 1:1
he commanded and they were **c**. ... Ps 148:5
LORD, who **c** the heavens and ... Is 42:5
For everything **c** by God is ... 1 Tm 4:4
who **c** heaven and what is in ... Rv 10:6

CREATION
work that he had done in **c**. ... Gn 2:3
For the **c** waits with eager ... Rom 8:19
he is a new **c**. The old has ... 2 Cor 5:17
uncircumcision, but a new **c**. ... Gal 6:15
God, the firstborn of all **c**. ... Col 1:15
the beginning of God's **c**. ... Rv 3:14

CREATOR
the **C** of the ends of the earth. ... Is 40:28
after the image of its **c**. ... Col 3:10
their souls to a faithful **C** ... 1 Pt 4:19

CREATURES
the earth is full of your **c**. ... Ps 104:24
c of instinct, born to be ... 2 Pt 2:12

CROOKED
The way of the guilty is **c**, ... Prv 21:8
and the **c** shall become straight, ... Lk 3:5
blemish in the midst of a **c** ... Phil 2:15

CROSS
himself and take up his **c** ... Lk 9:23
boast except in the **c** ... Gal 6:14
peace by the blood of his **c** ... Col 1:20

CROWN
An excellent wife is the **c** ... Prv
Grandchildren are the **c** ... Prv 17:6
wearing the **c** of thorns and ... Jn 19:5
there is laid up for me the **c**. ... 2 Tm 4:8
the test he will receive the **c**. ... Jas 1:12
receive the unfading **c** of glory. ... 1 Pt 5:4
and I will give you the **c** of life. ... Rv 2:10

CROWNED
the heavenly beings and **c** ... Ps 8:5
An athlete is not **c** unless he ... 2 Tm 2:5
you have **c** him with glory ... Heb 2:7

CRUCIFIED
but we preach Christ **c** ... 1 Cor 1:23
For he was **c** in weakness, ... 2 Cor 13:4

CRUCIFY
of whom you will kill and **c**, ... Mt 23:34
they kept shouting, "**C**, **c** him!" ... Lk 23:21
"Shall I **c** your King?" The ... Jn 19:15

CRUSHED
and saves the **c** in spirit. ... Ps 34:18
he was **c** for our iniquities; ... Is 53:5
but not **c**; perplexed, but not ... 2 Cor 4:8

CRY
to me and heard my **c**. ... Ps 40:1
the very stones would **c** out." ... Lk 19:40

CUNNING
deceived Eve by his **c**, ... 2 Cor 11:3
by human **c**, by craftiness in ... Eph 4:14

CUP
with oil; my **c** overflows. ... Ps 23:5
let this **c** pass from me; ... Mt 26:39
"This **c** is the new covenant ... 1 Cor 11:25

CURSE
"I will never again **c** the ... Gn 8:21
you today a blessing and a **c**: ... Dt 11:26
bless those who **c** you, pray ... Lk 6:28
bless and do not **c** them. ... Rom 12:14

CURSED
c is the ground because of ... Gn 3:17
"'**C** be the man who makes a ... Dt 27:15

CURTAIN
the **c** of the temple was torn ... Mt 27:51
inner place behind the **c**, ... Heb 6:19

DAGON
it into the house of **D**. ... 1 Sm 5:2

DAILY
and take up his cross **d** ... Lk 9:23
examining the Scriptures **d** ... Acts 17:11

DANCE
to mourn, and a time to **d**; ... Eccl 3:4
and you did not **d**; we sang a ... Mt 11:17

DANCING
for me my mourning into **d**; ... Ps 30:11
praise his name with **d**, ... Ps 149:3

DANGER
The prudent sees **d** and ... Prv 27:12
nakedness, or **d**, or sword? ... Rom 8:35

DARK
you have said in the **d** ... Lk 12:3
as to a lamp shining in a **d**. ... 2 Pt 1:19

DARKENED
They are **d** in their ... Eph 4:18

DARKNESS
separated the light from the **d**. ... Gn 1:4
follows me will not walk in **d**, ... Jn 8:12
and in him is no **d** at all. ... 1 Jn 1:5

in **d**. . . . 1 Jn 2:9
hates his brother... **d**. . . . Jude 1:6
chains und... was plunged into **d**. . . . Rv 16:10
kin...

DAUGHTERS
your sons and your **d** shall . . . . Jl 2:28
you shall be sons and **d** . . . . 2 Cor 6:18

DAVID
D took the lyre and played . . . . 1 Sm 16:23
and there they anointed **D** . . . . 2 Sm 2:4
D said to Nathan, "I have. . . . 2 Sm 12:13
D said to Solomon, "My . . . . 1 Chr 22:7
to the city of **D**, which is called . . . . Lk 2:4
Son of **D**, have mercy on me!" . . . . Lk 18:38
comes from the offspring of **D**, ... Jn 7:42

DAWN
righteous is like the light of **d**, ... Prv 4:18
at early **d**, they went to the . . . . Lk 24:1

DAY
God called the light **D**, and the. . . . Gn 1:5
for it is a **D** of Atonement, to . . . . Lv 23:28
in a pillar of cloud by **d** . . . . Nm 14:14
This is the **d** that the LORD . . . . Ps 118:24
Give us this **d** our daily bread, ... Mt 6:11
you do not know on what **d**. . . . Mt 24:42
the **d** is at hand. So then let. . . . Rom 13:12
when he comes on that **d**. . . . 2 Thes 1:10

DAYS
his **d** shall be 120 years." . . . . Gn 6:3
So teach us to number our **d** . . . . Ps 90:12
also your Creator in the **d**. . . . Eccl 12:1
and female servants in those **d**. . . . Jl 2:29
but in these last **d** he has. . . . Heb 1:2

DEACONS
with the overseers and **d**: . . . . Phil 1:1
D likewise must be dignified, ... 1 Tm 3:8
then let them serve as **d**. . . . 1 Tm 3:10

DEAD
that he has risen from the **d**, ... Mt 28:7
him who raised from the **d**. . . . Rom 4:24
And you were **d** in the . . . . Eph 2:1
the resurrection from the **d**. . . . Phil 3:11
judge the living and the **d**, ... 2 Tm 4:1
and him as good as **d**, were. . . . Heb 11:12

DEATH
murderer shall be put to **d**. . . . Nm 35:16
He will swallow up **d** forever . . . . Is 25:8
he poured out his soul to **d** . . . . Is 53:12
but has passed from **d** to life. . . . Jn 5:24
reconciled to God by the **d**. . . . Rom 5:10
point of **d**, even **d** on a cross. . . . Phil 2:8
is fully grown brings forth **d**. . . . Jas 1:15
And its rider's name was **D**, ... Rv 6:8
Over such the second **d** has no. . . . Rv 20:6

DEBT
I forgave you all that **d**. . . . Mt 18:32
by canceling the record of **d**. . . . Col 2:14

DEBTORS
we also have forgiven our **d**. . . . Mt 6:12
we are **d**, not to the flesh, to . . . . Rom 8:12

DECEIT
D is in the heart of those . . . . Prv 12:20

DECEITFUL
The heart is **d** above all . . . . Jer 17:9
d workmen, disguising . . . . 2 Cor 11:13

DECEITFULNESS
cares of the world and the **d** . . . . Mk 4:19
may be hardened by the **d** . . . . Heb 3:13

DECEIVE
Let no one **d** himself. If. . . . 1 Cor 3:18
Let no one **d** you with empty . . . . Eph 5:6
let no one **d** you. Whoever . . . . 1 Jn 3:7

DECEIVED
"The serpent **d** me, and I ate." . . . . Gn 3:13
care lest your heart be **d**, ... Dt 11:16
d me and through it killed me. . . . Rom 7:11
Do not be **d**: God is not mocked, ... Gal 6:7
Do not be **d**, my beloved brothers. . . . Jas 1:16

DECEIVER
the **d** of the whole world — . . . . Rv 12:9

DECEIVERS
empty talkers and **d**, especially . . . . Ti 1:10
For many **d** have gone out . . . . 2 Jn 1:7

DECLARE
The heavens **d** the glory of. . . . Ps 19:1
and new things I now **d**; . . . . Is 42:9
D these things; exhort and . . . . Ti 2:15

DEED
was a prophet mighty in **d** . . . . Lk 24:19
in word or talk but in **d** . . . . 1 Jn 3:18

DEEDS
in glorious **d**, doing wonders? . . . . Ex 15:11
performing **d** in keeping . . . . Acts 26:20
in mind, doing evil **d**, ... Col 1:21
according to each one's **d**, ... 1 Pt 1:17

DEFEND
d your cause; remember how . . . . Ps 74:22
d the rights of the poor and . . . . Prv 31:9

DEFILE
resolved that he would not **d** . . . . Dn 1:8
These are what **d** a person. . . . Mt 15:20

DELAY
will surely come; it will not **d**. . . . Hb 2:3
there would be no more **d**, ... Rv 10:6

DELIGHT
D yourself in the LORD, and he . . . . Ps 37:4
I **d** to do your will, O my God; . . . . Ps 40:8
For you will not **d** in. . . . Ps 51:16
to me a joy and the **d** . . . . Jer 15:16
For I **d** in the law of God, in. . . . Rom 7:22

DELIGHTS
rescue him, for he **d** in him!" . . . . Ps 22:8
drink from the river of your **d**. . . . Ps 36:8
because he **d** in steadfast love. . . . Mi 7:18

DELIVER
In your righteousness **d** me. . . . Ps 71:2
but **d** us from evil. . . . Mt 6:13

DELIVERED
who was **d** up for our. . . . Rom 4:25
He has **d** us from the domain . . . . Col 1:13

DELIVERER
the LORD raised up a **d** for the . . . . Jgs 3:9
and my fortress and my **d**, ... Ps 18:2
my stronghold and my **d**, ... Ps 144:2
"The **D** will come from . . . . Rom 11:26

DELIVERS
the LORD hears and **d** them. . . . Ps 34:17
but righteousness **d** from death. . . . Prv 10:2
when he **d** the kingdom to. . . . 1 Cor 15:24

DEMON
the spirit of an unclean **d**, ... Lk 4:33
"I do not have a **d**, but I honor . . . . Jn 8:49

DEMON-OPPRESSED
a **d** man who was mute was. . . . Mt 9:32
Then a **d** man who was blind . . . . Mt 12:22

DEMON-POSSESSED
came to Jesus and saw the **d**. . . . Mk 5:15
seen it told them how the **d**. . . . Lk 8:36

DEMONIC
but is earthly, unspiritual, **d**. . . . Jas 3:15
For they are **d** spirits, ... Rv 16:14

DEMONS
And if I cast out **d** by. . . . Mt 12:27
And they cast out many **d** . . . . Mk 6:13
spirits and teachings of **d**, ... 1 Tm 4:1

DEN
become a **d** of robbers in your . . . . Jer 7:11
brought and cast into the **d** . . . . Dn 6:16
but you make it a **d** of robbers." . . . . Mt 21:13

DENIED
Peter again **d** it, and at once a. . . . Jn 18:27
he has **d** the faith and is . . . . 1 Tm 5:8

DENIES
but whoever **d** me before. . . . Mt 10:33
No one who **d** the Son has. . . . 1 Jn 2:23

DENY
let him **d** himself and take up. . . . Lk 9:23
you will **d** me three times." . . . . Lk 22:61

DENYING
and **d** the LORD, and turning. . . . Is 59:13
d its power. Avoid such people. . . . 2 Tm 3:5
even **d** the Master who bought. . . . 2 Pt 2:1

DEPART
The scepter shall not **d** from. . . . Gn 49:10
when he is old he will not **d**. . . . Prv 22:6
'**D** from me, you cursed, into. . . . Mt 25:41

DEPARTED
"The glory has **d** from Israel, ... 1 Sm 4:22
nor have our steps **d** from . . . . Ps 44:18

DEPRIVE
partial to the wicked or to **d**. . . . Prv 18:5
and **d** the innocent of his right! . . . . Is 5:23
and to **d** the thirsty of drink. . . . Is 32:6

DEPTH
nor height nor **d**, nor . . . . Rom 8:39
Oh, the **d** of the riches and. . . . Rom 11:33
length and height and **d**, ... Eph 3:18

DEPTHS
from the **d** of the earth you . . . . Ps 71:20
even the **d** of God. . . . 1 Cor 2:10

DESCEND
"I saw the Spirit **d** from . . . . Jn 1:32
the Lord himself will **d** . . . . 1 Thes 4:16

DESCENDED
because the LORD had **d**. . . . Ex 19:18
for an angel of the Lord **d** . . . . Mt 28:2
For not all who are **d** from . . . . Rom 9:6

DESERT
He turns a **d** into pools of . . . . Ps 107:35
make straight in the **d** a. . . . Is 40:3

DESERVE
to the proud what they **d**! . . . . Ps 94:2
practice such things **d** to die, ... Rom 1:32

DESERVES
of you less than your guilt **d**. . . . Jb 11:6
for the laborer **d** his wages. Do. . . . Lk 10:7

DESIRE
Your **d** shall be for your . . . . Gn 3:16
Its **d** is for you, but you must . . . . Gn 4:7
For I **d** steadfast love and not. . . . Hos 6:6
'I **d** mercy, and not sacrifice.' . . . . Mt 9:13
My **d** is to depart and be with . . . . Phil 1:23
they **d** a better country, that. . . . Heb 11:16

DESIRED
More to be **d** are they than . . . . Ps 19:10
And whatever my eyes **d** . . . . Eccl 2:10
many prophets and kings **d** . . . . Lk 10:24

DESIRES
will is to do your father's **d**. . . . Jn 8:44
who **d** all people to be saved . . . . 1 Tm 2:4

DESP...
but not d...

DESPISE
therefore I **d** myself, and. . . . . Jb 42:6

DESPISED
Thus Esau **d** his birthright. . . . . .Gn 25:34
scorned by mankind and **d**. . . . . .Ps 22:6
chose what is low and **d**. . . . . .1 Cor 1:28

DESTINED
know that we are **d** . . . . 1 Thes 3:3
For God has not **d** us for . . . . 1 Thes 5:9
word, as they were **d** to do. . . . . .1 Pt 2:8

DESTITUTE
regards the prayer of the **d**. . . . . Ps 102:17
the rights of all who are **d**. . . . . .Prv 31:8
d, afflicted, mistreated — . . . . Heb 11:37

DESTROY
fear him who can **d** both soul. . . . . Mt 10:28
only to steal and kill and **d**. . . . . Jn 10:10
through death he might **d** . . . . Heb 2:14

DESTROYED
My people are **d** for lack of . . . . Hos 4:6
is **d**, we have a building. . . . . .2 Cor 5:1
who shrink back and are **d**, ... Heb 10:39

DESTRUCTION
way is easy that leads to **d**, ...Mt 7:13
of wrath prepared for **d**,. . . . . Rom 9:22
upon themselves swift **d**. . . . . 2 Pt 2:1

DETERMINED
Since his days are **d**, and the . . . . Jb 14:5
having **d** allotted periods . . . . .Acts 17:26

DEVIL
And yet one of you is a **d**." . . . . Jn 6:70
give no opportunity to the **d**. . . . . Eph 4:27
and the **d** who had deceived . . . . Rv 20:10

DEVOTE
But we will **d** ourselves to . . . . .Acts 6:4
d yourself to the public . . . . 1 Tm 4:13
And let our people learn to **d** . . . . Ti 3:14

DEVOUT
d men are taken away, while . . . . .Is 57:1
man was righteous and **d**, ... Lk 2:25

DIE
integrity? Curse God and **d**." . . . . Jb 2:9
and a time to **d**; a time to . . . . Eccl 3:2
is Christ, and to **d** is gain. . . . . Phil 1:21
it is appointed for man to **d** . . . . .Heb 9:27
that we might **d** to sin and. . . . . 1 Pt 2:24

DIED
at the right time Christ **d** . . . . Rom 5:6
that Christ **d** for our sins in . . . . .1 Cor 15:3
If we have **d** with him, we . . . . 2 Tm 2:11

DIES
When the wicked **d**, his hope . . . . .Prv 11:7
but if it **d**, it bears much fruit. . . . . Jn 12:24

DIFFERENT
because he has a **d** spirit . . . . Nm 14:24
Christ and are turning to a **d** . . . . Gal 1:6
If anyone teaches a **d**. . . . . 1 Tm 6:3

DIGNITY
Strength and **d** are her . . . . .Prv 31:25

...tegrity, **d**, ... Ti 2:7
. . . . Prv 21:5
. . . . 2 Pt 3:14
Who can **d** his errors . . .
you **d** my thoughts from afar. . . . . Ps 139:2
and try to **d** what is pleasing . . . . Eph 5:10

DISCIPLE
cold water because he is a **d**, ... Mt 10:42
life, he cannot be my **d**. . . . . Lk 14:26

DISCIPLES
Go therefore and make **d** . . . . Mt 28:19
my word, you are truly my **d**, ... Jn 8:31
know that you are my **d**, ... Jn 13:35

DISCIPLINE
therefore despise not the **d** . . . . Jb 5:17
do not despise the LORD's **d** . . . . .Prv 3:11
Do not withhold **d** from a. . . . . .Prv 23:13
D your son, and he will give . . . . .Prv 29:17
But I **d** my body and keep it . . . . 1 Cor 9:27
but bring them up in the **d**. . . . . Eph 6:4
I reprove and **d**, so be zealous . . . . Rv 3:19

DISCIPLINED
The LORD has **d** me severely, ... Ps 118:18
we are **d** so that we may . . . . 1 Cor 11:32
had earthly fathers who **d** . . . . Heb 12:9

DISCOURAGED
He will not grow faint or be **d** . . . . .Is 42:4
lest they become **d**. . . . . Col 3:21

DISCRETION
may the LORD grant you **d**. . . . . 1 Chr 22:12
knowledge and **d** to the youth — . . . . Prv 1:4
that you may keep **d**, and your. . . . . Prv 5:2

DISGRACE
honor, but fools get **d**. . . . . .Prv 3:35
that he may not fall into **d**,. . . . . 1 Tm 3:7

DISHONOR
counted worthy to suffer **d**. . . . . .Acts 5:41
You who boast in the law **d** . . . . Rom 2:23
It is sown in **d**; it is raised . . . . 1 Cor 15:43

DISHONORABLE
God gave them up to **d** . . . . Rom 1:26
honorable use, some for **d**. . . . . 2 Tm 2:20

DISOBEDIENCE
by the one man's **d** the many . . . . Rom 5:19
ready to punish every **d**, ... 2 Cor 10:6
every transgression or **d** received . . . . Heb 2:2

DISOBEDIENT
as you were at one time **d** . . . . Rom 11:30
d to their parents, ungrateful, ... 2 Tm 3:2
d, unfit for any good work. . . . . Ti 1:16

DISORDER
gossip, conceit, and **d**. . . . . 2 Cor 12:20
will be **d** and every vile practice. . . . . Jas 3:16

DISPERSED
of the whole earth were **d**. . . . . Gn 9:19
So the LORD **d** them from . . . . Gn 11:8

DISPERSION
of your slaughter and **d** . . . . .Jer 25:34
Does he intend to go to the **D** . . . . Jn 7:35
who are elect exiles of the **D** . . . . 1 Pt 1:1

DISQUALIFIED
corrupted in mind and **d**. . . . . 2 Tm 3:8

DISTINCTION
and he made no **d** between . . . . Acts 15:9
For there is no **d** between . . . . Rom 10:12

DISTINGUISH
You are to **d** between the. . . . . Lv 10:10
...other the ability to **d** . . . . 1 Cor 12:10
...practice to **d** . . . . Heb 5:14
. . . . Ps 18:6
. . . . Jon 2:2
. . . . Rom 8:35
by gifts of the Holy Spirit . . .

DIVIDED
and a **d** household falls. . . . . Lk 11:17
Is Christ **d**? Was Paul crucified . . . . 1 Cor 1:13

DIVINE
his eternal power and **d**. . . . . Rom 1:20
because in his **d** forbearance . . . . Rom 3:25
become partakers of the **d** . . . . 2 Pt 1:4

DIVISION
I tell you, but rather **d**. . . . . Lk 12:51
that there may be no **d** . . . . 1 Cor 12:25

DIVISIONS
out for those who cause **d** . . . . Rom 16:17
and that there be no **d**. . . . . 1 Cor 1:10
It is these who cause **d**, ... Jude 1:19

DIVORCE
He may not **d** her all his days. . . . . Dt 22:19
the husband should not **d** . . . . 1 Cor 7:11

DIVORCES
does not love his wife but **d**. . . . . Mal 2:16
whoever **d** his wife, except for . . . . Mt 19:9
"Everyone who **d** his wife. . . . . Lk 16:18

DOCTRINE
'My **d** is pure, and I am clean . . . . Jb 11:4
about by every wind of **d**, ... Eph 4:14
to give instruction in sound **d**. . . . . Ti 1:9

DOERS
but the **d** of the law who . . . . Rom 2:13
But be **d** of the word, and not . . . . Jas 1:22

DOMINION
and subdue it and have **d**. . . . . Gn 1:28
his **d** is an everlasting **d**, ... Dn 4:34

DOOR
sin is crouching at the **d**. Its . . . . Gn 4:7
I am the **d**. If anyone enters . . . . Jn 10:9
I stand at the **d** and knock. If. . . . . Rv 3:20

DOUBLE-MINDED
I hate the **d**, but I love. . . . . Ps 119:113
he is a **d** man, unstable in all . . . . Jas 1:8

DOUBT
little faith, why did you **d**?" . . . . Mt 14:31
and does not **d** in his heart, ... Mk 11:23
mercy on those who **d**; . . . . Jude 1:22

DOVE
And the **d** came back to him . . . . Gn 8:11
of God descending like a **d**. . . . . Mt 3:16

DOWNCAST
"Why are your faces **d** today?" . . . . Gn 40:7
God, who comforts the **d**, ... 2 Cor 7:6

DRAGON
and he will slay the **d** that is . . . . Is 27:1
a great red **d**, with seven . . . . Rv 12:3

DREAD
Whom did you **d** and fear, ... Is 57:11

they shall turn in **d** to the. . . . . Mi 7:17

DREAM

Now Joseph had a **d**, and. . .
Therefore show me the **d**. . .
your old men shall **d** dreams,. . .
appeared to Joseph in a **d**. . .

DRINK

D water from your own
let him come to me a. . .
you eat this bread. . .
being poured. . . . . Is 29:9

DRUNK

. . . are not **d**,. . . . . Acts 2:15
Be. . . not get **d** with wine,. . . . . Eph 5:18

DRUNKARD

for the **d** and the glutton . . . . Prv 23:21
not a **d**, not violent but . . . . 1 Tm 3:3

DRUNKENNESS

down with dissipation and **d** . . . . Lk 21:34
d, orgies, and things like . . . . Gal 5:21

DRY

God called the **d** land Earth,. . . . . Gn 1:10
plant, and like a root out of **d** . . . . Is 53:2
O **d** bones, hear the word of. . . . . Ez 37:4

DUE

in themselves the **d** . . . . Rom 1:27
one may receive what is **d** . . . . 2 Cor 5:10
d to their hardness of heart. . . . . Eph 4:18

DUST

LORD God formed the man of **d**. . . . . Gn 2:7
remembers that we are **d**. . . . . Ps 103:14
All are from the **d**, and to. . . . . Eccl 3:20

DUTY

for this is the whole **d** . . . . Eccl 12:13

DWELL

"But will God indeed **d** . . . . 2 Chr 6:18
so that Christ may **d** in your. . . . . Eph 3:17

DWELLING

"I will make my **d** among. . . . . 2 Cor 6:16
the **d** place of God is with . . . . Rv 21:3

DWELLS

God's Spirit **d** in you?. . . . . 1 Cor 3:16
Holy Spirit who **d** within us, ... 2 Tm 1:14

EAGER

So I am **e** to preach the gospel. . . . . . . Rom 1:15

EAGERLY

by faith, we ourselves **e** wait . . . . Gal 5:5
but to save those who are **e**. . . . . Heb 9:28

EAR

Incline your **e**, and hear . . . . Prv 22:17
And if the **e** should say, ... 1 Cor 12:16
He who has an **e**, let him hear . . . . Rv 2:7

EARNESTLY

Therefore pray **e** to the Lord . . . . Lk 10:2
Pursue love, and **e** desire . . . . 1 Cor 14:1
keep loving one another **e**, ... 1 Pt 4:8

EARTH

is your name in all the **e**! . . . . Ps 8:1
The **e** is the LORD's and the. . . . . Ps 24:1
I made the **e** and created . . . . Is 45:12
come, your will be done, on **e**. . . . . Mt 6:10
authority in heaven and on **e** . . . . Mt 28:18
I am lifted up from the **e**, ... Jn 12:32
and to the end of the **e**." . . . . Acts 1:8
a new heaven and a new **e**, ... Rv 21:1

EARTHLY

if the tent that is our **e**. . . . . 2 Cor 5:1
shame, with minds set on **e** . . . . Phil 3:19

. . . Ps 103:12
. . . Mt 2:1
gate is wide and the way is **e**. . . . . Mt 7:13
For my yoke is **e**, and my . . . . Mt 11:30

EAT

give him bread to **e**, and if he . . . . Prv 25:21
disciples, and said, "Take, **e**; . . . . Mt 26:26
as often as you **e** this bread . . . . 1 Cor 11:26

EDEN

God planted a garden in **E**,. . . . . Gn 2:8
makes her wilderness like **E**, ... Is 51:3
You were in **E**, the garden . . . . Ez 28:13

EFFECT

And the **e** of righteousness. . . . . Is 32:17
For a will takes **e** only at . . . . Heb 9:17
steadfastness have its full **e**, ... Jas 1:4

ELDERS

Let the **e** who rule well be . . . . 1 Tm 5:17
So I exhort the **e** among you, ... 1 Pt 5:1

ELECT

But for the sake of the **e** . . . . Mt 24:22
for the sake of the **e**, ... 2 Tm 2:10

ELECTION

that God's purpose of **e** . . . . Rom 9:11
But as regards **e**, they are . . . . Rom 11:28
to confirm your calling and **e**, ... 2 Pt 1:10

ELIJAH

Now **E** the Tishbite, of . . . . 1 Kgs 17:1
"Behold, I will send you **E** . . . . Mal 4:5
But I tell you that **E** has . . . . Mt 17:12
E was a man with a nature. . . . . Jas 5:17

ELISHA

spirit of Elijah rests on **E**." . . . . 2 Kgs 2:15

ELOQUENT

"Oh, my Lord, I am not **e**,. . . . . Ex 4:10
He was an **e** man, ... Acts 18:24
and not with words of **e**. . . . . 1 Cor 1:17

EMMAUS

going to a village named **E**, ... Lk 24:13

EMPTY

it shall not return to me **e**, ... Is 55:11
no one deceive you with **e** words, ... Eph 5:6
by philosophy and **e** deceit, ... Col 2:8

ENCOURAGE

Therefore **e** one another . . . . 1 Thes 5:11
rebuke an older man but **e** . . . . 1 Tm 5:1

ENCOURAGED

that we may be mutually **e**. . . . . Rom 1:12
may learn and all be **e**,. . . . . 1 Cor 14:31
that their hearts may be **e**, ... Col 2:2

ENCOURAGEMENT

and through the **e** . . . . Rom 15:4
refuge might have strong **e** . . . . Heb 6:18

END

right to a man, but its **e**. . . . . Prv 16:25
endures to the **e** will be saved. . . . . Mt 10:22
Then comes the **e**, when. . . . . 1 Cor 15:24
once for all at the **e** . . . . Heb 9:26

ENDURANCE

your **e** you will gain your lives. . . . . Lk 21:19
that suffering produces **e**, ... Rom 5:3
his glorious might, for all **e**. . . . . Col 1:11

. . . his . . . . Ps 72:17
. . . the day of his . . . . Mal 3:2
. . . we **e**, we will also reign . . . . 2 Tm 2:12

ENDURES

for his steadfast love **e**. . . . . 1 Chr 16:34
good, for his steadfast love **e** . . . . Ps 106:1
his righteousness **e** forever; . . . . Ps 112:9
But the one who **e** to the end . . . . Mt 24:13
things, hopes all things, **e**. . . . . 1 Cor 13:7

ENDURING

for he is the living God, **e**. . . . . Dn 6:26
I know you are **e** patiently and. . . . . Rv 2:3

ENEMIES

But love your **e**, and do good, ... Lk 6:35
I make your **e** your footstool.'. . . . . Lk 20:43
For if while we were **e** . . . . Rom 5:10

ENEMY

Do not rejoice when your **e** . . . . Prv 24:17
If your **e** is hungry, give . . . . Prv 25:21
the world makes himself an **e**. . . . . Jas 4:4

ENJOY

E life with the wife whom . . . . Eccl 9:9
us with everything to **e**. . . . . 1 Tm 6:17
the people of God than to **e**. . . . . Heb 11:25

ENLIGHTENED

those who have once been **e**,. . . . . Heb 6:4
when, after you were **e**, ... Heb 10:32

ENSLAVED

we would no longer be **e** . . . . Rom 6:6
we were children, were **e** . . . . Gal 4:3

ENTANGLED

No soldier gets **e** in civilian . . . . 2 Tm 2:4
Christ, they are again **e** . . . . 2 Pt 2:20

ENTER

Pharisees, you will never **e** . . . . Mt 5:20
of life and that they may **e**. . . . . Rv 22:14

ENTERS

since it **e** not his heart but . . . . Mk 7:19
If anyone **e** by me, he will be . . . . Jn 10:9

ENTHRONED

the LORD of hosts, who is **e**. . . . . 1 Sm 4:4
hosts, God of Israel, **e** above . . . . Is 37:16

ENTICE

My son, if sinners **e** you, do . . . . Prv 1:10
They **e** unsteady souls. They . . . . 2 Pt 2:14

ENTRUSTED

approved by God to be **e** . . . . 1 Thes 2:4
with which I have been **e**. . . . . 1 Tm 1:11
guard the deposit **e** to you. . . . . 1 Tm 6:20

ENVY

e, slander, pride, foolishness.. . . . . Mk 7:22
love does not **e** or boast; it. . . . . 1 Cor 13:4

EPHESUS

hear that not only in **E** . . . . Acts 19:26
fought with beasts at **E**? . . . . 1 Cor 15:32
the angel of the church in **E** . . . . Rv 2:1

EQUAL

But it is you, a man, my **e**, ... Ps 55:13
because they are **e** to angels . . . . Lk 20:36
Father, making himself **e**. . . . . Jn 5:18

EQUALITY

form of God, did not count **e** . . . . Phil 2:6

EQUIPPED

the God who **e** me with . . . . Ps 18:32
joint with which it is **e**,. . . . . Eph 4:16
of God may be complete, **e**. . . . . 2 Tm 3:17

ERROR
the due penalty for their **e**. . . . . Rom 1:27
from those who live in **e**. . . . . 2 Pt 2:18
of truth and the spirit of **e**. . . . . 1 Jn 4:6

ESCAPE
that you will **e** the judgment . . . . Rom 2:3
also provide the way of **e**, ... 1 Cor 10:13
how shall we **e** if we neglect . . . . Heb 2:3

ESTABLISH
But I will **e** my covenant with . . . . Gn 6:18
I will **e** his kingdom . . . . 1 Chr 28:7
of God, and seeking to **e** . . . . Rom 10:3

ETERNAL
The **e** God is your dwelling . . . . Dt 33:27
what must I do to inherit **e**. . . . . Mk 10:17
should not perish but have **e** . . . . Jn 3:16
believes in the Son has **e** life; . . . . Jn 3:36
You have the words of **e** life, ... Jn 6:68
I give them **e** life, and they. . . . . Jn 10:28
And this is **e** life, that they . . . . Jn 17:3
will from the Spirit reap **e** life. . . . . Gal 6:8
This was according to the **e** . . . . Eph 3:11
Take hold of the **e** life to . . . . 1 Tm 6:12
you an entrance into the **e** . . . . 2 Pt 1:11
Jesus Christ that leads to **e**. . . . . Jude 1:21

ETERNITY
lifted up, who inhabits **e**, ... Is 57:15

EVE
called his wife's name **E**, ... Gn 3:20
as the serpent deceived **E**. . . . . 2 Cor 11:3
was formed first, then **E**; . . . . 1 Tm 2:13

EVER
let them **e** sing for joy, and. . . . . Ps 5:11
No one has **e** seen God; if . . . . 1 Jn 4:12

EVERLASTING
be in your flesh an **e** . . . . Gn 17:13
earth and the world, from **e** . . . . Ps 90:2
Counselor, Mighty God, **E** . . . . Is 9:6
It shall be an **e** covenant . . . . Ez 37:26
His kingdom is an **e** kingdom, ... Dn 4:3

EVIDENCE
to death on the **e** of witnesses. . . . . . . Nm 35:30
established by the **e** of two or . . . . Mt 18:16
elder except on the **e** of two . . . . 1 Tm 5:19

EVIL
the knowledge of good and **e**. . . . . Gn 2:9
intention of man's heart is **e**. . . . . Gn 8:21
of the LORD is hatred of **e**. . . . . Prv 8:13
Hate **e**, and love good, and . . . . Am 5:15
If you then, who are **e**, know . . . . Mt 7:11
"Purge the **e** person from. . . . . 1 Cor 5:13
deliver us from the present **e** . . . . Gal 1:4
all the flaming darts of the **e** . . . . Eph 6:16
patiently enduring **e**, ... 2 Tm 2:24
Do not repay **e** for **e** or . . . . 1 Pt 3:9
Beloved, do not imitate **e**. . . . . 3 Jn 1:11

EXALT
E the LORD our God, and . . . . Ps 99:9
So also Christ did not **e** . . . . Heb 5:5
the Lord, and he will **e** you. . . . . Jas 4:10

EXALTED
blessed be my rock, and **e** . . . . 2 Sm 22:47
Be **e**, O God, above the . . . . Ps 108:5
and lifted up, and shall be **e**. . . . . Is 52:13
Therefore God has highly **e**. . . . . Phil 2:9

EXALTS
Righteousness **e** a nation, ... Prv 14:34
to you, and therefore he **e** . . . . Is 30:18

EXAMINE
Let us test and **e** our ways, ... Lam 3:40
Let a person **e** himself, ... 1 Cor 11:28
E yourselves, to see . . . . 2 Cor 13:5

EXAMPLE
give you in ourselves an **e** . . . . 2 Thes 3:9
his perfect patience as an **e** . . . . 1 Tm 1:16

EXCEL
of the Spirit, strive to **e** . . . . 1 Cor 14:12
But as you **e** in everything . . . . 2 Cor 8:7

EXCELLENT
praise him according to his **e** . . . . Ps 150:2
show you a still more **e** way. . . . . 1 Cor 12:31
you may approve what is **e**, ... Phil 1:10

EXCUSE
but now they have no **e** . . . . Jn 15:22
So they are without **e**. . . . . Rom 1:20

EXHORT
things; **e** and rebuke with all . . . . Ti 2:15
But **e** one another every day, ... Heb 3:13

EXHORTATION
one who exhorts, in his **e**; . . . . Rom 12:8
Scripture, to **e**, to teaching. . . . . 1 Tm 4:13
the **e** that addresses you . . . . Heb 12:5

EXIST
things and for whom we **e**, ... 1 Cor 8:6
and by whom all things **e**, ... Heb 2:10

EXPECTATION
as it is my eager **e** and hope . . . . Phil 1:20
but a fearful **e** of judgment, ... Heb 10:27

EXPOSED
lest his works should be **e**. . . . . Jn 3:20
But when anything is **e** . . . . Eph 5:13

EXTOL
"Remember to **e** his work, of . . . . Jb 36:24
I will **e** you, O LORD, for you . . . . Ps 30:1
and let all the peoples **e**. . . . . Rom 15:11

EXULT
and **e**, O earth; break forth, ... Is 49:13

EYE
He who formed the **e**, does he . . . . Ps 94:9
that is in your brother's **e**, ... Lk 6:41
a camel to go through the **e**. . . . . Lk 18:25

EYES
Open my **e**, that I may . . . . Ps 119:18
I lift up my **e** to the hills. . . . . Ps 121:1
For the **e** of the Lord are on . . . . 1 Pt 3:12

EYEWITNESSES
from the beginning were **e**. . . . . Lk 1:2
Jesus Christ, but we were **e** . . . . 2 Pt 1:16

FACE
God was hovering over the **f** . . . . Gn 1:2
"For I have seen God **f**. . . . . Gn 32:30
said, "you cannot see my **f**, ... Ex 33:20
the LORD make his **f** to shine. . . . . Nm 6:25
Lift up the light of your **f** upon . . . . Ps 4:6
mirror dimly, but then **f** to **f**. . . . . 1 Cor 13:12
But the **f** of the Lord is. . . . . 1 Pt 3:12

FAIL
flesh and my heart may **f**, ... Ps 73:26
that your faith may not **f**. . . . . Lk 22:32
unless indeed you **f** to meet . . . . 2 Cor 13:5

FAILED
the word of God has **f**. . . . . Rom 9:6
Israel **f** to obtain what it. . . . . Rom 11:7
received the good news **f** . . . . Heb 4:6

FAILS
See to it that no one **f** to . . . . Heb 12:15
right thing to do and **f** to do it, ... Jas 4:17

FAITH
If you are not firm in **f**, you . . . . Is 7:9
righteous shall live by his **f**. . . . . Hb 2:4
you afraid, O you of little **f**?" . . . . Mt 8:26
in Israel have I found such **f**." . . . . Lk 7:9
of Man comes, will he find **f** . . . . Lk 18:8
who are sanctified by **f**. . . . . Acts 26:18
righteous shall live by **f**." . . . . Rom 1:17
That is why it depends on **f**, ... Rom 4:16
So **f** comes from hearing, ... Rom 10:17
stand firm in the **f**, ... 1 Cor 16:13
of the law but through **f** in Jesus. . . . . Gal 2:16
in your hearts through **f** . . . . Eph 3:17
one Lord, one **f**, one baptism, ... Eph 4:5
take up the shield of **f**, ... Eph 6:16
about you through your **f**. . . . . 1 Thes 3:7
the race, I have kept the **f**. . . . . 2 Tm 4:7
that the testing of your **f** . . . . Jas 1:3
if someone says he has **f** . . . . Jas 2:14
are being guarded through **f**. . . . . 1 Pt 1:5
Resist him, firm in your **f**, ... 1 Pt 5:9
to you to contend for the **f**. . . . . Jude 1:3

FAITHFUL
the LORD your God is God, the **f** . . . . Dt 7:9
will raise up for myself a **f** . . . . 1 Sm 2:35
The LORD is **f** in all his . . . . Ps 145:13
own steadfast love, but a **f**. . . . . Prv 20:6
A **f** man will abound with. . . . . Prv 28:20
because of the LORD, who is **f**, ... Is 49:7
"One who is **f** in a very little . . . . Lk 16:10
But the Lord is **f**. He will. . . . . 2 Thes 3:3
sober-minded, **f** in all things. . . . . 1 Tm 3:11
are faithless, he remains **f**. . . . . 2 Tm 2:13
for he who promised is **f**. . . . . Heb 10:23
one sitting on it is called **F**. . . . . Rv 19:11

FAITHFULLY
"And if you **f** obey the voice of. . . . . Dt 28:1
LORD, but those who act **f**. . . . . Prv 12:22
my word speak my word **f**. . . . . Jer 23:28

FAITHFULNESS
A God of **f** and without . . . . Dt 32:4
LORD are steadfast love and **f**, ... Ps 25:10
his **f** is a shield and buckler. . . . . Ps 91:4
be the belt of his waist, and **f**. . . . . Is 11:5
morning; great is your **f**. . . . . Lam 3:23
kindness, goodness, **f**, ... Gal 5:22

FAITHLESS
I look at the **f** with disgust, ... Ps 119:158
Return, O **f** children, declares . . . . Jer 3:14
if we are **f**, he remains. . . . . 2 Tm 2:13

FALL
a haughty spirit before a **f**. . . . . Prv 16:18
For if they **f**, one will lift up . . . . Eccl 4:10
And not one of them will **f**. . . . . Mt 10:29
for all have sinned and **f** . . . . Rom 3:23

FALLEN
How the mighty have **f**! . . . . 2 Sm 1:19
"How you are **f** from heaven, ... Is 14:12
him those who have **f** . . . . 1 Thes 4:14

FALLS
rejoice when your enemy **f**, ... Prv 24:17
unless a grain of wheat **f** . . . . Jn 12:24

FALSE
"You shall not bear **f** witness . . . . Ex 20:16
A **f** witness will not go . . . . Prv 19:5
"Beware of **f** prophets, who . . . . Mt 7:15
does what is detestable or **f**, ... Rv 21:27

FALSEHOOD
Remove far from me **f** and . . . . Prv 30:8
having put away **f**, let each . . . . Eph 4:25

FAMILIES
curse, and in you all the **f**. . . . . Gn 12:3
to the LORD, and all the **f** . . . . Ps 22:27

FAMINE
will arise seven years of **f**, ... Gn 41:30

GIFT
So if you are offering your **g** ... Mt 5:23
receive the **g** of the Holy Spirit. ... Acts 2:38
then God gave the same **g** ... Acts 11:17
But the free **g** is not like the ... Rom 5:15
But each has his own **g** ... 1 Cor 7:7
doing; it is the **g** of God, ... Eph 2:8
Do not neglect the **g** you ... 1 Tm 4:14
have tasted the heavenly **g**, ... Heb 6:4
Every good **g** and every perfect ... Jas 1:17

GIFTS
your train and receiving **g**. ... Ps 68:18
know how to give good **g** ... Mt 7:11
concerning spiritual **g**, ... 1 Cor 12:1
of captives, and he gave **g** ... Eph 4:8

GIVE
"To your offspring I will **g** ... Gn 12:7
upon you and **g** you peace. ... Nm 6:26
"Thus, when you **g** to the ... Mt 6:2
A new commandment I **g** ... Jn 13:34
the Father, and he will **g** ... Jn 14:16
'It is more blessed to **g** ... Acts 20:35
So then each of us will **g** ... Rom 14:12
Each one must **g** as he has ... 2 Cor 9:7
a loud voice, "Fear God and **g** ... Rv 14:7
To the thirsty I will **g** from ... Rv 21:6

GIVEN
For they are wholly **g** to me ... Nm 8:16
a child is born, to us a son is **g**; ... Is 9:6
Holy Spirit who has been **g** ... Rom 5:5

GIVES
And whoever **g** one of these ... Mt 10:42
It is the Spirit who **g** life; the ... Jn 6:63
thanks be to God, who **g** ... 1 Cor 15:57
the presence of God, who **g** ... 1 Tm 6:13

GIVING
so that your **g** may be in secret ... Mt 6:4
bore witness to them, by **g** ... Acts 15:8

GLAD
let the many coastlands be **g**! ... Ps 97:1
Rejoice and be **g**, for your ... Mt 5:12

GLADNESS
anointed you with the oil of **g** ... Ps 45:7
Let me hear joy and **g**; let the ... Ps 51:8
Serve the LORD with **g**! Come ... Ps 100:2
give them **g** for sorrow ... Jer 31:13
you with the oil of **g** ... Heb 1:9

GLORIFIED
he justified he also **g** ... Rom 8:30
that day to be **g** in his saints, ... 2 Thes 1:10
in everything God may be **g** ... 1 Pt 4:11

GLORIFY
heart, and I will **g** your name ... Ps 86:12
in him, God will also **g** him ... Jn 13:32
see your good deeds and **g** God ... 1 Pt 2:12

GLORIOUS
On the **g** splendor of your ... Ps 145:5
LORD shall be beautiful and **g**, ... Is 4:2
his law and make it **g** ... Is 42:21

GLORY
The **g** of the LORD dwelt on ... Ex 24:16
But the **g** of the LORD ... Nm 14:10
doors, that the King of **g** may ... Ps 24:7
It is the **g** of God to conceal ... Prv 25:2
whole earth is full of his **g**!" ... Is 6:3
And behold, the **g** of the God ... Ez 43:2
Son of Man comes in his **g**, ... Mt 25:31
your own presence with the **g** ... Jn 17:5
The God of **g** appeared to our ... Acts 7:2
and fall short of the **g** of God, ... Rom 3:23
comparing with the **g** ... Rom 8:18
us an eternal weight of **g** ... 2 Cor 4:17
to the riches of his **g** ... Eph 3:16
will appear with him in **g** ... Col 3:4
to shine on it, for the **g** of God ... Rv 21:23

GNATS
so that it may become **g** in all ... Ex 8:16
came swarms of flies, and **g** ... Ps 105:31

GOAT
one male **g** for a sin offering; ... Nm 7:16
lie down with the young **g**, ... Is 11:6

GOATS
the sheep from the **g** ... Mt 25:32
by means of the blood of **g** ... Heb 9:12

GOD
In the beginning, **G** created the ... Gn 1:1
Enoch walked with **G** after he ... Gn 5:22
Abraham said, "**G** will provide ... Gn 22:8
evil against me, but **G** meant ... Gn 50:20
no one like the LORD our **G** ... Ex 8:10
"I am the LORD your **G**, who ... Ex 20:2
G is not man, that he should ... Nm 23:19
LORD your **G** is a consuming fire, ... Dt 4:24
You shall love the LORD your **G** ... Dt 6:5
A **G** of faithfulness and ... Dt 32:4
dismayed, for the LORD your **G** ... Jos 1:9
things that the LORD your **G** ... Jos 23:14
LORD and said, "O Lord **G**, ... Jgs 16:28
be my people, and your **G** ... Ru 1:16
there is no rock like our **G** ... 1 Sm 2:2
But **G** will not take away ... 2 Sm 14:14
And **G** gave Solomon ... 1 Kgs 4:29
of Israel, there is no **G** ... 1 Kgs 8:23
If the LORD is **G**, follow ... 1 Kgs 18:21
"O LORD, the **G** of Israel, ... 2 Kgs 19:15
for the footstool of our **G**, ... 1 Chr 28:2
LORD filled the house of **G** ... 2 Chr 5:14
He set himself to seek **G** ... 2 Chr 26:5
king, "The hand of our **G** ... Ezr 8:22
But you are a **G** ready to ... Neh 9:17
yet in my flesh I shall see **G**, ... Jb 19:26
my deliverer, my **G**, my rock, ... Ps 18:2
heavens declare the glory of **G**, ... Ps 19:1
My **G**, my **G**, why have you ... Ps 22:1
still, and know that I am **G** ... Ps 46:10
Your way, O **G**, is holy ... Ps 77:13
should set their hope in **G** ... Ps 78:7
O **G**, do not keep silence; do ... Ps 83:1
sing for joy to the living **G** ... Ps 84:2
Every word of **G** proves true; ... Prv 30:5
Mighty **G**, Everlasting Father, ... Is 9:6
LORD is the everlasting **G**, ... Is 40:28
And I will be their **G**, and ... Jer 31:33
If this be so, our **G** whom we ... Dn 3:17
that are Caesar's, and to **G** ... Mt 22:21
The Lord our **G**, the Lord is ... Mk 12:29
will be impossible with **G**." ... Lk 1:37
shall love the Lord your **G** ... Lk 10:27
No one is good except **G** ... Lk 18:19
"For **G** so loved the world, that ... Jn 3:16
him, "My Lord and my **G**!" ... Jn 20:28
not lied to men but to **G**." ... Acts 5:4
'To the unknown **g**.' What ... Acts 17:23
but **G** shows his love for us in ... Rom 5:8
If **G** is for us, who can be ... Rom 8:31
Therefore be imitators of **G**, ... Eph 5:1
And my **G** will supply every ... Phil 4:19
For there is one **G**, and the ... 1 Tm 2:5
lacks wisdom, let him ask **G**, ... Jas 1:5
You believe that **G** is one; you ... Jas 2:19
holy, holy, is the Lord **G** ... Rv 4:8
For the Lord our **G** the ... Rv 19:6

GODLINESS
truth, which accords with **g**, ... Ti 1:1
that pertain to life and **g**, ... 2 Pt 1:3
be in lives of holiness and **g**, ... 2 Pt 3:11

GODLY
the LORD has set apart the **g** ... Ps 4:3
a peaceful and quiet life, **g** ... 1 Tm 2:2
all who desire to live a **g** ... 2 Tm 3:12

GODS
you, O LORD, among the **g**? ... Ex 15:11
shall have no other **g** before me ... Ex 20:3
You shall not make **g** of silver ... Ex 20:23

GOLD
is better than silver or **g** ... Prv 22:1
For which is greater, the **g** ... Mt 23:17
said, "I have no silver and **g**, ... Acts 3:6
more precious than **g** that ... 1 Pt 1:7

GOLIATH
a champion named **G** of Gath, ... 1 Sm 17:4

GOOD
and behold, it was very **g** ... Gn 1:31
me, but God meant it for **g**, ... Gn 50:20
there is none who does **g** ... Ps 14:1
No **g** thing does he withhold ... Ps 84:11
Woe to those who call evil **g** ... Is 5:20
The LORD is **g**, a stronghold in ... Na 1:7
said to him, 'Well done, **g** ... Mt 25:21
"Why do you call me **g**? ... Mk 10:18
Love your enemies, do **g** to ... Lk 6:27
are evil, know how to give **g** ... Lk 11:13
things work together for **g**, ... Rom 8:28
but overcome evil with **g** ... Rom 12:21
us not grow weary of doing **g**, ... Gal 6:9
he who began a **g** work in you ... Phil 1:6
they may see your **g** deeds ... 1 Pt 2:12

GOODNESS
Surely **g** and mercy shall ... Ps 23:6
For how great is his **g**, and ... Zec 9:17
kindness, **g**, faithfulness, ... Gal 5:22

GOSPEL
and proclaiming the **g** ... Mt 4:23
the **g** must first be proclaimed ... Mk 13:10
it all for the sake of the **g**, ... 1 Cor 9:23
that we may preach the **g** ... 2 Cor 10:16
is preaching to you a **g** contrary ... Gal 1:9
from the hope of the **g** ... Col 1:23
to be entrusted with the **g**, ... 1 Thes 2:4
share in suffering for the **g** ... 2 Tm 1:8
overhead, with an eternal **g** ... Rv 14:6

GOSSIPS
maliciousness. They are **g**, ... Rom 1:29
not only idlers, but also **g** ... 1 Tm 5:13

GRACE
full of **g** and truth ... Jn 1:14
and are justified by his **g** ... Rom 3:24
not under law but under **g** ... Rom 6:14
But he said to me, "My **g** ... 2 Cor 12:9
you have fallen away from **g** ... Gal 5:4
But **g** was given to each one ... Eph 4:7
The **g** of our Lord Jesus ... 2 Thes 3:18
For the **g** of God has appeared, ... Ti 2:11
near to the throne of **g**, ... Heb 4:16
set your hope fully on the **g** ... 1 Pt 1:13
stewards of God's varied **g**: ... 1 Pt 4:10
But grow in the **g** and ... 2 Pt 3:18

GRACIOUS
And I will be **g** to whom I ... Ex 33:19
to shine upon you and be **g** ... Nm 6:25
But the LORD was **g** to ... 2 Kgs 13:23
are a God merciful and **g**, ... Ps 86:15
The LORD is merciful and **g**, ... Ps 103:8
G is the LORD, and righteous; ... Ps 116:5
the LORD waits to be **g** ... Is 30:18
the God of hosts, will be **g** ... Am 5:15
Let your speech always be **g**, ... Col 4:6

HEALING
shall rise with **h** in its wings. ... Mal 4:2
gospel of the kingdom and **h** ... Mt 4:23
then gifts of **h**, helping, ... 1 Cor 12:28
of the tree were for the **h**. ... Rv 22:2

HEALS
all your iniquity, who **h**. ... Ps 103:3
He **h** the brokenhearted and. ... Ps 147:3

HEALTH
you restore him to full **h**. ... Ps 41:3
sweetness to the soul and **h**. ... Prv 16:24
Oh restore me to **h** and make. ... Is 38:16

HEAR
In that day the deaf shall **h** ... Is 29:18
And how are they to **h**. ... Rom 10:14

HEARD
I had **h** of you by the hearing. ... Jb 42:5
Who has **h** such a thing? Who. ... Is 66:8
"You have **h** that it was said to ... Mt 5:21
no eye has seen, nor ear **h**, ... 1 Cor 2:9
of God, which you **h** from. ... 1 Thes 2:13

HEART
LORD your God with all your **h** ... Dt 6:5
to him freely, and your **h** ... Dt 15:10
to serve him with all your **h** ... Jos 22:5
a man after his own **h**, ... 1 Sm 13:14
the LORD looks on the **h**." ... 1 Sm 16:7
My eyes and my **h** will be. ... 2 Chr 7:16
give you the desires of your **h**. ... Ps 37:4
Create in me a clean **h**, O God, ... Ps 51:10
cherished iniquity in my **h**, ... Ps 66:18
in the LORD with all your **h**, ... Prv 3:5
A joyful **h** is good medicine, ... Prv 17:22
A wise man's **h** inclines him ... Eccl 10:2
The **h** is deceitful above all. ... Jer 17:9
I will give you a new **h**, ... Ez 36:26
treasure is, there your **h** will be ... Mt 6:21
this they were cut to the **h**, ... Acts 2:37
draw near with a true **h** ... Heb 10:22
he who searches mind and **h**, ... Rv 2:23

HEARTS
that he may incline our **h** ... 1 Kgs 8:58
for the LORD searches all **h** ... 1 Chr 28:9
"Let not your **h** be troubled. ... Jn 14:1
having cleansed their **h** ... Acts 15:9
law is written on their **h**, ... Rom 2:15
but on tablets of human **h**. ... 2 Cor 3:3
Christ may dwell in your **h** ... Eph 3:17

HEAVEN
"How you are fallen from **h**, ... Is 14:12
behold, with the clouds of **h**. ... Dn 7:13
enter the kingdom of **h**. ... Mt 19:23
to them, "All authority in **h** ... Mt 28:18
But our citizenship is in **h**, ... Phil 3:20
and unfading, kept in **h** for you, ... 1 Pt 1:4

HEAVENLY
him a little lower than the **h** beings ... Ps 8:5
can you believe if I tell you **h** ... Jn 3:12
seated us with him in the **h** ... Eph 2:6
better country, that is, a **h** ... Heb 11:16

HEAVENS
The **h** declare the glory of God, ... Ps 19:1
The **h** declare his righteousness ... Ps 50:6
love is great above the **h**; ... Ps 108:4
we are waiting for new **h** ... 2 Pt 3:13

HEAVY
and night your hand was **h**. ... Ps 32:4
like a **h** burden, they are too ... Ps 38:4
all who labor and are **h** ... Mt 11:28

HEIR
own son shall be your **h**." ... Gn 15:4
a son, and if a son, then an **h**. ... Gal 4:7
whom he appointed the **h** ... Heb 1:2
the world and became an **h** ... Heb 11:7

HEIRS
vessel, since they are **h** with. ... 1 Pt 3:7

HELL
will be liable to the **h** of fire. ... Mt 5:22
both soul and body in **h**. ... Mt 10:28
of life, and set on fire by **h**. ... Jas 3:6

HELMET
as a breastplate, and a **h** ... Is 59:17
faith and love, and for a **h** ... 1 Thes 5:8

HELP
is none like you to **h**, ... 2 Chr 14:11
to my God I cried for **h**. From ... Ps 18:6
strength, a very present **h**. ... Ps 46:1
H us, O God of our salvation, ... Ps 79:9
From where does my **h** come? ... Ps 121:1
will strengthen you, I will **h** ... Is 41:10
"I believe; **h** my unbelief!" ... Mk 9:24

HELPER
I will make him a **h** fit for him." ... Gn 2:18
have been the **h** of the fatherless. ... Ps 10:14
say, "The Lord is my **h**; I will. ... Heb 13:6

HID
and the man and his wife **h** ... Gn 3:8
And Moses **h** his face, for he ... Ex 3:6
shall live, because she **h**. ... Jos 6:17

HIDDEN
and search for it as for **h** ... Prv 2:4
to you new things, **h** things ... Is 48:6
God, and your sins have **h** ... Is 59:2
the mystery **h** for ages and. ... Col 1:26

HIDE
h me in the shadow of your wings, ... Ps 17:8
H your face from my sins, and ... Ps 51:9
And I will not **h** my face any. ... Ez 39:29

HIDING
You are a **h** place for me; you. ... Ps 32:7
You are my **h** place and my ... Ps 119:114

HIGH
name of the LORD, the Most **H**. ... Ps 7:17
called the Son of the Most **H**. ... Lk 1:32

HILL
shall dwell on your holy **h**? ... Ps 15:1
city set on a **h** cannot be hidden. ... Mt 5:14

HILLS
the cattle on a thousand **h**. ... Ps 50:10
I lift up my eyes to the **h**. ... Ps 121:1

HINDER
for us, for nothing can **h**. ... 1 Sm 14:6
come to me and do not **h**. ... Mt 19:14

HOLD
Keep **h** of instruction; do not ... Prv 4:13
For I, the LORD your God, **h**. ... Is 41:13
who, hearing the word, **h**. ... Lk 8:15

HOLINESS
the LORD in the splendor of **h**. ... Ps 29:2
bringing **h** to completion ... 2 Cor 7:1
in true righteousness and **h**. ... Eph 4:24
and for the **h** without which. ... Heb 12:14

HOME
come **h** with shouts of joy, ... Ps 126:6
come to him and make our **h** ... Jn 14:23
pure, working at **h**, kind, ... Ti 2:5

HOMES
"See, we have left our **h**. ... Lk 18:28
breaking bread in their **h**, ... Acts 2:46

HOMOSEXUALITY
nor men who practice **h**, ... 1 Cor 6:9
men who practice **h**, enslavers ... 1 Tm 1:10

HONEST
speaks the truth gives **h**. ... Prv 12:17
Whoever gives an **h** answer ... Prv 24:26

HONEY
land flowing with milk and **h**, ... Ex 3:8
sweeter also than **h** and. ... Ps 19:10
my taste, sweeter than **h** ... Ps 119:103

HONOR
"**H** your father and your. ... Ex 20:12
crowned him with glory and **h**. ... Ps 8:5
humility comes before **h**. ... Prv 15:33
For God commanded, '**H** your ... Mt 15:4
that a prophet has no **h**. ... Jn 4:44
"**H** your father and mother" ... Eph 6:2
worthy of double **h**, ... 1 Tm 5:17
Let marriage be held in **h**. ... Heb 13:4
creatures give glory and **h** ... Rv 4:9

HONORABLE
is true, whatever is **h**, ... Phil 4:8
wood and clay, some for **h** ... 2 Tm 2:20

HONORS
person is despised, but who **h** ... Ps 15:4
is generous to the needy **h**. ... Prv 14:31

HOPE
do I wait? My **h** is in you. ... Ps 39:7
H in God; for I shall again ... Ps 42:5
I **h** in your word. ... Ps 119:81
H deferred makes the heart ... Prv 13:12
We set our **h** on you, for you ... Jer 14:22
Rejoice in **h**, be patient in. ... Rom 12:12
So now faith, **h**, and love ... 1 Cor 13:13
On him we have set our **h** ... 2 Cor 1:10
eagerly wait for the **h**. ... Gal 5:5
and our boasting in our **h**. ... Heb 3:6
to be born again to a living **h**. ... 1 Pt 1:3

HORSE
the **h** and his rider he has ... Ex 15:1
not in the strength of the **h**, ... Ps 147:10
A whip for the **h**, a bridle. ... Prv 26:3
a man riding on a red **h**! He. ... Zec 1:8
looked, and behold, a white **h**! ... Rv 6:2
and behold, a white **h**! The. ... Rv 19:11

HOSANNA
the Lord! **H** in the highest!" ... Mt 21:9

HOSPITABLE
respectable, **h**, able to teach, ... 1 Tm 3:2
but **h**, a lover of good, ... Ti 1:8

HOSPITALITY
saints and seek to show **h**. ... Rom 12:13
up children, has shown **h**, ... 1 Tm 5:10

HOST
were finished, and all the **h** ... Gn 2:1
As the **h** of heaven cannot ... Jer 33:22
multitude of the heavenly **h** ... Lk 2:13

HOSTILE
that is set on the flesh is **h**. ... Rom 8:7
once were alienated and **h**. ... Col 1:21
from sinners such **h** ... Heb 12:3

HOUR
anxious can add a single **h**. ... Mt 6:27
But the **h** is coming, and is. ... Jn 4:23

HOUSE
But as for me and my **h**, ... Jos 24:15
and I shall dwell in the **h** ... Ps 23:6
the LORD builds the **h**, ... Ps 127:1
By wisdom a **h** is built, and by ... Prv 24:3
h shall be called a **h** of prayer ... Is 56:7
divided against itself, that **h** ... Mk 3:25
In my Father's **h** are many ... Jn 14:2

HOUSEHOLD
will be those of his own **h** ... Mt 10:36
He must manage his own **h** ... 1 Tm 3:4

HUMAN
"Whoever takes a **h** life shall ... Lv 24:17
a stone was cut out by no **h** ... Dn 2:34

HUMBLE
are called by my name **h** ... 2 Chr 7:14
he adorns the **h** with salvation ... Ps 149:4
he who is **h** and contrite in ... Is 66:2
walk in pride he is able to **h** ... Dn 4:37
but gives grace to the **h**." ... Jas 4:6
H yourselves before the Lord, ... Jas 4:10
H yourselves, therefore, ... 1 Pt 5:6

HUMBLED
exalts himself will be **h**, ... Mt 23:12
he **h** himself by becoming ... Phil 2:8

HUMILITY
in wisdom, and **h** comes ... Prv 15:33
h, meekness, and patience, ... Col 3:12
yourselves, all of you, with **h** ... 1 Pt 5:5

HUNGER
they shall not **h** or thirst, ... Is 49:10
"Blessed are those who **h** and ... Mt 5:6
comes to me shall not **h**, ... Jn 6:35
They shall **h** no more, neither ... Rv 7:16

HUNGRY
the longing soul, and the **h** ... Ps 107:9
who gives food to the **h** ... Ps 146:7
If your enemy is **h**, give ... Prv 25:21
gives his bread to the **h** and ... Ez 18:7
"Blessed are you who are **h** ... Lk 6:21
if your enemy is **h**, feed him ... Rom 12:20

HURT
the fire, and they are not **h**; ... Dn 3:25
who conquers will not be **h** ... Rv 2:11

HUSBAND
desire shall be for your **h**, ... Gn 3:16
wife is the crown of her **h**, ... Prv 12:4
I betrothed you to one **h**, ... 2 Cor 11:2

HUSBANDS
H, love your wives, as ... Eph 5:25
young women to love their **h** ... Ti 2:4
Likewise, **h**, live with your ... 1 Pt 3:7

HYMN
when they had sung a **h**, ... Mt 26:30
each one has a **h**, a lesson, ... 1 Cor 14:26

HYMNS
praying and singing **h** ... Acts 16:25
singing psalms and **h** and ... Col 3:16

HYPOCRISY
but within you are full of **h** ... Mt 23:28
of the Pharisees, which is **h** ... Lk 12:1
malice and all deceit and **h** ... 1 Pt 2:1

HYPOCRITE
You **h**, first take the log out of ... Mt 7:5

HYPOCRITES
nor do I consort with **h** ... Ps 26:4
you must not be like the **h** ... Mt 6:5
put me to the test, you **h**? ... Mt 22:18

IDLE
brothers, admonish the **i**, ... 1 Thes 5:14
because we were not **i** ... 2 Thes 3:7
from long ago is not **i**, ... 2 Pt 2:3

IDOL
it he makes into a god, his **i**, ... Is 44:17
"an **i** has no real existence," ... 1 Cor 8:4
is anything, or that an **i** ... 1 Cor 10:19

IDOLATER
or greed, or is an **i**, reviler, ... 1 Cor 5:11
an **i**), has no inheritance in ... Eph 5:5

IDOLATRY
my beloved, flee from **i** ... 1 Cor 10:14
i, sorcery, enmity, strife, ... Gal 5:20
and covetousness, which is **i** ... Col 3:5

IDOLS
concerning food offered to **i**: ... 1 Cor 8:1
you turned to God from **i** ... 1 Thes 1:9
keep yourselves from **i** ... 1 Jn 5:21

IGNORANT
being **i** of the righteousness ... Rom 10:3
with foolish, **i** controversies; ... 2 Tm 2:23

IGNORES
at once, but the prudent **i** ... Prv 12:16
disgrace come to him who **i** ... Prv 13:18
Whoever **i** instruction ... Prv 15:32

IMAGE
make for yourself a carved **i**, ... Ex 20:4
the glory of God for the **i** ... Ps 106:20
conformed to the **i** of his Son, ... Rom 8:29
we shall also bear the **i** ... 1 Cor 15:49
He is the **i** of the invisible ... Col 1:15

IMITATE
ourselves an example to **i** ... 2 Thes 3:9
of their way of life, and **i** ... Heb 13:7
do not **i** evil but **i** good ... 3 Jn 1:11

IMITATORS
And you became **i** of us and ... 1 Thes 1:6
may not be sluggish, but **i** ... Heb 6:12

IMMANUEL
and shall call his name **I** ... Is 7:14
call his name **I**" (which means, ... Mt 1:23

IMMORAL
everyone who is sexually **i** ... Eph 5:5
the sexually **i**, men who ... 1 Tm 1:10
the sexually **i**, sorcerers, ... Rv 21:8

IMMORALITY
evident: sexual **i**, impurity, ... Gal 5:19
you abstain from sexual **i**; ... 1 Thes 4:3

IMMORTAL
exchanged the glory of the **i** God ... Rom 1:23
To the King of ages, **i**, ... 1 Tm 1:17

IMMORTALITY
for glory and honor and **i**, ... Rom 2:7
who alone has **i**, who ... 1 Tm 6:16
and brought life and **i** ... 2 Tm 1:10

IMPERISHABLE
wreath, but we an **i** ... 1 Cor 9:25
body must put on the **i**, ... 1 Cor 15:53
of perishable seed but of **i**, ... 1 Pt 1:23

IMPORTANT
commandment is the most **i** ... Mk 12:28

IMPOSSIBLE
propose to do will now be **i** ... Gn 11:6
move, and nothing will be **i** ... Mt 17:20

IMPURITY
not repented of the **i**, ... 2 Cor 12:21
God has not called us for **i**, ... 1 Thes 4:7

INCENSE
put the golden altar for **i** ... Ex 40:5
my prayer be counted as **i** ... Ps 141:2
having the golden altar of **i** ... Heb 9:4

INCOME
trouble befalls the **i** of the wicked ... Prv 15:6
who loves wealth with his **i**; ... Eccl 5:10

INCREASE
if riches **i**, set not your ... Ps 62:10
said to the Lord, "**I** our faith!" ... Lk 17:5
He must **i**, but I must ... Jn 3:30

INCREASED
And Jesus **i** in wisdom and in ... Lk 2:52
word of God **i** and multiplied ... Acts 12:24
trespass, but where sin **i**, ... Rom 5:20

INCREASING
the disciples were **i** in number, ... Acts 6:1
in every good work and **i** ... Col 1:10
of you for one another is **i** ... 2 Thes 1:3

INEXPRESSIBLE
Thanks be to God for his **i** ... 2 Cor 9:15
and rejoice with joy that is **i** ... 1 Pt 1:8

INFANTS
of the mouth of babies and **i**, ... Ps 8:2
read, "'Out of the mouth of **i** ... Mt 21:16
Be **i** in evil, but in your ... 1 Cor 14:20
Like newborn **i**, long for the ... 1 Pt 2:2

INHERIT
But the meek shall **i** the land ... Ps 37:11
are the meek, for they shall **i** ... Mt 5:5

INHERITANCE
that I may glory with your **i** ... Ps 106:5
the riches of his glorious **i** ... Eph 1:18
you to share in the **i** ... Col 1:12
the promised eternal **i**, ... Heb 9:15

INIQUITIES
repay us according to our **i** ... Ps 103:10
he was crushed for our **i**; ... Is 53:5
be merciful toward their **i**, ... Heb 8:12

INIQUITY
of faithfulness and without **i**, ... Dt 32:4
me thoroughly from my **i**, ... Ps 51:2
of the Lord depart from **i**." ... 2 Tm 2:19

INJUSTICE
you do, for there is no **i** ... 2 Chr 19:7
Is there **i** on God's part? By ... Rom 9:14

INNOCENT
I shall be blameless, and **i** ... Ps 19:13
so be wise as serpents and **i** ... Mt 10:16
you may be blameless and **i**, ... Phil 2:15
priest, holy, **i**, unstained, ... Heb 7:26

INSOLENT
slanderers, haters of God, **i**, ... Rom 1:30
persecutor, and **i** opponent ... 1 Tm 1:13

INSTRUCT
I will **i** you and teach you in ... Ps 32:8
knowledge and able to **i** ... Rom 15:14
mind of the Lord so as to **i** ... 1 Cor 2:16

INSTRUCTION
Hear, O sons, a father's **i**, and ... Prv 4:1
so that he may be able to give **i** ... Ti 1:9

INSTRUMENTS
play my music on stringed **i** ... Is 38:20
If even lifeless **i**, such as ... 1 Cor 14:7

INSULT
who has avenged the **i** ... 1 Sm 25:39
the prudent ignores an **i** ... Prv 12:16
in saying these things you **i** ... Lk 11:45

INSULTS
whoever **i** his brother will be ... Mt 5:22
weaknesses, **i**, hardships, ... 2 Cor 12:10

INTEGRITY
your father walked, with **i** ... 1 Kgs 9:4
I die I will not put away my **i** ... Jb 27:5
I will walk with **i** of heart ... Ps 101:2
and in your teaching show **i**, ... Ti 2:7

INTELLIGENCE
of God, with ability and **i**, ... Ex 31:3

listens to reproof gains **i**. ... Prv 15:32

INTERCESSION
the sin of many, and makes **i** ... Is 53:12
he always lives to make **i** ... Heb 7:25

INTERESTS
and his **i** are divided. And ... 1 Cor 7:34
look not only to his own **i**, ... Phil 2:4

INTERPRET
You know how to **i** the ... Mt 16:3
if there is no one to **i**, ... 1 Cor 14:28

INTERPRETATION
tongues, to another the **i** ... 1 Cor 12:10
from someone's own **i**. ... 2 Pt 1:20

INVITE
But when you give a feast, **i** ... Lk 14:13

IRON
I sharpens **i**, and one man ... Prv 27:17
rule them with a rod of **i**. ... Rv 19:15

IRREVERENT
Have nothing to do with **i**, ... 1 Tm 4:7
But avoid **i** babble, for it ... 2 Tm 2:16

ISAAC
she tells you, for through **I** ... Gn 21:12
he was tested, offered up **I**, ... Heb 11:17

ISHMAEL
You shall call his name **I**, ... Gn 16:11

ISRAEL
spoke thus to the people of **I**, ... Ex 6:9
I was holy to the LORD, the ... Jer 2:3
lost sheep of the house of **I**. ... Mt 10:6
I failed to obtain what it ... Rom 11:7

JACOB
so his name was called **J**. ... Gn 25:26
Now the sons of **J** were twelve. ... Gn 35:22

JEALOUS
I the LORD your God am a **j** ... Ex 20:5
I am exceedingly **j** for Jerusalem ... Zec 1:14
to make my fellow Jews **j**, ... Rom 11:14

JEALOUSY
they moved him to **j**. ... Ps 78:58
For while there is **j** and ... 1 Cor 3:3

JERICHO
When Joshua was by **J**, he ... Jos 5:13
By faith the walls of **J** fell ... Heb 11:30

JERUSALEM
the ark of God back to **J**, ... 2 Sm 15:29
desired to build in **J**, ... 1 Kgs 9:19
He carried away all **J** ... 2 Kgs 24:14
So I went to **J** and was ... Neh 2:11
I create **J** to be a joy, and her ... Is 65:18
"O **J**, **J**, the city that ... Mt 23:37
boy Jesus stayed behind in **J**. ... Lk 2:43
the heavenly **J**, and to ... Heb 12:22
the new **J**, which comes down ... Rv 3:12

JESUS
and you shall call his name **J**, ... Mt 1:21
Then **J** was led up by the Spirit ... Mt 4:1
But **J** remained silent. And ... Mt 26:63
beginning of the gospel of **J** ... Mk 1:1
And at the ninth hour **J** ... Mk 15:34
and truth came through **J**. ... Jn 1:17
"I am **J**, whom you are persecuting ... Acts 9:5
"Believe in the Lord **J**, ... Acts 16:31
"This **J**, whom I proclaim to ... Acts 17:3
"**J** I know, and Paul ... Acts 19:15
J himself being the cornerstone, ... Eph 2:20
so that at the name of **J** ... Phil 2:10
in the name of the Lord **J**, ... Col 3:17
of our great God and Savior **J** ... Ti 2:13
J, the Son of God, let us hold ... Heb 4:14

and coming of our Lord **J** ... 2 Pt 1:16
The revelation of **J** Christ, ... Rv 1:1
soon." Amen. Come, Lord **J**! ... Rv 22:20

JEW
the **J** first and also to the Greek ... Rom 1:16
the Jews I became as a **J**, ... 1 Cor 9:20
There is neither **J** nor Greek, ... Gal 3:28

JEWELS
She is more precious than **j**, ... Prv 3:15
adorns herself with her **j**. ... Is 61:10
for like the **j** of a crown they ... Zec 9:16

JEWS
has been born king of the **J**? ... Mt 2:2
"Are you the King of the **J**?" ... Mt 27:11
for salvation is from the **J**. ... Jn 4:22
For **J** demand signs and ... 1 Cor 1:22

JOIN
and do not **j** with those who ... Prv 24:21
j in imitating me, and keep ... Phil 3:17
surprised when you do not **j** ... 1 Pt 4:4

JOINED
What therefore God has **j**, ... Mt 19:6
But he who is **j** to the Lord ... 1 Cor 6:17
being **j** together, grows into a ... Eph 2:21

JOY
the **j** of the LORD is your strength ... Neh 8:10
You have put more **j** in my ... Ps 4:7
you make him glad with the **j** ... Ps 21:6
to God my exceeding **j**, and I ... Ps 43:4
Shout for **j** to God, all the earth; ... Ps 66:1
take **j** in the God of my salvation ... Hb 3:18
in my womb leaped for **j**. ... Lk 1:44
you good news of great **j** ... Lk 2:10
j, peace, patience, kindness, ... Gal 5:22
with the **j** of the Holy Spirit, ... 1 Thes 1:6
Count it all **j**, my brothers, ... Jas 1:2
in him and rejoice with **j** ... 1 Pt 1:8

JOYFUL
Make a **j** noise to the LORD, all ... Ps 98:4

JUDGE
for he comes to **j** the earth ... 1 Chr 16:33
God is a righteous **j**, and a God ... Ps 7:11
he will **j** the peoples with equity ... Ps 96:10
for there I will sit to **j** all the ... Jl 3:12
for I did not come to **j** the ... Jn 12:47
a day on which he will **j** ... Acts 17:31

JUDGED
under the law will be **j** ... Rom 2:12
But if we **j** ourselves ... 1 Cor 11:31
that we who teach will be **j** ... Jas 3:1

JUDGES
Then the LORD raised up **j**, ... Jgs 2:16
surely there is a God who **j** ... Ps 58:11
call on him as Father who **j** ... 1 Pt 1:17

JUDGMENT
but it is God who executes **j**, ... Ps 75:7
bring every deed into **j**, ... Eccl 12:14
will the LORD enter into **j**, ... Is 66:16
but has given all **j** to the Son, ... Jn 5:22
a fearful expectation of **j**, ... Heb 10:27
Mercy triumphs over **j**. ... Jas 2:13
For it is time for **j** to begin at ... 1 Pt 4:17

JUST
iniquity, **j** and upright is he. ... Dt 32:4
his hands are faithful and **j**; ... Ps 111:7
so that he might be **j** and ... Rom 3:26

JUSTICE
He executes **j** for the ... Dt 10:18
You shall not pervert **j**. You ... Dt 16:19
j and abundant righteousness ... Jb 37:23
sing of steadfast love and **j**; ... Ps 101:1

are they who observe **j**, ... Ps 106:3
When **j** is done, it is a joy to ... Prv 21:15
men do not understand **j**, ... Prv 28:5
seek **j**, correct oppression; ... Is 1:17
And I will make **j** the line, ... Is 28:17
For I the LORD love **j**; I hate ... Is 61:8
and establish **j** in the gate; it ... Am 5:15
But let **j** roll down like ... Am 5:24
LORD require of you but to do **j**, ... Mi 6:8
j and mercy and faithfulness ... Mt 23:23
enforced **j**, obtained ... Heb 11:33

JUSTIFICATION
and raised for our **j**. ... Rom 4:25
many trespasses brought **j**. ... Rom 5:16

JUSTIFIED
so that you may be **j** in your ... Ps 51:4
you were **j** in the name of ... 1 Cor 6:11
it is evident that no one is **j** ... Gal 3:11
so that being **j** by his grace we ... Ti 3:7

JUSTIFIES
He who **j** the wicked and he ... Prv 17:15
work but believes in him who **j** ... Rom 4:5
elect? It is God who **j**. ... Rom 8:33

KEEP
of Eden to work it and **k** it. ... Gn 2:15
The LORD bless you and **k** ... Nm 6:24
to fear me and to **k** all my ... Dt 5:29
all evil; he will **k** your life. ... Ps 121:7
to **k** you from stumbling ... Jude 1:24

KEEPS
the faithful God who **k** ... Dt 7:9
commandments and **k** them, ... Jn 14:21

KEPT
For when I **k** silent, my ... Ps 32:3
k in heaven for you, ... 1 Pt 1:4

KEYS
I will give you the **k** of the ... Mt 16:19
and I have the **k** of Death ... Rv 1:18

KILL
a time to **k**, and a time to ... Eccl 3:3
and they will **k** him, and he ... Mt 17:23

KILLED
and you **k** the Author of ... Acts 3:15
we are being **k** all the day ... Rom 8:36

KILLS
and whoever **k** a person ... Lv 24:21
For the letter **k**, but the ... 2 Cor 3:6

KIND
his words and **k** in all his ... Ps 145:13
for he is **k** to the ungrateful ... Lk 6:35
Love is patient and **k**; love ... 1 Cor 13:4
pure, working at home, **k**, ... Ti 2:5

KINDNESS
"He who withholds **k** from a ... Jb 6:14
I led them with cords of **k**, ... Hos 11:4
but to do justice, and to love **k**, ... Mi 6:8
of his **k** and forbearance and ... Rom 2:4
fallen, but God's **k** to you, ... Rom 11:22
k, goodness, faithfulness, ... Gal 5:22
k, humility, meekness, ... Col 3:12

KINDS
produced in me all **k** of ... Rom 7:8
is a root of all **k** of evils. ... 1 Tm 6:10

KING
In those days there was no **k** ... Jgs 17:6
your God was your **k**. ... 1 Sm 12:12
that the **K** of glory may come ... Ps 24:7
the LORD sits enthroned as **k**. ... Ps 29:10
has been born **k** of the Jews? ... Mt 2:2
your **k** is coming to you, ... Mt 21:5
he himself is Christ, a **k**." ... Lk 23:2

You are the **K** of Israel!" Jn 1:49
"You say that I am a **k**. For Jn 18:37
"We have no **k** but Caesar." Jn 19:15
K of kings and Lord of lords. Rv 19:16

KINGDOM
and you shall be to me a **k** of. Ex 19:6
Yours is the **k**, O LORD, 1 Chr 29:11
His **k** is an everlasting Dn 4:3
"Repent, for the **k** of heaven is. Mt 3:2
Your **k** come, your will be Mt 6:10
But seek first the **k** of God Mt 6:33
And this gospel of the **k**. Mt 24:14
inherit the **k** prepared for Mt 25:34
for to such belongs the **k** of Mk 10:14
for behold, the **k** of God is Lk 17:21
he cannot enter the **k** of God. Jn 3:5
a **k** that cannot be shaken, Heb 12:28

KINGS
May all **k** fall down before Ps 72:11
and all the **k** of the earth Ps 102:15
is God of gods and Lord of **k**, Dn 2:47
for **k** and all who are in 1 Tm 2:2
and the ruler of **k** on earth. Rv 1:5

KISS
K the Son, lest he be angry, Ps 2:12
righteousness and peace **k** Ps 85:10
the Son of Man with a **k**?" Lk 22:48

KNEE
'To me every **k** shall bow, Is 45:23
not bowed the **k** to Baal." Rom 11:4
every **k** shall bow to me, Rom 14:11
Jesus every **k** should bow, Phil 2:10

KNEES
For this reason I bow my **k** Eph 3:14

KNEW
you in the womb I **k** you, Jer 1:5
For although they **k** God, Rom 1:21

KNOCK
seek, and you will find; **k**, and it. Mt 7:7
I stand at the door and **k**. Rv 3:20

KNOW
K then in your heart that, Dt 8:5
For I **k** that my Redeemer Jb 19:25
"I **k** that you can do all Jb 42:2
still, and **k** that I am God. Ps 46:10
And I applied my heart to **k** Eccl 1:17
saying, '**K** the LORD,' for they Jer 31:34
do not let your left hand **k** Mt 6:3
yet the world did not **k** him. Jn 1:10
therefore **k** for certain that Acts 2:36
part; then I shall **k** fully, 1 Cor 13:12
that I may **k** him and the Phil 3:10
yet you do not **k** what Jas 4:14

KNOWLEDGE
counsel by words without **k**? Jb 38:2
Such **k** is too wonderful for Ps 139:6
LORD is the beginning of **k**; Prv 1:7
loves discipline loves **k**, Prv 12:1
Desire without **k** is not good, Prv 19:2
be full of the **k** of the LORD. Is 11:9
the **k** of him everywhere. 2 Cor 2:14
of Christ that surpasses **k**, Eph 3:19
treasures of wisdom and **k**. Col 2:3
what is falsely called "**k**," 1 Tm 6:20

KNOWN
Make them **k** to your children. Dt 4:9
You make **k** to me the path Ps 16:11
or hidden that will not be **k**. Mt 10:26
"For who has **k** the mind Rom 11:34

KNOWS
But he **k** the way that I take; Jb 23:10
For he **k** the secrets of the Ps 44:21
he **k** those who take refuge in Na 1:7
"The Lord **k** those who are 2 Tm 2:19

LABOR
Six days you shall **l**, and do Ex 20:9
not run in vain or **l** in vain. Phil 2:16

LABORER
Sweet is the sleep of a **l**, Eccl 5:12
"The **l** deserves his wages." 1 Tm 5:18

LACK
the LORD **l** no good thing. Ps 34:10
of your **l** of self-control. 1 Cor 7:5

LACKS
worthless pursuits **l** sense. Prv 12:11
If any of you **l** wisdom, let Jas 1:5

LAMB
and kill the Passover **l**. Ex 12:21
said, "Behold, the **L** of God, Jn 1:29
like a **l** before its shearer Acts 8:32
like that of a **l** without 1 Pt 1:19
the elders I saw a **L** standing, Rv 5:6
"Worthy is the **L** who was Rv 5:12

LAMBS
I am sending you out as **l** in Lk 10:3
He said to him, "Feed my **l**." Jn 21:15

LAME
their sight and the **l** walk, Mt 11:5
to enter life **l** than with two Mk 9:45
so that what is **l** may not Heb 12:13

LAMP
For you are my **l**, O LORD, 2 Sm 22:29
Your word is a **l** to my Ps 119:105
For the commandment is a **l** Prv 6:23
Nor do people light a **l** and Mt 5:15
light, and its **l** is the Lamb. Rv 21:23

LAMPS
who took their **l** and went to Mt 25:1
and keep your **l** burning, Lk 12:35

LAND
and let the dry **l** appear." And Gn 1:9
offspring I will give this **l**." Gn 12:7
You shall not pollute the **l** Nm 35:33
their sin and heal their **l**. 2 Chr 7:14
LORD in the **l** of the living. Ps 116:9
upright will inhabit the **l**, Prv 2:21
off out of the **l** of the living, Is 53:8
bring you into your own **l**. Ez 36:24

LANGUAGE
had one **l** and the same Gn 11:1
them speak in his own **l**. Acts 2:6
tribe and **l** and people and Rv 5:9

LAST
first, and with the **l**; I am he. Is 41:4
"I am the first and I am the **l**; Is 44:6
raise him up on the **l** day." Jn 6:40

LAUGH
time to weep, and a time to **l**; Eccl 3:4
weep now, for you shall **l**. Lk 6:21

LAUGHS
He who sits in the heavens **l**; Ps 2:4
but the Lord **l** at the wicked, Ps 37:13

LAUGHTER
said, "God has made **l** for me; Gn 21:6
our mouth was filled with **l**, Ps 126:2
Let your **l** be turned to Jas 4:9

LAW
do all the words of this **l**. Dt 29:29
from the **L** of God, clearly, Neh 8:8
but his delight is in the **l** of Ps 1:2
for a **l** will go out from me, Is 51:4
I will put my **l** within them, Jer 31:33
abolish the **L** or the Prophets; Mt 5:17
for this is the **L** and the Mt 7:12
For the **l** was given through Jn 1:17
For the **l** brings wrath, Rom 4:15
is the fulfilling of the **l**. Rom 13:10
the power of sin is the **l**. 1 Cor 15:56
of the **l** but through faith Gal 2:16
For the whole **l** is fulfilled Gal 5:14
by abolishing the **l** of Eph 2:15
own that comes from the **l**, Phil 3:9
keeps the whole **l** but fails in Jas 2:10

LAWLESSNESS
us from all **l** and to purify Ti 2:14
of sinning also practices **l**; 1 Jn 3:4

LAYING
I am **l** in Zion a stone of. Rom 9:33
Do not be hasty in the **l** 1 Tm 5:22
not **l** again a foundation of Heb 6:1

LEAD
of cloud to **l** them along the Ex 13:21
L me, O LORD, in your Ps 5:8
L me in your truth and teach Ps 25:5
and a little child shall **l** them. Is 11:6
and gently **l** those that are Is 40:11
And if the blind **l** the blind, Mt 15:14
that we may **l** a peaceful 1 Tm 2:2

LEADS
He **l** me beside still waters. Ps 23:2
the way is hard that **l** to life, Mt 7:14
There is sin that **l** to death; 1 Jn 5:16

LEARN
l to do good; seek justice, Is 1:17
upon you, and **l** from me, Mt 11:29

LEARNED
What you have **l** and Phil 4:9
you have **l** and have firmly 2 Tm 3:14

LEAST
Yet the one who is **l** in the Mt 11:11
For I am the **l** of the 1 Cor 15:9
from the **l** of them to the Heb 8:11

LEAVE
Peace I **l** with you; my peace Jn 14:27
"I will never **l** you nor Heb 13:5

LED
like a lamb that is **l** to the Is 53:7
I **l** them with cords of Hos 11:4
For all who are **l** by the Rom 8:14
But if you are **l** by the Spirit, Gal 5:18

LEND
to him and **l** him sufficient for Dt 15:8
And if you **l** to those from Lk 6:34

LENDS
to the poor **l** to the LORD, Prv 19:17

LENGTH
l of days forever and ever. Ps 21:4
for **l** of days and years of life Prv 3:2
and **l** and height and Eph 3:18

LETTER
by the Spirit, not by the **l**. Rom 2:29
For the **l** kills, but the 2 Cor 3:6
what we say in this **l**, 2 Thes 3:14

LETTERS
For they say, "His **l** are 2 Cor 10:10
as he does in all his **l** when 2 Pt 3:16

LEVEL
My foot stands on **l** ground; Ps 26:12
The path of the righteous is **l**; Is 26:7
places shall become **l** ways, Lk 3:5

LIAR
poor man is better than a **l**. Prv 19:22

for he is a **l** and the father of ... Jn 8:44
hates his brother, he is a **l**; ... 1 Jn 4:20

LIBERTY
to proclaim **l** to the captives, ... Is 61:1
For why should my **l** be ... 1 Cor 10:29
the law of **l**, and perseveres, ... Jas 1:25

LIE
you shall not **l** to one ... Lv 19:11
not man, that he should **l**, ... Nm 23:19
He makes me **l** down in ... Ps 23:2
for a **l** and worshiped and ... Rom 1:25
Do not **l** to one another, ... Col 3:9

LIFE
his nostrils the breath of **l**, ... Gn 2:7
the way to the tree of **l**. ... Gn 3:24
then you shall pay **l** for **l**, ... Ex 21:23
For the **l** of the flesh is in ... Lv 17:11
known to me the path of **l**; ... Ps 16:11
me finds **l** and obtains favor ... Prv 8:35
and kindness will find **l**, ... Prv 21:21
delivered my **l** from the pit ... Is 38:17
not be anxious about your **l**, ... Mt 6:25
and to give his **l** as a ... Mt 20:28
It is better for you to enter **l** ... Mk 9:43
down his **l** for the sheep. ... Jn 10:11
way, and the truth, and the **l**. ... Jn 14:6
you may have **l** in his name. ... Jn 20:31
to eternal **l** believed. ... Acts 13:48
lead the **l** that the Lord ... 1 Cor 7:17
kills, but the Spirit gives **l**. ... 2 Cor 3:6

LIFT
the LORD **l** up his ... Nm 6:26
I **l** up my eyes to the hills. ... Ps 121:1
Let us **l** up our hearts and ... Lam 3:41

LIFTED
he shall be high and **l** up, ... Is 52:13
And I, when I am **l** up from ... Jn 12:32

LIGHT
And God said, "Let there be **l**," ... Gn 1:3
The LORD is my **l** and my ... Ps 27:1
I will make you as a **l** for the ... Is 49:6
"You are the **l** of the world. ... Mt 5:14
the **l** has come into the world, ... Jn 3:19
"I am the **l** of the world. ... Jn 8:12
"'I have made you a **l** for ... Acts 13:47
and put on the armor of **l**. ... Rom 13:12
himself as an angel of **l**. ... 2 Cor 11:14
the Lord God will be their **l**, ... Rv 22:5

LIGHTNING
face like the appearance of **l**, ... Dn 10:6
For as the **l** comes from the ... Mt 24:27
His appearance was like **l**, ... Mt 28:3

LIKENESS
in our image, after our **l**. ... Gn 1:26
or any **l** of anything that is ... Ex 20:4
be satisfied with your **l**. ... Ps 17:15
who are made in the **l** of God. ... Jas 3:9

LION
and the **l** shall eat straw like ... Is 11:7
around like a roaring **l**, ... 1 Pt 5:8
the **L** of the tribe of Judah, ... Rv 5:5

LIPS
grace is poured upon your **l**; ... Ps 45:2
he who opens wide his **l** ... Prv 13:3
honors me with their **l**, ... Mt 15:8

LISTEN
I am well pleased; **l** to him." ... Mt 17:5
and they will **l** to my voice. ... Jn 10:16

LISTENS
but a wise man **l** to advice. ... Prv 12:15
is of the truth **l** to my voice." ... Jn 18:37

Whoever knows God **l** to us; ... 1 Jn 4:6

LIVE
life and eat, and **l** forever — ... Gn 3:22
man does not **l** by bread alone, ... Dt 8:3
a man dies, shall he **l** again? ... Jb 14:14
hear, that your soul may **l**; ... Is 55:3
but the righteous shall **l** by ... Hb 2:4
"'Man shall not **l** by bread ... Mt 4:4
though he die, yet shall he **l**, ... Jn 11:25
does not **l** in temples ... Acts 17:24
"The righteous shall **l** by ... Rom 1:17
For if we **l**, we **l** to the Lord, ... Rom 14:8
It is no longer I who **l**, but ... Gal 2:20
For to me to **l** is Christ, ... Phil 1:21
one shall **l** by faith, ... Heb 10:38
L as people who are free, ... 1 Pt 2:16

LIVES
I know that my Redeemer **l**, ... Jb 19:25
since he always **l** to make ... Heb 7:25
down our **l** for the brothers. ... 1 Jn 3:16

LONG
"How **l** will you go ... 1 Kgs 18:21
O LORD — how **l**? ... Ps 6:3

LONGING
O Lord, all my **l** is before you; ... Ps 38:9
For he satisfies the **l** soul, ... Ps 107:9
eager **l** for the revealing ... Rom 8:19
For in this tent we groan, **l** ... 2 Cor 5:2

LOOK
evil and cannot **l** at wrong, ... Hb 1:13
L, I tell you, lift up your eyes, ... Jn 4:35
as we **l** not to the things ... 2 Cor 4:18

LOOKING
Turn my eyes from **l** at ... Ps 119:37
l to Jesus, the founder and ... Heb 12:2

LOOKS
but the LORD **l** on the ... 1 Sm 16:7
everyone who **l** at a woman ... Mt 5:28
to the plow and **l** back is fit ... Lk 9:62
that everyone who **l** on the ... Jn 6:40
he is like a man who **l** ... Jas 1:23

LORD (LORD; Hb., *Yahweh*)
in the day that the **L** God ... Gn 2:4
too hard for the **L**? ... Gn 18:14
But the **L** hardened the ... Ex 9:12
for I the **L** your God am holy. ... Lv 19:2
L our God, the **L** is one. ... Dt 6:4
for it is the **L** your God who ... Dt 31:6
house, we will serve the **L**." ... Jos 24:15
If the **L** is God, follow ... 1 Kgs 18:21
"You are the **L**, you alone. ... Neh 9:6
The **L** gave, and the Lord has ... Jb 1:21
I have set the **L** always ... Ps 16:8
The **L** is my shepherd; I shall ... Ps 23:1
Cast your burden on the **L**, ... Ps 55:22
that has breath praise the **L**! ... Ps 150:6
Trust in the **L** with all your ... Prv 3:5
The name of the **L** is a ... Prv 18:10
For the day of the **L** is great ... Jl 2:11
and what does the **L** require ... Mi 6:8
The **L** is slow to anger and ... Na 1:3
glory of the **L** as the waters ... Hb 2:14
The **L** your God is in your ... Zep 3:17

LORD (Lord; Hb., *'Adonay*)
Remember the **L**, who is ... Neh 4:14
'Behold, the fear of the **L**, ... Jb 28:28
the **L** is the upholder of my ... Ps 54:4
and that to you, O **L**, For you ... Ps 62:12
The LORD says to my **L**: "Sit ... Ps 110:1
died I saw the **L** sitting upon a ... Is 6:1

LORD (Lord; Gk., *Kyrios*)
'Prepare the way of the **L**; ... Mt 3:3
L,' will enter the kingdom of ... Mt 7:21
"'The **L** said to my **L**, ... Mt 22:44
O Israel: The **L** our God, ... Mk 12:29
"Believe in the **L** Jesus, ... Acts 16:31
Jesus is **L** and believe in ... Rom 10:9
crucified the **L** of glory. ... 1 Cor 2:8
"Jesus is **L**" except in the ... 1 Cor 12:3
the Spirit of the **L** is, ... 2 Cor 3:17
cross of our **L** Jesus Christ, ... Gal 6:14
one **L**, one faith, one baptism, ... Eph 4:5
that Jesus Christ is **L**, ... Phil 2:11
Rejoice in the **L** always; Rejoice ... Phil 4:4
received Christ Jesus the **L**, ... Col 2:6
as for the **L** and not for men, ... Col 3:23
day of the **L** will come like ... 1 Thes 5:2
tasted that the **L** is good. ... 1 Pt 2:3

LORD'S (LORD'S; Hb., *Yahweh*)
But the **L** portion is his ... Dt 32:9
The earth is the **L** and the ... Ps 24:1
the **L** discipline or be weary ... Prv 3:11

LORD'S (Lord's; Gk., *Kyrios*)
you proclaim the **L** death ... 1 Cor 11:26

LOSE
For it is better that you **l** one ... Mt 5:29
that I should **l** nothing of all ... Jn 6:39

LOSES
and whoever **l** his life for ... Mt 10:39
silver coins, if she **l** one coin, ... Lk 15:8
Whoever loves his life **l** it, ... Jn 12:25

LOSS
up, he will suffer **l**, though ... 1 Cor 3:15
I count everything as **l** ... Phil 3:8

LOST
For I am **l**; for I am a man of ... Is 6:5
I will seek the **l**, and I will ... Ez 34:16
"I was sent only to the **l** ... Mt 15:24
if he has **l** one of them, ... Lk 15:4
to seek and to save the **l**." ... Lk 19:10
gave me I have **l** not one." ... Jn 18:9

LOTS
for my clothing they cast **l**. ... Ps 22:18
among them by casting **l**. ... Mt 27:35
And they cast **l** for them, ... Acts 1:26

LOVE
but you shall **l** your ... Lv 19:18
You shall **l** the LORD your God. ... Dt 6:5
you, to **l** the LORD your God, ... Jos 22:5
for his steadfast **l** endures ... 2 Chr 5:13
his steadfast **l** endures ... Ps 100:5
and abounding in steadfast **l**. ... Ps 145:8
but **l** covers all offenses. ... Prv 10:12
and his banner over me was **l**. ... Sg 2:4
Many waters cannot quench **l**, ... Sg 8:7
steadfast **l** with those who ... Dn 9:4
with the bands of **l**, and I ... Hos 11:4
"You shall **l** the Lord your ... Mt 22:37
you, that you **l** one another: ... Jn 13:34
the fruit of the Spirit is **l**, ... Gal 5:22
speaking the truth in **l** ... Eph 4:15
that your **l** may abound more ... Phil 1:9
by God to **l** one another, ... 1 Thes 4:9
For the **l** of money is a ... 1 Tm 6:10
to **l** and good works, ... Heb 10:24
"You shall **l** your neighbor as ... Jas 2:8
for a sincere brotherly **l**, ... 1 Pt 1:22
since **l** covers a multitude of ... 1 Pt 4:8
Christ and **l** one another, ... 1 Jn 3:23
Beloved, let us **l** one another, ... 1 Jn 4:7
God is **l**, and whoever abides ... 1 Jn 4:16
By this we know that we **l** ... 1 Jn 5:2
— that we **l** one another. ... 2 Jn 1:5

soul and with all your **m**. . . . . Mt 22:37
by the renewal of your **m**, ... Rom 12:2
my spirit prays but my **m** . . . . 1 Cor 14:14
and will not change his **m**, ... Heb 7:21
have unity of **m**, sympathy, ... 1 Pt 3:8

MINDS
you who test the **m** and hearts, ... Ps 7:9
put my laws into their **m**, ... Heb 8:10

MINISTERING
and the angels were **m** to . . . . Mk 1:13
Are they not all **m** spirits . . . . Heb 1:14

MINISTRY
and to the **m** of the word." . . . . Acts 6:4
us the **m** of reconciliation; . . . . 2 Cor 5:18
an evangelist, fulfill your **m**. . . . . 2 Tm 4:5
Christ has obtained a **m** that . . . . Heb 8:6

MIRACLES
his **m** and the judgments . . . . 1 Chr 16:12
the working of **m**, ... 1 Cor 12:10
and various **m** and by gifts . . . . Heb 2:4

MIRROR
For now we see in a **m**. . . . . 1 Cor 13:12

MISERY
over the **m** of Israel. . . . . Jgs 10:16
their paths are ruin and **m**, ... Rom 3:16

MISLEADS
"'Cursed be anyone who **m** . . . . Dt 27:18
Whoever **m** the upright . . . . Prv 28:10

MIST
and a **m** was going up from . . . . Gn 2:6
a cloud and your sins like **m**; . . . . Is 44:22
For you are a **m** that . . . . Jas 4:14

MOCK
All who see me **m** me; they . . . . Ps 22:7
And they will **m** him and . . . . Mk 10:34

MOCKED
And at noon Elijah **m**. . . . . 1 Kgs 18:27
they **m** him, saying, "Hail, ... Mt 27:29
not be deceived: God is not **m**, ... Gal 6:7

MODESTY
treated with greater **m**, ... 1 Cor 12:23
with **m** and self-control, ... 1 Tm 2:9

MOMENT
joy of the godless but for a **m**? . . . . Jb 20:5
For his anger is but for a **m**, ... Ps 30:5
in a **m**, in the twinkling . . . . 1 Cor 15:52

MONEY
and he who has no **m**, come, ... Is 55:1
nor bag, nor bread, nor **m**; . . . . Lk 9:3
the gift of God with **m**! . . . . Acts 8:20
For the love of **m** is a root . . . . 1 Tm 6:10

MOON
fingers, the **m** and the stars, ... Ps 8:3
and the **m** will not give its . . . . Mt 24:29
and the **m** to blood, ... Acts 2:20

MORNING
evening and there was **m**, ... Gn 1:5
in the **m** you hear my voice; . . . . Ps 5:3
they are new every **m**; . . . . Lam 3:23
of David, the bright **m** star." . . . . Rv 22:16

MORTAL
'Can **m** man be in the right . . . . Jb 4:17
and the **m** puts on . . . . 1 Cor 15:54

MOSES
Now **M** was keeping the flock . . . . Ex 3:1
while **M** went up to God. . . . . Ex 19:3
just as **M** also was faithful in . . . . Heb 3:2
And they sing the song of **M**, ... Rv 15:3

MOTHER
and his **m** and hold fast . . . . Gn 2:24
because she was the **m** of all . . . . Gn 3:20
cursed his father or his **m**; . . . . Lv 20:9
foolish man despises his **m**. . . . . Prv 15:20
As one whom his **m** comforts, ... Is 66:13
When his **m** Mary had been . . . . Mt 1:18

MOTHER'S
my **m** womb, and naked shall . . . . Jb 1:21

MOUNTAIN
came to Horeb, the **m** of God. . . . . Ex 3:1
city of our God! His holy **m**, ... Ps 48:1
the Spirit to a great, high **m**, ... Rv 21:10

MOUNTAINS
How beautiful upon the **m** . . . . Is 52:7
the **m** and the hills before . . . . Is 55:12
faith, so as to remove **m**, ... 1 Cor 13:2

MOURN
and those who **m** are lifted to . . . . Jb 5:11
a time to laugh; a time to **m**, ... Eccl 3:4
God; to comfort all who **m**; . . . . Is 61:2
"Blessed are those who **m**, ... Mt 5:4

MOURNING
and your days of **m** shall be . . . . Is 60:20
I will turn their **m** into joy; . . . . Jer 31:13
neither shall there be **m**, nor . . . . Rv 21:4

MOUTH
shall not depart from your **m**, ... Jos 1:8
Let the words of my **m** and . . . . Ps 19:14
He put a new song in my **m**, ... Ps 40:3
in your **m** and covered you . . . . Is 51:16
of the heart the **m** speaks. . . . . Mt 12:34

MULTIPLY
"Be fruitful and **m** and fill . . . . Gn 1:22
they shall be fruitful and **m**. . . . . Jer 23:3
I will bless you and **m** you." . . . . Heb 6:14

MULTITUDE
and will cover a **m** of sins. . . . . Jas 5:20
since love covers a **m** of sins. . . . . 1 Pt 4:8
a great **m** that no one could. . . . . Rv 7:9

MURDER
"You shall not **m**. . . . . Ex 20:13
those of old, 'You shall not **m**; . . . . Mt 5:21
adultery, You shall not **m**, ... Rom 13:9

MURDERER
The **m** shall be put to death. . . . . Nm 35:16
you suffer as a **m** or a thief . . . . 1 Pt 4:15
hates his brother is a **m**, ... 1 Jn 3:15

MURDERERS
fathers and mothers, for **m**, ... 1 Tm 1:9
the detestable, as for **m**, ... Rv 21:8

MUSIC
you, O Lord, I will make **m**. . . . . Ps 101:1
and we will play my **m** on . . . . Is 38:20

MUSTARD
like a grain of **m** seed that a . . . . Mt 13:31
faith like a grain of **m** seed, ... Mt 17:20

MYSTERY
you to understand this **m**, ... Rom 11:25
I tell you a **m**. We shall. . . . . 1 Cor 15:51

MYTHS
truth and wander off into **m**. . . . . 2 Tm 4:4
Jewish **m** and the commands . . . . Ti 1:14
devised **m** when we made . . . . 2 Pt 1:16

NAKED
were both **n** and were not . . . . Gn 2:25
And he said, "**N** I came from . . . . Jb 1:21
house; when you see the **n**, ... Is 58:7

NAME
This is my **n** forever, and. . . . . Ex 3:15
"You shall not take the **n** of . . . . Ex 20:7
to put his **n** and make his. . . . . Dt 12:5
build the house for my **n**.' . . . . 1 Kgs 5:5
A good **n** is to be chosen . . . . Prv 22:1
my people shall know my **n**. . . . . Is 52:6
had concern for my holy **n**, ... Ez 36:21
everyone whose **n** shall be . . . . Dn 12:1
him, who believed in his **n**, ... Jn 1:12
Whatever you ask in my **n**, ... Jn 14:13
you may have life in his **n**. . . . . Jn 20:31
for there is no other **n** . . . . Acts 4:12
do everything in the **n** of . . . . Col 3:17
as the **n** he has inherited . . . . Heb 1:4
And if anyone's **n** was not . . . . Rv 20:15

NAME'S
for my **n** sake, and you have. . . . . Rv 2:3

NAMES
but rejoice that your **n** are . . . . Lk 10:20
earth whose **n** have not been. . . . . Rv 17:8

NATION
I will make of you a great **n**, ... Gn 12:2
Blessed is the **n** whose God . . . . Ps 33:12
a royal priesthood, a holy **n**, ... 1 Pt 2:9

NATIONS
father of a multitude of **n**. . . . . Gn 17:4
He makes **n** great, and he . . . . Jb 12:23
Behold, the **n** are like a drop . . . . Is 40:15
And the **n** will know that I . . . . Ez 36:23
kingdom, that all peoples, **n**, ... Dn 7:14
and make disciples of all **n**, ... Mt 28:19
first be proclaimed to all **n**. . . . . Mk 13:10
proclaimed among the **n**, ... 1 Tm 3:16

NATURAL
n relations for those. . . . . Rom 1:26
not spare the **n** branches, ... Rom 11:21
The **n** person does not . . . . 1 Cor 2:14
If there is a **n** body, ... 1 Cor 15:44

NATURE
by **n** do what the law. . . . . Rom 2:14
the exact imprint of his **n**, ... Heb 1:3

NEED
lend him sufficient for his **n**, ... Dt 15:8
to share with anyone in **n**. . . . . Eph 4:28
every **n** of yours according . . . . Phil 4:19
grace to help in time of **n**. . . . . Heb 4:16

NEEDY
out her hands to the **n**. . . . . Prv 31:20

NEGLECT
and be wise, and do not **n** it. . . . . Prv 8:33
Do not **n** to show hospitality . . . . Heb 13:2

NEIGHBOR
but you shall love your **n** . . . . Lv 19:18
Whoever despises his **n** is. . . . . Prv 14:21
Better is a **n** who is near . . . . Prv 27:10
Let each of us please his **n**. . . . . Rom 15:2
"You shall love your **n** as . . . . Gal 5:14
speak the truth with his **n**, ... Eph 4:25
each one his **n** and each . . . . Heb 8:11

NEIGHBOR'S
your **n** wife, or his male . . . . Ex 20:17
n landmark, which the men . . . . Dt 19:14
your **n** house, lest he have . . . . Prv 25:17

NEW
Sing to him a **n** song; play . . . . Ps 33:3
He put a **n** song in my mouth, ... Ps 40:3
and there is nothing **n** . . . . Eccl 1:9
"For behold, I create **n** . . . . Is 65:17
And I will give you a **n**. . . . . Ez 36:26
Neither is **n** wine put into. . . . . Mt 9:17

PATHS
he will make straight your **p**. . . . . Prv 3:6
the Lord; make his **p** straight.' . . . . Mt 3:3
and make straight **p** for . . . . Heb 12:13

PATIENCE
has endured with much **p**. . . . . Rom 9:22
peace, **p**, kindness, goodness, ... Gal 5:22
perfect **p** as an example . . . . 1 Tm 1:16

PATIENT
hope, be **p** in tribulation, ...Rom 12:12
Love is **p** and kind; love . . . . 1 Cor 13:4
Be **p**, therefore, brothers, until . . . . .Jas 5:7
but is **p** toward you, not. . . . . 2 Pt 3:9

PATIENTLY
I waited **p** for the LORD; he. . . . . Ps 40:1
to teach, **p** enduring evil, ... 2 Tm 2:24

PAUL
who was also called **P**, ...Acts 13:9

PAY
wrath will **p** the penalty, ... Prv 19:19
Is it lawful to **p** taxes to . . . . Mt 22:17
P to all what is owed to. . . . . Rom 13:7

PEACE
upon you and give you **p**. . . . . Nm 6:26
good; seek **p** and pursue it. . . . . Ps 34:14
for war, and a time for **p**. . . . . Eccl 3:8
Everlasting Father, Prince of **P**. . . . . .Is 9:6
You keep him in perfect **p**. . . . . .Is 26:3
We looked for **p**, but no good. . . . . Jer 8:15
come to bring **p** to the earth. . . . . Mt 10:34
that in me you may have **p**. . . . . Jn 16:33
preaching good news of **p** . . . . .Acts 10:36
we have **p** with God. . . . . Rom 5:1
God of confusion but of **p**. . . . . 1 Cor 14:33
joy, **p**, patience, kindness, ... Gal 5:22
of the Spirit in the bond of **p**. . . . . Eph 4:3
given by the gospel of **p**. . . . . Eph 6:15
And the **p** of God, which . . . . Phil 4:7
And let the **p** of Christ rule. . . . . Col 3:15
faith, love, and **p**, ... 2 Tm 2:22

PEACEMAKERS
"Blessed are the **p**, for they . . . . Mt 5:9

PEARL
who, on finding one **p** of . . . . Mt 13:46
the gates made of a single **p**, ... Rv 21:21

PEARLS
and do not throw your **p** . . . . .Mt 7:6
and gold or **p** or costly attire, ... 1 Tm 2:9

PENTECOST
When the day of **P** arrived, ...Acts 2:1

PEOPLE
"Behold, they are one **p**, ... Gn 11:6
take you to be my **p**, and I will be . . . . Ex 6:7
Your **p** shall be my **p**, and . . . . Ru 1:16
shall be shepherd of my **p** Israel, ... 2 Sm 5:2
The LORD is the strength of his **p**; . . . . Ps 28:8
the LORD will not forsake his **p**; . . . . Ps 94:14
know, my **p** do not understand." . . . . .Is 1:3
But my **p** have forgotten me; . . . . Jer 18:15
My **P**, for you are not my **p**, ... Hos 1:9
who will shepherd my **p** Israel.'" . . . . Mt 2:6
many in this city who are my **p**. . . . . . .Acts 18:10
purify for himself a **p** for his own . . . . Ti 2:14
propitiation for the sins of the **p**. . . . . . . Heb 2:17
a **p** for his own possession . . . . 1 Pt 2:9

PEOPLES
Clap your hands, all **p**! Shout. . . . . Ps 47:1
all nations! Extol him, all **p**! . . . . Ps 117:1
kingdom, that all **p**, nations, ...Dn 7:14
the hills; and **p** shall flow to it, ... Mi 4:1

PERFECT
My dove, my **p** one, is the only . . . . Sg 6:9
You keep him in **p** peace . . . . .Is 26:3
for my power is made **p** in . . . . 2 Cor 12:9
that you may be **p** and. . . . . .Jas 1:4
Every good gift and every **p** . . . . .Jas 1:17
but **p** love casts out fear. . . . . 1 Jn 4:18

PERFECTION
I have seen a limit to all **p**, ... Ps 119:96
Now if **p** had been attainable. . . . . Heb 7:11

PERISH
They will **p**, but you will . . . . Ps 102:26
you will all likewise **p**. . . . . Lk 13:3
life, and they will never **p**, ... Jn 10:28

PERISHABLE
For this **p** body must put . . . . 1 Cor 15:53
not with **p** things such as. . . . . 1 Pt 1:18

PERSECUTE
pray for those who **p** you, ... Mt 5:44
me, they will also **p** you. . . . . Jn 15:20
Bless those who **p** you; . . . . .Rom 12:14

PERSECUTED
bless; when **p**, we endure; . . . . 1 Cor 4:12
in Christ Jesus will be **p**, ... 2 Tm 3:12

PERSIST
P in this, for by so doing . . . . 1 Tm 4:16
As for those who **p** in sin, ... 1 Tm 5:20

PERVERT
in secret to **p** the ways of. . . . . .Prv 17:23
who **p** the grace of our God . . . . Jude 1:4

PERVERTS
"'Cursed be anyone who **p**. . . . . Dt 27:19

PHARISEE
You blind **P**! First clean the . . . . Mt 23:26
"Brothers, I am a **P**, a son . . . . .Acts 23:6
Hebrews; as to the law, a **P**; . . . . Phil 3:5

PHILOSOPHY
captive by **p** and empty deceit, ... Col 2:8

PIERCED
they have **p** my hands and . . . . Ps 22:16
on him whom they have **p**, ... Zec 12:10

PILATE
him over to **P** the governor. . . . . .Mt 27:2
P answered, "What I have . . . . Jn 19:22

PILLAR
and she became a **p** of salt. . . . . Gn 19:26
by day in a **p** of cloud to . . . . Ex 13:21
a **p** and buttress of the truth . . . . 1 Tm 3:15

PIT
He drew me up from the **p** of. . . . . Ps 40:2
your life from the **p**, ... Ps 103:4
and threw him into the **p**, ... Rv 20:3

PLACES
blessing in the heavenly **p**, ... Eph 1:3
once for all into the holy **p**, ... Heb 9:12

PLAGUE
"Yet one **p** more I will bring . . . . Ex 11:1
earth with every kind of **p**, ... Rv 11:6

PLAN
Do not **p** evil against your . . . . .Prv 3:29
p and foreknowledge of . . . . .Acts 2:23
as a **p** for the fullness of . . . . Eph 1:10

PLANNED
I **p** from days of old . . . . 2 Kgs 19:25
"As I have **p**, so shall it be, ...Is 14:24

PLANS
desire and fulfill all your **p**! . . . . Ps 20:4
the **p** of his heart to all . . . . Ps 33:11
P are established by. . . . . .Prv 20:18

But he who is noble **p** noble. . . . . .Is 32:8

PLANTS
vegetation, **p** yielding seed, ...Gn 1:11
So neither he who **p** nor. . . . . 1 Cor 3:7
Who **p** a vineyard without . . . . 1 Cor 9:7

PLAYED
"'We **p** the flute for you, ... Lk 7:32
anyone know what is **p**? . . . . 1 Cor 14:7

PLEAD
If you will seek God and **p** . . . . Jb 8:5
and to the Lord I **p** for mercy: . . . . Ps 30:8

PLEASANT
tree that is **p** to the sight . . . . .Gn 2:9
Behold, how good and **p** it is . . . . Ps 133:1
How beautiful and **p** you are, ... Sg 7:6

PLEASE
This will **p** the LORD more . . . . Ps 69:31
but to **p** God who tests our . . . . 1 Thes 2:4
since his aim is to **p** the one. . . . . 2 Tm 2:4

PLEASED
with whom I am well **p**." . . . . .Mt 3:17
commended as having **p** God. . . . . Heb 11:5

PLEASES
for this **p** the Lord. . . . . Col 3:20
and do what **p** him. . . . . 1 Jn 3:22

PLEASING
May my meditation be **p** to . . . . Ps 104:34
of the Lord, fully **p** to him, ... Col 1:10
for such sacrifices are **p** to . . . . Heb 13:16

PLEASURE
but the LORD takes **p** in . . . . Ps 147:11
lovers of **p** rather than . . . . 2 Tm 3:4

PLEASURES
cares and riches and **p** of life, ... Lk 8:14

POLLUTED
And they **p** the house of. . . . . 2 Chr 36:14
spring or a **p** fountain is a . . . . .Prv 25:26
from the things **p** by idols, ...Acts 15:20

POOR
But there will be no **p** among. . . . . Dt 15:4
The LORD makes **p** and . . . . 1 Sm 2:7
and the hope of the **p** shall . . . . Ps 9:18
delivering the **p** from him. . . . . Ps 35:10
who is generous to the **p**. . . . . .Prv 14:21
Better is a **p** person who . . . . .Prv 19:1
defend the rights of the **p** . . . . .Prv 31:9
"Blessed are the **p** in spirit, ...Mt 5:3
possess and give to the **p**, ... Mt 19:21
For you always have the **p** . . . . .Mt 26:11
for your sake he became **p**, ... 2 Cor 8:9
those who are **p** in the world . . . . .Jas 2:5

PORTION
my heart and my **p** forever. . . . . Ps 73:26
they shall possess a double **p**; . . . . .Is 61:7
"The LORD is my **p**," says . . . . .Lam 3:24

POSSESS
to give you this land to **p**." . . . . .Gn 15:7
the land to you to **p** it. . . . . Nm 33:53
and **p** the kingdom forever, ... Dn 7:18

POSSESSION
I will give it to you for a **p**. . . . . Ex 6:8
a better **p** and an abiding. . . . . Heb 10:34
a people for his own **p**, ... 1 Pt 2:9

POSSESSIONS
in the abundance of his **p**." . . . . Lk 12:15

POSSIBLE
with God all things are **p**." . . . . Mt 19:26
that by any means **p** I may. . . . . Phil 3:11

O LORD, my rock and my **r**. . . . . Ps 19:14
Holy One of Israel is your **R**, ...Is 54:5

REDEEMS
The LORD **r** the life of his . . . . Ps 34:22
who **r** your life from the pit, ... Ps 103:4
that **r** them from the . . . . Heb 9:15

REDEMPTION
then he shall give for the **r**. . . . . Ex 21:30
Take my right of **r** yourself, ...Ru 4:6
He sent **r** to his people; he . . . . Ps 111:9
because your **r** is drawing. . . . . Lk 21:28
through the **r** that is in. . . . . Rom 3:24
in whom we have **r**, the . . . . Col 1:14

REFUGE
to be cities of **r** for you, ... Nm 35:11
God is our **r** and strength, ... Ps 46:1
But the LORD is a **r** to his . . . . .Jl 3:16

REGARD
So do not let what you **r** . . . . .Rom 14:16
we **r** no one according to . . . . .2 Cor 5:16
"My son, do not **r** lightly the . . . . .Heb 12:5

REIGN
The LORD will **r** forever, ... Ps 146:10
Let not sin therefore **r** in . . . . Rom 6:12
For he must **r** until he. . . . . .1 Cor 15:25

REIGNS
The LORD **r**, let the earth. . . . . Ps 97:1
Lord our God the Almighty **r**. . . . . Rv 19:6

REJECTED
builders **r** has become the . . . . Ps 118:22
He was despised and **r** by. . . . . .Is 53:3
the stone that was **r** by you, ...Acts 4:11
and nothing is to be **r** if it is. . . . . 1 Tm 4:4

REJECTS
one who **r** me **r** him who sent . . . . Lk 10:16
The one who **r** me and does. . . . . Jn 12:48

REJOICE
let us **r** and be glad in it. . . . . Ps 118:24
and **r** in the wife of your . . . . .Prv 5:18
R with those who **r**, ...Rom 12:15
R in the Lord always; again . . . . Phil 4:4

REJOICES
is glad, and my whole being **r**; . . . . Ps 16:9
and my spirit **r** in God my. . . . . Lk 1:47
but **r** with the truth. . . . . .1 Cor 13:6

REJOICING
r that they were counted . . . . .Acts 5:41
as sorrowful, yet always **r**; . . . . .2 Cor 6:10

RELIGION
r and asceticism and . . . . Col 2:23
R that is pure and undefiled. . . . . .Jas 1:27

RELY
our God, for we **r** on you, ...2 Chr 14:11
But that was to make us **r** . . . . .2 Cor 1:9
For all who **r** on works of. . . . . Gal 3:10

REMEMBER
I will see it and **r** the . . . . .Gn 9:16
R also your Creator in the . . . . .Eccl 12:1
and I will not **r** your sins. . . . . .Is 43:25
and I will **r** their sin no. . . . . .Jer 31:34
they asked us to **r** the poor, ... Gal 2:10
and I will **r** their sins no . . . . .Heb 8:12

REMEMBERS
he **r** that we are dust. . . . . Ps 103:14
He **r** his covenant forever, ... Ps 105:8

REMEMBRANCE
for you. Do this in **r** of me." . . . . Lk 22:19
you. Do this in **r** of me." . . . . .1 Cor 11:24

REMNANT
for you a **r** on earth, ...Gn 45:7
A **r** will return, the **r**. . . . . .Is 10:21
I will gather the **r** of Israel; . . . . Mi 2:12
present time there is a **r**, ... Rom 11:5

RENEWAL
wait, till my **r** should come. . . . . Jb 14:14
but be transformed by the **r** . . . . Rom 12:2
regeneration and **r** of the Holy . . . . .Ti 3:5

RENEWED
youth is **r** like the eagle's. . . . . Ps 103:5
is being **r** day by day. . . . . .2 Cor 4:16

RENOUNCE
who does not **r** all that he . . . . Lk 14:33

REPAY
The LORD **r** you for what you. . . . . Ru 2:12
R no one evil for evil, but. . . . . .Rom 12:17
is mine; I will **r**." And . . . . Heb 10:30

REPENT
and **r** in dust and ashes." . . . . Jb 42:6
I tell you; but unless you **r**, ... Lk 13:3
And Peter said to them, "**R**. . . . . .Acts 2:38

REPENTANCE
righteous but sinners to **r**." . . . . Lk 5:32
and that **r** and forgiveness . . . . Lk 24:47
produces a **r** that leads to . . . . .2 Cor 7:10
but that all should reach **r**. . . . . .2 Pt 3:9

REPENTS
who **r** than over ninety-nine . . . . .Lk 15:7
him, and if he **r**, forgive him, ... Lk 17:3

REPROACH
overseer must be above **r**, ... 1 Tm 3:2
and bear the **r** he endured. . . . . Heb 13:13

REQUESTS
we have the **r** that we have . . . . 1 Jn 5:15

REQUIRE
the LORD your God **r** of you, ... Dt 10:12
and what does the LORD **r** of . . . . Mi 6:8

RESCUE
deliver me and **r** me; . . . . Ps 71:2
how to **r** the godly from . . . . .2 Pt 2:9

RESCUES
He delivers and **r**; he works . . . . .Dn 6:27

RESIST
R the devil, and he will flee . . . . .Jas 4:7
R him, firm in your faith, ...1 Pt 5:9

RESPECT
r to whom **r** is owed, ... Rom 13:7
brothers, to **r** those who labor . . . . . . 1 Thes 5:12
do it with gentleness and **r**, ...1 Pt 3:15

REST
is a Sabbath of solemn **r**, ... Ex 31:15
and find **r** for your souls. . . . . .Jer 6:16
laden, and I will give you **r**. . . . . Mt 11:28

RESTORE
R to me the joy of your . . . . Ps 51:12
spiritual should **r** him in a . . . . Gal 6:1

RESURRECTION
For in the **r** they neither . . . . Mt 22:30
I am the **r** and the life. . . . . Jn 11:25
So is it with the **r** of the . . . . .1 Cor 15:42
through the **r** of Jesus Christ . . . . .1 Pt 1:3

RETURN
For if you **r** to the LORD, ...2 Chr 30:9
it shall not **r** to me empty, ...Is 55:11
R to me, and I will **r** to you, ... Mal 3:7

REVEALED
but the things that are **r**. . . . . Dt 29:29
he has **r** his righteousness in . . . . Ps 98:2
glory that is to be **r** to us. . . . . Rom 8:18

REVELATION
according to the **r** of the . . . . .Rom 16:25
but I received it through a **r**. . . . . Gal 1:12

REVERENCE
and **r** my sanctuary: . . . . Lv 19:30
another out of **r** for Christ. . . . . Eph 5:21
worship, with **r** and awe, ... Heb 12:28

REVIVE
seek God, let your hearts **r**. . . . . Ps 69:32
and to **r** the heart of the . . . . .Is 57:15

REWARD
them there is great **r**. . . . . Ps 19:11
for your **r** is great in heaven, ...Mt 5:12
the inheritance as your **r**. . . . . Col 3:24
which has a great **r**. . . . . Heb 10:35

REWARDED
So the LORD has **r** me . . . . Ps 18:24
commandment will be **r**. . . . . .Prv 13:13
but the righteous are **r**. . . . . .Prv 13:21

RICH
hand of the diligent makes **r**. . . . . .Prv 10:4
let not the **r** man boast in . . . . .Jer 9:23
As for the **r** in this present . . . . 1 Tm 6:17

RICHES
Whoever trusts in his **r**. . . . . .Prv 11:28
Oh, the depth of the **r** and . . . . .Rom 11:33
that according to the **r** of. . . . . Eph 3:16
are the **r** of the glory . . . . Col 1:27

RIGHT
and do that which is **r** in . . . . Ex 15:26
And you shall do what is **r**. . . . . Dt 6:18
the precepts of the LORD are **r**, ... Ps 19:8
and renew a **r** spirit within. . . . . Ps 51:10
he gave the **r** to become . . . . .Jn 1:12
that is good and **r** and true), ... Eph 5:9
in the Lord, for this is **r**. . . . . .Eph 6:1
So whoever knows the **r**. . . . . .Jas 4:17

RIGHTEOUS
For the LORD is **r**; he loves. . . . . Ps 11:7
Let the **r** one rejoice in the. . . . . Ps 64:10
Surely the **r** shall give. . . . . Ps 140:13
but the desire of the **r** will . . . . .Prv 10:24
When the **r** increase, the . . . . .Prv 29:2
Surely there is not a **r** man. . . . . Eccl 7:20
and all our **r** deeds are like a . . . . .Is 64:6
but the **r** shall live by his faith. . . . . .Hb 2:4
but the **r** into eternal life." . . . . .Mt 25:46
as it is written: "None is **r**, ... Rom 3:10
is holy and **r** and good. . . . . Rom 7:12
This is evidence of the **r** . . . . 2 Thes 1:5
but my **r** one shall live by. . . . . Heb 10:38
The prayer of a **r** person has. . . . . .Jas 5:16

RIGHTEOUSNESS
but in **r** shall you judge . . . . Lv 19:15
his **r** and his faithfulness, ... 1 Sm 26:23
R and justice are the . . . . Ps 89:14
Whoever pursues **r** and . . . . .Prv 21:21
to bring in everlasting **r**, ...Dn 9:24
Sow for yourselves **r**; reap . . . . Hos 10:12
it was counted to him as **r**." . . . . Rom 4:3
so one act of **r** leads to . . . . Rom 5:18
to God as instruments for **r**. . . . . Rom 6:13
put on the breastplate of **r**, ... Eph 6:14
not produce the **r** of God. . . . . .Jas 1:20

RISE
live; their bodies shall **r**. . . . . .Is 26:19
For he makes his sun **r** on . . . . .Mt 5:45
dead in Christ will **r** first. . . . . 1 Thes 4:16

RISEN
'He has **r** from the dead,' . . . . Mt 27:64

"The Lord has **r** indeed, ... Lk 24:34
Christ, **r** from the dead, the ... 2 Tm 2:8

ROBBERS
become a den of **r** in your ... Jer 7:11
him they crucified two **r**, ... Mk 15:27
have made it a den of **r**." ... Lk 19:46
before me are thieves and **r**, ... Jn 10:8

ROCK
The LORD is my **r** and my ... Ps 18:2
bog, and set my feet upon a **r**, ... Ps 40:2
who built his house on the **r**. ... Mt 7:24
and on this **r** I will build ... Mt 16:18
and the **R** was Christ. ... 1 Cor 10:4
and a **r** of offense." They ... 1 Pt 2:8

ROD
Whoever spares the **r** ... Prv 13:24
I come to you with a **r**, ... 1 Cor 4:21

ROOM
go into your **r** and shut the ... Mt 6:6
went up to the upper **r**, ... Acts 1:13
Make **r** in your hearts for ... 2 Cor 7:2

ROOT
"The **r** of Jesse will come, ... Rom 15:12
of money is a **r** of all kinds ... 1 Tm 6:10

RUIN
companions may come to **r**, ... Prv 18:24
a **r**, without inhabitant. ... Jer 46:19

RUINS
And your ancient **r** shall be ... Is 58:12
make Jerusalem a heap of **r**, ... Jer 9:11
"Bad company **r** good ... 1 Cor 15:33
but only **r** the hearers. ... 2 Tm 2:14

RULE
his **r** shall be from sea to ... Zec 9:10
And let the peace of Christ **r** ... Col 3:15
and he will **r** them with a ... Rv 2:27

RULER
nor curse a **r** of your people. ... Ex 22:28
A **r** who lacks understanding ... Prv 28:16
land, and **r** is against **r**. ... Jer 51:46
'Who made you a **r** and a ... Acts 7:27

RULERS
and the **r** were gathered ... Acts 4:26
and blood, but against the **r**, ... Eph 6:12
submissive to **r** and authorities, ... Ti 3:1

RULES
and his kingdom **r** over all. ... Ps 103:19
r without prejudging, ... 1 Tm 5:21
competes according to the **r**. ... 2 Tm 2:5

RUN
running or had not **r** in vain. ... Gal 2:2
that I did not **r** in vain or ... Phil 2:16
and let us **r** with endurance ... Heb 12:1

SABBATH
"Remember the **S** day, to ... Ex 20:8
Son of Man is lord of the **S**." ... Mt 12:8
or a new moon or a **S**. ... Col 2:16

SACRIFICE
and Jacob offered a **s** in the ... Gn 31:54
you shall say, 'It is the **s** of ... Ex 12:27
ram as a **s** of peace offering ... Nm 6:17
to obey is better than **s**, ... 1 Sm 15:22
Offer to God a **s** of ... Ps 50:14
desire mercy, and not **s**.' For ... Mt 9:13
a fragrant offering and **s** to ... Eph 5:2

SACRIFICED
what has been **s** to idols, ... Acts 15:29
Passover lamb, has been **s**. ... 1 Cor 5:7

SACRIFICES
The **s** of God are a broken ... Ps 51:17
to offer gifts and **s** for sins. ... Heb 5:1
to offer spiritual **s** acceptable ... 1 Pt 2:5

SADDUCEES
of the Pharisees and **S**." ... Mt 16:6
The same day **S** came to ... Mt 22:23

SAFETY
O LORD, make me dwell in **s**. ... Ps 4:8
He redeems my soul in **s** ... Ps 55:18
of counselors there is **s**. ... Prv 11:14

SAINTS
preserves the lives of his **s**; ... Ps 97:10
LORD is the death of his **s**. ... Ps 116:15
But the **s** of the Most High ... Dn 7:18
done to your **s** at Jerusalem. ... Acts 9:13
for the **s** according to the ... Rom 8:27
the needs of the **s** ... 2 Cor 9:12
but now revealed to his **s**. ... Col 1:26
for all delivered to the **s**. ... Jude 1:3
the righteous deeds of the **s**. ... Rv 19:8

SAKE
Yet for your **s** we are killed ... Ps 44:22
I counted as loss for the **s** of ... Phil 3:7
suffer for righteousness' **s**, ... 1 Pt 3:14

SALT
she became a pillar of **s**. ... Gn 19:26
"You are the **s** of the earth, ... Mt 5:13
be gracious, seasoned with **s**, ... Col 4:6

SALVATION
I wait for your **s**, O LORD. ... Gn 49:18
and see the **s** of the LORD, ... Ex 14:13
scoffed at the Rock of his **s**. ... Dt 32:15
because I rejoice in your **s**. ... 1 Sm 2:1
and the horn of my **s**, my ... 2 Sm 22:3
LORD is my light and my **s**; ... Ps 27:1
song; he has become my **s**. ... Ps 118:14
Lord, the strength of my **s**, ... Ps 140:7
that my **s** may reach to the ... Is 49:6
pay. **S** belongs to the LORD!" ... Jon 2:9
will wait for the God of my **s**; ... Mi 7:7
And there is **s** in no one ... Acts 4:12
that you may bring **s** to ... Acts 13:47
truth, the gospel of your **s**, ... Eph 1:13
and take the helmet of **s**, ... Eph 6:17
work out your own **s** with ... Phil 2:12
for a helmet the hope of **s**. ... 1 Thes 5:8
may obtain the **s** that is in ... 2 Tm 2:10
those who are to inherit **s**? ... Heb 1:14
faith for a **s** ready to be ... 1 Pt 1:5
to you about our common **s**, ... Jude 1:3
"**S** belongs to our God who ... Rv 7:10

SAMARITAN
But a **S**, as he journeyed, ... Lk 10:33
The **S** woman said to him, ... Jn 4:9

SAME
of gifts, but the **s** Spirit; ... 1 Cor 12:4
joy by being of the **s** mind, ... Phil 2:2

SANCTIFICATION
righteousness leading to **s**. ... Rom 6:19
is the will of God, your **s**: ... 1 Thes 4:3
through **s** by the Spirit ... 2 Thes 2:13
Father, in the **s** of the Spirit, ... 1 Pt 1:2

SANCTIFIED
that they also may be **s** in ... Jn 17:19
those who are **s** by faith in ... Acts 26:18
s by the Holy Spirit. ... Rom 15:16
were washed, you were **s**, ... 1 Cor 6:11
s through the offering ... Heb 10:10

SANCTIFIES
I am the LORD who **s** you. ... Lv 20:8
For he who **s** and those ... Heb 2:11

SANCTIFY
know that I, the LORD, **s** you. ... Ex 31:13
S them in the truth; your ... Jn 17:17
that he might **s** her, having ... Eph 5:26
himself **s** you completely, ... 1 Thes 5:23

SANCTUARY
And let them make me a **s**, ... Ex 25:8
yet I have been a **s** to them ... Ez 11:16
and will set my **s** in their ... Ez 37:26

SAND
and as the **s** that is on ... Gn 22:17
shall be like the **s** of the sea, ... Hos 1:10
who built his house on the **s**. ... Mt 7:26

SANDALS
near; take your **s** off your feet, ... Ex 3:5
"Take off your **s** from your ... Jos 5:15
whose **s** I am not worthy to ... Mt 3:11

SARAH
Now Abraham and **S** were ... Gn 18:11

SATAN
and **S** also came among them. ... Jb 1:6
And the LORD said to **S**, "The ... Zec 3:2
said to him, "Be gone, **S**! For it ... Mt 4:10
crush **S** under your feet ... Rom 16:20
for even **S** disguises ... 2 Cor 11:14
is called the devil and **S**, ... Rv 12:9

SATISFIED
yet his appetite is not **s**. ... Eccl 6:7
soul he shall see and be **s**; ... Is 53:11
for they shall be **s**. ... Mt 5:6

SATISFIES
who **s** you with good so that ... Ps 103:5
For he **s** the longing soul, ... Ps 107:9

SATISFY
S us in the morning with ... Ps 90:14
for that which does not **s**? ... Is 55:2

SAUL
a son whose name was **S**, ... 1 Sm 9:2
And **S** approved of his ... Acts 8:1
But **S**, who was also called ... Acts 13:9

SAVE
our God, **s** us, please, ... 2 Kgs 19:19
s me in your steadfast love! ... Ps 31:16
warrior who cannot **s**? ... Jer 14:9
a mighty one who will **s**; ... Zep 3:17
for he will **s** his people from ... Mt 1:21
the world but to **s** the world ... Jn 12:47
is able to **s** to the uttermost ... Heb 7:25
Can that faith **s** him? ... Jas 2:14
And the prayer of faith will **s** ... Jas 5:15

SAVED
who **s** them out of the hand ... Jgs 2:16
Yet he **s** them for his name's ... Ps 106:8
"Turn to me and be **s**, all the ... Is 45:22
name of the LORD shall be **s**. ... Jl 2:32
endures to the end will be **s**. ... Mt 10:22
will those who are **s** be ... Lk 13:23
what must I do to be **s**?" ... Acts 16:30
much more shall we be **s** by ... Rom 5:9
the dead, you will be **s**. ... Rom 10:9
by which you are being **s**, ... 1 Cor 15:2
For by grace you have been **s** ... Eph 2:8
that they might be **s** — ... 1 Thes 2:16
the truth and so be **s**. ... 2 Thes 2:10
who **s** us and called us to a ... 2 Tm 1:9
he **s** us, not because of works ... Ti 3:5

SAVES
the LORD **s** not with sword ... 1 Sm 17:47
of pride'; but he **s** the lowly. ... Jb 22:29
who **s** the upright in heart. ... Ps 7:10
hears their cry and **s** them. ... Ps 145:19

A truthful witness **s** lives, ... Prv 14:25

SAVING
me in your **s** faithfulness. . . . . Ps 69:13
that you may know the **s** acts. . . . . Mi 6:5

SAVIOR
and my refuge, my **s**; . . . . 2 Sm 22:3
the LORD gave Israel a **s**, ... 2 Kgs 13:5
O **S** of those who seek refuge. . . . . Ps 17:7
They forgot God, their **S**, ... Ps 106:21
he will send them a **s** and . . . . Is 19:20
and besides me there is no **s**. . . . . Is 43:11
O God of Israel, the **S**. . . . . Is 45:15
its **s** in time of trouble, ... Jer 14:8
day in the city of David a **S**, ... Lk 2:11
is indeed the **S** of the world." . . . . Jn 4:42
who is the **S** of all people, ... 1 Tm 4:10
great God and **S** Jesus Christ, ... Ti 2:13

SCALES
and false **s** are not good. . . . . Prv 20:23
like **s** fell from his eyes, ... Acts 9:18
And its rider had a pair of **s** . . . . Rv 6:5

SCATTERED
'He who **s** Israel will. . . . . Jer 31:10
Now those who were **s**. . . . . Acts 8:4

SCEPTER
The **s** shall not depart from. . . . . Gn 49:10
is the **s** of your kingdom. . . . . Heb 1:8

SCHEMES
and the **s** of the wily are . . . . Jb 5:13
by craftiness in deceitful **s**. . . . . Eph 4:14
against the **s** of the devil. . . . . Eph 6:11

SCOFFERS
nor sits in the seat of **s**; . . . . Ps 1:1
How long will **s** delight in. . . . . Prv 1:22
last time there will be **s**, ... Jude 1:18

SCRIPTURE
"Today this **S** has been . . . . Lk 4:21
and **S** cannot be broken — . . . . Jn 10:35
to the public reading of **S**, ... 1 Tm 4:13
All **S** is breathed out by . . . . 2 Tm 3:16
royal law according to the **S**, ... Jas 2:8
that no prophecy of **S**. . . . . 2 Pt 1:20

SCRIPTURES
the **S** the things concerning . . . . Lk 24:27
You search the **S** because you. . . . . Jn 5:39
in accordance with the **S**, ... 1 Cor 15:3
as they do the other **S**. . . . . 2 Pt 3:16

SCROLL
Eat this **s**, and go, speak to the . . . . Ez 3:1
And he rolled up the **s** and. . . . . Lk 4:20
"Who is worthy to open the **s** . . . . Rv 5:2

SEA
and the LORD drove the **s** . . . . Ex 14:21
By his power he stilled the **s**; . . . . Jb 26:12
The **s** is his, for he made it, ... Ps 95:5
sins into the depths of the **s**. . . . . Mi 7:19

SEAL
God the Father has set his **s**." . . . . Jn 6:27
and who has also put his **s**. . . . . 2 Cor 1:22
Lamb opened the seventh **s**, ... Rv 8:1

SEARCH
if you **s** after him with all. . . . . Dt 4:29
"I the LORD **s** the heart and . . . . Jer 17:10
You **s** the Scriptures because . . . . Jn 5:39

SEARCHED
O LORD, you have **s** me and . . . . Ps 139:1
s and inquired carefully, ... 1 Pt 1:10

SEARCHES
for the LORD **s** all hearts . . . . 1 Chr 28:9

SEASON
For everything there is a **s**, ... Eccl 3:1
be ready in **s** and out of. . . . . 2 Tm 4:2

SEAT
You shall make a mercy **s** of . . . . Ex 25:17
the Ancient of Days took his **s**; . . . . Dn 7:9
the judgment **s** of God; . . . . Rom 14:10

SEATED
Son of Man **s** at the right. . . . . Mt 26:64
with him and **s** us with him . . . . Eph 2:6
one who is **s** at the right . . . . Heb 8:1

SECRET
"The **s** things belong to the . . . . Dt 29:29
our **s** sins in the light of your . . . . Ps 90:8
was kept **s** for long ages . . . . Rom 16:25

SECRETS
For he knows the **s** of the. . . . . Ps 44:21
to know the **s** of the kingdom . . . . Lk 8:10
God judges the **s** of men by . . . . Rom 2:16

SECURE
and set me **s** on the heights. . . . . Ps 18:33

SECURITY
and **s** within your towers!" . . . . Ps 122:7
"There is peace and **s**," . . . . 1 Thes 5:3

SEED
like a grain of mustard **s**, ... Mt 17:20
He who supplies **s** to the . . . . 2 Cor 9:10
not of perishable **s** but of. . . . . 1 Pt 1:23

SEEING
keep on **s**, but do not perceive.' . . . . Is 6:9
because **s** they do not see, ... Mt 13:13
to keep them from **s** the. . . . . 2 Cor 4:4

SEEK
If you **s** him, he will be. . . . . 1 Chr 28:9
and pray and **s** my face . . . . 2 Chr 7:14
when you **s** me with all . . . . Jer 29:13
s, and you will find; knock, ... Mt 7:7
Man came to **s** and to save . . . . Lk 19:10
a wife? Do not **s** a wife. . . . . 1 Cor 7:27
rewards those who **s** him. . . . . Heb 11:6

SEEKS
understanding **s** knowledge, ... Prv 15:14
As a shepherd **s** out his . . . . Ez 34:12
no one **s** for God. . . . . Rom 3:11

SEES
For the LORD **s** not as man . . . . 1 Sm 16:7
And whoever **s** me **s** him . . . . Jn 12:45
who hopes for what he **s**? . . . . Rom 8:24

SELF
We know that our old **s** was. . . . . Rom 6:6
and to put on the new **s**, ... Eph 4:24
off the old **s** with its practices. . . . . Col 3:9
people will be lovers of **s**, ... 2 Tm 3:2

SELF-CONTROL
A man without **s** is like a . . . . Prv 25:28
gentleness, **s**; against such . . . . Gal 5:23
apparel, with modesty and **s**, ... 1 Tm 2:9

SELF-CONTROLLED
a lover of good, **s**, upright, holy, ... Ti 1:8
therefore be **s** and . . . . 1 Pt 4:7

SELF-INDULGENCE
they are full of greed and **s**. . . . . Mt 23:25
the earth in luxury and in **s**. . . . . Jas 5:5

SELFISH
and not to **s** gain! . . . . Ps 119:36
and **s** ambition in your . . . . Jas 3:14

SEND
"Here am I! **S** me." . . . . Is 6:8
For God did not **s** his Son. . . . . Jn 3:17

if I go, I will **s** him to you. . . . . Jn 16:7

SENDING
"Behold, I am **s** you out as. . . . . Mt 10:16
me, even so I am **s** you." . . . . Jn 20:21
By **s** his own Son in the . . . . Rom 8:3

SENT
preach unless they are **s**? . . . . Rom 10:15
come, God **s** forth his Son, ... Gal 4:4
loved us and **s** his Son to . . . . 1 Jn 4:10

SEPARATE
Who shall **s** us from the. . . . . Rom 8:35
the wife should not **s** from . . . . 1 Cor 7:10

SEPARATED
at that time **s** from Christ, ... Eph 2:12
unstained, **s** from sinners, ... Heb 7:26

SEPARATES
and a whisperer **s** close. . . . . Prv 16:28
a shepherd **s** the sheep from . . . . Mt 25:32
the unbelieving partner **s**, ... 1 Cor 7:15

SERPENT
Now the **s** was more crafty. . . . . Gn 3:1
And as Moses lifted up the **s** . . . . Jn 3:14
the dragon, that ancient **s**, ... Rv 20:2

SERVANT
among you must be your **s**, ... Mt 20:26
done, good and faithful **s**. . . . . Mt 25:21
No **s** can serve two masters, ... Lk 16:13
I have made myself a **s** to. . . . . 1 Cor 9:19
taking the form of a **s**, ... Phil 2:7
And the Lord's **s** must not . . . . 2 Tm 2:24

SERVANTS
say, 'We are unworthy **s**; . . . . Lk 17:10
but as **s** of God we commend. . . . . 2 Cor 6:4
evil, but living as **s** of God. . . . . 1 Pt 2:16

SERVE
to **s** the LORD your God with. . . . . Dt 10:12
this day whom you will **s**, ... Jos 24:15
and him only shall you **s**.'" . . . . Mt 4:10
not to be served but to **s**, ... Mt 20:28
so that we **s** in the new way . . . . Rom 7:6
rather they must **s** all the . . . . 1 Tm 6:2

SEVEN
march around the city **s** times, ... Jos 6:4
s that are an abomination to . . . . Prv 6:16
him? As many as **s** times?" . . . . Mt 18:21
"I have kept for myself **s** . . . . Rom 11:4
who holds the **s** stars in his . . . . Rv 2:1
opened one of the **s** seals, ... Rv 6:1
and **s** trumpets were given to. . . . . Rv 8:2
And when the **s** thunders . . . . Rv 10:4
angels **s** golden bowls full . . . . Rv 15:7

SEVENTH
And on the **s** day God . . . . Gn 2:2
but on the **s** day you shall . . . . Ex 23:12

SEXUAL
except on the ground of **s** . . . . Mt 5:32
Flee from **s** immorality. . . . . 1 Cor 6:18
that you abstain from **s** . . . . 1 Thes 4:3

SEXUALLY
with **s** immoral people — . . . . 1 Cor 5:9
that everyone who is **s** . . . . Eph 5:5

SHADOW
the valley of the **s** of death, ... Ps 23:4
refuge in the **s** of your wings. . . . . Ps 36:7
These are a **s** of the things . . . . Col 2:17

SHADRACH
Hananiah he called **S**, ... Dn 1:7

SHAME
Then I shall not be put to **s**, ... Ps 119:6
the cross, despising the **s**, ... Heb 12:2

SHARE
word must s all good things . . . . Gal 6:6
to s with anyone in . . . . Eph 4:28
But rejoice insofar as you s. . . . . 1 Pt 4:13

SHEEP
and the s of his pasture. . . . . Ps 100:3
All we like s have gone . . . . Is 53:6
for my s and will seek . . . . Ez 34:11
I am sending you out as s . . . . Mt 10:16
The s hear his voice, and he . . . . Jn 10:3
He said to him, "Tend my s." . . . . Jn 21:16

SHELTER
under the s of your wings! . . . . Ps 61:4
He who dwells in the s of the. . . . . Ps 91:1

SHEOL
he brings down to S and . . . . 1 Sm 2:6
not abandon my soul to S, ... Ps 16:10
her steps follow the path to S; . . . . Prv 5:5
to the gates of S for the rest . . . . Is 38:10
them from the power of S? . . . . Hos 13:14

SHEPHERD
'You shall be s of my . . . . 1 Chr 11:2
and will keep him as a s. . . . . Jer 31:10
And he shall stand and s his . . . . Mi 5:4
I am the good s. The good . . . . Jn 10:11
the great s of the sheep, ... Heb 13:20
of the throne will be their s, ... Rv 7:17

SHEPHERDS
Should not s feed the sheep? . . . . Ez 34:2
region there were s out in the . . . . Lk 2:8
evangelists, the s and teachers . . . . Eph 4:11

SHIELD
"Fear not, Abram, I am your s; . . . . Gn 15:1
LORD is my strength and my s; . . . . Ps 28:7

SHINE
the LORD make his face to s . . . . Nm 6:25
make his face to s upon us, ... Ps 67:1
Arise, s, for your light has. . . . . Is 60:1

SHINES
of beauty, God s forth. . . . . Ps 50:2
The light s in the darkness, ... Jn 1:5

SHONE
of his face s because he had . . . . Ex 34:29
and his face s like the sun, ... Mt 17:2
and the glory of the Lord s. . . . . Lk 2:9

SHORT
those days will be cut s. . . . . Mt 24:22
and fall s of the glory of God, ... Rom 3:23

SHOW
s the immeasurable riches . . . . Eph 2:7
S me your faith apart from . . . . Jas 2:18
S hospitality to one another . . . . 1 Pt 4:9

SICK
deferred makes the heart s, ... Prv 13:12
but those who are s. . . . . Mt 9:12
s and in prison and you did . . . . Mt 25:43

SIGHT
Precious in the s of the . . . . Ps 116:15
we walk by faith, not by s. . . . . 2 Cor 5:7
and it is pleasing in the s of. . . . . 1 Tm 2:3
which in God's s is very . . . . 1 Pt 3:4

SIGN
The blood shall be a s for. . . . . Ex 12:13
You shall bind them as a s on. . . . . Dt 6:8
He received the s of . . . . Rom 4:11
This is the s of genuineness . . . . 2 Thes 3:17
Then I saw another s in . . . . Rv 15:1

SIGNS
Now Jesus did many other s. . . . . Jn 20:30
above and s on the earth . . . . Acts 2:19
by s and wonders and . . . . Heb 2:4

SILENCE
time to sew; a time to keep s, ... Eccl 3:7
put to s the ignorance of . . . . 1 Pt 2:15
there was s in heaven for. . . . . Rv 8:1

SILENT
Even a fool who keeps s is . . . . Prv 17:28
that before its shearers is s, ... Is 53:7
Be s before the Lord GOD! . . . . Zep 1:7

SILVER
if you seek it like s and . . . . Prv 2:4
The s is mine, and the gold is. . . . . Hg 2:8
said, "I have no s and gold, ... Acts 3:6
things such as s or gold, ... 1 Pt 1:18

SIN
s is crouching at the door. . . . . Gn 4:7
he shall confess his s that he . . . . Nm 5:7
their s and heal their . . . . 2 Chr 7:14
in my bones because of my s. . . . . Ps 38:3
and cleanse me from my s! . . . . Ps 51:2
you covered all their s. Selah . . . . Ps 85:2
that I might not s against. . . . . Ps 119:11
away, and your s atoned for." . . . . Is 6:7
ones who believe in me to s, ... Mt 18:6
"Temptations to s are sure to . . . . Lk 17:1
who takes away the s of the. . . . . Jn 1:29
but where s increased, ... Rom 5:20
For the wages of s is death, ... Rom 6:23
him to be s who knew no. . . . . 2 Cor 5:21
for those who persist in s, ... 1 Tm 5:20
conceived gives birth to s, ... Jas 1:15
fails to do it, for him it is s. . . . . Jas 4:17
He committed no s, neither . . . . 1 Pt 2:22
Son cleanses us from all s. . . . . 1 Jn 1:7

SINFUL
the world because of s desire. . . . . 2 Pt 1:4
following their own s desires; . . . . Jude 1:16

SING
I will s and make melody to . . . . Ps 27:6
S to the LORD with thanksgiving; . . . . Ps 147:7
cheerful? Let him s praise. . . . . Jas 5:13

SINGING
into his presence with s! . . . . Ps 100:2
s psalms and hymns and . . . . Col 3:16

SINGLE
them to remain s as I am. . . . . 1 Cor 7:8

SINNED
have I s and done what is . . . . Ps 51:4
for all have s and fall short. . . . . Rom 3:23

SINNER
but one s destroys much . . . . Eccl 9:18
over one s who repents." . . . . Lk 15:10

SINNERS
Let not your heart envy s, ... Prv 23:17
to call the righteous, but s." . . . . Mt 9:13
into the world to save s, ... 1 Tm 1:15

SINNING
Thus, s against your . . . . 1 Cor 8:12
of God does not keep on s, ... 1 Jn 5:18

SINS
are my iniquities and my s? . . . . Jb 13:23
our secret s in the light of . . . . Ps 90:8
for you have cast all my s. . . . . Is 38:17
save his people from their s." . . . . Mt 1:21
for the forgiveness of s. . . . . Mt 26:28
once to bear the s of many, ... Heb 9:28
Therefore, confess your s to . . . . Jas 5:16
also suffered once for s, ... 1 Pt 3:18
cleansed from his former s. . . . . 2 Pt 1:9
If we confess our s, he is . . . . 1 Jn 1:9

SIT
Lord: "S at my right hand, ... Ps 110:1
to give light to those who s . . . . Lk 1:79

SKIN
and I have escaped by the s . . . . Jb 19:20
change his s or the leopard . . . . Jer 13:23
and s had covered them. But . . . . Ez 37:8

SLANDER
who does not s with his. . . . . Ps 15:3
and whoever utters s is a . . . . Prv 10:18
hypocrisy and envy and all s. . . . . 1 Pt 2:1

SLANDERED
when s, we entreat. We . . . . 1 Cor 4:13
so that, when you are s, ... 1 Pt 3:16

SLAVE
among you must be your s, ... Mt 20:27
who practices sin is a s to sin. . . . . Jn 8:34
there is neither s nor free, ... Gal 3:28

SLAVERY
the spirit of s to fall back . . . . Rom 8:15
submit again to a yoke of s. . . . . Gal 5:1
were subject to lifelong s. . . . . Heb 2:15

SLAVES
you are s of the one whom. . . . . Rom 6:16
s to various passions and . . . . Ti 3:3

SLEEP
caused a deep s to fall upon . . . . Gn 2:21
will neither slumber nor s. . . . . Ps 121:4
Sweet is the s of a laborer, ... Eccl 5:12

SLOW
and gracious, s to anger, ... Ex 34:6
s to anger and abounding in . . . . Ps 103:8
Whoever is s to anger has . . . . Prv 14:29
The LORD is s to anger and . . . . Na 1:3
If it seems s, wait for it; it will . . . . Hb 2:3
The Lord is not s to fulfill . . . . 2 Pt 3:9

SNARE
which became a s to them. . . . . Ps 106:36
fall into temptation, into a s, ... 1 Tm 6:9
from the s of the devil, ... 2 Tm 2:26

SNOW
and I shall be whiter than s. . . . . Ps 51:7
they shall be as white as s; . . . . Is 1:18
and his clothing white as s. . . . . Mt 28:3

SOBER
but to think with s . . . . Rom 12:3
us keep awake and be s. . . . . 1 Thes 5:6

SOBER-MINDED
one wife, s, self-controlled, ... 1 Tm 3:2
Older men are to be s, ... Ti 2:2
for action, and being s, ... 1 Pt 1:13

SOLDIER
Who serves as a s at his. . . . . 1 Cor 9:7
fellow worker and fellow s, ... Phil 2:25
as a good s of Christ Jesus. . . . . 2 Tm 2:3

SON
He said, "Take your s, your . . . . Gn 22:2
said to me, "You are my S; . . . . Ps 2:7
and the s of man that you care . . . . Ps 8:4
A wise s hears his father's . . . . Prv 13:1
shall conceive and bear a s, ... Is 7:14
child is born, to us a s is given; . . . . Is 9:6
out of Egypt I called my s. . . . . Hos 11:1
said, "This is my beloved S, ... Mt 17:5
firstborn s and wrapped him. . . . . Lk 2:7
that he gave his only S, ... Jn 3:16
his own S but gave him . . . . Rom 8:32
a slave, but a s, and if a s, ... Gal 4:7
and this life is in his S. . . . . 1 Jn 5:11

SONG
is my strength and my **s**, … Ex 15:2
He put a new **s** in my mouth, … Ps 40:3

SONGS
who gives **s** in the night, … Jb 35:10
Shout to God with loud **s** of … Ps 47:1
and hymns and spiritual **s**, … Eph 5:19

SONS
your **s** and your daughters … Jl 2:28
that is, **S** of Thunder); … Mk 3:17
that you may become **s** of … Jn 12:36
and you shall be **s** and … 2 Cor 6:18
God is treating you as **s**. … Heb 12:7

SOON
The God of peace will **s** … Rom 16:20
things that must **s** take place. … Rv 1:1
"Surely I am coming **s**." … Rv 22:20

SORROW
knowledge increases **s**. … Eccl 1:18
give them gladness for **s**. … Jer 31:13
but your **s** will turn into joy. … Jn 16:20

SORROWS
rejected by men; a man of **s**, … Is 53:3
one endures **s** while suffering … 1 Pt 2:19

SOUL
heart and with all your **s**." … Jos 22:5
He restores my **s**. He leads me … Ps 23:3
so pants my **s** for you, O God. … Ps 42:1
The **s** who sins shall die. … Ez 18:20
with all your **s** and with all … Mt 22:37
piercing to the division of **s** … Heb 4:12

SOULS
in it, and find rest for your **s**. … Jer 6:16
faith, the salvation of your **s**. … 1 Pt 1:9

SOUND
heaven a **s** like a mighty … Acts 2:2
be able to give instruction in **s** … Ti 1:9

SOVEREIGN
to God and said, "**S** Lord, … Acts 4:24
is the blessed and only **S**, … 1 Tm 6:15
"O **S** Lord, holy and true, … Rv 6:10

SOW
Those who **s** in tears shall … Ps 126:5
"A sower went out to **s**. … Mt 13:3

SOWS
but one who **s** righteousness … Prv 11:18
'One **s** and another reaps.' … Jn 4:37

SPARE
For if God did not **s** the … Rom 11:21
For if God did not **s** angels … 2 Pt 2:4

SPEECH
understand one another's **s**." … Gn 11:7
Day to day pours out **s**, and … Ps 19:2
Let your **s** always be gracious, … Col 4:6

SPIRIT
And the **S** of God was … Gn 1:2
And the **S** of God came … Nm 24:2
The **S** of the LORD was upon … Jgs 3:10
Now the **S** of the LORD … 1 Sm 16:14
"The **S** of the LORD speaks … 2 Sm 23:2
and the **s** of God is in my … Jb 27:3
your hand I commit my **s**; … Ps 31:5
and the **s** returns to God … Eccl 12:7
and a new **s** I will put … Ez 36:26
and he saw the **S** of God … Mt 3:16
"Blessed are the poor in **s**, … Mt 5:3
God is **s**, and those who … Jn 4:24
Now this he said about the **S**, … Jn 7:39
them, "Receive the Holy **S**. … Jn 20:22
the Holy **S** and began to … Acts 2:4
might receive the Holy **S**, … Acts 8:15
The **S** himself bears … Rom 8:16
But the fruit of the **S** is love, … Gal 5:22
and the sword of the **S**, … Eph 6:17
with the joy of the Holy **S**, … 1 Thes 1:6
by the **S** and belief in … 2 Thes 2:13
By the Holy **S** who dwells … 2 Tm 1:14
And the Holy **S** also bears … Heb 10:15
in the sanctification of the **S**, … 1 Pt 1:2
carried along by the Holy **S**. … 2 Pt 1:21
faith and praying in the Holy **S**, … Jude 1:20

SPIRITS
and he cast out the **s** with a … Mt 8:16
and the evil **s** came out of … Acts 19:12
and the **s** of prophets are … 1 Cor 14:32
proclaimed to the **s** in prison, … 1 Pt 3:19
but test the **s** to see whether … 1 Jn 4:1

SPIRITUAL
share in their **s** blessings, … Rom 15:27
against the **s** forces of evil … Eph 6:12
s wisdom and understanding, … Col 1:9

SPLENDOR
S and majesty are before … 1 Chr 16:27
You are clothed with **s** and … Ps 104:1
On the glorious **s** of your … Ps 145:5

SPOT
without **s** or wrinkle or any … Eph 5:27
a lamb without blemish or **s**. … 1 Pt 1:19
him without **s** or blemish, … 2 Pt 3:14

SPRING
Branch to **s** up for David, … Jer 33:15
in him a **s** of water welling … Jn 4:14
give from the **s** of the water … Rv 21:6

STAFF
And Moses took the **s** of God … Ex 4:20
with me; your rod and your **s**, … Ps 23:4

STAND
the people, "Fear not, **s** firm, … Ex 14:13
S firm, hold your position … 2 Chr 20:17
of the righteous will **s**. … Prv 12:7
the wall and **s** in the breach … Ez 22:30
For we will all **s** before … Rom 14:10
that you may be able to **s**. … Eph 6:11

STANDING
you are **s** is holy ground." … Ex 3:5
where you are **s** is holy." … Jos 5:15
if you are **s** fast in the … 1 Thes 3:8

STANDS
The counsel of the LORD **s** … Ps 33:11
that he **s** take heed lest … 1 Cor 10:12

STAR
O Day **S**, son of Dawn! … Is 14:12
When they saw the **s**, they … Mt 2:10

STARS
as the **s** of heaven and … Gn 22:17
like the **s** forever and ever. … Dn 12:3
as the **s** of heaven and … Heb 11:12

STATUTES
and keep all his **s**, … Ex 15:26
walk in my **s** and be careful … Ez 36:27

STEADFAST
but showing **s** love to … Dt 5:10
For your **s** love is before my … Ps 26:3
For great is your **s** love … Ps 86:13
in the faith, stable and **s**, … Col 1:23

STEADFASTNESS
faith, love, **s**, gentleness. … 1 Tm 6:11
of your faith produces **s**. … Jas 1:3
and self-control with **s**, … 2 Pt 1:6

STEAL
"You shall not **s**. … Ex 20:15
Let the thief no longer **s**, … Eph 4:28

STEPHEN
as they were stoning **S**, … Acts 7:59

STEPS
Keep steady my **s** … Ps 119:133
the LORD establishes his **s**. … Prv 16:9
you might follow in his **s**. … 1 Pt 2:21

STEWARDS
as servants of Christ and **s** … 1 Cor 4:1
as good **s** of God's varied … 1 Pt 4:10

STEWARDSHIP
am still entrusted with a **s**. … 1 Cor 9:17
heard of the **s** of God's grace … Eph 3:2
to the **s** from God that … Col 1:25

STIFF-NECKED
and behold, it is a **s** people. … Ex 32:9
Do not now be **s** as your … 2 Chr 30:8
"You **s** people, uncircumcised … Acts 7:51

STILL
"Sun, stand **s** at Gibeon, … Jos 10:12
"Be **s**, and know that I am … Ps 46:10
The sun and moon stood **s** in … Hb 3:11

STING
O Sheol, where is your **s**? … Hos 13:14
death, where is your **s**?" … 1 Cor 15:55

STONE
strike your foot against a **s**. … Ps 91:12
and a **s** of offense and … Is 8:14
I will remove the heart of **s** … Ez 11:19
"'The **s** that the builders … Mt 21:42
strike your foot against a **s**.'" … Lk 4:11
I am laying in Zion a **s** of … Rom 9:33

STONES
the very **s** would cry out." … Lk 19:40
you yourselves like living **s** … 1 Pt 2:5

STORM
He made the **s** be still, and … Ps 107:29
a shelter from the **s** and a … Is 25:4
there arose a great **s** on the … Mt 8:24

STRAIGHT
make **s** in the desert a … Is 40:3
and make **s** paths for your … Heb 12:13

STRAINING
You blind guides, **s** out a … Mt 23:24
s forward to what lies ahead, … Phil 3:13

STRANGE
For by people of **s** lips and … Is 28:11
"By people of **s** tongues … 1 Cor 14:21

STRANGER
I was a **s** and you welcomed … Mt 25:35
A **s** they will not follow, but … Jn 10:5

STRANGERS
and **s** to the covenants … Eph 2:12
they were **s** and exiles on … Heb 11:13
to show hospitality to **s**, … Heb 13:2

STREAMS
He is like a tree planted by **s** … Ps 1:3
As a deer pants for flowing **s**, … Ps 42:1
like **s** of water in a dry place, … Is 32:2

STRENGTH
Blessed are those whose **s** is … Ps 84:5
Lord, the **s** of my salvation, … Ps 140:7
A wise man is full of **s**, and … Prv 24:5
as one who serves by the **s** … 1 Pt 4:11

STRENGTHEN
s me according to your … Ps 119:28
I will **s** you, I will help you, … Is 41:10

and s your weak knees, ... Heb 12:12

STRENGTHENED

to be s with power through ... Eph 3:16
You then, my child, be s by. ... 2 Tm 2:1
the heart to be s by grace, ... Heb 13:9

STRIFE

Hatred stirs up s, but love ... Prv 10:12
A man of wrath stirs up s, ... Prv 29:22
s, deceit, maliciousness. ... Rom 1:29

STRIKE

"S the shepherd, and the ... Zec 13:7

STRIKES

To one who s you on the ... Lk 6:29
airs, or s you in the face. ... 2 Cor 11:20

STRONG

Be s and courageous, for you ... Jos 1:6
Be s, and show yourself a. ... 1 Kgs 2:2
Be s and courageous. ... 1 Chr 22:13
a s tower against the enemy. ... Ps 61:3
but you are my s refuge. ... Ps 71:7
The name of the LORD is a s ... Prv 18:10
arm, for love is s as death, ... Sg 8:6
faith, act like men, be s. ... 1 Cor 16:13
are weak and you are s. ... 2 Cor 13:9

STRONGHOLD

The LORD is a s for the ... Ps 9:9
LORD, my strength and my s, ... Jer 16:19

STRUGGLE

how great a s I have for ... Col 2:1
you endured a hard s with ... Heb 10:32
In your s against sin you ... Heb 12:4

STUDY

set his heart to s the Law of. ... Ezr 7:10
and much s is a weariness ... Eccl 12:12

STUMBLE

in which they shall not s, ... Jer 31:9
They s because they disobey ... 1 Pt 2:8

STUMBLING

and a rock of s to both houses ... Is 8:14
put a s block or hindrance ... Rom 14:13
a s block to Jews and folly ... 1 Cor 1:23
become a s block to the ... 1 Cor 8:9
you from s and to present ... Jude 1:24

SUBJECT

Let every person be s to ... Rom 13:1
him even to s all things to ... Phil 3:21
Be s for the Lord's sake to ... 1 Pt 2:13

SUBJECTED

For the creation was s to ... Rom 8:20
and powers having been s ... 1 Pt 3:22

SUBJECTION

Therefore one must be in s, ... Rom 13:5
in s under his feet." ... 1 Cor 15:27
putting everything in s ... Heb 2:8

SUBMISSION

speak, but should be in s, ... 1 Cor 14:34
your s that comes from your ... 2 Cor 9:13
to them we did not yield in s ... Gal 2:5

SUBMISSIVE

keeping his children s, ... 1 Tm 3:4
Remind them to be s to rulers ... Ti 3:1

SUBMIT

and do not s again to a yoke ... Gal 5:1
Obey your leaders and s to ... Heb 13:17

SUBMITTING

s to one another out of ... Eph 5:21
by s to their own husbands, ... 1 Pt 3:5

SUCCESS

that you may have good s ... Jos 1:7
And David had s in all ... 1 Sm 18:14
favor and good s in the sight ... Prv 3:4

SUFFER

provided we s with him in ... Rom 8:17
suffers, all s together; ... 1 Cor 12:26
same sufferings that we s. ... 2 Cor 1:6
him but also s for his sake, ... Phil 1:29
Therefore let those who s ... 1 Pt 4:19

SUFFERED

himself has s when tempted, ... Heb 2:18
For Christ also s once for ... 1 Pt 3:18
And after you have s a little ... 1 Pt 5:10

SUFFERING

knowing that s produces ... Rom 5:3
but share in s for the gospel. ... 2 Tm 1:8

SUFFERINGS

and may share his s, ... Phil 3:10
Now I rejoice in my s for ... Col 1:24

SUN

From the rising of the s to ... Ps 113:3
For he makes his s rise on ... Mt 5:45
the s shall be turned to ... Acts 2:20
and his face was like the s ... Rv 1:16
need no light of lamp or s, ... Rv 22:5

SUPPER

it is not the Lord's s that ... 1 Cor 11:20
the cup, after s, saying, ... 1 Cor 11:25

SUPREME

For the word of the king is s, ... Eccl 8:4
it be to the emperor as s, ... 1 Pt 2:13

SURE

and be s your sin will find ... Nm 32:23
the testimony of the LORD is s, ... Ps 19:7
your commandments are s; ... Ps 119:86
of a s foundation: ... Is 28:16
For I am s that neither ... Rom 8:38
your calling and election s, ... 2 Pt 1:10

SUSTAIN

the LORD, and he will s you; ... Ps 55:22
who will s you to the end, ... 1 Cor 1:8

SWALLOWED

"Death is s up in victory." ... 1 Cor 15:54
mortal may be s up by life. ... 2 Cor 5:4

SWEAR

and does not s deceitfully. ... Ps 24:4
all, my brothers, do not s, ... Jas 5:12

SWEAT

By the s of your face you ... Gn 3:19
and his s became like great ... Lk 22:44

SWERVE

but I do not s from your ... Ps 119:157
Do not s to the right or to ... Prv 4:27
they do not s from their paths. ... Jl 2:7

SWORD

Gird your s on your thigh, ... Ps 45:3
come to bring peace, but a s. ... Mt 10:34
and the s of the Spirit, ... Eph 6:17
than any two-edged s, ... Heb 4:12
came a sharp two-edged s, ... Rv 1:16

SWORDS

Beat your plowshares into s, ... Jl 3:10
and they shall beat their s ... Mi 4:3

SYMPATHY

show him s and comfort him. ... Jb 2:11
of mind, s, brotherly love, ... 1 Pt 3:8

TABERNACLE

the pattern of the t, ... Ex 25:9
glory of the LORD filled the t. ... Ex 40:34

TABLE

You prepare a t before me in ... Ps 23:5
of the t of the Lord ... 1 Cor 10:21

TABLET

write them on the t of your ... Prv 3:3
on the t of their heart, ... Jer 17:1

TABLETS

that I may give you the t of ... Ex 24:12
and put the t in the ark ... Dt 10:5
not on t of stone but on ... 2 Cor 3:3

TAKE

"T your son, your only son ... Gn 22:2
Do not t us across the Jordan." ... Nm 32:5
t possession of the land ... Dt 9:23
shall not add to it or t from it. ... Dt 12:32
t not your Holy Spirit from me. ... Ps 51:11
T my instruction instead of silver, ... Prv 8:10
no longer knew how to t advice. ... Eccl 4:13
not t your stand in an evil cause, ... Eccl 8:3
iniquities, like the wind, t us away. ... Is 64:6
deny himself and t up his cross. ... Mk 8:34

TALENTS

To one he gave five t, to ... Mt 25:15

TALK

consist in t but in power. ... 1 Cor 4:20
let us not love in word or t. ... 1 Jn 3:18

TASTE

Oh, t and see that the LORD is ... Ps 34:8
"Do not handle, Do not t, ... Col 2:21

TASTED

who have t the heavenly gift, ... Heb 6:4
if indeed you have t that the ... 1 Pt 2:3

TAUGHT

for he t them as one who ... Mk 1:22
not t by human wisdom ... 1 Cor 2:13
the faith, just as you were t, ... Col 2:7

TAXES

Is it lawful to pay t to ... Mt 22:17
t to whom t are owed, ... Rom 13:7

TEACH

mouth and t you what you ... Ex 4:12
You shall t them diligently to ... Dt 6:7
So t us to number our days ... Ps 90:12
to him, "Lord, t us to pray, ... Lk 11:1
woman to t or to exercise ... 1 Tm 2:12

TEACHER

disciple is not above his t, ... Mt 10:24
If I then, your Lord and T, ... Jn 13:14
preacher and apostle and t, ... 2 Tm 1:11

TEACHERS

third t, then miracles, ... 1 Cor 12:28
evangelists, the shepherds and t, ... Eph 4:11
for themselves t to suit their ... 2 Tm 4:3

TEACHING

is a lamp and the t a light, ... Prv 6:23
t them to observe all that I ... Mt 28:20
by God and profitable for t, ... 2 Tm 3:16
and in your t show integrity, ... Ti 2:7
Whoever abides in the t has ... 2 Jn 1:9

TEARS

Those who sow in t shall ... Ps 126:5
wipe away t from all faces, ... Is 25:8

TEETH

he gnashes his t and melts ... Ps 112:10
weeping and gnashing of t." ... Mt 8:12

TEMPER

A man of quick t acts ... Prv 14:17
but he who has a hasty t ... Prv 14:29

TEMPEST
from the raging wind and **t**.” . . . Ps 55:8
and no small **t** lay on us, . . . Acts 27:20

TEMPLE
of the LORD filled the **t**. . . . 2 Chr 7:1
The LORD is in his holy **t**; the . . . Ps 11:4
But the LORD is in his holy **t**; . . . Hb 2:20
grows into a holy **t** in the . . . Eph 2:21
for its **t** is the Lord God the . . . Rv 21:22

TEMPTATION
And lead us not into **t**, but . . . Mt 6:13
you may not enter into **t**. . . . Mt 26:41
desire to be rich fall into **t**, . . . 1 Tm 6:9

TEMPTED
on yourself, lest you too be **t**. . . . Gal 6:1
help those who are being **t**. . . . Heb 2:18
Let no one say when he is **t**, . . . Jas 1:13

TEMPTER
And the **t** came and said to . . . Mt 4:3
the **t** had tempted you . . . 1 Thes 3:5

TEN
covenant, the **T** Commandments. . . . Ex 34:28
that is, the **T** Commandments, . . . Dt 4:13

TENDER
because of the **t** mercy of our . . . Lk 1:78
brotherly love, a **t** heart, . . . 1 Pt 3:8

TENT
about in a **t** for my dwelling. . . . 2 Sm 7:6

TERROR
You will not fear the **t** of the . . . Ps 91:5
For rulers are not a **t** to . . . Rom 13:3

TEST
me; **t** my heart and my mind. . . . Ps 26:2
the Lord your God to the **t**.’” . . . Mt 4:7
T yourselves. Or do you not . . . 2 Cor 13:5
it comes upon you to **t** you, . . . 1 Pt 4:12

TESTED
After these things God **t** . . . Gn 22:1
For you, O God, have **t** us; . . . Ps 66:10
and a man is **t** by his praise. . . . Prv 27:21

TESTIMONY
world as a **t** to all nations, . . . Mt 24:14
And this is the **t**, that God . . . 1 Jn 5:11

TESTING
For the LORD your God is **t** . . . Dt 13:3
that by **t** you may discern . . . Rom 12:2

TESTS
The LORD **t** the righteous, . . . Ps 11:5
gold, and the LORD **t** hearts. . . . Prv 17:3

THANK
Let them **t** the LORD for his . . . Ps 107:8
First, I **t** my God through . . . Rom 1:8

THANKFULNESS
If I partake with **t**, why . . . 1 Cor 10:30
with **t** in your hearts to God. . . . Col 3:16

THANKS
will give **t** to you forever; . . . Ps 79:13
But **t** be to God, who in . . . 2 Cor 2:14
give **t** in all circumstances . . . 1 Thes 5:18

THANKSGIVING
a sacrifice of **t** to the LORD, . . . Lv 22:29
I will magnify him with **t**. . . . Ps 69:30
Enter his gates with **t**, and . . . Ps 100:4
But I with the voice of **t** will . . . Jon 2:9
but instead let there be **t**. . . . Eph 5:4
wisdom and **t** and honor and . . . Rv 7:12

THIEF
the Lord will come like a **t**, . . . 2 Pt 3:10
I am coming like a **t**! Blessed . . . Rv 16:15

THIEVES
and where **t** do not break. . . . Mt 6:20
nor **t**, nor the greedy, nor . . . 1 Cor 6:10

THINK
you not to **t** of himself more . . . Rom 12:3
praise, **t** about these things. . . . Phil 4:8
T over what I say, for the . . . 2 Tm 2:7

THINKING
became futile in their **t**, . . . Rom 1:21
not be children in your **t**. . . . 1 Cor 14:20
with the same way of **t**, . . . 1 Pt 4:1

THINKS
If anyone **t** he is religious . . . Jas 1:26

THIRST
and for my **t** they gave me . . . Ps 69:21
and **t** for righteousness, . . . Mt 5:6
believes in me shall never **t**. . . . Jn 6:35

THIRSTS
My soul **t** for God, for the . . . Ps 42:2
“Come, everyone who **t**, come . . . Is 55:1

THIRSTY
hungry and **t**, their soul . . . Ps 107:5
I was **t** and you gave me . . . Mt 25:35
feed him; if he is **t**, give . . . Rom 12:20
And let the one who is **t** . . . Rv 22:17

THOUGHT
but the prudent gives **t** to . . . Prv 14:15
and take every **t** captive to . . . 2 Cor 10:5

THOUGHTS
intention of the **t** of his heart . . . Gn 6:5
knows the **t** of man, that . . . Ps 94:11
Try me and know my **t**! . . . Ps 139:23

THREE
‘After **t** days I will rise.’ . . . Mt 27:63
and love abide, these **t**; . . . 1 Cor 13:13
of two or **t** witnesses. . . . 2 Cor 13:1
For there are **t** that testify: . . . 1 Jn 5:7

THRONE
Your **t** shall be established . . . 2 Sm 7:16
Your **t**, O God, is forever and . . . Ps 45:6
then a **t** will be established in . . . Is 16:5
cast their crowns before the **t**, . . . Rv 4:10
Then I saw a great white **t** . . . Rv 20:11

TIME
for such a **t** as this?” . . . Est 4:14
to you at a **t** when you may . . . Ps 32:6
everything beautiful in its **t**. . . . Eccl 3:11
for it is the **t** to seek the . . . Hos 10:12
making the best use of the **t**, . . . Eph 5:16
for all **t** a single sacrifice . . . Heb 10:12
For it is **t** for judgment to . . . 1 Pt 4:17

TIMES
I will bless the LORD at all **t**; . . . Ps 34:1
“It is not for you to know **t** . . . Acts 1:7
will come **t** of difficulty. . . . 2 Tm 3:1

TITHE
“Every **t** of the land, whether . . . Lv 27:30
towns the **t** of your grain . . . Dt 12:17
Bring the full **t** into the . . . Mal 3:10

TODAY
as long as it is called “**t**,” . . . Heb 3:13
yesterday and **t** and forever. . . . Heb 13:8
Come now, you who say, “**T** . . . Jas 4:13

TOMB
Therefore order the **t** to be . . . Mt 27:64
stone rolled away from the **t**, . . . Lk 24:2
and his **t** is with us to this . . . Acts 2:29

TOMORROW
Do not boast about **t**, for you . . . Prv 27:1
eat and drink, for **t** we die.” . . . Is 22:13

do not be anxious about **t**, . . . Mt 6:34

TONGUE
and every **t** confess that . . . Phil 2:11
let him keep his **t** from evil . . . 1 Pt 3:10

TONGUES
to gather all nations and **t**. . . . Is 66:18
And divided **t** as of fire . . . Acts 2:3
in **t** and extolling God. . . . Acts 10:46
various kinds of **t**, . . . 1 Cor 12:10
not forbid speaking in **t**. . . . 1 Cor 14:39

TOOTH
eye for eye, **t** for **t**, hand . . . Ex 21:24
‘An eye for an eye and a **t** . . . Mt 5:38

TOUCH
“**T** not my anointed ones, . . . Ps 105:15

TOUCHED
whose hearts God had **t**. . . . 1 Sm 10:26
And as many as **t** it were . . . Mt 14:36

TOWER
a city and a **t** with its top . . . Gn 11:4
of the LORD is a strong **t**; . . . Prv 18:10

TRADITION
So for the sake of your **t** you . . . Mt 15:6
deceit, according to human **t**, . . . Col 2:8

TRADITIONS
maintain the **t** even as I . . . 1 Cor 11:2
to the **t** that you were . . . 2 Thes 2:15

TRAIN
T up a child in the way he . . . Prv 22:6
Rather **t** yourself for . . . 1 Tm 4:7

TRANCE
and in a **t** I saw a vision, . . . Acts 11:5
the temple, I fell into a **t** . . . Acts 22:17

TRANSFIGURED
And he was **t** before them, . . . Mt 17:2

TRANSFORMED
but be **t** by the renewal of . . . Rom 12:2
are being **t** into the same . . . 2 Cor 3:18

TRANSGRESSION
forgiving iniquity and **t** and . . . Ex 34:7
Blessed is the one whose **t** is . . . Ps 32:1
if anyone is caught in any **t**, . . . Gal 6:1

TRANSGRESSIONS
Deliver me from all my **t**. . . . Ps 39:8
so far does he remove our **t** . . . Ps 103:12
It was added because of **t**, . . . Gal 3:19

TRANSGRESSORS
Then I will teach **t** your . . . Ps 51:13
was numbered with the **t**; . . . Is 53:12

TREASURE
and you will have **t** in . . . Mt 19:21
But we have this **t** in jars . . . 2 Cor 4:7
thus storing up **t** for . . . 1 Tm 6:19

TREASURED
a people for his **t** possession, . . . Dt 7:6
But Mary **t** up all these . . . Lk 2:19

TREASURES
but lay up for yourselves **t** in . . . Mt 6:20
in whom are hidden all the **t** . . . Col 2:3

TREE
The **t** of life was in the midst . . . Gn 2:9
but of the **t** of the knowledge. . . . Gn 2:17
He is like a **t** planted by . . . Ps 1:3
Every **t** therefore that does . . . Mt 3:10
for the **t** is known by its . . . Mt 12:33
who is hanged on a **t**” — . . . Gal 3:13
the right to the **t** of life and . . . Rv 22:14

TREMBLING
with fear, and rejoice with **t**. . . . . Ps 2:11
salvation with fear and **t**, ... Phil 2:12

TRESPASSES
And you were dead in the **t** . . . . . Eph 2:1
having forgiven us all our **t**, ... Col 2:13

TRIAL
remains steadfast under **t**, ... Jas 1:12
at the fiery **t** when it comes . . . . . 1 Pt 4:12
the hour of **t** that is coming . . . . . Rv 3:10

TRIALS
been grieved by various **t**, ... 1 Pt 1:6
to rescue the godly from **t**, ... 2 Pt 2:9

TRIBES
All these are the twelve **t** . . . . . Gn 49:28
from all **t** and peoples and . . . . . Rv 7:9

TRIBULATION
then there will be great **t**, ... Mt 24:21
Shall **t**, or distress, or . . . . . Rom 8:35

TROUBLE
is few of days and full of **t**. . . . . Jb 14:1
a very present help in **t**. . . . . Ps 46:1
although man's **t** lies heavy . . . . . Eccl 8:6
a stronghold in the day of **t**; . . . . . Na 1:7

TRUE
not come to pass or come **t**, ... Dt 18:22
word of the LORD proves **t**; . . . . . 2 Sm 22:31
"I am the **t** vine, and my . . . . . Jn 15:1
serve the living and **t** God, ... 1 Thes 1:9
it is called Faithful and **T**, ... Rv 19:11

TRUMPET
For the **t** will sound, ... 1 Cor 15:52
the sound of the **t** of God. . . . . 1 Thes 4:16

TRUST
am afraid, I put my **t** in you. . . . . Ps 56:3
LORD, whose **t** is the LORD. . . . . Jer 17:7

TRUSTED
But I have **t** in your steadfast . . . . . Ps 13:5
his servants, who **t** in him, ... Dn 3:28

TRUSTS
"He **t** in the LORD; let him. . . . . Ps 22:8
Whoever **t** in his riches. . . . . Prv 11:28
but whoever **t** in the LORD . . . . . Prv 29:25

TRUSTWORTHY
Your decrees are very **t**; . . . . . Ps 93:5
just; all his precepts are **t**; . . . . . Ps 111:7
"These words are **t** and true. . . . . Rv 22:6

TRUTH
Lead me in your **t** and teach. . . . . Ps 25:5
the Father in spirit and **t**, ... Jn 4:23
and the **t** will set you free." . . . . . Jn 8:32
way, and the **t**, and the life. . . . . Jn 14:6
in the **t**; your word is **t**. . . . . Jn 17:17
said to him, "What is **t**?" . . . . . Jn 18:38
the **t** about God for . . . . . Rom 1:25
so that the **t** of the gospel . . . . . Gal 2:5
fastened on the belt of **t**, ... Eph 6:14
the knowledge of the **t**, ... Heb 10:26

TRUTHFUL
T lips endure forever, but a. . . . . Prv 12:19
A **t** witness saves lives, ... Prv 14:25
by **t** speech, and the power . . . . . 2 Cor 6:7

TURN
You shall not **t** aside to the . . . . . Dt 5:32
Do not **t** from it to the right . . . . . Jos 1:7
You **t** things upside down! . . . . . Is 29:16
And he will **t** the hearts of . . . . . Mal 4:6
let him **t** away from evil . . . . . 1 Pt 3:11

TWELVE
All these are the **t** tribes of. . . . . Gn 49:28
And he called to him his **t** . . . . . Mt 10:1

UNBELIEF
marveled because of their **u**. . . . . Mk 6:6
off because of their **u**, ... Rom 11:20
had acted ignorantly in **u**, ... 1 Tm 1:13

UNBELIEVER
has a wife who is an **u**, ... 1 Cor 7:12
believer share with an **u**? . . . . . 2 Cor 6:15

UNBELIEVERS
brother, and that before **u**? . . . . . 1 Cor 6:6
blinded the minds of the **u**, ... 2 Cor 4:4

UNBELIEVING
For the **u** husband is . . . . . 1 Cor 7:14
pure, but to the defiled and **u**, ... Ti 1:15
any of you an evil, **u** heart, ... Heb 3:12

UNBORN
to a people yet **u**, ... Ps 22:31
them, the children yet **u**, ... Ps 78:6

UNCHANGEABLE
But he is **u**, and who can . . . . . Jb 23:13
the **u** character of his . . . . . Heb 6:17

UNCIRCUMCISED
with the gospel to the **u**, ... Gal 2:7
and Jew, circumcised and **u**, ... Col 3:11

UNCLEAN
lost; for I am a man of **u** lips, ... Is 6:5
that nothing is **u** in itself, ... Rom 14:14
and touch no **u** thing; . . . . . 2 Cor 6:17

UNDERSTAND
uttered what I did not **u**, ... Jb 42:3
but **u** what the will of the . . . . . Eph 5:17
in them that are hard to **u**, ... 2 Pt 3:16

UNDERSTANDING
do not lean on your own **u**. . . . . Prv 3:5
he who keeps **u** will . . . . . Prv 19:8
and **u** to interpret dreams, ... Dn 5:12
Who is wise and **u** among . . . . . Jas 3:13

UNDERSTANDS
no one **u**; no one seeks for. . . . . Rom 3:11
with conceit and **u** nothing. . . . . 1 Tm 6:4

UNFRUITFUL
Take no part in the **u** . . . . . Eph 5:11

UNGODLINESS
u and unrighteousness of . . . . . Rom 1:18
into more and more **u**, ... 2 Tm 2:16

UNGODLY
him who justifies the **u**, ... Rom 4:5
time Christ died for the **u**. . . . . Rom 5:6
what will become of the **u** . . . . . 1 Pt 4:18

UNITE
u my heart to fear your . . . . . Ps 86:11
time, to **u** all things in him, ... Eph 1:10

UNITED
For if we have been **u** with. . . . . Rom 6:5
but that you be **u** in the . . . . . 1 Cor 1:10
because they were not **u** by . . . . . Heb 4:2

UNITY
is when brothers dwell in **u**! . . . . . Ps 133:1
eager to maintain the **u** of . . . . . Eph 4:3
until we all attain to the **u** . . . . . Eph 4:13
have **u** of mind, sympathy, ... 1 Pt 3:8

UNIVERSE
and he upholds the **u** by the. . . . . Heb 1:3
that the **u** was created by. . . . . Heb 11:3

UNJUST
rain on the just and on the **u**. . . . . Mt 5:45
of both the just and the **u**. . . . . Acts 24:15

UNLEAVENED
observe the Feast of **U** Bread, ... Ex 12:17

UNPUNISHED
evil person will not go **u**, ... Prv 11:21
false witness will not go **u**, ... Prv 19:5

UNRIGHTEOUSNESS
But if our **u** serves to show. . . . . Rom 3:5
but had pleasure in **u**. . . . . 2 Thes 2:12

UNSEARCHABLE
How **u** are his judgments . . . . . Rom 11:33
the **u** riches of Christ, ... Eph 3:8

UNWORTHY
say, 'We are **u** servants; . . . . . Lk 17:10
in an **u** manner will be. . . . . 1 Cor 11:27

UPHOLD
and **u** me with a willing . . . . . Ps 51:12
U me according to your . . . . . Ps 119:116
the contrary, we **u** the law. . . . . Rom 3:31

UPRIGHT
that man was blameless and **u**, ... Jb 1:1
For the word of the LORD is **u**, ... Ps 33:4
but the prayer of the **u** is . . . . . Prv 15:8
and to live self-controlled, **u**, ... Ti 2:12

URGE
u you to walk in a manner . . . . . Eph 4:1
Teach and **u** these things. . . . . 1 Tm 6:2
Beloved, I **u** you as. . . . . 1 Pt 2:11

UTTERANCE
as the Spirit gave them **u**. . . . . Acts 2:4
the Spirit the **u** of wisdom, ... 1 Cor 12:8

VAIN
of the LORD your God in **v**, ... Ex 20:7
unless you believed in **v**. . . . . 1 Cor 15:2
did not run in **v** or labor in. . . . . Phil 2:16

VALLEY
through the **v** of the shadow . . . . . Ps 23:4
is near in the **v** of decision. . . . . Jl 3:14
Every **v** shall be filled, and . . . . . Lk 3:5

VEIL
And the **v** shall separate for . . . . . Ex 26:33
he put a **v** over his face. . . . . Ex 34:33
that same **v** remains. . . . . 2 Cor 3:14

VENGEANCE
For the LORD has a day of **v**, ... Is 34:8
"**V** is mine, I will repay, ... Rom 12:19

VESSEL
lump one **v** for honorable use. . . . . Rom 9:21
he will be a **v** for honorable . . . . . 2 Tm 2:21

VICTORY
until he brings justice to **v**; . . . . . Mt 12:20
is swallowed up in **v**." . . . . . 1 Cor 15:54
And this is the **v** that has. . . . . 1 Jn 5:4

VINE
"I am the true **v**, and my . . . . . Jn 15:1

VIOLENCE
V shall no more be heard in . . . . . Is 60:18
Put away **v** and oppression, ... Ez 45:9

VIRGIN
Behold, the **v** shall conceive . . . . . Is 7:14
to a **v** betrothed to a man . . . . . Lk 1:27
to present you as a pure **v** . . . . . 2 Cor 11:2

VISIONS
your young men shall see **v**. . . . . Jl 2:28

VOICE
Today, if you hear his **v**, ... Ps 95:7
The sheep hear his **v**, and he . . . . . Jn 10:3
"Today, if you hear his **v**, ... Heb 3:7

VOW
If a man vows a **v** to the .... Nm 30:2
When you **v** a **v** to God, ... Eccl 5:4

WAGES
the laborer deserves his **w**. .... Lk 10:7
For the **w** of sin is death, ... Rom 6:23
laborer deserves his **w**." .... 1 Tm 5:18

WAIT
I **w** for your salvation, O. .... Gn 49:18
Be still before the LORD and **w** .... Ps 37:7
groan inwardly as we **w**. .... Rom 8:23
to eat, **w** for one another .... 1 Cor 11:33

WAITED
I **w** patiently for the LORD; .... Ps 40:1
when God's patience **w** in .... 1 Pt 3:20

WALK
You shall **w** in all the way .... Dt 5:33
from those who **w** uprightly. .... Ps 84:11
the good way is; and **w** in it, ... Jer 6:16
But I say, **w** by the Spirit, ... Gal 5:16
carefully then how you **w**, ... Eph 5:15
But if we **w** in the light, ... 1 Jn 1:7

WALKED
Enoch **w** with God, and he .... Gn 5:24
Noah **w** with God. .... Gn 6:9
the boat and **w** on the water .... Mt 14:29

WALKING
the LORD God **w** in the garden .... Gn 3:8
w blamelessly in all the .... Lk 1:6
you are no longer **w** in. .... Rom 14:15

WALKS
your God **w** in the midst .... Dt 23:14
Whoever **w** in uprightness .... Prv 14:2
Let him who **w** in darkness. .... Is 50:10
The one who **w** in the .... Jn 12:35

WALL
and the **w** fell down flat, ... Jos 6:20
Come, let us build the **w** of .... Neh 2:17
the dividing **w** of hostility. .... Eph 2:14
It had a great, high **w**, with .... Rv 21:12

WANT
is my shepherd; I shall not **w**. .... Ps 23:1
For I do not do what I **w**, ... Rom 7:15

WAR
a time to hate; a time for **w**, ... Eccl 3:8
neither shall they learn **w**. .... Is 2:4
to the end there shall be **w**. .... Dn 9:26

WARFARE
For the weapons of our **w** .... 2 Cor 10:4
you may wage the good **w**, ... 1 Tm 1:18

WARN
But if you **w** the wicked, and .... Ez 3:19
I **w** you, as I warned you .... Gal 5:21
but **w** him as a brother. .... 2 Thes 3:15

WARNED
by them is your servant **w**; .... Ps 19:11
him who **w** them on earth, ... Heb 12:25

WARS
He makes **w** cease to the end. .... Ps 46:9
And you will hear of **w** and .... Mt 24:6

WASH
W me thoroughly from my .... Ps 51:2
and **w** away your sins, ... Acts 22:16
Blessed are those who **w** .... Rv 22:14

WASHED
But you were **w**, you were .... 1 Cor 6:11
bodies **w** with pure water. .... Heb 10:22
They have **w** their robes and. .... Rv 7:14

WASHING
her by the **w** of water with. .... Eph 5:26
by the **w** of regeneration and .... Ti 3:5

WATCH
W therefore, for you know .... Mt 25:13
Keep **w** on yourself, lest you .... Gal 6:1
Keep a close **w** on yourself .... 1 Tm 4:16

WATCHFUL
Be **w**, stand firm in the. .... 1 Cor 16:13
being **w** in it with .... Col 4:2
Be sober-minded; be **w**. Your .... 1 Pt 5:8

WATER
I am poured out like **w**, ... Ps 22:14
give him **w** to drink, ... Prv 25:21
is like a tree planted by **w**, ... Jer 17:8
"I baptize you with **w** for. .... Mt 3:11
cup of cold **w** because he is .... Mt 10:42
unless one is born of **w** and .... Jn 3:5
will flow rivers of living **w**.'" .... Jn 7:38
formed out of **w** and through **w**. .... 2 Pt 3:5
them to springs of living **w**, ... Rv 7:17

WATERED
waters will himself be **w**. .... Prv 11:25
I planted, Apollos **w**, but .... 1 Cor 3:6

WATERS
over the face of the **w**. .... Gn 1:2
He leads me beside still **w**. .... Ps 23:2
water, whose **w** do not fail. .... Is 58:11
the fountain of living **w**, ... Jer 2:13

WAY
the **w** of the wicked will perish. .... Ps 1:6
Teach me your **w**, O LORD, that I ...... Ps 86:11
young man keep his **w** pure? .... Ps 119:9
there be any grievous **w** in me, ... Ps 139:24
There is a **w** that seems right .... Prv 16:25
Train up a child in the **w** he .... Prv 22:6
do not know the **w** the spirit .... Eccl 11:5
shall be called the **W** of Holiness; .... Is 35:8
— every one — to his own **w**; .... Is 53:6
'Prepare the **w** of the Lord; .... Mt 3:3
but truly teach the **w** of God. .... Lk 20:21
Jesus said to him, "I am the **w**, ... Jn 14:6
you, that according to the **W**, ... Acts 24:14
hindrance in the **w** of a brother. ...... Rom 14:13
you a still more excellent **w**. .... 1 Cor 12:31
We are afflicted in every **w**, ... 2 Cor 4:8
godliness is of value in every **w**, ... 1 Tm 4:8

WAYS
teach transgressors your **w**, ... Ps 51:13
neither are your **w** my **w**, ... Is 55:8
for the **w** of the LORD are .... Hos 14:9
how inscrutable his **w**! .... Rom 11:33

WEAK
willing, but the flesh is **w**." .... Mt 26:41
God chose what is **w** in .... 1 Cor 1:27
To the **w** I became **w**, ... 1 Cor 9:22
For when I am **w**, then. .... 2 Cor 12:10
strengthen your **w** knees, ... Heb 12:12

WEAKER
be **w** are indispensable, ... 1 Cor 12:22
the woman as the **w** vessel, ... 1 Pt 3:7

WEAKNESS
Spirit helps us in our **w**. .... Rom 8:26
he himself is beset with **w**. .... Heb 5:2

WEAKNESSES
not boast, except of my **w**. .... 2 Cor 12:5
to sympathize with our **w**, ... Heb 4:15

WEALTH
Honor the LORD with your **w**. .... Prv 3:9
who have **w** to enter the .... Mk 10:23

WEAPONS
with the **w** of righteousness .... 2 Cor 6:7
For the **w** of our warfare .... 2 Cor 10:4

WEARY
they shall run and not be **w**; .... Is 40:31
And let us not grow **w** of. .... Gal 6:9

WEDDING
who had no **w** garment. .... Mt 22:11
Jesus also was invited to the **w** .... Jn 2:2

WEEP
a time to **w**, and a time to .... Eccl 3:4
"Blessed are you who **w** now, ... Lk 6:21
w with those who **w**. .... Rom 12:15

WEEPING
W may tarry for the night, ... Ps 30:5
In that place there will be **w**. .... Mt 8:12

WEPT
When I **w** and humbled my .... Ps 69:10
Jesus **w**. .... Jn 11:35

WHIRLWIND
Elijah up to heaven by a **w**, ... 2 Kgs 2:1
Job out of the **w** and said: .... Jb 38:1
His way is in **w** and storm, ... Na 1:3

WHITE
they shall be as **w** as snow; .... Is 1:18
his clothing was **w** as snow, ... Dn 7:9
The hairs of his head were **w**, ... Rv 1:14

WHOLE
who seek him with their **w**. .... Ps 119:2
you the **w** counsel of God. .... Acts 20:27
For whoever keeps the **w** .... Jas 2:10

WICKED
Therefore the **w** will not stand .... Ps 1:5
the **w** will be no more; .... Ps 37:10
let the **w** forsake his way, ... Is 55:7
nor speak to warn the **w** .... Ez 3:18
in the death of the **w**, ... Ez 18:23
though I say to the **w**, ... Ez 33:14
For everyone who does **w**. .... Jn 3:20

WIDOW
for the fatherless and the **w**, ... Dt 10:18
and he saw a poor **w** put in. .... Lk 21:2

WIDOWS
Honor **w** who are truly. .... 1 Tm 5:3
to visit orphans and **w** in .... Jas 1:27

WIFE
and hold fast to his **w**, ... Gn 2:24
and rejoice in the **w** of your .... Prv 5:18
An excellent **w** is the crown .... Prv 12:4
a quarrelsome **w** are alike; .... Prv 27:15
An excellent **w** who can .... Prv 31:10
everyone who divorces his **w**, ... Mt 5:32
own **w** and each woman .... 1 Cor 7:2
should not divorce his **w**. .... 1 Cor 7:11
of the **w** even as Christ .... Eph 5:23
Bride, the **w** of the Lamb." .... Rv 21:9

WILL
the **w** of the LORD to crush him; .... Is 53:10
kingdom come, your **w** be done, ... Mt 6:10
does the **w** of my Father. .... Mt 12:50
anyone's **w** is to do God's **w**, ... Jn 7:17
who works in you, both to **w** .... Phil 2:13
captured by him to do his **w**. .... 2 Tm 2:26
and by your **w** they existed. .... Rv 4:11

WILLING
and uphold me with a **w** .... Ps 51:12
The spirit indeed is **w**, but .... Mt 26:41

WILLS
mercy on whomever he **w**, ... Rom 9:18
ought to say, "If the Lord **w**, ... Jas 4:15

WIN
that I might w more of. . . . 1 Cor 9:19
but may w a full reward. . . . 2 Jn 1:8

WIND
like a mighty rushing w, ... Acts 2:2
by every w of doctrine, ... Eph 4:14
is driven and tossed by the w. . . . Jas 1:6

WINE
W is a mocker, strong drink . . . . Prv 20:1
For your love is better than w; . . . . Sg 1:2
the water now become w, ... Jn 2:9
do not get drunk with w, ... Eph 5:18
but use a little w for the . . . . 1 Tm 5:23

WINGS
me in the shadow of your w, ... Ps 17:8
they shall mount up with w . . . . Is 40:31
her brood under her w, ... Lk 13:34

WIPE
and the Lord God will w. . . . . Is 25:8
He will w away every tear . . . . Rv 21:4

WISDOM
And God gave Solomon w . . . . 1 Kgs 4:29
Lord is the beginning of w; . . . . Ps 111:10
Lord is the beginning of w, ... Prv 9:10
Yet w is justified by her . . . . Mt 11:19
For the w of this world is . . . . 1 Cor 3:19
If any of you lacks w, let him . . . . Jas 1:5
But the w from above is first . . . . Jas 3:17

WISE
is sure, making w the simple; . . . . Ps 19:7
Be not w in your own eyes; . . . . Prv 3:7
A w son makes a glad father, ... Prv 10:1
silent is considered w; . . . . Prv 17:28
w men from the east came to. . . . . Mt 2:1
Claiming to be w, they. . . . . Rom 1:22
Never be w in your own. . . . . Rom 12:16
the world to shame the w; . . . . 1 Cor 1:27

WITNESS
"You shall not bear false w . . . . Ex 20:16
A truthful w saves lives, ... Prv 14:25
conscience also bears w, ... Rom 2:15
Jesus Christ the faithful w, ... Rv 1:5

WITNESSES
of two w or of three . . . . Dt 19:15
and you will be my w in. . . . . Acts 1:8
of two or three w. . . . . 1 Tm 5:19
by so great a cloud of w, ... Heb 12:1

WIVES
W, submit to your own. . . . . Eph 5:22

WOLF
The w shall dwell with the. . . . . Is 11:6
sees the w coming and . . . . Jn 10:12

WOMAN
into a w and brought her. . . . . Gn 2:22
that you are a worthy w. . . . . Ru 3:11
but a w who fears the Lord . . . . Prv 31:30
at a w with lustful intent . . . . Mt 5:28
For a married w is bound. . . . . Rom 7:2
but w is the glory of man. . . . . 1 Cor 11:7
sent forth his Son, born of w, ... Gal 4:4
Let a w learn quietly with. . . . . 1 Tm 2:11
showing honor to the w as. . . . . 1 Pt 3:7

WOMB
I came from my mother's w, ... Jb 1:21
together in my mother's w. . . . . Ps 139:13
his mother's w he shall go . . . . Eccl 5:15

WOMEN
"Blessed are you among w, ... Lk 1:42
likewise also that w should . . . . 1 Tm 2:9
Older w likewise are to be . . . . Ti 2:3

WONDERFUL
I will recount all of your w. . . . . Ps 9:1
and his name shall be called W . . . . Is 9:6
for you have done w things, ... Is 25:1

WONDERS
who alone does great w, ... Ps 136:4
"And I will show w in the. . . . . Jl 2:30
And I will show w in the . . . . Acts 2:19

WOOD
down before a block of w?" . . . . Is 44:19
stones, w, hay, straw — . . . . 1 Cor 3:12

WORD
After these things the w of. . . . . Gn 15:1
but man lives by every w that. . . . . Dt 8:3
his way is perfect; the w . . . . 2 Sm 22:31
For the w of the Lord is . . . . Ps 33:4
Every w of God proves true; . . . . Prv 30:5
In the beginning was the W, ... Jn 1:1
law is fulfilled in one w: . . . . Gal 5:14
preach the w; be ready in. . . . . 2 Tm 4:2
For the w of God is living. . . . . Heb 4:12
But be doers of the w, and. . . . . Jas 1:22
and the w of God abides in . . . . 1 Jn 2:14

WORDS
shall therefore lay up these w . . . . Dt 11:18
Give ear to my w, O Lord; . . . . Ps 5:1
Let the w of my mouth and the . . . . Ps 19:14
sweet are your w to my taste, ... Ps 119:103
My son, if you receive my w. . . . . Prv 2:1
but my w will not pass away. . . . . Mt 24:35
with w of eloquent wisdom, ... 1 Cor 1:17
the one who reads aloud the w . . . . Rv 1:3
the one who keeps the w of. . . . . Rv 22:7

WORK
finished his w that he had . . . . Gn 2:2
them, "This is the w of God, ... Jn 6:29
each one's w will become . . . . 1 Cor 3:13
according to the power at w . . . . Eph 3:20
w out your own salvation. . . . . Phil 2:12
which is at w in you. . . . . 1 Thes 2:13

WORKER
What gain has the w from . . . . Eccl 3:9
give to this last w as I give . . . . Mt 20:14
a w who has no need to . . . . 2 Tm 2:15

WORKS
Remember the wondrous w . . . . Ps 105:5
and let her w praise her in . . . . Prv 31:31
not justified by w of the law . . . . Gal 2:16
in Christ Jesus for good w, ... Eph 2:10
for it is God who w in you, ... Phil 2:13
good, to be rich in good w, ... 1 Tm 6:18
not because of our w but. . . . . 2 Tm 1:9
to be a model of good w, ... Ti 2:7
to love and good w, ... Heb 10:24
your faith apart from your w, ... Jas 2:18

WORLD
He will judge the w with . . . . Ps 98:9
was coming into the w. . . . . Jn 1:9
takes away the sin of the w! . . . . Jn 1:29
the w did not know God . . . . 1 Cor 1:21
whom also he created the w. . . . . Heb 1:2
with the w is enmity with. . . . . Jas 4:4
Do not love the w or the . . . . 1 Jn 2:15
of the w in the book . . . . Rv 13:8

WORSHIP
nations shall w before you. . . . . Ps 22:27
come, let us w and bow down; . . . . Ps 95:6
rose and have come to w him." . . . . Mt 2:2
him must w in spirit and . . . . Jn 4:24
offer to God acceptable w, ... Heb 12:28
throne and w him who lives. . . . . Rv 4:10
All nations will come and w. . . . . Rv 15:4

WORTH
Man does not know its w, ... Jb 28:13
of the wicked is of little w. . . . . Prv 10:20
w of knowing Christ. . . . . Phil 3:8

WORTHLESS
they have become w; . . . . Rom 3:12
they are unprofitable and w. . . . . Ti 3:9

WORTHY
Lord, who is w to be praised, ... Ps 18:3
so as to walk in a manner w . . . . Col 1:10
saying with a loud voice, "W . . . . Rv 5:12

WOUNDS
Faithful are the w of a . . . . Prv 27:6
'What are these w on your. . . . . Zec 13:6

WRATH
he will speak to them in his w, ... Ps 2:5
kings on the day of his w. . . . . Ps 110:5
this cup of the wine of w, ... Jer 25:15
by nature children of w, ... Eph 2:3

WRITE
You shall w them on the . . . . Dt 6:9
w them on the tablet of your . . . . Prv 3:3
and w them on their hearts, ... Heb 8:10

WRITINGS
if you do not believe his w, ... Jn 5:47
w has been made . . . . Rom 16:26
with the sacred w, ... 2 Tm 3:15

WRITTEN
shall be found w in the book. . . . . Dn 12:1
names are w in heaven." . . . . Lk 10:20
but these are w so that you . . . . Jn 20:31

WRONG
Love does no w to a . . . . Rom 13:10
back for the w he has done, ... Col 3:25

YEAR
once in the y because of all . . . . Lv 16:34
but in the seventh y there . . . . Lv 25:4
For a whole y they met. . . . . Acts 11:26
continually offered every y, ... Heb 10:1

YEARNS
My soul y for you in the. . . . . Is 26:9
Therefore my heart y for. . . . . Jer 31:20

YIELDS
of water that y its fruit in. . . . . Ps 1:3
He indeed bears fruit and y, ... Mt 13:23
but later it y the peaceful. . . . . Heb 12:11

YOKE
Take my y upon you, and . . . . Mt 11:29
submit again to a y of slavery. . . . . Gal 5:1
Let all who are under a y . . . . 1 Tm 6:1

YOUNG
How can a y man keep his. . . . . Ps 119:9
The glory of y men is their . . . . Prv 20:29
and your y men shall see . . . . Jl 2:28
and so train the y women to . . . . Ti 2:4

YOUTH
heart is evil from his y. . . . . Gn 8:21
in the days of your y, ... Eccl 12:1
to the wife of your y. . . . . Mal 2:15
one despise you for your y, ... 1 Tm 4:12

ZEAL
The z of the Lord of hosts will . . . . Is 9:7
"Z for your house will . . . . Jn 2:17
that they have a z for God, ... Rom 10:2
the one who leads, with z; . . . . Rom 12:8

ZEALOUS
being z for God as all of. . . . . Acts 22:3
who are z for good works. . . . . Ti 2:14
discipline, so be z and repent. . . . . Rv 3:19

TABLE OF
WEIGHTS AND MEASURES
AND MONETARY UNITS

The following table is based on the best generally accepted information available for biblical weights, measures, and monetary units. All equivalents are approximate. Weights and measures varied somewhat in different times and places in the ancient world. Most weights, measures, and monetary units are also explained in footnotes on the pages where they occur in the ESV text.

Biblical Unit	Approximate American and Metric Equivalents	Biblical Equivalent
bath	6 gallons or 22 liters	1 ephah
beka	1/5 ounce or 5.5 grams	10 gerahs
cor	6 bushels or 220 liters	10 ephahs
cubit	18 inches or 45 centimeters	6 handbreadths
daric	A coin of about 1/4 ounce or 8.5 grams	
denarius	A day's wage for a laborer	
ephah	3/5 bushel or 22 liters	10 omers
gerah	1/50 ounce or 0.6 gram	1/10 beka
handbreadth	3 inches or 7.5 centimeters	1/6 cubit
hin	4 quarts or 3.5 liters	1/6 bath
homer	6 bushels or 220 liters	10 ephahs
kab	1 quart or 1 liter	1/22 ephah
lethech	3 bushels or 110 liters	5 ephahs
log	1/3 quart or 0.3 liter	1/72 bath
mina	1 1/4 pounds or 0.6 kilogram	50 shekels
omer	2 quarts or 2 liters	1/10 ephah
pim	1/3 ounce or 7.5 grams	2/3 shekel
seah	7 quarts or 7.3 liters	1/3 ephah
shekel	2/5 ounce or 11 grams	2 bekas
span	9 inches or 22 centimeters	3 handbreadths
stadion	607 feet or 185 meters	
talent	75 pounds or 34 kilograms	60 minas

Colophon

The Crossway ESV Study Bible Publishing Team

Editorial Team

Lane T. Dennis	*Executive Editor, President and Publisher*
Justin Taylor	*Project Director, Managing Editor*
Bill Deckard	*Senior Project Editor*
Sherah Grose	*Assistant to the Project Director*

Design

Joshua Dennis	*Creative Director and Interior Design*
The Design Works Group	*Cover Design*

Typesetting

Raymond Elliott	*Information Systems Director, Senior Bible Typesetter*
David Eyk	*Bible Typesetter, Prepress Technician*

Proofreading Services

Peachtree Editorial and Proofreading Service

Production

Dallas Richards	*Bible Production Director*
Donald Jones	*Bible Project Manager*
Monica Gee	*Bible Production Coordinator*
Keane Fine	*Production Prepress Technician*

Management Leaders

Geoffrey L. Dennis	*Executive Vice President, Sales and Marketing*
Randall D. Jahns	*Senior Vice President, Bible Publishing*
Allan Fisher	*Senior Vice President, Book Publishing*
M. Ebeth Dennis	*Vice President, Publishing Ministry*
Paul K. Thomas	*Vice President, Finance*
Daniel J. Kok	*Vice President, Operations*

Acknowledgments

The publisher also wishes to express appreciation to the following persons for their assistance in copyediting, proofreading, and design: Dana Adams, Robert Barnes, Kris Bearss, Gloria Deckard, Candy DenOuden, Amy Donaldson, Suzanne Johnson, Karen Magnuson, Christopher Reese, and Allan Sholes.

ESV Study Bible Specifications and Production

Typefaces:	*Lexicon, Frutiger, and Helvetica*
Text paper:	*Thincoat Plus (28.5 gsm), delfortgroup, Tervakoski, Finland. Programme for the Endorsement of Forest Certification (PEFC), certificate number 5039-02.*
Binding type:	*Smyth Sewn*
Printing and binding:	*R. R. Donnelley & Sons*

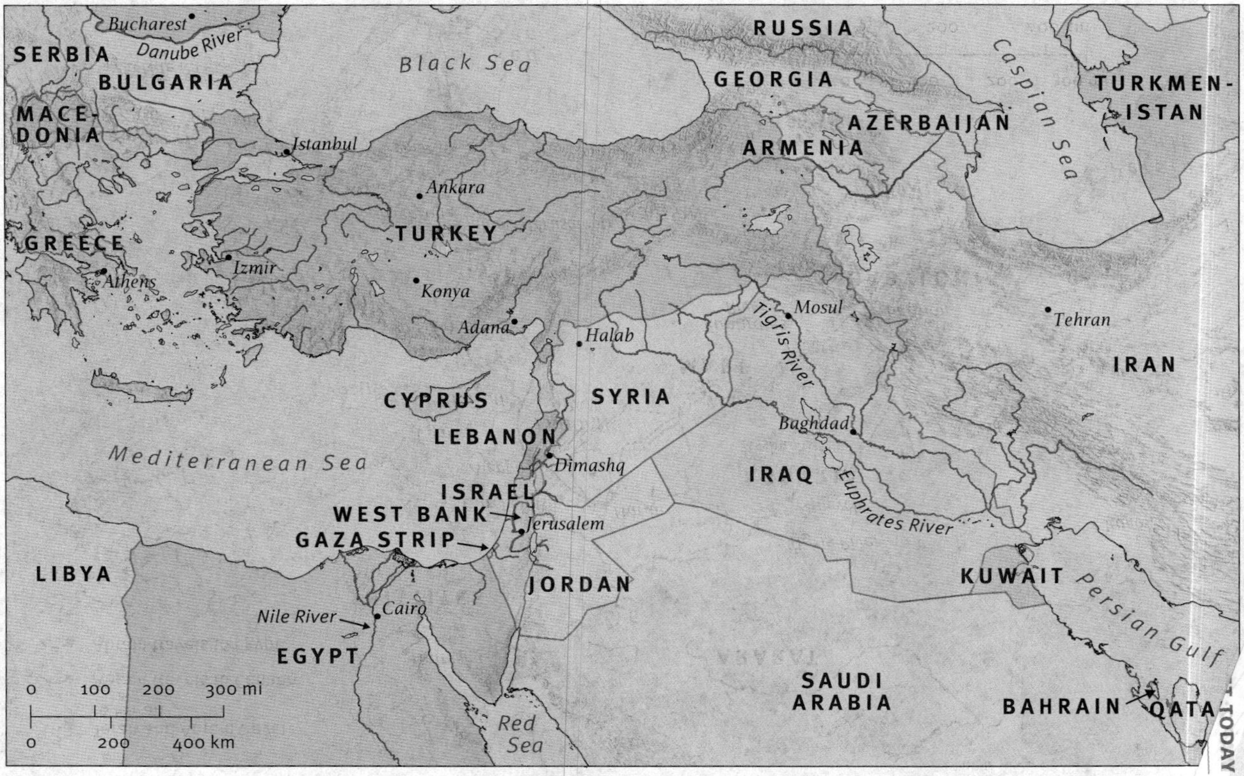
Bucharest
Danube River
SERBIA
BULGARIA
MACE-
DONIA
Black Sea
Istanbul
Ankara
TURKEY
GREECE
Izmir
Athens
Konya
Adana
Halab
RUSSIA
GEORGIA
AZERBAIJAN
ARMENIA
Caspian Sea
TURKMEN-
ISTAN
Mosul
Tigris River
Tehran
IRAN
CYPRUS
SYRIA
LEBANON
Dimashq
Baghdad
Mediterranean Sea
IRAQ
Euphrates River
ISRAEL
WEST BANK
Jerusalem
GAZA STRIP
LIBYA
JORDAN
KUWAIT
Persian Gulf
Nile River
Cairo
EGYPT
SAUDI
ARABIA
BAHRAIN
QATA
Red
Sea
0 100 200 300 mi
0 200 400 km

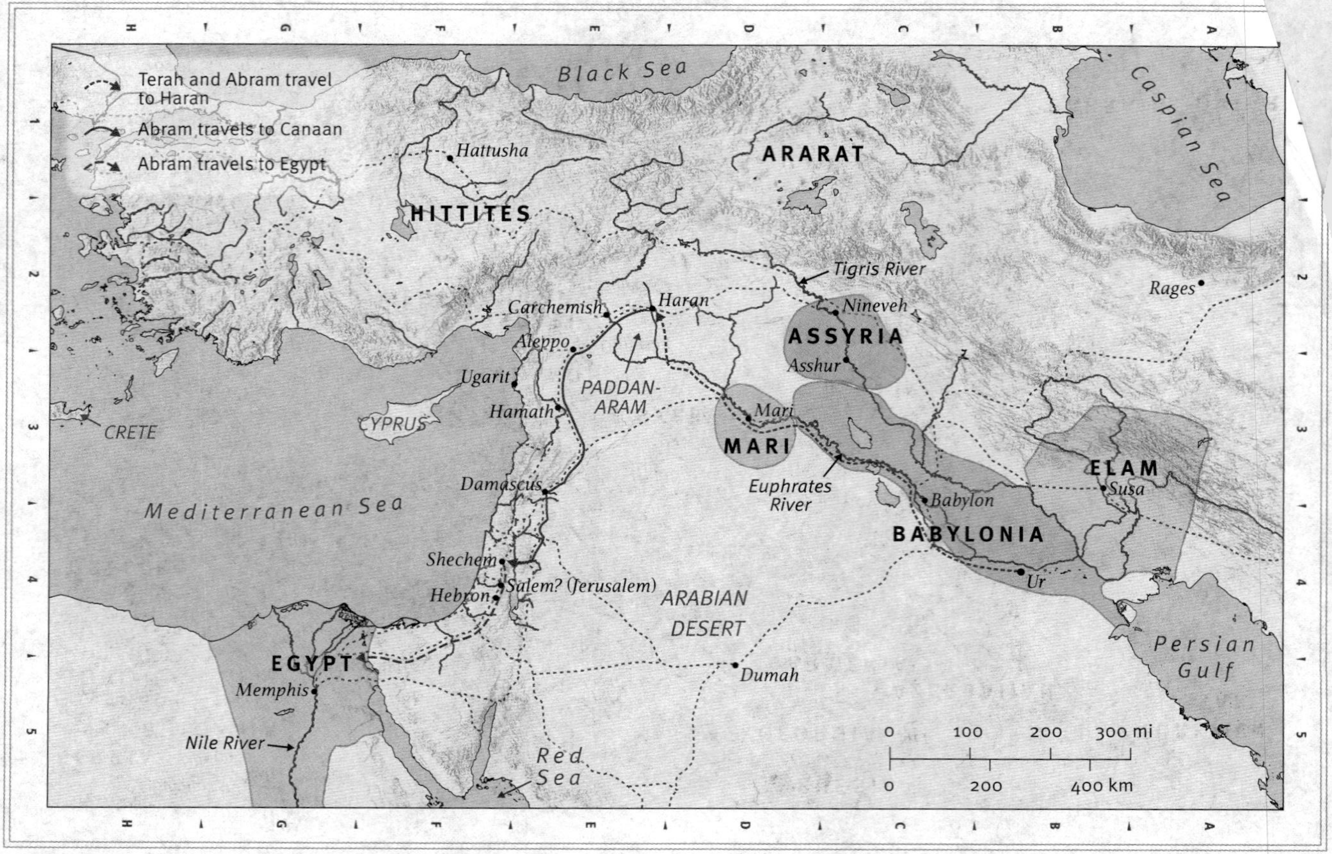
Terah and Abram travel to Haran
Abram travels to Canaan
Abram travels to Egypt
Black Sea
Caspian Sea
Hattusha
HITTITES
ARARAT
Tigris River
Rages
Carchemish
Haran
Nineveh
ASSYRIA
Asshur
Aleppo
PADDAN-ARAM
Ugarit
Hamath
Mari
MARI
CYPRUS
CRETE
Euphrates River
ELAM
Susa
Damascus
Babylon
Mediterranean Sea
BABYLONIA
Shechem
Salem? (Jerusalem)
Hebron
Ur
ARABIAN DESERT
Persian Gulf
EGYPT
Dumah
Memphis
Nile River
Red Sea
0 100 200 300 mi
0 200 400 km
H G F E D C B A
1 2 3 4 5